Corpus of Paintings Sold in the Netherlands during the Nineteenth Century 1801–1810

The *Corpus of Paintings Sold in the Netherlands during the Nineteenth Century* is a joint project of

RIJKSBUREAU VOOR KUNSTHISTORISCHE DOCUMENTATIE
Den Haag

THE NATIONAL GALLERY OF ART
Washington D.C.

THE PROVENANCE INDEX
THE GETTY INFORMATION INSTITUTE
Los Angeles

Other members of the Provenance Documentation Collaborative are

MUSÉES ROYAUX DES BEAUX-ARTS DE BELGIQUE
Bruxelles

PIETER BIESBOER
Haarlem

KUNSTHALLE
Hamburg

THE PAUL MELLON CENTRE FOR STUDIES IN BRITISH ART
London

THE FRICK ART REFERENCE LIBRARY
New York

INSTITUT NATIONAL D'HISTOIRE DE L'ART
Paris

HERMITAGE MUSEUM
St. Petersburg

FONDAZIONE DELL'ISTITUTO BANCARIO SAN PAOLO DI TORINO
Torino

Corpus of Paintings Sold in the Netherlands during the Nineteenth Century

Volume 1 1801–1810

Edited by
Burton B. Fredericksen

Archival contributions by
Ruud Priem

Assisted by
Julia I. Armstrong

The Provenance Index
of the Getty Information Institute

1998

THE GETTY
INFORMATION
INSTITUTE

Fredericksen, Burton B.
Corpus of paintings sold in The Netherlands during the nineteenth century / edited by Burton B. Fredericksen ; with archival contributions by Ruud Priem ; assisted by Julia I. Armstrong.
p. cm.
Contents: v. 1. 1801–1810
Includes bibliographical references and indexes.
ISBN 0-89236-532-3 (alk. paper)

1. Painting—Prices—Netherlands—Indexes. 2. Painting—Netherlands—Marketing—History—19th century—Indexes.
I. Fredericksen, Burton B. II. Priem, Ruud. III. Armstrong, Julia I. IV. Provenance Index of the Getty Information Institute.
ND47.C67 1998
750.75'09492—dc21 98–3757
CIP

Designed by Joe Molloy, Los Angeles, California, USA.
Composed by G&S Typesetters, Austin, Texas, USA in Times Roman.
Cover typography by Mondo Typo, Inc., Los Angeles, California, USA.
Printing and binding by Braun-Brumfield, Inc., Ann Arbor, Michigan, USA on acid-free 50# Glatfelter.
Cover bound in Holliston Roxite.

An automated version of this project is available on CD-ROM.

Contents

Preface and Acknowledgments

Scholars of Dutch art will know that, despite appearances, this is not an entirely new project. Beginning very early in this century with the work of Cornelis Hofstede de Groot, the contents of sale catalogues – primarily Dutch and French – have been excerpted in an attempt to document the provenance of Dutch and Flemish paintings. The cumulative card file, now almost a century old, resides in the Rijksbureau voor Kunsthistorische Documentatie in The Hague, and consists of about two million typed or handwritten fiches used by countless students and scholars compiling the history of individual paintings or, more often, the complete oeuvre of a given artist. The present book is simply a new phase of the same project, albeit cast in the form dictated by automation and embellished with some features not previously feasible. It has been undertaken in collaboration with the RKD and its staff, and although it is meant to gradually supplant the fiches, decades will be needed to replace the entire file, even if the participants are able to sustain the present momentum.

The original "excerpten," as they are still called at the RKD, were simply transcriptions taken from catalogues in the possession of that institution, the bulk of which had been assembled by Frits Lugt, the author of the *Répertoire des catalogues de ventes*, who has contributed more to their study than anyone else. Since the RKD has one of the largest and most complete collection of sale catalogues of any library in the world, it was an appropriate place to maintain such an ambitious project, and the RKD, to and including the present administration of Rudi Ekkart, has continued to build it through thick and thin.

However, automation has wreaked enormous changes in the world's libraries, and Dr. Ekkart and his staff understood that for the fiches to have their greatest possible utility, like the books in the library they would eventually have to be automated. The Getty Provenance Index had already embarked on an index to British sale catalogues of the nineteenth century (B. Fredericksen, *Index of Paintings Sold in the British Isles during the Nineteenth Century,* 1988+), followed later by one dedicated to those of France (B. Peronnet and B. Fredericksen, *Répertoire des tableaux vendus en France au XIXe siècle,* 1998+), so when we approached Dr. Ekkart in 1991 about a Dutch project, there was already a model to refer to. The goal of these projects was to include all paintings found in every known catalogue, both large and small, whereas the RKD had begun with just the most important sales, adding a second more comprehensive layer afterwards that carried up to the year 1825. It also concentrated on Dutch and Flemish paintings, the focus of the RKD's interests, although it did not limit itself to catalogues issued in the Netherlands. With our agreement in 1993 to collaborate on an index of just the Dutch catalogues of the nineteenth century, it was understood that, besides automating material that had previously resided on cards, we would carry the level of documentation a step further and make it as comprehensive as possible.

This attempt at comprehensiveness involved more than including catalogues not found in the RKD library, or minor sales previously ignored, or paintings other than from the Dutch and Flemish schools. Automation not only made it possible to include much more information than before, but also permitted greater insight into the individuals active in the art market at the time and the movements of individual paintings from city to city and country to country. By looking at the annotations in all extant catalogues, recording the buyers' names, the prices paid, and – whenever possible – any clues to the identity of the sellers, we could build an electronic archive that made it possible to identify individuals and establish basic biographies. Automation also allows one to match the vocabulary in the description of a painting with that of other paintings in diverse sales many years apart, permitting links in the provenance that previously had to be made much more laboriously. Of course, it takes time to assemble all of this data, and automation does little to hasten the process. However, it does guarantee that the results can be used more widely, and that interested parties anywhere in the world can contibute as though it were a communal project. Once done, the work never need be done again, except to add any material found at a later date.

This first volume of the *Corpus of Paintings Sold in the Netherlands during the Nineteenth Century* is meant to give an idea of what the automated material looks like in print. In this form, of course, it is not automated, and its use is therefore limited. We have elected to print at least this one volume in order to acquaint readers with the scope of the data and to indicate how it differs from the excerpten at the RKD. It follows the model of the British and French publications – others dedicated to Belgian and German sale catalogues are planned for 1999 – and so its form will come as no surprise to those who have used the earlier books. The community of art history scholars is just beginning to make use of such information in automated form, and the limits of this transitional phase demand that we make the material available both ways. Since the character and scope of the information differs somewhat from the excerpten at the RKD, with a book in hand one can better visualize what one can expect to find. It is likely that further segments will be made available only on CD-ROM or via the Internet.

Like the French series, this volume contains a full decade of data rather than just five years, as was necessary in the publication dedicated to the more numerous British catalogues. Of the 179 catalogues recorded in the Netherlands during this period, 59 are not in Lugt's *Répertoire*. The number of paintings found in these catalogues amounts to 17,245. This is not, of course, a definitive figure, since many catalogues have been completely lost, many lots contained more than one painting, and some paintings appeared two, three or more times during the same period. It is also possible that still other catalogues, though probably relatively minor ones, will be found in lesser-known libraries. Within the past year my colleague Ruud Priem found an interesting and unique catalogue from 1808 (no.128-A) at a public sale; it now resides in his personal library.

The catalogues are, of course, primarily in Dutch, but many of the most important were issued in both Dutch and French editions; a few were issued only in French. As with the other projects, we have transcribed the entries exactly as given in the catalogues, and whenever there were editions in two languages, we have included both. This was necessary because it was found that the information in one edition often varied significantly from that in the other, sometimes because of typographical errors, but more often because the information was simply different. These variations sometimes entailed the form of the artist's name, extended the description in the title, identified the support, or gave conflicting dimensions. The extent of these differences has also served to demonstrate, as forcefully as possible, the amount of error that occurred in catalogues of this period. This is most important in the recording of dimensions, which, from the days of C. Hofstede de Groot onward, have been so crucial in tracing Dutch pictures. We have often been able to link paintings in spite of conflicting dimensions, when it has become clear that the obstacle was simply a typographer's error.

For a variety of reasons, Dutch catalogues were more susceptible to error than was the case in England or France. First, the Dutch language has undergone continual orthographical changes that have kept it in constant flux; during the period in question it was not unusual for certain words to be spelled three or more ways. Second, Dutch command of French was understandably imperfect, so French texts tend to have still more irregularities. When combined in the catalogues with typographical errors, often involving letters put in upside down, like "u" or "n," achieving accuracy in the transcriptions becomes much more difficult. The latter have been read and re-read by both Dutch and French editors in an attempt to eliminate our own errors, and we have used the word "sic" often to show that an error was part of the original text. But we could not do this for every example of unorthodox spelling.

The work of compiling the information from these catalogues has been done primarily at the RKD, specifically by Ingrid van Beest in the Department of Archives and Excerpten. Miss van Beest has been personally responsible for the bulk of this labor, and there can be no doubt that the project would not have been attempted, much less succeeded, without her efforts. Because she also processed the *excerpten* and the collection of current sale catalogues at the RKD before the project took its present form, it was possible to maintain a certain continuity that would otherwise have been more difficult to achieve.

Her work, and the project in general, was overseen by Marcia Zaaijer, head archivist at the RKD and a gracious host and colleague on the many occasions when we visited The Hague. Miss Zaaijer has provided the administrative and organizational skills necessary to keep such an ambitious project on track, and her diplomacy and warmth have been crucial. While her name does not appear on the title page, we cannot overstate her importance to the project. We should also mention Mr. Gosem Dullaert, head librarian at the RKD, who has always been a kind and beneficial presence in making his books available.

Equally fundamental to the success of the project has been Rudi Ekkart, director of the RKD, who originally gave his blessing to the undertaking and has lent scholarly advice from time to time. The proposal to embark on this work came at a time when the status of the RKD was being reconsidered and funds were in very short supply. He has managed to launch this and other projects, somehow finding a way to fund them, and never doubting their eventual value to scholars and students. The debt we owe him is of a very great magnitude, and we hope that this book will justify his enthusiasm.

The character and quality of the research brought to bear on the material have been significantly improved by the inclusion of Ruud Priem, who agreed in 1996 to participate in the project. Mr. Priem, a graduate of Utrecht University specializing in the history of collecting in the Netherlands, has contributed more to the documentation in this book than anyone else; without him it would be a much less valuable publication. Mr. Priem has contributed most of the biographical information on individual dealers, auctioneers and collectors; he also assisted in tracing many of the paintings to their present location and gave extensive advice on the nature of the Dutch art market in the early nineteenth century. His importance to the scholarly aspects of the project has been considerable.

Other Dutch colleagues have been particularly helpful at various times. Marten Jan Bok has been a continual source of advice and valuable counsel over many years; S.A.C. Dudok van Heel has assisted us many times at the Gemeentearchief in Amsterdam; Peter Hecht and Annemieke Hoogenboom of Utrecht University were very helpful at a critical juncture, and brought us into contact with Ruud Priem; J.J. van Heel at the Meermanno-Westreenianum in The Hague has been most generous in making accessible the books in its precious library; and Geert-Jan Koot, librarian at the Rijksmuseum, has answered a number of queries and produced photocopies on various occasions. Numerous other librarians in other cities also deserve our thanks.

We are especially grateful to Catherine Hesterbeek-Bert and Joëlle Kinet of the library of the Musées Royaux des Beaux-Arts in Brussels, the repository for many rare catalogues. Besides making the books available to us, often on short notice, Mlle. Kinet has answered many questions during the last stages of the editing; her kindness is very much appreciated.

The efforts of Ingrid van Beest at the RKD were significantly augmented by those of Daniel Nolting at the National Gallery in Washington. Mr. Nolting was originally a contributor to the index of British sale catalogues, and at a moment when work on that undertaking seemed well in hand, he was asked to help out with the newer and still developing Dutch project. Although Dutch was not his native language, he managed to learn enough of it to make a very large contribution, aided by Inge Newstead, his colleague at the National Gallery, who was kind enough to assist with difficult Dutch vocabulary. Neal Turtell, head librarian at the National Gallery, has also been a most generous and consistent supporter in allowing his staff to participate in more than one project.

Among Provenance Index staff members, Julia Armstrong has taken responsibility for the final editing of the entire manuscript, searching out errors or inconsistencies at all levels, as she did for its British and French predecessors. In a book involving three languages and a number of contributors, this has not been an easy task, but we are confident that she has made it as clean and error-free as could be done. Patricia Teter has edited all of the artists' names in order to make them consistent with those in other projects, and in the process has identified a large number of artists whose names as given in the catalogue were not immediately familiar. Elizabeth Spatz has overseen the technical aspects of the project and guided the book through the entire production phase. Carol Togneri has acted as general manager, coordinating with the typesetters, the printer and the Getty Trust, among many others. Henriëtte Kets de Vries, Eric Hormell, Benjamin Peronnet, Trudy Kuijpers, Gerda Kleijkamp and Laura Pasquale have all helped with the final editing. Nancy Bryan of the Getty Information Institute has kindly read and skillfully edited all of the English text, for which we are immensely grateful. Finally, we want to thank Richard Kinney, Patrick Callahan, Karen Schmidt, Deenie Yudell, and Elizabeth Zozom of Getty Trust Publications Services for their help and support at many points along the way.

Burton B. Fredericksen

Introduction

The modern auction catalogue was born during the seventeenth century in the northern provinces of the Netherlands in conjunction with the early development there of an art market that initially rivalled that of London, its greatest competitor, in both size and sophistication. In spite of its relatively small size, not only did the Dutch art market export an inordinate number of paintings, but over time Dutch sale catalogues also established the highest standards for the description and authorship of individual objects put up for sale, which gives the catalogues permanent value as documents of the history of taste and collecting. During the eighteenth century, the French, while indulging a prodigious appetite for Dutch pictures, also imitated Dutch marketing methods, and French sale catalogues of this period, like those of the Dutch, are considered marvels of connoisseurship and refinement that warrant study even today. Across the Channel, the British, in the course of building their own more international market, and apparently more concerned with volume, were content to produce relatively brief lists of objects for sale which generally lacked evidence of the expertise that typified Dutch and French catalogues.

How much public auction catalogues were primarily a Dutch phenomenon is found in the two volumes published by the Dutch artist Gerard Hoet in 1752. His *Catalogus of Naamlyst van Schilderyen, met derzelver pryzen, zedert een langen reeks van Jaaren zoo in Holland als op andere Plaatzen in het openbaar verkogt* consisted of a faithful reprinting of the contents of 200 Dutch sale catalogues dating from the late seventeenth century to the middle of the next. This publication, while obviously reflecting the author's Dutch origins, also demonstrates an unusual preoccupation with the provenance of Dutch paintings and the history of collecting in the northern Netherlands. Eighteen years later another artist, Pieter Terwesten, issued a third volume consisting of 100 more catalogues, including a few from the period covered by Hoet. All three volumes boasted indexes of the artists' names, and the prices for the individual lots, whenever possible. No comparable book ever appeared in any other country.

Just before the turn of the century, when the northern provinces of the Netherlands were obliged to join the French bloc and change their name to the Batavian Republic, the taste for Dutch pictures had reached its apogee. For the past century contemporary taste in northern Europe had closely reflected French style in decoration, clothing, architecture, and a range of other areas, but collectors, including both the gentry and the middle classes, continued to prefer Dutch paintings, which constituted a large part of the works on the market. During the first decade of the new century, approximately 29 percent of the paintings sold publicly in France were Dutch; when combined with Flemish pictures, this figure rose to nearly 50 percent. Even in England, where Italian pictures could be more readily obtained, Dutch paintings – which accounted for approximately 25.4 percent of the market during the same decade – were among those bringing the highest prices, especially during the period when the Prince Regent – the future George IV – was most active; this predilection did not change until well into the new century. Of course, Italian pictures, when available, were still recognized as the most valuable of all, but since outstanding examples only rarely came onto the northern market, Continental auction rooms were normally dominated by the more numerous Dutch works.

In order to cope with the volume of Dutch paintings, certain tools were developed to help collectors sort out the work of different Dutch artists and to put some order into the connoisseurship devoted to them. The most notable was the *Catalogue Raisonné of the Works of the most eminent Dutch, Flemish, and French Painters* of John Smith, the English picture dealer, which began to appear in 1829 and did not conclude until 1842. This remarkable series of volumes attempted to provide definitive lists and descriptions of all of the known paintings of 33 Dutch, as well as four Flemish and three French painters. Nothing comparable was attempted for Italian painters or those of any other country until almost the end of the century. Smith's choice of artists no doubt reflected his own preferences, and especially his need to buy and sell such works to earn a living, but it also mirrored the northern art market of that time. It must also be admitted that such a task was easier to perform when it involved cabinet-size paintings that were often signed and widely dispersed, rather than the larger canvases and panels from Italy or Spain, the bulk of which remained in their native countries. Smith's books were an amazing feat of connoisseurship, completely original in their time, and an incentive for collectors who liked to find their paintings mentioned in print in the company of other works by the same artist. These publications represented the early phase of the artist monograph.

The Dutch Art Market

By the end of the eighteenth century, London had already replaced Paris as the hub of the European art trade, a process accelerated by the disorder on the Continent caused by the French Revolution and then by two decades of intermittent war. The Dutch market, concentrated primarily in Amsterdam, had served for a century or more as one of the principal sources of pictures for both London and Paris; its volume of business consistently qualified it as the third largest market, marginally ahead of that of Belgium, although it exported a great deal more than it imported. During the first decade of the new century the number of paintings sold publicly in London was approximately three times the number that passed through Paris and nearly four times that of the Netherlands. However, the Dutch market differed from the other two in that it consisted almost exclusively of pieces produced within its own borders, whereas the British market, and to a lesser degree the French, was largely composed of works produced in other countries. This was partially owing to topography, since the Low Countries were less centrally placed than London or Paris for pan-European trade, but it also resulted from the enormous volume of pictures produced in the Netherlands, coupled with a very limited taste among the Dutch for the art of other countries. Only German collectors sometimes found it advantageous to sell their paintings in the Netherlands, since their own markets were scattered and much less developed. Moreover, German collections were composed primarily of Dutch and Flemish paintings, which could be sold most profitably in their country of origin.

Because so little was being imported, over the course of the next 150 years the Dutch market for older pictures would slowly atrophy, but at least during the first half of the century the popularity of modern – i.e., eighteenth- and early nineteenth-century – Dutch artists working in the tradition of the seventeenth century was great enough to replenish a significant portion of the works leaving the country. The works of later Dutch painters never reached the same level of appreciation on foreign markets that the earlier paintings had achieved, and relatively few were ever exported, but their success with local collectors was considerable, and at local auctions they came to replace the older, more prized works that were being exported. Nonetheless, the enormous number of pictures produced during the seventeenth century was sufficient to feed a thriving market for many generations to come, albeit on a steadily decreasing scale.

Of course the years 1801–1810 cannot be considered typical for the history of collecting or the art market in Europe or the Netherlands because of the wars and reciprocal blockades that disrupted normal trade during this time. The French attempt to interdict all trade between the Continent and the British Isles was never entirely successful, largely because both French and British entrepreneurs were able to route their wares through the Netherlands which, though under French control, was less inclined to enforce the regulations than its French counterparts. Even incorporation into the French empire, accompanied in 1806 by the advent of a French king, Napoleon's younger brother Louis Bonaparte, did not alleviate the problem. The new king, just 28 years old when he ascended the throne, was admirably altruistic in his approach to his new subjects and was not inclined to do anything that would harm their commerce. He also bolstered the art market by making a number of expensive purchases at public auction of paintings intended for a new Royal Museum in Amsterdam, the eventual nucleus of the Rijksmuseum. As a result, the market remained active, and in spite of lessened trade with the British, especially during 1807 and 1808, the strong demand for Dutch pictures in France continued much as before.

Amsterdam had already become the center of the Dutch art market during the seventeenth century, and its dominance had only become more pronounced in the meantime. During the decade in question, 63, or nearly one-third, of the 179 sales for which catalogues have survived were held in Amsterdam. These sales were not only the most numerous, but also the longest, offering the largest number of objects. The second most active venue was The Hague, where 33 sales are recorded. Only one other city, Rotterdam, where 16 sale catalogues are still extant, deserves mention. (Although 25 sales are recorded at Middelburg, these were almost all book sales with very few pictures.) At this time, collections were as a rule sold in or near the city where they had been formed, and most of those sold in Amsterdam were from that city. But whenever a collection was judged important enough to warrant moving to a larger market, it was generally brought to Amsterdam.

With a few exceptions, such as the Gerrit van der Pot sale held in Rotterdam in 1808, virtually all of the most important and successful sales were held in Amsterdam by a group of dealers usually led by Philippus van der Schley (1724–1817). Most of these sales (37) were held in the so-called Trippenhuis, or Huis van Trip, at the Kloveniersburgwal, the premises of the dealer Cornelis Sebille Roos (1754–1820), another of the dealers who regularly participated in organizing the sales and whose annotated catalogues have been preserved at the Rijksbureau voor Kunsthistorische Documentatie in The Hague.

The dealers working with Van der Schley and Roos generally included Jan Yver (1747–1816), Jeronimo de Vries (1776–1853), Bernardus de Bosch Jeronimozoon II (1742–1816), Jan de Bosch Jeronimozoon (dates unknown), and Roelof Meurs Pruyssenaar (d. ca.1804). Members of the younger generation included Jacobus Vinkeles (dates unknown) and Theodorus Franciscus Spaan (1780–1811). Except for the latter, who died young, all of these men had long careers in the Amsterdam art market and seem to have functioned as a closely knit group, dominating the auctions during the late eighteenth century and well into the next. Many other dealers who were not involved in organizing sales, but whose names appear regularly as buyers, evidently kept very large stocks of paintings. After the death of Pierre Fouquet Jr. in 1800, the most active were Louis Bernard Coclers (1741–1817), Adriaan de Lelie (1755–1820), Matthias Ignatius van Iperen (1769–1822), Jan Hulswit (1766–1822), Willem de Gruyter Sr. (dates unknown), Jan Spaan (ca.1742–1828?), and François Jules Mensart (dates unknown). Besides this group, there were countless other dealers who dealt in less expensive, though sometimes numerous, pictures. A good example is Levy Pakker, who seems to have lived on the fringes of the market, buying large numbers of very cheap pictures, usually the uncatalogued or anonymous works found at the end of a catalogue. As in other major cities from the eighteenth century to the present, the buyers at auctions were almost exclusively such dealers, sometimes buying for others, but usually buying for stock to resell privately afterwards. This is especially true in Amsterdam, where one only rarely finds the name of a private collector buying for his own account.

The auctions in The Hague, dominated by booksellers, were generally very different. The most important auctioneers were Melis van Daalen Wetters (d.1803, succeeded by his son Pieter), Bernardus Scheurleer (1754–1828), Hendrik and Gerrit Bakhuysen (dates unknown), Johannes Immerzeel Jr. (1776–1841), and Frans Johannes Bosboom. The painter Dirk van der Aa (1731–1809) was also active in The Hague, but the most intriguing figure was a certain Teissier, probably the painter and restorer Jean George Teissier (1750–1821), whose name appears in a variety of forms. The Parisian dealer Jean-Baptiste-Pierre Lebrun used the firm Texier, Gerbet et Comp. to bid on his behalf at the important Smeth van Alphen sale in Amsterdam in 1810 as well as at a number of other lesser auctions, and it is thought that this firm's name referred to Teissier as well. It is not clear why Lebrun would use a relatively obscure painter/dealer from The Hague to bid for him in Amsterdam, but perhaps he preferred someone not so closely associated with the Amsterdam market and therefore less likely to have conflicting interests.

Although it held relatively few sales, the major auctioneering firm in Rotterdam was that of the Van Rijp brothers, who were responsible for the Gerrit van der Pot auction in 1808. This partnership consisted of Gerardus Constantinus van Rijp (1773–1815) and Petrus Eliza van Rijp (1775-?), the sons of Petrus Constantinus van Rijp, who managed the firm earlier. The presence in Rotterdam of major collectors, such as Van der Pot (1732–1807), Daniel de Jongh Adrszn. (1745–1809), and the Englishman George Craufurd (d.1809), indicates the vitality of the cultural life in that city, but this strength was not supported by an equally significant coterie of dealers. It is known that Van der Pot acquired his paintings in many places other than Rotterdam, including Amsterdam and Brussels; his chief supplier was the Brussels dealer Pieter Joseph Thijs. However, there were a few major dealers in Rotterdam, the best known of whom was probably the painter Willem van Leen of Delfshaven (1753–1825). Also based there were two younger dealers, namely a certain Dr. Luchtmans (identified by Ruud Priem as Dr. Cornelis Jan Luchtmans, 1777–1860), and the more elusive F.J. Noordwyck, whose dates are not known but whom contemporary sources describe as having sold primarily to the English (cf. R. van Eijnden and A. van der Willigen, *Geschiedenis der Vaderlandsche Schilderkunst*, III, 1820, p.481).

Imports and Exports

As mentioned earlier, relatively few paintings were imported to the Lowlands for sale; during the period in question only one sale is known to have included a significant number of items from a foreign collection. On September 7, 1803 and following days (cat. no.65), the paintings of an unidentified Cologne collector were sold in Amsterdam by Ph. van der Schley and his associates. The title page of the catalogue does not mention the collection's origins, but one copy is annotated with the name "Smidt de Cologne," and the existence of a French-language version printed in Cologne substantiates this claim. "Smidt" has not been identified – he might conceivably have been the painter Johann Jacob Schmitz (1724–1810), although Schmitz is not known to have had a collection of pictures – but his cabinet, consisting of numerous inexpensive Dutch, Flemish, and German landscapes and genre scenes, was in many ways typical of the sort formed during the eighteenth century in Germany. The political situation may have played a role in the owner's decision to send his possessions to Amsterdam to sell, but at this date it is more likely that simple economics determined the choice.

The collection was altogether unremarkable and prices were generally modest. A total of 82 lots were left unsold, including most of those knocked down for more than fl. 100. These unsold paintings were then taken to Paris, where they appeared in a sale held on February 22, 1808, organized by the expert Charles Elie. The latter upgraded many of the artists' names and may have succeeded in making the collection more attractive, since the prices at the second sale were generally higher than at the first. However, we do not know whether the later prices were genuine, and very few of the paintings can be traced.

One other sale, which included works of greater importance than those belonging to "Smidt," may have derived from a German collector, but there is proof that at least some of the pieces had never left the Netherlands. On June 16, 1802 (cat. no.34) Van der Schley and his colleagues auctioned a collection said to be the property of a "Buitenlands Kunst-Liefhebber." It can be demonstrated that some of these paintings had been acquired at recent Amsterdam auctions by a certain "Merrem," who was most probably of German origin. Since the sale included a large number of paintings, most of which cannot be traced to earlier auctions, it is possible that they had been brought to Amsterdam to be sold along with those that probably never left the city. There is, however, no firm proof of this supposition.

The presence of foreigners who came to the Netherlands to buy paintings is much easier to document. Some, such as the English banker George Craufurd, lived there for extended periods, but most were dealers, primarily French, who came only to attend the sales before returning home. The most successful of these was undoubtedly Pierre-Joseph Lafontaine, who made numerous excursions to the Lowlands, purchasing some of the most expensive pictures, which he then took either to Paris or to London for resale. The boldest of these forays was on the occasion of the Pieter de Smeth van Alphen sale in 1810 (cat. no.167). Apparently bidding by himself for some lots, but using two Dutch dealers, Wessel Rijers and Theodorus Spaan, to bid for others, Lafontaine bought a total of nine lots costing an astonishing fl. 68,000. (One further item, a landscape by Hobbema costing fl. 3250, was purchased by Lafontaine but conceded to his rival J.-B.-P. Lebrun after the sale.) Six of the most expensive, including Rembrandt's famous *Shipbuilder and His Wife*, were then taken to London, where they were sold en bloc in 1811 to the Prince of Wales, remaining in the Royal Collection to the present day. Thus Lafontaine's gamble ultimately proved very profitable, although he cannot have known in advance that Wales would agree to such an extravagance.

Similar buying trips were made by Lebrun, who also bought a large number of paintings at the De Smeth van Alphen sale, albeit at less lavish prices. These were promptly taken back to Paris where they were put up at auction in 1811 at one of Lebrun's own sales. This type of enterprise, however, belonged to an old tradition, followed since the mid-eighteenth century by numerous French dealers who strived to satisfy the insatiable demand for Dutch pictures in their homeland.

Many Dutch dealers also profited from the same kind of trade during the period in question. An early example is the purchase by the Dutch dealer L.B. Coclers of 26 paintings at the sale of Herman ten Kate's collection in Amsterdam on June 10/11, 1801 (cat. no.10). Most of these pictures were taken to Paris, where they appeared at auction under Coclers' own name a little more than two months later. Of the Dutch dealers, Coclers seems to have been the most ambitious in this type of trade. At the same time he was buying the Ten Kate paintings, he was also involved in a still larger undertaking, acquiring for 54,000 francs a group of 44 paintings that composed the important Amsterdam cabinet of Hendrik van Eyl Sluyter and exporting the entire group to Paris for resale on January 25/28, 1802 (see B. Peronnet and B. Fredericksen, *Répertoire des tableaux vendus en France au XIXe siècle*, I, 1998, no.19). The prices realized at this sale were generally impressive and the entire transaction seems to have been profitable, although we do not know how many of the paintings were left unsold. Coclers was also instrumental in another comparable scheme concerning the paintings belonging to Diderick, baron van Leyden. With two French associates, J.-A. Paillet and A.-L.-C.-H.-T. de Lespinasse de Langeac, he purchased the entire collection of 167 paintings in Amsterdam and put them up for sale in Paris on November 5/8, 1804 (Peronnet and Fredericksen, idem., no.80). Although the paintings were less choice than the collection of Van Eyl Sluyter, prices were equally good. However, many of the lots may have been left unsold. As far as we know, this was the last large-scale speculation Coclers undertook, perhaps because gambles of this kind had ceased being profitable enough to justify the risk.

Two further Dutch collections were sold in Paris during the period in question, though neither represents the type of speculation described above. The enormous and varied collection of baron Pieter-Nicolaas van Hoorn van Vlooswyck (1742–1809), including a spectacular collection of sculpture and rare objects as well as paintings, was sold in Paris on November 22/December 7, 1809. However, the owner, originally a resident of Amsterdam, had moved with his collection to Paris at an earlier date and the collection was sold in his Paris residence, apparently not having been taken there expressly for sale. The final instance concerns the collection of a certain Amman de Schwanberg, said to be from The Hague, who is supposed to have taken his possessions to Paris for sale; the auction, which took place on December 19/22, 1809, seems to have been reasonably successful, although only one of the 154 paintings in the sale has so far been identified. There were certainly many smaller examples of this migration to France that have yet to be documented. With the English dealers effectively blocked for the moment from participating, the way was left open for French, Dutch, and Belgian dealers to take advantage of the reduced competition.

The Organization of Dutch Sales

The major Amsterdam sales often consisted of thousands of items, ranging from the very expensive to the very cheap. A typical sale catalogue began with a few hundred paintings, followed by large numbers of drawings, both individual and in portfolios, followed in turn by still larger numbers of prints and occasionally by groups of miscellaneous items. The catalogues for these sales were usually organized by artist's name in alphabetical order without separating the various schools. Often a second category of less valuable, usually anonymous, works followed the first, and numerous items were almost always added to the sale after the catalogue was printed. These were listed by hand at the back of the catalogues belonging to the dealers coordinating the sale, such as C.S. Roos, but were completely lacking in the copies given or sold to the public.

This manner of organizing the sale differs from sales held in smaller cities, where it was more common to put the most valuable pieces at the head of the sale, leaving the less important pieces to bring up the rear. The British generally did the opposite, beginning with the least valuable and finishing with the most costly, a practice often followed today. French catalogues were organized by school, and within the school sometimes by alphabet or genre. But the lots in large French sales were not sold in the order of the catalogue but rather in a more random order, with major works scattered throughout the length of the sales, which sometimes lasted many days. The precise order of the French sales was to be found on the *Feuille de Vacation*, a list often issued just prior to the sale. No such lists for Dutch sales are known, which suggests that the paintings were sold in the same order as the catalogue, i.e., in alphabetical order. This is surprising, since it seems to indicate that no attempt was made either to manipulate the sale in order to build to a climax or to group works that might benefit from being sold together. Moreover, the larger Amsterdam sale catalogues generally do not tell us how long the sales were expected to last, and although many must have taken at least a week or two to run their course, there is no indication of the day on which a given lot might be sold. Presumably an interested bidder was required to follow the sale's progress in order to be present at the right time.

Because so many catalogues annotated by auctioneers have been preserved, the organization of Dutch sales can be studied most profitably using Amsterdam as the model. The relatively large amount of documentation does not simplify the task, however, as it normally would in Britain or France whenever the auctioneer's or expert's records have been preserved. In England, proprietors simply consigned their items to an auctioneer, such as James Christie or Harry Phillips, who then marked each lot in his catalogue with the owner's name. French sales tended to include the possessions of fewer proprietors, but whenever the records of an expert, such as F.-L. Regnault-Delalande, have been found, they are annotated in very much the same manner. However, the fact that so many different dealers participated in organizing Dutch sales makes them much more difficult to unravel. As mentioned above, the major Amsterdam sales were sometimes organized by just two or three "makelaars," but more commonly by six or more. Each dealer kept his own record of the sale, annotating his catalogue with letters next to each lot indicating the consignment to which it belonged. These letters were sometimes the first initial of the proprietor's name, but at other times they were assigned arbitrarily beginning with the letter "A." Many sales contained between ten and twenty consignments. Usually one or more of the extant catalogues lists the distribution of the sale's receipts among the various consigners, and sometimes the consigners are identified by name. However, these names were often those of the dealers who organized the sales, and in many instances they clearly represented still other collectors whose names are usually not given. So in spite of the fact that a given lot might be marked with an "R," and "R" can be identified as C.S. Roos, Roos was not necessarily the owner. The actual names of the proprietors are much more difficult to determine, and as a result only a small percentage of the real owners have been identified.

The Paintings in Dutch Auctions

During the decade under discussion, a total of 17,245 paintings are recorded in Dutch sale catalogues. (This is, of course, not a definitive figure because an unknown number of catalogues have been lost altogether, numerous lots consisted of more than one item, and many paintings appeared two, three, or more times before finding a buyer. However, since the same limitations apply to the statistics from other countries, the figure can at least be used to make comparisons or to give a rough idea of the overall volume of the market.) Of this amount, 10,131 were by artists who are generally classified as Dutch. Since 4678 were either by anonymous or unidentified artists whose nationality cannot be determined, one may conclude that roughly 80 percent of all paintings sold at public auction in the Netherlands were by artists from that country.

As might be expected, paintings from the Flemish (or Belgian) school were the second most common, with a total of 1251 works. To these might be added the 34 pieces that have been categorized as Netherlandish, i.e., fifteenth- and sixteenth-century Flemish. The latter do not, however, constitute a significant example of the still undeveloped taste for so-called "primitives." Most were evidently minor works, and only one, a picture sold with the Smeth van Alphen collection to Louis Bonaparte for the Royal Museum in Amsterdam as the work of Hubert and Jan van Eyck, can be counted as significant. It is now recognized as one of the masterpieces of Geertgen tot Sint Jans and it remains an exceptional purchase for the period.

By comparison the numbers of paintings from other schools were hardly significant: German, 363; Italian, 335; French, 123; British, 42; and Spanish, 18. Only one Italian picture, an unidentified depiction of the *Baptism* by Veronese from the collection of the gravin van Moens, managed to exceed fl. 200. Most surprising, perhaps, is the sparsity of works from the French school, which one might have expected to be more in evidence, given the general prevalence of French taste and style in northern Europe during this period. While many Dutch citizens supported the principles of the French Revolution, their Francophilia did not extend to collecting French paintings. Moreover, almost all of the French pictures that one finds in the Netherlands were by, or attributed to, seventeenth- or eighteenth-century artists, such as Poussin, Valentin, C.-J. Vernet or Hubert Robert. Modern French works were found in the Lowlands only rarely, and British paintings were almost completely unknown. A large proportion of the pictures classified as such were still lifes by the Scot William Gowe Ferguson, who was, in fact, active most of his life in the Netherlands and worked in a Dutch style.

The profile of Dutch sales during the first decade of the century differs from those in Britain or France during the same period. The volume of pictures passing through British auction houses generally rose in spite of the wars, and by 1810 the number of pictures recorded in British sales had almost doubled. Not surprisingly, the French market followed a more erratic course, with very little activity during 1804–1805 and with a low point in 1807, only to rise spectacularly by the end of the decade, reaching a figure four times that of 1801. The Netherlands, as part of the French bloc, tended to mirror more closely the fortunes of the French market, so 1805 and especially 1807 were the worst years for the Dutch market as well. By the end of the decade numbers were again on the upswing, but although they generally matched those from the first years of the century, they showed no significant increase. Viewed as a whole, this period of conflict seems to have strengthened the British and French art trade while weakening the Dutch. A similar result is found in Belgium, whose market volume had been roughly comparable to, and only marginally smaller than, that of the Netherlands.

The count of pictures sold year by year in the Netherlands reads as follows:

1801	*1802*	*1803*	*1804*	*1805*	*1806*	*1807*	*1808*	*1809*	*1810*
1881	2965	1748	1894	993	1263	802	1901	1367	2430

Such statistics may, however, be as much the result of the unpredictable passing of major collectors as the war and the resulting economic up- and downturns. The list of major sales – i.e., all of those that realized at least fl.15,000 – reads as follows:

Pierre Fouquet Jr. sale, April 13/14, 1801 (cat. 6)
Circumstances: death of owner
Auctioneer and results: Van der Schley, etc., fl. 24,400 (including drawings and prints)

Herman ten Kate sale, June 10/11, 1801 (cat. 10)
Circumstances: death of owner
Auctioneer and results: Van der Schley, etc., fl. 26,514

Anonymous sale, October 6ff., 1801 (cat. 17)
Circumstances: unknown
Auctioneer and results: Van der Schley, etc., fl. 17,395 (of which fl. 12,289 were from paintings)

Merrem sale, June 16ff., 1802 (cat. 34)
Circumstances: death of owner
Auctioneer and results: Van der Schley, etc., fl. 18,152 (mostly paintings)

Maria Magdalena van Sluypwyk, Gravinne van Moens sale, April 20/21, 1803 (cat. 54)
Circumstances: death of owner
Auctioneer and results: Van der Schley, etc., fl. 15,004

Aarnoud de Lange sale, December 12, 1803 (cat. 70)
Circumstances: death of owner
Auctioneer and results: Van der Schley, etc., fl. 16,022 (includes drawings and prints, etc.)

Jan de Groot sale, December 10, 1804 (cat. 88)
Circumstances: death of owner
Auctioneer and results: Van der Schley, etc., fl. 28,531 (includes drawings and prints, etc.)

Gerard Godart Baron Taets van Amerongen sale, July 3, 1805 (cat. 93)
Circumstances: death of owner
Auctioneer and results: Van der Schley, etc., fl. 16,133

Munnikhuizen, et al. sale, November 24, 1806 (cat. 109)
Circumstances: unknown
Auctioneer and results: Van der Schley, etc., fl. 15,054 (includes mostly drawings and prints, etc.)

Gerrit van der Pot sale, June 6, 1808 (cat. 126)
Circumstances: death of owner
Auctioneer and results: Gebroeders Van Rijp, fl. 127,037

E.M. Engelberts sale, June 13/14, 1808 (cat. 128)
Circumstances: death of owner
Auctioneer and results: Van der Schley, etc., fl. 19,036 (mostly paintings)

J. B. Bicker and Wijkerslooth sale, July 19, 1809 (cat. 146)
Circumstances: held while owners were still active
Auctioneer and results: Van der Schley, etc., fl. 18,412

Daniel de Jongh sale, March 26ff., 1810 (cat. 156)
Circumstances: death of owner
Auctioneer and results: Robert Muys and Gebroeders Van Rijp, fl. 28,750 (mostly drawings and prints)

Pieter de Smeth van Alphen sale, August 1/2, 1810 (cat. 167)
Circumstances: death of owner
Auctioneer and results: Van der Schley, etc., fl. 161,999

As will be seen, all but two of these sales were organized in Amsterdam by Philippus van der Schley and his associates. The two exceptions, both of which were very successful, were held in Rotterdam by the Gebroeders Van Rijp. Since one of these Rotterdam sales, that of Gerrit van der Pot in 1808, produced one of the two highest results for this period, it does not appear that holding it in Rotterdam, the home of the proprietor, significantly impaired the results.

Although the Van der Pot auction was on a level apart from the majority of auctions and the most profitable since the sale in 1800 dedicated to Jan Gildemeesteer's collection (whose receipts came to an extraordinary fl. 167,141), it was superseded only two years later by the Smeth van Alphen sale, which broke many records and established a still higher scale for the prices of Dutch pictures. These two sales were by far the high points of the first years of the century; between them they produced all ten of the most expensive lots sold during this period. The lots fetching fl. 5000 or more from this time were as follows:

Anthonie van Dyck, *Christ Healing the Paralytic*
1810/08/01 (Pieter de Smeth van Alphen sale)
Bought by P.-J. Lafontaine for fl. 19,200
Now in the British Royal Collection

Gerrit Dou, *Night School*
1808/06/06 (Gerrit van der Pot sale)
Bought by Louis Bonaparte for the Royal Museum for fl. 17,500
Now in the Rijksmuseum, Amsterdam

Rembrandt, *Portrait of the Master Shipbuilder and His Wife*
1810/08/01 (Pieter de Smeth van Alphen sale)
Bought by P.-J. Lafontaine for fl. 16,500
Now in the British Royal Collection

Paulus Potter, *Herdsmen with their Cattle*
1808/06/06 (Gerrit van der Pot sale)
Bought by A.J. van Lennep for the Royal Museum for fl. 10,050
Now in the Rijksmuseum, Amsterdam

Jan Both, *Landscape with Baptism of the Eunuch*
1810/08/01 (Pieter de Smeth van Alphen sale)
Bought by P.-J. Lafontaine for fl. 10,000
Now in the British Royal Collection

Willem van de Velde, *Two Scenes from the Second Anglo-Dutch War*
1808/06/06 (Gerrit van der Pot sale)
Bought by Louis Bonaparte for the Royal Museum for fl. 8,000
Now in the Rijksmuseum, Amsterdam

Adriaen van de Velde, *Peasants and Cattle Reposing*
1810/08/01 (Pieter de Smeth van Alphen sale)
Bought by P.-J. Lafontaine for fl. 7,650
Now in the British Royal Collection

Adriaen van der Werff, *Holy Family*
1808/06/06 (Gerrit van der Pot sale)
Bought by A.A. Stratenus for the Royal Museum for fl. 5,225
Now in the Rijksmuseum, Amsterdam

Isack van Ostade, *Halt at an Inn*
1810/08/01 (Pieter de Smeth van Alphen sale)
Bought by J.-B.-P. Lebrun for fl. 5,050
Present location unknown

Adriaen van Ostade, *Peasant Interior with Family and Child*
1810/08/01 (Pieter de Smeth van Alphen sale)
Bought by P.-J. Lafontaine for fl. 5,000
Now in the British Royal Collection

This list gives us a fairly accurate idea of which types of pictures were most highly valued in the Netherlands during the first decade of the new century. Most were small cabinet-size pictures of genre subjects or landscapes by artists known and appreciated for a high degree of finish. Except for its religious theme, the picture by Adriaen van der Werff would also fit this description. The two obvious exceptions are the double portrait by Rembrandt, considered then, as now, one of the artist's most impressive works, and especially the canvas by Van Dyck, the only non-Dutch painting to reach this level, but nonetheless fetching the highest price. Because the buyer was a Frenchman who exported the picture to England, it might not be seen as an example of Dutch taste, but it had belonged to Smeth van Alphen, a Dutch collector, and so does serve to remind us that Dutch collectors were hardly averse to including the odd Flemish or Italian picture if the opportunity presented itself. Alas, major examples of the best Italian or Flemish artists, especially Rubens and Van Dyck, were not readily available. Smeth van Alphen's collection also included a painting by Rubens that, given the price it fetched – fl. 2700 – was apparently viewed as an unusually rare opportunity to acquire such a piece. It was bought by Lucretia Johanna van Winter and later came into the Six van Vromade collection with the rest of her paintings, eventually passing to the Rijksmuseum, where, however, it is now recognized as a work of Rubens' studio. The canvas by Van Dyck has fared better at the hands of modern criticism and is still recognized as an authentic work by the master, though generally not ranked among his best works. Not having a wide range of paintings by such foreign masters to choose from, Dutch collectors were often led to overestimate the quality of those few that did appear.

Description of the Indexes

Index of Catalogues

This section lists every known sale that included paintings from the period 1801–1810 for which at least one catalogue has survived. (There are also a few for which the only recorded catalogue has been lost in recent years.) For each we have tried to include as much information in the entry as seemed potentially useful to the reader of this book. Because so many of the catalogues are not included in Lugt's *Répertoire des catalogues de ventes*, we have assigned original numbers – from 1 to 176 – and placed them in chronological order corresponding to the date on which the sale began.

Sale Dates

Immediately following the assigned number are given the starting and ending dates (if known) of the sale. In some cases the dates were changed, usually postponed, and it is not unusual to find the original printed dates on a catalogue struck through by hand and replaced by other dates. This means that not all copies of the catalogue will necessarily reflect the change. (And it is possible that a sale date was changed without any extant copy of the catalogue being so altered, which would probably cause the change to have escaped our notice.) However, whenever we were aware that a sale was postponed or changed, we adopted the date on which the sale finally took place, not the date for which it was first planned. This differs from Lugt's practice, and thus the order of the catalogues will occasionally differ from that in the *Répertoire*.

A few catalogues carry incomplete dates, lacking the day, but including the year and month. Unless some other clue could be found, we have listed these sales at the beginning of the period to which they belong. If, for example, a sale took place sometime in 1816, the entry will be found at the beginning of that year. If the sale took place sometime during May, 1816, it will be listed at the beginning of the entries for that month and year.

Lugt Number

Following the dates is the number assigned by Lugt to the sale, if it is included in his *Répertoire des catalogues de ventes*.

Auctioneer

The next lines record the auctioneer's name, rendered precisely as printed on the title page of the catalogue itself, and the location of the sale, either a public space used for such auctions or the residence of the owner, if the sale was held on the premises of the latter.

Sellers' Names

The next few lines list the sellers' names and their sources. The first category includes names printed on the catalogue. These are transcribed just as they appear on the title page, or, if the name is not given, we repeat whatever words were used by the auctioneer to describe the seller, such as "A gentleman, recently deceased." If there is no description whatsoever, we have stated "None." The second category gives the names of sellers identified from annotated auctioneers' catalogues, such as the set belonging originally to C.S. Roos and now kept at the Rijksbureau voor Kunsthistorische Documentatie in The Hague, if such a copy exists. The third category – which is also not present for every sale – gives sellers' names derived from other sources, either annotations from catalogues not belonging to auctioneers or through deductive methods of various kinds. The nature of these methods will always be explained in the Comments at the end of the entry, but we have assumed that it would be helpful to the reader to be able to ascertain at a glance the general source, and therefore the relative reliability, of the names used. A final line gives the complete authoritative form of the owners' names.

To explain this a bit further, the names printed on the title page are sometimes the only means we have of identifying the seller, but they are also the most unreliable for determining the owner of individual lots. That is to say, the name may apply to many or most of the lots in the sale, but it cannot be assumed to be correct for all of the lots since auctioneers often included works belonging to other owners whose names do not appear on the catalogue. Therefore, the reader should be cautious about assuming that names in this category which are not substantiated by an auctioneer's annotated copy in fact represent the actual seller of any given lot. We have generally used such names when giving the seller of individual paintings in the Index of Paintings by Artist because they are most often correct, but they cannot always be confirmed. If we have specific reason to believe that lots from other owners have been added into the sale, we have added the phrase "or others" after the name in the sellers column in the Index of Paintings by Artist.

Names taken from annotated auctioneers' catalogues can generally be assumed to be the most definitive for individual lots, and for this reason they have been separated from names derived from other sources. There are instances where information from other sources has proven to be more accurate than the auctioneer's record of the sale, but this is relatively rare.

Paintings Lots

The next item in the entry includes a count of the number of lots with paintings to indicate how large the sale was. Note that we have given the figure for paintings lots rather than the actual number of paintings. Lots often included two or more paintings, making it difficult to determine the total number of paintings in a sale.

Regarding our definition of a "painting," we have generally included any work described as a "Schildery" or "Tableau" unless the description clearly indicates the lot was something other than a painting, which we have defined as any picture painted in oil, whether on canvas, wood, glass, metal, or even paper. Today we would probably class most of the works on paper as drawings, but preferring to err on the side of caution, we have included them. Frescoes and paintings in distemper or tempera are also included, whereas paintings in watercolor, body color, gouache, and pastel, as well as enamels are excluded.

Miniature portraits are not included, as by modern definition they clearly constitute a separate category. Unfortunately, the catalogues of the time often do not distinguish between a miniature and a small painting. We have therefore generally restricted our definition of miniatures to portrait miniatures or small copies on ivory of famous paintings. We have tried to include any item, however, that appeared to be a small painting.

Catalogue Locations

Within the entry for each sale is found a list of all known extant copies of the catalogue, listed in the order of their importance. The catalogues at the top of the list are the best annotated, having the largest number of buyers and, secondarily, the most prices. Those at the bottom of the list have the fewest or no annotations at all.

At the left are listed the acronyms for the names of the institutions holding a copy of the catalogue and the cities in which they are located. Thus, CIL stands for Courtauld Institute, London, and RKDH for Rijksbureau voor Kunsthistorische Documentatie, Den Haag. The acronyms follow, so far as possible, those used by Lugt in his *Répertoire*. For institutions not found in his lists we have invented new ones following the same principles. A complete list of the acronyms used in this volume will be found on pp. xxii–xxiii.

An asterisk (*) appears next to the catalogues from which we have taken the prices. We have generally chosen one or two copies we regard as the most reliable – often the auctioneer's copy – because it is not feasible to reconcile the prices given in every extant copy of the catalogue.

In each instance we also record the nature of that catalogue's annotations and the name of the annotator, if known. Sometimes we are only able to say who owned the catalogue – owners' names are often written on their catalogues – without being certain whether that person was also the annotator. It was also a common practice of antiquarians and dealers to mark sets of catalogues at a later date, copying the information from other catalogues to which they had access. Therefore it is not always safe to assume that the annotator was also the original owner of the catalogue.

We have usually taken the names of buyers (and sometimes sellers) from the first copies on the list. However, for any given lot we have used the annotation with the most complete or authoritative form of a buyer's or seller's name, sometimes taking it from a less extensively annotated catalogue. For instance, the RKDH copy of a catalogue may list the buyer of a lot as "Burgrave," but if the EBNP copy gives it as "Burggraaff" – which is the preferred spelling – we have used that instead. If a third copy gives the buyer's first name, or an address as well, then we have preferred that one. A more extensive explanation of these procedures follows under the headings "Buyers" and "Sellers" in the section describing the Index of Paintings by Artist below.

Photocopies

We have also included a list of those institutions owning photocopies of original catalogues belonging to other libraries. We have indicated the location of the original whenever possible. It should be noted that the Provenance Index has photocopies of almost all of the catalogues – sometimes four or more different versions – including many of the annotated copies. We have not included our own photocopies in these lists because they are too numerous.

Comments

Finally, each sale entry concludes with a discussion of the nature of the sale and any relevant information that is not apparent from the title page. This may include speculation about the sellers' identities, the provenance of the paintings, subsequent sales in which groups of pictures reappeared, prices fetched at the sale and indications about the quality of the pictures.

Index of Paintings by Artist

The heart of this book is the listing of individual paintings sold during the period 1801–1810, indexed alphabetically by the name of the artist. In this volume there are 17,245 entries altogether.

A general note about the organization of this section is needed because of the problems inherent in rendering information from a wide variety of catalogues printed and composed in many different styles into a consistent and intelligible automated form. No program could duplicate precisely the pages as found in the catalogues because the catalogues themselves are disconcertingly inconsistent in format. The catalogues may list the artist's name above the lot, or at the end the title, etc., and we have not attempted to imitate these variations. All of the catalogues have been put into a consistent and uniform style.

Artist's Name

All paintings included in the *Corpus* are listed under the form of the artist's name which has come to be most accepted. In general, our usage agrees with *BHA* (*Bibliography of the History of Art*), but a variety of source books have been utilized to obtain the most authoritative spelling.

In cases where the catalogue does not provide the first name or initial of the artist and he or she belonged to a family of artists all having the same last name, we cannot always supply the full name. An example is the van Ostade family, for whom we have works listed under Ostade as well as Adriaen van Ostade and Isack van Ostade. In other instances we have assumed the identity of the intended family member. An example is Cuyp. It is likely that all references to "Cuyp" refer to Aelbert Cuyp rather than Benjamin or Jacob Gerritsz., both of whom were less well known. Unless the subject of the painting seems inappropriate for Aelbert alone, we have tended to put it under his name. To avoid propagating errors based on mistaken assumptions, we have included the form of the name exactly as given in the catalogue (see below under Verbatim Name of the Artist) in italics at the head of each title so the reader may compare and judge whether our identification is correct.

The principle guiding our choice of an artist's name was that of wanting to determine which artist the compiler of the catalogue had in mind, not necessarily the artist who painted the picture. In order to do this, we have referred to artists dictionaries which were in use at the time. From these sources we hoped to determine how much the compilers knew or thought they knew about each artist. Their understanding of the artists and their oeuvres at the beginning of the century was sometimes based upon erroneous tradition. However, with few exceptions we have not tried to correct the attributions. For example, pictures now known to be by Jacob Duck were at the time commonly attributed to Jacques Le Ducq, who was incorrectly assumed to be the same artist. Although the name is occasionally spelled in catalogues as "Le Duck," most often it is written as "Le Ducq," and we have assigned all pictures by artists of both names to Le Ducq because Jacob Duck was not known to the compilers.

Similarly, a "Moonlight Scene" attributed to E. (i.e., Eglon) van der Neer may be assumed to be by Aert van der Neer since Eglon did

Sample Entry

[1] **Rembrant Harmensz. van Rijn (manner)**

[2] 1810/[3] 07/[4] 23 [5] DO[6] LGI [7] 0073	[8] *Rembrandt* | [9] Twee stuks, een Sultan en Sultane, halver lijfs. Zeer uitvoerig en kunstig behandeld, in de manier, en als van Rembrandt, gem. Anno 1641 | [10] *This Lot:* Een Sultan, halver lijf [11] *Annots:* médiocre [12] (EBNP) [13] *Mat:* op koper [14] *Fmt:* ovaal [15] *Size:* ieder hoog 6 duim, breed 4 duim [16] *Inscr:* Anno 1641 (dated) [17] *Notes:* Lots 73 and 74 were printed in the catalogue as one item. [18] *Loc:* Paris, France. Private collection.	[19] Mr Pieter van den Santheuvel	[20] (Sold) [21] fl 3 for lots 73 & 74. [22] Strij [or] H

1 Artist	**7** Lot Number	**13** Materials	**19** Seller
2 Year	**8** Artist's Name from Catalogue	**14** Format	**20** Transaction
3 Month	**9** Title	**15** Size	**21** Price
4 Day	**10** Title Modifier	**16** Inscription	**22** Buyer
5 City Code	**11** Annotations	**17** Notes	
6 Auctioneer's Code	**12** Source of Annotation	**18** Present Location	

not paint moonlight scenes. However, we have not corrected these errors. Only in blatant instances of misattribution have we added a note to indicate the error. On the other hand, if the artist of the moonlight scene were given as "R. van der Neer" – an artist who does not exist – we have assumed this to be a typographical error and have listed the painting under Aert van der Neer. Mistakes of this kind have not been incorporated into the *Corpus*, because spelling and typographical errors were common and preserving them would have produced a bewildering proliferation of lists of pictures by nonexistent artists. Nevertheless, to reiterate, the form of the name as it is appears in the catalogue is retained in each entry and will be found in italics preceding the title.

There is at least one other notable exception to our practice of retaining the original attribution. This is the list of pictures by David Teniers the Younger. At the beginning of the nineteenth century there was a firm belief that the enormous number of pictures we now associate only with the younger David Teniers could in fact be divided between the elder and younger Teniers, and that their styles were readily distinguishable. Numerous paintings were accordingly attributed to each artist. Modern scholarship has shown that David Teniers the Elder did not paint genre scenes in the style of his son but rather was a painter whose style derived from Elsheimer and whose rare pictures were primarily landscapes with religious themes. We concluded that it would serve no real purpose to maintain the distinction between the elder and younger Teniers' works, not least because it would have resulted in three lists, one for each artist and another for the many pictures for which the catalogue did not specify either the father or the son.

It should be noted that paintings by two or more artists working together are not intermixed in the lists of each of those artists' paintings, but rather are found in separate lists where the two names are combined. For instance, paintings by both Jacob van Ruisdael and Adriaen van de Velde will appear twice, once following the list of works by Ruisdael and again following that of Van de Velde, but never intermixed. In fact all modified attributions, such as "school," "copy after," "manner," etc., are found in separate lists following the works given without qualification to that artist. That is to say, all of the pictures from the school of Rubens will be listed together following the pictures by Rubens himself.

Sale Date, Sale Code, and Lot Number

As will be quickly seen, our date format differs from that in other indexes in that the year is given first, followed by the month and then the day. This choice was made because dates listed chronologically are easier to scan in this style.

The date, given in the left column, is whenever possible the exact date on which the painting was put up for sale. For auctions, as opposed to other kinds of sales, this presents no difficulties. If a painting was sold on the third day of a sale that began on February 10, the sale date recorded for that painting in the *Corpus* is February 12.

The four- or five-character code that follows the date, when combined with the date itself, is meant to help establish a unique identifier for each sale. The first two letters are an abbreviation for the city where the sale took place (most often AM for Amsterdam) and the next two or three stand for the auctioneer (for example, SCH for Van der Schley). Each auctioneer has a unique code. Lists of codes for auctioneers and locations may be found on pp. xxiv–xxv. If an auctioneer held two sales on the same day, we have added the number "1" to the code for the earlier sale and the number "2" to the code for the later one (e.g., AMSCH2).

In the third column from the left, following the sale date and code, is the lot number. To facilitate computerized sorting they are given in four digits. If the number originally had just two digits, two aughts are added so that, for example, 24 would appear as 0024.

Yet another variation in the lot numbers in this *Corpus* occurs when items needed to be inserted in the catalogue after the original numbering had already been set. Such lots were often introduced into the numbering by repeating the number of the previous lot and adding an "a" or "bis." We have substituted the letter "a" for "bis."

We have normally split lots containing two or more paintings into separate entries and have added a letter in brackets following the lot number in order to distinguish them as multiple parts of one lot. For example, if lot 24 contained three paintings with three different artists, they would be numbered 0024[a], 0024[b], and 0024[c]. However, if all of the paintings in the lot are by the same artist and have the same title – e.g., *Two landscapes by Dughet* – we have left them together.

If a lot has been added by hand to the catalogue, we have appended an "[H]" (for handwritten) to the lot number. Thus, if a printed catalogue contained 94 lots, and a 95th lot containing two paintings has been added by hand at the end of the catalogue, they would be numbered 0095[a][H] and 0095[b][H] in this *Corpus*.

In a very few instances, a catalogue will have more than one set of numbers, each beginning with the number one. In this case we have placed a letter – i.e., "A", "B", "C", "D" or "E" – before each number in the second and following sets to distinguish them from the first.

Finally, there are occasional instances of catalogues – usually of book dealers' stock – in which the lots are not numbered at all. For these we have had to assign lot numbers, and they are denoted by brackets (e.g., [0001]).

Verbatim Name of the Artist

The wide column in the middle of the page begins with the name of the artist as it is given in the catalogue, in what we refer to as the "verbatim" form. This appears in our *Corpus* in italics. Whenever the catalogue has used the word "dito," "id.," or "denzelven" in place of the artist's name, we have repeated the name to which they refer. And if no artist's name is given, we have designated the artist as "[Anonymous]." (Anonymous pictures described as "anticq" or "antique" are termed by us "[Anonymous-Antique]." Pictures called "modern" in the catalogue are assigned as "[Anonymous-Modern]" in this *Corpus*.)

Title

Vertical bars enclose the title of the work and separate it from the verbatim artist's name which precedes it and any other information relating to the lot which follows. The title has been copied almost always exactly as it appears in the catalogue, including typographical errors and misspellings. It should be emphasized that the title as defined here includes everything written about the painting in the catalogue; we have not excluded (except in rare cases of unreasonable length) the sometimes extensive verbiage meant to raise a potential buyer's perception of the painting's value. This occasionally contains information on the artist, the subject, or something about the provenance, etc. As exceptions to this we have extracted dimensions and lengthy inscriptions from the main body of the title and listed them separately following the labels "Size" and "Inscr" (for both of which see below). An example of additions to the original title is the use of bracketed words to explain the meaning of "Dito." This word is frequently used in sale catalogues to avoid repeating words or phrases from the preceding lot. Since our *Corpus* is organized alphabetically by artist and does not necessarily list the paintings in lot number order, we have inserted into the title, in brackets, the words that were meant to be repeated.

There are a few instances in which information from extraneous sources has been inserted into the title. One of the more usual occurs when information about two or more lots – either pendants or pictures from a series sharing a common provenance – is printed in just one of the lots. In this case we have repeated the information in brackets in each pertinent lot and given the source in the Notes at the end of the entry. All of these additions should be self-explanatory.

For lots including two or more titles we have repeated all of the titles in each entry. This permits the reader to see everything the lot contained. We have also preserved an artist's name embedded in the text so that the reader can better understand the basis for our decisions where authorship is in question. Since each entry is restricted to just one painting, it is necessary to specify which of the works included in a multiple picture lot is the subject of the entry at hand. This is indicated by the "Title Modifier." (See the following section.) The end of the title is marked by a vertical line when it is followed by other categories of information.

Title Modifier

This segment includes information that explains some aspect of the title. The title modifier is most commonly used to specify which title in a compound lot is the one by the artist under which it is listed; such a note is signalled by the words "This Lot," which introduce the title of the picture in question. For example:

1810/10/11 AMSCH 0258[a] *H. Zagtleven* | Drie Stuks, twee Rijngezigten, door H. Zagtleven en een Landschapje door Everdingen | *This Lot*: Twee Rijngezigten; lot 258[b] by A. Everdingen

Any references to pendants or companion pictures are also recorded in this section. This information is always taken from the catalogue itself and is repeated here primarily to facilitate easy reference. The catalogues often indicate pendants in only one of the two lot entries, usually the second listed.

We do not indicate that a painting has a companion or is part of a pair unless it is specifically stated in the catalogue. In many instances it could be correctly assumed that two pictures, either consecutive lots or two parts of the same lot, by the same artist with related subjects – e.g., "Een Herder" and "Eene Herderin," or "Een Mans Pourtrait" en "Een Vrouwe Pourtrait" – were indeed pendants, but in keeping with our policy of avoiding editorializing, we have resisted the temptation to link them, and readers will be obligated to notice the connection themselves.

If the paintings in compound lots are by different artists, the title modifier for each is also used to record the names of the other artists. Excepting those with pendants, compound lots normally contained minor or less valuable paintings, and their association as parts of a single lot was often completely arbitrary. Nevertheless, the reader may want to know what other paintings were sold as part of the same lot. This information also tells the reader what other material was included in the quoted purchase price.

Whenever appropriate, the title modifier is also used to record the fact that the painting in question was called a copy by one artist after another.

Annotations (abbreviated Annots)

Handwritten annotations found in the catalogues have been included whenever we thought they would be useful in tracing or identifying the painting. In general we have retained any annotations that describe the paintings in more detail than the catalogue itself and those which give additional provenance information.

One type of annotation has been treated differently. Handwritten changes affecting the attribution or the lot's description have been treated as comparable to an author's alterations. If a clerk or some other person presumably acting on the firm's behalf has struck through the printed name of the artist and written in another, we have assumed the picture was sold as the work of the second artist. Similarly, a handwritten change in a title in an auctioneer's copy of the catalogue has been given precedence over the original printed one. We have also incorporated changes in instances in which no auctioneer's copy exists, but when certain copies of the catalogue seemed to reflect alterations made by the auctioneer at the time of the sale.

In cases where we have repeated an annotation we have also cited the copy of the catalogue from which it was taken. The acronyms identifying the source of these notes are the same as those used in the Index of Catalogues. A list of them appears on pp. xxii–xxiii.

Materials (abbreviated Mat)

Whenever the sale catalogue includes either the support (e.g., paneel, doek, koper, etc.) or the medium (e.g., olyverf, etc.) of a painting, it has been included in the materials section after the label "Mat."

Generally the information appears in the sale catalogue as part of the title, though many catalogues list such facts separately.

Format (abbreviated Fmt)

References in the catalogue to either the shape of the painting or its original function – such as an overdoor – have been included after the word "Fmt." These facts are almost always repeated from the title. In some instances the information is derived from a handwritten annotation or from a descriptive catalogue, and in the latter case the source is cited in the "Notes."

Size

As with materials, dimensions printed in the sale catalogue are extracted and appear after the label "Size." These are normally repeated exactly as given in the catalogue and have not been edited to put the height consistently first, or spell out "hoog," "breed," and "duimen." It should be noted that the Size section may include information extracted from handwritten annotations.

Inscriptions (abbreviated Inscr)

A few catalogues record inscriptions found on the paintings. Such notes have been repeated after the label "Inscr." Again, they are often derived from the title and therefore appear twice in the entry. In a few cases, we have excised very long inscriptions from the title, so that they appear only in the inscriptions section.

Notes

This section consists of miscellaneous comments explaining any item included in the entry. In general our notes explain anything that has been added, altered, or edited by us. They should be self-explanatory.

Present Location (abbreviated Loc)

Whenever we have been able to determine the present location of a given painting, we have included it following the label "Loc." This will normally include the name of the city (in the form used in that city) and the country (in the form used by the majority of the citizens of that country), followed by the name of the institution and the accession number. If the painting is now identified as the work of a different artist, or carries a different title, these are also given. We have generally not attempted to record the location of paintings in private collections.

Sellers

The names of the sellers of the paintings appear in the penultimate column in the Index of Paintings by Artist. They come primarily from two sources: the printed title pages of the sale catalogues and annotations made by the auctioneer or his clerk in their own catalogues. In addition we have obtained some sellers' names from contemporary inscriptions on individual catalogues, and a few have been arrived at through deduction.

Where no annotated set of auctioneers' catalogues has survived there is no authoritative source for the sellers' names. In general, only the sellers' names supplied by an auctioneer's annotated catalogue can be completely trusted. The names printed on the title page are not necessarily reliable, because it was common practice on the part of auctioneers to include the property of other owners in sales of pictures supposedly belonging to a single collector. The reader would be well advised, therefore, to check the Index of Catalogues to see whether the source for the seller is an auctioneer's copy. If the auctioneer's annotated copy is lacking, then the name may be suspect. The relative reliability of the sellers' names is often discussed in the Comments at the end of each entry in the Index of Catalogues.

If we had some reason to question whether a seller named on the title page of the catalogue was indeed the owner of the entire contents of the sale and the auctioneer's copy was lacking, we have added the qualifier "or others" in brackets after the name. This usually occurs when a few pictures in the sale can be traced definitively to some source other than the seller given on the title page. Again, the Comments in the Index of Catalogues explain the reasons for any such qualifications.

The names in the sellers column are given in their "verbatim" form, that is, exactly as they appear in the source. We have usually chosen the most complete – or what we believe to be the most accurate – version of the name available in the existing sources. (Names coming from the printed title page will correspond to those listed after "Seller(s) from Title Page" in the Index of Catalogues.) If the source is an annotation, the names are most often taken from the auctioneer's copy of the catalogue.

We have not edited or altered the form or spelling of the name except to drop the word "Heer" and periods after initials. If the best source available misspelled a name – giving, for example, "Sly" instead of "Schley" – we have retained the misspelling. However, the Index of Owners unites all transactions connected with a given collector under what we have determined to be the best spelling, and cross-references are provided for the variations.

One other form of editing has also been employed. Occasionally, the seller's name is given as a single letter, for instance "R." Whenever we can be certain that this refers to a particular name, such as "Rijfsnijder," we have supplied the missing letters in brackets: "R[ijfsnijder]." We have chosen this course to avoid confusion in the Index of Owners since "R" sometimes refers to more than one person.

In a few instances, conflicting annotations list different sellers for a given lot. Or, more commonly, a catalogue may have two sellers' names printed on the title page without specifying which lots belonged to each person. In those cases we have been obliged to include both names for each lot, joined by "[or]" or "[and]."

Transactions

The final column contains three kinds of information: the transaction, the price (if known), and the buyer (if known). The transaction may be one or a combination of four types: Sold, Bought In, Withdrawn, or Unknown. (Whenever catalogues suggested two conflicting transactions, both are given.) If we had no conclusive evidence to indicate what transpired, we have designated the transaction as "Unknown."

It is important to explain what the terms in the transaction field signify and how we have arrived at them. As applied in the present *Corpus* they have varying degrees of reliability and the reasons for using them differ from sale to sale. As always, the auctioneers' catalogues provide us with the most dependable information about what was sold and what was bought in. Their annotated copies are interleaved with lined pages upon which the clerk or the auctioneer recorded the price and buyer of each lot. If the painting was sold, the figure was placed in a column which could be added up at the bottom. Sometimes running totals appear at the top and bottom of each page. If a painting failed to sell, the final bid was placed outside the column, usually to the right, and the amount was not included in the sale's total receipts.

However, the presence of a price in the column of sale results does not guarantee that a picture was actually sold. There are numerous cases of pictures which are recorded by the auctioneer as having been sold but were in fact bought in. Sometimes other marks in the auctioneer's own catalogues note this, such as check marks by certain lots.

It is not uncommon for an auctioneer to record the price of a picture, putting the sum in the proper column, but leaving off the buyer's name. In such cases we record the picture as "Sold," unless there is some reason to question the outcome.

In the case of sales for which no auctioneer's catalogue has survived, another set of guidelines has been followed. If a buyer's name is given in any of the annotated copies of the catalogue, we have designated the picture as having been sold. Obviously, for the reasons given above, one cannot assume on this basis that the picture was indeed sold. We have made this choice in order to avoid confusing the reader by recording a buyer for a transaction given as "Unknown." (We do not, by the same token, record the fictitious buyers whose names are given for pictures bought in. Nor do we record highest bidders.) In other words, we have quoted the most reliable source available to us.

In all cases we have recorded the selling price – if one is known – no matter whether the picture was sold or bought in, on the assumption that it is invariably useful to know at what price a picture was knocked down, even if no one actually bought it. This figure is a gauge of the picture's importance and helpful in linking it to other sales. But we do not regard the presence of a price in a sale catalogue as proof that a picture actually sold. In other words, if an annotated catalogue other than the auctioneer's copy gives only a price and no buyer, we have listed the price but recorded the transaction as "Unknown."

Finally, we have taken as our sources only the catalogues themselves. If a buyer is recorded for a picture – and none of the other extant catalogues contradict it – we have designated the picture as "Sold" even when it reappears in a later sale belonging to the same owner. That is to say, we have not used any deductive process as a method of determining whether a picture was in fact sold or not.

Prices

For some of the major sales as many as a half dozen or more catalogues have survived that are thoroughly marked with prices. A comparison among them will always show minor – and sometimes even major – discrepancies. We have not attempted to reconcile these differences; instead we have followed the most authoritative catalogue (or catalogues), usually the auctioneer's copy, if it exists. In any case, the copies from which the prices were taken are marked with an asterisk (*) in the Index of Catalogues.

Buyers

The buyers' names are listed after the transaction and price in the final column in the Index of Paintings by Artist. Much of what has been said about the sellers is also true of the buyers. Of course, the printed title page is never a source for buyers; all of the names in this field are taken from annotations, or in just a few cases from published sources.

As with the sellers, buyers' names are repeated "verbatim," that is, as given in at least one annotated copy of the catalogue. If the name exists in several copies of the catalogue, we have chosen the most complete annotation or what we consider to be the most accurate spelling. However, if none of the catalogues provide us with the correct form of a name that is otherwise well known to us, we have resisted the temptation to change it.

As before, the names have been edited as little as possible, deleting only "Heer." In rare cases when only an initial is given, such as "R," we have sometimes supplied the remainder of the name in brackets, for example "R[ijfsnijder]," for the reasons explained under Sellers' Names, and if we were reasonably certain who was intended.

Commonly two different copies of a catalogue will give conflicting buyers. Sometimes the discrepancy is due to the fact that one buyer was representing the other, and one annotator, being aware of this, recorded the fact while the other did not. But more often one of the two annotators was simply mistaken. If we could not determine which was accurate, we included both names. This type of error sometimes occurred when the annotator accidently misaligned the names with the lots, putting a series of names one lot out of place. We have kept a record of the buyers' annotations in most copies of the catalogue, and by matching them we are usually able to pinpoint the error and what caused it.

We have not attempted to indicate which catalogue served as the source for any given annotation or why one source was chosen over another, believing that this would have rendered the *Corpus* clumsy and confusing to use. Readers wanting to know the source for the buyer of a given lot that cannot be ascertained from the Index of Catalogues can obtain the information from the compilers. We trust most readers will be content to know that the evidence is available on request if needed.

Index of Owners

This section lists all references to pictures bought or sold by a given owner under the most complete and authoritative form of the owner's name. The fullest entries include both the owner's first and last names, any titles, life or activity dates, and a brief description of the owner's profession, if known. The barest entries offer only an initial, presumably standing for the last name of an owner whom we have been unable to identify.

It will be remembered from the previous discussion that the sellers' and buyers' names cited in the Index of Paintings by Artist are recorded in their verbatim form, just as they appear printed on the catalogue or written in an annotation. These are, therefore, more likely to be misspelled or incomplete than the form given in the Index of Owners. To facilitate finding the "authoritative" form of the name in the Index of Owners from the "verbatim" form, there are cross-references for every variant of each name found in the buyers and sellers columns in the Index of Paintings by Artist.

In order to limit the size of the Index of Owners, we have given only the name of the artist of each picture bought or sold, and the date on which the sale took place. We have not included lot numbers or titles, nor have we indicated the number of pictures by the same artist bought or sold at the same sale by a given owner. It would have been desirable to indicate in this index which pictures were bought and which sold, and also which were by the artist and which were considered copies, or in the manner of the artist. Unfortunately, this has proved too difficult to achieve.

Index of Previous Owners

Many sale catalogues include information on the provenance of individual lots, usually referring to prominent collectors of the previous century. These references are sometimes incomplete or vague, and in a few cases they are clearly false. Their inclusion in this index should not be taken as confirmation of the provenance. As in the index devoted to the buyers and sellers at the sales, the information has been abbreviated for reasons of space. It includes only the name of the collector in its most authoritative form, followed by a list of the transactions (indicated by artist and sale date) where that name appears, either in the printed catalogue or in a handwritten annotation to that catalogue. We have not included references from later sources.

Material not Included in the Printed Index

Excluded from the present volume is any information concerning the subsequent provenance of the individual paintings – except when it is mentioned in handwritten annotations or when their present location in known. The Provenance Index staff has traced many of the paintings to subsequent sales, and as can be seen in the Comments on sales in the Index of Catalogues, many paintings already appear two or more times within a given half-decade. Failing to sell once, they were reoffered until they found a buyer, or the buyer at one sale may have attempted to realize a quick profit by putting the painting up for sale again shortly after having acquired it. This book makes no attempt to point out these links, because this type of information will continually be expanded and is subject to constant change.

In November, 1996, an automated version of this *Corpus* was made available commercially on compact disc (CD-ROM) along with other databases compiled by the Provenance Documentation Collaborative. (These consist of indexes to archival documents, primarily inventories of private collections of the seventeenth and eighteenth centuries, in Italy, Spain and the Netherlands, as well as paintings found in British sale catalogues for the years 1801–1825 and in French sale catalogues for 1801–1810.) The material from Dutch catalogues was not yet fully edited at that time, but the CD-ROM does offer the reader much more flexible searching options, as well as a few fields absent in this book, such as previous and subsequent provenance, if known. A new updated edition of the CD is planned for the Summer of 1999.

Catalogue Location Abbreviations

AA	Société Arti et Amicitiae, Amsterdam, Nederland
AAP	Bibliothèque d'Art et d'Archéologie, Paris, France
AKW	Akademie der bildenden Künste, Wien, Österreich
AMA	Gemeentearchief, Amsterdam, Nederland
AMH	Gemeentearchief, Den Haag, Nederland
AMR	Gemeentearchief, Rotterdam, Nederland
BG	Centrale Bibliotheek, Rijksuniversiteit, Gent, Belgique
BHm	Stadsbibliotheek, Haarlem, Nederland
BMB	Bibliothek der Staatlichen Museen, Berlin, Deutschland
BML	British Library, London, England, UK
BMPL	British Museum, Print Room, London, England, UK
BNP	Bibliothèque Nationale, Département des Imprimés, Paris, France
BPG	Bibliothèque Publique et Universitaire, Genève, Schweiz
BR	Bibliotheek, Rotterdam, Nederland
BRB	Bibliothèque Royale, Bruxelles, Belgique
CCPP	Service de Documentation, Compagnie des Commissaires-Priseurs de Paris, Paris, France
EBNP	Cabinet des Estampes, Bibliothèque Nationale, Paris, France
ESP	Ermitazh, Sankt-Peterburg, Rossiya
FLNY	Frick Art Reference Library, New York, NY, USA
IFP	Bibliothèque de l'Institut de France, Paris, France
INP	Institut Néerlandais, Fondation Custodia, Paris, France
JPGM	J. Paul Getty Library, formerly Malibu, CA, USA (now Los Angeles)
KBH	Koninklijke Bibliotheek, Den Haag, Nederland
KH	Hamburger Kunsthalle, Hamburg, Deutschland
KKB	Kupferstichkabinett, Berlin, Deutschland
KKD	Kupferstichkabinett, Dresden, Deutschland
KPL	Prentenkabinet der Rijksuniversiteit, Leiden, Nederland
LBDa	Hessische Landesbibliothek, Darmstadt, Deutschland
LCW	Library of Congress, Washington, DC, USA
LP	Bibliothèque du Musée du Louvre, Paris, France
LRB	Le Roy et Cie., Bruxelles, Belgique (formerly)
MA	Bibliotheek, Koninklijke Museum voor Schone Kunsten, Antwerpen, Belgique
MB	Bibliothèque des Musées Royaux des Beaux-Arts, Bruxelles, Belgique
MGD	Museum Mr. Simon van Gijn, Dordrecht, Nederland
MM	Bibliothèque Municipale, Mâcon, France

MPA	Museum Plantin-Moretus en Stedelijk Prentenkabinet, Antwerpen, Belgique
MR	Museum Boymans-van Beuningen, Rotterdam, Nederland
MWH	Rijksmuseum Meermanno-Westreenianum, Den Haag, Nederland
NGL	National Gallery, London, England, UK
NGW	National Gallery, Washington, D.C., USA
NOL	Nanne Ottema, Leeuwarden, Nederland (formerly)
OGA	Koninklijk Oudheidkundig Genootschap, Amsterdam, Nederland
RAU	Rijksarchief, Utrecht, Nederland
RKDH	Rijksbureau voor Kunsthistorische Documentatie, Den Haag, Nederland
RLM	Rylands Library, Manchester, England, UK
RMA	Rijksmuseum, Amsterdam, Nederland
RPUt	Ruud Priem, Utrecht, Nederland
SBB	Staatsbibliothek, Berlin, Deutschland
SIF	Städelsches Kunstinstitut und Städtische Galerie, Frankfurt am Main, Deutschland
SMLn	Stedelijke Musea, Leuven, Belgique
UBA	Universiteitsbibliotheek, Amsterdam, Nederland
UBL	Universiteitsbibliotheek, Leiden, Nederland
ULn	Universiteit, Leuven, Belgique
ULne	Bibliothèque de l'Université, Louvain-la-Neuve, Belgique
UU	Universiteit, Utrecht, Nederland
VAL	National Art Library, Victoria and Albert Museum, London, England, UK
VBBA	Vereeniging ter Bevordering van de Belangen des Boekhandels, Amsterdam, Nederland
WCL	Wallace Collection, London, England, UK
ZBM	Zeeuwse Museum, Middelburg, Nederland

City Abbreviations

AK	Alkmaar
AM	Amsterdam
AR	Arnhem
BD	Breda
DL	Delft
DO	Dordrecht
FK	Franeker
GD	Gouda
GR	Groningen
HA	Haarlem
HG	Den Haag
HH	Hertogenbosch
HO	Hoorn
HR	Harlingen
LN	Leiden
MG	Middelburg
RM	Rotterdam
UT	Utrecht

Auctioneer Abbreviations

AN	Anonymous
BAA	Baalen (Jacob)
BAE	Bauer
BAK	Bakhuysen (Hendrik & Gerrit)
BAU	Baur (Hendricus Johan Antonius)
BEE	Breebaart (Jan)
BEO	Benthem (Salomon)
BES	Besanger (Barent)
BLU	Blussé (Abraham)
BOL	Bolt (Johannes Henri)
BOS	Bosch (Jan)
BRA	Braam (Pieter)
BRK	Brinkman (Nicolaas)
BRU	Brussel (Hermanus)
BSM	Bosboom (Frans Johannes)
CIT	Citters (Caspar)
CLF	Cleef (J.)
CNL	Cornel (Nicolaas)
DAA	Daams (Pieter)
DAW	Daalen Wetters
DLS	Delfos (Abraham)
DRS	Dries (C.)
GRO	Groot (Jan)
GRW	Groenewold (A.)
HAA	Haas (Hendrik)
HDG	Hardenberg (Cornelis)
HRK	Horstok (J.P.)
HSN	Holsteyn (Pieter & Johannis)
HUY	Huysinga (Leonard)
IMM	Immerzeel
KAN	Kann (I.)
KLY	Kleijne (David)
LAC	La Cable (Willem)
LG	Logger (Hendrik)
LOO	Loosjes (Adriaan)
MUY	Muys (Robert)
NIJ	Nijhoff (Paulus)
NOM	Noman (D.)
OND	Onderdewyngaart Canzius (J.H.)
OTT	Otten (Theodorus)
POS	Posthumus (Pieter)
REB	Rebel (Willem)
RIJ	Rijp
ROM	Romar (Dionysius)
ROU	Roo (N.)
SAN	Sande (Johannes Jacobus)
SCH	Schley (Philippus)
SCR	Scheurleer (Bernardus)
STO	Stoopendahl (W.H.)
VIN	Vinne (Vincent)
VIS	Vis (D.)
VRS	Vries (Jeronimo)
WIN	Winter (Anthony Pieter)
WLD	Wild (Bartholomeus)
WUR	Wurfbain (Johannes Samuel)
YVR	Yver (Jan)

Index of Catalogues

1801–1810

1 1801/02/18 [Lugt 6200]

Jan Bosch; Amsterdam, Premises, op de hoek van de Geldersche Kaay, en Schreijershoek

Additional Auctioneers: Abel Langerhuizen; Lambertus van der Hans; Casparus Johannes Bon

Seller(s) from Title Page: Nagelaaten door Wylen J. Schonevelt

Seller Authority: Schonevelt, Jan J.

Paintings Lots: 78

Catalogue Locations:

FLNY	Not annot.

Comments: The sale consisted almost entirely of paintings – mostly landscapes – but there were a few lots of prints near the end. The owner, J. Schonevelt, is described as deceased at the time of the sale, and his premises were described as "op de hoek van de Geldersche Kaay, en Schreijershoek." His relatively large collection of paintings consisted primarily of works by contemporary artists working in Amsterdam, most notably Johann Heinrich Wüest (1741–1822), a Swiss landscape painter active in Amsterdam between 1760 and 1766. The fact that Schonevelt owned at least 42 of his paintings implies that the two men must have had a close relationship. An autobiographical memoir by Wüest makes reference to a certain "A. Schonenveld," described as a "Flachmaler," who had helped Wüest learn the trade in Amsterdam. (See *Oud Holland*, 26, 1908, p.247.) The differences in the spelling and first initial leaves the identification open to question, but there is another indication that J. Schonevelt was also a painter. Lot 56 in this sale is described as a copy after Jan van Goyen by "J. Schooneveld," almost certainly an alternative spelling of the collector's name. Documents found in the Amsterdam Gemeentearchief enable us to identify him with a certain Jan Schonevelt (1730–1800), a painter and glazier originally from Deventer who had settled in Amsterdam by 1756, living in the Geldersche Kaay. He was buried in the Oude Kerk in December, 1800. He was apparently a painter of wall decorations, which would also explain why the sale contained no other works by him. None of the pictures in the sale has been identified.

For some unexplained reason Lugt records that the sale contained 2633 lots, among which were 216 lots of paintings, 640 of drawings and 1767 of prints in a catalogue of 94 pages. This information was presumably taken from the LRB copy of the catalogue since it was the only copy known to Lugt. The LRB copy appears to be the one now at FLNY; it has only 8 pages and 82 lots, an appropriate number for a one-day sale. The source of this discrepancy is not apparent.

2 1801/02/24 and following days [Lugt 6206]

Theodorus van Otten; Amsterdam, Ten Huize van Carel Daniel Meerhoff, Castelein in 't Oudezyds Heeren Logement

Additional Auctioneers: Pieter Posthumus; Jacobus Pekkeren junior

Seller(s) from Title Page: None

Paintings Lots: 19

Catalogue Locations:

AMA	Not annot.

Comments: This anonymous sale consisted of a wide variety of objects, including furniture, porcelain and jewels as well as a few paintings and drawings. The latter are poorly described and were probably works of little interest.

3 1801/03/16 and following days [Lugt 6216]

Philippus van der Schley; Amsterdam, Ten Huize van C.S. Roos, op de Cloveniers Burgwal, in 't Huis van Trip

Additional Auctioneers: Jan de Bosch, Jeronimusz.; Bernardus de Bosch, Jeronimusz.; Jan Yver; Cornelis Sebille Roos; Roelof Meurs Pruyssenaar

Seller(s) from Title Page: Nagelaaten door Wylen den Kunst-minnaar, W.F. Taelman Kip, En een ander Kunst-Liefhebber

Seller(s) from Auctioneer's Copy: Schley; P[ruyssenaar]; R[oos]

Seller Authority: Kip, Willem Frederick Taelman; Schley, Philippus van der; Pruyssenaar, Roelof Meurs; Roos, Cornelis Sebille

Paintings Lots: 234

Catalogue Locations:

*RKDH	Auctioneer's copy, annot. with all buyers and prices on interleaved pages as well as letters for the names of the sellers. It belonged to the dealer C.S. Roos.
LBDa	Auctioneer's copy, annot. with all buyers and prices on interleaved pages as well as letters for the sellers. Some of the latter are also identified. It may have belonged to the dealer P. van der Schley.
EBNP	Auctioneer's copy, annot. with all buyers and prices on interleaved pages as well as letters for the names of the sellers.
FLNY	Annot. with many buyers and all prices for the paintings only. The annotations are often difficult to read.
MPA	Annot. in pencil with some prices for the drawings and prints but not the paintings.
ESP I	Not annot.
ESP II	Not annot.
BMB	Present location unknown. According to Lugt it is not annot.

Comments: The catalogue for this extended sale was issued in two parts, the first devoted to paintings, drawings, and prints, and the second to coins, musical and scientific instruments, naturalia, books and miscellanea. The title page, which indicates that the paintings were considered the most significant segment, mentions just two collectors: W.F. Taelman Kip, deceased, and an unidentified "Kunst-Liefhebber," neither of whom is necessarily connected with the paintings in the sale. Three extant copies of the catalogue that belonged to dealers who organized the sale are annotated with letters next to the individual lots, designating the consignments to which they belonged. Of the sixteen consignments, only six included paintings: E, K, P, R, S and Z. The largest number of paintings, 112 lots, belonged to "K," who was certainly W.F. Taelman Kip. Most of the remainder belonged to "P," who was almost certainly the dealer R.M. Pruyssenaar, since he is also given as the person buying in some of the same lots. The consigner "S" can be confidently identified as Ph. van der Schley, one of the co-organizers of the sale. This is confirmed by the LBDa copy of the catalogue, which probably belonged to Van der Schley and which has a brief list identifying some of the consigners, including F, G, H, M and S. Only the latter submitted paintings, and he is identified there as "Schley divers," meaning that he was representing a variety of other collectors, as was perhaps Pruyssenaar. Finally, we may assume that "R," who owned just seven lots, was the dealer C.S. Roos, leaving just "E" (one lot) and "Z" (four lots) unidentified.

Willem Frederick Taelman (or sometimes Taalman) Kip (1761–1800) was a wealthy collector who lived on the Herengracht during the last eight years of his life. Very little is known about how and where he acquired his paintings, but the collection seems to have been assembled during the decade preceding the sale. All of his 112 lots were sold, and the annotated catalogues record that his lots brought a total of fl. 974:4 altogether. The highest price was realized by a landscape painted by Jan Miel, which fetched fl. 54. Only one of Kip's lots has been identified: lot 14 by Adriaen van Gaesbeeck, *A Young Man in His Study*, which the Royal Museum (now the Rijksmuseum) acquired in 1808. At the present sale it brought fl. 47 from the dealer Roos.

The paintings consigned by P[ruyssenaar] did slightly better, although eight of his 97 lots were bought in. By far the largest amount was brought by the first two lots in the sale, described as portraits of a man and his wife by Metsu, for which the dealer Coclers paid fl. 219. (They cannot now be traced.) The next highest amount was fl. 68:10 paid for a satirical representation of *The Trial of Johan van Oldenbarneveld* by Cornelis Saftleven. (This painting is now also in the Rijksmuseum.) Pruyssenaar's paintings fetched a total of fl. 1568:15.

In spite of its size, the sale consisted primarily of inexpensive landscapes and genre pieces and does not seem to have included major works. The entire sale, including all categories, came to fl. 10,818:10.

4 1801/03/23–1801/03/31

J. van Cleef; Den Haag, Veenestraat

Additional Auctioneers: B. Scheurleer

Seller(s) from Title Page: Feu Monsieur H. van der Hoop, de son vivant Ministre Plénipotentiaire de LL.HH.PP. à la Cour de Liège &c. &c.

Seller Authority: Hoop, Hendrik van der

Paintings Lots: 12

Catalogue Locations:

*VBBA I	Annot. with some buyers and most prices for the art objects only.
MWH I	Annot. with a few prices for books only.
VBBA II	Not annot.
MWH II	Not annot.

Comments: The owner was Hendrik van der Hoop (1725–1800), who had served from 1783 until the French occupation as the Minister Plenipotentiary of the Dutch states at the court of Liège. He went into retirement in The Hague in 1795. The present eight-day sale, which followed his death by just a few months, was dedicated primarily to his library, which was quite large. There were also some miscellaneous "rariteiten," naturalia, prints, drawings and a few paintings. The latter consisted of genre pieces, still lifes and portraits sold on March 31, the last day of the sale. The highest price was fl. 11:10, fetched by a pair of peasant subjects by J.C. Janson.

5 1801/04/08–1801/04/09 [Lugt 6228]

Vincent van der Vinne; Haarlem, Burgerhof

Seller(s) from Title Page: None

Paintings Lots: 77

Catalogue Locations:

MB	Not annot.

Comments: This anonymous two-day sale in Haarlem consisted primarily of paintings, but also significant numbers of drawings, prints, sculpture, books, scientific instruments and miscellaneous objects. The paintings included many by local Haarlem artists, but the descriptions are very brief and neither dimensions nor provenance are included, making it difficult to identify them. Since the only extant copy of the catalogue is not annotated, we know virtually nothing of the results.

6 **1801/04/13–1801/04/14** [Lugt 6231]

Philippus van der Schley; Amsterdam, Ten Huize van C.S. Roos, op de Kloveniers Burgwal, in 't Huis van Trip

Additional Auctioneers: Jan de Bosch, Jeronimusz.; B. de Bosch, Jeronimusz.; Jan Yver; Cornelis Sebille Roos; R. Meurs Pruyssenaar

Seller(s) from Title Page: Alles nagelaten door Wylen den Kunsthandelaar Pierre Fouquet, junior

Seller Authority: Fouquet, Pierre, Jr.

Paintings Lots: 109

Catalogue Locations:

*RKDH	Auctioneer's copy, annot. with all buyers and prices on interleaved pages. It belonged to the dealer C.S. Roos.
FLNY	Auctioneer's copy, annot. with all buyers and prices on interleaved pages.
LBDa	Auctioneer's copy, annot. with all buyers and prices on interleaved pages. It may have belonged to the dealer P. van der Schley.
MA II	Annot. with all buyers and prices. It evidently belonged to the dealer B. Carli who has listed his purchases at the front.
BMPL	Annot. with all buyers and prices on interleaved pages. It belonged to Wm. Smith.
MA I	Annot. with all buyers and prices on interleaved pages.
BRB	Annot. with most buyers and all prices for the paintings only.
ESP I	Annot. with many buyers and all prices for the paintings. Some lots are also marked with pencilled letters which are probably bidding codes. The drawings and prints are priced through p.89.
AA	Annot. with some buyers and all prices, especially for the paintings which have all the buyers.
LRB	Present location unknown. According to Lugt it is annot. with buyers and prices.
NOL	Present location unknown. According to Lugt it is annot. with buyers and prices.
EBNP	Annot. with all prices.
ESP II	Annot. in pencil with all prices. This is the copy formerly at KKB.
BPG	Not annot. It belonged to the dealer J.B.P. Lebrun.
MPA	Not annot.
MB	Not annot.
INP	Not annot.
VBBA	Not annot.
JPGM	Not annot.
MR	Missing for many years and presumably lost. According to Lugt it is not annot.
RMA	Not seen. According to Lugt it is not annot.
MGD	Not seen. According to Lugt it is not annot.

Comments: Pierre (or Pieter) Fouquet (1729–1800) was the pre-eminent picture and print dealer in the Netherlands during the latter half of the eighteenth century. He was already active in 1753 when he registered in St. Luke's Guild as a painter and art dealer, and by 1760 he had also established himself as a major publisher of prints, most notably views of Amsterdam used to illustrate a luxurious atlas to the city. (See especially I.H. van Eeghen in *Amstelodamum*, 1960, pp.49–59.) He enjoyed an exceptionally good reputation as an expert and maintained connections with many dealers in France and England, whom he often represented in the Netherlands. In 1773 he organized an important sale of Dutch pictures in London that included numerous works of exceptional value.

The present sale, held just a few months after Fouquet's death at the age of 71, presumably included the remainder of his stock. He no longer possessed large numbers of major works, but his sale nonetheless included more than 2500 lots of prints, 600 lots of drawings, and 100 lots of paintings. Prices were generally good, though not exceptional, and none of the paintings were left unsold. The best result was realized by an interior scene depicting the workroom of a weaver by Cornelis Decker and Adriaen van Ostade, for which the dealer Jan Yver paid fl. 860. (It is now in the Brussels museum and attributed to Decker alone.) The next highest amount was fl. 775 paid by the dealer C.S. Roos for lot 61 by Rembrandt, which represented *Salome with the Head of St. John the Baptist*. (It is now in the Rijksmuseum, recognized as a work by Carel Fabritius.) Roos also bought an *Interior with a Man tuning a Violin and a Woman with Music* by Gabriel Metsu for fl. 670. (It is now in the National Gallery, London.) Aside from a pair of still lifes by P.T. van Brussel, which cost fl. 750, most of the remaining lots sold for much less, many bringing under fl. 50. The totals for all categories are recorded in the LBDa and RKDH copies of the catalogue as fl. 24,400:16, making it one of the most successful sales of the period, perhaps the result of the esteem in which Fouquet had been held during the previous four decades.

7 **1801/04/13–1801/04/22** [Lugt 6232]

M. van Daalen Wetters; Den Haag, Au Coin du Hof-Cingel

Seller(s) from Title Page: None

Paintings Lots: 4

Catalogue Locations:

VBBA	Annot. with a few prices, but not for the paintings.
MWH	Not annot.

Comments: This was a nine-day sale of books held by the Hague bookseller and print dealer Melis van Daalen Wetters. On the last two days there were some prints, drawings and "rariteiten," as well as a few anonymous paintings. The title page is in French, but the contents are a mixture of both Dutch and French.

8 **1801/04/21–1801/04/23**

Jan Yver; Amsterdam, Huis op den Binnen Amstel, tusschen de Heeren- en Keizersgragten

Additional Auctioneers: G.W. van Ophoven; J.A. Jourdany; G. Twisk, Cornelisz.; G. Steenhoff; J.G. Francken; G. Cluwen, Jacobz.; Hendrik Oyens; F. Leonhardt

Seller(s) from Title Page: None

Paintings Lots: 58

Catalogue Locations:

*MA	Incomplete, consisting only of the title page and pp.29–30, 41–48. Annot. with some buyers and many prices for the paintings only.

Comments: This was a three-day sale in Amsterdam consisting of miscellaneous objects, including clocks, medals, musical instruments, porcelain, glass, furniture and books. On the last day there were some drawings, prints and 60 lots of paintings. The latter are given very little prominence on the title page, and as might be expected in a sale of this kind, most brought low prices. However, a few lots were sold for surprisingly large amounts, which suggests they were of a quality normally found in important picture sales. The first three lots of paintings included works by Berchem, Lingelbach and Huchtenburgh, each of which fetched more than fl. 300. The painting by Lingelbach, depicting a *Landscape with Haywagon*, was bought by the dealer Jan Yver acting on behalf of Pieter van Winter, the wealthy Amsterdam merchant. The picture by Berchem, a *Landscape with Shepherds and Animals*, was sold for fl. 430 to "Farret," and the pair of landscapes by Huchtenburg were knocked down to the same person for fl. 335. A few other lots exceeded fl. 40, but the majority brought much less. The owner or owners at the time of the sale are still unknown.

9 **1801/05/11** and following days [Lugt 6261]

Philippus van der Schley; Amsterdam, Ten Huize van C.S. Roos, in het Huis van Trip

Additional Auctioneers: Jan de Bosch, Jeronimusz.; Bernardus de Bosch, Jeronimusz.; Jan Yver; Cornelis Sebille Roos; Roelof Meurs Pruyssenaar

Seller(s) from Title Page: Meerendeels Nagelaten door Wylen Giorgius Henricus Trochel, Med. Doctor

Seller(s) from Auctioneer's Copy: Elias; Pruyssenaar; Roos; Schley

Seller Authority: Elias; Pruyssenaar, Roelof Meurs; Roos, Cornelis Sebille; Schley, Philippus van der

Paintings Lots: 170

Catalogue Locations:

RKDH	Auctioneer's copy, annot. with all buyers and prices on interleaved pages as well as letters for the sellers. It belonged to the dealer C.S. Roos.
*EBNP	Auctioneer's copy, annot. with all buyers and prices on interleaved pages as well as letters for the sellers.
*FLNY	Auctioneer's copy, annot. with all buyers and prices on interleaved pages as well as letters for the sellers.
MA	Annot. with all buyers and prices.
ESP	Not annot.

Comments: The principal part of this sale was devoted to paintings, but there were also significant numbers of prints as well as scientific and musical instruments. The only collector mentioned in the catalogue is G.H. Trochel, a doctor of medicine whose name is given on the title page immediately following the description of the scientific and musical instruments, implying that his possessions were to be found in this part of the catalogue rather than among the paintings or drawings. This is confirmed by the three copies of the catalogue annotated by organizers of the sale, who marked the lots with the initials of the sellers; the letter "T" is exclusively associated with lots consisting of scientific instruments, so Trochel apparently submitted no paintings. There were six different consignments of pictures, designated E, P, PP, R, S, and V. The RKDH copy of the catalogue, which belonged to the dealer C.S. Roos, contains a list that identifies a few of the owners and shows how the profits were distributed. By far the largest amount was owing to "E," the proprietor of 51 lots, among which were many of the best paintings in the sale. He is identified there as "Elias." This is certainly a member of the prominent Amsterdam family of that name, most probably the former mayor – prior to the French occupation – Jacob Arnoudsz. Elias (1728–1800), who had died only a few months before the present sale. Since it is still unknown whether Elias owned a collection of paintings, his identity cannot be confirmed without further research in the Amsterdam archives. In any case, a few of the "Elias" paintings brought high prices: most notably Metsu's *The Usurer*, bought by the artist-dealer Cornelis Buijs for fl. 850. (It is now in the Boston Museum of Fine Arts.) A depiction of a marine storm by Backhuysen sold for fl. 751. Altogether Elias's pictures realized fl. 4711:18.

Only one other consigner is identified in the RKDH copy of the catalogue: "PP" was "Pruisse M," which presumably signifies R.M. Pruyssenaar acting on behalf of "M." "M" is still unidentified, but it is worth noting that one of his lots, no.48 by "De Delfsche van der Meer," was bought by his colleague Philippus van der Schley, also acting for "M." The latter can be identified as "Merrem," but there is no reason to assume that the two "M's" are the same person. The pictures in this consignment were sold for much lower amounts, fetching a total of just fl. 852:10. A landscape by Jacob van Ruisdael brought fl. 160, and the picture of *A Woman Weighing Gold* by Jan Vermeer of Delft reached only fl. 60. (This is the painting of that subject by Pieter de Hooch now in the Gemäldegalerie in Berlin rather than the one by Vermeer in Washington.)

Of the remaining consigners, "P" can certainly be identified as Pruyssenaar, "R" was no doubt C.R. Roos, and "S" was Ph. van der Schley. Only "V," who consigned eight paintings, cannot be named, although he was most probably the dealer Jacobus Vinkeles.

Altogether the sale realized fl. 12,298:16.

10 **1801/06/10–1801/06/11** [Lugt 6282]

Philippus van der Schley; Amsterdam, Ten Huize van C.S. Roos, in het Huis van Trip, op de Kloveniers Burgwal

Additional Auctioneers: Jan de Bosch Jeronimusz.; Bernardus de Bosch Jeronimusz.; Jan Yver; Cornelis Sebille Roos; Roelof Meurs Pruyssenaar

Seller(s) from Title Page: Nagelaaten door Wylen den Kunstminnaar Herman ten Kate

Seller(s) from Other Sources: [Doublet]

Seller Authority: Kate, Herman ten; Doublet, Pieter

Paintings Lots: 216

Catalogue Locations:

*RKDH	Auctioneer's copy, annot. with all buyers and prices on interleaved pages. Some lots are also marked with the letter B, evidently a seller. There is also some correspondance with the widow and various dealers from the time of the sale settling the costs, etc.
LBDa	Auctioneer's copy, annot. with all buyers and prices on interleaved pages. Some lots are also marked with the letter B, evidently a seller. It lacks a title page. It may have belonged to the dealer P. van der Schley.
AA	Annot. with all buyers and prices.
MA	Annot. with all buyers and prices.
MB	Annot. in pencil with most buyers and all prices. It is addressed to Heer Gt. van der Pot.
BRB	Annot. in ink and pencil with most buyers and prices.
KPL	Not seen. According to Lugt it is annot. with buyers and prices.
FLNY	Annot. with a few buyers and all prices.
MPA	Annot. in ink and pencil with a few buyers and all prices.
EBNP	Annot. with all prices.
ESP II	Not annot. excepting pencilled initials and figures by some lots which are apparently bidding codes.
MR	Not annot.
ESP I	Not annot.
BMB	Present location unknown. According to Lugt it is not annot.
MM	Not seen. According to Lugt it is not annot.

Comments: This two-day sale consisted of 216 lots of paintings, one of which was added after the catalogue was printed. Two lots containing artists' easels were also added *hors du catalogue*. The owner was Herman ten Kate (1731–1800), a wealthy cloth merchant and member of parliament, recently deceased. He is described in the catalogue only as a "kunstminaar." The ten Kate family enjoyed considerable prominence in Amsterdam, owing in large part to Lambert ten Kate (1674–1731), the famous philologist, also an important collector who corresponded with contemporary artists. Herman ten Kate was his nephew, but so far as is known he owned nothing from the earlier collection and seems to have built this collection from his own resources. His purchases were apparently made primarily during the 1780s and 1790s, often at public auction. Judging primarily from the prices his paintings realized, his collection contained many valuable works, although only a small portion has been identified so far. From a modern perspective, the most important was Vermeer's *Woman in Blue Reading a Letter* (now in the Rijksmuseum). However, this lot was sold for a mere fl. 110 and was not among the most expensive pieces. A landscape by Jan Both was sold for a surprising fl. 1600 and soon passed into the collection of Pieter van Winter. Two other paintings exceeded fl. 1000, including a *Hunting Still Life* by Jan Weenix which brought fl. 1055, and a landscape by Wijnants which was sold for fl. 1041. Nine further lots cost fl. 500 or more; the total for the sale was recorded as fl. 26,514, an impressive amount.

Two copies of the catalogue, those at RKDH and LBDa annotated by the dealers Roos and Van der Schley, indicate that 43 lots were consigned by "B" and apparently did not belong to Ten Kate. Six of the paintings can be traced to two sales in 1797 and 1800, at which time they were purchased by a certain "Doublet," who can probably be identified with Pieter Doublet (1766-?), an accountant who married Louise Marie ten Kate, Herman ten Kate's widow, in July, 1801, just one month after the present sale. He may, therefore, have been a family friend well before this time. His pictures were generally among the less important lots in the sale and did not fetch large amounts, totaling just fl. 940:5 altogether.

A total of twenty-six lots were purchased at this sale by the dealer L.B. Coclers, all but three of which had belonged to Ten Kate. Most of these were taken to Paris for resale and appeared at an auction held by J.B.P. Lebrun on August 26 ff., 1801. (See B. Peronnet & B. Fredericksen, *Répertoire des tableaux vendus en France au XIXe siècle*, I, 1997, cat. no.13.)

11 **1801/06/13** [Lugt 6283]

A. Delfos; Leiden, Op de Papegragt

Seller(s) from Title Page: None

Seller(s) from Other Sources: D. van R

Seller Authority: R., D. van

Paintings Lots: 97

Catalogue Locations:

*RKDH I	Auctioneer's copy, annot. with all buyers and prices on interleaved pages. There are also notes about expenses and total results.
ESP	Annot. with all buyers and prices.
MB II	Annot. in pencil with most buyers and prices. It belonged to the dealer Thijs and the annotations are his.
BMB	Present location unknown. According to Lugt it is annot. with buyers and prices.
MB I	Annot. in pencil with all prices.
RKDH II	Not annot.
MWH	Not annot.
KBH	Not annot.
MA	Not annot.

Comments: This sale in Leyden consisted entirely of paintings which, according to the title page of the catalogue, had been "in veele jaaren bijeen verzameld en nagelaten." This may indicate that all of the paintings belonged to a single collector, a conclusion confirmed by the annotations in the RKDH I copy of the catalogue which describe the contents as "Schilderijen Nagelaten door Wylen D. van R." The identity of this collector remains unknown, but since the pictures are described at some length and a few seem to have been valuable, it is to be hoped that his name will eventually be found. A few of the lots can be traced to later sales, including auctions in England and France, although very few can be identified in present-day collections.

Judging from the prices and the length of the entries, the best lots were apparently put at the beginning of the sale and the less important at the end. The highest price was supposedly fetched by the second lot, a *Landschap met geboomte en wooningen* by Isack van Ostade, which was knocked down for fl. 1725. However, the buyer was Abraham Delfos, the organizer of the sale, so it was perhaps bought in. The only other lots to exceed fl. 200 were also knocked down to Delfos, including lot 3, a landscape by Jacob van Ruisdael, which was sold for fl. 500, and lot 48, *Een Jongman, die als zingende op de Luit speelt* by Frans Hals, which brought fl. 281. Most other lots brought much less, the majority under fl. 40. The RKDH I copy of the catalogue records the total receipts as fl. 5204.

12 **1801/06/15–1801/06/23**

H. et G. Backhuysen; Den Haag, La Salle de la Cour

Seller(s) from Title Page: Delaissée par feu Monsieur T. Tamé, en son vivant Docteur en Medecine & d'un autre Amateur

Seller Authority: Tamé, T.

Paintings Lots: 137

Catalogue Locations:

MWH Not annot.

Comments: This was a book sale that also included a large number of drawings, prints and paintings that appeared on the last day of the sale. The latter were mostly anonymous, excepting only a few by the Hague painter Simon Besanger (active 1790–1795). The title page of the catalogue indicates that the principal owner was a medical doctor, T. Tamé, who may be identifiable as Tieleman Tamé, whose dissertation at Leyden University was written in 1751. He might in turn be the son or descendant of another T. Tamé, likewise a doctor but also known as a poet, whose dissertation at Leyden was written in 1722 and whose works include a poem written in 1725. (Cited by Abr. J. van der Aa, *Nieuw, biografish...woordenboek van Nederlandsche dichter*, v.3, 1846, p.93.)

However, Tamé was not the only collector whose property is found in this sale. The title page mentions one other unnamed consigner, and there may have been more, so it is uncertain whether any of the paintings were from Tamé's estate.

13 **1801/06/29–1801/07/06**

Joannem Jacobum van de Sande; Middelburg, Premises, Lange St. Pieterstraat

Additional Auctioneers: Anthonium Petrum de Winter

Seller(s) from Title Page: Gerardus de Wind, dum in vivis esset med: doct: anatomiae, chirug: et artis: obstetric: professor

Seller Authority: Wind, Gerard de

Paintings Lots: 1

Catalogue Locations:

*ZBM	Annot. with all buyers and prices on interleaved pages, although the single painting lacks the buyer.
ULn	Not annot. It is addressed to Mr van Hultem, and formerly belonged to the Bibliothèque Royale in Brussels.
MWH	Not annot.

Comments: The proprietor, Gerard de Wind, was a prominent medical doctor and professor in Middelburg with an extensive list of books to his credit. His impressive library was sold at a week-long auction the year following his death in 1800. One unnumbered lot with a painting by Droochsloot was included on the last day of the sale.

14 **1801/08/10–1801/08/14**

J. Kann; Den Haag, Groote Zaal van het Hoff

Seller(s) from Title Page: None

Paintings Lots: 1

Catalogue Locations:

MWH Not annot.

Comments: This five-day sale in The Hague consisted primarily of books but included also prints, frames, music and miscellaneous objects. One lot is described as containing nine anonymous paintings on canvas and panel. The owners are not identified.

15 **1801/08/19–1801/08/20** [Lugt 6302]

Philippus van der Schley; Amsterdam, Ten Huize van Cornelis Sebille Roos, op de Kloveniersburgwal, in het Huis van Trip

Additional Auctioneers: Jan de Bosch, Jeronimusz.; Bernardus de Bosch, Jeronimusz.; Jan Yver; Cornelis Sebille Roos; Roeloff Meurs Pruyssenaar

Seller(s) from Title Page: None

Seller(s) from Auctioneer's Copy: Van Forreest; Pruyssenaar; W. Wynen; etc.

Seller Authority: Foreest, van; Pruyssenaar, Roelof Meurs; Wynen, W.

Paintings Lots: 232

Catalogue Locations:

*RKDH	Auctioneer's copy, annot. with all buyers and prices on interleaved pages as well as letters for the sellers. The sellers are also identified.
EBNP	Auctioneer's copy, annot. with all buyers and prices on interleaved pages as well as letters for the sellers.
LBDa	Auctioneer's copy, annot. with all buyers and prices on interleaved pages as well as letters for the sellers. It may have belonged to the dealer P. van der Schley.

Comments: The catalogue of this two-day sale in Amsterdam describes 176 lots of paintings with six lots of drawings and miscellaneous objects. The RKDH and LBDa copies of the catalogue also list an additional 52 lots of paintings and three miscellaneous items that do not appear in the printed catalogue. As usual, these added lots are not described except to count the number of items they contained. The printed catalogue does not identify any of the owners, but all three extant catalogues place an letter next to each lot, and the RKDH copy has a list of their names that also tallies the amounts their lots fetched. The list reads as follows: A = Van Forreest fl. 1374:18; C = Mevr Hogguer fl. 80:10; D = Wolf fl. 3:00; E = W. Wynen fl. 412:01; F = van der Schly fl. 72:16; G = C.S. Roos fl. 118:15; P = Pruyssen^{r} fl. 192:09; Q = Pruyssen^{r} fl. 323:38. The principal consigner was "Van Forreest," who submitted a total of 58 lots. This is probably a misspelling of "Van Foreest," and therefore possibly a member of the Alkmaar family of that name. The second consigner is readily identified as Anna Maria Ebeling, the wife of Paul Iwan Hogguer, the Amsterdam banker. She consigned just four lots, apparently items that were considered inappropriate for her highly regarded collection. (It was later sold in 1817.) The identities of "Wolf," who was selling just one minor painting, and "W. Wynen," who sent 58 lots, are not known. The last three sellers are all dealers involved with organizing the sale; because the letters used are not their initials, one may assume that they were representing collectors other than themselves.

A few of the lots, especially some of those consigned by "Van Forreest," brought high prices, and all three of the most expensive lots were bought by the dealer Vinkeles. He paid fl. 330 for a seascape by Backhuysen, fl. 205 for a marine piece by Dubbels, and fl. 200 for an interior by de Hooch. The latter is thought to be the painting that went to the Speck van Sternberg collection in Lützschena and is now in the Leipzig museum. It is possible, but not certain, that some of the other lots bought by Vinkeles were also intended for this collection. The total receipts for the sale came to fl. 2578:7.

16 **1801/08/31–1801/09/04**

Anthony Pieter de Winter; Middelburg, Premises, Kortendelft over de St. Pieterstraat

Additional Auctioneers: Johannes Jacobus van de Sande

Seller(s) from Title Page: Nagelaten door wylen Pieter Gillissen, In leven Boekverkooper binnen deze Stad

Seller Authority: Gillissen, Pieter

Paintings Lots: 13

Catalogue Locations:

ULn	Not annot. It belonged formerly to the Bibliothèque Royale in Brussels.
VBBA	Not annot.

Comments: The owner is identified as the recently deceased bookseller from Middelburg, Pieter Gillissen. His five-day sale consisted primarily of his stock of books, but there were also prints, maps and some paintings. The latter were mostly anonymous, but a large *Nativity* attributed to Bloemaert was given prominence of place. The results of the sale are not known.

17 **1801/10/06** and following days [Lugt 6316]

Philippus van der Schley; Amsterdam, Ten Huize van C.S. Roos, op de Kloveniers Burgwal, in het Huis van Trip

Additional Auctioneers: Jan de Bosch, Jeronimusz.; Bernardus de Bosch, Jnz.; Jan Yver; Corn. Sebille Roos; R. Meurs Pruyssenaar

Seller(s) from Title Page: None

Seller(s) from Auctioneer's Copy: Y[ver]; etc.

Seller Authority: Yver, Jan

Paintings Lots: 119

Catalogue Locations:

LBDa	Auctioneer's copy, annot. with all buyers and prices on interleaved pages as well as letters for the sellers. Includes both parts. It may have belonged to the dealer P. van der Schley.
RKDH	Auctioneer's copy, annot. with all buyers and prices on interleaved pages as well as letters for the sellers.
*EBNP	Auctioneer's copy, annot. with all buyers and prices on interleaved pages as well as letters for the sellers.
BRB	Annot. with most buyers and all prices.
MB	Annot. in pencil with many buyers and most prices. It belonged to the dealer P.J. Thijs and the annotations are his.
MA	Annot. with all buyers and prices for the first part. The second part is not annot. It is addressed to "Tersmitten."
ESP	Not annot.
OGA	Not annot. Includes both parts.
AAP	Incomplete, second part only. Not annot.
JPGM	Incomplete, second part only. Not annot.
BMB	Present location unknown. According to Lugt it lacks the second part and is not annot.

Comments: The catalogue for this sale was published in two parts, the first dedicated to 101 lots of paintings and one lot of prints, and the second to coins and medals. According to the EBNP, LBDa and RKDH copies of the catalogue, all of which are annotated by different dealers who participated in organizing the sale, the paintings belonged to five consigners who are given the letters L, M, S, Y and Z. Their random nature implies that these letters correspond to the first initial of the consigners' names. "Y" is presumably the dealer Jan Yver, one of the co-organizers of the sale, but while it is tempting to suggest that "S" was Philippus van der Schley, another of the auctioneers – one of the two unsold lots belonging to "S" reappeared under Van der Schley's name in 1804 – this seems unlikely. This consignment was not only large (49 lots) but also valuable, including many of the most expensive lots in the sale, characteristics of a private collection rather than the unsold stock of a dealer. Their share of the proceeds was fl. 9603.13, or approximately three-fourths of the total realized by the paintings. If "S" was Van der Schley, he was probably acting on behalf of someone else. The remaining sellers are still unknown.

The range of prices in this sale was unusually wide, with a number of lots fetching very large amounts while the majority remained below fl. 50. The most impressive purchases were made by the dealer A.E. Sterk, who bought six of the most expensive lots, at least three of which were sold soon after to the English collector Francis Baring and from him passed to the British Royal Collection where they remain today. Sterk paid a surprising fl. 2075 for an interior scene by Adriaen van Ostade, fl. 1650 for a *Self Portrait* by Rembrandt, and fl. 1000 for a *Self Portrait* by Metsu. (The portrait by Rembrandt is now considered to be a later imitation.) Two other lots by Berchem and Wouwerman also reached fl. 1000. (Both are now untraced.) A number of others brought more than fl. 300. The total figures for the paintings came to fl. 12,829:10; the entire sale brought fl. 17,395:05.

18 1801/10/19 and following days [Lugt 6320]

Philippus van der Schley; Amsterdam, Ten Huize van Cornelis Sebille Roos, in het Huis van Trip, op de Kloveniersburgwal

Additional Auctioneers: Jan de Bosch, Jeronimusz.; Bernardus de Bosch, Jeronimusz.; Jan Yver; Cornelis Sebille Roos; Roeloff Meurs Pruyssenaar

Seller(s) from Title Page: Nagelaten door Wylen Jonkheer Menno Baron van Coehoorn, In deszelfs Leeven sesie gehad hebbende in onderscheiden Generaliteits-Collegien, in den Hage

Seller Authority: Coehoorn, Menno, Baron van

Paintings Lots: 91

Catalogue Locations:

BMPL	Auctioneer's copy, annot. with all buyers and prices on interleaved pages. It belonged later to Wm. Smith.
*LBDa	Auctioneer's copy, annot. with all buyers and prices on interleaved pages. It may have belonged to the dealer P. van der Schley.
RKDH	Auctioneer's copy, annot. with all buyers and prices on interleaved pages.
MA II	Annot. with all buyers and prices on interleaved pages.
MA I	Annot. with all buyers and prices.
EBNP I	Annot. with many buyers and all prices.
NGL	Annot. with all buyers and prices.
FLNY	Annot. with all buyers and prices.
BRB	Annot. in ink and pencil with all buyers and prices for the paintings only. It lacks a title page.
AA	Annot. with most buyers and all prices for the paintings. Some other parts have prices only.
LRB	Present location unknown. According to Lugt it is annot. with buyers and prices.
RMA	Annot. with all prices. It is addressed to A van Swieten[?].
EBNP II	Annot. with all prices.
ESP	Not annot. excepting some letters and figures by certain lots that are probably bidding codes. Two lots also have the dimensions added.
BMB	Not annot.
AAP	Not annot.
MWH	Not annot.
MB	Not annot.
MR	Missing for many years and presumably lost. According to Lugt it is not annot.
KKB	Present location unknown. According to Lugt it is not annot.

Comments: The relative importance of this sale notwithstanding, very little has been learned about the seller. Menno baron van Coehoorn was a member of the prominent Hague family whose most famous ancestor, also named Menno, was a noted military engineer in the late seventeenth century. The name was carried by at least three other members of the family, all known for their military careers. The present baron, described by the sale catalogue as a magistrate in The Hague, was the grandson and last male descendant of his more famous predecessor. He died in The Hague on Nov.20, 1800, and was best known as a collector of prints, more than 3500 lots of which are included in this sale. There were also 91 lots of paintings, some of which can be identified and which help to confirm that the collection was indeed of some importance. Nonetheless, there seems to be very little contemporary comment about the collection, and its reputation depends almost exclusively on the present catalogue. As far as can be determined, Coehoorn had acquired the paintings during the previous 25 years from public sales and local dealers. They were a mixture of landscapes, seascapes, still lifes and genre scenes. The most expensive lot was a stable scene by Wouwerman, which was sold for fl. 1810 and which passed shortly afterward to the collection of Lucretia Johanna van Winter in Amsterdam. (It is now in the Rijksmuseum.) The only other lot to exceed fl. 1000 was a landscape by Hobbema, which was sold for fl. 1710 to the dealer Coclers. (It is very tentatively identified as no.2570 in the London National Gallery.) Two lots purchased by the dealer A.E. Sterk were apparently acquired not much later by Francis Baring, from whom they were purchased by the English Prince Regent, later George IV. The first, a small interior with peasants by Adriaen van Ostade, cost fl. 800, and the other, a shore scene by Willem van der Velde the Younger brought fl. 500. (Both are still in the Royal Collection.) Nothing was left unsold, an indication that there were no reserves. The paintings sold for a total of fl. 16,974, while the entire sale brought nearly twice that amount, fl. 31,405:17.

A few additional paintings appeared in a sale of Coehoorn's books, prints and miscellaneous possessions which took place in The Hague on November 23 ff.(no.21). Finally, a segment of the print collection reappeared for sale in London about six months later, on April 28/29, 1802. This latter sale also included a few paintings, which, however, are unlikely to have come from Coehoorn. (See B. Fredericksen, *Index of Paintings Sold in the British Isles during the Nineteenth Century*, I, 1988, no.105.)

19 1801/11/10 and following days [Lugt 6324]

Pieter Posthumus; Amsterdam, Ten Huize van C.D. Meerhoff, Castelyn in 't O.Z. Heeren Logement

Seller(s) from Title Page: None

Paintings Lots: 59

Catalogue Locations:

AA	Not annot.

Comments: This was an anonymous sale of miscellaneous items, including jewelry, porcelain, clothing, furniture, paintings and prints. The paintings are unlikely to have been of much importance, given the humble nature of the sale; the only extant copy of the catalogue is not annotated, making it impossible to know what prices were realized. However, some of the paintings are attributed to artists of prominence, and the dates of a few are also recorded, although the descriptions are generally brief.

20 1801/11/16–1801/11/21

D. Vis; Rotterdam, Zaal boven de Beurs

Additional Auctioneers: C. van den Dries en Zoon

Seller(s) from Title Page: Nagelaten door wylen den Heer Gelinus van Spaan, Koopman te Rotterdam

Seller Authority: Spaan, Gelinus van

Paintings Lots: 11

Catalogue Locations:

MWH	Not annot. It is addressed to Heer van Westreenan.

Comments: The contents of this six-day sale in Rotterdam were primarily books, but there was also a large collection of music as well as some prints, paintings and miscellaneous items sold on the last day. The paintings are described very briefly, and the results of the sale are not recorded. Nothing is known about the owner except that he was described as a Rotterdam merchant.

21 1801/11/23–1801/12/01

M. van Daalen Wetters; Den Haag, Hof-Cingel

Seller(s) from Title Page: Nagelaaten door Wylen Jonkheer Menno Baron van Coehoorn

Seller Authority: Coehoorn, Menno, Baron van

Paintings Lots: 6

Catalogue Locations:

KBH	Not annot.
MWH I	Not annot.
MWH II	Not annot.

Comments: The more valuable paintings and prints belonging to baron van Coehoorn had been sold in Amsterdam on October 19 ff. (cat. no.18), presumably because a wider audience could be found there, but the lesser parts of his estate, consisting of his books, mathematical instruments, and miscellaneous objects, were sold in The Hague, where he lived. This sale also included a few prints and paintings, perhaps items that did not warrant being transported to Amsterdam to be sold. Whereas most Dutch sale catalogues during the period of French domination were in either Dutch or French, the present catalogue is a curious blend of French, Dutch and English. However, the description of the paintings is entirely in Dutch. The results of the sale are not recorded.

22 **1801/12/22** and following days [Lugt 6344]

Theodorus van Otten; Amsterdam, Ten Huize van C.D. Meerhoff, Castelein in 't O.Z. Heeren Logement

Additional Auctioneers: Pieter Posthumus; Johannes Buys

Seller(s) from Title Page: Paulus van den Bogaart, Voormalig Oud Schepen en Raad der Stad Delft; [en] Bartholomeus Ruloffs, In leven beroemd Organist en Orchestmeester binnen deeze Stad

Seller Authority: Ruloffs, Bartholomeus

Paintings Lots: 131

Catalogue Locations:

*AMA	Annot. with all prices.

Comments: As the title page of the catalogue indicates, the items in this sale belonged to two different collectors. The principal part consisted of scientific instruments and some items of naturalia belonging to Paulus van den Bogaart, whereas the second portion, containing musical instruments, paintings and prints, was the property of Bartholomeus Ruloffs (1741–1801), a well-known organist and composer in Amsterdam. The Gemeentearchief also possesses a manuscript inventory of Ruloffs's estate, which includes much of the same material found in the present sale catalogue. Judging only from the prices recorded in the AMA copy of the catalogue, the collection seems to have consisted primarily of lesser pieces, since most lots brought less than fl. 10. However, a few lots were sold for somewhat more. An interior scene by W.J. Laquy was knocked down for fl. 91, and another by Thomas Wyck depicting a chemist in his laboratory cost fl. 44:10.

23 **1802/02/16** and following days [Lugt 6359]

Philippus van der Schley; Amsterdam, Ten Huize van C.S. Roos, op de Kloveniers Burgwal, in het Huis van Trip

Additional Auctioneers: Jan de Bosch, Jeronimusz.; Bernardus de Bosch, Jnz.; Jan Yver; Corn. Sebille Roos; Roel. Meurs Pruyssenaar

Seller(s) from Title Page: Jacobus Buys, Jan Swart, en Leendert Viervant

Seller Authority: Buys, Jacobus

Paintings Lots: 99

Catalogue Locations:

*RKDH	Auctioneer's copy, annot. with all buyers and prices on interleaved pages as well as letters for the sellers. It belonged to the dealer C.S. Roos.
LBDa	Auctioneer's copy, annot. with all buyers and prices on interleaved pages as well as letters for the sellers. The title page is lacking. It may have belonged to the dealer P. van der Schley.
FLNY	Not annot.

Comments: The largest part of this sale was dedicated to drawings and prints, but there were also 99 lots of paintings as well as books, sculpture and artists' equipment of various kinds. The title page of the catalogue identifies three sellers, all deceased. The first, Jacobus Buys, was a painter who had died in 1801. The second was Jan Swart, a sculptor, who had died in 1793. The last, Leendert Viervant, was an architect who had died the year before. All were from Amsterdam. Both the RKDH and LBDa copies of the catalogue are annotated by the dealers who organized the sale, placing a letter next to each lot to designate the proprietors. (Contrary to normal procedure, the lots are generally grouped by consigner rather than listed alphabetically by artist.) They are A, B, C, CC, E, F, G, H, K, S, V and Z, implying that some may correspond to the first letters of the consigner's name and some may not. The principal consigner was "B," whose lots fetched a total of fl. 1981:5 and included the first 20 lots of paintings. These were clearly the property of Jacobus Buys, since the first five lots were also painted by him. Two more of the major consigners were "S" and "V," who must have been Swart and Viervant. However, neither of them owned any of the paintings. The consigners of the paintings were B[uys], C, E, F, G, H and Z; with the exception of Buys, none of them can be identified.

The prices realized by the sale were generally modest. Only one lot, a painting of *A Man Sitting at a Table Writing* attributed to Rembrandt, did reasonably well, fetching fl. 255 from the dealer Willem Gruyter. The first lot in the sale, consisting of two genre pictures by Buys, brought fl. 100. The total for the entire sale came to fl. 5587:9.

24 **1802/02/23** and following days [Lugt 6365]

Willem Rebel; Amsterdam, Premises, op de Binnen Amstel, by de Keizersgragt

Additional Auctioneers: Ab. Jacob Broes; A L Bs. van Riessen; Cornelis Sebille Roos; Willem van Orsoy; Isaak Esser

Seller(s) from Title Page: Nagelaaten door Wylen Mejuffrouw Margaretha Maria van Laar, Woduwe [sic] den Heer Johannes Esser

Seller Authority: Laar, Margaretha Maria van

Paintings Lots: 22

Catalogue Locations:

*RKDH I	Auctioneer's copy, annot. with all buyers and prices on interleaved pages as well as a few letters for the sellers.
RKDH II	Auctioneer's copy, annot. with all buyers and prices on interleaved pages as well as a few letters for the sellers.

Comments: The contents of this sale were a wide range of miscellaneous items, including porcelain, jewelry, clothing, furniture, books and some paintings. The recently deceased owner, Margaretha Maria van Laar, was the widow of Johannes Esser, an Amsterdam sugar refiner who had died in September, 1801. The paintings were mostly landscapes and portraits that generally fetched less than fl. 10, although one lot, consisting of two paintings on copper said to be by Elsheimer and Poelenburgh, brought fl. 31.

25 **1802/03/15–1802/03/18**

H. en G. Backhuyzen; Den Haag, Groote Zaal van het Hof

Additional Auctioneers: Wed. P. Wynands

Seller(s) from Title Page: Nagelaten door twee Liefhebbers

Paintings Lots: 2

Catalogue Locations:

MWH	Not annot.

Comments: This four-day anonymous sale in The Hague included books and musical instruments as well as a number of miscellaneous *rariteiten*, prints and three lots of paintings. One of the latter consisted of watercolors.

26 **1802/04/12–1802/04/14**

I. Kann; Den Haag, Groote Zaal van het Hof

Seller(s) from Title Page: None

Paintings Lots: 4

Catalogue Locations:

MWH	Not annot.

Comments: This book sale held in The Hague by the bookseller I. Kann also contained some precious stones, silver and prints, all sold on the last day. There were also four lots of anonymous paintings.

27 **1802/04/13–1802/04/14** [Lugt 6407]

Vincent van der Vinne; Haarlem, Burgerhof

Seller(s) from Title Page: Heer ****

Paintings Lots: 77

Catalogue Locations:

MB	Not annot.

Comments: During the first decade of the century the landscape painter Vincent van der Vinne III (1736–1811) was still the most active auctioneer in Haarlem, although he was by now very elderly. The present sale included a large number of paintings and drawings as well as some prints and miscellaneous items, most notably some musical instruments. The title page indicates that everything belonged to a single collector whose name is not revealed. His paintings included landscapes, still lifes, battle scenes and genre pieces, most of which are described very briefly and without dimensions. No results are recorded.

28 **1802/04/26–1802/05/01**

J. van Cleef; Den Haag, Veenestraat

Additional Auctioneers: B. Scheurleer

Seller(s) from Title Page: Feu Monsieur & Mr. B. de Moor van Immerzeel, dans son vivant conseiller & Bourguemaître de la Ville de Gouda

Seller Authority: Moor van Immerzeel, B. de, Mr.

Paintings Lots: 7

Catalogue Locations:

MWH	Not annot.

Comments: This six-day sale in The Hague contained mostly books, but on the last day there were also some drawings, medals and "curiosités." Among the latter were seven lots of poorly described paintings.

29 **1802/05/05–1802/05/06** [Lugt 6424]

Philippus van der Schley; Amsterdam, Ten Huize van Cornelis Sebille Roos, op de Kloveniersburgwal, in het Huis van Trip

Additional Auctioneers: Jan de Bosch, Jeronimusz.; Bernardus de Bosch, Jeronimusz.; Jan Yver; Cornelis Sebille Roos; Roelof Meurs Pruyssenaar

Seller(s) from Title Page: None

Paintings Lots: 323

Catalogue Locations:

RKDH	Auctioneer's copy, annot. with all buyers and prices on interleaved pages as well as letters for the sellers.
EBNP	Auctioneer's copy, annot. with all buyers and prices on interleaved pages as well as letters for the sellers.
*LBDa	Auctioneer's copy, annot. with all buyers and prices on interleaved pages, as well as letters for the sellers. The title page is lacking. It may have belonged to the dealer P. van der Schley.
JPGM	Annot. in ink and pencil with many buyers and all prices.
ESP	Not annot.
MA	Not annot.

Comments: This was one of the regular sales held in Amsterdam in the Huis van Trip, the premises of the dealer C.S. Roos, under the auspices of Philippus van der Schley, Roos and a group of their colleagues. It was almost entirely dedicated to paintings, of which 272 lots appeared in the printed catalogue and another 56 were added *hors du catalogue*. There were also some drawings. No proprietors are mentioned, but the EBNP, LBDa and RKDH copies of the catalogue, all of which must have belonged originally to dealers who helped organize the sale, are annotated with a letter next to each lot designating the consigners. A list of the consignments in the RKDH catalogue reveals how the proceeds were divided. The consigners are designated as A, B, BB, C, CC, D, E, F, G, H, J, K and R. The largest consignment, consisting of 80 lots, belonged to "J," but they were generally inexpensive paintings that realized a total of just fl. 1380:3. The most valuable items were those submitted by "D" whose 29 lots realized fl. 3248. None of the consigners have been identified, although it is likely that "R," who submitted just one lot, was Roos himself, since this letter falls outside the sequence. As was not unusual for a sale of this size, the pictures seem to have varied greatly in quality, with many bringing less than fl. 1 and others more than fl. 500. The highest price was paid for a pair of still lifes by Paul Theodor van Brussel belonging to "D," which cost fl. 1150. One of the paintings in the "J" consignment, a *Landscape with Riders and Animals* by Wouwerman, cost fl. 680, which was the best price for a single painting. Just one other lot exceeded fl. 500: a marine picture by Backhuysen was sold for fl. 565. None of these paintings has been traced, but a few of the less costly lots are known. An interior with the story of *The Satyr and the Peasant* by Jan Steen (lot 190) that was knocked down to Pruyssenaar for fl. 400 can be identified with one that reappeared in Paris in 1811 and was more recently in the Philips collection in Eindhoven. A small interior with a shoemaker by Brekelencam that was withdrawn from the sale is now in the Musée de Picardie in Amiens, and a scene with a *Woman Selling Vegetables to a Mother and Her Daughter* by Nicolas Maes is now in the Rijksmuseum. On the whole, however, the sale consisted primarily of minor landscapes and genre pieces. The total receipts for the sale came to fl. 8946:14.

30 1802/05/10–1802/05/11 [Lugt 6428]

J. van de Sande en Zoon; Middelburg, Op den Langenburgt, by de Groote Markt

Seller(s) from Title Page: Nagelaaten door wylen den Heer Johan Dirk Kruysse, in leven apothecar binnen deze stad

Seller Authority: Kruysse, Johan Dirk

Paintings Lots: 52

Catalogue Locations:

*RMA	Annot. with some buyers and most prices for the paintings only.
ULn	Not annot. It is addressed to Mr van Hultem and belonged formerly to the Royal Library in Brussels.

Photocopies : RKDH (of RMA)

Comments: The owner is described as an apothecary from Middelburg who had evidently died very recently. The two-day sale was devoted primarily to books, as was common in sales held in this city, but there were also 52 lots of paintings, some prints, drawings and miscellaneous objects. The paintings were mostly anonymous and clearly of no great importance, but a few brought higher prices and so may have been of above-average quality. The most expensive lot was a landscape with travelers by Lingelbach which brought £28. An architectural piece by Dirck van Delen was bought for £24. A number of paintings by the contemporary Flemish landscape painter Gerardus Dinter were present. The total receipts for the paintings came to £213.19.3.

31 1802/05/11 and following days

A. Groenewold; Groningen, not given

Additional Auctioneers: H.H. Bolt

Seller(s) from Title Page: Arnold. Sicco Werumeus, Amplissimo Senatui civitatis Groninganae

Seller Authority: Werumeus, Arnold Sicco

Paintings Lots: 81

Catalogue Locations:

*KBH	Annot. in pencil with most prices for the lots on pp.13–25, 31–34, 36–37 and 62–63.
MWH	Not annot.
BRB	Not annot.

Comments: The catalogue of this sale was issued in two parts; the first contained just books, while the second included manuscripts, maps, prints, paintings, naturalia and miscellaneous items as well as books. It also stipulates that the paintings were to be sold after May 15, but no more precise date is given. The proprietor, Werumeus, is described as having been a councillor in Groningen before his death, and the contents of his estate indicate that he was also a scholar of some breadth. Unfortunately, his paintings, which were quite numerous, are poorly described, making it difficult to judge their importance. They consisted of landscapes, genre pieces, a few portraits, and even fewer religious scenes. The results of the sale are unknown.

32 1802/05/18–1802/05/22 [Lugt 6438]

P. en J. Holsteyn; Rotterdam, Op de Zaal boven de Beurs

Seller(s) from Title Page: Nagelaten door den Heer Lambertus Bicker, In Leven Medicinae Doctor, Directeur van het Bataafsch Genootschap te Rotterdam, Lid van de Hollandsche Maatschappy te Haarlem, en van 't Zeeuwsch Genootschap te Vlissingen enz.

Seller Authority: Bicker, Lambertus

Paintings Lots: 30

Catalogue Locations:

VBBA	Not annot.

Comments: The owner, Lambertus Bicker, was a medical doctor in Rotterdam who had died the previous year. The five-day sale of his property included primarily his books, but there were also a number of paintings, drawings, prints, scientific instruments and miscellaneous *liefhebberyen*. His paintings were mostly anonymous landscapes and marine views, described briefly. The results are not recorded.

33 1802/05/24 [Lugt 6443]

H. en G. Backhuysen; Den Haag, Groote Zaal van 't Hof

Seller(s) from Title Page: Nagelaten door Mejuffrouw A. van der Mieden

Seller Authority: Mieden, A. van der, Mejuffrouw

Paintings Lots: 74

Catalogue Locations:

*MA	Annot. with most buyers and all prices. The annotations are difficult to read.
AMA	Not located, 1994. According to Lugt it is annot. with many prices.
MWH	Not annot.

Comments: The identity of the proprietor is still uncertain, but she may have been related to Adriaan van der Mieden (1702–1764), steward to the High Counsel in The Hague and from 1735 onward advisor to the stadholders Van Oranje. The books of A. van der Mieden were sold on May 3/6, 1802, by the same auctioneer. (A copy exists at MWH.) Most of the paintings were landscapes and genre scenes, but there were also a few religious subjects. The prices were generally modest, but with one exception: lot 23, described as "een drie Koningen vreugd" by Jan Steen, was sold for fl. 300 to the dealer Labouchere. None of the pictures has been identified. The MA copy of the catalogue gives the totals as fl. 1011:14.

34 1802/06/16 and following days [Lugt 6469]

Philippus van der Schley; Amsterdam, Ten Huize van C.S. Roos, op de Kloveniers Burgwal, in het van ouds genaamde Huis van Trip

Additional Auctioneers: Jan de Bosch, Jeronimusz.; Bernardus de Bosch, Jeronimusz.; Jan Yver; Cornelis Sebille Roos; Roelof Meurs Pruissenaar

Seller(s) from Title Page: Nagelaten door een Buitenlands Kunst:Liefhebber

Seller(s) from Other Sources: [Merrem]

Seller Authority: Merrem

Paintings Lots: 253

Catalogue Locations:

*RKDH	Auctioneer's copy, annot. with all buyers and prices on interleaved pages.
EBNP	Auctioneer's copy, annot. with all buyers and prices on interleaved pages.

LBDa	Auctioneer's copy, annot. with all buyers and prices on interleaved pages. The title page is lacking. There is also a handwritten list of pictures in pencil at the back which may be someone's purchases. It may have belonged to the dealer P. van der Schley.
MB	Annot. in pencil with a few buyers and prices.
FLNY	Annot. with all prices.
ESP	Not annot. excepting a few letters and figures that may be bidding codes.

Comments: It appears that all of the paintings in this sale, 253 lots altogether, were the property of a single person, described on the title page as a foreigner. None of the three annotated catalogues indicates that more than one seller was involved, and although the sale did contain seven lots of Italian paintings, an unusually high number for a Dutch sale, more than 80 percent of the remainder were in fact by Dutch artists, reason to think the owner was probably Dutch or German. In addition, at least fifteen lots can be traced to the time of their purchase at previous Amsterdam sales, one in 1800, seven at the Fouquet sale on April 13, 1801 (cat. no.6) and seven more at the anonymous sale on May 11, 1801 (cat. no.9). In all cases the buyer was the dealer Ph. van der Schley, and for all of those purchased during 1801, he was bidding on behalf of "M" or "Merrem." It is therefore certain that if a single proprietor was represented at this sale, he was Merrem, and he most probably resided in or near Amsterdam, at least temporarily. His full identity is yet to be discovered, however; because he evidently preferred to act through Van der Schley rather than representing himself at auctions, his name has so far escaped appearing in the literature. He might be a relative of the "Commerzian Rath" Gerhard Merrem (1729–1803) who died in Duisberg the following year.

As might be expected for a sale with so many pictures, the prices ranged widely, from fl. 2 to fl. 2600, although most were near the low end of this scale, and only two exceeded fl. 600. Only a few have been identified in their present locations. The highest amount, fl. 2600, was paid by Izaäk Schmidt for a landscape by Hobbema, implying that it was an unusually good example. The second highest price, fl. 860, was paid by the French dealer Lafontaine for a *Kermis* by Cornelis Dusart, a painting on copper that can be identified with one now in the Sinebrychoff Art Museum in Helsinki. Lot 99, described as *A Woman Weighing Gold* by Jan Vermeer of Delft, is certainly the painting of this subject by Pieter de Hooch now in Berlin. It had been purchased at the sale on May 11, 1801, for fl. 60 and was sold to the dealer Gruyter at the present sale for fl. 140. The total receipts are recorded as fl. 18,152.

35 1802/06/21–1802/06/29

M. van Daalen Wetters; Den Haag, Op den Hoek van de Hof-Cingel

Seller(s) from Title Page: None

Paintings Lots: 26

Catalogue Locations:

*BRB	Annot. with a few prices.
MWH	Not annot.

Comments: This was an anonymous seven-day sale of books held by the Hague bookseller Melis van Daalen Wetters. The last day of the sale also included naturalia, scientific instruments, "curiosités" and a number of paintings. The latter were mostly anonymous and very cursorily described. The results are largely unknown.

36 1802/06/28 and following days [Lugt 6473]

Philippus van der Schley; Amsterdam, Ten Huize van Cornelis Sebille Roos, op de Kloveniersburgwal, in het Huis van Trip

Additional Auctioneers: Jan de Bosch, Jeronimusz.; Bernardus de Bosch, Jeronimusz.; Jan Yver; Cornelis Sebille Roos; Roelof Meurs Pruyssenaar

Seller(s) from Title Page: Verzameld door Wylen de Heeren Hendrik en Gerard Elink, En laatstelyk nagelaaten door Wylen Mejuffrouw Anna Elink

Seller Authority: Elink, Anna, Mejuffrouw

Paintings Lots: 267

Catalogue Locations:

*RKDH	Auctioneer's copy, annot. with all buyers and prices on interleaved pages as well as a few letters for the sellers.
LBDa	Auctioneer's copy, annot. with all buyers and prices on interleaved pages as well as some letters for the sellers. The title page is lacking. It may have belonged to the dealer P. van der Schley.
MPA	Not annot.
MA	Not annot.

Comments: The title page of the catalogue tells us that this collection of 267 paintings belonged to a single person, Mejuffrouw Anna Elink, who had apparently inherited it from Hendrik and Gerard Elink, who had assembled the collection. Anna Elink died in January, 1802, at which time her residence was "op de Keysersgragt by de Runstraat." One of her executors was the dealer Augustus Elink Sterk. Gerard, possibly her father or an elder brother, had died already by 1773, and Hendrik, probably another brother, had died in 1794. Nine of the lots can be traced to the Fouquet sale of 1783, at which time they were purchased by Hendrik Elink; another was acquired in 1790. It appears that most of the paintings had been bought by Hendrik during the past twenty years or more from local auctions, generally at very modest prices. The results of the present sale reflect this as well. Only one lot, a scene with peasants outside an inn by Adriaen van Ostade, was sold for more than fl. 100. Most lots were well under fl. 30, and the collection seems to have lacked works of great significance. The first two lots, a pair of still lifes by Paul Theodor van Brussel, were knocked down as a pair for fl. 560. They may have been the most valuable items in the sale, but were bought in. Only a few lots in the sale have been tentatively traced to their present location. Lot 66, an interior scene with a still life by Jan van der Heyden, which sold for fl. 39, may be identical with a painting in the Budapest museum. (Although the description and dimensions correspond, the Elink painting is described as being on panel, while the one in Budapest is on canvas.) Lot 67, another interior by van der Heyden but of different dimensions, is apparently the one that later was in the Adolph Schloss collection in Paris. Some of the paintings in the sale apparently did not belong to the Elinks. Thirty-six lots are marked in the LBDa and RKDH copies of the catalogue with the letter "B" to indicate that they derived from a different proprietor, but he (or she) remains unidentified. The same catalogues give the total receipts for the sale as fl. 3513:12.

37 1802/07/06–1802/07/09 [Lugt 6478]

W.H. Stoopendahl; Amsterdam, P. Le Dantu en Comp., op de N.2 Voorburgwal, achter het Stadhuis, in No.215

Additional Auctioneers: etc.

Seller(s) from Title Page: None

Paintings Lots: 40

Catalogue Locations:

AMA	Not annot.

Comments: The contents of this four-day sale consisted of a wide variety of items, including furniture, porcelain, glass, silver, jewelry, prints and paintings. The proprietors are not recorded, and the only extant copy of the catalogue is not annotated with the results. The organizers of the sale were a group of 13 dealers, of whom W.H. Stoopendahl was only the first listed. The paintings were sold on the last day of the sale, and are very poorly described. Most are anonymous.

38 1802/07/20–1802/07/21 [Lugt 6482]

J. van de Sande en Zoon; Middelburg, Op den Langenburgt, by de Groote Markt

Seller(s) from Title Page: None

Paintings Lots: 61

Catalogue Locations:

BMB	Present location unknown. According to Lugt it is annot. with buyers and prices for the paintings but lacked some pages of the print section.
MWH	Not annot.

Comments: The catalogue for this anonymous Middelburg sale includes more information about the individual lots than was usual for sales held in this city, perhaps because it was devoted primarily to paintings rather than books. Both the author and dimensions are given for most lots, and the descriptions are ample enough to allow one to recognize the picture. Unfortunately, the only annotated catalogue has been lost, so the results of the sale are unknown. The proprietor(s) have not been identified.

39 1802/07/21 [Lugt 6482a]

I: Kann; Den Haag, Groote Zaal van het Hof

Seller(s) from Title Page: None

Paintings Lots: 119

Catalogue Locations:

MWH	Not annot.

Comments: The only extant catalogue of this sale is very poorly printed, with many letters either illegible or missing altogether. The sales organized by I. (or J.) Kann, the auctioneer, were primarily given over to books, but the present one was devoted entirely to paintings. Most were landscapes, genre scenes or portraits, but there were also a few "curiosités." Lot 46 is described as a picture by Hieronymus Bosch dated 1502 and depicting a group of monks and nuns singing, with other unusual details. Unfortunately it cannot be identified. Another painting, dated 1627, is said to be by "C. Bakker van Harlingen," who is otherwise unknown but might be related to the painter Jacob Backer, also from Harlingen. The proprietor(s) of these paintings are unknown and the results are not recorded.

40 1802/07/27 [Lugt 6484]

J.P. van Horstok; Alkmaar, Premises, aan de Z.Z. van de Langestraat

Seller(s) from Title Page: Nagelaaten door wijlen Maria Stategaart

Seller Authority: Stategaart, Maria

Paintings Lots: 105

Catalogue Locations:

MPA	Annot. in pencil with all buyers and prices.
*AA	Annot. with some buyers and all prices. Most of the annotations refer to the dealer Wm. Gruyter and the catalogue was probably his.
RKDH	Not annot. excepting a note by the first lot, which may be modern.

Comments: This is one of the few sales held in Alkmaar for which catalogues have survived. Excepting a few drawings, it consisted entirely of paintings, the property of the recently deceased Maria Stategaart, in whose home the sale took place. Nothing has been learned about the proprietor or how she acquired her paintings, but the collection included some works of more than average interest. The prize of the sale was apparently a group of four paintings by Jan Steen, lots 1–4, of which the first, *The Twelve-year-old Christ Disputing in the Temple*, brought the highest price, fl. 160, paid by the dealer Willem Gruyter. (This painting is now in the Kunstmuseum, Basel.) The other three works brought much less; one of them, lot 2, described as "een Vastenavonds," has been identified (by C. Hofstede de Groot, *Catalogue Raisonné*, I, 1907, under no.538) as a copy. (It is now in the Leipzig museum, no.556.) The presence of a fifth painting by "de Alkmaarsche Jan Steen," an eighteenth-century namesake, implies that the proprietor had some special interest in the subject. One further item, lot 6, *An Interior with an Old Woman Scaling a Fish* by Brekelencam is probably identical to a painting formerly in the Los Angeles County Museum of Art. (However, the dimensions are reversed and the last digit of the date is incorrect.) This lot, which fetched fl. 41, was also sold to Gruyter. Most of the remaining lots brought still lower prices, although a signed and dated *Portrait of an Anatomy Professor and His Family* by Gerbrand van den Eeckhout brought fl. 50. (It is now lost.) A number of works by eighteenth-century artists were also present.

41 1802/08/24 [Lugt 6488]

A. Delfos; Leiden, Op de Papegragt

Seller(s) from Title Page: Nagelaten door Wijlen den Wel-Eerw. Heere Leonardus Bouman, In Leven rustend Roomsch Pastoor, te Leyden: En een ander Liefhebber

Seller Authority: Bouman, Leonardus

Paintings Lots: 154

Catalogue Locations:

*RKDH I	Annot. in pencil with one buyer and most prices for the pictures only.
*RKDH II	Annot. in pencil with most prices for the pictures only.
BMB	Present location unknown. According to Lugt it is annot. with many buyers and prices.
FLNY	Annot. with the buyers and prices for the prints only. The paintings are not annot.
MGD	Not seen. According to Lugt it is not annot.
ESP	Not seen.

Comments: The principal part of the sale consisted of 154 lots of paintings, but there was also a collection of prints and drawings as well as some sculpture and miscellaneous items, such as a clavier. The title page of the catalogue describes the primary owner as Leonardus Bouman, a recently deceased priest, but also mentions that another unnamed amateur was involved. Very little is known about Bouman or where he acquired his collection, but it seems likely that at least some of the paintings in the sale belonged to the auctioneer, Abraham Delfos. At least four lots reappear as his property at a sale held in April, 1807 (no.110), then were finally sold in The Hague on June 10 of the same year (no.113). Another lot, no.36, an *Interior with a Slaughtered Pig* by Netscher, had been purchased by Delfos at a sale in 1788. So the "ander Liefhebber" referred to on the title page might be Delfos, or yet a third consigner. The sale was organized with the most expensive lots at the beginning; it is likely that these were Bouman's (if, indeed, any of them were). These were mostly landscapes and genre scenes with a few still lifes, although it appears that no major examples were present. The highest recorded price was fetched by a landscape by Pieter Janson at fl. 175, but two other lots brought similar amounts: a winter landscape by Jan Griffier cost fl. 150, and a flower piece by C.J. Schaalje was sold for fl. 130. The RKDH I copy of the catalogue puts the total for the paintings at fl. 2836:10.

42 1802/09/06 and following days [Lugt 6491]

Philippus van der Schley; Amsterdam, Ten Huize van Cornelis Sebille Roos, op de Kloveniersburgwal, in het van ouds genaamde Huis van Trip

Additional Auctioneers: Jan de Bosch, Jeronimusz.; Bernardus de Bosch, Jeronimusz.; Jan Yver; Cornelis Sebille Roos; Roelof Meurs Pruissenaar

Seller(s) from Title Page: Nagelaten, door wylen den Heer J.B.J. Achtienhoven

Seller(s) from Auctioneer's Copy: Mevrouw Achtienhoven; Wed. Grave; Hn Smit; etc.

Seller Authority: Witt, Aldegonda Maria Theresia de; Grave; Smit, Hn.

Paintings Lots: 297

Catalogue Locations:

LBDa	Auctioneer's copy, annot. with all buyers and prices on interleaved pages as well as letters for the sellers. The title page is lacking. It may have belonged to the dealer P. van der Schley.
RKDH	Auctioneer's copy, annot. with all buyers and prices on interleaved pages as well as letters for the sellers. It belonged to the dealer C.S. Roos.
BMB	Auctioneer's copy, annot. with all buyers and prices on interleaved pages as well as letters for the sellers. It lacks a title page.
FLNY	Auctioneer's copy, annot. with all buyers and prices – excepting lots 251–260 – on interleaved pages as well as letters for the sellers. However, it lacks the title page and introduction.
*EBNP	Auctioneer's copy. Part one is annot. with all buyers and prices on interleaved pages as well as letters for the sellers. Many of the owners are identifed at the back of the catalogue.
ESP II	Not annot. This is the copy formerly at KKB.
ESP I	Not annot.
MR	Missing for many years and presumably lost. According to Lugt it is not annot.
MGD	Not seen. According to Lugt it is not annot.

Comments: This sale, which certainly extended over a period of two weeks or more, was dedicated to paintings, drawings and prints as well as naturalia, optical instruments and a variety of miscellanea. The title page mentions just one owner, J.B.J. Achtienhoven, the Amsterdam dealer who had died in 1801, but at least five copies of the catalogue exist annotated with letters for various sellers, and the EBNP copy – which presumably belonged originally to one of the six dealers who organized the sale – lists the letters and the owners to which they were assigned. They are: A = Mevrouw Achtienhoven; B (not given); C = Wed. Grave en ander; CC = Wed. Grave; D, E and F (not given); G = Brave; H = Hanenberg; J (not given); K = Spaan; M = D H van der Meulen; N = Hn Smit; O = Wed. Flickarnis [?]; P = D W ten Houten; R = Hr Renselaar; V = Hr Voigt; X and Y (not given); Z = Hr Coclers. As will be seen, a few of the initials correspond to the names of the consigners but the majority do not. This list also includes the results of the sale (fl. 6583:6) broken down by seller: Achtienhoven's widow, who had submitted 59 lots, received the largest amount, fl. 1608:3. The second largest amount, fl. 743:13, was returned to Hn. Smit, who had consigned 16 lots. Numerically, the largest group was that of "J," which consisted of 80 lots, though they were generally not valuable items. The consignments designated as E, F, H, O, R, V, Y and Z did not include paintings. Overall, the sale evidently included few paintings of major importance and the prices were generally quite low, with most lots bringing less than fl. 10. Only three exceeded fl. 100: lot 103 by Jan Steen depicting the interior of an inn (and belonging to "D") was bought by the dealer C.H. Hodges for fl. 230, the highest price of the sale. (It brought fl. 313 when Hodges resold it in 1809, and was later in the Higginson collection at Saltmarshe.) Lot 48, a landscape by Jan Hackaert and Jan Lingelbach consigned by Hn. Smit, was bought by the dealer Izaäk Schmidt for fl. 131. Lastly a landscape by Willem Romeyn belonging to "B" was purchased by the dealer Pruyssenaar for fl. 122. None of these paintings has been traced.

43 1802/09/13–1802/09/15

I. Kann; Den Haag, Groote Zaal van het Hof

Seller(s) from Title Page: None

Paintings Lots: 8

Catalogue Locations:

MWH	Not annot.

Comments: This was a sale of books held in The Hague by the bookdealer I. Kann. As often occurred, some prints and paintings were included on the last day of the sale. These are likely to have been fairly minor works, but the results of the sale are unrecorded.

44 1802/09/18 [Lugt 6494]

C. van den Dries en Zoon; Rotterdam, Zaal boven de beurs

Seller(s) from Title Page: Nagelaaten door Casper de Haas, In leven Mr. Metselaar binnen de Stad Rotterdam

Seller Authority: Haas, Casper de

Paintings Lots: 123

Catalogue Locations:

*MB	Not annot., but there is a handwritten list of prices and buyers appended to the catalogue with a long note. This note was written

by Gerrit van der Pot and describes his activities at the sale, so the catalogue presumably belonged to him.

Comments: The proprietor, Casper de Haas, is described as a "master metselaar" active in Rotterdam; at the time of his death in May, 1802, he was 81 years old. The contents of his sale consisted of a library on architectural subjects as well as drawings and designs for a number of buildings, including a town hall intended for Rotterdam. However, the bulk of the sale was dedicated to his extensive collection of paintings, as well as a smaller collection of prints. The paintings consisted primarily of landscapes, among which are found some genre subjects, a few mythological pictures, and an occasional architectural piece. A number of artists were included, both modern and earlier, but the contemporary Leyden landscape painter B.H. Thier (1751–1814) was represented by 23 lots, indicating that he was held in particular favor. Thier's paintings were also among the most expensive lots in the sale, his copy after Potter's *Landscape with Cattle and Bathers* of 1648 in the Mauritshuis, fetching the highest price, fl. 90. It was purchased by the Rotterdam collector Gerrit van der Pot, and reappeared in the latter's sale in 1806 (cat. no.126) at which time it brought fl. 160. Altogether Pot acquired four items at this sale; the only extant copy of the catalogue appears to have belonged to him, since it contains a lengthy note to someone telling which lots he had bought and explaining that two of them, nos.44 and 60, had been bought on behalf of the unidentified addressee. Most of the paintings brought less than fl. 10.

45 1802/09/21 [Lugt 6495]

C. van Hardenberg; Utrecht, Op de kromme Nieuwe Gragt

Seller(s) from Title Page: None

Paintings Lots: 130

Catalogue Locations:

*OGA	Annot. with all buyers and prices on interleaved pages. There are also some added lots.
MPA	Annot. in pencil with all prices.
MB	Not annot.

Comments: The contents of this Utrecht sale were primarily paintings, but there were also a few drawings and prints. The sale was organized by the artist Cornelis van Hardenberg (1755–1843), who was active in Utrecht as a dealer and to whom some of the paintings may have belonged. A few of the lots were by Utrecht artists, such as Breenbergh, Honthorst, Poelenburgh and J.G. van Bronchorst, but the majority were landscapes by artists from Haarlem and elsewhere. Public picture sales were relatively rare in Utrecht during this period, and it is difficult to speculate about the source(s) for the paintings found in the present auction, but they presumably derived from local collections. At least eleven lots can be traced to the posthumous sale of the collection of J.W. Barchman Wuytiers held in Utrecht on September 17 ff., 1792, which was the last known sale of this kind recorded in that city. (A sale held in September, 1798, and listed by Lugt as perhaps containing works belonging to Barchman Wuytiers, consisted entirely of Italian paintings or copies after Italian paintings.) They had been knocked down on that occasion to at least three different buyers: Carseboom (three), Cotterel (five) and Roosje (one). Hardenberg, who is recorded as having bought other lots at the Barchman Wuytiers sale, is not known to have acquired any of these. It is possible that in 1802 they still belonged to the Barchman Wuytiers estate, but it is more likely that a variety of different consigners were involved. The prices were generally modest; according to the OGA copy of the catalogue, as many as 69 lots appear to have been bought in. The highest prices were paid for a few depictions of landscapes with hunting parties: lot 96 by Ph. Wouwerman was sold to Kobell for fl. 120, and the same buyer acquired one by Thos. Wyck and Dirk van Bergen for fl. 80. A third painting of the same subject by Wouwerman was knocked down for fl. 1450, but was evidently bought in by Hardenberg. The unsold paintings have not been traced.

46 1802/09/27–1802/09/30

H. en G. Backhuysen; Den Haag, Groote Zaal van 't Hof

Seller(s) from Title Page: Nagelaaten door wylen den wel Eerwaarde Heer Jacobus de Ryke, in Leven Predikant te Voorburg, Den Heer en Mr. Johannes van Assendelft en den Heer Arnoldus van Beek, in Leven Notaris en Makelaar in 's Hage

Paintings Lots: 26

Catalogue Locations:

MWH	Not annot.

Comments: This was a four-day sale of books that also included a few paintings, drawings, prints and miscellaneous objects on the last day. The title page stipulates the names of three different sellers without indicating which lots they owned. Since it is possible that further consigners were involved as well, we have not attempted to assign any given lot to any specific owner. The paintings, which were mostly anonymous, consisted of genre pieces and portraits as well as a few mythological and religious pictures. The results are not known.

47 1802/09/29 [Lugt 6498]

Philippus van der Schley; Amsterdam, Ten Huize van C.S. Roos, in het Huis van Trip, op de Kloveniers Burgwal

Additional Auctioneers: Jan de Bosch, Jeronimusz.; Bernardus de Bosch, Jeronimusz.; Jan Yver; Cornelis Sebille Roos; Roelof Meurs Pruyssenaar

Seller(s) from Title Page: Nagelaten door een Kunst-Liefhebber uit Friesland En een ander Liefhebber

Seller(s) from Auctioneer's Copy: Y[ver]

Seller(s) from Other Sources: [Labouchere?; Hendrik III, baron Fagel]

Seller Authority: Labouchere; Fagel, Hendrik III, baron; Yver, Jan

Paintings Lots: 75

Catalogue Locations:

*RKDH	Auctioneer's copy, annot. with all buyers and prices on interleaved pages as well as letters for the sellers. It belonged to the dealer C.S. Roos. (Dutch edition)
EBNP	Auctioneer's copy, annot. with all buyers and prices on interleaved pages as well as letters for the sellers. (Dutch edition)
BMB	Annot. with all buyers and prices on interleaved pages, as well as a few letters for the sellers. (Dutch edition)
FLNY	Annot. in ink and pencil with all buyers and prices. (Dutch edition)
MA I	Annot. with all buyers and prices. (Dutch edition)
MB	Annot. in pencil with a few buyers and prices. It also includes a handwritten list of many buyers and all prices taken from a copy belonging to the dealer van Giesen, evidently in the 19th century. (Dutch edition)
MPA	Annot. in pencil with the buyers for lots 1–3 and all prices. (French edition)
ESP I	Not annot. excepting a few initials by certain lots that may be bidding codes. (Dutch edition)
MA II	Not annot. (French edition)
MWH	Not annot. (French edition)
LBDa	Not annot. It may have belonged to the dealer P. van der Schley. (French edition)
ESP II	Not seen. It is supposed to be unannotated. (French edition)

Comments: The title page of the catalogue, which was issued in both Dutch and French editions, describes the contents of the sale, consisting entirely of paintings, as belonging to a "Kunst-Liefhebber uit Friesland en een ander Liefhebber." At least three extant copies of the catalogue were used by the dealers who organized the sale and are annotated with letters to identify the sellers, revealing that there six altogether, designated as A, B, C, D, E and Y. Their names are not given in any of the catalogues, but at least the two principal consigners can be identified with some certainty: the seller "A," who consigned 62 lots and whose receipts totaled fl. 6647:8, was evidently the dealer Labouchere. No fewer than fourteen lots can be traced to the sale of August 21 ff., 1799, where they were purchased by Labouchere; they appear to be paintings that he had failed to sell during the intervening three years. All were sold on this occasion, an indication that there were no reserves. The seller given as "B," who consigned just four lots and whose receipts came to fl. 4081, was certainly Hendrik III, baron Fagel (1765–1838) – or a representative – whose collection had been put up for sale in London on May 22/23, 1801 (Cf. B. Fredericksen, *Index of Paintings Sold in the British Isles during the Nineteenth Century*, I, 1988, no.40), at which time all four of these lots had been bought in. Three consigners have not yet been identified: "C," who submitted just three lots for a total of fl. 1116; "D," two lots for fl. 888 and "E," three lots for fl. 570. The consigner "Y" was probably the dealer Jan Yver, who was commonly designated with this letter. The majority of the paintings were landscapes by Dutch artists, among which are also found a few genre subjects. The prices were generally above average, and a number of valuable works were present. The most expensive lot was no.45, a *Landscape with Cattle by a Farmhouse* by Paulus Potter, which belonged to the Greffier Fagel and fetched fl. 2210. (It is now in the Rijksmuseum.) A beach scene with fishermen by Wouwerman that came from the "Labouchere" group brought fl. 1020. One of the two paintings submitted by "D" was an *Interior with a Young Woman Playing the Harpsichord with a Young Man* by Jan Steen which was sold for fl. 676. (It is now in the London National Gallery.) Among the remaining pictures that can be traced are a still life by Willem van Aelst (now in the Koninklijk Museum voor Schone Kunsten, Antwerp) and *Jacob's Dream* by Frans van Mieris (Rijksmuseum), which is now recognized as the work of Ary de Vois. The total receipts for the sale came to fl. 13,302:8. Just one lot was bought in.

48 1802/10/18 and following days

Salomon van Benthem; Middelburg, In het Burger Logement Antwerpen, staande in den Langendelft

Additional Auctioneers: Johannes Ooms

Seller(s) from Title Page: None

Paintings Lots: 44

Catalogue Locations:

*ZBM	Annot. with all buyers and prices on interleaved pages.

Comments: This was one of the regular book sales held in Middelburg by the bookdealers Salomon van Benthem and Johannes Ooms. In addition to books, the sale included drawings, prints, maps and miscellaneous items. The title page also refers to a small collection of paintings, drawings and prints that was apparently a separate consignment, but the contents of this latter group are not listed in the catalogue. On p.16 there is also a note: "NB. Voorts eenige Schilderyen, Teekeningen en Prenten, in Lysten met Glazen; waaronder uitmnnt [sic], een ryk te dier tyd gestoffeerde Danszaal, schoon en fiks gepenseeld, de naam des Meesters genoeg bekend; welke op hunne Nommers, volgens een geschreeven Lyst, zullen gepresenteerd worden." However, this list is not present, although there is an interleaved page titled "Schilderijen" which gives the buyers and the prices paid, but no titles. We have included these lots, although it is possible that drawings and prints were also among them. The totals for the sale without the added lots were £72.12.4. The additional paintings totaled £19.19.

49 1802/11/01 [Lugt 6511]

Pieter van Braam; Dordrecht, Berken Poort

Seller(s) from Title Page: Grootendeels nagelaaten door Paulus van der Spyk, In leeven Commijs ter Recherche

Seller Authority: Spyk, Paulus van der

Paintings Lots: 194

Catalogue Locations:

*FLNY	Annot. with all buyers and prices for lots 1–82 as well as some buyers and most prices for lots 144–197 in the supplement.
*MPA	Incomplete and mutilated, including only pp.1–12 and with pp.9–11 cut, causing the loss of many lots. Annot. in pencil with all buyers and prices, but the annotations are difficult to read. The supplement, which is bound elsewhere, is not annot.
MB	Not annot.

Comments: The catalogue for this sale was issued in two fascicles, the first consisting of 18 pages with 143 lots of paintings and 66 lots of prints, the second of 8 pages with paintings lots numbered 144 to 197 and a single lot of prints numbered 67. The first part stipulates that the paintings (but not necessarily the prints) belonged in large part ("grootendeels") to the deceased Paulus van der Spyk. It is printed with a break following lot 82 that might imply a division into two parts, and this is perhaps supported by the fact that the FLNY copy of the catalogue is fully annotated through the same lot, giving a total of fl. 969 for lots 1–82, while lots 83–143 are completely unannotated. If this interpretation is correct, then lots 1–82 may have been van der Spyk's, but this cannot be proven. The second part of the catalogue carries no name at all. At present nothing is known about Spyk beyond what is found on the title page, i.e., that he had been "Commijs ter Recherche," presumably in the city of Dordrecht. (The collection of a similarly named collector, Paulus van Spyk, a Leyden brewer, was sold in 1781 and again under the name of his widow in Rotterdam in 1783. Although Paulus van der Spyk may have been related, the two collections appear to have no connection with each other.) None of Spyk's paintings have been traced, but they seem to have consisted of relatively minor works, primarily genre pieces and landscapes, many of which were anonymous. The prices were generally not very high; only one lot brought more than fl. 100: lot 3, a portrait of a man by Arent de Gelder and dated 1687, was sold for fl. 150. (This might well be the painting now in the Detroit Institute of Arts, although the dimensions do not tally.) Two other lots by the same artist were sold for less than fl. 10.

50 1802/12/13 and following days [Lugt 6529]

Philippus van der Schley; Amsterdam, Ten huize van Cornelis Sebille Roos, op de Kloveniersburgwal, in het van ouds genaamde Huis van Trip

Additional Auctioneers: Jan de Bosch, Jeronimusz.; Bernardus de Bosch, Jeronimusz.; Jan Yver; Cornelis Sebille Roos; Roelof Meurs Pruissenaar

Seller(s) from Title Page: Naargelaaten door Wylen den Vermaarde Kunst-Schilder Jacobus Lauwers, en een ander Liefhebber

Seller(s) from Auctioneer's Copy: Pruyssenaar; Yver; etc.

Seller Authority: Lauwers, Jacobus Johannes; Pruyssenaar, Roelof Meurs; Yver, Jan

Paintings Lots: 267

Catalogue Locations:

*RKDH	Auctioneer's copy, annot. with all buyers and prices on interleaved pages as well as letters for the sellers. It belonged to the dealer C.S. Roos.
*LBDa	Auctioneer's copy, annot. with all buyers and prices on interleaved pages as well as letters for the sellers. The title page is lacking. It may have belonged to the dealer P. van der Schley.
FLNY	Auctioneer's copy, annot. with all buyers and prices on interleaved pages as well as letters for the sellers. However, it lacks the title page and the introduction.
EBNP	Auctioneer's copy; part one is annot. with letters for the sellers and all prices. Part two is annot. with letters for the sellers and in pencil with all prices. Some of the sellers and a few buyers are also identifed at the back of the catalogue.
MB	Annot. in pencil with some buyers and prices for the drawings. The paintings are not annot.
ESP	Lacks the title page. Not annot. excepting some initials by certain lots which may be bidding codes.
MPA	Not annot.
AA	Not annot.
MA	Not annot.
RMA	Incomplete, including part one only. Not annot.

Comments: This was a large sale of paintings, drawings, prints, and artists' materials which must have lasted approximately two weeks. The title page of the catalogue specifies just one seller, the painter Jacobus Lauwers (1753–1800), but also indicates that another anonymous collector was involved. There are at least four extant copies of the catalogue, used by the dealers who organized the sale; all are annotated with letters for the sellers. The EBNP copy of the catalogue identifies fourteen of these, ten of which submitted paintings. Four different groups, designated by the letters A, B, C and D, were consigned by the dealer Pruyssenaar, presumably representing four different persons. The letter "F" was assigned to Florijn [?]; "L" was the dealer Ph. van der Schley representing Lauwers; "N" was de Neufville; "O" was Stech [?]; "W" was Vermeulen; and "Y" was the dealer Yver. The largest single group (99 lots) was consigned by Pruyssenaar for A; at least two can be traced to previous sales, but it is not clear who their owner was. Other large consignments were those from Lauwers (43 lots) and Yver (32 lots). However, only two lots exceeded fl. 100 and the majority of the remainder brought modest prices, an indication that the sale was reserved for relatively unimportant pictures. The highest price was fl. 251, paid for a landscape with a battle scene by Huchtenburgh that belonged to Yver. Yver was also the source for the other successful lot, a church interior by Hendrik van Vliet, which sold for fl. 170. The totals for the auction were fl. 7829:6, and for the paintings fl. 2099:5, a low figure for a sale with 267 items. Thirteen lots were bought in.

51 1803/03/05–1803/03/08 [Lugt 6570]

Bauer; Amsterdam, In de Nes, in de Brakke Grond

Additional Auctioneers: van Leeuwen

Seller(s) from Title Page: None

Paintings Lots: 5

Catalogue Locations:

AA	Annot. in pencil with a few prices, but not for the paintings.

Comments: This three-day sale in Amsterdam consisted primarily of drawings and prints, in addition to musical and scientific instruments, miscellaneous items and a few minor paintings. The latter were mostly anonymous and the names of the owners are not recorded.

52 1803/04/04–1803/04/06 [Lugt 6593]

J. van de Sande en Zoon; Middelburg, Op den Langenburgt, by de Groote Markt

Seller(s) from Title Page: Nagelaaten door wylen Mr. Evert Clyver, in leven Oud Gecommitteerde Raad van Zeeland

Seller Authority: Clyver, Evert, Mr.

Paintings Lots: 21

Catalogue Locations:

VBBA	Not annot.

Comments: The contents of this three-day sale in Middelburg were primarily book and prints, the property of Evert Clyver, described as the "Oud Gecommitteerde Raad van Zeeland." His estate also contained a few miscellaneous items as well as some paintings, the majority of which were landscapes or topographical pieces. The most interesting lots were five still lifes by the relatively rare Middelburg artist Adriaen Coorte, which constituted one of the few assemblages of his work. Unfortunately, the prices are not recorded.

53 1803/04/12–1803/04/18

H. en G. Backhuysen; Den Haag, Groote Zaal van 't Hof

Seller(s) from Title Page: Wel Edele Gestrenge Heer Johan Pieter Reigersman, In leven Generaal Major van de Infanterie, en Collonel Commandant van het gelicentieerd Regiment Oranje Gelderland, ten dienste deezer Landen, &c. &c. en een ander Liefhebber

Seller Authority: Reigersman, Johan Pieter

Paintings Lots: 48

Catalogue Locations:

KBH	Annot. in pencil with a few prices, but not for the paintings.
MWH	Not annot.

Comments: The catalogue of this six-day sale in The Hague indicates that the contents belonged to the deceased Major-General Reigersman, as well as another collector whose name is not given. There may well have been still other consigners. The contents were primarily books, and small numbers of prints, drawings, paintings and miscellanea. Noteworthy are a group of eight landscapes and peasant scenes by Heinrich Wilhelm Schweickardt (1746–1797), the German painter who had been active in The Hague from 1775 until 1786, and probably acquired directly from the artist during this period. Much of the remainder consisted of anonymous landscapes and genre scenes, although the title page refers to a school scene by Jan Steen that was evidently considered to be the most important piece in the collection. The prices are not recorded.

54 1803/04/20–1803/04/21 [Lugt 6605]

Philippus van der Schley; Amsterdam, Ten Huize van C.S. Roos, op de Kloveniers Burgwal, in 't van ouds genaamde Huis van Trip

Additional Auctioneers: Jan de Bosch, Jeronimusz.; Jan Yver; Cornelis Sebille Roos; Roelof Meurs Pruyssenaar; Jacobus Vinkeles

Seller(s) from Title Page: De Hoog Welgeboorene Jonkvrouwe Maria Magdalena van Sluypwyk, Gravinne van Moens, Vry-Vrouwe van Vryenesse, Ambachtsvrouw van Sluypwyk, Ravensbergen en Gryssort, &c. &c.

Seller Authority: Moens, Maria Magdalena van Sluypwijk, gravin van

Paintings Lots: 158

Catalogue Locations:

LBDa	Auctioneer's copy, annot. with all buyers and prices on interleaved pages as well as letters for the sellers. The title page is lacking. It may have belonged to the dealer P. van der Schley. (Dutch edition)
*EBNP	Auctioneer's copy, annot. with all buyers and prices on interleaved pages as well as letters for some of the sellers. (Dutch edition)
RKDH	Auctioneer's copy, annot. with all buyers and prices on interleaved pages. A few lots are also marked with the letter B, evidently a seller. (Dutch edition)
MB	Annot. in pencil with many buyers and all prices. It belonged to the dealer P.J. Thijs and the annotations are his. (French edition)
MA I	Annot. with some buyers and many prices. Some of the latter are modern additions. (French edition)
AA II	Annot. in pencil with a few buyers and all prices. (French edition)
MA II	Annot. with all prices. (Dutch edition)
FLNY	Annot. in pencil with many prices. (Dutch edition)
AAP	Annot. with most prices for lots 1–106. (Dutch edition)
ESP	Not annot. excepting some initials which may be bidding codes. (French edition)
AA I	Not annot. (Dutch edition)
MPA	Not annot. (French edition)
MM	Not seen. According to Lugt it is not annot.

Comments: The contents of this two-day sale in Amsterdam were limited to paintings. The title page of the catalogue, issued in both Dutch and French versions, explicitly states that everything belonged to the estate of Maria Magdalena van Sluypwijk, countess of Moens, who had died the year before. This claim would appear to be contradicted by the three extant copies of the catalogue annotated for the use of the dealers who organized the sale, all of which have the letter "B" next to 24 lots, implying a different ownership than the majority of the lots, which are marked "A." The lots marked "B" are 2, 4, 6–7, 9, 13, 25, 43, 45, 68–69, 84, 90, 99, 101, 115, 117, 150–151, 153 and 155–158. There is reason to think, however, that these annotations may relate to a division of the estate rather than to different consigners. Lots 4 and 5 by J. Beschey, for instance, appear to be pendants (although they are described as such only in the French version of the catalogue), but the first is marked with a "B" and the second is not. The same is true for lots 7 and 8 by H. van Balen, also pendants, but with one marked "B" and the other with "A." Moreover, the auctioneers' catalogues fail to include a division of the receipts, as was normal for sales with more than one consigner. We have, therefore, left everything under the name of the countess. Unfortunately, very little is known about the origins of her collection. Maria Magdalena van Sluypwijk was the illegitimate daughter of Gerbrand, graaf van Moens (1680–1760), and lived at various times in two homes on the Herengracht in Amsterdam. She is thought to have acquired at least two of her paintings, a small oval portrait of a man at his desk by Gerrit Dou and a double portrait of a man and his wife by Dou and Nicolas Berchem, by inheritance from her father. These two paintings (now in the Rijksmuseum), tentatively identified as depicting members of the Wittert family, are supposed to have been family heirlooms that passed from Adriaen Wittert van der Aa to his wife, Anna Maria, later gravin van Moens, who left them to her brother, Gerbrand. (See *Het Rapenburg, Geschiedenis van een Leidse gracht*, IIIb, 1988, pp.461ff.) The Wittert family is known to have owned other paintings, and very possibly some of these were handed down to Maria Magdalena van Sluypwijk. However, none of the documents published so far substantiate this, and it is known that the bulk of the Wittert collection was sold to Pieter de la Court van der Voort in 1710. The pictures in that collection included many works by Leyden painters, such as Dou and both Frans and Willem van Mieris, as well as numerous pictures by Flemish and Utrecht painters, as does the present group. However, at least one of the present lots, a depiction of *Vertumnus and Pomona* by Willem van Mieris, is thought to have appeared in a sale in Amsterdam in August, 1799, and, if so, would have been acquired by the countess soon after. It is equally possible, therefore, that the collection could have been formed largely by the countess herself.

The most expensive lots in the sale were the two paintings by Dou. The double portrait was sold to the dealer Roos for fl. 3200, and the small oval was bought by the dealer Jan Spaan for fl. 1600. Other lots that brought high prices included an *Interior with Card Players* by Teniers, which was purchased by the dealer Gruyter for fl. 1340, and a small landscape by Adriaen van de Velde, for which the dealer Coclers paid fl. 1010. As was usual, virtually all of the lots were purchased by dealers, either for resale or on behalf of clients. Among the buyers were three whose names appear in the RKDH, LBDa, and EBNP catalogues as having requested the sale, evidently as executors or agents involved with the countess's estate. The inscription mentions "De Heeren J. Van Schornenbergh, C Van Cooth, D Lesscher, en Mr F. Horrius." The total receipts for the sale were fl. 15,004.

55 1803/04/27 [Lugt 6614]

Philippe van der Schley; Amsterdam, Maison de Trip, sur le Canal, dit Kloveniers Burgwal

Additional Auctioneers: Jean de Bosch, fils de Jer.; Jean Yver; Corneille Sebille Roos; Roelof Meurs Pruisenaar; Jacques Vinkeles

Seller(s) from Title Page: None

Paintings Lots: 211

Catalogue Locations:

*RKDH	Auctioneer's copy, annot. with all buyers and prices on interleaved pages as well as letters for the sellers. (French edition)
*LBDa	Auctioneer's copy, annot. with all buyers and prices on interleaved pages as well as letters for the sellers. The title page is lacking. It may have belonged to the dealer P. van der Schley. (French edition)
AA	Annot. in ink and pencil with some buyers and all prices. (French edition)
MB	Annot. in pencil with a few buyers and all prices. (French edition)
MA	Annot. with many prices. (French edition)
MPA	Annot. in pencil with a few prices. (French edition)
ESP	Not annot. (French edition)
MWH	Not annot. (French edition)

Comments: This was one of the most unusual sales held in Amsterdam during this period. The catalogue exists only in French and was apparently never issued in Dutch. The contents were primarily Italian and Flemish paintings with only a few by Dutch artists, in addition to which there were some Italian drawings and prints and a small group of ancient statues and "Etruscan" vases. Unfortunately nothing is known about the owners or the origins of the collection, although it would appear to have come from southern Italy, perhaps Naples. Among the attributed pictures are works by Luca Giordano, Jusepe Ribera, Vito d'Anna and Caravaggio. There were apparently four consigners, designated as A, B, C and G in the LBDa and RKDH copies of the catalogue, both of which belonged to dealers involved with the organization of the sale. The bulk of the paintings belonged to "A," none of whose lots were bought in, an indication that they had no reserves. The prices for these paintings were generally low, with just three lots fetching more than fl. 100. These included the first lot, a depiction of *The Annunciation to the Shepherds* by "Moréälese," which at fl. 151 was the most successful lot in the sale. (The artist was probably Pietro Novelli, il Monrealese, but it might also have been Paulus Moreelse.) Two more of his paintings are listed in the appendix of the catalogue, lots A and B, a *Mars and Venus* by Rubens and *Mercury and Herse* by Bertholet Flemal, brought fl. 129 and fl. 111, respectively. None of these can be traced, although the latter is known from an engraving. Most of the remainder brought well under fl. 20.

A much smaller group belonged to "B," whose possessions appear in the appendix as lots C through T. Two of these, lots C and D, a small landscape by Adriaen van de Velde and an altarpiece by Gaspar de Crayer, were knocked down for fl. 1500 and fl. 1200, by far the highest prices in the sale. However, both were bought in, as were eleven other lots from this group. Those belonging to "C" and "G" were added by hand to the catalogues and brought relatively low prices. The total receipts for the sale were fl. 3404:7, with the paintings accounting for fl. 2717:2.

56 1803/06/06–1803/06/07

Van Benthem en Ooms; Middelburg, Premises, ten Huize van voorn. Notaris Wagenaar, in de korte Noordstraat L.ª P. N.º 69

Seller(s) from Title Page: Nagelaten door wylen den Heer P. van Noemer; Nagelaten door wylen den Heer Notaris A. Wagenaar

Seller Authority: Wagenaar, A.

Paintings Lots: 5

Catalogue Locations:

*ZBM	Annot. with all buyers and prices on interleaved pages.

Comments: This was a two-day sale of books in Middelburg to which a small group of paintings, prints and miscellaneous objects was appended at the end. The title specifies that the paintings, of which there were just five anonymous lots, all belonged to the notary A. Wagenaar, in whose house the sale was also held.

57 1803/06/20 and following days [Lugt 6657]

Philippus van der Schley; Amsterdam, Ten Huize van C.S. Roos, op de Cloveniers Burgwal, in 't van ouds genaamde Huis van Trip

Additional Auctioneers: Jan de Bosch, Jeronimusz.; Jan Yver; Cornelis Sebille Roos; Jacobus Vinkeles

Seller(s) from Title Page: None

Seller(s) from Auctioneer's Copy: Schley; Roos

Seller Authority: Schley, Philippus van der; Roos, Cornelis Sebille

Paintings Lots: 108

Catalogue Locations:

*LBDa	Auctioneer's copy, annot. with all buyers and prices on interleaved pages as well as letters for the sellers. The sellers are also identified. The title page is lacking. It may have belonged to the dealer P. van der Schley.
*RKDH	Auctioneer's copy, annot. with all buyers and prices on interleaved pages as well as letters for the sellers. It belonged to the dealer C.S. Roos.
MA	Annot. with all buyers and prices on interleaved pages for the drawings and some other sections, but the paintings are not annot.
NOL	Present location unknown. According to Lugt it is annot. with buyers and prices.
BMPL	Annot. with the prices for the prints but not the paintings. It belonged to Wm. Smith.

Comments: The contents of this sale were primarily paintings, drawings and prints, but there were also significant numbers of precious objects, naturalia and musical instruments. No owner is given on the title page, but two extant copies of the catalogue, LBDa and RKDH, which belonged originally to two of the dealers who organized the sale, are both marked with letters for the consigners, from A through M and Z. The LBDa copy also identifies the consigners to whom these letters were assigned, although they were apparently only acting on the behalf of others. There were at least eight consignments of paintings, but since the owners for lots 82–107, which were added after the catalogue had been printed, have been lost, there may have been more. Lots designated as belonging to B, F, G, H and K were submitted by the dealer Philippus van der Schley; those marked C, E and L were associated with Cornelis Sebille Roos. Contrary to standard procedure, the different consignments were generally kept together in the catalogue rather than placed in alphabetical order. Thus the two largest groups, those marked "G" (27 lots) and "B" (17 lots), are found as lots 19–43a and 1–17, respectively. None of the collectors represented by the two dealers can yet be identified, with the possible exception of "B," who may have been Van der Schley himself. At least 15 of the 17 lots in this group can be traced to the sale of June 16, 1802, where nearly half of them were in fact purchased by Van der Schley. However, eight of them had been bought by two other dealers, Isaäk Schmidt and Hendrik de Valk, leading to the possibility that all three had been acting for someone else. We have, therefore, elected to leave "B" unidentified.

The sale contained very few expensive works; only four lots surpassed fl. 100, three of them in the "B" group consigned by Van der Schley. The best price was fl. 200 for lot 6, described as being "zoo goed als" Jan Vermeer which was bought by Van der Schley, apparently acting for "F." This painting had been bought by Izaäk Schmidt in 1802 for fl. 480 as the work of Vermeer himself, meaning that the owner had taken a significant loss. Presumably general opinion had rejected the attribution in the meantime. The second highest price was fl. 160, paid the dealer Gruyter for a landscape with hunters by Ludolf de Jongh, which is probably identical with one attributed to Waterloo and J.B. Weenix in the 1802 sale, for which Hendrik Valk had paid fl. 210. (Aside from the change of authorship – which is referred to in the entry for lot 6 – the chief obstacles to the identification are the dimensions, given as 51 x 16 duim in the 1802 catalogue, as opposed to 51 x 61 duim in the catalogue. It seems probable that the earlier figure was a misprint.) If the identification is correct, this also represented a drop in price. The third lot, a landscape by Jan and Andries Both, was sold for fl. 127 but had been bought by Valk for fl. 500 in 1802, a disastrous decrease. The total receipts for the sale were fl. 5304:18, of which fl. 2604:14 was realized by the paintings. Nearly half of this latter amount, fl. 1135, was derived from the B group of paintings. None of the pieces in this sale have yet been traced.

58 1803/06/27 and following days

Van Benthem en Ooms; Middelburg, In het Burger Logement Antwerpen, staande in den Langendelft

Seller(s) from Title Page: None

Paintings Lots: 16

Catalogue Locations:

*ZBM	Annot. with all buyers and prices on interleaved pages.

Comments: This Middelburg sale was devoted primarily to books, but there were also small groups of prints, maps, miscellaneous objects and both musical and scientific instruments. No owner is mentioned, but a note in the catalogue of the Zeeuws Bibliotheek in Middelburg indicates that the sale "Zeer waarschijnlijk betreft dit de nalatenschap van D. Radermacher." The reasons for this are not known to us. The title page of the sale catalogue and a note on page 83 state that a group of paintings was also to be included and that a list would be distributed at the time of the sale. The only extant copy of the catalogue does not include the list, although there is an interleaved page with the buyers and prices for 16 lots. We have, therefore, included the lots but without artists' names or titles.

59 1803/07/04–1803/07/07

I. Kann; Den Haag, Grande Salle de la Cour

Seller(s) from Title Page: None

Paintings Lots: 26

Catalogue Locations:

MWH	Not annot.

Comments: This was a four-day sale of books in The Hague that included some lots of paintings, prints, maps and "curiosités" on the last day. Most of the paintings were landscapes and genre pieces. The results of the sale are not known.

60 1803/07/14 [Lugt 6669]

D. Kleyne; Middelburg, Premises, Op de Haringplaats

Seller(s) from Title Page: Nagelaaten door Mr. Caspar Jacob van Citters

Seller Authority: Citters, Caspar Jacob van, Mr.

Paintings Lots: 39

Catalogue Locations:

RKDH	Not annot.

Comments: Caspar Jacob van Citters was a prominent official in Middelburg who had died in 1801. The collections put on sale at his home included paintings, drawings, prints and books. The paintings were mostly landscapes or sea pieces by lesser artists, a number of which are described as copies or in the manner of the artist given. A few were by contemporary local artists such as Willem Udemans or David Kleijne. Kleijne was also responsible for organizing the sale. The results of the sale are unrecorded, but since at least one of the lots, a depiction of *Mars and Venus* by Ottmar Elliger, reappeared in the lottery of the pictures belonging to Van Citters' son, Caspar, held on Oct.10, 1810 (cat. no.171), it seems that some lots may have been left unsold.

61 1803/07/18 and following days [Lugt 6670]

Philippus van der Schley; Amsterdam, Ten Huise van C.S. Roos, op de Cloveniers Burgwal, in 't Huis van Trip

Additional Auctioneers: Jan de Bosch, Jeronimusz.; Jan Yver; Cornelis Sebille Roos; R. Meurs Pruyssenaar; Jacobus Vinkeles

Seller(s) from Title Page: Nagelaaten door Wylen Vrouwe Maria Theresia Andrioli, Weduwe den Heere Jan Clicquet

Seller Authority: Andrioli, Maria Theresia

Paintings Lots: 65

Catalogue Locations:

LBDa	Auctioneer's copy, annot. with all buyers and prices on interleaved pages. It may have belonged to the dealer P. van der Schley. (Dutch edition)
*RKDH I	Auctioneer's copy, annot. with all buyers and prices on interleaved pages. It belonged to the dealer C.S. Roos. (Dutch edition)
AA	Annot. in pencil with all buyers and prices. There is a list of pictures at the back purchased by Hodges and he was evidently the owner of the catalogue. (French edition)
EBNP	Annot. with all buyers and prices. (Dutch edition)
MB	Annot. in pencil with most buyers and all prices. It belonged to the dealer P.J. Thijs and the annotations are his. (French edition)
MA II	Annot. with a few buyers and all prices. (Dutch edition)
RKDH II	Incomplete, consisting of pp.1–27 only. Annot. with most buyers and all prices.
NOL	Present location unknown. According to Lugt it is annot. with buyers and sellers.
MM	Not seen. According to Lugt it is annot. with buyers and sellers for the paintings.
MPA	Annot. in pencil with all prices. (French edition)

ESP	Not annot. excepting some letters by certain lots which may be bidding codes. (French edition)
MA I	Not annot. (French edition)

Comments: The deceased owner, Maria Theresia Andrioli (born 1734), was a member of a prominent Amsterdam family and the widow of Jean Clicquet, whom she had married in 1758. They lived at no.301 on the Herengracht, which had belonged to the Clicquet family since 1711. Their collection contained a number of good pictures, some of which can be identified, but it is not yet clear precisely how and when they were acquired. At least two lots (nos.38 by Adriaen van Ostade and 46 by Jan Steen) have been traced to sales held in the 1780s, and two others (lots 35 by Eglon van der Neer and 45 by Jan Steen) had appeared in sales in the 1760s. A fifth painting may have been purchased as recently as 1802. (Lot 34, *Rape of the Sabines* by Vincent Malo, corresponds to a painting sold on August 24, 1802, in Antwerp, but the dimensions are somewhat different.) From these few clues, it might appear that the collection had been assembled piecemeal during the last part of the preceding century rather than having been inherited within either the Clicquet or the Andrioli families. This has yet to be confirmed, however. The most expensive lot was an *Interior with a Man Playing the Violin* by Jan Steen that was bought by the dealer Pruyssenaar for fl. 1000, one of the highest prices brought by a work by this artist during this period. (It is now in the British Royal Collection.) The next highest amount, fl. 800, was paid for lot 19, an *Interior with a Woman and a young Child* by Pieter de Hooch, bought by the dealer Roos. (It is now in the Wallace Collection, London.) Many other lots surpassed fl. 500, making this one of the more important sales of the period. Only two lots were bought in. The total receipts were fl. 14,329:17, of which fl. 9832:10 were realized by the paintings. The catalogue was printed in both Dutch and French editions.

62 1803/08/01 [Lugt 6677]

Philippus van der Schley; Amsterdam, Ten Huize van C.S. Roos, op de Cloveniers Burgwal, in 't Huis van Trip

Additional Auctioneers: Jan de Bosch, Jeronimusz.; Jan Yver; Cornelis Sebille Roos; Jacobus Vinkeles

Seller(s) from Title Page: Nagelaten door een Voornaam Kunst-Liefhebber

Seller(s) from Auctioneer's Copy: Thoen; Y[ver]

Seller(s) from Other Sources: Vn Hoorn; Scheerenberg

Seller Authority: Thoen; Yver, Jan

Paintings Lots: 95

Catalogue Locations:

*LBDa I	Auctioneer's copy, annot. with all buyers and prices on interleaved pages as well as letters for the sellers. A few sellers are also identified. The title page is lacking. It may have belonged to the dealer P. van der Schley.
BMPL	Auctioneer's copy, annot. with all buyers and prices on interleaved pages. It belonged later to Wm. Smith.
RKDH	Auctioneer's copy, annot. with all buyers and prices on interleaved pages as well as letters for the sellers. It belonged to the dealer C.S. Roos.
EBNP	Auctioneer's copy, annot. with all buyers and prices on interleaved pages as well as letters for the sellers.
FLNY	Annot. with a few buyers and all prices as well as letters for the sellers.
LBDa II	Not annot.
MB	Not annot.
ESP	Not annot.
MA	Not annot.

Comments: The title page of the catalogue of this sale of paintings, drawings and prints implies that everything belonged to an unidentified "voornaam kunst-liefhebber." The MA copy of the catalogue is inscribed on the title page with two names: after the word "Schilderyen" the annotator has written "Van Secretaris Vn Hoorn" and after "Prent-Werken" he has added "van Scheerenberg." Four copies of the catalogue that belonged originally to the dealers who organized the sale are annotated with letters next to the individual lots: these indicate that there were eleven consignments, six of which included paintings. None of these can be associated with Van Hoorn and Scheerenberg, which suggests that the latter are erroneous. The largest consignments were those from "A," which consisted primarily of prints, and "T," whose lots were mostly drawings. The six consignments with paintings are marked C, H, J, R, S and Y. One of these, "S," is identified in the LBDa copy of the catalogue as "Thoen." His consignment consisted of just five relatively minor pictures, however, and his precise identity is still unknown. Oddly, in the same catalogue "S" is identified as "de Wed" in the case of five other lots (nos.31–34a; these lots are marked with a "Z" in the FLNY catalogue). This is probably an abbreviation for "weduwe," indicating perhaps that "S" was "de weduwe Thoen." One other consigner, "Y," was certainly the dealer Jan Yver, to whom at least one of the paintings can be traced. And "R," whose consignment was the largest (35 lots), was probably the dealer Roos. His paintings, which consisted mostly of untitled works *hors du catalogue*, fetched very small prices. The best results were realized by the four paintings – three marine pictures and a landscape – submitted by "H." One of the former, lot 40 by Willem van de Velde, was sold for fl. 1525, the highest price of the sale. Another from the same consignment, lot 7 by Jan van de Cappelle, brought fl. 350. But the vast majority brought much smaller amounts. The 32 lots consigned by "J" brought just average amounts, although a few exceeded fl. 100. The most expensive of these was no.51, a landscape by Herman Saftleven, which was sold for fl. 285. The total receipts for the sale came to fl. 11,094:5, of which the drawings and prints made up nearly two-thirds.

63 1803/08/17 [Lugt 6681]

Philippus van der Schley; Amsterdam, Ten Huize van C.S. Roos, in het Huis van Trip, op de Kloveniers Burgwal

Additional Auctioneers: Jan de Bosch, Jeronimusz.; Jan Yver; Cornelis Sebille Roos; Roelof Meurs Pruyssenaar; Jacobus Vinkeles

Seller(s) from Title Page: Nagelaaten door Wylen Jonkvrouwe Anna Catharina Putman

Seller Authority: Putman, Anna Catharina

Paintings Lots: 107

Catalogue Locations:

LBDa I	Auctioneer's copy, annot. with all buyers and prices on interleaved pages. The title page is lacking. It may have belonged to the dealer P. van der Schley.
RKDH	Auctioneer's copy, annot. with all buyers and prices on interleaved pages. It belonged to the dealer C.S. Roos.
*NGW	Auctioneer's copy, annot. with all buyers and prices on interleaved pages.
EBNP	Annot. with all buyers and prices.
AA	Annot. with most buyers and prices.
AAP	Annot. with many buyers and all prices.
MA	Annot. with a few buyers and all prices.
MPA	Annot. in pencil with a few buyers and all prices.
ESP	Not annot. excepting some numbers and letters that appear to be bidding codes.
MB	Not annot.
FLNY	Not annot.
LBDa II	Not annot.

Comments: The owner was Anna Catharina Putman, described as unmarried and recently deceased. Her burial in the Amsterdam Nieuwe Kerk is recorded on Dec.3, 1801, and her former address was "in de Warmoestraat shuyns over de Vissteeg." Little is known about the origins of her collection, but it appears that it was probably assembled in relatively recent times, presumably by Jonkvrouwe Putman herself, rather than by inheritance. At least three of her paintings have been traced to previous sales: two lots, an *Interior with Brawling Peasants* by Jan Steen and a church interior by Philips de Koninck, had both appeared in the Abraham Dijkman sale in Amsterdam on July 17/18, 1794, and so were presumably acquired sometime after that. (The painting by Steen, Hofstede de Groot no.770, was later in the collection of C.T.D. Crews in London, but its present location is unknown. The picture by de Koninck has not been traced since 1803.) Moreover, a sketch by Jan Lievens for the Amsterdam Stadhuis had appeared in a sale as recently as September 10, 1800. (Schneider, 1932, no.99a; later in the collection of H. Schneider.) However, all three of these paintings were relatively minor and their provenance may not be entirely typical. Oddly, the major pieces in the sale, or at least those that registered the highest prices, were mostly left unsold. Eleven lots, including almost all of those that were knocked down for more than fl. 100, were bought in and presumably sold at some later date, but their later history has yet to be found. Among these were a *Landscape with a Shepherd and Cattle* by Dujardin, for which a price of fl. 700 was registered, and a small landscape by Wouwerman knocked down for fl. 650. One of the few expensive lots that actually found a buyer was no.80, a depiction of *The Ratification of the Treaty of Münster* by Ter Borch for which the dealer Roos paid fl. 340 and which was subsequently sold to the National Museum in The Hague. It is now in the Rijksmuseum and considered a copy of the painting in the London National Gallery. In view of these results, it appears that the sale was not a success, and that the unsold lots had been given reserves they did not warrant. The total result of the sale of 107 lots was just fl. 2447:6.

64 1803/08/24 [Lugt 6684]

I. Kann; Den Haag, Groote Zaal van 't Hof

Seller(s) from Title Page: None

Paintings Lots: 148

Catalogue Locations:

*RKDH	Annot. in pencil with most buyers and all prices.
MWH	Not annot.

Comments: Although the catalogue was printed with the date of July 26, this was subsequently struck through and changed to August 24, indicating that the sale was postponed. The contents were limited to paintings, the principal part of the catalogue consisting of 111 lots, followed by an appendix with 32 further lots. Since the numbering of the appended lots begins again at no.1, we have added the prefix A to distinguish them from the others. This is the last recorded sale held by the Hague dealer I. Kann, who must have retired shortly afterward. His sales normally consisted primarily of books, although one previous auction (no.39) was also dedicated just to pictures. As usual, the individual lots were mostly landscapes and genre pieces with a few religious and mythological scenes, among them seven works by Italian artists. At least five lots in the sale can be traced to purchases made by the dealer Teissier (probably the Hague painter J.G. Teissier, 1749–1821) at Amsterdam auctions during 1802. If the first 111 lots all belonged to one seller, that person was probably Teissier. Moreover, at least seven lots were also knocked down to Teissier, including one of those purchased earlier by him, so he was clearly involved with the sale. (Two of these are later found in the sale of T.H. van Willigen held in The Hague on October 9, 1805, cat. no.98.) However, it is still possible that there were other consigners. But the paintings in the appendix certainly came from a different source or sources. Three of the less important lots had appeared in earlier sales held by Kann, and two of these were here knocked down to Kann. They may, therefore, have been his own possessions, or simply items left over from previous sales. However, the provenance of the bulk of the paintings in the appendix is unknown. Two of the most expensive lots in the sale, *An Italian Seaport* by Jacob van der Ulft and four landscapes by Gaspar van Wittel, were placed at the beginning and fetched fl. 110 and fl. 155, respectively. Just two other lots surpassed fl. 100: a battle scene by Huchtenburgh brought fl. 130, and a small landscape by Wouwerman cost fl. 101. However, the first three of these were knocked down to Kann himself and therefore may not represent bona fide transactions. Altogether, 25 lots are recorded as having been sold to Kann. At least four of these, including the battle scene by Huchtenburgh, reappeared in an Amsterdam sale on February 27, 1804 (no.73) as part of a consignment from "B," who might, therefore, have been Kann, but this is not certain. A very large proportion of the paintings sold for less than fl. 10. The RKDH copy of the catalogue records the total result for the sale as having been fl. 1410:16.

65 1803/09/07 and following days [Lugt 6690]

Philippus van der Schley; Amsterdam, Ten Huize van Cornelis Sebille Roos, op de Kolveniersburgwal [sic], in het Huis van Trip

Additional Auctioneers: Jan de Bosch, Jeronimusz.; Jan Yver; Cornelis Sebille Roos; Roelof Meurs Pruyssenaar; Jacobus Vinkeles

Seller(s) from Title Page: None

Seller(s) from Other Sources: Smidt de Cologne

Seller Authority: Schmidt

Paintings Lots: 291

Catalogue Locations:

RKDH I	Auctioneer's copy, annot. with all buyers and prices on interleaved pages as well as letters for the seller of two lots. The latter are in pencil. It may have belonged to the dealer C.S. Roos. (Dutch edition)
*FLNY	Auctioneer's copy, annot. with all buyers and prices on interleaved pages. It lacks the title page. (Dutch edition)
EBNP	Auctioneer's copy, annot. with all buyers and prices on interleaved pages. (Dutch edition)
MA II	Annot. with many buyers and all prices. (Dutch edition)
LBDa	Annot. with a few buyers and all prices. It may have belonged to the dealer P. van der Schley. (Dutch edition)
MB	Annot. in pencil with all prices. (Dutch edition)
RKDH II	Annot. in pencil with all prices. (French edition)
ESP	Not annot. (Dutch edition)
MA I	Not annot. (French edition)
MPA	Title page only; the remainder of the catalogue, to which it has been erroneously attached, is no.54.

Comments: The catalogue of this sale was published in both Dutch and French versions. The latter was printed in Cologne, lending some credence to an inscription on the MA I copy of the catalogue which identifies the seller as "Smidt de Cologne." The character of the collection also bears this out. Some works by German or Swiss artists were included, and the vast majority of the paintings were small in size, generally less than 25 duimen (63.5 cm.), a characteristic of many German collections. The precise identity of the owner is still unknown, but he might have been the Cologne painter Johann Jakob Schmitz (1724–1810). However, Schmitz is not known to have had a collection of pictures. Whoever the owner, he was no doubt consigning his pictures to Amsterdam because its art market was less affected by the French occupation than Cologne's and was altogether a more promising venue.

Judging only from the results of the sale, the paintings do not appear to have been of very great quality. A total of 82 lots were left unsold, and these included almost everything knocked down for more than fl. 100. The major exception was a *Landscape with a Stag Hunt* by Herman van Swanevelt which was bought by the dealer Theodorus Spaan for a surprising fl. 580, a price that finds no parallels among Swanevelt's works, perhaps indicating that the picture was a misattributed work by Claude. Another lot that sold reasonably well was no.206, a small landscape by Wouwerman that brought fl. 255. In the RKDH II copy of the catalogue many lots are marked with a second figure that seems to be estimates made before the sale. These are usually much higher than the figure at which the lot was eventually knocked down and are an indication of how drastically overvalued the collection was. The unsold paintings can be subsequently followed to Paris, where almost all of them reappeared in an anonymous sale ("Un Cabinet Etranger") on Feb.22, 1808 (Cf. B. Peronnet and B. Fredericksen, *Répertoire des tableaux vendus en France au XIXe siècle*, I, 1997, no.139). Many of the attributions were changed, generally for the better, and the prices were fairly high. However, it is not certain that they did in fact find buyers, and the prices may not be reliable. Some of the paintings bought by "Scheffer" at the present sale also reappear in the later one, and so were apparently bought in or perhaps returned by the buyer. It should be noted that the RKDH copy of the catalogue has the letter "T" marked next to two lots, nos.95 and 125a, which could signify that they had come from a different source. According to the FLNY and RKDH copies of the catalogue, the total receipts from the paintings that found buyers came to fl. 4155:19, whereas the unsold pieces came to fl. 7681:10.

66 1803/10/10 and following days

Van Benthem en Ooms; Middelburg, In het Burger Logement Antwerpen, staande in den Langendelft

Seller(s) from Title Page: None

Paintings Lots: 36

Catalogue Locations:

*ZBM	Auctioneer's copy, annot. with all buyers and prices on interleaved pages.

Comments: This sale in Middelburg consisted primarily of books and smaller numbers of drawings and prints. The title page of the catalogue also states that some paintings were to be included, and on p.91 there is the following note: "Voorts een Verzameling van Schilderyen; waaronder van goede Meesters, benevens eenige Prenten en Pourtraiten, in Lysten met Glazen; welke alle op hunne Nommers zullen gepresenteerd worden." There is no list of the paintings, however, although the auctioneer has annotated the ZBM copy of the catalogue with the names of the buyers and the prices. We have been forced to include them without artists' names or titles.

67 1803/10/17–1803/10/24 [Lugt 6695]

Pierre van Daalen Wetters; Den Haag, Premises, Coin du Hofcingel

Seller(s) from Title Page: M. van Daalen Wetters, en son vivant, Libraire et Négociant-d'Estampes

Seller Authority: Daalen Wetters, Melis van

Paintings Lots: 16

Catalogue Locations:

VBBA	Not annot.
MWH	Not annot.
BRB	Not annot.
KBH	Not annot.
LCW	Not seen, but apparently not annot.

Comments: Melis van Daalen Wetters was, until his death in January, 1803, the head of an old firm of booksellers in The Hague that bore the family name. He was succeeded by his son Pierre, who was responsible for selling his father's library and art collections at this six-day sale. The catalogue was issued in two parts: the first of 86 pages contained the books, and the second of 78 pages had works of art. The latter consisted primarily of prints, but there was also some sculpture and drawings. On the last day of the sale there were also a few mostly anonymous paintings. The only attributed pieces were by the Hague painter Nicolas Hooft (1664–1748) and the more prominent Aert Schouman, who was represented by two portraits of himself in the act of painting. The results are not recorded.

68 1803/10/20–1803/10/25 [Lugt 6699]

D. Noman en Zoon; Hertogenbosch, Vugterstraat in den Papier Molen

Seller(s) from Title Page: Nagelaaten door den Wel Ed. Gestrengen Heer en Mr. Stephanies Roosendaal, J.F.Z. in leven Oud President, Schepen en Raad dezer Stad 's Bosch

Seller Authority: Roosendaal, Stephanies, Mr.

Paintings Lots: 12

Catalogue Locations:

VBBA	Not annot.

Comments: Very few sale catalogues from Hertogenbosch have been preserved, and this is the only one from this period that included paintings. The sale lasted five days and contained primarily books, but on the last day there were some lots of maps, prints, paintings and miscellaneous items. The prints and paintings, listed together, constitute 24 lots, of which roughly half are clearly prints. The remainder are all by British artists such as Richard Westall and Henry Singleton, and are not described as either prints or paintings, although they fall under the rubric of "Prenten en Schilderijen." Some are given French titles and some English, implying that they might be prints. It is eminently possible that none are paintings, but we have included them in the off chance that they could be. The owner is described as having held a number of prominent positions in Hertogenbosch.

69 1803/11/28–1803/11/30

Van Benthem en Ooms; Middelburg, In het Burger Logement Antwerpen, staande in den Langendelft

Seller(s) from Title Page: Nagelaten door wylen den Heer Samuel de Wind, in leven Medicine Doctor

Seller Authority: Wind, Samuel de

Paintings Lots: 15

Catalogue Locations:

*RKDH	Annot. with all buyers and prices on interleaved pages.
ZBM I	Auctioneer's copy, annot. with all buyers and prices on interleaved pages.
ZBM II	Auctioneer's copy, annot. with all buyers and prices on interleaved pages.

Comments: The proprietor, Samuel de Wind (1742–1803), was a prominent doctor in Middelburg whose library made up the principal part of this three-day sale. Besides books there were also prints, maps, scientific instruments and some paintings, all of which were sold on the last day. These included a few with religious themes, as well as marine pictures and a bust of Seneca. Among the miscellaneous objects was a portrait of Voltaire in wax.

70 1803/12/12 and following days [Lugt 6718]

Philippus van der Schley; Amsterdam, Ten Huize van C.S. Roos, op de Kloveniers Burgwal, in 't van ouds genaamd Huis van Trip

Additional Auctioneers: Jan de Bosch, Jeronimusz.; Jan Yver; Cornelis Sebille Roos; Roelof Meurs Pruissenaar; Jacobus Vinkeles

Seller(s) from Title Page: Naargelaaten, door wylen den Kunst-beminnaar den Heer Arnoud de Lange

Seller(s) from Auctioneer's Copy: R[oos]; V[inkeles?]

Seller Authority: Lange, Aarnoud de; Roos, Cornelis Sebille; Vinkeles, Jacobus

Paintings Lots: 247

Catalogue Locations:

*LBDa	Auctioneer's copy, annot. with all buyers and prices on interleaved pages as well as letters for the sellers. It may have belonged to the dealer P. van der Schley.
RKDH	Auctioneer's copy, annot. with all buyers and prices on interleaved pages as well as letters for the sellers. It belonged to the dealer C.S. Roos.
NOL	Present location unknown. According to Lugt it is annot. with buyers and prices.
EBNP	Annot. with all prices.
ESP	Not annot.
MA	Not annot.
VBBA	Not annot. It lacks a title page.

Comments: Besides 247 lots of paintings (85 of which were added after the catalogue was printed), the sale contained large numbers of drawings and prints as well as a few pieces of sculpture and some musical instruments. The only proprietor mentioned by the catalogue is the recently deceased Aarnoud de Lange, a dealer and auctioneer in Amsterdam who had died in February, 1803. Besides the paintings in the present sale, he also owned a particularly important collection of engravings by Rembrandt that had previously belonged to Cornelis Ploos van Amstel (1726–1798) whose first wife, Elisabeth Troost, was Lange's cousin. (Cf. S.A.C. Dudok van Heel, "Rembrandt's etsen uit de verzameling van Cornelis Ploos van Amstel J. Czn.," *Maandblad Amstelodamum*, 64, 1977, pp.53–59.) One of De Lange's executors was the dealer Christian Josi, also a relation, who later organized the sale of his prints on July 31, 1810. His books were sold on Dec.27, 1803. The title page of the present catalogue does not specify, however, that everything in the sale derived from De Lange, and two extant copies of the catalogue that belonged to dealers who organized the sale are annotated with letters next to each lot indicating that 16 consignments were included, ten of which included paintings. They are A, B, C, D, E, F, H, R, V and W. Neither catalogue identifies any of the consigners, but given the distribution, one can probably assume that the first six letters were arbitrarily assigned, while the last four were the initials of their names. It was common to utilize "A" for the principal consigner, or the one named on the title page, and in this case the 20 pictures belonging to "A" were clearly the most valuable, fetching a total of fl. 6248:19. The identification of "A" with Aarnoud de Lange can be confirmed by the presence in this group of a sea piece by Willem van de Velde that had been purchased by De Lange at an Amsterdam sale on Aug.30, 1797. There were also two lots of paintings by Louis Chalon (1687–1741) who was De Lange's uncle. We have, therefore, put all of these lots under his name. They included three of the four most expensive lots in the sale, most notably an interior by Jan Steen showing *The Effects of Intemperance*, which was sold for fl. 1405 (present location unknown) and *The Geographer* by Jan Vermeer, which was sold to the dealer Coclers for fl. 360. (It is now in the Städelsches Institut, Frankfurt.) However, the most expensive lot in the sale was no.50, *A View of the Dam in Amsterdam* by Lingelbach which was sold to the dealer Van der Schley (apparently representing someone designated as "S") for fl. 1725. (It is now in the Historisch Museum in Amsterdam.) This painting was the only lot consigned by "C," who is still unidentified. It had been sold at auction in 1797 to a certain "van der Veurst" who might, therefore, have been the consigner in 1803, but this cannot be confirmed. The largest consignment consisted of 48 paintings belonging to "B," whose proceeds came to fl. 3201:6, the second highest share of the sale. His paintings brought lower prices; just three exceeded fl. 100, including a depiction of *Leda and the Swan* by Carel de Moor, which was bought in at fl. 250 and when put up again in 1808 fetched only fl. 31. Two other consignments, those belonging to "V" (46 lots) and "W" (44), were comparably large, but these both consisted of inexpensive pictures. The two consigners referred to as "R" and "V" can probably be identified as the dealers C.S. Roos and Jacobus Vinkeles, co-organizers of the sale. And we might speculate that "D," whose possessions included an unusually large number of pictures by French artists – such as Fragonard and Norblin – could have been a Frenchman. It is also possible that "E" may have been somehow associated with "Salcedo," who bought four of the seven lots in his consignment and whose name does not otherwise appear at any sale. The total receipts were fl. 16,022:14.

71 1803/12/13 [Lugt 6719]

v.d. Muelen; Amsterdam, unknown

Seller(s) from Title Page: None

Catalogue Locations:

Comments: Lugt lists this catalogue and cites a single copy at LBDa which, though lacking a title page, had been dated 1803. In fact, the year should be 1802, making it identical with Lugt's no.6529 (cat. no.50).

72 1803/12/15 [Lugt 6721]

Willem La Cable; Middelburg, Premises, op de Vlasmarkt

Seller(s) from Title Page: Hr. en Mr. L.H. de Haze Bomme

Seller Authority: Haze Bomme, Leendert Huibrecht de, Mr.

Paintings Lots: 63

Catalogue Locations:

FLNY	Not annot. It addressed to "de Heer Dan Le laar [or Caar]" by Willem La Cable.
RKDH	Not annot.

Comments: The owner was Leendert Huibrecht de Haze Bomme (1762–1837), a prominent official in Middelburg. He was the son of Huybrecht de Haze Bomme (1737–1821); his mother was Cornelia Maria van Citters (1742–1780), whose family included many collectors and from whom he may have inherited some pictures. Given his young age, it was probably financial need that forced him to sell his collection at this unpropitious moment. The paintings were mostly landscapes and genre pieces of small proportions. One of the few portraits, a depiction of Maria Anna, wife of Carlos II of Spain, by Schalcken can be traced to a sale held in The Hague in 1792, which means that it is likely to have been purchased some time afterward by Leendert Huibrecht himself. His mother had died well before this time, and his father was still alive in 1803, so it seems improbable that the painting would have passed to him by inheritance. However, one does not know whether this one painting was representative of the collection as a whole. The results of the sale are unknown.

73 1804/02/27 and following days [Lugt 6747]

Philippus van der Schley; Amsterdam, Ten Huize van C.S. Roos, op de Cloveniers Burgwal, in 't Huis van Trip

Additional Auctioneers: Jan de Bosch, Jeronimusz.; Jan Yver; Cornelis Sebille Roos; Roeloff Meurs Pruyssenaar; Jacobus Vinkeles

Seller(s) from Title Page: J.C. Pruyssenaar

Seller(s) from Auctioneer's Copy: R[oos]

Seller Authority: Pruyssenaar, J.C.; Roos, Cornelis Sebille

Paintings Lots: 190

Catalogue Locations:

*LBDa	Auctioneer's copy, annot. with all buyers and prices on interleaved pages as well as letters for the sellers. The title page is lacking. It may have belonged to the dealer P. van der Schley.

RKDH	Auctioneer's copy, annot. with all buyers and prices on interleaved pages as well as letters for the sellers. It belonged to the dealer C.S. Roos.
FLNY	Auctioneer's copy, annot. with all buyers and sellers on interleaved pages, as well as letters for the sellers. It consists of only the first part with 28 pages, although the annotations for many subsequent lots are also present.
MB	Annot. in pencil with most buyers and prices. It belonged to the dealer P.J. Thijs and the annotations are his.
AA	Annot. with some buyers and all prices.
EBNP	Auctioneer's copy, annot. with a few buyers, all prices and initials for the names of the sellers. Most of the annotations are in pencil.
MA	Not annot.
NGL	Not annot.

Comments: The contents of this sale were paintings, drawings and prints, as well as some scientific instruments and miscellaneous objects. Of these, the drawings constituted by far the largest portion. The title page of the catalogue gives the name of just one seller, J.C. Pruyssenaar, but three copies of the catalogue that belonged originally to the dealers who organized the sale are annotated with letters next to the individual lots indicating that six consignments were included. These are designated A, B, C, D, F and R. The title page of the catalogue mentions first "een fraaye verzameling Schilderyen" that was to be sold, in addition to which ("beneevens") there was "een keurige en uitgezochte collectie gekouleurde en ongekouleurde Teekeningen, en eenige Prent-Kunst... Rariteiten...in veele Jaaren by een vergaderd, door den Kunst Minaar J.C. Pruyssenaar." This seems to imply that Pruyssenaar was the owner of the drawings and prints rather than paintings, a conclusion supported by the fact that the largest consignment, the one designated "A," included no paintings. It seems probable, therefore, that "A" was J.C. Pruyssenaar and that none of the paintings in this sale were his. This is perhaps complicated by the fact that two of the paintings in the "B" consignment had been purchased by "Pruyssenaar" at a sale on August 17, 1803 (no.63), but none of the remaining 87 lots in this consignment can be associated with him, nor do the other 12 lots purchased by Pruyssenaar at the 1803 sale appear here. It is likely, moreover, that these transactions, as well as the more than 600 transactions recorded in the name of "Pruyssenaar" between 1801 and 1804, are attributable to Roeloff Meurs Pruyssenaar, one of the co-organizers of the sale and presumably a relation of J.C. Pruyssenaar. It is noteworthy that all but three of these transactions took place at sales at which R.M. Pruyssenaar was one of the organizers. (The only exceptions are two lots purchased in 1801 at an Amsterdam sale directed by the dealer Jan Yver, and a single painting purchased in Utrecht in 1802, where Pruyssenaar's name is followed by "Amst.") Further substantiation is provided by the fact that Pruyssenaar's name ceased to appear as either seller or buyer after 1804, when R.M. Pruyssenaar discontinued organizing sales, perhaps a result of retirement or death. The name of J.C. Pruyssenaar appears just once more, in association with a sale held on November 27ff., 1814, that again consisted primarily of drawings. Although the distribution of ownership at this latter sale is not yet clarified, it seems probable that J.C. Pruyssenaar was primarily a collector of drawings and prints, and that his activity extended at least ten years longer than that of R.M. Pruyssenaar.

Unfortunately, it is still not possible to identify the owners of most of the remaining consignments, four of which, B, C, D, and R, included paintings. The "B" consignment of 89 lots was the largest; besides the two paintings mentioned above that can be traced to [R.M.] Pruyssenaar, four other lots appear to derive from the sale held in The Hague on August 24, 1803 (no.64), at which time they were bought (or bought in) by I. Kann. The connection is tenuous, however. The "C" consignment, containing 62 lots, included five paintings that had been very recently purchased by three dealers, permitting no conclusions to be drawn. It is possible to suggest, however, that "R" was the dealer Cornelis Sebille Roos, in part because the major lot in this consignment, a depiction of *The Continence of Scipio* by Jan Steen, was bought in by Roos, and also because the letter "R" falls out of sequence, an indication that it was an initial and not arbitrarily selected. Judging from the prices, the sale contained few works of great value. Only three lots exceeded fl. 200, one of which, the picture by Jan Steen mentioned above, was bought in (at fl. 285). The highest price, fl. 700, was paid by the Brussels dealer Burggraaff for a *Falcon Hunt* by Philips Wouwerman, while an *Interior with Men and Women* by Ter Borch was sold for fl. 225. With the exception of the painting by Steen – which was on the London art market in 1970 – and a *Portrait of a Man* by Ferdinand Bol (now in the Rijksmuseum), hardly any of the pictures in the sale have been traced. The total receipts came to fl. 13538:15, of which fl. 8700:1 were dispersed to "A" and fl. 1116:15 to "F" for drawings and prints. The 190 lots of paintings, therefore, realized just fl. 3721:19.

74 1804/03/26 and following days [Lugt 6771]

J. van de Sande en Zoon; Middelburg, Op den Langenburgt, by de Groote Markt

Seller(s) from Title Page: None

Paintings Lots: 13

Catalogue Locations:

MWH Not annot.

Comments: The contents were primarily books, but there were also small numbers of prints, maps, paintings, coins and scientific instruments. The paintings were mostly anonymous, but included two pictures by Arnold Verbuys, whose subjects the auctioneer was unable to recognize, as well as five works that carried monograms but whose authors could not be identified. The results are not recorded.

75 1804/04/24–1804/04/25

B. Besanger; Den Haag, Veenestraat Lett. S. N. 185

Seller(s) from Title Page: None

Paintings Lots: 2

Catalogue Locations:

MWH Not annot.

Comments: In addition to books, this two-day sale in The Hague contained some paintings, prints and miscellaneous items. Unfortunately, the paintings and prints are grouped together and so poorly described that they are indistinguishable. We have included just two lots which may, in fact, be prints.

76 1804/04/28 [Lugt 6793]

A. Delfos; Leiden, Op de Papegraft [sic]

Seller(s) from Title Page: None

Seller(s) from Other Sources: [Abraham Delfos]

Seller Authority: Delfos, Abraham

Paintings Lots: 62

Catalogue Locations:

*MB	Auctioneer's copy, annot. with all buyers and prices on interleaved pages. Many lots are also marked with what are probably the reserves.

Comments: The Leyden artist and dealer, Abraham Delfos (1731–1820), held regular sales in his quarters on the Papegragt; the present sale, although preserved in just one copy, was one of the most important of his career. It contained 62 lots of paintings, 70 lots of drawings, and 172 lots of prints. The title page stipulates that the paintings had been "in veele jaaren by een Verzameld en Nagelaten," but does not name the deceased collector. It is not difficult to determine, however, that the paintings belonged primarily to Delfos himself. Five of the lots, including two sketches by Ferdinand Bol for paintings in the town halls in Amsterdam and Leyden, had been bought at a sale in Amsterdam on August 21, 1799. A marine picture by Everdingen had been purchased by Delfos at an Amsterdam sale on June 16, 1802. Moreover, all but two of the 23 paintings knocked down to Delfos, and both of those officially listed as bought in, reappeared in sales of his property in Leyden in April, 1807 (no.110) and on June 10, 1807 (no.113). It is likely, therefore, that all of the paintings – but perhaps not the drawings and prints – were his. However, it is also possible that he included works belonging to other collectors in the sale, and for this reason we have qualified his ownership throughout. Being a relatively small figure in the art market, Delfos did not deal in very major works, although he often had works of interest. The highest prices, fl. 100 and fl. 108, were registered for the sketch of *Moses and the Tablets of the Law* by Bol and a picture of poultry by Dirk Valckenburg. Both were knocked down to Delfos, however, and when resold in 1807, the Bol seems to have been bought in a second time (at the same price), while the picture by Valckenburg reached only fl. 24.

77 1804/05/07–1804/05/08 [Lugt 6799]

Philippus van der Schley; Amsterdam, Ten Huize van C.S. Roos, op de Cloveniersburgwal, in het Huis van Trip

Additional Auctioneers: Jan de Bosch, Jeronimusz.; Jan Yver; Cornelis Sebille Roos; Roelof Meurs Pruyssenaar; Jacobus Vinkeles

Seller(s) from Title Page: None

Seller(s) from Auctioneer's Copy: Vinkeles; Roos; Schley; Pruysnaar

Seller(s) from Other Sources: Haffner

Seller Authority: Roos, Cornelis Sebille; Schley, Philippus van der; Pruyssenaar, Roelof Meurs; Haffner

Paintings Lots: 252

Catalogue Locations:

LBDa	Auctioneer's copy, annot. with all buyers and prices on interleaved pages as well as letters for the sellers. The title page is lacking. It may have belonged to the dealer P. van der Schley.
*EBNP	Auctioneer's copy, annot. with all buyers and prices on interleaved pages as well as letters for the sellers. The latter are also identified at the back of the catalogue.
RKDH	Auctioneer's copy, annot. with all buyers and prices on interleaved pages as well as letters for the sellers. It belonged to the dealer C.S. Roos.
MB	Annot. with most buyers and all prices. It belonged to the dealer P.J. Thijs and the annotations are his.

MPA	Annot. in ink and pencil with many buyers and prices. The title page is from no.45 and is erroneously attached to this catalogue.
AAP	Annot. with some buyers and all prices.
MA	Annot. with some buyers and all prices.
AA	Annot. with a few buyers and some prices. Most of the annotations refer to the dealer Wm. Gruyter and the catalogue may have been his.
ESP	Not annot.
FLNY	Lugt lists a copy at this location, but it cannot be located and seems never to have been there.

Comments: The sale was anonymous and, excepting four lots of drawings and prints, contained only paintings. In addition to the 237 lots printed in the catalogue, 15 more were added at the time of the sale. Three extant copies of the catalogue originally belonged to dealers who helped organize the sale; all three are annotated with letters next to the individual lots indicating there were 13 different consignments. The EBNP copy of the catalogue also identifies the names of the consigners, although they are all dealers and co-organizers of the sale, who, in most cases, represented other collectors whose names are not given. The list reads as follows: A = Roos (52 lots); G = Y Vinkeles (45 lots); H = Y Vinkeles (20 lots); J = Vinkeles (33 lots); JJ = Y (22 lots); K = Roos (12 lots); P = Pruysnaar (5 lots); R = Roos (12 lots); S = Y Schley (17 lots); V = Y Vinkeles (8 lots); W = Y (15 lots); X = Vinkeles (4 lots); Y = Y (7 lots). Since the letters are not in sequence, it is probable that most are initials rather than being arbitrarily assigned letters, and this is borne out by the single identification made so far. It can be demonstrated that "H" was a certain Haffner, since all of the pictures sold in this consignment had been purchased earlier by him. (He was apparently represented at the sale by Jacobus Vinkeles, but the presence of the letter "Y" – presumably referring to the dealer Jan Yver – may indicate that the commission was supposed to be shared.) For three of the remaining consignments, those of R[oos], S[chley] and V[inkeles], initials were also employed rather than arbitrary letters, implying that this may also be true for the unidentified sellers. Similarly, it may be assumed that "Y" refers to Jan Yver.

By far the largest and most important consignment was that belonging to "A." The sale contained no works of exceptional value, but six lots did surpass fl. 200, and of these, five belonged to the A consignment. Unfortunately, the owner's identity remains unknown. Nine of his paintings were bought in and reappeared on August 8, 1804 (no.82), as the property of "F," but this has not led to his identification. The consigner "J" might be the dealer Christian Josi, but this is only speculation. The most expensive lot was no.145, which consisted of a pair of still lifes by J.C. Roedig and which cost fl. 475. A *Landscape with Resting Hunters* by Wouwerman belonging to Pruyssenaar was knocked down for fl. 1000, but was not sold. (When put up again in 1808 it brought fl. 455.) The total returns for the sale were fl. 6848:19, of which nearly half, fl. 3033:16, was paid out to "A."

78 **1804/06/18** and following days

Van Benthem en Ooms; Middelburg, In het Heeren Logement Antwerpen, staande in den Langendelft

Seller(s) from Title Page: None

Paintings Lots: 36

Catalogue Locations:

*ZBM	Annot. with all buyers and prices on interleaved pages.

Comments: This was one of the regular book sales held in Middelburg by the book dealers Salomon van Benthem and Johannes Ooms. The sale also contained some prints and drawings as well as a number of paintings, although the latter are not found in the printed catalogue. They are referred to on the title page, and a note on p.98 reads: "Voorts eenige Schilderyen; waaronder van goede Meesters, welke volgens hun Nommer zullen gepresenteerd worden." However, there is no list, only an interleaved page with the names of the buyers and the prices paid. We have included them, therefore, but without giving any artists' names or titles.

79 **1804/07/25** [Lugt 6846]

Philippus van der Schley; Amsterdam, Ten Huize van C.S. Roos, op de Cloveniersburgwal, in het Huis van Trip

Additional Auctioneers: Jan de Bosch, Jeronimusz.; Jan Yver; Cornelis Sebille Roos; Roelof Meurs Pruyssenaar; Jacobus Vinkeles

Seller(s) from Title Page: Een Kundig Liefhebber

Paintings Lots: 92

Catalogue Locations:

*LBDa	Auctioneer's copy, annot. with all buyers and prices on interleaved pages. The title page is lacking. It may have belonged to the dealer P. van der Schley.
RKDH	Auctioneer's copy, annot. with all buyers and prices on interleaved pages. It belonged to the dealer C.S. Roos.
MB	Annot. with all buyers and prices. It belonged to the dealer P.J. Thijs and the annotations are his.
AAP	Annot. with most buyers and all prices.
MA	Annot. with most buyers and all prices.
MPA	Annot. with most buyers and all prices.
AA	Annot. with many buyers and all prices.
EBNP	Annot. in pencil with a few buyers and all prices. The annotations are difficult to read.
ESP	Not annot.
MWH	Not annot.

Comments: The sale consisted of 92 lots of paintings, the property of "een kundig liefhebber" who is not identified. The LBDa and RKDH copies of the catalogue belonged originally to dealers who helped organize the sale; neither indicates that more than a single proprietor was represented. Judging primarily from the descriptions, the collection contained a number of interesting pictures, at least one of which, the *Allegory of Justice* by Metsu (now in the Mauritshuis), can also be identified. The painting is known to have come from the collection of Sara de Witte, the widow of the merchant Michiel van Peene, in Leyden, where it is documented in 1667. However, its subsequent history is unknown prior to the present sale, nor can any of the other paintings in the collection be traced to their earlier proprietors. As a result, the origins of the collection remain unknown. As was usual, the bulk of the individual paintings consisted of landscapes and genre scenes by Dutch artists, but there were also a few mythological and allegorical pieces, and, most notably, some seventeenth-century Italian pictures. There were also 14 paintings by C.W.E. Dietrich, an unusually large number for one collection. It is perhaps noteworthy that none of the lots were bought in, indicating that there were no reserves and that the owner, if he was still alive, was determined to sell everything. The prices realized at the sale were respectable without being unusually high. Eight lots exceeded fl. 300, and two surpassed fl. 400. The highest price was realized by lot 19, a depiction of the *Presentation in the Temple* by Dietrich, which was sold for fl. 435. (It is perhaps the same painting that was sold for fl. 450 at the Smeth van Alphen sale on August 1, 1810, cat. no.167). A landscape with poultry by Hondecoeter brought fl. 423. The allegory by Metsu was sold for just fl. 200. The totals for the sale amounted to fl. 8565:15. Twenty-one lots were purchased by the dealer C.S. Roos; of these ten or eleven appeared later in the Udink sale on October 18, 1810 (no.131).

80 **1804/07/25** [Lugt 6846a]

Weduwe Jan de Groot en Zoon; Delft, Premises, op de Voorstraat

Seller(s) from Title Page: Nagelaten door wylen den Wel Edele Geb. Heer Mr. Franc van der Burch Wz., Oud-Burgemeester der Stad Delft, &c. &c.

Seller Authority: Burch Wz., Franc van der, Mr.

Paintings Lots: 107

Catalogue Locations:

MWH	Not annot.

Comments: The proprietor was the recently deceased mayor of Delft, Franc van der Burch, whose collection consisted of 107 lots of paintings. The sale took place at his home in the Voorstraat, but did not include other types of items, such as furniture or drawings. With few exceptions, the paintings were all of small dimensions and generally depicted landscapes or genre subjects, although there were a few religious and mythological scenes. None of the lots is given special prominence, and none have been traced. The results are unknown.

81 **1804/08/02**

[Anonymous]; Breda, Premises, not given

Seller(s) from Title Page: Nagelaten door wylen de Heer J.G. Calckberner, te Breda

Seller Authority: Calckberner, Johan Caspar

Paintings Lots: 78

Catalogue Locations:

JPGM	Not annot. It belonged formerly to BRB.

Comments: This is the only sale of paintings held in Breda during this period for which a catalogue is known to survive. The owner can be identified as Johan Caspar Calckberner, who had died the previous December. The sale took place in his late residence, and besides paintings included a few coaches and wagons. In addition to the usual landscapes and genre scenes of modest size there was a significant number of religious scenes as well, some of them by artists active in Antwerp and of much larger dimensions. The collection does not appear, however, to have contained major works and nothing has been traced. The results are not known.

82 **1804/08/08–1804/08/09** [Lugt 6848]

Philippus van der Schley; Amsterdam, Ten Huize van Cornelis Sebille Roos, op de Cloveniersburgwal, in het Huis van Trip

Additional Auctioneers: Jan de Bosch, Jeronimusz.; Jan Yver; Cornelis Sebille Roos; Roelof Meurs Pruyssenaar; Jacobus Vinkeles

Seller(s) from Title Page: None

Seller(s) from Auctioneer's Copy: Schley; Vink[eles]; Pruys[senaar]; Roos

Seller(s) from Other Sources: [Willem Gruyter]

Seller Authority: Schley, Philippus van der; Vinkeles, Jacobus; Pruyssenaar, Roelof Meurs; Roos, Cornelis Sebille; Gruyter, Willem, Senior

Paintings Lots: 289

Catalogue Locations:

*LBDa	Auctioneer's copy, annot. with all buyers and prices on interleaved pages as well as letters for the sellers. A few sellers are also identified. The title page is lacking. It may have belonged to the dealer P. van der Schley.
RKDH	Auctioneer's copy, annot. with all buyers and prices on interleaved pages as well as letters for the sellers. It belonged to the dealer C.S. Roos.
EBNP	Auctioneer's copy, annot. with all buyers and prices on interleaved pages as well as letters for the sellers.
AA	Annot. with some buyers and prices. Most of the annotations refer to the dealer Wm. Gruyter and the catalogue may have been his.
MB	Annot. with many prices.
MA	Not annot.

Comments: Besides four lots of drawings and two of prints, this two-day sale in Amsterdam consisted entirely of paintings. No owner is mentioned, but three extant copies of the catalogue (LBDa, EBNP and RKDH) that belonged originally to dealers who were co-organizers of the sale are annotated with letters next to the individual lots indicating that a large number of consignments were included. One of the catalogues, EBNP, has the following list of seven consigners and the letters used to designate their lots: A = Schley; B = Schley; K = Vink[eles]; P = Pruys[senaar]; R = Roos; S = Vink[eles]; W = Vink[eles]. All of these were dealers who organized the sale, and we may assume that, excepting perhaps those whose first initials correspond with the letters assigned to them – i.e., P for Pruyssenaar and R for Roos – they were not the actual owners and were instead representing still other, unnamed collectors. It is also likely that both Pruyssenaar and Roos were representing others, as is testified to by the annotations in the RKDH copy of the catalogue, which belonged to C.S. Roos himself. In his catalogue, all of the lots marked with "R" have a second letter, no doubt representing the actual sellers who had submitted their possessions to Roos for sale. Altogether there are 13 letters in the group associated with Roos: a, C, D, E, F, G, H, J, K, L, M, N and O. (One of these, "K," who owned just one lot, is also found in the EBNP list associated with Vinkeles, and we have assumed that it refers to the same person, in part because Roos has apparently utilized a small "a" to distinguish his consigner from the "A" associated with Van der Schley.) So there were altogether at least 18 consignments to this sale; of these, only two can be identified with reasonable certainty. The largest single consignment, comprising 71 lots, belonged to "K," very likely the dealer Willem Gruyter. Ten of the pictures in this consignment can be traced to sales held between 1802 and 1804, whenever the earlier buyer is known, he was Gruyter. Two of these, lots 32 by Begeyn and 119 by Miereveld, had been purchased by Gruyter as recently as February 27, 1804 (cat. no.73), and three of the unsold lots reappeared at a sale on August 23, 1808 (cat. no.129), as the property of "D," who was also probably Gruyter. The fact that Gruyter is registered as the buyer of 17 of the 71 lots in the consignment might be seen as contradicting this identification, but at least nine of these same pictures reappeared in a sale on May 5, 1806 (cat. no.101) in the same consignment with four others that had been bought in at the present sale, and so it appears that Gruyter was probably bidding on his own pictures. As a result, we have attributed all of the paintings in this consignment to Gruyter with a question mark. The other large consignment was that of "a," which consisted of 47 lots of paintings. Two of these had been purchased by Roos in 1801; four of the unsold lots reappeared under his name at the sale on Aug.26, 1807 (cat. no.115). It appears, therefore, that Roos used the letter "a" to denote his own lots, so for these we have substituted his name. It must be noted, however, that three other lots, nos.171–173, which were added to the sale after the catalogue was printed, are marked with just the letter "R," and thus were probably also his own property, although this could constitute grounds for questioning the identity of "a" as Roos. Finally, it should be mentioned that all of the pictures consigned by "F" can been traced to the sale held on May 7, 1804 (cat. no.77) at which time they had been offered by "A" and bought in. He cannot be identified, however. Altogether, the sale contained few works of great value, and only two lots were sold for more than fl. 200. The highest price was fl. 300 paid by Gruyter for a marine scene by Willem van de Velde, and a *Penitent Magdalen* by Van Dyck, or in his manner, was sold to Gruyter for fl. 225. A picture by Wouwerman depicting a convoy being plundered was bought in at fl. 480. The EBNP copy of the catalogue gives the totals as just fl. 4201, a very low figure for a sale of 289 lots.

83 1804/10/01–1804/10/08

Cornel; Rotterdam, Op de Zaal boven de Beurs

Additional Auctioneers: van Baalen

Seller(s) from Title Page: Nagelaten door een voornaam Liefhebber to Rotterdam [en] door wylen de Heer, A. t'Hooft

Seller Authority: Hooft, A. t'

Paintings Lots: 74

Catalogue Locations:

MWH	Not annot.

Comments: This was an eight-day sale of books in Rotterdam that included a number of prints, paintings and miscellaneous objects offered on the last day. The title page of the catalogue indicates that the books belonged to an unidentified Rotterdam collector, but the works of art were the property of A. t'Hooft, recently deceased. Nothing is known about him. The paintings were mostly anonymous and very briefly described, often with ludicrous misspellings of proper names. The bulk of them were landscapes and genre scenes, but there were also a number of mythological and religious pictures. The results are not known, but it appears to have been a collection of relatively minor pieces.

84 1804/10/15–1804/10/20

J.H. Bolt; Groningen, In Academia Gron.

Seller(s) from Title Page: Joannis Cannegieteri, dum in vivis esset, J.U.D. et Juris Civilis in Academia Groningana Professoris Ordin.

Seller Authority: Cannegieter, Johannes, Mr.

Paintings Lots: 34

Catalogue Locations:

BRB	Not annot. It is addressed to Heer Musschenbroek.

Comments: The contents of this five-day sale in Groningen consisted primarily of books, but on the last day some lots of coins, paintings, maps and miscellaneous items were also included. The paintings, which were mostly landscapes and portraits of members of the house of Orange, are very poorly described. The owner, Johannes Cannegieter (1731–1804), was a native of Arnhem who later became professor of law in Groningen. His elder brother Hermannus Cannegieter was professor of law at Franeker University (see cat. no.97). The results of the sale are unknown.

85 1804/10/16 and following days [Lugt 6859]

J.H. Onderdewyngaart Canzius; Delft, Verwersdyk, door de Poort van Stads Doele

Seller(s) from Title Page: None

Paintings Lots: 346

Catalogue Locations:

*MB	Annot. with a few buyers and prices. It belonged to the dealer Thijs and the annotations are his.
MWH	Not annot.
MPA	Not annot.
BRB	Not annot.

Comments: This sale of paintings, drawings, prints, sculpture, maps and miscellanea was unusual in many respects. Auctions in Delft were relatively rare, and this one included an exceptionally large number of paintings. The catalogue was printed in Dutch, but a French translation is given for each lot. In addition to the catalogue number there is also a second number described as "No. ink." – for "inkoppen" ? – whose significance is not clear. These numbers are generally much higher than the lot numbers, between 1000 and 2000, but their origin is not known, and we have not included them. For some reason, three of the four extant copies of the catalogue are in Belgian libraries; although only one of them is annotated with just a few buyers' names, it appears that a number of Belgian dealers attended the sale. The individual paintings were mostly landscapes and genre scenes of small dimensions, and the prices, so far as they are known, were generally low. Among the few exceptions was lot 213a, a scene with *A Drunken Schoolmaster* by Jan Steen, which is supposed to have fetched fl. 600. A landscape by Dirk van Bergen was knocked down for fl. 400, but its buyer was apparently the auctioneer himself, so it may have been bought in.

86 1804/10/22 and following days

A.P. de Winter; Middelburg, Premises, Noordstraat

Additional Auctioneers: S. van Benthem

Seller(s) from Title Page: Heer F. Reytsma

Seller Authority: Reytsma, F.

Paintings Lots: 5

Catalogue Locations:

*ZBM	Annot. with all buyers and prices on interleaved pages.

Comments: The contents of this Middelburg sale were primarily books, but on the last day there were some prints and a few paintings.

87 1804/10/29–1804/11/02 [Lugt 6862]

H.A. Baur en Zoon; Harlingen, Premises, not given

Additional Auctioneers: V. van der Plaats

Seller(s) from Title Page: Nagelaaten door den Heer Simon Styl, Med. Doct.

Seller Authority: Stijl, Simon

Paintings Lots: 175

Catalogue Locations:

AMR	Not annot.
UBL	Not seen. According to Lugt it is not annot.

Comments: This is the only sale from this period to be held in Harlingen for which a catalogue has been found. The date is given only as October, 1804, and the day has been filled in by hand. The contents were primarily paintings, but there were also significant numbers of prints, drawings and sculpture. The owner was a prominent physician, statesman, poet, and historian who was also co-founder of the Harlinger Theatre. At his death in 1804 his estate was estimated at fl. 192,000, a very large sum for the time. His collection of paintings, however, appears to have been fairly modest. Most of the individual works were landscapes, seascapes or genre scenes of small dimensions, in addition to a few portraits, still lifes and religious subjects. There were just three pictures with mythological subjects, including a depiction of *Diana* thought to be by Parmigianino. The descriptions are fairly lengthy, but none of the paintings have yet been traced, and the results are not known.

88 1804/12/10 and following days [Lugt 6874]

Philippus van der Schley; Amsterdam, Ten Huize van Cornelis Sebille Roos, op de Cloveniers Burgwal, in 't Huis van Trip

Additional Auctioneers: Jan de Bosch Jeronimusz.; Jan Yver; Cornelis Sebille Roos; Roelof Meurs Pruyssenaar; Jacobus Vinkeles

Seller(s) from Title Page: Naargelaaten, door Wylen den Kunst-Minnaar den Heer Jan de Groot

Seller Authority: Groot, Jan de

Paintings Lots: 126

Catalogue Locations:

LBDa	Auctioneer's copy, annot. with all buyers and prices on interleaved pages. It may have belonged to the dealer P. van der Schley. (Dutch edition)
*RKDH	Auctioneer's copy, annot. with all buyers and prices on interleaved pages. It belonged to the dealer C.S. Roos. (Dutch edition)
FLNY	Annot. with all buyers and prices. (Dutch edition)
BMPL	Annot. with all buyers and prices. It belonged to Wm. Smith.
EBNP	Auctioneer's copy, annot. with all buyers and prices on interleaved pages. However, the drawings lots are annot. with only a few buyers.
NGW	Annot. with most buyers and prices.
MPA I	Annot. with many buyers and prices. (Dutch edition)
MA	Annot. with most buyers and prices for the paintings only.
MB	Annot. with some buyers and prices for the prints but not for the paintings. (Dutch edition)
AA	Annot. with a few buyers and prices. The annotations refer mostly to the dealer Wm. Gruyter and the catalogue may have been his.
NGL	Annot. in pencil with some prices but not for the paintings.
KPL	Not seen. According to Lugt it is annot. with prices for the drawings.
ESP	Not annot. excepting one note. (Dutch edition)
MPA II	Not annot. (French edition)
RMA	Incomplete, including only pp.37–96, and therefore lacking the paintings. Not annot.
BMB	Present location unknown. According to Lugt it is not annot.

Comments: The catalogue of this sale was published in two parts, the first devoted to paintings, drawings and a few prints, the second to prints and some miscellaneous furniture and telescopes, etc. The length of the sale is not known, but judging from the very large number of lots, it must have lasted at least two weeks. The identity of the owner, Jan de Groot, has never been conclusively established. He was very active in the Amsterdam art market over a long period, and it has been suggested that he was the painter Johannes (or Jan) de Groot who is recorded as having been a student of Jacob de Wit in The Hague in 1752 and whose activity as a painter is recorded until 1776. He is known to have taken over his father's printing business in 1755/57, including responsibility for the *Haagsche Courant*, which is supposed to have caused him to give up painting. This identification is lent some credence by the 1755 testament of his father, Anthony de Groot, in which a significant collection of drawings, prints, paintings and sculpture was left to his son. (Cf. A. Bredius, *Künstler-Inventare*, III, 1917, p.758.) If he is the same collector whose possessions appear in the present sale, he would have been about 70/75 years of age at the time of his death, which is presumed to have taken place in 1804. Seven of the paintings in the sale can be traced to auctions held between 1774 and 1781, at which time most were knocked down to "de Groot," perhaps indicating that his chief activity as a buyer of paintings had taken place two to three decades before his death. However, the sale consisted in large part of landscapes or topographical views by Dutch artists some of whom were active only during the second half of the century. There were, for instance, six paintings by Willem Joseph Laquy (1738–1798) and twelve by Johannes Christianus Janson (1763–1823), the latter a painter active in The Hague. Moreover, the collection of drawings was heavily weighted toward the modern Dutch school, and some of the prints, such as a group devoted to the French Revolution, reveal very recent activity. This taste for the work of contemporary artists might well be indicative of a painter who enjoyed patronizing his peers, but the identification remains unproven. If our Jan de Groot inherited a collection from his father, he had certainly added to it extensively during his lifetime. The most expensive lot was one of the early paintings, an *Interior with a Woman and a Child Playing with a Dog* by Metsu, for which the dealers Ph. van der Schley and C.S. Roos paid fl. 351. (Its subsequent history is unknown.) A marine picture by Backhuysen was sold for fl. 300 and a pair of flower and fruit paintings by Jan van Os brought fl. 605. The total receipts for the entire sale reached fl. 28,531:11, but the bulk of this amount was realized by the drawings and prints.

89 1805/02/07–1805/02/09

B. Besanger; Den Haag, Veenestraat Letter S. No.185

Seller(s) from Title Page: Twee voornaame Liefhebbers

Paintings Lots: 3

Catalogue Locations:

MWH	Not annot.

Comments: This was a three-day sale of books held by the Hague bookseller Barent Besanger (1781-after 1811) in his shop in the Veenestraat. It also included a collection of music, musical instruments, and a few paintings and miscellaneous items. All the paintings were anonymous.

90 1805/04/23–1805/04/24

Jan Breebaart; Hoorn, Zaal van St. Pieters Hoff

Seller(s) from Title Page: None

Paintings Lots: 4

Catalogue Locations:

VBBA	Not annot.

Comments: This is one of the few sales held in the city of Hoorn for which a catalogue has survived. It was held in the refectory of Sint Pietershof, a former monastery near the Munnickenveld and Gedempte Turfhaven. The sale, which lasted two days, consisted of books as well as a few paintings, prints, maps and miscellaneous objects. The owners are unidentified and the results are not recorded.

91 1805/06/24 and following days [Lugt 6981]

A. Blussé & Zoon; Dordrecht, Stads Venduhuis in de Wynstraat over de Nieuwbrug

Seller(s) from Title Page: Heer Mr. Willem Snellen, in leven Burgemeester &c. to Dordrecht; Heer F.R.E. Nibbelinck, in leven rustend Predikant te Dubbeldam; en Heer Gysbert Visser, in leven Makelaar te Dordrecht

Seller Authority: Snellen, Willem, Mr.; Nibbelinck, F.R.E.; Visser, Gysbert

Paintings Lots: 30

Catalogue Locations:

RKDH	Not annot. It is addressed to the Rev. Ewaldus Kist (1762–1822).
MWH	Not annot.

Comments: This is one of the sales held by the bookdealers Abraham Blussé en Zoon in Dordrecht that also included a few paintings, drawings, prints and miscellanea. In addition there was a collection of shells and a cabinet of medals, the latter described as the property of Gysbert Visser. The catalogue leaves it unclear as to which of the three collectors were the owners of the paintings, but since Visser was a broker, he is the best candidate. His premises had been in "op de Voorstraat tusschen de Kerkstraat en Toorenstraatje" and he was buried in the Grote Kerk in December, 1804 (GAD, Begraafboek Grote Kerk, Arch. 11, inv.54, folio 48V). The paintings are described very cursorily; many are anonymous.

92 1805/06/28–1805/06/29

N. Brinkman; Gouda, Ten Huize van N. Brinkman

Seller(s) from Title Page: None

Paintings Lots: 1

Catalogue Locations:

KBH Not annot.

Comments: This was a two-day sale of books, "rariteiten" and pictures held in Gouda. The title page of the catalogue refers prominently to the paintings in the sale, but within the catalogue proper there is no list of paintings, only a single unnumbered item on the last day which refers to 20 paintings by different artists and for which no further description is given.

92-A 1805/07/01 and following days

Van Benthem en Ooms; Middelburg, In het Heeren Logement Antwerpen, staande in den Langendelft

Seller(s) from Title Page: None

Paintings Lots: 6

Catalogue Locations:

*ZBM Auctioneer's copy, annot. with all buyers and prices on interleaved pages.

Comments: The contents were books, music, prints, drawings and miscellaneous items. No paintings are listed, but an interleaved page gives the buyers and prices for six lots of "schilderyen" which are otherwise not described.

93 1805/07/03 [Lugt 6985]

Philippus van der Schley; Amsterdam, Ten Huize van C.S. Roos, in 't Huis van Trip

Additional Auctioneers: Jan de Bosch, Jeronimusz.; Jan Yver; Cornelis Sebille Roos; Jacobus Vinkeles

Seller(s) from Title Page: Nagelaaten Door Wylen den Hoogh Edele Heere Gerard Godart Baron Taets van Amerongen, Heere van Oud Amélisweerd en Oud Marschalk van 't Neederquartier, 's Lands van Utrecht

Seller(s) from Auctioneer's Copy: R[oos]; V[inkeles]

Seller Authority: Roos, Cornelis Sebille; Vinkeles, Jacobus

Paintings Lots: 219

Catalogue Locations:

FLNY	Auctioneer's copy, annot. with all buyers and prices on interleaved pages, as well as letters for the sellers. (Dutch edition)
*RKDH	Auctioneer's copy, annot. with all buyers and prices on interleaved pages as well as letters for the sellers. It belonged to the dealer C.S. Roos. (Dutch edition)
AA	Annot. with all buyers and prices on interleaved pages. (Dutch edition)
AAP	Annot. with all buyers and prices. (French edition)
RMA	Annot. with most buyers and all prices. (Dutch edition)
MB II	Annot. with many buyers and all prices. It belonged to the dealer P.J. Thijs and the annotations are his. (Dutch edition)
EBNP	Annot. with many buyers and all prices. (Dutch edition)
ESP	Annot. in pencil with all prices. (Dutch edition)
MB I	Not annot. (French edition)

Comments: The catalogue for this sale was printed in both Dutch and French, but the French edition contained just the first 54 lots, described as the first part of the sale, while the Dutch edition contained 219 lots altogether. The contents were entirely paintings, described on the title page as belonging in part to Gerard Godart, baron Taets van Amerongen(1729–1804) and in part to other, unnamed collectors. The division of the catalogue corresponds to this description, with the first part consisting of lots 1–54 arranged in alphabetical order, described as "een fray Cabinet Schilderyen," and apparently meant to correspond to the "kabinet" belonging to Taets van Amerongen mentioned on the title page. The title page of the French edition, in fact, specifically describes the paintings in this part as being his. The second part, beginning with lot 55, is described simply as the "Vervolg van Schilderyen," leading one to presume that these were the paintings that did not derive from Taets van Amerongen. This interpretation, however, is contradicted by annotations in the RKDH and FLNY copies of the catalogue, both of which belonged to dealers who helped organize the sale. They are annotated with letters next to the individual lots indicating that there were seven consignments, designated C, D, G, R, S, V and Y (which, because of their sequence, appear to be initials rather than arbitrary letters), and that lots 1 through 54 belonged to four consigners, all but one of whom also owned paintings in the second part. (The exception is "D," who owned just three lots in part one.) This suggests that the catalogue was compiled to give the false impression that Taets van Amerongen owned lots 1–54 – which included the majority of the most valuable pictures – when in fact he apparently owned no more than a part of them. The only initial in the sequence that might apply to Taets van Amerongen is "G," which would correspond to his given names, Gerard Godart. "G" owned eight of the lots in the first section, but he is given as the source of 27 lots in the second part, which constitutes a major reason for questioning the identification. Nothing more about the nature of the paintings in this group – or any of the other groups – suggests an association with Taets van Amerongen, aside from the fact that they constituted the third-largest consignment in the sale and realized the second-largest return (fl. 3207:10). It is also noteworthy that none of these pictures has been traced to earlier sales from the last half of the previous century, and none were bought in at the present sale, as would be appropriate for works consigned by an owner now deceased. However, the connection is not proven.

There are also some, though less compelling, reasons for thinking that the paintings belonging to Taets van Amerongen were those marked with an "R." These were the most numerous (92 altogether) and they brought the highest total amount (fl. 9436:15). Thirty-nine of the first 54 lots belonged to this group. The initial "R" certainly refers to the dealer Cornelis Sebille Roos, one of the organizers of the sale, who might have been acting on behalf of Taets van Amerongen. Roos was also the original owner of the RKDH copy of the catalogue, but the annotations in his catalogue do not indicate, as they usually did, that he was representing someone else. Two of the lots can be traced to the Gildemeester sale of 1800, where one of them, lot no.43 by Schalcken depicting *An Old Woman with a Dog on Her Lap*, had been purchased by Roos. However, the second Gildemeester painting had been purchased by a different dealer, and other lots in the "R" consignment can also be traced to sales, sometimes recent, where they were acquired by a variety of people. Consequently, an association with Taets van Amerongen can be neither proven or disproven.

Unfortunately, nothing is presently known about the origins or composition of Taets van Amerongen's collection, and there is no record of his having acquired a painting under his own name. He was a native of Utrecht, the son of Leonard Godart (1700–1736) and Maria Jacoba Pynssen van der Aa, lady of Renswoude, Emmikhuijsen and Deijl. He was appointed judge at the court of Utrecht in 1751, a position he held until 1786. He lived in Utrecht at the Wittevrouwenstraat on the corner of the Rietsteeg, and in 1760 he acquired the country estate Oud-Amélisweerd near Utrecht. In 1751 he married Anna Susanna Hasselaer (1730–1788), daughter of the Amsterdam burgomaster Mr. Gerard Aarnout Hasselaer. After his death his books were sold in Utrecht on April 1, 1805 (a copy exists at VBBA), just three months before the present sale. In view of the discrepancy between the claims found in this catalogue and the annotations mentioned above, it seems likely that not only the size but also the importance of his collection of pictures was deliberately exaggerated for the purposes of this sale. However, documents in the Utrecht archives (GAU, Notarieel Archief, not. Jan de Wijs, archief 174, inv. U 315a003, d.d. Dec.17, 1806) indicate that Taets van Amerongen's estate did indeed include paintings which were sold in Amsterdam, and so one of the consignments in the present sale must have been his. Until some proof can be found of what his cabinet did in fact include, it seems hazardous to draw any conclusions about which consignment it was.

The consigners S, V and Y were not represented by paintings in the first part of the sale, and so can probably be excluded as having been associated with Taets van Amerongen. "V" can be identified as the dealer Jacobus Vinkeles, and "Y" may have been the dealer Jan Yver, although this is not certain. Three of the seven pictures belonging to "S" were also bought in by Vinkeles and later reappeared at the sale on August 13, 1806 (cat. no.103) as the property of "J" (represented by V[inkeles]). Two of them subsequently appeared a third time on June 13, 1808 (cat. no.128) as the property of "K," but his identity remains unknown.

The majority of the most expensive lots were among those consigned by R[oos]. The highest price, fl. 800, was fetched by lot 29, the panel depicting *A Man Offering Oysters to a Young Lady* by Frans van Mieris, which had been bought by Roos at the Gildemeester sale. A landscape by Jacob van Ruisdael from this group brought fl. 750, and a scene in Rome by Lingelbach was sold for fl. 720. A pair of Ruisdael landscapes consigned by "G" was sold for fl. 1500. Two higher prices were registered for a *Portrait of a Woman* by Van Dyck and a landscape by Hobbema, but both were bought in and cannot be traced. The total receipts for the sale came to fl. 16,133:5.

94 1805/07/10–1805/07/11 [Lugt 6987]

Philippus van der Schley; Amsterdam, Huize van C.S. Roos, in 't Huis van Trip

Additional Auctioneers: Jan de Bosch, Jeronimusz.; Jan Yver; Cornelis Sebille Roos; Jacobus Vinkeles

Seller(s) from Title Page: None

Seller(s) from Auctioneer's Copy: R[oos]; S[chley]; V[inkeles]; Y[ver]

Seller Authority: Roos, Cornelis Sebille; Schley, Philippus van der; Vinkeles, Jacobus; Yver, Jan

Paintings Lots: 313

Catalogue Locations:

RKDH	Auctioneer's copy, annot. with all buyers and prices on interleaved pages as well as letters for the sellers. It belonged to the dealer C.S. Roos.
EBNP	Auctioneer's copy, annot. with all buyers and prices on interleaved pages as well as letters for the sellers.

AA	Annot. with all buyers and prices on interleaved pages.
*FLNY	Auctioneer's copy, annot. with initials for the names of the sellers, as well as a few buyers and all prices. The latter are in pencil and in two columns, indicating which were sold and which bought in. Some of the sellers are identified at the back. It apparently belonged to the auctioneer Schley, whose name is written on the title page.
LBDa	Auctioneer's copy, annot. with some sellers, a few buyers and all prices. It apparently belonged to the dealer P. van der Schley.

Comments: This was a two-day sale that included a large number of inexpensive paintings evidently belonging to a number of collectors and dealers. Although the title page identifies none of the owners, four of the extant catalogues belonged originally to dealers who helped organize the sale, and all are annotated with letters next to the individual lots designating the various consigners. Two of the catalogues, EBNP and RKDH, show that there were seven different consignments, designated as H, R, S, V, X, Y and Z which, because of the sequence, were probably the owners' initials rather than arbitrary letters. Some of these can be readily identified as being the dealers who oversaw the sale: R[oos], S[chley], V[inkeles] and Y[ver]. The FLNY copy of the catalogue, however, which belonged to the dealer Van der Schley, substitutes nine different letters for most of the lots belonging to V[inkeles], as follows: C, G, H, J, K, L, M, N and P. These must stand for the collectors represented by Vinkeles at the sale. (The letter "H" appears both as one of this group and by itself, so it is uncertain whether it refers to the same person.) The FLNY catalogue also identifies "Z" as "MynH^{r} Temmink" (which is confirmed by the LBDa catalogue) and "X" as "Juff^{r} de Wed. Grave." In addition, a number of lots in Van der Schley's group are shown to belong to Doralle, Kliene[?], Bernard, Louis and "de Wed. Landers." Taken altogether, it appears that there were at least 23 consigners to the sale. The largest group, 55 lots, was consigned by R[oos], but we cannot be certain that he was not in turn representing yet other persons. His lots yielded fl. 1651:8 and just three were bought in. The dealer Jan Yver consigned 35 lots, many of which were *hors du catalogue* and anonymous, and which brought only fl. 553:6. Another relatively large consignment was that of "M," whose 29 lots were sold for modest amounts and of which six were bought in. Only one of the anonymous sellers represented by Vinkeles can be identified. The consigner "H" was certainly Haffner, whose pictures can be traced to earlier sales where they were recorded as his. Very few lots exceeded fl. 100, and just two surpassed fl. 200. A *Landscape with a Falcon Hunt* supposedly by Philips de Koninck and Lingelbach was bought by the dealer Hulswit for fl. 275, and a church interior by Neeffs was sold for fl. 220. The highest price, fl. 322, was registered for a *View of the Bleaching Grounds at Overveen* by Ruisdael which, however, was left unsold. The total receipts for the sale came to fl. 4066:15.

95 1805/09/23–1805/10/21

Joannem Henricum Bol; Groningen, Majori Academia Auditorio

Seller(s) from Title Page: Gerardus Nicolaus Heerkens, dum viveret, med. doctor, arcadum romanorum, acad. cortonensis, et societatum doctrinarum harlemensis et vlissinganae socii…

Seller Authority: Heerkens, Gerardus Nicolaus

Paintings Lots: 68

Catalogue Locations:

VBBA	Not annot.
MWH	Not annot.

Comments: The owner, Gerard Nicolaas Heerkens (1726–1801), was born in Kleine Meer (near Sappemeer), the son of Eppo Joannes Ignatius Heerkens (1692–1758) and Anna Maria Meijknecht (1703–1756). He studied at the Jesuit College in Meppen, Westphalia, and later as a student of law at Groningen. As a student he published several Latin poems under the pseudonym "Curillus" in which he attacked some prominent local dignitaries, causing him to leave Groningen for Leyden, where he took up the study of medicine. Subsequently he moved to France, where he became acquainted with Voltaire, Fontenelle and other writers. Eventually he returned to Groningen, where he practiced medicine until his death, but he often travelled to France and to Italy, where he was a member of various learned societies. The present sale lasted nearly a month and was largely dedicated to his library, but on the last day there were a number of paintings, drawings, prints and miscellaneous objects. The paintings, which are described with relatively few words, were predominantly landscapes and genre pieces, but there were also a few religious and mythological subjects as well. The results are unrecorded.

96 1805/09/23 and following days

Van Benthem en Ooms; Middelburg, In het Heeren Logement Antwerpen, staande in den Langendelft

Seller(s) from Title Page: Nagelaaten door Wylen den Heer Mr. P. Changuion, in Zyn Ed. Leven Oud Secretaris dezer Stad [en] N.N.

Seller Authority: Changuion, Paul, Mr.

Paintings Lots: 7

Catalogue Locations:

*ZBM	Auctioneer's copy, annot. with all buyers and prices on interleaved pages.

Comments: The contents of this Middelburg sale were primarily books, but a number of prints, drawings, maps and scientific instruments were also included. The owner of the principal part of the sale is described on the title page as Mr. P. Changuion who can be identified as Mr. Paul Changuion, director and later vice president of the Zeeuwsch Genootschap der Wetenschappen. The two subsequent parts are said to belong to "N.N." Two lots of paintings are described in the catalogue as the property of "N.N." and a note on p.82 states, "Nog eenige Schilderyen, waaronder van goede Meesters, welke volgens een geschreeven Lyst zullen verkocht worden." No list of these additional paintings is present, but an interleaved page of buyers and sellers for lots 5 through 9 indicates that five lots were added and sold, although there are no descriptions for them. It is unclear whether lots 3 and 4 were ever included. Apparently none of the paintings belonged to Changuion.

97 1805/09/24–1805/10/02

Dionysius Romar; Franeker, not given

Seller(s) from Title Page: Hermannus Cannegieter

Seller Authority: Cannegieter, Herman, Mr.

Paintings Lots: 1

Catalogue Locations:

KBH	Not annot. Addressed to J. Valckenaar, professor at Leiden.
BRB I	Not annot.
BRB II	Not annot.
MWH	Not annot.

Comments: This week-long sale of books in Franeker was devoted primarily to the library of Herman Cannegieter (1723–1804), professor of law at Franeker University. He was the son of Hendrik Cannegieter (1691–1770), also a professor of law, and Rachel Muys (1695–1777). He studied law at Leyden and was appointed professor at Franeker in 1750. He married Amarantia Susanna Gonggrijp (died 1806) in 1768. In 1795, during the unrest caused by the French Revolution, he was discharged from his position, but was reinstated in 1802. His younger brother was Johannes Cannegieter, professor law at Groningen (see cat. no.84). Included in his estate sale were some miscellaneous "rariteiten," among which was a lot containing "eenige Schilderyen."

98 1805/10/09 [Lugt 7000]

Frans Johannes Bosboom; Den Haag, Kunstkamer boven het Koornhuis op de Princegragt

Seller(s) from Title Page: Nagelaaten door wylen den wel edele gebooren Heer, de Heer T.H van Willigen, Regerings Raad en oud resident van zyne Keurvorstelyke Doorlugtigheid van Paltz-Beyeren, &c. &c. &c. en van meer anderen

Seller Authority: Willigen, T.H. van

Paintings Lots: 186

Catalogue Locations:

RKDH	Annot. with all buyers and prices. It includes the supplement.
*MWH	Annot. with all buyers and prices. The supplement has been incorrectly bound with no.104.
BMB	Present location unknown. According to Lugt it is annot. with buyers and prices.
MA	Annot. in red pencil with a few buyers and all prices. It is addressed to the painter Hendrik Carrée and the annotations are his.
MB	Not annot.

Comments: The catalogue of this sale was printed in two parts, the first containing 149 lots of paintings and the second, called an appendix, containing 41 additional lots of paintings as well as three lots of sculpture. The lot numbering in the appendix is highly idiosyncratic, beginning with A1, then B2, and concluding with QQ41. We have respected this system in spite of its absurd logic. The title page of the catalogue states that the paintings belonged to T.H. van Willigen, apparently deceased, and "meer anderen." There is no way to determine how many of the lots were van Willigen's, although some can be traced to an earlier sale held in The Hague on August 24, 1803 (cat. no.64) at which time they apparently belonged to the dealer Teissier and so can probably be excluded as belonging to van Willigen. The identity of T.H. van Willigen remains unresolved. Because of similarities in their professional careers, it is tempting to propose that the name found on the catalogue is a misprint and that Franciscus Antonius van Willigen was intended. The latter, born in 1738, was judge advocate of the court of Gelderland in Roermond and in 1768 was appointed counselor to the Elector of Bavaria, moving later to The Hague where he represented the Elector as chargé d'affaires from 1787 onwards. He was still at this post in 1802. He is referred to as a resident of the Palatinate and/or Bavaria but living in The Hague as late as 1806, but the date of his death is apparently unknown. (Cf. O. Schutte, *Repertorum der buitenlandse vertegenwoordigers residerende in Nederland, 1584–1810*, The Hague, 1982, pp.188–189.) With the exception of his first initials, the collector whose possessions were put up for sale at the present auction fits this description quite well, albeit that he was supposed to have died sometime earlier. His identity should eventually be found. In spite of its size, the sale did not contain paintings of exceptional value. Only two lots exceeded fl. 50, and the highest price, fl. 85, was paid for a genre scene by Hendrik Sorgh.

99 1805/12/16 and following days [Lugt 7013]

Philippus van der Schley; Amsterdam, Ten Huize van Cornelis Sebille Roos, op de Cloveniersburgwal, in 't Huis van Trip

Additional Auctioneers: Jan Yver; Cornelis Sebille Roos; Jacobus Vinkeles

Seller(s) from Title Page: None

Seller(s) from Auctioneer's Copy: Spaan; R[oos]; etc.

Seller Authority: Spaan; Roos, Cornelis Sebille

Paintings Lots: 153

Catalogue Locations:

*LBDa	Auctioneer's copy, annot. with all buyers and prices on interleaved pages as well as letters for the sellers. It may have belonged to the dealer P. van der Schley.
RKDH	Auctioneer's copy, annot. with all buyers and prices on interleaved pages as well as letters for the sellers. It belonged to the dealer C.S. Roos.
EBNP	Auctioneer's copy. Annot. with a few buyers and all prices as well as letters for some of the sellers. The prices are in pencil and some are difficult to read.
AA	Not annot.
NOL	Present location unknown. According to Lugt it is not annot.

Comments: This sale contained 153 lots of paintings, 137 printed in the catalogue and 16 added by hand. However, the drawings and prints constituted the largest sections, and in addition there were groups of sculpture, porcelain, optical and musical instruments and a number of miscellaneous items of various kinds. The catalogue mentions no sellers, but three of the extant catalogues belonged originally to dealers who helped organize the sale and are marked with letters next to the individual lots that pertain to different consigners. These catalogues also have lists showing how the proceeds were divided, and these reveal that nine consigners were represented, designated as C, O, R, S, V, W, X, Y and Z. Three of these, C, W and X, consigned no paintings. Of the remainder, "R" can be readily identified with C.S. Roos, one of the co-organizers of the sale. Two others, "V" and "Y" may be the dealers Jacobus Vinkeles and Jan Yver who were also involved with the sale, but these identifications are still uncertain. The EBNP catalogue is also annotated with the name "Spaan" next to those lots consigned by "S," and therefore identifiable with either Jan or Theodorus Spaan, both dealers. This leaves only "O," all of whose five lots were bought in, and "Z," who submitted just one lot with two anonymous and untitled paintings.

The largest consignment was that from R[oos], whose initial is found next to 102 lots. It is fairly certain, however, that in many if not all instances he was acting on behalf of others. Twenty-two of his lots were bought in, and five of these reappeared on November 24, 1806 (cat. no.109) as the property of "van den Bosch," to whom they probably also belonged at the time of the present sale. However, three others reappear under his name on June 20, 1810 (cat. no.163), and these are likely to have been his own property. With few exceptions, the prices were generally very low, and it is clear that the sale was dedicated to minor works. A few works were knocked down for reasonably good amounts, including fl. 260 for a *Crucifixion* by Jacob Maurer and fl. 180 for a pair of still lifes by Johannes Christianus Roedig. However, all of these were in fact bought in; the highest price paid for a lot that actually changed hands was fl. 95 for a small landscape by Jan Both. The totals for the sale were fl. 7244, with fl. 1868:15 bought in. These figures include all categories, not just the paintings.

100 1806/01/30 [Lugt 7022]

[Anonymous]; Rotterdam, In 't Rechthuis

Seller(s) from Title Page: Nagelaten door Dirk Langendijk

Seller Authority: Langendijk, Dirk

Paintings Lots: 10

Catalogue Locations:

MR	Not annot.

Comments: Dirk Langendijk was born in 1748 in Rotterdam where he eventually also worked as a painter, draftsman and etcher, mainly of military scenes. A number of local collectors were his patrons, including Gerrit van der Pot, who owned several of his works. He was married to Josina Margaretha van Doorn (1758–1804), who was independently wealthy and whose resources no doubt helped him assemble his collection. In 1795 he separated from his wife, and took up quarters in the Hoge Heul. His later years were marred by alcoholism, and in 1805 he drowned from falling into the harbor. The present sale was held at the request of Langendijk's only son, the painter and draftsman Jan Anthonie Langendijk (1780–1818), in order to pay his father's debts and funeral expenses. By approval of the bailiff and aldermen of Cool, the sale was held at the local Rechthuis; it included Langendijk's equipment, books, drawings and prints, as well as ten paintings. The paintings are poorly described and were probably of little interest. The total receipts for the sale (including the pictures) was just fl. 295:17:4, which was clearly insufficient to pay off Langendijk's creditors, among whom were the collectors Gerrit van der Pals (to whom fl. 700 was owed) and Daniel de Jongh Adrszn. (fl. 500).

101 1806/05/05 and following days [Lugt 7085]

Philippus van der Schley; Amsterdam, Ten Huize van Cornelis Sebille Roos, op de Cloveniers Burgwal, in 't Huis van Trip

Additional Auctioneers: Jan Yver; Cornelis Sebille Roos; Jacobus Vinkeles

Seller(s) from Title Page: Nagelaaten door wylen den Kunst-Oessenaar Jan Everhard Grave

Seller(s) from Auctioneer's Copy: R[oos]; S[chley]; V[inkeles]; etc.

Seller Authority: Roos, Cornelis Sebille; Schley, Philippus van der; Vinkeles, Jacobus

Paintings Lots: 276

Catalogue Locations:

RKDH	Auctioneer's copy, annot. with all buyers and prices on interleaved pages as well as letters for the sellers. It belonged to the dealer C.S. Roos.
EBNP	Auctioneer's copy, annot. with all buyers and prices on interleaved pages.
*FLNY	Auctioneer's copy, annot. with all buyers and prices on interleaved pages as well as letters for the sellers. It is incomplete, consisting of only pp.1–48, but this includes all of the paintings.
RMA	Annot. with a few prices for drawings and prints but not for the paintings.
LBDa	Not annot. It may have belonged to the dealer P. van der Schley.
ESP	Not annot. This is the copy formerly at KKB.

Comments: The title page of the catalogue describes the contents of the sale as paintings, drawings, prints, coins and musical instruments, etc., after which is mentioned "eenige rariteiten en kunstkasten," the property of Jan Everhard Grave. Therefore the latter, an amateur draftsman and etcher who had died in December of the previous year, owned none of the paintings; this is borne out by the FLNY and RKDH copies of the catalogue, which belonged to dealers who helped organize the sale and are annotated with letters next to each lot designating the different consignments: E, F, G, H, L, O, R, S, V, and Y. The only letter not associated with paintings is "G," who was clearly Grave. Three of the last four consigners can be identified as dealers responsible for the auction: R[oos], S[chley] and V[inkeles]. The consigner "Y" may be Jan Yver, another of the co-auctioneers, but this is less certain. It is likely, however, that in many cases they were only representing other anonymous individuals. A number of pictures belonging to V[inkeles], for instance, had been bought in earlier at the sale on August 8, 1804 (no.82), at which time they probably belonged to the dealer Willem Gruyter. Since all of these letters correspond to the names of the participants, the remaining five letters are probably also initials rather than arbitrarily assigned letters, but none of them can be identified conclusively. One lot consigned by "H," a self-portrait by Frans van Mieris, had been purchased at a sale in 1788 by "Hoefman," who might then be the current owner. Unfortunately, the association is too tenuous to adopt. The largest number of pictures, 67 altogether, were submitted by Roos, who also received the largest share of the receipts, fl. 1366:17. However, the sale contained no works of significant value, and very few lots brought more than fl. 100. The highest prices were fl. 181 paid for a pair of portraits attributed to Pieter van Miereveld and fl. 158 for two landscapes by Ommeganck. Considering the number of items in the sale, and the fact that relatively few lots were left unsold, the results were modest. The net income for all categories was fl. 5356:8.

101-A 1806/05/19 and following days

S. van Benthem; Middelburg, In het Heeren Logement Antwerpen, staande in den Langendelft

Seller(s) from Title Page: None

Paintings Lots: 6

Catalogue Locations:

*ZBM	Auctioneer's copy, annot. with all buyers and prices on interleaved pages.

Comments: This was one of the book sales held in Middelburg by Salomon van Benthem, which apparently also included a few paintings. The printed catalogue contained only books, maps, prints, drawings and miscellanea, but a note inside indicates that some paintings were to be added. No list of the paintings exists, although an interleaved page shows that six paintings were offered and then bought in. No description of individual pictures is given.

102 **1806/06/02–1806/06/07** [Lugt 7118]

P. en J. Holsteyn; Rotterdam, Zaal boven de Beurs

Seller(s) from Title Page: Hoog Eerw: Hoog Gel: Heere Dingeman Wouter Smits, Professor Honorair in de H: Godgeleerdheid en Predikant in de Hervormde Gemeente te Rotterdam; Heere J.P.H.V. en J.V.B.; [en] Heere A.E.K.L.

Seller Authority: Smits, Dingeman Wouter; L., A.E.K.

Paintings Lots: 132

Catalogue Locations:

*MB	Annot. in ink and pencil with a few buyers and prices. It includes only the last day of the sale. It belonged to the dealer P.J. Thijs and the annotations are his.
KBH	Not annot. excepting a note by lot 2.

Comments: This was a six-day sale of books that included some pictures, drawings and prints sold on the last day. One of the extant copies of the catalogue (MB) lists only the last day's lots and has its own title page, perhaps indicating it was issued as a separate catalogue. (Lugt in fact lists it only under the last day.) A number of owners are mentioned on the title page of the catalogue, where it is made clear that Dingeman Wouter Smits (1748–1806) and two of the owners identified only by their initials were the proprietors of the books. The paintings belonged to A.E.K.L., about whom nothing is known. His collection consisted mostly of landscapes and genre scenes with a few biblical subjects mixed in. The MB copy of the catalogue is annotated with just a few of the prices which, if representative, indicate that most lots brought less than fl. 60. None of the paintings has been conclusively identified.

103 **1806/08/13** and following days [Lugt 7143]

Philippus van der Schley; Amsterdam, Ten Huize van Cornelis Sebille Roos, op de Kloveniers Burgwal, in 't Huis van Trip

Additional Auctioneers: Jan de Bosch, Jeronimusz.; Jan Yver; Cornelis Sebille Roos; Jacobus Vinkeles

Seller(s) from Title Page: Nagelaaten door Wylen den Heere Daniel Mansveld

Seller(s) from Auctioneer's Copy: van der Voort; Coclers; Vinkeles; etc.

Seller Authority: Mansveld, Daniel; Voort, van der; Coclers, Louis-Bernard; Vinkeles, Jacobus

Paintings Lots: 400

Catalogue Locations:

*RKDH	Auctioneer's copy, annot. with all buyers and prices on interleaved pages as well as letters for the sellers. The latter are also identified. It belonged to the dealer C.S. Roos.
LBDa	Auctioneer's copy, annot. with all buyers and prices on interleaved pages as well as letters for the sellers. It may have belonged to the dealer P. van der Schley.
MA	Annot. with most buyers and all prices.
MB	Annot. in ink and pencil with many buyers and all prices. It belonged to the dealer P.J. Thijs and the annotations are his.
EBNP	Annot. with the names of a few buyers, and in pencil with all prices. There are also letters for the sellers.
JPGM	Annot. with letters for the sellers as well as the names of a few buyers and some prices in pencil. It belonged to the auctioneer Roos and the sellers' names are identified at the back.
ESP	Not annot.
AAP	Not annot.
BMB	Present location unknown. According to Lugt it is not annot.

Comments: The catalogue for this sale included 347 lots of paintings, to which 46 more were added *hors du catalogue*, making it one of the largest picture sales in the Netherlands during this period. There were also a few lots of drawings and prints. The only proprietor mentioned on the title page is Daniel Mansveld (1726–1806), a resident of Amsterdam whose profession remains unknown. At the time of his marriage in 1776 he was living "op de Agterburgwal" (GAA, DTB Ondertrouw inv. fol.566), and he was buried in the Westerkerk on April 28, 1806 (GAA, DTB Begraven inv.1106, fol.15). Three extant copies of the catalogue that belonged to co-organizers of the sale are annotated with letters next to the individual lots indicating that a number of other consigners were included; two copies, JPGM and RKDH, also identify them, but with slightly different results. The former lists just six owners, designated A, B, R, S, V, and Y, while the RKDH catalogue adds C and subdivides V into five groups. Most, but not all, of the letters correspond to the first letters of the names of the consigners, but the five owners represented by V (Jacobus Vinkeles) are not named. The full list from the RKDH catalogue reads as follows: A = Mansveld; B = Van der Voort; C = Coclers; D, E, F, G, J = Vinkeles; R = Roos; S = Van der Schley; and Y = Yver, the last four being dealers involved with the organization of the sale. The pictures consigned by Roos, Van der Schley and Yver, like Vinkeles, may have also belonged to still other collectors whose names are not recorded. In fact, the JPGM catalogue, which belonged originally to Roos, is annotated with a few secondary names, such as "Vos" by lot 6, "Flen"(?) by lot 66, and "Ruel"(?) by lot 121, who were no doubt the true owners. This might imply, in turn, that the other lots in the group were Roos's own property. Roos's consignment was the largest of the sale, comprising 141 lots altogether. However, the individual pictures were inexpensive and apparently old stock of which he wanted to dispose. The return from his lots came to just fl. 1498:16. The most valuable pictures were those belonging to Van der Voort. He submitted 26 lots altogether that fetched fl. 6272:15. Mansveld's consignment consisted of 23 lots that realized fl. 4394. One of Vinkeles's unnamed consigners can also be identified: "G" was certainly the dealer Willem Gruyter, and many of his paintings can be traced to earlier sales where he acquired them. His consignment included 68 paintings altogether, but brought only fl. 561:9.

The most expensive lot in the sale was no.49, a depiction of *Christ and the Adulteress* by Eeckhout that belonged to Mansveld and was bought by the French dealer Lafontaine for fl. 1430, an unusually high price for a work by this master. (This may be the painting later in the Six collection in Amsterdam, sold in 1923.) Another high price, fl. 1220, was paid by the dealer Van Iperen for lot 82, an Italian genre scene by Karel Dujardin consigned by Van der Voort. (It was most recently in the S. Steinberg collection in New York, from which it was sold in 1991.) Two marine pictures by Backhuysen and Van de Cappelle brought fl. 730 and fl. 760, respectively, but have not been traced. Among identifiable pictures from this sale are the *Marriage Contract of Tobias and Sarah* by Aert de Gelder (now in the Brighton Art Gallery and Museum) and the *Interior with a Still life* by Jan der Heyden (now in the Budapest museum). The total receipts were fl. 14,490:9, and the unsold lots came to fl. 2079:10.

104 **1806/08/20** [Lugt 7146]

Frans Johannes Bosboom; Den Haag, Kunstkamer boven het Koornhuis op de Prince Gragt

Seller(s) from Title Page: Heere Macalester Loup

Seller(s) from Auctioneer's Copy: Pompe van Meerdervoort; Pothoven; Teissier; etc.

Seller Authority: Macalester Loup, Duncan; Pompe van Meerdervoort; Pothoven

Paintings Lots: 226

Catalogue Locations:

*JPGM	Auctioneer's copy, annot. with all buyers and prices on interleaved pages. There is also a list of sellers.
MWH II	Annot. with all buyers and prices.
RKDH	Annot. with all buyers and prices.
MB	Annot. with many buyers and prices. It is addressed to "Hr Thijs by H G v d Pot S^{r} port."
LBDa	Incomplete, including only pp.1–24, lots 1–188. Annot. with all buyers and prices. It is addressed to "Myn Heer Vallette Konstschilder," i.e., Joseph Vallette.
AA	Incomplete, including only pp.1–24 and lots 1–188. Annot. in red pencil with one buyer and all prices.
MWH I	Not annot.
MM	Not seen. According to Lugt it is not annot.
MA	Lugt lists a copy at this location, but it is probably an error for MB.

Comments: The catalogue of this sale contained 188 lots of paintings followed by an appendix with lots 189–225, also consisting entirely of paintings. The owners are identified on the title page as Heere Macalester Loup and "andere Liefhebbers." A list of names found at the back of the JPGM copy of the catalogue identifies the sellers and describes how the receipts from the sale were divided, but does not reveal who owned the individual lots. The complete list reads as follows: Macalester 2700:5; Tendal 95:6; Temminch 5:15; Teissier 362:15; Pompe van Meerdervoort 2389:15; Renoud 21; Palairiet 118:11; Brink 17:3; Freule van Rechteren 13; Pothoven 442:5; Caan 2:18; Havel 2; krs[?] Haaf 29:12. These figures produced a total of fl. 6200:5; when this figure is combined with the unsold lots, the result comes to fl. 6942:17. From this we can deduce that Macalester Loup had probably consigned the largest number of paintings, since more than one-third of the revenue was returned to him. So far only eight paintings, purchased by "Macalester" at sales held in 1796 and 1797 by the same auctioneer, Bosboom, can be associated with this group. All of these are found in the present sale between lots 3 and 45, which might indicate that his pictures are generally among the first lots to be sold. However, lot 33 by Gerrit Berckheyde can be tentatively associated with the dealer Teissier, another of the consigners, so it seems hazardous to be too precise. Macalester Loup is probably to be identified with Duncan Macalester Loup (1751–1812), the son of Robert

Macalester Loup (1718–1800), who, like his son, had a career in the army. The family was of Scottish origin and is recorded living in the Netherlands from about 1707/09 onwards. Robert Macalester was born in Yperen, Belgium; from 1749–51 he is recorded in Gorinchem, where he married Levina van der Burch, and in Nijmegen in 1761 at the time of his wife's death. In 1782 he was living in The Hague, where he served as a colonel in the Scottish regiment stationed there, later as major-general. He was still in The Hague at the time of his death. It is uncertain whether it was Robert or his son who is recorded buying paintings in The Hague in 1796 and 1797, but it was presumably the son who decided to sell the collection since the father had died six years before. Duncan Macalester Loup was born in Gorinchem and reached the position of lieutenant-colonel in the Scottish brigade. In 1780 he married Maria Ouwens in The Hague and was still living there in 1810. In his later life he acted as an agent for the West Indies colony and he died in Guyana in 1812. His decision to sell the paintings may have been the result of his anticipated move. Many of the paintings purchased in the 1790s, as well as one recorded in 1804, do not appear in the present sale, so there may have been other dispersals (or perhaps Macalester was both buying and selling).

The other important consignment to the sale came from the Pompe van Meerdervoort family, which can be associated with at least lots 93 and 94, both by Cuyp, which brought the highest prices in the sale. The former is probably the painting now in the Wallace Collection in London, which is thought to depict members of the family standing in a road near the Huis te Meerdervoort. Until now the earliest record of that painting was thought to be its appearance in the De Séréville sale in Paris in 1812; the present painting was presumed to be a copy that later passed into a private collection in England. (Cf. Hofstede de Groot, *Catalogue Raisonné*, II, 1909, no.169.) However, since the Pompe van Meerdervoort family is now known to have consigned the painting to the sale, and given that it fetched fl. 960 from the French dealer Lafontaine, it is more likely to have been the original. Lafontaine must have sold the painting to De Séréville sometime between 1806 and 1812. A similar provenance can probably be attached to lot 94, described as a *Hunting Party with Three Men on Horses and a Hunter with Dogs in the Foreground*, which was also bought by Lafontaine for a high price, fl. 695. The description of the painting accords perfectly with the painting now in the Metropolitan Museum in New York, which has been identified as depicting *Michiel and Cornelis Pompe van Meerdervoort with their Tutor and Coachman*. The only obstacle to this identification is the difference in dimensions, given as 42 x 50 duim in the present catalogue, as against 43 ½ x 61 ½ inches for the Metropolitan Museum canvas. The discrepancy is probably a result of a typographical error in the sale catalogue. The Metropolitan Museum painting is next recorded in the Lapeyrière sale in Paris in 1829.

Since the two pictures by Cuyp were grouped together in the sale, one might speculate that lots 95 and 96, a pair of portraits by Rembrandt that were bought by Lafontaine for fl. 495, could also be from the same consignment. Unfortunately, this cannot yet be proved. The four following lots, nos.97–100, all depict members of the De Witt family of Dordrecht, including Cornelis de Witt, mayor of Dordrecht, and so presumably had a common provenance, perhaps via the Pompe van Meerdervoort family. (Three of them are now in the Rijksmuseum and are thought to be copies or replicas.)

The sale attracted a number of important dealers from other cities in addition to Lafontaine, among them L.J. Nieuwenhuysen, L.B. Coclers, C.J.F. Spruyt and P.J. Thijs. The prices were generally not very high, however, excepting the lots mentioned above. Lot 4, for instance, a painting of *Christ at Emmaus* by Jan Steen, was sold for just fl. 185. (It is also now in the Rijksmuseum.)

105 1806/09/22–1806/09/24

B. Besanger; Den Haag, not given

Seller(s) from Title Page: None

Paintings Lots: 5

Catalogue Locations:

MWH	Not annot.

Comments: This was a three-day sale of books held by the Hague bookseller and binder Barent Besanger (1781-after 1811) that also included a collection of medals, prints, musical instruments and eight lots of mostly anonymous paintings. Lot 4 consisted of seven portraits of members of the royal family by the Swiss painter Benjamin Bolomey (1739–1819), who was active in The Hague from 1763–1791, having been appointed official painter to the court of William V, prince of Orange.

106 1806/10/13–1806/10/17 [Lugt 7155]

B. Wild; Utrecht, Over de Domskerk

Additional Auctioneers: J. Altheer

Seller(s) from Title Page: Nagelaten door den Hoog Wel Geb. Heer Mr. P. de Malapert, Heere van Jutphaas en Canonik in 't Capittel van den Dom te Utrecht etc. en den Wel Edele Heer W. Beeldsnyder

Seller Authority: Malapert, Pieter de, Mr.; Beeldsnijder, Wolfert, Mr.

Paintings Lots: 25

Catalogue Locations:

VBBA	Not annot.
MWH	Not annot.

Comments: This was primarily a book sale (2005 lots), although many lots of prints and "curiosa" as well as some drawings were also included. Two owners are named on the title page of the catalogue, and it is uncertain which of the two is supposed to have owned the paintings. Mr. Pieter de Malapert (1740–1806) lived in a house called Plettenberg at Jutphaas near Utrecht, a possession of the Malapert family since the late sixteenth century, after inheriting it from his father, Louis de Malapert, in 1782. He had a law degree from Utrecht University and was canon at Utrecht cathedral. At his death his estate was estimated to be worth fl. 99,286:7:4. He seems to have been active primarily as a collector of naturalia, the bulk of which was described in the *Catalogus musei Malaperttiani* published in 1806. His heirs elected to sell Plettenberg, so the contents were removed, probably by his only brother and executor, Jan Jacob de Malapert (1743–1816), and given to the Utrecht booksellers Bartholomeus Wild and Johannes Altheer to sell. The other owner can be identified as the late Wolfert Beeldsnijder, an iron merchant and alderman of Ijsselstein who died in 1806. The paintings consisted mostly of landscapes and genre scenes, but the descriptions are too brief to allow them to be identified.

107 1806/10/13–1806/10/18 [Lugt 7156]

J.J. van de Sande; Middelburg, Korte St. Pieterstraat, La. B. No.8

Additional Auctioneers: D. Reghter

Seller(s) from Title Page: Nagelaten door Wylen de Heer Gerardus Beljard

Seller Authority: Beljard, Gerardus

Paintings Lots: 63

Catalogue Locations:

*ZBM	Annot. with all buyers and prices on interleaved pages.
MWH	Not annot.

Comments: Gerardus Beljard was a Middelburg notary whose supposed political sympathies provoked patriots to plunder his house during the riots of September, 1787. He is recorded as a buyer at three Middelburg sales between 1801 and 1803, invariably of works costing less than £ 1. This sale was devoted primarily to books in addition to some drawings, prints and miscellanea. The pictures, which were fairly numerous for a Middelburg collection, included mostly land- and seascapes, but there were also a few still lifes as well as religious and mythological subjects. Lots 63–131, lumped together as one item, were to be sold individually, but evidently did not warrant the time it would take to describe them, although 1799 lots of books are given full descriptions. This may reflect the expertise of the auctioneers, J.J. van de Sande, a bookseller, and D. Reghter, described as a maker of scientific instruments, rather than the quality of the paintings.

108 1806/10/20–1806/10/22

H. Bakhuysen; Den Haag, Hoogstraat E. No. 298

Seller(s) from Title Page: None

Paintings Lots: 12

Catalogue Locations:

MWH	Not annot.
KBH	Not annot.

Comments: This was one of the last sales held by the Hague bookseller Hendrik Bakhuysen (1729–1812), who apparently retired about this time. The sale contained primarily books, but there were also parts dedicated to prints, paintings and "rariteiten." The paintings ("schilderyen") are so poorly described that it is difficult to distinguish them from the prints and drawings, which are all merged under the single heading. Possibly only two or three lots may in fact have contained paintings.

109 1806/11/24 and following days [Lugt 7163]

Philippus van der Schley; Amsterdam, Ten Huize van Cornelis Sebille Roos, op de Cloveniers Burgwal, in 't Huis van Trip

Additional Auctioneers: Jan Yver; Cornelis Sebille Roos; Jacobus Vinkeles

Seller(s) from Title Page: None

Seller(s) from Auctioneer's Copy: Munnikhuizen; van den Bosch; de Flines; Ferguson

Seller Authority: Munnikhuizen, Frans; Flines, de; Bosch, van den

Paintings Lots: 105

Catalogue Locations:

*RKDH I	Auctioneer's copy, annot. with all buyers and prices on interleaved pages as well as letters for the sellers. It belonged to the auctioneer Roos.

LBDa	Auctioneer's copy, annot. with all buyers and prices on interleaved pages. The title page is lacking. It may have belonged to the dealer P. van der Schley.
MB I	Annot. on interleaved pages with all buyers and prices for the paintings and drawings. The prints are annot. with most prices. The title page is lacking and has been replaced with a handwritten transcription.
EBNP	Annot. in pencil with all prices.
AAP	Annot. with many prices, especially for the pictures and drawings. It belonged formerly to the Prentenkabinet in Leiden and later to the RKD in The Hague.
RKDH II	Auctioneer's copy, annot. with letters for the sellers but no buyers or prices. The sellers are also identified.
MB II	Annot. with a few prices.
ESP	Not annot.

Comments: The principal segments of this sale consisted of prints and drawings, although there was a sizeable group of paintings as well as smaller numbers of sculpture, optical instruments, lacquer work from the East Indies and miscellaneous objects. The title page of the catalogue mentions no sellers, but the RKDH I and RKDH II copies of the catalogue, both of which belonged to the dealer C.S. Roos, one of the co-organizers of the sale, are marked with letters next to each lot designating different consigners, and a list in the RKDH II copy also identifies them by name. Eleven consigners are included, four of whom submitted paintings. The largest group by far derived from "D^{o} Munnikhuizen," whose 92 lots of paintings were marked with the letter B. Five lots belonged to "Van den Bosch," five to "de Flines" (represented by Roos) and three to "Ferguson" (also represented by Roos). The eight paintings belonging to the last two were added by hand after the catalogue was printed and lack both artist and title, as a result of which the proprietors cannot be identified. The five paintings belonging to "Van den Bosch" had all been bought in at the sale held on December 16, 1805 (cat. no.99), at which time they had been consigned by Roos. No doubt they had been part of a larger collection belonging to Van den Bosch, but submitted to sale under the auspices of Roos, the bulk of which had been sold. The pictures in the sale were therefore primarily the property of "D^{o} Munnikhuizen," who can be identified as the Lutheran priest, the Rev. Frans Munnikhuizen (1742–1820). He was born in Amsterdam of German parents; after completing his theological studies in 1764, he became a minister in Schiedam. While there he married a wealthy widow, Lydia van Dobben, with whom he resettled in Rotterdam until her death in 1776. He remarried in 1784 and a short time later resigned his position in the church, returning to Amsterdam in 1800. In that same year he sold to the newly established Nationale Konst-Gallery two pairs of portraits of important naval figures by Bartholomeus van der Helst and Ludolph de Jongh, which later came into the collection of the Rijksmuseum. He died in Amsterdam on June 25, 1820, at which time his address was the Herengracht No.148. It is not known how or when he acquired his paintings, but the works by Van der Helst sold to the museum were probably among the best pieces he owned. The paintings in the present sale did not bring very high prices; the best price recorded was fl. 300 for a painting of *Two Soldiers Playing Cards and a Girl Filling a Pipe* by Pieter de Hooch, which, however, was only bought in. (It is now in a private collection in Switzerland.) The best price for a painting that was actually sold was fl. 120 for lot 41, an *Interior with a Woman Receiving a Letter from her Maid* by Metsu. The total revenue for the sale was fl. 15,054:5 with fl. 1738:8 bought in.

110 1807/04/00 dates unknown

Abraham Delfos; Leiden, not given

Seller(s) from Title Page: None

Seller(s) from Other Sources: [Abraham Delfos]

Seller Authority: Delfos, Abraham

Paintings Lots: 61

Catalogue Locations:

MB	Not annot.

Comments: The catalogue of this sale is known to exist in just a single copy at MB. It is not annotated, probably because the sale was never held. Its contents consisted of paintings, drawings and prints as well as a collection of atlases, the property of a proprietor or proprietors left unnamed by the auctioneer, Abraham Delfos. There is good reason to think that Delfos himself was the principal consigner. The first 60 lots of the sale are found again in precisely the same order and without change (excepting the addition of one lot) in a sale held in The Hague on June 10, 1807 (no.113) by the auctioneer F.J. Bosboom. The catalogue of the later sale identifies Delfos as the owner. This is confirmed by the fact that at least 15 of the paintings can be traced to the sale of April 28, 1804 (no.76), at which time they were probably already the property of Delfos. It is possible, however, that the possessions of other consigners were included in all three of these sales; for this reason we have qualified Delfos's ownership, although it is likely that the bulk, if not all, of the lots belonged to him. The reasons for cancelling the present sale are not known, but possibly Delfos concluded that the sale would be more successful if held in The Hague where the art market had a larger number of potential customers than in Leyden. For a discussion of the paintings, see the later sale.

111 1807/04/13 and following days [Lugt 7221]

Philippus van der Schley; Amsterdam, Ten Huize van Cornelis Sebille Roos, op de Kloveniers Burgwal, in 't Huis van Trip

Additional Auctioneers: Jan de Bosch Jeronimusz.; Jan Yver; Cornelis Sebille; Jacobus Vinkeles

Seller(s) from Title Page: Naargelaaten Door wijlen den Wel Edele Heer Everard de Burlett

Seller Authority: Burlett, Everard de

Paintings Lots: 12

Catalogue Locations:

RKDH I	Auctioneer's copy, annot. with all buyers and prices on interleaved pages. It belonged to the dealer C.S. Roos.
RMA	Annot. with all buyers and prices on interleaved pages.
*EBNP	Auctioneer's copy, annot. with all buyers and prices on interleaved pages.
AA	Not located. According to Lugt it is annot. with many buyers and prices for the drawings.
RKDH II	Auctioneer's copy, annot. with all prices on interleaved pages but no buyers.
LBDa	Annot. in pencil with all prices. It may have belonged to the dealer P. van der Schley.
BHm	Not seen. According to Lugt it is annot. with some prices.
FLNY	Annot. in pencil with some prices but not for the paintings.
MWH	Not annot.

Comments: The collector Everard de Burlett (1731–1806) was an Amsterdam corn merchant who also held a series of public offices between 1767 and 1788. In 1773 he was living in the Singel and in 1777, when he married the wealthy widow Anna Emerentia van Broyel (1731–84), he moved into her house at Herengracht 442. Burlett also owned, in his own right, the manor Groeneveld near Ouderkerk, valued in 1784 at fl. 8000. After his wife died he inherited Herengracht 442 and lived there until his death on October 4, 1806. His son, an Amsterdam merchant, carried the same name. The first sale of De Burlett's property, held on March 17 and following days, contained his library. The present sale, nearly one month later, consisted primarily of prints, drawings and a collection of atlases. There were just 12 lots of paintings, two of which, lots 1 and 2 (described as being either by Murillo or in his style), were bought by the dealer Coclers for fl. 900 and must have been considered the stars of the collection. These were evidently versions or copies of the two paintings which were already at that time in Munich depicting *An Old Woman Delousing a Young Boy* and *A Girl Buying Fruit from a Boy*. Both paintings reappeared at Coclers's sale on April 8, 1816, as by Murillo himself, and on that occasion they were bought by the dealer Jeronimo de Vries for fl. 815 and fl. 600, respectively. They are untraced after that sale. Although they are unlikely to have been superior to the versions in Munich, their prices reflect the fact that more than a few people thought highly of them. The remaining pictures, consisting of a few genre pieces and still lifes, brought much lower prices. The returns for the entire sale came to fl. 6825:7, with a larger amount, fl. 8560, left unsold.

112 1807/06/02 and following days [Lugt 7262]

Leonard Huysinga; Amsterdam, Premises, op de [nieuwe] Herregragt, tusschen de Binnen-Amstel en Houtmarkt, gemerkt No.24

Additional Auctioneers: Louis Garach; Joseph da Costa Athias; Gerrit Jansen; Joh. Arent Stoopendaal; Hermanus van Ophoven; Adrianus Portielje

Seller(s) from Title Page: None

Seller(s) from Other Sources: [Van Iperen]

Seller Authority: Iperen, Matthias Ignatius van

Paintings Lots: 44

Catalogue Locations:

RKDH	Not annot.

Comments: This was an estate sale that contained a wide variety of material, including porcelain, jewelry, books, furniture, prints and paintings, etc. (It took place in the home of the deceased owner on the Herengracht, described as no.24. A sale on September 28/30, 1807 (no.116) was held in the same location, but on this occasion it is described as the Nieuwe Herengracht rather than the more prestigious address.) The paintings consisted mostly of landscapes, but there were also a few still lifes and genre scenes as well as three biblical pictures, described as having been painted by an English artist. None of the paintings are identifiable and the results of the sale are not recorded. It appears, however, that at least a few of the paintings belonged to the dealer M.I. van Iperen, to whom they can be traced both before and after the sale.

113 1807/06/10 [Lugt 7267]

Frans Johannes Bosboom; Den Haag, Princegragt

Seller(s) from Title Page: Heer Konst-Graveerder Abraham Delfos en van meer andere Liefhebbers

Seller Authority: Delfos, Abraham

Paintings Lots: 219

Catalogue Locations:

*MWH	Annot. with all buyers and prices.
RKDH	Annot. with a few buyers and prices. It lacks the appendix.
ESP	Annot. with a few prices. It may lack the appendix. It was formerly at KKB.
MM	Not seen. According to Lugt it is not annot.

Comments: The catalogue of this sale consisted of 26 pages with 174 lots of paintings, plus an appendix of five pages that included lots 175–219. The MWH copy of the catalogue, which may be the only one that includes the appendix, also has four additional lots added by hand. The title page describes the owners as the Leyden engraver, dealer and auctioneer Abraham Delfos (1731–1820) and "meer andere Liefhebbers." Unfortunately, the catalogue does not specify which lots belonged to Delfos and which to others. Delfos had been active as a dealer in Leyden during the last three decades of the eighteenth century, and is recorded as a buyer at numerous sales in Amsterdam, The Hague and Soeterwoude as well as Leyden. At various times he owned works of considerable importance, and on occasion acted as agent for both Mr. Pieter Cornelis van Leyden (1717–1788) and his son Diderick, baron van Leyden (1744–1810). During the last twenty years of his career, however, he dealt in works of more modest value, as evidenced by the works in the present sale. At least 24 of the paintings offered here had already appeared at Delfos's auction in Leyden held on April 28, 1804 (no.76), at which time they had been bought in. Only five paintings in the present sale exceeded fl. 100, and the large majority were sold for less than fl. 20. It appears that Delfos was trying to dispose of his stock, perhaps in anticipation of his retirement, which occurred during 1808 or shortly thereafter.

Evidently Delfos had initially intended to hold the auction in Leyden under his own direction, and a catalogue exists dated April, 1807 (no.110), in which the first 60 lots are precisely the same as those found in the present catalogue. (The only change is the addition of a lot 14a.) The earlier sale was apparently cancelled and the paintings used as the nucleus of this much larger sale held by the auctioneer Bosboom in The Hague, perhaps because the latter city had a more prosperous art market that would attract more buyers. Perhaps the first 60 lots belonged to Delfos while subsequent lots were the property of others, but at least 12 of the later lots can be traced to Delfos's sale in 1804 (no.76), and although they are grouped in a way that suggests that a certain range of these later lots were also his, it is difficult to be certain.

The highest prices were paid for lots 87, 88 and 90, all of which were bought by a certain "LaCourt" who is unidentified. These were an Italian genre scene by Lingelbach (fl. 345, now in the Metropolitan Museum), a landscape by – or as good as – Jan Wijnants (fl. 352), and a scene with *Hermit in a Grotto* by Abraham van Dyck (fl. 350). In view of the modest descriptions, these prices appear excessive and may be the result of the owner bidding up his own possessions. The only other lots to fetch a reasonably good price were two of those added by hand at the end, nos.222 and 223, both of which were bought by "de Gelder" at fl. 290 each. Neither the artist nor the subject of these lots are known. The total receipts for the sale are recorded as fl. 3968:13.

114 1807/07/20 and following days [Lugt 7286]

Johannes Jacobus van de Sande; Middelburg, Op den Langenburgt by de Groote Markt

Seller(s) from Title Page: Mr. C.J. van den Helm Boddaert, In Zyn Wel Ed. Leven Griffier van Stads Thesaurie te Middelburg; [en] N.N.

Seller Authority: Helm Boddaert, Cornelis J. van den, Mr.

Paintings Lots: 4

Catalogue Locations:

MWH	Not annot.

Comments: Cornelis van den Helm Boddaert (1727–1800) was a native of Middelburg, where he held several public offices, including councillor, alderman, treasurer and burgomaster. He was also at one time a governor of the Dutch West India Company. Following his death a sale of his books was held in Middelburg on September 14, 1801, and the present sale, nearly six years later, contained more books as well as prints, paintings, medals and miscellaneous objects. However, the title page of the catalogue specifies that the property of another unnamed proprietor was also included, so we cannot be certain the paintings were Boddaert's. Three of the four paintings in the sale were anonymous. The fourth was an architectural piece by the Middelburg painter Daniel de Blieck, which is said to be dated 1649. If true, it would be his earliest painting, but its present location is not known.

115 1807/08/26 and following days [Lugt 7297]

Philippus van der Schley; Amsterdam, Ten Huize van Cornelis Sebille Roos, op de Kloveniers Burgwal, in 't Huis van Trip

Additional Auctioneers: Jan de Bosch, Jeronimusz.; Jan Yver; Cornelis Sebille Roos; Jeronimo de Vries

Seller(s) from Title Page: Nagelaten by Wylen de Heeren Joseph Vallette en een ander Kunst-Liefhebber

Seller(s) from Auctioneer's Copy: Roos; Helsdinge; etc.

Seller Authority: Vallette, Joseph; Roos, Cornelis Sebille; Helsdingen, Jacob van

Paintings Lots: 377

Catalogue Locations:

FLNY	Auctioneer's copy, annot. with all buyers and prices on interleaved pages, as well as letters for the sellers. There is also a list that identifies the sellers.
RKDH	Auctioneer's copy, annot. with all buyers and prices on interleaved pages as well as letters for the sellers. It belonged to the dealer C.S. Roos.
*EBNP	Auctioneer's copy, annot. with all buyers and prices on interleaved pages as well as letters for the sellers.
AA I	Annot. with some buyers and prices. Most of the annotated lots were bought by the dealer Wm. Gruyter and so the catalogue was probably his.
AA II	Annot. with a few buyers and some prices.
MB II	Annot. in pencil with all prices.
AAP	Annot. with most prices.
ESP	Not annot.
MB I	Not annot. The bottom has been damaged by water.

Comments: The catalogue of this sale, which included 344 lots of paintings plus 33 added after the catalogue had been printed, identifies the owners as Joseph Vallette and another "Kunst-Liefhebber." Three of the extant copies of the catalogue belonged originally to dealers associated with the sale and are annotated with letters next to each lot indicating the consignment to which they belonged; a list in the FLNY copy of the catalogue also identifies the proprietors, as follows: A = Roos; B = Vallette; H = Helsdinge; L = v d Schley; P = Roos; R = Roos; S = Yver; V = de Vries; Y = Coclers; Z = v d Schley. In addition, the EBNP copy of the catalogue identifies "Z" as "Smits Wed Schley" and the owner of lots 335–337 as "Schott." The first of these can be identified as the widow of Hn. Smit, at whose sale in 1802 (no.42) at least two of the pictures had been bought. Although some of the names in the list – notably Vallette, Helsdinge and Coclers – were the actual owners of the paintings, the others, such as Roos, Van der Schley and Yver, were dealers who probably represented other unnamed collectors. This is exemplified by "Z," the letter designating the widow Smit, whose paintings had been given to Van der Schley to sell at the auction. Roos represented two consigners besides himself and Van der Schley represented the widow Smit and one other. The dealer Jeronimo de Vries evidently submitted pieces that were his own, since the letter "V" corresponds to his initial. Four of the owners, A, L, P and S, remain unidentified, although the 16 lots belonging to "P," all of which were works by Jan van Gool (1685-1763/65), are described in the catalogue as having been until now in the possession of the artist's family. "P" might therefore be a descendant.

The largest consignment, 79 lots, belonged to Joseph Vallette (1740–1807), an upholsterer, master wallpaperer and dealer active in The Hague. He is recorded as an active buyer at auctions in both Amsterdam and The Hague from the 1780s to 1805, just two years before his death by stroke on March 9, 1807. Between 1781 and 1792 he is also known to have commissioned several paintings from the painter H.W. Schweickardt, which he presumably purchased for resale. (See *Oud Holland*, 89, 1975, pp.142–212.) Three works by the artist appear in the present auction, which presumably represented Vallette's stock at the time of his death. He apparently never married, and his last address is given as Hoogstraat E 338 in The Hague (GAG, Q.O.R.S., inv.2, fol.17, no.241). In his will (GAG, Not. Arch. notary Van Alphen, inv.4457, fol.36) he left fl. 600 to Schweickardt's widow, Magdalena Holst, an indication of the close relationship between Vallette and the artist. Vallette's drawings were sold in Amsterdam on October 26, 1807 (Lugt 7305). His paintings in the present sale, all of which were sold, realized a total of fl. 2167:17, and included most of those that brought more than fl. 100. One of them, a *Village Scene with Skittle Players* by Adriaen van Ostade, was sold for fl. 415, the best price at the sale. One of the paintings by Schweickardt, a small copy of a painting by Potter, reached fl. 171.

The consignment from Roos, consisting of 77 paintings, was nearly as large as Vallette's, but consisted generally of less expensive items and a number were bought in. The 47 pictures belonging to Helsdinge – presumably the Amsterdam dealer Jacob van Helsdingen (1736–1812) – were less numerous but brought the second largest dividend, fl. 1107:11. The total for the sale came to fl. 5780, with fl. 1132:10 (26 paintings) left unsold.

116 1807/09/28–1807/09/30 [Lugt 7301]

Johs. Samuel Wurfbain; Amsterdam, Op de nieuwe Heeregragt, tusschen de Binnen-Amstel en Houtmarkt, voor het Huis, geteekend No.24

Additional Auctioneers: L. van Olivier Boogmaker; Pierre Geraud; Jan van der Feen

Seller(s) from Title Page: None

Paintings Lots: 35

Catalogue Locations:

*AA	Annot. in pencil with a few buyers and some prices. It apparently belonged to a certain Andriessen, probably Juriaan.

Comments: This was an estate sale, consisting of a many different kinds of objects, including large numbers of naturalia, furniture and jewels, as well as many prints, some drawings and 35 lots of paintings. The owner is not identified. The sale of another estate had taken place in the same residence just four months earlier (cat. no.112), and since there was no apparent relation between the two properties, it appears that the site had been converted into a place to hold auctions of household goods. The paintings consisted mostly of landscapes and marine pieces as well as a few genre scenes, a large number of which are left anonymous. The prices were invariably modest.

117 1807/09/28 and following days [Lugt 7302]

Hendrik de Haas; Dordrecht, Premises, en deels in het Stads Venduhuis

Additional Auctioneers: Pieter van Braam

Seller(s) from Title Page: Nagelaten door den Heer Mattheus Westerouen van Meeteren, In leven Koopman te Dordrecht

Seller Authority: Westerouen van Meeteren, Mattheus

Paintings Lots: 32

Catalogue Locations:

MWH	Not annot.
VBBA	Not annot.

Comments: The seller Mattheus Westerouen van Meeteren (1765–1807) was a wealthy merchant from Dordrecht, who also held the offices of councillor and alderman in that city. In 1812 his daughter Margaretha married the Dordrecht collector Jhr. Etienne Jean de Court, heer van Valkenswaard (1784–1846). The present sale consisted primarily of books (2773 lots), a considerable number of scientific instruments, as well as curiosa and drawings. There were also some prints, musical instruments and a small music library. The paintings were mostly anonymous and predominantly landscapes or sea pieces, but there were also a few religious subjects. At least one reappears in the sale on June 4, 1810 (cat. no.161), of the estate of Hendrik de Haas, the bookdealer who organized the present sale, implying that at least some of the paintings belonged to Haas and not to Westerouen van Meeteren.

118 1807/10/12 and following days

S. van Benthem; Middelburg, Premises, in de Wagenaarstraat, by de Oude Kerk

Seller(s) from Title Page: Heer Hermannus Johannes Heyman, In zyn Wel Eerwaarde Leven Predikant binnen deze Stad

Seller Authority: Heyman, Hermannus Johannes

Paintings Lots: 9

Catalogue Locations:

*ZBM	Annot. with all buyers and prices on interleaved pages.

Comments: The seller is identified on the title page as the deceased Rev. Hermannus Johannes Heyman, a preacher from Middelburg. The sale of his books, maps, prints and paintings took place at his home in the Wagenaarstraat near the Oude Kerk. The paintings consisted of portraits, two genre scenes and a still life, the latter said to be by Adriaen van Utrecht. The descriptions are very brief.

118-A 1807/10/28–1807/10/29 [Lugt 7307]

C. van den Dries en Zoon; Rotterdam, Zaal boven de Beurs

Seller(s) from Title Page: Alles nagelaten door wyle den Wel Ed. Geb. Heer Gerrit van der Pot, Heer van Groeneveld

Seller Authority: Pot, Gerrit van der Pot, Heer van Groeneveld

Paintings Lots: 1

Catalogue Locations:

*AMR	Annot. with all prices.

Comments: This sale consisted of the books, drawings, prints, maps and miscellaneous items belonging to Gerrit van der Pot, the wealthy Rotterdam merchant and collector who had died in March, 1807. It did not include his paintings, which were sold separately by another group of dealers on June 6ff., 1808, but one of the lots added by hand and described as a "Schoorsteenstuk" was apparently a painting by Abraham Hondius that had been part of the furnishings Van der Pot acquired with the house. For a discussion of Van der Pot, see the later sale (no.126).

119 1807/11/23–1807/11/26

B. Besanger; Den Haag, not given

Seller(s) from Title Page: None

Paintings Lots: 1

Catalogue Locations:

MWH	Not annot.

Comments: This was a book sale that included a few lots of drawings, prints, medals, miscellaneous objects and a single painting, described as a *Portrait of a Turkish Empress* on copper.

120 1807/12/00 dates unknown

[Paulus Nijhoff]; Arnhem, unknown

Seller(s) from Title Page: Heer Meinsmaa[?] & Engelan

Seller Authority: Meinsmaa; Engelan

Paintings Lots: 6

Catalogue Locations:

*VBBA	Annot. with all buyers and prices on interleaved pages. It lacks the title page.

Comments: Because the title page of the only extant copy of the catalogue is lacking, the date of this sale is uncertain. A note in the catalogue, giving the owners as "Heer Meinsmaa[?] & Engelan," is dated December 28, 1807, so the sale was probably held about that time. We have assumed that the auctioneer was the Arnhem bookseller Paulus Nijhoff (1756–1832), since some lots were bought by him and because VBBA has another catalogue of his annotated in a similar way. If our assumption is correct, the sale probably took place at "De Crabbe," Nijhoff's bookshop and premises at the Bakkerstraat Wijk D no. 144 (the present Bakkerstraat 17) in Arnhem. The second of the two sellers mentioned above was probably J. Engelen, whose name appears as a seller at other sales held by Nijhoff. In 1809 he was apparently already deceased. (See W. Nijhoff, *De Arnhemsche boekverkoopers en uitgevers Nijhoff*, The Hague, 1934, pp.90, 94.) The other owner, Meinsmaa, is unidentified. As was usual in provincial book sales, the paintings were apparently of little importance. Three are described as being in the manner of Jan van Goyen.

121 1808/03/03 [Lugt 7345]

Vincent van der Vinne; Haarlem, Op 't Princenhof

Seller(s) from Title Page: Nagelaten door Wijle den Heere Jacobus Spillebout

Seller Authority: Spillebout, Jacobus

Paintings Lots: 38

Catalogue Locations:

*EBNP	Annot. in pencil and ink with many prices, especially for the paintings.
RMA	Annot. with a few prices for drawings. The paintings are not annot.
MB	Not annot.
RKDH	Not annot.

Comments: The contents of the sale were paintings, drawings, prints and "rariteiten" owned by Jacobus Spillebout (1733–1807), a native and long-time resident of Haarlem, where the sale was also held. His marriage to Christina van den Bosch is recorded in 1762 (he died a widower on September 20, 1807), but his profession is still unknown. At the time of his death he lived in the Oude Gracht (GAH, DTB, inv.102, fol.153). His collection of paintings consisted of both modern and older works, including some by Haarlem artists who were Spillebout's contemporaries, making it possible that he had commissioned them directly from the artists. One of these is Jan van der Vinne I, whose paintings brought some of the best prices at the sale. (His son, the Haarlem painter and dealer Vincent Jansz. van der Vinne (1736–1811), was the auctioneer at the present sale.) The highest price, fl. 61, was paid for two portraits by Johannes Cornelisz. Verspronck. Some biblical scenes by the contemporary Amsterdam painter and dealer Charles Howard Hodges (1764–1837) also fetched reasonably good amounts, but on the whole the sale contained no works of great value.

122 1808/04/26–1808/04/27 [Lugt 7386]

[Anonymous]; Gouda, Premises, not given

Seller(s) from Title Page: Nagelaten door den Heer Konst-Liefhebber G.H. Fortuyn

Seller Authority: Fortuyn, Gerrit Hendrik

Paintings Lots: 303

Catalogue Locations:

RKDH	Not annot.
MB	Not annot.

Comments: Very little is known about the owner, Gerrit Hendrik Fortuyn (1731–1807), except that he married Catharina van Eybergen in 1765 and that a child from their marriage was reported dead in 1771. At that time his premises were at the Botermarkt in Gouda, possibly the same premises he occupied at the time of his death on October 14, 1807 (GG, Gaardersarchief Overlijden, 1807, inv.326, nr.53) and where the present sale may have been held. The contents of the sale were 296 lots of paintings, to which an additional seven lots were appended with separate numbering (possibly because they came from a different source). This is the only significant sale of paintings held in Gouda during this period, and it was surprisingly large for a small city that must have lacked an art market of any size. The results of the sale are unrecorded, making it difficult to speculate about the value of the collection, but it may have contained some moderately important pieces. Two pictures by Jan Steen, *An Interior with a Man Blowing Smoke at a Sleeping Woman*, and a companion with *A Man Offering an Oyster to a Woman*, were probably the same two pictures that had been sold in Amsterdam on May 7, 1804, for fl. 39, meaning that Fortuyn had purchased them fairly recently. Four or five others can be traced to the Linden van Slingeland sale held in Dordrecht on August 22, 1785, where Fortuyn is recorded as having bought a dozen paintings, implying that he may have bought and sold on a regular basis. The collection, of which the large majority were landscapes, contained sizeable groups of pictures by certain artists: ten lots are given to Aelbert Cuyp, seven to Jan van Goyen, seven to Melchior d'Hondecoeter and seven to Jan Steen.

123 1808/05/17 [Lugt 7403]

[Anonymous]; Leiden, In het gewezen Fransche Koffijhuis in de Sint' Pieters Kerkstraat

Seller(s) from Title Page: None

Seller(s) from Other Sources: [Abraham Delfos]

Seller Authority: Delfos, Abraham

Paintings Lots: 41

Catalogue Locations:

*RKDH	Annot. with many buyers and prices. The annotations are difficult to read.
KKB	Present location unknown. According to Lugt it is annot. with buyers and prices.
MB	Not annot.

Comments: The contents of the sale were paintings, prints, drawings, sculpture and stuffed birds, described on the title page as having been "in vele jaren bijeenverzameld en nagelaten." This implies that there was a single deceased owner, but since none are identified or mentioned, it cannot be assumed to be accurate. The sale was held in Leyden in a coffee house, and the dealer Abraham Delfos and the bookseller Leendert Herdingh are mentioned as agents from whom the catalogue could be obtained, but no auctioneer is specified. In spite of these circumstances, it appears that some relatively valuable works were included. The Brussels dealer L.J. Nieuwenhuys purchased at least five lots, and four lots are recorded as having exceeded fl. 100. By far the most expensive was the first lot by Isack van Ostade depicting *A Frozen Canal with a Coach on a Road*, which was bought by Nieuwenhuys for fl. 860. (This appears to be the painting now in the Louvre, for whose collection Louis XVI purchased it in 1817.) Nieuwenhuys also bought lot 2 by Jan Steen, an exterior scene with numerous figures and a sign with the words *Het Misverstand,* for fl. 510. Lot 6, an *Interior with a Girl Plucking a Duck* by Domenicus van Tol, was sold for fl. 610, and another painting by Jan Steen, *Interior with a Doctor Writing a Prescription*, was bought for fl. 310. (It is now in the Boymans-Van Beuningen Museum, Rotterdam.) The remaining paintings, some of which can also be identified, brought much lower amounts. At least three of these, lots 3, 5 and 13, can be traced to earlier sales held by Abraham Delfos, and they were certainly his property at the present sale as well, strongly indicating that Delfos was also the organizer of the sale. No doubt he was asked to sell the property of a local collector and elected to include his own possessions as well. This is also the last sale where Delfos's name appears in any capacity; he apparently retired shortly thereafter.

124 1808/05/18 [Lugt 7404]

[Anonymous]; Leyderdorp, near Leiden, Voordorp te Leyderdorp

Seller(s) from Title Page: Nagelaten van Wijlen den Wel-Edelen Heer Mr. Cornelis Versluys

Seller Authority: Versluys, Cornelis, Mr.

Paintings Lots: 63

Catalogue Locations:

*RKDH	Annot. with a few prices. A number of artists' names have also been added.
RMA	Not annot.
MB	Not annot.

Comments: The catalogue of this unusual country sale held outside Leyden is not called a "catalogue" on the title page, but rather a "Notitie." No auctioneer is mentioned, and individual lots do not carry the names of the artists, as though it was meant to be a preliminary notice of the contents of the sale rather than a full catalogue. Fortunately, the RKDH copy of the catalogue is extensively annotated with the names of artists, which allows one to better assess the nature of the collection, but the descriptions are very brief and no dimensions are included, making identifications nearly impossible. Moreover, the RKDH catalogue is only partially annotated with prices. The highest price recorded there is fl. 101 paid for a *Landscape with Men and Women on Horseback* by Wouwerman. Most of the paintings were landscapes, but there were also a few still lifes. The last four lots in the sale consisted of prints. Nothing is known about the owner.

125 1808/05/30 and following days

S. van Benthem; Middelburg, In het Heeren Logement Antwerpen, staande in den Langendelft

Seller(s) from Title Page: None

Catalogue Locations:

ZBM	Not located, 1995.

Comments: A catalogue of this sale was and may still be preserved at ZBM. Its title page was photographed and included in *Veilingcatalogi Zeeland, 1731–1925* (Zeeuwse Bibliotheek, Middelburg, 1987, no.34), but it has since been misplaced. The title page indicates that it was a primarily a sale of books that also included prints and miscellaneous objects. Apparently a few paintings were also present, but we have been unable to list them in this index.

126 1808/06/06 and following days [Lugt 7424]

Gebroeders van Rijp; Rotterdam, Premises, op de Kortehoogstraat, Westzijde E. N° 288

Seller(s) from Title Page: Nagelaten door Wijlen den wel Edel-Geb. Heer Gerrit van der Pot, Heer van Groeneveld

Seller Authority: Pot, Gerrit van der, Heer van Groeneveld

Paintings Lots: 159

Catalogue Locations:

*RKDH I	Annot. with all buyers and prices as well as a few notes about the provenance of individual lots. There is also a printed list of results. (Dutch edition)
MR	Annot. in ink and pencil with all buyers and prices, as well as a few notes about the provenance and cost of certain lots. There is also a printed list of the results.
AMR I	Annot. with all buyers and prices. There is also a printed list of results bound separately. (Dutch edition)
BMPL	Annot. with all buyers and prices, but includes also a printed list of the buyers and prices for lots 1–74. It belonged to Wm. Smith. (Dutch edition)
RMA I	Annot. with all buyers and prices. There are also many pencilled notes about provenance which may be modern. Reference is often made to valuations made for tax purposes in 1807 and so the catalogue may have belonged to a member of the family or an executor. (Dutch edition)
VAL I	Annot. with all buyers and prices as well as some notes about provenance.
RKDH III	Annot. with all buyers and prices. (Dutch edition)
EBNP	Annot. with all buyers and prices. (Dutch edition)
FLNY	Annot. with all buyers and prices. (Dutch edition)
LBDa I	Annot. with all buyers and prices. It may have belonged to the dealer P. van der Schley. (Dutch edition)
ESP II	Annot. in pencil with all buyers and prices. (Dutch edition)
ESP III	Annot. with all buyers and prices. (Dutch edition)
MB II	Annot. in pencil with all buyers and prices. (Dutch edition)
MB III	Annot. with all buyers and prices. (Dutch edition)
SBB	Annot. in pencil with all buyers and prices. It is addressed to Heer J. Van Reijsewijk te Arnhem.
VAL II	Annot. with all buyers and prices.
SMLn	Annot. with all buyers and prices. (French edition)
BPG	Annot. with all buyers and prices. It belonged to the dealer J.B.P. Lebrun. (French edition)
AA	Annot. with all buyers and prices. There is also the printed list of results. (French edition)
RKDH II	Annot. with all buyers and prices. (French edition)

ESP I	Annot. with all buyers and prices. (French edition)
AAP	Annot. with all buyers and prices. (French edition)
BMB	Annot. with all buyers and prices. (French edition)
MA	Annot. with all buyers and prices. (French edition)
MB I	Annot. with all buyers and prices. (French edition)
ULne	Annot. with all buyers and prices. The buyers' names are given both in pencil and ink and often do not agree. The latter may have been taken from a printed list of buyers.
BNP	Not seen. According to Lugt it is annot. with buyers and prices.
KKD	Present location unknown. According to Lugt it is annot. with buyers and prices.
AMR III	Annot. in ink and pencil with some buyers and all prices. (Dutch edition)
NGW	Annot. with all prices. It includes the printed list of buyers and prices which is also marked with the lots bought for the king. A note by lot 132 indicates that the catalogue belonged to the French dealer Lafontaine. (French edition)
RMA II	Annot. with all prices. (Dutch edition)
UU	Annot. with all prices. (Dutch edition)
UBA	Annot. with all prices. (Dutch edition)
CCPP	Annot. with all prices. (French edition)
KBH II	Annot. with all prices. (French edition)
SIF	Annot. with all prices. (French edition)
AMR II	Not annot. It includes the printed list of results. (French edition)
BML	Not annot. excepting a few modern notes.
KBH I	Not annot. (Dutch edition)
JPGM	Not annot. (Dutch edition)
LBDa II	Not annot. It may have belonged to the dealer P. van der Schley. (Dutch edition)
BR	Not annot.
VAL III	Not annot.
INP	Not annot.
LP	Not annot.
NGL	Not annot. (French edition)
RKDH IV	This is a handwritten transcription in English, perhaps intended to serve for an English edition. Not annot.
ULn	Not seen.
MM	Not seen. According to Lugt it is not annot.
AKW	Not annot. (Dutch edition)

Comments: The sale of Gerrit van der Pot's collection of paintings was one of the most important events of its kind to take place in the Netherlands during the early decades of the nineteenth century. Van der Pot's cabinet was widely regarded as the finest in Rotterdam during the late eighteenth and early nineteenth century, and it certainly rivalled the best in Amsterdam as well. Gerrit Van der Pot (1732–1807) was born in Rotterdam, where he also lived and worked most of his life as a merchant and sugar refiner. The only exception were the years 1787–1795, which he spent as an émigré in Brussels. Since his strong political sympathy for the patriots was well known, he took refuge there when the Prussian armies came to the aid of the Prince of Orange during the 1787 riots. Subsequently Van der Pot was officially banished by the Court of Holland. During his absence, at least part of his collection must have remained in Rotterdam, since it was seen there by Samuel Ireland in 1789 (*A Picturesque Tour through Holland, Brabant, and part of France, Made in the Autumn of 1789*, 1796, p. 39). The advent of the French allowed him to return to Rotterdam in 1795, at which time he was appointed councillor and alderman, offices he held until 1797. He also purchased the monumental house at Korte Hoogstraat 288, where his collection was then hung and given an appropriate setting. The Belgian dealer P.J. Thijs was employed as his conservator, with the painter Nicolaas Muys overseeing the arrangement. Van der Pot died childless and a widower on March 19, 1807.

The origins and growth of the collection are well documented through the existence of an inventory, probably compiled by Van der Pot himself or Nicolaas Muys, which includes information on the provenance and other particulars of each painting (Rotterdam, Gemeentelijke Archiefdienst, Bibliotheek van Handschriften, nr.353; see *Oud Holland*, 48, 1931, pp.201–214). From this document we learn that his first purchase was a pair of small genre scenes by Sorgh (lot 152 in the present sale) for which he had paid fl. 334 at the Beyerman sale in Gouda on April 21/22, 1778. At the same sale he also purchased five portraits by Van der Helst (lots 50 and 51 in the present sale) and one or two other items as well. During the time he was forming his cabinet, Van der Pot sold or exchanged several paintings, and also commissioned a few from contemporary artists, such as Dirk Langendijk, Aert Schouman and his cousin Gerard van Nijmegen, although the latter is known to have given him at least three of the paintings found in this sale. A few were also acquired as gifts or by inheritance, and two pictures by E. van der Poel and Pynacker had even been left behind by the previous owner of the house he purchased, as was a mantle piece by Abraham Hondius. (The latter was included in a sale of Van der Pot's books, drawings and prints held in Rotterdam on October 28/29, 1807 (cat. no.118-A), which was the first auction of his property to take place.) Van der Pot was active as a buyer in Paris, Brussels, Rotterdam, The Hague, Leyden, Amsterdam and several other Dutch cities, often buying though his agents Thijs or Muys (the latter from about 1793 onward). We are informed about many of Van der Pot's purchases through his correspondence with Thijs between November, 1795, and December, 1802, which has been preserved (see *Rotterdamsch Jaarboekje*, 1932, pp. 4–17). He also bought several works directly from dealers and collectors, among them Fouquet Jr., Nyman, De Neufville, Van der Hooft, Lemmens and Thijs. After his death his paintings remained in his home for the 15 months prior to the sale. By order of the Rotterdam collector Gerrit van der Pals and the other executors of Van der Pot's will, his pictures were appraised on April 9ff. by Muys and Van Nijmegen. Between May 20 and the time of the sale the collection was on view at Van der Pot's premises. During this interval persistent rumors circulated that the paintings had already been sold *en bloc*, causing the executors to put several advertisements in the *Rotterdamsche Courant* firmly denying these reports and offering a reward of fl. 50,000 to anyone who could provide evidence to the contrary.

The catalogue of the sale, which attracted international attention, was printed in both Dutch and French editions; the existence of a handwritten transcription in English (RKDH IV) may indicate that an English edition was also considered but never printed. It was an enormous success, producing record prices that remained unsurpassed for many years. Louis Bonaparte, the King of Holland, was instrumental to the success of the sale, buying a total of 63 paintings through various agents. These purchases were organized by Johan Meerman (1753–1815), director-general of sciences and arts, to whom the King had provided a budget of fl. 100,000 to be used specifically for this sale. His purchases were brought to Amsterdam to be housed with the collection of the newly installed Koninklijk Museum (formerly the Nationale Konst-Gallery), which Bonaparte had moved from the Buitenhof in The Hague to Amsterdam's town hall on the Dam the same year. With the exception of some exchanges made with the Mauritshuis in 1825, all of these paintings are still in the Rijksmuseum. Among them is Dou's *Night School*, for which fl. 17,500 was paid, by far the highest price of the sale and also the highest for any painting during this period. In his report to the King, Meerman tried to put this excessive amount into perspective by pointing out that at one time Van der Pot had been offered fl. 50,000 for it. (See E.W. Moes and E. van Biema, *De Nationale Konstgallerij en het Koninklijk Museum*, 1909, pp.111–113.) Similarly large amounts were paid for Potter's *Herdsmen with their Cattle* (fl. 10,050), and two splendid marine paintings by Willem van de Velde (fl. 8000). Other major purchases by Bonaparte included *The Holy Kinship*, thought to be by Hubert and Jan van Eyck and now recognized as by Geertgen tot Sint Jans (fl. 210), *Isaac Blessing Jacob* by Flinck (fl. 1380), *The Leyden Baker Arent Oostwaard and his Wife Catharina Keizerswaard* by Steen (fl. 705), *The Painter's Studio* by A. van Ostade (fl. 600) and *Boatmen Moored on the Shore of an Italian Lake* by Pynacker (fl. 1800). One of the few expensive pictures that did not go to Bonaparte was an Italian landscape by Jan Both, which was bought by the dealer Coclers for an astounding fl. 4010 (it is now in the Mauritshuis). Some of the less costly purchases were also of good quality, such as the *Woman Reading a Letter by a Window* by De Hooch, sold to Allard for fl. 155 (now in the Budapest Museum). Altogether the amount spent by Bonaparte came to fl. 101,881, about four-fifths of the total. There is some uncertainty on the amount realized by the entire sale, since various catalogues give differing figures, ranging from a low fl. 94,650 (FDP) to a high fl. 134,696 (PKA). A list of the buyers and the prices paid for each lot was printed after the sale, and by adding these together one arrives at a figure of fl. 127,037, which is probably the most reliable. A further sale of Van der Pot's books was held in The Hague on October 17/21, 1808.

127 1808/06/11–1808/06/13 [Lugt 7429]

Gebroeders van Ryp; Rotterdam, In den Stads Doele

Seller(s) from Title Page: None

Paintings Lots: 128

Catalogue Locations:

*EBNP	Annot. in pencil with many buyers, especially for the paintings, and all prices. The annotations are difficult to read, however.
*MA	Annot. with all buyers and prices for the paintings only.
MB	Lugt lists a copy at this location which is supposed to be annot. with buyers and prices, but it cannot be located.
FLNY	Not annot.

Comments: This sale consisted of paintings, drawings and prints. No owners are mentioned. The auctioneers were Gerardus Constantinus van Rijp (1773–1815) and his younger brother Petrus Eliza (1775-?) who were charged with the direction of Rotterdam sales by the city council. As was sometimes done in smaller Dutch auctions, the best lot was placed at the head of the sale; in this instance it was a battle scene by Aelbert Cuyp that fetched fl. 610 from the Rotterdam dealer and physician Dr. Cornelis Jan Luchtmans (1777–1860). Luchtmans also bought lot 4, a *Landscape with Cattle* by Jan Kobell II, for the second highest price, fl. 370. Most of the paintings were landscapes, among which one finds a smaller number of genre pictures and a few portraits. Many are described as copies or in the manner of the artist in question, but on the whole the prices were reasonably good. A *Landscape with a River and Waterfall* by Everdingen, for instance, was sold for fl. 295, and an Italianate landscape by Asselyn was bought for fl. 151. None of these paintings has been identified. At least 22 lots were either bought in or withdrawn.

128 1808/06/13–1808/06/14 [Lugt 7430]

Philippus van der Schleij; Amsterdam, Ten Huize van C.S. Roos, in het van ouds genaamde Huis van Trip, op de Kloveniers Burgwal

Additional Auctioneers: Jan Ijver; Cornelis Sebille Roos; Jeronimo de Vries

Seller(s) from Title Page: Nagelaten door wijlen den Wel Eerw. Heer E.M. Engelberts, in leven Predikant te Hoorn…en wijlen den kunstminnende Heer Jan Tersteeg

Seller(s) from Auctioneer's Copy: R[oos]; etc.

Seller(s) from Other Sources: [Cattrop?]

Seller Authority: Engelberts, Engelbertus Matthias; Tersteeg, Jan; Roos, Cornelis Sebille

Paintings Lots: 331

Catalogue Locations:

FLNY	Auctioneer's copy, annot. with all buyers and prices on interleaved pages as well as letters for the sellers.
RKDH	Auctioneer's copy, annot. with all buyers and prices on interleaved pages as well as letters for the sellers. It belonged to the dealer C.S. Roos.
*EBNP	Auctioneer's copy, annot. with all buyers and prices on interleaved pages as well as letters for the sellers.
MB	Annot. in pencil with most buyers and all prices. At the back is a list of pictures purchased by the dealer P.J. Thijs, and the catalogue evidently belonged to him.
AA I	Annot. with most buyers and prices. It also has a few added lots.
MA	Annot. with most buyers and all prices.
AA II	Annot. with most buyers and prices.
MPA II	Annot. with many buyers and most prices.
AA III	Annot. in ink and pencil with all prices. Pages 33–36 are torn off.
MPA I	Not annot.

Comments: The contents of this sale were 250 lots of paintings, as well as nine lots of drawings and 20 of prints. A further 81 lots of paintings were added by hand after the catalogue was printed. The title page of the catalogue mentions two owners, E.M. Engelberts and Jan Tersteeg, both of whom were deceased. Three extant copies of the catalogue that originally belonged to dealers who helped organize the sale are annotated with letters next to each lot indicating to which consignment they belonged, and a list in the RKDH and FLNY copies of the catalogue also details how the receipts of the sale were distributed. There were altogether twelve consigners, designated A, B, E, G, K, L, R, V, W, X, Y and Z. None of the catalogues identifies them by name, but it is nonetheless possible to deduce some of the more important ones. Sometimes the letters correspond to the names of the sellers and sometimes they are simply taken from the beginning of the alphabet. In the latter case, the proprietor(s) on the title page are often assigned the first letters, A and B, and this appears to be the case with the present sale.

The identification of "A" with Engelberts is made possible because 12 of the 121 paintings consigned by "A" were purchased by the dealer Engelbert Michaël Engelberts, the son of the deceased proprietor. (He also bought one lot belonging to another consigner.) He was most probably the executor of his father's estate and was no doubt buying in lots that he felt had not fetched a sufficiently high price. Very little is known about how the father, the Rev. Engelbertus Matthias Engelberts (1732–1807), had assembled his collection. By 1763 he had already settled in Hoorn and he remained active there as a Protestant minister until his death. He wrote extensively on Dutch history, and besides being an amateur draftsman and etcher, he was a member of several scientific and literary societies in various cities. He was also in close contact with a number of dealers and collectors, most prominently Cornelis Ploos van Amstel (1726–1798), the eminent Amsterdam collector. Besides paintings, he owned a large collection of drawings and prints which was sold separately in Amsterdam on December 14ff., 1807. His pictures in the present sale numbered 121, more than one third of the total.

The consigner designated as "B" was the second collector mentioned on the title page, Jan Tersteeg. This is confirmed by the fact that he had purchased a number of the paintings in this group at earlier sales. Jan Tersteeg (1750–1807) was an Amsterdam merchant who sometimes called himself Jan Tersteeg Junior, to distinguish himself from his father of the same name, also a merchant. Like Engelberts, he was an amateur draftsman and etcher and a member of the Felix Meritis Society in Amsterdam. He is included in a group portrait of the Society painted in 1801 by Adriaan de Lelie (now in the Rijksmuseum). The name Tersteeg is found as a buyer in numerous sales beginning at least as early as 1761, but some of these must refer to his father. Only a small proportion of the paintings that the two men purchased have so far been identified in the present sale, suggesting that both of them were dealing in paintings as a business. Of those that can be traced with some probability, the most prominent are two by Pieter de Hooch and Jan Wijnants that had been purchased at the Pieter Pama sale on January 30ff., 1781 (see P. Sutton, *Pieter de Hooch*, 1980, no.C187, and C. Hofstede de Groot, *Catalogue Raisonné*, VIII, 1927, no.196). Further examples are four paintings by Ochtervelt, T. Wyck and J. Buys which had been purchased at the Calkoen sale on September 8, 1781. A small landscape by Jacob van Ruisdael (lot 130) may be identical with one bought at the Jacob van den Velden sale on December 3ff., 1781 (Hofstede de Groot, IV, 1928, nos.631b and 794); and a picture of *A Man Drinking Before a House* by Willem van Mieris has been associated with one bought at a sale in 1761 (Cf. C. Hofstede de Groot, X, no.263, although that date is apparently incorrect). Taken altogether, these provide sufficient confirmation of the identification.

Three of the remaining consigners can be readily identified with dealers active at the time. "R" is certainly C.S. Roos, "Y" is Jan Yver and "V" is Jacobus Vinkeles. (The latter was not one of the co-auctioneers of this sale and so "V" could plausibly be Jeronimo de Vries; however, one of the two lots consigned by "V" had appeared at a sale in 1806 under the name of Vinkeles and was bought in.) It is also likely that in some cases these three dealers were representing still other unnamed collectors rather than consigning their own paintings. The RKDH copy of the catalogue – which belonged to Roos – is annotated to show that lot one, marked with an "R," actually belonged to a certain "van Hall," and it is just possible that all of the "R" consignment were his. The identification of "X" can also be proposed, although with some hesitation. Just two paintings were in this consignment, both allegories dealing with the reformed church in the Lowlands. (One of them by Abraham van Eyk is now in the Musée des Beaux-Arts in Lyon.) Both had been purchased by a certain "Cattrop" (spelling uncertain) at a sale in Leyden on November 4, 1783, and although it is possible that they had changed hands during the intervening two and one half decades, we have elected to use this name, albeit with qualifications. The other consigners have not been identified. The four paintings belonging to "W" were sold for relatively high amounts, and it would useful to know their source. One of them, lot 167 by Wouwerman, had been bought at a sale in 1804 by the dealer Pruyssenaar, but there is no proof that he was still its owner. Another of his lots, no.11 by Jan and Andries Both, brought the highest price in the sale, fl. 850. The consigner "L" submitted nine paintings, five of which were supposed to be by an artist named J. Elfers, who is otherwise unknown. Finally, the consigner "Z" owned 61 paintings, the second largest group in the sale, but so far there is no clue as to his identity. Besides the picture by Both mentioned above, the most expensive lot in the sale was the so-called *Burgomaster of Delft* by Jan Steen (now in the Pennant collection at Penrhyn Castle, National Trust), which belonged to Engelberts and for which the dealer Nieuwenhuys paid fl. 750. Another high price, fl. 699, was paid for lot 4, a large marine picture by Backhuysen consigned by Roos. Overall, this was one of the more successful sales from this period; the results were fl. 19,036:15 with 29 lots (fl. 2579) left unsold.

128-A 1808/07/19 and following days

N. de Roo; Amsterdam, Premises, op de Buitenkant, tusschen de Bantemer- en Schipperstraaten

Additional Auctioneers: H. Winkelman; A.G. Pareau; D. Krayschot; etc.

Seller(s) from Title Page: None

Seller(s) from Auctioneer's Copy: Johannes Remmers; Abraham Bredius

Seller Authority: Remmers, Johannes; Bredius, Abraham

Paintings Lots: 31

Catalogue Locations:

RPUt	Annot. in pencil with figures that cannot be interpreted. It apparently belonged to the dealer Johannes Remmers.

Comments: This was an anonymous estate sale held in Amsterdam at the premises of the deceased. It consisted of virtually everything found in the household, including furniture, silver, jewelry, porcelain, clothing, carpets and a few paintings and prints. The only extant copy of the catalogue belonged to one of the consigners, Johannes Remmers, who was also one of the four people who requested the sale on behalf of the unidentified proprietor in whose house the sale was held. The other three were Cornelis Poortermans, Vrouwe J.J. Remmers, widow of Jacobus Remmers, and P.H. te Nuys, all of whom were presumably executors of the deceased. It has been suggested that the unidentified proprietor may have been Maria Remmers (1742–1808), who died in early March of the same year and who was related in one way or another to most, if not all, of the those persons mentioned above. However, at the time of her burial her address was given as being in the Singel rather than at the location given on the present catalogue, so the identification remains unresolved. Objects sold from the estate were marked with the letter "C" and altogether realized fl. 8082:3. In addition, some items were consigned by Johannes Remmers and his son-in-law, Abraham Bredius, who often bought and sold pictures in partnership. Their items were marked "N" and fetched a total of fl. 1301:19. However, in the only extant catalogue, none of the paintings lots are marked with either letter, so their ownership is unclear. There were 27 lots of paintings altogether, one of which, lot 6 by Jan Steen, improbably described as depicting *Jan Steen Offering a Ring to His Sister*, may be identical with the painting formerly in the

Bremen Kunsthalle (Cf. C. Hofstede de Groot, *Catalogue Raisonné*, I, 1907, no.787; it disappeared at the end of World War II). No dimensions are given for any of the lots, making it difficult to trace the remaining paintings, but it is possible that some reasonably valuable pieces were present.

129 1808/08/23–1808/08/24 [Lugt 7456]

Philippus van der Schleij; Amsterdam, Ten Huize van Carel Daniel Meerhoff, Castelein in 't Oudezijds Heeren Logement

Additional Auctioneers: Theodorus Spaan

Seller(s) from Title Page: None

Seller(s) from Other Sources: [Coclers, Gruyter?, Van Iperen?]

Seller Authority: Coclers, Louis-Bernard; Gruyter, Willem, Senior; Iperen, Matthias Ignatius van

Paintings Lots: 347

Catalogue Locations:

*EBNP	Auctioneer's copy, annot. with all buyers and prices on interleaved pages as well as letters for the sellers.
FLNY	Annot. with most buyers and prices.

Comments: The printed catalogue of this sale describes 290 lots of paintings and five lots of prints and drawings. Fifty-seven more lots were later added by hand; these are listed in the EBNP copy of the catalogue, though generally without titles or artists. No owners are mentioned on the title page of the catalogue, but the EBNP copy, which originally belonged to one of the dealers who organized the sale, is marked with letters next to each lot indicating the consignment to which each belonged. There is also a list showing how the receipts were distributed. The following letters were employed: A, C, D, E, H, J, R, S, T, X, Y and Z. Such letters sometimes corresponded to the names of the consigners, especially the group of dealers who regularly organized the sales, while others were assigned arbitrarily. The present sale had just two auctioneers, Ph. van der Schley and Theodorus Spaan, so the usual identifications are rendered more difficult. It is possible that "S" refers to either Van der Schley or Spaan, "R" might refer to the dealer C.S. Roos, and "Y" might be the dealer Jan Yver, but none of these can be confirmed. The earlier letters would appear to be assigned letters rather than initials. It can be demonstrated that "A" was the dealer L.B. Coclers, since a number of the paintings in this group can be traced to previous sales at which he had purchased them. The same is true of "D," whose 75 lots constituted the largest single consignment, and who was almost certainly the dealer Wm. Gruyter, as well as "T," who submitted 60 lots and was probably the dealer M.I. van Iperen. It is possible that "H" was the dealer Izaäk Schmidt, since two of the ten lots in this group were last recorded as being in his possession in 1801 and 1803, but this is less certain. The remaining consigners are not identified. Among them is "C," whose lots numbered 56 altogether, of which 18 were bought in only to reappear on August 6, 1810 (cat. no.168), as the property of "B." Unfortunately, this does not help to identify him.

The highest price, fl. 1055, was brought by lot 119, depicting an *Interior of a Stall with a Man Cutting Chaff* by Caspar Netscher, which was one of just two paintings belonging to "E." (It is now in the Johnson Collection at the Philadelphia Museum of Art.) The other expensive paintings both belonged to "X." One of these was a landscape by Hobbema, for which Coclers paid fl. 800. (It is now in the London National Gallery.) The other was a landscape by Jan Both (with figures by Poelenburgh) which was knocked down at fl. 760 but only bought in. (It is now in the Busiri-Vici collection in Rome.) The total revenue for the sale came to fl. 8593:10, with fl. 5023:10 left unsold.

130 1808/09/13 and following days [Lugt 7461]

H. van Brussel; Haarlem, Valkesteeg, No.399, bij de Koudenhoorn

Seller(s) from Title Page: None

Paintings Lots: 117

Catalogue Locations:

*EBNP	Annot. in pencil with all prices. It is addressed to the dealer Adriaan van der Willigen who has also marked some lots with his initials, probably those he purchased.
MB	Not annot.

Comments: This sale, consisting of paintings, drawings and prints, was organized by the Haarlem painter Hermanus van Brussel (1763–1815). As might be expected, the pictures offered included a large number attributed to local Haarlem painters, such as Frans and Dirck Hals, Adriaen and Isack van Ostade, as well as more obscure artists such as the still life painter Anthoni Bres to whom four paintings were assigned. There were also, however, some landscapes by Swiss and German artists. A few names are too garbled or obscure to permit identification, such as Le Compe, S. de Wett, Stube and Uijlenbroek. It is not likely that the sale included any major works. Lot 47, described as an altarpiece with the *Deposition* by Gaspar de Crayer, is described at much greater length than the other lots and so may have been considered the most important item, although it apparently fetched only fl. 50. The EBNP copy of the catalogue is annotated by the Haarlem dealer and auctioneer Adriaan van der Willigen (1766–1841), who bought at least four lots, all of which cost less than fl. 10. The highest recorded price was fl. 92 paid for a landscape by Van Goyen.

131 1808/10/28 [Lugt 7473]

Jeronimo de Vries; Amsterdam, Op de Westermarkt, still Zijde, No.2

Seller(s) from Title Page: Nagelaten door wijlen den Wel Ed. Heer Marten Udink

Seller Authority: Udink, Marten

Paintings Lots: 80

Catalogue Locations:

*EBNP	Auctioneer's copy, annot. with all buyers and prices on interleaved pages.
AA I	Annot. with many buyers and all prices.
MA	Annot. with all prices.
AA II	Incomplete, lacking pp.9–10 with lots 28–35. Annot. with all prices on interleaved pages but no buyers.
MPA	Not annot.
MB	Lugt lists an unannotated copy at this location but it cannot be located there.

Comments: The deceased, Marten Udink (1748–1808), was a native of Amsterdam, the son of wine merchant Barend Theunisz. Udink. In 1769, when he registered as a burgher, his profession is given as office clerk (Comptoirbediende) (GAA, Poorters bk. 25, p.309). At the time of his marriage to Lammerdina Kooij in 1774 his address is given as "Op de N:Z. Voorburgwal," but from 1775 until 1777 he lived at Herengracht 151, indicating that he had already risen well above the level of office clerk. His wife died a short time later, and in 1777 he married Cornelia Margaretha le Grand (GAA, DTB [Onder]trouwen, inv.619, fol.564; inv.622, fol.179). By 1805 he had become wealthy enough to rent the stables of Herengracht 165, in which he kept four horses. The sale of Udink's collection was limited to paintings. The prices were generally good, although the collection seems to have lacked outstanding pieces. The most expensive lot was an Italianate landscape by Lingelbach, for which the Amsterdam dealers Lourens Joukes and Hendrik Oyens paid fl. 700 (now in the Museum Boymans-Van Beuningen, Rotterdam). Two other lots exceeded fl. 500, a flower piece by Jan van Os was sold for fl. 560 and a market scene by Jan Steen brought fl. 506. The latter painting had recently appeared in the Pierre Fouquet sale in 1801 (cat. no.6), at which time it fetched fl. 430. Another painting by Steen, a *Village Scene with a Kermis and Numerous Figures* which brought just fl. 86, has been identified with one now in the Detroit Institute of Arts. Lot no.62, a church interior by Van Vliet, was bought by "T. Udink," who must have been Theunis Udink, the seller's brother. The total receipts for the sale were fl. 6719:10.

132 1808/11/07–1808/11/12 [Lugt 7474]

B. Scheurleer; Den Haag, Veenestraat Wyk S. No.152

Seller(s) from Title Page: Heer Mr. J. van Buren, Bailliuw van Noordwykerhout, Hillegom, Lisse en Voorhout

Seller Authority: Buren, J. van, Mr.

Paintings Lots: 23

Catalogue Locations:

*VBBA I	Annot. with all prices.
*BG	Annot. with all prices for the paintings and with some prices for the prints.
KBH	Annot. in pencil with a few prices.
AMH I	Incomplete, including only pp.1–158 which consist of book lots. Annot. with all buyers and prices on interleaved pages.
RKDH	Not annot.
RMA	Not annot.
MR	Not annot.
VBBA II	Not annot.
AMH II	Not annot.
MWH	Not annot.
UU	Not annot.
BRB	Not annot.
KPL	Not seen. According to Lugt it is not annot.
UBL	Not seen. According to Lugt it is not annot.

Comments: Three and one-half days of this six-day sale were devoted to books, with the remainder given over to drawings, prints and a wide variety of miscellaneous items. The paintings were scheduled to be sold on the last day. It appears, however, that the sale was postponed. The "Order der Verkoping" in the AMH I copy of the catalogue is annotated to show that the third through the sixth days were held on November 23/26 rather than November 9/12. This would indicate that the sale probably began on November 21 rather than

November 7. We have kept the original dating primarily because none of the other copies reflect this change.

The owner was J. van Buren, described as bailiff for Noordwijkerhout, Hillegom, Lisse and Voorhout. The sale was held on the premises of the Hague bookseller Bernardus Scheurleer (1754–1828), who also served as the auctioneer. Compared to the books, the paintings in the sale were not numerous, but the texts describing them are fairly long for a sale of this kind and some were apparently of good quality. Besides Dutch and Flemish pictures, there were also pictures from the German and Italian schools. From a modern point of view the most important item in the collection was lot 22, *A Woman in a Yellow Jacket Writing* by Johannes Vermeer (now in the National Gallery of Art, Washington), which was knocked down for just fl. 80. The preceding lot depicting *A Man and Two Women Conversing* by Pieter de Hooch (now in the Manchester City Art Museum) brought just fl. 66. Both of these were eclipsed in price by lot 4, a modern work in the same spirit as the other two showing *A Woman Feeding a Child with a Maid and a Young Boy on the Floor* by J.C. Janson. It was sold for fl. 210 (another catalogue gives the price as fl. 250) and can be identified as the painting now titled *Good Neighbors* in the Rijksmuseum.

133 1808/11/08–1808/11/11 [Lugt 7477]

[Anonymous]; Amsterdam, De Witte Molen, Op de Achterburgwal, by de Huiszittensteeg

Seller(s) from Title Page: None

Seller(s) from Auctioneer's Copy: IJ

Paintings Lots: 5

Catalogue Locations:

AMA Annot. with buyers and prices on interleaved pages for some parts; other parts are not annot. There are also letters for a few sellers. The pictures are not annot.

Comments: This sale took place at the former Amsterdam inn and lodging house "De Witte Molen," located at the present Spuistraat no.168 (then called the Nieuwezijds Achterburgwal), near the Korte Huiszittensteeg. Since the early eighteenth century it was used as a sale location and a meeting place for artists. From 1805 onward it was owned by the Amsterdam commissioners of bankrupt properties, and the offices of the Desolate Boedelskamer had been moved there shortly before the present sale. (See *Jaarboek Amstelodamum*, LVIII, 1965, p.93) No doubt items from a number of different estates were included in such a sale. The AMA copy of the catalogue is annotated with the buyers and prices for those items belonging to "IJ," but the other consignments are not identified. The cover of the catalogue indicates that the sale was to last just two days, but a list inside shows that it took four days. The paintings were sold on the third day, i.e., November 10. There were only five lots, and the individual paintings are only described as "Schilderyen" without titles.

134 1808/11/28 [Lugt 7479, 7483]

Scheurleer; Den Haag, Unknown

Seller(s) from Title Page: J.H. Colizzi

Seller Authority: Kauchlitz Colizzi, Johan Andrea

Catalogue Locations:

RKDH Not located, 1993.

Comments: The sale was originally scheduled to take place on November 14, but was postponed two weeks. The owner can be identified as the Czech musician Johan Andrea Kauchlitz (1742–1808), generally known as Johan Andrea Kauc(h)litz Colizzi. Besides being a musician, he was also active as a composer, herbalist, etcher and teacher in harpsichord and Italian. He is said to have added "Colizzi" to his name to support his qualifications as an Italian teacher – a practice not uncommon during the period (see *Mens & Melodie*, 30, 1975, pp.104–106, 151–154). Before moving to Leyden in 1766 he had lived for a time in Brunswick, Germany, where he was active as a composer. In Leyden, where he was registered at the university as a teacher of Italian, he became acquainted with the dealer and auctioneer Louis Bernard Coclers (1741–1817), who lived there from 1769 until 1787 and through whom he may have acquired some of his collection. Coclers also painted and engraved Colizzi's portrait. In 1777 Colizzi was appointed music teacher for the stadholder's daughter Frederica Louisa Wilhelmina (1770–1819), princess of Orange-Nassau, at which time he moved to The Hague and took a residence in the Hoge Nieuwstraat. From 1777–1790 he worked as a music teacher and harpsichordist at the court. In 1790 his student married a prince of Braunschweig-Wolfenbüttel and moved to Germany, upon which Colizzi was relieved of his posolation but given a substantial court pension. After 1793 he is recorded as living on his estate "Louisenburg" at the Bezuidenhout. He died aged 66 in August, 1808, just three months before the present sale. He left no descendants, so his estate was auctioned by the Hague bookseller Bernardus Scheurleer, probably at the latter's bookshop in the Veenestraat 152, although the catalogue does not say so. Colizzi's estate included 27 paintings. Unfortunately, the only copy of the catalogue has been misplaced and could not be consulted for the present index, but his collection presumably included J.F.A. Tischbein's portrait of Frederica Louisa Wilhelmina now at the MusE9e des Beaux-Arts in Bordeaux. It portrays the princess standing before a harpsichord, holding a sheet of piano sonatas composed for her by Colizzi. The RKDH copy of the catalogue is (or was) annotated with a note indicating that the sale realized a total of fl. 3534:90.

135 1808/11/28 and following days [Lugt 7482]

Philippus van der Schleij; Amsterdam, Ten Huize van C.D. Meerhoff, Kastelein in het O.Z. Heeren Logement

Additional Auctioneers: Theodorus Spaan

Seller(s) from Title Page: None

Seller(s) from Auctioneer's Copy: [Gruyter]

Seller Authority: Gruyter, Willem, Senior

Paintings Lots: 148

Catalogue Locations:

*EBNP Auctioneer's copy, annot. with all buyers and prices on interleaved pages as well as letters for the sellers. It may have belonged to the dealer Ph. van der Schley.

AA Annot. with all prices on interleaved pages but no buyers. It lacks a title page.

MWH Not annot.

Comments: This sale was one of many held in the Oudezijds Herenlogement at the Grimburgwal in Amsterdam. Since the seventeenth century it had been a lodging house for guests of the local government, but whenever it was vacant, the inner courtyard was used for auctions. Until 1811 it was the foremost sale location in Amsterdam, and so the present sale was nearly at the end of a long tradition. The catalogue was issued in two parts: the first consisted of paintings, drawings and prints; the second included coins and medals, sculpture, scientific instruments and a variety of miscellaneous items. No owner is given, but the EBNP copy of the catalogue, which evidently belonged to one of the dealers responsible for organizing the sale – most likely Philippus van der Schley – is annotated with letters next to each of the lots, indicating the consignment to which they belonged, as well as a list showing how the receipts were divided. From these one can determine that the paintings were divided into eight consignments, designated C, D, F, H, P. S, Y and Z. The largest consignment (60 lots) belonged to "D," who can be linked with the dealer Willem Gruyter Senior because many of the lots in this group can be traced to other sales at which he was either their owner or buyer. The other consigners remain unidentified, although it is likely that "S" was either Ph. van der Schley or Theodorus Spaan, i.e., one of the two dealers who served as co-auctioneers, and "Y" was probably the dealer Jan Yver. The paintings in the sale included no works of great value, and most lots were sold for less than fl. 10. The highest price was fl. 320 paid by the dealer L.B. Coclers for a painting by Jacob Jordaens that belonged to "Z" and is described only as depicting a Roman warrior. Because of its brief description and inauspicious location in the catalogue, the painting appears to have been either seriously underestimated by the auctioneer or overestimated by the purchaser. The only other lot to exceed fl. 100 was an *Interior with a Slaughtered Pig* by G. Lundens, which also belonged to "Z" and for which fl. 130 was paid. A relatively large number of lots, 31 altogether, were left unsold. According to the EBNP copy of the catalogue, a total of fl. 5538:11 was realized at the sale with fl. 937 bought in.

136 1808/12/12–1808/12/13

Hendrik de Haas; Dordrecht, Stads Venduhuis

Additional Auctioneers: Pieter van Braam

Seller(s) from Title Page: None

Paintings Lots: 10

Catalogue Locations:

VBBA Not annot.

Comments: The auctioneers for this sale were the Dordrecht booksellers Hendrik de Haas and Pieter van Braam, and the contents were primarily books. Special prominence was also given to a large French telescope. The paintings, included as lots 66–74 in the catalogue, were probably works of little interest. Besides three anonymous works and a copy after Rubens, the sale consisted primarily of paintings by Dordrecht or Hague artists, both contemporary and earlier. The results are not recorded.

137 1808/12/12–1808/12/19

B. Wild; Utrecht, Over de Domskerk

Additional Auctioneers: J. Altheer

Seller(s) from Title Page: Nagelaten door wylen den Wel Edele Gestr. Heer en Mr. D. Hoola van Nooten, In leven Oud Burgemeester en Raad in de Vroedschap, &c. &c. te Schoonhoven

Seller Authority: Hoola van Nooten, Dirk, Mr.

Paintings Lots: 19

Catalogue Locations:

VBBA	Not annot.

Comments: The seller was Mr. Dirk Hoola van Nooten (1747–1808), a native of Schoonhoven, where he was active later as a lawyer, alderman and burgomaster. The latter position had previously been held by his father, Mr. Jan van Nooten (1715–1760). Among his other public offices was membership in the Council of the States of Holland and West Frisia. He died in Gorinchem on January 30, 1808. This posthumous sale took place at the shop of the Utrecht bookseller Bartholomeus Wild, located at the south side of the cathedral's square, near the Domsteeg. It was primarily a book sale, with a few pictures sold on the last day. Most of the paintings were anonymous, but lot 8 was an unusual item, depicting *St. Augustine in a Landscape*, and evidently inscribed with the date 1562. Lots 18 and 19 were maps of Utrecht, perhaps in the form of paintings.

138 1808/12/27–1808/12/30

Immerzeel en Comp.; Den Haag, Venestraat No.147

Seller(s) from Title Page: None

Paintings Lots: 19

Catalogue Locations:

VBBA	Not annot.
MWH	Not annot.

Comments: The auctioneer of this sale was the Hague bookseller and publisher Johannes Immerzeel Junior (1776–1841). Immerzeel had become the associate of the Hague physician Jacob Lodewijk Kesteloot (1778–1852) in 1807, thus founding the firm of Immerzeel en Comp. The sale location was the firm's shop at Venestraat 147. Besides books the sale included paintings, drawings, prints and "rariteiten," but unfortunately the paintings are not described individually. An entry following the section of prints mentions only that "een exquis kabinetje Schilderijen van voorname Nederlandsche Meesters" was to be sold and lists 19 seventeenth-century painters, but no titles. It also indicates that a detailed list with descriptions of each painting was to be made available shortly before the sale, but no such list is known to exist. As a result one cannot readily determine the character of the individual works, although one of them by W.J. Laquy is described as " 't beste dat hij schilderde."

139 1808/12/27–1809/01/02

P. en J. Holsteyn; Rotterdam, Zaal boven de Beurs

Seller(s) from Title Page: Nagelaten door de Heeren G. Spanjaart, H. de Haas en C. van der Looy Lans

Seller Authority: Spanjaart, Govert; Haas, Hugo de; Looy Lans, Cornelis van der

Paintings Lots: 39

Catalogue Locations:

MWH	Not annot.

Comments: This was a book sale organized by the Rotterdam booksellers Pieter Holsteijn (1732–1813) and his son Johannes (1761–1822). It also included prints, drawings, medals, coins, numerous scientific instruments and machines as well as other miscellaneous items. The paintings were sold on December 31, the last day of the year, but it is not known exactly which pictures belonged to each of the three sellers mentioned on the title page. The sellers can be identified as Govert Spanjaart (1731–1807), Hugo de Haas Nicolaaszoon (1738–1808) and Cornelis van der Looy Lans (died 1808). The paintings are described very briefly and were probably of little importance, with the possible exception of the first item, described as a winter landscape by Isack van Ostade dated 1644.

140 1809/04/17–1809/04/18 [Lugt 7560]

Philippus van der Schleij; Amsterdam, Ten Huize van Carel Daniel Meerhoff, Castelein in 't Oudezijds Heeren Logement

Additional Auctioneers: Jan Ijver; Jeronimo de Vries; Theodorus Spaan

Seller(s) from Title Page: None

Seller(s) from Auctioneer's Copy: Crajenschot

Seller(s) from Other Sources: [Gruyter?]

Seller Authority: Crajenschot, B.J.; Gruyter, Willem, Senior

Paintings Lots: 210

Catalogue Locations:

AA	Annot. with many buyers and prices. Most of the annotations refer to the dealer Wm. Gruyter and the catalogue may have been his.
*EBNP	Auctioneer's copy, annot. with letters for the sellers as well as a few buyers and all prices.
MWH	Not annot.

Comments: The sale consisted primarily of paintings, but there was also a significant number of drawings and a few prints. The owners are not given, but the EBNP copy of the catalogue, which must have belonged to one of the dealers who organized the sale, is annotated with letters next to the individual lots, indicating to which consignment each belonged. These show that there were ten consignments of paintings, designated as A, C, D, H, O, R, S, T, Y and Z. The EBNP catalogue also identifies "O" as "Crajenschot," evidently the Amsterdam bookdealer B.J. Crajenschot, whose consignment consisted of just four lots of paintings. It is likely, though not entirely certain, that the largest consignment, consisting of 58 paintings belonging to "D," derived from the dealer Willem Gruyter Senior. This letter was often used for his consignments during this period, and one of the paintings, lot 57 by W. van Mieris, had been acquired by him in 1805. Moreover, 20 of these lots were knocked down to Gruyter, according to the AA copy of the catalogue, which probably belonged to him. It is likely that he was buying in his own paintings, as he apparently did on other occasions. Although this is not altogether conclusive, we have therefore tentatively identified him as their owner. The remaining consigners are not as yet identified. Of these, the consignments from "A" (40 lots) and "T" (32 lots) were the most important.

The sale consisted primarily of fairly inexpensive pictures, with most fetching less than fl. 10, but there were a number of notable exceptions. Lot 3, a marine picture by Backhuysen that belonged to "C," was knocked down for fl. 895, but was probably only bought in. Lot 79 from the "T" consignment, a landscape given to Jacob van Ruisdael and Ph. Wouwerman, was apparently sold for fl. 355. (In 1804 it had been bought in for fl. 275.) Four other lots surpassed fl. 200, although some of these may not have found buyers. So far, only one of the paintings in this sale has been identified. Lot 45 by Thomas de Keyser, described as *An Interior with a Man Receiving a letter from a Servant*, is clearly the *Portrait of Constantin Huygens and His Clerk* that had remained in the Huygens estate until 1785 and which is now in the London National Gallery. Although knocked down for fl. 214, it was apparently left unsold.

141 1809/04/22 and following days [Lugt 7570]

Jan Ijver; Amsterdam, Ten Huize van C.S. Roos, in het Trippenhuis

Additional Auctioneers: Cornelis Sebille Roos; Jeronimo de Vries

Seller(s) from Title Page: None

Seller(s) from Auctioneer's Copy: de Bruin; Juffr. Julikker; van den Bracke; Smit

Seller Authority: Bruin, de; Julikker, Juffr.; Bracke, van den; Smit

Paintings Lots: 218

Catalogue Locations:

*RKDH	Auctioneer's copy, annot. with all buyers and prices on interleaved pages as well as letters for the sellers.
MA	Annot. with some buyers and most prices.
AA	Annot. in pencil with a few buyers and all prices.
RMA	Annot. in pencil with a few prices.

Comments: The contents of this sale were 210 lots of paintings and two lots of musical instruments. Eight lots of paintings and three of "schilderkasjes" were added after the catalogue was printed. No sellers are mentioned, but the RKDH copy of the catalogue, which belonged originally to the dealer Roos, one of the organizers of the sale, is annotated with a letter next to each lot designating the consigner; there is also a list showing how the receipts were divided among the consigners, designated as A, C, D, R and V. At the back of the same catalogue is another list that apparently identifies the first four of these as A = de Bruin; C = Juffr. Julikker; D = van den Bracke (or Brocke); and R = Smit. As was often the case, the "A" consignment was the most important, consisting at this sale of 178 lots, for which a total of fl. 1387:15 was paid. The precise identity of "de Bruin" is not known, but it is certain that he had an association with the dealer Dupré. Many of the paintings in this consignment were purchased by Dupré at sales as late as 1806 and 1807, and fully 77 of them were knocked down to him in the present sale. If "de Bruin" is not an error of some sort, then it appears that Dupré was representing him at sales and may also have been buying in for him. A few of the pictures can also be traced to other dealers. The sale included no works of great value, and almost every lot that was knocked down for more than fl. 100 was bought in. A family portrait by Gonzales Coques, for instance, was left unsold at fl. 600. The highest price for a lot that did find a buyer was fl. 140 for an interior scene by the contemporary painter W.J. Laquy. This painting had been purchased in 1807 by Dupré for fl. 100. The total realized by the sale was just fl. 1849, and it is possible that the real figure was much lower still.

142 1809/05/26–1809/05/28 [Lugt 7595]

Pieter Daams; Haarlem, Op de Zaal van het Prinsenhof

Seller(s) from Title Page: Nagelaten door wijle Mejuffrouw de Wed. David Heemskerk en een ander Liefhebber

Seller Authority: Heemskerk, David, Mejuffrouw

Paintings Lots: 113

Catalogue Locations:

*EBNP	Annot. with a few prices.
MWH	Not annot.
MR	Missing for many years and presumably lost. According to Lugt it is not annot.

Comments: The contents were paintings, drawings, prints and "rariteiten," described on the title page of the catalogue as the property of the widow of David Heemskerk (1725–1794) and another unidentified person. Heemskerk's widow was Stijntje Verburg (1723–1809), who according to her death certificate was living on the Oude Gracht in Haarlem. Her deceased husband had been a wallpaper and ornamental painter, as well as a dealer whose collection was sold in Haarlem on April 26ff., 1796. The earlier sale consisted of approximately 35 paintings, 1365 drawings, 409 prints and 32 lots of "curiosa." Apparently the present sale included items retained by his widow and not put up for sale in 1796. Almost half of the sale consisted of either unattributed copies or works by anonymous artists, but there were several paintings by contemporary Haarlem artists, such as Jelgersma, Van Noorde, Van Brussel, etc. Among the older paintings were two river landscapes and a view of Utrecht by Van Goyen, the latter evidently the highlight of the collection. (It is now in the Johnson Collection in the Philadelphia Museum of Art.) In general, however, the descriptions are brief and lack dimensions, making it difficult to identify individual pictures. Moreover, we have the results for just three of the lots, all sold for well under fl. 10, but these were not among the more valuable pictures in the sale. The paintings are divided into two parts, the second consisting of 26 lots described as "nagekomen schilderijen." It is likely that these had not derived from Heemskerk's collection, and were those of the other unnamed collector.

143 1809/06/13–1809/06/14 [Lugt 7606]

Philippus van der Schley; Amsterdam, Ten Huize van Carel Daniel Meerhoff, Castelein in 't Oudezijds Heeren Logement

Additional Auctioneers: Jan Ijver; Jeronimo de Vries; Theodorus Spaan

Seller(s) from Title Page: None

Seller(s) from Auctioneer's Copy: Y[ver]; S[chley]

Seller(s) from Other Sources: [Gruyter; Hodges]

Seller Authority: Gruyter, Willem, Senior; Hodges, Charles Howard; Yver, Jan; Schley, Philippus van der

Paintings Lots: 253

Catalogue Locations:

*EBNP	Auctioneer's copy, annot. with all buyers and prices on interleaved pages as well as letters for the sellers.
*FLNY	Auctioneer's copy, annot. with a few buyers and all prices, as well as letters for the sellers. The prices are in two columns, the reason for which is not clear.
MA	Annot. in pencil with a few buyers and many prices. The annotations are difficult to read.
AA	Annot. with a few buyers and prices. The annotations refer most often to the dealer Wm. Gruyter and the catalogue was probably his.
RKDH	Annot. in pencil with a few prices.
AAP	Not annot. It belonged earlier to F. Lugt and RKDH.
BRB	Not annot.
RMA	Not annot.

Comments: The sale was devoted entirely to paintings, of which 246 lots were printed in the catalogue and seven more added later. No owners are mentioned, but the EBNP and FLNY copies of the catalogue, both of which must have belonged to dealers associated with the sale, are annotated with letters by the individual lots indicating that at least 12 consigners were involved. The EBNP catalogue also has a list showing how the receipts were distributed among them. The letters are A, B, D, E, H, M, P, R, Q, S, T and Y. One of these, "S," can be identified as the dealer Ph. van der Schley, who was among the co-auctioneers of the sale. The EBNP catalogue is marked with an "S" next to lot 40 whereas the FLNY copy has "Schley," and it is fair to presume that all of the "S" consignment, consisting of 24 lots, must have been his. It is also possible, but not certain, that "Y" was one of the other co-auctioneers, Jan Yver. His consignment of 62 lots was the largest in the sale, but even if it was Yver, it is likely that both he and Van der Schley were representing still other, unnamed collectors. Three other consigners can be identified with some degree of certainty. "D" was almost certainly the dealer Willem Gruyter Senior, since many of the 46 lots in his consignment can be traced to him, and he was, for some reason, commonly designated with this letter. "H" was the dealer Charles Howard Hodges, to whom four of the nine pictures can be traced. "R" was most probably a certain "Rijfsnijder," with whom three of the 14 lots can be directly associated. The remainder are still anonymous.

The sale was apparently dedicated to relatively minor paintings, and most of them fetched low prices. Only a few lots exceeded fl. 100, the most expensive of which was an interior with drinkers by Jan Steen, commonly referred to as *Het laatste drupje*, which belonged to Hodges and brought fl. 313. (Hodges had paid fl. 230 for it in 1802.) Another picture by Steen, depicting the interior of an inn, was sold for fl. 164. This was the only painting consigned by "B." One of the items left unsold was no.100, one of Gruyter's lots described as *A Woman Weighing Gold* by Vermeer of Delft, which was bought in at fl. 126. This is the painting by Pieter de Hooch of that subject now in the Gemäldegalerie in Berlin. The EBNP catalogue gives the total receipts as fl. 2681.9 with fl. 1551.5 left unsold.

144 1809/06/19 [Lugt 7611]

Philippus van der Schley; Amsterdam

Additional Auctioneers: Spaan

Seller(s) from Title Page: None

Catalogue Locations:

Comments: Lugt lists a sale held by the dealers Ph. van der Schley and Th. Spaan on June 19, 1809, but this was an error. The description applies to his no.723, which was held on July 19 rather than June 19. (See cat. no.146.)

145 1809/07/10–1809/07/13

Immerzeel & Comp.; Rotterdam, Zaal boven de Beurs

Seller(s) from Title Page: Grootendeels nagelaten door den weledelen Heer J. De Roo, In leven Ontvanger der Domeinen van Zijne Majesteit den Keizer van Oostenrijk

Seller Authority: Roo, J. De

Paintings Lots: 7

Catalogue Locations:

KBH	Not annot.

Comments: This was a sale of books which included a number of drawings, prints and paintings on the last day. The title page specifies that the books belonged largely to J. de Roo, but the pictures were evidently the property of someone whose name is not given. There were just seven lots of pictures, all left anonymous and very briefly described. Half were either flower pieces or paintings of birds.

146 1809/07/19 [Lugt 7623]

Philippus van der Schley; Amsterdam, Ten Huize van Carel Daniel Meerhof, Kastelein in het Oudezijds Heeren-Logement

Additional Auctioneers: Jan de Bosch, Jeronimusz.; Jan Yver; Jeronimo de Vries; Theodorus Spaan

Seller(s) from Title Page: Een Voornaam Liefhebber

Seller(s) from Other Sources: J.B. Bikker; Wijkersloot

Seller Authority: Bicker, Jan Bernd; Wijkersslooth van Grevenmachern, Hendricus Theodorus van

Paintings Lots: 90

Catalogue Locations:

*EBNP I	Auctioneer's copy, annot. with all buyers and prices on interleaved pages as well as letters for the sellers.
EBNP II	Auctioneer's copy, annot. with all buyers and prices on interleaved pages as well as letters for the sellers.
FLNY	Auctioneer's copy, annot. with all buyers and prices on interleaved pages as well as letters for the sellers.
AA	Annot. with all buyers and prices as well as some additional lots.
MB	Annot. with all buyers and prices.
BG	Annot. with most buyers and all prices.
RKDH	Annot. in pencil with all prices.
BMB	Present location unknown. According to Lugt it is annot. with prices.
BRB	Not annot.
MR	Missing for many years and presumably lost. According to Lugt it is not annot.

Comments: This sale was unusual for its relatively small size and the importance of the paintings included. The catalogue contained just 74 lots, and six more were added prior to the sale date. The latter are found – but not described – in the EBNP I and II and FLNY copies of the catalogue, all three of which must have belonged to dealers who helped organize the sale. The AA copy of the catalogue has ten additional unnumbered lots that may or may not duplicate those found in the other catalogues. We have included these lots but have preceded them with the letter "A."

The title page of the catalogue seems to indicate that everything in the sale belonged to a single "voornaam liefhebber" but the EBNP I and II and FLNY copies are annotated with letters next to each lot revealing that there were eight consigners. The EBNP I catalogue also has a list that indicates how the revenue from the sale was distributed. The consigners are designated A, B, C, E, F, G, V and Y. Only the first three submitted more than a few pictures, and they were clearly of more importance than the others. The title pages of three copies of the catalogue are inscribed with the name "Bicker" or "Bikker," indicating that the identity of the principal seller was well known. The MB catalogue is inscribed "Dr Heer Bikker," while the EBNP II copy has "J.B. Bikker," and on the RKDH copy one finds "Bicker en Wijkersloot." The first of these two names is confirmed by R. van Eijnden and A. van der Willigen (*Geschiedenis der vaderlandsche Schilderkunst*, III, 1820, p.439), who identify the owner as J. Bikker of Amsterdam whom they describe as being deceased at the time of the sale. They then identify some of the more important pieces in his collection, most of which can be associated with the "A" consignment. However, they also include a picture by Backhuysen (lot 2 in the sale), which belonged to a different consignment; since they apparently also did not know Bicker's full name, it is likely that their information was based primarily upon the present catalogue and may have been inaccurate. If the owner was indeed deceased, he would presumably have been Jan Bernd Bicker (1733–1774), a member of the prominent Amsterdam banking firm of Andries Pels en Soonen. Bicker married his cousin Catharina Boreel (1736–1780) in 1752, and after his death his widow remarried and moved to Geneva. It is unknown whether Bicker had a collection of paintings, but since he had been dead for more than a quarter-century, it is unlikely that he was the collector in question. If one disregards Van Eijnden and Van der Willigen's description of him as deceased, the reference could be to Bicker's nephew and namesake, Mr. Jan Bernd Bicker (1746–1812), who was also associated with the bank. The latter was a prominent politician and merchant who held many public offices between 1772 and 1796, among them chairman of the national assembly. He was the son of the merchant and banker Henrick Bicker (1722–1783) and Clara Magdalena Dedel (1727–1778). In 1778 he and his wife sat for portraits by L.B. Coclers (now in the Rijksmuseum). In 1780 he bought the monumental house at Herengracht 546 for the enormous sum of fl. 100,000. When his father died he also inherited his parents' premises at Herengracht 438. Together with his wife Catharina Six (1752–1793), he lived alternately at both addresses. He seems a more likely proprietor of the pictures in the present sale, although he still had approximately three years to live. Whatever his identification, it can be demonstrated that the paintings in the "A" consignment were those from Bicker. At least three of them can be traced to the time of their purchase in 1771 and 1777. Lot 23 by Dujardin had been acquired at the Oudermoole sale on July 25, 1771, by "Bikker," and lots 4 by G. Berckheyde and 34 by Metsu had been purchased at the Nieuhoff sale on April 14/17, 1777, by "H Bekker" or "Hy Bikker." (These annotations are found next to lots 18 and 117 in the French edition of the catalogue at RKDH. The Dutch edition has the name "JB Bikker" for lot 18 and "H Bikker" for lot 117.) This strongly implies that it was Henrick Bikker who had bought the paintings rather than his son (who would have been just 25 years old in 1771) or his brother Jan Bernd, as suggested by Van Eijnden and Van der Willigen. In this case the collection would have been inherited by the younger Jan Bernd, confirming that it was he who put the paintings up for sale on this occasion.

The second name found annotated on the title page of the RKDH catalogue, "Wijkersloot," presumably refers to a member of the family Wijkerslooth van Grevenmachern. By 1809 the families Bicker and Wijkerslooth van Grevenmachern had been acquainted with each other for over three decades, having been the owners of neighboring houses at Herengracht 438 and 436 in Amsterdam since 1777. The seller in question would then be jhr. Hendricus Theodorus (1780–1823), son of the recently deceased jhr. Cornelis Gerardus Josephus des H.R. Rijks, baron van Wijkerslooth van Grevenmachern (1749–1804). Like Bicker, the younger Van Wijkerslooth had probably inherited the paintings upon the death of his parents. His mother, Geertruida Maria Roest (1753–1807), had died just two years earlier. Wijkerslooth moved into the parental premises at Herengracht 436 in 1808. He also held public offices, including membership in the Amsterdam city council from 1808 until 1823. Both Bicker and Wijkerslooth were in close contact with several prominent Amsterdam collectors, some of whom were their neighbors in the Herengracht, such as Everhard de Burlett (1731–1806) at 442 and Lucretia Johanna van Winter (1785–1845) at 440. It is probable, but not demonstrable, that the Wijkerslooth paintings constituted the "B" consignment. This group contained works of greater importance than the "C" group; since the letters were evidently chosen without any relevance to the spelling of the name, it is likely that it would immediately follow the Bicker (A) consignment. We have, therefore, tentatively linked them. The other consigners remain unidentified with the exception of "Y," who was almost certainly the dealer Jan Yver, one of the organizers of the sale. The consignments designated E, G and V contained just two paintings each, and the "F" consignment consisted of just one, although some of these brought quite good prices and were clearly selected because of their value.

Taken as a whole, the sale included numerous works of importance, many of which were sold for record prices, although in many cases the same paintings were later unable to attain the levels established at the present sale and were sold for lesser amounts. Like the Pot sale from the year before, the results were no doubt stimulated in part by the participation of the king, Louis Bonaparte, on whose behalf Jan Yver was bidding. He acquired seven paintings that later passed to the Rijksmuseum. One of these, lot 3 by Berchem called *The Cattle Ferry* that belonged to Bicker, brought the highest amount at the sale, fl. 3040. The other six pictures were all much less expensive, but the total spent for the national collection on this occasion came to fl. 4375. A similarly high price, fl. 3000, was paid by another collector, D. Teengs, for lot 23, *A Mountainous Landscape with a Waterfall and Seven Pigs* by Dujardin that also belonged to Bicker. When Teengs's collection was sold just two years later the price dropped to fl. 2250. (It's present location is unknown.) Among other pictures from the Bicker collection that can be identified are *The Music Lesson* by Frans van Mieris which was bought for fl. 1625 by T. Spaan acting for the Amsterdam collector Pieter de Smeth van Alphen (and which fell to fl. 1320 when resold in 1810; it was last recorded ca.1928 in the collection of Anton Jurgens, Nijmegen), *The Marriage at Cana* by Jan Steen (now in the National Gallery of Ireland, Dublin), and *The Quack Doctor* by Adriaen van Ostade (Rijksmuseum). Among the paintings from the "B" (Van Wijkerslooth) consignment were Dujardin's *The Riding School* (National Gallery of Ireland) and Pieter de Hooch's *Interior with a Couple with a Parrot Cage* (Wallraf-Richartz Museum, Cologne). The EBNP I copy of the catalogue records the total for the sale as fl. 18,412:5 with just fl. 1080 (three lots) bought in.

147 1809/07/25–1809/07/26 [Lugt 7625]

Frans Johannes Bosboom; Den Haag, Kunst-Kamer boven het Koornhuis op de Princegragt

Seller(s) from Title Page: Nagelaten door wylen den Heer D. van der Aa, In leven beroemd Konst- en Rytuig-Schilder, En den Wel-Edele Heer E.B. ten Dall, In leven Procureur voor de respective Hoven van Justitie alhier

Seller Authority: Aa, Dirk van der; Dall, Egbertus Bernardus ten, Mr.

Paintings Lots: 306

Catalogue Locations:

*RKDH	Annot. with all buyers and prices. There are also some added lots.
NGW	Annot. with all buyers and prices.
AKW	Annot. with all buyers and prices.
FLNY	Annot. with all prices.
MWH	Not annot.
MR	Missing for many years and presumably lost. According to Lugt it is not annot.

Comments: Besides paintings, this sale contained 48 lots of plaster casts, molds and models. The title page of the catalogue identifies two sellers, Dirk van der Aa (1731–1809), a well-known coach painter, and Egbertus Bernardus ten Dall (1752–1802), an attorney, both from The Hague. The catalogue does not stipulate which or how many lots belonged to each person, but the plaster casts were certainly the property of Van der Aa (a few are also described as by him), and it appears that the majority of the paintings were also his. Besides those of which he was the author, there were works painted by Johann Heinrich Keller, Van der Aa's former teacher, as well as by Louis Moritz and Johannes Christianus Roedig, his former students. Moreover, there were a large number of pictures by his colleagues in the Hague drawing academy "Pictura," such as J.F. Valois, Heinrich Willem Schweickardt, Simon Besanger, and A.J. Besters, etc. If one can also assume that all of these lots, as well as those knocked down to "van der Aa" (or "Mes," who appears to have had an association with the buyer "van der Aa") were also from Dirk van der Aa's consignment, a total of 85 lots can be attributed to him. The preponderance of these pictures falls between lots 27 and 185, and it is possible that all of the lots within this range were his. It is perhaps also worthy of note that the annotator of the NGW copy of the catalogue has drawn a line between lots 26 and 27, possibly indicating a change of ownership. Furthermore, fully 23 of the first 26 – i.e., non Van der Aa – lots were knocked down to the Hague dealer/auctioneer Johannes van Eyk, implying that he may have been buying in for the proprietor. This is supported by the annotations in the NGW copy of the catalogue, which total up the results of the sale page by page and omit all of the 23 lots bought by Van Eyk. However, the same annotator also does not include the amounts paid for lots 28, 34–37, 39–43 and 45–51, most of which were not knocked down to Van Eyk. Assumptions about the significance of these annotations are further undermined by the reappearance of at least ten of the lots knocked down to Van Eyk in an auction held in The Hague on July 5, 1814, of which Van Eyk was the co-auctioneer. These lots include some of those from among lots 1–26 which one might suspect had been bought in, but also others from later parts of the sale which were presumably sold. As a result, one cannot make any firm generalizations about the activities of Van Eyk at this sale or about the ownership of the various lots, except to repeat that at least 85 can probably be associated with Van der Aa, and that the majority of the remainder were probably his as well.

Dirk van der Aa was a native of The Hague and achieved a considerable success there working for the court and several distinguished individuals. His financial success enabled him to live in a comfortable home and to move in the highest circles of society. Van Eijnden and Van der Willigen (*Geschiedenis der vaderlandsche schilderkunst*, II, 1817, p.213) refer to his collection in the following terms "Hij had zich eene fraaije Kunstverzameling aangeschaft, die hem ter verlustiging verstrekte tot in eenen zeer ver gevorderden leeftijd." He died a bachelor on February 23, 1809, about five months before the present sale.

The second proprietor associated with the sale was Mr. Egbertus Bernardus ten Dall, who worked in The Hague as an attorney at both the Court of

Justice of Holland and the High Courts of Generalities. He also served as an agent at the court for the cities of Hulst, Hulsterambacht (province of Zeeland Vlaanderen) and Maastricht. In 1778 he married Alida Visser, but it is not known whether she was still alive when he died in August, 1802. His collection of books, prints and drawings were sold on April 13/21, 1807, by Bernardus Scheurleer.

At least 12 lots are recorded as having been sold for more than fl. 100, but one cannot be certain that some were not bought in. A surprising number of modern works by artists such as Besanger, Moritz and Valois were among those that brought the best prices, but the most expensive lot in the sale was lot one, described as depicting *Alexander Prevented by Providence from Killing the Jews* by Jacob van der Ulft, which was knocked down to Van Eyk for fl. 276. A pair of small interiors with smoking and drinking peasants by Adriaen van Ostade cost fl. 170 and 156, respectively. The best price for a modern work was fl. 195 paid for a painting of *The Entombment* by Louis Moritz. Very few of the paintings in the sale have been conclusively identified.

148 1809/07/26–1809/07/27 [Lugt 7626]

Jan Yver; Amsterdam, Premises, op de Cingel, bij de Gasthuismolensteeg

Additional Auctioneers: Johannes Buys

Seller(s) from Title Page: Lieutenant Admiraal C. Schryver...Natgelaten by deszelfs eenige overgeblevene Dochter Jonkvrouwe Cornelia Haasje Schryver

Seller(s) from Auctioneer's Copy: H. Munk; T. van der Feen; G. de Hoeft, etc.

Seller Authority: Munk, Hendrik; Feen, Tjetse van der, Mr.; Hoeft, G. de

Paintings Lots: 4

Catalogue Locations:

*EBNP	Auctioneer's copy, annot. with all buyers and prices on interleaved pages as well as letters for the sellers.

Comments: The contents of this sale were primarily models of ships, navigational tools and maps, as well as a few drawings and paintings. The owner mentioned on the title page, Cornelis Schrijver (1687–1768), had been a prominent naval officer who rose to the rank of lieutenant-admiral and became an expert on nautical and military subjects as well as counsellor on marine matters to Willem IV, Prince of Orange Nassau. After his death his estate apparently remained intact in the possession of his daughter, Jkvr. Cornelia Haasje Schrijver, the seller on the present occasion. However, this collection included no paintings. The EBNP copy of the catalogue, which originally belonged to one of the dealers who organized the sale, is annotated with letters next to the individual lots indicating different consigners, and all the paintings belonged to "A." The same catalogue also identifies "A" as a group of three persons, "de Heerren H Munk, T van der Feen, en G. de Hoeft." The first of these was probably Hendrik Munk (1764–1825), collector of the state lottery at the Dam in Amsterdam. Following the death of his father, Pieter Munk, his mother had remarried the important collector Hendrik van Eyl Sluyter in 1792. Munk was also the son-in-law of the Amsterdam dealer and auctioneer Lourens Joukes, whose daughter he had married in 1787. T. van der Feen was probably the Amsterdam lawyer Mr. Tjetse van der Feen. The third participant, G. de Hoeft, is unidentified. It is not known how they came to be associated. The paintings they submitted totaled just four altogether, all of marine subjects in keeping with the nature of the Schrijver estate. None exceeded even fl. 4, so they are likely to have been rather poor specimens.

149 1809/09/06–1809/09/07 [Lugt 7632]

Philippus van der Schley; Amsterdam, Ten Huize van Carel Daniel Meerhof, Kastelein in het Oudezijds Heeren-Logement

Additional Auctioneers: Jan Yver; Cornelis Sebille Roos

Seller(s) from Title Page: Nagelaten door Wijlen den Heer Johannes Caudri, In leeven Oudste Soldy Boekhouder der voormalige Oost-Indische Compagnie

Seller Authority: Caudri, Johannes

Paintings Lots: 93

Catalogue Locations:

FLNY	Auctioneer's copy, annot. with all buyers and prices on interleaved pages.
RKDH	Auctioneer's copy, annot. with all buyers and prices on interleaved pages.
*EBNP	Auctioneer's copy, annot. with all buyers and prices on interleaved pages.
AAP I	Annot. with all buyers and prices.
AA	Annot. with most buyers and all prices.
MA	Annot. with most buyers and prices.
MPA	Annot. in pencil with many buyers and prices.
AAP II	Annot. in pencil with a few buyers and many prices.
BRB	Not annot.
LBDa	Not annot. It may have belonged to the dealer P. van der Schley.

Comments: The proprietor of the 93 lots of paintings in this sale is identified on the title page as Johannes Caudri (1723–1809). He was the son of the Amsterdam merchant David Caudri (1680–1748) and Petronella Elison; at the time of his father's death he was living at their home at the "Princegragt by de Vyzelgragt." By 1753 he was already an accountant of the Dutch East India Company (GAA, Poorters, bk.21, p.575). Although no marriage certificate has been found, the death certificate of "Suzanna van de Waereld, huisvrouw van Johannes Caudri," dated January 3, 1797, indicates that Caudri probably married and resided for some years away from Amsterdam. His address at that time was "op de Raamgragt en hoek van de Sanddwarsstraat." (GAA, DTB Begraven, inv.1051, fol. 74.) Caudri died in Amsterdam on June 9, 1809, at his premises "in de Spinhuyssteeg," leaving no descendants. According to inscriptions in the FLNY and EBNP copies of the catalogue, the sale of his paintings took place at the request of Pieter Swanenburg (1770–1843), probably the executor of Caudri's will. It included several works of value, but in general it is not known how or when they were acquired. Probably they had been purchased individually by Caudri over the course of many years. The prices realized at the present sale were reasonably good, but only one unusual figure was recorded, that of fl. 2225 paid for lot 84, *The March of an Army* by Philips Wouwerman, which was bought by the dealer Theodorus Spaan, possibly acting for the Amsterdam collector Hendrik Muilman. (It appeared in the latter's sale on April 12, 1812, fetching precisely the same price, and was last traced in the Baring collection in London, where it may have been destroyed by fire.) No other lot approached this amazing figure. A *Rustic Interior with Men Smoking and Drinking* by Adriaen van Ostade was sold to the dealer Gruyter for fl. 405. A few of the remaining pictures can be identified, including Vermeer's *Woman with a Pearl Necklace* (now in the Berlin GemE4ldegalerie), which was sold for just fl. 55. (When resold in 1811 it brought only fl. 36.) Pieter de Hooch's *Woman Receiving a Letter from a Man* (now in the Kunsthalle, Hamburg) was bought for fl. 31. Both of these were surpassed by an eighteenth-century work, Louis de Moni's *Old Woman in a Window* (now in the Museum Bredius, The Hague) which was acquired by Bredius for fl. 62. One of the more expensive pictures was the *Dutch Ship in a Foreign Bay* by Backhuysen, which brought fl. 109. (It is now in the Michaelis collection in the Old Town House, Cape Town, South Africa.) The total receipts for the sale are recorded as fl. 9014:5.

150 1809/10/16–1809/10/20 [Lugt 7640]

H. en G. Bakhuysen; Den Haag, Hoogstraat

Seller(s) from Title Page: Nagelaten door de Heer Konst Schilder D. van der Aa. en de Heer en Mr. P. v d. Heuvell, In Leven Advocaat voor de Respective. Hoven van Justitie

Seller Authority: Aa, Dirk van der; Heuvel, Petrus van den, Mr.

Paintings Lots: 7

Catalogue Locations:

VBBA I	Not annot.
VBBA II	Not annot.
MWH	Not annot.

Comments: This was a sale of books, prints, drawings, scientific instruments and miscellanea. The sellers mentioned on the title page are Dirk van der Aa (1731–1809), the Hague painter whose pictures had been sold three months earlier (cat. no.147), and a certain P. van den Heuvell, described as a lawyer at the Court of Justice in The Hague. The latter was probably Mr. Petrus van den Heuvel, who studied law at Harderwijk University and from 1783 onward practiced at the Court of Justice, but whose birth and death dates have not been found. The sale contained only a few, mostly anonymous, paintings that are very poorly described. The sale was held by the Hague booksellers Hendrik and Gerrit Bakhuysen, and at least three of the paintings appear to have been bought by them at the Van der Aa sale. Lot 180 depicting a bullfight, for instance, is certainly identical with lot 273 in the earlier sale. Therefore, the present ower was not Van der Aa, but the Bakhuysens, and the painter's name was being used to attract buyers. It is possible that all seven lots in the sale belonged to the auctioneers.

151 1809/10/16–1809/10/21

B. Wild; Utrecht, Premises, en face de l'Eglise du Dôme

Additional Auctioneers: J. Altheer

Seller(s) from Title Page: Delaissé par feu Messire J.J. van Rhyn, Dans son vivant Archeveque d'Utrecht

Seller Authority: Rhyn, Johannes Jacobus van

Paintings Lots: 40

Catalogue Locations:

MWH	Not annot. It is addressed to W.H.J. van Westreenen.

Comments: The seller can be identified as Johannes Jacobus van Rhijn (died 1808), archbishop of the Old Catholic Church, an independent denomination of Dutch Catholics who renounced the authority of the Pope and seceded from the

Roman Catholic Church in 1724. The Utrecht chapter – Utrecht was also the archiepiscopal seat – first appointed Van Rhijn vicar, and then archbishop, in 1797. His election and ordination were declared illegal by Pius VI, who subsequently excommunicated Van Rhijn and all those involved. In 1807 Van Rhijn successfully opposed the efforts of the Roman Catholic Louis Bonaparte, King of Holland – who was supported by some members of the group – to reunify the Catholic Church in the Netherlands. Upon Van Rhijn's death, Bonaparte promptly forbade the appointment of a successor.

The title page of the catalogue tells us that the sale, which included mostly books as well as a few prints, paintings, coins and "curiosités," was to take place "en face de l'Eglise du Dôme." However, it is unlikely that this was, in fact, on the premises of the archbishop, but rather at the bookshop of the auctioneers Wild and Altheer, located across from the cathedral at Domkerkhof F 304 (the present Domplein 1). The collection does not seem to have included any works of particular interest. Most paintings were anonymous, and it is striking that very few had religious subjects. The majority were genre scenes, with a few landscapes and portraits as well. It is entirely possible that many of them had come from other sources. The results are not recorded.

152 **1809/10/16** and following days

Paulus Nijhoff; Arnhem, not given

Seller(s) from Title Page: None

Seller(s) from Auctioneer's Copy: Wed N. Nijhoff

Seller Authority: Nijhoff, N.

Paintings Lots: 23

Catalogue Locations:

*VBBA Annot. with all buyers and prices on interleaved pages.

Comments: This was primarily a sale of books, to which a number of paintings, prints, drawings and miscellanea were added. The title page of the catalogue does not mention a seller, but some annotations at the front of the VBBA copy of the catalogue give the names of eight sellers (transcribed in W. Nijhoff, *De Arnhemsche boekverkoopers en uitgevers Nijhoff*, The Hague, 1934, pp. 92–94). These notes indicate that the paintings belonged to the "Wed. N. Nijhoff," who can probably be identified as the widow of Jacob Nijhoff (died 1794) who died in 1803, having outlived her husband by about nine years. This is borne out by the fact that the name of her son Johan Nijhoff (perhaps her executor) is found next to hers. The auctioneer was the Arnhem bookseller Paulus Nijhoff (1756–1832), another son of the presumed seller. The sale location is not given, but was probably the Nijhoff bookshop in the house called "De Crabbe" at the Bakkerstraat Wijk D no. 144 (the present Bakkerstraat 17). Most of the paintings, which may well have been inherited from her husband Jacob, were anonymous, although two are described as being the manner of Weenix and Van Goyen and three others are given to E. van der Poel, Droochsloot and a certain Van Ameron, who is unidentified. A number of lots were also added to the sale after the catalogue was printed, but they are not described. The items belonging to the widow Nijhoff fetched a total of fl. 285:4, while the entire sale brought fl. 1874:8.

153 **1810/02/26–1810/02/28**

J. van Baalen; Rotterdam, De Hoogstraat over de groote Markt

Seller(s) from Title Page: Nagelaten door een voornaam Liefhebber

Paintings Lots: 1

Catalogue Locations:

KBH Auctioneer's copy, annot. with some buyers and prices on interleaved pages, but not for the single painting.

Comments: This sale, consisting primarily of books as well as a piano and some miscellaneous scientific instruments, was held in the shop of the Rotterdam bookseller Jacob van Baalen (1775–1853). Just one painting, an anonymous depiction of a mill called "de Valk" (in Rotterdam?), was included.

154 **1810/03/05–1810/03/08** [Lugt 7715]

B. Wild; Utrecht, Premises, Nouveau Canal, vis-à-vis la Porte de la Cour de Justice

Additional Auctioneers: J. Altheer

Seller(s) from Title Page: Delaissé par feu Monsieur J.J. Woertman, en son Vivant, Conseiler & Echevin de la Ville à Utrecht &c. &c.

Seller Authority: Woertman, Johan Jacob, Mr.

Paintings Lots: 60

Catalogue Locations:

*EBNP Annot. only with the prices for the paintings.
BRB Not annot. It is addressed to Meinard Tydeman, a professor of law at Utrecht University.

Comments: The seller is Mr. Johan Jacob Woertman (1753–1809), councillor and alderman in Utrecht. He was born in Utrecht, the son of Jacob Gysberth Woertman and Beatrix Verwey, and died there, unmarried, on November 7, 1809. The sale of his books, naturalia, scientific instruments, paintings, drawings and prints was at his residence on the Nieuwe Gracht. The title page of the catalogue indicates that the house was located across from the Hofpoort, the Nieuwe Gracht gateway to the former abbey of St. Paul's, which in 1810 accommodated the Provincial Court of Justice. The auctioneers were the Utrecht booksellers Bartholomeus Wild and his cousin Johannes Altheer. The paintings were sold on the third day; judging only from the prices, they seem to have included a few items of more than average value. However, it is not known which lots were actually sold and which bought in. The highest price was paid for lot 52, a landscape by Wouwerman that brought fl. 370. A painting, described only as an interior with a man and a woman in the manner of Ter Borch, managed to reach fl. 230, implying that it had been underestimated by the auctioneers, who no doubt knew books better than paintings. A scene described as including a temple and some merchants – probably a scene in Italy – by Lingelbach was sold for fl. 200, and a scene with a military camp by Jan Wouwerman reached fl. 199. Unfortunately, the descriptions are too brief to allow the paintings to be identified, although it is possible that lot 7, a painting of *Children Playing with a Cat* by Jan Steen, is the painting now in the Landesmuseum in Mainz where it is catalogued as a copy after a painting in the Rijksmuseum. Lot 6 by Herman Saftleven depicting an historical event, the disbanding of the Waardgelders, a regiment of local militia, by Prince Maurits at Neude Square in Utrecht, can be identified as a painting that had belonged earlier to the famous Amsterdam collector Gerret Braamcamp. It had been sold with the Braamcamp collection in 1771 and had passed through at least five hands before reaching Woertman. (Its present location is unknown.)

155 **1810/03/23** and following days [Lugt 7736]

Vincent van der Vinne; Haarlem, Op 't Princenhof

Seller(s) from Title Page: Nagelaten door Wijle de Heere Rudolf Hendrik de Wetstein en ***

Seller Authority: Wetstein, Rudolf Hendrik de

Paintings Lots: 78

Catalogue Locations:

*EBNP Annot. with a few buyers (not for the paintings) and the prices for lots 1–9, 11 and 16.

Comments: This sale appears to have been of more than usual importance, but unfortunately little is known about the collector or the sale's results. The contents were paintings, drawings and prints as well as a few miscellaneous lots of "rariteiten." The owner is described on the title page of the catalogue as Rudolf Hendrik de Wetstein, recently deceased, and at least one other unnamed collector. As was often the case in smaller or provincial Dutch sales, the most important lots were placed at the beginning. The descriptions are lengthier than those found nearer the end, and the artists were more prominent. Moreover, the annotator of the only extant copy of the catalogue did not bother to record the prices for most of the lots following no.11.

Clearly, the highlight of the collection were three major pictures by Jan Steen that appeared as lots 1 through 3. The first, *St. Nicholas' Day* was knocked down for fl. 315. (It is now in the Museum Boymans-Van Beuningen, Rotterdam.) The second, which fetched the highest price, fl. 550, is described as *A Fortune Teller*, but from its description it can be identified as the so-called *Credit Book* (until recently on loan to the Walker Art Gallery in Liverpool from the Heywood-Lonsdale collection). The third, described as *De Pinkster Bloem voor een Huis*, is perhaps the original of *The Whitsuntide Flower* (known now only in copies), which was knocked down for fl. 400. At least two other lots also exceeded fl. 100: a landscape with figures and animals by Dirk van Bergen reached fl. 178, and an *Interior with Peasants by a Fire* by Isack van Ostade is recorded as having cost fl. 190. Other interesting pictures were also present, including two by Barent Graat depicting *Hercules and Dejanira* and *Manoah's Sacrifice* as well as six pictures by "Wulfraat," probably Matthijs Wulfraet, and one by his daughter Margaretha.

One may suggest that the major pictures at the head of the sale were those that belonged to Wetstein, but this cannot be proved. No earlier provenance is known for any of the paintings in the sale, including the three pictures by Jan Steen, but further research will no doubt eventually clarify the origins of the collection. (An inventory made in 1742 on the death of an earlier Rudolph Wetstein in Amsterdam contains a number of paintings, none of which are described. He may well have been an earlier ancestor of the present proprietor.)

156 **1810/03/26** and following days [Lugt 7739]

R. Muys; Rotterdam, In het Gebouw van het Teeken Genootschap, onder de Zinspreuk

Additional Auctioneers: W. van Leen; Gebroeders Van Ryp

Seller(s) from Title Page: Nagelaten door wijlen den wel Edelen Heer Daniel de Jongh Az.

Seller Authority: Jongh Adrszn., Daniël de

Paintings Lots: 89

Catalogue Locations:

ESP I	Annot. with all buyers and prices on interleaved pages. There are also a few notes about the cost of certain lots. (Dutch edition)
AMR	Annot. with all buyers and prices as well as some notes about the original cost of individual lots.
*AAP I	Annot. with all buyers and prices on interleaved pages. (Dutch edition)
RMA II	Annot. with all buyers and prices on interleaved pages.
RMA I	Annot. with all buyers and prices.
EBNP	Annot. with all buyers and prices. (Dutch edition)
RKDH I	Annot. with all buyers and prices. (Dutch edition)
BMPL	Annot. with all buyers and prices for the paintings. The remainder have many buyers and all prices. (Dutch edition)
NGW	Annot. with all buyers and prices for the paintings and drawings.
MPA	Annot. in pencil with all buyers and prices for the paintings. The prints and a few drawings also have prices.
BPG II	Annot. in pencil with most buyers and all prices as well as some comments for the paintings only. It belonged to the dealer J.B.P. Lebrun.
FLNY	Annot. with many buyers and all prices for the paintings only. It belonged to J.H. Cremer. (Dutch edition)
MR II	Annot. in ink and pencil with most buyers and prices for the lots on pp.1–176. (Dutch edition)
MA I	Annot. in pencil with all buyers and prices for lots 1–30 and the drawings.
LRB	Present location unknown. According to Lugt it is annot. with buyers and prices for the paintings.
KPL	Not seen. According to Lugt it is annot. with buyers and prices.
BMB	Incomplete, lacking a title page and pp.33 onwards. Annot. with a few buyers and all prices for the paintings only. (Dutch edition)
MR I	Annot. in pencil with a few buyers and many prices. (Dutch edition)
MA II	Annot. in pencil with a few buyers and prices.
ESP III	Annot. with all prices. This was formerly at KKB. (Dutch edition)
ESP II	Annot. in pencil with all prices for the paintings and some sections of the prints.
RKDH II	Annot. with all prices. (French edition)
NGL	Not annot. (Dutch edition)
AAP II	Not annot. (Dutch edition)
MB II	Not annot. (Dutch edition)
BPG I	Not annot. It belonged to the dealer J.B.P. Lebrun. (French edition)
MB I	Not annot. (French edition)
MWH	Not annot.
JPGM	Not annot.
VAL	Not annot.
SMLn	Not annot.
IFP	Not annot.
BRB	Not annot.

Comments: The proprietor was Daniël de Jongh Adrianuszoon (1745–1809), a copper merchant from Rotterdam. His Lutheran family was originally from Amsterdam but had already relocated in the late seventeenth century. Daniël was the only son of Adrianus de Jongh (1715–1777), also a copper merchant, and Anna Geertruy Croll (1727–1811). His father had been the partner of his younger brother, Daniël de Jongh (1721–1796), after whom our collector was named. Because of his political beliefs, Daniël de Jongh had gone into exile in Brussels in 1787, living there at the home of another Rotterdam exile, the collector Gerrit van der Pot (Cf. cat. no.126), and his nephew was called upon to govern his affairs while he was away. At his death Daniël de Jongh gave Van der Pot a painting by Backhuysen, *The Y at Amsterdam, Seen from the Mosselsteiger* (now in the Rijksmuseum), in payment for having been allowed to room with him (Cf. *Oud Holland*, 48, 1931, p. 212), but the bulk of his collection was willed to Daniël de Jongh Adrszn. and formed the core of the latter's collection.

Daniël de Jongh Adrszn. had married Lucia Maria Raeber (1754–1796), daughter of an equerry to the stadholder Willem V, Prince of Orange, and game warden at the royal estate Het Loo, in 1774. By 1778 the couple had already settled at Zuid Blaak B 39, near the Gapersteeg in Rotterdam. He entered into a partnership with two sons, Erdwin and Johan, and founded the copper firm and foundry Daniël de Jongh en Zoonen. Altogether he had seven children. It is still unclear to what extent he added to the collection inherited from his uncle; no purchases are recorded in the eight and one half years prior to his death on May 21, 1809.

The first sale of his property consisted of his books, prints and medals and was held in Rotterdam on October 30-November 7, 1809. The sale of his cabinet of paintings was held at the lower hall of the building used by the Rotterdam drawing society "Hierdoor tot Hooger" at the Oppert in Rotterdam. De Jongh and both auctioneers of the sale, Robert Muys (1742–1825) and Willem van Leen (1753–1825), had been members of "Hierdoor tot Hooger" and close friends. The paintings included several major works and were held in considerable esteem, attracting the interest of collectors and dealers throughout the country. The catalogue was issued in both Dutch and French. (The two editions differ slightly, and lots 69 through 76 are numbered differently.) Besides a number of prominent Dutch dealers, such as Aernout van Beeftingh (1759–1831), Gerrit van der Pals (1742–1839), Laurentius Bernardus de Wit van der Hoop (1781–1845) and Dr. Cornelis Jan Luchtmans (1777–1860), the famous Paris dealer J.-B.-P. Lebrun was in attendance. One of De Jongh's descendants is also found among the buyers, most probably the Rotterdam collector Erdwin Adrianus de Jongh (1777–1833), possibly buying for himself and/or for one of his brothers. The dealer M.I. van Iperen acted as an agent for the Amsterdam collectors Warnaar Wreesman Borghartszoon and Johannes Baptist Kobell (1778–1814). The paintings were not catalogued in alphabetical order as was normal for a large sale, nor in the order of importance as was sometimes the case. The highest prices were attained by the first lots, however, notably lot 3, a *Mountainous Landscape* by Jan Both, which sold for fl. 805. (There are several versions, but it may be the painting now in the Spencer Museum of Art, Lawrence, Kansas.) Nearly as expensive was lot 2 by G. de Lairesse, an *Ecce Homo* that cost fl. 705. This was the only painting mentioned by R. van Eijnden and A. van der Willigen (*Geschiedenis der Vaderlandsche Schilderkunst*, III, 1820, pp.440–441) in their discussion of the collection. (It is now at the Musées Royaux des Beaux-Arts in Brussels.) Lebrun purchased 22 lots altogether, nearly one-quarter of the entire sale, including three of the more expensive items, a *Landscape with a Waterfall* by Wouwerman (fl. 701), Metsu's *A Lady and a Gentleman Playing Cards* (fl. 600) and Dou's *A Woman Reading* (fl. 505). Among the works that can be identified are Willem van de Velde the Younger's *A Small Dutch Vessel Close-hauled in a Strong Breeze* (now National Gallery, London), *Cavalry Attack at Sunset* by Jan Asselyn (Rijksmuseum), *Samson and Delilah* by Jan Steen (Los Angeles County Museum of Art) and *The Writing Lesson* also by Jan Steen (Foundation Custodia, Paris). Three others are somewhat more tentative: Lot 8, a church interior by Saenredam described as being dated 1630, might be the *Interior of St. Bavo* now in the Louvre; lot 47, *A Young Woman with a Lighted Candle at a Window* said to be either by Dou or a copy after him, may well be the painting of this description now in the Thyssen Collection; and lot 17, a marine picture by Jan van de Cappelle, might be the panel now in the Harold Samuel Collection, Corporation of London, although the De Jongh picture is described as being on canvas.

Altogether the sale was very successful, and nothing was left unsold. The AAP I copy of the catalogue gives the totals as fl. 8461:3 for the paintings and fl. 22,927:2 for the entire sale. EBNP puts it higher, at fl. 8579:13 for the paintings and fl. 28,748.18 for everything. Van Eijnden and Van der Willigen, apparently agreeing with the EBNP catalogue, put the total at approximately fl. 28,750:18.

157 1810/03/27–1810/03/28 [Lugt 7740]

Nicolaas Cornel; Rotterdam, not given

Seller(s) from Title Page: Een Voornaam Liefhebber

Paintings Lots: 105

Catalogue Locations:

MR	Not annot.

Comments: Besides 105 lots of paintings, this Rotterdam sale included a group of prints and some miscellaneous items. A collection of books was sold on the second day. According to the title page of the catalogue everything belonged to a single "liefhebber," but he (or she) has not been identified. The paintings, mostly from the seventeenth century but including many from the eighteenth, were almost entirely genre scenes and still lifes. Although the artists are usually named, the dimensions are not included and the descriptions are too brief to allow for any identifications. We also do not know the results, since the only extant catalogue is not annotated. It is therefore difficult to speculate on the quality of the individual pieces. This was one of the few sales held by the bookseller Nicolaas Cornel (1756–1841) that included paintings. The location of the sale is not given, but it was presumably at Cornel's premises at the corner of the Meent and the second Lombardstraat, at no.253.

158 1810/04/17

S. van Benthem; Middelburg, Premises, in de Wagenaardstraat bij de Oude Kerk

Seller(s) from Title Page: Nagelaten door Wijlen den Heer Mr. J.H. Milet, In zijn Ed. Leven Raad in het Departementaal Gerichtshof van Zeeland

Seller Authority: Milet, Johannes Henricus, Mr.

Paintings Lots: 2

Catalogue Locations:

*ZBM	Annot. with all buyers and prices on interleaved pages.

Comments: The contents of this Middelburg sale were primarily books, at the end of which there was a small number of prints and miscellaneous items. Two anonymous paintings were also included, both of which were knocked down to

S. van Benthem, the auctioneer. The owner was Johannes Henricus Milet, a lawyer who was also a counsellor at the Court of Justice for the province of Zeeland. In 1796 he published some essays on national government. His father had also been a prominent lawyer, alderman and burgomaster in Veere.

159 **1810/05/16** and following days

P. Posthumus; Amsterdam, Princegragt, over het Amstelveld; voor het Huis getekend met No.852

Seller(s) from Title Page: None

Paintings Lots: 8

Catalogue Locations:

AMA	Not annot.

Comments: This was an estate sale consisting of porcelain, furniture, silver, jewelry, clothes, etc. as well as paintings. It was organized by a group of eight dealers of which Pieter Posthumus is just the first of eight listed on the title page. There were eight lots of paintings containing a total of 22 items, mostly landscapes and still lifes. All were anonymous and probably of little interest. The results are not recorded.

160 **1810/05/22** and following days [Lugt 7788]

Philippus van der Schleij; Amsterdam, Ten Huize van C:D: Meerhof, in het Oude Zijde Heeren Logement

Additional Auctioneers: Jan Ijver; Cornelis Sebille Roos; Jeronimo de Vries; Theodorus Franciscus Spaan

Seller(s) from Title Page: Nagelaten door Wijlen den Heer Johannes van de Putte, Nicolaasz.

Seller(s) from Auctioneer's Copy: Y[ver]

Seller Authority: Putte Nicolaasz., Johannes van de; Yver, Jan

Paintings Lots: 174

Catalogue Locations:

*EBNP I	Auctioneer's copy, annot. with all buyers and prices on interleaved pages as well as letters for the sellers.
MA	Annot. in ink and pencil with many buyers and prices for the paintings only.
*AA I	Annot. with some buyers and all prices for the pictures. The remainder has some prices.
AA II	Annot. with some buyers and prices.
EBNP II	Not annot.
RMA	Not seen. According to Lugt it is not annot.

Comments: The contents were paintings, drawings, prints and a few lots of miscellaneous items. The title page of the catalogue mentions just one owner, Johannes van de Putte Nicolaasz., implying that everything in the sale was his property. Not much is known about Van de Putte, except that he died in 1810 and according to the notice of his burial (GAA, DTB Begraven nr.1051, fol.178) his residence was at the "Oude Waal by de Kraansluys." His profession is not recorded.

However, the EBNP copy of the catalogue, which must have belonged originally to one of the five dealers who organized the sale, is annotated with letters next to each of the lots, indicating that there seven consignments rather than just one. They are designated A, D, F, R, S, T and Y. It can be demonstrated that Van de Putte was the owner of the "A" consignment, consisting of 96 lots of paintings, more than half of the sale. He had purchased five of them at public sales between 1801 and 1803 using the dealer Ph. van der Schley as his representative. Another had been knocked down to "P" in 1803, again with Van der Schley bidding. Ten others from this group had been purchased by "A," "B" or "Z" at five sales between the years 1801 and 1804, always with Van der Schley acting on his behalf. His activity before the turn of the century is also documented. He bought four paintings at the Jan Danser Nijman sale in Amsterdam on August 16ff., 1797, again with Van der Schley bidding on behalf of "P," and five others at an anonymous sale on June 21, 1797, all bought by Van der Schley. Finally, a pair of views by Jan van der Heyden had been acquired at the Ploos van Amstel sale on March 3, 1800, once more with Van der Schley acting as Van de Putte's agent.

All of the most expensive lots in the sale came from Van de Putte's consignment. Lot 89, a pair of flower pieces by Rachel Ruysch, brought the highest price, fl. 350, followed by a small landscape with figures by Dujardin that was sold for fl. 340. Three other lots also managed to exceed fl. 300. Van de Putte apparently had a taste for eighteenth-century genre pictures as well as landscapes from the previous century, since they made up a large proportion of his cabinet. Unfortunately, very few of the paintings can be identified with certainty. A small view with the Huis ten Bosch by Jan van der Heyden has been tentatively associated with one in the National Gallery in London, but the connection is uncertain. A painting by Jan Ekels the younger depicting *Wine Tasters* can be identified with one now in the Stedelijk Museum De Lakenhal in Leyden.

With the exception of "Y," who was presumably the dealer Jan Yver, none of the other consigners can be identified. The paintings submitted by "T," while only eight in number, included at least two lots that were knocked down at reasonably good figures. One of his pictures, a landscape by Salomon van Ruysdael, had been bought by the dealer M.I. van Iperen as recently as June 13, 1809 (cat. no.143), but since the remaining paintings cannot be associated with him, we have not assumed that he was their consigner on the present occasion.

161 **1810/06/04**

Pieter van Braam; Dordrecht, Stads Venduhuis

Additional Auctioneers: Pieter Blussé den Jongen

Seller(s) from Title Page: Nagelaten door den Heer Hendrik de Haas, In Leven Boekhandelaar in Dordrecht

Seller Authority: Haas, Hendrik de

Paintings Lots: 23

Catalogue Locations:

VBBA	Not annot.

Comments: The contents of the sale were primarily books, the property of the Dordrecht bookdealer Hendrik de Haas, who had died on January 2, 1810 (GAD, DTB Overlijden 1810, fol.2). The auctioneers were the bookdealers Pieter van Braam (1740–1817) and his son-in-law Pieter Blussé the younger (1786–1869); the former had occasionally organized sales jointly with De Haas. (Cf. nos.117 and 136.) At least one of the paintings in the present sale, lot 9 by Houbraken, had appeared at one of those earlier sales. Similarly, at least two of the lots in the present sale, the bulk of which consisted of landscapes and genre scenes, reappeared at a sale held by Van Braam and Blussé on December 3, 1810 (cat. no.176). Such pictures seem to have remained in circulation with local bookdealers over periods of months or years, giving the impression of having been of relatively minor importance. The results of the present sale are unknown.

162 **1810/06/06** and following days [Lugt 7803]

R. Muys; Rotterdam, Op de Zaal boven de Beurs

Additional Auctioneers: W. van Leen; Gebroeders Van Ryp

Seller(s) from Title Page: None

Paintings Lots: 233

Catalogue Locations:

*EBNP	Annot. with some buyers and all prices.
*MA	Annot. with a few buyers and all prices. The annotations are difficult to read.
MB	Not annot.
RMA	Not annot.
FLNY	Not annot.

Comments: Besides 233 lots of paintings, this Rotterdam sale included a single lot of frames, another with a watercolor and an unnumbered lot of sculpture said to be by Dürer. No owner is mentioned, although a number of the paintings can be traced to an earlier sale. At least 18 of them, and probably as many as 22, had come from the Linden van Slingeland sale held in Dordrecht on August 22ff., 1785, at which time they had been bought (or bought in) by the dealer Abraham Delfos, who was also involved in the organization of the sale. For such a large group of pictures to come from a single source implies that they had remained together for 25 years, although they may well have changed hands in the meantime. It is unlikely that Delfos was their proprietor, but possibly he had bought them for someone else, or they may have represented the residue of the Linden van Slingeland estate. Some valuable works were included, however, mostly placed at the head of the sale. Lot 8, for instance, a winter landscape by Philips Wouwerman, had been knocked down in 1785 for fl. 510 and reached fl. 440 on the present occasion. A painting by Cuyp said to depict the *Siege of Breda* had been knocked down for fl. 405 in 1785 and brought fl. 404 at this sale. A few other lots also exceeded fl. 100, but the great majority were well under that, and the latter part of the sale was devoted to copies and unattributed works that mostly fetched very small amounts. It seems likely that they came from a variety of sources. Very few have been identified, but lot 86, a depiction of *Moses and the Brazen Serpent* by Cornelis van Haarlem dated 1597, is presumably the painting now in the Hessisches Landesmuseum, Darmstadt. A very large *trompe-l'oeil* canvas of architecture and a young man reading by Samuel van Hoogstraten was bought by the "Teekengenootschap Pictura," possibly the drawing society in Dordrecht rather than the better known Confrerie Pictura in The Hague. This painting is probably a pendant to a similar painting in the Mauritshuis and was recently on the New York art market.

163 **1810/06/20** [Lugt 7817]

Philippus van der Schley; Amsterdam, Ten Huize van Carel Daniel Meerhoff, Kastelein in het Oudezijde Heeren-Logement

Additional Auctioneers: Jan Ijver; Cornelis Sebille Roos; Jeronimo de Vries; Theodorus Franciscus Spaan

Seller(s) from Title Page: None

Seller(s) from Auctioneer's Copy: R[oos]

Seller Authority: Roos, Cornelis Sebille

Paintings Lots: 211

Catalogue Locations:

*EBNP	Auctioneer's copy, annot. with all buyers and prices on interleaved pages as well as letters for the sellers.
AA	Annot. in ink and pencil with many buyers and all prices.
MA	Annot. with some buyers and most prices.
RMA	Not seen. According to Lugt it is not annot.

Comments: The sale consisted of 208 lots of paintings, 195 of which appear in the principal section of the catalogue and 13 in a "Verfolg der schilderijen." Three further lots were added by hand after the catalogue was printed. No owner is mentioned on the title page, but the EBNP copy of the catalogue, which must have belonged to one of the five dealers who organized the sale, is annotated with letters next to each of the lots indicating that there were 13 consignments designated A-D, K, N, Q-T, V, X and Y. A number of the paintings can be traced to earlier sales, and it is possible to speculate about who the consigners were, although in most cases there is room for doubt. The largest consigner was "A," who submitted 65 lots of paintings, five of which can be traced to "de Meijer," evidently one of the dealers of this name. The association seems tenuous. The consigner "B" owned 49 lots, four of which can be traced to the dealer Theodorus Spaan. As one of the dealers overseeing the sale, Spaan was also buying in these lots. Consigner "C" owned just three lots, one of which had been purchased as recently as June 13, 1808, by the dealer Jan Smit, who might then be the owner in question. The consigner "D" owned 18 lots, one of which had bought by the dealer Dupré on June 13, 1809, but the remainder cannot be traced to him. Somewhat more compelling is the identity of "S," two of whose 17 lots can certainly be traced to the dealer Frantzen. Finally, "Y" was probably the dealer Jan Yver. However, for all of these we have left the matter unresolved. The only consigner we have ventured to identify is "R," presumably the dealer C.S. Roos, who was one of the co-auctioneers of the sale and to whom at least one of the paintings can be traced.

The paintings were mostly inexpensive ones and the sale was evidently intended for minor works, although a few brought reasonably good prices. The highest was registered for lot 79 by Jan Steen, described as *Two Children Leaving a Shop with Sweets*, which belonged to "N" and was knocked down for fl. 300. However, it was only bought in, and when it reappeared at an anonymous sale in 1817 it was again bought in for the same price. What appears to be the same painting then appeared in the Everhardus Boers sale of 1818, where it fetched a mere fl. 9.10, an indication that the higher price was completely artificial. (It is presumably the painting now in the Hamburg Kunsthalle.) A large landscape with hunters by Wijnants and Lingelbach belonging to "D" was sold to the dealer J. de Vries for fl. 250 (the AA copy of the catalogue has fl. 275). Four months later De Vries put it up for sale again and knocked it down for double that amount, but he was apparently bidding on his own painting. Another successful lot was a painting of a riding school by Wm. Schellinks, also belonging to "D," that was sold for fl. 200. However, a very large proportion of the paintings were sold for less than fl. 5.

164 1810/07/23 [Lugt 7729]

Hendrik Logger; Dordrecht, Premises, not given [see below]

Seller(s) from Title Page: Nagelaten door den Wel-Edel Geboren Heer Mr. Pieter van den Santheuvel, Heer van Driel, In Leven Oud Burgemeester en Ontvenger van der Gemeenenlands Middelen

Seller Authority: Santheuvel, Pieter van den, Mr.

Paintings Lots: 84

Catalogue Locations:

*RMA	Annot. with all buyers and prices.
*RKDH	Annot. with most buyers and all prices.
EBNP	Not annot.
KH	Not seen.

Comments: This was the first of two sales held on the same day by the same auctioneer in Dordrecht. The catalogue indicates that it was originally scheduled to be held on March 20, and two of the extant catalogues have the date changed by hand. The contents were limited to paintings, the property of Mr. Pieter van den Santheuvel, lord of Driel (1732–1799). The Santheuvel family originated in Ghent and beginning in the seventeenth century produced several dignitaries active in the political life of Dordrecht. Pieter van den Santheuvel also held public offices, including those of councillor, provost marshal and burgomaster of Dordrecht. He was also a member and benefactor of the Dordrecht drawing society Pictura, and was close to local artists such as Aert Schouman and Jacob van Stry. His predilection for contemporary art is underlined by the presence of works by both Abraham and Jacob van Strij in his collection, but the bulk of his cabinet consisted of works by seventeenth-century artists, some of which he may well have inherited from his father Hendrik (1687–1747) or his grandfather Bartholomeus van den Santheuvel (1654–1718), both collectors. Pieter van den Santheuvel died in Dordrecht on August 20, 1799, leaving no descendants. His collection passed to his widow, Adriana Gevaerts (1736–1809), who apparently added a few works herself. After her death the collection was divided, with part eventually going to a cousin, Willem Bartholomeus van den Santheuvel (1796–1865), while a large part of the remainder was put up for sale on the present occasion. The paintings that failed to find buyers, as well as other works that were not put up for sale, were given for safekeeping to Jacob van Stry, the seller's friend and agent. These paintings were sold, along with others belonging to Van Stry, after the latter's death on April 14, 1816.

The present sale took place on the deceased widow's premises, which are mentioned in the registration of her burial as "Kerkbuurt by het Stadhuijs Letter A No.200" (GAD, Begraafboek Grote Kerk 1809, inv.54, fol. 132), i.e., Grotekerksbuurt no.200 not far from the Dordrecht town hall. The sale was organized by Hendrik Logger (1736–1820), "Stads Vendumeester," and was apparently one of the last held under his auspices. The prices ranged from small to reasonably good. The most successful lot was no.47, an exterior scene by Jan Steen depicting the artist asleep at a table with his wife, which was sold for fl. 365. Three other lots exceeded fl. 300, an *Italian Harbor Scene* by Lingelbach, and a pair of small canvases depicting *A Fisherman and His Wife*. Most of the paintings were marine- or landscapes and genre pieces.

165 1810/07/23 and following days [Lugt 7728, 7835]

Hendrik Logger; Dordrecht, Premises, same as preceding sale

Seller(s) from Title Page: Nagelaten door den Heer Pieter Quinting, in Leven Koopman

Seller Authority: Quinting, Pieter

Paintings Lots: 142

Catalogue Locations:

*RKDH	Annot. with many buyers and prices.
FLNY	Annot. in pencil with many buyers and prices.
RMA	Not annot. Addressed to H.J. Rombouts.
EBNP	Not annot.

Comments: Like the preceding sale, this auction was postponed from March 20 until July 23. It was the second of two sales held by the same auctioneer on the same day and at the same location, but continued for an undetermined number of days afterward, although the number of lots would indicate that it was probably not more than a two-day sale altogether. The owner is probably to be identified as the same Pieter Quinting who, together with his twin brother Johannes, was born in Dordrecht in 1770, the son of Jacob Quinting and Maria Sara van Pelt. He appears to have used his mother's name in addition to, or instead of, that of his father, since he is found recorded in the Dordrecht archives also as "Quintingh van Pelt" or "van Pelt." The notice of his intended marriage to Henrietta Anna Geertruida Hornman in Dordrecht in 1800 gives his name as "Pierre van Pelt" (GAD, DTB Ondertrouw inv.93). The same document indicates that notice of their marriage had been given earlier in Krefeld, Westphalia, in Germany, where they had evidently resided before returning to Dordrecht. Since Krefeld's economy largely depended on the manufacture of silks and velvets – begun by Protestant and Mennonite refugees in the seventeenth and eighteenth centuries – Quinting, who is referred to on the title page of the catalogue as a merchant, may well have been involved in that business. However, the presence of paintings by Dordrecht artists, such as Cuyp, Aert de Gelder, Aert Schouman and others, strongly indicates that the collection was formed in the local market rather than abroad. The results recorded for the sale are somewhat incomplete, but imply that prices were not very high. The most successful lot was apparently no.43, a small landscape by Pieter Bout (changed in the FLNY catalogue to read "Rombouts") that sold for fl. 50:10. Hardly any of the paintings have been identified, although lot 9, a painting by C. Lelienbergh of dead poultry hanging on the wall, is probably a painting now in the Rijksmuseum. At this sale it cost just fl. 4:5.

166 1810/07/26 [Lugt 7837]

Philippus van der Schleij; Amsterdam, Ten Huize van A. Poorters, Kastelein in het Wapen van Amsterdam, op de Kloveniersburgwal

Additional Auctioneers: Jan Ijver; Cornelis Sebille Roos; Jeronimo de Vries; Theodorus Franciscus Spaan

Seller(s) from Title Page: Een Kundig Liefhebber

Seller(s) from Other Sources: Cassino

Seller Authority: Cassino

Paintings Lots: 150

Catalogue Locations:

*FLNY	Auctioneer's copy, annot. with all buyers and prices on interleaved pages.

AA	Annot. with most buyers and all prices. It apparently belonged to "Andriessen" who bought lot 23.
MPA	Annot. with most buyers and prices.
MA	Annot. with most buyers and prices.
SMLn	Annot. in pencil with most buyers and prices. Some are difficult to read.
EBNP	Annot. with all prices. Some lots are marked with a line which may denote they were bought in.
RKDH	Not annot.
RMA	Not annot.

Comments: The sale consisted entirely of paintings, the property of an unidentified "Liefhebber." The AA copy of the catalogue is inscribed "Cassino" on the title page and the RKDH has "Casiner of Casseno." His ownership is confirmed by the fact that the unsold lots were bought in by Cassino. The only other record of such a collector occurs at the sale held on June 20, 1810 (no.163), at which Cassino bought ten lots of inexpensive paintings. One of these, a landscape with animals by Savery, appears in the present sale held just a month later. No trace of his activity is found afterward. The name suggests that he was of Italian origin, and this is also supported by the fact that 33 lots of Italian paintings were included, among them works by artists such as Titian, Veronese, Bassano and even Verrocchio ("Verdochio"). However, a note in the AA copy of the catalogue casts appropriate doubt on these claims: "NB: uyt de genoteerde pryzen zal men ligtelyk gewaar worden dat de stukken zelven veel scheelden by die beschryving daar van in deezen catalogus gemaakt." The prices were indeed modest and 67 lots – nearly half – of the lots were bought in, an indication that the offering was not well received. The highest prices were registered by a painting of *A Woman Cleaning a Calf's Head* by Teniers (fl. 200) and a depiction of the *Adoration of the Golden Calf* by Francisque Millet (fl. 71). However, both were bought in. The best price for a painting that actually changed hands was fl. 59 for a *Holy Family* by A. Carracci. The annotator of the AA copy of the catalogue, evidently Andriessen, gives the totals as fl. 1564:10 with fl. 434:16 left unsold. The sale took place in one of the large rooms of "Het Wapen van Amsterdam," an inn located on the Kloveniersburgwal at the corner of Het Rusland.

167 1810/08/01–1810/08/02 [Lugt 7842]

Philippus van der Schley; Amsterdam, In het Oude Zijds Heeren Logement te Amsterdam

Additional Auctioneers: Jan de Bosch, Jeronimusz.; Jan Yver; Cornelis Sebille Roos; Jan Wytman; Jeronimo de Vries; Theodorus Franciscus Spaan

Seller(s) from Title Page: Nagelaten door Den Hoog Edelen Gestrengen Heer M^{r}. Pieter de Smeth van Alphen, Groot Kruijs van de Koninklijke Orde der Unie, Staatsraad van Zijne Majesteit den Koning van Holland, en Vroedschap der Stad Amsterdam

Seller Authority: Smeth, Pieter de, heer van Alphen en Rietveld

Paintings Lots: 133

Catalogue Locations:

*LBDa	Auctioneer's copy, annot. with all buyers and prices on interleaved pages. There is also a printed list of the results. It may have belonged to the dealer P. van der Schley. (Dutch edition)
NGW I	Annot. with all buyers and prices as well as many notes. It also has a printed list of buyers and prices. (Dutch edition)
RKDH I	Auctioneer's copy, annot. with all buyers and prices on interleaved pages. It belonged to the dealer C.S. Roos. (Dutch edition)
BMB	Annot. with all buyers and prices. It belonged to the English dealer John Smith and later to RKDH. (Dutch edition)
MWH	Annot. with all buyers and prices. There is also a printed list of the results. (Dutch edition)
RKDH IV	Annot. with all buyers and prices. (Dutch edition)
AAP	Annot. with all buyers and prices. (Dutch edition)
MB	Annot. with all buyers and prices. (Dutch edition)
FLNY	Annot. with all buyers and prices. (Dutch edition)
VAL I	Annot. with all buyers and prices.
VAL II	Annot. with all buyers and prices.
RMA	Annot. with all buyers and prices.
SBB	Annot. in pencil with all buyers and prices.
ESP III	Annot. in ink and pencil with all buyers and prices. It was formerly at KKB. (Dutch edition)
NGW II	Annot. with all buyers and prices. (French edition)
SIF	Annot. with all buyers and prices. (French edition)
ESP I	Annot. in pencil with all buyers and prices. (French edition)
ESP II	Annot. with all buyers and prices. (French edition)
RKDH III	Annot. with most buyers and all prices. It also includes evaluations for tax purposes. However, the prices do not match those in other copies and may be erroneous.
RKDH II	Annot. with most buyers and prices. (French edition)
MR I	Annot. in ink and pencil with many buyers and all prices as well as many notes about the colors and quality. The latter are difficult to read. (Dutch edition)
BPG I	Annot. with many buyers and all prices as well as some comments. It lacks the title page. It belonged to the dealer J.B.P. Lebrun. (French edition)
UU	Annot. with all prices.
KBH	Annot. with all prices, also indicating which lots which were bought in. (French edition)
MA I	Annot. with all prices. (French edition)
SMLn	Annot. with some prices and notes. It also has the printed list of buyers and prices.
BPG III	Abridged edition that includes the results. It belonged to the dealer J.B.P. Lebrun. Not annot. (Dutch edition)
MR II	Abridged edition that also includes the printed results.
MR III	Abridged edition that also includes the printed results.
BPG IV	This is a printed list of the buyers and prices. It belonged to the dealer J.B.P. Lebrun who has corrected some of the results.
NGL	Not annot. Includes the printed list of buyers and prices. (Dutch edition)
EBNP	Not annot. It includes a printed summary of the sale's results with all buyers and prices as well as a list of just the prices.
MA II	Not annot. It includes two printed lists of the results. (Dutch edition)
INP	Not annot.
MPA	Not annot.
BPG II	Not annot. It belonged to the dealer J.B.P. Lebrun. (French edition)
BNP	Not annot. (French edition)
RKDH VI	This is a printed list of the buyers and sellers.
RKDH V	This is a handwritten list of the paintings with all buyers and prices.
AA	Includes the list of prices only and not the catalogue.

Comments: The sale of the De Smeth van Alphen paintings was by far the most spectacular sale held in the Netherlands during the first decade of the nineteenth century, overshadowing even the Van der Pot sale in Rotterdam of 1808 (cat. no.126). The seller, Pieter de Smeth, lord of Alphen and Rietveld (1753–1809), was a very wealthy Amsterdam merchant and banker. Besides holding numerous public offices, he was an associate in the prominent Amsterdam banking house of Raymond & Theodoor de Smith, founded by his uncle and father in 1736, which granted the Russian Czarist government its first foreign loans (of fl. 17 million) between 1769 and 1782. He inherited several titles from his father, Theodorus de Smeth, vrijheer of Deurne and Liesselt and lord of Alphen and Rietveld (1710–1772), who had been proclaimed a baron of the Russian empire by Tsarina Catharina II in 1772. Pieter de Smeth was born in Amsterdam in 1753; in 1774 he married Machtelina Christina Bregitta Warin, who died shortly afterward. In 1777 he married Sara Maria Graafland (1758–89), with whom he lived at Herengracht 508 from 1780–88 and Herengracht 554a from 1788–1802. After 1802 he lived at Doelenstraat 22. In 1807 De Smeth was appointed Extraordinary State Councillor to Louis Bonaparte, King of Holland. He died at his estate Vollenhoven in De Bilt (near Utrecht) on September 7, 1809. As a sign of his prestige, the King commissioned a full-length portrait of the deceased from the painter Charles Howard Hodges (1764–1837). His collection of paintings remained intact at his home, where it was on view until the time of the sale.

With the exception of ten mostly Flemish paintings, the collection consisted almost entirely of Dutch pictures of the seventeenth century, including numerous works of the first rank. De Smeth had acquired them individually from dealers or from sales over the course of the last two decades, in two cases as recently as 1803. The sale produced a large number of record prices, in spite of the fact that it was an inauspicious moment for such an event, given the European blockade that prevented British dealers from attending, and an unsettled political situation. The prices established at this sale proved to be the benchmark for the top of the Dutch art market for years to come, and a provenance from the De Smeth van Alphen collection was usually touted as an important selling point.

Besides the major Dutch dealers, the sale attracted the Parisian dealers J.-B.-P. Lebrun, P.-J. Lafontaine and A.-N. Pérignon, although it is uncertain whether they were there in person. Lafontaine, in one of the most audacious speculations ever witnessed on the European art market, acquired nine lots that included many of the most expensive in the sale, bidding for himself in some cases and using local dealers in others. The largest price was paid for lot 30, *Christ Healing the Paralytique* by Van Dyck, for which Lafontaine paid an astonishing fl. 19,200. De Smeth had bought this picture at the Pauwels sale in Brussels in 1803 for 25,000 frs., using Th. Spaan as his agent. Not long after the present sale, Lafontaine took it and five other De Smeth paintings to London, where all were bought by the Prince of Wales just prior to a sale to be held at Christie's on June 12, 1811 (Cf. B. Fredericksen, *Index of Paintings Sold in the British Isles during the Nineteenth Century*, 3, 1993, no.901). The second and third most expensive paintings were also in this shipment, namely Rembrandt's so-called *Master Ship-Builder* (fl. 16,500) and the *Landscape with the Baptism of the Moor* by Jan and Andries Both (fl. 10,000). Lafontaine could not have known in advance that his gamble would recoup his investment with such stunning success.

His rival, Jean-Baptiste-Pierre Lebrun, bought a total of 27 paintings using the dealer Teissier (Texier) to represent him. These were somewhat less expensive than those bought by Lafontaine, but often represented record prices nonetheless. The largest amounts were paid for a scene depicting the *Halt at an Inn* by Isack van Ostade (lot 74), which cost Lebrun fl. 5050, and an interior by Adriaen van Ostade (lot 71) at fl. 4600. Lebrun took all of these paintings to Paris, where he placed them in one of his own sales held on April 16ff., 1811. Other dealers buying actively at the sale included C.S. Roos, L.B. Coclers and M.I. van Iperen. The dealer Jeronimo de Vries bought nine paintings for Lucretia Johanna van Winter which later passed to the Six van Hillegom collection and a few of which eventually found their way to the Rijksmuseum. (See R. Priem, "The 'most excellent collection' of Lucretia Johanna van Winter," in *Simiolus*, 25, 1997, pp.103ff.) The most costly of this group was a flower piece by Jan van Huysum for which fl. 4500 was paid. (It is now in the Edw. Carter collection, Los Angeles.) Within a short time, a large number of the De Smeth paintings had been scattered to different parts of the continent, a few even going to Italy. An unusually large proportion can still be identified and are found in both European and North American museums. Apart from those already mentioned, the following are notable: *The Departure of Jacob from Laban* by Adriaen van de Velde (Wallace Collection, London); *The Artist's Studio* by Teniers and J.D. de Heem (Los Angeles County Museum of Art); *Interior with a Girl Interrupted at her Music* by Jan Vermeer (Frick Collection, New York); *Courtyard Scene* by Pieter de Hooch (National Gallery, London); *The Piebald Horse* by Potter (J. Paul Getty Museum, Los Angeles); *A Moor Presenting a Parrot to a Lady* by Berchem (Wadsworth Atheneum, Hartford, CT.); *Woman Selling Herring* by Metsu (Rijksmuseum, Amsterdam); and the *Village Wedding* by Jan Steen (Museum Boymans-Van Beuningen, Rotterdam). The full list would be much longer.

Another sign of the attention given this sale is the 20-page printed list of buyers and prices issued at its conclusion. The list does not indicate which lots were bought in, but this information is found in the RKDH I and LBDa copies of the catalogue. (The dealer J. de Vries was given the task of buying in the lots that did not meet their reserve.) According to the printed souvenir, the total receipts came to fl. 185,482, a figure repeated by other sources and annotators. Apparently a commission of 5 percent was also added to the price of all purchases, putting the final amount at approximately fl. 194,000. However, if this includes the unsold lots – eighteen are recorded as having been bought in – then the figure was obviously lower. The annotator of the LBDa copy of the catalogue, which probably belonged to Ph. van der Schley, one of the principal organizers of the sale, records the total as fl. 161,999 with fl. 23,160 left unsold. These are probably the most accurate figures. The unsold paintings reappeared at a sale in Amsterdam on September 18, 1811, that was devoted primarily to the collection of Hendrik Croese. De Smeth's books were sold on September 3/4, 1810, and his coins on September 5.

168 1810/08/06 and following days [Lugt 7844]

Philippus van der Schleij; Amsterdam, Ten Huize van C:D: Meerhof, Kastelein in het Oudezijds Heeren-Logement

Additional Auctioneers: Jan Ijver; Cornelis Sebille Roos; Jeronimo de Vries; Theodorus Franciscus Spaan

Seller(s) from Title Page: Een voornaam Liefhebber

Seller(s) from Auctioneer's Copy: V[ries]; R[oos]

Seller(s) from Other Sources: [J de Bos]

Seller Authority: Vries, Jeronimo de; Roos, Cornelis Sebille; Bos, J. de

Paintings Lots: 266

Catalogue Locations:

*EBNP I	Auctioneer's copy, annot. with all buyers and prices on interleaved pages as well as letters for the sellers.
AA I	Annot. with all buyers and prices.
MWH	Annot. in pencil with all buyers and prices.
AA II	Annot. with most buyers and prices.
MA	Annot. with most buyers and prices.
BPG I	Annot. in pencil with some buyers and most prices as well as a few comments. The annotations are hard to read. It belonged to the dealer J.B.P. Lebrun and at least some of the annotations are his.
RKDH	Annot. in pencil with a few buyers and prices. It belonged to Bredius.
BPG II	Not annot. It beloged to the dealer J.B.P. Lebrun.
BRB	Not annot.
FLNY	Not annot.
EBNP II	Not annot.
AAP	Incomplete, lacking pp.3–6, 11–14, 17–24, and 27–30. Not annot. It belonged previously to F. Lugt and RKDH.

Comments: The catalogue printed for this sale included 155 lots of paintings, but an unusually large number, 111 altogether, were added at the time of the sale, producing a total of 266 lots. The title page of the catalogue mentions only that the proprietor was "een vornaam liefhebber," but the EBNP copy of the catalogue, which must have belonged to one of the dealers who organized the sale, is annotated with letters next to each of the lots indicating that 13 consignments were included rather than just one. They are designated A-D, F-G, J, Q-S, U-V and X. From this sequence, one may assume that most, but probably not all, of the letters were arbitrarily chosen and did not represent the initials of the consigners' names. Probably the "A" pictures were those of the "vornaam liefhebber" mentioned on the title page, since that letter was often reserved for the most important consignment. This group consisted of 33 lots of paintings and also included all of the expensive items. The owner has not been identified, but a number of the paintings can be traced to sales held in the third quarter of the eighteenth century, and it appears to have been a cabinet formed during that period, not in more recent times. At least two of these paintings, a scene in a school by Jan Steen and a depiction of *Mercury, Argus and Io* by Adriaen van de Velde, had come from the P. Capello sale of May 6, 1767; a picture of a hermit by Dou (now in the Rijksmuseum) had earlier appeared in the Wierman sale on August 18, 1762; a scene of *Soldiers and a Girl Eating on an Ancient Tomb* by Dujardin (now in the Yale University Art Gallery, New Haven) had come from the Johan van der Marck sale of August 25, 1773; and lot 119, the *Calling of St. Matthew* by Weenix and Berchem (now in the Mauritshuis), had last appeared in an anonymous sale in Amsterdam on May 8, 1769. The provenance of these paintings during the fourth quarter of the century is unknown; possibly they remained in a single collection during most or all of that time. The painting by Adriaen van de Velde was the most successful lot in the sale, fetching fl. 3125, a surprisingly high price for this artist. (The painting is now lost.) At less than half this figure, fl. 1310, the painting by Dou was still an expensive piece. Five other lots from this group exceeded fl. 600, indicating that it was a cabinet of some importance whose identity should someday be found. A canal scene by Jan van der Heyden (now at Waddesdon Manor) also derives from this collection.

The "B" consignment consisted of 18 paintings, all of which had been bought in as the property of "C" on August 23, 1808 (cat. no.129). Eleven of these lots were bought in once more at the present sale at generally modest prices, indicating that they were less attractive than advertised. At least one can be identified: the depiction of *The Death of Ananias and Saphira*, possibly Jan Steen's earliest known painting, was in recent times in a private collection in the Netherlands. The "C" consigner is also unidentified, but it is worthy of note that nearly half of the lots in his group were purchased by W.H. Stoopendahl bidding for a client designated as "B."

Of the remaining consignments, three can be identified with some certainty. "R," who submitted 15 lots of paintings, is certainly the dealer C.S. Roos, and the pictures belonging to "V" can be traced to the dealer Jeronimo de Vries. The consigner "X" is somewhat more problematic, but can probably be identified with a certain J. de Bos. Three of his four lots were sold, but the fourth, a painting of *Rebecca and Abraham's Servant* by Ferdinand Bol, was bought in and reappeared as Bos's property on April 6, 1812, along with pictures that resembled in type those already sold. The totals for the sale are given in the EBNP I copy of the catalogue as fl. 1914:13.

169 1810/08/10 [Lugt 7848]

Gebroeders Van Ryp; Rotterdam, In den Stads Doele

Seller(s) from Title Page: None

Paintings Lots: 31

Catalogue Locations:

*EBNP	Annot. with all buyers and prices.
*RKDH	Annot. in pencil with all prices.
BPG	Not annot. It belonged to the dealer J.B.P. Lebrun.

Comments: This was a small sale of 31 lots of paintings held in Rotterdam by the brothers Van Rijp. No owner is mentioned, and it is possible that more than one was involved. Although some of the paintings are attributed to major artists, such as Jacob van Ruisdael, Nicolas Berchem, Paulus Potter, Gerard Dou, etc., the descriptions are very lackluster, and none of the pictures have been identified or traced to other sales. The most confusing aspect of the sale derives from the conflicting annotations in the two extant copies of the catalogue. Both have the prices of each lot, but they disagree with each other in all but one or two instances, and one of the two sets of annotations must be completely wrong. The EBNP copy of the catalogue is also annotated with the names of the buyers; these include some Rotterdam collectors, perhaps lending some credence to the prices found in that copy. The prices in the RKDH copy are generally, but not always, much lower, sometimes inexplicably so, making them more suspect. The last lot, for instance, described as representing *Bacchus and other Figures* by Honthorst, apparently was inscribed with the name "H Brugge" and the date 1628 (according to a note in the EBNP copy of the catalogue), meaning it was probably a signed work by Hendrick ter Brugghen that is now lost. The EBNP catalogue records the price as fl. 60, while the RKDH has just fl. 1.10. However, we have included both sets of prices, since it is impossible to determine conclusively which is correct. RKDH gives the total as fl. 644. Both catalogues agree that lot 2, a landscape by Pynacker which was sold for fl. 200, was the most successful lot.

169-A 1810/09/17–1810/09/18

S. van Benthem; Middelburg, In het Heeren Logement Antwerpen, staande in den Langendelft

Seller(s) from Title Page: Weleerw: Heer R. Engelberts, Emeritis Predikant te Oostsouburg [en] onderscheidene Liefhebbers

Seller Authority: Engelberts, R.

Paintings Lots: 17

Catalogue Locations:

*ZBM	Auctioneer's copy, annot. with all buyers and prices on interleaved pages.

Comments: This was a two-day sale of books in Middelburg that also included a few prints, medical instruments and miscellaneous objects. The catalogue does not include paintings, nor does the title page mention them, but the annotations in the ZBM copy of the catalogue list buyers and prices for some paintings without giving artists or titles. Just one lot, no.16, is described as "Brandspiegel."

170 1810/10/08–1810/10/13 [Lugt 7867]

P. van Daalen Wetters; Den Haag, Op den Hoek van het Hof-Cingel, Wyk K No.9

Seller(s) from Title Page: None

Paintings Lots: 16

Catalogue Locations:

MWH	Not annot.

Comments: This was a six-day sale of books in The Hague that included a number of paintings, drawings, prints, maps and miscellaneous items during the latter half of the sale. Sixteen lots of paintings were sold on the very last day. The auctioneer was Pieter van Daalen-Wetters, only 23 years old at the time, and the sale took place in the family bookshop on the Hofsingel. The paintings are reasonably well described for a book sale and the dimensions are also included. They consisted primarily of genre pieces, one of which, a self-portrait of the artist Aert Schouman playing with a cat, had appeared in a sale of the paintings belonging to Melis van Daalen Wetters held on October 24, 1803 (cat. no.67), and so was probably the property of the auctioneer. The results of the sale are not known.

171 1810/10/10 [Lugt 7868]

Caspar van Citters; Middelburg, Premises, not given

Seller(s) from Title Page: Caspar van Citters

Seller Authority: Citters, Caspar van

Paintings Lots: 165

Catalogue Locations:

BPG	Not annot. It belonged to the dealer J.B.P. Lebrun.
AAP	Not annot. The catalogue is addressed to "Mynheer Vorvier M.D. hoogstraete" who was evidently its original owner.
MA	Not annot. It is addressed to Mynheer Langenhaeke, lange Strandstraate.
RKDH	Not annot.
RAU	Not annot.

Comments: This was a lottery rather than an auction, organized by the collector Caspar van Citters (1746–1815), a resident of Middelburg. Citters was the son of Mr. Aernout van Citters and Sara Jacoba Ockerse of Middelburg. After an extended residence in the village of Tholen, he was delegated a councillor of Zeeland in 1782 and returned to live in Middelburg until his death there in 1815. In general it is not known how or where he acquired his paintings, but at least two of them, including a painting by Frans van Mieris (see below) that was considered to be one of the stars of the collection, and another by Ary de Vois, had come from the collection of W.A. Kien van Citters, presumably a relative, and had been bought in a sale of the latter's collection held in Amsterdam on August 21, 1798. At least one other, a depiction of *Mars and Venus* by Ottmar Elliger, had come from yet another relative, Caspar Jacob van Citters, and had appeared in the latter's sale in Middelburg on July 14, 1803 (cat. no.60).

In preparation for the lottery, which was to held at his home, Van Citters sold tickets and printed an extensive catalogue. In the introduction to the catalogue he mentions having been offered considerable sums for his paintings and having negotiated to sell his collection *en bloc*. However, the collection had remained intact and had even been augmented prior to the lottery. His old age, the worsened economic situation and an uncertainty about whether he would be able to maintain his residence are given as reasons for selling the paintings at this time. He also discusses how paintings had gained in popularity as investments and that their value had appreciated considerably in recent years.

As a condition for the sale, Van Citters states that he would proceed with the lottery only after 250 tickets, costing fl. 285 each, had been sold. The contents of the lottery were 165 numbers consisting of 188 paintings. The first prize consisted of the 71 finest paintings from the collection, and the second prize would be the remaining 117 pieces. The other prizes were various amounts of money, including 48 prizes of fl. 285, 50 prizes of fl. 142:50, and 25 prizes of fl. 100. However, the winner of the first prize was obligated to pay a surcharge of fl. 5000 to the seller, and the winner of the second prize would pay fl. 500. If the winners did not pay the surcharge, Van Citters reserved the right to retain 21 of the 71 paintings from the first prize and 17 of the 117 paintings from the second prize. These 38 paintings are enumerated in the "conditions" that follow the introduction to the catalogue. From the first prize, for instance, Van Citters intended to retain lot 33, described as depicting an old man and a young woman, which can be identified as a replica (or copy) of *The Wife of Jeroboam with the Prophet Ahijah* now in the Musée des Beaux-Arts in Lille. This painting was one of the two that Van Citters had inherited from W.A. Kien van Citters, and was apparently considered one of the highlights of the collection. (It had been bought in for fl. 200 at the sale in 1798.) Another item that he meant to retain was Cuyp's *Prince Frederick Henry at the Siege of Breda*. From the second prize he would retain, among others, *Lot and his Daughters* by Jordaens (lot 76) and two paintings by Ter Borch (lots 126 and 127). If the lottery had gone ahead as planned and Van Citters had succeeded in selling 250 tickets, he would have stood to gain over fl. 53,000. (See R. Kosse, *Een Raere Loterye*, 1992; and J.W. des Tombe, "Verloting van een Schilderijkabinet," *De Navorscher*, 546, 1906, pp.444–460.) However, it appears that the lottery did not take place, since virtually all of the paintings reappeared at an auction under Van Citters's name in Rotterdam on July 1, 1811. (A few of the minor and poorly described lots, including some landscapes and still lifes, cannot be identified in the later sale, but are probably there under different names.) At this later sale a number of the best lots brought reasonably good prices, with three lots exceeding fl. 200. However, the majority brought relatively small amounts, an indication that Van Citters had overvalued his cabinet.

172 1810/10/11 and following days [Lugt 7869]

Philippus van der Schleij; Amsterdam, Ten Huize van Carel Daniel Meerhof, Kastelein in het Oudezijds Heeren Logement

Additional Auctioneers: Jan Ijver; Cornelis Sebille Roos; Jeronimo de Vries; Theodorus Franciscus Spaan

Seller(s) from Title Page: None

Seller(s) from Auctioneer's Copy: R[oos]

Seller(s) from Other Sources: [Levy Pakker?]

Seller Authority: Roos, Cornelis Sebille; Pakker, Levy

Paintings Lots: 284

Catalogue Locations:

*EBNP	Auctioneer's copy, annot. with all buyers and prices on interleaved pages as well as letters for the sellers.
FLNY	Annot. with a few buyers and all prices.
RMA	Not annot.

Comments: This sale was dedicated entirely to paintings, 274 of which appear in the catalogue; ten more were added *hors du catalogue*. No owner is mentioned, but the EBNP copy of the catalogue is annotated with letters indicating the various consignments to which each lot belonged. There were ten consigners, designated as A-D, K, M, R, S, V and Y. The largest group, 95 lots, belonged to "A," and make up the "Vervolg der Schilderijen" at the back of the catalogue, lots 179–272. In contrast to most of the remainder of the catalogue, these lots are not given dimensions, and all brought very low prices; only three fetched more than fl. 10. The identity of the consigner is not known. The consignment "B" consisted of 23 lots of paintings, two or three of which had been acquired very recently. Lot 45a, a *View of Zoeterwoude* by Pieter van Liender, and perhaps a second lot by J. van Dregt, had been bought on August 6, 1810 (cat. no.168) by the dealer Levy Pakker, while lot 25, a depiction of *St. Ignatius* by Diepenbeeck, had been bought at the same sale either by Pakker or the dealer Dupré. (One of the six annotated catalogues gives the buyer as Pakker, while the remainder have Dupré.) Pakker normally dealt in very inexpensive paintings; most of those in this group would fit this description, so we have tentatively identified him as their owner. The 43 paintings in the "D" consignment probably belonged to the dealer Willem Gruyter Senior. Two of them can be traced to him and for some unexplained reason, he was commonly designated with this letter. The connection in this instance is, however, more tenuous than usual. All five of the paintings belonging to "K" had been bought by the dealer Ph. van der Schley at the sale held on July 25, 1804 (cat. no.79). It is doubtful, however, that they belonged to Van der Schley at the present sale. The use of this letter out of sequence implies that the owner's name did indeed begin with "K," and no doubt he had bought the paintings through Van der Schley. The five paintings belonging to "R" can be safely given to the dealer C.S. Roos, and those belonging to "V" surely came from Jeronimo de Vries, to whom one can be confidently traced. Both were among the co-auctioneers. The consigner "S" was probably the dealer Theodorus Spaan, another of the co-auctioneers, because four of the five unsold lots from this group of 26 lots were knocked down to him. However, the fifth was knocked down to Ph. van der Schley, so we have left their owner unidentified. Similarly, "Y" was probably Jan Yver, but it is not certain.

The sale was limited primarily to cheap pictures; only a small number were sold for more than fl. 10. Five lots exceeded fl. 100, and just one, lot 103, a landscape by Wijnants and Lingelbach, went much above that, reaching fl. 500. However, its consigner was "V," i.e. Jeronimo de Vries; since he was also its buyer, the price was most likely completely artificial.

173 1810/11/07 [Lugt 7876]

[B. Wild]; Utrecht, unknown

Seller(s) from Title Page: None

Paintings Lots: 68

Catalogue Locations:

*EBNP Incomplete, lacking a title page and including only pp.41–53. Annot. with all prices.

Comments: The only copy of the catalogue lacks the title page and pp.1–40, leaving just the section containing the paintings on pp.41–53, which, however, seems to be complete. The catalogue is inscribed "welke verkogt zyn op 7 November 1810 te Utrecht." The format conforms to that of other catalogues published by the auctioneer Bartholomeus Wild in Utrecht, and he was certainly responsible for the sale. The sale probably contained primarily books and perhaps other works of art as well. If the names of the owners were originally found on the title page, they are now lost. One may assume that he or they were from Utrecht or the neighborhood; this is borne out by the presence of six paintings by Willem Rutgaart van der Wall (1756–1813), an artist active only in Utrecht. Most of the paintings were landscapes, and although the dimensions are given, it is difficult to conclusively identify any of them. One unusual painting, lot 20, described as depicting an episode from Turkish history and as being signed "P. Lasman inv. D. Keyzer 1660," is certainly the painting by Thomas de Keyser now in the Fondation Custodia in Paris of *King Cyrus Returning the Vessels from the Temple to the Jews*, which De Keyser copied after a stained glass window by Lastman. (See *Gods, Saints & Heroes*, exhibition Washington, Detroit and Amsterdam, 1980, no.60.) This painting was sold for just fl. 16 on the present occasion. Another painting of *A Doctor and a Moorish Lady* by Reinier de La Haye (lot 65) closely resembles the description of a painting that appeared at an Amsterdam sale on November 28, 1808 (cat. no.135), but the dimensions differ. (It is probably the painting that was sold at Sotheby's in London on June 5, 1974, as lot 20.) The more important paintings in the sale, however, have not been identified. Two lots, no.5, a painting of poultry by Hondecoeter, and no.27, a landscape by Roelof van Vries, brought fl. 435 and fl. 431. A battle scene by Huchtenburgh is supposed to have brought fl. 300. Altogether it appears to have been an interesting collection whose owner may one day be identified.

174 1810/11/12–1810/11/14

G. Bakhuysen; Den Haag, Hoogstraat

Seller(s) from Title Page: Nagelaten door de Wel Edele Heer en Mr. J.N. Chanfleurij, in leven Advocaat voor de respective Hoven van Justicie, En de Heer L. Swanenburg

Seller Authority: Chanfleury, Jan Nicolaas, Mr.; Swanenburg, Leonard

Paintings Lots: 6

Catalogue Locations:

MWH Not annot.

Comments: This was a three-day sale of books held by the bookseller Gerrit Bakhuysen (1758–1823) at his premises in the Hoogstraat in The Hague. Some drawings, prints, scientific instruments and miscellanea were also included. The pictures were sold on the last day. The first seller can be identified as the unmarried Hague barrister Mr. Jan Nicolaas Chanfleury (1738–1810). Originally from Alphen, he studied law at Leyden University and became a barrister at the Court of Holland in 1761. At the time of his death he was living at the Tournooyveld [Wijk] J in The Hague (GAG, DTB Overlijden (Q.O.R.S.), inv.5, fol.13, nr.204). An inventory of his estate was made by the notary J.J. Verwoert. The second seller was Leonard Swanenburg (1730–1810), whose profession is unknown. It is possible that he is to be identified with the Leonardus Swanenburg who is recorded as a burgher in Amsterdam in 1798 and described as the son of the late Amsterdam broker Willem Swanenburg (GAA, Poortersboek 30, fol.184). At the time of his death his premises were Spuy P 294 in The Hague (GAG, DTB Overlijden (Q.O.R.S.), inv.5, fol.17, nr.291). The sale had just a few unattributed paintings of little importance, and the descriptions are so brief that in some cases one cannot be certain they are paintings and not prints.

175 1810/11/27–1810/11/29

A. Loosjes, Pz.; Haarlem, Zaal van het Prinsenhof

Seller(s) from Title Page: Nagelaten door wylen den Wel Eerwaarden en zeer Geleerden Heer Abraham Rutgers, In leven Bedienaar des H. Woords by de Nederd. Hervormde Gemeente te Haarlem

Seller Authority: Rutgers, Abraham, Ds.

Paintings Lots: 3

Catalogue Locations:

VBBA Not annot.

Comments: The contents of this three-day sale in Haarlem were primarily books. An appendix on the last day contained some maps, paintings and miscellanea. The seller was Abraham Rutgers (1751–1809), reverend of the Dutch Reformed Church in that city. A native of Aalsmeer and the son of the Rev. Paulus Rutgers (died 1801), he had resided in a number of cities before settling in Haarlem in 1779. He was an associate of the Hoorn preacher and collector Engelbertus Matthias Engelberts (1732–1807), with whom he had compiled a book of songs for the church. His portrait was painted by Wybrand Hendriks.

The sale was organized by the Haarlem bookseller, poet and novelist Adriaan Loosjes Pietersz. (1761–1818). It included just a few paintings of minor interest, none of which are attributed. The descriptions are very brief, and a few might be prints rather than paintings.

176 1810/12/03

Pieter van Braam; Dordrecht, Stads Venduhuis

Additional Auctioneers: Pieter Blussé, den Jongen

Seller(s) from Title Page: None

Paintings Lots: 76

Catalogue Locations:

VBBA Not annot.

Comments: This was a small sale of books organized by the Dordrecht booksellers Pieter van Braam and Pieter Blussé the Younger. At the conclusion of the sale there were some prints, drawings, paintings, musical instruments, etc. No owner is given, but some of the paintings had appeared in Van Braam and Blussé's sale of June 4/6, 1810 (cat. no.161) and so may have been part of their own stock. One of the paintings, lot one, signed and dated 1656 by Barent Fabritius and described as *A Slaughtered Pig*, can be identified with one now in the Gemäldegalerie in Berlin. The results of the sale are not recorded.

Index of Paintings

1801–1810

Sample Entry

[1] **Rembrant Harmensz. van Rijn (manner)**

[2]1810/[3]07/[4]23	[5]DOL[6]G1	[7]0073	[8]*Rembrandt* | [9]Twee stuks, een Sultan en Sultane, halver lijfs. Zeer uitvoerig en kunstig behandeld, in de manier, en als van Rembrandt, gem. Anno 1641 | [10]*This Lot:* Een Sultan, halver lijf [11]*Annots:* médiocre [12](EBNP) [13]*Mat:* op koper [14]*Fmt:* ovaal [15]*Size:* ieder hoog 6 duim, breed 4 duim [16]*Inscr:* Anno 1641 (dated) [17]*Notes:* Lots 73 and 74 were printed in the catalogue as one item. [18]*Loc:* Paris, France. Private collection.	[19]Mr Pieter van den Santheuvel	[20](Sold) [21]fl 3 for lots 73 & 74. [22]Strij [or] H

1 Artist
2 Year
3 Month
4 Day
5 City Code
6 Auctioneer's Code
7 Lot Number
8 Artist's Name from Catalogue
9 Title
10 Title Modifier
11 Annotations
12 Source of Annotation
13 Materials
14 Format
15 Size
16 Inscription
17 Notes
18 Present Location
19 Seller
20 Transaction
21 Price
22 Buyer

Aa, Dirk van der

1809/07/25	HGBSM	0112	*D. van der Aa* | Heracliet en Democriet | *Mat:* op doek *Size:* hoog 21, breed 17 en een half duim	D van der Aa	(Sold) fl 9:5 van Voorden
1809/07/25	HGBSM	0113	*D. van der Aa* | Een Apostel Petrus met den Haan | *Mat:* op doek *Size:* hoog 14 en een half, breed 11 en een half duim	D van der Aa	(Sold) fl 2:15 van der Aa
1809/07/25	HGBSM	0116	*D. van der Aa* | Twee Stuks, verbeeldende de Opstandinge van Christus | *Mat:* op paneel	D van der Aa	(Sold) fl 11 van der Aa
1809/07/25	HGBSM	0117	*D. van der Aa* | Rykdom en Overvloed door Kinderen verbeeld in Basrelief | *Mat:* op doek *Size:* hoog 36, breed 29 duim	D van der Aa	(Sold) fl 3:4 van der Aa
1809/07/25	HGBSM	0118	*D. van der Aa* | Een dito [Basrelief], verbeeldende de Sterrekunde | *Mat:* op doek *Size:* hoog 42, breed 29 en een half	D van der Aa	(Sold) fl 3:4 van der Aa [or] van Voorden
1809/07/25	HGBSM	0119	*D. van der Aa* | Een Dito [Basrelief], verbeeldende de Vryheid | *Mat:* op doek *Size:* hoog 36, breed 27 en een half duim	D van der Aa	(Sold) fl 3:6 van der Aa
1809/07/25	HGBSM	0120	*D. van der Aa* | Een Dito [Basrelief], zynde Zinnebeeldig | *Size:* hoog 34, breed 35 en een half duim	D van der Aa	(Sold) fl 4:2 ten Haaf
1809/07/25	HGBSM	0121	*D. van der Aa* | Een Offerhande in Canaé, en een dito onafgemaakt | *Mat:* op doek *Fmt:* ovaal *Size:* hoog 33, breed 43 duim	D van der Aa	(Sold) fl 7:5 Mes
1809/07/25	HGBSM	0122	*D. van der Aa* | Een Dito [Offerhande], met Danzende Kinderen | *Fmt:* ovaal *Size:* hoog 20 en een half, breed 27 duim	D van der Aa	(Sold) fl 9:5 Mes
1809/07/25	HGBSM	0123	*D. van der Aa* | Speelende Kindertjes op de wolken, verbeeldende de Zomer in 't Groen, geschildert door denzelven [D. van der Aa] | *Size:* hoog 23, breed 14 en een half duim	D van der Aa	(Sold) fl 1:2 Mes
1809/07/25	HGBSM	0185	*D. van der Aa* | Een kapitaal Autaerstuk [sic], verbeeldende de Verryzenis van Christus uit het Graf, door D. van der Aa 1790 | *Mat:* op doek *Size:* hoog 8 voet, breed 4 voet vier duim *Inscr:* D. van der Aa 1790 (signed and dated?) *Notes:* It is unclear whether the name and date are inscribed on the painting.	D van der Aa	(Sold) fl 100 van der Aa
1810/07/23	DOLGI	0001	*Dirk van der Aa* | Een Schoorsteenstuk, in 't graauw, zijnde Kindertjes, enz; eene Zinnebeeldige Ordonnantie op den Vrede | *Mat:* op doek *Fmt:* schoorsteenstuk *Size:* hoog 56, breed 32 duim	Mr Pieter van den Santheuvel	(Sold) fl 5 A van Wet Dordt

Aa, Dirk van der (copy by)

1809/07/25	HGBSM	0114	*D. van der Aa; P.P. Rubbens* | Een Heilige Famillie na P.P. Rubbens, door D. van der Aa | copy by Dirk Aa after Rubens *Mat:* op doek *Size:* hoog 36, breed 30 duim	D van der Aa	(Sold) fl 36 van der Aa
1809/07/25	HGBSM	0115	*D. van der Aa; J. de Wit* | Een Groep van Naakte Kinderen na J. de Wit, door D. van der Aa | copy by Dirk Aa after Jacob de Wit *Mat:* op doek *Size:* hoog 29 en een half, breed 24 duim	D van der Aa	(Sold) fl 12 van Eyk

Aalen, V. [Unidentified]

1810/10/10	MGCIT	0129	*v. Aalen* | Een Stukje, waarop eenige Groentens, Visch en Aardewerk, goed geschilderd	Caspar van Citters	(Unknown)

Aalst, van [Unidentified] (and Lingelbach, manner)

1802/11/01	DOBRA	0149	*van Aalst; Lingelbach* | Een Boomrijk Landschap, door van Aalst. De stoffagie als van Lingelbach | *Mat:* op paneel *Size:* hoog 15, br. 18 ½ duim		(Unknown) fl 40:10 for lots 149 & 150
1802/11/01	DOBRA	0150	*van Aalst; Lingelbach* | Een dito [Boomrijk Landschap], als boven [De stoffagie als van Lingelbach]; door van Aalst | *Mat:* op paneel *Size:* hoog 15, br. 18 ½ duim		(Unknown) fl 40:10 for lots 149 & 150

Accama

1801/04/23	AMYVR	0024	*Accama* | Het Pourtrait van den Kunstschilder Jan van Huysum, uitvoerig geschilderd		(Sold) fl 1 ¼ A Mayer
1804/10/29	HRBAU	0001	*Accama* | 't Pourtrait van W. C.H. Friso met den Staf van Commando | *Mat:* op doek *Size:* hoog 36, breed 28 duim	Simon Styl	(Unknown)
1804/10/29	HRBAU	0002	*Accama* | 't Pourtrait van H. K. H. Maria, Gemalin van Willem de derde, Koning van Engeland | *Mat:* op doek *Size:* hoog 36, breed 28 duim	Simon Styl	(Unknown)

Adolfi, Ciro

1802/07/20	MGSAN	0057	*C. Adolfie* | Een Medona [sic], op Doek | *Mat:* op doek *Size:* hoog duim 20, breed duim 16		(Unknown)

Adriaenssen, Alexander

1802/07/20	MGSAN	0060	*Adriaanssens* | Een Stuk, waarop Visch en verder Bywerk, op Paneel: zeer fraai | *Mat:* op paneel *Size:* hoog duim 28, breed duim 21		(Unknown)

Aelst, Evert van

1804/10/16	DLOND	0001	*E. van Aelst* | Ene Tafel met Vruchten. Quelques Fruits | *Mat:* op paneel *Size:* hoog 8, breed 11		(Unknown)

Aelst, Willem van

1801/03/16	AMSCH	0104	*van Aals* | Een stil leeven, natuurlyk	K[ip]	(Sold) fl 4:5 Cocler
1801/04/13	AMSCH	0001	*A. van Aalst* | Twee stuks stille leevens, zynde in het eene een hangende doode Haan, en dood Gevogelte, zo ook in het ander stuk; beide natuurlyk en uitvoerig gepenceeld | *Mat:* op doek *Size:* ieder hoog 33, breed 28 duim *Notes:* The artist's name was given as "A. van Aalst" but we have assumed this is an error.	Pierre Fouquet, junior	(Sold) fl 29 Lafontaine
1802/02/16	AMSCH	0011	*van Aalst* | Een stil Leeven fix gepenceeldt	B[uys]	(Sold) fl 2:5 van Dijl
1802/05/11	GRGRW	0011	*Van Aalst* | Een Bloemstuk in een Pot [Schilderijen met Olie-Verf; In zwarte Lijsten] | *Mat:* in olyverf *Notes:* The bracketed information in the title appears above lot 1 and refers to lots 1 to 79a.	Arnold Sicco Werumeus	(Unknown)
1802/05/11	GRGRW	0012	*Van Aalst* | Een dito [Bloemstuk] [Schilderijen met Olie-Verf; In zwarte Lijsten] | *Mat:* in olyverf *Notes:* The bracketed information in the title about the medium appears above lot 1 and refers to lots 1 to 79a.	Arnold Sicco Werumeus	(Unknown)
1802/08/24	LNDLS	0046	*G. van Aalst* | Een Patrijsvogel, rustende op een kleed dat op een steenen tafel ligt, boven hetzelve hangen Valken – kappen en Veldfluiten. Delicaat en uitvoerig geschilderd, door G. van Aalst, 1675 | *Mat:* op doek *Size:* hoog 18 ½, breed 15 ½ duimen *Inscr:* G. van Aalst, 1675 (signed and dated?) *Notes:* It is unclear whether the name and date are inscribed on the painting.	Leonardus Bouman [or others]	(Unknown) fl 11:10
1802/09/29	AMSCH	0001	*G. van Aelst* | Een Vrugtstuk. Hoog 32, breed 26 ½ duim, op Doek. In dit voortreffelyk Schildery, ziet men eenen steenen Baluster, gedeeltelyk bedekt met een carmosyn rood fluweel Kleed met goudene Franjen; waarop geplaatst zyn blaauwe en witte Druiven, met rank en bladeren, een Roemer met Rhynsche wyn, ter helfts gevult, en een zilver Bord met Persiken en geöpende gebradene Castagnien; onderscheide Insecten laten zig hier en daar bemerken; een afhangend bruin zyd Gordyn is met koorden en kwasten aan d'eene zyde opgenomen. Men ziet in dit Stuk de groote vermogens van der Konstenaar, alles evenaart de natuur, en de uitmuntende zuivere uitvoerigheid is gelyk aan zeer schoon Coloriet [Un des plus précieux Tableaux de cet artiste célébre, Tout y est rendu avec une verité Surprenante ; sur une Balustrade négligemment couverte d'un Tapis de velour [sic] cramoisy à franges d'or, sont placés un plat d'argent avec des Pêches & des chataignes, des raisins de differentes Espéces & un grand verre à moitié rempli de vin du Rhin, des Papillons & quelques Insectes, animent cette belle composition, un rideau d'Etoffe brune, relevé avec goût contraste avec le fond, à la beauté du Coloris.] | *Mat:* op doek *Size:* hoog 32, breed 26 ½ duim *Loc:* Antwerpen, Belgique. Koninklijk Museum voor Schone Kunsten. (729)	[Labouchere?]	(Sold) fl 71 Burtin
1802/09/29	AMSCH	0002	*G. van Aelst* | Dood Gevogelteu [sic]. Hoog 37, breed 30 ½ duim. Dit verwonderlyk schoone Schildery, waarin deezen grooten Konstenaar de natuur op eene onnavolgbaare wyze tot in het minste deel heeft nagebootst, doet meede zien, wat volmaaktheid in schilderkonst men kan bereiken; aan eenig touw en haak hangen een goud lakense bonten Haan, een spier witten Haan van een byzondere aart, en eenig ander klein Gevogelte. De twee Haanen zyn gedeeltelyk rustende op een marmere Tafel, met een Basrelief versierd [Le Tableau précedent mérita à tous Egards des éloges, celui-ci lui à èté mis de niveau par la plupart des curieux ; notre artiste heureux dans le beau choix de la nature Et inimatable [sic] dans ce genre, paroit par ce Tableau avoir trouvé un sujet, digne d'y employer ses plus grandes facultés. Deux coqs morts dont l'un d'un plumage varié des plus brillantes couleurs et l'autre a plûmes toutes blanches, d'une finesse singuliere, sont suspendus à des cordons & crochet ainsi que quelques beaux petits oiseaux ; ils reposont [sic] en partie sur, une Table de marbre, ornée d'un Basrelief antique : l'Illusion que produit ce beau morceau, fait qu'on l'admire sans-cesse, avec un nouveau plaisir.] | *Mat:* [sur toile] *Size:* hoog 37, breed 30 ¼ duim *Notes:* The material was given only in the French edition of the catalogue.	[Labouchere?]	(Sold) fl 44 de Roy
1802/11/01	DOBRA	0144	*Gillis van Aalst* | Een Marmeren Tafel, gedekt met een Fluweelen Kleed, waaröp blaauwe en witte Druiven, Persiken, Bladeren, en een glazen Pocaal; schoon en breed geschilderd door Gillis van Aalst, 1670 | *Mat:* op doek *Size:* hoog 28, breed 22 duim *Inscr:* Gillis van Aalst, 1670 (signed and dated?) *Notes:* The artist's name was given as "Gillis van Aalst" but we have assumed this is an error. It is unclear whether the name and date are inscribed on the painting.		(Unknown) fl 12:10
1802/12/13	AMSCH	0007	*G. van Aalst* | Twee stuks Tafels met Delicaaten Vrugten, als: Druyven, Persiken en Wyngaardsblaaden, waarop Insecten Aasen, uitvoerig gepenseeld | *Mat:* op doek *Size:* hoog 10, breed 12 ½ duim	Pruyssenaar [for] A	(Sold) fl 2 Gruiter
1803/07/18	AMSCH	0001	*Aalst. (W. van)* | Op een Marmere Tafel, gedeeltelyk met een Tapyten Kleed gedekt, staat een Zilvere Vaas, gevuld met verscheide geurige Bloemen, waarop eenige Insecten aazen, alles delicaat en uitvoerig geschilderd [Sur une table de marbre, garnie d'un tapis, est posé un Vase d'argent orné d'un bouquet de fleurs les plus brillantes ; la rose, l'oeuillet, la tilupe [sic], l'iris & autres fleurs s'y disputent la primautée [sic]. Nombre d'insectes ajoutent à l'agrément de cet ensemble. Le charme de la couleur, la netteté du pinceau, le fini des feuilles en font un morceau d'un vray mérite.] | *Mat:* op doek *Size:* hoog 38, breed 29 duim	Maria Theresia Andrioli	(Sold) fl 62 Thys

1804/05/07	AMSCH	0001	*Aalst (G. van)* | Een stil leeven; voor een steene Nis hangen twee doode Patrysen en verscheiden Vogeljachts-Tuig, beneevens en Blaashoorn, van onder staat een Marmere Tafel, waarop een blaauwe Wytasch met Goude Franje; alles zeer Natuurlyk Wytasch, met Goude Franje; alles zeer Natuurlyk, uitvoerig en fraai gepenceelt | *Mat:* op doek *Size:* hoog 25, breed 20 duim	Schley	(Sold) fl 101 Thais
1805/07/03	AMSCH	0001	*Aelst. (G. van)* | Op een Marmersteenen Tafel, staat een fles gevuld met fray geschakeerde Bloemen, waarop verscheide Insecten azen; alles dun en uitvoerig geschilderd | *Mat:* op doek *Size:* hoog 30 ½, breed 23 ½	R[oos]	(Sold) fl 60 Gruyter
1805/07/10	AMSCH	0004a	*A. van Aalst* | Op een Tafel met een Tapyt gedekt, staat een Porcelynen Kom, gevuld met delicate Vrugten, ter zyde een Goude Beeker, een Roemer, Broodje, enz. meesterlyk op Doek | *Mat:* op doek *Size:* hoog 51, breed 42 duim *Notes:* The artist's name was given as "A. van Aalst" but we have assumed this is an error.	R[oos]	(Sold) fl 14 Agina
1805/10/09	HGBSM	0042	*W. van Aalst* | Twee bloem stukken | *Mat:* op doek *Size:* byde hoog 19 breet 16 ½ duim	T H van Willigen [or others]	(Sold) fl 6 Ph Mey
1806/08/20	HGBSM	0034	*van Aelst* | Dit stuk, het welk door zijne waarheid en uitvoerigheid den aanschouwer tot zich lokt, verbeeld een doode Patrijs en eene rijke weitas op eene marmere tafel liggende: als mede eenige andere Vogels aan eene rits hangende en verder bijwerk | *Mat:* op doek *Size:* hoog 26, breed 21 duim *Notes:* This lot was misnumbered no. 35.	Macalester Loup [or others]	(Sold) fl 63 Thijs
1807/04/00	LNDLS	0043	*G. van Aalst* | Een dode vogel en een jachttuig, delicaat geschildert, door G. van Aalst, 1675 | *Mat:* op doek *Size:* hoog 18, breed 15 duim *Inscr:* G. van Aalst, 1675 (signed and dated?) *Notes:* It is unclear whether the name and date are inscribed on the painting.	[Abraham Delfos] [or others]	(Unknown)
1807/06/10	HGBSM	0043	*G. van Aalst* | Een dode vogel en een jachttuig, delicaat geschilderd, 1675 | *Mat:* op doek *Size:* hoog 18, breed 15 duim *Inscr:* 1675 (dated?) *Notes:* It is unclear whether the date is inscribed on the painting.	Abraham Delfos [or others]	(Sold) fl 1:12 Zwarts
1807/08/26	AMSCH	0001	*G. van Aalst* | Boven een Marmeren Tafel hangt dood Gevogelte, Jagthoorn, Valkenkappen, en ander Jagttuig; zeer natuurlyk en uitvoerig gepenceeld | *Mat:* op doek *Size:* hoog 29, breed 23 duim	Helsdinge	(Sold) fl 48 Coclair
1808/05/18	LNAN	0039	*van Aalst* | Eene doode hangende Patrijs-Vogel | *Notes:* The artist's name "van Aalst" was added in by hand in the RKDH copy of the catalogue.	Mr Cornelis Versluys	(Unknown)
1808/06/06	RMRIJ	0001	*Aalst. (Guillaume van)* | Eene glazen flesch, op eene marmeren Tafel staande, met een aantal differente soorten van Bloemen, op welke eenige Vlinders azen. Overheerlijk, uitvoerig en krachtig geschilderd [Dans un vase de cristal placé sur une Table de marbre s'offre aux regards un riche bouquet de belles Fleurs, sur lesquelles sont posé, ou voltigent plusieurs Papillons épars. Composition riche, d'une parfaite imitation de la nature, d'une couleur fraiche et du plus grand fini] | *Annots:* Aug. 1806 van P.J. Thys (f 160.-) (RMA I) *Mat:* op doek *Size:* Hoog 29 ½, en breed 22 ½ duim	Gerrit van der Pot, Heer van Groeneveld	(Sold) fl 300 van Beefting
1808/08/23	AMSCH	0002	*Aalst. (G. van)* | Op een Tafel met een Fluweel kleed bedekt, staat een zilveren Schotel, waar op twee Persiken, een tros Druiven en een Glas geplaatst is, ter zijde een Roemer met een geschilde Citroen en verder bijwerk; alles uitmuntend en van de beste behandeling van deeze Meester | *Mat:* op doek *Size:* hoog 28, breed 20 duim	H	(Bought In) fl 51
1809/04/17	AMSCH	0158	*van Aalst* | Een Steenen Tafel, waarop een Beker, gevuld met een menigte van geurige Bloemen, benevens eenige smakelijke Vruchten | *Mat:* op doek	[Gruyter?]	(Sold or Bought In) fl 2 Gruyter
1809/04/22	AMYVR	0001	*G. van Aalst* | In eene Nis ziet men eenige delikate Vruchten, zoo witte Druiven, Persiken, Peeren als anderen; smeltend gepenseelt | *Mat:* op doek *Size:* hoog 19, breed 18 duim	de Bruin	(Sold) fl 5:10 C S Roos
1809/04/22	AMYVR	0002	*G. Van Aalst* | Een Tafel, waarop een tros Druiven en een Persik | *Mat:* op doek *Size:* hoog 10, breed 12 duim	de Bruin	(Sold) fl 3:5 H G van Raan
1809/04/22	AMYVR	0003	*G. van Aalst* | Een stil leven | *Mat:* op doek *Size:* hoog 12, breed 10 duim	de Bruin	(Sold) fl 2:15 Yver
1810/03/26	RMMUY	0013	*Willem van Aalst* | Op eene marmere Tafel ligt eene fluweele Weijtas, daar op, en naastaan een goudlakensche inlandsche Faisant, boven dezelve een hangende Patrijs en ander gevogelte. Konstig natuurlijk en uitvoerig gepenceeld, en een der besten van dezen Meester [Sur un sôcle de marbre sont posés une Gibecière de velours, un Faisan doré d'Europe et une Gelinotte, une Perdrix attachée à une de ses pattes, et plusieurs petits Oiseaux de differentes espèces et suspendues, forment un bel ensemble. L'imitation des objets est parfaite, et précieusement fini, dans tout les details.] | *Mat:* op doek *Size:* hoog 34 ½, breed 26 ½ duimen	Daniel de Jongh Az	(Sold) fl 120 J W d Kock Rott[m]
1810/03/27	RMCNL	0057	*van Aalst* | Een klein, doch zeer netjes gepenseeld, Vruchtstukje, aardig behandeld		(Unknown)
1810/03/27	RMCNL	0087	*van Aalst* | Een klein Vrucht stukje, zeer delicaat gepenseeld		(Unknown)
1810/08/06	AMSCH	0001	*Aalst (G. van)* | Eene Tafel, gedekt met een Kleed, waarop geplaatst zijn Persiken, Druiven, enz. Zacht behandeld | *Mat:* op doek *Size:* hoog 19, breed 15 duimen	F	(Sold) fl 7 T Spaan
1810/10/10	MGCIT	0059	*G. v. Aalst* | Een Stuk, waarop verbeeld word een ongemeen fraai uitgevoerd Patrys, liggende met nog een Vogel op een steene Tafel; terwyl	Caspar van Citters	(Unknown)

			boven dezelve nog eenig Gevogelte aan een strik hangd; ongemeen delicaat behandeld		
1810/10/10	MGCIT	0094	*van Aalst* | Een fraai Stuk met Bloemen	Caspar van Citters	(Unknown)
1810/10/11	AMSCH	0001	*G. Van Aalst* | Op eene marmeren Tafel, met een zyd Kleed gedekt, staat een Mand, gevuld met blaauwe en witte Druiven, Persiken, Pruimen en andere Vruchten, waarop insekten azen; mals en zagt van schildering | *Mat:* op doek *Size:* hoog 30, breed 21 duimen	[Gruyter?]	(Sold or Bought In) fl 6 Gruiter
1810/10/11	AMSCH	0137	*V. Alst* | Een kapitaal Bloemstuk	[Gruyter?]	(Sold or Bought In) fl 2 Gruiter
			Aelst, Willem van (manner)		
1804/05/07	AMSCH	0223	*G. v. Aalst* | Twee hangende doode Vogels; in de manier van G. v. Aalst	Schley	(Sold) fl 0:8 Gruiter
1810/06/06	RMMUY	0056	*G. van Aelst* | Een hangende Patrys, Kruithoorn en Weytas, uitvoerig en natuurlijk geschilderd. Als door G. van Aelst | *Mat:* op doek		(Unknown) fl 6:10
			Aerk, R. [Unidentified]		
1802/05/10	MGSAN	0004	*R. Aerk* | Een Heuvelachtig Landschapje, waar op vertoond word, daar Venus met haar Nimphen den dooden Adonis beweenen, meesterachtig geschilderd, door R. Aerk: op Paneel | *Mat:* op paneel *Size:* hoog 29 duim, breed 40 duim	Johan Dirk Kruysse	(Unknown)
			Aertsen, Pieter (manner)		
1801/08/19	AMSCH	0150	*Lange Pier* | Een Keukenstuk; schoon gepenceeld, in de manier van Lange Pier	Van Forreest	(Sold) fl 0:10 Wijland
1810/06/06	RMMUY	0087[a]	*Langen Pier* | Een oud en raar stuk, verbeeldende eene Keuken, waar in verscheiden figuren goede cier maken, in 't verschiet eenigen die dansen en vrolijk zijn, in de manier of tijd van Langen Pier, geschilderd op Paneel. Op de achter zijde de lotgevallen van den Aartsvader Abraham, in 't graauw, in de manier van Frans Flores, zeer zuiver geconserveert | *This Lot:* Eene Keuken; lot 87[b] is manner of F. Floris (I) *Mat:* op paneel		(Sold) fl 3:10 for lots 87[a] & 87[b]. v Giesen
			Agricola, Christoph Ludwig		
1803/09/07	AMSCH	0005	*Agricola* | Twee stuks, met Heesters en Plantgewassen, alwaar verscheide Insecten op aasen, uitvoerig op Doek [Deux morceaux représentant des plantes et des buissons sur lesquels paturent diverses insectes ; peint avec beaucoup de détail] | *Mat:* op doek *Size:* hoog 18, breed 24 duim	Smidt	(Sold) fl 6 C S Roos
			Albani, Francesco (copy after)		
1803/04/27	AMSCH	0017	*P. d'Aquila; l'Albane* | La Sainte Vierge, l'Enfant Jésus, & St. Jean, belle Copie d'après l'Albane | copy by P. Aquila after Fr. Albani *Size:* h. 5, l. 3 ½ pieds	A	(Sold) fl 10:10 Esser
			Alcock		
1802/12/13	AMSCH	0008	*Alkok* | Twee stuks met cierlyke Vaasen, gevuld met een meenigte van geurige Bloemen, delicaat geschilderd, door Alkok, à London | *Mat:* op koper *Size:* hoog 12, breed 16 duim	Pruyssenaar [for] A	(Sold) fl 8:15 de Meijer
			Alcock, Edward		
1801/12/22	AMOTT	0074	*E. Alcock* | 1 Officier in een Leuningstoel, door E. Alcock, 1774 | *Inscr:* E. Alcock, 1774 (signed and dated?) *Notes:* It is unclear whether the name and date are inscribed on the painting.	Bartholomeus Ruloffs	(Unknown) fl 3
1803/12/15	MGLAC	0030	*Alcoek* | Een Mans Portrait met een Baard; kragtig geschilderd, als van Rembrand | *Mat:* op doek *Size:* hoog duim 14, breed duim 11	Mr L H de Haze Bomme	(Unknown)
1810/06/20	AMSCH	0002	*E. Alcok* | Een bejaard Krijgsman houdt een glas en degen in zijne handen | *Mat:* op koper *Size:* hoog 16, breed 12 duimen	A	(Sold) fl 4 Du Pree
			Alewyn, Abraham		
1805/10/09	HGBSM	0130	*A. Alewyn* | Een fraay landschap, ziet men op de voorgrond een staande en zittend beeldje, en verder stoffagie | *Mat:* op doek *Size:* hoog 24 breet 33 ½ duim	T H van Willigen [or others]	(Sold) fl 1:14 Van der Meer
			Ameron, van [Unidentified]		
1809/10/16	ARNIJ	0009	*Van Ameron* | Een binnen vertrek door van Ameron, in een goude Lijst	Wed N Nijhoff	(Sold) fl 6 v Leeuwen
			Amerongen, Jan van		
1810/03/27	RMCNL	0049	*Amerongen* | Een Binnenhuisje, waar in men een Boer aan Tafel ziet zitten, terwijl de Vrouw eene Fles op de Tafel brengt, aardig geschilderd		(Unknown)
			Amers, Piters (and Siberechts, J.)		
1809/04/22	AMYVR	0119	*Sibrechts; Amers* | In een Waterplas, omgeven met zwaar Geboomte, ziet men eene Boerin te Paard, met een Kopere Kan op haar schoot, eenig Vee voortdrijvende, schijnende te spreeken met eene andere Vrouw, welke haar voeten wascht, in de manier van A. Cuijp, door Sibrechts en Amers, 1672 | *Mat:* op doek *Size:* hoog 27, breed 23 duim *Inscr:* Sibrechts en Amers, 1672 (signed and dated?) *Notes:* It is unclear whether the names and date are inscribed on the painting.	de Bruin	(Sold) fl 14:10 du Pree

			Amigoni, Jacopo		
1801/04/13	AMSCH	0002	*Amiconi* | Een Sater een Bachante op den schoot houdende, waarby een Minnewigt; meesterlyk behandeld | *Mat:* op doek *Size:* hoog 82, breed 62 duim	Pierre Fouquet, junior	(Sold) fl 26 Texier
1803/04/27	AMSCH	0045	*Amiconi* | Venes [sic] & Cupidon | *Size:* h. 3 ½, l. 4 ½ pieds	A	(Sold) fl 2:15 Gruiter
1803/04/27	AMSCH	0093	*Amiconi* | Venus en Adonis | *Size:* h. 2 ½, l. 3 ½ pieds	A	(Sold) fl 2 Grimpen
1804/05/07	AMSCH	0003	*Amiconi* | Een Bybelsche Ordonantie, verbeelende Abraham zyn Zoon Isaäk willende offeren; meesterlyk behandeld | *Mat:* op doek *Size:* hoog 17, breed 14 duim	Y[ver] [for] JJ	(Sold) fl 5:10 Jan Spaan
1805/07/10	AMSCH	0004	*Amiconi* | Abraham Offerd zyn Zoon Isaäk; meesterlyk op Doek | *Mat:* op doek *Size:* hoog 17, breed 15 duim	V[inkeles] [for] M	(Sold) fl 14 Gruyter
			Andrea del Sarto		
1803/04/27	AMSCH	0074	*A. del Sarto* | La Sainte Vierge & l'Enfant Jésus, par A. del Sarto, peint sur bois | *Mat:* sur bois *Size:* h. 3, l. 2 pieds	A	(Sold) fl 4 L Pakker
1803/07/18	AMSCH	0050	*Sarto. (A. del)* | St. Jan den Dooper in zyn kindse jaaren, natuurlyk van grootte ten voeten uit, bezig zynde om uit een rots in een schaaltje water te tappen, voorts een bergachtig verschiet; de tekening is van een verheven styl, zoo ook het coloriet, en is wyders van een kloeke behandeling [St. Jean Baptiste dans son enfance : figure de proportion naturelle. Il se tient debout la tête tournée en face, tirant de l'eau d'une source sortant d'un rocher ; une draperie rouge flotte sur ses epaules. Le fond est terminé par un paysage largement traité. Cette figure d'essinée [sic] d'un grand stile unit à une couleur vigoureuse une exécution large & facile.] | *Mat:* op doek *Size:* hoog 44, breed 33 duim	Maria Theresia Andrioli	(Sold) fl 105 Hodges
1806/08/20	HGBSM	0092	*André Delsarto* | Een Heilige Famillie, zijnde Maria die het Kind Jesus liefkoosd, terwijl Joseph, in eene denkende houding, en twee Engelen zulks met diepe eerbied aanschouwen. Krachtig en schoon van coloriet | *Mat:* op koper *Size:* hoog 16 ¼, breed 14 duim	Macalester Loup [or others]	(Sold) fl 40 du Cloux
1809/06/13	AMSCH	0135	*A. del Sarto* | Een bevallig Kindje, verbeeldende St. Jan, staande in een Landschap, op de voorgrond een Mandje met twee Duiven; krachtig van koloriet, meesterlijk breed en fraai geschilderd | *Mat:* op doek *Size:* hoog 42, breed 32 duim	H[odges]	(Sold) fl 51 Spaan
			Andrea del Sarto (copy after)		
1808/06/13	AMSCH	0061	*Grandjean (J.); Andrea del Sarto* | Een Heilige Familie: zijnde een zeer fraaije Kopij, naar een zeer beroemd Schilderij van Andrea del Sarto, te Rome | copy by J. Grandjean after Andrea del Sarto *Size:* hoog 37, breed 36 duim	[Jan Tersteeg]	(Sold) fl 20 du Pré
1810/06/06	RMMUY	0003	*N. Pousijn; André del Sarto* | Een konstrijke Copij. Door N. Pousijn, naar André del Sarto. Verbeeldende eene heilige Familie, het origineel van dezelve grootte berust, in het Museum Napoléon te Parijs; en deze Copij besloeg wel eer eene aanzienlijke plaats in de eerste verzamelingen aldaar, en is gemonteerd in eene kostbare lijst | copy by N. Poussin after Andrea del Sarto *Mat:* op doek		(Sold) fl 200 Brunelli
			Anna, Vito d'		
1803/04/27	AMSCH	0026	*Vite D'Anna* | L'Ebauche d'un Tableau d'Autel, bien Composée, d'un bel effêt & largement peintre | *Size:* h. 2 ¼, l. 1 ½ pieds	A	(Sold) fl 81 Stevens
			Anne, P. d' [Unidentified]		
1803/04/27	AMSCH	0064[a]	*P. d'Anne* | Deux Esquisses de Tableaux dont l'une réprésente le Saveur Nourissant la Multitude, par P. d'Anne, & l'autre un Sujét historique | *This Lot:* Le Saveur Nourissant la Multitude; lot 64[b] by Anonymous	A	(Sold) fl 2 for lots 64[a] & 64[b]. Stevens
			Antonissen, Henricus Josephus		
1802/09/06	AMSCH	0002	*H. J. Antonissen* | In een Capitaal Heuvelagtig Landschap, met hoog Geboomten, ziet men op de voorgrond by een opgaande Wegh, een rustende Vrouw, als spreekende met een Huisman, die teegens een Os Leunt; verder vertoonen zig andere Reizigers, en een Rivier, waar by eenige Woningen; warm, zonagtig en meesterlyk gepenceeld | *Mat:* op doek *Size:* hoog 31, breed 43 duim	H^{n} Smit	(Sold) fl 66 W Reijers
1804/08/08	AMSCH	0001	*H J. Antonissen* | Op een met Gras en Kruiden bewassen Heuvel ziet men verscheide staande en leggende Ossen, Schapen en een Bokje, waarby een rustende Herder, met zyn Vrouw en Kind, als mede een Hond; verders een andere Herder, met twee Osjes, voorts een aangenaam verschiet, met Geboomte en een Watertje; zeer fraai geordineerd en van de beste schildering | *Mat:* op doek *Size:* hoog 30, breed 40 duim	Roos [for] C	(Bought In) fl 200 for lots 1 & 2
1804/08/08	AMSCH	0002	*H J. Antonissen* | Op een Heuvel staan twee Ossen, waarby eene leggende en verder een rustende Herder en Herderin, verders een Boomryk verschiet; in alles als de voorgaande behandeld | *Mat:* op doek *Size:* hoog 30, breed 40 duim	Roos [for] C	(Bought In) fl 200 for lots 1 & 2
1804/08/08	AMSCH	0003	*H J. Antonissen* | Twee stuks Bergachtige Landschappen, met hoog Geboomte, bevallig gestoffeerd met verscheide Beeldjes, Schapen, enz.; kragtig en zonachtig | *Mat:* op paneel *Size:* yder hoog 15, breed 18 duim	Roos [for] C	(Bought In) fl 120

1804/08/08	AMSCH	0004	*H J. Antonissen* | In een alleraangenaamst Boomryk en Bergachtig Landschap ziet men op 't Gebergte eenige capitaale Gebouwen en Boschadiën, op de voorgrond is de zandige Weg gestoffeerd met een Reiziger te Paard, die aan een daar passeerende Vrouw schynt naar den weg te vraagen; ter zyde op een grazige vlakte, onder 't zwaar opgaand Geboomte, zit een Landman met eenig Vée te rusten, van achteren een allerbevalligst verschiet; zonachtig en uitvoerig gepenceeld | *Mat:* op paneel *Size:* hoog 17 ½, br. 20 ½ duim	Vink[eles] [for] K[=Gruyter?]	(Bought In) fl 29 ½
1804/08/08	AMSCH	0005	*H J. Antonissen* | Een dito [alleraangenaamst] Boomryk Landschap, met een stil Water, meede geestig met Beeldjes en Beesjes gestoffeerd, en als de voorgaande geschilderd | *Mat:* op paneel *Size:* hoog 12, br. 16 duim	Roos [for] C	(Bought In) fl 50
1804/08/08	AMSCH	0006	*H J. Antonissen* | Op een Marmere Tafel staat een Vaas, gevuld met een ménigte geurige Bloemen, ter zyde legt een Tros Druiven en twee Persiken; delicaat en uitvoerig met de natuur overeenkomende gepenceeld | *Mat:* op doek *Size:* hoog 19, breed 15 duim	Roos [for] C	(Bought In) fl 20
1804/08/08	AMSCH	0007	*H J. Antonissen* | Op een dito [Marmere] Tafel staat een Schotel, gevuld met delicate Vruchten, als Persiken, blaauwe en witte Pruimen, ter zyde witte en blaauwe Druiven, een Glas met Wyn, geschilde Citroen, enz.; behandeld als de voorgaande | *Mat:* op doek *Size:* hoog 15, breed 18 duim	Roos [for] C	(Bought In) fl 32 for lots 7 & 8
1804/08/08	AMSCH	0008	*H J. Antonissen* | Een niet minder ryker Ordinantie, zynde meerendeels dezelfde Voorwerpen, in alles als de voorgaande | *Mat:* op doek *Size:* hoog 15, breed 19 duim	Roos [for] C	(Bought In) fl 32 for lots 7 & 8
1805/07/10	AMSCH	0003	*Antonissen* | Een fraay gestoffeert Landschapje; zonachtig op Paneel | *Mat:* op paneel	V[inkeles] [for] K	(Sold) fl 3:15 Gruyter
1806/08/20	HGBSM	0028	*S. J. Antonissen* | Een Landschap, met eene Herderin, rustende en staande Vee op de voorgrond, zeer uitvoerig en aangenaam van coloriet | *Mat:* op doek *Size:* hoog 22, breed 28 duim *Notes:* The artist's name was given as "S. J. Antonissen" but we have assumed this is an error.	Macalester Loup [or others]	(Sold) fl 40:10 Zwartsman
1807/08/26	AMSCH	0006	*H.J. Antonissen* | Een zon- en bergachtiig [sic] Landschap, op de voorgrond by een opgaande Weg ziet men een Man te Paard, die aan eene Vrouw, die nevens hem staat, de weg schynt te wyzen, verder een rustend Herder, by een Stam van een Boom, en Schapen en Bokken, benevens een aangenaam verschiet; | *Mat:* op paneel *Size:* hoog 17, breed 20 duim	de Vries	(Sold) fl 51 van Iperen
1809/06/13	AMSCH	0002	*J. Antonissen* | Twee stuks Duin- en Boomrijke Landschappen, met helder spiegelende Rivieren, beide rijk gestoffeerd met staand en leggend Vee, gaande en rustende Landlieden en Herders met Schapen; uitvoerig gepenceeld | *Mat:* op paneel *Size:* hoog 9, breed 12 duim	[Gruyter?]	(Sold) fl 20 Simon Heeren
1810/05/22	AMSCH	0003	*Antonissen (H. J.)* | In een Landzicht vertoonen zich twee bij elkander staande Beesten, zijnde een roskleurde Os en vaal bonte Koe; zeer uitvoerig van penceelbehandeling | *Mat:* op paneel *Size:* hoog 9, breed 12 duim	Johannes van de Putte Nicolaasz.	(Sold) fl 14:10 Jeronimo de Vries
			Appel		
1810/06/20	AMSCH	0184	*Appel* | Een Landschap, met grootsche Gebouwen en Ruine	A	(Sold) fl 10:10 van Iperen
			Appel, Jacob (I)		
1802/07/21	HGKAN	0044	*J. Appel den Ouden* | Een Binnenhuys waar in een Vrouw zich bezich houd met Groentens en Vrugten, terwyl de Man nevens haar zittende, een glas Bier in de hand hond. Voords een Dienstmaagd en Knegt de Groentens aan en wegbrengen, door J. Appel den Ouden, zwarte Lyst, op Doek | *Mat:* op doek		(Unknown)
1809/06/13	AMSCH	0004	*J. Appel* | In een sterk woelende Zee, ziet men een groot Schip, welk door een Lootsschuit gepraid [sic] word | *Size:* hoog 14, breed 17 ½ duim	Q	(Sold) fl 1:15 Meijer
			Appelman, Bartholomäus		
1802/05/05	AMSCH	0002	*Appelman* | Een gezicht op een Oud Kasteel, op de voorgrond Reizigers en eenige Beesten, die door een Water gaan | *Mat:* op paneel *Size:* hoog 16, breed 21 duim	G	(Sold) fl 8:10 Cocler
1803/08/17	AMSCH	0004	*Appelman. (B.)* | Een Gezicht op Ponte Molle by Romen, in de Rivier eenige Beesjes, ter zyde op het land twee Beeldjes, zoo ook op de Brug; zonachtig en bevallig behandeld. De Schilderyën van dezen Meester zyn zeldzaam | *Mat:* op doek op paneel *Size:* hoog 13, breed 17 duim	Anna Catharina Putman	(Bought In) fl 5:5
1810/03/26	RMMUY	0074	*Barent Appelman* | Een Italiaansch Land- en Water Gezigt. Warm van coloriet, en fix behandeld, in de manier van Asselijn [Un paysage Vue d'Italie, d'un joli ton, et dans la maniere d'Asselin.] | *Annots:* Ponte Molle (BPG) *Notes:* This lot was printed in the French edition of the catalogue as lot 75.	Daniel de Jongh Az	(Sold) fl 7 Le Brun Parys
			Apshoven		
1802/06/16	AMSCH	0003	*J. Abshoven* | Een Gezelschap van Boeren, zich vermaakende met Drinken en Rooken, verders eenig bywerk, breed behandeld | *Mat:* op doek *Size:* hoog 23 ½, breed 28 ½ duim	[Merrem]	(Sold) fl 5:5 H de Valk

1803/04/20	AMSCH	0001	*Abshoven* | In een Boere Doctor zyn Studeer Vertrek, zit den Medicus voor een tafel, waar op Boeken en flessen geplaatst zyn, houdende een Urinaal in de hand: ter zyde staat een bedaagde Vrouw, en verder eenige huislieden by een toonbank, gestoffeert met verder bywerk, meesterlyk gepenceeld [Un Medecin villageois assis dans son Laboratoire se voit occupé à examiner l'urine d'une vielle qui paroit le consulter ; d'utres [sic] personnages attendant devant la boutique qui est garnie de differens objets relatifs au sujet. Ce tableau est bien traité.] | *Mat:* op paneel *Size:* hoog 12, breed 15 duim	Maria Magdalena van Sluypwyk, gravinne van Moens	(Sold) fl 115 Pruijssenaar
1803/04/20	AMSCH	0002	*Abshoven* | Een Boere Binnenhuis waarin drie Boeren zich met rooken vermaken; een derzelven gaat met een kan de Deur uit; bevallig in de manier van D. Teniers gepenceeld [Dans l'interieur d'une habitation rustique sont trois hommes occupés à fumer ; l'un d'eux s'en allant tirer de la Bierre, très joliment peint dans la maniere de Teniers.] | *Mat:* op paneel *Size:* hoog 9, breed 8 duim	Maria Magdalena van Sluypwyk, gravinne van Moens	(Sold) fl 21 de Bie
1803/08/01	AMSCH	0001	*Van Abshoven. (J.)* | In een Binnenvertrek zitten twee Boeren by een bank, op de kaart te speelen, waarby twee anderen die het spel aanzien, in een ander Vertrek ziet men een Vuur, waarby zich eenige Huislieden staan te warmen, krachtig en natuurlyk gepenceeld | *Mat:* op koper *Size:* hoog 10, breed 12 ½ duim	J	(Sold) fl 40 J[b] Roelofs
1805/07/03	AMSCH	0056	*Abshoven* | Een zittende bedaagde Chimist, in zyn Laboratorium, by het Fournuis, bézig vuur onder een kroes aan te blaazen: verder ziet men werkende Bedienden; voorts gestoffeerd, met verscheide gereedschappen; alles is helder en bevallig van penceel behandeling | *Mat:* op paneel *Size:* hoog 15, breed 19 duim	R[oos]	(Sold) fl 36 T van Iperen
1805/07/10	AMSCH	0002	*Abshoven* | In een Boere Binnenhuys ziet men eenige vrolyke Lieden te Eeten en galantiseeren, &c. en verder bywerk; meesterlyk op Doek | *Mat:* op doek	V[inkeles] [for] K	(Sold) fl 29 L Pakker
1806/08/13	AMSCH	0002	*Abshoven* | In een Binnenvertrek, zit een studeerende Philosooph, in aloude kleeding, by een tafel, met een kleed bedekt, waar op boeken, zandloper, en doodschoofd geplaatst is, kragtig en uitvoerig gepenceeld | *Mat:* op paneel *Size:* hoog 14, breed 13 duim	Roos	(Sold) fl 6:10 van Iperen
1806/08/13	AMSCH	0245	*Abshoven* | Een Boerebinnehuis met rokende en drinkende Boeren	Vinkeles [for] G[ruyter]	(Sold) fl 4 Hafner
1808/11/28	AMSCH	0001	*Abshoven* | Twee stuks Boere Binnenhuijzen, met rokende, spelende en drinkende Huislieden en verder bijwerk, geestig | *Mat:* op paneel *Size:* hoog 10, breed 14 duim	[Gruyter?]	(Sold) fl 25 S M Levy
1809/04/22	AMYVR	0004	*Abshoven* | Twee stuks rijk met Beelden gestoffeerde Dorpgezichten; fraai | *Mat:* op doek *Size:* hoog 11, breed 15 duim	de Bruin	(Bought In) fl 35
1809/04/22	AMYVR	0005	*Abshoven* | Een Doktor in zijn Kamer, zittende te studeeren; geestig | *Mat:* op paneel *Size:* hoog 14, breed 13 duim	de Bruin	(Sold) fl 3:10 Duprée
1810/10/10	MGCIT	0068	*Abshoven* | Een Oud Man, zittende voor een Tafel, met een rood Kleed, lezende in een Boek; delicaat geschilderd	Caspar van Citters	(Unknown)
1810/10/11	AMSCH	0002	*Abshoven* | Het Binnengezigt van een Corps de Garde, vooraan ligt eene menigte Krijgstuig, verder rokende en op de kaart speelende Krijgslieden; bevallig en uitvoerig, als D. Teniers geschilderd | *Mat:* op paneel *Size:* hoog 25, breed 33 duimen	M	(Sold) fl 50 Roos
			Apshoven (manner)		
1801/03/16	AMSCH	0028	*Abshoven* | Een Boere Binnehuis met diverse Boeren, in de manier van Abshoven	K[ip]	(Sold) fl 2:5 Van Iperen
1801/03/16	AMSCH	0029	*Abshoven* | Een dito [een Boere Binnehuis] als dito [Abshoven]	K[ip]	(Sold) fl 7 Wijland
			Aquila, Pietro		
1803/04/27	AMSCH	0018	*P. d'Aquila* | Loth & ses filles | *Size:* h. 5 ¼, l. 5 ¼ pieds	A	(Sold) fl 8 H Pakker
			Aquila, Pietro (copy by)		
1803/04/27	AMSCH	0016	*P. d'Aquila; Titiën* | Une bonne Copie d'Après la Danäé du Titiën | copy by P. Aquila after Tiziano *Size:* h. 4 ½, l. 6 pieds	A	(Sold) fl 10:10 V d Brink
1803/04/27	AMSCH	0017	*P. d'Aquila; l'Albane* | La Sainte Vierge, l'Enfant Jésus, & St. Jean, belle Copie d'après l'Albane | copy by P. Aquila after Fr. Albani *Size:* h. 5, l. 3 ½ pieds	A	(Sold) fl 10:10 Esser
			Arends, Jan		
1804/10/16	DLOND	0002	*J. Arends* | Twee stukjens. Riviergezicht met verscheiden Schepen. Deux pièces. Vue de la Rivière & des Vaisseaux | *This Lot:* Een stukje. Riviergezicht *Mat:* op paneel *Size:* hoog 12, breed 16 *Notes:* Lots 2 and 3 were printed in the catalogue as one item.		(Unknown)
1804/10/16	DLOND	0003	*J. Arends* | Twee stukjens. Riviergezicht met verscheiden Schepen. Deux pièces. Vue de la Rivière & des Vaisseaux | *This Lot:* Een stukje. Riviergezicht. *Mat:* op paneel *Size:* hoog 12, breed 16 *Notes:* Lots 2 and 3 were printed in the catalogue as one item.		(Unknown)

Arthois, Jacques d'

1807/08/26	AMSCH	0002	*J. d'Arthois* | Een boomryk Bosch, gestoffeerd met Beeldjes; zynde zonachtig en meesterlyk op Doek behandeld | *Mat:* op doek *Size:* hoog 24, breed 35 duim	Roos	(Sold) fl 3 du Pree
1810/07/26	AMSCH	0088	*Van Artois* | Twee kleine Landschapjes, met Beeldjes gestoffeerd | *Mat:* op koper *Size:* hoog 6, breed 8 duimen	Cassino	(Sold) fl 0:18 Lohuys
1810/07/26	AMSCH	0089	*Van Artois* | Twee Landschapjes, als de voorgaande | *Mat:* op paneel *Size:* hoog 6, breed 7 duimen	Cassino	(Sold) fl 0:18 Immos

Asch, Pieter Jansz. van

1801/05/11	AMSCH	0003	*J. van Asch* | Een Dorpgezicht langs een stil Water, met Vaartuigen gestoffeerd, op de Voorgrond ziet men een grazige wyde, met Koeibeesten en twee Landlieden, alles is bevallig en natuurlyk geschilderd | *Mat:* op paneel *Size:* hoog 14, breed 19 duim *Notes:* The artist's name was given as "J. van Asch" but we have assumed this is an error.	P[ruyssenaar]	(Sold) fl 29 Pruijssenaar [for] R
1801/05/11	AMSCH	0004	*J. van As* | Twee stuks Hollandsche Landschappen, met beeldjes gestoffeerd, meesterlyk geschilderd | *Mat:* op paneel *Size:* hoog 7, breed 9 duim *Notes:* The artist's name was given as "J. van As" but we have assumed this is an error.	P[ruyssenaar]	(Sold) fl 9 C S Roos
1801/05/11	AMSCH	0005	*J. van As* | Een bevallig Landschap met hoog geboomte, op de Voorgrond ziet men Jagers met honden by zig, krachtig van coloriet en fix gepenceeld | *Mat:* op paneel *Size:* hoog 16, breed 22 duim *Notes:* The artist's name was given as "J. van As" but we have assumed this is an error.	P[ruyssenaar]	(Sold) fl 24:10 Rijnders
1802/05/05	AMSCH	0003	*P. van As* | Twee stuks aangenaame Land- en Dorpgezigten, met Waterplassen en fraaije stoffagie. Alles natuurlyk en bevallig gepenceeld | *Mat:* op paneel *Size:* hoog 7, breed 9 duim	A	(Sold) fl 10:10 Spruit
1802/05/05	AMSCH	0004	*P. van As* | Een Glas, staande op een Tafel, gevuld met verscheide fraaije Bloemen, zeer dun behandeld | *Mat:* op paneel *Size:* hoog 12, breed 14 duim	C	(Sold) fl 1 L^y Pakker
1802/05/05	AMSCH	0005	*P. van As* | Eenige fraaije Bloemen | *Mat:* op paneel *Size:* hoog 9, breed 7 duim	G	(Sold) fl 1 Gruiter
1802/09/21	UTHDG	0001	*P.J. van Asch* | Tusschen een Rivier, en eene hoogte met Ruïnes en geboomte, loopt een weg waarop twee Ossen en vier Schaapen worden voortgedreeven, verder eer Aak met volk, een Bosch, en een Bergagtig doorzigt. Zonägtig en helder | *Mat:* op paneel *Size:* hoog 9, breed 11 ½ duimen		(Sold) fl 28 J Niekerk Juffer Straat
1802/09/29	AMSCH	0003	*P. Jansz. van Asch* | Een Landschap. Hoog 21 ½, breed 16 duim. Paneel. Waarin eenig fraai geboomten langs het water, verders bevallig stoffagie; zonägtig en dun van Penceelbehandeling [Un beau Paysage, qu'une Eau traverse, entre des terrasses irrégulieres et des arbres de belle forme ; orné de quelques figures, les Effets du soleil y sont observés à produire l'Illusion.] | *Mat:* op paneel *Size:* hoog 21 ½, breed 16 duim	[Labouchere?]	(Sold) fl 20 C S Roos
1803/09/07	AMSCH	0004	*P. J. van Asch* | Een boomryk Landschap of Boschgezigt, gestoffeerd met verscheide wandelende Beeldjes; het Geboomte is zeer natuurlyk, de Lugt dun, en alles van een aangenaame behandeling [Un paysage enrichi d'arbres, ou vue d'un bois, vivifiée par diverses figures ambulantes ; la feuillée en est très naturelle, l'air est fluide et le tout traité d'une manière bien agréable] | *Mat:* op paneel *Size:* hoog 21, breed 32 duim	Smidt	(Bought In) fl 16
1804/02/27	AMSCH	0001	*Asch. (P. J. van)* | In een Boomryk Landschap, ziet men op den voorgrond een Heer te Paard, nevens hem een Bedelaar, Hond, enz; zonachtig en uitvoerig gepenceeld | *Mat:* op paneel *Size:* hoog 15, breed 13 duim	D	(Sold) fl 16:10 for lots 1 & 2. Coclers
1804/02/27	AMSCH	0002	*Asch. (P. J. van)* | Een dito [Boomryk] dito Landschap, op den voorgrond een Man en een Vrouw, verders een aangenaam verschiet, zynde niet minder dan de voorgaande | *Size:* hoog 15, breed 13 duim *Notes:* It is unclear what "dito" refers to in the title.	D	(Sold) fl 16:10 for lots 1 & 2. Coclers
1804/05/07	AMSCH	0002	*Asch. (P. van)* | Een Dorpgezicht, voorstellende een Boeren-Kermis en Paardenmarkt; vol gewoel en geestig behandeld | *Mat:* op paneel *Size:* hoog 18, breed 24 duim	Y[ver] [for] W	(Bought In) fl 6
1804/10/16	DLOND	0005	*P. van As* | Een stuk met Vruchten, Schulpen, Kapellen. Des Fruits, Coquilles & Papillons | *Mat:* op paneel *Size:* hoog 13, breed 18		(Unknown)
1804/10/16	DLOND	0006	*P. van As* | Een Landschap met Geboomte en gestoffeerd. Paysage avec des Figures de		(Unknown)
1805/07/10	AMSCH	0001	*P. J. van Asch* | Twee stuks Boomryke Landschappen, gestoffeert met allerhande soorten van Vee; zonachtig en uitvoerig op Paneel | *Mat:* op paneel	V[inkeles] [for] K	(Sold) fl 32 Gruyter
1806/08/20	HGBSM	0227[H]	*van As* | Een Landschap met veel geboomten V van As | *Notes:* This lot was added in by hand in the JPGM copy of the catalogue.	Macalester Loup [or others]	(Sold) fl 11:10 Spruyt
1807/08/26	AMSCH	0003	*P. v. As* | Een bevallig boomryk Landzicht, op de voorgrond twee Beesten by een Waterplas, verder eene Vrouw, eenig Vee voortdryvende, en een aangenaam verschiet; zonachtig behandeld | *Size:* hoog 10, breed 8 duim	Roos [for] A	(Sold) fl 10 T Spaan

1808/06/11	RMRIJ	0080	*P: van As* | Een aangenaam Boomryk Landschap, aartig gestoffeerd | *Mat:* op paneel *Size:* hoog 12 ½, breed 10 duim		(Sold) fl 14 Van Leen
1808/06/11	RMRIJ	0081	*P: van As* | Een dito [aangenaam Boomryk Landschap], als 't voorgaande | *Mat:* op paneel *Size:* hoog 6 ¾, breed 5 duim		(Sold) fl 9 Van Leen
1808/08/23	AMSCH	0198	*P. van Ast* | Een natuurlijk Land- en Watergezicht, met opgaande Geboomte en Stoffagie	[Gruyter?]	(Bought In) fl 9:10
1809/06/13	AMSCH	0195	*P. van Ast* | Een Boomrijk Landschap met stoffagie	Y	(Sold) fl 0:10 L Pakker
			Asch, Pieter Jansz. van (and Lingelbach)		
1810/06/06	RMMUY	0045	*P. van As; Lingelbach* | Een Landschapje, waar in een kerk, op den weg een Postwagen en verdere Figuren, fiks geschilderd. Door P. van As, en gestoffeerd door Lingelbach | *Mat:* op paneel		(Unknown) fl 10
			Asch, Pieter Jansz. van (and Palamedesz.)		
1804/10/16	DLOND	0004	*P. van As; Palamedes* | Een Landschap vol geboomte en gestoffeerd door Palamedes en anderen. Paysage avec des figures de Palamedes & d'autres | *Mat:* op paneel *Size:* hoog 23, breed 35		(Unknown)
			Asch, Pieter Jansz. van (and Schellinks, W.)		
1808/08/23	AMSCH	0003	*Asch (P. van); W. Schellings* | Een capitaal hoog bergachtig Landschap, met opgaand geboomten, ter zijde over een helderen Rivier een steene Sluis, gestoffeert met Heeren te Paard, rustende Reisigers, beladen Muil-Ezels en andere figuuren; zonachtig behandeld | *Mat:* op doek *Size:* hoog 28, breed 38 duim	[Gruyter?]	(Bought In) fl 19:10
			Asselyn, A. [Unidentified]		
1804/10/29	HRBAU	0003	*Asselyn, (A.)* | Een bevallig Zeegezigt, waar, voor aan op een zandbank, eenige Visschers in hun beroep bezig zyn; wyders ziet men een menigte dryvende Vaartuigen en Oorlogscheepen en in het verschiet een' Wal. Alles is zeer fraai behandeld | *Mat:* op paneel *Size:* hoog 14, breed 25 duim	Simon Styl	(Unknown)
			Asselyn, Jan		
1801/05/11	AMSCH	0001	*J. Asselyn, (bygenaamd Crabbetje)* | Voor een Rots ziet men een bruin en een wit Paard, nevens eenige Landlieden en Honden; alles zonachtig en krachtig geschilderd | *Mat:* op paneel *Size:* hoog 12, breed 14 duim	P[ruyssenaar]	(Sold) fl 161 v d Schley [for] Z[=Putte]
1801/05/11	AMSCH	0002	*J. Asselyn, (bygenaamd Crabbetje)* | Langs een stil Water, ziet men de ruïne van oude Gebouwen, gestoffeerd met beelden en beesten, verders een bergachtig verschiet, zonachtig behandeld | *Mat:* op doek *Size:* hoog 25, breed 29 duim	P[ruyssenaar]	(Sold) fl 14:10 Rijnders
1801/06/10	AMSCH	0001	*Asselyn, (J. alias Crabbetje)* | Deeze capitaale en ryke Ordonantie, stelt voor een bevrosen Rivier, langs een oud Kasteel, fraai gestoffeert; op den voorgrond ziet men drie Ezels, met hout en lammeren beladen, op een derzelven zit een bedaard Vrouwtje, agter dezelve een Landman en een Hond, ter zyde ziet men Visschers, een net uit het ys trekken, verders nog een menigte Beelden en Beesten, en een bergagtig verschiet. Dit uitmuntafreel [sic] is fraai van ligt en bruin, en een der beste van deezen Meester | *Mat:* op doek *Size:* hoog 28, breed 40 duim *Loc:* Amsterdam, Nederland. Rijksmuseum. (A 2112) as Wm. Schellinks	Herman ten Kate	(Sold) fl 716 J Ijver
1801/06/10	AMSCH	0002	*Asselyn, (J. alias Crabbetje)* | Dit niet minder, dan het voorgaande alleruitmuntend behandeld Meesterstuk, steld voor, eene warme Zomersche avond, in een aangegenaam [sic] bergachtig Landschap, meteen Rivier, waardoor eenig Vee waad, men ziet op de voorgrond eenige Herders, een belade Paard en een Dame op een Ezel. Alles meesterlyk behandeld | *Mat:* op doek *Size:* hoog 36, breed 48 duim	Herman ten Kate	(Sold) fl 600 J Ijver
1801/06/10	AMSCH	0003	*Asselyn, (J. alias Crabbetje)* | Een Grot, van binnen bevallig gestoffeerd, met een menigte Beeldjes en Beesten, verders een aangenaam verschiet. Fraai van ligt en uitvoerig geschilderd | *Mat:* op doek *Size:* hoog 18, breed 17 duim	Herman ten Kate	(Sold) fl 145 Thys
1801/06/10	AMSCH	0004	*Asselyn, (J. alias Crabbetje)* | Een Landschap op de voorgrond langs een stil Water, gestoffeerd met een Koey en Schaapen, nevens twee Ezels. Zonachtig behandeld | *Mat:* op paneel *Size:* hoog 7, breed 10 duim	Herman ten Kate	(Sold) fl 50 v d Schley [for] Pätte
1801/10/19	AMSCH	0001	*Asselyn. (J.)* | Een Italiaansch Landschap met een Ruïne, een Man te Paard, eenige rustende en wandelende Beelden, en belaade Ezels; van de beste zoort van Schildering | companion to lot 2, by D. Maes *Mat:* op paneel *Size:* hoog 7, breed 10 ½ duim	Jonkheer Menno Baron van Coehoorn	(Sold) fl 57 Hulswit
1802/05/05	AMSCH	0001	*Asselyn* | Een Bergachtig Landschap, met stoffagie van Beelden en Beesten, dun behandeld | *Mat:* op paneel *Size:* hoog 15, breed 12 duim	C	(Sold) fl 6:10 Claasens
1802/06/16	AMSCH	0002	*J. Asselyn* | Dit Capitaal stuk vertoond een Italiaansch Bergachtig Landschap, gedeeltelyk met klein Houtgewas: op de Voorgrond staat een Vééhoeder, verzeld van rustende en staande Schaapen, en een Ram; verder zit een Huisman, en op een gedeelten van een Berg staat een Gedenkteeken. Alles is Natuurlyk, zonachtig, en van een malsche Penceel-behandeling | *Mat:* op paneel *Size:* hoog 22, breed 19 duim	[Merrem]	(Sold) fl 37 J Yver

1802/09/06	AMSCH	0001	*J. Asselyn* | Twee stuks Italiaansche Landschappen, met vervallen Gebouwen en Bergachtige verschieten, gestoffeerd met Landlieden en onderscheiden Vee; meesterachtig geschilderd | *Mat:* op paneel *Size:* hoog 9, breed 8 duim	J	(Sold) fl 8:5 Abraham Schotte
1802/12/13	AMSCH	0001	*J. Asselyn* | In een Rotsagtig Landschap, ter zyden by een Waterval en een aangenaam verschiet, vertoonen zig zwemmende Jongens en andere Beeldjes, kragtig geschilderd | *Mat:* op doek *Size:* hoog 19, breed 25 ½ duim	Pruyssenaar [for] A	(Sold) fl 1 L Pakker
1802/12/13	AMSCH	0002	*J. Asselyn* | Een Wintergezicht met Gebouwen, by een Steene Brug, op de voorgrond een beladen Muil-Ezel, en andere stoffagie | *Mat:* op paneel *Size:* hoog 11, breed 10 duim	Pruyssenaar [for] D	(Sold) fl 6:10 L Pakker
1802/12/13	AMSCH	0003	*J. Asselyn* | Een Landschap, met verscheide stoffagie, door denzelven [J. Asselyn], fix behandeld	Pruyssenaar [for] B	(Sold) fl 8 Mensart
1803/08/17	AMSCH	0003	*Asselyn, (J.) alias Crabbetje* | In een rotsachtig Landschap, by een Fontyn, waar uit een wit Paard drinkt, staat een Heer en Dame, in deftige kleding, nevens dezelve twee Jagthonden; verders nog een Man te Paard, en twee Beeldjes in het verschiet: kragtig zonachtig en uitvoerig gepenceeld | *Mat:* op paneel *Size:* hoog 12, breed 12 duim	Anna Catharina Putman	(Sold) fl 7:10 Agina
1803/08/24	HGKAN	A0005	*Asselyn* | Een Berg en Rotz Gezigt met Geboomte en Gebouwen op de voorgrond eenige Schaapen en Beelden, origineel | *Mat:* op doek *Size:* breet 11, hoog 12 duim		(Sold) fl 6:5 van Giesen
1803/09/07	AMSCH	0001	*J. Asselyn* | Een uitmuntend capitaal Italiaansch Bergagtig Landschap, op de voorgrond vertoont zig een zwartbonte Os, door een Jongeling voortgedreeven, ter zyde twee Landvrouwen, verder een Vrouw op een Ezel, en een Huisman by een beladen Ezel, en eenige Schaapen, die door een Beekje waden; alles is zeer fraay, bevallig, zonagtig, en van een uitvoerige penceelsbehandeling [Tableau capital ; représentant un paysage d'Italie, riant et montueux. Sur le devant un boeuf blanc et noir conduit par un jeune pâtre ; à côté deux paysannes, plus loin une femme montée sur un âne et un paysan auprès d'un autre âne chargé ; enfin des brebis guéant à travers un petit ruisseau. L'ensemble est fort agréable et charmant ; il y règne un beau soleil et la touche en est très finie] | *Mat:* op doek *Size:* hoog 33, breed 30 duim	Smidt	(Bought In) fl 131
1803/09/07	AMSCH	0002	*J. Asselyn* | Een Gezicht op de Tempel te Tivoli, gestoffeerd met een Man op een wit Paard, en verders Ezeldryvers, Honden, en andere stoffagie van beeldjes; dun en warm behandeld [Vue sur le temple de Tivoli, animée par un homme monté sur un cheval blanc : des conducteurs d'ânes, de chiens et autres objets vivifians. Peint avec chaleur et rapidité] | *Mat:* op doek *Size:* hoog 19, breed 23 duim	Smidt	(Bought In) fl 250
1803/12/15	MGLAC	0044	*J. Asselyn* | Een Bergagtig Landschapje, met fraaie stoffagie | *Mat:* op doek *Size:* hoog duim 15, breed duim 17	Mr L H de Haze Bomme	(Unknown)
1804/07/25	AMSCH	0001	*Asselyn. (J.) alias Crabbetje* | Een gezicht aan de Tyber te Romen; by een vervallen Brug, ziet men een vierkante Toren en andere Gebouwen; in den Tyber ziet men een Pont, geladen met Goederen, een Ryziger te Paard en verscheide andere Beeldjes; aan den Oever een beladen Wagen, en een menigte andere Lieden; voorts een aangenaam bergachtig Verschiet; het licht en bruin, de spiegeling in het water, en het aangenaame Coloriet, maken dit stuk tot een der helderste en bevalligste van dezen Meester | *Mat:* op doek *Size:* hoog 26 ½, breed 35 duim		(Sold) fl 94 B[d] Kooij
1806/08/13	AMSCH	0001	*Asselyn. (J.)* | Twee stuks bergachtige Land- en Riviergezichten, met stoffagie van een houtvlot en andere vaartuigen en beeldjes; zonachtig geschilderd | *Mat:* op paneel *Size:* hoog 7, breed 8 duim	van der Voort	(Sold) fl 31 Spruyt
1806/08/20	HGBSM	0200[a]	*Asselijn* | Twee stuks agthoekige Lijsjes, waarin elk negen stuks aardige ovaale Landschapjes, op koper en in de midden Fruitstukjes, op paneel, de Landschapjes door Asselijn | *This Lot:* Negen stuks aardige ovaale Landschapjes; lot 200[b] by Anonymous *Mat:* op koper *Fmt:* ovaal	Macalester Loup [or others]	(Sold) fl 20:10 for lots 220[a] & 200[b]. Cocard
1806/11/24	AMSCH	0001	*Asselyn (J.)* | Een gezigt op een Italiaanschen Brug, waarby eenige Vissers op de wal, en in een schuit; verders een aangenaam verschiet, dun en kragtig behandeld | *Mat:* op paneel *Size:* hoog 10, breed 11 duim	Munnikhuizen	(Sold) fl 7 du Pree
1808/04/26	GDAN	0001	*Asselyn (J)* | Dit stuk vertoond een Fontijn, bij hoog Geboomte, waar eenige Jagers te Paard, hunne Paarden doen drinken, benevens eenige Menschen en Honden, wel gepenceeld | *Size:* hoog 12 ½, breed 17 duim	G H Fortuyn	(Unknown)
1808/04/26	GDAN	0002	*Asselyn (J)* | Een Grot en Kasteel Gezigt op een Heuvel, met Bomen gestoffeerd, met Beelden | *Size:* hoog 20, breed 32 duim	G H Fortuyn	(Unknown)
1808/04/26	GDAN	0003	*Asselyn (J)* | Een bergägtig Landschap, met Koeijen en Schapen, een Man en een Vrouw, elk op een Ezel rijdende, uitvoerig en fraai gepenseeld | *Size:* hoog 13, breed 16 duim	G H Fortuyn	(Unknown)
1808/05/18	LNAN	0013	*van Asselijn* | Een Landschap met een Man en een gezadeld Paard | *Notes:* The artist's name "van Asselijn" was added in by hand in the RKDH copy of the catalogue.	Mr Cornelis Versluys	(Unknown)
1808/06/11	RMRIJ	0012	*J: Asselyn* | Een Italiaansch Landschap, met Ruïnen en bevallige Stoffagie; uitvoerig en meesterlyk behandeld | *Mat:* op paneel *Size:* hoog 13 ¾, breed 14 ¾ duim		(Sold) fl 151 Noordwijk

1808/06/13	AMSCH	0001	*Asselijn, (J.) bijgenaamd Krabbetje* | In een bergachtig Landschap, aan eene Rivier, ziet men op den voorgrond een Grasnaald en Tombe, waarbij eenige Beeldjes en Munniken. Dit stuk is van eene meesterlijke penceelsbehandeling | *Mat:* op doek op paneel *Size:* hoog 16, breed 19 duim	R[oos] [for] van Hall	(Sold) fl 105 Glad
1808/08/23	AMSCH	0001	*Asselijn. (J.)* | Een Italiaansch Landgezigt, door eene opene Rots ziet men de ruïne van een aloud trotsch Gebouw, op de voorgrond gestoffeert met een Huisman, twee Muil-Ezels, met eenig Vee en andere Goederen beladen; verder eene Vrouw en Jongeling die door een beekje waden, in 't verschiet eenige Reisigers. Het zonlicht doet een aangenaame werking, en is fraai en uitvoerig gepenceeld | *Mat:* op doek *Size:* hoog 24, breed 21 duim	C	(Sold) fl 279 makelaar Spaan
1808/09/13	HABRU	0001	*J. Asselijn* | Een Italiaansch Landschap, met Ruïne aan een Water, waar door diversche Beesten gedreeven worden		(Unknown) fl 16:10
1808/09/13	HABRU	0002	*J. Asselijn* | Een dito [Italiaansch] Riviergezicht, met een drift Beestjes door het Water gaande		(Unknown) fl 1:12
1808/11/28	AMSCH	0002	*J. Asselijn* | Twee stuks Italiaansche Landschappen, met aloude Gebouwen en Ruïne, gestoffeerd met Huislieden bij hun Vee, en gaande en rustende Reizigers | *Mat:* op paneel *Size:* hoog 4, breed 6 duim	[Gruyter?]	(Sold or Bought In) fl 2 Gruyter
1809/04/17	AMSCH	0001	*J. Asselijn* | Deeze kapitaale Ordonantie, verbeeld een Italiaansch boom- en bergachtig Landschap, ter zijde bij een vervalle Steene Sluijs ziet men een sterk nederstortende Waterval, dewelke zig in een Rivier ontlast, waarin verscheide badende Lieden; de voorgrond gestoffeerd met wandelende en te Paard rijdende Heeren en Dames, waarbij verscheide Honden; het invallend zonlicht en de bevallige schildering maken dit stuk tot een der besten van deeze Meester | *Mat:* op doek *Size:* hoog 23, breed 17 duim	[Gruyter?]	(Sold or Bought In) fl 230 Spaan
1809/04/17	AMSCH	0002	*J. Asselijn* | Een hoog bergachtig Landschap, op de voorgrond tusschen het Gebergten ziet men eene opene Rots, gestoffeerd met eenige Landlieden, bij een menigte Vee, die door een Beekje waden; fraai en uitvoerig gepenceeld | *Mat:* op paneel *Size:* hoog 14, breed 16 duim	R	(Sold) fl 9:10
1809/07/19	AMSCH	0001	*Asselijn (J.)* | Dit aangenaam Schilderij vertoont een Italiaansch Landschap, bij een stille Rivier, op den voorgrond ter linker zijde bij de Ruïne van een oude Poort ziet men eenige rustende en staande Kooplieden bij Vaten en Balen met Goederen, en eene Vrouw op een Ezel rijdende; ter regter zijde zijn verscheide beladen Vaartuigen met Goederen, waar bij eenige Lieden, verder Gebergte. Het bevallige zonlicht, en de uitvoerige penceelsbehandeling maken dit stuk tot een der fraaiste van dezen Meester | *Mat:* op doek *Size:* hoog 18, breed 25 duim	[Bicker]	(Sold) fl 225 Gruyter
1809/09/06	AMSCH	0001	*Asselijn (J.)* | In een Italiaansch Bergachtig Landschap, ziet men door een stille Rivier een Herder en Herderin, zittende op Ezels door het Water waaden, en ander Vee voortdrijven; alles verbeeld bij een ondergaande Zon, en is van een bevallige schildering | *Mat:* op doek *Size:* hoog 20, breed 16 duim	Johannes Caudri	(Sold) fl 34 van Iperen
1810/03/26	RMMUY	0006	*Jan Asselyn, alias Crabbetje* | Eene rencontre van eenige Ruiters. In het midden ziet men een Officier op een wit paard in vollen galop aanrennen, terwijl er een te voet op hem aanlegt; verder eenige dooden en gekwetsten. In 't verschiet een Fort dat in brand geschoten is. Helder en delicaat geschilderd [Une rencontre de Cavallerie ; au milieu un officier qui, monte un cheval blanc, vient au galop à la rencontre d'un autre, qui est à terre et qui le couche en joue. Ils sont entourés de plusieurs combattans, et de blessés étendus a terre. Le devant est enrichi de plantes, et le lointain offre un Fort incendié : le courage et l'acharnement des guerriers est surprenant, le faire de [sic] plus savant et la touche la plus fine, font admirer cette savante production.] | *Mat:* op paneel *Size:* hoog 18 ½, breed 27 ½ duimen *Loc:* Amsterdam, Nederland. Rijksmuseum. (A5)	Daniel de Jongh Az	(Sold) fl 300 Rombouts a Dort
1810/03/26	RMMUY	0007	*Jan Asselyn, alias Crabbetje* | Eene Italiaansche Grot van binnen te zien, waarin een Man op een Ezel door een Heidin of waarzegster in de hand schijnt gezien te worden, ander bijwerk versiert den voorgrond, terwijl van achteren eenige geiten voort gedreven worden: zeer uitvoerig en krachtig geschilderd [Dans un souterrain (ou grotte Italienne) auprès d'une Fontaine, sont quelques figures, à pieds et à cheval ; une Bohémienne paroit leur dire la bonne avanture : plus loin des Patres conduisant un troupeau de chèvres ; sujet agréable, d'une touche fine et spirituelle.] | *Mat:* op doek *Size:* hoog 15, breed 14 duimen	Daniel de Jongh Az	(Sold) fl 71 D van Dongen Rott^{m}
1810/05/22	AMSCH	0001	*Asselijn. (J.)* | In een Bergachtig Landschap vertoont zich op den voorgrond een Heer op een wit Paard gezeeten, een ander maakt zich gereed, ter zijde denzelven staat een bruin Paard, waarbij twee Huislieden met Honden, verders eene gaande Vrouw; zonachtig en meesterlijk fraai gepenceeld | *Mat:* op doek op paneel *Size:* hoog 12, breed 14 duim	Johannes van de Putte Nicolaasz.	(Sold) fl 180 Gruyter [for] Dirkse
1810/05/22	AMSCH	0002	*Asselijn. (J.)* | Een dito [Bergachtig] Landschap aan een Rivier, op den voorgrond staand en liggend Vee, waarbij een Veehoeder met Ezels; in alles als de voorgaande behandeld | *Mat:* op paneel *Size:* hoog 6 ½, breed 9 ½ duim	Johannes van de Putte Nicolaasz.	(Sold) fl 19:10 Gruyter

1810/06/20	AMSCH	0001	*J. Asselijn* | Een Landschap, met een rustend Landman, bij twee staande Koeijen | *Mat:* op paneel *Size:* hoog 16, breed 13 duimen	B	(Sold) fl 2 L Pakker
1810/08/01	AMSCH	0001	*Asselijn (Jan)* | Een Italiaansch Landschap met eene groote Brug en Ruïne, voorzien van Reizigers en Muilezels [Un Paysage site d'Italie ; on y distingue un Pont, des Ruines et des Fabriques, étant orné de Voyageurs et de Mulets] | *Annots:* Bon (NGW I); Amsterdam 1769 à de Smeth 890 fl. (NGW II); Vente le Brun à Paris 4 Avril 1811 no.132 frncs 1800 (SMLN) *Mat:* op doek *Size:* hoog 25, breed 32 duimen *Loc:* Amsterdam, Nederland. Rijksmuseum. (C 89)	Mr Pieter de Smeth van Alphen	(Sold) fl 530 Texier, Gerbet en Comp [for] LeBrun de Paris
1810/08/01	AMSCH	0002	*Asselijn (Jan)* | Een Italiaansch Landschap, met eenen opgaanden Weg naar eene oude Poort; gestoffeerd met eenen Heer te Paard en andere Beeldjes [Un Site pris en Italie, ou l'on remarque un Chemin menant à une antique Porte. Il est orné d'un Cavalier à Cheval et d'autres figures] | *Annots:* Bon : mais rond et trop petit (NGW I); Même vente [le Brun à Paris 4 Avril 1811] no.133 fr 340 (SMLN) *Mat:* op paneel *Fmt:* rond *Size:* hoog 8, breed 8 duimen	Mr Pieter de Smeth van Alphen	(Sold) fl 150 Texier, Gerbet en Comp [for] LeBrun de Paris
1810/08/01	AMSCH	0003	*Asselijn (Jan)* | Een hoog bergachtig Landschap, met Gebouwen en eene steenen Brug over een stil Water; op den voorgrond eene Vrouw, zittende op eenen Ezel, waar bij twee Herders; verder beladene Muilezels, en Reizigers in het verschiet [Site de Paysage montueux, orné de Batiments et d'un Pont traversant une Riviere Limpide. Au premier plan l'on voit une Femme assise sur un Ane, ayant deux Pâtres à côté d'elle ; des Muletiers et des Mulets chargés ornent les plans reculés] | *Annots:* Vente le Brun sous nom C. duJardin No.130 fr 321 (SMLN); Dujardin uzé (BPG) *Mat:* op doek *Size:* hoog 20, breed 17 ½ duimen	Mr Pieter de Smeth van Alphen	(Sold) fl 165 Texier, Gerbet en Comp [for] LeBrun
1810/10/11	AMSCH	0003	*J. Asselijn* | Een Boom en Bergachtig Landschap, op den voorgrond een Landman, zittende op een Paard, schijnende in gesprek met eene nevens hem gaande Vrouw, verder, by een heldere Waterplas, een Herder met een drift Schapen | *Mat:* op paneel *Size:* hoog 18, breed 24 duimen	[Gruyter?]	(Bought In) fl 9:10

Asselyn, Jan (and Roghman, R.)

1810/10/10	MGCIT	0061	*Rogman; Asselyn* | Een Landschap, waarin het overblyfsel van een oud publiek Gebouw, door Rogman, en gestoffeerd door Asselyn: door beide Meesters wel behandeld	Caspar van Citters	(Unknown)

Asselyn, Jan (or Asselyn, manner)

1805/12/16	AMSCH	0001	*Asselyn* | Een Ruïne van een Antiek Gebouw, waar by een ménigte Beeldjes, uitvoerig op Paneel, door of in de manier van Asselyn | *Mat:* op paneel *Size:* hoog 11, breed 12 duim	R[oos]	(Sold) fl 17 Taxera
1808/08/23	AMSCH	0242	*Asselijn* | Een Grot, waar door een drift Beesten gedreeven word; goed geschilderd door of in de manier van Asselijn	S	(Sold) fl 10:10 Reydon

Asselyn, Jan (manner)

1802/02/16	AMSCH	0065	*J. Asselyn* | Een Italiaans Landschap, by een oude Poort ziet men een steene brug over een Rivier, waar in verschyde schuyten, op de voorgrond lieden die zig baden, zonachtig gepenceeld, als door J. Asselyn	G	(Sold) fl 6:10 T Spaan
1802/11/01	DOBRA	0007	*Asselyn* | Een landschap, waar in een ruïne; en eenige Cavaliers, Jagers, enz. als door Asselyn | *Mat:* op paneel *Size:* hoog circa 27 ½, breed 35 duim	Paulus van der Spyk [or others]	(Sold) fl 13:10 Randwijk
1804/02/27	AMSCH	0121	*J. Asselyn* | In een Italiaansch Rotsgezicht, ziet men op den voorgrond eenige Ryzigers met hunne Paarden, waarby een Hydin, die een derzelve schynt goeder geluk te zeggen; verders andere Lieden onder het verwulft; het is bevallig van licht en meesterlyk gepenceeld in de manier van J. Asselyn | *Mat:* op doek *Size:* hoog 31, breed 26 duim	B	(Bought In) fl 90

Assteyn, Bartholomeus Abrahamsz.

1803/09/07	AMSCH	0003	*B. Asstyn* | Een stil Leeven, zynde een Tafel met een ménigte Fruiten, en een Roemer Wyn, waarin een Citroenschil; alles met de natuur evenarende behandeld [Un intérieur représentant une table avec une quantité de fruits, et un verre à la romaine rempli de vin, dans lequel on voit une pelure de citron ; le tout traité au naturel] | *Mat:* op paneel *Size:* hoog 18, breed 21 duim	Smidt	(Sold) fl 3 Grimpen

Ast, Balthasar van der

1801/03/31	HGCLF	0384	*B. van der Ast* | Een Fruitstukje met eenige Insecten door B. van der Ast, in een vergulde lyst	H van der Hoop	(Unknown) fl 1
1801/03/31	HGCLF	0388	*van der Ast* | Drie stukjes met Bloemen, Insecten, Hoorns, &c. op koper door van der Ast, in swarte lystjes met vergulde binne randen | *Mat:* op koper	H van der Hoop	(Sold) fl 8 Heijns
1802/02/16	AMSCH	0055	*B. v. der Ast* | Twee stuks, den een vertoont een mand met verschyde soorten van fraaye Bloemen; en den andere een mand, waar in twee fraaye schootels met keurige Vrugten, uitvoerig behandeld	F	(Sold) fl 6 Levij Pakker
1802/09/18	RMDRS	0065	*van der Ast* | Een Vles, waarin een Tulp	Casper de Haas	(Unknown) fl 1:12
1809/06/13	AMSCH	0003	*B. van Ast* | Een Glaze Fles, staande op een Tafel, gevuld met geurige Bloemen | *Mat:* op paneel *Size:* hoog 14, breed 10 duim	P	(Sold) fl 1 Frantsen

1810/06/20	AMSCH	0002a	*Van Ast* | Een Glazen Fles, gevuld met geurige Bloemen, staande op eene Tafel. Uitvoerig | *Mat:* op paneel *Size:* hoog 14, breed 10 duimen	S	(Sold) fl 1 Reijers
1810/06/20	AMSCH	0143	*P. van Ast* | Een Fles, gevuld met onderscheidene Bloemen | *Mat:* op koper *Notes:* The artist's name was given as "P. van Ast" but we have assumed this is an error.	B	(Sold) fl 1:15 Focken
1810/10/10	MGCIT	0097	*van Ast* | Een dito [Stuk], met Bloemen, Vruchten, Hoorns en Schulpen	Caspar van Citters	(Unknown)
1810/10/11	AMSCH	0177	*Van Ast* | Een Vaas, met bloemen	[Levy Pakker?]	(Sold) fl 0:14 du Pree
			Ast, Balthasar van der (and Schellinks, W.)		
1809/06/13	AMSCH	0001	*B. van Ast; Schellinx* | Een kapitaal hoog Bergachtig Landschap, met hoog opgaand Geboomten, ter zijde over een klaar spiegelend Water een Steene Sluis, gestoffeerd met Heeren te Paard en gaande en rustende Reizigers; zonagtig en uitvoerig geschilderd, door B. van Ast en gestoffeerd door Schellinx | *Mat:* op doek *Size:* hoog 28, breed 38 duim *Notes:* The artist was presumably Pieter Jansz van Asch and not Balthasar van der Ast.	[Gruyter?]	(Sold) fl 10:10 Spaan
			Avercamp, Hendrick		
1801/03/16	AMSCH	0046	*H. Averkamp, de Stomme van Campen* | Een Ysgezicht ryk gestoffeerd met Arresleede Schaatseryders en wandelende Beeltjes, zeer uitvoerig	Z	(Sold) fl 2 Bouwer
1801/06/10	AMSCH	0005	*Avercamp. (H. van) bygenaamd de Stomme van Campen* | Een ryk gestoffeerd Wintergezicht, op e.n [sic] Rivier by een Dorp; zeer uitvoerig en natuurlyk behandeld | *Mat:* op paneel *Size:* hoog 12 ½, breed 20 duim *Notes:* Originally the artist's name was spelled "Avecamp." This error was corrected in an errata sheet located at the end of the catalogue.	Herman ten Kate	(Sold) fl 17 van der Vinne
1801/08/19	AMSCH	0001	*H. Averkamp* | Een Landgezigt, met een aloude Wagt Tooren, by een bevroosen Rivier; verbeeldende een besneeuwde Winter, daar verschyden Lieden zig op het Ys vermaaken, door H. Averkamp, op Paneel | *Mat:* op paneel *Size:* hoog 13, breed 19 duim	W Wynen	(Sold) fl 5:5 Le Dantú
1801/10/06	AMSCH	0001	*H. Averkamp, bygenaamd de stomme van Kampen* | Op een bevroosen Rivier, ziet men een menigte Lieden, van verschillende Rang en Staat, zig met wandelen en Schaatsen ryden vermaaken, waar by verscheide Marketenters: ter linker zyde aan den Oever, vertoonen zich Boeren Wooningen en Schuur by Dor Geboomte, alles is Natuurlyk, en Meesterlyk fraai gepenceeld | *Mat:* op paneel *Size:* hoog 13, breed 20 ½ duim	S	(Sold) fl 21 v d Schleij A [for] Ter Smitten
1801/12/22	AMOTT	0015	*Averkamp* | 1 Liereman, als ryziger in een Bosch wordende aangevallen; in zinnebeeldige ordonnantie	Bartholomeus Ruloffs	(Unknown) fl 2
1801/12/22	AMOTT	0098	*Averkamp* | 2 stuks, Zomer en Winter	Bartholomeus Ruloffs	(Unknown) fl 7:10
1802/02/16	AMSCH	0060	*H. Averkamp* | Een Wintergezigt, op een bevrosen Rivier ziet men verscheide Lieden, zig op het ys vermaken, verder vertoonen zig eenige Gebouwen, natuurlyk behandeld	G	(Sold) fl 1:15 Boelen
1802/12/13	AMSCH	0004	*A. Averkamp, bygenaamd de Stomme van Campen* | In een aangenaam Land- en Riviergezigt, ziet men 't Water ryk gestoffeerd, met een meenigte van Schuiten en Zylende Vaartuigen, ter zyde een Eende-Kooy, op de voorgrond eenige handeldryvende Lieden; uivoerig [sic] geschilderd | *Mat:* op paneel *Size:* hoog 21, breed 27 duim	Pruyssenaar [for] A	(Sold) fl 1:10 Theens
1802/12/13	AMSCH	0005	*A. Averkamp* | Op een breede Bevrosen Rivier, aan byden Oevers met Boere Woningen en Dor Geboomten; ziet men een ménigte Lieden, van verschillende rang, zig op het Ys vermaken, zoo met Wandelen als met Schaatseryden, helder en fix geschilderd | *Mat:* op paneel *Size:* hoog 20, breed 36 duim *Notes:* The artist's name was given as "A. Averkamp" but we have assumed this is an error.	Schley [for] Lauwers	(Sold) fl 10 Gruiter
1802/12/13	AMSCH	0006	*A. Averkamp* | Een ryk gestoffeerde Winter | *Mat:* op paneel *Size:* hoog 20, breed 37 duim *Notes:* The artist's name was given as "A. Averkamp" but we have assumed this is an error.	Pruyssenaar [for] A	(Sold) fl 0:12 Gruiter
1803/08/17	AMSCH	0001	*Avercamp, (H. van) bygenaamd de Stomme van Campen* | Op een bevrozen Rivier ziet men een menigte van Arresleden, Schaatseryders, Wandelaars, en eenige Visschers; meer agterwaards eenige Marketenters, en een Stad in het verschiet; dun en natuurlyk behandeld, zynde een der beste, welken van dezen Meester bekend zyn | *Mat:* op paneel *Size:* hoog 19, breed 35 duim	Anna Catharina Putman	(Sold) fl 27:10 Yver
1803/08/17	AMSCH	0002	*Avercamp, (H. van) bygenaamd de Stomme van Campen* | Een bevrozen Rivier, aan weerszyde met Gebouwen, Boere Woningen, en Geboomten; gestoffeerd met een menigte Schaatseryders, Kolvers en Wandelaars; niet minder behandeld als de voorgaande | *Mat:* op koper *Size:* hoog 10, breed 15 ½ duim	Anna Catharina Putman	(Sold) fl 8:5 Hodges
1804/04/28	LNDLS	0033	*Averkamp, genaamd de stomme van Kampe* | Een Wintergezicht op den Amstel, met veel gewoel van schaatsen ryders, narresleden, wandelende lieden, visschers, en andere die kolven, tenten, Dorpen en Steden in 't verschiet, uitvoerig op paneel, door Averkamp, genaamd de stomme van Kampe | *Mat:* op paneel	[Abraham Delfos] [or others]	(Bought In) fl 11
1805/07/03	AMSCH	0055	*H. Averkamp* | Op een Bevroozen Rivier, vertoonen zig een ménigte Lieden, zig met wandelen en schaatzryden vermakende, terzyde zier men	G	(Sold) fl 4 Gruyter

			Boere Woningen en Vaartuigen, aan den Oever; helder en natuurlyk gepenceeld | *Mat:* op paneel *Size:* hoog 10, breed 13 duim		
1806/08/13	AMSCH	0003	*Avercamp. (bygenaamd de Stomme van Campen)* | Een Winter, verbeeldende een Land- en Riviergezicht, ryk gestoffeerd met wandelende Heeren en Dames, schaatsenryders, arresleede, eenige vaartuigen en een aangenaam Dorpgezicht; delicaat van Penceelsbehandeling | *Mat:* op paneel *Size:* hoog 14, breed 18 duim	Vinkeles [for] F	(Sold) fl 30 Th Spaan
1806/08/20	HGBSM	0213	*Averkamp, bij genaamd de stomme van Kampen* | Een winter met Schaatserijders &c. uitvoerig geschilderd | *Mat:* op paneel *Size:* hoog 5, breed 9 ¾ duim	Macalester Loup [or others]	(Sold) fl 2:10 Cocard
1807/04/00	LNDLS	0037	*Averkamp* | Een Wintergezigt op den Amstel, vol gewoel van rijdende en wandelende beelden | *Mat:* op paneel *Size:* hoog 22, breed 37 duim	[Abraham Delfos] [or others]	(Unknown)
1807/06/10	HGBSM	0037	*Averkamp* | Een Wintergezigt op den Amstel, vol gewoel van rijdende en wandelende beelden | *Mat:* op paneel *Size:* hoog 22, breed 37 duim	Abraham Delfos [or others]	(Sold) fl 4 Colonbon
1807/06/10	HGBSM	0152	*Averkamp* | Een Ys vermaak vol gewoel, zeer uitvoerig geschilderd | *Mat:* op paneel *Size:* hoog 11 ½, breed 20 duim	Abraham Delfos [or others]	(Sold) fl 13 S T
1810/06/20	AMSCH	0117	*H. Averkamp* | Een bevrozen Rivier, ter zijde Boeren Woningen, rijk gestoffeerd met Schaatzerijders en andere voorwerpen	N	(Sold) fl 0:6 L Pakker
1810/07/23	DOLGI	0014	*(de Stomme) van Campen* | Een Ijsvermaak, met Schaatsrijders, rijk van figuren | *Mat:* op paneel *Size:* hoog 9 ½, breed 16 duim	Mr Pieter van den Santheuvel	(Sold) fl 7 van Braam Dordt
1810/08/06	AMSCH	0002	*Avercamp (H. van)* | Een rijk gestoffeerd Wintergezicht. Natuurlijk geschilderd | *Mat:* op paneel *Size:* hoog 15, breed 12 duimen	G	(Bought In) fl 1:5
			Avercamp, Hendrick (manner)		
1801/09/04	MGWIN	0004	*den stommen van Campen* | Een Winter, in de manier van den stommen van Campen, op Paneel, in een zwarte Lyst | *Mat:* op paneel *Size:* hoog 21 ½ en breed 56 duim	Pieter Gillissen	(Unknown)
1802/09/06	AMSCH	0226	*Averkamp* | Een natuurlyk ryk gestoffeerd Wintergezigt; in de manier van Averkamp	J	(Sold) fl 0:14 L Pakker
1807/08/26	AMSCH	0318	*de Stomme van Kampen* | Een Wintergezicht met Schaatsenryders; in de manier van de Stomme van Kampen	Joseph Vallette	(Sold) fl 0:10 L Pakker
1810/06/06	RMMUY	0173	*de Stomme van Kampen* | Een Winter. Als door de Stomme van Kampen | *Mat:* op paneel		(Sold) fl 4:5 Strikland
			Avont, Peeter van		
1807/08/26	AMSCH	0005	*P. van den Avond* | In een Landschap, vertoont zig Maria, houdende het Kindeken op de schoot, waar voor St. Jan, knielende met een schotel Vruchten in de handen, waar nevens St. Anna en ter andere zyde St. Joseph; het is uitvoerig en meesterlyk behandeld | *Mat:* op paneel *Size:* hoog 11 ½, breed 13 duim	v d Schley [for] L	(Sold) fl 7:10 Peeters
			B…., W.		
1803/09/07	AMSCH	0035	*W.B.… [B.W.…]* | Twee stuks bevallige Landschapjes, met Geboomten, gestoffeerd met verscheide gaande Huislieden, en andere Reizigers, verder aangenaame verschieten, beide zonagtig en uitvoerig geschilderd, op Koper, door W. B.… [Deux paysages montueux, garnis d'arbres, de paysans ambulans, de voyageurs et d'autres diversités agréables : il règne dans tous les deux, une belle lumière, et ils sont d'une exécution soignée] | *Mat:* op koper *Size:* ieder hoog 5, breed 6 duim *Notes:* The artist's initials differ in the Dutch and French editions of the catalogue.	Smidt	(Sold) fl 3:15 J Yver
			Baburen, Dirck van		
1810/06/06	RMMUY	0096	*Babuer* | Een Mans Pourtrait in Spaansche kleeding spelende op een Tromp | *Mat:* op doek		(Unknown) fl 2:4
			Backer		
1803/08/24	HGKAN	0066	*Bakker* | Een Vrouwe Portrait kragtig geschildert	[Teissier] [or others]	(Sold) fl 7 Kan
1803/12/12	AMSCH	0015	*Bakker* | In een Binnenvertrek, voor een Tafel, met een rood Kleed gedekt, ziet men een Bevallige Oude Vrouw, dewelke door een Jonger een tros Druiven aangeboden word, voor haar legt een Hond; meesterlyk op Doek | *Mat:* op doek *Size:* hoog 40, breed 51 duim	B	(Sold) fl 3 La Bouchere
1805/10/09	HGBSM	0139	*Bakker* | Een biddende Petrus, kragtig en uitvoerig en wel gecoloreerd | *Mat:* op doek *Size:* hoog 23 breet 20 duim	T H van Willigen [or others]	(Sold) fl 30 van den Broek
1809/05/26	HADAA	0009	*Bakker* | Het Portrait van eene Non houdende een Kerkboek in de hand, zeer natuurlijk en treffend | *Mat:* op doek *Size:* hoog 20 breed 21 ½ duimen	Mejuffrouw de Wed David Heemskerk [or others]	(Unknown)
1809/05/26	HADAA	0018	*Bakker* | Een Mans Portrait met een kraag, door …. Bakker	Mejuffrouw de Wed David Heemskerk [or others]	(Unknown)
1809/07/25	HGBSM	0054	*Bakker* | Een Capitaal Schildery verbeeldende de vier Evangelisten, zittende aan een Tafel te leezen waarby hunne teekens, kragtig en breed geschildert | *Mat:* op doek *Size:* hoog 5 voet 1 duim, breed 4 voet 2 duim	D van der Aa	(Sold) fl 25 van der Aa

1810/08/06	AMSCH	0006	*Bakker* | Een Regtsgeleerde in zijne Kamer, aan een met een Tapijt gedekte Tafel zittende, met pen en Papier in zijne handen. Gloeijend van koloriet, als Rembrand behandeld | *Mat:* op doek *Size:* hoog 48, breed 38 duimen	F	(Bought In) fl 17
1810/08/06	AMSCH	0007	*Bakker* | Eene jonge Vrouw, in deftige kleeding. Delicaat gepenceeld | *Mat:* op doek *Size:* hoog 33, breed 26 duimen	F	(Sold) fl 11 van Dijl
1810/10/11	AMSCH	0210	*Bakker* | Twee stuks; een Mans en Vrouwe Portret | *Mat:* op doek	A	(Sold) fl 1 Gruiter

Backer (manner)

1805/10/09	HGBSM	A0001	*Bakker* | Heracliet en Democriet, kragtig in de manier van Bakker | *Mat:* op doek *Size:* hoog 33 ½ breet 41 duim	T H van Willigen [or others]	(Sold) fl 7:5 Zwartsman

Backer, Adriaen

1803/04/20	AMSCH	0016	*Bakker. (H.)* | Twee stuks Afbeeldzels van een bevallige Dame, en een Heer, halver lyf levensgroote, beide zyn ze in ryke Deftige Kleeding; uitvoerig en meesterlyk fraay gepenceeld [Deux portraits, celui d'un Homme & l'autre d'une Dame, à mi-corps en costume Ancien ; ils sont traités avec beaucoup d'art & de delicatesse.] | *Mat:* op doek *Size:* ieder hoog 41, breed 35 duim	Maria Magdalena van Sluypwyk, gravinne van Moens	(Sold) fl 350 Hodges
1804/08/08	AMSCH	0028	*A. Bakker* | Het onderwerp van dit Schildery schynt een Famieljestuk te zyn, voorstellende een Gezelschap van eenige Herders en Herderinnen, by eenige Schaapen en verdere Stoffagie; breed en meesterlyk geschilderd | *Mat:* op doek *Size:* hoog 44, breed 49 duim	Vink[eles] [for] K[=Gruyter?]	(Sold) fl 5:10 Menzart
1809/06/13	AMSCH	0008	*A. Bakker* | Twee stuks, een Mans en Vrouwe Pourtrait, beide deftig in 't zwart gekleed en halver lijf; edel gepenceeld en meesterlijk als van der Helst behandeld, door A. Bakker | *Mat:* op doek *Size:* ieder is hoog 41, breed 35 duim	H[odges]	(Bought In) fl 200

Backer, Jacob Adriaensz.

1806/05/05	AMSCH	0014	*J. Bakker* | De oprechting Christi aan het Kruis, zynde een ryke ordinantie van verscheide beelden; kragtig gepenceeld op Doek | *Mat:* op doek *Size:* hoog 50, breed 43 duim	R[oos]	(Sold) fl 30 Roos
1808/06/13	AMSCH	0026	*Bakker (J.)* | Twee stuks: een Mans- en een Vrouwe-portret; krachtig geschilderd en van een schoone kleur | *Mat:* op paneel *Size:* ieder hoog 32, breed 25 duim	E M Engelberts	(Sold) fl 18 Simons
1808/08/23	AMSCH	0029	*Bakker. (J.)* | Twee stuks, een Mans en Vrouwe Pourtret in aloude Hollandsche Kleeding; beide stout en meesterlijk behandeld | *Mat:* op paneel *Size:* Ieder hoog 32, breed 25 duim	J	(Sold) fl 5 D Maijkel

Backer, Jacob Adriaensz. (manner)

1807/08/26	AMSCH	0258	*J. Bakker* | Een Vrouwe Pourtrait in ryke kleding, staande by een Fontyn; als van J. Bakker | *Mat:* op doek *Size:* hoog 44, breed 35 duim	de Vries	(Sold) fl 0:6 Levy Pakker

Backhuysen, Ludolf

1801/04/13	AMSCH	0004	*L. Backhuyzen* | Een woelend Water gestoffeerd met een Oorlogschip, Jagt en andere Vaartuigen, op de voorgrond een Sloep met Bootsgezellen; delicaat en van eene bevallige schildering | *Mat:* op doek *Size:* hoog 18, breed 23 duim	Pierre Fouquet, junior	(Sold) fl 250 Coclers
1801/04/13	AMSCH	0005	*L. Backhuyzen* | Een woelend Water met verscheide Oorlog- en andere Schepen, op de voorgrond twee Visschers, bezig eenige Korven te verwerken; natuurlyk behandeld | *Mat:* op doek op paneel *Size:* hoog 13, breed 15 duim	Pierre Fouquet, junior	(Sold) fl 100 Huijgens
1801/04/13	AMSCH	0006	*L. Backhuyzen* | Een woelend Water met zeilende Schepen en uitgestrekt verschiet; behandeld als de voorgaande | *Mat:* op doek op paneel *Size:* hoog 12, breed 14 duim	Pierre Fouquet, junior	(Sold) fl 20 Huijgens
1801/05/11	AMSCH	0006	*L. Backhuyzen* | Dit voortreffelyk Schildery verbeeld een woelend Water, ryk gestoffeerd, met een menigte Oorlog en andere Scheepen en Vaartuigen, zoo zeilende als ten anker leggende: de sombre Lucht geeft een frapant licht en bruin, over het dunne water, alles is delicaat behandeld, en van de beste tyd van deezen meester | *Mat:* op doek *Size:* hoog 43, breed 65 duim	E[lias]	(Sold) fl 751 Th Spaan
1801/06/10	AMSCH	0009	*Backhuysen. (L.)* | Een sterk woelende Zee, in het midden ziet men een Oorlogsschip, een Beurtman, een Visserspink, Schuiten en fraaije stoffage van Beeldjes, de Lucht, de woeling der Golven, en het Frappantelicht [sic] maken dit Stuk tot een der beste van deezen Meester | *Mat:* op doek *Size:* hoog 39, breed 50 duim	Herman ten Kate	(Sold) fl 520 Vreesman
1801/06/10	AMSCH	0010	*Backhuysen. (L.)* | Een golvende Zee, met zeylend Oorlogschip, Beurtman en andere Vaartuigen, 't Water is zeer dun, en uitvoerig behandeld | *Mat:* op paneel *Size:* hoog 19, breed 24 duim	Herman ten Kate	(Sold) fl 47 Spruit van Gend
1801/08/19	AMSCH	0002	*L. Bakhuizen* | Dit stuk verbeeld een woelend Water, ryk gestoffeerd met Oorlogscheepen, Jachten en andere Vaartuigen, voorts ryk met Beeldjes gestoffeerd, en delicaat gepenceeld op Doek | *Mat:* op doek *Size:* hoog 21, breed 30 duim	Van Forreest	(Sold) fl 330 Vinkeles

1801/10/06	AMSCH	0004	*L. Backhuysen* | Dit fraaije Stuk, verbeeld een woelende Zee, ryk gestoffeert met zylende Oorlog Scheepen, en andere Vaartuigen: op de voorgrond, ter regter zyde ziet men een Vissers Vaartuig, met eenige Lieden: en verder eenige Vissers in een Schuit, de golving van het Water, het dun en doorschynende, alles evenaart de Natuur, en is helder van Coloriet, en uitvoerig gepenceelt | *Mat:* op doek *Size:* hoog 29, breed 40 duim	S	(Sold) fl 500 Pruijssenaar [for] R
1801/10/19	AMSCH	0003	*Backhuyzen. (Ludolf)* | Een woelend Water, ter linkerzyde Visschers in hun schuit, beneevens een zeilend Driemast Schip en een Kaag dewelke daar voor heen zeild, in het verschiet nog eenige zeilende Scheepen; zeer dun, en delicaat behandeld | companion to lot 4 *Mat:* op doek *Size:* hoog 13 ½, breed 16 ¾ duim *Loc:* Amsterdam, Nederland. Rijksmuseum. (A2315)	Jonkheer Menno Baron van Coehoorn	(Sold) fl 535 for lots 3 & 4. Pruijssenaar
1801/10/19	AMSCH	0004	*Backhuyzen. (Ludolf)* | Een wéderga, verbeeldende een Cabbelend Water, op de linkerzyde een Scheepje, waar uit een Man met een Anker in de hand, door het water gaat, verder een zeilende Boeijer, en in het verschiet meer Scheepen; niet minder dan de voorgaande en van dezelve groote | companion to lot 3 *Mat:* op doek *Size:* hoog 13 ½, breed 16 ¾ duim *Loc:* Amsterdam, Nederland. Rijksmuseum. (A2316)	Jonkheer Menno Baron van Coehoorn	(Sold) fl 535 for lots 3 & 4. Pruijssenaar
1802/05/05	AMSCH	0006	*L. Bakhuyzen* | Een Woelend Water, met verscheide Oorlog- en Beurtscheepen en andere Vaartuigen, het Ligt en Bruin is frappant en de behandeling allerbevalligst | *Mat:* op doek *Size:* hoog 29, breed 37 duim	D	(Sold) fl 565 Pruijssenaar [for] R
1802/05/05	AMSCH	0007	*L. Bakhuyzen* | Een Onstuimige Zee, met een menigte Oorlog- en andere Scheepen, op de Voorgrond eenige Beeldtjes, zynde van de delicaatste schildering | *Mat:* op doek *Size:* hoog 26, breed 30 duim	D	(Bought In) fl 150
1802/05/05	AMSCH	0008	*L. Bakhuyzen* | Een gezicht op de Zuyder Zee, ryk met Beurtscheepen en Vissers Schuiten gestoffeerd; terzyde een Stadgezicht, fraai geördoneerd en behandeld als de Voorgaande | *Size:* hoog 21, breed 26 duim	E	(Sold) fl 265 Pruijssenaar [for] J
1802/06/16	AMSCH	0004	*L. Backhuysen* | In een Woelende Zée vertoond zich een Groenlands Visschers Schip, voor de Wind dryvende, en een zeilende Visschers Schuit en Sloep met Zeelieden; verder gestoffeerd met verscheiden andere Vaartuigen: het Water is Natuurlyk, dun en doorscheinend behandeld; het licht bevallig, en van een uitvoerige Penceelbehandeling | *Mat:* op doek *Size:* hoog 17 ½, breed 23 duim	[Merrem]	(Sold) fl 575 I Smit Gz
1802/06/16	AMSCH	0005	*L. Backhuysen* | Dit Voorwerp verbeeld een Storm op Zée, by een Rotsachtig Strand: op de voorgrond een Schip in gevaar van zich tegen de Rotzen te verbreizelen, terwyl eenige Zèelieden zich trachten te redden; verder werden andere Scheepen door de Baaren geslingert: de golving van 't Water, de verbolgen Lucht, alles evenaart de Natuur, en is Meesterlyk fraai gepenceelt | *Mat:* op doek *Size:* hoog 19, breed 25 duim	[Merrem]	(Sold) fl 135 v d Schleij
1802/06/16	AMSCH	0006	*L. Backhuysen* | Een Woelende Zée, op de voorgrond een zeilende Visschers Pink, wyders een Oorlogschip en andere Vaartuigen, ter zyde een Dorp: het Water is dun transparant, en zonachtig van Schildering | *Mat:* op paneel *Size:* hoog 12, breed 15 ½ duim	[Merrem]	(Sold) fl 20 Frantsen
1802/06/16	AMSCH	0007	*L. Backhuysen* | Een Strandgezicht langs een kabbelende Zée gestoffeerd met verscheiden Beelden; dun en meesterlyk behandeld | *Mat:* op paneel *Size:* hoog 11 ½, breed 16 duim	[Merrem]	(Sold) fl 4 v Dijl
1802/09/29	AMSCH	0005	*Lud^{lph.} Backhuysen* | Een Woelend Water. Hoog 20 ¼, breed 24 duim. Doek. In dit uitmuntende Kunst-Tafereel ziet men een Beurtman en verscheide andere Vaartuigen met opgespanne Zylen in een dun en transparant Water, als meede eenige Zwemmers, ziende verders op het Tolhuis aan het Y, over de Stad Amsterdam; de zonagtige Penceelbehandeling is verwonderlyk, als meede de schoon bewolkte Lucht; dit Schildery is van de allereerste qualiteit [On ne balancera pas de classer cette Peinture ravissante, parmi les ouvrages les plus distingués qui soient sortis du Pinceau de notre artiste unique dans ce genre, tant pour la finesse précieuse de touche, que pour le beau choix du sujet ou il à singulierement bien réussi, qui offre une vûe de la Riviere de l'Y, Et de la maison du Péage, vis à vis la ville d'Amsterdam, la quelle se distingue dans le lointain ; des voiliers de differentes formes, passent prés de quelques Pilotis et se mirent dans les vagues écumantes : Quelques baigneurs se font remarquer sur le rivage. – La disposition des beaux nuages et le soleil, produisent dans ce Tableau des Effets de clair-obscur admirables.] | *Mat:* op doek *Size:* hoog 20 ¼, breed 24 duim	[Labouchere?]	(Sold) fl 642 Yver
1802/09/29	AMSCH	0006	*Lud^{lph.} Backhuysen* | Een Watergezigt. Hoog 17, breed 24 ¾ duim Doek. Zynde het uitzigt op de Stad Delft; over de Trekvaart, tusschen het Geboomte in het kabbelende Waater, worden twee zeilende Schepen en Schuiten gezien beneevens een dryvend Vat; uitvoerig en bevallig behandelt [Une vüe du Canal qui conduit de la Haye à la ville de Delft en Hollande la quelle ville est vue dans l'eloignement ; des arbres agités par les vents bordent le rivage & quelques barques à pleines voiles, éclairées du soleil, produisent un Effet piquant : Ce Tableau est d'une touche facile & conforme à la verité.] | *Mat:* op doek *Size:* hoog 17, breed 24 ¾ duim	[Labouchere?]	(Sold) fl 19 L Pakker
1802/12/13	AMSCH	0027	*L. Bakhuizen* | Een woelende Zee met een Oorlogschip. en andere zeilende Vaartuigen, meesterlyk gepenceeld | *Mat:* op doek *Size:* hoog 38, breed 47 duim	Pruyssenaar [for] B	(Sold) fl 35 Gruiter

1803/06/20	AMSCH	0001	*L. Bakhuyzen* | Een Storm op Zee by een rotsachtig Strand, gestoffeerd met een menigte Schépen, welke in gevaar zyn, alles meesterlyk geschilderd, door L. Bakhuyzen, op Doek | *Mat:* op doek *Size:* hoog 19, breed 25 duim	Schley [for] B	(Sold) fl 70 V d Schleij [for] F
1803/08/17	AMSCH	0006	*Backhuyzen. (L.)* | Een kabbelend Water, met een opkomende Stormbuy, waarop een zylend en een ten anker leggend Oorlogschip, op de voorgrond een Sloep met eenige Visschers; verders in het verschiet nog een menigte Vaartuigen; alles dun en in den zilverachtigen toon van W. van de Velde gepenceeld | *Mat:* op paneel *Size:* hoog 16, breed 21 duim	Anna Catharina Putman	(Bought In) fl 170
1804/04/28	LNDLS	0026	*Ludolph Backhuyzen* | Een woelend Water, met verscheiden oorlog- en andere schepen, als met de pen op een witten grond geärceerd, door Ludolph Backhuyzen, op paneel | *Mat:* op paneel *Size:* hoog 15, breed 23 duim	[Abraham Delfos] [or others]	(Sold) fl 11 Tilyn
1804/05/07	AMSCH	0004	*Backhuyzen. (L.)* | Een woelend Water, ryk gestoffeerd met een ménigte Scheepen en andere Vaartuigen, Visschers in hun Schuit; de verbolgen lucht geeft een koele en zilverächtigen toon aan dit Schildery | *Mat:* op doek *Size:* hoog 21, breed 25 duim	Roos [for] A	(Sold) fl 101 Gruyter
1804/05/07	AMSCH	0005	*Backhuyzen. (L.)* | Een dito [woelend Water], zynde een Avondstond, met verscheide Zeilende en ten Anker leggende Scheepen, in het verschiet een Stad; meesterlyk behandeld | *Mat:* op doek op paneel *Size:* hoog 19, breed 29 duim	Roos [for] A	(Bought In) fl 15
1804/05/07	AMSCH	0006	*Backhuyzen. (L.)* | In een sterk woelend Ygezicht ziet men eenige zeilende en stilleggende Scheepen en Vaartuigen, ter zyde het Tolhuis, en de Stad Amsterdam in het verschiet; het door de betrokken lucht invallende zonlicht, stelt zeer Natuurlyk voor de opkomende buijen, die in dit stuk kunstig verbeeld zyn; hetzelve is meesterlyk geschilderd | *Mat:* op doek *Size:* hoog 21, breed 24 duim	Vinkeles [for] G	(Sold) fl 14:10 Tys
1804/05/07	AMSCH	0007	*Backhuyzen. (L.)* | Dit bevallig stukje verbeeld een Gezichtje aan een Rivier, op de voorgrond ziet men eenige Visschers, waarby een Boerin, welke een Visch uit de Ben neemt, waarby een Hond; verders eenige Zeilende en Roeijende Schuiten, en een alleraangenaamst verschiet; uitvoerig en tevens meesterlyk van behandeling | *Mat:* op doek *Size:* hoog 13, breed 15 duim	Vinkeles	(Sold) fl 57 Pruissenaar
1804/05/07	AMSCH	0008	*Backhuyzen. (L.)* | Een Dorpgezicht, gestoffeerd met een wandelend Heer en Dame, op de voorgrond by eenige Boomstammen en Tonnen diversche Lieden, verders in de Rivier, by een Brug, eenige Schuiten, en in 't verschiet verscheide Dorpen; zynde hetzelve van een dito [uitvoerig en tevens meesterlyk van] behandeling als de voorgaande | *Size:* hoog 12, breed 15 duim *Notes:* It is unclear what "dito" refers to in the title.	Vinkeles	(Bought In) fl 5
1804/07/25	DLGRO	0010	*L. Bakhuisen* | Een woelend Water, met verscheide Schepen, op de voorgrond ziet men een Beurtschip, agter hetzelve een Oorlogschip en andere Vaartuigen, fraai gepenceeld op Doek | *Mat:* op doek *Size:* hoog 25, breed 31 duim	Mr Franc van der Burch Wz.	(Unknown)
1804/08/08	AMSCH	0010	*L. Bakhuyzen* | In een capitaale sterk woelende Zee ziet men eenige zeilende en ten Anker leggende Scheepen en Vaartuigen; het by uitstek wel verkoozen Licht en de heldere en dunne schildering maaken dit tot een aangenaam Schildery | *Mat:* op doek *Size:* hoog 22, breed 27 duim	Vink[eles] [for] K[=Gruyter?]	(Sold) fl 17 Texier
1804/08/08	AMSCH	0011	*L. Bakhuyzen* | Een met verscheide zeilende en ten Anker leggende Scheepen, in een woelige Zee, zynde een Avondstond; meesterlyk behandeld | *Mat:* op doek op paneel *Size:* hoog 19, breed 29 duim	Roos [for] F	(Sold) fl 4:10 Kamphuizen
1804/10/16	DLOND	0007	*Lud. Bachuysen* | Een Zeegezicht met zeilende Schepen. Vue d'une Mer & des Vaisseaux qui font voile | *Mat:* op paneel *Size:* hoog 17, breed 19 *Notes:* The lot was changed from "Lud. Bachuysen, Een Zeegezicht met zeilende Schepen," to "J.G. Cuny," without giving a title, at the front of the catalogue.		(Withdrawn)
1804/10/16	DLOND	0008	*Lud. Bachuysen* | Riviergezicht met Jachten en Schepen voor ene Stad. Vue de quelques Vaisseaux devant une Ville | *Mat:* op paneel *Size:* hoog 26, breed 40		(Unknown)
1804/12/10	AMSCH	0002	*Ludolph Bakhuysen* | Een kabbelend Water, ryk gestoffeert met diverse vaartuigen, op de voorgrond, ziet men een zylend Jacht, dat het geschut lost, achter hetzelven diverse oorlogscheepen, in het verschiet eene Stad; het Water is dun en helder, en alles krachtig van schildering | *Mat:* op doek *Size:* Hoog 24, breed 26 duim	Jan de Groot	(Sold) fl 107 Jozi
1804/12/10	AMSCH	0003	*Ludolph Bakhuysen* | Deeze capitaale Ordinantie stelt voor een Gezicht aan strand, een menigte krygslieden, welke aanmarcheeren om ingescheept te worden, op de voorgrond ziet men een der opper-officieren met een Dame by zig, verders onderscheide oorlog- en transportscheepen; dit stuk is vol gewoel, en fraai gepenceeld | *Mat:* op doek *Size:* Hoog 35, breed 53 duim	Jan de Groot	(Sold) fl 300 Coclers
1805/07/10	AMSCH	0007	*L. Bakhuysen* | In een Kabbelend Water ziet men verscheide zylende Oorlog, Koopvaardy- en Beurtschepen Pinken, Jollen, enz. aller delicaast gepenceeld op Doek | *Mat:* op doek *Size:* hoog 17, breed 21 duim	V[inkeles] [for] J	(Sold) fl 20 Lafontaine
1805/07/10	AMSCH	0008	*L. Bakhuysen* | Een Onstuimige Zee met verscheide zylende Scheepen en Schuyten, in 't verschiet een Stad; fraay van licht, en meesterlyk van behandeling | *Mat:* op paneel *Size:* hoog 20, breed 16 duim	V[inkeles] [for] N	(Sold) fl 2:5 L Pakker

1805/07/10	AMSCH	0008a[H]	*L. Bakhuysen* | 1 Schildery | *Notes:* This lot was added in by hand in the EBNP, FLNY and RKDH copies of the catalogue.	Y[ver]	(Bought In) fl 25
1805/07/10	AMSCH	0024	*L. Bakhuizen* | Twee stuks, het Pourtrait van L. Bakhuizen, met deszelfs Huisvrouw; uitvoerig door hemzelven | *Mat:* op paneel *Size:* hoog 7, breed 6 duim	R[oos]	(Sold) fl 3:5 v den Brink
1805/07/10	AMSCH	0025	*L. Bakhuizen* | Een Dame met een Tros Druiven in de hand | *Mat:* op doek *Size:* hoog 12, breed 9 duim	R[oos]	(Sold) fl 6 L Pakker
1805/12/16	AMSCH	0003	*L. Backhuyzen* | Een Oorlogschip, dat zyn Bezaansmast vervoren heeft, ziet men in het midden van het stuk, zeilende met zyn Onderzeilen voor de Wind; en verder eenige andere Scheepen, kragtig en fraay op Doek | *Mat:* op doek *Size:* hoog 26, breed 34 duim	V	(Sold) fl 25 C S Roos
1805/12/16	AMSCH	0004	*L. Backhuyzen* | Een woelend Water, met een zeilend Jagt, en andere Vaartuigen, ter zyde een Hoofd van Paalwerk; meesterlyk op Doek | *Mat:* op doek *Size:* hoog 41, breed 56 duim	R[oos]	(Sold) fl 5:5 T van Iperen
1805/12/16	AMSCH	0005	*L. Backhuyzen* | Een Dorpgezicht, met verscheide Woningen by Geboomten, op de Voorgrond rustende en gaande Huislieden, verder de opgang naar een Brug, over een Rivier, gestoffeert met verscheide Scheepen en Trekschuit, by een Dorpgezicht, met Kerk en Woningen; zonagtig en fiks gepenceeld | *Mat:* op doek *Size:* hoog 12, breed 17 duim	Y	(Sold) fl 2:15 Yver
1806/05/05	AMSCH	0004	*L. Bakhuizen* | Een woelend Water, met onderscheiden zeilende Oorlog en andere Scheepen, en kleinder Vaartuigen. Het Water is dun, en het zonlicht maakt een aangename werking; zynde van een delicaate schildering op Doek | *Mat:* op doek *Size:* hoog 18, breed 22 duim	R[oos]	(Sold) fl 87 Hulswit
1806/05/05	AMSCH	0005	*L. Bakhuizen* | Een fraay en natuurlyk Gezicht aan de Buiten Amstel, op den voorgrond gestoffeerd met een Heer en twee Dames by een Visser in zyn Schuit, verder eenige Gebouwen, Molens, Lusthuis en zeilende Scheepen; bevallig en uitvoerig gepenceeld | *Mat:* op doek *Size:* hoog 22, breed 35 duimen	E	(Sold) fl 65 Josi
1806/05/05	AMSCH	0006	*L. Bakhuizen* | Een Gezichtje te Ouderkerk, ziende op de Brug, fraai gestoffeerd met Beeldjes, Schuiten &c.; delicaat gepenceeld op Doek | *Mat:* op doek *Size:* hoog 12, breed 17 duim	Y	(Sold) fl 3 Scheurleer
1806/08/13	AMSCH	0007	*Bakhuysen. (L.)* | In een woelende Zee, ziet men ter eene zyde op de voorgrond een zeilende Jol, en ter andere zyde een drie mast zeilend Oorlogschip; verders een ménigte van zeilende Oorlogscheepen, Pinken, Boeijers en roeijende vaartuigen; dit Schildery is uitmuntend van schildering, schoon van effect, 't water helder en dun, en van de beste behandeling van deeze voortreffelyke Meester | *Mat:* op doek *Size:* hoog 29, breed 40 duim	Coclers	(Sold) fl 730 C S Roos
1806/08/13	AMSCH	0008	*Bakhuysen. (L.)* | Een gezigt op 't Blaauwhoofd te Amsterdam, waar by eenige staande en zittende lieden, en een kanon; verders op 't water een menigte van zeilende en stilleggende vaartuigen, enz. delicaat gepenceeld | *Mat:* op doek *Size:* hoog 16, breed 19 duim	Vinkeles [for] D	(Sold) fl 5:5 van Iperen
1807/04/00	LNDLS	0055	*L. Bakhuyzen* | Een woelend water met zeilende schepen, uitvoerig als met de pen, op een witte grond	[Abraham Delfos] [or others]	(Unknown)
1807/06/10	HGBSM	0055	*L. Bakhuyzen* | Een woelend water met zeilende schepen, uitvoerig als met de pen, op een witte grond	Abraham Delfos [or others]	(Sold) fl 6 Ocke
1807/06/10	HGBSM	0131	*L. Bakhuizen* | Dit fraaij stukje verbeeld een Zeestrand, waarop een schip en eenige figuuren schijnende, op een vuur iets te kooken, op de voorgrond werd een visschers Schuitje in het water gewerkt, verders eenige zijlende Schepen, dit alles aangenaam geördonneerd en uitvoerig geschilderd | *Mat:* op doek *Size:* hoog 14 ½, breed 17 duim	Abraham Delfos [or others]	(Sold) fl 69 Tessier
1807/08/26	AMSCH	0007	*L. Bakhuysen* | Een sterk woelende Zee: ter regter zyde van een rotsachtig Strand ziet men een Man, gaande naast een Vrouw, die op een Muilezel is gezeten, verder in de branding der Zee een driemast Schip, by de wind zeilende, en in 't verschiet hoog Gebergte, benevens eenige Vaartuigen langs de kust: de sterk bewolkte Lugt geeft het onstuimige weder te kennen; zynde alles uitvoerig op Doek geschilderd | *Mat:* op doek *Size:* hoog 21, breed 26 duim	Coclers	(Bought In) fl 140
1807/08/26	AMSCH	0131[a]	*L. Bakhuysen* | Twee stuks stille Waters, by het opkomen der Zon, gestoffeerd met zylende en dryvende Vaartuigen, Visschers in hunne Schuiten, en ruime verschieten; zeer natuurlyk, de eene door L. Bakhuysen, en de ander door Maddersteg | *This Lot:* Een stil Water; lot 131[b] by Maddersteeg *Mat:* op doek *Size:* hoog 16, breed 16 duim	de Vries	(Sold) fl 14 for lots 131[a] & 131[b]. Spruit
1808/04/26	GDAN	0015	*Bakhuyzen (L.)* | Een woelende Zee, waar op een Oorlogschip in zijne Zeilen, in 't verschiet een Fregatschip voor anker leggende, met eenige Schoenders en andere Vaartuigen, uitmuntend geschilderd, eene zijner beste stukken | *Mat:* op doek *Size:* hoog 24 ½, breed 29 duim	G H Fortuyn	(Unknown)
1808/06/06	RMRIJ	0002	*Bakhuisen. (Ludolf)* | Dit Tafereel verbeeldt een gedeelte van het IJ, aan den Mosselsteiger te Amsterdam, vol Schepen en figuren, onder welke laatstgenoemde, op den voorgrond, de asbeelding van dien beroemden Zeeschilder, geheel in 't zwart gekleed, vertoond wordt. Alles zeer verstandig, schoon en kunstig behandeld [Ce Tableau represente le Mosselsteiger, situé sur l'Y á Amsterdam ; l'eau y est calme : plusieurs bâtiments, braques et chaloupes occupent les differents plans. On	Gerrit van der Pot, Heer van Groeneveld	(Sold) fl 1005 J J de Wit [for] le Roi d'Hol[lande]

			distingue, parmi les diverses figures du premier plan, le portrait du célèbre peintre costumé en noir. Ce morceau precieux et achevé dans ses détails, est d'un ton argentin et de son plus beau faire] | *Mat:* op doek *Size:* Hoog 30 ¼, en breed 25 duim *Loc:* Amsterdam, Nederland. Rijksmuseum. (A9)		
1808/06/06	RMRIJ	0003	*Bakhuisen. (Ludolf)* | Eene woelende Zee, waarin zich vertoonen zeilende en stil liggende groote en kleine Vaartuigen, over al het welke eene Onweersbui heen trekt. Op den voorgrond, ter zijde van het stuk, ziet men op het Strand een bevallig Vrouwtje bij een Schipper zitten, terwijl een ander Man, verzeld van zijnen hond, iets komt aanbrengen. Verder eenig paalwerk, enz. Eene wedergade, vertoonende mede een woelend Water met zeilende en stil liggende Vaartuigen: vooraan ziet men eene Sloep (achter op met den naam van Bakhuisen pronkende) in welke eenige Heeren zich naar een groot Oorlogschip laten voeren, dat hooger op voor anker ligt. Verder ziet men hier ook eenig paalwerk, enz. Deze beide stukken zijn meesterlijk geschilderd, en doen eer aan den, in dit vak, beroemden Meester [La prémiere represente l'entrée d'un port Hollandais, dont l'eau est agitée : un vaisseau de guerre est à l'ancre, et plusieurs bateaux sont à la voile. Au bord du rivage sont assis un Vieillard et une femme qui s'entretiennent avec un Pècheur accompagné de son chien, et le ciel paroit annoncer un orage. Le tout fait illusion et est de la plus grande vèrité. La Second Pièce represente la vue d'une eau fortement agitée : sur le devant, on voit une chaloupe, (portant en pouppe le nom de Bakhuisen) sur laquelle plusieurs personnes de distinction se font conduire à la rame vers un vaisseau de guerre, qui est à l'ancre plus loin, et qui porte Pavillon Hollandais. Divers bâtiments sont a la viole, et sous un beau ciel à l'horison, on distingue des bouts de rivage. Ce Tableau est d'une perfection égale au précédent tant par la beauté de l'Exécution que par le vrai du Coloris, et la précision dans tous les détails] | *Mat:* op doek *Size:* Twee Stukken. Hoog 20 ½, en breed 25 ¾ duim *Loc:* Amsterdam, Nederland. Rijksmuseum. (A 10)	Gerrit van der Pot, Heer van Groeneveld	(Sold) fl 3050 Johs Eck en Zoon [for] le Roi
1808/06/13	AMSCH	0004	*Bakhuizen (L.)* | Aan een Hooft ziet men in een kabbelend Water eenige Beurtschepen, Visschers en andere Vaartuigen, en in het verschiet eenige Oorlogs- en Koopvaardijschepen, zijnde eene rijke Ordonantie vol gewoel van Beelden enz.; meesterlijk behandeld | *Mat:* op doek *Size:* hoog 36, breed 40 duim	R[oos]	(Sold) fl 699 Coclers
1808/06/13	AMSCH	0005	*Bakhuizen (L.)* | Deze niet minder fraaije Ordonantie is een meerder woelend Water, aan een Dijk; in het midden ziet men een Oorlogsschip, verders Visschers en andere Vaartuigen, niet minder als de voorgaande | *Size:* hoog 36, breed 40 duim	R[oos]	(Sold) fl 400 Nieuwenhuis pour Henry
1808/06/13	AMSCH	0006	*Bakhuizen (L.)* | Een woelend Water, zijnde een IJgezicht, gestoffeert met zeilende Vaartuigen, verder een ten Anker liggend Oorlogschip, in 't verschiet de Oost-Indische en 's Lands Werven. Meesterlijk fraai van penceelbehandeling | *Mat:* op doek *Size:* hoog 11, breed 15 duim	[Jan Tersteeg]	(Sold) fl 100 for lots 6 & 7. Van Iperen
1808/06/13	AMSCH	0007	*Bakhuizen (L.)* | Een sterk woelende Zee, bij een rots- en bergachtig Strand, waarin zeilende Schepen, alles verbeeld bij een opkomend Onweder, verder bij Geboomte eenige Gebouwen. Mede zeer natuurlijk | *Mat:* op doek *Size:* hoog 11 ½, breed 16 ½ duim	[Jan Tersteeg]	(Sold) fl 100 for lots 6 & 7. Van Iperen
1808/06/13	AMSCH	0008	*Bakhuizen (L.)* | Een kabbelend Zeegezicht, op den voorgrond aan Strand vertoonen zich eenige Visschers, bij een opkomend Vaartuig, verder twee zeilende Oorlog- en andere Schepen; het water is dun, natuurlijk en doorschijnend behandeld, en uitvoerig gepenceeld | *Mat:* op doek *Size:* hoog 25 ½, breed 29 ½ duim	[Jan Tersteeg]	(Sold) fl 280 van Iperen
1808/06/13	AMSCH	0009	*Bakhuizen (L.)* | Deze uitmuntende Ordonantie stelt voor de Vischvangst van Petrus, Christus is zittende aan het Roer, terwijl de Visschers de Netten ophalen; het woelende water is zeer doorschijnend en de schildering uitnemend | *Mat:* op doek *Size:* hoog 26, breed 36 duim	[Jan Tersteeg]	(Sold) fl 250 Thaijs
1808/06/13	AMSCH	0010	*Bakhuizen (L.)* | In een woelende Zee ziet men in het midden een zeilend Schip, met verscheide Beeldjes, en in het verschiet nog verscheide Vaartuigen, fraai van licht, door de wolken, welken het water gedeeltelijk overschaduwen, en van zijne beste behandeling | *Mat:* op paneel *Size:* hoog 16, breed 13 duim	R[oos]	(Bought In) fl 130
1808/08/23	AMSCH	0005	*Bakhuizen. (L.)* | In een woelende Zee vertoond zich een driemast Oorlogschip voor de wind drijvende: ter zijde een stilleggend Beurtschip, waarbij een Visschuitje met twee Beeldjes, verder gestoffeert met verscheide andere Vaartuigen; de woeling van het water is natuurlijk, het licht bevallig, en van een uitvoerige penceelbehandeling | *Mat:* op doek *Size:* hoog 22, breed 31 duim	X	(Bought In) fl 280
1808/08/23	AMSCH	0006	*Bakhuizen. (L.)* | Een sterk woelende Zee, ter regter zijde bij een rotsachtig strand, ziet men een man, gaande naast eene Vrouw, die op een Muil-Ezel gezeten is, verder in de branding der Zee, een driemast Schip, bij de wind zeilende, in het verschiet hoog Gebergte, benevens eenige vaartuigen langs de kust; het water is dun en helder doorschijnend, en krachtig van schildering | *Mat:* op doek *Size:* hoog 21, breed 26 duim	[Coclers]	(Sold) fl 190 Hulswit
1808/11/28	AMSCH	0003	*L. Backhuijsen* | Een sterk woelende Zee, bij een vroege Morgenstond, zijnde een Gezicht aan de Engelsche Kust, gestoffeerd met een Oorlogschip voor Wind zeilende, verder bij de Wal een Schip ten Anker leggende en in 't verschiet een zeilende; de golving van het Water is	F	(Sold) fl 5:15 Rooijers

			natuurlijk, het Licht bevallig en van een fraaije Penceelsbehandeling | *Mat:* op doek *Size:* hoog 35, breed 44 duim		
1808/11/28	AMSCH	0004	*L. Backhuijsen* | Een capitaal woelend Water, met zeilende en ten Anker leggende Schepen en andere Vaartuigen, Meesterlijk behandeld | *Mat:* op paneel *Size:* hoog 12 ½, breed 14 ½ duim	[Gruyter?]	(Bought In) fl 15
1809/04/17	AMSCH	0003	*L. Backhuijsen* | In een sterk woelende Zee, ziet men op de voorgrond ter regter zijde een Veerman tegen de Wind opzeilen, in het midden een Driemast Oorlogschip, een Beurtman, een Visschers Pink en andere Vaartuigen; de woeling der Golven, de fraaije bewolkte Lucht, en het frapante Licht maken dit stuk tot een der beste van deeze groote Meester | *Mat:* op doek *Size:* hoog 26, breed 31 duim	C	(Sold or Bought In) fl 895
1809/07/19	AMSCH	0002	*Bakhuizen (L.)* | Een woelend Water of Zeegezicht, gestoffeerd ter linker zijde met een Kaag, liggende zo bij als teegens den Wind, waar nevens een Vaartuig, dat door gemelde Kaag schijnt overzeild te zijn, en waaruit eenige Goederen in de Kaag werden overgeladen, daarbij een Boot of Jol, waarin zig eenige Personen redden, ter regter zijde een Driemast Schip, zeilende voor den wind, verder ziet men nog andere Scheepen en Vaartuigen, en in het verschiet aan den Horisont ondekt men een Vuurtoren, Stad en Gebergte. De bewolkte Lucht, en het Water zijn dun en natuurlijk van kleur, alles is uitvoerig en fraai gepenceeld; het is een der beste Werken van dezen Meester | *Mat:* op doek *Size:* hoog 22, breed 27 duim	G	(Bought In) fl 400
1809/07/25	HGBSM	0259	*L. Bakhuizen* | Een woelende Zee met Oorlogscheepen and andere Vaartuigen, in 't grauw, kunstig behandelt, door L. Bakhuizen, 1658 | *Mat:* op paneel *Size:* hoog 15 en een half, breed 23 duim *Inscr:* L. Bakhuizen, 1658 (signed and dated?) *Notes:* It is unclear whether the name and date are inscribed on the painting.	D van der Aa [or] E B ten Dall	(Sold) fl 4:5 Bogaard
1809/09/06	AMSCH	0004	*Backhuizen (L.)* | Een Strandgezicht in Italiën, bij een hoogen Rots in Zee, gestoffeerd met Vaartuigen en Beelden, welk eenig Vaatwerk door een stil Water werken; dun behandeld en van de beste schildering van dezen Meester | *Mat:* op paneel *Size:* hoog 20, breed 17 duim *Loc:* Cape Town, South Africa. Old Town House (Michaelis Collection)	Johannes Caudri	(Sold) fl 109 Gruiter
1810/03/26	RMMUY	0068	*Ludolf Bakhuizen* | Op een wit paneel, ziet men met olijverf en als gewasschen in het zwart, een woelend Water, het Y, met een aantal zeilende Schepen, Schuiten en Sloepen. In het verschiet, de stad Amsterdam. Zeer konstig geordonneerd en behandeld [Une vue de l'Y à Amsterdam : plusieurs batiments et bateaux voguant et à l'ancre ; des chaloupes &c. et la dite ville à l'horizon, formant un bel ensemble. Peint en grisaille.] | *Annots:* [par] DVlen [?] (BPG) *Mat:* op paneel *Size:* hoog 14, breed 18 ½ duimen	Daniel de Jongh Az	(Sold) fl 20 Le Brun Parys
1810/07/23	DOLG1	0002	*Ludolph Backhuizen* | Aan 't inkomen van eene Reede, ziet men een Oorlogschip in volle Zeilen, met eenige andere Vaartuigen; op den voorgrond, eenige Visschers, waar onder een, bezig een Boot tegen den Wal optetrekken. Alles dun, kunstig en meesterlijk geschilderd | *Mat:* op doek *Size:* hoog 26, breed 23 ½ duim	Mr Pieter van den Santheuvel	(Sold) fl 260 Nieuwenhuizen van Brussel
1810/07/23	DOLG1	0003	*Ludolph Backhuizen* | Een woelig Water, met Zeilende Schepen, fix geschilderd | *Mat:* op doek *Size:* hoog 11, breed 17 duim	Mr Pieter van den Santheuvel	(Sold) fl 78 van den Einden Dordt
1810/08/01	AMSCH	0004	*Bakhuizen (Ludolph)* | Een woelend Water; zijnde een Gezigt in het IJ, met een groot Jagt, bij den Wind zeilende, verder Oorlogschepen, andere Vaartuigen en de Stad Amsterdam in het verschiet [Vue sur le Port d'Amsterdam, le Fleuve l'IJ étant agité. On y distingue un Jacht voilant sous le vent ; plus en arriere se trouvent des Vaisseaux de guerre et d'autres Batiments ; la Ville d'Amsterdam se presentant dans la perspective] | *Annots:* Passable (NGW); 1771, 31 Julij Amsterdam. Cat. van Braamcamp no.5–550 guld aan P. Calkoen 1781, 10 Sept. Amsterdam. Cat. van P. Calkoen no. 2–700 guld aan van der Schley 1822, 23 Martii London. Sale at Christie's, no. 63 £ 262.10 s. (VAL I) *Mat:* op doek *Size:* hoog 46, breed 68 duimen	Mr Pieter de Smeth van Alphen	(Sold) fl 805 C S Roos d'Amsterdam
1810/08/01	AMSCH	0005	*Bakhuizen (Ludolph)* | Eene sterk woelende Zee, met eene zwaar bewolkte Lucht, rijk gestoffeerd met Oorlog- en Beurt schepen, Visschersschuiten en andere Vaartuigen [Une Mer orageuse, le Ciel étant chargé d'epais nuages : Elle est richement ornée de Batiments de Guerre, de Vaisseaux Marchands, de Pêcheurs et d'autres Navires] | *Annots:* passable (NGW); Vente le Brun No. 141 fr. 2151 (SMLN) *Mat:* op doek *Size:* hoog 40, breed 53 duimen	Mr Pieter de Smeth van Alphen	(Sold) fl 950 Texier, Gerbet en Comp [for] LeBrun
1810/08/01	AMSCH	0006	*Bakhuizen (Ludolph)* | Een Strandgezigt met deftige Heeren, Vrouwen en Visschers. In Zee een groot Jagt en andere Vaartuigen [Vue sur le rivage de la Mer : on y voit des Seigneurs et des Dames aller le long de la côte, ainsi que des pauvres Pêcheurs. Sur la Mer se distinguent un Jacht et d'autres Navires] | possibly companion to lot 7 *Annots:* Excellent (NGW); Vente le Brun No.140 fr 7001 (SMLN) *Mat:* op doek *Size:* hoog 22, breed 33 duimen	Mr Pieter de Smeth van Alphen	(Sold) fl 1400 Texier, Gerbet en Comp [for] LeBrun
1810/08/01	AMSCH	0007	*Bakhuizen (Ludolph)* | Eene onstuimige Zee, met zeilende Schepen, in het verschiet Gebergte. Kunnende strekken tot eene wederga van de voorgaande [Representation d'une Mer orageuse ; ornée de Navires à la voile ; on y decouvre des Montagnes vèrs l'horison. Ce Tableau peut faire pendant au précédent] | possibly companion to lot 6 *Annots:* médiocre	Mr Pieter de Smeth van Alphen	(Sold) fl 550 C Josi

(NGW); 1822, 23 March. Sale at Christie's, London, no.44 £42 to Hamlet (VAL I) *Mat:* op doek *Size:* hoog 22, breed 33 duimen

Backhuysen, Ludolf (or Backhuysen, copy after)

1806/10/17	MGSAN	0008	*Bakhuizen* | Een woelend Zeetje, op de voorgrond een Boot, op 't Strand een laveerend Sprietschip, door of naar Bakhuizen | *Mat:* op paneel	Gerardus Beljard	(Unknown)
1806/10/17	MGSAN	0009	*Bakhuizen* | Een onstuimige Zee, op de voorgrond een laveerend Sprietschip, door denzelven [of naar Bakhuizen] | *Mat:* op paneel	Gerardus Beljard	(Unknown)

Backhuysen, Ludolf (or Backhuysen, manner)

1801/08/19	AMSCH	0003	*L. Bakhuizen* | Een woelende Zee met verscheide Oorlogscheepen en andere Vaartuigen, op de voorgrond een Man in een Boot, meesterlyk op doek, door of in de manier van dito [L. Bakhuizen] | *Mat:* op doek *Size:* hoog 24, breed 42 duim	Van Forreest	(Sold) fl 14:10 Wolft
1802/08/24	LNDLS	0121	*Bakhuyzen* | Een Gezigt op het Y, op den voorgrond eenige Heeren en Juffers van of in de manier van Bakhuyzen | *Mat:* op paneel	Leonardus Bouman [or others]	(Unknown) fl 14
1805/06/24	DOBLU	0028	*Bakhuyzen* | Een zeer fraai Watergezicht, door of in de Manier van Bakhuyzen	Willem Snellen [or] F R E Nibbelinck [or] Gysbert Visser	(Unknown)
1805/06/24	DOBLU	0029	*Bakhuyzen* | Een dito [zeer fraai Watergezicht], dito [door of in de Manier van Bakhuyzen	Willem Snellen [or] F R E Nibbelinck [or] Gysbert Visser	(Unknown)

Backhuysen, Ludolf (copy after)

1802/09/18	RMDRS	0055	*L. Bakhuizen* | Een Zeen met Scheepen, na L. Bakhuizen	Casper de Haas	(Unknown) fl 3
1806/10/17	MGSAN	0034	*Bakhuyzen* | Een woelend Zeetje, op de voorgrond een Schuit op strand, voorts gestoffeerd met Zee- en andere Schepen, naar Bakhuyzen | *Mat:* op paneel *Notes:* This lot was sold with lot 33 by an anonymous artist.	Gerardus Beljard	(Sold) £ 0.4.7 for lots 33 & 34. de Onde
1806/11/24	AMSCH	0040	*Langendyk (D.); L. Bakhuyzen* | Een kabbelend Water met zeilende Scheepen en andere Vaartuigen; het licht doet in dit stukje een byzondere werking en is kunstig gecopieerd naar L. Bakhuyzen | copy by D. Langendijk after Backhuysen *Mat:* op doek *Size:* hoog 13, breed 17 duim	Munnikhuizen	(Sold) fl 21 van Iperen

Backhuysen, Ludolf (manner)

1801/02/24	AMOTT	0007	*Bakhuisen* | 1 dito [Zeetje] als Bakhuisen		(Unknown)
1801/03/16	AMSCH	0138	*Bakhuizen* | Een onstuimige Zee met verscheide Schepen, in de manier van Bakhuizen	K[ip]	(Sold) fl 5:5 Koopman
1801/03/16	AMSCH	0203	*Bakhuyzen* | Een Zee met verscheide Schepen en Vaartuigen, in de manier van Bakhuyzen	K[ip]	(Sold) fl 4 Koopman
1801/03/16	AMSCH	0209	*Bakhuizen* | Een woelende Zee, in de manier van Bakhuizen	P[ruyssenaar]	(Sold) fl 2:15 Pruissenaar [for] R
1802/05/05	AMSCH	0248	*L. Bakhuyzen* | Een kabbelende Zee, met een Oorlogschip en andere Vaartuigen, op Strand twee Beelden, in de manier van L. Bakhuyzen | *Mat:* op doek *Size:* hoog 17, breed 22 duim	G	(Sold) fl 3 Spruit
1803/11/30	MGBEO	0008	*Bakhuizen* | Een woelende Zee, met Scheepen, in de manier van Bakhuizen | *Mat:* op paneel *Size:* hoog 18 duim, breed 24 duim	Samuel de Wind	(Sold) £ 0:7 Ad^n Tak
1804/12/10	AMSCH	0112	*Bakhuise* | Een woelend Water, ryk met diversche vaartuigen en in de manier van Bakhuise behandeld | *Mat:* op doek *Size:* hoog 18, breed 24 duim	Jan De Groot	(Sold) fl 9:15 Yver
1805/10/09	HGBSM	C0003	*L. Bakhuyzen* | Het opkoomen van storm op Zee, op de tweede grond ziet men een Haven, kragtig en natuurlyk, als door L. Bakhuyzen | *Mat:* op doek *Size:* hoog 23 ½ breet 31 duim	T H van Willigen [or others]	(Sold) fl 9 Uytenbogart
1808/08/23	AMSCH	0259	*L. Bakhuijsen* | Een woelend Water, in 't verschiet een Stad, op de voorgrond een zeilende Kaag, Oorlog en andere Scheepen; in de manier van L. Bakhuijsen	J	(Sold) fl 2 L Pakker
1810/05/22	AMSCH	0148	*L. Backhuisen* | Een Storm op Zee, gestoffeerd met verscheide Scheepen; fiks behandeld, in de manier van L. Backhuisen | *Notes:* This lot was sold with lot 147 by an anonymous artist.	D	(Sold) fl 1:10 for lots 147 & 148. Topher

Baden, Jan Juriaensz. van

1804/10/29	HRBAU	0004	*Baden* | In een' pragtigen Tempel ziet men Ananias en Sapphira, door Petrus en Johannes bestraft wordende, ter aarde vallen. Het Perspectief is regelmatig, en zeer zonagtig, in de manier van van Deelen behandeld | *Mat:* op paneel *Size:* hoog 16, breed 20 duim	Simon Styl	(Unknown)

Baeck, Johannes

1806/08/13	AMSCH	0027	*Baeck. (J.)* | Een musiceerend Gezelschap van Heeren en Dames, verders eenige liefkoozende; en verder bywerk; delicaat en uitvoerig gepenceeld | *Mat:* op doek *Size:* hoog 39, breed 46 duim	Vinkeles [for] D	(Sold) fl 6:10 Nieuwenhuijs

Baen, Jan de

1806/08/20	HGBSM	0097	*J. de Baan* | Een Schilderij verbeeldende de overwinning van Chattam in het jaar 1667, onder het beleid van Cornelis de Witt, Burgemeester der	Macalester Loup [or others]	(Bought In) fl 160

			Stad Dordrecht en Ruwaard van Putten, waarin Cornelis de Witt, naar het leven is geschilderd; terwijl het levendig pourtrait der Huisvrouw van dezen Held onder de gedaante van eene weldadige Godinne des overvloeds zich achter zijn beeltenis vertoont, zijnde in het verschiet de sterkte Charnesse bij Chattam afgebeeld met de Hollandsche en Vijandelijke Vlooten, als na het eindigen van den slag, waarvan sommige Schepen nog brandende vertoond worden. Helder van couleur, door J. de Baan, op doek, hoog 29, breed 38 duim. Dit stuk is het origineel model, op last der Regeering van Dordrecht vervaardigd, ter gelegenheid van de plegtige inhaling van dezen destijds nog naar waarde geëerde [sic] steun des Vaderlands om tot eene eeuwigduurende gedachtenis te verstrekken. Na het welk dan ook het groote stuk, het welk volgens Wagenaar Vaderlandsche Historie XIII.^{de} Deel, Bladzijde 478, te Dordrecht op het Stadhuis heeft te pronk gehangen, meer uitvoerig is geschilderd geworden; doch welk laatste bij de troebeles in later tijden is vernield, terwijl de plaat bij Wagenaar XIII.^{de} Deel, na dit stuk is gegraveerd geworden. De lijst van dit stuk, kostbaar van beeld en snijkunst, heeft boven aan, het Wapen der Stad Dordrecht en onder aan het Wapen Familie van de Wit, met een Latijnsch onderschrift, ter vereering van den Held dezer geschiedenis door de Regeering van Hollands oudste Stad uitgeven | *Mat:* op doek *Size:* hoog 29, breed 38 duim *Loc:* Amsterdam, Nederland. Rijksmuseum. (A 4648)		
1806/08/20	HGBSM	0098	*J. de Baan* | Het origineel Portrait van Jan de Witt, Raadpensiönaris van Holland, in het verschiet de Raadkamer | *Mat:* op doek *Size:* hoog 46 ½, breed 36 ½ duim *Loc:* Amsterdam, Nederland. Rijksmuseum. (A 13) as copy after Jan de Baen	Macalester Loup [or others]	(Sold) fl 81 for lots 98 & 99. Huybrechts
1806/08/20	HGBSM	0099	*J. de Baan* | Het origineel Portrait van Cornelis de Witt, oud Burgermeester van Dordrecht, gevolmagtigde van H. H. M. op 's Lands Vloot tot de Expeditie naar Chattam | *Mat:* op doek *Size:* hoog 46 ½, breed 36 ½ duim *Loc:* Amsterdam, Nederland. Rijksmuseum. (A 14) as copy after Jan de Baen	Macalester Loup [or others]	(Sold) fl 81 for lots 98 & 99. Huybrechts
1807/06/10	HGBSM	0217	*Jan de Baan* | Een vrouwe Portrait | *Mat:* op doek *Size:* hoog 23, breed 17 ½ duim	Abraham Delfos [or others]	(Sold) fl 3 Bogard

Bager, Johann Daniel

1802/06/28	AMSCH	0022	*Bager* | Twee stuks bevallige Voorwerpen, de eene verbeeld een Jongeling zittende te teekenen; en 't andere een Dame, zittende wol te winden; beide fiks behandeld door Bager, Panneel | *Mat:* op paneel *Size:* hoog 6, breed 6 duim	Anna Elink	(Sold) fl 3 van Iperen
1802/06/28	AMSCH	0023	*Bager* | Twee stuks met staande Beeldjes, fiks op Panneel | *Mat:* op paneel	Anna Elink	(Sold) fl 3 Vermeulen
1802/06/28	AMSCH	0024	*Bager* | Twee stuks bevallige Voorwerpen, de eene verbeeld een Leezend Meisje, en de andere verbeeld een Jongen met een Vogelnesje; fiks gepenceeld door Denzelven [Bager], Panneel | *Mat:* op paneel *Size:* hoog 9, breed 8 duim	Anna Elink	(Sold) fl 1:5 Vermeulen

Bakken, van [Unidentified] (and Carree, Hend. (I))

1804/07/25	DLGRO	0017	*van Bakken; Hendrik Carré* | Een Bergächtig Landschap, zeer uitvoerig geschilderd | *Mat:* op doek *Size:* hoog 32, breed 29 duim	Mr Franc van der Burch Wz.	(Unknown)

Bakker, C. [Unidentified]

1802/07/21	HGKAN	0048	*C. Bakker* | Een capitaal stuk, verbeeldende eenige Krygslieden, welke zich met eenige Vrouwen in een verliefde houding schynen te vermaaken, Teekening, Couleuren en Hartstogten, zyn zodanig geobserveerd, dat men ter niets in aantreft, het geen niet yders bewondering opwekt, door C. Bakker, van Harlingen, A^{o}. 1627, zwarte Lyst | *Inscr:* C. Bakker, van Harlingen, A^{o}. 1627 (signed and dated?) *Notes:* It is unclear whether the name and date are inscribed on the painting.		(Unknown)

Balen, van

1801/03/16	AMSCH	0129	*van Baalen* | Twee stuks Landschappen, ryk met Beelden gestoffeerd	P[ruyssenaar]	(Bought In) fl 43
1801/04/23	AMYVR	0012	*van Baalen* | Een Bybelsche Ordonantie, op Koper | *Mat:* op koper		(Sold) fl 5 Yperen
1806/05/05	AMSCH	0021	*van Baalen* | Den Berg Parnas, met Apollo en de Muzen, verzeld door Minerva en andere Nimphen; meesterlyk en delicaat gepenceeld door van Baalen | *Mat:* op paneel *Size:* hoog 33, breed 51 duim	V[inkeles]	(Sold) fl 2:15 Levy Pakker

Balen, van (manner)

1801/03/16	AMSCH	0062	*van Baalen* | Een Bagenaal [sic] van verscheide dansende Beelden en Kinderen, in de manier van van Baalen | *Notes:* This lot was sold with lot 63 by an anonymous artist.	P[ruyssenaar]	(Sold) fl 1:10 for lots 62 & 63. Gruiter
1806/10/16	UTWLD	0010	*van Balen* | Eenige spelende Cupido's en verder bywerk als van van Balen	Mr P de Malapert [or] W Beeldsnyder	(Unknown)
1809/04/22	AMYVR	0190	*van Balen* | Mozes met den Slangenstaf, waarbij eene groote menigte Volks; meesterlijk, als door van Balen	de Bruin	(Sold) fl 8 du Pree

Balen, Hendrik van (I)

1802/09/06	AMSCH	0003	*H. van Balen* | In een aangenaam Boomryk Landschap, vertoond zig de Fabelgeschiedenis van Euridice, de Echtgenoot van Orphéus, door een	Brave	(Sold) fl 31 for lots 3 & 4. van Iperen

<table>
<tr><td></td><td></td><td></td><td>Slang in de hiel gekwest, terwyl zy beezig was met haare Gezellinne Bloemen in Korfjes te vergaderen; bevallig van Coloriet, en meesterlyk van Penceelbehandeling | companion to lot 4 Mat: op koper Size: hoog 21, breed 16 duim</td><td></td><td></td></tr>
<tr><td>1802/09/06</td><td>AMSCH</td><td>0004</td><td>H. van Balen | De wéderga verbeeld in een dito [Boomryk] Landschap, Apollo de dood van Hyacintus beweenende, gestoffeerd met verder bywerk; in alles als de voorgaande meesterlyk gepenceeld | companion to lot 3</td><td>Brave</td><td>(Sold) fl 31 for lots 3 & 4. van Iperen</td></tr>
<tr><td>1802/12/13</td><td>AMSCH</td><td>0015</td><td>H. van Baalen | Een Zinnebeeldige Fabel Ordenantie in een Landschap, verbeeldende Orpheus op de Fiool speelende, waar voor verscheide Dansende Kindertjes met Bloemkranssen, gestoffeert met anderen rustende Beelden, met verder Bywerk, uitvoerig op Paneel geschilderd | Mat: op paneel Size: hoog 15, breed 19 duim</td><td>Yver</td><td>(Sold) fl 16 Coclers</td></tr>
<tr><td>1803/09/07</td><td>AMSCH</td><td>0006</td><td>H. v. Balen | Deeze ryke Ordenantie vertoont de ontdekking van den Held Achilles, onder de Maagden; op twee Tafels, en op de voorgrond, ziet men een ménigte kostbaare Cieraaden van Goude en Zilvere Vaaten, Musicq Instrumenten, en verscheide zeldzaamhéden, alles ongemeen uitvoerig en kunstig gepenceeld [Ce tableau d'une riche ordonnance représente la découverte d'Achille entre les filles : sur le devant on voit sur deux tables une quantité d'ornemens précieux, des vases d'or et d'argent, des instrumens de musique et des curiosités ; le tout peint avec beaucoup d'art et des profusion] | Mat: op paneel Size: hoog 22, breed 30 duim</td><td>Smidt</td><td>(Sold) fl 28 Jan Yver</td></tr>
<tr><td>1803/09/07</td><td>AMSCH</td><td>0007</td><td>H. v. Balen | Deeze Ryke Ordenantie, vertoont op zee, de Triomph van Nephtunus en Galathéa, op de Schulpwagen, door Zee Paarden getrokken, verzeld van een menigte Waternimphen, Naijaden, en Riviergoden; zeer delicaat en uitvoerig op Koper geschilderd [Cette riche ordonnance représente sur mer le triomphe de Neptune et de Galathée, assis sur un char de conque trainé par des chevaux marins, et accompagné d'un grand nombre de Néreides, de Nayades et de divinités riveraines ; peint avec délicatesse et beaucoup de fini] | Mat: op koper Size: hoog 12 ½, breed 17 duim</td><td>Smidt</td><td>(Sold) fl 7:5 Gruiter</td></tr>
<tr><td>1803/09/07</td><td>AMSCH</td><td>0008</td><td>H. v. Balen | Deeze Ordenantie in een Boomryk Landschap, vertoond den Parnasberg, met Apollo en de Musen, verzeld van Minerva, en andere Nimphen; meesterlyk en uitvoerig gepenceeld [Cette ordonnance, dans un paysage riche en arbres, représente le mont Parnasse, Apollon et les Muses accompagnées de Minerve et d'autres Nymphes ; peint et achevé en maître] | Mat: op paneel Size: hoog 33, breed 51 duim</td><td>Smidt</td><td>(Sold) fl 11:10 Gruiter</td></tr>
<tr><td>1804/07/25</td><td>AMSCH</td><td>0010</td><td>Baalen. (H. van) | De Romeinsche Kinderen Liefde; in een Kerker verbeeld; zynde Çimon door zyne Dochter met haar Borstgevoed; meesterlyk en fraay gepenceeld | Mat: op koper Size: hoog 10, breed 12 ½ duim</td><td></td><td>(Sold) fl 3:15 Yver</td></tr>
<tr><td>1804/08/02</td><td>BDAN</td><td>0024</td><td>H. van Balen | Een Maria-beeld in de Wolken, zeer delicaat geschildert | Mat: op koper Size: b. 10 en 1 half d. h. 13 en 1 half d.</td><td>J G Calckberner</td><td>(Unknown)</td></tr>
<tr><td>1804/08/08</td><td>AMSCH</td><td>0014</td><td>H. van Baalen | In een Boomryk Landschap vertoont zich de Parnasberg, met Apollo en de Muzen, verzeld van Minerva en andere Nimphen, en verder toepasselyk Bywerk; uitvoerig en meesterlyk gepenceeld | Mat: op paneel Size: hoog 33, breed 51 duim</td><td>Vink[eles] [for] K[=Gruyter?]</td><td>(Sold) fl 2:15 Gruiter</td></tr>
<tr><td>1805/07/03</td><td>AMSCH</td><td>0010</td><td>Balen (H. van) | Deeze ryke Ordinantie in een Boomryk Landschap, vol gewoel van een ménigte Beelden, vertoont een Goden-Maaltyd, waarby verscheide Minnewigten, en verder bywerk; Meesterlyk en bevallig geschilderd | Mat: op paneel Size: hoog 20, breed 29 duim</td><td>R[oos]</td><td>(Sold) fl 11 Lafontaine</td></tr>
<tr><td>1805/10/09</td><td>HGBSM</td><td>0077</td><td>H. van Balen | Danaë, met de goude regen | Mat: op koper Size: hoog 13 breet 10 ½ duim</td><td>T H van Willigen [or others]</td><td>(Sold) fl 8:5 Teissier</td></tr>
<tr><td>1807/08/26</td><td>AMSCH</td><td>0021</td><td>H. van Baalen | De Heilige Famielje, zittende in een Landschap by geboomte, Maria zit met het Kindeken op de schoot, waar voor St. Jan, hetzelven een korfje Bloemen aanbiedende, verder andere Engelen Bloemen vergaderende, om hoog een glorie van verscheide Engelen; uitvoerig gepenceeld | Mat: op koper Size: hoog 11, breed 9 ½ duim</td><td>v d Schley [for] L</td><td>(Sold) fl 1:5 v d Schley [for] A</td></tr>
<tr><td>1808/08/23</td><td>AMSCH</td><td>0013</td><td>Baalen. (H. van) | Dit rijk geordoneert Schilderstuk, vertoont Neptunus en zijne Gemalinne, zittende op een prachtige Zee-wagen, door Zeepaarden getrokken, omringt van eene menigte Naijaden en andere Water-Nimphen, Tritons op Kinkhoorns blazende, en verscheide Minnewigten op Dolphijnen drijvende, anderen zijn vliegende, verder een bergagtig Strand met eenige Lieden; het is bevallig van licht en koloriet, en uitvoerig gepenceeld | Mat: op koper Size: hoog 22, breed 28 duim</td><td>C</td><td>(Bought In) fl 40</td></tr>
<tr><td>1808/11/28</td><td>AMSCH</td><td>0006</td><td>H. van Baalen | Deeze rijke Ordonantie, verbeeld de Triump [sic] van Nepthunus en Galathéa, zittende op een pragtige Zeewagen, werdende door Zeepaarden getrokken, omringd van een menigte Naijaden, Waternimphen en andere Riviergoden, delicaat en uitvoerig gepenceeld | Mat: op koper Size: hoog 13, breed 17 duim</td><td>[Gruyter?]</td><td>(Bought In) fl 9:10</td></tr>
<tr><td>1810/06/20</td><td>AMSCH</td><td>0004</td><td>H. Van Baalen | Een Godenmaaltijd, met eene menigte Beelden, Meesterlijk | Mat: op koper Size: hoog 19, breed 26 duimen</td><td>A</td><td>(Sold) fl 30:10 Andriessen</td></tr>
<tr><td>1810/06/20</td><td>AMSCH</td><td>0004a</td><td>H. Van Baalen | Twee stuks Landschappen, beide met Fabelhistorien gestoffeerd en uitvoerig behandeld | Mat: op koper Size: Jeder is hoog 21, breed 16 duimen</td><td>T</td><td>(Sold) fl 11 du Pree</td></tr>
</table>

1810/07/26	AMSCH	0004	*Baalen (H. van)* | Een zamenkomst der Zanggodinnen. Schoon geschilderd | *Mat:* op koper *Size:* hoog 19, breed 25 duimen	Cassino	(Sold) fl 11:10 du Pree
1810/08/06	AMSCH	0005	*Baalen (H. van)* | Dit rijk geordonneerd Schilderstuk vertoont Neptunus en zijne Gemalinne, zittende op een prachtige Zeewagen, door Zeepaarden getrokken, omringd van Waternimfen, vliegende Minnewichten, enz. Krachtig en meesterlijk uitgevoerd | *Mat:* op koper *Size:* hoog 22, breed 28 duimen	B	(Bought In) fl 30
			Balen, Hendrik van (I) (and Brueghel, J. (I))		
1801/05/11	AMSCH	0013	*Van Balen; Breughel* | De historie van David en Abigaël, zynde een ryken Ordinantie, van verscheiden beelden en paarden, en andere stoffagie, fraay gepenceeld | *Mat:* op paneel *Size:* hoog 22, breed 33 duim	R[oos]	(Sold) fl 40 P M Levij
1801/08/19	AMSCH	0006	*van Balen; Breugel* | In een Landschap met geboomten, vertoont zig by een Tempel van Bachus, een groote ménigte Bachanten, die Dansende en musiceerende zig vermaaken; ryk gestoffeert met verder bywerk, zeer uitvoerig op Koper geschilderd | *Mat:* op koper *Size:* hoog 11, breed 16 duim	Van Forreest	(Sold) fl 22:10 Wed Achtienhoven
1802/06/16	AMSCH	0021	*Breugel; van Baalen* | Een fraai Egyptisch Landschap, met verscheiden soorten van Bloemen, op de voorgrond Maria met het Kindje: alles zeer uitvoerig en helder gepenceeld | *Mat:* op doek *Size:* hoog 14 ½, breed 18 ½ duim	[Merrem]	(Sold) fl 39 Pruijssenaar
1802/09/29	AMSCH	0012	*Hk. van Baalen; J. Breugel* | Een Historiëelen, hoog 10 ½, breed 8 ¼ duim. Paneel. Den God Pan word in dit Schilderstukje verbeeld, als vervolgende Syrinx, tot de Rivier Ladon, waarin zy zig werpende, in een Riet herschept wierd; de delicaate Penceelbehandeling, waarmeede dit Stukje is uitgevoerd, is zeer fraai en meesterlyk [Dans ce sujet de la Fable, Le Dieu Pan est représenté, comme poursuivant Syrinx, jusqu'au Fleuve Ladon, entre les bras du quel sejetta [sic] cette Nimphe, ou elle fut metamorphosée en Roseau. – La précision du dessin, un Pinceau délicat, caractére des beaux ouvrages de ces deux artistes, se remarquent dans ce petit Tableau.] | *Mat:* op paneel *Size:* hoog 10 ½, breed 8 ¼ duim	[Labouchere?]	(Sold) fl 8:10 Gruiter
1803/07/18	AMSCH	0005	*Balen, (J. van) [Baelen (H. van)]; J. Breughel* | Een Bachenaal met verscheide Nimphen, Saters en vliegende Kinderen, welke met Bloemen en Vrugten zich vermaaken. Het Landschap is even uitvoerig en delicaat als de Beelden gepenceeld [Une bacchanale. Deux Nimphes recevant des fruits & des fleurs de deux Genies & d'un troisieme voltigent [sic] en air. Vèrs la droite sont deux faunes. Breugel à orné ce tableau par un paysage & de jolis animaux formant un ensemble charment [sic], surtout par la belle fonte de couleur de la carnation des Nimphes.] | *Mat:* op koper *Size:* hoog 12, breed 15 duim *Notes:* The first artist's name differs in the Dutch and French editions of the catalogue.	Maria Theresia Andrioli	(Sold) fl 27:10 Coclers
1803/09/07	AMSCH	0009	*van Balen; Breugel* | Een Feest van Céres, zy zit op een pragtige Wagen, en word geleid van een menigte Beelden en Boeren, fraay op Paneel [Une fête de Cérés ; la déesse est montée sur un char magnifique et entourée d'une quantité de figures et de paysans ; beau tableau] | *Mat:* op paneel *Size:* hoog 14, breed 22 duim	Smidt	(Sold) fl 4:5 Gruiter
1803/09/07	AMSCH	0010	*van Balen; Breugel* | Een Landschap met veel Geboomte, gestoffeerd op de voorgrond met verscheide dansende kinderen, verder andere die musiseeren; uitvoerig op Koper geschilderd [Paysage avec beaucoup d'arbres ; relevé sur le devant par des groupes d'enfans, dont les uns dansent et les autres font de la musique] | *Mat:* op koper *Size:* hoog 14, breed 11 duim	Smidt	(Bought In) fl 11
1803/09/07	AMSCH	0011	*van Balen; Breugel* | Een zeer uitvoerig Rhyngezicht, gestoffeerd met Diana en hare Nimphen [Une très belle vue du Rhin ; animée par Diane et ses Nymphes] | *Mat:* op koper *Size:* hoog 11, breed 17 duim	Smidt	(Sold) fl 4 Gruiter
1804/08/02	BDAN	0004	*Flaelen Breugel; H. van Baelen* | Een Goode-Feest, vol gewoel van Beelden, schoon in Couleur, alles kunstig en uitvoerig geschildert | *Mat:* op koper *Size:* b. 19 d. h. 14 en 1 half d.	J G Calckberner	(Unknown)
1804/08/08	AMSCH	0013	*J. Breugel; H. van Baalen* | De Maagd Maria, met het Kind Jezus op de schoot, om dezelve een Feston met Bloemen; meesterlyk gepenceeld | *Mat:* op paneel *Size:* hoog 12, br. 9 ½ duim	Vink[eles] [for] K[=Gruyter?]	(Sold) fl 2 Gruyter
1805/10/09	HGBSM	0009	*Breugel; van Baalen* | Een thuin gezigt met een bad, waarin Susanna zit te baden, agter haar de twee ouden, benevens een ryke fontein, zeer uitvoerig | *Mat:* op koper *Size:* hoog 18 ½ breet 26 ½ duim	T H van Willigen [or others]	(Sold) fl 14 Ph Meij
1806/08/20	HGBSM	0091	*J. Breugel; H. van Balen* | Een Landschap, waarin een voorhof, beplant met veelerhande soort van bloemen, bij eene fontein, zijn Eenden, Paauwen en andere Vogels, in het zelven is verbeeld Christus, in de gedaante van een Hovenier; het Landschap, Vogels en ander bijwerk, is konstig en uitvoerig geschilderd, door J. Breugel, en de figuuren, door H. van Balen, op paneel uit een stuk | *Mat:* op paneel *Size:* hoog 24, breed 34 duim	Macalester Loup [or others]	(Sold) fl 30 Zwartsman
1807/06/10	HGBSM	0154	*H. van Baalen; J. Breugel* | Het Bad van Diana, met haare Nimphen bezig zijnde met baden, de voorgrond gestoffeerd met veelerhande dood wild enz., zeer uitvoerig gepenceeld, de figuuren door H. van Baalen, en het Landschap en bijwerk door J. Breugel, zijnde van het beste tijd der beide Meesters | *Mat:* op paneel *Size:* hoog 22 ½, breed 31 duim	Abraham Delfos [or others]	(Sold) fl 62 S T

1807/08/26	AMSCH	0017	*den Fluweelen Breugel; P. van Baalen* | In dit Tafreel, vertoont zig in een aangenaam Landschap, de ontdekking van Erichtonius, zoon van Vulcaan, in een korfje geleegen, dat de dochteren van Cecrops door Pallas was aanbevolen hetzelve zorgvuldig te bewaaren, zonder het te bezigtigen; de Beeldjes zyn wel geteekend, bevallig van koloriet, het licht en bruin doed eene goede werking, en is van eene uitvoerige penceel-behandeling, door den Fluweelen Breugel en P. van Baalen, op Koper, hoog 12, breed 9 duim; dit stukje is een der fraaiste die door beide deeze Meesters vervaardigd zyn | *Mat:* op koper *Size:* hoog 12, breed 9 duim *Notes:* The artist's name was given as "P. van Baalen" but we have assumed this is an error.	Helsdinge	(Bought In) fl 42
1808/08/23	AMSCH	0011	*Baalen (H. vam); J. Breugel* | Dit kunstrijk Tafereel vertoont in een heuvelagtig Landschap, de Reiniging der Joodsche Mannen en Vrouwen, verzelt van verscheide Kinderen, alle in bijzondere beweegingen; dit stuk is rijk geordoneert met een groote meenigte Beelden, bevallig van schikking, aangenaam van koloriet en licht, en meesterlijk fraai en uitvoerig gepenceeld | *Mat:* op paneel *Size:* hoog 37, breed 54 duim	C	(Bought In) fl 50
1808/08/23	AMSCH	0012	*Breugel (J); van Baalen* | Deeze kapitaale Ordonantie verbeeld de Dooping van Christus, waar bij verscheiden Vrouwen met Kinderen en andere Beelden; uitmuntend en krachtig van schildering | *Mat:* op paneel *Size:* hoog 59, breed 76 duim	C	(Bought In) fl 61
1809/04/17	AMSCH	0013	*Breugel; H. van Baalen* | Een boomrijk Landschap, op de voorgrond bij een Bad, zien men Diana met haare Nimphen, in 't verschiet Actéon; uitvoerig door Breugel en H. van Baalen | *Mat:* op koper *Size:* hoog 8, breed 10 duim	A	(Sold) fl 2:15 Gruyter
1809/06/13	AMSCH	0029	*Breugel; van Baalen* | In een Landschap, vertoond zig de Godin Céres, zittende op een pragtige Waagen, verzeld van eenige Lieden die de Staasie volgen, uitvoerig | *Mat:* op paneel *Size:* hoog 14, breed 22 duim	[Gruyter?]	(Sold or Bought In) fl 3:15 Gruiter
1810/06/06	RMMUY	0175	*van Baalen; Breugel* | Adam en Eva in 't Paradijs, met veel cierlijk bijwerk | *Mat:* op koper		(Sold) fl 9 V Leen
1810/07/26	AMSCH	0003	*Baalen (H. van); J. Breugel* | Een Godemaaltijd, waarbij eene menigte Vrouwen, Kinderen enz. Meesterlijk en uitvoerig | *Mat:* op paneel *Size:* hoog 13, breed 15 duimen	Cassino	(Sold) fl 30 C S Roos
1810/08/06	AMSCH	0003	*Baalen (H.van); J. Breugel* | Deze rijke Ordonnantie vertoont in een heuvelachtig Landschap de reiniging der Joodsche Mannen en Vrouwen, waarbij verscheidene Kinderen, alle in bijzondere bewegingen. Dit stuk is bevallig van koloriet, uitvoerig en fraai gepenceeld | *Mat:* op paneel *Size:* hoog 37, breed 54 duimen	B	(Sold) fl 50 Josi [for] Burtyn
1810/08/06	AMSCH	0004	*Baalen (H. van); J. Breugel* | Eene Bijbel-Ordonnantie, voorstellende de Dooping van Christus, waarbij verscheidene Vrouwen met Kinderen, en andere Beelden. Uitvoerig en krachtig van schildering | *Mat:* op paneel *Size:* hoog 59, breed 76 duimen	B	(Bought In) fl 15
1810/10/11	AMSCH	0015	*Breugel; Van Balen* | In een Boschachtig Landschap ziet men bij een heldere Beek de Jagtgodin Diana, verzeld van hare Nimfen, in 't verschiet Actéon; delikaat gepenseeld | *Mat:* op koper *Size:* hoog 8, breed 10 duimen	[Gruyter?]	(Sold) fl 10 T Spaan
			Balen, Hendrik van (I) (and Seghers, D.)		
1802/08/24	LNDLS	0023	*van Balen; D. Seegers* | Een Krans van veele Bloemen, rustende tegen Steenwerk. Delicaat en zeer konstig van schildering, door D. Seegers. In 't midden een Vrouw met Kinderen, verbeeldende de Liefde | *Mat:* op doek *Size:* hoog 31, breed 25 duimen	Leonardus Bouman [or others]	(Unknown) fl 16
			Balen, Hendrik van (II)		
1803/04/20	AMSCH	0007	*Baalen, (H. van) de Jonge* | Dit voorwerp vertoont de Ontmoeting van Maria by Elizabeth, zynde een ordenantie van vyf beelden, by den ingang van een treffelyk Gebouw, meesterlyk en uitvoerig gepenceeld [Sur un perron est representée la Visite de Marie à Elisabeth, occompagnées [sic] de Joseph, de Joachim & d'une femme Sainte. Ce morceau touché avec art est d'un beau Colories [sic].] | companion to lot 8 *Mat:* op steen *Size:* hoog 15, breed 13 duim	Maria Magdalena van Sluypwyk, gravinne van Moens	(Sold) fl 35 Pruijssenaar [for] R
1803/04/20	AMSCH	0008	*Baalen, (H. van) de Jonge* | Deeze Ordenantie verbeeld de Boodschap van den Engel aan Maria, het is in een Binnenkamer, waarin de Maagd ter zyde een Slaapplaats by een tafeltje op de kniën leggende, en als met verwondering omziende, de gezeegende Boodschap ontfangt, verders een glorie van Engelen; meesterlyk en uitvoerig als de voorgaande behandeld [Ce pendant du précedent offre l'annonciation de l'Ange Gabriel à L.V. Marie, elle est agenoullée en attitude respectueuse, dans une chambre à coucher ornée de meubles anologues : une gloire d'Anges termine la partie Supérieure de ce morceau également méritant que le premier.] | companion to lot 7 *Mat:* op steen *Size:* hoog 15, breed 13 duim	Maria Magdalena van Sluypwyk, gravinne van Moens	(Sold) fl 12:10 Lesscher
			Balen, Jan van		
1810/10/13	HGDAW	0003	*J. van Balen* | Een Vrouw met een staand Kindje op haar schoot, welke door twee anderen geliefkoosd wordt, in de hoogte een Kindje met een Lauwerkrans in de hand, schynende haar te kroonen, zeer delicaat en breed geschilderd | *Mat:* op paneel *Size:* hoog 11, breed 10 ½ duim		(Unknown)

Balen, Jan van (and Snyders, F. and Vinckeboons, D.)

1803/07/18	AMSCH	0004	*Balen, (J. van); F. Snyders; D. Vinkebooms* | Twee Nimphen van de Jagt komende met een menigte Wild, 't geen op de grond legt, schynende met elkander daarover te spreeken, een derde ter zyde hun in de schaduwe, voor dezelven verscheide Jagthonden; het Bosch door Vinkebooms, het Wild door Snyders, en de Beelden door van Balen, maaken een schoon geheel uit, en doen de talenten van deeze drie Meesters alle eer aan [Deux Nimphes, au retour d'une chasse abondante, s'entretiennent vèrs la droite, ayant cinq beaux chiens bracs auprès d'elles ; une troisieme Nimphe s'achemine vèrs la foret. A la gauche sont les animaux morts, couchés sur une légère élévation, c'est un sanglier, un loup, un liévre avec d'autres quadrupédes & de la volaille. Cette réunion de talens des trois artistes s'accorde parfaitement bien. Les figures sont belles & de couleur riche ; les animaux traités avec légereté & delicatesse, & le Paysage repond bien au sujet.] | *Mat:* op paneel *Size:* hoog 24, breed 33 duim	Maria Theresia Andrioli	(Sold) fl 52 Hulswit

Balestra, Antonio

1810/06/06	RMMUY	0207	*Balestra* | Twee spelende Kindertjes, levensgroote konstig behandeld | *Mat:* op doek		(Unknown) fl 3

Bandt [Unidentified]

1804/10/16	DLOND	0009	*Bandt* | Naakte Beelden. Des Nudités | *Mat:* op paneel *Size:* hoog 5, breed 6		(Unknown)

Banthem, J. van [Unidentified]

1804/05/07	AMSCH	0032	*Banthem (J. van)* | Een Protestante Kerk van binnen te zien, met een meenigte van Wandelende Heeren en Dames; uitvoerig gepenceeld | *Mat:* op doek *Size:* hoog 37, breed 52 duim	Roos [for] K	(Sold) fl 6 Lely

Barbiers, Pieter

1802/12/13	AMSCH	0222	*P. Barbiers* | Een Model, verbeeldende twee Kalfs-Koppen en eenige Pooten, zeer Natuurlyk en fiks geschilderd	Schley [for] Lauwers	(Sold) fl 1:5 van Dijl
1804/02/27	AMSCH	0007	*Barbiers. (P.)* | In dit bevallig Landschap, ziet men op den voorgrond een Brug, waar over een Huisman en een Kind ligt, achter hetzelve een Boerewoning, waarby hoog Geboomte, op den voorgrond by een Willige Boom, ziet men drie Schaapen, verders een aangenaam verschiet; alles is helder en krachtig gepenceeld | *Mat:* op paneel *Size:* hoog 15, breed 23 duim	B	(Sold) fl 60 Coclers
1804/02/27	AMSCH	0008	*Barbiers. (P.)* | Twee stuks bevalligen Duin en Boomryke Landschappen met Boerenwooningen en verderen stoffage; bevallig van licht en uitvoerig geschildert | *Mat:* op paneel *Size:* hoog 9, breed 10 duim	C	(Bought In) fl 16
1806/05/05	AMSCH	0018	*P. Barbiers* | Twee stuks bevallige duin en boomryke Landschappen, met Boeren wooninge en verdere stoffagie; uitvoerig geschilderd door P. Barbiers | *Mat:* op paneel *Size:* hoog 9, breed 10 duim	V[inkeles]	(Sold) fl 9 Rynberg
1808/08/23	AMSCH	0026	*Barbiers (P.)* | Aan den ingang van een Boere Werf staat eene Vrouwtje, benevens een Kind, als sprekende met een zittend man, in 't verschiet een Reisiger bij onderscheide Geboomten; alles zonachtig en schoon behandeld | *Mat:* op doek *Size:* hoog 11, breed 14 duim	J	(Bought In) fl 13:10
1808/11/28	AMSCH	0009	*P. Barbiers* | Voor een openstaand Vengster, vertoond zig een jeugdig bevallig Vrouwtje, in haar Nachtgewaad, zij is bezig een Wolle Kinderdekentje over eenige Stokken te hangen, ter zijde staat een Tobbetje, waarin een Pot met Bloemen en verder met een Wijngaard bewassen, dit Stukje is uitvoerig en malsch gepenceeld | *Mat:* op paneel *Size:* hoog 14, breed 12 duim	[Gruyter?]	(Sold) fl 55 S M Levy
1809/04/22	AMYVR	0024	*P. Barbiers* | Een aangenaam gestoffeerd Duinachtig Landschap, met Geboomte en Boerenwooningen; fraai behandeld | *Mat:* op paneel *Size:* hoog 12, breed 16 duim	de Bruin	(Sold) fl 6 van Raan

Barbiers, Pieter (I)

1801/03/16	AMSCH	0119	*P. Barbiers, de oude* | Twee stuks, in een opgeslagen Tent zit een Vrouw, bezig Plaatkoeken te bakken, ter zyde staat een Man by een vat, de andere een vrouw Darmen verkopende, alles natuurlyk verbeeld op doek | *Mat:* op doek	K[ip]	(Sold) fl 21 Cocler

Barocci, Federico

1805/07/10	AMSCH	0034	*Barotius* | St. Franciscus op zyn kniën, ontfangende de vyf Wonden van Christus, breed en fraay op Paneel | *Mat:* op paneel *Size:* hoog 24, breed 19 ½ duim	V[inkeles] [for] H[affner]	(Bought In) fl 9

Barrey, J. [Unidentified]

1803/10/25	HHNOM	0006	*J. Barrey* | L'Oiseleur [Prenten en Schilderijen, in extra schoone vergulde Lysten en Glazen] | *Notes:* The bracketed information in the title appears above lot 1 and refers to lots 1 to 24. It is uncertain whether this lot is a painting.	Mr Stephanies Roosendaal	(Unknown)
1803/10/25	HHNOM	0007	*J. Barrey* | Le Servolant achevé [Prenten en Schilderijen, in extra schoone vergulde Lysten en Glazen] | *Notes:* The bracketed information in the title appears above lot 1 and refers to lots 1 to 24. It is uncertain whether this lot is a painting.	Mr Stephanies Roosendaal	(Unknown)

			Bartels, Gerrit		
1804/10/16	DLOND	0010	*G. Bartels* | Een rokend Boertjen met een ton nevens zich. Un Paysan qui fume sa pipe | *Mat:* op paneel *Size:* hoog 12, breed 10		(Unknown)
			Bassano		
1801/10/06	AMSCH	0006	*Pontebassano* | Deeze Ordinantie vol gewoel, van verscheide Beelden, vertoont, de geboorten Christi, alwaar de Herders, het Kindeken met eerbied beschouwen en aanbidden, om hoog ziet men een glorie van Engelen, het Kaarslicht, doed een Natuurlyke werking, alles is kragtig en Meesterlyk gepenceelt | *Mat:* op doek *Size:* hoog 9 ½, breed 11 duim	S	(Sold) fl 31 Spruit van Gend
1802/06/16	AMSCH	0025	*P. Bassano* | In een Boschachtig Landschap vertoonen zich vier gewapende Struik-Rovers, met elkander Dobbelende, in 't verschiet een geplunderde Wagen; meesterlyk en fiks gepenceelt | *Mat:* op paneel *Size:* hoog 12 ½, breed 16 ½ duim	[Merrem]	(Sold) fl 4:5 Gruiter
1802/12/13	AMSCH	0014	*P. Bassano* | Een capitaale Bybel Ordenantie, ryk gestoffeert, met verschyde werkende Beelden, een menigte zoorten van verschillend Vée, en Huiselyke Gereedschappen, kragtig en meesterlyk gepenceelt | *Mat:* op doek *Size:* hoog 39, breed 53 duim	Yver	(Sold) fl 14:10 Jan Spaan
1803/04/20	AMSCH	0003	*Bassano (Ponto)* | Deeze ryke Ordenantie van meer dan vyftig Beelden, steld voor de Aanbidding der Herdets [sic], in de Stal te Bethelehem, in de Wolken een glorie van Engelen, de Ordenantie en het licht, zo wel als de bevallige schildering, maken dit stuk tot een Schildery van groote verdiensten [Cette Composition richement Ordonnée comprend plus de cinquante figures, elle expose l'adoration des Bergers dans l'etable de Bethleem ; du ciel descend une gloire d'Anges. Ce morceau très recommandable par la richesse de l'ensemble & par l'effet de la lumiere, l'est aussi pour la belle maniere de l'execution.] | *Mat:* op doek *Size:* hoog 57, breed 88 duim	Maria Magdalena van Sluypwyk, gravinne van Moens	(Sold) fl 15 Gruiter
1810/07/26	AMSCH	0002	*Bassano (P.)* | Een Kafsneider, met Kerven bezig zijnde; fraai geschilderd | *Mat:* op doek *Size:* hoog 25, breed 19 duimen	Cassino	(Bought In) fl 1
1810/07/26	AMSCH	0137	*Bassano (P.)* | Christus met de Discipelen van Emmaus, ter zijde andere Beelden en bijwerk. Meesterlijk geschilderd | *Mat:* op doek *Size:* hoog 32, breed 39 duim	Cassino	(Bought In) fl 16:10
			Bassano (copy after)		
1810/06/06	RMMUY	0167	*D. Teniers; Bassano* | Een Postishe. Door D. Teniers, naar Bassano | copy by Teniers after Bassano *Mat:* op paneel		(Sold) fl 4:10 Pot
			Bassano (manner)		
1802/11/01	DOBRA	0192	*Bassano* | Twee stuks historieele; als het bezoek der Herders by het Kindeke; en Herodias Dochter het hoofd van Johannes den Dooper op een schootel aan Herodes vertoonende; als Bassano | *Mat:* op koper *Size:* hoog 13, breed 10 ½ duim		(Unknown) fl 10:15
			Bassano, Jacopo (Jacopo da Ponte)		
1808/06/06	RMRIJ	0004	*Bassano. (Jacomo da Ponto)* | Een rustend Man in Spaansche kleeding, omringd van een Os, Bok, Schapen, Hond en verder bijwerk. In eene Italiaansche en trotsche manier meesterlijk geschilderd. Eene wedergade. Een Herder met Schapen, Bok en Hond, enz. In dezelfde manier behandeld [La prémiere represente un homme en costume Espagnol, qui est assis entouré d'un Boeuf, d'un Bouc, d'un Chien, de moutons etc. Peint en Maitre. La Seconde est de la même proportion et du même genre. Un pâtre avec des moutons et autres animaux etc. Egal au précédent] | *Annots:* Gillourd[?] 1794 van P.J. Thys (f 51.9) (RMA I) *Mat:* op doek *Size:* Twee Stukken. Hoog 23 ½, en breed 40 ¼ duim	Gerrit van der Pot, Heer van Groeneveld	(Sold) fl 21 Gebroeders Levy
1810/10/11	AMSCH	0004	*J. De Ponte Bassano* | Een Bijbel Ordonantie, voorstellende de Begraving van den Zaligmaker; meesterlijk behandeld | *Mat:* op doek *Size:* hoog 27, breed 29 duimen	M	(Sold) fl 42 T Spaan
			Bassen, Bartholomeus van		
1802/05/05	AMSCH	0024	*B. van Bassen* | Een Gezicht in een Roomsche Kerk, alwaar de Priester de Misse [sic] leest; zeer natuurlyk en dun gepenceeld | *Mat:* op paneel *Size:* hoog 20, breed 27 duim	C	(Sold) fl 42 Stevens
1802/05/05	AMSCH	0029	*B. van Bassen* | In een pragtig Gebouw ziet men de Historie van den Verlooren Zoon. Meesterlyk | *Mat:* op doek *Size:* hoog 43, breed 57 duim	E	(Sold) fl 0:10 L Pakker
1802/11/01	DOBRA	0037	*B. van Bassen* | Petrus en Johannes, in den Tempel den Kreupelen genezende, f. 1637 | *Mat:* op paneel *Size:* hoog 17 ½, breed 24 duim *Inscr:* f.1637 (dated?) *Notes:* It is unclear whether the date is inscribed on the painting.	Paulus van der Spyk [or others]	(Sold) fl 7:5 Baalen
1803/08/24	HGKAN	0057	*van Bassen* | Twee stuks prachtige Gebouwen, fraay van Perspectief	[Teissier] [or others]	(Sold) fl 4:5 van Giesen
1804/10/16	DLOND	0011	*B. van Bassen. 1653* | Een Kerkgebouw van binnen te zien. L'intérieur d'une Eglise | *Mat:* op paneel *Size:* hoog 21, breed 15 *Inscr:* B. van Bassen. 1653 (signed and dated?) *Notes:* It is unclear whether the name and date are inscribed on the painting.		(Sold) fl 5:10 Carre

1804/10/16	DLOND	0012	*B. van Bassen* | Het voorste gedeelte van een Tempel. Le devant d'un Temple | *Mat:* op doek *Size:* hoog 20, breed 20		(Unknown)
1805/07/10	AMSCH	0026	*B. van Bassen* | In een Prachtig aloud Vertrek, ryk met Schilderyen behangen, ziet men twee Lieden in Spaansche Kleeding, schynende te willen Duëlleeren, waarby een ander welke hem tegenhoud, enz.; uitvoerig van behandeling | *Mat:* op paneel *Size:* hoog 19, breed 25 duim	V[inkeles] [for] L	(Bought In) fl 6
1806/08/13	AMSCH	0236	*van Bassen* | Een Roomsche Kerk van binnen te zien; frapant van licht	Vinkeles [for] G[ruyter]	(Sold) fl 3 du Pre
1808/08/23	AMSCH	0021	*Bassen. (van)* | Een Roomsche Kerk van binnen te zien, gestoffeert met verscheide wandelende beeldjes, ter zijde een Altaar, waar bij een Priester die den Dienst leest; fraai van Perspectief, zonachtig en uitvoerig behandeld | *Mat:* op doek *Size:* hoog 43, breed 54 duim	C	(Bought In) fl 13
1809/06/13	AMSCH	0023	*B van Bassen* | Het Binnegezigt van een pragtige Tempel, rijk met Colommen, andere Sieraaden en Beelden gestoffeerd, fraai van doorzigt en uitvoerig van schildering | *Mat:* op paneel *Size:* hoog 29, breed 43 duim	Y	(Sold) fl 12 Eversdijk
1810/03/07	UTWLD	0055	*van Bassen* | Eene Kerk | *Size:* hoog 2 voet, breed 2 voet 9 duim	J J Woertman	(Unknown) fl 13
1810/08/06	AMSCH	0008	*Bassen (B. van)* | Eene Roomsche Kerk, van binnen te zien, gestoffeerd met wandelende lieden, ter zijde een Altaar, waarbij een Priester, die den dienst leest. Fraai van doorzigt en zonachtig behandeld | *Mat:* op doek *Size:* hoog 43, breed 54 duimen	B	(Sold) fl 12 T Spaan
1810/10/10	MGCIT	0124	*Bassan* | Twee kapitale Stukken, zijnde zeer grootsche Gebouwen, van een zeer fraaije Architectuur, Perspectif en Stoffage; meesterlijk en uitvoerig op paneel gebragt | *Mat:* op paneel	Caspar van Citters	(Unknown)
1810/10/11	AMSCH	0157	*Van Bassan* | Een Tempel	S	(Sold) fl 1 Gruiter
			Bassen, Bartholomeus van (and Franks, J.)		
1802/06/28	AMSCH	0009	*B. van Bassen; J. Franks* | In een prachtige Zaal, ziet men een groot Gezelschap, waarvan eenige Danssende; uitvoerig op Panneel, door B. van Bassen en J. Franks | *Mat:* op paneel *Size:* hoog 35, breed 45 duim	Anna Elink	(Sold) fl 7 Gruiter
			Bassen, Bartholomeus van (manner)		
1803/04/20	AMSCH	0115	*van Bassen* | Een Roomsche Kerk van binnen te zien; frappant van Zonlichten, en uitvoerig behandeld, in de manier van van Bassen [Une Eglise Catholique, d'un bel effet & bien executée dans la maniere de van Bassen.] | *Mat:* op paneel *Size:* hoog 12, breed 10 ½ duim	Maria Magdalena van Sluypwyk, gravinne van Moens	(Sold) fl 5 Gruiter
			Batist, Karel		
1802/06/16	AMSCH	0030	*C. Batist* | Twee stuks Fruitstukken, met onderscheiden soorten van Vruchten op een steenen rand, bevallig van Ordenantie en uitvoerig gepenceeld | *Mat:* op doek *Size:* ieder hoog 27, breed 22 duim	[Merrem]	(Sold) fl 5 Agina
			Battem, Gerrit van		
1802/09/18	RMDRS	0014	*J. van Battum* | Een capitaal Boschagtig Landschap, waarin een Waterval, een Hartejacht en verdere Stoffagie, uitvoerig geschilderd | *Annots:* voor Meubel buiten[?] (MB) *Size:* hoog 30 ½, breed 43 duim	Casper de Haas	(Sold) fl 27 v Pot
1802/09/18	RMDRS	0066	*van Battum* | Twee stuks Landschappen	Casper de Haas	(Sold) fl 3:5 V Giesen
1803/12/15	MGLAC	0038	*van Battem* | Een Binnenvertrek, waarin eenige Figuuren en dood Wild; zeer kragtig en fraai | *Mat:* op doek *Size:* hoog duim 19, breed duim 26	Mr L H de Haze Bomme	(Unknown)
1804/10/16	DLOND	0014	*Van Battem* | Een Landschap. Paysage | *Mat:* op paneel *Size:* hoog 10, breed 12		(Unknown)
1804/10/16	DLOND	0015	*Van Battem* | Een Bosch met Herten. Quelques Cerfs dans un Bois | *Mat:* op paneel *Size:* hoog 16, breed 21		(Unknown)
1806/06/07	RMHSN	0119	*Van Battem* | Een Stadgezigt, zynde een Besneeuwde Winter, met Schaatsryders &c.	A E K L	(Unknown)
1808/06/06	RMRIJ	0005	*Battem (J. van)* | Een Boschgezigt, met Rivier en Waterval, rijk gestoffeerd met eene Hertejagt; voorts een fraai verschiet. Helder en krachtig geschilderd [Une chasse au Cerf, dans un riche Paysage. On voit à droite l'Entrée d'un bois ; à gauche des Rochers et une Rivière forment de belles chûtes d'eau. Un beau lointain, un Ciel clair et agréable terminent la vue. Ce tableaux est traité avec beaucoup de goût et d'esprit] | *Annots:* Verk. Casper de Haas, Rotterdam 18 Sept 1802 (f 27.-) (RMA I) *Mat:* op doek *Size:* Hoog 30 ½, en breed 43 duim	Gerrit van der Pot, Heer van Groeneveld	(Sold) fl 70 P L Ellinkhuyzen
			Baur, Nicolaus		
1810/05/22	AMSCH	0014	*Baur. (N.)* | Een onstuimige Zee, met verscheide Vaartuigen, bij een Hoofd van Paalwerk, waarop twee Beelden; fiks gepenceeld | *Mat:* op doek *Size:* hoog 14, breed 17 duim	Johannes van de Putte Nicolaasz.	(Sold) fl 31 van Iperen
			Baur, W. [Unidentified]		
1802/09/06	AMSCH	0025	*W. Baur* | Een stil Water, bevallig gestoffeerd met ten anker leggende en dryvende Oorlogscheepen, kleinder Vaartuigen en Sloepen; zonachtig en uitvoerig gepenceeld | *Mat:* op doek *Size:* hoog 11, breed 14 duim	Wed Grave [or others]	(Bought In) fl 30 for lots 25 & 26

1802/09/06	AMSCH	0026	*W. Baur* | Een verbolgen Zée, waar in een Kaagh by de Wind zeilende, verder een Oorlogschip in gevaar; het Water is natuurlyk, dun en van een uitvoerigen Penceelbehandeling | *Mat:* op doek *Size:* hoog 11, breed 14 duim	Wed Grave [or others]	(Bought In) fl 30 for lots 25 & 26
1802/09/06	AMSCH	0027	*W. Baur* | Een besneeuwt Wintergezicht aan een Dorp, met Woningen, Molen en verder stoffagie, by een bevrosen Rivier, waar op Paard en Arresleeden, Schaatseryders en wandelaars zig vermaaken; natuurlyk en uitvoerig van Penceelbehandeling | *Mat:* op doek *Size:* hoog 11, breed 14 duim	Wed Grave [or others]	(Bought In) fl 12
			Beck [Unidentified] (and Lingelbach)		
1804/10/16	DLOND	0127	*J. Lingelbach; Beck* | Een Schermutseling met de Turken. Une Escarmouche avec les Turcs | *Mat:* op doek *Size:* hoog 21, breed 15		(Sold) fl 25 Thijs
			Becker, Johann Wilhelm		
1804/05/07	AMSCH	0020	*Becker (J.W.)* | Twee stuks Boom-, Duin- en Rotsachtige Landschappen; eigenaartig gestoffeerd, en breed en meesterlyk gepenceeld | *Size:* hoog 17, breed 14 duim	Vinkeles [for] J	(Bought In) fl 12
1804/05/07	AMSCH	0020a[H]	*Becker (J.W.)* | 2 Stux | *Notes:* This lot was added in by hand in the EBNP, LBDa and RKDH copies of the catalogue.	Vinkeles [for] J	(Sold) fl 15 van Iperen
			Beckeringh, Theodorus		
1802/05/11	GRGRW	0056	*Beckeringh* | Een gezicht buiten 't Kleine Poortje bij Groningen [Schilderijen met Olie-Verf; In zwarte Lijsten] | companion to lot 57 *Mat:* in olyverf *Notes:* The bracketed information in the title appears above lot 1 and refers to lots 1 to 79a.	Arnold Sicco Werumeus	(Unknown) fl 5:15 for lots 56 & 57
1802/05/11	GRGRW	0057	*Beckeringh* | Een dito [gezicht] van Warfum, tot een weerga [Schilderijen met Olie-Verf; In zwarte Lijsten | companion to lot 56 *Mat:* in olyverf *Notes:* The bracketed information in the title about the medium appears above lot 1 and refers to lots 1 to 79a.	Arnold Sicco Werumeus	(Unknown) fl 5:15 for lots 56 & 57
			Beeldemaker		
1801/03/16	AMSCH	0111	*Beeldemaker* | Een Landschap met verscheide jagthonden en andere stoffagie, fraai en uitvoerig gepenceeld	K[ip]	(Sold) fl 18:10 Koopman
1803/04/20	AMSCH	0015	*Beeldemaker* | Twee stuks Landschappen met vegtende Honden; beide fix gepenceeld [Ils ont pour sujets des chiens qui se battent. Ces deux tableaux ont du merite.] | *Mat:* op doek *Size:* ieder hoog 18, breed 23 duim	Maria Magdalena van Sluypwyk, gravinne van Moens	(Sold) fl 3 Grimpen
1803/07/14	MGKLY	0003	*Beeldemaker* | Twee stuks met Honden, goed geschildert	Mr Caspar Jacob van Citters	(Unknown)
1803/12/15	MGLAC	0045	*Beeldemaker* | Een Landschap, waarin eenige Honden; goed van teekening en wel geschilderd | *Mat:* op doek *Size:* hoog duim 18, breed duim 23	Mr L H de Haze Bomme	(Unknown)
1804/10/29	HRBAU	0012	*Beeldemaker* | Hier ziet men een Patryshond, levensgrootte, een Zwaan aanvallen, welke zig, door de kragt zyner vleugelen, schynt te verdeedigen, terwyl een ander agter de biezen zwemt; en nog een' anderen Hond, die met alle snelheid ter hulpe van zyn' makker komt aanloopen. Alles is kragtig, en de Honden zo natuurlyk geschilderd, dat zy schynen te leeven | *Mat:* op doek *Size:* hoog 49, breed 63 duim	Simon Styl	(Unknown)
1806/05/05	AMSCH	0172	*Beeldemaker* | Een Zwyn, door diverse Honden aangevallen wordende	R[oos]	(Sold) fl 0:14 Coclers
1806/06/07	RMHSN	0087	*Beeldemaker* | Een Jager met een Hond in een Landschap | *Mat:* op paneel	A E K L	(Unknown)
1806/08/20	HGBSM	0178	*Beeldemaaker* | Een Vossenjagt, met veel Honden | *Mat:* op doek	Macalester Loup [or others]	(Sold) fl 1 L Voerman voor Huibrechts
1807/06/10	HGBSM	0190	*Beeldemaker* | Een Landschap met beelden en honden | *Mat:* op doek *Size:* hoog 18 ½, breed 23 duim	Abraham Delfos [or others]	(Sold) fl 6 De Gelder
1807/08/26	AMSCH	0028	*Beeldemaker* | Een Landschap met Honden | *Mat:* op doek *Size:* hoog 17, breed 23 duim	de Vries	(Sold) fl 3:5 Coclair
1807/09/28	DOHAA	00XX	*Beeldemaker* | Een Schildery met Honden	Mattheus Westerouen van Meeteren	(Unknown)
1808/04/26	GDAN	0016	*Beeldemaler* | Een groot Hert dat door eenige Honden gevangen word, zeer goed geschilderd | *Mat:* op doek *Size:* hoog 48, breed 78 duim	G H Fortuyn	(Unknown)
1808/05/18	LNAN	0003	*Beeldemaker* | 2 Landschappen met aardige Hondjes | *This Lot:* Een Landschap met aardige Hondjes *Notes:* Lots 3 and 4 were printed in the catalogue as one item. The artist's name "Beeldemaker" was added in by hand in the RKDH copy of the catalogue.	Mr Cornelis Versluys	(Unknown)
1808/05/18	LNAN	0004	*Beeldemaker* | 2 Landschappen met aardige Hondjes | *This Lot:* Een Landschap met aardige Hondjes *Notes:* Lots 3 and 4 were printed in the catalogue as one item. The artist's name "Beeldemaker" was added in by hand in the RKDH copy of the catalogue.	Mr Cornelis Versluys	(Unknown)
1808/05/18	LNAN	0035	*Beeldemaker* | Een met differente Honden | *Notes:* The artist's name "Beeldemaker" was added in by hand in the RKDH copy of the catalogue.	Mr Cornelis Versluys	(Unknown)

1808/05/18	LNAN	0042	*Beeldemaker* | Een Rots Gezigt, met differente Honden op den Voorgrond | *Notes:* The artist's name "Beeldemaker" was added in by hand in the RKDH copy of the catalogue.	Mr Cornelis Versluys	(Unknown)
1808/09/13	HABRU	0111	*Beeldemaker* | Een met Honden		(Unknown) fl 0:8
1808/12/12	DOHAA	0067	*Beeldemaker* | Een Landschap met Honden | *Mat:* op doek		(Unknown)
1810/03/27	RMCNL	0015	*Beeldemaker* | Eenige Jagthonden, zeer schoon van koloriet en Penseel		(Unknown)
1810/06/04	DOBRA	0003	*Beeldemaker* | Een Landschap met Hondjes	Hendrik de Haas	(Unknown)
1810/06/04	DOBRA	0004	*Beeldemaker* | Een dito [Landschap] met dito [Hondjes]	Hendrik de Haas	(Unknown)
1810/07/23	DOLG2	000G	*Beeldemaker* | Een levensgroote Hond, benevens meer andere Honden, meesterlijk schoon geschilderd | *Mat:* op doek *Size:* hoog 47, breed 75 duim	Pieter Quinting	(Unknown) fl 1:10
1810/11/07	UTWLD	0042	*Beeldemaker* | Eenige te zamenspeelende Honden, op den tweeden grond een liggende Man, alles zeer kragtig door Beeldemaker op doek, 1 voet 10 duim hoog, 1 voet 8 duim breed, zwarte Lijst | *Mat:* op doek *Size:* 1 voet 10 duim hoog, 1 voet 8 duim breed		(Unknown) fl 4:10
			Beeldemaker (manner)		
1801/09/04	MGWIN	0006	*Beeldemaker* | Een groot Stuk, zynde een Wolven Jacht, in de manier van Beeldemaker, op Doek, zonder Lyst | *Mat:* op doek	Pieter Gillissen	(Unknown)
1802/05/22	RMHSN	0014	*Beeldemaker* | Een stuk met vegtende Honden, in de trant van Beeldemaker	Lambertus Bicker	(Unknown)
1802/08/24	LNDLS	0133	*Beeldemaker* | In een Landschap met Boomen zitten twee Heeren te paard, voor dezelven Jagt-honden, in de manier van Beeldemaker | *Mat:* op doek	Leonardus Bouman [or others]	(Unknown) fl 1:13
			Beeldemaker, Adriaen Cornelisz.		
1802/05/05	AMSCH	0025	*J. Beeldemaaker* | Een Dorp- en Strandgezicht, op de voorgrond eenige staande Vissers, een Boerewagen en verder Bywerk, zeer natuurlyk behandeld | *Mat:* op paneel *Size:* hoog 23, breed 69 duim	C	(Sold) fl 5:10 Vermeulen
1802/05/05	AMSCH	0026	*J. Beeldemaaker* | Een Strandgezicht, op de Voorgrond eenige Vissers, in 't verschiet een Dorpstooren | *Mat:* op paneel *Size:* hoog 26, breed 34 duim	G	(Sold) fl 20 Cocler
1802/11/01	DOBRA	0163	*A. Beeldemaker* | Twee stuks, verbeeldende Honden op de Eenden-Jagt		(Unknown) fl 6:15
1803/12/12	AMSCH	0009	*A. Beeldemaker* | In een Landschap ziet men op de voorgrond in een Water een Hert, door eenige Honden aangevallen, dewelke door Jagers agtervolgt worden; meesterachtig als Potter, op Doek geschilderd | *Mat:* op doek *Size:* hoog 51, breed 56 duim	B	(Sold) fl 45 Coclers
1804/07/25	DLGRO	0045	*A. Beeldemaker* | Een Jager met een Hond die een stuk Wild apporteerd, en verder bywerk | *Mat:* op paneel *Size:* hoog 28, breed 22 duim	Mr Franc van der Burch Wz.	(Unknown)
1804/08/08	AMSCH	0029	*A. Beeldemaker* | Twee stuks met verscheide Honden en Beelden; kragtig op Doek | *Mat:* op doek *Size:* hoog 18, breed 23 duim	Roos [for] M	(Sold) fl 0:10 L Pakker
1804/08/08	AMSCH	0030	*A. Beeldemaker* | Twee stuks met dito [verscheide Honden en Beelden] | *Size:* hoog 17, breed 23 duim	Roos [for] M	(Sold) fl 1 L Pakker
1804/10/16	DLOND	0016	*J. Beeldemaker. 1714* | Een Landschap met Koeien en Schapen. Paysage, des Vaches & Moutons | *Mat:* op paneel *Size:* hoog 11, breed 13 *Inscr:* J. Beeldemaker. 1714 (signed and dated?) *Notes:* It is unclear whether the name and date are inscribed on the painting.		(Unknown)
1807/06/10	HGBSM	0104	*J. Beeldemaker* | Een Vossen Jagt | *Mat:* op doek *Size:* hoog 18, breed 21 ½ duim	Abraham Delfos [or others]	(Unknown) fl 2:10
1810/07/23	DOLG1	0004	*A. Beeldemaker* | Een Mans Pourtrait, ten halven lijve, in eene Oud-Hollandsche kleding | *Mat:* op paneel *Size:* hoog 9, breed 7 duim	Mr Pieter van den Santheuvel	(Sold) fl 3:10 van den Einden
1810/07/23	DOLG1	0005	*A. Beeldemaker* | Een groep Honden | *Mat:* op doek *Size:* hoog 17 ½, breed 22 ½ duim	Mr Pieter van den Santheuvel	(Sold) fl 1 A van Strij
			Beelds, J. [Unidentified]		
1809/04/17	AMSCH	0019	*J. Beelds* | Een Gezicht op Strand bij het Dorp Katwijk, gestoffeerd met Vaartuigen en Beeldjes; fiks op Paneel | *Mat:* op paneel	T	(Sold) fl 1:5
1809/06/13	AMSCH	0244	*Beels* | Een Strandgezicht	Y	(Sold) fl 0:12 L Pakker
			Beelt, Cornelis		
1802/07/27	AKHRK	0024	*K. Beeld* | Een stuk vol gewoel, zijnde een Dorp, voor een Huis staan twee Musiekanten op de Fluit en Viöol, de Dorpelingen zijn zeer aandachtig en maaken in verschillende Actiën een fraaije Groep in dit Tafreel | *Mat:* op doek *Size:* hoog 20, breed 25 ½ duim	Maria Stategaart	(Sold) fl 18:10 Meyer
1802/07/27	AKHRK	0025	*K. Beeld* | Een Binnenhuis, men ziet een Wever op zijn Getouw, een ander staat 'er bij, en een rookend zittend Man; verder een Vrouw bezig met twee Kinderen, met het verder Bijwerk: krachtig geschilderd | *Mat:* op doek *Size:* hoog 18, breed 25 ½ duim	Maria Stategaart	(Sold) fl 21 V Iperen
1804/10/29	HRBAU	0011	*Beelt* | In een' Smitswinkel ziet men den Baas in zyn beroep bezig, nevens een' Jongen die het vuur aanblaast, terwyl een andere de deur schynt in te	Simon Styl	(Unknown)

			komen. Ryk met Gereedschap gestoffeerd, en kloek behandeld | *Mat:* op paneel *Size:* hoog 9 ½, breed 7 ½ duim		
			Beer [Unidentified]		
1803/12/12	AMSCH	0122	*de Beer* | Twee Bergachtige Landschappen	W	(Sold) fl 1 Yver
1808/09/13	HABRU	0016	*de Beer* | Een Dorpgezicht aan een Water, zijnde een Maneschijn		(Unknown) fl 3:15
			Beer, J. de [Unidentified]		
1804/05/07	AMSCH	0219	*J. de Beer* | Een Dorpgezicht aan een Rivier, zynde een Maneschyn, met Vaartuigen en verscheide andere Stoffagie; plaisant geschilderd op Doek | *Mat:* op doek	Roos [for] K	(Sold) fl 0:10 L Pakker
1805/12/16	AMSCH	0014	*J. de Beer* | Een Land- en Riviergezicht, met zylende Scheepen en andere Schuiten; alles verbeeld by helder Maanlicht | *Mat:* op paneel	R[oos]	(Sold) fl 0:8 du Pree
			Beerstraten		
1810/03/27	RMCNL	0100	*Burenstraaten* | Een Zeehaven, waar in men groote en kleine Zeilende Schepen ziet, het Water is woelig, fraaij behandelt		(Unknown)
1810/06/06	RMMUY	0194	*Beerestraten* | Eene Zeehaven | *Mat:* op doek		(Sold) fl 49 Dr Dalen
1810/10/10	MGCIT	0030	*H. Beerestraten* | Een zeer bevallig Schilderij, verbeeldende een soort van een Zeearm of Rheede, terwijl in een zeer stil Water een groot Schip legt en door een verafgelegen verschiet in Zee nog vele Schepen gezien worden; voorts is van wederzijde de wal beplant en met getimmerten voorzien, terwijl een aartig voorgrondje met gaande en leggende Figuurtjes aan dit stuk veel bevalligheid bijzet	Caspar van Citters	(Unknown)
1810/10/10	MGCIT	0125	*H. Beerestraten* | Een zeer schoon Schilderij, zijnde een stille Zee met een Stad in 't verschiet; voorts rijk van Schepen, zoo in de nabyheid als in eene verre afstand; meesterlyk behandeld	Caspar van Citters	(Unknown)
			Beerstraten (manner)		
1801/04/08	HAVIN	0073	*Beereustraten* | Een Zee, als van Beereustraten		(Unknown)
1802/05/22	RMHSN	0021	*Beerestraten* | Twee stuks Zeehavens in de trant van Beerestraten	Lambertus Bicker	(Unknown)
1802/09/06	AMSCH	0215	*Beerestraaten* | Een Zéehaven, met verscheide Scheepen; als door Beerestraaten	Mevrouw Achtienhoven	(Sold) fl 1:15 Baur
1805/07/10	AMSCH	0189	*Beerestraten* | Een Winter, als door Beerestraten	R[oos]	(Sold) fl 0:6 L Pakker
1809/05/26	HADAA	0049	*Beerestraten* | Een Winter op dito [doek] als door Beerestraten | *Mat:* op doek	Mejuffrouw de Wed David Heemskerk [or others]	(Unknown)
			Beerstraten, A.		
1802/05/05	AMSCH	0012	*A. Beerestraaten* | Een Bevrozen Rivier, met een menigte zich op het Ys vermakende Beeldjes; ter zyde een Opgaande Weg, met Geboomte, naar een Dorps Kerk gaande, in het verschiet verscheide Boere Woningen, het natuurlyke Koude en Sneeuwächtige is hier in wel waargenomen, en is van de beste schildering van A. Beerestraaten | *Mat:* op doek *Size:* hoog 34, breed 42 duim	H	(Sold) fl 61 Le Dantú
1802/09/06	AMSCH	0020	*A. Beerestraaten* | Een Gezicht van de groote Kerk op de Markt te Haarlem, ryk gestoffeerd met een ménigte karren, sleeden, te Paard rydende, en wandelende Beeldjes; fraay en zonachtig behandeld | *Mat:* op paneel *Size:* hoog 32, breed 30 duim	J	(Sold) fl 8:10 Gruiter
1804/05/07	AMSCH	0012	*Beerstraten. (A.)* | Dit Natuurlyk voorwerp vertoont een Winter, met besneeuwde Daken en Weegen, zynde een Gezicht te Amsterdam, uit het Y te zien, naar de Haringpakkers Tooren, en verdere Gebouwen naar de Oude Stads Herberg; ryk gestoffeerd met verscheide Scheepen, Schaatsenryders en Wandelaars; alles helder en bevallig gepenceeld | *Mat:* op doek *Size:* hoog 37, breed 50 duim	Schley	(Bought In) fl 39
1804/07/25	AMSCH	0009	*Beerstraaten. (A.)* | Dit allernatuurlykst Wintergezicht, vertoont het Dorp Dronsryk in Vriesland, ziende naar de Kerk, een Oud Kasteel en verscheide Wooningen, alles schynt met besneeuwde Daken, en Weegen, en het Ys is gestoffeert met Schaatzeryders, wandelende Lieden en Kinderen, die zig op het Ys vermaken; alles is bevallig van licht en uitvoerig gepenceelt | *Mat:* op doek *Size:* hoog 36, breed 50 duim		(Sold) fl 150 C S Roos
1804/10/16	DLOND	0017	*A. Beerstraten* | Ene onstuimige Zee met Schepen, die tegen ene rots stoten. Une Mer orageuse & des Vaisseaux brisans contre un rocher | *Mat:* op paneel *Size:* hoog 28, breed 41		(Unknown)
1805/07/03	AMSCH	0003	*Beerestraten. (A.)* | Een zeer fraai besneeuwd Dorpgezicht, met de Kerk, op een hoogte staande, omringd van verscheiden Woningen, aan een bevrozen Rivier welke gestoffeerd is met een ménigte Schaatseryders en wandelende Beelden; het licht en bruin, is hierin wel waargenomen, en is met regt een der frappanste stukken van dezen Meester | *Mat:* op doek *Size:* hoog 36, breed 51 duim	R[oos]	(Bought In) fl 81
1805/07/03	AMSCH	0060	*A. Beerestraten* | Een Onstuimige Zee, met eenige Scheepen, waar van 'er een tegens de klippen verbryzeld; zynde een ordinantie vol vuur, en is voorts meesterlyk op Doek geschilderd | *Mat:* op doek *Size:* hoog 37, breed 45 duim	C	(Sold) fl 3:10 Wynand Esser

1805/07/10	AMSCH	0015	*A. Beerestraten* | In een Levantsche Zeehaven ziet men by een prachtig Gebouw, Fontyn en andere Gebouwen, een ménigte stoffagie van Beeldjes, in 't Water verscheide Scheepen enz; fiks op Paneel | *Mat:* op paneel *Size:* hoog 23, breed 32 duim	V[inkeles] [for] M	(Sold) fl 12 Lafontaine
1805/07/10	AMSCH	0016	*A. Beerestraten* | Een gezicht op de groote Markt te Groningen; ryk gestoffeerd met Lieden te Paart en te Voet, Vrachtkarren enz., zonachtig en uitvoerig op Doek | *Mat:* op doek *Size:* hoog 36, breed 48 duim	V[inkeles] [for] M	(Sold) fl 26 van Iperen
1805/10/09	HGBSM	F0006	*A. Berestraaten* | Een gezicht in Amsterdam, langs, en op het rondeel na de munttoorn te zien, gestoffeerd met vaartuigen &c, uitvoerig en helder geschilderd | *Mat:* op doek *Size:* hoog 31 ½ breet 43 duim	T H van Willigen [or others]	(Sold) fl 9:10 Blommers
1805/12/16	AMSCH	0013	*A. Berestraten* | Een Italiaansche Zeehaven, vol gewoel van Scheepen en Beelden | *Mat:* op doek *Size:* hoog 21, breed 25 duim	R[oos]	(Bought In) fl 1:15
1806/11/24	AMSCH	0003	*Beerstraten (A.)* | Een gezigt op het Dorp Sloten, zynde een besneeuwde Winter; het Ys gestoffeerd met wandelende, schaatzenrydende Beeldjes; en Arresleden; allernatuurlykst, en fraay geschilderd | *Mat:* op doek *Size:* hoog 36, breed 50 duim	Munnikhuizen	(Sold) fl 65 Yver
1806/11/24	AMSCH	0004	*Beerstraten (A.)* | Een Italiaansche Zeehaven, vol gewoel van Scheepen en Beelden, fiks gepenceeld | *Mat:* op doek *Size:* hoog 21, breed 25 duim	van den Bosch	(Sold) fl 1 T Spaan
1807/08/26	AMSCH	0013	*A. Beerstraaten* | Een capitaal Ys- en Wintergezicht, by een Slot of Adelyk Huis. Het Ys is ryk gestoffeerd met Schaatseryders, Wandelaars en Kolvers, ter regter zyde ziet men over een Bruggetje naar een Dorp, met Kerk en Toren; de voorgrond en Daken der Huizen zyn alle met sneeuw bedekt. Alles is zeer kunstig en regt natuurlyk gepenceeld | *Mat:* op doek *Size:* hoog 33, breed 50 duim	de Vries	(Sold) fl 57 Gruiter
1808/08/23	AMSCH	0020	*Beerestraten. (A.)* | Een Gezigt uit de Stad ter Veere in Zeeland, naar de Haven te zien, gestoffeert met een Oorlogschip, verscheide andere Scheepen, en wandelende Lieden op een Brug, ter regter zijde vertoont zig een Rondel of Wagttooren, en andere Gebouwen binnen de Stad, in 't verschiet zeilende Vaartuigen; het bevallig zonlicht geeft een natuurlijke luister aan dit stuk, en is van eene uitvoerige penceelbehandeling | *Mat:* op doek *Size:* hoog 36, breed 50 duim	Z	(Sold) fl 31 van Iperen
1808/08/23	AMSCH	0206	*A. Beerestraaten* | Een Gezicht op de groote Mark te Haarlem, ziende langs de Kerk- en Vleeshal, rijk gestoffeerd met Heeren te Paard, Vragt-Karren, en een menigte Voetgangers; zonachtig en meesterlijk gepenceeld	[Gruyter?]	(Sold) fl 10:10 Jan Spaan
1808/08/23	AMSCH	0246	*A. Beerstraaten* | Een Zeehaven met Gebouwen en Beelden	S	(Sold) fl 1:5 van Os
1808/10/28	AMVRS	0001	*Beerestraten. (A.)* | Her [sic] Dorp Dronsrijk in Vriesland, bij den Winter. Men ziet naar de Kerk, het oud Kasteel en verscheidene Woningen. De besneeuwde Daken, het Ys gestoffeerd met Schaatserijders, Wandelaars, Kinderen, enz.; alles is natuurlijk en kunstig behandeld | *Mat:* op doek *Size:* hoog 36, breed 50 duimen	Marten Udink	(Sold) fl 110 Nijhof
1808/10/28	AMVRS	0002	*Beerestraten. (A.)* | Een Wintergezicht, aan de Buitekant te Amsterdam, met Brug en Toren. Alles is natuurlijk voorgesteld en rijk van Wandelende en Schaatserijdende Beelden | *Size:* hoog 33, breed 43 duim	Marten Udink	(Sold) fl 55 Du Pré
1809/04/22	AMYVR	0017	*A. Beerestraten* | Een Land- en Zeegezicht, met stoffagie van Beeldjes en Vaartuigen; warm en meesterlijk | *Mat:* op paneel *Size:* hoog 23, breed 14 duim	de Bruin	(Bought In) fl 30
1809/06/13	AMSCH	0005	*A. Beerstraten* | Dit fraaije Voorwerp verbeeld een aloud Gezigt binnen de Stad Delft, op de voorgrond in een Gragt ziet men twee Visschuiten, en bij de afgang van een Steene Trap eene Vrouw die goed spoelt, ter regter zijde een aloude Poort, verder een Plijn, gestoffeerd met speelende Kinderen en andere Beeldjes; dit stuk is bevallig van koloriet en allernatuurlijkst van penceelbehandeling | *Mat:* op doek *Size:* hoog 36, breed 35 ½ duim	[Gruyter?]	(Sold) fl 74 T Spaan
1810/07/23	DOLG1	0006	*A. Beerstraten* | Een Maanlicht, zijnde een Landschap, met een ouden Toren, en eenige bijstaande Gebouwen. Fraai van Teekening en Ordonnantie | *Mat:* op doek *Size:* hoog 24 ½, breed 13 ½ duim	Mr Pieter van den Santheuvel	(Sold) fl 28 van Eijk 's Hage
1810/07/23	DOLG1	0007	*A. Beerstraten* | Een Italiaansche Zeehaven, met Schepen, rijk gestoffeerd, uitvoerig en fix van behandeling | companion to lot 8 *Mat:* op paneel *Size:* hoog 22 ½, breed 12 duim	Mr Pieter van den Santheuvel	(Sold) fl 6 [Illegible]
1810/07/23	DOLG1	0008	*A. Beerstraten* | Een Italiaansche Zeehaven, pendant van no.7 | companion to lot 7 *Mat:* op paneel *Size:* hoog 22 ½, breed 32 duim	Mr Pieter van den Santheuvel	(Sold) fl 10 [or] 18 Van Braam Dordt
1810/08/06	AMSCH	0009	*Beerestraaten (A.)* | Een besneeuwde Winter, zijnde een oud Gezigt binnen Amsterdam, ziende op een der Stads Poorten, versierd met Schaatsenrijders en Wandelaars. Zeer natuurlijk verbeeld en fraai geschilderd | *Mat:* op doek *Size:* hoog 36, breed 50 duimen	C	(Sold) fl 100 Roelsema
1810/08/06	AMSCH	0010	*Beerestraaten (A.)* | Een sterk bevrozen Water, aan beide kanten Gebouwen en Geboomte, rijk met Schaatsenrijders, Kolvers en gaande Huislieden. Van gelijke schildering als de voorgaande | *Mat:* op doek *Size:* hoog 35, breed 50 duimen	C	(Sold) fl 65 van Leen

Beerstraten, A. (and Lingelbach)

1808/06/13	AMSCH	0013	*Beerestraten (A.); J. Lingelbag* | Deze Ordonantie verbeeldt het Stadhuis en de Markt te Kampen; rijk gestoffeerd door J. Lingelbag. Is zonachtig	E M Engelberts	(Sold) fl 380 O W J Berg

			en meesterlijk behandeld, en kan voor het beste van deze Meester gehouden worden | *Mat:* op doek *Size:* hoog 36, breed 50 duim		
1809/06/13	AMSCH	0006	*A. Beerstraten; J. Lingelbach* | In een kapitaale Winter, ziet men langs een sterk bevrozen Rivier, op een hoogte een Kerk en de ingang van een Dorp, verders een oud Adelijk Kasteel en andere Gebouwen, het IJs is rijk gestoffeerd met Schaatsenrijders, Kolvers, Wandelende Heeren en Dames en langs den Weg eenige na de Kerk gaande Dorpelingen, de voorgrond de Daken der Gebouwen en het Geboomten zijn alle als met Sneeuw bedekt; het is schoon van effect, konstig en natuurlijk gepenceeld, door A. Beerstraten en gestoffeerd door J. Lingelbach | *Mat:* op doek *Size:* hoog 36, breed 49 duim	[Gruyter?]	(Bought In) fl 125
1810/10/11	AMSCH	0005	*A. Beerstraten; J. Lingelbag* | Een kapitaal Wintergezigt, ziende over een Steenen Sluis, een Kerk, bij de ingang van een Dorp, benevens een sterk bevrozen Rivier, bij een Adelijk Slot, het is rijk gestoffeert met Schaatsenrijders, Wandelaars, en ter Kerk gaande Dorpelingen, de besneeuwde Daken en het Geboomte zijn natuurlijk, en de stoffagie uitvoerig geschilderd | *Mat:* op doek *Size:* hoog 33, breed 48 duimen	[Gruyter?]	(Bought In) fl 110
			Beerstraten, A. (and Velde, A.)		
1801/06/10	AMSCH	0013	*Beerestraten. (A.); A. v.d. Velde* | Een Venetiaansche Zeehaven, met hooge Gebouwen, waarby een Fontein, waaruit eenig Vee drinkt, verders een menigte Beeldjes, het water is ryk gestoffeerd met Scheepen en Schuiten, en is voorts van eene delicaate penseels behandeling | *Mat:* op doek *Size:* hoog 41, breed 34 duim	Herman ten Kate	(Sold) fl 255 C S Roos
			Beerstraten, J.		
1801/05/11	AMSCH	0014	*J. Beerstraaten* | Een Levandsche Zeehaven, ryk gestoffeert, met diversche Vaartuigen en handeldryvende Persoonen, uitvoerig en meesterlyk behandeld | *Mat:* op doek *Size:* hoog 26, breed 25 duim	E[lias]	(Sold) fl 8 Rijnders
1801/06/10	AMSCH	0014	*Beerestraten. (J.)* | Een gezicht op het Dorp Nukoop, zynde een besneeuwde Winter; op een Rivier ziet men enige Schaatseryders en wandelende Beelden, op het Kerkhoff de begraafnis van het Kind van den Schout, zynde op dien tyd naar het leeven meesterlyk geschilderd | *Mat:* op doek *Size:* hoog 36, breed 50 duim	Herman ten Kate	(Sold) fl 120 Pruyssenaar
1801/06/10	AMSCH	0015	*Beerestraten. (J.)* | Een gezicht van het Oude-Stadhuis van Amsterdam, gestoffeert met een menigte Beelden, alles is van natuurlyke en krachtige behandeling | *Mat:* op paneel *Size:* hoog 20, breed 23 duim	Herman ten Kate	(Sold) fl 115 J Yver
1801/06/10	AMSCH	0016	*Beerestraten. (J.)* | Een Bergachtig Landschap, op de voorgrond ziet men tusschen Rotsen een Waterval, verders Beeldjes en Gebouwen, krachtig behandeld | *Mat:* op paneel *Size:* hoog 23, breed 20 duim	[Doublet]	(Sold) fl 23 Teyler van Hall
1802/05/10	MGSAN	0008	*J. Beerstra* | Een fraaije Zeehaven, met een Havepoort, daarvoor verscheide Schepen en Schuiten, door J. Beerstra: op Paneel, in zwarte Lyst, met vergulde Binnenlyst | *Mat:* op paneel *Size:* hoog 36 duim, breed 49 duim	Johan Dirk Kruysse	(Unknown) £ 1:14
1802/06/28	AMSCH	0018	*J. Beerestraten* | Twee stuks Italiaansche Zeehavens	B	(Sold) fl 2:10 Geld
1802/09/21	UTHDG	0008	*J. Beerstraten* | Het oude Hoofd te Rotterdam in 1662, met een gezigt over de Maas bij stormagtig weer, rijk met Vaartuigen en Beelden gestoffeerd, helder en van de beste qualiteit | *Mat:* op paneel *Size:* hoog 17, breed 23 duimen *Inscr:* 1662 (dated?) *Notes:* It is unclear whether the date is inscribed on the painting.		(Sold) fl 54 Cobell
1802/12/13	AMSCH	0034	*J. Beerestraaten* | Een Levantsche Zeehaven	Pruyssenaar [for] B	(Sold) fl 14 C S Roos
1803/08/17	AMSCH	0007	*Berestraten. (J.)* | Twee woelende Zeeën, met een menigte Oorlog en andere Schepen, Vaartuigen en Beeldjes gestoffeerd, beide met Steeden in het verschiet; zonachtig en natuurlyk geschilderd | *Mat:* op paneel *Size:* ieder hoog 20, breed 24 duim	Anna Catharina Putman	(Sold) fl 20:10 Hodges
1803/12/12	AMSCH	0001	*J. Beerestraaten* | Een Winter, langs een bevrooze Rivier ziet men een besneeuwde Kerk, en verder eenige Huizen van een Dorp; gestoffeerd met Schaatzeryders en Wandelende Persoonen; dit stuk is van een fraai licht, en meesterlyk gepenceeld | *Mat:* op doek *Size:* hoog 37, breed 46 duim	B	(Sold) fl 38:10 C S Roos [for] N
1804/02/27	AMSCH	0009	*Beerstraaten. (J.)* | Een bevroozen Rivier, gestoffeerd met Schaatseryders en wandelen Persoonen, ter zyde een op een Heuvel besneeuwde Kerk; alles is zeer natuurlyk en byzonder fraai van licht en bruin, en een der fraaiste van deeze meester | *Mat:* op doek *Size:* hoog 36, breed 49 duim	B	(Sold) fl 136 Theengs
1804/02/27	AMSCH	0010	*Beerstraaten. (J.)* | Het gezigt van den Grooten Kerk en Vleeshal, op de Markt te Haarlem, ryk gestoffeerd met differenten stoffage, zonachtig en meesterlyk geschilderd | *Mat:* op paneel *Size:* hoog 33, breed 31 duim	C	(Bought In) fl 9
1804/05/07	AMSCH	0013	*Beerstraten. (J.)* | Dit bevallig en Natuurlyk Landschap steld voor, 't Dorp Maarsen; de Vegt, en de Weg, zyn beiden ryk gestoffeerd met onderscheiden Stoffagie; zonachtig en bevallig geschilderd | *Mat:* op doek *Size:* hoog 25, breed 37 duim	Vinkeles [for] G	(Bought In) fl 11 ½
1804/12/10	AMSCH	0004	*J. Beerstraaten* | Een kabbelend Water, met diverse vaartuigen, ter regter zyde een Jacht fraai gestoffeert met beelden; alles uitvoerig van Schildering | *Mat:* op paneel *Size:* Hoog 17, breed 30 duim	Jan de Groot	(Sold) fl 3:5 Uitenbogaard
1805/07/03	AMSCH	0059	*J. Beerestraten* | In een stil Water, ziet men by eenig Land en Paalwerk, een stil leggend Beurtschip, met verscheide Lieden, verzeld van twee	V[inkeles]	(Sold) fl 40 Reijers

			andere, eenige zylende en roeijende Scheepen en Vaartuigen; breed en meesterlyk op Paneel | *Mat:* op paneel *Size:* hoog 24, breed 32		
1806/05/05	AMSCH	0019	*J. Beerenstraeten* | 't Gezigt van de grooten Kerk en Vleeshal op de grooten Markt te Haarlem; ryk gestoffeerd en meesterlyk geschilderd door J. Beerenstraeten | *Mat:* op paneel *Size:* hoog 33, breed 31 duim	V[inkeles]	(Sold) fl 4 Gruyter
1808/06/06	RMRIJ	0006	*Beerestraten. (J.)* | De afbeelding van den Roemrijken Zeeslag tusschen den Hollandschen Luitenant Admiraal Hertog en Ridder Michiel Adriaansz. de Ruiter, en den Engelschen Admiraal Monk, Hertog van Albemarle; in welken de groote Steng van het Schip van de Ruiter word afgeschoten. Zijnde voorgevallen den 12 Junij 1666, den tweeden dag der vier dagen aangehoudene Bataille; waar van de verdere bijzonderheden te vinden zijn in de folio uitgave van 't leven van M. A. de Ruiter, door Gerard Brandt, pag. 486., en in de octavo uitgave bij Allart, 3 deel, pag. 53. Deze capitale en ongemeen rijke ordinantie, zoo van Schepen als groot aantal figuren, is een wonder van vinding en verbeeldingskracht, welks wedergade in dit opzigt niet bekend is. Zilveragtig van toon. Uitvoerig, meesterlijk en krachtig geschilderd [Ce Tableau magnifique represente la mémorable et glorieuse Bataille entre le Lieutenant Amiral Hollandais Duc et Chevalier Michiel Adriaansz. de Ruyter et l'Amiral Anglais Monk Duc d'Albemarle au moment ou le vaisseau Amiral Hollandais a son mât de hunes emporté. Cet Evenement eut lieu le 12 Juin 1666 et le 2d. jour de la Bataille, qui a duré pendant quatre jours, et dont les particularités se trouvent dans la vie de ce Héros par G. Brandt, Edition Hollandaise in folio page 486 et in 8°. vol. 3 page 53. La composition savante et riche, le grand fini, le ton vrai et argentin font de ce Morceau unique un chef-d'oeuvre de l'art et de l'imagination] | *Mat:* op doek *Size:* Hoog 66, en breed 106 duim *Loc:* Amsterdam, Nederland. Rijksmuseum. (A22)	Gerrit van der Pot, Heer van Groeneveld	(Sold) fl 540 van Lennep [for] le Roi
1808/06/06	RMRIJ	0007	*Beerestraten. (J.)* | Een aangenaam Wintergezigt, aan den IJ kant te Amsterdam, de Schippers Beurs en Nieuwe Brug voorstellende, vol Beelden en bijwerk. Zie Beschreibung der Stadt Amsterdam, bij Joachim Boschen 1664. pag. 175 en 176 [Imitation Pittoresque de la Bourse des Batteliers et de plusieurs autres bâtiments situés prés de l'Y à Amsterdam, et prise pendant l'hyver. On y voit beaucoup de figures occupées de differentes manières. Ce Tableau vigoureux et hardi est peint en Maitre] | *Mat:* op doek *Size:* Hoog 31 ½, en breed 37 ½ duim *Loc:* Amsterdam, Nederland. Rijksmuseum. (A20)	Gerrit van der Pot, Heer van Groeneveld	(Sold) fl 500 J M Jorissen [for] le Roi
1810/06/20	AMSCH	0007	*J. Beerstraten* | Een Venetiaansche Zeehaven, met grootsche Gebouwen, ter zijde zeilende Oorlogschepen, Jagten en andere Vaartuigen. Helder en vrolijk behandeld | *Mat:* op doek *Size:* hoog 27, breed 42 duimen	D	(Sold) fl 22 Coclers
1810/06/20	AMSCH	0192	*J. Beerstraten* | Een kabbelende Zee, met zeilende Oorlogschepen, roeijende Sloepen en andere Vaartuigen. Fiks geschilderd | *Mat:* op doek	A	(Sold) fl 1:5 Teerling
1810/10/11	AMSCH	0006	*J. Beerestraten* | Een Italiaansche Zeehaven, met prachtige Gebouwen, gestoffeerd met zeilende Schepen, Galeijen, Sloepen en andere Vaartuigen; helder en uitvoerig geschilderd | *Mat:* op doek *Size:* hoog 34, breed 46 duimen	Y	(Sold) fl 8:10 de Vries
1810/10/11	AMSCH	0007	*J. Beerestraten* | Een Italiaansche Zeehaven, met prachtige Gebouwen, Vaartuigen en Beeldjes gestoffeerd | *Size:* hoog 36, breed 50 duimen	[Levy Pakker?]	(Sold) fl 3 Vallee
			Beerstraten, J. (and Lingelbach)		
1809/04/17	AMSCH	0004	*J. Beerstraaten; J. Lingelbach* | Een kapitaal Wintergezicht, ziende over een bevrozen Rivier op een Dorp, met verscheide Wooningen, Kerk en Tooren, ter zijde een Slot of adelijk Huis, het IJs is rijk gestoffeerd met Schaatzenrijders, Wandelaars, Kolvers en Arresleeden: de voorgrond, het Geboomte en de Daken der Huizen zijn alle met Sneeuw bedekt; alles is zeer kunstig en natuurlijk door J. Beerstraaten en de stoffagie uitvoerig door J. Lingelbach, behandeld op Doek | *Mat:* op doek *Size:* hoog 36, breed 51 duim	C	(Sold) fl 275
			Beerstraten, Jan Abrahamsz.		
1803/08/01	AMSCH	0003	*Beerstraten. (J. A.)* | Een Amstelgezigt, gestoffeert op de voorgrond met zeilende Jagten en roeyende Vaartuigen, verder de twee Blokhuizen, en in 't verschiet de Zuyderkerks Tooren en andere Gebouwen binnen Amsterdam, zeer uitvoerig en natuurlyk behandeld | *Mat:* op paneel *Size:* hoog 24, breed 33 duim	H	(Sold) fl 39 Teengs
1803/08/01	AMSCH	0003a[H]	*Beerstraten. (J. A.)* | Een Stad gezigt | *Notes:* This lot was added in by hand in the EBNP, FLNY, LBDa and RKDH copies of the catalogue.	J	(Sold) fl 54 Pruijssenaar
			Beest, J. [Unidentified]		
1809/07/25	HGBSM	0255	*J. Beest* | Een Binnen-Stadsgezigt, verbeeldende een Groenmarkt, vol Figuren en Groente, door J. Beest, 1650 | *Mat:* op paneel *Size:* hoog 18 en een half, breed 24 duim *Inscr:* J. Beest, 1650 (signed and dated?) *Notes:* It is unclear whether the name and date are inscribed on the painting.	D van der Aa [or] E B ten Dall	(Sold) fl 13 Teissier
			Beest, Sybrand van		
1803/08/01	AMSCH	0006	*Beels. (S. V.)* | Een Gezicht in s'Gravenhage, alwaar het Kermis is, in het midden een Kwakzalver, waarby een menigte omstanders, op de	Thoen	(Sold) fl 9 Pruijssenaar

			voorgrond eenige Militairen, zonachtig en kragtig gepenceeld | *Mat:* op paneel *Size:* hoog 23, breed 33 duim		
1805/07/10	AMSCH	0037	*S. van Beest* | Een Stadgezigt, de voorgrond met een Quakzalver op zyn Theater; kragtig op Paneel | *Mat:* op paneel *Size:* hoog 28, breed 23 duim	R[oos]	(Sold) fl 2:10 Gruyter
			Beesten, Abraham Hendrik van		
1803/06/20	AMSCH	0050	*A.H. van Beesten* | Een Heilige Famiellie, op Doek | *Mat:* op doek *Size:* hoog 14, breed 12 duim	Roos [for] C	(Sold) fl 4 V d Schley [for] R[ijfsnijder]
1804/02/27	AMSCH	0133a	*van Beesten* | Twee stuks Basrelieven met Kindertjes	B	(Sold) fl 8 Cocler
			Beesten, J. van [Unidentified]		
1804/05/07	AMSCH	0026	*Beesten. (J. van)* | In een Stadgezicht ziet men een Groenmarkt, ryk gestoffeerd met een meenigte van allerhande Persoonen, Groentens, Fruiten, Manden, Kruiwagens, enz.; uitvoerig en zonachtig behandeld | *Mat:* op paneel	Vinkeles [for] J	(Sold) fl 9 Gruiter
			Bega, Cornelis Pietersz.		
1801/03/16	AMSCH	0097	*C. Bega* | Een Boer bezig zynde, een meisje te caresseeren, uitvoerig behandeld	K[ip]	(Sold) fl 4:5 Stevens
1801/06/10	AMSCH	0023	*Bega. (C.)* | Een binnen Huis, waarin verscheiden Boeren zig vrolyk makende, met drinken, verders eenig Huysraad; krachtig en uitvoerig geschilderd | *Mat:* op paneel *Size:* hoog 16, breed 14 duim	Herman ten Kate	(Sold) fl 100 Pruyssenaar
1801/10/19	AMSCH	0006	*Bega. (Cornelis)* | In dit fraaije stukje is verbeeld een Alchimist, zittende in een stook-vertrek met een tang in de hand, en een blaasbalk op zyn knie, voor hem eenige Boeken, Potten en disteleer Glazen op en by een steene Fournuis, met meer bywerk, zeer uitvoerig | *Mat:* op paneel *Size:* hoog 13 ½, breed 11 ½ duim	Jonkheer Menno Baron van Coehoorn	(Sold) fl 100 Coclers
1802/05/05	AMSCH	0022	*C. Bega* | Voor een Boere Buitenhuis, ziet men eenige Vrolyke Huislieden zich met Carresseeren en Danssen vermaken, delicaat | *Size:* hoog 21, breed 17 duim	E	(Sold) fl 50 Mensard
1802/05/24	HGBAK	0027	*Bega* | Een binnen vertrek, met een Boer en Boerinnen, zittende met een ontbloten boezem, door Bega, hoog 16 duim, breed 13 duim, op doek, zwarte lyst en bies | *Mat:* op doek *Size:* hoog 16 duim, breed 13 duim	Mejuffrouw A van der Mieden	(Sold) fl 10:10 Carré
1802/06/16	AMSCH	0020	*C. Bega* | In een Boere Binnenvertrek ziet men, behalven eenige andere Beeldjes, een Boer en Boerin, beezig zynde een bevallig Vrouwtje, op een galante wyze, een Roemer Wyn aan te bieden; alles delicaat en uitvoerig gepenceelt | *Mat:* op paneel *Size:* hoog 15 ½, breed 12 ½ duim	[Merrem]	(Sold) fl 74 van der Vinne
1802/06/28	AMSCH	0014	*C. Bega* | In een Binnenhuis ziet men eenige Boeren en een Boerin, zich met Roken en Drinken vermaken; meesterlyk op Panneel | *Mat:* op paneel *Size:* hoog 11, breed 9 duim	Anna Elink	(Sold) fl 5:15 Geld
1802/07/21	HGKAN	0075	*Bega* | Een Dame welke bezig is haar Toilet te manken, fraay geschildert, door Bega, op Doek, zwarte Lyst, vergulde binnen rand | *Mat:* op doek		(Unknown)
1802/09/06	AMSCH	0200	*C. Béga* | Een Boeren Buitenhuis	Spaan	(Sold) fl 6 Texier
1802/09/18	RMDRS	0003	*C. Bega* | Een Boere Binnehuis, waarin een Boerin zittende te zingen, by haar staat een Boer met een Kan in de eene en een Glas in de andere hand, verder nog een Boer en bywerk | companion to lot 4 *Annots:* Copie (MB) *Size:* hoog 14 ½, breed 12 ½ duim	Casper de Haas	(Sold) fl 20 v Wallen
1802/09/18	RMDRS	0004	*C. Bega* | Een dito [Boere Binnehuis], waar in een verliefde Boer en Boerin, en meerder Figuuren, door denzelven [C. Bega], tot een wederga | companion to lot 3 *Annots:* Copie (MB)	Casper de Haas	(Sold) fl 11:5 V Giesen
1802/09/18	RMDRS	0023	*C. Bega* | Een Doctor by een ziek Vrouwtje | *Size:* hoog 7 ½, breed 10 duim	Casper de Haas	(Sold) fl 21 V Beefting
1802/09/29	AMSCH	0007	*C. Bega* | Een Binnehuisje. Hoog 14 ¼, breed 11 ¾ duim. Paneel. Waarin men in een bevallig licht een interessant Vrouwtje by een Wieg ziet zitten, hebbende by haar twee Kinderen die met elkanderen speelen; nevens haar een oud Boertje, met dewelke zy in gesprek schynt, en aan de andere zyde zit een Boertje by den Haard; onderscheiden bywerk verreiken deeze fraaije Ordenantie, de Penceelbehandeling is uitmuntend, en van de beste van deezen verdienstlyken Meester [L'Artiste à représenté, par ce précieux Tableau dans l'interieur d'une maison rustique, une famille de villageois au sein du bonheur, une femme intèressante & un villageois sur l'âge, s'entretiennent et paroissent contens de leurs sort, tandis qu'un Paysan se chausse près de la Cheminée, deux Enfans, dont l'un est tenu de la mère, jouent ensemble à côté d'un Berceau ; divers accessoires ornent encore ce charmant sujet, qui est d'une finesse de touche et d'un Effet admirable.] | *Mat:* op paneel *Size:* hoog 14 ¼, breed 11 ¾ duim	[Labouchere?]	(Sold) fl 78 Vinkeles
1802/12/13	AMSCH	0012	*C. Béga* | In een Binnevertrek ziet men een Vrouw een Ketel schuuren by 't Licht van een Lamp, agter haar ziet men een Wieg, waarby twee Kinderen, 't Lamplicht doet een kragtig Effect en is konstig gepenceeld | *Mat:* op paneel *Size:* hoog 17, breed 13 duim	Pruyssenaar [for] A	(Bought In) fl 9:15
1802/12/13	AMSCH	0013	*C. Béga* | In een Binnehuis, ziet men een Boer zittende met een Pyp en Vuurtest in zyn Handen, als sprekende met en staande voor hem, met een Glas in de Hand, verder een andere Huisman en Vrouw, de Caracters zyn	Schley [for] Lauwers	(Sold) fl 12 Van Iperen

			geestig en meesterlyk van Penceel behandeling | *Mat:* op paneel *Size:* hoog 12 ½, breed 10 ½ duim		
1803/07/18	AMSCH	0002	*Bega. (Cornelis)* | Twee stuks, yder hoog 17, breed 14 duim, Paneel. In een Huismanswooning ziet men een Boer met een Kan en Glas, eenigzints door den Drank vervrolykt zynde, by hem zit een Vrouw, en agter hem ziet men nog drie Boeren en verder Huisraad. De tweede stelt mede een dito Binnenvertrek voor, waarin een Vrouw met haar Kind aan de Borst, naast haar een Wieg, waarop een Boer met een Pyp in de hand leund, schynende met haar te spreeken, agter hun zit een andere met de Meid te praaten, voorts een menigte bywerk. Deeze beide stukjes zyn helder, delicaat en van de beste schildering van dezen Meester [Dans une demeure rustique est un homme jovial tenant le verre & le pot de Bierre ; il est assi [sic] sur un Banc, son manteau sous lui, cajolant une Paysane ; trois autres rustres achevent ce groupe de Cinq figures. Quelques ustenciles ornent de plus ce morceau. Ce tableau excellent pour l'effet du clair obscur est d'un fini rare ; l'expression parfaitement rendue & les habillemens traités avec un soin particulier nous le fait exposer pour être de la meilleure qualité de cet Artiste. De même grandeur : Un sujet dans le genre du précedent peint pour second offre audevant du tableau une femme tenant un Enfant au Sein ; sur une berce qui est près d'elle s'appuyt un villageois qui semble lui parler la pipe à la main. Derriere eux est un autre courtisant la servante. Ce morceau d'egal merite au premier, réunit les mêmes qualitées, exprime avec autant de caractère que de finesse la vie champêtre, il ne peut être depareillé sans domage de son pandant.] | *Mat:* op paneel *Size:* yder hoog 17, breed 14 duim	Maria Theresia Andrioli	(Sold) fl 305 W Reijers
1803/08/17	AMSCH	0009	*Bega. (C.)* | Een liefkozende Boer en Boerin, in een Binnehuis, by de haard nog een staande Vrouw en zittende Boer, alles delicaat gepenceeld | *Mat:* op paneel *Size:* hoog 12, breed 11 duim	Anna Catharina Putman	(Sold) fl 89 Gruyter
1804/08/08	AMSCH	0026	*C. Bega* | In een Boeren Binnenhuis ziet men op de voorgrond eenige vrolyke Boeren en een Boerin, zich met speelen en zingen vermakende, ter zyde een Schoorsteen en ander toepasselyk Bywerk; helder en uitvoerig van penceelsbehandeling | *Mat:* op paneel *Size:* hoog 14, breed 13 duim	Vink[eles] [for] S	(Bought In) fl 29
1805/07/03	AMSCH	0058	*C. Béga* | Dit bevallig stukje steldt voor: een Boere Binnehuis, waarin op de Voorgrond twee Vrouwen, houdende den eene een jong Kind op de schoot, waarby een Wieg, agter hun een Boer, rustende tégen een hout schot, verders aan een Tafel eenige drinkende en praatende Boeren en eenig huisraad, alleruitvoerigst en delicaast gepenceeld | *Mat:* op doek *Size:* hoog 17, breed 14 duim *Loc:* Philadelphia, PA, USA. Museum of Art. (Johnson Coll. 527)	V[inkeles]	(Sold) fl 231 Th Spaan
1805/07/10	AMSCH	0027	*C. Béga* | In een Boere Binnehuis ziet men drie vrolyke Boeren, en een Boerin, rookende en drinkende, verders eenig Huisraad; breed en meesterlyk op Paneel | *Mat:* op paneel *Size:* hoog 13, breed 11 duim	V[inkeles] [for] L	(Sold) fl 20 Teengs
1805/07/10	AMSCH	0027a[H]	*Bega* | Schildery | *Notes:* This lot was added in by hand in the EBNP, FLNY and RKDH copies of the catalogue.	R[oos]	(Bought In) fl 81
1807/04/00	LNDLS	0026	*C. Bega* | Een vrouwtje met een kind aan haar borst, zittende nevens een tafel, daar een brandende kaars op staat, met een man agter haar | *Mat:* op doek	[Abraham Delfos] [or others]	(Unknown)
1807/06/10	HGBSM	0026	*C. Bega* | Een Vrouwtje met een kind aan haar borst, zittende nevens een tafel, daar een brandende kaars op staat, met een man agter haar | *Mat:* op doek	Abraham Delfos [or others]	(Sold) fl 4 de Gelder
1807/08/26	AMSCH	0008	*C. Béga* | Een Chimist in zyn Laboratorium, gezeten by een Tafel, waarop verscheidene Boeken, Potten, Flessen enz., de Chimie rakende gezien worden, hy is bezig een Urinaal met veel aandacht te beschouwen, die hem door eene Vrouw, naast hem staande, is aangebragt; alles is uitvoerig en fraai behandeld, en zeer natuurlyk van licht en donker | *Mat:* op doek *Size:* hoog 15 ½, breed 19 duim		(Withdrawn)
1808/06/06	RMRIJ	0008	*Béga. (Cornelis) 1663* | In eene gewulfde Studeerkamer ziet men, in eene overdenkende houding, een Astrologist, gezeten op een stoel, in de hand eene bril houdende, voor hem een opengeslagen boek met schrift en zinbeduidende figuren. Achter hem eene met een tapijt bedekte tafel, waar op eene Hemel-Globe, Boeken en Papieren; op den voorgrond nog eenige schilderachtige voorwerpen. Alles is uitmuntend helder en uitvoerig behandeld [On voit dans un souterrain vouté un Astrologue assis sur une chaise, tenant ses lunettes à la main, et méditant sur des caractéres qu'un livre ouvert et posé devant lui, offre à ses regards. Derrière lui, sur une table couverte d'un tapis, se trouve une Sphere Céleste avec des papiers, des livres etc., et sur le devant plusieurs accessoires Pittoresques. Le fini precieux et l'imitation éxacte de la nature, font honneur a la réputation de cet Artiste] | *Annots:* Thys berichte 22 Juli 1798, dat hij het te Brussel gekocht had. Juli 1799 van P.J. Thys (f 200.-) (RMA I) *Mat:* op paneel *Size:* Hoog 14 ¾, en breed 11 ¼ duim *Inscr:* Cornelis Bega. 1663 (signed and dated?) *Notes:* It is unclear whether the name and date are inscribed on the painting. *Loc:* London, England, UK. National Gallery. (1481)	Gerrit van der Pot, Heer van Groeneveld	(Sold) fl 605 M van Noort de Leyde
1808/06/06	RMRIJ	0009	*Béga. (Cornelis)* | Een Oud Man in eene overdenkende houding, in zijne Studeerkamer zittende, met aangenaam bijwerk. Bevallig verlicht;	Gerrit van der Pot, Heer van Groeneveld	(Sold) fl 195 Stratenus [for] le Roi

			uitvoerig en krachtig geschilderd [Un Vieillard dans son Cabinet d'Etude paroit être dans une méditation profonde, il est entouré de livres et d'autres objets. D'un grand fini, d'un effet piquant, et d'un ton vigoureux] | *Annots:* [door] S Koninck (RMA I) *Mat:* op paneel *Size:* Hoog 15 ¼, en breed 12 ¾ duim *Loc:* Amsterdam, Nederland. Rijksmuseum. (A23) as S. Koninck		
1808/06/11	RMRIJ	0070	*C: Bega* | Een uitmuntend Schilderytje, waar eene Vrouw, gezeten by de Wieg, haar Kind staande voor haar houd, een Rookend Man en verder Bywerk. Ovaal Paneel | *Mat:* op paneel *Fmt:* ovaal *Size:* hoog 5 ½, breed 4 duim		(Sold) fl 77 van Leen
1808/08/23	AMSCH	0008	*Bega. (C.)* | In een Boeren Binnenhuis zit een bedaagd Landman, houdende een Borrelflesje in de hand, schijnende te spreeken tegens eene bevallige Hospita, die nevens hem geplaast is, houdende een Bierkan in de hand, ter zijde ligt een Phiool, Verkeerbort, en verscheide Huisraad, verder zitten twee bejaarde Lieden; het licht is bevallig en van een uitvoerige penceelbehandeling | *Mat:* op paneel *Size:* hoog 15, breed 13 duim	[Coclers]	(Bought In) fl 285
1808/08/23	AMSCH	0009	*Bega. (C.)* | Een Doctor in zijn Laboratorium, zittende voor een Tafel, waar op Flessen, Boeken, en verschillende Papieren geplaatst zijn, houdende een Urinaal in de hand, en het met aandagt beschouwende, achter hem staat eene Landvrouw, als berigt afwagtende, verders gestoffeert met verschillende soorten van Chimicaale Gereedschappen; het ter zijde invallende licht doet een natuurlijke werking, en is fraai gepenceeld | *Mat:* op doek *Size:* hoog 16, breed 19 duim	[Coclers]	(Bought In) fl 130
1809/04/17	AMSCH	0008	*C. Bega* | In een Binnenvertrek zitten twee Vrouwen op een Kist voor een Bedsteede, zig met rooken en drinken vermakende, ter zijde liggen eenige Vaten en ander Bijwerk; geestig en natuurlijk verbeeld | *Mat:* op doek *Size:* hoog 14, breed 11 duim	C	(Sold) fl 33:10
1809/06/13	AMSCH	0021	*C. Bega* | Eene oude Boerin, een Meisje liefkoozende, ter zijde op een Bank, staat een Test met Vuur en Tabaksdoos; geestig | *Mat:* op paneel *Size:* hoog 9, breed 8 duim	Q	(Sold) fl 10:10 Gruyter
1809/06/13	AMSCH	0193	*C. Béga* | Een Binnenhuis met een vrolijke Boer en Boerin	Y	(Sold) fl 0:6 L Pakker
1810/03/27	RMCNL	0069	*Bega* | Men ziet in eene Keuken waarin eene meenigte Keuken-gereedschap, eene Meid aan 't Schuren, fraai en fix gepenseeld		(Unknown)
1810/05/22	AMSCH	0013	*Bega. (C.)* | In een Binnenhuis, zitten twee Vrouwen, nevens elkander, de eene heeft een Tinnen Kan in de hand en een Glas in de andere, de tweede houdt een Pijp in de hand, verders gestoffeerd met verscheide bijwerk; meesterlijk gepenceeld | *Mat:* op doek *Size:* hoog 13, breed 11 duim	F	(Sold) fl 36 van Iperen
1810/06/06	RMMUY	0162	*C. Bega* | Een Binnenhuis met Boertjes, fraaij | *Mat:* op paneel		(Unknown) fl 2:6
1810/06/06	RMMUY	0196	*C. Bega* | Twee stuks Boertjes | *Mat:* op paneel		(Sold) fl 5:10 V Dongen
1810/08/01	AMSCH	0012	*Bega (Cornelis)* | In eene Boerenwoning zitten op den voorgrond twee Vrouwen met een Kind, bij een Wieg; nevens haar staat een vergenoegd Huisman; achterwaarts andere Beelden [Dans une Habitation rustique l'on voit assises au devant du Tableau deux Femmes avec un Enfant, auprès d'un Berceau ; un Villageois se tient debout a côté d'elles. Vèrs le fond on remarque quelqu'autres figures] | *Annots:* assez bon (NGW) *Mat:* op paneel *Size:* hoog 16, breed 14 duimen *Loc:* Philadelphia, PA, USA. Museum of Art. (Johnson Coll. 527)	Mr Pieter de Smeth van Alphen	(Sold) fl 335 R Pot te Rotterdam
1810/08/06	AMSCH	0011	*Bega (C)* | Eene Boeren-woning of Herberg, in dezelve zit een vergenoegd Huisman, welken door eene Vrouw een Glas met Bier wordt aangeboden, waarbij een ander, die zijn pijp aansteekt, achterwaarts twee andere Lieden, bij den Haard. Meesterlijk en van de beste schildering | *Mat:* op paneel *Size:* hoog 14, breed 12 ½ duimen	A	(Sold) fl 381 Texier Gerbet en Comp [for] Librun

Bega, Cornelis Pietersz. (copy after)

1804/10/16	DLOND	0240a[b]	*C. Vermeulen; C. Bega* | [Een Stuk, bevattende 13 zeer schone Copiën van de volgende Meesters. Un Tableau, contenant 13 Copies très-belles des Peintres suivans.] 2. C. Bega. Vrolyk Gezelschap, Compagnie joyeuse | copy by Corn. Vermeulen (III) after Bega *Mat:* op paneel *Size:* hoog 41, breed 55 *Notes:* The bracketed information in the title appears above lot 240a[a] and refers to lots 240a[a-m].		(Sold) fl 150 for lots 240a[a-m]. Ond d Wyngaert
1804/10/16	DLOND	0263	*De With, naar Bega* | Twee Stukjens. Vuur-en Lamplichtjens. Deux pièces. Lumière de Feu & de Lampe | copy by Wit after Bega *Mat:* op paneel *Size:* hoog 10, breed 8		(Unknown)

Bega, Cornelis Pietersz. (manner)

1802/02/16	AMSCH	0063	*C. Béga* | Een Boere Binnehuys, waar in een geslagt varken op een Leer, ter zyde een vrouw die worst hakt, en een jongen met een blaas, kragtig gepenceeld, als door C. Béga	G	(Sold) fl 4:5 C Meijer
1803/09/07	AMSCH	0254	*C. Béga* | Twee stuks, zynde het éëne een Hofgezicht, en ander een Dorp, ryk gestoffeerd met Beelden; op Paneel geschilderd, in de manier van C. Béga [Deux tableaux, l'un représentant l'intérieur d'une basse cour, l'autre un village richement garni de figures, dans la manière de C. Bega] | *Mat:* op paneel *Size:* ieder hoog 20, breed 28 duim	Smidt	(Bought In) fl 11

1810/06/06	RMMUY	0036	*Bega* | Een klein fraaij Stukje, verbeeldende een haspelend Vrouwtje, bij Lamplicht. Als door Bega, in de trant van G. Dou | *Mat:* op paneel		(Unknown) fl 13:5
1810/12/03	DOBRA	0014	*Bega* | Drie vrolyke Boeren in een Binnenhuis, als door Bega		(Unknown)
			Begeyn, Abraham		
1801/03/16	AMSCH	0005	*A. Begeyn* | Een capitaal boomryk Landschap, gestoffeerd met grasende Bokjes, in 't verschiet een Fontein, alles zeer uitvoerig en fraai van schildering	P[ruyssenaar]	(Sold) fl 16:10 Cocler
1801/06/13	LNDLS	0024	*A. Begein* | Een Zeehaven met schepen, op de voorgrond eenige wandelende en handeldrijvende persoonen, konstig, fix en helder, op doek, door A. Begein 1659 | *Mat:* op doek *Size:* hoog 36, breed 52 duimen *Inscr:* A. Begein 1659 (signed and dated?) *Notes:* It is unclear whether the name and date are inscribed on the painting.	D van R	(Sold) fl 133 A Delfos [for] W
1801/08/19	AMSCH	0012	*A. Begyn* | Een Boomryk Landschap, op de voorgrond by eenige Planten, gestoffeerd met twee Vrouwen by eenige Bokken; meesterlyk gepenceeld als Berghem	Pruyssen^{r} [for] Q	(Sold) fl 7 Gruiter
1802/05/05	AMSCH	0020	*A. Begeyn* | Een Bergachtig Landschap, met een Rivier doorsneeden, gestoffeert met Beelden en Beesten | *Size:* hoog 32, breed 44 duim	J	(Sold) fl 7:10 Spruit
1802/09/06	AMSCH	0016	*A. Béga* | Een Hofgezicht met Beeldjes en Bokken gestoffeerd; uitvoerig | *Mat:* op doek *Size:* hoog 17, breed 21 duim	Mevrouw Achtienhoven	(Sold) fl 2:5 I^{c} Smit
1802/09/06	AMSCH	0017	*A. Begyn* | In een Landschap voor een Boere Herbergh, ververschen zig twee Krygslieden te Paard, verzelt van een Trompetter, ter zyde staat een bevallig Waardinnetje met een wynkan in de hand, en twee Beedelaars; voor de Herberg zitten eenige Boeren te drinken; plaisant geschilderd | *Size:* hoog 21, breed 29 duim	X	(Bought In) fl 6
1802/12/13	AMSCH	0010	*A. Begyn* | Een capitaal Landschap, ter linker zyde gestoffeerd met Herders by hun Vée, verders een stil Water en een Bergagtig verschiet, krachtig van Coloriet en meesterlyk gepenceeld in de manier van N. Berchem | *Mat:* op doek *Size:* hoog 54, breed 71 duim	Pruyssenaar [for] B	(Sold) fl 90 Coclers
1802/12/13	AMSCH	0011	*A. Begyn* | Een Zeehaven, gestoffeert op de voorgrond met Kooplieden, Slaven en beladene Vragtkar, en in 't verschiet Zylende Scheepen | *Mat:* op doek *Size:* hoog 33, breed 42 duim	Pruyssenaar [for] D	(Sold) fl 50 J Spaan
1803/08/17	AMSCH	0014	*Begyn. (A.)* | In het midden van een heuvelachtig Landschap staat een beladen Huiskar voor een Boere Herberg, een Vroaw [sic] te Paard, en andere Beelden te voet, schynen zich te ververschen, op de voorgrond een leggende Koe, Schapen, en een Bok; alles van een aangenaame ordonnantie en schildering | companion to lot 15 *Mat:* op doek *Size:* hoog 23, breed 22 duim	Anna Catharina Putman	(Sold) fl 189 for lots 14 & 15. Pruijssenaar
1803/08/17	AMSCH	0015	*Begyn. (A.)* | De wederga van het voorgaande Schildery, steld voor een rotachtig Landschap, met kreupelgewas en bergachtig Verschiet, ter zyde, voor een Smits Winkel, word een Paard beslagen, waarby een Vrouw met een Kind, op een Ezel; verders een leggende Koe en eenige Schapen, behandeld als de voorgaande | companion to lot 14 *Mat:* op doek *Size:* hoog 23, breed 22 duim	Anna Catharina Putman	(Sold) fl 189 for lots 14 & 15. Pruijssenaar
1803/12/12	AMSCH	0004	*A. Begyn* | Een Venétiaansche Zéehaven, ryk gestoffeert met een ménigte van Werkende en Handeldryvende Beelden; zonachtig en meesterlyk geschildert | *Mat:* op doek *Size:* hoog 26, breed 35 duim	B	(Sold) fl 1 L Pakker
1804/02/27	AMSCH	0013	*Begyn. (A.)* | In een Boomryk Landschap by eenige Gedenktekens, ziet men twee bevallige Landvrouwen, op den voorgrond by eenige Planten en Kruyden eenige Bokken | *Mat:* op doek *Size:* hoog 23, breed 19 duim	C	(Sold) fl 2:5 Gruiter
1804/04/28	LNDLS	0051	*J. Begein* | Een Italiaansche Zeehaven, op den voorgrond eene meenigte handelende en werkende persoonen by hunne pakken en koopgoederen, kragtig geschilderd, door J. Begein, als van T. Wyck	[Abraham Delfos] [or others]	(Sold) fl 10 Schouman
1804/07/25	AMSCH	0007	*Begyn. (A.)* | Een Italiaansch bergachtig Landschap, op de Voorgrond ryk gestoffeert met Huislieden, Mans en Vrouwen, belaaden Ezels en ander Vee; verder een aangenaam verschiet; alles is zonachtig, warm en van een uitvoerige penceelbehandeling | *Mat:* op doek *Size:* hoog 30, breed 36 duim		(Sold) fl 62 for lots 7 & 8. van der Schley
1804/07/25	AMSCH	0008	*Begyn. (A.)* | In een dito [Italiaansch] bevallig Landschap met eenig Boomgewas, vertoont zig op de Voorgrond een stil Waterbeekje, waar door eenig verschillend Vee gedreeven word, verzelt van eenige Veehoeders; het aangenaam zonlicht doet een natuurlyke werking, en is als de voorgaande meesterlyk en fraai behandeld | *Size:* hoog 30, breed 36 duim		(Sold) fl 62 for lots 7 & 8. van der Schley
1804/08/08	AMSCH	0032	*Begyn* | In een Boomryk Landschap zyn twee bevallige Landvrouwen by eenige Bokken en Planten; zonachtig en fraai geschilderd | *Mat:* op doek *Size:* hoog 23 ½, breed 19 ½ duim	Vink[eles] [for] K[=Gruyter?]	(Sold) fl 2:15 Gruyter
1804/10/29	HRBAU	0005	*Begyn, (A.)* | Op den Voorgrond by een' stam van een' Boom en Plantgewassen, ziet men twee Geiten, waar agter een bergagtig verschiet. Fiks geschilderd | *Mat:* op doek *Size:* hoog 14, breed 16 duim	Simon Styl	(Unknown)
1805/07/10	AMSCH	0029	*A. Begyn* | In een Boom- en Bergachtig Landschap, by een Waterval, ziet men op een Heuvel eenig staand en rustend Vee, verders by Geboomte	V[inkeles] [for] M	(Sold) fl 24 van Iperen

			een Herder en Herderin, Koe enz.; uitvoerig en zonachtig gepenceeld | *Mat:* op paneel *Size:* hoog 16, breed 13 ½ duim		
1806/05/05	AMSCH	0008	*A. Begyn* | Twee stuks Landschappen met Schapen, Bokken, Geboomten en Kruiden; kragtig op Doek | *Mat:* op doek *Size:* hoog 13, breed 15 duim	R[oos]	(Sold) fl 2:5 Mensart
1806/05/05	AMSCH	0020	*A. Begyn* | In een boomryk Landschap by eenige gedenktekens, zyn twee bevallige Vrouwen en eenige Bokjes by Planten en Kruiden | *Mat:* op doek *Size:* hoog 23, breed 19 duim	V[inkeles]	(Sold) fl 5:5 van Laar
1806/05/05	AMSCH	0026	*Begyn* | Twee Levensgroote Geiten, op een met kruiden en boomstammen bewassen Hoogten, in een aangenaam Landschap; meesteragtig in de manier van Berghem	V[inkeles]	(Bought In) fl 11
1806/06/07	RMHSN	0044	*A. Begyn* | En Zonachtig warm Landschap met Gebouwen, ryk van Beesten &c. door A. Begyn, van zyn beste soort | *Mat:* op doek	A E K L	(Unknown)
1806/08/13	AMSCH	0023	*Begyn. (A.)* | Een Rotsachtig Landschap, gestoffeerd met Herders by hun Vée, bestaande in een Paard, Koe, Schapen en Bokje, meesterlyk en zonachtig behandeld | *Mat:* op doek *Size:* hoog 20, breed 24 duim	Roos	(Sold) fl 3:5 Frantzen
1806/08/20	HGBSM	0057	*Begyn* | Een Kapitaal Landschap met Herders en Herderin, Koebeesten en Schaapen die een groot water doorwaaden, in de manier van Berghem | *Mat:* op doek *Size:* hoog 34, breed 31 duim	Macalester Loup [or others]	(Sold) fl 67 Lafontaine
1806/11/24	AMSCH	0005	*Begyn (A.)* | Een aangenaam Landgezigt by een Buitengoed, men ziet 'er een beladen Hooywagen met twee Paarden, Vee, en stoeijende Huislieden; dartel van Penceelsbehandeling | *Mat:* op doek *Size:* hoog 17 ½, breed 24 ½ duim	Munnikhuizen	(Sold) fl 6:5 Spaan
1806/11/24	AMSCH	0006	*Begyn (A.)* | Een Land- en Dorpgezigt, voor een Boere woning ziet men verscheiden Koeijen, waarvan 'er een gemolken word, ter zyde galantiseerende Beelden; kragtig gepenceeld | *Mat:* op doek *Size:* hoog 17, breed 22 duim	Munnikhuizen	(Sold) fl 5:5 du Pree
1808/04/26	GDAN	0009	*Begyn (A.)* | Een Boeren Binnenhuis verbeeldende, op den Voorgrond ziet men eenige Paarden en Koeijen, en verdere stoffage, zeer uitvoerig en goed behandeld | *Size:* hoog 30, breed 38 duim	G H Fortuyn	(Unknown)
1808/06/06	RMRIJ	0010	*Begijn. (Abraham)* | Op den voorgrond eene rijke Distelplant, Bloemen en Kruiden, waar op verscheidene Vlinders azen; terzijde een zittende Hond, en voor denzelven ligt eenig dood Gevogelte. Verder eene Balustrade, Vaas, Geboomte, en grootsch verschiet [Le devant du Tableau offre un chardon, des herbes et des fleurs, sur lesquelles sont posés, ou voltigent plusieurs papillons. A droite on voit un chien, et devant lui differents oiseaux morts etc. Le second plan est décoré d'une Balustrade et d'un vase, et est terminé par un riche lointain] | *Annots:* Verk. in den Doelen, Rotterdam, 5 Juli 1798 (f 12.-) (RMA I) *Mat:* op doek *Size:* Hoog 64, en breed 56 ½ duim	Gerrit van der Pot, Heer van Groeneveld	(Sold) fl 72 Allard
1808/06/13	AMSCH	0012	*Begijn (A.)* | Dit fraaije Schilderij stelt voor een Italiaansch Landschap, met eene Ruïne, in welker schaduw eene menigte Beesten en Schapen zich bevinden, op den voorgrond een Herder op een Ezel. sprekende met eene staande Vrouw; uitmuntend als N. Berchem behandeld | *Mat:* op doek *Size:* hoog 21, breed 26 duim	R[oos]	(Bought In) fl 105
1808/06/13	AMSCH	0213	*A. Begeijn* | Twee stuks met Kruiden en Insekten; meesterlijk	E M Engelberts	(Sold) fl 14 Gruiter
1809/04/22	AMYVR	0018	*A. Begijn* | Een aangenaam Italiaansch Landschapje, men ziet in hetzelve eenige Herders met Ossen en ander Vee; meesterlijk fraai | *Mat:* op paneel *Size:* hoog 12, breed 15 duim	de Bruin	(Sold) fl 5:15 du Pree
1809/07/25	HGBSM	0192	*Begyn* | Een Bergachtig Landschap, gestoffeert met een zittende Herderin en staande en rustende Schaapen en Bokken &c. | *Mat:* op doek *Size:* hoog 32, breed 39 duim	D van der Aa [or] E B ten Dall	(Sold) fl 6:10 van Eyk
1810/06/04	DOBRA	0016	*A. Bega* | Een Dorps Chirurgyn | *Notes:* The artist was presumably Cornelis Pietersz. Bega and not Abraham Begeyn.	Hendrik de Haas	(Unknown)
1810/06/04	DOBRA	0017	*Bega* | Een Landschap	Hendrik de Haas	(Unknown)

Begeyn, Abraham (changed from Marseus, O.)

1809/04/17	AMSCH	0065	*O. Marseus; Begyn* | In een Landschap, ziet men bij de Stam van een Boom, eenige Kruijden en Plantgewas, waarop onderscheidene Capellen aazen, op de grond een Kikvorsch en ander Gedierten; uitvoerig geschilderd | *Mat:* op doek *Size:* hoog 41, breed 35 duim *Notes:* The artist's name was changed by hand from "O. Marseus" to "Begyn" in the EBNP copy of the catalogue.	H	(Sold) fl 6:10

Begeyn, Abraham (or Begeyn, manner)

1810/11/07	UTWLD	0031	*Bagyn* | In een aangenaam Landschap ziet men Koeijen, Schapen, Bokken, enz. een Vrouwtje op een Koeij gezeten, in gesprek met eene Boerin, alles geestig geschilderd, door of in de manier van Bagyn, op doek, 2 voet 8 duim hoog, 2 voet 10 duim breed, zwarte Lijst | *Mat:* op doek *Size:* 2 voet 8 duim hoog, 2 voet 10 duim breed		(Unknown) fl 21

Begeyn, Abraham (manner)

1802/09/06	AMSCH	0252	*A. Begyn* | Een Italiaansch Landschap, met Ruïnen en stoffagie van beelden en beesten; in de manier van A. Begyn	Mevrouw Achtienhoven	(Sold) fl 1:15 Jan Spaan

Beham, Hans Sebald

1808/11/12 HGSCR 0016 — *H.S. Besam* | Keizer Trajanus yverig voorstander der wet, geeft zyn zoon met veele geschenken aan een arme vrouw in eigendom, in plaats van haare zoon die door dezelve te paard te velde trekkende was overleden, uitvoerig en fraai behandeld door H.S. Besam 1537. P. bekend door 't prentje van dezen meester | *Mat:* op paneel *Inscr:* H.S. Besam 1537. P. (signed and dated?) *Notes:* It is unclear whether the name and date are inscribed on the painting. — Mr J van Buren — (Unknown) fl 24

Beijer, Jan de

1809/06/13 AMSCH 0022 — *J. de Beijer* | Een Stadgezigt, met verscheide Gebouwen en een Brug; rijk met Beeldjes gestoffeerd, en zonachtig en uitvoerig behandeld | *Mat:* op paneel *Size:* hoog 12, breed 15 duim — S[chley] — (Sold) fl 15 van Iperen

1810/08/06 AMSCH 0023 — *Beijer (J. de)* | Een Gezigt op het Dorp Loenen aan de Vecht, gestoffeerd met Beeldjes en Vaartuigen. Natuurlijk voorgesteld | *Mat:* op doek *Size:* hoog 14, breed 17 duimen — G — (Sold) fl 26 Roos [for] L Bols

Belanger, B. [Unidentified]

1804/02/27 AMSCH 0005 — *Belanger. (B.)* | Door een steene Nis ziet men een bejaarde Vrouw bezig een Pot met Bloemen, welke voor dezelve op een Bank geplaast is te begieten, naast dezelve hangt een Mat en een Kwast, waarby een Wyngaardsrank en Mossepot, door den Nis ziet men in een ouwerwets Vertrek; dit allerfraaist kunstjuweel, is aller uitvoerigst en piquant van licht en bruin | *Mat:* op paneel *Size:* hoog 14, breed 11 duim — D — (Sold) fl 85 Gruiter

Bellevois, Jacob Adriaensz.

1804/10/29 HRBAU 0010 — *Bellevois, 1668* | Op den Voorgrond van dit Meergezigt, by een Ton, zeilt een pragtig Jagt, vol Passagiers, by den wind, als mede een Kaag van den wind, hun koers naar eene Stad zettende die in het verschiet ligt, waar by nog eenige Vaartuigen zyn; 't Water is helder en dun, en alles zeer uitvoerig gepenceeld | *Mat:* op doek *Size:* hoog 23, breed 30 duim *Inscr:* Bellevois, 1668 (signed and dated?) *Notes:* It is unclear whether the name and date are inscribed on the painting. — Simon Styl — (Unknown)

1806/05/05 AMSCH 0025 — *Bellevois* | Een woelende Zee | *Size:* hoog 23, breed 35 duim — V[inkeles] — (Sold) fl 2 L Pakker

1808/08/23 AMSCH 0212 — *J. Bellevois* | Een kabbelende Zee met zeilende Schepen, Jachten en anderen Vaartuigen, in 't verschiet een Sterk door de zon verlicht wordende de Stad; uitvoerig — [Gruyter?] — (Bought In) fl 4:15

1809/06/13 AMSCH 0192 — *Bellevois* | Twee stuks kabbelende Zeeën, met Vaartuigen en Beeldjes; uitvoerig — Y — (Sold) fl 1:5 Gruyter

Bellucci, Antonio

1803/09/07 AMSCH 0027 — *Belloutsi* | Twee stuks bevallige Vrouwe Pourtraiten, beide draagende Vruchten en Bloemen, breed en natuurlyk [Deux jolis portraits de femme, portant des fruits et des fleurs ; d'une exécution ample et naturelle] | *Mat:* op doek *Size:* ieder hoog 28, breed 21 duim — Smidt — (Bought In) fl 2 ¼

1803/09/07 AMSCH 0028 — *Belloutsi* | Een dito [bevallig] Vrouwe Pourtrait, niet minder dan de voorgaande [Un autre portrait de femme, dans le même goût et d'un mérite égal au précédent] | *Mat:* op doek *Size:* hoog 28, breed 20 duim [Haut 28, large 21 pouces] *Notes:* It is unclear what "dito" refers to in the title. The dimensions differ in the Dutch and French editions of the catalogue. — Smidt — (Sold) fl 0:10 L Pakker

Bemmel

1804/08/08 AMSCH 0031 — *van Bemmel* | In een Landschap ziet men van achteren een Boer eenig Vée dryven, op de voorgrond staat een Boerin met een Emmer in haar Hand, gereed een Koe te melken, neevens haar eenige Schaapen en Bokken; zonachtig en bevallig gepenceeld, als A. Cuyp, door van Bemmel | *Mat:* op paneel *Size:* hoog 17 ½, breed 25 ½ duim — Vink[eles] [for] K[=Gruyter?] — (Sold) fl 5:10 Menzart

1804/10/20 GRBOL 0007 — *Bommel* | Een Battaille — Joannis Cannegieteri — (Unknown)

1804/10/20 GRBOL 0008 — *Bommel* | Een dito [Battaille] — Joannis Cannegieteri — (Unknown)

1806/08/13 AMSCH 0316 — *Bemel (van)* | Een Landschap, met staand en leggend Vee; fiks gepenceeld | *Mat:* op doek *Size:* hoog 24, breed 30 duim — Vinkeles [for] G[ruyter] — (Sold) fl 0:10 L Pakker

Bemmel, J. van

1801/06/10 AMSCH 0030 — *Bemmel, (J. van) in de Manier van Cuyp.* | Een duinachtig Landschap met Boeren wooningen en hoog geboomte, ryk gestoffeert met Beesten en Schapen, welke door een Hek gedreven worden, ter zyde eenige rustende Beelden; zonachtig en meesterlyk geschilderd | *Mat:* op doek *Size:* hoog 33, breed 45 duim — Herman ten Kate — (Sold) fl 205 Jacob Roelofs

1802/12/13 AMSCH 0025 — *J. van Bemmel* | In een aangenaam zonachtig Landschap, is de voorgrond gestoffeert met een Vrouw die eenig Vee dryft; ter zyden een stil Water, drinkende Schapen, en een aangenaam verschiet, zonachtig geschilderd | *Mat:* op paneel *Size:* hoog 21, breed 28 duim — Pruyssenaar [for] A — (Sold) fl 6 Yver

1810/06/20 AMSCH 0005a — *J. Van Bemmel* | Een Veldgezigt, gestoffeerd met staand en rustend Vee. Zonachtig behandeld | *Mat:* op paneel *Size:* hoog 17, breed 21 duimen — Y — (Sold) fl 4:15 Rooijers

1810/10/11	AMSCH	0151	*J. Van Bemmel* | Een Landschap, met stoffagie van Beelden en Beesten	S	(Sold) fl 0:14 Singeling

Bemmel, Wilhelm von

1803/06/20	AMSCH	0044	*W. van Bemmel* | Een Landschap met Beelden en Beesten, aan een stile Rivier en een aangenaam bergachtig verschiet; door W. van Bemmel, op Doek | *Mat:* op doek *Size:* hoog 26, breed 31 duim	Roos [for] C	(Sold) fl 1 Th^{s} Spaan

Bendorp, Carel Frederik (I)

1810/06/06	RMMUY	0079	*C. F. Bendorp* | Twee stuks uitvoerige Land- en Water gezigten | *Mat:* op paneel		(Unknown) fl 6:15

Benets, R. [Unidentified]

1803/09/07	AMSCH	0032	*R. Benets* | Twee stuks, het eene een hévige Batailje, tusschen Turken en Ruiters, het andere een Legerplaats, alwaar verscheide Officieren by een Marketenter, en verder bywerk [Deux morceaux, dont l'un représente une bataille très vive entre des turcs et des cavaliers ; l'autre un camp, où plusieurs officiers sont rassemblés près d'un vivandier, plus loin quelques accessoires] | *Mat:* op koper *Size:* hoog 18, breed 24 duim	Smidt	(Bought In) fl 85

Bens, van der [Unidentified]

1802/05/05	AMSCH	0036	*van der Bens* | By Prachtige Gebouwen vertoond zich een Veneetsiaansche Zeehaven, op de Voorgrond ryk gestoffeerd, in de manier van Berghem | *Size:* hoog 46, breed 43 duim	J	(Sold) fl 4:5 v d Vinne
1802/05/05	AMSCH	0037	*van der Bens* | Een Capitaal Bergächtig Landschap, waar in de Overblyfsels van een fraai gebouw; op de Voorgrond een Plas Water, waar by een Veêhoeder en een Spinnende Vrouw, verzelt van Beesten, brillant van Ligt en Meesterlyk geschilderd | *Size:* hoog 40, breed 43 duim	J	(Sold) fl 18 Hulswit

Bent, Johannes van der

1801/03/16	AMSCH	0110	*van der Bent* | Een Manege met verscheide Heeren, Dames en Paarden, fiks	K[ip]	(Sold) fl 4:10 Valentijn
1802/02/16	AMSCH	0037	*J. van der Bent* | Een Italiaansch Landschap, by een Plysterplaats.ziet men een Hoef Smit, het Paard, van een Ryziger beslaan; verders eenige Schaapen, natuurlyk gepenceeld	G	(Sold) fl 31 Pruijssenaar
1802/07/20	MGSAN	0045	*v. d. Bent* | Een Landschap met Figuuren en Beesten, op Paneel | *Mat:* op paneel *Size:* hoog duim 15, breed duim 20		(Unknown)
1802/08/24	LNDLS	0080	*J. van der Bent* | Een Landschap met hooge Boomen, in 't midden staat een Fontein, op den Voorgrond een Vrouw en een Man bij hun Vee, terwijl een Meisje een Geit melkt | *Mat:* op doek *Size:* hoog 30, breed 26 duimen	Leonardus Bouman [or others]	(Unknown) fl 11:10
1802/09/06	AMSCH	0219	*v. d. Bent* | Een Landschap met Beelden en Beesten | *Mat:* op doek *Size:* hoog 24, breed 32 duim	J	(Sold) fl 4 Baur
1804/02/27	AMSCH	0138	*J. v. d. Bent* | Twee stuks Landschappen	B	(Sold) fl 2 van Iperen
1804/05/07	AMSCH	0018	*Bent. (J. van der)* | In dit bevallig Duinachtig Landschap ziet men op de voorgrond by eenig Geboomte verscheiden Veehoeders, met een menigte van staand en rustend Vee; breed en fiks van behandeling | *Mat:* op doek *Size:* hoog 31, breed 41 duim	Vinkeles [for] J	(Sold) fl 8 Gruiter
1804/05/07	AMSCH	0019	*Bent. (J. van der)* | In een aangenaam Boomryk Landschap vertoont zich een Rustende Véehoeder en Vrouw, verzeld van onderscheidene zoorten van Vée; Natuurlyk en bevallig gepenceeld | *Mat:* op doek *Size:* hoog 23, breed 39 duim	Roos [for] K	(Sold) fl 16:10 S^{n} Joseph
1804/08/08	AMSCH	0034	*van der Bent* | Een Landschap met Boomen en Planten, gestoffeerd met eenige Bokken en andere Stoffagie | *Mat:* op doek *Size:* hoog 25 ½, breed 21 ½ duim	Vink[eles] [for] K[=Gruyter?]	(Sold) fl 1:5 Gruyter
1805/07/10	AMSCH	0288[H]	*van der Bent* | 1 dito [Landschappen] | *Notes:* This lot was added in by hand in the AA, EBNP and RKDH copies of the catalogue.	V[inkeles]	(Bought In) fl 10
1805/10/09	HGBSM	0017	*J. van der Bendt* | Een landschap, met koebeesten, schaapen en verdere figuuren &c. in de manier van N. Berghem | *Mat:* op doek *Size:* hoog 39 breet 31 duim	T H van Willigen [or others]	(Sold) fl 15 Ph Mey
1805/12/16	AMSCH	0007	*J. van der Bent* | Voor de Ruïne van een Antiek Gebouw, ziet men een Vrouw op een Ezel, waarby een ander, staande by een roden Koe, verders een Ezel die beslagen word, op de Voorgrond twee Schapen, een Bok, en een Hond; kragtig op Doek, door J. van der Bent, na N. Berchem | *Mat:* op doek *Size:* hoog 32, breed 25 duim	V	(Sold) fl 24 C S Roos
1806/08/13	AMSCH	0026	*Bent. (J. van der)* | Een Boom- en Bergachtig Landschap, met staand en leggend Vée, waarby eenige Landlieden en Kinderen | *Mat:* op doek *Size:* hoog 32, breed 40 duim	Vinkeles [for] G[ruyter]	(Sold) fl 4 Gruiter
1806/11/24	AMSCH	0010	*Bent (J. van der)* | Een Boeren Deel of Stal, van binnen te zien, gestoffeerd met Huislieden, een Paard en onderscheide Vee; het invallend Zonlicht geeft een fraije werking in dit welgeschilderd stukje | *Mat:* op paneel *Size:* hoog 16, breed 22 duim	Munnikhuizen	(Sold) fl 9:5 T Spaan
1807/08/26	AMSCH	0031	*J. van der Bent* | Twee stuks capitaale Italiaansche Landschappen met Gebouwen, Fontyn, en Geboomten, beide gestoffeerd met Landlieden,	Yver [for] S	(Sold) fl 20 Coclair

			beladen Ezels en Vragtkar met Ossen bespannen, en verder Vee en bywerk; bevallig | *Mat:* op doek *Size:* ieder hoog 31, breed 39 duim		
1808/06/13	AMSCH	0028	*Bent (J. van der)* | Voor een Buitenplaats ziet men een Heer te paard, in gesprek zijnde met eene Dame; ter zijde Werklieden, welken hout op een Ezel laden; meesterlijk en zonachtig behandeld | *Mat:* op doek *Size:* hoog 36, breed 31 duim	E M Engelberts	(Sold) fl 30 Glad [or] Spaan
1808/06/13	AMSCH	0029	*Bent (J. van der)* | In een Italiaansch Landschap ziet men, voor een Smits woning, den Smit bezig een Ezel te beslaan; verder staand en rustend Vee, waarby een Vrouw te paard; in de stijl van N. Berchem geschilderd | *Mat:* op doek *Size:* hoog 42, breed 35 duim	E M Engelberts	(Sold) fl 51 Nieuwenhuisen
1808/06/13	AMSCH	0030	*Bent (J. van der)* | Een Italiaansch Landschap: op den voorgrond ziet men eene Vrouw te paard, met een ander in gesprek; verder een Herder met Ossen en Schapen; ter zijde een Wagen, met Ossen bespannen: als de voorgaande | *Mat:* op doek *Size:* hoog 23, breed 26 duim	E M Engelberts	(Sold) fl 91 Th Spaan
1808/06/13	AMSCH	0031	*Bent (J. van der* | Een Italiaansch Landschap, waarin eenig Vee staat te drinken, terwijl een Herder en Herderin bezig zijn goed te wasschen; mede als voren | *Size:* hoog 22, breed 26 duim	E M Engelberts	(Sold) fl 14:10 Nieuwenhuysen
1808/08/23	AMSCH	0025	*Bent. (J. van der)* | Een Hofgezigt, waar in een Heer en Dame te Paard, welke zig tot de Jagt schijnen te bereiden, op de voorgrond een Bok, eenig Gevogelten en bevallige Kruiden; fraai gepenceeld | *Mat:* op doek *Size:* hoog 30, breed 35 duim	S	(Sold) fl 14:10 Van Iperen
1808/08/23	AMSCH	0189	*J. van der Bent* | Een Bergachtig Landschap met hoog Geboomten en Gebouwen, op de voorgrond eenige Landlieden bij hun Vee; goed geschildert	[Gruyter?]	(Sold) fl 12:10 Vallée
1808/09/13	HABRU	0007	*van Bent* | Een Landschap, op de voorgrond een Muil-ezel, Kalf, &c.		(Unknown) fl 3:15
1808/11/28	AMSCH	0076	*J. van der Bent* | Een Italiaansch Landschap, gestoffeerd met staande en leggende Beesten	[Gruyter?]	(Sold or Bought In) fl 2 Gruyter
1809/04/17	AMSCH	0153	*van der Bent* | Een hoog Bergachtig Landschap, met staand en liggend Vee | *Mat:* op doek	[Gruyter?]	(Sold or Bought In) fl 0:14 Gruyter
1809/04/17	AMSCH	0159	*van der Bent* | Twee stuks kapitale Boomrijke Landschappen, met staand en liggend Vee; meesterlijk geschilderd | *Mat:* op doek	[Gruyter?]	(Sold) fl 10
1809/04/22	AMYVR	0016	*J. van der Bent* | Voor een Huismanswooning ziet men eene Boerin, bezig een roode Koe te melken, ter zijde twee caresseerende Beeldjes; fraai geschilderd | *Mat:* op doek *Size:* hoog 17, breed 23 duim	de Bruin	(Sold) fl 4:10 C S Roos
1810/05/22	AMSCH	0015	*Bent (J. van der)* | In een Stal is eene Boerin bezig Koeijen te melken, nevens haar eenige Bokken, een Schaap en liggende Varkens; kloek geschilderd | *Mat:* op doek *Size:* hoog 16, breed 19 duim	R	(Sold) fl 5:5 Rinkhuijzen
1810/06/06	RMMUY	0226	*J. van der Bent* | Een Landschap met Beelden en Dieren | *Mat:* op doek *Notes:* According to the MA copy of the catalogue, this lot was sold with lot 227, which is in the manner of Klomp, for fl. 2:16.		(Unknown) fl 7:16

Berchem, Nicolaes Pietersz.

1801/04/13	AMSCH	0003	*N. Berchem* | In een boom- en bergachtig Landschap, ziet men een Heer en Dame te paard, verzeld van eenige Jagers met hunne Honden, een Hart najagen; de behandeling is fraai en uitvoering, het coloriet behaaglyk, en is van eene delicaate penceelsbehandeling | *Mat:* op paneel *Size:* hoog 15, breed 19 duim	Pierre Fouquet, junior	(Sold) fl 460 Coclers
1801/04/23	AMYVR	0001	*N. Berchem* | In een Landschap ziet men eenige Herders en Herderinnen by een staande Koe, een Bok en Schaapen, dit Schildery is warm van couleur, fix en meesterlyk behandeld op Paneel | *Mat:* op paneel *Size:* hoog 26, breed 25 duim		(Sold) fl 430 Farret
1801/05/11	AMSCH	0009	*N. Berchem* | Twee stuks bevallige Landschapjes, met historiële stoffagie, waar by twee bokjes, alles is van een aangenaam coloriet, en fix gepenceeld | *Mat:* op paneel *Size:* yder hoog 7, breed 9 duim	P[ruyssenaar]	(Sold) fl 175 Allard
1801/06/10	AMSCH	0012	*Berchem. (N.)* | Een Landschap, agter hoog geboomte komt de Maan op, op de voorgrond ziet men eenig Vee, benevens een Herder, ter zyde een stil Water met een Pond, natuurlyk en kragtig uitgevoerd | *Mat:* op paneel *Size:* hoog 11, breed 14 duim	Herman ten Kate	(Sold) fl 109 Coclers
1801/10/06	AMSCH	0002	*N. Berchem* | Dit Uitmuntend Tafreel, vertoont in een Italiaansch Bergagtig Landschap, een vroege Morgenstond, op de voorgrond ryk gestoffeerd, met een Veehoeder op een Ezel gezeeten, schynende te spreeken met een gaande Landman, welke drie Ossen, eenige Schaapen, een Bok, en een belaaden Ezel voortdryft, ter zyde staat een Boere Jongen, dwingende met slagen een Roscouleurde Os, die, als op een blaffende Hond, verstoord is, verder aan den Oever, van een stille Rivier, zit een Vrouw op een Ezel, waar by een gaande Huisman, vier Ossen en eenige Schaapen voortdryvende, aan de overzyde ziet men eenige Wooningen, en verder hoog Gebergten, de schoone Ordinantie, aangenaam Zonlicht, het bevallig Coloriet, en uitvoerige Penceel behandeling: geeven een luister aan dit Stuk, van deeze beroemde Meester | *Mat:* op doek *Size:* hoog 27, breed 31 duim	S	(Sold) fl 1000 Coclers
1801/10/06	AMSCH	0003	*N. Berchem* | Deeze fraaije Ordinantie, verbeelt een Levantsche Zee-Haven, op de voorgrond gestoffeert met een Dame in deftige kleeding, waar by een Landloopster dezelve goeder geluk zeggende: verders	Z	(Sold) fl 800 A E Sterk

<table>
<tr><td></td><td></td><td></td><td>verscheide rustende Lieden van verschillende Natien, by Baalen en Pakken, met Koopmans Goederen, een gelaaden Schuit met verscheide Vee, en een Bergagtig verschiet, met Gebouwen, bevallig en Zonagtig, en Meesterlyk gepenceelt | Mat: op doek Size: hoog 21, breed 23 duim</td><td></td><td></td></tr>
<tr><td>1801/10/19</td><td>AMSCH</td><td>0005</td><td>Berchem. (N.) | Een heuvelägtig Landschap, in 't midden op de voorgrond rust een roode en een witte Koe, beneevens eenige Schapen, waar by een staande bruine Os; ter regterzyde een Rots, en ter linkerzyde een zittend Man met een Hond; konstig van Licht en bruin, en uitvoerig geschilderd | Mat: op paneel Size: hoog 14 ¾, breed 18 duim</td><td>Jonkheer Menno Baron van Coehoorn</td><td>(Sold) fl 425 J^b Roelofs (B^d Kooy)</td></tr>
<tr><td>1802/06/16</td><td>AMSCH</td><td>0008</td><td>N. Berchem | Een Levantsche Zéehaven, by een Bergachtig Strand, op de voorgrond zit een Dame, met een Valk op de hand, op een wit Paard, nevens dezelve staat een Levants Koopman, en een staand Heer, als spreekende tegen eenige Slaaven; verder gestoffeerd met Koopmans Goeden, en Scheepen in de Haven leggende; Meesterlyk gepenceelt | Mat: op paneel Size: hoog 13 ½, breed 18 duim</td><td>[Merrem]</td><td>(Sold) fl 40 Mensart</td></tr>
<tr><td>1802/06/16</td><td>AMSCH</td><td>0009</td><td>N. Berchem | Deeze Ordenantie stelt voor de aankondiging van den Engel aan de Herders, men ziet dezelve in een gloeijend licht in de Wolken, terwyl de Herders in een beängste houding hun gezicht Hemelwaarts wenden; verscheiden staand en leggend Vée verryken deeze Ordenantie; zynde van een voortreffelyke penceelbehandeling | Mat: op doek Size: hoog 27, breed 22 ½ duim</td><td>[Merrem]</td><td>(Sold) fl 100 LaFontaine</td></tr>
<tr><td>1802/06/16</td><td>AMSCH</td><td>0010</td><td>N. Berchem | Voor de Ruïne van een trots Gebouw, in een Italiaansch Bergachtig Landschap, ziet men een Vrouw op een Muil- Ezel, waarby Landlieden met verscheiden Vée, verder in het verschiet een Vrouw met een Kind op een Ezel, waarby een Herder met Schaapen; alles zonachtig geschilderd | Size: hoog 26 ½, breed 31 duim</td><td>[Merrem]</td><td>(Sold) fl 145 LaFontaine</td></tr>
<tr><td>1802/06/16</td><td>AMSCH</td><td>0011</td><td>N. Berchem | Deeze fraaije Ordenantie vertoond een Levantsche Zéehaven, op de voorgrond, by een prachtige Fontein, ziet men een Dame en Heer in treffelyke Kleeding, verders eenige vrouwen met groenten, een Man by een Ezel, en verscheiden rustende Slaaven, in 't verschiet ziet men een Galei in de Haven; alles krachtig en Meesterlyk breed gepenceelt | Mat: op doek Size: hoog 35, breed 48 ½ duim</td><td>[Merrem]</td><td>(Sold) fl 52 Coclers</td></tr>
<tr><td>1802/08/24</td><td>LNDLS</td><td>0010</td><td>Berghem | Een Berg – achtig Landschap, met een Man op een Ezel, nevens hem een ander te voet, voords Koeijen over eene hoogte gaande, in het verschiet eenige Gebouwen op een heuvel, gem. Berghem | Mat: op paneel Size: hoog 8, breed 11 duimen Inscr: Berghem (signed)</td><td>Leonardus Bouman [or others]</td><td>(Unknown) fl 8</td></tr>
<tr><td>1802/09/21</td><td>UTHDG</td><td>0003</td><td>N. Berghem | Jö in een Koe herschapen, en weidende onder het vee, word Argus, door Juno aanbevolen, zijnde inzonderheid de beesten, dun en natuurlijk geschildert | Mat: op paneel Size: hoog 9 ½, breed 11 ¾ duimen</td><td></td><td>(Bought In) fl 14</td></tr>
<tr><td>1802/09/21</td><td>UTHDG</td><td>000H[H]</td><td>Berchem | Een Maneschijn getekend Berchem | Inscr: Berchem (signed) Notes: This lot was added in by hand in the OGA copy of the catalogue.</td><td></td><td>(Bought In) fl 1</td></tr>
<tr><td>1802/09/29</td><td>AMSCH</td><td>0004</td><td>Nicolaas Berchem | Een Zeehaven. Hoog 20 ½, breed 24 duim. Doek. In Italien by hooge Rotzen. Op den Voorgrond ziet men twee bevallige Vrouwen, eene goede Gelukzegster met een Kind op haren rug, voorzegt aan eene derzelve haar lot; verscheide andere Figuren, waaronder eenige Kooplieden by hunne Goederen, een overvarende Pontschuit met Hoornvee, verreiken deeze schoone Ordenantie, zynde van eene delicate en meesterlyke Penceelsbehandeling [Le charme de cette composition, fait honneur au genie et aux rares Talens de ce Peintre aimable, il à fait choix pour sujet de ce Tableau, d'un beau site et d'un Port de Mer de l'Italie, ou des marchands de differens Païs, paroissent disposés à s'émbarquer, s'entretenant avec chaleur, d'autres se reposent pres de quelques Balots, mais ce qui intéresse davantage sont deux jeunes belles femmes, dans la partie la plus eclairée qui demandent à une Bohemienne Instruction sur leur sort futur : nombre d'autres figures dans des dispositions differentes ; un Passage de Bestiaux, un beau lointain méritent également de l'admiration, ainsi que la belle touche de Pinceau, dont ce morceau est exécuté.] | Mat: op doek Size: hoog 20 ½, breed 24 duim</td><td>[Labouchere?]</td><td>(Sold) fl 200 de Roy</td></tr>
<tr><td>1802/12/13</td><td>AMSCH</td><td>0033</td><td>N. Berchem | Zynde een fraay Model, van negen verschillende Bokkenkoppen, kragtig en meesterlyk gepenceelt</td><td>Schley [for] Lauwers</td><td>(Sold) fl 47 Coclers</td></tr>
<tr><td>1804/07/25</td><td>AMSCH</td><td>0003</td><td>Berchem. (N.) | Deeze ryke en uitmuntende Ordinantie vertoont in een Arcadisch Landschap, verscheiden vrolyke Bachanten, zoo Mans, Vrouwen als Kinderen; op de Voorgrond rusten ter wederzyde bevallige Vrouwen, verzelt van Kinderen, leggende en staande Bokken, en een Geit, waarby twee Kinderen, één derzelve schynt aan een der speunen te zuigen; verder staat een Bachant rustende tegen een Pedestal, waarop een cierlyke gewerkte Vaas geplaatst is; verder een staande Term van Priaap, waarby dansende Lieden; omhoog verscheide Minnewigten met Bloemen te strooijen zig vermakende; dit fraai Voorwerp is frappant van licht; meesterlyk geteekent, en van een bevallig Coloriet en uitvoerige penceelbehandeling | Mat: op doek Size: hoog 36, breed 34 duim</td><td></td><td>(Sold) fl 81 Jan Yver</td></tr>
<tr><td>1804/08/08</td><td>AMSCH</td><td>0009</td><td>N. Berghem | Dit stukje verbeeld, een aangenaam Boom- en Bergachtig Landschap, met Ruïnen, doorsneeden met een Rivier, gestoffeerd met een Vrouwtje op een Ezel, daarby een Man, voor hun eenig Vée, op de voorgrond een rustende Herder met een Hond; alleruitvoerigst op Doek | Mat: op doek Size: hoog 11, breed 13 duim</td><td>Roos a</td><td>(Sold) fl 64 Hulswit</td></tr>
</table>

1804/10/16	DLOND	0021	*Nicolaas Berghem* | Een Bosch, waarin enige Struikrovers, die een Wagen aanranden, en in gevegt zyn. Rencontre de quelques Voleurs de chemin dans un Bois | *Mat:* op doek *Size:* hoog 26, breed 31		(Sold) fl 99 Schol
1804/10/16	DLOND	0022	*Nicolaas Berghem* | Een Landschap met een vervallen Muur, Koeien, Schapen en Geiten, enz. Paysage avec une Ruine, des Vaches, Moutons, &c.		(Unknown)
1804/12/10	AMSCH	0001	*N. Berchem* | Dit geestelyk zinryk onderwerp uit de Openbaringe Joannes, vertoont een Vrouw met vleugelen, hebbende een krans met starren om het hoofd, zweevende op de wolken, en met de voeten de maan vertreedende; als vlugtende met schrik, voor de zevenhoofdige draak, die op de voorgrond stroomen van water uitblaast, en met zyn staart eenige starren met zig sleept; waar by de val der boozen, om hoog werd haar jong gebooren kind, door twee Engelen hemelwaards gevoerd, verzelt van een glorie van verscheiden anderen, alles is uitmuntend schoon van ordinantie, fraai van teekening, bevallig van coloriet, en van een uitvoerige penceel behandeling, door die beroemde Meester | *Mat:* op doek *Size:* Hoog 43, breed 35 duim	Jan de Groot	(Sold) fl 150 van Iperen
1805/12/16	AMSCH	0006	*N. Berchem* | In een Heuvelagtig Landschap, met eenig Geboomten, ziet men verscheide Huislieden, met staand en rustend Vée, meesterlyk op Paneel behandeld | *Mat:* op paneel *Size:* hoog 20, breed 15 duim	R[oos]	(Bought In) fl 156
1806/11/24	AMSCH	0002	*Berghem (N.)* | Een Boomryk Landschap, op de voorgrond een menigte Vee, zo Ossen, Schapen, en een Hond en verscheiden Herders door een waterplas gaande, zynde van de vroege tyd van deezen meester, en geteekend den Jongen Berghem | *Mat:* op doek *Size:* hoog 19, breed 28 duim	Munnikhuizen	(Sold) fl 61 Josi
1808/04/26	GDAN	0014	*Berchem (N.)* | Een overheerlijk Zon- en Bergägtig Landschap, met een Brug en Ruïne, verder gestoffeerd met Koeijen en ander Vee, &c., zeer uitmuntend geschilderd | *Mat:* op doek *Size:* hoog 25, breed 29 duim	G H Fortuyn	(Unknown)
1808/05/18	LNAN	0050	*Berghem* | Een konstig uitvoerig Landschap, met Beelden en Beesten | *Notes:* The artist's name "Berghem" was added in by hand in the RKDH copy of the catalogue.	Mr Cornelis Versluys	(Unknown)
1808/06/06	RMRIJ	0011	*Berchem. (Nicolaas)* | Een Landschap met hoog opgaande Gebergte en Geboomte. Aan de eene zijde ziet men eene drift Koeijen en Schapen, geleid door een herder op een Ezel zittende, vergezeld door een te voet gaanden Jongen. Aan de andere zijde eene kudde Schapen door een Jongen voortgedreven. Zonachtig, uitvoerig, geestig en meesterlijk behandeld [Paysage Montagneux. A gauche sur un grand chemin, et à travers un terrain inégal, on voit un homme monté sur un Mulet et accompagné d'un garcon et d'un chien, qui conduit un troupeau de bétail ; à droite sur un terrain élevé, un Berger secondé de son chien, paroit Chasser devant lui un troupeau de moutons. Plus loin on voit une femme montée sur un Mulet, et plusieurs animaux et autres objets. De beaux arbres, des Sites et des fabriques agréables, un ton chaud, la touche spirituelle et le grand fini rendent ce Tableau un des plus beaux de ce grand Artiste] | *Mat:* op paneel *Size:* Hoog 16 ½, en breed 25 duim *Loc:* Amsterdam, Nederland. Rijksmuseum. (A29)	Gerrit van der Pot, Heer van Groeneveld	(Sold) fl 3025 J J de Wit [for] le Roi
1808/06/06	RMRIJ	0012	*Berchem. (Nicolaas)* | Een Italiaansch Berg- en Rotsachtig Landschapje Op den voorgrond ziet men twee rustende beelden, wat verder eene Ossendrift, verzeld door een man op een Ezel. Op den tweeden grond is eene brug, waarover eenige beesten en figuren enz. gaan. Dit stukje is een der fijnste en krachtigste van dezen Meester [Ce petit Tableau offre une Perspective de hautes montagnes, au bas des quelles on voit serpenter une Rivière. Le Premier plan est enrichi de figures et d'animaux etc. Ce Bijou d'une touche aussi fine que spirituelle est un chef-d'oeuvre dans son genre] | *Mat:* op koper *Size:* Hoog 5 ¼, en breed 6 ¼ duim *Loc:* Amsterdam, Nederland. Rijksmuseum. (A26)	Gerrit van der Pot, Heer van Groeneveld	(Sold) fl 345 Stratenus [for] le Roi
1808/06/06	RMRIJ	0013	*Berchem. (Nicolaas)* | In een Italiaansch Landschap, waarin op den tweeden grond zich eene Schaapskooi en een gedeeltelijk gebouw voordoet, ziet men eenige Schapen, een Hond, twee Figuren en een Ezel. Op den voorgrond eene op de knien liggende Geitenmelkster, rustende met de linkerhand op eene graauw gekleurde Geit, met de andere in eene koperen Melk-Emmer tastende; bezijden haar ligt een Schaap bij eenige Planten. Wel gekleurd, uitvoerig en fiks geschilderd [Paysage. A gauche on voit une Paysane à genoux, et auprés d'elle une chêvre et d'autres animaux ; à droite un Berger s'appuyant sur son âne, semble s'entretenir avec elle, son chien le regarde, et plusieurs brebis l'environnent, tandis qu'un vieux paysan à barbe blanche s'occupe à éxaminer la toison d'un mouton etc. Ce Tableau savamment peint est d'un coloris brillant et d'une agréable composition] | *Annots:* 12 Aug. 1795 van E. Arents te Brussel (f. 336.-) (RMA I) *Mat:* op paneel *Size:* Hoog 9, en breed 11 ½ duim	Gerrit van der Pot, Heer van Groeneveld	(Sold) fl 1160 Noortwyk
1808/06/13	AMSCH	0002	*Berchem (N.)* | In dit aangenaam Tafreel, zijnde een kapitaal heuvel- en bergachtig Landschap, vertoont zich op een zandigen voorgrond eene bevallige Dame in rijke kleeding, met pluimen op het hoofd versierd, houdende in de regterhand een schulp met water, schijnende het ontvangen te hebben van een Veehoeder, die, halverlijf met een bonte vacht omgord, op eene knie rustende, in een nederige houding voor haar ligt; achter hun staat een gezadeld bruin Paard, door een jonge Neger		(Withdrawn)

			vastgehouden wordende, verzeld van twee Jagthonden; een weinig voorwaarts ter regterzijde vertoonen zich vier rustende en twee staande Schapen, allen in bijzondere houding, daar nevens liggen afgebroken Stammen van Boomen bij eenig Plantgewas; ter linkerzijde staat een zwarte Bok, iets verder twee rustende Schapen en een wit- en zwart-bonte Bok: voor het Gebergte, het geen met Geboomte en Kreupelbosch beplant is, ziet men eene staande Herderin, met een Stroohoedje op 't Hoofd, met Bloemen omvlochten, houdende een Herdersstaf in de hand, als sprekende met eene zittende Vrouw, verzeld van vier rustende en twee staande Schapen, een derzelven schijnt uit een Beekje te drinken; aan de regterzijde op den tweeden grond staat een roskleurde en een vaalkleurige Os, verder op een Heuvel zeven zoo grazende als liggende Schapen, en bij een afkomende Weg van 't Gebergte een op de Fluit speelend Veehoeder, met een troep Schapen bij weelderig Geboomte en laag Houtgewas, en een bergachtig verschiet. Het aangenaam zonlicht, alomme natuurlijk verspreid, de warme heldere lucht, de verschillende kleuren van 't Gebergte, doen alle de voorwerpen in dit stuk bevallig voorkomen, het Vee evenaart de Natuur, en alles is van eene uitvoerige penceelsbehandeling | *Mat:* op doek *Size:* hoog 50, breed 69 duim		
1808/06/13	AMSCH	0003	*Berchem (N.)* | In een Landschap vertoonen zich op den voorgrond in een Waterbeekje drie Ossen van verschillende kleur en houding, drie Bokken en een Schaap, zijnde waarschijnlijk naar het leven vervaardigd, en meesterlijk schoon en breed gepenceeld | *Mat:* op doek op paneel *Size:* hoog 17 ½, breed 24 ½ duim	[Jan Tersteeg]	(Sold) fl 130 van den Berghe de Gand
1808/08/23	AMSCH	0004	*Berchem. (N)* | Dit kapitaal gezicht, verbeeld het Slot te Heemsteede, ter zijde en van vooren te zien, naar den ingang en steene borstweering aan den vijver; gestoffeert met Beeldjes, een Bok en eenige Honden, en in de Vijver zwemmende Zwaanen en een Schuitje; alles verwonderlijk natuurlijk, zonachtig en uitvoerig gepenceeld | *Mat:* op doek *Size:* hoog 42, breed 66 duim	[Coclers]	(Sold) fl 49 Josi
1809/04/17	AMSCH	0005	*N. Berghem* | In een hoog boschagtig Landschap, ziet men bij een heldere Waterplas, een Landman eenig Vee voortdrijvende, op de voorgrond eene Vrouw zittende op een Ezel, nevens haar een gaande Landman, verder een Man en Jongen te Paard en een aangenaam verschiet, zonachtig en uitvoerig behandeld | *Mat:* op paneel *Size:* hoog 11, breed 13 ½ duim	C	(Sold) fl 47 Van Jepren
1809/06/13	AMSCH	0013	*N. Berchem* | In een Landschap ziet men op een Heuvel bij Boere Woningen en Geboomten, rustende Landlieden bij staand en liggend Vee, ter zijden Bokken en Schapen, verders een aangenaam verschiet; zonachtig en uitvoerig geschilderd | *Mat:* op paneel *Size:* hoog 11, breed 14 duim	[Gruyter?]	(Sold) fl 23:5 du Pree
1809/07/19	AMSCH	0003	*Berchem (N.)* | Dit voortreffelijk kunstjuweel, verbeelt een Italiaansch Bergachtig Landschap, met een Rivier doorsneden, in het midden ziet men eene Vrouw, zittende op een wit Paard, zij schijnt in gesprek met eene andere Vrouw over eenige Lieden, welke met hun Vee in een Pontschuit gereed zijn over te varen, op den voorgrond een Man bij een beladen Muilezel, verder eenige Landlieden, staande en liggende Koeijen, Bokken en Schapen. Dit stuk is zonachtig, warm van koloriet, en in den besten tijd van dezen beroemden Meester geschilderd | *Mat:* op doek *Size:* hoog 32, breed 41 duim *Loc:* Amsterdam, Nederland. Rijksmuseum. (A31)	[Bicker]	(Sold) fl 3040 J^{n} Yver voor Z H den Koning
1810/03/27	RMCNL	0074	*van Berghem* | Een klein doch zeer aardig Landschapje, met eene liggende Koe, zeer fix geschilderd		(Unknown)
1810/05/22	AMSCH	0004	*Berchem. (N.)* | In een Bergachtig Landschap vertoont zich eene Vrouw op een Ezel zittende, ter zijde staat een Huisman, verders gestoffeerd met verscheide Vee; zonagtig en meesterlijk gepenceeld | *Mat:* op paneel *Size:* hoog 14, breed 19 duim	F	(Sold) fl 25 van Iperen
1810/08/01	AMSCH	0008	*Berchem (Nicolaas)* | Op eenen grazigen Heuvel, bij eenig staand en rustend Vee, ziet men twee bevallige Landmeisjes, waar van de eene bezig is eene Geit te melken [Sur une Eminence fertille [sic] l'on voit quelques Animaux couchés, et quelq'autres paturans ; deux jeunes Veillageoises [sic] paroissent garder ce troupeau, une des deux s'occupant traire une Chèvre] | possibly companion to lot 9 *Annots:* passable (NGW) *Mat:* op paneel *Size:* hoog 11 ½, breed 14 ½ duimen *Loc:* Amsterdam, Nederland. Rijksmuseum. (C 98)	Mr Pieter de Smeth van Alphen	(Bought In) fl 1000
1810/08/01	AMSCH	0009	*Berchem (Nicolaas)* | Een Italiaansch Land en Watergezigt met hoog Gebergte, gestoffeerd met twee Landlieden en eene Vrouw, bij eene rustende Koe, twee Schapen en een Hond. Kunnende dit strekken tot eene wederga van de voorgaande [Un Paysage Site d'Italie, coupé par une Rivière ; il est varié par des arbres de forme pittoresque, et orné par deux Pâtres et par une Villageoise qui se trouve auprès d'une Vache couchée, de deux Brebis, et d'un Chien. Ce Tableau peut servir de pendant au précédent] | possibly companion to lot 8 *Annots:* médiocre (NGW) *Mat:* op paneel *Size:* hoog 11 ½, breed 14 ½ duimen	Mr Pieter de Smeth van Alphen	(Bought In) fl 800
1810/08/01	AMSCH	0010	*Berchem (Nicolaas)* | Een Italiaansch bergachtig Landschap met een breed Water doorsneden, waar in verscheide Vee waadt; op den voorgrond een Herder, zittende op een bruin Paard, waar bij een staande Os en Hond [Un Site de Paysage indiquant le Sol de l'Italie, coupé par une grande Riviere, dans laquelle le Bêtail s'abreuve à gué. Sur le premier plan est un	Mr Pieter de Smeth van Alphen	(Sold) fl 2500 Texier, Gerbet en Comp [for] LeBrun

			Pâtre assis sur un Cheval bai, attenant un Boeuf et un Chien] | *Annots:* Bon (NGW); Vente le Brun No. 104 fr 6050 (SMLN) *Mat:* op paneel *Size:* hoog 14, breed 20 ½ duimen		
1810/08/01	AMSCH	0011	*Berchem (Nicolaas)* | Voor een grootsch Gebouw, met Standbeelden versierd, ziet men, op eenen steenen Trap, eene rijk gekleede Vrouw, aan welke door eenen Moor een Papegaai wordt aangeboden; ter zijde andere Beelden, twee Honden, en een Zeehaven in het verschiet [Audevant du Perron d'une vaste Batiment, orné de Statues, se presente une Dame magnifiquement costumée, à laquelle un Négre presente un Peroquet ; ce groupe est accompagné par quelqu'autres figures, et par deux Chiens. Un Port de Mer terminant la perspective] | *Annots:* Bon ; mais hors de Son Stijle (NGW) *Mat:* op doek *Size:* hoog 36, breed 34 duimen *Loc:* Hartford, CT, USA. Wadsworth Atheneum. (1961.29)	Mr Pieter de Smeth van Alphen	(Sold) fl 1625 J^{mo} de Vries
1810/08/10	RMRIJ	0001	*N. Berchem* | Een Landschap, waar in Bokjes, Figuren, Planten en Kruiden. Meesterlijk en Piquant geschilderd van de beste classe | *Mat:* op doek *Size:* hoog 30 ¾ duim, breed 37 ½ duim		(Sold) fl 25 [or] 28 Dr Dalen
1810/10/11	AMSCH	0008	*N. Berchem* | Een Fabel-Ordonantie, zeer uitvoerig en fraai geschilderd | *Mat:* op paneel *Size:* hoog 11 ½, breed 14 duimen	C	(Sold) fl 195 Posthumus
1810/10/11	AMSCH	0009	*N. Berchem* | Een aangenaam Boomrijk Landschap, gestoffeerd met een Landman en een Jongen bij een Ploeg, met twee Ossen bespannen; meesterlijk gepenseeld | *Mat:* op paneel *Size:* hoog 15, breed 20 duimen	C	(Sold) fl 35 Posthumus

Berchem, Nicolaes Pietersz. (and Dou)

1803/04/20	AMSCH	0020	*Dou (G.); N. Berchem* | Dit voortreffelyk Tafreel, vertoond in een Boomryk Landschap, een staand Heer met een Wandelstok in de hand; neevens hem zit zyne Gemalinne, zy zyn beiden in ryke Deftige Kleeding uitgedost, ter zyde op de grond staat een Hondje, en op de voorgrond legt een Capiteel van de Corintische Order, waar in het Portrait van G. Dou geplaast is, de Hoofd-Personaadie is het Afbeeldzel van den Roemwaardigen Pieter van de Werve, Burgemeester der Stad Leyden, die in de zwaare Beleegering door de Spanjaarden in den Jaren 1574, en in de grootste Hongersnoot zyn Vaderlyke Liefde aan zynen Medeburgers Edelmoedig te kennen gaf, met zyn eigen Vleesch tot Spys aan te bieden; dit stuk is bevallig van Ordenantie, het Coloriet aangenaam, en van een uitvoerige Penceelbehandeling [Ce morceau très intéressant pour l'histoire de la Hollande, represente les portraits du Bourgemêtre Pierre van der Werve & de son Epouse. Cet homme célèbre par sa fermeté & son courage (* Footnote: Il étoit Bourgemêtre gouvernant la ville de Leyde en 1574, lorsque les Espagnols sous la conduite de Baldeus reduisirent cette ville aux dernieres extremitées [sic] de la famine, cet homme ferme s'offrit plutot pour nourriture que de souscire [sic] à la reddition de la place ; enfin après la mort de la moitié de ses concitoyens & des efforts, & de patience dont l'histoire fournit peu d'exemples! il sauva sa ville & l'independance de sa Patrie. Il mourut en 1604. G. Dou aura probablement pris les sujets de sa composition dans les portraits de la famille qui étoient anterieurs à son tems.), se voit debout tenant une longue canne à la main ; il est habillé d'un riche costume à l'ancienne Espagnolle. La Dame est assise, ses habillemens correspondant pour le tems & pour l'ornement avec ceux de son Epoux. N. Berchem en a peint le paysage qui designe la partie d'un Parc ou d'une avenue ; il y a jouté un beau chien brac [sic] qui est à gauche, & vers la droite se voit un chapiteau Corinthien, renversé, ou se trouve le buste de G. Dou. Ce tableau rare & précieux, est d'un beau fini, les figures en sont d'un dessin gracieux ; le paysage & l'animal sont touchés avec cet esprit fin & leger que l'on sait être propre à N. Berchem.] | *Mat:* op paneel *Size:* hoog 30, breed 24 duim *Loc:* Amsterdam, Nederland. Rijksmuseum. (A 90) as Portraits of Adriaen Wittert van der Aa and his wife Maria Knotter	Maria Magdalena van Sluypwyk, gravinne van Moens	(Sold) fl 3200 C S Roos

Berchem, Nicolaes Pietersz. (and Heusch, Jacob)

1802/06/16	AMSCH	0077	*J. de Heusch; N. Berchem* | Een Italiaansch Boom- en Bergachtig Landschap, met een aangenaam verschiet, Waterplatsen [sic] en uitmuntende Stoffagie op de voorgrond, zynde een Man en een Vrouw op een Ezel, verders nog verscheide andere Stoffagie; alles zonachtig en meesterlyk behandeld | *Mat:* op doek *Size:* hoog 26, breed 32 duim	[Merrem]	(Sold) fl 190 Agina

Berchem, Nicolaes Pietersz. (and Moucheron, F.)

1809/04/17	AMSCH	0054	*F. de Moucheron; N. Berchem* | Dit fraaije Schilderijtje verbeeld een Italiaansch Hoog Boschachtig Landschap, met een aanzienlijke Brug en Gebouwen, op de voorgrond een helder spiegelend Water, waar door eenige Beesten waaden, benevens een Landman zittende op een Ezel; voorts een aangenaam verschiet, het zonlicht doet een schoone werking, en is uitmuntend en van de beste behandeling, door F. de Moucheron, gestoffeerd door N. Berchem | *Mat:* op doek *Size:* hoog 15, breed 19 duim	C	(Sold or Bought In) fl 285

Berchem, Nicolaes Pietersz. (and Weenix, J.B.)

1810/08/06	AMSCH	0119	*Weenix (G.B.); Gestoffeerd door N. Berchem* | Dit fraaije kapitale Tafreel verbeelt eene ruime Plaats, met grootsche Gebouwen, ter regterzijde bij den opgang van eenen prachtigen Tempel ziet men den Zaligmaker, voor	A	(Sold) fl 765 J Spaan

wien eenige Schriftgeleerde en andere Personen elkander de Cijnspenning vertoonende, op den voorgrond op een Steenen Trap een zittende Jongeling, houdende een Paauw, waarbij drie staande Honden, verder een Landman en Vrouw bij onderscheiden Vee en een Zeehaven in het verschiet; dit stuk is bevallig van schikking, krachtig en schoon geschilderd en zeldzaam zoo fraai voorkomende | *Mat:* op paneel *Size:* hoog 37, breed 45 duimen *Loc:* Den Haag, Nederland. Mauritshuis. (1058)

Berchem, Nicolaes Pietersz. (or Berchem, N.P., manner)

1801/05/11	AMSCH	0010	*N. Berchem (of in de manier.)* | Een Landschap, op de Voorgrond met een menigte beesten gestoffeerd, waar by Herders en andere Landlieden, verders een bergachtig verschiet, zonachtig behandeld | *Mat:* op doek *Size:* hoog 29, breed 32 duim	Pruisse [for] M	(Sold) fl 105 Cocler
1801/05/11	AMSCH	0011	*N. Berchem (of in de manier)* | Een diergelyke Ordonantie, men ziet verscheide beesten door een plas Water dryven, in alles niet minder dan de vorige | *Mat:* op doek *Size:* hoog 29, breed 32 duim	Pruisse [for] M	(Sold) fl 80 Gruiter
1801/11/10	AMPOS	0002	*van Berghein* | 1 Ezeldrift door Rotsen naar een aangenaam Landschap, door een stil Water, als of door van Berghein		(Unknown)
1802/08/24	LNDLS	0011	*Berghem* | Een Landschap met Geboomte, op den Voorgrond is een Vrouw en Man te Paard, een ander die met zijn Vee door 't Water gaat, en meer Stoffage. van of in den trant van denzelven [Berghem] | *Mat:* op doek *Size:* hoog 25, breed 31 duimen	Leonardus Bouman [or others]	(Unknown) fl 63
1802/12/13	AMSCH	0009	*N. Berchem* | Dit aangenaam voorwerp verbeeld een Italiaansch Berghagtig Landschap, met een klaar Waterbeekje; op de voorgrond gestoffeert met een rustende Vrouw, houdende een Spinrok in de Hand, als spreekende tegen een Landman, daar névens zit een Vrouw op een Ezel, met eenig Hout belaaden, waar by een staande Landloopster met twee Kinderen, een Boere Jongen met een Mand aan den Arm schynt met een Hond te speelen; waarby Bokjes en Schaapen, zoo rustende als loopende, en verder andere Huislieden met Vée, alles evenaart de Natuur, het Zonlicht doet een bevallige Werking, en is meesterlyk fraay en uitvoerig van Penseel behandeling, als of het door N. Berchem vervaardigd was | *Mat:* op paneel *Size:* hoog 19, breed 15 duim	Schley [for] Lauwers	(Bought In) fl 30
1803/08/01	AMSCH	0002	*N. Berchem, of in de Manier* | Twee stuks Italiaansche Landschappen, gestoffeed [sic] met staande en leggende Beesten, beneevens rustende Herders en Herderinnen, warm van coloriet, en aangenaam behandeld | *Mat:* op paneel *Size:* ieder hoog 11, breed 10 duim	J	(Sold) fl 20:10 Pruijssenaar
1804/08/02	BDAN	0022	*Berghem, of in zyne manieren* | Een aangenaam Landschap, waarin verbeeld word Argus en Mercurius, voorts eenige Koeijen en Schaapen | *Mat:* op paneel *Size:* b. 26 d. h. 20 en 1 half d.	J G Calckberner	(Unknown)

Berchem, Nicolaes Pietersz. (copy after)

1801/03/16	AMSCH	0072	*Berchem* | Een dito [Landschap] met Beelden en Beesten, naa Berchem	P[ruyssenaar]	(Bought In) fl 2
1802/02/23	AMREB	0030	*N. Berchem* | 2 stuks Landschappen met Beesten, op Doek na N. Berchem | *Mat:* op doek	Margaretha Maria van Laar	(Sold) fl 8:5 A van Houten
1802/02/23	AMREB	0031	*N. Berchem* | 2 stuks dito [Landschappen] na dito [N. Berchem]	Margaretha Maria van Laar	(Sold) fl 8:15 A van Houten
1802/07/27	AKHRK	0076	*Na N. Berghem* | Een Landschapje met Figuuren en Ossen; zeer goed geschilderd | *Mat:* op paneel *Size:* hoog 7 ¼, breed 9 ¾ duim	Maria Stategaart	(Sold) fl 5 for lots 76 & 77. De Ruyd
1802/07/27	AKHRK	0077	*Na N. Berghem* | Een Herderin te Paard, een drinkende Boer, met een Ezel en Schaapen	Maria Stategaart	(Sold) fl 5 for lots 76 & 77. De Ruyd
1802/09/06	AMSCH	0146	*N. Berghem* | Een Italiaansche Zéehaven, ryk gestoffeerd met Gallyen, een meenigte Beelden, Paarden en ander Vée; bevallig gepenceeld na N. Berghem	Mevrouw Achtienhoven	(Sold) fl 76 Pruijssenaar
1804/08/02	BDAN	0042	*Na Berghem* | Twee Landschappen met Figuren en Koeyen | *Mat:* op doek *Size:* b. 14 d. h. 11 d.	J G Calckberner	(Unknown)
1804/10/16	DLOND	0047	*M. Carre; naar Berchem* | Een Landschap met Herders en Vee. Paysage, des Bergers & du Betail | copy by M. Carree after N.P. Berchem *Mat:* op doek *Size:* hoog 23, breed 27		(Unknown)
1804/10/16	DLOND	0239	*C. Vermeulen; naar Berghem* | Ene zeer schone en allernaauwkeurigste Copy naar N. Berghem, verbeeldende een Hertenjacht. Une Copie superbe & très-exacte d'après N. Berghem, repres. une Chasse de Cerf | copy by Corn. Vermeulen (III) after N.P. Berchem *Mat:* op paneel *Size:* hoog 15, breed 20		(Sold) fl 28 O D Wyngaert
1804/10/29	HRBAU	0153	*Berchem* | Een Landschap, met Beestjens. Na Berchem | *Mat:* op paneel *Size:* hoog 12, breed 15 duim	Simon Styl	(Unknown)
1804/10/29	HRBAU	0160	*Berchem* | Een Landschap met Beesten. Na Berchem | *Mat:* op paneel *Size:* hoog 27, breed 35 duim	Simon Styl	(Unknown)
1806/05/05	AMSCH	0251	*N. Berghem* | Twee stuks met dito [staand en leggend Vee], na N. Berghem | *Notes:* It is unclear what "dito" refers to in the title.	R[oos]	(Sold) fl 12 Vermeulen
1807/09/28	DOHAA	00SS	*N. Berghem* | Een dito [Landschap] met Koebeestjes, naar N. Berghem	Mattheus Westerouen van Meeteren	(Unknown)

1810/03/07	UTWLD	0004	*Berghem* | Twee Landschappen naar Berghem | *Size:* hoog 3 voet, breed 3 voet 6 duim	J J Woertman	(Unknown) fl 14:10
1810/06/04	DOBRA	0001	*Berchem* | Een Landschap met Beesten; naar Berchem	Hendrik de Haas	(Unknown)
			Berchem, Nicolaes Pietersz. (manner)		
1802/02/16	AMSCH	0066	*N. Berchem* | Een dito [Italiaans] Landschap, gestoffeerd met een huisman en een vrouw, verzelt van verschyde Vee, kragtig gepenceeld, in de manier van N. Berchem	G	(Sold) fl 11 Gruiter
1802/09/06	AMSCH	0245	*N. Berchem* | Twee stuks Italiaansche Landzichten, in de eene staat een Véehoeder, rustende op zyn Stok, ter zyde ziet men een Os, en rustende Schaapen; den andere verbeeld een Landvrouw, op een Ezel rydende, by een Waterput, verzelt van een Huisman en belaaden Ezel, verders eenige Schaapen; beide plaisant geschilderd, in de manier van N. Berchem | *Size:* ieder hoog 11, breed 13 duim	Brave	(Sold) fl 17:10 de Meijer
1803/09/07	AMSCH	0226	*N. Berchem* | Twee stuks Landschappen met stille Waterbeeken, waarin verscheide Vee, door Huislieden op Ezels gezéten, gelyd worden; fix van Penceelbehandeling, in de manier van N. Berchem [Deux paysages avec des étangs, auxquels plusieurs paysans montés sur des ânes conduisent leurs bestiaux pour les y abreuver ; d'un fini délicat et d'une belle exécution dans le genre de N. Berchem] | *Mat:* op paneel *Size:* yder hoog 12, breed 25 duim	Smidt	(Bought In) fl 4
1804/10/16	DLOND	0279	*In de manier van N. Berchem* | Een Landschap met Vee. Paysage & du Betail | *Mat:* op doek op paneel *Size:* hoog 16, breed 18		(Unknown)
1805/07/10	AMSCH	0204	*Berghem* | Een Boom- en Bergachtig Landschap, met een Rivier doorsneeden, met een ménigte Vee, verzeld van hunne Herders; meesterlyk als Berghem gepenceeld	V[inkeles] [for] J	(Sold) fl 14 Gruyter
1805/07/10	AMSCH	0243	*N. van Berchem* | In een Italiaansch Heuvelachtig Landschap, ziet men verscheide Huislieden, met Belaaden Muilëzels, Schaapen, en ander Vee; plaisant geschildert op Doek, in de manier van N. van Berchem | *Mat:* op doek	Wed Grave	(Sold) fl 1:5 L Pakker
1806/05/05	AMSCH	0177[a]	*Berghem* | Drie stuks Landschappen; als Wynands en Berghem | *This Lot:* Landschap[pen]; lot 177[b] is manner of Wijnants	R[oos]	(Sold) fl 4:10 for lots 177[a] & 177[b]. Scheurleer
1806/08/20	HGBSM	0072	*Berghem* | Een heuvelachtig Landschap, met verschillende soort van Vee gestoffeerd, op de voorgrond is een Landman gezeten op een wit Paard met bruine bonte vlakken, benevens een Jongen, en eenige Honden; fraai in de manier van Berghem geordonneerd, en door een goed meester geschilderd | *Mat:* op paneel *Size:* hoog 15, breed 19 duim	Macalester Loup [or others]	(Sold) fl 17 Lafontaine
1806/08/20	HGBSM	0198	*N. Berghem* | Een Capitaal Landschap, waarin een Herder die een Herderinne liefkoost en verder met Bokken en Schaapen, &c., de beesten zijn in de trand van N. Berghem | *Mat:* op doek *Size:* hoog 48, breed 52 ½ duim	Macalester Loup [or others]	(Sold) fl 18:10 Cocard
1807/06/10	HGBSM	0093	*Berghem* | Een Landschap, bij een Fontein zit een Herderinne bij eenige Koeijen, Schaapen, Hond en een Ezel, Zonagtig, in de trant van Berghem | *Mat:* op paneel *Size:* hoog 15, breed 21 duim	Abraham Delfos [or others]	(Sold) fl 6 Tessier
1808/05/17	LNAN	0023	*Berghem* | Een warm Landschap, als van Berghem		(Sold) fl 7:10 Thomasse
1808/08/23	AMSCH	0235	*Berchem* | Een Heuvelachtig Landzigt, gestoffeert met eene Landvrouw bij rustende en gràsende Beesten; kloek geschildert in de manier van Berchem	C	(Sold) fl 7:5 du Prée
1809/04/22	AMYVR	0161	*N. Berchem* | Een Landschap met Beelden en Beesten; als N. Berchem	de Bruin	(Sold) fl 9:10 du Pree
1810/03/26	RMMUY	0080	*Berchem* | Twee Bergachtige Landschappen, met Beelden en Beesten. In de manier van Berchem [Deux Paysages, avec Figures et Animaux, dans la manière de Berchem.] | *This Lot:* Een Bergachtig Landschap, met Beelden en Beesten *Annots:* 2 Copies de Berchem (BPG) *Notes:* Lots 80 and 81 were printed in the catalogue as one item.	Daniel de Jongh Az	(Sold) fl 27:10 for lots 80 & 81. H Rochussen a Rott[m]
1810/03/26	RMMUY	0081	*Berchem* | Twee Bergachtige Landschappen, met Beelden en Beesten. In de manier van Berchem [Deux Paysages, avec Figures et Animaux, dans la manière de Berchem.] | *This Lot:* Een Bergachtig Landschap, met Beelden en Beesten *Annots:* 2 Copies de Berchem (BPG) *Notes:* Lots 80 and 81 were printed in the catalogue as one item.	Daniel de Jongh Az	(Sold) fl 27:10 for lots 80 & 81. H Rochussen a Rott[m]
1810/06/20	AMSCH	0173	*Berchem* | Een Bergachtig Landschap, met Landlieden en Vee, in de manier van Berchem	A	(Sold) fl 15 T Spaan
			Berckheyde		
1801/03/16	AMSCH	0108	*Berkheyden* | Twee stuks, een Gezicht op den Dam te Amsterdam, gestoffeerd met een menigte Beelden, en de weerga zynde een Gezicht op de groote Kerk te Haarlem, natuurlyk	K[ip]	(Sold) fl 30 Wijland
1801/03/16	AMSCH	0171	*Berckheyden* | Twee Binnenhuizen | *Notes:* This lot was sold with lot 172 by J. Reigenbach.	P[ruyssenaar]	(Sold) fl 3:5 for lots 171 & 172. van Iperen
1802/05/11	GRGRW	0024	*Berckheijde* | Ene dito [Herderin] [Schilderijen met Olie-Verf; In zwarte Lijsten] | *Mat:* in olyverf *Notes:* The bracketed information in the title about the medium appears above lot 1 and refers to lots 1 to 79a.	Arnold Sicco Werumeus	(Unknown)

1802/12/13	AMSCH	0017	*Berckheyden* | In een Studeervertrek ziet men een Man, voor een met een Kleed bedekte Schryftafel zitten, hy schynt om te zien na iemand die hy een Brief wil overhandigen; door een openstaande Deur ziet men in een Welgemeubeld ander Vertrek, zonachtig en fix geschilderd | *Mat:* op doek *Size:* hoog 22, breed 19 duim	Pruyssenaar [for] A	(Sold) fl 0:10 L Pakker
1806/08/20	HGBSM	0033	*F. Berkheijden* | Het gezicht van de grote Kerk te Haarlem, rijk gestoffeerd | *Mat:* op paneel *Size:* hoog 15, breed 21 ½ duim	[Teissier]	(Sold) fl 53 Nieuwenhuys
1808/06/11	RMRIJ	0078	*Berkheiden* | Twee Stuks aangename en duinachtige Landschappen, fraai gestoffeerd | *Mat:* op paneel *Size:* hoog 12 ½, breed 17 ½ duim		(Sold) fl 13 Noordwyk
1810/10/13	HGDAW	0010	*Berkhuizen* | Een Boeren Binnenvertrek, waarin een Boertje de Courant zit te lezen, waarby een ander met een Kan in de hand, staat te luisteren, fiks gepenseeld | *Mat:* op paneel *Size:* hoog 8 ¾, breed 11 ¼ duim		(Unknown)

Berckheyde, Gerrit Adriaensz.

1801/04/08	HAVIN	0044	*G. Berkheide* | Een gezigt op Haarlem, verbeeldende een Winter		(Unknown)
1801/05/11	AMSCH	0007	*G. Berckheyden* | Een Gezicht op het Binnenhof in den Haag, ryk gestoffeerd, met een menigte beeldjes en rytuigen, natuurlyk en zonachtig behandeld | *Mat:* op paneel *Size:* hoog 13, breed 18 duim	E[lias]	(Sold) fl 50 P Le Dantú
1801/05/11	AMSCH	0008	*G. Berckheyden* | Een Gezicht op het Stadhuis te Amsterdam, zynde den Dam, bevallig met beeldjes, diversche kooplieden en rytuigen gestoffeerd, aangenaam van licht en bruin, en meesterlyk gepenceeld | *Mat:* op doek *Size:* hoog 21, breed 24 duim	E[lias]	(Sold) fl 87 Bern^{d} de Bosch
1801/06/10	AMSCH	0024	*Berkheyden. (G.)* | Een gezicht van het binne Spaare te Haarlem, gestoffeerd met een menigte Beelden, verders diverse Schuyten en Jagten, Zonachtig, en uitvoerig van Schildering | *Mat:* op paneel *Size:* hoog 17, breed 24 duim	Herman ten Kate	(Sold) fl 100 van der Vinne [and] Schleij
1801/06/10	AMSCH	0025	*Berkheyden. (G.)* | Een dito [gezicht], zynde een gezicht op de Markt, en groote Kerk te Haarlem, langs het Stadhuys te zien, gestoffeert met wandelende Beelden, alles delicaat en Zonachtig behandeld | *Mat:* op paneel *Size:* hoog 17, breed 25 duim	Herman ten Kate	(Sold) fl 205 Jan Spaan
1801/06/10	AMSCH	0026	*Berkheyden. (G.)* | Een Landschap, op de voorgrond ziet men een Geytemelkster, verders een staande en leggende Koey, ter zyde een Fontein, verder een bergachtig verschiet, fraai van ligt en bruin en helder van schildering | *Size:* hoog 13, breed 17 duim	Herman ten Kate	(Sold) fl 75 for lots 26 & 27. C S Roos
1801/06/10	AMSCH	0027	*Berkheyden. (G.)* | Een gezicht op de Baan te Haarlem met de groote Kerk in 't verschiet te zien, op de voorgrond verscheide staande en leggende Beesten en Paarden; zonachtig behandeld | *Mat:* op paneel *Size:* hoog 12, breed 17 duim	Herman ten Kate	(Sold) fl 75 for lots 26 & 27. C S Roos
1801/06/10	AMSCH	0028	*Berkheyden. (G.)* | Gezicht van de Markt en groote Kerk te Haarlem, gestoffeert met een aantal Beelden; zeer natuurlyk behandeld | *Mat:* op paneel *Size:* hoog 25, breed 32 duim	[Doublet]	(Sold) fl 81 Van Iperen
1801/06/10	AMSCH	0029	*Berkheyden. (G.)* | Twee fraaije en zonachtige Gezichten van de Heerengragt te Amsterdam, beiden met Beeldjes gestoffeert en uitvoerig gepenceeld | *Mat:* op paneel *Size:* hoog 11, breed 14 duim	[Doublet]	(Sold) fl 50 Van Dijl
1801/10/19	AMSCH	0011	*Berkheiden. (G.)* | Een Gezigt binnen de Stad Haarlem van de Markt op de groote Kerk ziende, zeer ryk gestoffeerd met een Rytuig en Beelden, fraay en zonagtig behandeld | *Mat:* op paneel *Size:* hoog 15, breed 21 ½ duim	Jonkheer Menno Baron van Coehoorn	(Sold) fl 61 Tessier
1802/05/05	AMSCH	0016	*G. Berkheide* | Een Gezicht op het Huis te Heemstede, gestoffeerd met Heeren, Dames en Jagers met Honden, Zonächtig | *Mat:* op doek *Size:* hoog 19, breed 22 duim	A	(Sold) fl 86 for lots 16 & 17. Le Dantú
1802/05/05	AMSCH	0017	*G. Berkheide* | Een Gezicht op de Vyverberg en Groene Zootje in den Haag, gestoffeerd met een Uittogt te Paard, behandeld als de Voorgaande | *Mat:* op doek *Size:* hoog 19, breed 22 duim	A	(Sold) fl 86 for lots 16 & 17. Le Dantú
1802/06/16	AMSCH	0018	*G. Berckheyden* | Een Binnengezicht van een Protestante Kerk, gestoffeerd met wandelende Dames en Heeren: de Perspectief is wel waargenomen, zonachtig en bevallig gepenceelt | *Mat:* op doek *Size:* hoog 16, breed 14 duim	[Merrem]	(Sold) fl 33 v d Vinne
1802/06/28	AMSCH	0013	*G. Berkheide* | Een gezicht op het Spaarn en de Waag te Haarlem, gestoffeert met Schuiten, Beeldjes en Paarden; zonachtig behandeld door G. Berkheide | *Mat:* op paneel *Size:* hoog 13, breed 18 duim	Anna Elink	(Sold) fl 48 van Iperen
1802/12/13	AMSCH	0028	*G. Berkheyden* | Een gezicht binnen Parys, ryk gestoffeerd, met Beelden en Vaartuigen | *Mat:* op paneel *Size:* hoog 14 ½, breed 14 ½ duim	Pruyssenaar [for] A	(Sold) fl 0:14 Gruiter
1804/05/07	AMSCH	0015	*Berkheyde. (G.)* | Een Gezicht aan de Ingang van een Kerk, vol gewoel van Heeren en Dames, Bedelaars, enz.; fiks van behandeling en meesterlyk gepenceeld | *Mat:* op doek *Size:* hoog 21, breed 28 duim	Vinkeles [for] J	(Sold) fl 16:10 Pruissenaar
1804/05/07	AMSCH	0016	*Berkheyde. (G.)* | Door een oude Poort ziet men op een Markt, alwaar het Kermis schynt te weezen, mede vol gewoel van Beelden enz.; niet minder dan de voorgaande | *Size:* hoog 21, breed 28 duim	Vinkeles [for] J	(Sold) fl 16:10 Pruissenaar
1804/08/08	AMSCH	0012	*G. Berckheiden* | Een Gezicht binnen Rome, gestoffeerd met een beladen Kar, bespannen met een wit Paard, ter zyde, by een Fontyn drie Vrouwen, een Ezel en verdere Stoffagie; kragtig en zonachtig | *Mat:* op doek *Size:* hoog 19, br. 16 duim	Roos a	(Sold) fl 47 van Iperen

1804/10/16	DLOND	0023	*Ger. Berkheyden* | De Grote Markt te Zwolle, met veel gewoel. La Grande Place de Zwolle & beaucoup de figures | *Mat:* op doek *Size:* hoog 19, breed 22		(Unknown)
1804/10/29	HRBAU	0006	*Berkheiden, (G.)* | Dit allerbevalligst Tafereel stelt ons een fraai Italiaansch bergagtig Landschap voor oogen; op den Voorgrond van hetzelve zit een Vrouwtje op een Ezel, spreekende met eene andere Vrouw, welke naast haar gaat, vergezeld door een Man paard; nevens nog een Vrouwtje, welke een Pak op heur hoofd draagt, voor zig eenige Koeijen, Schaapen en Geiten door eene Beek dryvende; wat verder, by een Steenklip, is een Herder en Vrouw, welke hunne Kudde naar agteren naar het Gebergte dryven, en een zeer uitgestrekt verschiet. Dit Schildery is zeer fraai geordineerd, de Couleur smeltend, en alles zeer uitvoerig, en in een' grootschen trant behandeld | *Mat:* op paneel *Size:* hoog 24, breed 34 duim	Simon Styl	(Unknown)
1804/12/10	AMSCH	0005	*G. Berkheyden* | Een capitaal Gezicht langs de Kloveniers Burgwal te Amsterdam, ziende naar het Huis van Trip en andere Woningen, verder de Nieuwe Markt en Waag, gestoffeert met verscheide beeldjes, jacht en ander bywerk; zonachtig en meesterlyk behandeld | *Mat:* op doek *Size:* Hoog 20 ½, breed 24 duim	Jan de Groot	(Sold) fl 24:10 Coclers
1804/12/10	AMSCH	0006	*G. Berkheyden* | Een Gezicht op het Binnenhof in den Haag, fraay en ryk gestoffeerd, meesterlyk van perspectief en zonachtig geschilderd | *Mat:* op doek *Size:* Hoog 19, breed 26 duim	Jan de Groot	(Sold) fl 41 Reijers
1805/07/03	AMSCH	0006	*Berckheyden, (G.)* | Een gezicht op de kleine Houtpoort te Haarlem, gestoffeerd met een Herder, welke eenig Vee dryft, het water met Zwaanen; alles delicaat behandeld en van een bevallig licht en bruin | *Mat:* op doek *Size:* hoog 21, breed 25 duim	G	(Sold) fl 48 Tessier
1805/07/10	AMSCH	0014	*G. Berkheyden* | De Beurs van Amsterdam, zynde 't aangaan derzelven, met een ménigte Beelden; zonachtig en fraay gepenceeld | *Mat:* op doek *Size:* hoog 38, breed 48 duim	V[inkeles] [for] H[affner]	(Sold) fl 17:10 Parker Hodges
1806/05/05	AMSCH	0013	*G. Berkheiden* | Een gezicht te Romen met een ménigte stoffagie van Beeldjes en Ezels; zonachtig op Doek | *Mat:* op doek *Size:* hoog 11, breed 13 duim	H	(Sold) fl 10 van Iperen
1806/08/13	AMSCH	0011	*Berkheiden. (G.)* | Een gezicht op een Stad en Kasteel aan den Rhyn, de voorgrond gestoffeerd met een ménigte beelden te paard en te voet, als mede een beladen wagen door Ossen en een paard voortgetrokken wordende; meesterlyk behandeld | *Mat:* op doek *Size:* hoog 30, breed 51 duim	van der Voort	(Sold) fl 62 Roos
1806/08/13	AMSCH	0012	*Berkheiden. (G.)* | Deeze ordinantie vol gewoel van Beelden, steld voor 't verjaagen der Spanjaarden, door 't volk te Haarlem; alles eigenaartigst en de caracters vol uitdrukking; en meesterlyk van schildering | *Mat:* op doek *Size:* hoog 26, breed 42 duim	Vinkeles [for] D	(Sold) fl 42 Pr Swanenburgh
1808/04/26	GDAN	0010	*Berkheiden (G.)* | Men ziet hier een gedeelte der Stad Utrecht, als: de Vismarkt, 't Stadhuis, met de Huizen daar naast, voorts de Kraan en de Doms Toren, gestoffeerd met een aantal werkzame en wandelende Menschen, alles zeer fraai uitvoerig en meesterlijk geschilderd | *Size:* hoog 80, breed 61 duim	G H Fortuyn	(Unknown)
1808/06/06	RMRIJ	0014	*Berkheijden. (Gerard)* | Een gezigt binnen Keulen, met aangename Gebouwen en Geboomte, bevallig gestoffeerd. Breed en goed geschilderd. Eene wedergade, dito gezigt binnen Keulen, als boven behandeld [Vue dans la Ville de Cologne representant plusieurs bâtiments, figures, animaux, arbres etc. Le second Tableau (autre vue dans Cologne) est de la même dimension et du même genre que le précèdent] | *Annots:* afk uit coll Pieter Calkoen Wmz Amst 10 Sept 1781 (f 163) (RKDH I) *Mat:* op doek *Size:* Twee stukken. Hoog 20, en breed 24 duim	Gerrit van der Pot, Heer van Groeneveld	(Sold) fl 300 J Havelaar
1808/06/13	AMSCH	0016	*Berckheijden (G.)* | Een Gezicht op het Binnen-Sparen te Haarlem, zijnde het water met onderscheidene Vaartuigen en Zwanen, en de wal met Beeldjes gestoffeerd; zonachtig gepenceeld | *Mat:* op doek *Size:* hoog 19, breed 22 duim	[Jan Tersteeg]	(Sold) fl 71 Roos P [for] v d Palts
1808/06/13	AMSCH	0017	*Berckheijden (G.)* | Een Gezicht binnen Amsterdam, ziende langs de Prinsengragt naar het N. Z. Huiszittenhuis, Leliëgragt, Wester Kerk en Tooren, en andere Gebouwen; gestoffeerd met verscheidene Beeldjes, Schepen en Schuiten. Zonachtig en natuurlijk behandeld | *Mat:* op doek *Size:* hoog 26, breed 35 duim	[Jan Tersteeg]	(Bought In) fl 16
1809/04/22	AMYVR	0010	*G. Berkheiden* | Voor een Buitenhuis staat een Jongen op de Fiool te speelen voor eene menigte Aanhoorers [sic]; krachtig | *Mat:* op paneel *Size:* hoog 19, breed 14 duim	de Bruin	(Sold) fl 16 Dupré
1809/07/19	AMSCH	0004	*Berckheijden (G.)* | Een aangenaam Gezicht, in de Stad Haarlem, langs het binnen-Spaarn, waar verscheide Woningen en Geboomten, een Brouwerij, verders gestoffeerd met Beeldjes en Vaartuigen, in 't verschiet een gedeelte der groote-Kerk. Alles is zonagtig, natuurlijk en uitvoerig gepenceeld | *Mat:* op paneel *Size:* hoog 15, breed 19 duim	[Bicker]	(Sold) fl 199 J^{mo} de Vries
1809/07/25	HGBSM	0009	*G. Berkheyden* | Een Gezigt binnen Haarlem langs het Spaaren, met Schepen en Figuuren gestoffeerd, helder en uitvoerig geschildert | *Mat:* op paneel *Size:* hoog 12 ½, breet 17 ½ duim	D van der Aa [or] E B ten Dall	(Sold) fl 62 van Eijk

1809/09/06	AMSCH	0005	*Berkheijden (G.)* | Gezicht op het Binnenspaarn te Haarlem, ziende naar de Waag en Kraan, op de voorgrond gestoffeerd met verscheide Lieden en Speelschuitje, verder vertoond zig een gedeelten der groote Kerk; alles zonagtig en uitvoerig behandeld | *Mat:* op paneel *Size:* hoog 19, breed 24 duim	Johannes Caudri	(Sold) fl 36 van Iperen
1810/07/26	AMSCH	0005	*Berckheiden (G.)* | Een Markt of Plijn, met groote Gebouwen. Gestoffeerd met Lieden te Voet en te Paard | *Mat:* op doek *Size:* hoog 16, breed 25 duimen	Cassino	(Sold) fl 14:10 de Vries
1810/08/06	AMSCH	0012	*Berckheijden (G.)* | Een Gezigt in den Haag, ziende langs den Vijverberg, op den voorgrond eenige Vorstelijke Personen te Paard, verzeld van Pages, en een Jager, met Honden. Helder en uitvoerig gepenceeld | *Mat:* op paneel *Size:* hoog 13, breed 15 ½ duimen	A	(Sold) fl 43 Van Iperen [for] Vriesman
1810/08/06	AMSCH	0013	*Berckheijden (G.)* | Twee stuks Gezigten: het eene buiten Leijden, ziende op een der Stads Poorten; het andere de groote Markt te Haarlem. Beide eigenaardig gestoffeerd en uitvoerig geschilderd | *Mat:* op paneel *Size:* ieder hoog 13, breed 17 duimen	A	(Sold) fl 51 Gruyter
1810/08/06	AMSCH	0014	*Berckheijden (G.)* | Een Markt of Plein, met Gebouwen, op den voorgrond ziet men eenen Kwakzalver op zijn Theater, waarbij eene menigte Aanschouwers. Zonachtig behandeld | *Mat:* op doek *Size:* hoog 17 ½, breed 21 duimen	C	(Sold) fl 24 L Pakker
1810/10/11	AMSCH	0010	*G. Berckheiden* | In een Landschap ziet men een Heer te Paard, voor een Stal, benevens een Paard dat gezadeld wordt, verder Honden en andere Stoffage; natuurlijk | *Mat:* op doek *Size:* hoog 16, breed 28 duimen	Y	(Sold) fl 12 Gruiter
1810/10/11	AMSCH	0011	*G. Berckheiden* | Twee stuks bevallige Land- en Watergezigten, met Boerenwoningen, Geboomte, Beelden en Beesten gestoffeerd; zeer natuurlijk | *Mat:* op doek *Size:* hoog 25, breed 30 duimen	Y	(Sold) fl 21 Gruiter

Berckheyde, Gerrit Adriaensz. (and Moucheron, I.)

1807/08/26	AMSCH	0014	*G. Berkheide; J. de Moucheron* | Op een Pleisterplaats ziet men verscheiden Reizigers te Paard, zich ververschende; by een Put staat eene Vrouw met een Koperen Kan, terwyl een andere eene Geit melkt, verders nog verscheiden Paarden, Honden, enz.; fraai geschilderd | *Mat:* op doek *Size:* hoog 22, breed 27 duim	de Vries	(Bought In or Withdrawn)

Berckheyde, Gerrit Adriaensz. (manner)

1803/08/17	AMSCH	0101	*G. Berkheiden* | Twee stuks, met naakte en gekleede Beelden, als door G. Berkheiden | *Mat:* op paneel *Size:* hoog 14, breed 12 duim	Anna Catharina Putman	(Sold) fl 9 Gruyter

Berckheyde, Job Adriaensz.

1801/05/11	AMSCH	0017	*Job Berkheyden* | Een gezelschap van vier Persoonen, in een binnehuis, meesterlyk geschilderd | *Mat:* op paneel *Size:* hoog 10, breed 8 duim	P[ruyssenaar]	(Sold) fl 3 van Iperen
1802/02/16	AMSCH	0045	*J. Berkheiden* | Een gezigt by de Vestmuur van een Stadt, op de Voorgrond gestoffeert, met een belaaden Ryskar, en eenige Huislieden, zonachtig behandeld	G	(Sold) fl 8:10 Gruiter
1802/05/05	AMSCH	0013	*J. Berkheyde* | Een Bergachtig Landschap, op de Voorgrond een Herder, welke een Os Voortdryft; verders eenige Leggende Schapen, in 't verschiet, een Oud Kasteel en verder Bywerk; zeer natuurlyk | *Mat:* op paneel *Size:* hoog 14, breed 19 duim	C	(Sold) fl 3 Spruit
1802/05/05	AMSCH	0014	*J. Berkheyde* | Een Dorpgezicht, van Binnen te zien, gestoffeerd met een Paardemarkt, vol gewoel, van een menigte Wandelende Heeren en Dames, fiks gepenceeld | *Mat:* op doek *Size:* hoog 33, breed 40 duim	C	(Sold) fl 41 Hulswit
1802/05/05	AMSCH	0015	*J. Berkheyde* | Een Boere Binnenhuis, met verscheide Speelende Boeren en Boerinnen, fiks behandeld | *Mat:* op paneel *Size:* hoog 12, breed 9 duim	R	(Sold) fl 0:10 Van Iperen
1802/06/16	AMSCH	0019	*J. Berckheyden* | Een Capitaal Boomryk Landschap, waar achter zich vertoond een trots Gebouw met Toorens, op de Voorgrond ziet men een Jager, verders een aangenaam Verschiet: zonachtig en krachtig behandeld | *Mat:* op doek *Size:* hoog 17, breed 23 ½ duim	[Merrem]	(Sold) fl 14 Yver
1802/06/28	AMSCH	0012	*Joh. Berkheiden* | Een Binnenhuis, waarin een Man, die een Haring schoon maakt, voor hem een stuk Brood en Boter; meesterlyk gepenceelt door Joh. Berkheiden | *Mat:* op doek *Size:* hoog 14, breed 11 duim	Anna Elink	(Sold) fl 15 Jan Spaan
1802/09/21	UTHDG	0011	*J. Berkheide* | De Historie in welke Joseph zijne nedergeknielde Broederen den Beeker vertoond, fraai van licht en kragtig behandelt | *Mat:* op paneel *Size:* hoog 28, breed 36 duimen		(Bought In) fl 10
1803/04/27	AMSCH	000Z[H]	*J Berkijden* | Een met Muijlezels door J Berkhijden | *Notes:* This lot was added in by hand in the LBDa and RKDH copies of the catalogue.	G	(Sold) fl 14 Stevens
1803/06/20	AMSCH	0028	*J. Berkheiden* | Een gezicht van de Geldersche Kaay op de Waag, Nieuwenmarkt en Zuyderkerk te Amsterdam te zien; gestoffeerd met Scheepen en Beeldjes; zonagtig op Doek | *Mat:* op doek *Size:* hoog 24, breed 30 duim	Schley [for] G	(Sold) fl 9:10 Gruiter
1803/08/01	AMSCH	0005	*Berkheiden (H.)* | Een Gezicht op de Beurs te Amsterdam, gestoffeert met verscheide Beelden, van verscheide Natien, kragtig en zoo zonachtig als 'er van dien Meester bekend zyn | *Mat:* op doek *Size:* hoog 37, breed 47 duim	Thoen	(Sold) fl 35 Haffner

1803/08/17	AMSCH	0010	*Berkheiden. (J.)* | Twee stuks Italiaansche Landschappen, met Gebouwen, Ruïnes, hoog Geboomte en Bergachtige Verschieten, beide ryk gestoffeerd met Muilezels, Paarden, Ossen en Schaapen, met hunne Hoeders, en verdere Stoffagie, beide van een kragtige behandeling, zynde een Morgen- en Avondstond | *Mat:* op doek *Size:* ieder hoog 21, breed 24 duim	Anna Catharina Putman	(Sold) fl 43 W Reijers
1804/02/27	AMSCH	0012	*Berckheiden. (JOB.)* | De Uitplundering van een Dorp door Krygslieden, meesterlyk verbeeld | *Mat:* op doek *Size:* hoog 26, breed 33 duim	B	(Sold) fl 1 L Pakker
1804/05/07	AMSCH	0017	*Berkheyden. (J.)* | Het Gezicht langs de Trippenburgwal, naa de Nieuwmarkt, te Amsterdam; ryk gestoffeerd en zonachtig geschilderd	Vinkeles [for] G	(Sold) fl 11:10 van Iperen
1805/07/03	AMSCH	0005	*Berkheyden, (J.)* | In een Boeren Herberg, zyn eenige Huislieden lustig aan het drinken, rooken en vrolyk te zingen; de voorgrond is met onderscheiden huisraad voorzien; de penceels behandeling is van de beste van deezen Meester | *Mat:* op doek *Size:* hoog 20, breed 31 duim	R[oos]	(Sold) fl 62 Lafontaine
1805/07/10	AMSCH	0023	*J. Berkheiden* | Een gezicht binnen Romen, gestofferd met Heeren te Paard, een Jager met Honden, Herders met Schapen, enz.; fraay en zonachtig op Doek | *Mat:* op doek *Size:* hoog 21, breed 24 duim	R[oos]	(Sold) fl 10 L Pakker
1805/10/09	HGBSM	0101	*J. Berkheyden* | Een gezelschap op het verkeerd bord speelende, onder een priëel fix en natuurlyk | *Mat:* op paneel *Size:* hoog 13 breet 11 duim	T H van Willigen [or others]	(Sold) fl 24:5 for lots 101 & 102. Teissier
1805/10/09	HGBSM	0102	*J. Berkheyden* | Een dito gezelschap, zittende te praaten, voor een buitenhuis, niet minder als de voorgaande | *Size:* hoog 13 breet 11 duim *Notes:* It is unclear what "dito" refers to in the title.	T H van Willigen [or others]	(Sold) fl 24:5 for lots 101 & 102. Teissier
1806/11/24	AMSCH	0007	*Berkheiden (J.)* | Eenige rokende en caresseerende Boeren en Boerinnen in een binnenhuis; zynde van een breede schildering | *Mat:* op doek *Size:* hoog 12, breed 10 duim	Munnikhuizen	(Sold) fl 2:10 Levy Pakker
1808/08/23	AMSCH	0202	*J. Berkheyden* | Een Italiaans Landschap met Gebouwen en Ruïne, gestoffeerd met Reizigers en Landlieden bij hun Vee; krachtig op Doek | *Mat:* op doek	[Gruyter?]	(Sold) fl 1:10 Maas [or] Mayken
1809/05/26	HADAA	0042	*J. Berkheyde* | Een Gezicht op de Kleine Houtpoort te Haarlem, zonachtig | *Mat:* op paneel	Mejuffrouw de Wed David Heemskerk [or others]	(Unknown)
1810/06/06	RMMUY	0161	*Job Berkheiden* | Een Binnenhuis met spelende en andere Figuren		(Unknown) fl 5

Berckheyde, Job Adriaensz. (and Neeffs, P. (I))

1806/11/24	AMSCH	0047	*Neefs (P.); J. Berkheiden* | Een gezigt in de groote Kerk te Rotterdam, gestoffeerd met verscheidene Wapenborden, Heeren en Dames, welke in dezelve wandelen; het zonligt is'er kragtig in werking, en is voorts delicaat geschildert | *Mat:* op doek *Size:* hoog 24, breed 24 duim	Munnikhuizen	(Sold) fl 70 Engelberts

Berg (Bergh)

1804/02/27	AMSCH	0019	*Berg. (V.)* | Een Zinnebeeldige Ordonantie, uitvoerig geschilderd | *Mat:* op paneel *Size:* hoog 22, breed 16 duim	D	(Sold) fl 0:14 L Pakker
1804/03/27	MGSAN	0008	*v. Bergh* | Een fraai Stuk, vertoonende de Begraving van Christus door Joseph van Arimathea en Nicodemus, met het gezigt van de Grafkelder en de daarby staande Vrouwen en Discipelen, zeer uitvoerig en krachtig geschilderd in de manier van P.P. Rubens, door v. Bergh, in vergulde Lyst | *Mat:* op paneel *Size:* hoog 20 duim x breed 26 duim		(Unknown)

Bergen, Dirk van

1801/04/08	HAVIN	0031	*D. van den Berge* | Een Landschap met Beesten		(Unknown)
1801/05/11	AMSCH	0012	*D^k van Bergen* | Een grazige wyde, met geboomten en bevallige stoffagie, van Koeijen en Schapen, fraay van coloriet en delicaat behandeld | *Mat:* op paneel *Size:* hoog 11, breed 12 ½ duim	P[ruyssenaar]	(Sold) fl 100 Isak Smit
1801/10/06	AMSCH	0007	*D. van Bergen* | Een Heuvelagtig Landschap, op de voorgrond twee staande en een rustende Koe, benevens Schaapen en Varkens; voor een Stal, schynt een Vrouw beezig een Geit te melken, bevallig en uitvoerig geschilderd | *Mat:* op doek *Size:* hoog 15 ½, breed 18 ½ duim	M	(Sold) fl 101 Coclers
1801/10/19	AMSCH	0010	*Bergen. (D. van)* | Een fraay Landschap met Ossen, Paarden, Schapen en Bokken; verder een Herder en Herderin by een Ruïne, uitvoerig gepenceeld | *Mat:* op paneel *Size:* hoog 12 ¼, breed 14 ½ duim	Jonkheer Menno Baron van Coehoorn	(Sold) fl 130 Pruijssenaar R [for] Reynders
1802/07/20	MGSAN	0044	*D. v. d. Berge* | Een dito [fraai] dito [Stukje], mer dito [Beestjes] | *Mat:* op paneel *Size:* hoog duim 14 ½, breed duim 13		(Unknown)
1804/10/16	DLOND	0018	*Dirk van Bergen* | Een zeer schoon Landschap, waar in, op den voorgrond, eenige Koeien en Schapen. Ter rechterzyde een Stal onder een Rietendak, waarin een Paard. De Herder zit agter de Koeien op enen Heuvel. Paysage très-beau avec des figures. Sur le devant se voient quelques Vaches & des Moutons qui paissent; à la droite est une écurie sous un toict de chaume, dans laquelle on voit un Cheval gris. Le Berger est assis derrière les Vaches sur une Colline | *Mat:* op doek *Size:* hoog 18, breed 20		(Sold) fl 400 O D Wyngaerts
1804/10/16	DLOND	0019	*Dirk van Bergen* | Een Landschap met Koeien. Paysage & des Vaches | *Mat:* op paneel *Size:* hoog 9, breed 12		(Unknown)
1804/10/16	DLOND	0020	*Dirk van Bergen* | Uts^a [Een Landschap met Koeien. Paysage & des Vaches]		(Unknown)

1806/05/05	AMSCH	0016	*D. van Bergen* | In een boomryk Landschap op een grazige Vlakten vertoond zig een Landman, met een Hond, en een Vrouw die een Koe melkt; ter zyden staand en leggend Vee; uitvoerig en bevallig gepenceeld door D. van Bergen | *Mat:* op doek *Size:* hoog 13, breed 16 duim	V[inkeles]	(Bought In) fl 15:10
1806/08/13	AMSCH	0239	*D. van Bergen* | Een Boomryk Landschap, met Beelden en Beesten	Vinkeles [for] G[ruyter]	(Sold) fl 3:10 Gruyter
1806/08/20	HGBSM	0040	*D. van Bergen* | Een Landschap, met een roode en blaauw bonte Koei, en Schaap met twee Lammetjes; op de tweede grond, een Herder met een Ezel en ander Vee. In de manier van van de Velde | *Mat:* op doek *Size:* hoog 14, breed 18 duim	Macalester Loup [or others]	(Sold) fl 84 Nieuwenhuys
1808/06/13	AMSCH	0014	*Bergen (D. van)* | In een boomryk Landschap, ziet men eenige staande en rustende Beesten, Schapen, een Bok en een Paard, waarby eene rustende en eene staande Vrouw; zacht en teder als A. van de Velde behandeld | *Mat:* op doek *Size:* hoog 14, breed 18 duim	R[oos]	(Sold) fl 200 Van den Bergen van Gent
1808/08/23	AMSCH	0209	*D. van Bergen* | Een aangenaam Hollands Landschap, met opgaand Geboomte en staand en rustend Vee	[Gruyter?]	(Sold) fl 2:5 Spaan
1809/04/17	AMSCH	0006	*D. van Bergen* | In een aangenaam Landschap, zit op een grasige vlakte, onder de Schaduwe van een Boom eene Boerin bezig een Koe te Melken, nevens haar een rustend Landman bij eenige Beesten, verder op een hoogte verscheide grasende Schapen | *Mat:* op paneel *Size:* hoog 12, breed 16 duim	C	(Sold) fl 19
1809/04/17	AMSCH	0156	*D. van Bergen* | Een Boomrijk Landschap, met staand en liggend Vee | *Mat:* op doek	[Gruyter?]	(Sold or Bought In) fl 2 Gruyter
1809/04/22	AMYVR	0188	*D. van Bergen* | Een Landschap met verscheiden Vee	de Bruin	(Sold) fl 3:15 du Pree
1809/07/25	HGBSM	0146	*D. v. Bergen* | Een Landschap met Koebeesten, Paarden en Schaapen, en een Herder en Herderin | *Mat:* op doek *Size:* hoog 20 en een half, breed 17 en een half duim	D van der Aa [or] E B ten Dall	(Sold) fl 8 Vermeulen
1810/03/23	HAVIN	0004	*D. van den Bergen* | Aan een water zit een Vrouw bij een witte Os en een Kalf, waar agter een Man met een Ezel, en een Kar met twee Ossen en een Man te paard. Op de voorgrond eenige Schapen en een Bok, uitmuntend fraai in de manier van A. v. d. Velde door D. van den Bergen | *Size:* hoog 24 breet 29 d.	Rudolf Hendrik de Wetstein [or others]	(Unknown) fl 178
1810/03/27	RMCNL	0011	*van Bergen* | Een fraai Bergachtig Landschap met Koeijen, Schapen en verder gedierte, uitmuntend behandeld		(Unknown)
1810/05/22	AMSCH	0011	*Bergen. (D. van)* | In een Boomrijk Landschap, ziet men twee rosbonte Koeijen en eenige Schapen; zijnde zonachtig behandeld en uitvoerig gepenceeld | *Mat:* op doek *Size:* hoog 10, breed 12 duim	Johannes van de Putte Nicolaasz.	(Sold) fl 137 Hulswit
1810/05/22	AMSCH	0012	*Bergen. (D. van)* | Een Landschapje met een Herder bij Koeijen en Schapen; krachtig geschilderd | *Mat:* op paneel *Size:* hoog 5, breed 6 ½ duim	Johannes van de Putte Nicolaasz.	(Sold) fl 12 Gruyter
1810/06/20	AMSCH	0005	*D. Van Bergen* | In een aangenaam Landschap zit op een grazige Vlakte, onder de schaduwe van een Boom, eene Boerin, bezig eene Koe te melken; nevens haar een Landman bij eenige Beesten. Bevallig | *Mat:* op paneel *Size:* hoog 12, breed 16 duimen	B	(Bought In) fl 12
1810/07/26	AMSCH	0006	*Bergen (D. van)* | Een Landschap, met Geboomte, staande en liggende Koeien en Schapen. Als A. van de Velde | *Mat:* op doek *Size:* hoog 12, breed 18 duimen	Cassino	(Sold) fl 8:10 de Vries

Bergen, Dirk van (and Koninck, P.)

1808/06/06	RMRIJ	0066	*Koning. (Philip de); Bergen. (Dirk van)* | Deze schoone en krachtige Schilderij vertoont op den voorgrond den ingang van een Bosch, waarin zich voordoet een Ossendrift, Veehoeder, Jonge en Hond, het Bosch uitkomende. De tweede grond verbeeldt eene Rivier met een uitgestrekt rijk en vlak verschiet. Meesterlijk behandeld [On découvre d'abord l'Entrée d'une belle forêt bien garnie d'arbres touffus, d'où sort un troupeau de Boeufs, conduit par un Pâtre, un Garçon, et un Chien. Le second plan offre une belle Rivière et un lointain d'une immense Etendue. Ce Tableau vrai, savant et hardi fait honneur aux Artistes qui l'ont composé] | *Mat:* op doek *Size:* Hoog 52, en breed 63 duim. *Loc:* Amsterdam, Nederland. Rijksmuseum. (A207) as P. Koninck	Gerrit van der Pot, Heer van Groeneveld	(Sold) fl 310 Johs Eck en Zoon [for] le Roi

Bergen, Dirk van (and Wyck, T.)

1802/09/21	UTHDG	0009	*Th. Wijk; Th. van Bergen* | Een Voerman laat de hoef van zijn paard voorzien, dit geschied bij een Herberg, uit welke de vrouw langs een steene trap, met een kan in de hand nederklimt, verder een Valkenier, komende door een poort: op de voorgrond Schapen, Ploeg en Planten, zeer zonägtig en fiks behandeld | *Mat:* op paneel *Size:* hoog 20, breed 15 ½ duimen		(Sold) fl 80 Cobell

Bergen, Dirk van (copy after)

1804/10/16	DLOND	0280	*Naar Dirk van Bergen* | Een Landschap met Koeien en Schapen. Paysage avec des Vaches & Moutons | *Mat:* op paneel *Size:* hoog 13, breed 11		(Unknown)

Bergen, Dirk van (manner)

1810/10/11	AMSCH	0226	*D. van Bergen* | Een Landschap met Herders en Vee; als D. van Bergen | *Notes:* This lot was sold with lot 212 by an anonymous artist.	A	(Sold) fl 0:6 for lots 212 & 226. T Spaan

			Bergen, Dirk van (manner; and Moucheron, F., manner)		
1809/04/22	AMYVR	0178	*F. de Moucheron; D. van Bergen* | Een Landschap met Boerenwooningen en stoffagie van Beelden en Beesten, als door F. de Moucheron en D. van Bergen	de Bruin	(Sold) fl 2:5 du Pree
			Bergh, R.V. [Unidentified]		
1810/06/20	AMSCH	0010	*R. V. Bergh* | Twee stuks; Steenen Tafels, waarop Flessen met geurige Bloemen. Zacht en teder gepenceeld | *Mat:* op doek *Size:* ieder hoog 19, breed 16 duimen	A	(Sold) fl 1:5 Eversdijk
			Berghe, Christoffel van den		
1810/10/10	MGCIT	0143	*Berg* | Een Stil Leven, waarop een menigte van Voorwerpen van allerhanden aart; kunstig op paneel gebragt | *Mat:* op paneel	Caspar van Citters	(Unknown)
			Berkenkamp		
1803/08/01	AMSCH	0054	*Berkenkamp* | 't Portrait van J. Reynolds en twee anderen	Ij[ver]	(Sold) fl 1:5 Gruiter
			Berninck, H.		
1801/02/18	AMBOS	0050	*J. Bernink* | Een Ordonnantie van Vrugten, verbeeldende een Persik met blaauwe Druiven, zeer natuurlyk en fraay geschilderd	J Schonevelt	(Unknown)
1801/02/18	AMBOS	0051	*Bernink* | Twee stuks, een met een Vaas met Bloemen en een met Vrugten in een Nis, uitvoerig geschilderd	J Schonevelt	(Unknown)
1802/05/05	AMSCH	0023	*J. Bernink* | Een steene Vaas, staande op een Tafel, gevuld met verscheide fraaije geschakeerde Bloemen, op de rand van de Tafel legt een Vogelnestje; zeer natuurlyk en fraai geschilderd | *Mat:* op doek *Size:* hoog 14, breed 15 duim	C	(Sold) fl 8 Gruiter
1802/12/13	AMSCH	0024	*J. Bernink* | In een fraay Steene Vaas, staande op een Marmeren Tafel, ziet men een ménigten van Welgeschakeerde Bloemen, op de rand van de Tafel een nesje met Eijeren, zeer natuurlyk en fraay geschilderd | *Mat:* op doek *Size:* hoog 19, breed 15 duim	Pruyssenaar [for] A	(Sold) fl 9:15 v d Schley [for] R[ijfsnijder]
1807/08/26	AMSCH	0024	*H. Bernink* | Op een Marmeren Tafel ziet men een tros witte en blaauwe Druiven leggen, benevens Persiken en andere Vrugten, als mede een roode Roos; alleruitvoerigst gepenceeld | *Mat:* op doek *Size:* hoog 15, breed 12 duim	Roos	(Sold) fl 9:15 Jozi
			Besanger, Simon		
1801/06/23	HGBAK	0109	*S. Besanger* | Een Schildery verbeelden een Polak [Schilderyen in Olyverf] | *Mat:* in olyverf *Notes:* The bracketed information in the title appears above lot 1 and refers to lots 1 to 163.	T Tamé [or others]	(Unknown)
1801/06/23	HGBAK	0110	*S. Besanger* | Een dito [Schildery] verbeelden een Ram [Schilderyen in Olyverf] | *Mat:* in olyverf *Notes:* The bracketed information in the title appears above lot 1 and refers to lots 1 to 163.	T Tamé [or others]	(Unknown)
1801/06/23	HGBAK	0111	*S. Besanger* | Een dito [Schildery] verbeelden een Grysaart [Schilderyen in Olyverf] | *Mat:* in olyverf *Notes:* The bracketed information in the title about the medium appears above lot 1 and refers to lots 1 to 163.	T Tamé [or others]	(Unknown)
1801/06/23	HGBAK	0112	*S. Besanger* | Een dito [Schildery] verbeelden een Spanjaart [Schilderyen in Olyverf] | *Mat:* in olyverf *Notes:* The bracketed information in the title about the medium appears above lot 1 and refers to lots 1 to 163.	T Tamé [or others]	(Unknown)
1801/06/23	HGBAK	0113	*S. Besanger* | Twee kleine dito [Schilderyen] [Schilderyen in Olyverf] | *Mat:* in olyverf *Notes:* The bracketed information in the title about the medium appears above lot 1 and refers to lots 1 to 163.	T Tamé [or others]	(Unknown)
1801/06/23	HGBAK	0114	*S. Besanger* | Vier defecte stukken [Schilderyen in Olyverf] | *Mat:* in olyverf *Notes:* The bracketed information in the title appears above lot 1 and refers to lots 1 to 163.	T Tamé [or others]	(Unknown)
1802/09/29	AMSCH	0008	*S. Besanger* | Hoog 14, breed 11 duim. Paneel. Dit fraaije Stukje verbeeld een oude Vrouw, die door een Nis, met een geele aarde Kan een Pot met Bloemen begiet, en na iets met aandagt is omziende; de Nis is met een Wyngaardsrank en Bladeren gecierd, en verders eenig bywerk; men ziet door de Nis in een Keukenvertrek. Dit Stukje heeft veel verdiensten, en benevens het volgende zynde een wederga; de beste werken van dezen Konstenaar, vroegtydig overleden [La mort enleva cet artiste à la fleur de son âge il donna deja très jeune des marques d'un génie superieur ; – Ce Tableau et le suivant sont des morceaux de sa composition, en prenant la nature pour modéle : il donna tous ses soins a les exécuter ce sont les meilleurs qui soient connus de lui : – on voit dans l'Embrasure d'une niche ornée d'une vigne. Une vielle [sic] inquiéte qui arrose un pôt de fleurs cette Peinture est fine et délicate et à bien du mérite.] | companion to lot 9 *Mat:* op paneel *Size:* hoog 14, breed 11 duim *Notes:* The information given in the French text of the title concerns lots 8 and 9.	[Labouchere?]	(Sold) fl 138 J Spaan
1802/09/29	AMSCH	0009	*S. Besanger* | Hoog 14, breed 11 duim. Paneel. Het voorwerp van dit Schilderytje is een bejaard Man, leunende op de rand van een Nis, en rokende met smaak een pyp Tabak, hy is in aandagtige beschouwingen; voor de Nis ziet men een Pot met Bloemen, en boven dezelve een Wyngaardsrank en bladeren, benevens een Vogel-kooitje. Eenig ander toepasselyk bywerk verreiken deeze fraaije Ordenantie; alles is met de grootste uitvoerigheid delicaat, gelyk het voorgaande, en zonägtig	[Labouchere?]	(Sold) fl 58 L Pakker

			behandelt [Ce Tableau et le precédent donnent de l'embarras dans le choix, celui-ci offre le sujet d'un homme sur l'age d'un caractére satisfait, qui fûme sa pipe dans l'Embrasure d'une niche ornée d'une vigne et d'une cage d'oiseau. Il à prés de lui un pôt de fleurs, et d'autres accessoires ornent cette aimable composition qui sera toujours regretter les Talens de l'artiste. [Ce Tableau et le suivant sont des morceaux de sa composition, en prenant la nature pour modéle : il donna tous ses soins a les exécuter ce sont les meilleurs qui soient connus de lui]] | companion to lot 8 *Mat:* op paneel *Size:* hoog 14, breed 11 duim *Notes:* The bracketed information within the French text of the title appears in lot 8 and concerns lots 8 and 9.		
1802/09/29	AMSCH	0010	*S. Besanger* | Een Pourtrait. Hoog 7 ¼, breed 6 duim. Paneel. Zynde het Afbeeldzel van deezen Konstenaar Dertien jaaren oud, fraai en bevallig gepenceeld [Le Portrait de ce Peintre agé de treize ans faisant la grimace, traité d'un Pinceau agréable.] | *Mat:* op paneel *Size:* hoog 7 ¼, breed 6 duim	[Labouchere?]	(Sold) fl 5 V^n Dijl
1809/07/25	HGBSM	0037	*Simon Besanger* | Twee uitvoerige Cabinet-Stukjes, het eene steld voor een Scheevelinger uit zyn vengster leggende zyn pypje rookende, voor het vengster staat een Bank waar op een Pot met een een [sic] Bloemeplant, Mes en verder bywerk, de muur gesiert met een Wyngaartrank waar aan een Net hangt, dit alies [sic] uitmuntend geschildert. Het andere verbeeld een Scheevelings-Vrouwtje met een Mand, door een Doek gedekt, voor het vengster is wederom een Bank met een omgekeerde Kan en de Muur gesiert als de voorgaande, beide natuurlyk en fraay van Couleur | *Mat:* op paneel *Size:* hoog 12 ½, breed 10 duim	D van der Aa	(Sold) fl 200 Ponse [or] Stees

Beschey

1801/12/22	AMOTT	0034	*Beschay* | Het Historieel van Philemon en Bauses [sic], in een Binnenvertrek, zeer uitvoerig	Bartholomeus Ruloffs	(Unknown) fl 20:10
1803/06/20	AMSCH	0037	*Beschay* | Twee stuks, en eene verbeeld de Aanbidding der Koningen aan het Kind Jesus, op de schoot van den H. Maagd, de andere steld voor, Maria door haar Ouders, aan den Hogenpriester in den Tempel aangeboden; beide meesterlyk op Koper | *Mat:* op koper *Size:* hoog 30, breed 23 duim	Schley [for] G	(Sold) fl 91 Gruiter

Beschey (copy by)

1810/06/06	RMMUY	0092	*Bescheij; A. van Dijk* | Eene uitvoerige Copij. Door Bescheij, naar het altaar stuk van A. van Dijk, verbeeldende de Gekruiste Christus tusschen de Moordenaren, waar bij Maria, Johannes, en Maria Magdalena | copy by Beschey after Anth. van Dyck *Mat:* op paneel		(Unknown) fl 43

Beschey (or Beschey, manner)

1803/06/20	AMSCH	0020	*Beschay* | Christus aan het Kruis, waarby Johannes, Maria en eenige andere Vrouwen, in weenende gestalten; fix op Doek, door of in de manier van Beschay | *Mat:* op doek *Size:* hoog 35, breed 30 duim	Schley [for] G	(Bought In) fl 3
1803/06/20	AMSCH	0021	*Beschay* | Abraham vergast drie Engelen, zynde een ryke Ordenantie, behandeld als de voorgaande, door denzelven [of in de manier van Beschay] | *Mat:* op paneel *Size:* hoog 26, breed 45 duim	Schley [for] G	(Sold) fl 6:15 V d Schleij [for] R[ijfsnijder]

Beschey (manner)

1805/07/03	AMSCH	0201	*Beschay* | Twee stuks, de Trouw van Maria, en de Aanbidding van het Kindeken door de Koningen; kragtig geschilderd, in de manier van Beschay | *Mat:* op doek	R[oos]	(Sold) fl 30 Zurmuklen

Beschey, Balthasar

1802/09/18	RMDRS	0027	*Beschey* | Een zeer uitvoerig stukje, verbeeldende Christus aan het Kruis, tusschen de Moordenaaren, beneden aan hetzelve, zyne Moeder en Joannes &c. | *Size:* hoog 15, breed 12 duim	Casper de Haas	(Sold) fl 64 Frets
1803/09/07	AMSCH	0017	*B. Beschay* | Twee stuks Bybelsche Historiën, zynde het eene Pharao in de roode zee verdrinkende, en het andere de Aanbidding van het Gulden Kalf, ryk van ordenantie, bevallig van coloriet, delicaat en uitvoerig gepenceeld [Deux sujets tirés de la bible : l'un représente Pharaon périssant dans la mer rouge, l'autre l'idolatrie du veau d'or ; l'ordonnance en est riche, le coloris brillant, délicat et d'un bel effet dans tous ses détails] | *Mat:* op paneel *Size:* ieder hoog 16, breed 21 duim	Smidt	(Bought In) fl 181
1808/11/28	AMSCH	0008	*B. Bescheij* | Deeze Ordonantie verbeeld Christus aan Tafel, met de Discipelen van Emaus, het brood brekende en zegenende, agterwaards komt een Bediende de Trap af, kragtig en meesterlijk uitgevoerd | *Mat:* op doek *Size:* hoog 28, breed 21 duim	S	(Sold) fl 39:10 Smit
1809/04/17	AMSCH	0015	*B. Bescheij* | Een Bijbel-Ordonantie, voorstellende David met het Hoofd van Goliath, waar bij verscheide Vrouwen; meesterlijk uitgevoerd | *Mat:* op koper *Size:* hoog 17, breed 22 duim	[Gruyter?]	(Sold or Bought In) fl 2:15 Gruyter
1809/09/06	AMSCH	0010	*Bescheij (B.)* | Deze Ordinantie vertoond in een Landschap bij een Rots, den doode Christus, door zijne Dicipelen en andere Godvrugtige Lieden in een Linnen Kleed naar het Graf gebragt, waar bij verscheide weenenden Lieden; het is bevallig van koloriet en van een uitvoerige penceelbehandeling | *Mat:* op paneel *Size:* hoog 15, breed 12 duim	Johannes Caudri	(Sold) fl 23 Tomassen
1810/05/22	AMSCH	0136	*B. Bescheij* | Eene Binnenkamer met eene jonge Dame, Dienstmaagd en Kind	Johannes van de Putte Nicolaasz.	(Sold) fl 2:5 T Spaan

Beschey, Balthasar (copy by)

1805/10/09	HGBSM	0129	*Beschaey; Rubbens* | Christus aan het kruis tusschen de moordenaars, naar het groote schildery van Rubbens | copy by B. Beschey after Rubens *Mat:* op koper *Size:* hoog 9 ½ breet 7 duim	T H van Willigen [or others]	(Sold) fl 50 De Gelder, R

Beschey, Charles

1802/07/27	AKHRK	0055	*C. Bescheij* | Een Brabandsch Dorpgezicht: men is hier bezig om den Meijboom te dansen, op het geluit van den Liereman, met menigte van Beelden en Rijtuigen, de Figuuren zeer netjes geschilderd | *Mat:* op paneel *Size:* hoog 11 ½, breed 15 ½ duim	Maria Stategaart	(Sold) fl 9 for lots 55 & 56. Stroo
1802/07/27	AKHRK	0056	*C. Bescheij* | Een uitgestrekt Dorp- en Watergezicht, met Sneeuw en IJs, bedekt met Schaatsrijders, Voetgangers en Wagens, als boven	Maria Stategaart	(Sold) fl 9 for lots 55 & 56. Stroo

Beschey, J.

1801/06/10	AMSCH	0032	*Beschaay. (I.)* | Een Nimph door een Sater vervolgd wordendende [sic]; uitvoerig van penceel | *Mat:* op paneel *Size:* hoog 11, breed 9 duim *Notes:* This lot was misnumbered no. 3.	Herman ten Kate	(Sold) fl 5 Stevens
1801/06/10	AMSCH	0033	*Beschaay. (I.)* | Twee stuks Bybelsche Ordonnantien, zynde het eene, waar Christus de Sleutels aan Petrus geeft, en het andere, waar Christus door Maria en Johannes beweend wotd [sic]; fraai van Hartstogten en Schildering | *Mat:* op doek *Size:* yder hoog 29, breed 23 duim	[Doublet]	(Sold) fl 20 Reynders
1802/06/28	AMSCH	0019	*J. Beschay* | Elias door de Raven gevoed wordende; zeer natuurlyk door J. Beschay, Panneel | *Mat:* op paneel *Size:* hoog 24, breed 19 duim	Anna Elink	(Sold) fl 16:10 Reyers
1802/06/28	AMSCH	0020	*J. Beschay* | Een Historieëele [sic] Ordonnantie, ryk van Beelden en kragtig gepenceeld gepenceeld door Denzelven [J. Beschay], op Doek | *Mat:* op doek *Size:* hoog 35, breed 43 duim	Anna Elink	(Sold) fl 8 van Iperen
1802/06/28	AMSCH	0021	*J. Beschay* | Een Bybelsche Ordonnantie, verbeeldende de Boodschap aan Marie; meesterlyk gepenceeld door Denzelven [J. Beschay], Panneel | *Mat:* op paneel *Size:* hoog 15, breed 12 duim	Anna Elink	(Sold) fl 5:5 Jan Spaan
1803/04/20	AMSCH	0005	*Beschay. (J.)* | Christus aan zyne Dicipelen het laatste Avondmaal uitdeelende, den Heiland zit met het Brood in zyne handen, en met de oogen hemelwaards als tot zynen Vader spreekende, terwyl de Dicipelen, behalven Judas in een verrukkende houding zich vertonen; zynde in allen deele als de vooraande behandeld [Pour pendant l'artiste a pris le sujet de la derniere Cene, au moment que J.C. rompt le pain ; les caracteres des Apôtres, la couleur, & l'effet y sont très bien rendus de même que dans le morceau précedent.] | companion to lot 4, copy by J. Beschey after Rubens *Size:* hoog 23, breed 19 duim	Maria Magdalena van Sluypwyk, gravinne van Moens	(Sold) fl 30 B^{d} Kooij
1803/04/20	AMSCH	0006	*Beschay. (J.)* | Maria met het Kind Jesu op haar Schoot, zittende in een Landschap; delicaat en bevallig gepenceeld [La Vierge Marie tenant l'enfant Jesus sur son giron est assise dans un paysage agréable ; ce petit morceau est touché & collorié avec art.] | *Mat:* op koper *Size:* hoog 7, breed 5 duim	Maria Magdalena van Sluypwyk, gravinne van Moens	(Sold) fl 4:15 Lesscher
1803/09/07	AMSCH	0018	*J. Beschay* | St. Catharina, gekroond wordende door het Kind Jesus, op de Schoot der H. Maagd zittende; nog twee Vrouwen en eenige Ceraphynen, alles delicaat [Ste.-Catherine, couronnée par l'enfant Jésus assis sur les genoux de la Ste.-Vierge, deux femmes et plusieurs séraphins remplissent ce tableau, dont l'ensemble est d'une exécution délicate] | *Mat:* op paneel *Size:* hoog 18, breed 15 duim	Smidt	(Sold) fl 126 for lots 18 & 19. Rijnders
1803/09/07	AMSCH	0019	*J. Beschay* | De oprichting van Christus aan het Kruis, door de Beulen, waarby eenige Krygsknegten te Paard, in alles als de voorgaande behandeld [L'élèvation de Jésus-Christ à la croix, par ses bourreaux ; on y voit quelques gens de guerre à cheval. L'exécution est semblable au tableau précédent.] | *Size:* hoog 17, breed 13 duim	Smidt	(Sold) fl 126 for lots 18 & 19. Rijnders
1803/09/07	AMSCH	0020	*J. Beschay* | De doode Christus, verzeld van Joseph van Arimathéa, beneevens St. Jan en de Heilige Vrouwen; zeer fraay en delicaat gepenceeld, door denzelven [J. Beschay], in de manier van de Ridder van der Werf [Un Christ mort, auprès duquel Joseph d'Arimathée, St-Jean et la Ste.-Vierge ; d'une exécution très agréable et d'une touche délicate, dans la manière du chevalier Van der Werft] | *Mat:* op doek *Size:* hoog 25, breed 21 duim	Smidt	(Sold) fl 23 C S Roos
1807/08/26	AMSCH	0025	*J. Beschay* | In een Landschap met Geboomten, onder het lommer derzelve zit Maria, houdende het kindeken slaapende op de schoot, en rustende tegen haar borst; ter zyde staat St. Joseph, het als met aandagt beschouwende; bevallig op Paneel geschilderd | *Mat:* op paneel *Size:* hoog 12, breed 10 duim	v d Schley [for] L	(Sold) fl 15 v d Schley [for] Ryfsnyder
1810/08/10	RMRIJ	0012	*J. Bescheij* | Een Filosoof, een Pen versnijdende, gezeten aan eene Tafel waar op boeken en verder bijwerk. Uitvoerig en van eene aangename couleur | *Mat:* op paneel *Size:* hoog 11 ½ duim, breed 9 duim		(Sold) fl 6 [or] 17 v d Bosch

Beschey, J. (copy by)

1803/04/20	AMSCH	0004	*Beschay. (J.); Rubens* | Christus aan het Volk vertoond wordende, staat op een Bordes met den purperen mantel omhangen, ter zyde ziet men Pilatus, benevens eenige krygsknegten en een der moordenaren, op de voorgrond een menigte Jooden: als roepende Kruist hem; de hartstogten zyn zeer wel waargenomen, en is voorts van een meesterlyke behandeling [Le	Maria Magdalena van Sluypwyk, gravinne van Moens	(Sold) fl 31 Theijs

			sujet de ce tableau est J.C. exposé sur le perron du Juge Pilate devant une multitude de Juifs & de Romains : c'est une bonne imitation d'après Rubens dont la belle estempe [sic] par Bolswert est assez connue.] | copy by J. Beschey after Rubens; companion to lot 5, by J. Beschey *Mat:* op doek *Size:* hoog 23, breed 19 duim		
			Bestens, C. [Unidentified]		
1808/10/28	AMVRS	0003	*Bestens. (C.)* | Twee stuks bevallige Land- en Watergezichten met Boerewooningen en Hooi-bergen, gestoffeerd met gaande en rustende Reizigers, en in 't verschiet een Dorpgezicht. Uitvoerig van Penceel | *Mat:* op paneel *Size:* hoog 10, breed 13 duim	Marten Udink	(Sold) fl 34:10 M Kooij
			Besters, Albertus Johannes		
1802/06/16	AMSCH	0027	*A. J. Bester* | Een Natuurlyk Landgezicht, met een Boere Woning en Geboomten, op de voorgrond een stil Water, waarin twee Ossen waden; verder een rustend Huisman en staande Vrouw met een Kind: zonachtig en fiks gepenceeld | *Mat:* op paneel *Size:* hoog 9, breed 12 ½ duim	[Merrem]	(Sold) fl 6:10 Gruiter
1805/07/10	AMSCH	0022	*Bestér* | Een Boomryk Landschapje, met Beeldjes, Beesjes en Woningen; uitvoerig op Paneel | *Mat:* op paneel	V[inkeles] [for] H[affner]	(Sold) fl 3:15 Boelen
1809/07/25	HGBSM	0040	*A.J. Besters* | Een Winter met Schaatseryders en andere Figuren, de eene zyde is een weg met een brug, waar een Kar over reid, voor aan legt een Schuit met eenige Figuren, natuurlyk geschildert | *Mat:* op paneel *Size:* hoog 17, breed 22 en een half duim	D van der Aa	(Sold) fl 28 Ponse [or] van der Burg
1809/07/25	HGBSM	0041	*A.J. Besters* | Voor een Boerewoning staat een Herder met een troep Schaapen, zyn Pyp aansteekende, het verschiet is een uitgestrekt Landschap, op een weg een Hooywagen, ryk van ordonnantie, door denzelven [A.J. Besters], op Paneel, hoog en breed als de voorgaande, kunnende dienen tot een weerga | *Mat:* op paneel *Size:* hoog 17, breed 22 en een half duim	D van der Aa	(Sold) fl 28 Ponse [or] Stees
1809/07/25	HGBSM	0042	*A.J. Besters* | Een Boomryk Duinachtig Landschap, gestoffeert met Figuren en een Mannetje te Paard | *Mat:* op paneel *Size:* hoog 14, breed 13 duim	D van der Aa	(Sold) fl 15 Ponse
1809/07/25	HGBSM	0043	*A.J. Besters* | Een Land- en Water-Gezigt, met een Molen in het verschiet, en gestoffeerd met Figuren en een Schuit &c. | *Mat:* op paneel *Size:* hoog 13 en een half, breed 12 duim	D van der Aa	(Sold) fl 20 Ponse
1809/07/25	HGBSM	0044	*A.J. Besters* | Een Landschap, waarin een Herder met Schapen, en in het verschiet een Boerewoning aan 't water | *Mat:* op paneel *Size:* hoog 12, breed 10 en een halve duim	D van der Aa	(Sold) fl 23 van Ijperen
1809/07/25	HGBSM	0045	*A.J. Besters* | Een Landschap, zynde een storm met een betrokken lugt, op de voorgrond een Man te paard en meer Figuren | *Mat:* op paneel *Size:* hoog 17, breed 19 duim	D van der Aa	(Sold) fl 25 Ponse [or] Stees
1809/07/25	HGBSM	0046	*A.J. Besters* | Een Gezigt van een Boerewoning, op de voorgrond eenige Koeyen en een Boerinnetje met een Emmer aan de hand, schynende te gaan melken, in 't verschiet een Dorps-Kerk &c., ryk van ordonnantie | *Mat:* op paneel *Size:* hoog 16 en een half, breed 22 duim	D van der Aa	(Sold) fl 76 Ponse [or] Stees
1809/07/25	HGBSM	0047	*A.J. Besters* | Een Boomryk Duinachtig Landschap, op de voorgrond staat een Boerewoning, de weg gestoffeert met een paar Figuren, zynde Vogelvangers, een Hond en verder stoffage; de Lugt, Boomen en verder bywerk is Zonachtig en uitmuntend Geschildert | *Mat:* op paneel *Size:* hoog 17 en een half, breed 16 en een half duim	D van der Aa	(Sold) fl 115 Ponse [or] de Zwart
1810/03/27	RMCNL	0032	*Besters* | Een dito Landschapje, fraai gepenceeld | *Notes:* It is unclear what "dito" refers to in the title.		(Unknown)
1810/03/27	RMCNL	0079	*J. A. Besters* | Een Landschapje met een Koeijendrift, zeer aardig behandeld, warm van coloriet		(Unknown)
			Besters, C. [Unidentified]		
1810/05/22	AMSCH	0016	*Besters (C.)* | Een stil Water langs een Weg, gestoffeerd met Hengelaars en andere Beeldjes; bevallig gepenceeld | *Mat:* op paneel *Size:* hoog 8, breed 9 duim	R	(Sold) fl 5:5 Topher
			Beurs, Willem		
1806/05/05	AMSCH	0028	*Beurs* | Een Landschap met onderscheiden Riviervis en Viswand gestoffeerd; meesterlyk geschilderd door Beurs | *Mat:* op doek *Size:* hoog 26, breed 33 duim	O [or] V[inkeles]	(Sold) fl 1 van Laar
			Beyeren, Abraham Hendricksz. van		
1804/02/27	AMSCH	0015	*Beyeren. (A. van)* | Een Vischbank, ryk voorzien met een meenigte differenten zoorten van Visch, agter dezelve een Mand met gesneden Schelvisch, Kopere Schaalen en verder Bywerk; meesterlyk geschilderd | *Mat:* op doek *Size:* hoog 42, breed 49 duim	B	(Sold) fl 5:10 Coclers
1804/02/27	AMSCH	0016	*Beyeren. (A. van)* | Een Tafel met onderscheiden zoorten van Zeevis, agter dezelve een Ben met dito, en verder Bywerk | *Mat:* op doek *Size:* hoog 45, breed 68 duim	B	(Sold) fl 0:6 L Pakker
1808/06/06	RMRIJ	0015	*Beijeren (J).* | Eene Tafel, waarop eene Visben met Schelvisschen en eene moot Zalm; wijders Platvisschen, Mosselen en verder bijwerk. Dit stuk is schoon en krachtig geschilderd [Differents Poissons de mer arrangés avec	Gerrit van der Pot, Heer van Groeneveld	(Sold) fl 25 Stratenus, A.A.

			art dans un panier et d'autres accessoires, le tout posé sur une table et naturellement imité forme un ensemble parfait dans ce genre] | *Annots:* Pour le Musée d'Amsterdam (NGW) *Mat:* op doek *Size:* Hoog 27 ½, en breed 32 duim *Notes:* The artist's name was given as "Beijeren (J)." but we have assumed this is an error. *Loc:* Amsterdam, Nederland. Rijksmuseum. (A25)		
1808/06/11	RMRIJ	0041	*Jan van Beieren* | Eenige Zeevis en verder bywerk, meesterlyk en schoon geschilderd | *Mat:* op doek *Notes:* The artist's name was given as "Jan van Beieren" but we have assumed this is an error.		(Sold) fl 11:10 Koning
1808/08/23	AMSCH	0032	*Beijere (A. van)* | Op een houten bank ziet men verschillende zoorten van Zeevisch, als Cabeljauw, Schelvis, Bot, Zalm, enz.; natuurlijk geschilderd | *Mat:* op doek *Size:* hoog 42, breed 49 duim	[Coclers]	(Sold) fl 7 L Pakker
1810/06/06	RMMUY	0133	*van Beijeren* | Een stuk met Vrugten | *Mat:* op doek		(Unknown) fl 2
1810/06/06	RMMUY	0134	*van Beijeren* | Een dito [stuk] met verscheiden soorten van Visschen | *Mat:* op doek		(Unknown) fl 7:5
1810/06/06	RMMUY	0164	*A. van Beijeren* | Een Keuken stuk, fraaij en rijk van allerlei voorwerpen | *Mat:* op doek		(Unknown) fl 6:15
1810/06/20	AMSCH	0193	*van Beijeren* | Een groot stuk met verschillende Visschen	A	(Sold) fl 6 Boelhouwer
			Bierweiler		
1808/03/03	HAVIN	0039	*Bierweiler* | De Graflegging | *Notes:* This lot was sold with lot 38 by C.H. Hodges.	Jacobus Spillebout	(Unknown) fl 31 for lots 38 & 39
			Bijlert, Jan Hermansz. van		
1802/11/01	DOBRA	0076	*J. v. Bylert* | Een Zinnebeeldig stuk door J. v. Bylert; vertoonende de vergankelykheid des Leevens, en 's Waerelds ijdelheden | *Mat:* op doek *Size:* breed ruim 5, hoog ruim 4 voet	Paulus van der Spyk [or others]	(Sold) fl 2:5 Faessen
1803/04/20	AMSCH	0011	*Beylert. (J.)* | Deeze Ordenantie met leevensgroote Beelden tot aan de Knien; vertoont de Heilige Familietje: Maria zit met het Kindeken op de Schoot, voor deze staat St. Joseph, het met aandagt beschouwende; de Caracters zyn natuurlyk, de Teekening en het Coloriet bevallig, en van eene schoone meesterlyke penceelsbehandeling [La Vierge Marie ténant l'enfant Jesus & St. Joseph qui est au devant du tableau Composent ce morceau de merite, qui est traité de grandeur naturelle : la vierge est vue jusq'aux genoux. La delicatesse de la couleur, le choix des drapperies, & la maniere delicate de l'execution meritent l'attention des amateurs.] | *Mat:* op doek *Size:* hoog 48, breed 40 duim	Maria Magdalena van Sluypwyk, gravinne van Moens	(Sold) fl 112 Gruiter
			Bijlert, Jan Hermansz. van (manner)		
1810/06/06	RMMUY	0198	*van den Bylaart* | Een Mans en Vrouwen Pourtrait, twee stuks. Als door van den Bylaart | *Mat:* op paneel		(Unknown) fl 1:4
			Biltius		
1805/09/23	MGBEO	0001	*Van der Bilt* | Een Patrys, extra fraai gepenseeld, door van der Bilt, op Paneel, zwarte Lyst | *Mat:* op paneel		(Withdrawn)
1808/06/13	AMSCH	0245	*Billius* | Eene dooden Haas en drie doode Vinken, benevens een Hond, boven een hangende Trompet; fraai geschilderd	K	(Bought In) fl 21
			Bino, H. [Unidentified]		
1802/07/27	AKHRK	0061	*H. Bino* | Een Boeren Kermis, fraai geschilderd | *Mat:* op doek *Size:* hoog 41 ½, breed 31 ½ duim	Maria Stategaart	(Sold) fl 3:10 Zanegeest
			Biset, Charles Emmanuel		
1801/02/24	AMOTT	0005	*Biset* | 1 Heidensche Historie		(Unknown)
1804/08/08	AMSCH	0037	*Bisset* | In een prachtige Zaal ziet men een Masquerade Bal, vol gewoel van Beelden; geestig op Doek | *Mat:* op doek *Size:* hoog 24, breed 33 duim	Roos [for] C	(Sold) fl 51 Coclers
			Biset, Jean Andreas		
1805/10/09	HGBSM	0133	*J. Biset* | Een portret van een dame, staande voor een gebouw &c. | *Mat:* op doek *Size:* hoog 26 breet 19 ½ duim	T H van Willigen [or others]	(Sold) fl 1:4 Carré
			Bisraat [Unidentified]		
1801/12/22	AMOTT	0051[a]	*Bisraat* | 2 stuks oude Historieele Ordonnantien, door Bisraat, 1703 en 1704 | *This Lot:* 1 stuk oude Historieele Ordonnantie *Inscr:* Bisraat, 1703 (signed and dated?) *Notes:* It is unclear whether the name and date are inscribed on the painting.	Bartholomeus Ruloffs	(Unknown) fl 5:10 for lots 51[a] & 51[b]
1801/12/22	AMOTT	0051[b]	*Bisraat* | 2 stuks oude Historieele Ordonnantien, door Bisraat, 1703 en 1704 | *This Lot:* 1 stuk oude Historieele Ordonnantie *Inscr:* Bisraat, 1704 (signed and dated?) *Notes:* It is unclear whether the name and date are inscribed on the painting.	Bartholomeus Ruloffs	(Unknown) fl 5:10 for lots 51[a] & 51[b]
			Bisschop, Abraham		
1806/05/05	AMSCH	0009	*A. Busschop* | Een Menagerie met uitlandsche Vogelen, meesterlyk in de manier van Hondekoeter | *Mat:* op doek *Size:* hoog 43, breed 55 duim	R[oos]	(Sold) fl 1:5 Coclers

1806/05/05	AMSCH	0010	*A. Busschop* | Een dito [Menagerie] dito [met uitlandsche Vogelen], niet minder als de voorgaande | *Size:* hoog 49, breed 42 duim	R[oos]	(Sold) fl 1:10 Gruyter
1806/05/05	AMSCH	0011	*A. Busschop* | Een niet minder fraije dito [Menagerie] | *Size:* hoog 34, breed 46 duim *Notes:* It is unclear what "dito" refers to in the title.	R[oos]	(Sold) fl 1:5 Gruyter
1806/05/05	AMSCH	0012	*A. Busschop* | Een Vogelen Concert als de voorgaande | *Mat:* op doek *Size:* hoog 39, breed 46 duim	R[oos]	(Sold) fl 0:12 Driesseler
1810/07/23	DOLG2	000V	*A. de Bisschop* | Een levensgroote fraai gekleurde Haan, benevens eenige Hennen, bizonder krachtig geschilderd | *Mat:* op doek *Size:* hoog 30, breed 47 duim	Pieter Quinting	(Sold) fl 22 P de Heere Dordt
1810/10/10	MGCIT	0072	*A. Bisschop* | Een Capitaal Stuk, waarop verbeeld is een Zwaan, volgens deszelfs houding schijnende te komen uit het water, waarin een Gans ligt te flodderen; voorts vertoond zich op den grond een Taling, alsmede een Goudlakensche Phaisant; achter dit alles een Landschap met laag en hoog Geboomte, op welk laatste een fraaije blaauwe Raaf; alles schoon behandeld	Caspar van Citters	(Unknown)
1810/10/11	AMSCH	0165	*A. De Bisschop* | Een Hofgezigt, met Vogels, Vrugten en bijwerk | *Mat:* op doek	[Levy Pakker?]	(Sold) fl 3:5 Vallee
1810/10/11	AMSCH	0166	*A. De Bisschop* | Twee stuks Fabel-Ordonantien | *Mat:* op doek	[Levy Pakker?]	(Sold) fl 3:5 Vallee
			Bisschop, Abraham (copy after)		
1810/07/23	DOLG2	0006	*de Bisschop* | Op den voorgrond, op een bewerkt voetstuk, zit een Pauw, bij denzelven een witte Hen met hare Kiekens; naar de Bisschop | *Mat:* op doek *Size:* hoog 30, breed 34 duim	Pieter Quinting	(Sold or Bought In) fl 3 Quin van Dordt
			Bisschop, Abraham (manner)		
1807/09/28	DOHAA	00AA	*Bisschop* | Een stukje met Vogels, in de manier van Bisschop | *Mat:* op doek	Mattheus Westerouen van Meeteren	(Unknown)
			Bisschop, Jan de		
1802/06/16	AMSCH	0028	*J. de Bischop* | Een bevallig Boomryk Landschap, aan een stille Rivier, op de voorgrond een rustende Huisman met eenig Vée: zeer Natuurlyk en Meesterlyk behandeld | *Mat:* op paneel *Size:* hoog 16 ½, breed 22 duim	[Merrem]	(Sold) fl 15:10 Agina
1810/07/23	DOLG1	0010	*J. den Bisschop* | Een Landschap, met drie naar 't leven geschilderde Jagthonden, waar van een enen Haas draagt. Goed van Ordonnantie, en kragtig van Coloriet | *Mat:* op doek *Size:* hoog 36, breed 47 duim	Mr Pieter van den Santheuvel	(Sold) fl 13 van Eijk 's Hage
1810/07/23	DOLG1	0011	*J. den Bisschop* | Een Hond eenige Vogels verjagende, waar bij een witte Haan. Zeer uitvoerig, dun en meesterlijk behandeld | *Mat:* op doek *Size:* hoog 23, breed 19 duim	Mr Pieter van den Santheuvel	(Sold) fl 11:10 van Eijk 's Hage
			Blaauw		
1802/12/13	AMSCH	0035	*Blauw* | Een dito [Levantsche Zeehaven], met verscheide Oorlogscheepen	Pruyssenaar [for] B	(Sold) fl 2 van Iperen
1806/05/05	AMSCH	0024	*Blaauw* | Een kabbelende Zee, met verscheidende zeilende Scheepen en Schuiten; breed en meesterlyk gepenceeld door Blaauw | *Mat:* op doek *Size:* hoog 18, breed 25 duim	E	(Sold) fl 4:10 Vermeulen
1808/09/13	HABRU	0008	*Blauw* | Een stil Water, met differente Vaartuigen		(Unknown) fl 1:4
			Blaauw, Johannes de		
1802/06/28	AMSCH	0025	*J. Blaauw* | Twee stuks, verbeeldende de Groenlandsche Visserye, ryk gestoffeerd met Vaartuigen; door J. Blaauw, hoog 20, breed 23 duim. Doek | *Mat:* op doek *Size:* hoog 20, breed 23 duim	Anna Elink	(Sold) fl 7:10 Mensart
1804/05/07	AMSCH	0031	*Blauw (J. de)* | Een Ygezicht, zynde een woelend Water, gestoffeerd met zeilende Oorlogscheepen en andere Vaartuigen; plaisant geschilderd | *Mat:* op doek *Size:* hoog 18, breed 21 duim	Schley	(Sold) fl 0:8 Harbome
			Blanckerhoff, Jan Theunisz.		
1801/03/16	AMSCH	0180	*Blanckenhagen* | Een Zee	P[ruyssenaar]	(Sold) fl 2 Cocler
1801/04/08	HAVIN	0062	*J. Maat* | Twee Zeën		(Unknown)
1801/05/11	AMSCH	0059	*Jan Maat* | Een woelend Water, met een Oorlogschip en andere Vaartuigen, ter zyden het strand, zeer natuurlyk en dun gepenceeld | *Mat:* op doek *Size:* hoog 38, breed 50 duim	Pruisse [for] M	(Sold) fl 18 Coclers
1801/06/10	AMSCH	0035	*Blankenhagen. (J.) alias Jan Maat* | Een kabbelende Zee, op dezelve ziet men een Zeeslag tusschen verscheide Oorlogschepen; natuurlyk behandeld | *Size:* hoog 39, breed 50 duim	Herman ten Kate	(Sold) fl 15 C S Roos
1802/05/05	AMSCH	0139	*J. Maat* | Een hevige Zeebatailje van verscheiden Oorlogscheepen voor een Fort, zeer natuurlyk behandeld | *Mat:* op doek *Size:* hoog 38, breed 51 duim	A	(Sold) fl 7 Mensard
1804/02/27	AMSCH	0014	*Blankenhagen* | In een Stormende Zee, ziet men eenige Scheepen in gevaar van te vergaan, terwyl reeds eenige tegens de Klippen verbryselt werden; schoon van Effect en meesterlyk geschilderd | *Mat:* op doek *Size:* hoog 27, breed 42 duim	C	(Sold) fl 0:6 V d^{n} Brink
1804/10/29	HRBAU	0013	*Blankhof, (J.) Alias Maat* | Een Storm op Zee; voor aan ziet men een Driemast voor de wind lensen, waar agter een ander zyn' koers naar de Kust zet, die in het verschiet te zien is, en door de zon verlicht wordt; met	Simon Styl	(Unknown)

			meer andere Vaartuigen. Zeer uitvoerig behandeld | *Mat:* op doek *Size:* hoog 28, breed 41 duim		
1805/07/10	AMSCH	0033	*J.T. Blankhoff, bygenaamt J. Maat* | Een kabbelende Zee, by een bergachtig Strand, gestoffeert met een zylend Oorlogschip en een dryvend Vissers Vaartuig met eenige lieden, het Water is doorschynend en dun behandeld, en meesterlyk gepenceeld | *Mat:* op doek *Size:* hoog 24, breed 34 duim	Temmink	(Sold) fl 13 L Pakker
1805/07/10	AMSCH	0033a[H]	*J.T. Blankhoff, bygenaamt J. Maat* | 1 dito [Schildery] | *Notes:* This lot was added in by hand in the EBNP and RKDH copies of the catalogue.	V[inkeles]	(Bought In) fl 3:15
1808/03/03	HAVIN	0021	*J. Maat* | Een Woelend Water	Jacobus Spillebout	(Unknown) fl 6:5
1808/06/13	AMSCH	0032	*Blankenhagen, (H.) bijgenaamd Jan Maat* | Een onstuimige Zee, waarin een Schip hetwelk bij een Noordsche Haven gestrand is, waar men bezig is eenige goederen te bergen; alles natuurlijk behandeld | *Mat:* op doek *Size:* hoog 39, breed 55 duim	E M Engelberts	(Sold) fl 30 Coclers
1808/06/13	AMSCH	0235	*J. Maat* | Een Strandgezicht, waarop een Schip dat gekalfaterd wordt, verder een woelende Zee met Schepen, in het verschiet een Stad en Fort op eene Berg	Z	(Sold) fl 14 J Spaan
1808/08/23	AMSCH	0027	*Blankenhagen. (H.)* | Een woelende Zee met verscheide Schepen en andere Vaartuigen, en een bergachtig strand Gezigt; natuurlijk en schoon gepenceeld | *Mat:* op doek *Size:* hoog 44, breed 60 duim	J	(Sold) fl 2:15 Reyers
1808/08/23	AMSCH	0028	*Blankenhagen. (H.)* | Een dito Ordonantie als de voorgaande, met verscheide Schepen, Vaartuigen en Beeldjes gestoffeert; mede natuurlijk en fraai geschilderd | *Mat:* op paneel *Size:* hoog 28, breed 38 duim *Notes:* It is unclear what "dito" refers to in the title.	[Van Iperen?]	(Sold) fl 12 Tessier
			Blanckerhoff, Jan Theunisz. (manner)		
1803/04/06	MGSAN	0005	*Jan Maat* | Een Zeegevecht, vol gewoel, fiks behandeld in de manier van Jan Maat	Mr Evert Clyver	(Unknown)
			Bleeker, A. [Unidentified]		
1804/05/07	AMSCH	0028	*Bleeker. (A.) Ao. 1628* | In dit zoo bevallig als aangenaam Boomryk Landschap ziet men eenige Ruiters te Paard en te voet, waarby op de voorgrond en drift Ossen, verders in 't verschiet eenige Boerewooningen, Kerktooren, hoog Geboomte, enz; uitvoerig en zonachtig gepenceeld | *Mat:* op paneel *Size:* hoog 30, breed 51 duim *Inscr:* A. Bleeker Ao. 1628 (signed and dated?) *Notes:* It is unclear whether the name and date are inscribed on the painting.	Vinkeles	(Sold) fl 5:5 Gruyter
1806/05/05	AMSCH	0017	*A. Bleeker* | Een boomryk Landschap met eenige Ruiters te paard en te voet, waar by op de voorgrond een drift Ossen, verders een aangenaam verschiet; meesterlyk door A. Bleeker op Paneel | *Mat:* op paneel *Size:* hoog 30, breed 51 duim	V[inkeles]	(Sold) fl 3 L Pakker
			Bleeker, J. de [Unidentified]		
1801/10/06	AMSCH	0008	*J. de Bleeker* | Een Historieelen Ordinantie, alwaar eenige Vrouwen, hunne Mannen uit de Stad draagen, in 't gezicht van een Veld Overste te Paard, helder en kragtig gepenceeld | *Mat:* op doek *Size:* hoog 28, breed 52 duim	M	(Sold) fl 9 Jan Spaan
			Bleker, Dirck		
1804/10/16	DLOND	0024	*D. Bleker* | Ene Boetvaerdige Vrouw in een Rots, met een Crucifix in de hand, sterk van hartstocht. Une Femme penitente, dans un rocher | *Mat:* op doek *Size:* hoog 43, breed 32		(Unknown)
			Blieck, Daniel de		
1802/05/10	MGSAN	0031	*D. D. Bliek* | Een fraai Tempelstukje, met Beeldjes, door D. D. Bliek: op Paneel, in vergulde Lyst | *Mat:* op paneel *Size:* hoog 13 ½ duim, breed 15 duim	Johan Dirk Kruysse	(Unknown) £ 0:12
1803/07/18	AMSCH	0007	*Bleek (D. de)* | Een Protestantsche Kerk van binnen te zien, gestoffeerd met een menigte Beeldjes en Wapenborden, zeer bevallig van zonlight en schildering [L'intérieur d'une Eglise protestante, dont le point de vue donne sur la chaire : differents blasons & armories sont suspendus aux colonnes gothiques du temple. Le pavé est orné de jolies figures bien disposées. Ce petit morceau clair, lumineux, est du plus charmant effet ; il atteint d'aussi près à la nature qu'aucune production en ce genre.] | *Mat:* op paneel *Size:* hoog 17, breed 13 duim	Maria Theresia Andrioli	(Sold) fl 38 Haffner
1803/11/30	MGBEO	0007	*D.D. Blieck* | Een gedeelte van den Tempel, van Binnen te zien | *Mat:* op paneel *Size:* hoog 12 duim, breed 14 duim	Samuel de Wind	(Sold) £ 0:14 G M Petersen
1803/12/15	MGLAC	0058	*Blieck* | Een fraai Architectuur, met verscheide Beelden; zeer schoon en uitvoerig geschilderd | *Mat:* op doek *Size:* hoog duim 65, breed duim 90	Mr L H de Haze Bomme	(Unknown)
1804/05/07	AMSCH	0029	*Bleek. (P. de)* | Een Protestante Kerk van binnen te zien, gestoffeerd met een meenigte van Rustende en Wandelende Beelden en eenige Honden; zonachtig en alleruitvoerigst van penceelbehandeling | *Mat:* op paneel *Size:* hoog 17, breed 14 duim *Notes:* The artist's name was given as "Bleek. (P. de)" but we have assumed this is an error.	Vinkeles [for] H[affner]	(Bought In) fl 25

1805/07/10	AMSCH	0035	*P. de Bleek* | Een Protestante Kerk van binnen te zien, ryk gestoffeerd met een ménigte Beelden, Wapenborden, enz.; krachtig en fraay van schildering | *Mat:* op paneel *Size:* hoog 16, breed 12 ½ duim *Notes:* The artist's name was given as "P. de Bleek" but we have assumed this is an error.	V[inkeles] [for] H[affner]	(Sold) fl 41 Gruyter
1807/07/20	MGSAN	0001	*D.D. Bliek* | Een fraai Tempelstuk, de voorgrond gestoffeerd met Beelden, 1649 | *Mat:* op paneel *Inscr:* 1649 (dated?) *Notes:* It is unclear whether the date is inscribed on the painting.	C J van den Helm Boddaert [or others]	(Unknown)
1810/03/26	RMMUY	0022	*De Bliek* | Eene oude Protestantsche Kerk, naar het Koor te zien, met veel figuren van Heeren en Dames. Uitvoerig en konstig geschilderd [L'intérieur d'une ancienne Eglise protestante, où plusieurs personnes se promênent, d'un bon effet et soigneusement traité.] | *Mat:* op doek *Size:* hoog 22, breed 28 duimen	Daniel de Jongh Az	(Sold) fl 19:10 van Eyk s'Hage
1810/10/10	MGCIT	0064	*Bliek* | Een zeer schoon en uitmuntend Gebouw, zynde eene Inlandsche Kerk, kenbaar aan de onderscheiden Wapens van aanzienlyke Familien, daarin afgebeeld; voorts zoo ten aanzien der Bouworde als de werking van Ligt, kunstig en meesterlyk uitgevoerd	Caspar van Citters	(Unknown)
1810/10/10	MGCIT	0151	*Bliek* | Een Capitaal Stuk, verbeeldende een zeer spatieus Plein of Bassecour, waarop een Prachtig Gebouw, schoon van bouworde, en achter hetzelve een Landschap; meesterlijk nevens de stoffage uitgevoerd	Caspar van Citters	(Unknown)
			Blinkvliet, M.		
1804/10/16	DLOND	0025	*Blinckvliet* | Een Landschap, waarin een Herder met Vee en twee Paerden aan een hek. Paysage, un Berger, du Betail & des Chevaux | *Mat:* op paneel *Size:* hoog 12, breed 17		(Sold) fl 10:5 Thijs
1807/08/26	AMSCH	0032	*Blinkvliet* | Een Italiaansch Land- en Watergezigt, gestoffeerd met Rysigers en Vee, verder een Zeehaven; kragtig geschilderd | *Mat:* op doek	Yver [for] S	(Sold) fl 0:6 Levij Pakker
1809/07/25	HGBSM	0151	*Bluikvliet* | Een Landschap met Figuuren, Paarden en Koeyen en Schaapen, in de trant van Berchem, door Bluikvliet 1727 | *Mat:* op doek *Size:* hoog 21 en een half, breed 25 en een half duim *Inscr:* Bluikvliet 1727 (signed and dated?) *Notes:* It is unclear whether the name and date are inscribed on the painting.	D van der Aa [or] E B ten Dall	(Sold) fl 3:5 Vermeulen
1810/06/06	RMMUY	0078	*M. Blinkvliet* | Een Landschap met stoffagie van Koeijen, Schapen, en Bokken, verder een water &c. goed geschilderd. Door M. Blinkvliet 1716 | *Mat:* op doek *Inscr:* M. Blinkvliet 1716 (signed and dated?) *Notes:* It is unclear whether the name and date are inscribed on the painting.		(Unknown) fl 4:5
			Block, J. van [Unidentified]		
1802/07/09	AMSTO	0002	*J. van Block* | 1 Boom en Bergagtig Landschap, op de voorgrond met staande en leggende Beesten		(Unknown)
			Bloemaert		
1801/05/11	AMSCH	0018	*F. Bloemaart* | Een biddende Petrus, fraay en meesterlyk behandeld | *Mat:* op doek *Size:* hoog 39, breed 31 duim	Pruisse [for] M	(Sold) fl 1:15 Gruiter
1804/02/27	AMSCH	0018	*Bloemaert* | In een Boomryk Landschap by eenige Woningen, ziet men eenige Boeren en Boerinnen, en verder Bywerk | *Mat:* op paneel *Size:* hoog 22, breed 25 duim	B	(Sold) fl 1 L Pakker
1806/05/05	AMSCH	0242	*Bloemaert* | Een Herder en Herderin, liefkoozende, in een Landschap	V[inkeles]	(Sold) fl 2 Grauu
1806/06/07	RMHSN	0106	*Bloemaert* | Een Man met zyn Hand op zyn Borst | *Mat:* op doek	A E K L	(Unknown)
1810/03/07	UTWLD	0049	*Bloemart* | Een levensgroot Borstbeeld, verbeeldende een drinkenden Man, konstig behandeld | *Size:* hoog 4 duim, breed 3 voet 2 duim	J J Woertman	(Unknown) fl 20
1810/07/26	AMSCH	0008	*Bloemaert* | De Aanbidding der Herders, een fraai samenstel van Beelden | *Mat:* op doek *Size:* hoog 19, breed 13 duimen	Cassino	(Bought In) fl 3:5
1810/07/26	AMSCH	0009	*Bloemaert* | Een Gezigt op een Scheeps Timmer-Werf, met eigenaartige Voorwerpen | *Mat:* op doek *Size:* hoog 27, breed 31 duimen	Cassino	(Bought In) fl 10:15
1810/07/26	AMSCH	0133	*Bloemaert* | Loth met zijne Dochter, wordende uit Sodom geleid. Schoon geschilderd | *Mat:* op paneel *Size:* hoog 31, breed 38 duimen	Cassino	(Bought In) fl 11
1810/10/11	AMSCH	0250	*Bloemaert* | De Herders aanbidden het Kind	A	(Sold) fl 4 L Pakker
1810/10/11	AMSCH	0251	*Bloemaert* | Maria, hebbende het Kind aan de borst	A	(Sold) fl 0:8 du Pree
			Bloemaert (and Delen)		
1810/10/10	MGCIT	0121	*v. Deelen; Bloemaart* | Een fraai Antiek Gebouw, door v. Deelen; waar achter is geplaatst een zeer bevallig Landschap, door Bloemaart	Caspar van Citters	(Unknown)
			Bloemaert (manner)		
1806/06/07	RMHSN	0047	*Bloemaert* | Een Mans en Vrouwe Beeld, Levensgroote, Halflyfs &c, als door Bloemaert | *Mat:* op doek	A E K L	(Unknown)
1806/06/07	RMHSN	0048	*Bloemaert* | Een Man zyn Handen Warmende over een Test met Vuur en een Jongeling daar by staande, met Bywerk, als door denzelven [Bloemaert] | *Mat:* op doek	A E K L	(Unknown)
1807/08/26	AMSCH	0026	*Bloemaard* | Een Grysaard met een groote baard, en een stok in de hand; in de manier van Bloemaard | *Mat:* op doek *Size:* hoog 28, breed 24 duim	de Vries	(Sold) fl 1 Coclair

Bloemaert, Abraham

1801/03/16	AMSCH	0050	*A. Bloemaart* | Een heuvelagtig Landschap, op de voorgrond een Herder en een Herderin, fiks van schildering	P[ruyssenaar]	(Sold) fl 9:10 Coclers
1801/10/06	AMSCH	0009	*A. Bloemaart* | Een Boomryk Landschap, de voorgrond gestoffeert, met een Historieele Ordinantie, fraai van Coloriet en uitvoerig behandeld | *Mat:* op doek *Size:* hoog 34, breed 27 duim	M	(Sold) fl 31 Van Dijl
1801/11/10	AMPOS	0011	*A. Bloemaart* | De Ryze naar Bethlehem		(Unknown)
1802/05/05	AMSCH	0028	*A. Bloemäart* | Een Keukenstuk, met verscheide smakelyke Spyzen, waar by de Kok en Keukenmeid. Alles zeer natuurlyk en kragtig | *Mat:* op doek *Size:* hoog 35, breed 45 duim	B	(Sold) fl 3:5 Gruiter
1802/05/22	RMHSN	0001	*A. Bloemaert* | Twee stuks Boer en Boerinnetje, in een Landschap door A. Bloemaert	Lambertus Bicker	(Unknown)
1802/06/28	AMSCH	0010	*A. Bloemaert* | Twee stuks, een Mans en Vrouwe Pourtrait, door A. Bloemaert, Panneel | *Mat:* op paneel *Size:* hoog 15, breed 11 duim	B	(Sold) fl 1:10 Van Iperen
1802/06/28	AMSCH	0011	*A. Bloemaert* | Maria met het Kindje op de Wolken, verzeld van een menigte Engelen, door Denzelven [A. Bloemaert], op Doek | *Mat:* op doek *Size:* hoog 62, breed 47 duim	Anna Elink	(Sold) fl 90 Gruiter
1802/09/06	AMSCH	0018	*A. Bloemaert* | Een Italiaansch Landzicht, op de voorgrond gestoffeerd met een zittende Vrouw, by een staand oud Man, ter zyde op een Heuvel, ziet men eenige Bokjes en verder de Ruïne van een Poort en andere Gebouwen; meesterlyk fix | *Mat:* op paneel *Size:* hoog 11, breed 17 duim	H^n^ Smit	(Sold) fl 0:14 van Iperen
1802/09/06	AMSCH	0180	*A. Bloemaert* | Maria zittende met het Kindje op de schoot, waar by St. Catharina, de Trouwring ontvangende; meesterlyk geschilderd	Spaan	(Sold) fl 1 Th^s^ Spaan [or] Jan Spaan
1802/09/06	AMSCH	0181	*A. Bloemaert* | Deeze Ordenantie verbeeld de Kroning van Maria; meesterlyk	Spaan	(Sold) fl 2 Th^s^ Spaan
1803/04/20	AMSCH	0009	*Bloemaert. (A.)* | Twee stuks: een Boer met een Kan in de hand en een Vrouw met een korf met Eyeren; fix op Paneel geschilderd [Deux sujets pour pendans dont l'un offre un villageois la canette à la main, l'autre represente une femme tenant un pannier avec des Oeufs : largement peints.] | *Mat:* op paneel *Size:* ieder is hoog 15, breed 12 duim	Maria Magdalena van Sluypwyk, gravinne van Moens	(Sold) fl 8 C S Roos
1803/08/17	AMSCH	0013	*Bloemmaert. (A.)* | Christus met zyne Discipelen, aan Tafel zittende, den Beker zeegenende; dit stukje is vol uitdrukking, schoon van couler, en kragtig en meesterlyk van schildertrant | *Mat:* op paneel *Size:* hoog 16, breed 11 duim	Anna Catharina Putman	(Sold) fl 48 Gruyter
1803/12/12	AMSCH	0014	*A. Bloemaart* | In een Landschap met zwaar Geboomte ziet men een staande en leggende Herder, met Bokken en Schaapen; zonachtig meesterlyk op Doek | *Mat:* op doek *Size:* hoog 21, br. 17 duim	Arnoud de Lange	(Sold) fl 2 V^n^ Dijl
1804/08/02	BDAN	0027	*A. Blommaert* | De Predicatie van Johannes in de Woestyne, met veele Figuren | *Mat:* op doek *Size:* b. 40 d. h. 29 en een half d.	J G Calckberner	(Unknown)
1805/10/09	HGBSM	0026	*A. Bloemaart* | Een boer met een mand met eijeren, hoenders, boter, kaas, en een kopere melkkan &c. | *Mat:* op doek *Size:* hoog 33 breet 46 duim	T H van Willigen [or others]	(Sold) fl 7:10 Ph Mey
1805/10/21	GRBOL	0012	*A. Bloemaart* | Een Landschap, waar in een Herder en Herderin	Gerardus Nicolaus Heerkens	(Unknown)
1806/08/13	AMSCH	0022a	*Bloemaert. (A.)* | Een Boomryk Landschap met Boerewoningen en andere Gebouwen, vol stoffagie; fiks van schildering | *Size:* hoog 15, breed 18 duim	Vinkeles [for] G[ruyter]	(Sold) fl 2:5 Gruyter
1806/08/20	HGBSM	0002	*A. Bloemaart* | De Aanbidding der Herders, in den Stal; zijnde eene ordonnantie van zeven beelden, waar van de meesten vol godsdienstige uitdrukking, zeer krachtig van Coloriet, en schoon van Draperijen, in eenen Italiaanschen trant | *Mat:* op doek *Size:* hoog 37 ½, breed 28 ½ duim	Macalester Loup [or others]	(Sold) fl 13:10 Praison
1806/08/20	HGBSM	0021	*A. Bloemaart* | Een groep van verscheide Menschen, alwaar een Vrouwtje met een pan in de hand zit koeken te bakken, met verder bijwerk | *Mat:* op doek *Size:* hoog 11 ¼, breed 15 duim	Macalester Loup	(Sold) fl 19 Zwartsman
1806/11/24	AMSCH	0008	*Bloemaert (A.)* | Elias in een woest Landschap, door de Raven gespysd wordende; kloek en meesterlyk behandeld | *Mat:* op doek *Size:* hoog 40, breed 50 duim	Munnikhuizen	(Bought In) fl 8:10
1806/11/24	AMSCH	0009	*Bloemaert (A.)* | Een Vrouw zig kammende, naast haar een Kat; behandeld als de voorgaande [kloek en meesterlyk] | *Mat:* op paneel *Size:* hoog 14, breed 12 duim	Munnikhuizen	(Sold) fl 1:15 Dusart
1807/04/00	LNDLS	0018	*Abraham Bloemaert* | Een biddende Petrus halverlijf met te zamen gevouwen handen, en omhangen met een blaauwe mantel, uitvoerig en kragtig behandelt, op doek hoog 23 en een half, breed 19 en een half duim zijnde een weerga van Pellegrini | companion to lot 17, by Pellegrini *Mat:* op doek *Size:* hoog 23 en een half, breed 19 en een half duim	[Abraham Delfos] [or others]	(Unknown)
1807/06/10	HGBSM	0018	*Abraham Bloemaert* | Een biddende Petrus halverlijf met te zamen gevouwen handen, en omhangen met een blaauwe mantel, uitvoerig en kragtig behandelt, op doek hoog 23 en een half, breed 19 en een half duim zijnde een weerga van Pellegrini | companion to lot 17, by Pellegrini *Mat:* op doek *Size:* hoog 23 ½, breed 19 ½ duim	Abraham Delfos [or others]	(Sold or Bought In) fl 21 D

1808/08/23	AMSCH	0023	*Bloemaart. (A.)* | Een weenende Petrus met zaamgevouwe handen en de Oogen hemelwaarts, voor hem ligt een opengeslagen boek; krachtig en meesterlijk behandeld | *Mat:* op doek *Size:* hoog 33, breed 28 duim	[Coclers]	(Sold) fl 14:10 David Maijkel
1808/08/23	AMSCH	0024	*Bloemaart. (A.)* | Een Bijbelsche Ordonantie, voorstellende de Geboorte Christi te Bethlehem, alwaar de Herders het Kind aanbidden, en geschenken brengen; meesterlijk gepenceeld | *Mat:* op doek *Size:* hoog 55, breed 66 duim	C	(Sold) fl 4 L Pakker
1808/11/12	HGSCR	0003	*Abr. Bloemhart* | Een capitaal landschap, waar in verbeeld de prediking van Johannes den Dooper, ten aanhoren van een menigte menschen van verschillende rang en houdingen, dit wel geconserveerde stuk is van een schoone ordonnantie, wel getekend, kragtig van koloriet en uitvoerig behandeld door Abr. Bloemhart en kan voor een der beste van deze meester gehouden worden	Mr J van Buren	(Unknown) fl 100
1808/11/28	AMSCH	0010	*A. Bloemaert* | Een Bijbel-ordonantie, voorstellende St. Jan, Predikende in de Woestijne, meesterlijk behandeld | *Mat:* op doek *Size:* hoog 30, breed 38 duim	H	(Sold) fl 5:10 van der Schley (P) [for] E van Dijk
1809/04/17	AMSCH	0121	*A. Bloemaert* | De Godin Diana, verzeld van eenige Nimphen; meesterlijk	T	(Sold) fl 1:5
1809/04/17	AMSCH	0155	*A. Bloemaert* | Een kapitaal Landschap, met Boerenwooningen en Geboomten | *Mat:* op doek	[Gruyter?]	(Sold) fl 2:15
1809/06/13	AMSCH	0027	*A. Bloemaert* | Twee stuks, Maria met het Kindje en St. Joseph; beide meesterlijk behandeld | *Mat:* op paneel *Size:* hoog 25, breed 21 duim	T	(Sold) fl 4 van Dijl
1809/06/13	AMSCH	0028	*A. Bloemaert* | Christus met zijn Dicipelen aan Tafel zittende; schoon van koloriet en uitdrukking, kragtig en meesterlijk geschilderd | *Mat:* op paneel *Size:* hoog 16, breed 11 duim	[Gruyter?]	(Sold) fl 49:10 van Iperen
1810/03/07	UTWLD	0008	*A. Bloemart* | Een Schildery, voorstellende eene zwaare brand, op de voorgrond, menschen die hun goed en vee redden, meesterlyk behandeld | *Size:* hoog 3 voet 4 duim, breed 4 voet 5 duim	J J Woertman	(Unknown) fl 12
1810/06/20	AMSCH	0011	*A. Bloemaert* | Een bergachtig Landschap, met een Rivier doorsneden, gestoffeerd met Jagers, gaande en rustende Reizigers | *Mat:* op paneel *Size:* hoog 18, breed 23 duimen	A	(Sold) fl 1 L Pakker
1810/07/23	DOLG1	0009	*Abraham Bloemaart* | De Uitdrijving van Hagar, door Abraham | *Mat:* op doek *Size:* hoog 63, breed 65 duim	Mr Pieter van den Santheuvel	(Sold) fl 6 van der Hegge
1810/07/26	AMSCH	0007	*Bloemaert (A.)* | Jacob slapende onder een Boom, terwijl de Engelen op een Ladder op en neder klimmen. Goed geschilderd | *Mat:* op doek *Size:* hoog 43, breed 32 duimen	Cassino	(Bought In) fl 3:15
1810/08/06	AMSCH	0017	*Bloemaert (A.)* | Elias door de Raven gespijzigd wordende. Meesterlijk behandeld | *Mat:* op doek *Size:* hoog 40, breed 51 duimen	R[oos]	(Sold) fl 6:15 Van Iperen
1810/10/11	AMSCH	0184	*A. Bloemaert* | Eene Bijbelvoorstelling, zijnde de Wijzen, welke het Kind Jezus aanbidden en geschenken brengen; schoon als Rubbens geschilderd	A	(Sold) fl 10:10 Menzart

Bloemaert, Abraham (or Bloemaert, A., manner)

1801/09/04	MGWIN	0001	*A. Bloemaart* | Verbeeldende de Geboorte van Christus, meesterlyk geschilderd, door of in de manier van A. Bloemaart, op doek, in een vergulde Lyst | *Mat:* op doek *Size:* hoog 67 en breed 84 duim	Pieter Gillissen	(Unknown)
1805/12/16	AMSCH	0061	*A. Bloemmaert* | Een ryke Ordinantie, voorstellende de Aanbidding der Herders; meesterlyk op Doek, door of in de manier van A. Bloemmaert | *Mat:* op doek	R[oos]	(Sold) fl 3:5 Jozi
1806/05/05	AMSCH	0226	*A. Blommaert* | Een dito [ryk gekleedde Dame] door of in de manier van A. Blommaert | *Notes:* It is unclear what "dito" refers to in the title.	O	(Sold) fl 1:10 de Flines

Bloemaert, Abraham (copy after)

1806/05/05	AMSCH	0259[a]	*A. Bloemaert* | Een Kaarslicht; na A. Bloemaert en een Bloemstukje | *This Lot:* Een Kaarslicht; lot 259[b] by Anonymous	R[oos]	(Sold) fl 1:10 for lots 259[a] & 259[b]. L Pakker

Bloemaert, Abraham (manner)

1802/05/05	AMSCH	0027	*A. Bloemäart* | De Aanbidding der Herders, zeer natuurlyk in de manier van A. Bloemäart | *Size:* hoog 22, breed 25 duim	G	(Sold) fl 2 Spruit
1803/04/20	AMSCH	0146	*A. Bloemaert* | Een ryke Ordenantie vol gewoel, verbeeldende de Geboorte Christi, daar de Herders het Kindeken aanbidden en geschenken offeren; meesterlyk geschilderd op Doek, in de manier van A. Bloemaert [Une Composition bien entendue de la naissance de J.C. ou les Pasteurs viennent faire leur offrande & leur adoration, artistement traitée dans la maniere d'A. Blommaert.] | *Mat:* op doek	Maria Magdalena van Sluypwyk, gravinne van Moens	(Sold) fl 19 Gruiter
1804/08/08	AMSCH	0249	*A. Bloemaert* | Een Bejaard Man, welke aan een Jonge Vrouw een Gouden Ketting aanbied; meesterlyk op Doek, als door A. Bloemaert | *Mat:* op doek	Roos [for] J	(Sold) fl 5:10 Toselli

Bloemaert, Cornelis (II)

1802/09/06	AMSCH	0019	*C. Bloemaert* | Een aangenaam Bergachtig Landschap met een Heidensche Historie | *Mat:* op doek *Size:* hoog 30, breed 26 duim	J	(Sold) fl 2:5 Wepner
1810/12/03	DOBRA	0067	*Cornelis Bloemaart* | Diana met hare Nymphen, in een Landschap, door Cornelis Bloemaart, op Doek, in een zwarte Lyst | *Mat:* op doek		(Unknown)

Bloemaert, Hendrick

1810/06/06	RMMUY	0089	*H. Bloemaart* | Twee stuks, het eene eene Jonge Vrouw, het andere een Oud Man. Uitvoerig en meesterlijk | *Mat:* op doek		(Sold) fl 14 Strikland

Bloemaert, Hendrick (or Bloemaert, H., manner)

1810/06/06	RMMUY	0001	*Hendrik Bloemaart* | Deze konstige Schilderij, stelt voor, den Bisschop Athanasius in zijn Pontificaal gewaad, nevens hem een Oudvader, een boek vertonende waar op te lezen staat Qui Conceptus est de Spiritus Sancti, natus ex Maria Virgina. Boven dien ziet men de Heilige Maagd met het kind Jezus op haren Schoot, ter linkerzijde St. Jan Evangelist, met een boek waar op men leest In principio erat Verbu et Verbum, et Deus erat verbum, et verbum Caro Factu est: achter hem een Oudvader, in 't verschiet en in de lucht twee kindertjes; waar van het eene St. Jan verbeeld met het Agnus Dei, allen levensgroote, konstig en meesterlijk geschilderd. Door of in de manier van Hendrik Bloemaart, op doek. Hoog 79, breed 60 duimen. NB. Dit stuk is zeer geschikt voor een Altaar | *Mat:* op doek *Size:* hoog 79, breed 60 duimen		(Sold) fl 50 Muller

Bloemen

1801/04/08	HAVIN	0026	*van Blommen* | Eenige Ruiters te Paard by een Tent		(Unknown)
1801/12/22	AMOTT	0039	*van Blomme* | Legertenten, Paarden en Beesten, met Beelden, in een Campement	Bartholomeus Ruloffs	(Unknown) fl 15:10
1802/09/21	UTHDG	000P[H]	*Bloemen* | Een Kloek Landschap van Bloemen | *Notes:* This lot was added in by hand in the OGA copy of the catalogue.		(Sold) fl 4:5 J Niekerk
1809/10/19	HGBAK	0179	*Van Blomme* | Een Ruyter te paart	D van der Aa [or] P v d Heuvell	(Unknown)
1810/07/26	AMSCH	0105	*van Blommen* | Een besneeuwd Wintergezigt, met Paarden, Sleeden en Beelden | *Mat:* op doek	Cassino	(Sold) fl 0:10 L Pakker

Bloemen (manner)

1806/01/30	RMAN	0004	*Van Blommen* | Een Landschap in de manier van Van Blommen	Dirk Langendyk	(Unknown)

Bloemen (manner; copy by)

1803/12/12	AMSCH	0148	*Blommen; Wouwerman* | Twee ryk met Paarden en Beelden gestoffeerde Landschappen; als van Blommen, naar Wouwerman | copy in the manner of Bloemen after Wouwerman *Mat:* op paneel *Size:* hoog 13, breed 17 duim	D	(Sold) fl 30 Coclers

Bloemen, Jan Frans van (Orizzonte)

1808/06/13	AMSCH	0025	*Blommen (Horisonti van)* | Een Italiaansch boomryk Landschap, gestoffeerd met eene menigte Beelden en Beesten; zijnde van eene meesterlijke schildering | *Size:* hoog 26, breed 33 duim	[Jan Tersteeg]	(Sold) fl 16 Glad

Bloemen, Norbert van

1802/02/16	AMSCH	0074[a]	*N. van Bloemen* | Twee stuks Arcadische Landschapjes, gestoffeerd met Beeldjes, Gebouwen en Geboomten, uitvoerig op koper geschilderd, door N. van Bloemen, en een Trouwverbond, op koper, ovaal formaat, 3 stuk | *This Lot:* Twee stuks Arcadische Landschapjes, gestoffeerd met Beeldjes, Gebouwen en Geboomten; lot 74[b] by Anonymous *Mat:* op koper	C	(Sold) fl 1:15 for lots 74[a] & 74[b]. L Pakker
1802/02/16	AMSCH	0078	*N. van Bloemen* | In een Italiaansch Landschap met een Boerehut en geboomten, op de voorgrond gestoffeerd met verschyde soort van rustend Vee, verder een huisman Lammeren leggende op een Ezel, en een bergachtig verschiet; kragtig van coloriet, en meesterlyk gepenceeld	C	(Sold) fl 25 Coclers
1804/02/27	AMSCH	0017	*Blommen (N. van)* | In een Landschap voor een Boerewoning ziet men eenige Huislieden, waarby een Vrouw welke de courant leest, waar naar zy aandachtig luisteren verders een Bergachtig verschiet; en fraai van behandeling | *Mat:* op doek *Size:* hoog 19, breed 22 duim	D	(Sold) fl 0:14 du Pree
1808/08/23	AMSCH	0022	*Blommem (N. van)* | Twee stuks Landschappen, beide gestoffeert met vrolijke Arbeidslieden, welke zig met rooken, drinken en speelen vermaaken, verder speelende Kinderen, en eigenaartig bijwerk; helder en plaisant geschilderd | *Mat:* op doek *Size:* Ieder hoog 23, breed 27 duim	Z	(Sold) fl 41 Van Iperen

Bloemen, Pieter van (Stendardo)

1802/05/05	AMSCH	0030	*P. van Bloemen* | Twee stuks Italiaansche Landschappen, beide ryk gestoffeert met Paarden, Koeybeesten en Ezels, waar by eenige Landlieden. Krachtig en breed gepenceeld | *Mat:* op doek *Size:* hoog 27, breed 23 duim	E	(Sold) fl 25 Rigters
1802/05/05	AMSCH	0031	*P. van Bloemen* | Twee stuks Markten in Roomen, beide gestoffeerd met Quackzalvers op hun Théâter, met Hansworsten, Pierots en andere Commique Voorwerpen, waar naar een menigte Aanschouwers staan te kyken. Meesterlyk | *Mat:* op doek *Size:* ieder hoog 21, breed 25 duim	E [or] BB	(Bought In) fl 47
1802/06/16	AMSCH	0029	*P. van Blommen* | Een Bergachtig Landschap: op de voorgrond ziet men een Ploeg, waar voor twee Ossen en een Ezel, ter zyde een Man te Paard, en een rustende Vrouw: fiks behandeld | *Mat:* op doek *Size:* hoog 19 ½, breed 24 ½ duim	[Merrem]	(Sold) fl 18:10 Th Spaan

1802/09/29	AMSCH	0011	*P. van Bloemen* | Een Italiaans Landschap, hoog 22, breed 33. Doek. In dit uitmuntend Schildery, ziet men langs een Rivier, verscheiden Gebouwen en Ruïnen; op de Voorgrond werkende Lieden by een Vaartuig, beneevens twee Paarden op een Heuvel, en verder anderen die in de Rivier geleid worden; alles is kloek en meesterlyk behandeld, en voorts bevallig en kragtig van couleur [Vue en Italie, ce site garni de fabriques est coupé par une rieviere [sic] dans laquelle, au premier plan, differens hommes menent des chevaux pour abreuver. La gauche offre une motte de terre ou l'on decharge des objets hors d'une chaloupe, des baigneurs, deux chevaux bruns et des personnages diversement occupés terminent cette partie. Ce morceau que l'on peut donner comme un de ses meilleurs, est au dessus de la reputation de l'auteur.] | *Mat:* op doek *Size:* hoog 22, breed 33 duim	C	(Sold) fl 345 Pruijssenaar
1802/12/13	AMSCH	0029	*P. van Blommen* | Een aangenaam Italiaansch Landschap, ryk gestoffeerd met Beelden en Beesten en breet geschilderd | *Mat:* op doek *Size:* hoog 19, breed 25 duim	Pruyssenaar [for] A	(Sold) fl 1:10 Van Iperen
1803/08/17	AMSCH	0017	*Blommen. (P. van)* | Een Gezigt by Romen, by de Triumphboog van Titus ziet men een menigte Ossen, Koeijen, Schapen, Paarden en Ezels, welke zich in een plas ververschen, met hunne Dryvers, alles meesterlyk geschilderd | *Mat:* op doek *Size:* hoog 23 ½, breed 29 ½ duim	Anna Catharina Putman	(Sold) fl 40:10 Hodges
1803/08/17	AMSCH	0018	*Blommen. (P. van)* | Voor eenige Legertenten ziet men een Ruiter en een Trompetter, zich schynende te ververschen, fix uitgevoerd | *Mat:* op koper *Size:* hoog 13, breed 15 ½ duim	Anna Catharina Putman	(Sold) fl 14:10 Hodges
1803/12/12	AMSCH	0007	*P. van Blommen* | Een Pleisterplaats, met Lieden te Paard; fix gepenceeld | *Mat:* op paneel *Size:* hoog 13, breed 11 duim	H	(Sold) fl 1:5 Coclers
1804/05/07	AMSCH	0025	*Blommen. (P. van)* | Twee stuks, het eene verbeelende een Smits Winkel, en het andere een Campement, gestoffeerd met Legerwagens en Officieren te Paard; fiks behandeld | *Size:* yder hoog 15, breed 12 ½ duim	Y[ver] [for] JJ	(Sold) fl 7:15 T van Iperen
1804/05/07	AMSCH	0027	*Blommen. (P. van)* | Een Bergachtig Landschap, op de voorgrond ziet men een Ploeg, waar voor twee Ossen en een Ezel, ter zyde een Man te Paard, en een rustende Vrouw; fiks behandeld | *Mat:* op doek *Size:* hoog 19, breed 24 duim	Y[ver] [for] JJ	(Bought In) fl 14 ½
1804/07/25	AMSCH	0011	*Blommen. (P. van)* | Voor een Romeinsche Poort ziet men St. Marten op een wit Paard gezéten, met zyn Zwaard een stuk van zyn Mantel snydende, om aan eenige behoeftigen uit te deelen, op de voorgrond een blaffende Hond, klock, en van een meesterlyke penceelsbehandeling | *Mat:* op doek *Size:* hoog 29, breed 25 duim		(Sold) fl 51 B[d] Kooy
1805/07/03	AMSCH	0008	*Blommen (P. van)* | Twee stuks Landschappen, met Gebouwen en Reizigers, met verscheide Paarden, en ander Vee; kragtig en Meesterlyk van Schildering | *Mat:* op doek *Size:* yder hoog 13, breed 12 duim	R[oos]	(Sold) fl 25 Tozelli
1805/07/03	AMSCH	0009	*Blommen (P. van)* | Twee stuks, een Smitswinkel; en eenige Ryzigers te paard en verdere stoffagie; als de voorgaande behandeld | *Size:* hoog 13, breed 12 duim	R[oos]	(Sold) fl 21:10 Vallet
1805/07/10	AMSCH	0030	*P. van Blommen* | In een Boom- en Duinryk Landschap, ziet men by een plas Water een Landman met twee Ossen en een Ezel, verzeld van een ander te Paard, en aan de Voet van een boom een rustende Vrouw, waarby een Jongen en Hond; meesterlyk op Doek | *Mat:* op doek *Size:* hoog 19 ½, breed 24 duim	V[inkeles] [for] M	(Sold) fl 9 van Iperen
1805/10/09	HGBSM	0069	*P. van Blomme* | Een leggend koeitje | *Mat:* op doek *Size:* hoog 5 ½ breet 7 ½ duim	T H van Willigen [or others]	(Sold) fl 3 van der Aa
1807/08/26	AMSCH	0011	*P. van Blommen* | Twee stuks Romeinsche Landschappen met antique Gebouwen, zynde de eene een Beestenmarkt, en het andere eenige Krygslieden, met hunne Paarden voor een Smits Winkel staande, en verdere stoffage; meesterlyk fraai op Doek geschilderd en aangenaam verlicht | *Mat:* op doek *Size:* hoog 46, breed 37 duim	Joseph Vallette	(Sold) fl 42 H Jansen
1807/08/26	AMSCH	0012	*P. van Blommem* | Twee stuks Landschappen, gestoffeerd met een Smits Wiukel [sic], waarby Paarden en Beelden, de andere met Paarden en Vee; beide krachtig | *Mat:* op doek *Size:* hoog 14, breed 12 duim	Joseph Vallette	(Sold) fl 20 A Rynders
1808/06/13	AMSCH	0024	*Blommen (P. van)* | Twee stuks Landschappen: in de eene wordt een Postwagen door Rovers aangevallen, en in den anderen ziet men eenige Beesten door een water drijven, waarbij Krijgslieden te paard. De schildering is kloek | *Mat:* op koper *Size:* hoog 13, breed 17 duim	[Jan Tersteeg]	(Sold) fl 101 Glad
1808/08/23	AMSCH	0186	*P. van Blommen* | Twee stuks Bergachtige Landschappen, met aloude Gebouwen, beide met Beelden en Beesten gestoffeerd	[Gruyter?]	(Sold) fl 12:10 Spruit
1809/07/25	HGBSM	0239	*P. van Blommen* | Twee Stuks met Figuuren en Paarden | *Mat:* op doek *Size:* hoog 15, breed 12 duim	D van der Aa [or] E B ten Dall	(Sold) fl 11:5 Hassevoord
1810/10/11	AMSCH	0153	*P. Van Blommen* | Een Landschap, met stoffagie	S	(Sold) fl 0:12 Singeling

Blok, H. [Unidentified]

1804/10/16	DLOND	0026	*H. Blok* | Ene Vrouw die Appelen verkoopt aan Jongens. Des Garçons qui achettent des Pommes d'une Femme | *Mat:* op doek *Size:* hoog 13, breed 11		(Sold) fl 7:5 Mahy

Blom, Jan

1805/07/03	AMSCH	0069	*J. Blom* | Een Boom- en Bergachtig Landschap, met diverse stoffagie van Beelden te paard en te voet; kragtig en zonachtig op Doek | *Mat:* op doek *Size:* hoog 33, breed 39 duim	C	(Sold) fl 15 Nieuwenhuis

Blom, P. [Unidentified]

1801/04/13	AMSCH	0106	*P. Blom* | Aan een Fontein in een bergachtig Landschap ziet men Reizigers te paard, zich verfrissen, verder nog een menigte stoffagie van Beelden en Beesten; meesterlyk geschilderd, door P. Blom, in de manier van T. Wyk, op Doek | *Mat:* op doek *Size:* hoog 18, breed 23 duim	Pierre Fouquet, junior	(Sold) fl 28 Lafontaine

Bloos, P. de [Unidentified]

1802/08/24	LNDLS	0049	*P. de Bloos* | Dit Stuk verbeeld een Stil Leven, met eene menigte Huisraad van differente soort; alles zoo konstig en uitvoerig behandeld, dat het de Natuur evenaart | *Mat:* op paneel *Size:* hoog 18 ½, breed 25 ½ duimen	Leonardus Bouman [or others]	(Unknown) fl 28

Bloot, Pieter de

1801/03/16	AMSCH	0094	*P. de Bloot* | Een Boere Binnehuis met diverse Stoffagie en een Varken op de leer, natuurlyk behandeld	K[ip]	(Sold) fl 7 Wijland
1801/06/10	AMSCH	0036	*Bloot. (P. de)* | In een Binnenhuis ziet men een Vrouw met een Kind op de schoot, verders andere Huislieden; kragtig gepenceeld | *Mat:* op paneel *Size:* hoog 14, breed 13 duim	[Doublet]	(Sold) fl 22 Stevens
1802/06/16	AMSCH	0023	*P. de Bloot* | In een zeer Natuurlyk Landzicht, vertoonen zich eenige Boere Woningen, by een Moolen; verders by een Water leggen eenige Scheepen, op de voorgrond zyn twee Wandelaars, en verder een Huisman, Beesten voortdryvende: verwonderlyk, natuurlyk en meesterlyk gepenceeld | *Mat:* op paneel *Size:* hoog 12, breed 16 duim	[Merrem]	(Sold) fl 40 van der Schley
1802/06/28	AMSCH	0008	*P. de Bloot* | Twee stuks rykgestoffeerde Binnehuizen, waarin eenige Lieden aan Tafel zitten te Eeten, en andere zich met Drinken en Stoeijen vermakende, verders een menigte Huisraad, zeer natuurlyk gepenceeld door P. de Bloot, op Koper | *Mat:* op koper *Size:* hoog 25, breed 35 duim	Anna Elink	(Sold) fl 91 Jan Spaan
1803/06/20	AMSCH	0047	*P. de Bloot* | In een Binnenschuur ziet men een Valken op de Leer en een menigte Bywerk, een Vrouw aan een Put en andere Beelden | *Mat:* op paneel *Size:* hoog 15, breed 17 duim	Roos [for] C	(Sold) fl 2 Plux
1803/09/07	AMSCH	0026	*P. de Bloot* | Een Binnenhuis, alwaar een Man en Vrouw beezig zyn hun Glaasje in te schenken, en een ander over een Schut, verders eenig Huisraad, geestig op Paneel [L'intérieur d'un maison ; une homme et une femme se versent à boire ; un autre qui repand la boisson par dessus le verre ; on voit encore quelques meubles ; il règne dans l'ensemble un ton spirituel] | *Mat:* op paneel *Size:* hoog 12, breed 10 duim	Smidt	(Sold) fl 9 Teengs
1803/12/15	MGLAC	0049	*P. de Bloodt* | Een Boere Kermis in een Dorp; zeer kragtig en breed behandeld | *Mat:* op paneel *Size:* hoog duim 14, breed duim 13	Mr L H de Haze Bomme	(Unknown)
1804/10/16	DLOND	0027	*P. de Bloot* | Een Boeren Gevegt. Combat entre quelques Paysans | *Mat:* op doek *Size:* hoog 13, breed 16		(Unknown)
1805/10/09	HGBSM	0013	*P. de Bloot* | Een boeren gezelschap | *Mat:* op paneel *Size:* hoog 8 breet 10 ½ duim	T H van Willigen [or others]	(Sold) fl 5:5 Roedig
1808/04/26	GDAN	0006	*Bloot (P. de)* | Een zonägtig Landschap met Boere Woningen, en verdere stoffagie, wel gedaan | *Size:* hoog 14, breed 18 ½ duim	G H Fortuyn	(Unknown)
1808/04/26	GDAN	0007	*Bloot (P.de)* | Een Herberg, waar voor een groot gezelschap Boeren en Boerinnen zich vermaken, heel fraai konstig en uitvoerig geschilderd, dit uitmuntend stuk is of 't van D. Teniers was | companion to lot 8 *Size:* hoog 16, breed 20 duim	G H Fortuyn	(Unknown)
1808/04/26	GDAN	0008	*Bloot (P. de)* | Een dito [Herberg], tot een wederga, waar bij een Paardrijder iets uitdeeld aan een menigte Volks, alles als het vorige [heel fraai konstig en uitvoerig geschilderd] | companion to lot 7 *Size:* hoog 16, breed 20 duim	G H Fortuyn	(Unknown)
1809/04/17	AMSCH	0009	*P. de Bloot* | Het Binnengezicht van een Boeren Wooning, gestoffeerd met een Huisman en Vrouw, verscheide Hennen en verder Huisraad; fiks geschilderd | *Mat:* op paneel *Size:* hoog 19, breed 25 duim	A	(Sold) fl 14:10
1809/04/17	AMSCH	0010	*P. de Bloot* | Een Boeren Binnenhuis, met drie Beelden gestoffeerd en verder Bijwerk, geestig | *Mat:* op paneel *Size:* hoog 19, breed 22 duim	A	(Sold) fl 2:10
1809/04/17	AMSCH	0010a[H]	*P. de Bloot* | Twee Stuk | *Notes:* This lot was added in by hand in the EBNP copy of the catalogue.	A	(Sold) fl 9
1809/04/22	AMYVR	0008	*P. de Bloot* | In een Dorp ziet men voor een Boerenwooning een Varkenmarkt met eene menigte Huislieden, welken schijnen te negotiëeren; de uitvoering is van de beste van deezen Meester | *Mat:* op paneel *Size:* hoog 23, breed 30 duim	de Bruin	(Bought In) fl 14
1809/07/19	AMSCH	[A0009][H]	*P de Bloot* | 1 Land[schap] | *Notes:* This lot was added in by hand in the AA copy of the catalogue. Because it was not numbered, we have assigned the number.		(Unknown)

Blyhooft, Zacharias

1802/05/10	MGSAN	0049	*Z. Blyhooft* | Een fraaije Battaille, waarover een zwaar Onweder; op de voorgrond verscheide Dooden en Gekwesten, krachtig geschilderd, door	Johan Dirk Kruysse	(Unknown) £ 1:9

			Z. Blyhooft: op Paneel, in vergulde Lyst | *Mat:* op paneel *Size:* hoog 14 duim, breed 21 duim		
			Boet, J.		
1803/07/14	MGKLY	0022	*J. Boets, 1658* | De vier Elementen in een geestige en ryke ordonnantie verbeeld, goed en kunstig gepenseeld | *Inscr:* J. Boets, 1658 (signed and dated?) *Notes:* It is unclear whether the name and date are inscribed on the painting.	Mr Caspar Jacob van Citters	(Unknown)
			Bogaert, Hendrick Hendricksz.		
1802/05/11	GRGRW	0051	*Boqaarts* | Een Werkende Kuiper [Schilderijen met Olie-Verf; In zwarte Lijsten] | *Mat:* in olyverf *Notes:* The bracketed information in the title appears above lot 1 and refers to lots 1 to 79a.	Arnold Sicco Werumeus	(Unknown) fl 1:8
1804/10/16	DLOND	0028	*H. Bogert, 1673* | Een Boeren Kermis, waarop enige Heren en Dames in gezelschap die ververschingen gebruiken. Familie Portraitten. Une foire de Village; on y voit une Compagnie de quelques Messieurs & Dames prendre des rafraichissemens. Portraits de Famille | *Mat:* op doek *Size:* hoog 42, breed 56 *Inscr:* H. Bogert, 1673 (signed and dated?) *Notes:* It is unclear whether the name and date are inscribed on the painting.		(Sold) fl 13:10 v Giesen
			Bogaert, Iemant		
1806/08/20	HGBSM	0157	*J. Bogert 1649* | Een binnehuis met Boere huisraad, door J. Bogert 1649 | *Mat:* op paneel *Size:* hoog 20 ½, breed 31 ½ duim *Inscr:* J. Bogert 1649 (signed and dated?) *Notes:* It is unclear whether the name and date are inscribed on the painting.	Macalester Loup [or others]	(Sold) fl 13:15 Gram
			Bogdany, Jakob		
1808/06/06	RMRIJ	0016	*Bogdani. (J.)* | Een Bloem- en Fruitstuk met Gevogelte, voor een Schoorsteenstuk geschikt. Goed geschilderd [Cette Pièce represente un Groupe de fleurs, de fruits et d'oiseaux, et est propre à être placée devant une cheminée] | *Mat:* op doek *Fmt:* schoorsteenstuk *Size:* Hoog 62, en breed 43 ¼ duim	Gerrit van der Pot, Heer van Groeneveld	(Sold) fl 12 Coclers
			Boijer, H. de [Unidentified]		
1808/09/13	HABRU	0012	*H. de Boijer* | Een vegtende Partij		(Unknown) fl 2:15
			Bol, Ferdinand		
1801/04/13	AMSCH	0007	*F. Bol* | De Koning David zittende in een mediteerende gestalte, hy is gekleed in een met bond gevoerde rok, nevens hem ligt zyn kroon, in de eene hand heeft hy een pen, terwyl de andere op een Boek ligt; de houding is brillant en de schildering kragtig en meesterlyk | *Mat:* op doek *Size:* hoog 50, breed 38 duim	Pierre Fouquet, junior	(Sold) fl 81 v d Schley [for] M[errem]
1801/04/13	AMSCH	0008	*F. Bol* | Een Romeinsche historieele Ordonantie, alwaar aan een Krygsoverste door een menigte in ryke Oostersche kleding gekleede personen, kostbare geschenken worden aangebragt; meesterlyk behandeld | *Mat:* op doek *Size:* hoog 33, breed 32 duim *Loc:* Worcester, MA, USA. Art Museum. (1961–39) as A Roman Consul refusing gifts	Pierre Fouquet, junior	(Sold) fl 102 Pruyssenaar
1801/06/10	AMSCH	0020	*Boll. (F.)* | Een model van het Capitaal stuk op het Raadhuis dezer Stad berustende, voorstellende het Paleis van Pyrrhus, hy is bezig met den Romeinschen Veldheer Fabricius te handelen. De verdere aanschouwers zo in krygs als burgerlyke gewaden, schynen zig over de standvastigheid van den Romeinschen Held te verwonderen, alles is by uitstek krachtig en tevens helder gepenseeld | *Mat:* op doek op paneel *Size:* hoog 27, breed 22 duim *Loc:* Amsterdam, Nederland. Historisch Museum. (A 35807)	[Doublet]	(Sold) fl 34 Van Dijl
1801/06/10	AMSCH	0021	*Boll. (F.)* | In een Landschap ziet men zeven Kinderen speelen, met een met Bloemen bekransde Bok, aangenaam van Coloriet en penceels behandeling | *Mat:* op doek *Size:* hoog 51, breed 61 duim	Herman ten Kate	(Sold) fl 80 Pruyssenaar
1801/06/10	AMSCH	0022	*Boll. (F.)* | In dit Stuk zit de Liefde verzeld van vier Kinderen, in eene graaselyke houding, twee derzelven houden den hoorn des Overvloeds in hunne handen, meesterlyk gepenseeld | *Mat:* op doek *Size:* hoog 94, breed 70 duim	Herman ten Kate	(Sold) fl 24:10 C S Roos
1801/10/19	AMSCH	0012	*Bol. (F.)* | Een bejaard Mans Pourtrait met een groene muts op, gekleed met een geel bruine Rok en roode Mantel; zeer kragtig en uitvoerig behandeld | *Mat:* op doek *Size:* hoog 22 ¼, breed 18 duim	Jonkheer Menno Baron van Coehoorn	(Sold) fl 19:10 v d Schleij M [for] Merrem
1802/05/05	AMSCH	0035	*F. Bol* | Een Capitaal Historiëel Onderwerp	J	(Sold) fl 5:10 Spruit
1802/05/10	MGSAN	0041	*F. Bol* | Een Philosooph in zyn Kamer, zittende aan een Tafel, waarop een Globe; op de voorgrond een Kaart, en ander Bywerk, uitvoerig, door F. Bol: in vergulde Lyst | *Size:* hoog 9 ½ duim, breed 7 ½ duim	Johan Dirk Kruysse	(Unknown) £ 1
1802/06/16	AMSCH	0016	*Ferdinand Bol* | Het Afbeeldsel van David, zittende voor een Tafel, waarop een Boek geplaatst; dit stuk is krachtig en meesterlyk gepenceelt | *Mat:* op doek *Size:* hoog 49, breed 37 duim	[Merrem]	(Sold) fl 87 H de Valk
1802/06/16	AMSCH	0017	*Ferdinand Bol* | Een Gryzaard met een Muts op 't Hoofd, zynde van een meesterlyke penceelbehandeling | *Size:* hoog 22 ½, breed 18 ½ duim	[Merrem]	(Sold) fl 25:10 Van Iperen
1802/09/21	UTHDG	0010	*F. Bol* | Een vrolijke knaap, houdende de vinger aan de mond, schijnt voorwaarts te gaan, om iets te bespieden of om te verrassen, natuurlijk en meesterlijk | *Mat:* op paneel *Size:* hoog 23 ½, breed 18 duimen		(Sold) fl 32 G Roelands

1803/07/07	HGKAN	0003	*F. Bol* | Een Philosooph in Studie, door F. Bol, op Doek [Schilderyen in Olyverf] | *Mat:* in olyverf op doek *Notes:* The bracketed information in the title appears above lot 1 and refers to lots 1 to 25.		(Unknown)
1803/08/17	AMSCH	0012	*Bol. (F.)* | De verschyning van den Engel by Maria, de heerlykheid van den Engel, en de verwondering van Maria, zyn schoon; zoo wel de fixe behandeling, als het fraaije ligt en bruin, geeven een bewijs der kunde van deezen Meester | *Mat:* op paneel *Size:* hoog 21, breed 17 duim	Anna Catharina Putman	(Sold) fl 20 Pruijssenaar
1803/09/07	AMSCH	0022	*F. Boll* | Een Vrouwe Pourtrait, welke met haar regterhand een Gordyn open schuift [Un portrait de femme, qui de la main droite rélève un rideau] | *Mat:* op paneel *Size:* hoog 15 ½, breed 12 duim	Smidt	(Bought In) fl 20 for lots 22 & 23
1803/09/07	AMSCH	0023	*F. Boll* | Een Jonge Krygsheld, met een Ringkraag om den hals, en een Pluim op den Hoed, meesterlyk als Rembrandt [Un jeune chevalier, orné d'un haussecol, ayant un plumet au chapeau ; exécuté en maître dans la manière de Rembrant] | *Mat:* op paneel *Size:* hoog 15, breed 12 duim	Smidt	(Bought In) fl 20 for lots 22 & 23
1803/12/12	AMSCH	0008	*F. Boll* | Deeze capitaale Ordonnantie stelt voor, den Fabel van Virtumnis en Pomona, in een Landschap; de téekening en schildering van beide deeze figuuren zyn meesterlyk en van de delicaatste Penceelbehandeling van F. Boll | *Mat:* op doek *Size:* hoog 45, breed 49 duim	B	(Bought In) fl 105
1804/02/27	AMSCH	0004	*Boll. (F.)* | Dit uitmuntend Pourtrait, zeer ryk gekleed, met een purpere Mantel omhange; vertoond zich voor een Gebouw met Colommen, hy rust met de Linkerhand op een Leuning en wyst met de rechter na den Aanschouwer; de dunheid en fraaie Tusschentinten welke men in dit Pourtrait ontdekt; zyn meesterlyk gepenceeld, en is alles van een krachtig Effect | *Mat:* op doek *Size:* hoog 50, breed 40 duim *Loc:* Amsterdam, Nederland. Rijksmuseum. (A 43)	B	(Sold) fl 101 van Iperen
1804/04/28	LNDLS	0002	*F. Bols* | Dit Konststuk, verbeeldende Moses met de tafelen der Wet, van den berg Sinai afkomende, daar de joodsche mannen, vrouwen en kinderen met eerbied en ootmoed [sic] zig voor nederbuigen en aanbidden; zeer konstig van ordonnantie, colloriet en fix van schildering, door F. Bols, op paneel, hoog 28, breed 20 duim. Hetzelve ontwerp is op het Raadhuis der Stad Amsterdam geplaatst, door denzelven in 't groot geschildert | *Mat:* op paneel *Size:* hoog 28, breed 20 duim *Loc:* St. Bonaventure, NY, USA. St. Bonaventure University.	[Abraham Delfos] [or others]	(Bought In) fl 100
1804/04/28	LNDLS	0003	*F. Bols* | De Godinne der Wysheid, met den schepter in de rechter, en het roer van den staat in de andere hand, nevens haar den zuil van standvastigheid, zy word gekroond met de onsterflykheid, voor haar zetel ziet men de godinne der rykdom, een weduwvrouw streelen, daar geregtigheid, overvloed en welvaard, benevens speer en hoed der vryheid, door kinderen verbeeld zyn, door denzelven [F. Bols], op paneel, hoog 28 breed 20 duim. Deze ordonnantie is door denzelven meester in 't groot geschildert, en berust voor de schoorsteen, op de Raadkamer van 't Raadhuis der Stad Leyden | *Mat:* op paneel *Size:* hoog 28, breed 20 duim	[Abraham Delfos] [or others]	(Bought In) fl 51
1804/07/25	AMSCH	0005	*Boll. (F.)* | In een capitaal boomryk Landschap, ziet men een wandelend Heer, in deftig Oostersch gewaad, verzelt van een Dame in ryke Satyne kleeding; ter linkerzyde op een Heuvel, onder het Geboomte, schynt een Veehoeder te rusten, waarby eenige Schaapen en een Bok; ter andere zyde vertoont zig een aangenaam Verschiet; het is van een bevallige en uitvoerige behandeling | *Mat:* op doek *Size:* hoog 47, breed 67 duim		(Sold) fl 28 Hulswit
1804/10/16	DLOND	0132a	*F. Bol* | [Untitled] | *Notes:* The lot was changed from "Nic. Maas en J.H. Nickelen, Het Raadhuis te Amsterdam, met de Waag, en veel gewoel," to "F. Bol," without giving a title, at the front of the catalogue.		(Unknown)
1805/07/10	AMSCH	0005	*F. Boll* | Dit Capitaal Schildery stelt voor een Professor met zyn Vrouw, beide in deftige aloude Kleeding, zittende voor een Tafel, hy rust met de eene hand op een Doodshoofd, en met de andere op de Armstoel; en zy houd in de eene hand een Bloem; achter hun een Steene Kolom, waarvoor een groen Kleed hangt, &c. allerdelicaast [sic] en fraay gepenceeld | *Mat:* op doek *Size:* hoog 43, breed 54 duim	V[inkeles] [for] C	(Sold) fl 5 v der Schley [for] R[ijfsnijder]
1805/07/10	AMSCH	0006	*F. Boll* | Een deftig Heer, gekleed in een bonte Pels en een Muts met bond op zyn Hoofd, met zyn regter hand leunende op de Stoel; meesterlyk fraay op Doek | *Mat:* op doek *Size:* hoog 45, breed 36 duim	R[oos]	(Sold) fl 20:10 Hulsewit
1806/05/05	AMSCH	0015	*F. Bol* | Een Ordinnantie van drie bevallige Vrouwen, dewelke zig met een hond schynen te vermaken en verdere bywerk; meesterlyk gepenceeld door F. Bol | *Mat:* op doek *Size:* hoog 50, breed 63 duim	V[inkeles]	(Bought In) fl 12
1806/05/05	AMSCH	0027	*F. Bol* | Diana als vermoeid van de Jagt, in een bosch rustende, verzeld van staande en leggende honden; byna levensgroote	V[inkeles]	(Sold) fl 1 Willem van der Schley
1806/08/13	AMSCH	0006	*Bol. (F.)* | Maria met het kind Jesus, waarby Johannes; zynde een treffelyke Ordinantie, uitmuntend van drapperie, teekening, coloriet en meesterlyke penceelsbehandeling | *Mat:* op doek *Size:* hoog 50, breed 48 duim	Roos [for] Vos	(Sold) fl 20:10 Verhoesen
1807/06/10	HGBSM	0069	*F. Boll* | Dit konststuk verbeeld , daar Moses met de Tafelen der Wet, van den berg Sinaï afkomt, en het Joodsche volk zich eerbiedig nederbuigen, fix behandeld, door F. Boll, op paneel, hoog 28 breed 20 duim. Een ordonnantie voor een vertrek in 't Stadshuis te Amsterdam | *Mat:* op paneel *Size:* hoog 28 breed 20 duim *Loc:* St. Bonaventure, NY, USA. St. Bonaventure University.	Abraham Delfos [or others]	(Sold or Bought In) 100 D

1807/06/10	HGBSM	0070	*F. Boll* | De Godinne der Wijsheid, word gekroond met de Onsterflijkheid, en meer zinnebeeldige figuren, dito [fix] behandeld, door denzelven [F. Boll], op paneel, hoog 28 breed 20 duim. Konstig geördonneerd, voor de Raadkamer der Stad Leyden. | *Mat:* op paneel *Size:* hoog 28 breed 20 duim	Abraham Delfos [or others]	(Sold or Bought In) fl 45 D
1809/04/22	AMYVR	0007	*F. Bol* | Vertumnus en Pomona in een Landschap; meesterlijk geschilderd | *Mat:* op doek *Size:* hoog 49, breed 50 duim	van den Bracke	(Sold) fl 110 Coclers
1809/06/13	AMSCH	0011	*F. Boll* | Een Bijbel-Ordonantie, verbeeldende de Droom van Jacob, waar bij een staande Engel en eene Vrouw; fraai van licht en bruin en meesterlijk geschilderd | *Mat:* op doek *Size:* hoog 29, breed 26 duim	E	(Sold) fl 29 Buck
1809/06/13	AMSCH	0012	*F. Boll* | Een Ordonantie van vier Beelden, verbeeldende Meleager, het Zwijnshoofd Athalante aanbiedende; meesterlijk geschilderd | *Mat:* op doek *Size:* hoog 59, breed 64 duim	S[chley]	(Sold) fl 2 Gruyter
1810/08/01	AMSCH	0013	*Boll (Ferdinand)* | Eene deftige Vrouw, zittende in een Armstoel; voor haar staat een Kind, hetwelk haar eenige Bloemen aanbiedt [Le Portrait d'une Femme distingué assise dans un fauteul. Elle a devant elle un Enfant qui lui presente des Fleurs] | *Annots:* médiocre (NGW) *Mat:* op doek *Size:* hoog 48, breed 39 duimen	Mr Pieter de Smeth van Alphen	(Sold) fl 70 Coclers d'Amsterdam
1810/08/06	AMSCH	0015	*Bol (F.)* | Rebecca geeft den dienaar van Abraham te drinken, terwijl hare Dienstmaagd het Vee drenkt. Alles is zeer krachtig en natuurlijk, als van Rembrand | *Mat:* op doek *Size:* hoog 64, breed 64 duimen	[J de Bos?]	(Bought In) fl 40
1810/08/06	AMSCH	0016	*Bol (F.)* | Twee stuks fraaije Mans en Vrouwe Portretten, tot de knieën te zien. Meesterlijk als Rembrand geschilderd | *Mat:* op doek *Size:* ieder hoog 49, breed 35 duimen	G	(Bought In) fl 50
1810/10/10	MGCIT	0052	*Fr. Bol* | Een Jongen halver Lijve, in eene hoog bruine kleding, en blond gekruld Hair, met veel graagte een Koek eetende, natuurlijk en stout behandeld	Caspar van Citters	(Unknown)
1810/10/11	AMSCH	0136a[H]	*Bol* | Een oud Manshooft | *Notes:* The lot was changed by hand from "Een Paardenkop; krachtig op Doek, door G. Van Den Eekhout" to "Een oud Manshooft, door Bol" in the FLNY copy of the catalogue.	[Gruyter?]	(Bought In) fl 7

Bol, Ferdinand (or Bol, F., manner)

1802/05/05	AMSCH	0034	*F. Bol* | Een Deftig Oud Man, leunende op een Boek, houdende in de Hand een Pen, door, of als F. Bol | *Size:* hoog 50, breed 37 duim	J	(Sold) fl 4:15 Ackina
1804/05/07	AMSCH	0022	*Boll. (F.) of in de manier* | Een Schildery, daar een Proffessor aan een Tafel zit, rustende met de eene Hand op een Bekkeneel, over hem deszelfs Huisvrouw, enz.; dit stuk is uitmuntend geschilderd, en van een meesterlyke penceelsbehandeling | *Mat:* op doek *Size:* hoog 42, breed 25 duim	Y[ver] [for] W	(Bought In) fl 60

Bol, Ferdinand (manner)

1805/12/16	AMSCH	0066	*F. Bol* | Een Vrouw met drie Kinderen, zinspeelende op de Liefde, als F. Bol, meesterlyk behandeld	R[oos]	(Sold) fl 0:14 L Pakker
1805/12/16	AMSCH	0086	*F. Bol* | Een Vorstelyk Personaadje, in prachtige Kleeding, als door F. Bol	R[oos]	(Sold) fl 3:10 Hulswit
1808/06/11	RMRIJ	0060	*Als door F: Bol* | Een Oosters Vorst ligt in een prachtig Ledikant, een Kamerling gezeten voor hetzelve, terwyl een jonge Neger met eene toors by hun staat, voorts op den tweede grond Lyfwacht en andere personen, Wapenrusting, Kroon en verder Bywerk versieren dit Schildery; Transpirant, gloeiend en meesterlyk behandeld | *Mat:* op paneel *Size:* hoog 34, breed 46 duim		(Bought In) fl 25

Bola, F. [Unidentified]

1801/03/16	AMSCH	0131	*F. Bola* | Een stil Leven	P[ruyssenaar]	(Sold) fl 10 Van Dijl

Boldeker [Unidentified]

1802/07/09	AMSTO	0062	*Boldeker* | 1 vrouwe Portrait, op doek | *Mat:* op doek		(Unknown)

Bolff, C. [Unidentified]

1805/10/09	HGBSM	0058	*C. Bolff* | Een keuken stuk met kopere ketels &c., verwonderlyk natuurlyk | *Mat:* op paneel *Size:* hoog 26 breet 39 duim	T H van Willigen [or others]	(Sold) fl 23:10 Zwartsman

Bollongier, Hans

1809/05/26	HADAA	0067	*H. Bollongier* | Een Brand buiten de Schalkwijker Poort te Haarlem, natuurlijk en meesterachtig op Paneel door H. Bollongier, A$^{o.}$ 1648 | *Mat:* op paneel *Inscr:* H. Bollongier, A$^{o.}$ 1648 (signed and dated?) *Notes:* It is unclear whether the name and date are inscribed on the painting.	Mejuffrouw de Wed David Heemskerk [or others]	(Unknown)
1809/05/26	HADAA	A0011	*H. Bollongier* | Een Brand buiten de Schalkwijker Poort, te Haarlem, natuurlijk | *Mat:* op paneel *Size:* hoog 15, breed 10 duimen	Mejuffrouw de Wed David Heemskerk [or others]	(Unknown)

Bolomey, Benjamin Samuel

1802/12/13	AMSCH	0016	*Boulomy* | De Doghters van 't Heilig Eiland offeren huune [sic] Gordels op het Altaar, in de Tempel van Minerva; meesterlyk en uitvoerig gepenseelt | *Mat:* op doek *Size:* hoog 22, breed 18 duim	Yver	(Sold) fl 3:10 Gruiter

1804/08/08	AMSCH	0036	*Boulomy* | De Dochters van 't Heilige Eiland offeren hunne Gordels op het Altaar, in de Tempel van Minerva; meesterlyk en bevallig van schildering | *Mat:* op doek *Size:* hoog 22, breed 18 duim	Vink[eles] [for] K[=Gruyter?]	(Sold) fl 4 Coclers
1806/08/20	HGBSM	0185	*B. S. Bolemey* | Het Portrait van Z. D. H. den Heere Prins Willem den Vijfde, levensgroot ten voeten uit, in het Harnas, met een Vorstelijke Mantel omhangen, rustende met zijne rechterhand op het gevest zijns Degen, in het verschiet een Vloot, en verder bijwerk | *Mat:* op doek *Size:* hoog 84, breed 60 duim	Macalester Loup [or others]	(Sold) fl 13 Zwartsman
1806/09/24	HGBES	0004	*Bolomy* | Het Vorstelyke Huisgezin 7 st. door Bolomy, Zwarte Lyste en Glazen		(Unknown)

Bon, C. de [Unidentified]

1804/07/25	DLGRO	0029	*C. de Bon* | Een Landschapje met twee Boeren Huizen, en verder bywerk | *Mat:* op paneel *Size:* hoog 14, breed 12 duim	Mr Franc van der Burch Wz.	(Unknown)

Boon, H. [Unidentified]

1801/04/08	HAVIN	0060	*H. Boon* | Twee Landschappen		(Unknown)
1801/04/08	HAVIN	0061	*H. Boon* | Twee dito [Landschappen]		(Unknown)

Boon, H. [Unidentified] (copy by)

1801/04/08	HAVIN	0059	*H. Boon; Jordaans* | Een Hist: na Jordaans | copy by H. Boon after J. Jordaens (I)		(Unknown)

Boonen, Arnold

1801/10/19	AMSCH	0013	*Bonen. (Arnoldus)* | Voor een open steene Nis, ziet men een bevallige Dame, houdende in de hand een Mandtje met verscheiden vrugten; neevens dezelve staat een vriendelyk Jongetje, schynende na het Fruit te grypen; verder is een Tuingezigt: dit stukje is fraay van Ordonnantie, aangenaam van Coloriet, en zeer uitvoerig gepenseeld | *Mat:* op doek *Size:* hoog 17 ½, breed 14 duim	Jonkheer Menno Baron van Coehoorn	(Sold) fl 34 B[d] Kooy
1802/06/28	AMSCH	0007	*A. Boonen* | In eene steene Nis ziet men het Pourtrait van W. J. Koster, oud 111 Jaar, fiks gepenceeld | *Size:* hoog 20, breed 16 duim	Anna Elink	(Sold) fl 2 Yver
1803/12/12	AMSCH	0011	*A. Bonen* | Een Pourtrait van een Kunstliefhebber, met eenige Kunstboeken voor zich, en een Tekening in zyn Hand houdende, delicaat op Doek | *Mat:* op doek *Size:* hoog 17, br. 14 duim	F	(Sold) fl 4 Bergh
1804/08/08	AMSCH	0025	*A. Bonen* | Een Heer in zyn Japon, aan een Tafel zittende met aandacht, by een brandende Kaars, een Medailje te beschouwen; het licht is frappant, en de uitvoering als J. Schalken, door A. Bonen | *Mat:* op paneel *Size:* hoog 7 ½, breed 6 ½	Roos a	(Sold) fl 7 Gruyter
1806/08/20	HGBSM	0020	*A. Boonen* | Een Heer met een Patrijs in de hand tegen een boom zittende, helder geschilderd door A. Boonen | *Mat:* op doek *Size:* hoog 16, breed 13 duim	Macalester Loup [or others]	(Sold) fl 1:8 Schouman
1806/08/20	HGBSM	0128	*A. Boone* | Twee stuks dito Portraiten | *Mat:* op paneel *Notes:* It is unclear what "dito" refers to in the title.	Macalester Loup [or others]	(Sold) fl 1 Heijmans
1807/08/26	AMSCH	0015	*A. Boonen* | Het Pourtret van den Konsthandelaar Jan Pietersz. Soomer, die bezig is om Teekeningen te bezien; zeer fraai en uitvoerig behandeld | *Mat:* op doek *Size:* hoog 17, breed 13 duim	de Vries	(Sold) fl 2:10 J de Vries
1807/08/26	AMSCH	0016	*A. Boonen* | Een vergenoegde Jongeling voor een Nes, met een Roemer Wyn in de hand | *Mat:* op doek *Size:* hoog 12, breed 10 duim	de Vries	(Sold) fl 1 Coclair
1808/08/23	AMSCH	0030	*Boonen. (A.)* | Eene bejaarde Vrouw, zittende aan een Tafel, waar boven een brandende lamp geplaatst is; het licht doet een schoone werking, en is uitvoerig gepenceeld | *Mat:* op paneel *Size:* hoog 8, breed 6 duim	H	(Bought In) fl 27
1809/04/22	AMYVR	0009	*A. Boonen* | Twee stuks: een Jongeling met een Hondje, en een Meisje met een Schotel met Vruchten; delicaat | *Mat:* op doek *Size:* hoog 13, breed 11 duim	Juff[r] Julikker	(Sold) fl 10:10 C S Roos
1809/09/06	AMSCH	0007	*Boonen (A.)* | Dit bevallig stukje verbeeld, bij een open Steenen Nis, eene Dame in deftige Kleeding, houdende op de eene hand een Cacetou-vogel; schijnende met de andere hem eenig eeten te geeven, ter zijde staat een aardige Jongeling, met een Zilver Schoteltje in de handen, waar op eenig Spijs ligt; alles uitvoerig en meesterlijk gepenceeld | *Mat:* op doek *Size:* hoog 16, breed 13 duim	Johannes Caudri	(Sold) fl 12:10 Tomassen
1810/05/22	AMSCH	0009	*Boonen (A.)* | Een Heer in deftige Kleeding, rustende op eene Borstweering met den regterarm, houdende een Pijp in de Hand, in de linker heeft hij een Roemer Wijn, schijnende derzelver helderheid tegens de Dag te beschouwen, nevens hem staat een Tabaksdoos, Komvoir, enz.; zeer natuurlijk en uitvoerig van penceelbehandeling | *Mat:* op doek op paneel *Size:* hoog 11 ½, breed 9 duim	Johannes van de Putte Nicolaasz.	(Sold) fl 21 Hulswit

Boonen, Arnold (copy by)

1802/05/05	AMSCH	0195	*A. Boonen; G. Schalken* | In een Binnenvertrek by een Kaarslicht, ziet men een bevallige Dame voor haar Toilet, verzeld van een Dienstmaagd, welke een Spiegel vast houd, beneevens een Jongeling die achter haar staat, zeer natuurlyk en warm van Coloriet, door A. Boonen na G. Schalken | copy by A. Boonen after Schalcken *Mat:* op paneel *Size:* hoog 16, breed 13 duim	C	(Sold) fl 8 Rigters

			Boonen, Arnold (or Boonen, A., manner)		
1805/07/03	AMSCH	0068	*A. Boonen* | Een jonge Vrouw, houdende een brandende Kaars in de hand; de reflectie van het licht, doed een natuurlyke werking, meesterlyk en kragtig geschilderd, op Paneel, door of in de manier van A. Boonen | *Mat:* op paneel *Size:* hoog 11, breed 9 duim	R[oos]	(Sold) fl 50 Lafontaine
			Boonen, Arnold (copy after)		
1809/04/22	AMYVR	0175	*A. Boonen* | Een met twee Beelden; naar A. Boonen	de Bruin	(Sold) fl 1:10 van Iperen
			Boonen, Arnold (manner)		
1805/07/10	AMSCH	0031	*A. Boonen* | Het Portrait van den Kunsthandelaar J. P. Zoomer; meesterlyk op Doek geschilderd, als door A. Boonen | *Mat:* op doek	S[chley] [for] Doralle	(Sold) fl 1:10 Jan Yver
			Borch, Gerard ter (II)		
1801/05/11	AMSCH	0087	*G. Terburg* | Een bevallig Meisje aan een Tafel zittende te schryven, een uitmuntend bewerkt Tapytenkleed, legt als opgeschoven, en fraai geplooyd, zynde dit stukje van een bevallig penceel | *Mat:* op paneel *Size:* hoog 15, breed 11 duim	E[lias]	(Sold) fl 205 Bern de Bosch
1801/05/11	AMSCH	0088	*G. Terburg* | Een deftig Man in een kamer staande met handschoenen in zyn hand, delicaat behandeld | *Mat:* op doek *Size:* hoog 25, breed 21 duim	P[ruyssenaar]	(Sold) fl 40 Allard
1801/06/13	LNDLS	0047	*G. Terburg* | Een Binnenvertrek, waarin een zittende juffer, met een jakje met bont, en een satijne rok aan, bij een tafel, benevens twee heeren die musiceeren, en meer bijwerk, op doek geschilderd | *Mat:* op doek *Size:* hoog 28, breed 22 duimen	D van R	(Sold) fl 100 A Delfos [for] W
1802/05/05	AMSCH	0208	*Ter Burg* | Een Mans Pourtrait, ten voeten uit	J	(Withdrawn)
1802/06/16	AMSCH	0024	*G. ter Burg* | Het Afbeeldsel van een Geleerd Geestelyk Persoon, halver lyf, in deftige houding: meesterlyk fraai en krachtig gepenceelt | *Mat:* op doek op paneel *Size:* hoog 11 ½, breed 9 ½ duim	[Merrem]	(Sold) fl 10:10 Reijers
1802/08/24	LNDLS	0005	*G. Terburg* | Een Dame in wit satyn gekleed, staande voor een Tafel, die met een Tapijt-kleed gedekt is, waar een zilveren doos en een spiegel op geplaatst is, agter hetzelve een stoel daar een Patrijshondje op rust, verder een Ledikant, alles in een Binnen-vertrek. Konstig op doek | *Mat:* op doek *Size:* hoog 25, breed 20 duimen	Leonardus Bouman [or others]	(Unknown) fl 59
1803/08/17	AMSCH	0080	*Terburg. (G.)* | Deeze ryke Ordonnantie van meer dan zeventig Beelden, steld voor de Vredehandeling te Munster, dit stuk is van een aller-uitvoerigste behandeling, en bekend, door de Prent van J. Suyderhoef, welke naar dit Schildery gegraveerd is. Hierby de Prent | *Mat:* op koper *Size:* hoog 18, breed 23 ½ duim *Loc:* Amsterdam, Nederland. Rijksmuseum. (A 405) as copy after Ter Borch	Anna Catharina Putman	(Sold) fl 340 C S Roos
1803/09/07	AMSCH	0182	*G. Terburch* | Een Binnenhuis, waarin een Arme Jongeling, staande met een Schotel in zyn handen, by eene oude Vrouw, zittende by den Haard; zeer fraai, fix en uitvoerig behandelt [Un intérieur représentant un jeune mendiant qui tient un plat dans ses mains auprès d'une vieille femme assise près du feu ; belle composition et peint avec beaucoup de soin et d'effet] | *Mat:* op paneel *Size:* hoog 11, breed 9 duim	Smidt	(Bought In) fl 41
1803/12/12	AMSCH	0095	*G. Terburg* | Dit stukje steld voor een Heer en Dame, op de Kaart spelende, welke door een ander Heer geholpen word; bevallig geordoneerd, delicaat en uitvoerig behandeld | *Mat:* op paneel *Size:* hoog 10, breed 9 duim	Arnoud de Lange	(Sold) fl 225 Josi
1804/02/27	AMSCH	0003	*Burch. (G. ter)* | Een Binnenvertrek; in hetzelve bevind zich een gezelschap van twee Dames en twee Heeren, zeer ryk gekleed; een Dame met een bruin fluweel jak en bonte rand, zit op den voorgrond, houdende een brief in de hand, waarover zy met de overige van het gezelschap schynd te spreeken, voor haar ziet men een staande Dame in het wit zatyn; 't welk zo fraay gepenceeld is, dat het de natuur evenaard, alles is voor het overige van een krachtig coloriet en meesterlyk behandeld | *Mat:* op doek *Size:* hoog 28, breed 24 duim	B	(Sold) fl 225 Jozi
1804/07/25	DLGRO	0073	*Ter Burgh* | Een Juffrouw in het Wit Satyn, voor een Tafel zittende waarop een Heer over haar legt te slaapen, terwyl zy uit een Wynglas drinkt, en met haar andere hand een Kruikje op haar schoot houd, fraai geschilderd door Ter Burgh | *Mat:* op doek *Size:* hoog 13 ½, breed 12 duim	Mr Franc van der Burch Wz.	(Unknown)
1804/08/08	AMSCH	0183	*G. Terburg* | In een Gemeubileerde Binnenkamer zit een Deftig Heer, met een Zyden Tabbaard, de Courant te leezen, voor een Tafel met een Tapyten Kleed gedekt, waarop een opengeslagen Kaartenboek; de uitvoerigheid van dit fraaije Kabinetstukje is te bewonderen, zynde van de beste schildering van G. Terburg | *Size:* hoog 19, breed 15 duim	Roos a	(Bought In) fl 70
1804/08/08	AMSCH	0184	*G. Terburg* | Willem de Derden, ten voeten uit, in 't Harnas, voor hem een Tafel met een Tapyt Kleed gedekt, waarop zyn Helm en verder Bywerk; uitvoerig gepenceeld | *Mat:* op doek *Size:* hoog 31 ½, breed 25 duim	Vink[eles] [for] K[=Gruyter?]	(Sold) fl 0:14 L Pakker
1804/08/08	AMSCH	0185	*G. Terburg* | Twee stuks, een Mans en een Vrouwen Pourtrait, in oude deftige Kleeding; zeer fraai gepenceeld | *Mat:* op doek *Size:* hoog 20, breed 16 duim	Pruys[senaar]	(Withdrawn)
1804/10/20	GRBOL	0003	*ter Burg* | Een Landschap met Water	Joannis Cannegieteri	(Unknown)

1804/10/20	GRBOL	0004	*ter Burg* | Een dito [Landschap]	Joannis Cannegieteri	(Unknown)
1805/07/03	AMSCH	0045	*Terburgh. (G.)* | Deeze Capitalen Ordinantie vertoont, in een Binnenvertrek, ter eener zyde, een Officier in aloude kleeding, met een Borst-harnas, schynende een glaaze fluit met wyn te leedigen, hy leunt teegen een vat; waarop een test met vuur geplaatst is, en voor dezelve op de grond, een wynkan; ter andere zyde zit een Trompetter, lustig opblaazende, verder staat een Krygsman, als met de Hospes spreekende, en op de Voorgrond een slaapend Hondje; het is Meesterlyk fraai, en van een uitvoerige penceel behandeling | *Mat:* op doek *Size:* hoog 38, breed 32 duim *Loc:* Philadelphia, PA, USA. Museum of Art. (Johnson Coll. 504)	R[oos]	(Sold) fl 650 Reijers
1805/07/03	AMSCH	0046	*Terburgh. (G.)* | Twee stuks, zynde het Afbeeldzel van een Dame en Heer, beide in aloude deftige Kleeding, in alles als de voorgaande, bevallig en zeer uitvoerig gepenceeld | *Mat:* op paneel *Size:* yder hoog 16, breed 11 duim	C	(Sold) fl 90 L Pakker
1805/07/03	AMSCH	0067	*G. Terburg* | Een bevallig Vrouwe pourtrait, halverlyf, in deftige aloude Kleeding, staande by een Tafel; fraay en uitvoerig van schildering | *Mat:* op doek *Size:* hoog 17, breed 13 duim	S	(Sold) fl 4:15 Agina
1806/01/30	RMAN	0010	*Terburgh* | Een Vrolyk Gezelschap	Dirk Langendyk	(Unknown)
1806/05/05	AMSCH	0001	*G. ter Burg* | Een Dame in deftige zwarte zyde kleding met een wit satyne Rok, kante doek en bevallig kapsel; uitvoerig op Doek | *Mat:* op doek *Size:* hoog 22, breed 16 duim	R[oos]	(Sold) fl 38 Hulswit
1806/05/05	AMSCH	0002	*G. ter Burg* | Een Mans Pourtret, halverlyf staande in deftige aloude kleeding in een prachtig Voorportaal; delicaat en fiks gepenceeld door denzelven [G. ter Burg] | *Mat:* op doek *Size:* hoog 18, breed 14 ½ duim	V[inkeles]	(Sold) fl 50:10 Coclers
1806/05/05	AMSCH	0003	*G. ter Burg* | In een Binnenkamer voor een Tafel met een rood kleed gedekt, staat een Heer in een peinsende houding, en verder bywerk; uitvoerig gepenceeld door denzelven [G. ter Burg] | *Size:* hoog 32, breed 26 duim	V[inkeles]	(Sold) fl 3:5 H^{S} Dekker
1806/08/13	AMSCH	0004	*Burgh. (G. ter)* | Dit bevallig tafreel, verbeeld een zittende Dame in wit Satyne kleeding, met een wit kapje op 't hoofd, schynende een glaasje wyn te drinken, en in de regter hand een Porcelyn Wynkannetje houdende, ter zyde legt een Heer op zyn armen rustende op een tafel, in diepe slaap; zeer fraai en uitvoerig geschilderd | *Mat:* op doek op paneel *Size:* hoog 16, breed 14 duim	Roos	(Sold) fl 83 Gruiter
1806/08/13	AMSCH	0005	*Burgh. (G. ter)* | In een deftig gemeubileerd Binnenvertrek, ziet men een bevallige Dame, staande voor haar toilet, gekleed met een rood Jakje met bont, en witte Satyne Rok, welke door een trompetter een brief word aangeboden, achter haar staat een Dienstmaagd met een zilver Schenkbord in de hand, en een Moor, welke haar beveelen schynen aftewachten; de fraaije ordinantie en de delicaate penceelsbehandeling, maken dit stuk tot een fraai Schildery | *Mat:* op doek *Size:* hoog 30, breed 31 duim	Vinkeles [for] G[ruyter]	(Sold) fl 161 Schumacher
1806/10/16	UTWLD	0015	*Gerard Ter Burg* | Een Landschap met een Heer te Paard	Mr P de Malapert [or] W Beeldsnyder	(Unknown)
1808/04/26	GDAN	0011	*Borgh (G. ter)* | Zijnde een uitmuntend geschilderd gemeubileerd Binnenvertrek, waar een Dame zittende, op een Guitar speeld, wordende door een Jongeling in 't Portaal geaccompagneerd door een Bas, waar in men door een deur in een ander gemeubileerd Vertrek een Naaistertje ziet zittende te naaijen, konstig en kragtig geschildert | *Size:* hoog 29, breed 37 duim	G H Fortuyn	(Unknown)
1808/06/06	RMRIJ	0123	*Terburg. (Gerard)* | Een Corps-de-Garde, waarin, aan eene, met een tapijt overdekte tafel, twee Heeren op het verkeerbord zitten te spelen, benevens een daarbij staande Officier, die men achter tegen den rug beschouwt, en een vierde eene pijp rookende. Op den tweeden grond zit een Man en Vrouw bij 't vuur. De teekening der Beelden, het Koloriet, de Satijnen, Linnen en anderen Stoffen, die zich in dit stuk voordoen, zijn fraai en uitvoerig geschilderd [Dans l'intérieur d'une chambre Hollandaise, deux personnes sont assises à une table couverte d'un tapis et jouent au Trictrac ; un troisième fume sa pipe, tandis qu'un Officier debout et appuyé sur la table, paroit regarder leur jeu. Dans le fond, un homme et une femme sont assis près du feu. On voît differents Meubles et autres accessoires, qui enrichissent ce Tableau, dont la Composition est agréable et la couleur vraie. On y distingue bien le Satin et les differentes étoffes. Le tout est d'un grand fini] | *Annots:* Gek. van Thijs, April 1805 (f 400.-) (RMA I) *Mat:* op paneel *Size:* Hoog 16, en breed 21 duim	Gerrit van der Pot, Heer van Groeneveld	(Sold) fl 325 Steenstra van Harlinge
1808/06/06	RMRIJ	0124	*Terburg. (Gerard)* | Een, door slaap overvallen, zittend Krijgsman, een Cuiras aanhebbende, dewelke door een daarbij staanden Jongeling met tabaksrook in het gezigt geblazen wordt; een ander, voor een ton zittende, beschouwt dit bedrijf met genoegen. Breed, uitvoerig en meesterlijk geschilderd [Dans une Tabagie, un Militaire dort assis devant un tonneau, tandis qu'un jeune homme debout lui souffle la fumée dans la figure, et un troisième les regarde avec contentement. Cette composition sage et harmonieuse, est d'un beau fini] | *Annots:* Van Jan de Neufville, Sept. 1782 (f 450.-) (RMA I) *Mat:* op paneel *Size:* Hoog 18, en breed 14 ¼ duim	Gerrit van der Pot, Heer van Groeneveld	(Sold) fl 330 P Roelszema

1808/11/28	AMSCH	0005	*G. ter Burg* | Het Afbeeldsel van een geleerd Persoon, in het zwart gekleed en in deftige houding, halver lijf, houdende Handschoenen in de hand, meesterlijk fraai en uitvoerig gepenseeld | *Mat:* op paneel *Size:* hoog 11, breed 9 duim	C	(Sold) fl 40 T Spaan
1809/06/13	AMSCH	0007	*G. Terburg* | In een Binnevertrek, zit op de voorgrond eene Vrouwtje in het Fluweel, met Bont gekleed, nevens haar staat een Heer, verder drie Officieren, bij een Kist, die eenig Goed welke zij Buit gemaakt hebben, schijnen te deelen; uitvoerig en fraai geschilderd | *Mat:* op doek *Size:* hoog 12, breed 11 duim	T	(Sold) fl 36 Gruyter
1809/07/19	AMSCH	0006	*Burgh (G. ter)* | In een Gemeubileerde Kamer ziet men bij eene Tafel, met een Kleed bedekt, twee Krijgs-Officieren in 't Verkeerbord speelen, terwijl een ander het spel met aandagt beschouwt. De karacters zijn natuurlijk, het is van eene fraaije en zeer uitvoerige penceelsbehandeling | *Mat:* op doek *Size:* hoog 16, breed 14 duim	[Bicker]	(Sold) fl 635 Nieuwenhuys
1809/09/06	AMSCH	0002	*Burg (G. ter)* | In een Binnenvertrek staat eene in het wit Satijn gekleede Dame, boven een Zilvere Lampetschotel haar handen te wasschen, de Dienstmaagd houd den Kan, ter zijde zit een Hondje bij een Tafel, welke met een Tapijtkleedje gedekt is; alles is delicaat gepenceeld | *Mat:* op doek *Size:* hoog 20, breed 17 duim	Johannes Caudri	(Sold) fl 31 Gruyter
1810/03/27	RMCNL	0047	*ter Burch* | Men ziet in een Binnenhuis eene Vrouw versche Zalm kopen; bij uitnemenheid mooi gepenseeld		(Unknown)
1810/06/20	AMSCH	0003	*G. Ter Burg* | Een bevallig Vrouwtje, zittende voor eene Tafel, houdende een Wijnkan en Glas in de handen; nevens haar een bejaard Man, en een slapend Officier. Delikaat en uitvoerig gepenceeld | *Mat:* op paneel *Size:* hoog 14, breed 11 duimen	N	(Sold) fl 26 Coclers
1810/07/23	DOLGI	0056	*Gerard Terburgh* | Een deftig Binnenvertrek, waar in eene jonge Dame, gekleed in zwart Satijn, zit een Brief te lezen. Op een Tafel, welke met een rood kleed gedekt is, staat een gouden Lampet-Schotel en Kan, benevens een Kandelaar. Delikaat van teekening en penceelsbehandeling | *Mat:* op doek *Size:* hoog 16 ½, breed 14 ½ duim	Mr Pieter van den Santheuvel	(Sold) fl 85 A van Strij
1810/07/23	DOLGI	0057	*Gerard Terburgh* | In een Wachtkamer zit een Officier een Brief te schrijven, en voor de Tafel staat een Trompetter ten voeten uit, naar dien Brief te wachten. Uitmuntend van teekening en behandeling | *Mat:* op doek *Size:* hoog 19, breed 14 ½ duim	Mr Pieter van den Santheuvel	(Sold) fl 115 P de Heere à Dordt
1810/08/01	AMSCH	0100	*Terburg (Gerard)* | In eene Binnenkamer ziet men eene jonge bevallige Vrouw, met een geel fluweelen Jakje met Bont en wit satijnen Rok gekleed, zittende bij eene Tafel; zij heeft op den schoot een Luit, welke zij met de linkerhand vast houdt, terwijl zij met de regter op een Muzijkboek rust; over haar zit een Krijsman [sic], nevens wien een staand Heer [Dans un intérieur d'apartement s'assit une jeune et gracieuse Femme, habillée d'un Casaquin de Velours jaune, bordé d'un passepoil, et d'un Jupon de Satin blanc : elle a une Table audevant d'elle et un Luth est sur ses genoux. Elle tient l'instrument de la main gauche et appuye sa droite sur un Livre de Musique. En face de la Dame s'assit un Cavalier, et à son côté se tient un second] | *Annots:* fort bon. (NGW) *Mat:* op paneel *Size:* hoog 22, breed 18 duimen	Mr Pieter de Smeth van Alphen	(Sold) fl 2000 Jan Yver
1810/08/01	AMSCH	0101	*Terburg (Gerard)* | In een Vertrek zit op den voorgrond eene deftig Vrouw, nevens een Wieg; zij is bezig Linnen te naaijen; achterwaarts eene Dienstmaagd bij eene Haardstede [Un intérieur de Chambre, où l'on distingue audevant du Tableau une Dame assise à côté d'un berceau : elle est occupée à coudre. En arriere se tronve [sic] une Servante auprès de la cheminée] | *Annots:* NB : tout repeint. (NGW) *Mat:* op paneel *Size:* hoog 17 ½, breed 14 ½ duimen	Mr Pieter de Smeth van Alphen	(Sold) fl 510 T Spaan [for] Croese
1810/10/10	MGCIT	0127	*Terburg* | Twee zeer vrolyke Stukken op ieder van welken een musicerend Mans en Vrouwspersoon in eene in allen opzigte zeer vergenoegde houding; expressif en met een meesterlyk en stout penceel behandeld	Caspar van Citters	(Unknown)

Borch, Gerard ter (II) (and Ruisdael, J.)

1803/08/17	AMSCH	0072	*Ruysdaal (J.); G. Terburg* | Een gezicht van de Dam, op het Damrak en Water te Amsterdam, te zien, het Water vol Scheepen en den Dam ryk van Beeldjes, door G. Terburg gestoffeerd, het ligt en bruin is frappant, en is voorts van de beste behandeling van dezen Meester | *Mat:* op doek *Size:* hoog 21, breed 29 duim	Anna Catharina Putman	(Sold) fl 76 W Reijers

Borch, Gerard ter (II) (or Borch, G. ter (II), manner)

1802/09/06	AMSCH	0241	*ter Burgh* | In een Gemeubileerde Kamer, ziet men een bevallige Vrouw met een Kind op haar schoot, neevens haar een wieg met een Kind, door een openstaande Deur, ziet men in een ander Vertrek, een Man by 't vuur een Pyp rooken; door of als ter Burgh | *Mat:* op paneel *Size:* hoog 19, breed 23 duim	J	(Sold) fl 3 van Cooth

Borch, Gerard ter (II) (copy after)

1806/06/07	RMHSN	0078	*Terburg* | Een Drinkende Juffrouw, na Terburg | *Mat:* op doek	A E K L	(Sold) fl 3 Thijs

Borch, Gerard ter (II) (manner)

1802/09/06	AMSCH	0160	*G. ter Burgh* | In een Gemeubileerde Kamer, zit een bevallige Dame in zatyne kleeding, op de Guithar speelende, naast dezelve een staand Heer	X	(Sold) fl 6:5 van Cooth

<table>
<tr><td></td><td></td><td></td><td>by een tafel, waarop een Musiekboek en verder bywerk geplaatst is; bevallig van licht en uitvoerig geschilderd op Doek, als door G. ter Burgh | *Mat:* op doek *Size:* hoog 27, breed 21 duim</td><td></td><td></td></tr>
<tr><td>1803/06/20</td><td>AMSCH</td><td>0056</td><td>*G. ter Burch* | Een bedaagd Heer in oude Hollansche Kleeding, zittende naast een Tafel, met een Kleed bedekt, waar op een Lessenaar, Boek, Papier en Inktkoker geplaatst zyn in zyn Studeérkamer, houdende de linker hand aan een opengeslagen Boek, verders eenige Boeken, Musiek-Instrumenten en verder bywerk, uitvoerig op Koper geschilderd in de manier van G. ter Burch | *Mat:* op koper *Size:* hoog 15 ½, breed 11 duim</td><td>Schley [for] H</td><td>(Sold) fl 5 Pruijssenaar</td></tr>
<tr><td>1805/07/10</td><td>AMSCH</td><td>0242</td><td>*G. Terburg* | Een Corps de Guarde, waarin verscheide Officieren, waarby een Vaandrager; zig met drinken, en eeten verlustende, alle in oude Hollandsche Kleeding; kragtig op Doek geschilderd, in de manier van G. Terburg | *Mat:* op doek</td><td>Wed Grave</td><td>(Bought In) fl 85</td></tr>
<tr><td>1805/07/10</td><td>AMSCH</td><td>0278</td><td>*G. ter Burg* | Een Binnevertrek, met Kaartspeelende Heeren en Dames; fiks en breed op Paneel, als G. ter Burg | *Mat:* op paneel</td><td>V[inkeles] [for] L</td><td>(Bought In) fl 7</td></tr>
<tr><td>1805/07/10</td><td>AMSCH</td><td>0281</td><td>*G. Terburg* | Twee Herderinen in een Landschap, by eenige Schaapen; in de manier van G. Terburg</td><td>V[inkeles] [for] H[affner]</td><td>(Bought In) fl 1</td></tr>
<tr><td>1806/08/13</td><td>AMSCH</td><td>0273</td><td>*G. ter Burg* | Een deftig Mans Pourtrait; als G. ter Burg | *Notes:* This lot was sold with lot 274, which is in the manner of J.M. Molenaer.</td><td>Vinkeles [for] D</td><td>(Sold) fl 3:5 for lots 273 & 274. Yver [for] G</td></tr>
<tr><td>1807/06/10</td><td>HGBSM</td><td>0211</td><td>*Terborg* | Een Jongeling zittende te studeeren, met verder bijwerk zijnde een lamp licht, schoon van Effech en Couleur, zo goed als Terborg | *Mat:* op doek *Size:* hoog 26, breed 22 ½ duim</td><td>Abraham Delfos [or others]</td><td>(Sold) fl 8:5 Tessier</td></tr>
<tr><td>1807/08/26</td><td>AMSCH</td><td>0308</td><td>*ter Burgh* | In een Binnenvertrek zit een Heer, met een Glas Wyn in de hand, by een Tafel, vergezeld van eene Jufvrouw, gestoffeerd met verder bywerk; in de manier van ter Burgh | *Mat:* op paneel</td><td>Yver [for] S</td><td>(Sold) fl 4:5 H Jansen</td></tr>
<tr><td>1807/10/12</td><td>MGBEO</td><td>0004</td><td>*Terburg* | Een Heer, die verbeeld van de Jagt te komen, by een Dame, medebrengende eenig Wild, in de manier van Terburg | *Mat:* op doek</td><td>Hermannus Johannes Heyman</td><td>(Sold) £ 0:2 Hardegai</td></tr>
<tr><td>1808/08/23</td><td>AMSCH</td><td>0275</td><td>*G. ter Burg* | Een Manspourtret in het zwart gekleed; uitvoerig op Paneel in de manier van G. ter Burg | *Mat:* op paneel</td><td>Y</td><td>(Sold) fl 1 D Maijkel</td></tr>
<tr><td>1809/10/20</td><td>UTWLD</td><td>0015</td><td>*Terburg* | Een Dame uit een roemer wyn drinkende in de manier van Terburg</td><td>J J van Rhyn</td><td>(Unknown)</td></tr>
<tr><td>1809/10/20</td><td>UTWLD</td><td>0016</td><td>*Terburg* | Een dito [Dame], schryvende dito [in de manier van Terburg]</td><td>J J van Rhyn</td><td>(Unknown)</td></tr>
<tr><td>1810/03/07</td><td>UTWLD</td><td>0043</td><td>*ter Burg* | Een Heer en Dame in een binnenvertrek in de smaak van ter Burg | *Size:* hoog 1 voet 3 duim, breed 1 voet 1 duim</td><td>J J Woertman</td><td>(Unknown) fl 230</td></tr>
</table>

Borkeloo, J. van [Unidentified]

<table>
<tr><td>1805/07/03</td><td>AMSCH</td><td>0004</td><td>*Borkeloo (J. van)* | Twee stuks Capitaale Bergachtige Landschappen, met Geboomte en Rivieren doorsnéden, bevallig gestoffeerd met Beeldjes te paard en te voet, zoo ook met Vaartuigen; zonachtig en fix gepenceeld. Zynde de stukken van dezen Meester zeer zeldzaam voorkomende | *Mat:* op doek *Size:* yder hoog 23, breed 30 duim</td><td>R[oos]</td><td>(Sold) fl 20:10 Vallet</td></tr>
<tr><td>1807/08/26</td><td>AMSCH</td><td>0027</td><td>*Borkulo* | Twee stuks Bergachtige Landschappen, met Rivieren doorsneeden en gestoffeerd met Beelden | *Mat:* op doek *Size:* hoog 23, breed 30 duim</td><td>Joseph Vallette</td><td>(Sold) fl 4:10 du Pree</td></tr>
</table>

Borman, Johannes

<table>
<tr><td>1810/07/23</td><td>DOLG2</td><td>0013</td><td>*J. Bornman* | Op een tafel, welke gedekt is met een groen kleed, vertoont zich een tinnen bord met Vruchten. Geschilderd | *Mat:* op doek *Size:* hoog 29, breed 24 duim</td><td>Pieter Quinting</td><td>(Sold) fl 15 van Leen</td></tr>
</table>

Borrekens, Jean Pierre

<table>
<tr><td>1806/11/24</td><td>AMSCH</td><td>0011</td><td>*Borrekens (J.P.)* | Een zeer schoon Boom- en bergachtig Landschap, met een Rivier en aangenaam verafwykend verschiet, gestoffeerd met eenige Herders met Koeijen en Schapen, zynde van een bevallige schildering | possibly companion to lot 65, by P. Regemorter *Mat:* op doek *Size:* hoog 40, breed 49 duim</td><td>Munnikhuizen</td><td>(Sold) fl 32 Engelbert</td></tr>
</table>

Borssom, Anthonie van

<table>
<tr><td>1801/08/19</td><td>AMSCH</td><td>0016</td><td>*A. van Borsum* | Een fraai en natuurlyk Landschap aan een Water, waar in men bézig is te vissen</td><td>Pruyssen^{r} [for] Q</td><td>(Sold) fl 6 Gruiter</td></tr>
<tr><td>1802/12/13</td><td>AMSCH</td><td>0026</td><td>*A. van Borssum* | Een natuurlyk Land- en Watergezicht, gestoffeerd met een gaanden en een Vissend Beeltje, alles zeer natuurlyk by een opkoomende Morgen verbeeld | *Mat:* op doek *Size:* hoog 10, breed 14 duim</td><td>Pruyssenaar [for] A</td><td>(Sold) fl 1:15 Van Dijl</td></tr>
<tr><td>1804/02/27</td><td>AMSCH</td><td>0011</td><td>*Borssum. (A. van)* | Een boomryk Landschap, gestoffeerd met een Haan en eenige Hennen, op de voorgrond by een Piedestal een goudlakense Kloek met zyn Kuikens; meesterlyk geschilderd | *Mat:* op doek *Size:* hoog 53, breed 61 duim</td><td>B</td><td>(Sold) fl 4 Coclers</td></tr>
<tr><td>1804/05/07</td><td>AMSCH</td><td>0021</td><td>*Borsum. (A. van)* | Een Heuvelachtig Landschap, met Ruïne en Geboomte, op de voorgrond gestoffeerd met vier staande en een leggende Koe en twee Schaapen, verders een Man te Paard, waarby twee Honden, en een aangenaam verschiet; zonachtig en meesterlyk gepenceeld | *Mat:* op doek *Size:* hoog 26, breed 24 ½ duim</td><td>Y[ver] [for] JJ</td><td>(Sold) fl 52 Kooy</td></tr>
</table>

1805/07/03	AMSCH	0070	*van Borsum* | Een Hofgezicht, met een ménigte Kippen, Kiekens en Haan; breed en meesterlyk gepenceeld | *Mat:* op doek *Size:* hoog 53, breed 62 duim	V[inkeles]	(Sold) fl 1 L Pakker
1806/08/13	AMSCH	0021	*Borsum. (A. van)* | Een natuurlyk Boomryk Landschap, met een Rivier, waarby eenige Huislieden met hun Vée; zonachtig en fraai van behandeling | *Mat:* op paneel *Size:* hoog 30, breed 62 duim	Roos	(Sold) fl 5:10 du Pre
1806/08/13	AMSCH	0022	*Borsum. (A. van)* | Aan het Hek van een Grasweide, aan een Sloot, zitten twee Boeren by eenige Varkens en Eenden, verders een aangenaam verschiet; natuurlyk uitgevoerd | *Mat:* op paneel *Size:* hoog 14, breed 18 duim	Roos	(Sold) fl 36 Hulswit
1806/08/13	AMSCH	0259	*van Borssum* | Een Menagerie van Gevogelte; fiks op Doek | *Mat:* op doek	Roos	(Sold) fl 3 Schumacher
1808/09/13	HABRU	0015	*van Bassum* | Een Bosch- en Bergachtig Landschap, met een drift Beesten op den voorgrond		(Unknown) fl 1:4
1809/04/22	AMYVR	0025	*A. van Borsum* | Een liggende Koe, waarbij eenige Schapen, in een Landschap; meesterlijk | *Mat:* op paneel *Size:* hoog 14, breed 12 duim	de Bruin	(Sold) fl 4 C S Roos
1809/04/22	AMYVR	0026	*A. van Borsum* | Een kapitaal Boomrijk Landschap, met een Rivier en Melkboer en Boerin bij eenig Vee; als de voorgaande | *Mat:* op paneel *Size:* hoog 37, breed 62 duim	de Bruin	(Sold) fl 9 du Pree
			Borssom, Anthonie van (manner)		
1802/02/16	AMSCH	0046	*van Borsum* | Een bevallig Landzigt, gestoffeert met staand, en rustend Vee, verzelt van een Boerin, dragende een emmer aan de hand, natuurlyk en meesterlyk gepenceeld, als door van Borsum	G	(Sold) fl 4:5 Gruiter
1803/12/12	AMSCH	0137	*v. Borsum* | Een Land- en Watergezigt, met een Molen, zynde een Winter; op Doek, als v. Borsum | *Mat:* op doek *Size:* hoog 33, breed 38 duim	V[inkeles?]	(Sold) fl 1 L Pakker
1806/05/05	AMSCH	0174	*van Borssum* | Een Landschap met Beesten, aan een Rivier; in de manier van van Borssum	R[oos]	(Sold) fl 3 Jan Smit
			Bos, N. [Unidentified]		
1805/10/09	HGBSM	0117	*N. Bos* | In een binne kaamer zit een vrouw te slaapen met een kind op haar schoot, benevens nog een meisje met een lepel in de hand. Een spinnewiel en verder huisraad versieren dit stukje, dat aangenaam geschildert is door N. Bos | *Mat:* op doek op paneel *Size:* hoog 14 breet 11 duim	T H van Willigen [or others]	(Sold) fl 3 Teissier
			Bos, Pieter van den		
1807/06/10	HGBSM	0182	*P. van den Bos* | Een Vasten Avondfeest, daar ze zich bij een vuur vermaaken, in open lucht | *Mat:* op paneel *Size:* hoog 15, breed 18 ½ duim	Abraham Delfos [or others]	(Sold) fl 7 Zwarts
			Bosch, A. ten [Unidentified]		
1804/07/25	AMSCH	0006	*Bosch (A. ten)* | In een bevallig boomryk Landschap, op de Voorgrond by een stil Waterbeekje, vertoont zich de Fabelgeschiedenis van Pan, Syringa vervolgende, die in een biesch-bos herschept werd; alles is bevallig en meesterlyk gepenceelt | *Mat:* op doek *Size:* Jeder hoog 39, breed 44 duim		(Sold) fl 7:15 C S Roos
1808/10/28	AMVRS	0004	*Bosch (A.)* | Een Boomrijk Landschap, gestoffeerd met eene Nijmf, welke door een Sater vervolgd wordt. Meesterlijk gepenceeld | *Mat:* op doek *Size:* hoog 34, breed 46 duim	Marten Udink	(Sold) fl 3 van Iperen
			Bosch, Hieronymus (Hieronymus van Aken)		
1802/07/21	HGKAN	0046	*Hieronimus de Bosch* | Een Gezelschap Monniken en Nonnen, in een zingende houding, hebbende eene derzelve een open Kisje voor zich waar uit iemand schynt ontsnapt te zyn, terwyl wat laager een ander bezig is om Eyeren onder een op het Nest zittende Zwaan weg te haalen, dit is een zeer oud stuk, door Hieronimus de Bosch, geschildert in A°. 1502. en schynt te zinspeelen, op de toen opkomende Reformatie, zwarte Lyst | *Inscr:* 1502 (dated?) *Notes:* It is unclear whether the date is inscribed on the painting.		(Unknown)
			Bosch, Jan Hendrik van den		
1806/08/20	HGBSM	0065	*J. H. van den Bos* | Een Landschap, met een drift Beesten, die door het water waaden, vrolijk en uitvoerig geschilderd | *Mat:* op paneel *Size:* hoog 13 ½, breed 17 duim	Macalester Loup [or others]	(Sold) fl 31 Zwartsman
			Bosman, Maria [Unidentified]		
1804/10/16	DLOND	0029	*Maria Bosman* | Ene Vrouw bezig met naar een Pleisterbeeld te tekenen. Une Femme occupée à dessiner d'après une statue | *Mat:* op doek *Size:* hoog 19, breed 17		(Unknown)
1809/04/17	AMSCH	0018	*Maria Bosman* | In een Binnenvertrek zit eene bevallige Vrouw naar het Plijster te Teekenen, nevens haar een Heer het zelve met aandacht beschouwende, bevallig gepenceeld | *Mat:* op doek *Size:* hoog 20, breed 27 duim	S	(Sold) fl 6:5
			Bosschaert		
1804/08/02	BDAN	0075	*Bosschaert* | Een Bloem-stuk door Boschaert	J G Calckberner	(Unknown)

Bosschaert, Ambrosius

1807/08/26	AMSCH	0004	*Ambrosius* | Op een Steenen Tafel staat een Fles, gevuld met onderscheidene soorten van bevallige Bloemen, waarop Insecten aazen; het koloriet is bevallig en van een ongemeen uitvoerige penceelsbehandeling, door den beroemden Ambrosius | *Mat:* op koper *Size:* hoog 13, breed 9 duim	Helsdinge	(Sold) fl 12 Jozi

Both, Andries Dirksz.

1801/06/10	AMSCH	0008	*Both. (And.)* | Een Landschap, op de voorgrond voor een grot, Ziet men eenige Landlopers, een derzelven is bezig, spys te kooken op een Kachel, in 't verschiet eenig Vee, allee fraai en kragtig van Schildering | *Mat:* op doek *Size:* hoog 23, breed 19 duim	Herman ten Kate	(Sold) fl 305 Pruyssenaar
1804/10/16	DLOND	0030	*Andr. Both* | Een Landschap met veel Geboomte. Paysage ombragé | *Mat:* op paneel *Size:* hoog 9, breed 11		(Unknown)
1807/08/26	AMSCH	0022	*A. Both* | In een Landschap ziet men een Kwakzalver op zyn Theater, zyn Koopwaren aanpryzen, verzelt van een meenigte aanschouwers; fiks van Penceelbehandeling | *Mat:* op paneel *Size:* hoog 21, breed 18 duim	Helsdinge	(Sold) fl 4:10 Spruit
1809/07/25	HGBSM	0023	*A. Bot* | Eenige Jagers in een Grot | *Mat:* op doek *Size:* hoog 14 en 1 half, breed 12 duim	D van der Aa [or] E B ten Dall	(Sold) fl 5:5 van Eyk
1810/03/23	HAVIN	0062	*A. Both* | De Groote Markt te Haarlem alwaar bij de vrede Piktonnen gebrand worden	Rudolf Hendrik de Wetstein [or others]	(Unknown)
1810/07/23	DOLGI	0012	*A. Both* | Een Bergächtig Landschap, zijnde een Avondstond, met Beeldtjes en Beesten gestoffeerd, kragtig van Coloriet, en meesterlijk geschilderd | *Mat:* op doek *Size:* hoog 33, breed 22 duim	Mr Pieter van den Santheuvel	(Sold) fl 54 [or] 50 Nieuwenhuizen van Brussel

Both, Andries Dirksz. (and Both, J.)

1801/06/10	AMSCH	0006	*Both (Jan); Both (Andries)* | Een bergachtig Landschap, ter linker zyde op de voorgrond ziet men, Visschers bezig het net intehalen, verders, een man te paard, waar nevens twee Landlieden en een beladen Ezel, in 't verschiet eenige Ossen die door een Veehoeder voortgedreven worden; alles zonachtig en delicaat van penceels behandeling | *Mat:* op doek *Size:* hoog 22, breed 31 duim	Herman ten Kate	(Sold) fl 1600 Coclers
1801/06/10	AMSCH	0007	*Both (Jan); Both (Andries)* | Een Bergachtig Landschap, gestoffeert met een man op een Ezel, nevens hem een voetganger, ter zyde. Over een vallend Water, ziet men een brug, en verder hoog geboomte, alles is Zonachtig, en van een uitvoerige en delicaate penceels behandeling | *Mat:* op paneel *Size:* hoog 17, breed 16 duim *Loc:* Hamburg, Deutschland. Kunsthalle. (22)	Herman ten Kate	(Sold) fl 835 Coclers
1802/06/16	AMSCH	0012	*Jan Both; Andries Both* | Een Bergachtig Landschap met hoog Geboomten en dartel Kreupelgewas, gestoffeerd met een Man welke twee beladen Ezels dryft; voorts een aangenaam Verschiet: het Coloriet is gloeijend, het geval en de behandeling zyn allerbevalligst voorgesteld | *Mat:* op doek *Size:* hoog 25, breed 31 duim	[Merrem]	(Sold) fl 500 H de Valk
1802/06/16	AMSCH	0013	*Jan Both; Andries Both* | Een Heuvelachtig Zonachtig Landschap, met hoog Geboomten, op de voorgrond een stille Rivier; door een vervallen Poort ziet men eenig Vée dryven: alles transparant en uitvoerig behandeld | *Mat:* op paneel *Size:* hoog 18, breed 14 duim	[Merrem]	(Sold) fl 151 Cobel
1803/06/20	AMSCH	0007	*J. Both; A. Both* | En Boom- en Bergachtig Landschap, op de voorgrond eenig kreupel gewas, gestoffeerd met een Man, welke twee beladen Muilëzels dryft, warm van colriet en fix getoest [sic], op Doek, door J. en A. Both | *Mat:* op doek *Size:* hoog 25, breed 31 duim	Schley [for] B	(Sold) fl 127 Hulswit
1805/07/10	AMSCH	0009	*J. Both; A. Both* | Een Capitaal Bergachtig Landschap, met hoog Geboomte, Kreupelgewas, Watervallen en Beekjes, gestoffeerd met Beelden, Ezeldryvers en andere stoffagie; meesterlyk en zonachtig op Doek | *Mat:* op doek *Size:* hoog 44, breed 45 duim	R[oos]	(Sold) fl 65 Gruyter
1808/06/13	AMSCH	0011	*Both (Jan); Both (Andries)* | Een hoog bergachtig Landschap, met een Rivier doorsneden, ter linkerzijde gestoffeert met beladene Muilezels en Reizigers, ter rechterzijde, hoog Gebergte, op den voorgrond bijeen Stam van een Boom eenige Kruiden en Plantgewassen; zonachtig en zeer uitvoerig | *Mat:* op doek *Size:* hoog 37, breed 42 duim	W	(Sold) fl 850 C S Roos
1810/06/06	RMMUY	0007	*Jan Both; Andries Both* | In een Bergachtig Landschap, word verbeeld de Fabel van Iö; Mercurius is gereed om met het zwaard den slapenden Argus het hoofd af te slaan; ter zijde staat Iö, in eene witte Koe herschapen. Dit stuk is van een warm coloriet, krachtig en meesterlijk uitgevoerd | *Mat:* op paneel		(Sold) fl 62 Vermeulen
1810/08/01	AMSCH	0014	*Both (Jan); Both (Andries)* | Een wijd uitgestrekt hoog bergachtig Landschap met eenen opgaanden Weg, helder Water en Geboomte, gestoffeerd met eene voorstelling van de dooping des Moormans door den Apostel Philippus [Une vaste Paysage, richement boisé et varié par des Monticules et par une Riviere. On remarque sur une large route une representation du Baptème de l'Enuque [sic] de la Reine de Candace, par l'Apôtre Philippe] | *Annots:* Très bon; sans l'habit trop rouge de Nègre (NGW) *Mat:* op doek *Size:* hoog 49, breed 62 duimen *Loc:* London, England, UK. Royal Collection (Windsor Castle) Inv.3216. as by Jan Both	Mr Pieter de Smeth van Alphen	(Sold) fl 10,000 Reijers voor la Fontaine

1810/08/01	AMSCH	0015	*Both (Jan); Both (Andries)* | Een Italiaansch Landschap, met hoog Geboomte en Kruiden op den voorgrond, versierd met eene Vrouw, zittende op eenen Ezel, wordende door eenen Landman geleid; hier by een Reiziger met zijnen Muilezel; verder een bergachtig verschiet [Un site pittoresque pris en Italie, orné d'Arbres et de Plantes : on distingue au premier plan une femme assise sure un Ane, accompagnée par un Villageois, un Muletier et son Mulet. La perspective montueuse va se terminer à l'horison] | *Annots:* terminé avec soin. vendu fl:4000, dans la vente de Debruin 1798 à Amsterd: (NGW) *Mat:* op koper *Size:* hoog 16, breed 21 duimen	Mr Pieter de Smeth van Alphen	(Bought In) fl 2900
			Both, Andries Dirksz. (manner)		
1802/11/01	DOBRA	0008	*Andries Both* | De Ruïne van eenen antiekschen Tempel, in een Italiaansch heuvelagtig Landschap op den voorgrond, en verder mannen te voet en te paard, by belaaden Muilezels, enz. als door Andries Both | *Size:* hoog 43, breed 58 duim	Paulus van der Spyk [or others]	(Sold) fl 38 Boercoert
1804/10/16	DLOND	0281	*In de manier van And. Both* | Een heuvelig Landschap met Koeien, Ezels enz. Paysage collineux avec des Vaches, Anes &c. | *Mat:* op doek *Size:* hoog 40, breed 34		(Unknown)
1804/10/16	DLOND	0282	*In de manier van And. Both* | Uts[a]. [Een heuvelig Landschap] met Geboomte en Menschen. Uts[a]. [Paysage collineux] avec des Arbres & figures | *Mat:* op doek *Size:* hoog 22, breed 26		(Unknown)
			Both, Jan		
1801/10/06	AMSCH	0005	*J. Both* | In een aangenaam Landschap, ziet men een Man, die een beladen Ezel te drinken geeft, verder een rustend Ryziger by een Heuvel, en een Veehoeder, die eenige Beesten voortdryft, warm en bevallig, van Coloriet en Penceel behandeling | *Mat:* op paneel *Size:* hoog 19, breed 22 duim	M	(Sold) fl 200 Makelaar A E Sterk
1802/05/05	AMSCH	0008a	*J. Both* | Een Boom- en Bergächtig Landschap, gestoffeerd met Gaande en Rustende Reizigers, warm van Coloriet en Zonächtig behandeld | *Mat:* op doek op paneel *Size:* hoog 17, breed 21 duim	C	(Sold) fl 16:10 Claasens
1802/09/06	AMSCH	0006	*J.A. Both* | Een Berghagtig Landschap, met eenig Geboomten en stille Rivier, langs een opgaande Wegh, ziet men een Huisman op een Ezel, verder gaande Landlieden met Vée, en andere Reizigers; natuurlyk en bevallig behandeld, gemerkt J. A. Both | *Mat:* op doek *Size:* hoog 17, breed 22 duim *Inscr:* J.A. Both (signed)	Brave	(Sold) fl 4 Oostwijn
1804/10/16	DLOND	0031	*J. Both* | Een Bergagtig Landschap. Paysage Montagneux | *Mat:* op paneel *Size:* hoog 13, breed 13		(Unknown)
1805/12/16	AMSCH	0002	*J. Both* | Een Bergachtig Landschapje, met een vervallen Poort, op de Voorgrond by een stortend Beekje, ziet men eenige Reizigers, en andere stoffagie, warm en dun op Paneel behandeld | *Mat:* op paneel *Size:* hoog 13, breed 10 duim	R[oos]	(Sold) fl 95 Versteegh
1808/04/26	GDAN	0004	*Both (Jan)* | Een heuvelägtig Landschap, gestoffeerd met een ploegend Paard, en verdere Werklieden, fiks gedaan | *Size:* hoog 23 ½, breed 29 duim	G H Fortuyn	(Unknown)
1808/04/26	GDAN	0005	*Both (Jan)* | Een zonägtig Landschap, met hoog Geboomte, in het verschiet ziet men een Brug, aan de linkerzijde ziet men een Vrouwtje op een Ezel gezeten, met verder schoone stoffagie van Beelden, heel uitvoerig geschilderd | *Size:* hoog 22 ½, breed 29 ½ duim	G H Fortuyn	(Unknown)
1808/06/06	RMRIJ	0018	*Both. (Jan)* | Een bergachtig en boomrijk Landschap, doorsneden met eene Rivier, wordende, zoo als ook de lucht en wolken, door de ondergaande Zon, op eene aangename wijze, verlicht. Op den rijk versierden voorgrond vertoont zich, bij het aankomen van eene Schuit met beesten, eene Dame te paard, door een Heer wordende aangesproken, terwijl een Muil-Ezel wordt weg geleid, enz. Dit alles is zeer schoon voorgesteld en behandeld. Van deze Schilderij vindt men eene prent onder het bekende geetste werk van dezen meester [Ce Tableau admirable represente un magnifique Paysage où l'on apperçoit, dans toute la partie gauche d'un terrein élevé, des Broussailles et une belle masse d'arbres ; à droite une Perspective de Rivière, sur la quelle se trouve un Ponton chargé de Passagers et de Bétail. On voit sur le rivage une Dame à cheval, qui s'entretient avec un Cavalier debout auprès d'elle, et un Garçon qui tient un Mulet par la bride. Ce Tableau pris à l'heure du Soleil Couchant, est d'un ton riche, d'une touche brillante, et un chef-d'oeuvre dans son genre. On en trouve la gravure à l'eau-forte dans la Collection gravée par cet Artiste] | *Mat:* op doek *Size:* Hoog 28, en breed 33 ½ duim *Loc:* Amsterdam, Nederland. Rijksmuseum. (A52)	Gerrit van der Pot, Heer van Groeneveld	(Sold) fl 3690 J J de Wit [for] le Roi
1808/06/06	RMRIJ	0019	*Both. (Jan)* | Een bergachtig Landschap, aan welks eene zijde men opgaande hoog Geboomte en Gewassen ziet; in 't verschiet hoog en laag Gebergte, een Water, Brug en Ruine; op den voorgrond vertoont zich een Vrouwtje, zittende op een Ezel, vergezeld van een jongen Boer, welke ontmoet worden door een Ezeldrijver met twee beladen Ezels. De lucht en alles, wat zich in dit stuk voordoet, is Zonachtig, uitvoerig en schoon behandeld. Mede te vinden in de geëtste prenten van dien meester [Ce magnifique Tableau represente un Paysage Italien. On voit sur le devant des Broussailles et un beau groupe d'arbres, à droite dans le lointain plusieurs sites et fabriques. Un Pont sur une Rivière et des Montagnes	Gerrit van der Pot, Heer van Groeneveld	(Sold) fl 4010 Coclers

			terminent la vue. Au milieu du Tableau, une femme montée sur un Mulet et un jeune Paysan sont rencontrés par un Muletier qui conduit deux Mulets chargés. Le Ciel et tout ce qu'on voit dans ce Morceau préciéux, est d'un ton agréable et piquant, d'un grand fini et de son meilleur faire] | *Annots:* 14 Aug. 1785 van P. Fouquet Jr te Amsterdam (f 1620.-) (RMA I) *Mat:* op koper *Size:* Hoog 20, en breed 26 ½ duim *Loc:* Den Haag, Nederland. Mauritshuis. (21)		
1809/07/19	AMSCH	0005	*Both (J.)* | Een Bergachtig Landschap, met Ruïne en Geboomte, gestoffeerd op den voorgrond met de Heilige Familelle, vlugtende naar Egipte. Zonachtig en in de stijl van Breenberg geschilderd | *Mat:* op paneel *Size:* hoog 29, breed 42 duim	[Wijkersloot?]	(Sold) fl 7 Gruyter
1810/03/26	RMMUY	0003	*Jan Both* | Een Bergachtig Landschap. Op den rijk versierden voorgrond, hoog geboomte, een grooten weg in 't midden, waar op een staand en een zittend Man, wat verder een wagen getrokken wordende door twee Ossen, in 't verschiet nog eenige stoffagie, krachtig uitvoerig en zonachtig gepenceeld en een der capitaalsten van dezen Meester. In zijn eigen geëtst werk is deze ordonnantie te vinden [Au milieu d'un riant paysage, passe une grande route, où sur le devant sont deux figures, l'une debout et l'autre assise ; un gros-chariot surmonté de son conducteur, attellé de deux boeufs, vient a leur rencontre ; plus loin sont en differents endroits plusieurs figures et animaux. Le second plan offre de belles masses d'arbres, sites et fabriques. Des hautes montagnes qui se perdent à fleur d'eau, dans une vaste plage, forment le plus agréable lointain. Le devant est enrichi d'arbres, de haute futaille, de plantes et de broussailles, un bel ensemble, un ton clair, doré et harmonieux, une touche piquante et franche, font considérer ce tableau, pur et bien conservé, parmi les plus belles productions de cet habile artiste. Parmi ses gravures à l'eau forte, se trouve cette composition.] | *Mat:* op doek *Size:* hoog 42 ¼, breed 39 ½ duim *Loc:* Lawrence, KA, USA. Kansas University. Spencer Museum of Art (86.35) (?)	Daniel de Jongh Az	(Sold) fl 805 van Iperen Amsterdam voor Vreesman
1810/10/10	MGCIT	0044	*J. Both* | Een Stuk, verbeeldende een lieflijke Morgenstond; wijders een zeer bekoorlijk Landschap, als mede Boomen en Gebergten, tusschen welken en den Voorgrond een Watervliet, terwijl langs een daar over geslagen Brug twee Menschen Ezels drijven; voorts is zoo dit, als alles, in den aan den Meester gewonen regt kunstigen, helderen en natuurlijken trant behandeld	Caspar van Citters	(Unknown)
1810/10/11	AMSCH	0012	*J. Both* | Een Italiaansch Landschap met Watervallen, gestoffeerd met Koeijen, een Hond enz | *Mat:* op doek *Size:* hoog 25, breed 30 duimen	C	(Sold) fl 6:10 Posthumus
			Both, Jan (and Both, A.)		
1801/06/10	AMSCH	0006	*Both (Jan); Both (Andries)* | Een bergachtig Landschap, ter linker zyde op de voorgrond ziet men, Visschers bezig het net intehalen, verders, een man te paard, waar nevens twee Landlieden en een beladen Ezel, in 't verschiet eenige Ossen die door een Veehoeder voortgedreven worden; alles zonachtig en delicaat van penceels behandeling | *Mat:* op doek *Size:* hoog 22, breed 31 duim	Herman ten Kate	(Sold) fl 1600 Coclers
1801/06/10	AMSCH	0007	*Both (Jan); Both (Andries)* | Een Bergachtig Landschap, gestoffeert met een man op een Ezel, nevens hem een voetganger, ter zyde. Over een vallend Water, ziet men een brug, en verder hoog geboomte, alles is Zonachtig, en van een uitvoerige en delicaate penceels behandeling | *Mat:* op paneel *Size:* hoog 17, breed 16 duim *Loc:* Hamburg, Deutschland. Kunsthalle. (22)	Herman ten Kate	(Sold) fl 835 Coclers
1802/06/16	AMSCH	0012	*Jan Both; Andries Both* | Een Bergachtig Landschap met hoog Geboomten en dartel Kreupelgewas, gestoffeerd met een Man welke twee beladen Ezels dryft; voorts een aangenaam Verschiet: het Coloriet is gloeijend, het geval en de behandeling zyn allerbevalligst voorgesteld | *Mat:* op doek *Size:* hoog 25, breed 31 duim	[Merrem]	(Sold) fl 500 H de Valk
1802/06/16	AMSCH	0013	*Jan Both; Andries Both* | Een Heuvelachtig Zonachtig Landschap, met hoog Geboomten, op de voorgrond een stille Rivier; door een vervallen Poort ziet men eenig Vée dryven: alles transparant en uitvoerig behandeld | *Mat:* op paneel *Size:* hoog 18, breed 14 duim	[Merrem]	(Sold) fl 151 Cobel
1803/06/20	AMSCH	0007	*J. Both; A. Both* | En Boom- en Bergachtig Landschap, op de voorgrond eenig kreupel gewas, gestoffeerd met een Man, welke twee beladen Muilëzels dryft, warm van colriet en fix getoest [sic], op Doek, door J. en A. Both | *Mat:* op doek *Size:* hoog 25, breed 31 duim	Schley [for] B	(Sold) fl 127 Hulswit
1805/07/10	AMSCH	0009	*J. Both; A. Both* | Een Capitaal Bergachtig Landschap, met hoog Geboomte, Kreupelgewas, Watervallen en Beekjes, gestoffeerd met Beelden, Ezeldryvers en andere stoffagie; meesterlyk en zonachtig op Doek | *Mat:* op doek *Size:* hoog 44, breed 45 duim	R[oos]	(Sold) fl 65 Gruyter
1808/06/13	AMSCH	0011	*Both (Jan); Both (Andries)* | Een hoog bergachtig Landschap, met een Rivier doorsneden, ter linkerzijde gestoffeert met beladene Muilezels en Reizigers, ter rechterzijde, hoog Gebergte, op den voorgrond bijeen Stam van een Boom eenige Kruiden en Plantgewassen; zonachtig en zeer uitvoerig | *Mat:* op doek *Size:* hoog 37, breed 42 duim	W	(Sold) fl 850 C S Roos
1810/06/06	RMMUY	0007	*Jan Both; Andries Both* | In een Bergachtig Landschap, word verbeeld de Fabel van Iö; Mercurius is gereed om met het zwaard den slapenden Argus het hoofd af te slaan; ter zijde staat Iö, in eene witte Koe		(Sold) fl 62 Vermeulen

			herschapen. Dit stuk is van een warm coloriet, krachtig en meesterlijk uitgevoerd | *Mat:* op paneel		
1810/08/01	AMSCH	0014	*Both (Jan); Both (Andries)* | Een wijd uitgestrekt hoog bergachtig Landschap met eenen opgaanden Weg, helder Water en Geboomte, gestoffeerd met eene voorstelling van de dooping des Moormans door den Apostel Philippus [Une vaste Paysage, richement boisé et varié par des Monticules et par une Riviere. On remarque sur une large route une representation du Baptème de l'Enuque [sic] de la Reine de Candace, par l'Apôtre Philippe] | *Annots:* Très bon; sans l'habit trop rouge de Nègre (NGW) *Mat:* op doek *Size:* hoog 49, breed 62 duimen *Loc:* London, England, UK. Royal Collection (Windsor Castle) Inv.3216. as by Jan Both	Mr Pieter de Smeth van Alphen	(Sold) fl 10,000 Reijers voor la Fontaine
1810/08/01	AMSCH	0015	*Both (Jan); Both (Andries)* | Een Italiaansch Landschap, met hoog Geboomte en Kruiden op den voorgrond, versierd met eene Vrouw, zittende op eenen Ezel, wordende door eenen Landman geleid; hier by een Reiziger met zijnen Muilezel; verder een bergachtig verschiet [Un site pittoresque pris en Italie, orné d'Arbres et de Plantes : on distingue au premier plan une femme assise sure un Ane, accompagnée par un Villageois, un Muletier et son Mulet. La perspective montueuse va se terminer à l'horison] | *Annots:* terminé avec soin. vendu fl:4000, dans la vente de Debruin 1798 à Amsterd: (NGW) *Mat:* op koper *Size:* hoog 16, breed 21 duimen	Mr Pieter de Smeth van Alphen	(Bought In) fl 2900

Both, Jan (and Poelenburgh, C.)

1808/08/23	AMSCH	0007	*Both (J); C. Poelenburg* | Een bergachtig Landschap met geboomte en dartel Kreupelgewas, ter zijde met een loopend water doorsneeden, gestoffeerd op den voorgrond met drie Vrouwen benevens een Jongen, en in het verschiet drie andere Beeldjes; het Landschap is zonachtig en warm van Coloriet, en de Beeldjes zijn delicaat en uitvoerig gepenceeld | *Mat:* op doek *Size:* hoog 38, breed 46 duim *Loc:* Roma, Italia. Busiri-Vici collection.	X	(Bought In) fl 760

Both, Jan (and Wyck, T.)

1808/08/23	AMSCH	0171	*Wijk (Th.); J. Both* | Een kapitaal Heuvel en Bergachtig Landschap, ter rechterzijde van hetzelven ziet men voor een groot Gebouw eene Vrouw van eene Trap afkomende, onder aan dezelven zit eene Vrouw, waar bij een oud Man en twee staande Kinderen, meerder op den voorgrond eenige grasende Bokken en Schaapen, ter linker zijde op een Heuvel, een staande en een leggende Koe, benevens een Ram bij de stam van een Boom, en eenig Plantgewas; dit stuk is schoon van koloriet, en van een meesterlijke penceelbehandeling | *Mat:* op doek *Size:* hoog 36, breed 43 duim	[Coclers]	(Sold) fl 61 Dupré
1809/04/22	AMYVR	0143	*T. Wijk; J. Both* | Een kapitaal Heuvelachtig Landschap: van de Trap van een groot Gebouw komt eene Vrouw nederwaarts, onder aan dezelve zit eene andere Vrouw, daarbij een oud Man en twee Kinderen, verders eenige Koeijen en Schapen; meesterlijk fraai gepenseeld, door T. Wijk en J. Both | *Mat:* op doek *Size:* hoog 36, breed 43 duim	de Bruin	(Sold) fl 51 C S Roos

Both, Jan (or Both, J., manner)

1805/06/24	DOBLU	0023	*Both* | Een zeer fraai Bergachtig Landschap en Waterval, met Koetjes, &c., door of in de Manier van Both	Willem Snellen [or] F R E Nibbelinck [or] Gysbert Visser	(Unknown)
1808/04/26	GDAN	0268	*Both* | Door of in de manier van Both, en zon en bergagtig Landschap, met hoog Geboomte, gestoffeerd met eenige Menschen op Ezels gezeeten, voorts eenig Vee | *Size:* hoog 49, breed 65 duim	G H Fortuyn	(Unknown)

Both, Jan (copy after)

1802/09/18	RMDRS	0060	*J. Both* | Een Landschap, na J. Both | *Annots:* zeer goed (MB) *Notes:* A ms. note in the MB copy of the catalogue indicates that the buyer, G. van der Pot, was acting on behalf of someone else.	Casper de Haas	(Sold) fl 7 v Pot

Both, Jan (manner)

1802/05/05	AMSCH	0039	*Both* | Een Land- en Watergezicht, in de manier van Both | *Mat:* op paneel *Size:* hoog 19, breed 18 duim	G	(Sold) fl 3 Rigters
1802/05/22	RMHSN	0006	*Bot* | Een Landschap met Geboomten, waarin Reizigers met een Ezel &c., in de trant van Bot	Lambertus Bicker	(Unknown)
1802/07/21	HGKAN	0091	*Both* | Een groot Landschap, manier van Both		(Unknown)
1803/12/12	AMSCH	0124	*Both* | Twee stuks dito [Boom] dito [en Bergachtig Italiaansch Landschap], op Doek, in de manier van Both | *Mat:* op doek *Size:* hoog 33, breed 44 duim *Notes:* It is unclear what "dito" refers to in the title.	V[inkeles?]	(Sold) fl 10:10 Hodges
1804/08/08	AMSCH	0240	*J. Both* | Een Boom- en Bergachtig Landschap, met Watervallen en Beeldjes; warm en zonachtig, in de manier van J. Both | *Mat:* op doek *Size:* hoog 24, breed 30 duim	Roos a	(Sold) fl 18:10 Van Iperen
1804/10/29	HRBAU	0146	*Both* | Een zeer bevallig bergagtig Landschap; op den Voorgrond gestoffeerd met een Mannetjen, welk op een' Ezel rydt, schynende met een ander te spreeken, die een met Pakken belaaden Muildier voor zig heen dryft; waar by een rustend Landman. Zeer zonagtig in de manier van Both behandeld | *Mat:* op paneel *Size:* hoog 14, breed 17 duim	Simon Styl	(Unknown)

1806/05/05	AMSCH	0007	*J. Both* | Een fraai bergachtig en boomryk Landschap, gestoffeerd met Jagers, Paarden en Honden; dun en warm behandeld als J. Both | *Mat:* op paneel *Size:* hoog 31, breed 41 duim	R[oos]	(Sold) fl 6:15 Mensart
1806/06/07	RMHSN	0074	*Both* | Twee Stuks Moderne Landschappen, in den trant van Both, door een goed Meester | *Mat:* op doek	A E K L	(Unknown)
1806/08/20	HGBSM	0214	*J. Both* | Een Italiaansch Landschapje, in de manier van J. Both | *Mat:* op paneel *Size:* hoog 8 ½, breed 11 ¾ duim	Macalester Loup [or others]	(Sold) fl 13 Lafontaine
			Boucher, François		
1805/06/24	DOBLU	0024	*Boucher* | Een Fabelsche Historie, zeer goed	Willem Snellen [or] F R E Nibbelinck [or] Gysbert Visser	(Unknown)
1805/07/10	AMSCH	0036	*Boucher* | Pan en Syringa; meesterlyk op Paneel | *Mat:* op paneel *Size:* hoog 12, breed 19 duim	V[inkeles] [for] H[affner]	(Sold) fl 0:6 L Pakker
			Boucher, François (or Boucher, manner)		
1809/06/13	AMSCH	0024	*F. Boucher* | Deeze Ordonantie, verbeeld in een bevallig Landschap Vénus en Bachus, verselt van Cupido en andere Minnewigten, gestoffeerd met verscheide bijwerk; het is aangenaam van koloriet en van een uitvoerige penceelsbehandeling, door of in de manier van F. Boucher | *Mat:* op doek *Size:* hoog 23, breed 28 duim	Q	(Bought In) fl 19
			Boudewyns, Adriaen Frans		
1801/04/23	AMYVR	0020	*Boudewyns* | Een Boschgezicht met een Hartenjagt gestoffeerd		(Sold) fl 13 Coclaire
1801/04/23	AMYVR	0029	*Boudewyn* | Twee stuks zynde een Zomer- en Wintergezicht		(Sold) fl 5 Coclaire
1801/08/19	AMSCH	0013	*J. Boudewyns* | Een Bergagtig Landschap, gestoffeerd met Reizigers, zoo te paard, als te voet; door J. Boudewyns, op Doek | *Mat:* op doek *Size:* hoog 24, breed 28 duim *Notes:* The artist's name was given as "J. Boudewyns" but we have assumed this is an error.	van der Schly [for] F	(Sold) fl 1:10 Gruiter
1804/07/25	DLGRO	0075	*Baudewins* | Een Bergächtig Landschap, met eenige oude Ruines en Beeldjes, beneffens een Water gezicht met Scheepen of Schuiten | *Mat:* op paneel *Size:* hoog 11, breed 13 ½ duim	Mr Franc van der Burch Wz.	(Unknown)
1804/07/25	DLGRO	0076	*Baudewins* | Een dito [Bergächtig] dito [Landschap], met een Cascade of Waterval | *Mat:* op paneel *Size:* hoog 11, breed 13 ½ duim	Mr Franc van der Burch Wz.	(Unknown)
1805/07/03	AMSCH	0063	*Boudouin* | Twee stuks aangenaame Land- en Riviergezichtten, met Geboomten, Gebergten, antique Gebouwen, stoffagie van Beeldjes enz.; beide zonachtig gepenceeld | *Mat:* op doek *Size:* hoog 13, breed 15 duim	V[inkeles]	(Sold) fl 6:10 Hardenberg
1806/06/07	RMHSN	0054	*Boudewyns* | Twee dito [Stuks] Arkadische Landschapjes, ryk met Beeldjes | *Mat:* op paneel	A E K L	(Unknown)
1810/07/26	AMSCH	0011	*Boudewijns* | Een dergelijk Landschap, met stoffagie van Beelden. Goed van schildering | *Mat:* op doek *Size:* hoog 14, breed 19 duimen	Cassino	(Sold) fl 4 Dupré
1810/07/26	AMSCH	0012	*Boudewijns* | Een Landschap. In alles als de voorgaande | *Mat:* op doek *Size:* hoog 25, breed 32 duimen	Cassino	(Bought In) fl 0:18
1810/10/11	AMSCH	0190	*Boudewijns* | Een Landschap, met Beelden en Beesten gestoffeerd	A	(Sold) fl 0:6 Gruiter
			Boudewyns, Adriaen Frans (and Bout, P.)		
1810/07/26	AMSCH	0010	*Bout; Boudewijns* | Een Landschap, met Geboomte, Landlieden, Vee enz. Zeer fraai | *Mat:* op doek *Size:* hoog 18, breed 22 duimen	Cassino	(Sold) L Pakker
1810/07/26	AMSCH	0096	*Bout; Boudewijns* | Twee fraaije Landschappen. Fraai | *Mat:* op doek	Cassino	(Bought In) fl 1:15
			Boudewyns, Adriaen Frans (and Schoevaerdts, M.)		
1803/07/18	AMSCH	0006	*Boudewyns, (F.); M. Schoevaerts* | Twee stuks aangenaame Brabandsche Landschappen, met Rivieren doorsneeden, gestoffeerd met verscheide Beeldjes en Paarden, warm van coloriet en uitvoerig geschilderd [Deux Jolis paysages traversés par des rivieres : ils sont ornés de figures & animaux spirituellement touchés, de la meilleure maniere des deux peintres.] | *Mat:* [sur bois] *Size:* yder hoog 12, breed 16 duim *Notes:* The material was given only in the French edition of the catalogue.	Maria Theresia Andrioli	(Sold) fl 17 Teissier
			Bourdon, Sébastien		
1801/04/13	AMSCH	0012	*S. Bourdon* | Deeze uitmuntende Ordonantie steld voor de Opwekking van Lazarus, men ziet Christus in een biddende gestalte, verders eenige Beelden, alle als in verrukking; de drappery is breed, en alles is meesterlyk fix behandeld | *Mat:* op doek *Size:* hoog 21, breed 25 duim	Pierre Fouquet, junior	(Sold) fl 76 B Wolft
			Boursse, Esaias		
1801/12/22	AMOTT	0019	*E. Boursse* | 1 oppassende Maagd, voor het Bedde van een stervende Vrouw, door E. Boursse, 1655 | *Inscr:* E. Boursse, 1655 (signed and dated?) *Notes:* It is unclear whether the name and date are inscribed on the painting.	Bartholomeus Ruloffs	(Unknown) fl 4
1809/04/22	AMYVR	0013	*E. Boursse* | Een Militair, zittende te rooken aan eene Tafel, waarop een Kan, Test en Verkeerbord; uitvoerig op Doek, door E. Boursse, in de manier van Terburg | *Mat:* op doek *Size:* hoog 17, breed 15 duim	de Bruin	(Sold) fl 10:5 J de Vries

			Bout, Peeter		
1802/05/05	AMSCH	0032	*P. Bout* | Een Bergächtig Landschap, op de Voorgrond ziet men een Herder zittende op een Paard, verzeld van een menigte Veê; verders een vervallen Kasteel, zeer dun van penceelbehandeling | *Mat:* op paneel *Size:* hoog 15, breed 12 duim	BB	(Sold) fl 18:10 Vermeulen
1803/08/01	AMSCH	0004	*Bouts. (P.)* | Twee stuks Brabandsche Dorpgezichten, in de eene is verbeeld een Kermis, en in de andere een Beestenmarkt, beide vol gewoel van beelden en andere stoffagie, uitvoerig gepenceeld | *Mat:* op doek *Size:* ieder hoog 17, breed 23 duim	C	(Sold) fl 33:10 Pruijssenaar
1803/09/07	AMSCH	0021	*P. Bout* | Twee stuks Italiaansche Kermissen, vol gewoel van Kwakzalvers en andere Kooplieden, van diverse Natien, bevallig van Coleur en Schildering [Deux kermesses italiennes ; grande foule, dans laquelle on remarque des charlatans et des marchands de différentes nations : d'un coloris agréable et d'une touche charmante] | *Mat:* op doek op paneel *Size:* hoog 14, breed 18 duim	Smidt	(Sold) fl 13:10 Scheffer
1804/08/08	AMSCH	0033	*P. Bout* | Een Bergachtig Landschap, ryk gestoffeerd met Heeren te Paard, belaaden Muilezels en andere Stoffagie; meesterlyk gepenceelt | *Mat:* op doek *Size:* hoog 24, breed 29 duim	Vink[eles] [for] K[=Gruyter?]	(Sold) fl 1:10 Gruyter
1806/08/13	AMSCH	0249	*P. Bout* | Een Bergachtig Landschap, met Heeren en Dames te paard	Vinkeles [for] G[ruyter]	(Sold) fl 1:5 Gruiter
1808/11/28	AMSCH	0011	*P. Bout* | Een Gezicht op Strand aan de Noordzee, rijk gestoffeerd met wandelende Heeren en Dames, Viswagens en Dorppelingen [sic], verder zeilende en stilleggende Schepen en Visschers Vaartuigen, meesterlijk | *Mat:* op doek *Size:* hoog 32, breed 55 duim	[Gruyter?]	(Bought In) fl 5:10
1810/07/23	DOLG2	0018	*P. Bout* | In een Bergachtig Landschap, ziet men door een vervallen Poort Runderen en Schapen drijven. Voords een beladen Ezel, Paarden en Beesten. Dun en breed geschilderd | *Mat:* op paneel *Size:* hoog 23, breed 31 duim	Pieter Quinting	(Sold) fl 21:10 van Eyk 's Hage
1810/07/26	AMSCH	0013	*Bout* | Een Boomrijk Landschap, met Gebouwen, Beelden en Beesten gestoffeerd | *Mat:* op doek *Size:* hoog 10, breed 14 duimen	Cassino	(Sold) fl 3:15 Dupré
1810/10/11	AMSCH	0013	*P. Bout* | Een Strand- en Zeegezigt, gestoffeerd met zeilende en ten anker liggende Vaartuigen, Heeren, Dames, en Visschers; kloek geschilderd | *Mat:* op doek *Size:* hoog 38, breed 57 duimen	[Gruyter?]	(Withdrawn)
1810/12/03	DOBRA	0060	*P. Bout* | Twee Boeren in een Drinkgelag, door P. Bout, in een zwarte Lyst		(Unknown)
			Bout, Peeter (and Boudewyns)		
1810/07/26	AMSCH	0010	*Bout; Boudewijns* | Een Landschap, met Geboomte, Landlieden, Vee enz. Zeer fraai | *Mat:* op doek *Size:* hoog 18, breed 22 duimen	Cassino	(Sold) L Pakker
1810/07/26	AMSCH	0096	*Bout; Boudewijns* | Twee fraaije Landschappen. Fraai | *Mat:* op doek	Cassino	(Bought In) fl 1:15
			Bout, Peeter (changed to Rombouts)		
1810/07/23	DOLG2	0043	*P. Bout; Rombout* | Een Boomrijk Landschap, krachtig van coloriet, en wel geschilderd | *Mat:* op paneel *Size:* hoog 15, breed 19 duim *Notes:* The artist's name was changed by hand from "P. Bout" to "Rombout" in the FLNY copy of the catalogue.	Pieter Quinting	(Sold) fl 50:10 Blijk
			Bouts, F. [Unidentified]		
1806/08/13	AMSCH	0333	*Bout (F.)* | In een gemeubileerd Binnevertrek, ziet men een Heer aan een Tafel zitten, bézig zynde te rooken waarnaast een ander staande, verders toepasselyk bywerk; delicaat en fraai van behandeling | *Mat:* op doek *Size:* hoog 17, breed 15 duim	Vinkeles [for] J	(Sold) fl 3:10 du Pree
			Bovette, Simone [Unidentified]		
1803/04/27	AMSCH	0029	*Simone Bovette* | Loth & ses filles, ce Tableau, est d'un bon effêt, la couleur en est vigoureuse & il est peint avec beaucoup de Franchise | *Size:* h. 3 ½, l. 4 ½ pieds *Notes:* The artist was presumably Simon Vouet and not Simone Bovette.	A	(Sold) fl 65 Hulswit
			Braccioli		
1804/10/16	DLOND	0036	*Bratchioli* | Twee Mans- en Vrouwe Pourtraitten. Deux Portraits d'Homme & Femme | *Mat:* op paneel *Size:* hoog 12, breed 9		(Unknown)
			Brakenburg, Richard		
1801/10/19	AMSCH	0009	*Braakenburg. (R.)* | Een Binnevertrek, waar in een Matroos met twee Meisjes, en een Oude Vrouw, die hem een glas wyn brengt, konstig geschilderd | *Mat:* op paneel *Size:* hoog 15, breed 12 duim	Jonkheer Menno Baron van Coehoorn	(Sold) fl 106 van der Schley [for] A
1802/05/05	AMSCH	000A	*R. Brakenburg* | In een burger Binnevertrek ziet men een Dokter by een zieke Vrouw, haar de Pols voelen, ter zyde een oude Vrouw, en agter haar een jong Meisje, delicaat gepenceeld | *Mat:* op paneel *Size:* hoog 13, breed 10 duim	A	(Sold) fl 71 Pruijssenaar [for] R
1802/06/28	AMSCH	0003	*R. Brakenburg* | Een Kraamkamer, vol gewoel van Beelden, de Vader des Huisgezins, met een Kind in den Arm, krabt zyn hoofd, over het aanbieden van een Tweede; alles delicaat gepenceeld, op Doek, door R. Brakenburg | *Mat:* op doek *Size:* hoog 16, breed 19 duim	Anna Elink	(Sold) fl 13 Reijers

1802/06/28	AMSCH	0004	*R. Brakenburg* | Twee stuks Binnehuizen, gestoffeert met verscheide eetende, drinkende en musiceerende Lieden, zoo Mans, Vrouwen, als Kinderen. Natuurlyk en geestig behandeld, op Panneel | *Mat:* op paneel *Size:* hoog 11, breed 13 duim	B	(Sold) fl 40 Texier
1802/06/28	AMSCH	0005	*R. Brakenburg* | Een Doktor by een Zieke Vrouw, op Panneel | *Mat:* op paneel *Size:* hoog 13, breed 10 duim	Anna Elink	(Sold) fl 5:5 T Spaan
1802/07/21	HGKAN	0031	*Brakenburg* | Een Boeren Binnenhuys, met eenige drinkende en rookende Boeren, op de Voorgrond een oude Boerin met een Kind en verder bywerk, vergulde Lyst, paneel door Brakenburg, van zyn beste tyd | *Mat:* op paneel		(Unknown)
1802/12/13	AMSCH	0022	*R. Brakenburg* | In een Landschap ziet men voor een Herberg, eenigen Boeren met elkander Vegten, de Hartstogten zyn zeer wel waargenomen, zonachtig en meesterlyk gepenseeld | *Mat:* op doek *Size:* hoog 24, breed 32 duim	Pruyssenaar [for] A	(Sold) fl 6:5 de Meijer
1803/06/20	AMSCH	0046	*R. Brakenburg* | Een Kraamkamer, alwaar de Vroedvrouw de Vader twee Kinderen in den Arm geeft, waar mede hy niet in zyn schik schynt te zyn, een meenigte Vrouwen zyn te Gast, alles is zoo geestig behandeld als J. Steen, zynde dit Stukje een der bevalligste van R. Brakenburg | *Mat:* op doek *Size:* hoog 20, breed 25 duim	Roos [for] C	(Sold) fl 16 Hafner
1803/07/18	AMSCH	0003	*Brakenburg. (R.)* | Twee stuks, yder hoog 19, breed 22 duim, Doek. In een Boerewooning ziet men een geslagt Varken op de Ladder hangen, een menigte Gasten vermaaken zich met eeten en drinken, terwyl de Kinderen beezig zyn de Blaas op te blaazen, ter linkerzyde tapt de Knegt Bier, wordende het Vat door de Meid geligt, een Patryshond legt op de voorgrond, naast eenig Gereedschap tot de Slagt behoorende. De andere steld voor een voornaam Heer met zyn Vrouw op een Binnenplaats zittende, terwyl een aantal Kinderen zich vermaaken met Belleblaazen! voorts twee speelende Honden, eenige Fruiten, Speelgoed, en ander bywerk. Dezelve zyn beide van een veelbeduidende expressie, helder van ligt en aangenaam van behandeling [Dans l'Interieur d'une ferme ou l'on s'apprête au repas du Porc tuè, l'on voit differens personnages rangés autour d'une table, tandis que trois enfans s'amusent à souffler la vessie de l'Animal tué. A la gauche, se voyent un Homme & une Femme à tirer de la Bierre, & à droite est une servante occupée au Porc. Nombre d'ustenciles & un Gros matou couché sur le devant du tableau achevent cet ensemble de dixsept figures. Ce sujet souvent repeté, mais souvent desagréablement est dans ce tableau-ci très intéressant le peintre n'ayant pas exposé l'animal mort d'une maniere ostencible. La disposition en est bien entendue ! A une belle fonte de couleurs s'unit l'expression naive des figures & un bel Effet de lumière. Le second de même grandeur : Dans une Cour intérieure est assis un personnage distingué, & une Dame ténant un Jeune Enfant ; plus avant est une servante & quelques Enfans qui s'amusent à faire des boules de Savon. Vers la Maison & le Jardin sont differentes personnes : tout y est naturellement rendu ainsi que deux Jolis chiens en quérelle. Ce tableau faisant pendant au précedent est d'un même mérite, & d'un même Eclat.] | *Mat:* op doek *Size:* yder hoog 19, breed 22 duim	Maria Theresia Andrioli	(Sold) fl 110 Gruyter
1803/08/24	HGKAN	0010	*Reynier Brakenburg* | Een vrolyk Boeren Binnehuis met verscheide figuuren en Kinderen, uitvoerig en van de beste Schildering | *Mat:* op paneel *Size:* hoog 10, breet 13 duim	[Teissier] [or others]	(Sold) fl 42 Cuylenburg
1803/09/07	AMSCH	0031	*R. Brakenburg* | Twee stuks Binnehuizen, ryk gestoffeerd met verscheide Huislieden en Kinderen, dewelken zig met Spys en Drank vermaken; uitvoerig op Paneel geschilderd [Deux intérieurs, remplis d'habitans et d'enfans qui se régalent et s'amusent à manger et boire ; excellente composition] | *Mat:* op paneel *Size:* ieder hoog 16, breed 20 duim	Smidt	(Bought In) fl 100
1803/12/12	AMSCH	0013	*R. Brakenburg* | Een Binnenvertrek, waarin een ménigte Spelende Kinderen; uitvoerig op Paneel | *Mat:* op paneel *Size:* hoog 10, breed 7 duim	W	(Sold) fl 3:5 Ijver
1804/02/27	AMSCH	0006	*Brakenburg. (R.)* | Deeze ryke ordonnantie van twintig Beelden, stelt voor een Binnenhuis, waar verscheide Boeren en Boerrinnen, zich vermaaken met zingen en drinken, men ziet een bevallig jong Meisje welke door een Boer gecarresseerd word en een ander hebbende een glas bier in de hand, ter zyde een oude Huisman, welke lustig een vrolyke Meid het glas vol schenkt; alles is zo geestig en uitvoerig behandeld van Teekening, helder en tevens krachtig van Coloriet, dat men met recht mag zegge [sic] dat dit een der allersfraaiste van deeze meester is | *Mat:* op doek *Size:* hoog 16, breed 19 duim	B	(Sold) fl 105 Burggraaff
1804/05/07	AMSCH	0023	*Brakenburg. (R.)* | In een Binnenhuis vertoont zich een vrolyke op de Phiool speelende Huisman, neevens hem twee met aandagt luisterende Landlieden en een oude Boerin, op de voorgrond een bevallige Vrouw, met een Kom met Brandewyn in haar Handen, voor haar een Vat met een Test en eenige Kaarten, en verder Huisraad; dit stuk is als J Steen gepenceeld | *Mat:* op doek *Size:* hoog 27, breed 21 ½ duim	Vinkeles [for] G	(Bought In) fl 11
1804/08/08	AMSCH	0018	*R. Brakenburg* | Twee stuks Boeren Binnenhuizen, in de eene een Galantiseerende Boer en Boerin; in de andere Huislieden met hun Kinderen; beiden van de uitvoerigste zoort van R. Brakenburg | *Mat:* op paneel *Size:* hoog 9, breed 6 ½ duim	Roos a	(Sold) fl 32 Gruyter

1804/08/08	AMSCH	0019	*R. Brakenburg* | In een Binnehuis zitten verscheiden vrolyke Munneken en Nonnetjes, zich met musiceeren en drinken vermaakende; bevallig gepenceeld | *Mat:* op paneel *Size:* hoog 14, br. 18 duim	Schley [for] A	(Sold) fl 66 van Iperen
1804/10/16	DLOND	0033	*R Brakenburg* | Een Binnenvertrek met ene Vrouw agter een Tafel, waarop een Tapyt, benevens verscheiden Beelden. Une Chambre dans laquelle, entre beaucoup de Figures, une Femme derriere une Table couverte d'un Tapis | *Mat:* op doek *Size:* hoog 17, breed 15		(Sold) fl 8 Brerkhuis
1804/10/29	HRBAU	0007	*Brakenburg, (R.) 1669* | In een ryk gemeubileerd Binnenvertrek wordt eene bevallige Dame adergelaten, welke eenigzins schynt te bezwymen, wordende het bekken door een Jongetje gehouden; hier by zit een oud Heer en Dame, benevens een staande jonge Dame, welke verslagen schynen, terwyl een andere Heer en Dame daar over glimlagchen [sic]; ter linkerzyde staat een Tafel met een Turks Tapyt overdekt, waar by een Meid staat, welke, op eene comique wyze, de ziekte heurer Juffer schynt te willen aanwyzen. Dit Stuk is van de heldere soort, uitvoerig, en teffens zeer mals behandeld, zynde een der besten van dezen Meester | *Mat:* op paneel *Size:* hoog 29, breed 36 duim *Inscr:* R. Brakenburg, 1669 (signed and dated?) *Notes:* It is unclear whether the name and date are inscribed on the painting.	Simon Styl	(Unknown)
1804/10/29	HRBAU	0008	*Brakenburg, (R.)* | In het midden van dit Stuk, op een helder licht, zit een bevallige Moeder zeer vergenoegd het spel aan te zien van heure Kinderen, welken zeer gretig naar de Nooten verlangen, welken een jonge Dame by een plank laat neêrrollen, om die op te raapen, en in hunne zakken te steeken; waar by een Heer en Dame, welken met elkander in gesprek zyn; wat verder by een venster, waar door het licht valt, en waar door twee Jongens naar binnen zien, zitten een Heer en Dame elkander te caresseeren; terwyl agter aan zig verscheiden Mans en Vrouwen onder het gespeel der fiool verlustigen. Fraai van licht en bruin, en zeer uitvoerig in de manier van Jan Steen behandeld | *Mat:* op doek *Size:* hoog 24, breed 31 duim	Simon Styl	(Unknown)
1804/10/29	HRBAU	0009	*Brakenburg, (R.)* | Dit grappig Schilderytje vertoont een aartige Hospita, welke een Boertje, dat met een ander op de Kaart schynt te speelen, eens ter deegen in de oogen kykt, terwyl hy haar by het boeselaar vat; waar by nog twee Boeren zyn, welken zig by het vuur warmen; op den grond staat een Hond die de pot uitlikt, en een aarden Bierkan. Dit Stukje is zeer bevallig, delicaat en uitvoerig in de manier als het voorgaande [Jan Steen] behandeld | *Mat:* op paneel *Size:* hoog 13 ½, breed 10 ½ duim	Simon Styl	(Unknown)
1805/07/03	AMSCH	0066	*R. Brakenburg* | Twee stuks Voorwerpen, met galantiseerende figuren; kragtig en geestig op Koper | *Mat:* op koper *Size:* hoog 4, breed 4 duim	C	(Sold) fl 3:5 L Pakker
1805/07/10	AMSCH	0019	*R. Brakenburg* | Een Vertrek met een ménigte vrolyke Heeren en Dames; delicaat en uitvoerig op Doek | *Mat:* op doek	V[inkeles] [for] K	(Sold) fl 3:5 Boelen
1805/07/10	AMSCH	0020	*R. Brakenburg* | Een Kraamkamer, alwaar de Baker de Vader de Jonggeboorene aanbied, verders een ménigte andere Beelden en Huisraad; delicaat en meesterlyk op Paneel | *Mat:* op paneel *Size:* hoog 13, breed 17 duim	V[inkeles] [for] H[affner]	(Bought In) fl 6
1805/07/10	AMSCH	0021	*R. Brakenburg* | In een Kraamkamer ziet men de Baker twee Jonggeboornen aan de Vader aanbieden; verders een ménigte andere Beelden en verder bywerk; geestig en fraay van schildering | *Mat:* op doek *Size:* hoog 20, breed 24 duim	V[inkeles] [for] H[affner]	(Sold) fl 20 L Pakker
1805/07/10	AMSCH	0200	*R. Brakenburg* | Een Biddend Huisgezin	R[oos]	(Sold) fl 2 Agina
1805/12/16	AMSCH	0011	*R. Brakenburg* | Twee stuks Binnehuizen, met rokende, en drinkende Huislieden, kragtig op Paneel | *Mat:* op paneel *Size:* hoog 13, breed 10 duim	R[oos]	(Sold) fl 9:10 Vinkeles
1805/12/16	AMSCH	0012	*R. Brakenburg* | Een Vasten-Avond Vreugd, alwaar de Koning drinkt; geestig op Doek | *Mat:* op doek *Size:* hoog 16, breed 19 duim	V	(Sold) fl 3:5 Van Dijl
1806/08/13	AMSCH	0019	*Brakenburg. (R.)* | Een Boeren School, vol gewoel van Kinderen; geestig geschilderd | *Mat:* op paneel *Size:* hoog 10, breed 13 duim	Roos	(Sold) fl 8:5 Verhoesen
1808/06/11	RMRIJ	0030	*A: Brakenburgh* | Een Kraamkamer, vol Gewoel, van meer dan Dertig Beelden en een aantal verschilderd Bywerk, aangenaam, geestig, dun en helder geschilderd | *Mat:* op doek *Size:* hoog 32, breed 37 ½ duim *Notes:* The artist's name was given as "A: Brakenburgh" but we have assumed this is an error.		(Withdrawn)
1808/08/23	AMSCH	0031	*Brakenburg. (R.)* | Een Binnehuis, met een Heer en Dame, zittende bij een Tafel, waar bij eene bejaarde Vrouw en verder bijwerk; natuurlijk en fiks behandeld | *Mat:* op koper *Size:* hoog 8, breed 6 duim	Y	(Sold) fl 14.10 Spruit
1808/09/13	HABRU	0013	*R. Brakenburg* | Een Binnenhuis, met vrolijke kaartspeelende Boeren en Boerinnen | companion to lot 14		(Unknown) fl 7
1808/09/13	HABRU	0014	*R. Brakenburg* | Een dito [Binnenhuis], zijnde een weergaa, door denzelven; fraai geschilderd | companion to lot 13		(Unknown) fl 20
1808/10/28	AMVRS	0005	*Brakenburg. (R.)* | Een rijk gemeubileerd Binnehuis, waarin verscheide bejaarde en jonge Lieden van verschillende standen bezig met het uitdeelen en ontvangen van Nieuwejaarsgeschenkjes. De harstochten, vooral der Kinderen, zijn zeer natuurlijk uitgedrukt, en alles is zeer geestig en levendig behandeld | *Mat:* op doek *Size:* hoog 30, breed 34 duim	Marten Udink	(Sold) fl 305 Spaan

1809/06/13	AMSCH	0014	*R. Brakenburg* | In een Bovenkamer ziet men een menigte vergenoegde Huislieden, zich met Eeten, Drinken, Zingen, Speelen en Liefkoozen vermaaken, verders eenig toepasselijk bijwerk, en Keukengereedschap; fraai gecaracteriseerd en meesterlijk geschilderd | *Mat:* op doek *Size:* hoog 34, breed 44 duim	[Gruyter?]	(Bought In) fl 12:10
1809/06/13	AMSCH	0015	*R. Brakenburg* | Een Kaartspeelend Gezelschap, eene oude Vrouw ziet hetzelve aandachtig aan, terwijl een Deftig Heer, zijn Pijp rookt, een Kind en andere Beelden, stoffeeren verder dit Binnevertrek; het geen geestig en uitvoerig geschilderd is | *Size:* hoog 19, breed 16 duim	Y	(Sold) fl 3:5 Gruyter
1809/09/06	AMSCH	0008	*Brakenburg (R.)* | Deze rijke Ordinantie vol gewoel van Beelden, vertoond den Wijsgeer Diogenes in zijn Ton, op de Markt van Atheenen, vrijmoedig spreekende teegens de Keijser, die hen met verwondering beschouwd, verder gestoffeerd met Gebouwen en Standbeelden; het is kragtig van koloriet en meesterlijk fraai behandeld | *Mat:* op doek *Size:* hoog 24, breed 30 duim	Johannes Caudri	(Sold) fl 8:5 Tomassen
1809/09/06	AMSCH	0009	*Brakenburg (R.)* | Dit Voorwerp verbeeld in een Bergachtig Landschap, Jupiter in zijne jonge Jaren aan de Maagden ter opvoeding overgeeven, zijnde een Ordonantie van verscheide Vrouwenbeelden; het is kragtig en meesterlijk geschilderd | *Mat:* op doek *Size:* hoog 24, breed 30 duim	Johannes Caudri	(Sold) fl 7:5 Tomassen
1810/06/06	RMMUY	0015	*Reinter Brakenburg* | Vijf kleine Kabinet Stukjes, verbeeldende de Zinnen, in eene vrolijke manier, aller aangenaamst en uitvoerig behandeld. Door Reinter Brakenburg, van zijn besten tijd | *Mat:* op koper *Size:* hoog 5, breed 3 ½ duim		(Sold) fl 90 Pot
1810/06/20	AMSCH	0008	*R. Brakenburg* | Twee stuks grappige Voorwerpen: beide zeer geestig en uitvoerig geschilderd | *Mat:* op doek *Size:* Jeder is hoog 11, breed 13 duimen	B	(Sold) fl 14:10 Boelhouwer
1810/06/20	AMSCH	0009	*R. Brakenburg* | Eene Kraamkamer, rijk met Beelden gestoffeerd. Geestig van ordonnantie | *Mat:* op doek *Size:* hoog 34, breed 43 duimen	A	(Sold) fl 6 du Pree
1810/08/06	AMSCH	0018	*Brakenburg (R.)* | Een Binnenvertrek, waarin een Kaartspelend Gezelschap, op den voorgrond spelende Kinderen. Uitvoerig behandeld | *Mat:* op doek *Size:* hoog 19, breed 16 duimen	C	(Sold) fl 3:10 Stoopendaal [for] B

Brakenburg, Richard (or Brakenburg, manner)

1809/07/25	HGBSM	0085	*Brakenburg* | Een vrolyk Boeregezelschap in een Binnen-Vertrek, zig vermakende met eeten, drinken, speelen enz., door of in de manier van Brakenburg | *Mat:* op doek *Size:* hoog 25, breed 30 duim	D van der Aa	(Sold) fl 3:10 van der Aa

Brakenburg, Richard (copy after)

1804/10/16	DLOND	0240a[l]	*C. Vermeulen; Brakenburg* | [Een Stuk, bevattende 13 zeer schone Copiën van de volgende Meesters. Un Tableau, contenant 13 Copies très-belles des Peintres suivans.] 12. Brakenburg. Enige Boeren, des Paysans | copy by Corn. Vermeulen (III) after Brakenburg *Mat:* op paneel *Size:* hoog 41, breed 55 *Notes:* The bracketed information in the title appears above lot 240a[a] and refers to lots 240a[a-m].		(Sold) fl 150 for lots 240a[a-m]. Ond d Wyngaert

Brakenburg, Richard (manner)

1805/12/16	AMSCH	0060	*R. Brakenburg* | Twee stuks, het eene een Kaartspeelend, en het andere een Gezelschap hetwelk Oesters Eet, geestig op Doek, in de manier van R. Brakenburg | *Mat:* op doek	R[oos]	(Bought In) fl 20
1805/12/16	AMSCH	0106	*Brakenburg* | Twee stuks, met vrolyke en galantiseerende Gezelschappen; in de manier van Brakenburg | *Notes:* This lot was sold with lot 107 by an anonymous artist.	V	(Sold) fl 0:6 for lots 106 & 107. L Pakker
1806/05/05	AMSCH	0164	*R. Brakenburg* | Een Chirurgyn een Man zyn hoofd verbindendende [sic], waar by een Vrouw, en verder bywerk; geestig op Paneel, als R. Brakenburg | *Mat:* op paneel	R[oos]	(Sold) fl 8:5 Coclers
1807/08/26	AMSCH	0311	*R. Brakenburg* | Een Binnenhuis, met verscheiden Vrouwen en verder bywerk; als door R. Brakenburg | *Mat:* op paneel	Yver [for] S	(Sold) fl 1:5 Gruiter

Brakenburg, W. [Unidentified]

1810/11/07	UTWLD	0021	*W. Brakenburg* | Een Vette Keuken, een bejaard Man van een stuk Vleesch snijdende, dat voor hem op een tafel staat, met eenige eetende Boertjes, terwijl een dik Vrouwtje er voor zit, met een glas met wijn, naast haar een tinne wijnkan, op de voorgrond twee jongens met een hond, bezig zijnde de pot schoon te maken, de tekening en groupeering zeer nauwkeuring, natuurlijk en klaar geschilderd door W. Brakenburg 1665 op doek, 11 en een half duim hoog, 9 duim breed, zwarte Lijst | companion to lot 22 *Mat:* op doek *Size:* 11 en een half duim hoog, 9 duim breed *Inscr:* W. Brakenburg 1665 (signed and dated?) *Notes:* It is unclear whether the name and date are inscribed on the painting.		(Unknown) fl 52 for lots 21 & 22
1810/11/07	UTWLD	0022	*W. Brakenburg* | Een pendant, de Magere Keuken, een Boertje voor een Tafel gezeten, waar op een pot, waar uit hij schijnt te eeten, – een Vrouwtje met een lepel een Kind voerende, een ander met eeten bezig, terwijl één een ledige pot schijnt te ontrukken aan een nevens hem staande meisje – op den agtergrond een Schilder voor zijn Ezel – dit alles tot onderwerp nemende – door denzelven [W. Brakenburg] | companion to lot 21 *Notes:* It is unclear whether the date is inscribed on the painting.		(Unknown) fl 52 for lots 21 & 22

Bramer, Leonard

1801/08/19	AMSCH	0015	*L. Bramer* | Deeze Ordenantie verbeeld de Besnydenis van Christus, in den Tempel, gestoffeert met verscheide Tempeldienaaren, het natuurlyk licht der Flambouwen, geeft een byzondere houding; en is meesterlyk gepenceeld, op Doek | *Mat:* op doek *Size:* hoog 27, breed 40 duim	C S Roos [for] G	(Sold) fl 5 J Spaan
1802/05/05	AMSCH	0038	*Bramer* | Een Man, staande in 't Harnas, met een Purpere Mantel omhangen | *Mat:* op paneel *Size:* hoog 25, breed 18 duim	G	(Sold) fl 4 Spruit
1802/12/13	AMSCH	0031	*L. Bramer* | Een Biddende Heremiet in een Binnenvertrek, met bywerk | *Mat:* op paneel *Size:* hoog 19, breed 15 duim	Pruyssenaar [for] D	(Sold) fl 2:15 Gruiter
1803/06/20	AMSCH	0005	*L. Bramer* | Een Manspourtrait men een Pluim op de Muts, omkleed met Goude en Zilvere Franjes, en een Keeten met een Medailje om den Hals, alles meesterlyk, door L. Bramer, in de manier van Rembrand, op Paneel | *Mat:* op paneel *Size:* hoog 37, breed 29 duim	Schley [for] B	(Sold) fl 81 Hodges
1803/09/07	AMSCH	0033	*L. Bramer* | Een Man en Vrouw, in een Binnenhuis, speelende met een Hond, verders een Spinnewiel; kragtig op Paneel [Un homme et une femme dans l'intérieur d'une maison jouant avec un chien ; plus loin un rouet à filer ; touche vigoureuse] | *Mat:* op paneel *Size:* hoog 20, breed 18 duim	Smidt	(Bought In) fl 19
1804/02/27	AMSCH	0139	*Bramer* | Een Historiele Ordonantie	B	(Sold) fl 0:18 for lots 139 & 140. Gruiter
1804/02/27	AMSCH	0140	*Bramer* | Een dito [Historiele Ordonantie]	B	(Sold) fl 0:18 for lots 139 & 140. Gruiter
1804/10/16	DLOND	0034	*L. Bramer* | De wyze en dwaze Maagden. Schoon Lamplicht. Les Vierges Sages & Folles. Lumière de Lampe très belle | *Mat:* op paneel *Size:* hoog 20, breed 29		(Unknown)
1804/10/16	DLOND	0035	*L. Bramer* | De Tegemoetkoming van den Bruidegom. Uts[a] [Schoon Lamplicht]. L'Arrivée de l'Epoux. Utsa [Lumière de Lampe très belle] | *Mat:* op paneel *Size:* hoog 20, breed 29		(Unknown)
1806/08/13	AMSCH	0020	*Bramer. (L.)* | Een Bybel Ordinantie van twee Figuuren, in een Binnenvertrek, verbeeldende een Vorstelyk Persoon, op een knie leggende, ter zyde een Tafel, waarop een Leesenaar en Boek geplaatst is, ter zyde op wolken staat een Engel; kragtig en meesterlyk geschilderd | *Mat:* op doek *Size:* hoog 50, breed 43 duim	van der Voort	(Sold) fl 18:10 Richter
1806/10/16	UTWLD	0006	*Braamer* | Een Philosooph in zyne studeerkamer zittende in een boek te lezen	Mr P de Malapert [or] W Beeldsnyder	(Unknown)
1808/06/11	RMRIJ	0053	*Leonard Bramer* | Simeon, het Kind Jezus offerende in den Tempel, zeer fraai en meesterlyk geschilderd | *Mat:* op paneel *Size:* hoog 20, breed 27 ½ duim		(Sold) fl 17 van Leen
1809/04/22	AMYVR	0021	*L. Bramer* | Een grootsch Binnenvertrek, waarin bij kaarslicht eenige Beelden bij 't Vuur zitten; geestig van licht | *Mat:* op paneel *Size:* hoog 14, breed 20 duim	de Bruin	(Sold) fl 7:15 du Pree
1809/04/22	AMYVR	0022	*L. Bramer* | Een Paus als in verrukking, niet minder als de voorgaande | *Mat:* op doek *Size:* hoog 21, breed 15 duim	de Bruin	(Sold) fl 1 van Dyl
1809/04/22	AMYVR	0023	*L. Bramer* | Een Goudweeger, mede als de voorgaande | *Mat:* op paneel *Size:* hoog 20, breed 16 duim	de Bruin	(Sold) fl 4:15 du Pree
1810/03/07	UTWLD	0020	*J. Bramer* | Een historie stuk, konstig en breed behandeld | *Size:* hoog 4 voet 2 duim, breed 6 voet 6 duim *Notes:* The artist's name was given as "J. Bramer" but we have assumed this is an error.	J J Woertman	(Unknown) fl 18:5

Bramer, Leonard (manner)

1806/11/24	AMSCH	0089	*G. Bramer* | Een Beedelaars gezelschap by kaarslicht; als G. Bramer | *Notes:* The artist's name was given as "G. Bramer" but we have assumed this is an error.	Munnikhuizen	(Sold) fl 1:10 L Pakker

Brassauw, Melchior

1802/02/16	AMSCH	0054	*M. Brassau* | By een steene Baluster met een basrelief versiert, staat een Heer, welke een Dame in ryke kleeding met bont, een Horologie aanbied; uitvoerig gepenceeld	F	(Sold) fl 2 Vink & Fitsing

Bray (manner)

1808/09/13	HABRU	0009	*de Braij* | De Dochter haar Vader lavende door de Borsten, in de Gevangenis, als van de Braij		(Unknown) fl 3:15

Bray, Jan de

1804/10/16	DLOND	0032	*J. de Braay* | Een Vrouwen Portrait. Portrait de Femme | *Mat:* op paneel *Size:* hoog 62, breed 27		(Unknown)
1808/03/03	HAVIN	0007	*J. de Bray* | De H. Familie Wandelende, konstig	Jacobus Spillebout	(Unknown) fl 7:5
1808/03/03	HAVIN	0008	*J. de Bray* | Hager in de Woestijne	Jacobus Spillebout	(Unknown) fl 3:15
1808/08/23	AMSCH	0010	*Braij. (J. de)* | Dit fraai Tafereel, bij Campo Wijerman beschreven, stelt voor, den Koninklijken Propheet David, staande in plechtig Koorgewaad, speelende op zijn Harp voor den Bondkist, verzelt met den Priesterlijken Trein, van veele zingende en op kunstwerktuigen speelende Livieten, en	[Coclers]	(Sold) fl 105 Jan Spaan

			andere die Kandelaaren aanbrengen; de Beelden zijn levensgrootte tot de kniën, het is schoon geteekent, krachtig van koloriet, en van een zuivere penceelbehandeling | *Mat:* op doek *Size:* hoog 57, breed 62 duim *Loc:* Gosford House, East Lothian, Scotland, UK. Earl of Wemyss and March.		
1809/05/26	HADAA	0015	*J. de Bray* | De Smidse van Vulkaan	Mejuffrouw de Wed David Heemskerk [or others]	(Unknown)

Bray, Salomon de

1801/02/18	AMBOS	0007	*S. de Bray* | De twee Hoeren twistende over het doode Kind, uitmuntend fix geteekend en geschilderd, en schoon van hartstogt	J Schonevelt	(Unknown)
1803/04/20	AMSCH	0012	*Bray. (S. de)* | Twee stuks bevallige Portraiten van Jonge Jnffrouwen [sic], ryk met Kant, Paerlen en Goude Ornamenten vercierd, meesterlyk behandeld [Deux charmans portraits de jeunes Demoiselles en costume ancien, portant chacune une fraise rabattue de dentelle, avec des chaines & des ornemens d'or. Les chairs d'un ton clair sont de la couleur la plus attrayante, & d'une touche fixe.] | *Mat:* op doek *Size:* ieder hoog 21, breed 18 duim	Maria Magdalena van Sluypwyk, gravinne van Moens	(Sold) fl 85 Theijs
1804/08/08	AMSCH	0016	*S. de Bray* | De Besnydenis Christi in den Tempel, men ziet 'er Maria met haare Moeder, en een ménigte Hogepriesters; de ordinantie, het licht en bruin, en 't coloriet zyn allerfraaist, zoo ook de behandeling | *Mat:* op paneel *Size:* hoog 11, breed 9 duim	Roos [for] D	(Sold) fl 99 Hulswit
1804/08/08	AMSCH	0017	*S. de Bray* | Twee Vrouwen twistende om het Doode Kind; krägtig op Doek | *Mat:* op doek *Size:* hoog 40, breed 37 duim	Roos [for] O	(Sold) fl 1 Gruyter
1805/07/03	AMSCH	0002	*Bray. (S. de)* | Dit stuk in Campo Wyerman beschreven en voorstellende de Koning David, in ryke kleeding, voor de Bondkist staande, verzelt van den Priesterlyken Treyn, van veele zingende en op instrumenten spelende Levieten, en andere, welken de kandelaren aanbrengen; zynde konstig geteekend, en kragtig en zuiver gepenceeld | *Mat:* op doek *Size:* hoog 57, breed 62 duim *Loc:* Gosford House, East Lothian, Scotland, UK. Earl of Wemyss and March	C	(Sold) fl 100 Coclers
1806/08/13	AMSCH	0242	*S. de Bray* | Een Historiëele Ordinantie; meesterlyk door S. de Bray	Vinkeles [for] G[ruyter]	(Sold) fl 3:15 Verhoesen
1807/04/00	LNDLS	0001	*S. de Braay* | Een heerlijke Ordonnantie, verbeeldende, daar Cornelius den Hooftman van Cesareen, en zijn huisgezin door den Apostel Petrus gedoopt worden, en den H. Geest ontvangen, rijk van beelden; op de voortreden van een gebouw staat een hond, konstig en kragtig op doek | *Mat:* op doek *Size:* hoog 56, breed 71 duim	[Abraham Delfos] [or others]	(Unknown)
1807/06/10	HGBSM	0001	*S. de Braay* | Een heerlijke Ordonnantie, verbeeldende, daar Cornelius den Hooftman van Cesareen en zijn huisgezin door den Apostel Petrus gedoopt worden, en den H. Geest ontvangen, rijk van beelden; op de voortreden van een gebouw staat een hond, konstig en kragtig | *Mat:* op doek *Size:* hoog 56, breed 71 duim	Abraham Delfos [or others]	(Sold) fl 20:10 Spruit
1807/08/26	AMSCH	0009	*S. de Bray* | Deze grootsche Ordonnantie met verscheidene Beelden vertoont in een prachtig Gebouw de ontdekking van Achilles onder de Maagden, gestoffeerd met verscheide bywerk; de hartstogten zyn natuurlyk en bevallig van koloriet, schoon van teekening, en de kleederen van verschillenden aard der stoffen meesterlyk behandeld, en treffelyk en uitvoerig gepenceeld | *Mat:* op doek *Size:* hoog 51, breed 70 duim	Joseph Vallette	(Sold) fl 11 Hend^{k} Jansen
1807/08/26	AMSCH	0010	*S. de Bray* | Een Ordonnantie van Neptunus en eene Watergodin; zynde meesterlyk geschilderd en fraai geteekend | *Mat:* op doek *Size:* hoog 54, breed 51 duim	Roos	(Bought In) fl 10
1808/08/23	AMSCH	0191	*S. de Braij* | Twee Vrouwen, om een dood Kind twistende; krachtig op Doek | *Mat:* op doek	[Gruyter?]	(Sold) fl 5 Spruit
1810/08/06	AMSCH	0019	*Braij (S. de)* | De Martelisatie van eenen Heiligen, zijne oogen ten Hemel heffende, twee Jongelingen en een Meisje staan er met ontroering naar te kijken. Dit stuk is fraai van licht, en van eene meesterlijke penceelsbehandeling | *Mat:* op doek *Size:* hoog 60, breed 52 duimen	F	(Bought In) fl 20
1810/10/10	MGCIT	0073	*S. de Braai* | Samson, liggende in den schoot van Delila, vertonende zich daarbij nog eenige Personen, alsmede het een en ander Bijwerk, zeer kragtig behandeld	Caspar van Citters	(Unknown)

Bray, Salomon de (or Bray, S., manner)

1806/06/07	RMHSN	0002	*S: de Bray* | Een kapitaal Stuk, zynde de Vinding van Moses, met uitmuntende schoone Beelden in een Landschap, door of in de manier van S: de Bray, op Doek, Vergulde Lyst | *Mat:* op doek *Notes:* The artist's last name was changed by hand from "Berg" to "Bray" in the MB copy of the catalogue.	A E K L	(Unknown)

Bredael

1803/08/24	HGKAN	0011	*Breydel* | Twee stuks Boomryke Lantschapjes, ryk gestoffeerd met figuuren en Paarde | *Mat:* op paneel *Size:* hoog 5, breet 7 ½ duim	[Teissier] [or others]	(Sold) fl 4:10 Carre
1806/11/24	AMSCH	0012	*Breydel* | Twee stuks hévige Rencontres tusschen Cavallerie in boomryke Landschappen; uitvoerig geschilderd | *Mat:* op paneel *Size:* Yder hoog 9, breed 11 duim	Munnikhuizen	(Sold) fl 6 Vermunt

1809/04/17	AMSCH	0017	*Brijdel* | Een hevige Bataille tusschen Ruiterij en Voetvolk, in een bergachtig Landschap; kragtig geschilderd | *Mat:* op doek *Size:* hoog 19, breed 21 duim	[Gruyter?]	(Sold or Bought In) fl 4 Gruyter
1810/06/06	RMMUY	0062	*Breidel* | Eene Pleisterplaats met veel Paarden en Figuren, uitvoerig en verdienstlijk gepenceeld | companion to lot 63 *Mat:* op paneel *Notes:* This lot was sold with lot 63 by an anonymous artist.		(Unknown) fl 29:5 for lots 62 & 63
1810/06/06	RMMUY	0064	*Bredaal* | Een Land en Watergezigt met een aantal Figuren, Schuiten en meer Bijwerk, aller uitvoerigst en fraaij | companion to lot 65 *Mat:* op koper		(Unknown) fl 6:10 for lots 64 & 65
1810/06/06	RMMUY	0065	*Bredaal* | Eene Wedergade, Landschap als het vorige, en niet minder van verdienste | companion to lot 64 *Mat:* op koper		(Unknown) fl 6:10 for lots 64 & 65

Bredael (or Brueghel)

1810/06/06	RMMUY	0060	*van Bredaal; Breugel* | Een Land en Watergezigt, gestoffeerd met Schuiten en Figuren, konstig en plaisant. Door van Bredaal of Breugel | companion to lot 61 *Mat:* op paneel *Notes:* This lot was sold with lot 61 by an anonymous artist.		(Unknown) fl 14:10 for lots 60 & 61

Bredael (copy after)

1805/10/09	HGBSM	BB0027	*Bredael* | Een batailje, na Bredael | *Mat:* op paneel *Size:* hoog 7 breed 8 ½ duim	T H van Willigen [or others]	(Sold) fl 2 van der Linden

Bredael (manner)

1802/04/13	HAVIN	0072	*Breda* | Een Landschap, als van Breda		(Unknown)
1806/06/07	RMHSN	0121	*Bredaal* | Twee Stuks Italiaansche Zeehavens, met Schepen en Beelden &c. in de manier van Bredaal	A E K L	(Unknown)

Bredael, J. van

1801/10/06	AMSCH	0012	*J. Brydel* | Een Landschap, gestoffeert met verscheide Ruiters, en een Man die op de Phiool speelt, Natuurlyk behandelt | *Mat:* op paneel *Size:* hoog 4 ½, breed 6 duim	M	(Sold) fl 3:10 Wed Achtienhoven
1802/09/06	AMSCH	0151	*J. Brydel* | Twee stuks bevallige gestoffeerde Landschapjes | *Mat:* op koper *Size:* ieder hoog 7, breed 8 duim	B	(Sold) fl 1:10 Gruiter
1805/07/03	AMSCH	0061	*J. Breidel* | Een hévige Batalje, tusschen Turken en ander Krygsvolk te paard; vol hartstogt, fraay geordineerd en geschilderd | *Mat:* op paneel *Size:* hoog 18, breed 24 duim	R[oos]	(Sold) fl 20 Agina
1805/10/09	HGBSM	0084	*J. Bredaal* | Een landschap met wagens en paarden, en verder gestoffeerd met veel figuuren, zeer uitvoerig | *Mat:* op koper *Size:* hoog 7 ½ breet 10 ½ duim	T H van Willigen [or others]	(Sold) fl 16 for lots 84 & 85. Roedig
1805/10/09	HGBSM	0085	*J. Bredaal* | Een dito [landschap] met een rivier gezigt, niet minder als de voorgaande, door denzelven [J. Bredaal], eender grooten | *Size:* hoog 7 ½ breet 10 ½ duim	T H van Willigen [or others]	(Sold) fl 16 for lots 84 & 85. Roedig
1807/08/26	AMSCH	0030	*J. Brydel* | Twee stuks Boomryke Landschappen, met Waterbeekjes, gestoffeerd met reizende Huislieden, met verscheiden Vee; uitvoerig | *Mat:* op paneel	Roos [for] A	(Sold) fl 3 Gruiter
1810/08/06	AMSCH	0021	*Bredael (J. van)* | Twee stuks hevige Batailles tusschen Ruiterij en Voetvolk. Fraai behandeld | *Mat:* op doek *Size:* Jeder hoog 11, breed 15 duimen	F	(Sold) fl 7 Roelsma

Bredael, Jan Frans van (copy by)

1804/10/16	DLOND	0037	*F.J. Breda; naar Breugel* | Twee Landschappen, het een met een Pont by een Overvaarplaats, het andere met een Postwagen. Deux Paysages, dans la premiere une Gondole, dans l'autre un Chariot de Poste | *This Lot:* Een Landschap; copy by J.F. Bredael after Brueghel *Mat:* op koper *Size:* hoog 9, breed 12 *Notes:* Lots 37 and 38 were printed in the catalogue as one item.		(Unknown)
1804/10/16	DLOND	0038	*F.J. Breda; naar Breugel* | Twee Landschappen, het een met een Pont by een Overvaarplaats, het andere met een Postwagen. Deux Paysages, dans la premiere une Gondole, dans l'autre un Chariot de Poste | *This Lot:* Een Landschap; copy by J.F. Bredael after Brueghel *Mat:* op koper *Size:* hoog 9, breed 12 *Notes:* Lots 37 and 38 were printed in the catalogue as one item.		(Unknown)

Bredael, Peeter van

1801/06/10	AMSCH	0034	*Bredaal. (P.)* | Twee stuks Brabantsche Landschappen, met danssende en speelende Huislieden; uitvoerig geschildert | *Mat:* op paneel *Size:* yder hoog 9, breed 13 duim	[Doublet]	(Sold) fl 12 Stevens
1802/09/06	AMSCH	0024	*P. van Breda* | Een Italiaansch Landschap met Gebouwen, gestoffeerd met Beelden en Beesten	Mevrouw Achtienhoven	(Sold) fl 12 van Iperen
1803/04/20	AMSCH	0013	*Bredael. (P. van)* | Twee stuks Brabandsche Landschappen met Gebouwen en stille Waters, ryk gestoffeerd met een meenigte Beelden en Beesten; warm en zonachtig gepenceeld [Deux pendans : ce sont deux jolis paysages ayant vue sur des Rivieres & des Fabriques, ils sont ornés par une multitude de figures & d'animaux, traités d'un bon ton de couleur &	Maria Magdalena van Sluypwyk, gravinne van Moens	(Sold) fl 14 C S Roos

<table>
<tr><td></td><td></td><td></td><td>touchés avec esprit.] | *Mat:* op doek op paneel *Size:* ieder hoog 7 ½, breed 10 duim</td><td></td><td></td></tr>
<tr><td>1803/08/17</td><td>AMSCH</td><td>0016</td><td>*Breidel. (P.)* | Twee stuks hevige Batailles, tusschen Cavalerie, zynde vol vuurs behandeld | *Mat:* op doek *Size:* ieder hoog 14, breed 18 duim</td><td>Anna Catharina Putman</td><td>(Sold) fl 12 Agina</td></tr>
<tr><td>1803/12/12</td><td>AMSCH</td><td>0010</td><td>*P. van Bredael* | Een Levantsche Zéehaven, vol gewoel van Schépen, Beelden en Beesten; fix gepenceeld | *Mat:* op doek *Size:* hoog 46, breed 66 duim</td><td>F</td><td>(Bought In) fl 10</td></tr>
<tr><td>1806/08/20</td><td>HGBSM</td><td>0088</td><td>*P. van Bredaal* | Een Brabansch Landschap met Gebouwen, op den voorgrond een Postwagen halte houdende voor eene Herberg, verders rijk gestoffeerd met Heeren te Paard, wandelende Heeren en Dames. – En menigte andere figuuren en beesten. Konstig geschilderd in de manier van Breugel | companion to lot 89 *Mat:* op paneel *Size:* hoog 11 ½, breed 15 duim</td><td>Macalester Loup [or others]</td><td>(Sold) fl 40 for lots 88 & 89. Zwartsman</td></tr>
<tr><td>1806/08/20</td><td>HGBSM</td><td>0089</td><td>*P. van Bredaal* | Een dito [Brabansch Landschap] wederga, en niet minder als het voorgaande, van dezelve groote | companion to lot 88 *Mat:* op paneel *Size:* hoog 11 ½, breed 15 duim *Notes:* It is unclear what "dito" refers to in the title.</td><td>Macalester Loup [or others]</td><td>(Sold) fl 40 for lots 88 & 89. Zwartsman</td></tr>
<tr><td>1809/04/17</td><td>AMSCH</td><td>0016</td><td>*P. van Bredael* | Een Brabandsch Dorpgezicht, gestoffeerd met Heeren te Paard en Reizigers; fiks | *Mat:* op paneel</td><td>Y</td><td>(Sold or Bought In) fl 2:10</td></tr>
<tr><td></td><td></td><td></td><td>**Breenbergh, Bartholomeus**</td><td></td><td></td></tr>
<tr><td>1801/04/13</td><td>AMSCH</td><td>0013</td><td>*B. Breemberg* | David met het Hoofd van Goliath op zyn zwaard, in het verschiet eenige Gebouwen en Beelden; fix gepenceeld | *Mat:* op paneel *Size:* hoog 10, breed 8 duim</td><td>Pierre Fouquet, junior</td><td>(Sold) fl 10:10 B Carli</td></tr>
<tr><td>1801/05/11</td><td>AMSCH</td><td>0015</td><td>*J. Breenberg* | Een Landschap by de ruïne van een oud Gebouw, ziet men eenige beeldjes, krachtig van coloriet en zonachtig behandeld | *Mat:* op doek *Size:* hoog 17, breed 20 duim *Notes:* The artist's name was given as "J. Breenberg" but we have assumed this is an error.</td><td>P[ruyssenaar]</td><td>(Sold) fl 13 Boelen</td></tr>
<tr><td>1801/06/10</td><td>AMSCH</td><td>0017</td><td>*Breenberg. (B.)* | In een Italiaansch Landschap, met grootsche Gebouwen, ziet men een Bybelsche geschiedenis, in allen deele meesterlyk gepenceeld | *Mat:* op paneel *Size:* hoog 28, breed 36 duim *Notes:* Originally the artist's name was spelled "Breemberg." This error was corrected in an errata sheet located at the end of the catalogue.</td><td>Herman ten Kate</td><td>(Sold) fl 60 Reynders</td></tr>
<tr><td>1801/06/10</td><td>AMSCH</td><td>0018</td><td>*Breenberg. (B.)* | Deeze ordonantie steld voor, de Geboorte van den Heiland, alles is, zoo van ordonantie als van schildering, een der beste van deezen Meester | *Mat:* op paneel *Size:* hoog 23, breed 18 duim *Notes:* Originally the artist's name was spelled "Breemberg." This error was corrected in an errata sheet located at the end of the catalogue.</td><td>Herman ten Kate</td><td>(Sold) fl 40 Taijs</td></tr>
<tr><td>1801/06/10</td><td>AMSCH</td><td>0019</td><td>*Breenberg. (B.)* | Loth met zyne Dogters in het gras zittende, in het verschiet ziet met Sodom in vollen vlam, uitvoerig en meesterlyk van Schildering | *Mat:* op paneel *Size:* hoog 18, breed 24 duim *Notes:* Originally the artist's name was spelled "Breemberg." This error was corrected in an errata sheet located at the end of the catalogue.</td><td>[Doublet]</td><td>(Sold) fl 19 Stevens</td></tr>
<tr><td>1802/04/13</td><td>HAVIN</td><td>0015</td><td>*B. Breenberg* | Een Landschap met Ruines, en een Fontyn, waarby een Man staat, ziende na eenige slaapende Beelden, extra uitvoerig</td><td></td><td>(Unknown)</td></tr>
<tr><td>1802/07/20</td><td>MGSAN</td><td>0025</td><td>*Breenberg* | Twee Stuks Ruïnen, met Figuurtjes en ander Bywerk, op Paneel | *Mat:* op paneel *Size:* hoog duim 7, breed duim 5 ⅜</td><td></td><td>(Unknown)</td></tr>
<tr><td>1802/09/06</td><td>AMSCH</td><td>0014</td><td>*B. Bréenberg* | Een Landschap met overblyfzels van aloude Gebouwen en rustende Reizigers; zonachtig gepenceeld | *Mat:* op paneel *Size:* hoog 20, breed 16 duim</td><td>J</td><td>(Sold) fl 1 Vermeulen</td></tr>
<tr><td>1802/09/06</td><td>AMSCH</td><td>0015</td><td>*B. Bréenberg* | Een Italiaansch Landschap met Ruïne, op de voorgrond een Vrouwtje met een Ezel; meesterlyk behandeld | *Mat:* op paneel *Size:* hoog 7, breed 6 duim</td><td>W ten Houten</td><td>(Sold) fl 1 Gruiter</td></tr>
<tr><td>1802/09/21</td><td>UTHDG</td><td>0014</td><td>*B. Breemberg* | Overblijfzelen van prachtige Gebouwen in een Italiaansch Landschap, op den voorgrond Beelden enz. | *Mat:* op paneel *Size:* hoog 26, breed 35 duimen</td><td></td><td>(Sold) fl 9:10 Van Toll Lange N Straat</td></tr>
<tr><td>1803/06/20</td><td>AMSCH</td><td>0077</td><td>*B. Breenberg* | Twee Zaters met een Nimph, in een Landschap | *Size:* hoog 9 ¾, breed 16 ½ duim</td><td>Roos [for] L</td><td>(Sold) fl 28:10 Hulswit</td></tr>
<tr><td>1803/08/17</td><td>AMSCH</td><td>0008</td><td>*Breenberg. (B.)* | Een Landschap met Ruïnes, Gedenktekens, Geboomten en Bergachtig verschiet, ter regter zyde een Waterplas, waar in zich iemand baad; verders nog verscheiden Beelden, uitvoerig helder en van een aangenaame schildering | *Mat:* op paneel *Size:* hoog 15, breed 18 duim</td><td>Anna Catharina Putman</td><td>(Sold) fl 41 Gruyter</td></tr>
<tr><td>1804/07/25</td><td>AMSCH</td><td>0004</td><td>*Breenberg. (B.)* | In dit uitmuntend Schildery, ziet men den Heiland, genezende eene blinde; de bewondering der groote menigte omstanders is klaarblykelyk in hun te zien; het bergachtig Landschap, de Gebouwen, en dunne verschiet is helder, het coloriet behaaglyk, en de Ordinantie zo wel als de penceelsbehandeling van de beste van deezen voortreffelyken Meester | *Mat:* op paneel *Size:* hoog 18, breed 24 duim</td><td></td><td>(Sold) fl 300 Theod^{s} Spaan</td></tr>
<tr><td>1804/08/08</td><td>AMSCH</td><td>0024</td><td>*B. Breenberg* | In een Grot ziet men een jongen Heremiet, knielende voor een Boek, Doosdhoofd [sic], Kruis, enz., in het verschiet een leezende Munnik en fraaije Gebergtens met Ruïnen; dit uitmuntend Schildery behoeft in uitvoerigheid voor niemand te wyken, zynde daarby delicaat gepenceeld | *Mat:* op doek *Size:* hoog 17, br. 14 duim</td><td>Roos a</td><td>(Sold) fl 126 Hulswit</td></tr>
</table>

1804/12/10	AMSCH	0007	*J. Breenberg* | Een Grot van binnen te zien, ryk met diverse beelden gestoffeerd; krachtig van penceels behandeling | *Mat:* op paneel *Size:* Hoog 23, breed 33 duim *Notes:* The artist's name was given as "J. Breenberg" but we have assumed this is an error.	Jan de Groot	(Sold) fl 9:10 van der Linden
1805/07/03	AMSCH	0057	*B. Bréenberg* | Dit allerfraaist Duinryk Landschap, stelt voor: een Bybelsche Ordinantie van drie Beelden, be de Ruïnen van een aloud prachtig Gebouw; verder ziet men door een oude Poort, by eenige Gebouwen en Geboomten een Markt en een Duin- en Bergachtig verschiet; dit stuk is allerfrapanst van licht, en delicaat gepenceeld, door den beroemden B. Bréenberg | *Mat:* op paneel *Size:* hoog 28, breed 32 duim	V[inkeles]	(Sold) fl 82 van Iperen
1805/10/09	HGBSM	0012	*Breemberg* | Een bergagtig landschap met badende Nimphen | *Mat:* op paneel *Size:* hoog 10 breet 13 duim	T H van Willigen [or others]	(Sold) fl 2 van der Vin
1806/06/07	RMHSN	0129	*B. Breenberg* | Een Zittend Heer in een Kamer by een Tafel, lezende een Brief, in een Oud Hollandsche Zwarte Kleeding, op de Tafel eenige Boeken en een Globe &c.	A E K L	(Unknown) fl 43
1806/08/13	AMSCH	0025	*Breenberg. (B.)* | Een Bybelsche Ordinantie, in een Landschap met verscheiden Beelden; fix gepenceeld | *Mat:* op paneel *Size:* hoog 7, breed 8 duim	van der Voort	(Sold) fl 1:5 Jansen [for] P
1808/06/13	AMSCH	0018	*Breenberg (B.)* | Een Gezicht te Rome met Ruïnes; op den voorgrond eenige rustende Beeldjes, verder Reizigers. Zeer zonachtig uitgevoerd | *Mat:* op doek *Size:* hoog 43, breed 54 duim	E M Engelberts	(Sold) fl 19:10 Th^{s} Spaan
1808/06/13	AMSCH	0019	*Breenberg (B.)* | Twee stuks met Ruïnes te Rome, gestoffeerd met verschillende Beeldjes; krachtig en zonachtig | *Mat:* op doek *Size:* ieder hoog 25, breed 20 duim	E M Engelberts	(Sold) fl 26 Thaijs
1809/04/22	AMYVR	0014	*R. Breenberg* | De Geboorte van den Zaligmaker, zijnde een Ordonantie van verscheidene Beelden | *Mat:* op paneel *Size:* hoog 17, breed 12 duim *Notes:* The artist's name was given as "R. Breenberg" but we have assumed this is an error.	Juff^{r} Julikker	(Sold) fl 3:10 du Pree
1809/04/22	AMYVR	0015	*R. Breenberg* | De Steniging van St. Stephanus, als de voorgaande | *Mat:* op doek *Size:* hoog 19, breed 16 duim *Notes:* The artist's name was given as "R. Breenberg" but we have assumed this is an error.	Juff^{r} Julikker	(Sold) fl 1 van Iperen
1809/06/13	AMSCH	0179	*B. Breenberg* | Een Landschap met aloude Ruïne, gestoffeerd met eene Vrouw, welke eenige Beesten voortdrijft	T	(Sold) fl 1:15 van Iperen
1810/10/10	MGCIT	0110	*Breenberg* | Een Landschapje | *Notes:* In the original title the words "Een Landschapje" were printed as "Een dito Landschap doch kleinder." This error was corrected in an errata sheet located at the front of the catalogue.	Caspar van Citters	(Unknown)
1810/11/07	UTWLD	0014	*Breyenburg* | Een Italiaansch Landschap met eenige Antieke gebouwen en Ruines, verders eenige stoffagie, zeer geestig en warm geschilderd door Breyenburg op paneel, 1 voet 1 duim hoog, 1 voet 5 duim breed, zwarte Lijst | *Mat:* op paneel *Size:* 1 voet 1 duim hoog, 1 voet 5 duim breed		(Unknown) fl 6

Breenbergh, Bartholomeus (and Poelenburgh, C.)

1804/10/16	DLOND	0136a	*C. Polenburg; B. Breenburg* | [Untitled] | *Notes:* The lot was changed from "G. Metzu, Een Meisjen, liggende over de deur bij enige Wyngaardranken," to "C. Polenburg en B. Breenburg," without giving a title, at the front of the catalogue.		(Unknown)

Breenbergh, Bartholomeus (manner)

1801/10/06	AMSCH	0094	*Bréénbergh* | Een Bergagtig Landschap met Ruïne en andere aloude Gebouwen, gestoffeerd met Beeldjes en verder bywerk, in de manier van Bréénbergh | *Mat:* op paneel	S	(Sold) fl 3 V^{n} Dijl
1804/12/10	AMSCH	0117	*Breenberg* | Een Bybelsche Ordonnantie, in een landschap, fraai en meesterlyk gepenceeld, als Breenberg | *Mat:* op paneel *Size:* hoog 17, breed 18 duim	Jan De Groot	(Sold) fl 10 Coclers
1806/05/05	AMSCH	0180	*B. Breenberg* | Een Italiaansch Landschap, met een Rivier, waar by een Ruïnen en Geboomten, gestoffeert met Reisigers, en Huislieden met Vee; meesterlyk geschilderd op Koper, als door B. Breenberg | *Mat:* op koper	S[chley]	(Bought In) fl 1:10
1808/06/11	RMRIJ	0118	*Als Breenberg* | Een Landschap net Ruïne en Stoffagie | *Mat:* op doek		(Unknown) fl 1:15
1810/10/10	MGCIT	0133	*Breenberg* | Een Landschapje op koper, in de manier van Breenberg | *Mat:* op koper	Caspar van Citters	(Unknown)

Brekelencam, Quiringh Gerritsz. van

1801/08/19	AMSCH	0010	*Q. Breckelenkamp* | In een Binnenhuis, voor een Openstaande Vengster, ziet men een Schoenmaker by zyn Tafel met Gereedschappen zyn werk verrichten, terwyl een Vrouw bézig is brood te snyden; alles fraai behandeld	Pruyssen^{r} [for] Q	(Sold) fl 10:10 V d^{r} Vinne
1801/10/19	AMSCH	0007	*Breekelenkamp. (Q)* | In een Binnenvertrek zit een oud Wyfje in een matte Stoel by den haard, daar een Ketel over het vuur hangt; neevens haar staat een Stoel met een Schotel daaröp, voor dezelve een Vergiet-test met een Moot Zalm, een bak met Brood, een Bierkan en verders eenig huisraad, zeer fraay | *Mat:* op paneel *Size:* hoog 16 ½, breed 14 duim	Jonkheer Menno Baron van Coehoorn	(Sold) fl 101 Spruit van Gend
1801/10/19	AMSCH	0008	*Breekelenkamp. (Q.)* | In een Binnenvertrek zit een Dame met een rood fluweel Jakje aan, dat met Bond gevoerd is, wordende door een oude Vrouw gekopt, verder eenige huisraad en ander bywerk, zeer kragtig en	Jonkheer Menno Baron van Coehoorn	(Sold) fl 355 Theod Spaan

			uitvoerig geschilderd, en zo goed als van dien meester bekend is | *Mat:* op paneel *Size:* hoog 18 ½, breed 14 ½ duim *Notes:* In the original title the word "gekopt" was printed as "gekapt." This error was corrected in an errata sheet located at the end of the title. *Loc:* Den Haag, Nederland. Mauritshuis. (562)		
1801/11/21	RMVIS	0001	*Q. Brekelencamp* | Een Heremiet, zittende in een Grot te lezen, hebbende voor zich staan een Christusbeeld	Gelinus van Spaan	(Unknown)
1802/05/05	AMSCH	0018	*G. Brekelenkamp* | In een Binnevertrek zit een Bejaarde Schoenmaker op zyn Driestal Schoenen te Lappen, in het Vengster legt een Boer, agter hem zit de Vrouw Appelen te Schillen. Alles Meesterlyk en bevallig van Licht | *Mat:* op paneel *Size:* hoog 23, breed 32 duim *Loc:* Amiens, France. Musée de Picardie. (M.P. 894–3)	A	(Withdrawn)
1802/06/16	AMSCH	0014	*Q. Breekelenkamp* | Dit bevallig Voorwerp, in een Binnenhuis, verbeeld een Jeugdige Vrouw, in aloude Hollandsche kleeding, voor een Toonbank zittende, met een ongemeene aandacht te Speldewerken, op de bank leggen Boeken, daar nevens staat een Inktkooker: verder gestoffeerd met verscheiden Bywerk: het Natuurlyk Caracter, en het Licht geeft een aangenaame werking, en is van een Meesterlyk fraaije Penceelbehandeling | *Mat:* op paneel *Size:* hoog 22, breed 17 duim	[Merrem]	(Sold) fl 103 J Yver
1802/06/16	AMSCH	0015	*Q. Brekelenkamp* | Een Chirurgyns Winkel, waarin de Heelmeester bézig is een Vrouw het been te verbinden; natuurlyk en meesterlyk van Schildering | *Mat:* op paneel *Size:* hoog 19, breed 15 duim	[Merrem]	(Sold) fl 30 v d Schley
1802/07/20	MGSAN	0050	*Q. Brekehecamp* | Een zeer schoon Stuk, verbeeldende een Vischverkooper, aan een Dame, zittende Kant te werken, zyn Visch te Koop presenteerende, op Paneel: extra uitvoerig | *Mat:* op paneel *Size:* hoog duim 20, breed duim 14		(Unknown)
1802/07/27	AKHRK	0006	*Quirijn Brekelenkamp, 1661* | In dit meesterlijk kundig en uitmuntend fraai stukje ziet men een oude Vrouw zitten, met een aartig Mutsje op haar Hoofd, en gekleed met een zwart Jak met roode Mouwen en gedeeltelijk hier over grijze Morsmouwen. Zij heeft een Bril op, en een Plankje op haar Schoot, bezig zijnde met een Baarsje te kerven. Voor haar staat een Driestal met een Gatepetiel, met schoon gemaakte en gekorven Baars, een kopere Ketel staat nevens haar. De grond achter haar, de Kas en Schoorsteen is verstandig en stil met gebroken couleuren bedommeld: 'er spreekt hier in niet meer als het voornaamste, vol gloed en natuurlijke tederheid, en roept den kundigen kenner tot zich, of men 'er wel te veel van gezegd hebbe [sic] | *Mat:* op paneel *Size:* hoog 14, breed 18 duim *Inscr:* Quirijn Brekelenkamp, 1661 (signed and dated?) *Notes:* It is unclear whether the name and date are inscribed on the painting. *Loc:* Los Angeles, CA, USA. Los Angeles County Museum (52.14.1) (formerly)	Maria Stategaart	(Sold) fl 41 Gruyter
1802/07/27	AKHRK	0007	*Quirijn Brekelenkamp* | Een rookend zittend oud Mannetje voor een Tafel, met een Bierkruik, Test en Tabaksdoos op dezelve. Dit eenvouwdig stukje is meesterlijk geschilderd en getoetst, in een luchtiger trant als het voorige | *Mat:* op paneel *Size:* hoog 7 ¼, breed 8 ½ duim	Maria Stategaart	(Sold) fl 12 Juffr Boerse
1802/08/24	LNDLS	0017	*Q. Brekelenkamp* | Een Binnen-vertrek; in het midden staat een vergiettest met Vis, en emmers, benevens een kind die een Visje aan een staanden Man aanbiedt, daar bij een zittend Vrouwtje die Vis schrapt bij een Kind in een Kinderstoel. Op paneel | *Mat:* op paneel *Size:* hoog 18, breed 22 duimen	Leonardus Bouman [or others]	(Unknown) fl 26
1802/09/06	AMSCH	0013	*Breekelenkamp* | In een Binnehuis, ziet men op de voorgrond een Tafel, waar op een kopere keetel, Water-Emmer, roode kool en uijen geplaatst is, verder zit een bedaagde Vrouw met een Lépel in de hand uit een Pot Eetende; meesterlyk gepenceeld | *Mat:* op paneel *Size:* hoog 9, breed 7 duim	Wed Grave [or others]	(Bought In) fl 8
1802/09/21	UTHDG	0004	*Q. Brekelenkamp* | Een bejaarde Schoenmaker, bezig met lappen, word over de onderdeur door eene oude vrouw, schoenen toegereikt; het licht krachtig door de geopende deur in het vertrek vallende, geeft dit stukje een aangenaame werking. Zijnde alles breed en helder behandeld | *Mat:* op paneel *Size:* hoog 11 ½, breed 9 duimen		(Sold) fl 38 Cobell
1802/09/21	UTHDG	0005	*Q. Brekelenkamp* | Een oude vrouw, koeken bakkende, verzeld van drie kinderen. Fraai en natuurlijk geschilderdt | *Mat:* op paneel *Size:* hoog 16, breed 23 duimen		(Bought In) fl 29
1802/09/21	UTHDG	0006	*Q. Brekelenkamp* | Een man in het zwart, zit in eene losse en vrolijke houding bij een vrouwtje, gekleed in een rood jak met wit bont. Dit stukje fraaij van Couleur, is uitvoerig geschilderdt door denzelven [Q. Brekelenkamp] | *Mat:* op paneel *Size:* hoog 14, breed 11 ½ duimen		(Bought In) fl 20
1803/06/20	AMSCH	0002	*Q. Breekelenkamp* | Een Chirurgyns Winkel, waarin den Heelmeester bézig is een Vrouw het Been te verbinden, natuurlyk van licht en meesterlyk gepenceeld	Schley [for] B	(Sold) fl 20 Gruiter
1803/06/20	AMSCH	0023	*Q. Breekelenkamp* | In een deftige gemeubileerde Kamer, ter zyde een opgeslagen Tapytenkleed zit een Vrouw gekleed met een bont Jakje, een klyn Kind op schoot hebbende, het geen zy de Borst wil geeven, een Meisje agter haar, speelt met het Kind, voor haar staat de Wieg en verder een menigte bywerk, uitvoerig behandeld op Doek | *Mat:* op doek *Size:* hoog 19, breed 14 duim	Schley [for] G	(Sold) fl 42 Hodges

1803/06/20	AMSCH	0060	*Q Brékenlenkamp* | In een Gemeubileerd Vertrek, zit een Vrouwtje in oude Hollandsche Kleeding, met een Speldewerk Kussen op de schoot, voor een Tafel, waarop een Aarde Bierkan geplaatst is, op de Grond staat een Marktëmmer, zeer natuurlyk en bevallig gepenceelt, door Q Brékenlenkamp, op Paneel | *Mat:* op paneel *Size:* hoog 14, breed 13 duim	Schley [for] H	(Sold) fl 20:10 Gruiter
1803/08/24	HGKAN	0047	*Breekelenkamp* | Een Herremiet in een Rots, zittende aandagtig te schryven in een Boek, verders toepasselyk bywerk, kragtig gepenseelt | *Mat:* op paneel *Size:* hoog 26, breet 21 duim	[Teissier] [or others]	(Sold) fl 23 Kan
1803/09/07	AMSCH	0024	*G. Brekelenkamp* | Een Schoolmeester, beezig zynde een Meisje te onderwyzen, agter in het Vertrek zit de Moeder te spinnen, op de voorgrond een Gatepetiel en ander bywerk, meesterlyk op Paneel [Un maître d'école, occupé à instruire une jeune fille ; dans l'arrière fond, la mère assise qui file, sur le devant un passoire de cuisine et autres ustensiles de menage. Tableau de maître] | *Mat:* op paneel *Size:* hoog 19, breed 14 ½ duim	Smidt	(Sold) fl 91 J Spaan
1803/12/12	AMSCH	0002	*Q. Brekelenkamp* | Een Herremiet, zittende met een Boek op zyn Schoot; fraai gepenceeld | *Mat:* op paneel *Size:* hoog 27, breed 22 duim	B	(Sold) fl 37 Hijm Pakker
1803/12/12	AMSCH	0003	*Q. Brekelenkamp* | Een Bevallige Oude Vrouw, met een Bril op haar Neus, zy is bézig Groote Boonen te doppen, ter zyde staan eenige Manden en Bakken met diverse Groentens; bevallig van licht en uitvoerig geschildert | *Mat:* op paneel *Size:* hoog 17 ½, breed 14 duim	B	(Sold) fl 7 Theod[S] Spaan
1804/04/28	LNDLS	0021	*Q. Brekelenkamp* | Een Mannetje, zittende baars te schrappen, by een tafel, daar een schotel met baars op legt, en eenig huisraad, door Q. Brekelenkamp, op paneel | *Mat:* op paneel *Size:* hoog 18, breed 15 duim	[Abraham Delfos] [or others]	(Sold) fl 40 Jan Landa
1804/05/07	AMSCH	0009	*Breekelenkamp. (Q)* | In een Keuken ziet men een Dienstmaagd, bezig eenige Wortelen schoon te maken, waar naast een Emmer en Vergiettest, waarop zy dezelve legt, achter haar een Jongen, met zyn Hoed in de eene en een Appel in de andere hand, op de voorgrond eenige Groentens, Hakmes en ander Huisraad; uitvoerig en allernatuurlykst van behandeling | *Mat:* op paneel *Size:* hoog 11, breed 9 Duim	Vinkeles [for] J	(Sold) fl 53 J Bolten
1804/05/07	AMSCH	0010	*Breekelenkamp. (Q)* | In een dito [Keuken] Vertrek ziet men een Vrouw eenige Groentens schoon maaken, welke op een Tafel voor haar liggen, ter zyde een Jongeling, en op de voorgrond eenig dood Wild; zynde van behandeling niet minder als de voorgaande | *Mat:* op paneel *Size:* hoog 3 ½, breed 6 ½ duim	Vinkeles [for] J	(Sold) fl 81 Pruyssenaar
1804/05/07	AMSCH	0011	*Breekelenkamp. (Q)* | In een Binnenvertrek ziet men een Schoenmaker, bézig Schoenen te lappen, waarby een onder Vrouw aan 't Spinnen, verders by een vuur eenige Boeren, welken zich warmen; meesterlyk en fiks gepenceeld | *Mat:* op doek *Size:* hoog 29, breed 37 duim	Vinkeles [for] J	(Sold) fl 6:5 van der Schley [for] R[ijfsnijder]
1804/07/25	DLGRO	0036	*G. van Breekelenkamp* | Een Oude Vrouw, op een Stoel zittende, voor haar staat een Jonge die zy onderwyst, met verder bywerk | *Mat:* op paneel *Size:* hoog 23, breed 17 duim	Mr Franc van der Burch Wz.	(Unknown)
1804/08/08	AMSCH	0022	*Q. Breekelenkamp* | In een Boerenwooning ziet men een bejaarde Vrouw, zittende voor een Vuur, bézig Koeken te bakken, naast haar staat een Pot met Beslag, op de Tafel eenig ander Huisraad; fraai en meesterlyk van schildering | *Mat:* op paneel *Size:* hoog 22, breed 18 duim	Vink[eles] [for] W	(Sold) fl 22:10 Jacob Roelofs
1804/08/08	AMSCH	0023	*Q. Breekelenkamp* | In een Boeren Binnenhuis ziet men een Boerin aan een Tafel zitten, met een Pyp in de hand, waar naast een Meisje, welke 'er om schynt te lagchen, op de Tafel een Kan, Glas, Papier met Tabak en Pyp, door een open Vengster ziet men op eenige Wooningen; fiks en breed gepenceeld | *Mat:* op paneel *Size:* hoog 12 ½, breed 11 duim	Vink[eles] [for] S	(Sold) fl 4 de Harde Swart
1805/04/23	HOBEE	0001	*Brekelenkamp* | Een oud Vrouwen Pourtrait, zeer natuurlyk en uitvoerig geschilderd op Paneel | *Mat:* op paneel		(Unknown)
1805/07/03	AMSCH	0062	*G. Breekelenkamp* | In een Boere Binnehuis, zit een bejaarde Vrouw voor een Schoorsteen, bézig zynde vis te kooken, terzyde op een Emmer een Vergiet-test, waarop eenige Vissen, achter een gedekte Tafel en verder huisraad; fiks en breed gepenceeld | *Mat:* op paneel *Size:* hoog 20, breed 14 duim	V[inkeles]	(Sold) fl 20 Cremer
1805/07/10	AMSCH	0012	*Q. Breekelenkamp* | In een Boere Binnenhuys ziet men een bejaard Man, bézig een Haring Schoon te maaken voor een Ton, waarop eenig Huisraad, op de Aanregtbank, voor een open Raam een half Brood en Bord met Boter, enz. zonachtig en meesterlyk op Paneel | *Mat:* op paneel *Size:* hoog 14, breed 11 ½ duim	V[inkeles] [for] M	(Sold) fl 25:10 Gruyter
1805/07/10	AMSCH	0013	*Q. Breekelenkamp* | In een Keuken, ziet men een jonge Meid, staande voor een Tafel Groenten schoon te maaken, verders een Vergiet-test met Baars, waarby een Kat en verder Huisraad; breed en fiks op Paneel | *Mat:* op paneel *Size:* hoog 25, breed 19 duim	V[inkeles] [for] L	(Withdrawn)
1805/10/09	HGBSM	0001	*Q. Breekelekamp* | Een Hermiet in zyn Grot zittende te schryven in een boek, op zyn schoot, benevens hem eenig bywerk, als boek, zandlooper, doodshoofd &c. natuurlyk geschildert | *Mat:* op paneel *Size:* hoog 24, breet 18 duim	T H van Willigen [or others]	(Sold) fl 18:5 Ph Meij
1805/10/09	HGBSM	0002	*Q. Breekelekamp* | Een dito [Hermiet] knielende, in devotie, en dito [eenig] bywerk | *Mat:* op paneel *Size:* hoog 24, breet 18 duim	T H van Willigen [or others]	(Sold) fl 21:15 Ph Meij
1805/10/09	HGBSM	0006	*Q. Breekelekamp* | Een vrouwtje in een nis, bezig zynde vis te schrappen, nevens haar een meisje, op de rand van de nis een vergiettest met vis, en	T H van Willigen [or others]	(Sold) fl 21:10 Ph Meij

			verder bywerk, helder en aangenaam geschildert | *Mat:* op paneel *Size:* hoog 17 ½ breet 13 ½ duim		
1805/10/09	HGBSM	R0017	*Q. Brekelekamp* | Een binnen vertrek, waarin een zittende dame naast haar staat, een meit met een marktemmer aan den arm | *Mat:* op paneel *Size:* hoog 19 breet 15 duim	T H van Willigen [or others]	(Sold) fl 5:5 De Gelder
1806/08/13	AMSCH	0013	*Brekelencamp. (Q.)* | In een Binnenvertrek ziet men een bejaarde Vrouw zitten, ter zyde een Spinnewiel, houdende een stoof met een test op haar schoot, schynende haar handen over dezelve te warmen; dun en delicaat gepenceeld | *Mat:* op paneel *Size:* hoog 11, breed 13 duim	Vinkeles [for] J	(Sold) fl 35 Verhoesen
1806/08/13	AMSCH	0244	*Q. Brekelencamp* | Een Binnekamer, waar een Vrouw zit Kant te werken	Vinkeles [for] G[ruyter]	(Sold) fl 1:10 Nieuwenhuys
1806/10/16	UTWLD	0017	*Boekelenkamp* | Een binnenhuys met een Vrouwtje by een tafel en een staande Jongen door Boekelekamp	Mr P de Malapert [or] W Beeldsnyder	(Unknown)
1808/06/06	RMRIJ	0020	*Brekelenkamp. (Quirijn)* | In een Binnenhuis zit een Grijsaard aan 't Spinnewiel; een Visscher schijnt binnen te treden en hem te onderhouden. Uitvoerig en naar waarheid behandeld. Een wedergade. Een Binnenhuis, waarin een Man, eene Kruik in de hand houdende, bij het Vuur zit; een tweede persoon is bezig zijne Pijp te ontsteken. Als boven behandeld [Dans l'intérieur d'une Cabane, un vieillard assis devant un Rouet à filer, semble s'entretenir avec un Pêcheur qui entre avec un Panier rempli de Poissons. Le Pendant, qui est de la même dimension, represente un homme assis prés du feu et tenant une cruche à la main, tandis qu'une autre personne allume sa pipe. Ces deux Tableaux sont peints avec verité et éxactitude] | *Mat:* op paneel *Size:* Twee stukken. Hoog 23, en breed 17 ½ duim *Loc:* Amsterdam, Nederland. Rijksmuseum. (A60)	Gerrit van der Pot, Heer van Groeneveld	(Sold) fl 850 Stratenus [for] le Roi
1808/06/11	RMRIJ	0085	*Quiryn Brekelenkamp* | Twee Kinderen zich vermakende met een Muis in de Val zynde, ongemeen natuurlyk en fraai geschilderd | *Mat:* op paneel *Size:* hoog 6 ½, breed 6 duim		(Sold) fl 21 van Leen
1808/08/23	AMSCH	0019	*Brekelenkamp. (Q.)* | In een oud Hollandsch Binnevertrek zit eene bevallige Vrouw, gekleed met een rood fluweel Jakje met een bonte rand, houdende eenig naaiwerk op haare schoot, zij schijnt in gesprek met eene oude Vrouw en Kind, die nevens haar zitten, agterwaards een deftig gekleed Man, en verder bijwerk; natuurlijk en meesterlijk van schildering | *Annots:* [door] H. Bogert 1672 (FLNY) *Mat:* op doek *Size:* hoog 29, breed 32 duim *Inscr:* [H. Bogert 1672] (signed and dated?) *Notes:* It is unclear whether the name and date are inscribed on the painting.	[Gruyter?]	(Bought In) fl 11
1808/09/13	HABRU	0003	*Q. Breekelenkamp* | Een Binnenvertrek, waarin een opgaande Trap, ter zijde een Zieke op het Ledikant leggende, welke door de Doctor de Pols werd gevoeld, met verder veel Bijwerk; natuurlijk		(Unknown) fl 12:5
1808/09/13	HABRU	0004	*Q. Breekelenkamp* | Twee Pourtraitjes, halver lijf		(Unknown) fl 2:8
1808/10/28	AMVRS	0006	*Brekelenkamp. (Q.)* | In een Keukenvertrek zit eene bevallige Vrouw bij een Tafel groente te verlezen, nevens haar staat een Emmer en verder bijwerk. Natuurlijk voorgesteld | *Mat:* op paneel *Size:* hoog 12, breed 10 duim	Marten Udink	(Sold) fl 34 J Twisk
1809/04/17	AMSCH	0007	*Q. Brekelenkamp* | In een Boeren Binnehuis, ziet men op de voorgrond een bedaagd man, bezig een Haring schoon te maaken, voor hem staat een Ton waar op een Bord en Bierglas geplaatst is, verder bij een openstaand Vengster een Aanregtbank, waar op een Schotel met Boter en ander Bijwerk, agterwaards ziet men door een open Deur in een Keukenvertrek; uitvoerig in de stijl van G. Metzu, door Q. Brekelenkamp | *Mat:* op paneel *Size:* hoog 14, breed 11 ½ duim	C	(Sold) fl 42
1809/04/22	AMYVR	0011	*Q. Breekelenkamp* | Een oud Man, bezig zijnde een Baarsje schoon te maken; uitvoerig | *Mat:* op paneel *Size:* hoog 12, breed 9 duim	de Bruin	(Sold) fl 5:10 C S Roos
1809/04/22	AMYVR	0012	*Q. Breekelenkamp* | Eene Vrouw bezig zijnde Appelen te schillen, op de Tafel een Rist Uijen en ander bijwerk; krachtig | *Mat:* op doek *Size:* hoog 23, breed 19 duim	Smit	(Sold) fl 15 Bonte
1809/05/26	HADAA	0007	*Brekelenkamp* | Een Speldewerkster in oud Hollandsche Kleding, met een omgeknoopten Halsdoek. Zeer natuurlijk en geestig | *Mat:* op paneel *Size:* hoog 10 breed 7 duimen	Mejuffrouw de Wed David Heemskerk [or others]	(Unknown)
1809/05/26	HADAA	A0002	*Q. Brekelenkamp* | Een Schoenmakers Winkel, op den voorgrond zien men de Schoenmaker aan zijn Handwerk bezig, te gelijk in gesprek met een Meid die door het vengster ligt, nevens hem een oude Vrouw die Appelen schilt, alles breed en meesterlijk geschilderd | *Mat:* op paneel *Size:* hoog 19 breed 23 duimen	Mejuffrouw de Wed David Heemskerk [or others]	(Unknown)
1809/06/13	AMSCH	0017	*Q. Breekelenkamp* | Agter een Visbank staat eene oude Boerin, met een Mes in de eene en een Moot Zalm in de andere Hand, dewelken zij aan eene Dame die voor de Bank staat, schijnt aan te bieden, verder toepasselijk bijwerk; helder en kragtig geschilderd | *Mat:* op paneel *Size:* hoog 19, breed 14 duim	[Gruyter?]	(Sold) fl 9 van Dijl
1809/06/13	AMSCH	0018	*Q. Breekelenkamp* | Eene oude Vrouw, zittende voor een Tafel, waarop Honing, Brood en verder bijwerk geplaatst is; uitvoerig geschilderd | *Mat:* op paneel *Size:* hoog 10, breed 8 duim	Y	(Sold) fl 1 Gruyter
1809/06/13	AMSCH	0019	*Q. Breekelenkamp* | In een Ouderwetsche gemeubileerde Kamer, zit eene bevallige Vrouw; gekleed met een rood Fluweel Jak, met een bonte Rand,	[Gruyter?]	(Bought In) fl 9:10

			houdende eenig Naaijwerk op haar schoot, zij schijnt in gesprek met eene oude Vrouw en Kind die nevens haar zitten, agterwaards een deftig gekleed Man en verder bijwerk; bevallig van licht, en uitvoerig geschilderd | *Mat:* op doek *Size:* hoog 29, breed 32 duim		
1809/06/13	AMSCH	0020	*Q. Breekelenkamp* | In een Binnehuis zit een bejaard Schoenmaker te arbeiden, nevens hem zit een oude Vrouw bij een Spinnewiel, verder drie anderen Beelden en Gereedschappen; natuurlijk | *Mat:* op doek *Size:* hoog 30, breed 37 duim	R[ijfsnijder]	(Sold) fl 2 L Pakker
1809/06/13	AMSCH	0203	*Q. Brékelenkamp* | Bij een Visbank staat eene Dienstmaagd, verzeld van een Kind, en twee andere Lieden	P	(Sold) fl 2:15 de Gruiter
1810/03/07	UTWLD	0002	*Q. Brekelenkamp* | Een kapitaal binnen huis, waar in een man by het vuur zit te leezen, op de voorgrond eene vrouw en twee kinderen, zeer natuurlyk en helder van coloriet | *Size:* hoog 2 voet, drie duim, breed 3 voet en een half duim	J J Woertman	(Unknown) fl 61
1810/03/07	UTWLD	0022	*Q. Brekelenkamp* | Een Schoolmeester bezig met onderwyzen, fraay behandeld | *Size:* hoog 1 voet 2 duim, breed 1 voet	J J Woertman	(Unknown) fl 70
1810/03/07	UTWLD	0023	*Brekelenkamp* | Een oud Heer bezig met een pen te vermaken konstig en uitvoerig behandeld | *Size:* hoog 1 voet 2 duim, breed 1 voet	J J Woertman	(Unknown) fl 50
1810/03/26	RMMUY	0026	*Quirijn Brekelenkamp* | Een Boeren Keuken, waarin eene bedaagde Vrouw aan den haard bezig is koeken te bakken, waarvan zij er een uit de pan ligt, en die aan een bij haar zittend Jongeling schijnt te zullen geven. Een Spinnewiel, Potten en ander Huisraad verrijken deze ordonnantie. Krachtig en bevallig van effect [L'intérieur d'une maison rustique ; une vieille femme est occupée à faire des gateaux, dont elle paroit vouloir en donner à un jeune homme assis auprès d'elle ; plusieurs ustenciles de menage l'entourent : l'ensemble est bien entendu, d'un ton léger et transparent, et d'un bon effet.] | *Mat:* op paneel *Size:* hoog 22 ½, breed 19 ½ duimen	Daniel de Jongh Az	(Sold) fl 101 van Eyk s'Hage
1810/03/26	RMMUY	0027	*Quirijn Brekelenkamp* | In een binne Vertrek, zit een Heer en Dame met de Kaart te spelen aan een met Tapijt bedekte Tafel (waarop een Schotel, Kan en Vruchten staan); voor dezelve een Tabouret, waarop een Viool ligt. Fraaij geschilderd [Une ancienne Chambre hollandoise ; un officier et une dame jouent aux cartes, à une table couverte d'un tapis, sur laquelle sont posés un linge, un plat et des fruits ; près d'éux est placé un tabouret, un violon, et autres accessoires, d'un beau faire, et d'un bon effet.] | *Mat:* op paneel *Size:* hoog 18, breed 19 duimen	Daniel de Jongh Az	(Sold) fl 41 Doctor Luchtmans a Rott[m]
1810/03/27	RMCNL	0021	*Brekelenkamp* | Men ziet in een Binnenvertrek een Doctor, aan eene Zieke Vrouw, de Pols voelen, alles vol uitdrukking, netjes en fraai behandeld		(Unknown)
1810/03/27	RMCNL	0022	*Brekelenkamp* | Een Vrouwtje achter eene Tafel zittende, waarop Brood enz., geschilderd		(Unknown)
1810/06/20	AMSCH	0006	*G. Brekelenkamp* | Eene bejaarde Vrouw, bezig Boonen te doppen; nevens haar Manden met Aardvruchten | *Mat:* op paneel *Size:* hoog 11, breed 9 duimen	A	(Sold) fl 4:5 Sardet
1810/07/23	DOLGI	0013	*Quirijn Brekelenkamp* | Een Boeren Binnenvertrek, alwaar eene Vrouw de Klederen van eenen daar bij staanden Jongen zit te reinigen, en een Meisje staande bij een Kindje in de Wieg. Het Vertrek is verder met allerlei eigenäardig Huisraad gestoffeerd. Zeer natuurlijk en fraai van Teekening, Ordonnantie, en Penseels-Behandeling | *Mat:* op paneel *Size:* hoog 18, breed 27 duim	Mr Pieter van den Santheuvel	(Sold) fl 110 H
1810/08/01	AMSCH	0016	*Brekelenkamp (Quirijn)* | In een Binnenvertrek zit eene Vrouw in deftig Hollandsch Gewaad, welke door eene oude Vrouw, die over haar zit, op den Arm gekopt wordt; verder eenig Huisraad [Dans un intérieur de Chambre est assise une Femme en Costume à l'ancienne Hollandoise : une Vielle paroit vouloir lui faire une ventouse sur le bras. Il est orné de Meubles et d'accessoires analogues à ce sujet] | *Annots:* passable (NGW) *Mat:* op paneel *Size:* hoog 17 ½, breed 14 ½ duimen *Loc:* Den Haag, Nederland. Mauritshuis. (562)	Mr Pieter de Smeth van Alphen	(Sold) fl 275 Van Iperen
1810/08/06	AMSCH	0020	*Brekelenkamp (Q)* | In een Binnenvertrek, bij een open Venster, zit eene bejaarde Vrouw, voor een Spinnewiel; zij schijnt in gesprek met eene andere Vrouw, die over haar zit, en welke een marktemmer aan haar arm houdt; verder eenig Huisraad. Krachtig geschilderd | *Mat:* op paneel *Size:* hoog 19, breed 15 duimen	S[paan]	(Sold) fl 69 J Spaan
1810/10/10	MGCIT	0028	*Q. van Brekelencamp* | Een Vrouwtje, op een stoel en met de eene voet op een stoof zittende, houdende een Kind aan de Borst, en een Wieg naast haar zijde staande; lieflijk geschildert	Caspar van Citters	(Unknown)
1810/10/11	AMSCH	0014	*Q. Brekelenkamp* | In een Grot, bij de Ruïne van een oud Gebouw, ziet men een knielende Monnik, in eerbiedige houding, voor hem bij de stam van een boom, ligt een opengeslagen boek, krusifix, watervles en ander bijwerk; fraai van licht, en in de manier van G. Dou geschilderd, door Q. Brekelenkamp | *Mat:* op paneel *Size:* hoog 20, breed 16 duimen	[Gruyter?]	(Bought In) fl 13:10
1810/12/03	DOBRA	0041	*Brekelenkamp* | Een rookend Boertje		(Unknown)
			Brekelencam, Quiringh Gerritsz. van (or Brekelencam, Q., manner)		
1802/06/28	AMSCH	0006	*Breckelenkamp* | Een Schoenmakers Winkel, men ziet op de Voorgrond de Huisbaas, schynende te spreeken tegen een Vrouw, die in de Deur	Anna Elink	(Sold) fl 22 van Iperen

			staat; kragtig op Doek, door Breckelenkamp, of in de manier | *Mat:* op doek *Size:* hoog 29, breed 33 duim		
1808/06/11	RMRIJ	0016	*Brekelenkamp, of in zyn manier* | Een Oud Man zyn Pyp aanstekende en verder Bywerk; stout en meesterlyk geschilderd | *Mat:* op paneel *Size:* hoog 9, breed 8 duim		(Sold) fl 10:10 Van Dongen
			Brekelencam, Quiringh Gerritsz. van (copy after)		
1804/10/16	DLOND	0240a[k]	*C. Vermeulen; Brekelenkamp* | [Een Stuk, bevattende 13 zeer schone Copiën van de volgende Meesters. Un Tableau, contenant 13 Copies très-belles des Peintres suivans.] 11. Brekelenkamp. Een Vertrek, une Chambre | copy by Corn. Vermeulen (III) after Q. Brekelencam *Mat:* op paneel *Size:* hoog 41, breed 55 *Notes:* The bracketed information in the title appears above lot 240a[a] and refers to lots 240a[a-m].		(Sold) fl 150 for lots 240a[a-m]. Ond d Wyngaert
1810/06/06	RMMUY	0212	*Brekelenkamp* | Een Man die Visch schoon maakt, van achteren een Kinderschool. Naar Brekelenkamp | *Mat:* op doek		(Unknown) fl 1:15
1810/07/23	DOLG1	0083	*Brekelenkamp* | Een Kledermakers Winkel, naar Brekelenkamp	Mr Pieter van den Santheuvel	(Sold) fl 3:10 Nieuwenhuizen van Brussel
1810/07/23	DOLG1	0084	*Brekelenkamp* | Een Schoenmakers Winkel, naar dito [Brekelenkamp]	Mr Pieter van den Santheuvel	(Sold) fl 1:5 Nieuwenhuizen van Brussel
			Brekelencam, Quiringh Gerritsz. van (manner)		
1801/03/16	AMSCH	0143	*Brekelenkamp* | Een oud Man met een boek in zyn hand, als Brekelenkamp	K[ip]	(Sold) fl 0:10 Gruiter
1801/03/16	AMSCH	0164	*G. Brekelenkamp* | Een Vrouw bij den haard zittende, naast haar een Gatepetiel met Bot, in de manier van G. Brekelenkamp	K[ip]	(Sold) fl 10 Rijnders
1801/04/08	HAVIN	0064	*Brekelenkamp* | Een Naaister, als van Brekelenkamp | *Notes:* In the original title the word "Naaister" was printed as "Landschap." This error was corrected at the front of the catalogue.		(Unknown)
1801/04/23	AMYVR	0039	*Brekelenkamp* | Het Pourtrait van Annetje Caspers Laringer, en Michiel van Huysum in de manier van Brekelenkamp		(Sold) fl 3 ½ Hulswit
1801/08/19	AMSCH	0011	*Q. Breckelenkamp* | Een Heer zittende te roken in zyn Studeerkamer; in de manier van dito [Q. Breckelenkamp] | *Mat:* op paneel *Size:* hoog 13, breed 10 duim	Van Forreest	(Sold) fl 6:10 Wed Achtienhoven
1802/02/16	AMSCH	0032	*Q. Breekelenkamp* | Een Hermiet in een Rotz, met devotie ziende naar een kruisifiks, het geen hy met zaamgevouwen handen vast houd, gestoffeert met verder bywerk kragtig geschilderd als door Q. Breekelenkamp	H	(Sold) fl 2 J Royers
1802/05/11	GRGRW	0040	*Brekelenkamp* | Ene Bezige Keukenmeid, in den smaak van Brekelenkamp [Schilderijen met Olie-Verf; In zwarte Lijsten] | *Mat:* in olyverf *Notes:* The bracketed information in the title appears above lot 1 and refers to lots 1 to 79a.	Arnold Sicco Werumeus	(Unknown)
1802/06/16	AMSCH	0240	*Breekelenkamp* | Een bedaagde Vrouw in aloude Kleeding, in diepe aandagt, met zaamgevouwen handen biddende voor een Crufix [sic]: daar nevens leggen eenige Boeken, het Caracter is zeer natuurlyk en uitvoering gepenceeld, op Paneel, hoog 15 ½, breed 13 ½ duim, als door Breekelenkamp | *Mat:* op paneel *Size:* hoog 15 ½, breed 13 ½ duim	[Merrem]	(Sold) fl 3 Van Dijk
1802/09/06	AMSCH	0145	*Brékelenkamp* | Een Vrouw, zittende in een Binnevertrek, beezig Linnen te Naaijen, neevens haar een Hond; op Paneel, in de manier van Brékelenkamp | *Mat:* op paneel	Mevrouw Achtienhoven	(Sold) fl 11:10 van Iperen
1802/09/06	AMSCH	0237	*Breekelenkamp* | In een Binnehuis zit een Vrouw appelen te schillen, daar nevens een kind en andere stoffagie, in de manier van Breekelenkamp	J	(Sold) fl 0:12 Boelen
1804/04/28	LNDLS	0053	*Brekelenkamp* | Een Vrouwtje, zittende in een binnenvertrek knollen te schillen, en een ander, die by een tobben staat, met meer bywerk, door .... als van Brekelenkamp	[Abraham Delfos] [or others]	(Sold) fl 21 Rigter [for] G
1806/06/07	RMHSN	0102	*Brekelenkamp* | Een Vrouw die een Jonge Onderwyst, in de manier van Brekelenkamp | *Mat:* op paneel	A E K L	(Unknown)
1808/04/26	GDAN	0255	*Brekelenkamp* | In de manier van Brekelenkamp een Binnenhuis met eetende Menschen | *Size:* hoog 18, breed 24 duim	G H Fortuyn	(Unknown)
1808/04/26	GDAN	0296	*Brekelenkamp* | In de manier van Brekelenkamp, een Vrouwtje dat Kool zit schoon te maken | *Size:* hoog 16, breed 20 duim	G H Fortuyn	(Unknown)
1809/04/22	AMYVR	0177	*Brekelenkamp* | Een Speldenwerkster; als Brekelenkamp	de Bruin	(Sold) fl 4:5 J^n de Vries
1809/06/13	AMSCH	0212	*Q. Brékelenkamp* | Het Binnengezigt van een Boeren Wooning met Huislieden en Bijwerk gestoffeerd, in de manier van Q. Brékelenkamp	E	(Sold) fl 2 T Spaan
1810/07/23	DOLG2	0021	*Brekelenkamp* | In een Keukenvertrek vertoont zich een zittend oud man, benevens eene vrouw aan het Spinnewiel; in de manier van Brekelenkamp | *Annots:* [door] Marseus (EBNP) *Mat:* op paneel *Size:* hoog 18, breed 24 duim	Pieter Quinting	(Sold) fl 3:15 Visser
1810/07/23	DOLG2	0076	*Brekelenkamp* | Een Kluizenaar, in een grot, te lezen zittende. Wel geteekend, en gepenseeld als Brekelenkamp | *Mat:* op paneel *Size:* hoog 11, breed 10 Duim	Pieter Quinting	(Unknown)

Bres, Anthoni

1808/09/13	HABRU	0106	*A. Bres* | Een Bloemstuk		(Unknown) fl 5:10 for lots 106 & 107
1808/09/13	HABRU	0107	*A. Bres* | Een dito [Bloemstuk]		(Unknown) fl 5:10 for lots 106 & 107
1808/09/13	HABRU	0108	*A. Bres* | Een met dood Wild		(Unknown) fl 1:4 for lots 108 & 109
1808/09/13	HABRU	0109	*A. Bres* | Een dito [met dood Wild]		(Unknown) fl 1:4 for lots 108 & 109

Bresser, A. [Unidentified]

1808/03/03	HAVIN	0026	*A. Bresser* | Twee Landschappen	Jacobus Spillebout	(Unknown) fl 0:5

Breydel, Karel

1801/08/19	AMSCH	0014	*C. Breydel* | Twee stuks Dorpgezichten, ryk gestoffeerd met een menigte Huislieden, Postwagens en wandelende Persoonen; uitvoerig geschilderd	Pruyssen[r] [for] Q	(Bought In) fl 19 ¾

Bril, Paul

1802/06/28	AMSCH	0016	*P. Bril* | Twee stuks, het eene verbeeld een boschachtig Landschap; en het andere een Ysgezicht, beide fiks gepenceeld door P. Bril, Panneel | *Mat:* op paneel *Size:* hoog 8, breed 10 duim	Anna Elink	(Sold) fl 1 Gruiter
1802/06/28	AMSCH	0017	*P. Bril* | Twee stuks, Boom- en Bergachtige Landschappen, gestoffeerd met rustende Reizigers en andere stoffagie, krachtig gepenceeld, door Denzelven [P. Bril], Panneel | *Mat:* op paneel *Size:* hoog 18, breed 14 duim	Anna Elink	(Sold) fl 1 Coclers
1802/07/20	MGSAN	0006	*P. Bril* | Een zeer uitvoerig Landschapje, op Paneel | *Mat:* op paneel *Size:* hoog duim 9, breed duim 13		(Unknown)
1802/09/06	AMSCH	0012	*P. Bril* | Een gestoffeerd Landschap met Gebouwen; uitvoerig | *Mat:* op paneel *Size:* hoog 11, breed 15 duim	Mevrouw Achtienhoven	(Sold) fl 0:10 L Pakker
1803/06/20	AMSCH	0040	*P. Bril* | Een besneeuwd Brabands Dorpgezigt, ryk met Wagens, Paarden en Beelden gestoffeerd, en natuurlyk behandeld, op Paneel | *Mat:* op paneel *Size:* hoog 18, breed 29 duim	Schley [for] G	(Sold) fl 10:10 J Spaan
1803/08/24	HGKAN	0092	*Paul Brill* | Een fraay Landschapje	[Teissier] [or others]	(Sold) fl 4 C [?]
1805/07/03	AMSCH	0071	*P. Bril* | Een Bergachtig Landzicht, by een stille Rivier, gestoffeerd met Rysigers en Paarden, eenige Bokjes en Wooningen; kragtig gepenceeld | *Mat:* op paneel *Size:* hoog 18, breed 26 duim	R[oos]	(Sold) fl 13 H Zurmuklen
1805/10/09	HGBSM	0082	*P. Bril* | Een smeedery van binnen te zien | *Mat:* op koper *Size:* hoog 8 breet 11 ½ duim	T H van Willigen [or others]	(Sold) fl 3 Carré
1810/10/11	AMSCH	0020	*P. Bril* | Een Bergachtig Landschap met zwaar Geboomte, Heeren te Paard, en Jagers met hunne Honden | *Mat:* op koper *Size:* hoog 7 ½, breed 10 duimen	C	(Sold) fl 1:15 Posthumus

Bril, Paul (and Brueghel, J. (I))

1808/08/23	AMSCH	0014	*Breugel (J.); P. Bril* | Een hoog bergachtig Landschap, met een Rivier doorsneeden, gestoffeert met een beladen Vrachtwagen, Arbeidslieden, gaande en rustende Reisigers, natuurlijk behandeld | *Mat:* op paneel *Size:* hoog 19, breed 33 duim	C	(Sold) fl 1 Boelhouwer
1810/07/26	AMSCH	0093	*J. Breugel; P. Bril* | Een Landschap met Beelden | *Mat:* op paneel	Cassino	(Sold) fl 1:5 Geld

Bril, Paul (and Carracci, A.)

1808/06/13	AMSCH	0027	*Bril (P.); A. Carats* | Een Landschap, op den voorgrond een Heremiet; op zijn knieën voor een Christusbeeld liggende, fraai behandeld | *Mat:* op koper *Size:* hoog 5, breed 6 duim	R[oos]	(Bought In) fl 30

Bril, Paul (and Rottenhammer, H. (I))

1805/10/09	HGBSM	0094	*H. Bottenhamer; P. Bril* | Een landschap daar Christus een blinde aan de weg geneest, door H. Bottenhamer, en het landschap door P. Bril | *Mat:* op koper *Size:* hoog 13 breet 18 duim	T H van Willigen [or others]	(Sold) fl 7:15 Teissier

Bril, Paul (manner)

1801/04/23	AMYVR	0048	*Poulie Bril* | 1 Landschap als van Poulie Bril | *Notes:* This lot was sold with lot 47, which is in the manner of Rubens.		(Unknown) fl 5 for lots 47 & 48

Brinckmann, Philipp Hieronymus

1803/09/07	AMSCH	0034	*P. H. Brinkman* | Twee stuks bevallige Noordsche Landschapjes, x door P. H. Brinkman [Deux paysages montagneux de la Nord-Hollande] | *Mat:* op paneel *Size:* hoog 3, breed 5 duim	Smidt	(Sold) fl 2 J Yver

Broeck, Elias van den

1802/07/27	AKHRK	0051	*Elias van den Broek* | Een Tafel, waarop een Fles met Bloemen, dun geschilderd | *Mat:* op doek *Size:* hoog 15, breed 12 ½ duim	Maria Stategaart	(Sold) fl 0:10 Son Meyer
1802/09/06	AMSCH	0023	*E. van den Broek* | Een zeer uitvoerig op Doek geschilderd Bloemstuk | *Mat:* op doek *Size:* hoog 27, breed 20 duim	Mevrouw Achtienhoven	(Sold) fl 4 Jan Spaan

1802/09/29	AMSCH	0013	*E. van den Broek, Dicipel van J. D. de Heem* | Een Bloemstuck, hoog 26, breed 21 duim. Doek. Op een steenen Tafel is geplaatst een glaze Fles met onderscheidene bevallige Bloemen, als roode, geele en andere Roozen, Africanen, Papaver, Anemonen en schoone Bladeren en Kroppen; zeer delicaat en natuurlyk verbeeld [Des Fleurs d'un beau choix, groupées avec intelligénce, sont placés, dans une Bouteille de verre, sur une Table de marbre traité en maitre avec beaucoup de délicatesse et de vérité.] | *Mat:* op doek *Size:* hoog 26, breed 21 duim	[Labouchere?]	(Sold) fl 11:10 Coclers
1802/12/13	AMSCH	0030	*E. van der Broek* | Op een Steene rand staat een Fles met diverse zoorten van Bloemen | *Mat:* op doek *Size:* hoog 23, breed 19 duim	Pruyssenaar [for] D	(Sold) fl 1:15 Van der Schley [for] R[ijfsnijder]
1804/05/07	AMSCH	0030	*Broek. (E. van den)* | Den eene verbeeld in een Landschap een Stam van een Boom, waarop een Nesje met Vogeleijeren, onder op een Steen legt een Oranjeappel, met takbloeisem en bladeren, verders verscheide vliegende en andere Insecten; den ander verbeeld een Vaas met Bloemen op den Steen Tafel, waar op eenige Insecten aazen; beiden bevallig en uitvoerig gepenceeld | *Mat:* op doek *Size:* hoog 23, breed 20 duim	Schley	(Sold) fl 4 Menzart
1804/08/08	AMSCH	0027	*E. van den Broek* | Op een Steene Tafel staat een Pot, gevuld met geurige Bloemen van allerlei soort; uitvoerig op Doek | *Mat:* op doek *Size:* hoog 27, breed 22 duim	Roos [for] G	(Bought In) fl 1
1805/07/10	AMSCH	0032	*E. van der Broek* | Twee stuks, de eene verbeeld op een steene Voetstuk een Fles, gevuld met verscheide zoorten van fraaije Bloemen; den anderen vertoont in een Landschap by de stam van een Boom, eenige keurige Bloemen by Plantgewas, waarop insecten Aasen, beide bevallig en uitvoerig gepenseeld | *Mat:* op doek *Size:* ieder hoog 24, breed 21 duim	Temmink	(Sold) fl 51 Lafontaine
1805/07/10	AMSCH	0032a[H]	*E. van der Broek* | 1 dito [Schildery] | *Notes:* This lot was added in by hand in the EBNP and RKDH copies of the catalogue.	V[inkeles]	(Sold) fl 14:10 Gruyter
1807/04/13	AMSCH	0006	*E. van den Broek* | Op een steene Rand ziet men een Fles met diverse soorten van welriekende Bloemen, als roode en witte Roozen, Tulpen, Hiacinten, Auriculaars, beneevens Insecten, delicaat en uitvoerig gepenseeld | *Mat:* op doek *Size:* hoog 24, breed 20 ½ duim	Everard de Burlett	(Sold) fl 12 Coclers
1807/06/02	AMHUY	0032	*van den Broek* | Op een Marmersteene Tafel staat een Fles gevuld met fraaije Bloemen, waar op verscheide Insecten aasen; alles is dun en uitvoerig geschilderd		(Unknown)
1807/06/02	AMHUY	0033	*van den Broek* | Twee dito dito [Op een Marmersteene Tafel staat een Fles gevuld met fraaije Bloemen, waar op verscheide Insecten aasen; alles is dun en uitvoerig geschilderd]		(Unknown)
1807/06/02	AMHUY	0036	*E. van den Broek* | Op een Marmersteene Tafel staat een Fles met verscheide Bloemen en Insecten; uitvoerig geschilderd		(Unknown)
1808/06/13	AMSCH	0208	*van den Broek* | Een kapitaal en teder gewerkt Bloemstuk	E M Engelberts	(Sold) fl 5:5 Th Spaan
1808/06/13	AMSCH	0214	*van den Broek* | Eenige stuks met Kruiden en Insekten; als de voorgaande	E M Engelberts	(Sold) fl 3:10 Gruiter
1809/04/17	AMSCH	0011	*E. van den Broek* | Op een Steene Tafel staat een Vaas, gevuld met onderscheidene zoorten van Bloemen; zacht en teder gepenceeld | *Mat:* op doek *Size:* hoog 31, breed 25 duim	A	(Sold) fl 1:10
1809/04/17	AMSCH	0012	*E. van den Broek* | Een dito Ordonantie in alles als de voorgaande | *Mat:* op doek *Size:* hoog 18, breed 14 duim *Notes:* It is unclear what "dito" refers to in the title.	A	(Sold) fl 3:10
1809/06/13	AMSCH	0218	*E. van den Broek* | Een Bloemstuk	E	(Sold) fl 0:6 L Pakker
1810/10/10	MGCIT	0095	*van den Broecke* | Een fraai Stuk met Bloemen	Caspar van Citters	(Unknown)
			Bronchorst, Jan Gerritsz. van		
1802/09/21	UTHDG	0002	*J. van Bronkhorst* | Jacob droomende dat de Engelen tot hem van den Hemel nederklimmen, door J. van Bronkhorst, hoog 30, breed 23 duimen, op doek. De schoone Ordonnantie van dit kragtig en natuurlijk schilderij is bekent door de zwarte konstplaat van Blooteling | *Mat:* op doek *Size:* hoog 30, breed 23 duimen		(Sold) fl 72:10 Venhouse
1805/07/10	AMSCH	0028	*Bronkhorst* | Maria Magdaléna in berouw; meesterlyk op Doek | *Mat:* op doek *Size:* hoog 32, breed 25 duim	V[inkeles] [for] N	(Sold) fl 5:5 Menzard
1810/03/07	UTWLD	0054	*Bronkhorst* | Eenige muziek makende Nimphen | *Size:* hoog 4 voet 9 duim, breed 6 voet	J J Woertman	(Unknown) fl 20
			Bronzino, Agnolo		
1810/07/26	AMSCH	0001	*Agnolo Bronzino* | Eene Bijbel-Ordonantie, voorstellende Christus, gekruist tusschen de Moordenaars; dit stuk is rijk met eene menigte Beelden en uitmuntend geschilderd | *Mat:* op paneel *Size:* hoog 44, breed 36 duimen	Cassino	(Bought In) fl 60
			Brouwer, Adriaen		
1801/02/18	AMBOS	0038	*A. Brouwer* | Een Boer met zyn regter hand op een Tafel leunende, in de linker hand een Pyp houdende	J Schonevelt	(Unknown)
1801/06/10	AMSCH	0011	*Brouwer. (A.)* | In een Boere-Binnehuis, zitten een menigte Huislieden, zich met musiceeren, roken en drinken te vermaaken, verder een menigte huisraad, alles is fraai van hartstochten, en meesterlyk behandeld | *Mat:* op koper *Size:* hoog 20, breed 24 duim	Herman ten Kate	(Sold) fl 115 Wreesman

1802/05/05	AMSCH	0021	*A. Brouwer* | In een Boere Binnenhuis, ziet men een Huisman, beezig zynde een Pyp op te steken, door een Vengster komt een Boer kyken en verder Bywerk, geestig gepenceeld | *Mat:* op paneel *Size:* hoog 11, breed 14 duim	A	(Sold) fl 26:10 W Reijers
1802/12/13	AMSCH	0023	*A. Brouwer* | Voor een Schutting van een Buitenhuis, zitten eenige drinkende en slaapende Boeren, geestig gecaractriseerd, en bevallig geschilderd | *Mat:* op paneel *Size:* hoog 12, breed 16 duim	Pruyssenaar [for] A	(Sold) fl 1:15 Daame
1803/09/07	AMSCH	0025	*A. Brouwer* | In een Chirurgynswinkel word een Boer verbonden aan zyn Arm, hy schynt zeer pynlyk, en de Barbier zeer voorzigtig, waarna een derde staat te kyken, verder eenig bywerk; geestig en malsch behandeld [La chambre d'un chirurgien, occupé à panser le bras d'un paysan ; ce dernier paroit beaucoup, souffrir tandis que le barbier semble opérer avec précaution ; à côté un tiers qui le regarde, puis quelques accessoires. Tableau d'une touche delicate et spirituelle] | *Mat:* op koper *Size:* hoog 12, breed 8 ½ duim	Smidt	(Bought In) fl 13 ½
1804/05/07	AMSCH	0014	*Brouwer. (A.)* | Een Boeren Binnenhuis, waarin een Boer zit te rooken, terwyl een ander van een Meisje een glas Bier ontfangt; geestig behandeld | *Mat:* op paneel *Size:* hoog 13, breed 11 duim	Roos [for] A	(Sold) fl 19:10 Haffner
1804/07/25	DLGRO	0009	*A. Brouwer* | Een dito [Boerer binnen Huis] met een Oude Vrouw, die een Jonge 't Hoofd reinigd, en een paar Boertjes aan den Haard zittende | *Mat:* op paneel *Size:* hoog 8, breed 7 duim	Mr Franc van der Burch Wz.	(Unknown)
1804/08/08	AMSCH	0020	*A. Brouwer* | In een Binnenhuis ziet men drie Boeren, bézig zich met rooken te vermaaken, ter zyde een Bierkan; dun en warm van schildering | *Mat:* op paneel *Size:* hoog 11, breed 8 duim	Roos [for] C	(Sold) fl 22 Gruyter
1804/08/08	AMSCH	0021	*A. Brouwer* | In een Boeren Binnenhuis ziet men aan een wèl voorziene Tafel eenigé eetende en vrolyke Gasten, terwyl eenige zich met zingen en danssen vermaaken, ziet men andere zich van 't overtollige ontlasten; schoon gecaracteriseert en meesterlyk geschilderd | *Mat:* op paneel *Size:* hoog 13 ½, breed 16 ½ duim	Vink[eles] [for] K[=Gruyter?]	(Sold) fl 9 Texier
1805/07/10	AMSCH	0017	*A. Brouwer* | Een Boere Bruiloft, vol gewoel in een Binnennenhuis [sic] zich vermaakende met dansen, speelen, drinken, galantiseeren enz.; allernatuurlykst en fraay gepenceeld | *Mat:* op doek *Size:* hoog 38, breed 51 duim	V[inkeles] [for] P	(Sold) fl 14 Gruyter
1805/07/10	AMSCH	0018	*A. Brouwer* | In een Binnevertrek ziet men twee Boeren; zittende by een Ton, de eene met een Glas in de Hand, en de andere zyn Pyp opsteekende, agter hun een Meid; dit Stukje is fraay gepenceeld | *Mat:* op paneel *Size:* hoog 13 ½, breed 11 duim	V[inkeles] [for] H[affner]	(Sold) fl 20 Lafontaine
1805/10/09	HGBSM	K0010	*A. Brouwer* | Een gezelschap met boertjes | *Mat:* op paneel *Size:* hoog 8 ½ breet 7 duim	T H van Willigen [or others]	(Sold) fl 3:10 Blommers
1805/10/21	GRBOL	0035	*A. Brouwer* | Een Binnenkamer, waar in een Vrouwtje, wyzende op een stuk goud geld, het welk zy in hare linker hand houdt; verder enige slapende en andere Figuren, meesterlyk geschilderd	Gerardus Nicolaus Heerkens	(Unknown)
1806/08/13	AMSCH	0013a	*Brouwer. (A.)* | Een Boerebruiloft vol gewoel in een Binnehuis, zich vermakende met Danzen, zingen, speelen en galantiseeren, meesterlyk en fiks geschilderd | *Mat:* op doek *Size:* hoog 38, breed 51 duim	Vinkeles [for] G[ruyter]	(Bought In) fl 14
1807/08/26	AMSCH	0023	*A. Brouwer* | Een vrolyke Boer, halverlyf, met een Bierkan in de hand, schynende Tabakrook uit de mond te blazen; ter zyde zit een andere Boer, rookende; het karacter is geestig, en meesterlyk uitgevoerd | *Mat:* op paneel *Size:* hoog 7, breed 6 duim	Helsdinge	(Sold) fl 26 Coclair
1808/05/18	LNAN	0031	*Brouwer* | Een Man halverlijf te zien, uitvoerig behandeld | *Notes:* The artist's name "Brouwer" was added in by hand in the RKDH copy of the catalogue.	Mr Cornelis Versluys	(Unknown) fl 21
1808/05/18	LNAN	0037	*Brouwer* | Een met vrolijke Boertjes | *Notes:* The artist's name "Brouwer" was added in by hand in the RKDH copy of the catalogue.	Mr Cornelis Versluys	(Unknown)
1808/06/13	AMSCH	0020	*Brouwer (A.)* | In een binnenvertrek is een Chirurgijn bezig een Boer de kies te trekken, daar achter een Vrouw en een Jongen; geestig gepenceeld | *Mat:* op paneel *Size:* hoog 10, breed 12 duim	R[oos]	(Bought In) fl 86
1808/09/13	HABRU	0005	*Brouwer* | Een met rokende Boertjes		(Unknown) fl 1:4
1808/09/13	HABRU	0006	*Brouwer* | Een leggende Boer in de Kan kijkende		(Unknown) fl 0:13
1808/11/28	AMSCH	0007	*A. Brouwer* | In een Binnenvertrek zit een groot Gezelschap aan een Tafel, zig met eeten en drinken vermaakende, ter zijde speelende, zingende, drinkende en liefkoosende Lieden, allernatuurlijkst en fraai gepenceeld | *Mat:* op doek *Size:* hoog 38, breed 51 duim	[Gruyter?]	(Sold) fl 16:10 Spaan
1810/10/10	MGCIT	0111	*Brouwer* | Een vrolyk Boertje, spelende op een Viool	Caspar van Citters	(Unknown)
			Brouwer, Adriaen (or Brouwer, Adr., manner)		
1802/06/16	AMSCH	0026	*A. Brouwer, of in de Manier* | In een Binnenhuis zit een Boer smakelyk zyn Pyp rookende: Meesterlyk en bevallig geschilderd | *Mat:* op paneel *Size:* hoog 11, breed 9 duim	[Merrem]	(Sold) fl 12 Boelen
1810/03/26	RMMUY	0058	*A. Brouwer, of in zijn manier* | Een dronke zingende Boer, verzeld van twee andere Boeren en eenig bijwerk [Un Paysan, ivre et chantant, accompagné de deux autres, et de quelques accessoires.] | *Annots:* Copie (BPG)	Daniel de Jongh Az	(Sold) fl 7 Le Brun Parys

Brouwer, Adriaen (or Monogrammist C.B.)

1802/08/24	LNDLS	0091	*C.B.; Brouwer* | Een Oud Man, zittende bij een kaars met Kan en Glas in de handen, en meer bijwerk. Gemerkt C.B. of Brouwer | *Mat:* op paneel *Size:* hoog 19, breed 15 duimen *Inscr:* C. B. (marked)	Leonardus Bouman [or others]	(Unknown) fl 20

Brouwer, Adriaen (copy after)

1802/07/21	HGKAN	0011[b]	*Brouwer* | Een stuk na Dusart en een naar Brouwer | *This Lot:* Een stuk; lot 11[a] is copy after Dusart		(Unknown)

Brouwer, Adriaen (manner)

1802/05/11	GRGRW	0070	*Brouwer* | Vijf Stukjes, verbeeldende de Vijf Zinnen, door vijf Werkende personen, in den smaak van Brouwer [Schilderijen met Olie-Verf; In Vergulde Lijsten] | *Mat:* in olyverf *Notes:* The bracketed information in the title appears above lot 1 and refers to lots 1 to 79a.	Arnold Sicco Werumeus	(Unknown) fl 8
1802/06/28	AMSCH	0258	*Brouwer* | Twee stuks Dorpgezigten, met vrolyke Dansende en Drinkende Huislieden, fiks gepenceelt in de manier van Brouwer	B	(Sold) fl 3 Vermeulen
1803/09/07	AMSCH	0233	*Brouwer* | Een vrolyke knaap, houdende in de eene hand een Schaaltje en in de andere een Borrelflesje, schynende al zingende, zig te vermaken; fix en meesterlyk geschilderd, op Doek, in de manier van Brouwer [Un garçon d'une mine joyeuse, tenant dans une main une tasse et dans l'autre une bouteille semble chanter et s'égaier [sic] ; d'une belle exécution, sur toile, dans la manière de Brouwer.] | *Mat:* op doek *Size:* hoog 29, breed 24 duim	Smidt	(Sold) fl 16 de Meijer
1805/10/21	GRBOL	0044	*A. Brouwer* | Een Boer, Tabak Rokende, in de manier van A. Brouwer	Gerardus Nicolaus Heerkens	(Unknown)
1806/08/13	AMSCH	0271	*A. Brouwer* | Twee Boertjes in een Binnehuis tabak rokende; in de manier van A. Brouwer | *Mat:* op paneel	Roos	(Sold) fl 7 du Pree
1807/08/26	AMSCH	0306	*A. Brouwer* | In een Binnenhuis vertoonen zich vechtende Boeren; in de manier van A. Brouwer | *Mat:* op paneel	Yver [for] S	(Sold) fl 1:10 Levy Pakker
1809/05/26	HADAA	0060	*Brouwer* | Twee Binnenhuizen, in de manier van Brouwer	Mejuffrouw de Wed David Heemskerk [or others]	(Unknown)
1809/05/26	HADAA	0061	*Brouwer* | Twee Binnenhuizen, in de manier van Brouwer	Mejuffrouw de Wed David Heemskerk [or others]	(Unknown)
1810/03/26	RMMUY	0052	*maniere de Brouwer* | Een rookende Boer, met een Kan in de hand [Un Paysan fumant sa pipe et tenant une cruche à la main.] | *Annots:* Genre de Brawer (BPG) *Notes:* The Dutch edition of the catalogue gives the artist as "Onbekend."	Daniel de Jongh Az	(Sold) fl 4 LeBrun Parys
1810/11/07	UTWLD	0066	*A. Brouwer* | Een vrolijk boertje met een tinne kan, zeer geestig behandeld, in de manier van A. Brouwer, op paneel, 7 duim hoog, 6 duim breed, zwarte Lijst | *Mat:* op paneel *Size:* 7 duim hoog, 6 duim breed		(Unknown) fl 12

Brouwer, J.

1801/05/11	AMSCH	0016	*J. Brouwer* | Een Mans Pourtret, meesterlyk geschilderd | *Mat:* op paneel *Size:* hoog 4, breed 4 duim	P[ruyssenaar]	(Sold) fl 0:18 Gruiter
1804/10/29	HRBAU	0014	*Brouwer, (J)* | Dit verbeeldt een Rencontre tusschen Cavallerie, waar van reeds eenige, zo Menschen als Paarden, dood, of gekwetst op den grond liggen, terwyl anderen zich door de vlugt zoeken te redden. Meesterlyk behandeld | *Mat:* op paneel *Size:* hoog 21, breed 31 duim	Simon Styl	(Unknown)

Bruegel, Pieter (the elder)

1802/05/24	HGBAK	0026	*Boeren Breugel* | Vier stuks, verbeeldende de vier getyden des jaars, door de Boeren Breugel, allen hoog 15 duim, breed 21 ½ duim paneel, zwarte lysten met verg. binnenranden | *Mat:* op paneel *Size:* hoog 15 duim, breed 21 ½ duim	Mejuffrouw A van der Mieden	(Sold) fl 21 Boscet
1802/07/21	HGKAN	0053	*Boere Breugel* | Een Kwakzalver, bezig om een Boer de Tand te trekken, door een Boere Breugel | companion to lot 54		(Unknown)
1802/07/21	HGKAN	0054	*Boere Breugel* | Een tot een weerga, daar de Boer de Kop gesleepen word | companion to lot 53		(Unknown)
1803/08/17	AMSCH	0019	*Breugel. (Boere)* | Een Gezelschap Geestelyken, op Krukken, geestig behandeld | *Mat:* op paneel *Size:* hoog 7, breed 8 duim	Anna Catharina Putman	(Sold) fl 0:14 Yver
1804/08/08	AMSCH	0015	*Boeren Breughel* | Een Bergachtig Landschap, met Geboomte, Boerenwooningen, en een Gevecht tusschen Boeren en Militairen; uitvoerig op Paneel | *Mat:* op paneel *Size:* hoog 20, breed 20 duim	Roos [for] D	(Sold) fl 2:10 Pieterse
1806/10/16	UTWLD	0012	*De Boeren Breugel* | Een Binnenhuis met verscheide Beelden door de Boeren Breugel	Mr P de Malapert [or] W Beeldsnyder	(Unknown)
1807/06/10	HGBSM	0173	*De Boeren Breugel* | Het Gezigt van het wegspoelen van de 72 Dorpen voor Dordrecht | *Mat:* op doek	Abraham Delfos [or others]	(Sold) fl 4:5 de Gelder
1807/08/26	AMSCH	0018	*De Boeren Breugel* | Twee stuks Zomer en Wintergezichten, ryk gestoffeert met vrolyke Huislieden in Landschappen, met verder bywerk; kragtig op paneel geschilderd | *Mat:* op paneel *Size:* hoog 16, breed 22 duim	Yver [for] S	(Sold) fl 2:5 Levij Pakker

1807/08/26	AMSCH	0019	*Boeren Breugel* | Twee dito [stuks] dito [Zomer en Wintergezichten] als de voorgaande, mede ryk gestoffeerd en van verschillende Ordonnantie | *Size:* hoog 16, breed 22 duim	Yver [for] S	(Sold) fl 2:5 Gruiter
			Brueghel		
1803/09/07	AMSCH	0012	*Breughel* | Twee stuks bevallige Wintertjes, gestoffeerd met eene menigte Beeldjes, Beestjes enz, krachtig op Paneel [Deux pièces représentant des scènes d'hyver bien agréables, relevées par une quantité de figures, d'animaux etc. ; peint avec beaucoup de vigueur] | *Mat:* op paneel *Size:* hoog 6 ½, breed 8 ½ duim	Smidt	(Sold) fl 16 W Reijers
1803/09/07	AMSCH	0013	*Breughel* | Een Boomryk en Duinachtig Landschap, gestoffeerd met een menigte Beeldjes enz, krachtig op Paneel [Un paysage parsemé d'arbres et d'une quantité de figures ; tableau d'une touche forte] | *Mat:* op paneel *Size:* hoog 9, breed 12 duim	Smidt	(Sold) fl 3:10 Grimpen
1803/09/07	AMSCH	0014	*Breughel* | Een hevige Bataille, tusschen Ruitery en Voetvolk, in een Boom- en Bergagtig Landschap, helder en meesterlyk [Une bataille très vive, entre de la cavalerie et de l'infanterie, dans un paysage montagneux et chargé d'arbres ; jour serein, exécuté en maître] | *Mat:* op koper *Size:* hoog 9, breed 12 duim	Smidt	(Sold) fl 12 de Lafontaine
1803/09/07	AMSCH	0015	*Breughel* | Twee stuks boomryke Landschappen, vol gewoel van beeldjes, beestjes, verders Gebouwen en Schuiten, natuurlyk gepenceeld [Deux paysages enrichis d'arbres, pleins de mouvement et d'une infinité de figures, de bestiaux, de batimens et de nacelles ; peint au naturel] | *Mat:* op koper *Size:* hoog 10, breed 15 duim	Smidt	(Sold) fl 36:10 Gruiter
1804/07/25	DLGRO	0054	*Breugel* | Een Winter gezicht verbeeldende een Bosch met verscheide Boomen, Reizigers te Paard en verder bywerk, fraai geschilderd door Breugel | *Mat:* op paneel *Size:* hoog 12, breed 24 duim	Mr Franc van der Burch Wz.	(Unknown)
1805/10/09	HGBSM	0032	*Breugel* | Een landschap, waarin men ziet een harte jagt, door Breugel, agtkant formaat op koper | *Mat:* op koper *Fmt:* agtkant *Size:* hoog 22 breet 28 duim	T H van Willigen [or others]	(Sold) fl 5:10 Ph Mey
1806/05/05	AMSCH	0236[a]	*Breugel* | Twee diversche Landschappen, door Breugel en Poelenburg | *This Lot:* Landschap; lot 236[b] by C. Poelenburgh	V[inkeles]	(Sold) fl 0:8 for lots 236[a] & 236[b]. Gruyter
1807/04/00	LNDLS	0049	*Breugel* | Maria met het kind, in een toog met bloemen	[Abraham Delfos] [or others]	(Unknown)
1807/06/10	HGBSM	0049	*Breugel* | Maria met het kind, in een toog met bloemen	Abraham Delfos [or others]	(Sold) fl 3 Nootwyk
1808/09/13	HABRU	0011	*Breugel* | Een Boere Gezelschap		(Unknown) fl 1:2
1809/05/26	HADAA	A0019	*Breugel* | Een Land- en Dorpgezigt, vol stoffagie | *Mat:* op paneel	Mejuffrouw de Wed David Heemskerk [or others]	(Unknown)
1810/06/20	AMSCH	0013	*Breugel* | Een Brabandsch Landschap, rijk met Beeldjes gestoffeerd | *Mat:* op paneel *Size:* hoog 8, breed 12 duimen	B	(Sold) fl 0:6 L Pakker
			Brueghel (and Elsheimer, A.)		
1805/10/09	HGBSM	0010	*Breugel; Elshaimer* | Andromeda verlost wordende door Perseus, uitvoerig | *Mat:* op koper *Size:* hoog 7 ½ breet 10 duim	T H van Willigen [or others]	(Sold) fl 4:15 Teissier
			Brueghel (or Bredael)		
1810/06/06	RMMUY	0060	*van Bredaal; Breugel* | Een Land en Watergezigt, gestoffeerd met Schuiten en Figuren, konstig en plaisant. Door van Bredaal of Breugel | companion to lot 61 *Mat:* op paneel *Notes:* This lot was sold with lot 61 by an anonymous artist.		(Unknown) fl 14:10 for lots 60 & 61
			Brueghel (or Brueghel, copy after)		
1806/10/17	MGSAN	0036	*Breugel* | Een Boerenvreugd, vol gewoel, door of naar Breugel | *Mat:* op paneel	Gerardus Beljard	(Sold) £ 0.2.7 for lots 36 & 37. de Onde
1806/10/17	MGSAN	0037	*Breugel* | Een Dorpgezigt, op de voorgrond een Wagen met Gras, door of naar denzelven [Breugel] | *Mat:* op paneel	Gerardus Beljard	(Sold) £ 0.2.7 for lots 36 & 37. de Onde
			Brueghel (or Brueghel, manner)		
1808/05/17	LNAN	0015	*Breugel* | Een stads Gezigt vol gewoel, door of in de manier van Breugel		(Unknown)
			Brueghel (copy after)		
1804/10/16	DLOND	0037	*F.J. Breda; naar Breugel* | Twee Landschappen, het een met een Pont by een Overvaarplaats, het andere met een Postwagen. Deux Paysages, dans la premiere une Gondole, dans l'autre un Chariot de Poste | *This Lot:* Een Landschap; copy by J.F. Bredael after Brueghel *Mat:* op koper *Size:* hoog 9, breed 12 *Notes:* Lots 37 and 38 were printed in the catalogue as one item.		(Unknown)
1804/10/16	DLOND	0038	*F.J. Breda; naar Breugel* | Twee Landschappen, het een met een Pont by een Overvaarplaats, het andere met een Postwagen. Deux Paysages, dans la premiere une Gondole, dans l'autre un Chariot de Poste | *This Lot:* Een Landschap; copy by J.F. Bredael after Brueghel *Mat:* op koper *Size:*		(Unknown)

			hoog 9, breed 12 *Notes:* Lots 37 and 38 were printed in the catalogue as one item.		
			Brueghel (manner)		
1802/05/22	RMHSN	0003	*Breugel* | Een Boer en Boerinne vrolyke Maaltyd in de trant van Breugel	Lambertus Bicker	(Unknown)
1803/11/30	MGBEO	0004	*Breugel* | Een dito [Binnen-Vertrek], verbeelende [sic] een Keuken, waar in een Kok bezig is met Wild aan het Spit te braaden, wyl hy met zyn andere hand een Meid liefkoosd, in de manier van Breugel | *Mat:* op paneel *Size:* hoog 27 duim, breed 40 duim	Samuel de Wind	(Sold) £ 0:5 Ad^{n} Tak
1803/12/12	AMSCH	0135	*Breughel* | Een uitgestrekt Boom- en Bergachtig Landschap met Koorn-äkkers, en een ménigte stoffagie; meesterlyk op Doek; als Breughel | *Mat:* op doek *Size:* hoog 52, breed 40 duim	V[inkeles?]	(Sold) fl 2 Van Iperen
1804/04/28	LNDLS	0036	*Breugel* | Een boere Kermis, vol gewoel, in die trant van Breugel | *Mat:* op doek *Size:* hoog 26, breed 37 duim	[Abraham Delfos] [or others]	(Sold) fl 2 Jan Landa
1804/10/08	RMCNL	0011	*Breugel* | Pomone en Vestumnus [sic] in Tuingezigt, in de manier van Breugel	A t'Hooft	(Unknown)
1804/10/08	RMCNL	0016	*Breugel* | Een Brabandsch Landschap met stoffagie in de manier van Breugel | *Mat:* op koper	A t'Hooft	(Unknown)
1804/10/29	HRBAU	0159	*Breugel* | Een Brabandsch Landschapjen, ryk gestoffeerd, en in de manier van Breugel behandeld | *Mat:* op koper *Size:* hoog 9 ½, breed 12 duim	Simon Styl	(Unknown)
1805/07/03	AMSCH	0191	*Breugel* | Twee stuks Boomryke Landschapjes, met Boerewoningen en stoffagie van Beeldjes, als Breugel	C	(Sold) fl 12 van Iperen
1805/12/16	AMSCH	0070	*Breugel* | Een Landschap in de manier van Breugel | *Notes:* This lot was sold with lot 83, which is in the manner of Goyen.	R[oos]	(Sold) fl 1 for lots 70 & 83. L Pakker
1805/12/16	AMSCH	0105	*Breugel* | Twee stuks, een Dorpgezicht vol gewoel, en een Land- en Watergezicht, uitvoerig op Paneel geschilderd, in de manier van Breugel | *Mat:* op paneel	V	(Sold) fl 2 Yver
1807/06/10	HGBSM	0167	*Breugel* | Twee stuks Stads gezigten vol gewoel, met figuuren en vaartuigen, in de trant van Breugel | *Mat:* op doek	Abraham Delfos [or others]	(Sold) fl 2 Noordwyk
1807/08/26	AMSCH	0020	*Breugel* | Twee stuks Land- en Watergezigten, gestoffeerd met Boerenwoningen, Vaartuigen en Beelden; in de manier van Breugel | *Mat:* op koper *Size:* ieder hoog 5 ½ en breed 8 duim	de Vries	(Sold) fl 1:5 A Rynders
1808/05/17	LNAN	0016	*Breugel* | Een boomrijk Landschap, als van Breugel		(Unknown)
1808/05/17	LNAN	0030	*Breugel* | Een rond land en water Gezigt, uitvoerig als van Breugel		(Unknown)
1809/07/25	HGBSM	0162	*Breugel* | Twee dito [Landschapjes met stoffage], in de trant van Breugel | *Mat:* op paneel *Size:* hoog 5, breed 6 en een half duim	D van der Aa [or] E B ten Dall	(Sold) fl 2:4 Bakhuyzen
1809/07/25	HGBSM	0274	*Breugel* | Twee Landschapjes, in de manier van Breugel, op paneel, rond formaat | *Mat:* op paneel *Fmt:* rond	D van der Aa [or] E B ten Dall	(Sold) fl 1:2 A Vermeulen
			Brueghel, Jan (the elder)		
1801/06/10	AMSCH	0031	*Breughel de Fluweele* | Een Brabandsch Landschap, ryk gestoffeert met Reizigers in wagens, te paard enandere [sic] te voet; alles zonachtig en uitvoerig behandeld | *Mat:* op koper *Size:* hoog 11, breed 17 duim	Herman ten Kate	(Sold) fl 55 de Roy
1801/08/19	AMSCH	0004	*J. Breughel* | Een Brabandsch Landschap, ryk gestoffeerd met een Postwagen en Beeldjes, uitvoerig op Koper | *Mat:* op koper *Size:* hoog 6, breed 8 duim	Van Forreest	(Sold) fl 6:5 for lots 4 & 5. Roos
1801/08/19	AMSCH	0005	*J. Breughel* | Een dito [Brabandsch] Land- en Watergezigt, in alles behandeld als de voorgaande, door dito [J. Breughel] | *Mat:* op koper *Size:* hoog 5, breed 8 duim	Van Forreest	(Sold) fl 6:5 for lots 4 & 5. Roos
1801/08/19	AMSCH	0007	*J. Breugel* | Een Strand- Gezicht aan Zee, waar by een Ruïne van een oud gebouw, op de voorgrond gestoffeert met verschyde Beeldjes, Scheepen en Schuyten; fraay op Paneel | *Mat:* op paneel *Size:* hoog 5, breed 7 duim	Van Forreest	(Sold) fl 0:6 D^{k} Nieuland
1801/08/19	AMSCH	0008	*J. Breugel* | Een Landschap met een Rivier doorsneeden en met Beeldjes gestoffeerd	Pruyssen^{r} [for] Q	(Bought In) fl 7
1801/08/19	AMSCH	0009	*J. Breugel* | Een digt Boschachtig Landschap met een Ryziger, die door Rovers word aangevallen	Pruyssen^{r} [for] Q	(Sold) fl 3:10 Wolft
1802/05/05	AMSCH	0019	*J. Brenghel* | Twee stuks Brabandsche Land- en Dorpgezichten, ryk gestoffeerd met een menigte Beeldjes, Postwagens en andere Reizigers, verbeeldende een Winter; zynde het Ys vol stoffagie van Beeldjes, Arresleden, enz. Alles zeer uitvoerig | *Mat:* op paneel *Size:* ieder is hoog 10, breed 12 duim	A	(Sold) fl 16 Auber
1802/05/24	HGBAK	0040	*de fluweele Breugel* | Een Land en Dorpgezicht, op de voorgrond een Herberg met Boertjes, Paarden en Wagens, gestoffeerd door de fluweele Breugel, hoog 8 ¾ duim, breed 11 ¼ duim, op koper, zwarte lyst en vergulde rand | *Mat:* op koper *Size:* hoog 8 ¾ duim, breed 11 ¼ duim	Mejuffrouw A van der Mieden	(Sold) fl 7 Takséra
1802/06/16	AMSCH	0022	*J. Breugel* | Een aangenaam Landzicht: ter zyde op een Heuvel, ziet men verscheiden Huislieden, verder by Geboomten, een beladen Vragtkar: het Licht is bevallig, en van een uitvoerige penceelbehandeling | *Mat:* op koper *Size:* hoog 3 ¼, breed 5 ¼ duim	[Merrem]	(Sold) fl 2 Wed Achtienhoven
1802/09/06	AMSCH	0008	*J. Breughel* | Een Boschgezicht met een Rivier doorsnéden, en met Beeldjes gestoffeerd | *Mat:* op paneel *Size:* hoog 17, breed 16 duim	Mevrouw Achtienhoven	(Sold) fl 3 Gruiter

1802/09/06	AMSCH	0009	*J. Breughel* | Een Brabandsch gestoffeerd Landschap	B	(Sold) fl 0:10 Van Iperen
1802/09/06	AMSCH	0010	*J. Breughel* | Een dito [Brabandsch gestoffeerd] dito [Landschap] | *Size:* hoog 5, breed 5 duim	J	(Sold) fl 1 A Schotte
1802/09/06	AMSCH	0011	*J. Breughel* | Twee Brabandsche Landschappen; ryk gestoffeerd | *Mat:* op koper	J	(Sold) fl 1:15 Baur
1802/09/21	UTHDG	0013	*J. Breugel* | Een Brabandsch Dorp, Land- en Watergezigt, zeer rijk, met eene menigte fraaije Beeldjes, Beestjes, Rijtuigen enz. gestoffeerd, alles uitvoerig | *Mat:* op koper *Size:* hoog 10, breed 14 ½ duimen		(Bought In) fl 8:10
1802/12/13	AMSCH	0019	*J. Breugel* | In een aangenaam Landschap met verscheide Woningen, ziet men op de voorgrond, verscheide Beeldjes by eenige Koopgoederen, uitvoerig en zonagtig gepenceelt | *Mat:* op koper *Size:* hoog 4 ½, breed 6 duim	Schley [for] Lauwers	(Sold) fl 0:10 L Pakker
1802/12/13	AMSCH	0020	*J. Breugel* | Twee stuks Berghagtige gestoffeerde Landschappen, verbeeldende van ter zyde te zien twee Mans hoofden, fix geschilderd | *Mat:* op paneel *Size:* yder hoog 22, breed 29 duim	Yver	(Sold) fl 1:15 L Pakker
1802/12/13	AMSCH	0021	*J. Breugel* | Twee stuks Brabandse Landschappen ryk gestoffeerd | *Size:* hoog 15 ½, breed 21 duim	Pruyssenaar [for] A	(Sold) fl 3 Ijver
1803/04/18	HGBAK	0009	*de Fluweele Breugel* | Een Kabinetstukje zynde een Boeren vreugd, vol gewoel van dansende en gastereerenden Boeren en Boerinnen met veel bywerk, zeer kragtig en ryk van Ordonantie, door de de Fluweele Breugel, op koper, hoog 12 breed 15 d. vergulde lyst [Schilderyen in Olyverf] | *Mat:* in olyverf op koper *Size:* hoog 12 breed 15 duim *Notes:* The bracketed information in the title appears above lot 1 and refers to lots 1 to 48.	Johan Pieter Reigersman [or others]	(Unknown)
1803/04/20	AMSCH	0014	*Breugel. (J.)* | Een Winter, verbeeldende een Boere Dorp, alwaar de Krygslieden bézig zyn de Boeren te Plunderen; vol gewoel en meesterlyk gepenceeld [Un Hyver ou est representé le pillage d'un bourg rempli de figures, bien traité.] | *Mat:* op paneel *Size:* hoog 30, breed 41 duim	Maria Magdalena van Sluypwyk, gravinne van Moens	(Sold) fl 2:5 Mensard
1804/04/28	LNDLS	0017	*J. Breugel* | Een Watergezicht met vaartuigen met volk, benevens een heuvel, met veel stoffagie van beelden, extra uitvoerig behandelt, door J. Breugel, op koper | *Mat:* op koper *Size:* hoog 10 ½, breed 13 ½ duim	[Abraham Delfos] [or others]	(Bought In) fl 24:5
1804/05/07	AMSCH	0024	*Breughell. (J) de Fluweele* | Een Brabandsch Dorpgezicht, ryk gestoffeerd met een meenigte van Lieden, Paarden, Karren eenige Vée met hunne Hoeders, enz.; verders by eenige Wooningen by Geboomte een alleraangenaamst verschiet; dit stukje is alleruitvoerigst gepenceeld | *Mat:* op paneel *Size:* hoog 10, breed 14 duim	Roos [for] A	(Sold) fl 18 Van der Schley [for] A[=Putte]
1804/10/16	DLOND	0039	*Jan Breughel* | Twee Landschappen, onderwerp als van de vorige. Deux Paysages, sujet comme des precedens | *This Lot:* Een Landschap *Mat:* op doek *Size:* hoog 7, breed 8 *Notes:* Lots 39 and 40 were printed in the catalogue as one item.		(Unknown)
1804/10/16	DLOND	0040	*Jan Breughel* | Twee Landschappen, onderwerp als van de vorige. Deux Paysages, sujet comme des precedens | *This Lot:* Een Landschap *Mat:* op doek *Size:* hoog 7, breed 8 *Notes:* Lots 39 and 40 were printed in the catalogue as one item.		(Unknown)
1804/10/16	DLOND	0041	*Jan Breughel* | Dode Visschen, Vogelen enz. Des Poissons, Oiseaux &c. morts | *Mat:* op paneel *Size:* hoog 6, breed 8		(Unknown)
1804/10/16	DLOND	0042	*Jan Breughel* | Twee Landschapjens, het ene de Kruisdraging en het andere de Kruissiging. Deux Paysages, l'un repres. J. C. mené au Calvaire, l'autre le Crucifiement | *Mat:* op koper *Size:* hoog 4, breed 7		(Unknown)
1804/10/16	DLOND	0043	*Jan Breughel* | Een Landschap. Paysage | *Mat:* op koper *Size:* hoog 15, breed 24		(Unknown)
1804/10/16	DLOND	0044	*Jan Breughel* | Uts[a] [Een Landschap. Paysage] | *Mat:* op koper *Size:* hoog 19, breed 28		(Unknown)
1805/07/03	AMSCH	0007	*Breugel. de Fluweele* | Twee stuks aangename Land- en Dorpgezichten, met Boere Woningen, Kerkgebouwen, en een ménigte stoffagie van vrolyke, dansende en andere Beeldjes, Post- en Vragtwagens enz. beide zeer uitvoerig gepenceeld | *Mat:* op koper *Size:* yder hoog 10, breed 13 duim	R[oos]	(Sold) fl 50 L Pakker
1805/07/03	AMSCH	0064	*J. Breughel* | Twee stuks bevallige Dorpgezichten, zynde een Zomer en een Winter, byde met Geboomte en Rivieren, ryk gestoffeerd met Landlieden, Paarden, Wagens, Vrachtgoederen, enz.; beide uitvoerig en zonachtig behandeld | *Mat:* op paneel *Size:* hoog 23, breed 32 duim	V[inkeles]	(Bought In) fl 28
1805/07/03	AMSCH	0065	*J. Breughel* | Een Dorpgezicht met een Rivier doorsnéden, waarin Vaartuigen en Beeldjes; als de voorgaande op Paneel | *Mat:* op paneel *Size:* hoog 5, breed 6 duim	C	(Sold) fl 3:5 J Yver
1805/07/10	AMSCH	0010	*J. Breugel* | Een bevallig Boom- en Duinryk Landschapje, met stoffagie van Beeldjes, Waagens, enz. uitvoerig en fraay gepenceeld | *Mat:* op paneel *Size:* hoog 9, breed 12 duim	V[inkeles] [for] G	(Sold) fl 6:10 Tozelli
1805/12/16	AMSCH	0008	*J. Breugel* | Een Brabandsch Dorpgezigt, op het Land verscheide stoffagie, zoo ook in het Water een Schuit met Beeldjes; uitvoerig op Koper | *Mat:* op koper *Size:* hoog 11, breed 16 duim	V	(Sold) fl 4 Rookmans

1805/12/16	AMSCH	0009	*J. Breugel* | Een dito [Brabandsch] Dorpgezicht, in alles als de voorgaande | *Mat:* op paneel *Size:* hoog 10, breed 13 duim	V	(Sold) fl 2 v der Schley [for] A
1805/12/16	AMSCH	0010	*J. Breugel* | Een dito [Brabandsch Dorpgezigt], mede als de vorige | *Mat:* op koper *Size:* hoog 4, breed 6 ½ duim *Notes:* It is unclear what "dito" refers to in the title.	V	(Sold) fl 1:10 Muller
1806/05/05	AMSCH	0022	*J. Breughel* | Twee stuks Boschgezichten, ryk gestoffeerd met Jagers en Honden; breed en bevallig gepenceeld door J. Breughel | *Mat:* op paneel *Size:* hoog 8, breed 6 ½ duim	E	(Sold) fl 6:15 van Iperen
1806/05/05	AMSCH	0023	*J. Breughel* | Twee stuks Dorpgezichten aan stille waters, ryk gestoffeerd met Beeldjes, Woningen, Schepen, Vrachtkarren enz.; beiden zeer delicaat behandeld door denzelven [J. Breughel] | *Mat:* koper op paneel *Size:* yder hoog 8, breed 8 duim	E	(Sold) fl 15 Mensard
1806/08/13	AMSCH	0015	*Breugel. (J.)* | Twee stuks, zynde een Zomer en een Winter, beide Brabandsche Landschappen en Dorpgezichten, de Zomer gestoffeerd met een Postwagen en andere Reizigers te paard en te voet; de Winter met Schaatsenryders en andere Beelden; beide van een meesterlyke schildering | *Mat:* op doek *Size:* Ieder hoog 40, breed 64 duim	Roos	(Sold) fl 50 Schumacher
1806/08/13	AMSCH	0016	*Breugel. (J.)* | Een bevallig Boomryk Brabandsch Landzicht, gestoffeerd met verscheiden reizende lieden, zoo te Paard als te Voet, ter zyde vertoont zich een waterbeekje; zonachtig en van een alleruitvoerigste penceelsbehandeling | *Mat:* op paneel *Size:* hoog 12, breed 17 duim	Roos	(Sold) fl 18 Th Spaan
1806/08/13	AMSCH	0017	*Breugel (J.)* | Een Brabandsch Landschap, met zwaar opgaand geboomte en gebouwen, gestoffeerd met Postwagens, Lieden te paard enz.; delicaat en uitvoerig gepenceeld | *Mat:* op koper *Size:* hoog 9, breed 11 ½ duim	Vinkeles [for] G[ruyter]	(Sold) fl 7 Th Spaan
1806/08/13	AMSCH	0018	*Breugel. (J.)* | Twee stuks bevallige Zomer- en Wintergezichtjes; ryk gestoffeerd en fraai behandeld | *Mat:* op koper *Size:* Ieder hoog 4, breed 5 duim	Vinkeles [for] D	(Sold) fl 2 Yver
1806/08/20	HGBSM	0073	*J. Breugel* | Een Landschapje uitvoerig geschilderd | *Mat:* op paneel *Size:* hoog 5 ¾, breed 8 duim	Macalester Loup [or others]	(Sold) fl 8 Zwartsman
1806/08/20	HGBSM	0074	*J. Breugel* | Een uitgestrekt Landschap, gestoffeerd met eene menigte kleine Figuurtjes, uitvoerig geschilderd door J. Breugel | companion to lot 75 *Mat:* op paneel *Size:* hoog 9, breed 14 duim	Macalester Loup [or others]	(Sold) fl 9:5 for lots 74 & 75. Gram
1806/08/20	HGBSM	0075	*J. Breugel* | Een dito [uitgestrekt Landschap] wederga, zijnde een Winter insgelijks gestoffeerd | companion to lot 74	Macalester Loup [or others]	(Sold) fl 9:5 for lots 74 & 75. Gram
1807/04/00	LNDLS	0014	*Jan of de Fluele Breugel* | Een Land- en Watergezigt; ter regterzijde ziet men eenige heeren en juffers, verder werkende en handeldrijvende persoonen bij een hoogte daar een molen op staat, een vaartuig met volk schijnt aan land te komen, voorts meer bijwerk en in 't verschiet een stads gezigt; alleruitvoerigst op koper geschilderd, door Jan of de Fluele [sic] Breugel | *Mat:* op koper *Size:* hoog 10 en een half, breed 13 en een half duim	[Abraham Delfos] [or others]	(Unknown)
1807/06/10	HGBSM	0014	*Jan of de Fluele Breugel* | Een Land- en Watergezigt; ter regterzijde ziet men eenige heeren en juffers, verder werkende en handeldrijvende persoonen bij een hoogte daar een molen op staat, een vaartuig met volk schijnt aan land te komen, voorts meer bijwerk en in 't verschiet een stads gezigt; alleruitvoerigst op koper geschilderd | *Mat:* op koper *Size:* hoog 10 ½, breed 13 ½ duim	Abraham Delfos [or others]	(Sold) fl 5:15 Tessier
1807/06/10	HGBSM	0014a	*Jan of de Fluele Breugel* | Een dito [Land- en Watergezigt] Landschapje met veel Figuurtjes zeer uitvoerig | *Mat:* op paneel *Size:* hoog 4 ½, breet 6 ½ duim	Abraham Delfos [or others]	(Sold) fl 3 de Gelder
1808/06/06	RMRIJ	0021	*Breugel. (Fluweelen)* | Een Land en Watergezigtje, vol Schepen en Beelden: in zijne gewone uitvoerige manier behandeld. Eene wedergade, in alles als boven [Paysage prés d'un village Flamand au bord d'une Rivière, rempli de figures et autres objets. Très fini et de la meilleure qualité. Un pendant dans le même genre et égal en mérite au précédent] | *Mat:* op koper *Size:* Twee stukjes. Hoog 5 ½, en breed 8 duim *Loc:* Amsterdam, Nederland. Rijksmuseum. (A66 & A67)	Gerrit van der Pot, Heer van Groeneveld	(Sold) fl 180 Johs Eck en Zoon [for] le Roi
1808/08/23	AMSCH	0015	*Breugel. (J.)* | Twee stuks Brabandsche Dorp-gezichten, beide rijk gestoffeerd met Postwagens, Vragtkarren, gaande en rustende Huislieden en andere bijwerk; uitvoerig en fraai gepenceeld | *Mat:* op koper *Size:* Ieder hoog 10, breed 11 duim	C	(Sold) fl 33 Swanenburg
1808/08/23	AMSCH	0016	*Breugel. (J.)* | Een Brabandsch Landschap, gestoffeert op den voorgrond met twee Heeren te Paard, ter zijde eenige Vragtwagens en andere figuuren; plaisant en uitvoerig behandeld | *Mat:* op koper *Size:* hoog 7, breed 10 duim	C	(Sold) fl 4:5 Jan Spaan [or] Pakker
1808/08/23	AMSCH	0017	*Breugel. (J.)* | Een stille Rivier, ter zijde een Boschgezigt, gestoffeerd met verscheide Beeldjes; fiks gepenceeld | *Mat:* op koper *Size:* hoog 6, breed 7 duim	C	(Sold) fl 2 Dupré
1808/08/23	AMSCH	0018	*Breugel. (J.)* | Twee stuks, het eene verbeeld een Brabands Landschap met Beeldjes en Vragtwagen gestoffeert; het andere een Boschgezigt, met de dood van Adonis, welke door twee Jongelingen ondersteund word; beide uitvoerig en fraai van behandeling | *Mat:* op paneel *Fmt:* rond *Size:* hoog 8, breed 8 duim	C	(Sold) fl 4:5 Dupré

<table>
<tr><td>1809/04/22</td><td>AMYVR</td><td>0019</td><td>*J. Breugel* | Twee stuks: in een Brabandsch Landschap ziet men twee Postwagens met Paarden en een menigte Beeldjes; de wederga verbeeld een Winter, mede als de voorgaande | *Mat:* op paneel *Size:* hoog 10, breed 13 duim</td><td>de Bruin</td><td>(Sold) fl 9 C S Roos</td></tr>
<tr><td>1809/04/22</td><td>AMYVR</td><td>0020</td><td>*J. Breugel* | Een gestoffeerd Wintertje | *Mat:* op paneel *Size:* hoog 6, breed 9 duim</td><td>Juff[r] Julikker</td><td>(Sold) fl 0:6 van der Schley</td></tr>
<tr><td>1809/05/26</td><td>HADAA</td><td>0036</td><td>*De Fluelle Breugel* | Twee stuks zeer uitvoerige Landschapjes, rijk van stoffagie | *Mat:* op paneel</td><td>Mejuffrouw de Wed David Heemskerk [or others]</td><td>(Unknown)</td></tr>
<tr><td>1809/09/06</td><td>AMSCH</td><td>0003</td><td>*Breugel (De Fluweele)* | Twee stuks aangename Brabandsche Dorpgezichten; rijk gestoffeerd met een menigte Beelden, Paarden, Wagens, Vaartuigen enz. alleruitvoerigst behandeld | *Mat:* op koper *Size:* ieder hoog 11, breed 15 duim</td><td>Johannes Caudri</td><td>(Sold) fl 82 Izaac Smit</td></tr>
<tr><td>1810/03/27</td><td>RMCNL</td><td>0051</td><td>*de Fluweele van Breugel* | Een dito klein Landschapje, netjes behandeld | *Mat:* op koper *Notes:* It is unclear what "dito" refers to in the title.</td><td></td><td>(Unknown)</td></tr>
<tr><td>1810/05/22</td><td>AMSCH</td><td>0005</td><td>*Breugel. (De Fluweele)* | Een Brabandsch Dorpgezicht, gestoffeerd met eene menigte Beelden, Paarden en Karren; zijnde uitvoerig geschilderd | *Mat:* op paneel *Size:* hoog 10, breed 14 duim</td><td>Johannes van de Putte Nicolaasz.</td><td>(Sold) fl 14:10 van der Schleij [for] Ryfsnyder</td></tr>
<tr><td>1810/06/06</td><td>RMMUY</td><td>0057</td><td>*Den Fluweelen Breugel* | Een Bloemkrans, in het Midden eene heilige Familie, uitvoerig en net behandeld. Door den Fluweelen Breugel | *Mat:* op paneel</td><td></td><td>(Unknown) fl 6:10</td></tr>
<tr><td>1810/06/06</td><td>RMMUY</td><td>0058</td><td>*Den Fluweelen Breugel* | Eene Fles met Bloemen. Door denzelven [Fluweelen Breugel] | *Mat:* op paneel</td><td></td><td>(Unknown) fl 2:10</td></tr>
<tr><td>1810/07/26</td><td>AMSCH</td><td>0092</td><td>*J. Breugel* | Een Landschap, met stoffagie van Beelden en Beesten | *Mat:* op paneel</td><td>Cassino</td><td>(Sold) fl 0:6 Lohuijs</td></tr>
<tr><td>1810/07/26</td><td>AMSCH</td><td>0111</td><td>*J. Breugel* | Een Brabandsch Landgezigt, met Reizigers gestoffeerd | *Mat:* op paneel</td><td>Cassino</td><td>(Sold) fl 2 Immos</td></tr>
<tr><td>1810/07/26</td><td>AMSCH</td><td>0112</td><td>*J. Breugel* | Twee ronde Landschapjes | *Mat:* op paneel *Fmt:* rond</td><td>Cassino</td><td>(Bought In) fl 0:18</td></tr>
<tr><td>1810/08/06</td><td>AMSCH</td><td>0022</td><td>*Breugel (J.)* | Een Strand- en Zeegezigt, met eene menigte Beeldjes, Paarden, Vaartuigen en andere voorwerpen gestoffeerd. Helder en zuiver van schildering | *Mat:* op koper *Size:* hoog 11, breed 14 duimen</td><td>C</td><td>(Sold) fl 25:10 Burtin</td></tr>
<tr><td>1810/10/11</td><td>AMSCH</td><td>0016</td><td>*J. Breugel* | Een Bergachtig Landschapje, met eene Rivier doorsneden | *Mat:* op koper *Size:* hoog 5 ½, breed 7 ½ duimen</td><td>C</td><td>(Sold) fl 1 Posthumus</td></tr>
<tr><td>1810/10/11</td><td>AMSCH</td><td>0017</td><td>*J. Breugel* | Twee stuks Landschappen met Geboomte en Woningen, achterwaards Visschers bij een Water | *Mat:* op paneel *Size:* hoog 7, breed 9 duimen</td><td>C</td><td>(Sold) fl 3 Posthumus</td></tr>
<tr><td>1810/10/11</td><td>AMSCH</td><td>0018</td><td>*J. Breugel* | Een Brabansch Landschap, met Boerenwoningen en Dorpen in 't verschiet, gestoffeerd met eene menigte vrolijke dansende en andere Lieden | *Mat:* op paneel *Size:* hoog 16, breed 21 duimen</td><td>C</td><td>(Sold) fl 4 Posthumus</td></tr>
<tr><td>1810/10/11</td><td>AMSCH</td><td>0019</td><td>*J. Breugel* | Een Landschap met Gebouwen, Geboomte en Stoffage van Beelden | *Mat:* op koper</td><td>Y</td><td>(Sold) fl 2:15 Gruiter</td></tr>
<tr><td>1810/10/11</td><td>AMSCH</td><td>0229</td><td>*J. Breugel* | Twee Brabandsche Land- en Watergezigten, uitvoerig | *Mat:* op koper</td><td>A</td><td>(Sold) fl 2 L Pakker</td></tr>
</table>

Brueghel, Jan (the elder) (and Balen, H. (I))

<table>
<tr><td>1801/05/11</td><td>AMSCH</td><td>0013</td><td>*Van Balen; Breughel* | De historie van David en Abigaël, zynde een ryken Ordinantie, van verscheiden beelden en paarden, en andere stoffagie, fraay gepenceeld | *Mat:* op paneel *Size:* hoog 22, breed 33 duim</td><td>R[oos]</td><td>(Sold) fl 40 P M Levij</td></tr>
<tr><td>1801/08/19</td><td>AMSCH</td><td>0006</td><td>*van Balen; Breugel* | In een Landschap met geboomten, vertoont zig by een Tempel van Bachus, een groote ménigte Bachanten, die Dansende en musiceerende zig vermaaken; ryk gestoffeert met verder bywerk, zeer uitvoerig op Koper geschilderd | *Mat:* op koper *Size:* hoog 11, breed 16 duim</td><td>Van Forreest</td><td>(Sold) fl 22:10 Wed Achtienhoven</td></tr>
<tr><td>1802/06/16</td><td>AMSCH</td><td>0021</td><td>*Breugel; van Baalen* | Een fraai Egyptisch Landschap, met verscheiden soorten van Bloemen, op de voorgrond Maria met het Kindje: alles zeer uitvoerig en helder gepenceeld | *Mat:* op doek *Size:* hoog 14 ½, breed 18 ½ duim</td><td>[Merrem]</td><td>(Sold) fl 39 Pruijssenaar</td></tr>
<tr><td>1802/09/29</td><td>AMSCH</td><td>0012</td><td>*Hk. van Baalen; J. Breugel* | Een Historiëelen, hoog 10 ½, breed 8 ¼ duim. Paneel. Den God Pan word in dit Schilderstukje verbeeld, als vervolgende Syrinx, tot de Rivier Ladon, waarin zy zig werpende, in een Riet herschept wierd; de delicaate Penceelbehandeling, waarmeede dit Stukje is uitgevoerd, is zeer fraai en meesterlyk [Dans ce sujet de la Fable, Le Dieu Pan est représenté, comme poursuivant Syrinx, jusqu'au Fleuve Ladon, entre les bras du quel sejetta [sic] cette Nimphe, ou elle fut metamorphosée en Roseau. – La précision du dessin, un Pinceau délicat, caractére des beaux ouvrages de ces deux artistes, se remarquent dans ce petit Tableau.] | *Mat:* op paneel *Size:* hoog 10 ½, breed 8 ¼ duim</td><td>[Labouchere?]</td><td>(Sold) fl 8:10 Gruiter</td></tr>
<tr><td>1803/07/18</td><td>AMSCH</td><td>0005</td><td>*Balen, (J. van) [Baelen (H. van)]; J. Breughel* | Een Bachenaal met verscheide Nimphen, Saters en vliegende Kinderen, welke met Bloemen en Vrugten zich vermaaken. Het Landschap is even uitvoerig en delicaat als de Beelden gepenceeld [Une bacchanale. Deux Nimphes recevant des fruits & des fleurs de deux Genies & d'un troisieme voltigent [sic] en air.</td><td>Maria Theresia Andrioli</td><td>(Sold) fl 27:10 Coclers</td></tr>
</table>

			Vèrs la droite sont deux faunes. Breugel à orné ce tableau par un paysage & de jolis animaux formant un ensemble charment [sic], surtout par la belle fonte de couleur de la carnation des Nimphes.] | *Mat:* op koper *Size:* hoog 12, breed 15 duim *Notes:* The first artist's name differs in the Dutch and French editions of the catalogue.		
1803/09/07	AMSCH	0009	*van Balen; Breugel* | Een Feest van Céres, zy zit op een pragtige Wagen, en word geleid van een menigte Beelden en Boeren, fraay op Paneel [Une fête de Cérés ; la déesse est montée sur un char magnifique et entourée d'une quantité de figures et de paysans ; beau tableau] | *Mat:* op paneel *Size:* hoog 14, breed 22 duim	Smidt	(Sold) fl 4:5 Gruiter
1803/09/07	AMSCH	0010	*van Balen; Breugel* | Een Landschap met veel Geboomte, gestoffeerd op de voorgrond met verscheide dansende kinderen, verder andere die musiseeren; uitvoerig op Koper geschilderd [Paysage avec beaucoup d'arbres ; relevé sur le devant par des groupes d'enfans, dont les uns dansent et les autres font de la musique] | *Mat:* op koper *Size:* hoog 14, breed 11 duim	Smidt	(Bought In) fl 11
1803/09/07	AMSCH	0011	*van Balen; Breugel* | Een zeer uitvoerig Rhyngezicht, gestoffeerd met Diana en hare Nimphen [Une très belle vue du Rhin ; animée par Diane et ses Nymphes] | *Mat:* op koper *Size:* hoog 11, breed 17 duim	Smidt	(Sold) fl 4 Gruiter
1804/08/02	BDAN	0004	*Flaelen Breugel; H. van Baelen* | Een Goode-Feest, vol gewoel van Beelden, schoon in Couleur, alles kunstig en uitvoerig geschildert | *Mat:* op koper *Size:* b. 19 d. h. 14 en 1 half d.	J G Calckberner	(Unknown)
1804/08/08	AMSCH	0013	*J. Breugel; H. van Baalen* | De Maagd Maria, met het Kind Jezus op de schoot, om dezelve een Feston met Bloemen; meesterlyk gepenceeld | *Mat:* op paneel *Size:* hoog 12, br. 9 ½ duim	Vink[eles] [for] K[=Gruyter?]	(Sold) fl 2 Gruyter
1805/10/09	HGBSM	0009	*Breugel; van Baalen* | Een thuin gezigt met een bad, waarin Susanna zit te baden, agter haar de twee ouden, benevens een ryke fontein, zeer uitvoerig | *Mat:* op koper *Size:* hoog 18 ½ breet 26 ½ duim	T H van Willigen [or others]	(Sold) fl 14 Ph Meij
1806/08/20	HGBSM	0091	*J. Breugel; H. van Balen* | Een Landschap, waarin een voorhof, beplant met veelerhande soort van bloemen, bij eene fontein, zijn Eenden, Paauwen en andere Vogels, in het zelven is verbeeld Christus, in de gedaante van een Hovenier; het Landschap, Vogels en ander bijwerk, is konstig en uitvoerig geschilderd, door J. Breugel, en de figuuren, door H. van Balen, op paneel uit een stuk | *Mat:* op paneel *Size:* hoog 24, breed 34 duim	Macalester Loup [or others]	(Sold) fl 30 Zwartsman
1807/06/10	HGBSM	0154	*H. van Baalen; J. Breugel* | Het Bad van Diana, met haare Nimphen bezig zijnde met baden, de voorgrond gestoffeerd met veelerhande dood wild enz., zeer uitvoerig gepenceeld, de figuuren door H. van Baalen, en het Landschap en bijwerk door J. Breugel, zijnde van het beste tijd der beide Meesters | *Mat:* op paneel *Size:* hoog 22 ½, breed 31 duim	Abraham Delfos [or others]	(Sold) fl 62 S T
1807/08/26	AMSCH	0017	*den Fluweelen Breugel; P. van Baalen* | In dit Tafreel, vertoont zig in een aangenaam Landschap, de ontdekking van Erichtonius, zoon van Vulcaan, in een korfje geleegen, dat de dochteren van Cecrops door Pallas was aanbevolen hetzelve zorgvuldig te bewaaren, zonder het te bezigtigen; de Beeldjes zyn wel geteekend, bevallig van koloriet, het licht en bruin doed eene goede werking, en is van eene uitvoerige penceel-behandeling, door den Fluweelen Breugel en P. van Baalen, op Koper, hoog 12, breed 9 duim; dit stukje is een der fraaiste die door beide deeze Meesters vervaardigd zyn | *Mat:* op koper *Size:* hoog 12, breed 9 duim *Notes:* The artist's name was given as "P. van Baalen" but we have assumed this is an error.	Helsdinge	(Bought In) fl 42
1808/08/23	AMSCH	0011	*Baalen (H. vam); J. Breugel* | Dit kunstrijk Tafereel vertoont in een heuvelagtig Landschap, de Reiniging der Joodsche Mannen en Vrouwen, verzelt van verscheide Kinderen, alle in bijzondere beweegingen; dit stuk is rijk geordoneert met een groote meenigte Beelden, bevallig van schikking, aangenaam van koloriet en licht, en meesterlijk fraai en uitvoerig gepenceeld | *Mat:* op paneel *Size:* hoog 37, breed 54 duim	C	(Bought In) fl 50
1808/08/23	AMSCH	0012	*Breugel (J); van Baalen* | Deeze kapitaale Ordonnantie verbeeld de Dooping van Christus, waar bij verscheiden Vrouwen met Kinderen en andere Beelden; uitmuntend en krachtig van schildering | *Mat:* op paneel *Size:* hoog 59, breed 76 duim	C	(Bought In) fl 61
1809/04/17	AMSCH	0013	*Breugel; H. van Baalen* | Een boomrijk Landschap, op de voorgrond bij een Bad, zien men Diana met haare Nimphen, in 't verschiet Actéon; uitvoerig door Breugel en H. van Baalen | *Mat:* op koper *Size:* hoog 8, breed 10 duim	A	(Sold) fl 2:15 Gruyter
1809/06/13	AMSCH	0029	*Breugel; van Baalen* | In een Landschap, vertoond zig de Godin Céres, zittende op een pragtige Waagen, verzeld van eenige Lieden die de Staasie volgen, uitvoerig | *Mat:* op paneel *Size:* hoog 14, breed 22 duim	[Gruyter?]	(Sold or Bought In) fl 3:15 Gruiter
1810/06/06	RMMUY	0175	*van Baalen; Breugel* | Adam en Eva in 't Paradijs, met veel cierlijk bijwerk | *Mat:* op koper		(Sold) fl 9 V Leen
1810/07/26	AMSCH	0003	*Baalen (H. van); J. Breugel* | Een Godemaaltijd, waarbij eene menigte Vrouwen, Kinderen enz. Meesterlijk en uitvoerig | *Mat:* op paneel *Size:* hoog 13, breed 15 duimen	Cassino	(Sold) fl 30 C S Roos
1810/08/06	AMSCH	0003	*Baalen (H.van); J. Breugel* | Deze rijke Ordonnantie vertoont in een heuvelachtig Landschap de reiniging der Joodsche Mannen en Vrouwen, waarbij verscheidene Kinderen, alle in bijzondere bewegingen. Dit stuk is	B	(Sold) fl 50 Josi [for] Burtyn

			bevallig van koloriet, uitvoerig en fraai gepenceeld | *Mat:* op paneel *Size:* hoog 37, breed 54 duimen		
1810/08/06	AMSCH	0004	*Baalen (H. van); J. Breugel* | Eene Bijbel-Ordonnantie, voorstellende de Dooping van Christus, waarbij verscheidene Vrouwen met Kinderen, en andere Beelden. Uitvoerig en krachtig van schildering | *Mat:* op paneel *Size:* hoog 59, breed 76 duimen	B	(Bought In) fl 15
1810/10/11	AMSCH	0015	*Breugel; Van Balen* | In een Boschachtig Landschap ziet men bij een heldere Beek de Jagtgodin Diana, verzeld van hare Nimfen, in 't verschiet Actéon; delikaat gepenseeld | *Mat:* op koper *Size:* hoog 8, breed 10 duimen	[Gruyter?]	(Sold) fl 10 T Spaan
			Brueghel, Jan (the elder) (and Bril, P.)		
1808/08/23	AMSCH	0014	*Breugel (J.); P. Bril* | Een hoog bergachtig Landschap, met een Rivier doorsneeden, gestoffeert met een beladen Vrachtwagen, Arbeidslieden, gaande en rustende Reisigers, natuurlijk behandeld | *Mat:* op paneel *Size:* hoog 19, breed 33 duim	C	(Sold) fl 1 Boelhouwer
1810/07/26	AMSCH	0093	*J. Breugel; P. Bril* | Een Landschap met Beelden | *Mat:* op paneel	Cassino	(Sold) fl 1:5 Geld
			Brueghel, Jan (the elder) (and Momper, J. (II))		
1804/08/02	BDAN	0018	*J. Momper; Breughel* | Twee bergachtige Landschappen, vol gewoel, van de besten door deezen Meester gemaakt | *Mat:* op paneel *Size:* b. 24 en een half d. h. 17 d.	J G Calckberner	(Unknown)
1804/08/02	BDAN	0038	*Momper; Breugel* | Een schoon bergachtig Landschap, rykelyk gestoffeert | *Mat:* op paneel *Size:* b. 25 d. h. 17 en een half d.	J G Calckberner	(Unknown)
1805/07/10	AMSCH	0011	*Breugel; Momper* | Een besneeuwd Brabandsch Dorpgezicht, ryk gestoffeerd met Wagens, Paarden en Beelden; natuurlyk en fiks | *Size:* hoog 18, breed 29 duim	V[inkeles] [for] M	(Sold) fl 14 Lafontaine
1805/10/09	HGBSM	0092	*Momper; J. Breugel* | Een landschap door Momper, gestoffeerd, door J. Breugel | *Mat:* op paneel *Size:* hoog 18 breet 27 duim	T H van Willigen [or others]	(Sold) fl 3:8 Carré
1807/04/00	LNDLS	0028	*Momper; Breugel* | Een helder bergagtig Landschap met geboomte, ter regterzijde jagerspaarden, eu [sic] jagthonden, gevolgd van andere lieden, en beladen ezels, en heeren te paard | *Mat:* op paneel *Size:* hoog 30, breed 42 duim	[Abraham Delfos] [or others]	(Unknown)
1807/06/10	HGBSM	0028	*Momper; Breugel* | Een helder bergagtig Landschap met geboomte ter regterzijde jagerspaarden, en jagthonden, gevolgd van andere lieden, en beladen ezels en heeren te paard | *Mat:* op paneel *Size:* hoog 30, breed 42 duim	Abraham Delfos [or others]	(Sold) fl 2 de Gelder
1807/08/26	AMSCH	0128	*Momper; Breugel* | Twee stuks, verbeeldende Zomer en Winter. Den eene vertoont een Brabandsch Landschap, met Geboomte, op den voorgrond rydende Postwagens en vrolyke Huislieden, verders Graanlanden en een aangenaam verschiet. De wederga verbeeld een heuvelachtig Landgezigt, met besneeuwde Daken en Wegen, by dor en ander Geboomte; gestoffeerd met wandelende en rustende Lieden, op de bevrozen Rivier verscheiden Schaatsenryders, in het verschiet en Stadzigt beide natuurlyk, en uitvoerig van penceelsbehandeling | *Mat:* op paneel *Size:* ieder hoog 9 ½, breed 13 ½ duim	v d Schley [for] L	(Sold) fl 7:5 du Pree
1808/08/23	AMSCH	0196	*Momper; Breägel* | Een natuurlijk Wintergezicht, met stoffagie van Beeldjes	[Gruyter?]	(Sold) fl 3 L Pakker
1809/06/13	AMSCH	0216	*Momper; Breugel* | Een Wintergezigt met Schaatserijders gestoffeerd, door Momper en Breugel	E	(Sold) fl 0:6 L Pakker
			Brueghel, Jan (the elder) (and Rottenhammer, H. (I))		
1801/08/19	AMSCH	0096	*Rottenhamer; Breugel* | Een zinryke Ordenantie, in een Boomryk Landschap, met een stille Rivier, op de voorgrond ziet men drie Nimphen, een Net met verschillende Visschen, uitschudden, verders op de voorgrond leggen viervoetige Dieren en verscheide Vogels, waar by eenige staande Jagthonden; meesterlyk en uitvoerig op Paneel geschilderd | *Mat:* op paneel *Size:* hoog 25, breed 32 duim	W Wynen	(Sold) fl 19 Gruiter
1803/07/18	AMSCH	0042	*Rottenhamer. (J.); J. Breugel* | Het Paradys alwaar God den Vader in zyn Glorie aan Adam en Eva zyn bevelen geeft, welke zy met veel aandagt aanhooren, ter linkerzyde ziet men hun van den verboden Boom plukken, in het verschiet worden zy door een Engel verjaagd: op de voorgrond twee Tygers en een groot aantal andere Gediertens, alles is zeer uitvoerig door deeze beide voortreffelyke Meesters gepenceeld [Ce tableau est le Paradis terrestre, ou le Pere éternel accompagné de sa gloire préscrit à Adam & à Eve sa volonté, qu'ils ecoutent en attitude de prosternation. Au devant & un peu vèrs la gauche est assi [sic] le Pere Adam prenant de la main de sa moitié une pomme de l'arbre fatal ! tandis qu'elle a le bras levé pour en ceuillir davantage. Dans l'eloignement sont representés d'autres épisodes de la génèse, mais par de petittes figures. Le paysage de Breugel richement boisé & très varié, est surtout enrichi d'une multitude de quadrupédes & d'oiseaux d'une finesse d'execution admirable. Quant aux figures elles sont d'un excellent dessin, & d'une fonte de couleur si belle ! que l'Albane même ne les desavoueroit pas.] | *Mat:* op paneel *Size:* hoog 23, breed 37 duim	Maria Theresia Andrioli	(Sold) fl 125 Thys
1810/06/06	RMMUY	0059	*Rottenhamer; Breugel* | Eene heilige Familie, zeer uitvoerig | *Mat:* op koper		(Unknown) fl 16

Brueghel, Jan (the elder) (and Rubens)

1806/08/13	AMSCH	0150	*Rubbens. (P. P.); J. Breugel* | Dit kunstryk Tafreel steld voor: de drie Gratien, door drie bevallige naakte Vrouwen-beelden in een Landschap, welke een korf met bloemen omhoog ophouden; achter hun is een rood kleed aan de boomen vastgehegt, waartegen de voorwerpen helder uitkomen; het Landschap en de Bloemen, zyn door J. Breugel, de ordinantie en couleur der Vrouwen is uitmuntend schoon, en van een uitvoerige penceelbehandeling; dit heerlyk Cabinetstukje, is een der uitmuntendste, welke van beide deeze beroemden Meesters bekend zyn | *Mat:* op koper *Size:* hoog 18, breed 13 ½ duim	van der Schley	(Sold) fl 400 Jan Spaan
1806/08/13	AMSCH	0151	*Rubbens (P. P.); J. Breugel* | Een Boom- en Bergachtig Landschap, met een Rivier doorsneeden, gestoffeerd met Herders met hun Vee, kragtig van penceelsbehandeling | *Mat:* op doek *Size:* hoog 39, breed 52 duim	Roos	(Sold) fl 41 Du Pré

Brueghel, Jan (the elder) (and Steenwyck, Hend.)

1802/09/29	AMSCH	0051	*H. van Steenwyk; Fluweele Breugel* | Een Roomsche Kerk in Braband, hoog 14, breed 21 duim. Koper. Dezelve is verbeeld uit het Middenruim te zien, naar het Choor en den Hoogen Altaar, ryk gestoffeerd met een ménigte Persoonen, zoo Vrouwen als Mannen, waar onder eenige Geestelyken; ter zyde op de Voorgrond vertoond zig een Dame, met een Kindje op by de handen dragende, welke plechtig ter Doop gebragt word; by het hooge Choor werd de Ceremonie verrigt voor een Overleedene; verders ziet men verscheiden Altaaren, Orgel en Schilderstukken; de Perspectief, de vermindering van Lichten, de zuivere omtrek van Lysten en Gewelven, zyn 'er kunstig in waargenomen, en alles is van een uitvoerige Penceelbehandeling, door beide deeze Meesters [Une Eglise Catholique. Dont le point de Vue est pris de la grande nef sur le maitre autel ou l'on fait l'office des morts, parmi le nombre de belles figures de tout étàt qui ornent ce morceau, l'on distingue sur le devant un groupe portant un enfant à baptiser ; des autels, les orgues et des peintures achevent ce joli morceau dont la perspective et la gradation de lumiere sont parfaitement observés.] | *Mat:* op koper *Size:* hoog 14, breed 21 duim	D	(Sold) fl 212 Vinkeles
1810/11/07	UTWLD	0001	*H. v. Steenwijk; Breugel* | Een Kerk waarin het de perspectief wel geobserveerd is, en zeer geestig gestoffeerd zo met staande als zittende beeldjes, zijnde het licht zeer fraai genomen, en formeert een Capitale Schilderdij door H. v. Steenwijk en Breugel, op paneel, 2 voet 3 duim hoog, 3 voet 3 duim breed in een vergulde Lijst | *Mat:* op paneel *Size:* 2 voet 3 duim hoog, 3 voet 3 duim breed		(Unknown) fl 105

Brueghel, Jan (the elder) (changed to Elsteijn)

1802/05/24	HGBAK	0007	*de fluweele Breugel; Elsteijn* | Een fraay stukje, verbeeldende Maria met het Kindeke, ontfangende van Johannis ook nog een Kind zynde een druiftros, aan de voeten het lam, als ook een mand met vruchten, bloemen en kruiden, in een Landschap, door Elsteijn, hoog 12 ½ duim, breed 18 ½ duim, zwarte lyst en vergulde bies | *Size:* hoog 12 ½ duim, breed 18 ½ duim *Notes:* The artist's name was changed by hand from "de fluweele Breugel" to "Elsteijn" in the MA copy of the catalogue.	Mejuffrouw A van der Mieden	(Sold) fl 7:5 te ché

Brueghel, Jan (the elder) (manner)

1808/06/11	RMRIJ	0088	*In de manier van den Fluweelen Breugel* | Twee Brabandsche Landschappen, met veel Stoffagie, zeer net uitgevoert | *Mat:* op koper *Size:* hoog 10 ¾, breed 19 ½ duim		(Sold) fl 12:10 van Yperen

Brueghel, Pieter

1802/09/06	AMSCH	0007	*P. Breugel* | Een Wintergezicht in een Dorp, met verscheide Woningen met besneeuwde Daken en Weegen, waar in verbeeld de drie Koningen, het Kindeken aanbidden en geschenken offerende, zynde ryk gestoffeerd met andere Lieden, Lastdragende Ezels, en verder bywerk; krachtig gepenceeld, door P. Breugel, 1632 | *Mat:* op paneel *Size:* hoog 15, breed 20 duim *Inscr:* P. Breugel, 1632 (signed and dated?) *Notes:* It is unclear whether the name and date are inscribed on the painting.	Brave	(Sold) fl 2 Ph van der Schley [for] G
1803/11/30	MGBEO	0003	*P. Breugel* | Een Binnen-Vertrek verbeeldende een Vastenavond Vreugd | *Mat:* op paneel *Size:* hoog 29 duim, breed 39 duim	Samuel de Wind	(Sold) £ 0:7 Ad^n Tak
1803/12/12	AMSCH	0005	*P. Breughel* | Een Brabandsche Stad, aan een Rivier, de voorgrond gestoffeerd met een ménigte Beelden, welken ter Markt gaan, by verscheiden Visch- en Fruitverkopers; uitvoerig op Koper | *Mat:* op koper *Size:* hoog 20, breed 29 duim	D	(Sold) fl 16:10 Hijm Pakker
1804/10/16	DLOND	0045	*P. Breughel* | Een Gevegt tusschen Marodeurs en Boeren. Combat entre des Marodeurs & Paysans | *Mat:* op paneel *Size:* hoog 16, breed 22		(Unknown)
1806/10/17	MGSAN	0006	*P. Breugel* | Een Wintergezigt | *Mat:* op paneel	Gerardus Beljard	(Unknown)
1810/12/03	DOBRA	0058	*P. van Breugel* | Vier-en twintig Hollandsche Spreekwoorden, in zwarte lysten, door P. van Breugel. zeer raar		(Unknown)

Brueghel, Pieter (the younger)

1801/02/18	AMBOS	0074	*Helschen Breugel* | Een Schildery waarop diverse Helsche Furien	J Schonevelt	(Unknown)
1802/11/01	DOBRA	0038	*De Helsche Breugel* | Een St. Anthonies temtatie | *Mat:* op paneel *Size:* breed ruim 17, hoog 13 duim	Paulus van der Spyk [or others]	(Bought In) fl 1:10

1802/12/13	AMSCH	0018	*De Helsche Brengel* | Deezen Ordenantie steld voor 't Voorburg van de Hel, waar Caron, met een lading schynt aan te komen; vervolgens is dit stuk ryk gestoffeerd, van differenten zoorten van Wanschepsels en Gedrogten, en zeer uitvoerig geschilderd | *Mat:* op doek *Size:* hoog 15, breed 18 duim	Pruyssenaar [for] A	(Sold) fl 1:15 Gruiter
1809/07/25	HGBSM	0279	*De Helsche Breugel* | De Temtatie van St. Antonius | *Mat:* op paneel *Size:* hoog 5 en een half, breed 8 en een half duim	D van der Aa [or] E B ten Dall	(Sold) fl 1:18 Teissier
			Brueghel, Pieter (the younger) (manner)		
1804/08/08	AMSCH	0260	*de Helsche Breugel* | Een Stukje met Spookeryën; als de Helsche Breugel	Roos [for] O	(Sold) fl 1 Coclers
			Brugghen, Hendrick ter		
1803/04/20	AMSCH	0010	*Brugghen. (H. ter)* | Voor een Open Nis, vertoont zig een Zanger, houdende met de Linkerhand een Musicqboek en met de Regterhand als de Maat slaande; hy ziet opwaarts als in verrukking, op de Rand des Nis legt een Boek en Musicqpapier; het is kragtig en Coloriet van meesterlyk gepenceeld [Dans une embrasure se montre un Chanteur, comme en extase, d'une main il tient de la musique, & de l'autre il bat la mesure ; des accessoires de musique se voyent sur l'entablure [sic] de la niche. Ce tableau est traité avec beaucoup de force & d'eclât.] | *Mat:* op doek *Size:* hoog 41, breed 33 duim	Maria Magdalena van Sluypwyk, gravinne van Moens	(Sold) fl 68 Coclers
			Brugghen, Hendrick ter (changed from Honthorst, G.)		
1810/08/10	RMRIJ	0030	*Honthorst; H Brugge 1628* | Bachus en andere Figuren. Kloek en verdienstelijk behandelt | *Inscr:* H Brugge 1628 (signed and dated?) *Notes:* The artist's name was changed by hand from "Honthorst" to "H Brugge 1628" in the EBNP copy of the catalogue. It is unclear whether the name and date are inscribed on the painting.		(Sold) fl 1:10 [or] 60 v Ryp
			Brugman, N. [Unidentified]		
1810/10/11	AMSCH	0021	*N. Brugman* | Een hevig Gevecht tusschen Ruiterij | *Mat:* op paneel *Size:* hoog 16, breed 20 duimen	C	(Sold) fl 2:5 Posthumus
			Brukkerhoofd [Unidentified]		
1802/07/21	HGKAN	0006	*Brukkerhoofd* | Niche door Brukkerhoofd		(Unknown)
			Brussel, Hermanus van		
1808/06/13	AMSCH	0015	*Brussel (T. van)* | Twee stuks duinachtige Landschapjes met hoog geboomte, en Dorpen in het verschiet; geestig gestoffeerd met Beelden en Beesten: zijnde deze stukjes van de weinige Landschappen, die van deze Meester bekend zijn, wel de beste | *Mat:* op paneel *Size:* hoog 12 ½, breed 14 ½ duim *Notes:* The artist's name was given as "Brussel (T. van)" but we have assumed this is an error.	[Jan Tersteeg]	(Sold) fl 80 van Iperen
1809/05/26	HADAA	0023	*H. van Brussel* | Een Landschap, zijnde een Storm	Mejuffrouw de Wed David Heemskerk [or others]	(Unknown)
1809/05/26	HADAA	A0012	*H. van Brussel* | Een bevallig Landschap | *Mat:* op paneel	Mejuffrouw de Wed David Heemskerk [or others]	(Unknown)
1809/05/26	HADAA	A0013	*H. van Brussel* | Een dito [bevallig Landschap]	Mejuffrouw de Wed David Heemskerk [or others]	(Unknown)
			Brussel, Paul Theodor van		
1801/04/13	AMSCH	0009	*P.T. van Brussel* | Op een marmere Tafel, staat een cierlyke Vaas, gevuld met uitmuntend geschilderde Bloemen van allerlei zoort: een Vogelnestje met eijeren, eenige Insecten en Waterdroppen vercieren verder dit Tafreel, zo wel als het verschiet, het geen een gezicht op een Hofstede voorsteld; de behandeling is dun en behaaglyk, zynde van de beste van deezen meester | *Mat:* op paneel *Size:* hoog 28, breed 22 duim	Pierre Fouquet, junior	(Sold) fl 750 for lots 9 & 10. Wreesman
1801/04/13	AMSCH	0010	*P.T. van Brussel* | Op een marmere Tafel ligt een menigte Fruit, als witte en blaauwe Druiven, Persiken, Pruimen, Kanteloepen, Mispelen, Quépeeren, en andere smakelyke Vrugten, waarop verscheide Insecten azen, eenige Papavers, Rozen en andere Bloemen versieren voorts dit Tafreel; het geen in allen deele behandeld is als het voorgaande | *Mat:* op paneel *Size:* hoog 28, breed 22 duim	Pierre Fouquet, junior	(Sold) fl 750 for lots 9 & 10. Wreesman
1801/05/11	AMSCH	0018a	*T. van Brussel* | Eenige fraay geschakeerde Bloemen, alle zeer dun en konstig gepenceeld | *Mat:* op doek *Size:* hoog 14, breed 12 duim	P[ruyssenaar]	(Sold) fl 70 Van Iperen
1802/05/05	AMSCH	0009	*P.T. van Brussel* | Op een marmere Tafel staat een Vaas, gevuld met een menigte Bloemen, als: geele, witte en roode Roozen, Nageltakken en een menigte andere geurige Bloemen; terzyde een Vogelnestje, met Eijeren. Alles van de beste schildering, ordonnantie en couleur | companion to lot 10 *Mat:* op paneel *Size:* hoog 27, breed 21 duim	D	(Sold) fl 1150 for lots 9 & 10. B[d] Kooij
1802/05/05	AMSCH	0010	*P.T. van Brussel* | Op een marmere Tafel ziet men een menigte Fruiten, als: blaauwe en witte Druiven, Persiken, Abrikoozen, Canteloepen, Annanas, Pruimen, Bessen en andere smakelyke Vrugten; voorts, eenige Bloemen. In alles behandeld als de Voorgaande, door Dezelven; zynde een geschikte Wedergade | companion to lot 9 *Mat:* op paneel *Size:* hoog 27, breed 21 duim	D	(Sold) fl 1150 for lots 9 & 10. B[d] Kooij

1802/05/05	AMSCH	0011	*P.T. van Brussel* | Een prachtig Bloem- en Fruitstuk, zynde een ryke Ordonantie van Bloemen en smakelyke Vrugten: van Druiven en Canteloepen, een Vogelnestje, met Eijeren en een Spin en Spinnewebbe. Meede behandeld als de Voorgaande | *Mat:* op doek *Size:* hoog 32, breed 29 duim	D	(Sold) fl 320 Gruiter
1802/06/28	AMSCH	0001	*P.T. van Brussel* | Dit capitaal en aangenaam Voorwerp, verbeeld een cierlyke gewerkte Vaas, staande op een gecouleurd marmer Voetstuk, gevuld met een menigte keurige Bloemen, als roode, geele en witte Roozen, blaauwe Hiacinth, Tulpen, Auriculaas, Papaver en andere soorten, met steel en bladeren; waarop verscheide Insecten aazen; alles is kunstig van schikking en groeping, de harmonie der couleuren, en de bevallige losheid, zeer natuurlyk; het werd als door een krachtig Licht bescheenen, de achtergrond verbeeld een Landschap, en is alleruitvoerigst gepenceeld door P. T. van Brussel, op Panneel | companion to lot 2 *Mat:* op paneel *Size:* hoog 21, breed 15 ½ duim	Anna Elink	(Bought In) fl 560 for lots 1 & 2
1802/06/28	AMSCH	0002	*P.T. van Brussel* | Dit fraaye Stuk zynde een wederga van 't voorgaande, verbeeld een dito [cierlyke gewerkte] Vaas, staande op een marmer Voetstuk, ter zyde leggen verscheide soorten van smaakelyke Vruchten, als Persiken, Abricoosen, Pruimen, verschillende Druiven, Bramboozen, Tak met Vruchten, Turkstarw [sic], waar boven diversche bevallige Bloemen en Bladeren, waarop verschillende Insecten aazen; alles in dun en doorschynend behandeld, en op het allernatuurlykst en uitvoerigst gepenceeld | companion to lot 1 *Size:* hoog 21, breed 15 ½ duim	Anna Elink	(Bought In) fl 560 for lots 1 & 2
1806/08/13	AMSCH	0009	*Brussel. (P.T. van)* | Dit uitmuntend tafreel, steld voor een capitaal Bloem en Fruitstuk, met fraai geschakeerde bloemen, als: Roode en witte Roosen, Hiacinten, Auriculaas en een menigte van vrugten, als: blaauwe en witte Druiven, Persiken, Annassen [sic], Canteloepen, Pruimen, enz. alles voorgesteld op een marmeren rand, waarop een vogelnestje geplaatst is; dit stuk is aller delicaatst uitvoerig en van de beste behandeling van deeze verdienstelyke Meester | *Mat:* op paneel *Size:* hoog 31, breed 24 duim	Vinkeles [for] J	(Bought In) fl 405
1806/08/13	AMSCH	0010	*Brussel. (P.T. van)* | Op een Steene Rand ziet men een Vaas, gevult met een ménigte van sierlyke geschakeerde Bloemen, beneevens op de Steene Rand eenige Blaauwe en witte Druiven en Canteloep, fiks en meesterlyk van behandeling | *Mat:* op doek *Size:* hoog 32, breed 26 duim	Vinkeles [for] F	(Sold) fl 30 van Iperen
1809/04/22	AMYVR	0006	*P.T. van Brussel* | Dit uitmuntend Tafreel steld voor een magnifieke Bloem- en Fruitstuk, men ziet op een Marmere Tafel geplaatst eenige wélgeschakeerde Bloemen, als witte Roozen, Hyacinten, Auricula's, Papavers en andere, omgeeven van eenige trossen witte en blaauwe Druiven, Persiken, Pruimen, Canteloepen en andere Vruchten, waarop eenige Insekten azen, als mede een Vogelnestje met Eijertjes; de uitvoering en het coloriet zijn allerschoonst, en is delicaat geschilderd in de beste tijd van P.T. van Brussel, hoog 21, breed 34 duim, hetzelve is geplaatst in een zeer kunstig gemaakte Maghoniehoute Kast, met een Cylinderdeur | *Size:* hoog 21, breed 34 duim	de Bruin	(Bought In) fl 425
1809/06/13	AMSCH	0010	*P.T. van Brussel* | In dit fraaije stukje, ziet men op een Marmere Tafel, eenige delikaaten Vrugten, als witte en blaauwe Druiven, Persiken, Abrikosen, Canteloup en anderen, liggende tegens Wijngaardranken; het koloriet is schoon en de schildering uitvoerig | *Mat:* op doek *Size:* hoog 17, breed 14 duim	T	(Bought In) fl 127
1809/09/06	AMSCH	0006	*Brussel (P.T. van)* | Op een couleurde Marmere Tafel, liggen verscheide smakelijke Vrugten, als blauwe en witte Druiven, Persik, Abricoosen, Pruimen, met Steel en Bladeren, Bramboosen, verders witte Stokroos en andere Bloempjes, waarop verschillende Insecten azen; alles evenaart de Natuur, bevallig van licht en koloriet en van een uitvoerige penceel-behandeling | *Mat:* op doek *Size:* hoog 19, breed 15 ½ duim	Johannes Caudri	(Sold) fl 180 Izaac Smit
1810/05/22	AMSCH	0006	*Brussel (P.T. van)* | Op eene Tafel staat een Vaas gevuld met geurige Bloemen, ter zijde liggen blaauwe en witte Druiven, Kerssen en andere Vrugten; alles uitvoerig behandeld | *Mat:* op paneel *Size:* hoog 11, breed 9 ½ duim	Johannes van de Putte Nicolaasz.	(Sold) fl 61 Gruyter
1810/05/22	AMSCH	0007	*Brussel (P.T. van)* | Een Fruitstukje, in dezelfde manier als de voorgaande; uitvoerig gepenceeld | *Mat:* op paneel *Size:* hoog 8, breed 6 duim *Notes:* This lot was sold with lot 158 by an anonymous artist.	Johannes van de Putte Nicolaasz.	(Sold) fl 41 for lots 7 & 158. Twisk [?]
1810/05/22	AMSCH	0008	*Brussel (P.T. van)* | Twee stuks bevallige Duingezichten, met Dorpen in het verschiet; geestig gestoffeerd met verscheide Beelden en behandeld als de voorige | *Mat:* op paneel *Size:* Jeder hoog 11, breed 13 duim	Johannes van de Putte Nicolaasz.	(Sold) fl 27:10 van Iperen

Brussel, Paul Theodor van (manner)

1807/06/10	HGBSM	0133	*van Brussel* | Op een marmersteene Voetstuk, staat een barnsteene Vaas, gevuld met velerhande Bloemen, als roode, witte en geele Roozen, Hijacinten, Auriculaas, &c., benevens de vaas ligt een Vogelnestje met eijertjes, alles uitvoerig gepenceelt, in de trant van van Brussel | *Mat:* op paneel *Size:* hoog 20, breed 16 ½ duim	Abraham Delfos [or others]	(Sold) fl 24 Tessier

Bruyn, Theodor de

1810/06/20	AMSCH	0012	*Theod. De Bruin* | Een Arkadisch Landschap, rijk gestoffeerd en uitvoerig behandeld | *Mat:* op doek *Size:* hoog 17, breed 20 duimen	A	(Sold) fl 1:15 Gruiter

Bryer, C. de

1803/09/07	AMSCH	0030	*C. de Briers* | Op een Steene Tafel, staat een gevlogte Bennetje, gevuld met onderscheidene zoorten van smakelyke Vrugten, met Steel en Bladeren, ter zyde een Porcelyne Kom, met diversche Pruimen, meesterlyk geschilderd [Sur une table de pierre est une corbeille d'osier remplie de différentes espèces de fruits très appétissans, avec leurs tiges et des feuilles ; à côté une écuelle de porcelaine, avec des prunes. Exécution parfaite] | *Mat:* op doek *Size:* hoog 23, breed 33 duim	Smidt	(Sold) fl 3:15 Gruiter

Bucker [Unidentified] (copy by)

1810/10/10	MGCIT	0150	*Bucker; Corregio* | Twee zeer aardige uitgevoerde Stukjes, in eenen goeden Trand behandeld, zijnde twee leggende Vrouwe Figuuren, in eene leezende houding, met eenig Bijwerk; gecopiëerd door Bucker; de Origineelen van beide door Corregio geschildert | copy by Bucker after Correggio	Caspar van Citters	(Unknown)

Buma, Johannes

1804/10/29	HRBAU	0015	*Buma* | Een Land- en Watergezigt, waar het Stormt. Zonagtig en uitvoerig behandeld | *Mat:* op doek *Size:* hoog 21, breed 23 duim	Simon Styl	(Unknown)

Burch, Hendrick van der

1805/10/09	HGBSM	0050	*H. van der Burgh* | Een boere binnehuis, waarin op de voorgrond verscheide soorten van groentens, een tobbe met potten, kopere ketel, en andere gereedschappen, op de tweede grond twee figuuren by een vuur zittende &c., zeer natuurlyk fraay en uitvoerig geschilderd | *Mat:* op paneel *Size:* hoog 12 ½ breet 14 ½ duim	T H van Willigen [or others]	(Sold) fl 22:10 Carré (de Secretaris)
1806/08/13	AMSCH	0014	*Burgh. (H. van der)* | Een Binnenhuis, in hetzelve zit een Vrouw Appelen te schillen, een jongen met een mand met turf komt dezelve aandragen, verders een ménigte huisraad; zynde van een kragtige en zeer uitvoerige behandeling | *Mat:* op paneel *Size:* hoog 11, breed 13 duim	Roos	(Bought In) fl 30
1809/06/13	AMSCH	0009	*H. van der Burch* | In het Binnengezigt van een Corps de Garde, zitten drie Officieren te rooken en te drinken, agter hun een ander Krijgsman, in een vrolijke houding met een Glas in de hand, vier andere Beelden en eigenaartig bijwerk, stoffeeren verder dit Schilderij; het geen meesterlijk en breed gepenceeld is | *Mat:* op doek *Size:* hoog 23, breed 29 duim	T	(Sold) fl 75 Reijers
1809/07/25	HGBSM	0069	*H. v.d. Burgh* | Een Boeren Binnenhuis, waar in een Meid die een Keetel schuurt, het invallend ligt door een openstaande deur doet een aangename werking, kunstig en uitvoerig geschildert | *Mat:* op paneel *Size:* hoog 12, breed 15 duim	D van der Aa	(Sold) fl 32 van der Aa

Burg (Burgh)

1804/07/25	DLGRO	0050	*Van der Burgh* | Een Jongeling voor een Tafel zittende op de Guithare te speelen, met eenige Muziekboeken voor zig, zeer fraai door Van der Burgh | *Mat:* op paneel *Size:* hoog 15, breed 13 duim	Mr Franc van der Burch Wz.	(Unknown)
1806/08/20	HGBSM	0049	*van der Burg* | Maria Magdalena, uitvoerig geschilderd | *Mat:* op paneel *Size:* hoog 9 ¼, breed 8 ¼ duim	Macalester Loup [or others]	(Sold) fl 14 Teissier

Burg (Burgh) (copy after)

1805/06/24	DOBLU	0021	*v.d. Burg* | Twee kleine Stukjes, naar v.d. Burg; het eene een Boertje, en het andere een Haringvrouwtje	Willem Snellen [or] F R E Nibbelinck [or] Gysbert Visser	(Unknown)

Burg, Adriaan van der

1801/10/19	AMSCH	0014	*Burgh. (A. van der)* | Een slaapend Vrouwtje, waar agter een Man die haar lagchend aanziet, neevens haar een Jonge die met de hand na haar wyst, en in de andere hand een Vogel op een kruk houd, verder een Uil op een kruk by een Tafel, waaröp een Schotel met Oesters enz; zeer uitvoerig en helder geschildert van zyn beste tyd | *Mat:* op paneel *Size:* hoog 24 ¼, breed 15 ¾ duim	Jonkheer Menno Baron van Coehoorn	(Sold) fl 80 B^{d} Kooy
1802/11/01	DOBRA	0039	*A. van der Burg* | Jupiter by Calisto, onder de gedaante van Diana | *Mat:* op paneel	Paulus van der Spyk [or others]	(Sold) fl 3:5 Randwyk
1802/11/01	DOBRA	0040	*A. van der Burg* | Een slaapend Meisje	Paulus van der Spyk [or others]	(Sold) fl 3:10 Schouman
1802/11/01	DOBRA	0093	*A. v. Burgh* | Een ruim Italiaansch bergagtig Landschap; op den voorgrond een Herderin schaapen melkende, gemerkt A. v. Burgh. f. | *Mat:* op doek *Size:* breed 3 voet en 6 duim, hoog 2 voet 5 duim *Inscr:* A. v. Burgh. f. (signed)	Paulus van der Spyk [or others]	(Unknown)
1803/06/20	AMSCH	0022	*A. van der Burg* | Christus gebonden door de Krygsknegten, word gebragt voor Pilatus, welke op zyn Troon zit, een groote menigte Jooden ziet men om hem heenen, de Ordenantie is grootsch en de Schildering delicaat op Doek | *Mat:* op doek *Size:* hoog 22, breed 28 duim	Schley [for] G	(Sold) fl 29:10 Gruiter
1806/06/07	RMHSN	0124	*A. van der Burg* | Twee Stuks, Pomona en Virtumus [sic], en Diana met haar Nymphen	A E K L	(Unknown)
1810/12/03	DOBRA	0017	*A. van der Burg* | In een Binnen-Vertrek zit een slapende Vrouw; breed geschilderd		(Unknown)

Burg, Dirk van der

1802/05/05	AMSCH	0033	*D. v. Burgh* | Een Aangenaam Landschap, met een Rivier; ryk gestoffeert met een menigte Vaartuigen en Beelden. Als Wynands, door D. v. Burgh	J	(Sold) fl 3 Spruit
1802/09/06	AMSCH	0021	*D. van Burch* | Een natuurlyk Landschap, op de voorgrond een Overvaarende Pontschuit, verder een Dorpgezicht en andere stoffagie | *Mat:* op paneel *Size:* hoog 28, breed 40 duim	J	(Sold) fl 0:10 Levy Pakker
1802/09/06	AMSCH	0022	*D. van Burch* | Een dito [natuurlyk] Landschap, in de manier van Wynants | *Size:* hoog 16, breed 20 duim	J	(Sold) fl 0:10 Levy Pakker

Burg, M. van den [Unidentified]

1802/06/28	AMSCH	0015	*M. van den Burg* | Een Kwakzalver, waarby een Jonge, dragende een Wapenschild, verders eenig Bywerk | *Mat:* op doek *Size:* hoog 21, breed 17 duim	Anna Elink	(Sold) fl 3:5 de Meyer

Burgs, J.V.H. [Unidentified]

1810/11/07	UTWLD	0012	*J. v. H. Burgs* | Een Landschap, aan den ingang van een Bosch een Postwagen door te paard en te voet zijnde struikrovers aangevallen, die te paard schijnen door hunne Carabijnen tot de overgave te noodzaken, op den voorgrond ziet men eenige liggende beeldjes, alles zeer klaar en krachtig geschilderd, de stoffagie ferm getekend, en wel geordonneerd door J. v. H. Burgs op doek 1 en een half voet hoog, 1 voet 9 duim breed, zwarte Lijst | *Mat:* op doek *Size:* 1 en een half voet hoog, 1 voet 9 duim breed *Notes:* The artist may have been Jan van Huchtenburgh.		(Unknown) fl 9

Buys, Jacobus

1802/02/16	AMSCH	0001	*J. Buys* | Twee stuks bevallige Voorwerpen, zynde beiden voor Buitenhuyzen; in de eene ziet men een Vogel-Verkoopster; en in het andere, een Fruit Vrouw zitten, beezig om geld te ontvangen van twee Vrouwen, voor gekogte waaren; benevens een Jongeling en Hond; de verdere stoffagie, als mede de aangenaame Zonachtige verschieten; maken deeze stukjes; van de fraayste van dezen Meester; zynde bevallig, en kragtig op paneel geschilderd | *Mat:* op paneel	B[uys]	(Sold) fl 100 Van der Schley [for] A[=Putte]
1802/02/16	AMSCH	0002	*J. Buys* | De Tartuffe voorgesteld in een gemeubileerd Binnenhuys; meesterlyk op paneel | *Mat:* op paneel	B[uys]	(Sold) fl 12:15 J^{b} Roeloffs
1802/02/16	AMSCH	0003	*J. Buys* | Twee stuks Bybelsche Ordenantiën de eene verbeeld de uitdryving van Hagar en Ismaël, en de andere Naomi haar Dochter vertroostende; krachtig en fraay gepenceeld op paneel | *Mat:* op paneel	B[uys]	(Sold) fl 44 S M Levy
1802/02/16	AMSCH	0004	*J. Buys* | Dito [een stuk Bybelsche] Ordonantie verbeeld een onderwerp uit het Teneelspel [sic], het Coffyhuys | *Notes:* It is unclear what "dito" refers to in the title.	B[uys]	(Sold) fl 2:5 Gruiter
1802/02/16	AMSCH	0005	*J. Buys* | Twee stuks Boere binnehuyzen gestoffeerd met vrolyke Huislieden; delicaat in de manier van A. V. Ostade	B[uys]	(Sold) fl 25:10 J Smit
1802/12/13	AMSCH	0032	*J. Buis* | Het Afbeeldzel van den Kunstschilder D. Dalens, zittende voor zyn Schilder Ezel; houdende in de Hand een Teekening, meesterlyk van Penceel behandeling | *Mat:* op paneel *Size:* hoog 11, breed 9 ½ duim	Schley [for] Lauwers	(Sold) fl 1:10 v d^{r} Schley
1804/10/16	DLOND	0046	*Buys* | Het Engelen Gezang. Chant des Anges | *Mat:* op doek *Size:* hoog 35, breed 43		(Unknown)
1808/06/13	AMSCH	0021	*Buys (J.)* | Dit Voorwerp verbeeld een der Tooneelen uit het Blijspel Lubbert Lubbertsen. Op den Voorgrond, ter zijde, voor een treffelijk Gebouw, staat eene Dame met een fier gelaat, in deftige kleeding; voor dezelve ligt een bedaagd Heer op eene knie, als woedend van spijt, die door den ouden Vader en Moeder wordt aangespoord, zijne Huisvrouw vergiffenis te vragen. In de deur der woning staat een beminnelijk Dienstmeisje, met een spottend gelaad, houdende een blaker met een brandende kaars in de hand; verder een Jongeling, een lantaarn dragende. De karakters zijn geestig en natuurlyk, en de beide kaarslichten doen eene bevallige werking. Alles is van een uitvoerige penceelbehandeling | *Mat:* op paneel *Size:* hoog 22, breed 17 ½ duim	[Jan Tersteeg]	(Bought In) fl 50
1808/06/13	AMSCH	0022	*Buys (J.)* | Deze Ordonantie stelt voor het uitgaan van den ouden Schouwburg. Het Kaarslicht doet hierin eene natuurlijke werking, en is fraai geschilderd	G	(Sold) fl 7 van Dyl
1810/05/22	AMSCH	0010	*Buijs. (J.)* | Twee stuks bevallige Voorwerpen, zijnde beide verbeeld voor Buitenhuizen, een Vogelkoopster en het andere eene Fruitvrouw, bezig hunne Waren uit te venten; zijnde van eene delikate behandeling | *Mat:* op paneel *Size:* hoog 17, breed 13 duim	Johannes van de Putte Nicolaasz.	(Sold) fl 46 Van Iperen

Buys, Jacobus (and Ouwater, Isaak)

1808/10/28	AMVRS	0047	*Ouwater (J.); J. Buys* | Een Gezicht te Utrecht met den Dom en Kerk, ter linkerzijde een Smits Winkel. Zeer zonachtig en uitvoerig | *Size:* hoog 20, breed 22 ½ duim	Marten Udink	(Sold) fl 51 Stopendaal

Bys, Johann Rudolf

1802/06/16	AMSCH	0031	*J. R. Bys* | Een Zwitsers Landschap, doorsneede met een Water, waarby eenige Landlieden, ter zyde eenig hoog Geboomten; helder en natuurlyk behandeld | *Mat:* op doek *Size:* hoog 24, breed 12 ½ duim	[Merrem]	(Sold) fl 9:10 Agina

Cabbaey, Michiel

1806/05/05	AMSCH	0036	*M. Cabbay* | Een Italiaansch Landschapje met Geboomte, Rivieren, stoffagie van Beeldjes enz.; delicaat op Paneel | *Mat:* op paneel	L	(Sold) fl 0:10 L Pakker

Cabel, Adrian van der

1810/07/26	AMSCH	0043	*Kabel (van der)* | Een Wintergezigt met een bevrozen Water, waarop Boeren met Sleden, welke hun Goederen ter Markt brengen | *Mat:* op paneel *Size:* hoog 16, breed 21 duimen	Cassino	(Bought In) fl 2:15
1810/07/26	AMSCH	0146	*Kabel (van der)* | Twee Landschappen, met stoffagie van Beelden enz. | *Mat:* op doek *Size:* hoog 10, breed 18 duimen	Cassino	(Sold) fl 8 T Spaan
1810/10/11	AMSCH	0199	*Van Der Kabel* | Een Winter met Schaatsenrijders, enz.	A	(Sold) fl 0:6 L Pakker

Cagnacci, Guido (or Cagnacci, manner)

1801/10/06	AMSCH	0013	*Guido Cagnacci, of in de manier* | Deeze Capitaale Ordinantie van drie leevensgroote Beelden, tot aan de Knien, vertoont Susanna zig Badende, en door de twee Oude verrast, de byzondere hartstogten, zyn natuurlyk verbeeld, het is kunstig van Teekening, kragtig van Coloriet, en van een Meesterlyke breede Penceelbehandeling. NB. Dit Stuk gaat in Prent uit door C. de Visscher, in het Werk van Reynst | *Mat:* op doek *Size:* hoog 60, breed 54 duim *Notes:* The print referred to in the title reproduced a painting thought to be by G. Reni.	M	(Bought In) fl 41

Camphuysen

1801/03/16	AMSCH	0051	*Camphuysen* | Een Bergagtig Landschap, op de voorgrond met staande en leggende Beesten	P[ruyssenaar]	(Sold) fl 17 Pruysenaar [for] R
1801/04/08	HAVIN	0030	*Camphuizen* | Een Landschap met een drift Beesten		(Unknown)
1804/02/27	AMSCH	0022	*Camphuysen* | In een Stal staat een oude Boer, met één bevallige Myd te praaten, terwyl ze door een oude Vrouw die de Deur inkomd [sic], schyne beluisterdt te worden; voorts wel voorzien van Stal- en Keukengereedschap | *Size:* hoog 21, breed 25 duim	C	(Sold) fl 1:15 Gruiter
1808/08/23	AMSCH	0182	*Camphuisen* | Een Landschap met staande en liggende Koeijen en Schaapen, en een Bergachtig verschiet; krachtig op Doek | *Mat:* op doek	[Van Iperen?]	(Sold or Bought In) fl 10:10 Van Iperen
1808/09/13	HABRU	0054	*Kamphuizen* | Een Landschap, gestoffeerd met Koeijen en Schapen		(Unknown) fl 11
1808/12/30	HGIMM	[0071i]	*Kamphuyzen* | Voorts een exquis kabinetje Schilderijen van voorname Nederlandsche Meesters, welke uit hoofde van de kortheid des tijds niet stuk voor stuk kunnen beschreven worden; doch waarvan de beschrijving op den Kijkdag zal voorhanden zijn. Dus wij hier alleen de namen van eenige dier Meesters laten volgen, als: A. Kuyp, Ruysdaal, Karel du Jardyn, Loqwi ('t beste dat hij schilderde) Hondekoeter, van Dyk, Janson, Moesgever, Kamphuyzen, van Gooijen, A. van der Neer, T. Wyk, Huchtenburgh, Zolemaker, van Hassel, A. Vermeulen, van Dongen, Scheffer, van Os enz. | *This Lot:* Een Schilderij, Kamphuyzen *Notes:* Because this lot was not numbered in the catalogue, we have assigned the number.		(Unknown)
1809/04/22	AMYVR	0065	*Kamphuizen* | In een Stal staat een Paard aan de Ruif, tegen een witten Muur uitkomende; krachtig | *Mat:* op paneel *Size:* hoog 15, breed 19 duim	de Bruin	(Sold) fl 11 C S Roos
1809/05/26	HADAA	A0006	*Kamphuyzen* | Een Landschap	Mejuffrouw de Wed David Heemskerk [or others]	(Unknown)
1810/03/27	RMCNL	0035	*Kamphuizen* | Een Koeijenstal van binnen te zien, zeer aardig geschilderd		(Unknown)
1810/03/27	RMCNL	0055	*Kamphuizen* | Een Stalletje, van binnen te zien, met eenige Koebeesten, aardig behandeld		(Unknown)
1810/03/27	RMCNL	0096	*Kamphuizen* | Steld een Visboertje voor, allerlei soort van Rivier Vis uit eene Mand stortende		(Unknown)

Camphuysen, Dirck Raphaelsz.

1804/10/29	HRBAU	0046	*Kamphuisen, (D. R.)* | In een ryk gemeubileerd Binnenvertrek, by een Clavier, en een Tafel, waar op een Boek ligt en eene Bierkan staat, zit eene Juffer, welke bezig is Raapen te schillen; naast haar staat een Emmer en Marktemmer, nevens een Hond; welk alles door een helder zonlicht, dat door de vensters in het vertrek valt, bescheenen wordt, en eene frappante uitwerking doet tegens de stilte van den agtergrond; welk alles zeer uitvoerig behandeld is | *Mat:* op paneel *Size:* hoog 19, breed 25 duim	Simon Styl	(Unknown)
1805/10/09	HGBSM	0016	*D. R. Kamphuyzen* | Een boeren stal, met koebeesten &c. natuurlyk geschildert | *Mat:* op doek *Size:* hoog 16 breet 21 duim	T H van Willigen [or others]	(Sold) fl 7:5 Regters
1806/08/13	AMSCH	0034	*Camphuysen. (D. R.)* | In een vlak Landgezicht ziet men by een Boom een ménigte van staand grazend en rustend Vee, verders een aangenaam verschiet; breed en meesterlyk van schildering | *Mat:* op doek *Size:* hoog 19, breed 22 duim	Vinkeles [for] F	(Sold) fl 2 L Pakker

Camphuysen, Govert (Godefridus)

1808/07/19	AMROU	0019	*Godefridus Camphuyze* | 2 stuks, zynde een Mans en Vrouwe Pourtrait, in eene deftige Kleding		(Unknown)

			Camphuysen, Govert Dircksz.		
1802/06/28	AMSCH	0036	*G. Camphuysen* | In een Boeren Schuur, ziet men een Meisje bezig Linnen te wasschen, nevens haar leggen eenige rustende Koeijen, verder een menigte Huisraad; het Licht is zeer bevallig, en verders van een fraai Coloriet, door G. Camphuysen, op Panneel | *Mat:* op paneel *Size:* hoog 16, breed 21 duim	Anna Elink	(Sold) fl 8 Coclers
			Camphuysen, J.		
1810/06/20	AMSCH	0036	*J. Kamphuizen* | Een Landschap met Geboomte en een Rivier, door dewelke eenige Herders, zoo te paard als te voet, eene menigte Vee drijven. Zijnde van een fraaije schildering | *Mat:* op doek *Size:* hoog 33, breed 42 duimen	X	(Sold) fl 17:10 Pantijn
			Camphuysen, Rafel Govertsz.		
1802/12/13	AMSCH	0039	*R. Camphuisen* | In een Boeren Stal, ziet men een bevallige Meid een Boer een Ey aanbieden, terwyl een oud Besje door een half open Deur haar schynt te bespieden, de Voorgrond is ryk voorzien, van diverssen zoorten van Keukengereedschappen, meesterlyk gepenceeld | *Mat:* op paneel *Size:* hoog 22, breed 25 duim	Pruyssenaar [for] A	(Sold) fl 1 Gruiter
1805/07/03	AMSCH	0072	*R. Camphuizen* | In een Grazige Weiden, met Geboomten, ziet men eenige jonge Huislieden stoeijen, verders onder het Geboomten een drinkende Koe, in 't verschiet een Jonge met een Bul; meesterlyk behandeld | *Mat:* op paneel *Size:* hoog 20, breed 25 duim	C	(Sold) fl 63 H Pakker
1806/08/13	AMSCH	0250	*R. Camphuizen* | Een aangenaam Land- en Watergezicht	Vinkeles [for] G[ruyter]	(Sold) fl 9:10 Schumacher
			Camsen, J. van [Unidentified]		
1804/08/08	AMSCH	0038	*J. van Camsen* | Op een Weg met eenige Wooningen zit een bedaagde Vrouw, in oude Hollandsche Kleeding, schynende Groentens en Fruit te verkoopen, een Jongeling staat voor dezelve, met een Bennetje Vruchten in de Hand, welke zy een Boodschap geeft, ter zyde staat een Mand met Appelen, en op de Grond leggen andere Groentens, verders gaat een Vrouw met een Bosch Wortelen, en in 't verschiet een Landschap; de caracters zyn natuurlyk en bevallig van coloriet, en meesterlyk gepenceeld, in de manier van Metzu, door J. van Camsen | *Mat:* op doek *Size:* hoog 47, breed 39, duim	Schley [for] B	(Sold) fl 32 Bernard
			Canaletto (Giovanni Antonio Canal)		
1805/10/09	HGBSM	0131	*Canalettie* | Een gezigt in Venetien met grootsche gebouwen aan 't water, ryk gestoffeerd met beelden en schuitjes, fix en helder geschilderd | *Mat:* op doek *Size:* hoog 18 breet 27 ½ duim	T H van Willigen [or others]	(Sold) fl 5:5 Valette
1805/12/16	AMSCH	0064	*Canaletti* | Twee stuks Romynsche Gezichten, bevallig op Doek | *Mat:* op doek	R[oos]	(Sold) fl 1:15 Gruiter
1805/12/16	AMSCH	0065	*Canaletti* | Twee dito [stuks Romynsche Gezichten] | *Notes:* It is unclear what "dito" refers to in the title.	R[oos]	(Sold) fl 1:5 Gruiter
1806/01/30	RMAN	0002	*Canaletti* | Een Venetiaansch Gezigt	Dirk Langendyk	(Unknown)
1807/08/26	AMSCH	0033	*Canaletti* | Vier stuks gezigten in Venetien vol stoffagie van Beelden, Schepen and andere Vaartuigen; op Doek, geestig gepenceeld | *Mat:* op doek *Size:* hoog 21, breed 31 duim	Joseph Vallette	(Sold) fl 7:5 van Iperen
1807/08/26	AMSCH	0034	*Canaletti* | Een dito [gezigt], te dito [Venetien] | *Size:* hoog 18, breed 28 duim	Joseph Vallette	(Sold) fl 2 Hooft
1807/08/26	AMSCH	0034a	*Canaletti* | Een dito [gezigt] met een pragtig Gebouw | *Size:* hoog 20, breed 23 duim	Joseph Vallette	(Sold) fl 3:5 van Dyk
1808/08/23	AMSCH	0179	*Canaletti* | Twee stuks Italiaansche Zeehavens, met Ruïne en oude Gedenkteekens, beide rijk gestoffeerd met Lieden te Paard, rustende en gaande Reizigers, uit verschiet een woelend Zee met Scheepen; krachtig en meesterlijk gepenceeld op Doek | *Mat:* op doek	Y	(Sold) fl 9:10 Levie Pakker
1810/07/26	AMSCH	0019	*Canaletti* | Een Zeehaven, met Gebouwen, Vaartuigen en Beelden versierd | *Mat:* op doek *Size:* hoog 39, breed 47 duimen	Cassino	(Bought In) fl 2:5
			Cappelle, Jan van de		
1801/05/11	AMSCH	0019	*J. Capelle* | Een stil Water, waar op verscheiden zeilende Schepen, ter zyde ziet men een weg, waar op eenige beeldjes geplaast zyn, alles zeer uitvoerig en zonachtig gepenceeld | *Mat:* op doek *Size:* hoog 24, breed 33 duim	Pruisse [for] M	(Sold) fl 48 Rijers
1801/05/11	AMSCH	0020	*J. Capelle* | Een woelend Water, op de Voorgrond ziet men een Schuit, welke aan een paal vastgebonde word, natuurlyk behandeld | *Mat:* op doek *Size:* hoog 16, breed 16 duim	P[ruyssenaar]	(Sold) fl 11 van Iperen
1801/06/10	AMSCH	0037	*Capelle. (J. van)* | Een capitaal stil Water, met verscheiden Beurtschepen, Roeischuiten en andere Vaartuigen, ter linkerzyde ziet men het Bothuisje, de opkomst der Zon doet in het Water een natuurlyk effect en is van een fraaije schildering | *Mat:* op paneel *Size:* hoog 26, breed 34 duim	Herman ten Kate	(Sold) fl 95 Pruyssenaar
1801/06/10	AMSCH	0038	*Capelle. (J. van)* | Aan een hoofd en paalwerk legd een Visschers Schuit, verder een menigte Beeldjes, en in 't verschiet eenige Vaartuigen; alles dun en bevallig gepenceeld | *Mat:* op doek *Size:* hoog 22, breed 27 duim	Herman ten Kate	(Sold) fl 200 Pruyssenaar

1802/05/05	AMSCH	000D	*J. van Capelle* | Een bevrozen Rivier aan een tusschen hoog geboomte leggend Dorp, het Ys is gestoffeerd met verscheide Schaatzeryders en Yssleeden, zeer natuurlyk | *Mat:* op paneel *Size:* hoog 16, breed 17 duim	A	(Sold) fl 30 Cocler
1802/05/05	AMSCH	0040	*J. van Capellen* | Een Stil Water, met een menigte Vaartuigen, schoon van Ligt en Meesterlyk geschilderd | *Mat:* op paneel *Size:* hoog 39, breed 48 duim	J	(Sold) fl 5:5 v d Vinne
1802/06/16	AMSCH	0034	*J. van Cappelle* | Een stil Water, met een meenigte zeilree leggende Vaartuigen, met Beeldjes, en een Stad in het verschiet: alles dun en spiegelend behandeld | *Mat:* op doek *Size:* hoog 30, breed 38 duim	[Merrem]	(Sold) fl 9 Teyssier
1802/07/09	AMSTO	0005	*Capello* | 1 Riviergezigt met zylende Schepen		(Unknown)
1802/12/13	AMSCH	0040	*Cappellen* | In een natuurlyk Wintergesigt, ziet men 't Ys, en de met Sneeuw bedekte Weg, gestoffeerd met gaande en rydende Beeldjes, natuurlyk geschilderd | *Mat:* op paneel *Size:* hoog 14, breed 20 duim	Pruyssenaar [for] A	(Sold) fl 2:5 Wolft
1803/07/18	AMSCH	0008	*Capelle. (J. van)* | Een stil Water met verscheide Vaartuigen en Beeldjes gestoffeerd, de spiegeling in 't water is geestig, het verschiet dun, en de penceelsbehandeling als W. van de Velde [Une Mer Calme. Audevant sont deux barques de Pêcheurs avec deux chaloupes garnies de monde ; vers la droite se distinguent des vaisseaux sous voiles, & la perspective offre une langue de terre, & quelqu'autres navires. Un beau ciel bien nuagé ajoute infiniment à la vérite & l'éclat de ce tableau. La couleur en [sic] si vraye & si fraiche ! & la composition si ressemblante à Guil. van de Velde qu'un premier coup-d'oeuil pourroit la faire attribuer à ce Maître.] | *Mat:* op doek *Size:* hoog 33, breed 41 duim	Maria Theresia Andrioli	(Sold) fl 155 Josi
1803/08/01	AMSCH	0007	*Cappelle. (J. van de)* | Een stil Water, ryk gestoffeert met een groot aantal verschillende Scheepen en andere Vaartuigen, beneevens een Staaten Jagt, een Sloup met Volk, enz.; dit Schildery is zeer fraay en zonachtig behandeld, en voorts frapant en aangenaam van coloriet | *Mat:* op paneel *Size:* hoog 28, breed 36 duim	H	(Sold) fl 350 C S Roos
1803/12/12	AMSCH	0022	*A. van Capellen* | Een aangenaam stil Water, ter zyden de Stad Dord, ryk gestoffeerd met een beladen Pontschuit en een ménigte van zeilende en stil liggende Scheepen; bevallig van licht en meesterlyk gepenceeld | *Mat:* op paneel *Size:* hoog 29, breed 12 duim *Notes:* The artist's name was given as "A. van Capellen" but we have assumed this is an error.	B	(Sold) fl 30 Coclers
1804/02/27	AMSCH	0020	*Capellen (A.)* | In een aangenaam stil Water ziet men eenigen zylende en stilleggende Vaartuigen, op den voorgrond aan 't Strand zyn eenige Visschers bezig de Zylen te bergen van hun Vaartuig, en van agteren een Stad; bevallig van licht en als door W. van der Velde, geschilderd | *Mat:* op paneel *Size:* hoog 16, breed 21 ½ duim *Notes:* The artist's name was given as "Capellen (A.)" but we have assumed this is an error.	B	(Bought In) fl 14
1804/02/27	AMSCH	0148	*Cappelle* | Twee stuks Winters; meesteragtig geschilderd	B	(Sold) fl 1:5 Hulswit
1805/07/03	AMSCH	0011	*Capelle. (J. van)* | Een Aangenaam stil Water, met een ménigte Scheepen, en klyndere Vaartuigen vol Beelden, op de voorgrond op een zandbank ziet men een Visserschuit welke tot de vangst gereed gemaakt word: de aangenaame warme toon in dit stuk, en de spiegeling in het water, maken het tot een aangenaam en lieflyk behandeld Schildery | *Mat:* op doek *Size:* hoog 23, breed 29 duim	G	(Sold) fl 170 Hulswit
1806/05/05	AMSCH	0030	*Capellen* | Een stil Water, gestoffeerd met zeilende en leggende Schepen, Vissers in hun Schuiten, by eenig Paalwerk en anderen stoffagie; zonagtig en uitvoerig gepenceeld door Capellen | *Mat:* op doek *Size:* hoog 33, breed 46 duim	V[inkeles]	(Sold) fl 28:10 Vinkeles [for] S
1806/05/05	AMSCH	0031	*Capellen* | Een stil Water, met zeilende en stil leggende Vaartuigen, op de voorgrond Visschers bézig hunne netten en zeillagien te bergen | *Mat:* op paneel *Size:* hoog 16, breed 22 duim	V[inkeles]	(Sold) fl 6:5 du Pree
1806/08/13	AMSCH	0028	*Capelle. (J. van de)* | Dit capitaale Stuk verbeeld een stil Water, ryk gestoffeerd met verschillende Vaartuigen, in het midden vertoont zich een groot Jacht, waarop verscheide Lieden, leggende hetzelve voor anker: ter eener zyde ziet men een Pontschuit met passagiers en pakgoederen, ter andere zyde een zeilende Pontschuit, met Reizigers, eenig Vée en andere koopwaaren, verder andere Jachten Sloepen en een ménigte dryvende en zeilende Scheepen; het bevallig licht, de spiegeling in het water, en de meesterlyke penceelsbehandeling, maken hetzelve tot een behaagelyk Schildery | *Mat:* op doek *Size:* hoog 42, breed 52 duim	van der Voort	(Sold) fl 488 Lafontaine
1806/08/13	AMSCH	0029	*Capelle. (J. van de)* | Dit alles Overtreffend Kunstgewrocht verbeeld een helder kabbelend Water, met een ménigte welgeordineerde zo zeilende als stilleggende Vaartuigen, roeijende Jachten, met onderscheiden Beelden, een Hooipont enz.; het natuurlyke licht, de spiegeling in het dunne water, en de aangename Horisont zyn gepaard met een bevallige penceelsbehandeling | *Mat:* op doek *Size:* hoog 42, breed 52 duim	Daniel Mansveld	(Sold) fl 760 Haffner
1806/08/13	AMSCH	0030	*Capelle. (J. van de)* | Een ryk met Scheepen en Schuiten gestoffeerd stil Water, op de voorgrond een jacht met een ménigte lieden, als mede een Pont met Vée, alles zeer natuurlyk en delicaat geschilderd | *Mat:* op paneel *Size:* hoog 30, breed 42 duim	Daniel Mansveld	(Sold) fl 102 Van Iperen
1806/11/24	AMSCH	0015	*Capelle (J.v.)* | Een kabbelend Water met zeilende Scheepen, ter zyde een hoofd van Paalwerk; zonagtig gepenceeld | *Mat:* op paneel *Size:* hoog 14, breed 20 duim	Munnikhuizen	(Sold) fl 2:10 du Pree

1807/04/00	LNDLS	0057	*Cappelle* | Een stil water met vele jagten en schepen, die zijlree leggen, en booten met volk, verbeeldende, het vertrek van Koning Willem de 3, naar Engeland | *Mat:* op doek	[Abraham Delfos] [or others]	(Unknown)
1807/06/10	HGBSM	0057	*Cappelle* | Een stil water met vele jagten en schepen, die zijlree leggen, en booten met volk, verbeeldende, het vertrek van Koning Willem de 3de, naar Engeland | *Mat:* op doek	Abraham Delfos [or others]	(Sold) fl 6 Bogart
1808/04/26	GDAN	0087	*Kapelle (J. v.d.)* | Een stil Watergezigtje met considerabel veel zeilende en leggende Schepen, uitmuntend geschildert of het van W. van de Velden was | *Mat:* op paneel *Size:* hoog 13 ½, breed 15 duim	G H Fortuyn	(Unknown)
1808/06/13	AMSCH	0033	*Capelle (J. van)* | Deze uitmuntende Ordonantie stelt voor de Rivier de Maas, waarop verschillende Schepen; in het midden een Pont; op den voorgrond een Sloep, welke een Admiraal aan boord brengt: alles natuurlijk en doorschijnend in de stijl van A. Cuijp geschilderd | *Mat:* op doek *Size:* hoog 34, breed 46 duim	E M Engelberts	(Sold) fl 31 P G van Os
1810/03/26	RMMUY	0017	*J. van Capelle* | Een Rivier Gezigt. Op den voorgrond een Markt Schuit. Met een Boot schijnen eenige passagiers aangebragt te worden. Eenige schuiten, schepen, en een aangenaam verschiet, versieren dit natuurlijk en konstig schilderij [Une Rivière garnie de plusieurs bateaux et barques. Sur le devant est une chaloupe avec plusieurs figures, qui paroissent vouloir aborder une barque marchande. D'une grande vérité et d'un ton argentin.] | *Mat:* op doek *Size:* hoog 29, breed 40 ¾ duimen *Loc:* London, England, UK. Corporation of London. (Howard Samuel Collection) (?) as follower of Cappelle	Daniel de Jongh Az	(Sold) fl 125 Josi Amsterdam
1810/08/01	AMSCH	0017	*Capelle (Jan)* | Een stil Water, zijnde een Riviergezigt, rijk voorzien van zeilende, drijvende en stil liggende Schepen, waar van sommigen met Hooi geladen liggen bij eene versterkte Schans; op den voorgrond twee Sloepen met Krijgsvolk [La Vue sur une Riviere representée au plein calme, ornée de Navires dont les uns sont à la Voile et d'autres attachés. On en distingue quelques uns chargés de foin auprès d'un Fort. Vèrs le premier plan on voit deux Chaloupes chargées de Militaires] | *Annots:* Bon : sauf les ombres trop rousses. (NGW) *Mat:* op doek *Size:* hoog 48, breed 59 duimen	Mr Pieter de Smeth van Alphen	(Sold) fl 1000 T Spaan [for] Croes d'Amsterdam
1810/08/01	AMSCH	0018	*Capelle (Jan)* | Een besneeuwd Wintergezigt met Boerenwoningen en eene Brug over bevrozen Water, gestoffeerd met Schaatserijders, Kolvers en andere Beeldjes [Paysage representé en Hyver, il est orné de Fabriques et d'un Pont traversant un ruisseau gelé ; la neige naturellement rendue couvre ce Site. Des Patineurs et des Joueurs à la Crosse, avec d'autres Figures achevent l'embellisement] | *Annots:* médiocre (NGW) *Mat:* op paneel *Size:* hoog 15 ½, breed 14 ½ duimen	Mr Pieter de Smeth van Alphen	(Sold) fl 145 [or] 150 Van Ijperen pour Wreesman
1810/10/11	AMSCH	0022	*J. Van Capellen* | Een bevallig stil Water, met zeilende en stilliggende Schepen, en Visschers in Schuiten; uitvoerig geschilderd | *Mat:* op paneel *Size:* hoog 17, breed 23 duimen	[Gruyter?]	(Sold) fl 6:5 van Leen
			Cappelle, Jan van de (manner)		
1801/06/10	AMSCH	0215	*Capelle* | Een stil Water met zeilende en dryvende Scheepen en Schuiten, zonachtig behandeld, op Doek, in de manier van Capelle | *Mat:* op doek *Size:* hoog 30, breed 38 duim	[Doublet]	(Sold) fl 6:10 A Meijer
1801/10/19	AMSCH	0090	*J. v. Cappelle* | Een zeer schoon Zeegezicht of stil Water met verscheiden Scheepen en andere Vaartuigen, breed en aangenaam geschilderd, als door J. v. Cappelle | *Mat:* op doek *Size:* hoog 14 ⅞, breed 20 duim	Jonkheer Menno Baron van Coehoorn	(Sold) fl 76 Hulswit
			Caravaggio, Michelangelo Merisi da		
1802/06/16	AMSCH	0001	*M. Angelo da Caravagio* | De Heilige Franciscus, in een biddende gestalte met toegevouwe Handen; voor hem een Doodshoofd op een Boek op Tafel leggende; zynde van een Meesterlyke behandeling, breede plooijing en fixe Schildering | *Mat:* op doek *Size:* hoog 31 ½, breed 26 duim	[Merrem]	(Sold) fl 81 Pruijssenaar
1803/04/27	AMSCH	0056	*Carravage* | La mort d'Abel | *Size:* h. 4, l. 6 pieds	A	(Sold) fl 7 Roselli
1803/04/27	AMSCH	0105	*Carravage* | St. Bartolomée | *Size:* h. 3 ¼, l. 3 ½ pieds	A	(Sold) fl 9:5 de Meijer
1810/10/10	MGCIT	0014	*Caravagio* | Een ongemeen stout behandeld Mans Figuur halver lijf, gloeiënd van couleur, met zwart hair en baard, in een lezende gestalte; fix gepenceeld	Caspar van Citters	(Unknown)
			Caravaggio, Michelangelo Merisi da (copy after)		
1810/10/11	AMSCH	0071	*Parenti; Michel Angelo de Caravachio* | De Kaartspeelers, op Doek, door denzelven [Parenti], naar Michel Angelo de Caravachio | copy by Parenti after Caravaggio *Mat:* op doek *Size:* hoog 29, breed 38 duimen	M	(Sold) fl 10 du Pree
			Caravaggio, Michelangelo Merisi da (school)		
1803/04/27	AMSCH	0054	*Caravage* | Un Tableau représentant une veille femme qui arrange les cheveux à une Jeune fille ; de l'Ecole du Caravage | *Size:* h. 6, l. 4 ½ pieds	A	(Sold) fl 60 Th Spaan
			Cari, A. [Unidentified]		
1810/03/07	UTWLD	0029	*A. Cari* | Een vrouwtje dat visch te koop aanbiedt, konstig en uitvoerig | *Size:* hoog 1 voet 3 duim, breed 1 voet 1 duim	J J Woertman	(Unknown) fl 51

Carpioni, Giulio (I)

1802/06/16	AMSCH	0035	*G. Corpioni* | Twee stuks Bybelsche Ordenantien, de eene voorstellende Christus by de Emausgangers, en de andere aan de Tafel zittende, brekende het Brood: Meesterlyk geschilderd | *Mat:* op doek *Size:* hoog 27, breed 36 duim	[Merrem]	(Sold) fl 14 Teyssier
1803/08/24	HGKAN	0013	*G. Corpioni* | Twee Italiaansche Stukken, zynde Bybelsche Ordonnantien, de eene voorstellende Christus by de Emausgangers en de andere aan de Tafel zittende brekende het Brood, Meesterlyk geschildert | *Mat:* op doek *Size:* hoog 27, breet 36 duim	[Teissier] [or others]	(Sold) fl 12 van Giesen

Carracci

1803/12/12	AMSCH	0153	*Carrats* | Een Heilige Famillie | *Size:* hoog 8, breed 6 duim	D	(Sold) fl 1:10 Scheffers

Carracci (copy after)

1803/04/27	AMSCH	0038	*Carrache* | Un Ecce homo, d'après le Carrache	A	(Sold) fl 4:10 Yver
1806/05/05	AMSCH	0044	*van Dorne; Carats* | Maria met het Kindje, verzeld van St. Jan; allerdelicaatst geschilderd na Carats | copy by F. Dorne after Carracci *Mat:* op paneel *Size:* hoog 15, breed 17 ½ duim	L	(Sold) fl 9 Van Laar
1810/07/26	AMSCH	0094	*D. Teniers; Caracci* | De afneming van het Kruis, bestaande in acht Beeldjes. Zeer uitvoerig op agaat, door D. Teniers, naar Caracci | copy by Teniers after Carracci *Mat:* op agaat	Cassino	(Bought In) fl 6

Carracci (manner)

1802/06/28	AMSCH	0250	*Carrats* | Een Nimph op een Rustbed, waarby een Satyr; als door Carrats | *Mat:* op paneel *Size:* hoog 13, breed 10 duim	B	(Sold) fl 17:15 Royers

Carracci, A.

1801/10/06	AMSCH	0014	*A. Carrats* | Deeze fraaije Ordinantie stelt voor Galathea op haare Zee-Wagen, verzelt van Cupido, en verscheide Water Nimphen, en Triton blazers, om hoog ziet men vliegende Minnewigten: alles is schoon geteekent, het Coloriet bevallig, en van een kunstige Penceelbehandeling | *Mat:* op koper *Size:* hoog 16, breed 21 duim	S	(Sold) fl 28 Jan Spaan
1810/07/26	AMSCH	0014	*Caracci (A.)* | De Maagd Maria, hebbende het Kind Jesus voor zich, ter zijde St. Joseph, benevens een Engel. Zijnde een fraai zamenstel | *Mat:* op doek *Size:* hoog 46, breed 36 duimen	Cassino	(Sold) fl 59 T Spaan
1810/07/26	AMSCH	0015	*Caracci (A.)* | De Negen Zanggodinnen. Fraai geschilderd | *Mat:* op doek *Size:* hoog 7, breed 25 duimen	Cassino	(Bought In) fl 6:15
1810/07/26	AMSCH	0017	*Caracci (A.)* | Eene Heilige Familje. Meesterlijk schoon geschilderd | *Mat:* op paneel *Size:* hoog 15, breed 12 duimen	Cassino	(Bought In) fl 4

Carracci, A. (and Bril, P.)

1808/06/13	AMSCH	0027	*Bril (P.); A. Carats* | Een Landschap, op den voorgrond een Heremiet; op zijn knieën voor een Christusbeeld liggende, fraai behandeld | *Mat:* op koper *Size:* hoog 5, breed 6 duim	R[oos]	(Bought In) fl 30

Carracci, A. (copy after)

1801/08/19	AMSCH	0019	*A. Carrats* | St. Rochus, aan behoeftige Lieden Aalmoesen uitdeelende, vol gewoel, naar A. Carrats | *Mat:* op doek *Size:* hoog 32, breed 44 duim	C S Roos [for] G	(Sold) fl 1:5 Wijland

Carracci, Agostino

1808/11/12	HGSCR	0023	*Augustyn Carrats* | Venus wordende door een sater geliefkoosd waar by een slapende Cupido, zeer fraai en uitvoerig op een toetsteen geschilderd, extra raar	Mr J van Buren	(Unknown) fl 40

Carracci, Annibale

1802/07/20	MGSAN	0054	*H. Carats* | Een extra fraai Schildery, verbeeldende de Aanbidding der Herders, op Doek: extra schoon en breed gepenceeld | *Mat:* op doek *Size:* hoog duim 42, breed duim 53		(Unknown)

Carracci, Ludovico

1803/04/27	AMSCH	000I	*L. Carrache* | Moise recevant les Tables de la Loix [sic], des mains du Pere Eternel, accompagné des anges | *Size:* h. 50, l. 37 pouces	B	(Bought In) fl 50
1803/04/27	AMSCH	0055	*Louis Carrache* | Le Sauveur guerissant un auveugle | *Size:* h. 4 ½, l. 5 ½ pieds	A	(Sold) fl 11 Hodges
1810/07/26	AMSCH	0016	*Caracci (L.)* | Hercules den Draak dodende. Zijnde een zeer schoon stuk | *Mat:* op doek *Size:* hoog 16, breed 13 duimen	Cassino	(Sold) fl 1 Boelhouwer

Carree

1802/05/05	AMSCH	0045	*Carré* | Een Italiaansch Landschap, met Veê	J	(Sold) fl 2:5 Rigters
1803/08/24	HGKAN	0046	*Carré* | Twee stuks Lantschappen, Ryk gestoffeerd | *Mat:* op doek *Size:* hoog 33, breet 27 duim	[Teissier] [or others]	(Sold) fl 16:10 Carre
1804/08/02	BDAN	0029	*Carré* | Circé in een Landschap met anderhande soorten van Dieren, zeer fraay van Couleur | *Mat:* op doek *Size:* b. 22 d. h. 18 en een half d.	J G Calckberner	(Unknown)

1804/08/08	AMSCH	0049	*Carré* | Europa, zittende op een Stier, in een Landschap, met hoog Geboomte, meesterlyk behandeld | *Mat:* op doek *Size:* hoog 38 ½, breed 32 duim	Pruys[senaar]	(Bought In) fl 10
1805/07/03	AMSCH	0184	*Carré* | Een Landschap met Vee	R[oos]	(Sold) fl 4:10 Agina
1809/04/17	AMSCH	0181	*Carreé* | In een Landschap, ziet men eenige Reizigers, door Roovers aangevallen | *Mat:* op doek	[Gruyter?]	(Sold) fl 1:10
1809/05/26	HADAA	0064	*Carré* | Een Landschap met Beestjes door het water gaande	Mejuffrouw de Wed David Heemskerk [or others]	(Unknown)
1810/03/27	RMCNL	0042	*Careé* | Een zeer fraai en net Landschapje, met Koeijen; op den tweeden grond eene Boerderije, enz. zeer warm geschilderd		(Unknown)
1810/03/27	RMCNL	0046	*Carée* | Een zeer fraai Landschap met Koeijen		(Unknown)
1810/10/11	AMSCH	0242	*Carree* | Een Buitenhuis, waarvoor een Os geslagt wordt	A	(Sold) fl 0:8 T Spaan
			Carree, Abraham		
1803/08/24	HGKAN	0014	*A. Carré* | Een vrolyk Boere Binnehuis | *Mat:* op doek op paneel *Size:* hoog 12, breet 15 duim	[Teissier] [or others]	(Sold) fl 4:5 van Giesen
1807/08/26	AMSCH	0036	*A. Carré* | Twee stuks Italiaansche Landschapjes, geestig gestoffeerd met Ossen en Schapen, met hunne Herders; meesterlyk | *Mat:* op paneel *Size:* hoog 12, breed 10 duim	Roos	(Sold) fl 14:10 S Levy
			Carree, Franciscus		
1802/05/24	HGBAK	0041	*F. Carré* | Een Nagtgezicht, verbeeldende een Vrouw met een Jongetje aan de eene hand, en in de andere een Lantaarn, door F. Carré, hoog 8 ¼ duim, breed 8 ¼ duim, paneel, zwarte lyst en vergulde binnenrand | *Mat:* op paneel *Size:* hoog 8 ¼ duim, breed 8 ¼ duim	Mejuffrouw A van der Mieden	(Sold) fl 7 Carré jr
1802/07/27	AKHRK	0060	*F. Carree, 1654* | Een Binnenhuis, waarin een Vrouwtje zit te Naaijen; goed gepenceeld | *Mat:* op paneel *Size:* hoog 12, breed 10 duim *Inscr:* F. Carree, 1654 (signed and dated?) *Notes:* It is unclear whether the name and date are inscribed on the painting.	Maria Stategaart	(Sold) fl 3 Hellingwerf
1802/09/06	AMSCH	0184	*F. Carrée* | Twee stuks, voor open Nissen, ziet men vrolyke Liefkoozende Boeren en Boerinnen; plaisant behandeld	Spaan	(Sold) fl 3:10 Barteling
1810/10/10	MGCIT	0120	*F. Carrée* | Een Mannetje, rokende een Pyp, in eene vergenoegde houding, rondsom hem eenig Bywerk; zeer verdienstig in de manier van A. Ostade behandeld, door F. Carrée	Caspar van Citters	(Unknown)
			Carree, Hendrik (I)		
1801/03/16	AMSCH	0123	*H. Carre* | Vrolyke Boeren en een Boerin, voor een Buitenhuis in een Dorpgezicht, bevallig op paneel geschilderd | *Mat:* op paneel	K[ip]	(Sold) fl 3:5 Pruisenaar [for] L
1801/03/16	AMSCH	0127	*H. Carre* | Een verliefde Boer en Boerinnetje, bevallig geschilderd op paneel | *Mat:* op paneel	K[ip]	(Sold) fl 10:10 J Yver
1802/09/18	RMDRS	0017	*H. Carree* | Een capitaal Landgezicht, waarin een Boerin bezig is met een Koe te melken, en de Melk een boere Knaap in de oogen spuit, terwyl een andere Boer daarom schynt te lachen, zeer uitvoerig geschilderd | *Annots:* voor Meubel voor een Vriend (MB) *Size:* hoog 14 ½, breed 19 ½ duim	Casper de Haas	(Sold) fl 69 Van Leen
1802/09/18	RMDRS	0024	*H. Carree* | Een fraay Bosch gezicht, waarin een Vorstelyke Hartejacht, in de manier van D. Vinkeboom, op koper | *Mat:* op koper *Size:* hoog 13 ½, breed 16 ½ duim	Casper de Haas	(Sold) fl 9 Gruiter
1802/12/13	AMSCH	0038	*H. Carré* | In een Landschap, zit teegens de Stam van een Boom, een ter halver Lyf gekleeden Vénus, verseld van een der Minnewichten, uitvoerig gepenceeld | *Mat:* op paneel *Size:* hoog 11, breed 8 ½ duim	Pruyssenaar [for] C	(Sold) fl 1:15 Frantze
1803/04/18	HGBAK	0023	*H. Carré* | Een Dame zittende aan een Tafel in een zieklyke houding, en een Doctor de Urin beziende, zeer natuurlyk en kragtig door H. Carré, hoog 28, breed 24 duim, op doek, zwarte lyst [Schilderyen in Olyverf] | *Mat:* in olyverf op doek *Size:* hoog 28 breed 24 duim *Notes:* The bracketed information in the title appears above lot 1 and refers to lots 1 to 48.	Johan Pieter Reigersman [or others]	(Unknown)
1804/10/16	DLOND	0050	*H. Carre* | Een Boeren Gezelschap. Quelques Paysans en Compagnie | *Mat:* op paneel *Size:* hoog 10, breed 22		(Unknown)
1805/07/03	AMSCH	0073	*H. Carré* | In een Boere Binnehuis, ziet men eenige vrolyke Boeren en Boerinnen, zich met dansen, speelen drinken en galantiseeren vermaken; fraay en meesterlyk op Doek | *Mat:* op doek *Size:* hoog 14, breed 17 duim	Y	(Sold) fl 33 Lafontaine
1805/07/03	AMSCH	0074	*H. Carré* | Een grazige Weide, waarin men twee staande Ossen, een Herder en Hond gewaar word, verders een Bergachtig verschiet, door H. Carré, als K. du Jardin | *Mat:* op paneel *Size:* hoog 14, breed 17 duim	R[oos]	(Sold) fl 8:10 Nieuwenhuis
1805/10/09	HGBSM	0079	*H. Carré* | Een zingende boer en boerinne, met een man die op de fiool speelt, door H. Carré, op paneel, hoog 7 breet 5 duim, ovaal formaat | *Mat:* op paneel *Fmt:* ovaal *Size:* hoog 7 breet 5 duim	T H van Willigen [or others]	(Sold) fl 4:5 van der Aa
1805/10/09	HGBSM	0149	*H. Carrée* | Een kapitaal bergagtig landschap, op de voorgrond met hoog geboomte, en gestoffeerd met eenige visschers | *Mat:* op doek *Size:* hoog 43 breet 42 duim	T H van Willigen [or others]	(Sold) fl 4 Mutters

1807/10/12	MGBEO	0008	*Hendrik Carrée* | Een Mans en Vrouwe Potrait [sic] door Hendrik Carrée; 2 stuks	Hermannus Johannes Heyman	(Sold) £ 0:4 Ooms
1809/04/17	AMSCH	0021	*H. Carrée* | In een aangenaam Landschap, ziet men op de voorgrond, een Herder twee Koeijen en eenige Schapen voortdrijven; zonagtig en bevallig gepenceeld | *Mat:* op paneel *Size:* hoog 9, breed 11 duim	A	(Sold) fl 13:10
1809/07/25	HGBSM	0172	*H. Carré* | Twee Musiceerende Boeren en een Boerin | *Mat:* op paneel *Fmt:* ovaal *Size:* hoog 7, breed 5 duim	D van der Aa [or] E B ten Dall	(Sold) fl 7:5 Nieuwenhuis
			Carree, Hendrik (I) (and Bakken)		
1804/07/25	DLGRO	0017	*van Bakken; Hendrik Carré* | Een Bergächtig Landschap, zeer uitvoerig geschilderd | *Mat:* op doek *Size:* hoog 32, breed 29 duim	Mr Franc van der Burch Wz.	(Unknown)
			Carree, Hendrik (I) (copy by)		
1801/06/13	LNDLS	0026	*H. Carre; G. Dou* | Een Chirurgijn in zijn Winkel, daar een man, zijn been gekwest zijnde, geholpen wordt, in 't bijzijn van zijn vrouw, met veel bijwerk, op paneel naar G. Dou, door H. Carre | copy by Hend. Carree (I) after Dou *Mat:* op paneel *Size:* hoog 23, breed 18 duimen	D van R	(Sold) fl 17 de Roy
			Carree, Johannes		
1801/03/16	AMSCH	0098	*J. Carré* | Een zittende Boer met een kan in de hand, naast hem een hond, bevallig	K[ip]	(Sold) fl 10 Rijnders
1806/08/13	AMSCH	0037	*Carre. (J.)* | Twee stuks bevallige Landschapjes, met staand en leggend Vee; fiks gepenceeld | *Mat:* op doek *Size:* hoog 12, breed 14 duim	Vinkeles [for] E	(Sold) fl 14:10 du Pré
1806/08/13	AMSCH	0038	*Carre. (J.)* | Twee dito [stuks] dito [bevallige Landschapjes], in alles als vooren | *Mat:* op doek *Size:* hoog 9, breed 11 duim	Vinkeles [for] E	(Sold) fl 11 Wed Achtienhoven
			Carree, Michiel		
1801/03/16	AMSCH	0113	*M. Carrë* | Twee stuks heuvelagtige Landschappen met geboomte en Veehoeders met Vee, natuurlyk behandeld op doek | *Mat:* op doek	K[ip]	(Sold) fl 18 Cocler
1801/08/19	AMSCH	0017	*M. Carré* | Twee stuks Boom- en Bergachtige Landschappen, bevallig met Koeijen, Schaapen, Bokken en Beesten gestoffeert, door M. Carré, op Doek | *Mat:* op doek *Size:* hoog 14, breed 19 duim	W Wynen	(Sold) fl 20:10 Le Dantú
1802/07/27	AKHRK	0032	*M. Carre* | Een bergachtig Landschap, waarin een Boer, lijdende een Paard bij de Toom, en een Boerin, zittende op een Ezel, met hun Koeijen en Schaapen, waadende door een Rivier; in een goede trant gepenceeld | *Mat:* op doek *Size:* hoog 13 ¾, breed 18 ¾ duim	Maria Stategaart	(Sold) fl 6:5 Brouwer
1802/09/06	AMSCH	0030	*M. Carré* | Twee stuks bevallige Landschappen met Beesten; natuurlyk	J	(Sold) fl 3:15 A Schotte
1802/09/21	UTHDG	0018	*M. Carré* | Groot en klein vee, rustende bij een Herder en een vrouwtje, in een Landschap, fraaij van schildering | *Mat:* op doek *Size:* hoog 16 ½, breed 20 ½ duimen		(Bought In) fl 12:10
1802/12/13	AMSCH	0037	*M. Carré* | In een hoog bergagtig Landschap, by eenige overblyfsels van alouden Gebouwen, ziet men een bevallige Herderin by een witte Stier, en een meenigte van ander Vee; schoon van Licht en breed gepenceeld | *Mat:* op doek *Size:* hoog 34, breed 39 duim	Pruyssenaar [for] A	(Sold) fl 10 Yver
1803/09/07	AMSCH	0036	*M. Carre* | Een Aangenaam Landschap, met een Rivier doorsneeden, op de voorgrond een menigte staand en rustend Vee, door de Rivier vaart een Pont, met een Herder, Herderin, benevens eenige Ossen, verder een aangenaam Boom- en Duinachtig verschiet, meesterlyk en natuurlyk gepenceeld [Un beau paysage, traversé par une rivière ; sur le devant une multitude de bétail couché et de bout [sic] ; un ponton avec un berger et une bergère et quelques boeufs passent la rivière ; le fond du tableau présente une agréable perspective à travers les arbres ; peint au naturel et de main de maître] | *Mat:* op doek *Size:* hoog 30, breed 36 duim	Smidt	(Sold) fl 31 Teengs
1803/09/07	AMSCH	0037	*M. Carre* | Twee stuks Boom- en Bergachtige Landschappen, gestoffeerd met divers staand en leggend Vee, behandeld als de voorgaande [Deux paysages relevés par des montagnes et des bois, du bétail couché et débout forme une agréable diversité ; d'une ordonnance et d'une exécution semblable au précédent] | *Mat:* op doek *Size:* ieder hoog 22, breed 28 duim	Smidt	(Sold) fl 14 Toselli
1804/02/27	AMSCH	0147	*M. Carré* | Twee stuks Schilderyen	B	(Sold) fl 8:10 La Bouchere
1804/05/07	AMSCH	0035	*Carré. (M.)* | In een Straat in den Haag ziet men oude Visboerin Schelvis aan een Juffrouw, op een Stoep staande verkopen, naast haar een jong Boertje, verders de Dienstmeid, op de voorgrond zit een Schoenlapper in zyn Pothuis, de Visch met oplettendheid aan te zien; bevallig van coloriet en meesterlyk gepenceeld | *Mat:* op doek *Size:* hoog 26, breed 19 duim	Roos [for] A	(Sold) fl 188 Theijs
1804/05/07	AMSCH	0036	*Carré. (M.)* | Twee stuks aangenaame Landschappen, ryk gestoffeerd met een meenigte van stand en rustend Vée, waarby eenige Boomen en Boerenschuuren; deeze ryke Ordonantiën zyn beide van de beste schildering van deeze Meester | *Size:* yder hoog 18, breed 17 duim	Vinkeles [for] J	(Sold) fl 12 Wed Achtienhoven
1804/05/07	AMSCH	0037	*Carré. (M.)* | In een Boomryk Landschap, by Maaneschyn, ziet men op de voorgrond eenige Lieden, bézig by een vuur zich te warmen; breed en fiks van behandeling | *Mat:* op paneel *Size:* hoog 10, breed 8 ½ duim	Vinkeles [for] H[affner]	(Bought In) fl 1 ½

1804/10/16	DLOND	0048	*M. Carre* | Twee Stukken. Het Oordeel van Paris en Midas. Deux Pièces. Les Jugemens de Paris & Mida [sic] | *This Lot:* Het Oordeel van Paris *Mat:* op doek *Size:* hoog 19, breed 25 *Notes:* Lots 48 and 49 were printed in the catalogue as one item.		(Unknown)
1804/10/16	DLOND	0049	*M. Carre* | Twee Stukken. Het Oordeel van Paris en Midas. Deux Pièces. Les Jugemens de Paris & Mida [sic] | *This Lot:* Het Oordeel van Midas *Mat:* op doek *Size:* hoog 19, breed 25 *Notes:* Lots 48 and 49 were printed in the catalogue as one item.		(Unknown)
1805/07/10	AMSCH	0042	*M. Carreé* | Een Maneschyn in een Bergachtig Landschap, op de voorgrond verscheide Lieden, welke zich by een Vuur warmen; natuurlyk op Paneel | *Mat:* op paneel *Size:* hoog 10, breed 9 duim	V[inkeles] [for] H[affner]	(Sold) fl 0:10 L Pakker
1805/12/16	AMSCH	0016	*M. Carré* | Een capitale Ordinantie, van verscheide Kinderen, speelende met een Bok, daar by eenige Lammeren, in het verschiet een Herder met Vée by een Fontyn; zeer fraay op Doek behandeld | *Mat:* op doek *Size:* hoog 54, breed 56 duim	R[oos]	(Bought In) fl 3
1806/08/13	AMSCH	0317	*Carre. (M.)* | Twee stuks Riviergezichten, met Gebergtens, Ruïnes, Houtvlotten, Ponten, zeilende Scheepen, Beelden en Beesten; zonachtig en fiks gepenceeld | *Mat:* op doek *Size:* Ieder hoog 13, breed 15 duim	Vinkeles [for] G[ruyter]	(Sold) fl 2:15 Gruiter
1808/06/13	AMSCH	0034	*Carré (M.)* | Eene Offerhande, waarbij eenige Maagden met een witte Stier, op den voorgrond een roode Os, benevens Schapen en Bokken. Zacht geschilderd | *Mat:* op doek *Size:* hoog 23, breed 46 duim	E M Engelberts	(Sold) fl 31 van Drielst
1808/06/13	AMSCH	0035	*Carré (M.)* | Eene Vrouw op een Ezel zittende, met een Herder in gesprek, eenig Vee voortdrijvende: behandeld als voren | *Mat:* op doek *Size:* hoog 16, breed 19 duim	E M Engelberts	(Sold) fl 15 Engelberts
1808/06/13	AMSCH	0037	*Carré (M.)* | Twee stuks boomrijke Landschappen, met staand en liggend Vee, Herders enz. krachtig behandeld | *Mat:* op doek *Size:* ieder hoog 16, breed 19 duim	Z	(Sold) fl 47 Reyers pour Allard
1808/08/23	AMSCH	0203	*M. Carree* | Twee stuks Italiaansche Landschappen, met Landlieden en Vee gestoffeerd, meesterlijk op Doek | *Mat:* op doek	[Gruyter?]	(Sold) fl 4:15 van Iperen
1809/04/22	AMYVR	0027	*M. Carré* | Eene Herderin op een Ezel, met een Kind, wordt door een Jongen, benevens eenig Vee, door eene Waterplas geleid, voorts eenig zwaar Geboomte en aangenaam Bergachtig verschiet; meesterlijk | *Mat:* op doek *Size:* hoog 12, breed 16 duim	de Bruin	(Bought In) fl 23
1809/04/22	AMYVR	0028	*M. Carré* | Twee stuks Landschappen, gestoffeerd met staand en liggend Vee, Beelden, enz., geestig | *Mat:* op doek *Size:* hoog 12, breed 14 duim	de Bruin	(Sold) fl 9:15 du Pree
1809/04/22	AMYVR	0029	*M. Carré* | Twee stuks rijk met Beesten gestoffeerde Berg- en Boomrijke Landschappen; zonachtig behandeld | *Mat:* op doek *Size:* hoog 19, breed 22 duim	de Bruin	(Sold) fl 20 C S Roos
1809/07/25	HGBSM	0234	*M. Carré* | Twee stuks bergachtige Landschappen, ryk met verschillend soort van Vee gestoffeert | *Mat:* op doek *Size:* hoog 21 en een half, breed 18 duim	D van der Aa [or] E B ten Dall	(Sold) fl 30 de Gelder
1810/06/06	RMMUY	0158	*M. Carrée* | Twee fraaije Landschappen met Koeijen Schapen en andere Figuren, zonachtig en goed geschilderd | *Mat:* op doek		(Sold) fl 16:10 Brunelli
1810/06/20	AMSCH	0014	*M. Carré* | In een Landschap ziet men eenige Kinderen, spelende met Bokjes; verder Schapen and ander Vee. Bevallig behandeld | *Mat:* op doek *Size:* hoog 52, breed 56 duimen	R[oos]	(Sold) fl 2 du Pree
1810/08/10	RMRIJ	0016	*M. Carreé* | Een Landschap, waar in een drift Beesten en Figuren. Kloek en meesterlijk geschilderd | *Mat:* op doek *Size:* hoog 24 duim, breed 29 ½ duim		(Sold) fl 20 [or] 36 de Bruin
			Carree, Michiel (copy by)		
1804/10/16	DLOND	0047	*M. Carre; naar Berchem* | Een Landschap met Herders en Vee. Paysage, des Bergers & du Betail | copy by M. Carree after N.P. Berchem *Mat:* op doek *Size:* hoog 23, breed 27		(Unknown)
1806/11/24	AMSCH	0013	*Carré (M.); P. Potter* | Dit stuk is een accurate Copy na de beroemde Ossendrift van P. Potter, voormaals toebehorende aan de Heer G. Braamkamp, en ook van dezelfde groote, zynde een Ordinnantie van tien Beesten, waar agter een Boer en aangenaam verschiet; fraai gepenceeld | copy by M. Carree after Paulus Potter *Mat:* op doek *Size:* hoog 54, breed 78 duim	Munnikhuizen	(Sold) fl 21 Sukerbekker
			Carree, Michiel (manner)		
1801/03/16	AMSCH	0190	*M. Carré* | Twee stuks Landzichten, gestoffeerd met staand en rustend Vee, op paneel, in de manier van M. Carré | *Mat:* op paneel	K[ip]	(Sold) fl 2:15 Roelofs
			Carriera, Rosalba		
1808/11/12	HGSCR	0007	*Rosalba* | Twee stuks bevallige pourtraitten zynde de een een man en 't ander een vrouw, zeer fraai en uitvoerig geschildert | *Mat:* op paneel	Mr J van Buren	(Unknown) fl 5:5
			Casanova, Francesco Giuseppe		
1803/04/27	AMSCH	0096	*Casanova* | Deux Batailles | *Size:* h. 2 ¼, l. 4 ½ pieds	A	(Sold) fl 2:15 L Pakker
1803/12/12	AMSCH	0020	*Casanove* | Een Ezeldryver en eenige Schaapen in een Landschap; meesterlyk op Paneel | *Mat:* op paneel *Size:* hoog 7, breed 10 duim	D	(Sold) fl 12:10 Coclers

1810/07/26	AMSCH	0114	*Cassanova* | Eene Bataille | *Mat:* op paneel	Cassino	(Sold) fl 0:14 L Pakker
			Casteels, Pieter (III)		
1801/10/06	AMSCH	0019	*P. Casteels* | Op een Steene Voetstuk, staat een cierlyke gewerkte Vaas, omslingerd met een Rank van onderscheidene zoorten van fraaije Bloemen, zeer natuurlyk en kragtig gepenceeld | *Mat:* op doek *Size:* hoog 43, breed 31 duim	L	(Sold) fl 3:10 Van Houten
1807/08/26	AMSCH	0035	*Casteels* | Een bevallige Dame, staande voor eene Tafel, op welke een Pot met Bloemen staat; helder en krachtig | *Mat:* op doek *Size:* hoog 46, breed 39 duim	de Vries	(Sold) fl 0:6 Dirk Nuland
1810/10/10	MGCIT	0155	*Casteels* | Een Capitaal Stuk met Bloemen	Caspar van Citters	(Unknown)
			Castiglione, Giovanni Benedetto (Il Grechetto)		
1803/09/07	AMSCH	0039	*B. Castillione* | Verscheide Schaapen en een Bokje, voor een Waterplas, waarin een zwemmende Hond, meesterlyk op Doek [Des moutons et des chevres devant une nape d'eau dans laquelle nage un chien, d'une parfaite exécution] | *Mat:* op doek *Size:* hoog 13, breed 17 duim	Smidt	(Sold) fl 1:15 Van den Brink
1808/06/06	RMRIJ	0022	*Castiglione. (Jean Benedette)* | Eene meesterlijke schets, de Heilige Maagd voorstellende, dewelke, knielende in eene gebogene houding, het kind Jezus, in eene kribbe gelegen, omhelst. In den achtergrond twee Engelen. Fraai van kleur en uitwerking [Esquisse representant la Sainte Vierge embrassant l'enfant Jézus couché dans la Crêche. On voit deux Anges dans le fond] | *Annots:* Verk. pastoor Bruiuslean[?] te St. Nicolaas (f 240.-) Verk. E A J v d Meersche, Gent 4 Juli 1791 (f 60.-) (RMA I); NB ca no.22 n'est qu'une esquisse toute ruinée et raplâtrée, achetée par feu Mr v der Pot pour 10 # de gros, dans la vente du comte Berlaar à Gand, sous la no.133 en 1791 (MA) *Mat:* op doek *Size:* Hoog 13 ¼, en breed 15 ¾ duim	Gerrit van der Pot, Heer van Groeneveld	(Sold) fl 55 R Pott
			Cats, Jacob		
1809/06/13	AMSCH	0033	*J. Cats* | Twee stuks Hollandsche Landschappen, met Post- en Boerenwagens, gaande en rustende Rijzigers en Dorpen in 't verschiet; fiks geschilderd | *Mat:* op doek *Size:* hoog 19, breed 16 duim	S[chley]	(Sold) fl 8:10 Gruiter
			Cavedone, Giacomo		
1803/08/17	AMSCH	0020	*Cavedone* | Het Pourtrait van den beruchten Napolitaansche Muiteling, Masaniello, kragtig, stout en vol uitdrukking geschilderd | *Mat:* op doek *Size:* hoog 25, breed 19 duim	Anna Catharina Putman	(Sold) fl 7 de Lelie
			Cerquozzi, Michelangelo (Michelangelo delle Battaglie)		
1802/04/13	HAVIN	0036	*M. Angelo de la Bataille* | Twee Battailles vol vuur		(Unknown)
1804/07/25	AMSCH	0002	*Angelo. (M.) de la Bataille* | In dit stuk ziet men ter regterzyde een Legertent, waarin een gekwetste werd verbonden, terwyl een andere ter hulpen werd aangebragt, en in 't verschiet vertoonen zig eenige vegtende en vlugtende Ruiters en Voetknegten; op de voorgrond ter linkerzyde liggen verscheide Wapentuig, Trommels en Kleederen; alles is fix en kragtig gepenceeld | *Mat:* op doek *Size:* hoog 22, breed 30 duim		(Sold) fl 22 Gruiter
1804/10/16	DLOND	0013	*De la Batailly* | Een Grot, waarin verscheiden Personen. Une Grotte dans laquelle beaucoup de Personnes | *Mat:* op doek *Size:* hoog 26, breed 22		(Sold) fl 22 Mahy
1810/08/10	RMRIJ	0017	*Michel Angelo de la Battaille* | Voor een Italiaansch Gebouw, ziet men eenige Beelden, en eene Smederij in 't verschiet. Krachtig en aangenaam van effect | *Mat:* op doek *Size:* hoog 24 ½ duim, breed 19 ½ duim		(Sold) fl 30 [or] 40 de Bruin
1810/08/10	RMRIJ	0018	*Michel Angelo de la Battaille* | Een Italiaansch Landschap, op den voorgrond zijn dansende, drinkende en spelende Figuren. Zeer konstig en meesterlijk gepenceeld | *Mat:* op doek *Size:* hoog 19 ½ duim, breed 25 ½ duim		(Sold) fl 50 [or] 100 R Pot
			Ceulen, Jan Jansz. van		
1804/05/07	AMSCH	0094	*Keulen (J. Janse van)* | Een Manspourtret in deftige Kleeding, meesterlyk behandeld | *Mat:* op doek *Size:* hoog 44, breed 35 duim	Y[ver] [for] JJ	(Sold) fl 1:5 A van der Hagen
			Chalon, Louis		
1801/10/06	AMSCH	0017	*L. Chalon* | Twee stuks Gezichten aan den Rhyn, – byden gestoffeert met Hout-Vlotten, 3 Aken en andere Vaartuigen, helder en plaisant geschilderd | *Mat:* op doek *Size:* yder hoog 15, breed 12 ½ duim	M	(Sold) fl 10:10 J^n Yver
1801/12/22	AMOTT	0007	*L. Chalon* | 2 aangenaam voordoende Gezigten aan den Rhyn, met steenagtige Gebouwen, Beelden in onderschydene actien, Vaartuigen en andere playsante stoffagien, door L. Chalon, 1736 | *Inscr:* L. Chalon, 1736 (signed and dated?) *Notes:* It is unclear whether the name and date are inscribed on the painting.	Bartholomeus Ruloffs	(Unknown) fl 10:10
1801/12/22	AMOTT	0041	*L. Chalon* | 2 aangenaame Ryngezigten, met Kooplieden en Vaartuigen	Bartholomeus Ruloffs	(Unknown) fl 9
1801/12/22	AMOTT	0066	*Chalon* | Handeldryvende Kooplieden, met veelerly Vaartuigen, by een bergachtig Landschap aan den Rhyn	Bartholomeus Ruloffs	(Unknown) fl 12
1801/12/22	AMOTT	0099	*Challon* | 2 fraaie dito [stuks] Gezigten	Bartholomeus Ruloffs	(Unknown) fl 2:5

1801/12/22	AMOTT	0100[a]	*Challon* | 2 stuks, een Landschapje, door denzelven [Challon], en een Binnenvertrek | *This Lot:* Een Landschapje; lot 100[b] by Anonymous	Bartholomeus Ruloffs	(Unknown) fl 7:10 for lots 100[a] & 100[b]
1802/02/16	AMSCH	0062	*L. Chalon* | Een natuurlyk Wintergezigt, gestoffeert met Schaatseryders, en diverse Sleeden	G	(Sold) fl 0:10 Vink & Fitsing
1802/06/28	AMSCH	0032	*L. Chalon* | Twee stuks, ryk met Vaartuigen en Beelden, gestoffeerde Rhyngezigten; natuurlyk op Doek | *Mat:* op doek *Size:* hoog 10, breed 13 duim	Anna Elink	(Sold) fl 12:10 Mensart
1802/12/13	AMSCH	0046	*L. Chalon* | Een Binnegezigt, op de Plaats van 't Leproosenhuis, gestoffeert met verscheide wandelende Beeldjes, plaisant behandeld | *Mat:* op doek *Size:* hoog 16, breed 20 duim	Florijn [?]	(Sold) fl 1 B^n Abrahams
1803/07/18	AMSCH	0009	*Chalon. (Louis)* | Twee stuks ryk met Gebouwen, Gebergtens, Beelden en Schepen gestoffeerde Rhyngezigten, zonachtig en uitvoerig behandeld [Deux Paysages & vues sur les deux rives du Rhin. La riviere qui serpente au millieu de ces Sites est garnie de nacelles & de Jolies figures. Ils ont l'agrement d'une belle couleur & d'un faire facile.] | *Mat:* op doek *Size:* yder hoog 16, breed 13 duim	Maria Theresia Andrioli	(Sold) fl 14:10 Theens
1803/08/24	HGKAN	0012	*L. Chalon* | Twee stuks Rhyn Gezigten, ryk gestoffeerd met figuuren en Schuitjes, in de manier van Griffier, door L. Chalon | *Mat:* op paneel *Size:* hoog 12 ½, breet 15 duim	[Teissier] [or others]	(Sold) fl 14 Pulver
1803/12/12	AMSCH	0017	*L. Chalon* | Twee stuks ryk gestoffeerde Rhyngezichten; geestig op Doek | *Mat:* op doek *Size:* hoog 24, breed 29 duim	Arnoud de Lange	(Sold) fl 15 Uselino
1803/12/12	AMSCH	0018	*L. Chalon* | Twee dito [stuks] dito [ryk gestoffeerde Rhyngezichten]; uitvoerig | *Mat:* op doek *Size:* hoog 9, breed 12 duim *Notes:* It is unclear what "dito" refers to in the title.	Arnoud de Lange	(Sold) fl 5:5 Ijver
1804/02/27	AMSCH	0023	*Chalon. (L.)* | Twee stuks bevallige Boom- en Duinachtige Landschappen, voorstellende beide vrolyke Boeren Kermissen; aller natuurlykst en fraai gepenceeld | *Mat:* op doek *Size:* ieder hoog 28, breed 33 duim	D	(Sold) fl 5 de Veer
1804/10/29	HRBAU	0016	*Chalon, (Louis)* | Een zeer fraai Gezigt over eene Rivier, met Gebouwen en hoog Gebergte voorzien; op den Voorgrond by een' Weg, waar op een menigte Beeldtjes zyn, ligt een Pont die belaaden wordt; en aan de overzyde des waters, aan den voet van het Gebergte, ligt eene Stad, waar agter zig een verrukkelyk gezigt in het Gebergte opdoet. Zeer uitvoerig in de manier van Griffier behandeld | *Mat:* op doek *Size:* hoog 21, breed 25 duim	Simon Styl	(Unknown)
1806/08/13	AMSCH	0035	*Chalon. (L.)* | Twee stuks Rhyngezichten, vol gewoel van Beeldjes, Schuitjes en aangenaame Bergachtige verschieten; fiks van behandeling | *Mat:* op doek *Size:* Ieder hoog 13, breed 18 duim	Vinkeles [for] F	(Sold) fl 25 Schumacher
1806/08/13	AMSCH	0036	*Chalon. (L.)* | Een Rhyngezichtje, met Geboomten, Gebergten en stoffagie van Beeldjes; delicaat en uitvoerig gepenceeld | *Mat:* op paneel *Size:* hoog 6, breed 7 duim	Vinkeles [for] F	(Sold) fl 1:10 Yver
1807/08/26	AMSCH	0037	*L. Chalon* | Een gezigt aan den Rhyn, de voorgrond gestoffeerd met Ryzigers en andere Beelden | *Mat:* op doek *Size:* hoog 16 ½, breed 18 ½ duim	de Vries	(Sold) fl 2 Gruiter
1807/08/26	AMSCH	0304	*L. Chalon* | Twee stuks gestoffeerde Rhyngezichten | *Mat:* op doek	Yver [for] S	(Sold) fl 1:5 T Spaan
1808/03/03	HAVIN	0034	*Chalon* | Een Zomer en Winter, met Coul.	Jacobus Spillebout	(Unknown) fl 2:2
1810/10/11	AMSCH	0123	*Chalon* | Een Bergachtig Rhijngezigt, met Beelden en Vaartuigen | *Mat:* op doek	[Gruyter?]	(Sold or Bought In) fl 2 Gruiter

Chalon, Louis (manner)

1801/12/22	AMOTT	0004	*Chalon* | Onderscheidene Lieden welke hunne Koopwaaren, in Scheepen en Vaartuigen, laaden en lossen, by een bergachtig Landschap aan den Rhyn, in bevallige smaak, als Chalon	Bartholomeus Ruloffs	(Unknown) fl 7
1801/12/22	AMOTT	0017	*Chalon* | 1 Poort- en Riviergezigt, met bywerk, als Chalon	Bartholomeus Ruloffs	(Unknown) fl 1
1801/12/22	AMOTT	0028	*Chalon* | 1 Bergachtig en Ryngezigt, als Chalon	Bartholomeus Ruloffs	(Unknown) fl 0:12

Chalons, F. [Unidentified]

1802/07/21	HGKAN	0019	*F. Chalons* | Twee dito [Schilderyen], zynde Italiaansche Zeehaavens, rykelyk gestoffeerd met scheepen en Beelden, waar van eenige bezig zyn met Laaden en ontlaaden der Scheepen, terwyl een ander gedeelte, zich vermaaken met Zwemmen en Baaden		(Unknown)

Champaigne, Philippe de

1810/07/26	AMSCH	0022	*Champagne (Ph. de)* | Een fraai stuk van vijf Beelden, in onderscheidene houding | *Mat:* op doek *Size:* hoog 26, breed 32 duimen	Cassino	(Sold) fl 30 T Spaan

Chapman, J. [Unidentified]

1806/08/20	HGBSM	0181	*J. Chapman* | Een Italiäansch Land- en Zeegezicht; rijk gestoffeerd, in de manier van Salvator Rosa, door J. Chapman 1690 | companion to lot 182 *Mat:* op doek *Size:* hoog 17 ½, breed 36 ½ duim *Inscr:* J. Chapman 1690 (signed and dated?) *Notes:* It is unclear whether the name and date are inscribed on the painting.	Macalester Loup [or others]	(Sold) fl 0:14 for lots 181 & 182. Abr Salomon
1806/08/20	HGBSM	0182	*J. Chapman* | Een dito [Italiäansch Land-] gezicht tot wederga | companion to lot 181 *Notes:* It is unclear what "dito" refers to in the title.	Macalester Loup [or others]	(Sold) fl 0:14 for lots 181 & 182. Abr Salomon

Cignani, Carlo

1803/04/27	AMSCH	0120[b]	*Carlo Cignani* | Deux tableaux, la pentecôte d'après Rafaël, & la Chasteté | *This Lot:* La Chasteté; lot 120[a] is copy after Raffaello Santi	A	(Sold) fl 2 for lots 120[a] & 120[b]. L Pakker
1810/07/26	AMSCH	0140	*Carlo Cignani* | De Godin Flora, omgeeven van eene menigte Bloemen en Vrugten. Zeer schoon geschilderd, als Titiano | *Mat:* op doek *Size:* hoog 43, breed 60 duimen	Cassino	(Bought In) fl 3

Claude Lorrain (Claude Gellée)

1810/07/26	AMSCH	0047	*Laurain (Claude de)* | De Heilige Familje, rustende in een Landschap met oude Ruïne. Zijnde een bijzonder fraai stuk | *Mat:* op doek *Size:* hoog 18, breed 24 duimen	Cassino	(Bought In) fl 61

Claude Lorrain (Claude Gellée) (and Lauri, F.)

1810/10/11	AMSCH	0046	*C. De Lorrain; Ph. Lauri* | Een fraai Boschgezigt, met hoog Geboomte, Kreupelgewassen en Beeldjes gestoffeerd | *Mat:* op doek *Size:* hoog 24, breed 20 duimen	C	(Bought In) fl 40

Claude Lorrain (Claude Gellée) (manner)

1805/07/10	AMSCH	0215	*C. de Lorrain* | Een Zeehaven in de Levant, met eenige Scheepen, Lieden, enz.; in de manier van C. de Lorrain	V[inkeles] [for] H[affner]	(Bought In) fl 2:5

Claude Lorrain (Claude Gellée) (style)

1810/07/26	AMSCH	0144	*Claude Lorrain (In den stijl van)* | Een Gezigt buiten Rome, zijnde een Landschap, met Beelden gestoffeerd. Een schoon stuk | *Mat:* op doek *Size:* hoog 45, breed 63 duimen	Cassino	(Sold) fl 23:10 van Iperen

Cleve, Joos van

1806/05/05	AMSCH	0193	*Zotte van Kleef* | Een met twee Vrouwen hoofden; door de Zotte van Kleef	H	(Sold) fl 1:10 Gruyter

Coclers

1810/03/27	RMCNL	0045	*Coceler* | In een Binnenhuis zit een Vrouwtje te Naaijen, terwijl zij inmiddels uit haren mond eene Kanarievogel op hare schouder gezeten voedt, zeer aardig en netjes behandeld		(Unknown)

Coclers, Bernard (copy by)

1808/06/06	RMRIJ	0023	*Coclers. (Bernard); naar Metzu* | Eene Vrouw aan eene Waschtobbe. Getrouw gevolgd en aangenaam geschilderd [Une Blanchisseuse occupée devant son Cuvier. Cette Copie est fidelle et bien traitée] | copy by B. Coclers after Metsu *Annots:* Verk. P. Spyk 23 Avril 1781 (f 50.-) Verk Drk Haak, Leiden, 8 April 1782 (f 17.-) (RMA I) *Mat:* op paneel *Size:* Hoog 8 ¾, en breed 7 ¾ duim	Gerrit van der Pot, Heer van Groeneveld	(Sold) fl 53 W van der Pot

Coclers, Jean Baptiste

1807/04/00	LNDLS	0027	*J. B. Coclers* | Een studeerend man, zittende voor een tafel met een boek voor hem | *Mat:* op paneel	[Abraham Delfos] [or others]	(Unknown)
1807/06/10	HGBSM	0027	*J.B. Coclers* | Een studeerende man, zittende voor een tafel met een boek voor hem | *Mat:* op paneel	Abraham Delfos [or others]	(Sold) fl 3:2 V Giesen

Coclers, Jean Baptiste Bernard (Louis Bernard)

1802/06/28	AMSCH	0033	*L. B. Coclers* | Een Dame, met een Kind by zich, bezig zynde Koussen te stoppen; alles by een helder Kaarslicht, natuurlyk op Panneel | *Mat:* op paneel *Size:* hoog 12, breed 10 duim	Anna Elink	(Sold) fl 10:10 T Spaan
1802/08/24	LNDLS	0076	*L.B. Coclers* | Een Juffertje, zittende naast een Tafel daar een Vogelkooi op staat, terwijl zij een doek naait, agter haar een Ledikant, en meer Bijwerk. Uitvoerig op paneel, hoog 10, breed 8 duimen, door L.B. Coclers, 1775 | *Mat:* op paneel *Size:* hoog 10, breed 8 duimen *Inscr:* L.B. Coclers, 1775 (signed and dated?) *Notes:* It is unclear whether the name and date are inscribed on the painting.	Leonardus Bouman [or others]	(Unknown) fl 6:10
1802/08/24	LNDLS	0077	*L.B. Coclers* | Een Binnen-huis met caresserende Jongelingen en Meisjes, terwijl een derzelve zit te rusten. Helder van coloriet en plaizant | *Mat:* op paneel *Size:* hoog 12 ½, breed 10 ½ duimen	Leonardus Bouman [or others]	(Unknown) fl 10:5

Codanelli, P. [Unidentified]

1804/08/08	AMSCH	0048	*P. Codanelli* | Op een Steenen Aanregtsbank legt eenig dood Wild en Gevogelte, achter dezelve een Jager, met een Geweer in zyn Hand; fiks en breed geschilderd | *Mat:* op doek *Size:* hoog 47, breed 65 duim	Vink[eles] [for] K[=Gruyter?]	(Sold) fl 1:10 L Pakker

Codde, Pieter Jacobs

1804/10/16	DLOND	0051	*P. Codde* | Een Boerenhuis, waar in de Boer en zyn Vrouw door Soldaten worden aangerand. L'Interieur d'une Maison de Paysan, dans la quelle des Soldats attaquent les habitans | *Mat:* op paneel *Size:* hoog 16, breed 20		(Unknown)
1806/06/07	RMHSN	0035	*P. Kodde* | Een dito [Corps du Garde] met Kaartspelers en anderen | *Mat:* op paneel	A E K L	(Unknown)

Coecke van Aelst, Pauwels

1803/08/17	AMSCH	0005	*Aalst. (P. van)* | Op een Steene Tafel staat een Porcelyne Schaal, gevuld met diversche Fruiten, uitvoerig geschilderd | *Mat:* op doek *Size:* hoog 25, breed 21 duim	Anna Catharina Putman	(Sold) fl 2:15 LaBouchere

Coelenbier, Jan

1801/04/08	HAVIN	0039	*Coelombie* | Een Land en Watergezigt		(Unknown)
1810/08/06	AMSCH	0056	*Koelenbier* | Een kabbelend Water, ter zijde een Stad, gestoffeerd met een overvarende Pontschuit en andere Vaartuigen; natuurlijk behandeld | *Size:* hoog 26, breed 37 duimen	C	(Sold) fl 12 Stoopendaal [for] B
1810/10/11	AMSCH	0192	*J. Koelenbier* | Eene stille Rivier, ter zijde Woningen en een oude Toren, gestoffeerd met Visschers in hunne Schuiten; natuurlijk geschilderd | *Mat:* op doek	A	(Sold) fl 4:10 Gruiter

Coelmans, J. [Unidentified]

1802/05/11	GRGRW	0050	*Coelmam* | Een Oud Kasteel [Schilderijen met Olie-Verf; In zwarte Lijsten] | *Mat:* in olyverf *Notes:* The bracketed information in the title appears above lot 1 and refers to lots 1 to 79a.	Arnold Sicco Werumeus	(Unknown) fl 0:10
1805/10/21	GRBOL	0015	*J. Coelmans* | Een Landschap, Ryk gestoffeerd, met Beelden en Beesten, zoo goed, als J. van Goojen	Gerardus Nicolaus Heerkens	(Unknown)
1805/10/21	GRBOL	0028	*J. Coelmans* | Een Watergezicht met een Molen en Kalkovens	Gerardus Nicolaus Heerkens	(Unknown)

Coesermans, Johannes

1804/10/16	DLOND	0120	*J. Koeserman* | Een Kerk van binnen. L'Interieur d'une Eglise | *Mat:* op paneel *Size:* hoog 18, breed 20		(Unknown)

Cok, Jan Matthias

1802/06/28	AMSCH	0034	*J. M. Cok* | Twee stuks bevallige Landzigten, beide gestoffeert met Huislieden, staand en rustend Vee; meesterlyk behandeld | *Size:* hoog 9, breed 11 duim	B	(Sold) fl 6 Roos [for] A
1802/06/28	AMSCH	0035	*J. M. Cok* | Een Jongeling, leunende op de rand van een steene Nis; fiks behandeld, door Denzelven [J. M. Cok], Panneel | *Mat:* op paneel *Size:* hoog 11, breed 9 duim	B	(Sold) fl 2 Roos [for] A
1804/02/27	AMSCH	0024	*Cok. (J. M.)* | Twee stuks Grazige Weiden, met verscheiden Vee, Beeldjes en Honden; delicaat en uitvoerig behandeld | *Size:* hoog 10, breed 11 duim	R[oos]	(Sold) fl 6:15 van Iperen
1804/05/07	AMSCH	0040	*Cok. (J. M.)* | Een Dame aan een Tafel zittende, waarop Chocolade, ter zyde een Papagaai in zyn Kooi, en ander bywerk; uitvoerig behandeld | *Mat:* op paneel *Size:* hoog 20, breed 16 duim	R[oos]	(Sold) fl 6:15 Sal Joseph

Colaert, Johannes (Landscape Painter)

1801/03/16	AMSCH	0179	*Coller* | Een bevallig Landschap	P[ruyssenaar]	(Sold) fl 3 Roelofs
1802/05/05	AMSCH	0046	*Coller* | Een Duin- en Boomryk Landschap, gestoffeerd met rustende Reizigers | *Size:* hoog 11, breed 14 duim	J	(Sold) fl 2:5 Ackina
1808/10/28	AMVRS	0007	*Collard. (J.)* | Een Bergachtig Landschap met een Boere Schuur, daarnevens ziet men een loopend en zeer natuurlijk stuivend Water en Watermolen. Zeer treffend en fraai behandeld | *Mat:* op paneel *Size:* hoog 31, breed 22 duim	Marten Udink	(Sold) fl 20 du Pré

Colonia, Adam

1805/10/21	GRBOL	0046	*A. Colona* | Een Brantje: op de Voorgrond ziet men enige Romeinsche Soldaten, en verder Bywerk, uitvoerig geschilderd	Gerardus Nicolaus Heerkens	(Unknown)
1806/11/24	AMSCH	0016	*Colonia* | Een Herder, leunende tegen een staketzel by een Boom, waarby twee staande en leggende Beesten; kragtig als P. Potter behandeld | *Mat:* op paneel *Size:* hoog 9, breed 8 duim	Munnikhuizen	(Sold) fl 1:10 Levy Pakker
1808/04/26	GDAN	0018	*Collonia* | Zijnde een Landschap met Koeijen en Schapen | *Size:* hoog 9 ½, breed 12 duim	G H Fortuyn	(Unknown)
1808/06/13	AMSCH	0219	*Collonia* | Een Maneschijn, waarbij eenige Visschers op het Strand; natuurlijk	E M Engelberts	(Sold) fl 14 Gruiter
1808/12/31	RMHSN	0021	*Colonia* | Een Kersnagt | *Mat:* op paneel	G Spanjaart [or] H de Haas [or] C van der Looy Lans	(Unknown)
1810/10/11	AMSCH	0207	*A. Colonia* | Een Landschap met Ruïne, op de voorgrond Landlieden en Vee	A	(Sold) fl 1:5 Mensart
1810/10/11	AMSCH	0217	*A. Colonia* | De Boodschap aan de Herders | *Mat:* op paneel	A	(Sold) fl 3:15 Mensart

Colyer, Edwaert

1804/08/02	BDAN	0009	*E. Colleyen* | Een Tafel waarop zyn eenige Boeken, Doods hoofd en ander bywerk, dienende tot eene verbeelding van een Vanitas, zeer uitvoerig geschildert | *Mat:* op paneel *Size:* b. 8 en 1 half d. h. 10 en 1 half d.	J G Calckberner	(Unknown)
1804/10/16	DLOND	0052	*E. Colier* | Twee Stukjens, op ieder van welken een zittende Boer. Deux Pièces. Chacune represente un Paysan assis | *This Lot:* Een Stuk *Mat:* op		(Unknown)

			paneel *Size:* hoog 9, breed 8 *Notes:* Lots 52 and 53 were printed in the catalogue as one item.		
1804/10/16	DLOND	0053	*E. Colier* | Twee Stukjens, op ieder van welken een zittende Boer. Deux Pièces. Chacune represente un Paysan assis | *This Lot:* Een Stuk *Mat:* op paneel *Size:* hoog 9, breed 8 *Notes:* Lots 52 and 53 were printed in the catalogue as one item.		(Unknown)
1806/10/17	MGSAN	0022	*C. Coljer* | Een stil Leven, verbeeldende een omgekeerde Kroon en Scepter op een Tafel, waarop een Doodschoofd | *Mat:* op paneel *Notes:* The artist's name was given as "C. Coljer" but we have assumed this is an error.	Gerardus Beljard	(Unknown)
1809/07/25	HGBSM	0230	*P. Colier* | Een Vanitas met een Doodshoofd, Lamp en Orlogie, kunstig geschildert | *Mat:* op paneel *Size:* hoog 15 en een half, breed 23 en een half duim *Notes:* The artist's name was given as "P. Colier" but we have assumed this is an error.	D van der Aa [or] E B ten Dall	(Sold) fl 3:2 de Gruyter
1810/10/10	MGCIT	0160	*Coliert* | Een oud Man met grijs Hair en Baard, zittende in zijn Studeerkamer, voor een Tafel, gedekt met een Tapijt, en waarop leggen verscheide Boeken, Papieren en Documenten; uitvoerig behandelt | *Notes:* This lot was misnumbered no. 161 and changed in an errata sheet located at the front of the catalogue.	Caspar van Citters	(Unknown)
			Compe, Jan ten		
1801/05/11	AMSCH	0020a	*J. ten Compe* | Twee stuks Gezichten op de geweezene Lustplaats Rynhof, buiten Amsterdam, op de Slooterweg, ziende naar het Heerenhuis en andere Woningen; en het ander vertoond het Gezicht over de Vyver, naar het huis van agteren, beiden ryk gestoffeerd, met beeltjes en vee, zonachtig en plaisant geschilderd | *Mat:* op paneel *Size:* yder hoog 15, breed 20 duim	S[chley]	(Bought In) fl 32
1801/06/10	AMSCH	0039	*Compe. (J. ten)* | Dit bevallig Stukje verbeeld een Gezicht op de Montalbaans Tooren te Amsterdam, het Water gestoffeerd met Jachten, Schuiten en Beelden; uitvoerig en zonachtig behandeld | *Mat:* op doek *Size:* hoog 18, breed 22 duim	Herman ten Kate	(Sold) fl 77 C S Roos
1801/10/06	AMSCH	0015	*J. ten Compe* | Een gezigt op de Neu te Utrecht, gestoffeert met verscheide Beeldjes, een Smit is beezig een Paard te beslaan, in 't verschiet vertoont zig de Dom-Tooren, en andere Gebouwen, helder en aangenaam van Coloriet | *Mat:* op paneel *Size:* hoog 15, breed 19 duim	M	(Sold) fl 20 Tersmitten
1801/10/06	AMSCH	0016	*J. ten Compe* | Twee stuks Stads-Gezichten, gestoffeert met Wandelaars, Gebouwen en Vaartuigen, Zonagtig en plaisant geschilderd | *Mat:* op paneel *Size:* yder hoog 8, breed 10 duim	M	(Sold) fl 35 Theijs
1801/10/19	AMSCH	0016	*Compe. (J. ten)* | Een Gezicht van de witte Vrouwe Poort te Utrecht, gestoffeerd met Beeldjes en ander bywerk | companion to lot 17 *Mat:* op paneel *Size:* hoog 15 ½, breed 20 duim	Jonkheer Menno Baron van Coehoorn	(Sold) fl 90 for lots 16 & 17. Gruyter
1801/10/19	AMSCH	0017	*Compe. (J. ten)* | Een weederga, zynde een Gezicht van de Rotterdamsche Poort te Delft, zeer uitvoerig en fraay gestoffeerd met Beeldjes en ander bywerk | companion to lot 16 *Mat:* op paneel *Size:* hoog 15 ½, breed 20 duim	Jonkheer Menno Baron van Coehoorn	(Sold) fl 90 for lots 16 & 17. Gruyter
1801/10/19	AMSCH	0018	*Compe. (J. ten)* | Een Gezicht op het Stadhuis te Haarlem, ryk gestoffeerd en zonagtig behandeld | companion to lot 19 *Mat:* op paneel *Size:* hoog 11, breed 14 duim	Jonkheer Menno Baron van Coehoorn	(Sold) fl 31 for lots 18 & 19. De Roy
1801/10/19	AMSCH	0019	*Compe. (J. ten)* | Een weederga van de voorgaande, zynde het Stadhuis te Delft | companion to lot 18 *Mat:* op paneel *Size:* hoog 11, breed 14 duim	Jonkheer Menno Baron van Coehoorn	(Sold) fl 31 for lots 18 & 19. De Roy
1802/06/28	AMSCH	0027	*J. ten Compe* | Twee stuks, zynde het eene een gezicht op de Stad Kleef, men ziet op de Voorgrond een Weyland, waarin eenige leggende en graazende Beesten, ter zyde op de Weg een belaaden Kar en twee Monniken; in het verschiet ziet men boven het geboomten de Stad. De weerga stelt voor een gezicht buiten den Haag, mede zeer ryk gestoffeert met Beelden en Beesten; beide deeze Schilderyen, zyn van de uitvoerigste en bevalligste schildering van J. ten Compe | *Mat:* op paneel *Size:* hoog 12, breed 15 duim	Anna Elink	(Sold) fl 28 Texier
1802/06/28	AMSCH	0028	*J. ten Compe* | Een gezicht op de O. Z. Achterburgwal, door de Straat ziet men de Waag op de Nieuwe Markt, bevallig en zonachtig geschilderd door Denzelven [J. ten Compe] | *Mat:* op paneel *Size:* hoog 16, breed 19 duim	Anna Elink	(Sold) fl 10:10 Reyers
1802/06/28	AMSCH	0029	*J. ten Compe* | Een natuurlyk besneeuwt Wintergezicht; op het bevroozen Water, aan de Vestmuur der Stad Utrecht, ziet men verscheide Schaatsenryders en wandelende Lieden: meesterlyk fraai en bevallig gepenceelt, door Denzelven, hoog 7, breed 9 duim. Panneel | *Mat:* op paneel *Size:* hoog 7, breed 9 duim	Anna Elink	(Sold) fl 20 for lots 29 & 30. Texier
1802/06/28	AMSCH	0030	*J. ten Compe* | Een bevallig gezicht op een Stads Poort buiten Utrecht, gestoffeerd met een menigte Beelden en Beesten, door denzelven, Panneel | *Mat:* op paneel *Size:* hoog 7, breed 9 duim	Anna Elink	(Sold) fl 20 for lots 29 & 30. Texier
1802/12/13	AMSCH	0041	*J. ten Compe* | Een Gezicht van de Amsterdamsche Poort der Stad Haarlem, bevallig gestoffeerd en uitvoerig geschilderd | *Mat:* op doek *Size:* hoog 9 ½, breed 11 ½ duim	Pruyssenaar [for] A	(Sold) fl 4:15 Gruiter
1802/12/13	AMSCH	0042	*J. ten Compe* | Een dito [Gezicht] zynde het Gezicht van de O: Z: Achterburgwal, te zien na de Nieuwmarkt | *Mat:* op paneel *Size:* hoog 16, breed 19 duim	Pruyssenaar [for] A	(Bought In) fl 19:10

1803/12/15	MGLAC	0008	*Ten Compe* | Een zeer aangenaam Landschapje, waar by een Stads Gezicht; zeer delicaat | companion to lot 9 *Mat:* op paneel *Size:* hoog duim 13, breed duim 15	Mr L H de Haze Bomme	(Unknown)
1803/12/15	MGLAC	0009	*Ten Compe* | Een dito [zeer aangenaam Landschapje], weêrgaê; zynde niet minder dan de voorgaande | companion to lot 8 *Mat:* op paneel *Size:* hoog duim 13, breed duim 15 *Notes:* It is unclear what "dito" refers to in the title.	Mr L H de Haze Bomme	(Unknown)
1804/05/07	AMSCH	0038	*Compe. (J. ten)* | Twee stuks, het eene een Gezicht te Alkmaar, en het andere de Witte Vrouwen-Poort te Utrecht; beide gestoffeerd met een ménigte Beeldjes en andere Stoffagie, en altoos bekend geweest voor de beste van deezen Meester | *Mat:* op paneel *Size:* yder hoog 16, breed 21 duim	Roos [for] A	(Bought In) fl 190
1804/05/07	AMSCH	0039	*Compe. (J. ten)* | Dit aangenaam Landschap steld voor, het Gezicht van een der Stads Poorten der Stad Haarlem; zonachtig en uitvoerig geschilderd | *Mat:* op paneel *Size:* hoog 9 ½, breed 11 ½ duim	Vinkeles [for] G	(Sold) fl 8:10 Gruyter
1804/07/25	AMSCH	0014	*Compe. (J. ten)* | Dit zonachtig Schilderytje stelt voor, een gezicht naar 't Huis in 't Bosch, buiten s'Hage, met verscheide wandelende Heeren en Dames; het zonlicht geeft een bevallige werking en is uitvoerig gepenceeld | *Mat:* op paneel *Size:* hoog 10 ½, breed 14 ½ duim		(Sold) fl 19 van der Schley
1804/08/08	AMSCH	0046	*J. ten Compe* | Een Gezicht aan de Schans, ziende na de Weesper en Utrechtsche Poort, te Amsterdam; ryk gestoffeerd met wandelende Lieden, een Vrouw, welke Goed schynt te bleeken, Soldaten, enz.; zynde hetzelve zonachtig en van eene uitvoerige penceelsbehandeling | *Mat:* op paneel *Size:* hoog 18, breed 24 duim	Vink[eles] [for] S	(Sold) fl 21:10 Van Iperen
1804/08/08	AMSCH	0047	*J. ten Compe* | Twee stuks, het eene een Gezicht te Alkmaar, en het andere de Witte Vrouwen-Poort te Utrecht; beiden gestoffeerd met een ménigte Beeldjes en andere Stoffagie, zynde bekend voor het beste soort van dezelfde Meester [J. ten Compe] | *Mat:* op paneel *Size:* hoog 16 breed 21 duim	Roos [for] F	(Sold) fl 130 Van Iperen
1804/12/10	AMSCH	0008	*J. ten Compe* | Twee stuks Gezichten van buiten te zien, naar 's Hage, verbeeldende zomer en winter, beiden natuurlyk gestoffeert, naar de eigenschap van het saisoen, met verscheide wandelende, en op schaatze rydende lieden; uitvoerig en bevallig gepenceelt | *Mat:* op paneel *Size:* Ieder hoog 9 ¼, breed 11 ½ duim	Jan de Groot	(Sold) fl 12:10 van Iperen
1804/12/10	AMSCH	0009	*J. ten Compe* | Twee stuks Gezichten buiten en binnen de Stad Leyden, beide gestoffeerd met wandelende en werkende persoonen; helder, krachtig en bevallig van ordinantie en schildering | *Mat:* op paneel *Size:* Hoog 11, breed 15 duim	Jan de Groot	(Sold) fl 35 Coclers
1804/12/10	AMSCH	0010	*J. ten Compe* | Twee stuks, een Gezicht buiten de Poort te Utrecht, en het andere buiten Rotterdam; fiks en krachtig gepenceeld | *Mat:* op paneel *Size:* Hoog 13, breed 12 duim	Jan de Groot	(Sold) fl 25:10 van Iperen
1804/12/10	AMSCH	0011	*J. ten Compe* | Een Gezicht te Amsterdam, op de Oude Schans, na de Montalbaanstooren, gestoffeerd met wandelaars en andere persoonen; zonachtig en uitvoerig behandeld | *Mat:* op paneel *Size:* Hoog 14, breed 17 duim	Jan de Groot	(Sold) fl 60 Coclers
1804/12/10	AMSCH	0012	*J. ten Compe* | Een Gezicht op een Adelyk Kasteel, leggende rondsom in zyn gragt, waarby hoog geboomte, en wandelende Heeren en Dames; fraai en bevallig geordineerd | *Mat:* op paneel *Size:* Hoog 11, breed 14 duim	Jan de Groot	(Sold) fl 14:10 Roelofs
1804/12/10	AMSCH	0013	*J. ten Compe* | Een fraai Landschap, in 't verschiet het Huis te Kleef, aangenaam en uitvoerig gestoffeerd met wandelende persoonen; en zonachtig gepenceeld | *Mat:* op paneel *Size:* Hoog 12, breed 15 duim	Jan de Groot	(Sold) fl 16:10 T van Iperen
1805/07/03	AMSCH	0077	*J. ten Compe* | Een gezicht op de Haarlemmer Poort en Plyn; gestoffeerd met Beeldjes; zonachtig op Paneel | *Mat:* op paneel *Size:* hoog 16, breed 16 duim	G	(Sold) fl 62 Th Spaan
1805/07/10	AMSCH	0038	*J. ten Compe* | Een deftige Dame, wandelende in een Tuin, verder een aangenaam verschiet; uitvoerig op Paneel | *Mat:* op paneel *Size:* hoog 12, breed 9 duim	R[oos]	(Sold) fl 1 v der Schley [for] R[ijfsnijder]
1805/12/16	AMSCH	0015	*J. ten Compe* | Twee stuks, het eene een Gezicht op de Nieuwe Kerk in den Haag; en het andere een Gezicht van de Vaart op den Haag te zien; beide eigenaartig gestoffeerd, en zonachtig behandeld | *Mat:* op paneel *Size:* hoog 11, breed 14 duim	R[oos]	(Sold) fl 20 T van Iperen
1806/05/05	AMSCH	0035	*J. ten Compe* | Het gezigt langs de Wallen en een der Stads Poorten van Leyden, zonagtig en uitvoerig door J. ten Compe | *Mat:* op paneel *Size:* hoog 9 ½, breed 11 ½ duim	V[inkeles]	(Sold) fl 6:5 du Pree
1806/08/13	AMSCH	0318	*Compe. (J. ten)* | Een gezicht van een gedeelte der Binne-Amstel, ziende na het Diaken Weeshuis; delicaat en uitvoerig van schildering | *Mat:* op doek *Size:* hoog 19, breed 25 duim	Vinkeles [for] G[ruyter]	(Sold) fl 4:10 Gruiter
1807/06/10	HGBSM	0105	*J. ten Compe* | Het Gezicht van het Huis in 't Bosch, gestoffeerd met wandelende Heeren en Dames, natuurlijk | *Mat:* op doek *Size:* hoog 23, breed 33 ½ duim	Abraham Delfos [or others]	(Sold) fl 8:5 Tessier
1807/06/10	HGBSM	0106	*J. ten Compe* | Een dito zijnde het Gezicht van de nieuwen Tol, voorbij de Geestbrugge, gestoffeerd met een Marktschuit en verdere figuren, mede natuurlijk | *Mat:* op doek *Size:* hoog 23, breed 33 ½ duim *Notes:* It is unclear what "dito" refers to in the title.	Abraham Delfos [or others]	(Sold) fl 7 Tessier

1807/06/10	HGBSM	0107	*J. ten Compe* | Een dito Gezicht op het Moletje bij de Hoornbrugge, gestoffeerd met Visschers, een Trekschuit een andere figuren | *Size:* hoog 23, breed 33 ½ duim *Notes:* It is unclear what "dito" refers to in the title.	Abraham Delfos [or others]	(Sold) fl 4:5 Tessier
1807/06/10	HGBSM	0108	*J. ten Compe* | Een Gezicht op den Leidschendam. van de kant van Leyden te zien, waarin een zeilend Jacht en verder stoffagie | *Mat:* op doek *Size:* hoog 23, breed 33 ½ duim	Abraham Delfos [or others]	(Sold) fl 10 Colonbon
1807/06/10	HGBSM	0109	*J. ten Compe* | Het Gezigt van het vaarwater op den Lijdschendam te zien, waarin een speel Jachje, Trekschuit en verder figuuren | *Mat:* op doek *Size:* hoog 23, breed 33 ½ duim	Abraham Delfos [or others]	(Sold) fl 11:10 Colonbon
1807/06/10	HGBSM	0110	*J. ten Compe* | Een Gezigt op het Huis ter Werven in de Laan van nieuw Oostindiën bij Voorburg, met stoffagie | *Mat:* op doek *Size:* hoog 23, breed 33 ½ duim	Abraham Delfos [or others]	(Sold) fl 6:15 Carré
1807/06/10	HGBSM	0111	*J. ten Compe* | Een dito Gezigt van het Huis ter Noot, op de Bezuijdenhoutscheweg, met stoffagie | *Mat:* op doek *Size:* hoog 23, breed 33 ½ duim *Notes:* It is unclear what "dito" refers to in the title.	Abraham Delfos [or others]	(Sold) fl 5:10 Nes [?]
1808/06/13	AMSCH	0092	*Kompe (J. ten)* | Twee stuks gezichten binnen Amsterdam, zijnde Zomer en Winter. Het eene ziende van de Geldersche Kaai naar de Nieuwe Markt, Anthonis Waag en Zuiderkerk-Tooren, gestoffeerd met Beeldjes en Vaartuigen. Het invallend zonlicht is bevallig. Den anderen verbeeld van den Binnen-Amstel te zien naar de Halvemaans Brug, Munttooren en andere Gebouwen. Alles met besneeuwde daken en wegen: gestoffeerd met Schaatzenrijders en wandelende Beeldjes. Zeer natuurlijk gepenceeld | *Mat:* op paneel *Size:* ieder hoog 11 ½, breed 16 duim	[Jan Tersteeg]	(Sold) fl 40 Boelen T
1808/06/13	AMSCH	0182	*J. ten Compe* | Het Dorp Leiderdorp aan den Rhijn; zeer natuurlijk en zonachtig	E M Engelberts	(Sold) fl 5 Simons
1808/08/23	AMSCH	0036	*Compe. (J. ten)* | Een Gezigt op de Nieuwe Stads Herberg aan het IJ, te Amsterdam, rijk gestoffeert met verschillende Vaartuigen, op de voorgrond een Plaisier Schuitje, waarin een Heer en Dame, en twee andere Beeldjes, zonachtig, uitvoerig en van de beste schildering | *Mat:* op paneel *Size:* hoog 16, breed 20 duim	[Coclers]	(Bought In) fl 55
1809/04/22	AMYVR	0205	*J. ten Compe* | Een Kasteel	de Bruin	(Sold) fl 1:15 du Pree
1809/06/13	AMSCH	0031	*J. ten Compe* | Een Gezigt buiten Leyden, ziende van de buiten Cingel op een der Stads Poorten, gestoffeerd met een Landman bij drie Koebeesten, wandelende Heeren en Dames en andere Beeldjes; uitvoerig en zonachtig van behandeling | *Mat:* op paneel *Size:* hoog 12, breed 15 duim	S[chley]	(Sold) fl 31 van Iperen
1809/07/19	AMSCH	0007	*Compe (J.ten)* | Een Gezicht van het Buiten-Spaarn, op den voorgrond een Roeischuitje met Heeren en Dames, benevens twee zeilende Boeijers, ter zijde op den weg een Huisman met eenig Vee, verder eenige Heeren-Huizing, Koepels en de Stad Haarlem in 't verschiet. Helder, zonachtig en uitvoerig van schildering | *Mat:* op paneel *Size:* hoog 12 ½, breed 25 duim	[Bicker]	(Sold) fl 40 Bredius
1809/07/19	AMSCH	0008	*Compe (J. ten)* | De Overhaal buiten de Wetering Poort te Amsterdam, men ziet van den Buiten-Singel langs den Wetering, op de hooge Brug en Witloot-Molen, gestoffeerd met Vaartuigen en onderscheidene Beeldjes. Bevallig verbeeld en als voorgaande behandeld | *Size:* hoog 12 ½, breed 25 duim	[Bicker]	(Sold) fl 269 J^{mo} de Vries
1809/07/19	AMSCH	0009	*Compe (J. ten)* | Een Gezigt binnen Amsterdam, ziende langs de Raamgragt. Rijk met Beeldjes gestoffeerd en zonachtig behandeld | *Mat:* op paneel *Size:* hoog 14, breed 17 ½ duim	C	(Sold) fl 16 van Iperen
1809/09/06	AMSCH	0012	*Compe (J. ten)* | Twee stuks Gezichten binnen Amsterdam, het eene op het Diaken Huis en 't ander op het Korvers-hof te zien; geestig gestoffeerd, warm en zonagtig gepenceeld | *Mat:* op doek *Size:* ieder hoog 16, breed 20 duim	Johannes Caudri	(Sold) fl 61 van Iperen
1810/05/22	AMSCH	0017	*Compe. (J. ten)* | Gezicht binnen s' Hage, ziende langs den Vijverberg, naar het Hof en Fransche Kerk, verder naar het Plijn, verscheide Gebouwen en Kerktoren; zonachtig en uitvoerig van penceelbehandeling | *Mat:* op paneel *Size:* hoog 10, breed 14 duim	Johannes van de Putte Nicolaasz.	(Sold) fl 22 B Kooij
1810/05/22	AMSCH	0018	*Compe. (J. ten)* | Twee stuks bevallige Gezichten, van buiten naar 's Hage ziende, rijk gestoffeerd met verscheide wandelende Beeldjes; eenig Vee en verder bijwerk; zeer uitvoerig en fraai gepenceeld | *Mat:* op paneel *Size:* Jeder hoog 10, breed 14 duim	Johannes van de Putte Nicolaasz.	(Sold) fl 12 de Gruiter
1810/05/22	AMSCH	0019	*Compe. (J. ten)* | Gezicht binnen Amsterdam, ziende van de Geldersche Kaai naar de Nieuwe Markt en verdere Woningen, rijk gestoffeerd met verscheide Vaartuigen en Beeldjes; zonachtig en uitvoerig geschilderd | *Mat:* op paneel *Size:* hoog 16, breed 20 duim	Johannes van de Putte Nicolaasz.	(Sold) fl 76 for lots 19 & 20. Van Iperen
1810/05/22	AMSCH	0020	*Compe. (J. ten)* | Een dito [binnen Amsterdam] Gezicht, langs de Heeregracht, bij de Leidschegracht, gestoffeerd met Rijtuig en verscheide Beeldjes; in alles als de voorgaande uitvoerig behandeld | *Mat:* op paneel *Size:* hoog 16, breed 20 duim	Johannes van de Putte Nicolaasz.	(Sold) fl 76 for lots 19 & 20. Van Iperen
1810/08/01	AMSCH	0019	*Compe (Jan ten)* | Een Gezigt op het Slot Heemstede, van achteren te zien, verlevendigd door eenen Hengelaaren zwemmende Zwanen; verder Geboomte [Vue perspective sur le Chateau d'Heemstede, vû du côté anterieur, étant ornée par des Arbres, et par un Pêcheur à la Ligne, ainsi que par des Cignes dans le fossé] | *Annots:* médiocre (NGW) *Mat:* op paneel *Size:* hoog 12, breed 15 duimen	Mr Pieter de Smeth van Alphen	(Sold) fl 99 Schouman te Dorth

Compe, Jan ten (and Dietrich, Chr.)

1804/07/25	AMSCH	0013	*Compe, (J. ten); C. W. E. Ditrich* | Een gezicht naar de Stad en het Slot te Kleef, van de Land zyde te zien; de Voorgrond gestoffeerd met eenige Dames en Heeren, een Kind en een Hond, verders een Huifkar en twee Munniken, in het verschiet den Eltenberg, alles zonachtig en delicaat behandeld | *Mat:* op paneel *Size:* hoog 24 ½, breed 32 duim		(Sold) fl 105 C S Roos
1808/10/28	AMVRS	0008	*Compe. (J. ten); C. W. E. Ditrich* | Een Gezicht naar de Stad Kleef, met de Eltenberg in het verschiet, gestoffeerd met Heeren, Juffrouwen, een Kind, Hond, enz. Alles is helder, teder en zonachtig | *Mat:* op paneel *Size:* hoog 24 ½, breed 32 duim	Marten Udink	(Sold) fl 80 Josi

Conca, Sebastiano

1803/04/27	AMSCH	0024[a]	*Seb: Conca* | Deux Tableaux, dont l'un réprésente l'ascention de la Sainte Vierge, par Seb: Conca, & l'autre une Sainte, entre deux Anges | *This Lot:* L'ascention de la Sainte Vierge; lot 24[b] by Anonymous *Mat:* sur bois	A	(Sold) fl 11 for lots 24[a] & 24[b]. Stevens

Coninck, David de

1808/06/06	RMRIJ	0024[a]	*Coninck. (David de)* | Vier kapitale Stukken. N° 1. Eene Hertejagt. 2. Eene Beerejagt. 3. Dood Wild, Jagttuig, Honden en verder bijwerk. 4. Eenden door Honden en roofvogels gestoord. Alle stout van Ordinantie en fiks geschilderd [Quatre Tableaux capitaux representant. N°. 1. Une Chasse au Cerf. 2. Une Chasse d'Ours. 3. Du gibier mort, des Chiens et divers accessoires. 4. Des Canards troublés par des Chiens et des Oiseaux de proie] | *This Lot:* N° 1. Eene Hertejagt, 2. Eene Beerejagt *Mat:* op doek *Size:* Hoog 71 ½, en breed 70 duim *Notes:* Although lots 24[a] and 24[b] were catalogued as one lot, they were sold separately. *Loc:* Amsterdam, Nederland. Rijksmuseum. (A72 & A73) destroyed in World War II	Gerrit van der Pot, Heer van Groeneveld	(Sold) fl 280 Johs Eck en Zoon [for] le Roi
1808/06/06	RMRIJ	0024[b]	*Coninck. (David de)* | Vier kapitale Stukken. N° 1. Eene Hertejagt. 2. Eene Beerejagt. 3. Dood Wild, Jagttuig, Honden en verder bijwerk. 4. Eenden door Honden en roofvogels gestoord. Alle stout van Ordinantie en fiks geschilderd [Quatre Tableaux capitaux representant. N°. 1. Une Chasse au Cerf. 2. Une Chasse d'Ours. 3. Du gibier mort, des Chiens et divers accessoires. 4. Des Canards troublés par des Chiens et des Oiseaux de proie] | *This Lot:* 3. Dood Wild, Jagttuig, Honden en verder bijwerk, 4. Eenden door Honden en roofvogels gestoord *Mat:* op doek *Size:* Hoog 71 ½, en breed 70 duim *Notes:* Although lots 24[a] and 24[b] were catalogued as one lot, they were sold separately. *Loc:* Amsterdam, Nederland. Rijksmuseum. (A617 & A618) destroyed in World War II	Gerrit van der Pot, Heer van Groeneveld	(Sold) fl 285 Johs Eck en Zoon [for] le Roi

Coninxloo, Gillis van

1810/10/11	AMSCH	0147	*Koningsloo* | Een Landschap, met naakte Figuuren | *Mat:* op paneel	C	(Sold) fl 2 Posthumus

Coopse, Pieter

1801/06/10	AMSCH	0041	*Coops. (P.)* | Een woelend Water, zynde een gezicht in 't Y, by Amsterdam, gestoffeert met zeylende Scheepen, Sloepen en andere Vaartuygen, plaisant en natuurlyk van schildering | *Mat:* op doek *Size:* hoog 27, breed 34 duim	[Doublet]	(Sold) fl 3:15 Gruyter
1801/10/06	AMSCH	0018	*P. Coops* | Een Woelende Zee, met zeilende en dryvende Scheepen, en andere Vaartuigen, helder en aangenaam gepenceeld | *Mat:* op doek *Size:* hoog 29, breed 44 duim	M	(Sold) fl 8 v d Schleij A [for] Rijt

Coorte, Adriaen S.

1802/07/20	MGSAN	0032	*Koerten* | Een Fruitstukje | *Mat:* op doek *Size:* hoog duim 8, breed duim 6		(Unknown)
1802/07/20	MGSAN	0036	*Koerten* | Een fraai Stukje, waarin op een bord een Haring, Brood en Bierglas &c. op Doek | *Mat:* op doek *Size:* hoog duim 14, breed duim 17		(Unknown)
1803/04/06	MGSAN	0015	*A. Coerte* | Een dito [Stuk], met Abricoozen, fraai behandeld | companion to lot 16	Mr Evert Clyver	(Unknown)
1803/04/06	MGSAN	0016	*A. Coerte* | Een Stuk, met Persiken, tot een Pendant | companion to lot 15	Mr Evert Clyver	(Unknown)
1803/04/06	MGSAN	0017	*A. Coerte* | Een dito [Stuk], met Kruisbezien	Mr Evert Clyver	(Unknown)
1803/04/06	MGSAN	0018	*A. Coerte* | Een dito [Stuk], met Pruimen	Mr Evert Clyver	(Unknown)
1803/04/06	MGSAN	0019	*A. Coerte* | Een dito [Stuk], met Aardbezien	Mr Evert Clyver	(Unknown)

Coosemans, Alexander

1806/08/13	AMSCH	0033	*Coosemans. (A.)* | Een Feston met onderscheide vrugten als Druiven, Petsiken [sic], Granaat-Appelen, enz.; delicaat gepenceeld | *Mat:* op paneel *Size:* hoog 23, breed 28 duim	Roos	(Sold) fl 6 de Meijer

Coques, Gonzales

1809/04/22	AMYVR	0044	*Gonzalos, de Quokos* | Een overschoon Schilderij, voorstellende een Heer en eene Dame, zittende in een Bosch, de Vrouw heeft een Kind op haar schoot, het geen met een Jongetje speelt, en wel met den Hoed van zijn Vader, een oude Dienstmaagd biedt hun een Bloem aan; de hartstochten zijn overheerlijk, en is meesterlijk gepenceelt | *Mat:* op paneel *Size:* hoog 34, breed 33 duim	de Bruin	(Bought In) fl 600

Cornelisz. van Haarlem, Cornelis

1801/04/13	AMSCH	0037	*van Haarlem* | Een Historiële Ordonnantie van verscheide Beelden, uitvoerig behandeld en fraaije Tekening | *Mat:* op paneel *Size:* hoog 26, breed 22 duim	Pierre Fouquet, junior	(Sold) fl 10 Lafontaine
1801/06/10	AMSCH	0085	*Haerlem. (C. van)* | Een Bybelsche Ordonnantie, voorstellende de geneezing van den blinden op den weg van Jericho, met verscheide Beelden, kragtig en uitvoerig geschilderd | *Mat:* op paneel *Size:* hoog 45, breed 59 duim	Herman ten Kate	(Sold) fl 10 C S Roos
1801/06/13	LNDLS	0028	*C. van Haarlem* | Venus en Cupido, halverlijf, op paneel, door C. van Haarlem, 1602 | *Mat:* op paneel *Size:* hoog 20, breed 14 ½ duimen *Inscr:* C. van Haarlem, 1602 (signed and dated?) *Notes:* It is unclear whether the name and date are inscribed on the painting.	D van R	(Sold) fl 8 Spruyt
1801/06/13	LNDLS	0073	*C. van Haarlem* | Het Oordeel van Pares [sic], konstig	D van R	(Sold) fl 7:15 Richter G [for] v Giezen
1802/07/21	HGKAN	0083	*C. van Haarlem* | Een Zeetriumph, ryk van Oordonnantie		(Unknown)
1802/12/13	AMSCH	0084	*C. van Haarlem* | Een Man aan een jong Meisje een Beurs met Geld aanbiedende; fraay van Teekening en Coloriet | *Mat:* op paneel *Size:* hoog 29, breed 27 duim	Yver	(Sold) fl 30 J^n Spaan
1803/08/24	HGKAN	0019	*C. van Haarlem* | Twee figuuren in een omhelsende gestalte verbeeld Céres en Bacchus beide Borststukken in een Italiaansche manier | *Mat:* op paneel *Size:* hoog 20, breet 16 duim	[Teissier] [or others]	(Sold) fl 2:4 van Giesen
1804/10/16	DLOND	0089	*C. van Haarlem* | De Broedermoord van Cain. La Mort d'Abel | *Mat:* op doek *Size:* hoog 65, breed 84		(Unknown) fl 7
1804/10/16	DLOND	0090	*C. van Haarlem* | Spelende Kinders. Des Enfans jouans | *Mat:* op paneel *Size:* hoog 8, breed 10		(Unknown)
1806/06/07	RMHSN	0017	*C: van Haarlem* | Twee Stuks, een Mans- en Vrouwekop | *Mat:* op paneel	A E K L	(Unknown)
1808/06/11	RMRIJ	0099	*Cornelis van Haarlem* | Nepthunus staande op twee Dolphynen, meesterlyk | *Mat:* op paneel *Size:* hoog 18, breed 12 duim		(Sold) fl 8:10 V Dongen
1808/06/13	AMSCH	0084	*Haarlem (C. van)* | Adam en Eva in het Paradijs, hunne zonde bewenende, voor hun ligt eene doode Slang. Alleruitvoerigst gepenceeld | *Mat:* op paneel *Size:* hoog 8, breed 6 duim	R[oos]	(Bought In) fl 32
1809/05/26	HADAA	0087[H]	*Corn. van Haarlem* | [Untitled] | *Notes:* This lot was added in by hand in the EBNP copy of the catalogue, but without giving a title.	Mejuffrouw de Wed David Heemskerk [or others]	(Unknown) fl 3:14
1810/06/06	RMMUY	0086	*C.C. van Haarlem* | De oprigting van de Kopere Slang in de Woestijn. Door C.C. van Haarlem, 1597. De Naakten hier in voorkomende zijn verwonderlijk schoon geschilderd | *Inscr:* C.C. van Haarlem, 1597 (signed and dated?) *Notes:* It is unclear whether the name and date are inscribed on the painting. *Loc:* Darmstadt, Deutschland. Hessisches Landesmuseum.		(Unknown) fl 4:5
1810/10/10	MGCIT	0051	*C. v. Haarlem* | Het Figuur van een Jongeling meesterlijk gepenceeld	Caspar van Citters	(Unknown)
1810/10/11	AMSCH	0183	*C. Van Haarlem* | Eene kapitale Ordonantie, voorstellende de aanbidding der Herders; meesterlijk en breed geschilderd | *Mat:* op doek	A	(Sold) fl 4:15 Ijver
1810/10/11	AMSCH	0204	*C. Van Haarlem* | Verscheide Goden in een Landschap | *Mat:* op paneel	A	(Sold) fl 9:5 Bochaut

Cornelisz. van Haarlem, Cornelis (and Savery, R.)

1803/12/12	AMSCH	0090	*R. Savery; C. van Haarlem* | Het Paradys waarin Adam en Eva gezeten zyn, met den Appel, omgeeven van een groot aantal viervoetige en vliegende Gediertens; alles zeer uitvoerig op Paneel, door R. Savery, en de Beelden door C. van Haarlem | *Mat:* op paneel *Size:* hoog 32, breed 54 duim	E	(Sold) fl 42 Salsedo

Cornelisz. van Haarlem, Cornelis (manner)

1805/10/09	HGBSM	0100	*C. van Haarlem* | Een geestelyk perzoon in een boek leezende natuurlyk, kragtig en uitvoerig geschilderd, in de trand en niet minder als C. van Haarlem | *Mat:* op paneel *Size:* hoog 21 ½ breet 21 ½ duim	T H van Willigen [or others]	(Sold) fl 25:10 Valette
1806/06/07	RMHSN	0018	*C: van Haarlem* | Een Vrouwe Pourtrait, zynde een Borststuk met los Hair, verbeeldende Diana, schoon geschilderd, in de manier van C: van Haarlem, zonder Lyst	A E K L	(Unknown)

Correggio (Antonio Allegri)

1808/04/26	GDAN	0019	*Corregio* | Een aller uitmuntendst Schildery, verbeeldende Joseph en Maria met elkander sprekende, terwijl 't Kind Jezus op de schoot zijner Moeder is slapende, wordende door een Engel 't Laken van 't Kind, waar mede het gedekt was, zagtjes opgeligt, om het Kind met veel oplettenheid te bezigtigen, alles pragtigst gepenseeld | *Mat:* op doek *Size:* hoog 34, breed 48 duim	G H Fortuyn	(Unknown)
1810/07/26	AMSCH	0018	*Correggio* | Maria vergezelschapt van twee Engelen. Zijnde een Meesterstuk | *Mat:* op doek *Size:* hoog 39, breed 29 duimen	Cassino	(Bought In) fl 5

Correggio (Antonio Allegri) (copy after)

1803/04/27	AMSCH	0035[b]	*Corrége* | Trois morceaux differens, dont l'un est une ébauche par Serenasio, le Second une Copie de la Cingarella du Corrége, & le	A	(Sold) fl 5 for lots 35[a-c]. Stevens

			troisiéme Socrate avec ses Disciples | *This Lot:* Une Copie de la Cingarella du Corrége; lots 35[a] by Serenacio & 35[c] by S. Rosa		
1803/04/27	AMSCH	0100	*Corrége* | Sainte Marie Madelaine, copie d'après le Corrége | *Size:* h. 2 ¾, l. 3 ¼ pieds	A	(Sold) fl 3:10 I^{c} Moses
1806/11/24	AMSCH	0057	*Poorter (W. de); Corégio* | De Herders aanbidden het Kindeken Jesus en offeren geschenken, zynde een Navolging van de beroemde Nagt van Corégio; zeer bevallig en uitvoerig van penceel | copy by W. Poorter after Correggio *Mat:* op paneel *Size:* hoog 8 ½, breed 11 duim	Munnikhuizen	(Sold) fl 8:10 Van Iperen
1810/10/10	MGCIT	0150	*Bucker; Corregio* | Twee zeer aardige uitgevoerde Stukjes, in eenen goeden Trand behandeld, zijnde twee leggende Vrouwe Figuuren, in eene leezende houding, met eenig Bijwerk; gecopiëerd door Bucker; de Origineelen van beide door Corregio geschildert | copy by Bucker after Correggio	Caspar van Citters	(Unknown)
1810/10/11	AMSCH	0117	*Corregio* | Kupido, rustende in een Landschap, nevens hem een Pijlkoker en ander bijwerk; zagt en uitvoerig gepenseeld, op Doek, door een Italiaansch Meester, naar Corregio | *Mat:* op doek *Size:* hoog 29, breed 24 duimen	M	(Sold) fl 9:10 Spaan
1810/10/11	AMSCH	0118	*Corregio* | Een Kindje, liggende te Slapen, onder een Boom; als de voorgaande geschilderd, naar denzelven [Corregio] | *Mat:* op doek *Size:* hoog 29, breed 24 duimen	M	(Sold) fl 12 T Spaan
			Correggio (Antonio Allegri) (manner)		
1807/08/26	AMSCH	0038	*Coreggio* | De Heilige Familelje in een Landschap. Maria als in verwondering opwaarts ziende, houd het Kindeken op de schoot, hetwelk Joseph die ter zyde staat het schynt te liefkoozen; het is van een kragtig en bevallig koloriet, in de manier van Coreggio | *Mat:* op paneel *Size:* hoog 25, breed 28 duim	Joseph Vallette	(Sold) fl 34 van Iperen
1808/06/13	AMSCH	0036	*Corregio (als)* | Maria met het kind Jezus, slapende op haar schoot, terwijl een Engeltje bezig is biezen te plukken: fraai van penceelbehandeling en kleur | *Mat:* op doek *Size:* hoog 18, breed 15 duim	E M Engelberts	(Sold) fl 50 Simons
			Cort, Hendrik Frans de		
1806/10/17	MGSAN	0023	*H. Coorte* | 4 Stuks met Steene Tafels, waarop Hoorns en Schulpen, door H. Coorte, op geschildert en gefernist Papier in Olieverw, op Paneel en Doek geplakt | *Mat:* gefernist papier in olyverf op paneel en doek geplakt	Gerardus Beljard	(Unknown)
			Corvi, Domenico		
1808/06/06	RMRIJ	0025	*Corvé. (Dominico)* | Amor slapende op een rustbed; door Psyché bij Lamplicht bespied wordende. Goed geteekend en breed geschilderd [Psyché une lampe à la main s'approche avec curiosité de l'Amour, qui est endormi sur un lit de repos] | *Annots:* Verk. te Utrecht Sept. 1798 (RMA I) *Mat:* op doek *Size:* Hoog 12 ½, en breed 17 duim	Gerrit van der Pot, Heer van Groeneveld	(Sold) fl 25 Coclers
			Cossiers, Jan		
1804/08/02	BDAN	0026	*Coessiers* | De Aanbidding van de Herders | *Mat:* op doek *Size:* b. 64 d. h. 44 d.	J G Calckberner	(Unknown)
			Coster, F. [Unidentified]		
1805/10/21	GRBOL	0011	*F. Coster* | Loth in Zoar	Gerardus Nicolaus Heerkens	(Unknown)
			Courtois, Jacques (Il Borgognone)		
1802/09/06	AMSCH	0005	*J. Bourgignon* | Een ryke Ordenantie vol gewoel, verbeeldende een heevige Bataille, tusschen Ruitery en Voetvolk, op de voorgrond ziet men de Veld-Overstens met de Zabel in de vuist, het Volk ten kryg aanmoedigen, op de grond leggen Dooden en Gekwetsten, verder schynen onder het Kanonneeren de beide Leegers in gevegt; de caracters zyn natuurlyk, en kragtig gepenceeld | *Mat:* op paneel *Size:* hoog 19, breed 28 duim	Brave	(Sold) fl 20 Van Iperen
1803/09/07	AMSCH	0029	*Bourgignon* | Een Batailje, tusschen Ruitery en Voetvolk, vol gewoel, meesterlyk op Doek [Une bataille entre gens de guerre à pied et à cheval ; travaillée en maître] | *Mat:* op doek *Size:* hoog 25, breed 35 duim	Smidt	(Sold) fl 4 Toselli
1805/10/09	HGBSM	0033	*Bourguion* | Een heevige bataille van cavallerie, op de voorgrond, en op de tweede grond op een brug, vertoond zig een dito heevige met minder, fix geschildert door Bourguion | *Mat:* op doek *Size:* hoog 27 breet 37 duim	T H van Willigen [or others]	(Sold) fl 15:5 Roedig
1805/10/21	GRBOL	0045	*Bourgonjon* | Een Romeinsche Batalje	Gerardus Nicolaus Heerkens	(Unknown)
1808/08/23	AMSCH	0033	*Bourgignon. (J. de)* | Twee stuks hevige Batailles tusschen Turksche en andere Ruiterij, op de voorgrond en ter zijde leggen verscheide dooden en gekwetsten; meesterlijk en stout behandeld | *Mat:* op doek *Size:* hoog 47, breed 67 duim	C	(Sold) fl 12:10 Gruyter
1808/08/23	AMSCH	0034	*Bourgignon. (J. de)* | Twee stuks Batailles, in alles als de voorgaande behandeld [meesterlijk en stout] | *Size:* hoog 47, breed 67 duim	C	(Sold) fl 14 D Maijkel
1809/07/25	HGBSM	0005	*J. Bourgignon* | Een hevige Rencontre van Cavallerie, daar zy een Standaart ontweldigen, op een hoogte is een Molen in brand, de	D van der Aa [or] E B ten Dall	(Sold) fl 165 van Eijk

hartstogten en woeden is in de vegtende partyen, treffend verbeeld, en konstig geschildert | *Mat:* op doek *Size:* hoog 22, breed 28 duim

1810/06/20 AMSCH 0137
Bourgignon | Twee stuks: het eene verbeelt een Plein met groote Gebouwen en eene Masquerade op den voorgrond. Het andere eenige Krijgslieden voor eene Herberg
S
(Sold) fl 4 de Pree

1810/10/10 MGCIT 0074
Bourguignon | Een St. Christoffel, dragende den Heiland over het water; stout uitgevoerd
Caspar van Citters
(Unknown)

Courtois, Jacques (Il Borgognone) (manner)

1803/09/07 AMSCH 0273
Bourgignon | Twee stuks Batailjes; in de manier van Bourgignon [Deux batailles, dans le genre de Bourguignon] | *Mat:* op doek *Size:* hoog 22, breed 31 duim
Smidt
(Sold) fl 1:15 van den Brink

Coxie, Anthonie

1806/08/13 AMSCH 0319
Coxie. (A. D.) | Een Historiëele Ordinantie, in de manier van A. van Dyk; breed en meesterlyk van schildering | *Mat:* op doek *Size:* hoog 34, breed 65 duim
Vinkeles [for] G[ruyter]
(Sold) fl 0:14 L Pakker

Coxie, Michiel (I)

1803/04/20 AMSCH 0017
Coxie. (M.) | De Exce [sic] Homo, halver lyf, met gebonden handen in welk de Rietstok geplaats is; meesterlyk kragtig gepenceeld [J.C. couronné d'epines tenant un roseau à la main ; d'un beau dessin & d'une couleur vigoureuse.] | *Mat:* op paneel *Size:* hoog 21, breed 15 duim
Maria Magdalena van Sluypwyk, gravinne van Moens
(Sold) fl 4 Gruiter

Coypel

1804/07/25 AMSCH 0012
Coypel | Deeze ryke en bevallige ordinantie, verbeeld de Triomph van de schoone Galathéa, zy is zittende op haar Zeewagen, en omringd van Tritons, Naijade, Minnewigten en Dolphynen, verder ziet men Polyphémus; speelende op zyn Fluit en zittende tegens het hoog Gebergten, en in 't verschiet een ruim Zeegezigt; zynde schoon van Coloriet, kragtig en uitvoerig gepenceeld | *Mat:* op doek *Size:* hoog 29, breed 35 ½ duim
(Sold) fl 72 Thais

Coypel, Antoine

1801/04/13 AMSCH 0014
A. Coypel | Pallas verbeeld op een draagbaar liggende, wordende door zyn Vader omhelsd, een menigte krygsknegten met toortzen verlichten het hoofdpunt van dit Tafreel, en maken het tot een grootsche ordonantie; zynde breed geschilderd | *Mat:* op doek *Size:* hoog 20 ½, breed 29 duim
Pierre Fouquet, junior
(Sold) fl 10 Yver

Craen, Laurens

1801/09/04 MGWIN 0002
Craane | Twee Fruit- en Bloemenstukken, door Craane, op Paneel, in vergulde Lysten | *Mat:* op paneel *Size:* hoog 30 ½ en breed 41 duim
Pieter Gillissen
(Unknown)

Craesbeeck, Joos van

1804/05/07 AMSCH 0071
Graesbeek. (J. van) | In een ouwerwets Vertrek ziet men een Oud Man, zittende op een Stoel, houdende op zyn kniën een groot Boek, waarin hy schynt te Leezen; uitvoerig en fraai gepenceeld | *Mat:* op paneel *Size:* hoog 14, breed 11 duim
Vinkeles [for] J
(Bought In) fl 29 ½

1804/10/16 DLOND 0088
Joost van Graesbeek | Eenige Drinkende Boeren. Des Paysans Buveurs | *Mat:* op paneel *Size:* hoog 15, breed 17
(Unknown)

Cramer, Petrus

1803/12/12 AMSCH 0119
Cramer | Een Heer zittende te slapen, terwyl zyn Liefje de Kan lédigd, ligt een oude Matrone hem van zyn Beurs; delicaat op Doek | *Mat:* op doek *Size:* hoog 19, breed 18 duim
W
(Sold) fl 14:10 V^{n} Iperen

Cranach, Lucas (the elder)

1802/09/06 AMSCH 0028
L. Cranach | Deeze Ordonnantie verbeeld Christus gekruist, tusschen de Moordenaaren, aan de voet van 't Kruis, ziet men Maria ondersteunt door Godvrugtige Vrouwen, ter zyde zyn de Krygsknegten beezig het Lot op de Kleederen te werpen, verders een meenigte andere te voet en te Paard; de onderscheide Hartstochten, zyn natuurlyk, en van een uitvoerige behandeling | *Mat:* op paneel *Size:* hoog 47, breed 32 duim
Brave
(Sold) fl 1 L Pakker

1803/09/07 AMSCH 0040
L. Cranach | Maria met het Kindje; zynde door deszelfs oudheid zeer raar, uitvoerig op Paneel [Une Ste.-Vierge avec l'enfant Jésus ; d'un mérite très rare par son antiquité, très bien peint] | *Mat:* op paneel *Size:* hoog 13 ½, breed 11 ½ duim
Smidt
(Sold) fl 4:15 Gruiter

1808/11/28 AMSCH 0086
L. Cranach | Maria met het Kindje, zijnde door deszelfs Oudheid, zeer raar en uitvoerig
[Gruyter?]
(Sold) fl 4 van der Schley [for] E v Dijk

1809/07/25 HGBSM 0246
L. Kranach | Een Heilige Famielie | *Mat:* op paneel *Fmt:* boogsgewys *Size:* hoog 9 en een half, breed 8 duim
D van der Aa [or] E B ten Dall
(Sold) fl 3 Teissier

1810/07/26 AMSCH 0021
Cranach (L.) | De Maagd Maria, houdende het Kind Jesus in haar Armen. Zeer fraai geschilderd | *Mat:* op paneel *Size:* hoog 24, breed 19 duimen
Cassino
(Sold) fl 8 Spaan

Cranach, Lucas (the elder) (or Cranach, L. (I), manner)

1803/04/20 AMSCH 0118
L. Cranach | In een Landschap ziet men de Heilige Familie,, verzelt van St. Jan, zittende in een Tempel; zeer uitvoerig en fraay van Coloriet, door of in de manier van L. Cranach [Un tableau gothique dans la maniere de
Maria Magdalena van Sluypwyk, gravinne van Moens
(Sold) fl 4:10 Gruiter

			L. Cranach, l'on y voit un batiment dans lequel est une Ste. Famile [sic]. Cette piéce est très finie & elle a du merite pour l'age & la conservation.] | *Mat:* op paneel *Size:* hoog 36, breed 25 duim		
1810/05/22	AMSCH	0021	*Cranach. (L. of in de manier)* | Deze rijke Ordonnantie vol gewoel verbeeldt daar de Koningen het Kind Jezus aanbidden en Geschenken offeren. Maria zit met het Kind op de Schoot, verzelt van Joseph en andere Lieden; meesterlijk en uitvoerig van penceelbehandeling | *Mat:* op doek *Size:* hoog 22, breed 17 duim	F	(Sold) fl 9:5 Otten
			Crari, Guilio Bapt. [Unidentified]		
1809/07/25	HGBSM	0058	*Guilio Bapt. Crari* | Een Italiaans Landschap, verbeeldende een zwaare storm, op de voorgrond een Man die een Eezel voortdryft, het verschiet gestoffeerd met Gebouwen en Figuuren, meesterlyk geschildert | *Mat:* op doek *Size:* hoog 27, breed 32 duim	D van der Aa [or] E B ten Dall	(Sold) fl 57 for lots 58 & 59. L Voerman
1809/07/25	HGBSM	0059	*Guilio Bapt. Crari* | Een dito [Italiaans Landschap] met een Waterval en Rivier, waar in een Schuit waar in Beesten geladen worden, de voorgrond gestoffeerd met een Pelgrim en een Hond | *Mat:* op doek *Size:* hoog 27, breed 32 duim	D van der Aa [or] E B ten Dall	(Sold) fl 57 for lots 58 & 59. L Voerman
			Crayer, Gaspar de		
1801/05/11	AMSCH	0041	*G. de Kraayer* | Een Christus beeld, ter halver lyven, met het kruis in den arm, de expressie in dit stuk is konstig, en alles van eene meesterlyke schildering | *Mat:* op doek *Size:* hoog 32, breed 28 duim	Pruisse [for] M	(Bought In) fl 21
1802/12/13	AMSCH	0043	*G. de Craijer* | Deeze Ordenantie verbeeld het doode Lichaam Christi van het Kruys afgelaaten, meesterlyk, fiks en kragtig gepenceelt: het heeft waarschynlyk gediend, als model voor een Altaarstuk | *Mat:* op paneel *Size:* hoog 14, breed 10 duim	Schley [for] Lauwers	(Sold) fl 1:10 van Dijl
1803/04/27	AMSCH	000D	*G. de Craayer* | Un magnifique Tableau d'Autel ; representent, le Martire de St. Denis, richement composé, fierement peint, & d'un bon ton de couleur	B	(Bought In) fl 1200
1803/08/24	HGKAN	0071	*G. de Kraayer* | Twee stuks de eene den Zaligmaker met een Doorne Kroon en de andere Maria in devotie, beide in een Bloemkrans	[Teissier] [or others]	(Sold) fl 9:5 van der A
1808/09/13	HABRU	0047	*C. de Kraijer* | Een Altaarstuk, verbeeldende, daar het doode Ligchaam van den Zaligmaker van het Kruijs is afgenoomen, leggende nederwaards uitgestrekt tegen de schoot van Maria, die met innige aandoening haar gezicht ten Hemel heft, Nicodemus neemt voorzichtig den Doornkroon af van het verwonde Hoofd, en Joseph van Armethia, schijnt terwijl het Ligchaam met wit Lijnwaadt te bedekken. Johannes legt geknield aan de zij, de wonden van zijn geliefde Heer in treurige betragtinge, terwijl Maria Magdalena vol heilige drift op den grond de doorboorde voeten, van den Heiland kust, twee Vrouwen agter Joseph beschouwen het Lijk met veel aandoening, het welke zeer kragtig door uitgeweende oogen en gelaat getroffen is, dit Schilderij is over het geheel meesterlijk behandeld | *Size:* hoog 8 voet, 6 duim, breed 6 voet		(Unknown) fl 50
1810/07/26	AMSCH	0020	*Craijer (G. de)* | De Heilige Laurentius, in eene Bisschoppelijke Kleeding. Krachtig en schoon geschilderd | *Mat:* op paneel *Size:* hoog 13, breed 9 duimen	Cassino	(Sold) fl 20 Hulswit
			Croos		
1804/10/20	GRBOL	0006	*Croos* | Een dito [Landschap] met Water	Joannis Cannegieteri	(Unknown)
1807/06/02	AMHUY	0008	*Croos* | Een Riviergezicht, waarin een Schuitje met Boeren die vissen, in het verschiet ziet men een hooge Brug en een Landschap met hoog Geboomte		(Unknown)
1808/12/31	RMHSN	0020	*Kroos* | Dito [Een Landschapje] | *Mat:* op paneel	G Spanjaart [or] H de Haas [or] C van der Looy Lans	(Unknown)
1810/03/27	RMCNL	0002	*Kroos* | Een groot Landschap, verbeeldende een Dorp langs het Water, een der beste van dien Meester, geheel behandeld in de smaak van S. Ruisdaal		(Unknown)
1810/07/23	DOLG2	0079	*Croos* | Een Landschap, met Beeldtjes | *Mat:* op paneel *Size:* hoog 13, breed 18 duim	Pieter Quinting	(Unknown)
			Croos (manner)		
1805/10/09	HGBSM	0143	*Kroos* | Een landschap met een waterval, gestoffeerd met herders en schaapen, in de manier van Kroos | *Mat:* op doek *Size:* hoog 31 breet 22 duim	T H van Willigen [or others]	(Sold) fl 3:2 van den Broek
1808/04/26	GDAN	0260	*Croost* | Een Landschap, in de manier van Croost	G H Fortuyn	(Unknown)
			Croos, Anthony Jansz. van der		
1806/08/13	AMSCH	0031	*Croos. (A. V.)* | Een Gezicht van de Stad Rhénen, van den Rhyn af te zien, welke met een Schuit en Beelden fraai gestoffeerd is; alles zeer natuurlyk behandeld | *Mat:* op doek *Size:* hoog 43, breed 80 duim	Roos	(Sold) fl 1:10 L Pakker
1809/07/25	HGBSM	0207	*A Croos* | Een Winter, voorstellende een gezigt van den Haag over't Veld-Ys te zien, gestoffeerd met een menigte Schaatsryders en andere Figuuren op de voorgrond, konstig geschildert, en eene der beste van deze Meester, door A. Croos 1654 | *Mat:* op doek *Size:* hoog 35 en een half, breed 44	D van der Aa [or] E B ten Dall	(Sold) fl 3:10 van Eyk

			duim *Inscr:* A. Croos 1654 (signed and dated?) *Notes:* It is unclear whether the name and date are inscribed on the painting.		

Croos, N. van [Unidentified]

1802/08/24	LNDLS	0059	*N. Croos* | Een Gezicht op een gedeelte der Stad Haarlem, op den Voorgrond eenige Beelden en Beesten bij een Water, nevens hoog Geboomte. Zoo goed als van J. van Goyen | *Mat:* op paneel *Size:* hoog 19, breed 25 duimen *Notes:* The artist was presumably Anthony Jansz. van der Croos and not N. van Croos.	Leonardus Bouman [or others]	(Unknown) fl 19
1804/04/28	LNDLS	0025	*N. van Kroos* | Een Gezicht langs het water, op de stad Haarlem, op den voorgrond eenige koeijen, en visschers by haar vaartuig, helder en uitvoerig op paneel geschilderd, door N. van Kroos, 1653 | *Mat:* op paneel *Size:* hoog 19, breed 26 duim *Inscr:* N. van Kroos, 1653 (signed and dated?) *Notes:* The artist was presumably Anthony Jansz. van der Croos and not N. van Croos. It is unclear whether the name and date are inscribed on the painting.	[Abraham Delfos] [or others]	(Bought In) fl 13
1804/04/28	LNDLS	0027	*N. van Kroos* | Twee stuks Landschappen, met boomen en gezichten op steden, op paneel, door N. van Kroos, 1652 | *Mat:* op paneel *Inscr:* N. van Kroos, 1652 (signed and dated?) *Notes:* The artist was presumably Anthony Jansz. van der Croos and not N. van Croos. It is unclear whether the name and date are inscribed on the painting.	[Abraham Delfos] [or others]	(Sold) fl 3:5 Richters [for] G
1807/04/00	LNDLS	0022	*N. Croos* | Een gezigt op de stad Haarlem, op de voorgrond beelden en beesten bij een water, en hoog geboomte, zoo goed als van J. van Goyen | *Size:* hoog 19, breed 25 duim *Notes:* The artist was presumably Anthony Jansz. van der Croos and not N. van Croos.	[Abraham Delfos] [or others]	(Unknown)
1807/06/10	HGBSM	0022	*N. Groos* | Een gezigt op de stad Haarlem, op de voorgrond beelden en beesten bij een water, en hoog geboomte, zoo goed als van J van Goyen | *Size:* hoog 19, breed 25 duim *Notes:* The artist was presumably Anthony Jansz. van der Croos and not N. van Croos.	Abraham Delfos [or others]	(Sold) fl 6:5 Heyman
1809/07/25	HGBSM	0067	*N. Croos* | Twee Land- en Watergezichten met de Stad Haarlem in 't verschiet, door N. Croos 1661 | *Mat:* op paneel *Size:* hoog 8, breed 10 duim *Inscr:* N. Croos 1661 (signed and dated?) *Notes:* The artist was presumably Anthony Jansz. van der Croos and not N. van Croos. It is unclear whether the name and date are inscribed on the painting.	D van der Aa [or] E B ten Dall	(Sold) fl 4:5 van Eyk

Croos, Pieter van der

1802/05/05	AMSCH	0043	*P. Croos* | Een Dorpgezicht aan een Rivier, met verscheide Beeldjes gestoffeerd | *Mat:* op doek *Size:* hoog 41, breed 56 duim	E	(Sold) fl 0:10 Vermeulen
1802/05/05	AMSCH	0044	*P. Croos* | Langs een Stil Water ziet men een Stads Gezicht, de Voorgrond en het Water is ryk gestoffeerd met Beelden en Vaartuigen. Fraai behandeld | *Mat:* op doek *Size:* hoog 39, breed 52 duim	J	(Sold) fl 3:5 Levÿ Pakker
1802/05/05	AMSCH	0095	*P. Kroos* | Een gezicht op eenige Koornlanden, in 't verschiet een Bergächtig Landschap, Zeer natuurlyk gepenceeld | *Size:* hoog 16, breed 23 duim	G	(Sold) fl 5:10 Hulswit
1803/08/17	AMSCH	0021	*Croos. (P.)* | Een zeer natuurlyk Land- en Watergezigtje, gestoffeerd met Visschers in hun Schuit, zeer natuurlyk verbeeld | *Mat:* op paneel *Size:* hoog 5, breed 7 duim	Anna Catharina Putman	(Sold) fl 3 for lots 21 & 22. Yver
1803/08/17	AMSCH	0022	*Croos. (P.)* | Een heuvelagtig Landschap, met Boere Woningen en Stoffagie, als vooren | *Mat:* op paneel *Size:* hoog 4 ½, breed 5 ½ duim	Anna Catharina Putman	(Sold) fl 3 for lots 21 & 22. Yver
1803/09/07	AMSCH	0038	*P. Croos* | Dit natuurlyk Schildery steld voor een stille Rivier, aan welkers overzyde een Boschgezigt, gestoffeerd met Beelden en Beesten; de Schildering is zoo fraay, dat het voor het beste gehouden kan worden [Tableau représentant au naturel une rivière tranquille à l'autre côté de laquelle s'offre une forêt, ainsi que des figures et des bestiaux ; ce tableau peut être regardé comme le chef-d'oeuvre de ce maître] | *Mat:* op paneel *Size:* hoog 16, breed 25 duim	Smidt	(Sold) fl 30 I^c Smit
1803/12/12	AMSCH	0016	*P. Croos* | Een bevallig Land- en Watergezicht, gestoffeerd met Visschers in een Schuit, door een Brug ziet men een aangenaam verschiet; natuurlyk op Paneel | *Mat:* op paneel *Size:* hoog 17, breed 13 duim	W	(Bought In) fl 8
1805/07/03	AMSCH	0075	*P. Croos* | In een Riviergezicht, ziende na een Stad; ziet men verscheide zylende en stillegende Schuiten, gestoffeerd met Beeldjes, enz.; natuurlyk en fraay van licht | *Mat:* op doek *Size:* hoog 39, breed 58 duim	S	(Sold) fl 1 L Pakker
1805/07/10	AMSCH	0039	*P. Croos* | Een bevallig Dorpgezichtje aan een Rivier, met Geboomte, Boerewoningen, Schuuren, stoffagie van Beeldjes enz.; zonachtig en fiks op Paneel | *Mat:* op paneel *Size:* hoog 10, breed 12 duim	V[inkeles] [for] P	(Sold) fl 1 Gruyter
1805/07/10	AMSCH	0040	*P. Croos* | Een Land- en Riviergezicht, op de voorgrond twee Vissers in een Schuit, verders Geboomte, Wooningen, Brug enz.; zonachtig op Paneel | *Mat:* op paneel *Size:* hoog 17, breed 13 duim	V[inkeles] [for] L	(Bought In) fl 5
1808/06/13	AMSCH	0198	*P. Croos* | Een als voren [Italiaansch Landschap]	E M Engelberts	(Sold) fl 4 Thais
1809/06/13	AMSCH	0032	*P. Croos* | Een Gezigt op de Stad Weezel, met stoffagie van Beelden; allernatuurlijkst voorgesteld | *Mat:* op doek *Size:* hoog 39, breed 54 duim	Y	(Sold) fl 2:15 Gruiter
1809/06/13	AMSCH	0196	*P Croos* | Een Landschap met een opgaande Weg, gestoffeerd met Huislieden	Y	(Sold) fl 0:10 Jan Spaan

Croos, Pieter van der (manner)

1805/07/03	AMSCH	0076	*P. Croos* | Een dito [Rivier] gezicht on een Stad, in de Rivier een Overvarende Pont, met een Postwagen en Passagiers, als de voorgaande | *Size:* hoog 44, breed 61 duim	C	(Sold) fl 3:5 van Giesen

Croos, R. [Unidentified]

1803/04/20	AMSCH	0019	*Croos. (R.)* | Een bevallig Landschap met verscheide Geboomten, ter wederzyde met stille Waters waar by Hengelaars, gestoffeerd met diverse wandelende Beeldjes en Dorpgezigten in 't verschiet; zonagtig behandeld [Un bon Paysage d'effet, orné de figures & d'un ruisseau ; très bien touché.] | *Mat:* op paneel *Size:* hoog 26, breed 35 duim	Maria Magdalena van Sluypwyk, gravinne van Moens	(Sold) fl 50 C S Roos

Croos, S. [Unidentified]

1808/06/11	RMRIJ	0033	*S: Croos* | Een Boomryk Landschap, Gebouwen en Figuren | *Mat:* op doek		(Sold) fl 1 Bogaart

Croos, W. [Unidentified]

1803/04/06	MGSAN	0002	*W. Kroos* | Een Land- en Waterzicht met Schepen en Figuuren	Mr Evert Clyver	(Unknown)
1810/06/20	AMSCH	0146	*W. Croos* | Een Landschap met stoffage	B	(Sold) fl 0:14 L Pakker
1810/10/11	AMSCH	0208	*W. Croos* | Een Veld- en Stadgezigt, met Beelden gestoffeerd en natuurlijk geschilderd	A	(Sold) fl 1 Frantzen

Cuny, J.G. [Unidentified]

1804/10/16	DLOND	0007a	*J.G. Cuny* | [Untitled] | *Notes:* The lot was changed from "Lud. Bachuysen, Een Zeegezicht met zeilende Schepen" to "J.G. Cuny," without giving a title, at the front of the catalogue.		(Unknown) fl 14:10

Cuylenborch, Abraham van

1801/03/16	AMSCH	0052	*Cuylenburg* | Een Grotgezicht met badende Nimphen	P[ruyssenaar]	(Sold) fl 3:10 Gruiter
1801/03/16	AMSCH	0200	*Cuylenburgh* | De Engelen verschynen by het Graf van Christus aan de Godvrugtige Vrouwen, fiks en meesterlyk behandeld, op paneel | *Mat:* op paneel	K[ip]	(Sold) fl 3:10 Gruiter
1802/05/11	GRGRW	0014	*Cuilenborg* | Een groot Stuk met zich badende Nijmphen [Schilderijen met Olie-Verf; In zwarte Lijsten] | *Mat:* in olyverf *Notes:* The bracketed information in the title appears above lot 1 and refers to lots 1 to 79a.	Arnold Sicco Werumeus	(Unknown)
1805/07/10	AMSCH	0043	*A. Cuylenburg* | In een Binnengezicht van een Rots, met aloude Gedenkteekens, ziet men in klaaren Waterbeeken, de Godin Diana met deszelfs Jaght-nimphen, zig Badende; uitvoerig gepenceeld | *Mat:* op paneel *Size:* hoog 20, breed 29 duim	Temmink	(Sold) fl 23 Lafontaine
1806/06/07	RMHSN	0049	*Cuylenburg* | Een Grot, waar iu [sic] eenige Beelden | *Mat:* op paneel	A E K L	(Unknown)
1806/08/13	AMSCH	0032	*Cuylenburg* | Door een Rotsgezicht ziet men een Anticq Landschap met verscheiden Ruïnen en andere Gedenkteekens; zonachtig en meesterlyk behandeld | *Mat:* op paneel *Size:* hoog 25, breed 21 duim	Roos	(Sold) fl 0:10 L Pakker
1808/04/26	GDAN	0017	*Cuylemburg* | Verbeeldende een Graftombe, waar bij een Bad, in 't zelve eenige badende Nimphen, wel gepenseeld | *Size:* hoog 33, breed 39 duim	G H Fortuyn	(Unknown)
1809/04/17	AMSCH	0022	*Cuijlenburg* | In een Grot met oude Ruïne en Gedenkteekens, ziet men twee slaapende Lieden bij een Graftombe, waar bij een Vrouw met een Kind en een staande Jongeling; meesterlijk | *Mat:* op doek *Size:* hoog 35, breed 44 duim	T	(Sold) fl 5
1809/07/25	HGBSM	0083	*C. van Cuilenborch* | Een Italiaans Rotsachtig Landschap met een Houte Brug over een Rivier, op de voorgrond eenige overblyfzels van een antiek Gebouw, door C. van Cuilenborch, Ao. 1641 | *Mat:* op doek *Size:* hoog 34 en een half, breed 45 en een half *Inscr:* C. van Cuilenborch, Ao. 1641 (signed and dated?) *Notes:* The artist's name was given as "C. van Cuilenborch" but we have assumed this is an error. It is unclear whether the name and date are inscribed on the painting.	D van der Aa [or] E B ten Dall	(Sold) fl 1:12 Bakhuizen

Cuylenburg, Cornelis van

1803/04/20	AMSCH	0018	*Cuylenburg. (C.)* | In een Rotsagtig Landschap met Geboomten en een Waterval, vertoonen zig op de voorgrond Badende Nimphen, gestoffeerd met verder Bywerk; kragtig gepenceeld [Dans un site Coupé par des Rochers & une Cascade sont representées, au devant du tableau, quelques Nimphes se baignant. Composition agréable ornée de differens accessoires, dont l'ensemble plait par la charmante exécution.] | *Mat:* op paneel *Size:* hoog 36, breed 28 duim *Notes:* The artist was presumably Abraham van Cuylenborch and not Cornelis van Cuylenburg.	Maria Magdalena van Sluypwyk, gravinne van Moens	(Sold) fl 1 L Pakker
1806/08/20	HGBSM	0037	*C. Cuylenburg* | De Godin Diana, zich badende met verscheide Nijmphen, in de smaak van Poelenburg | *Mat:* op doek *Size:* hoog 20, breed 23 ¼ duim *Notes:* The artist was presumably Abraham van Cuylenborch and not Cornelis van Cuylenburg.	Macalester Loup [or others]	(Sold) fl 8:10 Spruyt
1810/03/27	RMCNL	0025	*Cuilenburg* | Een Binnenhuisje, waarin men een Militair met eene Boeremeid vrolijk ziet stoeijen; alles is vol uitdrukking, zeer geestig en schoon geschilderd		(Unknown)
1810/03/27	RMCNL	0026	*Cuilenburg* | Een dito Binnenhuis, waar men eene menigte Boeren en Boerinnen ziet dansen, terwijl andere Kaart spelen; vol werking, schoon van Penseel | *Notes:* It is unclear what "dito" refers to in the title.		(Unknown)

Cuylenburg, Cornelis van (manner)

1809/07/25	HGBSM	0195	*C van Cuilenborgh* | Diana met hare Nimphen in een grot, in de manier van C. van Cuilenborgh | *Mat:* op paneel *Size:* hoog 23 en een half, breed 32 en een half duim *Notes:* The artist was presumably Abraham van Cuylenborch and not Cornelis van Cuylenburg.	D van der Aa [or] E B ten Dall	(Sold) fl 4 Bogaard

Cuyp

1801/04/08	HAVIN	0053	*Cuyp* | 't Pourtrait van een Jongeling in aardige Kleeding		(Unknown)
1810/10/11	AMSCH	0023	*R. Cuip* | Eenige Kwakzalvers, welke hunne Waren aanprijzen | *Mat:* op paneel *Size:* hoog 17, breed 21 duimen	C	(Sold) fl 1 Posthumus

Cuyp (manner)

1803/08/24	HGKAN	A0029	*Kuyp* | Twee dito [Bataille Stukken] met Paarden, als door Kuyp		(Sold) fl 11 Hoven

Cuyp, Aelbert

1801/03/16	AMSCH	0015	*A. Cuyp* | Een Bergachtig Landschap, met een opgaande weg naar een brug, op de voorgrond ziet men eenige staande en leggende Beesten nevens een Herder, meesterlyk gepenceeld	P[ruyssenaar]	(Sold) fl 13:10 Stevens
1801/10/19	AMSCH	0015	*Cuyp. (A.)* | Een staande Roode bonte Os, en een zwart leggende Koe by een Boere Schuur; op de voorgrond drie Duifjes, verder twee leggende Koeijen aan een stok, en een Dorp in 't verschiet; uitvoerig en kragtig geschildert | *Mat:* op paneel *Size:* [hoog] 15 ½, breed 21 ¼ duim *Loc:* Amsterdam, Nederland. Rijksmuseum. (C 122) as Calraet	Jonkheer Menno Baron van Coehoorn	(Sold) fl 110 Jan Spaan
1802/06/16	AMSCH	0032	*A. Cuyp* | Een Heuvelachtig Landschap, op de voorgrond een Man, Vrouw en Jongen, welke beladene Ezels voortdryven, in het verschiet, op een Berg, ziet men een Kasteel: het Kreupelgewas, de Kruiden en de klikachtige behandeling, maaken dit stuk tot een aangenaam Schildery | *Size:* hoog 19 ½, breed 24 duim	[Merrem]	(Sold) fl 50 Agina
1802/06/16	AMSCH	0033	*A. Cuyp* | Op een Tafel, met een wit kleed bedekt, ziet men een Tinnen Schotel, waarop een geschilde Citroen, daar nevens een Roemer met Rhynsche Wyn, waarin een Citroen hangt: uitvoerig krachtig en natuurlyk behandeld | *Mat:* op paneel *Size:* hoog 16, breed 20 ½ duim	[Merrem]	(Sold) fl 3:10 Grimpe
1802/06/28	AMSCH	0031	*A. Cuyp, de Oude* | Een Bataille, op de Voorgrond ziet men eenige Krygsknegten te Paard, welke elkander hevig te keer gaan, verders vol gewoel; op Panneel | *Mat:* op paneel *Size:* hoog 29, breed 45 duim	Anna Elink	(Sold) fl 3 Royers
1802/07/20	MGSAN	0061	*A. Cuip* | Een krachtig Stuk, verbeeldende Venus, die onder een Boom liggende te slaapen, door de Liefde doorschooten word, op Paneel | *Mat:* op paneel *Size:* hoog duim 26, breed duim 20		(Unknown)
1802/09/21	UTHDG	0015	*A. Cuip* | Een leggend Koeitje, en Hoenders in een Stalling, fiks en natuurlijk | *Mat:* op paneel *Size:* hoog 9, breed 11 duimen		(Bought In) fl 30
1802/09/21	UTHDG	0016	*A. Cuip* | Een rustende Haan en Hen, goed en breed | *Size:* hoog 23, breed 28 duimen		(Bought In) fl 24
1802/09/21	UTHDG	0017	*A. Cuip* | Een staande Stier in een Landschap, krachtig geschilderd en gem. A. Cuip | *Size:* hoog 6 ½, breed 12 duimen *Inscr:* A. Cuip (signed)		(Bought In) fl 21
1802/11/01	DOBRA	0001	*A. Cuip* | Een stukje, verbeeldende een staanden Ram met vier hoorens, en twee liggende Schaapjes; uitvoerig geschilderd | *Mat:* op paneel *Size:* hoog circa 12, breed 13 ½ duim	Paulus van der Spyk [or others]	(Sold) fl 51 Schouman
1802/11/01	DOBRA	0002	*A. Cuip* | Drie herkaauwende Koetjes, liggende aan den voet van een dijk; op den voorgrond eenige planten, lies en biezen; kragtig geschilderd | *Mat:* op paneel *Size:* hoog ruim 10, breed ruim 13 duim	Paulus van der Spyk [or others]	(Sold) fl 55 M Versteegh
1802/12/13	AMSCH	0036	*A. Cuip* | In een natuurlyk verbeeldende Winter, ziet men langs een met Sneeuw bedekte Weg, een Moolen en eenige Wooningen, verders een Dorp, in 't verschiet; de Weg en 't Ys zyn byde ryk gestoffeerd, met gaande en rydende Figuuren, 't Licht doet een bezonder Effect, breet en meesteragtig geschilderd | *Mat:* op doek *Size:* hoog 33, breed 38 duim	Pruyssenaar [for] A	(Sold) fl 13 Yver
1802/12/13	AMSCH	0220	*A. Cuip* | Een Ossekop, van vooren te zien, zeer natuurlyk en uitvoerig gepenceeld	Schley [for] Lauwers	(Sold) fl 6:15 Schouman
1803/12/15	MGLAC	0040	*A. Cuip* | Een capitaale Zee met Schepen; zeer natuurlyk en kragtig geschilderd | *Mat:* op paneel *Size:* hoog duim 23, breed duim 29	Mr L H de Haze Bomme	(Unknown)
1804/05/07	AMSCH	0033	*Cuip. (A.)* | Een capitaal kabbelend Maasgezicht, gestoffeerd met zeilende Scheepen en Vissers Vaartuigen, agterwaards de Stad Dorth in 't verschiet; meesterachtig geschilderd | *Mat:* op doek *Size:* hoog 35, breed 36 duim	Vinkeles [for] G	(Sold) fl 14 Reijers
1804/05/07	AMSCH	0034	*Cuip. (A.)* | In een hoog Bergachtig Landschap ziet men de voorgrond ryk gestoffeerd met eenige Jaagers en een meenigte van Honden, boven op 't Gebergte eenige van de Jagt terug koomende Lieden, te voet en te Paard, verzeld van hunne Honden, achterwaards een Bergachtig verschiet; warm en meesterlyk gepenceeld | *Mat:* op doek *Size:* hoog 31, breed 41 duim	Vinkeles [for] G	(Sold) fl 8:15 Theijs
1804/07/25	DLGRO	0015	*A. Cuip* | Een Corps de Guarde, met eenige Soldaten op den grond liggende Kaart te Speelen, en eenige toekykers | *Mat:* op paneel *Size:* hoog 14, breed 17 duim	Mr Franc van der Burch Wz.	(Unknown)
1804/08/08	AMSCH	0039	*A. Cuyp* | In een Slagters Winkel hangt een vette geslagte Os aan een Balk, ter zyde voor twee openstaande Vengsters, waar voor een Tafel	Vink[eles] [for] K[=Gruyter?]	(Bought In) fl 10

			en Aanregtbank, legt een Karrewy, Mout, Tobben, Mes, twee Blaazen, en ander Gereedschap, op de voorgrond een afgehaalde Huid; het invallende licht, de stoute, vette en breede schildering, maaken dit tot een verdienstelyk stuk | *Mat:* op paneel *Size:* hoog 35, br. 47 duim		
1804/08/08	AMSCH	0040	*A. Cuyp* | In een Boomryk en Bergachtig Landschap ziet men op de voorgrond in het Water twee zwemmende Zwaanen; breed en meesterlyk geschilderd | *Mat:* op doek *Size:* hoog 40 ½, br. 43 duim	Vink[eles] [for] K[=Gruyter?]	(Sold) fl 3 Gruiter
1804/08/08	AMSCH	0041	*A. Cuyp* | In een sterk woelend Gezicht op Zuider Zee ziet men onderscheide zeilende Scheepen en Visschers Vaartuigen; de sterk betrokken lucht en 't invallende zonlicht maaken dit tot een Schildery vol effect, meesterlyk geschilderd | *Mat:* op doek *Size:* hoog 35, breed 45 duim	Vink[eles] [for] K[=Gruyter?]	(Sold) fl 4:10 Gruiter
1804/10/16	DLOND	0054	*A. Cuyp* | Een Kinder Portrait. Portrait d'Enfant | *Mat:* op paneel *Size:* hoog 9, breed 7		(Unknown)
1804/10/16	DLOND	0055	*A. Cuyp* | Een Landschap met Schapen, Boer en Boerin. Paysage, des Moutons, Paysan & Paysane | *Notes:* The lot was changed from "A. Cuyp, Een Landschap met Schapen, Boer en Boerin," to "F. Sneyders," without giving a title, at the front of the catalogue.		(Withdrawn)
1804/10/16	DLOND	0056	*A. Cuyp* | Een Landschap met Koeien en Schapen. Paysage des Vaches & Moutons | *Mat:* op paneel *Size:* hoog 10, breed 13		(Unknown)
1805/07/10	AMSCH	0041	*Cuip* | Een Strandgezicht met een ménigte Beelden te Paard, en te Voet; breed op Paneel | *Mat:* op paneel *Size:* hoog 12, breed 17 duim	V[inkeles] [for] L	(Bought In) fl 7
1805/10/09	HGBSM	0018	*A. Cuyp* | Het gezigt van de stad Dordrecht, aan de waterkant te zien, ryk gestoffeerd, met verscheide vaartuigen, en natuurlyk | *Mat:* op paneel *Size:* hoog 23 breet 32 duim	T H van Willigen [or others]	(Sold) fl 38 Roedig
1806/05/05	AMSCH	0032	*A. Cuip* | In een Slagters Winkel, hangt een vetten geslagten Os, op een bank legt een Karwey, Mout, Tobben en ander gereedschap, op den voorgrond een afgehaalden Huid; de breede schildering maakt dit tot een verdienstelyk stuk door A. Cuip | *Mat:* op paneel *Size:* hoog 40 ½, breed 43 duim	V[inkeles]	(Sold) fl 4:15 Van Dyl
1806/05/05	AMSCH	0033	*A. Cuip* | Een sterk woelende Zee met onderscheiden Scheepen en Visschers Vaartuigen; het zonligt maakt een schoon effect in dit stuk | *Mat:* op doek *Size:* hoog 35, breed 45 duim	V[inkeles]	(Sold) fl 2:5 Gruyter
1806/05/05	AMSCH	0034	*A. Cuip* | In een boomryk en bergagtig Landschap, ziet men op de voorgrond twee zwemmende Zwaanen, meesterlyk geschilderd door denzelven [A. Cuip] | *Mat:* op doek *Size:* hoog 40 ½, breed 43 duim	V[inkeles]	(Sold) fl 3 Vermeulen
1806/05/05	AMSCH	0250	*A. Cuyp* | Een bergachtig Landschap, met staand en leggend Vee; meesterlyk door A. Cuyp	R[oos]	(Sold) fl 6 Josi
1806/08/13	AMSCH	0092	*Kuip. (de oude A. C.)* | Op een open Landgezicht ziet men een talryke Familie op een Pastoraale en Emblematische wyze voorgesteld; helder en meesterlyk van schildering | *Mat:* op doek *Size:* hoog 39, breed 59 duim	Vinkeles [for] J	(Sold) fl 0:18 Cl Scholten
1806/08/20	HGBSM	0064	*A. Cuijp* | Een Maas gezicht omstreeks Dordrecht, rijk gestoffeerd, met zijlende en ten anker leggende Scheepen, op den voorgrond een Sloep met Passagiers; aangenaam en zeer natuurlijk | *Mat:* op paneel *Size:* hoog 17, breed 24 duim	Macalester Loup [or others]	(Sold) fl 39:15 Teissier
1806/08/20	HGBSM	0093	*A. Cuyp* | Een fraai Schilderij, zijnde het gezicht van eene Buitenplaats, op den eersten grond ziet men eene Laan met opgaande Boomen, aan den voorgrond is een Lijfknegt die twee Rijpaarden vast houdt, nevens hun legt eene roode Koei, en eene zwarte die naar eene laagte gaat, in het midden der Laan is een Heer te Paard, en aan het einde derzelve een Dame met Kinderen. – Aan de regterzijde van het stuk op den tweeden grond is het Kasteel van de plaats te zien, aan de linkerzijde veel stoffagie, en in het verschiet de stad Dordrecht over de Rivier, die rijk met Scheepen gestoffeerd is. – Alles natuurlijk uitvoerig geschilderd en fraai van Coloriet, en wel van den besten tijd van A. Cuyp | *Mat:* op doek *Size:* hoog 26 ½, breed 38 duim *Loc:* London, England, UK. Wallace Collection. (P51)	[Pompe van Meerdervoort]	(Sold) fl 960 Lafontaine
1806/08/20	HGBSM	0094	*A. Cuyp* | Een kapitaal stuk, verbeeldende eene Jagtpartij van drie Heeren te Paard, met een Jager en Honden op den voorgrond. – Op den tweeden grond nog een Heer te Paard met een Jager die bezig zijn, met de lange Honden te jagen; verders een aangenaam verschiet, alles natuurlijk en krachtig geschilderd | *Mat:* op doek *Size:* hoog 42, breed 50 duim *Loc:* New York, NY, USA. Metropolitan Museum of Art. (32.100.20)	[Pompe van Meerdervoort]	(Sold) fl 695 Lafontaine
1806/08/20	HGBSM	0160	*A. Cuyp* | Een Boer die een Os leidt, in een Landschap, gemerkt A. Cuyp | *Mat:* op doek *Size:* hoog 34, breed 47 duim *Inscr:* A. Cuyp (signed)	Macalester Loup [or others]	(Sold) fl 30 Zwartsman
1808/04/26	GDAN	0020	*Cuyp (A.)* | Een overheerlijk bergägtig Landschap met eene Boere Woning, waar voor een hogen Boom, op de voorgrond vyf leggende, staande en grazende Koeijen, bij een Rivier, in het verschiet, een Veehoeder met eenig grazend Vee, en een Hond | *Size:* hoog 37, breed 49 duim	G H Fortuyn	(Unknown)
1808/04/26	GDAN	0021	*Cuyp (A.)* | Een zeilende Dordsche Marktschuit, met eenige stoffage | *Size:* hoog 22, breed 19 duim	G H Fortuyn	(Unknown)
1808/04/26	GDAN	0022	*Cuyp (A.)* | Een Landschap met hoog Geboomte, en eenige Beelden, wel geschilderd | *Size:* hoog 39, breed 48 duim	G H Fortuyn	(Unknown)

1808/04/26	GDAN	0023	*Cuyp (A.)* | Een uitmuntend Schilderij, verbeeldende een Paarde Wedde, op de voorgrond twee lieden te Paard uit het Wedde komende, in 't verschiet drie Paarden badende, konstig en gloeijend behandeld | *Mat:* op paneel *Size:* hoog 17, breed 20 duim	G H Fortuyn	(Unknown)
1808/04/26	GDAN	0024	*Cuyp (A.)* | Een bevroren Water, met verscheidene Paarden rijdende, op de voorgrond een Marketenter voor dezelve Tent, eenige Paarden met Sleeden, en een menigte Schaatsenrijders, goed geschilderd | *Size:* hoog 22, breed 32 duim	G H Fortuyn	(Unknown)
1808/04/26	GDAN	0025	*Cuyp (A.)* | Een zeer goed geschilderd Landschap, met Gebouwen, waar in een Jongen met drie schoone Paarden aan de toom, zonägtig en kragtig behandeld | *Size:* hoog 13 ½, breed 18 duim	G H Fortuyn	(Unknown)
1808/04/26	GDAN	0026	*Cuyp (A.)* | Een Watergezigtje, waar bij zich vyf Koeijen aan den Dijk vertoonen, één leggende en vier staande, konstig geschilderd | *Size:* hoog 15, breed 22 duim	G H Fortuyn	(Unknown)
1808/04/26	GDAN	0027	*Cuyp (A.)* | Een uitmuntend Schilderij, zijnde een Landschap met fraaije Boomen, op de voorgrond één leggende Koey, twee Schapen en drie Bokken, op de tweede grond, een Man en Vrouwtje met elkander sprekende, verder een staanden Ezel op een Dyk, en voorts eenige Schapen, Bokken, &c., konstig geschildert | *Size:* hoog 19, breed 27 duim	G H Fortuyn	(Unknown)
1808/04/26	GDAN	0028	*Cuyp (A.)* | Een fraai Strandgezigt, waar op de voorgrond een Heer op een fraai bruin Paard is rijdende, bij hem lopende een grooten Hond; op de tweede grond een Heer en een Dame wandelende, eenige Vissers op het Strand, in het verschiet een Vissers Schuit zeilende, alles kragtig geschilderd | *Size:* hoog 34, breed 45 duim	G H Fortuyn	(Unknown)
1808/04/26	GDAN	0029	*Cuyp (A.)* | Een groote Familie met een Jager, Honden, en een geschoten Haas, met verder bijwerk, konstig geschildert | *Size:* hoog 75, breed 91 duim	G H Fortuyn	(Unknown)
1808/06/06	RMRIJ	0026	*Cuijp. (Albert)* | Een Land- en Riviergezigt, zijnde een Morgenstond. Op den voorgrond vertoont zich eene drift Beesten, geleid door een Veehoeder en Boerin, beiden op Ezels gezeten, waarbij een Boeren jongen te voet gaat; verder ziet men Gewassen, hoog Geboomte en Bergen, alles schoon en breed behandeld [Paysage representant une fraiche Matinée. Sur le devant richement orné de plantes, de Broussailles et d'une belle Touffe d'arbres, on voit un troupeau de Boeufs conduit par un homme et une femme montés sur des Mulets. Le premier semble s'entretenir avec un paysan qui les suit à pied. Une Rivière, des Montagnes etc. terminent un agrèable lointain. La couleur vraie, la touche large et facile, et tout l'Ensemble forment un Tableau superbe composé dans le genre de Jean Both] | *Mat:* op doek *Size:* Hoog 40, en breed 38 ¼ duim *Loc:* Amsterdam, Nederland. Rijksmuseum. (A78)	Gerrit van der Pot, Heer van Groeneveld	(Sold) fl 3860 Stratenus [for] le Roi
1808/06/11	RMRIJ	0001	*Albert Cuyp* | Een ongemeen ryk Schildery, verbeeldende een hevige Rencontre tusschen Cavallerie, in een boomryk en heuvelachtig Landschap, op den Voorgrond ziet men eenige Kruiden en Planten; uitmuntend schoon en meesterlyk gepenceeld | *Mat:* op doek *Size:* hoog 50, en breed 61 duim		(Sold) fl 610 Luchtmans
1808/06/11	RMRIJ	0110	*Gemerkt A: Cuyp* | Een Jager ten Voeten uit, het Jagtroer in de eene hand houdende, terwyl hy met de andere zyn geschoten Wild aan eene Dame aanbied, verzeld van Honden enz. enz. in een aangenaam Landschap, fraai en zeer natuurlyk | *Mat:* op doek *Size:* hoog 29, breed 37 duim *Inscr:* A: Cuyp (signed)		(Bought In) fl 10
1808/08/23	AMSCH	0035	*Cuijp. (A.)* | In een heuvelachtig Landschap ziet men op de voorgrond een bevallig Landmeisje, waar bij een Jongeling, rustende bij hun Schaapen, verder een gaande Huisman, en in 't verschiet Boeren Wooningen en Geboomten; meesterlijk gepenceeld | *Mat:* op doek *Size:* hoog 52, breed 69 duim	C	(Sold) fl 19 T van Iperen
1808/09/13	HABRU	0017	*A. Cuijp* | Een Watergezicht, met Vaartuigen op de Stad Leijden		(Unknown) fl 3:10
1808/11/28	AMSCH	0085	*A. Cuijp* | Een Jongeling, halver lijf, houdende zijn Hoed in de Hand, meesterlijk | *Mat:* op doek	[Gruyter?]	(Bought In) fl 3:15
1808/12/30	HGIMM	[0071a]	*A. Kuyp* | Voorts een exquis kabinetje Schilderijen van voorname Nederlandsche Meesters, welke uit hoofde van de kortheid des tijds niet stuk voor stuk kunnen beschreven worden; doch waarvan de beschrijving op den Kijkdag zal voorhanden zijn. Dus wij hier alleen de namen van eenige dier Meesters laten volgen, als: A. Kuyp, Ruysdaal, Karel du Jardyn, Loqwi ('t beste dat hij schilderde) Hondekoeter, van Dyk, Janson, Moesgever, Kamphuyzen, van Gooijen, A. van der Neer, T. Wyk, Huchtenburgh, Zolemaker, van Hassel, A. Vermeulen, van Dongen, Scheffer, van Os enz. | *This Lot:* Een Schilderij, A. Kuyp *Notes:* Because this lot was not numbered in the catalogue, we have assigned the number.		(Unknown)
1809/04/17	AMSCH	0020	*A. Cuijp* | Een stille Rivier, met verscheide zijlende en stilleggende Scheepen, ter zijde een Dijk met Arbeiders en Visschers gestoffeerd; zonagtig behandeld | *Mat:* op paneel *Size:* hoog 12, breed 25 duim	H	(Sold) fl 17
1809/04/17	AMSCH	0147	*A. Cuijp* | Voor een Herberg zit een Heer op een wit Paard, welke door een Waard een glas drank gegeven word | *Mat:* op paneel	[Gruyter?]	(Sold or Bought In) fl 0:14 Gruyter
1809/04/22	AMYVR	0030	*A. Cuijp* | Een Heer, zittende te Paard, word door een Meisje met een Lam gevraagd om een Aalmoes; meesterlijk | *Mat:* op paneel *Size:* hoog 11, breed 12 duim	de Bruin	(Sold) fl 13 du Pree

1809/06/13	AMSCH	0031a	*A. Cuijp* | Een Protestante Kerk van binnen te zien, gestoffeerd met een menigte Beelden, Wapenborden en Gedenktekens; zonagtig en kragtig geschilderd | *Mat:* op doek *Size:* hoog 30, breed 40 duim	[Gruyter?]	(Bought In) fl 3
1809/09/06	AMSCH	0011	*Cuijp (A.)* | In een Bergachtig Landschap ziet men een rustend Man, Vrouw, en een Meisje, ter zijde verscheide Vee, in het verschiet word het Graan inge oogst [sic]; is voorts uitvoerig van schildering | *Mat:* op paneel *Size:* hoog 23, breed 32 duim	Johannes Caudri	(Sold) fl 7 P Swanenburg
1810/03/27	RMCNL	0024	*A. Cuip* | Een Landschap met staande en liggende Beesten; Meesterachtig van Penseel		(Unknown)
1810/06/04	DOBRA	0014	*A. Cuyp* | Een Landschap met Koeijen, get. A. Cuyp | *Inscr:* A. Cuyp (signed)	Hendrik de Haas	(Unknown)
1810/06/06	RMMUY	0010	*Albert Cuijp* | Een Kampement voor eene Belegerde Stad (waarschijnlijk Breda,) op den voorgrond schijnt een Officier in onderhandeling te zijn; verder twee afgevaardigden, waar bij een Officier, en Trompetter, eenig krijgsvolk en andere personen op den voorgrond geplaatst; verder eenige Tenten &c. Alles uitvoerig en smeltend geschilderd | *Mat:* op paneel *Size:* hoog 15 ½, breed 41 ½ duimen		(Sold) fl 404 Luchtmans
1810/06/06	RMMUY	0011	*Albert Cuijp* | Een Dorp en Watergezigt, met verscheide Schepen en Schuiten, zeer natuurlijk | *Mat:* op paneel		(Bought In) fl 70
1810/07/23	DOLG1	0015	*Aalbert Cuyp* | Een Bergachtig Landschap, op den voorgrond rijk gestoffeerd met Runderbeesten en Beeldtjes, goed van Ordonnantie en aangenaam van Coloriet | *Mat:* op paneel *Size:* hoog 16, breed 20 duim	Mr Pieter van den Santheuvel	(Sold) fl 170 Beekmans van Antwerpen
1810/07/23	DOLG1	0016	*Aalbert Cuyp* | Een liggende Eend, en bij dezelve een nest met vier Eijëren, naar het leven, meesterlijk geteekend, en geschilderd | *Mat:* op paneel *Size:* hoog 17, breed 21 duim	Mr Pieter van den Santheuvel	(Sold) fl 9 Disconi [or] de Senrie
1810/07/23	DOLG1	0017	*Aalbert Cuyp* | Een Landschap. Op den voorgrond een gezadeld Paard met witte en grijze vlekken, bij hetzelve, een Heer met een Bedienden; en verder nog twee Heeren te Paard, eene hoogte afrijdende. Alles keurig van behandeling | *Mat:* op paneel *Size:* hoog 16, breed 20 duim	Mr Pieter van den Santheuvel	(Sold) fl 262 van Eijk a 's Hage
1810/07/23	DOLG2	0022	*A. Cuyp* | Een levensgroote witte Haan en Hen; meesterlijk geschilderd | *Mat:* op paneel *Size:* hoog 22, breed 21 duim	Pieter Quinting	(Sold) fl 6 J Meurens
1810/07/23	DOLG2	00LL[H]	*A. Cuyp* | Een Schilderij | *Notes:* This lot was added in by hand in the RKDH copy of the catalogue.	Pieter Quinting	(Sold) fl 6 A van Strij
1810/08/01	AMSCH	0020	*Cuip (Aalbert)* | Een bergachtig Landschap met een Water doorsneden, op den voorgrond op een Heuvel twee liggende Koeijen, en een staand Kalf bij Geboomte [Une Site de Paysage montueux, coupé par une Riviere. Le premier plan presentant une eminence, est garni de deux Vaches couchées, et d'un Veau sur pieds auprès de quelques Arbres] | *Annots:* passable (NGW) *Mat:* op paneel *Size:* hoog 13, breed 21 duimen *Loc:* London, England, UK. Wallace Collection. (P180) as Calraet	Mr Pieter de Smeth van Alphen	(Sold) fl 1005 T Spaan [for] Coclers
1810/08/01	AMSCH	0021	*Cuip (Aalbert)* | Een ruim heuvelachtig Landschap, met eenen Landman en eene Vrouw, bij rustende Beesten; verder twee Heeren te paard [Paysage étendu, coupé par des collines. Ce Tableau est orné par un Pâtre, et par une Villageoise gardant des Bestiaux couchés : deux Cavaliers à Cheval terminent cet ensemble] | *Annots:* mauvais et pesant, je le crois copie. (NGW) *Mat:* op doek *Size:* hoog 21, breed 29 duimen	Mr Pieter de Smeth van Alphen	(Sold) fl 600 C Josi
1810/10/10	MGCIT	0065	*A. Cuip* | Een zeer bevallig Cabinetstuk, verbeeldende een Campement in de nabyheid van eene Stad; apparent Breda; terwyl op eene fraaije Voorgrond verrykt door eene opgerigte Tent en velerhande Figuren in verschillende werkzaamheden bezig, zig den Prins Frederik Hendrik te Paard vertoond, vergezeld door twee voorname Generaals Personen; alles zeer uitvoerig en delicaat behandeld	Caspar van Citters	(Unknown)
1810/12/03	DOBRA	0053	*A. Cuyp* | Een met Paartjes, get. A. Cuyp | *Inscr:* A. Cuyp (signed)		(Unknown)
1810/12/03	DOBRA	0055	*Cuyp* | Een Zeestrant, ryk gestoffeerd, met een menigte Visschers		(Unknown)
1810/12/03	DOBRA	0056	*Cuyp* | Een Landschap, met een vervallen Boeren-Woning		(Unknown)
			Cuyp, Aelbert (or Cuyp, A., copy after)		
1808/06/11	RMRIJ	0020	*Door of na A: Cuyp* | Een aangenaam Land- en Watergezicht, met Schepen, Schuiten en Beelden | *Mat:* op doek *Size:* hoog 23, breed 28 duim		(Sold) fl 52 Noordwyk
			Cuyp, Aelbert (or Cuyp, A., manner)		
1810/07/23	DOLG2	0011	*A. Cuyp* | Een Jongeling, ten halven lijve te zien, gekleed in een bijzonder gewaad, en rijk versierd met goud, zilver en gesteenten. Geschilderd door, of in de manier van A. Cuyp | *Mat:* op paneel *Size:* hoog 29, breed 22 duim	Pieter Quinting	(Sold) fl 47 van Leen van Delfshaven
			Cuyp, Aelbert (copy after)		
1802/08/24	LNDLS	0144	*A. Cuyp* | Twee gestoffeerde Landschapjes, helder en uitvoerig, na A. Cuyp | *Mat:* op paneel	Leonardus Bouman [or others]	(Unknown) fl 2:4
1804/10/16	DLOND	0242	*C. Vermeulen; naar Cuyp* | Een Pleisterplaats. Le devant d'une Auberge | copy by Corn. Vermeulen (III) after A. Cuyp *Mat:* op paneel *Size:* hoog 15, breed 19		(Unknown)

1804/10/16	DLOND	0283	*Naar A. Cuyp* | Twee Heren te Paerd. Deux Messieurs Cavalliers | *Mat:* op doek *Size:* hoog 26, breed 34		(Unknown)
1807/09/28	DOHAA	00PP	*Meulemans; A. Cuyp* | Een Landschap, op den voorgrond gestoffeerd met Koebeesjes [sic], naar A. Cuyp, door Meulemans | copy by Meulemans after A. Cuyp	Mattheus Westerouen van Meeteren	(Unknown)
1807/09/28	DOHAA	00QQ	*A. Cuyp* | Een bruin en wit Paard, met Beeltjes, waar van het eene uit een Emmer drinkt, naar A. Cuyp	Mattheus Westerouen van Meeteren	(Unknown)
1807/09/28	DOHAA	00RR	*A. Cuyp* | Een Landschap met twee Koebeestjes, waar van 't eene door een Boerenmeid word gemolken, naar A. Cuyp	Mattheus Westerouen van Meeteren	(Unknown)
1808/06/11	RMRIJ	0084	*A: Vermeulen; A. Cuyp* | Een Copy na A. Cuyp | copy by A. Vermeulen after A. Cuyp *Mat:* op paneel		(Sold) fl 7:15 van Yperen
1808/09/13	HABRU	0018	*A. Cuijp* | Een Landschap, met Beesten, naar denzelven [A. Cuijp]		(Unknown) fl 4:15
1809/07/25	HGBSM	0134	*A. Vermeulen; A. Cuyp* | Een uitgestrekt Landschap, waar in Heeren te Paard, en voorts gestoffeert met leggende Koebeesten en Schaapen &c., na A. Cuyp, door A. Vermeulen | copy by A. Vermeulen after A. Cuyp *Mat:* op doek *Size:* hoog 38, breed 59 duim	D van der Aa [or] E B ten Dall	(Sold) fl 12:10 A Vermeulen
1810/03/07	UTWLD	0060	*Kuip* | Een Schildery met drie rustende Koeiën, naar Kuip	J J Woertman	(Unknown) fl 4
1810/07/23	DOLG1	0060	*Andries Vermeulen; naar A. Cuip* | Een Landschap, in het zelve een bruin Paard, met witte Manen, en drie liggende Runderbeesten. Goed van tekening en coloriet, en zeer wel dezen grooten meester gevolgd | copy by A. Vermeulen after A. Cuyp *Size:* hoog 11, breed 15 duim	Mr Pieter van den Santheuvel	(Sold) fl 14:10 van der Hegge
1810/07/23	DOLG2	0101	*A. Lamme; A. Cuyp* | Liggende en staande Koebeesten; door A. Lamme, naar A. Cuyp | copy by A. Lamme after A. Cuyp	Pieter Quinting	(Sold) fl 1:14 v Meulen Dordt
			Cuyp, Aelbert (manner)		
1801/03/16	AMSCH	0117	*A. Cuyp* | Een heuvelagtig Landzicht by een Boere Stal ziet men Huislieden by staand en rustend Vee, bevallig op koper geschilderd, in de manier van A. Cuyp | *Mat:* op koper	K[ip]	(Sold) fl 1:15 Koopman
1802/06/28	AMSCH	0235	*A. Cuyp* | Twee stuks met Paarden en Bokken; op Panneel als A. Cuyp | *Mat:* op paneel *Size:* hoog 10, breed 10 duim	Anna Elink	(Sold) fl 1:15 Gruiter
1803/08/17	AMSCH	0100	*A. Cuyp* | Een Pleisterplaats, op de Voorgrond een gezadeld Paard en vier Beelden, kragtig als A. Cuyp | *Mat:* op paneel *Size:* hoog 11, breed 12 duim	Anna Catharina Putman	(Sold) fl 7:5 Haffner
1805/12/16	AMSCH	0017	*A. Cuyp* | Een Heuvelagtig Landschap, gestoffeerd met staand en rustend Vée, verzeld van een Landvrouw, ter zyde staat een Boere Woning; bevallig op Paneel geschilderd, in de manier van A. Cuyp | *Mat:* op paneel *Size:* hoog 9, breed 12 duim	V	(Sold) fl 1:15 Graffelman
1806/08/13	AMSCH	0267	*A. Cuyp* | Eenige Jagers te paard en te voet met hun Honden, in een Landschap; zeer zonachtig, als A. Cuyp	Roos	(Sold) fl 4:10 Menzart
1806/08/13	AMSCH	0286	*Cuip* | Een Landschap, met een pissend Paard en een slapende Man; breed gepenceeld, als Cuip	Vinkeles [for] D	(Sold) fl 4:5 Wed Achtlenhoven
1807/06/10	HGBSM	0139	*A. Cuyp* | Een Landschap met Koebeesten gestoffeerd, op de voorgrond een man te paard voor een hek, verders een hond, als door A. Cuyp | *Mat:* op paneel *Size:* hoog 18, breed 22 ½ duim	Abraham Delfos [or others]	(Sold) fl 12 Spruit
1808/04/26	GDAN	0256	*Kuyp* | In de manier van Kuyp, een reizende Paardrijder die naar de weg vraagt | *Size:* hoog 12, breed 16 duim	G H Fortuyn	(Unknown)
1808/04/26	GDAN	0257	*A Kuyp* | In de manier van A Kuyp, een Landschapje met een Vee-Herder en eenig Vee, en een dito tot een wederga	G H Fortuyn	(Unknown)
1808/06/11	RMRIJ	0015	*Als door A: Cuyp* | Een fraai Mans Pourtrait met een Hand | *Mat:* op paneel *Size:* hoog 27 ½, breed 22 ½ duim		(Bought In) fl 3
1810/12/03	DOBRA	0009	*A. Cuyp* | Een Landschap, waar in een liggend en een staande Koebeest; agter dezelve twee zittende beeldjes. Fraai geschilderd, in de manier van A. Cuyp		(Unknown)
			Cuyp, Benjamin Gerritsz.		
1802/09/06	AMSCH	0029	*B. Cuip* | In een Landschap met een Water, waar over een Brug, ziet men twee Blinden, elkander geleiden; meesterlyk gepenceeld | *Size:* hoog 29, breed 29 duim	J	(Sold) fl 3 Gruiter
1802/11/01	DOBRA	0050	*B. Kuip* | De Afwenteling van den Steen van 't Graf door den Engel | *Size:* breed 5 v. 7 d. hoog 3 voet 5 d.	Paulus van der Spyk [or others]	(Sold) fl 3:10 Randwyk
1802/11/01	DOBRA	0117	*B. Cuip* | Een Strandgezigt met Visschers enz. | *Mat:* op paneel *Size:* hoog 27, breed 35 duim	Paulus van der Spyk [or others]	(Unknown)
1804/08/08	AMSCH	0045	*B. Cuyp* | De Verkondiging aan de Herders, zy zien met een ontzag hebbende houding Hemelwaards; dit stuk is fraai van licht, en als Rembrand | *Mat:* op paneel *Size:* hoog 27, breed 32 duim	Roos [for] C	(Sold) fl 13 de Harde Swart
1805/10/09	HGBSM	Q0016	*B. Cuyp* | De boodschap aan de Herders | *Mat:* op paneel *Size:* hoog 32 ½ breet 44 ½ duim	T H van Willigen [or others]	(Sold) fl 3:2 Voerman
1805/10/09	HGBSM	X0023	*B. Cuyp* | De aanbidding van de herders | *Mat:* op paneel *Size:* hoog 27 breet 33 ½ duim	T H van Willigen [or others]	(Sold) fl 7 van der Linden

<table>
<tr><td>1807/09/28</td><td>DOHAA</td><td>00GG</td><td>*B. Cuyp* | De Verryzing</td><td>Mattheus Westerouen van Meeteren</td><td>(Unknown)</td></tr>
<tr><td>1808/04/26</td><td>GDAN</td><td>0029a</td><td>*Cuyp (Benjamin)* | Een hevige Schermutseling van Cavallerie, &c. zeer fraai geschildert | companion to lot 30 *Size:* hoog 38, breed 50 duim</td><td>G H Fortuyn</td><td>(Unknown)</td></tr>
<tr><td>1808/04/26</td><td>GDAN</td><td>0030</td><td>*Cuyp (Benjamin)* | Een tot een wederga, zijnde een Strandgezigt van Scheveningen, waar op eenige Heeren te Paard, en eenige Vissers met Visch | companion to lot 29a *Size:* hoog 38, breed 50 duim</td><td>G H Fortuyn</td><td>(Unknown)</td></tr>
<tr><td>1808/12/12</td><td>DOHAA</td><td>0071</td><td>*B. Cuyp* | Een Legerplaats vol Paarden en Krygsvolk | *Mat:* op doek *Size:* hoog 36 duimen en breed 52 duimen</td><td></td><td>(Unknown)</td></tr>
<tr><td>1809/07/25</td><td>HGBSM</td><td>0076</td><td>*B. Cuyp* | Een Strand-Gezigt, Schestgewys [sic] met veel Figuren | *Mat:* op paneel *Size:* hoog 16, breed 23 duim</td><td>D van der Aa</td><td>(Sold) fl 8 van der Aa</td></tr>
<tr><td>1809/07/25</td><td>HGBSM</td><td>0077</td><td>*B. Cuyp* | Een invallend Zonneligt in een Boeren-Schuur, met veel Boeren | *Mat:* op doek *Size:* hoog 18 en een half, breed 18 en een half duim</td><td>D van der Aa [or] E B ten Dall</td><td>(Sold) fl 6:5 Heymans [for] G</td></tr>
<tr><td>1810/07/23</td><td>DOLG2</td><td>0010</td><td>*B. Cuyp* | De geboorte van den Zaligmaker; zeer krachtig en meesterlijk gepenseeld | *Mat:* op paneel *Size:* hoog 43, breed 29 duim</td><td>Pieter Quinting</td><td>(Sold) fl 2:10 A v Stry</td></tr>
<tr><td>1810/07/23</td><td>DOLG2</td><td>0046</td><td>*B. Cuyp* | Binnen's huis gebruiken eenige lieden geweld aan eenige Boeren en Boerinnen; meesterlijk geschilderd | *Mat:* op paneel *Size:* hoog 19, breed 25 duim</td><td>Pieter Quinting</td><td>(Sold) fl 4 Nieuwenhuys</td></tr>
<tr><td>1810/07/23</td><td>DOLG2</td><td>0051</td><td>*B. Cuyp* | Een Historie | *Mat:* op paneel *Size:* hoog 18, breed 17 duim</td><td>Pieter Quinting</td><td>(Sold) fl 4:14 Visser</td></tr>
<tr><td>1810/08/10</td><td>RMRIJ</td><td>0019</td><td>*Benjemin Cuijp* | Eene rijke Bataille. Piquant van effect, en geestig geschilderd</td><td></td><td>(Sold) fl 20 [or] 5 v Dyk</td></tr>
<tr><td>1810/08/10</td><td>RMRIJ</td><td>0020</td><td>*Benjemin Cuijp* | De Boodschap aan de Herders</td><td></td><td>(Sold) fl 3 [or] 2 Baast [?]</td></tr>
<tr><td>1810/12/03</td><td>DOBRA</td><td>0023</td><td>*B. Cuyp* | Een Historie</td><td></td><td>(Unknown)</td></tr>
<tr><td></td><td></td><td></td><td>**Cuyp, Benjamin Gerritsz. (manner)**</td><td></td><td></td></tr>
<tr><td>1810/07/23</td><td>DOLG2</td><td>0020</td><td>*B. Cuyp* | Eenige vrolijke Boeren, raar gepenseeld; in de manier van B. Cuyp | *Mat:* op doek *Size:* hoog 21, breed 30 duim</td><td>Pieter Quinting</td><td>(Unknown) fl 20</td></tr>
<tr><td></td><td></td><td></td><td>**Cuyp, Jacob Abrahamsz.**</td><td></td><td></td></tr>
<tr><td>1806/11/24</td><td>AMSCH</td><td>0014</td><td>*Cuyp (J.A.)* | Een boomryk Landschap, gestoffeerd met een Man, Vrouw en Jongen by eenige Schapen en Bokken; meesterlyk van schildering | *Mat:* op paneel *Size:* hoog 19, breed 25 duim</td><td>Munnikhuizen</td><td>(Sold) fl 8:5 Levy Pakker</td></tr>
<tr><td></td><td></td><td></td><td>**Cuyp, Jacob Gerritsz.**</td><td></td><td></td></tr>
<tr><td>1801/06/10</td><td>AMSCH</td><td>0040</td><td>*Cuyp de Oude* | Dit Stuk stelt voor de Bekeering van Paulus zynde een Ordonnantie van verscheiden Beelden, krachtig en meesterlyk gepenceeld | *Mat:* op paneel *Size:* hoog 31, breed 46 duim</td><td>[Doublet]</td><td>(Sold) fl 8 J Yver</td></tr>
<tr><td>1801/06/13</td><td>LNDLS</td><td>0030</td><td>*de Oude Cuyp* | Eenige op de kaart speelende Soldaaten, in een oud gebouw, fix op paneel geschilderd, door de Oude Cuyp, rond formaat | *Mat:* op paneel *Fmt:* rond *Size:* hoog en breed 19 duimen</td><td>D van R</td><td>(Sold) fl 8:15 Bryan</td></tr>
<tr><td>1804/08/08</td><td>AMSCH</td><td>0042</td><td>*de oude J. Cuyp* | Een stil Watergezicht op de Rivier de Merwe, gestoffeerd met een prachtig zeilend Jagt, verzeld van verscheide andere zeilende en dryvende Scheepen en Sloepen, met blazende Trompetters, in 't verschiet de Stad Dordrecht; helder en plaisant geschilderd | *Mat:* op paneel *Size:* hoog 36, breed 60 duim</td><td>Schley [for] A</td><td>(Sold) fl 3:5 de Meijer</td></tr>
<tr><td>1804/08/08</td><td>AMSCH</td><td>0043</td><td>*de oude J. Cuyp* | De Boodschap van 's Heilands Geboorte aan de Herders, ryk gestoffeerd met Paarden, Koeijen, Schaapen, Bokken, enz.; frappant van licht, en breed en meesterlyk gepenceeld | *Mat:* op paneel *Size:* hoog 18, breed 26 duim</td><td>Vink[eles] [for] S</td><td>(Sold) fl 4:15 Menzart</td></tr>
<tr><td>1804/08/08</td><td>AMSCH</td><td>0044</td><td>*de oude J. Cuyp* | Een Strandgezicht met verscheide Pinken, Visschers, gaande en rydende Lieden, ziende na 't Dorp; breed en fiks | *Mat:* op paneel *Size:* hoog 12, breed 17 ½ duim</td><td>Vink[eles] [for] W</td><td>(Sold) fl 2 Van Iperen</td></tr>
<tr><td>1806/08/20</td><td>HGBSM</td><td>0101</td><td>*J.G. Cuyp* | Een Mans Portrait in het zwart gekleed, meesterlijk geschilderd, door J.G. Cuyp 1626 | *Mat:* op paneel *Size:* hoog 26 ½, breed 23 duim *Inscr:* J.G. Cuyp 1626 (signed and dated?) *Notes:* It is unclear whether the name and date are inscribed on the painting.</td><td>Macalester Loup [or others]</td><td>(Sold) fl 20:10 for lots 101 & 102. Spruyt</td></tr>
<tr><td>1806/08/20</td><td>HGBSM</td><td>0102</td><td>*J.G. Cuyp* | Een vrouwe Portrait, door denzelven [J.G. Cuyp] 1647 | *Size:* hoog 26 ½, breed 23 duim *Inscr:* 1647 (dated?) *Notes:* It is unclear whether the date is inscribed on the painting.</td><td>Macalester Loup [or others]</td><td>(Sold) fl 20:10 for lots 101 & 102. Spruyt</td></tr>
<tr><td>1806/08/20</td><td>HGBSM</td><td>0103</td><td>*J. G. Cuyp* | Een mans Portrait in het zwart | *Size:* hoog 26 ½, breed 23 duim</td><td>Macalester Loup [or others]</td><td>(Sold) fl 9:10 for lots 103 & 104. Spruyt</td></tr>
<tr><td>1806/08/20</td><td>HGBSM</td><td>0104</td><td>*J.G. Cuyp* | Een vrouwe Portrait | *Size:* hoog 26 ½, breed 23 duim</td><td>Macalester Loup [or others]</td><td>(Sold) fl 9:10 for lots 103 & 104. Spruyt</td></tr>
<tr><td>1806/08/20</td><td>HGBSM</td><td>0105</td><td>*J. G. Cuyp* | Een mans portrait | *Size:* hoog 26 ½, breed 23 duim</td><td>Macalester Loup [or others]</td><td>(Sold) fl 5:5 Loef</td></tr>
<tr><td>1807/04/00</td><td>LNDLS</td><td>0029</td><td>*De oude Cuijp* | Een Gampement [sic] van Ruiters bij haar tenten en ander krijgsvolk, fix behandelt op doek | *Mat:* op doek *Size:* hoog 34, breed 58 duim</td><td>[Abraham Delfos] [or others]</td><td>(Unknown)</td></tr>
<tr><td>1807/06/10</td><td>HGBSM</td><td>0029</td><td>*De oude Cuijp* | Een Campement van Ruiters by haar tenten en ander krijgsvolk, fix behandelt | *Mat:* op doek *Size:* hoog 34, breed 58 duim</td><td>Abraham Delfos [or others]</td><td>(Sold) fl 7 v Olden</td></tr>
</table>

1809/04/22	AMYVR	0031	*J. Cuijp* | Twee stuks: een Man met een Gans, en eene Vrouw met een Haan | *Mat:* op paneel *Size:* hoog 11, breed 8 duim	de Bruin	(Sold) fl 5 van Iperen
1810/06/06	RMMUY	0179	*Den Ouden Cuyp* | Een Herder en Herderin, verzeld van een Hond, Koeijen, Schapen &c. Door den Ouden Cuyp | *Mat:* op doek		(Unknown) fl 3:5
1810/07/23	DOLG2	000B	*J.G. Cuyp* | Een Man te Paard, benevens meer andere Paarden | *Mat:* op doek *Size:* hoog 59, breed 52 duim	Pieter Quinting	(Unknown) fl 2:10
1810/08/06	AMSCH	0142	*Den ouden Kuip* | Een Bataille tusschen Kavallerie en Infanterie	F	(Sold) fl 1 T Spaan

Cuyp, Jacob Gerritsz. (or Cuyp, J.G., manner)

1808/06/13	AMSCH	0239	*den Ouden Kuijp* | In een bergachtig Landschap (zijnde een zinrijke spotverbeelding), ziet men op eene open Boerenwagen onderscheidene Gezindheden, zijnde het Rijtuig van voren en achter met vier Paarden bespannen, ieder met hun Voerman, die de eene voorwaarts, en de andere achterwaarts trekken; het is geestig geordoneerd en fiks op Doek geschilderd, door of in de manier van den Ouden Kuijp | *Mat:* op doek	[Cattrop?]	(Sold) fl 34 O W J Berg

Cuypers (Kuypers)

1805/06/24	DOBLU	0008	*Kuipers* | Een Maaneschyn	Willem Snellen [or] F R E Nibbelinck [or] Gysbert Visser	(Unknown)

Dalens, Dirck

1801/10/06	AMSCH	0021	*D. Dalens* | Twee stuks Land en Watergezichten, byde gestoffeert met Beeldjes, Beesten, Gebouwen en Gebergten, helder en aangenaam gepenceeld | *Mat:* op paneel *Size:* yder hoog 8, breed 12 duim	M	(Sold) fl 38 Theijs
1801/12/22	AMOTT	0072	*D. Dalens* | 1 Ossen en Schapendrift, Boere Kar en stil Water by een Bosch	Bartholomeus Ruloffs	(Unknown) fl 2:10
1802/08/24	LNDLS	0106	*D. Dalens* | Een Gezigt langs een Water met zeilende Schepen en Schuiten met Vischers, op den voorgrond eenige die den Zegen trekken en Koopieden in Visch | *Mat:* op paneel *Size:* hoog 6, breed 13 duimen	Leonardus Bouman [or others]	(Unknown) fl 3:5
1803/04/20	AMSCH	0023	*Dalens. (D.)* | Twee stuks, ryk met Scheepen, Vaartuigen en Beeldjes, gestoffeerde Rhyngezichten; bevallig van licht en bruin en delicaat gepenceeld [Deux vues sur le Rhin & sur les Collines des deux rives, ornées de barques & de figures, peints d'une maniere Spirituelle & d'un bon effet.] | *Mat:* op paneel *Size:* ieder hoog 9, breed 11 duim	Maria Magdalena van Sluypwyk, gravinne van Moens	(Sold) fl 19 Texier
1803/12/12	AMSCH	0024	*D. Dalens* | Een Capitaal Boomryk Landschap, op de voorgrond een aangenaam Water, verders ryk gestoffeerd met gaande, rydende en rustende Beelden; zonachtig en bevallig gepenceeld | *Mat:* op doek *Size:* hoog 44, breed 57 duim	B	(Sold) fl 18:10 V^{n} Dijl
1804/04/28	LNDLS	0031	*D. Dalens* | Een Landschap met geboomten en kruiden en harten-beesten, door D. Dalens; op paneel | *Mat:* op paneel *Size:* hoog 10 ½, breed 13 duim	[Abraham Delfos] [or others]	(Bought In) fl 3
1805/07/03	AMSCH	0079	*D. Dalens* | Een Bergachtig Land- en Riviergezicht, gestoffeerd met Herders met hun Vee, de Rivier met Vaartuigen; warm van coloriet | *Mat:* op doek *Size:* hoog 17, breed 21 duim	C	(Sold) fl 6 Vallet
1805/07/10	AMSCH	0052	*D. Dalens* | Een Boom-, Rotsch- en Bergachtig Landschap met een ménigte gaande en rustende Lieden, Paarden, Honden enz.; breed en meesterlyk op Doek | *Mat:* op doek *Size:* hoog 34, breed 36 duim	V[inkeles] [for] M	(Sold) fl 1:5 Isaac Smit
1806/08/13	AMSCH	0041	*Dalens. (D.)* | Een Berg en Rotsachtig Landschapje, met Rivieren doorsneeden, Schuiten, stoffagie van Beeldjes, en een aangenaam verschiet | *Mat:* op paneel *Size:* hoog 12, breed 15 duim	Vinkeles [for] F	(Sold) fl 7:15 du Pré
1806/10/16	UTWLD	0007	*D. Dalens* | Een Land en Water gezicht met een Overhaal Pont, en eenige beesten door D. Dalens	Mr P de Malapert [or] W Beeldsnyder	(Unknown)
1807/04/00	LNDLS	0053	*D. Dalens* | Een Landschap met geboomte, op de voorgrond kruiden en hartebeesten, door D. Dalens, op paneel | *Mat:* op paneel *Size:* hoog 10 en een half, breed 13 duim	[Abraham Delfos] [or others]	(Unknown)
1807/06/10	HGBSM	0053	*D. Dalens* | Een Landschap met geboomte, op den voorgrond kruiden en hartebeesten | *Mat:* op paneel *Size:* hoog 10 ½, breed 13 duim	Abraham Delfos [or others]	(Sold) fl 4 Guicherit
1807/08/26	AMSCH	0049	*D. Dalens* | Twee stuks Landschappen met stoffage	Joseph Vallette	(Sold) fl 5:10 Coclair
1807/08/26	AMSCH	0050	*D. Dalens* | Een gestoffeerd Rhyngezigt	Joseph Vallette	(Sold) fl 4:10 Hooft
1810/03/26	RMMUY	0079	*D. Dalens* | Een Hof Gezigt [Une Maison de Campagne, avec Figures par Dalens.] | *Annots:* [par] Moucheron (BPG)	Daniel de Jongh Az	(Sold) fl 4 Le Brun Parys
1810/05/22	AMSCH	0023	*Dalens (D.)* | Twee stuks bevallige Landschappen, met Geboomten, beide gestoffeerd met Paarden en rustende Reizigers; zonachtig en aangenaam van schildering | *Mat:* op doek *Size:* Jeder hoog 20, breed 13 duim	D	(Sold) fl 3:5 Neelmeyer
1810/06/20	AMSCH	0015	*D. Dalens* | Een Boschachtig Landschap, gestoffeerd met Heeren te Paard, Jagers met hunne Honden; achterwaards, gaande Huislieden en Herders met Schapen. Kloek geschilderd | *Mat:* op doek *Size:* hoog 45, breed 59 duimen	S	(Sold) fl 1 L Pakker
1810/06/20	AMSCH	0170	*D. Dalens* | Twee stuks Duinachtige Landschappen, met Heeren te Paard, Jagers, Honden en Reizigers	A	(Sold) fl 1 L Pakker

Dalens, Dirck (manner)

1805/10/09	HGBSM	0146	*D. Daalens* | Een bergagtig landschapje, in de manier van D. Daalens | *Mat:* op paneel *Size:* hoog 8 breet 11 duim	T H van Willigen [or others]	(Sold) fl 4:5 van den Broek
1808/06/13	AMSCH	0247	*Dalens* | Twee Landgezichten, met Boerenwoningen, rijk gestoffeerd met staand en liggend Vee; op Doek, in de manier van Dalens | *Mat:* op doek	Y[ver]	(Sold) fl 1 C S Roos

Dalens, Dirck (I)

1805/07/10	AMSCH	0053	*de oude Dalens* | In een Landschap met Geboomten, ziet men verschyde Vée, zoo staande als rustende; meesterlyke behandeld, door de oude Dalens | *Mat:* op doek	S[chley]	(Sold) fl 2:10 Agina

Dame, A. [Unidentified]

1802/09/06	AMSCH	0036	*A. Dame* | Op een marmersteene Tafel, staat een Vaas, met onderscheidene zoorten van Bloemen, als roode en witte Roozen, Tulpen, en verscheide andere; voor dezelve leggen diversche vrugten, Persikken, Druyven &c., en Vogelnesje met Eyertjes, bevallig en plaisant geschilderd | *Mat:* op doek	H van der Meulen	(Bought In) fl 1
1802/09/06	AMSCH	0037	*A. Dame* | Op een dito [marmersteene Tafel] staat een Vaas en een Bennetje, met verscheide Bloemen en Vrugten, waarop eenige Insecten aazen, ter zyde legt een Vogelnesje in alles als de voorige; bevallig geschilderd | *Mat:* op doek	H van der Meulen	(Bought In) fl 4 ¼ for lots 37 & 38
1802/09/06	AMSCH	0038	*A. Dame* | Op een dito [marmersteene Tafel] staat een mandje met verschillende zoort van Bloemen, ter zyde legt een Cantaloup en andere vrugten; in alles als de voorige behandeld	H van der Meulen	(Bought In) fl 4 ¼ for lots 37 & 38
1809/06/13	AMSCH	0040	*A. Dame* | Op een Marmersteene Tafel, liggen verscheide zoorten van smaakelijke Vruchten, en ter zijde een Vogelnesje met Eijertjes, verder een Vaas met verscheide verschillende geurige Bloemen; het is van een meesterlijke penceelbehandeling | *Mat:* op doek	S[chley]	(Sold) fl 0:12 van der Schleij [for] A

Dattan [Unidentified]

1802/05/10	MGSAN	0033	*Dattan* | Een dito [Kabinetstukje], vertoonende daar Joseph het Wyf van Pothifar, op haar Rustbed leggende, ontvlucht, uit eene Binnenzaal, gloeiënd en malsch gepenseeld, als van van der Werf, door Dattan: in een vergulde Lyst dit Stuk is geconserveerd in een bruin geboend kasje, met een Glas over het Stuk	Johan Dirk Kruysse	(Sold) £ 21 Pr Ackermans

David

1803/04/27	AMSCH	0077	*David* | Deux Tableaux représentant Abel mort, & Goliath Vaincu | *Size:* h. 2 ¼, l. 2 ¾ pieds	A	(Sold) fl 5:15 Pruijssenaar [for] L

Deane

1810/07/26	AMSCH	0025	*Deane* | Een Bergachtig Landschap, met Geboomte, op den voorgrond eenige Beesten bij een helder Water | *Mat:* op doek *Size:* hoog 27, breed 36 duimen	Cassino	(Sold) fl 1:10 Spaan

Decker

1801/03/16	AMSCH	0177	*Decker* | Een Landschap	P[ruyssenaar]	(Sold) fl 2:10 Wijland
1805/07/10	AMSCH	0049	*Th. Dekker* | In een Boere Binnehuis ziet men in 't midden op de voorgrond een geslachten Os, met verder bywerk, ter zyde een Meid, en agter haar by een Vuur twee Boeren en een Boerin; breed en meesterlyk op Paneel | *Mat:* op paneel *Size:* hoog 28 ½, breed 40 ½ duim	V[inkeles]	(Sold) fl 35 Gruyter
1809/05/26	HADAA	A0007	*Dekker* | Een dito [Landschap]	Mejuffrouw de Wed David Heemskerk [or others]	(Unknown)
1810/07/26	AMSCH	0116	*Deker* | Een Landschap, met Figuren | *Mat:* op doek	Cassino	(Sold) fl 1 Lohuijs

Decker (and Palamedesz., A.)

1810/06/06	RMMUY	0149	*Dekker; Palamedes* | Een Boschrijk Landschap. Door Dekker, gestoffeerd met Figuren. Door Palamedes | *Mat:* op paneel		(Unknown) fl 5:10

Decker (manner)

1802/09/06	AMSCH	0167	*Decker* | In een bevallig boomryk Landschap, waar in huislieden, die verscheide Vée door een beekje dryven, verders wooningen en rivieren; zonagtig en meesterlyk behandeld als door Decker | *Size:* hoog 12, breed 15 duim	Wed Grave [or others]	(Sold) fl 4:5 de Meijer
1802/11/01	DOBRA	0017	*Dekker* | Het gezigt op een stadsgragt, vestmuur; rondeel en poort, als door Dekker | *Mat:* op paneel *Size:* breed circa 19, hoog 16 duim	Paulus van der Spyk [or others]	(Sold) fl 20 Schouman
1808/04/26	GDAN	0246	*Dekker* | In de manier van Dekker, eenige Boere Woningen, en in 't verschiet een Dorp | *Size:* hoog 17, breed 15 duim	G H Fortuyn	(Unknown)
1810/06/06	RMMUY	0154	*Dekker* | Een Landschap bij maaneschijn, op den voorgrond een vuur, krachtig en van een goed effect. Als door Dekker | *Mat:* op paneel		(Unknown) fl 1

Decker, Cornelis Gerritsz.

1801/05/11	AMSCH	0022	*C. Dekker* | Een boomryk Landschap aan een stille Rivier, waar in Visschers in een Schuit, de frappant verlichte Boerewoning en Schuur,	E[lias]	(Sold) fl 51 C S Roos

			maken dit stuk bevallig; zynde van een meesterlyke behandeling | *Mat:* op paneel *Size:* hoog 18, breed 22 duim		
1801/06/10	AMSCH	0053	*Dekker. (C.)* | Een bevallig Hollandsch Landschap, op den voorgrond een stil Water, waarby een Overhaal, ter zyde een Hengelaar en andere Lieden, bizonder helder en natuurlyk behandeld | *Mat:* op paneel *Size:* hoog 16, breed 19 duim	Herman ten Kate	(Sold) fl 115 Wreesman
1801/08/19	AMSCH	0023	*C. Dekker* | Dit fraai en natuurlyk voorwerp, verbeeld een Boere Woning, waarvoor een Waterput by hoog Geboomten; gestoffeert met een vrouw by de ingang der Deur, en op de Voorgrond eenige Hoenders; de Steene Muur, en verder Bywerk, is van een kunstige en uitvoerige penceel behandeling, op Doek | *Mat:* op doek *Size:* hoog 32, breed 26 duim	C S Roos [for] G	(Sold) fl 36 v d Schleij [for] Merrem
1802/06/16	AMSCH	0039	*C. Decker* | Een gemetzelde Boere Stulp, waarby een Put, Hooggeboomte, Stoffagie van Beeldjes; alles meesterlyk fix geschilderd | *Mat:* op doek *Size:* hoog 32, breed 26 ½ duim	[Merrem]	(Sold) fl 51 Cobel
1804/10/16	DLOND	0057	*C. Decker* | Een helder Landschap, gestoffeerd. Paysage Clair avec des Figures | *Mat:* op doek *Size:* hoog 25, breed 31		(Sold) fl 30:5 Mahy
1806/08/13	AMSCH	0043	*Dekker. (C.)* | Een natuurlyk Wintergezicht, op de Voorgrond eenige rustende Lieden by een ontspannen Vragtslee en Paard, verders eenige rydende en gaande Beeldjes en een aangenaam verschiet | *Mat:* op paneel *Size:* hoog 13, breed 11 ½ duim	Vinkeles [for] G[ruyter]	(Sold) fl 15:10 Schumacher
1806/08/13	AMSCH	0044	*Dekker. (C.)* | Een Boomryk Landschap, by een oud vervallen Casteel, verders een aangenaam verschiet; zonachtig en meesterlyk van schildering | *Mat:* op paneel *Size:* hoog 7, breed 9 duim	Vinkeles [for] F	(Sold) fl 1:5 Th Spaan
1806/11/24	AMSCH	0021	*Dekker (C.)* | Een Boeren Dorp, met zwaar Geboomte en Woningen, met Beeldjes gestoffeerd, en kragtig behandeld | *Mat:* op paneel *Size:* hoog 17, breed 20 duim	Munnikhuizen	(Sold) fl 9:10 T Spaan
1808/06/11	RMRIJ	0079	*C. Dekker* | Een fraai Landschap, Heuvel, Boomen enz. natuurlyk geschilderd | *Mat:* op paneel *Size:* hoog 11 ½, breed 10 ½ duim		(Sold) fl 31:10 van Giesen
1808/06/13	AMSCH	0039	*Dekker (C.)* | Bij een stil Water, staat een vervallen Gebouw; geestig en fraai van schildering | *Mat:* op paneel *Size:* hoog 16, breed 14 duim	G	(Sold) fl 31 J Smit
1808/09/13	HABRU	0020	*C. Dekker* | Een Boere Woning, bij Geboomte aan het Water		(Unknown) fl 8:10
1808/09/13	HABRU	0021	*C. Dekker* | In een Binnenvertrek, een Wever, op Getouw zittende, waar nevens een ander iets lezende		(Unknown) fl 2:4
1808/10/28	AMVRS	0009	*Decker. (C.)* | In een Binnehuis ziet men een Weever, arbeidende bij het Weefgetouw, ter zijde een zittende Jongen, verder eenige Aardvrugten bij een Waterpomp. Natuurlijk behandeld | *Mat:* op paneel *Size:* hoog 12, breed 16 duim	Marten Udink	(Sold) fl 15:10 Gruyter
1808/10/28	AMVRS	0010	*Decker. (C.)* | Een Boomrijk Landschap aan een stille Rivier, waarin Visschers in een Schuit. De fraai verlichte Boere Woningen en Schuur maken dit stuk bevallig | *Mat:* op paneel *Size:* hoog 18, breed 22 duim	Marten Udink	(Sold) fl 21 Coclers
1809/04/17	AMSCH	0023	*C. Dekker* | Dit bevallig Schilderijtje verbeeld een stil Water, ter zijde eenig Geboomte bij een vervallen Schuur, in 't verschiet een Schuitje met twee Visschers; allernatuurlijkst en zuiver van Penceelbehandeling | *Mat:* op paneel *Size:* hoog 16, breed 14 duim	A	(Sold) fl 43
1809/04/22	AMYVR	0032	*C. Dekker* | Een oude vervallen Poort, aan een Vestmuur; geestig met Visschers gestoffeerd, en meesterlijk op Paneel geschilderd | *Mat:* op paneel *Size:* hoog 14, breed 18 duim	de Bruin	(Sold) fl 14 du Pree
1809/06/13	AMSCH	0035	*C. Dekker* | Een Boschgezigt met wandelende Lieden, ter zijde een stille Rivier, met Visschers in een Schuit; zonagtig en natuurlijk behandeld | *Mat:* op paneel *Size:* hoog 20, breed 30 duim	Q	(Sold) fl 43:10 van Iperen
1810/06/20	AMSCH	0017	*C. Dekker* | Een boschachtig Landschap: op den voorgrond een helder spiegelend Water, gestoffeerd met Visschers in hunne Schuiten, en langs den weg gaande Reizigers. Helder en zonachtig behandeld | *Mat:* op paneel *Size:* hoog 21, breed 17 duimen	B	(Bought In) fl 7:5
1810/06/20	AMSCH	0018	*C. Dekker* | Een Landschap, met Geboomte en een Gebouw: op den voorgrond een rustend Reiziger | *Mat:* op paneel *Size:* hoog 6, breed 8 duimen	B	(Sold) fl 2:10 Cassino
1810/07/26	AMSCH	0028	*Decker (C.)* | Een Boomrijk Landschap, met oude vervallen Woningen en Huislieden gestoffeerd. Natuurlijk geschilderd | *Mat:* op doek *Size:* hoog 24, breed 20 duimen	Cassino	(Sold) fl 7:15 van Iperen
1810/11/07	UTWLD	0029	*C. Dekker* | Een zeer geestig boomrijk Landschap, ziende over een voorbij lopende stroom, waaraan eenige vervallen boeren woningen, die de hoofdzaak van dit stuk uitmaken, zeer klaar en meesteragtig behandeld door C. Dekker op doek, 1 voet 5 duim hoog, 1 voet 8 duim breed, zwarte Lijst | *Mat:* op doek *Size:* 1 voet 5 duim hoog, 1 voet 8 duim breed		(Unknown) fl 101

Decker, Cornelis Gerritsz. (and Ostade, A.)

1801/04/13	AMSCH	0018	*C. Decker; A. van Ostade* | In een Binnevertrek ziet men een Weefgetouw, ter zyde het zelve zit een Boer een pyp te roken, daar by een Vrouw met een Kind op de schoot, terwyl een ander aan de broodkast staat, een Hond en een menigte boere Meubelen maken dit tot een bevallig schildery; het geen zonachtig en meesterlyk behandeld is | *Mat:* op paneel *Size:* hoog	Pierre Fouquet, junior	(Sold) fl 860 Yver

			18, breed 22 duim *Loc:* Bruxelles, Belgique. Musées Royaux des Beaux Arts. (inv. 3061) as C.G. Decker		
1809/04/17	AMSCH	0024	*C. Dekker; A. van Ostade* | Een kapitaal boschagtig Landschap, op de voorgrond met een helder Spiegelend Water, gestoffeerd met gaande Reizigers en Visschers in hunne Schuiten; helder en zonagtig behandeld, door denzelven [C. Dekker], gestoffeerd door A. van Ostade | *Mat:* op paneel *Size:* hoog 21 ½, breed 17 duim	[Gruyter?]	(Sold) fl 18 Spaan

Decker, Cornelis Gerritsz. (or Ruisdael, J.)

1810/03/26	RMMUY	0019	*C. Dekker; J. Ruisdaal* | Een Heuvelachtig Landschap, met boerenwooningen en hoog geboomte. Op den voorgrond, Boomstammen, Planten en Kruiden. Krachtig en piquant geschilderd [Un Paysage rustique, plusieurs masures et belles masses d'arbres, des plantes et herbes, forment le devant. Le lointain est agréable ; vigoureusement traîté, et d'une bonne pate, digne de Ruisdaal.] | *Mat:* op paneel *Size:* hoog 18, breed 24 duimen *Notes:* The French edition of the catalogue gives only "C. Dekker" as the artist.	Daniel de Jongh Az	(Sold) fl 50 van Eyk s'Hage

Decker, Cornelis Gerritsz. (copy after)

1808/09/13	HABRU	0088	*H. Tuijlen; C. Dekker* | Een Landschap, met Boere Woningen, naar C. Dekker, door H. Tuijlen | copy by H. Tuijlen after C. Decker		(Unknown) fl 13

Decker, Frans

1801/03/16	AMSCH	0008	*F. Dekker* | Een Land- en Watergezicht langs Boerenwoningen, gestoffeerd met Vissers in hunnen Schuiten; krachtig en natuurlyk behandeld	P[ruyssenaar]	(Sold) fl 7 Rijnders
1802/09/06	AMSCH	0034	*F. Dekker* | In een aangenaam Landschap ziet men ter zyde een klaar water, eenig hoog geboomte, en boerenwoning, en verders een boomryk verschiet; aangenaam van Licht en bruin | *Mat:* op paneel *Size:* hoog 7, breed 9 duim	J	(Sold) fl 5:5 Croese
1804/08/08	AMSCH	0055	*F. Dekker* | In een Riviergezicht, by een oud vervallen Kasteel, en een Steene Brug, waar over eenige Lieden gaan, eenige andere Wooningen en een Kerktooren, ziet men eenige Visschende Lieden, by eenig Land, en Waterval; uitvoerig en fraai gepenceeld | *Mat:* op doek *Size:* hoog 26, breed 20 duim	Vink[eles] [for] W	(Bought In) fl 15
1804/08/08	AMSCH	0056	*F. Dekker* | Een bevallig Land- en Watergezicht; zonachtig en bevallig geschilderd | *Mat:* op doek *Size:* hoog 24, breed 33 duim	Vink[eles] [for] K[=Gruyter?]	(Sold) fl 1:10 Menzart

Decker, Jan

1804/05/07	AMSCH	0043	*Dekker (J.)* | In een aangenaam Land- en Riviergezicht, ziet men by een oud vervallen Gebouw en eenige andere Woningen, eenige Lieden in hunne Schuyten, ter zyde by eenig Paalwerk, twee Lieden in een Boot, schynende hun Netten na te zien, verders eenige zylende Schuyten, en in 't verschiet hoog Geboomte; dit allerzonachtigst en bevallig Stukje is uitvoerig en een der beste van deeze Meester | *Mat:* op paneel *Size:* hoog 17, breed 20 duim	Vinkeles [for] X	(Sold) fl 77 Moll
1804/05/07	AMSCH	0044	*Dekker (J.)* | Een Land- en Watergezicht, by Boere Woningen gestoffeerd met een Hengelaar en Visschers in hunne Schuiten; zeer natuurlyk geschilderd | *Mat:* op paneel *Size:* hoog 19, breed 21 duim	Y[ver] [for] JJ	(Sold) fl 83:15 Jan Spaan
1808/06/11	RMRIJ	0011	*J: Dekker* | Een aangenaam Landschap, waar in een Huis, Schuur, Water en verdere Stoffagie; zeer goed en natuurlyk geschilderd | *Mat:* op paneel *Size:* hoog 15, breed 13 duim		(Sold) fl 62 Noordwijk

Decker, Jan (manner)

1808/06/11	RMRIJ	0075	*Als J: Dekker, of in zyn manier* | Een Landschap, Maanlicht, op den Voorgrond by 't Water schynen eenige Stoppels te branden, fiks en natuurlyk geschilderd | *Mat:* op paneel		(Bought In) fl 15:10

Defrance, Léonard

1808/10/28	AMVRS	0013	*France, (P. la) bijenaamd Frans de Liege* | In een Luiksche Herberg ziet men Lieden aandachtig luisteren naar het leezen der Nieuwspapieren. Dit stukje is geestig en fiks van penceelsbehandeling | *Mat:* op paneel *Size:* hoog 12 ½, breed 16 duim *Loc:* Den Haag, Nederland. Museum Bredius. (47–1946)	Marten Udink	(Sold) fl 90 J Smit
1809/06/13	AMSCH	0048	*De La France, bijgenaamd Frans de Liege* | In een Luikse Herberg, ziet men eenige Lieden aandachtig luisteren, naar het leezen der Nieuwspapieren; dit stukje is bevallig van koloriet en van een zuivere penceelbehandeling, door De La France, bijgenaamd Frans De Liege | *Mat:* op paneel *Size:* hoog 13, breed 16 duim *Loc:* Den Haag, Nederland. Museum Bredius. (47–1946)	A	(Sold) fl 81 R[emmers] Bredius
1809/06/13	AMSCH	0049	*De La France, bijgenaamd Frans de Liege* | Twee stuks, het eene verbeeld een Smitswinkel, waarin verscheide Lieden staan te arbeiden, het andere een Binnehuis, waarin eenige Vrouwen bezig Linnen te Wasschen; beide bevallig | *Mat:* op paneel *Size:* hoog 8 ½, breed 11 duim	T	(Sold) fl 25 Buck

Delanes, J. [Unidentified]

1802/07/09	AMSTO	0001	*J. Delanes* | 1 Bybelsche Ordenantie, verbeelende de Kindertjes koomende tot den Zaligmaaker, zeer fraay geschildert		(Unknown)

Delcloche

1810/03/23	HAVIN	0073	*Delcloche* | Twee Historien [In Lysten met Glasen] | *Notes:* The bracketed information in the title appears above lot 63 and refers to lots 63 to 79.	Rudolf Hendrik de Wetstein [or others]	(Unknown)

Delcloche, Paul Joseph

1808/03/03	HAVIN	0011	*Delcloche Junior* | Twee Historiestukken, fraai geschildert	Jacobus Spillebout	(Unknown) fl 4

Delen, Dirck van

1801/03/16	AMSCH	0025	*D. van Deelen* | By een pragtig Gebouw wandeld een Heer en Dame, uitvoerig	K[ip]	(Sold) fl 28 v d Schley [for] S
1801/03/16	AMSCH	0056	*van Deelen* | Een capitaale ryk geordoneerde Kerk van binnen te zien, gestoffeerd met het Vrouwtje in overspel bevonden, fraai van perspectief en bevallig van ligt	P[ruyssenaar]	(Sold) fl 2 Croese
1802/05/05	AMSCH	0047	*D. van Deelen* | Het Voorportaal van een Prachtig Gebouw, met Colonades, gestoffeerd met een menigte Beelden, in het verschiet een Hofgezicht, dun en bevallig van Zonligt | *Mat:* op paneel *Size:* hoog 25, breed 41 duim	J	(Bought In) fl 26
1802/05/05	AMSCH	0048	*D. van Deelen* | Een Binnegezicht in een Prachtig Paleys, waarin een Historiëele Ordonnantie, verbeeldende Simion, houdende het Kind Jesus in zyne Armen. Meesterlyk en kloek geschilderd | *Mat:* op paneel *Size:* hoog 42, breed 52 duim	C	(Sold) fl 14:10 B^{d} Kooij
1802/05/10	MGSAN	0017	*D. v. Deelen* | Een extra fraai Tempelstuk, ryk gestoffeerd met onderscheide staande en wandelende Beeldjes, waaronder schynt verbeeld te worden, de Pharizeen, welke het Vrouwtje in Overspel bevonden, aan Christus voorstelde, door D. v. Deelen: op Paneel: in vergulde Lyst | *Mat:* op paneel *Size:* hoog 26 duim, breed 28 duim	Johan Dirk Kruysse	(Sold) £ 24 D Klyné
1803/12/12	AMSCH	0023	*D. van Deelen* | Op de Stoep van een prachtig Gebouw staat een Heer en Dame, met een ander pratende, waarby twee Honden, en een Laan in het verschiet; zonachtig behandeld | *Mat:* op paneel *Size:* hoog 27, breed 23 duim	W	(Sold) fl 16:10 W^{l} Reijers
1803/12/15	MGLAC	0023	*D. van Deelen* | Een Heerlyke Tempel van binnen te zien, met extra schoone Figuuren en zeer schoon van Architectuur | *Mat:* op paneel *Size:* hoog duim 24, breed duim 29	Mr L H de Haze Bomme	(Unknown)
1804/08/08	AMSCH	0052	*D. van Deelen* | Een prachtig Gebouw, van buiten te zien, by hetzelve eenige wandelende Beelden, in het verschiet een fraai Hofgezicht; delicaat op Paneel | *Mat:* op paneel *Size:* hoog 25, breed 42 duim	Roos a	(Bought In) fl 15
1804/12/10	AMSCH	0014	*D. van Deelen* | Een Roomsche Kerk van binnen te zien, met onderscheide Altaaren, deeze tempel is fraai van perspectief, vol gewoel en kragtig van schildering | *Mat:* op doek *Size:* Hoog 27, breed 34 duim	Jan de Groot	(Sold) fl 185 Gruyter
1804/12/10	AMSCH	0015	*D. van Deelen* | Het Gezicht van een prachtig Gebouw, gestoffeerd met wandelende heeren en dames, fraay van perspectief en krachtig gepenceeld | *Mat:* op doek *Size:* Hoog 27, breed 34 duim	Jan de Groot	(Sold) fl 40 Coclers
1805/07/10	AMSCH	0044	*D. van Deelen* | In een Pragtige Gemeubileerde Zaal, ziet men verscheide Dames aan een Tafel zitten, bezig zynde Bouquetten te formeeren, op de voorgrond een Hond blaffende tegen een Kat, uitvoerig behandeld op Paneel | *Mat:* op paneel *Size:* hoog 37, breed 56 duim	R[oos]	(Sold) fl 10 E Seeburgh
1805/07/10	AMSCH	0045	*D. van Deelen* | Een Prachtig Gebouw, van binnen te zien, met verscheide wandelende Heeren en Dames, Bedelaars enz.; door de Poort ziet men in een Tuyn na een ander cierlyk Gebouw, uitvoerig en fraay van behandeling | *Size:* hoog 33, breed 40 duim	V[inkeles] [for] M	(Sold) fl 2 Agina
1805/07/10	AMSCH	0193	*van Deelen* | Een verwulfd Gebouw	R[oos]	(Sold) fl 23 Gruyter
1806/11/24	AMSCH	0017	*Deelen (D. van)* | Dit voorwerp vertoont den Ingang naar een pragtig Paleis, in een Hofgezigt, gestoffeert met verscheiden Beeldjes; het is bevallig van licht, en uitvoerig gepenceelt | *Mat:* op paneel *Size:* hoog 21, breed 28 duim	Munnikhuizen	(Sold) fl 20 Yver
1807/08/26	AMSCH	0040	*D. van Deelen* | Een pragtig Paleis en Hofgezigt, gestoffeerd met Beelden; dit stuk is fraai van perspectief, bouwkunstig en zonachtig behandeld | *Mat:* op paneel *Size:* hoog 25, breed 42 duim	Roos	(Sold) fl 10 v d Schley A [for] Helsding
1808/06/13	AMSCH	0040	*Deelen (D. van)* | Een prachtig Hofgezicht: op den voorgrond een Gebouw, waarbij twee Heeren hun aandacht op een opkomend Onweder vestigen, fraai van uitdrukking en verschiet | *Mat:* op paneel *Size:* hoog 22, breed 29 duim	G	(Sold) fl 16 du Pré
1809/06/13	AMSCH	0036	*D. van Deelen* | Een Roomsche Kerk, van binnen gestoffeerd met Altaaren en Beeldjes; fraai van doorzicht en zonagtig behandeld | *Mat:* op paneel *Size:* hoog 13, breed 20 duim	T	(Sold) fl 7:10 du Pree
1809/06/13	AMSCH	0037	*D. van Deelen* | Een Hofgezicht, van binnen met pragtige Gebouwen, gestoffeerd met wandelende Dames en Heeren, door een verwulfde Poort ziet men in een Tuin, met een Fontijn en groene Wandelweegen, het zonlicht doet een natuurlijke werking en is uitvoerig van penceelbehandeling | *Size:* hoog 16, breed 17 duim	R[ijfsnijder]	(Sold) fl 1 L Pakker
1810/06/06	RMMUY	0020	*Dirk van Delen* | Een Prachtig Gebouw, konstig van Perspectief, op den voorgrond eene deftig gekleede Dame spelende op een Guitarre, terwijl		(Unknown) fl 14:10

			een Hondje voor haar loopt, delicaat behandeld, en zeer uitvoerig geschilderd | *Mat:* op paneel *Size:* hoog 18 ½, breed 15 ½ duim		
			Delen, Dirck van (and Bloemaert)		
1810/10/10	MGCIT	0121	*v. Deelen; Bloemaart* | Een fraai Antiek Gebouw, door v. Deelen; waar achter is geplaatst een zeer bevallig Landschap, door Bloemaart	Caspar van Citters	(Unknown)
			Delen, Dirck van (and Ducq, Johan le)		
1804/10/29	HRBAU	0017	*Deelen (D. van); J. le Duc* | Voor aan op eene hoogte, waar een Obelisque geplaatst is, by eene pragtige Gallery, staat een Gezelschap van vier Heeren met elkander te raisonneeren, waar by een Heer en Dame komen aanwandelen, nevens nog eenige Heeren die den trap opkomen; op den tweeden grond in de diepte, by een uitmuntend Paleis, zyn een menigte Heeren en Dames, welken zig met wandelen vermaaken; wordende deze plaats door een kostbaar Gebouw ingesloten, waar door men door de Poort in een' fraaien Tuin ziet. Dit Tafereel is zo zonagtig en uitvoerig behandeld, als men maar zeer zelden te zien zal krygen, en is de eer dezes Meesters waardig | *Mat:* op paneel *Size:* hoog 20 ½, breed 27 duim	Simon Styl	(Unknown)
			Delen, Dirck van (and Francken or Vrancx)		
1802/07/20	MGSAN	0007	*D. van Deelen; Francq* | In dit fraaije Stuk vertoont zich in een prachtige Zaal, een zeer aanzienlyk Gezelschap aan een Tafel te eeten; in het verschiet ziet men een Vorstelyk Collonade en Tuin, alles helder en krachtig geschilderd door D. van Deelen en Francqu | *Mat:* op paneel *Size:* hoog duim 25, breed duim 33		(Unknown)
			Delen, Dirck van (and Franks, St.)		
1810/10/10	MGCIT	0040	*D. v. Deelen; St. Franks* | Een schoon Kerk Gebouw op koper, waar in alles wat tot zoo een Gesticht behoord, naar de Kunst is geobserveerd, door D. v. Deelen en fraai gestoffeerd, door St. Franks: doende dit Stuk in zijn soort in allen opzigten eer aan beide Meesters | *Mat:* op koper	Caspar van Citters	(Unknown)
1810/10/10	MGCIT	0041	*D. v. Deelen; St. Franks* | Nog een Schilderij, zijnde een statelijk Gebouw van een aanzienlijke bouwörde en vercierd door een ongemeen fraai Perspectif, met uitmuntende stoffage, en van evengelijke waarde als 't vorige	Caspar van Citters	(Unknown)
			Delen, Dirck van (or Delen, manner)		
1803/07/14	MGKLY	0013	*Van Deele of zyn manier* | Een fraay Architectuur ryk gestoffeert	Mr Caspar Jacob van Citters	(Unknown)
1810/10/10	MGCIT	0157	*van Deelen* | Een Schilderij, zynde een statig Gebouw, en voor het zelve een Ruïne en bevloerde Plaats in de opene Lucht, alwaar eenige aanzienelijke Heeren en Dames, in eene antique kleeding, met dansen als andersints zig diverteren; door van Deelen, of in zijn Manier	Caspar van Citters	(Unknown)
			Delen, Dirck van (manner)		
1802/04/13	HAVIN	0073	*van Deelen* | Een Tempel, de manier van van Deelen		(Unknown)
1806/08/13	AMSCH	0269	*van Deelen* | Een Kerk van Binnen, met Tombes; als van Deelen	Roos	(Sold) fl 1 Boelen
			Delff, Cornelis Jacobsz.		
1802/06/29	HGDAW	0025	*van Delf* | Een groot Keuken Stuk door de beroemde van Delf. zeer uitvoerig		(Unknown)
1802/06/29	HGDAW	0026	*van Delf* | Een dito [Keuken Stuk] door dezelve [van Delf]		(Unknown)
1802/06/29	HGDAW	0027	*van Delf* | Een dito [Keuken Stuk] door dezelve [van Delf]		(Unknown)
1806/11/24	AMSCH	0022	*Delf* | Een Tafel, daarop een brandende Lamp, Koper en Aardewerk; fraai gepenceeld | *Mat:* op koper *Size:* hoog 16, breed 19 duim	Munnikhuizen	(Sold) fl 7:5 Meulie
			Denens, Jan		
1810/10/10	MGCIT	0113	*J. Deenens* | Een Slapend Kind, liggende gedekt op een Bed; goed behandeld	Caspar van Citters	(Unknown)
			Denick [Unidentified]		
1806/06/07	RMHSN	0080	*Denick* | Twee Stuks met Vrugten &c. | *Mat:* op doek	A E K L	(Unknown)
			Denies, Isaac		
1802/08/24	LNDLS	0024	*J. Denise* | Een Patrijsvogel, Valkenkap en Jachthoorn, hangende aan den tak van een Boom, nevens een distelplant, Insecten en doode Vogels. Delicaat op doek geschilderd | *Mat:* op doek *Size:* hoog 23 ½, breed 28 duimen	Leonardus Bouman [or others]	(Unknown) fl 9:10
1804/05/07	AMSCH	0045	*Denies. (J.)* | Op een Tafel waarop een groen Kussen legt een doode Patrys, waarby eenig Jagttuig hangt; uitvoerig gepenceeld | *Mat:* op doek *Size:* hoog 20, breed 17 duim	Roos [for] A	(Sold) fl 20 Thais
			Denner, Balthasar		
1801/04/08	HAVIN	0017	*Denner* | Twee, een ouden Man met een Baard en een Vrouw		(Unknown)
1801/05/11	AMSCH	0021	*B. Denner* | Een bevallig Vrouwe Pourtret, met een sluyer om 't hoofd, extra uitvoerig gepenceeld | *Mat:* op paneel *Size:* hoog 26, breed 21 duim	P[ruyssenaar]	(Sold) fl 21 Allard

1802/06/28	AMSCH	0043	*Denner* | Twee stuks, een bedaagde Vrouw en Man, in deftige aloude kleeding, halver lyf; zeer uitvoerig gepenceeld, door Denner | *Mat:* op paneel *Size:* ieder hoog 15, breed 12 duim	Anna Elink	(Sold) fl 24:15 Roijers
1802/06/28	AMSCH	0044	*Denner* | Een zittende Oude Philosooph, ter zyde by een Tafel, waarop een open Boek; meesterlyk fraai gepenceelt, door Denzelven [Denner] | *Mat:* op doek *Size:* hoog 13, breed 10 duim	Anna Elink	(Sold) fl 14:10 Gruiter
1803/09/07	AMSCH	0050	*Denner* | Een bedaagde Vrouw, met een witte Kraag om haar hals, uitvoerig op Paneel [Une femme agée, ayant une fraise blanche au col ; belle exécution] | *Mat:* op paneel *Size:* hoog 20, breed 15 duim	Smidt	(Sold) fl 2:5 Gruiter
1804/04/28	LNDLS	0014	*B. Denner* | Een Mans Borststuk met een gryze baard, eel van schildering; door B. Denner, op doek | companion to lot 15 *Mat:* op doek *Size:* hoog 17, breed 13 duim	[Abraham Delfos] [or others]	(Sold) fl 35 Gruyter
1804/04/28	LNDLS	0015	*B. Denner* | Een dito [Mans Borststuk], met een muts op 't hooft, weêrga | companion to lot 14 *Size:* hoog 17, breed 13 duim	[Abraham Delfos] [or others]	(Unknown)
1806/05/05	AMSCH	0038	*B. Denner* | Een bejaarde Grysaart, halverlyf met éen lange witte Baard en gevouwen handen, in een Landschap; 't character allernatuurlykst en van een een [sic] uitvoerige schildering | *Mat:* op doek *Size:* hoog 30, breed 25 duim		(Withdrawn)
1806/05/05	AMSCH	0039	*B. Denner* | Een Mans Pourtret met witte Hairen en Baard, met een rood Kleed met Bont; mede in alles als de voorgaande | *Mat:* op doek *Size:* hoog 14, breed 15 duim		(Withdrawn)
1806/05/05	AMSCH	0040	*B. Denner* | Een Grysaard met een lange witte Baard, met een zwart Kleed met een bonte Kraag; mede in alles als de voorgaande | *Mat:* op doek *Size:* hoog 14, breed 11 ½ duim		(Withdrawn)
1808/08/23	AMSCH	0043	*Denner. (B.)* | Het Afbeeldzel van een bedaagd Heer, ter halve lijf, in aloude deftige Kleeding, het Hoofd gedekt met een Mezetijne Muts met een Pluim; natuurlijk en krachtig van penceelbehandeling | *Mat:* op paneel *Size:* hoog 17, breed 12 duim	C	(Sold) fl 3:5 Gruyter
1808/08/23	AMSCH	0281	*Denner* | Een Mans Pourtret in deftige Kleeding | *Notes:* This lot was sold with lot 282, which is in the manner of Vertangen.	Z	(Sold) fl 2 for lots 281 & 282. L Pakker
1810/06/20	AMSCH	0016	*Denner* | Een Oud Mans Hoofd, zeer fraai en uitvoerig van schildering | *Mat:* op koper *Size:* hoog 16, breed 13 duim	D	(Sold) fl 15 Reijers

Denner, Balthasar (manner)

1806/10/16	UTWLD	0013	*Denner* | Het Portrait van Vader van Hoorn, in de manier van Denner	Mr P de Malapert [or] W Beeldsnyder	(Unknown)

Deuren, Olivier van

1810/08/01	AMSCH	0022	*Deuren (Otto van)* | In eene Nis ziet men eene oude Vrouw, houdende met de eene hand eenen Sluijer [Autravers d'une embrasure en forme de Niche, se presente une Femme agée, tenant un Voile à la main] | *Annots:* assez bon. Vendu fl: 120 ½ chez Pauwelsen 1803. (NGW); Vente le Brun No. 162 fr 99 (SMLN) *Mat:* op paneel *Size:* hoog 7 ½, breed 6 ½ duimen	Mr Pieter de Smeth van Alphen	(Sold) fl 100 Texier, Gerbet en Comp [for] Le Brun

Diepenbeeck, Abraham Jansz. van

1802/07/21	HGKAN	0013	*Diepenbroek* | Een Historieel		(Unknown)
1803/09/07	AMSCH	0046	*A. Diepenbeek* | Christus speelende met St. Jan, meesterlyk fraay [L'enfant Jésus, jouant avec St.-Jean, jolie composition] | *Mat:* op doek *Size:* hoog 34, breed 27 duim	Smidt	(Sold) fl 35:10 Gruiter
1804/02/27	AMSCH	0028	*Diepenbeek* | Joannes speelende met een Lam; breed gepenceeld | *Size:* hoog 29, breed 33 duim	C	(Sold) fl 0:8 Oostwijn
1804/08/08	AMSCH	0057	*A. van Diepenbeek* | De Boodschap aan Maria, met een Glorie van Engelen omhoog; alleruitvoerigst en fraai gepenceeld | *Mat:* op koper *Size:* hoog 15, breed 12 duim	Vink[eles] [for] S	(Sold) fl 2:5 Gruyter
1804/08/08	AMSCH	0058	*A. van Diepenbeek* | Een naakt Kind en verder Bywerk; kragtig en meesterlyk geschilderd | *Size:* hoog 26, breed 18 duim	Vink[eles] [for] K[=Gruyter?]	(Sold) fl 0:10 L Pakker
1809/04/17	AMSCH	0026	*A. van Diepenbeek* | Een geestelijke Ordonnantie, verbeeldende St. Rochus, op de voorgrond ziet men verscheide gebrekkelijke Lieden; meesterlijk geschilderd | *Mat:* op paneel	Y	(Sold or Bought In) fl 6
1810/08/06	AMSCH	0024	*Diepenbeek (A.)* | De Heiligen Ignatius, in eene devote gestalte. Schoon van teekening en penceelsbehandeling | *Mat:* op doek *Size:* hoog 48, breed 38 duimen	F	(Sold) fl 1:15 Dupre
1810/10/11	AMSCH	0024	*A. Diepenbeek* | De Edelmoedigheid van Scipio | *Mat:* op paneel *Size:* hoog 23, breed 32 duimen	C	(Sold) fl 7:10 Posthumus
1810/10/11	AMSCH	0025	*A. Diepenbeek* | St. Ignatius, in eerbiedige houding | *Mat:* op doek	[Levy Pakker?]	(Sold) fl 2:15 Gruiter

Diepenbeeck, Abraham Jansz. van (and Seghers, D.)

1808/06/13	AMSCH	0155	*Seegers (P.); A. Diepenbeek* | Eene Buste in 't graauw, omgeven met Guirlandes van Bloemen. Fraai van koloriet en uitvoerig gepenceelt | *Mat:* op koper *Size:* hoog 34, breed 24 duim	E M Engelberts	(Sold) fl 26 Simons
1809/06/13	AMSCH	0231	*P. Zeegers; A. Diepenbeek* | Maria met het Kind, in een Bloemkrans, uitvoerig door P. Zeegers en A. Diepenbeek | *Mat:* op paneel *Size:* hoog 12, breed 10 duim	[Gruyter?]	(Sold or Bought In) fl 3 de Gruiter

Diepenbeeck, Abraham Jansz. van (and Utrecht, Adr.)

1803/04/20	AMSCH	0022	*Diepenbeek (A.); A. van Utrecht* | In een Krans en Feston van Bloemen en Vrugten, welke allernatuurlykst voorgesteld zyn, ziet men Maria met het Kind Jesu op haar schoot zittende, waarby drie Kinderen; de Drapperie, en het Coloriet zyn van de beste Schildering van die meester [Au milieu de quelques guirlandes de fruits & de fleurs l'artiste a place [sic] L.V.M. avec l'enfant Jesus, accompagnés de trois Anges, cette representation est très bien rendue avec franchise & de l'éclât.] | *Mat:* op doek *Size:* hoog 45, breed 61 duim	Maria Magdalena van Sluypwyk, gravinne van Moens	(Sold) fl 48 Hodges

Diepenbeeck, Abraham Jansz. van (manner)

1806/06/07	RMHSN	0130	*Diepenbeek* | Sante Hubert, knielende voor een Hart, van het Paard gekomen, dat door een Knegt word vastgehouden, &c. in de manier van Diepenbeek	A E K L	(Unknown)

Diepraem, Abraham

1802/11/01	DOBRA	0024	*Abraham Diepraam* | Twee rookende Boertjes	Paulus van der Spyk [or others]	(Sold) fl 8 Boercoert
1802/11/01	DOBRA	0025	*Abraham Diepraam* | Twee Boertjes	Paulus van der Spyk [or others]	(Sold) fl 3 v Leen
1802/11/01	DOBRA	0026	*Abraham Diepraam* | Een Toebaks-Mannetje	Paulus van der Spyk [or others]	(Sold) fl 3 Randwyk
1803/12/15	MGLAC	0052	*Diepraam* | Een lezend oud Man; zeer breed geschilderd | *Mat:* op paneel *Size:* hoog duim 19, breed duim 14	Mr L H de Haze Bomme	(Unknown)
1804/10/29	HRBAU	0018	*Diepraam, (A.)* | In een Boeren Binnenhuis ziet men vier Boertjes zig met drinken en rooken vermaaken; terwyl een ander zyn Wyfje caresseert, en een Boer de deur komt inloopen om dat spel te beschouwen. Dit Schildery is schoon van licht en bruin, fiks getoetst, en meesterlyk in den trant van A. Brouwer behandeld | *Mat:* op paneel *Size:* hoog 13 ½, breed 19 duim	Simon Styl	(Unknown)
1807/09/28	DOHAA	00CC	*A. Diepraam* | Gezelschap van drinkende Boeren	Mattheus Westerouen van Meeteren	(Unknown)
1810/07/23	DOLG2	0081	*Diepram* | Een rookende Boer; door den beruchten Diepram | *Mat:* op paneel *Size:* hoog 8, breed 6 duim	Pieter Quinting	(Unknown)

Diepraem, Abraham (manner)

1810/06/06	RMMUY	0150	*Diepraam* | Twee stuks met Boertjes. Als door Diepraam | *Mat:* op doek		(Unknown) fl 3:4

Diest, Willem van

1807/04/00	LNDLS	0041	*W. van Diest* | Een stil water met Scheepen | *Mat:* op paneel *Size:* hoog 15, breed 23 duim	[Abraham Delfos] [or others]	(Unknown)
1807/06/10	HGBSM	0041	*W. van Diest* | Een stil water met Schepen | *Mat:* op paneel *Size:* hoog 15, breed 23 duim	Abraham Delfos [or others]	(Sold) fl 2:2 Temmink

Dietrich, Christian Wilhelm Ernst

1803/09/07	AMSCH	0048	*Ditricy* | Twee stuks zeer fraije Bergachtige Landschapjes, met Water-vallen, Kasteelen, Boerewoningen, Beeldjes en Vée gestoffeerd, de schildering is bevallig [Deux jolis paysages avec des montagnes garnies de chateaux, de cascades, de chaumières, de figures et de bestiaux ; la touche en est agréable et douce] | *Mat:* op paneel *Size:* yeder hoog 9, breed 12 duim	Smidt	(Sold) fl 26 J Yver
1803/09/07	AMSCH	0049	*Ditricy* | Twee Kinderen, speelende met een Vogelnesje, geestig op Doek [Deux enfans jouant avec un nit [sic] d'oiseaux ; composition très spirituelle] | *Mat:* op doek *Size:* hoog 24, breed 21 duim	Smidt	(Sold) fl 9 C S Roos
1804/07/25	AMSCH	0017	*Diterich. (C. W. E.)* | De wyzen uit het Oosten, komen Geschenken brengen, en aanbidden het Kind Jesus, in de Stal te Betlehem; ryk van ordenantie, fix en kragtig gepenceeld | companion to lot 18 *Mat:* op doek *Size:* ieder hoog 18, breed 25 duim		(Sold) fl 250 B^{d} Kooy
1804/07/25	AMSCH	0018	*Diterich. (C. W. E.)* | Deeze ryke Ordinantie van eene menigte Beelden, vertoond aan den Aanschouwer, Christus die de Kreupelen en Lammen geneest, waarby verscheiden Schriftgeleerden, en anderen Persoonen, aan den Ingang van de Tempel; dit stukje is als de voorgaande behandeld, en kan tot een wederga van 't zelven verstrekken | companion to lot 17 *Mat:* op doek *Size:* hoog 18, breed 25 duim		(Sold) fl 301 Gruiter
1804/07/25	AMSCH	0019	*Diterich. (C. W. E.)* | De voorstelling in den Tempel, Simeon ziet men geknield, en houdende het Kind Jesus, in zyne Armen, waarby de Heylige Maagd Maria, St. Joseph, en de Prophetesse Anna gezien worden, beneevens verscheide Priesters en Schriftgeleerden; en in 't verschiet een Offerhanden; dit fraaije Cabinetstuk is ryk van Ordinantie, uitvoerig gepenceeld, en schoon van Coloriet | *Mat:* op doek *Size:* hoog 18, breed 24 ½ duim		(Sold) fl 435 Jan Spaan
1804/07/25	AMSCH	0020	*Diterich. (C. W. E.)* | In een Rotsgezigt ziet men den Doode van het Kruis afgenomen Christus, leggende in de Schoot van zyne bedroefde Moeder de Maagd Maria, waarby de andere Heilige Vrouwen, en Johannes, die alle door hunne houdingen, hunne droefheid, en aandoeninge te kenne		(Sold) fl 107 Gruiter

			geeven, verder beschouwd men, Joseph van Arimathéa, en twee andere Discipelen; dit treffend Schildery is uitvoerig geschilderd, en van een kragtig coloriet | *Mat:* op doek *Size:* hoog 25, breed 31 ½ duim		
1804/07/25	AMSCH	0021	*Diterich. (C. W. E.)* | Dit frappant Voorwerp verbeeld een Hermiet in zyn Kluis, eerbiedig op zyn kniën leggende met saamgevouwen handen, als aandagtig mediteerende; op een steene Altaar staan twee Kandelaars en een afbeeldzel van den gekruiste Heiland en verder bywerk; de hartstogt is natuurlyk, en van een ongemeen meesterlyke penceelbehandeiing [sic] | *Mat:* op doek *Size:* hoog 25, breed 31 ½ duim		(Sold) fl 80 van der Schley
1804/07/25	AMSCH	0022	*Diterich. (C. W. E.)* | Op de Voorgrond aan strand vertoont zig St. Jacob, knielende in devote houding, voor een opgerecht steene Kruis; verder ziet men eenige Mooren, als met verwondering hem in die gestalten beschouwende, en een Schip in Zee; alles is als de vorige meesterlyk gepenceeld | *Size:* hoog 25, breed 31 ½ duim		(Sold) fl 19 van der Schley
1804/07/25	AMSCH	0023	*Diterich. (C. W. E.)* | Een Heremiet in zyn Kluis, zittende in een Boek te leezen, terzyde een Christus-beeld en Doodshoofd; het licht en bruin doet een frapante uitwerking, de teekening en schildering is van de fraaiste van dezen Meester | *Mat:* op paneel *Size:* hoog 12, breed 9 duim		(Sold) fl 150 van der Schley
1804/07/25	AMSCH	0024	*Diterich. (C. W. E.)* | In een Arcadisch boomryk Landschap, ziet men eenige Nimphen en danssende Cupidoos; verders eenige staande en leggende Koeijen en Schapen en een bevallig verschiet; kragtig en fix, in de manier van Salvator Rosa geschilderd | *Mat:* op paneel *Size:* hoog 27, breed 40 duim		(Sold) fl 41 Gruiter
1804/07/25	AMSCH	0025	*Diterich. (C. W. E.)* | Een aangenaam heuvelachtig Landschap, op de voorgrond een Rivier, waarover een Brug, by Boerewoningen en Geboomten, gestoffeerd met verscheide Beeldjes; voorts een dun en aangenaam verschiet, zynde in de trant van Jan Wouwerman; uitvoerig behandeld | *Mat:* op paneel *Size:* hoog 13 ½, breed 16 ½ duim		(Sold) fl 69 C S Roos
1804/07/25	AMSCH	0026	*Diterich. (C. W. E.)* | Een Rivier aan een Stads Muur, met Gebouwen en stoffagie van Beeldjes; alles verlicht wordende door de Maan, welke een aangenaame glans verspreid; allernatuurlykst in de manier van A. van der Neer | *Mat:* op doek *Size:* hoog 18, breed 24 duim		(Sold) fl 23 C S Roos
1804/07/25	AMSCH	0027	*Diterich. (C. W. E.)* | In een aangenaam Thuingezigt, by een springende Fontyn, ziet men eenige Dames en Heeren in treffelyke kleeding, benevens een bevallig Kindje; fix behandeld in de manier van Watteau | *Mat:* op doek *Size:* hoog 35, breed 26 duim		(Sold) fl 20 Mensart
1804/07/25	AMSCH	0028	*Diterich. (C. W. E.)* | In een aangenaame Hofstéde ziet men een menigte Dames, Heeren en Kinderen zich vermaken; Cupido in de midden van hun, schynt aan een Dame goeder geluk te zeggen; uitvoerig en bevallig in de manier van Watteau | *Mat:* op doek *Size:* hoog 20, breed 27 duim		(Sold) fl 62 C Burggraaf
1804/07/25	AMSCH	0029	*Diterich. (C. W. E.)* | Twee stuks Gezichten by Tivoli; in het eene ziet men de Tempel der Cibille, en in de anderen de Watervallen, beide van een bevallig licht en een natuurlyke en meesterlyke schildering | *Mat:* op paneel *Size:* hoog 14 ½, breed 11 duim		(Sold) fl 68 Coclers
1805/07/03	AMSCH	0015	*Ditricy (J. W.)* | Twee stuks, een Rots, Boom- en Bergachtig Landschap, terzyden een Waterval, in het midden ziet men een Heremiettage, waarin een Heremiet en verder bywerk, voorts een Bergachtig verschiet; het ander een aangenaam Bergachtig Landschap met hoog opgaand Geboomte, en gestoffeerd met een Herder welke een Os dryft, verders diverse werkende Beelden, achterwaarts een stille Beek, waarby op een hoogte een Klooster; beide zonachtig en Meesterlyk behandeld | *Mat:* op doek *Size:* yder hoog 21 ½, breed 28 ½ duim *Notes:* The artist's name was given as "Ditricy (J. W.)" but we have assumed this is an error.	G	(Sold) fl 305 Gruyter
1806/05/05	AMSCH	0048	*Ditriesie* | Hagar en Ismaël door Abraham weggezonden; schoon van effect en fix gepenceeld door Ditriesie | *Mat:* op paneel *Size:* hoog 12, breed 10 duim	V[inkeles]	(Sold) fl 2:15 J Yver
1807/08/26	AMSCH	0046	*Ditrici* | Twee stuks ovale, zynde een Vrouw en Manspourtrait, door Ditrici, op Koper, fraai geschilderd | *Mat:* op koper *Fmt:* ovaal	de Vries	(Sold) fl 9:5 Spruit
1807/08/26	AMSCH	0047	*Ditrici* | Twee dito [stuks ovale], zynde Manspourtraitjes | *Fmt:* ovaal	de Vries	(Sold) fl 5 Gruiter
1807/08/26	AMSCH	0048	*Ditrici* | Drie dito [stuks ovale], alle Manspourtraitjes, door denzelven [Ditrici], verbeeldende Rubbens, van Dyk en G. Flink | *Fmt:* ovaal	de Vries	(Sold) fl 15 Jeronimo de Vries
1808/10/28	AMVRS	0011	*Ditrich. (C. W. E.)* | Een aangenaam Landschap, op den voorgrond een Rivier, waarover een Brug bij Boere woningen en Geboomte met een aangenaam verschiet en stoffage. In den trant van J. Wouwerman | *Mat:* op paneel *Size:* hoog 13 ½, breed 16 ½ duim	Marten Udink	(Sold) fl 81 Gruyter
1809/05/26	HADAA	0021	*Ditrici* | Een bergachtig Landschap, warm en fiks geschilderd	Mejuffrouw de Wed David Heemskerk [or others]	(Unknown)
1809/07/19	AMSCH	0012	*Dietricij (C.G.)* | In een Italiaansch Bergachtig Landschap ziet men een rustende Os, twee Schapen en een Bok, waar bij twee Veehoeders. Bevallig van koloriet en van eene meesterlijke behandeling | *Mat:* op doek *Size:* hoog 11, breed 15 duim	[Bicker]	(Sold) fl 14 Gruyter
1810/07/26	AMSCH	0026	*Dietrich* | Een Zee- en Bergachtig Strandgezigt. Met Schepen gestoffeerd | *Mat:* op koper *Size:* hoog 10, breed 14 duimen	Cassino	(Sold) fl 5:5 Spruyt

1810/08/01	AMSCH	0023	*Dietrich (Christoffel Ernest)* | Simeon in den Tempel, houdende het Kind Jezus in zijne armen, waar bij Schriftgeleerden en andere Beelden [Siméon ténant l'Enfant Jesus dans le Temple ; il est accompagné par des Scribes, des Rabins, et par d'autres Personnages] | *Annots:* mauvaise copie. (NGW) *Mat:* op doek *Size:* hoog 17, breed 24 duimen	Mr Pieter de Smeth van Alphen	(Sold) fl 450 T Spaan
			Dietrich, Christian Wilhelm Ernst (and Compe, Jan ten)		
1804/07/25	AMSCH	0013	*Compe, (J. ten); C. W. E. Ditrich* | Een gezicht naar de Stad en het Slot te Kleef, van de Land zyde te zien; de Voorgrond gestoffeerd met eenige Dames en Heeren, een Kind en een Hond, verders een Huifkar en twee Munniken, in het verschiet den Eltenberg, alles zonachtig en delicaat behandeld | *Mat:* op paneel *Size:* hoog 24 ½, breed 32 duim		(Sold) fl 105 C S Roos
1808/10/28	AMVRS	0008	*Compe. (J. ten); C. W. E. Ditrich* | Een Gezicht naar de Stad Kleef, met de Eltenberg in het verschiet, gestoffeerd met Heeren, Juffrouwen, een Kind, Hond, enz. Alles is helder, teder en zonachtig | *Mat:* op paneel *Size:* hoog 24 ½, breed 32 duim	Marten Udink	(Sold) fl 80 Josi
			Dietrich, Christian Wilhelm Ernst (or Dietrich, Chr., manner)		
1807/08/26	AMSCH	0045	*Ditrici* | Twee stuks Italiaansche Bergachtige Landschappen met antique Tempels, Watervallen en stoffagie van Beelden en Beesten; warm van koloriet en meesterlyk behandeld, op Doek, door of in de manier van Ditrici | *Mat:* op doek *Size:* hoog 21, breed 27 duim	Roos	(Bought In) fl 14
			Dietzsch, Johann Christoph		
1806/11/24	AMSCH	0023	*Dietz (J.C.)* | Een gestoffeerd Boom- en bergachtig Landschap; zonachtig en uitvoerig behandeld | *Mat:* op koper *Size:* hoog 9, breed 7 duim	Munnikhuizen	(Sold) fl 5:5 du Pree
			Dinter, Gerardus		
1802/05/10	MGSAN	0018	*Dinter* | Een extra fraai Landschap met Koebeesten, waarby een Vrouw met een Korf aan de hand, daarby een rustend Manspersoon; verder een Haven met Schepen; in 't verschiet een Dorpgezigt, krachtig geschilderd, door Dinter: op Paneel, in vergulde Lyst | *Mat:* op paneel *Size:* hoog 16 duim, breed 21 duim	Johan Dirk Kruysse	(Unknown) £ 3:5
1802/05/10	MGSAN	0021	*van Dinter* | Een dito [fraai] dito [Land- en Boschgezit], waarop een Drift met Beesten, daarby een Herderin, in sierlyke Kleeding; verder een Berg, daarop een Ruïne, en anders, door van Dinter: op Paneel, in vergulde Lyst | *Mat:* op paneel *Size:* hoog 20 duim, breed 24 duim *Notes:* It is unclear what "dito" refers to in the title.	Johan Dirk Kruysse	(Unknown) £ 3:1
1802/05/10	MGSAN	0022	*van Dinter* | Een dito [fraai] Bergachtig Landschap met Beestjes, en een Herderin, door als boven: op Paneel, in vergulde Lyst | *Mat:* op paneel *Size:* hoog 15 duim, breed 20 duim *Notes:* It is unclear what "dito" refers to in the title.	Johan Dirk Kruysse	(Unknown) £ 1:19
1802/05/10	MGSAN	0026	*van Dinten* | Een dito [meesterachtig Stuk], daarop een Man, met een bruine Koe staande, en daarby twee wit bonte liggende dito; verder een rustend Vrouwtje, daarby een Bok; in 't verschiet eenige Gebouwen, door van Dinten: op Paneel, in vergulde Lyst | *Mat:* op paneel *Size:* hoog 21 duim, breed 25 ½ duim *Notes:* It is unclear what "dito" refers to in the title.	Johan Dirk Kruysse	(Sold) £ 6:15 Cosoly
			Does		
1802/07/21	HGKAN	0094	*van der Does* | Een Landschap met Schaapen		(Unknown)
1802/11/01	DOBRA	0140	*van der Does* | Een Mans-Portraitje, uitvoerig geschilderd; agter op staat geschreeven van der Does, Schilder in Landschappen en Schaapen | *Mat:* op koper *Fmt:* ovaal *Size:* hoog 3 duim	Paulus van der Spyk [or others]	(Unknown)
1802/12/13	AMSCH	0050	*G. van der Does* | Een Duinagtig Landschap ryk gestoffeerd, met een Herder, met een meenigte staande en rustende Schaapen en Bokken en een aangenaam verschiet | *Mat:* op doek *Size:* hoog 15, breed 18 duim	Pruyssenaar [for] A	(Sold) fl 4 Yver
1802/12/13	AMSCH	0051	*G. van der Does* | In een Landschap ziet men een Veehoeder, met een Doedelzak, verzelt van een staande Os, een staand en een rustend Schaap, fiks geschildert | *Mat:* op doek *Size:* hoog 24, breed 18 duim	Yver	(Sold) fl 0:10 L Pakker
1806/05/05	AMSCH	0049	*van der Does* | In een Landschap voor een Schuur ziet men eenige Schapen, Bokken en een Herder met zyn Hond | *Mat:* op doek *Size:* hoog 22, breed 29 duim	V[inkeles]	(Sold) fl 3:5 Boelen
1809/07/25	HGBSM	0173	*van der Does* | Een Schaap met een Lam, levensgroote | *Mat:* op doek *Size:* hoog 28, breed 23 duim	D van der Aa [or] E B ten Dall	(Sold) fl 11 van Eyk
1810/03/07	UTWLD	0061	*A. v. d. Does* | Een Schildery, zynde studiën met schaapen en schaape kopjes	J J Woertman	(Unknown) fl 8
1810/10/10	MGCIT	0008	*van der Does* | Een zeer aangenaam Landschap, op hetwelke een Koe, eenige Schapen en twee Bokken; alsmede een Mansfiguur, daar over de wacht houdende: voorts een zeer fraai verschiet; zonachtig en in alle opzigte goed behandeld	Caspar van Citters	(Unknown)
			Does (manner)		
1802/05/10	MGSAN	0023	*van der Does* | Een Landschapje met een Boerewooning, daarby verscheide Schaapjes; in 't verschiet een Kerkgebouw, in de manier van van der Does | *Size:* hoog 10 duim, breed 8 duim	Johan Dirk Kruysse	(Unknown) £ 0:11

1810/07/23	DOLG2	0063	*van der Does* | Bij eenige antieksche Gebouwen, vertonen zich Runderen, Schaapjes en Beelden; in de manier van van der Does | *Mat:* op paneel *Size:* hoog 13, breed 18 duim	Pieter Quinting	(Sold) fl 3 A v Strij

Does, Jacob van der (the elder)

1801/06/10	AMSCH	0042	*Does. (J. van der)* | Een heuvelachtig Landschap, gestoffeert met verscheiden Schaapen, Bokken; benevens een Ezel, verders Bergen in 't verschiet, krachtig en meesterlyk geschilderd | *Mat:* op paneel *Size:* hoog 12, breed 13 duim	Herman ten Kate	(Sold) fl 31 Stevens
1802/05/10	MGSAN	0025	*J. van der Does* | Een meesterachtig Stuk, daarop een Jongen, staande by een bruine Koe, en een zittend Meisje, by een Drift met Schaapen, aan een Ruïne; in 't verschiet een Berggezigt, en anders, alles zeer bevallig gepenseeld, door J. van der Does: op Paneel, in vergulde Lyst | *Mat:* op paneel *Size:* hoog 18 duim, breed 16 duim	Johan Dirk Kruysse	(Sold) £ 6:5 L. H. de Hare Bourne [?]
1802/06/16	AMSCH	0037	*J. van der Does* | In een heuvelagtig Landschap, vertoont zich op de voorgrond een zittend Meisje, verzelt van een staande Os, rustende Schaapen en staande Bokken: verder een bergagtig verschiet; alles uitvoerig behandeld | *Mat:* op paneel *Size:* hoog 13, breed 10 duim	[Merrem]	(Sold) fl 46 H de Valk
1802/07/20	MGSAN	0040	*J. van der Does* | Een fraai Landschap, met Schaapen, op Paneel | *Mat:* op paneel *Size:* hoog duim 17, breed duim 14		(Unknown)
1802/09/29	AMSCH	0018	*J. van der Does* | Een Landschap, hoog 14 ½, breed 13 duim. Doek. Men ziet in dit bevallig Schilderstukje eenige rustende en grazende Schaapen en Bokjes by een Schaapstal onder het geboomte; zeer uitvoerig konstig en zonagtig behandelt, door dezen beroemden Meester [Cet artiste fameux à peindre les chevres & les moutons en à placés quelques-uns dans ce paysage avec beaucoup de vérité & d'un Pinceau léger. Prés d'eux sont une petite fille & un petit garçon, avec des bottes de paille, c'est un des Tableaux les plus fins et des plus agréables de cet artiste.] | *Mat:* op doek *Size:* hoog 14 ½, breed 13 duim	[Labouchere?]	(Sold) fl 70 Coclers
1803/06/20	AMSCH	0011	*J. van der Does* | In een heuvelachtig Landschap vertoond zich op de voorgrond een zittend Meisje, verzelt van een staande Hond, rustende Schapen en Bokken, verder een bergachtig verschiet; alles uitvoerig behandeld, door J. van der Does, op Paneel | *Mat:* op paneel *Size:* hoog 13, breed 19 duim	Schley [for] B	(Sold) fl 60 V d Schley [for] F
1803/09/07	AMSCH	0047	*J. van der Does* | In een Landschap, by Geboomten, ziet men op een graazige Heuvel een rustend Kalf en Ram, ter zyde staat een Ram en witte Bok, verder een Véehoeder met Schaapen; alles Natuurlyk gepenceeldt [Un paysage, où l'on voit sur une colline garnie d'arbres un veau et un bélier se reposant ; à côté un bouc blanc et un bélier de bout [sic], plus loin un berger gardant des moutons ; le tout très naturel] | *Mat:* op paneel *Size:* hoog 11, breed 9 duim	Smidt	(Sold) fl 21 Gruiter
1804/04/28	LNDLS	0052	*J. van der Does* | Een juffer, ten voeten uit, zittende voor een Landschap met beeldwerk, konstig en kragtig, door J. van der Does, 1679 | *Inscr:* J. van der Does, 1679 (signed and dated?) *Notes:* It is unclear whether the name and date are inscribed on the painting.	[Abraham Delfos] [or others]	(Sold) fl 2:18 Rigter [for] G
1804/08/08	AMSCH	0050	*J. van der Does* | In een Italiaansch Landschap ziet men by een Fontyn een Herder, Herderin, met een Muil-Ezel, Ossen en Schaapen, welken zich schynen te drenken, kragtig op Paneel | *Mat:* op paneel *Size:* hoog 29, breed 22 duim	Roos [for] G	(Sold) fl 9 de Harde Swart
1804/08/08	AMSCH	0051	*J. van der Does* | In een Landschap ziet men voor een Schuur eenige Bokken, een Schaap en een Hond, waarby een Herder; als de voorgaande behandeld | *Mat:* op doek *Size:* hoog 22, breed 29 duim	Roos [for] G	(Sold) fl 4:5 Gruyter
1805/07/10	AMSCH	0047	*J. van der Does* | Een Bergachtig Landschap, met een Herderin met diverse Schapen; fraay op Paneel | *Mat:* op paneel *Size:* hoog 9, breed 10 duim	R[oos]	(Sold) fl 1 Reyers
1807/08/26	AMSCH	0039	*J. van der Does* | In een Italiaansch Landschap, met Geboomten by een Ruïne, vertoont zig op de voorgrond eene Vrouw met een Kind op de arm, te paard rydende, vergezeld van een gaande Veehoeder, die eenige Schapen, Ram en Bokken voortdryft, en gevolgt wordt door verscheide ander Vee, in 't verschiet Gebergten; alles evenaard de natuur, en is van een Meesterlyke schoone Penceelsbehandeling | *Mat:* op doek *Size:* hoog 26, breed 26 duim	Joseph Vallette	(Sold) fl 56 H^{k} Jansen

Does, Jacob van der (the elder) (manner)

1802/02/16	AMSCH	0067	*J. van der Does* | In een dito [Italiaans] Landschap, vertoont zig op de voorgrond een rustende vrouw, waar by een jongeling met een Lam onder de arm, verders eenige Schaapen, Geboomten en aloude Gedenkteekens en een bevallig verschiet; plaisant geschilderd, als door J. van der Does	G	(Sold) fl 10:10 Hulswit

Does, Simon van der

1801/06/13	LNDLS	0017	*S. van der Does* | Een Landschap, op den voorgrond bokken, schaapen en een rustend kalf, verder meer stoffage, op doek, door S. van der Does, 1696 | *Mat:* op doek *Size:* hoog 21, breed 18 duimen *Inscr:* S. van der Does, 1696 (signed and dated?) *Notes:* It is unclear whether the name and date are inscribed on the painting.	D van R	(Sold) fl 51 Richter S [for] Stevens
1801/06/13	LNDLS	0018	*S. van der Does* | Een Landschap met Gebouwen, op de voorgrond een rustende Os, bij schaapen en lammeren, verder beelden en beesten, op	D van R	(Sold) fl 106 Thys

			doek, door S. van der Does, 1707 | companion to lot 19 *Mat:* op doek *Size:* hoog 17, breed 20 duimen *Inscr:* S. van der Does, 1707 (signed and dated?) *Notes:* It is unclear whether the name and date are inscribed on the painting.		
1801/06/13	LNDLS	0019	*S. van der Does* | Een Weêrga, op den voorgrond een slapend meisje bij een jonge, benevens een staande koe, bij rustende schaapen en lammeren, verder een water met vaartuigen, door denzelven [S. van der Does] | companion to lot 18 *Mat:* op doek *Size:* hoog 17, breed 20 duimen	D van R	(Sold) fl 106 Richter S [for] Stevens
1801/10/19	AMSCH	0021	*Does. (S. van der)* | Eenige staande Schaapjes, waar by een leggende Ram in een boomryk Landschap; extra kunstig en helder gepenseeld | *Mat:* op paneel *Size:* hoog 13 ½, breed 16 ½ duim	Jonkheer Menno Baron van Coehoorn	(Sold) fl 170 C S Roos
1802/05/05	AMSCH	0049	*S. van der Does* | Een Bergächtig Landschap, op de Voorgrond ziet men eenige Schapen, een Bok en een Hond, beneevens een Herder en een Herderin; verders eenig Bywerk, zeer krachtig en fiks geschilderd | *Mat:* op doek *Size:* hoog 23, breed 30 duim	C	(Sold) fl 20 Ackina
1802/08/24	LNDLS	0018	*S. van der Does* | In een Landschap bij een Gebouw zit een Meisje op den kant van een Waterput, nevens haar eenige vruchten, terwijl zij een Schaap Koolbladen aanbiedt, benevens eenige rustende Bokken en Schaapen. Konstig op doek | *Mat:* op doek *Size:* hoog 24 ½, breed 22 duimen	Leonardus Bouman [or others]	(Unknown) fl 8
1802/09/21	UTHDG	0024a	*S. van der Does* | Door de poort van een vervallen gebouw, loopt een weg na voren, op welke vee word gedreven. Verder een ruim verschiet, fraaij geschildert | *Mat:* op paneel *Size:* hoog 10, breed 6 duimen *Notes:* There are two lots with the number 24; this lot has been changed to 24a.		(Bought In) fl 9:5
1802/12/13	AMSCH	0217	*S. van der Does* | Twee stuks fraaije Modellen van zes diversche Ramskoppen; kragtig en natuurlyk gepenceeld	Schley [for] Lauwers	(Sold) fl 0:16 van Dijl
1803/07/18	AMSCH	0013	*Does. (S. van der)* | In een Italiaansch Bergachtig Landschap met Geboomten en Ruïnes, ziet men op den voorgrond een Vrouw met een slaapend Kind op haar schoot, nevens haar zit een Jongen, agter haar by een Fontyn ziet men een leggende Koe, verders eenige staande en leggende Schaapen; een aangenaam Lugtje en een ver uitgestrekt verschiet, maaken dit stukje, het welk tevens helder en zonachtig behandeld is, tot een der beste van deezen Meester [Dans un site de paysage d'Italie est assise une bonne Mere, tenant un enfant endormi & un petit garçon à côté d'elle : un bellier & deux moutons sont au devant ; une vache prés d'une fontaine est couchée derriere la femme. A des Distances l'on voit quelques animaux, des ruines, & vèrs l'orison des collines bleuâtres. Un beau ciel acheve cette composition. L'on connoit le talent singulier de cet artiste pour representer la laine des moutons ; en effet ce morceau en est une autre preuve qui par sa parfaite conservation met en evidence tout le talent de son auteur.] | *Mat:* op paneel *Size:* hoog 16, breed 23 duim	Maria Theresia Andrioli	(Sold) fl 88 Thys
1806/06/07	RMHSN	0007	*S: van der Does* | Een Italiaansche Binneplaats met Schapen en Geiten, aangenaam en warm geschilderd | *Mat:* op paneel	A E K L	(Unknown)
1806/08/20	HGBSM	0042	*S. van der Does* | Twee Kinderen die met een Hond speelen, en eenige Schaapen, zeer natuurlijk en uitvoerig geschilderd | companion to lot 43 *Mat:* op doek op paneel *Size:* hoog 13, breed 10 ½ duim	Macalester Loup [or others]	(Sold) fl 65 for lots 42 & 43. Huybrechts
1806/08/20	HGBSM	0043	*S. van der Does* | Een dito [Kinderen die met een Hond speelen] wederga, even schoon als de voorgaande, door denzelven [S. van der Does], doek op paneel, eener groote | companion to lot 42 *Mat:* op doek op paneel *Size:* hoog 13, breed 10 ½ duim *Notes:* It is unclear what "dito" refers to in the title.	Macalester Loup [or others]	(Sold) fl 65 for lots 42 & 43. Huybrechts
1806/08/20	HGBSM	0199	*S. van der Does* | Een Landschap waarin een zittende Herderinne met eenige Schaapen en Geiten, verder een gelaaden Muil-Ezel, fraai en natuurlijk door S. van der Does | *Mat:* op doek *Size:* hoog 24, breed 28 duim	Macalester Loup [or others]	(Sold) fl 35 L Voerman voor Huibrechts
1808/04/26	GDAN	0031	*Does (S. van der)* | Een Herder, staande by een Waterput, met eenig Vee, extra fraai en uitvoerig geschildert | *Size:* hoog 16, breed 18 duim	G H Fortuyn	(Unknown)
1808/04/26	GDAN	0032	*Does (S. van der)* | Een goed Landschap, met een leggende Koe, en eenige Schapen, en bywerk, uitvoerig behandeld | *Size:* hoog 6, breed 8 duim	G H Fortuyn	(Unknown)
1808/04/26	GDAN	0033	*Does (S. van der)* | Een uitmuntend Landschap, waar in een Vrouwtje met Schapen en Bokken onder 't geboomte, zonägtig behandeld | *Size:* hoog 10, breed 9 duim	G H Fortuyn	(Unknown)
1808/06/06	RMRIJ	0027	*Does. (Simon van der)* | Een Italiaansch Landschap, gestoffeerd met Schapen, Lammeren en andere beesten; voorts eene Vrouw met een Kind aan de borst, omziende naar een Jongen, welke haar eenen jongen Hond vertoont; verder Geboomte en 't Standbeeld van een Faunus. Zijnde een der kapitale stukken van dezen Meester [Paysage Italien orné de plusieurs animaux domestiques. Sur le devant une femme assise donne le sein à son enfant, et regarde un garçon qui lui montre un petit Chien. On voit derrière eux de beaux arbres, une partie d'Architecture et la statue d'un Faune ; plus loin des Montagnes et un agréable lointain] | *Mat:* op doek *Size:* Hoog 30 ¾, en breed 36 duim *Loc:* Amsterdam, Nederland. Rijksmuseum. (A84)	Gerrit van der Pot, Heer van Groeneveld	(Sold) fl 325 van Lennep [for] le Roi
1808/06/13	AMSCH	0038	*Does (S. van der)* | Eene Herderin, zittende te zingen bij een roodbonte Koe; op den voorgrond een pissend en een liggend Schaap: allerfraaist van behandeling | *Mat:* op doek *Size:* hoog 40, breed 32 duim	E M Engelberts	(Sold) fl 31 J Schuman

1808/08/23	AMSCH	0037	*Does. (S. van der)* | In een heuvelachtig Landschap met Geboomte, zit op de voorgrond een bevallig Landmeisje, nevens dezelve een staande Jongeling, schijnende vrolijk een Liedje te zingen, voor dezelve staat een Ram, een grazend Schaap en een rustende, verder een leggende Os, bij een Vee-hut en Bergachtig verschiet; het zonlicht doet een bevallige werking, alles evenaart de Natuur, en van een uitmuntende penceelbehandeling | *Mat:* op doek *Size:* hoog 21, breed 17 duim	[Coclers]	(Bought In) fl 205
1808/08/23	AMSCH	0038	*Does. (S. van der)* | Een kapitaal Italiaansch bergachtig Landschap, op de voorgrond hoog Geboomten bij een steene Zuil, gestoffeert met een roscouleurde Os en twee Schaapen, verder een Veehoeder bij een Hut, verzelt van verscheide Vee bij een stil Water; het is meesterlijk en krachtig gepenceeld | *Mat:* op doek *Size:* hoog 32, breed 37 duim	[Van Iperen?]	(Sold or Bought In) fl 34 T van Iperen
1808/08/23	AMSCH	0039	*Does. (S. van der)* | Een Italiaansch Landschap, op de voorgrond een Herder, die eene rood bonte Koe en twee Schaapen voortdrijft, ter zijde op een Muur een zwartbonte Bok; meesterlijk behandeld | *Mat:* op doek *Size:* hoog 44, breed 35 duim	[Van Iperen?]	(Sold or Bought In) fl 73 Van Iperen
1809/04/17	AMSCH	0025	*S. van der Does* | Een duin- en boomrijk Landschap, gestoffeerd met grasende en liggende Schapen; uitvoerig geschilderd | *Mat:* op paneel *Size:* hoog 10, breed 11 ½ duim	[Gruyter?]	(Sold) fl 10 Spaan
1809/06/13	AMSCH	0034	*S. van der Does* | In een Bergachtig Landschap bij Geboomten, ziet men op eene grazige Heuvel een rustend Kalf, ter zijde staat een Ram en witte Bok, verder een Veehoeder met Schaapen en ee [sic] Bergachtig verschiet; warm en uitvoerig geschilderd | *Mat:* op paneel *Size:* hoog 11, breed 9 duim	[Gruyter?]	(Sold) fl 29 T Spaan
1809/07/19	AMSCH	0010	*Does (S. van der)* | Dit bevallig Schilderijtje vertoont een bergachtig Landschap, ter zijde bij een Veehut zit eene bevallige Vrouw met een Kind aan de borst, meerder op den voorgrond een staand Kalf en eenige grazende en rustende Bokken en Schapen, in 't verschiet oude Ruïnen. Het is aangenaam van koloriet en van eene zuivere en uitvoerige penceelsbehandeling | *Mat:* op paneel *Size:* hoog 12 ½, breed 16 duim *Loc:* Amsterdam, Nederland. Rijksmuseum. (A 83)	[Bicker]	(Sold) fl 320 Jan Yver voor Z H den Koning
1809/07/19	AMSCH	0011	*Does (S. van der)* | In een Heuvelachtig Landschap met Geboomte zit op den voorgrond een bevallig Landmeisje, nevens haar een staand Jongeling, schijnende zamen een liedje te zingen, voor hun staat een Ram, een grazend en een rustend Schaap, verder een liggende Os bij een Veehut, en een bergachtig verschiet. Het zonlicht doet eene bevallige werking; alles evenaart de natuur, het is van eene zachte penceelsbehandeling | *Mat:* op doek *Size:* hoog 21, breed 17 duim *Loc:* Amsterdam, Nederland. Rijksmuseum. (A82)	E	(Sold) fl 205 Jan Yver voor Z H den Koning
1809/07/25	HGBSM	0016	*S. van der Does* | Een Herder, een Koe en eenige Schapen voortdryvende, natuurlyk en fraay geschildert | *Mat:* op doek *Size:* hoog 42 ½, breed 37 duim	D van der Aa [or] E B ten Dall	(Sold) fl 50 van Eyk
1810/03/07	UTWLD	0005	*S. van der Does* | Een zeer schoon Landschap, op den voorgrond een Os, die zich tegen een boom schuurt, op de tweede grond, een herder, bezig met een schaap te scheeren, schoon van coloriet en breed behandeld | *Size:* hoog 3 voet, breed 3 voet 7 duim	J J Woertman	(Unknown) fl 67
1810/03/26	RMMUY	0061	*Simon van der Does* | Een Landschap. Op den voorgrond, drie Schapen, in het verschiet eene Vrouw, Geit, &c. [Un petit Paysage ; sur le devant trois moutons et une femme, un lointain et quelques objets.]	Daniel de Jongh Az	(Sold) fl 4 Esser S'Hage
1810/05/22	AMSCH	0022	*Does. (S. van der)* | Een Heuvelachtig Landschap, met Geboomten, op den voorgrond een Waterput, waarbij Landlieden en eene menigte Bokken en Schapen; meesterlijk van behandeling | *Mat:* op doek *Size:* hoog 14, breed 17 duim	Johannes van de Putte Nicolaasz.	(Sold) fl 155 Hulswit
1810/06/20	AMSCH	0019	*S. Van Der Does* | Een Duin- en Boomrijk Landschap, gestoffeerd met grazende en liggende Schapen. Uitvoerig geschilderd | *Mat:* op paneel *Size:* hoog 16, breed 14 duimen	B	(Bought In) fl 10
1810/10/11	AMSCH	0026	*S. Van Der Does* | Een Landschap, gestoffeerd met Schapen en een Bok | *Mat:* op paneel *Size:* hoog 8 ½, breed 10 duimen	C	(Sold) fl 3:15 Posthumus
1810/10/11	AMSCH	0027	*S. Van Der Does* | Voor eene Hut, bij hoog Geboomte, ziet men staande en liggende Beesten, waarbij eenige Landlieden; krachtig geschilderd | *Mat:* op doek *Size:* hoog 27, breed 32 duimen	[Gruyter?]	(Sold or Bought In) fl 2 Gruiter
			Does, Simon van der (manner)		
1802/08/24	LNDLS	0019	*S. van der Does* | Een Landschap, met een staande Koe, twee Schaapen en een zittend Vrouwtje. Uitvoerig in de manier van denzelven [S. van der Does] | *Mat:* op doek *Size:* hoog 13, breed 11 duimen	Leonardus Bouman [or others]	(Unknown) fl 11
			Dolci, Carlo		
1802/12/13	AMSCH	0047	*C. Dolce* | Een Vrouwenhoofd in antique kleeding, met Starren vercierd, uitmuntend van Coloriet en schoon van Teekening | *Mat:* op steen *Size:* hoog 23, breed 17 duim	Yver	(Sold) fl 23:10 Th[s] Spaan
1809/07/25	HGBSM	0209	*C. Dolci* | Een wenende Vrouw, fraai geschildert | *Mat:* op doek *Size:* hoog 31, breet 26 duim	D van der Aa [or] E B ten Dall	(Sold) fl 9:5 de Gruyter
1810/07/26	AMSCH	0023	*Dolce (C.)* | Het Borstbeeld van Magdalena. Zijnde een meesterstuk van dezen Kunstenaar | *Mat:* op doek *Size:* hoog 19, breed 16 duimen	Cassino	(Sold) fl 6 Andriessen

Dolci, Carlo (or Dolci, C., manner)

1804/05/07	AMSCH	0041	*Dolci. (C.) of in de manier* | Dit voorwerp verbeeld Maria Magdaléna in Berouw, houdende het Gezicht Heemelwaards [sic], en de beide Handen kruislings op de Borst, als met aandacht meditéerende; de hartstocht is natuurlyk, het coloriet bevallig, en van een uitvoerige penceelbehandeling | *Mat:* op paneel *Size:* hoog 23, breed 20 duim	Roos [for] A	(Bought In) fl 8

Dolci, Carlo (manner)

1803/04/27	AMSCH	000M	*C. Dolce* | Une Sainte Vierge en Meditation, dans la maniere de C. Dolce | *Size:* h. 14, l. 12 pouces	B	(Sold) fl 50 Stevens
1804/08/08	AMSCH	0239	*C. Dolci* | Maria Magdaléna in Berouw, haar Gezicht Hemelwaards, en de Handen kruislings over elkander, in een smeekende houding zich vertoonende; de behandeling is edel, als C. Dolci | *Mat:* op paneel *Size:* hoog 23, breed 20 duim	Roos [for] F	(Sold) fl 12:10 Gruiter

Domenichino (Domenico Zampieri)

1802/06/16	AMSCH	0041	*Dominiquino* | Een geestlyke zinnebeeldige Ordenantie, met verscheide Beelden, vertoonende de Paus zittende op een verheeven Zeetel, voor hem leggen verscheide Vorsten en ander Geestelyke op hunne kniën; om hoog ziet men een Glorie van Engelen, met de teekens der Pausselyke waardigheid, kragtig en fiks gepenceeld | *Mat:* op paneel *Size:* hoog 15 ½, breed 22 duim	[Merrem]	(Sold) fl 9:10 Gruiter
1803/04/27	AMSCH	0122	*le Dominiquain* | Une ébauche en grisaille, par le Dominiquain, réprèsentant la Vierge & l'enfant Jésus	A	(Sold) fl 4 Pruijssenaar [for] V

Donck, G.

1808/08/23	AMSCH	0045	*Donk. (J.)* | Een zinspeelende Ordonantie, voorstellende eene bevallige Vrouw, houdende in beide handen een Doodshoofd, nevens haar een Tafel, waar op eenige Instrumenten geplaatst zijn; krachtig geschilderd | *Mat:* op paneel *Size:* hoog 20, breed 23 duim	J	(Sold) fl 10 Van Iperen

Dongen, Dionys van

1801/04/23	AMYVR	0013	*J. van Dongen* | Twee stuks bevallige Landschappen, gestoffeerd met staand en leggend Vee, verder een Herder die twee Ossen voortdryft, en een Boer die een Koe melkt, zeer aangenaam van coloriet | *Notes:* The artist's name was given as "J. van Dongen" but we have assumed this is an error.		(Sold) fl 20 Coclaire
1801/06/10	AMSCH	0054	*Dongen. (D. van)* | Voor een Boeren Schuur ziet men een staande en liggende Koey, benevens een Bok; natuurlyk breed van behandeling | *Mat:* op paneel *Size:* hoog 10, breed 13 duim	Herman ten Kate	(Sold) fl 36 Gruyter
1801/06/13	LNDLS	0053	*van Dongen* | Twee Stuks Landschappen, met koeijen en ossen, op heuvelen in 't verschiet, op paneel | *Mat:* op paneel *Size:* ieder hoog 10, breed 12 duimen	D van R	(Sold) fl 10:10 Richter [for] S[tevens]
1802/05/05	AMSCH	0053	*D. van Dongen* | Langs een Bevroozen Rivier ziet men eenige Lieden zig op het Ys vermaaken, uitvoerig | *Size:* hoog 9, breed 13 duim	J	(Sold) fl 3:5 Gruiter
1802/06/16	AMSCH	0044	*D. van Dongen* | Een Natuurlyk Rivier en Landzicht, met eenige Geboomten en Woningen; gestoffeert met een Overvarende Pontschuit en zeilend Vaartuig: op de voorgrond een Heer te Paard en een gaand Man; helder en fiks gepenceeld | *Mat:* op paneel *Size:* hoog 9 ½, breed 12 duim	[Merrem]	(Sold) fl 4:5 Agina
1802/06/16	AMSCH	0045	*D. van Dongen* | In een Landschap staat een Bonte Os op een Heuvel, verder rust een ander by een Beesten Hut; natuurlyk en fiks behandeld | *Mat:* op paneel *Size:* hoog 10 ½, breed 8 ½ duim	[Merrem]	(Sold) fl 11:10 LaFontaine
1802/06/28	AMSCH	0045	*D. J. van Dongen* | Twee stuks Landschappen, gestoffeert met onder-scheide Beesten, waarby rustende Herders; zeer uitvoerig gepenceelt | *Size:* hoog 12, breed 15 duim	Anna Elink	(Sold) fl 11:15 de Meyer
1802/09/18	RMDRS	0012	*van Dongen* | Een Landschap met verscheide Koeyen en Schapen, zeer aangenaam geschilderd | *Size:* hoog 12, breed 15 duim	Casper de Haas	(Unknown) fl 20 for lots 12 & 13
1802/09/18	RMDRS	0013	*van Dongen* | Een dito [Landschap met verscheide Koeyen en Schapen], van dezelve groote als 't voorgaande | *Size:* hoog 12, breed 15 duim	Casper de Haas	(Unknown) fl 20 for lots 12 & 13
1802/09/18	RMDRS	0020	*H. van Dongen* | Een woelend Water, met verscheide Scheepen | *Size:* hoog 18, breed 24 duim *Notes:* The artist's name was given as "H. van Dongen" but we have assumed this is an error.	Casper de Haas	(Sold) fl 7:10 V Giesen
1802/09/18	RMDRS	0033	*H. van Dongen* | Een Zee, met eenige Schepen | *Size:* hoog 17 ½, breed 23 ½ duim *Notes:* The artist's name was given as "H. van Dongen" but we have assumed this is an error.	Casper de Haas	(Unknown) fl 5:5
1804/10/16	DLOND	0058	*Dion. van Dongen* | Een Landschap met Koeien. Paysage & des Vaches | *Mat:* op paneel *Size:* hoog 12, breed 15		(Unknown)
1808/04/26	GDAN	0043	*Dongen (D. van)* | Zynde een Zon en Bergägtig Landschap, met Ruïne, in de manier van Berghem, fraai gestoffeerd met Koeijen, Ezels en Schapen | *Size:* hoog 7, breed 9 ½ duim	G H Fortuyn	(Unknown)
1808/06/11	RMRIJ	0023	*D: van Dongen, 1799* | Een zonachtig Landschap, met kloeke Dieren op den Voorgrond en een aangenaam en ryk Verschiet; uitvoerig, breed en stout geschilderd | *Mat:* op paneel *Size:* hoog 25, breed 29 ½ duim *Inscr:*		(Sold) fl 30:10 v Yperen [or] Du Preé

			D: van Dongen, 1799 (signed and dated?) *Notes:* It is unclear whether the name and date are inscribed on the painting.		
1808/06/11	RMRIJ	0024	*D: van Dongen* | Een heuvelachtig Landschap, met drie staande Koeijen en twee leggende Geitjes op de Voorgrond, voorts een bevallig en schoon gestoffeerd Verschiet, dunne en heldere Lucht; zeer uitvoerig en fraai behandeld | *Mat:* op paneel *Size:* hoog 10 ½, breed 13 duim		(Sold) fl 30:10 v Dullev [?]
1808/06/11	RMRIJ	0025	*D: van Dongen* | Een Landschap met twee Koeijen, in de manier van Cuyp, meesterlyk aangezet. Paneel, hoog 1 ½, breed 13 ¾ duim. Een Wedergade met Paard en Koe en in alles als de voorgaande; zullende in een Koop geveild worden | *Mat:* op paneel *Size:* hoog 1 ½, breed 13 ¾ duim		(Sold) fl 21:10 v Yperen
1808/06/11	RMRIJ	0026	*D: van Dongen* | Een fraai Heuvelagtig Landschap met Koeijen, Schapen en Figuren | *Mat:* op paneel *Size:* hoog 14 ½, breed 18 duim		(Sold) fl 12:10 Kok
1808/06/11	RMRIJ	0027	*D: van Dongen* | Een Wintergezigt met veel Stoffagie, helder en natuurlijk | *Mat:* op doek *Size:* hoog 14, breed 19 ½ duim		(Sold) fl 9:10 v Yperen
1808/12/30	HGIMM	[0071q]	*Van Dongen* | Voorts een exquis kabinetje Schilderijen van voorname Nederlandsche Meesters, welke uit hoofde van de kortheid des tijds niet stuk voor stuk kunnen beschreven worden; doch waarvan de beschrijving op den Kijkdag zal voorhanden zijn. Dus wij hier alleen de namen van eenige dier Meesters laten volgen, als: A. Kuyp, Ruysdaal, Karel du Jardyn, Loqwi ('t beste dat hij schilderde) Hondekoeter, van Dyk, Janson, Moesgever, Kamphuyzen, van Gooijen, A. van der Neer, T. Wyk, Huchtenburgh, Zolemaker, van Hassel, A. Vermeulen, van Dongen, Scheffer, van Os enz. | *This Lot:* Een Schilderij, Van Dongen *Notes:* Because this lot was not numbered in the catalogue, we have assigned the number.		(Unknown)
1809/07/25	HGBSM	0247	*van Dongen* | Een Land- en Watergezigt, waar in verbeeld een Dorp in brand by maneschyn, uitvoerig | *Mat:* op paneel *Size:* hoog 7 en een half, breed 9 en een half duim	D van der Aa [or] E B ten Dall	(Sold) fl 6:5 Heijmans

Dongen, Dionys van (copy by)

1806/11/24	AMSCH	0019	*Dongen (van); J. van Goyen* | Een stil Riviergezigt, aan de Haven van een Stad; op de voorgrond gestoffeert met rustend en staand Vee; verder eenige Scheepen; bevallig gepenceelt, naar J. van Goyen | copy by Dionys Dongen after Goyen *Mat:* op paneel *Size:* hoog 12, breed 16 duim	Munnikhuizen	(Sold) fl 12:5 Scheurleer
1810/06/06	RMMUY	0157	*van Dongen; Potter* | Een stuk met Beesten, zijnde eene Copij naar Potter. Door van Dongen | copy by Dionys Dongen after Paulus Potter *Mat:* op doek		(Unknown) fl 13:5

Doomer, Lambert

1801/06/13	LNDLS	0068	*N. Doomer* | De wegjaaging van den Verloren Zoon | *Notes:* The artist's name was given as "N. Doomer" but we have assumed this is an error.	D van R	(Sold) fl 7:10 De Roy
1805/07/10	AMSCH	0048	*Domer* | Een Bergachtig Landschap, op de voorgrond een Herberg, een man met een Paard, een Ezeldryfster, en Munnikken, op 't Gebergte een Kasteel | *Mat:* op doek *Size:* hoog 26, breed 37 duim	Y[ver]	(Bought In) fl 12
1805/07/10	AMSCH	0217	*Doomer* | Twee jonge Lieden een Aard-Globen bekykende; geestig	Y[ver]	(Sold) fl 26:10 Gruyter
1805/07/10	AMSCH	0232	*Domer* | Een Kraaijende Haan | *Notes:* This lot was sold with lot 233 by an anonymous artist.	Y[ver]	(Bought In) fl 10 for lots 232 & 233

Doornik, Jan van

1802/08/24	LNDLS	0086	*J. v. Doornik* | Een Landschap met Boomen en Gebouwen, op den voorgrond een Vrouwtje met Koeijen en Schapen door het Water gaande | *Mat:* op paneel *Size:* hoog 12, breed 17 duimen	Leonardus Bouman [or others]	(Unknown) fl 2

Dorasse, C. [Unidentified]

1805/07/10	AMSCH	0051	*Dorasse* | Twee stuks aangenaame Duinachtige Landschappen met Geboomten, gestoffeert met Huislieden te Paard, en andere rustende; beide plaisant geschilderd op Paneel, door .... Dorasse | *Mat:* op paneel	Schley [for] Doralle	(Sold) fl 6 v d Schley
1810/05/22	AMSCH	0025	*Dorasse (C.)* | Een Dorpgezicht, met Woningen en Kerk aan een stil Water, waarbij eenig Vee, ter andere zijde aan den Oever een Molen, verder een zeilend Vaartuig, alles verbeeld bij helder Maanlicht; meer natuurlijk behandeld | *Mat:* op paneel *Size:* hoog 10, breed 13 duim	Johannes van de Putte Nicolaasz.	(Sold) fl 4:5 Masse
1810/05/22	AMSCH	0026	*Dorasse. (C.)* | Een Land en Watergezicht, met verscheide stoffagie, bij helder Maanlicht; als de voorgaande meesterlijk behandeld | *Mat:* op paneel *Size:* hoog 10, breed 13 duim	Johannes van de Putte Nicolaasz.	(Sold) fl 6:5 Topher

Dorne, François van

1806/05/05	AMSCH	0041	*van Dorne, Discipel van David* | Cajus Marius te Minturne, fraai van Teekening en meesterlyk gepenceeld door van Dorne, Discipel van David | *Mat:* op doek *Size:* hoog 36, breed 46 duim	L	(Sold) fl 19 van Laar

Dorne, François van (copy by)

1806/05/05	AMSCH	0042	*van Dorne, Discipel van David; Rembrand* | Het afbeeldsel van den Kunstschilder Rembrand; meesterlyk na Rembrand door Denzelven [van	L	(Sold) fl 5 van Laar

			Dorne, Discipel van David] | copy by F. Dorne after Rembrandt *Mat:* op doek *Size:* hoog 32, breed 24 duim		
1806/05/05	AMSCH	0043	*van Dorne; Raphael* | Raphael met zyn Schermmeester; alles meesterlyk en breed gepenceeld door van Dorne na Raphael | copy by F. Dorne after Raffaello Santi *Mat:* op doek *Size:* hoog 36, breed 31 duim	L	(Sold) fl 12 van Laar
1806/05/05	AMSCH	0044	*van Dorne; Carats* | Maria met het Kindje, verzeld van St. Jan; allerdelicaatst geschilderd na Carats | copy by F. Dorne after Carracci *Mat:* op paneel *Size:* hoog 15, breed 17 ½ duim	L	(Sold) fl 9 Van Laar
1806/05/05	AMSCH	0045	*van Dorne; A. van Dyk* | Een bevallig jong Meisje in aloude deftige Kleeding; meesterlyk gepenceeld door denzelven [van Dorne] na A. van Dyk | copy by F. Dorne after Anth. van Dyck *Mat:* op doek *Size:* hoog 22, breed 18 duim	L	(Sold) fl 10 Coclers
			Dorne, Martin van		
1806/05/05	AMSCH	0046	*van Dorne de Oude* | Op een Tafel, vercierd met een menigte van verschillende Vruchten, ziet men een Vaas, gevuld met verscheiden welriekende bloemen; allerdelicaatst op Doek door van Dorne de Oude | *Mat:* op doek *Size:* hoog 22, breed 32 duim	L	(Sold) fl 6:5 Graffelman
			Dorne, Martin van (copy by)		
1806/05/05	AMSCH	0047	*van Dorne de Oude; A. van Ostade* | Een bevallig Boere Binnenhuis met een zittende rookende Boer, en divers bywerk; meesterlyk na A. van Ostade | copy by M. Dorne after A. Ostade *Mat:* op doek *Size:* hoog 12 ½, breed 11 duim	L	(Sold) fl 6 van Iperen
			Dou, Gerard		
1801/04/13	AMSCH	0015	*G. Douw* | Een bejaarde Vrouw, met een kaper op haar hoofd, de handen onder haar voorschoot houdende; uitvoerig gepenceeld | *Mat:* op paneel *Size:* hoog 9, breed 7 duim	Pierre Fouquet, junior	(Sold) fl 36 Reynders
1801/10/06	AMSCH	0020	*Gerard Dou* | Het Afbeeldzel van een bejaarde Dame, halver lyf in ryke deftige aloude Kleeding, met Bont gevoerd; zy schynt als iets, met veel aandagt te beschouwen; het caracter is verwonderlyk natuurlyk, en van een uitmuntende Penceelbehandeling | *Mat:* op paneel *Fmt:* ovaal *Size:* hoog 10, breed 7 ½ duim	S	(Sold) fl 120 Jan Spaan
1802/06/16	AMSCH	0038	*G. Douw* | Het Afbeeldzel van de geleerde en kunstryke Anna Maria Schuurman, halver lyf, gekleed in een Jakje met bont gevoerd, en het hoofd gedekt met een wit Kapje, zeer fraay en uitvoerig gepenceelt | *Mat:* op paneel *Size:* hoog 6, breed 5 duim *Loc:* London, England, UK. National Gallery. (1415) (?) as Frans van Mieris I	[Merrem]	(Sold) fl 75 Coclers
1802/06/28	AMSCH	0037	*G. Dou* | Een biddende Heeremiet, op de knieën leggende, voor hem een Boek, Lantaarn, Zandloper, en verder Stilleven; alles delicaat en uitvoerig op Panneel | *Mat:* op paneel *Size:* hoog 17, breed 14 duim	Anna Elink	(Sold) fl 49 Van Iperen
1803/04/20	AMSCH	0021	*Dou (G.)* | Dit Kunstjuweel verbeeld in een aloude Deftige Binnenkamer, een Heer in Oud Hollandsche Kleeding, zittende aan een Tafel met een Fluweel Kleed gedekt, waarop hy met zyn linker hand rust, in zyn rechter houd hy zyn Handschoenen, en op de Tafel legd zyn Hoed en verder Bywerk; het licht en bruin, gepaard met een uitvoerige en delicate Penceelsbehandeling maken dit Schilderytje tot een der uitmundtendste gewrogten van dezen voortreffelyken meester [Cet excellent morceau a pour sujet le portrait d'un homme de Robe assis devant une table couverte d'un tapis de velours verd, ou se trouve son chapeau rond ; sa position est tournée à trois quarts de face, assis dans un ancien fauteuil, appuyant la main gauche sur la table & tenant ses gands de la droite. Le fond designe une salle appuyée sur des colonnes dont celle qui est avancée vèrs la lumiere, est ornée par des enfans sculptés en pierre. Nous trouvons réunis dans ce precieux tableau, l'effet le plus magique à la couleur la plus vraye ; ajoutons que l'élégance de la position, le dessin gracieux des mains & la touche la plus delicate & la finie en font un objet très rare! à rencontrer de cette conservation.] | *Mat:* op paneel *Fmt:* ovaal *Size:* hoog 11, breed 9 ½ duim *Loc:* Amsterdam, Nederland. Rijksmuseum. (A 686) as Portrait of Johan Wittert van der Aa	Maria Magdalena van Sluypwyk, gravinne van Moens	(Sold) fl 1600 Jan Spaan
1803/08/17	AMSCH	0023	*Douw. (G.)* | Het Pourtrait van deezen voortreffelyken Meester, met een fluweele muts op zyn hoofd, om het welke bevallige hairlokken zwieren, verders met een witte Kraag en een bruine Mantel gekleed, delicaat en uitvoerig gepenceeld, en van een effect, als of het van Rembrand was | *Mat:* op paneel *Size:* hoog 7, breed 5 ½ duim *Loc:* London, England, UK. National Gallery. (192) (?)	Anna Catharina Putman	(Bought In) fl 180
1803/08/17	AMSCH	0024	*Douw. (G.)* | Een Grysaard, met een bonte muts op zyn hoofd, zittende aan een Tafel, waarop een menigte Schryftuig geplaatst is, aandagtig een brief te leezen; agter hem een bevallig Meisje, in een lagchende houding, verders een Plank met Boeken, enz. zynde van een vroegere tyd, als het voorgaande behandeld | *Mat:* op paneel *Size:* hoog 14, breed 11 duim	Anna Catharina Putman	(Sold) fl 26 Gruyter
1803/09/07	AMSCH	0041	*G. Douw* | Twee stuks, zynde het eene een Grysaard en het andere een oude Vrouw, de Man met een Mantel met Bond, en de Vrouw met een rood fluweele Mantel, en een Handschoen aan haar hand, beide zeer uitvoerig en van een delicaate penceels-behandeling [Deux pendants ; l'un un vieillard avec un manteau garni de fourrures ; l'autre un vieille	Smidt	(Bought In) fl 150

			femme, ayant un manteau de velours rouge et des gants aux mains ; tous les deux d'une belle ordonnance et d'une exécution délicate] | *Mat:* op paneel *Size:* yder is hoog 7, breed 5 ½ duim		
1804/07/25	DLGRO	0007	*Gerard Douw* | Een binnen Huis, waarin een Oud Vrouwtje met een Mantel met een bonte rand om, aan den Haard zit Appelen te schillen, op de voorgrond een Kopere Ketel en verder bywerk, zeer fraai geschilderd door Gerard Douw | *Mat:* op paneel *Size:* hoog 12 ½, breed 16 duim	Mr Franc van der Burch Wz.	(Unknown)
1804/10/16	DLOND	0059	*G. Douw* | Een Studerend Man voor een Tafel, waarop een Pleyster Groupe. De Tafel is behangen met een groen Kleed, en meer Bywerk. Un Homme etudiant devant une Table couverte d'un Tapis verd. Sur la quelle on voit place une Groupe de Plâtre | *Size:* hoog 20, breed 15		(Sold) fl 23 Huijbregts
1805/07/03	AMSCH	0012	*Dou. (G.)* | Voor een Open Steene Nis, met verscheiden Basrelieven vercierd: ziet men een mediteerende Oudvader, het boek ligt op de rand der Nis, waarin hy aandachtig schynt te leezen, terzyde staat een pot met bloemen; de harstogt is zeer natuurlyk, het naakt en coloriet is fraai, en alles van een uitvoerige penceel behandelding [sic], door deeze beroemde Meester | *Mat:* op paneel *Size:* hoog 20, breed 17 duim	D	(Sold) fl 405 Josi
1805/07/03	AMSCH	0013	*Dou. (G.)* | Het afbeeldsel van een bevallige Vrouw, in treffelyke Kleeding, halver lyf, zy houd de linker hand op de borst, en schynt iets als met aandagt te beschowen, het caracter is natuurlyk, en als de voorgaande, aller uitvoerigst gepenceeld | *Mat:* op paneel *Size:* hoog 5 ½, breed 4 duim	D	(Sold) fl 220 Vaillant
1806/08/13	AMSCH	0039	*Dou. (G.)* | 't Afbeeldsel van een bejaard Man, met een witte baard en halfkaal hoofd met witte hairen, gekleed met een bruin Op- en Onderkleed en wit halsdoek, halverlyf met één hand; alleruitvoerigst, helder en delicaat van penceel behandeling | *Mat:* op paneel *Size:* hoog 6, breed 5 duim	Coclers	(Bought In) fl 265
1808/04/26	GDAN	0041	*Dou (G.)* | Een fraai Jongens Pourtretje	G H Fortuyn	(Unknown)
1808/04/26	GDAN	0042	*Dou (G.)* | Verbeeldende een Chirurgijns Winkel, waar in een Vrouwtje op een Stoel zit, die een ongemak in de keel schijnt te hebben, waarom de Chirurgijn, bij 't ligten met een kaars haar in de keel ziet, met de grootste oplettenheid, op de grond staat in een Lantaarn een Kaars te branden, doende de ligten een zeer goed effect, alles konstig en uitvoerig geschilderd | *Mat:* op doek *Size:* hoog 18 ½, breed 13 ½ duim	G H Fortuyn	(Unknown)
1808/06/06	RMRIJ	0028	*Dou. (Gerard)* | Dit, in allen opzigte beroemd, tafereel stelt voor eene Avondschool: de Meester, gezeten aan eene tafel, waarop zijn Lessenaar staat, schijnt eene ernstige vermaning te geven aan eenen Jongeling, welke hij, met het Schoolbord onder den arm, uit de school zendt; terwijl een bevallig jong Meisje, met alle aandacht, hare les opzegt. Voor op de tafel staat een Zandlooper, en eene Kaars, welke deze groep verlicht. Wat meer voorwaarts zit een Jongeling, met eene Schrijflei op den schoot, te cijferen; bij denzelven staat een jong lagchend Meisje, dat eene brandende kaars in de hand houdt, en hem bijlicht. De uitwerking en harmonie dezer twee lichten zijn uitmuntend. Op den voorgrond staat een open lantaarn, waarin eene brandende kaars, wier licht zich kunstig op de daarbij zijnde voorwerpen verspreidt. Op den derden of achtergrond vertoont zich eene tafel, waarop eene kaars staat, en waaraan eenige kinderen van beiderlei kunne gezeten zijn, bezig hunne lessen te leeren. Wat verder komt nog een Jongeling, eene kaars in de hand houdende, den Trap af. Een breed en ten deele opgehaald Gordijn, grootsch en natuurlijk geplooid, strekt ten voorhangsel aan dit tooneel. Vijf Lichten – twaalf Figuren, ziet men hier verstandig geplaatst, uitmuntend geteekend, schoon van hartstogten, krachtig en gloeijend gekleurd, in een woord een wonder der Schilderkunst in dit vak. Dit stuk is, na het verlies van de beroemde kraamkamer, eertijds in het Kabinet van wijlen den Heere G. Braamcamp berustende, doch naar Rusland overgebragt, en op Zee verongelukt, het allerrijkste en schoonste, dat van dezen Phenix bekend is [Ce Tableau si renommé en Europe, represente l'Intérieur d'une Ecole du soir. Le Maitre assis à son Pupitre, menace de la main un jeune Ecolier, qui debout le regarde avec soumission. Une petite fille paroit dire sa leçon, et près d'elle est un sablier et une lumière qui éclaire ce Groupe. Plus avant sur la droite, une autre jeune fille debout tient une chandelle à la main, et s'entretient avec un Garçon assis, qui s'occupe sur un ardoise. Ces deux Lumières parfaitement entendues éclairent les Groupes principaux, et produisent un brillant effet. A travers la feuille de corne d'une Lanterne entr'-ouverte et posée sur le devant, on apperçoit une lumière, qui éclaire le plus savamment en demi-teintes tout le bas du Tableau. Dans le fond plusieurs écoliers étudient à une table éclairée par une chandelle, tandis qu'un d'eux descend un Escalier une lumière a la main. Une large draperie arrangée avec art, sert d'ouverture à cette Scéne, et contraste agrèablement avec le sujet. Cinq differentes Lumières, et douze figures forment cette Composition riche et savante ; elles sont toutes du plus grand fini et de la plus grande vérité, et produisent une Illusion parfaite. Depuis la perte par un naufrage du Tableau de ce grand Peintre connu sous le nom de la Chambre de l'Accouchée, et acheté a la vente du Cabinet de Mr. Braamcamp pour la collection Impériale de St. Petersbourg, on peut considerer ce magnifique Tableau comme le chef-d'oeuvre Capital éxistant de cet Artiste célébre] | *Mat:* op paneel *Size:* Hoog 20, en breed 15 ½ duim *Loc:* Amsterdam, Nederland. Rijksmuseum. (A87)	Gerrit van der Pot, Heer van Groeneveld	(Sold) fl 17,500 Johs Eck en Zoon [for] le Roi

1808/06/06	RMRIJ	0029	*Dou. (Gerard)* | Een biddende Monnik, in eene Grot, op zijne armen rustende en tusschen zijne zaamgevouwen handen een Pater noster houdende, vestigt met aandacht zijne oogen op een voor hem liggend Crucifix. Schoon en meesterlijk geschilderd [Ce Tableau du même Artiste represente un Moine dans un Souterrain vu à mi-corps, dans une attitude dévote. Il tient un chapelet dans les mains jointes, et a les yeux fixés sur un Crucifix qui est devant lui. Ce Morceau est fini et touché en Maitre] | *Mat:* op paneel *Size:* Hoog 9 ¼, en breed 7 ¼ duim *Loc:* Amsterdam, Nederland. Rijksmuseum. (A88)	Gerrit van der Pot, Heer van Groeneveld	(Sold) fl 1100 J M Jorissen [for] le Roi
1808/08/23	AMSCH	0040	*Douw. (Gemerkt G.)* | Voor een open steenen Nis, om hoog met een opgeschoven Gordijn, zit een Astrologist voor een Tafel, waarop een Hemel Globe geplaatst is, hij schijnt in diepe overweging, houdende een brandende Kaars in de hand, voor zig ligt een opengeslagen Boek en een Kandelaar, de brandende Kaars verlicht zeer natuurlijk het voorwerp; en is uitvoerig gepenceeld | *Mat:* op paneel *Size:* hoog 14, breed 12 duim *Inscr:* G. Douw (signed)	H	(Bought In) fl 39
1808/08/23	AMSCH	0041	*Douw. (G.)* | Eene jeugdige Vrouw in aloude Hollandsche Kleeding, zittende voor een Tafel, halver Lijf, schijnende aandagtig te leezen in een boek, dat zij met beide handen vasthoud; het is meesterlijk en van eene schoone penceelbehandeling | *Mat:* op doek *Size:* hoog 21, breed 13 duim	[Coclers]	(Sold) fl 15 Dupré
1808/08/23	AMSCH	0268	*Douwe* | Voor een Tent ziet men Heeren te Paard, die zig ververschen, in het verschiet eenig Gebergte bij de Zeestrand; kloek behandeld	[Van Iperen?]	(Sold or Bought In) fl 16 Van Iperen
1809/09/06	AMSCH	0013	*Dou (G.)* | Een oud Mans Hoofd, met een grijzen Kruin, gekleed in een Bonte Pels; het zelve is van een allerdelicaatste penceelsbehandeling | *Mat:* op paneel *Size:* hoog 8, breed 7 duim	Johannes Caudri	(Sold) fl 32 Weyland
1810/03/26	RMMUY	0028	*Gerard Dou* | Eene Dame van middelbaren ouderdom, gezeten op een stoel; met haare rechter hand schijnt zij een blad van een boek dat op haar schoot ligt te zullen omslaan; haare linkerhand en arm, rust op eene naast haar staande met tapijt bedekte tafel, waarop twee boeken geplaatst zijn. In den helderen achtergrond ziet men een gottischen trap, een colom, en groen opgehaald gordijn. Uitvoerig, natuurlijk en ongemeen verdienstelijk geschilderd [Ce morceau précieux répresente une Dame de moyën âge, assise et costumée à l'ancienne mode, tenant sur ses genoux un livre, dont elle paroit vouloir tourner une feuille de la main droite. Son bras et sa main gauche s'appuient sur une table couverte d'un tapis placé à côté d'elle, et sur laquelle sont posés deux livres : le fond clair, offre un escalier tournant, un fut de colonne, et un rideau retroussé, d'un fini, et d'un effet admirable, púr, et de son meilleur temps.] | *Mat:* op paneel *Size:* hoog 10, breed 7 ¼ duimen [haut 10, large 7 ½ pouces] *Notes:* The dimensions differ in the Dutch and French editions of the catalogue.	Daniel de Jongh Az	(Sold) fl 505 Le Brun Parys
1810/03/26	RMMUY	0062	*Dow* | Een Vrouwtje voor een open Nis, houdende in de linkerhand eene brandende Kaars, gemerkt Dow.f: Natuurlijk en verdienstelijk geschilderd [Dans une ouverture en forme de niche, se presente une jeune personne, tenant un bout de chandelle allumée à la main, signé Dou. Ce petit tableau est d'une belle exécution.] | *Inscr:* Dow. f: (signed)	Daniel de Jongh Az	(Sold) fl 36 Spaan Amsterdam
1810/08/01	AMSCH	0024	*Dou (Gerard)* | Een Jongeling zittende voor eene Tafel naar het Pleisterbeeld te teekenen, op de Tafel eene brandende Kaars en Teekengereedschap [Sujet à l'effet de la lumiere, étant un jeune Homme occupé à dessiner d'après la bosse. Sur la Table qui est devant lui se trouvent la lumiere et les outils du Dessinateur] | *Annots:* fort médiocre et douteux (NGW); de la vente Sclingerlande à Dort Paillet (BPG) *Mat:* op paneel *Size:* hoog 12, breed 9 ½ duimen	Mr Pieter de Smeth van Alphen	(Bought In) fl 2500
1810/08/01	AMSCH	0025	*Dou (Gerard)* | In een Vertrekje staat een bevallig Meisje aan eene Tafel te schuren, nevens haar een Jongeling. Alles is verrijkt met Huisraad, Spinnewiel, Stoel en Tobbe met Keukengereedschap, verder een Katje [Dans un intérieur de Chambre l'on voit une jeune Fille occupée à recurer devant une Table : elle a un jeune Homme à côté d'elle. Ce morceau est orné d'accessoires, comme d'un Rouet à filer, d'une Chaise, et de plusieurs Meubles de Ménage ; on y distingue de plus un Chat] | *Annots:* fort médiocre (NGW) *Mat:* op paneel *Fmt:* boven rond *Size:* hoog 12 ½, breed 11 duimen	Mr Pieter de Smeth van Alphen	(Bought In) fl 1050
1810/08/06	AMSCH	0025	*Dou (G.)* | Dit fraaije stukje verbeeld een eerwaardig Grijsaard, zittende in een Kluis, houdende een Krucifix in zijne zamengevouwene handen, waarmede hij op een opengeslagen Boek rust, voor hem staat een Zandlooper, Watervat en ander bijwerk. Het licht en koloriet is bevallig, het is alleruitvoerigst gepenceeld | *Mat:* op paneel *Size:* hoog 13, breed 10 ½ duimen *Loc:* Amsterdam, Nederland. Rijksmuseum. (C 128)	A	(Sold) fl 1310 Texier Gerbet en Comp [for] Lebrun
1810/08/06	AMSCH	0026	*Dou (G.)* | Eene jonge bevallige Vrouw, in rijke kleeding, zittende nevens eene Tafel, en spelende op de Luit; zij heeft een Muziekboek op haar schoot. Het is delikaat en alleruitvoerigst van penceelsbehandeling | *Mat:* op paneel *Fmt:* ovaal *Size:* hoog 8 ½, breed 7 ½ duimen	C	(Sold) fl 150 Coclers
1810/08/06	AMSCH	0027	*Dou (G.)* | Een biddend Kluizenaar, in een Grot, voor hem ligt een open Boek en Paternoster, hij vestigt in eerbiedige houding zijne aandacht op een Kruisbeeld; verder is dit stukje versierd met een Doodshoofd, Zandlooper en ander toepasselijk bijwerk. Uitmuntend bewerkt | *Mat:* op paneel *Size:* hoog 15, breed 11 duimen	V[ries]	(Sold) fl 95 Roelsma

1810/08/10	RMRIJ	0003	*Gerard Dou* | Een rusticq Binnenvertrek, waarin twee Biddende Figuren en ander bijwerk. Uitmuntende van caracters, en alleruitvoerigst en krachtig geschilderd | *Mat:* op paneel *Size:* hoog 25 duim, breed 23 duim		(Sold) fl 25 [or] 180 de Bruin

Dou, Gerard (and Berchem, N.P.)

1803/04/20	AMSCH	0020	*Dou (G.); N. Berchem* | Dit voortreffelyk Tafreel, vertoond in een Boomryk Landschap, een staand Heer met een Wandelstok in de hand; neevens hem zit zyne Gemalinne, zy zyn beiden in ryke Deftige Kleeding uitgedost, ter zyde op de grond staat een Hondje, en op de voorgrond legt een Capiteel van de Corintische Order, waar in het Portrait van G. Dou geplaast is, de Hoofd-Personaadie is het Afbeeldzel van den Roemwaardigen Pieter van de Werve, Burgemeester der Stad Leyden, die in de zwaare Beleegering door de Spanjaarden in den Jaren 1574, en in de grootste Hongersnoot zyn Vaderlyke Liefde aan zynen Medeburgers Edelmoedig te kennen gaf, met zyn eigen Vleesch tot Spys aan te bieden; dit stuk is bevallig van Ordenantie, het Coloriet aangenaam, en van een uitvoerige Penceelbehandeling [Ce morceau très intéressant pour l'histoire de la Hollande, represente les portraits du Bourgemêtre Pierre van der Werve & de son Epouse. Cet homme célèbre par sa fermeté & son courage (* Footnote: Il étoit Bourgemêtre gouvernant la ville de Leyde en 1574, lorsque les Espagnols sous la conduite de Baldeus reduisirent cette ville aux dernieres extremitées [sic] de la famine, cet homme ferme s'offrit plutot pour nourriture que de souscire [sic] à la reddition de la place ; enfin après la mort de la moitié de ses concitoyens & des efforts, & de patience dont l'histoire fournit peu d'exemples! il sauva sa ville & l'independance de sa Patrie. Il mourut en 1604. G. Dou aura probablement pris les sujets de sa composition dans les portraits de la famille qui étoient anterieurs à son tems.), se voit debout tenant une longue canne à la main ; il est habillé d'un riche costume à l'ancienne Espagnolle. La Dame est assise, ses habillemens correspondant pour le tems & pour l'ornement avec ceux de son Epoux. N. Berchem en a peint le paysage qui designe la partie d'un Parc ou d'une avenue ; il y a jouté un beau chien brac [sic] qui est à gauche, & vers la droite se voit un chapiteau Corinthien, renversé, ou se trouve le buste de G. Dou. Ce tableau rare & précieux, est d'un beau fini, les figures en sont d'un dessin gracieux ; le paysage & l'animal sont touchés avec cet esprit fin & leger que l'on sait être propre à N. Berchem.] | *Mat:* op paneel *Size:* hoog 30, breed 24 duim *Loc:* Amsterdam, Nederland. Rijksmuseum. (A 90) as Portraits of Adriaen Wittert van der Aa and his wife Maria Knotter	Maria Magdalena van Sluypwyk, gravinne van Moens	(Sold) fl 3200 C S Roos

Dou, Gerard (or Dou, copy after)

1810/03/26	RMMUY	0047	*Door of naar Gerard Dou* | Voor een open hardsteenen Kozijn, staat eene bevallige jonge Vrouw, in de eene hand eene Kaars houdende en met de andere een Gordijn opligtende. Onder op het voetstuk van het Kozijn, is een Basrelief met speelende Kindertjes verbeeld. Alles natuurlijk en konstig [Dans une embrasure de fenêtre, ouverte en forme de niche, se presente une jeune personne, tenant d'une main une chandelle allumée, et relêvant de l'autre main, un rideau. Plus bas un bas relief d'enfants, en pierre de taille, d'un ton chaud et vigoureux. Nous croyons ce tableau originairement de Dou, mais repeint dans plusieurs endroits.] | *Mat:* op paneel *Size:* hoog 9 7/8, breed 7 1/4 duimen *Loc:* Madrid, España. Thyssen Collection.(1930.21) (?)	Daniel de Jongh Az	(Sold) fl 101 W v Leen Delfshaven

Dou, Gerard (or Dou, manner)

1802/06/28	AMSCH	0038	*G. Dou* | Een bevallig Meisje met een Lamp; uitvoerig en natuurlyk van Licht; door of in de manier van G. Dou | *Size:* hoog 8, breed 6 duim	Anna Elink	(Sold) fl 13:10 Texier
1802/09/21	UTHDG	0020	*G. Dou* | Een bejaarde vrouw voor een nis, houdende een kan, uit welke zij voornemens schijnt bloemen te begieten, groeiënde in een pot ter linkerzijde geplaatst buiten de nis, langs welke eene wijngaard opklimt. Dit, en veel bijwerk is uitvoerig helder en natuurlijk gepenceeld door of zoo goed als G. Dou | *Mat:* op paneel *Size:* hoog 14, breed 10 ½ duimen		(Bought In) fl 32
1810/10/11	AMSCH	0028	*G. Douw* | Het Binnengezigt van een Woning, gestoffeerd met eene Dienstmaagd en verschillende Keukengereedschappen; op Paneel, door G. Douw, of in de manier | *Mat:* op paneel *Size:* hoog 13, breed 15 duimen	C	(Sold) fl 16:10 Posthumus

Dou, Gerard (copy after)

1801/03/16	AMSCH	0120	*G. Dou* | Voor een open Steene Nis, op de borstweering zit een aardig Jongeling in deftige kleeding, op een tapytkleeed [sic] bezig waterbellen te blaazen, ter zyde staat een pot met bloemen en omhoog een Wyngaardrank; verder ziet men in een gemeubileerd Vertrek, alles is uitvoerig en bevallig gepepceeld [sic] op koper, naar G. Dou | *Mat:* op koper	K[ip]	(Sold) fl 14:10 Koopman
1801/03/16	AMSCH	0166	*G. Dou* | Een Meisje bezig zynde melk uit een kan te gieten en verder bywerk, uitvoerig, naar G. Dou	K[ip]	(Sold) fl 19 van Iperen
1801/06/13	LNDLS	0026	*H. Carre; G. Dou* | Een Chirurgijn in zijn Winkel, daar een man, zijn been gekwest zijnde, geholpen wordt, in 't bijzijn van zijn vrouw, met veel bijwerk, op paneel naar G. Dou, door H. Carre | copy by Hend. Carree (I) after Dou *Mat:* op paneel *Size:* hoog 23, breed 18 duimen	D van R	(Sold) fl 17 de Roy

1802/02/16	AMSCH	0009	*G. Douw* | Een Meisje, met een brandende kaars in de hand; uitvoerig op paneel na G. Douw | *Mat:* op paneel	B[uys]	(Sold) fl 11 Roelofs
1802/06/28	AMSCH	0218	*G. Dou* | Een bevallig Meisje in een Nis, met een Marktëmmer, Phaisant, een Pot met Anjelieren, en ander bywerk; uitvoerig op Panneel, naar G. Dou | *Mat:* op paneel *Size:* hoog 17, breed 10 duim	Anna Elink	(Sold) fl 22 van Iperen
1802/06/28	AMSCH	0221	*G. Dou* | Twee stuks na G. Dou, hoog 7, breed 6 duim, plaisant geschilderd | *Size:* hoog 7, breed 6 duim	Anna Elink	(Sold) fl 4 van Iperen
1802/06/28	AMSCH	0234	*G. Dou* | Het Haring Vrouwtje, na G. Dou | *Size:* hoog 16, breed 13 duim	Anna Elink	(Sold) fl 4 Balkenschooten
1802/09/06	AMSCH	0254	*G. Dou* | Een Jongeling speelende met een Vogelkooy; na G. Dou	Mevrouw Achtienhoven	(Sold) fl 6 Boelen
1802/09/18	RMDRS	0068	*Douw* | Twee stuks, een Mannetje die Vis schoonmaakt, en een haspelend Vrouwtje, na Douw	Casper de Haas	(Sold) fl 3:8 V Giesen
1803/04/20	AMSCH	0117	*G. Dou* | Een oude Vrouw met een Kan in de hand, schynt een Pot met Bloemen te willen begieten, met verder Bywerk; aartig gecoppieerd [sic], naar het beroemde Schildery van G. Dou [Une Vielle [sic] venant pour arroser un pot à fleurs, orné d'accéssoires, étant une imitation d'après G. Dou, qui n'est pas Sans merite.]	Maria Magdalena van Sluypwyk, gravinne van Moens	(Sold) fl 15 Theijs
1805/07/03	AMSCH	0195	*G. Dou* | Een meditérende Heremiet, met Kruis en Zandloper; zeer fraai na G. Dou	C	(Sold) fl 3:10 Menzart
1806/08/13	AMSCH	0314	*G. Douw* | Een Vrouw by een Lamplicht, in een Nis; na G. Douw	Roos	(Sold) fl 2:5 du Pree
1808/06/06	RMRIJ	0082	*Monni. (Louis de); naar Gerard Dou* | In een binnenvertrek zit, voor eene tafel, in een armstoel, eene slapende Vrouw, welke door eenen Krijgsman een rookende zwavelstok wordt onder den neus gehouden; op de tafel staat in eenen koperen kandelaar eene brandende Kaars, waaraan een ander Krijgsman zijne Pijp ontsteekt; in den achtergrond ziet men eene Vrouw het vertrek intreden, in de eene hand eene brandende lamp, in de andere eene kan houdende. Op den voorgrond staat eene licht inhoudende lantaarn, alles op eene aangename en verstandige wijze verlichtende. Eene roode Gordijn versiert het bovenste gedeelte van deze waarlijk uitvoerige, gloeijende en zeer natuurlijke schilderij [Dans l'Intérieur d'une Chambre, une femme est assise et endormie dans un fauteuil devant une table. Un Officier lui tient une allumette sous le nez, tandis que son camarade allume sa pipe à une chandelle, qui est sur la Table. Dans le fond on voit une jeune fille, qui entre, et qui tient d'une main un pot à bière, et de l'autre une Lampe. Une Lanterne, dont la lumière se répand sur le devant, est admirablement Imitée. Un Rideau artistement retroussé décore le haut de ce Tableau harmonieux et rempli de mérite] | copy by L. de Moni after Dou *Annots:* Verk coll B Kley, den Haag 10 Mei 1781 (RMA I) *Mat:* op koper *Size:* Hoog 11 en breed 8 ¾ duim	Gerrit van der Pot, Heer van Groeneveld	(Sold) fl 200 la Coste
1808/06/06	RMRIJ	0155	*Gerard Dou* | Een Portret van eenen Schilder in een boek bladende en zijn Ezel en Gereedschap bij zich hebbende. Eene Kopij, waarvan het origineele van Gerard Dou in de Gallerij te Dresden berustende is. Gaat ook in Plaat uit met het onderschrift L'Amateur des Arts et Sciences, door Tardieu [Un Peintre dans son Attelier. Copie d'après l'original de Gérard Dou, qui se trouve à la galerie de Dresde, et qui est connu par la gravure de Tardieu avec la Souscription : *L'Amateur des Arts et des Sciences*] | *Mat:* op paneel *Size:* Hoog 12 ¼, en breed 8 ½ duim	Gerrit van der Pot, Heer van Groeneveld	(Sold) fl 13:10 Nieuwenhuys
1809/04/22	AMYVR	0199	*G. Douw* | Een Vrouwtje met een Lamp; naar G. Douw	de Bruin	(Sold) fl 3:5 du Pree
			Dou, Gerard (manner)		
1801/03/16	AMSCH	0132	*G. Dou* | Een Chirurgyn bezig een Vrouw in haar mond te zien, met een kaars; uitvoerig behandeld, in de manier van G. Dou	K[ip]	(Sold) fl 22 Coclers
1802/06/28	AMSCH	0039	*G. Dou* | Een Jongeling met een Vogelkooy, als dito [in de manier van G. Dou] | *Notes:* It is unclear what "dito" refers to in the title.	Anna Elink	(Sold) fl 4 Van Iperen
1802/06/28	AMSCH	0254	*G. Douw* | Een oud Vrouwtje over de Deur leggende; in de manier van G. Douw | *Mat:* op paneel	B	(Sold) fl 1:10 van Iperen
1807/06/10	HGBSM	0178	*G. Dou* | Een biddende Hermiet in een grot, zeer uitvoerig geschilderd, in de manier van G. Dou | *Mat:* op paneel *Size:* hoog 12 ½, breed 10 ½ duim	Abraham Delfos [or others]	(Sold) fl 5:5 Spruit
1808/06/11	RMRIJ	0066	*In de manier van G: Dou* | Een Philosoof in zyn Studeerkamer, omringd van Boeken en meer Bywerk | *Mat:* op paneel *Size:* hoog 12 ½, breed 12 ½ duimen		(Sold) fl 4:5 V Giessen
1808/06/11	RMRIJ	0126	*Als door G: Douw* | Een keurig uitgevoerd Stil Leven, by Lamplicht | *Mat:* op paneel		(Unknown) fl 1:10
1810/06/06	RMMUY	0037	*G. Dou* | Een bevallig Vrouwtje word in de hand gezien, door een ouden Gelukzegger, eene brandende kaars in de hand houdende, krachtig en zeer natuurlijk, in de manier van G. Dou | *Mat:* op paneel		(Unknown) fl 52
1810/06/06	RMMUY	0107	*G. Dou* | Een Meisje, voor eene Nis staande, met een Muisenval in de hand, als naar G. Dou | *Mat:* op paneel		(Unknown) fl 2
			Dou, Gerard (manner; or Monogrammist A.S.H.)		
1804/10/16	DLOND	0284	*Niet minder, zelfs geheel als G. Douw; A.S.H.* | Een Keukenmeid met een Tobbe en Hakmes voor zich, staande aan een Tafel voor een open Raam,		(Sold) fl 104 Verbuyl [?]

nevens ene Pomp, omringd van Keukengereedschap enz. De tekening A. S. H. doet alleen twyffelen. Une Cuisinière occupée à hacher dans une Etuve sur une Table. Elle est debout devant une fenetre ouverte, à côté d'une Pompe, & entourée d'Ustensiles de Cuisine &c. Il n'y à que la seule marque A. S. H., laquelle fait douter | *Mat:* op paneel *Size:* hoog 19, breed 14 *Inscr:* A. S. H. (initialed)

Doudijns (Doedyns), Willem

1801/04/13	AMSCH	0020	*Dodyns* | Maria Magdalena met een Doodshoofd en Kruis, op een boek leunende, met de Ogen hemelwaarts geheven; meesterlyk breed gepenceeld | *Mat:* op doek *Size:* hoog 48, breed 38 duim	Pierre Fouquet, junior	(Sold) fl 4 C S Roos
1801/06/10	AMSCH	0055	*Doudyns* | Een ryke zinspeelende Ordonnantie van verscheide Vrouwen en Kinderen, meesterlyk behandeld | *Mat:* op doek *Size:* hoog 85, breed 70 duim *Notes:* Originally the artist's name was spelled "Doudias." This error was corrected in an errata sheet located at the end of the catalogue.	Herman ten Kate	(Sold) fl 1:10 Pruyssenaar
1805/10/09	HGBSM	0098	*G. Douden* | De tyd die de waarheid ontdekt | companion to lot 99 *Mat:* op doek *Size:* hoog 58 breet 42 duim	T H van Willigen [or others]	(Sold) fl 4:5 Valette
1805/10/09	HGBSM	0099	*G. Douden* | Een dito [tyd die de waarheid ontdekt], zinnebeeldige, zynde een weerga door denzelven [G. Douden], geschilderd A°. 1664 | companion to lot 98 *Inscr:* 1664 (dated) *Notes:* It is unclear what "dito" refers to in the title.	T H van Willigen [or others]	(Sold) fl 3:10 Valette

Douien [Unidentified]

1804/08/02	BDAN	0006	*Douien* | Een Heer speelende op een Viool in een Nisje, voor hem leggende een Musicq-boek, en beneevens hem een Tapyt, alles zeer uitvoerig geschildert en delicaat behandelt | *Mat:* op koper *Size:* b. 9 d. h. 12 d.	J G Calckberner	(Unknown)

Douw, Simon Johannes van

1802/07/21	HGKAN	0016	*S.Y. Dou* | Een extra fraay Schildery, verbeeldende een Plaats aan de voet van een Berg, alwaar eenige Reyzigers beezig zyn hunne Paarden Voeder te geeven, door S.Y. Dou, 1655, zwarte Lyst, op Doek met vergulde binnen rand | *Mat:* op doek *Inscr:* S.Y. Dou, 1655 (signed and dated?) *Notes:* It is unclear whether the name and date are inscribed on the painting.		(Unknown)
1802/09/18	RMDRS	0089	*S. van Dou* | Een dito [groot stuk], verbeeldende Moses en Aron, biddende op den Berg, terwyl Israël Amalec verslaat	Casper de Haas	(Sold) fl 5 V Giesen
1802/11/01	DOBRA	0116	*P. Dauw* | Een Kampement | *Mat:* op doek *Size:* hoog 12 breed 15 duim *Notes:* The artist's name was given as "P. Dauw" but we have assumed this is an error.	Paulus van der Spyk [or others]	(Unknown)
1803/08/24	HGKAN	A0027[a]	*Dou* | Twee Bataille Stukken | *This Lot:* Bataille Stuk *Mat:* op paneel		(Sold) fl 2:2 for lots A27[a] & A27[b]. Giesen
1803/08/24	HGKAN	A0027[b]	*Dou* | Twee Bataille Stukken | *This Lot:* Bataille Stuk *Mat:* op doek		(Sold) fl 2:2 for lots A27[a] & A27[b]. Giesen
1803/08/24	HGKAN	A0028	*Dou* | Twee dito [Bataille Stukken] Ovaal | *Mat:* op paneel *Fmt:* ovaal		(Sold) fl 0:18 Gesen
1803/12/15	MGLAC	0050	*S. van Dou* | Twee stuks Batailles; zeer kragtig en stout geschilderd | *Mat:* op paneel *Size:* hoog duim 11, breed duim 16	Mr L H de Haze Bomme	(Unknown)
1807/09/28	DOHAA	00HH	*Douw* | Een Battaille	Mattheus Westerouen van Meeteren	(Unknown)
1810/06/06	RMMUY	0233	*van Douwe* | Twee Batailles te Paard | *Mat:* op paneel		(Unknown) fl 4:5
1810/11/07	UTWLD	0002	*S. v. Douw* | Een prachtig Italiaansch gebouw, voor 't welke een zeer woelende Paardemarkt. – Een Boer op een Os gezeten, speelt op een dwarsfluit, en een danzend Vrouwtje, op de voorgrond een Heer met een Koopman, schijnende accoord te zijn, alles zeer kunstig gegroupeerd, kragtig geschilderd en meesterachtig getekend door S. v. Douw, op paneel, 2 voet 7 duim breed, 1 voet 10 duim hoog, in een zwarte Lijst | companion to lot 3 *Mat:* op paneel *Size:* 2 voet 7 duim breed, 1 voet 10 duim hoog		(Unknown) fl 21
1810/11/07	UTWLD	0003	*S. v. Douw* | Een pendant, zijnde eene Ruine, en voor dezelve een Beestenmarkt vol gewoel, op de voorgrond Schapen, Bokken etc. in de voorschreve manier door denzelve [S. v. Douw] | companion to lot 2		(Unknown) fl 21

Draaijenburg, W. [Unidentified]

1803/04/20	AMSCH	0156	*W. Draaijenburg* | Een Schynbedrieger, van verscheide Prenten; Tekeningen en Geschriften, zeer bedrieglyk geschilderd [Un Sujet de differens objets comme estampes, dessins & ecritures, paroissant legerement posés les uns sur les autres par l'effet des ombres, bien rendu par W. Draayenburg.] | *Mat:* op paneel *Size:* hoog 24, breed 19 duim	Maria Magdalena van Sluypwyk, gravinne van Moens	(Sold) fl 2:5 Hankock

Dregt, Johannes van

1808/11/28	AMSCH	0015	*J. van Drecht* | Twee stuks Duinachtige Geldersche Landschappen, zijnde een Morgen- en Avondstond, gestoffeerd met gaande en rustende	Z	(Sold) fl 18:10 Kits

			Huislieden, zonachtig en uitvoerig behandeld | *Mat:* op doek *Size:* hoog 10, breed 14 duim		
1808/11/28	AMSCH	0016	*J. van Drecht* | Twee stuks Rhijngezichten, gestoffeerd met Vaartuigen, Kooplieden en Rijzigers, in het verschiet een Stad op het Gebergten, helder en plaisant behandeld | *Mat:* op doek *Size:* hoog 13, breed 18 duim	Z	(Bought In) fl 24:10
1808/11/28	AMSCH	0017	*J. van Drecht* | Twee stuks Italiaansche Landschappen, met aloude Gedenkteekens, gestoffeerd met verscheide Landlieden, in het verschiet vertoond zig de Berg Vesuvius; natuurlijk gepenceeld | *Mat:* op doek *Size:* hoog 15, breed 19 duim	Z	(Bought In) fl 33
1808/11/28	AMSCH	0018	*J. van Drecht* | Twee stuks Hoogduitsche Landschappen, met Beeldjes en Beesten gestoffeerd | *Size:* hoog 15, breed 19 duim	Z	(Bought In) fl 26
1808/11/28	AMSCH	0019	*J. van Drecht* | Een natuurlijk Landschap, met Geboomte gestoffeerd, met een gaande Man en Vrouw | *Mat:* op doek *Size:* hoog 10, breed 16 duim	Z	(Bought In) fl 5
1808/11/28	AMSCH	0020	*J. van Drecht* | Een zinspeelende Ordonantie van verscheide Kindertjes, zacht en uitvoerig | *Mat:* op doek	Z	(Bought In) fl 15:10
1809/04/17	AMSCH	0029	*J. van Drecht* | Een Gezicht langs den Rhijn, rijk gestoffeerd met wandelende Heeren en Dames, rustende Rijzigers en zijlende Vaartuigen; fiks van Penceel | *Mat:* op doek *Size:* hoog 11, breed 14 duim	[Gruyter?]	(Sold or Bought In) fl 1:10 Gruyter
1810/08/06	AMSCH	0147	*J. van Dreght* | Een bevallig Hofgezigt	G	(Sold) fl 2:10 L Pakker
1810/10/11	AMSCH	0169	*J. Van Dregt* | Een Hofgezigt, met Gebouwen en Beeldjes | *Mat:* op doek	[Levy Pakker?]	(Sold) fl 3 du Pree
			Drielenburch, Willem van		
1801/03/16	AMSCH	0181	*Drillenburgh* | Een Landschap	P[ruyssenaar]	(Sold) fl 2 van der Schley [for] A
1802/09/21	UTHDG	000F[H]	*Drillenburg* | Een Avondstond door Drillenburg | *Notes:* This lot was added in by hand in the OGA copy of the catalogue.		(Bought In) fl 6
1802/09/21	UTHDG	0025	*Drillenburg* | Een natuurlijk en wel uitgevoerd maaneschijntje | *Mat:* op paneel *Size:* hoog 7 ½, breed 10 ½ duimen		(Sold) fl 3:3 De Munnick
			Drielenburch, Willem van (copy by)		
1810/12/03	DOBRA	0046	*Drillenburg; P. Wouerman* | Een Landschap, door Drillenburg, naar P. Wouerman | copy by W. Drielenburch after P. Wouwerman		(Unknown)
			Drielst, Egbert van		
1801/03/16	AMSCH	0006	*E. van Drielst* | Een Bosch en Boomryk Landschap, gestoffeerd met een Man die een beest dryft, en een hond, warm van coloriet	P[ruyssenaar]	(Sold) fl 7:10 van der Schley [for] S
1802/09/06	AMSCH	0035	*E. van Drielst* | Een Arcadisch Landschap met een rivier doorsneeden, by den ingang van een bosch, ziet men een gedenkteken, gestoffeerd met beelden; bevallig gepenceeld	J	(Sold) fl 20 van Iperen
1802/12/13	AMSCH	0056	*E. van Drielst* | Een Landschap met een stil Water, welke door een helder Maanlicht bescheenen word, op de voorgrond ziet men eenige Vissers, welke bézig zyn het Net optehalen, verders zylende Scheepen en een aangenaam verschiet; alles is bevallig en krachtig gepenceeld | *Mat:* op doek *Size:* hoog 37, breed 48 duim	Pruyssenaar [for] B	(Sold) fl 44 van Iperen
1803/12/15	MGLAC	0043	*van Drielst* | Een aangenaam Landschapje, waarin eenige Figuuren en Beesje; zeer warm en fraai | *Mat:* op doek *Size:* hoog duim 16, breed duim 21	Mr L H de Haze Bomme	(Unknown)
1804/12/10	AMSCH	0017	*E. van Drielst* | Twee stuks, bevallige Landschappen, met hoog geboomte en gebergten, in de eene ziet men op de voorgrond een helder spiegelend water, waardoor een herder en herderin met twee koeyen beneevens een Bok gaan: verders op een berg, twee lieden en een oud vervallen kasteel; en de anderen verbeeld een dito landschap gestoffeerd, met een rysiger te paard, waar tevens een vrouw met een kind, welke hem om een Aalmoes vraagt, zy zit voor de stam van een hoog opgaande boom, verders over een brug ziet men een landman met een belaaden Ezel, en geboomte en gebergten; deeze beide Schilderytjes, zyn zonachtig piquant van licht en fraay gepenceeld | *Size:* beide hoog 19, breed 16 duim	Jan De Groot	(Sold) fl 92 Josi
1808/06/13	AMSCH	0041	*Drielst (E. van)* | Een aangenaam bevallig Landgezicht, met Boeren-woningen en Geboomten, op den voorgrond gestoffeert met eene Vrouw, twee beladen Ezels voortdrijvende, en verzeld van eenige Schapen, waarbij een rustend Veehoeder, ter zijde ziet men een Dorp in 't verschiet. Alles is zonachtig en zeer uitvoerig van penceelbehandeling | *Mat:* op doek *Size:* hoog 13, breed 20 duim	[Jan Tersteeg]	(Sold) fl 65 Gruiter
1808/06/13	AMSCH	0042	*Drielst (E. van)* | Een aangenaam Nederlandsch Landschap, op den voorgrond een Boer, een Ezel voortdrijvende, benevens eenige Schapen, verders Arbeiders in 't Koorn. Zonachtig en allernatuurlijkst | *Mat:* op doek *Size:* hoog 19, breed 16 duim	E M Engelberts	(Sold) fl 64 Schuman
1808/08/23	AMSCH	0044	*Drielst. (E. van)* | Een Arcadisch Landschap, ter zijde bij een klaar spiegelend Water, ziet men voor een prachtig geordoneerde Tempel, eenige bevallige Vrouwen schijnende te offeren, agterwaards onder het Geboomten, verscheidene Nimphen, waar bij een musiceerende Zater, zonachtig en meesterlijk gepenceeld | *Mat:* op doek *Size:* hoog 27, breed 34 duim	[Gruyter?]	(Sold or Bought In) fl 1:5 Gruyter

1808/11/28	AMSCH	0087	*van Drielst* | Twee met speelende Kindertjes, fiks | *Mat:* op paneel	[Gruyter?]	(Sold) fl 1 du Pree
1808/11/28	AMSCH	0088	*van Drielst* | Maria met het Kindje, waar bij St. Joseph, meesterlijk | *Mat:* op doek	Z	(Sold) fl 2:5 T Spaan
1808/11/28	AMSCH	0089	*van Drielst* | Een Fabel-Historie in een Landschap	Z	(Sold) fl 0:14 Klynveld
1808/11/28	AMSCH	0090	*van Drielst* | Een Eerzuil op Burgemeester H. Hooft, waar bij verscheide Kindertjes | *Mat:* op doek	Z	(Bought In) fl 7
1808/11/28	AMSCH	0091	*van Drielst* | Een Onix [sic], met verscheide Beelden	Z	(Sold) fl 36 T Spaan
1808/11/28	AMSCH	0092	*van Drielst* | Een dito [Onix] dito [met verscheide Beelden]	Z	(Sold) fl 20 A Kits
1808/11/28	AMSCH	0093	*van Drielst* | Een Medaillon, in graauw	Z	(Bought In) fl 5:10
1808/11/28	AMSCH	0094	*van Drielst* | Een dito [Medaillon] dito [in graauw]	Z	(Sold) fl 12 Welmeer
1808/11/28	AMSCH	0095	*van Drielst* | Een staand Studiebeeld in een Landschap, Levensgroote	Z	(Sold) fl 1 L Pakker
1809/06/13	AMSCH	0041	*E van Drielst* | Een Arcadiesch Landschap, gestoffeerd met een pragtige Tempel, waarbij eenige bevallige Vrouwen Offeren, verder onder het Geboomten eenige Nimfen, waarbij musiceerende Zaaters; zonachtig behandeld | *Mat:* op doek *Size:* hoog 27, breed 34 duim	[Gruyter?]	(Sold or Bought In) fl 1 Gruyter
1810/08/01	AMSCH	0026	*Drielst (Egbert van)* | Een Landschap in Drenthe met vervallene Boeren-woningen, Geboomte en andere Voorwerpen [Site de Paysage pris au Pays de Drenthe, orné de Chaumieres, de Figures et d'Animaux] | possibly companion to lot 27 *Annots:* fort peu méritant (NGW) *Mat:* op paneel *Size:* hoog 12 ½, breed 18 duimen	Mr Pieter de Smeth van Alphen	(Sold) fl 131 for lots 26 & 27. Th Spaan
1810/08/01	AMSCH	0027	*Drielst (Egbert van)* | Een Landschap in Drenthe met Geboomte en Beeldjes. Kunnende strekken tot eene wederga van de voorgaande [Une autre Vue dans la contrée de Drenthe, ornée d'Arbres, et correspondante à la précédente dont elle peut faire pendant] | possibly companion to lot 26 *Annots:* fort peu digné d'une telle collection. (NGW) *Mat:* op paneel *Size:* hoog 12 ½, breed 18 duimen	Mr Pieter de Smeth van Alphen	(Sold) fl 131 for lots 26 & 27. Th Spaan

Droman, F. [Unidentified]

1802/06/28	AMSCH	0046	*F. Droman* | Op eene steene Rand staat een Glas met verscheide fraaye geschakeerde Bloemen; door F. Droman, Doek op Panneel | *Mat:* op doek op paneel *Size:* hoog 22, breed 16 duim	Anna Elink	(Sold) fl 7:10 Texier

Droochsloot, Abraham [Unidentified]

1802/11/01	DOBRA	0069	*A. Droogsloot* | Een stroopende party, een Dorp uirplonderende [sic] | companion to lot 70 *Mat:* op paneel *Size:* 2 voet breed, 18 d. hoog	Paulus van der Spyk [or others]	(Sold) fl 7:15 for lots 69 & 70. J Meulemans
1802/11/01	DOBRA	0070	*A. Droogsloot* | Een dito [stroopende] party, naar 't schynt door de boeren afgeslaagen | companion to lot 69 *Mat:* op paneel *Size:* 2 voet breed, 18 d. hoog	Paulus van der Spyk [or others]	(Sold) fl 7:15 for lots 69 & 70. J Meulemans
1802/11/01	DOBRA	0071	*A. Droogsloot* | Twee Boertjes | *Notes:* This lot was sold with lot 72 by an anonymous artist.	Paulus van der Spyk [or others]	(Bought In) fl 4:5 for lots 71 & 72
1809/04/22	AMYVR	0035	*A. Droogsloot* | Een rijk gestoffeerde Kermis, in een Boerendorp, zonachtig | *Mat:* op paneel *Size:* hoog 11, breed 15 duim	de Bruin	(Sold) fl 3 C S Roos
1810/07/23	DOLGI	0020	*Abraham Droogsloot* | Het Bad van Bethesda | *Mat:* op paneel *Size:* hoog 23, breed 37 duim	Mr Pieter van den Santheuvel	(Sold) fl 9 Nieuwenhuizen van Brussel
1810/07/23	DOLGI	0021	*Abraham Droogsloot* | Een Hospitaal | *Mat:* op doek *Size:* hoog 36, breed 54 duim	Mr Pieter van den Santheuvel	(Sold) fl 21 P de Heere Dordt
1810/07/23	DOLGI	0022	*Abraham Droogsloot* | Een Boeren-Kermis | *Mat:* op doek *Size:* hoog 37, breed 28 duim	Mr Pieter van den Santheuvel	(Sold) fl 7 Gansewinkel Dordt
1810/07/23	DOLGI	0023	*Abraham Droogsloot* | Een dito [Boeren-Kermis] | *Mat:* op paneel *Size:* hoog 36, breed 23 duim	Mr Pieter van den Santheuvel	(Sold) fl 7 Nieuwenhuizen Brussel
1810/12/03	DOBRA	0050	*A. Droogsloot* | Een schoon Dorpgezicht, 't welk uitgeplunderd wordt; vol stoffagie en van de beste schildering		(Unknown)

Droochsloot, Cornelis (Nicolaes)

1802/11/01	DOBRA	0185	*C. Droogsloot* | De Zeven Werken van Barmhartigheid | *Mat:* op paneel *Size:* breed 32 ¾, hoog 23 duim		(Unknown) fl 3:5
1802/11/01	DOBRA	0186	*C. Droogsloot* | Een Boerekermis, vol gewoel | *Mat:* op paneel *Size:* breed 25 ½, hoog 18 ½ duim		(Unknown) fl 3:5
1802/11/01	DOBRA	0187	*C. Droogsloot* | Een Boerekermis | *Mat:* op paneel *Size:* hoog 28, breed circa 19 duim		(Unknown) fl 3:5
1810/06/06	RMMUY	0118	*K. Droogsloot* | Een Landschap met eene menigte Figuren | *Mat:* op paneel		(Unknown) fl 5:5
1810/06/06	RMMUY	0119	*K. Droogsloot* | Een Gezelschap van Heeren en Dames | *Mat:* op doek		(Unknown) fl 8:10

Droochsloot, Joost Cornelisz.

1801/03/16	AMSCH	0105	*Droogsloot* | Eenige vegtende Bedelaars in een Landschap, fiks	K[ip]	(Sold) fl 3:10 Koopman

1801/04/23	AMYVR	0017	*J. Droogsloot* | Een stuk verbeeldende de Werken van Barmhartigheid		(Sold) fl 1 ½ Yperen
1801/07/06	MGSAN	[0018]	*Droogsloot* | Een schoone Schildery, verbeeldende een Hospital, waarin veele Kreupelen, Zieken, en anderen; voorts is dit Stuk ryk gestoffeerd met extra veel Bywerk: wordende dit Schildery gehouden voor een der beste Sukken [sic] van Droogsloot | *Size:* breed circa 10 voet, en hoog 3 voet *Notes:* Because this lot was not numbered in the catalogue, we have assigned the number.	Gerardus de Wind	(Unknown) £ 4:15
1801/10/06	AMSCH	0022	*J. Droogsloot* | Een Land en Watergezicht, gestoffeerd met Boeren Wooningen, een Overhaal Pont en andere Schuiten, helder en aangenaam geschilderd | *Mat:* op doek *Size:* hoog 28, breed 38 duim	M	(Sold) fl 8 Th Spaan
1801/10/06	AMSCH	0023	*J. Droogsloot* | Een Gezicht op een der Markten te Utrecht, ryk gestoffeert met Krygsvolk, Bagagie Wagens, en Wandelaars, natuurlyk behandeld | *Mat:* op doek *Size:* hoog 42, breed 66 duim	M	(Sold) fl 11 Van Houten
1801/12/01	HGDAW	0002	*Doorsloten* | Een dito [Schildery] kleinder zynde een Boere Kermis door Doorsloten	Jonkheer Menno Baron van Coehoorn	(Unknown)
1802/02/16	AMSCH	0081	*Droogsloot* | Een Dorpgezigt by een Klooster, alwaar brood uitgedeeld word, op paneel | *Mat:* op paneel	E	(Sold) fl 6 Coclers
1802/04/13	HAVIN	0057	*Droogsloot* | Een Buytenhuis		(Unknown)
1802/05/05	AMSCH	0052	*J. Droogsloot* | Deeze ryke Ordonantie stelt voor 't Bad van Betzaïda. Fraai en Meesterlyk gepenceeld | *Mat:* op doek *Size:* hoog 40, breed 59 duim	C	(Sold) fl 14 B[d] Kooij
1802/05/10	MGSAN	0007	*Droogsloot* | Een extra fraai Stuk, vertoonende een Hospitaal, waar binnen en buiten zich veele Kranken en andere zich vertoonen; voorts is dit Stuk meesterlyk gestoffeerd, en word voor een der beste gehouden, door Droogsloot: op Paneel: in zwarte Lyst | *Mat:* op paneel *Size:* hoog 36 duim, breed 70 duim	Johan Dirk Kruysse	(Sold) £ 5:1 Jan Fahn [?]
1802/06/16	AMSCH	0043	*J. C. Droogsloot* | Deeze Ordonantie steld voor, daar de kreupelen naar de Beek Getzemané door een Engel begeleid worden, zynde geestig geordeneerd en bevallig geschilderd | *Mat:* op doek *Size:* hoog 40, breed 60 duim	[Merrem]	(Sold) fl 16 Delfos
1802/07/20	MGSAN	0033	*Droogsloot* | Een Dorpgezigt; vol Figuuren &c. op Paneel | *Mat:* op paneel *Size:* hoog duim 20, breed duim 27		(Unknown)
1802/09/21	UTHDG	000Q[H]	*Droogsloot* | Een Landschap | *Notes:* This lot was added in by hand in the OGA copy of the catalogue.		(Sold) fl 5 J Niekerk Juffer Str
1803/12/12	AMSCH	0025	*Droogsloot* | Twee stuks Dorpgezichten, met Gebouwen, Boeren-woningen en stoffagie van Beelden; alles kragtig op Paneel | *Mat:* op paneel *Size:* hoog 16, breed 25 duim	Arnoud de Lange	(Sold) fl 1:10 L Pakker
1804/07/25	DLGRO	0052	*J. Droogsloot* | Een Dorp gezicht, verbeeldende een Boeren Kermis vol gewoel, fraai geschilderd door J. Droogsloot | *Mat:* op paneel *Size:* hoog 19, breed 25 duim	Mr Franc van der Burch Wz.	(Unknown)
1804/08/02	BDAN	0028	*Droogsloot* | Twee aangenaame Landschappen, zynde Dorpgezigten vol gewoel | *Mat:* op paneel *Size:* b. 29 d. h. 21 d.	J G Calckberner	(Unknown)
1804/10/08	RMCNL	0013	*Droogsloot* | Een Boere Kermis	A t'Hooft	(Unknown)
1804/10/16	DLOND	0060	*Droogsloot* | Verscheiden Kreupelen en Ellendigen, die voor een Gebouw verkwikkingen ontfangen. Divers Boiteux & Miserables qui recoivent des rafraichissemens devant une maison | *Mat:* op doek *Size:* hoog 39, breed 65		(Unknown)
1804/10/16	DLOND	0061	*Droogsloot* | Twee Landschapjens. Deux Paysages | *Mat:* op paneel *Size:* hoog 9, breed 11		(Unknown)
1804/10/16	DLOND	0062	*Droogsloot* | Een Boeren Dorp vol gewoel. Un Village rempli de Figures | *Mat:* op paneel *Size:* hoog 18, breed 27		(Unknown)
1804/10/16	DLOND	0063	*Droogsloot* | Uts[a] [Een Boeren Dorp vol gewoel. Un Village rempli de Figures] | *Mat:* op paneel *Size:* hoog 13, breed 19		(Unknown)
1804/10/16	DLOND	0064	*Droogsloot* | Een Boeren Kermis, zynde een Schildery met zeer veel gewoel. Une Foire de Village; Tableau avec toutes sortes de figures | *Mat:* op doek *Size:* hoog 39, breed 58		(Unknown)
1804/10/16	DLOND	0065	*Droogsloot* | Uts[a] [Een Boeren Kermis, zynde een Schildery met zeer veel gewoel. Une Foire de Village; Tableau avec toutes sortes de figures] | *Mat:* op doek *Size:* hoog 17, breed 23		(Unknown)
1804/10/16	DLOND	0066	*Droogsloot* | Een Dorps Kerk in Brand, met veel Ruitery. L'Eglise d'un Village en Feu, & beaucoup de Cavallerie | *Mat:* op paneel *Size:* hoog 27, breed 42		(Unknown)
1804/10/20	GRBOL	0001	*Droogsloot* | Een boere Kermis vol gewoel	Joannis Cannegieteri	(Unknown)
1805/06/24	DOBLU	0001	*Droogsloot* | Twee Kermissen	Willem Snellen [or] F R E Nibbelinck [or] Gysbert Visser	(Unknown)
1805/10/09	HGBSM	0056	*Droogsloot* | Een dorp gezigt ryk van figuuren | companion to lot 57 *Mat:* op doek *Size:* hoog 24 breet 41 duim	T H van Willigen [or others]	(Sold) fl 4 De Gelder
1805/10/09	HGBSM	0057	*Droogsloot* | Een dito [dorp gezigt] zynde een weerga | companion to lot	T H van Willigen [or others]	(Sold) fl 2 Carré

			56 *Size:* hoog 24 breet 41 duim *Notes:* It is unclear what "dito" refers to in the title.		
1805/10/09	HGBSM	0090	*Droogsloot* | Een boeren kermis in een dorp gezigt | *Mat:* op paneel *Size:* hoog 34 ½ breet 47 duim	T H van Willigen [or others]	(Sold) fl 3 Carré
1806/06/07	RMHSN	0092	*Droogsloot* | Een Landschap vol Beeldjes | *Mat:* op paneel	A E K L	(Unknown)
1806/06/07	RMHSN	0123	*Droogsloot* | Het Badwater te Bethesda	A E K L	(Unknown)
1806/08/13	AMSCH	0045	*Droogsloot. (J.)* | Een hévige Brand in een Stad, vol gewoel van Beelden, Paarden, Goederen, enz.; allernatuurlykst van behandeling en breed gepenceeld | *Mat:* op doek *Size:* hoog 30, breed 41 duim	Vinkeles [for] D	(Sold) fl 15 Hafner
1806/08/13	AMSCH	0299	*Droogsloot* | Een aangenaam Land- en Riviergezicht; met Boere Woningen, Molen en stoffagie van Beeldjes	Vinkeles [for] F	(Sold) fl 6:10 Reydon
1806/11/24	AMSCH	0020	*Droogsloot (J.)* | Een Boeren Dorp; ryk van stoffagie en aangenaam van schildering | *Mat:* op paneel *Size:* hoog 12, breed 17 duim	Munnikhuizen	(Sold) fl 2 Yver
1807/04/00	LNDLS	0030	*Droogsloot* | Een winter met schaatzerijders, en houthakkers op 't ijs, verders een dorp in 't verschiet | *Mat:* op doek *Size:* hoog 26, breed 45 duim	[Abraham Delfos] [or others]	(Unknown)
1807/04/00	LNDLS	0031	*Droogsloot* | Een Capitaal stuk vol beelden, daar den engel nederdaalt om het water van Behtheza [sic] te beroeren | *Mat:* op doek	[Abraham Delfos] [or others]	(Unknown)
1807/06/10	HGBSM	0030	*Droogsloot* | Een winter met schaatzerijders, en houthakkers op 't ijs, verders een dorp in 't verschiet | *Mat:* op doek *Size:* hoog 26, breed 45 duim	Abraham Delfos [or others]	(Sold) fl 3 Carré
1807/06/10	HGBSM	0031	*Droogsloot* | Een Capitaal stuk vol beelden, daar den engel nederdaald om het water van Behtheza [sic] te beroeren | *Mat:* op doek	Abraham Delfos [or others]	(Sold) fl 7 Margadont [?]
1807/06/10	HGBSM	0113	*Droogsloot* | De zeven Werken van Barmhartigheid | *Mat:* op doek *Size:* hoog 39, breed 58 duim	Abraham Delfos [or others]	(Sold) fl 2 Carré
1807/08/26	AMSCH	0043	*J. Droogsloot* | Een capitaal Wintergezigt, ziende op een bevroozen Rivier, ter wederzyde aan den Oever met Boerenwoningen: op de voorgrond verscheide wandelende Lieden, en een Houthakker, verder een meenigte Schaatzeryders, Arresleeden, en Wandelaars die zig op het Ys vermaaken, in 't verschiet een Stadgezigt, meesterlyk gepenceeld | *Mat:* op doek *Size:* hoog 43, breed 67 duim	Yver [for] S	(Bought In) fl 3
1808/06/13	AMSCH	0043	*Droogsloot* | Een Gezicht op een Boerenwerf bij Haarlem, aan een Watertje, in 't verschiet de Duinen. Schoon van werking | *Mat:* op doek *Size:* hoog 21, breed 25 duim	E M Engelberts	(Sold) fl 70 J du Pree
1808/08/23	AMSCH	0046	*Droogsloot. (J.)* | Een Dorpgezigt, op de voorgrond voor een Tent ziet men twee Heeren, beiden met een roemer Wijn in de hand, nevens hun eenige Werklieden bij eenig Vaatwerk, verder gaande en rustende Reisigers; fiks gepenceeld | *Mat:* op doek *Size:* hoog 49, breed 44 duim	C	(Sold) fl 5:10 D Maijkel
1808/08/23	AMSCH	0201	*J. Droogsloot* | In een welbebouwd Dorp, ziet men de Werken van bermhertigheid aan verscheide gebrekkelijke Lieden uitoeffenen; fiks op Paneel | *Mat:* op paneel	[Gruyter?]	(Sold) fl 2 J Spaan
1809/06/13	AMSCH	0042	*J. Droogsloot* | Voor een Buitenhuis, staat een Man die op de Lier, en twee andere die op de Doedelzak speelen | *Mat:* op paneel *Size:* hoog 13, breed 20 duim	T	(Sold) fl 10 Buck
1809/07/25	HGBSM	0212	*Droogsloot* | Een Boeren Kermis, ryk gestoffeert met Figuuren | *Mat:* op paneel *Size:* hoog 20, breet 32 duim	D van der Aa [or] E B ten Dall	(Sold) fl 5 L Voerman
1809/07/25	HGBSM	0272	*Droogsloot* | Een Landschap en Boeren Kermis | *Mat:* op paneel	D van der Aa [or] E B ten Dall	(Sold) fl 0:18 L Voerman
1809/07/25	HGBSM	0285	*J.C. Droogsloot* | Een Gezigt op een groot Plyn in een Stad van binnen te zien, daar troepen in de Wapens staan geinspecteerd worden, vol Figuren, door J.C. Droogsloot 1625 | *Mat:* op doek *Size:* hoog 35, breed 60 duim *Inscr:* J.C. Droogsloot 1625 (signed and dated?) *Notes:* It is unclear whether the name and date are inscribed on the painting.	D van der Aa [or] E B ten Dall	(Sold) fl 30 Stratenus
1809/10/16	ARNIJ	0007	*Droogsloot* | Een boere kermis	Wed N Nijhoff	(Sold) fl 11 Tulleken
1810/03/07	UTWLD	0040	*Droogsloot* | Een boere Kermis | *Size:* hoog 3 voet 9 duim, breed 2 voet 6 duim	J J Woertman	(Unknown) fl 15
1810/06/20	AMSCH	0134	*J. Droogsloot* | Een natuurlijk Land- en Watergezigt, gestoffeerd met een overvarende Pontschuit	S	(Sold) fl 1 L Pakker
1810/08/06	AMSCH	0028	*Droogsloot (D.)* | Een Driekonings Maaltijd, zijnde eene geestige Ordonnantie van eene menigte Beelden. Krachtig gepenceeld | *Mat:* op doek *Size:* hoog 23, breed 32 duimen	G	(Sold) fl 11 L Pakker
1810/10/10	MGCIT	0122	*Droogsloot* | Twee zeer vrolijke Stukjes, met veelerhande zoo staande als zittende Figuren; zeer goed behandeld	Caspar van Citters	(Unknown)
1810/11/07	UTWLD	0062	*Droogsloot* | Een Riviergezichtje vertoonende een Kasteel, ophaalbrug voor de fortresse, een schuitje, waarin een visscher bezig met roeijen en verder eenige stoffagie door Droogsloot, op paneel, 1 voet 3 duim hoog, 2 voet 1 en een half duim breed, zwarte Lijst | *Mat:* op paneel *Size:* 1 voet 3 duim hoog, 2 voet 1 en een half duim breed		(Unknown) fl 3
1810/12/03	DOBRA	0002	*Droogsloot* | De Schilder Droogsloot voor den Ezel, zittende te schilderen; breed behandeld, door hem zelf 1630 | *Inscr:* 1630 (dated?)		(Unknown)

			Notes: It is unclear whether the date is inscribed on the painting. *Loc:* Macon, France. Musée Municipal des Ursulines.		
1810/12/03	DOBRA	0057	*Droogsloot* | Een geplunderd Dorp, ryk gestoffeerd		(Unknown)
			Dubbels, Hendrik Jacobsz.		
1801/03/16	AMSCH	0102	*Dubbels* | Een stil Water met verscheide Vaartuigen, zynde een avondstond, natuurlyk	K[ip]	(Sold) fl 6:5 Th Spaan
1801/03/16	AMSCH	0114	*D. Dubbels* | Een woelend Water met zylende Scheepen en Visschers in een schuit, helder en bevallig gepenceeld | *Mat:* op doek *Notes:* The artist's name was given as "D. Dubbels" but we have assumed this is an error.	K[ip]	(Sold) fl 6:5 Th Spaan
1801/03/16	AMSCH	0126	*D. Dubbels* | Een stil Water, met verscheide zeilende en dryvende Scheepen, ter zyde een Dorpgezicht, zeer natuurlyk en bevallig gepenceeld, op doek | *Mat:* op doek *Notes:* The artist's name was given as "D. Dubbels" but we have assumed this is an error.	K[ip]	(Sold) fl 5:10 Croese
1801/04/13	AMSCH	0019	*H. Dubbels* | Een gezigt op het Y, ziende op het Galgeveld, zynde een hobbelend water, gestoffeerd met een menigte Vaartuigen, op de voorgrond Visscher in hun schuit, het water, de lugt en het ver schiet, is dun, aangenaam van coloriet en uitvoerig van behandeling | *Mat:* op paneel *Size:* hoog 15, breed 22 duim	Pierre Fouquet, junior	(Sold) fl 69 Lafontaine
1801/06/10	AMSCH	0043	*Dubbels. (J.)* | Een Strand gezicht, by het zelve ziet men twee Visschers Pinken, benevenseenige [sic] Lieden aan 't Strand, verders een woelende Zee, natuurlyk en dun van schildering | *Mat:* op paneel *Size:* hoog 18, breed 22 duim	Herman ten Kate	(Sold) fl 135 I^{c} Smit
1801/06/10	AMSCH	0044	*Dubbels. (J.)* | Een Strand gezicht by Texel, ter regter zyde ziet men een Visscher, het Anker van een Pink lichten, in 't verschiet verscheyde Oorlogscheepen, 't Water is dun en alles van de fraaiste Penceels behandeling | *Mat:* op doek op paneel *Size:* hoog 28, breed 34 duim	Herman ten Kate	(Sold) fl 300 C S Roos
1801/06/10	AMSCH	0045	*Dubbels. (J.)* | Een woelende Zee, waarin een Oorlogschip ten Anker, verders andere zeylende Vaartuigen, natuurlyk behandeld | *Size:* hoog 31, breed 38 duim	[Doublet]	(Sold) fl 12 Pruissenaar
1801/08/19	AMSCH	0022	*J. Dubbels* | Een zeer fraai en uitvoerig kabbelend Water, met zeilende Vaartuigen | *Size:* hoog 19, breed 26 duim	Van Forreest	(Sold) fl 205 Vinkeles
1802/05/05	AMSCH	0050	*Dubbels* | Een Gedeelte van 't Eiland Texel; de Lugt vertoond eene opkoomende Onweêrsbuî, aan 't Strand een Hoofd van Paalwerk, verders in Zee ziet men eenige Zeilende Scheepen, waarvan eene bezig is, zyne Zeilen voor de opkoomende Buî te Reeven. Natuurlyk en uitvoerig gepenceeld	J	(Sold) fl 3:10 Spruit
1802/05/05	AMSCH	0051	*Dubbels* | Een Onstuimige Zee, met een Zeilend Beurtschip en Oorlogscheepen. Zeer natuurlyk geschilderd | *Mat:* op doek *Size:* hoog 26, breed 31 duim	C	(Sold) fl 4:15 Spruit
1802/06/16	AMSCH	0042	*J. Dubbels* | Een woelende Zee met een Beurtschip, verders een Oorlogschip en een ander Vaartuig, in 't verschiet een Stad; meesterlyk behandeld | *Mat:* op paneel *Size:* hoog 11, breed 17 duim	[Merrem]	(Sold) fl 24 La Fontaine
1802/07/20	MGSAN	0038	*Dubbels* | Een Winterstuk, zynde een party Schepen, die omtrent een Scheepswerf in 't Ys bevroozen liggen; op den voorgrond ziet men een Man in het Ys liggen, die door twee anderen daaruit geholpen word; verder nog eenige Schaatsryders &c. malsch en delicaat geschilderd, in de manier van W. v. d. Velde: door den beroemden Zee- en Scheepschilder Dubbels | *Size:* hoog duim 15 ½, breed duim 19 ½		(Unknown)
1802/09/29	AMSCH	0014	*H. Dubbels* | Een Zeegezigt, hoog 19, broed 26 duim. Doek. Een onstuimig weder is in dit fraaije stuk verbeeld. Twee Visschers tragten een Visschers Pink op strand te haalen; verders een Heer te Paard met zyn Hond, verscheide Visschers, en Paalwerk, tegen 't welk het schuimende Water aanstuifd; dit Schildery is zeer fyn en delicaat behandelt, en fraai van ligt en bruin [La Fin d'une Tempête, beau Tableau de ce celébre Peintre de marines ; l'on y remarque le jeu des Elémens, une grande Lumiere perce les nuages et éclaire. une partié de la mer en tourmente et qnelques [sic] Piloties [sic]. Des Pécheurs tachent de Sauver une Barque de la force des vagues ; Plusieurs autres figures donnent de l'intéret à ce morceau, qui par sa touche délicate & précieuse est estimé être une des belles productions du Pinçeau de cet artiste.] | *Mat:* op doek *Size:* hoog 19, breed 26 duim	[Labouchere?]	(Sold) fl 61 Pruijssenaar
1802/11/01	DOBRA	0018	*Dubbels* | Twee stuks, zynde een woelend, en een stil water | *Mat:* op doek	Paulus van der Spyk [or others]	(Sold) fl 12 v d Blijk
1802/12/13	AMSCH	0052	*J. Dubbels* | Een Cabbelend- Water, met een meenigte van zylende en ten anker leggende Scheepen, uitvoerig geschilderd | *Mat:* op doek *Size:* hoog 30, breed 41 duim	Pruyssenaar [for] A	(Sold) fl 2 Gruiter
1802/12/13	AMSCH	0054	*Dubbels* | Een stil Water, met zylende en dryvende Scheepen, op de voorgrond Visschers in een Schuit | *Mat:* op paneel *Size:* hoog 16, breed 14 ½ duim	Pruyssenaar [for] D	(Sold) fl 3:5 B Boelen
1804/02/27	AMSCH	0029	*Dubbels. (H.)* | In een kabbelende Zee, ziet men eenige zeilende Scheepen en Schuiten, enz; uitvoerig van behandeling | *Mat:* op doek *Size:* hoog 13, breed 19 duim	D	(Bought In) fl 10

<table>
<tr><td>1804/10/29</td><td>HRBAU</td><td>0019</td><td>*Dubbels, (H.)* | Een allerbevalligst stil Water, verbeeld op het oogenblik dat de zon de kimmen gepasseerd is; gestoffeerd voor aan met een Pont, waar in een Rydtuig, Paarden en Passagiers zyn, welken overgehaald worden; nevens een Jagt en eenige Kaagen die ten anker liggen; wat verder ligt een Oorlogschip, een Driemast en andere Vaartuigen, welken zig in groepen tot aan den horison verspreiden. Het licht doet in dit Stuk eene frapante en aangenaame werking, het water is dun, en alles zeer uitvoerig behandeld | *Mat:* op doek *Size:* hoog 20, breed 26 duim</td><td>Simon Styl</td><td>(Unknown)</td></tr>
<tr><td>1805/12/16</td><td>AMSCH</td><td>0020</td><td>*J. Dubbels* | Een stil Water, gestoffeerd met verscheide Vaartuigen, Scheepen en Beelden, kragtig op Doek | *Mat:* op doek *Size:* hoog 29, breed 30 duim</td><td>R[oos]</td><td>(Sold) fl 1:15 T van Iperen</td></tr>
<tr><td>1805/12/16</td><td>AMSCH</td><td>0074</td><td>*Dubbels* | Een stil Water, met dieversse [sic] Vaartuigen, in 't verschiet een Stad, bevallig door Dubbels</td><td>R[oos]</td><td>(Sold) fl 7:5 Graffelman</td></tr>
<tr><td>1806/08/13</td><td>AMSCH</td><td>0042</td><td>*Dubbels (J.)* | Een kabbelend Water, met zylende Scheepen en Schuiten; dun en fiks gepenceeld | *Mat:* op paneel *Size:* hoog 13, breed 17 duim</td><td>Vinkeles [for] F</td><td>(Sold) fl 12:10 Swanenburg</td></tr>
<tr><td>1806/08/13</td><td>AMSCH</td><td>0308</td><td>*Dubbels* | Een stil Water, met zeilende en stilleggende Vaartuigen</td><td>Vinkeles [for] F</td><td>(Sold) fl 0:6 L Pakker</td></tr>
<tr><td>1806/10/16</td><td>UTWLD</td><td>0005</td><td>*J. Dubbels* | Een besneeuwd Winter gezicht, met schaatsenryders en Arresleden door J. Dubbels</td><td>Mr P de Malapert [or] W Beeldsnyder</td><td>(Unknown)</td></tr>
<tr><td>1808/06/13</td><td>AMSCH</td><td>0193</td><td>*H. Dubbels* | Een kabbelend Water, met zeilende Schepen</td><td>E M Engelberts</td><td>(Sold) fl 25 Schuman</td></tr>
<tr><td>1808/10/28</td><td>AMVRS</td><td>0012</td><td>*Dubbels. (J.)* | Een Strand-Gezicht op Texel, ter rechter zijde ziet men een Visscher het Anker van een Pink lichten; in het verschiet verscheide Oorlogschepen. 't Water is dun en alles zeer fraai geschilderd | *Mat:* op doek op paneel *Size:* hoog 28, breed 34 duim</td><td>Marten Udink</td><td>(Sold) fl 200 Gruyter</td></tr>
<tr><td>1808/11/28</td><td>AMSCH</td><td>0012</td><td>*Dubbels* | Een Strandgezigt, met zeilende en ten Anker leggende Vaartuigen, op de voorgrond eenige Visschers bij hunne Schuiten, kloek gepenceeld | *Mat:* op paneel *Size:* hoog 10, breed 14 duim</td><td>[Gruyter?]</td><td>(Sold) fl 12:10 van Os</td></tr>
<tr><td>1809/04/17</td><td>AMSCH</td><td>0027</td><td>*H. Dubbels* | Een Strand- en Zeegezicht, met zijlende en ten Anker leggende Schepen, en Visschers Pinken; meesterlijk geschilderd | *Mat:* op doek *Size:* hoog 23, breed 27 duim</td><td>[Gruyter?]</td><td>(Sold or Bought In) fl 2:5 Gruyter</td></tr>
<tr><td>1809/04/17</td><td>AMSCH</td><td>0028</td><td>*H. Dubbels* | Een Strand- en Zeegezicht, met Vaartuigen en Beeldjes; zonagtig geschilderd | *Mat:* op doek *Size:* hoog 13, breed 15 duim</td><td>R</td><td>(Sold) fl 2:5</td></tr>
<tr><td>1809/04/22</td><td>AMYVR</td><td>0033</td><td>*J. Dubbels* | Twee stuks stille Zeegezichten, met een menigte Vaartuigen en Beeldjes; natuurlijk | *Mat:* op doek *Size:* hoog 14, breed 16 duim</td><td>de Bruin</td><td>(Sold) fl 13 du Pree</td></tr>
<tr><td>1809/04/22</td><td>AMYVR</td><td>0034</td><td>*J. Dubbels* | Twee stuks stille Waters met Schepen; dun behandeld | *Mat:* op doek *Size:* hoog 14, breed 17 duim</td><td>Juff[r] Julikker</td><td>(Sold) fl 4:10 du Pree</td></tr>
<tr><td>1809/06/13</td><td>AMSCH</td><td>0039</td><td>*H. Dubbels* | Een Gezigt van een Hollands Dorp aan de Noordzee, rijk gestoffeerd met Heeren en Dames te Paard, rijdende Viswagens, en een menigte Dorpelingen; zonachtig en uitvoerig geschilderd | *Mat:* op doek *Size:* hoog 16, breed 24 duim</td><td>[Gruyter?]</td><td>(Bought In) fl 20:10</td></tr>
<tr><td>1809/07/19</td><td>AMSCH</td><td>0013</td><td>*Dubbels* | Een stil Water, zijnde een Riviergezicht, met drijvende en stil liggende Vaartuigen; aan beide oevers Geboomte en Woningen. Het is zonagtig en bevallig geschilderd | *Mat:* op paneel *Size:* hoog 15, breed 19 duim *Loc:* Amsterdam, Nederland. Rijksmuseum. (A92)</td><td>[Bicker]</td><td>(Sold) fl 200 Yver voor Z H den Koning</td></tr>
<tr><td>1810/10/10</td><td>MGCIT</td><td>0007</td><td>*H. Dubbels* | Een holle en onstuimige Zee, door een felle Wind tegen een ongemeen fraai bewerkt Strand aangedreven wordende, voorts naar den eisch gestoffeerd en in allen opzigten kragtig uitgevoerd</td><td>Caspar van Citters</td><td>(Unknown)</td></tr>
<tr><td>1810/10/11</td><td>AMSCH</td><td>0029</td><td>*H. Dubbels* | Dit kapitaal Schilderij stelt voor een ruim kabbelend Water, vooraan een zeilende Beurtman, waar achter een Oorlogschip, ter linker zijde een Jagt, waarbij een Schuit, waarin Visschers, bezig hunne netten op te halen, verder eene menigte verschillende Vaartuigen en een Stad in het verschiet; dit stuk is fraai van Ordonantie, en van de beste schildering van H. Dubbels | *Mat:* op doek *Size:* hoog 39, breed 50 duimen</td><td>[Gruyter?]</td><td>(Bought In) fl 180</td></tr>
</table>

Dubbels, Hendrik Jacobsz. (manner)

<table>
<tr><td>1802/12/13</td><td>AMSCH</td><td>0053</td><td>*Dubbels* | Een Strand Gezigt, op de voorgrond gestoffeerd met een Postwagen, Vissers en andere Figuuren; als door Dubbels | *Mat:* op doek *Size:* hoog 13, breed 16 duim</td><td>Pruyssenaar [for] D</td><td>(Sold) fl 1:5 Hulswit</td></tr>
</table>

Dubois, Guillam

<table>
<tr><td>1803/08/17</td><td>AMSCH</td><td>0011</td><td>*Boys. (C. de)* | Twee stuks gestoffeerde Boomryke Landschappen, in de eene een Water, waar in een Schuitje en andere Stoffagie van Beelden, beide zeer natuurlyk en geestig geschilderd | *Mat:* op paneel *Size:* ieder hoog 13, breed 14 duim</td><td>Anna Catharina Putman</td><td>(Sold) fl 20 Gruyter</td></tr>
<tr><td>1804/08/08</td><td>AMSCH</td><td>0035</td><td>*C. du Boi* | In een wyd uitgestrekt Landschap vertoond zich op een hoogten een Moolen, waarby een Vrouw en eenige Schaapen, ter zyde, tusschen het Geboomte, een Boerenwooning, en langs de zwaar gespoorde Weg eenige gaande en rustende Reizigers; zonachtig en bevallig geschilderd | *Mat:* op doek *Size:* hoog 11, breed 14 duim</td><td>Vink[eles] [for] K[=Gruyter?]</td><td>(Sold) fl 2 Gruyter</td></tr>
<tr><td>1805/12/16</td><td>AMSCH</td><td>0069</td><td>*du Bois* | Een Boschgezicht</td><td>R[oos]</td><td>(Sold) fl 0:6 L Pakker</td></tr>
<tr><td>1806/06/07</td><td>RMHSN</td><td>0056</td><td>*Dubois* | Een Landschap met een Boerenhuis en eenige Beeldjes | *Mat:* op paneel</td><td>A E K L</td><td>(Unknown)</td></tr>
</table>

1806/08/13	AMSCH	0024	*Bois. (C. du)* | Een aangenaam Landschap met een Dorp-Tooren in 't verschiet, gestoffeerd met Paarden en Beelden; bevallig van licht en bruin, en natuurlyk voorgesteld | *Size:* hoog 16, breed 22 duim	Roos	(Sold) fl 41 Th Spaan
1809/06/13	AMSCH	0016	*C. Du Bois* | Twee stuks duinachtige Landschappen, met Boere Wooningen en Geboomten, gestoffeerd met Landlieden en Vee, rustende Reizigers en bevallig verschiet; als J. Ruisdaal, geschilderd door C. Du Bois | *Mat:* op paneel *Size:* ieder is hoog 10, breed 14 duim	E	(Sold) fl 35 van Iperen
1810/06/20	AMSCH	0013a	*C. Du Bois* | Een boomrijk Landschap met een opgaande Weg, waarop een Reiziger bij een Vragtkar. Natuurlijk geschilderd | *Mat:* op doek *Size:* hoog 41, breed 31 duimen	K	(Sold) fl 12:10 Hulswit
1810/06/20	AMSCH	0013b	*C. Du Bois* | Een dito [boomrijk] Landschap met Landlieden en Vee | *Mat:* op doek *Size:* hoog 35, breed 24 duimen	K	(Sold) fl 1:10 L Pakker
			Dubois, Guillam (manner)		
1804/02/27	AMSCH	0135	*du Boi* | Twee stuks Landschappen; als du Boi	B	(Withdrawn)
			Dubois, H. [Unidentified] (copy by)		
1809/06/13	AMSCH	0026	*H. Du Bois; J. Wijnands* | Een Heuvelagtig Landschap met Geboomten, Kruidgewas en Koornakker, gestoffeerd met rustende en staande Landlieden; bevallig en uitvoerig geschilderd, naar J. Wijnands, door H. Du Bois | copy by H. Dubois after Wijnants *Mat:* op paneel *Size:* hoog 14, breed 19 duim	M	(Sold) fl 16:5 van Iperen
			Dubois, J. [Unidentified]		
1802/05/05	AMSCH	000B	*J. de Bois* | Een boomryk Landschap aan een Waterplas, met Beelden en Beesten, uitvoerig | *Mat:* op paneel *Size:* hoog 16, breed 15 duim	A	(Sold) fl 54 Pruijssenaar [for] R
1802/05/05	AMSCH	000C	*J. de Bois* | Een niet minder fraay Landschap | *Mat:* op paneel *Size:* hoog 15, breed 13 duim	A	(Sold) fl 51 Gruiter
1802/09/21	UTHDG	0012	*J. du Bois* | Een Boschagtig Landschapje met voetgangers gestoffeerd, kragtig | *Mat:* op paneel *Size:* hoog 12, breed 13 duimen		(Bought In) fl 10
1803/06/20	AMSCH	0052	*J. du Bois* | Twee Stuks boom, en bergachtige Landschappen, gestoffeerd met Beeldjes, op Doek | *Mat:* op doek *Size:* hoog 16, breed 22 duim	Roos [for] E	(Sold) fl 4:15 Pruijssenaar
1807/08/26	AMSCH	0029	*J. du Bois* | Een Bergachtig Landschap met twee Ryzigers op een Berg, en op de voorgrond een Man op een Ezel | *Mat:* op paneel *Size:* hoog 8, breed 11 duim	de Vries	(Sold) fl 1:5 H Rynders
			Dubordieu, Pieter (and Steenwyck, Hend.; copy by)		
1808/06/06	RMRIJ	0017	*Bordieu. (du); Steenwijk. (H. J. van); A. Durer; Holbeijn* | Eene zeer getrouwe kopij naar de origineele Schilderij van A. Durer en H. Holbeijn, Desiderius Erasmus verbeeldende. Het bijwerk door H. J. van Steenwijk. Alles zeer uitvoerig behandeld [Copie fidelle du Portrait de Désiré Erasme d'aprés l'original d'Albert Durer et H. Holbeyn. Les accessoires sont peints par van Steenwyk] | copy by P. Dubordieu and Hend. Steenwyck after Dürer and H. Holbein (II) *Annots:* Geschenk Teding Berkhout (RMA I) *Mat:* op paneel *Size:* Hoog 9 ½, en breed 7 ½ duim	Gerrit van der Pot, Heer van Groeneveld	(Sold) fl 21 du Pré
			Dubourg, Louis Fabritius		
1801/10/06	AMSCH	0010	*L. F. du Bourg* | Deeze Ordinantie verbeeld, de wegzending van Hagar en Ismaël, uit het Huis van den Aartsvader Abraham, zynde Meesterlyk fraai van Teekening, aangenaam van Coloriet en uitvoerig gepenceeld | *Mat:* op doek *Size:* hoog 14, breed 11 duim	S	(Sold) fl 45 for lots 10 & 11. Theijs
1801/10/06	AMSCH	0011	*L. F. du Bourg* | In een Landschap, vertoont zich Vertumnis in de gedaante van een oude Vrouw by Pomona, verzelt van Cupido, zynde fraai geordineert, en als de voorige, van een bevallige en uitvoerige Penceel behandeling | *Mat:* op doek *Size:* hoog 14, breed 11 duim	S	(Sold) fl 45 for lots 10 & 11. Theijs
1801/12/22	AMOTT	0027	*du Bourg* | Door Cupidoos verzelde Venussen, in een Landschap, door du Bourg, 1761 | *Inscr:* du Bourg, 1761 (signed and dated?) *Notes:* It is unclear whether the name and date are inscribed on the painting.	Bartholomeus Ruloffs	(Unknown) fl 2:5
1806/08/13	AMSCH	0247	*L. F. de Bourg* | 't Vrouwtje in Overspel	Vinkeles [for] G[ruyter]	(Sold) fl 3 v d Schleij
1807/08/26	AMSCH	0331	*L. F. du Bourg* | Een Bybel-Ordonnantie: het Vrouwtje in overspel bevonden, gestoffeerd met verscheiden Beelden | *Mat:* op doek	v d Schley [for] L	(Sold) fl 6:5 Yver
1808/06/13	AMSCH	0023	*Bourg (L.F. du)* | Dit Voorwerp verbeeld vrolijke Bacchanten in een aangenaam Landschap, met verschillende geboomte, als een Feest van Pomona; in het midden staat een steenen Term, waarbij verscheiden Mannen en Vrouwen, die het met kransen van onderscheidene vruchten versieren; Kindertjes dragen korfjes met fruit, die zij eene Nimf aanbieden. Op den voorgrond ligt eene Vrouw en Kinderen, als door den drank in slaap gevallen, en andere beschouwen die vermaken: in 't verschiet ziet men danssende Nimfen. Het is bevallig van licht en koloriet, en meesterlijk gepenceeld | *Mat:* op doek *Size:* hoog 26, breed 35 duim	[Jan Tersteeg]	(Sold) fl 40 van Iperen
1808/11/28	AMSCH	0109	*L.F. du Bourg* | Een Schoorsteenstuk, verbeeldende de Afgezant van Abraham bij Rebecca, haar Geschenken aanbiedende, krachtig op Doek geschilderd | *Mat:* op doek *Fmt:* schoorsteenstuk	F	(Sold) fl 2 v der Schley [for] Myn

1809/06/13	AMSCH	0025	*L F. Du Bourg* | Een Bijbel-Ordonantie, voorstellende de Offerhande van Jephta, vol gewoel van een menigte Beelden, zo mannen als Vrouwen; kragtig | *Mat:* op doek *Size:* hoog 24, breed 30 duim	E	(Sold) fl 3:15 Gruiter

Ducq, Johan le

1801/08/19	AMSCH	0020	*J. le Ducq* | Een Corps de Garde, in dezelven zit op de voorgrond, een Krygsbevelhebber zyn Pyp te rooken, by hem staat een bevallige Dame, daar nevens leggen Trommels, Vaandels, en ander Krygsgeweer, uitvoerig van penceelbehandeling	Pruyssen^{r} [for] Q	(Bought In) fl 100
1801/10/19	AMSCH	0020	*Ducq. (J. le)* | Een Binnenhuis, waar in twee Heeren en een Dame in Spaansche kleeding zittende met de kaart te speelen by een Tafel, ter zyde een zittende Hond | *Mat:* op paneel *Size:* hoog 10 ¾, breed 12 ¾ duim	Jonkheer Menno Baron van Coehoorn	(Sold) fl 35 van der Schley [for] A
1802/06/16	AMSCH	0040	*J. le Ducq* | Een Gezelschap van Heeren en Dames, waar een goede Gelukzegster aan een Dame schynt geluk te zeggen; bevallig behandeld | *Mat:* op paneel *Size:* hoog 16, breed 18 duim	[Merrem]	(Sold) fl 40 LaFontaine
1802/06/28	AMSCH	0040	*J. le Duc* | In een Heuvelagtig Landschap, ziet men ter zyde by een Boom, een staande rosbonte Os en een rustende dito; op de grond leggen, en rusten drie Schaapen; meesterlyk gepenceelt door J. Le Duc | *Mat:* op doek *Size:* hoog 12, breed 10 duim	Anna Elink	(Sold) fl 5:15 Gruiter
1802/07/27	AKHRK	0009	*C. le Ducq* | In een deftige gemeubileerde zaal zitten twee in 't Satijn gekleede Dames, de oudste derzelve werd door de Kamenier in het hair gekapt, met een Paerelsnoer, zij is in het zwart gekleed, met een groen gegalloneerd Rokje; de andere Dame heeft een geele Kleeding, witte Mantel en Boezelaar, zij reikt een verzegeld briefje aan de Dame nevens haar, tusschen beiden staat een jonge Dame, mede zeer bevallig gekleed; verders aangenaam Bijwerk, een Tafel waarop een prachtig uitgewerkt Tapijt; een Stoel, met een uitgewerkt Mandje en Musiek- Instrumenten: benevens een goede houding, is het alles zoo uitvoerig en kunstig geschilderd, als mogelijk kan zijn | *Mat:* op paneel *Size:* hoog 15, breed 23 duim *Notes:* The artist's name was given as "C. le Ducq" but we have assumed this is an error.	Maria Stategaart	(Sold) fl 34 Regter Schagen
1802/09/06	AMSCH	0031	*J. le Ducq* | In een Corps de Garde, speelen twee Krygslieden met de kaart, terwyl een derde zittende zyn pyp schynt te rooken, verder ziet men een Haardsteede; alles geestig en fraay van Penceelbehandling | *Mat:* op paneel *Size:* hoog 11 ½, breed 12 duim	H^{n} Smit	(Sold) fl 5 van der Schley [for] S[mits wed]
1802/09/21	UTHDG	0022	*J. le Duiq* | Eene op de Guitar speelende Dame, zittende naast een Edelman, die haar met de Viool accompagneerd, zij schijnen te zingen, bij hun op den grond een open verkeerbord, omgevallen kan, enz. Verder drie persoonen, bij het vuur kaart speelende, dit aangenaam schilderij is goed van licht en hartstochten, zijnde uitvoerig en helder geschildert | *Mat:* op paneel *Size:* hoog 22 ½, breed 19 duimen		(Bought In) fl 77
1802/09/21	UTHDG	0023	*J. le Duiq* | Een vrolijk vrouwtje kaart speelende met een bejaard krijgsman, die door iemand agter hem staande, iets ontfusseld word. Aan den ingang der kamer een Officier, aandagtig toeziende. Verder twee personen bij het vuur, voor aan harnassen, enz. in alles niet minder dan het voorgaande behandeld | *Mat:* op paneel *Size:* hoog 17 ½, breed 22 duimen		(Sold) fl 60 G Roelands
1802/09/21	UTHDG	0024	*J. le Duiq* | Twee bruinbonte Patrijs-Honden, de een drinkende, verder Ruine en Landschap, zeer excellent, uitvoerig en natuurlijk geschildert | *Mat:* op paneel *Size:* hoog 12, breed 6 ½ duimen		(Bought In) fl 27
1802/09/29	AMSCH	0015	*J. le Ducq* | Een Landschap, hoog 19 ½, breed 17 duim. Doek. In een Itallaansche Bergagtige Landstreek by oude en vervallene muuren ziet men twee Honden, die om een stuk Vleesch vegten, eenige lieden schynen dit geval met vermaak aantezien, te meer daar een Boerenknaap deeze Dieren tegens elkanderen aanhitst. Een vaal zwart Schaap, en een gevlakt Bokje, leggen als in tegenoverstelling rustig aan de andere zyde; dit Stukje is fyn van qualiteit, en een der besten van deezen Meester [Un combat de deux Chiens pour un morceau de Viande plusieurs personnes s'en divertissent, d'autant plus qu'on Rustre se plait à les agasser, cette scene se passe près d'une masure, dans un site de l'Italie. Ce Tableau est executé avec une délicatesse de touche & une finesse qui font plaisir.] | *Mat:* op doek *Size:* hoog 19 ½, breed 17 duim	[Labouchere?]	(Sold) fl 46 W Reijers
1802/12/13	AMSCH	0055	*J. Le Ducq* | In een Binnekamer ziet men eenige Heeren en Dames met de Kaart speelen, op de voorgrond voor een met een Tapyt bedekten Tafel zit een Officier, op de schoot van een bevallige Vrouw, ter zyden derzelven een dienstmaagd, die een Glas Wyn inschenkt, en verder Bywerk, bevallig en uitvoerig geschilderd | *Mat:* op doek *Size:* hoog 16, breed 18 duim	Pruyssenaar [for] A	(Sold) fl 3:5 Theens
1803/07/18	AMSCH	0014	*Ducq. (J. le)* | In een Stal ziet men een aantal Militairen welke hunne Vrouwen de buit gemaakte Kleinodiën aanbieden, welke met greetigheid ontfangen worden, ter regterzyde ziet men een Man en Vrouw schynende beschonken te zyn, de ordonantie is ryk en de schildering delicaat [Dans une vaste Ecurie est representé un Partage de Bijoux entre quelques groupes de guerriers ; ils ont Partagé des Coliers de Perles, d'or & autres objets que leurs femmes ôtent des Cassettes & qu'elles examinent avec avidité. Le detail entier de cette riche Composition de vingt quatre figures seroit long & diffus, nous nous bornerons donc à observer qu'il paroit	Maria Theresia Andrioli	(Sold) fl 199 Josi

			que le Ducq ait Epuisé tout son talent & toute sa patience à Produire ce tableau : en effet l'on en trouveroit difficilement un qui seroit aussi composé & aussi fini. Les figures bien dessinées & pittoresquement costumées, sont Pleines de Caractère ; une touche spirituelle & un coloris frais ajoutent à son mérite.] | *Mat:* op paneel *Size:* hoog 18, breed 29 duim		
1803/09/07	AMSCH	0045	*J. le Ducq* | Een zittend Krygsman, in aloude Kleeding, bevallig en meesterlyk gepenceeld [Un guerrier assis et noblement habillé ; d'une touche excellente et d'une belle exécution] | *Mat:* op paneel *Size:* hoog 15, breed 12 duim	Smidt	(Sold) fl 4:10 Toselli
1803/09/07	AMSCH	0098	*J. Leduc* | Een Italiaans Landschap met hoog Geboomte en Ruïnen, op de Voorgrond legd een roodbonte Koe en verscheide Schapen, waarby een Hond, verder een Herderin met een Lam; alles van een delicaate behandeling [Un paysage d'Italie avec des hauts arbres et des ruines ; sur le devant, une vache tachetée de rouge, plusieurs brebis et un chien : plus loin une bergère avec un agneau ; le tout d'une exécution délicate] | *Mat:* op doek *Size:* hoog 19, breed 25 duim	Smidt	(Sold) fl 64 W Reijers
1804/02/27	AMSCH	0027	*Ducq. (J. le)* | In een Binnenvertrek ziet men van achteren aan een tafel, eenige Militairen met de Kaart speelen, meer voorwaards aan een tafel, met een kleed bedekt, zitten eenige bevallige Vrouwen met Officiers te speelen, den voorgrond is ryk voorzien met Vaandels, Trommels, Harnassen en andere Oorlogs-Amminutie [sic]; bevallig van licht en meesterlyk gepenceeld | *Mat:* op doek *Size:* hoog 24, breed 29 ½ duim	C	(Sold) fl 25 de Meijer
1804/05/07	AMSCH	0042	*Duc. (J. le)* | In een Vertrek ziet men op de voorgrond en Heer in deftige Kleeding, waarby een bevallige Jonge Dame, beneevens een zittende Boer, welke een Harnas schoonmaakt, iets achterwaards by een Deur twee galantiseerende Lieden enz.; uitvoerig en fraay gepenceeld	Vinkeles [for] H[affner]	(Bought In) fl 6
1804/07/25	DLGRO	0002	*A. le Duck* | Een Corps de Guarde met Spaansche Soldaten, waar onder eenen die flaauw [sic] legt en door anderen geholpen word, met veel bywerk | *Mat:* op paneel *Size:* hoog 15, breed 21 duim *Notes:* The artist's name was given as "A. le Duck" but we have assumed this is an error.	Mr Franc van der Burch Wz.	(Unknown)
1804/08/02	BDAN	0013	*J. Le Duc* | Een Corps-de-garde met eenige Soldaaten, in Spaansche Kleederen | *Mat:* op paneel *Size:* b. 16 d. h. 12 en 1 half d.	J G Calckberner	(Unknown)
1804/08/08	AMSCH	0053	*A. le Ducq* | Deze zinryke Ordonantie vertoond op de voorgrond, ter rechter zyde, een Landzicht, met Geboomten en Rivieren, by een Strandgezicht, gestoffeerd met een-en-twintig Persoonen, in deftige Kleeding, als Opper-Zeebevelhebbers, eenigen zyn béezig een Net met Visch op strand te haalen, terwyl anderen die in Korf en Mand inzamelen, een derzelven, ter linker zyde, houd in de ééne hand zyn Hoed, en in de andere een Both, verder zeilende Scheepen en een Stadgezicht; kragtig een meesterlyk gepenceeld | *Mat:* op doek *Size:* hoog 46, breed 66 duim *Notes:* The artist's name was given as "A. le Ducq" but we have assumed this is an error.	Schley [for] A	(Sold) fl 13:10 Van Iperen
1804/08/08	AMSCH	0054	*J. le Ducq* | In een Corps de Guarde van Officiers ziet men twee Krygslieden aan een Tafel zitten, speelende op 't Verkeerbord, waarna twee andere aandachtig zien, van achteren by een Vuur een Man en een Vrouw, schynende zich te warmen, en verder eenig Wapentuig, Kleederen, enz.; alleruitvoerigst en fraai van schildering | *Mat:* op paneel *Size:* hoog 17, br. 22 duim	Vink[eles] [for] W	(Bought In) fl 65
1804/10/16	DLOND	0068	*Le Duc* | Een Binnenwacht, waarin een Slapende Tambour, die door een Vrouw gewekt wordt met een brandende Zwavelstok. Un Corps de Guarde. On y voit un Tambour en sommeil; tandis qu' une Femme tient sous son nez une allumette | *Mat:* op paneel *Size:* hoog 16, breed 22		(Sold) fl 51 Thijs
1805/07/03	AMSCH	0078	*J. le Ducq* | In een Kraamkamer, ziet men ter zyde by een Schoorsteen twee Heeren, verzeld van een jonge Maagd, verders eenige Dames, de Kraamvrouw en 't Kindje, en verder bywerk; delicaat gepenceeld | *Mat:* op paneel *Size:* hoog 20, breed 28 duim	V[inkeles]	(Sold) fl 41 Gruyter
1805/07/10	AMSCH	0046	*J. le Ducq* | Een Heer en Dame by een Man, welke een Harnas schoon maakt, waarachter een andere welke een Meisje op de arm houdt, en verder bywerk; fiks op Paneel | *Mat:* op paneel *Size:* hoog 22 ½, breed 17 ¼ duim	V[inkeles] [for] H[affner]	(Sold) fl 1:10 Gruyter
1805/10/09	HGBSM	0115	*J. le Duc* | Een heer een meisje carresseerende in een binne vertrek met veel bywerk, konstig geschilderd op paneel | *Mat:* op paneel *Size:* hoog 16 breet 13 duim	T H van Willigen [or others]	(Sold) fl 5:10 Teissier
1806/06/07	RMHSN	0034	*A. le Duc* | Een Corps du Garde met Officiers, Soldaten &c. | *Mat:* op paneel *Notes:* The artist's name was given as "A. le Duc" but we have assumed this is an error.	A E K L	(Sold) fl 26 Thijs
1806/08/13	AMSCH	0042a	*Duc. (Le)* | Een uitgestrekt Landschap met Heeren en Dames te Paard, verbeeldende een Valkenjacht; meesterlyk van schildering | *Size:* hoog 25, breed 68 duim	Vinkeles [for] G[ruyter]	(Sold) fl 0:10 Gruiter
1807/06/10	HGBSM	0137	*J. le Duc* | Een Binnevertrek, waar in een Heer met een vrolijk meisje, de Heer op de Viool speelende, fraai | *Mat:* op paneel *Size:* hoog 16, breed 13 duim	Abraham Delfos [or others]	(Sold) fl 6 de Gelder
1807/06/10	HGBSM	0151	*J. le Duc* | In een Vertrek zijn eenige militairen bezig een roof te deelen, aan de voorgrond ziet men eene Dame in een smeekende houding op de	Abraham Delfos [or others]	(Sold) fl 18 S T

			kniën leggen voor een officier, fraai geschilderd | *Mat:* op paneel *Size:* hoog 10, breed 13 ½ duim		
1808/04/26	GDAN	0036	*Ducq (J. le)* | Een Binnenhuis of Corp de Garde, waar in een Officier die door een Vrouwtje iets word afgebeden, in 't verschiet, een Man en Vrouw zich bij by 't Vuur warmende, alles overheerlijk geschilderd | *Size:* hoog 14, breed 18 duim	G H Fortuyn	(Unknown)
1808/04/26	GDAN	0037	*Ducq (J. le)* | Een dito [Binnenhuis of Corp de Garde] uitmuntend, waar in een Krijgsgevangenen met eenige Koffers, voor den Commandant gebragt is en een voetval doet, waar bij eene Dame die over het geval zeer schijnt aangedaan te wezen, in 't verschiet, door een open deur, ziet men een aantal Krijgslieden in de Wapenen, terwijl den Oversten in eene woedende houding gereed is den gevangenen een vuistslag te geven, extra fraai gepenseeld | *Mat:* op paneel *Size:* hoog 13, breed 15 ½ duim	G H Fortuyn	(Unknown)
1808/04/26	GDAN	0038	*Ducq (J. le)* | Een Vorstelijke Famille, dun en fraai geschilderd | *Size:* hoog 7, breed 7 duim	G H Fortuyn	(Unknown)
1808/04/26	GDAN	0039	*Ducq (J. le)* | Een Binnenhuis waar een Heer aan een Tafel zit te slapen, agter staat een Dame die zich in een Spiegel bezigtigd, op de Tafel is een Bas met eenig Musiek en een Globe, in 't verschiet ziet men een Officier om de hoek van een deur kyken, om te zien wat er in 't Vertrek omgaat, zeer konstig en fiks geschildert | *Size:* hoog 19, breed 13 duim	G H Fortuyn	(Unknown)
1808/04/26	GDAN	0040	*Ducq (J. le)* | Een dito Binnenhuis waar in een Heer en Dame, die zeer fraai gekleed zijn, de Dame op een Stoel gezeten zijnde, word door den Heer iets aangeboden, op de Tafel staat een Kan en een Glas met roode Wijn, als ook een witte Hoed met een pluim, fiks gedaan | *Size:* hoog 12, breed 10 ½ duim	G H Fortuyn	(Unknown)
1808/06/06	RMRIJ	0030	*Ducq. (Johan le)* | Een Krijgsman, door een Moor en twee Vrouwen gevolgd, treedt een Corps de Garde binnen, waarin slapende en andere figuren zich bevinden. Verrijkt met aangenaam bijwerk en uitvoerig geschilderd [Un guerrier entre dans un Corps de Garde, suivi d'un Nègre et de deux femmes. On voit des personnes endormies et d'autres. Plusieurs accessoires décorent ce Tableau qui est d'une éxécution soignée] | *Annots:* Verk. Pictura, den haag 18 Sept 1781 (f 40.-) (RMA I) *Mat:* op paneel *Size:* Hoog 18 ¾, en breed 24 ¼ duim	Gerrit van der Pot, Heer van Groeneveld	(Sold) fl 200 Allard
1809/04/17	AMSCH	0175	*Le Ducq* | Een Binnenhuis, met twee Beelden, fiks | *Mat:* op paneel	H	(Sold) fl 0:16
1809/04/22	AMYVR	0036	*J. le Ducq* | Eenige Krijgslieden, bezig zijnde op het Verkeerbord te speelen; meesterlijk | *Mat:* op paneel *Size:* hoog 37, breed 28 duim	de Bruin	(Bought In) fl 20
1809/04/22	AMYVR	0037	*J. le Ducq* | Een Krijgsman, aan een Tafel zittende | *Mat:* op paneel *Size:* hoog 11, breed 9 duim	Juff^{r} Julikker	(Sold) fl 1:10 du Pree
1809/05/26	HADAA	A0003	*Leducq* | De Historie van Loth en zijne Dochters, krachtig en van een meesterachtige behandeling | *Mat:* op paneel *Size:* hoog 19 breed 25 duimen	Mejuffrouw de Wed David Heemskerk [or others]	(Unknown)
1809/09/06	AMSCH	0016	*Ducq (J. le)* | In een Binnenhuis vertoont zich in het midden eene zittende Dame, verzeld van eene staande, beide in deftige kleeding, waarbij eene Landloopster of Goedergelukzegster en andere Lieden; ter eene zijde staat een Heer in deftig gewaad, ter andere zijde een Paard bij een Kreb: dit voorwerp is bekend onder de benaming van het Spaansch Heidinnetje; het is helder en bevallig van schildering en coloriet | *Mat:* op paneel *Size:* hoog 18, breed 26 duim	Johannes Caudri	(Sold) fl 70 Gruyter
1810/03/07	UTWLD	0028	*le Duck* | Een binnekamer, alwaar een Heer en Dame musiek maaken, konstig en delicaat behandeld | *Size:* hoog 2 voet 2 duim, breed 2 voet	J J Woertman	(Unknown) fl 23
1810/06/20	AMSCH	0020	*J. Le Ducq* | In een Binnenkamer, zitten twee Officieren en eene Dame bij eene Tafel, ter zijde staat eene Dienstmaagd, met eene Kan en Roemer in de handen. Krachtig geschilderd | *Mat:* op doek *Size:* hoog 31, breed 39 duimen	A	(Sold) fl 12:10 Cassino
1810/06/20	AMSCH	0020a	*J. Le Ducq* | Een zich met Muziek vermakend Gezelschap, zittende voor eene Tafel. Kloek en vrolijk geschilderd | *Mat:* op doek *Size:* hoog 31, breed 37 duimen	K	(Sold) fl 1:15 du Pree
1810/08/10	RMRIJ	0004	*J. Le Ducq* | Een Binnenvertrek, waarin twee Figuren, met veel cierlijk bijwerk; zijnde een zinnebeeld op de verganglijkheid des Menschelijken Levens. Delicaat uitvoerig en overschoon geschilderd | *Mat:* op paneel *Size:* hoog 22 duim, breed 27 ½ duim		(Sold) fl 45 [or] 218 v Dyk
1810/10/13	HGDAW	0009	*J. le Ducq* | Een Corps du Garde, waarby eenige Officiers, in het verschiet een Krygsman, zittende op een Mande een Pyp aan te steken, fraay geschilderd | *Mat:* op paneel *Size:* hoog 9 ¾, breed 13 ¼ duim		(Unknown)

Ducq, Johan le (and Delen)

1804/10/29	HRBAU	0017	*Deelen (D. van); J. le Duc* | Voor aan op eene hoogte, waar een Obelisque geplaatst is, by eene pragtige Gallery, staat een Gezelschap van vier Heeren met elkander te raisonneeren, waar by een Heer en Dame komen aanwandelen, nevens nog eenige Heeren die den trap opkomen; op den tweeden grond in de diepte, by een uitmuntend Paleis, zyn een menigte Heeren en Dames, welken zig met wandelen vermaaken; wordende deze plaats door een kostbaar Gebouw ingesloten, waar door men door de Poort in een' fraaien Tuin ziet. Dit Tafereel is zo zonagtig en uitvoerig	Simon Styl	(Unknown)

behandeld, als men maar zeer zelden te zien zal krygen, en is de eer dezes Meesters waardig | *Mat:* op paneel *Size:* hoog 20 ½, breed 27 duim

Ducq, Johan le (copy after)

1804/10/16	DLOND	0240a[i]	*C. Vermeulen; Le Duc* | [Een Stuk, bevattende 13 zeer schone Copiën van de volgende Meesters. Un Tableau, contenant 13 Copies très-belles des Peintres suivans.] 9. Le Duc. Een Binnenwacht, un Corps de Garde | copy by Corn. Vermeulen (III) after Johan le Ducq *Mat:* op paneel *Size:* hoog 41, breed 55 *Notes:* The bracketed information in the title appears above lot 240a[a] and refers to lots 240a[a-m].		(Sold) fl 150 for lots 240a[a-m]. Ond d Wyngaert
1808/12/31	RMHSN	0023	*Le Duc* | Een Slapend Vrouwtje met Kindertjes, na Le Duc | *Mat:* op doek	G Spanjaart [or] H de Haas [or] C van der Looy Lans	(Unknown)

Ducq, Johan le (manner)

1801/08/19	AMSCH	0021	*le Ducq* | Twee stuks Binnenvertrekken, met Officieren en andere Beelden, zich, met speelen en drinken vermakende, fix gepenceeld, in de manier van le Ducq | *Mat:* op doek *Size:* hoog 30, breed 25 duim	W Wynen	(Sold) fl 16 Gruiter
1802/07/20	MGSAN	0011	*le Ducq* | Een Binnenvertrek, waarin eenige Krygsknechten, schoon geteekend, en fiks geschilderd, in de manier van le Ducq | *Mat:* op paneel *Size:* hoog duim 16, breed duim 21		(Unknown)
1803/06/20	AMSCH	0041	*le Ducq* | Eenige geharnasde Militaire in een Binnenvertrek, op de voorgrond eenige Harnassen en Trommels, behandeld in de manier van le Ducq | *Mat:* op paneel *Size:* hoog 23, breed 18 duim	Schley [for] G	(Sold) fl 1 Yver
1805/07/10	AMSCH	0190	*Le Ducq* | Een Studérend Man, aan een Tafel zittende en verder bywerk, als door Le Ducq	R[oos]	(Sold) fl 0:12 Royers
1806/10/16	UTWLD	0019	*Le Ducq* | Een Musiceerend gezelschap in de manier van le Ducq, ovaal | *Fmt:* ovaal	Mr P de Malapert [or] W Beeldsnyder	(Unknown)

Dughet, Gaspard (Gaspard Poussin)

1802/06/16	AMSCH	0137	*C. Poussin* | Een Bergachtig Landschap, doorsneeden met een Waterval, op de voorgrond met Beelden gestoffeerd, in 't verschiet eenige Gebouwen; fiks behandeld | *Mat:* op doek *Size:* hoog 22 ½, breed 27 ½ duim	[Merrem]	(Sold) fl 50 Gruiter
1803/04/27	AMSCH	0021	*G. Poussin* | Deux beaux païsages, par G. Poussin, avec des figures | *Size:* h. 4 ¼, l. 6 ¼ pieds	A	(Sold) fl 16:5 Hodges
1803/04/27	AMSCH	0022	*G. Poussin* | Deux dito [beaux païsages] dito [par G. Poussin, avec des figures] | *Size:* h. 3 ½, l. 5 pieds *Notes:* It is unclear what "dito" refers to in the title.	A	(Sold) fl 13 Gruiter
1803/04/27	AMSCH	0023	*G. Poussin* | Un dito [beau païsage] dito [par G. Poussin, avec des figures] | *Size:* h. 3 ½, l. 4 ½ pieds *Notes:* It is unclear what "dito" refers to in the title.	A	(Sold) fl 9:10 Gruiter
1810/07/26	AMSCH	0058	*Poussin (G.)* | Een Landschap, met Bergen en een Waterval. Meesterlijk geschilderd | *Mat:* op doek *Size:* hoog 13, breed 18 duimen	Cassino	(Sold) fl 20 J^{mo} de Vries [and] Hulswit
1810/07/26	AMSCH	0059	*Poussin (G.)* | Een fraai Landschap, met Geboomte en stoffagie. Als de voorgaande | *Mat:* op doek *Size:* hoog 23, breed 29 duimen	Cassino	(Bought In) fl 6:15
1810/07/26	AMSCH	0060	*Poussin (G.)* | Een Landschap als de voorgaande | *Mat:* op doek *Size:* hoog 12, breed 15 duimen	Cassino	(Sold) fl 1 Van Iperen

Duigenberg [Unidentified] (copy by)

1804/10/16	DLOND	0067	*Duigenberg; naar van Thol* | Een oud Vrouwtje uit een Vengster ene Waterpot uitgietende, toogsgewys. Une vieille Femme dans une fenetre. Elle vuide son pot de Chambre | copy by Duigenberg after D. Tol *Mat:* op doek op paneel *Size:* hoog 9, breed 7		(Unknown)

Dujardin, Karel

1801/05/11	AMSCH	0034	*K. du Jardin* | Voor een Herberg by een antiecq Gebouw, zit een Man te paard, schynende een glas drank van een Jonge aantenemen, ter zyde een staand Man en twee Honden, krachtig en zonachtig gepenceeld | *Size:* hoog 14, breed 12 duim *Loc:* Hamburg, Deutschland. Kunsthalle. (180)	E[lias]	(Sold) fl 455 Jan Spaan
1801/05/11	AMSCH	0035	*K. du Jardin* | Een Italiaansch boomryk Landschap, met een Waterplas, waarin twee Vissers bezig zyn met vissen, zynde mede als de voorgaande behandeld | *Mat:* op paneel *Size:* hoog 16, breed 12 duim	E[lias]	(Sold) fl 165 Coclers
1801/05/11	AMSCH	0036	*K. du Jardin* | Een Vanitas, men ziet een bevallige Jongeling, staande met de linker voet op een waterbel, welke in een schulp, op een woelende zee dryft, houdende in de eene hand een schulp, met waterbellen, ziende zeer vergenoegt na eenige geblaasene bellen, die voor hem zweeven, alles is van eene delicaaten en uitvoerige penceel behandeling | *Mat:* op doek *Size:* hoog 45, breed 36 duim *Loc:* København, Danmark. Statens Museum for Kunst. (195)	P[ruyssenaar]	(Sold) fl 140 Pruijssenaar [for] R
1801/06/10	AMSCH	0090	*Jardin. (K. du)* | Een Landschap, op de voorgrond een Landloopster met een Jonge, een Ezel benevens een wit Bokje, alles is Zonachtig en van een fyne penceels behandeling | *Mat:* op paneel *Size:* hoog 9, breed 10 duim	Herman ten Kate	(Sold) fl 100 Spruit van Gend
1802/05/24	HGBAK	0033	*K. du Jardin* | Een Stal met Runderen, een gezadeld Paard, een Schaap en Geit &c. door K. du Jardin, hoog 9 ½ d., breed 14 duim, op doek, zwarte	Mejuffrouw A van der Mieden	(Sold) fl 10 Te Ché

			lyst en vergulde binnenrand | *Mat:* op doek *Size:* hoog 9 ½ duim, breed 14 duim		
1802/06/16	AMSCH	0084	*K. du Jardin* | By de Ruïne van een trots Gebouw, ziet men eenige Herders met een menigte Osen, Schapen, Bokken en beladen Muil- Ezels, als meede een aangenaam verschiet; alles delicaat en Zonachtig behandeld | *Mat:* op paneel *Size:* hoog 27 ½, breed 22 ½ duim	[Merrem]	(Sold) fl 156 Reijers
1802/06/16	AMSCH	0085	*K. du Jardin* | In een Landschap, op de voorgrond een grazige Heuvel, gestoffeerd en met een graazend Paard, staande Ossen, Schaap en Ram; verder een Veehoeder met een Hond speelende; zonachtig en uitvoering van Penceel behandeling | *Mat:* op doek *Size:* hoog 12, breed 10 ½ duim	[Merrem]	(Sold) fl 42 Reijers
1802/09/06	AMSCH	0055	*K. du Jardin* | In een Bergachtig Landschap met Geboomten, vertoont zig op de voorgrond, een gaande Vrouw en Jongeling, die twee Ossen en eenige Schaapen door een Waterbeekje dryven; zonachtig en meesterlyk fix van Penceelbehandeling | *Mat:* op doek op paneel *Size:* hoog 15, breed 20 duim	H[n] Smit	(Sold) fl 60 van der Schley [for] S[mits wed]
1802/09/29	AMSCH	0023	*K du Jardin* | Een Landschap, hoog 17 ¼, breed 22 duim. Doek. Zynde een Italiaansch gezigt met Bergen en Geboomten, Gebouwen en Waterval, gestoffeerd met Beelden en Beelden; van eene aangename Ordenantie, en zonagtig van Coloriet [Un Paysage d'Italie avec figures & animaux l'ordonnance en est agréable & la couleur vraie.] | companion to lot 24 *Mat:* op doek *Size:* hoog 17 ¼, breed 22 duim	[Labouchere?]	(Sold) fl 30 C S Roos
1802/09/29	AMSCH	0024	*K du Jardin* | Een Land- en Watergezigt, hoog 17 ¼, breed 22 duim. Doek. Dit Schildery verbeeld gelyk het voorgaande, een aangenaam Italiaansch bergagtig Landschap, met Gebouwen en bevallige Stoffagie; in en omtrent een groote Waterplas; zeer zonagtig en meesterlyk behandelt [Ce Tableau fait pendant au precédent. On y remarque une Eau qu'une Bergere passe avec des animaux, plusieurs autres figures & du Bétail enrichissent cette belle composition. Le soleil produit dans ces deux Tableaux beaucoup d'Effet.] | companion to lot 23 *Mat:* op doek *Size:* hoog 17 ¼, breed 22 duim	[Labouchere?]	(Sold) fl 28 C S Roos
1802/11/01	DOBRA	0195	*C. du Jardin* | Twee landschappen met Beesten, gemerkt C. du Jardin | *Mat:* op paneel *Inscr:* C. du Jardin (signed)		(Unknown) fl 2:5
1802/12/13	AMSCH	0218	*K. du Jardin* | Twee stuks voorwerpen, verbeelde twee staande Ezels; meesterlyk en fiks gepenceeld	Schley [for] Lauwers	(Sold) fl 2 van Dijl
1803/08/17	AMSCH	0040	*Jardin. (C. du)* | Dit uitmuntend kunstjuweel steld voor, op een grazigen heuvel een roodbonte staande Os, en een leggende Koe, waarby een witte Patryshond met een bruin gevelkte kop, agter den heuvel staat een jonge Herder, leunende op zyn stok, omkleed met een Schapenvagt; voorts een menigte Kruiden en aangenaam bergachtig Verschiet; het luchtje is dun, het zonligt frappant, en de schildering van zyn allerdelicaatste behandeling | *Mat:* op paneel *Size:* hoog 9, breed 10 duim	Anna Catharina Putman	(Bought In) fl 700
1803/08/17	AMSCH	0041	*Jardin (C. du)* | Voor een Schuur, waarby een opgaande Boom, staat een Herder, waarby eenige Bokjes en Schapen, delicaat en uitvoerig gepenceeld | *Mat:* op paneel *Size:* hoog 6, breed 8 duim	Anna Catharina Putman	(Sold) fl 30 for lots 41 & 42. Pruijssenaar
1803/08/17	AMSCH	0042	*Jardin (C. du)* | Voor een dito Schuur staat een Ezel, behandeld als de voorgaande | *Mat:* op paneel *Size:* hoog 6, breed 8 duim *Notes:* It is unclear what "dito" refers to in the title.	Anna Catharina Putman	(Sold) fl 30 for lots 41 & 42. Pruijssenaar
1803/08/17	AMSCH	0043	*Jardin. (C. du)* | Een Manspourtrait met een Hoed en Bef, zynde van een behaagelyke behandeling | *Mat:* op paneel *Size:* hoog 23, breed 18 ½ duim	Anna Catharina Putman	(Sold) fl 17 Yver
1803/12/12	AMSCH	0045	*C. du Jardin* | Voor een Stal ziet men een Man, névens hem eenige Schaapen en een Bokje; zeer fraai gepenceeld | *Size:* hoog 7, breed 8 duim	B	(Sold) fl 12:10 Jozi
1804/02/27	AMSCH	0059	*Jardin. (C. du)* | In een Italiaansch Landschap, vertoont zig voor een oud Gebouw twee Ezels en eenige Hoenders, door een open Deur ziet men een Smit, bezig aan zyn smeeden; meesterlyk geschilderd | *Mat:* op paneel *Size:* hoog 10, breed 8 duim	C	(Sold) fl 12 Coclers
1804/05/07	AMSCH	0087	*Jardyn. (C. du)* | In een natuurlyk Landschap, by eenig Geboomte legt een Koe en Bok, terzyden op een hoogten een rustende Landman, en agterwaards een bevallig verschiet; bevallig geschildert | *Mat:* op paneel *Size:* hoog 8, breed 10 ½ duim	Vinkeles [for] G	(Sold) fl 9:10 van der Schley A [for] Van der Vinne
1804/08/08	AMSCH	0093	*C. du Jardin* | In een Landschap voor een Schuur, by eenig Geboomte, ziet men eenige staande en leggende Schaapen, en een rustende Herder, achterwaards eenige Gebouwen, zonachtig geschilderd | *Size:* hoog 8, breed 7 duim	Vink[eles] [for] K[=Gruyter?]	(Sold) fl 2 Izaac Smit
1805/12/16	AMSCH	0032	*K. du Jardin* | Een Italiaansch Landschap, gestoffeerd met Huislieden, en verschillende zoorten van Vée, verder een Bergachtig verschiet; fiks op Doek geschilderd | *Mat:* op doek *Size:* hoog 20, breed 22 duim	R[oos]	(Sold) fl 9 Spaan
1806/08/13	AMSCH	0082	*Jardin. (K. du)* | In een Italiaansch Landschap, voor een Herberg vertoont zich een Jongeling op een Ezel zittende; verzelt van op de Phiool speelende Land-jongens en danzende Boeren Kinderen; dit stukje is geestig geordineert, bevallig van coloriet en uitvoerig gepenceeld | *Mat:* op doek *Size:* hoog 20, breed 18 duim	van der Voort	(Sold) fl 1220 Van Iperen
1808/05/18	LNAN	0046	*Dujantijn* | Een Bergachtig Landschap, met veel Beelden en Beesten | *Notes:* The artist's name "Dujantijn" was added in by hand in the RKDH copy of the catalogue.	Mr Cornelis Versluys	(Unknown)

1808/06/06	RMRIJ	0061	*Jardijn. (Karel du)* | Een Italiaansch bergachtig Landschap. Op den voorgrond vertoont zich een roodbonte Os; hierbij een bruin Paard van achteren in 't verkort te zien; vooraan een liggend Schaap, benevens twee Herders-jongens; nog voor den voorgrond een stronk van een boom, waarbij een hond, enz. Helder, uitvoerig en schoon behandeld [Paysage Italien. Sur le devant d'une Prairie émaillée, où l'on croît voir la rosée sur l'herbe, est couché un beau Mouton, derrière lui sont des Brebis, un Boeuf et un Cheval, dont le raccourci est parfaitement imité. Du côté opposé vers la droite, on apperçoît un Chien, un Tronc d'arbre et quelques Plantes etc. Le beau lointain, et le ciel clair et argentin indiquent parfaitement la fraicheur d'une matinée dudit Pays. Ce Tableau savamment traité, et de la plus belle exécution, est dans toute sa pureté, et fait honneur à cette Collection] | *Annots:* Coll Marquis de Breteuil. Gek. Juli 1790 van Fouquet te Ny'ann[?] (f 1600.-) (RMA I) *Mat:* op doek op paneel *Size:* Hoog 10 ¼ en breed 12 ¾ duim	Gerrit van der Pot, Heer van Groeneveld	(Sold) fl 1525 Josi
1808/08/23	AMSCH	0083	*Jardin (K. du)* | Twee stuks Italiaansche Bergachtige Landschapen, beide gestoffeert met Huislieden, en verschillende soorten van Vée, die door een Beekje gedreeven worden; in den andere grazende en rustende Beesten; meesterlijk en kunstig behandeld | *Mat:* op doek *Size:* Ieder hoog 20, breed 26 duim	C	(Sold) fl 30 Th Spaan
1808/09/13	HABRU	0043	*K. du Jardin* | Een Landschap, waar een Vrouw nevens een Hond uit het Water stapt, agter haar een Ezel		(Unknown) fl 25
1808/12/30	HGIMM	[0071c]	*Karel du Jardyn* | Voorts een exquis kabinetje Schilderijen van voorname Nederlandsche Meesters, welke uit hoofde van de kortheid des tijds niet stuk voor stuk kunnen beschreven worden; doch waarvan de beschrijving op den Kijkdag zal voorhanden zijn. Dus wij hier alleen de namen van eenige dier Meesters laten volgen, als: A. Kuyp, Ruysdaal, Karel du Jardyn, Loqwi ('t beste dat hij schilderde) Hondekoeter, van Dyk, Janson, Moesgever, Kamphuyzen, van Gooijen, A. van der Neer, T. Wyk, Huchtenburgh, Zolemaker, van Hassel, A. Vermeulen, van Dongen, Scheffer, van Os enz. | *This Lot:* Een Schilderij, Karel du Jardyn *Notes:* Because this lot was not numbered in the catalogue, we have assigned the number.		(Unknown)
1809/07/19	AMSCH	0023	*Jardin (K. du)* | Dit uitmuntend Kabinetstukje verbeelt een aangenaam duinachtig Landschap, ter regterzijde bij zwaar Geboomte ziet men een Boeren-Schuur, waar bij een Watermolen, benevens een Put, waaraan een Huisman bezig Water te scheppen, verder op den voorgrond een staande Ezel, vier liggende en drie staande Varkens en twee Hennen. De onbegrijpelijke uitvoerigheid, en het invallend zonlicht, gepaard met een bevallig koloriet, maken dit stukje zeer behaaglijk, en tot een der beste van dezen groten Meester | *Mat:* op doek *Size:* hoog 17, breed 15 duim *Loc:* Oxford, England, UK. Ashmolean Museum. (A665)	[Bicker]	(Sold) fl 3000 Teengs
1809/07/19	AMSCH	0024	*Jardin (K. du)* | In een Italiaansch Landschap ziet men op den voorgrond een jongeling, leidende een wit gezadeld Paard bij den Toom, verder eene Rijschool, bij Gebouwen en Geboomte. Krachtig en breed geschilderd | *Mat:* op doek *Size:* hoog 23, breed 28 duim *Loc:* Dublin, Eire. National Gallery of Ireland. (544)	[Wijkersloot?]	(Sold) fl 190 Coclers
1809/07/19	AMSCH	0025	*Jardin (K. du)* | In een Italiaansch Bergachtig Landschap zit op den voorgrond eene bevallige Vrouw, verseld van twee Kinderen, waar bij eene staande Koe en een Schaap. Meesterlijk als het voorgaande behandeld | *Mat:* op doek *Size:* hoog 23, breed 28 duim	[Wijkersloot?]	(Sold) fl 40 Gruyter
1810/03/26	RMMUY	0084	*K. du Jardin* | Een Hollandsch Landschap, met Schapen, figuur en bijwerk. Gemerkt K. du Jardin [Un Paysage, avec un Berger, et plusieurs Moutons, dans le genre de C. du Jardin ; un joli tableau.] | *Annots:* Genre duJardin Perdu (BPG) *Inscr:* K. du Jardin (signed)	Daniel de Jongh Az	(Sold) fl 40 van Eyk s'Hage
1810/05/22	AMSCH	0042	*Jardin. (K. du)* | Op een Heuvel met Geboomten ziet men eenen Heer op een Paard, voorts twee zittende Mannen, welke bezig zijn te vinken; geestig en uitvoerig behandeld | *Mat:* op paneel *Size:* hoog 9, breed 11 duim	Johannes van de Putte Nicolaasz.	(Sold) fl 340 Hulswit
1810/08/01	AMSCH	0049	*Jardin (Karel du)* | Een Heuvelachtig Landschap met een Water doorsneden, verlevendigd door Visschers, en eenig Vee; men ziet Geboomte in het verschiet [Point de vue donnant sur une Colline, coupé par une Riviere ; il est orné de Pêcheurs et d'Animaux ; vèrs l'horison on apperçoit quelques Arbres] | *Annots:* Bagatelle insignifiante. NB : ce n'est qu'une vraie babiole. (NGW); Vente le Brun No. 128. fr. 1555 (SMLN) *Mat:* op koper *Fmt:* rond *Size:* hoog 9, breed 9 duimen	Mr Pieter de Smeth van Alphen	(Sold) fl 500 Texier, Gerbet en Comp [for] Le Brun
1810/08/06	AMSCH	0051	*Jardin (K. du)* | Op eene Plaats met groote Gebouwen en Gedenktekens zit op den voorgrond bij een bank, waarop Brood en een Fles, zijn geplaats een jong Officier, over hem bij een steenen voetstuk zitten twee Savoijards, waar agter een staand bevallig Meisje, houdende een Schotel met Gebraad; het is bevallig van koloriet en fraai geschilderd | *Annots:* De Choiseul [incorrect] (BPG) *Mat:* op doek *Size:* hoog 34, breed 28 duimen *Loc:* New Haven, CT, USA. Yale University. Art Gallery. (1966.84)	A	(Sold) fl 385 van Iperen [for] Vriesman
1810/08/06	AMSCH	0052	*Jardin (K. du)* | Diana bij Endijmion, in een Landschap met Honden en Jachtgereedschap | *Annots:* Venus Adonis (BPG) *Mat:* op doek *Size:* hoog 33, breed 58 duimen	R[oos]	(Sold) fl 40 Van Leen

Dujardin, Karel (copy after)

1804/08/08	AMSCH	0152	*P. G. van Os; K. du Jardin* | In een Landschap ziet men een staande Vrouw, névens dezelve een witte Os, een rustend Ezel, en twee Schaapen; zonachtig en bevallig geschilderd, door denzelven [P. G. van Os], op Doek, naar een Schildery door K. du Jardin | copy by Pieter G. Os after K. Dujardin *Mat:* op doek *Size:* hoog 13, breed 16 duim	Schley [for] B	(Sold) fl 3:5 Graffelman
1805/07/10	AMSCH	0235	*C. du Jardin* | Een Quakzalver op zyn Theater, na C. du Jardin	Y[ver]	(Bought In) fl 1:5

Dujardin, Karel (manner)

1803/09/07	AMSCH	0228	*C. du Jardin* | Voor een Stal staat een wit Paard, en een jonge Ezel, verder een slapende Vrouw, fix behandeld in de manier van C. du Jardin [Devant une écurie, un cheval blanc et un jeune ânon ; au fond une femme endormie ; dans la manière de C. du Jardin] | *Mat:* op paneel *Size:* hoog 9 ½, breed 12 ½ duim	Smidt	(Sold) fl 26 v der Schleij
1806/08/13	AMSCH	0297	*C. du Jardin* | Een Boom- en Bergachtige Landschapje, met staand en rustend Vée; als C. du Jardin	Vinkeles [for] F	(Sold) fl 1:10 L Pakker
1807/08/26	AMSCH	0106	*C. du Jardin* | Twee stuks, zynde Boomryke Landschappen, de eene met staand en leggend Vee, waarby eene Boerin; de andere met Herders, die Vee door een Rivier dryven; fraai gestoffeerd, en geestig als C. du Jardin behandeld | *Mat:* op doek *Size:* hoog 21, breed 24 duim	Joseph Vallette	(Sold) fl 11 Gruiter
1807/08/26	AMSCH	0279	*K. du Jardin* | Een Italiaansch Landschap met een Ruïne, waar in een Huisman met verscheiden Vee; in de manier van K. du Jardin | *Mat:* op paneel	Roos [for] A	(Sold) fl 1:5 Coclair
1809/05/26	HADAA	0046	*C. du Jardin* | Een Landschap met Koeijen en Schapen, breed en kloek geschilderd als door C. du Jardin	Mejuffrouw de Wed David Heemskerk [or others]	(Unknown)
1809/07/25	HGBSM	0024	*Dujardin* | Een Landschap met Koeyen en Schapen, waarby een Boer die op de Hoorn blaast, in de trant van Dujardin geordonneert | *Mat:* op paneel *Size:* hoog 9 en 1 half, breed 12 en 1 half duim	D van der Aa [or] E B ten Dall	(Sold) fl 40 de Gruijter
1810/03/26	RMMUY	0059	*K. du Jardijn* | Een Hollandsch Landschap, met Koeijen, Schaap en Bok. In het verschiet een Dorp en eenige stoffagie; als door K. du Jardijn, maar veel overschilderd [Un Paysage hollandois, plusieurs animaux, et un village dans le lointain ; dans le gout de C. du Jardin.] | *Annots:* Copie vandevelde [i.e., Van de Velde] (BPG)	Daniel de Jongh Az	(Sold) fl 17 Le Brun Parys
1810/05/22	AMSCH	0141	*K. du Jardin* | Voor een open Stal staat een wit Paard en eene Ezel; in de manier van K. du Jardin geschilderd	Johannes van de Putte Nicolaasz.	(Sold) fl 34 Gruyter [for] Dirkse
1810/06/20	AMSCH	0157	*K. du Jardin* | Twee stuks Landschappen, met Beelden en Beesten, in de manier van K. du Jardin	B	(Sold) fl 0:16 du Pree

Dujardin, Karel (style)

1808/10/28	AMVRS	0076	*K. du Jardin* | Op een heuvel ligt een roskleurige Koe met eenige Schapen, waarbij een slapende Jongen. Natuurlijk in den stijl van K. du Jardin	Marten Udink	(Sold) fl 7 Coclers

Dupré, Daniel

1803/08/01	AMSCH	0028	*Du Pre. (D.)* | Een bevallig, zonagtig en boomryk Italiaans Landschap, zynde een Gezigt op de Wildbaan te Larriccia, en in het verschiet op een hoogte vertoond zig 't Pallazzo Chigi, zynde de voorgrond gestoffeerd met eenige reizigers en andere Figuuren, aangenaam van coloriet en uitvoerig gepenceeld | *Mat:* op doek *Size:* hoog 23, breed 29 duim	H	(Sold) fl 47 Yver
1803/08/01	AMSCH	0029	*Du Pre (D.)* | Een aangenaam Landschap, met hoog Geboomte en Boerewoningen, gestoffeerd met een belaaden Hessekar, eenige Beelden en Schaapen, alles zeer uitvoerig en warm gepenceeld | *Mat:* op doek *Size:* hoog 16 ½, breed 21 duim	R	(Sold) fl 70 v d Schleij [for] P[utte]
1805/07/03	AMSCH	0134	*D. du Pré* | Twee stuks aller aangenaamste Boom- en Duinryke Landschapjes met Rivieren, beide ryk gestoffeerd met Herders en Herderinnen, met hun Vee, Vrachtkarren met Paarden bespannen, enz.; aller zonachtigst en uitvoerig gepenceeld | *Mat:* op doek *Size:* hoog 21, breed 29 duim	Y	(Sold) fl 36 Josi
1806/05/05	AMSCH	0114	*D. du Pré* | Twee stuks zeer fraaije berg en boomryke Zwitsersche Landschappen; geestig gestoffeerd en zonachtig behandeld door D. du Pré | *Mat:* op doek *Size:* hoog 16, breed 21 duim	R[oos]	(Bought In) fl 77
1810/05/22	AMSCH	0024	*Dupré (D.)* | Een aangenaam Landschap, met Geboomte en Boere Woningen, gestoffeerd met een beladen Hessekar, Beelden en Schapen; zonachtig en meesterlijk fraai gepenceeld | *Mat:* op doek *Size:* hoog 16 ½, breed 21 duim	Johannes van de Putte Nicolaasz.	(Sold) fl 19:10 Yver

Dürer, Albrecht

1802/12/13	AMSCH	0049	*A. Durer* | Deeze fraaije Ordenantie, verbeeld de Koningen die het Kind Jesu aanbidden, en geschenken offeren, de Caracters zyn natuurlyk verbeeld, de schikking en Coloriet is bevallig en van een uitvoerige penceel behandeling, door A. Durer, Ao. 1512 | *Mat:* op paneel *Size:* hoog 17, breed 13 ½ duim *Inscr:* A. Durer, Ao. 1512 (signed and dated?) *Notes:* It is unclear whether the name and date are inscribed on the painting.	Schley [for] Lauwers	(Sold) fl 20:10 Yver

1805/10/21	GRBOL	0001	*A. Durer* | Een Capitaal Stuk met Beelden	Gerardus Nicolaus Heerkens	(Unknown)
1806/05/05	AMSCH	0192	*A. Durer* | Een Vrouw met een Anjelier in de hand; door A. Durer, zynde van agteren met een doodshoofd	H	(Sold) fl 4:5 Josi
1808/04/26	GDAN	0034	*Duren (A.)* | Een Autaar [sic] stuk, verbeeldende de Wijzen uit het Oosten, komende om 't Kind Jezus te aanbidden, brengende met zich kostbare Geschenken, fraai en uitvoerig geschilderd | *Size:* hoog 36, breed 48 duim	G H Fortuyn	(Unknown)
1808/06/11	RMRIJ	0034	*Albert Durer, 1539* | Het Laatste Avondmaal, in de manier van Leonard da Vinci, ongemeen zuiver en schoon van coleur, gaaf en wel geconserveert | *Mat:* op paneel *Size:* hoog 24, breed 31 ¼ duim *Inscr:* Albert Durer, 1539 (signed and dated?) *Notes:* It is unclear whether the name and date are inscribed on the painting.		(Sold) fl 7:5 v Yperin [or] V Giesen
1808/09/13	HABRU	0022	*A. Durer* | Een Boer en Boerin		(Sold) fl 1:2 V D W[illigen]
1810/07/26	AMSCH	0027	*Durer (A.)* | Joachim houdende een Schaap in zijn Arm, waarbij andere Beelden enz | *Mat:* op paneel *Size:* hoog 25, breed 16 duimen	Cassino	(Sold) fl 17 Boelhouwer
			Dürer, Albrecht (and Holbein, H. (II); copy after)		
1808/06/06	RMRIJ	0017	*Bordieu. (du); Steenwijk. (H. J. van); A. Durer; Holbeijn* | Eene zeer getrouwe kopij naar de origineele Schilderij van A. Durer en H. Holbeijn, Desiderius Erasmus verbeeldende. Het bijwerk door H. J. van Steenwijk. Alles zeer uitvoerig behandeld [Copie fidelle du Portrait de Désiré Erasme d'aprés l'original d'Albert Durer et H. Holbeyn. Les accessoires sont peints par van Steenwyk] | copy by P. Dubordieu and Hend. Steenwyck after Dürer and H. Holbein (II) *Annots:* Geschenk Teding Berkhout (RMA I) *Mat:* op paneel *Size:* Hoog 9 ½, en breed 7 ½ duim	Gerrit van der Pot, Heer van Groeneveld	(Sold) fl 21 du Pré
			Dürer, Albrecht (or Dürer, manner; or Lucas van Leyden, or Lucas van Leyden, manner)		
1810/06/06	RMMUY	0088	*Lucas van Leiden; Albert Durer* | Een doode Christus, Maria en een Heilige. Ongemeen uitvoerig en raar. Door of als Lucas van Leiden, of Albert Durer | *Mat:* op paneel		(Sold) fl 5 Luchtmans
			Dürer, Albrecht (school)		
1802/06/29	HGDAW	0031	*Albert Durer* | Een Spotstuk op de Reformateurs uit het School van Albert Durer		(Unknown)
			Dusart		
1810/03/07	UTWLD	0026	*Dusart* | Twee extra fraaye Schilderstukjes zeer fix en uitvoerig behandeld | *Size:* hoog 8 duim, breed 6 duim	J J Woertman	(Unknown) fl 122
			Dusart (or Dusart, copy after)		
1802/05/11	GRGRW	0046	*Dusjaard* | Een Oud Besje, hare Familie voorlezende, door of naar Dusjaard [Schilderijen met Olie-Verf; In zwarte Lijsten] | *Mat:* in olyverf *Notes:* The bracketed information in the title appears above lot 1 and refers to lots 1 to 79a.	Arnold Sicco Werumeus	(Unknown) fl 1:2
			Dusart (copy after)		
1802/07/21	HGKAN	0011[a]	*Dusart* | Een stuk na Dusart en een naar Brouwer | *This Lot:* Een stuk; lot 11[b] is copy after Adr. Brouwer		(Unknown)
			Dusart, A. [Unidentified]		
1808/12/31	RMHSN	0028	*A. Dusart* | Een Groot Stuk, waar in Vier Beelden die Musiceeren, uitvoerig behandeld door A. Dusart | *Mat:* op doek	G Spanjaart [or] H de Haas [or] C van der Looy Lans	(Unknown)
			Dusart, Cornelis		
1801/04/13	AMSCH	0017	*C. Dusart* | In een boere Binnenhuis ziet men een oude vrouw, eenige speelende Kinderen, en andere huislieden, in 't verschiet, voorts een slapende hond, huisraad, en andere, als door A. van Ostade gepenceelde onderwerpen, die dit stukje bevallig maken | *Mat:* op paneel *Size:* hoog 16, breed 14 duim	Pierre Fouquet, junior	(Sold) fl 63 Spruit v Gend
1801/06/10	AMSCH	0046	*Dusart. (C.)* | In een Binnehuis zit een Boer de Courant te leezen, by een driestal, waarop een Tabaks-Comvoir, alles is breed behandeld | *Mat:* op paneel *Size:* hoog 12 ½ breed 10 duim	Herman ten Kate	(Sold) fl 75 C S Roos
1801/06/10	AMSCH	0047	*Dusart. (C.)* | Deeze Ryke ordonantie, verbeeld een Boere-Binnehuis, op de voorgrond zit een vrolyke Gast, waar by een staande Hospes hem een glas Bier schenkende, veele speelen, eenige andere Boeren in 't verkeerbort, terwyl twee andere Huyslieden by den Haart een Pyp rooken, geestig gestoffeert met verscheide Huisraad, alles is natuurlyk en Meesterlyk behandeld | *Mat:* op doek *Size:* hoog 46 breed 58 duim	Herman ten Kate	(Sold) fl 65 Van Iperen
1801/06/10	AMSCH	0048	*Dusart. (C.)* | Een Boeren Buiten-Huis, voor het zelve ziet men eenige Landlieden met elkander in gesprek, op de voorgrond eenige varkens, alles zeer natuurlyk en meesterlyk van penceel | *Mat:* op paneel *Size:* hoog 11, breed 14 duim	Herman ten Kate	(Sold) fl 100 Spruit van Gend
1801/06/10	AMSCH	0049	*Dusart. (C.)* | Voor een Boeren-Buitenhuis, ziet men verscheide Huys-lieden, op den voorgrond een Vrouw met een Glas en een Kan in de	Herman ten Kate	(Sold) fl 49 Stevens

			Hand, schynende aan een Man nevens haar te zullen aangeeven, natuurlyk behandeld | *Mat:* op doek *Size:* hoog 14, breed 12 duim		
1801/06/10	AMSCH	0050	*Dusart. (C.)* | In een Binnenhuis ziet men voor een Tafel, een bedaagd Man, een Kind pap gevende, op de Tafel ziet men een opgesneden Haring en Uijen; geestig en kragtig van penceels behandeling | *Mat:* op paneel *Size:* hoog 13, breed 11 duim	Herman ten Kate	(Sold) fl 86 C S Roos
1801/06/10	AMSCH	0051	*Dusart. (C.)* | Een dito [Boeren?] Binnenhuis, waar in verscheide vrolyke Huislieden; helder en fraai van schildering | *Mat:* op doek op paneel *Size:* hoog 13, breed 11 duim	Herman ten Kate	(Sold) fl 95 Pruyssenaar
1801/06/10	AMSCH	0052	*Dusart. (C.)* | Een Boeren Binnenhuis, gestoffeerd met verscheide Beelden, op den voorgrond ziet men twee derzelve in het verkeerbord speelen, verders een Hond en eenig Huisraad, uitvoerig gepenceeld | *Mat:* op paneel *Size:* hoog 19, breed 14 duim	Herman ten Kate	(Sold) fl 97 Taijs
1801/10/19	AMSCH	0022	*Dusart (C)* | Een Mannetje met een Beuling in de eene hand en een brief in de andere; zeer aardig verbeeld en uitvoerig geschildert | *Mat:* op paneel *Fmt:* ovaal *Size:* hoog 5, breed 4 duim	Jonkheer Menno Baron van Coehoorn	(Sold) fl 9 Van Dijl
1802/06/16	AMSCH	0036	*C. Dusart* | Dit uitmuntend Tafreel, vol gewoel van vrolyke Huislieden, vertoont een Boere Kermis in een Dorp: op de voorgrond voor een Herberg danst een Boer en Boerinnetje, terwyl een ander Huisman met een Bierkan in de hand en een pyp, zich Danzende schynt te vermaken, onder het speelen van Phiool en Doedelzak, een menigte zoo Mans, Vrouwe en Kinderen zyn aanschouwers van deeze vreugd; verders ziet men spellen, Kwakzalvers op het Theater en Koekkramen, waar by verscheiden vrolyke Lieden: verder een aangenaam verschiet van een Kerkgebouw en andere Woningen. De Caracters zyn verwonderlyk Natuurlyk, het Licht en Coloriet bevallig, en van een aller uitvoerigste Penceel behandeling, en kan met regt voor een der Capitaalste van deeze meester gehouden werden | *Mat:* op koper *Size:* hoog 16 ½, breed 19 duim *Loc:* Helsingfors, Suomen. Sinebrychoffin Taidemuseo. (S 116)	[Merrem]	(Sold) fl 860 LaFontaine
1802/06/28	AMSCH	0041	*C. Dusart* | Voor een Boeren Buitenhuis, ziet men eenige Vastenavond-gekken; bevallig geordonneerd door C. Dusart | *Mat:* op paneel *Size:* hoog 11, breed 13 duim	Anna Elink	(Sold) fl 20:10 Kamphuis
1802/06/28	AMSCH	0042	*C. Dusart* | Twee stuks met Boeren gestoffeerde Binnehuizen, uitvoerig op Koper | *Mat:* op koper *Size:* hoog 7, breed 6 duim	Anna Elink	(Sold) fl 3:10 Texier
1802/07/27	AKHRK	0008	*Cornelis Duzart, 1686* | In dit bevallig stukje ziet men buiten een Herberg een menigte rookende en drinkende Boeren, die aandachtig zien en hooren na een Liereman, op de voorgrond op een Bank zit een zich niet wel bevindend en aartig gekleed Vrouwtje, hebbende te veel gedronken van een zeker vogt, welk zij in een vol Glas op haar Schoot houdt; een bejaard Boertje ondersteunt haar, terwijl zijn rechte hand haare linker hand vast houd. Alles is keurlijk behandeld en van een smeltend Penceel | *Mat:* op paneel *Size:* hoog 11 ½, breed 14 ½ duim *Inscr:* Cornelis Duzart, 1686 (signed and dated?) *Notes:* It is unclear whether the name and date are inscribed on the painting.	Maria Stategaart	(Sold) fl 38 Juffr Boerse
1802/09/06	AMSCH	0032	*C. Dusart* | Een staande Lierman, meesterlyk gepenceeld | *Mat:* op paneel *Size:* hoog 9, breed 8 duim	W ten Houten	(Sold) fl 16 Texier
1802/09/06	AMSCH	0033	*C. Dusart* | In een Binnenvertrek voor een tafel, waarop een test, zwavelstok en kleed, zit een Vrouw met een glas wyn in de hand, en een wafel op haar schoot; agter dezelve een Boer met een kan en pyp in de hand, fix gepenceelt | *Mat:* op paneel *Size:* hoog 17, breed 14 duim	J	(Sold) fl 2:15 Gruiter
1802/09/29	AMSCH	0016	*Corn$^{S.}$ Dusart* | Een Vischboerinnetje, hoog 10, breed 8 duim. Paneel. Het voornaamste onderwerp van dit Stukje is een Visch-boerinnetje, houdende met haar regter hand een Mandje, waarop een gesneeden en een ongesneeden Schelvis; in haar linker hand houd zy 'er een ander ongesneeden, die zy als te koop aanbied, zy is gekleed met een olyf bruin Jakje, met roode mouwen en met zwart uitgemonstert, waar over een losse witte Doek; agter haar ziet men een Burger Huis en een Vischmarkt onder het geboomte; dit Stukje is zeer fyn en fraai behandeld, zynde de natuur in alles stiptelyk met smaak waargenomen [Une marchande de Poissons, en costume Hollandois offre à en acheter quelques-uns quelle a sur un petit pagnier, ce charmant petit Tableau de cet habile artiste est peint avec beaucoup de delicatesse & de verité.] | possibly companion to lot 17 *Mat:* op paneel *Size:* hoog 10, breed 8 duim	[Labouchere?]	(Sold) fl 40 Coclers
1802/09/29	AMSCH	0017	*Corn$^{S.}$ Dusart* | Een Visch-boer, hoog 10, breed 8 duim. Paneel. Men ziet in dit Stukje een Visch-boer, die al gaande op een mandje twee schoone Schelvissen te koop aanbied, zynde de eene daarvan gesneeden en de anderen ongesneden, aan zyn linker arm heeft hy een bruin en wit Hengselmandje met meerdere Visch; op de tweede grond zyn verbeeld een Vischmarkt by oude Stads Gebouwen, en in 't verschiet eenige Huismans woningen by geboomten; de qualiteit van dit Stukje is met het vorige gelyk [Ce joli Tableau peut servir de pendant au précédent. C'est un marchand de Poisson qui offre sa marchandise d'une mine engageante. La vérité dont les divers objéts sont rendus est surprenante, ce qui le mêt au rang des beaux ouvrages de ce génre.] | possibly companion to lot 16 *Mat:* op paneel *Size:* hoog 10, breed 8 duim	[Labouchere?]	(Sold) fl 42 C S Roos
1803/07/18	AMSCH	0012	*Dusart. (C.)* | Op een Boere Dorp voor een Herberg ziet men eenige Kermisgasten zich met danssen en drinken vermaaken, in het verschiet	Maria Theresia Andrioli	(Sold) fl 560 Pruijssenaar

			eenige Kraamen, een Kar en Paard, en een groote menigte Beeldjes, zynde dit stuk een der capitaalste van deezen Meester, en behoefd niet te wyken voor zyn Meester A. van Ostade [Dans un Excellent paysage audevant d'un Cabaret est representée un fête Village [sic] ; nous ne pouvons detailler en entier toutes les parties de ce morceau capital, un des plus consequens de ce maître, étant une composition de plus de Cinquante figures, dont les principales sont attroupées audevant du Cabaret de Village & autour des Musiciens, à dancer, à boire, ou à carresser. Nous observerons en peu de mots que le beau fini du faire, l'eclât du paysage, & la vérité des Caractéres le font presq'égaler à Ad. van Ostade son maitre. C'est une representation vraye & caractérisée de la vie champâitre [sic], unisant [sic] à une couleur forte une variété infinie & un êclât imposant.] | *Mat:* op doek *Size:* hoog 39, breed 31 duim [haut 29, large 31 pouces] *Notes:* The dimensions differ in the Dutch and French editions of the catalogue.		
1803/08/24	HGKAN	A0010	*Cornelis Dusart* | Dit Capitaal Schildery verbeelt Abrahams Offerhande, door Cornelis Dusart, iets zeldzaams van deeze groote Meester schoon van Coloriet en breet geschildert. N.B. Dit Schildery schynt gedient te hebben voor een Deurstuk waar toe een Stuk aangezet is, dat men kan afneemen als men wil | *Mat:* op doek *Size:* breet 48, hoog 36 duim		(Sold) fl 6 van Giesen
1804/02/27	AMSCH	0025	*Dusart. (C.)* | Voor een Buitenhuis ziet men een vrolyke Huisman, speelende op de Fiool, een Jongen welke een Hond laat danzen is voor hem, en op den voorgrond zit een Vrouw en een Kind, verders een verschiet met zes beelden, waarby een Vrouw die vruchten weegt; dit stukje is zeer fraai, en in de trant van A. van Ostade gepenceeld | *Mat:* op doek *Size:* hoog 17, breed 14 duim	B	(Bought In) fl 70
1804/02/27	AMSCH	0026	*Dusart. (C.)* | In een Binnenhuis ziet men een Boerin, met een Glas in haar hand, by een tafel, achter dezelve staat een Boer, met een Kan en Pyp in de hand; en verder bywerk; fiks geschilderd | *Mat:* op paneel *Size:* hoog 17, breed 14 duim	C	(Sold) fl 3 van den Brink
1805/07/10	AMSCH	0050	*C. Dusart* | Een Vasten-avondfeest: in een Boere Dorp, vol gewoel, met Beeldjes, enz.; allernatuurlykst en uitvoerig gepenceeld | *Mat:* op paneel *Size:* hoog 11, breed 13 ½ duim	V[inkeles] [for] N	(Sold) fl 20 Lafontaine
1805/10/09	HGBSM	0113	*C. Dusart* | Een vrolyk mannetje, speelende op de lier, uitvoerig geschildert op paneel | *Mat:* op paneel *Size:* hoog 9 breet 8 duim	T H van Willigen [or others]	(Sold) fl 10:15 Basemoine
1805/12/16	AMSCH	0018	*C. Dusart* | Een zittend Vrouwtje, met een Flesje in de eene, en een Glaasje in de andere hand; uitvoerig op Paneel geschilderd | *Mat:* op paneel *Size:* hoog 6 ½, breed 5 ½ duim	Spaan	(Sold) fl 1 T van Iperen
1805/12/16	AMSCH	0019	*C. Dusart* | Een Boere Binnehuis, met vrolyke Huislieden, delicaat op Paneel | *Mat:* op paneel *Size:* hoog 12, breed 10 duim	R[oos]	(Bought In) fl 1:15
1806/11/24	AMSCH	0018	*Dusart (C.)* | Een Boeren Binnenhuis met vrolyke Huislieden; meesterlyk geschilderd | *Mat:* op paneel *Size:* hoog 12, breed 10 duim	van den Bosch	(Sold) fl 6:10 Van Dyl
1807/08/26	AMSCH	0041	*C. Dusart* | Een Boerevreugd in een Dorp, op de voorgrond een Kwakzalver en Hansworst, waarby een menigte aanschouwers; geestig geordonneerd en uitvoerig gepenceeld | *Mat:* op doek *Size:* hoog 29, breed 34 duim	Joseph Vallette	(Sold) fl 23 Spruyt
1808/04/26	GDAN	0035	*Dusart (C.)* | Verbeeldende een Militair Wachthuis in den Nagt, in 't zelve eenige Persoonen, goed geschilderd | *Size:* hoog 21, breed 19 ½ duim	G H Fortuyn	(Unknown)
1808/06/06	RMRIJ	0031	*Dusart. (Cornelis)* | Een Dorpgezigt, waarin zich op den voorgrond vertoont eene Zeevischmarkt met vele soorten van Visch, gestoffeerd met een aantal figuren en bijwerk. Rijk van ordinantie, uitvoerig, helder en krachtig behandeld, en een der kapitaalste stukken van dezen Meester [L'Intérieur d'un village. Sur le premier plan on voit une Poisonnerie [sic] rempli d'une Marée fraiche. Plusieurs figures en differentes actions forment une Composition riche et d'une grande vérité. Un beau fini, un coloris brillant, vigoureux et bien soutenu font regarder ce Tableau comme un chef-d'oeuvre de cet Artiste] | *Mat:* op doek *Size:* Hoog 25, en breed 33 ¾ duim *Loc:* Amsterdam, Nederland. Rijksmuseum. (A98)	Gerrit van der Pot, Heer van Groeneveld	(Sold) fl 1665 Stratenus [for] le Roi
1808/06/06	RMRIJ	0032	*Dusart. (Cornelis)* | Voor een Buitenhuis zit een vergenoegde Boer aan eene tafel met verscheidene spijzen gedekt; benevens hem een Jongen met een Hond spelende. Wijders een Vrouwtje met een pot de deur uitkomende. Zijnde de woning door een wijngaard aangenaam gedekt. Verder rijk van bijwerk, breed en uitvoerig geschilderd [Un Paysan est devant une Maison rustique assis prés d'une Table Couverte de plusieurs plats. Auprés de lui, un Enfant joue avec un Chien, tandis qu'une femme sort de la maison. Ce Tableau fait honneur au Peintre] | *Annots:* Verk. Dirk Haak Leiden 8 April 1782 (f 50.-) (RMA I) *Mat:* op paneel *Size:* Hoog 14, en breed 11 duim	Gerrit van der Pot, Heer van Groeneveld	(Sold) fl 255 Allard
1808/11/28	AMSCH	0013	*C. Dusart* | Een zittend Vrouwtje, houdende een Vles in de eene en een Glaasje in de andere Hand, uitvoerig geschilderd | *Mat:* op paneel *Size:* hoog 7, breed 6 duim	[Gruyter?]	(Sold or Bought In) fl 1:15 Gruyter
1809/09/06	AMSCH	0015	*Dusart (C.)* | In een Boere Binnenvertrek zit eene Vrouw een Kind pap gevende, ter zijde een liggende Kat met Jongen, voorts een menigte bywerk: in het verschiet ziet men voor de deur een Boer en Boerin te zamen praten; delicaat van penceelbehandeling | *Mat:* op doek *Size:* hoog 19, breed 16 duim	Johannes Caudri	(Sold) fl 193 van Iperen

1810/06/06	RMMUY	0171	*C. Dusart* | Drie Figuren		(Unknown) fl 3:2
1810/07/23	DOLGI	0018	*Cornelis Dusart* | Een Visscher, aan eene Vrouw Schol of Bot te koop aanbiedende, benevens eenige andere Stoffagie; zeer keurig getekend en uitmuntend fraai geschilderd. Een der beste stukken, van dezen groten Meester | *Mat:* op doek *Size:* hoog 13, breed 15 duim	Mr Pieter van den Santheuvel	(Sold) fl 301 van Leen a Delfsthaven
1810/07/23	DOLGI	0019	*Cornelis Dusart* | Een Visschers Vrouw, biedende gesneden Kabeljauw te koop, aan eene Vrouw door een Venster-Raam liggende; en verdere Beeldtjes. In alles niet minder behandeld als het vorige stuk | *Mat:* op doek *Size:* hoog 13, breed 15 duim	Mr Pieter van den Santheuvel	(Sold) fl 301 van Leen a Delfsthaven
1810/08/01	AMSCH	0028	*Dusart (Cornelis)* | Eene Boerenkermis, vol gewoel; op den voorgrond voor eene Herberg zijn eenige vrolijke Boeren en Boerinnen, die in het rond dansen, terwijl anderen het met vermaak aanschouwen, en twee op de Viool en de Lier spelen; in het verschiet Kramen, en een Kerktoren bij Geboomte [Le sujet d'une Foire de Village, orné de nombre de Figures. On distingue au premier plan, des Villageois dansans à la ronde audevant d'un Cabaret, tandis que les Spectateurs paroissent participer à la joye ; deux joueurs, l'un du Violon, et l'autre de la Vielle animent cette Scène. Dans la perspective on apperçoit des Boutiques, et le chocher [sic] au milieu d'un massif d'arbres] | *Annots:* peu soigné, mais d'un très bon effet. (NGW); Vente le Brun No. 108 fr 1345 (SMLN) *Mat:* op doek *Size:* hoog 33, breed 54 duimen	Mr Pieter de Smeth van Alphen	(Sold) fl 660 Texier, Gerbet en Comp [for] LeBrun
1810/08/01	AMSCH	0029	*Dusart (Cornelis)* | Eene Kermis in een Dorp; op den voorgrond voor een Buitenhuis ziet men, onder een Wijngaard, vrolijke Huislieden, welke zich op onderscheidene wijzen vermaken [Autre Fête de Village. Audevant du Tableau se presente une Maison de Campagne, dont le devant est ombragé par une Vigne ; audessous de ce feuillé on voit la joye naïve de nombre de Villageois] | *Annots:* Soigné, mais de peu d'effet. (NGW) *Mat:* op doek *Size:* hoog 25 ½, breed 22 duimen	Mr Pieter de Smeth van Alphen	(Sold) fl 760 R Pot te Rotterdam
			Dusart, Cornelis (manner)		
1801/04/08	HAVIN	0027	*Dusart* | Een Boere Binnenhuis gestoffeerd met Huisraad en een Vrouw met een Kind op de schoot in de manieren van Dusart		(Unknown)
1807/08/26	AMSCH	0042	*C. Dusart* | Een Boeren vreugd, of een Binnenhuis, waar in zig dezelve met zingen en dansen vermaaken; kragtig op geschilderd, in de manier van denzelven [C. Dusart] | *Mat:* op paneel	Helsdinge	(Sold) fl 3:15 du Pree
			Duynen, Isaac van		
1802/11/01	DOBRA	0014	*Izaak van Duinen* | Een Duingezicht. Op den voorgrond ziet men veelerly soorten van Zee- Visschen, Kreeften en andere Schelpvisschen, byna leevens grootte afgebeeld | *Size:* breed 57, hoog 42 duim	Paulus van der Spyk [or others]	(Sold) fl 7:5 v Braam
1807/09/28	DOHAA	00YY	*J. van Duinen* | Een dito [Schildery] met Vissen	Mattheus Westerouen van Meeteren	(Unknown)
1808/05/17	LNAN	0022	*van Duynen* | Een tafel met een kan enz. enz.		(Sold) fl 1 van Os
1808/06/13	AMSCH	0215	*J. van Duijven* | Eene Vrouw, welke van eene andere Schelvisch koopt; geestig	E M Engelberts	(Sold) fl 10 Simons
1810/08/06	AMSCH	0135	*J. Duivens* | Eene Vrouw over de Deur liggende, in gesprek met eene Vischmeid, welke een Ben met Visch in hare hand heeft. Zeer natuurlijk | *Mat:* op doek *Size:* hoog 24, breed 16 duimen		(Withdrawn)
			Dyck, Abraham van		
1807/06/10	HGBSM	0090	*A. v. Dyk* | Een Hermiet in een Grot zittende te leezen, nevens hem eenige Boeken, Inktkoker, Flesschen, Kruicifix, &c. breed en kragtig in de trant van Eekhoud, gemerkt A. v. Dyk | *Mat:* op paneel *Fmt:* ovaal *Size:* hoog 31, breed 25 duim *Inscr:* A. v. Dyk (signed)	Abraham Delfos [or others]	(Sold) fl 350 LaCourt
1808/06/11	RMRIJ	0058	*A: van Dyck van Alkmaar* | Een Gezelschap van Heeren en Dames, in de manier van Terburgh, fraai gepenceeld | *Mat:* op doek *Size:* hoog 25 ¾, breed 22 ½ duim		(Sold) fl 68 v Yperen [or] V Giesen
1810/06/06	RMMUY	0081	*Den Alkmaarschen Van Dyk* | Een Binnen vertrek waarin verscheide Figuren zig vermaken, met rooken, muziceeren en drinken, schoon en natuurlijk geschilderd. Door den Alkmaarschen Van Dyk | *Mat:* op paneel		(Unknown) fl 69
			Dyck, Abraham van (manner)		
1808/06/11	RMRIJ	0059	*Als door A: van Dyck* | Een schoon Mans Pourtrait met een kante kraag | *Size:* hoog 18, breed 15 duim		(Sold) fl 13:5 van Giesen
			Dyck, Anthonie van		
1801/04/13	AMSCH	0016	*A. van Dyk* | De heilige Franciscus in een devote gestalte, met een gekruist Christusbeeld in zyn handen op de knien leggende, voor hem een Doodshoofd en Boek, wordende door een Hemels licht bestraald; dit stuk is meesterlyk fraai geschilderd | *Mat:* op doek *Size:* hoog 39, breed 30 duim	Pierre Fouquet, junior	(Sold) fl 18 Coclers
1802/07/21	HGKAN	0030	*A. van Dyk* | Een zeer kragtig geschildert en zeer uitvoerig behandelt, dito [stuk] verbeeldende eenige Lieden, welke een Mensch gevangen neemen | *Notes:* It is unclear what "dito" refers to in the title.		(Unknown)

1802/07/21	HGKAN	0062	*van Dyk* | Twee Pourtraiten in ovaale zwarte Lysten | *Fmt:* ovaal		(Unknown)
1802/07/21	HGKAN	0089	*A. van Dyk* | Een Mans Pourtrait met twee handen		(Unknown)
1802/09/21	UTHDG	0019	*A. van Dijk* | Eene voor den maaltijd biddende oude vrouw, zittende aan een gedekte tafel, waarop vleesch, brood, enz. Haar bovenkleed is met bont, en den doek om haar hoofd, tot op de schouders nederhangende, is met goud omboord, zeer natuurlijk en schoon van uitvoering, gemerkt A. van Dijk | *Mat:* op paneel *Size:* hoog 18, breed 16 ½ duimen *Inscr:* A. van Dijk (signed)		(Sold) fl 71 La Maine
1802/12/13	AMSCH	0048	*A. van Dyk* | Een jonge Dame in cierlyke kleeding, staande by een Pot met Bloemen in een Landschap, uitvoerig en kragtig gepenceeld | *Mat:* op doek *Size:* hoog 40, breed 33 duim	Yver	(Sold) fl 11 Jan Spaan
1803/07/18	AMSCH	0010	*Dyk. (A. van)* | Dit bevallige Schilderytje steld voor den Heiland en St. Jan als Kinderen voorgesteld, zich omhelzende in een verrukkende houding! de tekening het coloriet zyn van een alleruitmuntendste aart en fixe schildering [Le Sauveur & St. Jean Baptiste representés comme Enfans ; Jesus paroit relever le précurseur qui est dans une attitude d'adoration. La force & l'Eclat de la Carnation vraye comme la Nature, de ces deux Enfans, de Proportion à peu près Naturelle est au plus haut degrè ; une fonte de couleur, touchée d'une maniere grasse, & un contour facile distingueront ce Morceau.] | *Mat:* op paneel *Size:* hoog 26, breed 21 duim	Maria Theresia Andrioli	(Sold) fl 150 C S Roos
1803/08/17	AMSCH	0025	*Dyck. (A. van)* | Een Mans Pourtrait, van ter zyde te zien, kragtig en meesterlyk geschilderd | *Mat:* op paneel *Size:* hoog 21, breed 16 duim	Anna Catharina Putman	(Sold) fl 3:10 van Dijl
1803/09/07	AMSCH	0042	*A. van Dyck* | Het Pourtrait van een Vorstelyke Dame, prachtig gekleed en gehuld met Paarlen en Juweelen, zynde van de Delicaatste behandeling van A. van Dyck [Portrait d'une dame de distinction ; fastueusement habillée et garnie de diamans et de perles ; l'exécution en est de la plus grande délicatesse] | *Mat:* op paneel *Size:* hoog 27, breed 20 duim	Smidt	(Bought In) fl 86
1803/09/07	AMSCH	0043	*A. van Dyck* | Een Bad van Diana met hare Nimphen, zynde een bevallige Ordenantie van verscheide Beelden, het Landschap is meede in een meesterlyke trant, in de manier van Rubbens [Diane au bain avec ses Nimphes ; d'une ordonnance charmante par la diversité des figures : ce paysage est d'ailleurs d'une exécution parfaite et dans la manière de Rubens] | *Mat:* op paneel *Size:* hoog 24, breed 34 duim	Smidt	(Bought In) fl 100
1804/07/25	AMSCH	0015	*Dyk. (A. van)* | Het Afbeeldsel van een bevallige Dame, in aloude treffelyke zwarte Satyne Kleeding, zittende in een Armstoel, houdende de Linkerhand op de Borst, en rustende met de Rechterarm op de Leuning van de Stoel; het coloriet en de penceel behandeling, zyn meesterlyk fraai | *Mat:* op doek *Size:* hoog 44, breed 36 duim		(Sold) fl 155 Thais
1805/07/03	AMSCH	0014	*Dyk (A. van)* | Een Vorstelyke Dame, zittende in een armstoel in een gracelyke houding, leevens groote tot de kniën, uitgedoscht in ryke Spaansche zyde Kleeding, met een kante Kraag om haar hals alsmede kante Lubmouwen aan haar handen; zoowel de de Teekening als het Coloriet, zyn van de beste Penceel werken van dezen voortreflyke Meester | *Mat:* op doek *Size:* hoog 46, breed 38 duim	D	(Bought In) fl 975
1806/08/13	AMSCH	0040	*Dyk. (A. van)* | Deeze Ordinantie, vol gewoel van Beelden, vertoont de Opwekking van Lazarus; meesterlyk in 't graauw geschilderd | *Mat:* op paneel *Size:* hoog 11, breed 13 duim	Roos	(Sold) fl 10 Josi
1808/06/06	RMRIJ	0033	*Dijck. (Anthonij van)* | Eene Dame in de gedaante van de Heilige Maagd het kind Jezus op haren schoot houdende; voor dewelke een persoon (zijnde de afbeelding van den Abt Caesar Alexander Scaglia) met gevouwen handen, in eene biddende houding zich vertoont. Schoon geordineerd en geschilderd. Dit tafereel gaat in plaat uit door J. Meijsens [Une Dame representant la Sainte Vierge, tient l'Enfant Jésus sur ses genoux, on voit devant lui une figure (le portrait de l'Abbé César Alexandre Scaglia) qui, les mains jointes, est dans une attitude d'adoration. On reconnoit dans ce Tableau la touche de ce grand Artiste] | *Annots:* 2 Maart 1800 Verouden[?] door Thys voor f 160.- Thys had het par jeders hort (RMA I); Copie (SMLN) *Mat:* op paneel *Size:* Hoog 12 ¾, en breed 17 ¾ duim	Gerrit van der Pot, Heer van Groeneveld	(Sold) fl 215 Coclers
1808/08/23	AMSCH	0042	*Dijck. (A. van)* | Een deftig mans Pourtret, halver lijf, in het zwart gekleed, en een kanten Kraag om de hals; krachtig van koloriet, stout en meesterlijk gepenceeld | *Mat:* op doek *Size:* hoog 28, breed 24 duim	[Coclers]	(Sold) fl 24:10 D Maijkel
1808/09/13	HABRU	0113	*van Dijk* | Een dito [Pourtraitje] | *Notes:* This lot was sold with lot 112 by Rembrandt.		(Unknown) fl 4 for lots 112 & 113
1808/11/28	AMSCH	0014	*A. van Dijk* | Een Mans Hoofd, meesterlijk en breed behandeld | *Mat:* op doek *Size:* hoog 19, breed 15 duim	H	(Sold) fl 0:6 Cocler
1808/12/30	HGIMM	[0071f]	*Van Dyk* | Voorts een exquis kabinetje Schilderijen van voorname Nederlandsche Meesters, welke uit hoofde van de kortheid des tijds niet stuk voor stuk kunnen beschreven worden; doch waarvan de beschrijving op den Kijkdag zal voorhanden zijn. Dus wij hier alleen de namen van eenige dier Meesters laten volgen, als: A. Kuyp, Ruysdaal, Karel du Jardyn, Loqwi ('t beste dat hij schilderde) Hondekoeter, van Dyk, Janson, Moesgever, Kamphuyzen, van Gooijen, A. van der Neer, T. Wyk, Huchtenburgh, Zolemaker, van Hassel, A. Vermeulen, van Dongen, Scheffer, van Os enz. | *This Lot:* Een Schilderij, Van Dyk *Notes:* Because this lot was not numbered in the catalogue, we have assigned the number.		(Unknown)

1809/09/06	AMSCH	0014	*Dyk (A. van)* | Het Pourtret van den grooten Schilder P.P. Rubbens, met een hoed op het hoofd; meesterlijk schoon gepenceeld | *Mat:* op doek *Size:* hoog 30, breed 24 duim	Johannes Caudri	(Sold) fl 15 Weyland
1810/03/27	RMCNL	0091	*van Dyk* | De Heilige Famillie, zeer delicaat en levendig van Penseel		(Unknown)
1810/08/01	AMSCH	0030	*Dijk (Anthonij van)* | De Bijbelsche voorstelling van eenen Melaatschen, zijnen dank betuigende voor genezing aan den Zaligmaker; nevens Jezus staat een Apostel, achterwaarts twee Schriftgeleerden [Un Sujet de l'Histoire Sacrée, representant Jesus Christ guerissant un Paralitique : le Sauveur est accompagné d'un Disciple et de deux Scribes. On y voit le Malade guèri exprimer énergiquement sa reconnoissance. Ce Sujet est gravé par Pierre de Jode, portant le titre *Tolle Grabatum* &c] | *Annots:* assez bon, mais le Christ et St. Jan paroissent indignes du pinceau de V. Dijk, ou de Rubens. Vendu 3300 fl: chez Robijns, 4500 chez Verhulst, et 11812 ½ chez Pauwels. (NGW) *Mat:* op doek *Size:* hoog 45, breed 56 duimen *Loc:* London, England, UK. Royal Collection (Buckingham Palace) (146)	M[r] Pieter de Smeth van Alphen	(Sold) fl 19,200 T Spaan voor Lafontaine
1810/08/01	AMSCH	0031	*Dijk (Anthonij van)* | Een Heer, spelende op een Luit en gezeten voor eene Tafel, waarop een Muzijkboek en Fluit geplaatst zijn; nevens hem een Jongeling, die op de Fluit speelt [Representation d'un Homme assis devant une Table, jouant du Luth ; il a devant lui de la Musique et une Flûte. A son côté se tient un jeune Homme qui l'accompagne de la Flûte Traversiere] | *Annots:* fort inferieur à Van Dijck. (NGW); [par] J vanloo (BPG) *Mat:* op doek *Size:* hoog 43, breed 36 duimen	Mr Pieter de Smeth van Alphen	(Bought In) fl 700
1810/10/10	MGCIT	0001	*A. van Dijk* | Een Maria met het kind Jezus op haar schoot, drukkende zijn vleesch zagtjes met de vingeren, houdende een linnen doek in de hand, en met Moederlijke tederheid op het kind nederziende; ongemeen delicaat behandeld	Caspar van Citters	(Unknown)
			Dyck, Anthonie van (or Dyck, Anth. van, manner)		
1801/06/13	LNDLS	0055	*van Dyck* | Een Vrouw, met eenige Kinderen, verbeeldende de liefde, konstig op doek, door of in de manier van van Dyck | *Mat:* op doek *Size:* hoog 50, breed 48 duimen	D van R	(Sold) fl 11:10 Thomasse
1803/09/07	AMSCH	0044	*van Dyk* | Een Graflegging Christi, zynde een ryke Ordenantie, en op een schetsachtige manier, door of als van Dyk [L'ensevelissement de Jésus-Christ ; d'une ordonnance riche, peint en esquisse] | *Mat:* op doek *Size:* hoog 10, breed 7 duim	Smidt	(Sold) fl 4:10 Gruiter
1804/07/25	AMSCH	0016	*Dyk (A. v.) of in de manier* | Dit voorwerp verbeeld de Liefde, door een zittende Vrouw, houdende op de Schoot een slaapend Kindje, nevens dezelve twee met elkander liefkoozende Kinderen; alles is van een krachtige en teffens uitvoerige penceel behandeling | *Mat:* op doek *Size:* hoog 52, breed 55 duim		(Sold) fl 5 Lelie
1804/08/08	AMSCH	0242	*A. van Dyk* | Maria Magdaléna in Berouw, met een Doodshoofd in de Hand; kragtig op Paneel, door of in de manier van A. van Dyk | *Mat:* op paneel	Roos [for] C	(Sold) fl 225 Gruiter
1805/07/03	AMSCH	0216	*van Dyk* | Maria Magdaléna in berouw; in de Lugt eenige Seraphynen; door of in de manier van van Dyk	C	(Sold) fl 135 Nieuwenhuys
1809/04/17	AMSCH	0139	*van Dijk* | Een Boetvaardige Magdaléna, door of als van Dijk | *Mat:* op doek	[Gruyter?]	(Sold) fl 0:5
1809/06/13	AMSCH	0038	*A. van Dijk* | Eene bevallig Meisje, halver lijf, in deftige Kleeding, zij rust met haar Arm op een Leuningstoel; meesterlijk schoon geschilderd, door of als A. van Dijk | *Mat:* op doek *Size:* hoog 50, breed 34 duim	H[odges]	(Bought In) fl 46
			Dyck, Anthonie van (copy after)		
1802/04/13	HAVIN	0067	*van der Myn; van Dyk* | Maria met het Kindje, na van Dyk | copy by H. Myn after Anth. van Dyck		(Unknown)
1802/09/06	AMSCH	0242	*A. van Dyk* | Een oud Mans Beeld, zinspeelende op de Tyd; meesterlyk naar A. van Dyk | *Mat:* op doek	J	(Sold) fl 2:5 van Dijl
1803/04/27	AMSCH	0062[b]	*le Chevaliér van Dyk* | Deux morceaux, dont l'un est l'esquisse d'un Tableau d'Autel, par Serenado, & l'autre une Copie d'après le Chevaliér van Dyk, réprésentant St. Augustin présenté par deux Anges à Jesus Christ | *This Lot:* St. Augustin présenté par deux Anges à Jesus Christ; lot 62[a] by Serenado	A	(Sold) fl 36 for lots 62[a] & 62[b]. V[n] Iperen
1803/08/24	HGKAN	0087	*van Dyk* | Jesus, Maria, Joseph in een Landschap, na van Dyk	[Teissier] [or others]	(Unknown) fl 4:5
1803/08/24	HGKAN	0098	*van Dyk* | Jesus en Johannes, na van Dyk	[Teissier] [or others]	(Unknown)
1803/09/07	AMSCH	0260	*A. van Dyk* | St. Augustinus, in verrukking, verzeld van twee Engelen, en boven hem een glorie; meesterlyk op Paneel geschilderd, door een goed Meester, naar A. van Dyk [St. Augustin paroissant inspiré, accompagné de deux anges et entouré d'une gloire ; parfaitement peint par un bon maître, et dans le goût de Van Dyk.] | *Mat:* op paneel *Size:* hoog 20, breed 14 duim	Smidt	(Bought In) fl 19 ½
1805/12/16	AMSCH	0090	*A. van Dyk* | De Tyd, kortwiekende de Vleugels van Cupido, naar A. van Dyk	R[oos]	(Sold) fl 0:14 L Pakker
1806/05/05	AMSCH	0045	*van Dorne; A. van Dyk* | Een bevallig jong Meisje in aloude deftige Kleeding; meesterlyk gepenceeld door denzelven [van Dorne] na A. van	L	(Sold) fl 10 Coclers

			Dyk | copy by F. Dorne after Anth. van Dyck *Mat:* op doek *Size:* hoog 22, breed 18 duim		
1806/06/07	RMHSN	0066	*van Dyk* | Een Heilige Familie, na van Dyk | *Mat:* op koper	A E K L	(Unknown)
1808/03/03	HAVIN	0036	*Hodges; van Dyk* | De Kruisiging, na van Dyk, door Hodges | copy by C.H. Hodges after Anth. van Dyck *Notes:* This lot was sold with lot 37 by C.H. Hodges.	Jacobus Spillebout	(Unknown) fl 28 for lots 36 & 37
1810/06/06	RMMUY	0092	*Bescheij; A. van Dijk* | Eene uitvoerige Copij. Door Bescheij, naar het altaar stuk van A. van Dijk, verbeeldende de Gekruiste Christus tusschen de Moordenaren, waar bij Maria, Johannes, en Maria Magdalena | copy by Beschey after Anth. van Dyck *Mat:* op paneel		(Unknown) fl 43
1810/06/06	RMMUY	0199	*D. van Nymegen; A. van Dyk* | Een Mans Pourtrait, zijnde het afbeeldsel van Q. Mathijs. Naar A. van Dyk, door D. van Nymegen | copy by D. Nijmegen after Anth. van Dyck *Mat:* op doek		(Sold) fl 7 Brunelli
1810/06/20	AMSCH	0175	*A. van Dijk* | Christus in den Schoot van Maria; meesterlijk naar A. van Dijk	A	(Sold) fl 1:10 Andriessen
1810/07/23	DOLG2	000Ca[H]	*vandyck* | Venus naer vandyck | *Notes:* This lot was added in by hand in the FLNY copy of the catalogue and purchased by the anonymous annotator.	Pieter Quinting	(Sold) fl 7
1810/12/03	DOBRA	0048	*A. van Dyk* | Een, Zinnebeeld van Christus Liefde, naar A. van Dyk		(Unknown)
			Dyck, Anthonie van (manner)		
1801/12/22	AMOTT	0122	*van Dyk* | 1 mans Pourtrait op koper, als van Dyk | *Mat:* op koper	Bartholomeus Ruloffs	(Unknown) fl 5
1803/09/07	AMSCH	0243	*A. van Dyk* | Een Manspourtrait, in Spaansche Kleeding, uitvoerig en meesterlyk fraay gepenceeld, in de manier van A. van Dyk [Un portrait d'homme habillé à l'Espagnole ; d'une touche bien agréable et d'une exécution finie, dans le goût de Van Dyck] | *Mat:* op doek *Size:* hoog 30, breed 23 duim	Smidt	(Sold) fl 3:5 Frantszen
1804/10/16	DLOND	0285	*In de manier en zo goed als Van Dyk* | Ene Vrouw in gesprek met een Man agter zich die de handen om hoog houdt. Une Femme en discours avec un Homme qui leve ses mains & vers lequel elle tourne sa tête | *Mat:* op doek *Size:* hoog 33, breed 11		(Unknown)
1805/07/10	AMSCH	0181	*A. van Dyk* | Den dooden Christus, door zyne Discipelen aan Maria vertoond wordende, welke met aandoening hetzelve beschouwd; het naakt is uitnemend geschildert, en word gehouden voor A. van Dyk | *Mat:* op paneel *Size:* hoog 41, breed 28 duim	R[oos]	(Sold) fl 30:10 Gruyter
1805/07/10	AMSCH	0293[H]	*Van Dyk* | Een Vrouwe Pourtrait als Van Dyk | *Notes:* This lot was added in by hand in the AA, EBNP and RKDH copies of the catalogue.	V[inkeles] [for] Menzard	(Sold) fl 9:10 Parker Hodges
1805/12/16	AMSCH	0079	*A. van Dyk* | Een Mans Pourtrait, als door A. van Dyk	R[oos]	(Sold) fl 0:6 Yver
1806/08/13	AMSCH	0277	*A. van Dyk* | Een jong Meisje met een Tulp in de hand, ten voeten uit; in de manier van A. van Dyk	Vinkeles [for] D	(Sold) fl 0:10 L Pakker
1806/08/20	HGBSM	0113	*A. van Dyk* | Een portrait van een Heer, met eene zijde mantel en eene hand, fraai geschilderd in de manier van A. van Dyk | *Mat:* op doek	Macalester Loup [or others]	(Sold) fl 20 L Voerman voor Huibrechts
1807/08/26	AMSCH	0044	*A. van Dyk* | Twee stuks Pourtraiten, een Heer en Dame, verbeeldende Vorstelyke Persoonaadien in treffelyke kleeding; meesterlyk gepenceeld, in de manier van A. van Dyk | *Mat:* op paneel *Size:* ieder hoog 19, breed 16 duim	Helsdinge	(Sold) fl 2:10 Spruyt
1809/04/17	AMSCH	0152	*A. van Dijk* | De Tyd kort Cupido de vleugels; meesterlijk als A. van Dijk | *Mat:* op doek	[Gruyter?]	(Sold or Bought In) fl 0:8 Gruyter
1810/03/07	UTWLD	0041	*van Dyk* | Eene jonge Dame speelende op de Guitaar, konstig en uitvoerig behandeld in de smaak van van Dyk | *Size:* hoog 5 voet, breed 4 voet 3 duim	J J Woertman	(Unknown) fl 22
1810/10/10	MGCIT	0154	*A. van Dijk* | Een Stuk, waarop een Wagentje, door twee Bokken voortgetrokken, en bestuurd wordende door twee naakte en ongemeen delicaat geschilderde Kindertjes; alles vertoond in een Landschap, in de trant van A. van Dijk behandelt, goed uitgevoerd, door een voornaam Meester	Caspar van Citters	(Unknown)
1810/10/11	AMSCH	0209	*van Dyk* | Eene bevallige Vrouw; krachtig op Doek, in de manier van van Dyk | *Mat:* op doek	A	(Sold) fl 15 Gruiter
			Dyck, Anthonie van (school)		
1803/04/27	AMSCH	0080	*Chévalier van Dyk* | Le Portrait d'un Savant, par un éléve du Chévalier van Dyk | *Mat:* sur bois *Size:* h. 1 ½, l. 1 pieds	A	(Sold) fl 15 Gruiter
1803/07/18	AMSCH	0011	*Dyk. (uit het school van A. van)* | Een Ordonnantie van verscheide Beelden, alwaar een Nimph door de Musen gekroond word, dit stuk is van een schoone couleur meesterlyke behandeling [Une grande composition au milieu de laquelle l'on distingue une Nimphe couronnée par l'Amour. Sur le devant sont les Muses en attitudes de repos, le fond est un paysage d'une maniere large. Ce tableau est d'une belle fonte de couleurs, très approchante de celle de van Dyck, l'execution est facile, elle ne se ressent pas de la gène d'une imitation. Picot a gravé ce sujet.] | *Mat:* op doek *Size:* hoog 46, breed 54 duim	Maria Theresia Andrioli	(Sold) fl 96 Gruyter

Dyck, Anthonie van (style)

1808/06/13	AMSCH	0191	*A. van Dijk* | Een Mansportret; in den stijl van A. van Dijk	E M Engelberts	(Sold) fl 3:5 Gruiter

Dyck, J. van [Unidentified]

1803/07/07	HGKAN	0024	*J. van Dyk* | Een Pourtrait, door J. van Dyk [Schilderyen in Olyverf] | *Mat:* in olyverf *Notes:* The bracketed information in the title appears above lot 1 and refers to lots 1 to 25.		(Unknown)

Dyk, F.H. van [Unidentified]

1802/05/10	MGSAN	0043	*F.H. van Dyk* | Een Mansportrait, met een Jachthond; in 't verschiet een Landschap, door F. H. van Dyk: op Doek, in vergulde Lyst | *Mat:* op doek *Size:* hoog 17 duim, breed 13 duim	Johan Dirk Kruysse	(Unknown) £ 0:5

Dyk, Philip van

1802/05/10	MGSAN	0032	*P. van Dyk* | Een Kabinetstukje, vertoonende een weenende Vrouw, in eene buitengemeene Passie, in een blaauw kleed, voor haar eene als wit marmere Tafel, met een groen fluweel kleed bedekt, waarop een Kistje met Paarlen en anders, houdende in haar hand een gouden Beker, zynde dit Stuk in alles delicaat behandeld, door P. van Dyk: op Paneel, in vergulde Lyst | *Mat:* op paneel *Size:* hoog 8 ½ duim, breed 7 duim	Johan Dirk Kruysse	(Sold) £ 36 Caspar van Citters
1804/12/10	AMSCH	0016	*Ph. van Dyk* | Het Pourtrait van een geleerde in oude deftige kleeding; zeer fraai en uitvoerig gepenceeld | *Mat:* op doek *Size:* Hoog 20, breed 16 duim	Jan de Groot	(Sold) fl 14:10 Coclers
1806/08/20	HGBSM	0081	*P^{h}. van Dyk* | Voor eene steene borstweering staat eene jonge Dame, haar hand uitstrekkende aan eene Waarzegster die een Kind op de rug draagt. Een Heer over de schouder van de Dame ziende, schijnt de Waarzegster iets aantewijzen; verders is dit schilderij verzierd op den voorgrond met een Hondje en omgevallen Mandtje, de borstweering met een Bas-relief van speelende Kindertjes, en in het verschiet een Tuingezicht; dit alles uitvoerig en fraai geschilderd | *Mat:* op doek *Size:* hoog 19, breed 16 duim	Macalester Loup [or others]	(Sold) fl 71 Lafontaine
1806/08/20	HGBSM	0191	*Ph. van Dijk* | Een Vrolijk Gezelschap, zijnde een Kabinetstuk, zeer delicaat geschilderd door Ph. van Dijk, 1738 | *Mat:* op paneel *Size:* hoog 18, breed 14 duim *Inscr:* Ph. van Dijk, 1738 (signed and dated?) *Notes:* It is unclear whether the name and date are inscribed on the painting.	Macalester Loup [or others]	(Sold) fl 46 Cocard
1806/08/20	HGBSM	0192	*Ph. van Dijk* | Eene Dame voor haar Toilet zittende zig te paleeren bij kaarslicht, natuurlijk geschilderd | *Mat:* op doek *Size:* hoog 14, breed 10 ½ duim	Macalester Loup [or others]	(Sold) fl 10 Spruyt

Dyk, Philip van (or Dyk, P., manner)

1803/12/15	MGLAC	0003	*Ph. von Dyk, of in de Manier* | Een fraai en delicaat Schildery, verbeeldende de Historie van Sophonisba | *Mat:* op doek *Size:* hoog duim 30, breed duim 25	Mr L H de Haze Bomme	(Unknown)

Eckhard, C. [Unidentified]

1803/12/12	AMSCH	0028	*C. Eckhard* | Een fraai Landschap, met hoog Geboomte en stoffagie van Beelden en Beesten; zonachtig op Paneel | *Mat:* op paneel *Size:* hoog 19, breed 24 duim	D	(Sold) fl 17 Blaauwpot
1803/12/12	AMSCH	0029	*C. Eckhard* | Een met Schuiten en Beeldjes gestoffeerde Rivier, aan een Stads Wal | *Mat:* op paneel *Size:* hoog 13, breed 21 duim	D	(Sold) fl 3:5 Berg
1803/12/12	AMSCH	0030	*C. Eckhard* | Een Hartejagt, met verscheide Honden; meesterlyk op Doek | *Mat:* op doek *Size:* hoog 28, breed 23 duim	E	(Sold) fl 1:5 Salcedo

Eckhardt

1809/04/22	AMYVR	0040	*Eckhard* | Een vrolijke dronken Boer; geestig | *Mat:* op paneel *Size:* hoog 7, breed 5 duim	de Bruin	(Sold) fl 1:10 du Pree

Eeckhout, Gerbrand van den

1801/04/13	AMSCH	0021	*G. van den Eekhout* | Hagar in de Woestyne door den Engel vertroost wordende, voor wien zy op de kniën legd in een devote gestalte; het licht en bruin is frappant, en meesterlyk behandelt | *Mat:* op doek *Size:* hoog 31, breed 26 duim	Pierre Fouquet, junior	(Sold) fl 36 Rijnders
1801/04/13	AMSCH	0022	*G. van den Eekhout* | Deeze Ordonantie verbeeld mede Hagar in de Woestyne door een Engel in 't wit gekleed gestroost wordende, terwyl Ismaël legt te slaapen; dit stuk is zoo frappant van licht, en behandeld, als of het van Rembrand geschilderd was | *Mat:* op doek *Size:* hoog 42, breed 39 duim	Pierre Fouquet, junior	(Sold) fl 49 Coclers
1801/04/13	AMSCH	0023	*G. van den Eekhout* | Deeze ryke Ordonantie verbeeld de Edelmoedigheid van Scipio, gevende de Bruid de schatten te rug, zy legt voor hem met haar Bruidegom op de kniën; behandeld als de voorgaande | *Mat:* op doek *Size:* hoog 53, breed 66 duim	Pierre Fouquet, junior	(Sold) fl 40 Hulswit
1801/05/11	AMSCH	0024	*G. van den Eekhout* | Deeze bybelsche Ordonnantie, steld voor de betraffing [sic] van Nathan aan David, de uitdrukking der carakters zyn treffend, en als door Rembrand gepenceeld | *Mat:* op doek	P[ruyssenaar]	(Sold) fl 165 Rijnders
1801/05/11	AMSCH	0025	*G. van den Eekhout* | Een Ordonnantie van drie beelden, in een Landschap, fix gepenceeld | *Mat:* op paneel *Size:* hoog 7, breed 7 duim	P[ruyssenaar]	(Sold) fl 3:5 Gruiter

1801/06/10	AMSCH	0056	*Eekhout. (G. van den)* | Een Heremiet voor een Kluis zittende te leezen, ter zyde hem een ben met Groenten; dit stuk is zeer frapant van licht en breed gepenceeld | *Mat:* op doek *Size:* hoog 37, breed 34 duim	Herman ten Kate	(Sold) fl 145 C S Roos
1801/11/10	AMPOS	0010	*G. v. Eeckhout* | 1 rustend Jager, met de Honden en Jachttuig		(Unknown)
1802/06/16	AMSCH	0054	*G. van den Eeckhout* | Een Corps de Guarde, waar in eenige Officieren kaartspeelen, een ander ziet men een glas uitdrinken; alles krachtig van Colloriet en meesterlyk behandeld | *Mat:* op doek op paneel *Size:* hoog 18 ½, breed 14 ½ duim	[Merrem]	(Sold) fl 39 v d Schley
1802/07/27	AKHRK	0010	*Gerbrand van den Eekhout, 1662* | Men ziet in het Vertrek en Studieplaats een Professor in de Heel- en Medicijnkunde zitten, voor een met Tapijt overdekte Tafel, op dezelve staan en liggen Boeken met Plaaten van de Anatomie en Kruidkunde &c. De Doctor is in het zwart gekleed, zwenkt zich om, op het zien naderen van eene innerlijke bedroefde Vrouw, met een Kind aan de hand, 't welk een Urinaal aan zijn Armtje heeft hangen. Hetzelve is overheerlijk en kragtig geschilderd; en zilverachtig in zijn Tinten, en de stilte en schemering die in hetzelve heerscht, ook de Expressie, is 'er verstandig in waargenomen. Het is beslooten in een bruin Ovaal, met een Trophée van Anatomische Schiletten [sic], en geen van de minste van dezen Meester | *Mat:* op doek *Fmt:* ovaal *Size:* hoog 30, breed 26 duim *Inscr:* Gerbrand van den Eekhout, 1662 (signed and dated?) *Notes:* It is unclear whether the name and date are inscribed on the painting.	Maria Stategaart	(Sold) fl 50 Gruyter
1802/09/06	AMSCH	0039	*G. v. d. Eekhout* | In een Oostersch Landschap ziet men Jacob, 't voorstel aan zyn beide vrouwen Léa en Rachel doende, om 't huis van haare Vader Laban te verlaaten, en na Cana te vertrekken; schoon van licht en meesterlyk gepenceeld | *Size:* hoog 48, breed 73 duim	J	(Sold) fl 12 Th^{S} Spaan
1802/09/21	UTHDG	0026	*G. van den Eekhout* | Twee Kaartspeelders, de voorste (ter zijde te zien, en geplaatst in het beste licht,) schijnt te winnen, de andere betoond spijt over zijn verlies, op tafel een glas, drank enz. De hartstogten zijn wel uitgedrukt, en alles is meesterlijk en uitvoerig behandeld | *Mat:* op paneel *Size:* hoog 11, breed 9 ¾ duimen		(Sold) fl 19 La Maine
1803/08/01	AMSCH	0008	*Eekhout. (G. van den)* | In een Binnenvertrek ziet men een Man, Vrouw en Kind, zittende aan een Tafel te spyzen, waarby een Sater, schynende met dezelven te spreeken, voorts ziet men een Schoorsteen met een brandend vuur, op de voorgrond eenige Boere Gereedschappen, ter regterzyde ziet men in een Stal, waarin eenige Beesten, natuurlyk en fix behandeld | *Mat:* op doek *Size:* hoog 22, breed 25 duim	J	(Sold) fl 76 Gruiter
1804/04/28	LNDLS	0006	*G. v. d. Eekhout* | Den Aardsvader Abraham, staande nevens zyn Zoon Izaäk op den berg, rustende tegen een heuvel, daar het hout en mes om te offeren oplegt, door G. v. d. Eekhout, op doek | *Mat:* op doek *Size:* hoog 38, breed 34 duim	[Abraham Delfos] [or others]	(Bought In) fl 40:10
1804/07/25	AMSCH	0030	*Eeckhout. (G. van)* | Deeze Ordinantie vertoont de Koningen, die het Kind Jezus aanbidden en geschenken offeren; Maria zit in zeedige houding met het Kindje op de schoot; voor dezelve legt een der Vorsten, in treffelyk gewaad op zyn knien nedergeboogen, tot geschenk een Goude Vaas aanbiedende, verzelt van zyn gevolg, het welk Joseph, een weinig agterwaards, met aandagt beschouwt; verder verscheide Krygslieden en eenige Gebouwen; alles is van een meesterlyke fraaije penceelbehandeling | *Mat:* op paneel *Size:* hoog 23, breed 18 duim		(Sold) fl 47 C S Roos
1804/07/25	AMSCH	0031	*Eeckhout. (G. van)* | Een Bybel-Ordenantie van vier Beelden voor een Buitenhuis, in een Landschap, verbeeldende de Geschiedenis van Ruth en Boas, gestoffeert met verder bywerk; de teekening, het natuurlyk licht, en de kunstige penceelbehandeling, maken dit Voorwerp een bevallig schildery | *Mat:* op paneel *Size:* hoog 14 ½, breed 12 ½ duim		(Sold) fl 100 Gruyter
1805/07/03	AMSCH	0080	*G. van den Eckhoudt* | In een Bybelsche Ordinantie ziet men een Engel, voor de welke een Vrouw geknield legt; meesterlyk en fiks op Doek | *Mat:* op doek *Size:* hoog 32, breed 21 duim	V[inkeles]	(Bought In) fl 25
1805/07/10	AMSCH	0054	*G. van den Eekhout* | Dit Capitaal Schildery, verbeeld in een Landschap met Geboomten, een zittend bevallig Jongeling, met de regterhand houd hy vast een der Hoornen van een Ram: die 'er van vier voorzien is, en ter zyde van hem staat; in de linker hand heeft hy een Schulp met Water; dit Stuk is meesterlyk behandeld, kragtig en teffens uitvoerig gepenceeld | *Mat:* op doek *Size:* hoog 52, breed 61 duim	Wed Grave	(Bought In) fl 160
1806/08/13	AMSCH	0046	*Eeckhout. (G. v. d.)* | Twee stuks, den eene verbeeld de Geboorte Christi te Bethleëm, daar de Herders het Kindeken aanbidden en geschenken brengen; den andere vertoont den Heiland in 't Hof Getzemané, nedergeknield in zyn smeekgebed, en door een Engel ondersteunt; op de voorgrond en terzyde ziet men de slapende Discipelen; beiden van een meesterlyke penceel behandeling | *Mat:* op doek *Size:* Ieder hoog 19, breed 24 duim	Daniel Mansveld	(Sold) fl 54 Swanenburg
1806/08/13	AMSCH	0047	*Eeckhout. (G. v. d.)* | Deeze Bybel-Ordinantie vertoont de jongeling Salomon, door zyn Ouders aan den Hogenpriester ter zeegening voorgestelt; het is schoon van Ordinantie en van een kragtig dog teffens uitvoerig Penceel | *Mat:* op doek *Size:* hoog 43, breed 54 duim	van der Voort	(Sold) fl 114 Schumacher
1806/08/13	AMSCH	0048	*Eeckhout. (G. v. d.)* | Denzelven Bybel-Geschiedenis [de jongeling Salomon, door zyn Ouders aan den Hogenpriester ter zeegening	Daniel Mansveld	(Sold) fl 202 Van Iperen

			voorgestelt], anders van Ordinantie, voorgesteld; in alles als de vorige meesterlyk fraai en uitvoerig van behandeling | *Mat:* op doek *Size:* hoog 25, breed 27 duim		
1806/08/13	AMSCH	0049	*Eeckhout. (G. v. d.)* | Deeze fraaije Ordinantie vertoont het Vrouwtje in Overspel bevonden voor Christus gebragt, waarby verscheide Schriftgeleerden, en Phariseen; de Caracters zyn natuurlyk, bevallig van licht en Coloriet en alleruitvoerigst gepenceeld | *Mat:* op doek *Size:* hoog 25, breed 31 duim	Daniel Mansveld	(Sold) fl 1430 Lafontaine
1806/08/13	AMSCH	0050	*Eeckhout. (G. v. d.)* | Een Bybel-Ordinantie van twee Beelden, in een Binnevertrek, een Vorstelyk Persoon legt eerbiedig nedergeknielt, voor een nederdalende Engel; in alles als de voorgaande, en van een meesterlyke fraaije schildering | *Mat:* op doek *Size:* hoog 36, breed 49 duim	Daniel Mansveld	(Sold) fl 41 Riemsdijk
1806/08/13	AMSCH	0051	*Eeckhout. (G. v. d.)* | In een Oostersch Landschap, voor een oud Gebouw, ziet men aan een beryde Tafel, den Aartsvader Abraham de Engelen te gast hebben, verzelt van Sara; schoon van licht en breed geschilderd | *Mat:* op doek *Size:* hoog 32, breed 51 duim	Vinkeles [for] G[ruyter]	(Sold) fl 2:15 Gruyter
1807/04/00	LNDLS	0002	*G. v. d. Eechout* | Een capitaal Schilderij, verbeeeldende [sic], een Herder en Herderin in 't wit satijn gekleed, versiert met, en dragende een mantje bloemen; benevens dezelve op de voorgrond twee kinderen die met een appel spelen in een landschap met schapen en bokken bij een fontein, extra konstig op doek | *Mat:* op doek *Size:* hoog 60, breed 54 duim	[Abraham Delfos] [or others]	(Unknown)
1807/04/00	LNDLS	0015	*G. v. d. Eekhout* | Den Aartsvader Abraham, staande nevens zijn zoon Izaak op den berg, hem als onderwijzende en gereed om te offeren, met het mes en hout op een heuvel rustende, zeer konstig en kragtig van schildering | *Mat:* op doek *Size:* hoog 39, breed 36 duim	[Abraham Delfos] [or others]	(Unknown)
1807/06/10	HGBSM	0002	*G. v.d. Eechout* | Een capitaal Schilderij, verbeeldende, een Herder en Herderin in 't wit satijn gekleed, versiert met, en dragende een mantje bloemen; benevens dezelve op de voorgrond twee kinderen die met een appel spelen in een landschap met schapen en bokken bij een fontein, extra konstig | *Mat:* op doek *Size:* hoog 60, breet 54 duim	Abraham Delfos [or others]	(Sold) fl 10:10 Spruit
1807/06/10	HGBSM	0015	*G. v.d. Eekhout* | Den Aartsvader Abraham, staande nevens zijn zoon Izaak op den berg, hem als onderwijzende en gereed om te offeren, met het mes en hout op een heuvel rustende, zeer konstig en kragtig van schildering | *Mat:* op doek *Size:* hoog 39, breed 36 duim	Abraham Delfos [or others]	(Sold) fl 11:10 van Os
1807/06/10	HGBSM	0134	*G. van den Eekhout* | Een historiëel Schilderij verbeeld Venus, en Adonis met eenige Jagthonden, helder en fraaij geschilderd | *Mat:* op doek *Size:* hoog 60, breed 61 duim	Abraham Delfos [or others]	(Sold) fl 23 Spruit
1808/04/26	GDAN	0044	*Eekhout (G. van den)* | Een uitmuntend oude Rijk Gekleeden Heer op een Stoel zittende te lezen, met veel gepeins | *Size:* hoog 13, breed 11 duim	G H Fortuyn	(Unknown)
1808/06/06	RMRIJ	0034	*Eekhout. (Gerbrand van den)* | Dit tafereel verbeeldt Eliäzer, Afgezant van Abraham, levensgrootte ten voeten uit, staande in gesprek met Rebekka, welke eene koperen kan in de hand heeft; ter linkerzijde twee staande Maagden; op den tweeden grond eenige knechten bij een put, werkende en hunne Kemels drenkende. Verder ziet men twee beladen Kemels, figuren, enz. Deze uitmuntende Schilderij is verstandig, krachtig en uitvoerig in de manier van Rembrand behandeld [Cette noble Composition represente Eliézer envoyé d'Abraham, de grandeur naturelle, qui debout, s'entretient avec Rebecca, qui tient un vase de cuivre dans ses mains. A gauche sont deux de ses suivantes. Du côté opposé plusieurs personnes de la suite d'Eliézer s'occupent à abreuver leurs chameaux, et dans le fond on voit deux de ces animaux chargés et plusieurs figures. Les Caractères sont admirablement exprimés, le Coloris bien soutenu, et l'Exécution d'une manière savante et vigourense [sic] dans le style de Rembrand, font honneur au Peintre] | *Annots:* Verk. by Roos, Amst 13 Sept. 1797 (f 165.-) (RMA I) *Mat:* op doek *Size:* Hoog 79, en breed 76 duim *Loc:* Praha, Ceská Republika. Národni Galerie.	Gerrit van der Pot, Heer van Groeneveld	(Sold) fl 830 Allard
1808/06/13	AMSCH	0044	*Eekhout (G. van den)* | Eene kapitale Bijbelsche Ordonantie van zes Beelden, in een prachtig Gebouw, het Koloriet, Kleeding der Beelden, en de meesterlijke penceelbehandeling maken dit tot een voortreffelijk Tafereel | *Mat:* op doek *Size:* hoog 42, breed 51 duim	[Jan Tersteeg]	(Sold) fl 70 van Drielst
1808/06/13	AMSCH	0045	*Eekhout (G. van den)* | Dit uitmuntende Schilderij stelt voor de Voetwassching van Christus, zijnde eene rijke Ordonantie; fraai van licht en bruin, en zoo meesterlijk behandeld, als of het door Rembrand geschilderd was | *Mat:* op paneel *Size:* hoog 18, breed 24 duim	R[oos]	(Bought In) fl 88
1808/08/23	AMSCH	0047	*Eeckhout. (G. van den)* | Dit bevallig stuk verbeeld in een Landschap met Geboomten een zittende Jongeling, met de regterhand vasthoudende een der Hoornen van een Ram, die 'er van vier voorzien is, en ter zijde bij hem staat, in de linkerhand heeft hij een Schulp met water; het is meesterlijk, kragtig, en tevens uitvoerig van penceelbehandeling | *Mat:* op doek *Size:* hoog 52, breed 61 duim	Z	(Bought In) fl 25
1808/11/28	AMSCH	0021	*G. van Eekhout* | Deeze capitaale Ordonantie, verbeeld het wegzenden van Hagar en Ismaël, door Abraham, agterwaards ziet men Sara, meesterlijk en schoon geschilderd | *Mat:* op doek *Size:* hoog 50, breed 62 duim	S	(Bought In) fl 25
1809/04/17	AMSCH	0150	*G. van den Eekhout* | In een Landschap vertoont zich de Barmhartige Samaritaan, zijn hulp de Ongelukkige bewijzende; krachtig en meesterlijk | *Mat:* op doek	[Gruyter?]	(Sold) fl 2:5

1809/06/13	AMSCH	0043	*G. van den Eekhoud* | Deeze capitaale Ordonantie, verbeeld den Berg Moria, alwaar den Aartsvader Abraham gereed is zijn Zoon Izaak op te offeren, in de laagten ziet men verscheide Knegten, het bevel van den Aartsvader afwagtende; krachtig en vol effect, in de stijl van Rembrand, geschilderd, door G. van den Eekhoud | *Mat:* op doek *Size:* hoog 40, breed 32 duim	[Gruyter?]	(Sold) fl 25 Rijers
1809/07/25	HGBSM	0188	*G. van den Eekhout* | Een kapitaal Stuk, verbeeldende de Historie daar aan Jacob de bebloede Rok van Joseph vertoond word, waar van de hartstogten in de Figuren, byzonder wel zyn uitgedrukt | *Mat:* op doek *Size:* hoog 59 en een half, breed 71 duim	D van der Aa [or] E B ten Dall	(Sold) fl 6:5 van Eyk
1809/09/06	AMSCH	0017	*Eeckhout (G. van den)* | De Opwekking van Lazarus door Christus, verzelt van zijne Dicipelen, die alle met verwondering deze Gebeurtenis beschouwen: alles verbeeld in een duister Rotsgezigt; de hartstogten zijn treffelijk verbeeld en van een meesterlijke penceelsbehandeling, in de manier van Rembrand | *Mat:* op paneel *Size:* hoog 32, breed 23 duim	Johannes Caudri	(Sold) fl 31 Coclers
1809/09/06	AMSCH	0018	*Eeckhout (G. van den)* | De Historie van Meléagar en Athalante, voorgesteld door verscheidene Beelden in een Landschap, met verscheiden Jagers, Honden en ander bijwerk; delicaat gepenceelt | *Mat:* op doek *Size:* hoog 30, breed 26 duim	Johannes Caudri	(Sold) fl 70 T Spaan
1810/06/20	AMSCH	0022a	*G. Van Den Eechout* | In een boomrijk Landschap rust eene bevallige Vrouw, in deftige kleeding; zij schijnt te leunen tegen een Heuveltje, waarop een Koker met Pijlen en een Boog ligt; op den voorgrond ligt een Zwijnskop, Piek en Jagthoorn; verder rustende Jagers met hunne Honden en een Heer te Paard. Alles van een meesterlijke penceelsbehandeling | *Mat:* op doek *Size:* hoog 33, breed 44 duimen	V	(Sold) fl 1 van der Schleij
1810/10/11	AMSCH	0136	*G. Van Den Eekhout* | Een Paardenkop; krachtig | *Mat:* op doek *Notes:* The lot was changed by hand from "Een Paardenkop; krachtig op Doek, door G. Van Den Eekhout" to "Een oud Manshooft, door Bol" in the FLNY copy of the catalogue.	[Gruyter?]	(Withdrawn)
			Eeckhout, Gerbrand van den (or Eeckhout, G., manner)		
1802/04/13	HAVIN	0037	*Eekhout* | Een leezende Eremiet, verstandig geschilderd; door of in de manier van Eekhout		(Unknown)
1802/09/06	AMSCH	0243	*G. van den Eeckhout* | Een Mans Hoofd, omhangen met een bonte Mantel; breed gepenceeld door G. van den Eeckhout, of in zyn manier | *Mat:* op paneel *Size:* hoog 12, breed 9 duim	J	(Sold) fl 1:15 Hulswit
1802/09/06	AMSCH	0244	*G. van den Eeckhout* | Een Historieele Ordenantie, voorstellende een van de Mirakelen; uitmuntend van effect door of in de manier van denzelven [G. van den Eeckhout] | *Size:* hoog 23, breed 32 duim	J	(Sold) fl 2 Hulswit
			Eeckhout, Gerbrand van den (manner)		
1803/12/12	AMSCH	0032	*G. van den Eckhout* | Christus, 12 jaaren oud zynde, leerende in den Tempel; meesterlyk geschilderd, als G. van den Eckhout | *Mat:* op doek *Size:* hoog 57, breed 61 duim	B	(Sold) fl 1:15 Roos [for] N
1809/06/13	AMSCH	0178	*G. v. den Eekhout* | Een Historieele Ordonantie met verscheiden Beelden, als G. v. den Eekhout	S[chley]	(Sold) fl 2 Gruyter
			Ekels, Jan (the elder)		
1801/03/16	AMSCH	0183	*J. Ekels* | Een gezicht binnen Amsterdam, ziende naar de Lydsche Poort, gestoffeerd met verscheide Beeldjes, bevallig op doek geschilderd | *Mat:* op doek	K[ip]	(Sold) fl 4:5 Boelen
1801/12/22	AMOTT	0043	*J. Ekels* | De Ossemarkt en Gezigt van en door de Utrechtsche Poort in Amsterdam	Bartholomeus Ruloffs	(Unknown) fl 10:10
1802/05/05	AMSCH	0056	*de Oude Ekels* | Een Gezicht langs de Haarlemmer Weg, na het Dorp Sloterdyk, ryk gestoffeerd met wandelende en rydende Beelden, een menigte staande en leggend Veê, bevallig van Ligt en uitvoerig geschilderd | *Size:* hoog 18, breed 23 duim	J	(Sold) fl 14 Ackina
1802/06/28	AMSCH	0047	*J. Ekels* | Twee stuks gezichten te Amsterdam aan de Halvemaansbrug; ryk gestoffeerd met Beeldjes en Vaartuigen; zonachtig op Panneel | *Mat:* op paneel *Size:* hoog 11, breed 14 duim	Anna Elink	(Sold) fl 12 Van Iperen
1802/06/28	AMSCH	0048	*J. Ekels* | Een gezicht na de Weesper Poort te zien, gestoffeerd met een menigte wandelende Lieden; fiks behandeld door Denzelven [J. Ekels], op Panneel | *Mat:* op paneel *Size:* hoog 10, breed 13 duim	Anna Elink	(Sold) fl 4:10 Vermeulen
1802/06/28	AMSCH	0049	*J. Ekels* | Twee stuks gezichten op Adelyke Huizen in een Landschap; zeer natuurlyk door Denzelven [J. Ekels], op Doek | *Mat:* op doek *Size:* hoog 10, breed 12 duim	Anna Elink	(Sold) fl 5:5 Van Iperen
1804/05/07	AMSCH	0049	*Ekels. (J.)* | Twee stuks bevallige Stadsgezichten, voorstellende Gezichten op de Joode en Portugeessche Kerken, te Amsterdam, ziende de eene na de Weesperstraat en de andere na de Plantagie, ryk gestoffeerd met een ménigte van Wandelende, Veedryvende en andere Lieden; deze byde Kunststukken zyn aller zonachtigst en van de beste penceelbehandeling van deze Meester | *Mat:* op doek *Size:* hoog 18 ½, breed 23 ½ duim	Vinkeles	(Bought In) fl 71
1804/05/07	AMSCH	0050	*Ekels. (J.)* | Dit aangenaam en zonächtig Schildery verbeeld een Gezicht na de Haringpakkerstooren, ziende na de kleine Vismarkt, vol gewoel van	Vinkeles	(Bought In) fl 8

			Beeldjes, Rytuigen, Schuiten, enz.; zynde hetzelve niet minder dan de voorgaande | *Mat:* op paneel *Size:* hoog 15 ½, breed 18 ½ duim		
1804/05/07	AMSCH	0051	*Ekels. (J.)* | Twee stuks, een Gezigt van binnen en buiten de Muiderpoort te Amsterdam te zien, gestoffeerd met verscheide Beeldjes, en behandeld als de voorgaande | *Mat:* op paneel *Size:* hoog 14, breed 19 duim	R[oos]	(Sold) fl 19 Coclers
1804/05/07	AMSCH	0052	*Ekels. (J.)* | Een Gezicht op de groote Kerk te Arnhem, gestoffeerd met verscheiden Stoffagie; en als J. van der Heyden behandeld | *Mat:* op doek *Size:* hoog 14, breed 19 duim	Roos [for] A	(Bought In) fl 14
1804/08/08	AMSCH	0063	*J. Ekels* | Een Gezicht op de Groote Kerk te Arnhem, met diversche Stoffagie, zynde als J. van der Heyden, behandeld door J. Ekels | *Mat:* op doek *Size:* hoog 14, breed 19 duim	Roos [for] F	(Sold) fl 25:10 Moll
1806/08/13	AMSCH	0054	*Ekels. (J.)* | Twee stuks, zynde Gezichten van de Muyderpoort, de ééne binnen de Stad en de anderen van buiten te zien, ryk gestoffeerd met wandelende Heeren en Dames, Schaapherder met Schaapen, enz.; beide zonachtig en uitvoerig uitgevoerd | *Mat:* op paneel *Size:* Ieder hoog 19, breed 26 duim	Vinkeles [for] D	(Sold) fl 36 Gruyter
1806/08/20	HGBSM	0205	*J. Ekels* | Een Stadsgezicht van binnen te zien, langs een Gragt waar over een Hardsteenebrug, in 't verschiet een Kerk, en aangenaam gestoffeerd met Figuuren, in de manier van J. van der Heiden | *Mat:* op paneel *Size:* hoog 12 ½, breed 15 duim	Macalester Loup [or others]	(Sold) fl 33 Zwartsman
1807/08/26	AMSCH	0054	*J. Ekels den oude* | By een Boeren Woning en Schuur, waar voor een ledige Kar, ziet men een Vrouw bezig te melken, verder staand Vee en rustende Schapen; zonachtig behandeld | *Mat:* op paneel *Size:* hoog 13, breed 18 duim	Helsdinge	(Sold) fl 10 Spaan
1808/08/23	AMSCH	0051	*Ekels, (J) de oude* | Een Gezigt binnen Amsterdam, ziende van de Kalverstraat langs den Dam, naar een gedeelte van de voorgevel van het Stadhuis, naar de Nieuwe Kerk, Waag, Nieuwendijk en Damrak, rijk gestoffeert met Beeldjes en Rijtuigen; het zonlicht is natuurlijk, en de schildering uitvoerig | *Mat:* op paneel *Size:* hoog 19, breed 24 duim	[Coclers]	(Sold) fl 280 Jan Spaan
1808/11/28	AMSCH	0022	*J. Ekels, de Oude* | Twee stuks Gezichten op de Joden Kerken en Houtmarkt te Amsterdam, gestoffeerd met wandelende Heeren en Dames, Kooplieden, Vragtsleeden en andere Voorwerpen, zonachtig behandeld | *Mat:* op doek *Size:* ieder hoog 19, breed 24 duim	S	(Sold) fl 26 Gruyter
1808/11/28	AMSCH	0023	*J. Ekels* | Een Gezicht binnen Amsterdam, ziende van de Nieuwe Stads Herberg, op de Haringpakkerij, de Tooren en Haarlemmersluijs, rijk gestoffeerd met Beeldjes, Vragtsleeden en Vaartuigen, helder en plaisant voorgesteld | *Mat:* op paneel *Size:* hoog 18, breed 16 duim	S	(Sold) fl 6 T Spaan
1809/06/13	AMSCH	0046	*J. Ekels* | Twee stuks Gezichten, van den Muiderpoort, te Amsterdam, den eenen ziende langs de Plantagie na de Heertjes Lijnbaan en Funie, en den anderen van den Buitensingel langs het Bosch naar de Houtwaalderweg, beide rijk gestoffeerd met wandelende Heeren en Dames en andere Beeldjes; zonachtig en uitvoerig op Paneel geschilderd | *Mat:* op paneel *Size:* hoog 19, breed 25 duim	[Gruyter?]	(Bought In) fl 43
1809/06/13	AMSCH	0047	*J. Ekels* | Een stille Zee, met onderscheidene Vaartuigen en op het strand met Visschers gestoffeerd; helder en bevallig | *Mat:* op paneel *Size:* hoog 13, breed 19 duim	M	(Bought In) fl 8
1810/05/22	AMSCH	0028	*Ekels. (J.) de oude* | Een Gezicht op de Botermarkt te Amsterdam, van de Utrechtschestraat te zien, met stoffagie van Beeldjes; uitvoerig behandeld | *Mat:* op doek *Size:* hoog 16, breed 21 duim	Johannes van de Putte Nicolaasz.	(Sold) fl 36 Van Iperen
1810/05/22	AMSCH	0029	*Ekels. (J.) de oude* | Een Gezicht binnen Amsterdam, ziende langs het Singel op de Reguliers-Breestraat en Munt-toren; rijk met Beeldjes gestoffeerd en zonachtig geschilderd | *Mat:* op doek *Size:* hoog 11, breed 16 ½ duim	Johannes van de Putte Nicolaasz.	(Sold) fl 8:10 Van Iperen
1810/06/20	AMSCH	0025	*J. Ekels De Oude* | Een Gezigt binnen Utrecht, rijk met Beeldjes gestoffeerd | *Mat:* op paneel *Size:* hoog 12, breed 9 duimen	A	(Sold) fl 10 J Twisk
			Ekels, Jan (the elder) (copy by)		
1802/12/13	AMSCH	0059	*Jan Eekels; A. van der Neer* | Op een Bevroozen Rivier in de nabyheid van een Stad, ziet men een meenigte van Lieden, die zig met Reyden en Kolven op het Ys vermaaken, uitvoerig geschilderd, door Jan Eekels, naar A. van der Neer | copy by Jan Ekels (I) after A. Neer *Mat:* op doek *Size:* hoog 19, breed 21 duim	Pruyssenaar [for] A	(Bought In) fl 8
1805/12/16	AMSCH	0021	*J. Ekels; W. van de Velde* | Twee stuks woelende Zeegezichten, met zylende Oorlogscheepen, en Vissers Vaartuigen; uitvoerig behandeld door J. Ekels, naar W. van de Velde | copy by Jan Ekels (I) after W. Velde *Size:* yder hoog 9, breed 13 duim	R[oos]	(Sold) fl 2:5 L Pakker
1805/12/16	AMSCH	0022	*J. Ekels; W. van de Velde* | Twee stuks stille Zeegezichten, aan Strand, gestoffeerd met verscheide Vissers Scheepen, en andere Vaartuigen; bevallig geschilderd, op paneel, door dito [J. Ekels], naar dito [W. van de Velde] | copy by Jan Ekels (I) after W. Velde *Mat:* op paneel *Size:* yder hoog 11, breed 15 duim	R[oos]	(Sold) fl 3 T van Iperen
			Ekels, Jan (the younger)		
1801/05/11	AMSCH	0023	*Jan Ekels, de jonge* | Een Binnenvertrek, in hetzelven ziet men een Jongman by een tafel zitten, waar op een kom met punsch geplaast is,	V	(Sold) fl 101 Rijnders

			krachtig en van de beste schildering van deeze meester | *Mat:* op doek *Size:* hoog 22, breed 19 duim		
1801/08/19	AMSCH	0024	*Jan Ekels, de Jonge* | Circe by Ulyssis, verzeld van Mercuur op de Wolken, ter Zyden in een Landschap de Gezellen van Ulyssis in Varkens verandert, met verder Bywerk, uitvoerig gepenceeld	Pruyssen^{r}	(Sold) fl 7:5 Gruiter
1801/08/19	AMSCH	0025	*Jan Ekels, de Jonge* | In een Landschap, by de Stam van een Boom, legt een Nimph, op een wit Kleed, met een vriendelyk gelaat schynt zy iets te beschouwen	Pruyssen^{r}	(Sold) fl 6 Gruiter
1801/12/22	AMOTT	0026	*J. Eekels* | 1 bergachtig Landschap, met Beelden en Beesten, door J. Eekels, 1783 | *Inscr:* J. Eekels, 1783 (signed and dated?) *Notes:* It is unclear whether the name and date are inscribed on the painting.	Bartholomeus Ruloffs	(Unknown) fl 2:5
1802/05/05	AMSCH	0054	*J. Ekels* | In een Deftig Gemeubileert Binnenvertrek staat een Aanvallig Vrouwtje, met een bont Jakje, welke aan twee Heeren een Glaasje Wyn presenteerd. Alles zeer natuurlyk en aangenaam voorgesteld | *Mat:* op doek *Size:* hoog 25, breed 23 duim	D	(Sold) fl 89 B^{d} Kooij
1802/05/05	AMSCH	0055	*J. Ekels* | In een Gemeubileerde Kamer, ziet men een Bevallig Meisje, in een met bond gevoerd zyd Kleedje, schynende Onderwezen te worden door haare Meester. Alles delicaat geschilderd | *Size:* hoog 23, breed 18 duim	D	(Bought In) fl 35
1802/09/06	AMSCH	0041	*J. Ekels de jonge* | In een gemeubileerde Zaal, zit een jonge Dame, in een galante Zatyne Kleeding, houdende een Musicq-Papier in de hand, by een tafel met een groen kleed bedekt; schynende met een Heer te musiceeren, die voor dezelve staat op de Fiool speelende; ter andere zyde zit een Heer met een glas wyn in de hand, als met aandagt luisterende; de Caracters zyn natuurlyk, het Coloriet bevallig, en uitvoerig gepenceeld | *Size:* hoog 25, breed 23 duim	H^{n} Smit	(Sold) fl 81 van der Schley [for] S[mits wed]
1802/09/06	AMSCH	0042	*J. Ekels de jonge* | In een Keukenvertrek, vertoont zig een Vrouw, staande voor een tafel, bezig linnen te stryken: verders gestoffeerd met een linnenkast, eenige groentens en huizelyk gereedschap; alles natuurlyk en van een uitvoerige penceel-behandeling | *Mat:* op paneel *Size:* hoog 20 ½, breed 16 ½ duim	H^{n} Smit	(Sold) fl 73 Hulswit
1804/02/27	AMSCH	0032	*Ekels. (J.)* | Een Jager van een Trekschuit zyn pyp opsteekende, hy zit aan een Tafel, waarop een Glas met bier; dit stukje is zeer fraai van coloriet, krachtig gepenceeld, en eene van de beste van dezen Meester | *Mat:* op paneel *Size:* hoog 10, breed 9 duim	B	(Sold) fl 45 van Iperen
1804/05/07	AMSCH	0053	*Ekels. (J.) de Jonge* | Twee stuks, in het eene zit een bevallig Meisje in een Jakje met bonte rand, en een witte Satyne Rok gekleed, met aandacht een Brief te lezen; in de andere zit een Heer in gepyne aan een Schryftafel; het Satyn en ander bywerk is natuurlyk en delicaat geschilderd | *Mat:* op doek *Size:* hoog 23, breed 18 duim	Roos [for] A	(Sold) fl 91 B^{d} Kooy
1806/05/05	AMSCH	0050	*J. Ekels* | Een Dienstmaagd aan een Tafel, staat een Kétel te schuren, en verder bywerk; kragtig op Doek | *Mat:* op doek *Size:* hoog 23, breed 18 duim	R[oos]	(Sold) fl 21 van Iperen
1806/08/13	AMSCH	0334	*Ekels, de jonge. (J.)* | In een aangenaam Landschap by een Boomstam, ziet men een leggende naakte Vénus; fraai van teekening en uitvoerig van schildering | *Mat:* op paneel *Size:* hoog 20, breed 25 duim	Vinkeles [for] J	(Sold) fl 11:10 Riemsdyk
1806/08/13	AMSCH	0335	*Ekels, de jonge. (J.)* | Een Ordinantie van drie Figuuren; als de voorgaande van behandeling | *Mat:* op paneel *Size:* hoog 21, breed 18 duim	Vinkeles [for] J	(Sold) fl 10 van Iperen
1807/06/02	AMHUY	0010	*Jan Ekels* | Een Historiëele Ordonantie van drie Beelden		(Unknown)
1808/06/13	AMSCH	0047	*Ekels, (J.) de Jonge* | In een gemeubileerde Kamer zit eene bedaagde Juffrouw voor eene Tafel, met een Kleed bedekt, waarop eene Kandelaar met brandend Licht geplaatst is, schijnende bezig Linnen te naaijen; het kaarslicht doet eene natuurlijke werking, en is van eene uitvoerige penceelbehandeling | *Mat:* op doek *Size:* hoog 22, breed 17 duim	[Jan Tersteeg]	(Bought In) fl 25
1808/06/13	AMSCH	0048	*Ekels, (J.) de Jonge* | In een Binnenvertrek ziet men een bejaard Man en eene bevallige Vrouw, bezig te lezen: een Jager met een lans, geweer, enz. komt het Vertrek in, waarop de Man als in verwondering van zijn Stoel opstaat. Alles is vol van uitdrukking en uitneemend behandeld | *Mat:* op doek *Size:* hoog 26, breed 24 duim	K	(Sold) fl 102 Jan Smit
1808/06/13	AMSCH	0049	*Ekels, (J.) de Jonge* | In een Binnenvertrek zitten twee Heeren bij een Tafel, met een Kleed bedekt, als ijverig met de Kaart spelende, de Verliezer schijnt mismoedig, terwijl zijn partij toont het Spel gewonnen te hebben; achter deze staat een Heer als aanschouwer, en verder eene Hospita, met Kelken Wijn op een Schenkbord. De karakters zijn natuurlijk en van een meesterlijke penceelbehandeling | *Mat:* op doek *Size:* hoog 29, breed 33 duim	[Jan Tersteeg]	(Bought In) fl 49
1808/06/13	AMSCH	0050	*Ekels, (J.) de Jonge* | In deze twee fraaije voorwerpen verbeeld het eene eene bevallige jonge Dame, in galante Kleeding, zittende voor een Tafel, met een Tapijtkleed bedekt, waarop een Pleisterhoofd en Teekengereedschap geplaatst is, schijnende in diepen aandacht: Het ander vertoont een jong Heer, ziitende [sic] ter zijde een Tafel, waarop eenig Schrijftuig geplaatst is, en als met veel aandacht eene pen versnijdende; de karakters zijn natuurlijk, het licht en coloriet aangenaam en alleruitvoerigst	[Jan Tersteeg]	(Sold) fl 50 O W J Berg

			gepenceelt. Deze twee stukjes zijn het laatste penceelwerk geweest van dezen verdienstelijken Kunstschilder | *Mat:* op paneel *Size:* ieder hoog 6 ½, breed 5 ½ duim		
1808/08/23	AMSCH	0052	*Ekels, (J.) de jonge* | In een Keukenvertrek staat eene Vrouw, zij geeft geld aan een Boer, van wien zij eenige Both, welke voor haar op een bak geplaatst is schijnt gekocht te hebben, achterwaards bij den haardstede zit eene Dienstmaagd groente schoon te maken; verders zeer natuurlijk gestoffeert met verscheiden Keukengereedschappen, en van een uitvoerige penceelbehandeling | *Mat:* op doek *Size:* hoog 24, breed 29 duim	[Coclers]	(Bought In) fl 90
1808/08/23	AMSCH	0053	*Ekels, (J.) de jonge* | Een zinnebeeldige Ordonantie van drie Beelden, benevens toepasselijk bijwerk; meesterlijk behandeld | *Mat:* op paneel *Size:* hoog 21, breed 18 duim	[Van Iperen?]	(Sold or Bought In) fl 5 Van Iperen
1810/05/22	AMSCH	0027	*Ekels. (J) de jonge* | In een gemeubileerd Binnenvertrek, ziet men een vrolijk Gezelschap van twee Heeren met eene Dame, hun Glaasje Wijn drinkende; dit voorwerp is teder van penceelsbehandeling | *Mat:* op doek *Size:* hoog 26, breed 23 duim *Loc:* Leiden, Nederland. Stedelijk Museum De Lakenhal. (88)	Johannes van de Putte Nicolaasz.	(Sold) fl 33 Van Iperen
1810/06/20	AMSCH	0023	*J. Ekels De Jonge* | In een Binnenvertrek ziet men een bejaard Man en eene Vrouw, aan een Tafel zittende te lezen, terwijl een Jager met een Haas aan de hand het Vertrek binnenkomt, waarvan de Heer van verwondering als opspringt. Vol uitdrukking geschilderd | *Mat:* op doek *Size:* hoog 26, breed 24 duimen	C	(Sold) fl 51 van Iperen
1810/06/20	AMSCH	0024	*J. Ekels De Jonge* | In eene Kamer ziet men drie Perzonen aan een Tafel, waarvan een Heer staat op de Viool te spelen, terwijl eene Jufvrouw zit te zingen, een ander Heer zit met een Glaasje Wijn in de hand. Alles is regt natuurlijk en uitnemend behandeld | *Mat:* op doek *Size:* hoog 26, breed 24 duimen	C	(Sold) fl 37:10 Gruyter
			Elfers, J. [Unidentified]		
1808/06/13	AMSCH	0051	*Elfers (J.)* | Een doode Haas, benevens eenig dood Gevogelte, en een Jachtgeweer; uitnemend krachtig bewerkt en fraai van penceelbehandeling | *Mat:* op doek *Size:* hoog 39, breed 34 duim	L	(Sold) fl 19:10 Th Spaan
1808/06/13	AMSCH	0052	*Elfers (J.)* | Twee Boschgezichten, in het eene een Heer, met dood Wilt, tegen een ander sprekende. In het ander een Landman en Boerin, met Ossen en Schapen, beide Gezichten bij Zutphen. Natuurlijk en meesterlijk behandelt | *Mat:* op doek *Size:* hoog 26, breed 33 duim	L	(Sold) fl 11:10 du Pré
1808/06/13	AMSCH	0053	*Elfers (J.)* | Twee Gezichten in het Landschap Drenthe, met aartig Stoffage; natuurlijk en helder behandeld | *Mat:* op doek *Size:* hoog 15, breed 18 duim	L	(Sold) fl 9:5 Jan Spaan
1808/06/13	AMSCH	0054	*Elfers (J.)* | Twee Gezichten te Metman, boven Dusseldorp, zijnde Boerenwoningen, met opgaande hooge Trappen en Vrouwen gestoffeert; zonachtig en natuurlijk behandeld | *Mat:* op paneel *Size:* hoog 13, breed 10 duim	L	(Sold) fl 22 van Drielst
1808/06/13	AMSCH	0243	*Elfers* | Een woelige Zee, met eene Baak en twee Beelden, op den voorgrond met onderscheidene Vaartuigen; fiks en krachtig	L	(Sold) fl 40 Nieuwenhuisen
			Elliger		
1805/07/10	AMSCH	0291[H]	*Elliger* | Twee door Elliger | *Notes:* This lot was added in by hand in the AA, EBNP and RKDH copies of the catalogue.	V[inkeles]	(Sold) fl 1:5 Boelen
			Elliger, Antoni		
1804/12/10	AMSCH	0019	*A. Elliger* | Een Bybel-Ordinantie in een Landschap, met verscheide figuuren voor een pragtig gebouw, meesterlyk geschilderd | *Mat:* op paneel *Size:* Hoog 23, breed 17 duim	Jan De Groot	(Sold) fl 2 Yver
			Elliger, Ottmar (the elder)		
1802/02/16	AMSCH	0073	*oude Elliger* | Een oud Man met een jong Meisje voor een Nis, schynende iets te verrigten, over een cierlyk gewerkt Vuur-Comvoir, gestoffeerd met verder bywerk, door de oude Elliger	C	(Sold) fl 0:16 Grimpen
1802/07/21	HGKAN	0050	*O. Elger* | Een stil Leven, door O. Elger, op Doek, vergulde Lyst | *Mat:* op doek		(Unknown)
			Elliger, Ottmar (the younger)		
1801/04/13	AMSCH	0024	*O. Elliger* | Deeze fraaije Ordonantie verbeeld de Maaltyd van Cleopatra in een prachtig Gebouw, de rykheid der beelden, maakt dit stuk zo wel als de schildering tot een der beste van deezen Meester | *Mat:* op doek *Size:* hoog 47, breed 57 duim	Pierre Fouquet, junior	(Sold) fl 34 Reynders
1802/06/28	AMSCH	0050	*O. Elliger* | Twee stuks Historieele Ordonnantien	B	(Sold) fl 21:10 Texier
1802/06/28	AMSCH	0051	*O. Elliger* | Pallas, in 't graauw geschilderd door Denzelven [O. Elliger], Doek | *Mat:* op doek *Size:* hoog 64, breed 32 duim *Notes:* This lot was sold with lot 135 by Aug. Nicodemo.	Anna Elink	(Sold) fl 0:6 for lots 51 & 135. L Pakker
1802/09/06	AMSCH	0191	*O. Elliger* | Een zinnebeeldige Ordenantie	Spaan	(Sold) fl 2:15 van Iperen
1802/12/13	AMSCH	0061	*O. Elliger* | Twee stuks Ordenantien, verbeeldende de eene Zusanna door de oude verrast, en de anderen, Sophonisba de Béker met vergift	Florijn [?]	(Sold) fl 7:15 Van Iperen

			aanneemende, meesterlyk geschilderd | *Mat:* op doek *Size:* yder hoog 15, breed 12 duim		
1803/07/14	MGKLY	0009	*O. Ellinger* | Mars by Venus kunstig gepenseeld	Mr Caspar Jacob van Citters	(Unknown)
1803/07/18	AMSCH	0015	*Elliger (O.)* | Twee stuks, in het eene ziet men een Toveres verzeld van eenige Nimphen, het tweede steld voor de Bruiloft van Cupido en Psiche; de Goden en Tovergodinnen van den Olimpus, benevens eenige Cupidootjes, woonen dit Feest by. Deeze beide ryke Ordonantiën zyn in magnifique Paleizen verbeeld en meesterlyk geschilderd [Dans un Palais richement decoré se distingue au milieu une Magicienne ; elle est entourrée de Nimphes, & paroit occupée a quelque charme en faveur d'un jeune Guerrier. Près d'un autel Antique & entre les collonades sont d'autres nimphes. Pour Pandant le Peintre à choisi le sujet des Nôces de Cupidon & de Psichée. Les Dieux & Déesses de l'Olimpe assis au festin dans un magnifique Palais enchanté, sont entourrés d'amours faisans les honneurs de la fête. Ces tableaux sont d'une imagination fertile, ils ont une bonne couleur & beaucoup d'eclat.] | *Mat:* op doek *Size:* hoog 29, breed 33 duim	Maria Theresia Andrioli	(Sold) fl 74 Thys
1803/12/12	AMSCH	0026	*O. Elliger* | Een zinspelende Ordenantie van verscheide Beelden | *Mat:* op doek *Size:* hoog 21, breed 16 duim	W	(Sold) fl 2 Gruiter
1803/12/12	AMSCH	0027	*O. Elliger* | Een Historiëele Ordonantie, in een prachtig Paleis; meesterlyk door denzelven [O. Elliger] | *Mat:* op doek *Size:* hoog 23, breed 27 duim	W	(Sold) fl 2 v d Schleij
1804/05/07	AMSCH	0056	*Elliger. (O.)* | Deze Historieele Ordonantie vertoond in een prachtige Zaal, verscheide vorstelyke Persoonen en andere Lieden; ryk gestoffeert, met verder bywerk en bevallig van schildering | *Mat:* op doek *Size:* hoog 23, breed 27 duim	Schley	(Bought In) fl 2 ¾
1805/07/10	AMSCH	0059	*M. Elliger* | Twee stuks, Susanna met de Boeven, en Hypermenestra; beide breed op Doek | *Mat:* op doek *Size:* hoog 15, breed 14 duim *Notes:* The artist's name was given as "M. Elliger" but we have assumed this is an error.	V[inkeles] [for] L	(Sold) fl 3 Isaac Smit
1806/05/05	AMSCH	0052	*Elliger* | Een zinnebeeldige Ordinnantie door Elliger	V[inkeles]	(Sold) fl 1:15 Van Stroom
1806/08/13	AMSCH	0336	*Elliger (O)* | Door een Steene Nis, ziet men een bevallige jonge Dame; met een Roemer in de eene en eenige Vrugten in de andere hand; uitvoerig van penceelsbehandeling | *Mat:* op doek *Size:* hoog 15, breed 13 duim	Vinkeles [for] J	(Sold) fl 20 Schumacher
1807/08/26	AMSCH	0053	*O. Elliger* | In twee stuks bevallige Landschappen met Geboomte vertoonen zich de Fabelgeschiedenissen van Diana by Endiméon, en Bachus by Ariadne, verders gestoffeerd met verscheiden Minnewigten; meesterlyk op Doek geschilderd | *Mat:* op doek *Size:* ieder hoog 20, breed 16 duim	Roos [for] A	(Sold) fl 11 v der Schley [for] A
1808/06/06	RMRIJ	0035	*Elliger. (Ottomar)* | De afbeelding van Maria de Medicis ten voeten uit, met een Hofgezigt, zeer uitvoerig en aangenaam geschilderd [Marie de Médicis se proméne sous un Portique. On apperçoit la partie d'un jardin dans le fond de ce Tableau précieux] | *Annots:* Verk. C. Groeninx[?], Rotterdam 25 Juni 1800 (f 9.-) (RMA I) *Mat:* op paneel *Size:* Hoog 15, en breed 10 ¼ duim	Gerrit van der Pot, Heer van Groeneveld	(Sold) fl 42 Noordwyck
1810/10/10	MGCIT	0104	*Ellinger* | Mars, liggende met Venus; zeer voluptueus behandeld, en met 't een en ander voortreflyk Bywerk voorzien	Caspar van Citters	(Unknown)
1810/10/11	AMSCH	0030	*O. Elliger* | Twee stuks met bevallige Vrouwen, Kindertjes en bijwerk | *Mat:* op paneel *Size:* hoog 18, breed 13 duimen	[Levy Pakker?]	(Sold) fl 2:15 Vallee
1810/10/11	AMSCH	0112	*O. Elliger* | Twee stuks Fabel-Historiën | *Mat:* op doek	Y	(Sold) fl 1 Ijver [for] Mensart
			Elliger, Ottmar (the younger) (manner)		
1805/07/10	AMSCH	0285	*Eliger* | Een Historieele Ordinantie van twee Beelden; fiks op Doek, als door Eliger | *Mat:* op doek *Notes:* This lot was sold with lot 286 by an anonymous artist.	V[inkeles] [for] N	(Sold) fl 0:14 for lots 285 & 286. Agina
			Elsheimer, Adam		
1801/10/06	AMSCH	0024	*A. Elshaimer* | hoog Bergagtig Landschap, gestoffeert op de voorgrond: met een Bybel Ordinantie, verders een Ruwien, en aangenaam verschiet, uitvoerig en fraai behandeld | *Mat:* op koper *Size:* hoog 15, breed 19 duim	M	(Bought In) fl 14
1802/02/23	AMREB	0027[a]	*A. Elsheimer* | 2 stuks zynde het eene den jongen Tobias, door den Engel geleid wordende en het andere een Landschap, met Ruïnes, gestoffeerd met Nimphen, fraay op Koper | *This Lot:* Den jongen Tobias, door den Engel geleid wordende; lot 27[b] by C. Poelenburgh *Mat:* op koper	Margaretha Maria van Laar	(Sold) fl 31 for lots 27[a] & 27[b]. J Rooyers
1802/06/16	AMSCH	0051	*A. Elshaimer* | In een bergagtig Landschap, met eenige Gebouwen en Geboomten, vertoont zich de vlucht naar Egypten; Maria ryd op een Ezel, houdende het Kindeken in de Arm, ter zyde wandeld Joseph; alles is verbeeld by helder Maanlicht, en zeer natuurlyk en uitvoerig gepenceeld | *Mat:* op paneel *Size:* hoog 14, breed 19 duim	[Merrem]	(Sold) fl 9 Coclers
1802/06/16	AMSCH	0052	*A. Elshaimer* | Den Apostel Petrus, door Krygslieden bewaakt in de gevangenis; word door een Engel verlost: meesterlyk gepenceeld | *Mat:* op paneel *Size:* hoog 6 ½, breed 8 duim	[Merrem]	(Sold) fl 6 v d Schley

1802/06/16	AMSCH	0053	*A. Elshaimer* | Een Historiëele Ordenantie van drie Beelden, in een Landschap, by een Kaarsligt verbeeld | *Mat:* op koper *Size:* hoog 11 ½, breed 8 ½ duim	[Merrem]	(Sold) fl 4:5 Cobel
1803/08/17	AMSCH	0026	*Elsheimer. (A.)* | Een Landschap, met hoog Geboomte, bergachtig verschiet en badende Nimphen, kragtig behandeld | *Mat:* op paneel *Size:* hoog 12, breed 13 duim	Anna Catharina Putman	(Sold) fl 3 Gruyter
1805/10/09	HGBSM	0078	*A. Elshaimer* | Een slaapende nimph, in een landschap, in 't verschiet eenige satyrs | *Mat:* op paneel *Size:* hoog 6 ½ breet 9 duim	T H van Willigen [or others]	(Sold) fl 2 Teissier
1806/05/05	AMSCH	0051	*Elsheimer* | Twee stuks Bybelsche Historien, het eene Christus in den Hof van Getzemané, en het andere de gevangeneeming van denzelven; schoon van Licht en meesterlyk geschilderd door Elsheimer | *Mat:* op paneel *Size:* hoog 15 ½, breed 19 duim	V[inkeles]	(Sold) fl 9:5 Scheurleer
1806/08/20	HGBSM	0167	*Elsheimer* | Een Historieel stuk | *Mat:* op paneel	Macalester Loup [or others]	(Sold) fl 2 Guicherit
1807/08/26	AMSCH	0051	*A. Elshaimer* | De gekruiste Heiland tusschen de Moordenaren. Onder het Kruis staat de bedroefde Moeder met andere godvruchtige Vrouwen, en ter zyde eenige Soldaten, die het lot om het kleed werpen; zeer uitvoerig op Koper gepenceeld | *Mat:* op koper *Size:* hoog 14, breed 11 duim	Helsdinge	(Bought In) fl 12:10
1808/08/23	AMSCH	0049	*Elshaimer. (A.)* | In een Boomrijk Landschap, ziet men verbeeld de Fabel-historie van Latona met hare Kinderen, bij de onbarmhartige Boeren, aan een stille Waterbeek; het is kragtig en meesterlijk geschilderd | *Mat:* op koper *Size:* hoog 9, breed 11 duim	C	(Bought In) fl 68
1808/08/23	AMSCH	0050	*Elshaimer. (A.)* | Een Maneschijn over een Rivier, ter zijde eenig Geboomten, gestoffeert op de voorgrond met een Bijbelsche Historie, verbeeldende de H. Familie, vluchtende naar Egypte; fraai en uitvoerig behandeld | *Mat:* op koper *Size:* hoog 12, breed 17 duim	C	(Bought In) fl 11
1808/08/23	AMSCH	0192	*A. Elshaimer* | Twee stuks Bijbelsche Ordonantie, het eene verbeeld Christus in Gethzemané; en het andere de verraderij van Judas; zacht gepenceeld op Paneel | *Mat:* op paneel	[Gruyter?]	(Sold) fl 13 Van Iperen
1809/04/17	AMSCH	0030	*A. Elshaimer* | Bij een helder Maanlicht ziet men de Heilige Familelje, vlugtende na Egijpten; fraai en uitvoerig van schildering | *Mat:* op paneel *Size:* hoog 17, breed 14 duim	[Gruyter?]	(Sold or Bought In) fl 2 Gruyter
1809/04/22	AMYVR	0153	*Elsheimer* | Een Maneschijn	Juff^{r} Julikker	(Sold) fl 1:10 Andriessen
1810/08/06	AMSCH	0029	*Elshaimer (A.)* | In een Boomrijk Landschap ziet men de Fabel-Historie van Latona, met hare Kinderen, bij de onbarmhartige Boeren. Het is krachtig en meesterlijk geschilderd | *Mat:* op koper *Size:* hoog 9, breed 11 duimen	B	(Sold) fl 16:10 Gruyter
1810/08/06	AMSCH	0030	*Elshaimer (A.)* | Een Maneschijn, over een Rivier, ter zijde eenig Geboomte, gestoffeerd op den voorgrond met de Heilige Familie, vlugtende naar Egijpte. Fraai en uitvoerig behandeld | *Mat:* op koper *Size:* hoog 12, breed 17 duimen	B	(Bought In) fl 8
1810/10/11	AMSCH	0031	*A. Elsheymer* | Een Bergachtig Landschap, met eene Rivier doorsneden, gestoffeerd met de Heilige Familie | *Mat:* op koper *Size:* hoog 7, breed 9 duimen	C	(Sold) fl 5 Posthumus

Elsheimer, Adam (and Brueghel)

1805/10/09	HGBSM	0010	*Breugel; Elshaimer* | Andromeda verlost wordende door Perseus, uitvoerig | *Mat:* op koper *Size:* hoog 7 ½ breet 10 duim	T H van Willigen [or others]	(Sold) fl 4:15 Teissier

Elsheimer, Adam (or Elsheimer, A., manner)

1807/08/26	AMSCH	0286	*A. Elsheimer* | Een Ordonnantie, zynde een Nachtlicht; fraai op Koper, door of in de manier van A. Elsheimer | *Mat:* op koper	Joseph Vallette	(Sold) fl 5:15 Jozi

Elsheimer, Adam (copy after)

1804/10/08	RMCNL	0020	*Elskamer* | Eres [sic] haar Dogter Prosenpina [sic] zoekende na Elskamer	A t'Hooft	(Unknown)

Elsheimer, Adam (manner)

1801/04/13	AMSCH	0104	*A. Elsheimer* | Een boom- en bergachtig Landschap, op den voorgrond een Offerhande; meesterlyk gepenceeld in de manier van A. Elsheimer | *Mat:* op paneel *Size:* hoog 12, breed 13 duim	Pierre Fouquet, junior	(Sold) fl 12 Coclers
1801/08/19	AMSCH	0026	*A. Elshaimer* | In een heuvelagtig Landschap, met Riviere en Geboomte, rust op de Voorgrond een Man en Vrouw, verder Lieden met Vee, krachtig geschilderd, op paneel, als door A. Elshaimer | *Mat:* op paneel *Size:* hoog 14, breed 17 Duim	W Wynen	(Sold) fl 9:10 Le Dantú

Elsheimer, Johann (or Elsheimer, Joh., manner)

1804/08/08	AMSCH	0062	*J. Elshaimer* | Twee Bybelsche Ordinantiën, in het éene is Christus in den Hof van Gethsémané, en in 't andere wordt Christus door Judas verraaden; warm en delicaat geschilderd, door of als J. Elshaimer | *Mat:* op paneel *Size:* hoog 8, breed 12 duim	Vink[eles] [for] K[=Gruyter?]	(Sold) fl 2:10 Gruyter

Elsteijn [Unidentified] (changed from Brueghel, J. (I))

1802/05/24	HGBAK	0007	*de fluweele Breugel; Elsteijn* | Een fraay stukje, verbeeldende Maria met het Kindeke, ontfangende van Johannis ook nog een Kind zynde een	Mejuffrouw A van der Mieden	(Sold) fl 7:5 te ché

			druiftros, aan de voeten het lam, als ook een mand met vruchten, bloemen en kruiden, in een Landschap, door Elsteijn, hoog 12 ½ duim, breed 18 ½ duim, zwarte lyst en vergulde bies | *Size:* hoog 12 ½ duim, breed 18 ½ duim *Notes:* The artist's name was changed by hand from "de fluweele Breugel" to "Elsteijn" in the MA copy of the catalogue.		

Engels, Bartholomeus

1803/08/24	HGKAN	0072	*B. Enger* | Twee Italsaansche [sic] Landschappen	[Teissier] [or others]	(Sold) fl 6 Giesen

Ermels, Johann Franciscus

1807/06/10	HGBSM	0135	*Ermels* | Twee stuks arcadische Landschappen, met figuurtjes gestoffeerd, in de manier van J. van Huyzem | *Mat:* op doek *Size:* hoog 13, breed 16 duim	Abraham Delfos [or others]	(Sold) fl 7 v d Aa
1809/07/25	HGBSM	0068	*Ermels* | Twee Stuks Italiaansche Landschappen, in de trant van van Huisum, door Ermels | *Mat:* op doek *Size:* hoog 12 en 1 half, breed 16 duim	D van der Aa	(Sold) fl 17:5 Nieuwenhuis
1810/10/13	HGDAW	0007	*J.F. Ermel* | Een Rotsachtig Landschap, zwaar met Geboomte, op de voorgrond een Herderin, speelende op een Tambourain, waarna een Jongen agter een boom schynt te luisteren, in het verschiet een Behugt by een Water, Zonachtig en breed behandeld | *Mat:* op doek op paneel *Size:* hoog 12, breed 15 ½ duim		(Unknown)
1810/10/13	HGDAW	0008	*J.F. Ermel* | Een dito [Rotsachtig Landschap], op de Voorgrond, een zittende Reiziger, waarby een staand Mannetje, in het verschiet twee Wandelaars, niet minder als de voorgaande, door denzelfden Meester [J.F. Ermel] | *Mat:* op doek op paneel *Size:* hoog 12, breed 15 ½ duim		(Unknown)

Erp, van [Unidentified]

1804/08/02	BDAN	0019	*Van Erp* | Een aangenaam Landschap, in het midden een Water, waar inne eenige Beesten, en op den voorgrond Twee Figuren, schoon gecoloreerd | *Mat:* op paneel *Size:* b. 20 d. h. 13 d.	J G Calckberner	(Unknown)

Esselens, Jacob

1802/09/06	AMSCH	0040	*J. Esselens* | Een boomryk Landschap aan een waterplas, gestoffeerd met beeldjes en honden; meesterlyk | *Mat:* op doek *Size:* hoog 20, breed 18 duim	Mevrouw Achtienhoven	(Sold) fl 1:5 Gruiter
1803/08/24	HGKAN	0015	*J. Esselens* | Een Boomryk Lantschap en Hofgezigt, gestoffeerd met Heeren en Dames en verdere figuuren, konstig en uitvoerig geschildert | *Mat:* op doek *Size:* hoog 31, breet 25 duim	[Teissier] [or others]	(Sold) fl 24 Huybregts
1803/09/07	AMSCH	0053	*J. Esselens* | Een Bevroozen Rivier, gestoffeerd met een meenigte stoffagie van Beeldjes, welke zich met schaatzenryden, kolven en wandelen vermaken, verders eenige Arresleeden, Ysschuitje, enz.; op de voorgrond een gezakte Schuit, alles is zoo Natuurlyk behandeld, als of men de Natuur zelve beschouwd [Une rivière engelée [sic] ; l'on voit sur la glace une multitude de figures, qui s'amusent à courir à patins, à jouer à la crosse et à se promener ; dans le fond quelques traineaux etc. sur le devant une nacelle enfoncée dans la glace, l'ensemble est si frappant qu'on croit voir l'objet dans la nature] | *Mat:* op paneel *Size:* hoog 20, breed 29 duim [Haut 20, large 26 pouces] *Notes:* The dimensions differ in the Dutch and French editions of the catalogue.	Smidt	(Sold) fl 43 Gruiter
1804/05/07	AMSCH	0048	*Esselens. (J.)* | Een bevallig Landschap, doorsneede met een stuk Water, op de Voorgrond ziet men eenige Heeren en Dames, welke elkander verwelkomen en schynen te zullen gaan Vaaren; verders een aangenaam verschiet, en alles meesterlyk gepenceeld | *Mat:* op doek *Size:* hoog 23, breed 26 duim	Pruysnaar	(Sold) fl 132 C S Roos
1807/06/02	AMHUY	0004	*Esellens* | Een Gezicht aan het Strand, in het verschiet ziet men eenige Pinken, op de voorgrond een Heer te Paard, en verdere stoffagie		(Unknown)
1809/06/13	AMSCH	0044	*J. Esselens* | Een hoog Bergachtig Landschap, gestoffeerd op de voorgrond bij eene Poort met eene Vrouw en Kind, verder eenige Rijsigers en een bevallig verschiet, zonachtig en uitvoerig behandeld | *Mat:* op doek *Size:* hoog 22, breed 26 duim	H[odges]	(Bought In) fl 50

Esselens, Jacob (and Lingelbach)

1807/06/02	AMHUY	0017	*Esselens; Lingelbach* | Een Landschap, by een Boerewoning eenige Bomen, ter zyde een Brug, waar over een Man ligt, benevens een Heer en Dame met de Knecht daar agter, aan de andere zyde eenige Schapen, waarby de Herder ligt te rusten, meesterlijk geschilderd door Esselens, gestoffeerd door Lingelbach		(Unknown)

Essen, Cornelis van

1801/03/16	AMSCH	0075	*C. van Essen* | Twee capitaale Landschappen	P[ruyssenaar]	(Sold) fl 1:15 Wijland
1801/03/16	AMSCH	0096	*C. van Essen* | Twee stuks. een ryk gestoffeerd Dorpgezicht en een Harte-Jagt	K[ip]	(Sold) fl 2:5 Gruiter
1801/03/16	AMSCH	0101	*C. van Essen* | Een Batailje in een boomryk Landschap, meesterlyk	K[ip]	(Sold) fl 6 Koopman
1801/06/10	AMSCH	0058	*Essen. (C. van)* | Een Dorpgezicht, voor een Herberg staan twee Paarden voor een Krib, verders eenige Boeren eu Boerinnen, fyn en bevallig gepenceelt | *Mat:* op doek *Size:* hoog 17, breed 22 duim	[Doublet]	(Sold) fl 9 Pruyssenaar

1801/12/22	AMOTT	0006	*C. van Essen* | Eetende Paardjes voor een boere Herberg, in een zandig Landschap	Bartholomeus Ruloffs	(Unknown) fl 10:10
1801/12/22	AMOTT	0090	*C. van Essen* | Vrolyke Boeren voor een Buitenhuis	Bartholomeus Ruloffs	(Unknown) fl 5:15
1802/05/24	HGBAK	0009	*C. van Essen* | Een Landschap, op de voorgrond eenige Jagers te paard stygende, door C. van Essen, hoog 17 ½ duim, breed 24 duim, op doek, zwarte lyst en vergulde binnenrand | *Mat:* op doek *Size:* hoog 17 ½ duim, breed 24 duim	Mejuffrouw A van der Mieden	(Sold) fl 5:10 Kirderberg
1802/09/06	AMSCH	0043	*C. van Essen* | Twee stuks, een Plysterplaats, en een Batailje; fraay | *Mat:* op paneel *Size:* hoog 9, breed 10 duim	Mevrouw Achtienhoven	(Sold) fl 3:5 Yver
1802/12/13	AMSCH	0060	*C. van Essen* | Een Landschap; voor een Boere Wooning, ziet men een Bruin en wit Paard, terzyde eenige Huislieden, in alles krachtig en van de beste Schildering | *Mat:* op doek *Size:* hoog 17, breed 22 duim	Pruyssenaar [for] B	(Sold) fl 8:10 Gruiter
1803/09/07	AMSCH	0052	*C. van Essen* | Twee stuks Boere Herbergen, waarvoor een Varken- en een Vogelmarkt, met verscheide Beeldjes gestoffeerd en kloek behandeld [Deux tableaux représentant des auberges de village, devant lesquelles un marché de cochons et d'oiseaux, animé par diverses figures ; peint avec discernement] | *Mat:* op paneel *Size:* hoog 7, breed 9 duim	Smidt	(Sold) fl 2:15 L Pakker
1803/12/12	AMSCH	0031	*C. van Essen* | Voor een Boeren Herberg ziet men eenige Reizigers te paard en te voet; natuurlyk op Doek | *Mat:* op doek *Size:* hoog 9, breed 11 duim	Arnoud de Lange	(Sold) fl 4:10 Josi
1804/05/07	AMSCH	0054	*Essen. (C. van)* | Een Plysterplaats, voor een Boerewoning en Hooyschuur ziet men een belaaden Kar, waarby eenige Lieden, op de voorgrond twee Paarden by een Ruif; verders een aangenaam verschiet, zonachtig en uitvoerig gepenceeld | *Mat:* op doek *Size:* hoog 21, breed 40 duim	Roos [for] A	(Sold) fl 10 Pruissenaar
1804/05/07	AMSCH	0055	*Essen. (C. van)* | Twee stuks Boere Dorpgezichten, verbeeldende de eene een Paardenmarkt en de andere alwaar een Gans getrokken wordt; beide zeer natuurlyk en geestig, en fiks gepenceeld | *Mat:* op doek *Size:* hoog 31, breed 45 duim	Pruysnaar	(Bought In) fl 19
1804/10/16	DLOND	0070	*C. van Essen* | Een Gezelschap. Une Compagnie | *Mat:* op doek *Size:* hoog 14, breed 11		(Unknown)
1804/10/16	DLOND	0071	*C. van Essen* | Een Wintervermaak. Tableau d'Hyver | *Mat:* op doek *Size:* hoog 14, breed 18		(Unknown)
1804/10/16	DLOND	0072	*C. van Essen* | Een Boeren Gezelschap onder een Boom. Quelques paysans sous un Arbre | *Mat:* op koper *Size:* hoog 23, breed 11		(Unknown)
1804/10/16	DLOND	0073	*C. van Essen* | Een Pleister Plaats. Le Devant d'une Auberge | *Mat:* op doek *Size:* hoog 18, breed 15		(Unknown)
1805/07/03	AMSCH	0081	*C. van Essen* | Een Dorpgezicht met een Herberg op de Voorgrond, alwaar eenige Lieden zich met hunne Paarden ververschen; kragtig op Doek | *Mat:* op doek *Size:* hoog 21, breed 25 duim	C	(Sold) fl 9:10 Hardenberg
1805/07/03	AMSCH	0188	*C. van Essen* | Twee stuks, een Jagtparty en een Plysterplaats | *Mat:* op paneel	C	(Sold) fl 5 Hardenberg
1805/07/10	AMSCH	0057	*C. van Essen* | Langs een Weg, vertoont zig een Boeren Herberg of Plyster plaats, by Geboomten, waarvoor een Reiziger, met een gezadeld wit Paard, verders Huislieden en Kinderen; zonagtig behandeld	S[chley] [for] Doralle	(Sold) fl 1:15 Gruyter
1805/07/10	AMSCH	0058	*C. van Essen* | Een ryke Ordinantie, verbeeldende eene Plundering door Soldaaten, in een Boere Dorp, meesterlyk geschilderd | *Mat:* op doek	Wed Grave	(Sold) fl 7 Agina
1806/08/13	AMSCH	0052	*Essen. (C. van)* | In een Dorp, voor een Boeren Herberg, ziet men ryzende Lieden by gezadelde Paarden, terwyl andere zig ververschen, verders een Kerk en andere Woningen; plaisant behandeld | *Mat:* op doek *Size:* hoog 13, breed 15 duim	Roos	(Sold) fl 3 Th Spaan
1807/08/26	AMSCH	0055	*C. van Essen* | Twee stuks Landschappen, een Hartenjagt en een Pleisterplaats, beide met Beeldjes en Paarden gestoffeerd | *Mat:* op paneel	Roos [for] A	(Sold) fl 2:15 Gruiter
1807/08/26	AMSCH	0056	*C. van Essen* | Een met Paarden en Beeldjes ryk gestoffeerd Dorpgezigt; kloek | *Mat:* op paneel	Roos	(Sold) fl 4:10 Levy Pakker
1807/08/26	AMSCH	0057	*C. van Essen* | Een Postwagen voor een Herberg staande	Roos	(Sold) fl 5:10 A Rynders
1808/03/03	HAVIN	0019	*van Essen* | Een Pleisterplaats	Jacobus Spillebout	(Unknown)
1809/04/22	AMYVR	0038	*C. van Essen* | Voor een Boeren-Herberg ziet men een menigte vrolijke Gasten, welke zich met drinken en danssen vermaken; geestig | *Mat:* op paneel *Size:* hoog 12, breed 14 duim	de Bruin	(Sold) fl 5:5 du Pree
1809/04/22	AMYVR	0039	*C. van Essen* | Een Pleisterplaats | *Mat:* op doek *Size:* hoog 12, breed 15 duim	Juff^{r} Julikker	(Sold) fl 1:5 C S Roos
1809/06/13	AMSCH	0211	*C. van Essen* | Twee stuks, een Duinachtig Landschap en een Land- en Watergezigt	E	(Sold) fl 2 Gruiter
			Everbroeck, Frans van		
1802/06/16	AMSCH	0055	*F. v. Everbroeck* | In een Krans en Festoen met diversche Vruchten, ziet men een Roemer Rhynschen Wyn geplaatst; alles zeer natuurlyk en dun gepenceeld | *Mat:* op doek *Size:* hoog 62, breed 45 duim	[Merrem]	(Sold) fl 10:10 van Dijl

Everdingen, Allart van

1801/06/10	AMSCH	0057	*Everdingen. (A. van)* | Een Noorsch bergachtig Landschap met een Waterval en Gebouwen; allernatuurlykst van licht en meesterlvk [sic] behandeld | *Mat:* op paneel *Size:* hoog 25, breed 22 duim	Herman ten Kate	(Sold) fl 50:10 Wolft
1802/06/16	AMSCH	0046	*A. van Everdingen* | Een Bergagtig Landschap met hoog Geboomte, in het midden ziet men een Waterval en stroomend Beekjen, een Zwitsersche Brug en stoffagie van Beeldjes en een Ezel; zonachtig en dun, als J. Ruysdaal behandeld | *Mat:* op doek *Size:* hoog 44, breed 56 duim	[Merrem]	(Sold) fl 60 H de Valk
1802/06/16	AMSCH	0047	*A. van Everdingen* | Een Noordsch bergachtig Landschap met eene fraaije Sparreboom, op de voorgrond by een stil Watertje, voorts een menigte Kreupelgewas en gestoffeerd met een rustende Ryziger; alles behandeld als de voorgaande | *Mat:* op paneel *Size:* hoog 19 ½, breed 15 ½ duim	[Merrem]	(Sold) fl 41 Th Spaan
1802/06/16	AMSCH	0048	*A. van Everdingen* | Een sterk woelend Water met verscheide zeilende Scheepen; verder ziet men een Dorpkerk en Tooren, helder en bevallig gepenceeld | *Mat:* op paneel *Size:* hoog 13 ½, breed 19 duim	[Merrem]	(Sold) fl 8 Delfos
1802/06/16	AMSCH	0049	*A. van Everdingen* | Een woelende Zee gestoffeerd met verscheide zeilende Scheepen; zeer natuurlyk en fraay geschilderd | *Mat:* op paneel *Size:* hoog 17, breed 24 ½ duim	[Merrem]	(Sold) fl 14 Reijers
1802/12/13	AMSCH	0057	*A. van Everdingen* | In een onstuimige Zee, ziet men eenige Scheepen in Gevaar van te vergaan, beneffens eenige Wrakken, waarop zig eenig Volk schynt te redden, de branding van de Zee en 't Licht, zyn zeer wel waargenomen | *Mat:* op doek *Size:* hoog 27, breed 41 duim	Pruyssenaar [for] A	(Sold) fl 0:12 Gruiter
1803/06/20	AMSCH	0009	*A. v. Everdingen* | Een Noords bergachtig Landschap, met hoog gebergten en divers opgaand geboomte, in de midden ziet men een waterval, op een brug ziet men eenige Ezeldryvers; de Schildering is de natuur evenarende behandeld, op Doek | *Mat:* op doek *Size:* hoog 44, breed 36 duim	Schley [for] B	(Sold) fl 95 Pruijssenaar
1803/09/07	AMSCH	0051	*A. van Everdingen* | Twee stuks woelende Waters, met zylende Schépen en andere Vaartuigen, Natuurlyk op Paneel [Deux tableaux représentant la mer agitée, avec diverses bateaux à pleines voiles et d'autres batimens ; peint au naturel] | *Mat:* op paneel *Size:* hoog 7, breed 10 duim	Smidt	(Bought In) fl 10
1804/02/27	AMSCH	0030	*Everdingen. (A. van)* | Een capitaale Winter, ryk gestoffeerd met gaande en rydende Beeldjes, fiks en meesterlyk geschilderd | *Mat:* op doek *Size:* hoog 37, breed 53 duim	C	(Sold) fl 1 Theengs
1804/02/27	AMSCH	0031	*Everdingen. (A. van)* | By een opkomende Storm, ziet men in een sterk woelende Zee, eenige zeilende Vaartuigen; de betrokken lucht en het invallend zonlicht, doen een byzonder effect in dit natuurlyk Schildery, en is allerschoonst van penceelsbehandeling | *Mat:* op doek *Size:* hoog 15, breed 21 duim	C	(Bought In) fl 26
1804/04/28	LNDLS	0043	*Everdingen* | Een woelend Water, met zeilende schepen, en een dorp in 't verschiet, helder en konstig, door Everdingen, op paneel | *Mat:* op paneel *Size:* hoog 13, breed 18 duim	[Abraham Delfos] [or others]	(Sold) fl 8:10 Gerrit Mulder
1804/05/07	AMSCH	0046	*Everdingen. (A. van)* | In een Rotsächtig Landschap, ziet men by eenig Geboomte, een ménigte Beelden, Postwagens Paarden, enz.; breed meesterlyk gepenceeld | *Mat:* op doek *Size:* hoog 22, breed 27 duim	Vinkeles [for] H[affner]	(Bought In) fl 5
1804/05/07	AMSCH	0047	*Everdingen. (A. van)* | Op een Heuvel ziet men een Boerewooning, en Stoffagie van Beeldjes, voorts een aangenaam verschiet; meesterlyk behandeld | *Mat:* op doek *Size:* hoog 17, breed 24 duim	Y[ver] [for] JJ	(Sold) fl 7:15 L Pakker
1804/08/08	AMSCH	0059	*A. van Everdingen* | Een Noordsch Bergachtig Landschap, met een Waterval, een Schuit, en verdere Stoffagie, meesterlyk op Doek | *Mat:* op doek *Size:* hoog 24, breed 27 duim	Roos a	(Sold) fl 56 Hulswit
1804/08/08	AMSCH	0060	*A. van Everdingen* | Een Noordsch Bergachtig Landschap, met hoog Geboomte en een Waterval; zonachtig en fraai van schildering | *Mat:* op doek *Size:* hoog 44, breed 56 duim	Pruys[senaar]	(Sold) fl 54 de Harde Swart
1804/10/16	DLOND	0074	*Everdingen* | Een Arcadisch Landschap. Paysage d'Arcadie | *Mat:* op paneel *Size:* hoog 15, breed 18		(Unknown)
1804/10/29	HRBAU	0020	*Everdingen, (A. van)* | Op den Voorgrond van dezen Zeestorm, by een Steenklip, staat een zwaare Branding, waar agter een Driemast in groot gevaar ten anker ligt; wyders zyn er nog eenige Vaartuigen, welken poging doen, den laagen wal te ontzeilen. Zeer bevallig van licht, en de schuim der Branding zeer natuurlyk behandeld | *Mat:* op doek *Size:* hoog 19, breed 23 duim	Simon Styl	(Unknown)
1805/07/10	AMSCH	0055	*A. van Everdingen* | In een Bergachtig Landschap ziet men by een hoog opgaande Boom en helder spiegelende Rivier eenige rustende Schapen met hunne Herders, verder Geboomte en Gebergten; meesterlyk op Paneel | *Mat:* op paneel *Size:* hoog 20, breed 16 duim	V[inkeles] [for] M	(Sold) fl 80 L Pakker
1805/07/10	AMSCH	0056	*A. van Everdingen* | Twee stuks Noordsche Boomryke Landschappen, met stoffagie; zonachtig op Paneel | *Mat:* op paneel *Size:* hoog 16, breed 13 duim	V[inkeles] [for] N	(Sold) fl 3 L Pakker
1806/08/13	AMSCH	0053	*Everdingen. (A. van)* | Een Noordsch Berg- en Boomryk Landschap, Landschap, op de Voorgrond eenige Lieden in een Schuitje; dit stukje is in allendeelen [sic] de natuur gelyk, en bevallig gepenceeld | *Mat:* op doek *Size:* hoog 15, breed 19 duim	Daniel Mansveld	(Sold) fl 51 T Spaan

1807/06/02	AMHUY	0013	*Everdingen* | Een hoog bergachtig Landschap, met Geboomte en Waterval, op de voorgrond zit een Vrouw met een Kind aan de Borst, waarby staat een Landman, zonachtig en krachtig gepenceeld		(Unknown)
1808/06/11	RMRIJ	0054	*A: van Everdingen, zoo goed als van Ruisdaal* | Een welverkozen bergachtig Landschap, Rivier en Waterval, gestoffeerd met Figuren, als door Lingelbach, alles meesterlyk en vast geschilderd | *Mat:* op doek *Size:* hoog 51, breed 39 ½ duim		(Sold) fl 295 Rohan
1808/06/13	AMSCH	0046	*Everdingen (A. van)* | Een Noordsch boom- en bergachtig Landschap, met een Waterval en stoffage van Herders en Schapen. Kragtig behandeld | *Mat:* op doek *Size:* hoog 20, breed 25 duim	E M Engelberts	(Sold) fl 46 Nieuwenhuisen
1808/06/13	AMSCH	0202	*A. van Everdingen* | Een Noordsch Landschap	E M Engelberts	(Sold) fl 45 J Schuman
1809/04/17	AMSCH	0031	*A. van Everdingen* | Een bergachtig Landschap, ter zijde een Waterval, gestoffeerd met gaande en rustende Rijzigers; meesterlijk | *Mat:* op doek *Size:* hoog 47, breed 37 duim	T	(Sold) fl 4:10
1809/06/13	AMSCH	0045	*A. van Everdingen* | Een Boomrijk Landschap, met een Rivier doorsneeden, gestoffeerd met Beeldjes en Schaapen, agterwaards een groot Kasteel; natuurlijk | *Mat:* op doek *Size:* hoog 30, breed 37 duim	T	(Sold) fl 22 Hulswit
1810/06/06	RMMUY	0048	*A. van Everdingen* | Een Waterval. Door A. van Everdingen stout en natuurlijk geschilderd | *Mat:* op doek		(Unknown) fl 53:10
1810/06/20	AMSCH	0021	*A. Van Everdingen* | Een aangenaam Landschap, met Geboomte en een helder Water op den voorgrond, gestoffeerd met gaande en rustende Reizigers en een Herder met Schapen. Het is zonachtig en bevallig van schildering | *Mat:* op doek *Size:* hoog 18 ½, breed 24 duimen	D	(Sold) fl 141 Jan Ijver
1810/06/20	AMSCH	0022	*A. Van Everdingen* | Dit natuurlijk Schilderij verbeelt een Duinrijk Landschap met Geboomte, ter zijde een opgaande Weg naar een Boeren Woning, gestoffeerd met gaande Huislieden en een Hond. Warm en zuiver van schildering | *Mat:* op paneel *Size:* hoog 31, breed 35 duimen		(Sold or Withdrawn) fl 95 Spaan
1810/07/23	DOLG2	0059	*Everdingen* | Een Boomrijk Landschap, meesterlijk geschilderd | *Mat:* op doek *Size:* hoog 17, breed 27 duim	Pieter Quinting	(Sold) fl 8:10 Spruijt van Gent
1810/08/06	AMSCH	0031	*Everdingen (A. van)* | Voor eene Ruïne van een oud Gebouw ziet men verscheidene rustende en staande Beelden, bij een Paard en Muilezel. Warm van koloriet, en delicaat in de manier van Asselijn geschilderd | *Mat:* op doek *Size:* hoog 28, breed 30 duimen	F	(Sold) fl 61 van Leen
1810/10/11	AMSCH	0238	*A. Van Everdingen* | Een Noordsch Bergachtig Landschap	A	(Sold) fl 0:6 Gruiter
1810/10/11	AMSCH	0258[b]	*Everdingen* | Drie stuks, twee Rijngezigten, door H. Zagtleven en een Landschapje door Everdingen | *This Lot:* Een Landschapje; lot 258[a] by H. Saftleven	A	(Sold) fl 1:10 for lots 258[a] & 258[b]. L Pakker
			Everdingen, Allart van (and Lingelbach)		
1808/08/23	AMSCH	0048	*Everdingen (A. van); J. Lingelbagh* | Een Noords bergachtig Landschap, met hoog Geboomte en nederstortende Watervallen, gestoffeert op de voorgrond met twee beladen Muil-Ezels, op de eene zit een Huisman, nevens hem eene gaande Vrouw en Hond, en ter zijde drie Vissers; het bruischen van het Water is natuurlijk verbeeld, en meesterlijk schoon geschilderd | *Mat:* op doek *Size:* hoog 42, breed 45 duim	X	(Bought In) fl 50
			Everdingen, Allart van (or Everdingen, A., manner)		
1806/08/13	AMSCH	0312	*Everdingen* | Een Strandgezichtje, met verscheide Scheepen en Schuiten; door of als Everdingen	Vinkeles [for] F	(Sold) fl 1 Yver
			Everdingen, Allart van (manner)		
1802/05/05	AMSCH	0057	*A van Everdingen* | Een Rotsächtig Landschap, met een Waterval en verder hoog Geboomte. Zeer natuurlyk in de manier van A van Everdingen | *Mat:* op doek *Size:* hoog 25, breed 18 duim	BB	(Sold) fl 10:10 Stevens
			Everdingen, Cesar Boetius van		
1802/06/16	AMSCH	0050	*C. van Everdingen* | Op een Heuvel ziet men een Boerewooning en stoffagie van Beeldjes, op de voorgrond een Waterplas, voorts een aangenaam verschiet; meesterlyk behandeld | *Mat:* op doek *Size:* hoog 17, breed 24 duim	[Merrem]	(Sold) fl 11:10 Spaan
1802/09/21	UTHDG	0027	*Cesar van Everdingen* | St. Hieronymus in devotie, 't halve lijf naakt, verzeld door een Leeuw enz. Alles, inzonderheid het hoofd, schoon van licht en bruin, en in een stoute manier behandeld | *Mat:* op doek *Size:* hoog 47, breed 56 duimen		(Bought In) fl 14
1802/12/13	AMSCH	0058	*C. van Everdingen* | Op een Heuvel; ziet men een Boere Wooning en Stoffagie van Beeldjes, op de voorgrond een Waterplas | *Mat:* op doek *Size:* hoog 17, breed 24 duim	Pruyssenaar [for] A	(Bought In) fl 12
1804/08/08	AMSCH	0061	*C. van Everdingen* | Een Gezicht op de Waal voor Nymeegen, ziende na de Stad en Dyk, waarin verscheide zeilende en stil leggende Vaartuigen; fiks gepenceeld | *Mat:* op doek *Size:* hoog 19, breed 25 duim	Vink[eles] [for] S	(Sold) fl 2:10 de Harde Swart
1804/12/10	AMSCH	0018	*C. van Everdingen* | Een Historieele Ordinantie van onderscheide figuuren, fraay van teekening en krachtig geschilderd | *Mat:* op doek *Size:* Hoog 28, breed 24 duim	Jan De Groot	(Sold) fl 10 Vallet

1807/08/26	AMSCH	0052	*C. van Everdingen* | Een fraaije Ordonnantie van vyf Vrouwen aan een Bad, waarvan de eene zich wascht. Het naakt is schoon, de plooijing der gekleede Beelden is fraai, en de schildering delicaat, zynde zonachtig gedaagd, en van een uitmuntende behandeling | *Mat:* op doek *Size:* hoog 29, breed 25 duim	Joseph Vallette	(Sold) fl 20 S M Levy
			Everdingen, Pieter van		
1805/10/21	GRBOL	0023	*P. V. Everdingen* | Een Rotsich Landschap en Waterval	Gerardus Nicolaus Heerkens	(Unknown)
			Eych, J.F. [Unidentified]		
1809/05/26	HADAA	0058	*J.F. Eych* | Een schoon geschilderd mans Pourtreit	Mejuffrouw de Wed David Heemskerk [or others]	(Unknown)
1809/05/26	HADAA	0059	*J.F. Eych* | Een dito [mans Pourtreit], in de manier van Rembrand	Mejuffrouw de Wed David Heemskerk [or others]	(Unknown)
			Eyck, Hubert van (and Eyck, J.)		
1808/06/06	RMRIJ	0036	*Eijck. (Huibert van); Eijck. (Jan van)* | In eenen Gottischen tempel vertoont zich een op het oude en nieuwe Verbond zinspelend tafereel, rijk van ordinantie, ongemeen uitvoerig en fraai geschilderd. De werken van deze Meesters zeldzaam voorkomende, moet dit stuk, als iets bijzonders, aangemerkt worden [Dans l'intérieur d'un Temple Gothique, sont representées deux Allégories tirées du vieux et du nouveau Testament. Cette Production des Inventeurs de la Peinture à l'huile, est un chef-d'oeuvre en ce genre. Une composition agréable, un dessin correct et de la fraicheur dans le Coloris, font de ce morceau antique et bien conservé, un objet rare et qui mérite l'attention des amateurs] | *Mat:* op paneel *Size:* Hoog 51 ¾, en breed 40 duim *Loc:* Amsterdam, Nederland. Rijksmuseum. (A500) as Geertgen tot Sint Jans	Gerrit van der Pot, Heer van Groeneveld	(Sold) fl 210 van Lennep [for] le Roi
			Eyck, Jan van (and Eyck, H.)		
1808/06/06	RMRIJ	0036	*Eijck. (Huibert van); Eijck. (Jan van)* | In eenen Gottischen tempel vertoont zich een op het oude en nieuwe Verbond zinspelend tafereel, rijk van ordinantie, ongemeen uitvoerig en fraai geschilderd. De werken van deze Meesters zeldzaam voorkomende, moet dit stuk, als iets bijzonders, aangemerkt worden [Dans l'intérieur d'un Temple Gothique, sont representées deux Allégories tirées du vieux et du nouveau Testament. Cette Production des Inventeurs de la Peinture à l'huile, est un chef-d'oeuvre en ce genre. Une composition agréable, un dessin correct et de la fraicheur dans le Coloris, font de ce morceau antique et bien conservé, un objet rare et qui mérite l'attention des amateurs] | *Mat:* op paneel *Size:* Hoog 51 ¾, en breed 40 duim *Loc:* Amsterdam, Nederland. Rijksmuseum. (A500) as Geertgen tot Sint Jans	Gerrit van der Pot, Heer van Groeneveld	(Sold) fl 210 van Lennep [for] le Roi
			Eyk, Abraham van der		
1808/06/13	AMSCH	0240	*A. van den Eijck* | In een Binnenvertrek, verbeeldende een zinspelende Ordonantie, op de Politieke Weegschaal, ziet men vier-en-twintig onderscheidene Persoonen, zijnde alle bekende Portretten; het is van eene uitvoerige penceelsbehandeling | *Mat:* op paneel *Loc:* Lyon, France. Musée des Beaux-Arts. (H-1151)	[Cattrop?]	(Sold) fl 85 Moll
			Faber, J.H. [Unidentified]		
1804/05/07	AMSCH	0060	*Faber (J. H.)* | Twee stuks, het eene steld voor in een Boerewoning de werving van een Jonge Boer, waar over de Ouders en verdere Vrienden zich zeer schynen te bedroeven, in de weerga komt hy als Generaal in de armen zyner Vader en Famielie terug; beide van een bevallige schildering | *Mat:* op doek *Size:* hoog 29, breed 36 duim	Roos [for] A	(Sold) fl 34 Teengs
			Fabritius, Barent		
1810/12/03	DOBRA	0001	*B. Fabritius* | In een Keuken staat een geslagt Varken op de ladder, waar agter een Meisje met de blaas in de hand. Verder zit een Vrouw darmen schoon te maken, nevens haar een kind, agter dezelve een man aan den haart een pyp te rooken; uitvoerig en delikaat geschilderd, door B. Fabritius, 1656 | *Inscr:* B. Fabritius, 1656 (signed and dated?) *Notes:* It is unclear whether the name and date are inscribed on the painting. *Loc:* Berlin, Deutschland. Gemäldegalerie. (819 B)		(Unknown)
			Fabritius, Carel		
1810/07/23	DOLGI	0024	*Fabritius* | De Strafóeffening aan den Balliuw van Zuid-Holland, om het roven van een Koe; onder Willem den Goeden, Graaf van Holland. Fraai van Teekening, en wel gepenseeld | *Mat:* op paneel *Size:* hoog 13, breed 18 duim	Mr Pieter van den Santheuvel	(Sold) fl 10 [or] 20 Disconi [or] De Senrie
			Faistenberger, Anton		
1803/09/07	AMSCH	0061	*A. Feystenberg* | Een capitaal Italiaansch Bergagtig ryk gestoffeerd Landschap, met Gebouwen, Geboomten en springende Fontyn, by een Waterbeekje, waar in een Man, met twee Ezels, op de voorgrond Huislieden, met Schaapen en ander Vée; alles is zonagtig, bevallig en	Smidt	(Sold) fl 16 for lots 61 & 62. Scheffer

			Meesterlyk gepenceeld [Un paysage montagneux d'Italie ; tableau capital et richement garni d'arbres, de jardins et de jets d'eau ; un petit ruisseau dans lequel est un homme avec deux ânes, sur le devant des campagnards avec du bétail, l'ensemble est d'un excellent effet ; d'une exécution soignée et précieuse] | companion to lot 62 *Mat:* op doek *Size:* hoog 28, breed 39 duim		
1803/09/07	AMSCH	0062	*A. Feystenberg* | Een dito [capitaal Italiaansch Bergagtig ryk gestoffeerd Landschap], zynde de wéderga, verbeeld een Boomryk Landschap, op de voorgrond gestoffeerd met verscheide Huislieden, met verschillende soorten van Vée, verder een Rivierzicht en hoog Gebergten; in alles als de voorige [Paysage semblable au précédent ; sur le devant quelques paysans avec différentes espèces de bétail ; dans le fond la vue d'une rivière serpentant au pied de hautes montagnes ; l'exécution et l'ordonnance ont le mérite du précédent tableau.] | companion to lot 61 *Mat:* op doek *Size:* hoog 28, breed 39 duim *Notes:* It is unclear what "dito" refers to in the title.	Smidt	(Sold) fl 16 for lots 61 & 62. Scheffer
			Fargue		
1802/07/21	HGKAN	0026	*la Fargue* | Twee stuks kleine dito [Schilderyen], zynde een Jongens en Meisjens Pourtrait		(Unknown)
1802/07/21	HGKAN	0071	*la Fargue* | Een zeer accurate afbeelding van het Binnen en Buyten-Hoff in 's Hage, met veel Bywerk, door La Fargue, vergulde Lyst		(Unknown)
1802/07/21	HGKAN	0078	*la Fargue* | Het Dorp Overschie		(Unknown)
1806/08/20	HGBSM	0156	*la Fargue* | Eene Boerewoning | *Size:* hoog 10, breed 13 ½ duim	Macalester Loup [or others]	(Sold) fl 1:10 Gram
			Fargue, J.C. la [Unidentified]		
1805/12/16	AMSCH	0104	*J. C. la Fargue* | Een bevallig Gezicht, uit het Haagsche Bosch, naar het Vorstelyk Huis te zien, en de verdere Gebouwen, gestoffeerd met verscheide wandelende Lieden; zonachtig en plaisant op Paneel geschilderd | *Mat:* op paneel *Size:* hoog 9, breed 13 duim	V	(Sold) fl 4:5 T van Iperen
			Fargue, Karel la		
1804/12/10	AMSCH	0020	*K. la Fargue* | Een Hollandsch Landschap, by verscheide Boeren Woningen ziet men koeijen en bokken in een weide; alles natuurlyk en fiks behandeld | *Mat:* op paneel *Size:* Hoog 10, breed 14 duim	Jan De Groot	(Sold) fl 5 Coclers
			Fargue, Maria la		
1801/03/16	AMSCH	0007	*M. la Fargue* | Twee stuks, het eene een Fruitverkoopster, en het andere een Hoenderverkoopster; beide uitvoerig gepenceeld	P[ruyssenaar]	(Sold) fl 30 Rijnders
1801/06/10	AMSCH	0063	*Fargue. (M. la)* | Een Binnenhuis, door een openstaande deur ziet men een Vrouw Garnaalen verkoopen, in 't Voorhuis een Dienstmeid met een Kind op den arm, bevallig en uitvoerig behandeld | *Mat:* op paneel *Size:* hoog 12, breed 9 duim	Herman ten Kate	(Sold) fl 15:10 Taijs
1801/06/13	LNDLS	0085	*M. la Fargue* | Een Juffertje, staande voor een thuin, nevens een voetstuk, zich opsierende met bloemen, op paneel | *Mat:* op paneel	D van R	(Sold) fl 6:5 A Delfos [for] W
1802/06/28	AMSCH	0056	*M. M. la Fargue* | Voor een Buitenhuis zit een oude Vrouw, op de Stoep ter zyde, een andere Vrouw met een Kind, en over de Onderdeur een Meid; verder en Dansende Jongen, met een Hond, en een Man met een Stok; plaisant geschilderd door M. M. la Fargue, | *Mat:* op paneel *Size:* hoog 13, breed 14 duim	Anna Elink	(Sold) fl 7 Van der Schley [for] Ryfsnyder
1802/09/18	RMDRS	0050	*M. la Farge* | Een Dame in een Voorportaal, terwijl haar Meid van een Vrouw, voor het huis Aalbessen koopt; zeer aangenaam geschilderd | *Size:* hoog 12, breed 9 duim	Casper de Haas	(Sold) fl 10:5 Abresch
1802/11/01	DOBRA	0175	*Maria La Fargue* | Een gemeubileerd Binnen-Vertrek. Een Heer zittende te leezen, terwyl hy Toebak rookt, voor een opgeschooven raam, aan een tafel waar Theegoed op staat; benevens drie Juffers, terwyl een dienstmeid met een kind op den arm de deur inkoomt | *Mat:* op paneel *Size:* hoog 15, breed 18 duim		(Sold) fl 5 Belaerts [?]
1803/08/24	HGKAN	0056	*M. La Fargue* | Twee stuks Buitehuysen, zeer bevallig van Ordonnantie en Geestig gestoffeerd | *Mat:* op paneel *Size:* hoog 9, breet 10 duim	[Teissier] [or others]	(Sold) fl 11 Kan
1804/02/27	AMSCH	0036	*Fargue. (M. la)* | Twee stuks Buitenhuizen, het eene een Zalmboer, en het andere een Boerin met Eyeren; bevallig van Ordonantie | *Mat:* op paneel *Size:* hoog 9, breed 10 duim	B	(Sold) fl 10:5 Van Iperen
1805/07/10	AMSCH	0061	*Maria la Fargue* | In een Binnekamer zit een zieke Vrouw in een Armstoel, neffens haar een Dame; welke haar een bezoek geeft; en in 't Portaal een Dienstmaagd met een Vuurmand, en verder Huisraad; uitvoerig en delicaat gepenceeld | *Mat:* op paneel *Size:* hoog 17, breed 14 duim	Y[ver]	(Sold) fl 10 L Pakker
1809/04/22	AMYVR	0041	*Juffrouw lu Fargue* | In een Binnenvertrek staat een Meisje in een Boek voor haar Moeder te leezen; ter zijde een Wieg en ander bijwerk; uitvoerig | *Mat:* op paneel *Size:* hoog 10, breed 12 duim	de Bruin	(Bought In) fl 21
1809/04/22	AMYVR	0042	*Juffrouw lu Fargue* | In een moderne Kamer zit eene Dame met een Kind op haar Schoot, waarbij een Meisje met een Pop, door de Deur ziet men in het Voorhuis de Dienstmaagd, waarbij een Jongetje; zonachtig, als de voorgaande | *Mat:* op paneel *Size:* hoog 13, breed 14 duim	de Bruin	(Bought In) fl 23

Fargue, Paulus Constantijn la

1801/12/22	AMOTT	0040	*P. C. la Fargue* | 2 stuks gestoffeerde fraaije Gezigten, in 's Hage	Bartholomeus Ruloffs	(Unknown) fl 19:10
1802/07/20	MGSAN	0003	*C. C. de la Fargue* | Een extra plaisant Landschap, gestoffeerd met Figuuren en Beesten, en verder Bywerk, op Paneel | *Mat:* op paneel *Size:* hoog duim 16, breed duim 23 *Notes:* The artist's name was given as "C. C. de la Fargue" but we have assumed this is an error.		(Unknown)
1803/08/24	HGKAN	0058	*P.C. La Fargue* | Een Gezicht op Halfweegen Haarlem, ryk gestoffeerd, en Meesterlyk geschildert | *Mat:* op paneel *Size:* hoog 13, breet 15 duim	[Teissier] [or others]	(Sold) fl 14:15 Kan
1804/05/07	AMSCH	0062	*Fargue. (P. C. la)* | Twee aangenaamen Gezichten binnen Schravenhaagen, byde ryk gestoffeerd met Heeren en Dames en Rytuigen; bevallig en uitvoerig geschildert | *Mat:* op paneel *Size:* hoog 10, breed 13 ½ duim	Vinkeles [for] G	(Sold) fl 3 L Pakker
1804/05/07	AMSCH	0063	*Fargue. (P. C. la)* | Twee Gezichten, te Haarlem den Dam, en de Damstraat, byde zeer natuurlyk en zonachtig geschilderd | *Mat:* op doek *Size:* hoog 10, breed 13 duim	Y[ver] [for] W	(Sold) fl 37 Ferguson
1804/10/16	DLOND	0075	*P. C. la Fargue* | Een Landschap, gestoffeerd. Paysage avec des figures | *Mat:* op paneel *Size:* hoog 10, breed 14		(Unknown)
1804/10/16	DLOND	0076	*P. C. la Fargue* | Uts[a] [Een Landschap, gestoffeerd. Paysage avec des figures] | *Mat:* op doek *Size:* hoog 16, breed 19		(Unknown)
1806/11/24	AMSCH	0026	*Fargue (P.C. La)* | Een gezigt op de Broeksloot by 't Huis te Werve, het Land is met den Hooibouw gestoffeerd; zonagtig geschilderd | *Mat:* op doek *Size:* hoog 25, breed 30 duim	Munnikhuizen	(Sold) fl 3:10 v d Schley [for] Ryfsneyder
1807/06/10	HGBSM	0127	*P.C. la Fargue* | Het gezigt van het Nagttegaalspad na de Kloosterkerk te zien in den Haag | *Mat:* op doek *Size:* hoog 13, breed 16 duim	Abraham Delfos [or others]	(Sold) fl 25:10 Oosterwyk
1809/06/13	AMSCH	0050	*P.C. La Fargue* | Een Gezicht aan de Broeksloot, ziende op het Huis te Merwe, gestoffeerd met eenige in het Hooi arbeidende Huislieden; zonachtig | *Mat:* op doek *Size:* hoog 22, breed 30 duim	R[ijfsnijder]	(Sold) fl 1:5 L Pakker
1809/07/25	HGBSM	0215	*P.C. la Fargue* | Een Gezigt over 't Buitenhof naar het Stadhouders quartier te zien, met een menigte Figuuren gestoffeerd | *Mat:* op paneel *Size:* hoog 22 en een half, breed 27 duim	D van der Aa [or] E B ten Dall	(Sold) fl 12:5 for lots 215 & 216. van Eyk
1809/07/25	HGBSM	0216	*P.C. la Fargue* | Een dito Gezigt van de Kneuterdyk door de Gevange Poort te zien, als de voorgaande | *Mat:* op paneel *Size:* hoog 22 en een half, breed 27 duim *Notes:* It is unclear what "dito" refers to in the title.	D van der Aa [or] E B ten Dall	(Sold) fl 12:5 for lots 215 & 216. van Eyk

Ferg, Franz de Paula

1803/09/07	AMSCH	0059	*Ferch* | Twee stuks Boom en Bergachtige Landschappen, ryk gestoffeerd met Beeldjes en Beestjes, uitvoerig en helder gepenceeld, door Ferch [Deux paysages montueux, riches en arbres, en figures et en bestiaux ; excellemment travaillé et d'une belle ordonnance] | *Mat:* op paneel *Size:* hoog 16, breed 13 duim	Smidt	(Sold) fl 14:10 de Lafontaine
1803/09/07	AMSCH	0060	*Ferch* | Twee stuks Gezichten binnen Rome, gestoffeerd met een ménigte Beelden, Paarden, Ezels, Kwakzalvers, en andere stoffagie; zonagtig en uitvoerig op Paneel [Deux points de vue de Rome ; enrichies d'un grand nombre de figures, de chevaux, d'ânes et de charlatans etc. ; il règne un ton saillant dans ce tableau, qui est bien exécuté] | *Mat:* op paneel *Size:* hoog 20, breed 25 duim	Smidt	(Bought In) fl 61
1810/07/26	AMSCH	0029	*Ferg (P.)* | Een schoon Landschap, met eene Caravane van Reizigers | *Mat:* op doek *Size:* hoog 16, breed 12 duimen	Cassino	(Sold) fl 12 Spaan
1810/07/26	AMSCH	0030	*Ferg (P.)* | Een Wintergezigt, met Beelden and andere eigenaartige Voorwerpen | *Mat:* op doek *Size:* hoog 16, breed 12 duimen	Cassino	(Sold) fl 5:5 T Spaan

Ferguson, William Gowe

1801/03/16	AMSCH	0077	*Ferguzon* | Een schoone Ordonnantie van dood Gevogelte | *Notes:* This lot was sold with lot 78 by N. Maes.	P[ruyssenaar]	(Sold) fl 4:5 for lots 77 & 78. Coclers
1801/08/19	AMSCH	0029	*W. G. Ferguson* | Twee stuks met dood Gevogelte, op steene Tafels leggende, uitvoerig op Doek | *Mat:* op doek *Size:* hoog 25, breed 21 Duim	Van Forreest	(Sold) fl 16 V[n] Dijl
1802/05/05	AMSCH	0061	*Ferguson* | Een Tafel, met Dood Gevogeltje en Jagtgereedschap | *Size:* hoog 24, breed 19 duim	J	(Sold) fl 1:5 Gruiter
1802/06/29	HGDAW	0028	*Ferguson* | Een stuk met dood Wild van Vogels zeer uitvoerig door Ferguson		(Unknown)
1802/12/13	AMSCH	0065	*Ferguson* | Eenig Dood Gevogelte en Jachtgereedschappen | *Mat:* op doek *Size:* hoog 25, breed 21 duim	Pruyssenaar [for] A	(Sold) fl 1:15 Gruiter
1804/02/27	AMSCH	0035	*Ferguson* | Een Tafel met Jagtgereedschap en dood Gevogelten | *Mat:* op doek *Size:* hoog 25, breed 21 duim	C	(Sold) fl 1 de Meijer
1804/10/29	HRBAU	0021	*Fergison* | Een Patrys, gedeeltelyk liggende en aan zyn' poot hangende, waar by meer klein Gevogelte en Jagtgereedschappen. Zeer natuurlyk en uitvoerig geschilderd | *Mat:* op doek *Size:* hoog 22, breed 16 duim	Simon Styl	(Unknown)
1804/10/29	HRBAU	0022	*Fergison* | Een Duif, mede aan zyn' poot hangende, benevens eenige Vinken; op het Voetstuk ligt een Seisje en Jagtgereedschap. Als het voorige behandeld | *Mat:* op doek *Size:* hoog 22, breed 16 duim	Simon Styl	(Unknown)

1805/07/03	AMSCH	0083	*Ferguson* | Twee stuks, met Dood Gevogelten, leggende op steene Tafels, met Tapyten en Jagtgereedschap; delicaat op Doek | *Mat:* op doek *Size:* hoog 25, breed 21 duim	C	(Sold) fl 6 Teissier
1806/08/20	HGBSM	0085	*Ferguson* | Eene doode hangende Patrijs, benevens eenig klein Gevogelte, verders een Hoorn en eenige Netten, Valkekappen &c. dit alles rust op eene marmer steene Tafel, gedeeltelijk met een zijde kleed met Franje bedekt, delicaat en uitvoerig geschilderd door Ferguson | *Mat:* op doek *Size:* hoog 24, breed 20 duim	Macalester Loup [or others]	(Sold) fl 20 Lafontaine
1810/06/20	AMSCH	0166	*W. Ferguson* | Op eene Tafel ligt eenig Jagttuig en dood Gevogelte	A	(Sold) fl 1:10 Koopman
1810/10/10	MGCIT	0087	*Ferguson* | Een Tafel, waarop een doode Duif en verder Bywerk; goed behandeld	Caspar van Citters	(Unknown)

Ferguson, William Gowe (manner)

1801/04/08	HAVIN	0041	*Fergeson* | Een dito [Tafel] met Vrugten van of in de Manier van Fergeson		(Unknown)
1802/09/06	AMSCH	0163	*Ferguson* | Hangende doode Vogels, boven een tafel, waar op eenig Jagttuig geplaatst is; fiks geschilderd in de manier van Ferguson | *Mat:* op doek	X	(Sold) fl 1:15 A Schotte

Ferri, Ciro

1803/04/27	AMSCH	0048	*Ciroferri* | Samson & Dalila, bien composé & largement peint | *Size:* h. 5 ½, l. 7 pieds	A	(Sold) fl 18 Th Spaan

Filippo Napoletano (Filippo d'Angeli)

1803/12/12	AMSCH	0155	*Napolitain* | Twee Bataitjes | *Size:* hoog 7, breed 9 duim	D	(Sold) fl 3 Coclers
1810/07/26	AMSCH	0031	*Filippo Napolitano* | Twee stuks hevige Gevechten. Vol uitdrukking en stout geschilderd | *Mat:* op doek *Size:* hoog 16, breed 28 duimen	Cassino	(Sold) fl 0:14 L^y Pakker

Finjé, A. [Unidentified]

1804/10/22	MGWIN	0003	*A. Finjé* | Een dito [extra fraaië] Fruit- en Bloemstuk, door A. Finjé, in vergulde Lysten, op Glas geschilderd | *Mat:* op glas	F Reytsma	(Sold) £ 1:7 Abr Buford

Flemal, Bertholet (I)

1803/04/27	AMSCH	000B	*Bertholet* | Mercure devenant amoureux d'Hersé, ce tableau de Bertholet, est connu par une des Estampes du Cabinet de Mr. le Brun, gravé par J. de Wit	A	(Sold) fl 111 Th Spaan

Flinck, Govert

1801/06/10	AMSCH	0059	*Flink. (G.)* | Een slapende Cupido, in een Landschap, in het verschiet eenige Nimphen, zich badende, meesterlyk gepenceelt | *Mat:* op doek op paneel *Size:* hoog 26, breed 32 duim	Herman ten Kate	(Sold) fl 35 J^b Roeloffs
1801/08/19	AMSCH	0027	*G. Flink* | Een bevallige Vrouw, halver Lyf: rustende met de Rechter Arm, op een Baluster, houde de Linker Hand op de Borst, verder vertoont zich Cupido, met Pyl en Boog, uitvoerig op Doek behandeld | *Mat:* op doek *Size:* hoog 32, breed 26 duim *Loc:* Tel Aviv, Israel. Museum. (?)	W Wynen	(Sold) fl 6 J Spaan
1802/02/16	AMSCH	0028	*G. Flink* | Een Diana en ander bywerk, op doek | *Mat:* op doek	E	(Sold) fl 2 L Pakker
1802/12/13	AMSCH	0062	*G. Flinck* | Voor een Baluster ziet men een bevallige Vrouw in ryke Kleeding, verseld met Cupido; door G. Flinck, op Doek, hoog 32, breed 26 duim, van boven toogs gewys | *Mat:* op doek *Fmt:* van boven toogs gewys *Size:* hoog 32, breed 26 duim *Loc:* Tel Aviv, Israel. Museum. (?)	Pruyssenaar [for] D	(Sold) fl 20 Coclers
1802/12/13	AMSCH	0063	*G. Flinck* | Een Mans Pourtrait, meesterlyk gepenceeld	Pruyssenaar [for] B	(Sold) fl 2:5 Gruiter
1803/04/20	AMSCH	0027	*Flink. (G)* | Twee stuks, het Afbeeldzel van een Dame en Heer in ryke Deftige Kleeding; bevallig en meesterlyk fraay gepenceeld [Deux Portraits : un Homme & une Dame vus à mi-corps, peints d'une maniere large & vigoureuse.] | *Mat:* op doek *Size:* ieder hoog 34, breed 27 duim	Maria Magdalena van Sluypwyk, gravinne van Moens	(Sold) fl 50 Coclers
1803/08/01	AMSCH	0009	*Flinck. (G.)* | Twee stuks, zynde een Mans- en Vrouwe Pourtrait, halverlyf, beide in eenvoudige kleeding, krachtig en meesterlyk behandeld | *Mat:* op doek *Size:* ieder hoog 30, breed 24 duim	J	(Bought In) fl 14:10
1804/08/08	AMSCH	0064	*G. Flink* | AEneas by de Brand van Troijen, hy heeft zyn Vader en zyn Zoon névens hem, en is in vreesachtige houding; alles zeer fraai behandeld | *Mat:* op doek *Size:* hoog 43, br. 50 duim	Pruys[senaar]	(Sold) fl 20 Bd de Harde Swart
1804/10/29	HRBAU	0023	*Flink, (G.)* | Een Oud Mans Hoofd, ter linkerzyde in profil en tot den Borst te zien: zyne gryze lokken zyn met een roode muts gedekt. Hy is gekleed met een groene rok en een lederen schootsvel. Alles zeer natuurlyk en byzonder meesterlyk geschilderd | *Mat:* op paneel *Size:* hoog 23 ½, breed 19 duim	Simon Styl	(Unknown)
1806/08/13	AMSCH	0055	*Flinck. (G.)* | Dit overheerlyk Schildery, stelt voor: Christus dood leggende in de schoot van Maria, verzeld van godvruchtige Vrouwen, treurende en andere Apostelen, terzyde Bediendens en achterwaards 't Kruis, verders een Boom en Bergachtig verschiet; de hartstogten zyn natuurlykst 't effect frapant en van de beste Schildering van deeze beroemde Meester | *Mat:* op doek *Size:* hoog 43, breed 28 duim	Coclers	(Sold) fl 230 P Swanenburg
1806/08/20	HGBSM	0005	*Govert Flink* | Het Borstbeeld van den Apostel Paulus met het zwaard in de hand. – Dit Schilderij verdient alle lof, zo voor de uitdrukking, als wonderbaare kragt van Coloriet, en evenaard een besten Rembrand | *Mat:* op doek *Size:* hoog 28, breed 23 duim	Macalester Loup [or others]	(Sold) fl 42 Teissier

1807/04/00	LNDLS	0036	*G. Flink* | Het Pourtrait van .... met twee handen, tot de knieën, konstig in de manier van Rembrandt | *Mat:* op doek *Size:* hoog 46, breed 38 duim	[Abraham Delfos] [or others]	(Unknown)
1807/06/10	HGBSM	0036	*G. Flink* | Het Pourtrait van .... met twee handen, tot de knieën, konstig in de manier van Rembrandt | *Mat:* op doek *Size:* hoog 46, breed 31 duim	Abraham Delfos [or others]	(Sold) fl 2:2 Bogart
1807/08/26	AMSCH	0058	*G. Flink* | Diana met hare Nimphen, zich badende aan een Waterplas, onder hoog Geboomte; meesterlyk fraai op Doek gepenceeld | *Mat:* op doek *Size:* hoog 25, breed 32 duim	Joseph Vallette	(Sold) fl 35 S M Levij
1807/08/26	AMSCH	0059	*G. Flink* | Een fraai Mans-Pourtret, fiks | *Mat:* op doek *Size:* hoog 29, breed 25 duim	Roos	(Sold) fl 7:5 van Iperen
1808/04/26	GDAN	0049	*Flinck (G.)* | Een dorre Heijgezigt met fraaije Beekers, Pourtretten, en een gekranst Schaap, meesterlijk geschildert | *Size:* hoog 34 ½, breed 36 duim	G H Fortuyn	(Unknown)
1808/06/06	RMRIJ	0037	*Flinck. (Govert)* | De Zegening van Jakob door Izaak voorstellende. Men ziet de twijfeling in het gelaat van den Aartsvader, het verlangen van Rebekka, en de begeerte van Jakob, overschoon uitgedrukt. Dit konststuk, alleszins van ordinantie, behandeling en costume in de manier van Rembrand, doet eer aan dezen Meester [Isaac donnant la Bénédiction à son fils Jacob. La Patriarche, dans son lit et sur son séant, semble se douter de la supercherie de son Epouse et de son fils. Le desir de Rebecca, et la crainte d'être découvert dans la figure de Jacob, sont admirablement exprimés. Ce Tableau magnifique et digne de Rembrand, est un chef-d'oeuvre] | *Mat:* op doek *Size:* Hoog 44, en breed 53 duim *Loc:* Amsterdam, Nederland. Rijksmuseum. (A 110)	Gerrit van der Pot, Heer van Groeneveld	(Sold) fl 1380 J J de Wit [for] le Roi
1808/08/23	AMSCH	0054	*Flinck. (G.)* | Eene staande Vénus, halver-lijf naakt, gedeelte-lijk met een' wit linnen en blaauwe zijde Sluijer omhangen, zij houdt den regter arm en hand omhoog, waarin zij een Pijl vasthoudt, voor haar staat Cupido, als met een uitgestrekten arm naar dezelve grijpende; meesterlijk fraai en krachtig gepenceeld | *Mat:* op doek *Size:* hoog 45, breed 34 duim	H	(Bought In) fl 195
1808/11/28	AMSCH	0075	*G. Flink* | Een capitaale Historiëele Ordonanrie [sic], meesterlijk geteekend en schoon geschilderd	[Gruyter?]	(Sold) fl 1:15 W v d Schley
1810/03/23	HAVIN	0072	*G. Flink* | Een oud Man leezende in een Boek [In Lysten met Glasen] | *Notes:* The bracketed information in the title appears above lot 63 and refers to lots 63 to 79.	Rudolf Hendrik de Wetstein [or others]	(Unknown)
1810/08/01	AMSCH	0032	*Flinck (Govert)* | Een deftig Heer, met zijn Hoed in de hand, staande voor eene Tafel [Un Homme de distinction, tenant son chapeau à la main, ayant un Table audevant de lui, la figure étant vue jusqu'aux genoux] | possibly companion to lot 33 *Annots:* médiocre (NGW) *Mat:* op doek *Size:* hoog 48, breed 39 duimen	Mr Pieter de Smeth van Alphen	(Sold) fl 120 for lots 32 & 33. Roelsma de Groningen
1810/08/01	AMSCH	0033	*Flinck (Govert)* | Eene deftige Vrouw met eenen Waaijer in de hand en staande voor eene Tafel. Kunnende strekken tot eene wederga van de voorgaande [Une Dame en beau Costume, tenant son Evanteil [sic] à la main : elle se voit debout devant sa Table. Cette pièce peut servir de pendant à la précédente] | possibly companion to lot 32 *Annots:* médiocre (NGW) *Mat:* op doek *Size:* hoog 48, breed 39 duimen	Mr Pieter de Smeth van Alphen	(Sold) fl 120 for lots 32 & 33. Roelsma de Groningen

Flinck, Govert (manner)

1801/03/16	AMSCH	0152	*G. Flink* | Een lagchende Jonge, allerbevalligst geschilderd, in de manier van G. Flink	K[ip]	(Sold) fl 39 C S Roos
1801/04/13	AMSCH	0096	*G. Flink* | Een bejaarde Vrouw zittende op een Leuningstoel; in de manier van G. Flink | *Mat:* op doek *Size:* hoog 32, breed 26 duim	Pierre Fouquet, junior	(Sold) fl 13 Coclers
1802/05/05	AMSCH	0058	*G. Flink* | Het Pourtrait van P. P. Rubbens, in Alöude Kleeding, fiks gepenceeld in de manier van G. Flink | *Mat:* op doek *Size:* hoog 26, breed 21 duim	G	(Sold) fl 8 Cocler
1806/08/13	AMSCH	0234	*G. Flink* | Een Mans Pourtrait, levensgrooten halverlyf, in treffelyke Kleeding, in de manier van G. Flink | *Mat:* op doek	Roos	(Sold) fl 1 Du Pre
1807/08/26	AMSCH	0333	*G. Flink* | Hes [sic] Pourtret van een jong bevallig Meisje, in een ryke Kleeding; meesterlyk als de vorige behandeld [fiks geschilderd], als G. Flink | *Mat:* op doek op paneel	v d Schley [for] L	(Sold) fl 1 T Spaan

Floris, Frans (I)

1803/09/07	AMSCH	0063	*Frans Floris* | Twee stuks, Vénus en Cupido, en Mars en Vénus; beide Delicaat gepenceeld [Deux tableaux ; l'un représentant Venus et Cupidon, l'autre Mars et Venus ; tous les deux pleins de graces et de finesse] | *Mat:* op paneel [sur toile] *Size:* hoog 9, breed 6 duim *Notes:* The materials differ in the Dutch and French editions of the catalogue.	Smidt	(Sold) fl 3:5 Gruiter
1804/08/08	AMSCH	0068	*F. Flores* | Twee Koppen; meesterlyk geschilderd | *Mat:* op paneel *Size:* hoog 18, breed 13 duim	Vink[eles] [for] K[=Gruyter?]	(Sold) fl 1:5 Coclers
1809/04/17	AMSCH	0145	*F. Flores* | Twee stuks, Vénus en Cupido en Mars en Vénus; delicaat geschilderd | *Mat:* op paneel	[Gruyter?]	(Sold or Bought In) fl 2 Gruyter

Floris, Frans (I) (manner)

1810/06/06	RMMUY	0087[b]	*Frans Flores* | Een oud en raar stuk, verbeeldende eene Keuken, waar in verscheiden figuren goede cier maken, in 't verschiet eenigen die dansen en vrolijk zijn, in de manier of tijd van Langen Pier, geschilderd op Paneel. Op de achter zijde de lotgevallen van den Aartsvader Abraham, in 't		(Sold) fl 3:10 for lots 87[a] & 87[b]. v Giesen

			graauw, in de manier van Frans Flores, zeer zuiver geconserveert | *This Lot:* De lotgevallen van den Aartsvader Abraham; lot 87[a] is manner of Aertsen *Mat:* op paneel		

Fock, Harmanus

1801/08/19	AMSCH	0030	*Hs. Fok* | Twee stuks Arcadische Landschappen met oude Gedenktekens ryk gestoffeerd, en zonachtig geschilderd	Pruyssen^{r}	(Bought In) fl 15
1804/02/27	AMSCH	0034	*Fok. (H.)* | In twee Aangenaame Boome- en Bergachtige Landschappen, ziet men by de overblyfzels van pragtige Gebouwen en opgerigte Gedenktekens, eenige bevallige staande en rustende Beeldjes, en een aangenaam verschiet; warm van kleur en fraai geschilderd | *Mat:* op paneel *Size:* hoog 16, breed 13 duim	C	(Sold) fl 30 I^{c} Smit
1804/08/08	AMSCH	0065	*H. Fok* | By een helder schynende Maan ziet men een aangenaam Land- en Watergezicht, gestoffeerd met zeilende en stil leggende Vaartuigen, ter zyde eenig zwaar Geboomte en een aangenaam verschiet; bevallig geschilderd | *Mat:* op paneel *Size:* hoog 10, breed 14 ½ duim	Vink[eles] [for] K[=Gruyter?]	(Sold) fl 5 for lots 65 & 66. Graffelman
1804/08/08	AMSCH	0066	*H. Fok* | By een bewolkte Maan ziet men in een Land- en Riviergezicht een Overhaalpond, met Menschen en Beesten; ter zyde, op een hoogte, eenig dartel Geboomte, waarby twee Landlieden met Schaapen; niet minder dan de voorige | *Mat:* op paneel *Size:* hoog 10, breed 14 ½ duim	Vink[eles] [for] K[=Gruyter?]	(Sold) fl 5 for lots 65 & 66. Graffelman
1804/08/08	AMSCH	0067	*H. Fok* | In een Boom- en Bergachtig Landschapje ziet men twee Landlieden met elkander praaten, ter zyde een Koornakker, onder 't opgaand Geboomte eenige grazende Schaapen en Bokken, en een bevallig verschiet | *Mat:* op paneel *Size:* hoog 5 ½, breed 7 ½ duim	Vink[eles] [for] K[=Gruyter?]	(Sold) fl 1:15 Graffelman

Forman, L. [Unidentified]

1801/04/13	AMSCH	0025	*L. Forman* | Voor een Buitenhuis zitten eenige vrolyke Gasten met wyn, een Vrouw in 't wit gekleed heeft de Kan in de hand; het licht en bruin is wel waargenomen, de schildering is in den aart van G. Metzu | *Mat:* op paneel *Size:* hoog 15, breed 12 duim	Pierre Fouquet, junior	(Sold) fl 200 Carli

Fourdrier [Unidentified]

1810/03/26	RMMUY	0089	*Fourdrier* | Twee stuks zeer fraai moderne Landschappen, met konstige figuren. Uitvoerig en zeer verdienstelijk geschilderd [Deux tableaux modernes des Paysages, avec figures, tres fin et d'un jolie genre.] | *This Lot:* Een zeer fraai modern Landschap *Annots:* 2 ferm effrayer Exple d'echolle (BPG) *Notes:* Lots 89 and 90 were printed in the catalogue as one item. The French edition of the catalogue does not include an artist for this lot.	Daniel de Jongh Az	(Sold) fl 30 for lots 89 & 90. Van Iperen Amsterdam [for] Wreesman
1810/03/26	RMMUY	0090	*Fourdrier* | Twee stuks zeer fraai moderne Landschappen, met konstige figuren. Uitvoerig en zeer verdienstelijk geschilderd [Deux tableaux modernes des Paysages, avec figures, tres fin et d'un jolie genre.] | *This Lot:* Een zeer fraai modern Landschap *Annots:* 2 ferm effrayer Exple d'echolle (BPG) *Notes:* Lots 89 and 90 were printed in the catalogue as one item. The French edition of the catalogue does not include an artist for this lot.	Daniel de Jongh Az	(Sold) fl 30 for lots 89 & 90. Van Iperen Amsterdam [for] Wreesman

Fournier

1806/05/05	AMSCH	0160	*Fourniers* | Een Dame, met een tak Druiven over Balustrade	R[oos]	(Sold) fl 4:15 Graffelman

Fragonard, Jean Honoré

1803/12/12	AMSCH	0033	*Fragonard* | Een Historieele Ordenantie van drie Beelden; meesterlyk op Doek | *Mat:* op doek *Size:* hoog 12, breed 9 duim	D	(Sold) fl 1:5 Gruiter

Franck, Johan Willem

1802/09/18	RMDRS	0028	*W. Frank* | Een Tafel, waarop een Vaas met een menigte Bloemen en Vogelnesje, uitvoerig geschilderd | *Size:* hoog 33, breed 25 duim	Casper de Haas	(Unknown) fl 5:10
1803/06/20	AMSCH	0029	*J. W. Frankx* | In een Boekenkamer zit een bejaard Heer in zyn Japon aan een Tafel, met een Bril in zyn Hand, en bonte Muts op zyn Hoofd, verders een Hond en ander bywerk; uitvoerig op Doek | *Mat:* op doek *Size:* hoog 18, breed 15 duim	Schley [for] G	(Sold) fl 6 Hafner
1804/02/27	AMSCH	0033	*Frankx. (J. W.)* | Twee stuks Binnenhuizen, de eene verbeeld een Teekenaar, bezig iets na te teekenen, en de andere een Geleerde in zyn Studeerkamer; beide alleruitvoerigst van schildering | *Mat:* op paneel *Size:* hoog 18, breed 16 duim	D	(Sold) fl 6:10 V^{n} d^{r} Schleij [for] R[ijfsnijder]
1808/08/23	AMSCH	0055	*Frank. (J. W.)* | Op een steene Rand ziet men een fraai gewerkte Vaas, gevuld met onderscheidene zoorten van van Bloemen, als roode, witten en geele Roosen, Angelieren, Tulpen, Hyacinthen, Papavers en anderen, ter zijde ligt een Vogelnesje; schoon geordoneerd en delicaat van penceelbehandeling | companion to lot 56 *Mat:* op paneel	C	(Sold) fl 44 for lots 55 & 56. Dupré
1808/08/23	AMSCH	0056	*Frank. (J. W.)* | Deeze Ordonantie verbeeld een sierlijke Vaas, met onderscheiden bloemen, waarop Infecten aazen; zacht en uitvoerig gepenceeld, zijnde dit stuk de wederga van het voorgaande | companion to lot 55	C	(Sold) fl 44 for lots 55 & 56. Dupré

Francken

1803/12/15	MGLAC	0041	*Franck, (den ouden)* | Een Danszaal, waarin eenige dansende en andere vroolyke [sic] Figuuren; goed van ordonnantie en coloriet | *Mat:* op paneel *Size:* hoog duim 19, breed duim 26	Mr L H de Haze Bomme	(Unknown)
1808/09/13	HABRU	0023	*Franken* | Een Zeestrand vol gewoel		(Unknown) fl 1:6

Francken (or Francken, manner; or Vrancx, or Vrancx, manner)

1805/12/16	AMSCH	0135	*Francx* | Een Bybelsche Ordinantie, van een ménigte Beelden; op Doek, door of als Francx | *Mat:* op doek	Y	(Sold) fl 0:10 Yver

Francken (or Vrancx)

1801/03/16	AMSCH	0084	*Franks* | Een capitaale Bybelsche Ordonnantie, stellende voor, daar Christus 12 jaaren oud zynde, zig in den Tempel bevond, uitvoerig geschilderd	P[ruyssenaar]	(Sold) fl 19 Coclers
1801/08/19	AMSCH	0028	*Franks* | Een Capitaal Boomryk Landschap, gestoffeert met Christus, daar hy de Blinde Ziende maakt, onder een ménigte Aanschouwers	W Wynen	(Sold) fl 6 Yver
1802/02/16	AMSCH	0010	*Franks* | Twee stuks Bybelsche Ordenantiën op koper | *Mat:* op koper	B[uys]	(Sold) fl 2:5 Coclers
1802/05/05	AMSCH	0060	*Franks* | Een afgelaaten Christus van 't Kruis en verdere Beelden | *Size:* hoog 12, breed 15 duim	J	(Sold) fl 14:10 Spruit
1802/07/09	AMSTO	0009	*Franck* | 2 dito [stuks] dito [Binnenhuyzen]		(Unknown)
1804/08/02	BDAN	0048	*Franc* | Maria met het Kind | *Mat:* op koper *Size:* b. 6 d. h. 8 en een half d.	J G Calckberner	(Unknown)
1806/05/05	AMSCH	0234	*Francks* | Een Muziseerend Gezelschap | *Mat:* op koper *Size:* hoog 5, breed 4 duim	V[inkeles]	(Sold) fl 0:14 van Iperen
1806/08/20	HGBSM	0154	*Frank* | Een Zee triumf | *Mat:* op paneel *Size:* hoog 18, breed 25 duim	Macalester Loup [or others]	(Sold) fl 5 Smeets
1808/04/26	GDAN	0045	*Frank* | Verbeeldende de Steeniging van Stephanus, met veele Beelden, wel geschilderd | *Mat:* op koper *Size:* hoog 14 ½, breed 11 ½ duim	G H Fortuyn	(Unknown)
1808/04/26	GDAN	0046	*Frank* | De Wetgeving op Sinaï, de verëering van 't Goude Kalf, waarom de Israeliten zijn dansende, dus een groot aantal Beelden, zeer uitvoerig en fraai geschilderd | *Size:* hoog 19, breed 28 duim	G H Fortuyn	(Unknown)
1808/04/26	GDAN	0047	*Frank* | Zijnde de allerprachtigste Roomsche lieve Vrouwe Kerk van Antwerpen, met een overheerlijk verschiet, aan de Pijlaren een aantal schoone Beelden, en Altaaren, waar in verscheidene Geestelijken in hun gewaad werkzaam zijn, brandende Kaarsen ziet men hier en daar in 't verschiet, en een Lamptaarn, waar in licht brand, door een Geestelijk Persoon gedragen wordende, alles zo uitvoerig en vol gewoel en overheerlijk geschilderd | *Size:* hoog 31, breed 43 duim	G H Fortuyn	(Unknown)
1808/04/26	GDAN	0048	*Frank* | Zijnde de Kruisiging van Christus, vol gewoel, uitvoerig geschildert | *Size:* hoog 24 ½, breed 29 duim	G H Fortuyn	(Unknown)
1809/07/25	HGBSM	0170	*Frank* | De Dood van Cleopatra | *Mat:* op koper *Size:* hoog 5 en een half, breed 7 en een half duim	D van der Aa [or] E B ten Dall	(Sold) fl 2 de Gruyter
1809/07/25	HGBSM	0208	*Franck* | Dit onderwerp vertoond de Verloren Zoon, in zyn wellustigen stand verbeeld, en omringt met verscheiden Gebeurtenissen uit diergelyk leven voordgevloeid; het middenvak is in 't Coloriet, en de omringende vakjes zyn in 't grauw geschildert | *Mat:* op doek *Size:* hoog 26 en een half, breed 33 duim	D van der Aa [or] E B ten Dall	(Sold) fl 1:12 Bogaard
1809/07/25	HGBSM	0213	*Francks* | De Bataille van Lekkerbeetje | *Mat:* op paneel *Size:* hoog 21, breet 31 en een half duim	D van der Aa [or] E B ten Dall	(Sold) fl 1:4 A Vermeulen

Francken (or Vrancx and Delen)

1802/07/20	MGSAN	0007	*D. van Deelen; Francq* | In dit fraaije Stuk vertoont zich in een prachtige Zaal, een zeer aanzienlyk Gezelschap aan een Tafel te eeten; in het verschiet ziet men een Vorstelyk Collonade en Tuin, alles helder en krachtig geschilderd door D. van Deelen en Francqu | *Mat:* op paneel *Size:* hoog duim 25, breed duim 33		(Unknown)

Francken (manner; or Vrancx, manner)

1802/12/13	AMSCH	0200	*Franx* | Een ryke Ordenantie, zinspeelende op het Oude en Nieuwe Verbondt, in 't midden vertoond zig de Boodschap van den Engel aan Maria, en omhoog een glorie van een meenigte Musiceerende Engelen op de Wolken; uitvoerig op Koper geschilderd, in de manier van Franx | *Mat:* op koper	Florijn [?]	(Sold) fl 8 Jan Spaan

Francken, Ambrosius (I)

1805/07/03	AMSCH	0019	*Francken. (A.)* | Dit fraay Tafreel, vertoont de wellustige Zoon in weelde; zittende by een gedekte Tafel met spys, verzelt van een wel opgecierde Dame, een Zanger en Musicanten; in 't verschiet, word hy berooft van zyne goederen, en de deur uitgejaagt; dit stukje is geestig geordineert, aangenaam van coloriet, en van een uitvoerige behandeling | *Mat:* op koper *Size:* hoog 17, breed 14 duim	R[oos]	(Sold) fl 28 Coclers

Francken, Frans

1807/04/00	LNDLS	0003	*F. Frank* | Een capitale Ordonnantie met een menigte beelden, waarin op de voorgrond verbeeld is, daar Scipio voor zijn tent staande, de bruid aan	[Abraham Delfos] [or others]	(Unknown)

			hare vrienden wedergeeft, dewelke alle voor hem geknield nederbukken en een menigte kostbare geschenken aanbieden; in 't verschiet gebouwen en legertenten, krijgsknegten te paard en te voet; alleruitvoerigst behandeld en zeer konstig van teekening en hartstogten | *Mat:* op paneel *Size:* hoog 37, breed 57 duim		
1807/06/10	HGBSM	0003	*F. Frank* | Een capitale Ordonnantie met een menigte beelden, waarin op de voorgrond verbeeld is, daar Scipio voor zijn tent staande, de bruid aan hare vrienden wedergeeft, dewelke alle voor hem geknield nederbukken en een menigte kostbare geschenken aanbieden; in 't verschiet gebouwen en legertenten, krijgsknegten te paart en te voet; alleruitvoerigst behandeld en zeer konstig van teekening en hartstogten | *Mat:* op paneel *Size:* hoog 37, breed 67 duim	Abraham Delfos [or others]	(Sold) fl 5:10 V Giesen

Francken, Frans (II)

1803/07/18	AMSCH	0016	*Francks (D.)* | Een geblesseerde Generaal voor zyn Legertent zittende, omgeeven van een menigte Krygsknegten; een Geneesheer is beezig een Pyl uit zyn wond te trekken, voor hem een Tafel met kostbaarheden en in 't verschiet een Gevegt; de hartstogten zyn fraai, zo ook de schildering [Un Général blessé, entourré par nombre de Guerriers est ramené audevant de sa tente ; un esculape lui ôte une fleche de la jambe. A côté sur une table sont des vases précieux, & un combat se voit au fond. Ce tableau à de l'expression & fait un bon effet.] | *Mat:* op paneel *Size:* hoog 14, breed 18 duim	Maria Theresia Andrioli	(Sold) fl 8 Grimpen
1803/07/18	AMSCH	0017	*Francks. (D.) [Franck. (Don Francisque)]* | Voor een Autaar [sic] ziet men een Concilie van verscheide Prelaaten afgebeeld, bevallig van couleur en penceelsbehandling [Devant l'exposition de l'Eucharistie est representé un Concile de Prèlats : composition nombreuse, d'une belle couleur & touchée avec esprit.] | *Mat:* op koper *Size:* hoog 16, breed 20 duim *Notes:* The artist's name differs in the Dutch and French editions of the catalogue.	Maria Theresia Andrioli	(Sold) fl 19 Coclers
1804/05/07	AMSCH	0057	*Franks. (D.)* | Deze ryke Ordonantie steld voor de edelmoedigheid van Scipio, hy is zittende op een Throon, waarby verscheide Beelden enz.; dit Schildery is fraai en meesterlyk geschilderd | *Mat:* op paneel *Size:* hoog 23, breed 29 duim	Y[ver] [for] W	(Sold) fl 22 Hulswit
1804/05/07	AMSCH	0058	*Franks. (D.)* | Epaminondas, voor zyn Legertent zittende, omgeeven van een meenigte Krygsknechten, een Geneesheer is beezig een Pyl uit zyn Wond te trekken, voor hem een Tafel met eenige Kostbaarheeden, en in 't verschiet een Gevecht; de hartstochten zyn fraai en van een dito [dit Schildery is fraai en meesterlyk geschilderd] schildering als de voorgaande | *Mat:* op paneel *Size:* hoog 13, breed 18 duim	Y[ver] [for] W	(Sold) fl 8 Gruiter
1804/05/07	AMSCH	0059	*Franks. (D.)* | Een Bybelsche Ordonantie, verbeeldende de aanbidding der Koningen aan het Kind Jesus, op de schoot van den H. Maagd; meesterlyk gepenceeld | *Mat:* op koper *Size:* hoog 13 ½, breed 10 ½ duim	Y[ver] [for] W	(Sold) fl 17 J Spaan
1805/07/03	AMSCH	0016	*Francks (Don F.)* | In een Hydensche Temple, vertoont zich Salomon nedergeknielt, eerbiedig wierook toezwaaijende aan den Afgod, die op een verheeven Altaar geplaatst is; en met Vorstelyke Kleeding, zoo als het gevolg zyner Vrouwen vercierd is; verders verscheide aanschouwers, die deze plechtigheid bywoonen, de caracters zyn natuurlyk, en Meesterlyk fraai van coloriet, en penceel behandeling | *Mat:* op paneel *Size:* hoog 23, breed 43 duim	R[oos]	(Sold) fl 36 L Pakker

Franco, Battista

1804/10/16	DLOND	0077	*Franco* | De Bruiloft te Canaan. Les Noces de Canaan | *Mat:* op koper *Size:* hoog 21, breed 28		(Unknown)

Franks, J. [Unidentified]

1801/10/06	AMSCH	0025	*J. Franks* | Een Dorp Gezicht, verbeeldende een Kermis, ryk gestoffeert met Beelden, die zig met dansen en drinken vermaaken; in 't verschiet de Kerk en Tooren, plaisant geschilderd | *Mat:* op paneel *Size:* hoog 28, breed 53 duim	M	(Sold) fl 5:10 Tersmitten

Franks, J. [Unidentified] (and Bassen)

1802/06/28	AMSCH	0009	*B. van Bassen; J. Franks* | In een prachtige Zaal, ziet men een groot Gezelschap, waarvan eenige Danssende; uitvoerig op Panneel, door B. van Bassen en J. Franks | *Mat:* op paneel *Size:* hoog 35, breed 45 duim	Anna Elink	(Sold) fl 7 Gruiter

Franks, J. [Unidentified] (manner)

1802/06/16	AMSCH	0242	*J. Franks* | Een Kunstzaal behangen met een menigte Schilderyen en andere Kunstwerken, in een tweede Vertrek ziet men eenige Geleerden; zeer uitvoerig behandeld, als J. Franks | *Mat:* op paneel *Size:* hoog 23, breed 31 duim	[Merrem]	(Sold) fl 11 Coclers

Franks, St. [Unidentified] (and Delen)

1810/10/10	MGCIT	0040	*D. v. Deelen; St. Franks* | Een schoon Kerk Gebouw op koper, waar in alles wat tot zoo een Gesticht behoord, naar de Kunst is geobserveerd, door D. v. Deelen en fraai gestoffeerd, door St. Franks: doende dit Stuk in zijn soort in allen opzigten eer aan beide Meesters | *Mat:* op koper	Caspar van Citters	(Unknown)
1810/10/10	MGCIT	0041	*D. v. Deelen; St. Franks* | Nog een Schilderij, zijnde een statelijk Gebouw van een aanzienlijke bouwörde en vercierd door een ongemeen fraai	Caspar van Citters	(Unknown)

			Perspectif, met uitmuntende stoffage, en van evengelijke waarde als 't vorige		
			Fredriks, Johannes Hendrik		
1805/07/03	AMSCH	0182	*J. H. Fredriks* | Een Watergezigt, met een Man, Vrouw en Jonge in een Schuitje; geestig door J. H. Fredriks	R[oos]	(Sold) fl 2 J Yver
1808/11/28	AMSCH	0024	*H. Fredrik* | In een Landschap, vertoond zig op een Marmere Tafel, een cierlijke Vaas, met Basrelieven, gevuld met verscheide zoort van keurige Bloemen, waarop Kapelletjes aasen, ter zijde op de Tafel ligt eene Vogelnesje en daar nevens Torren, ter wederzijde eenige Vruchten, alles evenaart de Natuur en van een uitvoerige Penceelsbehandeling | *Mat:* op paneel *Size:* hoog 17, breed 14 ½ duim	F	(Sold) fl 33 Gruyter
1810/03/26	RMMUY	0025	*H. Frederiks* | Op een Marmer Voetstuk, ligt een blaauw fluweel Kleed, waarop verscheiden uitgeleezene Vruchten en Bloemen. Welge-ordonneerd, uitvoerig en natuurlijk behandeld [Sur un sôcle de marbre, couvert en partie d'un tapis de velours bleu, sont posés plusieurs fruits exquis, et quelques belles fleurs, forment un ensemble agréable et artistement composé, très fini et d'une imitation parfaite.] | *Mat:* op doek *Size:* hoog 28 ½, breed 22 duimen	Daniel de Jongh Az	(Sold) fl 76 H Broekhinkel Delfshaven
			Frey, Anna de		
1810/05/22	AMSCH	0030	*Frij. (Anna de)* | Een Heer, zittende aan eene Tafel, waarop Tabaks-gereedschap, bezig zijnde de Courant te lezen, in 't verschiet eene Dienstmaagd; uitvoerig gepenceeld, zijnde het eenigste in olijverf geschilderde stukje van deeze Kunst-Teekenaresse | *Mat:* in olyverf op doek *Size:* hoog 14, breed 11 duim	Johannes van de Putte Nicolaasz.	(Sold) fl 9:10 du Pree
			Friedrich, J.D. [Unidentified]		
1802/09/21	UTHDG	0028	*J.D. Friedrich* | Twee stuks bergagtige Landschappen met gebouwen en geboomte. In het eerste een Waterval en wassende vrouwtjes, in de wederga, op den voorgrond, een Boerenwoning en Beelden, beiden rijk met staand en rustend Vee, en uitvoerig geschildert | *Mat:* op doek *Size:* hoog 20, breed 27 ½ duimen		(Bought In) fl 20
			Fris		
1804/05/07	AMSCH	0061	*Frys* | 't Afbeeldsel van Hugo de Groot, bezich zynde in een Boek te Studeeren, fiks en van een fraaije penceelbehandeling | *Mat:* op doek *Size:* hoog 31, breed 28 duim	Vinkeles [for] H[affner]	(Sold) fl 9 Leelie
			Fris, Jan (Johannes)		
1802/07/27	AKHRK	000M	*J. Fris, 1658* | Een lachgende Jongen, houdende met beide zijne Handen een groote Bokaal met Wijn; op de Tafel staat een Porcelijne Schotel met Citroenen, een Zilvere Schotel met Perziken, en een Schotel met een Orange – Appel en een geschilde Citroen; kunstig fraai geschilderd | *Mat:* op doek *Size:* hoog 47 ½, breed 38 duim *Inscr:* J. Fris, 1658 (signed and dated?) *Notes:* It is unclear whether the name and date are inscribed on the painting.	Maria Stategaart	(Sold) fl 11:10 Juffr Boersen
			Frytom, Frederick van		
1806/06/07	RMHSN	0072	*Fryton* | Een Landschap met Geboomten | *Mat:* op paneel	A E K L	(Unknown)
1810/10/10	MGCIT	0058	*Freton* | Een dito [treflyk] Landschap, zynde in een smaak niet geheel van het vorige afwykende: mede in een goede trant geschilderd	Caspar van Citters	(Unknown)
			Fyt, Jan		
1802/12/13	AMSCH	0064	*Fyt* | Een Stuk met divers dood Wild | *Mat:* op doek *Size:* hoog 36, breed 54 duim	Pruyssenaar [for] D	(Sold) fl 1 L Pakker
1803/06/20	AMSCH	0043	*J. Fyt* | Twee stuks Landschappen, de voorgrond gestoffeerd met een menigte dood Gevogelte en Jagtgereedschappen, in de eene een Hond, en in de andere een Valk, beide meesterlyk op Doek | *Mat:* op doek *Size:* hoog 22, breed 32 duim	Schley [for] G	(Sold) fl 28:10 Gruiter
1803/12/15	MGLAC	0034	*Fyt* | Een zeer uitvoerig stukje met doode Vogels | *Mat:* op paneel *Size:* hoog duim 15, breed duim 12	Mr L H de Haze Bomme	(Unknown)
1806/08/13	AMSCH	0056	*Fyt. (J.)* | Op de Voorgrond van een Boomryk Landschap legt by een Korf een Haas, Kalkoen en een ménigte ander dood gevogelte, meesterlyk behandeld | *Mat:* op doek *Size:* hoog 64, breed 72 duim	Roos	(Sold) fl 17 Th Spaan
1808/05/18	LNAN	0033	*Feijt* | 2 Stuks met different dood Gevogelte, uitvoerig geschilderd door een voornaam Meester | *This Lot:* Een stuk met different dood Gevogelte *Notes:* Lots 33 and 34 were printed in the catalogue as one item. The artist's name "Feijt" was added in by hand in the RKDH copy of the catalogue.	Mr Cornelis Versluys	(Unknown)
1808/05/18	LNAN	0034	*Feijt* | 2 Stuks met different dood Gevogelte, uitvoerig geschilderd door een voornaam Meester | *This Lot:* Een stuk met different dood Gevogelte *Notes:* Lots 33 and 34 were printed in the catalogue as one item. The artist's name "Feijt" was added in by hand in the RKDH copy of the catalogue.	Mr Cornelis Versluys	(Unknown)

1808/06/13	AMSCH	0055	*Fijt (J.)* | Een uitgestrekte doode Haas, waar naast een Eendvogel is hangende, op de voorgrond Duiven en ander Gevogelte; in een meesterlijke stijl geschilderd | *Size:* hoog 37, breed 29 duim	E M Engelberts	(Sold) fl 32 Engelberts

Fyt, Jan (or Fyt, manner)

1805/10/09	HGBSM	0055	*Fyt* | Een stuk met dood wild, meesterlyk geschilderd door of in de manier van Fyt | *Mat:* op doek *Size:* hoog 40 ½ breet 53 ½ duim	T H van Willigen [or others]	(Sold) fl 3:10 Zwarts

Fyt, Jan (manner)

1806/08/13	AMSCH	0259a	*Fyt* | Twee stuks met dood Wild; in de manier van Fyt	Roos	(Sold) fl 1:10 Boelen
1807/08/26	AMSCH	0284	*Fyt* | Een Stuk met dood Gevogelte, in een Landschap; in de manier van Fyt	Joseph Vallette	(Sold) fl 18 Coclair

Gaal, Pieter

1810/10/10	MGCIT	0036	*P. Gaal* | Een capitaal Landschap, waar op zich op den voorgrond bevind, een leggend Schaap en Geijtjen, en agter dezelve eene staande blaauwe bonte Koe en tegen dezelve nog een liggend Lammetjen; ter zijden deze voorwerpen, zit tegen een groen bewassen Heuvel, onder de Lommer van het Geboomte een Meisje, dat breid en het oog op het voors. weidend Vee schijnd te houden; voorts voltooid een fraaije voorgrond en een bevallig Verschiet, dit schoon van schildering en ordonnantie en tevens zeer uitvoerig stuk	Caspar van Citters	(Unknown)

Gael, Barend

1801/04/08	HAVIN	0038	*B. Gaal* | Twee Boere Plaisterplaatsen		(Unknown)
1801/04/23	AMYVR	0014	*B. Gual* | Een Wintergezicht, met een Marketenter, Arresleeden en Schaatseryders		(Sold) fl 8 Coclaire
1801/04/23	AMYVR	0015	*B. Gaal* | Een Rencontre tusschen eenige Ruiters		(Sold) fl 1 Yperen
1801/05/11	AMSCH	0028	*B. Gaal* | Een Landschap, by een Boerenhuis, ziet men twee ryzigers te paard, zig ververen, krachtig van schildering | *Mat:* op doek op paneel *Size:* hoog 10, breed 12 duim	E[lias]	(Sold) fl 15 Gruiter
1801/06/10	AMSCH	0070	*Gaal. (B.)* | Twee stuks aangename Land en Dorp gezichten, ryk gestoffeerd met Reizigers te Paard, kloek en natuurlyk geschilderd | *Mat:* op paneel *Size:* hoog 17, breed 22 duim	[Doublet]	(Sold) fl 38 Jan Yver
1801/06/13	LNDLS	0062	*B. Gael* | Twee Stuks Dorpgezichten, met veel beelden en beesten op den voorgrond, krachtig, op paneel | *Mat:* op paneel *Size:* hoog 10, breed 13 duimen	D van R	(Sold) fl 20 P Koppeschaar
1801/08/19	AMSCH	0033	*B. Gaal* | Twee stuks, een Zomer, en een Wintergezicht beiden met Beelden en Beesjes gestoffeert, uitvoerig en van de beste Schildering van B. Gaal	Pruyssen[r] [for] Q	(Sold) fl 30 Le Dantú
1801/10/19	AMSCH	0023	*Gaal (B.)* | Een heuvelächtig Landschap met een stroomend Water op de voorgrond, gestoffeerd met Jagers te paard en te voet; zeer fraay uitvoerig en kragtig gepenseeld | *Mat:* op paneel *Size:* hoog 1 v. 6 ½, breed 2 voet	Jonkheer Menno Baron van Coehoorn	(Sold) fl 75 Jan Spaan
1802/05/05	AMSCH	0068	*B. Gaas* | Een Landschap, met hoog Geboomte, met verscheide Paarden en Reizigers. Zeer natuurlyk | *Mat:* op paneel *Size:* hoog 6, breed 8 duim	BB	(Sold) fl 8 Spruit
1802/05/11	GRGRW	0041	*Berend Gaal* | Een uitvoerig Landschapje [Schilderijen met Olie-Verf; In zwarte Lijsten] | *Mat:* in olyverf *Notes:* The bracketed information in the title appears above lot 1 and refers to lots 1 to 79a.	Arnold Sicco Werumeus	(Unknown) fl 10:10
1802/05/11	GRGRW	0045	*B. Gaal* | Een Marketenter [Schilderijen met Olie-Verf; In zwarte Lijsten] | *Mat:* in olyverf *Notes:* The bracketed information in the title appears above lot 1 and refers to lots 1 to 79a.	Arnold Sicco Werumeus	(Unknown) fl 1
1802/05/24	HGBAK	0052	*B. Gaal* | Een Paardenmarkt, vol gewoel, door B. Gaal, 1667, hoog 3 voet, breed 3 ½ voet, op doek, vergulde lyst | *Mat:* op doek *Size:* hoog 3 voet, breed 3 ½ voet *Inscr:* B. Gaal, 1667 (signed and dated?) *Notes:* It is unclear whether the name and date are inscribed on the painting.	Mejuffrouw A van der Mieden	(Sold) fl 30 Zwarte [?]
1802/06/16	AMSCH	0057	*B. Gaal* | In een Dorp voor een Boeren Woning ziet men een menigte Boeren en Boerinne, waar by een Kar en een wit Paard, fiks en breed behandeld | *Mat:* op paneel *Size:* hoog 17, breed 22 duim	[Merrem]	(Sold) fl 20 Coclers
1802/06/16	AMSCH	0058	*B. Gaal* | In een Dorpgezicht by een Boere Plysterplaats, staat een wit gezadeld Paard, by een Kreb, en verder een dito bruin Paard, en een Heer daar nevens; verder eenige Huislieden en bevallig verschiet; kragtig gepenceeld | *Mat:* op paneel *Size:* hoog 13 ½, breed 16 duim	[Merrem]	(Sold) fl 14:10 Coclers
1802/07/27	AKHRK	0013	*B. Gaal* | Een Landgezicht, op de voorgrond waar op een Herberg, zitten koutende Boertjes, schijnende een Boerin te plaagen, met een Kan in de hand; verders een Paard dat gevoederd word; en twee zittende Kindertjes, de Figuurtjes zijn als van Ostade behandeld en van een warm coloriet | companion to lot 14 *Mat:* op paneel *Size:* hoog 18, breed 22 duim	Maria Stategaart	(Sold) fl 10:10 for lots 13 & 14. Gruyter
1802/07/27	AKHRK	0014	*B. Gaal* | Denzelve wedergaa. In dit Landgezicht ziet men een oud Huis, voor hetzelve eenige Vrouwen en Kinderen, luisterende aandachtig na een Speelman op de Viöol. Mede als de voorige, goed geschilderd | companion to lot 13	Maria Stategaart	(Sold) fl 10:10 for lots 13 & 14. Gruyter
1802/09/06	AMSCH	0203	*B. Gaal* | Twee stuks, een Jachtparty en een Pleister-plaats; bevallig | *Size:* hoog 6, breed 8 duim	J	(Sold) fl 6:5 Texier

1802/11/01	DOBRA	0058	*B. Gaal* | Een Pleisterplaats van Cavaliers, enz. | *Size:* breed 13 d. h. 11 d.	Paulus van der Spyk [or others]	(Sold) fl 5:10 Randwyk
1802/11/01	DOBRA	0096	*B. Gaal* | Een rencontre van Ruitery in een boomryk Landschap by een gehugt | companion to lot 97 *Mat:* op doek *Size:* breed 9 ½ duim hoog 7 ½ duim	Paulus van der Spyk [or others]	(Sold) fl 11 for lots 96 & 97. Rander [?]
1802/11/01	DOBRA	0097	*B. Gaal* | De wedergaade, zynde een Pleisterplaats | companion to lot 96 *Mat:* op doek *Size:* breed 9 ½ duim hoog 7 ½ duim	Paulus van der Spyk [or others]	(Sold) fl 11 for lots 96 & 97. Rander [?]
1802/12/13	AMSCH	0066	*B. Gaal* | Langs een Weg met veel Geboomten, ziet men op de voorgrond Krygslieden, by een wit en een Bruin Paard; verder eenige Huislieden. van een fix penceel behandeling | *Mat:* op paneel *Size:* hoog 7 ½, breed 11 duim	Schley [for] Lauwers	(Sold) fl 0:6 L Pakker
1802/12/13	AMSCH	0067	*B. Gaal* | In een Dorpgezicht, voor een Plyster Plaats, ziet men een Heer te Paard, verders twee anderen, op de voorgrond een Vrouw die Waterput en een Man die het wegdraagt; zonachtig en uitvoerig van penceel behandeling | *Size:* hoog 8, breed 7 duim	Schley [for] Lauwers	(Sold) fl 4:15 Gruiter
1802/12/13	AMSCH	0068	*B. Gaal* | Een Historieele Ordennantie, breed en meesterachtig geschilderd | *Mat:* op doek *Size:* hoog 21, breed 18 duim	Pruyssenaar [for] A	(Sold) fl 0:16 Gruiter
1802/12/13	AMSCH	0069	*B. Gaal* | Een Plyster Plaats met verschyde Stoffagie | *Mat:* op doek *Size:* hoog 14, breed 12 duim	Pruyssenaar [for] A	(Bought In) fl 12:10
1802/12/13	AMSCH	0070	*B. Gaal* | Een Dorpgezicht met Lieden te Paard voor een Herberg, die zig ververschen | *Mat:* op paneel *Size:* hoog 17, breed 20 duim	Pruyssenaar [for] D	(Sold) fl 7 de Meijer
1803/08/24	HGKAN	0016	*B. Gaal* | Twee stuks Lantschappen den eene gestoffeerd met Jagers te Paard en Honden die een Hart vervolgen, 't andere daar 't Hart reeds Gevangen is, en door de Jagers zoo te Paard als te Voet beschouwt werd, kragtig en uitvoerig geschildert | *Mat:* op doek op paneel *Size:* hoog 6 ½, breet 8 ½ duim	[Teissier] [or others]	(Sold) fl 16 Cuylenburg
1804/04/28	LNDLS	0030	*B. Gaal* | Een Landschap met geboomte, en mannen te paard, benevens een zittend vrouwtjen en jongen, door B. Gaal; op paneel | *Mat:* op paneel *Size:* hoog 16, breed 21 duim	[Abraham Delfos] [or others]	(Sold) fl 4:15 Rigters
1804/05/07	AMSCH	0065	*Gaal. (B.)* | Twee stuks Plysterplaatsen, gestoffeerd met een ménigte van Ruiters te paard en te voet en eenige andere Lieden, piquant van licht en meesterlyk gepenceeld | *Mat:* op doek *Size:* hoog 17, breed 21 duim	Vinkeles	(Sold) fl 36 Thais
1804/10/16	DLOND	0078	*Barend Gael* | Een Heuvelig Landschap met Lieden te Paard en te Voet. Paysage Collineux; on y voit des Personnes a Cheval & a Pied | *Mat:* op doek *Size:* hoog 35, breed 42		(Sold) fl 15:15 Huijbregts
1804/10/29	HRBAU	0024	*Gaal, (Barend)* | Een fraai Wintergezigt by een Stads Vest, gestoffeerd met een wit Paard voor een Sleede, waar by eenige Menschen op schaatsen, en nog meer Sleeden gezien worden. Dit Schilderytje is zeer klikkig, doch tevens in een' zagten toon behandeld | *Mat:* op paneel *Size:* hoog 11, breed 9 duim	Simon Styl	(Unknown)
1805/07/10	AMSCH	0067	*B. Gaal* | Langs een Weg ziet men voor eenige Boerewoningen, eenige rustende Reizigers, met hun Paarden en Goederen, fiks op Doek | *Mat:* op doek *Size:* hoog 14, breed 12 duim	V[inkeles] [for] M	(Sold) fl 4 Vallette
1805/07/10	AMSCH	0068	*B. Gaal* | Een Campement met een ménigte Ruiters te Paart en te Voet, Marquetenters, enz.; breed en fiks gepenceeld | *Mat:* op paneel *Size:* hoog 18, breed 21 ½ duim	V[inkeles] [for] M	(Sold) fl 52 L Pakker
1805/07/10	AMSCH	0234	*B. Gaal* | Twee stuks, met Paarden en Beelden	Y[ver]	(Sold) fl 1:15 Gruyter
1806/08/13	AMSCH	0063	*Gaal. (B.)* | In een Landschap met Geboomten en Boerewoning ziet men een Slager bézig een Varken te slagten, verders eenige Huislieden en Kinderen; zonachtig en fiks gepenceeld | *Mat:* op paneel *Size:* hoog 10, breed 8 duim	Vinkeles [for] D	(Sold) fl 15:10 T Spaan
1806/08/13	AMSCH	0063a[H]	*Gaal. (B.)* | 1 Schilderij | *Notes:* This lot was added in by hand in the MA and RKDH copies of the catalogue.	Vinkeles [for] D	(Sold) fl 21:10 T Spaan
1806/08/13	AMSCH	0063b[H]	*Gaal. (B.)* | 1 dito [Schilderij] | *Notes:* This lot was added in by hand in the MA and RKDH copies of the catalogue.	Vinkeles [for] D	(Sold) fl 3 T Spaan
1806/11/24	AMSCH	0029	*Gaal (B.)* | Twee stuks Pleisterplaatzen, met verscheide Reizigers te paard en te voet, en verdere stoffagie; zynde van zyn beste behandeling | *Mat:* op doek *Size:* Yder hoog 16, breed 19 duim	Munnikhuizen	(Sold) fl 13:10 Scheurleer
1807/08/26	AMSCH	0078	*B. Gaal* | Een Boomryk Landschap, alwaar een Postwagen door Rovers aangevallen word | *Mat:* op paneel *Size:* hoog 18, breed 21 duim	Roos	(Sold) fl 3:5 A Rynders
1807/08/26	AMSCH	0296	*B. Gaal* | Een Pleisterplaats	Joseph Vallette	(Sold) fl 0:6 Coclair
1807/09/28	AMWUR	0029	*B. Gall* | Een dito [stuk] op Doek, verbeeldende een Herberg, met drinkende Ruiters en verscheiden anderen Beelden, zeer fraay in zwarte Lyst, met vergulde sponning | *Mat:* op doek *Notes:* This lot was sold with lot 30 by an anonymous artist.		(Unknown) fl 30 for lots 29 & 30
1807/09/28	DOHAA	000C	*B. Gaal* | Twee Schilderstukjes, door B. Gaal. Boeren Woningen met Paardjes | *Size:* hoog circa 14 d. breed 11 d.	Mattheus Westerouen van Meeteren	(Unknown)
1808/06/06	RMRIJ	0039	*Gaal. (Barend)* | Eene Pleisterplaats met paarden en figuren. Fraai geschilderd [Des Cavaliers s'arrêtant devant un Auberge, et plusieurs autres figures etc. D'une belle Touche] | *Annots:* Verk. Pictura, den	Gerrit van der Pot, Heer van Groeneveld	(Sold) fl 24 R Pott

			Haag, 18 Sept. 1781 (f 20.-) (RMA I) *Mat:* op paneel *Size:* Hoog 9 ½, en breed 13 duim		
1808/06/13	AMSCH	0063	*Gaal (B.)* | Een vrolijke Ordonantie, zijnde een Boere Kermis: bij een Herberg ziet men Ruiters te Paard; in het Dorp staan verscheidene Kramen, waarbij eene menigte Omstanders. Helder en zonachtig behandeld | *Mat:* op doek *Size:* hoog 37, breed 48 duim	E M Engelberts	(Sold) fl 36 O W J Berg
1808/09/13	HABRU	0026	*Goaels* | Een Arcadisch Landschap		(Unknown) fl 51
1808/11/28	AMSCH	0079	*B. Gaal* | Een Landschap, met hoog opgaand Geboomte bij eenige Gebouwen | *Mat:* op paneel	[Gruyter?]	(Sold) fl 1 L Pakker
1808/11/28	AMSCH	0080	*B. Gaal* | Een dito Landschap, gestoffeerd met een Postwagen, welke door Rovers geplunderd word | *Notes:* It is unclear what "dito" refers to in the title.	[Gruyter?]	(Sold) fl 1 van der Schley [for] E v Dijk
1809/04/17	AMSCH	0033a[H]	*Gaal* | [Untitled] | *Notes:* This lot was added in by hand in the EBNP copy of the catalogue, but without giving a title.		(Sold) fl 14:10
1809/07/25	HGBSM	0019	*B. Gaal* | Een Landschap met een plyster plaats, waar by eenige Figuuren en Paarden | *Mat:* op paneel *Size:* hoog 11, breed 13 duim	D van der Aa [or] E B ten Dall	(Sold) fl 9 van Eyk
1809/07/25	HGBSM	0203	*B. Gaal* | Een Landschap waarin een Boere Herberg, benevens eenige Tenten daar zig eenige Cavaliers met hunne Paarden ververschen, verders gestoffeerd met veel Figuren, konstig gepenseelt | *Mat:* op doek *Size:* hoog 18 en een half, breed 23 en een half duim	D van der Aa [or] E B ten Dall	(Sold) fl 22:15 Teissier
1809/07/25	HGBSM	0223	*B. Gaal* | Een Boere Kermis met veel figuuren gestoffeerd, goed geschildert | *Mat:* op doek *Size:* hoog 18 en een half, breed 23 en een half duim	D van der Aa [or] E B ten Dall	(Sold) fl 7:10 Nieuwenhuyzen
1810/03/07	UTWLD	0003	*B. Gaal* | Twee Landschappen | *Size:* hoog 1 voet, 4 duim, breed 1 voet 8 duim	J J Woertman	(Unknown) fl 16:10
1810/03/26	RMMUY	0043	*Barend Gaal* | Twee Pleisterplaatsen, rijk van Beelden, Paarden, Honden, en verder bijwerk. Krachtig en meesterlijk geschilderd [Deux Paysages, faisant pendants. Des chevaux qui s'arrêtent, devant un cabaret de village et plusieurs figures, diversement occupées ; d'une touche ferme, vigoureuse et d'une savante composition.] | *This Lot:* Een Pleisterplaats *Mat:* op paneel *Size:* hoog 15, breed 18 ½ duimen *Notes:* Lots 43 and 44 were printed in the catalogue as one item.	Daniel de Jongh Az	(Sold) fl 33 for lots 43 & 44. F Kamerman Rott[m]
1810/03/26	RMMUY	0044	*Barend Gaal* | Twee Pleisterplaatsen, rijk van Beelden, Paarden, Honden, en verder bijwerk. Krachtig en meesterlijk geschilderd [Deux Paysages, faisant pendants. Des chevaux qui s'arrêtent, devant un cabaret de village et plusieurs figures, diversement occupées ; d'une touche ferme, vigoureuse et d'une savante composition.] | *This Lot:* Een Pleisterplaats *Mat:* op paneel *Size:* hoog 15, breed 18 ½ duimen *Notes:* Lots 43 and 44 were printed in the catalogue as one item.	Daniel de Jongh Az	(Sold) fl 33 for lots 43 & 44. F Kamerman Rott[m]
1810/06/06	RMMUY	0129	*B. Gaal* | Een Pleister Plaatsje | *Mat:* op paneel		(Unknown) fl 9
1810/06/20	AMSCH	0030	*B. Gaal* | Twee stuks Buitenhuizen, waarvoor spelende Kinderen en andere Beeldjes. Natuurlijk | *Mat:* op paneel *Size:* hoog 10, breed 11 duimen	B	(Bought In) fl 9:10
1810/10/11	AMSCH	0158	*B. Gaal* | Twee stuks, met Paarden, enz.	S	(Sold) fl 1:15 du Pree
			Gael, Barend (manner)		
1803/07/14	MGKLY	0006	*Als B. Gaal* | Twee Landschapjes, met Stoffasie	Mr Caspar Jacob van Citters	(Unknown)
1805/12/16	AMSCH	0091	*B. Gaal* | Een Landschap met Reisigers, als B. Gaal	R[oos]	(Sold) fl 1 L Pakker
			Gaelen, Alexander van		
1810/11/07	UTWLD	0044	*A. v. Galon* | Een hevig gevecht door Cavallerie en Infanterie voor een Vesting, welke bedreigd word – zeer helder en uitvoerig op doek geschilderd door A. v. Galon, 1 voet 5 en een half duim breed, 1 voet 2 duim hoog, zwarte Lijst | *Mat:* op doek *Size:* 1 voet 5 en een half duim breed, 1 voet 2 duim hoog		(Unknown) fl 5:5
			Gaesbeeck, Adriaen van		
1801/03/16	AMSCH	0014	*A. van Graasbeek* | Een Jongeling staande by een tafel, waarop een globe Boeken, Kaart en andere Instrumenten, aan een colom hangt een Pourtret van een Meisje, in 't verschiet komt een Dienstmaagd de trappen af; dit stuk is zonachtig en uitvoerig gepenceeld | *Loc:* Amsterdam, Nederland. Rijksmuseum. (A 113)	K[ip]	(Sold) fl 41 C S Roos
1801/06/10	AMSCH	0068	*Gaesbeek. (A. van)* | Een deftige Vrouw in een ouderwetsch Binnevertrek op een Stoel zittende aan een Tafel, waarop eenige Boeken en Papieren, alles is krachtig en overeenkomstig de Natuur verlicht en kragtig behandeld | *Mat:* op paneel *Size:* hoog 25, breed 21 duim	Herman ten Kate	(Sold) fl 204 C S Roos
1801/06/10	AMSCH	0069	*Gaesbeek. (A. van)* | Een Binnenvertrek, in het zelve ziet men een Vrouw, schynende een Kleed te verstellen; nevens haar een Kind in een wieg, verders twee speelende Jongens, benevens eenig Huisraad, kragtig en fyn behandeld | *Mat:* op paneel *Size:* hoog 22, breed 28 duim	Herman ten Kate	(Sold) fl 99 Coclers
1802/06/28	AMSCH	0063	*Gaasbeek* | Een Heilige Famillie in een Binnenhuis; kragtig op Panneel | *Mat:* op paneel *Size:* hoog 13, breed 17 duim	Anna Elink	(Sold) fl 2 Brouwer

1806/11/24	AMSCH	0027	*Gaasbeek (A. van)* | In een Binnenvertrek zit een bedaagde Vrouw, in oude hollandsche Kleeding, met een Speldewerk kussen op de schoot, ter zyde staat een Jongeling, en voor haar zit een jong Meisje pap te eeten, verzelt met een Hondje; alles is natuurlyk en fraai van penceelbehandeling | *Mat:* op paneel *Size:* hoog 14, breed 12 duim	Munnikhuizen	(Sold) fl 11:10 du Pree
1808/10/28	AMVRS	0014	*Gaesbeek. (A. van)* | Eene deftige Vrouw in een ouderwetsch Binnehuis op een Stoel aan Tafel zittende met een Boek in de Hand. Op de Tafel liggen Boeken, Hoorntjes, enz; aan den wand een Schilderij. Treffend van licht en krachtig van uitdrukking | *Mat:* op paneel *Size:* hoog 25, breed 21 duim	Marten Udink	(Sold) fl 131 Van Iperen
1809/04/22	AMYVR	0045	*Gaasbeek* | Eene Vrouw, in oude Hollandsche Kleeding, bezig zijnde Wortelen te schrapen, ter zijde haar een Kat, Emmer, Mand en doode Eend; krachtig en natuurlijk | *Mat:* op paneel *Size:* hoog 17, breed 16 duim	de Bruin	(Sold) fl 30:10 C S Roos

Gagneraux, Bénigne

1810/08/06	AMSCH	0035	*Gagneraux* | Een prachtige Tempel, waarin eene Historieele Ordonnantie van verscheidene Beelden is voorgesteld. Meesterlijk behandeld | *Mat:* op doek *Size:* hoog 23, breed 32 duimen	A	(Sold) fl 17:10 Coclers

Galle, Hieronymus (I)

1803/09/07	AMSCH	0068	*G. Galles* | Twee stuks stil levens, met Bloemen en Gevogelte, alles van een aangename Schildering [Deux intérieurs, avec des fleurs et de la volaille ; l'ensemble est d'un fini agréable et d'un très bel effet] | *Mat:* op doek *Size:* hoog 33, breed 25 duim	Smidt	(Sold) fl 12 C S Roos

Geel, Joost van

1808/06/06	RMRIJ	0040	*Geel. (Joost van)* | De Vrouws moeder van den heiligen Petrus, voor aan op een rustbed krank liggende, wordt met de eene hand, door den daarbij staanden Heiland, het hoofd ondersteund, terwijl hij met zijne regterhand de hare schijnt vast te houden. Petrus, en nog drie van des Heilands Discipelen vestigen hunne aandacht op beiden. Deze schoone Schilderij, alleszins in de manier van Metzu, is heerlijk van effect, schildering en koloriet, en als het beste bekend van dezen verdienstelijken Schilder. Is ook in Plaat gebragt [Ce Tableau represente la Belle-Mère de St. Pierre couchée sur son lit et à l'agonie. Le Sauveur auprés d'elle, lui soutient la tête de la main gauche, et de l'autre semble lui tâter le Poulx [sic]. St. Pierre et trois Disciples regardent attentivement. Cette Production rare de ce Peintre, (éléve de Metzu) est d'un beau coloris, d'une Composition savante, et mérite de grands éloges] | *Mat:* op doek *Fmt:* toogsgewijze *Size:* hoog 19 ¾, en breed 16 ¾ duim	Gerrit van der Pot, Heer van Groeneveld	(Sold) fl 410 R Pott
1808/06/06	RMRIJ	0041	*Geel. (Joost van)* | In een rijk versierd vertrek, omringd van prachtig bijwerk en wapenrusting, zit Delila voor een Lit d'Ange, hebbende Simson liggende op haren schoot en aan een inkomend persoon te kennen gevende zich stil te houden. Uitvoerig geschilderd [Dans un Appartement décoré de beaux meubles, et de belles armures etc., Dèlila est assise devant un Lit d'Ange ; Samson est couché auprés d'elle, et a la tête posée sur ses genoux. Il paroit être au moment de perdre la tresse de ses cheveux, tandis qu'il entre une personne qui semble d'intelligence avec la Courtisane. Tableau d'un précieux fini, et d'un ton chaud et vigoureux] | *Mat:* op doek *Size:* Hoog 22, en breed 23 ½ duim	Gerrit van der Pot, Heer van Groeneveld	(Sold) fl 145 Allard
1808/06/06	RMRIJ	0042	*Geel. (Joost van)* | Het Portret van den konstschilder Joost van Geel, door hem zelven zeer schoon, uitvoerig en meesterlijk geschilderd. Bekend door de Plaat van J. Houbraken [Le Portrait du Peintre Joost van Geel avec plusieurs accessoires peints avec art par lui-même. Connu par la Gravure de J. Houbraken] | *Mat:* op doek *Size:* Hoog 31 ¼, en breed 27 ¼ duim *Loc:* Amsterdam, Nederland. Rijksmuseum. (A 115)	Gerrit van der Pot, Heer van Groeneveld	(Sold) fl 265 van Lennep [for] le Roi
1808/06/06	RMRIJ	0043	*Geel. (Joost van)* | Eene oude vrouw (de moeder van den Schilder voorstellende) zittende in eene overdenkende houding, met eene bril in de hand, en een boek op den schoot. Zeer verdienstelijk en in de manier van Metzu geschilderd [Une vieille Dame (la Mére du Peintre) assise tenant un livre sur ses genoux et ses Lunettes a la main, semble méditer sur ce qu'elle a lu. Peint avec mèrite] | *Mat:* op paneel *Size:* Hoog 7, en breed 6 ¼ duim	Gerrit van der Pot, Heer van Groeneveld	(Sold) fl 37 R Pott
1810/03/26	RMMUY	0012	*Joost van Geel* | Dit stukje verbeelt de Herstelling van de Vrouws Moeder van Petrus door den Zaligmaker. De ordonnantie, en de uitdrukking, in de persoonen, zijn schoon en dezen Meester waardig [La belle Mère de Saint Pierre guerie par le Seigneur. La composition et les expressions sont pleines de mérites, d'un ton de couleur soutenu et vigoureux.] | *Mat:* op doek *Size:* hoog 16 ¼, breed 14 duimen	Daniel de Jongh Az	(Sold) fl 71 Wm Baartz Rott^{m}

Geel, Joost van (copy after)

1810/06/06	RMMUY	0209	*J. van Geel* | Petrus Vrouws Moeder, door den Zaligmaker hersteld. Naar J. van Geel | *Mat:* op doek		(Unknown) fl 2:10

Geel, N. van [Unidentified]

1802/06/16	AMSCH	0064	*N. van Geel* | Een Heuvelagtig Boomryk Landschap; ter zyde met een Rivier doorsneeden: het verschillend Geboomten is natuurlyk en zeer uitvoerig behandeld | *Mat:* op koper *Size:* hoog 6, breed 9 duim	[Merrem]	(Sold) fl 3 Teyssier

Geelen, Christiaan van (I)

1810/03/07	UTWLD	0027	*C. van Geelen* | Een Landschap alwaar op de voorgrond by een bosch een Jagthond staat | *Size:* hoog 1 voet 1 duim, breed 2 voet 2 duim	J J Woertman	(Unknown) fl 13

Gelder, Arent de

1801/05/11	AMSCH	0029	*A. de Gelder* | 't Pourtret van een Jongeling, staande by een tafel, waar op een tapyt legt, krachtig, fix en meesterlyk behandeld | *Mat:* op paneel *Size:* hoog 33, breed 33 duim	P[ruyssenaar]	(Sold) fl 40 Gruiter
1802/05/05	AMSCH	0063	*A. de Gelder* | De Dooping van den Moorman, zynde een Ordonnantie van verscheide Beelden in een Landschap, men ziet dezelven in een nedrige Gestalte den Doop ontfangen, boven op een Heuvel staat een prachtige Wagen. Alles Meesterlyk geschilderd | *Mat:* op paneel *Size:* hoog 45, breed 38 duim	A	(Sold) fl 58 Coclers
1802/11/01	DOBRA	0003	*A. de Gelder* | Een deftig Man in zonderling ouderwets gewaad, houdende een rotting in de hand; als door Rembrand. A. de Gelder. f. 1687 | *Mat:* op paneel *Size:* breed 27, hoog 34 d. *Inscr:* A. de Gelder. f. 1687 (signed and dated?) *Notes:* It is unclear whether the name and date are inscribed on the painting. *Loc:* Detroit, MI, USA. Institute of Arts. (49.531) (?)	Paulus van der Spyk [or others]	(Sold) fl 150 M Versteegh
1802/11/01	DOBRA	0004	*A. de Gelder* | Een deftig Man en Vrouw, als in een ernstig gesprek bij een taafel zittende | *Size:* hoog circa 20, breed 21 duim	Paulus van der Spyk [or others]	(Sold) fl 8:10 Meloen
1802/11/01	DOBRA	0005	*A. de Gelder* | Een historiele met gebouwen, en vol gewoel van beelden | *Size:* hoog 3 v. 2 d., breed 4 ½ voet	Paulus van der Spyk [or others]	(Sold) fl 6:5 Boercoert
1803/12/12	AMSCH	0034	*A. de Gelder* | Een Bybelsche Ordonantie van vyf Beelden, fraai van licht en meesterlyk, in de manier van Rembrand, behandeld door A. de Gelder | *Mat:* op doek *Size:* hoog 47, breed 38 duim	F	(Sold) fl 326 Gruiter
1803/12/12	AMSCH	0035	*A. de Gelder* | In een Landschap, by eenige Oude prachtige Gebouwen, ziet men een Historie verbeeld; als Rembrand, op Doek, meesterachtig gepenceeld | *Mat:* op doek *Size:* hoog 36, breed 50 duim	B	(Sold) fl 1:10 Gruiter
1803/12/12	AMSCH	0036	*A. de Gelder* | Een Goede-Gelukzegster, welke in de hand van eene Jongeling ziet, névens hem een jonge Dame, welke aandachtig toeziet; dit stuk is meesterlyk van Coloriet en schildering | *Mat:* op doek *Size:* hoog 34, breed 43 duim *Loc:* Den Haag, Nederland. Dienst Verspreide Rijkscollecties. (NK 1909) on loan to Utrecht, Catharijneconvent	B	(Sold) fl 99 Josi
1804/02/27	AMSCH	0042	*Gelder. (A. de)* | In een Landschap by oude Gebouwen, ziet men een Historie verbeeldt, in de manier van Rembrant | *Size:* hoog 36, breed 50 duim	C	(Sold) fl 0:4 Mets
1804/02/27	AMSCH	0145	*de Gelder* | Een cierlyk gekleed Pourtrait	B	(Sold) fl 0:6 Hulswit
1806/05/05	AMSCH	0056	*A. de Gelder* | Een Mans Pourtret in Turksche Kleeding | *Mat:* op doek *Size:* hoog 35, breed 29 duim	V[inkeles]	(Sold) fl 0:8 Vermeulen
1806/08/13	AMSCH	0060	*Gelder. (A. de)* | Een Ordinnantie van vyf Beelden, verbeeldende een Notaris bézig zynde een huwelyks voorwaarde te schryven, verzeld van Bruid en Bruidegom, beneevens de Wederzydsche Ouders; breed en fiks geschilderd | *Mat:* op doek *Size:* hoog 37, breed 55 duim *Loc:* Brighton, England, UK. Art Gallery and Museum. (14)	Coclers	(Sold) fl 61 Wed Achtienhoven
1810/03/26	RMMUY	0056	*Arent de Gelder* | De Besnijdenis van den Zaligmaker. Eene ordonnantie van verscheide figuren, in de manier van Rembrandt zijn meester, en van een groot effect [La Circoncision ; composition de plusieurs figures, d'un grand effet, dans la maniere de Rembrandt son maitre.] | *Mat:* op doek *Size:* hoog 35 ½, breed 43 ½ duimen	Daniel de Jongh Az	(Sold) fl 26 LeBrun Parys
1810/07/23	DOLG2	0001	*A. de Gelder* | Een oud Man, in een Oostersche kleding, benevens twee Vrouwen, rijk gekleed, en versierd met Parelen en Diamanten, bijna levens grootte; meesterlijk en stout; volkomen in den smaak van Rembrand. Geschilderd door A. de Gelder | *Mat:* op doek *Size:* hoog 59, breed 56 duim	Pieter Quinting	(Sold) fl 30 A v Strij

Gelder, Arent de (manner)

1810/06/04	DOBRA	0006	*de Gelder* | Twee Pourtretten, als door de Gelder	Hendrik de Haas	(Unknown)
1810/10/11	AMSCH	0205	*de Gelder* | Christus aan het Kruis, waarbij eene menigte Beelden, als de Gelder	A	(Sold) fl 1 van der Schleij

Genoels, Abraham (Archimedes)

1810/07/26	AMSCH	0036	*Genoels* | Een Landschap met Beelden en andere Voorwerpen | *Mat:* op doek *Size:* hoog 10, breed 10 duimen	Cassino	(Sold) fl 41 Spruyt
1810/07/26	AMSCH	0037	*Genoels* | Een Landschap als het voorgaande, en van gelijke schildering | *Mat:* op doek *Size:* hoog 12, breed 16 duimen	Cassino	(Sold) fl 2 Levie Pakker
1810/07/26	AMSCH	0145	*Genoels* | Een Bergachtig Landschap, met stoffage van Beeldjes | *Mat:* op doek *Size:* hoog 21, breed 32 duimen	Cassino	(Sold) fl 4 L Pakker

Gérard, Marguerite

1808/08/23	AMSCH	0066	*Gerards. (M.)* | In een Binnenkamer zit eene Dame, en Heeren met de Kaart speelende, waarbij andere aanschouwers; meesterlijk geschilderd | *Mat:* op doek op paneel *Size:* hoog 16, breed 12 duim	[Van Iperen?]	(Sold or Bought In) fl 11 van Iperen
1809/06/13	AMSCH	0057	*M. Gerards* | Eene Dame en twee Heeren met de Kaart speelende, waarbij eenige aanschouwers; bevallig geschilderd | *Mat:* op paneel *Size:* hoog 16, breed 12 duim	M	(Bought In) fl 10

Gérard, Marguerite (changed to Zyl, G.)

1806/08/13	AMSCH	0059	*Gerards. (M.); G P Zijl* | Dit bevallig Voorwerp, verbeeld een Musiceerend Gezelschap, voor een Buitenwoning, waar in twee Dames en vier Heeren, zig met Speel-Instrumenten en zingen vermaaken, zeer uitvoerig gepenceeld | *Mat:* op doek *Size:* hoog 16, breed 15 duim *Notes:* The artist's name was changed by hand from "Gerards. (M.)" to "G P Zijl" in the RKDH copy of the catalogue.	van der Voort	(Sold) fl 70 T Spaan

Gerards

1801/10/06	AMSCH	0026	*J. Gerards* | Een Gemeubileerd Binnenvertrek, in 't zelve ziet men by een Tafel, eenige Dames en Heeren, Musiceeren, verder een Knegt die Wyn in schenkt, gestoffeert met verder bywerk, fiks en bevallig gepenceeld | *Mat:* op doek *Size:* hoog 19, breed 24 duim	M	(Sold) fl 26 Spruit van Gend
1802/06/28	AMSCH	0059	*Gerards* | In een gemeubileerd Binnenvertrek, ziet men een Dame, welke een Musiekblad in haar Hand houd, verzeld van een Heer, welke op de Fiool speelt; zeer natuurlyk gepenceelt door Gerards. Doek | *Mat:* op doek *Size:* hoog 16, breed 14 duim	Anna Elink	(Sold) fl 4:5 Gruiter
1802/06/28	AMSCH	0060	*Gerards* | Een Heer en twee Dames, zittende aan Tafel te Speelen; delicaat op Doek | *Mat:* op doek *Size:* hoog 15, breed 14 duim	Anna Elink	(Sold) fl 4 Vermeulen
1802/06/28	AMSCH	0061	*Gerards* | Twee stuks, voor een steene Baluster, met een Basrelief, vertoont zig een bevallige jonge Juffrouw, met een Hondje speelende, waar by een Jongeling, en de ander een dito met een Papegaay, in een Binnevertrek; plaisant geschilderd | *Size:* hoog 12, breed 11 duim	Anna Elink	(Sold) fl 1:15 Vermeulen
1803/08/24	HGKAN	0031	*Gerarda* | Voor een Buitenhuis bevind zig een vrolyk Gezelschap van Heeren en Dames aan een Collation, uitvoerig en delicaat geschildert | *Mat:* op doek *Size:* hoog 24, breet 21 duim	[Teissier] [or others]	(Sold) fl 7 Teissier
1803/09/07	AMSCH	0071	*Gerards* | Twee stuks Hofgezichten, met Heeren, Dames en Kinderen, welken zich met Eten en Spelen vermaken, op een meesterlyke manier gepenceeld [Deux tableaux offrant l'aspect d'une cour ; des seigneurs et des dames assis et se promenant, les uns s'amusent à manger, les autres à jouer ; la touche de ces deux morceaux ne laisse rien à désirer soit pour le fini, soit pour l'agréable.] | *Size:* hoog 11, breed 14 duim	Smidt	(Bought In) fl 10
1804/08/08	AMSCH	0071	*F. Gerards* | Een Musicant in zyn Studeervertrek; met een Guitar op zyn Schoot, op de Tafel leunende, om te schryven; bevallig gepenceeld | *Mat:* op paneel *Size:* hoog 12, br. 10 duim	Roos a	(Sold) fl 8:5 van Iperen
1805/07/10	AMSCH	A0007	*Gerards* | Een Zinspeelende Ordinantie door Kinderen, afgebeeld in 't graauw, door Gerards, hoog 3 voet, 2 duim, breed 5 voet, 2 duim, zynde een Suporte [sic] [Fraaije geschilderde Kamer-Behangsels] | *Size:* hoog 4 voet, 2 duim, breed 5 voet, 2 duim *Notes:* The bracketed information in the title appears above lot A1 and refers to lots A1 to A8.	R[oos]	(Sold) fl 11 Gruyter
1805/10/09	HGBSM	0106	*G. Gerards* | Voor de deur van een buitenhuis onder een priëel, zit een gezelschap van dames en heeren by een gedekte tafel, ziende, als met verlangen naar een heer die vrugten plukt, gestoffeerd met verder bywerk, fraay en uitvoerig op doek geschilderd | *Mat:* op doek *Size:* hoog 24 breet 21 duim	T H van Willigen [or others]	(Sold) fl 11:5 Vallette
1807/06/02	AMHUY	0007	*Geerards* | In een Binnenvertrek ziet men eenige Heeren en Dames aan een Tafel zitten Kaart te spelen		(Unknown)
1807/08/26	AMSCH	0077	*Gerards* | Een vrolyk Gezelschap aan een Tafel zittende voor een Buitenhuis; zynde een aangenaam sujet, delicaat | *Mat:* op doek *Size:* hoog 24, breed 22 duim	Joseph Vallette	(Sold) fl 10 Gruiter
1808/06/13	AMSCH	0064	*Gerards* | In een Binnenvertrek, zit eene bevallige jonge Dame in rood satijne kleeding, op de cither spelende; achter haar staat een Heer, met een Muziekboek in de hand; verder voor het open vengster een afhangend gordijn. Alles aangenaam van kleur en uitvoerig gepenceeld | *Mat:* op paneel *Size:* hoog 10, breed 8 duim	[Jan Tersteeg]	(Bought In) fl 52
1809/04/22	AMYVR	0053	*Gerards* | Een Musiceerend Gezelschap; delicaat geschilderd | *Mat:* op doek *Size:* hoog 30, breed 39 duim	Juff^{r} Julikker	(Sold) fl 3:10 du Pree
1810/07/23	DOLG1	0025	*B. Gerards* | Een vrolijk Gezelschap, goed van Ordonnantie, Teekening en behandeling | *Mat:* op doek op paneel *Size:* hoog 16 ½, breed 14 duim	Mr Pieter van den Santheuvel	(Sold) fl 20 Spruijt van Gent

Gerards (manner)

1807/08/26	AMSCH	0303	*Gerards* | Een Voorportaal van een Gebouw, gestoffeerd met Heeren en Dames; fiks op Doek geschilderd, als door Gerards | *Mat:* op doek	Yver [for] S	(Sold) fl 2:10 T Spaan
1808/06/13	AMSCH	0223	*Gerardi* | Eene Goedegelukzegster [sic] bij eene in wit Satijn gekleede jonge Dame; zacht en teder, op Paneel, als door Gerardi | *Mat:* op paneel	[Jan Tersteeg]	(Sold) fl 12:10 Glad

Ghersi, T. [Unidentified]

1801/05/11	AMSCH	0030	*T. Ghersi* | Een zinbeteekende Ordonnantie, uit verschillende zoort van voorwerpen, krachtig gepenceeld | *Mat:* op paneel *Size:* hoog 26, breed 24 duim	E[lias]	(Sold) fl 8:10 Allard

Gheyn, Jacob de (II)

1805/10/21	GRBOL	0007	*J. de Ghein* | Een Schoon Stuk, zynde het Oordeel van Paris, stout geschilderd	Gerardus Nicolaus Heerkens	(Unknown)

Giesel, Johann Ludwig

1801/02/18	AMBOS	0020	*J.L. Giesel* | Twee stuks Gezigten, naar het leven, in Saxen, fraai geschilderd	J Schonevelt	(Unknown)
1801/02/18	AMBOS	0021	*J.L. Giesel* | Twee stuks dito [Gezigten], ook zeer natuurlyk, een Morgen- en Avondstond	J Schonevelt	(Unknown)
1808/09/13	HABRU	0024	*Giesel* | Een Boschgezicht; natuurlijk en uitvoerig		(Unknown)
1808/09/13	HABRU	0025	*Giesel* | Een dito [Boschgezicht] als voren		(Unknown) fl 4:16

Gillemans, Jan Pauwel

1802/07/20	MGSAN	0017	*Gilleman* | Een Bloem- en Fruitstukje, zeer fraai en uitvoerig op Doek | *Mat:* op doek *Size:* hoog duim 12, breed duim 16		(Unknown)
1802/07/20	MGSAN	0018	*Gilleman* | Een dito [Een Bloem- en Fruitstukje] als 't voorgaande | *Size:* hoog duim 12, breed duim 16 *Notes:* It is unclear what "dito" refers to in the title.		(Unknown)
1810/10/10	MGCIT	0079	*Guilemans* | Een Capitaal Schilderij met allerhande Vruchten, alsmede een groote Kreeft, liggende op een Schotel; het een en ander zoo wel als het Porcelein en Mandewerk, natuurlijk behandeld	Caspar van Citters	(Unknown)
1810/10/10	MGCIT	0080	*Guilemans* | Nog twee dito [Capitale Schilderijen], doch kleiner, waarop een menigte van Bloemen en Vruchten van allerlei soort; uitvoerig en delikaat samengesteld.	Caspar van Citters	(Unknown)
1810/10/10	MGCIT	0134	*Guillemans* | Een Stukje met Vruchten, door Guillemans, zonder Lijst	Caspar van Citters	(Unknown)

Gillig, Jakob

1803/04/20	AMSCH	0031	*Gillig. (J.)* | Twee stuks met Vissen; uitvoerig gepenceeld [Deux sujets composés de differens poissons : bien finis.] | *Mat:* op paneel *Size:* ieder hoog 10, breed 16 duim	Maria Magdalena van Sluypwyk, gravinne van Moens	(Sold) fl 1 Gruiter

Giordano, Luca

1801/04/13	AMSCH	0026	*L. Giordano* | Deeze ryke Ordonantie steld voor, de Kindermoord te Bethlehem; de hartstogten zyn 'er wonderbaarlyk in waargenomen, en is voorts van een meesterlyk penceel | *Mat:* op doek *Size:* hoog 19, breed 25 duim	Pierre Fouquet, junior	(Sold) fl 15 Yver
1803/04/27	AMSCH	0003	*Luca Giordano* | L'Adoration des bergers ; ce beaux Tableau de Luca Giordano, est d'une belle Composition, le clair-obscur en est fort picquant & les figures ont beaucoup d'expression | *Size:* h. 7, l. 9 pieds	A	(Sold) fl 18:10 Andriessen
1803/04/27	AMSCH	0004	*Luca Giordano* | Repos en Egypte, du même maitre [Luca Giordano], ce morceau peint largement, & avec beaucoup de franchise | *Size:* h. 7, l. 9 pieds	A	(Sold) fl 16 Th Spaan
1803/04/27	AMSCH	0098	*Luca Guordano* | Deux tableaux de Luca Guordano, dont l'un répresente la mort de Sophonisbe, & l'autre la mort de Caton | *Size:* h. 4 ½, l. 3 ½ pieds	A	(Sold) fl 24:15 Th[s] Spaan
1804/07/25	AMSCH	0044	*Jordano. (L.)* | In deeze capitaale Ordinantie, van zes Beelden leevens groote, ruim halver Lyf, ziet men den Heldhaftige Tomyris, Koningin der Massagéten, naar den Persische Koning Cyrus overwonnen te hebben, bevel geeven, om zyn afgehouwe Hoofd in een Leederen Zak, met Menschenbloed gevuld te dompelen; de Hartstogten zyn treffend verbeeld, het licht, het ongemeen kragtig coloriet en de stoute penceelbehandeling, geeven alle lof aan deeze voortreflyke meester | *Mat:* op doek *Size:* hoog 50, breed 66 duim		(Sold) fl 101 van der Schley
1804/07/25	AMSCH	0045	*Jordano. (L.)* | In een capitaal Landschap, vertoont zich leevens grooten, de Fabelgeschiedenis, Apollo de Nimph Daphné vervolgende, welke in een Laurierboom herschept werd; de Caracters zyn natuurlyk verbeeld, het licht en coloriet bevallig en van een meesterlyke en uitvoerige penceel behandeling | *Mat:* op doek *Size:* hoog 72, breed 84 duim		(Sold) fl 50 Jan Ijver
1804/10/16	DLOND	0113	*Luc. Jordaens 1622* | Marodeurs met de Buit te huis komende. Des Marodeurs revenans avec le Butin | *Mat:* op paneel *Size:* hoog 11, breed 16 *Inscr:* Luc. Jordaens 1622 (signed and dated?) *Notes:* It is unclear whether the name and date are inscribed on the painting.		(Unknown)
1810/08/06	AMSCH	0054	*Jordano (Luca)* | Deeze Ordonantie stelt voor, Apollo en Daphné de Tekening en het Coloriet zijn beide overschoon, en is voorts van een delicate behandeling | *Mat:* op doek *Size:* hoog 70, breed 80 duimen	R[oos]	(Bought In) fl 14
1810/10/11	AMSCH	0040	*L. Jordano* | Een Historiëele Ordonnantie, verbeelende de heldhaftige Tomyris, bevel gevende het hoofd van Cyrus in een lederen Zak te dompelen; krachtig van kleur, stout en meesterlijk gepenceeld | *Mat:* op doek *Size:* hoog 55, breed 60 duimen	K	(Sold) fl 19 Mensart

Giorgione (Giorgio da Castelfranco)

1802/12/13	AMSCH	0072	*Georgione* | Het Afbeeldzel van Hertog Karel de Stoute, kragtig en meesterlyk gepenceelt | *Mat:* op doek *Size:* hoog 36, breed 29 duim	Yver	(Sold) fl 39:10 Pruijssenaar [for] R
1803/04/27	AMSCH	0050	*Giorgione* | Deux Philosophes | *Size:* h. 6, l. 4 ½ pieds	A	(Sold) fl 9:5 Th Spaan

Giulio Romano (Giulio Pippi)

1803/04/27	AMSCH	0073	*Julio Romano* | L'Adoration des Bergers | *Size:* h. 2 ¼, l. 1 ¾ pieds	A	(Sold) fl 8:15 Pruijssenaar [for] L

			Glauber, Johannes (Polidoro)		
1802/05/05	AMSCH	0069	*Glauber* | Een Arcadisch Landschap, gestoffeert en Meesterlyk geschilderd | *Size:* hoog 40, breed 53 duim	J	(Sold) fl 6 v d Vinne
1802/08/24	LNDLS	0028	*Glauber* | Een Arcadiesch Landschap gestoffeerd met Herders en Schaapen, in het verschiet Gebouwen en Gebergte. Konstig | *Mat:* op doek *Size:* hoog 13, breed 16 duimen	Leonardus Bouman [or others]	(Unknown) fl 17
1803/09/07	AMSCH	0064	*J. Glauber* | Een Grot, van binnen te zien, gestoffeerd met Gedenktékens, en een Vrouw op een Paard, door een opening ziet men een aangenaam verschiet; zonagtig en op een klikagtige manier behandeld [L'intérieur d'une grotte ; on y remarque quelques monumens [sic] d'une belle architecture. Une ouverture pratiquée dans le roc laisse voir une perspective très agréable ; les reflets de la lumière sont fortement exprimés et d'un effet naturel] | *Mat:* op koper *Size:* hoog 12, breed 15 duim	Smidt	(Sold) fl 16 Scheffer
1804/08/08	AMSCH	0075	*J. Glauber* | Twee stuks Fabelgeschiedenissen, in fraaije Hofgezichten | *Mat:* op paneel *Size:* hoog 10, breed 12 duim	Roos [for] J	(Sold) fl 2:10 Pieterse
1809/09/06	AMSCH	0020	*Glauber (J.)* | Twee stuks Arcadische Landschappen, met Historieele stoffagie; uitvoerig gepenceeld | *Mat:* op paneel *Size:* ieder hoog 18, breed 22 duim	Johannes Caudri	(Sold) fl 36 Coclers
1810/03/23	HAVIN	0017	*Glauber* | Een Landschap door Glauber | *Size:* h. 36 ½ b. 46 d.	Rudolf Hendrik de Wetstein [or others]	(Unknown)
1810/05/22	AMSCH	0153	*J. Glauber* | Een Boom- en Bergachtig Landschapje, met rustende Beeldjes | *Notes:* This lot was sold with lot 154, which is in the manner of A. Ostade.	F	(Sold) fl 1:5 for lots 153 & 154. Geld
1810/06/20	AMSCH	0141	*J. Glauber* | Twee stuks Landschappen met Beelden en Beesten	B	(Sold) fl 8 Gruiter
			Glauber, Johannes (Polidoro) (and Lairesse, G.)		
1804/07/25	AMSCH	0049	*Lairesse. (G. de); J. Glauber* | Diana en Endimion in een boomryk Landschap by een Fontyn, omgeven van een menigte Minnewigten; beide Meesters hebben hunne talenten in dit stukje bevallig aan den dag gebragt, door een aangenaam en meesterlyk penceel | *Mat:* op doek *Size:* hoog 18, breed 22 duim		(Sold) fl 31 Gruiter
1806/08/20	HGBSM	0197	*J. Glauber; G. de Lairesse* | Een Arcadisch Landschap, door J. Glauber, en gestoffeerd door G. de Lairesse | *Mat:* op doek *Size:* hoog 14, breed 12 duim	Macalester Loup [or others]	(Sold) fl 19 Lafontaine
1808/08/23	AMSCH	0057	*Glauber (J.); G. de Lairesse* | Twee stuks kapitaale boomrijke Arcadische Landschappen, gestoffeert met Fabel-geschiedenissen uit Ovidius, waar bij verscheiden Minnewigten; beide meesterlijk fraai van penceelbehandeling | *Mat:* op doek *Size:* Ieder hoog 25, breed 34 duim	C	(Sold) fl 62 Gruyter
			Glauber, Johannes (Polidoro) (manner)		
1802/05/22	RMHSN	0028	*Glauber* | Een Arkadiesch Landschap, ryk en uitvoerig in de manier van Glauber	Lambertus Bicker	(Unknown)
			Glimes, Pierre de		
1802/12/13	AMSCH	0073	*P. de Glim* | In een Landschap ziet men een Vrouw, haar Hoofd bedekt met een Zonnehoed, houdende in haar Hand een Vogeltje; uitvoerig gepenseeld | *Mat:* op paneel *Size:* hoog 12, breed 8 ½ duim	Pruyssenaar [for] C	(Sold) fl 12 de Meijer
1810/06/20	AMSCH	0029	*P. De Glim* | Een bevallig Meisje, houdende een Vogel op de hand | *Mat:* op paneel *Size:* hoog 11, breed 9 duimen	A	(Sold) fl 7:10 J Twisk
			Goerier [Unidentified]		
1802/07/09	AMSTO	0003	*Goerier* | 2 stuks gesigte op de Scene a Paris, zynde le Pont-Neuf, gestoffeerd met Beelden en Vaartuigen		(Unknown)
			Goltzius, Hendrick		
1801/04/08	HAVIN	0001	*Goltius* | Een fraai Zinnebeeld op de ontdekking der Waarheid uitmuntend geschilderd		(Unknown)
1802/06/28	AMSCH	0064	*H. Goltzins* | Een Keuken, voorzien van allerhande Eetwaren, waarby eenige Beelden, door H. Goltzins, op Doek | *Mat:* op doek *Size:* hoog 24, breed 37 duim	Anna Elink	(Sold) fl 3:5 Gruiter
1802/09/06	AMSCH	0222	*Goltzius* | St. Sebastiaan met pylen doorschoten	J	(Sold) fl 1 Gruiter
1802/09/21	UTHDG	0034	*H. Goltzius* | De boodschap, meesterlijk en krachtig geschilderd | *Mat:* op paneel *Size:* hoog 66, breed 46 duimen *Loc:* Moskva, Rossiya. Muzei imeni Pushkina. (1944) (?)		(Bought In) fl 39
1804/02/27	AMSCH	0043	*Goltsius. (H.)* | Het bezoek der Herders in de Stal te Bethlehem; ryk geordoneerd en bevallig geschilderd | *Size:* hoog 25, breed 21 duim *Notes:* This lot was sold with lot 44 by Graat.	C	(Sold) fl 1:15 for lots 43 & 44. du Pree
1804/08/08	AMSCH	0069	*H. Goltzius* | Dit voorwerp verbeeld Christus in den Hof Gethsémané, neder geknield in een biddende gestalte, met zaamgevoude Handen, om hoog vertoont zich een Engel, als hem vertroostende; de hartstocht is natuurlyk, het coloriet kragtig, en van een meesterlyke penceelbehandeling | *Mat:* op doek *Size:* hoog 34, br. 26 duim	Schley [for] A	(Sold) fl 18 Jan Spaan

1804/10/16	DLOND	0079	*Goltzius* | De Hoop in 't midden der Gevaren, Zinnebeeldig Stuk. L'Esperance au millieu des Dangers, pièce Emblematique | *Mat:* op paneel *Size:* hoog 35, breed 27		(Unknown)
1805/07/10	AMSCH	0062	*Goltzius* | Een Oude Boer, welke een jong Meisje liefkoosd; uitvoerig op Koper | *Mat:* op koper *Size:* hoog 4, breed 5 duim	V[inkeles] [for] N	(Sold) fl 1 Tozelli
1806/06/07	RMHSN	0058	*Goltzius* | Een Heilige Familie | *Mat:* op koper	A E K L	(Unknown)
1806/06/07	RMHSN	0059	*Goltzius* | Twee dito [Heilige] Bybelsche Historien | *Mat:* op koper *Notes:* It is unclear what "dito" refers to in the title.	A E K L	(Unknown)
1806/06/07	RMHSN	0060	*Goltzius* | Adam en Eva, door dito [Goltzius], in 't rond | *Mat:* op paneel *Fmt:* rond	A E K L	(Unknown)
1806/06/07	RMHSN	0105	*Goltzius* | Een Schoone Mans Kop met een Baard | *Mat:* op paneel	A E K L	(Unknown)
1806/08/13	AMSCH	0246	*H. Goltzius* | 't Afbeeldzel van Coornhert	Vinkeles [for] G[ruyter]	(Sold) fl 0:16 Yver
1807/04/00	LNDLS	0024	*Goltius* | Een Vanitas, een kind dat bellen blaast, rustende op een doodshoofd | *Mat:* op paneel	[Abraham Delfos] [or others]	(Unknown)
1807/06/10	HGBSM	0024	*Goltius* | Een Vanitas, een kind dat bellen blaast, rustende op een doodshoofd | *Mat:* op paneel	Abraham Delfos [or others]	(Sold) fl 1:2 Van Zante
1807/08/26	AMSCH	0081	*H. Goltsius* | In een groote Keuken ziet men Koks en Meiden, een menigte Spyzen gereed maken; bevallig op Doek geschilderd | *Mat:* op doek *Size:* hoog 24, breed 37	Joseph Vallette	(Sold) fl 22 Jozi
1809/04/17	AMSCH	0033	*H. Goltzius* | Deeze Ordonantie verbeeld een naakte Vénus, liggende op een Rustbed, waarbij twee worstelende Zaters; meesterlijk | *Mat:* op doek	T	(Sold) fl 1:10 Gruyter
1810/10/11	AMSCH	0187	*Goltius* | Batseba zich badende werd door David bespied; krachtig geschilderd | *Mat:* op doek	A	(Sold) fl 11 Boelhouwer
			Goltzius, Hendrick (manner)		
1802/04/13	HAVIN	0070	*Goltius* | Een H: Familie, als van Goltius		(Unknown)
1802/11/01	DOBRA	0064	*H. Goltius* | Susanna met de Boeven, als door H. Goltius | *Mat:* op paneel *Size:* hoog 15 breed 11 duim	Paulus van der Spyk [or others]	(Sold) fl 4 Meloen
1803/04/27	AMSCH	000N	*Goltsius* | La Grossesse de Calisto, decouverte par Deanc [sic], riche composition, dans la maniere de Goltsius | *Size:* h. 63, l. 94 pouces	B	(Bought In) fl 1
1805/07/03	AMSCH	0218	*Goltius* | Een Zinspelende Ordinantie, aan 't Strand ziet men verscheide Watergodinnen. Vissen, Hoorns, enz.; in de manier van Goltius, geschilderd	R[oos]	(Sold) fl 2:15 Reyers
1807/08/26	AMSCH	0082	*H. Goltsius* | Een dikke Geestelyke, in een Boek lezende, als door denzelven [H. Goltsius] | *Mat:* op paneel *Size:* hoog 22, breed 22 duim	Joseph Vallette	(Sold) fl 2:10 Coclair
			Goltzius, Hendrick (style)		
1810/10/11	AMSCH	0116	*Goltius* | Een Keukenvertrek, waarin eenige Lieden, benevens eenig Huisraad, en een menigte verschillend bijwerk; krachtig op Doek, in den Stijl van Goltius | *Mat:* op doek *Size:* hoog 28, breed 39 duimen	M	(Sold) fl 9:15 G Pakker
			Gonzalet [Unidentified]		
1802/05/10	MGSAN	0019	*Gonzalet* | Een Stuk, vertoonende de Bruiloft te Kanaän, waar het water in wyn wordt veranderd, door Gonzalet: op Paneel, in zwarte Lyst | *Mat:* op paneel *Size:* hoog 19 duim, breed 18 duim	Johan Dirk Kruysse	(Unknown) £ 2
			Gool, Jan van		
1801/10/06	AMSCH	0027	*J. van Gool* | Een Aangenaam Landschap, de voorgrond gestoffeert met graazende Koeijen, Schaapen en Bokken, waar by een Veehoeder en Vrouw, helder van Coloriet, en fraai behandeld | *Mat:* op paneel *Size:* hoog 20, breed 28 duim	M	(Sold) fl 30:10 Frantsen
1803/08/17	AMSCH	0029	*Gool. (J. van)* | Twee stuks grazige Weiden met Geboomte, gestoffeerd met een menigte staand en leggend Vee, uitvoerig gepenceeld | *Mat:* op paneel *Size:* ieder hoog 11, breed 16 duim	Anna Catharina Putman	(Sold) fl 14:10 Pruijssenaar
1804/04/28	LNDLS	0022	*J. van Gool* | Een Landschap, met ossen en bokken, geboomten en kruiden, met een landschap en dorp in 't verschiet, zeer uitvoerig door J. van Gool, op paneel, hoog 17, breed 24 duim geheel in de manier van P. Potter | companion to lot 23 *Mat:* op paneel *Size:* hoog 17, breed 24 duim	[Abraham Delfos] [or others]	(Bought In) fl 24
1804/04/28	LNDLS	0023	*J. van Gool* | Een Weêrga, met staande en rustende stier, koeijen, bokken en schaapen, en een aangenaam verschiet, door denzelven [J. van Gool], grootte en behandeling | companion to lot 22 *Size:* hoog 17, breed 24 duim	[Abraham Delfos] [or others]	(Bought In) fl 24
1804/12/10	AMSCH	0022	*J. van Gool* | Twee stuks, een grazige Wyde en een Landschap, doorsneede met een stil water, beide gestoffeerd met koeijen en schapen en bevallige verschieten; fiks en meesterlyk gepenceeld | *Mat:* op paneel *Size:* Hoog 12, breed 17 duim	Jan De Groot	(Sold) fl 26 J Spaan
1804/12/10	AMSCH	0023	*J. van Gool* | Een Landschap, in een Grot ziet men diverse honden, koeijen, bokken en een paard; fiks geschilderd | *Mat:* op paneel *Size:* Hoog 20, breed 29 duim	Jan De Groot	(Sold) fl 31 J Spaan

1805/07/03	AMSCH	0085	*J. van Gool* | In een Landschap met Geboomten, by een stil Water, ziet men twee Huislieden, verschillende zoort van Vee voortdryven, een derzelve drinkt aan een Waterplas: verder een Bergachtig verschiet; kragtig en bevallig geschilderd op Doek | *Mat:* op doek *Size:* hoog 28, breed 48 duim	R[oos]	(Sold) fl 9 H Zurmuklen
1805/10/09	HGBSM	0086	*J. van Gool* | Een drift van koebeesten en ander vee, die door een bergagtig landschap gedreeven word, van de allerbesten tyd van J. van Gool | companion to lot 87 *Mat:* op paneel *Size:* hoog 16 ½ breet 24 duim	T H van Willigen [or others]	(Sold) fl 13:5 Ponse
1805/10/09	HGBSM	0087	*J. van Gool* | Een dito [drift van koebeesten en ander vee, die door een bergagtig landschap gedreeven word] niet minder als de voorgaande, zynde een pendant | companion to lot 86 *Size:* hoog 16 ½ breet 24 duim *Notes:* It is unclear what "dito" refers to in the title.	T H van Willigen [or others]	(Sold) fl 14 Ponse
1806/08/13	AMSCH	0061	*Gool. (J. van)* | Twee stuks aangenaame Boomryke Landschappen, ryk gestoffeerd met staand en rustend Vee, verders Boeren en Boerinnen en bevallige verschieten; zonachtig gepenceeld | *Mat:* op paneel *Size:* Ieder hoog 14, breed 19 duim	Vinkeles [for] E	(Sold) fl 12 Van Iperen
1806/08/13	AMSCH	0062	*Gool. (J. van)* | Twee stuks dito [aangenaame] dito [Boomryke Landschappen] in alles als de voorgaande | *Mat:* op doek *Size:* Ieder hoog 12, breed 16 duim *Notes:* It is unclear what "dito" refers to in the title.	Vinkeles [for] E	(Sold) fl 15:10 du Pre
1807/04/00	LNDLS	0007	*J. v. Gool* | Een uitmuntend Landschap met geboomte, op den voorgrond een grazend paard, verder koeijen schapen en bokken, benevens een water daar beesten in waden, en meer stoffagie, geheel in de trant van Ad. van de Velde | *Size:* hoog 24, breed 32 duim	[Abraham Delfos] [or others]	(Unknown)
1807/04/00	LNDLS	0008	*J. v. Gool* | Een capitaal Landschap met geboomte; op de voorgrond een vrouwtje te paard, en twee landlieden, die een menigte koeijen, bokken en schapen langs den weg drijven; verder op een heuvel meer beelden en beesten,jagers met haar jagthonden en bergen in 't verschiet, alles is met veel geduld konstig en kragtig uitgewerkt, en een der beste van dezen meester	[Abraham Delfos] [or others]	(Unknown)
1807/04/00	LNDLS	0019	*J. van Gool* | Een Landschap met vele beesten, bij her [sic] opkomen van een onweersbui, daar een vrouw een koe melkt, en een landman die dat aanwijst. Benevens een klimmende stier en meer beesten zeer konstig in de trant van P. Potter | companion to lot 20 *Size:* hoog 18, breed 24 duim	[Abraham Delfos] [or others]	(Unknown)
1807/04/00	LNDLS	0020	*J. van Gool* | Een weerga niet minder van konst, met vele differente beesten, en beelden, en een aangenaam verschiet | companion to lot 19 *Size:* hoog 18, breed 24 duim	[Abraham Delfos] [or others]	(Unknown)
1807/06/10	HGBSM	0007	*J. v. Gool* | Een uitmuntend Landschap met geboomte; op den voorgrond een grazend paard, verder koeijen schapen en bokken, benevens een water daar beesten in waden, en meer stoffagie, geheel in de trant van Ad. van de Velde | *Size:* hoog 24, breed 32 duim	Abraham Delfos [or others]	(Sold) fl 17:10 Tessier
1807/06/10	HGBSM	0008	*J. v. Gool* | Een capitaal Landschap met geboomte; op de voorgrond een vrouwtje te paard, en twee landlieden, die een menigte koeijen, bokken en schapen langs den weg drijven; verder op een heuvel meer beelden en beesten, jagers met haar jagthonden en bergen in 't verschiet, alles is met veel geduld konstig en kragtig uitgewerkt, en een der beste van dezen meester	Abraham Delfos [or others]	(Sold) fl 13 Dupré
1807/06/10	HGBSM	0019	*J. van Gool* | Een Landschap met vele beesten, bij het opkomen van een onweersbui, daar een vrouw een koe melkt, en een landman die dat aanwijst. Benevens een klimmende stier en meer beesten zeer konstig in de trant van P. Potter | companion to lot 20 *Size:* hoog 18, breed 24 duim	Abraham Delfos [or others]	(Sold) fl 10:5 Dupré
1807/06/10	HGBSM	0020	*J. v. Gool* | Een weerga niet minder van konst, met vele differente beesten, en beelden, en een aangenaam verschiet | companion to lot 19 *Size:* hoog 18, breed 24 duim	Abraham Delfos [or others]	(Sold) fl 12:15 Tomas
1807/08/26	AMSCH	0060	*J. van Gool* | Twee stuks: het eerste stelt voor een groote party Koeijen die gemolken worden, en andere die staan en liggen, verders Schapen en Bokken, ter zyde een Boeren Woning en Beelden, op de weg een Herder met Vee, en aangenaam verschiet: de wederga is een drift Ossen, Schapen, Bokken en Geitjes, die op den voorgrond spelen, op de tweede grond Jagers met Honden; beide van de beste en uitvoerigste. [NB. Alle deeze gemelde 30 stukken, door den vermaarden Kunst-Schilder J. van Gool vervaardigd, zyn nimmer verkogt geweest, en komen nu eerst uit zyne nalaatenschap, tot heden berustende geweest in zyne familje.] | *Mat:* op paneel *Size:* hoog 22, breed 30 duim *Notes:* The bracketed information in the title appears below lot 75 and refers to lots 60 to 75.	Roos [for] P	(Sold) fl 67 Jozi
1807/08/26	AMSCH	0061	*J. van Gool* | Twee stuks: voor een Herberg leggen op een grazigen grond verscheiden Beesten, Bokken en Schapen. Ter zyde zitten Lieden te drinken, verders een aangenaam verschiet, in de tweede ziet men een Pont vol Vee met hunnen Herder, ter zyde op een Heuvel met hoog Geboomte nog verscheiden staande en leggende Beesten, en eenige Beeldjes; niet minder als de voorgaande. [NB. Alle deeze gemelde 30 stukken, door den vermaarden Kunst-Schilder J. van Gool vervaardigd, zyn nimmer verkogt geweest, en komen nu eerst uit zyne nalaatenschap, tot heden berustende geweest in zyne familje.] | *Mat:* op paneel *Size:* hoog 21, breed 30 duim *Notes:* The bracketed information in the title appears below lot 75 and refers to lots 60 to 75.	Roos [for] P	(Sold) fl 67 Jozi

1807/08/26	AMSCH	0062	*J. van Gool* | Twee stuks: beide grazige Weiden, vol onderscheiden Vee, met Beelden, hoog Geboomte en aangename verschieten; zynde fraaije Ordonnantiën, uitvoerig behandeld. [NB. Alle deeze gemelde 30 stukken, door den vermaarden Kunst-Schilder J. van Gool vervaardigd, zyn nimmer verkogt geweest, en komen nu eerst uit zyne nalaatenschap, tot heden berustende geweest in zyne familelje.] | *Mat:* op paneel *Size:* hoog 17, breed 26 duim *Notes:* The bracketed information in the title appears below lot 75 and refers to lots 60 to 75.	Roos [for] P	(Sold) fl 50 T Spaan
1807/08/26	AMSCH	0063	*J. van Gool* | Twee dito [stuks]: de eene met Vee dat door een Water gaat en daarin spiegelt; in de wederga ziet men op een Heuvel eenig ander Vee, beide met Beelden, Honden, hoog Geboomte en bevallige verschieten; niet minder fraai van uitvoering als de voorgaande. [NB. Alle deeze gemelde 30 stukken, door den vermaarden Kunst-Schilder J. van Gool vervaardigd, zyn nimmer verkogt geweest, en komen nu eerst uit zyne nalaatenschap, tot heden berustende geweest in zyne familelje.] | *Mat:* op paneel *Size:* hoog 17, breed 24 duim *Notes:* The bracketed provenance information in the title appears below lot 75 and refers to lots 60 to 75.	Roos [for] P	(Sold) fl 54:10 T Spaan
1807/08/26	AMSCH	0064	*J. van Gool* | Deze twee zyn beide bergachtige Landschappen, fraai gestoffeerd met een menigte staand en leggend Vee, hoog Geboomte, Waterval en liefkozende Landlieden; zonachtig en delicaat behandeld. [NB. Alle deeze gemelde 30 stukken, door den vermaarden Kunst-Schilder J. van Gool vervaardigd, zyn nimmer verkogt geweest, en komen nu eerst uit zyne nalaatenschap, tot heden berustende geweest in zyne familelje.] | *Mat:* op paneel *Size:* hoog 17, breed 22 duim *Notes:* The bracketed information in the title appears below lot 75 and refers to lots 60 to 75.	Roos [for] P	(Sold) fl 51 du Pree
1807/08/26	AMSCH	0065	*J. van Gool* | Twee andere dito [Landschappen]. Het eene een Morgenstond voorstellende, alwaar veel onderscheiden Vee uit de Stal gedreven wordt, veel Geboomte en een aangenaam Stadgezigt in 't verschiet. De tweede is mede ryk van Beesten, die door een Water waden, in 't verschiet zwemmende Jongens; beide met Geboomte, Boeren Woningen en Beeldjes gestoffeerd en als de vorige geschilderd [zonachtig en delicaat]. [NB. Alle deeze gemelde 30 stukken, door den vermaarden Kunst-Schilder J. van Gool vervaardigd, zyn nimmer verkogt geweest, en komen nu eerst uit zyne nalaatenschap, tot heden berustende geweest in zyne familelje.] | *Mat:* op paneel *Size:* hoog 17, breed 24 duim *Notes:* The bracketed provenance information in the title appears below lot 75 and refers to lots 60 to 75.	Roos [for] P	(Sold) fl 56 Tebbetman
1807/08/26	AMSCH	0066	*J. van Gool* | Twee stuks: de eene met een Herder met Vee, die van een hoogte afkomt, en door een Water waad. De wederga stelt voor het aan Wal komen en lossen van een Pont met Koeijen en Schapen, en Bokken, verders aangename verschieten; als vooren [zonachtig en delicaat behandeld]. [NB. Alle deeze gemelde 30 stukken, door den vermaarden Kunst-Schilder J. van Gool vervaardigd, zyn nimmer verkogt geweest, en komen nu eerst uit zyne nalaatenschap, tot heden berustende geweest in zyne familelje.] | *Mat:* op paneel *Size:* hoog 14, breed 19 duim *Notes:* The bracketed provenance information in the title appears below lot 75 and refers to lots 60 to 75.	Roos [for] P	(Sold) fl 32:10 H G van Raan
1807/08/26	AMSCH	0067	*J. van Gool* | Twee stuks grazige Heuvels. De een met staand en leggend Vee, de andere met divers Vee dat door een Herder van een hoogte gedreven word; verders hoog Geboomte en mede behandeld als de voorgaande [zonachtig en delicaat]. [NB. Alle deeze gemelde 30 stukken, door den vermaarden Kunst-Schilder J. van Gool vervaardigd, zyn nimmer verkogt geweest, en komen nu eerst uit zyne nalaatenschap, tot heden berustende geweest in zyne familelje.] | *Mat:* op paneel *Size:* hoog 14, breed 19 duim *Notes:* The bracketed provenance information in the title appears below lot 75 and refers to lots 60 to 75.	Roos [for] P	(Sold) fl 24 Van Iperen
1807/08/26	AMSCH	0068	*J. van Gool* | Twee dito [stuks] bevallige Landzigten, op de voorgrond een rustende Veehoeder, op de Fluit speelende, vergezeld van zyne Vrouw, verders twee rustende Koeijen en een staande roskleurige Os op een Heuvel, en verder onder Geboomte eenig Vee. De wederga vertoont op den voorgrond een Huisman, die drie Koeijen, waarby een Bul, een Bok, Schapen en zwarte Hond, naar een Brug dryft, en een Man, eenige Schapen voortdryvende; in alles als de vorige van behandeling [zonachtig en delicaat]. [NB. Alle deeze gemelde 30 stukken, door den vermaarden Kunst-Schilder J. van Gool vervaardigd, zyn nimmer verkogt geweest, en komen nu eerst uit zyne nalaatenschap, tot heden berustende geweest in zyne familelje.] | *Size:* ieder hoog 14, breed 19 duim *Notes:* The bracketed provenance information in the title appears below lot 75 and refers to lots 60 to 75.	Roos [for] P	(Sold) fl 29 Jozi
1807/08/26	AMSCH	0069	*J. van Gool* | Twee stuks aangename Landschappen, een met Boeren Woning, Schuur en Geboomten, op de voorgrond ryk gestoffeerd met Ossen, Koeijen en Schapen; verder eene Vrouw te Paard, als sprekende met een Man die naar den Weg vraagt, verder een bevallig verschiet. De wederga vertoont voor een Huismans Woning by Geboomte een Heer te Paard; op de voorgrond drie Jagers, met verscheiden soort van Jagthonden, verder een grazige Weide met eenig Vee, en een Vinkenbaan, beide deze voorwerpen verbeelden vroege Morgenstonden; het Vee is natuurlyk, en alles is van eene uitvoerige penceelbehandeling. [NB. Alle deeze gemelde 30 stukken, door den vermaarden Kunst-Schilder J. van	Roos [for] P	(Sold) fl 45 Coclair

			Gool vervaardigd, zyn nimmer verkogt geweest, en komen nu eerst uit zyne nalaatenschap, tot heden berustende geweest in zyne famielje.] | *Mat:* op paneel *Size:* ieder hoog 16, breed 24 duim *Notes:* The bracketed information in the title appears below lot 75 and refers to lots 60 to 75.		
1807/08/26	AMSCH	0070	*J. van Gool* | Twee dito [stuks] bevallige dito [Landschappen]; zynde de eene het Gezigt aan een stil Water, waar een Pontschuit met verscheiden Vee en een Heer te Paard wordt overgehaald, op de voorgrond staat een Os, Ram en Hond, in 't verschiet eene Weide met eenig Vee. In de andere ziet men voor een Boeren Herberg een Heer te Paard, als sprekende tegen een Jager, van verscheiden Honden vergezeld. Een zittend Heer schynt de Hospita te betalen, een Knegt haalt een gezadeld Paard van Stal, verder een Landman, Vee voortdryvende; in alles als de voorgaande. [NB. Alle deeze gemelde 30 stukken, door den vermaarden Kunst-Schilder J. van Gool vervaardigd, zyn nimmer verkogt geweest, en komen nu eerst uit zyne nalaatenschap, tot heden berustende geweest in zyne famielje.] | *Mat:* op paneel *Size:* ieder hoog 17, breed 24 duim *Notes:* The bracketed provenance information in the title appears below lot 75 and refers to lots 60 to 75.	Roos [for] P	(Sold) fl 42 Graffelman
1807/08/26	AMSCH	0071	*J. van Gool* | Is een Italiaansch Langezigt met Geboomte by een Rots, waaronder een wyde opening, daar verscheiden Vee door gedreven wordt, vergezeld van eene Vrouw te Paard en eenen gaande Veehoeder, verder een aangenaam verschiet; het koloriet is bevallig, het zonlicht geeft een natuurlyke werking. Het is van een alleruitvoerigste penceelsbehandeling. [NB. Alle deeze gemelde 30 stukken, door den vermaarden Kunst-Schilder J. van Gool vervaardigd, zyn nimmer verkogt geweest, en komen nu eerst uit zyne nalaatenschap, tot heden berustende geweest in zyne famielje.] | *Size:* hoog 17, breed 26 duim *Notes:* The bracketed information in the title appears below lot 75 and refers to lots 60 to 75.	Roos [for] P	(Sold) fl 28 Graffelman
1807/08/26	AMSCH	0072	*J. van Gool* | In dit capitaal en bevallig Landgezigt, met fraai Geboomte, vertoont zich een Heer te Paard, vergezeld van een Jager, met een menigte Jagthonden, van verschillende kleuren, alle naar het leven geschilderd, in verscheiden actien, in 't verschiet een grazige Weide, met een menigte Vee, en een Boerin die een Koe melkt; het is van een warm koloriet, en een allerbevalligste behandeling. [NB. Alle deeze gemelde 30 stukken, door den vermaarden Kunst-Schilder J. van Gool vervaardigd, zyn nimmer verkogt geweest, en komen nu eerst uit zyne nalaatenschap, tot heden berustende geweest in zyne famielje.] | *Mat:* op paneel *Size:* hoog 21, breed 30 duim *Notes:* The bracketed information in the title appears below lot 75 and refers to lots 60 to 75.	Roos [for] P	(Sold) fl 30 van Iperen
1807/08/26	AMSCH	0073	*J. van Gool* | Twee stuks aangename Landschappen met Geboomte, op de voorgrond twee leggende en een rosbonte Os, die zich tegen een Willigeboom vryft, waarby staande en rustende Bokken, en een Veehoeder die op een Dwarsfluit speelt, en een Hond, verder onder het lommer der Boomen een Huisman met Vee. De wederga verbeeld een drift Beesten op de voorgrond, en verder eenige volgende, die over een Brug gedreven worden, waarby een Heer te Paard en een Landman; beide van een bevallig penceel. [NB. Alle deeze gemelde 30 stukken, door den vermaarden Kunst-Schilder J. van Gool vervaardigd, zyn nimmer verkogt geweest, en komen nu eerst uit zyne nalaatenschap, tot heden berustende geweest in zyne famielje.] | *Mat:* op paneel *Size:* hoog 14, breed 19 duim *Notes:* The bracketed information in the title appears below lot 75 and refers to lots 60 to 75.	Roos [for] P	(Sold) fl 36 Zonnenbergh
1807/08/26	AMSCH	0074	*J. van Gool* | Twee dito [stuks] dito [aangename Landschappen], op een grazige Heuvel ziet men een rustende en twee staande Koeijen, drie Schapen, twee Geiten en een Hond, waar by een zittende Vrouw en een staande Veehoeder, leunende tegen de stam van een Boom, verder een bergachtig verschiet. De wederga vertoont op de voorgrond drie Ossen, waarvan een zich te weer stelt tegen een blaffenden Hond, die van een Landman met een stok teruggestooten wordt, verder vertoont zich verscheiden Vee, van een Berg afkomende; beide zonachtig en uitvoerig gepenceeld. [NB. Alle deeze gemelde 30 stukken, door den vermaarden Kunst-Schilder J. van Gool vervaardigd, zyn nimmer verkogt geweest, en komen nu eerst uit zyne nalaatenschap, tot heden berustende geweest in zyne famielje.] | *Size:* ieder hoog 12, breed 17 duim *Notes:* The bracketed provenance information in the title appears below lot 75 and refers to lots 60 to 75.	Roos [for] P	(Sold) fl 50 Jozi
1807/08/26	AMSCH	0075	*J. van Gool* | Twee capitalen Bloem en Fruitstukken: in de eene vertoont zig op een Steene Voetstuk, een Bennetje met blaauwe Druiven en Vrugten, voor hetzelve leggen verscheide zoorten van Fruit, als Kantaloup, Persikken, Abricoosen, Pruimen en Druiven, verders diversche Bloemen, waarop Insecten aazen, en by de stam van een Boom twee Vogeltjes. De wederga verbeelt mede op een Steenen Tafel, verscheide zoort van Vrugten en Bloemen, waar by eenige vliegende Kapelletjes; beide kragtig en met de Natuur overeenkomende behandeld, en Meesterlyk fraai gepenceeld. NB. Alle deeze gemelde 30 stukken, door den vermaarden Kunst-Schilder J. van Gool vervaardigd, zyn nimmer verkogt geweest, en komen nu eerst uit zyne nalaatenschap, tot heden berustende geweest in zyne famielje. | *Mat:* op doek *Size:* ieder hoog 26, breed 23 duim *Notes:* The information at the end of the title refers to lots 60 to 75.	Roos [for] P	(Sold) fl 40 H G van Raan

1808/05/18	LNAN	0005	*van Gool* | Een Helder Landschap met Koeijen, Schapen en Beeldjes | companion to lot 6 *Notes:* The artist's name "van Gool" was added in by hand in the RKDH copy of the catalogue.	Mr Cornelis Versluys	(Unknown)
1808/05/18	LNAN	0006	*van Gool* | Een Weêrga | companion to lot 5 *Notes:* The artist's name "van Gool" was added in by hand in the RKDH copy of the catalogue.	Mr Cornelis Versluys	(Unknown)
1808/05/18	LNAN	0007	*van Gool* | Een dito [Helder Landschap] met differente Beesten | *Notes:* The artist's name "van Gool" was added in by hand in the RKDH copy of the catalogue.	Mr Cornelis Versluys	(Unknown)
1808/08/23	AMSCH	0059	*Gool. (J. van)* | Twee stuks bevallige Landschappen, een met een Boeren Wooning, Schuur en Geboomten, op de voorgrond rijk gestoffeert men Ossen, Koeijen en Schaapen, waar bij eene Vrouw te Paard, als spreekende met een Man die naar den weg vraagd, verder een aangenaam verschiet; de wederga vertoont voor een Huismans Wooning een Heer te Paard, op de voorgrond drie Jagers met verscheiden Jagthonden, verder een grazige Weiden met eenig Vee en een Vinkebaan; het Vee is natuurlijk, en alles is van eene uitvoerige penceelbehandeling | *Mat:* op paneel *Size:* hoog 17, breed 24 duim	[Coclers]	(Sold) fl 37 Dupré
1809/04/22	AMYVR	0046	*J. van Gool* | Twee stuks: een Morgen- en een Avondstond, zijnde Landschappen met Boerenwooningen, gestoffeerd met Jagers, Beesten en Honden; delicaat | *Mat:* op paneel *Size:* hoog 18, breed 25 duim	de Bruin	(Bought In) fl 36
1809/04/22	AMYVR	0047	*J. van Gool* | Twee stuks Landschappen, met eene menigte onderscheiden Vee en stoffagie van Beelden; krachtig | *Mat:* op paneel *Size:* hoog 17, breed 24 duim	de Bruin	(Sold) fl 18 Rijfsnijder
1809/06/13	AMSCH	0051	*J. van Gool* | In een aangenaam Boomrijk Landschap, is de voorgrond rijk gestoffeerd met Landlieden en Vee, en Herders met Schaapen, agterwaards Heeren te Paard, waar bij Jagers, Honden en een fraai verschiet; zijnde dit een van de beste stukken | *Mat:* op paneel *Size:* hoog 19, breed 25 duim	[Gruyter?]	(Bought In) fl 22
1809/07/25	HGBSM	0048	*J. van Gool* | Een Drift van differente soorten van Vee in een Bergachtig Landschap, helder en uitvoerig geschildert | companion to lot 49 *Mat:* op paneel *Size:* hoog 16 en een half, breed 24 duim	D van der Aa [or] E B ten Dall	(Sold) fl 21:5 for lots 48 & 49. van Eyk
1809/07/25	HGBSM	0049	*J. van Gool* | Een Dito [Drift van differente soorten van Vee], zynde niet minder als de voorgaande, dienende tot een weerga | companion to lot 48 *Mat:* op paneel *Size:* hoog 16 en een half, breed 24 duim	D van der Aa [or] E B ten Dall	(Sold) fl 21:5 for lots 48 & 49. van Eyk
1809/07/25	HGBSM	0050	*J. van Gool* | Een Koeye-Stal, van binnen te zien, met veel Koeyen daar in, aan de regter zyde gestoffeerd met zittende Boeren en een Boerin, en verder Huisraad, ryk van Ordonnantie, door denzelven [J. van Gool], zynde een van de beste tyd van dien Meester | *Mat:* op paneel *Size:* hoog 18 en een half, breed 25 duim	D van der Aa [or] E B ten Dall	(Sold) fl 55 Ponse [or] Stees
1809/07/25	HGBSM	0278	*J. van Gool* | Twee stuks Landschappen met verschillende soort van Vee gestoffeert | *Mat:* op paneel *Size:* hoog 12, breed 15 en een half duim	D van der Aa [or] E B ten Dall	(Sold) fl 10:10 Pulver
1810/03/27	RMCNL	0039	*van Gool* | Een Landschap, waarop men een Boer uit eene pont Koeijen, Schapen, enz. ziet drijven, op de voorgrond een Hond, welke een Bok tegenblaft, fraai geschilderd		(Unknown)
1810/03/27	RMCNL	0084	*van Gool* | Twee Stuks, zeer uitvoerig behandelde Landschappen, bij uitnemenheid fraaij en netjes gepenseeld en onder de beste van dien Meester te tellen		(Unknown)
1810/08/10	RMRIJ	0028	*Jan van Gool* | Twee Landschappen met Beesten. Uitvoerig en natuurlijk behandeld		(Sold) fl 20 [or] 17 Haas

Gossaert, Jan

1803/09/07	AMSCH	0115	*M. de Maubuge* | Diana onder een Boom zittende, met haar Honden, meesterlyk in 't grauw [Diane assise sous un arbre et entourée de ses chiens ; d'une belle exécution en gris] | *Mat:* op paneel *Size:* hoog 8, breed 5 ½ duim *Notes:* The artist's name was given as "M. de Maubuge" but we have assumed this is an error.	Smidt	(Bought In) fl 9
1810/08/01	AMSCH	0055	*Mabuge (Jean de)* | Maria, houdende het Kind op haren Schoot, zij is gezeten op de Plint eener Nis, hebbende eene Voetbank onder hare voeten [La Vierge Marie tenant l'Enfant Jesus sur son giron. Elle est assise sur une partie d'architecture formant cintre. Ce morceau porte la date de 1527] | *Annots:* fort médiocre. (NGW) *Mat:* op paneel *Fmt:* boven rond *Size:* hoog 12, breed 9 ½ duimen *Inscr:* A^{o}. 1527 (dated)	Mr Pieter de Smeth van Alphen	(Sold) fl 85 Remmers Bredius

Govaerts, Jan Baptist

1803/09/07	AMSCH	0065	*J. B. Gevaerts* | Vertumnus en Pomona, zy heeft een Mandje met Fruiten in haar handen, zynde van een delicate behandeling [Vertumne et Pomone, portant des mains une corbeille de fruits ; peinture délicate et agréable] | *Mat:* op paneel *Size:* hoog 18, breed 14 duim	Smidt	(Sold) fl 44 J Yver
1803/09/07	AMSCH	0069	*J. B. Govaerts* | Twee stuks, het eene verbeeld een bevallig Fruitvrouwtje, welke een tros Druiven aan een bejaarde Vrouw schynt te verkoopen; het tweede steld voor een Visvrouw, welke haar Waar aan een Kok verkoopt, het Bywerk in deeze stukjes is zoo uitvoerig als Mieris, en meriteeren onder de beste Meesters geplaatst te worden, zynde zeer fray geschilderd [Deux tableaux, l'un représentant un aimable fruitière, qui semble vendre une grappe de raisin à une vieille femme ; l'autre une poissarde qui vend	Smidt	(Sold) fl 150 C S Roos

			sa marchandise à un cuisinier ; les accessoires dans ces deux morceaux sont parfaitement bien traités dans le genre de Mieris, ; et dignes d'être placés parmi les oeuvres des meilleurs maîtres] | *Mat:* op doek *Size:* hoog 21, breed 16 duim		
			Goyen, Jan Josephsz. van		
1801/03/16	AMSCH	0044	*J. van Gooyen* | Een Wintergezicht met verscheiden Schaatseryders en Arresleede, natuurlyk geschilderd	P[ruyssenaar]	(Sold) fl 10:10 Mensart
1801/03/16	AMSCH	0103	*J. van Goyen* | Een Gezicht op het Valkenhof te Nymeegen, natuurlyk	K[ip]	(Sold) fl 10:10 Roelofs
1801/03/16	AMSCH	0173	*J. van Goyen* | Een Land- en Watergezicht	P[ruyssenaar]	(Sold) fl 1:15 Geld
1801/03/16	AMSCH	0174	*J. van Goyen* | Een dito dito [Land- en Watergezicht]	P[ruyssenaar]	(Sold) fl 2:10 Stevens
1801/05/11	AMSCH	0026	*Jan van Goyen* | Een woelend Water, met een zeilend Beurtschip, langs 't strand ziet men de Toren van de Kerk, natuurlyk en fix behandeld | companion to lot 27 *Mat:* op paneel *Size:* hoog 14, breed 19 duim	E[lias]	(Sold) fl 22 Coclers
1801/05/11	AMSCH	0027	*Jan van Goyen* | Een dergelyke Ordonnantie, zynde een weerga van de voorgaande | companion to lot 26 *Mat:* op paneel *Size:* hoog 14, breed 19 duim	E[lias]	(Sold) fl 40 Jozi
1801/06/10	AMSCH	0066	*Goyen. (J. van)* | By een Dorp ziet met op een stille bevrozen Rivier een menigte Schaatzeryders, Arresleeden, en Wandelaars, dit Stukje is van de keurigste, welke van deezen Meester bekend zyn | *Mat:* op paneel *Size:* hoog 15 ½, breed 24 duim	Herman ten Kate	(Sold) fl 51 Barent Kooij
1801/06/10	AMSCH	0067	*Goyen. (J. van)* | Een Dorpgezicht, aan een stille Rivier, gestoffeert met Scheepen en Visschers Schuiten, natuurlyk gepenceeld | *Mat:* op paneel *Size:* hoog 27, breed 36 duim	[Doublet]	(Sold) fl 19:10 J Yver
1801/06/13	LNDLS	0033	*J. van Goijen* | Een Wintergezicht, met Schaatsen-rijders op 't Ys, bij een Stadspoort, rond formaat, op paneel, door J. van Goijen, 1627 | *Mat:* op paneel *Fmt:* rond *Size:* hoog en breed 12 ½ duimen *Inscr:* J. van Goijen, 1627 (signed and dated?) *Notes:* It is unclear whether the name and date are inscribed on the painting.	D van R	(Sold) fl 12:10 Richter S [for] Stevens
1801/08/19	AMSCH	0031	*J. van Goijen* | Een Duin en Boomryk Landschap, met Boerewooningen, en Stoffagie van Beeldjes, Warm en Zonachtig geschilderd op Paneel | *Mat:* op paneel *Size:* hoog 16, breed 24 duim	Mevr Hogguer	(Sold) fl 20:10 Le Dantú
1801/08/19	AMSCH	0032	*J. van Goijen* | Een Land- en Riviergezicht, met Vissers in hun Schuiten, dun op Paneel | *Mat:* op paneel *Size:* hoog 24, breed 34 duim	Van Forreest	(Sold) fl 9:10 v d Vinne
1802/04/13	HAVIN	0048	*van Gooyen* | Een Landschap		(Unknown)
1802/05/05	AMSCH	0064	*J. van Gooijen* | Twee stuks Stille Waters, met een menigte Vaartuigen, Paalwerken en Visschers; voorts, veruitgestrekte Verschieten, natuurlyk | *Mat:* op paneel *Size:* ieder hoog 19, breed 4 duim	H	(Sold) fl 70 W Reijers
1802/05/24	HGBAK	0001	*J van Gooijen* | Een Rhyn-Gezicht, op de voorgrond een vervallen Toorn en figuuren, in 't verschiet eenige Scheepjes, door J van Gooijen, hoog 13 ½ duim, breed 22 duim, penant [sic], zwarte lyst en vergulde binnenrand | companion to lot 2 *Size:* hoog 13 ½ duim, breed 22 duim	Mejuffrouw A van der Mieden	(Unknown) fl 15 for lots 1 & 2
1802/05/24	HGBAK	0002	*J van Gooijen* | Een dito [Rhyn-Gezicht] tot een weerga, en gelyk het voorgaande geordonneerd door denzelve Meester [J van Gooijen], hoog en breed als vooren, en in dezelve lyst | companion to lot 1 *Size:* hoog 13 ½ duim, breed 22 duim	Mejuffrouw A van der Mieden	(Unknown) fl 15 for lots 1 & 2
1802/06/16	AMSCH	0059	*J. van Goijen* | Een Landschap, op de voorgrond ziet men eenig staand en rustend Vee; verders over een stil water ziet men een Stad nevens een aangenaam verschiet, fraay van Schildering | *Mat:* op paneel *Size:* hoog 16 ½, breed 23 ½ duim	[Merrem]	(Sold) fl 33 J Yver
1802/06/16	AMSCH	0060	*J. van Goijen* | Een Dorpgezicht met Boere Woningen, by Geboomtens, langs een opgaande weg; gestoffeerd met staande en rustende Landlieden, zeer natuurlyk en meesterlyk fiks gepenceeld | *Mat:* op paneel *Size:* hoog 10, breed 13 ½ duim	[Merrem]	(Sold) fl 10 J Yver
1802/06/16	AMSCH	0061	*J. van Goijen* | Langs een weg, met een Boere Woning, by Geboomten, ziet men een rydende Wagen met verscheide Lieden; zonagtig en natuurlyk behandeld | *Mat:* op paneel *Size:* hoog 10 ½, breed 16 ½ duim	[Merrem]	(Sold) fl 10 J Yver
1802/06/16	AMSCH	0062	*J. van Goijen* | Een Cabbelend Water langs een strand, waarby een arbeider bezig is Zand te kruyen, meesterlyk geschilderd | *Mat:* op paneel *Size:* hoog 11 ½, breed 21 duim	[Merrem]	(Sold) fl 2 Levij Pakker
1802/06/16	AMSCH	0063	*J. van Goijen* | Een woelend Water met verscheiden zeilenden Scheepen: ter zyde op de voorgrond by een gedeelte van Strand ziet men Visschers in een Schuit; natuurlyk en fiks gepenceeld | *Mat:* op paneel *Size:* hoog 14, breed 12 duim	[Merrem]	(Sold) fl 2:5 Delfos
1802/06/28	AMSCH	0062	*J. van Goijen* | Twee stuks Wintergezigtjes, met stoffagie van Beeldjes; uitvoerig op Panneel | *Mat:* op paneel *Size:* hoog 5, breed 5 duim	Anna Elink	(Sold) fl 4:5 Vermeulen
1802/07/20	MGSAN	0004	*J. van Gooijen* | Een Stads Poort by een Rivier, vol gewoel van leggende en zeilende Schepen, helder van coloriet, ovaal formaat, op Paneel | companion to lot 5 *Mat:* op paneel *Fmt:* ovaal *Size:* hoog duim 19, breed duim 25		(Unknown)

1802/07/20	MGSAN	0005	*J. van Gooijen* | Zynde de Pendent van 't voorgaande, verbeeldende een Landgezigt, waarin een Herberg, waarvoor eenige Beeldjes en verdere Stoffagie, op Paneel | companion to lot 4 *Mat:* op paneel *Size:* hoog duim 19, breed duim 25		(Unknown)
1802/07/21	HGKAN	0037	*A. van Goeyen* | Een stil Water met eenige Scheepjes en Schuytjes, in het Verschiet eenige Dorp Gezichten, zeer fiks geschildert, door A. van Goeyen, paneel zwarte Lyst | *Mat:* op paneel *Notes:* The artist's name was given as "A. van Goeyen" but we have assumed this is an error.		(Unknown)
1802/07/21	HGKAN	0101	*J. van Gooyen* | Een Zomertje en een Wintertje, met een meenigte van Beeltjens, door J. van Gooyen, twee stuks		(Unknown)
1802/08/24	LNDLS	0025	*J. van Goyen* | Een heuvelachtig landschap met Boeren woningen en Geboomte, in het midden is eene Vrouw met een Jongen die water put, met meer persoonen en Boeren gereedschap op den Voorgrond. Konstig op paneel | *Mat:* op paneel *Size:* hoog 14 ½, breed 21 duimen	Leonardus Bouman [or others]	(Unknown) fl 26:10
1802/08/24	LNDLS	0048	*J. van Goyen* | Langs een Water met Vaartuigen, een Landgezicht met Geboomte en Boeren Wooningen. Uitvoerig op paneel | *Mat:* op paneel *Size:* hoog 14, breed 15 ½ duimen	Leonardus Bouman [or others]	(Unknown) fl 8
1802/08/24	LNDLS	0053	*J. van Goyen* | Een Gezicht langs de Rivier de Merwede op de Stad Dordrecht, met veele zeilende Schepen en vaarende Schuiten, op den Voorgrond rustende en staande Koeijen bij een Visschers Schuit die aan land komt. Zeer plaisant, konstig en krachtig op doek | *Mat:* op doek *Size:* hoog 36, breed 54 duimen	Leonardus Bouman [or others]	(Unknown) fl 99
1802/08/24	LNDLS	0054	*J. van Goyen* | Een aangenaam Land – en Water – Gezicht; ter regter zijde Geboomte en Woningen, ter linker zijde een Trekschuit met Volk en een Jager te paard, en meer Stoffagie. Door denzelven [J. van Goyen], 1635. van zijn beste soort | *Mat:* op paneel *Size:* hoog 13 ½, breed 25 duimen *Inscr:* 1635 (dated?) *Notes:* It is unclear whether the date is inscribed on the painting.	Leonardus Bouman [or others]	(Unknown) fl 40
1802/09/06	AMSCH	0044	*J. van Goyen* | Aan een stille Rivier, vertoonen zig boerewooningen en schnuren [sic] by geboomten, gestoffeerd met huislieden, op de voorgrond zyn visschers in een schuit; zeer natuurlyk en bevallig gepenceeld | *Mat:* op paneel *Size:* hoog 15, breed 19 duim	Baur	(Sold) fl 22 Pruijssenaar
1802/09/06	AMSCH	0045	*J. van Goyen* | Een dito [stille Rivier]; verschillende van ordenantie, met boerewooningen, schuuren en geboomten, aan een Rivier, gestoffeerd met verscheide huislieden en hengelaars, zonagtig en meesterlyk gepenceeld | *Mat:* op paneel *Size:* hoog 11, breed 17 duim	Baur	(Sold) fl 23 Jan Spaan
1802/09/06	AMSCH	0046	*J. van Goyen* | Langs een weg met geboomte, by een Bruggetje aan een stil water, ziet men een visser in zyn schuit, op den weg eenige huislieden; zonagtig en natuurlyk van Coloriet, behandeld | *Mat:* op paneel *Size:* hoog 13, breed 21 duim	W ten Houten	(Sold) fl 9:10 T van Iperen
1802/09/06	AMSCH	0047	*J. v. Goyen* | In een aangenaam stil water, ziet men een menigte van zeilende en stilleggende Vaartuigen, dun en helder | *Mat:* op paneel *Size:* hoog 13, breed 17 duim	J	(Sold) fl 9:5 van Cooth
1802/09/18	RMDRS	0064	*J. van Goyen* | Een klein Watergezigt	Casper de Haas	(Sold) fl 6 V Giesen
1802/09/21	UTHDG	0029	*J.J. van Gooijen* | Een woelende Rivier, met veelerhande vaartuigen vooraan een boot met scheepsvolk, in het verschiet een Kasteel, Dorp, enz. fraaij van licht en couleur en meesterlijk geschildert | *Mat:* op paneel *Size:* hoog 10 ½, breed 15 ½ duimen		(Bought In) fl 21
1802/09/21	UTHDG	0030	*J.J. van Gooijen* | Een kabbelend water, gestoffeerd met een zeilend vaartuig, en Visschers in een schuit bezig hunne netten optehaalen, als de voorgaande | *Mat:* op paneel *Size:* hoog 12 ½, breed 14 ½ duimen		(Bought In) fl 24:10
1802/09/21	UTHDG	0032	*J. van Goijen* | Een Hoofd, waarbij vaartuigen, in het verschiet een Dorp, fraaij met werkende beeldtjes gestoffeerd | *Size:* hoog 6, breed 9 duimen		(Sold) fl 10:15 De Munnick
1802/09/21	UTHDG	0033	*J. van Goijen* | Een Vestgezicht van eene oude Stad, liggende aan een Rivier, met veele Vaartuigen enz. gestoffeert | *Size:* hoog 13, breed 16 duimen		(Bought In) fl 13
1802/11/01	DOBRA	0010	*J. v. Gooyen* | Een dito [Dorpsgezicht] | *Size:* hoog 12, breed 29 d.	Paulus van der Spyk [or others]	(Sold) fl 11:15 v Braam
1802/11/01	DOBRA	0011	*J. v. Gooyen* | Een Riviergezigt, door denzelven [J. v. Gooyen] 1653 | *Size:* breed 17, hoog 12 ½ duim *Inscr:* 1653 (dated?) *Notes:* It is unclear whether the date is inscribed on the painting.	Paulus van der Spyk [or others]	(Sold) fl 12:5 Parees
1802/11/01	DOBRA	0012	*J. v. Gooyen* | Een dito [Riviergezigt], door denzelven [J. v. Gooyen] 1650. in een rond | *Fmt:* rond *Inscr:* 1650 (dated?) *Notes:* It is unclear whether the date is inscribed on the painting.	Paulus van der Spyk [or others]	(Sold) fl 9:5 M v Steeg
1802/11/01	DOBRA	0013	*J. v. Gooyen* | Een Stad, gelegen aan een rivier, waar de veerpont over vaart. De Voorgrond gestoffeerd met Beeldjes; voords Scheepjes, enz. | *Mat:* op paneel *Size:* breed 3 hoog 2 voet	Paulus van der Spyk [or others]	(Sold) fl 35 Lamme
1802/11/01	DOBRA	0120	*J. van Gooyen* | Een Watergezigt	Paulus van der Spyk [or others]	(Unknown)
1802/11/01	DOBRA	0145	*J. van Gooijen* | Een gezicht langs een Stads Vest, vol Gebouwen, en een Moolen; van den besten tyd | *Mat:* op paneel *Size:* hoog 25, br. 37 d.		(Unknown) fl 21

1803/04/20	AMSCH	0029	*Goyen. (J. van)* | Een stille Rivier, gestoffeerd met een ménigte Vaartuigen, op de voorgrond zyn eenige Vissers zoo op het Land als in hun Schuiten beezig met hunne netten op te haalen, aan de overzyde der Rivier ziet men een Molen, Boerewoningen, en hoog Geboomte; alles is volmaakt met de Natuur overeenkomstig behandeld, en van de beste van dezen Meester [Aux bords d'une riviere garnie d'une multitude de barques & de navires l'on voit des pêcheurs occupés de leur étât ; des habitations & ce qui se presente de plus dans un paysage riant, y est rendu d'une maniere si vraye & si naturelle! qu'on ne balancera pas a mettre ce tableau parmi les meilleurs de cet artiste.] | *Mat:* op doek *Size:* hoog 44, breed 69 duim	Maria Magdalena van Sluypwyk, gravinne van Moens	(Sold) fl 280 Josi
1803/04/20	AMSCH	0030	*Goyen. (J. van)* | Twee stuks, het eene verbeeld een Duinachtig Landschap, met een Jager te Paard en te voet, in het verschiet een Stad, de andere verbeeld een stil Water, met verscheide Vaartuigen, en eenige Vissers in hun Schuit een net op te haalen; beide zeer natuurlyk geschilderd [Deux pieces dont une represente une partie de dunes, ornée de chasseurs & d'un point de vue sur une ville, l'autre est une vue de riviere garnie de barques & de pêcheurs. Ces pieces ont le merite d'être traitées d'une maniere très naturelle.] | *Mat:* op paneel *Size:* ieder hoog 14, breed 13 duim	Maria Magdalena van Sluypwyk, gravinne van Moens	(Sold) fl 18 Hodges
1803/04/27	AMSCH	000T	*J. van Gooijen* | Une Riviere avec un Village, dans le Loingtains [sic]. Orné de plusieurs Bateaux | *Size:* h. 15, l. 22 pouces	B	(Bought In) fl 5
1803/08/01	AMSCH	0010	*Gooyen. (J. van)* | Een Riviergezigt, gestoffeerd op de voorgrond met Visschers in een Schuit, verders eenige Boomen, langs een weg, en in 't verschiet een Kasteel, natuurlyk daargesteld | *Mat:* op paneel *Size:* hoog 23, breed 26 duim	J	(Sold) fl 11:10 Pruijssenaar
1803/08/17	AMSCH	0028	*Goyen. (J. van)* | Een Riviergezicht met zeilende Schepen, ter zyde een Landgezigt, met hoog Geboomte, en Stoffagie van Beeldjes, natuurlyk behandeld | *Mat:* op paneel *Size:* hoog 23, breed 33 duim	Anna Catharina Putman	(Sold) fl 5:10 v^{n} Dijl
1803/08/24	HGKAN	0055	*van Gooyen* | Het Gezicht langs een hoofd op een Stil Water	[Teissier] [or others]	(Sold) fl 8 van Giesen
1803/09/07	AMSCH	0070	*J. van Goijen* | Een Zeehaven, met verscheide Schepen en Vaartuigen [Un port de mer, contenant plusieurs navires et des batimens de différentes grandeurs] | *Mat:* op paneel *Size:* hoog 15, breed 19 duim	Smidt	(Sold) fl 5:5 de Lafontaine
1803/12/12	AMSCH	0037	*J. van Goijen* | Een stil Water, met een ménigte Visschers en Vaartuigen, en een Stad in het verschiet; meesterlyk op Paneel | *Mat:* op paneel *Size:* hoog 19, breed 25 duim	E	(Sold) fl 18:10 W Reijers
1803/12/15	MGLAC	0010	*J. van Gooyen* | Een fraai en aangenaam Landschapje; zeer helder geschilderd en schoon van coloriet | *Mat:* op paneel *Size:* hoog duim 13, breed duim 25	Mr L H de Haze Bomme	(Unknown)
1803/12/15	MGLAC	0011	*J. van Gooyen* | Een dito [fraai en aangenaam Landschapje], Stad- en Watergezigt; zeer fraai | *Mat:* op paneel *Size:* hoog duim 20, breed duim 31 *Notes:* It is unclear what "dito" refers to in the title.	Mr L H de Haze Bomme	(Unknown)
1804/02/27	AMSCH	0038	*Goyen. (J. van)* | In dit capitaale Schildery, ziet men by een Rivier waarin een Schuitje met twee Lieden, een oud vervallen Cassteel, waarby een menigte Beelden, verder achter eenig hoog Geboomte een aangenaam verschiet; zynde dit stuk delicaat en zonachtig gepenceeld en een der beste van deze meester | *Mat:* op doek *Size:* hoog 50, breed 39 duim	D	(Bought In) fl 20
1804/02/27	AMSCH	0039	*Goyen. (J. van)* | Langs een stil Water, waarin in eenige Visschers in een Schuit, ziet men eenige Boerewoningen en Geboomte; zeer natuurlyk behandeld | *Mat:* op paneel *Size:* hoog 15, breed 21 duim	B	(Bought In) fl 1:5
1804/02/27	AMSCH	0040	*Goyen. (J. van)* | Een gezicht op een Kerktooren aan een Rivier; waarby eenige Visschers met hunne Schuiten | *Mat:* op paneel *Size:* hoog 20, breed 16 duim	D	(Sold) fl 2 Van Dijl
1804/04/28	LNDLS	0032	*J. van Goyen* | Een kabbelent Water, met zeilende schepen en andere vaartuigen, en dorpen in 't verschiet, konstig, en kragtig door J. van Goyen, op paneel | *Mat:* op paneel *Size:* hoog 15, breed 23 duim	[Abraham Delfos] [or others]	(Sold) fl 28 Macalester
1804/04/28	LNDLS	0049	*J. v. Goyen* | Een Landschap met boomen en wooningen langs een water met schuiten, door J. v. Goyen, op paneel | *Mat:* op paneel *Size:* hoog 12, breed 17 duim	[Abraham Delfos] [or others]	(Sold) fl 4:14 Bake
1804/04/28	LNDLS	0050	*J. v. Goyen* | Twee Stuks, Land- en Watergezichten, door denzelven [J. v. Goyen], in 't graauw, op paneel | *Mat:* op paneel	[Abraham Delfos] [or others]	(Sold) fl 3 Jan Landa
1804/05/07	AMSCH	0066	*Goijen. (J. van)* | Een Dorpgezicht, met Kerk en Tooren, en verscheide Gebouwen, aan een Rivier, gestoffeerd met diversche Scheepen en Visschersschuiten, fiks en Meesterlyk geschilderd | *Mat:* op paneel *Size:* hoog 18, breed 26 duim	Schley	(Bought In) fl 6
1804/05/07	AMSCH	0067	*Goijen. (J. van)* | Een Duinächtig Landschap, met Boere Wooningen, Geboomte en Stoffagie van Beeldjes; natuurlyk behandeld | *Mat:* op paneel *Size:* hoog 13, breed 18 duim	Y[ver] [for] JJ	(Sold) fl 12 Roelofs
1804/05/07	AMSCH	0068	*Goijen. (J. van)* | In een Kabbelende Zee ziet men eenige zylende Scheepen en Schuiten, fiks en fraai gepenceeld | *Mat:* op doek *Size:* hoog 15, breed 23 duim	Roos [for] A	(Sold) fl 23 Hulswit
1804/05/07	AMSCH	0069	*Goijen. (J. van)* | In een Kabbelend Water, by eenig Latwerk en houte Trap, ziet men een Visser in een Schuit, in 't verschiet by eenige Boere	Roos [for] A	(Sold) fl 4 Coclers

			Woningen eenige Zylende Schuiten; fraai en natuurlyk behandeld | *Mat:* op paneel *Size:* hoog 11, breed 13 duim		
1804/05/07	AMSCH	0070	*Goijen. (J. van)* | In een Landschap by eenig Duin, ziet men eenige Boerewoningen, waarby eenige Lieden, in 't verschiet een Strant enz., zonachtig en breed gepenceeld | *Mat:* op paneel *Size:* hoog 17, breed 22 duim	Roos [for] A	(Sold) fl 12 Roelofs
1804/07/25	DLGRO	0006	*J. van Goijen* | Een Water gezicht, met eenige Zeilende Scheepen, Visschers, &c. fraai en uitvoerig geschilderd door J. van Goijen | *Mat:* op paneel *Size:* hoog 22, breed 32 duim	Mr Franc van der Burch Wz.	(Unknown)
1804/07/25	DLGRO	0018	*J. van Goijen* | Een woelig Water gezicht, zynde een Veer of Overvaart, met een Pont of Veerschuit vol Menschen en Paarden; voorts een Dorp of Stads gezicht, uitvoerig op Doek geschilderd | *Mat:* op doek *Size:* hoog 10, breed 15 duim	Mr Franc van der Burch Wz.	(Unknown)
1804/07/25	DLGRO	0023	*Jan van Goijen* | Een stil Water, op den voorgrond eenige ViSschers in een Schuit, in 't verschiet Boere Woningen, en hoog Geboomte op Paneel | *Mat:* op paneel *Size:* hoog 15, breed 18 duim	Mr Franc van der Burch Wz.	(Unknown)
1804/07/25	DLGRO	0041	*J. van Goijen* | Een Winter gezicht, verbeeldende de bevrozen Rhyn of Galgenwater, met Sleeden en Paarden, en een menigte van Schaatze Ryders, en de Stad Leiden in 't verschiet, zeer uitvoerig en fraai geschilderd door J. van Goijen | *Mat:* op paneel *Size:* hoog 18, breed 28 duim	Mr Franc van der Burch Wz.	(Unknown)
1804/07/25	DLGRO	0042	*J. van Goijen* | Een Strand gezicht, met eenige Pinken op Strand liggende, een menigte Visschers en Vrouwen die Visch opladen en dragen, voorts eenige Persoonen te Paard, en verder Dorps gezicht, zeer uitvoerig | *Mat:* op paneel *Size:* hoog 18, breed 28 duim	Mr Franc van der Burch Wz.	(Unknown)
1804/07/25	DLGRO	0055	*J. van Goijen* | Een Land en Water gezicht, verbeeldende een Veer of Overvaart, en een Herberg waar voor een Wagen met Paarden staat: op den voorgrond een Visscher in een Schuitje, en verder bywerk, zeer fraai door J. van Goijen | *Mat:* op paneel *Size:* hoog 15, breed 22 duim	Mr Franc van der Burch Wz.	(Unknown)
1804/07/25	DLGRO	0056	*J. van Goijen* | Een woelend Water gezicht, verbeeldende de Rivier de Merwede, met het oude Huis of Slot in 't verschiet, en verder bywerk, mede fraai door denzelfde [J. van Goijen] | *Mat:* op paneel *Size:* hoog 11, breed 16 duim	Mr Franc van der Burch Wz.	(Unknown)
1804/07/25	DLGRO	0057	*J. van Goijen* | Een Rhyn gezicht voor de Stad Rheenen, met een Schuit of Pont vol met Menschen en Koeijen, voorts verscheide Scheepen en Visschers; zeer uitvoerig en fraai geschilderd door denzelfde [J. van Goijen] op Doek | *Mat:* op doek *Size:* hoog 34 duim, breed 4 voet 2 duim	Mr Franc van der Burch Wz.	(Unknown)
1804/07/25	DLGRO	0058	*J. van Goijen* | Een Zeedorp en Strand, verbeeldende de aankomst der Pinken, het lossen en opladen van Visch &c., zeer uitvoerig en fraai door denzelfde [J. van Goijen] op Doek | *Mat:* op doek *Size:* hoog 34 duim, breed 4 voet 2 duim	Mr Franc van der Burch Wz.	(Unknown)
1804/08/08	AMSCH	0072	*J. van Goyen* | Een stil Water, met diverse Vaartuigen en Beeldjes, bézig met roeijen, ter zyde een Landgezicht; dun op Paneel | *Mat:* op paneel *Size:* hoog 19, breed 27 duim	Roos [for] D	(Sold) fl 1 Gruyter
1804/08/08	AMSCH	0073	*J. van Goyen* | In een Riviergezicht ziet men langs een oud Kasteel een ménigte van zeilende en stil leggende Vaartuigen; fraai gepenceeld | *Mat:* op paneel *Size:* hoog 19, breed 24 duim	Vink[eles] [for] W	(Sold) fl 4 van Iperen
1804/08/08	AMSCH	0074	*J. van Goyen* | Een Duin- en Boomryk Landschap, met Boerenwooningen en differente Stoffagie; warm en zonachtig geschilderd | *Mat:* op paneel *Size:* hoog 20 ½, breed 21 ½ duim	Vink[eles] [for] K[=Gruyter?]	(Sold) fl 0:6 L Pakker
1804/10/16	DLOND	0080	*J. van Goyen* | Een Landschap. Paysage | *Mat:* op paneel *Size:* hoog 14, breed 16		(Unknown)
1804/10/16	DLOND	0081	*J. van Goyen* | Een Winter Gezicht. Tableau d'Hyver | *Mat:* op paneel *Size:* hoog 10, breed 13		(Unknown) fl 3:10
1804/10/16	DLOND	0082	*J. van Goyen* | Uts[a] [Een Winter Gezicht. Tableau d'Hyver] | *Mat:* op paneel *Size:* hoog 10, breed 13		(Unknown)
1804/10/16	DLOND	0083	*J. van Goyen* | Een Stil Water Gezicht. Vue d'une Calme | *Mat:* op paneel *Size:* hoog 15, breed 20		(Unknown)
1804/10/16	DLOND	0084	*J. van Goyen* | Uts[a] [Een Stil Water Gezicht. Vue d'une Calme] | *Mat:* op paneel *Size:* hoog 7, breed 12		(Unknown)
1804/10/16	DLOND	0085	*J. van Goyen* | Een Landschap. Paysage | *Mat:* op paneel *Size:* hoog 11, breed 15		(Unknown)
1804/10/16	DLOND	0086	*J. van Goyen* | Het Dorp Scheveningen in deszelfs eersten stand. Scheveningen dans son état primitif | *Mat:* op paneel *Size:* hoog 9, breed 13		(Unknown)
1804/10/29	HRBAU	0026	*Goyen, (Jan van)* | Een Gezigt van een Kerk, staande langs een Watertje, waar by Visschers in hunne schuitjes, nevens een aangenaam verschiet. Zeer tekenagtig behandeld | *Mat:* op paneel *Size:* hoog 14, breed 13 duim	Simon Styl	(Unknown)
1804/10/29	HRBAU	0027	*Goyen, (Jan van)* | Een fraai stil Watertje, met Scheepen en Schuiten bezet, waar agter in het verschiet een Kust ontdekt wordt. Dit Stukje is niet minder bevallig als het voorgaande | *Mat:* op paneel *Size:* hoog 14, breed 13 duim	Simon Styl	(Unknown)

1805/07/03	AMSCH	0084	*J. van Gooijen* | In een Riviergezicht, ziet men een ménigte van zylende en stillegende Vaartuigen, terzyde op 't Land eenige Gebouwen, Molen, Kerktooren; fiks en natuurlyk | *Mat:* op paneel *Size:* hoog 17, breed 22 duim	V[inkeles]	(Sold) fl 50 Reyers
1805/07/10	AMSCH	0063	*J. van Goijen* | Een gezicht op den Haag, zynde de Vaart gestoffeert met een Trekschuit en andere Vaartuigen, op de voorgrond eenige Beeldjes en Beesten; natuurlyk op Paneel | *Mat:* op paneel *Size:* hoog 15, breed 19 duim	R[oos]	(Bought In) fl 60
1805/07/10	AMSCH	0064	*J. van Goijen* | Een gezicht op een Rivier langs een Stad, het Water gestoffeerd met Vissers in hunne Schuit; niet minder als de voorgaande | *Size:* hoog 10, breed 14 duim	R[oos]	(Sold) fl 6:10 Boelhouwer
1805/07/10	AMSCH	0065	*J. van Goijen* | In een Wintergezicht ziet men op 't Ys op de voorgrond eenige Kolvende Lieden, verders Schaatseryders, Wandelaars, Paarden, Arren-Sleede, enz. op 't Land hoog Geboomten, Woningen en Molens; breed en meesterlyk gepenceeld | *Mat:* op paneel *Size:* hoog 23, breed 28 duim	V[inkeles] [for] M	(Bought In) fl 41
1805/07/10	AMSCH	0066	*J. van Goijen* | Een Land- en Watergezicht, met verscheide Visschers in Scheepen, en andere Schuiten; natuurlyk behandeld | *Mat:* op paneel	S[chley] [for] Louis [?]	(Bought In) fl 3
1805/10/09	HGBSM	E0005	*J. van Gooyen* | Een Stad en Water gezigt, gestoffeerd met visschers &c | *Mat:* op paneel *Size:* hoog 18 ½ breet 24 ½ duim	T H van Willigen [or others]	(Sold) fl 6 Blommers
1805/12/16	AMSCH	0024	*J. van Goyen* | Een Gezicht op de Haarlemer Meer, ziende op 't Huis te Heemsteden, ryk gestoffeerd met Vaartuigen en Beelden | *Size:* hoog 36, breed 43 duim	R[oos]	(Bought In) fl 3
1805/12/16	AMSCH	0025	*J. van Goyen* | Ruïne van het Huis te Merwe, waarby verscheide Beelden, meesterlyk op Doek | *Mat:* op doek *Size:* hoog 39, breed 52 duim	R[oos]	(Sold) fl 1 L Pakker
1806/05/05	AMSCH	0054	*J. v. Goyen* | Een kabbelend Water met verscheiden zeilende Scheepen, roei en andere Vaartuigen, vol stoffagien van Beelden, en een Dorp in het verschiet; natuurlyk op Paneel | *Mat:* op paneel *Size:* hoog 20, breed 28 duim	R[oos]	(Sold) fl 34 Roos
1806/06/07	RMHSN	0011	*J: van Gojen* | Een Watergezigt met Zeilende Scheepjes, aangenaam en helder geschilderd | *Mat:* op paneel	A E K L	(Sold) fl 28 Thijs
1806/06/07	RMHSN	0023	*J: v: Gojen* | Een Land- en Watergezigt met Schepen en een Pont die Overvaart, aangenaam van Coleur	A E K L	(Unknown)
1806/06/07	RMHSN	0024	*J: v: Gojen* | Een Wintervermaak met Schaatseryders &c. | *Mat:* op paneel	A E K L	(Sold) fl 26 Thijs
1806/06/07	RMHSN	0025	*J: v: Gojen* | Een Water met Zeilende Schepen, en Gezigt op het Huis de Merwe | *Mat:* op paneel	A E K L	(Unknown)
1806/06/07	RMHSN	0026	*J: v: Gojen* | Een Woelend Water met Zeilende Schepen | *Mat:* op paneel	A E K L	(Unknown)
1806/06/07	RMHSN	0027	*J: v: Gojen* | Een Zeestrand met Visschers en anderen | *Mat:* op paneel	A E K L	(Sold) fl 11 Thijs
1806/06/07	RMHSN	0028	*J: v: Gojen* | Een met Zeilende Schepen, Papier op Paneel | *Mat:* op papier op paneel	A E K L	(Unknown)
1806/06/07	RMHSN	0120	*Van Gojen* | Een Stil Water by een Stadsgezigt, met Schuiten en Schepen	A E K L	(Unknown)
1806/08/13	AMSCH	0064	*Goijen. (J. van)* | Een Gezicht op 't Slot Loevestyn, 't Water met Visschers in hunne Schuiten en een aangenaam verschiet | *Mat:* op paneel *Size:* hoog 27, breed 39 duim	Vinkeles [for] J	(Sold) fl 11 Van Dijll
1806/08/13	AMSCH	0241	*van Gooijen* | Een gezicht op de Zuiderzee, met zeilende Scheepen en Vissers in hun Schuiten	Vinkeles [for] G[ruyter]	(Sold) fl 5:5 Weyland
1806/08/20	HGBSM	0090	*J. van Gooyen* | Een Landschap met Boerewoningen en Geboomte, gestoffeerd met eenige figuuren, helder van couleur en breed van licht en bruin | *Mat:* op paneel *Size:* hoog 17, breed 23 duim	Macalester Loup [or others]	(Sold) fl 20 Teissier
1806/11/24	AMSCH	0028	*Goyen (J. van)* | Een gezigt op de Haarlemmer Meer, ziende op het Huis te Heemsteden, ryk gestoffeerd, met zeilende Scheepen en andere Schuiten, met Lieden; meesterlyk geschilderd | *Mat:* op paneel *Size:* hoog 36, breed 43 duim	Munnikhuizen	(Sold) fl 14 Coclers
1807/04/00	LNDLS	0021	*Jan van Goyen* | Een gezigt langs de Merwede op de stad Dordrecht, met veel schepen en vaartuigen, op den voorgrond rustende vee, een der beste stukken van dien meester | *Mat:* op doek *Size:* hoog 36, breed 54 duim	[Abraham Delfos] [or others]	(Unknown)
1807/04/00	LNDLS	0025	*J. v. Goyen* | Een gezigt langs het water met visschers in haar schuit | *Mat:* op paneel	[Abraham Delfos] [or others]	(Unknown)
1807/04/00	LNDLS	0032	*J. van Goyen* | Een gezigt op 't Belvidère te Nymegen, langs een water met vaartuigen | *Mat:* op paneel	[Abraham Delfos] [or others]	(Unknown)
1807/04/00	LNDLS	0045	*J. van Goyen* | Een Landschap | *Size:* hoog 13, breed 16 duim	[Abraham Delfos] [or others]	(Unknown)
1807/06/02	AMHUY	0014	*van Gooyen* | Een Riviergezicht by een Boeren Dorp, met eenige Vissers in haar Schuiten		(Unknown)
1807/06/02	AMHUY	0031	*van Gooyen* | Een Rivier agter een Boere Dorp, met verscheide Vissers in Schuiten en andere Vaartuigen, zonachtig en krachtig geschilderd		(Unknown)
1807/06/10	HGBSM	0021	*Jan van Goyen* | Een gezigt langs de Merwede op de stad Dordrecht, met veel schepen en vaartuigen, op den voorgrond rustend vee, een der beste stukken van dien meester | *Mat:* op doek *Size:* hoog 36, breed 54 duim	Abraham Delfos [or others]	(Sold) fl 20 Tomas

1807/06/10	HGBSM	0025	*J. v. Goyen* | Een gezigt langs het water met visschers in haar schuit | *Mat:* op paneel	Abraham Delfos [or others]	(Sold) fl 8:5 Uitbogert
1807/06/10	HGBSM	0032	*J. van Goyen* | Een gezigt op 't Belvidère te Nymegen, langst een water met vaartuigen | *Mat:* op paneel	Abraham Delfos [or others]	(Sold) fl 22 v Olden
1807/06/10	HGBSM	0045	*J. van Goyen* | Een Landschap | *Size:* hoog 13, breed 16 duim	Abraham Delfos [or others]	(Sold) fl 2:10 Temmink
1807/06/10	HGBSM	0153	*J. van Gooyen* | Een Land en Water gezigt met eenige Boeren wooningen, gestoffeerd met figuuren en schuitjes, zeer natuurlijk | *Mat:* op paneel *Size:* hoog 15, breed 20 duim	Abraham Delfos [or others]	(Sold) fl 10 S T
1807/06/10	HGBSM	0179	*J. van Goojen* | Het Gezicht van Schevening aan het Strand vol gewoel, met figuren en schepen | *Mat:* op paneel *Size:* hoog 15, breed 20 duim	Abraham Delfos [or others]	(Sold) fl 3:4 Zeppel
1807/06/10	HGBSM	0180	*J. van Goojen* | Een dito Rivier gezigt, gestoffeerd met vaartuigen, &c. in het verschiet een Dorp | *Mat:* op paneel *Size:* hoog 13, breed 18 ½ duim *Notes:* It is unclear what "dito" refers to in the title.	Abraham Delfos [or others]	(Sold) fl 11:10 Uittenbogart
1807/08/26	AMSCH	0084	*J. van Goyen* | Een Watergezigt by een Kasteel, geestig met Beeldjes en Vaartuigen gestoffeerd | *Mat:* op paneel *Size:* hoog 18, breed 23 duim	Joseph Vallette	(Sold) fl 6:10 du Pree
1807/08/26	AMSCH	0086	*J. van Goyen* | Een Riviergezigt, met Vaartuigen gestoffeerd	Joseph Vallette	(Sold) fl 1:5 Graffelman
1807/09/28	DOHAA	00FF	*J. van Gooijen* | Watergezigt op 't Huis de Merwede | *Mat:* op paneel	Mattheus Westerouen van Meeteren	(Unknown)
1808/04/26	GDAN	0050	*Goyen (J van)* | Een Watergezigt met een Kasteel, en bywerk | *Size:* hoog 15 ½, breed 20 ½ duim	G H Fortuyn	(Unknown)
1808/04/26	GDAN	0051	*Goyen (J van)* | Een fraai Watergezigtje met eenige zeilende Scheepjes en Vissers | *Size:* hoog 5, breed 8 duim	G H Fortuyn	(Unknown)
1808/04/26	GDAN	0052	*Goyen (J van)* | Een Watergezigtje met een Huis, en eenig Geboomte, en verder bywerk | *Size:* hoog 12, breed 15 duim	G H Fortuyn	(Unknown)
1808/04/26	GDAN	0053	*Goyen (J van)* | Een stil Water met zeilende Schepen | *Size:* hoog 42, breed 54 duim	G H Fortuyn	(Unknown)
1808/04/26	GDAN	0054	*Goyen (J van)* | Een woelend Water bij een Hoofd, fiks en wel geschildert | *Size:* hoog 26, breed 29 duim	G H Fortuyn	(Unknown)
1808/04/26	GDAN	0055	*Goyen (J van)* | Een aangenaam Watergezigtje met een Kasteel in 't gezigt, waar bij een aantal leggende, en in het verschiet eenige zeilende Schepen, fiks gepenseeld | *Size:* hoog 17, breed 29 duim	G H Fortuyn	(Unknown)
1808/04/26	GDAN	0056	*Goyen (J van)* | Een woelend Water met zeilende Schepen en Schuiten, bij een Paalwerk, met veel Menschen, zeer goed geschilderd | *Size:* hoog 31, breed 46 duim	G H Fortuyn	(Unknown)
1808/05/17	LNAN	0005	*Jan van Gooyen* | Een Gezigt lang het Water op de stad Dordrecht, met zeilende schepen en schuiten met volk; op den voorgrond rustende en staande koeijen, en een aangenaam verschiet; kunstig op doek geschilderd en aangenaam van kleur, een der capitaalste en beste stukken | *Mat:* op doek *Size:* hoog 36, breed 54 duim	[Abraham Delfos]	(Sold) fl 50 Sluyter
1808/06/06	RMRIJ	0044	*Gooijen. (Jan Josephz. van)* | Een aangenaam Rivier- en Landgezigt. Rijk gestoffeerd, ongemeen schoon van kleur, kloek en meesterlijk geschilderd [Ce Tableau represente une partie d'un Village situé au bord d'une Rivière. On voit sous un beau ciel plusieurs Bateaux à la voile et barques à la rame, et beaucoup de figures. Ce Morceau Peint avec art est d'un beau Coloris, d'un bel effet, et un chef-d'oeuvre de cet Artiste] | *Mat:* op doek *Size:* Hoog 49 ¼, en breed 62 ½ duim *Loc:* Amsterdam, Nederland. Rijksmuseum. (A 120)	Gerrit van der Pot, Heer van Groeneveld	(Sold) fl 160 Stratenus [for] le Roi
1808/06/11	RMRIJ	0007	*Jan van Goijen* | Een fraai en schilderachtig Stad- Land- en Watergezicht, ryk gestoffeerd; breed en meesterlyk geschilderd | *Mat:* op paneel *Size:* hoog 26 ½, breed 37 duim		(Bought In) fl 15
1808/06/13	AMSCH	0065	*Goijen (J. van)* | Een heuvelachtig Landschap met Geboomte, Boere Woningen en stoffage van Beeldjes. Meesterlijk geschilderd | *Mat:* op paneel *Size:* hoog 12, breed 21 duim	[Jan Tersteeg]	(Bought In) fl 5
1808/08/23	AMSCH	0060	*Gooijen. (J. van)* | Een stille Rivier, ter zijde eenige Boeren Wooningen en Geboomten, gestoffeert met een Visscher in een Schuit en andere figuuren; zeer natuurlijk en bevallig voorgesteld | *Mat:* op paneel *Size:* hoog 12, breed 18 duim	X	(Bought In) fl 20
1808/08/23	AMSCH	0061	*Gooijen. (J. van)* | Een Gezigt op de Haarlemmer Meer, met verscheiden zeilende Visschers Schuiten en andere Vaartuigen; natuurlijk geschilderd | *Mat:* op paneel *Size:* hoog 16, breed 22 duim	J	(Sold) fl 25 Reydon
1808/08/23	AMSCH	0062	*Gooijen. (J. van)* | Een Land en Watergezigt, waarin Visschers in Schuiten, verder Geboomten, Kerk en Wooningen; fiks op Paneel behandeld | *Mat:* op paneel	Z	(Sold) fl 0:6 W van der Schley
1808/08/23	AMSCH	0063	*Gooijen. (J. van)* | Een ruim Gezigt, ziende van de Landzijde naar de Willemstad, gestoffeert met Beeldjes	Z	(Sold) fl 1:5 Boulhouwer
1808/09/13	HABRU	0027	*J. van Goijen* | Een Land- en Watergezicht		(Unknown) fl 4:13
1808/09/13	HABRU	0028	*J. van Goijen* | Een dito [Land- en Watergezicht]		(Unknown) fl 92 [?]
1808/09/13	HABRU	0029	*J. van Goijen* | Een dito Landgezicht | *Notes:* It is unclear what "dito" refers to in the title.		(Unknown) fl 1:8 [?]

1808/09/13	HABRU	0030	*J. van Goijen* | Een Heijgezicht, met een Molen, natuurlijk		(Unknown) fl 3:10
1808/09/13	HABRU	0031	*J. van Goijen* | Een Watergezicht aan een Stadsvest, waar een Pont overvaarende		(Sold) fl 4:15 V D W[illigen]
1808/09/13	HABRU	0032	*J. van Goijen* | Een Watergezicht, aan een oude Tooren		(Unknown) fl 2:10
1808/11/28	AMSCH	0084	*J. van Goijen* | Twee stuks Duinachtige Landschappen, met vervallen Boeren Wooningen en stoffage, natuurlijk	[Gruyter?]	(Sold) fl 19 van der Schley [for] E v Dijk
1808/12/30	HGIMM	[0071j]	*Van Gooijen* | Voorts een exquis kabinetje Schilderijen van voorname Nederlandsche Meesters, welke uit hoofde de van kortheid des tijds niet stuk voor stuk kunnen beschreven worden; doch waarvan de beschrijving op den Kijkdag zal voorhanden zijn. Dus wij hier alleen de namen van eenige dier Meesters laten volgen, als: A. Kuyp, Ruysdaal, Karel du Jardyn, Loqwi ('t beste dat hij schilderde) Hondekoeter, van Dyk, Janson, Moesgever, Kamphuyzen, van Gooijen, A. van der Neer, T. Wyk, Huchtenburgh, Zolemaker, van Hassel, A. Vermeulen, van Dongen, Scheffer, van Os enz. | *This Lot:* Een Schilderij, Van Gooijen *Notes:* Because this lot was not numbered in the catalogue, we have assigned the number.		(Unknown)
1809/04/17	AMSCH	0169	*J. van Goijen* | Een Land en Watergezicht, met Vaartuigen gestoffeerd; fiks | *Mat:* op paneel	H	(Sold) fl 1:5 Gruyter
1809/04/22	AMYVR	0048	*J. van Goijen* | Een Land- en Riviergezicht, gestoffeerd met Beelden en Vaartuigen; meesterlijk | *Mat:* op paneel *Size:* hoog 16, breed 24 duim	de Bruin	(Sold) fl 12:10 du Pree
1809/04/22	AMYVR	0049	*J. van Goijen* | Aan een Vestmuur ziet men eene menigte Visschers, zoo op de Wal als in hunne Schuiten; als de voorgaande | *Mat:* op paneel *Size:* hoog 18, breed 23 duim	de Bruin	(Sold) fl 10:10 C S Roos
1809/04/22	AMYVR	0050	*J. van Goijen* | Een Dorp- en Riviergezicht, met een Pont en andere Vaartuigen; fiks | *Mat:* op paneel *Size:* hoog 11, breed 17 duim	de Bruin	(Sold) fl 6 fl for lots 50 & 51. Coclers
1809/04/22	AMYVR	0051	*J. van Goijen* | Een dito [Dorp- en Rivier-] Gezicht; niet minder | *Size:* hoog 11, breed 17 duim	de Bruin	(Sold) fl 6 fl for lots 50 & 51. Coclers
1809/04/22	AMYVR	0052	*J. van Goijen* | Een Stad- en Riviergezicht; als de voorgaande | *Mat:* op paneel *Size:* hoog 8, breed 10 duim	de Bruin	(Sold) fl 0:6 v d Schley
1809/05/26	HADAA	0041	*Jan van Goijen* | Een Gezicht binnen Utrecht na den Dom, op Paneel door Jan van Goijen, A^{o}: 1646 | *Mat:* op paneel *Inscr:* Jan van Goijen, A^{o}: 1646 (signed and dated?) *Notes:* It is unclear whether the name and date are inscribed on the painting. *Loc:* Philadelphia, PA, USA. Museum of Art. (Johnson Coll. 463)	Mejuffrouw de Wed David Heemskerk [or others]	(Unknown)
1809/05/26	HADAA	A0015	*J. van Gooyen* | Een Land- en Watergezigt	Mejuffrouw de Wed David Heemskerk [or others]	(Unknown)
1809/05/26	HADAA	A0016	*J. van Gooyen* | Een dito [Land- en Watergezigt], dito [door J. van Gooyen]	Mejuffrouw de Wed David Heemskerk [or others]	(Unknown)
1809/06/13	AMSCH	0052	*J. v. Gooijen* | Een aangenaam Land- en Watergezicht, met Boeren Woningen en Geboomten, gestoffeerd met staand en liggend Vee, zeilende Scheepen, Visschers en andere Vaartuigen en verdere stoffagie; helder van koloriet en meesterlijk geschilderd | *Mat:* op paneel *Size:* hoog 19, breed 25 duim	[Gruyter?]	(Bought In) fl 6
1809/06/13	AMSCH	0053	*J. v. Gooijen* | Een Duinachtig Landschap, voor een Herberg ziet men Wagens met Huislieden, welken zich ververschen en andere Figuuren | *Mat:* op paneel *Size:* hoog 14, breed 22 duim	Y	(Sold) fl 3:5 van Dijl
1809/06/13	AMSCH	0054	*J. v. Gooijen* | Een Kasteel of Slot, aan een stille Rivier, ter zijde een opgaande Weg; eigenaartig gestoffeerd | *Mat:* op paneel *Size:* hoog 14, breed 21 duim	Y	(Sold) fl 1 L Pakker
1809/06/13	AMSCH	0055	*J. v. Gooijen* | Een sterk woelend Water, gestoffeerd met Visschers in hunne Schuiten, ter zijde met een Vesting, natuurlijk behandeld | *Size:* hoog 19, breed 25 duim	Y	(Sold) fl 1 L Pakker
1809/06/13	AMSCH	0056	*J. v. Gooijen* | Een Land- en Watergezigt, met Boere Woningen, een Houte Brug en Beeldjes gestoffeerd | *Mat:* op paneel *Size:* hoog 16, breed 21 duim	Y	(Sold) fl 1 L Pakker
1809/07/19	AMSCH	0018	*Gooien (J. van)* | Een Riviergezigt, met verscheiden Vaartuigen, ter zijde een Dijk, gestoffeerd met eenige Postwagens, bij Boere Huizen. Fiks behandeld | *Mat:* op paneel *Fmt:* ovaal *Size:* hoog 26, breed 36 duim	C	(Sold) fl 1 Nieuwenhuys
1809/07/25	HGBSM	0063	*J. van Goyen* | Een Heuvelachtig Landschap, waarop een Postwagen daar eenige Reizigers zig ververschen, breed geschildert | *Mat:* op paneel *Size:* hoog 17, breed 23 d.	D van der Aa [or] E B ten Dall	(Sold) fl 9:5 Teissier
1809/07/25	HGBSM	0064	*J. van Goyen* | Een Watergezigt | *Mat:* op paneel *Size:* hoog 8 en 1 half, breed 12 en 1 half duim	D van der Aa [or] E B ten Dall	(Sold) fl 3 ten Haaf
1809/07/25	HGBSM	0086	*J. van Goyen* | Een Landschap, waar van de voorgrond gestoffeert met een Kar en eenige Figuren, door J. van Goyen, 1638 | *Mat:* op doek *Size:* hoog 28, breed 25 en een half duim *Inscr:* J. van Goyen, 1638 (signed and dated?) *Notes:* It is unclear whether the name and date are inscribed on the painting.	D van der Aa [or] E B ten Dall	(Sold) fl 10:15 Hassevoord

1809/07/25	HGBSM	0149	*J. van Goyen* | Een Ruine aan een Rivier, vol stoffage | *Mat:* op paneel *Size:* hoog 17, breed 25 duim	D van der Aa [or] E B ten Dall	(Sold) fl 5:15 Hassevoord
1809/07/25	HGBSM	0160	*J. van Goyen* | Een Landschapje | *Mat:* op paneel *Size:* hoog 10 en een half, breed 14 duim	D van der Aa [or] E B ten Dall	(Sold) fl 1:4 ten Haaf
1809/07/25	HGBSM	0206	*J. Van Gooyen* | Een Land- en Watergezigt, konstig gestoffeerd met zeilende en stil leggende Vaartuigen | *Mat:* op doek *Size:* hoog 41, breed 57 en een half duim	D van der Aa [or] E B ten Dall	(Sold) fl 2 Uijttenbogaard
1809/07/25	HGBSM	0219	*J. van Gooyen* | Een Gezigt van de Delftsche Vaart op den Haag te zien, ryk gestoffeerd met figuuren en vaartuigen, fraay gepenseelt, en een der beste stukken | *Mat:* op paneel *Size:* hoog 17 en een half, breed 22 en een half duim	D van der Aa [or] E B ten Dall	(Sold) fl 14 Teissier
1809/07/25	HGBSM	0232	*J. van Gooyen* | Een Watergezigt langs een Vest te zien, met Vaartuigen enz. | *Mat:* op paneel *Size:* hoog 16, breed 25 en een half duim	D van der Aa [or] E B ten Dall	(Sold) fl 1 Zwarts
1810/03/26	RMMUY	0010	*Jan van Goijen* | Een gezigt op eene Oude Stads Poort, Wallen en Paalhoofd, langs eene rivier met zeilende en stilliggende Vaartuigen. In 't verschiet een Dorp, van eene fraaije couleur en behandeling [La partie pittoresque d'une ancienne Ville située au bord d'une rivière, garnie de plusieurs bateaux, figures et chaloupes, d'un joli ton de couleur.] | *Mat:* op paneel *Size:* hoog 13 ½, breed 19 ½ duimen	Daniel de Jongh Az	(Sold) fl 20 van Eyk S'Hage
1810/03/27	RMCNL	0004	*van Goijen* | Een zeer fraai Landschap, de Stad Gorinchem voorstellende, langs de Maas te zien; op den voorgrond ziet men eene groote Pont, waar mede eene Koets met vier Paarden bespannen wordt overgevoerd, alles fix geschilderd		(Unknown)
1810/03/27	RMCNL	0005	*van Goijen* | Een Landschap, verbeeldende een Stadgezigt, mede langs eene Rivier, fraai geschilderd		(Unknown)
1810/03/27	RMCNL	0006	*van Goijen* | Een Land- en Watergezigt		(Unknown)
1810/03/27	RMCNL	0007	*van Goijen* | Twee Landschapjes, het eene Bergachtig, het andere langs een Watertje verbeeldende, aardig en fraai behandeld		(Unknown)
1810/03/27	RMCNL	0008	*van Goijen* | Een woelig Watertje, zeer fix en fraai gepenceeld		(Unknown)
1810/03/27	RMCNL	0067	*van Goijen* | Een woelig Watertje, waarop men eenige kleine Scheepjes ziet zeilen, zeer aardig geschilderd, in den smaak van S. Ruisdaal		(Unknown)
1810/03/27	RMCNL	0082	*van Gooyen* | Een zeer vrolijk Dorpgezichtje langs het Warer, warm en krachtig geschildert		(Unknown)
1810/05/22	AMSCH	0033	*Goijen. (J. van)* | Een stil Water, ter zijde Boeren Woningen en Geboomten, gestoffeerd met Visschers in hunne Schuiten en gaande Huislieden; natuurlijk gepenceeld | *Mat:* op doek *Size:* hoog 19, breed 25 duim	T	(Sold) fl 4:15 Rutte
1810/06/06	RMMUY	0075	*J. van Goijen* | Een Gezigt op eene Stad (als Rheenen) aan den Rhijn, met veel Stoffage, als Schepen, Schuiten en Figuren, aangenaam van kleur en meesterlijk behandeld | *Mat:* op paneel		(Unknown) fl 21
1810/06/06	RMMUY	0076	*J. van Goijen* | Een wel gekouleurd Landschap | *Mat:* op paneel		(Unknown) fl 14
1810/06/20	AMSCH	0028	*J. Van Goijen* | Een Hollandsch Zeedorp, gestoffeerd met Visschers en gaande Dorpelingen. Natuurlijk | *Mat:* op paneel *Size:* hoog 9, breed 11 duimen	B	(Sold) fl 1:10 Coclers
1810/06/20	AMSCH	0188	*J. van Goijen* | Een natuurlijk Land- en Watergezigt	A	(Sold) fl 1:10 Royers
1810/07/23	DOLG1	0026	*Jan van Goijen* | Een Boomrijk Landschap, gestoffeerd met Beeldtjes en Vaartuigen. Zeer naïf van Ordonnantie, en goed geschilderd | *Mat:* op paneel *Size:* hoog 13 ½, breed 20 duim	Mr Pieter van den Santheuvel	(Sold) fl 24 van Eijk 's Hage
1810/07/23	DOLG2	0044	*J. van Gooijen* | Een Landschap, vol stoffagie, luchtig en dun geschilderd | *Mat:* op paneel *Size:* hoog 15, breed 21 duim	Pieter Quinting	(Sold) fl 5:5 Schalk
1810/07/23	DOLG2	0050	*J. van Gooijen* | Een Land- en Watergezicht, vrolijk en wel | *Mat:* op paneel *Size:* hoog 26, breed 21 duim	Pieter Quinting	(Sold) fl 14 P de Heere Dordt
1810/07/23	DOLG2	0054	*J. van Gooijen* | Een zeer natuurlijk en wel geordoneerd Watergezicht | *Size:* hoog 14, breed 20 duim	Pieter Quinting	(Sold) fl 29 Blijk
1810/07/23	DOLG2	0065	*J. van Gooijen* | Een Watergezicht, met Schepen | *Mat:* op paneel *Size:* hoog 14, breed 16 duim	Pieter Quinting	(Sold) fl 8 Blijk
1810/07/23	DOLG2	00FF	*J. van Gooijen* | Een Land- en Watergezicht | *Mat:* op paneel *Size:* hoog 8, breed 8 duim	Pieter Quinting	(Unknown)
1810/08/06	AMSCH	0037	*Goijen (J. van)* | Een bevallig Land- en Watergezigt, met Boerenwoninge en Geboomten, gestoffeerd met Huislieden en Vissers in een Schuit; natuurlijk en zuiver van schildering | *Mat:* op paneel *Size:* hoog 14 ½, breed 19 ½ duimen	A	(Sold) fl 18:10 Texier Gerbet en Comp [for] Le Gran
1810/10/11	AMSCH	0129	*J. Van Goien* | Een Landschap, met Boerenwoningen en Geboomte | *Mat:* op doek	[Gruyter?]	(Sold or Bought In) fl 1:10 Gruiter
1810/10/11	AMSCH	0134	*J. Van Gojen* | Een Land- en Watergezigt, gestoffeerd met Visschers in Schuiten en andere stoffagie | *Mat:* op paneel	[Gruyter?]	(Sold or Bought In) fl 1:10 Gruiter
1810/10/11	AMSCH	0182	*J. Van Goijen* | Een Rivier, met verscheide Vaartuigen gestoffeerd, en in het verschiet een Dorpgezigt; natuurlijk behandeld	A	(Sold) fl 1:5 Ijver

1810/12/03	DOBRA	0025	*van Gojen* | Een Strandgezicht, ryk gestoffeerd, door van Gojen 1634 | *Inscr:* van Gojen 1634 (signed and dated?) *Notes:* It is unclear whether the name and date are inscribed on the painting.		(Unknown)
1810/12/03	DOBRA	0047	*J. van Gooijen* | Twee Watertjes		(Unknown)

Goyen, Jan Josephsz. van (or Goyen, copy after)

1803/03/07	AMBAE	0129	*J. van Goyen* | Gezigt van een oud Kasteel aan een Rivier, naar of door J. van Goyen		(Unknown)
1806/10/17	MGSAN	0038	*van Gooyen* | Een Stadgezigt aan de Vaart, door of naar van Gooyen | *Mat:* op paneel	Gerardus Beljard	(Sold) £ 0.2.1

Goyen, Jan Josephsz. van (or Goyen, manner)

1805/07/03	AMSCH	0207	*J. van Gooijen* | Een Boom- en Duinryk Landschap, by eenige oude Gebouwen, twee Beeldjes en aangenaam verschiet; door of in de manier van J. van Gooijen	V[inkeles]	(Sold) fl 9 Lafontaine
1805/07/10	AMSCH	0251	*J. van Goijen* | Een Land- en Watergezicht, op de Voorgrond Visschers bézig hun Net op te haalen, verder een Dorpgezicht en eenig Vee- en zylende Scheepen; door of in de manier van J. van Goijen	Wed Grave	(Sold) fl 1 Gruyter
1807/12/00	ARNIJ	0001	*van Goijen* | Twee Fraaije Dorp- en Stadgezichten, door of in de Manier van van Goijen	Meinsmaa [or] Engelan	(Unknown) fl 0:2

Goyen, Jan Josephsz. van (copy after)

1801/02/18	AMBOS	0056	*J. Schooneveld; J. van Goyen* | Een Stadt aan een groote Rivier, waarop zeilende Scheepen, naar J. van Goyen | copy by J.J. Schonevelt after Goyen	J Schonevelt	(Unknown)
1803/04/27	AMSCH	000W[H]	*Ven. J. Gooyen* | Een Land + Watergesigt na Ven. J. Gooyen | *Notes:* This lot was added in by hand in the LBDa and RKDH copies of the catalogue.	G	(Sold) fl 4:15 Stevens
1803/07/14	MGKLY	0005	*Na van Goyen* | Een fraay Winter Stukje	Mr Caspar Jacob van Citters	(Unknown)
1806/10/17	MGSAN	0032	*van Gooyen* | Een Stadgezigt aan de Vaart, de voorgrond gestoffeerd met Visschers, naar van Gooyen | *Mat:* op doek	Gerardus Beljard	(Sold) £ 0.3.1 Traayerhaven [?]
1806/10/17	MGSAN	0055	*van Gooyen* | Een Landschap, naar van Gooyen, en een ander | *Mat:* op paneel *Notes:* This lot was sold with lot 56 by an anonymous artist.	Gerardus Beljard	(Sold) £ 0.6.7 for lots 55 & 56
1806/11/24	AMSCH	0019	*Dongen (van); J. van Goyen* | Een stil Riviergezigt, aan de Haven van een Stad; op de voorgrond gestoffeert met rustend en staand Vee; verder eenige Scheepen; bevallig gepenceelt, naar J. van Goyen | copy by Dionys Dongen after Goyen *Mat:* op paneel *Size:* hoog 12, breed 16 duim	Munnikhuizen	(Sold) fl 12:5 Scheurleer
1810/03/23	HAVIN	0042	*J.N. Gooijen* | Een gezigt aan den Rhijn op de Stad Rhenen gestoff. met Scheepen, na J.N. Gooijen	Rudolf Hendrik de Wetstein [or others]	(Unknown)

Goyen, Jan Josephsz. van (manner)

1801/03/16	AMSCH	0167	*J. van Goyen* | Twee stuks, gestoffeerde Land- en Riviergezichten, in de manier van J. van Goyen	K[ip]	(Sold) fl 3:15 Valentijn
1801/03/16	AMSCH	0202	*van Goyen* | Een Dorpgezigt aan een Rivier, als van Goyen	K[ip]	(Sold) fl 5:15 Roelofs
1801/04/23	AMYVR	0055	*van Gooijen* | 2 Land- en Watergezichten in de manier van van Gooijen		(Sold) fl 3 Coclaire
1801/05/11	AMSCH	0127[a]	*van Gooyen* | Twee stuks Landschappen, een in de manier van van Gooyen, en een ander | *This Lot:* Een Landschap; lot 127[b] by Anonymous	E[lias]	(Sold) fl 2:15 for lots 127[a] & 127[b]. Coclers
1801/06/13	LNDLS	0080	*van Goyen* | Een Landschap, als van van Goyen | *Notes:* This lot was sold with lot 79 by an anonymous artist.	D van R	(Sold) fl 0:8 for lots 79 & 80. Richter
1802/05/05	AMSCH	0065	*J. van Gooijen* | Twee stuks, een Stil en een Woelend Water, in de manier van Dezelven [J. van Gooijen] | *Mat:* op paneel *Size:* hoog 10, breed 14 duim	G	(Sold) fl 4 A Schotte
1802/05/11	GRGRW	0019	*Van Gooijen* | Een Landschap, in den smaak van Van Gooijen [Schilderijen met Olie-Verf; In zwarte Lijsten] | *Mat:* in olyverf *Notes:* The bracketed information in the title appears above lot 1 and refers to lots 1 to 79a.	Arnold Sicco Werumeus	(Unknown)
1802/11/01	DOBRA	0009	*J. van Gooyen* | Een Dorpsgezicht langs een Binnenrivier, met hoog geboomte, gestoffeerd met vaartuigen, en vol gewoel van Boeren, enz. gemt. v.g.f. als door J. van Gooyen | *Mat:* op doek *Size:* hoog 41, breed 60 duim *Inscr:* v.g.f. (marked)	Paulus van der Spyk [or others]	(Sold) fl 59 Randwyk
1803/09/07	AMSCH	0227	*J. van Goijen* | Een woelend Water met verscheide Zylende Vaartuigen, op Paneel, in de manier van J. van Goijen [Une mer agitée ; différens navires et autres batimens à pleines voiles ; sur bois d'après J. van Goyen.] | *Mat:* op paneel *Size:* hoog 15, breed 19 duim [Haut 15, large 16 pouces] *Notes:* The dimensions differ in the Dutch and French editions of the catalogue.	Smidt	(Sold) fl 2 Van Iperen
1803/09/07	AMSCH	0256	*J. van Goijen* | Twee stuks Gezichten op Nymeegen, en een andere Stad, het Water gestoffeerd met een ménigte Beeldjes in diverse Vaartuigen, als J. van Goijen [Deux vues de Nimegue et d'une autre ville ; les plages d'eau qui avoisinent ces villes sont chargées de bateaux et de differens objets ; dans le goût de Goyen] | *Mat:* op doek *Size:* ieder hoog 17, breed 22 duim	Smidt	(Sold) fl 26:10 Frantszen

1805/10/09	HGBSM	0019	*J. van Goyen* | Een stads gezigt aan een rivier, daar een pont met volk overgaat, in de trant van J. van Goyen | *Mat:* op doek *Size:* hoog 25 breet 35 duim	T H van Willigen [or others]	(Sold) fl 7:10 Roedig
1805/10/09	HGBSM	B0002	*J. van Gooyen* | Een gezigt van een Zeedorp langs strand vol stoffagie, niet minder als J. van Gooyen | *Mat:* op doek *Size:* hoog 36 breet 53 duim	T H van Willigen [or others]	(Sold) fl 7 Blommers
1805/12/16	AMSCH	0083	*J. van Goyen* | Een Land- en Watergezicht, bevallig gestoffeerd, als door J. van Goyen | *Notes:* This lot was sold with lot 70, which is in the manner of Brueghel.	R[oos]	(Sold) fl 1 for lots 70 & 83. L Pakker
1807/08/26	AMSCH	0085	*J. van Goyen* | Een met Schepen gestoffeerd Watergezigt, als denzelven [J. van Goyen]	Roos	(Sold) fl 1:5 Graffelman
1807/08/26	AMSCH	0087	*J. van Goyen* | Een bevallig Land- en Watergezigt, ter zyde vertoonen zig eenige Wooningen by Geboomten, en in de Rivier een zeilend Vaartuig; fiks geschilderd, in de manier van denzelven [J. van Goyen] | *Mat:* op paneel *Size:* hoog 16, breed 23 duim	Yver [for] S	(Sold) fl 4:15 du Pree
1807/08/26	AMSCH	0268	*J. van Goijen* | Een Land- en Watergezicht, met Woningen, Geboomte en Huislieden; als door J. van Goijen, ovaal formaat | *Fmt:* ovaal	Roos [for] A	(Sold) fl 1 A Rynders
1807/12/00	ARNIJ	0002	*van Goijen* | Een Landschap, in de Manier van denzelven [van Goijen]	Meinsmaa [or] Engelan	(Unknown) fl 0:2
1808/08/23	AMSCH	0287	*J. v. Goijen* | Een stil Rivier-gezicht, met zeilende Scheepen, en Vissers in Schuiten, als door J. v. Goijen | *Mat:* op paneel	Z	(Sold) fl 1:15 Gruyter
1809/04/17	AMSCH	0178	*van Goijen* | Een natuurlijk Land en Watergezigt, als van Goijen	H	(Sold) fl 1:5
1809/10/16	ARNIJ	0008	*Van Gooijen* | Een groot Landschap in de manier van van Gooijen	Wed N Nijhoff	(Sold) fl 6 v Leeuwen
1810/06/20	AMSCH	0114	*van Goijen* | Een kabbelende Zee, met Vaartuigen; als van Goijen	N	(Sold) fl 0:10 L Pakker
			Graat, Barent		
1801/11/10	AMPOS	0007	*B. Graat, 1674* | Venus met speelende Cupidoos en bywerk, door B. Graat, 1674 | *Inscr:* B. Graat, 1674 (signed and dated?) *Notes:* It is unclear whether the name and date are inscribed on the painting.		(Unknown)
1802/05/05	AMSCH	0062	*B. Graat* | Een Historiëele Ordonantie, waar in Venus en Cupido wyzende op Jupiter, gezeeten op zyn Zeegenwagen, delicaat gepenceeld | *Mat:* op doek *Size:* hoog 48, breed 66 duim	B	(Sold) fl 8:10 Stevens de wd Ploos
1802/08/24	LNDLS	0055	*B. Graat* | In een Landschap zit Maria met het Kind op haar schoot, benevens Elisabeth, Johannes en het Lam, bij de staanden Joseph | *Mat:* op doek *Size:* hoog 40, breed 35 duimen	Leonardus Bouman [or others]	(Unknown) fl 8
1802/09/06	AMSCH	0188	*B. Graat* | Een Historieele Ordenantie	Spaan	(Sold) fl 0:8 L Pakker
1803/08/17	AMSCH	0027	*Graat. (B.)* | Pandora tusschen de Deugd en Ondeugd, door twee Genietjes verbeeld, de Drapperie is meesterlyk en het naakt, geheel in de couleur van Titiaan uitgedtukt [sic] | *Mat:* op paneel *Size:* hoog 44, breed 32 duim	Anna Catharina Putman	(Sold) fl 31 Coclers
1804/02/27	AMSCH	0044	*Graad. (B.)* | Twee Landschappen, met Hisstorien [sic] gestoffeerd | *Mat:* op doek *Size:* hoog 14, breed 13 duim *Notes:* This lot was sold with lot 43 by Hend. Goltzius.	C	(Sold) fl 1:15 for lots 43 & 44. du Pree
1804/10/16	DLOND	0087	*Barend Graat. 1682* | Mars en Venus | *Mat:* op doek *Size:* hoog 56, breed 48 *Inscr:* Barend Graat. 1682 (signed and dated?) *Notes:* It is unclear whether the name and date are inscribed on the painting.		(Unknown) fl 3
1806/05/05	AMSCH	0053	*B. Graat* | Deeze Ordinnantie van vier Beelden levensgrooten vertoont: Bachus zittende in een Landschap, met zyn gezellen; Een bevallige Nimph schynt hem met een Wyngaard Rank te vercieren. op de grond ligt een bennetje met trosse druiven, en een omgevallen Wynkan; alles is kragtig en bevallig van Coloriet, en van een uitvoerig penceel behandeling door B. Graat | *Mat:* op doek *Size:* hoog 9 voet 5 duim, breed 5 voet 5 duim	R[oos]	(Sold) fl 1:15 Wm van der Schley
1809/04/17	AMSCH	0032	*B. Graat* | In een Landschap zit eene bevallige Dame, verseld van drie Kinderen; meesterlijk | *Mat:* op doek *Size:* hoog 20, breed 18 duim	T	(Sold) fl 20
1809/07/25	HGBSM	0266	*B. Grent* | Een Mans Portrait, ten voeten uit in 't zwart gekleed, leunende met de Hand op een Steene Plint, in 't verschiet een Tuin | *Mat:* op doek *Size:* hoog 43, breed 36 duim	D van der Aa [or] E B ten Dall	(Sold) fl 2:10 van Zanten
1810/03/23	HAVIN	0006	*B. Graat* | Hercules bij Dianire, toond grimmig aan Achelous zijn vuist, schoon geschilderd door B. Graat | *Size:* hoog 30 breet 34 d.	Rudolf Hendrik de Wetstein [or others]	(Unknown) fl 10:10
1810/03/23	HAVIN	0007	*B. Graat* | Manoach verzoekt den Engel te vertoeven om de Offerhande te zien, fraai door denzelven [B. Graat] | *Size:* hoog 27 ½ breet 21 d.	Rudolf Hendrik de Wetstein [or others]	(Unknown) fl 7
1810/10/10	MGCIT	0029	*B. Graat* | Een Man en Vrouw bij een brandende Lantaarn, Koeken zittende te bakken, zijnde alle de Voorwerpen op hetzelve door den Schilder verstandig gekozen en van een zeer goed en natuurlijk effect over het geheel	Caspar van Citters	(Unknown)
			Graat, Barent (manner)		
1804/10/16	DLOND	0286	*In de manier van Barend Graat* | Diana zich badende met hare Nymphen. Diane se baignant avec ses Nymphes | *Mat:* op doek *Size:* hoog 29, breed 36		(Unknown)

Graef, Timotheus de

1804/10/29	HRBAU	0025	*Graaf, (T. de)* | Een Italiaansch bergagtig Landschap met een Rivier doorsneeden, waar over eene Steenen Brug ligt, waar agter Gebergte. Warm en uitvoerig geschilderd | *Mat:* op doek *Size:* hoog 37, breed 47 duim	Simon Styl	(Unknown)
1805/10/21	GRBOL	0024	*De Graaf* | Een Schoon Landschap, waar in een Gezelschap ter Jagt gaande	Gerardus Nicolaus Heerkens	(Unknown)
1807/08/26	AMSCH	0083	*T. de Graaf* | Een gezigt binnen Amsterdam, op de Nieuw Markt, ziende naar een gedeelte der St. Anthonies Waag en Boomsloot, naar de Geldersche Kaay, gestoffeert met verscheide Lieden, Sleepers met Paarden en diversche Woningen; zonachtig behandeld | *Mat:* op doek *Size:* hoog 20, breed 25 duim	Yver [for] S	(Sold) fl 4:15 van Iperen
1808/06/13	AMSCH	0201	*F. de Graaf* | Een als voren [Italiaansch Landschap], met eene Rivier | *Notes:* The artist's name was given as "F. de Graaf" but we have assumed this is an error.	E M Engelberts	(Sold) fl 4:5 Th Spaan

Grandjean, Jean

1802/05/05	AMSCH	0067	*J. Grandjean* | Een Egiptisch Landschap, met Geboomte, Gedenktekens en fraaije stoffagie, schynende een Bachus Feest, ryk van Ordonnantie, bevallig van Coloriet en aangenaam gepenceeld | *Mat:* op paneel *Size:* hoog 16, breed 19 duim	A	(Sold) fl 17:10 Gruiter
1804/02/27	AMSCH	0037	*Grandjean. (J.)* | Deeze ryke Ordonantie vertoond den gestorven Heiland, door Godvuchtige [sic] Mannen van het Kruis afgenoomen, die hetzelve eerbiedig in Lynwaad omvangen, schynen te willen nederleggen, verders verscheide Godvruchtige Mannen en Vrouwen, die door hun gelaat en houding hunne Zielsdroefheid te kennen geeven; de Hartstochten zyn natuurlyk verbeeld, meesterlyk geteekend, kragtig van coloriet, en van een uitvoerige penceelsbehandeling | *Mat:* op doek *Size:* hoog 56, breed 42 duim	B	(Sold) fl 50 Gruyter
1805/12/16	AMSCH	0026	*J. Grandjean* | Een Christushoofd, aller uitmuntend gepenceeld | *Mat:* op doek *Size:* hoog 30, breed 24 duim	R[oos]	(Bought In) fl 25
1808/06/13	AMSCH	0057	*Grandjean (J.)* | Dit kunstrijk Tafereel vertoond een aanlokkelijk denkbeeld der Gulde Eeuw: in de aangename en vruchtbare Velden van Enna, met verschillend Geboomte, Kruidjes en Bloemplanten bewasschen, ziet men de Godin Céres en de jeugdige Bacchus, omringt van eene menigte Mannen, Vrouwen, Kinderen en Saters; alles schijnt in volle vreugde: verscheidene Nimfen vermaken zich met danssen, spelen en liefkoozen, andere dragen korfjes met bloemen en vruchten; verder bij geboomte een aloude Tempel, alwaar plegtig geöffert wordt; in het verschiet Akkerlieden, het land beploegende. Alles is schoon geördoneert, bevallig van licht en kleur, en van eene uitvoerige penceelbehandeling | *Mat:* op doek *Size:* hoog 27, breed 35 duim	[Jan Tersteeg]	(Bought In) fl 100
1808/06/13	AMSCH	0058	*Grandjean (J.)* | Dit Historieel Voorwerp vertoond, in een prachtig Paleis, de eenige Zoon van de Syrische Koning Seleukus, op een vorstelijk rustbedde liggende, als in eene doodelijke krankte, veroorzaakt door een heimelijke liefde tot zijne Schoonmoeder Stratonice, die, ter zijde staande, hem met medelijden beschouwd; de Vorst zit als in zwaarmoedige gedachten, die de oorzaak der ziekte door zijn' Geneesmeester vernomen hebbende, niet alleen zijne Gemalinne aan zijn' Zoon tot Vrouw geeft, maar tevens zijn geheele Koningrijk. Dit stuk is grootsch geördoneerd, de hartstochten zijn natuurlijk, het licht en kleur bevallig, en uitvoerig gepenceeld | *Mat:* op doek *Size:* hoog 23, breed 32 duim	[Jan Tersteeg]	(Bought In) fl 130
1808/06/13	AMSCH	0059	*Grandjean (J.)* | Twee stuks kapitale Landschappen, met hoog Gebergte en Watervallen, zijnde Gezichten te Tivoli; op het Gebergte ziet men eenige aloude Gebouwen; op den voorgrond gestoffeerd met Reizigers: alles vertoond de Natuur: beide aangenaam van licht, en uitvoerig gepenceeld | *Mat:* op doek *Size:* ieder hoog 23, breed 28 duim	[Jan Tersteeg]	(Bought In) fl 155
1808/06/13	AMSCH	0060	*Grandjean (J.)* | In een Arkadisch boomrijk Landschap, ziet men, op den voorgrond, een Graftombe, waarbij drie Lieden, eerbiedig nedergeknield, ter gedachtenisse schijnen te offeren, waarbij twee muziek spelende; verder ziet men verscheidene Nimfen, die manden met bloemen en vruchten dragen; gestoffeerd met prachtige Tempels, Standbeelden en andere Gedenkteekens: mede als de voorgaande | *Mat:* op doek *Size:* hoog 36, breed 50 duim	[Jan Tersteeg]	(Sold) fl 30 Hoogers
1808/06/13	AMSCH	0061a[H]	*Grandjean (J.)* | Een heilige famille | *Notes:* This lot was added in by hand in the AA I copy of the catalogue.		(Sold) fl 6 de Gruiter
1808/06/13	AMSCH	0062	*Grandjean (J.)* | Zestien stuks, zijnde de Historie van Germanicus; alle zacht in het graauw geschilderd, en genoeg bekend door de Prenten, welken door Garreau en andere na dezelven gegraveerd zijn | *Size:* ieder hoog 7, breed 5 ½ duim (4 stuks in een Lijst.)	[Jan Tersteeg]	(Bought In) fl 80

Grandjean, Jean (copy by)

1808/06/13	AMSCH	0061	*Grandjean (J.); Andrea del Sarto* | Een Heilige Famielle: zijnde een zeer fraaije Kopij, naar een zeer beroemd Schilderij van Andrea del Sarto, te Rome | copy by J. Grandjean after Andrea del Sarto *Size:* hoog 37, breed 36 duim	[Jan Tersteeg]	(Sold) fl 20 du Pré

Grasdorp, Jan Gerrit

1801/12/22	AMOTT	0033	*J. Graesdiep* | 1 Duin en Heuvelachtig dito [gezigt], met een Waterval | *Notes:* It is unclear what "dito" refers to in the title.	Bartholomeus Ruloffs	(Unknown) fl 9

Grasdorp, Willem

1802/07/27	AKHRK	0047	*W. Grandor* | Op een Tafel ligt een Kanteloep, een Bord met een Kreeft met twee Perziken; en aan een Lint hangt een schoone Tros Druiven, en verder Bijwerk, kunstig uitgevoerd | companion to lot 48 *Mat:* op doek *Size:* hoog 29, breed 20 ½ duim	Maria Stategaart	(Sold) fl 5:10 for lots 47 & 48. Gruyter
1802/07/27	AKHRK	0048	*W. Grandor* | Dito de wederga. Op de grond liggen Druiven, Perziken, een Queepeer en Hazelnooten, verders een Puttertje, op de agtergrond een sierlijke Pot en een Landschap, alles goed gepenseeld | companion to lot 47 *Notes:* It is unclear what "dito" refers to in the title.	Maria Stategaart	(Sold) fl 5:10 for lots 47 & 48. Gruyter
1802/12/13	AMSCH	0071	*W. Grasdorp* | Twee capitaale Stukken, met diverse soorten van keurige Vrugten, als: blaauwe en witte Druiven, Persiken, Canteloupen, Quépeeren, en verder Bywerk, kunstig en meesterachtig gepenceeld | *Mat:* op doek *Size:* hoog 24, breed 21 duim	Pruyssenaar [for] A	(Sold) fl 3 Gruiter
1804/08/08	AMSCH	0076	*W. Grasdorp* | Twee capitaale Ordinantiën, van een ménigte van smakelyke Vruchten, als Druiven, Persiken, Canteloupen, Quépeeren, Nooten en andere Vruchten; meesterlyk geschilderd | *Mat:* op doek *Size:* hoog 29, breed 20 ½ duim	Vink[eles] [for] K[=Gruyter?]	(Sold) fl 1:15 Oortwijn

Grebber

1802/04/13	HAVIN	0039	*de Grebber* | Vertuminus [sic] en Pomona		(Unknown)

Grebber, Anthony Claesz.

1804/07/25	AMSCH	0032	*Grebber. (A. de)* | Deeze ryke Ordinantie, vol gewoel van een meenigte Beelden, steld voor de Geboorte Christi, Maria zit in een eerbiedige houding, met het jong gebooren Kindeken op de schoot; verscheide Veehoeders, Mans en Vrouwen, komen alle met yver hun geschenken aanbieden; omhoog vertoont zig een Glorie van verscheide Engelen; verder gestoffeert met een meenigte bywerk; de caracters zyn natuurlyk, het licht bevallig, en van een uitvoerige penceelbehandeling | *Mat:* op doek *Size:* hoog 67, breed 68 duim		(Sold) fl 12 Van der Schleij
1810/10/11	AMSCH	0033	*A. De Grebber* | Eene rijke Ordonantie, vol gewoel van eene menigte Beelden, voorstellende de Geboorte van Christus, – Maria zit in eene eerbiedige houding, hebbende het Kind op de schoot, voor hun de Herders, welken hunne Geschenken aanbieden, en in de lucht een Glorie van Engelen; bevallig van licht en uitvoerig van penseelbehandeling | *Mat:* op doek *Size:* hoog 67, breed 68 duimen	K	(Sold) fl 5:15 du Pree

Grebber, Frans Pietersz. de

1804/08/08	AMSCH	0070	*F. De Grebber* | Het capitaale Pourtrait van Oldenbarneveld, ten voeten uit, rustende met zyne rechterhand op de Leuning van zyn Stoel, en met de linker op een Doodshoofd, dat voor hem op een Tafel, met een Tapyt Kleed gedekt legt; meesterlyk geschilderd | *Size:* hoog 61, breed 47 duim	Vink[eles] [for] K[=Gruyter?]	(Sold) fl 0:10 L Pakker

Grebber, Pieter Fransz. de

1801/04/08	HAVIN	0010	*P. de Grebber* | Een Historiestuk konstig		(Unknown)
1803/04/20	AMSCH	0028	*Grebber, 1629. (P. de)* | Deeze capitaale Ordenantie vertoont Maria, zittende op de Wolken, houdende het Kind Jesu op de Schoot, welke een Ring aan de Vinger van St. Catharina, die kuielende [sic] voor dezelve geplaatst is, steekt, agter dezelve staat een Engel, ter zyde zitten de Apostelen Petrus en Paulus, hoger eenige vliegende Engelen; alles is bevallig van Coloriet en van een alleruitvoerigste penceelsbehandeling [Ce tableau dont l'ordonnance est bien disposée represente les epousailles de Ste. Catharine ; ce sujet mistique est traité dans les neués : la vierge tenant l'enfant Jesus aux pieds du quel St. Catharine recoit l'anneau, le groupe est terminé par un Seraphin qui est en arriere. Aux côtés sont St. Pierre & St. Paul, & vers le haut quelques Anges. La couleur en est pleine de charme & l'execution des plus Soignées.] | *Mat:* op paneel *Size:* hoog 56, breed 77 duim *Inscr:* P. de Grebber, 1629 (signed and dated?) *Notes:* It is unclear whether the name and date are inscribed on the painting.	Maria Magdalena van Sluypwyk, gravinne van Moens	(Sold) fl 7:15 v^n Iperen
1804/05/07	AMSCH	0072	*Grebber. (P. de)* | Een Historieele Ordonantie, voorstellende de Bootschap aan Maria, door den Engel; bevallig geschildert | *Mat:* op doek *Size:* hoog 60, breed 54 duim	Vinkeles [for] G	(Sold) fl 1:10 Van Iperen

Greenwood (copy by)

1801/03/16	AMSCH	0073	*Greenwood; Rembrand* | 'T Poutrait [sic] van een Jongeling na Rembrand | copy by Greenwood after Rembrandt	P[ruyssenaar]	(Withdrawn)

Gregoor, Pieter Martinus

1810/05/22	AMSCH	0031	*Gregoor. (P. M.)* | Een kapitaal Landgezicht, met Boeren Woningen en Geboomten, rijk gestoffeerd met staand en rustende Vee; natuurlijk van licht en koloriet, en van eene uitvoerige penceelbehandeling | *Mat:* op paneel *Size:* hoog 20, breed 26 duim	D	(Sold) fl 44 van Iperen

1810/05/22	AMSCH	0032	*Gregoor. (P. M.)* | Twee stuks bevallige Landschappen, met Geboomten, rijk gestoffeerd met staande en rustende Schapen en Bokken; in alles als de voorgaande, uitvoerig en meesterlijk behandeld | *Mat:* op paneel *Size:* Jeder hoog 32, breed 24 duim	D	(Sold) fl 58 van Iperen

Greuze, Jean Baptiste (manner)

1809/04/22	AMYVR	0165	*Greuze* | Een Meisje met een Bosch Stroo; als Greuze	de Bruin	(Sold) fl 1:10 van der Schley

Griffier

1801/06/13	LNDLS	0016	*Griffier* | Een Landschap met Anticque Ruïnes en Beeldwerk, gestoffeerd met beelden, alleruitvoerigst, op paneel geschilderd | *Mat:* op paneel *Size:* hoog 14, breed 19 duimen	D van R	(Sold) fl 43 Texier
1803/12/15	MGLAC	0053	*Griffier* | Een fraai Ysgezigt, met veel Figuuren; zeer natuurlyk geschilderd | *Mat:* op doek *Size:* hoog duim 21, breed duim 28	Mr L H de Haze Bomme	(Unknown)
1804/05/07	AMSCH	0064	*Griffier* | Een Rhyngezicht, voorstellende een Winter, alwaar verscheide Lieden zich op 't Ys met Schaatseryden, Wandelen enz. vermaken, ter zyde eenige Woningen, een Kraam waarin een Vrouw welke Koekenbakt, welke verscheide Menschen en Kinderen aandachtig beschouwen, verders een aangenaam verschiet; dit Schildery is aller natuurlykst, bevallig van licht en van de beste penceelbehandeling van deze Meester | *Mat:* op doek *Size:* hoog 19, breed 25 duim	Vinkeles [for] H[affner]	(Sold) fl 63 Thais
1804/12/10	AMSCH	0021	*Griffier* | Een bevroosen Rivier, ryk gestoffeerd met wandelaars en schaatseryders, ter zyde aan de voet van een berg een Stad; uitvoerig behandeld | *Mat:* op koper *Size:* Hoog 16, breed 21 duim	Jan De Groot	(Sold) fl 68 Josi

Griffier, Jan (I)

1801/06/13	LNDLS	0014	*J. Griffier* | Een Gezicht langs een Vaarwater, met veel vaartuigen, tusschen gebergtens, zeer uitvoerig, op paneel | *Mat:* op paneel *Size:* hoog 14, breed 19 duimen	D van R	(Sold) fl 60 A Delfos [for] W
1802/08/24	LNDLS	0008	*Jan Griffier* | Dit Kabinetstuk verbeeld een Winter, in 't midden vertoont het een bevroren Rivier, met eene ontelbaare menigte Schaatsen-rijders, Narren en Boeren-Sleeden met Paarden, voords Tenten, met rustende en drinkende personen, ter regter zijde een Herberg en veele Gebouwen, ter linker zijde een Kasteel bij een weg, met veel gewoel van Volk, in 't verschiet een Dorp en een Stad, bij een uitgestrekt Landschap. Alles zoo uitvoerig en delicaat op een koperen plaat geschilderd, dat het de beste Miniatuur-stukken evenaart | *Mat:* op koperen plaat *Size:* hoog 19 ½, breed 22 ½ duimen	Leonardus Bouman [or others]	(Unknown) fl 150
1804/07/25	AMSCH	0033	*Griffier (J.)* | Een Rhyn gezicht, voorstellende een Winter, ryk gestoffeerd met een ménigte van rydende en wandelende Persoonen, Arresleeden, Zeilschuiten, enz. Op de Voorgrond ter eene zyde by eenig Geboomte een Tent, waarin eenige Lieden zich warmen, en ter andere zyde by eenige Gebouwen, twee wandelende Lieden; dit Schilderytje is alleruitvoerigst en van de beste schildering van deeze meester | *Mat:* op paneel *Size:* hoog 11, breed 14 ½ duim		(Sold) fl 39 Gruyter
1808/08/23	AMSCH	0065	*Griffier. (J) de oude* | Een Italiaansch Landschap met Geboomten, gestoffeert op de voorgrond met een gaand Huisman bij een beladen Ezel, verzeld van een Os en verscheide Schaapen; kragtig en meesterlijk behandeld | *Mat:* op doek *Size:* hoog 32, breed 38 duim	C	(Sold) fl 6:10 D Maykel

Griffier, Jan (I) (and Poelenburgh, C.)

1810/10/10	MGCIT	0010	*J. Griffier; C. Poelenburg* | Een schoon Stuk met Ruïnen, door J. Griffier, en gestoffeerd met Figuuren en Gewassen, door C. Poelenburg; zijnde deze Schilderij door beide Meesters keurig en in een geëmailleerde trant behandeld	Caspar van Citters	(Unknown)

Griffier, Jan (I) (manner)

1806/08/13	AMSCH	0256	*Griffier* | Een aangenaam Rhyngezicht, waarin eenige Vaartuigen en verscheide Beeldjes op de voorgrond, verder een Kasteel op een Heuvel en een Stadgezicht; uitvoerig en zonachtig behandeld op Koper, in de manier van Griffier | *Mat:* op koper	Roos	(Sold) fl 5:5 Th Spaan

Griffier, Robert

1801/06/10	AMSCH	0064	*Griffier. (R.)* | Een capitaal Ryngezicht, ryk gestoffeerd met Beeldjes en een menigte Vaartuigen, het Gebergte verliest zich in 't dunne verschiet, zynde fraai van coloriet, uitvoerig van penceel | *Mat:* op paneel *Size:* hoog 19, breed 24 duim	Herman ten Kate	(Sold) fl 75 C S Roos
1801/06/10	AMSCH	0065	*Griffier. (R.)* | Deeze Ordonantie is in allen deelen eene geschikte weergade van de voorgaande en van gelyke schildering | *Size:* hoog 19, breed 24 duim	Herman ten Kate	(Sold) fl 75 C S Roos
1801/10/19	AMSCH	0024	*Griffier. (Robbert)* | Een Gezicht aan den Rhyn, op de voorgrond, ter regterzyde ziet men een Boere Herberg, waar by verscheiden Personen zo te voet als te paard halte houden, en zich ververschen; de Rivier is ryk gestoffeerd met diversche Vaartuigen, aan den Oever en boven op de Bergen ontdekt men veele gebouwen, en verder een aangenaam verschiet; dit stuk is van een ryke Ordonantie, bevallig van couleur, en verdienstig geschildert | *Mat:* op paneel *Size:* hoog 17, breed 21 duim	Jonkheer Menno Baron van Coehoorn	(Sold) fl 100 Vallette

1802/06/28	AMSCH	0057	*R. Griffier* | Een Wintergezicht, gestoffeerd met een menigte Schaatsenryders en Marketenters; uitvoerig op Doek | *Mat:* op doek *Size:* hoog 20, breed 27 duim	Anna Elink	(Sold) fl 24:10 Texier
1802/06/28	AMSCH	0058	*R. Griffier* | Een bevroozen Rivier, ryk gestoffeerd met Schaatsenryders en wandelende Beelden; bevallig gepenceelt door Denzelven [R. Griffier], hoog 23, breed 27 duim. Doek | *Mat:* op doek *Size:* hoog 23, breed 27 duim	Anna Elink	(Sold) fl 5:15 Texier
1802/07/20	MGSAN	0047	*R. Griffier* | Een uitvoerig Stukje, zynde een Rhyngezigt, op Doek | *Mat:* op doek *Size:* hoog duim 19, breed duim 15 ½		(Unknown)
1803/06/20	AMSCH	0025	*R. Griffier* | Een Rhyngezicht met hoog gebergten, besneeuwde Gebouwen en Geboomtens, het Ys gestoffeerd met verscheide wandelende Beeldjes en Schaatzeryders; alles zeer uitvoerig en natuurlyk verbeeld door R. Griffier, op doek | *Mat:* op doek *Size:* hoog 18, breed 25 duim	Schley [for] G	(Sold) fl 60 Hafner
1803/07/18	AMSCH	0018	*Griffier. (R.)* | Een Rhyngezicht, zynde een besneeuwde Winter. Het Land en het Ys gestoffeerd met een menigte Beeldjes, zich vermakende met Arren en Schaatsenryden, op de voorgrond een Marketenter; alles, zo wel het veruitgestrekt Gebergte als de verdere stoffagie, is zeer uitvoerig en natuurlyk behandeld [Ce Tableau dun [sic] fini & d'une richesse peu communs offre une partie du Rhin au milieu des rigeurs [sic] de l'Hiver ; la riviere est Chargée ainsi que les parties de terre d'une multitude de figures atachées aux amusemens differens de la saison. Au devant est une tente de vivendieres & vèrs la gauche une auberge egalement bien visitée. Cette representation n'a rien du triste qui souvent est le defaut de ces sujets. La grande varietée des figures animées & spirituelles, des montagnes & des collines à perte de vue, & un [sic] charmante couleur le rendent très intéressent [sic].] | *Mat:* op koper *Size:* hoog 16, breed 21 duim	Maria Theresia Andrioli	(Sold) fl 90 Josi
1804/02/27	AMSCH	0041	*Griffier. (R.)* | Een aangenaam Ryngezicht, ryk gestoffeerd met een menigte van Vaartuigen en Beeltjes; zonachtig en uitvoerig geschilderd | *Mat:* op doek *Size:* hoog 19, breed 22 duim	B	(Bought In) fl 12 ½
1806/05/05	AMSCH	0055	*R. Griffier* | Een Rhyngezigt, gestoffeerd met Vaartuigen en Beeldjes; uitvoerig geschilderd door R. Griffier | *Mat:* op doek *Size:* hoog 19, breed 21 duim	V[inkeles]	(Sold) fl 14:10 van Laar
1807/08/26	AMSCH	0076	*R. Griffier* | Een Rhyngezicht, gestoffeerd met een menigte Vaartuigen en Beeldjes, op de weg by een Herberg verscheide Heeren te Paard en andere stoffage; natuurlyk | *Mat:* op paneel *Size:* hoog 17, breed 21 duim	Joseph Vallette	(Sold) fl 101 Jozi
1808/10/28	AMVRS	0015	*Griffier. (R.)* | Twee uitneemende Rijngezichten, rijk gestoffeerd met Menschen en Vaartuigen; het Gebergte verliest zich in het verschiet. Alles is dun en fraai van kleur en van eene zeer uitvoerige penceelsbehandeling | *Mat:* op paneel *Size:* hoog 19, breed 24 duim	Marten Udink	(Sold) fl 205 Van Iperen
1809/07/19	AMSCH	0016	*Griffier (R)* | Een kapitaal Rhijngezigt, rijk gestoffeerd met Huislieden, overvarende Pontschuiten, Aken, en gaande en rustende Lieden, het hoog Gebergte is in 't verschiet. Fraai, zonachtig, en alleruitvoerigst gepenceeld | companion to lot 17 *Mat:* op paneel *Size:* hoog 20, breed 25 duim	[Bicker]	(Sold) fl 117 for lots 16 & 17. van Iperen
1809/07/19	AMSCH	0017	*Griffier (R)* | Een dito [kapitaal] Rhijngezigt met stoffage van Beeldjes, zijnde een wederga van de voorgaande en van gelijke Schildering | companion to lot 16 *Size:* hoog 20, breed 25 duim	[Bicker]	(Sold) fl 117 for lots 16 & 17. van Iperen
1809/09/06	AMSCH	0019	*Griffier (R.)* | Een Heeremiet, zittende voor zijn Kluis in een Boek te leezen, voor hem staat een Kruisbeeld, en achter hem een stam van een dooden Boom; alleruitvoerigst in de manier van G. Dou behandeld | *Size:* hoog 14 ½, breed 12 duim	Johannes Caudri	(Sold) fl 59 van Iperen
1810/06/20	AMSCH	0026	*R. Griffier* | Een hoog bergachtig Landschap, met een Rivier doorsneden, gestoffeerd met verscheidene Arbeiders bij Vaartuigen, ter zijde rustende Krijgslieden, en op het Gebergte een biddende Heremiet. Uitvoerig behandeld | *Mat:* op paneel *Size:* hoog 19, breed 16 duimen	D	(Sold) fl 25 T Spaan
1810/06/20	AMSCH	0027	*R. Griffier* | Een Rhijngezigt, ter zijde ziet men voor Boeren Woningen dansende Huislieden, in het verschiet hoog Gebergte. Als de voorgaande behandeld | *Mat:* op paneel *Size:* hoog 10, breed 12 duimen	D	(Sold) fl 13:10 Roos
1810/08/06	AMSCH	0038	*Griffier (R.)* | Een Rhijngezigt, ter zijde een Dorp, alwaar het kermis is, rijk gestoffeerd met Kramen, een menigte Beeldjes, Vaartuigen en hoog Gebergte in 't verschiet; konstig en zeer uitvoerig geschilderd | *Mat:* op koper *Size:* hoog 15, breed 19 ½ duimen	A	(Sold) fl 41 de Vries
1810/10/11	AMSCH	0034	*R. Griffier* | Twee stuks kapitale Rhijngezigten, rijk gestoffeerd met Schepen, Schuiten, Aken en andere Vaartuigen, op den voorgrond, voor eene Herberg, eene menigte drinkende, spelende en dansende Huislieden, en in 't verschiet hoog Gebergte; zeer dun en uitvoerig geschilderd | *Mat:* op koper *Size:* hoog 13, breed 17 duimen	[Gruyter?]	(Bought In) fl 41
1810/10/11	AMSCH	0035	*R. Griffier* | Twee stuks Rhijngezigten, met Stoffage van Beeldjes | *Mat:* op paneel *Size:* hoog 6 ½, breed 8 duimen	C	(Sold) fl 3:15 Posthumus
			Groenewegen, Gerrit		
1808/06/06	RMRIJ	0045	*Groeneweegen. (Gerrit)* | Een gezigt van de Leuvehaven van de Vischmarkt af te zien. Uitvoerig behandeld en eene wedergade van N° 88.	Gerrit van der Pot, Heer van Groeneveld	(Sold) fl 130 Cremer

			door N. Muijs [Vue d'un Canal appellé le Leuvehaven dans la Ville de Rotterdam. Pendant du Numero 88 par Nicolas Muys] | companion to lot 88, by Nic. Muys *Annots:* Verk. op de Leuvehaven Sept. 1802 (f.25-) (RMA I) *Mat:* op paneel *Size:* Hoog 14 ½, en breed 18 ½ duim		

Groenhagen, F. [Unidentified]

1802/06/29	HGDAW	0011	*F. Groenhagen* | De Maaltyd van Joseph met zyn Broeders door F. Groenhagen, 1740 | *Inscr:* F. Groenhagen, 1740 (signed and dated?) *Notes:* It is unclear whether the name and date are inscribed on the painting.		(Unknown)

Groot, Johannes de

1807/06/10	HGBSM	0114	*J. de Groot* | De gekruiste Heijland, 1759 | *Mat:* op doek *Size:* hoog 29 ½, breed 23 duim *Inscr:* 1759 (dated?) *Notes:* It is unclear whether the date is inscribed on the painting.	Abraham Delfos [or others]	(Sold) fl 5:15 v Giese

Gryef, Adriaen de

1802/06/16	AMSCH	0056	*N. Gryff* | Twee stuks, verbeeldende de eene in een Landschap een zittende Boer zyn Pyp rookende voor een buitenwoning; voor zich staat een omgekeerde Ton, waar op een Bierkan, daar neevens een Kruiwagen met verschillende Groentens, waar by Potten, Pannen, een doode Vogei [sic] en een rustende Kat: den ander verbeeld een Binnehuis, waar in een zittende Boer met een glas Bier in de hand: nevens hem staat een Ton, waar op een doode Vogel en een aarde Kan geplaatst is; in 't verschiet drie Boeren by een Tafel; verders op de voorgrond gestoffeert met kopere Ketel, Groentens en een rustende Hond, beide deeze stukken zyn verwonderlyk natuurlyk en bevallig gepenceeld | *Mat:* op doek *Size:* ieder hoog 12, breed 15 duim *Notes:* The artist's name was given as "N. Gryff" but we have assumed this is an error.	[Merrem]	(Sold) fl 42 Agina
1803/09/07	AMSCH	0066	*Gryff* | Twee stuks met dood Wild en Gevogelte, waarby eenige Jagthonden en rustende Jagers, uitvoerig op Paneel geschilderd [Deux morceaux de chasse, représentant du gibier et différentes espèces de volailles tuées ; quelques chasseurs avec leurs chiens : d'un beau fini] | *Mat:* op paneel *Size:* ieder hoog 11, breed 14 duim	Smidt	(Sold) fl 6:5 J Yver
1803/09/07	AMSCH	0067	*Gryff* | Twee Landschappen, ryk gestoffeerd met dood Wild, dood Gevogelte, Jagtgereedschap en Honden [Deux paysages, dans lesquels des chasseurs, du gibier tué, et tous les accessoires d'une partie de chasse forment les principaux objets] | *Mat:* op paneel *Size:* hoog 17, breed 21 duim	Smidt	(Sold) fl 10 de Lafontaine
1810/10/11	AMSCH	0036	*A. Grijft* | Voor een Buitenhuis of Herberg zit een Jager, in deftige kleeding, met een Roemer Wijn in de eene, en eene Pijp in de andere hand, voor eene Tafel, waarop Brood, Tabaksdoos, Vuurtest en ander bijwerk geplaatst is, achter dezelve staat een Knecht met een Snaphaan en Jagthond, daar nevens ligt verscheiden dood Wild, en op den voorgrond een rustende Hond, doode Vogel en eenig Jagtgereedschap; het is van eene meesterlijke penseelbehandeling | *Mat:* op doek *Size:* hoog 29, breed 24 duimen	S	(Sold) fl 14:10 van der Schley [for] R[ijfsnijder]

Grypmoed, Geerlig

1801/03/16	AMSCH	0088	*Grypmoet* | Twee bevallige Landschappen | *Notes:* This lot was sold with lot 89 by an anonymous artist.	P[ruyssenaar]	(Sold) fl 1 for lots 88 & 89. Gruiter

Guercino (Giovanni Francesco Barbieri)

1803/04/27	AMSCH	0097	*Guerchin* | Loth avec ses Filles | *Size:* h. 2 ½, l. 3 ½ pieds	A	(Sold) fl 3:15 Stevens
1803/04/27	AMSCH	0110	*Guerchin* | Hérodias Présentant la tête de Saint Jean Batiste, beau Tableau du Guerchin bien composé & biën colorie | *Size:* h. 4 ¼, l. 7 pieds	A	(Sold) fl 13:10 V^{n} Brink
1810/07/26	AMSCH	0035	*Guercino* | Eene weenende Magdalena, houdende een doek in hare hand. Bijzonder fraai geschilderd | *Mat:* op doek *Size:* hoog 27, breed 38 duimen	Cassino	(Bought In) fl 16

Guercino (Giovanni Francesco Barbieri) (copy after)

1810/10/11	AMSCH	0069	*Parenti; Guerchino* | Het Afbeeldsel van Sybilla Samia, halver Lijf, en in rijke kleeding, rustende met hare handen op een Boek; meesterlijk geschilderd, op Doek, door denzelven [Parenti], naar het schilderij van Guerchino | copy by Parenti after Guercino *Mat:* op doek *Size:* hoog 45, breed 37 duimen	M	(Bought In) fl 9

Guercino (Giovanni Francesco Barbieri) (manner)

1803/04/27	AMSCH	0129	*Guerchin* | Moise encore enfant mangeant du feu en présence de Pharaön, dans la maniére du Guerchin | *Size:* h. 45, l. 54 pouces	A	(Sold) fl 25:10 Hodges
1803/04/27	AMSCH	0137	*Guerchin* | Une tête de Bachus, dans la maniére du Guerchin | *Size:* h. 28, l. 22 pieds	A	(Sold) fl 52 Th Spaan

Guichardino [Unidentified]

1805/10/09	HGBSM	0036	*Guichardino* | Een gezelschap op het dambord speelende, by kaarsligt | *Mat:* op doek *Size:* hoog 41 breet 48 duim	T H van Willigen [or others]	(Sold) fl 6 Ph Mey

Gulck, A. [Unidentified]

1805/06/24	DOBLU	0015	*A. Gulck* | Een met Vissen, 1664 | *Inscr:* 1664 (dated?) *Notes:* It is unclear whether the date is inscribed on the painting.	Willem Snellen [or] F R E Nibbelinck [or] Gysbert Visser	(Unknown)

Gulik, R. van [Unidentified]

1802/07/27	AKHRK	0021	*R. van Gulik* | Een Campement, alwaar eenige Krijgslieden bij een Soetelaars Tent hun met speelen vermaaken. Goed gepenseeld | *Mat:* op paneel *Size:* hoog 15 ½, breed 20 ½ duim	Maria Stategaart	(Sold) fl 6:10 Sonnevelt

Gyselaer, Nicolaes de

1808/08/23	AMSCH	0064	*Gieselaer (N.D.)* | Een Roomsche Kerk van binnen te zien, gestoffeert met verscheiden Altaaren, wandelende Heeren en Dames, zittende Jongens en andere Beeldjes; fraai van doorzicht, zonachtig en uitvoerig gepenceeld | *Mat:* op paneel *Size:* hoog 13, breed 17 duim	C	(Bought In) fl 30
1810/08/06	AMSCH	0036	*Gieselaar (N.D.)* | Een Roomsche Kerk, van binnen met verscheide Altaaren, wandelende Heeren en Dames, zittende Jongens, en andere stoffage; fraai van zonlicht en uitvoerig gepenceeld | *Mat:* op paneel *Size:* hoog 13, breed 17 duimen	B	(Bought In) fl 30

Gysels, Peeter

1802/05/05	AMSCH	0066	*J. Gyzen* | Twee stuks, zynde een Man en een Vrouw, beide met een Mand met Vrugten, Gevoogelte en eenige Groentens. Alles zeer met de natuur overëenkomstig geschilderd | *Mat:* op doek *Size:* hoog 38, breed 47 duim *Notes:* The artist's name was given as "J. Gyzen" but we have assumed this is an error.	B	(Sold) fl 3 Van Seest
1807/08/26	AMSCH	0079	*P. Gysens* | Het Paradys met Adam en Eva, staande by de Boom des Levens, en een menigte van Gedierte; uitvoerig | companion to lot 80 *Mat:* op koper *Size:* hoog 7, breed 9 duim	de Vries	(Sold) fl 2 Yver
1807/08/26	AMSCH	0080	*P. Gysens* | Een Boomryk Landschap, gestoffeerd met Struikrovers die een Rytuig overvallen, ter linker zyde een verschiet met hooggebergten, door denzelven [P. Gysens], zynde een wederga | companion to lot 79 *Size:* hoog 7, breed 9 duim	de Vries	(Sold) fl 3 Yver
1810/06/06	RMMUY	0021	*Pieter Gijzels* | In dit Tafreel ziet men een dooden Haas, hangende met zijn Looper aan een Jachtroer 't welk tegen een boom rust, bij hetzelve veelerlei dood Gevogelte, en een staande Hond; op den voorgrond eene Distelplant, in 't verschiet een Landschap; verwonderlijk uitvoerig geschilderd | *Mat:* op koper *Size:* hoog 13, breed 10 ½ duim		(Sold) fl 68 Hachefort

Haag, Tethart Philip Christian

1804/12/10	AMSCH	0029	*P.C. Haag* | Een Stal van binnen te zien, een Chais met twee geele paarden, waar op een heer en dame zit, ryd uit dezelve, ter zyde ziet men een Heer op een paard, welke van de waardin een glas liqueur gepresenteerd word, verder is dit stukje vol gewoel, en bevallig behandeld | *Mat:* op paneel *Size:* Hoog 16, breed 19 duim	Jan De Groot	(Sold) fl 40 Gruyter
1807/08/26	AMSCH	0097	*P.C. Haag* | Een Plysterplaats, waarby eenige Heeren en een Dame te Paard, eenige Honden en Kippen, zynde een Duinachtig Landschap; bevallig gepenceeld | *Mat:* op paneel *Size:* hoog 17, breed 23 duim	Joseph Vallette	(Sold) fl 30 van Iperen
1808/11/28	AMSCH	0032	*P.C. Haag* | In een open Stal, ziet men een Chais met twee geele Paarden waar op een Heer en Dame zit, dezelve uitrijdende, ter zijde een Heer te Paard, welke door eene bevallige Waardin een Glas Liqeur gepresenteerd word, verder een Wagen met vrolijke Lieden en verscheide Paarden bij een Kreb, zonachtig en uitvoerig gepenceeld | *Mat:* op paneel *Size:* hoog 16, breed 19 duim	C	(Bought In) fl 54
1808/12/12	DOHAA	0073	*T.P.C. Haag* | Een in 't graauw lang ovaal zinnebeeldig Stuk, op de Botanie, op doek, door T.P.C. Haag, met een fraai vergulden gesneden Lyst | *Mat:* op doek *Fmt:* ovaal		(Unknown)

Haan, C. de [Unidentified]

1802/11/01	DOBRA	0028	*C. de Haan* | Een Biervliegje, item een Boertje	Paulus van der Spyk [or others]	(Sold) fl 1:15 v Leen

Haar, C. van [Unidentified]

1802/09/21	UTHDG	0039	*C. van Haar* | Een partij Schaapen en ander Vee, wordende gedreven door vrouwen, enz. in een fraai Landschap. Helder en aangenaam | *Mat:* op doek *Size:* hoog 15, breed 19 duimen		(Bought In) fl 29

Haastert, Izaak van

1804/07/25	DLGRO	0080	*Van Haastert* | Eene Bybelsche Geschiedenis | *Mat:* op doek *Size:* hoog 11, breed 14 duim	Mr Franc van der Burch Wz.	(Unknown)
1804/07/25	DLGRO	0081	*Van Haastert* | Een Tafel met allerleij Rivier Visch, en een Kat die 'er op zit te loeren | *Size:* hoog 11, breed 14 duim	Mr Franc van der Burch Wz.	(Unknown)

Hackaert

1802/05/05	AMSCH	0073	*Hakkert* | Een Boom- en Bergachtig Landschap, met een Waterval, ziet men eenige door de zon snel verligt wordende Gebouwen langs een	J	(Sold) fl 8:10 Stevens

			Opgaande Weg, een speelende Herder, met Schaapen en andere stoffagie, fraai gepenceeld | *Size:* hoog 20, breed 30 duim		
1802/09/21	UTHDG	0035	*Hackert* | Hoog geboomte welker stammen hier en daar belicht, een goede uitwerking doen. Vooraan een moerassig water; in het verschiet een Stad aan den voet eens Bergs, gestoffeerd met Reizigers, en natuurlijk geschildert | *Mat:* op doek *Size:* hoog 43, breed 36 duimen		(Bought In) fl 36
1803/12/12	AMSCH	0159	*Hakkert* | Twee stuks met Schaapen en Bokkken [sic] | *Mat:* op koper *Size:* hoog 8, br. 10 duim	D	(Sold) fl 5:10 Mensart
			Hackaert (or Hackaert, manner)		
1802/09/06	AMSCH	0204	*Hakkaert* | Een Aangenaam en bevallig Landschap, op de voorgrond eenige Reizigers; picant van Licht, door of in manier van Hakkaert | *Mat:* op doek *Size:* hoog 24, breed 32 duim	J	(Sold) fl 3:15 Hulswit
			Hackaert (manner)		
1803/12/12	AMSCH	0147	*Hakkert* | Twee Duitsche gestoffeerde Landschappen; als Hakkert | *Size:* hoog 11, breed 14 duim	D	(Sold) fl 8 Coclers
1804/02/27	AMSCH	0137	*Hakkart* | Een Landschap, fraai gestoffeerd, als Hakkart	B	(Sold) fl 2 Thais
			Hackaert, Jan		
1801/08/19	AMSCH	0034	*J. Hackart* | Een zeer natuurlyk Heuvelagtig Landschap met Geboomten: by een stil Water, ziet men Hengelaars, en een Visser in zyn Schuit; ter linker zyde een Heer te Paard, waar neevens een gaande Huisman, alles zonachtig en fraai van penceel behandeling op Doek | *Mat:* op doek *Size:* hoog 31, breed 39 Duim	Mevr Hogguer	(Sold) fl 60 Pruijssenaar [for] R
1801/08/19	AMSCH	0035	*J. Hackart* | Een Bosch en Bergachtig Landschap, gestoffeerd met Landlieden, met belaaden Muil Ezels verders een ménigte staand en leggend Vee	Pruyssen^{r} [for] Q	(Sold) fl 11 v d Schley [for] Merrem
1802/06/16	AMSCH	0078	*J. Hackert* | Een aangenaam Landschap met hoog Geboomten Gebergtens, gestoffeerd met een Ezel op de voorgrond; verders by een Waterplas een menigte Vee met hunne Hoeders; alles breed behandeld | *Mat:* op doek *Size:* hoog 32, breed 43 duim	[Merrem]	(Sold) fl 31 Teyssier
1803/08/17	AMSCH	0032	*Hakkert. (J.)* | Door een Laan met hoog Geboomten, ziet men op een pragtig Gebouw, de voorgrond gestoffeerd met Heeren te Paard, zonachtig uitgevoerd | *Mat:* op paneel *Size:* hoog 10, breed 7 ½ duim	Anna Catharina Putman	(Sold) fl 3:5 Camphuijsen
1803/08/24	HGKAN	0017	*J. Hakkert* | Een aangenaam Lantschap met hoog Geboomte en Gebergtens gestoffeerd met een Ezel op de voorgrond, verders by een Waterplas een menigte Vee met hunne Hoeders, alles breet Behandelt | *Mat:* op doek *Size:* hoog 32, breet 43 duim	[Teissier] [or others]	(Sold) fl 10 Teissier
1805/07/10	AMSCH	0081	*J. Hakkaert* | Een bevallig Boomryk Landschapje, met Lieden te Paard, Rytuigen enz.; zonachtig en fiks gepenceeld | *Mat:* op paneel *Size:* hoog 10, breed 8 duimen	V[inkeles] [for] N	(Sold) fl 1 L Pakker
			Hackaert, Jan (and Lingelbach)		
1802/09/06	AMSCH	0048	*J. Hackaert; J. Lingelbach* | Een Boschachtig Landschap, met een Rivier doorsneeden, waarin verbeeld een Hartejacht, op de voorgrond, en in 't verschiet, Heeren te Paard, en Jagers te voet, met verscheide Honden, die het wild vervolgen; het natuurlyk zonlicht, doet een fraaye werking, is kragtig van Coloriet, en meesterlyk gepenceeld, door J. Hackaert, en de Stoffagie door J. Lingelbach | *Mat:* op paneel *Size:* hoog 17, breed 12 ½ duim	H^{n} Smit	(Sold) fl 131 Izaac Smit
1802/09/06	AMSCH	0049	*J. Hakkert; J. Lingelbach* | Een Boom- en bergachtig Landschap, met een stille Rivier, gestoffeerd met danssende beelden; uitvoerig en zonachtig | *Mat:* op paneel *Size:* hoog 16, breed 21 duim	Mevrouw Achtienhoven	(Sold) fl 10:10 van Iperen
1802/12/13	AMSCH	0078	*J. Hackaert; J. Lingelbagh* | In een Italiaansch bevallig Landschap, met hoog Geboomten, by een Rivier, waar over een Steene Brug en aloude Poort, ziet men op de voorgrond een Heer te Paard, gevolgt van een Jager met Honden: in 't verschiet eenige Gebouwen en Gebergtens, dit voorwerp is natuurlyk warm en zonagtig gepenceelt | *Mat:* op paneel *Size:* hoog 13, breed 17 duim	Schley [for] Lauwers	(Sold) fl 24 J^{n} Yver
1809/04/22	AMYVR	0054	*J. Hakkert; J. Lingelbach* | Een fraai Boom- en Bergachtig Landschap, aan een Rivier, gestoffeerd met een Heer te Paard; het zonlicht doet een uitmuntende werking, en is meesterlijk gepenceelt door J. Hakkert en J. Lingelbach | *Mat:* op doek *Size:* hoog 50, breed 58 duim	van den Bracke	(Sold) fl 56 C S Roos
			Hackaert, Jan (and Velde, A.)		
1801/04/13	AMSCH	0029	*J. Hackaert; A. van de Velde* | Een alleraangenaamst Italiaansch Landschap met hoog Geboomte, ter regter zyde de Ruïne van eene Collonnade, waar by een Fontein, een Jager met zyn Hond, verfrisschen zig aan dezelve, voorts nog een Heer en Dame te paard, verders Jagers, Honden, Koeijen en Schapen; over een Rivier ziet men een aangenaam bergachtig verschiet; alles is zonachtig en transperant behandeld | *Mat:* op doek *Size:* hoog 22, breed 31 duim	Pierre Fouquet, junior	(Sold) fl 200 Pruyssenaar
1804/05/07	AMSCH	0076	*Hakkert (J.); A. van de Velde* | Een aangenaam Landschap, met een Waterplas op de voorgrond, waar by een Vrouw, die een Beest voort dryft,	Y[ver]	(Sold) fl 13 Reijers

			verder een opgaande Weg met Geboomte en een drift Beesten en voorts een aangenaam verschiet, zonachtig en bevallig gepenceeld | *Mat:* op doek *Size:* hoog 19 ½, breed 23 duim		
1804/05/07	AMSCH	0077	*Hakkert (J.); A. van de Velde* | Een aangenaam Boom en Bergächtig Landschap, op de voorgrond gestoffeerd, met rustende Landlieden, verders een Herder eenig Vee langs den weg dryvenden, hooger op ziet men een vlietend Watertje, de toppen van Ruigbegroeide Bergen en aengenaam verschiet, warm en zonachtig van penceelbehandeling | *Mat:* op doek *Size:* hoog 32, breed 43 duim	Vinkeles [for] G	(Sold) fl 89 Thys
1808/06/06	RMRIJ	0047	*Hakkert. (Jan); Velde. (Adriaan van de)* | Een zeer aangenaam Landschap, rijk in hoog opgaande verschillende soorten van boomen. Op den voorgrond van eenen weg, welke met eene bogt langs een water loopt, ziet men een Heer op een Bruin Vos-Paard, daarnevens eene rijk gekleede Dame op een Wit Paard; uit de poort van een Oud Slot trekken eenige Jagers en Bedienden, met een groot aantal Honden, ter jagt. Alles zeer natuurlijk en allerschoonst door beide deze groote Meesters behandeld. Is in Plaat te vinden in het Prentwerk van het Kabinet van Mr. Le Brun [Sur le devant d'un chemin courbé, enrichi de beaux hêtres de haute futaie, et qui borde un Canal, on voit un Cavalier, dont le Cheval Alezan se cabre ; une Dame richement costumée et montée sur un Cheval blanc, se trouve prés de lui : ils sont suivis par un fauconnier accompagné d'un Chasseur, avec une meute de Chiens. Dans le fond, auprés de la Porte d'un Enclos, un Cavalier prend congé d'un Seigneur, deux Chasseurs et des Chiens sont auprés d'eux ; vers la gauche et sur le devant au bord du Canal, on voit un Chien qui aboye des Cignes. De beaux arbres, l'Effet de la Réverberation du Soleil dans l'eau, la Perspective Aérienne, l'harmonie bien sentie, tout cela joint aux figures et aux Animaux supériéurement peints par le célébre van den Velde, forme un Ensemble gracieux et par fait. Nous pouvons dire de ce superbe morceau qu'on chercheroit en vain son pareil. On trouve dans le Cabinet de Mr. le Brun une gravure de ce Tableau par Daudet] | *Mat:* op doek *Size:* Hoog 25, en breed 20 ⅛ duim *Loc:* Amsterdam, Nederland. Rijksmuseum. (A 130)	Gerrit van der Pot, Heer van Groeneveld	(Sold) fl 3005 Johs Eck en Zoon [for] le Roi
1810/03/26	RMMUY	0020	*Jan Hakkert; gestoffeerd door Adriaan van de Velde* | Een Italiaansch Bergachtig Landschap, met hoog en laag Geboomte. Op den breeden weg een Herder zijne Schapen drijvende, en op den voorgrond een Man te Paard, dat aan een Water staat te drinken. Krachtig, zonachtig en meesterlijk behandeld [Un Paysage, site de l'Italie, au milieu un large chemin, bordé de montagnes et de beaux arbres : occupé par un berger conduisant ses moutons, sur le devant un homme monté sur son cheval, qui s'abreuve à une mare d'eau, d'un ton chaud, d'un beau faire et d'un brillant effet.] | *Mat:* op doek *Size:* hoog 23 ½, breed 28 ½ duimen	Daniel de Jongh Az	(Sold) fl 505 Van Iperen Amsterdam
1810/07/26	AMSCH	0041	*Hakkaert (J.); A. van de Velde* | Een aangenaam boomrijk Landschap bij een opgaanden Weg, waarop een Heer te Paard, verzeld van Jagers en Honden. Zonachtig en uitvoerig behandeld | *Mat:* op doek *Size:* hoog 17, breed 22 duimen	Cassino	(Sold) fl 20 Dupré
1810/08/01	AMSCH	0034	*Hakkaert (Jan); Adriaan van de Velde* | Een hoog bergachtig Landschap, op den voorgrond met eene Rivier doorsneden, verder een Waterval bij eene Brug, en hoog opgaand Geboomte, voorzien van Hengelaars, gaande en rustende Reizigers [Un Site de Paysage montueux, coupé par une Riviere au premier plan ; on y observe une Chutte [sic] d'Eau auprès d'un Pont de Pierres, et une variété d'Arbres et de Broussailles, ainsi que des Pécheurs, et d'autres qui semblent faire route] | *Annots:* médiocre. (NGW) *Mat:* op doek *Size:* hoog 26 ½, breed 20 ½ duimen	Mr Pieter de Smeth van Alphen	(Sold) fl 400 Hulswit
1810/08/01	AMSCH	0035	*Hakkaert (Jan); Adriaan van de Velde* | Een aangenaam zonachtig Landschap, met Beeldjes en Schapen, ter zijde een Water [Un Site agréable doré des Rayons de la lumiere, orné de Figures et de Moutons. On y distingue une marre d'eau sur le côté] | *Annots:* médiocre. (NGW) *Mat:* op doek *Size:* hoog 20 ½, breed 26 duimen	Mr Pieter de Smeth van Alphen	(Sold) fl 315 Van Iperen [for] Wreesman
1810/10/10	MGCIT	0004	*Jan Hakkert; A. van de Velde* | Een overheerlijk boschächtig Gezigt, door Jan Hakkert, en met eene fraaije Hertenjagt gestoffeerd, door A. van de Velde; meesterlijk door beide Kunstenaars geschilderd en uitgevoerd; zijnde het Daglicht door het Geboomte heen, alsmede een Waterplas waarin een Hert door de Honden word aangevallen, van een ongemeene schoone werking: Nota: Dit voortreffelijk Stuk is met veel waarschijnlijkheid de Pendant van dat het welk word gevonden in de verkogte Verzameling van wijlen de Heer van der Pot. Pag. 21. No. 47.	Caspar van Citters	(Unknown)

Hackert, Jacob Philipp

1804/10/29	HRBAU	0028	*Hackert, (J. P.)* | Een Riviergezigt; op den Voorgrond, die steenagtig is en met boomgewassen beplant, zyn eenige Reizigers, en aan de overzyde van het Water een fraai bergagtig verschiet. Helder en uitvoerig geschilderd | *Mat:* op doek *Size:* hoog 14, breed 18 duim	Simon Styl	(Unknown)
1810/07/26	AMSCH	0139	*Hakkaert (De Berlijnsche)* | Een Italiaansch Landschap, met Gebouwen, Geboomte en Beelden | *Mat:* op doek *Size:* hoog 21, breed 37 duimen	Cassino	(Sold) fl 3 van Iperen
1810/08/01	AMSCH	0036	*Hakkaert (De Italiaansche)* | Een Italiaansch Landschap, met eene Rivier, Geboomte en Gebouwen, gestoffeerd met eenen Herder bij onderscheide Vee [Une Site de Paysage pris en Italie, varié par plusieurs espèces d'Arbres, une Riviere et des Batiments. Il est orné de plus d'un Pâtre	Mr Pieter de Smeth van Alphen	(Sold) fl 255 for lots 36 & 37. Texier, Gerbet en Comp [for] LeBrun

			et de different Bêtail] | possibly companion to lot 37 *Annots:* froid et sans vérité (NGW) *Mat:* op doek *Size:* hoog 38, breed 52 duimen		
1810/08/01	AMSCH	0037	*Hakkaert (De Italiaansche)* | Een Landschap met Water en Geboomte. Kunnende strekken tot eene wederga van de voorgaande [Un Sujet correspondant pouvant servir de pendant, étant également un Paysage orné d'une Riviere et de Figures] | possibly companion to lot 36 *Annots:* froid et sans vérité (NGW) *Mat:* op doek *Size:* hoog 38, breed 52 duimen	Mr Pieter de Smeth van Alphen	(Sold) fl 255 for lots 36 & 37. Texier, Gerbet en Comp [for] LeBrun
1810/08/06	AMSCH	0039	*Hakkaert (De Berlijnsche)* | Een Italiaans Landschap met Geboomte, Gebouwen en een Rivier doorsneden; gestoffeerd op den voorgrond met Reizigers met hunne Muil-Ezels, agterwaards bij een Steenen Brug eene Vrouw zittende op een Ezel, waarbij een Landman, die eenig Vee drijft; kragtig van koloriet, helder en uitvoerig gepenceeld | possibly companion to lot 40 *Mat:* op doek *Size:* hoog 31, breed 42 duimen	A	(Sold) fl 130 T Spaan
1810/08/06	AMSCH	0040	*Hakkaert (De Berlijnsche)* | Een dergelijk Landschap met een Herder en Herderin, bij grazende Bokken en Schapen, in 't verschiet hoog Gebergte; van gelijke schildering als de voorgaande, kunnende strekke tot eene wederga | possibly companion to lot 39 *Size:* hoog 31, breed 42 duimen	A	(Sold) fl 150 Coclers

Haen, Anthony de

1804/10/16	DLOND	0091	*A. de Haen* | Een Landschap, waarin een Herberg met een Groep Paerden. Paysage avec des Chevaux devant une Auberge | *Mat:* op paneel *Size:* hoog 36, breed 31		(Unknown)

Haensbergen, Johan van

1801/06/10	AMSCH	0088	*Hansbergen. (J.)* | Een Goden Hemel, met verscheide Goden en Godinnen, zittende op de Wolken | *Mat:* op paneel *Size:* hoog 11, breed 13 duim	Herman ten Kate	(Sold) fl 20:10 Stevens
1802/05/05	AMSCH	0077	*Haensbergen* | Door een Nis ziet men eenige Beelden, een derzelven, die vooraan geplaatst is, heeft in de Linkerhand een fraai gedreeven Schotel en in de Regterhand een Lepel, die hy aan een ander aanbied, zinspeelende op het geen onder de Balustrade geschreeven staat: Men had veel Bry van doen; zo me Elk de Mond zou stoppen. Dit stuk is als van Schalken of Mieris gepenceeld door Haensbergen | *Size:* hoog 23, breed 19 duim	J	(Sold) fl 65 Le Dantú
1803/08/17	AMSCH	0037	*Haensbergen. (J. van)* | De aanbidding der Herders in de Stal, te Betlehem, boven dezelve een glorie van Engelen, alles delicaat en uitvoerig geschilderd | *Mat:* op paneel *Size:* hoog 16, breed 22 duim	Anna Catharina Putman	(Sold) fl 67:10 W Reijers
1804/10/29	HRBAU	0032	*Hansbergen, (J.)* | Op den Voorgrond ligt Venus en Cupido te slaapen, welke door een Satyr bespied wordt; nevens een aangenaam bergagtig verschiet. Zeer delicaat behandeld | *Mat:* op paneel *Size:* hoog 7 ½, breed 10 duim	Simon Styl	(Unknown)
1807/06/10	HGBSM	0146	*Haansbergen* | Een Grot met naakte Nimphen en ander bijwerk, door Haansbergen, op paneel, rond formaat | *Mat:* op paneel *Fmt:* rond *Size:* 10 duim diameter	Abraham Delfos [or others]	(Sold) fl 16 de Gelder
1808/06/13	AMSCH	0081	*Haansbergen (J. van)* | In een heuvelachtig Landschap vertoond zich de Heilige Famielle, zijnde een rust in de vlucht naar Egypte; om hoog een Glorie van Engelen; verder een boomrijk Landschap. Alles bevallig van kleur, en van een uitvoerige penceelsbehandeling | *Mat:* op paneel *Size:* hoog 14 ½, breed 12 duim	[Jan Tersteeg]	(Sold) fl 60 Nieuwenhuys voor Henry
1808/06/13	AMSCH	0082	*Haansbergen (J. van)* | Deze rijke Ordonantie vertoond de Geboorte van Christus, alwaar de Herders het Kindje aanbidden, in de kribbe liggende; om hoog eene Glorie van Engelen. In alles als de vorige en van een uitvoerige penceelsbehandeling | *Mat:* op paneel *Size:* hoog 14 ½, breed 11 duim	[Jan Tersteeg]	(Sold) fl 141 T Boelen pour Henry
1808/10/28	AMVRS	0016	*Haensbergen. (J. v.)* | In een Landschap ziet men op den voorgrond de H. Maagd Maria, houdende het Kindje op de Schoot, agter haar staat St. Joseph en in de Lugt eene glorie van Engelen. Zacht en uitvoerig gepenceeld | *Mat:* op paneel *Size:* hoog 14, breed 12 duim	Marten Udink	(Sold) fl 20 van Ensten Dijk [or] van Dyl

Haensbergen, Johan van (manner)

1801/03/16	AMSCH	0161	*Haensbergen* | Een Landschap met badende Nimphen gestoffeerd, in de manier van Haensbergen	K[ip]	(Sold) fl 6:5 Gruiter
1807/08/26	AMSCH	0104	*van Haansbergen* | Onder de boog van een Oud vervallen Ruïne zitten twee Vrouwen Beeldtjes, en ter linker zyde een Kasteel op een Berg; helder gepenceeld als van Haansbergen | *Mat:* op paneel *Size:* hoog 9, breed 12 duim	de Vries	(Sold) fl 4:10 Coclair

Haer, C. van [Unidentified]

1804/10/16	DLOND	0092	*C. van Haer. 1661* | Een Landschap met Beelden. Paysage avec des figures | *Mat:* op paneel *Size:* hoog 13, breed 17 *Inscr:* C. van Haer. 1661 (signed and dated?) *Notes:* It is unclear whether the name and date are inscribed on the painting.		(Sold) fl 7 Noortwyk

Hagen, Joris van der

1802/06/28	AMSCH	0077	*J. van der Hagen* | Twee stuks boomryke Landschappen; meesterlyk door J. van der Hagen, op Panneel | *Mat:* op paneel	Anna Elink	(Sold) fl 1 Boelen

1803/09/07	AMSCH	0090	*J. van der Hagen* | Twee stuks Dorpgezichten met Geboomten en Boerewoningen en Rivieren, bevallig en kragtig op Paneel [Deux points de vue de campagne, entremelés d'arbres, de chaumières et de ruisseaux] | *Mat:* op paneel *Size:* hoog 10, breed 14 duim	Smidt	(Sold) fl 5:10 Gruiter
1804/02/27	AMSCH	0050	*Hagen. (J. van der)* | In een Boomryk Landschap met een Rivier doorsneeden, ziet men eenige wandelende Lieden, in 't verschiet hoog Gebergte en Geboomte; zonachtig geschilderd | *Mat:* op doek *Size:* hoog 29, breed 25 duim	D	(Bought In) fl 2:10
1806/06/07	RMHSN	0004	*J. van der Hagen* | Een Arkadisch Landschap, vol Geboomte en Water, met een drift Schapen | *Mat:* op doek	A E K L	(Unknown)
1808/06/06	RMRIJ	0046	*Hagen. (J. van der)* | Een Land- Dorp- en Watergezigt. Op den rijk versierden voorgrond vertoont zich een schilderachtige Heul en Overhaal. Een schoone lucht en een fraai verschiet veraangenamen dit natuurlijk en konstig behandeld tafereel [Magnifique Paysage Hollandais. Prés d'un Village sur un terrain en pente, on voit un Pont et une Roue d'Ecluse, dont on se sert pour faire passer des Barquettes d'un Canal à l'autre. Un Ciel clair, de beaux arbres, un grand Canal, et un Lointain agréablement terminé, font une Illusion si par faite, qu'on croiroit voir la Réalité] | *Mat:* op doek *Size:* Hoog 44 ¾, en breed 64 duim *Loc:* Amsterdam, Nederland. Rijksmuseum. (A 132) as North Netherlands, ca.1655	Gerrit van der Pot, Heer van Groeneveld	(Sold) fl 1405 van Lennep [for] le Roi
1808/06/11	RMRIJ	0051a	*J: van der Hagen* | Een Boomryk Landschap met stoffagie, fraai geschilderd | *Mat:* op paneel *Size:* hoog 21, breed 28 duim		(Sold) fl 13:10 Van Zanten [?] [or] Coclairs
1808/09/13	HABRU	0094	*Verhagen* | Een Dorpgezicht, natuurlijk		(Unknown) fl 1:16
1808/11/28	AMSCH	0026	*van der Haagen* | Een capitaal Boomrijk Landschap, ter zijde bij een klaar spiegelend Water, ziet men eenige Gebouwen op de voorgrond onder zwaar Geboomte, gestoffeerd met gaande en rustende Landlieden, verder Visschers in Schuiten en zeilende Vaartuigen, schoon van effect en natuurlijk voorgesteld | *Mat:* op doek *Size:* hoog 52, breed 63 duim	[Gruyter?]	(Sold) fl 11 T Spaan
			Hagen, Joris van der (and Lingelbach)		
1805/07/03	AMSCH	0025	*Hagen (J. van der); J. Lingelbagh* | Dit magnifique Schildery steld voor: het gezicht van de Rhynkant op de Stad Arnhem, den Rhyn met Vaartuigen, en de op de voorgrond geleegene Weg, met Huifkarren, Paarden en Reisigers gestoffeerd; het Geboomten, de Zandgronden en het dynzend verschiet, doen een uirmuntend [sic] effect; zynde van een kloeke penceels behandeling | *Mat:* op doek *Size:* hoog 46, breed 68 duim	G	(Sold) fl 50 C S Roos
			Hagen, Joris van der (and Wouwerman)		
1808/04/26	GDAN	0077	*Hagen (J van der); Wouerman* | Een Bos- en Boomrijk Landschap, door Wouerman gestoffeerd, met eenige Jagers te Paard en te Voet met hunne Honden, schoon geschildert | *Size:* hoog 58, breed 54 duim	G H Fortuyn	(Unknown)
			Hagen, Joris van der (manner)		
1806/06/07	RMHSN	0073	*van der Hagen* | Een Boomryk Landschap waar in een Harte Jagt, in de manier van van der Hagen | *Mat:* op doek	A E K L	(Unknown)
			Hagins, M. [Unidentified]		
1805/10/21	GRBOL	0059	*M. Hagins* | Een Stuk met dode Vogels	Gerardus Nicolaus Heerkens	(Unknown)
			Halen, J. van [Unidentified]		
1801/02/24	AMOTT	0006	*J. van Halen* | 1 Zeetje		(Unknown)
			Halleman, Thomas		
1803/07/14	MGKLY	0002	*T. Halleman* | Twee stuks, een Jong Heer en een Dame in een Nis, fraay gepenseelt	Mr Caspar Jacob van Citters	(Unknown)
			Hals		
1801/04/08	HAVIN	0016	*Hals* | Een Tafel met Stilleveen [sic], hierby een Vrouw met een Vis		(Unknown)
1807/06/02	AMHUY	0025	*de Hals* | Een Landschap met Geboomte, in het verschiet een Kerktoren, gestoffeerd met verscheide Beelden, uitvoerig geschilderd		(Unknown)
			Hals (and Nickelen)		
1801/04/08	HAVIN	0002	*van Nikkelen; Hals* | Een gezigt in de Groote Kerk te Haarlem, na 't Choor te zien extra fraai door van Nikkelen and door Hals gestoff:		(Unknown)
			Hals, Dirck		
1803/04/20	AMSCH	0034	*Hals. (D.)* | In een Hofgezicht ziet men een gedekte Tafel met Spys, waarby verscheide Dames en Heeren zitten, in aloude Spaansche kleeding, zig met Musiceeren vermaaken: ter zyde staat een Jongeling, met een Schenkbord met Glaazen, verders een bevallig verschiet; meesterlyk en bevallig gepenceeld [Sous une Collonade est répresenté n festin dont les convives sont costumés à l'ancienne Espagnolle ; ils sont occupés à faire de la musique, tandis qu'un page presente du rafraichissement. Le fond est terminé par une prespective agréable. Ce	Maria Magdalena van Sluypwyk, gravinne van Moens	(Sold) fl 71 Coclers

			morceau artistement touché, ajoute à l'agrement du sujet.] | *Mat:* op paneel *Size:* hoog 13 ½, breed 24 duim		
1803/12/15	MGLAC	0051	*D. Hals* | Een vrolyk Gezelschap van Dames en Officiers; zeer goed geschilderd | *Mat:* op paneel *Size:* hoog duim 16, breed duim 24	Mr L H de Haze Bomme	(Unknown)
1805/07/10	AMSCH	0198	*D. Hals* | Twee Vrouwen en een Man, zittende op de kaart te speelen; geestig op Paneel | *Mat:* op paneel	R[oos]	(Sold) fl 14 Lafontaine
1808/06/13	AMSCH	0233	*D. Hals* | Een Binnenhuis met drie Beelden; meesterlijk	Z	(Sold) fl 0:14 L Pakker
1808/09/13	HABRU	0041	*D. Hals* | Eenige Krijgslieden op de Kaart speelende, op de voorgrond Trom, Harnasse, &c.		(Unknown) fl 0:7
1808/09/13	HABRU	0042	*D. Hals* | Een rokende Boer		(Unknown) fl 0:8

Hals, Dirck (manner)

1803/04/20	AMSCH	0108	*D. Hals* | In een Binnenhuis zit een Heer en Dame, in aloude Spaansche Kleeding, als elkander de Liefde openbaarende, verder ziet men een Thuingezicht, fiks gepenceeld, als door D. Hals [Deux Amans en declaration d'Amour, sont vus dans une Coupole donnent sur le Jardin ; ils portent l'ancien costume Espagnol, ce tableau d'une touche fixe paroit être l'oeuvre de D. Hals.] | *Mat:* op paneel *Size:* hoog 11, breed 8 duim	Maria Magdalena van Sluypwyk, gravinne van Moens	(Sold) fl 0:10 Dekker
1805/07/10	AMSCH	0268	*D. Hals* | Een staande Juffrouw in aloude Hollandsche Kleeding, speelende op een Clavier, in een gemeubileerd Vertrek; fiks gepenceeld, als door D. Hals | *Mat:* op paneel	S[chley] [for] Jult Mann	(Bought In) fl 2
1809/04/17	AMSCH	0073a[H]	*als D Hals* | [Untitled] | *Notes:* This lot was added in by hand in the EBNP copy of the catalogue, but without giving a title.		(Sold) fl 14:5

Hals, Frans (I)

1801/05/11	AMSCH	0031	*Frans Hals* | Een Mans-Pourtret, halver lyf, houdende in de linkerhand zyn handschoene; en een dito Vrouwe Pourtret, alles is meesterlyk fix en krachtig geschilderd | *Mat:* op doek *Size:* hoog 37, breed 21 duim	Pruisse [for] M	(Withdrawn)
1801/05/11	AMSCH	0032	*Frans Hals* | Twee stuks, een Man en een Vrouwe Pourtret, beide fix en meesterlyk behandeld | *Mat:* op doek *Size:* hoog 32, breed 26 duim	P[ruyssenaar]	(Sold) fl 14 Pruijssenaar [for] R
1801/06/13	LNDLS	0048	*Frans Hals* | Een Jongman, die als zingende op de Luit speelt, fix en konstig, op paneel | *Mat:* op paneel *Size:* hoog 17, breed 13 duimen	D van R	(Sold) fl 281 A Delfos
1802/05/05	AMSCH	0082	*F. Hals* | Twee stuks, een Leggende Jongeling, met een Fluit en een Leggende dito, fiks gepenceeld | *Size:* hoog 13, breed 11 duim	J	(Sold) fl 3:15 A Schotte
1802/06/16	AMSCH	0074	*F. Hals* | Het Afbeeldzel van een bedaagd Leeraar, zittende in een Leuning-Stoel, ter zyde een Tafel, waarop Inktkooker en Papier leggen; zeer fraay en meesterlyk gepenceeld | *Mat:* op paneel *Size:* hoog 13, breed 10 ½ duim	[Merrem]	(Sold) fl 46 H de Valk
1802/06/16	AMSCH	0075	*F. Hals* | Het Pourtrait van een bekend Koopman in Bokkens, hebbende in zyn linker arm een strootje Bokkens, terwyl hy in zyn rechter een andere vertoond, als roepende Wie Begeert: zynde van een meesterlyke fixe Penceels-behandeling | *Mat:* op paneel *Size:* hoog 33, breed 26 ½ duim	[Merrem]	(Sold) fl 55 B^{d} Kooij
1802/06/16	AMSCH	0076	*F. Hals* | Een vrolyke Gast, halver lyf, in een lagchend Caracter: geestig en meesterlyk gepenceeld | *Mat:* op paneel *Size:* hoog 10 ½, breed 9 duim	[Merrem]	(Sold) fl 3:15 P M Levij
1802/09/06	AMSCH	0050	*F. Hals* | Dit stuk verbeeld Jonker Ram, houdende in zyn opgeheeven regterhand een wynglas, en met de linkerhand zyn Jagthond carresseerende, terwyl een bevallig meisje hem streeld; meesterlyk | *Mat:* op doek *Size:* hoog 41, breed 31 duim	D	(Bought In) fl 50
1802/09/06	AMSCH	0051	*F. Hals* | Een Manspourtrait, met de eene hand op de borst, en in de andere een ledere handschoen; breed geschilderd | *Size:* hoog 33, breed 27 duim	J	(Sold) fl 10:10 van Iperen
1802/11/01	DOBRA	0015	*Frans Hals* | Een Toebaksrooker | *Size:* hoog 27 breed 24 duim	Paulus van der Spyk [or others]	(Sold) fl 10 M v Steegh
1802/12/13	AMSCH	0086	*F. Hals* | Een Vrouwe Portrait, zittende op een bekleede Stoel, met de byde Handen over elkander, in een van dezelven heeft zy een Handschoen meesteragtig geschilderd | *Mat:* op doek *Size:* hoog 33, breed 27 duim	Pruyssenaar [for] A	(Sold) fl 1 Gruiter
1804/07/25	AMSCH	0035	*Hals. (F.)* | Het afbeeldzel van een Dame staande, en ter halver Lyf te zien, houdende byde de Handen in elkander, zy is in deftige aloude zwarte Satyne Kleeding, Meesterlyk en kragtig van penceel behandeling | *Mat:* op doek *Size:* hoog 40, breed 29 duim		(Sold) fl 45 Coclers
1804/07/25	DLGRO	0086	*F. Hals* | Een Boeren binnen Huis, met allerlei Boerengereije, en een Stal met een Koe en Geiten &c. | *Mat:* op paneel *Size:* hoog 18, breed 27 duim	Mr Franc van der Burch Wz.	(Unknown)
1804/08/08	AMSCH	0087	*F. Hals* | Een Vrouwen Pourtrait, zittende op een bekleede Stoel, met de beide Handen over elkander, in een van dezelve heeft zy een Handschoen; fiks en breed geschilderd | *Mat:* op doek *Size:* hoog 33, breed 27 duim	Vink[eles] [for] K[=Gruyter?]	(Sold) fl 4:15 Gruiter
1804/10/16	DLOND	0093	*Frans Hals* | Een Lagchend Kinderhoofd. La tête d'un Enfant joyeux | *Mat:* op paneel *Size:* hoog 13, breed 11		(Unknown)
1804/10/16	DLOND	0094	*Frans Hals* | Dito [Een Lagchend Kinderhoofd], met een Hond. Dito [La Tête d'un Enfant joyeux], avec un Chien | *Mat:* op paneel *Size:* hoog 13, breed 11 *Notes:* It is unclear what "dito" refers to in the title.		(Unknown)

1804/10/29	HRBAU	0042	*Hals, (Frans)* | Een Jongeling tot de borst te zien; hy verbeeldt in een comicq gelaat, de Lier te speelen, en daar by te zingen. Dit Stukje is fiks behandeld | *Mat:* op paneel *Size:* hoog 8, breed 7 ½ duim	Simon Styl	(Unknown)
1806/05/05	AMSCH	0059	*Frans Hals* | Een vrolyke Gast met een Pyp in zyn hand; meesterlyk op Paneel | *Mat:* op paneel *Size:* hoog 12, breed 10 duim	H	(Sold) fl 20 Roos
1806/05/05	AMSCH	0060	*Frans Hals* | Een Vrouwen Pourtret, zittende op een Stoel, met de handen over elkander; fiks en breed geschilderd door denzelven [Frans Hals] | *Mat:* op doek *Size:* hoog 33, breed 26 duim	V[inkeles]	(Sold) fl 2 Gruyter
1806/08/13	AMSCH	0070	*Hals. (F.)* | 't Afbeeldsel van den Dichter J. Hoornbeek, halverlyf, houdende een boek in de hand, in 't zwart fluweel gekleed met een witte kraag; allermeesterlykst van behandeling | *Mat:* op doek *Size:* hoog 31, breed 27 duim	Coclers	(Bought In) fl 61
1806/08/13	AMSCH	0071	*Hals. (F.)* | In een Zaal ziet men een gezelschap Heeren en Dames, zich vermakende met het spel handje plak; krachtig geschilderd | *Size:* hoog 29, breed 41 duim	Roos	(Sold) fl 7:5 Theins
1806/08/13	AMSCH	0323	*Hals. (F.)* | Een Fruit en Groenteverkoopster; meesterlyk geschilderd | *Size:* hoog 38, breed 58 duim	Vinkeles [for] G[ruyter]	(Sold) fl 2 Yver [for] G
1807/08/26	AMSCH	0098	*F. Hals* | Een vrolyke Visboer, zittende in een Landschap; meesterlyk | *Mat:* op doek *Size:* hoog 33, breed 29 duim	Joseph Vallette	(Sold) fl 21 du Pree
1807/08/26	AMSCH	0099	*F. Hals* | Een Man welke vol pynlyke trekken zyn arm wryft; kragtig | *Mat:* op doek *Size:* hoog 30, breed 26 duim	Joseph Vallette	(Sold) fl 61 H^k Jansen
1808/04/26	GDAN	0073	*Hals (Frans)* | Een Mans Kop, &c. | *Size:* hoog 22, breed 17 duim	G H Fortuyn	(Unknown)
1808/04/26	GDAN	0074	*Hals (Frans)* | Een Viool spelende Jongeling | *Size:* hoog 34, breed 26 duim	G H Fortuyn	(Unknown)
1808/04/26	GDAN	0075	*Hals (Frans)* | Een Pourtret in Manskleeding, zeer goed geschildert | *Size:* hoog 12, breed 8 duim	G H Fortuyn	(Unknown)
1808/04/26	GDAN	0076	*Hals (Frans)* | Een Binnenhuis waar in zich een Gezelschap vermaakt met het zingen van Musiek, dit is konstig geschildert | *Size:* hoog 18, breed 12 duim	G H Fortuyn	(Unknown)
1808/08/23	AMSCH	0073	*Hals. (F.)* | Een deftig Mans Pourtret, in 't zwart gekleed, met een wit linnen Kraag om de Hals, en zijn Hoed in de hand; meesterlijk behandeld en van de beste schildering | *Mat:* op paneel *Size:* hoog 43, breed 34 duim	[Coclers]	(Sold) fl 121 for lots 73 & 74. Van Iperen
1808/08/23	AMSCH	0074	*Hals. (F.)* | Een dito [deftig] Vrouwe Pourtret, mede in 't zwart gekleed, zij is gezeeten in een Armstoel, en als de voorgaande behandeld | *Mat:* op doek *Size:* hoog 43, breed 34 duim	[Coclers]	(Sold) fl 121 for lots 73 & 74. Van Iperen
1808/08/23	AMSCH	0207	*F. Hals* | Eene bevallige oude Vrouw, in aloude Hollandsche Kleeding; meesterlijk op doek | *Mat:* op doek	[Gruyter?]	(Sold or Bought In) fl 1:5 Gruyter
1808/09/13	HABRU	0035	*F. Hals* | Een Mans Pourtrait		(Unknown) fl 2
1808/09/13	HABRU	0036	*F. Hals* | Een Visboer		(Unknown) fl 1:18
1808/11/28	AMSCH	0029	*F. Hals* | Een Mans Portret, in deftige Kleeding met een witte Linne Kraag om de Hals, houdende Handschoenen in zijn Hand, kragtig geschilderd | *Mat:* op doek *Size:* hoog 33, breed 26 duim	H	(Sold) fl 6:5 du Pree
1809/04/22	AMYVR	0060	*F. Hals* | Een vrolijke Vischboer; meesterlijk | *Mat:* op doek *Size:* hoog 32, breed 26 duim	de Bruin	(Bought In) fl 10
1809/05/26	HADAA	0010	*Frans Hals* | Twee Kinderen, bezig Pap te eten	Mejuffrouw de Wed David Heemskerk [or others]	(Unknown)
1809/07/25	HGBSM	0222	*F. Hals* | Een Binnenhuis, waar in twee Vrouwen, en verder gestoffeerd met doode Vogels, Groentens en meer bywerk, gemerkt F. Hals | *Mat:* op paneel *Size:* hoog 21 en een half, breed 15 en een half duim *Inscr:* F. Hals (signed)	D van der Aa [or] E B ten Dall	(Sold) fl 33:5 van Eijk
1810/03/27	RMCNL	0020	*Frans Hals* | Twee Pourtraitten, fix gepenceeld		(Unknown)
1810/06/20	AMSCH	0163	*F. Hals* | Een bedaagd Man, houdende een Fles en Bakje in de hand	A	(Sold) fl 3 Cassino
1810/10/11	AMSCH	0125	*F. Hals* | Een Man met een Kan in zijn hand | *Mat:* op paneel	[Gruyter?]	(Sold or Bought In) fl 1:10 Gruiter

Hals, Frans (I) (and Heussen, N.)

1810/08/06	AMSCH	0041	*Hals (F.); G Heusen* | Eene Fruitvrouw, bezig eenige Vrugten te wegen, verders eene menigte Vrugten op Tafels en in Manden; meesterlijk behandeld | *Mat:* op doek *Size:* hoog 60, breed 74 duimen *Loc:* Bridgnorth, Shropshire, England, UK. Viscount Boyne.	R[oos]	(Bought In) fl 50

Hals, Frans (I) (and Snyders, F.)

1801/04/13	AMSCH	0072	*F. Snyders; F. Hals* | Een Fruit- en Vogelverkoopster, voor haar hangt een hart en ander gedierten, nevens haar een meid met druiven, verder musicant en andere zingende gasten; meesterlyk gepenceeld | *Mat:* op doek *Size:* hoog 59, breed 80 duim	Pierre Fouquet, junior	(Sold) fl 30 Spruit van Gend

Hals, Frans (I) (or Hals, F. (I), manner)

1801/06/13	LNDLS	0020	*F. Hals* | Een lagchend Man, met een tabakspijp in zijn hand, van of zoo goed als van F. Hals | *Mat:* op paneel *Size:* hoog 11 ½, breed 9 ½ duimen	D van R	(Sold) fl 16 Dibbets

1805/12/16	AMSCH	0089	*F. Hals* | Een Binnehuis, met een gezelschap van Heeren en Dames, door of als F. Hals	R[oos]	(Sold) fl 4:5 van Iperen

Hals, Frans (I) (or Hals, F. (I), manner; and Seghers, D.)

1810/07/26	AMSCH	0091	*F. Hals; Zegers (P.)* | Een fraai geschakeerde Krans, van onderscheidene keurige en uitvoerig geschilderde Bloemen, in het midden een vrolijk Mans Pourtrait, door of als F. Hals geschilderd	Cassino	(Bought In) fl 16

Hals, Frans (I) (attributed)

1810/10/10	MGCIT	0117	*F. Hals* | Een Gezelschap van Heeren en Dames, spelende met de Kaart; zeer meesterlyk behandeld, niet onwaarschynlyk eene Schets van F. Hals	Caspar van Citters	(Unknown)

Hals, Frans (I) (manner)

1801/06/13	LNDLS	0086	*F. Hals* | Den Schrijfmeester la Chambre, in de manier van F. Hals	D van R	(Sold) fl 4:5 Ryers
1804/02/27	AMSCH	0161	*F. Hals* | Voor een Tafel waarop eenige Vruchten geplaatst zyn, ziet men een vrolyke Jongen, met een tros Druiven in zyn hand; bevallig gepenceeld in de manier van F. Hals	B	(Sold) fl 1:15 de Veer
1806/11/24	AMSCH	0087	*F. Hals* | Een Man, met een roode Kan in zyn handen, en een Hooivork op zyn Schouder; breed als F. Hals	Munnikhuizen	(Sold) fl 4:15 L Pakker
1809/07/25	HGBSM	0155	*Frans Hals* | Een lachende Man, zittende voor een tafel met een fles in de hand, in de manier van Frans Hals | *Mat:* op paneel *Size:* hoog 16, breed 14 en een half duim	D van der Aa	(Sold) fl 2:2 van der Aa
1810/06/06	RMMUY	0213	*F. Hals* | Een Lagchende Jongen. In de manier van F. Hals | *Mat:* op paneel		(Unknown) fl 0:6
1810/12/03	DOBRA	0038	*Frans Hals* | Een oude Vrouwepourtret, in de manier van Frans Hals		(Unknown)

Hamilton, Philipp Ferdinand de

1803/09/07	AMSCH	0087	*P. F. Hamilton* | Twee stuks met dood Gevogelte en Landschappen in het verschiet, uitvoerig op Doek [Deux tableaux, avec de la volaille tuée sur le devant et de beaux paysages en perspective ; largement peint] | *Mat:* op doek *Size:* hoog 14, breed 18 duim	Smidt	(Sold) fl 2:5 C S Roos
1803/09/07	AMSCH	0088	*P. F. Hamilton* | Twee stuks Landschappen met divers dood Gevogelte, delicaat als Wenix, op Doek geschilderd [Deux paysages avec de la volaille de differentes espèces ; d'une exécution aussi delicate que Wenix] | *Mat:* op doek *Size:* hoog 13, breed 17 duim	Smidt	(Sold) fl 3:5 Teengs

Hanneman, Adriaen

1810/06/06	RMMUY	0082	*J. Hanneman* | Twee Jongelingen bezig met Waterbellen te blazen. Meesterlijk en vast geschilderd | *Mat:* op doek		(Unknown) fl 12:5

Hannot, Johannes

1804/10/16	DLOND	0095	*J. Hannot* | Een Bloemstuk met Kapellen. Des Fleurs & des Papillons | *Mat:* op paneel *Size:* hoog 19, breed 15		(Unknown)

Hansen, Carel Lodewijk

1801/03/16	AMSCH	0012	*O.L. Hanzen* | Een Landschap, verbeeldende een gezicht te Eckst in Drenthe, gestoffeerd met een Vrouw by eenige Schaapen, meesterlyk behandeld | *Notes:* The artist's name was given as "O.L. Hanzen" but we have assumed this is an error.	P[ruyssenaar]	(Sold) fl 10:10 Valentijn
1802/05/05	AMSCH	0078	*C. L. Hansen* | Twee fraaije Ruïnes, de eene verbeeld de Abdy te Rhynsberg, de andere die van Brederode, gestoffeerd met Beelden en Schaapen, zonachtig geschilderd | *Size:* hoog 15, breed 20 duim	J	(Bought In) fl 8
1802/09/06	AMSCH	0054	*C. L. Hansen* | Twee Gezichten in 't Landschap Drenthe, fraay van licht en natuur | *Mat:* op doek *Size:* hoog 19, breed 19 duim	J	(Sold) fl 25:10 van Iperen
1802/12/13	AMSCH	0085	*C.L. Hanssen* | Twee stuks aangenamen Duinagtigen Landschappen, met Geboomten en Boere Wooningen, ryk gestoffeert met gaande en rustende Landlieden, aangenaam van Coloriet, zonagtig en uitvoerig gepenceeld | *Mat:* op paneel *Size:* hoog 9, breed 10 duim	Pruyssenaar [for] A	(Bought In) fl 20:10
1804/02/27	AMSCH	0055	*Hanssen. (C. L.)* | Twee stuks aangenaamen Landschappen, zynde Gezigten van de Ruïne, van 't Huys van Breedenrooden, en van d'Abdy van Rynsburg, byde ryk gestoffeert en zonachtig geschilderd | *Mat:* op doek *Size:* hoog 15, breed 20 duim	B	(Bought In) fl 9:10
1806/05/05	AMSCH	0065	*C. L. Hanssen* | Twee aangenaame Landschappen, zynde gezigten van de ruine van 't Huis Bredenroode, en van de Abtdy van Rhynsburgh; beide ryk gestoffeerd en bevallig geschildert door C. L. Hanssen | *Mat:* op doek *Size:* hoog 15, breed 20 duim	V[inkeles]	(Sold) fl 2:5 Gruyter

Hardimé

1802/11/01	DOBRA	0122	*Hardinier* | Twee met Bloemen | *Mat:* op doek *Size:* hoog 23, br. 16 duim	Paulus van der Spyk [or others]	(Unknown)

Hassel, van [Unidentified]

1808/12/30	HGIMM	[0071o]	*Van Hassel* | Voorts een exquis kabinetje Schilderijen van voorname Nederlandsche Meesters, welke uit hoofde van de kortheid des tijds niet		(Unknown)

stuk voor stuk kunnen beschreven worden; doch waarvan de beschrijving op den Kijkdag zal voorhanden zijn. Dus wij hier alleen de namen van eenige dier Meesters laten volgen, als: A. Kuyp, Ruysdaal, Karel du Jardyn, Loqwi ('t beste dat hij schilderde) Hondekoeter, van Dyk, Janson, Moesgever, Kamphuyzen, van Gooijen, A. van der Neer, T. Wyk, Huchtenburgh, Zolemaker, van Hassel, A. Vermeulen, van Dongen, Scheffer, van Os enz. | *This Lot:* Een Schilderij, Van Hassel *Notes:* Because this lot was not numbered in the catalogue, we have assigned the number.

Hauck, J.L. [Unidentified]

1802/05/11	GRGRW	0064	*J.L. Hauck* | De Gevangenneming van Koning Lodewijk den XVI [Deze zes door den beroemden Schilder J.L. Hauck] [Schilderijen met Olie-Verf; In Vergulde Lijsten] | *Mat:* in olyverf *Notes:* The bracketed information in the title about the artist appears in lot 69 and refers to lots 64 to 69. The bracketed information in the title about the medium appears above lot 1 and refers to lots 1 to 79a.	Arnold Sicco Werumeus	(Unknown) fl 43 for lots 64–69
1802/05/11	GRGRW	0065	*J.L. Hauck* | Deszelfs Verhoor voor de Nationale Conventie [Deze zes door den beroemden Schilder J.L. Hauck] [Schilderijen met Olie-Verf; In vergulde Lijsten] | *Mat:* in olyverf *Notes:* The bracketed information in the title about the artist appears in lot 69 and refers to lots 64 to 69. The bracketed information in the title about the medium appears above lot 1 and refers to lots 1 to 79a.	Arnold Sicco Werumeus	(Unknown) fl 43 for lots 64–69
1802/05/11	GRGRW	0066	*J.L. Hauck* | Zijn laatste Afscheid van de Familie [Deze zes door den beroemden Schilder J.L. Hauck] [Schilderijen met Olie-Verf; In Vergulde Lijsten] | *Mat:* in olyverf *Notes:* The bracketed information in the title about the artist appears in lot 69 and refers to lots 64 to 69. The bracketed information in the title about the medium appears above lot 1 and refers to lots 1 to 79a.	Arnold Sicco Werumeus	(Unknown) fl 43 for lots 64–69
1802/05/11	GRGRW	0067	*J.L. Hauck* | Zijne Terechtstelling [Deze zes door den beroemden Schilder J.L. Hauck] [Schilderijen met Olie-Verf; In Vergulde Lijsten] | *Mat:* in olyverf *Notes:* The bracketed information in the title about the artist appears in lot 69 and refers to lots 64 to 69. The bracketed information in the title about the medium appears above lot 1 and refers to lots 1 to 79a.	Arnold Sicco Werumeus	(Unknown) fl 43 for lots 64–69
1802/05/11	GRGRW	0068	*J.L. Hauck* | De Wegvoering van den Dauphin uit de armen zijner Moeder [Deze zes door den beroemden Schilder J.L. Hauck] [Schilderijen met Olie-Verf; In Vergulde Lijsten] | *Mat:* in olyverf *Notes:* The bracketed information in the title about the artist appears in lot 69 and refers to lots 64 to 69. The bracketed information in the title about the medium appears above lot 1 and refers to lots 1 to 79a.	Arnold Sicco Werumeus	(Unknown) fl 43 for lots 64–69
1802/05/11	GRGRW	0069	*J.L. Hauck* | De Wegvoering van Madame Elizabeth. Deze zes door den beroemden Schilder J.L. Hauck [Schilderijen met Olie-Verf; In Vergulde Lijsten] | *Mat:* in olyverf *Notes:* The information in the title about the artist refers to lots 64 to 69. The bracketed information in the title appears above lot 1 and refers to lots 1 to 79a.	Arnold Sicco Werumeus	(Unknown) fl 43 for lots 64–69

Heck, C. van der

1802/07/27	AKHRK	0037	*C. Heck* | De vermaarde Abtdij van Egmond in zijn volkomende welstand, met de Buurtkerk; met Figuurtjes gestoffeerd en zeer uitvoerig gepenseeld | *Mat:* op paneel *Size:* hoog 13 ½, breed 23 duim	Maria Stategaart	(Unknown) fl 34:10 for lots 37–39
1802/07/27	AKHRK	0038	*C. Heck* | Het slot van dien op den Hoef en Egmond Binnen, mede in zijn welstand en zeer uitvoerig | *Mat:* op paneel *Size:* hoog 13 ½, breed 23 duim	Maria Stategaart	(Unknown) fl 34:10 for lots 37–39
1802/07/27	AKHRK	0039	*C. Heck* | Egmond aan Zee, met de voormaalige Kerk | *Mat:* op paneel *Size:* hoog 13 ½, breed 23 duim	Maria Stategaart	(Unknown) fl 34:10 for lots 37–39
1802/07/27	AKHRK	0040	*C. Heck* | Een excellent en zeer bevallig Wintergezicht, zijnde een Stad en Dorpgezicht, met een groot Water, een menigte van Schaatsrijders op het IJs zich vermakende, zeer keurig en net geschilderd | *Mat:* op paneel *Size:* hoog 11 ¾, breed 16 ¾ duim	Maria Stategaart	(Sold) fl 12 for lots 40 & 41. Stroo
1802/07/27	AKHRK	0041	*C. Heck* | Een bergachtig Rhijnegezicht, waar in Watermolens, en een overvarende Pont, in dezelve Menschen en Melkvee, en beladen Ezel, voorts Wandelaars; aangenaam gestoffeerd | *Mat:* op paneel *Size:* hoog 11 ¾, breed 16 ¾	Maria Stategaart	(Sold) fl 12 for lots 40 & 41. Stroo
1802/07/27	AKHRK	0042	*C. Heck* | Een zeer bevallig Land en Watergezicht, op de voorgrond de barmhartige Samaritaan | *Size:* hoog 12, breed 17 duim	Maria Stategaart	(Sold) fl 6:5 for lots 42 & 43. Stad Loon
1802/07/27	AKHRK	0043	*C. Heck* | Een uitgestrekt Berg-en Rotsachtig Landschap, op de voorgrond het Bad van Diana, met de naakte Nimphen door Axtion bespied	Maria Stategaart	(Sold) fl 6:5 for lots 42 & 43. Stad Loon

Hecke, Jan van den (I)

1802/07/21	HGKAN	0116	*van der Hecke* | Een Schildery op paneel, verbeeldende een Jagtparty, door van der Hecke | *Mat:* op paneel *Size:* hoog 10 à 11 duym en breed 1 voet		(Unknown)
1804/10/16	DLOND	0096	*J. v. Hecke* | Een Tafel met een Smirna's Tapyt, waarop dood Wild. Du Gibier mort sur une Table couverte d'un Tapis de Smirne | *Mat:* op doek *Size:* hoog 29, breed 39		(Unknown)

			Heda		
1804/10/16	DLOND	0097	*Heda* | Een Gebraden Ham, met Brood, Beker, Mes, enz. Un Jambon avec du Pain, Verre, Couteau &c. | *Mat:* op paneel *Size:* hoog 18, breed 24		(Unknown)
1809/04/22	AMYVR	0172	*Heda* | Een fraai stil Leven	de Bruin	(Sold) fl 1 C S Roos
			Heda (manner)		
1803/04/20	AMSCH	0111	*Heda* | Een stil Leeven, op een Tafel staan Schootels met Vrugten en Spys, een Roemer met Wyn, en Zilvere Drinkschaal; fiks geschilderd als door Heda [Un composé d'objets inanimés comme plats avec fruit, coupe d'argent, vases à boire & autres objets, naturellement representés par Héda ou sa maniere.] | *Mat:* op paneel *Fmt:* rond	Maria Magdalena van Sluypwyk, gravinne van Moens	(Sold) fl 0:6 L Pakker
			Heda, Gerrit Willemsz.		
1802/06/16	AMSCH	0083	*J. Heda* | Een stil Leeven; op een Tafel, met een blauw Kleed en Linne Tafellaken gedekt, vertoond zich een Venezoen, Zilvere-Schootels met Oesters, Haring, geschilde Citroen en Brood: verder Zilver Schenkkan, Mostertpot, Zoutvat en gedreeven Beeker, Glaase, Roemer met Rhynse Wyn, en ander bywerk; alles ongemeen fraay, natuurlyk en uitvoerig gepenceeld | *Mat:* op doek *Size:* hoog 36, breed 46 duim	[Merrem]	(Sold) fl 41 B[d] Kooij
1802/06/28	AMSCH	0079	*G. Heda* | Een stil Leeven, fiks gepenceeld door G. Heda, op Panneel | *Mat:* op paneel	B	(Sold) fl 0:16 L Pakker
			Heem		
1801/08/19	AMSCH	0044	*de Heem* | Een stil Leeven; uitvoerig op Paneel | *Mat:* op paneel *Size:* hoog 9, breed 8 duim	Van Forreest	(Sold) fl 1 Pruijssenaar [for] R
1808/09/13	HABRU	0103	*de Heem* | Een Fles, in dezelve verscheide soort van Bloemen		(Unknown) fl 1:14
			Heem (copy after)		
1803/04/27	AMSCH	00GG[H]	*De Heem* | Een Stil Leven na de Heem | *Notes:* This lot was added in by hand in the LBDa copy of the catalogue.	C	(Sold) fl 5 Vermeulen
			Heem (manner)		
1801/10/19	AMSCH	0091	*de Heem* | Een Vruchtstukje, waarin een Oranje-Appel, Druive en roode Aalbessen, met Vlindertjes, als door de Heem | *Mat:* op paneel *Size:* hoog 10, breed 9 duim	Jonkheer Menno Baron van Coehoorn	(Sold) fl 1:15 Pruijssenaar
1802/09/06	AMSCH	0232	*de Heem* | Twee stuks een Bloem, en een Fruitstuk; als door de Heem	J	(Sold) fl 2:15 Boelen
1805/07/10	AMSCH	0185	*de Heem* | Een stil leven; op Paneel, als de Heem | *Mat:* op paneel *Notes:* This lot was sold with lot 186 by H. Witmont.	R[oos]	(Sold) fl 0:8 for lots 185 & 186. W[m] v d Schley
1807/08/26	AMSCH	0334	*de Heem* | Voor een Steenen Nis staat op de Rand een gedreven sierlyke Schaal, waarin een Tros witte Druiven en een Persik, waar nevens een Roemer met Wyn, ter zyde leggen eenige Vruchten en een Horologie; in de manier van de Heem	v d Schley [for] L	(Sold) fl 1:5 Levij Pakker
			Heem, Cornelis de		
1802/09/21	UTHDG	0045	*C. de Heem* | Blauwe en witte Druiftrossen, hangen de aan wijngaarden, langs een der Ranken klimt een Muis op. Natuurlijk geschildert		(Sold) fl 1:8 G Bierman Jacobie burg
1803/06/20	AMSCH	0027	*C. de Heem* | Op eene steene Balustrade, leggen verscheide Vrugten, als: Druiven, Granaatappelen, Vygen, Mispelen, en op een Tin Bord een geschilde Citroen; kragtig behandeld op Doek | *Mat:* op doek *Size:* hoog 25, breed 20 duim	Schley [for] G	(Sold) fl 15:10 De Meyer
1803/06/20	AMSCH	0039	*C. de Heem* | Aan een zyden Strik hangen een menigte fraaije Bloemen; alle zeen uitvoerig gepenceeld, op Doek | *Mat:* op doek *Size:* hoog 24, breed 20 duim	Schley [for] G	(Sold) fl 8 Gruiter
1803/09/07	AMSCH	0078	*C. de Heem* | Een Bloem- en Fruitstuk, op een Tafel staat een Kom, gevuld met verscheide Vruchten, op de Tafel op een blaauw kleed leggen drie Roosen, &c. fix en natuurlyk behandeld [Un assemblage de fleurs et de fruits sur une table, où l'on voit une soucoupe remplie de fruits et trois roses sur une draperie bleue etc. dessin bien ordonné, et peint au naturel] | *Mat:* op paneel *Size:* hoog 14, breed 16 duim	Smidt	(Sold) fl 12 Toselli
1804/08/08	AMSCH	0086	*C. de Heem* | Aan een Zyde Strik hangt een welgeördineerde party van schoone Bloemen; alleruitvoerigst geschilderd | *Mat:* op doek *Size:* hoog 24, breed 20 duim	Vink[eles] [for] K[=Gruyter?]	(Sold) fl 10:10 Kamphuizen
1805/10/09	HGBSM	0043	*C. de Heem* | Twee dito fruit stukken | *Mat:* op doek *Size:* hoog 17 breet 13 duim *Notes:* It is unclear what "dito" refers to in the title.	T H van Willigen [or others]	(Sold) fl 6 Van Giesen
1806/08/13	AMSCH	0073	*Heem. (C. de)* | Op een stenen Tafel gedeeltelyk met een Tapyt bedekt, staat een zilvere Schotel met diverse Vrugten, als Druiven, Persiken enz.; delicaat van penceelsbehandeling | *Mat:* op doek *Size:* hoog 28, breed 24 duim	Roos	(Bought In) fl 20
1806/08/20	HGBSM	0150	*C. de Heem* | Een Fruit Stuk | *Mat:* op doek op paneel *Size:* hoog 21 ½, breed 16 duim	Macalester Loup [or others]	(Sold) fl 1:10 Coclers
1806/08/20	HGBSM	0151	*C. de Heem* | Een Bloem Stuk met Vruchten en Insecten | *Mat:* op doek *Size:* hoog 26, breed 21 duim	Macalester Loup [or others]	(Sold) fl 1:2 Coclers

1806/11/24	AMSCH	0034	*Heem (C. de)* | Op een steene Tafel staat een Tinne schotel, waarop een Rivierkreeftje; terzyde een geschilde Citroen, eenige Druiven, Moerbeyen en Karssen; delicaat gepenceeld | *Mat:* op paneel *Size:* hoog 11, breed 15 duim *Notes:* This lot was misnumbered no. 24.	Munnikhuizen	(Sold) fl 10:10 Hulswit
1808/10/28	AMVRS	0017	*Heem. (C. de)* | Op een Tafel liggen verscheide zoorten van smakelijke Vrugten, als Kanteloep, witte en blaauwe Druiven, enz. benevens eenige keurige Bloemen, terzijde bij een Spiegel twee Vinken, zittende op een Wijngaard Rank. Zacht en teder gepenceeld | *Mat:* op doek *Size:* hoog 36, breed 46 duim	Marten Udink	(Sold) fl 20 Gruyter
1810/03/07	UTWLD	0035	*C. de Heem* | Een zeer uitvoerig bloemstuk | *Size:* hoog 2 voet 8 duim, breed 2 voet 3 duim	J J Woertman	(Unknown) fl 9:10
1810/06/06	RMMUY	0190	*C. de Heem* | Een stuk met Vrugten		(Unknown) fl 6:15
1810/06/20	AMSCH	0034a	*C. De Heem* | Op eene Tafel, met een Tapijt Kleed gedekt, staat een Porceleinen Pot en Schaal, waarbij verscheidene smakelijke Vruchten. Mals gepenceeld | *Mat:* op doek *Size:* hoog 46, breed 53 duimen	Y	(Sold) fl 31:10 Roos

Heem, Cornelis de (manner)

1802/11/01	DOBRA	0087	*Corn. de Heem* | Een Fruitstuk als Corn. de Heem | *Mat:* op doek	Paulus van der Spyk [or others]	(Sold) fl ¾ Rijswijk

Heem, David de

1802/09/06	AMSCH	0052	*D. de Heem* | In een capitaal Bloem- en Fruitstuk, ziet men blaauwe en witte Druyven, en andere smakelyke Vrugten, voorts roode Roozen en andere Bloemen, waarop Insecten aazen; delicaat | *Mat:* op doek *Size:* hoog 26, breed 22 duim	J	(Sold) fl 19 van Iperen
1808/06/13	AMSCH	0083	*Heem (D. de)* | Op een Tafel staat een Schotel met Oesters, en een met een Kreeft, ter zijde een Glas, met een geschilde Citroen en verder bijwerk. Alles uitmuntend en van de beste behandeling van dezen Meester | *Mat:* op doek *Size:* hoog 29, breed 34 duim	E M Engelberts	(Sold) fl 72 van Os
1808/08/23	AMSCH	0079	*Heem. (D. de)* | Voor een Nis staat een steene Voetstuk, waar op geplaast is een zilver Schenkbord, met verschillende soorten van geurige Bloemen, met Steel en Bladeren, en eenige Karssen, waar op verscheiden Insecten aazen; zeer natuurlijk en uitvoerig gepenceeld | *Mat:* op doek *Size:* hoog 25, breed 20 duim	[Van Iperen?]	(Sold) fl 31 Th Spaan
1810/10/11	AMSCH	0132	*D. De Heem* | Een Tafel, waarop een Mand met Vruchten | *Mat:* op doek	[Gruyter?]	(Sold) fl 0:10 L Pakker

Heem, David de (and Schut, C. (I))

1808/06/13	AMSCH	0149	*Heem (D. de); J. Schut* | Christus in de schoot van Maria, waarbij eenige Engelen: deze Ordonantie is omgeven met Guirlandes van Bloemen, allen toepasselijk op het Lijden. Dit Stuk is even grootsch van onderwerp als behandeling | *Mat:* op doek *Size:* hoog 53, breed 47 duim *Notes:* The second artist's name was given as "J. Schut" but we have assumed this is an error.	E M Engelberts	(Sold) fl 30 Engelberts
1808/08/23	AMSCH	0078	*Heem. (D. de); J. Schut* | Eene schoone en bevallige Ordonantie van onderscheidene soorten van Bloemen, kunstig en met smaak zamengeschikt, en in het midden een Bijbelsche Ordonantie, door de beroemde J. Schut geschilderd, versierd dit heerlijk schilderij | *Mat:* op doek *Size:* hoog 53, breed 47 duim *Notes:* The second artist's name was given as "J. Schut" but we have assumed this is an error.	J	(Sold) fl 11 Hulswit

Heem, G. de [Unidentified]

1805/07/10	AMSCH	0071	*G. de Heem* | Een Tafel met een ménigte Vrugten | *Mat:* op doek	V[inkeles] [for] K	(Sold) fl 16 L Pakker

Heem, Jan Davidsz. de

1801/04/23	AMYVR	0007	*J. de Heem* | Een stil Leeven, op Tafel met een Tapyt bedekt, ziet men eenige Vruchten, een Bord met Garnaalen en ander Bywerk, benevens, twee Glaase Roemers, zeer fraay en natuurlyk op Paneel | *Mat:* op paneel *Size:* hoog 34, breed 24 duim		(Sold) fl 39 ½ Coclaire
1801/08/19	AMSCH	0043	*J. D. de Heem* | Op een Tafel met een kleed gedeeltelyk bedekt, staat een Porceleine Kom en zilver Bord, waar op verscheide zoorten van Vruchten, Bocaal en verder bywerk; uitvoerig gepenceeld, op Doek | *Mat:* op doek *Size:* hoog 19, breed 25 duim	Mevr Hogguer	(Bought In) fl 36
1802/04/13	HAVIN	0020	*J. D. de Heem* | Een steene Tafel met vrugten, en een Roemer, extra fraai en uitvoerig		(Unknown)
1802/07/27	AKHRK	0046	*J. D. de Heem* | Een Tafel waar op liggen verschillende zoorten van Bloemen, alle op de aangenaamste wijze, geschikt en goed geschilderd | *Mat:* op doek *Size:* hoog 25 ½, breed 20 ¾ duim	Maria Stategaart	(Sold) fl 10 Meyer
1802/09/29	AMSCH	0020	*J. D. de Heem* | Een Fruitstuk, hoog 39, breed 30 ½ duim. Doek. Dit Tafereel is van de beste Penceelbehandeling van deezen beroemden Konstenaar. By eenig geboomten ziet men voor een vervallene muur, op eenige Steenen van onderscheiden couleuren geplaatst, witte Paarl en lange roode Muscadel Druiven, met rank en bladeren, groote Noten en Haselnoten, een Tak Moerbesiën, eenige Bloemen, Turkse Tarwe, onderscheide andere Vrugten, Koornäiren, Eyke Takken met couleurige	[Labouchere?]	(Sold) fl 260 Pruijssenaar

			bladeren, Champignonts. Voorts eenige Insecten, een fraai Vogeltje, een Slang, Hagedis, Slakken, Sprinkhanen, enz. Alles als de natuur zelve met de zuiverste uitvoerigheid verbeeld; dit Stuk is capitaal en van eene schoone Ordenantie [L'oeuil des Curieux & des naturalistes trouvent ample matiere à satisfaire leurs inclinations chéries, dans la contemplation de ce chef d'oeuvre de l'art. – Ce qui le fait surtout admirer, comme un Tableau râre & trés précieux, c'est la parfaite exécution de cette riche composition, une des plus belles & des plus capitales de cet artiste. Les Fruits les plus exquis y ont servis de modele, ainsi que des Insectes de divers genres & une infinité d'autres objets qui sont groupés au bas du Tableau sur des pierres de diverses couleurs contre une muraille derriere la quelle quelques arbres, se détachent sur un ciel nuageux.] | *Mat:* op doek *Size:* hoog 39, breed 30 ½ duim		
1802/09/29	AMSCH	0021	*J. D. de Heem* | Een Bloemstuk, hoog 32, breed 26 duim. Doek. Op eenen steenen Tafel ziet men eenen geribde glaze Caraf geplaatst, met schoone bevallige Bloemen, als roode, witte en geele Roozen, met knop en bladeren, Pioen Rozen, Tulpen, Papaveren, Iriassen, Angelieren, enz. waarop Insecten; alles is byzonder natuurlyk verbeeld, door een zeer delicaat en uitvoerig Penceel; zynde dit Schildery mede als het voorgaande, van de beste Werken van dezen kunstryken Meester [Ce Tableau exécuté avec une delicatesse râre offre les plus belles fleurs comme Roses de différentes Espéces Tulipes, Pavôts, oeuillets & plusieurs autres, placées avec intelligence, dans une Bouteille de verre, sur une Table de pierre grise ; l'on remarque encore différentes Insectes, voltigeans & attachés sur les feuilles & les fleurs. Ce sujet fait le plus grand plaisir étant rendu avec beaucoup de vérité. C'est une des plus belle productions de cet Habile artiste.] | *Mat:* op doek *Size:* hoog 32, breed 26 duim	[Labouchere?]	(Sold) fl 295 Coclers
1802/11/01	DOBRA	0165	*Jan Davidsz. de Heem* | Een Taafel, waar op een Porcelaine Schotel, met Vrugten; op den kant der Tafel het Portrait van den Meester; door Jan Davidsz. de Heem. 1628 | *Mat:* op paneel *Size:* hoog 12 ½, breed 15 ½ duim *Inscr:* Jan Davidsz. de Heem. 1628 (dated?) *Notes:* It is unclear whether the name and date are inscribed on the painting.		(Sold) fl 2:10 Hofman
1802/12/13	AMSCH	0076	*J. de Heem* | Op een Tafel ziet men een meenigte keurigen Vrugten, als: blaauwe en witte Druyven, Citroen en Carstanjes en verder Bywerk, delicaat gepenceeld | *Mat:* op doek *Size:* hoog 20, breed 26 duim	Pruyssenaar [for] A	(Sold) fl 0:6 L Pakker
1803/06/20	AMSCH	0019	*J. D. de Heem* | Op een Steene Tafel staat een Fles, gevuld met éen ménigte geurige Bloemen, waarop verscheiden Insecten geplaatst zyn, eenige Karssen, Bessen en Brambozen verceiren dit in alle deelen delicaat gepenceelde Schildery, door J. D. de Heem, vervaardigd op Doek | *Mat:* op doek *Size:* hoog 29, breed 23 duim	Schley [for] G	(Sold) fl 99 Pruijssenaar
1803/09/07	AMSCH	0076	*J. D. de Heem* | Een stil leeven, op een Tafel met een kleed bedekt, staat een Porcelyne Schootel, met verscheide Vrugten, daar neevens een Porcelyne Pot en Bocaal, ter zyde een Zilver Schenkbord, waar op eenige Vrugten, Brood en Roemer met Wyn geplaatst is, alles is Natuurlyk, en van een uitvoerige penceel behandeling [Un intérieur, représentant une table, sur laquelle un plat de porcelaine rempli de differentes espèces de fruits, à côté un pot et un bocal ; une soucoupe d'argent, chargée de quelques fruits et de pain avec un verre à la Romaine plein de vin : le tout est d'une touche naturelle, largement peint et d'un très bon effet] | *Mat:* op doek *Size:* hoog 29, breed 41 duim	Smidt	(Sold) fl 68 Jan Yver
1803/09/07	AMSCH	0077	*J. D. de Heem* | Twee stuks Stilleevens, zynde Tafels waarop Roemers met Wyn, een menigte smakelyke Vruchten, Oesters, Citroenen, &c. alles met de natuur overeenkomende, gepenceeld op paneel [Deux intérieurs, offrant des tables chargées de verres à la Romaine et pleins de vin, de fruits appetissans, des citrons etc. le tout peint au naturel et du plus bel effet] | *Mat:* op paneel *Size:* yder hoog 18, breed 13 ½ duim *Notes:* The dimensions are given in the French edition as "Hauts 18, larges 33 1/4 pouces"; the width has been changed by hand to "13 ½" in the RKDH copy of the catalogue.	Smidt	(Bought In) fl 110
1803/12/15	MGLAC	0001	*J. D. de Heem* | Een extra fraay en uitvoerig Stuk, met Vrugten en Oesters, op een Steene Tafel | *Mat:* op paneel *Size:* hoog duim 24, breed duim 29	Mr L H de Haze Bomme	(Unknown)
1804/02/27	AMSCH	0053	*Heem. (Jan de)* | Op een Tafel met een kleed bedekt, staat een Porcelynen Schotel met een Kreeft en eenige Crabben, neffens dezelve een Kan en Roemer en eenigen Vrugten, waar achter een Vaas met Bloemen, en verder bywerk; meesterlyk geschilderd | *Mat:* op doek *Size:* hoog 41, breed 54 duim	B	(Sold) fl 3:5 Oostwijn
1804/02/27	AMSCH	0054	*Heem. (J. D. de)* | Eenige wel geschakeerde Bloemen op een Zilver Schenkbord; fraai gepenceeld | *Mat:* op doek *Size:* hoog 25, breed 20 duim	B	(Sold) fl 11 La Bouchere
1804/07/25	AMSCH	0040	*Heem. (J. D. de)* | Op een Tafel met een blaauw Kleed bedekt ziet men een menigte van Vruchten, als blaauwe en witte Druiven, Kersen, Appelen, Citroenen en Vygen, op een Tinne Schootel leggen; alles is natuurlyk, delicaat en uitvoerig gepenceeld | *Mat:* op paneel *Size:* hoog 19 ½, breed 17 duim		(Sold) fl 40 Vinkeles
1804/07/25	AMSCH	0041	*Heem (J. D. de)* | Op een met een groen Kleed gedekte Tafel, staat een opengesneden Ham, Oesters, een Citroen en eenige Vrugten op Zilvere		(Sold) fl 50 C S Roos

			Schotelen, agter dezelve een Mand met Vrugten, een Zilvere Kan en Beeker, door een opening ziet men een Zeegezicht by een Stads Tooren; alles is meesterlyk fraai en met de natuur overeenkomend gepenceeld | *Mat:* op doek *Size:* hoog 23, breed 35 duim		
1804/07/25	AMSCH	0042	*Heem (J. D. de)* | Op een dito [met een groen Kleed gedekte] Tafel ziet men mede een Mand met Vrugten, gevuld met Druiven, Granaatappelen, Citroenen enz. een Zilvere Schotel met Oesters, een Broodje, en Drinkschalen; niet minder fraai van schildering als de voorgaande | *Mat:* op doek *Size:* hoog 23, breed 32 duim *Notes:* It is unclear what "dito" refers to in the title.		(Sold) fl 121 Izaac Smit
1804/10/16	DLOND	0098	*J. de Heem* | Enige Vruchten, met een Papegaay. Un Perroquet & quelques Fruits | *Mat:* op paneel *Size:* hoog 11, breed 16		(Unknown)
1805/07/10	AMSCH	0072	*J. D. de Heem* | Aan een fraaije Strik ziet men eenige fraay geschakelde Bloemen, als roode en witte Roosen, Linten, enz.; delicaat op Doek | *Mat:* op doek *Size:* hoog 26, breed 21 duim	V[inkeles] [for] N	(Sold) fl 14:10 Hulswit
1805/10/09	HGBSM	0024	*J. de Heem* | Een groot stuk, waarin een tafel met allerley fruit, muziek instrumenten, goude en zilvere beekers, koelvat met flesje, een landschap in 't verschiet, zeer fraay geschildert | *Mat:* op doek *Size:* hoog 58 breet 79 duim	T H van Willigen [or others]	(Sold) fl 30 Ph Mey
1805/10/09	HGBSM	0119	*J. D. de Heem* | In een steene nis staat een paarlemoure schaal, cierlyk met zilver beslagen, waar op eenige vrugten en bloemen onder op de nis leggen, roode en witte druiven, en andere vrugten waar op insecten aasen, uitvoerig geschildert door J.D. de Heem | *Mat:* op paneel *Size:* hoog 29 breet 22 duim	T H van Willigen [or others]	(Sold) fl 10 Ph Mey
1806/08/13	AMSCH	0072	*Heem. (J. D. de)* | Op een steenen Tafel, ziet men een zilvere Schotel met eenige Oesters, een Orange-appel, Citroen, Druiven, Karsen en andere Vrugten, waarop Insecten aazen; zeer natuurlyk, en uitvoerig gepenceeld | *Mat:* op doek *Size:* hoog 16 ½, breed 14 duim	Yver	(Bought In) fl 18:10
1806/08/13	AMSCH	0337	*Heem. (J. D. de)* | Op een Tafel met een Tapyt Kleed bedekt, ziet men een ménigte van Vruchten waarby een Bord, Roemer Wyn; en divers; delicaat en meesterlyk geschilderd | *Mat:* op paneel *Size:* hoog 20, breed 18 duim	Vinkeles [for] J	(Sold) fl 21 Scheepens
1807/08/26	AMSCH	0094	*J.D. de Heem* | Op een Tafel, gedeeltelyk met een groen Kleed bedekt, staat een Zilveren Schootel, waar op een Kreeft, open Granaat Appel en Citroen geplaast zyn, verder Zilvere Beeker, Druiven, Oesters, Brood, Roemer en Wynschaal; uitvoerig van Penceelsbehandeling | *Mat:* op paneel *Size:* hoog 18, breed 28 duim	Helsdinge	(Sold) fl 31 Spruit
1807/08/26	AMSCH	0095	*J.D. de Heem* | In een Landschap met Geboomte, by de stam van een Boom leggen verscheide Vrugten, als: Kantaloup, Persikken, Druiven, Pruimen, en andere Vrugten, en Plantgewas, waarop Insecten aazen, natuurlyk, kragtig en meesterlyk fraai gepenceeld | *Mat:* op doek *Size:* hoog 35, breed 28 duim	Helsdinge	(Sold) fl 23 Jozi
1807/08/26	AMSCH	0096	*J.D. de Heem* | Op een Tafel ziet men een Zilver Bord, benevens een Zilveren Wynkan, een omgevallen Houten Bierkan, Wyn Roemer en verder bywerk; uitvoerig van schildering	Helsdinge	(Sold) fl 8:10 Coclair
1808/06/06	RMRIJ	0048	*Heem. (Jan Davidsz. de)* | Eene ongemeen rijke en prachtige Schilderij met een aantal differente uitgelezene Vruchten, Insekten en meerder bijwerk op eene blaauwe marmeren tafel. Alleruitvoerigst en schoon geschilderd [Ce Tableau offre une Composition choisie et riche de toutes fortes de fruits, d'insectes et d'autres accessoires. Du plus grand fini, et un des plus beaux le cet Artiste] | *Mat:* op doek *Size:* Hoog 32, en breed 24 ½ duim *Loc:* Amsterdam, Nederland, Rijksmuseum, (A 139)	Gerrit van der Pot, Heer van Groeneveld	(Sold) fl 385 Johs Eck en Zoon [for] le Roi
1808/06/06	RMRIJ	0049	*Heem. (Jan Davidsz. de)* | Eene tafel, waarop eene Porceleinen Schaal met differente Vruchten, benevens eene Kreeft. Insekten en verder bijwerk. Krachtig, uitvoerig en gloeijend geschilderd [Autre Tableau du même genre, representant de beaux fruits bien choisis, arrangés sur un plat de porcelaine posé sur une Table de marbre. Des Insectes, un Homar etc. ornent cette belle Composition d'un fini précieux] | *Mat:* op doek *Size:* Hoog 27, en breed 22 ¼ duim	Gerrit van der Pot, Heer van Groeneveld	(Sold) fl 460 J M Jorissen [for] le Roi
1808/10/28	AMVRS	0018	*Heem (J. de)* | Op een Houten Tafel, met een groen Fluweel Kleed overdekt, ziet men verscheide Vruchten, benevens een opgesneden Ham, Kreeft, Schotel met Garnalen en Krab, een Zilveren Drenkschaal, Roemer met Wijn, en andere Glazen. Alles is natuurlijk, en op het naauwkeurigste uitgedrukt | *Mat:* op doek *Size:* hoog 29, breed 40 duim	Marten Udink	(Sold) fl 71 Van Iperen
1808/11/28	AMSCH	0027	*J. de Heem* | Op een Tafel, gedeeltelijk met een Paars Kleed bedekt, staat een Zilvere Schotel, waaar [sic] op een geschilde Citroen en Abrikosen geplaast zijn, agter dezelven staat een Porcelijne Kom en Schaal, waar op Druiven, Pruimen, Nooten en andere Vrugten, ter zijde een Glaze Fluit en ander bijwerk, uitvoerig en van de beste Penceelsbehandeling | *Mat:* op doek *Size:* hoog 18, breed 25 duim	C	(Sold) fl 40 du Pree
1810/06/06	RMMUY	0055	*J. Davidz de Heem* | Eene steene Tafel, op dezelve blaauwe en witte Druiven, Abricoosen en Pruimen, benevens een porcelleine Kan, een Glas en een Schotel met een geschilde Citroen &c, alles delicaat behandeld | *Mat:* op paneel		(Unknown) fl 28
1810/07/23	DOLG1	0027	*J.D. de Heem* | Een Fruitstuk. Op- en nevens een Zilveren Fruit-Schaal liggen onderscheidene Vruchten, op welke hier en daar eenige Insecten	Mr Pieter van den Santheuvel	(Sold) fl 45 P de Heere à Dordt

			gevonden worden. Zeer kunstig en delicaat geschilderd | *Mat:* op paneel *Size:* hoog 23, breed 17 ½ duim		
1810/07/23	DOLG1	0028	*J.D. de Heem* | Een Bloemstuk. In eene glazen Vaas zijn onderscheiden soorten van Bloemen. Niet minder dan 't vorige stuk [nr.27] | *Mat:* op paneel *Size:* hoog 20, breed 15 duim	Mr Pieter van den Santheuvel	(Sold) fl 50 J de Visser
1810/07/23	DOLG2	0036	*J.D. de Heem* | Op een tafel ziet men een tinnen bord, waar op liggen gekookte Krabben. Verder bij een groen zijden kleed Vruchten, een glazen Pokaal, en verdere Sieraden. Zeer uitvoerig geschilderd | *Mat:* op paneel *Size:* hoog 19, breed 15 duim	Pieter Quinting	(Unknown) fl 13:15
1810/08/06	AMSCH	0042	*Heem (J.D. de)* | Op eene Tafel, met een opgeschoven Kleed gedekt, staat een Porcelijnen Pot, een dito Schotel met onderscheidene Vrugten, en een Roemer Rijnsche Wijn; alles is van eene delicate penceels behandeling | *Mat:* op doek *Size:* hoog 29, breed 40 duimen	F	(Bought In) fl 29

Heem, Jan Davidsz. de (and Teniers)

1810/08/01	AMSCH	0099	*Teniers (David); Jan Davidszoon de Heem* | Een Boerenschuur, waarin onderscheiden voorraad van Aard- en Boomvruchten, Vaatwerk, koperen Ketels, Koornmaat en verdere voorwerpen, verlevendigd met eenen Landman, Jongeling en eene Vrouw [Vue intérieure d'une grange, dans laquelle on voit un nombre de differents Fruits et de Légumes, ainsi que des ustenciles et des Meubles de Ménage. Cet ensemble est embelli par trois figures, étant un Cultivateur, un Jeunehomme et une Femme sortant par la porte] | *Annots:* Passable. (NGW) *Mat:* op paneel *Size:* hoog 19, breed 24 duimen *Loc:* Los Angeles, CA, USA. Los Angeles County Museum of Art. (M.72.67.1)	Mr Pieter de Smeth van Alphen	(Bought In) fl 1000

Heemskerck

1801/02/18	AMBOS	0068	*Heemskerk* | Een Gezelschap van Boeren	J Schonevelt	(Unknown)
1801/12/22	AMOTT	0030	*Heemskerk* | 2 stuks, een Groenteverkooper en een Binnestalling met Beesten, georneerd door veelerhande Keukengereedschap	Bartholomeus Ruloffs	(Unknown) fl 6
1802/06/28	AMSCH	0078	*Heemskerk* | Twee stuks gestoffeerde Boeren Binnehuizen, op Panneel | *Mat:* op paneel *Size:* hoog 13, breed 10 duim	Anna Elink	(Sold) fl 2 Boelen
1802/08/24	LNDLS	0047	*Heemskerk* | In een Binnen-vertrek zit een Vrouwtje met een Kind op haar schoot, nevens een Wieg, terwijl een Man nevens haar zijn pijp rookt, agterwaards eenigen die bij het vuur zitten | *Mat:* op doek *Size:* hoog 10, breed 13 duimen	Leonardus Bouman [or others]	(Unknown) fl 22
1802/09/21	UTHDG	0041	*Heemskerk* | Een Boer met zijn gezin, bid voor de Maaltijd die op een omgekeerde Tob gereed staat. Goed geschildert | *Mat:* op doek *Size:* hoog 9, breed 7 duimen		(Sold) fl 5:10 Verhoude
1802/11/01	DOBRA	0045	*Heemskerk* | Twee stukjes met Boertjes, enz.	Paulus van der Spyk [or others]	(Bought In) fl 13
1802/11/01	DOBRA	0046	*Heemskerk* | Twee dito [stukjes met Boertjes]	Paulus van der Spyk [or others]	(Sold) fl 14 M v Steegh
1802/11/01	DOBRA	0109	*Heemskerk* | Een Boeren binnenhuis, met rookende en drinkende Boeren, fraay van Ordonnantie | *Mat:* op doek *Size:* hoog 23 breed 33 ½ duim	Paulus van der Spyk [or others]	(Unknown)
1803/07/07	HGKAN	0005	*Heemskerk* | Vyf stuks zynde de vyf Zinnen, door Heemskerk, op Paneel [Schilderyen in Olyverf] | *Mat:* in olyverf op paneel *Notes:* The bracketed information in the title appears above lot 1 and refers to lots 1 to 25.		(Unknown)
1803/09/07	AMSCH	0089	*Heemskerk* | Twee stuks met vrolyke Boeren; fix en natuurlyk op Paneel [Deux tableaux représentant des villageois qui s'égaient ; d'une touche legère naturelle et vraie] | *Mat:* op paneel *Size:* hoog 9, breed 8 duim	Smidt	(Sold) fl 5:10 Gruiter
1804/02/27	AMSCH	0057	*Heemskerk* | Twee stuks Landschappen, by Ruine ziet men een menigte Vee, waarby hun Herders, verders een aangenaam verschiet | *Mat:* op doek *Size:* ieder hoog 15, breed 18 duim	D	(Sold) fl 10 De Meijer
1806/05/05	AMSCH	0066	*Heemskerck* | Twee stuks met zingende en drinkende Boertjes en dito Huisraad; uitvoerig behandeld door Heemskerck op Paneel | *Mat:* op paneel *Size:* hoog 9, breed 8 duim *Notes:* It is unclear what "dito" refers to in the title.	V[inkeles]	(Sold) fl 3:10 Grauu
1806/06/07	RMHSN	0040	*Heemskerk* | Een Keuken waar in allerlei Groentens, Beelden &c. | *Mat:* op doek	A E K L	(Unknown)
1806/06/07	RMHSN	0122	*Heemskerk* | Een met Rookende en Drinkende Boeren	A E K L	(Unknown)
1808/06/11	RMRIJ	0089	*Heemskerk* | Een Leering zegt by den Meester zyn Les op | *Mat:* op paneel *Size:* hoog 6 ¾, breed 6 duim		(Sold) fl 7:10 Rohan [or] Van Leen
1808/11/28	AMSCH	0036	*Heemskerk* | Een Boeren Chirurgijns Winkel, met verscheide Huislieden gestoffeerd, op de voorgrond zit een Patient, welke het Hoofd verbonden word, geestig behandeld | *Mat:* op paneel *Size:* hoog 16, breed 21 duim	S	(Sold) fl 16:10 J Smits
1810/06/06	RMMUY	0197	*Heemskerk* | Twee, met Figuren | *Mat:* op paneel		(Unknown) fl 5:10
1810/06/06	RMMUY	0230	*Heemskerk* | Twee met Boeren | *Mat:* op paneel		(Unknown) fl 1:10
1810/06/20	AMSCH	0150	*Heemskerk* | Twee stuks Boeren Huisgezinnen, met verscheidene Lieden	B	(Sold) fl 0:8 T Spaan
1810/06/20	AMSCH	0180	*Heemskerk* | Een Boer, houdende eene Kat in den Arm	A	(Sold) fl 1 J Stam
1810/10/11	AMSCH	0176	*Heemskerk* | Een Boer	[Levy Pakker?]	(Sold) fl 1:10 Vallee

Heemskerck (manner)

1807/10/12	MGBEO	0005	*Heemskerk* | Een Verbeeldende eenige Liedjeszangers, in de manier van Heemskerk | *Mat:* op paneel	Hermannus Johannes Heyman	(Sold) £ 0:11 Meertens

Heemskerck, Bastiaan

1802/09/06	AMSCH	0199	*de Boeren Heemskerk* | Twee stuks Binnenhuizen, gestoffeerd met vrolyke Huislieden	Spaan	(Sold) fl 0:6 L Pakker
1803/08/17	AMSCH	0038	*Heemskerk (S.)* | Twee Landschappen met Ruïnes en Geboomten, ryk gestoffeerd met Beelden en Beesten, meesterlyk behandeld | *Mat:* op doek *Size:* ieder hoog 14, breed 17 duim	Anna Catharina Putman	(Sold) fl 18 Haffner
1803/08/17	AMSCH	0039	*Heemskerk (S.)* | Twee dito [Landschappen] Voorwerpen, in alles als de voorgaande | *Mat:* op doek *Size:* ieder hoog 17, breed 22 duim *Notes:* It is unclear what "dito" refers to in the title.	Anna Catharina Putman	(Sold) fl 12 Hodges
1805/07/03	AMSCH	0183	*de Boere Heemskerk* | Twee stuks Boere Binnenhuizen, geestig geordineerd en geschilderd op Paneel | *Mat:* op paneel	R[oos]	(Sold) fl 15:10 L Pakker
1808/08/23	AMSCH	0267	*de boere Heemskerk* | Twee stuks Binnenhuisen met vrolijke Boeren Boeren en Boerinnen, welke zig met dansen rooken en drinken vermaken, geestig door de boere Heemskerk	[Van Iperen?]	(Sold or Bought In) fl 6:10 Van Iperen

Heemskerck, Bastiaan (manner)

1801/03/16	AMSCH	0150	*de Boere Heemskerk* | Twee stuks, met rokende Boer en drinkende Boerin, als de Boere Heemskerk	K[ip]	(Sold) fl 0:18 Roelofs
1802/09/06	AMSCH	0248	*de Boere Heemskerk* | Eenige vrolyke Boeren, en een Boerin in een Binnenhuis, zittende by een tafel; in de manier van de Boere Heemskerk	Wed Grave [or others]	(Sold) fl 0:18 L Pakker

Heemskerck, Jan

1806/10/16	UTWLD	0009	*J. Heemskerk* | Twee stuks Landschappen, met staande en leggende Ossen, Bokken en Schapen door J. Heemskerk	Mr P de Malapert [or] W Beeldsnyder	(Unknown)
1808/06/11	RMRIJ	0043	*J: Heemskerk* | Een Binnehuis, waar in een menigte van drinkende-dronken- speelende en danzende Boeren en Boerennen [sic], breed geschilderd en van een goede koleur en effect | *Mat:* op doek *Size:* hoog 29, breed 25 duim		(Sold) fl 22 Thomas

Heemskerck, Maerten van

1804/07/25	DLGRO	0034	*M. Heemskerk* | Een Boeren binnen Huis vol gewoel, met een vrolyk gezelschap om den Haard staande en zittende, een Boer die een Boerin wil zoenen; in 't geheel negen Beelden, op de voorgrond een Haan en twee Hennen, een party Wortelen, Kool en andere Groentens, fraai en uitvoerig geschilderd door M. Heemskerk | *Mat:* op doek *Size:* hoog 11, breed 13 duim *Notes:* The artist was presumably Egbert van Heemskerck (I) and not Maerten van Heemskerck.	Mr Franc van der Burch Wz.	(Unknown)
1804/10/16	DLOND	0099	*M. van Heemskerk* | Een Vrouwe Portrait met een Kraag. Un Portrait de Femme avec un Collet | *Mat:* op paneel *Size:* hoog 14, breed 11		(Unknown)
1805/10/09	HGBSM	0059	*M. Heemskerk* | Een gezelschap van vrolyke boeren, in een binnehuis | *Mat:* op paneel *Size:* hoog 29 ½ breet 25 ½ duim *Notes:* The artist was presumably Egbert van Heemskerck (I) and not Maerten van Heemskerck.	T H van Willigen [or others]	(Sold) fl 4 Zwartsman
1805/10/09	HGBSM	0060	*M. Heemskerk* | Een dito [boeren] vrolyk gezelschap | *Mat:* op doek *Size:* hoog 29 ½ breet 25 ½ duim *Notes:* The artist was presumably Egbert van Heemskerck (I) and not Maerten van Heemskerck. It is unclear what "dito" refers to in the title.	T H van Willigen [or others]	(Sold) fl 4 Basemoine
1806/08/20	HGBSM	0022	*M. Heemskerk* | Een Boeren gezelschap zittende te zingen | companion to lot 23 *Mat:* op doek *Size:* hoog 8 ¾, breed 11 ½ duim *Notes:* The artist was presumably Egbert van Heemskerck (I) and not Maerten van Heemskerck.	Macalester Loup [or others]	(Sold) fl 25:5 for lots 22 & 23. Gram
1806/08/20	HGBSM	0023	*M. Heemskerk* | Een dito [Boeren gezelschap] | companion to lot 22 *Mat:* op doek *Notes:* The artist was presumably Egbert van Heemskerck (I) and not Maerten van Heemskerck. It is unclear what "dito" refers to in the title.	Macalester Loup [or others]	(Sold) fl 25:5 for lots 22 & 23. Gram

Heemskerk, H. van [Unidentified]

1804/07/25	DLGRO	0077	*H. van Heemskerk* | Een stuk met Vruchten | *Mat:* op doek *Size:* hoog 9, breed 12 duim	Mr Franc van der Burch Wz.	(Unknown)

Heer, Gerrit Adriaensz. de (manner)

1808/06/13	AMSCH	0244	*de Heer* | Eene Tafel, waarop onderscheidene voorwerpen, als een Doodshoofd, Vazen, Globe, en eenig toebereid Gevogelte; fraai, als door de Heer	K	(Sold) fl 6 Glad

Heeremans, Thomas

1801/04/08	HAVIN	0035	*Heeremans* | Een Gezigt op de Stad Leyden		(Unknown)
1801/04/08	HAVIN	0051	*Heeremans* | Twee Gezigten, Overschie en .... plaisant		(Unknown)
1801/12/22	AMOTT	0053	*Heeremans* | 1 Brug over een stil water, in een boere Landschap	Bartholomeus Ruloffs	(Unknown) fl 2
1802/04/13	HAVIN	0031	*F. Heeremans* | Een Zomer en Winter, plaizant		(Unknown)

1802/05/11	GRGRW	0027	*P. Heermans* | Een Boerendorp aan strand [Schilderijen met Olie-Verf; In zwarte Lijsten] | companion to lot 28 *Mat:* in olyverf *Notes:* The artist's name was given as "P. Heermans" but we have assumed this is an error. The bracketed information in the title appears above lot 1 and refers to lots 1 to 79a.	Arnold Sicco Werumeus	(Unknown)
1802/05/11	GRGRW	0028	*P. Heermans* | Een dito [Boerendorp], tot een weerga [Schilderijen met Olie-Verf; In zwarte Lijsten] | companion to lot 27 *Mat:* in olyverf *Notes:* The artist's name was given as "P. Heermans" but we have assumed this is an error. The bracketed information in the title about the medium appears above lot 1 and refers to lots 1 to 79a.	Arnold Sicco Werumeus	(Unknown)
1802/05/11	GRGRW	0030	*Frans Heermans* | Een dito [deel Volks bij ene Herberg] [Schilderijen met Olie-Verf; In zwarte Lijsten] | *Mat:* in olyverf *Notes:* The bracketed information in the title about the medium appears above lot 1 and refers to lots 1 to 79a.	Arnold Sicco Werumeus	(Unknown)
1802/05/24	HGBAK	0045	*F. Mans* | Een Boeren Kermis, op een Dorp in de Veenen, daar de Gans getrokken word, fraay en ryk van ordonnantie, door F. Mans 1678, hoog 1 voet 10 duim, breed 2 v. 7d., panneel, ebbenh. lyst | companion to lot 46 *Mat:* op paneel *Size:* hoog 1 voet 10 duim, breed 2 voet 7 duim *Inscr:* F. Mans 1678 (signed and dated?) *Notes:* It is unclear whether the name and date are inscribed on the painting.	Mejuffrouw A van der Mieden	(Sold) fl 12:5 for lots 45 & 46. Ondorp
1802/05/24	HGBAK	0046	*F. Mans* | Een dito [Boeren Kermis] tot een weerga, vol gewoel van vegtende Boeren als anderen, door denzelven Meester [F. Mans 1678], hoog en breed als vooren [hoog 1 voet 10 duim, breed 2 v. 7d.], dito [ebbenh.] lyst | companion to lot 45 *Size:* hoog 1 voet 10 duim, breed 2 voet 7 duim	Mejuffrouw A van der Mieden	(Sold) fl 12:5 for lots 45 & 46. Ondorp
1802/06/28	AMSCH	0071	*Heeremans* | Twee stuks, de eene verbeeld een Schoenmakers Winkel, en de andere een Haspelaaster; beide zeer dun en uitvoerig gepenceeld door Heeremans, op Doek | *Mat:* op doek *Size:* hoog 23, breed 19 duim	Anna Elink	(Sold) fl 14:10 De Meyer
1802/06/28	AMSCH	0127	*F. Mans* | Een Land- en Watergezicht, men ziet eenige Boeren in Schuiten, verders nog een aantal Huislieden; zeer natuurlyk en bevallig | *Mat:* op doek *Size:* hoog 17, breed 22 duim	Anna Elink	(Sold) fl 5 Vermeulen
1802/07/21	HGKAN	0014	*Mans* | Een Harten Jagt		(Unknown)
1802/07/21	HGKAN	0060	*F. Mans* | Een Boeren Kermis, op een Dorp in de Veenen, daar de Gans getrokken wordend, fraay en ryk van ordonnantie, door F. Mans, 1678, paneel zwarte Lyst | companion to lot 61 *Mat:* op paneel *Inscr:* F. Mans, 1678 (signed and dated?) *Notes:* It is unclear whether the name and date are inscribed on the painting.		(Unknown)
1802/07/21	HGKAN	0061	*F. Mans* | Een dito [Boeren Kermis] tot een weerga, vol gewoel van vegtende Boeren als anderen, door denzelven Meester [F. Mans], hoog en breed als vooren, dito [zwarte] Lyst | companion to lot 60		(Unknown)
1802/07/21	HGKAN	0065	*Mans* | Een uitmuntend wel geschildert onde [sic] Vrouwe Pourtrait in een bindende houding, zittende voor een met Tapyt gedekte Tafel, op dezelve staande eenige zaaken toepasselyk op den tyd, door Mans, op Doek, zwarte Lyst | *Mat:* op doek		(Unknown)
1802/07/21	HGKAN	0105	*Mans* | Een Boere Kermis		(Unknown)
1802/09/06	AMSCH	0073	*H. Mans* | Twee stuks, een Dorpgezicht met Woningen, aan een stil Water, gestoffeerd met verscheide Vissers in Schuiten, en andere Lieden, verbeeldende een Zomer; den andere vertoond een besneeuwt Wintergezicht, aan de Vestmuur van een Stad; op de Rivier ziet men verscheide Lieden, zig op het Ys vermaken; natuurlyk behandeld | *Mat:* op doek	Wed Grave [or others]	(Sold) fl 6 Bauer
1802/09/21	UTHDG	0064	*H. Mans* | Boeren zich vermakende met het Gans trekken. Rijk met Beelden en Gebouwen gestoffeerd | *Mat:* op doek *Size:* hoog 14, breed 16 ½ duimen		(Bought In) fl 10:5
1802/11/01	DOBRA	0031	*T.H. Mans* | Een ijsgezichtje by een Stads Wal; gestoffeert met sleeden, paarden, schaatsenryders enz. | *Mat:* op paneel *Size:* hoog 17, breed 21 duim	Paulus van der Spyk [or others]	(Sold) fl 10:15 Baalen
1802/11/01	DOBRA	0032	*T.H. Mans* | Een dito [ijsgezichtje], als 't voorige, door denzelven [T.H. Mans], 1638 | *Mat:* op paneel *Size:* hoog 11, breed 14 duim *Inscr:* 1638 (dated?) *Notes:* It is unclear whether the date is inscribed on the painting.	Paulus van der Spyk [or others]	(Sold) fl 7 Schouman
1802/11/01	DOBRA	0033	*T.H. Mans* | Een wintertje | *Mat:* op doek	Paulus van der Spyk [or others]	(Sold) fl 7:5 Schouman
1802/12/13	AMSCH	0125	*Mans* | Een ryk gestoffeerd Wintergezicht | *Size:* hoog 23, breed 28 duim	Pruyssenaar [for] A	(Sold) fl 0:6 L Pakker
1803/07/14	MGKLY	0001	*T. Mans* | Een fraay Landschap, ryk gestoffeert met figuuren te Voet en te Paard	Mr Caspar Jacob van Citters	(Unknown)
1803/08/17	AMSCH	0035	*Heeremans. (F.)* | Twee stuks Strandgezichten, by Scheveningen, ryk gestoffeerd met een menigte Wandelaars, en Visschers welke hunne Vis uitventen; verders eenige Pinken, Wagens en Zeegezichten, met Schepen in 't verschiet, natuurlyk verbeeld | *Mat:* op paneel *Size:* ieder hoog 12, breed 13 ½ duim	Anna Catharina Putman	(Sold) fl 19 Yver
1803/12/12	AMSCH	0044	*F. Heeremans* | Twee stuks Dorpgezichten, gestoffeerd met Heeren te Paard, die zich ververschen, en meer andere figuuren | *Mat:* op paneel *Size:* hoog 16, breed 14 ½ duim	H	(Sold) fl 14:10 Hijm Pakker

1803/12/15	MGLAC	0039	*F. Mans* | Een Winter, met een menigte Schaatsryders en Sleden, waarby een Stads Gezicht; zeer natuurlyk en schoon behandeld | *Mat:* op paneel *Size:* hoog duim 25, breed duim 31	Mr L H de Haze Bomme	(Unknown)
1804/02/27	AMSCH	0056	*Heeremans (F.)* | In dit aangenaam Landschap, ziet men een Gezicht op eenige Bleekeryen; by eenigen Woningen en een Kerktooren, een Kar met drie Paarden, waarin verscheide Lieden, verder eenige gaande Beelden, en een aller bevalligst verschiet | *Mat:* op paneel *Size:* hoog 24, breed 33 duim	B	(Sold) fl 26 Thais
1804/02/27	AMSCH	0144	*Heeremans* | Twee stuks Schilderyen	B	(Sold) fl 0:6 L Pakker
1804/07/25	DLGRO	0103	*F. Mans* | Een Strand gezicht, met een meenigte Vischers en Vrouwen, uitvoerig geschilderd door F. Mans, 1669 op Paneel | *Mat:* op paneel *Size:* hoog 11, breed 14 duim *Inscr:* F. Mans, 1669 (signed and dated?) *Notes:* It is unclear whether the name and date are inscribed on the painting.	Mr Franc van der Burch Wz.	(Unknown)
1804/07/25	DLGRO	0104	*F. Mans* | Een dito [Strand] dito [gezicht], door denzelfde [F. Mans] 1670, op Paneel | *Mat:* op paneel *Size:* hoog 11, breed 14 duim *Inscr:* F. Mans, 1670 (signed and dated?) *Notes:* It is unclear whether the name and date are inscribed on the painting.	Mr Franc van der Burch Wz.	(Unknown)
1804/10/29	HRBAU	0055	*Mans, (Frans)* | Dit Schildery verbeeldt een Kerk op een Dorp, ryk gestoffeerd met eene menigte Menschen der beide sexe, welke aldaar Feest schynen te houden. Plaisant behandeld | *Mat:* op paneel *Size:* hoog 24, breed 34 duim	Simon Styl	(Unknown)
1804/10/29	HRBAU	0056	*Mans, (Frans)* | Voor aan, by een Kasteel, ziet men eene menigte Menschen zich op het Ys vermaaken; waar agter een aangenaam verschiet. Als het voorige behandeld | *Mat:* op paneel *Size:* hoog 24, breed 34 duim	Simon Styl	(Unknown)
1804/10/29	HRBAU	0057	*Mans, (Frans)* | Op den Voorgrond wandelen een Heer en een Dame op het Ys, benevens een Paard en Sleede, en eenige Schaatsenryders; waar agter een Kasteel en bevallig verschiet. Uitvoerig en dun behandeld | *Mat:* op paneel *Size:* hoog 18, breed 14 duim	Simon Styl	(Unknown)
1805/07/03	AMSCH	0117	*H. Mans* | Twee stuks aangename Dorpgezichten, in de eene met een Rivier, ziet men een ménigte Menschen; en, in de andere de fiere Pinxterblom, door Kinderen, voor een Boerewoning verbeeld; geestig geordineerd | *Mat:* op doek *Size:* hoog 16, breed 18 duim	C	(Sold) fl 20 Halingins
1805/07/10	AMSCH	0082	*F. Heeremans* | Een Boere Dorpgezicht, alwaar het Kermis is, vol gewoel van Heeren en Dames, te Paard en en te Voet, Boeren, Boerinnen, enz.; meesterlyk geschilderd | *Mat:* op paneel *Size:* hoog 19, breed 25 duim	V[inkeles] [for] G	(Sold) fl 3:5 v der Schley [for] R[ijfsnijder]
1805/07/10	AMSCH	0083	*F. Heeremans* | Een Plysterplaats voor een Boere Woning, kragtig op Paneel | *Mat:* op paneel *Size:* hoog 11, breed 14 duim	V[inkeles] [for] G	(Sold) fl 2:10 Gruyter
1806/11/24	AMSCH	0043	*Mans (F.)* | Een Strandgezigt, vol gewoel van Vissers, Pinken en Wagens, terzyde het Dorp, breed geschilderd | *Mat:* op paneel *Size:* hoog 28, breed 36 duim	Munnikhuizen	(Sold) fl 3 L Pakker
1807/08/26	AMSCH	0100	*F. Heermans* | Een Strandgezigt by een Dorp aan Zee, gestoffeerd met een menigte Vissers, met hun Koopwaren en andere wandelende Lieden, zoo te voet als te paard; natuurlyk behandeld | *Mat:* op paneel *Size:* hoog 28, breed 36 duim	Yver [for] S	(Sold) fl 4:10 Gruiter
1807/08/26	AMSCH	0101	*F. Heermans* | Een aangenaam Dorpgezigt aan een Rivier: de Weg gestoffeerd met wandelende Beeldjes, en het Water met Vaartuigen en andere stoffage; natuurlyk geschilderd | *Mat:* op paneel *Size:* hoog 10, breed 13 duim	Helsdinge	(Sold) fl 4:10 Levij Pakker
1807/08/26	AMSCH	0143	*H. Mans* | Twee stuks Dorpgezigten aan de Vegt, beide ryk gestoffeerd met Schepen, Jagten, Plaisier-Schuitjes met een menigte Lieden, die zig vermaken, verders Heere Huizingen en andere Woningen en Dorpkerk; plaisant op Doek geschilderd | *Mat:* op doek *Size:* ieder hoog 33, breed 43 duim	Yver [for] S	(Sold) fl 8 Coclair
1808/03/03	HAVIN	0012	*Heeremans* | Een Wintergezicht	Jacobus Spillebout	(Unknown) fl 7
1808/06/13	AMSCH	0188	*F.H. Mans* | Twee stuks Dorpgezichten, zijnde Pleisterplaatzen; geestig	E M Engelberts	(Sold) fl 26 Nieuwenhuisen
1808/06/13	AMSCH	0189	*F.H. Mans* | Twee stuks als voren [Dorpgezichten, zijnde Pleisterplaatzen]; natuurlijk	E M Engelberts	(Sold) fl 15 Engelberts
1808/08/23	AMSCH	0185	*F. Mans* | Twee stuks bevallige Land- en Watergezichten, met gaande en rustende Lieden gestoffeerd; fiks op Doek | *Mat:* op doek	[Gruyter?]	(Sold) fl 12 Spaan
1808/08/23	AMSCH	0270	*Mans* | Een Strandgezicht met verscheide Beeldjes	[Van Iperen?]	(Sold or Bought In) fl 3 Van Iperen
1808/11/12	HGSCR	0019	*F. Mans* | Een winter gezigt met diverse schaatzenryders en andere stoffagie, zeer natuurlyk behandeld door F. Mans 1686 | *Mat:* op doek *Inscr:* F. Mans 1686 (signed and dated?) *Notes:* It is unclear whether the name and date are inscribed on the painting.	Mr J van Buren	(Unknown) fl 7
1808/11/28	AMSCH	0097	*F. Mans* | Een Boeren Kermis, vol gewoel, fiks | *Mat:* op doek	Z	(Sold) fl 1:15 Klynveld
1809/06/13	AMSCH	0111	*F. Mans* | Een Dorpgezigt langs een stille Rivier, gestoffeerd met een menigte Huislieden, zoo op de Wal als in Schuiten, welke zich op	Q	(Sold) fl 3:10 du Pree

			onderscheide wijze vermaaken; natuurlijk verbeeld | *Mat:* op doek *Size:* hoog 20, breed 23 duim		
1809/06/13	AMSCH	0112	*F. Mans* | Een Land- en Watergezicht, rijk met Beeldjes gestoffeerd, en als de voorgaande behandeld | *Mat:* op doek *Size:* hoog 20, breed 23 duim	Q	(Sold) fl 4:10 du Pree
1809/07/25	HGBSM	0150	*F. Mans* | Een Boere Vreugd in een Dorp | *Mat:* op doek *Size:* hoog 16, breed 13 duim	D van der Aa [or] E B ten Dall	(Sold) fl 5 van Zanten
1810/06/20	AMSCH	0064	*F. Mans* | Een Dorp aan een stille Rivier, gestoffeerd met eene menigte Huislieden, zoo op den Wal als in de Schuiten. Natuurlijk voorgesteld | *Mat:* op doek *Size:* hoog 20, breed 24 duimen	D	(Sold) fl 6:15 J de Vries
1810/06/20	AMSCH	0065	*F. Mans* | Twee stuks bevallige Land- en Watergezigten, met gaande en rustende Lieden gestoffeerd; fiks | *Mat:* op doek *Size:* Jeder hoog 9, breed 11 duimen	B	(Sold) fl 3:5 T Spaan
1810/06/20	AMSCH	0066	*F. Mans* | Een Kermis in een Dorp, vol gewoel | *Mat:* op paneel *Size:* hoog 18, breed 24 duimen	A	(Sold) fl 8:5 Focken
1810/06/20	AMSCH	0116	*F. Mans* | Twee stuks Dorpgezigten aan stille Rivieren, met eene menigte Beeldjes enz.	N	(Sold) fl 2:15 J de Vries
1810/06/20	AMSCH	0156	*F. Mans* | Twee stuks Zeedorpen, met eene menigte Beeldjes	B	(Sold) fl 2 Teerling
1810/07/23	DOLG2	0049	*H. Mans* | Een Gezicht langs strand; rijk gestoffeerd, met Beeldjes, fix geschilderd, door H. Mans 1671 | *Mat:* op paneel *Size:* hoog 15, breed 22 duim *Inscr:* H. Mans 1671 (signed and dated?) *Notes:* It is unclear whether the name and date are inscribed on the painting.	Pieter Quinting	(Sold) fl 5:5 Visser
1810/07/23	DOLG2	0053	*H. Mans* | Een Strandgezicht zeer rijk gestoffeerd | *Mat:* op paneel *Size:* hoog 15, breed 20 duim	Pieter Quinting	(Sold) fl 5 Gansewinkel
1810/07/23	DOLG2	0056	*H. Mans* | Een Winter- en IJsgezicht, langs eenige Stads Gebouwen, vol beelden, paarden en Schaatsrijders. Zeer uitvoerig gepenseeld | *Mat:* op paneel *Size:* hoog 12, breed 14 duim	Pieter Quinting	(Sold) fl 11 P de Heere Dordt
1810/07/23	DOLG2	0057	*H. Mans* | Een dito Zomergezicht | *Mat:* op doek *Size:* hoog 14, breed 20 duim *Notes:* It is unclear what "dito" refers to in the title.	Pieter Quinting	(Sold) fl 2:10 A van Strij
1810/07/23	DOLG2	0080	*H. Mans* | Een Landschap, met Gebouwen en Beeldtjes | *Size:* hoog 12, breed 16 duim	Pieter Quinting	(Unknown)
1810/07/23	DOLG2	0095	*H. Mans* | Een Landschap | *Mat:* op paneel *Size:* hoog 8, breed 6 duim	Pieter Quinting	(Unknown)
1810/08/06	AMSCH	0068	*Mans (F.)* | Twee stuks Strandgezichten, rijk gestoffeerd met Visschers-Pinken, Visschers, onderscheidene Rijtuigen en Wandelaars; natuurlijk geschilderd | *Mat:* op paneel *Size:* ieder hoog 12, breed 14 duimen	F	(Sold) fl 19 Coclers
1810/10/10	MGCIT	0162	*Mans* | Twee Stukjes, zijnde Dorpgezigtjes aan de Zee gelegen, het Strand gestoffeerd met een veeltal van Figuuren, uitvoerig en aardig behandeld | *Notes:* This lot was misnumbered no. 163 and changed in an errata sheet located at the front of the catalogue.	Caspar van Citters	(Unknown)

Heerschop, Hendrik

1802/12/13	AMSCH	0083	*H. Heerschop* | In een verwulft Keukenvertrek, staat een Meid beesig Koper en Thin Huisraat te schuuren, verder door een open Nis, ziet men een Jongeling in een ander Vertrek, om hoog hangt een Ysere Kroon met dood Wilt, gestoffeert met verscheide Bywerk, fix gepenceelt | *Mat:* op paneel *Size:* hoog 21, breed 18 duim	Florijn [?]	(Sold) fl 8:10 v^{n} Iperen

Heerswijk, H.F. [Unidentified]

1808/06/13	AMSCH	0190	*H.F. Heerswijk* | Eene stervende Vrouw, te bed liggende, daarbij een bedrukte Man en Vrouw; geestig	E M Engelberts	(Sold) fl 7 Engelberts

Helmbreker, Dirk

1806/08/13	AMSCH	0080	*Helmbreeker. (T.)* | Een Man in een vrolyke gestalte gecarresseerd wordende door een Patryshond; de behandeling is breed en bevallig | *Mat:* op doek *Size:* hoog 34, breed 27 duim	Roos	(Sold) fl 7:10 Richter

Helmont, Mattheus van

1803/09/07	AMSCH	0081	*M. van Hilmont* | Een Boeren Binnenhuis met verscheide Beelden, welke zig met Roken en Drinken vermaken; meesterlyk op Doek [L'intérieur d'une chaumière avec differentes figures occupées à fumer et à boire ; exécuté en maître.] | *Mat:* op doek *Size:* hoog 16, breed 22 duim	Smidt	(Sold) fl 2:5 de Lafontaine
1803/09/07	AMSCH	0082	*M. van Hilmont* | Een Binnehuis, waarin vier Boeren, by een Tafel, bezig met Rooken en Drinken, verder een Vrouw by een Tobben; natuurlyk en meesterlyk van penceel behandeling [Un intérieur, représentant quatre villageois à table, s'amusant à boire et à fumer, dans le fond une femme occupée près d'une cuve ; ce tableau est plein de vérité et d'une très belle ordonnance] | *Mat:* op paneel *Size:* hoog 14, breed 19 duim	Smidt	(Sold) fl 8 Toselli
1804/08/08	AMSCH	0082	*M. Van Helmond* | In een ryk gestoffeerd Laborotorium zit een oude Philosooph met aandacht een Glas te beschouwen, dat hy in zyn Hand heeft, voor hem op een Tafel vindt men een ménigte Boeken en Papieren, Globe, differente Potten en Flessen, en andere kleinigheeden, op de voorgrond is een Jongen bézig een Fournuis in brand te maaken, van achteren zyn verscheide Lieden bézig met stooken en andere werkzaamheeden te verrichten; brillant van licht en meesterlyk gepenceelt | *Mat:* op doek *Size:* hoog 22 ½, breed 32 ½ duim	Vink[eles] [for] K[=Gruyter?]	(Bought In) fl 35

1807/08/26	AMSCH	0102	*Helmont* | In een Chirurgyns Winkel, ziet men door den Meester, een Patiënt een kwetsuur op den rug verbinden, op de tweede grond word een Man ader gelaten, verders twee Vrouwen, en een menigte bywerk | *Mat:* op doek *Size:* hoog 22, breed 32 duim	Joseph Vallette	(Sold) fl 9:10 du Pree
1808/08/23	AMSCH	0076	*Helmondt. (M. van)* | Een oude Philosoof, zittende in zijn Laboratorium met aandacht een Glas te beschouwen, voor hem op een Tafel staat een Globe en eenige Boeken, op de voorgrond een Jongen bij een Fournuis, bézig het vuur aan te blaazen, agterwaards verscheiden Lieden, bézig met stooken en andere werkzaamheden; brillant van licht en meesterlijk gepenceeld | *Mat:* op doek *Size:* hoog 22, breed 32 duim	[Gruyter?]	(Bought In) fl 31
1809/07/25	HGBSM	0233	*Helmond* | Een Boeren-Gezelschap in een Binnenvertrek in de trant van Teniers, door Helmond | *Mat:* op doek *Size:* hoog 14 en een half, breed 21 duim	D van der Aa [or] E B ten Dall	(Sold) fl 4 van Zanten

Helst, A. van [Unidentified]

1802/05/05	AMSCH	0076	*A. van Helst* | Een Wintergezicht, met eenige Schaatseryders en andere Lieden, zeer natuurlyk | *Mat:* op paneel *Size:* hoog 10, breed 16 duim	G	(Sold) fl 4:10 Spruit

Helst, Bartholomeus van der

1801/02/18	AMBOS	0018	*van der Helst* | Een mans Hoofd, uitmuntend fraai en natuurlyk geschilderd	J Schonevelt	(Unknown)
1801/08/19	AMSCH	0049	*B. van der Helst* | Een Mans Portrait in oude hollandsche kleeding	Pruyssen^{r} [for] Q	(Bought In) fl 5
1801/08/19	AMSCH	0050	*B. van der Helst* | Een dito Vrouwe Pourtrait | *Notes:* It is unclear what "dito" refers to in the title.	Pruyssen^{r} [for] Q	(Bought In) fl 5
1802/06/16	AMSCH	0082	*B. v. der Helst* | Een Mans Poutret, houdende in de rechterhand een rol Papier, krachtig en breed geschilderd | *Mat:* op doek *Size:* hoog 24, breed 20 duim	[Merrem]	(Sold) fl 14:10 Agina
1802/09/29	AMSCH	0019	*Barth$^{s.}$ van der Helst* | De Schilderyen van deezen beroemden Konstenaar komen zeer zelden voor, vooral die van uitmuntende qualiteit en bevollige [sic] Ordenantien zyn als deeze; in een Thuingezigt onder eenen Wyngaard, ziet men een schoon Jongman, met los bruin hair, ter halver lyf, levensgroote, in ryke oude Hollandsche kleeding, leunende met zyn regter arm op een steenen Baluster, en wyzende na zyn hond, schynende den Aanschouwer daar over te willen onderhouden. Het character is goedäartig; het naakt, de kleederen, het linnengoed, alles is volmaakt na de natuur gevolgd; zynde een Kabinetstuk van de eerste verdiensten [Il est connu combien les ouvrages de ce célêbre artiste sont rares, en ce qu'il à peint trés peu de Tableaux de Cabinet : et ceux qui les possedent les conservent précieusement, les vantans avec enthousiasme ; il y en à peu qui soient d'une aussi belle ordonnance que celle-ci. C'est un beau jeune Homme à cheveux bruns flottans, vu à mi corps de grandeur naturelle, dans le riche costume ancien de la Hollande. Il s'appuye du bras droit sur une Balustrade de pierre sur laquelle est son Chapeau et paroit entretenir le spectateur touchant son chien qui est prés de lui. Une vigne ornée d'Insectes, passe derriere et audessus de sa tête, le fond représente des arbres de differentes espéces ; Le Caractere de la Tête est trés beau & d'un bon naturel ; Les chairs Les Etoffes, Le Linge, tout y est conforme à la belle nature. l'Execution en est audela de l'Expression c'est à tous Egards. Un Chef d'oeuvre de Peinture.] | *Mat:* op doek *Size:* hoog 37 ½, breed 44 duim	[Labouchere?]	(Sold) fl 360 Coclers
1802/12/13	AMSCH	0079	*B. van der Helst* | Een oude Vrouw, zittende in een Leuningstoel met een rood Kussen, met byde Handen over de Leuning van de zelven, ter zyden een Tafel met een Kleed bedekt, waar op Handschoenen en in 't verschiet een Hofgezigt, uitmuntend geschilderd | *Mat:* op doek *Size:* hoog 49, breed 40 duim	Pruyssenaar [for] A	(Sold) fl 1:10 Gruiter
1804/07/25	AMSCH	0034	*Helst. (B. van der)* | Een bevallige vrolyke Jongeling in ryke Kleeding, het Hoofd gedekt met een roode Fluweel Mezetyne Muts, houdende in de Linkerhand een Schulp, en in de andere een Blaaspypje, zig vermakende met Waterbellen te blaazen, hy vertoont zig in een Landschap, en tot de Kniën te zien, het is kragtig van coloriet en zeer uitvoerig gepenceeld | *Mat:* op doek *Size:* hoog 32, breed 28 duim		(Sold) fl 35 Van der Schleij
1804/08/08	AMSCH	0085	*B. van der Helst* | Een oude Vrouw, zittende op een Leuningstoel, met een Rood Kussen, met de beide Handen over de Leunings van dezelve, ter zyde een Tafel met een Kleed gedekt, waarop Handschoenen, in het verschiet een Hofgezicht; meesterlyk gepenceelt | *Mat:* op doek *Size:* hoog 49, breed 40 duim	Vink[eles] [for] K[=Gruyter?]	(Sold) fl 0:4 Pieterse
1806/08/13	AMSCH	0065	*Helst (B. van der)* | Een bejaarde Dame met een zwarte sluijer om haar Hoofd, gekleed in een rood fluweel Jak met bond, heeft in haar regterhand een boek en met de linker stoot zy een Vengster open, waardoor zy in de kamer ziet, meesterlyk gepenceeld | *Mat:* op doek *Size:* hoog 38, breed 33 duim	van der Voort	(Sold) fl 332 Thais
1806/08/13	AMSCH	0066	*Helst. (B. van der)* | Een deftige Dame in zwarte zeide kleeding, zittende in een Stoel, leunende met de linkerhand, op deszelfs leuning; zynde ryk met Paerlen en Juweelen versierd; door een opgehaald gordyn ziet men een Kasteel; behandeld als de voorgaande | *Mat:* op doek *Size:* hoog 48, breed 40 duim	Roos [for] Flen [?]	(Bought In) fl 50

1808/06/06	RMRIJ	0050[a]	*Helst. (Bartholomeus van der)* | Drie Stukken. N°. 1. Een bejaard Mansportret. 2. Wedergade. Een bejaard Vrouweportret, van voren gedaagd. 3. Wedergade. Een jong Vrouweportret. Allen Borststukken, en in deftige Oud-Hollandsche kleeding. Vast geteekend, heerlijk en uitvoerig geschilderd [Trois Portraits par ce célébre Artiste, tous en anciens Costumes Hollandais et d'une même famille. N°. 1. Portrait d'un Vieillard vu à mi-corps. Bien dessiné, d'un beau faire et trés fini. Digne ouvrage de ce grand Artiste. 2. Une femme âgée et vue à mi-corps. Un chef-d'oeuvre. 3. Portrait d'une jeune femme vue à mi-corps. D'un grand fini] | *This Lot:* 1. Een bejaard Mansportret 2. Wedergade. Een bejaard Vrouweportret, van voren gedaagd *Annots:* [portret van] Lansbergen (RMA I) *Mat:* op paneel *Size:* Hoog 25 ½ en breed 21 ½ duim *Notes:* Although lots 50[a] and 50[b] were catalogued as one lot, they were sold separately. *Loc:* Amsterdam, Nederland. Rijksmuseum. (A 143 & A 144)	Gerrit van der Pot, Heer van Groeneveld	(Sold) fl 480 J J de Wit [for] le Roi
1808/06/06	RMRIJ	0050[b]	*Helst. (Bartholomeus van der)* | Drie Stukken. N°. 1. Een bejaard Mansportret. 2. Wedergade. Een bejaard Vrouweportret, van voren gedaagd. 3. Wedergade. Een jong Vrouweportret. Allen Borststukken, en in deftige Oud-Hollandsche kleeding. Vast geteekend, heerlijk en uitvoerig geschilderd [Trois Portraits par ce célébre Artiste, tous en anciens Costumes Hollandais et d'une même famille. N°. 1. Portrait d'un Vieillard vu à mi-corps. Bien dessiné, d'un beau faire et trés fini. Digne ouvrage de ce grand Artiste. 2. Une femme âgée et vue à mi-corps. Un chef-d'oeuvre. 3. Portrait d'une jeune femme vue à mi-corps. D'un grand fini] | *This Lot:* 3. Wedergade. Een jong Vrouweportret. Allen Borststukken, en in deftige Oud-Holandsche kleeding *Mat:* op paneel *Size:* Hoog 25 ½ en breed 21 ½ duim *Notes:* Although lots 50[a] and 50[b] were catalogued as one lot, they were sold separately.	Gerrit van der Pot, Heer van Groeneveld	(Sold) fl 110 Steenstraat
1808/06/06	RMRIJ	0051	*Helst. (Bartholomeus van der)* | Een kloek Jongmans-Portret, een open boek in de regterhand houdende. Achter hem een Gordijn, en boeken in 't verschiet. Eene wedergade, zijnde het Portret eener jonge Vrouw, de handen op elkaar houdende; in den achtergrond eene stemmige Architectuur. Beiden kloek geteekend, breed en meesterlijk geschilderd ten halven lijve [N°. 1. Portrait d'un Jeune homme vu à mi-corps, et tenant à sa main droite un livre ouvert. On apperçoit dans le fond un rideau et une Bibliothéque. 2. Pendant du prêcêdent. Portrait d'une Jeune femme, qui a les mains croisées l'une sur l'autre. Le fond presente une Architecture simple et noble] | *Mat:* op paneel *Size:* Twee Stukken. Hoog 28, en breed 22 ¾ duim	Gerrit van der Pot, Heer van Groeneveld	(Sold) fl 150 Coclers
1808/06/11	RMRIJ	0063	*B: van der Helst* | Een schoon Mans Pourtrait, levensgroote, Borststuk. Ovaal Paneel | *Mat:* op paneel *Fmt:* ovaal		(Bought In) fl 21
1808/06/11	RMRIJ	0064	*B: vander Helst* | Het Pourtrait van een Krygsoverste | *Mat:* op doek		(Sold) fl 4:10 Dupree
1808/08/23	AMSCH	0072	*Helst. (B. van der)* | In een Landschap zit op de voorgrond een Heer en eene Dame, beide deftig in het zwart gekleed ter zijde voor een Tafel, waar op Handschoenen en een Hoed geplaatst is, verders drie Jagthonden, in het verschiet een Meid met een Kind, en ander bywerk; uitmuntend schoon gepenceeld | *Mat:* op doek *Size:* hoog 52, breed 62 duim	Y	(Sold) fl 91 Gruyter
1808/09/13	HABRU	0039	*van der Helst* | Een Mans Pourtrait		(Unknown) fl 1:10
1810/06/06	RMMUY	0039	*B. van der Helst* | Twee Stuks Ovalen, een Mans en een Vrouwe Pourtrait, uitvoerig en schoon geschilderd | *Mat:* op paneel *Fmt:* ovaal		(Unknown) fl 75
1810/08/01	AMSCH	0039	*Helst (Bartholomeus van der)* | Een deftig Man met ronden Hoed en eenen Stok, staande in een Landschap, nevens hem een Hond [Un Homme de distinction ayant un Chapeau rond sur la tête et une Canne à la main ; un gros chien se voit à son côté. Cette representation se detache sur un fond de Paysage] | *Annots:* peu digne d'un tel pinceau (NGW) *Mat:* op doek *Size:* hoog 49, breed 37 duimen	Mr Pieter de Smeth van Alphen	(Sold) fl 105 T Spaan
1810/12/03	DOBRA	0039	*van der Elst* | Een Vrouwe Pourtret		(Unknown)
			Helst, Bartholomeus van der (or Helst, B., manner)		
1806/05/05	AMSCH	0067	*B. van der Helst* | Een Heer en een Dame, zittende in een pragtig Hofgezigt, levensgrooten tot de kniejen toe verbeeld; heerlyk en stout geschilderd door of in de manier van B. van der Helst	V[inkeles]	(Sold) fl 2:10 L Pakker
			Helst, Bartholomeus van der (copy after)		
1802/02/16	AMSCH	0038	*B. v. der Helst* | Eenige Burger Officieren in een Binnevertrek, staande den Capityn in volle Wapenrusting, met een Roemer Wyn, in de hand, ter zyde staat de Vaandrager, en mindere Bevelhebbers, zig met drinken vermakende, kragtig gepenceeld, na een schildery van B. v. der Helst, door een goed meester	G	(Bought In) fl 80
			Helst, Bartholomeus van der (manner)		
1802/05/05	AMSCH	0075	*B. van der Helst* | Een Deftig Man, in het Zwart Gekleed, als sprekende tegen den Beschouwer. Meesterlyk op Doek, als van B. van der Helst | *Mat:* op doek *Size:* hoog 32, breed 26 duim	B	(Sold) fl 12:10 Ackina
1810/06/20	AMSCH	0035a	*B. Van Der Helst* | Twee stuks: een Mans en eene Vrouwe Pourtrait, beide in deftige kleeding. Schoon geschilderd op doek, als B. Van Der Helst | *Mat:* op doek *Size:* hoog 26, breed 31 duimen	K	(Sold) fl 79 de Vries

1810/10/11	AMSCH	0122	*B. van der Helst* | Twee stuks, eens Mans en een Vrouwe Portret, beide in deftige kleeding; op Paneel, als B. van der Helst geschilderd | *Mat:* op paneel *Size:* hoog 28, breed 34 duimen	M	(Sold) fl 15:10 Gruiter

Helst, Jeronimus van der

1802/06/16	AMSCH	0081	*J. v. der Helst* | Aan een Dorp ziet men op een bevroozen Rivier, een Marketenter en een menigte Schaatzeryders, en andere met Ys en Priksleeden; alles fiks en bevallig gepenceeld | *Mat:* op doek *Size:* hoog 42, breed 53 duim	[Merrem]	(Sold) fl 42 Vermeulen
1804/10/29	HRBAU	0033	*Helst, (van der)* | Voor aan, in een plas Water, ziet men vier Eendvogels in verschillende gestalten; waar agter een Bosch- en bergagtig verschiet | *Mat:* op doek *Size:* hoog 33, breed 43 duim	Simon Styl	(Unknown)

Helt, F. van [Unidentified]

1808/04/26	GDAN	0057	*Helt (F. van)* | Een bergägtig Landschap, in de manier van Berghem, gestoffeerd met Koeijen, Paarden en Beelden, zeer uitvoerig en wel behandeld | *Size:* hoog 28 ½, breed 24 ½ duim	G H Fortuyn	(Unknown)

Helt Stockade, Nicolaes van

1810/12/03	DOBRA	0068	*Helt Stocade* | de Historie van Coriolanus, daar zyn moeder, vrouw, en andere vrouwen, hem bidden, om het behoud van Romen | possibly companion to lot 69		(Unknown)
1810/12/03	DOBRA	0069	*Helt Stocade* | De Historie van Ulysses, Koning van Ithaca, en Nausicaa, daar zy hem naakt in een Bosch vindende, van klederen voorziet, door denzelven [Helt Stocade], op Doek, in een zwarte Lyst, zynde een wederga van No. 12 | possibly companion to lot 68 *Mat:* op doek *Notes:* In the title we have assumed the reference to lot no. 12 was a misprint and should be lot no. 68, which has the same artist.		(Unknown)

Hendriks, Wijbrand

1801/04/08	HAVIN	0004	*W. Hendriks* | Een Boere Binnenhuis met een Varken aan de ladder, waarby een Man en Vrouw vergenoegd staan te praaten, konstig en uitvoerig		(Unknown)
1801/10/06	AMSCH	0034	*W. Hendriks* | Een Pot met verschillende zoorten van keurige Bloemen, staande op een steene Tafel, daar nevens legt een tros Druyven en andere Vrugten, bevallig Geordineert en fraay geschilderd | *Mat:* op doek *Size:* hoog 31, breed 27 duim	M	(Sold) fl 34 Gruyter
1802/06/28	AMSCH	0068	*W. Hendriks* | Op een marmere Tafel, ziet men een Pot met verscheide fraaye geschakeerde Bloemen, als Roozen, Tulpen, Hiacinten, enz. zeer natuurlyk, fiks en dun gepenceeld | companion to lot 69 *Size:* hoog 26, breed 21 duim	Anna Elink	(Sold) fl 85 for lots 68 & 69. Gruiter
1802/06/28	AMSCH	0069	*W. Hendriks* | Een wederga van de voorgaande, verbeeldende op de Rand van eene marmere Tafel, eenige fraaye Bloemen en Fruiten, als fraaye blaauwe en witte Druyven, Annanas, enz. zeer fraai en dun van Coloriet | companion to lot 68 *Size:* hoog 26, breed 21 duim	Anna Elink	(Sold) fl 85 for lots 68 & 69. Gruiter
1802/06/28	AMSCH	0074	*W. Hendriks* | Een Binnehuis, in dezelve ziet men een bevallige Dame, met een blad Musiek, nevens haar een Heer die zyn Fiool stelt; door W. Hendriks | *Mat:* op doek *Size:* hoog 18, breed 14 duim	Anna Elink	(Sold) fl 49 van der Schley [for] Putte
1802/09/06	AMSCH	0053	*W. Hendriks* | Op een steene Tafel ziet men een Pot, gevuld met verscheide zoorten van bloemen, als roode en witte Roozen, Nageltakken en andere geurige bloemen; ter zyde de Pot leggen eenige Druiven en andere vrugten, bevallig en fraay geordeneert | *Mat:* op doek *Size:* hoog 31, breed 27 duim	J	(Sold) fl 36 van Iperen
1803/12/12	AMSCH	0041	*W. Hendriks* | Een Boerenkamer, voor een gedekte Tafel ziet men een Vrouw, gereed Eeten op te zetten, terwyl de Man bézig is Brood te snyden, ter zyde twee Biddende Kinderen, op de voorgrond een Hond, die een Pot uitlekt, van achteren, door een openstaande Deur, ziet men een zonachtig Landschap; bevallig van licht en meesterachtig | *Mat:* op doek *Size:* hoog 17 ½, br. 14 duim	B	(Sold) fl 7 v d Schley [for] R[ijfsnijder]
1804/02/27	AMSCH	0052	*Hendriks. (W.)* | Twee stuks, een Kantewerkster, en een Jager, byde in een Binnenvertrek, met zeer natuurlyke doorzichten, het toepasselyk bywerk, en bevallige Ordonantie zyn zeer wel gevolgd en als de Delfsche van der Meer behandeld | *Mat:* op doek *Size:* hoog 17, breed 14 duim	B	(Sold) fl 103 Thys
1804/12/10	AMSCH	0026	*Wyb. Hendriks* | Aan de tak van een Boom, ter zyde een steene vaas met basrelieven, hangt een doode Haas aan zyne looper; op de grond legt verschillend dood Gevogelte, en ter zyde een Korfje met smakelyke vrugten, in 't verschiet een Hofgezicht: alles evenaart de natuur, en is bevallig van colriet en uitvoerig gepenceeld | companion to lot 27 *Mat:* op doek *Size:* Hoog 36, breed 31 duim	Jan De Groot	(Sold) fl 205 for lots 26 & 27. Reijers
1804/12/10	AMSCH	0027	*Wyb. Hendriks* | De wederga, vertoont in een landschap, by de stam van een Boom en steene vaas, een leggende doode Pauw en verscheide ander Gevogelten; op de voorgrond legt een Tak met roosen en bladeren, en ander Plantgewas, verder een Hofgezicht en Vyver; in alles als de voorgaande behandeld, en meesterlyk gepenceeld | companion to lot 26 *Mat:* op doek *Size:* Hoog 36, breed 31 duim	Jan De Groot	(Sold) fl 205 for lots 26 & 27. Reijers

1805/07/03	AMSCH	0097	*W. Hendriks* | Twee stuks Huislyke Voorwerpen, zynde het eene een Huishouden dat aan een Tafel zit te Bidden; en het andere daar de uchtend mede verbeeld word, zynde de Vrouw bézig coffy te malen, een Kind word gekleed, terwyl de Man een pypje rookt; geestig geordineerd, en geschilderd op Doek | *Mat:* op doek *Size:* hoog 18, breed 14 duim	G	(Sold) fl 31 van Iperen
1805/07/10	AMSCH	0077	*W. Hendriks* | Twee stuks, een staand Bloemstuk, versierd met een Vaas op een Marmere Tafel, staande gevuld met geurige fraay geschakeerde Bloemen, terzyde een Vogelnesje; in het ander een Fruitstuk, ziet men mede op een Tafel witte en blaauwe Druiven, Persiken, Pruimen, enz.; beide deeze stukken zyn van de aller besten en uitvoerigste van W. Hendriks | *Mat:* op paneel *Size:* hoog 23, breed 19 ½ duim	R[oos]	(Sold) fl 136 T van Iperen
1806/05/05	AMSCH	0062	*W. Hendriks* | Op een marmere Tafel ziet men een cierelyke Vaas, met differenten keurige Bloemen, als roode, geelen, bonten en witten Roosen, Hyacinten en andere welriekende Bloemen, waar op Insectens aazen; schoon geordineerd en meesterlyk geschilderd door W. Hendriks | *Mat:* op doek *Size:* hoog 22, breed 33 duim	V[inkeles]	(Bought In) fl 9
1806/05/05	AMSCH	0063	*W. Hendriks* | Twee stuks dito, op de eene vertoond zig een glas, gevuld met onderscheiden welriekende Bloemen, en op de andere eenige smakelyke Vrugten; meesterlyk gepenceeld door denzelven [W. Hendriks] | *Mat:* op paneel *Size:* hoog 12, breed 9 duim *Notes:* It is unclear what "dito" refers to in the title.	V[inkeles]	(Sold) fl 10 Josi
1808/06/13	AMSCH	0079	*Hendriks (W.)* | Een doode Haas, hangende aan den tak van een boom, bij eene sierlijk Vaas, waarvoor een Faisante Haan, een Snip, een koppel Patrijzen en een Tros witte Druiven liggen; voorts een Schietgeweer en Jagthoorn; verder eenige Jagers in een duinachtig verschiet. Dit stuk is in kracht, teekening en ordonantie evenarende aan J. Wenix | *Mat:* op doek *Size:* hoog 48, breed 38 duim	[Jan Tersteeg]	(Sold) fl 290 J Yver
1808/06/13	AMSCH	0080	*Hendriks (W.)* | In een Boere Binnenvertrek zitten vier Huislieden, zich met zingen, drinken en fioolspelen vermakende; op den voorgrond zit een Kat, bij haar Jongen; verder eene menigte Huisraad. Alles zacht en uitvoerig behandeld | *Mat:* op paneel *Size:* hoog 14, breed 19 duim	R[oos]	(Sold) fl 253 J Spaan [or] T Spaan
1808/08/23	AMSCH	0082	*Hendriks. (W.)* | Op een steene Tafel staat een cierlijke gewerkte Vaas, gevuld met een menigte welriekende Bloemen, als roode, witte en geele Roosen, Tulpen, Iriassen, Angelieren, Papavers en anderen, voor de Vaas ligt een tak Roosen, waar op Insectens aazen; schoon geordoneerd en mals gepenceeld | *Mat:* op doek *Size:* hoog 33, breed 38 ½ duim	[Gruyter?]	(Sold) fl 20:10 Van Iperen
1809/04/17	AMSCH	0038	*W. Hendriks* | Op een Steene Tafel staat een cierlijk gewerkte Vaas, gevuld met onderscheidene soorten van keurige Bloemen, waarop Insectens Azen, voor dezelve liggen eenige smakelijke Vrugten; meesterlijk uitgevoerd | *Mat:* op doek *Size:* hoog 24, breed 19 duim	[Gruyter?]	(Sold) fl 4:10
1809/06/13	AMSCH	0063	*W. Hendriks* | Op een Marmere Tafel, staat een cierlijke gewerkte Vaas, gevuld met fraaije keurige Bloemen, ter zijde ligt een Tros witte Druiven, Oranje Appelen, en andere Vruchten; fraai van Ordonantie en delicaat geschilderd | *Mat:* op doek *Size:* hoog 35, breed 29 duim	H[odges]	(Bought In) fl 26
1809/06/13	AMSCH	0230	*W. Hendriks* | Tulpen, Papavers en anderen, waarop Insecten aazen; helder en meesterlijk geschilderd | *Mat:* op doek	[Gruyter?]	(Sold) fl 2:10 J d Vries
1809/09/06	AMSCH	0026	*Hendriks (W.)* | Twee stuks, zijnde het eene een Bloem- en het andere een Fruitstuk, beide met de geurigste Bloemen en delicaten Vrugten; fraai geordineerd en uitvoerig gepenceeld | *Mat:* op paneel *Size:* ieder hoog 24, breed 20 duim	Johannes Caudri	(Sold) fl 101 Yver
1810/05/22	AMSCH	0040	*Hendriks (W.)* | Twee stuks kapitale Bloem en Fruitstukken, zijnde in het Bloemstuk een Vaas vol geurige Bloemen, waarbij een Vogelnesje met Eijertjes, in het Fruitstuk ziet men de smakelijkste Vrugten; beide van een uitvoerige en fraaije behandeling | *Mat:* op paneel *Size:* Jeder hoog 23, breed 20 duim	Johannes van de Putte Nicolaasz.	(Sold) fl 52 van Iperen
1810/05/22	AMSCH	0041	*Hendriks. (W.)* | In een Binnenvertrek zit een Dame aan eene Tafel, schijnende te zingen, agter de Tafel staat een Heer met zijn Fiool te acompagneeren, door de Deur ziet men in een Tuinhuis; bevallig gepenceeld | *Mat:* op doek *Size:* hoog 17, breed 14 duim	Johannes van de Putte Nicolaasz.	(Sold) fl 58 Yver
1810/08/06	AMSCH	0155	*Hendriks* | Een Schoorsteen Bloemstuk	V[ries]	(Sold) fl 2 van Dijl
			Hennekyn, Paulus		
1802/05/24	HGBAK	0070	*Paulus Hennekyn* | Een zittende oude Dame in ouwerwetsche kleeding, met een boek in de hand, door Paulus Hennekyn 1649, zeer krachtig, hoog 31 ½ duim, breed 25 duim, doek, zwarte lyst | *Mat:* op doek *Size:* hoog 31 ½ duim, breed 25 duim *Inscr:* Paulus Hennekyn 1649 (signed and dated?) *Notes:* It is unclear whether the name and date are inscribed on the painting.	Mejuffrouw A van der Mieden	(Sold) fl 19 v Gieze
			Henning		
1802/02/16	AMSCH	0094	*Henning* | Twee stuks Landzigten, ryk gestoffeert met In- en Uitlandsche Water- en Landgevogelten, plaisant geschildert op doek | *Mat:* op doek	Z	(Sold) fl 3 Gruiter
1805/12/16	AMSCH	0028	.... *Henning* | Twee stuks Landschappen, met Water- en Land- gevogelten; plaisant op Doek geschilderd | *Mat:* op doek *Size:* yder hoog 22, breed 31 duim	Spaan	(Sold) fl 4:5 du Pree

Henning, Godfried

1801/02/18	AMBOS	0048	*God Henning* | Een Landschap met Vogels, aangenaam en natuurlyk geschilderd, in zyn vroege Jaaren	J Schonevelt	(Unknown)

Henstenburgh, Herman

1801/10/06	AMSCH	0036	*J. Henstenburgh* | Dit Aangenaam Bevallig voorwerp vertoont een hangende Feston, met verschillende zoorten van smaaklijke Vrugten met steel en bladeren, als Persiken, Pruimen, Abricosen, Mispelen, en witte Druiven, Canteloup en andere, alles is verwonderlyk natuurlyk en ongemeen delicaat en uitvoerig met zapverven [sic] geteekent, in een lyst met glas	S	(Sold) fl 106 Van Iperen

Herp, Willem van (I)

1802/07/20	MGSAN	0027	*Herp* | Een Musiceerend Gezelschap, op Paneel | *Mat:* op paneel *Size:* hoog duim 10, breed duim 13 ½		(Unknown)

Herp, Willem van (I) (manner)

1801/03/16	AMSCH	0163	*van Harp* | Een dito [Binnehuis] met Kaartspelende Boeren, als van Harp	K[ip]	(Sold) fl 2 v d Schley [for] Ryfsnyder

Herrlein, Johann Andreas

1803/09/07	AMSCH	0083	*A. Herlin* | Twee stuks aangenaame Boomryke Landscappen, gestoffeerd met verscheide Huislieden en Vee, en Watervallen, verder bevallig Veeschieten; zonachtig en zeer uitvoerig gepenceeld [Deux paysages charmans, bocageux et artistement melés de paysans, de bétail, de cascades et terminé par une perspective superbe ; la lumière et l'ordonnance qui regnent dans ce tableau lui donnent beaucoup de merite] | *Mat:* op paneel *Size:* yder hoog 11, breed 14 duim	Smidt	(Sold) fl 14:10 de Lafontaine
1804/12/10	AMSCH	0030	*J. A. Herleyn* | Twee stuks Boeren Kermissen, beide vol gewoel, in het een ziet men de boeren zig vermaaken met dansen, in het ander een kwakzalver; beide uitvoerig gepenceeld | *Mat:* op paneel *Size:* Hoog 11, breed 14 duim	Jan De Groot	(Sold) fl 20 Vallette

Heusch

1802/11/01	DOBRA	0182	*S. de Heus* | Een Landschapje, met een Herder en Herderin, verzeld van eenige beesten | *Mat:* op paneel		(Unknown) fl 2:5
1802/12/13	AMSCH	0080	*C. de Heus* | Een Bosch en Bergagtig Landschap, gestoffeerd met een Landman met Schaapen, op de voorgrond eenige Rysigers, warm van Coloriet en uitvoerig geschilderd | *Mat:* op paneel *Size:* hoog 15, breed 19 duim	Pruyssenaar [for] A	(Sold) fl 0:18 L Pakker
1802/12/13	AMSCH	0081	*C. de Heus* | Een Boom en Bergagtig Landschap, gestoffeerd met gaande en rustende Beeldjes, fix geschilderd | *Mat:* op paneel *Size:* hoog 20, breed 26 duim	Pruyssenaar [for] A	(Sold) fl 1 L Pakker
1802/12/13	AMSCH	0082	*C. de Heus* | Een hoog Bergagtig Landschap, ryk gestoffeerd en zonagtig geschilderd | *Mat:* op paneel *Size:* hoog 10 ½, breed 12 ½ duim	Pruyssenaar [for] A	(Sold) fl 3 Gruiter
1804/07/25	DLGRO	0068	*de Heus* | Een Italiaansch Landschap, met Bergen &c. fraai geschilderd door de Heus | *Mat:* op paneel *Size:* hoog 9, breed 10 duim	Mr Franc van der Burch Wz.	(Unknown)
1804/08/08	AMSCH	0084	*P. de Heusch* | Een Bergachtig Boomryk Landschap, ter zyde een klaar spiegelende Rivier, gestoffeerd met zwemmende Beeldjes, op de voorgrond eenige Lieden te Paard en anderen, by belaaden Muilezels; warm van coloriet | *Mat:* op paneel *Size:* hoog 14, breed 17 ½ duim	Vink[eles] [for] K[=Gruyter?]	(Sold) fl 5:10 Texier
1808/05/18	LNAN	0028	*de Heus* | Eene Duinachtig Landschap met Beelden en Beesten | *Notes:* The artist's name "de Heus" was added in by hand in the RKDH copy of the catalogue.	Mr Cornelis Versluys	(Unknown)
1808/06/11	RMRIJ	0006	*P: de Heus* | Een kapitaal helder en bevallig Italiaansch Landschap, met onderscheidene Stoffagie, in de manier van Jan Both | *Size:* hoog 25 ½, breed 30 ½ duim		(Sold) fl 62 V D Wal
1810/03/07	UTWLD	0047	*de Heus* | Twee Italiaansche Landschappen | *Size:* hoog 2 voet 2 duim, breed 3 voet 2 duim	J J Woertman	(Unknown) fl 84
1810/03/27	RMCNL	0065	*de Heuz* | Een Bergachtig Landschap, op den voorgrond eenige reizigers; in 't verschiet een Slot, Bergen, enz. zeer warm van Penseel		(Unknown)

Heusch (manner)

1808/06/11	RMRIJ	0093	*de Heus* | Een zeer goed Warm en Zonachtig Landschap, aangenaam gestoffeerd, in de trant van de Heus | *Mat:* op doek op paneel *Size:* hoog 16 ½, breed 20 ½ duim		(Sold) fl 10:10 Coclers
1809/06/13	AMSCH	0189	*de Heus* | Een aangenaam Landschap met hoog opgaand Geboomten, gestoffeerd met Landlieden en Beesten, in de manier van de Heus	Y	(Sold) fl 10 Reijers
1810/11/07	UTWLD	0055	*de Heus* | Twee stuks bergagtige Landschapjes doorsneden met rivieren, met eenige antike gebouwen verder gestoffeerd, in de manier van de Heus, op paneel 8 en een half duim hoog, 11 duim breed, zwarte Lijst | *Mat:* op paneel *Size:* 8 en een half duim hoog, 11 duim breed		(Unknown) fl 15

Heusch, Jacob de

1801/06/10	AMSCH	0082	*Heus. (J. de)* | Dit Boom en Bergachtig Landschapje, zynde bevallig gestoffeerd met Jagers te Paard en te voet, met enige Honden, is Zonachtig en uitvoerig geschilderd | *Mat:* op paneel *Size:* hoog 11, breed 13 duim	Herman ten Kate	(Sold) fl 64 W Rijers
1801/06/10	AMSCH	0083	*Heus. (J. de)* | Een grootsch Bergachtig Landschap, met Watervallen, en Kreupelgewas, de voorgrond gestoffeerd met twee Tekenaars, fraay van Licht en Bruin, en kloek gepinseeld | *Mat:* op doek *Size:* hoog 77, breed 90 duim *Notes:* In the original title the words "fraay van Licht en Bruin, en kloek gepinseeld" were printed as "fraay van licht, bruin en kloek gepenceeld." This error was corrected in an errata sheet located at the end of the catalogue.	Herman ten Kate	(Sold) fl 36 C S Roos
1801/06/10	AMSCH	0084	*Heus. (J. de)* | Een Italiaansch Boomryk Landschap, met hoog Gebergte, en dun verschiet fraai gestoffeerd met een Vrouw by een belade Muilezel, Zonagtig en delicaat behandeld | *Mat:* op koper *Size:* hoog 14, breed 17 ½ duim	Herman ten Kate	(Sold) fl 220 W Reijers
1801/10/19	AMSCH	0025	*Heus (Jacob de)* | Een Italiaans Landschap, op de voorgrond van het zelve vertoonen zich verscheide Reizigers en paarden, die halte houden by een Herberg: wyders eenige Ruïnes en gebouwen; dit stuk is warm van Coloriet en kragtig geschildert | *Mat:* op doek *Size:* hoog 20, breed 26 duim	Jonkheer Menno Baron van Coehoorn	(Sold) fl 71 Jan Spaan
1802/02/16	AMSCH	0048	*J. de Heus* | Een boomryk Landschap met een stille Rivier, op de voorgrond Ryzigers, verder een bergachtig verschiet, zonachtig en uitvoerig gepenceeld	G	(Sold) fl 51 Coclers
1802/09/29	AMSCH	0022	*J. de Heusch* | Een Italiaansch Landschap, hoog 20, breed 26 duim. Doek. Voor een groot Italiaans Gebouw en Ruïne, ziet men eenige Muilëezels by een Smits Winkel: Voorts een Paard, dat uit de haud [sic] beslaagen word, en daar de Ruiter naar schynt te wagten; verder een Heer te Paard, en een Jongen die een Paard, en een Jongen die een Paard vasthoud; ter regter zyde vertoond zig den Tyber en Ponte Molo, en hoog Gebergte in 't verschiet; zynde dit Schildery van een warm en aangenaam Coloriet, zeer konstig en delicaat geschilderd [Envirron [sic] de Rome au devant de quelques batisses Italiennes, dont une partie sert de forge, sont artistement disposé plusieurs groupes de figures avec des chevaux et d'autres avec des mulets, occupés à faire ferrer ces montures ; un beau cheval gris ténu par un garçon, et un chien sont au devant dans la partie éclairée du Tableau, ce groupe est opposé à un cavalier monté sur un cheval brun ; vers la gauche sont deux forgerons à ferrer un cheval noir à la vue de son maitre ; les autres occupés des mulets sont au second plan en mi-teinte. Le fond agréable offre le ponte mole et ce qui appartient à cet envirron [sic]. Ce Tableau d'un ton de couleur chaud est traité avec beaucoup d'art et ne cede en rien aux belles productions de J. Lingelbach.] | *Mat:* op doek *Size:* hoog 20, breed 26 duim	C	(Sold) fl 275 Pruijssenaar
1804/07/25	AMSCH	0043	*Heusch. (J. de)* | Twee stuks aangenaame Italiaansche Land- en Watergezichten, byde ryk gestoffeerd met verschillende Beeldjes, Gebouwen en Geboomte, in een derzelve vertoont zich een brandende Berg en in byde bevallige Verschieten; alles is zonachtig, warm en van een fraaije penceel behandeling | *Mat:* op doek *Size:* ieder hoog 22, breed 29 duim		(Sold) fl 58 C S Roos
1804/08/08	AMSCH	0083	*J. de Heusch* | Dit fraaije Boom- en Bergachtige Landschap is met opgaand Geboomte, Kreupelgewas, heldere Beek, en fraaije Watervallen voorzien, verders een zeer aangenaam verschiet, gestoffeerd met verscheiden Beelden, dun, in de manier van J. Both | *Mat:* op doek *Size:* hoog 39, breed 63 duim	Roos a	(Bought In) fl 44
1805/07/03	AMSCH	0022	*Heus. (J. de)* | Deeze beide stukken verbeelden Gezichten te Romen aan den Tyber, de voorgronden ryk gestoffeerd met Beelden in onderscheide kleeding en werking, Paarden, Ezels, enz het Water met diverse Vaartuigen; terwyl een aangenaam zonlicht zo wel de kragtige gebouwen als de andere voorwerpen verlicht zynde alleruitmuntenst behandeld | *Mat:* op doek *Size:* yder hoog 22, breed 33 duim	R[oos]	(Sold) fl 320 Josi
1805/07/03	AMSCH	0093	*J. de Heusch* | In een Italiaansche Landzicht, vertoont zig over den Tyber, een aloude Brug en Poort; op de Voorgrond gestoffeerd, met gezadelde Ryspaarden, waarby Rysigers en een zittende Vrouw met een Kind, aan den Oever der Rivier leggen Vragtschuiten, verder Ezels en Paarden, die met Vragt beladen worden, en eenige rustende Bokken en Ezel; het zonlicht doed een aangenaame werking, en is van een uitvoerige penceel behandeling | *Mat:* op doek *Size:* hoog 20, breed 29 duim	R[oos]	(Sold) fl 155 Agina
1808/09/13	HABRU	0033	*J. de Heus* | Een Landschap		(Unknown) fl 3
1808/09/13	HABRU	0034	*J. de Heus* | Een Italiaansch Landschap		(Unknown) fl 1
1808/10/28	AMVRS	0019	*Heus (J. de)* | Twee stuks aangename Italiaansche Land- en Watergezichten, beide gestoffeerd met Beelden, Gebouwen enz., met bevallige verschieten | *Mat:* op doek *Size:* ieder hoog 22, breed 29 duim	Marten Udink	(Sold) fl 50 Josi
1808/10/28	AMVRS	0020	*Heus (J. de)* | Een hoog Bergachtig Landschap, met een Rivier doorsneden; gestoffeerd met een Fabel-Historie. Zonachtig behandeld | *Mat:* op paneel *Size:* hoog 31, breed 40 duim	Marten Udink	(Sold) fl 25:10 Gruyter

1808/10/28	AMVRS	0021	*Heus (J. de)* | Een aangenaam Landschap, op den voorgrond gestoffeerd met eene Vrouw, zittende op een Ezel, waarbij twee gaande Huislieden, met eenige Bokken en Schapen, verder hoog Gebergte. Meesterlijk en fraai behandeld | *Mat:* op paneel *Size:* hoog 13, breed 17 duim	Marten Udink	(Sold) fl 19 Van Iperen
1809/04/17	AMSCH	0034	*J. de Heus* | In een Landschap ziet men op de voorgrond de overblijfsels van een pragtig gebouw, waar bij eene Vrouw, zittende op een Ezel, benevens een Herder, rustende bij Bokken en Schapen; bevallig van kleur en licht en kloek geschilderd | *Mat:* op doek *Size:* hoog 27, breed 22 duim	A	(Sold) fl 49
1809/06/13	AMSCH	0064	*J. de Heus* | Twee stuks Bergachtige Landschappen, met Watervallen en Geboomtens, gestoffeerd met Heeren te Paard, rustende Reisigers en Landlieden met Vee | *Mat:* op doek *Size:* ieder is hoog 30, breed 24 duim	E	(Sold) fl 13:10 T Spaan
1810/06/20	AMSCH	0169	*J. de Heus* | Een Italiaansch Landschap met een Heer te Paard en rustende Lieden gestoffeerd	A	(Sold) fl 1 L Pakker

Heusch, Jacob de (and Berchem, N.P.)

1802/06/16	AMSCH	0077	*J. de Heusch; N. Berchem* | Een Italiaansch Boom- en Bergachtig Landschap, met een aangenaam verschiet, Waterplatsen [sic] en uitmuntende Stoffagie op de voorgrond, zynde een Man en een Vrouw op een Ezel, verders nog verscheide andere Stoffagie; alles zonachtig en meesterlyk behandeld | *Mat:* op doek *Size:* hoog 26, breed 32 duim	[Merrem]	(Sold) fl 190 Agina

Heusch, Jacob de (manner)

1802/09/21	UTHDG	0044	*J. de Heusch* | Een Rotsagtig Landschapje met stoffagie, en warm geschildert, in de man. van J. de Heusch | *Mat:* op paneel *Size:* hoog 9, breed 12 duimen		(Bought In) fl 6:10

Heusch, Willem de

1801/06/13	LNDLS	0004	*G. de Heusch* | Een warm en boomrijk Landschap met Gebergte, op de voorgrond beelden en beesten op den weg; zoo goed als van Both, door G. de Heusch, op paneel geschilderd | *Mat:* op paneel *Size:* hoog 22, breed 28 duimen	D van R	(Sold) fl 125 A Delfos [for] W
1801/08/19	AMSCH	0041	*G. de Heus* | Een aangenaam Boom en Bergachtig Landschap met bevallige stoffagie, geestig op Paneel | *Mat:* op paneel *Size:* hoog 11, breed 14 duim	W Wynen	(Sold) fl 22:10 Coclers
1801/08/19	AMSCH	0042	*G. de Heus* | Twee dito [aangenaam] dito [Boom en Bergachtig Landschap], niet minder als de voorgaande | *Size:* hoog 14, breed 18 duim	W Wynen	(Sold) fl 15 Gruiter
1803/06/20	AMSCH	0054	*G. de Heusch* | Twee stuks Italiaansche Landschappen met Geboomten, beide gestoffeerd met Veehoeders, en verscheiden zoorten van Vee; meesterlyk behandeld, door G. de Heusch, op Paneel | *Mat:* op paneel	Schley [for] F	(Sold) fl 5:5 Grimpen
1803/08/17	AMSCH	0034	*Heus. (G. de)* | Twee stuks Boom- en Bergachtige Landschapjes, met kreupel gewas, stille Rivier, en veruitgestrekte Verschieten, gestoffeerd met Beeldjes, een Vrouwtje te Paard, en eenige Ezeldryvers, warm en uitvoerig behandeld | *Mat:* op paneel *Size:* ieder hoog 7, breed 9 ½ duim	Anna Catharina Putman	(Sold) fl 20:10 Yver
1804/05/07	AMSCH	0081	*Heus. (G. de)* | In een hoog Bergachtig Landschap, ziet men een Vrouw een beladen Ezel dryven, op de voorgrond eenige rustende Ryzigers; zonachtig en bevallig gepenceeld | *Mat:* op paneel *Size:* hoog 10, breed 13 ½ duim	Vinkeles [for] G	(Sold) fl 6:10 Gruyter
1806/05/05	AMSCH	0069	*G. de Heus* | Een bergagtig Landschap met Ruine. Geboomten en anderen stoffagie; warm en meesterlyk geschilderd door G. de Heus | *Mat:* op doek *Size:* hoog 38, breed 33 duim	V[inkeles]	(Sold) fl 1:10 Boelen
1806/08/13	AMSCH	0075	*Heus. (G. de)* | Een Bergachtig en Boomryk Landschap, met capitaale Gebouwen, ryk gestoffeerd met gaand en rustende Jagers en Vee; warm en bevallig gepenceeld | *Mat:* op paneel *Size:* hoog 7 ½, breed 9 ½ duim	Vinkeles [for] G[ruyter]	(Sold) fl 1:5 Gruyter
1806/08/13	AMSCH	0322	*Heus. (G. de)* | Een fraai Boom- en Bergachtig Landschap, gestoffeerd met Beelden en Beesten; zonachtig en piquant van schildering | *Mat:* op doek *Size:* hoog 38, breed 54 duim	Vinkeles [for] G[ruyter]	(Sold) fl 1:10 du Pree
1806/08/20	HGBSM	0047	*G. de Heus* | Een Landschap | companion to lot 48 *Mat:* op paneel *Size:* hoog 11 ½, breed 15 duim	Macalester Loup [or others]	(Sold) fl 20 for lots 47 & 48. Zwartsman
1806/08/20	HGBSM	0048	*G. de Heus* | Een dito [Landschap] wederga, door denzelven [G. de Heus], op paneel, eender groote | companion to lot 47 *Mat:* op paneel *Size:* hoog 11 ½, breed 15 duim	Macalester Loup [or others]	(Sold) fl 20 for lots 47 & 48. Zwartsman
1808/06/06	RMRIJ	0052	*Heus. (Guillaume de)* | Een aangenaam bergachtig en boomrijk Landgezigt, waarin eenige Beesten, Schapen en Beelden. Uitvoerig en in de manier van Jan Both geschilderd [Paysage pittoresque. Sur le devant d'un grand chemin, on voit des figures conduisant un troupeau de Boeufs etc. De beaux arbres, un lointoin [sic] agréable, et un ciel clair forment un Ensemble bien fini, et dans la manière de Jean Both] | *Annots:* vd Pot kocht op veiling P. Calkoen W^{Z} Amst. 10 Sept 1781: ... Landschap fl 100 (RKDH I) *Mat:* op paneel *Size:* Hoog 18 ¼, en breed 24 ¼ duim	Gerrit van der Pot, Heer van Groeneveld	(Sold) fl 400 Coclers
1808/06/13	AMSCH	0068	*Heusch (G. de)* | Een Italiaansch bergachtig Landschap, fraai van Geboomte; in het verschiet een wagen, met twee ossen bespannen; ter zijde eenige Reizigers: op den voorgrond een Boer, met twee beladen Muilezels. Teder en zonachtig, als door J. Both behandeld | *Mat:* op paneel *Size:* hoog 34, breed 42 duim	E M Engelberts	(Sold) fl 50 Engelberts

1808/06/13	AMSCH	0068a[H]	*Heusch (G. de)* | 1 dito [Italiaansch] dito [bergachtig Landschap] [or] 1 fruitstuk | *Notes:* This lot was added in by hand in the AA I, EBNP and RKDH copies of the catalogue, with variations in the title as shown above.		(Sold) fl 30 Roos
1808/06/13	AMSCH	0070	*Heusch (G. de)* | Een Italiaansch Landschap, waarin een grootsche Waterval; ter regter zyde eenige Visschers; verder een alleraangenaamst verschiet. Als door J. Both behandeld | *Mat:* op doek *Size:* hoog 39, breed 63 duim	E M Engelberts	(Sold) fl 40 Glad
1808/08/23	AMSCH	0075	*Heus. (G. de)* | In een bergachtig Landschap vertoond zich onder een houten Brug een sterk stroomende Waterval, welke zich in een Beek ontlast, gestoffeert met een Landman bij eenig Vee, op de Brug eene Vrouw zittende op een Ezel, en een gaande Huisman; alles doorschijnend en natuurlijk behandeld | *Mat:* op paneel *Size:* hoog 15, breed 19 duim	[Gruyter?]	(Sold) fl 16 Texier
1809/04/22	AMYVR	0057	*G. de Heus* | Een Gezicht op een Steenen Brug over een Rivier, waar eenige Visschers bezig zijn met visschen; bevallig van schildering | *Mat:* op paneel *Size:* hoog 10, breed 11 duim	de Bruin	(Sold) fl 7:5 J de Vries
1809/06/13	AMSCH	0065	*G. de Heus* | Een hoog Bergachtig Boomrijk Landschap, met een klaarspiegelende Rivier, gestoffeerd met een Fabel-Historie uit Ovidius; warm en uitvoerig geschilderd | *Mat:* op paneel *Size:* hoog 31, breed 40 duim	[Gruyter?]	(Bought In) fl 10
1810/06/06	RMMUY	0071	*G. de Heus* | Een Landschap met Koeijen, en eene badende Vrouw | *Mat:* op paneel		(Unknown) fl 1:4
1810/06/06	RMMUY	0072	*G. de Heus* | Een bergachtig Landschap | *Mat:* op paneel		(Unknown) fl 9
1810/08/06	AMSCH	0045	*Heusch (G. de)* | Een Bergachtig Landschap met Gebouwen en een Water doorsneden, op den voorgrond eene Vrouw, zittende op een wit Paard, nevens haar een gaand Landman, bij een beladen Paard, en voor hun Bokken en Schapen; het is als de voorgaande van schildering, kunnende strekken tot eene wederga | possibly companion to lot 44, by Wm. Heusch and G. Lairesse *Mat:* op doek *Size:* hoog 58, breed 66 duimen	A	(Sold) fl 41 van Iperen
1810/08/06	AMSCH	0046	*Heusch (G. de)* | Een hoog Bergachtig Landschap met Water doorsneden, het welk zig op den voorgrond in een Beek ontlast, gestoffeerd met twee Tekenaaren en een Herder met Schapen; zonachtig en meesterlijk behandeld | *Annots:* [par] Both (BPG) *Mat:* op doek *Size:* hoog 77, breed 90 duimen	R[oos]	(Sold) fl 50 Texier Gerbet en Comp
1810/08/06	AMSCH	0047	*Heusch (G. de)* | Een Bergachtig Landschap met hoog Geboomte, gestoffeerd ter regter zijde een Man met een Ezel en ter linker zijde met Herders met Vee; alles is uitvoerig in de manier van Both geschilderd | *Mat:* op paneel *Size:* hoog 34, breed 42 duimen	G	(Sold) fl 200 Texier Gerbet en Comp [for] Lebrun

Heusch, Willem de (and Lairesse, G.)

1810/08/06	AMSCH	0044	*Heusch (G. de); G. de Lairesse* | Een hoog Bergachtig Landschap met Geboomte, op den voorgrond gestoffeerd met de Fabel Historie van Latona met hare Kinderen, agterwaards Herders met hunne Schapen; warm van koloriet zonachtig en fraai behandeld | possibly companion to lot 45, by Wm. Heusch *Mat:* op doek *Size:* hoog 58, breed 64 duimen	A	(Sold) fl 80 Coclers

Heusch, Willem de (and Lingelbach)

1808/06/13	AMSCH	0069	*Heusch (G. de); J. Lingelbach* | Een Italiaansch bergachtig Landschap, waarin eenige Reizigers, zoo te voet als te paard, van een Brug komen; op den voorgrond twee Muilezels. Rijk uitgedoscht, zonachtig en uitmuntend gestoffeerd, door J. Lingelbach | *Mat:* op doek *Size:* hoog 37, breed 58 duim	E M Engelberts	(Sold) fl 60 Glad

Heusch, Willem de (manner)

1810/06/06	RMMUY	0070	*G. de Heus* | Een schoon Landschap met Ruïnen en Stoffage van Beelden en Dieren, meesterlijk en konstig geschilderd. Als door G. de Heus | *Mat:* op doek		(Unknown) fl 8

Heussen, Nicolaas van (and Hals, F. (I))

1810/08/06	AMSCH	0041	*Hals (F.); G Heusen* | Eene Fruitvrouw, bezig eenige Vrugten te wegen, verders eene menigte Vrugten op Tafels en in Manden; meesterlijk behandeld | *Mat:* op doek *Size:* hoog 60, breed 74 duimen *Loc:* Bridgnorth, Shropshire, England, UK. Viscount Boyne.	R[oos]	(Bought In) fl 50

Heuvel, P. van den [Unidentified]

1805/07/03	AMSCH	0180[a]	*P. van den Heuvel* | Een Bloemstuk, door P. van den Heuvel, en een ander dito | *This Lot:* Een Bloemstuk; lot 180[b] by Anonymous	R[oos]	(Sold) fl 1:5 for lots 180[a] & 180[b]. Agina

Heyden, Jan van der

1801/04/13	AMSCH	0030	*J. van der Heyden* | Een Stadgezicht met verscheide Gebouwen, en een Kerktoren in het verschiet, gestoffeerd met een menigte beeldjes; de uitvoerigheid van het metzelwerk, maakt dit stuk tot een der beste van deezen Meester, zynde het licht en bruin zeer natuurlyk in dit stuk waargenomen | *Mat:* op paneel *Size:* hoog 23, breed 28 ½ duim	Pierre Fouquet, junior	(Sold) fl 200 Pruyssenaar
1801/06/10	AMSCH	0076	*Heyden. (J. van der)* | Een Dorpgezicht, met Gebouwen, Geboomten en stoffage van Beeldjes, Zonachtig, en natuurlyk gepenceeld | *Mat:* op paneel *Size:* hoog 17, breed 19 duim	Herman ten Kate	(Sold) fl 125 Wreesman

1802/06/28	AMSCH	0065	*J. van der Heyden* | Een fraay Heuvelachtig Landzigt, met een Waterval, op de Voorgrond gestoffeerd met Beeldjes, Woningen en verder bywerk; meesterlyk gepenceelt door J. van der Heyden | *Mat:* op paneel *Size:* hoog 19, breed 23 duim	Anna Elink	(Sold) fl 20 Reijers
1802/06/28	AMSCH	0066	*J. van der Heyden* | In een Binnenvertrek, vertoont zig een Tafel met een tapyt Kleed bedekt, waar op twee Globes en een opengeslaagen Boek, ter zyde op een Armstoel legt een Bybel, verder ter zyde een Schoorsteen met een Schilderstukje en een Rariteit-Kabinetje; alles uitneemend uitvoerig gepenceeld, door Denzelven [J. van der Heyden], hoog 30 , breed 24 duim. Panneel | *Mat:* op paneel *Size:* hoog 30, breed 24 duim *Loc:* Budapest, Magyarország. Szépmüvészati Múzeum. (201) (?)	Anna Elink	(Sold) fl 39 J^n Yver
1802/06/28	AMSCH	0067	*J. van der Heyden* | Een stil Leeven, verbeeld in een Binnenvertrek een Tafel, met een tapyt Kleed bedekt, waar op een Globe, opengeslagen Boek, Drinkschaal en andere Boeken, verder een Rariteit-Kabinetje; uitneemend fraai behandeld, door Denzelven [J. van der Heyden] | *Mat:* op paneel *Size:* hoog 20, breed 17 duim	Anna Elink	(Sold) fl 51 T Spaan
1802/12/13	AMSCH	0213	*J. van der Heyde* | Het Afbeeldzel van den vermaarde Kunstschilder J. van der Heyde; meesterlyk geschilderd op een Zilverde Plaat | *Mat:* op een zilverde plaat *Size:* hoog 5 ½, breed 4 duim	Schley [for] Lauwers	(Sold) fl 7 Coclers
1803/07/18	AMSCH	0020	*Heyde (Jan van der)* | Op een groote Markt, bebouwt met verscheide Gebouwen, ziet men in het verschiet een Kerk en Kerkhof, waarop een menigte Geboomtens, de straaten zyn gestoffeerd met verscheide figuuren, het zonligt is bevallig, en de behandeling van het Metzelwerk zoo uitvoerig als 'er ooit van deezen Meester gezien is [Sur une grande place envirronnée de batimens, d'un semitiere [sic] planté d'arbres dont les rues sont egalement garnies, le point de vue va se porter sur une vaste eglise & sur un couvent ; vérs la droite la perspective perce plus avant dans les rues. Le pavé est orné par de jolies figures & une pompe & une loge remplissent le vuide du milieu de la place. Rien n'est concevable audessus du fini de ce morceau ! Le detail en est immense, aucun tableau ne lui a couté plus de travail ; l'oeuil ne suit qu'a peine le travail des murs & des autres parties de batimens, ainsi que le feuille des arbres. Un ciel azuré repond à cette representation claire, lumineuse. L'on pourroit supposer de la dureté par un travail aussi opiniâtre, rien n'est cependant plus naturel que cette perspective d'une vérité de couleur ravissante.] | *Mat:* op paneel *Size:* hoog 20, breed 24 duim	Maria Theresia Andrioli	(Bought In) fl 445
1803/08/24	HGKAN	0051	*J. van der Heyde* | Een Lantschap met een vliedend water doorsneeden, gestoffeerd met verscheiden Bovenwoningen en Huislieden | *Mat:* op paneel *Size:* hoog 18, breet 15 duim	[Teissier] [or others]	(Sold) fl 11 Cuylenburg
1804/07/25	AMSCH	0036	*Heyden (J. van der)* | Een gezicht op een ruime Markt in een Duitsche Stad, ter zyde eenige aloude keurige gemetzelde Huizen, verders een Kerk met twee Torens, een ménigte andere Gebouwen, en diverse Stoffagie van Beeldjes, en Geboomten; warm, zonachtig en uitvoerig gepenceeld | *Mat:* op paneel *Size:* hoog 18, breed 22 duim		(Sold) fl 95 Vinkeles
1805/07/03	AMSCH	0095	*J. van der Heyden* | Een stil leeven, op een Tafel, by een Schoorsteen, met een rood Tapyt bedekt, legt een opengeslaagen Boek, waarby twee Globes en een klyn Rariteit Cabinet, voor de Tafel een rood bekleede Armstoel, waarop een Opengeslagen Bybel, verders in de Schoorsteen een historiëele Ordinantie, enz.; alleruitvoerigst en fraai gepenceeld | *Mat:* op doek *Size:* hoog 30, breed 24 duim *Loc:* Budapest, Magyarország. Szépmüvészati Múzeum. (201)	S	(Bought In) fl 41
1806/08/13	AMSCH	0321	*Heyden. (J. van der)* | Een stil Leven, op een Tafel met een rood Kleed bedekt, waarnaast een rood Damast bekleede Stoel, ziet men een opengeslagen Bybel, waarby twee Globes en achter dezelve een Rariteit-Kabinetje, verders in de Schoorsteen een Historiëele Ordinantie, alleruitvoerigst gepenceeld | *Mat:* op doek *Size:* hoog 30, breed 24 duim *Loc:* Budapest, Magyarország. Szépmüvészati Múzeum. (201)	Vinkeles [for] J	(Bought In) fl 33
1808/06/13	AMSCH	0066	*Heijden (J. van der)* | Een fraai Stadgezicht: in het midden een schoon Kerkgebouw, omgeven met Geboomte; ter zijde ziet men door een straat, gestoffeerd met verscheidene wandelende en rustende Beelden. Het metzelwerk is zeer uitvoerig, en is voorts van een zeer zachte penceelsbehandeling | *Mat:* op paneel *Size:* hoog 13, breed 17 duim	R[oos]	(Bought In) fl 150
1808/06/13	AMSCH	0067	*Heijden (J. van der)* | Eene Ordonantie, waarin opengeslagene Boeken; Aard- en Hemelglobe, Rariteitkast en andere Voorwerpen. Natuurlijk en uitvoerig behandeld, en fraai van kleur | *Mat:* op doek *Size:* hoog 29, breed 25 duim *Loc:* Budapest, Magyarország. Szépmüvészati Múzeum. (201)	K	(Sold) fl 25:10 Allard

Heyden, Jan van der (and Velde, A.)

1801/06/10	AMSCH	0075	*Heyden. (J. van der); A. v. Velde* | Een Stadgezicht gestoffeerd met hoog Geboomte, Schuiten en Beeldjes, Zonachtigen uitvoerig behandeld | *Mat:* op paneel *Size:* hoog 14, breed 18 duim	Herman ten Kate	(Sold) fl 390 W Reijers
1802/05/05	AMSCH	0070	*J. van der Heyden; A. van de Velde* | Een Binnegezicht in een Oude Stad, voorzien van een Prachtige Tempel en andere Grootsche Gebouwen, staande op een Markt; op de Voorgrond een steene Brug en Cappelletje, ryk gestoffeert met verscheide Werkende en Gaande Beeldjes.	J	(Bought In) fl 505

			Uitmuntend fraai uitvoerig en zonachtig gepenceeld | *Mat:* op doek *Size:* hoog 20 ½, breed 25 ½ duim		
1804/02/27	AMSCH	0045	*Heide (J. van der); A. van de Velde* | Een zeer aangenaam Landschap, met hoog opgaand Geboomte, op den voorgrond een stil Water, waarby een Hengelaar, ter zyde een Huysmanswoning, verders een Heer en een Dame Wandelende, en een bevallig verschiet; zeer uitvoerig van schildering | *Mat:* op paneel *Size:* hoog 9, breed 12 duim	B	(Sold) fl 67 Jozi
1805/07/03	AMSCH	0021	*Heyden. (J. van der); A. van de Velde* | Een Landschap met Gebergtens en een Waterval ontwaard men op de voorgrond, op de tweede grond ziet men een Stads Poort en verdere Gebouwen, Geboomten en een ménigte Beeldjes; kragtig en zonachtig en tevens uitvoerig gepenceeld | *Mat:* op paneel *Size:* hoog 12, breed 11 duim	G	(Sold) fl 30 Wed Achtienhoven
1808/06/06	RMRIJ	0053	*Heijden. (Joan van der); Velde. (Adriaan van de)* | Eenige fraaije Gebouwen, eene Valbrug en Boomen, langs waterachtige grachten. Lezende, Visschende en werkende figuren beschouwt men op dit in alle opzigten konstig en verwonderlijk uitgevoerd tafereel. Eene wedergade. In dit tafereel ziet men prachtige Gebouwen, rijk Geboomte en aangename Figuren, waaronder eene Vrouw met een Emmer eenen trap afgaande, terwijl een Heer, vergezeld van een Hond, een Heer en Dame schijnt te groeten. In alles gelijk aan het voorgaande [L'Intérieur d'une Ville Hollandaise. Un Canal bordé par des quais, un Pont-levis, des Bâtiments d'un bon gout, et plusieurs Figures admirablement peintes et du plus grand fini, décorent ce charmant Tableau Pendant au Précédent. Un Canal bordé d'un quai et traversé par un Pont-vouté, des joli Bâtiments, de beaux arbres et plusieurs figures agréables ornent cette belle Production] | *Mat:* op koper *Size:* Twee stukken. Hoog 13 ½, en breed 16 ¾ duim. *Loc:* Amsterdam, Nederland. Rijksmuseum. (A 152 & A 153)	Gerrit van der Pot, Heer van Groeneveld	(Sold) fl 1045 Johs Eck en Zoon [for] le Roi
1809/07/19	AMSCH	0020	*Heijden (J. van der); Velde (A. v. de)* | Dit fraai kapitaal Tafreel vertoont in een Heuvelachtig Landschap met Geboomte het Gezigt naar een aloud Kasteel, op den voorgrond gestoffeerd met twee Heeren te Paard, verzeld van een Valkenier en Jagthonden; by een opgaande Weg eenige Jagers en op een grazig Heuveltje eenig rustend Vee, verder een Riviergezicht naar een Dorp met Woningen en een gaand Rijziger. Het natuurlijk zonlicht, het bevallige koloriet, en de uitvoerige Penceelsbehandeling geven lof aan beide deze Meesters | *Mat:* op paneel *Size:* hoog 19, breed 26 duim	[Bicker]	(Sold) fl 255 T Spaan
1809/09/06	AMSCH	0021	*Heijden (J vam der); A. van de Velde* | In een Binnengezigt van een voorname Stad, op een ruim Plijn of Markt, vertoont zich op een Heuvel een groote Kerk, en verder andere Gebouwen; het is uitmuntend gestoffeert met wandelende Beeldjes, Rijtuigen en eenig Vee. Alles is ongemeen helder, zonachtig en van een uitvoerige penceelbehandeling door beide deze beroemde Meesters vervaardigd | *Mat:* op paneel *Size:* hoog 15, breed 17 duim *Loc:* Nieuwersluis, Nederland. B. de Geus van den Heuvel collection.	Johannes Caudri	(Sold) fl 81 Gruyter
1810/05/22	AMSCH	0035	*Heiden (J. van der); A. van de Velde* | Een fraai Boomrijk Landschap, op den voorgrond bij een Water een opgaande Weg naar een Gebouw, gestoffeerd met een Landman, eenig Vee voortdrijvende, verder een Heer te Paard en Reizigers; uitvoerig en zuiver van schildering | *Mat:* op paneel *Size:* hoog 11, breed 13 duim	Johannes van de Putte Nicolaasz.	(Sold) fl 122 Gruyter
1810/05/22	AMSCH	0036	*Heiden. (J. van der); A. van de Velde* | Twee stuks Gezichten buiten den Haag, verbeeldende het eene het Huis in het Bosch; het andere de Koekamp; beide met Beeldjes gestoffeerd en zeer uitvoerig van penceelbehandeling | *Mat:* op paneel *Size:* hoog 8 ½, breed 11 duim *Loc:* London, England, UK. National Gallery. (1914) (?)	Johannes van de Putte Nicolaasz.	(Sold) fl 256 Gruyter
1810/08/01	AMSCH	0038	*Heiden (Jan van der); Adriaan van de Velde* | Een Stadsgezigt met eene Brug bij een grootsch Gebouw, versierd met een Meisje, dat linnen spoelt, en andere zoo gaande als staande lieden [Vue intérieure de Ville prise sur un Canal, auprès d'un grand Batiment, contre lequel se trouve un pont. On observe au bord de l'eau une Fille blanchissant du linge et plusieurs Figures cheminans dans la rue] | *Annots:* Bon, mais nullement éminent. (NGW) *Mat:* op paneel *Size:* hoog 19, breed 22 duimen *Loc:* Waddesdon Manor, Bucks., England, UK. National Trust. (WI/60/9)	Mr Pieter de Smeth van Alphen	(Sold) fl 2999 J Yver
1810/08/06	AMSCH	0043	*Heiden (J. van der); Gestoffeerd door A. van de Velde* | Een oud Gezigt binnen Amsterdam, zijnde een gedeelte van de Heeregragt naar de Leliegragt te zien, gestoffeerd met onderscheidene Beeldjes en Vaartuigen; het is zonachtig en zeer uitvoerig door beide Meesters behandeld | *Mat:* op paneel *Size:* hoog 14, breed 17 duimen *Loc:* Waddesdon Manor, Bucks., England, UK. National Trust. (WI/60/8)	A	(Sold) fl 300 de Vries
			Heyden, Jan van der (manner)		
1804/10/29	HRBAU	0164	*J. v. d. Heiden* | Een stil Leven. Zeer natuurlyk en uitvoerig in de manier van J. v. d. Heiden gepenceeld | *Mat:* op paneel *Size:* hoog 16, breed 14 ½ duim	Simon Styl	(Unknown)
			Hellegaert, Pauwels van (I)		
1805/07/03	AMSCH	0096	*P. van Hellegaert* | Een Hartejacht in een Landschap, vol expresie en breed en breed geschilderd | *Mat:* op doek *Size:* hoog 22, breed 27 duim	Y	(Sold) fl 13 Agina

Himpel, Aarnout ter

1802/09/06	AMSCH	0201	*ter Himpel* | Een Paardestal, van binnen te zien	Spaan	(Sold) fl 1:5 Oostwijn

Hobbema, Meindert

1801/10/06	AMSCH	0033	*M. Hobbema* | In een Boschagtig Landschap ziet men ter regter zyde by een afgaande weg, een vrouw zittende op een Ezel, verder een Veehoeder eenige Beesten voortdryvende, op de voorgrond eenige Plantgewassen, het verschiet vertoont hoog Gebergte, zonagtig en fraay behandeld | *Mat:* op doek *Size:* hoog 42 breed 52 duim	M	(Sold) fl 20 Spruit van Gend
1801/10/19	AMSCH	0027	*Hobbema. (M.)* | Een extra fraay en natuurlyk Landschap met zwaare Boomen, Boerewoningen en Beelden; uitneemend breed en schoon geschildert | *Mat:* op paneel *Size:* hoog 20 ½, breed 26 duim *Loc:* London, England, UK. National Gallery. (2570) (?)	Jonkheer Menno Baron van Coehoorn	(Sold) fl 1710 Coclers
1802/05/05	AMSCH	0074	*M. Hobbema* | Een gezicht van het Duin, ziende over de Bleekerijen op de Stad Haarlem, bevallig van Ligt en stoffagie en Meesterlyk op Panneel geschilderd | *Mat:* op paneel *Size:* hoog 13, breed 16 duim	C	(Sold) fl 17 Spruit
1802/06/16	AMSCH	0065	*M. Hobbema* | Dit uitmuntend Kabinetstuk vertoont een Boomryk Landschap: op de voorgrond ziet men een helder Waterbeekje, waar by een Man, Vrouw en Jongen, en ter zyde een gaande Huisman; het verschillend Geboomten, en de onderscheiden aart der Stamme en Bladeren, zyn verwonderlyk natuurlyk, het aangenaam Zonlicht, de bevallige doorzichten, het Dun en spiegelend Beekje, alles evenaart de Natuur, en is van een aller uitvoerigste Penceel-behandeling en zeldzaam zoo voorkomende | *Mat:* op paneel *Size:* hoog 12, breed 15 ½ duim	[Merrem]	(Sold) fl 2600 I Smit Gz
1802/06/16	AMSCH	0066	*M. Hobbema* | Een dito [Kabinetstuk] als de voorgaanden, verbeeldende een aller Natuurlykst Boomryk Landschap, gestoffeerd met Boere Woningen en Hut, ter wederzyde, by een opgaande weg: waar op gaande Huislieden; de onderscheide aart der Stammen, het dartel speelend Geboomten en natuurlyk invallend Zonlicht, geeven een luister aan dit fraaije stuk, en is niet minder bevallig en uitvoerig als de voorgaande behandeld | *Mat:* op paneel *Size:* hoog 12, breed 15 ½ duim	[Merrem]	(Withdrawn)
1802/06/16	AMSCH	0067	*M. Hobbema* | Een Capitaal Landschap, gestoffeerd met eenig Geboomten; op de voorgrond ter zyde ziet men een Bruggetje en Voorpoort, gaande naar een Boere Woning, waar by een Vrouw aan de Deur staande; het invallende Zonlicht geeft een verwonderlyke natuurlyke werking, het Coloriet is kragtig, en meesterlyk breed gepenceeld | *Mat:* op doek *Size:* hoog 38, breed 46 duim	[Merrem]	(Sold) fl 200 I Smit Gz
1802/06/16	AMSCH	0068	*M. Hobbema* | Een Gezicht op de Stad Haarlem van de Duine te zien, op de voorgrond by verscheide Boere Woningen en Geboomte ziet men twee Landlieden, fiks en helder van Penceel-behandeling | *Mat:* op paneel *Size:* hoog 19, breed 25 duim	[Merrem]	(Sold) fl 38 LaFontaine
1802/06/16	AMSCH	0069	*M. Hobbema* | Een boomryk Landschap met Boerewooningen en stoffagie van Beeldjes, zonachtig en meesterlyk van de vroege tyd, van deezen voortreffelyken lyke Meester gepenceeld | *Size:* hoog 12, breed 17 duim	[Merrem]	(Sold) fl 39 Hulswit
1802/07/21	HGKAN	0099	*M. Hobbema* | Een Bergagtig Landschap, zeer piquant geschildert		(Unknown)
1803/06/20	AMSCH	0015	*M. Hobbema* | Een capitaal Landschap, gestoffeerd met eenig Geboomte op de voorgrond, ter zyde ziet men een Bruggetje en Voorpoort, gaande naar een Boere Woning, waarby een Vrouw aan de Deur staande, het invallende zonlicht, geeft een natuurlyke werking, en is krachtig van coloriet en breed gepenceelt, door M. Hobbema, op Doek | *Mat:* op doek *Size:* hoog 38, breed 46 duim	Schley [for] B	(Sold) fl 86 Pruijssenaar
1804/05/07	AMSCH	0078	*Hobbema. (M.)* | Een Gezicht op de Bleekeryen buiten de stad Leiden, gestoffeerd met een Heer te Paard en en twee gaande Huislieden; natuurlyk behandeld | *Mat:* op doek *Size:* hoog 12, breed 15 ½ duim	Y[ver] [for] JJ	(Sold) fl 8 Pruyssenaar
1805/07/03	AMSCH	0020	*Hobbema. (M.)* | Dit voortreffelyk Landschap steld voor, een opgaande Weg met zwaar Geboomten en stoffagie van Beelden, terzyde een helder spiegelende Water, waarover een Vonder; gaande over dezelve een Man naar het Dorp, hetgeen men agter een Kreupelbosch ontwaar word; het frapante zonlicht en de spiegeling der voorwerpen in het heldere Water, maken dit stuk, 't welk tevens Meesterlyk van penceels behandeling is tot een byzonder aangenaam Schildery | *Mat:* op doek *Size:* hoog 19, breed 25 duim	R[oos]	(Bought In) fl 1075
1808/08/23	AMSCH	0067	*Hobbema. (M.)* | Dit uitmuntend Kabinetstukje, steld voor een Boomrijk Landschap, op de voorgrond ziet men een helder Waterbeekje, waar bij een Man, Vrouw en Jongeling, ter zijde een gaande Huisman, het verschillend Geboomte en de onderscheiaart der Stammen, zijn verwonderlijk natuurlijk, het aangenaam zonlicht, het dun en spiegelend beekje, alles evenaart de Natuur; en is van een alleruitvoerigste penceelbehandeling | *Mat:* op paneel *Size:* hoog 12, breed 15 ½ duim *Loc:* London, England, UK. National Gallery. (833)	X	(Sold) fl 800 Coclers
1808/08/23	AMSCH	0068	*Hobbema. (M.)* | Dit fraai en zeer natuurlijk Landschap, vertoont langs een opgaande Weg met hoog Geboomten, eenige gaande Huislieden, ter eener zijde een stil Watertje, in 't verschiet een Molen; het invallend zonlicht doet een aangenaame werking en is van een meesterlijke penceelbehandeling | *Mat:* op paneel *Size:* hoog 13, breed 21 duim	H	(Bought In) fl 190

1809/04/17	AMSCH	0037	*M. Hobbema* | Een Landschap met Boere Woningen, op de voorgrond een Waterval; eigenaartig gestoffeerd en zonachtig behandeld | *Mat:* op paneel *Size:* hoog 14, breed 12 duim	T	(Sold) fl 35 [?]
1809/05/26	HADAA	0013	*M. Hobbema* | Een Landschap	Mejuffrouw de Wed David Heemskerk [or others]	(Unknown)
1809/06/13	AMSCH	0058	*M. Hobbema* | Dit eenvoudig dog zeer natuurlijk Schilderij, verbeeld een Land- en Watergezigt, gestoffeerd met een Roeischuit met verscheide Lieden; de spiegeling in het Water, en de onderscheiden Geboomtens zijn zeer natuurlijk verbeeld | *Size:* hoog 12, breed 15 duim	[Gruyter?]	(Sold) fl 15:5 van Iperen
1810/06/20	AMSCH	0033	*M. Hobbema* | Een stille Rivier en langs Boeren-Woningen eene Kerk en Geboomte. Het is gestoffeerd met Werklieden, en Visschers in hunne Vaartuigen. Natuurlijk verbeeld en zuiver van schildering | *Mat:* op paneel *Size:* hoog 20, breed 27 duimen	B	(Sold) fl 8:15 Boelhouwer
1810/08/01	AMSCH	0040	*Hobbema (Meindert)* | Een boomrijk Landschap, met een breed Water, Landweg en Boerenwoningen, verlevendigd door eenen Hengelaar en onderscheidene Huislieden [Un beau Paysage, richement boisé, coupé par une large plage d'eau, et varié par des Chaumieres ; Les Figures sont un Pêcheur et quelques Paysans] | *Annots:* très bon, mais les contours un peu durs. Lafontaine en revision avec LeBrun, qui l'a obtenu. (NGW); Vente le Brun retiré à fr. 10,000 (SMLN) *Mat:* op doek *Size:* hoog 37, breed 50 duimen *Loc:* London, England, UK. Wallace Collection. (P75)	Mr Pieter de Smeth van Alphen	(Sold) fl 3250 Lafontaine
1810/08/01	AMSCH	0041	*Hobbema (Meindert)* | Een Gezigt, binnen Amsterdam, van den Singel op de Schutsluis, Wipbrug en Haringpakkers-Toren, gestoffeerd met Beeldjes; verder schepen in het verschiet [Une Perspective dans l'interieur de la Ville d'Amsterdam du côté du port. On remarque le Pont et l'Ecluse tels qu'ils se trouvoient du tems de l'Auteur, ainsi que la tour qui est au bord du fleuve. Le fond est terminé par le fleuve l'Y. Ce tableau est orné de figures] | *Annots:* mauvais (NGW); [par] Kessel (BPG) *Mat:* op doek *Size:* hoog 30, breed 39 duimen *Loc:* London, England, UK. National Gallery. (6138)	Mr Pieter de Smeth van Alphen	(Bought In) fl 1000
1810/10/10	MGCIT	0031	*Hobbema* | Een extra fraai bergagtig Landschapje, waar in men tusschen het Geboomte een boeren Woning ziet, voorts een zeer aangenaam verschiet aan de linkerzijde; wijders eene welgekozene stoffage	Caspar van Citters	(Unknown)
			Hobbema, Meindert (or Hobbema, manner)		
1808/04/26	GDAN	0278	*Hobbema* | Een goed Landschap, door of in de manier van Hobbema, met goede stoffage | *Size:* hoog 25, breed 26 ½ duim	G H Fortuyn	(Unknown)
			Hobbema, Meindert (copy after)		
1809/04/22	AMYVR	0137	*A. Vermeulen; M. Hobbema* | Een Boomrijk Landschap, aan eene Waterplas; zonachtig behandeld, naar M. Hobbema, door A. Vermeulen | copy by A. Vermeulen after Hobbema *Size:* hoog 29, breed 41 duim	de Bruin	(Sold) fl 14:15 du Pree
			Hobbema, Meindert (manner)		
1805/07/10	AMSCH	0273	*Hobbema* | Een Boomryk Landschap met Boere Woningen stoffagie van Beeldjes en Beestjes, enz.; zonachtig op Doek, in de manier van Hobbema | *Mat:* op doek	V[inkeles] [for] K	(Bought In) fl 6:10
1806/05/05	AMSCH	0253	*Hobbema* | Een fraai natuurlyk Landschapje; in de manier van Hobbema	R[oos]	(Sold) fl 4:15 van Laar
1806/08/13	AMSCH	0300	*Hobbema* | Twee stuks aangenaam Boomryke Landschappen, met Rivieren doorsneeden en stoffagie van Beeldjes; in de manier van Hobbema	Vinkeles [for] F	(Sold) fl 22 T Spaan
1808/04/26	GDAN	0239	*Hobbema* | Een Zwitzersch bergägtig Gezigt, met eene Waterval, fraai gestoffeerd in de manier van Hobbema | *Size:* hoog 66, breed 68 duim	G H Fortuyn	(Unknown)
			Hochecker, Franz		
1805/10/09	HGBSM	0052	*F. Hocheker* | Twee stuks, rhyn gezigten met stoffagie, in de manier van Grefier | *Mat:* op doek *Size:* hoog 18 ½ breet 24 ½ duim	T H van Willigen [or others]	(Sold) fl 16:5 De Gelder
			Hodges, Charles Howard		
1808/03/03	HAVIN	0035	*Hodges* | De Geboorte, zeer fraai met Coul.	Jacobus Spillebout	(Unknown) fl 8:10
1808/03/03	HAVIN	0037	*Hodges* | De Afdoening | *Notes:* This lot was sold with lot 36, which is a copy by C.H. Hodges after Anth. van Dyck.	Jacobus Spillebout	(Unknown) fl 28 for lots 36 & 37
1808/03/03	HAVIN	0038	*Hodges* | De Verrijzenis | *Notes:* This lot was sold with lot 39 by Bierweiler.	Jacobus Spillebout	(Unknown) fl 31 for lots 38 & 39
			Hodges, Charles Howard (copy by)		
1808/03/03	HAVIN	0036	*Hodges; van Dyk* | De Kruisiging, na van Dyk, door Hodges | copy by C.H. Hodges after Anth. van Dyck *Notes:* This lot was sold with lot 37 by C.H. Hodges.	Jacobus Spillebout	(Unknown) fl 28 for lots 36 & 37
			Hoecke, Jan van den		
1803/07/18	AMSCH	0023	*Hoek (J. van)* | De Maagd Maria zittende op de Wolken, houdende het Kind Jesus op haar schoot, in zyn hand hebbende een Appel en onder zyne voeten een Slang, brillant van couleur, en zoo schoon gepenceeld als of het door Rubbens: vervaardigd was [La vierge Marie Assise dans une	Maria Theresia Andrioli	(Sold) fl 58 Gruyter

			Gloire ténant l'Enfant Jesus sur ses Genoux, dans sa Main il tient une Pomme & sous ses pieds le serpent destructeur. Ce Tableau d'une couleur aussi brillante & aussi vigoureuse que celle de Rubbens même, peut être compté parmi les Meilleures productions de van Hoeck son Eleve.] | *Mat:* op paneel *Size:* hoog 24, breed 18 duim		
1805/10/09	HGBSM	0075	*J. van Hoek* | Pallas, die de voorzigtigheid omhelst | *Mat:* op doek *Size:* hoog 14 ½ breet 17 duim	T H van Willigen [or others]	(Sold) fl 6:10 Van der Vin
			Hoecke, Jan van den (copy by)		
1804/08/02	BDAN	0012	*J. van Hoek; Rubens* | Venus Lusthof na Rubens, schoon in Couleur | copy by J. Hoecke after Rubens *Mat:* op paneel *Size:* b. 52 d. h. 36 d.	J G Calckberner	(Unknown)
			Hoecke, Robert van den		
1803/04/18	HGBAK	0033	*v. Hoeck* | Een Zee met Scheepen door v. Hoeck, op doek, hoog 23, breed 29 duim, bruine lyst [Schilderyen in Olyverf] | *Mat:* in olyverf op doek *Size:* hoog 23, breed 29 duim *Notes:* The bracketed information in the title appears above lot 1 and refers to lots 1 to 48.	Johan Pieter Reigersman [or others]	(Unknown)
1803/08/24	HGKAN	0018	*van Hoek* | Een Bataille vol gewoel van Krygslieden, verbeelt een allerhevigst Gevegt tusschen Ruitery die woedende op elkander Vuuren | *Mat:* op doek	[Teissier] [or others]	(Unknown) fl 5:5
1809/04/17	AMSCH	0174	*C. Hoek* | Een hevige Bataille tusschen Ruiterij | *Notes:* The artist's name was given as "C. Hoek" but we have assumed this is an error.	H	(Sold) fl 3
			Hoek, J. van [Unidentified]		
1802/04/13	HAVIN	0074	*J. van Hoek* | Twee met Stilleevens		(Unknown)
			Hoet, Gerard (I)		
1801/08/19	AMSCH	0046	*G. Hoet* | Twee stuks fraaije Bybel – Ordenantiën, verbeeldende de eene de vinding van Mozes, en den anderen, Christus op de weg met de Dicipelen naar Emaus, byde in bevallige Landschappen; meesterlyk en uitvoerig op Paneel | *Mat:* op paneel *Size:* hoog 13, breed 16 duim	W Wynen	(Sold) fl 15 Gruiter
1801/10/19	AMSCH	0026	*Hoet. (G.)* | Een Offerhande aan Diana, ryk gestoffeerd met Beelden en danzende Vrouwen, in een bergachtig Landschap met geboomten; uitvoerig behandeld | *Mat:* op doek *Size:* hoog 20, breed 24 ¼ duim	Jonkheer Menno Baron van Coehoorn	(Sold) fl 51 W[l] Reijers
1802/04/13	HAVIN	0026	*G. Hoed* | De Maaltyt van …., schoon van ordonantien en schildering		(Unknown)
1802/06/16	AMSCH	0079	*G. Hoet* | Deeze Ryke Ordenantie vol gewoel, verbeeld de viering van het Feest van Flora, verscheide Nimphen en Bachanten vermaken zich met op Instrumenten te speelen, andere vlegten Kransen van Bloemen en vercieren het afbeeldsel der Goden; verders vertoonen zich treffelyke Gebouwen, alles is kunstig en zeer uitvoerig gepenceeld | *Mat:* op doek op paneel *Size:* hoog 20, breed 24 duim	[Merrem]	(Sold) fl 60 Pruijssenaar
1802/06/28	AMSCH	0072	*G. Hoed* | Venus en Adonis, in een Landschap, verzelt van eenige Nimphen; kragtig geschilderd, door G. Hoed, op Panneel | *Mat:* op paneel *Size:* hoog 8, breed 11 duim	B	(Sold) fl 7 Royers
1802/06/28	AMSCH	0073	*G. Hoed* | Een hevige Rencontre van Cavallerie, op de Voorgrond ziet men eenige Stroopers; helder en meesterlyk gepenceelt, door Denzelven [G. Hoet], op Doek | *Mat:* op doek *Size:* hoog 23, breed 34 duim	Anna Elink	(Sold) fl 4 Mensart
1802/08/24	LNDLS	0068	*G. Hoet* | Een Heilige Familie; Maria zit met het Kind op haar schoot, benevens Joseph met een Boek voor zich, agter hem een Gebouw. Konstig, krachtig en delicaat | *Mat:* op paneel *Size:* hoog 10, breed 12 duimen	Leonardus Bouman [or others]	(Unknown) fl 25
1802/09/21	UTHDG	0042	*G. Hoet* | Twee stuks, in het eerste een jong meisje, liefkozende een wit Konijn, in de wederga een Maagd spelende met een wite [sic] Duif. Beide stukjes, die de onnoozelheid en oprechtheid schijnen voortestellen, zijn aangenaam geschildert | *Mat:* op paneel *Size:* hoog 11, breed 8 duimen		(Sold) fl 5:10 J La Maine
1803/08/24	HGKAN	0038	*G. Hoet* | Drie stuks differente Historieele Ordonnantien | *Mat:* op doek	[Teissier] [or others]	(Sold) fl 9 van Giesen
1803/09/07	AMSCH	0079	*G. Hoet* | De Steniging van Stefanus, zynde omgeven van een menigte Vrouwen, welke hetzelve met medelyden beschouwen, het coloriet en de schildering is allerbevalligst [La lapidation de St. Etienne ; le saint est entouré de plusieurs femmes qui le regardent avec compassion ; le coloris et l'ordonnance de ce morceau sont excellens] | *Mat:* op doek *Size:* hoog 21, breed 26 duim	Smidt	(Sold) fl 37 Gruiter
1803/12/12	AMSCH	0043	*G. Hoet* | Twee stuks, een Diana met haar Honden, en Flora in een Landschap; uitvoerig op Paneel | *Mat:* op paneel *Size:* hoog 8, breed 9 duim	D	(Sold) fl 30 Coclers
1803/12/15	MGLAC	0020	*G. Hoedt* | Een Landschap, waarin Ruïnen en eenige Figuuren; zeer delicaat geschilderd | *Mat:* op doek *Size:* hoog duim 17, breed duim 15	Mr L H de Haze Bomme	(Unknown)
1804/10/16	DLOND	0100	*G. Hoet* | Twee Stukjens, de Emmausgangers en de Samaritaansche Vrouw. Deux piéces. J. C. avec ses Disciples en chemin á Emmaus, & la Samaritaine | *Mat:* op koper *Size:* hoog 5, breed 7		(Unknown)
1804/10/29	HRBAU	0034	*Hoet, (G.)* | Door een steenen Nis ziet men een Musikant zeer gratieus op de viool speelen; waar agter een gordyn en basrelieven te zien zyn. Zeer delicaat en uitvoerig behandeld | *Mat:* op koper *Size:* hoog 10, breed 8	Simon Styl	(Unknown)

1804/12/10	AMSCH	0028	*G. Hoet* | Deeze ryke Ordinantie vol gewoel, van beelden, in een prachtig paleis; voor een cierlyk ledikant vertoont zig een Vorstin, grootmoedig een beeker aanneemende, welke haar door een held, in romeinsche kleeding word overgeleevert, zy is verzeld van een menigte andere vrouwen, waar onder die bloemen zamelen, eenige toonen hun droefheid, andere hun verwondering; het is bevallig van licht, en coloriet, en uitvoerig gepenceeld | *Mat:* op doek *Size:* Hoog 25, breed 31 duim	Jan De Groot	(Sold) fl 126 Reijers
1805/07/03	AMSCH	0026	*Hoet. (G.)* | Deeze ryke Ordinantie, in een bevallig Egyptisch Landschap, verbeeld de vinding van Mozes; de Dochter van Pharao, verzelt van haare Hofstoet van Vrouwen, die alle met verwondering het gevonden Kind beschouwen, hetwelk door een jonge Dochter, uit het biesen korfje genoomen word; alles is kragtig en van een uitvoerige penceel behandeling | *Mat:* op paneel *Size:* hoog 30, breed 42 duim	R[oos]	(Sold) fl 180 L Pakker
1805/07/03	AMSCH	0027	*Hoet. (G.)* | Een zinspeelende Ordinantie, in een prachtig Palys, vyf bevallige Vrouwen, offeren geschenken, verzelt van twee Minnewigten; op een verheeven Piedestal, zit een Godin, in een vorstelyk kleeding, houdende een Hoorn waaruit geld gestort is, en met de regter hand, schynt ze kleinodien uit te deelen; dit stuk is een der uitvoerigste van schildering van deze Meester | *Mat:* op doek *Size:* hoog 15, breed 19 duim	R[oos]	(Sold) fl 55 Hulswit
1805/10/09	HGBSM	0121	*G. Hoet* | Een historiëel stuk, verbeeld de fabelgeschiedenis van den boschgod Pan, die Siringa [sic] vervolgt, in een fraay landschap, konstig geschildert door G. Hoet | *Mat:* op paneel *Size:* hoog 23 breet 29 duim	T H van Willigen [or others]	(Sold) fl 1:18 Carré
1805/10/09	HGBSM	0122	*G. Hoet* | Voor een cierlyke fontein met een waterbak zit Narcissus, zig in 't water spiegelende, boven hem zweeft een cupido, helder en fraay geschilderd | *Mat:* op paneel *Size:* hoog 23 breet 32 duim	T H van Willigen [or others]	(Sold) fl 1:15 Teissier
1805/10/09	HGBSM	0123	*G. Hoet* | Een dito [historiëel stuk] van denzelven meester [G. Hoet], verbeeld den dooden Adonis, betreurd werdende voor Venus, niet minder als de voorgaande op paneel | *Mat:* op paneel	T H van Willigen [or others]	(Sold) fl 1:5 Carré
1805/10/09	HGBSM	N0013	*Hoet* | Eenige ruïnes met figuurtjes, door Hoet in de trant van Poelenburg | *Mat:* op paneel *Size:* hoog 9 ½ breet 12 duim	T H van Willigen [or others]	(Sold) fl 5 Huybrechts
1809/06/13	AMSCH	0067	*G. Hoed* | In een prachtige Zaal, ziet men eene bevallige naakte Vrouw, nevens haar voor een fraaije Canepé een oude Matrone, die haar schijnt het Bed gespreid te hebben, agterwaards een Turk hun bespiedende; delicaat gepenceeld | *Mat:* op doek *Size:* hoog 14, breed 19 duim	[Gruyter?]	(Sold or Bought In) fl 3 Gruyter
1810/03/27	RMCNL	0092	*Hoedt* | Een Stuk, verbeeldende Jezus in den Hof, zeer fijn en natuurlijk gepenceeld		(Unknown)
1810/06/20	AMSCH	0035	*G. Hoet* | Op eene Tafel staat een Mand met Vruchten, een Emmer met Visch en een Aarden Pot, ter zijde eene Kat en twee Hennen. Fiks gepenceeld | *Mat:* op doek *Size:* hoog 34, breed 42 duimen	A	(Sold) fl 7 J Twisk
1810/10/10	MGCIT	0101	*G. Hoet* | Twee fraaije Landschapjes | *Mat:* op koper	Caspar van Citters	(Unknown)
1810/10/10	MGCIT	0114	*G. Hoet* | Een uitvoerig Landschap met Figuren, ontleend uit de Fabelkunde, en ander Bywerk	Caspar van Citters	(Unknown)

Hoet, Gerard (I) (or Hoet, G. (I), manner)

1808/12/31	RMHSN	0010	*G. Hoet* | Een Landschap met Saters en Bachanten, op Paneel, door of in de Manier van G. Hoet | *Mat:* op paneel	G Spanjaart [or] H de Haas [or] C van der Looy Lans	(Unknown)

Hoet, Gerard (I) (manner)

1802/04/13	HAVIN	0050	*Hoed* | Een, daar Christus de Kindre [sic] tot zig laat koomen, als van Hoed		(Unknown)
1802/09/21	UTHDG	0043	*G. Hoet* | Twee stuks moderne Kinderhoofdjes, als de voorgaande [G. Hoet]		(Sold) fl 1:10 Gevaerts
1803/12/12	AMSCH	0154	*Hoet* | Twee stuks met Beelden; als Hoet | *Mat:* op paneel *Size:* hoog 10, breed 13 duim	D	(Sold) fl 3 Coclers
1807/08/26	AMSCH	0093	*G. Hoet* | Een Bybel Ordonnantie vol gewoel, verbeeldende de plegtige omlyding van Mordechaï te paard gezeeten, het geen door Haman geleid word, verder een menigte aanschouwers; gestoffeerd met pragtige Gebouwen; meesterlyk behandeld, in de manier van G. Hoet | *Mat:* op doek *Size:* hoog 28, breed 35 duim	Helsdinge	(Sold) fl 4 Levij Pakker

Hoet, Hendrik Jacob

1802/11/01	DOBRA	0190	*H.J. Hoet* | Een uitvoerig Landschap | *Mat:* op koper *Size:* breed 21, hoog 9 ½ duim		(Unknown) fl 11

Hoet, J. [Unidentified]

1801/12/22	AMOTT	0005	*J. Hoet* | 1 Gezigt binnen de Stad Utrecht, met gewapende Jongelingen en Beelden	Bartholomeus Ruloffs	(Unknown) fl 14

Hoffman, Martin

1802/02/16	AMSCH	0052	*M. Hoffman* | Twee dito [stuks], de eene verbeeld een Dame, welke by 't kaarslicht, dat voor haar op een gerridon geplaatst is, een brief leest; het andere een jongeling in Pelgrimskleeding, houdende een Staf in de hand uitvoerig behandeld	F	(Sold) fl 2 Sappé

			Hoffmann, Samuel		
1803/09/07	AMSCH	0075	*S. Hoffman [signé 1646]* | Een deftig Heer Staande by een Colom met zyn Hoed in de linkerhand en in de regter zyn Handschoenen, kragtig als van Dyk, op Doek, door S. Hoffman, 1646 [Un seigneur ayant une physionomie et une attitude respectables, s'appuie sur une colonne ; il tient d'une main son chapeau et de l'autre ses gants ; ce tableau est d'une expression forte et caractéristique, la touche en est vigoureuse, dans la manière de Van Dyck.] | *Mat:* op doek *Size:* hoog 47, breed 37 duim *Inscr:* S. Hoffman, 1646 (signed and dated) *Notes:* The information about the signature and date appears only in the French edition of the catalogue.	Smidt	(Sold) fl 43 C S Roos
			Hofman, Pieter (Giannizzero)		
1810/07/23	DOLG2	00BB	*P. Hofman* | Een Landschap met Schaapjes | *Mat:* op paneel *Size:* hoog 8, breed 11 duim	Pieter Quinting	(Sold) fl 7 A v Strij
			Hoge, J. van der [Unidentified]		
1804/10/16	DLOND	0102	*J. van der Hoge* | Een Landschap. Paysage | *Mat:* op paneel *Size:* hoog 18, breed 16		(Unknown)
			Holbein, Hans (the younger)		
1802/07/21	HGKAN	0012	*Holbeen* | Een Pourtrait		(Unknown)
1802/07/21	HGKAN	0090	*Holbeen* | Een Portrait		(Unknown)
1803/09/07	AMSCH	0091	*H. Holbein* | Een Man een Meisje een Ring aan de Pink doende zynde van een ouden aart van schildering [Un homme mettant un anneau au petit doigt d'une fille ; manière antique] | *Mat:* op paneel *Size:* hoog 8, breed 6 duim	Smidt	(Sold) fl 1:5 Camphuijsen
1804/02/27	AMSCH	0058	*Holbeyn. (H.)* | Een Altaarstuk met twee Deuren, fraai geschilderd | *Fmt:* een altaarstuk met twee deuren	B	(Sold) fl 2 L Pakker
1804/08/08	AMSCH	0088	*H. Holbein* | Het Afbeeldzel van een oude Geleerde, met een zwarte Muts op 't Hoofd, en een zwarte Mantel, met Rood gevoerd, omhangen; uitvoerig gepenceeld | *Mat:* op paneel *Size:* hoog 3 ½, breed 7 duim	Vink[eles] [for] S	(Bought In) fl 29:10
1805/07/10	AMSCH	0079	*H. Holbeyn* | Een Oud Man, welke een Meisje carresseerd delicaat en uitvoerig gepenceeld | *Size:* hoog 8, breed 6 duimen	V[inkeles] [for] N	(Sold) fl 7:10 Agina
1806/08/20	HGBSM	0203	*H. Holbein* | Hendrik den Agtste | *Mat:* op paneel *Size:* hoog 6 ½, breed 5 ⅔ duim	Macalester Loup [or others]	(Sold) fl 5 Praiston
1808/09/13	HABRU	0040	*Holbein* | Een dito [Mans] Pourtraitje		(Unknown) fl 0:10
			Holbein, Hans (the younger) (and Dürer; copy after)		
1808/06/06	RMRIJ	0017	*Bordieu. (du); Steenwijk. (H. J. van); A. Durer; Holbeijn* | Eene zeer getrouwe kopij naar de origineele Schilderij van A. Durer en H. Holbeijn, Desiderius Erasmus verbeeldende. Het bijwerk door H. J. van Steenwijk. Alles zeer uitvoerig behandeld [Copie fidelle du Portrait de Désiré Erasme d'aprés l'original d'Albert Durer et H. Holbeyn. Les accessoires sont peints par van Steenwyk] | copy by P. Dubordieu and Hend. Steenwyck after Dürer and H. Holbein (II) *Annots:* Geschenk Teding Berkhout (RMA I) *Mat:* op paneel *Size:* Hoog 9 ½, en breed 7 ½ duim	Gerrit van der Pot, Heer van Groeneveld	(Sold) fl 21 du Pré
			Holbein, Hans (the younger) (or Holbein, H. (II), manner)		
1803/04/20	AMSCH	0119	*H. Holbein* | Een Mans Pourtrait ter halver Lyf, in aloude Kleeding, houdende met beide Handen een Paar Handschoenen; breed en fiks gepenceeld, door of in de manier van H. Holbein [Un portrait d'homme a mi-corps tenant des gands traité d'une bonne maniere, comme H. Holbein.] | *Mat:* op paneel *Size:* hoog 29, breed 24 duim	Maria Magdalena van Sluypwyk, gravinne van Moens	(Sold) fl 0:10 Van Cooth
			Holbein, Hans (the younger) (manner)		
1801/08/19	AMSCH	0149	*H. Holbein* | Twee stuks, rond formaat, zynde een Mans- en een Vrouwe Hoofd, als door H. Holbein | *Fmt:* rond	Van Forreest	(Sold) fl 2:5 Roos
1803/08/24	HGKAN	0088	*Holbeyn* | Een Portrait in de trant van Holbeyn	[Teissier] [or others]	(Unknown) fl 2
1808/11/12	HGSCR	0006	*Holbein* | Het pourtrait van D. Erasmus uitvoerig geschildert als door Holbein | *Mat:* op paneel	Mr J van Buren	(Unknown) fl 4
			Holf, N. [Unidentified]		
1804/08/02	BDAN	0017	*N. Holf* | Twee stuks verbeelende Batailjes, zeer schoon geteekend op de manier van Palamedes | *Mat:* op paneel *Size:* b. 26 d. h. 19 d.	J G Calckberner	(Unknown)
			Holsteijn, Cornelis		
1802/12/13	AMSCH	0087	*J. Holstyn* | Een Triomph van Bachus, in een Landschap | *Mat:* op doek *Size:* hoog 37, breed 50 duim *Notes:* The artist's name was given as "J. Holstyn" but we have assumed this is an error.	Pruyssenaar [for] D	(Sold) fl 8:10 Gruiter
1803/11/30	MGBEO	0012	*Holsteyn* | Een Stukje met Vogels | *Mat:* op paneel *Size:* hoog 10 ½ duim, breed 14 ½ duim *Notes:* This lot was sold with lot 13 by an anonymous artist.	Samuel de Wind	(Sold) £ 0:4 for lots 12 & 13. van Benthem
1804/04/28	LNDLS	0011	*Holstein* | In een Landschap zit Maria, met het Kind staande op haar schoot, verzelt van eenige engelen en Joseph; konstig geschildert door	[Abraham Delfos] [or others]	(Sold or Bought In) fl 7 A Delfos

			Holstein 1651, op doek | *Mat:* op doek *Size:* hoog 41, breed 33 duim *Inscr:* Holstein 1651 (signed and dated?) *Notes:* It is unclear whether the name and date are inscribed on the painting.		
1807/04/00	LNDLS	0016	*Holstyn* | Maria zittende met het staande kind, op haar schoot, omringt van Engelen en Joseph agter haar, in een Landschap met geboomte zeer konstig van tekening en schildering | *Mat:* op doek *Size:* hoog 42, breed 33 duim	[Abraham Delfos] [or others]	(Unknown)
1807/06/10	HGBSM	0016	*Holstyn* | Maria zittende met het staande kind, op haar schoot, omringd van Engelen en Joseph agter haar, in een Landschap met geboomte zeer konstig van tekening en schildering | *Mat:* op doek *Size:* hoog 42, breed 33 duim	Abraham Delfos [or others]	(Sold) fl 5 Tomas
1808/05/17	LNAN	0012	*Holstyn* | In een Landschap zit Maria met het kind Jezus, staande op haar schoot, verzeld van Joseph en eenige Engelen bij en boven haar, kunstig geteekend en geschilderd | *Mat:* op doek *Size:* hoog 42, breed 33 duim		(Bought In) fl 14
1810/07/23	DOLG2	00DD	*Holsteen* | In een Landschap vertonen zich een spelend en twee dansende Kinderen; helder en goed geschilderd | *Mat:* op paneel *Size:* hoog 9, breed 12 duim	Pieter Quinting	(Sold) fl 6:5 Vrouw de Visser

Hondecoeter

1807/12/00	ARNIJ	0004	*Hondekoeter* | Een Haan, met eenige Hennen, door Hondekoeter, een weinig defect	Meinsmaa [or] Engelan	(Unknown) fl 0:14
1808/03/03	HAVIN	0022	*de Oude Hondekoeter* | Een Landschap	Jacobus Spillebout	(Unknown)
1808/09/13	HABRU	0038	*Hondekoeter* | Een Hen met Kuijkens, Haas, &c.		(Unknown) fl 8:5
1808/12/30	HGIMM	[0071e]	*Hondekoeter* | Voorts een exquis kabinetje Schilderijen van voorname Nederlandsche Meesters, welke uit hoofde van de kortheid des tijds niet stuk voor stuk kunnen beschreven worden; doch waarvan de beschrijving op den Kijkdag zal voorhanden zijn. Dus wij hier alleen de namen van eenige dier Meesters laten volgen, als: A. Kuyp, Ruysdaal, Karel du Jardyn, Loqwi ('t beste dat hij schilderde) Hondekoeter, van Dyk, Janson, Moesgever, Kamphuyzen, van Gooijen, A. van der Neer, T. Wyk, Huchtenburgh, Zolemaker, van Hassel, A. Vermeulen, van Dongen, Scheffer, van Os enz. | *This Lot:* Een Schilderij, Hondekoeter *Notes:* Because this lot was not numbered in the catalogue, we have assigned the number.		(Unknown)
1809/04/17	AMSCH	0039a[H]	*Hondekoeter* | [Untitled] | *Notes:* This lot was added in by hand in the EBNP copy of the catalogue, but without giving a title.		(Sold) fl 1:5
1809/07/25	HGBSM	0218	*De oude Hondekoeter* | Een Stuk met Hoenderen en Kuikens | *Mat:* op doek *Size:* hoog 23 en een half, breed 20 en een half duim	D van der Aa [or] E B ten Dall	(Sold) fl 2:18 Bakhuizen
1809/10/20	UTWLD	0004	*Hondekoeter* | Een stuk met Kippen enz. door Hondekoeter	J J van Rhyn	(Unknown)
1809/10/20	UTWLD	0005	*Hondekoeter* | Een dito [stuk] met Eenden door dito [Hondekoeter]	J J van Rhyn	(Unknown)
1810/10/10	MGCIT	0153	*Hondekoeter* | Een Schilderij, waarop een schoone Haan, alsmede Hoenders en andere Vogels; natuurlijk behandeld en gemerkt Hondekoeter | *Inscr:* Hondekoeter (signed)	Caspar van Citters	(Unknown)

Hondecoeter (or Hondecoeter, manner)

1801/12/22	AMOTT	0063	*Hondekoeter* | 1 Haan met de Hen, Kiekens en Gevogeltens, door of als Hondekoeter	Bartholomeus Ruloffs	(Unknown) fl 15:10
1810/03/07	UTWLD	0019	*Hondekoeter* | Een zeer schoon geschilderd stuk, verbeeldende eene menagerie met divers gevogelte door of in de smaak van Hondekoeter | *Size:* hoog 6 voet 4 duim, breed 7 voet 7 duim	J J Woertman	(Unknown) fl 7
1810/10/10	MGCIT	0081	*Hondekoeter* | Twee Stukken, verbeeldende een groote quantiteit van levendige Land- en Watervogels, als: Hoenders, Paauwen, Eenden, enz: alles besloten in een Warande, waarachter een fraai Thuinverschiet; alles kunstig en uitvoerig behandeld, door Hondekoeter, of in zyn Manier. Twee dito kleiner, door denzelven.	Caspar van Citters	(Unknown)

Hondecoeter (manner)

1801/04/23	AMYVR	0027	*Hondekoeter* | Eenige doode Vogels, in een Hofgezicht, in de manier van Hondekoeter | *Notes:* This lot was sold with lot 26, which is in the manner of Schalcken.		(Sold) fl 27 for lots 26 & 27. Gruijter
1806/08/13	AMSCH	0294	*Hondekoeter* | Een Ménagerie van Gevogelte als Hondekoeter	Vinkeles [for] F	(Sold) fl 0:14 Yver [for] G

Hondecoeter, G.

1802/02/16	AMSCH	0034	*G. de Hondekoeter* | Een Bergachtig Landschap met verschillend Geboomte en een Waterval, gestoffeerd met verschyden zoorten van Beesten, by een stil water beekje kragtig gepenceeld	H	(Sold) fl 30 Coclers
1803/04/20	AMSCH	0112	*G. de Hondekoeter* | Een Gestoffeert Landschap, met Geboomten, eenige Bokken en Vogels [Un Paysage orné d'animaux par G. Hondekoeter ; bien touché.] | *Mat:* op paneel *Size:* hoog 10, breed 16 duim	Maria Magdalena van Sluypwyk, gravinne van Moens	(Sold) fl 1 Palmhoff
1803/09/07	AMSCH	0084	*G. de Hondekoeter* | Een Duinachtig Landschap, gestoffeerd met verscheide Beestjes, Boerewoningen en Geboomte; zonachtig op Paneel [Un paysage melé de differentes espèces de betail, de chaumières et de	Smidt	(Sold) fl 1 Gruiter

			bocages ; il y regne un beau soleil] | *Mat:* op paneel *Size:* hoog 8, breed 14 duim		
1804/10/29	HRBAU	0031	*Hondekoeter, (G. de)* | In een Landschap ziet men de uitdryving van Hagar met heur' zoon Ismaël verbeeld. Zeer uitvoerig geschilderd | *Mat:* op paneel *Size:* hoog 23, breed 28 duim	Simon Styl	(Unknown)
1805/07/10	AMSCH	0069	*G. de Hondecoeter* | Een gezicht na de Zeylpoort te Haarlem, te zien, met een ménigte stoffagie met Beeldjes, enz.; meesterlyk op Paneel | *Mat:* op paneel *Size:* hoog 14, breed 18 duim	V[inkeles] [for] M	(Sold) fl 4:15 Gruyter
1805/07/10	AMSCH	0070	*G. de Hondecoeter* | Twee stuks Boom- en Duynryke Landschappen, met Woningen, Gevogelte en Gedierten, zonachtig en delicaat gepenceeld | *Mat:* op paneel *Size:* hoog 14, breed 13 duim	V[inkeles] [for] L	(Sold) fl 1:10 L Pakker
1806/08/13	AMSCH	0081	*Hondekoeter, (G. de)* | Een Boomryk Landschap met Boerewoningen en stoffagie van Beelden; zonachtig behandeld | *Mat:* op doek *Size:* hoog 31, breed 39 duim	Roos	(Sold) fl 3 Boelen

Hondecoeter, Gillis Claesz. d'

1810/08/10	RMRIJ	0015	*Gilles de Hondecoutre* | Een Landschap, in de manier van Vinkeboom | *Mat:* op paneel *Size:* hoog 13 duim, breed 22 ½ duim		(Sold) fl 2:10 [or] 3 v Dongen

Hondecoeter, Gysbert Gillisz. de

1806/08/20	HGBSM	0159	*G. de Hondekoeter* | Een stuk met een Haan, Hennen, Kalkoen en eene Eend, door G. de Hondekoeter 1627 | *Mat:* op paneel *Size:* hoog 23, breed 33 ½ duim *Inscr:* G. de Hondekoeter 1627 (signed and dated?) *Notes:* It is unclear whether the name and date are inscribed on the painting.	Macalester Loup [or others]	(Sold) fl 0:12 Abr Salomons
1810/03/23	HAVIN	0008	*G. de Hondekoeter* | Een Haan en eenige Hennen, als ook Kruiden, helder en uitmuntend geschilderd | *Size:* hoog 35 ½ breet 47 ½ d.	Rudolf Hendrik de Wetstein [or others]	(Unknown) fl 26:10

Hondecoeter, Melchior d'

1801/03/16	AMSCH	0033	*M. de Hondekoeter* | Een Hofgezicht, op de voorgrond een Kroonvogel, Inkhoorntje, verders een leggende spaansche Hond	P[ruyssenaar]	(Sold) fl 1:15 Coclers
1801/04/13	AMSCH	0032	*M. de Hondekoeter* | Op een prachtige Hofstede ziet men een menigte uit-en inlandsche Gevogeltens, als Paauwen, Pelicaanen, Duiven, Eenden en anderen; dit stuk is bevallig geordoneerd, en zonachtig behandeld | *Mat:* op doek *Size:* hoog 70, breed 71 duim	Pierre Fouquet, junior	(Sold) fl 82 Coclers
1801/04/13	AMSCH	0033	*M. de Hondekoeter* | Een niet minder fraaije Ordonantie van diverse Gevogelten, op de voorgrond een Pelicaan, Eenden in een Vyver, en verders een aangenaam verschiet; behandeld als de voorgaande | *Mat:* op doek *Size:* hoog 71, breed 72 duim	Pierre Fouquet, junior	(Withdrawn)
1801/06/10	AMSCH	0080	*Hondekoeter. (M. de)* | Een witte Hen, met hare Kiekens, eenige Duiven en een Pauw, geestig en natuurlyk geschilderd, zynde dit Stuk een der bevalligste van deezen Meester | *Mat:* op doek *Size:* hoog 27, breed 23 duim	Herman ten Kate	(Sold) fl 185 Coclers
1801/06/10	AMSCH	0081	*Hondekoeter. (M. de)* | Een witte Hen, met eenige Kiekens, een van dezelven is bezig met Graan te pikken, natuurlyk en ktagtig [sic] behandeld | *Mat:* op doek *Size:* hoog 19, breed 22 duim	Herman ten Kate	(Sold) fl 75 Coclers
1801/10/06	AMSCH	0032	*M. de Hondekoeter* | Op een steene Balustrade vertoont zig een schreeuwende Paauw, en een rustende Pauwin, verder vliegende Duiven en een Uyl, op een kruk, in 't verschiet ziet men de Tooren van 't Stadhuis van Amsterdam, zynde alles fraay en uitvoerig gepenceeld | *Mat:* op doek *Size:* hoog 70 breed 62 duim	M	(Sold) fl 46 C S Roos
1802/05/05	AMSCH	0071	*M. de Hondekoeter* | Op de Voorgrond van dit fraaije Schildery zit een witte Kloek, omgeeven van zyne Kiekens; terzyde een roodbonte Haan, goudlakensche Hen, een Duif en Paauw, verders fraai Geboomte. Alles delicaat en natuurlyk behandeld | *Mat:* op doek *Size:* hoog 42, breed 52 duim	D	(Sold) fl 355 Pruijssenaar [for] R
1802/05/05	AMSCH	0072	*M. de Hondekoeter* | In een Hofgezicht ziet men op een Balustrade eenige Hennen, voorts op de Voorgrond een Paauw, Eenden en Kloekhen, met zyn Kiekens. Alles Meesterlyk kragtig behandeld | *Mat:* op doek *Size:* hoog 50, breed 60 duim	H	(Sold) fl 330 Th^{S} Spaan
1802/12/13	AMSCH	0088	*M. de Hondekoeter* | Een doode Duif met uitgestrekte Vlerken; delicaat | *Size:* hoog 18, breed 13 duim	Yver	(Sold) fl 10 Th^{S} Spaan
1803/08/01	AMSCH	0011	*Hondekoeter (M. de)* | In een boomryk Landschap ziet men op de voorgrond een zwemmende Eend met zyne jongen, benevens een zwart bonte Kuifhen, een Eend en vliegende Roofvogel, en in 't verschiet over eenig Geboomte een Dorptooren, alles is kragtig en uitvoerig gepenceeld | *Mat:* op doek *Size:* hoog 39, breed 46 duim	J	(Sold) fl 140 C S Roos
1803/08/17	AMSCH	0030	*Hondekoeter. (M. de)* | Op de voorgrond van dit fraaye Schildery, staat een goudlakensche Haan, in een kraaijende gestalte, ter zyde en agter hem twee Hennen met Kuiven, benevens eenige Kuikens, op een steen zit een Duif, en in 't Landschap in het verschiet zyn eenige Eenden en een Zwaan in een Vyver, alles delicaat en uitvoerig behandeld, van de beste aart van schilderen van deeze meester | *Mat:* op doek *Size:* hoog 35, breed 43 duim	Anna Catharina Putman	(Bought In) fl 300

1803/08/17	AMSCH	0031	*Hondekoeter. (M. de)* | Een Vogele Conçert, alwaar de Uyl Orchest-meester schynt te zyn, alzo 'er een Muzykboek voor hem geplaatst is, een menigte gevogelte zoo op de grond als in de Boomen accompagneeren, dit luisteryk Concert zynde in alles als de voorgaande behandeld | *Mat:* op doek *Size:* hoog 29, breed 33 duim	Anna Catharina Putman	(Sold) fl 49:10 Hodges
1803/09/07	AMSCH	0072	*M. de Hondkoeter* | In een Boomryk Landschap ziet men een groote menigte Gevogelte, formerende een Concert, de Uil in het midden zittende, fungeerd als Orchestmeester, alles geestig en kragtig gepenceeld [Au milieu d'un paysage, riche en arbres et arbustes, dans lequel un grand nombre d'oiseaux sont rassemblés et font un concert ; le hibou qui est au milieu d'eux représente le directeur de l'orchestre ; composition très spirituelle, d'une touche forte et expressive] | *Mat:* op doek *Size:* hoog 55, br. 70 duim	Smidt	(Bought In) fl 50
1803/12/12	AMSCH	0038	*M. de Hondekoeter* | Op een Steen Voetstuk is geplaast een Pot, gevuld met differente soorten van welriekenke Bloemen, ter zyde een Kind, speelende met een Aap, by eenige vruchten, op de voorgrond een Paauw en een vliegende Duif; meesterlyk op Doek | *Mat:* op doek *Size:* hoog 50, breed 38 duim	B	(Sold) fl 3:5 Hodges
1803/12/12	AMSCH	0039	*M. de Hondekoeter* | In een Land ziet men eenige Hennen met een Haan, op de voorgrond, by een Bak met Eeten, een witte Klokhen met haar Kiekens, ter zyde een Aap; meesterlyk op Doek | *Mat:* op doek *Size:* hoog 33, br. 46 duim	B	(Sold) fl 6:5 Gruiter
1804/05/07	AMSCH	0082	*Hondekoeter. (M. de)* | Op een Steene Ballustraade ziet men een witte Hoen, een Paauw en kraijende Haan; krachtig van coloriet en fiks geschilderd | *Mat:* op doek *Size:* hoog 57, breed 66 duim	Pruysnaar	(Bought In) fl 19
1804/05/07	AMSCH	0083	*Hondekoeter. (M. de)* | Een doode Duif met uitgestrekte Vlerken, leggende op een Tafel, waarby Jagtgereedschap; delicaat behandeld | *Mat:* op paneel *Size:* hoog 18, breed 13 duim	Y[ver] [for] JJ	(Sold) fl 13 Hulswit
1804/07/25	AMSCH	0039	*Hondekoeter (M. de)* | In een Landschap ziet men op de Voorgrond by de Stam van een Boom, een stil Water waarin eenige Eenden met hunne Kiekens Swemmen, waarnevens by een Steene Muur een Spaansche Haan, en een leggende Hen, waarby eenige jonge Eenden en een vliegende Vogel, verders een aangenaam Boomryk verschiet; deeze ryke ordenantie, is piquant van licht, fraai gepenceeld, en aller natuurlykst behandeld | *Size:* hoog 44, breed 55 ½ duim		(Sold) fl 423 Izaac Smit
1804/10/29	HRBAU	0029	*Hondekoeter, (M. de)* | Op den Voorgrond, by een boomstam, ziet men een doode Duif, benevens een Specht en twee Vinken liggen, waar by eenig Jagtgereedschap. Extra natuurlyk en uitvoerig gepenceeld | *Mat:* op doek *Size:* hoog 19, breed 16 duim	Simon Styl	(Unknown)
1804/10/29	HRBAU	0030	*Hondekoeter, (M. de)* | Op den Voorgrond, by eene Waterplas en Plantgewassen, zyn drie bonte Eenden by hunne Jongen, terwyl een ander komt aanvliegen; waar agter een bergagtig verschiet. Zeer natuurlyk en uitvoerig behandeld | *Mat:* op doek *Size:* hoog 37, breed 31 duim	Simon Styl	(Unknown)
1804/12/10	AMSCH	0024	*M. de Hondekoeter* | Deeze fraaije Ordinantie van deeze groote meester, stelt voor een witte Klokhen met zyn Kiekens, waarby een goudlakense Kip en Haan, op de voorgrond drie Eenden; alles even fiks en dun van schildering, kragtig van coloriet en meesterlyk gepenceeld | *Mat:* op doek *Size:* Hoog 47, breed 53 duim	Jan De Groot	(Sold) fl 175 Hulswit
1805/07/03	AMSCH	0023	*Hondekoeter. (M. de)* | Dit zeldzaam voorkomend geval steld voor, een doode hangende Patrys en een ménigte ander dood Gevogelte tegen een balustrade waarop een Snaphaan, Hoorn en ander Jagttuig, alles zeer dun en uitvoerig behandeld als J. Wénix | *Mat:* op doek *Size:* hoog 22, breed 18 duim	R[oos]	(Sold) fl 326 Iz Smit
1805/07/03	AMSCH	0086	*M. de Hondekoeter* | In een Boom- en Bergachtig Landschap, ziet men op de Voorgrond een Beekje, waarin eenige Eenden met hun Kiekens, op de tweede grond een Pelicaan en ander vreemd Gevogelten, verders een aangenaam verschiet; het Geboomten en de Kruiden op de Voorgrond, zyn zoo wel als het Gevogelten van de beste penceelbehandeling van M. de Hondekoeter | *Mat:* op doek *Size:* hoog 75, breed 53 duim	R[oos]	(Sold) fl 65 Agina
1806/08/13	AMSCH	0074	*Hondekoeter. (M. de)* | By een zwaaren Boomstam en eenige Planten, terzyde aan een Water vertoont zich eenig Watergevogelte; schoon van licht en meesterlyk geschilderd | *Mat:* op doek *Size:* hoog 38, breed 31 duim	Vinkeles [for] G[ruyter]	(Bought In) fl 9
1806/08/20	HGBSM	0052	*M. D. Hondekoeter* | Deeze schoone Menagerie, bestaande uit een Paauw en Paauwin, een goudlakensche en witte Haan, Eenden, Watervogelen en diverse anderen, is krachtig en zeer natuurlijk geschilderd | *Mat:* op doek *Size:* hoog 41, breed 48 duim	Macalester Loup [or others]	(Sold) fl 175 Schouman
1806/08/20	HGBSM	0066	*M. D. Hondekoeter* | Een Stuk met een Faisant en verschillende Vogelen, gemerkt M. D. Hondekoeter | *Mat:* op doek *Size:* hoog 40 ½, breed 33 duim *Inscr:* M. D. Hondekoeter (signed)	Macalester Loup [or others]	(Sold) fl 2:6 Praiston
1807/08/26	AMSCH	0089	*M. de Hondekoeter* | In een Landschap ziet men een Haan, eene Hen met heure Kiekens, en twee Duiven op een Steen zittende; zynde fraai geordonneerd en meesterlyk geschilderd | *Mat:* op doek *Size:* hoog 35, breed 28 duim	Joseph Vallette	(Sold) fl 131 du Pree

1808/04/26	GDAN	0058	*Hondekoeter (M. de)* | Eene der beste van dezen Meester, bestaande uit Hennen, Haanen Kalkoenen, en ander Gevogelte, alles fraai en uitvoerig geschildert | *Size:* hoog 46, breed 63 duim	G H Fortuyn	(Unknown)
1808/04/26	GDAN	0059	*Hondekoeter (M. de)* | Op den voorgrond twee staande Kippen in het groen, op den tweeden grond een staande Haan en Paauw, en in de Lucht een vliegende Duif, met bijwerk, mede zeer uitmuntend gepenseeld | *Size:* hoog 43, breed 59 duim	G H Fortuyn	(Unknown)
1808/04/26	GDAN	0060	*Hondekoeter (M. de)* | Een Broedsche Hen op het Nest zittende, &c. | *Size:* hoog 18, breed 23 duim	G H Fortuyn	(Unknown)
1808/04/26	GDAN	0061	*Hondekoeter (M. de)* | Een Hen met eenige Kuikens, en bijwerk, mede zeer goed gepenseeld | *Size:* hoog 43, breed 37 duim	G H Fortuyn	(Unknown)
1808/04/26	GDAN	0062	*Hondekoeter (M. de)* | Met vliegende Eenden en ander Gevogelte, en bywerk | *Size:* hoog 36, breed 30 duim	G H Fortuyn	(Unknown)
1808/04/26	GDAN	0063	*Hondekoeter (M. de)* | Een dito met Watergevogeltes en andere | *Size:* hoog 40, breed 50 duim *Notes:* It is unclear what "dito" refers to in the title.	G H Fortuyn	(Unknown)
1808/04/26	GDAN	0064	*Hondekoeter (M. de)* | Een kraaijende Haan, en een Kip met Kuiken, en verder staande en vliegend Gevogelte, ook konstig behandeld | *Size:* hoog 40, breed 50 duim	G H Fortuyn	(Unknown)
1808/06/06	RMRIJ	0054	*Hondekoeter. (Melchior de)* | In een aangenaam Landschap op den voorgrond zijn twee Turksche Ganzen, twee Eenden en een Waard; in het bovenste gedeelte eene vliegende Duif; in het verschiet eenig Gevogelte. Breed en meesterlijk uitgevoerd [Paysage sur le devant duquel on voit des Canards, des Oies, des Pigeons etc. Le tout traité grandement et peint en Maître] | *Annots:* vd Pot Kocht uit coll. P. Calkoen, Wz Amst 10 Sept 1781: M. Hondicoeter Eenden[?] enz. fl 115 (RKDH I) *Mat:* op doek *Size:* Hoog 35, en breed 43 ¾ duim *Loc:* Amsterdam, Nederland. Rijksmuseum. (A172)	Gerrit van der Pot, Heer van Groeneveld	(Sold) fl 115 Johs Eck en Zoon [for] le Roi
1808/06/06	RMRIJ	0055	*Hondekoeter. (Melchior de)* | Eene Klokhen met hare kiekens, benevens een Hopvogel, en verder bijwerk. Zeer natuurlijk en fraai geschilderd [Une belle Poule blanche avec ses Poussins, et une Huppe perchée sur une Branche d'arbre. Dans le même Style que le Tableau précédent] | *Mat:* op doek *Size:* Hoog 35, en breed 24 ¾ duim	Gerrit van der Pot, Heer van Groeneveld	(Sold) fl 110 van Lennep [for] le Roi
1808/06/11	RMRIJ	0018	*M: de Hondekoeter* | Eenig Gevogelte, als Hoenders, Eenden en Kuikens; verder aangenaam Bywerk; meesterlyk geschilderd | *Mat:* op doek *Size:* hoog 30 ½, breed 26 ½ duim		(Sold) fl 46 Luchtmans [or] Rohan
1808/06/13	AMSCH	0071	*Hondekoeter (M. de)* | Deze rijke Ordonantie verbeeld eene Verzameling van de meest belangrijkste Inlandsche Vogelen, waar onder een Paauw, met zijn pronkende staart. Voor het overige overtreft dit Schilderij, zoo in uitwerking als behandeling, de meeste Schilderstukken van dezen Meester, en kan als een der beste van hem gehouden worden | *Mat:* op doek *Size:* hoog 64, breed 86 duim	E M Engelberts	(Sold) fl 570 Allard
1808/06/13	AMSCH	0072	*Hondekoeter (M. de)* | Een Landschap met Watergevogelte. Op den voorgrond eenige Eenden met hunne Jongen, in een Waterplas; ter zijde, bij den stam van een boom, een staande en liggende Gans. Zeer bevallig van ordonantie, meesterlijk en uitvoerig | *Size:* hoog 48, breed 60 duim	W	(Sold) fl 260 Coclers
1808/08/23	AMSCH	0070	*Hondekoeter. (M. de)* | In een aangenaam Landschap vertoond zig op de voorgrond een staande Haan, met een Graankorl [sic] in de Bek, daar nevens een Hen met haare Kiekens, ter zijde voor een Staketsel drie bonten Hennen, voorts eenige Duiven en ander Gevogelten; dit Schilderij is bevallig van Ordonantie, meesterlijk en uitvoerig, en kans als een der beste van deeze beroemde Kunstschilder gehouden worden | *Mat:* op doek *Size:* hoog 38, breed 46 duim	[Coclers]	(Bought In) fl 395
1808/08/23	AMSCH	0071	*Hondekoeter. (M. de)* | Een Hof-gezigt, op de voorgrond twee Paauwen, benevens twee liggende Hennen, en op de Takken van een Boom twee Duiven; meesterlijk geschilderd | *Mat:* op doek *Size:* hoog 55, breed 60 duim	[Van Iperen?]	(Sold or Bought In) fl 39 van Iperen
1808/11/28	AMSCH	0030	*M. Hondekoeter* | Een Hofgezigt, op de voorgrond een Bank, waar op een Vaas met Bloemen geplaast is, waar bij een Jongeling, beneevens een staande Paauw en een zittende Aap, natuurlijk behandeld | *Mat:* op doek *Size:* hoog 50, breed 38 duim	H	(Sold) fl 0:8 Oosterman
1808/11/28	AMSCH	0031	*M. Hondekoeter* | Een Boomrijk Hofgezigt, gestoffeerd met een menigte In- en Uitlands Gevogelte, meesterlijk | *Mat:* op doek *Size:* hoog 54, breed 66 duim	[Gruyter?]	(Sold) fl 10:15 du Pree
1809/04/17	AMSCH	0039	*M. Hondekoeter* | In een Landschap ziet men bij een oude Muur, een staande Haan, waarbij liggende Hennen, en ter zeide twee Paauwen, meesterlijk geschilderd | *Mat:* op doek *Size:* hoog 37, breed 39 duim	S	(Sold) fl 20:15
1809/04/22	AMYVR	0056	*M. de Hondekoeter* | Op een Balustrade zitten eenige Duiven, op de voorgrond een Haan en Hen met hun Kiekens; meesterlijk | *Mat:* op doek *Size:* hoog 34, breed 29 duim	de Bruin	(Sold) fl 92 Remmers Bredius
1809/06/13	AMSCH	0061	*M. de Hondekoeter* | In een Landschap ziet men op de voorgrond een staande Haan en drie Hennen, ter zijde een rustende Klokhen, met haare	E	(Sold) fl 22 Reyers

			Kiekens, en op een Schutting twee Duiven; bevallig van koloriet en natuurlijk behandeld | *Mat:* op doek *Size:* hoog 33, breed 44 duim		
1809/07/19	AMSCH	0022	*Hondekoeter (M. de)* | In een Hofgezicht ziet men een Steenen Balustrade, waar op een zittend Aapje, nevens een sierlijk gewerkte Vaas, voor dezelve twee vegtende Haanen en eene Klokhen met haare Kiekens, verder ter linkerzijde verscheide ander Gevogelte bij een Vijver, en een pragtig Gebouw in 't verschiet. Dit uitmuntend Schilderij is zeer schoon van koloriet, kragtig en uitvoerig geschilderd, en kan voor een der fraaiste van dezen Konstenaar gehouden worden | *Mat:* op doek *Size:* hoog 48, breed 43 duim	C	(Sold) fl 180 Reijers
1809/07/25	HGBSM	0055	*M. Hondekoeter* | Een Capitaal Stuk met onderscheiden soorten van Vogelen | *Mat:* op doek *Size:* hoog 4 voet 6 duim, breed 4 v. 10 d.	D van der Aa [or] E B ten Dall	(Sold) fl 10:5 van Eyk
1809/07/25	HGBSM	0056	*M. Hondekoeter* | Een dito [Capitaal Stuk] met Gevogelte, een Hond en twee Schapen en verder gediertens, met de Arke Noach in 't verschiet | *Mat:* op doek *Size:* hoog 5 v. 6 d., breed 4 v. 9 d.	D van der Aa [or] E B ten Dall	(Sold) fl 22:5 van Eyk
1809/07/25	HGBSM	0057	*M. Hondekoeter* | Een dito [Capitaal Stuk] met Kloek met jongen, een Haan en andere Gevogelte | *Mat:* op doek *Size:* hoog 33, breed 37 duim	D van der Aa	(Sold) fl 20 van der Aa
1810/03/07	UTWLD	0039	*M. de Hondecoeter* | Eene Ruine, op de voorgrond gevogelte konstig en breed uitgevoerd | *Size:* hoog 4 voet 7 duim, breed 5 voet 7 duim	J J Woertman	(Unknown) fl 140
1810/06/06	RMMUY	0022	*Melchior de Hondekoeter* | Eene kapitale Ordonnantie van Vogelen: als witte en andere Hennen, Haan, Pauwen, Eendvogels, en een Duif. Door Melchior de Hondekoeter, van zijn allerbesten tijd | *Mat:* op doek		(Bought In) fl 450
1810/06/06	RMMUY	0145	*M. de Hondekoeter* | Eene Kapitale ordonnantie, van Hoenders, Eenden &c. Meesterlijk geschilderd | *Mat:* op doek		(Unknown) fl 42
1810/06/20	AMSCH	0031	*M. De Hondekoeter* | In een Hofgezigt, voor een groot Gebouw, ziet men eene Pauwin, die door een Klokhen wordt aangevallen, ter zijde een Haan en eenige Kiekens. Het is krachtig en meesterlijk uitgevoerd | *Mat:* op doek *Size:* hoog 40, breed 39 duimen	D	(Sold) fl 103 Hulswit
1810/06/20	AMSCH	0031a	*M. De Hondekoeter* | In een prachtig Hofgezicht ziet men ter regterzijde, op een Steenen Balustrade, een staande Paauw en zittende Paauwin; op den voorgrond verschillende Eenden, Duiven, Klokhen met Kiekens en ander Gevogelte. Dit kapitale stuk is schoon van kleur, krachtig en meesterlijk geschilderd | *Mat:* op doek *Size:* hoog 60, breed 77 duimen	Y	(Sold) fl 150 Roos
1810/06/20	AMSCH	0031b	*M. De Hondekoeter* | In een Landschap vertoont zich een groote Roofvogel, houdende gretig met zijne klaauwen een Haan, en grimmig ziende naar eene witte Hen met hare Kiekens, die ter zijde bij een Houten Hek en Geboomte met ander Gevogelte geplaatst is; in het verschiet een Land- en Riviergezigt, waarbij eenige Watervogels. Het is meesterlijk en kloek gepenceeld | *Mat:* op doek *Size:* hoog 55, breed 77 duimen	V	(Sold) fl 8:10 Boelhouwer
1810/06/20	AMSCH	0194[H]	*Hondekoeter* | De paauw [?] van hondekoeter | *Notes:* This lot was added in by hand in the AA and EBNP copies of the catalogue.	A	(Sold) fl 180 Roos
1810/08/01	AMSCH	0042	*Hondekoeter (Melchior de)* | Eene Menagerie, waar in een schreeuwende Paauw, voor denzelven eene witte Gans, eene drinkende en eene staande Eend, ter zijde eene Hen met hare Kiekens; op een Baluster zitten eenige Hoenders [Sujet d'une Menagerie, dans laquelle on distingue un Paon ; au devant de cet Oiseau se trouve une Oye blanche, un Canard plongeant et un autre vû hors de l'eau ; sur le côté est une Poule avec ses Poussins, et sur la balustrade on voit des Poules perchées] | *Annots:* bien peint, mais mal compose. (NGW) *Mat:* op doek *Size:* hoog 50, breed 60 duimen	Mr Pieter de Smeth van Alphen	(Sold) fl 250 M Schouman
1810/08/01	AMSCH	0043	*Hondekoeter (Melchior de)* | In een Landschap ziet men op den voorgrond ter linkerzijde eenen Vos met zijne Prooi voor zich, aan de andere zijde eene Hen met hare Kiekens, in het midden eene roepende Eend, verder vliegend en ander Gevogelte [La vue sur un Parc, dont le premier plan offre un renard emportant sa proye ; d'autre part se trouve une Poule avec ses Poussin ; au milieu on voit un Canard appellant, et plusieurs Oiseaux qui sont repartis dans ce composé] | *Annots:* composition fort mal groupée (NGW) *Mat:* op doek *Size:* hoog 58, breed 66 duimen	Mr Pieter de Smeth van Alphen	(Sold) fl 340 C S Roos
1810/08/06	AMSCH	0048	*Hondekoeter (M. de)* | Op een Steenen Balustrade ziet men twee Pauwen, Duiven en andere Gevogelte; meesterlijk gepenceeld | *Mat:* op doek *Size:* hoog 70, breed 64 duimen	R[oos]	(Sold) fl 41 Coclers
1810/11/07	UTWLD	0005	*M. Hondekoeter* | Eene uitmuntende Schilderij verbeeldende op den voorgrond een moedig opziende Haan, na iets dat hij schijnt te hooren, daarnevens een staande Klock en aazende Kiekens, verders een liggende Hen, wijders een Duif op een schutting waar over eenig groen en boomstam te zien is, met eenig bijwerk, alles uitvoerig bewerkt door M. Hondekoeter op doek, 3 voet 2 en een half duim breed, 2 en een half voet hoog in een vergulde Lijst | companion to lot 6, by J.J.I. Straaten *Mat:* op doek *Size:* 3 voet 2 en een half duim breed, 2 en een half voet hoog		(Unknown) fl 435
			Hondecoeter, Melchior d' (copy after)		
1806/05/05	AMSCH	0058	*M. de Hondekoeter* | Een Menagerie met een Pelicaan, Eenden met hunne Kiekens, een Duif op een balustrade en andere Gevogelte in het verschiet; meesterlyk na M. de Hondekoeter | *Mat:* op doek *Size:* hoog 52, breed 65 duim	R[oos]	(Bought In) fl 1:5

			Hondecoeter, Melchior d' (manner)		
1801/03/16	AMSCH	0061	*Hondekoeter* | Een Vaas, gevuld met verscheide soorten van Bloemen, op de voorgrond een Pauw, in de manier van Hondekoeter	P[ruyssenaar]	(Sold) fl 2:10 Jan Spaan
1803/09/07	AMSCH	0236	*M. de Hondekoeter* | In een Hofgezicht ziet men op de Voorgrond, een staande Haan, drie Hennen, Duiven en een Berg Eend, zeer kragtig en natuurlyk, op Doek geschilderd, zoo goed als van M. de Hondekoeter [L'intérieur d'une basse cour, sur le devant un cocq, trois poules, des pigeons et un canard ; tableau plein de vérité et d'intérêt, sur toile et d'un mérite égal au genre de Hondekoeter.] | *Mat:* op doek *Size:* hoog 39, breed 53 duim	Smidt	(Bought In) fl 12
			Hondius, Abraham		
1804/10/16	DLOND	0103	*A. Hondius* | Een witte Zwaan, verstoord door twee Honden. Une Cygne blanche attaquée par deux Chiens | *Mat:* op paneel *Size:* hoog 9, breed 13		(Unknown)
1804/10/16	DLOND	0104	*A. Hondius* | Een Jager met zyn Hond. Un Chasseur & son Chien | *Mat:* op paneel *Size:* hoog 14, breed 12		(Unknown)
1806/10/17	MGSAN	0042	*A. Hondius* | Twee Jagthonden, door A. Hondius | *Mat:* op paneel	Gerardus Beljard	(Unknown)
1810/06/06	RMMUY	0025	*Abraham Hondius* | Eene Herte Jagt met verscheiden Honden, ongemeen stout behandeld | *Annots:* extra goost (EBNP) *Mat:* op doek		(Unknown) fl 52
			Hondt		
1810/10/10	MGCIT	0139	*Hont* | Twee aardige Bloemstukjes	Caspar van Citters	(Unknown)
			Honthorst, Gerrit van		
1801/04/13	AMSCH	0034	*G. Hondhorst* | Een geharnast Krygsman zittende, met zyn arm op een Trommel leunende, te slapen; dit stuk is zo meesterlyk en breed behandeld, als of het door A. van Dyk geschilderd was | *Mat:* op doek *Size:* hoog 46, breed 33 duim	Pierre Fouquet, junior	(Sold) fl 19:10 C S Roos
1801/06/10	AMSCH	0086	*Hondhorst. (G.)* | Simson, rustende in de schoot van Delila, meesterlyk behandeld | *Mat:* op doek *Size:* hoog 41, breed 50 duim	Herman ten Kate	(Sold) fl 9 Mensart
1801/06/13	LNDLS	0022	*Honthorst* | Een Man, die een Vrouw wil omhelzen, krachtig en levens-groote, op doek geschilderd | *Mat:* op doek *Size:* hoog 43, breed 50 duimen	D van R	(Sold) fl 4 Spaan
1801/08/19	AMSCH	0039	*C. Honthorst* | Een Ordenantie, van twee Beelden levensgrooten tot aen de kniën, verbeeldende een Heer die een Dame liefkoost, op Doek, kragtig geschilderd | *Mat:* op doek *Size:* hoog 44, breed 50 duim *Notes:* The artist's name was given as "C. Honthorst" but we have assumed this is an error.	van der Schly [for] F	(Sold) fl 12:10 Wolft
1801/08/19	AMSCH	0040	*C. Honthorst* | Een capitaale Ordenantie van vier Figuuren levensgrooten, verbeeldende Pétrus, door den Engel, uit de gevangenis verlost: schoon en kragtig van Coloriet, en van een breede penceelsbehandeling | *Mat:* op doek *Size:* hoog 52, breed 74 duim *Notes:* The artist's name was given as "C. Honthorst" but we have assumed this is an error.	C S Roos [for] G	(Sold) fl 3:10 Yver
1802/09/21	UTHDG	0040	*G. Hondhorst* | De dogter van Herodes, dragende het hoofd van Johannes den Dooper op eene schotel. Meesterlijk geschildert | *Mat:* op doek *Size:* hoog 28 ½, breed 23 duimen		(Bought In) fl 14
1802/11/01	DOBRA	0006	*Honthorst* | Een jonge Vrouw, speelende op een Viool di gamba | *Size:* hoog circa 31, breed 25 duim	Paulus van der Spyk [or others]	(Sold) fl 11:10 Randwyk
1802/11/01	DOBRA	0044	*Hondhorst* | Een Bruidegom en Bruid in een genoeglyke houding aan de Tafel zittende; een Cyterspeelder, en ander vrolyk gezelschap, byna Levensgroote | *Mat:* op doek *Size:* breed ruim 7 en hoog 9 voet	Paulus van der Spyk [or others]	(Sold) fl 30 Veldhoven
1802/12/13	AMSCH	0089	*Hondhorst* | David met 't Hoofd en Zwaard van Goliath in de Hand, meesteragtig geschilderd | *Mat:* op doek *Size:* hoog 49, breed 40 duim	Pruyssenaar [for] A	(Sold) fl 1 L Pakker
1803/04/20	AMSCH	0032	*Honthorst. (G.)* | Voor een Open Vengster, staat een vrolyke Muzikant, houdende een Fiool en Strykstok in de eene, en een Roemer met Wyn in de andere hand, hy is gekleed in aloude Spaansche kleeding, omhoog en ter zyde hangt een Tapytkleed; het Caracter is geestig verbeeld, en van een meesterlyke schoone penceelsbehandeling [Devant une fénêtre ouverte vient se montrer un musicien jovial, tenant son violon d'une main & de l'autre un verre de vin ; il est costumê d'une maniere pittoresque, & à sont côté est pendu un tapis. Ce morceau traité avec beaucoup de franchise a du caractère & une très bonne couleur.] | *Mat:* op doek *Size:* hoog 42, breed 34 duim	Maria Magdalena van Sluypwyk, gravinne van Moens	(Sold) fl 500 Josi
1803/04/20	AMSCH	0033	*Honthorst. (G.)* | Een oude Vrouw, houdende in de eene hand een brandende Kaars, en in de andere een Beurs; kragtig behandeld [Une vielle [sic] vue à mi-corps, tenant d'une main une chandelle & une bourse de l'autre. L'effet de la lumiere y est bien rendu & le faire en est d'une maniere très facile.] | *Mat:* op paneel *Size:* hoog 27, breed 12 duim	Maria Magdalena van Sluypwyk, gravinne van Moens	(Sold) fl 9 Theijs
1803/04/27	AMSCH	00CC[H]	*Hondhorst* | Een brede[?] vrouw door Hondhorst | *Notes:* This lot was added in by hand in the LBDa copy of the catalogue.	C	(Sold) fl 2 Grimpen
1803/08/24	HGKAN	0101	*G. Hondhorst* | Een Dame speelende op de Guitar, krachtig geschilderd	[Teissier] [or others]	(Sold) fl 0:12 Tessier
1803/09/07	AMSCH	0073	*G. Hondhorst* | Een Binnehuis, waarin een Dame, zittende op de Guitar te speelen, waarby twee anderen, en een Krygsman, met een Kan in zyn	Smidt	(Bought In) fl 170

			hand, alles word door een brandende Kaars verligt, kragtig en Natuurlyk op Doek [L'intérieur d'une salle représentant une dame assise près de deux autres, et pinçant de la guittarre ; un guerrier est à leur côté tenant une cruche à la main ; une chandelle alumée éclaire l'ensemble du sujet. Tableau d'une touche expressive et mâle, peint au naturel] | *Mat:* op doek *Size:* hoog 51, breed 63 duim		
1803/09/07	AMSCH	0074	*G. Hondhorst* | Een Gevangene voor een Koning en zyne Raad geleid wordende; meesterlyk op Doek [Un prisonnier amené devant un roi et son conseil, l'exécution de ce tableau est de main de maître] | *Mat:* op doek *Size:* hoog 49, breed 66 duim	Smidt	(Bought In) fl 22
1804/04/28	LNDLS	0037	*Hondhorst* | Een Jongman, die een flambouw aanblaast, door Hondhorst, op doek | *Mat:* op doek *Size:* hoog 31, breed 26 duim	[Abraham Delfos] [or others]	(Sold) fl 2 Jan Landa
1804/05/07	AMSCH	0084	*Hondhorst. (G.)* | Een muciceerend Gezelschap, de Dame speeld op de Guitar en zingt met een Heer en andere Dame welk een Glas wyn in de hand heeft, meesterlyk behandeld | *Mat:* op doek *Size:* hoog 44, breed 54 duim	R[oos]	(Bought In) fl 3
1805/07/10	AMSCH	0074	*G. Honthorst* | Deeze Capitaale Ordinantie stelt voor, daar Esau zyn Geboorte-recht aan zyn broeder Jacob verkoopt, aller fraayst van Teekening en coloriet, en uitvoerig gepenceeld | *Mat:* op doek *Size:* hoog 54, breed 67 duim	V[inkeles] [for] P	(Bought In) fl 7
1805/07/10	AMSCH	0075	*G. Honthorst* | Een musiceerend Gezelschap, op Speel-Instrumenten, zynde een Ordinantie van vyf Beelden, ruim halver lyf, levengrooten [sic]; de caracters zyn natuurlyk, en meesterlyk gepenceeld | *Mat:* op doek *Size:* hoog 50, breed 72 duim	Temmink	(Sold) fl 8:10 Gruyter
1805/07/10	AMSCH	0076	*G. Honthorst* | Twee stuks Pourtraiten, 't eene een Herderin, en 't ander een Herder; beide breed op Doek | *Mat:* op doek *Size:* hoog 44, breed 34 duim	V[inkeles] [for] M	(Sold) fl 6 Agina
1805/10/21	GRBOL	0003	*Hondhorst* | Een dito [Capitaal] Schoon Stuk, met drie Vrouwen Beelden, van de Jagt komende	Gerardus Nicolaus Heerkens	(Unknown)
1805/12/16	AMSCH	0133	*Honthorst* | Een Ordinantie van drie Beelden; by kaarslicht, meesterlyk en fraay op Doek | *Mat:* op doek	Y	(Sold) fl 2 Yver
1806/08/13	AMSCH	0079	*Honthorst. (G.)* | Dit voorwerp verbeeld twee figuuren, leevensgrootе halver lyf, zynde een oude Vrouw, met een brandende flambouw in de hand, verzelt van een bedaagd Man, op een Trommel en Fluit speelende; van een kragtige en meesterlyke penceelbehandeling | *Mat:* op doek *Size:* hoog 33, breed 36 duim	Roos	(Sold) fl 1:10 L Pakker
1806/08/20	HGBSM	0010	*G. Hondthorst* | Een Bacchanaal, bestaande uit eene uitmuntende Groep van Mans en Vrouwen meest allen naakt, zijnde zeer uitvoerig, natuurlijk en bijzonder aangenaam geschilderd, verzeldt van alderfraaijst bijwerk als Druiven, goude Beekers en Paarlemoere Hoorns. – Dit Schilderij is eenig in zijn soort, terwijl de Figuuren zelden zo uitvoerig en van die kleinte door die meester zijn voortgebragt | *Mat:* op doek *Size:* hoog 32 ½, breed 28 duim	Macalester Loup [or others]	(Sold) fl 41 Teissier
1806/08/20	HGBSM	0063	*J. Hondhorst* | Vier stuks levensgroote Portraitten, van de Famillie van het Huis van Orange | *Mat:* op doek	Macalester Loup [or others]	(Sold) fl 1:10 Carré
1806/08/20	HGBSM	0068	*G. Hondhorst* | Lot, met zijne Dogters; levens groote, krachtig geschilderd | *Mat:* op doek *Size:* hoog 42, breed 58 ½ duim	Macalester Loup [or others]	(Sold) fl 4:10 Schouman
1808/07/19	AMROU	0015	*Hondhorst* | Het Pourtrait van den Admiraal J. de Ruiter, in zyn Harnas kleeding		(Unknown)
1809/06/13	AMSCH	0226	*G. Hondhorst* | Maria, Joseph en het Kind; helder en krachtig geschilderd | *Mat:* op doek *Size:* hoog 42, breed 34 duim	[Gruyter?]	(Bought In) fl 2:10
1809/10/20	UTWLD	0001	*Honthorst* | Een vrolyk gezelschap door of in de manier van Honthorst	J J van Rhyn	(Unknown)
1810/05/22	AMSCH	0151	*J. Hondhorst* | Twee stuks met Beelden	R	(Sold) fl 0:6 du Pree
1810/06/06	RMMUY	0006	*G. Honthorst* | De Zangstrijd tusschen Apollo en Marsias, met eene menigte leevens groote Beelden, meesterlijk en schoon geschilderd | *Mat:* op doek		(Sold) fl 51 Pot
1810/07/26	AMSCH	0135	*Hondhorst (G.)* | Een Binnenvertrek, in het midden zit eene bevallige Vrouw bij eene Tafel, speelende met een Officier op het Verkeerbord, ter zijde anderen die Muziceeren en drinken. Een der beste stukken van dezen Meester | *Mat:* op doek *Size:* hoog 27, breed 35 duimen	Cassino	(Bought In) fl 11
1810/08/01	AMSCH	0044	*Hondhorst (Gerard)* | Een bevallig Meisje, aan wie door een bejaard Man eene beurs met Geld wordt aangeboden, achterwaarts eene oude Vrouw [Representation d'un Viellard offrant sa bourse à une gentille fille, derriere ce groupe on apperçoit une Vielle Femme] | *Annots:* passable (NGW) *Mat:* op doek *Size:* hoog 32, breed 39 duimen	Mr Pieter de Smeth van Alphen	(Sold) fl 360 Cremer
1810/08/06	AMSCH	0049	*Hondhorst (G.)* | Een Krijgsman rustende met zijn hand onder zijn hoofd op een Trommel en schijnende rustig te slapen; alles is met de natuur overeenkomstig op een meesterlijke wijze geschilderd | *Mat:* op doek *Size:* hoog 46, breed 33 duimen	F	(Sold) fl 9:10 van Dijl
1810/08/06	AMSCH	0050	*Hondhorst (G.)* | Een bejaard Man, houdende een groot Boek, waar uit hij een Jongeling die nevens hem staat schijnt te onderwijzen, ter zijde twee andere, waar van de een een brandende kaars vast houd; kragtig geschilderd | *Mat:* op paneel *Size:* hoog 34, breed 44 duimen	C	(Sold) fl 73 Pot van Rotterdam

<table>
<tr><td>1810/12/03</td><td>DOBRA</td><td>0035</td><td>Hondhorst | Venus en Cupido, door Hondhorst; met de Prent van Verkolje | This Lot: Venus en Cupido</td><td></td><td>(Unknown)</td></tr>
<tr><td></td><td></td><td></td><td>Honthorst, Gerrit van (or Honthorst, G., manner)</td><td></td><td></td></tr>
<tr><td>1801/05/11</td><td>AMSCH</td><td>0033</td><td>G. Hondhorst, (of in de manier) | Een bedaagde Vrouw, met een mand, waar by een haas, alles zeer natuurlyk verbeeld | Mat: op doek Size: hoog 33, breed 27 duim</td><td>Pruisse [for] M</td><td>(Sold) fl 35 Hulswit</td></tr>
<tr><td>1803/04/06</td><td>MGSAN</td><td>0006</td><td>Honthorst | Een Kaarslicht met twee Beelden levensgrootte, stout gepenceeld, door of in de manier van Honthorst</td><td>Mr Evert Clyver</td><td>(Unknown)</td></tr>
<tr><td></td><td></td><td></td><td>Honthorst, Gerrit van (changed to Brugghen, Hendrick ter)</td><td></td><td></td></tr>
<tr><td>1810/08/10</td><td>RMRIJ</td><td>0030</td><td>Honthorst; H Brugge 1628 | Bachus en andere Figuren. Kloek en verdienstelijk behandelt | Inscr: H Brugge 1628 (signed and dated?) Notes: The artist's name was changed by hand from "Honthorst" to "H Brugge 1628" in the EBNP copy of the catalogue. It is unclear whether the name and date are inscribed on the painting.</td><td></td><td>(Sold) fl 1:10 [or] 60 v Ryp</td></tr>
<tr><td></td><td></td><td></td><td>Honthorst, Gerrit van (manner)</td><td></td><td></td></tr>
<tr><td>1803/04/27</td><td>AMSCH</td><td>000O</td><td>Honthorst | Un Consert de trois figures, dans la maniere de Honthorst | Size: h. 46, l. 36 pouces</td><td>B</td><td>(Bought In) fl 4:10</td></tr>
<tr><td>1803/08/24</td><td>HGKAN</td><td>0083</td><td>Hondhorst | Een Borsstuk verbeeldende een Herderin met der Herderstaf, als Hondhorst</td><td>[Teissier] [or others]</td><td>(Unknown) fl 1:8</td></tr>
<tr><td>1803/09/07</td><td>AMSCH</td><td>0244</td><td>Honthorst | Dit Voorwerp vertoont een Jongman, in Spaansche Kleeding, zittende voor een Tafel, schynende iets aandagtigs [sic] te beschouwen, ter zyde staat een ander, een Brief léezende; de Caracters zyn Natuurlyk, het Coloriet bevallig, en meesterlyk fraai gepenceeld, op Doek, in de manier van Honthorst [Le sujet de ce tableau est un jeune homme habillé à l'espagnole, et assis à une table sur laquelle il paroît considerer quelque chose avec la plus grande attention ; à côté, un autre occupé à lire une lettre. Les caractères de ces figures sont exprimés au naturel, le coloris agréable et l'exécution parfaite ; sur toile, dans la manière de Honthorst.] | Mat: op doek Size: hoog 34, breed 27 duim</td><td>Smidt</td><td>(Sold) fl 18:10 Haffner</td></tr>
<tr><td>1805/07/10</td><td>AMSCH</td><td>0214</td><td>G. Hondhorst | Drie Kaartspeelders, zittende aan een Tafel; in de manier van G. Hondhorst</td><td>V[inkeles] [for] H[affner]</td><td>(Bought In) fl 2</td></tr>
<tr><td>1806/05/05</td><td>AMSCH</td><td>0228</td><td>Honthorst | Eenige Kaartspeelers; als door Honthorst, en een Historieele Ordinantie</td><td>Y</td><td>(Sold) fl 2:5 Boelen</td></tr>
<tr><td>1807/06/10</td><td>HGBSM</td><td>0171</td><td>Hondhorst | Een Gezelschap aan een tafel zittende, in de smaak van Hondhorst | Mat: op doek</td><td>Abraham Delfos [or others]</td><td>(Unknown) fl 5</td></tr>
<tr><td></td><td></td><td></td><td>Hooch, Carel Cornelisz. de</td><td></td><td></td></tr>
<tr><td>1807/08/26</td><td>AMSCH</td><td>0103</td><td>C. de Hooch | Een Italiaansch Landgezigt, ter zyde ziet men een Ruïne van een groot Gebouw, waar voor eene Vrouw met een Spinrok in de handen, verder eenige Woningen en Huislieden met Vee; zonagtig behandeld, 1631 | Mat: op paneel Size: hoog 25, breed 29 duim Inscr: 1631 (dated?) Notes: It is unclear whether the date is inscribed on the painting.</td><td>Yver [for] S</td><td>(Sold) fl 1 Levij Pakker</td></tr>
<tr><td></td><td></td><td></td><td>Hooch, Gerrit de</td><td></td><td></td></tr>
<tr><td>1802/05/05</td><td>AMSCH</td><td>0080</td><td>G. de Hoogh | Een Rotsächtig Landschap, met Oude Casteelen, op de Voorgrond by een Beekje, een Rustende Jager en eenig Grazend en Leggend Veê. Meesterlyk behandeld | Mat: op paneel Size: hoog 10, breed 14 duim</td><td>C</td><td>(Sold) fl 6:5 Cocler</td></tr>
<tr><td>1804/10/16</td><td>DLOND</td><td>0105</td><td>Gev. de Hoogh | Een Landschap. Paysage | Mat: op paneel Size: hoog 9, breed 11</td><td></td><td>(Unknown)</td></tr>
<tr><td></td><td></td><td></td><td>Hooch, Pieter de</td><td></td><td></td></tr>
<tr><td>1801/04/13</td><td>AMSCH</td><td>0031</td><td>P. de Hooghe | Een Binnevertrek waar in een Vrouw bezig is een Eendvogel te plukken, agter haar een Dienstmaagd bezig een Ketel over een brandend vuur te hangen, voor het Vengster komt een helder zonligt op de muur vallen; alles is van een bevallige en natuurlyke penceels-behandeling | Mat: op doek Size: hoog 21, breed 25 duim</td><td>Pierre Fouquet, junior</td><td>(Sold) fl 63 Lafontaine</td></tr>
<tr><td>1801/06/10</td><td>AMSCH</td><td>0089</td><td>Hooge. (Pieter de) | In een Binnevertrek, ziet men een Vrouw voor een Waschtobben, door een openstaande Deur, ziet men een binnenplaats waarop een Dienstmaagd, alles zeer naatuurlyk [sic] van schildering | Mat: op paneel Size: hoog 23, breed 18 duim Loc: Richmond, VA, USA. Virginia Museum of Fine Arts. (51−1) as copy after de Hooch.</td><td>[Doublet]</td><td>(Sold) fl 21 Jozi</td></tr>
<tr><td>1801/08/19</td><td>AMSCH</td><td>0037</td><td>P. de Hooge | In een gemeubileerd Vertrek, zit een Dame in al oude Hollandsche Kleeding, houdende op de Schoot een Mandje met Appelen, waarvan zy 'er een aan een Kindje Schynt te geeven, die door een andere Juffer aan de Lybant gehouden wordt, gestoffeert met verder Bywerk; het bevallig Zonlicht doet een natuurlyke werking, en is van een uitvoerige penceel behandeling op Doek | Mat: op doek Size: hoog 26, breed 23 duim Loc: Leipzig, Deutschland. Museum der bildenen Künste (1558)</td><td>Van Forreest</td><td>(Sold) fl 200 Vinkeles</td></tr>
<tr><td>1801/08/19</td><td>AMSCH</td><td>0038</td><td>P. de Hooge | Voor de Deur van een Huis, ziet men een Dienstmaegt met een Kopere Emmer aan de Arm, en een moot Zalm in de andere Hand, terzyde het Huis een Hond, fraai van licht en bevallig gepenceeld</td><td>Pruyssen[r]</td><td>(Sold) fl 30 Frantszen</td></tr>
</table>

1801/10/19	AMSCH	0028	*Hoge. (P. de)* | In een Binnenvertrek zit een Officier beneevens een Vrouwtje aan een Tafel, waar op een Verkeer-Bord, voor het zelve staat een Krygsman, als de steenen in 't bord werpende | companion to lot 29 *Mat:* op paneel *Size:* hoog 18, breed 13 duim *Loc:* Dublin, Eire. National Gallery of Ireland. (322)	Jonkheer Menno Baron van Coehoorn	(Sold) fl 102 for lots 28 & 29. Coclers
1801/10/19	AMSCH	0029	*Hoge. (P. de)* | Een dito [Binnenvertrek] zynde een weederga, waar in een krygsman op een bank zit in 't harnasch, by dezelve staat een vrolyk Vrouwtje, met een kan en een glas in haar hand, verder twee mannen die op de kaart speelen; helder van Coloriet en kragtig geschildert | companion to lot 28	Jonkheer Menno Baron van Coehoorn	(Sold) fl 102 for lots 28 & 29. Coclers
1802/12/13	AMSCH	0074	*P. de Hooge* | Een Dame in witte Satyne Kleeding, staande voor een Clavercimbaal, nevens haar een Heer die op de Fluit speelt, en 2 dansende Hondjes; door een openstaande Deur ziet men in de Tuin, meesterlyk behandeld | *Size:* hoog 24, breed 20 duim	Pruyssenaar [for] B	(Sold) fl 16 Hulswit
1803/07/18	AMSCH	0019	*Hooge. (P. de)* | Dit betoverend Schildery steld voor een Binnenvertrek; zyn uitgang hebbende op een Binnenplaats, in de Deur staat een Vrouw welke van een Jongen een Mandje met Brood aanneemt, zy is in oude Hollandsche Kleeding, met een roode Rok en zwart Fluweele Jak gekleed; over den zonachtig verlichte Binnenplaats ziet men door de Gang van het Voorhuis tot aan de overzyde der Gragt, alwaar uit een der Huisen een Vrouw over de Deur legt: de fraaie perspectief en het frapante zonligt, zoo eigenaartig aan deezen Meester, is hier zeer wel in waargenomen, en is voorts delicaat gepenceeld [Ce tableau vrayment magique represente l'intérieur d'une chambre ; dont la porte ouverte donne entrée à un jeune homme apportant une corbeille remplie de pain. Il la remet à une femme costumée d'un habillement court & d'un jupon rouge ; le jeune homme est également vetu à la mode du tems de l'auteur : cet appartement meublé d'un ancien fauteuil est eclairé par une fenêtre gothique. Par la porte l'on voit dans une cour intérieure donnant sur un corps de batiment percé d'une longue allée qui aboutit à la rue & sur un canal ; ce point de vue finit par la maison du côté opposé du canal, sur la porte de laquelle se tient une femme. L'on connoit le talent supérienr [sic] de cet artiste pour l'effet frappant & la vérité de sa couleur, celui dont nous presentons le detail est un des [plus] picquans pour l'effet de lumiere & l'illusion de la perspective.] | *Mat:* op doek *Size:* hoog 28, breed 23 duim *Loc:* London, England, UK. Wallace Collection. (P27)	Maria Theresia Andrioli	(Sold) fl 800 C S Roos
1803/12/12	AMSCH	0042	*P. de Hooghe* | In een Gemeubileerd Binnenvertrek zit een Heer en een Dame aan een Tafel, waar achter een ander Heer, de Dame de hand gevende, en gezondheid schynt te wenschen, een andere Dame, met een Mandje met Appelen, staat op de voorgrond; dit stukje is van een bevallige en zonachtige behandeling | *Mat:* op paneel *Size:* hoog 23, breed 19 duim	W	(Sold) fl 86 Mensard
1804/05/07	AMSCH	0073	*Hooghe. (P. de)* | In deeze ryke Ordonantie van tien Beelden, ziet men in een Gemeubileerde Kamer, op de voorgrond voor een opgeslaagen groen Gordyn, een Heer met een bevallige Jonge Dame, byde in deftige Kleeding; waarachter voor een open Raam eenige Muciceerende Lieden, waarby een Vrouw met een Kan en Glas in de Hand, ter zyde by een Portaal welke door een Gang in een andere Kamer ziet, een Heer en Dame; dit uitmuntend Tafreel is aller piquant van licht, uitvoerig gepenceeld en van de beste schildering van deeze Meester | *Mat:* op doek *Size:* hoog 28, breed 26 duim *Loc:* København, Danmark. Statens Museum for Kunst. (Sp.615)	Vinkeles [for] J	(Sold) fl 181 Pruissenaar
1804/05/07	AMSCH	0074	*Hooghe. (P. de)* | In een Binnenvertrek ziet met aan een Tafel zitten, een Heer welke een Pyp rookt, waar naast een bevallige jonge Damen, welke een Papegaay te eeten geeft, wiens Kooy een Moor na beneeden doet zakken, ter zyde een Dienstmaagd met een Bord en Fles in de hand, en op de Tafel legt een rood Kleed, en staat een Kan en Glas; dit schildery is allernatuurlykst van licht en van een dito [uitvoerig gepenceeld en van de beste schildering van deeze Meester] behandeling als de voorgaande | *Mat:* op doek *Size:* hoog 25, breed 25 duim *Notes:* It is unclear what "dito" refers to in the title.	Vinkeles [for] J	(Sold) fl 92 Van Iperen
1804/05/07	AMSCH	0075	*Hooghe (P. de)* | Een Binnekamer, alwaar een Dienstmaagd beezig is de vloer te veegen, ziende men verder door een Raam, in een tweede Vertrek en ter zyde door een Deur in een andere Kamer, daar een Dame voor haar Toilet staat een Brief te leezen, 't onderscheide zon- en daglicht geeven een allernatuurlykste nitwerking [sic] en 't zelve is meesterlyk en krachtig gepenceeld | *Mat:* op doek *Size:* hoog 31, breed 25 duim	Y[ver] [for] W	(Sold) fl 60 Jan Spaan
1804/07/25	DLGRO	0089	*Pieter de Hooghe* | Een binnen Vertrek, waarïn twee Heeren op het Verkeer Bord zitten te speelen en een derde over de leuning van een Stoel zyn Pyp staat te rooken; met verder bywerk, zeer fraai geschilderd door Pieter de Hooghe | *Mat:* op paneel *Size:* hoog 20, breed 22 duim	Mr Franc van der Burch Wz.	(Unknown)
1804/08/08	AMSCH	0077	*P. de Hooge* | In een Gemeubileerde Kamer zit een Dame en Heer, in deftige alöude Hollandsche Kleeding, by een Tafel, met een Tapyt Kleed bedekt, zy houd in de éene hand een Glas Wyn, een andere Juffer speelt op de Bas, verder voor een openstaande Deur ziet men een Heer, en aan de overzyde der Gragt eenige treffelyke Gebouwen; het zonlicht doet eene natuurlyke aangenaame werking, en is uitvoerig van penceelbehandeling | *Mat:* op doek *Size:* hoog 32, breed 27 duim	Schley [for] A	(Sold) fl 151 Reyers

1804/12/10	AMSCH	0025	*P. de Hooge* | In een ryk gemeubileerd Vertrek, met goudleeder behangsel, ziet men een deftig Heer, houdende een roemer in de hand, naast hem een bevallig Vrouwtje; ter zyde ziet men door een openstaande deur, in een ander vertrek een Vrouw zitten; alles is fraay van effect en uitvoerig van penceel behandeling | *Mat:* op doek *Size:* Hoog 22, breed 25 duim *Loc:* Philadelphia, PA, USA. Museum of Art. (E24-3-51) as Hendrick van der Burch	Jan De Groot	(Sold) fl 67 Coclers
1805/07/03	AMSCH	0024	*Hooge (P. de)* | In een gemeubileerd Binnen-Vertrek, zit een Heer by een helder brandende kaars aan een Tafel met een boek voor hem, terwyl de Vrouw zit te naaijen, en de Dienstmaagd met een Kind by een helder-brandend Vuur is; hetgeen een eclatanten uitwerking doed | *Mat:* op paneel *Size:* hoog 14, breed 16 duim	C	(Sold) fl 106 C S Roos
1806/05/05	AMSCH	0057	*P. de Hooge* | In een gemeubileerd Binnenvertrek; ziet men een jonge bevallige Dame in deftige Kleeding, houdende een glas Wyn in de hand, achter haar op een Tafel met een Tapyt Kleed, een Bierkan, Pyp enz., een Heer met een Fluit in de hand, ter zyde een openstaande Raam, en verder bywerk; allerpiquantst van licht en delicaat gepenceeld door P. de Hooge | *Mat:* op doek *Size:* hoog 18, breed 18 duim	E	(Sold) fl 90 B Tedeman
1806/05/05	AMSCH	0068	*P. de Hoog* | Een Hofgezigt, waar in een Jager en een rustende Dame, op de voorgrond een Patryshondje by Rietgewas	V[inkeles]	(Sold) fl 1 L Pakker
1806/06/07	RMHSN	0022	*P: de Hoog* | Een Gezelschap van Officiers die Rooken, Drinken en Spelen in een Binnenvertrek tegen een witte Muur | *Mat:* op paneel	A E K L	(Sold) fl 6 v Sartin [?]
1806/08/13	AMSCH	0067	*Hooge (P. de)* | In een Binnenkamer ziet men een gezelschap van Dames en Heeren zich met musiceeren verlustigen, op de Vootgrond [sic] een Patryshond, door een openstaande deur ziet men in een andere kamer waarin een Heer en Dame; zonachtig en van een delicaate penceels-behandeling | *Mat:* op doek *Size:* hoog 35, breed 42 duim	van der Voort	(Sold) fl 40 Gruiter
1806/08/13	AMSCH	0068	*Hooge. (P. de)* | In een gemeubileerd Binnenvertrek ziet men een bevallige Vrouw, zittende naast een Wieg waar een Kind in legt, achter dezelve een Dienstmaagd met een Papkommetje in de Hand, en verder bywerk; aller zonachtig en piquant van licht en van de beste schildering van deze Meester | *Mat:* op doek *Size:* hoog 20 ½, breed 23 duim *Loc:* Moskva, Rossiya. Muzei imeni Pushkina. (2030)	Vinkeles [for] D	(Bought In) fl 149
1806/08/13	AMSCH	0069	*Hooge. (P. de)* | In een Binnenvertrek ziet men twee Heeren, de eene slapende en de andere rokende aan een Tafel, waarop geplaast een bierkan en comvoir, verders een doorzigt in een andere Kamer waarin een Heer met een mantel, en verder bywerk; breed en meesterlyk gepenceeld | *Mat:* op doek *Size:* hoog 27, breed 33 duim	Vinkeles [for] E	(Sold) fl 18 Schumacher
1806/11/24	AMSCH	0030	*Hooge (P. de)* | In een gemeubileerde Kamer, by een Tafel met een kleedje bedekt, zitten twee Krygslieden, als met yver op de kaart speelende; verder staat een Vrouw; het zydelings invallende Licht door een vengster, doed een fraaije natuurlyke werking, en is van een uitvoerig penceel | *Mat:* op paneel *Size:* hoog 20, breed 18 duim	Munnikhuizen	(Bought In) fl 300
1808/06/06	RMRIJ	0056	*Hooge. (Pieter de)* | Een deftig Binnenvertrek, alwaar eene zittende Vrouw eenen brief leest; verder eene tafel, waarop een tapijt ligt, en meerder bijwerk. Door een open venster ziet men een aangenaam verschiet van Boomen, Huizen, Toren, Lucht, enz. Alles zeer konstig geschilderd [Une femme occupée à lire est assis dans un Appartement Hollandais, où l'on voit differents meubles et une Table couverte d'un Tapis. A Travers une croisée ouverte, on découvre un agréable lointain. Ce Tableau produit un effet admiràble et piquant, et fait illusion] | *Annots:* Gek. van Thys, Juli 1800 (f.60-) was door Thÿs 1800 gekocht (RMA I) *Mat:* op doek *Size:* Hoog 21, en breed 22 duim *Loc:* Budapest, Magyarország. Szépmüvészati Múzeum. (5933)	Gerrit van der Pot, Heer van Groeneveld	(Sold) fl 155 Allard
1808/06/13	AMSCH	0073	*Hooghe (P. de)* | In eene gemeubileerde Kamer zit eene bevallige Dame, in satijnen kleeding, met een Muziekboek op den schoot; ter zijde bij een open vengster zit een bedaagd Heer, op het Klavier spelende, waarbij een oude Dame met een Guitard. Uit het Voorvertrek komt eene Dienstmaagd met een roemer wijn. Door de openstaande deur ziet men uit het Voorhuis, naar de overzijde der gragt, eenige Woningen. De invallende lichten zijn natuurlijk, en alles is meesterlijk gepenceeld | *Mat:* op doek *Size:* hoog 25, breed 29 duim	[Jan Tersteeg]	(Sold) fl 121 van Iperen
1808/06/13	AMSCH	0074	*Hooghe (P. de)* | In een ouderwetsche Kamer zit eene Dame 'aan een' tafel, schijnende aan een in de kamer komend Kind een perzik te willen geven; achter de tafel staat de Vader, en op den voorgrond een Hond. Door de openstaande deur ziet men de overzijde der gragt, door een helder zonlicht beschenen. Mede natuurlijk als voren | *Mat:* op doek *Size:* hoog 33, breed 30 duim	[Jan Tersteeg]	(Sold) fl 235 van Drielst
1808/06/13	AMSCH	0225	*P. de Hooghe* | Voor eene Tafel staat eene Dame een Glas Wijn in te schenken voor een Heer, welke achter de Tafel zit, waarop eene Schotel met Oesters; krachtig | *Mat:* op paneel	[Jan Tersteeg]	(Sold) fl 51 Allard
1808/08/23	AMSCH	0069	*Hooghe, (P. de)* | In een Binnengezigt van een Woning, zit eene Juffrouw, in oude Hollandsche Kleeding, bij de openstaande Voordeur bézig een jong Kind te reinigen, verder een bedaagd Heer de Trap afkomende; het zonlicht doet een bevallige natuurlijke uitwerking, en is fraai gepenceeld | *Mat:* op doek *Size:* hoog 25, breed 21 duim	[Van Iperen?]	(Bought In) fl 100

1808/09/13	HABRU	0037	*P. de Hooch* | Een zittend Meisje, in oude Hollandsche Kleding, agter haar een Manspersoon, schijnende haar te verrassen		(Unknown) fl 10 [?]
1808/11/12	HGSCR	0021	*P. de Hooge* | Een binnenvertrek waar in een heer zit zyn pyp te roken by het vuur en een vrouwtje aan een tafel gezeten en ten andere zyde een dienstmaagd staande met een kan in haar hand, men ziet verder door een ander vertrek op de straat, het invallend zonligt doed een zeer natuurlyke uitwerking in dit stuk, 't welk uitvoerig en meesterlyk is behandeld | *Mat:* op doek *Loc:* Manchester, England, UK. City Art Museum. (Assheton Bennett collection)	Mr J van Buren	(Unknown) fl 66
1808/11/28	AMSCH	0025	*P. de Hoogh* | In een rijk gemeubileerde Kamer, vertoond zig een musiceerend Gezelschap van Heeren en Dames, verder ziet men door een openstaande Deur in een ander Vertrek, waar in een Officier met een Dame in gesprek; het invallend zonlicht doet een schoon effect en is van een meesterlijke Penceelsbehandeling | *Mat:* op doek *Size:* hoog 35, breed 52 duim	[Gruyter?]	(Bought In) fl 45
1809/05/26	HADAA	0035	*P. de Hoge* | Een Binnenvertrek, waar in eene Dame met eenig handwerk bezig is, kloek van behandeling | *Mat:* op paneel	Mejuffrouw de Wed David Heemskerk [or others]	(Unknown)
1809/06/13	AMSCH	0060	*P. de Hooge* | In een Binnevertrek ziet men eene bevallige Dame, speelende op de Guitar, een andere Dame speelt op het Clavier, terwijl een Heer schijnt te zingen, voorts een Hond en bijwerk; het invallend licht geeft een natuurlijke werking, en de schildering is uitvoerig | *Mat:* op doek *Size:* hoog 22, breed 24 duim	E	(Sold) fl 15:10 Eversdijk
1809/07/19	AMSCH	0021	*Hooge (P. de)* | Door een open Deur uit een Gang of Binnenvertrek ziet men in eene andere Kamer eene bevallige rijk gekleede Dame, zittende voor een Tafel, met een Tapijt bedekt, zij is bezig een Papegaai eeten te geeven, nevens haar een staand Heer, de Kooi vast houdende, verder ziet men door een Gang op een Gracht. Het invallend licht geeft eene schoone werking, het is uitvoerig en fraai gepenceeld | *Mat:* op doek *Size:* hoog 30, breed 26 duim *Loc:* Köln, Deutschland. Wallraf-Richartz Museum. (Dep. 239)	[Wijkersloot?]	(Sold) fl 145 D Teengs
1809/09/06	AMSCH	0024	*Hooge (Pieter de)* | In een Voorhuis, bij een openstaande Deur, schijnt een Bediende een brief te overhandigen aan eene jonge Dame, in satijnen kleeding, houdende een Hondje onder den arm, en een andere op den grond loopende. Door een open Deur ziet men in een gemeubileerde Kamer, en door de Voordeur eenige Woningen op de Gragt; de natuurlijk invallende zonlichten, zoo eigen aan deze Meester, zijn bevallig verbeeld, en zeer uitvoerig van penceelbehandeling | *Mat:* op doek *Size:* hoog 22, breed 20 ½ duim *Loc:* Hamburg, Deutschland. Kunsthalle.	Johannes Caudri	(Sold) fl 31 Dupre
1810/05/22	AMSCH	0034	*Hooghe (P. de)* | In een Binnenvertrek ziet men eene bevallige Vrouw, staande met een Glas met Wijn gevuld in haar Hand bij een Tafel, waarop een Tapijtkleedje en Wijnkan, agter de Tafel zit een Heer met een Fluit in zijn Handen, verder ziet men door een Glas Raam eene andere Vrouw in een tweede Vertrek; dit stukje is zeer fraai en uitvoerig gepenceeld en treffend van licht en donker | *Mat:* op doek *Size:* hoog 18, breed 17 ½ duim	Ij[ver]	(Sold) fl 101 van Iperen
1810/06/20	AMSCH	0032	*P. De Hooge* | Een Gezelschap van Heeren en Dames, welke zich met de Muziek vermaken. Allerfraaist | *Mat:* op doek *Size:* hoog 26, breed 30 duimen	X	(Sold) fl 26 Hulswit
1810/08/01	AMSCH	0045	*Hooge (Pieter de)* | In een Voorhuis, met roode en blaauwe Bakken bevloerd, ziet men ter linkerzijde eenen Kelder, waar uit eene Dienstmaagd gekomen is, houdende eene Bierkan, welke zij aan een Kind, dat voor haar staat, toereikt, en ter regterzijde een gestoffeerd Vertrek, waar in men door een open Venster op de Straat ziet [Dans un Vestibule pavé en bricques rouges et bleux on voit à la gauche l'entrée d'une Cave, dout [sic] est sortie une Servante tenant un pot à bierre ; elle est dans l'attitude de remettre la boisson à un Enfant qui se presente devant elle ; à droite est un appartement meublé ayant une fenêtre ouverte donnant sur la rue] | *Annots:* assez bon. vendu en 1798, fl: 2600, chez de Bruin à Amsterdam. (NGW) *Mat:* op doek *Size:* hoog 23, breed 24 duimen *Loc:* Amsterdam, Nederland. Rijksmuseum. (A 182)	Mr Pieter de Smeth van Alphen	(Sold) fl 3025 Izaac Smit voor Mev Huguer
1810/08/01	AMSCH	0046	*Hooge (Pieter de)* | Op eene Binnenplaats ziet men eene Vrouw en Kind, komende van eenen steenen Trap, en terzijde in eenen Gang of Doorloop eene andere Vrouw, gaande naar eene tweede opene Plaats [Sujet d'effet étant une Cour interieure de Maison, dans laquelle on voit une Femme et un Enfant descendant d'un escalier de pierres ; sur le côté se trouve une allée de Maison, conduisant à une seconde Cour ouverte, dans laquelle allée paroit cheminer une Femme] | *Annots:* vraiment magique et étonnant. (NGW) *Mat:* op doek *Size:* hoog 26, breed 23 duimen *Loc:* London, England, UK. National Gallery. (835)	Mr Pieter de Smeth van Alphen	(Sold) fl 2075 Van Ijperen pour Backer

Hooch, Pieter de (or Hooch, P., manner)

1803/06/20	AMSCH	0067	*P. de Hoge* | In een Binnenvertrek zit een Vrouw by het Vuur waarby een Dienstmaagd en een Hond, in 't verschiet een Heer die de Courant leest; zonachtig door of in de manier van P. de Hoge | *Mat:* op doek *Size:* hoog 29, breed 33 duim	Schley [for] K	(Sold) fl 107 Gruiter

1808/06/11	RMRIJ	0124	*Door of in de manier van Pieter de Hooge* | Een Binnenkamer met verscheide Doorzichten, waar in twee Musicerende Personen, met aangenaam Bywerk, zonachtig van effect | *Mat:* op doek		(Sold) fl 30:10 Allard [?] [or] Rohan
			Hooch, Pieter de (manner)		
1801/04/13	AMSCH	0107	*P. de Hooghe* | Een Binnenvertrek waarin een Vrouw by den haard zit te naaijen, verders een kind, en een menigte huisraad; kragtig in de manier van P. de Hooghe | *Mat:* op doek *Size:* hoog 20, breed 23 duim	Pierre Fouquet, junior	(Sold) fl 33 Spruit van Gend
1805/07/10	AMSCH	0254	*P. de Hooge* | Een Vrouw, zittende in een Binnevertrek by een Haardstee, houdende een Kind op de Schoot, gestoffeert met verder bywerk; op Doek geschilderd, in de manier van P. de Hooge | *Mat:* op doek *Size:* hoog 12, breed 2 duim	Temmink	(Sold) fl 2:5 Isaac Smit
1808/06/11	RMRIJ	0057	*Als door P: de Hooge* | Een Kindje, gezeten op eene Stoep, een Hondje zit voor hetzelve op, verders aangenaam Bywerk, alles verdienstig geschilderd | *Mat:* op doek *Size:* hoog 45 ½, breed 35 ½ duim		(Bought In) fl 20
1810/05/22	AMSCH	0131	*P. de Hooghe* | In een Binnenhaard van eene Herberg, zit op de voorgrond eene oude Vrouw, bezig zijnde te spinnen bij eene Tafel, voor een open Venster, ter zijde bij de Haard zit een oud Man te rooken, verder ziet men de Hospita in een Voorhuis, wordende door eenen Heer geliefkoosd; uitvoerig en krachtig behandeld. In de manier van P. de Hooghe | *Mat:* op doek *Size:* hoog 14, breed 20 duim	Ij[ver]	(Sold) fl 40 Mensart
1810/10/11	AMSCH	0193	*P. de Hooge* | Een Binnenvertrek, waarin eene Dame, welke door haare Dienstmaagd gekapt wordt, op Doek, in de manier van P. de Hooge | *Mat:* op doek	A	(Sold) fl 1:10 Yver
			Hooft, Nicolas		
1803/10/24	HGDAW	0003	*N. Hooft* | Een stuk met nakende Nimphen in een Landschap, door N. Hooft, in een zwarte lyst met vergulde binnen bies [Schilderyen in Olyverw] | *Mat:* in olyverf *Notes:* The bracketed information in the title appears above lot 1 and refers to lots 1 to 16.	M van Daalen Wetters	(Unknown)
1803/10/24	HGDAW	0004	*N. Hooft* | Een dito [stuk met nakende Nimphen in een Landschap, door N. Hooft] in een zwarte lyst [Schilderyen in Olyverw] | *Mat:* in olyverf *Notes:* The bracketed information in the title appears above lot 1 and refers to lots 1 to 16.	M van Daalen Wetters	(Unknown)
			Hoogerheyden, Engel		
1803/11/30	MGBEO	0009	*E. Hoogerheiden* | Een Storm en een Stil Zeetje, in 't verschiet de Stad Veere | *Mat:* op doek *Size:* hoog 15 duim, breed 20 duim	Samuel de Wind	(Sold) £ 2.12 Lambrechtsen
1803/11/30	MGBEO	0010	*E. Hoogerheiden* | Een dito [Storm] en een woelend Zeetje, op Paneel, door denzelven [E. Hoogerheiden] | *Mat:* op paneel *Size:* hoog 5 ½ duim, breed 7 duim	Samuel de Wind	(Sold) £ 1.3 Lambrechtsen
1806/10/17	MGSAN	0010	*E. Hogerbeiden* | Het Uitzeilen van twee O.I. Scheepen | *Mat:* op doek	Gerardus Beljard	(Unknown)
1806/10/17	MGSAN	0047	*E. Hogerbeiden* | Gezigt in de Kil by Dort, vol Zee- en andere Schepen | *Mat:* op paneel	Gerardus Beljard	(Sold) £ 0.7.7 for lots 47 & 48
1806/10/17	MGSAN	0048	*E. Hogerbeiden* | Een Stadgezigt aan Zee met Schepen | *Mat:* op paneel	Gerardus Beljard	(Sold) £ 0.7.7 for lots 47 & 48
1807/08/26	AMSCH	0105	*E. Hogerheyde* | Een Zeegezigt, met verscheide zeilende Oorlogschepen en andere Vaartuigen; fiks op Doek geschilderd | *Mat:* op doek	Roos	(Sold) fl 0:10 L Pakker
1807/09/28	AMWUR	0013	*E. Hogerheide* | Een dito [stuk] op Doek, zynde 't gezicht van 't Kasteel van Rammekens, door E. Hogerheide, 1793 | *Mat:* op doek *Inscr:* E. Hogerheide, 1793 (signed and dated?) *Notes:* It is unclear whether the name and date are inscribed on the painting.		(Unknown) fl 0:10
1807/09/28	AMWUR	0014	*E. Hogerheide* | Een dito [stuk] 't gezicht van Hellevoetsluis, door denzelfden [E. Hogerheide], 1791 | *Inscr:* E. Hogerheide, 1791 (signed and dated?) *Notes:* It is unclear whether the name and date are inscribed on the painting.		(Unknown) fl 7
1807/09/28	AMWUR	0015	*E. Hogerheide* | Een dito [stuk] onstuimige Zee, met in gevaar zynde Scheepen, door denzelfden [E. Hogerheide], 1793 | *Inscr:* E. Hogerheide, 1793 (signed and dated?) *Notes:* It is unclear whether the name and date are inscribed on the painting.		(Unknown) fl 7
1807/09/28	AMWUR	0021	*E. Hogerheide, 1792* | Een dito [stuk] op Paneel, verbeeldende een Deining der Zee na eenen Storm, door E. Hogerheide 1792, in vergulde Lyst | *Mat:* op paneel *Inscr:* E. Hogerheide, 1792 (signed and dated?) *Notes:* It is unclear whether the name and date are inscribed on the painting.		(Unknown) fl 8:10
			Hoogsaat, Jan Cornelisz.		
1802/05/05	AMSCH	0079	*Hoogzaat* | Een Historiëele Ordonnantie uit Ovidius, zynde een Prachtig Paleis, met verscheide Beelden, fraai en delicaat gepenceeld | *Mat:* op doek *Size:* hoog 22, breed 40 duim	C	(Sold) fl 4:5 Mensard
1802/09/06	AMSCH	0172	*Hoogzaat* | Christus voor den Rechter Pilatus; fix geschilderd	Spaan	(Sold) fl 0:8 C Deppe
1810/03/26	RMMUY	0024	*J. Hoogzaat* | De Slaapende Reinoud, door Armida betoverd, vergezeld door Cupido's, en ander bijwerk. Stout en meesterachtig gepenceeld	Daniel de Jongh Az	(Sold) fl 10 de Jongh [for] A

[L'enchantement d'Arnaud par Armide, &c. accompagné des amours, et plus haut dans les nues son char, peint en maître.] | *Annots:* Copie du N. Poussin (BPG) *Mat:* op doek *Size:* hoog 36 ½, breed 46 ¾ duimen

Hoogstraten, Jan van

1801/03/16	AMSCH	0153	*J. van Hoogstraten* | De uitdryving van Hagar, fraai geordonneerd en fix geschilderd	K[ip]	(Sold) fl 8 Pruisenaar [for] D
1801/06/10	AMSCH	0087	*Hoogstraaten. (J. van)* | Een bevallig jong Meisje, nevens een Tafel zittende, met een Hond in haarschoot, uitvoerig en kragtig gepenceeld | *Mat:* op doek *Size:* hoog 11, breed 8 duim	Herman ten Kate	(Sold) fl 9 van der Schley [for] Uylenburg

Hoogstraten, Samuel van

1802/08/24	LNDLS	0030	*Hoogstraten* | De kwijnende Schilderkonst, door de hoop opgebeurd, verbeeld door een Vrouw, liggende bij eene Graftombe en weenende Kinderen, met een Latijnsch Vaers op de Tombe. Door | *Mat:* op paneel *Size:* hoog 16, breed 13 ½ duimen	Leonardus Bouman [or others]	(Unknown) fl 6:15
1804/08/08	AMSCH	0089	*S. van Hoogstraten* | Een ryke Historiëele Ordinantie, zynde het Bruidje van Scipio; dit Schildery is zoo fraai, als men van deezen Meester zien kan | *Mat:* op doek *Size:* hoog 23, br. 30 duim	Roos [for] C	(Sold) fl 46 Gruyter
1804/08/08	AMSCH	0090	*S. van Hoogstraten* | Johannes predikt in de Woestyn, fiks en breed gepenceelt | *Mat:* op doek *Size:* hoog 21, breed 18 duim	Vink[eles] [for] K[=Gruyter?]	(Sold) fl 1 L Pakker
1805/07/10	AMSCH	0078	*S. van Hoogstraaten* | In een Kraamkamer ziet men een Vrouw, houdende een jong Gebaakert Kindje op de Schoot, waarby een Wieg, Tafel, Dienstmaagd, enz; uitvoerig op Doek, door S. van Hoogstraaten, in de manier van P. de Hooge | *Mat:* op doek *Size:* hoog 13, breed 16 duim	V[inkeles] [for] M	(Bought In) fl 13
1806/08/20	HGBSM	0117	*S. van Hoogstraaten* | Een jonge Dame, als een jagt Godin verbeeld, in het satijn gekleed, met boog en pijl in de handen, nevens haar een jagt hond, door S. van Hoogstraaten 1676 | *Mat:* op doek *Inscr:* S. van Hoogstraaten 1676 (signed and dated?) *Notes:* It is unclear whether the name and date are inscribed on the painting.	Macalester Loup [or others]	(Sold) fl 2:18 Spruyt
1806/08/20	HGBSM	0134	*S. van Hoogstraaten* | Twee dito [Stuks Mans en Vrouwe Portraiten] | *Mat:* op doek	Macalester Loup [or others]	(Sold) fl 1:8 Scheltema
1808/08/23	AMSCH	0211	*S. van Hoogstraten* | In een sterk woelende Zee, ziet men St. Petrus door Christus geroepen, op de Zee wankelen, schoon van efect en meesterlijk geschildert	[Gruyter?]	(Sold or Bought In) fl 2:5 Gruyter
1809/06/13	AMSCH	0062	*S. van Hoogstraaten* | In een Kraamkamer zit eene Vrouwtje, met een Kind aan de Borst, ter zijde eene Dienstmaagd, bij de Haardsteede, verder ziet men een Wieg, Vuurmand, enz.; delicaat gepenceeld | *Mat:* op doek *Size:* hoog 13, breed 15 duim	E	(Sold) fl 6:5 du Pree
1810/06/06	RMMUY	0005	*Samuel van Hoogstraten* | Een Voorportaal, Trap &c. van eene schoone Bouworde met verscheide doorzichten, waar in een Lezend Jongman; op den voorgrond een Hond. Ongemeen natuurlijk en konstig geschilderd. Door Samuel van Hoogstraten, op doek, zijnde dit eene wedergade, van dat het welk zich voor heen in de Gallerij van den Stadhouder bevond, en thans in 't Muséum te Parijs | *Mat:* op doek		(Sold) fl 30 Teekengenootschap Gen Pictura

Hoogstraten, Samuel van (manner)

1806/05/05	AMSCH	0207	*Hoogstraaten* | De Verhooging van Mordechay; fraai geordineerd en meesterlyk als van Hoogstraaten | *Mat:* op doek *Size:* hoog 47, breed 58 duim	V[inkeles]	(Sold) fl 15:10 T van Iperen

Hooren, J. van [Unidentified]

1801/08/19	AMSCH	0048	*J. van Hooren* | Virtumnus en Pomona, in een Boomryk Landschap, op Paneel | *Mat:* op paneel *Size:* hoog 21, breed 27 duim	Van Forreest	(Sold) fl 3:15 Wed Achtienhoven

Hoorn, Jordanus

1804/05/07	AMSCH	0085	*Hoorn. (J.)* | Twee stuks het eene Poort te Utrecht en het andere te Haarlem, beide fraai gestoffeerd met een ménigte Beeldjes en andere Stoffagie, zonachtig en bevallig gepenceeld | *Mat:* op paneel *Size:* hoog 13, breed 18 duim	Roos [for] A	(Sold) fl 101 Gruyter

Horemans, Jan Joseph (I)

1801/03/16	AMSCH	0106	*Horremans* | Een Binnehuis met een eetend Gezelschap, uitvoerig	K[ip]	(Sold) fl 1:5 J v d Bergh
1801/03/16	AMSCH	0112	*Horremans* | Een Heer zittende een meisje te galantiseeren, geestig	K[ip]	(Sold) fl 1:5 Clement
1801/03/16	AMSCH	0185	*J. Horremans* | Twee stuks, voor de Deur van een Hoefsmit staat een Paard dat beslagen word, verder ziet men eenige andere, en de wederga Eetende Lieden voor een Buitenhuis, plaisant geschilderd op doek | *Mat:* op doek	K[ip]	(Sold) fl 3 Pruisenaar [for] R
1801/03/16	AMSCH	0186	*J. Horremans* | Een Binnenvertrek, waarin een Huisgezin Eetende aan een gedekte tafel, natuurlyk op doek | *Mat:* op doek	K[ip]	(Sold) fl 1 van Iperen
1801/08/19	AMSCH	0047	*J. Horemans* | Twee stuks Binnenhuisen, met aanzienlyke Gezelschappen, uitvoerig op Doek | *Mat:* op doek	van der Schly [for] F	(Sold) fl 7 Le Dantú
1801/10/06	AMSCH	0035	*J. Hooremans* | Twee stuks Binnehuyzen, in het eene een Chirurgyn die een patient het been verbind, en het andere een musiceerend Gezelschap,	M	(Sold) fl 14:10 Van Houten

			helder en bevallig geschilderd | *Mat:* op doek *Size:* yder hoog 15, breed 12 duim		
1802/07/09	AMSTO	0008	*Hooremans* | 2 stuks Binnenhuyzen		(Unknown)
1803/04/20	AMSCH	0113	*J. Horemans* | Twee stuks Binnenhuizen, verbeeldende Kinderen Schoolen, gestoffeert met verder Bywerk [Deux tableaux par J. Horemans, dont les Sujets sont des Ecoles d'enfans.] | *Mat:* op doek *Size:* ieder hoog 20, breed 22 duim	Maria Magdalena van Sluypwyk, gravinne van Moens	(Sold) fl 1:5 L Pakker
1803/12/15	MGLAC	0060	*Hooremans* | Twee stuks zeer fraaie Binnenvertrekken, met vrolyke Gezelschapjes | *Mat:* op doek *Size:* hoog duim 20, breed duim 23	Mr L H de Haze Bomme	(Unknown)
1803/12/15	MGLAC	0062	*Hooremans* | Twee Binnenhuizen | *Size:* hoog duim 22, breed duim 19	Mr L H de Haze Bomme	(Unknown)
1804/04/28	LNDLS	0048	*Horremans* | Twee Stuks vrolyke Gezelschappen, door Horremans, op doek | *Mat:* op doek	[Abraham Delfos] [or others]	(Bought In) fl 2:10
1804/08/08	AMSCH	0091	*J. Horemans* | Twee stuks, een Schilder en een Beeldhouwer, yder in hunne Studeervertrekken, met hunne Leerlingen verzeld; deeze stukjes zyn van een kragtige behandeling, op Doek | *Mat:* op doek *Size:* hoog 19, breed 23 duim	Roos a	(Sold) fl 38 Coclers
1804/08/08	AMSCH	0092	*J. Horemans* | Twee stuks, de eene een Schoenmaaker met zyn Knegt, waarby een Vrouw met een paar Schoenen in de Hand; de andere een Spinnende Vrouw en verdere Beelden; kragtig op Doek | *Mat:* op doek *Size:* hoog 25, breed 12 duim	Roos [for] N	(Withdrawn)
1804/10/16	DLOND	0106	*N. Horremans* | Een Vrolyk Gezelschap. Une Compagnie joyeuse | *Size:* hoog 19, breed 23 *Notes:* The artist's name was given as "N. Horremans" but we have assumed this is an error.		(Unknown)
1805/07/10	AMSCH	0080	*Horemans* | Een Schoolmatres, bézig om een Kind te bestraffen, waarby drie Ouderen; dun en uitvoerig op Paneel | *Mat:* op paneel *Size:* hoog 10, breed 9 duimen	V[inkeles] [for] N	(Sold) fl 3:5 Gruyter
1805/12/16	AMSCH	0030	*Horremans* | Twee stuks Burger Gezelschappen van Mannen en Vrouwen, welke drinken en roken; geestig op Doek | *Mat:* op doek *Size:* hoog 13, breed 15 duim	R[oos]	(Bought In) fl 6
1805/12/16	AMSCH	0031	*Horremans* | Twee dito [stuks] Boere Gezelschappen, niet minder als de voorige | *Size:* hoog 11, breed 10 duim	R[oos]	(Bought In) fl 6
1806/05/05	AMSCH	0070	*J. Hooremans* | Een Landschap, gestoffeerd met eenige speelende Kinderen | *Mat:* op doek *Size:* hoog 27, breed 33 duim	V[inkeles]	(Sold) fl 2:10 L Pakker
1807/04/00	LNDLS	0054	*Horremans* | Twee stuks vrolijke gezelschappen | *Mat:* op doek	[Abraham Delfos] [or others]	(Unknown)
1807/06/10	HGBSM	0054	*Horremans* | Twee stuks vrolijke gezelschappen | *Mat:* op doek	Abraham Delfos [or others]	(Sold) fl 2 Carré
1808/06/13	AMSCH	0227	*Horremans* | Twee stuks, een Regter en een Geneesheer in hun vertrek, met eenige verdere Beelden en Gereedschappen; geestig geschilderd	R[oos]	(Sold) fl 19:10 Du Pré
1810/03/23	HAVIN	0026	*Hormans* | Twee stuks, zijnde een Kraamkamer, en een groot getal persoonen ter maaltijd zijnde, plaizant door Hormans | *Size:* h: 27 b: 33 ½ d.	Rudolf Hendrik de Wetstein [or others]	(Unknown)
1810/06/20	AMSCH	0034	*J. Hoornmans* | Twee stuks Binnenhuizen; in het eene zitten twee Schoenmakers te werken, waarbij eene Vrouw met een Kind; in het andere eene Vrouw, zittende bij een Spinnewiel, benevens drie rokende Huislieden. Bevallig geschilderd | *Mat:* op doek *Size:* Jeder hoog 14, breed 12 duimen	A	(Sold) fl 5:15 Focken
			Horemans, Jan Joseph (I) (copy by)		
1806/10/17	MGSAN	0018	*J. Horemans; Troost* | De Corps de Guarde van Hollandsche Officiers, naar Troost, door J. Horemans | copy by J.J. Horemans (I) after C. Troost *Mat:* op doek	Gerardus Beljard	(Unknown)
			Horemans, Jan Joseph (I) (manner)		
1801/04/23	AMYVR	0036	*Hovemans* | Een Binnenhuis met een Kaartspeelend Gezelschap in de manier van Hovemans | *Notes:* This lot was sold with lot 35 by Dionijs Verburgh.		(Sold) fl 1 ¼ for lots 35 & 36. A Maijer
			Horstink, Warner		
1809/09/06	AMSCH	0027	*Horstink (W.)* | Op een Heuvel met Geboomten, ziet men Koeijen, Schapen en Beelden, uitvoerig behandeld | *Mat:* op paneel *Size:* hoog 20, breed 12 duim	Johannes Caudri	(Sold) fl 7 Th[s] Spaan
			Houbraken, Arnold		
1802/11/01	DOBRA	0061	*Houbraken* | Een Bijbelsche Historie | *Mat:* op doek *Size:* hoog 11 duim, breed 9 ½ duim	Paulus van der Spyk [or others]	(Sold) fl 2:10 A v Well
1803/08/17	AMSCH	0036	*Houbraken (A.)* | De Fabel van Vertumnus en Pomona, in een Hofgezicht voorgesteld; de kleding is bevallig, zoo ook de behandeling | *Mat:* op doek *Size:* hoog 18, breed 15 duim	Anna Catharina Putman	(Sold) fl 11 Hodges
1808/10/28	AMVRS	0022	*Houbraken, (A.)* | Twee Bijbelsche Ordonantiën, met Beelden en toepasselijk bijwerk. Uitvoerig behandeld | *Mat:* op paneel *Size:* ieder hoog 12, breed 14 duim	Marten Udink	(Sold) fl 8 Gruyter

1810/06/04	DOBRA	0009	*A. Houbraken* | Joseph, Maria, en 't kindje	Hendrik de Haas	(Unknown)
1810/06/04	DOBRA	0010	*A. Houbraken* | Christus en Maria in den Hof	Hendrik de Haas	(Unknown)
1810/07/23	DOLG2	000F	*A. Houbraken* | Venus en Adonis, bijna levensgrootte | *Mat:* op doek *Size:* Hoog 52, breed 71 duim	Pieter Quinting	(Unknown)
1810/07/23	DOLG2	0038	*A. Houbraken* | In het binnenst van een Grot zit eene biddende Vrouw, geschilderd | *Mat:* op doek *Size:* hoog 18, breed 14 duim	Pieter Quinting	(Sold) fl 2:10 A van Strij
1810/07/23	DOLG2	00EE	*A. Houbraken* | Twee rookende en drinkende Boertjes; geestig en vrolijk geschilderd | *Mat:* op paneel *Size:* hoog 10, breed 7 ½ duim	Pieter Quinting	(Sold) fl 10:10 A v Strij
			Houbraken, Arnold (or Houbraken, Arn., manner)		
1807/09/28	DOHAA	00DD	*A. Houbraken* | Maria, Joseph en 't Kindje, door of in de manier van A. Houbraken	Mattheus Westerouen van Meeteren	(Unknown)
			Houbraken, H. [Unidentified]		
1808/04/26	GDAN	0072	*Houbraken (H.)* | Verbeeldende in een Landschap een Graftombe, waar bij zich eenige Herders met hun Vee zich ophouden, vrij goed geschildert | *Size:* hoog 25, breed 20 ½ duim	G H Fortuyn	(Unknown)
			Houckgeest, Gerard		
1803/12/15	MGLAC	0002	*G. Hoekgeest* | Een extra fraai Tempelgezigt; schoon van Architectuur en gestoffeerd | *Mat:* op paneel *Size:* hoog duim 27, breed duim 33 ½	Mr L H de Haze Bomme	(Unknown)
			Houckgeest, Gerard (and Palamedesz., A.)		
1808/11/28	AMSCH	0028	*G.J. Houckaerts; Palamedes* | Een pragtig Paleijs- en Hofgezicht, gestoffeerd met de Bijbel-ordonantie van Lazarus en de Rijke Man, dit stuk is fraai van perspectief en bouwkundig behandeld, op Paneel, door G.J. Houckaerts, 1646 en gestoffeerd door Palamedes | *Mat:* op paneel *Size:* hoog 31, breed 34 duim *Inscr:* G.J. Houckaerts, 1646 (signed and dated?) *Notes:* It is unclear whether the name and date are inscribed on the painting.	C	(Sold) fl 19 T Spaan
			Houten, F. van [Unidentified]		
1808/04/26	GDAN	0065	*Houten (F. van)* | Verbeeldende een Binnenhuis met eenig Huisraad, waar een bevallig Vrouwtje Uijen zit te schellen, konstig geschilderd | *Size:* hoog 12, breed 9 duim	G H Fortuyn	(Unknown)
1808/04/26	GDAN	0066	*Houten (F. van)* | Een dito Binnenhuis met eenig Keukengereedschap, een Vrouwtje Knollen zittende te schellen, en bij het Vuur staan eenige Menschen te kijken, mede kragtig | *Mat:* op paneel *Size:* hoog 14 ½, breed 21 ½ duim	G H Fortuyn	(Unknown)
			Houtstrom [Unidentified]		
1801/12/22	AMOTT	0069	*Houtstrom* | 1 arcadisch Hofgezigt	Bartholomeus Ruloffs	(Unknown) fl 1
			Huchtenburgh, Jan van		
1801/03/16	AMSCH	0003	*J. Hugtenburg* | Een Landschap met Colonnades en Gebouwen, ryk gestoffeerd met Dames en Heeren als van de Jagt komende met hunne Paarden en Honden, delicaat behandeld	S[chley]	(Sold) fl 38 Gruiter
1801/03/16	AMSCH	0043	*J. vn Hugtenburg* | Het Pourtret van een Generaal te paard, beneevens een Kampement, en in 't verschiet een Bataille; krachtig uitgevoerd	P[ruyssenaar]	(Sold) fl 6:5 C S Roos
1801/04/13	AMSCH	0035	*J. van Huchtenburg* | Een hevige Bataille tusschen Ruitery, men ziet 'er verscheide Dooden en Gekwetsten op den voorgrond liggen; dit stukje is meesterlyk behandeld | *Mat:* op paneel *Size:* hoog 10, breed 14 duim	Pierre Fouquet, junior	(Sold) fl 101 I^{C} Smit
1801/04/23	AMYVR	0003	*J. Huchtenburg* | Twee stuks fraaije Land- en Watergezichten, gestoffeerd met verscheiden Krygslieden en Paarden, benevens eenige andere figuuren, zeer schoon van couleur, uitvoerig en krachtig op Doek geschilderd | *Mat:* op doek *Size:* yder hoog 22, breed 25 duim		(Sold) fl 335 Farret
1801/06/10	AMSCH	0077	*Hugtenburg. (J. van)* | Een heevige rencontre, tusschen Ruitery en Voetvolk, in een Boom- en Bergachtig Landschap, delicaat en fraay van licht en bruin | *Mat:* op paneel *Size:* hoog 16 ½, breed 20 duim	Herman ten Kate	(Sold) fl 95 C S Roos
1801/06/10	AMSCH	0078	*Hugtenburg. (J. van)* | Een Landschap, voor een Boerenwoning ziet men twee Heeren, nevens een Dame te Paard, schyneude zig te ververschen, verders een menigte Beelden, krachtig en meesterlyk van schildering | *Mat:* op doek *Size:* hoog 20, breed 17 duim	Herman ten Kate	(Sold) fl 38 Taijs
1801/06/10	AMSCH	0079	*Hugtenburg. (J. van)* | Een rencontre van Cavallerie, ter zyde over een Brug, ziet men van een Wagen op eenige Jagers vuuren, in 't verschiet een Stad en een Bergachtig verschiet, helder en uitvoerig van penceels behandeling | *Mat:* op doek *Size:* hoog 12, breed 14 duim	Herman ten Kate	(Sold) fl 36 Stevens
1801/08/19	AMSCH	0036	*J. van Huchtenburg* | In een Landschap vertoond zich op de voorgrond een Dame en een Heer te Paard rydende ter Jacht, verzeld van Jagers en Honden, alles zonachtig en krachtig geschilderd	Pruyssen^{r} [for] Q	(Bought In) fl 30
1801/10/06	AMSCH	0030	*J. Hughtenburg* | Twee stuks, het eene verbeeld in een Landschap een Heer en andere Lieden te paard, zig ververschende by een Marquetenter, verder ziet men een Klooster en een koets met paarden en andere Ryzigers; het andere verbeeld een rustend man, by de stam van een boom,	S	(Sold) fl 12 Theijs

			het toom vasthoudende van een gezadeld Bruin Paard, verders twee Jagers op vogelen schietende, by een boere wooning, zeer uitvoerig geschilderd | *Mat:* op doek *Size:* yder hoog 5, breed 6 ½ duim		
1801/10/06	AMSCH	0031	*J. v. Hughtenburg* | Twee stuks ryk gestoffeerde Ordinantien, vol gewoel van Krygslieden en Paarden, verbeeldende de Veldslagen van Prins Eugeen, by Torino 1706. en by Malplaquet 1709. zynde byde meesterlyk fraay gepenseeld | *Mat:* op doek *Size:* yder hoog 17, breed 26 duim	L	(Sold) fl 50 Coclers
1801/10/19	AMSCH	0030	*Hugtenburg. (J van)* | Twee stuks op Doek, Een keurlyk en woelig Stadgezicht by het overryden van een Brug, zynde als een intreede in een Poort, men ziet verscheide wagens ryden, en in rust: ryk gestoffeerd met mans en vrouwen Beelden, in zeer leevende actiën. En een gevegt van Ruitery in het gezicht van een Stad, ter zyden ziet men eenige beladen Karren met Paarden enz beiden deezen stukken zyn zeer uitvoerig en fraay behandeld | *Mat:* op doek *Size:* yder hoog 20 ½, breed 24 ½ duim	Jonkheer Menno Baron van Coehoorn	(Sold) fl 152 Gruyter
1801/10/19	AMSCH	0031	*Hugtenburg. (J van)* | Een Bataille van Ruitery, in een heevige actie verbeeld, op den voorgrond drie voornamen Figuren in gevecht; zynde een uitmuntend Schildery; zeer ryk van Ordonantie en uitvoerig behandeld | *Mat:* op doek *Size:* hoog 20 ⅜, breed 24 duim	Jonkheer Menno Baron van Coehoorn	(Sold) fl 365 Coclers
1801/10/19	AMSCH	0032	*Hugtenburg. (J van)* | Een Rust van een Leeger, aan de linkerzyde vertoonen zich eenige Officieren, waar onder zoo het schynt de Generaal van Coehoorn, de Ordres vragende van de Veldmarschalk van Marlbourg; – aan de regterzyde eenige Tenten en ander Leegertuig, waar voor verscheiden rustende Figuren; helder en uitvoerig geschilderd | *Mat:* op doek *Size:* hoog 15 ½, breed 19 ½ duim	Jonkheer Menno Baron van Coehoorn	(Sold) fl 51 Gruiter
1802/04/13	HAVIN	0005	*Huchtenburg* | Een Rencontre, tusschen Cavallery, extra fraai en verstandig | companion to lot 6		(Unknown)
1802/04/13	HAVIN	0006	*Huchtenburg* | Een Manege, zeer plaisant, uitvoerig tot een weerga | companion to lot 5		(Unknown)
1802/04/13	HAVIN	0017	*Hugtenburg* | Een Belegering, zynde voor in een Battaille, waar in wreed gevogten word		(Unknown)
1802/05/24	HGBAK	0022	*J. v. Hughtenburgh* | Een Campement, op de voorgrond eenige Krygslieden, waarvan eenige met de kaart speelen, voorts eenige Paarden &c., in 't verschiet een opgeslagen Leger &c., meesterlyk door J. v Hughtenburgh, hoog 17 ½ duim, breed 21 duim, op doek, zwarte lyst met vergulde binnenrand | *Mat:* op doek *Size:* hoog 17 ½ duim, breed 21 duim	Mejuffrouw A van der Mieden	(Sold) fl 9 Ondorp
1802/06/16	AMSCH	0070	*J. van Huchtenburg* | In dit uitmuntend Schildery ziet men de Elende des Oorlogs op een treffende wyze afgebeeld; op de voorgrond leggen eenige doode Menschen én Paarden, by dewelke een wit geappeld Paard Predomineerd, boven een aantal andere; welke zoo met geplunderde goederen als krygsvolk beladen zyn; eenige Munnikken, Vrouwen en Kinderen smeeken om lyfsgenade, terwyl men in 't verschiet hunne Woningen ziet Plunderen en Branden; alles delicaat en uitvoerig behandeld | *Mat:* op doek *Size:* hoog 27 ½, breed 32 ½ duim	[Merrem]	(Sold) fl 475 de Lelie
1802/06/16	AMSCH	0071	*J. van Huchtenburg* | Deeze ryke Ordenantie, vol gewoel van Krygslieden; verbeeld een allerheevigst gevegt tusschen Ruitery, die woedende op elkander Vuuren; andere met de Zabel in de hand; op de voorgrond leggen verscheide gesneuvelde Lieden, Paarden en Wapens: verders ziet men eenige vlugtende; en in 't verschiet een brandend Dorp | *Mat:* op doek op paneel *Size:* hoog 17, breed 23 duim	[Merrem]	(Sold) fl 265 I^{c} Smit
1802/06/16	AMSCH	0072	*J. van Huchtenburg* | In een bevallig heuvelagtig Landschap, vertoond zich op de voorgrond een Harte Jagt, Heeren en een Dame te Paard, en Jagers met Honden, vervolgen het Wild; ter zyde ziet men een stil Water, en verder een Ruwien; alles is zeer fraay en natuurlyk verbeeld, en van een uitvoerige penceel-behandeling | *Mat:* op koper *Size:* hoog 11 ½, breed 13 ½ duim	[Merrem]	(Sold) fl 70 v d Schleij [for] Putte
1802/06/16	AMSCH	0073	*J. van Huchtenburg* | Dit stuk verbeeld een Campement by een Dorp; men ziet in het midden een Vorstelyk Persoon, omringe van een ménigte voornamen Officieren alle te Paard; ter zyde en op de voorgrond zyn een groote menigte zo rydende, rustende als marcheerende, Militairen, Marquetenters en Bagagiewagens; in het verschiet een Stad en Zeehaven: die stuk is van een der beste van deezen Meester | *Mat:* op doek *Size:* hoog 25, breed 31 duim	[Merrem]	(Sold) fl 80 LaFontaine
1802/06/28	AMSCH	0075	*J. Huchtenburg* | Een hevige Rencontre van Ruytery en Voetvolk; fiks gepenceeld door J. Huchtenburg, Panneel | *Mat:* op paneel *Size:* hoog 19, breed 25 duim	B	(Sold) fl 33 Texier
1802/07/09	AMSTO	0012	*Hugtenburg* | 1 hevige Rencontre tusschen Cavalarie, in een Landschap		(Unknown)
1802/07/21	HGKAN	0057	*J. v. Huchtenburtch* | Een Campement, op de Voorgrond, eenige Krygslieden, waar van eenige met de Kaart speelen voorts eenige Paarden, en in het verschiet een opgeslagen Leeger &c. Meesterlyk door J. v. Huchtenburch, hoog 17 ¾[?] duym, en breed 21 duym, op Doek, zwarte Lyst, vergulde binnen rand | *Mat:* op doek *Size:* hoog 17 ¾[?] duym, en breed 21 duym		(Unknown)
1802/07/21	HGKAN	0110	*J. Huchtenburg* | Een Origineel Schilderstuk, gedaan door J. Huchtenburg, verbeeldende een Manege waarin 7 Paarden, waar onder een Vos, door		(Unknown)

			een Piquer gedresseerd wordende, en verders eenige Beeldjes, zeer kragtig en fraay, op Doek geschildert | *Mat:* op doek *Size:* hoog 1 voet 9 duym en breed 2 voet		
1802/08/24	LNDLS	0069	*J. van Hugtenburgh* | Twee stuks Batailjes van Ruiters voor een Stad, vol gewoel | *Mat:* op paneel *Size:* ieder hoog 9 ½, breed 13 ½ duimen	Leonardus Bouman [or others]	(Unknown) fl 13:10
1802/12/13	AMSCH	0077	*J. Hugtenburg* | Die Stuk verbeeld in een Berg en Boomryk Landschap een heevige Rencontre van Ruitery; de hartstogten zyn hier meesterlyk in waar genomen, en is voorts fraay op Doek behandeld | *Mat:* op doek *Size:* hoog 22, breed 27 duim	Yver	(Sold) fl 251 Pruijssenaar [for] R
1803/07/18	AMSCH	0021	*Hughtenburg (J. van)* | Twee stuks, yder hoog 25, breed 31 duim, op Doek. Het eerste een bevallig Schildery verbeeld een Manége in de open lugt, by eenige Gebouwen en Geboomtens; verscheide Heeren te Paard, een Koets met Paarden en een menigte Beeldjes te voet, maaken te zaamen een bevallige groeping en een goed geheel. In de tweede word een Convooy geattacqueerd door eenige Ruiters, in het verschiet ziet men de beladene Wagens langs een Fort defileeren. Deeze beide stukjes zyn van een schoone couleur, fraaye tekening, en delicaat penceelsbehandeling [Dans un paysage montagneux, d'un ton de couleur clair, est representé au premier plan l'abreuvage d'une partie de chevaux d'hussards ; un homme tenant un enfant en croupe mène son cheval dans la même marre d'eau, ou se trouvent des nageurs, devant une hotellerie à gauche du tableau sont des personnages & des voitures attelées. Le second offre sur le penchant d'une colline un rassemblement d'officiers Généraux & Subalternes montés sur de beaux chevaux ; nombre d'autres personnes & de chevaux tenus par la bride sont repartis parmi cette foule. Vèrs la gauche défile une partie de Cavallerie, & à droite arrive une voiture à six chevaux. La perspective est terminée par une ville dont on fait le siége. Ces tableaux ont de l'éclat, un beau ciel & des chevaux d'un très beau dessin ; l'execution en est facile & soignée.] | *Mat:* op doek *Size:* yder hoog 25, breed 31 duim	Maria Theresia Andrioli	(Sold) fl 255 Teissier
1803/07/18	AMSCH	0022	*Hughtenburg (J. van)* | Twee stuks, yder hoog 25, breed 31 duim, op Doek. De eerste verbeeld een Berg- en Boomryk Landschap, op de voorgrond eenige Husaaren, beezig zynde hunne Paarden naar het Wet te brengen, op de tweede grond ziet men een Plysterplaats voor dewelke een Koets met zes Paarden en andere Reizigers zig ververschen. De tweede steld voor een afhellende Berg alwaar een aantal Opper Officieren verzameld zyn op hunne Paarden; eenige Dames, een Koets met zes Paarden, en een menigte Militairen, maken dit stuk ryk van Ordonnantie, in het verschiet ziet men de belegerde Stad; zy zyn beide van een zeer goede qualiteit van deezen Meester [Un très joli morceau étant un manège à ciel decouvert, environné de batimens & de quelques arbres. Des cavaliers montés & d'autres descendus de leurs chevaux, ainsi qu'une voiture attelée forment une masse bien entendue. Des figures & des chevaux sur differens plans, sous un ciel bien nuagé achevent ce bel emsemble. Pour second l'artiste a pris le sujet d'un Convoi attaqué par un partis de Cavallerie : à côté d'une colline l'on voit defiler, les chariots vérs un fort qui termine le point de vue du paysage. Ces deux tableaux d'un vray mérite sont du meilleur faire de l'auteur [;] à une couleur brillante & vigoureuse ils réunissent un beau dessin pour la forme & la variété des chevaux ; l'agrément du sujet du premier est balancé par le feu & le le [sic] caractére expressif repandu dans le second.] | *Mat:* op doek *Size:* yder hoog 25, breed 31 duim [hauts 16, larges 19 pouces] *Notes:* The dimensions differ in the Dutch and French editions of the catalogue.	Maria Theresia Andrioli	(Sold) fl 170 Thys
1803/08/01	AMSCH	0012	*Hugtenburg. (J. van)* | Een hevige Rencontre, tusschen Ruitery, op de voorgrond ziet men eenige dooden en gekwetsten ter neder leggen, fraay van Hartstochten en uitmuntend van Schildering | *Mat:* op paneel *Size:* hoog 11, breed 13 ½ duim	J	(Bought In) fl 71
1803/08/17	AMSCH	0033	*Huchtenburg (J. van)* | Een hevige Rencontre tusschen Ruitery, by een gefortificeerde Stad, uit dewelke hevig geschoten word op het daarby zynde Leger, alles vol expressie, en van een meesterlyke schildering | *Mat:* op doek *Size:* hoog 26, breed 33 duim	Anna Catharina Putman	(Sold) fl 64 W Reijers
1803/08/24	HGKAN	0042	*Hughtenburg* | Een Hevige Bataille tusschen Cavallerie, op de voorgrond zit een Ruyter op een wit Paard die door een ander gewond, van zyn Paard valt, ter zyde ziet men verscheide Vlugten met hun Huisraad, dit stuk is vol Expressie omgeeven, en van een fraaye Couleur en Tekening, en een van de beste stukken van Hughtenburg | *Mat:* op doek *Size:* hoog 21, breet 26 duim	[Teissier] [or others]	(Sold) fl 130 Kan
1803/09/07	AMSCH	0080	*J. Hugtenburg* | Twee stuks heuvelachtige Landschappen, gestoffeerd met Ryzigers te Paard en te Voet, als mede eenige Jagers met hunne Honden, Bedelaars en andere stoffagie, beide van een delicate behandeling [Deux paysages riches et d'une finesse précieuse ; des collines, des voyageurs à pied et à cheval, quelques chasseurs en train avec leurs chiens, le tout de la plus belle ordonnance.] | *Mat:* op doek *Size:* hoog 19, breed 16 duim	Smidt	(Sold) fl 40 van Iperen
1803/12/15	MGLAC	0027	*Hugtenburg* | Een hevige Rencontre van Ruitery; stout en kragtig geschilderd | companion to lot 28 *Mat:* op doek *Size:* hoog duim 20, breed duim 26	Mr L H de Haze Bomme	(Unknown)
1803/12/15	MGLAC	0028	*Hugtenburg* | Een dito [hevige Rencontre van Ruitery] weêrga; niet minder dan de voorgaande | companion to lot 27 *Mat:* op doek *Size:*	Mr L H de Haze Bomme	(Unknown)

			hoog duim 20, breed duim 26 *Notes:* It is unclear what "dito" refers to n the title.		
1804/02/27	AMSCH	0046	*Huchtenburg. (J. van)* | Een hevige Bataille tusschen Cavallerie, op den voorgrond ziet men een Ruiter op een wit Paard, welke door een ander met een Pistool van het Paard geschoote word, verders een menigte Dooden en Gekwesten; alles is fraai van coloriet uitvoerig en meesterlyk gepenceeld | *Mat:* op doek *Size:* hoog 21, breed 25 duim	B	(Sold) fl 152 Thais [or] Theengs
1804/02/27	AMSCH	0047	*Huchtenburg. (J. van)* | Deze Ordonantie stelt voor een Harte Jacht, op de voorgrond ziet men eenige Heerente Paard, waarby Jagers en Honden, in het verschiet een prachtig Jachthuis; dit stuk is fraai geteekend, en niet minder van schildering | *Mat:* op doek *Size:* hoog 31, breed 39 duim	B	(Bought In) fl 6:10
1804/02/27	AMSCH	0048	*Huchtenburg. (J. van)* | In een Stal of Posthuis, ziet men eenige Heeren en Dames, Paarden en Rytuigen, dit alles schynt zich tot uitreiden gereed te maaken; bevallig van licht en breed geschilderd | *Mat:* op doek *Size:* hoog 25, breed 30 duim	C	(Sold) fl 4:15 van den Brink
1804/02/27	AMSCH	0049	*Huchtenburg. (J. van)* | Een Italiaansch Bergachtig Landschap, met diverse Gebouwen, ryk gestoffeerd met Beelden en Beestjes; meesterlyk gepenceeld | *Mat:* op doek *Size:* hoog 15, breed 19 duim	B	(Bought In) fl 25
1804/05/07	AMSCH	0079	*Huchtenburg. (J. van)* | Twee stuks Campementen, zynde byde ryk gestoffeerd met Ruyters te paard en te voet, Marqetenters [sic], Ezels, Veehoeders, Honden, enz., in 't verschiet eenig Gebergte, byde zonachtig en van een der uitvoerigste penceelbehandeling van deze Meester | *Mat:* op paneel *Size:* hoog 16, breed 20 duim	Vinkeles [for] X	(Sold) fl 220 Josi
1804/05/07	AMSCH	0080	*Huchtenburg. (J. van)* | Een hevige Batalje tusschen Cavallerie, in een boomryk Landschap, op de voorgrond een ménigte doode Militairen en Paarden; kragtig behandeld | *Mat:* op doek *Size:* hoog 21, breed 29 duim	Roos [for] A	(Sold) fl 57:10 van Iperen
1804/07/25	AMSCH	0037	*Hughtenburg. (J. van)* | Deeze ryke ordinantie vol gewoel, in een Bergachtig Landschap, vertoont een heevige Rencontre tusschen Kyzerlyke, en Turksche Ruitery en eenig Voetvolk, op de Voorgrond schynt het heevigst Gevecht, en men ziet verscheiden Gekwesten en Gesneuvelden, verder schynen de Turken een uitval uit hunne beleegerde Vesting te doen, alles ziet men in woeden; de Hartstogten zyn natuurlyk en meesterlyk fraai en uitvoerig van penceel behandeling | *Mat:* op doek *Size:* hoog 34, breed 32 duim		(Sold) fl 200 C S Roos
1804/07/25	AMSCH	0038	*Hughtenburg. (J. van)* | Een Schermutseling van eenige Ruiters in een Landschap, verder in het Koorenland, een Gevegt van Voetvolk, in het verschiet een heevig Vuur, ter zyde een oude Stad; dit stukje is van de fraaiste schildering van dezen meester [Hughtenburg, (J. van)] | *Mat:* op doek *Size:* hoog 16 ½, breed 24 duim		(Sold) fl 345 C S Roos
1804/07/25	DLGRO	0024	*Huchtenburg* | Een Italiaansch Landschap, ryk gestoffeerd met Beeldjes | *Size:* hoog 16, breed 18 duimen	Mr Franc van der Burch Wz.	(Unknown)
1804/08/02	BDAN	0034	*Huchtenburg* | Een Batailje, zeer schoon van behandeling | *Mat:* op doek *Size:* b. 21 en een half d. h. 14 d.	J G Calckberner	(Unknown)
1804/08/08	AMSCH	0078	*J. van Huchtenberg* | Twee stuks aangenaame Boomryke Landschappen, in de éène ziet men op de voorgrond een Heer en Dame te Paard, waarby een andere met een Paard, rustende tegen de Stam van een Boom, verzeld van een ménigte Jachthonden, schynende zy lieden ter Jacht te gaan, verders een aangenaam Boom- en Duinryk Landschap; en in de andere ziet men op de voorgrond twee Krygslieden te Paard en te voet, waar névens eenige andere Lieden en Honden, verders een Schermutzeling, tusschen Ruitery, en een Boomryk verschiet; beiden frappant van licht en uitvoerig geschilderd | *Mat:* op doek *Size:* hoog 12 ½, breed 15 duim	Vink[eles] [for] W	(Sold) fl 74 Hulswit
1804/08/08	AMSCH	0079	*J. van Huchtenberg* | Twee stuks Campementen, in de éène ziet men by een Rivier, een ménigte Ruiters, te Paard en te voet, verdere eenige Tenten, een Stad en Gebergtens; en in de andere ziet men meede in een Rivier eenige Ruiters, welke hunne Paarden laaten drinken, waarby eenige andere Ruiters, te Paard en te voet, een Trompetter, Marquetenter, en een Bergachtig verschiet; beiden alleruitvoerigst, en van de beste penceels-behandeling | *Mat:* op doek *Size:* hoog 12 ½, breed 15 ½ duim	Vink[eles] [for] W	(Bought In) fl 69
1804/08/08	AMSCH	0080	*J. van Huchtenberg* | Op het Voorplein van een prachtige Hofsteede ziet men eenige Dames en Heeren, zoo te Paard als te voet, zich gereed maakende om ter Jacht te gaan, met hunne Jagers en Honden; de schildering is uitmuntend | *Mat:* op doek *Size:* hoog 25, breed 30 duim	Roos [for] G	(Bought In) fl 72
1804/10/16	DLOND	0107	*J. van Hugtenburg* | De Slag van Ramellies, A°. 1707. Da [sic] Bataille de Ramellies | *Mat:* op doek *Size:* hoog 35, breed 44 *Inscr:* 1707 (dated?) *Notes:* It is unclear whether the date is inscribed on the painting.		(Unknown)
1804/10/16	DLOND	0108	*J. van Hugtenburg* | De Slag van Pont à Pierre A°. 1706. La Bataille de Pont à Pierre | *Mat:* op doek *Size:* hoog 35, breed 44 *Notes:* It is unclear whether the date is inscribed on the painting.		(Unknown)
1804/10/16	DLOND	0109	*J. van Hugtenburg* | Een Schermutseling. Une Escarmouche | *Mat:* op doek *Size:* hoog 32, breed 44		(Unknown)
1804/10/29	HRBAU	0035	*Huchtenburg* | Op den Voorgrond van dit fraai Schildery is een Gevegt tusschen Paardenvolk, dat verwoed malkander aanvalt, en waar van reeds eenige, benevens hunne Paarden, dood, of gekwetst ter aarde liggen; wat	Simon Styl	(Unknown)

			verder by een Kasteel schynt een corps Cavallerie in het vyandelyk Voetvolk te willen doordringen, dat met alle kragt van vuur zich tegen hetzelve verdedigt, terwyl eenigen reeds de wyk naar een nabuurig Dorp zoeken, en hun leven door de vlugt schynen te redden. Zynde in dit Stuk de ordinantie zo als het licht en bruin treffend, de verwoedheid, zo van menschen als paarden, byzonder wel uitgedrukt, helder, kragtig, en zeer stout behandeld | *Mat:* op doek *Size:* hoog 44, breed 58 duim		
1804/10/29	HRBAU	0036	*Huchtenburg* | Dit Stuk is van een' meer bevalligen aart. Voor aan by den ingang van een Bosch ziet men eene Dame, nevens drie Heeren te paard, vergezeld van hunne Honden, een Hert door eene beek vervolgen; wat verder zyn eenige Koetzen en Wagens, welken tot dat Gezelschap schynen te behooren; waar agter eene pragtige Hofsteede, en een verlustigend wyd uitgestrekt bergagtig verschiet. Alles ongemeen delicaat, zonagtig en zeer uitvoerig gepenceeld. Zynde een Cabinetstuk van dezen Meester | *Mat:* op doek *Size:* hoog 22, breed 25 duim	Simon Styl	(Unknown)
1804/10/29	HRBAU	0037	*Huchtenburg* | Een capitaal Wintergezigt by een Stads Vest, ryk gestoffeerd met Arresleeden, wandelende Heeren en Dames, Schaatsenryders, Houtdraagers en meer andere Figuuren. Zonagtig behandeld | *Mat:* op doek *Size:* hoog 30, breed 43 duim	Simon Styl	(Unknown)
1805/07/03	AMSCH	0087	*J. van Huchtenburg* | Twee stuks Capitaale Ordinantiën, vol gewoel, verbeeldende in Landschappen, hévige Schermutselinge tusschen Ruitery, die elkander als woedende aanvallen; doode Paarden, en gekwetste Krygslieden leggen op de grond; andere vervolgt en zyn vlugtende door een Rivier, in 't verschiet, ziet men hévige Gevegten en Bergachtig Landzigt; de hartstochten zyn treffend verbeeld en van een uitvoerige behandeling | *Mat:* op doek *Size:* hoog 25, breed 30 duim	R[oos]	(Sold) fl 505 den Achtienhoven
1805/07/03	AMSCH	0088	*J. van Huchtenburg* | In een Heuvelachtig Landzicht, met eenig Geboomten, ziet men een hévig Gevecht tusschen Ruitery, die elkander, al vlugtende vervolgen, op de Voorgrond leggen gesneuvelde Kygslieden en Paarden, verders vlugtende Bagagiewagens en Voetvolk; alles is krachtig en meesterlyk gepenceeld | *Mat:* op doek *Size:* hoog 28, breed 35 duim	R[oos]	(Sold) fl 60 Jan Yver
1805/07/03	AMSCH	0089	*J. van Huchtenburg* | In een Landschap, ziet men een Uittogt ter Valkenjacht, gestoffeerd met Dames, Heeren, en Jagerstepaard [sic], verder by Geboomten, andere zig reisvaardig maakende; het is bevallig en uitvoerig gepenceeld | *Mat:* op paneel *Size:* hoog 11, breed 14 duim	R[oos]	(Sold) fl 55 J Yver
1805/07/03	AMSCH	0090	*J. van Huchtenburg* | Een Boomryk Landschap, met een stille Rivier, waarin zig eenige Jongelingen baden; op de Voorgrond een springend Paard, welke door een Jongeling en een klynder ander, op een bruin Paard gezéten, voort gedreeven word, verder een Vaartuig, waaruit Goederen gelaaden worden; bevallig van coloriet en penceel | *Mat:* op doek *Size:* hoog 20, breed 21 duim	R[oos]	(Sold) fl 20 Zurmuklen
1805/07/03	AMSCH	0091	*J. van Huchtenburg* | In een Landschap vertoont zig een Campement, gestoffeert met Opper-Bevelhebbes te Paard, verders Soldaaten en verscheide Paarden, Marquetenters, rydende Koets, verder een Dorpkerk op een Heuvel; uitvoerig en zonachtig gepenceeld | *Mat:* op doek op paneel *Size:* hoog 19, breed 22 duim	G	(Sold) fl 42 Gruiter
1805/10/09	HGBSM	0007	*J. van Hugtenburg* | Een rencontre van cavallerie, fix en kragtig geschildert | *Mat:* op doek *Size:* hoog 15 ½ breet 18 ½ duim	T H van Willigen [or others]	(Sold) fl 14:5 Roedig
1805/10/21	GRBOL	0008	*J. V. Huchtenberg* | Een Batalje te Paard	Gerardus Nicolaus Heerkens	(Unknown)
1805/12/16	AMSCH	0029	*J. Huchtenburg* | In een Landgezicht, by een Rivier, ziet men op de Voorgrond een heevig gevegt tussen Ruitery, die woedende elkander aanvallen, enverder [sic] andere vegtende partyen, het verschiet is een Bergachtig Landschap; kragtig en fiks gepenceeld | *Mat:* op doek op paneel *Size:* hoog 22, breed 24 duim	R[oos]	(Bought In) fl 20
1806/05/05	AMSCH	0061	*J. Hugtenburgh* | By een Stad ziet men voor en op deszelfs bevroozen Vest een menigte Arresleeden, rydende en wandelende Lieden, agterwaards eenige capitaale Gebouwen; meesterlyk geschildert door J. Hugtenburgh | *Mat:* op doek *Size:* hoog 30, breed 42 duim	V[inkeles]	(Sold) fl 11:10 Mensart
1806/08/20	HGBSM	0013	*J. van Huchtenburgh* | Dit uitmuntend Schilderij, steld voor, eene hevige Actie van Cavallerij die verwoedt op elkander aanvallen. – Is schoon, krachtig fraaij van Coloriet en uitvoerig geschilderd; dit onderwerp hoe verwoestend ook; is echter aangenaam te beschouwen, door de Genie van den meester die er in heerscht. Zijnde van zijn besten tijd | *Mat:* op doek *Size:* hoog 24 ½, breed 30 duim	Macalester Loup [or others]	(Sold) fl 225 Teissier
1806/08/20	HGBSM	0014	*J. van Huchtenburgh* | Eene Belegerde Stad, op den voorgrond zijn verscheide figuuren, Paarden en Wagens, zeer krachtig en aangenaam geschilderd | *Mat:* op doek *Size:* hoog 12, breed 15 ½ duim	Macalester Loup [or others]	(Sold) fl 50 Nieuwenhuys
1806/10/16	UTWLD	0002	*Hugtenburg* | Een Landschap, op de Voorgrond een hevige Rencontre van Ruyters door Hugtenburg	Mr P de Malapert [or] W Beeldsnyder	(Unknown)
1806/11/24	AMSCH	0031	*Hugtenburg (J.)* | Een Italiaansche Stad, waarin een zeer fraaije stoffagie van Beeldjes, Muil-ezels die met Vragtgoederen beladen zyn, Koeijen, Schapen en een Hond; hetzelve is van een goede houding en delicaat geschilderd | *Mat:* op doek *Size:* hoog 15, breed 19 duim	Munnikhuizen	(Sold) fl 68:10 Reyers

1806/11/24	AMSCH	0032	*Hugtenburg (J.)* | Een bergachtig Landschap; by een Rivier, op de Voorgrond een hévig gevegt tusschen Ruitery, die als woedende elkander aanvallen; kragtig en meesterlyk gepenceeld | *Mat:* op doek op paneel *Size:* hoog 22, breed 24 duim	van den Bosch	(Sold) fl 11 Van Iperen
1808/03/03	HAVIN	0003	*Hugtenburg* | De Battaille te Mons, door Prins Eugeen, uitvoerig	Jacobus Spillebout	(Unknown) fl 6
1808/04/26	GDAN	0067	*Hugtenburg (J. van)* | Zijnde eene zwaare Bataille bij het Fort | *Size:* hoog 21, breed 24 duim	G H Fortuyn	(Unknown)
1808/04/26	GDAN	0068	*Hugtenburg (J. van)* | Een overheerlijk Schilderij, verbeeldende eene Markt, waar op een Huigkar, met een Boere Kar met Paarden, op de Markt ziet men eenige Koopwaren der Boeren en Boerinnen uitventen, terwijl men in de Gracht eenige Schuiten ziet varende en leggende, over welke Gracht eene zeer lange Brug legt waar over Paardrijders, en een Kar door twee Paarden getrokken word, in het verschiet ziet men een Kerk en Tooren, het opdoen van Hooij op een Zolder, voorts eenige Huizen en Menschen, alles uitvoerig en konstig gedaan | companion to lot 69 *Size:* hoog 20, breed 25 duim	G H Fortuyn	(Unknown)
1808/04/26	GDAN	0069	*Hugtenburg (J. van)* | Tot een wederga, eene hevige Bataille, waarin de Actien uitmuntend zijn geobserveerd, bij een Kasteel op de tweede grond ziet men Legerkarren die door Paarden getrokken worden, voorts ziet men in het verschiet eene zeer groote Stad met derzelver Kerken en Torens, alles uitmuntend gedaan | companion to lot 68	G H Fortuyn	(Unknown)
1808/04/26	GDAN	0070	*Hugtenburg (J. van)* | Dit uitmuntend Schilderij is zo schoon als er van hem immer geweest is, en niet minder dan van Ph. Wouerman; zijnde twee groote Legers waar in hevig van weerskanten gestreden word, de Paarden der Cavallerie zijn fraaij en uitvoerig, in een woord, alles is meesteragtig gedaan en geobserveerd | *Size:* hoog 43, breed 53 ½ duim	G H Fortuyn	(Unknown)
1808/04/26	GDAN	0071	*Hugtenburg (J. van)* | Een bergägtig Landschap, en een Thuingezigt bij een Fontein, waar eene Jagtpartij is door eenige Heeren en Dames te Paard, met verdere stoffage | *Size:* hoog 30, breed 35 ½ duim	G H Fortuyn	(Unknown)
1808/06/06	RMRIJ	0057	*Huchtenburg. (Johan van)* | Eene Bataille tusschen Oostenrijksche en Turksche Kavallerij, vol gewoel; benevens eene Vesting in 't verschiet. Rijk van ordinantie, stout en meesterlijk geschilderd [Bataille entre les Turcs et les Autrichiens. Belle, riche et savante Composition, traitée dans la manière de van de Meulen] | *Annots:* Verk Jac. J Velden 3 Dec 1781 (f 27.-) (RMA I) *Mat:* op doek *Size:* Hoog 50 ½ en breed 57 duim	Gerrit van der Pot, Heer van Groeneveld	(Sold) fl 340 Allard
1808/06/13	AMSCH	0075	*Hugtenburg (J. van)* | Deze rijke Ordonantie verbeeld eene Buitenplaats, waarop eenige Heeren en Dames te paard; voorts een Rijdschool, alwaar een Paard gedresseerd wordt, verder een Koets, met zes Paarden bespannen; op den voorgrond Jagers met hunne Honden. Fraai van kleur en zacht gepenceeld | *Mat:* op doek *Size:* hoog 26, breed 32 duim	E M Engelberts	(Sold) fl 186 Hulswit
1808/06/13	AMSCH	0076	*Hugtenburg (J. van)* | In een Italiaansch Landschap ziet men aan een Waterplas rustende Reizigers; ter zijde een Man, die een Ezel uit het water trekt. Mede als de voorgaande | *Mat:* op doek *Size:* hoog 35, breed 42 duim	E M Engelberts	(Sold) fl 33 Coclers
1808/06/13	AMSCH	0077	*Hugtenburg (J. van)* | In een Hofgezicht, met prachtige Gebouwen en een Fontijn, ziet men op den voorgrond ter zijde een Liquerverkooper bij een tafeltje, waarbij een Heer en Jufvrouw, een slapend Landman, en twee zittende Vrouwen, met een beladen Ezel; verder Heeren en een Dame te Paard, en andere wandelende Lieden. Zonachtig en uitvoerig van penceelbehandeling | *Mat:* op doek *Size:* hoog 25, breed 30 duim	Z	(Sold) fl 48 J Schuman
1808/06/13	AMSCH	0077a[H]	*Hugtenburg (J. van)* | 1 dito dito [Hofgezicht] | *Notes:* This lot was added in by hand in the EBNP, FLNY and RKDH copies of the catalogue.	Z	(Bought In) fl 18
1808/08/23	AMSCH	0077	*Hugtenburg. (J. van)* | In een Manége ziet men op de voorgrond, een bruin en een zwart gezadeld Paard, beiden aan een Paal vastgebonden, agterwaards een Heer te Paard, benevens een Piqueur met een zweep in de hand; krachtig en meesterlijk behandeld | *Mat:* op doek *Size:* hoog 21, breed 25 duim	Y	(Sold) fl 42 Dupré
1808/08/23	AMSCH	0077a[H]	*Hugtenburg. (J. van)* | Een paard markt | *Notes:* This lot was added in by hand in the EBNP and FLNY copies of the catalogue.	Y	(Sold) fl 14:10 Vallée
1808/08/23	AMSCH	0247	*Hugtenburg* | Een Campement met verscheide Ruiters, Tenten enz, in het verschiet een Batterij, krachtig geschilderd	S	(Sold) fl 12:10 Spruit
1808/10/28	AMVRS	0023	*Hugtenburg, (J. van)* | Een hevig Gevegt tusschen Ruiterij en Voetvolk in een Boom- en Bergachtig Landschap. Uitneemend fraai van licht en bruin en vol uitdrukking geschilderd | *Mat:* op paneel *Size:* hoog 16 ½, breed 20 duim	Marten Udink	(Sold) fl 100 B Kooij
1808/10/28	AMVRS	0024	*Hugtenburg, (J. van)* | Een Schermutseling van eenige Ruiters in een Landschap, verder in het Koorenland een Gevecht van Voetvolk, in het verschiet een hevig vuur, ter zijde een oude Stad. Dit stuk is van de fraaiste van dezen Meester | *Mat:* op doek *Size:* hoog 16 ½, breed 24 duim	Marten Udink	(Sold) fl 200 M Kooij
1808/10/28	AMVRS	0025	*Hugtenburg, (J. van)* | Deze hevige strijd, tusschen Keizerlijke en Turksche Ruiterij, met eenig Voetvolk, in een Bergachtig Landschap, is vol gewoel; op den voorgrond is de strijd op zijn hevigst, men ziet verscheide gekwesten en gesneuvelde. Verder schijnen Turken een uitval	Marten Udink	(Sold) fl 101 Van Iperen

			uit hunne vesting te doen. De hartstochten zijn zeer natuurlijk, de woede is krachtig geteekend, alles is uitvoerig geschilderd | *Mat:* op doek *Size:* hoog 34, breed 32 duim		
1808/11/28	AMSCH	0033	*J. Hugtenburg* | Een capitaal hoog Bergachtig Landschap, met opgaand Geboomte en Gebouwen, rijk met Beelden en Beesten gestoffeerd en uitvoerig behandeld | *Mat:* op paneel *Size:* hoog 17, breed 21 duim	[Gruyter?]	(Sold) fl 16:10 T Spaan
1808/11/28	AMSCH	0034	*J. Hugtenburg* | Twee stuks Boom- en Bergachtige Landschappen, beide gestoffeerd met Heeren en Dames te Paard, beneevens Jagers die met hunne Honden eenig Wild vervolgen, zonachtig en kloek uitgevoerd | *Mat:* op paneel *Size:* ieder hoog 13, breed 15 duim	[Gruyter?]	(Bought In) fl 14
1808/12/30	HGIMM	[0071m]	*Huchtenburgh* | Voorts een exquis kabinetje Schilderijen van voorname Nederlandsche Meesters, welke uit hoofde van de kortheid des tijds niet stuk voor stuk kunnen beschreven worden; doch waarvan de beschrijving op den Kijkdag zal voorhanden zijn. Dus wij hier alleen de namen van eenige dier Meesters laten volgen, als: A. Kuyp, Ruysdaal, Karel du Jardyn, Loqwi ('t beste dat hij schilderde) Hondekoeter, van Dyk, Janson, Moesgever, Kamphuyzen, van Gooijen, A. van der Neer, T. Wyk, Huchtenburgh, Zolemaker, van Hassel, A. Vermeulen, van Dongen, Scheffer, van Os enz. | *This Lot:* Een Schilderij, Huchtenburgh *Notes:* Because this lot was not numbered in the catalogue, we have assigned the number.		(Unknown)
1809/04/17	AMSCH	0035	*J. Hugtenburg* | Een Italiaansche Markt of Plein, met grootsche Gebouwen, rijk gestoffeerd met Beeldjes, Muil Ezels en andere Figuuren; zonachtig en bevallig gepenceeld | *Mat:* op doek *Size:* hoog 11, breed 13 duim	A	(Sold) fl 39:10 Gruyter
1809/04/17	AMSCH	0036	*J. Hugtenburg* | Een hevige Bataille tusschen Turksche en andere Ruiterij en Voetvolk; krachtig geschilderd | *Mat:* op doek *Size:* hoog 12, breed 17 duim	T	(Sold) fl 5:10
1809/04/22	AMYVR	0055	*J. Hugtenberg* | In een Manege ziet men eenige schoone Paarden, welke gedresseerd worden, terwijl een Heer te Paard de Manege rondreid; fiks behandeld | *Mat:* op doek *Size:* hoog 21, breed 24 duim	de Bruin	(Bought In) fl 38
1809/06/13	AMSCH	0059	*J. Hugtenburg* | Dit kapitaal Schilderij, verbeeld in een Boom- en Bergachtig Landschap een hévige Bataille, tusschen Spaansche en andere Krijgsknegten, op de voorgrond ziet men eenige Ruiters, die elkander woedende aanvallen, ter zijde leggen verscheide dooden en gekwesten, en in 't verschiet Gebouwen; de groeping der Beelden en de fraaije schildering, maken dit stuk tot een der beste | *Mat:* op doek *Size:* hoog 42, breed 56 ½ duim	[Gruyter?]	(Bought In) fl 130
1809/06/13	AMSCH	0066	*J. Hugtenburg* | Een Duin- en Boomrijk Landschap, op de voorgrond gestoffeerd met Heeren en Dames te Paard, die zich tot den Jagt gereed maaken, verzeld van Honden, agterwaards eenige in 't Koorn arbeidende Lieden; zonachtig en krachtig geschilderd | *Mat:* op doek *Size:* hoog 14, breed 17 duim	[Gruyter?]	(Bought In) fl 20:10
1809/07/25	HGBSM	0006	*J. v. Hugtenburg* | Een dito Onderwerp als voren, zynde een scher-mutzeling of attakke [sic] op eenige Bagagie Wagens, uitvoerig gepenseelt | companion to lot 7 *Mat:* op doek *Size:* hoog 20 ½, breed 24 ½ duim *Notes:* It is unclear what "dito" refers to in the title.	D van der Aa [or] E B ten Dall	(Sold) fl 130 for lots 6 & 7. van Eijk
1809/07/25	HGBSM	0007	*J. v. Hugtenburg* | Een weerga van de voorgaande steld, voor een weg langs een Rivier waar over eenige Bruggen daar Karren en Paarden overtrekken, de Weg is ryklyk gestoffeerd met Figuren, Wagens en Paarden, als voren, uitvoerig geschildert | companion to lot 6 *Mat:* op doek *Size:* hoog 20 ½, breed 24 ½ duim	D van der Aa [or] E B ten Dall	(Sold) fl 130 for lots 6 & 7. van Eijk
1809/09/06	AMSCH	0025	*Huchtenburg (J.)* | Twee stuks, voor een Boeren Herberg, ziet men eenige Heeren en Dames, als van de Jagt komende eenige ververschinng gebruiken; de weerga vertoond een heevige Batalje van Ruiterij; meesterlijk fraai geschilderd | *Mat:* op paneel *Size:* ieder hoog 15, breed 13 duim	Johannes Caudri	(Sold) fl 70 van Iperen
1810/03/27	RMCNL	0060	*Huchtenburg* | Een Kapitaal Stuk, verbeeldende eene Bataille, op den voorgrond ziet men alles in de hevigste wanorde, dooden, gekwetsten onder elkander liggen, terwijl men in 't verschiet op eenen Berg een Kasteel in Brand geschoten ziet; alles vol werking		(Unknown)
1810/05/22	AMSCH	0038	*Hugtenburg. (J. van)* | Een Bergachtig Landschap, met een Hartejagt van Heeren en Dames, met Jagers en Honden; geestig uitgevoerd en meesterlijk geschilderd | *Mat:* op koper *Size:* hoog 11, breed 13 duim	Johannes van de Putte Nicolaasz.	(Sold) fl 40 van Iperen
1810/05/22	AMSCH	0039	*Hugtenburg. (J. van)* | Een Gezicht op een Marktplijn binnen Romen, vol stoffage van Beeldjes; delikaat gepenceeld | *Size:* hoog 12, breed 10 duim	Johannes van de Putte Nicolaasz.	(Sold) fl 30 van Iperen
1810/06/06	RMMUY	0044	*J. van Huchtenburgh* | Eene hevige Bataille, voor aan in 't midden een Krijgsman, welke van een ander geschooten zijnde, van het paard tuimeld, op den voorgrond gekwetste, stervende en dooden, verder eene menigte in gevegt zijnde Ruiters, van achteren schijnt de Slag algemeen, in 't verschiet een Burgt op 't Gebergte, dit Stuk is helder van kleur, krachtig en meesterlijk. Door J. van Huchtenburgh, van zijnen besten tijd | *Mat:* op doek		(Unknown) fl 97
1810/06/20	AMSCH	0168	*J. Hugtenburg* | In een Landschap ziet men op den voorgrond eene hevige Schermutseling tusschen Ruiterij | *Mat:* op doek	A—	(Sold) fl 5:10 Gela

1810/10/10	MGCIT	0023	*J. v. Huchtenburg* | Een Schilderij, vertoonende een Rencontre tusschen twee vijandelijke Leger-corps, waar in de hevige Weerstand van beide partijen op het levendigst word uitgedrukt, schoon van teekening voorts zeer Martiaal, doch tevens met een malsch penseel behandeld	Caspar van Citters	(Unknown)
1810/11/07	UTWLD	0024	*Huchtenburg* | Een bataille waar Prins Eugenius 't Commando voert, op den agtergrond een hevige attaque, door Infanterie en Cavallerie, een brandend Dorp toont de overblijfselen van schrijk en verwoesting, terwijl men op de voorgrond een hevige schermutzeling ontwaard, tusschen eenige Huzaren met zabels en pistolen, terwijl de Commandant voort blijft Commandeeren, de schoonheid der ordonnantie, de uitmuntende plaatzing van bruin en licht, kenschest [sic] des makers groote kennis in tekening en Coloriet – door Huchtenburg op doek, 4 doet 6 duim hoog, 5 voet 2 duim breed, verg. Lijst | *Mat:* op doek *Size:* 4 doet 6 duim hoog, 5 voet 2 duim breed		(Unknown) fl 300
			Huchtenburgh, Jan van (and Piemont)		
1807/08/26	AMSCH	0088	*J. van Hugtenburg; G. Piemont* | In een aangenaam Bergachtig en Boomryk Landschap, ziet men op den voorgrond een hevige schermutseling van Ruiters en Voetvolk, terwyl anderen een Convooy en beladene Muil-Ezels aanvallen; alles is met veel vuur en levendigheid verbeeld, door J. van Hugtenburg en G. Piemont, in hunnen besten tyd | *Mat:* op doek *Size:* hoog 25, breed 30 ½ duim *Notes:* The artist's name was given as "G. Piemont" but we have assumed this is an error.	Coclers	(Bought In) fl 140
			Huchtenburgh, Jan van (or Huchtenburgh, Jan, manner)		
1802/06/28	AMSCH	0076	*J. Huchtenburg* | Een hevige Rencontre tusschen Ruyters te Paard en Voetvolk; zeer natuurlyk door of in de manier van Denzelven [J. Huchtenburg] | *Mat:* op paneel *Size:* hoog 21, breed 25 duim	Anna Elink	(Sold) fl 5:5 van Iperen
			Huchtenburgh, Jan van (copy after)		
1806/08/20	HGBSM	0215	*J. Hugtenburg* | Een schermutseling van Ruiterij, na J. Hugtenburg | *Mat:* op doek *Size:* hoog 27 ½, breed 33 duim	Macalester Loup [or others]	(Sold) fl 7:10 Gram
			Huchtenburgh, Jan van (manner)		
1801/03/16	AMSCH	0204	*Hugtenburg* | Een hevige Batalje in de manier van Hugtenburg	K[ip]	(Sold) fl 4 Mensart
1801/04/13	AMSCH	0109	*Hugtenburg* | Twee stuks, het eene met Legertenten en Krygslieden te paard, en het andere een Manege voor een grootsch Gebouw; beide plaisant in de manier van Hugtenburg | *Mat:* op doek *Size:* ieder is hoog 34, breed 41 duim	Pierre Fouquet, junior	(Sold) fl 26 v d Schley [for] S
1802/08/24	LNDLS	0123	*Hugtenburg* | Een Manege met Ruijters en Paarden, als door Hugtenburg	Leonardus Bouman [or others]	(Unknown) fl 1:6
1802/09/06	AMSCH	0164	*Huchtenburg* | Een hévige Batalje tnsschen [sic] ruitery, vol gewoel, op de grond leggen dooden en gekwesten, zoo krygslieden als Paarden; fiks geschilderd op Doek, in de manier van Huchtenburg | *Mat:* op doek *Size:* hoog 21, breed 25 duim	X	(Sold) fl 1:15 van Cooth
1802/11/01	DOBRA	0110	*Hugtenburg* | Twee stuks, zynde Veldbatailjes fiks Geschildert en ryk van Ordonnantie, in de manier van Hugtenburg | *Mat:* op doek *Size:* hoog 19, br. 21 ½ d.	Paulus van der Spyk [or others]	(Sold) fl 6 ¾ v d Blyk
1803/06/20	AMSCH	0068	*J. van Hugtenburg* | Een hevige Bataille tusschen Ruytery, in een Boomryk Landschap, in een verschiet een Fort, meesterlyk op Doek als J. van Hugtenburg | *Mat:* op doek *Size:* hoog 26, breed 33 duim	Schley [for] K	(Sold) fl 14:10 V^{n} Iperen
1803/09/07	AMSCH	0239	*Huchtenburg* | Een hevige Bataille tusschen Ruitery, meesterlyk gepenceeld in de manier van Huchtenburg [Une action de cavalerie très animée ; tableau peint de main de maître, dans le goût de Huchtenburg] | *Mat:* op doek *Size:* hoog 30, breed 46 duim	Smidt	(Bought In) fl 11
1806/08/13	AMSCH	0231	*Hugtenburg* | Een hévige Schermutzeling tusschen Ruytery en Voetvolk, vol gewoel; in de manier van Hugtenburg | *Mat:* op paneel	Roos	(Sold) fl 3 Richters
1806/08/13	AMSCH	0281	*Hugtenburg* | Een hévige Rencontre tusschen Ruitery; als Hugtenburg	Daniel Mansveld	(Sold) fl 2 Reydon
1808/03/03	HAVIN	0029	*van Hugtenburg* | Twee Battailles, als van Hugtenburg	Jacobus Spillebout	(Unknown) fl 2
1808/08/23	AMSCH	0272	*Hugtenburg* | In een Manege ziet men op de voorgrond een zwart en een bruin gezadeld Paard, agterwaards een Heer te Paard, waar bij een Piqueur met de Zweep in de hand; kloek geschilderd in de manier van Hugtenburg	Y	(Sold) fl 17:10 Vallé
			Hulft, T.M. [Unidentified]		
1809/04/22	AMYVR	0058	*T.M. Hulft* | Een Wintergezicht, met stoffagie van Arresleeden, Schaatsenrijders, en andere Beelden; meesterlijk | *Mat:* op paneel *Size:* hoog 13, breed 21 duim	de Bruin	(Sold) fl 1:5 Andriessen
			Hulk, A. Pietersz.		
1809/04/22	AMYVR	0059	*A. Hulk, Pietersz.* | Een Historieele Ordonantie; delicaat en geestig | *Mat:* op doek *Size:* hoog 16, breed 12 duim	de Bruin	(Sold) fl 4:5 Ijver
			Hulsdonck, Jacob		
1804/08/08	AMSCH	0253	*Hulsdonk* | Op een Tafel ziet men eenige Fruiten, Kreeft en ander stil Leeven; uitvoerig gepenceeld	Roos a	(Sold) fl 1:15 Graffelman

Hulst

1809/07/25	HGBSM	0070	*van Hulst* | Twee Stuks Dorpgezigten, verbeeldende het eene een Boere Kermis, en het andere een Veemarkt, beide vol gewoel, helder en uitvoerig geschildert | *Mat:* op paneel *Size:* hoog 10 en 1 half, breed 14 duim	D van der Aa	(Sold) fl 66:10 van der Aa [or] Mes

Hulst (copy after)

1810/07/23	DOLG2	0017	*A. Lamme; van Hulst* | In een water, langs eenen stads toren, en verdere gebouwen, vertoonen zich Schuiten en Schepen. Naar van Hulst, door A. Lamme | copy by A. Lamme after Hulst *Mat:* op doek *Size:* hoog 21, breed 28 duim	Pieter Quinting	(Sold) fl 2:15 Visser

Hulst, Franz de

1804/10/16	DLOND	0110	*F. d. Hulst* | Een Landschap en Ruïne. Paysage & Ruine | *Mat:* op paneel *Fmt:* rond *Size:* 15 diam.		(Unknown)
1804/10/16	DLOND	0111	*F. d. Hulst* | Een dito [Landschap] en Storm. Dito [Paysage] & Orage | *Mat:* op paneel *Fmt:* rond *Size:* 15 diam.		(Unknown)
1804/10/29	HRBAU	0039	*Hulst, (F. D.)* | Een fraai uit het water opgebouwd en met boomgewas versierd Kasteel vertoont zig ter regterzyde, gestoffeerd met Schepen en Schuiten. Zeer zonagtig; in de manier van van Goijen behandeld | *Mat:* op paneel *Size:* hoog 18, breed 27 duim	Simon Styl	(Unknown)
1804/10/29	HRBAU	0040	*Hulst, (F. D.)* | Een zeer bevallig Gezigt langs eene Kerk in het Dorp, ryk gestoffeerd met Beeldtjes en Beesjes; waar agter een aangenaam verschiet. Niet minder dan het voorige behandeld | *Mat:* op paneel *Size:* hoog 18, breed 27 duim	Simon Styl	(Unknown)
1804/10/29	HRBAU	0041	*Hulst, (F. D.)* | Een bevallig boomryk Landschap, met Boerenwooningen langs een' zandigen Weg; ziende men in 't verschiet eene Stad. Alles in de manier als het voorige behandeld | *Mat:* op paneel *Size:* hoog 19, breed 25 duim	Simon Styl	(Unknown)
1810/06/04	DOBRA	0013	*F. van Hulst* | Twee Land en Watergezichten	Hendrik de Haas	(Unknown)
1810/07/23	DOLG2	0052	*F. Hulst* | Een Watergezicht, met Schepen en een Stads Toren | *Mat:* op paneel *Size:* hoog 14, breed 22 duim	Pieter Quinting	(Unknown) fl 4:10

Hulst, J. van der [Unidentified]

1808/05/17	LNAN	0004	*J. van der Hulst* | Een Gezigt langs het water op eene woning met geboomte, nevens hetzelve varende schuiten, en een dorp in 't verschiet; zeer natuurlijk en kunstig | *Mat:* op doek *Size:* hoog 49, breed 59 duim		(Sold) fl 14:10 Thomasse

Hulswit, Jan

1804/02/27	AMSCH	0051	*Hulswit. (J.)* | In een hoog Bergachtig Landschap, vertoont zich op een grazige vlakte, een Herder met Schaapen, op den tweede grond een Vrouw te Paard, en een Man met een Hond, en een bevallig verschiet; warm van coloriet en uitvoerig van schildering | *Mat:* op paneel *Size:* hoog 10, breed 10 duim	B	(Sold) fl 7:10 Gruiter
1806/05/05	AMSCH	0064	*Jan Hulswit* | In een hoog bergagtig Landschap, vertoond zig op een grasige vlakten een Herder met Schapen op de voorgrond, een Vrouw te Paard, by een Man met een Hond, verders een bergagtig verschiet; warm van coloriet door Jan Hulswit | *Mat:* op paneel *Size:* hoog 10, breed 10 duim	V[inkeles]	(Sold) fl 7:5 Gruiter
1808/08/23	AMSCH	0080	*Hulswit. (J.)* | In een hoog Bergachtig Landschap, vertoont zig op een grasige vlakte een Herder met Schaapen, op de tweede grond eene Vrouw te Paard, benevens een Man met een Hond, voorts een bevallig verschiet; warm van koloriet en zonachtig behandeld | *Mat:* op paneel *Size:* hoog 10, breed 10 duim	[Gruyter?]	(Sold) fl 7:15 Frantzen
1808/08/23	AMSCH	0081	*Hulswit. (J.)* | Aan een spiegelend Water ziet men een Landman bij eenige Ossen, die zig een den oever drenken, voorts onder de schaduwe van oude Willige Boomen, grasende Schaapen, en een aangenaam verschiet; uitvoerig en bevallig gepenceeld | *Mat:* op paneel *Size:* hoog 10, breed 12 duim	J	(Sold) fl 25 Th Spaan

Huysmans, Cornelis

1803/09/07	AMSCH	0085	*Huisman van Mechelen* | In een Boomryk Landschap, met een Bergachtig verschiet, ziet men Christus tusschen de Emausgangers, dit stukje is van een aangename Schildering [Jesus-Christ, au milieu de ses disciples, allant à Emaus. Ce sujet est traité dans un paysage, présentant une diversité agréable d'arbres et de collines] | *Mat:* op paneel *Size:* hoog 11, breed 14 duim	Smidt	(Sold) fl 9:10 I^{c} Smit
1803/09/07	AMSCH	0086	*Huisman van Mechelen* | Een Gezicht op de Stad Brussel, by maanligt voorgesteld, als de voorgaande [Vue de la ville de Bruxelles au clair de la lune ; d'un mérite égal au précédent] | *Mat:* op paneel *Size:* hoog 8, breed 10 duim	Smidt	(Sold) fl 1 I^{c} Smit
1805/07/10	AMSCH	0192	*Huismans* | Een dito [Boomryk] Landschapje	R[oos]	(Sold) fl 4:10 Nieuwenhuis
1806/08/13	AMSCH	0076	*Huismans van Mechelen* | Een Italiaansch Bergachtig Landschap met een Rivier doorsneeden, en verscheide Boomgewas, vertoont zich op de	Roos	(Sold) fl 10:5 Boelhouwer

			voorgrond verscheide rustende en gaande Ryzigers, verder een aangenaam verschiet; dit voorwerp is zonagtig, natuurlyk en meesterlyk gepenceeld | *Mat:* op doek *Size:* hoog 27, breed 33 duim		
1806/08/13	AMSCH	0077	*Huismans van Mechelen* | Een Gezicht in Italiën, zynde een Boom- en Bergachtig gestoffeerd Landschap; meesterlyk geschilderd | *Size:* hoog 19, breed 25 duim *Notes:* The artist's name "G Poussin" was added in by hand in the JPGM copy of the catalogue.	Roos	(Sold) fl 330 Van Iperen
1806/08/13	AMSCH	0078	*Huismans van Mechelen* | Een Arcadiesch Landschap met fraaije stoffagie mede als de voorgaande behandeld | *Mat:* op doek *Size:* hoog 24, breed 19 duim	Roos	(Bought In) fl 1
1807/08/26	AMSCH	0134	*Huisman van Mechelen* | Een Boomryk Landschap, met Reizigers gestoffeerd, en met een Zonlicht verlicht | *Mat:* op doek *Size:* hoog 23, breed 32 duim	Joseph Vallette	(Sold) fl 6:5 van Iperen
1809/04/17	AMSCH	0040	*Huismans van Mechelen* | Een hoog Bergachtig Landschap, met een Rivier doorsneeden, gestoffeerd met eene gaande Vrouw en rustende Beesten | *Mat:* op doek	T	(Sold) fl 1:15
1810/06/20	AMSCH	0111	*Huismans van Mechelen* | Een bevallig Boomrijk Landschap	R[oos]	(Sold) fl 1:15 Cassino
1810/07/26	AMSCH	0038	*Huismans van Mechelen* | Een Boomrijk Landschap, met Beelden en Beesten. Meesterlijk geschilderd | *Mat:* op doek *Size:* hoog 22, breed 22 duimen	Cassino	(Sold) fl 1 Boelhouwer
1810/07/26	AMSCH	0039	*Huismans van Mechelen* | Een zeer schoon Landschap. Zijnde een fraai stuk | *Mat:* op doek *Size:* hoog 39, breed 50 duimen	Cassino	(Bought In) fl 2
1810/07/26	AMSCH	0040	*Huismans van Mechelen* | Een Landschap met een Waterval en Beelden | *Mat:* op doek *Size:* hoog 28, breed 44 duimen	Cassino	(Bought In) fl 2:15
1810/10/13	HGDAW	0013	*C. Huisman* | Een vrolyk Landschap, waarin een vervallen Gebouw, voor hetzelve een gezelschap drinkende Boeren en Boerinnen, in het verschiet ziet men een Brug, waarover twee Ezels gedreven worden, extra uitvoerig en delicaat behandeld | *Mat:* op paneel *Size:* hoog 11 ¾, breed 16 ½ duim		(Unknown)
			Huysmans, Cornelis (manner)		
1801/03/16	AMSCH	0135	*Huisman van Mechelen* | Twee stuks Landschappen als Huisman van Mechelen	K[ip]	(Sold) fl 1 van Iperen
1805/12/16	AMSCH	0073	*Huismans* | Een gestoffeerd Landschap, als Huismans	R[oos]	(Sold) fl 0:8 van Eyk
1805/12/16	AMSCH	0080	*Huismans* | Twee Landschappen, als door Huismans	R[oos]	(Sold) fl 0:6 L Pakker
			Huysmans, P.J.		
1801/03/16	AMSCH	0010	*P.J. Huisman* | Een Brabandsch Landschap, by een oud Gebouw ziet men een Beek, waar door de Landman eenig Vee dryft; konstig van behandeling	P[ruyssenaar]	(Sold) fl 31 Rijnders
			Huysum		
1801/04/23	AMYVR	0021	*Josua van Huysum* | Een Borstbeeld met Bloemen omslingerd, waarby Hoorns en Schelpen		(Sold) fl 1 ¼ Gruyter
			Huysum, Jan van		
1801/03/16	AMSCH	0024	*J. van Huizum* | Een fraai gestoffeerd Arcadisch Landschap, zonagtig en uitvoerig	K[ip]	(Sold) fl 50 Cocler
1801/04/13	AMSCH	0036	*J. van Huyzum* | Twee stuks Arcadische Landschappen, met Geboomte, Gebouwen, Rivieren, en stoffage van Beeldjes en Schapen, warm van coloriet en uitvoerige geschilderd | *Mat:* op paneel *Size:* yder hoog 9, breed 10 duim	Pierre Fouquet, junior	(Sold) fl 24 v d Vinne
1801/04/23	AMYVR	0005	*J. van Huysum* | Een Vaas met verscheiden zoorten van Bloemen op een Steene Tafel in een Hofgezicht, fix gepenceeld op Doek | *Mat:* op doek *Size:* hoog 31, breed 24 duim		(Sold) fl 8 Reyers
1801/04/23	AMYVR	0006	*J. van Huysum* | Een Italiaansch Landschap met verscheiden Geboomte, en andere Stoffagie, uitvoerig op Doek geschilderd | *Mat:* op doek *Size:* hoog 16, breed 20 duim		(Sold) fl 27 Pruijssenaar
1801/04/23	AMYVR	0008	*J. van Huysum* | Een Pot met diverse zoorten van Bloemen, staande op een Tafel, meesterlyk in het graauw, op Paneel | *Mat:* op paneel		(Sold) fl 4 ¾ Dyl
1801/04/23	AMYVR	0022	*J. van Huysum* | Een Schets of Model tot een Fruitstuk, door J. van Huysum aangelegt, doch niet afgemaakt, zynde het laatste werk van deze Schilder		(Sold) fl 2 ¾ Van Dyl
1801/06/10	AMSCH	0071	*Huysum. (Jan van)* | Een capitaale Ordonnantie, van fraaije geschakeerde Bloemen, een geboetseerde Vaas staande op een steene Balustrade, is gevuld met witte, roode en geele Roosen, en andere uitgezogte Bloemen, alle in de beste order geschikt ter zyde deeze Vaas legt een Vogelnestje met Eyeren, verders verscheide Insectens die op de Bloemen aasen; alles is zeer dun, krachtig en van delicaat penceel | companion to lot 72 *Mat:* op paneel *Size:* hoog 23, breed 19 duim	Herman ten Kate	(Sold) fl 810 Coclers
1801/06/10	AMSCH	0072	*Huysum. (Jan van)* | Dit niet minder fraaye Stuk, verbeeld een fraaije gevlogte Mand, waar diverse Vrugten geplaatst zyn, als witte en blaauwe Druiven, Persiken en andere Fruiten, op de steene Rand waarop deeze Mand geplaatst is, liggen Nooten en Karssen, dit stuk is een weedergaa	Herman ten Kate	(Sold) fl 810 Coclers

			van de voorige en in alles als de voorgaande | companion to lot 71 *Mat:* op paneel *Size:* hoog 23, breed 19 duim		
1801/06/10	AMSCH	0073	*Huysum. (Jan van)* | Een Arcadiesch Landschap, met hoog Geboomte, Gebouwen, Waterval, en stoffage van Beelden en Schapen, uitvoerig van penceel en warm van Coloriet | *Mat:* op doek *Size:* hoog 21, breed 27 duim	Herman ten Kate	(Sold) fl 135 C S Roos
1801/06/10	AMSCH	0074	*Huysum. (Jan van)* | Een Vaas gevuld met verscheide soorten van Bloemen, fraai geschakeerd, en dun van schildering | *Mat:* op doek *Size:* hoog 43, breed 32 duim	Herman ten Kate	(Sold) fl 13 Coclers
1801/08/19	AMSCH	0045	*J. van Huisum* | Een Arcadisch Landschap met Beelden en Beesjes gestoffeerd	Pruyssen^{r} [for] Q	(Sold) fl 6 Wolft
1801/10/06	AMSCH	0028	*J. van Huysum* | In dit Aangenaam, Boomryk Arcadisch Landschap, vertoont zich op de voorgrond, by een Steene Voetstuk op een Altaar een Standbeeld van de Godin Flora; een Hydens Priester in plegt gewaad, verzelt van een Offerdienaar, schynt bevel te geeven twee Biggen te slagten, verder ziet men eenige Nimphen, al met elkander spreekende, andere vlegten Bloemen, in 't verschiet ziet men een omgang van verscheide Lieden, als naar een Tempel gaande; en verder flauw Gebergten, ter zyde staat een Gedenkzuil by een Begraafplaats, en ander treffelyke Gebouwen: het bevallige Zonlicht, door het gantsche Stuk verspreid, geeft een fraaije uitwerking, het verschillend geboomten, kruiden en andere Planten; alles is ongemeen uitvoerig en delicaat gepenceeld, en van de schoonste ordinantien van dezen Beroemde Meester | companion to lot 29 *Mat:* op doek *Size:* hoog 15, breed 21 duim	S	(Sold) fl 200 for lots 28 & 29. Ter Smitten
1801/10/06	AMSCH	0029	*J. van Huysum* | In een dito [Arcadisch] bevallig Landschap, zynde de wederga, ziet men op een cierlijk voetstuk het Standbeeld van de God Bachus, verscheide Nimphen zijn bézig plegtig te Offeren; ter linker zijde bij een boom, ziet men een oude Sileen, zig aan een tak vasthoudende om op zijn Ezel te stijgen, verder zit een bedaagde vrouw bij een Marmer-steen, met gebakken Spys, ter zijde vertoont zich een aangenaam verschiet met Gebouwen en Gebergten, het Geboomte, de verschillende gronden, het streelend Zonlicht, alles geeft luister aan dit schoon tafreel, en is als de vorige, aller uitvoerigst van penceel behandeling | companion to lot 28 *Mat:* op doek *Size:* hoog 15, breed 21 duim	S	(Sold) fl 200 for lots 28 & 29. Ter Smitten
1802/06/16	AMSCH	0080	*J. van Huysun* | Op een Tafel, ziet men een Vaas gevuld met verscheide soorten van fraay geschakeerde Bloemen, ter zyde een Vogelnesje met Eijeren; alles is meesterlyk van Ordenantie en Penseel-behandeling | *Mat:* op paneel *Size:* hoog 17, breed 13 duim	[Merrem]	(Sold) fl 104 C S Roos
1802/06/28	AMSCH	0070	*J. van Huysem* | Twee stuks prachtige Hofgezichten, met verscheide hoog Geboomten, Fontyn en andere stoffagie; zeer natuurlyk door J. van Huysem, Panneel | *Mat:* op paneel *Size:* hoog 10, breed 8 duim	Anna Elink	(Sold) fl 3:5 Gruiter
1802/09/21	UTHDG	0036	*Jan van Huysem* | Een Arcadisch Landschap met gebouwen en geboomte, rijk gestoffeerd met Reizigers, Herders, en Schaapen, zijnde grootsch van ordonnantie en uitvoerig geschildert | *Mat:* op doek *Size:* hoog 18 ½, breed 25 duimen		(Bought In) fl 40
1803/09/07	AMSCH	0238	*J. van Huysum* | Verscheide Vrugten, als Persiken, Druiven, enz. op een Steenen Tafel; fix geschilderd, op Doek, en gemerkt J. van Huysum [Un assemblage de fruits, tels que des pêches, des raisins etc. artistement grouppés sur une table de pierre ; d'une belle composition, sur toile et signé J. Van Huysum] | *Mat:* op doek *Size:* hoog 16, breed 13 duim *Inscr:* J. van Huysum (signed)	Smidt	(Sold) fl 3:5 Camphuijsen
1803/12/12	AMSCH	0040	*J. van Huysum* | Op een Steene Voet ziet men een Vaas, wel geschakeert met onderscheide soorten van Bloemen; meesterachtig gepenceeld | *Mat:* op paneel *Size:* hoog 17, breed 13 duim *Loc:* Troyes, France. Musée des Beaux-Arts. (D 872–3) (?)	B	(Sold) fl 80 Josi
1804/08/08	AMSCH	0081	*J. van Huyzum* | Een Landschap met hoog Geboomte, gestoffeerd met een Harte-Jacht; fraai gepenceeld | *Mat:* op doek *Size:* hoog 32, breed 38 duim	Pruys[senaar]	(Bought In) fl 6
1804/10/29	HRBAU	0038	*Huisum, (Jan van)* | Op den Voorgrond van dit bevallig Boschgezigt, by eene stroomende Beek, zit Diana, met haare Jagtnymph in gesprek, vergezeld van heure Jagthonden, op het heldere licht geplaatst, welk een heerlyke vertooning maakt tegens het aangenaame lommer der boomen van den tweeden grond, waar men nog eenige Nymphen by een kudde Schaapen ontdekt, nevens een bergagtig verschiet. Alles is zeer smeltend en uitvoerig geschilderd | *Mat:* op doek *Size:* hoog 31, breed 43 duim	Simon Styl	(Unknown)
1805/07/03	AMSCH	0094	*J. van Huyzum* | Twee stuks Arcadische Landschappen, in de eene een Hartejagt; en de andere met antique, Beelden; zonachtig op Doek | *Mat:* op doek *Size:* hoog 19, breed 22 duim	G	(Sold) fl 46 Josi
1805/07/10	AMSCH	0073	*J. van Huysum* | Op een Steene Tafel, leggen eenige smakelyke Vrugten, als Druyven, Persiken, en meer anderen; fiks op Doek | *Mat:* op doek *Size:* hoog 16, breed 13 duim	V[inkeles] [for] N	(Sold) fl 4 Zonnenberg
1805/10/09	HGBSM	0088	*J. van Huyzum* | Een kapitaal landschap, op de voorgrond, ziet men een waterval, waar in een hartenjagt, warm en meesterlyk geschilderd | *Mat:* op doek *Size:* hoog 33 breet 39 ½ duim	T H van Willigen [or others]	(Sold) fl 4:6 Heijmans

1805/12/16	AMSCH	0027	*J. van Huysum* | Twee stuks Arcadische Landschappen, gestoffeerd met speelende en dansende Nimphen, by Geboomten; bevallig op Doek geschilderd | *Mat:* op doek *Size:* yder hoog 21, breed 25 duim	Spaan	(Sold) fl 2:5 ter Maat
1806/11/24	AMSCH	0033	*Huysum (J. van)* | Een Italiaansch Landschap aan een Rivier, op de Voorgrond een Waterval en eenige Vissers; warm van coloriet, en bevallig van schildering | *Mat:* op doek *Size:* hoog 23, breed 19 duim	Munnikhuizen	(Sold) fl 4:5 Dusart
1807/08/26	AMSCH	0090	*J. van Huysum* | Twee stuks, zynde antique Vaazen, staande op Marmere Tafels, gevuld met de geurigste Bloemen van allerleie kleur, delicaat en dun op Doek gepenceeld | *Mat:* op doek *Size:* hoog 46, breed 36 duim	Roos	(Sold) fl 14:10 Gruiter
1807/08/26	AMSCH	0091	*J. van Huysum* | Een dito [antique] Vaas, mede met Bloemen gevuld en behandeld als de voorgaande [delicaat en dun gepenceeld] | *Mat:* op doek *Size:* hoog 25, breed 21 duim	Roos	(Sold) fl 4 Coclair
1807/08/26	AMSCH	0092	*J. van Huysum* | Een Italiaansch Landschap, gestoffeerd met een Herder met Schapen, over een Brug gaande; aangenaam geschilderd | *Mat:* op doek *Size:* hoog 9, breed 11 duim	Helsdinge	(Sold) fl 6:5 Spruit
1808/06/06	RMRIJ	0058	*Huijsum. (Jan van)* | Op een marmeren Voetstuk liggen eenige uitgelezen Vruchten, als witte Druiven, eene opengesneden Meloen, een Granaat-Appel, Perziken, Pruimen, enz. geschakeerd met Bladeren, Bloemen, Vlinders, Vliegen en Waterdroppels. Alles uitkomende tegen eenen lichten achtergrond. Dit tafereel is een der uitvoerigsten en in alle opzigten bevalligsten en heldersten van dezen grooten Meester [Plusieurs fruits exquis sont placés sur une Table de marbre. Une belle Grappe de Raisins blancs, des Pêches, des Prunes, une Pomme de Grenade et un Mélon entamés font briller cette savante et agréable Composition. Des feuilles de Vigne, une branche de framboises, quelques fleurs, des Papillons et plusieurs autres Insectes varient embellissent ce morceau délicat. Un fond clair et chaud, la plus belle harmonie, la Transparence, et le précieux fini de ce Tableau, en font un des chef-d'oeuvres de ce fameux Artiste] | *Mat:* op koper *Size:* Hoog 19, en breed 16 duim *Loc:* Amsterdam, Nederland. Rijksmuseum. (A187)	Gerrit van der Pot, Heer van Groeneveld	(Sold) fl 3610 J M Jorissen [for] le Roi
1808/06/06	RMRIJ	0059	*Huijsum. (Jan van)* | Een bergachtig, met een water doorsneden Landschap, vol Gebouwen, Beelden en Beesten. Zeer uitvoerig en delicaat geschilderd. Eene wedergade, met een Waterval en verdere rijke stoffering. Als boven behandeld [Un Paysage d'Arcadie. D'une Composition agréable et enrichie de Statues et de beaucoup de figures etc. d'un grand fini et de son meilleur faire. Le Pendant, où l'on voit une chûte d'eau et beaucoup de figures etc. Egal en mérite au Précédent] | *Annots:* 10 April 1783 van P. Fouquet (f.32-) (RMA I) *Mat:* op doek *Size:* Twee stukken. Hoog 20 en breed 23 ¼ duim	Gerrit van der Pot, Heer van Groeneveld	(Sold) fl 200 Allard
1808/06/13	AMSCH	0078	*Huijsum (J. van)* | In dit aangenaam Italiaansch bergachtig Landschap, met een stille Rivier doorsneden, vertoond zich op den voorgrond een stroomende Waterval, in het midden drie Visschers op een Heuvel; verder ter zijde een Huisman, met beladen Muilezel; aan de overzijde bij Geboomte een Klooster; achter ziet men Gebergte: verder over een houten Brug een Veehoeder met Schapen, en gestoffeerd met verscheidene Beeldjes en Geboomte. Warm en bevallig van kleur, en uitvoerig geschilderd | *Mat:* op doek *Size:* hoog 22, breed 27 ½ duim	[Jan Tersteeg]	(Bought In) fl 50
1809/09/06	AMSCH	0022	*Huijzum (J. van)* | Op een marmer Voetstuk in een Nis, ziet men een Pot, gevuld met welgeschakeerde Bloemen, als Roozen, Tulpen, Auriculaas, Papavers en andere geurige Bloemen: op de Tafel ligt een Vogelnesje met Eijeren; alles delicaat en welgeordoneerd behandeld | *Mat:* op paneel *Size:* hoog 31, breed 24 duim	Johannes Caudri	(Sold) fl 215 Roos
1809/09/06	AMSCH	0023	*Huijzum (J. van)* | Op een steenen Voetstuk staat een Vaas met Bloemen van allerlei aart; is niet minder van Ordonantie, maar op een schetsachtige wijze en meesterlyk gepenceeld | *Mat:* op paneel *Size:* hoog 32, breed 24 duim	Johannes Caudri	(Sold) fl 300 de Lelie
1810/05/22	AMSCH	0037	*Huijsum. (J. van)* | Dit kapitaal Tafreel vertoont een sierlijk gewerkte Vaas, staande op een kouleurde Marmeren Tafel, gevuld met eene menigte onderscheidene zoorten van keurige Bloemen, als verschillende Roozen, Hijacinten, Kroon-Imperiaalen, Tulpen en Auriculaas, waarop eenige Insecten aazen; alles evenaart de Natuur, bevallig van koloriet en meesterlijk fraai gepenceeld | *Mat:* op doek *Size:* hoog 31, breed 24 duim	Johannes van de Putte Nicolaasz.	(Sold) fl 301 van Iperen
1810/08/01	AMSCH	0047	*Huijsum (Jan van)* | Op een marmer Voetstuk staat eene met Kindertjes uitvoerig gewerkte steenen Vaas, sierlijk gevuld met Nagelen, Tulp, gele en roode Rozen; Bloembollen en andere keurige Bloemen; geschilderd tegen eenen lichten grond [Sur un Socle de Marbre est posé un Vase de Jaspe, sculpté et orné d'un basrelief offrant des Enfans, dans lequel on voit un riche groupe des plus belles Fleurs : on y distingue différentes Roses, les Iacinthes, la Tulipe et plusieurs autres espèces. Ce Bouquet est opposé à un fond clair et léger] | *Annots:* froid, sans clair obscur ni magie. (NGW) *Mat:* op paneel *Size:* hoog 31 ½, breed 23 ½ duimen *Loc:* Los Angeles, CA, USA. Edward Carter collection.	Mr Pieter de Smeth van Alphen	(Sold) fl 4500 J^{mo} de Vries
1810/08/01	AMSCH	0048	*Huijsum (Jan van)* | Eene met Beelden versierde Vaas, staande op eene marmeren Tafel en gevuld met roode en witte Rozen, Anjelieren en andere Bloemen; mede tegen eenen lichten grond [Sur une Table de Marbre est posé un Vase, figuré et orné de Sculptures, il est embelli d'un	Mr Pieter de Smeth van Alphen	(Bought In) fl 1340

			Bouquet des plus brillantes Fleurs, comme les Roses rouges et blanches, les Oëillets et plusieurs autres espèces, faisant opposition comme le précédent à un fond léger] | *Annots:* Boutique de couleurs crues. (NGW) *Mat:* op doek *Size:* hoog 31, breed 23 duimen		
1810/08/06	AMSCH	0050a[H]	*Van Huysum* | [Untitled] | *Notes:* This lot was added in by hand in the AA II and MA copies of the catalogue, but without giving a title.		(Sold) fl 255 van Leen
			Huysum, Jan van (and Moucheron)		
1801/03/16	AMSCH	0069	*Moucheron; van Huysum* | Een Boomryk Landschap met Beeldjes gestoffeerd, door Moucheron en van Huysum	P[ruyssenaar]	(Sold) fl 8 Stevens
			Huysum, Jan van (or Huysum, Jan, manner)		
1801/04/23	AMYVR	0009	*J. van Huysum* | Twee dito [Potten] met Vruchten en Bloemen, door of in de manier van denzelven [J. van Huysum]		(Sold) fl 3 ¼ A Maijer
1802/12/13	AMSCH	0075	*J. van Huysum* | Twee Arcadische Landschappen, met Beeltjes gestoffeert, door of in de manier van J. van Huysum | *Mat:* op doek *Size:* hoog 19, breed 24 duim *Notes:* This lot was misnumbered no. 74.	Pruyssenaar [for] B	(Sold) fl 10:10 Gruiter
1808/06/13	AMSCH	0194	*J. van Huizum* | Twee Landschapjes; door of in de manier van J. van Huizum	E M Engelberts	(Sold) fl 16 Schuman
			Huysum, Jan van (manner)		
1808/08/23	AMSCH	0236	*J. v. Huijsum* | Op een steene Borstweering staat een cierlijke Vaas, gevuld met onderscheiden soorten van fraaije Bloemen, benevens anderen die ter zijde afhangen; het is meesterlijk en fiks gepenceeld op Doek, in de manier van J. v. Huijsum | *Mat:* op doek	C	(Sold) fl 7 Th Spaan
			Huysum, Justus van (I)		
1801/04/23	AMYVR	0028	*Justus van Huysum* | Twee stuks gestoffeerde Wintergezichten		(Sold) fl 1 Bronsteede
1801/04/23	AMYVR	0032	*Justus van Huysum* | Een Land- en Watergezicht, gestoffeerd met een Hartenjagt		(Sold) fl 1 Maynzart
1802/09/21	UTHDG	0037	*Justus van Huysem* | Twee stuks, op ieder eene losse geschikt bouquet, bloemen in potten, met basrelief, beiden uitvoerig en natuurlijk geschildert | *Mat:* op doek *Size:* hoog 19 ½, breed 15 ½ duimen		(Bought In) fl 22
			Huysum, Michiel van		
1801/04/23	AMYVR	0023	*M. van Huysum* | Een Hofgezicht met verscheiden In- en Uitlandsche Vogelen		(Sold) fl 2 ¼ Gruijter
1802/05/05	AMSCH	0081	*M. van Huyzum* | Een Hofgezicht, met verscheiden In- en Uitlandsch Gevogelte | *Size:* hoog 19, breed 16 duim	J	(Sold) fl 2:5 Rigters
			Iserman		
1801/04/08	HAVIN	0055	*Yzerman* | Een schryvende Grysaart		(Unknown)
			Isretman [Unidentified]		
1809/07/19	AMSCH	[A0004][H]	*Isretman* | 1 Blomstukkie | *Notes:* This lot was added in by hand in the AA copy of the catalogue. Because it was not numbered, we have assigned the number.		(Unknown)
			Jacht, J. van der [Unidentified]		
1802/09/21	UTHDG	0051	*J. van der Jacht* | Een Landschap, rijk gestoffeerd met Rijmijen, Jagers, Wandelaars, en een menigte andere voorwerpen. Uitvoerig en fraai geschildert | *Mat:* op doek *Size:* hoog 17, breed 21 ½ duimen		(Bought In) fl 14
			Jacobsz., Juriaen		
1801/06/10	AMSCH	0091	*Jacobs. (J.)* | Eenige Jagers te paard en te voet; met hunne Honden vervolgende een Hart, meesterlyk behandeld | *Mat:* op doek *Size:* hoog 34, breed 55 duim	Herman ten Kate	(Sold) fl 13:10 Spruit van Gend
1803/08/24	HGKAN	0053	*Jacobson* | Het Afbeedzel [sic] van een Geleerde, zittende voor een Tafel met verscheiden Boeken, een Globe, en verder Bywerk | *Mat:* op paneel *Size:* hoog 24, breet 19 duim	[Teissier] [or others]	(Sold) fl 11:5 Teissier
1805/10/09	HGBSM	0116	*Jacobsen* | In een binne vertrek zit een oude grysaard, neevens hem een tafel met boeken en papier, uitvoerig geschildert op paneel | *Mat:* op paneel *Size:* hoog 24 breet 18 duim	T H van Willigen [or others]	(Sold) fl 8:5 De Gelder
			Jacobsz., Lambert		
1802/07/27	AKHRK	0044	*Lambert Jacobs, 1628* | De boetvaardige Magdalena, zeer beweeglijk en fraai geschilderd | *Mat:* op doek *Size:* hoog 23 ½, breed 18 ½ duim *Inscr:* Lambert Jacobs, 1628 (signed and dated?) *Notes:* It is unclear whether the name and date are inscribed on the painting.	Maria Stategaart	(Sold) fl 20:10 for lots 44 & 45. Meyer
1802/07/27	AKHRK	0045	*Lambert Jacobs, 1628* | De berouwhebbende Petrus, de Gemoedsbeweging is zeer wel uitgedrukt | *Inscr:* 1628 (dated?) *Notes:* It is unclear whether the date is inscribed on the painting.	Maria Stategaart	(Sold) fl 20:10 for lots 44 & 45. Meyer
			Jagt, Martinus van der (copy by)		
1806/11/24	AMSCH	0036	*Jaght (M. van der); A. v. Ostade* | Een Boeren Binnenhuis, gestoffeert men Mans, Vrouw, en Kinderen, zich met eeten en drinken vermaakende;	Munnikhuizen	(Sold) fl 14 du Pree

			verders vertoont zig verscheide Huisraad; alles uitvoerig behandeld naar A. v. Ostade | copy by M. Jagt after A. Ostade *Mat:* op paneel *Size:* hoog 11, breed 9 duim		

Jansen

1802/07/20	MGSAN	0063	*Jansens* | Een fraai Schildery, op Doek | *Mat:* op doek *Size:* hoog duim 23 ½, breed duim 21		(Unknown)
1808/12/30	HGIMM	[0071g]	*Janson* | Voorts een exquis kabinetje Schilderijen van voorname Nederlandsche Meesters, welke uit hoofde van de kortheid des tijds niet stuk voor stuk kunnen beschreven worden; doch waarvan de beschrijving op den Kijkdag zal voorhanden zijn. Dus wij hier alleen de namen van eenige dier Meesters laten volgen, als: A. Kuyp, Ruysdaal, Karel du Jardyn, Loqwi ('t beste dat hij schilderde) Hondekoeter, van Dyk, Janson, Moesgever, Kamphuyzen, van Gooijen, A. van der Neer, T. Wyk, Huchtenburgh, Zolemaker, van Hassel, A. Vermeulen, van Dongen, Scheffer, van Os enz. | *This Lot:* Een Schilderij, Janson *Notes:* Because this lot was not numbered in the catalogue, we have assigned the number.		(Unknown)

Jansen (or Jansen, manner)

1803/07/14	MGKLY	0029	*Janse* | Twee stuks een met Muziek, en een met dood Wild en Vrugten, extra ryk van ordonnantie en uitvoerig geschilderd, door Janse of in zyn Manier	Mr Caspar Jacob van Citters	(Unknown)

Jansen, R. [Unidentified]

1809/07/25	HGBSM	0141	*R. Jansen* | Een Attaque van Ruitery | *Mat:* op paneel *Size:* hoog 10 en een half, breed 20 en een half duim	D van der Aa [or] E B ten Dall	(Sold) fl 1:8 Penning

Janson, Johannes

1801/04/08	HAVIN	0014	*Janson* | Een Landschap met Koeijen en Schapen		(Unknown)
1801/05/11	AMSCH	0038	*J. Janson* | Twee stuks, een zomer en een winter, fraay met beelden en beesten gestoffeerd, bevallig van ordinantie en zonachtig behandeld | *Mat:* op paneel *Size:* hoog 12, breed 15 duim	P[ruyssenaar]	(Sold) fl 43 van Iperen
1801/10/19	AMSCH	0033	*Janson. (J.)* | Een fraay duynächtig Landschap met Geboomte, Beelden, Koeijen en Schaapen; zeer uitvoerig geschilderd | companion to lot 34 *Mat:* op paneel *Size:* hoog 13, breed 17 duim	Jonkheer Menno Baron van Coehoorn	(Sold) fl 80 for lots 33 & 34. van der Schleij [for] A
1801/10/19	AMSCH	0034	*Janson. (J.)* | Een dito [Landschap], zynde een weederga, meede zeer uitvoerig gepenseeld | companion to lot 33 *Mat:* op paneel *Size:* hoog 13, breed 17 duim	Jonkheer Menno Baron van Coehoorn	(Sold) fl 80 for lots 33 & 34. van der Schleij [for] A
1801/10/19	AMSCH	0035	*Janson. (J.)* | Een fraay Landschapje met een drinkende Koe, Schaap en Bokjes, en in 't verschiet een Herder | companion to lot 36 *Mat:* op paneel *Size:* hoog 8 ½, breed 7 ½ duim	Jonkheer Menno Baron van Coehoorn	(Sold) fl 40 for lots 35 & 36. van der Schleij [for] A
1801/10/19	AMSCH	0036	*Janson. (J.)* | Een dito [Landschap] tot een weederga, zynde een bergachtig Landschap | companion to lot 35 *Mat:* op paneel *Size:* hoog 8 ½, breed 7 ½ duim	Jonkheer Menno Baron van Coehoorn	(Sold) fl 40 for lots 35 & 36. van der Schleij [for] A
1802/05/05	AMSCH	0084	*J. Jansson* | Een Gezicht in de Stad Leyden, zynde een Besneeuwde Winter, bevallig en eigenaartig gestoffeerd en zonächtig | *Mat:* op paneel *Size:* hoog 12, breed 16 duim	A	(Sold) fl 22:10 for lots 84 & 85. v d^{r} Schleij [for] Rijfsnijder
1802/05/05	AMSCH	0085	*J. Jansson* | Een Bevroozen Rivier, met verscheide Schaatzeryders en Yssleeden gestoffeerd, bevallig | *Mat:* op paneel *Size:* hoog 12 ½, breed 16 ½ duim	A	(Sold) fl 22:10 for lots 84 & 85. v d^{r} Schleij [for] Rijfsnijder
1802/05/05	AMSCH	0086	*J. Jansson* | Een Gezicht aan de Leydsche Vaart, gestoffeerd, met een Herder, met Schaapen en andere Beestjes, zonachtig | *Mat:* op koper *Size:* hoog 10, breed 14 duim	A	(Sold) fl 8:10 Spruit
1802/05/05	AMSCH	0087	*J. Jansson* | Twee stuks bevallige Land- en Watergezichtjes, zynde het eene een Maneschyn, uitvoerig | *Mat:* op paneel *Size:* hoog 6, breed 8 duim	A	(Sold) fl 13 Ackina
1802/05/05	AMSCH	0088	*J. Jansson* | Een Gezicht op het Slot te Heemstede, gestoffeerd met Beeldjes en Rydtuigen, uitvoerig | *Mat:* op doek *Size:* hoog 26, breed 34 duim	A	(Bought In) fl 31
1802/05/05	AMSCH	0089	*J. Janson* | Een Gezicht op Halfweg Haarlem, van den Huizen Zwanenburg naar Haarlem ziende, gestoffeerd met een menigte Beesten, uitvoerig | *Mat:* op paneel *Size:* hoog 14, breed 17 duim	D	(Sold) fl 32 B^{d} Kooij
1802/05/05	AMSCH	0090	*J. Janson* | Een stil Water, met een Hooischip en verscheide andere Vaartuigen, zeer natuurlyk en fiks geschilderd | *Mat:* op doek *Size:* hoog 16, breed 19 duim	D	(Bought In) fl 27
1802/06/28	AMSCH	0087	*J. Jansson* | Een stil Water met Scheepen en Vissers, zynde een natuurlyk Maanligt; op Panneel | *Mat:* op paneel *Size:* hoog 11, breed 12 duim	Anna Elink	(Sold) fl 9:10 Geld
1802/08/24	LNDLS	0033	*De Oude J. Janzon* | Een Bergächtig Landschap met Geboomte, ter regter zijde een rustend Mannetje en een Hond bij een rustende Koe, ter linker zijde eenige Koeijen en Schaapen die door het Water gaan, en een aangenaam verschiet. Helder en plaisant op Mahonyhout paneel, door den Ouden J. Janzon, 1781 | *Mat:* op mahoniehout paneel *Size:* hoog 16, breed 21 ½ duimen *Inscr:* J. Janzon, 1781 (signed and dated?) *Notes:* It is unclear whether the name and date are inscribed on the painting.	Leonardus Bouman [or others]	(Unknown) fl 37

1802/08/24	LNDLS	0034	*De Oude J. Janzon* | Een Bergächtig Landschap met antique Gebouwen op eene hoogte, ter linker zijde langs een Rivier een weg daar een man te paard zittende, gevolgd van een ander te voet, eenige Koeijen en Schaapen voordrijft. Krachtig, in den trant van de Heus | *Mat:* op paneel *Size:* hoog 11 ½, breed 15 ½ duimen *Notes:* It is unclear whether the date is inscribed on the painting.	Leonardus Bouman [or others]	(Unknown) fl 13:10
1802/08/24	LNDLS	0035	*De Oude J. Janzon* | Twee stuks Landschapjes, met rustende en staande Koeijen en een Paard. Uitvoerig op paneel | *Mat:* op paneel *Size:* hoog 7, breed 8 duimen	Leonardus Bouman [or others]	(Unknown) fl 12:10
1802/08/24	LNDLS	0073	*J. Janzon* | Een aangenaam Landschap met Boomen, langs dezelve een Watertje, op den Voorgrond een Man die Koeijen en Schaapen langs den Weg drijft. Zeer uitvoerig, door J. Janzon, gestoffeerd op doek | *Mat:* op doek *Size:* hoog 12 ½, breed 14 ½ duimen	Leonardus Bouman [or others]	(Unknown) fl 15
1802/08/24	LNDLS	0074	*J. Janzon* | Een Hollandsch Landschap met Willig Geboomte, op den Voorgrond een fraai rood-bonte Koe, en een Dorp in 't verschiet. Zeer uitvoerig op paneel | *Mat:* op paneel *Size:* hoog 9 ½, breed 12 ½ duimen	Leonardus Bouman [or others]	(Unknown) fl 10:5
1802/08/24	LNDLS	0075	*J. Janzon* | Een Bergächtig Landschap met hooge Boomen, op den Voorgrond staat een rood – bond gevlekten Os, benevens een liggend Schaap. Uitvoerig op doek, door denzelven [J. Janzon], 1766 | *Mat:* op doek *Size:* hoog 19, breed 15 duimen *Inscr:* 1766 (dated?) *Notes:* It is unclear whether the date is inscribed on the painting.	Leonardus Bouman [or others]	(Unknown) fl 14:10
1802/09/21	UTHDG	0046	*J. Janson* | Aan den waterkant, bij een Wilgenboom, ligt een witte, en staat een rood bonte Koe, verder Schapen en een aangenaam verschiet. Uitvoerig, zonägtig, en van de beste zoort van J. Janson | *Mat:* op paneel *Size:* hoog 13 ½, breed 10 ½ duimen		(Sold) fl 28 Niekerk
1802/09/21	UTHDG	0047	*J. Janson* | Twee stuks. In het eerste ziet men op een ruim veld eenige beesten weiden, de voorsten zijn een staande Koe, twee Schapen en een Bok: in de wederga wordt een Koe gemolken bij een Boerewoning enz. Beiden niet minder dan het voorgaande | *Mat:* op paneel *Size:* hoog 11 ½, breed 13 ½ duimen		(Sold) fl 50 G Bierman
1802/09/21	UTHDG	0048	*J. Janson* | Een leggende en een grazende Koe en Schaap in een Weiland, als voren door denzelven [J. Janson] | *Mat:* op doek *Size:* hoog 14, breed 18 ½ duimen		(Bought In) fl 21
1802/09/21	UTHDG	0049	*J. Janson* | Hoog geboomte aan den oever eener Rivier, op welken tegens den voorgrond een Visschers Schuit enz. Dit stukje, zijnde een Maaneschijn, is natuurlijk geschildert | *Mat:* op paneel *Size:* hoog 13 ⅓, breed 17 ½ duimen		(Sold) fl 9 Proff Bleuland
1802/09/21	UTHDG	0050	*J. Janson* | Koebeesten in een Land, vooraan een Man over het hek leunende		(Bought In) fl 2
1802/11/01	DOBRA	0029	*J. Janson* | Een zonnig Landschapje, met beestjes; uitvoerig | *Mat:* op paneel	Paulus van der Spyk [or others]	(Sold) fl 6:5 Randwyk
1802/11/01	DOBRA	0170	*Jacobus Janson* | Een maaneschyn in een landschap met geboomte en boeren wooningen, verbeeldende het gezigt van den Doorslag, by Utrecht, komende van Ysselstein | *Mat:* op paneel *Size:* hoog 13, breed 18 ½ duim		(Unknown) fl 6
1802/11/01	DOBRA	0172	*J. Janson* | Twee stuks plaisante bergagtige en boomryke Landschapjes, en een Waterval, met Beelden en Beesten, uitvoerig en helder | *Mat:* op paneel *Size:* hoog 8 ½, breed 11 ½ duim		(Unknown) fl 18:10
1802/11/01	DOBRA	0174	*Jacobus Janson* | Een weerga tot het voorige, verbeeldende een rustende, en twee staande Koeijen, op een heuvel in een Landschap, met een Dorp in 't verschiet | copy by J. Janson after Paulus Potter; companion to lot 173 *Notes:* This lot was sold with lot 173, which is a copy by J. Janson after Paulus Potter.		(Unknown) fl 22 for lots 173 & 174
1802/11/01	DOBRA	0179	*J. Janson* | Twee stuks gestoffeerde Gezigten, het eene het Dorp Vlijmen, het andere het Dorp Engelen | *Mat:* op paneel *Size:* hoog 9 ½, breed 12 ½ duim		(Unknown) fl 8:10
1802/11/01	DOBRA	0181	*J. Janson* | Een Winter: ter regterzyde een weg langs Boeren and andere woningen, by een brug; gestoffeerd met een Wagen en Narresleeden. Wyders op het besneeuwde Ys een meenigte wandelende, en op de geveegde baan Schaatsen rydende Lieden. In het verschiet een Dorp | *Mat:* op paneel *Size:* hoog 15, breed 21 duim		(Sold) fl 18 Braam
1802/11/01	DOBRA	0183	*J. Janson* | Een Riviergezigtje, met zeilende en andere Vaartuigen, by Maanligt | *Mat:* op paneel *Size:* hoog 7 ½, breed 9 duim		(Unknown) fl 3
1804/02/27	AMSCH	0060	*Janson. (J.)* | In een aangenaam besneeuwd Wintertje, ziet men een menigte van Schaatzerydende en wandelende Perzoonen; uitvoerig gepenceeld | *Mat:* op paneel *Size:* hoog 8, breed 11 duim	D	(Sold) fl 1 J Yver
1804/08/08	AMSCH	0094	*J. Janson* | In een met hoog Geboomte grazige Weide staat een Boer met een Bul, ter zyde eenig grazend en leggend Vée, en een Dorp in het verschiet; kragtig op Koper | *Mat:* op koper *Size:* hoog 16, breed 22 duim	Roos a	(Sold) fl 24 Salomon Joseph
1804/08/08	AMSCH	0095	*J. Janson* | In een Veldgezicht met een stil Water, waarin drie Eenden zwemmen, ziet men een ménigte van staand en rustend Vée, waarby hunne Herder, by eenig Geboomte; verders een Boomryk verschiet; uitvoerig en zonachtig | *Mat:* op paneel *Size:* hoog 11 ½, breed 14 duim	Vink[eles] [for] W	(Sold) fl 3 Van Iperen

1804/10/29	HRBAU	0043	*Janson, (J.)* | Een zeer fraai Hollandsch Land- en Watergezigt, met boomgewassen beplant; ziende men, onder een' Flapbrug door in een aangenaam verschiet; rykelyk gestoffeerd met Visschers- en andere Schuitjes, Koetjes en Wandelaars. Alles is zeer helder en uitvoerig behandeld | companion to lot 44 *Mat:* op paneel *Size:* hoog 15, breed 19 duim	Simon Styl	(Unknown)
1804/10/29	HRBAU	0044	*Janson, (J.)* | Is mede een zeer bevallig Gezigt, over een' Flapbrug, langs een buurt Huizen, naar een' Moolen en Dorp; aan de overzyde van het water is een Weiland, waar agter een boomagtig verschiet. Alles is als het voorgaande gestoffeerd en niet minder fraai behandeld | companion to lot 43 *Mat:* op paneel *Size:* hoog 15, breed 19 duim	Simon Styl	(Unknown)
1804/10/29	HRBAU	0045	*Janson, (J.)* | Een zeer aardig Landschap by den Winter; het Ys is ryk gestoffeerd met Schaatsenryders en Wandelaars. Zeer natuurlyk en uitvoerig geschilderd | *Mat:* op doek *Size:* hoog 16, breed 20 duim	Simon Styl	(Unknown)
1804/12/10	AMSCH	0031	*J. Janson* | Twee stuks Landschappen, het eene eengrazige Wyde, met koeijen en schaapen, in het andere een Gezicht langs de Vaart na den Haag; beide zonachtig en uitvoerig geschildert | *Mat:* op doek op paneel *Size:* Hoog 18, breed 23 duim	Jan De Groot	(Sold) fl 72 Coclers
1804/12/10	AMSCH	0032	*J. Janson* | Dit bevallig Landschap langs een stil water, is gestoffeerd met een witte en roobonte koei, staande in het water, ter zyde een boere wooning, waar een huisman over de deur ligt, verders hoog geboomte, en een aangenaam verschiet | *Mat:* op paneel *Size:* Hoog 17, breed 22 duim	Jan De Groot	(Sold) fl 39 Coclers
1805/07/03	AMSCH	0098	*J. Janson* | Een Jonge met een Bul voor een Hek staande; uitvoerig op Paneel | *Mat:* op paneel *Size:* hoog 10, breed 12 duim	R[oos]	(Sold) fl 5:10 Tessier
1805/07/10	AMSCH	0085	*J. Janson* | Een bevallig Boomryk Landgezicht, met een helder spiegelend Water, gestoffeerd met een ménigte van staand en rustend Vee, verzelt van een Boer, verders een aangenaam verschiet; en zonachtig behandeld | *Mat:* op paneel *Size:* hoog 12, breed 14 duim	V[inkeles] [for] L	(Bought In) fl 8
1805/12/16	AMSCH	0033	*J. Jansson* | Een Gezicht op den Poort te Haarlem, gestoffeerd met Herders, hun Vée dryvende langs de buitencingel; uitvoerig en zonachtig | *Mat:* op paneel *Size:* hoog en breed 14 duim	R[oos]	(Sold) fl 31 v der Schley [for] R[ijfsnijder]
1806/05/05	AMSCH	0071	*J. Janson* | Op een bevroozen Rivier ziet men een ménigte gaande en rydende Lieden, Marketenters en andere stoffagie; uitvoerig geschildert door J. Janson | *Mat:* op doek *Size:* hoog 17, breed 14 duim	V[inkeles]	(Bought In) fl 11
1806/05/05	AMSCH	0072	*J. Janson* | Een boomryk Landschap, met staand en leggend Vee; zonagtig en uitvoerig behandeld door denzelven [J. Janson] | *Mat:* op paneel *Size:* hoog 17, breed 14 duim	V[inkeles]	(Sold) fl 2:15 du Pree
1806/08/13	AMSCH	0087	*Janson. (J.)* | In een graazigen Weide staat een rosbonte Koe, verder een ander rustende by twee Schaapen, terzyde een hooge willige Boom, in 't verschiet een Boerin met een Melkëmmer en ander grazend Vée; zonachtig en uitvoerig gepenceeld | *Mat:* op paneel *Size:* hoog 12 ½, breed 15 ½ duim	Roos	(Sold) fl 19 Rynbergh
1806/08/13	AMSCH	0088	*Janson. (J.)* | Dit natuurlyk voorwerp verbeeld een Wintergezicht, met besneuwde [sic] Daken en Weegen, gestoffeerd met een Landman en Vée, en eenige Schaatzeryders; uitvoerig gepenceeld | *Mat:* op paneel *Size:* hoog 12, breed 16 duim	Roos	(Sold) fl 20 van Iperen
1806/11/24	AMSCH	0035	*Janson (J.)* | Een Boom- en bergachtig Landschap, met een Waterplas, waarby een Herder, Herderin en verscheide Ossen en Schapen; alles in een warmen toon in de manier van J. Both, zonagtig behandeld | *Mat:* op paneel *Size:* hoog 17, breed 22 duim	Munnikhuizen	(Sold) fl 32:10 du Pree
1807/04/00	LNDLS	0009	*J. Janzon* | In een aangenaam helder Landschap, staat een blaauw bonte koe uit een beekje te drinken, nevens een rood bonte en geele ruetende koe, bij geboomte, en in 't verschiet meer stoffagie, van de uitvoerigste en beste soort van schildering op paneel | companion to lot 10 *Mat:* op paneel *Size:* hoog 9 en een half, breed 11 en en half duim	[Abraham Delfos] [or others]	(Unknown)
1807/04/00	LNDLS	0010	*J. Janzon* | Een weerga niet minder van konst, op de voorgrond rust een rood bont koetje, nevens dezelve een hek bij een water, daar twee koeijen en eenige schapen bij staan, verders geboomte en verschiet op paneel | companion to lot 9 *Mat:* op paneel	[Abraham Delfos] [or others]	(Unknown)
1807/06/10	HGBSM	0009	*J. Janzon* | In een aangenaam helder Landschap, staat een blaauw bonte koe uit een beekje te drinken, nevens een rood bonte en geele rustende koe, bij geboomte, en in 't verschiet meer stoffagie, van de uitvoerigste en beste soort van schildering | companion to lot 10 *Mat:* op paneel *Size:* hoog 9 ½, breed 11 ½ duim	Abraham Delfos [or others]	(Sold) fl 26 Tessier voor Valois
1807/06/10	HGBSM	0010	*J. Janzon* | Een weerga niet minder van konst, op de voorgrond rust een rood bont koetje, nevens dezelve een hek bij een water, daar twee koeijen en eenige schapen bij staan, verders geboomte en verschiet | companion to lot 9 *Mat:* op paneel	Abraham Delfos [or others]	(Unknown)
1807/06/10	HGBSM	0098	*J. Janson* | Een Duinagtig Landschapje, gestoffeerd met een Karretje en meer figuurtjes van de beste tijd | *Mat:* op paneel *Size:* hoog 10, breed 13 duim	Abraham Delfos [or others]	(Sold) fl 9 Tallée
1807/06/10	HGBSM	0099	*J. Janson* | Een Bergagtig Landschapje, gestoffeerd met Koeitjes en Schaapjes, niet minder | *Mat:* op paneel *Size:* hoog 9, breed 11 ½ duim	Abraham Delfos [or others]	(Sold) fl 8:5 Ten Haaf

1807/06/10	HGBSM	0187	*J. Janson* | Een Winter gezichtje met Schaatsereiders | *Mat:* op paneel *Size:* hoog 7 ½, breed 10 duim	Abraham Delfos [or others]	(Sold) fl 3:4 Noordwyk
1808/04/26	GDAN	0079	*Jonson (J.)* | Zijnde een Landschap, rijk met Koeijen en Schapen en ander Vee, gestoffeerd in de manier van Potter, te gelyk het gezigt op de Stad Dordrecht, fraai gedaan | *Size:* hoog 24, breed 31 duim	G H Fortuyn	(Unknown)
1808/04/26	GDAN	0080	*Jonson (J.)* | Een dito Gezigt op Dordrecht, bij 't Magazijn, en de Kraam, waar men eenig Oorlogstuig, Slypsteenen &c ziet, vol gewoel van Menschen, zeer lief gepenseeld | *Size:* hoog 24, breed 31 duim *Notes:* It is unclear what "dito" refers to in the title.	G H Fortuyn	(Unknown)
1808/06/06	RMRIJ	0060	*Janson. (Jacobus)* | Een heuvelachtig Landschap. In hetzelve eene Herberg, een Heer te paard en een Veedrijvende Boer; verder Jagers met Honden, enz. Uitvoerig geschilderd [Paysage Montagneux. Un Cavalier se trouve devant un Cabaret, et un Paysan conduit un Troupeau de Boeufs. Des Chasseurs et des Chiens varient et composent l'Ensemble de ce joli Tableau] | *Annots:* Verk. P. Spyk, Leiden 23 April 1781 (f 45.-) (RMA I) *Mat:* op mahonie paneel *Size:* Hoog 12 ½ en breed 16 ½ duim	Gerrit van der Pot, Heer van Groeneveld	(Sold) fl 70 Netscher
1808/06/11	RMRIJ	0013	*J: Janson, 1775* | Een Hollandsch Landschap, met Koeijen, Bok, Schapen en Figuur; natuurlyk, aangenaam en zeer uitvoerig geschilderd. Op Mahognie Paneel, hoog 17, breed 22 ½ duim. Een Wedergade, in alles als de voorgaande; zullen in eene Koop geveild worden | *Mat:* op mahonie paneel *Size:* hoog 17, breed 22 ½ duim *Inscr:* J: Janson, 1775 (signed and dated?) *Notes:* It is unclear whether the name and date are inscribed on the painting.		(Sold) fl 104 Rohan
1808/06/13	AMSCH	0086	*Jansson (J.)* | Een bergachtig Landschap: op den voorgrond, bij eenig staand en liggend Vee, ziet men een Herder, die met eene Vrouw in gesprek is. Alles doorschijnend en natuurlijk behandeld | *Mat:* op paneel *Size:* hoog 26, breed 23 duim	E M Engelberts	(Sold) fl 82 Th[s] Spaan
1808/06/13	AMSCH	0209	*J. Jansson* | Het Dorp Soeterwoude; uitvoerig	E M Engelberts	(Sold) fl 7 Simons
1808/06/13	AMSCH	0210	*J. Jansson* | Een grazige Weide, waarin een staand en twee liggende Beesten; zonachtig	E M Engelberts	(Sold) fl 14 van Drielst
1808/06/13	AMSCH	0211	*J. Jansson* | Een Duingezicht, met Stoffage van Herders en Vee	E M Engelberts	(Sold) fl 13:10 du Pree
1808/08/23	AMSCH	0084	*Janson. (J.)* | Een grazige Weiden, gestoffeert met Koeijen en Schaapen, ter zijde een zittend Landman aan de kant van een stil Water; bevallig en natuurlijk verbeeld | *Mat:* op paneel *Size:* hoog 11, breed 14 duim	[Van Iperen?]	(Sold or Bought In) fl 12 Van Iperen
1808/11/12	HGSCR	0017	*J. Janzon de Vader* | Twee stuks duinagtige landschappen met geboomte gestoffeerd met beelden en beesten, uitvoerig en fraai geschilderd | *Mat:* op paneel	Mr J van Buren	(Unknown) fl 3
1809/04/22	AMYVR	0061	*J. Jansson* | Een Italiaansch Boom- en Bergachtig Landschap, ter zijde een Water, waarin eenig Vee zich waad, op de voorgrond staande en liggende Beesten, waarbij twee Beeldjes; zonachtig | *Mat:* op paneel *Size:* hoog 17, breed 21 duim	de Bruin	(Sold) fl 30 Remmers Bredius
1809/04/22	AMYVR	0062	*J. Jansson* | Een dito [Italiaansch Boom- en Bergachtig] Landschap, met staand en liggend Vee; als de voorgaande | *Mat:* op doek *Size:* hoog 19, breed 15 duim	de Bruin	(Sold) fl 12 van Raan
1809/06/13	AMSCH	0069	*J. Janson* | Een aangenaam vlak Hollandsch Landschap, met opgaand Geboomten bij Boeren Wooningen, op de voorgrond gestoffeerd met een Landman, die eenig Vee drijft, verders een Boer op een Kar, ter zijde staand en liggend Vee, en een Dorp in het verschiet; zonachtig en uitvoerig geschilderd | *Mat:* op paneel *Size:* hoog 12, breed 16 duim	[Gruyter?]	(Bought In) fl 9
1809/06/13	AMSCH	0069a[H]	*J. Janson* | [Illegible] | *Notes:* This lot was added in by hand in the FLNY copy of the catalogue, but the title is illegible.	Y	(Unknown) fl 1:5
1809/09/06	AMSCH	0028	*Janson (J.)* | Een Boom- en Bergachtig Landschap, met stoffagie van Beelden en Beesten; als de vorige behandeld | *Mat:* op paneel *Size:* hoog 14, breed 12 duim	Johannes Caudri	(Sold) fl 13:10 Thomassen
1809/09/06	AMSCH	0029	*Janson (J.)* | Een grazige Weide, met weelig Geboomten; staand en leggend Vee; uitvoerig van penceelsbehandeling | *Mat:* op koper *Size:* hoog 13, breed 17 duim	Johannes Caudri	(Sold) fl 5:10 L Pakker
1810/03/27	RMCNL	0014	*J. Janssen* | Een Landschap met eene Koe en een Schaap		(Unknown)
1810/03/27	RMCNL	0023	*J. Janssen* | In een Binnenhuisje, zit een Vrouwtje te Naaijen, in eene houding als iets in de Kamer ziende komen, zeer aardig behandeld		(Unknown)
1810/03/27	RMCNL	0048	*J. Janssen* | Een Landschapje; Bergachtig, op den voorgrond Koeijen, Schapen, enz. op den tweeden grond eene oude Burgt, en in 't verschiet den Toorn van een Dorp, tusschen de Bergen gelegen, alles zeer warm en net geschilderd		(Unknown)
1810/05/22	AMSCH	0043	*Janson. (J.)* | Eene grazige Weide, waarin staande en liggende Koeijen, ter zijde voor eene Herberg een Boeren Wagen met twee Paarden bespannen, waarop eene Vrouw en Kind, verder een Hooiberg bij geboomten; warm en uitvoerig geschilderd | *Mat:* op paneel *Size:* hoog 20, breed 24 duim	Johannes van de Putte Nicolaasz.	(Sold) fl 50 T Spaan
1810/05/22	AMSCH	0044	*Janson. (J.)* | Een Wintergezicht langs den Buitensingel, ziende naar een der Poorten der Stad Leyden, met besneeuwde Daken en Wegen, gestoffeerd met wandelende en op Schaatsen-rijdende Lieden; natuurlijk gepenceeld | *Mat:* op paneel *Size:* hoog 12, breed 13 duim	Johannes van de Putte Nicolaasz.	(Sold) fl 9:15 Gruyter

1810/05/22	AMSCH	0045	*Janson. (J.)* | Een Wintergezicht buiten de Muiderpoort te Amsterdam; rijk met Beeldjes gestoffeerd, en natuurlijk behandeld | *Mat:* op paneel *Size:* hoog 12, breed 14 duim	Johannes van de Putte Nicolaasz.	(Sold) fl 15 T Spaan
1810/05/22	AMSCH	0046	*Janson. (J.)* | Een bevrozen Water langs de Vestmuur, buiten de Stad Leyden; rijk met onderscheidene Voorwerpen gestoffeerd, en uitvoerig geschilderd | *Mat:* op paneel *Size:* hoog 9, breed 12 duim	Johannes van de Putte Nicolaasz.	(Sold) fl 4 Gruyter
1810/05/22	AMSCH	0047	*Janson. (J.)* | Een Wintergezicht; eigenaartig gestoffeerd, en als de voorgaande behandeld | *Size:* hoog 9, breed 12 duim	Johannes van de Putte Nicolaasz.	(Sold) fl 5:5 van Iperen
1810/06/06	RMMUY	0126	*J. Janson* | Een uitvoerig Landschap, goed gestoffeerd met Figuren en Beesten | *Mat:* op mahoniehout paneel		(Unknown) fl 7
1810/06/06	RMMUY	0128	*Den ouden Janson* | Een Landschap. Door den ouden Janson | *Mat:* op paneel		(Unknown) fl 1:5
1810/10/11	AMSCH	0037	*J. Janson* | Een Landschap met staande en liggende Beesten bij een Hek en Geboomte | *Mat:* op paneel *Size:* hoog 15, breed 12 duimen	S	(Sold) fl 3:10 Gruiter
1810/10/11	AMSCH	0038	*J. Janson* | Een aangenaam Landschap met Boeren-Woningen en Geboomten, rijk gestoffeerd met Landlieden en Vee; zonachtig en uitvoerig gepenceeld | *Mat:* op paneel *Size:* hoog 14, breed 17 duimen	[Gruyter?]	(Sold) fl 8:10 van Leen
1810/10/11	AMSCH	0039	*J. Janson* | Twee stuks, een Zomer- en Wintergezigt, beide eigenaartig gestoffeerd en uitvoerig geschilderd | *Mat:* op paneel *Size:* hoog 10, breed 9 duimen	[Levy Pakker?]	(Sold) fl 7 van Iperen
1810/11/07	UTWLD	0009	*Janson* | Twee stuks zeer geestige Landschapjes met staande en liggende Koejen en rijzend geboomte, zeer uitvoerig en helder door Janson op paneel, ieder 6 en een half duim hoog, 7 en een half duim breed, verg. Lijsten | *Mat:* op paneel *Size:* ieder 6 en een half duim hoog, 7 en een half duim breed		(Unknown) fl 13:10

Janson, Johannes (and Monte)

1810/03/27	RMCNL	0031	*J. Janssen; Monté* | Een Landschapje, geschilderd door J. Janssen, en gestoffeerd door Monté		(Unknown)

Janson, Johannes (copy by)

1802/11/01	DOBRA	0173	*Jacobus Janson; Paulus Potter* | Een bruinbonte Koe, grazende, benevens een roodbonte, rustende; wat verder een witte, die door een meisje gemolken word, by hoog geboomte; kunstig gevolgd naar het Schildery van Paulus Potter, door Jacobus Janson | copy by J. Janson after Paulus Potter; companion to lot 174 *Mat:* op paneel *Size:* hoog 16 ½, breed 14 duim *Notes:* This lot was sold with lot 174 by J. Janson.		(Unknown) fl 22 for lots 173 & 174
1809/09/06	AMSCH	0030	*Janson (J.); P. Potter* | Een bevallige Copij naar een stukje van P. Potter, zijnde een Ordinantie van twee staande en een leggend Koebeest; uitvoerig en zonagtig gepenceeld | copy by J. Janson after Paulus Potter *Mat:* op doek *Size:* hoog 16, breed 14 duim	Johannes Caudri	(Sold) fl 41 Gruyter

Janson, Johannes (or Janson, J., manner)

1810/06/06	RMMUY	0124	*den Ouden Janson* | Een Landschap, met Koeijen en Schapen, uitvoerig geschilderd. Door of als den Ouden Janson | companion to lot 125 *Mat:* op paneel		(Unknown) fl 91 for lots 124 & 125
1810/06/06	RMMUY	0125	*den Ouden Janson* | Een Wedergade, als boven behandeld [Door of als den Ouden Janson] | companion to lot 124 *Mat:* op paneel		(Unknown) fl 91 for lots 124 & 125

Janson, Johannes (copy after)

1801/03/16	AMSCH	0133	*J. Jansson* | Twee stuks Landschappen met Beesten, na J. Jansson	K[ip]	(Sold) fl 5 van Iperen

Janson, Johannes Christianus

1801/03/31	HGCLF	0385	*J.C. Janson* | Twee stuks zynde een Boertje en Boerinne over de onderdeur leggende door J.C. Janson, swarte lyste met vergulde binne rande	H van der Hoop	(Sold) fl 11:10 van d[r] Foorn
1802/08/24	LNDLS	0038	*J.C. Janzon* | Een Binnenhuisje daar een Vrouw met een kind op haar schoot bij een Wieg zit, als sprekende tegen een Vrouwtje die nevens haar staat, verder eenig huisraad aan den wand; door een deur ziet men in een ander Vertrek. Alles zeer uitvoerig door J. C. Janzon, op paneel | *Mat:* op paneel *Size:* hoog 13, breed 11 ½ duimen	Leonardus Bouman [or others]	(Unknown) fl 32
1804/12/10	AMSCH	0033	*J. C. Janson* | In een grazige Wyde, by een stil water, staat een ros-bonte koe te drinken, daar neven een rustende, verder zit een Boerin te melken, waar by een Huisman met een emmer aan de hand, en ter zyde een Boere Woning by geboomten; zonachtig en uitvoerig gepenceeld | *Mat:* op paneel *Size:* Hoog 12 ½, breed 14 duim	Jan De Groot	(Sold) fl 37 Josi
1804/12/10	AMSCH	0034	*J.C. Janson* | Voor een Open steenen Nis staat een Keukenmeisje, houdende een doode Haas in de hand, verders een haardsteede en gestoffeert met verscheide huisselyk gereedschap; plaisant behandeld | *Mat:* op paneel *Size:* Hoog 11, breed 10 duim	Jan De Groot	(Sold) fl 46 Moll
1804/12/10	AMSCH	0035	*J. C. Janson* | Twee stuks Landgezichten, beide gestoffeerd met grazende en rustende koeijen en schaapen; zonachtig en bevallig van penceels behandeling | *Size:* Hoog 12, breed 15 duim	Jan De Groot	(Sold) fl 48 van Iperen
1804/12/10	AMSCH	0036	*J. C. Janson* | Twee stuks Wintergezichten, met bevrooze rivieren en verscheide beeldjes gestoffeerd, in het eene ziet men een maaneschyn;	Jan De Groot	(Sold) fl 29 Gruyter

			beide plaisant van schildering | *Mat:* op paneel *Size:* Hoog 11, breed 13 duim		
1804/12/10	AMSCH	0037	*J. C. Janson* | By een boere woning en hoog geboomte ziet met een Wegh, waar op een Jongeling met een Bul, hy blaast op zyn hoorn, ter zyde een Landgezicht met rustend Vee, en een bevallig verschiet, alles is zonagtig en uitvoerig geschilderd | *Mat:* op paneel *Size:* Hoog 13, breed 15 duim	Jan De Groot	(Sold) fl 27 Coclers
1804/12/10	AMSCH	0038	*J. C. Janson* | Een zonachtig Landschap, ryk gestoffeerd met Koeijen en Schaapen, ter zyde een boeren Wooning; alles uitvoerig behandeld | *Mat:* op paneel *Size:* Hoog 16, breed 22 duim	Jan De Groot	(Sold) fl 25 van Iperen
1804/12/10	AMSCH	0039	*J. C. Janson* | Een Gezicht buiten Haarlem, met een drift Beesten gestoffeerd; zonachtig van schildering | *Mat:* op paneel *Size:* Hoog 16, breed 21 duim	Jan De Groot	(Sold) fl 19:15 J Spaan
1804/12/10	AMSCH	0040	*J. C. Janson* | Een Landgezicht met twee staande en een leggende Koey, en bevallig verschiet; fiks en uitvoerig gepenceeld | *Mat:* op paneel *Size:* Hoog 13, breed 16 duim	Jan De Groot	(Sold) fl 21 Joh[s] Remmers
1808/11/12	HGSCR	0004	*J.C. Janzon* | Een burgerwoning van binnen te zien, waar in een vrouwtje zittende met haar kind aan de borst, aan wien door een andere vrouw nevens haar staande een glas bier word aangeboden, een jonge zit op de voorgrond te leezen en op een stoel een hond, het ligt en donker doet in dit schildery een zeer schone uitwerking, al de voorwerpen en huisraad zyn kunstig, uitvoerig en kragtig geschilderd door J.C. Janzon en een der fraaiste van deze meester | *Mat:* op paneel *Loc:* Amsterdam, Nederland. Rijksmuseum. (A 1052)	Mr J van Buren	(Unknown) fl 210
1810/05/22	AMSCH	0048	*Janson. (J. C.)* | Voor een Boeren Woning op een Steenen Bank zit een vergenoegd bejaard Huisman zijn Pijp te rooken, voor hem staat eene Vrouw, houdende een Kind aan de hand, voorts eenige Hoenders en verder bijwerk; bevallig en natuurlijk voorgesteld | *Mat:* op paneel *Size:* hoog 13 ½, breed 12 duim	Johannes van de Putte Nicolaasz.	(Sold) fl 36 van Iperen
1810/05/22	AMSCH	0049	*Janson. (J. C.)* | Een bevrozen Rivier, ter zijde Boeren Woningen en een Brug, gestoffeerd met Schaatsenrijders, IJssleeden, Paarden en andere Voorwerpen; natuurlijk behandeld | *Mat:* op paneel *Size:* hoog 15, breed 18 ½ duim	Johannes van de Putte Nicolaasz.	(Sold) fl 9:5 Rutten
1810/06/06	RMMUY	0123	*Janson* | Een Binnenvertrek, waar eene zittende Vrouw een boterham snijd; een biddend Jongetje staat nevens haar aan eene Tafel, verzeld van een Hond. Uitvoerig en natuurlijk | *Mat:* op paneel		(Sold) fl 67 v Dongen
			Janson, Johannes Christianus (and Janson, P.)		
1810/06/06	RMMUY	0127	*de Gebroeders Janson* | Een Landschap, op den voorgrond een Man den Hoorn blazende, daar bij een kloeken Stier; verder een aangenaam en veerijk verschiet. Konstig en krachtig. Door de Gebroeders Janson | *Mat:* op mahoniehout paneel		(Unknown) fl 63
			Janson, Pieter		
1801/03/16	AMSCH	0057	*P. Janson* | Een Landschap, gestoffeerd met staande en leggende Beesten	P[ruyssenaar]	(Sold) fl 10:10 Roelofs
1801/12/22	AMOTT	0075	*P. Jansen* | Weidende Koeitjes en Schaapen in het Land by een Boere wooning	Bartholomeus Ruloffs	(Unknown) fl 9
1802/08/24	LNDLS	0037	*Pieter Janzon* | Een Hollandsch Landschap met hoog Geboomte en Boeren Woningen, op den Voorgrond een Man die zes Koeijen van differente couleur langs den weg drijft, in 't verschiet meer Vee. Dit stuk is zeer konstig, krachtig, vet in de verw, en geheel in de manier der Ossendrift van Paulus Potter | *Mat:* op paneel *Size:* hoog 21, breed 28 duimen	Leonardus Bouman [or others]	(Unknown) fl 175
1808/06/11	RMRIJ	0021	*P: Janson, in de manier van J: van Ostade* | Een plaisant Landgezicht, verbeeldende een Winter, met fraaije Stoffagie; zeer natuurlyk, uitvoerig en verdienstelyk | *Mat:* op paneel *Size:* hoog 15 ¾, breed 20 duim		(Sold) fl 36:10 Thomassen
1808/06/11	RMRIJ	0096	*P: Janson, 1793* | Een Hollands Landschap vol Beesten en Figuren, in de manier van Potter, extra uitgevoerd, zonachtig en verdienstig geschilderd | *Mat:* op paneel *Size:* hoog 15 ½, breed 21 ½ duim *Inscr:* P: Janson, 1793 (signed and dated?) *Notes:* It is unclear whether the name and date are inscribed on the painting.		(Sold) fl 31:10 Thomas [or] Van Giesen
1808/11/12	HGSCR	0002	*P. Janzon* | Een landschap met een opgaande weg en brug by den vroege morgenstond, gestoffeerd met vyf koeijen in verschillende actien, welke door een Huisman gedreeven worden, uitmuntend, uitvoerig en natuurlyk gepenseeld, door P. Janzon een der beste stukken van deezen meester | *Mat:* op paneel	Mr J van Buren	(Unknown) fl 120
1809/04/17	AMSCH	0042	*P. Janson* | In een Hollandsch Landschap ziet men op de voorgrond een grasende rood bonte Os en twee zwart bonte liggende Koeijen, verder bij de Stam van een Boom eenige Schapen, agterwaarts aan een Water eenige Boere Woningen; uitvoerig van penceel behandeling | *Mat:* op paneel *Size:* hoog 17 ½, breed 14 duim	[Gruyter?]	(Sold) fl 20
1809/04/17	AMSCH	0151	*P. Janson* | Een Boomrijk Landschap, met Boerenwoningen en staand en liggend Vee; zonachtig en uitvoerig | *Mat:* op paneel	[Gruyter?]	(Sold) fl 3
			Janson, Pieter (and Janson, J.C.)		
1810/06/06	RMMUY	0127	*de Gebroeders Janson* | Een Landschap, op den voorgrond een Man den Hoorn blazende, daar bij een kloeken Stier; verder een aangenaam en		(Unknown) fl 63

veerijk verschiet. Konstig en krachtig. Door de Gebroeders Janson | *Mat:* op mahoniehout paneel

Janssens, Hieronymus

1804/03/27	MGSAN	0007	*G. Janssens* | Een extra schoon en plaisant Stuk, verbeeldende een Tuingezigt met veele Tuincieraden, verder een grootsch Gebouw, waaraan een Gaandery door Pylaaren ondersteund, voor het Gebouw een als met steenen belegde Vloer, waarop eenige zittende en staande Heeren en Dames, zich onder elkanderen amuseerende met het speelen van Handje-plak en het Dansen van een Ballet, waarby een Fiool- en Basspeelder, alles zeer krachtig doch zacht gepenseeld, door G. Janssens, in vergulde Lyst | *Mat:* op doek *Size:* hoog 24 ½ duim x breed 31 duim		(Unknown)

Jelgersma, Tako Hajo

1809/05/26	HADAA	0070	*Tako Jelgersma* | Twee Grauwtjes	Mejuffrouw de Wed David Heemskerk [or others]	(Unknown)
1809/05/26	HADAA	0083	*Tako Jelgersma* | Twee ten voeten uit, in het grauw, zijnde Bacchus en Venus	Mejuffrouw de Wed David Heemskerk [or others]	(Unknown)

Jelgersma, Tako Hajo (copy by)

1802/06/16	AMSCH	0086	*J.H. Jelgersma; na C. Saftleven* | Dit stuk stelt voor den Olden Barnevelt onder zyn Rechters voorgesteld; en verscheiden soorten van Gediertens, fiks en zeer natuurlyk na het Orgineel behandeld | copy by T.H. Jelgersma after C. Saftleven *Mat:* op doek *Size:* hoog 25, breed 31 ½ duim	[Merrem]	(Sold) fl 14 de Meijer

Jode, Pieter de

1803/08/01	AMSCH	0013	*Jode. (P. de)* | Twee stuks, een Bybelsche en een andere Ordonantie, ryk gestoffeerd met beelden en ander bywerk, kragtig gepenceeld | *Mat:* op paneel *Size:* ieder hoog 17, breed 10 duim	J	(Sold) fl 18 Haffner
1805/07/10	AMSCH	0084	*P. de Jode* | Twee stuks Bybelsche Ordinantiën, vol gewoel van Beelden, lugtig op Doek, fraay gepenceeld | *Mat:* op paneel *Size:* hoog 17 ½, breed 10 ½ duim	V[inkeles] [for] H[affner]	(Bought In) fl 3

Johnson, Cornelius (I)

1802/09/21	UTHDG	0052	*Janson van Keulen* | Het afbeeldzel eener aanzienelijke vrouw, bevallig van voorkomen, en deftig gekleed, zijnde met beide de handen en meest van voren gekozen. Dit helder schilderij is malsch, krachtig en uitvoerig behandeld | *Mat:* op doek *Size:* hoog 32, breed 26 duimen		(Bought In) fl 25
1806/08/13	AMSCH	0085	*C. Jansens. (van Kleef)* | 't Pourtrait van Burgemeester N. Tulp, Professor in de genees- en ontleedkunde en Oprichter van 't Collégium Medicum, halverlyf, zittende voor een Tafel, waarop een doodshoofd geplaatst is; delicaat en uitvoerig en van de beste schildering van deeze meester | *Mat:* op paneel *Size:* hoog 30, breed 27 duim	Vinkeles [for] J	(Bought In) fl 14
1806/08/13	AMSCH	0086	*C. Jansens. (van Kleef)* | 't Afbeeldzel van den beroemde Dichter Overbeek; fraai van Teekening en meesterlyk van schildering | *Mat:* op doek *Size:* hoog 39, breed 31 duim	Vinkeles [for] J	(Sold) fl 1:10 Yver [for] G
1808/06/13	AMSCH	0087	*Janzon van Cleef* | Het Afbeeldsel van den Burgemeester en Hoogleeraar Nikolaas Tulp, Oprigter van het Collegium Medicum alhier: rustende met zijn eene hand op een Doodshoofd, en houdende de andere op de borst. Allerkrachtigst en meesterlijk geschilderd, in de manier van Rembrandt | *Mat:* op paneel *Size:* hoog 31, breed 27 duim	V[inkeles]	(Sold) fl 22 Nieuwenhuisen

Jong, A.P.L. de [Unidentified]

1805/10/21	GRBOL	0032	*A. P. L. de Jong* | Een Binnenvertrek, waar in op de Kaart gespeeld, en gedronken wordt, uitvoerig geschilderd	Gerardus Nicolaus Heerkens	(Unknown)

Jong, J. de [Unidentified]

1809/07/25	HGBSM	0269	*J. de Jong* | De Kruisdraging Christi, ryk gestoffeert met Figuren en vol gewoel | *Mat:* op koper *Size:* hoog 19, breed 25 duim	D van der Aa [or] E B ten Dall	(Sold) fl 11:10 Bakhuyzen

Jonge, M. de [Unidentified]

1804/07/25	DLGRO	0096	*M. de Jonge* | Een fraai stukje, verbeeldende de ontmoeting van David en Abigaël, door M. de Jonge, 1633 op Paneel | *Mat:* op paneel *Size:* hoog 6 ½, breed 9 duim *Inscr:* M. de Jonge, 1633 (signed and dated?) *Notes:* It is unclear whether the name and date are inscribed on the painting.	Mr Franc van der Burch Wz.	(Unknown)
1804/07/25	DLGRO	0097	*M. de Jonge* | Een Boomryk Landschap, met een paar rustende Reizigers &c. door denzelfde [M. de Jonge] op Paneel | *Mat:* op paneel *Size:* hoog 6 ½, breed 9 duim	Mr Franc van der Burch Wz.	(Unknown)
1806/06/07	RMHSN	0093	*M. de Jonge* | De Ontmoeting van David en Abigaël | *Mat:* op paneel	A E K L	(Unknown)

Jongejan, J. [Unidentified]

1802/03/18	HGBAK	0079	*J. Jongejan* | 2 Stuks met Jagers en Honden		(Unknown)
1802/03/18	HGBAK	0080	*J. Jongejan* | 1 Dito [Stuk], verbeeldende eens Mans Hoofd		(Unknown)

Jongh, Claude de

1809/04/17	AMSCH	0041	*C. de Jongh* | Een natuurlijk Land- en Watergezigt, ter zijde een opgaande Weg, naar een oude Poort, gestoffeerd met een Heer te Paard, een gaande Huisman en twee Visschers in een Schuit; natuurlijk geschilderd, door C. de Jongh, 1650 | *Mat:* op paneel *Inscr:* C. de Jongh, 1650 (signed and dated?) *Notes:* It is unclear whether the name and date are inscribed on the painting.	Y	(Sold or Bought In) fl 13

Jongh, Ludolf de

1803/06/20	AMSCH	0008	*L. de Jong* | Een Boschgezicht, ryk van opgaand geboomte, kreupelgewas en aangenaam verschiet; de voorgrond gestoffeert met eenige rustende Jagers, met hunne Paarden en honden, meesterlyk als Waterlo gepenceeld, door L. de Jong, op Doek | *Mat:* op doek *Size:* hoog 51, breed 61	Schley [for] B	(Sold) fl 160 Gruiter
1804/10/16	DLOND	0112	*De Jong* | Een Schermutseling. Une Escarmouche | *Mat:* op paneel *Size:* hoog 11, breed 17		(Unknown)
1805/07/10	AMSCH	0139	*de Jong* | Een hévige Batailje tusschen Paard en Voetvolk | *Mat:* op paneel	V[inkeles] [for] K	(Sold) fl 8 Boelen
1805/07/10	AMSCH	0191	*L. de Jong* | Een Boomryk Landschap aan een Watertje; helder op Paneel | *Mat:* op paneel	R[oos]	(Sold) fl 13:10 Rooyers
1807/06/02	AMHUY	0012	*de Jong* | Een hevige Bataille tusschen Ruitery		(Unknown)
1808/06/11	RMRIJ	0014	*Ludolf de Jongh, 1655* | Een Vrouwe Pourtrait, schoon geschilderd | *Mat:* op paneel *Size:* hoog 27, breed 23 ½ duim *Inscr:* Ludolf de Jongh, 1655 (signed and dated?) *Notes:* It is unclear whether the name and date are inscribed on the painting.		(Sold) fl 9 Luchtmans
1810/06/06	RMMUY	0083	*L. de Jong* | Een kind, dat een Hondje op doet zitten | *Mat:* op doek		(Sold) fl 1:10 Luchtmans

Jongh, W. de [Unidentified]

1801/03/16	AMSCH	0009	*W. de Jongh* | Een Dorpgezicht op de voorgrond, voor een Herberg ziet men een Heer by een gezadeld Paard, die aan een Vrouw een aalmoes geeft; uitvoerig gepenceeld	P[ruyssenaar]	(Bought In) fl 28
1808/10/28	AMVRS	0026	*Jong, (W. de)* | Twee stuks Duinachtige Landschappen, met Wooningen en Geboomte, gestoffeerd met Reizigers en andere Beeldjes. Fiks behandeld | *Mat:* op paneel *Size:* ieder hoog 6 ½, breed 7 ½ duim	Marten Udink	(Sold) fl 17 J de Vries
1810/08/06	AMSCH	0053	*Jongh (W. de)* | Twee aangename en Duinachtige Landschappen, met fraaije stoffage; alles is zeer natuurlijk | *Mat:* op paneel *Size:* Jeder hoog 6 ½, breed 7 ½ duimen	V[ries]	(Bought In) fl 16

Jonkers [Unidentified]

1802/12/13	AMSCH	0208	*Jonkers* | Twee stuks, op Steene Tafels, ziet men verscheide zoorten van Vrugten en Bloemen, op Paneel, krachtig behandeld | *Mat:* op paneel	Florijn [?]	(Sold) fl 1:5 Geld

Jordaens, Hans

1802/08/24	LNDLS	0022	*H. Jordaans* | Eene hevige Bataille, verbeeldende den Strijd van Jason tegen de Amazonen, daar de Koningin van het paard valt in het midden van eene menigte geharnaste Krijgsknechten, strijdende vrouwen en verslagene dooden, bij een Brug, door welkers boog men de Stad der Amazonen in brand ziet. Konstig van Tekening en Schildering | *Mat:* op doek *Size:* hoog 25, breed 32 duimen	Leonardus Bouman [or others]	(Unknown) fl 6:5

Jordaens, Jacob (I)

1801/02/18	AMBOS	0001	*J. Jordaans* | Een fraai en meesterachtig Schildery, verbeeldende de vier Evangelisten met malkander discourerende, meesterachtig en fix geteekend en geschilderd	J Schonevelt	(Unknown)
1801/04/13	AMSCH	0038	*J. Jordaans* | Een Sater met een Nimph, houdende in zyn handen een Mand met Druiven en andere Vrugten, meesterlyk geschilderd | *Mat:* op doek *Size:* hoog 38, breed 31 duim	Pierre Fouquet, junior	(Sold) fl 15 Spruit v Gent
1801/04/13	AMSCH	0039	*J. Jordaans* | Een zingende Sater met korf Druiven in de hand, waarby een blaazende Jongeling, en een jonge Vrouw, behandeld als de voorgaande | *Mat:* op doek *Size:* hoog 56, breed 48 duim	Pierre Fouquet, junior	(Sold) fl 45 Coclers
1801/05/11	AMSCH	0037	*Jordaans* | Een bybelsche Ordonnantie, voorstellende Salomons eerste recht, met een menigte beelden gestoffeert, krachtig van coloriet en meesterlyk van schildering | *Mat:* op doek *Size:* hoog 56, breed 68 duim	P[ruyssenaar]	(Bought In) fl 10
1801/10/06	AMSCH	0037	*J. Jordaans* | Een hevige Batailje, verbeeldende de stryd der Amazoonen [sic], kragtig en meesterlyk gepenceeld | *Mat:* op paneel *Size:* hoog 15, breed 20 duim	M	(Sold) fl 13 Theijs
1802/07/21	HGKAN	0102	*Jordaens* | Een Historieel stuk		(Unknown)
1802/09/29	AMSCH	0074	*J. Jordaans* | Een Bachanaal, hoog 49 ½, breed 47 duim. Doek. Bachus, Ceres, de Liefde, en een Moor; levensgroote, Kniestuk, in een Landschap verbeeld door J. Jordaans [Une Bacchanale représentêe par Bacchus Céres l'amour & un nègre de grandeur naturelle vus à mi corps portants des Raisins & d'autres Fruits de l'automne, le fond offre un Paysage par J. Jordaans.] | *Mat:* op doek *Size:* hoog 49 ½, breed 47 duim	[Labouchere?]	(Sold) fl 0:18 L Pakker
1802/11/01	DOBRA	0034	*Jordaans* | Een Vrouw, staande voor een Tafel, waar op eenige moten Zalm, Vischketel, benevens andere keukengereedschappen; gemerkt	Paulus van der Spyk [or others]	(Sold) fl 6:15 Randwyk

			Jordaans. f. | *Size:* hoog 3 voet 6 duim, breed 3 voet *Inscr:* Jordaans f. (signed)		
1802/11/01	DOBRA	0049	*Jac. Jordaans* | Het bezoek van de Herders in de stal te Bethlehem, ryk van Ordonnantie, vol beelden | *Size:* breed ruim 6, hoog 4 v.	Paulus van der Spyk [or others]	(Sold) fl 50 de Gruijter
1804/07/25	AMSCH	0046	*Jordaans. (J.)* | De Herders aanbidden het Kindje te Betlehem, de Heilige Maagd ziet men zittende, en houdende het Kind Jesus, slapende in haare Armen, waarop zy zeer aandagtig neder ziet, en rondsom dezelven zyn de Herders, die hunnen verwondering en Eerbied door hunne houdingen te kennen geeven; de fraaiheid der Teekening, het kragtige en schoone coloriet, en het frapante licht, makende dit stuk tot een der beste van deeze beroemde meester | *Mat:* op doek *Size:* hoog 48, breed 37 duim		(Sold) fl 75 C S Roos
1804/08/02	BDAN	0007	*J. Jourdaens* | Een zittende Vrouw met een Kind op de schoot, agter haar staande een Man, houdende een brandende Kaars in de hand, waardoor het stuk verligt word, zeer kragtig in Couleur en groots behandelt | *Mat:* op paneel *Size:* b. 20 d. h. 32 d.	J G Calckberner	(Unknown)
1804/10/16	DLOND	0114	*J. Jordaens* | Enige Satyrs, Nymphen, Vruchten en verdere Beelden. Quelques Satyrs, des Nymphes, Fruits & autre Figures | *Mat:* op doek *Size:* hoog 60, breed 70		(Sold) fl 2:5 v Giesen
1806/08/13	AMSCH	0083	*Jordaans. (J.)* | Een Bachenaal van drie Beelden; fraai van coloriet en meesterlyk gepenceeld | *Mat:* op doek *Size:* hoog 53, breed 45 duim	Roos	(Sold) fl 3 Van Iperen
1806/08/13	AMSCH	0084	*Jordaans. (J.)* | Een Vasten Avond vreugd, daar de Koning drinkt, behandeld als de voorgaande | *Mat:* op doek *Size:* hoog 46, breed 65 duim	Roos	(Sold) fl 4:5 L Pakker
1806/08/13	AMSCH	0324	*Jordaans. (J.)* | Een capitaale Ordinantie van vier Beelden en eenig bywerk; schoon van coloriet en schildering | *Mat:* op doek *Size:* hoog 39, breed 35 duim	Vinkeles [for] G[ruyter]	(Sold) fl 2:5 Gruiter
1808/04/26	GDAN	0078	*Jordans (J.)* | Dit uitmuntend Schilderij verbeeld Seneca die met zijn Voeten in een koper Bekken met Vergif staat, en alzo op den linker arm word dood gelaten, terwijl er iemand met opmerkzaamheid op de verandering zyns gelaats, dat zoo zigtbaar is, met de laatste stervende woorden zit op te tekenen, zijnde het bloed dat uit den arm vloeid zeer natuurlyk, de Beelden in 't ligt en bruin meesterlijk getroffen | *Size:* hoog 63, breed 44 duim	G H Fortuyn	(Unknown)
1808/06/13	AMSCH	0085	*Jordaans (J.)* | Silenus zittende op een Ezel, zich vasthoudende aan twee Saters, ter zijde naakte Vrouwen en Kinderen. Alleruitmuntend behandeld | *Mat:* op paneel *Size:* hoog 13, breed 18 duim	R[oos]	(Bought In) fl 99
1808/09/13	HABRU	0044	*Jordaans* | De vier Euangelisten [sic]; meesterlijk en breed behandeld		(Unknown) fl 31
1808/09/13	HABRU	0045	*Jordaans* | Een Satar [sic] en Bachant		(Unknown) fl 9
1808/09/13	HABRU	0046	*Jordaans* | De Heet- en Koudblazers, in 't grauw		(Unknown) fl 0:8
1808/11/28	AMSCH	0096	*J. Jordaans* | Een Romijnsche Krijgsheld, met een Bont Kleed omhangen, houdende een Standaart in de Hand, meesterlijk geschilderd	Z	(Sold) fl 320 Coclers
1809/04/17	AMSCH	0044	*J. Jordaans* | St. Pétrus word in de Gevangenis door de Engelen bezocht; meesterlijk en breed geschilderd | *Mat:* op doek	T	(Sold) fl 10:10 Gruyter
1809/06/13	AMSCH	0068	*J. Jordaans* | Eene deftige gekleeden Vrouw, rijk met Sieraaden omhangen, zij houdt een Medaillon, waarop een Borstbeeld in de hand, hetzelve vertoonende; krachtig, uitvoerig en van de beste schildering | *Mat:* op doek *Size:* hoog 30, breed 25 duim *Loc:* Wien, Oesterreich. Akademie der bildenden Künste. (640) (?)	H[odges]	(Sold) fl 50 Yver
1810/07/23	DOLG2	00HH	*Jordaans* | Een Historie Stuk, door Jordaans, op Doek, in vergulden Lijst | *Mat:* op doek *Size:* Hoog 26, Breed 34 Duim	Pieter Quinting	(Sold) fl 35 A van Strij
1810/07/26	AMSCH	0042	*Jordaens (J.)* | Een Bacchushoofd: meesterlijk geschilderd | *Mat:* op paneel *Size:* hoog 12, breed 10 duimen	Cassino	(Sold) fl 3 Spaan
1810/10/10	MGCIT	0076	*Jordaans* | Loth met zijn Dochters, eerstgemelde in dronkenschap, en met een Beker in de Hand, meesterlijk uitgevoerd	Caspar van Citters	(Unknown)
1810/10/10	MGCIT	0158	*Jordaans* | Een Schilderij, zijnde een Bijbelsche Historiëel; verdienstig geschilderd, en gemerkt Jordaans | *Inscr:* Jordaans (signed) *Notes:* This lot was misnumbered no. 159 and changed in an errata sheet located at the front of the catalogue.	Caspar van Citters	(Unknown)
1810/10/11	AMSCH	0041	*J. Jordaans* | De ontdekking van Calisto, door Diana | *Mat:* op paneel *Size:* hoog 20, breed 27 ½ duimen	C	(Sold) fl 12 Posthumus
1810/10/11	AMSCH	0130	*J. Jordaans* | Een Sater, dragende een Mand met Vruchten, waarbij eene bevallige Nimf | *Mat:* op doek	[Gruyter?]	(Sold) fl 1:10 L^{y} Pakker

Jordaens, Jacob (I) (and Snyders, F.)

1802/05/05	AMSCH	0199	*F. Snyders; Jordaans* | Een Tafel met diverse soorten van Vrugten en Groentens, agter dezelven een bevallige Vrouw, die door een Jongeling geliefkoosd word, meesterlyk geschilderd | *Size:* hoog 68, breed 77 duim	J	(Sold) fl 20 v d Vinne

Jordaens, Jacob (I) (and Utrecht, Adr.)

1808/03/03	HAVIN	0001	*van Utrecht; Jordaans* | Een Tafel met Vrugten en Groentens, als ook dood Wild, waarbij een Man die een Meid tracht te liefkoozen, uitmuntend, door van Utrecht, en de Beelden waarschijnelijk [sic], door Jordaans	Jacobus Spillebout	(Unknown) fl 20

Jordaens, Jacob (I) (or Jordaens, J. (I), manner)

1810/07/23	DOLG2	000W	*Jordaans* | Een levensgroot Manshoofd, verbeeldende een Heiligen, door- of in de manier van Jordaans | *Mat:* op doek *Size:* hoog 30, breed 23 duim	Pieter Quinting	(Sold) fl 2:10 A van Strij

Jordaens, Jacob (I) (copy after)

1801/04/08	HAVIN	0059	*H. Boon; Jordaans* | Een Hist: na Jordaans | copy by H. Boon after J. Jordaens (I)		(Unknown)
1802/09/06	AMSCH	0205	*Jordaans* | Een ryke Ordenantie, voorstellende een drie Konings-Feest; fix gepenceeld naar Jordaans | *Mat:* op doek *Size:* hoog 25, breed 34 duim	J	(Sold) fl 6:10 Van Dijl
1807/06/10	HGBSM	0117	*Jordaans* | Een Silenus op de fluit speelende. na Jordaans | *Mat:* op doek *Size:* hoog 27 ½, breed 21 ½ duim *Notes:* This lot was misnumbered no. 177.	Abraham Delfos [or others]	(Sold) fl 5:10 Colonbon
1807/08/26	AMSCH	0107	*J. Jordaans* | Een Historieele Ordonnantie in een Landschap, zynde de Fabelgeschiedenis van Mercuur en Argus, verders gestoffeerd met eenig Vee; krachtig op Doek geschilderd, naar J. Jordaans | *Mat:* op doek *Size:* hoog 34, breed 42 duim	Yver [for] S	(Sold) fl 4:5 Sardet

Jordaens, Jacob (I) (manner)

1802/05/05	AMSCH	0083	*Jordaans* | Een Capitaale Ordonnantie van een menigten Goden en Godinnen en Nimphen. Meesterlyk geschilderd als Jordaans | *Size:* hoog 59, breed 84 duim	J	(Sold) fl 3:15 Pruijssenaar [for] J
1802/06/28	AMSCH	0086	*Jordaans* | De aanbidding der Herders, meesterlyk als Jordaans | *Mat:* op paneel *Size:* hoog 20, breed 29 duim	B	(Sold) fl 4 Yver
1810/05/22	AMSCH	0143	*Jordaans* | Deze Ordonantie vertoont het Spaansch Heidinnetje, waarbij verscheide Beelden, levensgrooten ter halver lijf; meesterlijk en kloek geschilderd, op Doek, als door Jordaans | *Mat:* op doek	D	(Sold) fl 6 Otte

Josepho [Unidentified]

1809/05/26	HADAA	0050	*Josepho* | Een Bloemstuk, uitvoerig en helder op Paneel door .... Josepho, A^{o} 1661 | *Mat:* op paneel *Inscr:* Josepho, A^{o} 1661 (signed and dated?) *Notes:* It is unclear whether the name and date are inscribed on the painting.	Mejuffrouw de Wed David Heemskerk [or others]	(Unknown)

Juncker, Justus

1805/10/09	HGBSM	0030	*Juncker* | Een oud man, zittende aan een tafel met een tapyt bedekt, waarop een boek, doodshoofd, zandloper &c. extra uitvoerig geschildert | *Mat:* op paneel *Size:* hoog 21 breet 17 duim	T H van Willigen [or others]	(Sold) fl 32:10 Ph Mey
1805/10/09	HGBSM	0041	*Juncker* | Een tafel waarop een mande met vrugten, en een vles met bloemen | *Mat:* op paneel *Size:* hoog 22 breet 32 ½ duim	T H van Willigen [or others]	(Sold) fl 3:8 Zwartsman
1809/04/17	AMSCH	0043	*Juncker* | In een Keukenvertrek zit eene bevallige Dienstmaagd bij de Haardsteede; verder eigenaartig gestoffeerd | *Mat:* op paneel *Size:* hoog 14, breed 12 duim	R	(Sold) fl 3:5

Juweel, Nicolaes

1809/04/22	AMYVR	0063	*N. Juweel* | Een Dame, met zinspeelend bijwerk | *Mat:* op doek *Size:* hoog 15, breed 13 duim	Juff^{r} Julikker	(Sold) fl 0:8 van der Schley

Kalf, Willem

1802/05/05	AMSCH	0096	*W. Kalf* | Op de Binneplaats van een Boerewerf ziet men twee Beelden en verder Bywerk | *Mat:* op paneel *Size:* hoog 11, breed 9 duim	BB	(Sold) fl 7 Stevens
1802/05/11	GRGRW	0034	*W. Kalf* | Een Stil leven [Schilderijen met Olie-Verf; In zwarte Lijsten] | *Mat:* in olyverf *Notes:* The bracketed information in the title appears above lot 1 and refers to lots 1 to 79a.	Arnold Sicco Werumeus	(Unknown)
1803/07/18	AMSCH	0024	*Kalf. (W.)* | Op een Marmere Tafel is geplaatst een Porcelyne Schotel met Vrugten, eenige Metaale Vaasen en ander bywerk, natuurlyk gevolgd en uitvoerig geschilderd [Sur une table de marbre est posée une jatte de porcelaine avec du fruit ; de beaux vases en metail [sic] embellissent ce composé, qui est traité d'une maniere large & facile, produisant un très bel effet.] | *Mat:* op doek *Size:* hoog 33, breed 27 duim	Maria Theresia Andrioli	(Sold) fl 8:10 Menli
1803/09/07	AMSCH	0095	*Kalf* | Een stil Leeven, waarin een Glas, Zilvere Schaal, Bord met Oranje-Appel en Broodje, konstig [Un intérieur, artistement composé d'un verre, d'une tasse d'argent, de petits pains, d'oranges etc.] | *Mat:* op paneel *Size:* hoog 18 ½, breed 13 duim	Smidt	(Sold) fl 1:15 C S Roos
1806/08/20	HGBSM	0179	*W. Kalf* | Een Tafel met een Tapijt bedekt, waar op eene Schotel met Sitroen en Oranje-Appel; verders een Parel d'Amoure Drinkbeker, glaaze Bocaal en ander Bijwerk; zeer natuurlijk door W. Kalf | companion to lot 180 *Mat:* op doek *Size:* hoog 28 ½, breed 24 ½ duim	Macalester Loup [or others]	(Sold) fl 8 Ph Meij
1806/08/20	HGBSM	0180	*W. Kalf* | Een dito Tafel, waar op eene Silvere Schotel en gesneeden Sitroen, tot een wederga | companion to lot 179 *Notes:* It is unclear what "dito" refers to in the title.	Macalester Loup [or others]	(Sold) fl 5:15 Ph Meij
1810/10/10	MGCIT	0093	*Kalf* | Twee Stukken, zynde Hoorns, Schulpen en ander Zeegewas; naar de natuur behandeld.	Caspar van Citters	(Unknown)
1810/10/11	AMSCH	0228	*Kalf* | Een Stil leven	A	(Sold) fl 0:12 Gruiter

1810/12/03	DOBRA	0011	*Kalf* | Een Stilleven, waar in een gekookte Kreeft op een schotel ligt, zilveren Schenkkan en Romers, Wittebrood, enz.; uitvoerig en delikaat geschilderd		(Unknown)
			Kalraet		
1802/09/21	UTHDG	0055	*J. Kalraat* | Een Manege, waarin veele Paarden-Piqueurs en verscheidene andere persoonen. Uitvoerig geschildert		(Sold) fl 9 Niekerk
1802/12/13	AMSCH	0044	*J. Calraat* | Voor een Herberg, ziet men Lieden te Paard en een beladen Vragtkar | *Mat:* op paneel *Size:* hoog 11, breed 14 duim	Pruyssenaar [for] D	(Sold) fl 9:15 P M Levy
1807/08/26	AMSCH	0109	*J. v. Kalraet* | Twee stuks Landschappen, beide gestoffeerd met Heeren te Paard, Huislieden met Paarden by een Waterbeek, en reizende Lieden te voet; zynde bevallig van penceelsbehandeling en koloriet | *Mat:* op paneel *Size:* ieder hoog 13, breed 15 duim	Roos [for] A	(Sold) fl 28 du Pree
1808/04/26	GDAN	0085	*Kalrath* | Een Pleisterplaatsje met Paarden | companion to lot 86 *Size:* hoog 8 ½, breed 9 duim	G H Fortuyn	(Unknown)
1808/04/26	GDAN	0086	*Kalrath* | Een dito [Pleisterplaatsje met Paarden] tot een wederga | companion to lot 85	G H Fortuyn	(Unknown)
1810/07/26	AMSCH	0044	*Kalraat* | Een Landgezigt: op den Voorgrond bij een Heuvel Lieden te Paard, benevens losse Paarden en andere Afbeeldingen, als Ph. Wouwerman behandeld | *Mat:* op paneel *Size:* hoog 14, breed 16 duimen	Cassino	(Sold) fl 3:15 Dupré
			Kalraet, Abraham Pietersz. van		
1810/07/23	DOLG1	0029	*A. Kalraad* | Een Landschap met Paarden | *Mat:* op paneel *Size:* hoog 19 ½, breed 26 ½ duim	Mr Pieter van den Santheuvel	(Sold) fl 1:16 Nieuwenhuizen van Brussel
			Kalraet, Barend van		
1802/11/01	DOBRA	0188	*B. van Calraat* | Twee stuks, zynde, het eene een Paarden-Wed, het ander een strandje; wederga | *Mat:* op paneel *Size:* breed 15, hoog 13 ½ duim		(Sold) fl 6:10 Lamme
1806/06/07	RMHSN	0014	*Calraat* | Een Rencontre in een Grot met Krygsvolk | *Mat:* op paneel	A E K L	(Unknown)
1807/09/28	DOHAA	00EE	*B. Kalraad* | 't Berouw van Petrus, door B. Kalraad, in de manier van T. Rechters, op panneel | *Mat:* op paneel	Mattheus Westerouen van Meeteren	(Unknown)
1810/10/10	MGCIT	0069	*Calrat* | Een Schildery, verbeeldende Prins Willem de Derde, aan het hoofd van eene Armée, en vergezeld van twee Generaals Personen; wel behandeld, en een der beste Stukken	Caspar van Citters	(Unknown)
1810/12/03	DOBRA	0015	*B. Kalraat* | Een Schermutseling in een Landschap; breed en uitvoerig behandeld, door B. Kalraat, in den trant van A. Cuyp		(Unknown)
1810/12/03	DOBRA	0016	*B. Kalraat* | Een Dame op een wit Paard, rydende naar de Valke-Jagt. Verder Heerente paard en te voet		(Unknown)
			Kamper, Godaert		
1809/07/25	HGBSM	0199	*G. Kamper* | Een hobbelend Watergezigt met eenige Scheepjes, op de voorgrond twee Figuren, in de trant van van Goyen, door G. Kamper | *Mat:* op paneel *Size:* hoog 18, breed 21 en een half duim	D van der Aa [or] E B ten Dall	(Sold) fl 2 Zwarts
			Kaukerk, P. [Unidentified]		
1810/08/10	RMRIJ	0009	*P. Kaukerk* | Voor een Huis, zitten eenige Figuren, zig vermakende met Speelen en Drinken. krachtig en geestig geschildert | *Mat:* op paneel *Size:* hoog 13 ½, breed 19 ½ duim		(Sold) fl 12 [or] 38 v Ryp
			Keirincx, Alexander		
1801/06/10	AMSCH	0094	*Keerings. (A.)* | Een Heuvelachtig Landschap met Geboomte, verders gestoffeerd met Reiziers [sic], meesterlyk en Zonachtig behandeld | *Mat:* op paneel *Size:* hoog 9, breed 13 duim	[Doublet]	(Sold) fl 7 Van Iperen
1802/05/05	AMSCH	0093	*J. Keerings* | Een Boom en Bergächtig Landschap, by een Steene Brug ziet men eenige Schaapen, waarby een Herderin, gezeeten op een Ezel, die dezelve Voordryft, verders in 't verschiet eenig Hoog Gebergte zeer delicaat en fiks geschilderd | *Mat:* op paneel *Size:* hoog 35, breed 31 duim	C	(Sold) fl 41 Auber
1802/05/05	AMSCH	0094	*J. Keerings* | Een Boomryk Landschap, op de Voorgrond een Herder, welke eenige Beesten voortdryft | *Mat:* op doek *Size:* hoog 32, breed 26 duim	G	(Sold) fl 12:10 Cocler
1802/06/16	AMSCH	0094	*A. Keerinx* | Een aangenaam Landschap, op de voorgrond gestoffeerd met een Jager en Honden, ter Valkenjaght uitgaande, by hoog Geboomten, en een bevallig verschiet: zonachtig en bevallig gepenceeld | *Mat:* op paneel *Size:* hoog 11, breed 9 duim	[Merrem]	(Sold) fl 11:10 Croesen
1802/09/06	AMSCH	0062	*A. Keerinx* | Twee stuks Boomryke Landschappen, gestoffeerd met Véehoeder en Jager; zonachtig behandeld	X	(Sold) fl 3 van Iperen
1803/08/01	AMSCH	0015	*Keerings. (A.)* | Een Bergachtig Landschap, op de voorgrond met een stille Rivier, waarby een Hengelaar, verder eenige staande en leggende Schaapen, en twee rustende Landlieden, en op een Berg weeldrig Geboomte, zeer natuurlyk behandeld | *Mat:* op paneel *Size:* hoog 19, breed 21 duim	J	(Sold) fl 2 Pruijssenaar
1803/08/01	AMSCH	0016	*Keerings. (A.)* | Twee stuks Boomryke Landschappen, met stoffagie van	J	(Sold) fl 5 Haffner

			Beeldjes, natuurlyk behandeld | *Mat:* op koper *Size:* ieder hoog 8, breed 10 duim		
1803/09/07	AMSCH	0093	*A. Keerings* | Een Boschgezigt, vol Geboomten, ter zyde een Waterplas, gestoffeerd met Beeldjes, uitvoerig op Paneel [La vue d'une forêt, à côté de laquelle se voit un étang et differentes figures ; parfaitement bien peint] | *Mat:* op paneel *Size:* hoog 17, breed 25 duim	Smidt	(Bought In) fl 15
1803/09/07	AMSCH	0094	*A. Keerings* | Een Bevallig Landschapje, met hoog Geboomten, Gebouwen, enz. zonachtig en meesterlyk op Paneel [Un charmant petit paysage ; avec des arbres de toutes grandeurs, des bâtimens etc. ; il y règne un beau soleil et toute l'exécution en est excellente] | *Mat:* op paneel *Size:* hoog 7 ½, breed 10 duim	Smidt	(Bought In) fl 3
1803/12/12	AMSCH	0048	*A. Kerings* | Een Boom- en Bergachtig Landschap, met een heldere Beek en een ménigte Beeldjes; alles uitvoerig op Paneel | *Mat:* op paneel *Size:* hoog 22, breed 34 duim	D	(Sold) fl 1:15 Oortwijn
1804/02/27	AMSCH	0063	*Keerings* | Twee stuks bevallige Boomryke en Rotsächtige Landschappen, ryk gestoffeerd met Beeldjes; en natuurlyk van licht | *Mat:* op koper *Size:* ieder hoog 7, breed 8 duim	D	(Sold) fl 9 Coclers
1804/05/07	AMSCH	0091	*Keerings. (J.)* | Twee stuks bevallige Boom, Duin en Bergachtige Landschapjes; eigenaartig gestoffeerd en uitvoerig geschilderd | *Mat:* op paneel *Size:* ieder hoog 12, breed 15 duim	Vinkeles [for] J	(Sold) fl 8 Gruyter
1805/12/16	AMSCH	0081	*Kerings* | Een gestoffeerd Landschap	R[oos]	(Sold) fl 1:15 du Pree
1809/06/13	AMSCH	0073	*A. Keerings* | Een Boschgezicht, met een Rivier doorsneeden, gestoffeerd met Jagers en Honden, in het verschiet bij een Valbrug, Visschers in een Schuit, natuurlijk | *Mat:* op paneel *Size:* hoog 15, breed 19 duim	Y	(Sold) fl 7:5 van Iperen
1810/06/20	AMSCH	0037	*A. Kerings* | Twee stuks Landschappen, met hoog Geboomte en stoffage van Beelden en Beesten. Natuurlijk behandeld | *Mat:* op paneel *Size:* hoog 25, breed 19 duimen	X	(Sold) fl 4 L Pakker
1810/10/11	AMSCH	0222	*Kerings* | Een boomrijk Landschap, met stoffagie | *Notes:* This lot was sold with lot 213 by an anonymous artist.	A	(Sold) fl 0:8 for lots 213 & 222. Gruiter
			Keirincx, Alexander (and Liss)		
1809/04/17	AMSCH	0048	*Keerings; Lis* | Een Boomrijk Landschap, ter zijde een stille Rivier, met verscheidene Badende Nimphen; fiks geschilderd | *Mat:* op paneel *Size:* hoog 21, breed 28 duim	T	(Sold) fl 6
			Keirincx, Alexander (and Vertangen)		
1801/03/16	AMSCH	0032	*Keerings; Vertangen* | Een heuvelachtig Landschap, doorsneede met een stil Water, met badende Nimphen en Saters, alles krachtig behandeld, door Keerings en Vertangen	P[ruyssenaar]	(Sold) fl 1:15 Gruiter
			Keirincx, Alexander (manner)		
1809/06/13	AMSCH	0199	*Keerings* | Een Landschap met naakte Beelden, als Keerings	Y	(Sold) fl 0:6 L Pakker
			Keller, Johann Heinrich (II)		
1802/11/01	DOBRA	0036	*Keller* | Twee Arkadische Landschappen vol Beelden | *Mat:* op doek	Paulus van der Spyk [or others]	(Bought In) fl 6
1803/12/12	AMSCH	0046	*Keller* | Twee stuks woelende Waters, met zeilende Schepen; dun op Paneel | *Mat:* op paneel *Size:* hoog 11, breed 14 duim	W	(Sold) fl 4 Ijver
1804/05/07	AMSCH	0093	*Keller. (J. H.)* | Drie speelende Kindertjes met bywerk, meesterlyk in 't graauw | *Mat:* op doek *Size:* hoog 47, breed 47 duim	Y[ver] [for] JJ	(Sold) fl 2 Jan Spaan
1806/08/20	HGBSM	0012	*H. Keller* | Eene Allegorie op de zeven Provintien, verbeeld door zeven danzende Vrouwen om de Vrijheidshoed, ieder het wapen van eene Provintie in de hand hebbende, verders eenige speelende kindertjes aangenaam en vrolijk | *Mat:* op koper *Size:* hoog 16, breed 19 ½ duim	Macalester Loup	(Sold) fl 15 Nieuwenhuis
1809/07/25	HGBSM	0096	*H. Keller* | Eenige Nymphen in een Landschap, welke door Saters bespied werden | *Mat:* op doek *Size:* hoog 20, breed 25 duim	D van der Aa	(Sold) fl 1:2 A Vermeulen
1809/07/25	HGBSM	0097	*H. Keller* | Twee Stuks Landschappen met overblyfzels van Gebouwen en eenige Figuren | *Mat:* op doek *Size:* hoog 20, breed 29 duim	D van der Aa	(Sold) fl 3:2 Mes
1809/07/25	HGBSM	0098	*H. Keller* | De Opstandinge van den Heiland uit het Graf | *Mat:* op doek *Size:* hoog 34 en 1 half, breed 32 duim	D van der Aa	(Sold) fl 6 van Eyk
1809/07/25	HGBSM	0099	*H. Keller* | Een Zinnebeeldig Stuk | *Mat:* op doek *Size:* hoog 47, breed 37 duim	D van der Aa	(Sold) fl 5:15 Mes
1809/07/25	HGBSM	0100	*H. Keller* | Een Historie uit Ovidius | companion to lot 101 *Mat:* op doek *Size:* hoog 38, breed 30 duim	D van der Aa	(Sold) fl 9:10 van Eijk
1809/07/25	HGBSM	0101	*H. Keller* | Een dito [Historie uit Ovidius], zynde een Pendant | companion to lot 100 *Size:* hoog 38, breed 30 duim	D van der Aa	(Sold) fl 3:10 Heymans [for] G
1809/07/25	HGBSM	0102	*H. Keller* | De Historie van Argus en Io | *Mat:* op doek *Size:* hoog 31, breed 38 duim	D van der Aa	(Sold) fl 5 van Eyk
1809/07/25	HGBSM	0103	*H. Keller* | Venus en Adonis | *Mat:* op doek *Size:* hoog 28, breed 37 en een half duim	D van der Aa	(Sold) fl 4:2 Mes
1809/07/25	HGBSM	0104	*H. Keller* | Een dito, zynde Diana &c. | *Mat:* op doek *Size:* hoog 23, breed 37 duim *Notes:* It is unclear what "dito" refers to in the title.	D van der Aa	(Sold) fl 1:10 Mes

1809/07/25	HGBSM	0105	*H. Keller* | Een Bergachtig Landschap | *Mat:* op doek *Size:* hoog 30, breed 38 en een half duim	D van der Aa	(Sold) fl 3:10 van der Aa
1809/07/25	HGBSM	0106	*H. Keller* | Twee stuks, zynde het een een Herder en Herderinne, in een Bosch gezigt, en het andere met musiceerende Figuuren &c. | *Mat:* op doek *Size:* hoog 21, breed 29 en een half duim	D van der Aa	(Sold) fl 3:10 van der Aa
1809/07/25	HGBSM	0107	*H. Keller* | Twee Stuks, zynde het eene Appollo op de Lier speelende voor zaters, en het andere Venus met haare Nymphen &c. | *Mat:* op doek *Size:* hoog 18, breed 15 duim	D van der Aa	(Sold) fl 4:4 van Voorden
1809/07/25	HGBSM	0108	*H. Keller* | Twee stuks Bachanaalen | *Mat:* op doek *Size:* hoog 25, breed 31 duim	D van der Aa	(Sold) fl 2 Vermeulen
1809/07/25	HGBSM	0109	*H. Keller* | Twee stuks Historieele stukken | *Mat:* op doek *Size:* hoog 31 en een half, breed 26 duim	D van der Aa	(Sold) fl 0:16 van Eyk
1809/07/25	HGBSM	0110	*H. Keller* | Een Schoorsteen Stuk | *Mat:* op doek	D van der Aa	(Sold) fl 0:10 Heymans
1809/07/25	HGBSM	0111	*H. Keller* | Twee Deurstukken | *Mat:* op doek	D van der Aa	(Sold) fl 1:2 A Vermeulen
1810/06/04	DOBRA	0022	*Keller* | Twee stuks met Beelden, enz.	Hendrik de Haas	(Unknown)
1810/07/23	DOLG2	000U	*H. Keller* | Een Historiestuk, meesterlijk geschilderd | *Mat:* op doek *Size:* hoog 39, breed 38 duim	Pieter Quinting	(Unknown) fl 3
			Kerckhoff, Frans		
1802/07/27	AKHRK	0052	*F. Kerkhof* | Een Tafel waarop doode Vogels liggen, als een Patrijs, Veldhoen, Lijster, IJsvogel en Chijsje, verders een Snip hangende aan zijn Poot, fraai geschilderd | *Mat:* op paneel *Size:* hoog 24 ½, breed 18 ½ duim	Maria Stategaart	(Sold) fl 2:5 Son Meyer
			Kessel		
1804/10/16	DLOND	0115	*Van Kessel* | Een Vrouwtjen, met een Papegaay boven zich, bezig om Groentens schoon te maken. Une Femme avec un Perroquet, occupée à preparer des legumes | *Mat:* op doek *Size:* hoog 13, breed 10		(Unknown)
1804/10/16	DLOND	0116	*Van Kessel* | Utsa. [Een Vrouwtjen, met een Papegaay boven zich, bezig om Groentens schoon te maken.] Bis. [Une Femme avec un Perroquet, occupée à preparer des legumes] | *Mat:* op doek *Size:* hoog 13, breed 10		(Unknown)
1804/10/16	DLOND	0117	*Van Kessel* | Twee Stukjens. Een Vrouwtjen met Naaiwerk, en ene andere schurende. Deux pièces. Une Femme avec quelqu'ouvrage de Couture; une autre occupée à écurer | *Mat:* op doek *Size:* hoog 13, breed 10		(Unknown)
			Kessel, Ferdinand van		
1802/09/06	AMSCH	0057	*F. van Kessel* | Twee stuks Boere Binnehuizen met verscheiden vrolyke Huislieden, zoo Eetende, drinkende, als danssende; uitvoerig | *Mat:* op paneel *Size:* hoog 11, breed 16 duim	B	(Sold) fl 11 A Baur
			Kessel, Jan van (I)		
1801/03/16	AMSCH	0026	*J. van Kessel* | Twee stuks met Gevogelten, uitvoerig gepenceeld	K[ip]	(Sold) fl 4:5 Stevens
1801/08/19	AMSCH	0145a	*J. van Kessel* | Op een Tafel ziet men een Kat, béezig van een Haring te Snoepen, verders Brood, eenige Kannen en een Rist Uijen; fraai en natuurlyk op Doek | *Mat:* op doek *Size:* hoog 32, breed 27 duim	van der Schly [for] F	(Bought In) fl 6 ½
1802/05/24	HGBAK	0047	*J. van Kessel* | Een stuk met veelerhande soorten van vrugten, door J. van Kessel, hoog 2 v. 7 d. breed 2 v. 3 d. op doek, in zwarte lyst met verg. bies | *Mat:* op doek *Size:* hoog 2 voet 7 duim, breed 2 voet 3 duim	Mejuffrouw A van der Mieden	(Sold) fl 4 van Giesen
1803/07/14	MGKLY	0038	*V. Kessel* | Een Landschap met Vogels	Mr Caspar Jacob van Citters	(Unknown)
1804/08/02	BDAN	0049	*Van Kessel* | Een stukje met Bloemen | *Size:* h. 19 en een half d. b. 12 d.	J G Calckberner	(Unknown)
1808/11/12	HGSCR	0012	*van Kessel* | Een klein stukje verbeeldende een vogel concert, zeer uitvoerig behandeld | *Mat:* op koper	Mr J van Buren	(Unknown) fl 3
1810/10/10	MGCIT	0096	*van Kessel* | Twee dito [Stukken met Bloemen]	Caspar van Citters	(Unknown)
			Kessel, Jan van (III)		
1801/10/06	AMSCH	0038	*J. van Kessel* | Een natuurlyk Landschap by een Oude vervalle Tooren, is de voorgrond gestoffeerd met Beeldjes en stammen van boomen, fiks en meesterlyk behandeld | *Mat:* op doek *Size:* hoog 20, breed 24 duim	M	(Sold) fl 49 Theijs
1802/05/05	AMSCH	0099	*van Kessel* | Een Gezicht binnen den Haag, ryk gestoffeerd met een menigte van Beelden en Rytuigen, meesterlyk behandeld | *Size:* hoog 36, breed 37 duim	J	(Sold) fl 7 Spruit
1802/05/05	AMSCH	0100	*van Kessel* | Een Bergachtig Landschap, gestoffeerd met Heeren en Jagers, verzeld van hunne Honden | *Size:* hoog 38, breed 45 duim	J	(Sold) fl 4:10 Spruit
1802/06/16	AMSCH	0088	*J. van Kessel* | Een Capitaal Landschap met verschillend zwaar Geboomte; op de voorgrond een klaare Waterbeek, ter zyde gestoffeerd met een Huisman, gaande over een Brugetje naar een Boere Woning, waar by een Vrouw op een Stygertje staande; het natuurlyk zonlicht, en de spiegeling der Boomen in het water zyn kunstig verbeeld; kragtig van Coloriet en meesterlyk schoon gepenceeld | *Mat:* op doek *Size:* hoog 42,	[Merrem]	(Sold) fl 205 Pruijssenaar [for] R

			breed 63 duim		
1802/09/06	AMSCH	0207	*J. van Kessel* | Een Boomryk Landschap, op de voorgrond een Vrouw te Paard, neevens een gaande dito, verders een Adelyk Huis aan een stil Water; zonachtig behandeld als van Hobbema, door J. van Kessel | *Mat:* op doek *Size:* hoog 27, breed 32 duim	J	(Sold) fl 4:10 van Iperen
1802/11/01	DOBRA	0094	*v. Kessel* | Een Land- en Rivier gezigt, gestoffeert met veelerly soorten van land- en water-gevoogelte, door v. Kessel 1681 | companion to lot 95 *Mat:* op koper *Size:* hoog 11 duim, breed 12 duim *Inscr:* v. Kessel 1681 (signed and dated?) *Notes:* It is unclear whether the name and date are inscribed on the painting.	Paulus van der Spyk [or others]	(Unknown)
1802/11/01	DOBRA	0095	*v. Kessel* | Een dito [Land- en Rivier gezigt] met dito [veelerly soorten van land- en water-gevoogelte], als een weerga | companion to lot 94	Paulus van der Spyk [or others]	(Unknown)
1802/12/13	AMSCH	0092	*J. van Kessel* | Twee stuks natuurlyke Landschappen, gestoffeerd met Beelden en Beesten, uitvoerig geschilderd | *Mat:* op paneel *Size:* hoog 14, breed 13 duim	Pruyssenaar [for] A	(Sold) fl 1:10 van Iperen
1802/12/13	AMSCH	0093	*J. van Kessel* | Een natuurlyk zonagtig Landschap | *Mat:* op paneel *Size:* hoog 11, breed 13 duim	Pruyssenaar [for] A	(Sold) fl 2:10 van Dijl
1804/02/27	AMSCH	0061	*Kessel. (J. van)* | Een Landschap, ter linkerzyde een Huismanswooning, waar voor een Ophaalbrug, welke beide door de zon sterk verlicht zyn, op den voorgrond is dit stuk gestoffeerd met een Reiziger te Paard en rustende Beelden; alles zeer natuurlyk gepenceeld | *Mat:* op doek *Size:* hoog 33, breed 40 duim	B	(Sold) fl 35 Gruiter
1804/05/07	AMSCH	0088	*Kessel. (J. van)* | Een Heuvelachtig Landschap aan een Rivier met zwaar Geboomte, Ruïnes en Stoffagie van Beeldjes; kragtig en natuurlyk behandeld | *Mat:* op doek *Size:* hoog 24, breed 32 duim	R[oos]	(Sold) fl 181 Thais
1804/05/07	AMSCH	0089	*Kessel (J. van)* | In een capitaal Bosch en Duinryk Landschap, zit voor een Staketzel onder het Geboomten een rustende Vrouw, langs de zwaar gespoorde weg, en twee met elkander in gesprek zynde Lieden, verzeldt van een Hondt; tusschen 't Geboomte een Kerk en Tooren; alles zeer natuurlyk geschildert als Hobbema | *Mat:* op doek *Size:* hoog 33, breed 33 duim	Vinkeles [for] G	(Bought In) fl 22
1804/08/08	AMSCH	0098	*J. van Kessel* | In een capitaal Boomryk Landschap ziet men op een grazige Vlakte, onder het Geboomte, een Herder met Schaapen, op de voorgrond een Vrouw te Paard en een gaande Man, met een Hond, dryvende een belaaden Muil-Ezel en eenige Schaapen; de bevallige couleur, het snelle zonlicht en breede schildering maaken dit tot een aangenaam Schildery | *Mat:* op paneel *Size:* hoog 23 ½, breed 23 duim	Vink[eles] [for] K[=Gruyter?]	(Bought In) fl 11
1804/08/08	AMSCH	0099	*J. van Kessel* | Twee stuks, verbeeldende Zomer en Winter, beiden gestoffeerd met eenige Beeldjes; fiks gepenceelt | *Mat:* op paneel *Size:* yder hoog 11, breed 24 duim	Schley [for] A	(Sold) fl 40 Jan Spaan
1805/07/03	AMSCH	0099	*J. van Kessel* | Een Boomryk Landschap met een Rivier doorsneeden, waarin twee Lieden bézig zyn een Visnet op te haalen, verder hoog Geboomten en een Duinachtig, verschiet; krachtig en Meesterlyk gepenceeld | *Mat:* op paneel *Size:* hoog 22, breed 28 duim	V[inkeles]	(Sold) fl 65 for lots 99 & 100. L Pakker
1805/07/03	AMSCH	0100	*J. van Kessel* | een Boom- en Duinryk Landschap, by een helder spiegelend Water; ryk gestoffeerd met gaande Landlieden; verders een aangenaam zonachtig verschiet en allerfraaist gepenceeld | *Mat:* op paneel *Size:* hoog 22, breed 28 duim	V[inkeles]	(Sold) fl 65 for lots 99 & 100. L Pakker
1806/05/05	AMSCH	0073	*J. van Kessel* | In een boomryk Landschap, ziet men op een grasige vlakten een Herder met Schapen, op de voorgrond een Vrouw te Paard en een gaande Man, dryvende een belaaden Muil Ezel en eenige Schapen; bevallig van schildering door J. van Kessel | *Mat:* op paneel *Size:* hoog 23 ½, breed 28 duim	V[inkeles]	(Sold) fl 9 van Laar
1806/05/05	AMSCH	0258	*S. van Kessel* | Een Landschapje | *Notes:* The artist's name was given as "S. van Kessel" but we have assumed this is an error.	R[oos]	(Sold) fl 0:14 L Pakker
1806/08/13	AMSCH	0325	*Kessel. (van)* | Een aangenaam Boom- en Heuvelachtig Landschap met een Rivier doorsneeden waarby een Visser bézig zynde te hengelen; zonachtig en meesterlyk behandeld | *Mat:* op paneel	Coclers	(Bought In) fl 81
1808/06/06	RMRIJ	0062	*Kessel (Jan van)* | Een Landschap, waarin op den voorgrond een bovenlandsche Watermolen, Waterval en Muurwerk; verder eenige Gebouwen en Geboomten. Allerkonstigst en zoo goed als door Jacob Ruijsdaal geschilderd [Ce Tableau represente, sur le premier plan, la Roue d'un moulin à eau avec sa Chûte, le bout d'une muraille, quelques fabriques et plusieurs figures etc. le tout forme un ensemble agréable et savammant peint, dans le genre, et avec autant de mérite que J. Ruisdaal] | *Annots:* 1781 gekregen van syn vader W.J. Pot (RMA I) *Mat:* op doek *Size:* Hoog 33 ½ en breed 40 duim	Gerrit van der Pot, Heer van Groeneveld	(Sold) fl 200 Cremer
1808/06/13	AMSCH	0088	*Kessel (J. van)* | Een aangenaam Wintergezicht aan de wal te Amsterdam, zijnde een gezicht op de Heiligewegs Poort. Op het IJs zijn eene menigte Schaatzenrijders, Wandelaars en Arresleden. Helder en zonachtig, en van een aangename penceelbehandeling | *Mat:* op doek *Size:* hoog 38, breed 50 duim	E M Engelberts	(Sold) fl 146 P G van Os
1808/06/13	AMSCH	0089	*Kessel (J. van)* | In een bergachtig Landschap vertoond zich een sterkstroomende Waterval, waarbij afgebroken Stammen van Boomen en	Z	(Sold) fl 350 Jan Spaan

			Aardkluiten; verder hoog Geboomte en aangenaam verschiet. Het bruischen van het water is zoo verwonderlijk natuurlijk verbeeld en zoo meesterlijk behandeld, als of het door J Ruisdaal vervaardigd was | *Mat:* op doek *Size:* hoog 36, breed 29 duim		
1808/06/13	AMSCH	0089a[H]	*Kessel (J. van)* | Stadgesicht | *Notes:* This lot was added in by hand in the AA I, EBNP, FLNY, and RKDH copies of the catalogue.	Z	(Sold) fl 49:10 J[mo] de Vries
1808/06/13	AMSCH	0090a[H]	*Kessel (J. van)* | Landscap met beesten | *Notes:* This lot was added in by hand in the AA I, EBNP, FLNY and RKDH copies of the catalogue.	Z	(Sold) fl 46 Reyers voor Allard
1808/06/13	AMSCH	0091	*Kessel (J. van)* | Een duin- en boomrijk Landschap, ter zijde een Water met twee Visschers: op den voorgrond eene Vrouw met een' Jonge. Zonachtig en kloek geschilderd | *Mat:* op paneel *Size:* hoog 23, breed 29 duim	E M Engelberts	(Sold) fl 250 Boelen
1808/08/23	AMSCH	0085	*Kessel (J. van)* | Een kapitaal Boomrijk Landschap, ter linker zijde eenige Boeren Wooningen, waar voor een Ophaalbrug over een klaar spiegelend Water, gestoffeert met Lieden te Paard, vissende Boeren, en gaande en rustende Reisigers; fraai en meesterlijk, als Hobbema geschildert | *Mat:* op doek *Size:* hoog 33, breed 40 duim	[Gruyter?]	(Sold) fl 75 Th Spaan
1808/10/28	AMVRS	0027	*Kessel, (J. van)* | De Dam, het Stadhuis, de Waag en een gedeelte van de Nieuwe Kerk met de Damrak en Vischmarkt, rijk gestoffeerd met Beelden en Vaartuigen, en natuurlijk geschilderd | *Mat:* op doek *Size:* hoog 39, breed 50 duim	Marten Udink	(Sold) fl 201 B Kooij
1809/04/17	AMSCH	0046	*J. van Kessel* | Een Gezicht op de Stad Haarlem, met Woningen en onderscheiden Geboomten, natuurlijk | *Mat:* op paneel *Size:* hoog 8, breed 10 duim	[Gruyter?]	(Sold or Bought In) fl 0:5 Gruyter
1809/04/17	AMSCH	0047	*J. van Kessel* | Langs een Zandigen Weg met opgaand Geboomte, ziet men over een Steene Sluijs de Opgang van een Buitenplaats, gestoffeerd met rijdende en wandelende Heeren en Dames; krachtig en zonachtig behandeld | *Mat:* op doek *Size:* hoog 31, breed 26 duim	[Gruyter?]	(Sold or Bought In) fl 1:5 Gruyter
1809/06/13	AMSCH	0071	*J. van Kessel* | Een Gezicht van Oud Ouwerkerk, aan den Amstel, met een Heer te Paard, Hengelaars en andere Figuuren gestoffeerd, aller natuurlijkst | *Mat:* op doek *Size:* hoog 19, breed 23 duim	Q	(Bought In) fl 4:5
1809/06/13	AMSCH	0072	*J. van Kessel* | Een Gezigt binnen Amsterdam, ziende van de Brouwerij de Haan, over de Nieuwmarkt, op de Joode Breestraat, en Zuiderkerk, gestoffeerd met Vaartuigen en Beeldjes, natuurlijk behandeld | *Mat:* op doek *Size:* hoog 25, breed 30 duim	T	(Sold) fl 9
1809/07/19	AMSCH	0027	*Kessel (J. van)* | Een fraai Stadsgezicht binnen Amsterdam, verbeeldende de Raamgracht, met een gedeelte der Verwersgragt, de Raamgragt met Wandelaars en andere Lieden gestoffeerd, van achteren ziet men de Zuiderkerkstoren, de Woningen, Stoepen, de Brug, het Water, de Schaduw zijn zeer treffend, en zeer natuurlijk van uitdrukking | *Mat:* op doek *Size:* hoog 39, breed 37 duim	V	(Bought In) fl 20
1810/08/06	AMSCH	0055	*Kessel (J. van)* | Een aangenaam natuurlijk en treffend Stadgezicht van een der Grachten binnen Amsterdam, te zien van de overzijde; het Zonlicht doet eene krachtige werking | *Mat:* op doek *Size:* hoog 26, breed 22 ½ duim	V[ries]	(Sold) fl 40 Texier Gerbet en Comp
			Kessel, Jan van (III) (and Lingelbach)		
1808/08/23	AMSCH	0086	*Kessel (J. van); Lingelbag* | Aan den ingang van een schilderachtig bosch, zit in de schaduwe van een Eiken Boom, eene rustende Landvrouw met een Jongen, verder ziet men over een heldere Waterplas een Heer te Paard, en een gaande Man bij een gedeelte Graanland; natuurlijk zonachtig en van een fraaije penceelbehandeling | *Mat:* op doek	J	(Sold) fl 230 Jan Spaan
			Kessel, Jan van (III) (and Schellinks, Daniel)		
1808/06/13	AMSCH	0090	*Kessel (J. van); D. Schellings* | Een boom- en heuvelachtig Landschap: op den voorgrond een dooden Boom aan een Watertje, gestoffeerd met Jagers te paard en te voet, welke een Hert vervolgen. Zonachtig en meesterlijk gepenceeld | *Mat:* op doek *Size:* hoog 29, breed 41 duim	Z	(Sold) fl 20 Glad [or] Carré
			Kessel, Jan van (III) (and Wouwerman)		
1801/08/19	AMSCH	0051	*van Kessel; Wouwerman* | Een Gezigt langs de Vaart, voor 't huis Overmeer, ryk gestoffeerd met een ter Jagt reidend Gezelschap, verder wandelende Persoonen; bevallig van licht, en schoon gepenceeld, door van Kessel, gestoffeerd door Wouwerman	Pruyssen[r] [for] Q	(Sold) fl 10 v d Vinne
			Kessel, Jan van (III) (and Wouwerman, J.)		
1808/03/03	HAVIN	0017	*van Kessel; J. Wouwerman* | Een Gezicht op de Buitenplaats Overmeer aan den Amstel, door van Kessel gestoffeerd	Jacobus Spillebout	(Unknown) fl 5
			Kessel, Jan van (III) (or Kessel, J. (III), manner)		
1802/06/16	AMSCH	0089	*J. van Kessel, of in zyn manier* | Een heuvelachtig Landschap met zwaar Geboomte en een uitgestrekt verschiet, aan een Rivier legt een Dorp, de voorgrond met een werkend beeld gestoffeerd, alles meesterlyk en met de natuur overeenkomende, behandeld | *Mat:* op doek *Size:* hoog 43, breed 52 duim	[Merrem]	(Sold) fl 38 Wolft

Kessel, Jan van (III) (manner)

1808/08/23	AMSCH	0262	*van Kessel* | Een Boschgezicht, in de manier van van Kessel	J	(Sold) fl 1:5 Hulswit

Kett, Willem

1810/10/13	HGDAW	0014	*W. Kett* | Een woedende Zee, waarin eenige Visschers in een Boot zich schynen te redden by een Dyk, waarop men een Gehugt ziet met Geboomte, op de Voorgrond twee Mannen bezig aan een mast op te halen, zeer natuurlyk geschilderd in de manier van Swykhard | *Mat:* op paneel *Size:* hoog 16, breed 23 duim		(Unknown)

Keun, Hendrik

1801/03/16	AMSCH	0083	*Kuhn* | Twee stuks, zynde 't eerste een Gezicht boven Haarlem in den Hout; en 't ander een Watergezicht, ryk gestoffeerd en uitvoerig geschilderd	P[ruyssenaar]	(Sold) fl 30 v d Schley [for] S
1801/04/08	HAVIN	0043	*H. Keun* | Twee gezigten de Lydse Poort en by de Haarlemmerpoort te Amsterdam		(Unknown)
1802/06/28	AMSCH	0088	*H. Keun* | Een gezicht op de Keizersgragt, by 't Molenpad, gestoffeerd met een menigte wandelende Beelden; fiks behandeld, door H. Keun | *Mat:* op doek *Size:* hoog 21, breed 17 duim	Anna Elink	(Sold) fl 7:5 Van Iperen
1802/06/28	AMSCH	0089	*H. Keun* | Twee stuks gezichten in en omtrent Haarlem, aan 't Spaaren; uitvoerig op Doek | *Mat:* op doek *Size:* hoog 13, breed 17 duim	Anna Elink	(Sold) fl 12 Van Iperen
1802/06/28	AMSCH	0090	*H. Keun* | Twee stuks, een gezicht op het Spaare te Haarlem, en het andere op de Cingel na de Munt te Amsterdam, door Denzelven [H. Keun] | *Mat:* op doek *Size:* hoog 19, breed 25 duim	Anna Elink	(Sold) fl 39 Van Iperen
1802/06/28	AMSCH	0091	*H. Keun* | Een gezicht op de groote Markt te Haarlem, met verscheide Beeldjes; zonachtig, op Doek | *Mat:* op doek *Size:* hoog 15, breed 11 duim	Anna Elink	(Sold) fl 6:10 de Meyer
1802/06/28	AMSCH	0092	*H. Keun* | Een Dorpgezicht aan een stille Rivier, met verscheide Stoffagie, door Denzelven [H. Keun], op Doek | *Mat:* op doek *Size:* hoog 21, breed 15 duim	Anna Elink	(Sold) fl 2:10 Risch
1802/06/28	AMSCH	0093	*H. Keun* | Een gezicht op een Poort van een Stad	Anna Elink	(Sold) fl 0:12 de Meyer
1803/12/12	AMSCH	0121	*Kuen* | Een Gezicht op de Doelen en Cloveniers-Burgwal | *Size:* hoog 13, br. 18 duim	W	(Sold) fl 4:15 Van Iperen
1804/02/27	AMSCH	0062	*Keun. (H.)* | Een Gezicht langs de Keizersgragt, voorby 't Moolenpad, gestoffeerd met differente Beelden en Rytuigen; bevallig van licht en fraai van schildering | *Mat:* op doek *Size:* hoog 21, breed 17 duim	C	(Sold) fl 14:10 de Meijer
1804/08/08	AMSCH	0100	*H. Keun* | Een Gezicht op de groote Houtpoort, buiten Haarlem, gestoffeerd met rydende, wandelende, werkende en vaarende Lieden; zonachtig en fraai gepenceeld | *Mat:* op paneel *Size:* hoog 18, breed 24 duim	Vink[eles] [for] S	(Sold) fl 10:10 Jan Spaan
1804/12/10	AMSCH	0041	*H. Keun* | Een zeer natuurlyk Gezicht langs een opgaande wegh, met verschillend hoog Geboomten, gestoffeert met Huislieden met Kar en Paard, gaande en rustende Landlieden en Hengelaars; zonagtig en bevallig geschilderd | *Mat:* op doek *Size:* Hoog 20, breed 27 ½ duim	Jan De Groot	(Sold) fl 7:5 van Iperen
1804/12/10	AMSCH	0042	*H. Keun* | Twee stuks Landschappen, het eene een gezicht op de Tolbrug by den Haag, en het andere de kleine Houtpoort te Haarlem; byde bevallig gestoffeerd en zonachtig gepenceeld | *Mat:* op paneel *Size:* Hoog 14, breed 19 duim	Jan De Groot	(Sold) fl 24:10 van Iperen
1807/08/26	AMSCH	0291	*H. Keun* | Een Zeegezicht, met verscheide Schepen	v d Schley [for] [Smits Wed]	(Sold) fl 2:5 du Pree
1807/08/26	AMSCH	0305a	*H. Keun* | Twee stuks Gezichten buiten Amsterdam, met verscheiden stoffage | *Mat:* op doek	Yver [for] S	(Sold) fl 2 Graffelman
1809/06/13	AMSCH	0085	*H. Keun* | Een Gezicht binnen Amsterdam, ziende op het Haarlemmerplein en Poort, met gaande en rustende Beeldjes gestoffeerd, en zonachtig behandeld | *Mat:* op doek *Size:* hoog 16, breed 22 duim	E	(Sold) fl 7 Van Iperen
1809/09/06	AMSCH	0031	*Keun (H.)* | Twee stuks, een Gezicht op de Weesper Poort en een ander op 't Diakenhuis; beide rijk gestoffeerd en zonachtig behandeld | *Mat:* op doek *Size:* ieder hoog, 12, breed 16 duim	Johannes Caudri	(Sold) fl 10 van Iperen
1809/09/06	AMSCH	0032	*Keun (H.)* | Een Gezicht uit de Zijlstraat op de groote Markt te Haarlem; als de voorgaande | *Mat:* op paneel *Size:* hoog 17, breed 12 duim	Johannes Caudri	(Sold) fl 2:10 van Iperen
1809/09/06	AMSCH	0033	*Keun (H.)* | Een Gezicht te Amsterdam, van den Binnen Amstel ziende op de Munt-Tooren; als de vorige behandeld | *Mat:* op paneel *Size:* hoog 16, breed 14 duim	Johannes Caudri	(Sold) fl 8:10 van Iperen
1809/09/06	AMSCH	0034	*Keun (H.)* | Een Gezicht op een Dorp, met stoffagie van Beeldjes; meede zeer uitvoerig gepenceeld | *Mat:* op paneel *Size:* hoog 16, breed 14 duim	Johannes Caudri	(Sold) fl 7 Th[s] Spaan

Keyser, H. de

1807/08/26	AMSCH	0108	*H. de Keyzer* | Een deftig Heer in een Kamer, zittende aan een Tafel, met een Tapyten Kleed gedekt, waarop een Kunstboek en een Beeldje geplaatst is, aan de Wand hangt een Guitar en Dégen; zynde in alle deelen fraai gepenceeld | *Mat:* op paneel *Size:* hoog 29, breed 22 duim	Helsdinge	(Sold) fl 60 Gruyter

Keyser, Thomas de

1804/10/16	DLOND	0119	*Keyzer* | Twee klene Stukjens, een Mans en een Vrouwen Borstbeeld, beiden in 't Bont gekleed. Deux petits Tableaux. Buste d'Homme & Femme en Pelterie [sic] | *Mat:* op paneel *Size:* hoog 6 ½, breed 5 ½		(Unknown)
1806/05/05	AMSCH	0244	*de Keyser* | Een Famielje stuk, van onderscheiden Beelden; konstig gepenceeld door de Keyser	V[inkeles]	(Sold) fl 1:10 van Laar
1806/05/05	AMSCH	0245	*De Keyser* | Een Mans Pourtrait	V[inkeles]	(Sold) fl 1 L Pakker
1806/10/16	UTWLD	0016	*T. de Keyser* | Een binnen vertrek met een Heer zittende voor een Clavier en een Dame by een tafel	Mr P de Malapert [or] W Beeldsnyder	(Unknown)
1808/07/19	AMROU	0017	*A. de Kyzer* | 1 deftig Binnenvertrek, waarin een Tafel met Tapyt bekleed, daar aan zittende een Heer en Dame, houde een Boek in de hand, en de Heer, leunende op de Tafel, in de hand hebbende een Passer rustende op een Tekenboek | *Notes:* The artist's name was given as "A. de Kyzer" but we have assumed this is an error.		(Unknown)
1808/07/19	AMROU	0018	*A. de Kyzer* | 1 Bosachtig Landscap, op de voorgrond staat een Heer en een Dame, waar by een Kind, en in het verschiet ziet men op een Boere Dorp, krachtig gepenseeld | *Notes:* The artist's name was given as "A. de Kyzer" but we have assumed this is an error.		(Unknown)
1809/04/17	AMSCH	0045	*Th. de Keijser* | Dit voortreffelijk Schilderij, verbeeld een prachtige Zaal of Binnenvertrek, met een rijk Tapijt behangen, in het zelve zit een deftig gekleed Heer bij een Tafel, waar op twee Globens, een open Landkaart en andere Instrumenten geplaatst zijn, agter hem staat een Bedienden, welke hem een Brief overhandigd en zijn bericht schijnt aftewachten; dit stuk is heerlijk van schildering, krachtig van koloriet en zeldzaam zo voorkomende | *Mat:* op paneel *Size:* hoog 36, breed 24 duim *Loc:* London, England, UK. National Gallery. (212) as Portrait of Constantin Huygens & his clerk.		(Sold or Bought In) fl 214

Keyser, Thomas de (and Lastman, P.P.)

1810/11/07	UTWLD	0020	*P. Lastman; D. Keyzer* | Een kapitale Schilderij, steld voor een Turksche historie, staande een Visier voor een Mosquée, aan wien een Turk iets geknield aanbied, verder Turksche stoffering van reukvaten etc. alles meesteragtig behandeld, (getekend P. Lastman inv. D. Keyzer 1660) op doek, 3 voet 8 duim hoog, breed 2 voet 10 duim, zwarte Lijst | *Mat:* op doek *Size:* 3 voet 8 duim hoog, breed 2 voet 10 duim *Inscr:* P. Lastman inv. D. Keyzer 1660 (signed and dated) *Loc:* Paris, France. Institut Néerlandais, Fondation Custodia. (6781)		(Unknown) fl 16

Kick, Cornelis

1808/07/19	AMROU	0008	*C. Kik* | 2 Fruitstukjes, op een steene Tafel ziet men leggen, een tros Druiven, waarby een Persik, en op de andere een Oranje Appel en twee fraaije Roosse, en verder bywerk		(Unknown)

Kieft, Pieter

1805/12/16	AMSCH	0034	*P. Kieft* | Een Land- en Watergezicht, met Vissers en Schuiten, nayuurlyk op Paneel | *Mat:* op paneel *Size:* hoog 14, breed 15 duim	R[oos]	(Sold) fl 4:15 Spaan

Kips, J. [Unidentified]

1810/10/11	AMSCH	0253	*J. Kips* | Twee stuks, Maria met het Kind en een Vrouwe-Portretje	A	(Sold) fl 1 L Pakker

Kipshaven, Isaack van

1802/06/28	AMSCH	0099	*J. V. Kipshaven* | Op een Tafel ziet men eenig dood Wild, en verder Jachtuig [sic], fiks gepenceeld, door J. V. Kipshaven, op Doek | *Mat:* op doek *Size:* hoog 25, breed 22 duim	Anna Elink	(Sold) fl 1 Coolers

Kleijne, David

1802/05/10	MGSAN	0051	*D. Klyne* | Een fraaije woelende Zee, met onderscheidene Schepen; in 't verschiet een Dorpgezigt, krachtig geschilderd, door D. Klyne: op Paneel, in vergulde Lyst | *Mat:* op paneel *Size:* hoog 17 duim, breed 23 duim	Johan Dirk Kruysse	(Sold) £ 4:10 Waterlander
1802/07/20	MGSAN	0015	*D. Klyne* | Een woelend Zeetje, met Schepen, op Paneel | *Mat:* op paneel *Size:* hoog duim 7, breed duim 9		(Unknown)
1802/07/20	MGSAN	0016	*D. Klyne* | Een dito [Zeetje], zynde een stil Watertje, op Paneel | *Mat:* op paneel *Size:* hoog duim 7, breed duim 9		(Unknown)
1802/07/20	MGSAN	0037	*D. Klyne* | Een stil Water, vol gewoel, met Schepen en Sloepen; op de voorgrond vertoont zich een Roeisloep vol Volk; aan de linkerzynde legt een Driemastschip ten anker, zyn zeilen te droogen; verder verscheide dryvende en ten anker liggende Schepen: alles uitvoerig, transpirant en kunstig gepenseeld, in de manier van W. v. d. Velde | *Size:* hoog duim 9 ½, breed duim 12 ½		(Unknown)
1802/07/21	HGKAN	0024	*Kleiné* | Een dito [Schildery] met Scheepjes, in een stil Water		(Unknown)
1803/07/14	MGKLY	0007	*D. Kleine* | Twee Stille Waters met Scheepen	Mr Caspar Jacob van Citters	(Unknown)
1803/08/24	HGKAN	0020	*D. Kleyne* | Twee stuks Stille Waters Ryk gestoffeerd, met diverse soort van Scheepen, uitvoerig en delicaat geschildert | *Mat:* op paneel *Size:* hoog 11, breet 14 duim	[Teissier] [or others]	(Sold) fl 17:10 Teissier

1803/11/30	MGBEO	0011	*D. Kleyne* | Een woelend Zeetje met Scheepen | *Mat:* op paneel *Size:* hoog 11 ½ duim, breed 15 ½ duim	Samuel de Wind	(Sold) £ 0:17 Lambrechtsen
1803/12/15	MGLAC	0054	*D. Kleyné* | Een woelend Zeetje met Schepen; zeer net en uitvoerig geschilderd | *Mat:* op paneel *Size:* hoog duim 19, breed duim 23	Mr L H de Haze Bomme	(Unknown)
1805/10/09	HGBSM	0047	*D. Klyne* | Een woelende zee, aan de voorgrond een Hollandsch driemast schip, en meer andere scheepen | *Mat:* op paneel *Size:* hoog 28 breet 40 ½ duim	T H van Willigen [or others]	(Sold) fl 5:10 Ph Mey
1806/08/13	AMSCH	0093	*Kleyne. (D.)* | Twee stuks stille Waters, gestoffeert met zylende Jagten en Scheepen, verder Dorpgezichten; uitvoerig gepenceeld | *Mat:* op paneel *Size:* Ieder hoog 14, breed 17 duim	Roos	(Sold) fl 8 Du Pre
1806/10/17	MGSAN	0014	*D. Kleine* | Een dito [woelende Zee], op de voorgrond het Wachthuis op Dishoek, gestoffeerd met Zee- en andere Schepen | *Mat:* op paneel	Gerardus Beljard	(Unknown)
1806/10/17	MGSAN	0015	*D. Kleine* | Een dito [woelende Zee] met Zee- en Sprietscheepen, van het groote Hooft te Vlissingen te zien | *Mat:* op paneel	Gerardus Beljard	(Unknown)
1806/10/17	MGSAN	0044	*D. Kleine* | Een Woelend Zeetje, op de voorgrond een Poon en een Jagt | *Mat:* op paneel *Notes:* This lot was sold with lot 43 by Monogrammist R.K.B.	Gerardus Beljard	(Sold) £ 0.4.1 for lots 43–45
1806/10/17	MGSAN	0045	*D. Kleine* | Een Stil Zeetje, op de voorgrond een Spriet- en Gaffelschip | *Mat:* op paneel *Notes:* This lot was sold with lot 43 by Monogrammist R.K.B.	Gerardus Beljard	(Sold) £ 0.4.1 for lots 43–45
1807/06/10	HGBSM	0132	*D. Kleyné* | Een storm op Zee, waarop verbeeld 's lands oorlog Schip den Hercules, gecommandeerd door Capitein Melville in 't jaar 1794, verliest zijn tuig en wand in de golf van Nerbonne [sic], uitvoerig geschilderd | *Mat:* op paneel *Size:* hoog 10, breed 13 duim	Abraham Delfos [or others]	(Sold) fl 13 Tessier
1807/09/28	AMWUR	0031	*D. Kleine* | Een dito [stuk] op Paneel, zynde een Zee Gezichtje, met verscheiden Scheepjes, in vergulde Lyst | *Mat:* op paneel		(Unknown) fl 8

Kleur, S. [Unidentified]

1803/06/20	AMSCH	0024[a]	*S. Kleur* | Op een Marmere Tafel staat een Glas, gevuld men een menigte geurige Bloemen, delicaat en uitvoerig gepenceeld | *Mat:* op koper *Size:* hoog 15 ½, breed 13 duim	Schley [for] G	(Sold) fl 14:10 for lots 24[a] & 24[b]. Mensard
1803/06/20	AMSCH	0024[b]	*S. Kleur* | Op een dito [Marmere] Tafel leggen eenige Trossen witte en blaauwe Druiven, Persiken en Hazenooten, waarop twee Vlinders Azen, behandeld als de voorgaande, door denzelven [S. Kleur], van gelyke grootte | *Size:* hoog 15 ½, breed 13 duim	Schley [for] G	(Sold) fl 14:10 for lots 24[a] & 24[b]. Mensard

Kloet, J. van der

1805/07/10	AMSCH	0188	*J. van Kloot* | Een Schynbedrieger	R[oos]	(Sold) fl 0:6 L Pakker

Klomp, Albert Jansz.

1801/02/18	AMBOS	0002	*A. Klomp* | Een Landgezigt, fraai gestoffeerd met Koebeesten, en een Vrouw zynde bezig een Koe te melken, en in de voorgrond twee leggende Koebeesten welke herkaauwen, alles zeer natuurlyk en fraai geschilderd | companion to lot 3	J Schonevelt	(Unknown)
1801/02/18	AMBOS	0003	*A. Klomp* | Een dito [Landgezigt], zynde een weerga, waarin een staande Os met een leggend Kalf en Geiten, niet minder als het voorgaande | companion to lot 2	J Schonevelt	(Unknown)
1801/04/23	AMYVR	0004	*A. Klomp* | Een Landschap met eenige Schaapen op de voorgrond, verders een Koe die gemolken word, op Doek geschilderd | *Mat:* op doek *Size:* hoog 27, breed 23 duim		(Sold) fl 85 Pruijssenaar
1801/05/11	AMSCH	0042	*A. Klomp* | Een hollandsch Landschap, met een staande koey en schaapen, ter zyde twee hengelaars, natuurlyk van penceel behandeling | *Mat:* op paneel *Size:* hoog 14, breed 12 duim	E[lias]	(Sold) fl 50 Allard
1801/06/10	AMSCH	0093	*Klomp. (A.)* | Twee stuks grazige Weiden, geboomte en aangenaame verschieten, bevallig gestoffeerd met Ossen, Koeijen en Schapen, zynde van de beste schildering van deezen Meester | *Mat:* op paneel *Size:* yder hoog 15, breed 12 ½ duim	Herman ten Kate	(Sold) fl 100 Pruijssenaar
1801/08/19	AMSCH	0053	*Klomp* | Twee bevallige Landschappen; gestoffeerd met Ossen en Schaapen	Pruyssen^{r}	(Sold) fl 7 Gruiter
1801/08/19	AMSCH	0054	*Klomp* | Een dito [bevallige Landschappen] met dito [Ossen en Schaapen]	Pruyssen^{r}	(Sold) fl 5:10 Coclers
1802/05/05	AMSCH	0097	*A. Klomp* | Een Landschap, met staande en leggende Beesten, benevens een Rustende Herder | *Mat:* op doek *Size:* hoog 14, breed 17 duim	G	(Sold) fl 5:10 Spruit
1802/05/05	AMSCH	0098	*A. Klomp* | Een Landschap, met staand en leggend Vee | *Size:* hoog 16, breed 14 duim	J	(Sold) fl 29 Cocler
1802/06/16	AMSCH	0090	*A. Klomp* | Voor een Boere Woning met hoog geboomte, ziet men in een grazige Weide, een menigte Koeijen, Schapen en Bokken, ter zyde twee Boeren welke een Hond doen opzitten; in 't vorschiet [sic] Vissers aan een Rivier, bevallig behandeld | *Mat:* op doek *Size:* hoog 19, breed 24 duim	[Merrem]	(Sold) fl 85 Reijers
1802/06/16	AMSCH	0091	*A. Klomp* | In een grazige wyde, met Boere Schuuren en Geboomten, vertoont zich op de voorgrond verscheide soorten van staand en rustend Vée: als Ossen, Koeijen, Schaapen en Bokjes; verder een aangenaam Landschap, zonachtig en bevallig gepenceeld | companion to lot 92 *Mat:* op paneel *Size:* hoog 13 ½, breed 16 ½ duim	[Merrem]	(Sold) fl 20:10 La Fontaine

1802/06/16	AMSCH	0092	*A. Klomp* | In een dito [aangenaam] Landzicht, met Boere Woningen en Geboomten, mede als de voorgaande, ryk gestoffeerd met een menigte Vée, zoo staande als rustende; zynde de wederga en niet minder uitvoerig behandeld als de vorige | companion to lot 91 *Size:* hoog 13 ½, breed 16 ½ duim	[Merrem]	(Sold) fl 10 La Fontaine
1802/09/06	AMSCH	0060	*A. Klomp* | Een Landschap met staand en leggend Vée, beneevens een Boerin die een Koe melkt, verders eenig Geboomte en Boerewoning | *Mat:* op paneel *Size:* hoog 19, breed 14 duim	J	(Sold) fl 5:10 A Schotte
1802/09/06	AMSCH	0061	*A. Klomp* | In een grazige Wyde, vertoont zig verscheide staand en rustend Vée, verzelt van twee Huislieden; fix geschilderd | *Mat:* op doek	Wed Grave [or others]	(Sold) fl 6 Jan Spaan
1802/09/06	AMSCH	0206	*A. Klomp* | Een allerbevalligst Landschap, op de voorgrond een Vrouw, beezig zynde een rood bonte Koe te melken, daar neevens een Landman en eenige rustende Schaapen; natuurlyk en in de smaak van P. Potter, door A. Klomp | *Mat:* op doek *Size:* hoog 25, breed 23 duim	J	(Bought In) fl 10 ½
1802/09/21	UTHDG	0053	*A. Klomp* | Een grazend rood bont Osje, leggend Kalf, Schapen, en verder op, staand en rustend Vee, twee beelden, een Bosch uit het welke den top van een Kasteel gezien word. Uitvoerig en natuurlijk | *Mat:* op doek *Size:* hoog 16, breed 13 duimen		(Sold) fl 38 Niekerk
1802/09/21	UTHDG	0054	*A. Klomp* | Een leggende herkauwende Koe, en een zwart bonten Bok in een Duinagtig Landschap, als voren, door denzelven [A. Klomp] | *Mat:* op doek *Size:* hoog 7, breed 9 duimen		(Bought In) fl 6
1802/09/29	AMSCH	0025	*A. Klomp* | Een Landschap, hoog 13 ¾, breed 16 ½ duim. Panel. In dit fraije Landschap zo van verkiesing als uitvoering, zyn op de voorgrond verbeeld tweeliggende Ros couleurige Koeien, terwyl een ander van een hoger coleur als voorgaande door een Boerinnetje gevolgd word. Dezen word tegen de Lucht gezien; – verders eenig klein Vee, als een liggend Kalf, grasende en leggende Schapen, een Ram; op de derde grond eenige Boerewoningen, tusschen het geboomten en drie staande en leggende Koebeesten op den Dyk by het water; dit stuk is zeer zonagtig, uitvoerig en tevens krachtig behandelt, en een der besten van deezen verdienstlyken meester [Un des plus heureux sites de Paysages de ce grand artiste, offrant le point de vüe d'une route prés de la riviére, au delà sont des chaumiéres et des arbres ; du gros & du menu Bétail, d'un beau choix et disposés avec varieté sur le premier plan. Ce Tableau est une representation fidele de la nature, par la simplicité du ton général de la couleur, et se distingue encore par une touche délicate & precieuse.] | *Mat:* op paneel *Size:* hoog 13 ¾, breed 16 ½ duim	[Labouchere?]	(Sold) fl 43 Yver
1802/09/29	AMSCH	0026	*A. Klomp* | Een Landschap, hoog 13 ¾, breed 16 ½ duim. Paneel. Dit bevallige Stukje is niet minder als het voorgaande, op eenen Dyk ziet men tegen de Lucht, twee staande Ros couleurige Koeiën, waarby een zwarte rustende Koe, een vaal couleurig Gytje met haar Jongen en eenige staande en rustende Schaapen en Bokjes, men ziet verders in 't verschiet by het waater, eenige staande en leggende Koebeesten, een heining, waaragter geboomten en Boerewoningen [Un autre beau Tableau de ce Peintre encore très piquant par l'Eclat de la couleur et rendu avec cette intelligence qui lui est connue offrant le point de vue d'une digue ornée de Boeufs, vâches, moutons & chévres, au delà, de la digue sont des arbres & des cabânes, l'on trouve par tout dans ce Tableau cette touche fine & précieuse qui caracterisent les plus beaux ouvrages de cet habile artiste.] | *Mat:* op paneel *Size:* hoog 13 ¾, breed 16 ½ duim	[Labouchere?]	(Sold) fl 25 J van Eyk
1802/09/29	AMSCH	0027	*A. Klomp* | Een Landschap, hoog 9, breed 11 ¼ duim. Paneel. Een zeer bevallig Landschapje met geboomte by het water, waar agter een adelyk Huys: op den zandigen grond gedeeltelyk met Gras en Planten bewassen, zyn twee staande jonge Ossen, waarvan de eene Ros, de andere Bont, beneevens een grazend en enige rustende Schaapen; zeer delicaat gepenceeld en zonagtig behandelt [Un Joli Tableau de Paysage avec deux boeufs & des montons [sic] sur une digue en vüe d'une chateau derriere quelques arbres et prés de l'Eau, d'un Pinceau delicat & d'un bon coloris.] | companion to lot 28 *Mat:* op paneel *Size:* hoog 9, breed 11 ¼ duim	[Labouchere?]	(Sold) fl 21 A Schotte
1802/09/29	AMSCH	0028	*A. Klomp* | Een Landschap, hoog 9, breed 11 ¼ duim. Paneel. Dit Schilderytje van de eige qualiteit van uitvoerige penceelbehandeling als het voorgaande, is meede bevallig van ordenantie, verbeeld een Landschap met een Ros Koeitje, en een zwart jong Osje, benevens staande en rusrende [sic] Schaapen; verders eenig geboomten, by de uitstek van een Huis; dit stukje is zoagtig [sic] en van een natuurlyk coloriet [Un pendant au precedent : une grande pleine avec quelques arbres, une vâche, une jeune Taureau & quelques montons [sic] sur le devant. de la même touche de Pinceau & de la même couleur, Egal à la nature.] | companion to lot 27 *Mat:* op paneel *Size:* hoog 9, breed 11 ¼ duim	[Labouchere?]	(Sold) fl 11:10 Roelofs
1802/11/01	DOBRA	0051	*A. Klomp* | Een Boeren Werf met Koeijen en Schaapen, door A. Klomp. 1680 | *Mat:* op doek *Size:* breed ruim 4 voet en hoog 3 v. 5 d. *Inscr:* A. Klomp. 1680 (signed and dated?) *Notes:* It is unclear whether the name and date are inscribed on the painting.	Paulus van der Spyk [or others]	(Sold) fl 83 Gruiter
1803/08/17	AMSCH	0044	*Klomp, in de manier van P. Potter* | Op een Heuvel by een Boomstam, staan twee Ossen, verder een leggende Koe, benevens drie Schapen, en een Boerewoning in 't verschiet, fix geschilderd | *Mat:* op doek *Size:* hoog 27, breed 34 duim	Anna Catharina Putman	(Sold) fl 44 Gruyter

1803/12/12	AMSCH	0047	*A. Klomp* | Twee stuks Landschapjes, met Geboomte, Boerenwoningen, en Beesten; bevallig op Doek | *Mat:* op doek *Size:* hoog 16, breed 21 duim	Arnoud de Lange	(Sold) fl 6:10 Jozi
1804/02/27	AMSCH	0021	*Clomp. (A.)* | Twee aangenaame Landschappen, met staand en leggend Vee; bevallig gepenceeld | *Size:* hoog 18, breed 15 ½ duim	C	(Sold) fl 4:10 van Iperen
1804/04/28	LNDLS	0024	*A. Klomp* | Een Landschap, met geboomte en veele beesten, als koeijen, kalveren, schaapen en bokken, zeer konstig en uitvoerig van schildering, in de manier van Potter, door A. Klomp, op doek, hoog 23, breed 28 duim, ovaal | *Mat:* op doek *Fmt:* ovaal *Size:* hoog 23, breed 28 duim	[Abraham Delfos] [or others]	(Sold) fl 60 Parker
1804/05/07	AMSCH	0090	*Klomp. (A.)* | In een ruim Veldgezicht ziet men by een Hek een staande Os en Koe, welke door een Boer gemolken wordt; uitvoerig en fraai gepenceeld | *Mat:* op paneel *Size:* hoog 10, breed 14 duim	Vinkeles [for] H[affner]	(Sold) fl 9:5 S Joseph
1804/10/16	DLOND	0118	*N. Klomp* | Een Landschap. Paysage | *Mat:* op paneel *Size:* hoog 10, breed 13 *Notes:* The artist's name was given as "N. Klomp" but we have assumed this is an error.		(Sold) fl 3:5 v Giesen
1804/10/29	HRBAU	0047	*Klomp, (A.)* | Deeze twee Schilderytjes verbeelden ieder, op een' heuvel, een Koetjen en eenige Schaapen, in onderscheidene houdingen staande en liggende; waar agter in 't verschiet Weiland en Boschadien. Zeer natuurlyk behandeld | *Mat:* op paneel *Size:* hoog 6, breed 7 duim	Simon Styl	(Unknown)
1805/12/16	AMSCH	0034a	*A. Klomp* | Dit bevallig en aangenaam Schildery, stelt voor een Duinryk Landschap, met Geboomte, Gebouwen en helder spiegelend Water, ryk gestoffeerd met staand en rustend Vée, als Ossen, Koeijen, Schaapen, Varkens, en een Boer en Boerin, welke een Koe melkt, verders een Duinachtig verschiet, met een oud Casteel en Geboomte; aller delicaats en uitvoerig gepenceeld, en fraay van licht | *Mat:* op doek *Size:* hoog 29, breed 36 duim	O	(Bought In) fl 30
1806/05/05	AMSCH	0077	*A. Klomp* | Een aangenaam Landschap met staand en leggend Vee; uitvoerig geschildert door A. Klomp | *Mat:* op doek *Size:* hoog 13, breed 14 duim	V[inkeles]	(Sold) fl 16 van Dijl
1806/08/13	AMSCH	0090	*Klomp. (A.)* | Een Boomryk Landschap, op de Voorgrond eenige Herders, met een ménigte Vee, krachtig en natuurlyk geschilderd | *Mat:* op doek *Size:* hoog 29, breed 36 duim	van der Voort	(Sold) fl 16:10 Thais
1808/04/26	GDAN	0081	*Klomp (A.)* | Zijnde een Boomrijk Landschap met drie Koeijen | *Size:* hoog 12, breed 14 duim	G H Fortuyn	(Unknown)
1808/04/26	GDAN	0082	*Klomp (A.)* | In een Landschap, een staande en leggend Koeitje met Schapen, zeer uitvoerig behandeld | *Size:* hoog 15, breed 11 duim	G H Fortuyn	(Unknown)
1808/08/23	AMSCH	0087	*Klomp. (A.)* | In een aangenaam Landgezigt met eenig Geboomten, ziet men op de voorgrond eene Boerin een Koe melken, verzelt van twee Huislieden, met een Hondje speelende, verders rustende Koeijen en Schaapen; natuurlijk en fiks gepenceelt | *Mat:* op doek *Size:* hoog 22, breed 28 duim	C	(Sold) fl 81 Coclers
1808/08/23	AMSCH	0088	*Klomp. (A.)* | Een aangenaam Landschap, de voorgrond gestoffeert met eene Vrouw, die bézig is een rood bonte Koe te melken, op de tweede grond een staande Koe bij verscheiden rustende Schaapen; meesterlijk en schoon geschilderd | *Mat:* op doek *Size:* hoog 24, breed 22 duim	J	(Sold) fl 15 van Iperen
1808/08/23	AMSCH	0089	*Klomp. (A.)* | Een grasige Weiden, waar in eenige staande Beesten bij de stam van een oude Boom; uitvoerig in de manier van Potter behandeld | *Mat:* op paneel *Size:* hoog 12, breed 15 duim	J	(Bought In) fl 14
1808/08/23	AMSCH	0090	*Klomp. (A.)* | Op een Heuvel bij de stam van een Boom, staan twee Ossen, verder een rustende Koe, benevens drie Schaapen, en eenige Boeren Wooningen in het verschiet; fiks geschilderd | *Mat:* op doek *Size:* hoog 27, breed 34 duim	[Gruyter?]	(Bought In) fl 49
1808/08/23	AMSCH	0194	*A. Klomp* | In een Boomrijk Landschap, zit op de voorgrond op een grasige Vlakte bij eenig rustend Vee eene Boerin een Koe melken, benevens twee Jongens, die een Hond laten opzitten; meesterlijk behandeld op Doek | *Mat:* op doek	[Gruyter?]	(Sold) fl 9 Spruit
1808/09/13	HABRU	0048	*Klomp* | Een Landschap, met Koebeesten, &c.		(Unknown) fl 19
1809/04/22	AMYVR	0064	*A. Klomp* | Een Landschap, met staand en liggend Vee; in 't verschiet eenige Beeldjes; zonachtig | *Mat:* op doek *Size:* hoog 16, breed 13 duim	de Bruin	(Sold) fl 7:15 C S Roos
1810/03/07	UTWLD	0011	*Klomp* | Twee bergachtige Landschappen, gestoffeerd met Schapen en Koeyen | *Size:* hoog 3 voet 8 duim, breed 3 voet 5 duim	J J Woertman	(Unknown) fl 72
1810/03/27	RMCNL	0012	*Klomp* | Een dito [fraai Bergachtig Landschap] met Koeijen en Schapen		(Unknown)
1810/03/27	RMCNL	0034	*Klomp* | Een Bergachtig Landschap met Koeijen en Schapen, zoo liggende als staande, zeer fraai behandeld		(Unknown)
1810/10/11	AMSCH	0042	*A. Klomp* | Een hoog Bergachtig en Boomrijk Landschap, met staand en liggend Vee; warm en uitvoerig geschilderd | *Mat:* op doek *Size:* hoog 27, breed 23 duimen	[Gruyter?]	(Sold) fl 8:10 Boelhouwer
1810/11/07	UTWLD	0032	*Klomp* | Eenige staande en rustende beeltjes, ten deelen schuilende onder de schaduw van eenig reijzend geboomte, achter dezelve het gezicht op eenige gebouwen en verder over een rivier, alles zeer geestig en kragtig behandeld door Klomp op doek, 2 voet hoog, 2 en een half voet breed, zwarte Lijst | *Mat:* op doek *Size:* 2 voet hoog, 2 en een half voet breed		(Unknown) fl 10

Klomp, Albert Jansz. (copy after)

1808/06/11	RMRIJ	0082	*C: Vermeulen; na A: Klomp* | Een aangenaam Landschap, met ryke Stoffagie van Vee enz., goed gedaan | copy by Corn. Vermeulen (III) after Klomp *Mat:* op paneel *Size:* hoog 5, breed 4 ½ duim		(Bought In) fl 9:10

Klomp, Albert Jansz. (manner)

1802/06/16	AMSCH	0248	*A. Klomp* | Een Heuvelachtig Landzicht met Geboomten, op de voorgrond een rustende en een staande Koe, verzelt van twee Schaapen; krachtig geschilderd op Doek, in de manier van A. Klomp | *Mat:* op doek *Size:* hoog 15 ½, breed 19 ½ duim	[Merrem]	(Sold) fl 10:10 Agina
1802/09/06	AMSCH	0147	*A. Klomp* | Twee stuks Landgezichten met Woningen en Geboomte, gestoffeerd met verschillende zoorten van Vée; plaisant geschilderd op Doek, in de manier van A. Klomp | *Mat:* op doek	B	(Sold) fl 12:10 Pruijssenaar
1802/09/06	AMSCH	0233	*Klomp* | Twee stuks aangenaame Landschappen, gestoffeerd met staand en leggend Vée; in de manier van Klomp	J	(Sold) fl 1:5 Vermeulen
1807/06/02	AMHUY	0003	*Klomp* | Twee bevallige Landschappen, met eenige staande en leggende Koejen en Schapen, zonachtig gepenceeld in de manier van Klomp		(Unknown)
1807/06/10	HGBSM	0144	*A. Klomp* | Twee stuks Landschappen met Koebeesten en Schapen, in de manier van A. Klomp | *Mat:* op paneel *Size:* hoog 10 ½, breed 14 duim	Abraham Delfos [or others]	(Sold) fl 2:12 Carré
1810/06/06	RMMUY	0227	*Klomp* | Een Landschap met Koeijen en Schapen, als door Klomp | *Notes:* According to the MA copy of the catalogue, this lot was sold with lot 226 by J. Bent for fl. 2:16.		(Unknown) fl 3:14

Klootwijk [Unidentified]

1810/07/23	DOLGI	0030	*Klootwijk* | Een rustend Jager bij eenig geschoten Wild | *Mat:* op paneel *Size:* hoog 17 ½, breed 15 ½ duim	Mr Pieter van den Santheuvel	(Sold) fl 2:7 van Dongen van Rotterdam [or] Schalk

Knip, Nicolaas Frederik (I)

1802/07/27	AKHRK	0016	*Knip, de oude* | De Verkondiging van de Geboorte des Heilands aan de Herders, die de Nachtwagt over hun Vee hadden, men ziet een glorie van Engelen nederdaalen, en de verwondering en verbaastheid in de Herders. Zeer dun, fix en zacht geschilderd | *Mat:* op paneel *Fmt:* rond *Size:* hoog 30, breed 30 [duim]	Maria Stategaart	(Sold) fl 22 Bruys

Knupfer, Nikolaus

1803/08/17	AMSCH	0046	*Knupfer. (N.)* | Daniel in de Leeuwenkuil geworpen, word van de Leeuwen in plaats van verslonden, integendeel bevyligt [sic], het welk door den Koning en zyn gevolg met verwondering beschouwt word, meesterlyk geschilderd | *Mat:* op doek *Size:* hoog 31, breed 40 ½ duim	Anna Catharina Putman	(Sold) fl 5 Gruyter
1809/07/19	AMSCH	0028	*Knupser (N.)* | Een rijke zinnebeeldige Ordonnantie, zinspeelende op de Vrede en Welvaart des Koophandels, bevallig van koloriet, krachtig en uitvoerig geschilderd | *Mat:* op doek *Size:* hoog 36, breed 32 duim	[Wijkersloot?]	(Sold) fl 3:15 Dupré
1809/07/19	AMSCH	0029	*Knupser (N.)* | Eene pragtig gekleede Vrouw, zittende nevens eene Tafel, waarop eenige Kostbaarheden, zij schijnt zig van haare Cieraaden te willen ontdoen, nevens haar staat een Engel, haar een Palmtak en Lauërkroon aanbiedende. Bevallig van koloriet en teder geschilderd | *Mat:* op doek *Size:* hoog 17, breed 12 ½ duim	C	(Sold) fl 7:10 T Spaan
1810/05/22	AMSCH	0052	*Knuffer (N.)* | Een zinrijke Geestelijke Ordonantie van twee Beelden, omhoog vertoonen zich eenige Engelen, gestoffeerd met verder bijwerk; bevallig van koloriet en uitvoerig van penceelbehandeling | *Mat:* op paneel *Size:* hoog 16, breed 12 duim	D	(Sold) fl 7 Yver

Kobell, Hendrik

1801/06/10	AMSCH	0095	*Kobell. (H.)* | Twee stuks, een woelende en een onstuimige Zee, beiden met Oorlogscheepen en andere Vaartuigen, konstig gepenceeld | *Mat:* op paneel *Size:* hoog 12, breed 17 duim	[Doublet]	(Sold) fl 30 Spruit van Gend
1808/06/06	RMRIJ	0063	*Kobell. (Hendrik)* | Een woelend Water met vele Schepen. Natuurlijk behandeld. Eene wedergade. Een stil Water met vele Schepen. Als boven [Une Mer agitée, sur laquelle on voit plusieurs Bateaux à la voile. Le Pendant. Une eau calme et plusieurs Bateaux à la rame etc. Ces deux Morceaux font honneur au Peintre, dont les Tableaux sont rares, et dont les talents ont été trop tôt moissonnés] | *Annots:* van Pehallis[?] 1780 (f 75.-) (RMA I) *Mat:* op paneel *Size:* Twee stukken. Hoog 13 ¾ en breed 18 ½ duim	Gerrit van der Pot, Heer van Groeneveld	(Sold) fl 205 van Yperen
1808/06/06	RMRIJ	0064	*Kobell. (Hendrik)* | Een woelend Water met Schepen. Eene wedergade. Zijnde een stil Water met vele Schepen [Une eau agitée, ou l'on voît des Bateaux etc. d'une belle et vraie exécution. Le Pendant. Une eau calme etc. Egal en mérite au précédent] | *Annots:* van Jan de Neufville te Amst. Sept. 1782 (f 250-) (RMA I) *Mat:* op paneel *Size:* Twee Stukken. Hoog 9 ½ en breed 13 ½ duim	Gerrit van der Pot, Heer van Groeneveld	(Sold) fl 165 van Dongen
1808/06/06	RMRIJ	0065	*Kobell. (Hendrik)* | Een Storm, waar in eenige Schepen in gevaar zijn [Un Orage. On voît la Mer fortement agitée, et deux Vaisseaux prêts à faire naufrage. Un ciel imposant, de la chaleur et de Génie Caracterisent ce Tableau] | *Mat:* op pergament *Size:* Hoog 18 en breed 24 ½ duim	Gerrit van der Pot, Heer van Groeneveld	(Sold) fl 50 Dr Luchtmans

1810/05/22	AMSCH	0050	*Kobell (H.) junior* | Een woelend Water, voor aan met een zeilende Kaag, verder Oorlogschepen, Visschers Pinken en andere Vaartuigen; fiks geschilderd | *Mat:* op paneel *Size:* hoog 16, breed 22 duim	Johannes van de Putte Nicolaasz.	(Sold) fl 47 Yver
1810/05/22	AMSCH	0051	*Kobell (H.) junior* | Een kabbelend Water, met eene menigte Vaartuigen en Beeldjes gestoffeerd, en van de beste schildering van dezen Meester | *Mat:* op paneel *Size:* hoog 16, breed 21 duim	Johannes van de Putte Nicolaasz.	(Sold) fl 22:10 van Iperen

Kobell, Jan (II)

1808/06/11	RMRIJ	0004	*J: Kobell* | Een aangenaam en welverkozen Hollandsch Landgezicht, waar in onderscheiden soorten van Hoornvee; alleruitvoerigst zonachtig en konstig geschilderd | *Mat:* op paneel *Size:* hoog 19, breed 26 duim		(Sold) fl 370 Luchtmans
1808/06/11	RMRIJ	0005	*J: Kobell* | Een aangenaam boomryk Landschap, met Koeijen, Schapen en Beelden; uitvoerig, kragtig en warm geschilderd | *Mat:* op mahonie paneel *Size:* hoog 13, breed 11 duim		(Sold or Bought In) fl 85 [or] 100 Bogaart
1810/08/01	AMSCH	0050	*Kobell (Jan)* | Eene grazige Weide, waarin op den voorgrond eene staande en eene rustende Koe bij eenen Wilgenboom; in het verschiet ander grazend Vee [Dans un gras Paturage auprès d'un Saule on voit une Vache sur pieds, à côté d'une autre qui est couchée ; dans la perspective se trouve du Bêtail à la pature] | *Annots:* crud et dur, comme Potter son modèle. (NGW) *Mat:* op paneel *Size:* hoog 24, breed 18 duimen	Mr Pieter de Smeth van Alphen	(Sold) fl 455 T v Iperen [voor] Wreesman
1810/08/01	AMSCH	0051	*Kobell (Jan)* | Een Landgezigt met eene liggende en twee staande Koeijen; van de laatsten wrijft zich eene tegen het Staketsel van eene Brug over een Water. Verder ziet men grazend en liggend Vee, en een Heerenhuis in het verschiet [Paysage orné de deux Vaches sur pieds et d'une troisième qui est couchée ; une des premieres se froissant contre la palisade d'un Pont qui traverse un Ruisseau. Au second plan se trouve different Bêtail, et un Chateau termine la perspective] | *Annots:* crud et dur. (NGW) *Mat:* op paneel *Size:* hoog 23, breed 28 duimen	Mr Pieter de Smeth van Alphen	(Sold) fl 415 T v Iperen voor Wreesman
1810/08/01	AMSCH	0051a[H]	*J. Kobel* | Eene grazige Weide, waar in op de voorgrond eenige staande en rustende Koeyen door J. Kobel | *Annots:* crud et dur. (NGW) *Notes:* This lot was added in by hand in the FLNY, NGW I and VAL I copies of the catalogue.	Mr Pieter de Smeth van Alphen	(Sold) fl 350 Van Iperen [for] Wreesman
1810/11/07	UTWLD	0033	*J. Kobell* | Twee losse Paarden in een Weiland, waar agter eenig boomgewas – verder een stil verschiet door J. Kobell op doek, 1 voet 1 en een half duim hoog, 1 voet 5 en een half duim breed, zwarte Lijst | companion to lot 34 *Mat:* op doek *Size:* 1 voet 1 ½ duim hoog, 1 voet 5 ½ duim breed		(Unknown) fl 5:5
1810/11/07	UTWLD	0034	*J. Kobell* | Een pendant | companion to lot 33		(Unknown) fl 22

Kobell, Jan (II) (copy by)

1810/11/07	UTWLD	0028	*J. Kobell; Ruisdael* | Een Copie van een der Kapitaalste Schilderijen van Ruisdael, verbeeldende een met geweld afkomenden Waterval, welks kracht aangezet word door een stuk Rots dat op onderscheiden kanten doorklieft is, op een verdere afstand ziet men op een duinagtige grond een Kloostergebouw, waaragter eenig geboomt en bergagtig verschiet in een bruine parthij: op een overhellende Rots eenige boomen, alles zeer klaar en kragtig, het water zeer vloeiend en schoon geschilderd door J. Kobell op doek, 2 voet 2 duim hoog, 1 voet 8 duim breed, zwarte Lijst | copy by Jan Kobell (II) after J. Ruisdael *Mat:* op doek *Size:* 2 voet 2 duim hoog, 1 voet 8 duim breed		(Unknown) fl 31

Koedijck, Isaac

1806/05/05	AMSCH	0029	*Coedyk* | In een oud Hollandsch Binnenvertrek zit op de voorgrond een oude Vrouw, bézig zynde een pot uit te schrapen, op de tafel staat eenig huisraad, nevens een houte Tobbe met Groentens; kragtig en natuurlyk op Paneel | *Mat:* op paneel *Size:* hoog 20, breed 24 duim	V[inkeles] [or] O	(Sold) fl 82 Jan Smit
1809/06/13	AMSCH	0030	*N. Coedijk* | In een Binnevertrek zit op de voorgrond eene bejaarde Vrouw, in oude Hollandsche Kleeding, zij houd een Aarde Pot op haar Schoot, welke zij met een Lepel schijnt uit te schraapen, voor haar op de Tafel staat een Kan, Mand en een Bak met Aardvruchten; dit stuk is fraai van licht en bruin en uitvoerig geschilderd | *Size:* hoog 20, breed 25 duim	A	(Sold) fl 152 de Lely

Koets

1802/04/13	HAVIN	0038	*Koets* | Een Tafel met vrugten		(Unknown)

Koller, Johann Jakob

1801/12/22	AMOTT	0037	*Koller* | 1 Boom- en Bergachtig Landschap, met een Rivier	Bartholomeus Ruloffs	(Unknown) fl 1
1801/12/22	AMOTT	0097	*J. Koller* | 2 plaisante Landschapjes	Bartholomeus Ruloffs	(Unknown) fl 1:5
1802/05/05	AMSCH	0102	*J. Koller* | Een Gezicht in de Moolebuurt te Zaandam, ziende op eenige Huizen en verdere stoffagie, zeer natuurlyk | *Mat:* op paneel *Size:* hoog 11, breed 15 duim	C	(Sold) fl 3:5 Vermeulen
1802/06/28	AMSCH	0094	*J. Koller* | Een gezicht op de Muntstooren [sic] te Amsterdam, ryk van Stoffagie, zonachtig behandeld | *Size:* hoog 15, breed 20 duim	Anna Elink	(Sold) fl 19:10 for lots 94 & 95. van Iperen
1802/06/28	AMSCH	0095	*J. Koller* | Een gezicht op de Joode Kerken binnen Amsterdam, zeer natuurlyk gepenceeld, door Denzelven [J. Koller], panneel | *Mat:* op paneel *Size:* hoog 15, breed 19 duim	Anna Elink	(Sold) fl 19:10 for lots 94 & 95. van Iperen

1802/06/28	AMSCH	0096	*J. Koller* | Een bevallig Dorpgezigt, op de voorgrond gestoffeerd met wandelende Boeren, en in het water een schuitje met een Melkboer, en verder bywerk, fiks, door Denzelven [J. Koller], op panneel | *Mat:* op paneel *Size:* hoog 7, breed 8 duim	Anna Elink	(Sold) fl 1:10 Yver
1802/12/13	AMSCH	0045	*Koller* | Een hoog bergagtig Zwitsers Landschap, met een Waterval, gestoffeerd met Beelden en Beesten | *Mat:* op paneel *Size:* hoog 14, breed 11 duim	Pruyssenaar [for] A	(Sold) fl 2 L Pakker
1805/07/10	AMSCH	0086	*J. J. Koller* | Een Boom- en Bergachtig Landschap, met een Watermolen, en fraay verschiet, gestoffeerd met verscheide Beeldjes; zonachtig op Paneel | *Mat:* op paneel *Size:* hoog 16, breed 21 duim	Y[ver]	(Sold) fl 8:5 Van Iperen
1808/09/13	HABRU	0049	*J. Koller* | Een Bergachtig Landschap, in de Contrij van Zurich, natuurlijk | companion to lot 50		(Unknown)
1808/09/13	HABRU	0050	*J. Koller* | Een dito [Bergachtig Landschap], zijnde een weerga | companion to lot 49		(Unknown) fl 24
1808/09/13	HABRU	0051	*J. Koller* | Een Rhijngezicht		(Unknown) fl 4:13
1808/09/13	HABRU	0052	*J. Koller* | Een dito [Rhijngezicht]		(Unknown) fl 3:15
1810/05/22	AMSCH	0135	*J. Koller* | Twee stuks Duitsche Landschappen, met Woningen, Geboomte en Beeldjes	R	(Sold) fl 9 Ringhuysen
1810/06/20	AMSCH	0187	*J. Koller* | Een Landschap, waarin eenige Beesten door een water waden	A	(Sold) fl 2:10 Focken
			Koninck		
1802/06/28	AMSCH	0098	*Koninck* | Een bedaagd Mansportrait met gevouwen handen, meesterlyk gepenceeld | *Mat:* op paneel *Size:* hoog 25, breed 19 duim	Anna Elink	(Sold) fl 2:5 Taak
1804/07/25	DLGRO	0082	*Koning* | Een fraai oud Mans Hoofd | *Mat:* op paneel *Size:* hoog 9, breed 8 duim	Mr Franc van der Burch Wz.	(Unknown)
1804/07/25	DLGRO	0083	*Koning* | Een dito [fraai] Borstbeeld, met een Boek in de hand, fraai geschilderd door denzelfde [Koning] | *Mat:* op paneel *Size:* hoog 9, breed 8 duim	Mr Franc van der Burch Wz.	(Unknown)
			Koninck (or Koninck, manner)		
1810/11/07	UTWLD	0017	*de Koning* | De begroeting van de drie Wijzen uit het Oosten, op de schoot van Maria 't Kindje spelende met de geschenken, die een derzelven knielend aanbied, de andere staan met groote inspanning 't Kindje aan te zien, verders veel beeldjes, alles zeer geestig geordineerd, ficks [sic] en schetsgewijs geschilderd, door of in de manier van de Koning, op doek, 1 voet 7 duim hoog 2 voet breed, zwarte Lijst | *Mat:* op doek *Size:* 1 voet 7 duim hoog 2 voet breed		(Unknown) fl 3
			Koninck (manner)		
1804/10/20	GRBOL	0013	*Koning* | Een oude Kop, in de Trant van Koning	Joannis Cannegieteri	(Unknown)
1810/12/03	DOBRA	0012	*Koning* | Een bedaagde Vrouw, halverlvf [sic], lezende in een boek; kragtig en uitvoerig geschilderd, als door Koning | *Notes:* In lot 69 by Helt Stockade, this lot was given as the companion; we have assumed this is an error and that lot 68 by Helt Stockade was intended.		(Unknown)
			Koninck, Jacob		
1802/05/05	AMSCH	0101	*J. D. Koonig* | Een Woelende Zee, waarin een Hollands Oorlogschip voor een Fort ten Anker komt, verders een zeilende Loodsbood, en Barkas, zeer natuurlyk en bevallig gepenceeld	J	(Sold) fl 7:5 Frantszen
1802/09/06	AMSCH	0056	*J. de Koning* | In een uitgestrekt Landschap, ziet men een ménigte van Geboomte en Gebouwen, doorsneeden met Rivieren, ryk gestoffeerd met Heeren en Dames te Paard, die ter Jacht ryden, beneevens een Koets met zes Paarden, en een ménigte anderen Figuuren; schoon van licht en meesterachtig gepenceeld | *Mat:* op doek *Size:* hoog 25, breed 30 duim	J	(Sold) fl 16 van Iperen [and] Ths Spaan
1802/12/13	AMSCH	0094	*J. D. Koning* | Een woelende Zee, op de voorgrond een zeilende Loots Boot en roeijende Barcas, wyders een Fort waar voor een Oorlogschip ten Anker komt, dun en zonagtig gepenceeld | *Mat:* op paneel *Size:* hoog 13, breed 16 ½ duim	Pruyssenaar [for] C	(Sold) fl 3 L Pakker
			Koninck, Philips de		
1801/05/11	AMSCH	0039	*P. Koning* | Een Man met een ring in de hand, fix behandeld | *Mat:* op paneel *Size:* hoog 7, breed 6 duim	P[ruyssenaar]	(Sold) fl 2:5 Gruiter
1801/05/11	AMSCH	0040	*P. Koning* | 't Pourtret van een bedaagde Vrouw, in prachtige hollandsche kleeding, meesterlyk en krachtig gepenceeld | *Mat:* op doek *Size:* hoog 27, breed 22 duim	P[ruyssenaar]	(Sold) fl 13 Gruiter
1801/06/10	AMSCH	0092	*Koning. (P.)* | Deeze uitmundtende Ordonantie, verbeeld den Hogenpriester den Cynspenning van den Heiland ontfangende, zynde een ryke Ordonantie van acht Beelden, bevallig geordoneerd fraai van licht en bruin, meesterlyk gepenceeld | *Mat:* op paneel *Size:* hoog 40, breed 32 duim	Herman ten Kate	(Sold) fl 475 T van Iperen
1802/06/16	AMSCH	0087	*P.H. Koning* | Deeze schoone Ordenantie verbeeld, alwaar de Godvrugtigen Mannen het doode Lichaam van Christus van het Kruis aflaaten; aan de voet des Kruis legt Maria Magdaléna, de voeten	[Merrem]	(Sold) fl 405 B^{d} Kooij

			omhelzende: ter zyde op de voorgrond ziet men Maria in zwym leggende, verzelt van Vrouwen, haar hulp en bystand biedenden: om hoog vertoonen zich eenige Engelen: de Hartstogten zyn treffende verbeeld; het Coloriet kragtig en van eene uitvoerige Penceel-behandeling | *Mat:* op doek *Fmt:* van boven tooggewyze *Size:* hoog 41, breed 35 duim		
1802/12/13	AMSCH	0091	*P. Koning* | In een Binnevertrek van een oud Gebouw, zit een Grysaard by een Tafel, waarop een Globe en verscheide Boeken, het licht door het Vengster geeft een kragtige werking op de Voorwerpen en is voorts meesterlyk op Paneel geschilderd | *Mat:* op paneel *Size:* hoog 24, breed 20 duim	Yver	(Sold) fl 44 Gruiter
1803/08/01	AMSCH	0014	*Koning. (Ph. de)* | Den Apostel Petrus, halverlyf, met zyne oogen hemelwaarts en zaamgevouwen handen, in de welke hy de Sleutels vasthoud, krachtig en meesterlyk gepenceeld | *Mat:* op doek *Size:* hoog 26, breed 21 ½ duim	J	(Sold) fl 46 Hodges
1803/08/17	AMSCH	0045	*Koning. (P.)* | Een, met een Man en Vrouw, gestoffeerde hoek van een Kerkgebouw, welke door een helder zonligt gedaagd worden, meesterlyk daargesteld | *Mat:* op paneel *Size:* hoog 9, breed 7 ½ duim	Anna Catharina Putman	(Sold) fl 7:10 van Dijl
1803/09/07	AMSCH	0092	*P. Koning* | Een Philosoof ter halver lyf, met een gryzen Baard, meesterlyk op Paneel [Un philosophe à demi-corps, ayant une longue barbe grise ; d'une vérité d'expression frappante] | *Mat:* op paneel *Size:* hoog 23, breed 16 duim	Smidt	(Bought In) fl 2
1804/08/08	AMSCH	0097	*Ph. Koning* | In een Kamer zit een ryk gekleede Vrouw, voor haar legt een Meid met eene Spiegel op haare Knieën, achter haar een Moor met een Koffertje met Kostbaarheeden en verder Bywerk; als Rembrand | *Mat:* op doek *Size:* hoog 66, breed 60 duim	Vink[eles] [for] K[=Gruyter?]	(Sold) fl 1 Toselli
1804/10/29	HRBAU	0048	*Kooning, (P.)* | Dit Stuk verbeeldt een zeer bevallig Oude Mans Hoofd; met hairen en een' zwaaren baard, zeer oplettend ziende naar een Landkaart, waar in hy iets schynt af te meeten, hy is in 't zwart gekleed, met een' gouden keten om den hals, en met een' Mantel met bont omhangen. Dit Schildery is zeer kunstig en meesterlyk behandeld | *Mat:* op doek *Size:* hoog 35, breed 29 duim	Simon Styl	(Unknown)
1805/07/10	AMSCH	0086a	*P. de Koning* | Een prachtig Gekleede Dame aan een Tafel zittende, waarop geplaatst zyn verscheide Zilvere Drinkschaalen, Muziek-Instrumenten, Globes, Boek, en andere Instrumenten, meesterlyk op Doek | *Mat:* op doek *Size:* hoog 54, breed 54 duim	R[oos]	(Sold) fl 17:10 Gruyter
1806/05/05	AMSCH	0075	*P.H. de Koningh* | Een boomryk Landschap met Gebouwen en andere stoffagie; zeer natuurlyk als door Ruisdaal, door P.H. de Koningh | *Mat:* op doek *Size:* hoog 22, breed 26 duim	V[inkeles]	(Sold) fl 34 Roos
1806/05/05	AMSCH	0076	*P. H. de Koningh* | Een levensgroot Mans Pourtret, zittende in een Armstoel in een peinsende houding, met een bonte Muts op 't hoofd in aloude Kleeding; kragtig en kunstig geschildert	V[inkeles]	(Bought In) fl 9
1808/09/13	HABRU	0053	*Ph. Koning* | Een Boomrijk Landschap, op een Dorp ziende		(Unknown) fl 5
1809/04/17	AMSCH	0049	*Ph. Koning* | Een Mans Pourtret, met de Muts op het Hoofd en een Purpere Mantel omhangen; meesterlijk en breed geschilderd | *Mat:* op doek *Size:* hoog 29, breed 24 duim	A	(Sold) fl 5:10
1809/04/17	AMSCH	0050	*Ph. Koning* | Een vergenoegd oud Man, houdende een Glas in de Hand, schoon geschilderd | *Mat:* op paneel	A	(Sold) fl 3 Gruyter
1809/04/17	AMSCH	0051	*Ph. Koning* | Een vlak Duinachtig Landschap, met Stoffagie van Beeldjes | *Mat:* op paneel	A	(Sold) fl 1
1809/06/13	AMSCH	0070	*Ph. de Koning* | Een vergenoegd Huisman, zit bij een Ton, bezig zijn Pijp aan te steeken, terwijl eenige anderen zich met Rooken en Drinken vermaaken; natuurlijk voorgesteld | *Mat:* op paneel *Size:* hoog 13, breed 12 duim	E	(Sold) fl 21 Buck
1809/07/19	AMSCH	0026	*Koning (P.)* | Dit uitmuntend kunstjuweel stelt voor de Roeping van Mattheus den Tollenaar. Dit voorval is verbeeld in een grootsch Gebouw, ter regter zijde bij het inkomen van gemelde Gebouw, ziet men den Heiland, verzeld van Petrus en een ander Discipel, Mattheus tot zich roepen, deze is gezeten nevens een Tafel, waarbij verscheide Personen of Tolbediendens zeer aandagtig werkzaam zijn ter ontfangst van Penningen, en aantekeningen te maken. Dit stuk is in den stijl van Rembrand geordonneerd, en zijn de uitvoerigste partijen zoo schoon en delicaat behandeld, als of het door G. Douw geschilderd was | *Mat:* op doek *Size:* hoog 19 ½, breed 24 ½ duim	G	(Bought In) fl 660
1810/06/20	AMSCH	0038	*P. De Koning* | Een Binnenhuis, met vrolijke, drinkende en liefkoozende Boeren en Boerinnen, benevens eenig Huisraad. Uitvoerig | *Mat:* op paneel *Size:* hoog 15, breed 18 duimen	A	(Sold) fl 4 J de Vries
1810/08/06	AMSCH	0057	*Koning (Ph. de)* | Een aangenaam vlak Landschap met Geboomte en verscheide Wegen, op den voorgrond een Vaart, waarin een Jaagschuit, verder gaande en rustende Lieden, en een ruim verschiet; aller natuurlijkst behandeld | *Mat:* op doek *Size:* hoog 60, breed 73 duimen	U	(Sold) fl 151 Texier Gerbet en Comp

Koninck, Philips de (and Bergen, D.)

1808/06/06	RMRIJ	0066	*Koning. (Philip de); Bergen. (Dirk van)* | Deze schoone en krachtige Schilderij vertoont op den voorgrond den ingang van een Bosch, waarin	Gerrit van der Pot, Heer van Groeneveld	(Sold) fl 310 Johs Eck en Zoon [for] le Roi

zich voordoet een Ossendrift, Veehoeder, Jonge en Hond, het Bosch uitkomende. De tweede grond verbeeldt eene Rivier met een uitgestrekt rijk en vlak verschiet. Meesterlijk behandeld [On découvre d'abord l'Entrée d'une belle forêt bien garnie d'arbres touffus, d'où sort un troupeau de Boeufs, conduit par un Pâtre, un Garçon, et un Chien. Le second plan offre une belle Rivière et un lointain d'une immense Etendue. Ce Tableau vrai, savant et hardi fait honneur aux Artistes qui l'ont composé] | *Mat:* op doek *Size:* Hoog 52, en breed 63 duim. *Loc:* Amsterdam, Nederland. Rijksmuseum. (A207) as P. Koninck

Koninck, Philips de (and Lingelbach)

1805/07/10	AMSCH	0086b	*P. de Koning; J. Lingelbach* | Een gezicht na het Leeven, zeer natuurlyk van lieht [sic] en bruin, en gestoffeerd met een uittogt ter Valken-Jagt, op Doek, door denzelven [P. de Koning] en J. Lingelbach | *Mat:* op doek *Size:* hoog 52, breed 62 duim	R[oos]	(Sold) fl 275 Hulswit

Koninck, Philips de (and Velde, A.)

1802/05/05	AMSCH	0091	*P. Koning; A. van de Velde* | Een Bergachtig Landschap, op de Voorgrond Boeren Wooningen, een Heer te Paard en eenige Hoenders. Natuurlyk en fraai behandeld | *Mat:* op paneel *Size:* hoog 19, breed 16 duim	C	(Sold) fl 7 Spruit
1804/08/08	AMSCH	0096	*Ph. Koning; A. van de Velde* | In een vlak en wyduitgestrekt Landzicht, met eenige Wooningen en Geboomte, vertoont zich een Vorstelyk Lusthuis en Thuin, by een Riviergezicht, waarin een Plaisierschuitje geplaatst is, op de voorgrond, by een opgaande Weg, ryk gestoffeerd met een Landman, een Drift Beesten voortdryvende, ter linker zyde een grazende en een rustende Os en Schaap; alles zonachtig en helder, en bevallig van coloriet, door Ph. Koning, en de Stoffagie door A. van de Velde | *Mat:* op doek *Size:* hoog 36, breed 42 duim *Loc:* Bruxelles, Belgique. Musées royaux des Beaux-Arts. (54)	Schley [for] A	(Sold) fl 36 Reyers
1806/08/13	AMSCH	0089	*Koning. (Ph. de); A. van de Velden* | In een uitgestrekt Landschap, ziet men over een klaar spiegelend Water een Stad, op de voorgrond by opgaand Geboomten eenige Gebouwen, verders Landlieden die eenig Vée dryven en een bevallig verschiet; zonachtig en meesterlyk geschildert | *Mat:* op doek *Size:* hoog 17, breed 21 duim	Vinkeles [for] G[ruyter]	(Sold) fl 25:10 van Iperen

Koningh, Leendert de

1809/07/25	HGBSM	0137	*L.D. Koning* | Een Maasgezigt met de Stad Dordrecht in het verschiet, met diverse Vaartuigen | *Mat:* op paneel *Size:* hoog 16 en een half, breed 27 duim	D van der Aa [or] E B ten Dall	(Sold) fl 6 van Eyk
1810/07/23	DOLG1	0031	*L. de Koning* | Een Zeehaven. Op den voorgrond een Zee-Officier, eenige Matrozen, en andere Stoffering. Verder een onttuigd Oorlogschip, en meerder Vaartuigen. Alles zeer uitvoerig van Teekening, en kragtig geschilderd | *Mat:* op paneel *Size:* hoog 13, breed 19 duim	Mr Pieter van den Santheuvel	(Sold) fl 25 A van Strij à Dordt [or] H
1810/07/23	DOLG1	0032	*L. de Koning* | Een stil Water, zijnde een Gezicht voor de Stad Dordrecht. Een Zeeschip ligt voor anker op den stroom; in eene Roeischuit laten zich eenige Heeren, met hunne Honden van de Jagt terug komende, over de Rivier zetten. Mede zeer uitvoerig, delicaat behandeld, en van een aangenaam coloriet | *Mat:* op paneel *Size:* hoog 10, breed 14 duim	Mr Pieter van den Santheuvel	(Sold) fl 17 van Eijk a 's Hage

Kool, N. [Unidentified]

1802/06/16	AMSCH	0093	*N. Kool* | In dit Natuurlyk Strandgezicht by een stille Zee, ziet men op de voorgrond Vissers met hun Vrouwen, en hun koopwaren, verder een Wagen waar op Visch geladen word: en andere Lieden by Zee wandelende; ter zyde vertoont zich de Dorpkerk en Tooren, in 't verschiet Visschersvaartuituigen [sic]; alles zeer natuurlyk en van een meesterlyke penceel-behandeling | *Mat:* op paneel *Size:* hoog 15 ½, breed 23 ½ duim	[Merrem]	(Sold) fl 18 La Fontaine

Koormans [Unidentified]

1802/09/18	RMDRS	0122	*Koormans* | Twee dito [Boere binnen huizen]	Casper de Haas	(Unknown) fl 5

Kooten, J. [Unidentified]

1804/10/29	HRBAU	0049	*Kooten, (J.)* | Op den Voorgrond, by een Soetelaars-tent, staat een Hessenkar, met vier paarden bespannen, die belaaden wordt; waar by verscheiden Mannen en Vrouwen, die zich ververschen, en een bergagtig verschiet. Plaisant behandeld | *Mat:* op doek *Size:* hoog 27, breed 38 duim	Simon Styl	(Unknown)

Kraft, J.

1804/08/08	AMSCH	0251	*J. Kraft* | Een Dorpgezicht, alwaar eenige Militairen gruwelyk plunderen, en de Boeren gevanglyk weg voeren; geestig op Paneel, als Teniers, door J. Kraft | *Mat:* op paneel	Roos a	(Sold) fl 4 Gruiter

Kraul, Karl Franz

1808/03/03	HAVIN	0013	*Kraul* | Een Landschap, uitvoerig	Jacobus Spillebout	(Unknown) fl 4:10

Kroost, C. [Unidentified]

1808/04/26	GDAN	0083	*Kroost (C.)* | Een fraai Dorp Gezigt, met eenige Gebouwen en wandelende Menschen, zeer goed geschildert | *Size:* hoog 18, breed 24 ½ duim	G H Fortuyn	(Unknown)

1808/04/26 GDAN 0084 *Kroost (C.)* | Een fraai Stads Gezigt, met eenige Beelden | *Size:* hoog 43, breed 65 duim — G H Fortuyn — (Unknown)

Kruger, Jacob

1801/03/16 AMSCH 0170 *Creuger* | Twee capitaalen Landschappen met Beesten — P[ruyssenaar] — (Sold) fl 6:5 Boelen

1802/06/28 AMSCH 0097 *J. Kruger* | Twee Landschappen ryk met Beesten en Beeldjes gestoffeerd, en fiks behandeld | *Size:* hoog 14, breed 18 duim — Anna Elink — (Sold) fl 3 van Iperen

1804/05/07 AMSCH 0092 *Kreuger. (J.)* | In een Landschap by eenig Geboomte, ziet men een ménigte van staand, rustend en gapend Vee, waarby een Boer, Boerin en een Jongen, fiks gepenceeld | *Mat:* op doek *Size:* hoog 28, breed 25 duim — Roos [for] A — (Sold) fl 0:14 L Pakker

Kuijper, J. [Unidentified]

1808/06/13 AMSCH 0093 *Kuijper (J.)* | Eene Ruïne van het Huis Brederode, van binnen te zien, waarin een Hond en twee Schapen; in het verschiet zit een Teekenaar. Het invallend zonlicht doet eene treffende uitwerking; en is meesterlijk geschilderd | *Mat:* op doek *Size:* hoog 16 ½, breed 13 duim — [Jan Tersteeg] — (Sold) fl 65 C S Roos

Kuik, J. van [Unidentified]

1802/05/05 AMSCH 0041 *J. van Cuik* | Een Land en Watergezicht, op de Voorgrond gestoffeerd met een leggend en een rustend Beest, benevens een groote Willige Boom en een Hengelaar. Zeer natuurlyk | *Mat:* op doek *Size:* hoog 19, breed 23 duim — F — (Sold) fl 1:15 van Iperen

1802/05/05 AMSCH 0042 *J. van Cuik* | Twee stuks Boomryke Landschappen; in de eene, ziet men langs een Weg, twee Beladen Hessen Karren en andere stoffagie; en de andere, verbeeld eenige rustende Huislieden, beide zeer natuurlyk gepenceeld | *Mat:* op paneel *Size:* ieder hoog 16, breed 21 duim — F — (Sold) fl 6:10 Auber

1809/06/13 AMSCH 0074 *J. van Kuik* | Een Landschap, met een Rivier doorsneeden, gestoffeerd met een Landman en Vrouw, bij staande en rustende Beesten, in de manier van Wijnands, door J. van Kuik | *Mat:* op doek *Size:* hoog 32, breed 39 duim — S[chley] — (Sold) fl 4:5 T Spaan

1809/06/13 AMSCH 0075 *J. van Kuik* | Een Boschgezicht, met Watervallen en Houthakkers gestoffeerd | *Mat:* op doek *Size:* hoog 30, breed 39 duim — S[chley] — (Sold) fl 1:5 Bulhouwer

1809/06/13 AMSCH 0076 *J. van Kuik* | Eenige staande en liggende Beesten, bij een Schuur, waarbij rustende Landlieden, als van der Does, door denzelven [J. van Kuik] | *Mat:* op doek *Size:* hoog 28, breed 33 duim — S[chley] — (Sold) fl 1:10 Gruiter

1809/06/13 AMSCH 0077 *J. van Kuik* | Een Heuvelachtig Landschap, met Huislieden en Vee gestoffeerd | *Mat:* op doek *Size:* hoog 24, breed 29 duim — S[chley] — (Sold) fl 1:15 Keurvorst

1809/06/13 AMSCH 0078 *J. van Kuik* | Een Duinachtig Landschap, met beladen Vragtwagens en Reizigers | *Mat:* op doek *Size:* hoog 34, breed 39 — S[chley] — (Sold) fl 3 van Iperen

1809/06/13 AMSCH 0079 *J. van Kuik* | Een Land- en Watergezicht, met Hooiwagens, Scheepen en Beeldjes, gestoffeerd | *Size:* hoog 38, breed 49 duim — S[chley] — (Sold) fl 2:5 van Iperen

1809/06/13 AMSCH 0080 *J. van Kuik* | Een Landschap met hoog Geboomten, gestoffeerd met Jongens, bij Schapen en Jagers, met Honden, in 't verschiet een Dorp, natuurlijk | *Mat:* op doek *Size:* hoog 40, breed 48 duim — S[chley] — (Sold) fl 7 T Spaan

1809/06/13 AMSCH 0081 *J. van Kuik* | Een Hofgezicht, met Colommen en Standbeelden en Wandelende Heeren en Dames, gestoffeerd | *Size:* hoog 43, breed 57 duim — S[chley] — (Sold) fl 2:15 T Spaan

1809/06/13 AMSCH 0082 *J. van Kuik* | Een vlak Landschap, met Beelden en Beesten gestoffeerd | *Mat:* op doek *Size:* hoog 33, breed 39 duim — S[chley] — (Sold) fl 2 Gruiter

1809/06/13 AMSCH 0083 *J. van Kuik* | Twee stuks, een Fabel-Ordonantie en een Landschap | *Mat:* op doek *Size:* hoog 35, breed 23 duim — S[chley] — (Sold) fl 0:6 Boelhouwer

1809/06/13 AMSCH 0084 *J. van Kuik* | Een Land- en Watergezicht | *Mat:* op doek *Size:* hoog 22, breed 26 duim — S[chley] — (Sold) fl 0:6 T Spaan

Kuster

1801/08/19 AMSCH 0052 *Kuster* | Een hoog Bergachtig Zwitzers Landschap met een sterk stortende Waterval, op de voorgrond ziet men een Teekenaar, verzelt van twee andere Reizigers; natuurlyk behandeld door Kuster — Pruyssen[r] [for] Q — (Bought In) fl 25

1803/12/12 AMSCH 0049 *Kuster* | Een Duinachtig Landschap; zeer bevallig gepenceeld | *Mat:* op doek *Size:* hoog 15, breed 18 duim — B — (Sold) fl 14 Blaauwpot

1808/10/28 AMVRS 0028 *Kuster* | Een Boomrijk Landschap met een Waterval, op den voorgrond twee Visschers. Natuurlijk behandeld | *Mat:* op doek *Size:* hoog 23, breed 19 duim — Marten Udink — (Sold) fl 4:5 Gruiter [or] Rosekrans

1808/11/28 AMSCH 0098 *Kuster* | Een Boomrijk Landschap, met stoffage — Z — (Sold) fl 1:10 A Kits

1809/07/25 HGBSM 0200 *Kuster* | De groote Waterval by Schafhausen, door Kuster 1785 | *Mat:* op paneel *Size:* hoog 20, breed 30 duim *Inscr:* Kuster 1785 (signed and dated?) *Notes:* It is unclear whether the name and date are inscribed on the painting. — D van der Aa [or] E B ten Dall — (Sold) fl 3:5 Teissier

Kuster, H. [Unidentified]

1802/02/16 AMSCH 0064 *H. Kuster* | Een Zwitsers heuvelachtig Landschap met geboomten en stroomende waters over een kluitachtige grond, verder op een heuvel, een Landman en vrouw; natuurlyk gepenceeld — G — (Sold) fl 5 Vermeulen

Kuster, J.

1802/09/06	AMSCH	0058	*J. Kuster* | Een Italiaansch Bergachtig Landschap, gestoffeerd met verscheide Reizigers en Vée, Gebouwen en Waterval, plaisant geschilderd | *Mat:* op doek *Size:* hoog 19, breed 22 duim	Wed Grave [or others]	(Sold) fl 11:5 for lots 58 & 59. de Meijer
1802/09/06	AMSCH	0059	*J. Kuster* | Een dito [Italiaansch Bergachtig Landschap], gestoffeerd met rustende, gaande en rydende Huislieden, ter zyde onder een Steene Brug een Watervalletje; in alles de voorige behandeld | *Size:* hoog 19, breed 23 duim	Wed Grave [or others]	(Sold) fl 11:5 for lots 58 & 59. de Meijer
1803/08/17	AMSCH	0047	*Kuster (J.)* | Daniel in de Leeuwenkuil geworpen, word van de Leeuwen Twee stuks hooge bergachtige Landschappen met kreupel Gewas, Watervallen en stoffagie van beeldjes, meesterlyk geschilderd | *Mat:* op paneel *Size:* ieder hoog 25, breed 19 duim	Anna Catharina Putman	(Sold) fl 20 Coclers
1803/08/17	AMSCH	0048	*Kuster. (J.)* | Een aangenaam bergachtig Landschap met Geboomte en Watervallen, gestoffeerd met Schapen en Beedjes, warm van coloriet en fix geschilderd | *Mat:* op doek *Size:* hoog 15, breed 19 duim	Anna Catharina Putman	(Sold) fl 10:10 Pruijssenaar
1806/05/05	AMSCH	0074	*J. Kuster* | Een bergagtig Landschap met laag Houtgewas, gestoffeerd met Huislieden, en verder Vee; zonachtig en uitvoerig gepenceeld door J. Kuster | *Mat:* op paneel *Size:* hoog 17 ½, breed 14 ½ duim	E	(Sold) fl 11 van Iperen

Kuster, Johann Kaspar

1810/08/06	AMSCH	0058	*Kuster (J.C.)* | Twee stuks Boomrijke Landschappen met Watervallen, Beelden en Beesjes gestoffeerd; fiks gepenceeld | *Mat:* op paneel *Size:* ieder hoog 13, breed 11 duimen	A	(Sold) fl 10 Coclers [for] T

Kuyper, Jacques

1802/05/05	AMSCH	0092	*J. Kuyper* | Twee stuks Bevallige Ordonnantien, zynde de Mercurius en Archus, in Boomryke Landschappen, met Antiquiteiten voorzien. Alles Meesterlyk | *Mat:* op doek *Size:* hoog 27, breed 22 duim	D	(Bought In) fl 140

Kyckenburgh, Dirck Nicolaesz. van

1806/08/13	AMSCH	0091	*Kyckenburg. (J. V.)* | In een Binnevertrek zit een Dame in prachtige kleeding aan een Tafel met een Tapyte Kleed, zy schynt een brief ontfangen te hebben door een Trompetter; delicaat en in de manier van G. Terburg behandeld | *Mat:* op paneel *Size:* hoog 17, breed 12 duim	van der Voort	(Sold) fl 116 van Iperen

Laaredam[?] [Illegible]

1809/07/19	AMSCH	[A0002][H]	*Laaredam [?]* | 1 hert | *Notes:* This lot was added in by hand in the AA copy of the catalogue. Because it was not numbered, we have assigned the number.		(Unknown)

La Baze [Unidentified]

1803/12/12	AMSCH	0006	*la Baze* | Twee stuks, een Maaneschyn en een Land- en Watergezicht | *Mat:* op paneel *Size:* hoog 4, breed 6 duim	D	(Sold) fl 0:10 L Pakker

Lacroix

1803/12/12	AMSCH	0021	*la Croix* | In een heuvelachtig Landschap ziet men op de voorgrond een Huzaar te Paard, waarby nog een ander, verder een grote party Bagagiewagens en Krygslieden; delicaat op Paneel | *Mat:* op paneel *Size:* hoog 14, br 16 duim	E	(Sold) fl 30 Coclers

La Croix, P. de [Unidentified]

1809/06/13	AMSCH	0232	*P. de la Croix* | Een Ordonantie, voorstellende de Vader door zijn Dochter in de Gevangenis gevoed; fiks geschilderd | *Mat:* op doek	Y	(Sold) fl 0:10 L Pakker
1809/06/13	AMSCH	0233	*P. de la Croix* | Eene Dame, speelende op de Bas | *Notes:* This lot was sold with lot 245 by an anonymous artist.	Y	(Sold) fl 0:6 for lots 233 & 245. L Pakker
1809/06/13	AMSCH	0234	*P. de la Croix* | Twee stuks met Beelden	Y	(Sold) fl 1:10 for lots 234 & 235. van Iperen
1809/06/13	AMSCH	0235	*P. de la Croix* | Een Historiëele Ordonantie	Y	(Sold) fl 1:10 for lots 234 & 235. van Iperen
1809/06/13	AMSCH	0236	*P. de la Croix* | Een vorstelijk Persoon, te Paard	Y	(Sold) fl 0:6 L Pakker
1809/06/13	AMSCH	0237	*P. de la Croix* | Het Afbeeldsel van Hendrik de vierden	Y	(Sold) fl 0:6 L Pakker

Laen, Dirk Jan van der

1801/03/16	AMSCH	0011	*V. der Laan* | Een Duinachtig Landschap, ryk met Beelden en Beesten gestoffeerd	P[ruyssenaar]	(Sold) fl 9:10 Coclers
1801/06/10	AMSCH	0107	*Laan. (D. J. van der)* | Een Bergachtig Landschap, op de voorgrond vertoont zich een bedaagd Man in Oostersche kleeding, nevens hem een bevallig Vrouwtje, alles helder en uitvoerig van penceels behandeling | *Mat:* op paneel *Size:* hoog 17, breed 13 duim	[Doublet]	(Sold) fl 17 Taijs
1802/06/16	AMSCH	0097	*J. van der Laan* | Een Landschap ter rechter zyde met hoog Geboomte, waar by een Reiziger te Paard, verders een aangenaam verschiet; en helder gepenceeld | *Mat:* op paneel *Size:* hoog 13, breed 17 ½ duim *Notes:* The artist's name was given as "J. van der Laan" but we have assumed this is an error.	[Merrem]	(Sold) fl 9:5 Boelen

			Laer, Pieter van (Bamboccio)		
1801/06/10	AMSCH	0106	*Laer (P. de) alias Bomboots* | In een Landschap, langs een Ruïne ziet men een Reiziger te paard, waarby een wit Paard, in 't verschiet ziet men eenige Schaapen en ander Vee voortdryven, warm en krachtig geschilderd | *Annots:* [door] H V: Lin (BRB) *Mat:* op paneel *Size:* hoog 12, breed 16 duim	Herman ten Kate	(Sold) fl 65 De Lelie
1801/10/06	AMSCH	0039	*P. de Laar* | In een Landschap, op de voorgrond voor een Stal, staat een wit Paard, daar nevens een man, die uit een kan drinkt, en een vrouw met een kind, natuurlyk behandeld | *Mat:* op paneel *Size:* hoog 30, breed 23 duim	M	(Sold) fl 8:5 Bron
1802/06/16	AMSCH	0096	*P. de Laar* | Voor een Italiaansch Gebouw ziet men een menigte Beedelaars, welke uit een Klooster spyzen worden toegedeeld; alles meesterlyk behandeld | *Mat:* op doek *Size:* hoog 13 ½, breed 17 ½ duim	[Merrem]	(Sold) fl 24:10 Wed Achtienhoven
1802/12/13	AMSCH	0106	*P. de Laar, Alias Bamboots* | Een Duinachtig Landschap met Beelden, Paarden en Ezels, krachtig | *Mat:* op paneel *Size:* hoog 10, breed 10 ½ duim	Yver	(Sold) fl 4:10 Gruiter
1802/12/13	AMSCH	0107	*P. de Laar, Alias Bamboots* | Twee stuks Binnehuisen, byde ryk gestoffeert met vrolyke Italiaansche Landlieden, zingende en musiceerende, waarby eenige Masquerade, fix en meesterlyk gepenceelt | *Mat:* op doek *Size:* yder hoog 6 ½, breed 12 duim	Schley [for] Lauwers	(Sold) fl 2 L Pakker
1802/12/13	AMSCH	0108	*P. de Laar, Alias Bamboots* | In een Stal, ziet men een wit gezadeld Paard, by een Kreb, waarby een Stalknegt, meesterlyk fix gepenceeld | *Mat:* op paneel *Size:* hoog 4, breed 6 ½ duim	Schley [for] Lauwers	(Sold) fl 0:10 v[n] Limmen
1802/12/13	AMSCH	0109	*P. de Laar, Alias Bamboots* | In een dito [Stal], staat een Bond en Bruin Paard aan een Ruyf, fix en kragtig gepenseelt	Schley [for] Lauwers	(Sold) fl 1:15 van Dijl
1804/08/08	AMSCH	0105	*P. de Laar* | Een Boomryk Landschap, gestoffeerd met een Man, twee Paarden en een Hond; vlak en breed geschilderd | *Mat:* op paneel *Size:* hoog 8, breed 10 ½ duim	Vink[eles] [for] K[=Gruyter?]	(Sold) fl 1 Gruyter
1804/10/16	DLOND	0121	*P. de Laar* | Een donker Landschap met een wit Paard. Paysage très ombragé avec un Cheval blanc | *Mat:* op paneel *Size:* hoog 8, breed 10		(Unknown)
1806/10/16	UTWLD	0003	*Pieter de Laar* | Voor een Buitenhuis ziet men een Man die zyne Laarsen aantrekt by een gezadelt Wit Paard door Pieter de Laar	Mr P de Malapert [or] W Beeldsnyder	(Unknown)
1809/04/17	AMSCH	0164	*P. de Laar* | In een Landschap ziet men een Man met een wit Paard, rustende bij een Waterput | *Mat:* op paneel	R	(Sold) fl 5
			Laer, Pieter van (Bamboccio) (or Laer, P., manner)		
1801/03/16	AMSCH	0147	*P. de Laar* | Een Grot waarin Paarden en Beelden, natuurlyk van ligt en bruin, door of in de manier van P. de Laar	K[ip]	(Sold) fl 3 Stevens
			Laer, Pieter van (Bamboccio) (manner)		
1803/12/12	AMSCH	0138	*P. de Laar* | Voor een Smits Winkel word een Paard beslagen, verders eenige andere stoffagie; alles meesterlyk, als door P. de Laar | *Mat:* op paneel *Size:* hoog 13, breed 17 duim	Arnoud de Lange	(Sold) fl 17 Josi
1806/11/24	AMSCH	0097	*P. de Laar* | Een Pleisterplaats; als P. de Laar	Munnikhuizen	(Sold) fl 10 Reyers
1810/05/22	AMSCH	0152	*P. de Laar* | In een Bergachtig Landschap ziet men eene menigte Krijgslieden, op elkander vuurende, waarbij eenige Bevelhebbers te Paard; meesterlijk gepenceeld, in de manier van P. de Laar | *Mat:* op paneel	F	(Sold) fl 1:10 Levij Pakker
			Lafage, Raymond de (manner)		
1804/10/29	HRBAU	0138	*La Fage* | Twee Stuks Bacchanten Feesten. Fiks in den trant van la Fage behandeld | *Mat:* op doek *Size:* hoog 15, breed 24 duim	Simon Styl	(Unknown)
			Lagoor, Johan		
1808/03/03	HAVIN	0014	*Lagoor* | Een dito [Landschap]	Jacobus Spillebout	(Unknown) fl 1:18
			La Haye, Reinier de		
1802/08/24	LNDLS	0006	*de la Haye* | In een ruim Binnen-vertrek staat een Juffer, in een rood jakje met witte bonte randen, en een witte satijne rok, nevens haar een Dienstmaagd met lampet, kan en schotel, de hand der Dame begietende, benevens een Tafel gedekt met een Tapijt-kleed, waar op een spiegel, een doos en een paarlsnoer, terwijl een Trompetter haar een brief brengt. Delicaat op doek geschilderd, als van G. Terburgh, door de la Haye | *Mat:* op doek *Size:* hoog 29 ½, breed 31 duimen	Leonardus Bouman [or others]	(Unknown) fl 33
1803/12/15	MGLAC	0033	*la Haye* | Een fraai stukje met twee Figuuren | *Mat:* op paneel *Size:* hoog duim 12, breed duim 9	Mr L H de Haze Bomme	(Unknown)
1804/05/07	AMSCH	0086	*Haye. (De La)* | Twee stuks Binnenhuizen met zittende Dames, voor Tafels, waarop Oesters, Brood and ander bywerk; fiks behandeld | *Size:* hoog 12, breed 11 duim	Y[ver] [for] JJ	(Sold) fl 1:15 A van der Hagen
1805/06/24	DOBLU	0017	*de la Heye* | Twee stuks	Willem Snellen [or] F R E Nibbelinck [or] Gysbert Visser	(Unknown)
1807/06/02	AMHUY	0024	*de la Hayen* | In een Binnenvertrek ziet men een Gezelschap van Heeren en Dames die zich vermaken		(Unknown)

1808/11/28	AMSCH	0035	*de la Haije* | Door een Nis ziet men een Doctor, zittende aan een Tafel, waar op een Globe, Papieren en eenige Boeken geplaast zijn, hij houd een Urinaal in de Hand, nevens hem staat een Moor, schijnende bericht af te wagten, delicaat gepenceeld | *Mat:* op doek *Size:* hoog 24, breed 19 duim	[Gruyter?]	(Sold) fl 15:10 T Spaan
1809/07/19	AMSCH	0019	*Haaije (de la)* | In een gemeubileerd Binnevertrek zit eene bevallige Dame, in Satijnen kleeding, bij een Tafel met een Tapijtkleed bedekt, schijnende kant te werken, nevens haar op een Stoel ligt een Hondje. Zacht en uitvoerig van penceelsbehandeling | *Mat:* op paneel *Size:* hoog 15, breed 12 duim	[Bicker]	(Sold) fl 112 Gruyter
1810/08/10	RMRIJ	0024	*R. La Haije* | Een Persoon in zijn Japonsche Tabbaerd, staande aan eene Tafel		(Unknown) fl 1 [or] 3:5
1810/10/11	AMSCH	0171	*De La Haije* | Eene Binnekamer, waarin twee Dames en een Heer | *Notes:* This lot was sold with lot 172 by Jan Porcellis.	[Levy Pakker?]	(Sold or Bought In) fl 0:6 for lots 171 & 172. L Pakker
1810/10/13	HGDAW	0004	*La Haye* | Een Dame met een rood fluweel Kleed met bont gevoerd, en een Satyne Rok, staande by een springend Fontein, waarby twee Hondjes, in het verschiet een Terras met Bloemen, natuurlyk geschilderd | *Mat:* op paneel *Size:* hoog 15, breed 13 ½ duim		(Unknown)
1810/11/07	UTWLD	0065	*R. de la Haye* | Voor een Nis zittend Doctor, het water in een Vles beziende, dat hem door een Negerin schijnt aangebragt, die met ingespanne verwagting zijn oordeel wagt, verder een Globe, Boeken en ander bijwerk, expressief en geestig behandeld door R. de la Haye, op doek, 1 voet 5 en een half duim hoog, 1 voet 2 en een half duim breed, zwarte Lijst | *Mat:* op doek *Size:* 1 voet 5 ½ duim hoog, 1 voet 2 ½ duim breed		(Unknown) fl 7:15
			Lairesse, Gerard de		
1801/06/10	AMSCH	0102	*Lairesse. (G. de)* | Een Ordonantie van vier Beelden by een Fontein, kragtig en breed gepenceeld | *Mat:* op doek *Size:* hoog 23, breed 27 duim	Herman ten Kate	(Sold) fl 33:10 Wolft
1801/10/06	AMSCH	0040	*G. de Lairesse* | In een Landschap, ziet men Vénus en Adonis, rustende, elkander Liefkoosen, verzelt van verscheide Minnewigten, alles is van een meesterlyke penceel behandeling | *Mat:* op doek *Size:* hoog 32, breed 66 duim	S	(Sold) fl 28:10 C S Roos
1801/10/06	AMSCH	0041	*G. de Lairesse* | Deze ryke Ordonantie, verbeeld de Graflegging van Christus, vergezeld van een menigte Godvrugtige Lieden, schoon van Teekening en uitvoerig gepenceeld | *Mat:* op doek *Size:* hoog 14, breed 19 duim	M	(Sold) fl 60 Isak Smit
1802/05/05	AMSCH	0105	*G. de Lairesse* | In een Hofgezicht ziet men een Heer, zittende te Tekenen, voor hem een Dame en twee speelende Kindertjes by een Fontyn, delicaat gepenceeld | *Size:* hoog 43, breed 53 duim	J	(Sold) fl 39 v d Vinne
1802/05/05	AMSCH	0106	*G. de Lairesse* | Een Historiëele Ordonnantie, fraai gepenceeld	J	(Bought In) fl 27
1802/07/21	HGKAN	0096	*Lairesse* | Een Rustende Narcisse		(Unknown)
1802/09/18	RMDRS	0115	*G. de Laresse* | Een Ordonnantie met naakte Figuuren	Casper de Haas	(Unknown) fl 6
1802/09/21	UTHDG	0057	*G. de Lairesse* | In een Tempel word aan eene Priesteres door een Held, een kind aangeboden. Dit, nevens meerder figuuren is schoon van ordonnantie en behandeling | *Mat:* op doek *Size:* hoog 28, breed 23 duimen		(Sold) fl 13 La Maine
1802/09/29	AMSCH	0029	*G. de Lairesse* | Een Historieele Ordenantie, hoog 26, breed 28 duim. Doek. Aan den ingang van een pragtig Paleis ziet men Paris de schoone Heléna by de hand leidende, werdende gevolgt door verscheiden van haare Maagden; eenige Krygslieden, Mannen, Vrouwen en Kinderen vertoonen zig op de voor- en agtergrond van dit Stuk; op de voorgrond ter linker zyde liggen eenige Scheepen en een Boot, waar in een der Scheepelingen, die zig daar mede van den oever schynt te verwyderen; de rykheid der Ordenantie, de groeping der Figuren, de plooijing der Kleederen, en de delicaate Penceelsbehandeling, doen dit Schildery onder de beste werken van deeze groote Meester uitmunten [Descendant d'un riche vaisseau l'on voit Paris conduisant la belle Hélene vers un magnifique palais, ils sont suivis et entourrés par un nombre de femmes et de Guerriers ; un groupe d'hommes et de femmes rangés devant le portique voit avec étonnement passer les Heros, au devant du vaisseau se trouve une chaloupe avec des marins qui semblent s'éloigner. L'ordonnance de ce morceau est imposante, elle est riche sans être chargée ni diffuse, les figures en sont d'un dessin svelte, et en gênéral il est harmonieux et d'un bon effet.] | *Mat:* op doek *Size:* hoog 26, breed 28 duim	E	(Sold) fl 185 Pruijssenaar
1802/09/29	AMSCH	0030	*G. de Lairesse* | Dansende Nimphen in een Landschap, hoog 24, breed 29 duim. Doek. In een Arcadiesch Landschap, by hoog Geboomten en een fraay gewerkte Vaas, ziet men vier dansende Nimphen, waarvan een het hooft met Bloemen en een ander met Koornayren verziert is, eene jeugdige Bachante speeld op de Rinkeltrom, tusschen het geboomte; ter regter zyde op de tweede grond, is eene andere Nimph gezeeten met de Lier van Apollo, en agter haar nog twee Bachante, een Colom Geboomte, en Gebergte, besluiten dit uitmuntend Stuk, dat in alle deelen nietminder [sic] dan het voorgaande is, en waarin het Zonlicht een schoone uitwerking doet [Près de quelques arbres élevés et d'un grand vase de	E	(Sold) fl 385 Yver

			belle scupture [sic] sont quatre nimphes formant une danse au son du tambourin d'une cinquieme : vers le second plan, près d'une figure en pierre l'artiste a disposê un groupe de trois autres nimphes dont une tient une lire. Le sujet paroit faire allusion aux saisons ; il est traité avec une delicatesse singuliere, et la couleur y produit un charme qui plait, il se distingue parmi les ouvrages de ce peintre en ce qu'il l'à composé entierement dans la maniere du Poussin.] | *Mat:* op doek *Size:* hoog 24, breed 29 duim		
1802/09/29	AMSCH	0031	*G. de Lairesse* | Een zinspelende Ordenantie, hoog 29, breed 22 duim. Doek. Men ziet op de voorgrond in dit Schildery in een bedrukten gestalte als in wanhoop nedergezeegen, de Schilderkunst hebbende nevens haar leggen, verscheide verbrokene Schildergereedschappen: een Romynsche Messénas met een Lauwerkrans op het hoofd, en een zak met Geld onder zyn arm, (waaruit eenige stukken vallen,) geeft haar den rechterhand, en schynt haar op te beuren, verder op eene Tombe, ziet met borstbeeld van Minerva, die door een bevallig Kindje aangeweezen [sic] word, in het verschiet, het standbeeld van Hercules, en eenige andere beelden zynde, de Drapperien edel en breed behandeld, en voorts in alles als de voorgaande geschilderd [La Peinture en defaillance. Elles est assise à terre dans une attitude languissante, ténant sa main droite sur ses attributs ; un Mecène en costume Romain lui tend la main et semble voulour la relever à la vue de l'argent qu'il laisse echapper, derriere ce groupe est un mausolé sur lequel est posé le buste de Minerve qu'un génie rappelle à la Peinture, la statue antique d'Hercule et un artiste Grec terminent le fond. Ce Tableau à de l'éclat et il est recommandable à tous égard.] | *Mat:* op doek *Size:* hoog 29, breed 22 duim	E	(Bought In) fl 81
1802/12/13	AMSCH	0103	*G. de Lairesse* | Een Historieele Ordennantie, verbeeldende de Schoone Herse op het Paradebed, meesterlyk van Schildering | *Mat:* op doek *Size:* hoog 19, breed 24 duim	Pruyssenaar [for] B	(Sold) fl 13 W Reijers
1803/07/07	HGKAN	0002	*Lairesse* | Hercules in de Wieg, twee Slangen doodende, door de Lairesse, op doek [Schilderyen in Olyverf] | *Mat:* in olyverf op doek *Notes:* The bracketed information in the title appears above lot 1 and refers to lots 1 to 25.		(Unknown)
1803/08/17	AMSCH	0049	*Lairesse. (G. de)* | Acht stuks ryke Ordonnantiën, voorstellende de Triumph van Kyzer Trajanus binnen Romen, met al deszelfs gevolg: als Zangers, Musicanten, vercierde Offerbeesten, gevolgd door de Priesteren, Romeinsche Krygshelden te paard en te voet, anderen dragen in Triumph den gewonnen buit en kostbaarheden, als Standaarden, Vaandelen en andere Krygstekenen, alle zyn ze konstig, meesterlyk, fraai en kragtig gepenceeld | *Mat:* op doek *Size:* ieder hoog 19, breed 31 duim	Anna Catharina Putman	(Bought In) fl 259
1803/08/17	AMSCH	0050	*Lairesse. (G. de)* | De Graflegging van een voornaam Persoon, verzeld wordende van een menigte Beelden, welke deeze begraving met veel aandoening beschouwen; de Ordonnantie is ryk, en de schildering meesterlyk, in het grauw | *Mat:* op doek *Size:* hoog 13, breed 50 duim	Anna Catharina Putman	(Sold) fl 24:10 Hodges
1803/08/17	AMSCH	0051	*Lairesse. (G. de)* | Een Schoorsteenstuk, zynde een Kind, by een Vaas met Bloemen | *Mat:* op doek *Fmt:* schoorsteenstuk *Size:* hoog 70, breed 28 duim	Anna Catharina Putman	(Sold) fl 0:18 Vinkeles
1803/08/24	HGKAN	0065	*G. de Lairesse* | Een Alegorie toepasselyk op de Koophandel van Amsterdam | *Mat:* op doek *Size:* hoog 21, breet 25 duim	[Teissier] [or others]	(Sold) fl 39 Cuylenburg
1804/02/27	AMSCH	0068	*Lairesse. (G. de)* | Een capitaale Zinnebeeldige Ordonantie, breed en bevallig gepenceeld | *Mat:* op doek *Size:* hoog 57, breed 57 duim	B	(Sold) fl 3:10 Gruiter
1804/02/27	AMSCH	0069	*Lairesse. (G. de)* | Joannes predikt in de Woesstyn; meesterlyk geschilderd | *Size:* hoog 21, breed 18 duim	C	(Sold) fl 0:10 Gruiter
1804/05/07	AMSCH	0096	*Lairess. (G. de)* | Een capitale zinnebeeldige Ordonantie; breed en meesterlyk geschilderd | *Mat:* op doek *Size:* hoog en breed 57 duim	Vinkeles [for] G	(Sold) fl 1 Van Iperen
1804/07/25	AMSCH	0048	*Lairesse. (G. de)* | Deeze capitaale Ordinantie steld voor, in een Landschap met zwaar Geboomte, een slaapende Bachante, meer dan levensgrootte; zy rust op een paarscouleurd en een wit kleed; terzyde by eenig Plantgewas legt een omgevallen steene Kruik; zy word bespied door een oude Bachant; verder by de stam van een Boom vertoonen zich twee Minnewigten, waarby een stok met Wyngaardranken omvlogten, waaraan een Drinkkannetje gehegt is; het licht doet een schoone werking, het Coloriet is kragtig en bevallig, en van een uitvoerige perceelbehandeling | *Mat:* op doek *Size:* hoog 57, breed 74 duim		(Sold) fl 70 van der Schley
1804/07/25	AMSCH	0050	*Lairesse. (G. de)* | Voor een steene Nis vertoont zig een Pedestal, op dezelve staat een cierlyk gewerkte Vaas; op de voorgrond ziet men een Jongeling, en een Meisje, houdende een Zilvere Doos in de hand; van boven hangt een Lauriertak, het is van een bevallig Coloriet, en meesterlyke behandeling | *Mat:* op doek *Size:* hoog 72, breed 27 duim		(Sold) fl 10:10 Van Dijl
1804/08/08	AMSCH	0101	*G. de Lairesse* | Deze capitaale Historiëele Ordinantie vertoond een schoone en bevallige Vrouw, in Vorstelyk Gewaad, en met edele Gesteentens en Paarlen vercierd, zittende in een prachtig Vertrek, verzeld van een jeugdige Gezellin; zy rykt de Hand aan haare Minnaar, die ter zyde, in een edele Houding en Kleeding, in een Armstoel gezéeten is, dezelve als met verwondering beschouwende, terwyl Cupido hem schynt aan te pryzen; achter deze staat Minerva, met een Flesje in de hand, hem	Schley [for] A	(Bought In) fl 60

			als welriekende Balsem op het Hoofd gietende; de Beelden zyn fraai geteekend, de caracters natuurlyk, den aart der Satyne en andere Stoffen der Kleederen eigenaartig verbeeld, en breed geplooit, het licht en coloriet aangenaam, en van een uitvoerige penceelbehandeling | *Mat:* op doek *Size:* hoog 57, breed 78 duim		
1804/08/08	AMSCH	0102	*G. de Lairesse* | In een prachtig Paleis ziet men Vénus, verzeld van een ménigte Minnewichtjens, Mars word in 't verschiet door een Nimph geweerd; delicaat op Doek | *Mat:* op doek *Size:* hoog 33, breed 29 duim	Roos [for] J	(Sold) fl 1 Gruyter
1804/08/08	AMSCH	0103	*G. de Lairesse* | Twee stuks, Jupiter in de gedaante van een Gouden Regen, verzeld van Minnewichten enz. en een wederga; beiden als dito | *Mat:* op doek *Size:* hoog 19, breed 16 duim *Notes:* It is unclear what "dito" refers to in the title.	Roos [for] J	(Sold) fl 3 Gruyter
1804/10/16	DLOND	0122	*G. de Lairesse* | Twee Kinders, verbeeldende J.C. en Johannes. Deux Enfans J. C. & St. Jean | *Mat:* op doek *Size:* hoog 31, breed 46		(Unknown)
1805/07/03	AMSCH	0102	*G. de Lairesse* | Een Zinnebeeldige Ordinantie, van drie Beelden, met twee Genien; kragtig op Doek | *Mat:* op doek *Size:* hoog 27, breed 23 duim	C	(Sold) fl 10 Gruyter
1805/07/10	AMSCH	0091	*G. de Lairesse* | De Zabynsche Maagderoof; meesterlyk en breed gepenceeld | *Mat:* op paneel *Size:* hoog 20, breed 29 duim	V[inkeles] [for] N	(Sold) fl 1:15 Menzard
1805/12/16	AMSCH	0068	*de Lairesse* | Een Schoorsteenstuk | *Fmt:* schoorsteenstuk	R[oos]	(Sold) fl 0:16 van Dijl
1806/08/20	HGBSM	0003	*G. de Lairesse* | De barmhartige Samaritaan, een gewondt man verbindende, dit stuk in allen opzichte zijn meester waardig, bestaat uit drie figuuren, alle even keurlijk geteekend en vol uitdrukking | *Mat:* op doek *Size:* hoog 20, breed 25 duim	Macalester Loup	(Sold) fl 73 Schouwman A
1806/11/24	AMSCH	0037	*Lairesse (G. de)* | Maria met het Kind Jesus, welke met een Duif speeld, Joseph, Johannes en zyne Moeder zyn in volle aandagt op het Kind; meesterlyk fraai geschilderd | *Mat:* op doek *Size:* hoog 19, breed 24 duim	Munnikhuizen	(Sold) fl 13 Coclers
1807/08/26	AMSCH	0116	*G. de Lairesse* | Deze capitaale Ordonnantie, in een Landschap met Geboomten by een Fontein, vertoont de Fabelgeschiedenis van Narcissus, op zig zelf verlievende; vergezelt van verscheide Minnewigten en een Jachthond; bevallig van koloriet en van een uitvoerige schildering | *Mat:* op doek *Size:* hoog 66, breed 51 duim	Helsdinge	(Sold) fl 7:10 van Dijl
1807/09/28	AMWUR	0011	*G. Lairesse* | Twee dito [stuks] zynde Historien uit Ovidius door G. Lairesse, in zwarte Lyst, met vergulde Sponnings		(Unknown) fl 1:10
1808/04/26	GDAN	0090	*Lairesse (G. de)* | Een bij den Avond prachtige Maaltijd van een groot aantal Persoonen, die verzogt zijn bij den Koning Herodes, alle in statieuse kleding, na dezelve Danst het Dochterke van Herodias, die daar voor het Hoofd van Johannes den Doper eischt, wordende gemusiceerd op differente Instrumenten, uitvoerig en konstig behand [sic] | *Size:* hoog 20, breed 26 duim	G H Fortuyn	(Unknown)
1808/04/26	GDAN	0091	*Lairesse (G. de)* | Zijnde de verschijning der Engelen aan de Herders in de Velden van Ephrata, bekend makende de Geboorte van den Zaligmaker | *Size:* hoog 15, breed 11 ½ duim	G H Fortuyn	(Unknown)
1809/09/06	AMSCH	0039	*Lairesse (G. de)* | Dit Tafereel steld voor de Vergasting van Abraham aan de Engelen, welke voor een prachtig Huis onder een Priëel gezeeten zijn, en door den Aardsvader gulhartig de Spijzen aangebragt worden; de Ordinantie is treffend, het koloriet aangenaam en de schildering van de beste van dezen voortreffelijken Meester | *Mat:* op doek *Size:* hoog 47, breed 54 duim	Johannes Caudri	(Sold) fl 53 Reyers
1809/09/06	AMSCH	0040	*Lairesse (G. de)* | Eene schoone Vrouw, verzeld van twee Kinderen, welken met Bloemen speelen; niet minder van schildering als de voorgaande | *Mat:* op doek *Size:* hoog 35, breed 45 duim	Johannes Caudri	(Sold) fl 9 Hulswit
1809/09/06	AMSCH	0041	*Lairesse (G. de)* | Dit Kabinetstukje, vertoond in een Binnenvertrek den Koning Lijncus, met een Dolk in de opgeheven hand, om den slaapende Triptolémus den Doodsteek te geeven, dog door de Godin Céres belet, die de Vorst in een Lijnx herschept; het is schoon geordineerd en van een kunstige uitvoerige penceelbehandeling | *Mat:* op doek *Size:* hoog 14, breed 17 duim	Johannes Caudri	(Sold) fl 30 C Buijs
1810/03/26	RMMUY	0002	*Gerard de Lairesse* | Christus op bevel van Pilatus aan het Joodsche Volk overgeleverd. De schikking en ordonnantie van dit konststuk is voortreffelijk, de onschuld in het gelaat van den Zaligmaker verwonderlijk doorstralende, contrasteert zeer schoon met de uitgedrukte dolle woede der Jooden zijne beschuldigers. Den achtergrond is verrijkt met grootsche architectuur en waar in men Pilatus ziet zijne handen in onschuld wasschende [Cette belle et savante composition répresente le Sauveur exposé aux insultes du peuple, devant le palais de Pilate. Deux soldats Romains armés de faisceaux d'armes, le tiennent lié entr'eux, tandis que trois autres le hûent, deux figures près d'une collonade dorique, contrastent avec force, contre le groupe précédent, qui est éclairé. Deux autres figures avancées, expriment les ménaces et l'insulte ; tandis que plusieurs, élevés sur une partie du [sic] balustrade, témoignent l'ivresse du desir de le voir crucifier, ainsi qu'une multitude au bas des dégrés apportent une croix. La partie supérieure de ce tableau est d'une riche architecture ; où Pilate se lavant les mains, est entouré de quelques	Daniel de Jongh Az	(Sold) fl 705 van Eyk S'Hage

			Romains ; et sous la balustrade de cette partie sont des rabins et quelqu'autres juifs. Lairesse paroit s'être surpassé dans ce morceau, qui réünit un dessein correct, et des expressions vraies, à un coloris suave et harmonieux ; l'ensemble est traité d'une manière aussi spirituelle, que l'effet en est piquant.] | *Mat:* op doek *Size:* hoog 49, breed 41 duimen *Loc:* Bruxelles, Belgique. Musées Royaux des Beaux-Arts. (3126)		
1810/06/20	AMSCH	0039	*G. De Lairesse* | Eene Historieele Ordonnantie van verscheidene Beelden, benevens Kupido's en toepasselijk bijwerk. Meesterlijk breed geschilderd op doek, en van den besten tijd van G. De Lairesse | *Mat:* op doek *Size:* hoog 22, breed 27 duimen	D	(Sold) fl 61 Reijers
1810/06/20	AMSCH	0040	*G. De Lairesse* | St. Jan, zittende bij een oud Gebouw, in eene peinzende houding. Meesterlijk geschilderd | *Mat:* op doek *Size:* hoog 35, breed 30 duimen	S	(Sold) fl 7:5 Twisk
1810/08/01	AMSCH	0052	*Lairesse (Gerard de)* | Een Italiaansch bergachtig Landschap met Gebouwen, op den voorgrond bij Geboomte eenige Herders, die een Vaartuig met muziceerende Nimfen bespieden [Un Site montueux pris en Italie, varié par des Batisses. Sur le devant du Tableau on voit un Massif d'Arbres auprès duquel se trouvent des Bergers qui semblent épier des Nimphes occupées à faire de la musique dans une Chaloupe] | *Annots:* faible et sans effet. (NGW) *Mat:* op doek *Size:* hoog 18 ½, breed 23 duimen	Mr Pieter de Smeth van Alphen	(Sold) fl 200 Nieuwenhuyse te Gent
1810/08/06	AMSCH	0059	*Lairesse (G. de)* | Deze overheerlijke Ordonnantie stelt in een pragtigen Tempel voor Simeon, het Kind Jesus op de armen ten hemel verheffende, voor hem liggen in eene nederige gestalte Maria en de overige heilige Mannen en Vrouwen; dit stuk is van de beste schildering van dezen voortreffelijken Meester | *Mat:* op doek *Size:* hoog 57, breed 53 duimen	[J de Bos?]	(Sold) fl 265 Texier Gerbet en Comp
1810/10/11	AMSCH	0043	*G. De Lairesse* | In een Landschap met zwaar geboomte, ziet men eene slapende Nimf, levens groote, zij rust op een paers en wit kleed, en wordt bespied door eenen ouden Bachant, verder bij een Boom twee Minnewigten en ander bijwerk; zeer fraai, en van den besten tijd van G. De Lairesse | *Mat:* op doek *Size:* hoog 57, breed 74 duimen	K	(Sold) fl 61 Gruiter

Lairesse, Gerard de (and Glauber, J.)

1804/07/25	AMSCH	0049	*Lairesse. (G. de); J. Glauber* | Diana en Endimion in een boomryk Landschap by een Fontyn, omgeven van een menigte Minnewigten; beide Meesters hebben hunne talenten in dit stukje bevallig aan den dag gebragt, door een aangenaam en meesterlyk penceel | *Mat:* op doek *Size:* hoog 18, breed 22 duim		(Sold) fl 31 Gruiter
1806/08/20	HGBSM	0197	*J. Glauber; G. de Lairesse* | Een Arcadisch Landschap, door J. Glauber, en gestoffeerd door G. de Lairesse | *Mat:* op doek *Size:* hoog 14, breed 12 duim	Macalester Loup [or others]	(Sold) fl 19 Lafontaine
1808/08/23	AMSCH	0057	*Glauber (J.); G. de Lairesse* | Twee stuks kapitaale boomrijke Arcadische Landschappen, gestoffeert met Fabel-geschiedenissen uit Ovidius, waar bij verscheiden Minnewigten; beide meesterlijk fraai van penceel-behandeling | *Mat:* op doek *Size:* Ieder hoog 25, breed 34 duim	C	(Sold) fl 62 Gruyter

Lairesse, Gerard de (and Heusch, Wm.)

1810/08/06	AMSCH	0044	*Heusch (G. de); G. de Lairesse* | Een hoog Bergachtig Landschap met Geboomte, op den voorgrond gestoffeerd met de Fabel Historie van Latona met hare Kinderen, agterwaards Herders met hunne Schapen; warm van koloriet zonachtig en fraai behandeld | possibly companion to lot 45, by Wm. Heusch *Mat:* op doek *Size:* hoog 58, breed 64 duimen	A	(Sold) fl 80 Coclers

Lairesse, Gerard de (or Lairesse, G., copy after)

1808/12/12	UTWLD	0001	*Lairesse* | De genezing van den Blinden, door of na Lairesse [Alle in swarte Lysten en wel geconserveerd.] | *Mat:* op doek *Size:* hoog 12 duim, breed 15 duim *Notes:* The bracketed information in the title appears above lot 1 and refers to lots 1 to 19.	Mr D Hoola van Nooten	(Unknown)

Lairesse, Gerard de (or Lairesse, G., manner)

1804/02/27	AMSCH	0152	*G. Lairesse* | Een Zinnebeeldige Ordonantie; meesterlyk op Doek, door of in de manier van G. Lairesse | *Mat:* op doek *Size:* hoog 14, breed 17 duim	B	(Sold) fl 3 Theys

Lairesse, Gerard de (copy after)

1810/06/06	RMMUY	0098	*Gerard de Lairesse* | Simion in den Tempel, eene zeer goede Copij. Naar Gerard de Lairesse | *Mat:* op doek		(Unknown) fl 2:14

Lairesse, Gerard de (manner)

1801/06/10	AMSCH	0207	*G. de Lairesse* | St. Jan, zittende by een Antiek Gebouw in een peinzende houding, meesterlyk als G. de Lairesse | *Mat:* op doek *Size:* hoog 35, breed 30 duim	Herman ten Kate	(Sold) fl 21 Frantsen
1802/09/06	AMSCH	0246	*G. de Lairesse* | Een Historieele Ordenantie van twee beelden; meesterlyk in de manier van G. de Lairesse | *Mat:* op doek *Size:* hoog 48, breed 54 duim	J	(Sold) fl 2:15 Wolft
1803/08/24	HGKAN	0033	*G. de Lairesse* | Een Historieel Schildery Ryk geordonneerd met figuuren, in de trant van G. de Lairesse | *Mat:* op doek	[Teissier] [or others]	(Unknown) fl 1:4

1804/08/08	AMSCH	0254	*G. de Lairesse* | Een Historiëele Ordinantie, van verscheide Beelden, zinspeelende op de Liefde; delicaat en meesterlyk, op Doek, zoo fraai als G. de Lairesse | *Mat:* op doek	Roos a	(Sold) fl 6:10 Toselli
1805/07/10	AMSCH	0231	*G. de Luiresse* | Een Ordinantie uit Ovidius, als G. de Luiresse	Y[ver]	(Sold) fl 0:12 van Iperen
1806/05/05	AMSCH	0176	*Lairesse* | Een Historiele Ordinantie; als Lairesse	R[oos]	(Sold) fl 4:5 Coclers
1810/03/23	HAVIN	0039	*Laires* | Het Kind Eurichthonius in zijn Mand, schoon geschilderd, door .... als van Laires	Rudolf Hendrik de Wetstein [or others]	(Unknown)
			Lairesse, Jan de		
1801/06/10	AMSCH	0105	*Lairesse. (J. de)* | Twee Ordonantien, yder van drie Beelden, in Binnevertrekken, meesterlyk gepenceeld | *Mat:* op paneel *Size:* hoog 10, breed 8 duim	[Doublet]	(Sold) fl 6 Menlie
1802/05/05	AMSCH	0107	*Jan de Lairesse* | Twee Stuks prachtige Ordonnantiën, met musiceerende Beelden, meesterlyk | *Mat:* op paneel *Size:* hoog 16, breed 14 duim	B	(Sold) fl 6:5 Pruijssenaar [for] R
1802/07/21	HGKAN	0040	*J. la Lairesse* | Een Dame welk bezig is om Spyze uit te deelen. met eenige Kindertjes en Dienstmaagden, zeer fraay geschildert, door J. la Lairesse, zwarte Lyste, vergulde binnen rand		(Unknown)
1802/09/06	AMSCH	0067	*J. de Lairesse* | Twee stuks Bybelsche Ordonantiën	B	(Sold) fl 1:10 Barteling
1803/04/20	AMSCH	0035	*Lairesse. (J. de)* | Twee stuks bevallige Schilderytjes met Kinderen, welke met Vogels, Bloemen, Vrugten, en een Hondje speelen, verbeeld in Nissen, met keurlyke gewerkte Tapyten behangen; delicaat behandeld [Deux pieces agréables dont les sujets sont des enfans qui s'amusement [sic] avec des oiseaux, des fruits, des fleurs, & un chien : ces petits tableaux composés en forme de niche sont ornés de plus avec des tapis également bien finis que le reste, dont l'ensemble plaira aux amateurs.] | *Mat:* op doek *Size:* ieder hoog 12 ½, breed 9 duim	Maria Magdalena van Sluypwyk, gravinne van Moens	(Sold) fl 88 Hodges
1803/08/01	AMSCH	0019	*Lairesse. (J. de)* | Een Bybelsche Ordonantie, waarin Christus de Kinderen tot zich doet koomen, meesterlyk behandeld | *Mat:* op doek *Size:* hoog 26, breed 33 duim	J	(Sold) fl 2:15 J Spaan
1806/08/13	AMSCH	0243	*J. de Lairesse* | Een Historiële Ordinantie	Vinkeles [for] G[ruyter]	(Sold) fl 1:5 Nieuwenhuys
1806/08/20	HGBSM	0152	*J. de Lairesse* | Salomon de Afgoden Aanbiddende | *Mat:* op doek *Size:* hoog 22, breed 25 duim	Macalester Loup [or others]	(Sold) fl 3:10 Gram
1806/11/24	AMSCH	0038	*Lairesse (J. de)* | Twee stuks historieele Ordinantiën van verscheiden Beelden; zynde zo fraai gepenceeld als of het van zyn Broeder was | *Mat:* op doek *Size:* Yder hoog 26, breed 32 duim	Munnikhuizen	(Sold) fl 4 Levie Pakker
1807/08/26	AMSCH	0117	*J. de Lairesse* | Een Jongeling en twee Meisjes, in een Hofgezigt met een Tolletje spelende | *Mat:* op doek *Size:* hoog 16, breed 13 duim	Helsdinge	(Sold) fl 3:15 du Pree
1807/08/26	AMSCH	0118	*J. de Lairesse* | Een dito dito [Een Jongeling en twee Meisjes, in een Hofgezigt], in alles als de voorgaande | *Mat:* op doek *Size:* hoog 16, breed 13 duim *Notes:* It is unclear what "dito" refers to in the title.	Helsdinge	(Sold) fl 1:5 Levy Pakker
1809/04/22	AMYVR	0076	*J. de Lairesse* | Den Heiligen Sebastiaan, met Pijlen doorschoten wordende; meesterlijk | *Mat:* op doek *Size:* hoog 19, breed 16 duim	Juff^{r} Julikker	(Sold) fl 0:8 du Pree
1810/06/20	AMSCH	0147[b]	*J. de Lairesse* | Twee stuks: een met Paarden, door van der Neer, en het andere met Beelden | *This Lot:* Het andere met Beelden; lot 147[a] by A. Neer	B	(Sold) fl 0:16 for lots 147[a] & 147[b]. du Pree
1810/06/20	AMSCH	0164	*J. de Lairesse* | Twee stuks Historieele Ordonantien, beide breed en meesterlijk geschilderd	A	(Sold) fl 1 Eekhof
1810/10/11	AMSCH	0223	*J. De Lairesse* | De ontmoeting van Maria en Elisabeth | *Notes:* This lot was sold with lots 214 by N. Verkolje and 224 by Abr. Storck.	A	(Sold) fl 8 for lots 214, 223 & 224. Yver
			Lakeman, H. [Unidentified]		
1809/10/20	UTWLD	0030	*H. Lakeman* | Een Noordhollander met zyn Vrouw in een prieeltje door H. Lakeman	J J van Rhyn	(Unknown)
			Lambrechts, Jan Baptist		
1801/04/08	HAVIN	0018	*Lambregs* | De vyf Zinnen plaizant en uitvoerig		(Unknown)
1802/04/13	HAVIN	0075	*Lambrechts* | Twee met gereedschappen		(Unknown)
1803/12/12	AMSCH	0054	*Lambregts* | Twee stuks bevallige Ordenantiën, zynde het ééne een Groen- en het andere een Fruitverkopers Winkel; beide plaisant van schildering | *Mat:* op paneel *Size:* hoog 10, breed 9 duim	W	(Sold) fl 10:10 Ijver
1807/06/10	HGBSM	0125	*Lambregts* | Een vrolijke Boeren danspartij voor een buiten huijs | companion to lot 126 *Mat:* op doek *Size:* hoog 17 ½, breed 22 duim	Abraham Delfos [or others]	(Sold) fl 7 Oosterwyk
1807/06/10	HGBSM	0126	*Lambregts* | Een dito weerga daar met de kaart gespeeld word, en meer bijwerk | companion to lot 125 *Mat:* op doek *Size:* hoog 17 ½, breed 22 duim *Notes:* It is unclear what "dito" refers to in the title.	Abraham Delfos [or others]	(Sold) fl 10 Oosterwyk
1809/07/25	HGBSM	0243	*Lambrechts* | Twee stuks Binnen-Vertrekken met figuren, groenten en fruit, uitvoerig | *Mat:* op paneel *Size:* hoog 10, breed 8 en een half duim	D van der Aa [or] E B ten Dall	(Sold) fl 6:5 Dupré

Lamen, Christoph Jacobsz. van der

1803/12/15	MGLAC	0007	*van der Laan* | Twee Stuks Conversatien; kragtig geschilderd, en zeer schoon van werking | *Mat:* op paneel *Size:* hoog duim 19, breed duim 25	Mr L H de Haze Bomme	(Unknown)
1810/03/07	UTWLD	0018	*van der Lamen* | Een Buitenhuis, met Heeren en Dames, die aan eene tafel zitten | *Size:* hoog 2 voet, breed 3 voet	J J Woertman	(Unknown) fl 25:10

Lamme, A.

1802/11/01	DOBRA	0193	*A. Lamme* | In een Boeren Binnenhuis hangt een geslagt Varken op de leer, waarby een Vrouw en Kind; verder een Jongen met de blaas. Aan den haard een Man | *Mat:* op paneel *Size:* breed 31, hoog 22 duim		(Unknown) fl 15:15
1806/01/30	RMAN	0005	*Lamme* | Een Vrouwe Hoofd	Dirk Langendyk	(Unknown)
1809/04/22	AMYVR	0070	*Lamme* | Een IJsgezicht, ziende op het Slot de Merwe, gestoffeerd met Marketenters, Schaatsenrijders, en eene menigte Beeldjes; meesterlijk | *Mat:* op doek *Size:* hoog 22, breed 31 duim	de Bruin	(Sold) fl 5 du Pree
1809/04/22	AMYVR	0071	*Lamme* | Twee stuks: een Landschap, met stoffagie van Ezeldrijvers, en een ander met staand en liggend Vee; geestig als de voorgaande | *Size:* hoog 22, breed 31 duim	de Bruin	(Sold) fl 10:10 C S Roos
1809/04/22	AMYVR	0072	*Lamme* | Een andere dito [Landschap], aan den oever van een Rivier, mede als voren | *Mat:* op paneel *Size:* hoog 20, breed 26 duim	de Bruin	(Sold) fl 6:10 Remmers Bredius
1810/07/23	DOLG2	0067	*A. Lamme* | Een Landschapje, met Beeldtjes | *Mat:* op paneel *Size:* hoog 13, breed 18 duim	Pieter Quinting	(Unknown) fl 5:10
1810/07/23	DOLG2	0091	*A. Lamme* | Een Watergezicht | *Mat:* op paneel *Size:* hoog 10, breed 12 duim	Pieter Quinting	(Unknown) fl 1
1810/12/03	DOBRA	0008	*A. Lamme* | Een Landschap, waar in een Koe, Schaap en Gyt; breed geschilderd		(Unknown)

Lamme, A. (copy by)

1810/07/23	DOLG2	0017	*A. Lamme; van Hulst* | In een water, langs eenen stads toren, en verdere gebouwen, vertoonen zich Schuiten en Schepen. Naar van Hulst, door A. Lamme | copy by A. Lamme after Hulst *Mat:* op doek *Size:* hoog 21, breed 28 duim	Pieter Quinting	(Sold) fl 2:15 Visser
1810/07/23	DOLG2	0101	*A. Lamme; A. Cuyp* | Liggende en staande Koebeesten; door A. Lamme, naar A. Cuyp | copy by A. Lamme after A. Cuyp	Pieter Quinting	(Sold) fl 1:14 v Meulen Dordt

Lamme, Arie

1807/09/28	DOHAA	000A	*Ary Lammen* | Een Zwitsersch Landschap | *Size:* breed 29. hoog 25 duim	Mattheus Westerouen van Meeteren	(Unknown)
1807/09/28	DOHAA	000B	*Ary Lammen* | Een dito [Zwitsersch Landschap] | *Size:* breed 29. hoog 25 duim	Mattheus Westerouen van Meeteren	(Unknown)

Lancret, Nicolas (copy after)

1802/09/18	RMDRS	0079	*Lankret* | Vier stuks, na Lankret, in lyste en glasen	Casper de Haas	(Unknown) fl 2:8

Lancret, Nicolas (manner)

1804/12/10	AMSCH	0111	*N. Lancret* | Twee stuks, in aangenaame boomryke Landschappen vertoonen zig Pastoraalen Voorwerpen, van Jongmans en jonge Dochters, verzelt van hunne schaapen; in een derzelve ziet men 'er een goeder geluk zeggen, zy zyn beide bevallig van coloriet en uitvoerig gepenceeld, als door N. Lancret | *Size:* ieder hoog 14, breed 12 duim	Jan De Groot	(Sold) fl 16:10 Coclers

Lange

1810/10/10	MGCIT	0137	*de Lange* | Een Schildery, zijnde een Historiëel	Caspar van Citters	(Unknown)

Langendijk, Dirk

1803/08/24	HGKAN	0091	*D. Langendyk* | Aeneas met de Sibyllen	[Teissier] [or others]	(Sold) fl 1:16 Carre
1806/01/30	RMAN	0003	*Dr. Langendyk* | Een Hondekop, door D: Langendyk	Dirk Langendyk	(Unknown)
1806/05/05	AMSCH	0079	*D. Langendyk* | Een hévig gevegt tusschen Ruitery, daar Christenen de Turken op de vlugt dryven, vol gewoel en gesneuvelden; kragtig gepenceeld op Doek | *Mat:* op doek *Size:* hoog 17, breed 25 duim	S[chley]	(Sold) fl 6 Isaac Smit
1808/06/06	RMRIJ	0067	*Langendijk. (Dirk)* | Eene Militaire Pleisterplaats. Een Officier zijn paard bij eene tent water gevende, waarvoor een groot gezelschap zich vrolijk maakt, en verder eenige Ruiters. Zeer rijk gestoffeerd, uitvoerig, dun en delicaat geschilderd [Un Officier abreuve son Cheval devant la tente d'un Vivandier, où plusieurs personnes sont en ribote. Au second plan de la Cavalerie, un horison et un Ciel agréable terminent ce précieux Morceau dans le gout de Philippe Wouwerman. Ce grand Génie, dont les Tableaux sont rares, ne travailloit qu'à des Dessins précieux au Lavis] | *Annots:* voor hem 1782 geschilderd (f 200.-) (RMA I) *Mat:* op paneel *Size:* Hoog 17 ¼ en breed 15 ½ duim	Gerrit van der Pot, Heer van Groeneveld	(Sold) fl 140 Roelfzema de Groeginge
1808/06/06	RMRIJ	0068	*Langendijk. (Dirk)* | Eene Rencontre, waarin de Kavallerij vlugtende is. Op den voorgrond een Cornet op een bruin Paard, enz. Zeer uitvoerig geschilderd. Eene wedergade. Eene overrompeling van Grenadiers door Ruiterij en Voetvolk wadende door een Moeras. Als boven behandeld [Une rencontre Militaire, où la Cavalerie est en retraite précipitée. Sur le	Gerrit van der Pot, Heer van Groeneveld	(Sold) fl 270 van Yperen

devant un Porte-Etendard monté sur un Cheval brun fuit à toute bride etc. D'un beau fini, et d'un ton fin et agréable. Le Pendant represente une surprise de Grenadiers par la Cavalerie à travers un Endroit marécageux. Egal en mérite au précédent] | *Annots:* voor hem 1782 geschilderd (f 200.-) (RMA I) *Mat:* op mahonie paneel *Size:* Twee Stukken. Hoog 15 ¾ en breed 18 duim

1808/06/06 RMRIJ 0069 *Langendijk. (Dirk)* | Eene Rencontre tusschen een Pauker, zijnde een Moor, en een Ruiter. Zeer delicaat en konstig behandeld. In Plaat gebragt door J. Beeme [Rencontre entre un Timbalier Négre et un Cavalier. Supérieurement peint, et plein de mérite] | *Annots:* voor hem 1782 geschilderd (f 200.-) (RMA I) *Mat:* op paneel *Size:* Hoog 13 en breed 10 ½ duim — Gerrit van der Pot, Heer van Groeneveld — (Sold) fl 160 van Beefting

1810/03/26 RMMUY 0085 *Dirk Langendyk* | Twee uitvoerige Landschapjes; het eene met Koeijen, het andere met Paarden. Uitvoerig en konstig geschilderd [Deux Paysages : l'un avec des Boeufs, et l'autre des Boeufs et Chevaux ; très fini et d'un mérite distingué. Les tableaux sont rares de ce grand dessinateur de batailles, ayant peu peint a l'huile.] | *This Lot:* Een uitvoerig Landschapje met Koeijen *Annots:* 2 pendants Jenrede[?] Janson[?] (BPG) *Notes:* Lots 85 and 86 were printed in the catalogue as one item. — Daniel de Jongh Az — (Sold) fl 33 for lots 85 & 86. van Eyk s'Hage

1810/03/26 RMMUY 0086 *Dirk Langendyk* | Twee uitvoerige Landschapjes; het eene met Koeijen, het andere met Paarden. Uitvoerig en konstig geschilderd [Deux Paysages : l'un avec des Boeufs, et l'autre des Boeufs et Chevaux ; très fini et d'un mérite distingué. Les tableaux sont rares de ce grand dessinateur de batailles, ayant peu peint a l'huile.] | *This Lot:* Een uitvoerig Landschapje met Paarden *Notes:* Lots 85 and 86 were printed in the catalogue as one item. — Daniel de Jongh Az — (Sold) fl 33 for lots 85 & 86. van Eyk s'Hage

Langendijk, Dirk (copy by)

1806/11/24 AMSCH 0040 *Langendyk (D.); L. Bakhuyzen* | Een kabbelend Water met zeilende Scheepen en andere Vaartuigen; het licht doet in dit stukje een byzondere werking en is kunstig gecopieerd naar L. Bakhuyzen | copy by D. Langendijk after Backhuysen *Mat:* op doek *Size:* hoog 13, breed 17 duim — Munnikhuizen — (Sold) fl 21 van Iperen

Langenhöffel, Johann Joseph Friedrich

1803/09/07 AMSCH 0102 *Proffessor Langenhoffel* | Dit Voorwerp vertoond Cupido en Psiche; uitvoerig op Doek geschilderd [Ce sujet représente Psiché et Cupidon] | *Mat:* op doek *Size:* hoog 19, breed 27 duim — Smidt — (Sold) fl 6 Scheffer

Lapotteren [Unidentified]

1809/04/17 AMSCH 0140 *Lapotteren* | Een Akadémie, rijk gestoffeerd met Studiën en Studerende Konstenaars; uitvoerig geschilderd | *Mat:* op doek — [Gruyter?] — (Sold) fl 0:12

Laquy, Willem Joseph

1801/12/22 AMOTT 0012 *Laquy* | 1 gestoffeerd Binnevertrek, daar in een Dienstmaagd Wafelen bakt voor twee bevallige jonge Lieden by een Tafel, een jonge Dochter is bezig voor dezelven Suyker te raspen, terwyl verder een ander nadert met byhebbende Vrugten; in vrolyke actien behandelt door Laquy, 1775 | *Inscr:* Laquy, 1775 (signed and dated?) *Notes:* It is unclear whether the name and date are inscribed on the painting. — Bartholomeus Ruloffs — (Unknown) fl 91

1801/12/22 AMOTT 0047 *Laquy* | 1 Krygsoverste met een balorige Boer op de Kaart speelende, in 't verschiet een Trap en aanschouwende Boerin; zeer konstig — Bartholomeus Ruloffs — (Unknown) fl 16

1802/05/05 AMSCH 0108 *W. J. Laqui* | Dit meesterstuk verbeeld een bevallig Vrouwtje, in een Binnevertrek, met een rood zyd Jakje met bond, beezig zynde appelen te schillen, naast hear [sic] een kopere Emmer met appelen, en andere Groentens, voor haar een Kind in de Wieg, waarmede een Meisje speeld; een Jager ziet men van agteren de deur inkomen, zynde alles delicaat en uitvoerig | *Mat:* op paneel *Size:* hoog 24, breed 20 duim — D — (Bought In) fl 190

1802/05/05 AMSCH 0109 *W. J. Laqui* | Een Binnenvertrek, alwaar een jonge Juffrouw aan een Tafel zit Tee te drinken, welke haar door een Dienstmaagd word geschonken, verscheiden Huisraad en een frappant ligt en bruin maken dit Stukje zeer bevallig, en is door Denzelfden Meester fraai gepenceeld | *Mat:* op paneel *Size:* hoog 21, breed 18 duim — D — (Bought In) fl 92

1802/05/05 AMSCH 0110 *W. J. Laqui* | Een Keuken, waarin een Dienstmaagd aan een Tafel staat Yeren [sic] in een roode Pot te breeken, een Korf en Booterschotel staan nevens haar, verders een menigte Keukengereedschap, alles door een aangenaam zonligt beschenen wordende, meesterlyk | *Mat:* op doek *Size:* hoog 21, breed 18 duim — D — (Sold) fl 99 v d Schleij [for] A[=Putte]

1802/06/28 AMSCH 0100 *W. J. Lagny* | Dit bevallig voorwerp, in een gemeubileerd Vertrek, vertoond een bevallige Dame, ter zyde een Tafel met een Tapytkleed bedekt, waar op een Kom met Punch [sic] geplaatst is, met een officier op het Schaakbord speelende, ter zyde staan twee andere Militairen het aanschouwende; de Caracters zyn natuurlyk en uitvoerig van penceel behandeling | *Mat:* op paneel *Size:* hoog 19, breed 15 duim — Anna Elink — (Sold) fl 17 Gruiter

1802/09/06 AMSCH 0065 *J. Laquy* | In een fraay Gemeubileerde Kamer, ziet men een bevallige Dame, in een deftige Negligé Kleeding, als met beide handen reikende naar een Kindje in de wieg leggende, welke mede beide de handjes — H^{n} Smit — (Sold) fl 94 van der Schley [for] S[mits wed]

			opheft, ter zyde by een glaase Raam, staat een Tafeltje met een Kleedje bedekt, waar op een Lampetkan en Schotel geplaast is, en ter zyde een Ledikant, Stoelen en verder bywerk; alles evenaart de natuur, en is van een uitvoerige Penceelbehandeling | *Mat:* op paneel *Size:* hoog 22, breed 18 duim		
1802/09/06	AMSCH	0066	*J. Laquy* | In een dito [Gemeubileerde Kamer] als het Voorige, zit een jonge Dame in geheele Zatyne Kleeding op een Canapé, verzelt van een Hondje, voor dezelve legt op een knie een Schoenmaker, als beezig de maat te neemen, verder ziet men een Clavier, en door de openstaande Deur, een Dienstmeisje de trap opgaande; mede als de voorige van een uitvoerige Penceelbehandeling | *Mat:* op paneel *Size:* hoog 22 ½, breed 18 ½ duim	H^{n} Smit	(Sold) fl 87 van der Schley [for] S[mits wed]
1804/05/07	AMSCH	0097	*Laqui. (W. I.)* | Aan een Tafel zit een Officier een brief te leezen een Dame over hem zittende schynt zeer bedroefd te zyn, getroost wordende door een Meisje; agter de Tafel staat een andere Militair, en op de grond zit een Jongeling, met een Trommel te speelen; aangenaam en geestig geschilderd | *Mat:* op paneel *Size:* hoog 19, breed 15 duim	Roos [for] A	(Sold) fl 66 Roelofs
1804/12/10	AMSCH	0043	*J. Laquy* | In een gemeubileerde Zaal vertoont zig een jeugdige bevallige Dame, in satyne negligée kleeding, houdende een jong vogeltje op de hand, ter zyde zit een Heer, in zyn japon, by een Tafel met een tapyt kleedje bedekt, waarop een kandelaar, inktkoker en papieren geplaatst zyn, hy houd in de eene hand een chocolaadkop, terwyl hy met den andere het vogeltje, in een lepeltje, eenig spys toerykt, verders een Dienstmysje [sic] met een klyn Kind aan de lyband, en een Jongeling de deur uitgaande; alles is natuurlyk, en van een uitvoerige penceel-behandeling | *Mat:* op doek *Size:* Hoog 21 ½, breed 18 duim	Jan De Groot	(Sold) fl 45 Numan
1804/12/10	AMSCH	0044	*J. Laquy* | In een aangenaam Thuingezicht, by een waterkom en fontyn onder geboomten, ziet men een jonge Dame, in bevallige galante negligée Kleeding, houdende in de handen een koopere gieter, waar meede zy een oranjeboom besproeit, ter zyde zit een andere Dame, beezig zig de voeten te baaden, en agter dezelve een jong Meisje met een korfje met bloemen, verder vertoont zig een treffelyk Gebouw en cierlyke Vaasen, op Piedestallen; alles bevallig en van een uitvoerig penceel behandeling | *Mat:* op doek *Size:* Hoog 21, breed 17 duim	Jan De Groot	(Sold) fl 18:10 Numan
1804/12/10	AMSCH	0045	*J. Laquy* | Een bevallige jonge Dame voor haar Toilet, zy heeft een mandje met bloemen op de schoot, en is bézig een brief te leezen, achter haar de Kamenier, bézig haar hair met bloemen te vlegten, op haar toilet ziet men een zilvere lampet en een doos met paerlen en andere ingredienten; dit stukje is zeer plaisant en van de beste schildering | *Mat:* op doek *Size:* Hoog 20, breed 17 duim	Jan De Groot	(Sold) fl 39 M Kooij
1804/12/10	AMSCH	0046	*J. Laquy* | In een Keukenvertrek zit een bevallige Dame, in deftige negligé kleeding, schynende bézig appelen te schillen, achter dezelve staat een Dienstmeisje, houdende met beide handen een Eend-vogel, die door een Jongeling met een mandje aan den arm gebragt is, op de grond staat een kopere markt-emmer, daar nevens ligt een kool; ter zyde om hoog ziet men een opgehaalt tapyt-gordyn en gestoffeert met verder bywerk; alles is zeer uitvoerig en van een kunstige penceel behandeling | *Mat:* op paneel *Size:* Hoog 22, breed 18 ½ duim	Jan De Groot	(Sold) fl 70 van Iperen
1804/12/10	AMSCH	0047	*J. Laquy* | Een bevallig Dienstmeisje ziet men bézig te schuuren aan een koper gatepetiel, zy heeft onderscheide keukengereedschap by haar, men ziet door de nis een kast en ander huisraad; en is fiks gepenceeld en niet minder dan de voorige | *Mat:* op paneel *Size:* Hoog 18, breed 13 duim	Jan De Groot	(Sold) fl 140 C S Roos
1804/12/10	AMSCH	0048	*J. Laquy* | Een Keuken, waar in een bevallig Vrouwtje met een Kind aan de borst, naast haar een Jonge met een trekpot, 't vertrek is ryk van huisraad gestoffeerd en alles van een zeer bevallige ordinantie | *Mat:* op paneel *Size:* Hoog 17, breed 20 duim	Jan De Groot	(Sold) fl 150 J Spaan
1805/12/16	AMSCH	0035	*J. W. Laquy* | Voor een open Steene Nis, onder de Rand versiert met speelende Kindertjes, als in Basrelief, vertoont zich in een Gemeubileerd Vertrek, een bevallige Dienstmaagd, beezig met verscheide Koper en Thin Huisraat te schuuren, het geen op de Rand der Nis geplaast is, ter zyde een opgeschoven Tapyt-Gordyn; alles natuurlyk en zeer uitvoerig gepenceeld | *Mat:* op paneel *Size:* hoog 18, breed 13 duim	R[oos]	(Bought In) fl 100
1806/05/05	AMSCH	0080	*J. Laquy* | Een gemeubileerde Kamer, voor een Tafel met een tapyt Kleed bedekt, zit een bevallige Moeder met een Kind op haar schoot, dewelken de complimenten schynt te ontfangen, van een in de Kamer komende Dame; en eenige andere Perzoonen, en verdere stoffagie; delicaat en uitvoerig geschilderd door J. Laquy | *Mat:* op paneel *Size:* hoog 20, breed 27 duim	V[inkeles]	(Bought In) fl 50 for lots 80 & 81
1806/05/05	AMSCH	0081	*J. Laquy* | In een niet minder sierelyk Vertrek, ziet men eenige musiceerende Heeren en Dames; in alles als de voorige behandeld	V[inkeles]	(Bought In) fl 50 for lots 80 & 81
1806/11/24	AMSCH	0039	*Laquy (W.J.)* | Voor een open steene Nis, onder de rand verciert met speelende Kindertjes als in Basrelief, vertoont zig in een gemeubileerd vertrek, een bevallig Dienstmeisje, schynende beezig met koper en thin Huisraat te schuuren, het geen op de rand der Nis geplaatst is, ter zyde hangt een opgeschoven Gordyn; zeer natuurlyk en uitvoerig van penceelbehandeling | *Mat:* op paneel *Size:* hoog 18, breed 13 duim	van den Bosch	(Sold) fl 97 B^{d} Kooy

1807/06/10	HGBSM	0155	*Laqui* | Een Binnevertrek, waarin een gezelschap van Officiers zittende met de kaart te speelen, met twee Dames en meer bijwerk | *Mat:* op doek *Size:* hoog 23, breed 27 ½ duim	Abraham Delfos [or others]	(Sold) fl 4:15 S T
1807/08/26	AMSCH	0110	*W.J. Laquy* | In een fraai gemeubileerde Kamer, ziet men eene bevallige Dame, in deftige Neglige-Kleeding, als met beide handen reikende naar een Kindje, in de Wieg leggende, welke mede de beide handjes opheft; ter zyde by een glaze Raam, staat een Tafeltje met een Kleedje bedekt, waarop een Lampetkan en Schotel geplaatst is, en ter zyde een Ledikant, Stoelen en verder bywerk; alles evenaard de Natuur, en is van een uitvoerige Penceelsbehandeling | *Mat:* op paneel *Size:* hoog 22, breed 18 duim	v d Schley [for] [Smits Wed]	(Sold) fl 95 van Iperen
1807/08/26	AMSCH	0111	*W.J. Laquy* | In een dito [fraai gemeubileerde] Vertrek als het voorige, zit eene jonge Dame, in geheele Satyne Kleeding op een Canapee, vergezelt van een Hondje, voor dezelve ligt op een knie, een Schoenmaker, als bezig de maat te neemen, verder ziet men een Clavier, en door een openstaande Deur, een Dienstmeisje de trap opgaande; mede als de vorige van behandeling | *Mat:* op paneel *Size:* hoog 22 ½, breed 18 ½ duim	v d Schley [for] [Smits Wed]	(Sold) fl 75 du Pree
1807/08/26	AMSCH	0112	*W.J. Laquy* | In een gemeubileerde Kamer zit een bevallig Vrouwtje aan een Spinnewiel, een ander Vrouwtje heeft een Kind 't welk zy op de Tafel zet om te speelen, met een Jongetje, met een Vogeltje; alle de voorwerpen zyn van een bevallig en aangename behandeling | *Mat:* op paneel *Size:* hoog 18, breed 21 duim	Joseph Vallette	(Sold) fl 100 du Pree
1808/06/13	AMSCH	0095	*Laquy (W.J.)* | In een gemeubileerd Vertrek zit eene bevallige Dame, in een Nachtgewaad, omhebbende een Manteltje met Bont gevoerd, en in een witte Satijne Rok, op de Schoot heeft zij een Bennetje met Appelen, zij schijnt geld te willen geven aan eene Dienstmaagd, nevens haar staande, die een dooden Haas in de hand houdt; verder staat een Vogelkopers Jongen, met een doode Vogel in een Mandje, op den grond staat eene Koperen Marktemmer, met eenige Vruchten. Het zonlicht, door het zijvenster invallende, doet eene natuurlijke werking, en alles is uitvoerig geschilderd | *Mat:* op paneel *Size:* hoog 22, breed 18 duim	[Jan Tersteeg]	(Sold) fl 122 J Twisk Cz
1808/08/23	AMSCH	0097	*Laqui. (J.)* | Twee stuks rijk gemeubileerde Kamers, in de eene eenige musiceerende Heeren en Dames; en het andere een Famieljegezelschap; beide fraai en uitvoerig gepenceeld | *Mat:* op paneel *Size:* Ieder hoog 20, breed 26 duim	[Gruyter?]	(Bought In) fl 78
1808/12/30	HGIMM	[0071d]	*Loqwi* | Voorts een exquis kabinetje Schilderijen van voorname Nederlandsche Meesters, welke uit hoofde van de kortheid des tijds niet stuk voor stuk kunnen beschreven worden; doch waarvan de beschrijving op den Kijkdag zal voorhanden zijn. Dus wij hier alleen de namen van eenige dier Meesters laten volgen, als: A. Kuyp, Ruysdaal, Karel du Jardyn, Loqwi ('t beste dat hij schilderde) Hondekoeter, van Dyk, Janson, Moesgever, Kamphuyzen, van Gooijen, A. van der Neer, T. Wyk, Huchtenburgh, Zolemaker, van Hassel, A. Vermeulen, van Dongen, Scheffer, van Os enz. | *This Lot:* Een Schilderij, Loqwi *Notes:* Because this lot was not numbered in the catalogue, we have assigned the number.		(Unknown)
1809/04/22	AMYVR	0066	*W.J. Laqui* | In een rijk gemeubileerd Vertrek zit eene bevallige Vrouw naast een Tafel te spinnen, eene andere Vrouw met een Kind, en een Jongeling met een Vogel op de Kruk, stoffeeren verder dit bevallig geschilderde stukje | *Mat:* op paneel *Size:* hoog 18, breed 21 duim	de Bruin	(Sold) fl 140 Remmers Bredius
1809/04/22	AMYVR	0067	*W.J. Laqui* | In een Binnenvertrek ziet men eene Dame, welke een Officier schaakmat schijnt gezet te hebben, twee anderen schijnen 'er met attentie naar te zien; dit stuk is vol caracter, en als de voorgaande behandeld | *Mat:* op paneel *Size:* hoog 19, breed 15 duim	de Bruin	(Bought In) fl 51
1809/04/22	AMYVR	0068	*W.J. Laqui* | Eene jonge Dame zit in een deftig gemeubileerde Kamer op een Canappé, terwijl de Schoenmaker haar de maat voor Schoenen meet; niet minder als het voorgaande | *Mat:* op paneel *Size:* hoog 22, breed 19 duim	de Bruin	(Bought In) fl 55
1809/04/22	AMYVR	0069	*W.J. Laqui* | Een bevallig Boerinnetje met een Kan en Muziekblad in de hand | *Mat:* op paneel *Size:* hoog 7, breed 6 duim	de Bruin	(Sold) fl 3:15 du Pree
1809/06/13	AMSCH	0086	*J. Laqui* | In een deftig gemeubileerde Kamer, zit eene jonge Dame, in wit Satijne Kleeding, voor een Borduur-raam, waarop eenig Werk begonnen is naar een Schilderstuk met Bloemen, hetwelk op een Canapé ter zijde geplaast is, daar nevens zit eene andere Dame, in een Jakje met Bont gevoerd, als in gesprek met een staande Krijgsoversten, die een Glas Wijn in de Hand heeft, door een openstaande Deur, ziet men in een andere Kamer, waarin eenige Krijgslieden zig met Drinken vermaken, verders gestoffeerd met Muziek-Instrumenten en ander bijwerk, ter zijde een weggeschooven Tapijtgordijn; het licht en koloriet is bevallig, en van een uitvoerige penceelbehandeling | *Mat:* op doek *Size:* hoog 25, breed 20 duim	Q	(Bought In) fl 50
1809/06/13	AMSCH	0087	*J. Laqui* | Deeze bevallige Ordonantie vertoont in een deftige gemeubileerde Binnekamer, een Sint Nicolaas-feest, verscheide Kindertjes beijveren zich om eenig Lekkernij, het geen door de Schoorsteen geworpen word, op te zamelen, de Moeder houd een kleinder Kind bij de Lijband, terwijl de Vader ter zijde zittende, het als met vreugde beschouwd, verder komt een Meid de Deur in met een Kaars;	P	(Sold) fl 38 van Iperen

			alles vertoont zich bij Kaars- en Lamplicht, en gestoffeerd met verscheide bijwerk, en is van een fraaije uitvoerige penceelbehandeling | *Mat:* op doek *Size:* hoog 28, breed 24 duim		
1809/06/13	AMSCH	0088	*J. Laqui* | Dit voorwerp vertoont eene jonge Dame, zittende met een Muziek-papier in de handen, voor een Tafel met een Tapijtkleedje bedekt, waarop een Schotel met verschillende Fruit geplaast is, daar nevens zit een Heer, met veel aandagt op de Fiool speelende; de karacters zijn natuurlijk en uitvoerig gepenceeld | *Mat:* op paneel *Size:* hoog 9, breed 8 duim	P	(Sold) fl 39 for lots 88 & 89. T Spaan
1809/06/13	AMSCH	0089	*J. Laqui* | Een verliefde Jager, zittende bij een Tafel, met verscheide Spijs voorzien, hij schijnt de jonge Hospita te liefkoozen, die al wijkende zich van hem zoekt te ontslaan; in alles als de voorgaande uitvoerig behandeld | *Mat:* op paneel *Size:* hoog 9, breed 8 duim	P	(Sold) fl 39 for lots 88 & 89. T Spaan
1809/06/13	AMSCH	0090	*J. Laqui* | Maria met het Kind, zittende in een Landschap, waarbij St. Joseph, als de voorgaande behandeld | *Mat:* op paneel *Size:* hoog 10, breed 8 ½ duim	P	(Sold) fl 6 Jan Yver
1809/06/13	AMSCH	0091	*J. Laqui* | Twee stuks, den eene vertoont in een gemeubileerde Kamer, eene Juffrouw in Negligee Kleding, zittende voor een Wieg, een jong Kindje op de Schoot houdende, schijnende het de Borst te willen geeven, ter zijde staat een aardig Jongetje, houdende een Vogeltje op een Krukje in de Hand; den anderen verbeeld in een dito Vertrek eene bevallig Vrouwtje, bij een openstaande Vengster, als een Brief leezenden, op de Schoot ligt een Naaikussen, agter dezelve staat een Dienstmeisje met een Marktëmmer aan den Arm, en op de grond een Mandje met eenig Goed; beide geestig geordoneert en meesterlijk fiks gepenceeld | *Mat:* op paneel *Size:* ieder hoog 6, breed 5 duim	P	(Sold) fl 16 T Spaan
1809/06/13	AMSCH	0092	*J. Laqui* | In een Binnevertrek zit een Heer bij een Lessenaar, bézig een Pen te snijden, nevens hem een Tafel, waarop Sandlooper en Inktkooker, bij het Kaarschlicht verbeeld | *Mat:* op paneel *Size:* hoog 16, breed 11 duim	P	(Sold) fl 6:5 van Dijl
1809/07/25	HGBSM	0018	*J. Lakis* | Een deftig gemeubileerd Binnenvertrek, waar in een staande Dame by een Kind in de Wieg, en verder ryk gestoffeert met ander bywerk | *Mat:* op paneel *Size:* hoog 22, breed 18 duim	D van der Aa [or] E B ten Dall	(Sold) fl 51 van Eyk
1810/05/22	AMSCH	0056	*Laquij. (W. J.)* | In een Keukenvertrek staat eene bevallige Vrouw bij een Tafel, bezig Eijeren in een Aarde Pot te breeken, een Korf en Boterschootel staan nevens dezelven, verder gestoffeerd met verscheide Keukengereedschap; alles word door een aangenaam zonlicht beschenen, en zeer uitvoerig van penceelbehandeling | *Mat:* op doek *Size:* hoog 22, breed 18 duim	Johannes van de Putte Nicolaasz.	(Sold) fl 80 Roos
1810/05/22	AMSCH	0057	*Laquij. (W. J.)* | In een Binnenhuis of Herberg, ziet men een Jager eene bevallig Meisje liefkoosen en zamen met een Roemer Wijn klinken, eene bedaagde Vrouw is bezig Wijn uit een Vat te tappen, verder twee Lieden in het Verkeerbord spelende; het Vertrek is rijkelijk met Meubelen en ander bijwerk gestoffeerd, en meesterlijk fraai gepenceeld | *Mat:* op paneel *Size:* hoog 18, breed 16 duim	Johannes van de Putte Nicolaasz.	(Sold) fl 46 Yver
			Laquy, Willem Joseph (copy by)		
1808/11/28	AMSCH	0038	*J. Laquij; P. Potter* | Langs een opgaande vlakte, ziet men een Landman, een drift van tien Beesten voortdrijvende, nevens hem een Hond, agterwaards grazige Weiden en een Dorp in 't verschiet, meesterlijk op Doek, door J. Laquij. Hoog 49, breed 76 duim, zijnde dit stuk een Copij na de beroemde Ossedrift van P. Potter | copy by W.J. Laquy after Paulus Potter *Mat:* op doek *Size:* hoog 49, breed 76 duim	[Gruyter?]	(Sold) fl 16:10 du Pree
			Largillière, Nicolas de		
1803/08/24	HGKAN	0022	*Largiliere* | Een Portrait van een gedistingeerde Dame, Ryk gekleed 't by werk steld voor, een Hof Gezigt met een Fontein, konstig geschildert | *Mat:* op doek	[Teissier] [or others]	(Sold) fl 5:10 Giesen
1803/09/07	AMSCH	0101	*N. Largilliere* | Een Pourtrait van een Vorstelyk Perzoon, in een rooden Mantel met Goude franjes; delicaat op Koper in 't Ovaal [Le portrait d'une personne de qualité, portant un manteau rouge à franges d'or ; peinture délicate] | *Mat:* op koper *Fmt:* ovaal *Size:* hoog 23, breed 17 duim	Smidt	(Bought In) fl 85
			Lastman, Pieter Pietersz.		
1801/05/11	AMSCH	0045	*P. Lastman* | Deeze Ordonnantie verbeeld, alwaar Boas bevel geeft, om de Ninnanitische Dochter vryheid te laaten met het geen zy in 't Land opzamelt, meesterlyk en krachtig van penceel behandeling | *Mat:* op doek *Size:* hoog 29, breed 34 duim	E[lias]	(Sold) fl 4 v d Schley [for] R[ijfsnijder]
1801/06/10	AMSCH	0104	*Lastman. (P.)* | Een Bybelsche Ordonantie, verbeeldende een Offerhande van Koning Jerobeam: de Hartstochten zyn natuurlyk en verder meesterlyk geschildert | *Mat:* op doek *Size:* hoog 62, breed 77 duim	[Doublet]	(Sold) fl 10 Pruijssenaar
1802/06/28	AMSCH	0105	*P. Lastman* | Een Bybelsche Ordonantie, voorstellende David met 't Hoofd van Goliat, verzeld van een menigte Beelden op Doek | *Mat:* op doek *Size:* hoog 36, breed 60 duim	Anna Elink	(Sold) fl 5 L Pakker
1805/07/03	AMSCH	0103	*P. Lastman* | In een Duin- en Boomryk Landschap, ziet men een Heydensche Offerhande, van een zeer groote ménigte Menschen,	V[inkeles]	(Sold) fl 60 Tozelli

			Rundervee, Paarden, oude Gothische Gebouwen, goude en zilvere Drinkbeekers, Schaalen, Bloemen, &c.; allerfraaist en uitvoerig gepenceeld | *Mat:* op paneel *Size:* hoog 29, breed 43 ½ duim		
1805/07/03	AMSCH	0104	*P. Lastman* | Een ryke Ordinantie van een ménigte Beelden, voorstellende een dito [Heydensche] Offerhanden, meede in een Bergachtig Landschap, met een Temple, en in alles als de voorgaande behandeld | *Mat:* op paneel *Size:* hoog 33, breed 49 duim	V[inkeles]	(Sold) fl 13 Tozelli
1806/08/13	AMSCH	0100	*Lastman. (P.)* | Hagar in een Bosch haar Kind beweenende word door den Engel getroost; meesterlyk geschilderd | *Mat:* op paneel *Size:* hoog 20, breed 18 duim	Roos	(Sold) fl 5 Riemsdijk
1806/08/13	AMSCH	0101	*Lastman. (P.)* | In een gemeubileerde Kamer, zit Delila, en Samson, slapende en rustende teegen haar schoot, terwyl een bediende hem het hair afknipt, verder een andere met een ketting in de handen en andere gewapende Soldaten; fraai van coloriet, en uitvoerig gepenceeld | *Mat:* op paneel *Size:* hoog 14, breed 19 duim	Roos	(Sold) fl 11 Lafontaine
1807/06/10	HGBSM	0210	*Lasman* | Een Historieel stuk verbelende eene Offerhande | *Mat:* op paneel *Size:* hoog 19 ½, breed 26 duim	Abraham Delfos [or others]	(Sold) fl 3:6 Spruit
1807/08/26	AMSCH	0121	*P. Lastman* | In een Boomryk bergachtig Landschap vertoont zich een Rust der Heilige Familie, in de vlugt naar Egypte; meesterlyk en bevallig gepenceeld | *Mat:* op paneel *Size:* hoog 13, breed 20 duim	Helsdinge	(Sold) fl 3:15 van Iperen
1810/10/11	AMSCH	0150	*J. Lastman* | Eene Historiëele Ordonantie, met eene menigte Beelden; fiks geschilderd	S	(Sold) fl 3:5 v d^{r} Schley [for] R[ijfsnijder]
1810/10/11	AMSCH	0198	*Lastman* | In een Landschap ziet men vooraan Joseph, welke door zijne Broeders in de Put gelaten werd | *Mat:* op doek	A	(Sold) fl 1 Yver

Lastman, Pieter Pietersz. (and Keyser, Thos. de)

1810/11/07	UTWLD	0020	*P. Lastman; D. Keyzer* | Een kapitale Schilderij, steld voor een Turksche historie, staande een Visier voor een Mosquée, aan wien een Turk iets geknield aanbied, verder Turksche stoffering van reukvaten etc. alles meesteragtig behandeld, (getekend P. Lastman inv. D. Keyzer 1660) op doek, 3 voet 8 duim hoog, breed 2 voet 10 duim, zwarte Lijst | *Mat:* op doek *Size:* 3 voet 8 duim hoog, breed 2 voet 10 duim *Inscr:* P. Lastman inv. D. Keyzer 1660 (signed and dated) *Loc:* Paris, France. Institut Néerlandais, Fondation Custodia. (6781)		(Unknown) fl 16

Lauri, Filippo

1801/04/13	AMSCH	0041	*P. Lanri* | De geboorte van Adonis in een Landschap, verzeld van een menigte Nimphen, de ordonantie is fraay en de behandeling bevallig | *Mat:* op doek *Size:* hoog 20, breed 25 duim	Pierre Fouquet, junior	(Sold) fl 10 Gruyter
1808/08/23	AMSCH	0100	*Lauri. (P.)* | De geboorte van Adonis, in een Landschap voorgesteld, waar bij eenige Nimphen; schoon geordoneert, en meesterlijk geschilderd | *Mat:* op doek *Size:* hoog 20, breed 25 duim	[Gruyter?]	(Sold) fl 11:10 van Iperen [or] Th Spaan
1808/08/23	AMSCH	0101	*Lauro. (Ph.)* | In een Landschap ziet men de H. Maagd Maria met het Kindje op haar knïen, zittende en rustende tegens een Boom, agterwaards St. Joseph, benevens knielende en staande Engelen; schoon van couleur en meesterlijk gepenceeld | *Mat:* op doek *Size:* hoog 15, breed 12 duim	C	(Sold) fl 25 Jan Spaan
1810/07/26	AMSCH	0045	*Lauri (Ph.)* | De verschijning van Christus aan Maria Magdalena. Fraai geschilderd | *Annots:* 2 Stuk (EBNP) *Mat:* op koper *Size:* hoog 10, breed 9 duimen	Cassino	(Bought In) fl 2
1810/07/26	AMSCH	0045a[H]	*Lauri (Ph.)* | 1 dito [De verschijning van Christus aan Maria Magdalena] | *Notes:* This lot was added in by hand in the EBNP and FLNY copies of the catalogue.	Cassino	(Sold) fl 4:15 Spruit

Lauri, Filippo (and Claude Lorrain)

1810/10/11	AMSCH	0046	*C. De Lorrain; Ph. Lauri* | Een fraai Boschgezigt, met hoog Geboomte, Kreupelgewassen en Beeldjes gestoffeerd | *Mat:* op doek *Size:* hoog 24, breed 20 duimen	C	(Bought In) fl 40

Lauwers, Jacobus Johannes

1802/06/28	AMSCH	0101	*J. Lauwers* | Twee stuks, voor open steene Nissen, ziet men in de eene een gemeubileerd Vertrek, waar in een ziek Man, in een armstoel zitten, voor zig op de rand der Nis staat een Tafelschel [sic], Soupkommetje en Caraf, hoger hangt een Vogeltje in een Kooy; den andere verbeeld een bevallig Meisje, in een Keukenvertrek, bezig water in een emmer te pompen; gestoffeerd met verder bywerk, beide deeze voorwerpen zyn bevallig en uitvoerig van penceel-behandeling | *Mat:* op paneel *Size:* ieder hoog 15, breed 11 duim	Anna Elink	(Sold) fl 20 Gruiter
1802/06/28	AMSCH	0102	*J. Lauwers* | Een modern Binnevertrek, waar in een bevallige Dame bezig zig te kleeden, verder eenig toepasselyk bywerk; hoog 22, breed 18 duim, op Doek, in alles als de voorige, uitvoerig gepenceeld | *Mat:* op doek *Size:* hoog 22, breed 18 duim	Anna Elink	(Sold) fl 10:10 van der Schleij [for] Mijn
1802/06/28	AMSCH	0103	*J. Lauwers* | Twee stuks plaisante Dorpgezichten, met verscheide Boeren Woningen, stoffagie van Beelden, Boeren Wagens, enz. fiks en uitvoerig geschilderd, door Denzelven [J. Lauwers], op Panneel | *Mat:* op paneel *Size:* hoog 8, breed 10 duim	Anna Elink	(Sold) fl 2 van Iperen

1802/06/28	AMSCH	0104	*J. Lauwers* | Twee stuks bevallige Dorpgezichten, met verscheide stoffagie van Beelden, Beesten, enz. fiks behandeld, door Denzelven [J. Lauwers], op Panneel | *Mat:* op paneel *Size:* hoog 10, breed 7 duim	Anna Elink	(Sold) fl 7:15 De Meyer
1802/12/13	AMSCH	0099	*J. Lauwers* | In een modern Gemeubileerden Kamer, ziet men een bevallige Dame eenige Bloemen Vlechten. terwyl een jong Meisje, haar een Roos aanbiet, verders eenig toepasselyk Bywerk; bevallig en uitvoerig geschilderd | companion to lot 100 *Mat:* op doek *Size:* hoog 13, breed 15 duim	Pruyssenaar [for] A	(Sold) fl 80 for lots 99 & 100. Van Iperen
1802/12/13	AMSCH	0100	*J. Lauwers* | Deezen weerga, steld voor een Keuken, waarin een Meid bézig is Groentens te verleezen, neffens haar een Jongen die op een Stoof zit, niet minder dan de voorgaanden | companion to lot 99 *Size:* hoog 13, breed 15 duim	Pruyssenaar [for] A	(Sold) fl 80 for lots 99 & 100. Van Iperen
1802/12/13	AMSCH	0101	*J. Lauwers* | Dit bevallig voorwerp vertoont een vrolyk Heer in deftige kleeding, zittende in een Gemeubileerd Vertrek, ter zyde een Tafel, waar op een Kom met Punsch, een Pyp en Kandelaar geplaatst is. Hy houd in de regter hand een Wynglas, het vergenoegd gelaat is zeer Natuurlyk verbeeld, en zeer uitvoerig van Penceel behandeling | *Mat:* op paneel *Size:* hoog 12, breed 9 ½ duim	Schley [for] Lauwers	(Bought In) fl 55
1802/12/13	AMSCH	0102	*J. Lauwers* | Dit Stukje verbeeld een bedaagde Vrouw, in oude hollandsche kleeding, als beezig voor een openstaande vengster een wolle Deeken te reinigen, ter zyde op de borstweering legt een slaapend Katje, en ter andere zyde ziet men een Wyngaard rank met bladeren, het aandachtig gelaat is natuurlyk, en zonagtig, en uitvoerig gepenceelt | *Mat:* op paneel *Size:* hoog 13 ½, breed 11 ½ duim	Schley [for] Lauwers	(Bought In) fl 70
1804/12/10	AMSCH	0049	*Jacobus Lauwers* | In een Keukenvertrek staat een bevallig vrouwtje by een aanregtbank voor een vengster, schynende beezig groente te hakken, ziende naar een jongetje die op de grond nederzit, met een hondje speelende; aan den haartsteede hangt een keetel over het vuur, door een open deur ziet men in een ander vertrek, verders zeer natuurlyk gestoffeert, met verscheiden keukengereedschappen; en van een uitvoerige penceel behandeling | *Mat:* op doek *Size:* Hoog 12 ½, breed 14 ½ duim	Jan De Groot	(Sold) fl 51 Moll
1804/12/10	AMSCH	0050	*Jacobus Lauwers* | In een modern vertrek, ziet men een dame, welke in onderhandeling schynt met een printe koopman, het vertrek is zeer ryk gestoffeert, met muziek en schilder gereedschap, door een open vengster ziet men in de tuin; dit schildery is zeer ryk van Ordinantie en niet minder uitvoerig behandeld | *Mat:* op doek *Size:* Hoog 28, breed 24 duim	Jan De Groot	(Sold) fl 39 Gruyter
1808/08/23	AMSCH	0098	*Lauwers. (J.)* | In een gemeubileerd Keukenvertrek zit eene Vrouw Groenten te verleesen bij een Tafel, waar op een kopere Markt-Emmer, en Schootel met Visch geplaatst is; ter zijde bij den Haardsteede een Jongetje met een Appel in de hand, door den openstaande deur ziet men in een ander Vertrek naar een Tuingezicht; het is van een bevallige penceel-behandeling | *Mat:* op doek *Size:* hoog 13, breed 15 duim	[Van Iperen?]	(Sold or Bought In) fl 82 van Iperen
1808/08/23	AMSCH	0099	*Lauwers. (J.)* | In een deftig gemeubileerde Kamer zit eene Dame in Negligée Kleeding, bij een Tafel, met een Kleed bedekt, waar bij een jonge Juffrouw zich met Bloemen vermakende, verder door een openstaande Deur, ziet men in een ander Vertrek; het is als de vorige, zonachtig en bevallig gepenceeld | *Size:* hoog 13, breed 15 duim	[Van Iperen?]	(Sold or Bought In) fl 50 van Iperen
1809/04/22	AMYVR	0074	*J. Lauwers* | Een Meisje dat geschaakt wordt; geestig | *Mat:* op doek *Size:* hoog 15, breed 12 duim	de Bruin	(Sold) fl 10 Rijfsnijder
1810/05/22	AMSCH	0058	*Lauwers (J.)* | Voor een Huismans Woning, staat een bevallig Boerinnetje bij een gemetzelde Put, houdende in de Hand een Aarden Kruik, als gereed om Water te scheppen, op den Grond staat een Pot en ter zijde eenig Aardgewas, op de voorgrond zit een Jongeling met een Hond onder den arm en hooger ligt een slaapend Katje, verders gestoffeerd met een Varkenskot en ander bijwerk; dit stukje is aangenaam van koloriet en licht, en van een uitvoerige penceelbehandeling | *Mat:* op paneel *Size:* hoog 17, breed 14 duim	Johannes van de Putte Nicolaasz.	(Sold) fl 141 van der Schleij
1810/05/22	AMSCH	0059	*Lauwers. (J.)* | Aan een treffelijk Gebouw bij een open Vengster, voor een IJzeren Baluster, vertoont zig eene bevallige Dame, in galante witte Kleeding, houdende een aardig jong Kindje op de Schoot, op den voorgrond staat een Marskramer, met eenige Galanterien, schijnende zijn Koopwaaren aan te bieden, ter zijde staat een Hond; het licht en koloriet doet een goede werking, en is zeer uitvoerig gepenceeld | *Mat:* op paneel *Size:* hoog 22 ½, breed 18 ½ duim	Johannes van de Putte Nicolaasz.	(Sold) fl 111 van der Schleij

Lauwers, Jacobus Johannes (copy by)

1802/12/13	AMSCH	0098	*J. Lauwers; A. van Ostade* | Een zittend vergenoegd Boertje, in een Binnehuis, houdende in de regter Hand een Pyp, en met de linker, rustende op zyn Hoed, die op zyn Knie voor hem legt, het caracter is natuurlyk; de penceelbehandeling bevallig, naar een Schildery, van A. van Ostade, door J. Lauwers | copy by J.J. Lauwers after A. Ostade *Mat:* op paneel *Size:* hoog 6 ½, breed 15 [duim]	Schley [for] Lauwers	(Sold) fl 11:10 Frantze
1804/02/27	AMSCH	0064	*Lauwers. (J.); na G. Metzu* | Deze bevallige Ordonantie steld voor een Vrouwtje, bezig een Schelvis schoon te maken, nevens haar een Kopere Ketel, waarop een jong Katje; dit stukje is byzonder uitvoerig, zeer	B	(Sold) fl 104 I^c Smit

accuraat en meesterlyk gevolgd na het orgineel, berustende in het Kabinet van den Heer Hk. Muylman | copy by J.J. Lauwers after Metsu *Mat:* op doek *Size:* hoog 11, breed 10 duim

Le Brun, Charles

1801/04/13	AMSCH	0011	*C. le Brun* | Een stervende Cleopatra in de armen van haare Maagden; de Ordonantie is grootsch en van een fraai penceel | *Mat:* op doek *Size:* hoog 50, breed 31 duim	Pierre Fouquet, junior	(Sold) fl 22 Mensard
1802/09/18	RMDRS	0118	*le Brun* | Twee Prenten op doek geplakt | *Mat:* op doek	Casper de Haas	(Unknown) fl 0:6
1808/04/26	GDAN	0012	*Brun (Le)* | Een Boomryk Landschap met veel badende Nimphen, allerheerlijkst en uitvoerig geschilderd | *Size:* hoog 18 ½, breed 24 ½ duim	G H Fortuyn	(Unknown)
1808/04/26	GDAN	0013	*Brun (Le)* | De Strijd der Amazonen, waar in een aantal met woede te Paard op een hogen Brug vegtende Menschen, door een Brug ziet men de brand van Troijen, en onder dezelve eenige overvarende Amazonen, terwijl eenige doode en stervende Menschen en Paarden op den grond en in 't Water leggen, alles extra uitvoerig en schoon geschilderd, terwijl de hartstogten klaar kunnen onderscheiden worden | *Size:* hoog 47, breed 64 duim	G H Fortuyn	(Unknown)

Le Clair [Unidentified]

1806/05/05	AMSCH	0037	*le Clair* | Twee stuks bevallige Landschappen, met Rivieren, Ruine van Gebouwen, badende Nimphen enz.; zonachtig op Paneel | *Mat:* op paneel *Size:* hoog 13, breed 16 duim	E	(Sold) fl 8 van Laar

Leclerc, Sebastien (II)

1803/12/12	AMSCH	0019	*S. le Clercq* | Twee stuks Italiaansche Hofgezichten, gestoffeerd met Dames en Heeren, zo te paard als te voet, welke zich gereed maken om ter Jagt te gaan; delicaat op Paneel | *Mat:* op paneel *Size:* hoog 10, breed 14 duim	D	(Sold) fl 6:10 Coclers [or] Gruiter

Le Compe [Unidentified]

1808/09/13	HABRU	0019	*Le Compe* | Een Landschap, met Gebouwen gestoffeerd; uitvoerig		(Unknown) fl 50

Leemans

1806/06/07	RMHSN	0127	*Leemans* | Een Stilleven met Jagttuig	A E K L	(Unknown)

Leemans, Anthony

1801/11/10	AMPOS	0001	*A. Leemans, 1667* | Honden en verder Jachttuig, in een boschachtig Landschap, zeer natuurlyk, door A. Leemans, 1667 | *Inscr:* A. Leemans, 1667 (signed and dated?) *Notes:* It is unclear whether the name and date are inscribed on the painting.		(Unknown)

Leemans, Johannes

1802/05/24	HOBAK	0051	*J. Leemans* | Een stuk met Jagt-tuig, door J. Leemans, hoog 2 voet 8 duim, breed 3 voet 3 duim, op doek | *Mat:* op doek *Size:* hoog 2 voet 8 duim, breed 3 voet 3 duim	Mejuffrouw A van der Mieden	(Sold) fl 1:10 H Carre

Leemans, T. [Unidentified]

1804/10/16	DLOND	0123	*T. Leemans 1675* | Eenig Jachttuig. Des Ustensiles de Chasse | *Mat:* op paneel *Size:* hoog 25, breed 22 *Inscr:* T. Leemans 1675 (signed and dated?) *Notes:* It is unclear whether the name and date are inscribed on the painting.		(Unknown)
1804/10/16	DLOND	0124	*T. Leemans 1675* | Uts^{a} [Eenig Jachttuig. Des Ustensiles de Chasse] | *Mat:* op doek *Size:* hoog 38, breed 51 *Inscr:* T. Leemans 1675 (signed and dated?) *Notes:* It is unclear whether the name and date are inscribed on the painting.		(Unknown)

Leen, Willem van

1802/04/13	HAVIN	0010	*van Leen* | Een Steen met een Mand met Druiven en twee Tortelduiven, op de Steen leggen Granaatappelen, uitvoerig en fraai		(Unknown)
1802/05/05	AMSCH	0113	*van Leen* | Op een steene Balustrade staat een koopere Vaas, gevuld met diversche schoone Bloemen, zeer uitvoerig gepenceeld	J	(Sold) fl 9 Gruiter
1804/02/27	AMSCH	0067	*Leen (van)* | Op een Steenen Tafel ziet men een Kopere fierlyk [sic] bewerkten Vaas, gevuldt met een meenigte zoorten van welrikende [sic] Bloemen, als bonte en witte Roozen, Tiloosen, Papavers, en andere geurige Bloemen; schoon geordoneert en meesterlyk geschilderd | *Mat:* op paneel *Size:* hoog 19 ½, breed 15 ½ duim	C	(Sold) fl 25:10 Josi
1808/08/23	AMSCH	0096	*Leen. (van)* | Een capitaal Bloemstuk, verbeeldende een cierlieke Vaas, gevult met onderscheiden soorten van keurige Bloemen, als roode en witte Roosen, Tulpen, Pioenroosen, Auriculaas en anderen, staande op een marmere Tafel, ter zijde legt een Vogelnesje met eijeren; alles evenaart de natuur, en de bevallige losheid en koloriet geeven verdiensten aan deeze Meester | *Mat:* op doek *Size:* hoog 35, breed 27 duim	[Van Iperen?]	(Bought In) fl 98
1810/06/06	RMMUY	0151	*W. van Leen* | Een hangend mandje, met Bloemen gevuld		(Sold) fl 55 V d Hoop
1810/06/06	RMMUY	0152	*W. van Leen* | Eene luchtige Bloem Schets | *Mat:* papier opgeplakt op paneel		(Sold) fl 32 V d Hoop

1810/06/06	RMMUY	0170	*W. van Leen* | Twee Paneelen van een Rijtuig, met Vrugten en doode Vogels | *Mat:* op paneel		(Unknown) fl 5

Leen, Willem van (and Versteeg)

1801/08/19	AMSCH	0131	*W. van Leen; M. Versteegh* | Een Italiaansch Landschap met een drift Beesten, waar by een Vrouw op een Ezel; helder en bevallig gepenceeld door W. van Leen, en gestoffeerd door M. Versteegh	Pruyssen^r	(Sold) fl 2:10 Pruijssenaar [for] R

Leent, van [Unidentified]

1802/12/13	AMSCH	0104	*van Leent* | Teegens 't Voetstuk van een Colom, legt een doode Duif, en ander gevogelten, benevens een Kruithoorn, uitvoerig gepenceeld | *Mat:* op doek *Size:* hoog 13 ½ breed 17 duim	Pruyssenaar [for] C	(Sold) fl 5:10 L Pakker

Leeuw, van der

1801/03/16	AMSCH	0016	*J. de Leone* | Een aangenaam Landschap, ter linker zyde by een hoog gebergte ziet men een Gebouw, op de voorgrond een Beekje, waarby een Herder die eenig Vee voordryft, nevens een Vrouw te Paard, alles natuurlyk geschilderd	P[ruyssenaar]	(Sold) fl 20:10 Coclers
1802/06/16	AMSCH	0095	*De Leone* | In een Italiaansch Landschap met eenig Geboomten, en een Ruïen, vertoont zich op de voorgrond een Rosbonte Koe, gevolgd door een Vrouw met een Emmer aan de hand; Natuurlyk, bevallig en uitvoerig van penceel behandeling | *Mat:* op doek op paneel *Size:* hoog 9 ½, breed 12 duim	[Merrem]	(Sold) fl 50 Royers
1803/09/07	AMSCH	0100	*J. de Leone* | Twee stuks grazige Weyden, byde gestoffeerd met staande en rustende Ossen en Schaapen; meesterlyk fraai en kragtig gepenceeld [Deux prairies, animées par plusieurs bêtes à cornes et de brebis, tant debout que couchées ; beaux tableaux, peints en maître, d'une touche forte] | *Mat:* op doek *Size:* yder hoog 13, breed 15 duim *Notes:* The dimensions are given in the French edition as "Haut 12, large 13 pouces"; this has been changed by hand to read "Haut 13, large 15 pouces" in the RKDH copy of the catalogue.	Smidt	(Sold) fl 24:10 W Reijers
1808/08/23	AMSCH	0219	*de Leone* | Een Italiaansch Bergachtig Landschap, waar in Huislieden, die verscheide Vée voortdrijven; krachtig op Doek geschilderd | *Mat:* op doek	R	(Sold) fl 10 Coclers
1810/07/23	DOLGI	0034	*De Leeuw, gezegt Lion* | Een Landschap met Runderbeesten en Beeldtjes | *Mat:* op doek *Size:* hoog 13, breed 15 ½ duim	Mr Pieter van den Santheuvel	(Sold) fl 24 [or] 25 P de Heere à Dordt
1810/10/11	AMSCH	0133	*Leeuw, van der; De Leeuw* | Een Boomrijk Landschap, met Beelden en Beesten	[Gruyter?]	(Sold) fl 5 Royere

Leeuw, Govert van der

1808/08/23	AMSCH	0094	*Leeuw (G. de) of de Leone* | Aan de kant van een spiegelend Water, zit eene bevallige Vrouw met een Kind, benevens een Jongeling die met een Hond speeld, bij rustende Schaapen, verder staande Beesten, en een bevallig verschiet; fraai in de manier van A. van de Velde | *Mat:* op doek *Size:* hoog 14, breed 17 duim	J	(Sold) fl 26:10 Th Spaan
1808/08/23	AMSCH	0095	*Leeuw (G. de) of de Leone* | Een aangenaam Landschap, ter zijde op een heuvel zit een bedaagd Landman, zijnde in gesprek met eene Vrouw die nevens hem zit, verder een rood bonte Koe, en grasende en rustende Bokken en Schaapen; warm van koloriet en uitvoerig gepenceeld | *Mat:* op paneel *Size:* hoog 8, breed 10 duim	C	(Sold) fl 20 Gruyter

Leeuw, Pieter van der

1803/08/01	AMSCH	0017	*Leeuw. (P. van der)* | Een aangenaam zonachtig Landschap, gestoffeerd op de voorgrond met drie roodbonte Koeyen, waar van een uit een beekje drinkt, daar nevens een staande Bok, en drie leggende Schaapen, voorts een zittende Herder en Herderin, en een ruim en aangenaam verschiet, dit stukje is bevallig van coloriet en uitvoerig behandeld | *Mat:* op doek *Size:* hoog 19, breed 14 ½ duim	J	(Sold) fl 50 Gruiter
1804/05/07	AMSCH	0095	*Leeuw. (P. de)* | Twee stuks bevallige Boomryke Landschappen, ryk gestoffeerd met staand en leggend Vee, met hunne Herders en Herderinnen, verders Geboomte, Gebergte enz; allerfraayst van penceelbehandeling, in de manier van A. v. d. Velde | *Mat:* op doek *Size:* hoog 14, breed 17 duim	Vinkeles [for] J	(Sold) fl 5 van Iperen
1805/07/10	AMSCH	0089	*P. de Leeuw* | Twee stuks bevallige Boomryke Landschapjes, met een ménigte van staand en rustend Vée, verzeld van hun Herders; als A. v. d. Velde, door P. de Leeuw | *Mat:* op paneel *Size:* hoog 10, breed 12 duim	V[inkeles] [for] J	(Sold) fl 37 L Pakker
1805/12/16	AMSCH	0037a	*P. de Leeuw* | Een aangenaam Boom- en Bergachtig Landschap, op de Voorgrond by een Grasige Weide, met Geboomte, een rustende Herderin, en een ménigte van staand, rustend en grasend Vée, ziet men by een helder spiegelende Rivier, waarin een Koe waad, verders een bevallig Duin en Boomryk verschiet, helder, zonachtig en meesterlyk geschilderd | *Size:* hoog 29, breed 36 duim	O	(Bought In) fl 43
1807/08/26	AMSCH	0119	*P. de Léone* | In een Italiaansch Landschap, ziet men op de voorgrond, een staande Rosbonte Koey, ter zyde onder Geboomten by een Fontyn en Waterbak, om Vee te drinken; zit eene Vrouw met een Kindje op de schoot, aan de borst leggende, en voor dezelve eenige rustende Schapen, verder een heuvelachtig verschiet; het is van een bevallige en uitvoerige Penceelsbehandeling | *Mat:* op paneel *Size:* hoog 10, breed 13 duim	Smits Wed [through] Schley	(Sold) fl 23:10 Gruiter

1809/06/13	AMSCH	0099	*P. de Leone* | Een Landschap, met staande Koeien en Schapen | *Mat:* op doek *Size:* hoog 13, breed 15 duim	E	(Sold) fl 3:5 Gruyter
			Lelie, Adriaan de		
1801/04/23	AMYVR	0040	*A. de Lely* | Het Pourtrait van den Burgemeester H. Hooft, Danielsz uitvoerig geschilderd op Doek | *Mat:* op doek		(Sold) fl 11 Endemann
1802/05/05	AMSCH	0111	*A. de Lely* | Het origineele Pourtrait van Burgemeester H. Hooft Daniëlsz., waarna de prent van Schiavonetty gegraveerd is, fraai | *Mat:* op doek *Size:* hoog 18, breed 14 duim	D	(Withdrawn)
1802/05/05	AMSCH	0112	*A. de Lely* | Het Pourtrait van den Baron van Pallant, in alles als de voorgaande | *Mat:* op doek *Size:* hoog 18, breed 14 duim	D	(Withdrawn)
1808/06/06	RMRIJ	0070	*Lelie. (A. de) 1796* | In eene Binnenkeuken een aan de tafel zittend Werkman zijne Pijp stoppende, die in eene lagchende houding schijnt te spreken met een tegen hem overstaand Meisje, dat een glas bier aan den mond brengt en eene aarden bierkan in de andere hand houdt; bij haar staat een kleine bevallige Jongen, een Komfoor met Vuur aanbrengende. Op den voorgrond ziet men eenige manden met verscheiden Groenten; verder eene Haardstede en Huisraad. Alles zeer uitvoerig, schoon van kleur en behandeling [L'Intérieur d'une Cuisine Hollandaise. Un jardinier assis à une table et occupé à Emplir sa Pipe, semble en souriant jaser avec une jeune servante, qui de bout, tient d'une main un verre à biére, et de l'autre une Cruche ; un gentil Garçon est à côté d'elle. Des Paniers et differents légumes ornent le devant. Ce Tableau dans le genre de Metzu, d'un Coloris agréable, et d'une touche facile et légére, fait honneur au Peintre] | *Mat:* op mahonie paneel *Size:* Hoog 19 ¾, en breed 15 ¾ duim. *Inscr:* A. de Lelie. 1796 (signed and dated?) *Notes:* It is unclear whether the name and date are inscribed on the painting. *Loc:* Amsterdam, Nederland. Rijksmuseum. (A 1075)	Gerrit van der Pot, Heer van Groeneveld	(Sold) fl 395 van Lennep [for] le Roi
			Lelienbergh, Cornelis		
1801/04/08	HAVIN	0036	*Lelienberg* | Doode Vogels		(Unknown)
1802/08/24	LNDLS	0095	*C. Lelyenberg* | Op een Steenen Voetstuk ligt eenig dood Gevogelte, en boven dezelve hangen twee wilde Duiven | *Mat:* op doek *Size:* hoog 23, breed 19 duimen	Leonardus Bouman [or others]	(Unknown) fl 1
1802/08/24	LNDLS	0107	*C. Lelyenberg* | Twee stuks met dood Gevogelte dat op Tafels ligt. Uitvoerig op paneel | *Mat:* op paneel *Size:* ieder hoog 7, breed 10 duimen	Leonardus Bouman [or others]	(Unknown) fl 2:4
1802/11/01	DOBRA	0054	*C. van Lelienbourg* | Eenig dood gevogelte, een Haas, Jagttuig, enz. | *Mat:* op doek *Size:* hoog 2 v. 8 d. breed 2 v. 3 d.	Paulus van der Spyk [or others]	(Sold) fl 2 A v Well
1803/08/24	HGKAN	A0007	*Lelienberg* | Een fraai Jagt Stuk met een doode Haas en ander Wildt, Ryk van Ordonantie, natuurlyk en zeer uitvoerig | *Mat:* op doek *Size:* hoog 34, breet 28 duim		(Sold) fl 5:5 Kan
1805/10/09	HGBSM	0105	*Lelienberg* | Een doden haas, snaphaan en jachthoorn, hangende aan een lint, verders op te tafel gedeeltelyk met een tapytkleed gedekt, leggen verscheide doode vogelen, kruithoorn, wytas, extra konstig geschilderd | *Mat:* op doek *Size:* hoog 35 breet 28 duim	T H van Willigen [or others]	(Sold) fl 7 De Gelder
1808/05/17	LNAN	0020	*Lelienberg* | Dood gevogelte		(Sold) fl 2:3 du Pré
1808/12/31	RMHSN	0018	*Lelienburg* | Een Land- en Water Gezicht, met Zes Koeitjes, door Lelienburg, 1648 | *Mat:* op paneel *Inscr:* Lelienburg, 1648 (signed and dated?) *Notes:* It is unclear whether the name and date are inscribed on the painting.	G Spanjaart [or] H de Haas [or] C van der Looy Lans	(Unknown)
1809/04/22	AMYVR	0073	*C. Lelienburg* | Een hangende doode Haas, een Patrijs, en eenig Jagtgereedschap; uitvoerig | *Mat:* op doek *Size:* hoog 29, breed 23 duim	de Bruin	(Sold) fl 2:10 du Pree
1809/06/13	AMSCH	0097	*P. Lelienberg* | Aan een Haak, hangt een doden Haas, Rijger en Faisant, voor dezelven op een Steene Baluster, ligt een Duif, ander Gevogelten en eenig Jagtgereedschap; meesterlijk geschilderd | *Mat:* op doek *Size:* hoog 42, breed 34 duim *Notes:* The artist's name was given as "P. Lelienberg" but we have assumed this is an error.	E [or] [Gruyter?]	(Sold or Bought In) fl 50 Gruiter
1810/07/23	DOLG2	0009	*C. Lelienberg* | Tegen een witten Muur hangt een zwarte Haan; een weinig ter zijde liggen in een Nis twee Konijnen. Krachtig gepenseeld | *Mat:* op doek *Size:* hoog 36, breed 32 duim *Notes:* The artist's last name was changed by hand from "Selnuburgh" to "Lelienberg" in the EBNP copy of the catalogue. *Loc:* Amsterdam, Nederland. Rijksmuseum. (A 1710)	Pieter Quinting	(Sold) fl 4:5 Visser
1810/08/10	RMRIJ	0027	*Leijenbergh* | Eenige doode Vogels, en verder bijwerk		(Sold) fl 6 [or] 4:10 v Dyk
1810/10/10	MGCIT	0022	*Lelienberg* | Een menigte van onderscheide Vogeltjes, op elkanderen liggende op een steene Tafel, terwijl alle deze voorwerpjes, op dat Schilderijtje geplaatst, ongemeen natuurlijk en teder zijn geschildert door .... Lelienberg	Caspar van Citters	(Unknown)
			Lelienbergh, Cornelis (manner)		
1802/04/13	HAVIN	0045	*Lelienberg* | Een Hangende Haas, als van Lelienberg		(Unknown)
			Lely, Peter		
1806/05/05	AMSCH	0078	*P. Lely* | Het Pourtret van Koningin Anna in Vorstelyke Kleeding; meesterlyk op Doek | *Mat:* op doek *Size:* hoog 30, breed 25 duim	R[oos]	(Bought In) fl 5

Lens, André Corneille

1805/12/16	AMSCH	0036a	*Lens* | In een Landschap met Geboomte, ziet men by een Heuvel een slaapende Vénus, met twee Cupidoos, delicaat gepenceeld | *Mat:* op doek *Size:* hoog 23, breed 29 ½ duim	O	(Bought In) fl 10:10
1809/07/25	HGBSM	0078	*A. Lens* | Een Jufvrouw die een Kind haar les op doet zeggen, natuurlyk Geschilderd, door A. Lens, 1762 | *Mat:* op doek *Size:* hoog 24, breed 20 en een half duim *Inscr:* A. Lens, 1762 (signed and dated?) *Notes:* It is unclear whether the name and date are inscribed on the painting.	D van der Aa [or] E B ten Dall	(Sold) fl 7:5 Heymans [for] G

Leonardo da Vinci

1803/04/27	AMSCH	0085	*Léonardo da Vinci* | La Sainte Vierge avec l'Enfant, peint sur bois par Léonardo da Vinci. Ce Tableau a de l'effêt & est d'un bon ton de couleur | *Mat:* sur bois *Size:* h. 3, l. 2 pieds	A	(Sold) fl 7 Stevens
1805/07/10	AMSCH	0147	*L. da Vinci* | Een Kinderen-Dans van veertien Kinderen; fraai van Teekening en coloriet | *Mat:* op doek *Size:* hoog 23, breed 44 duim	V[inkeles] [for] H[affner]	(Sold) fl 7:10 van Iperen

Leonardo da Vinci (or Leonardo da Vinci, manner)

1803/09/07	AMSCH	0264	*L. Da Vinci* | Een Kinderdans van veertien Kinderen; kragtig en meesterlyk op Doek, door of in de manier van L. da Vinci [Un danse figurée par quatorze enfans ; d'une touche expressive et d'un coloris agréable, dans la manière de Da Vinci] | *Mat:* op doek *Size:* hoog 21, breed 46 duim [Haut 27, large 46 pouces] *Notes:* The dimensions differ in the Dutch and French editions of the catalogue.	Smidt	(Sold) fl 34:10 Haffner
1805/10/09	HGBSM	0034	*L. Davinci* | Maria met het kind Jezus op den arm, zeer uitvoerig, door of in de manier van L. Davinci | *Mat:* op paneel *Size:* hoog 17 ½ breet 13 duim	T H van Willigen [or others]	(Sold) fl 57 Ph Mey

Leonardo da Vinci (copy after)

1810/07/26	AMSCH	0130	*Leonard da Vinci* | De Kopij van de vermaarde Joconda van Leonard da Vinci	Cassino	(Sold) fl 3 Yver

Leyden, J. van [Unidentified]

1810/10/11	AMSCH	0044	*J. Van Leyden* | Een Gezelschap van vrolijke Speelers | *Mat:* op paneel *Size:* hoog 8 ½, breed 12 duimen	C	(Withdrawn)

Liender, Pieter van

1804/12/10	AMSCH	0051	*P. van Liender* | Twee stuks Gezigten; een binnen Utrecht agter den Dom; en den andere ziende van buiten af, naar het Kasteel van Vianen, met verscheide Stofagie [sic]; zonagtig en uitvoerig gepenceelt | *Mat:* op paneel *Size:* Ieder hoog 10, breed 14 duim	Jan De Groot	(Sold) fl 17:10 Numan
1808/06/13	AMSCH	0218	*P. van Liender* | Een Dorpgezicht met eenige Trekschuiten, ter zijde eene Boerin met een Beest; uitvoerig	E M Engelberts	(Sold) fl 3 Simons
1810/06/06	RMMUY	0208	*Liender* | Vijf differente Stads Gezigten | *Mat:* op paneel		(Unknown) fl 15:10
1810/08/06	AMSCH	0062	*Liender (P. van)* | Het Dorp Soeterwouw, gestoffeerd met Beelden, Beesten en Schuiten; natuurlijk behandeld | *Mat:* op paneel *Size:* hoog 12, breed 16 duimen	G	(Sold) fl 6:10 L Pakker
1810/08/06	AMSCH	0063	*Liender (P. van)* | Een aangenaam lommerrijk Dorpgezigt, gestoffeerd met verscheide Vaartuigen en Beeldjes; behandeld als de voorgaande | *Mat:* op paneel *Size:* hoog 8, breed 11 duimen	G	(Sold) fl 4:15 F du Pree
1810/10/11	AMSCH	0045a	*P. Van Liender* | Het Dorp Zoeterwoude, gestoffeerd met Beelden, Beesten en Schuiten; natuurlijk | *Mat:* op paneel *Size:* hoog 12, breed 16 duimen	[Levy Pakker?]	(Sold) fl 4 du Pree

Lievens, Jan (I)

1803/08/17	AMSCH	0052	*Lievens (J.)* | Brunio, Veldoverste der Caninefaten, op een Schild gedragen wordende, zynde een modél van een der Stukken op het Stadhuis te Amsterdam, kragtig gepenceeld | *Mat:* op doek *Size:* hoog 22, breed 21 ½ duim	Anna Catharina Putman	(Sold) fl 0:10 Yver
1803/09/07	AMSCH	0097	*J. Lievens* | In een pragtige Antique Zaal, zit een Vorstin aan een Tafel, op dewelke eenige fraaije Kostbaarheden en Geld, een Oud Man schynt haar aan te spreken, hetzelve is van een kragtige schildering op Paneel [Dans une salle antique est assise une princesse, à une table chargée de bijoux et d'argent ; un vieillard a l'air de l'accoster. Ce tableau est d'une touche vigoureuse] | *Mat:* op paneel *Size:* hoog 20, breed 18 duim	Smidt	(Sold) fl 7 Gruiter
1808/11/28	AMSCH	0040	*J. Lievens* | Een Oud Mans Hoofd, met een Baard en Linne Kraag om de Hals, het Hoofd gedekt met een zwart Calotje, meesterlijk gepenceeld | *Mat:* op paneel *Size:* hoog 27, breed 23 duim	F	(Sold) fl 2:5 Cocler
1810/06/20	AMSCH	0042	*J. Lievens* | Een jong bevallig Meisje, meesterlijk geschilderd | *Mat:* op paneel *Size:* hoog 18, breed 15 duimen	B	(Sold) fl 1 T Spaan

Lievens, Jan (I) (or Anonymous)

1804/07/25	DLGRO	0101	*Jan Lievens; een ander oud Meester* | Een oude Boertje, zittende met een Bierkan in de eene, en een Glas in de ander hand, door Jan Lievens, of een ander oud Meester | *Mat:* op paneel *Size:* hoog 7 ½, breed 6 ½ duim	Mr Franc van der Burch Wz.	(Unknown)

Limborch, Hendrik van

1801/05/11	AMSCH	0043	*Limburgh* | Twee stuks bybelsche Ordonnantien, het eene verbeeld Christus by de Samaritaansche Vrouw, en het andere, waar Christus voor de Hovenier word aangezien, meesterlyk geschilderd | *Mat:* op paneel *Size:* hoog 23, breed 17 duim	Pruisse [for] M	(Sold) fl 25 Van Iperen
1801/05/11	AMSCH	0044	*Limburgh* | Een Bachenaal van vier beelden, in een Landschap, fix en meesterlyk behandeld | *Mat:* op doek *Size:* hoog 26, breed 30 duim	P[ruyssenaar]	(Sold) fl 5:5 Gruiter
1802/09/18	RMDRS	0080	*H. van Limborg* | Een groote Ordonnantie, verbeeldende Diana met haar Nimphen zig badende, en door Action ontrust wordende, door H. van Limborg, op paneel | *Mat:* op paneel *Size:* hoog 2 voet, breet 2 voet 9 ½ duim	Casper de Haas	(Sold) fl 21:10 V Giesen
1808/08/23	AMSCH	0102	*Limburg. (H.)* | Twee stuks bevallige Vrouwe Hoofden, beide in eene zedige houding; zacht en uitvoerig gepenceeld | *Mat:* op paneel *Size:* Ieder hoog 8, breed 6 duim	C	(Bought In) fl 1:5
1808/08/23	AMSCH	0103	*Limburg. (H.)* | Twee dito [stuks bevallige Vrouwe Hoofden], als de voorgaande behandeld | *Mat:* op paneel *Size:* Ieder hoog 5, breed 4 duim *Notes:* It is unclear what "dito" refers to in the title.	C	(Bought In) fl 2:5
1808/11/28	AMSCH	0037	*J. v. Limborch* | De Godin Vénus, zittende op de Wolken, werdende door Cupido gekroond, verder eenige Minnewigten, zacht en uitvoerig gepenceeld | *Mat:* op doek *Size:* hoog 11, breed 8 duim *Notes:* The artist's name was given as "J. v. Limborch" but we have assumed this is an error.	C	(Sold) fl 41 T Spaan
1810/07/26	AMSCH	0101	*J. van Limburg* | Venus en Cupido in een Landschap. Op paneel, rond formaat | *Annots:* Leda (EBNP) *Mat:* op paneel *Fmt:* rond *Notes:* The artist's name was given as "J. van Limburg" but we have assumed this is an error.	Cassino	(Sold) fl 5 Geld
1810/08/06	AMSCH	0065	*Limburg (H)* | Twee stuks bevallige Vrouwen-Hoofden, beide in zedige houding; zacht en uitvoerig gepenceeld | *Mat:* op paneel *Size:* ieder hoog 8, breed 6 duimen	B	(Bought In) fl 1:10
1810/08/06	AMSCH	0066	*Limburg (H)* | Twee dito [bevallige Vrouwen-Hoofden], als de voorgaande behandeld | *Mat:* op paneel *Size:* ieder hoog 5, breed 4 duimen	B	(Bought In) fl 1:5
1810/10/10	MGCIT	0017	*Hendrik van Limburg* | Een schoon Tafereel, vercierd door een menigte van Beelden en andere Voorwerpen, ontleend uit de Mijthologie, met ongemeen fraai en uitvoerig Bijwerk, tot het gekozen onderwerp betreklijk, door Hendrik van Limburg. [Nota: De twee bovengem. Schilderijën dragen in allen opzigte de bewijzen van de groote Talenten, vanvoorn. Meester; weleer den voornaamsten Leerling van den alom beroemden Ridder A. van der Werff: men vind ze beiden aangehaald bij. J. van Gool, *de Nieuwe Schouwburg der Nederlandsche Schilders &c.* id. p.453.] | companion to lot 18 *Notes:* The bracketed information in the title appears in lot 18 and refers to lots 17 and 18.	Caspar van Citters	(Unknown)
1810/10/10	MGCIT	0018	*Hendrik van Limburg* | Een wederga, insgelijks genomen uit voors. Fabelkunde, even voortreflijk op het paneel gebragt, door denzelven [Hendrik van Limburg]. Nota: De twee bovengem. Schilderijën dragen in allen opzigte de bewijzen van de groote Talenten, vanvoorn. Meester; weleer den voornaamsten Leerling van den alom beroemden Ridder A. van der Werff: men vind ze beiden aangehaald bij J. van Gool, *de Nieuwe Schouwburg der Nederlandsche Schllders &c.* id. p.453. | companion to lot 17 *Mat:* op paneel	Caspar van Citters	(Unknown)
1810/10/10	MGCIT	0089	*Limburg* | Een Hangende Patrys, alsmede een liggende Haas, fix en natuurlyk, nevens al het Bywerk behandeld	Caspar van Citters	(Unknown)

Limburg, N.N. [Unidentified]

1810/10/10	MGCIT	0075	*N.N. Limburg* | Een hangende Haas in een groot Nis, in het welk een steenen Tafel, waarop een Buste; voorts twee Zeehoorns, liggende op een blaauw kleed, alsmede Wijtas, Patrijs en Kruidhoorn; alles zeer natuurlijk geschilderd	Caspar van Citters	(Unknown)

Lin, Herman

1804/10/16	DLOND	0125	*H. van Lin* | Paerden, Ruiters en Gekwetsten. Des Chevaux, Cavalliers & Blessés | *Mat:* op paneel *Size:* hoog 14, breed 17		(Unknown) fl 37:5
1809/07/25	HGBSM	0140	*H. van Lin* | Een hevige Bataille van Cavallerie | *Mat:* op doek *Size:* hoog 14, breed 17 duim	D van der Aa [or] E B ten Dall	(Sold) fl 7:5 van Eyk

Lingelbach, Johannes

1801/04/13	AMSCH	0040	*J. Lingelbach* | Een gezicht op een der Markten te Rome, met Gebouwen, Fonteinen, Gedenkzuilen, en een menigte stoffage van Beelden, Kramers, Kwakzalvers en Bedelaars, fraay geordoneerd, zonachtig en breed gepenceeld | *Mat:* op doek *Size:* hoog 30, breed 26 duim	Pierre Fouquet, junior	(Sold) fl 100 Lafontaine
1801/04/23	AMYVR	0002	*J. Lingelbach* | Een Landgezicht, gestoffeerd met Hooywagen, een Valkenier, en eenige rustende Landlieden, op de voorgrond; zeer uitvoerig en fraay gepenceeld op Doek | *Mat:* op doek *Size:* hoog 22, breed 17 duim		(Sold) fl 350 Yver [for] Van Winter

1801/06/10	AMSCH	0096	*Lingelbach. (J.)* | Deeze fraaije Ordonantie, vol gewoel, stelt voor een Kwakzalver, in een Landschap; men ziet op den voorgrond onder een Boom, een Tent opgeslagen, waarby eenige musiceerende en danzende Beelden, dit stuk is fraai van ordonantie en uitvoerig van penceel | *Mat:* op doek *Size:* hoog 34, breed 32 duim	Herman ten Kate	(Sold) fl 325 Pruijssenaar
1801/06/10	AMSCH	0097	*Lingelbach. (J.)* | Op een Heuvel ziet men een Hooiwagen met een wit en bruin Paard bespannen, welke beladen word, ter zyde zitten eenige Landlieden te rusten, verders een uitgestrekt verschiet, alles is dun en van geen mindere schildering | *Mat:* op doek op paneel *Size:* hoog 13 ½, breed 11 ½ duim	Herman ten Kate	(Sold) fl 95 Pruijssenaar
1801/06/10	AMSCH	0098	*Lingelbach. (J.)* | In een Italiaansche plaats, ziet men voor een boere Herberg, een menigte drinkende, dansende, stoeijende en vrolyke Lieden, zynde van een kloeke eu breede penceels behandeling | *Mat:* op doek *Size:* hoog 21, breed 25 duim	Herman ten Kate	(Sold) fl 100 Pruijssenaar
1801/06/10	AMSCH	0099	*Lingelbach. (J.)* | Op den voorgrond vertonen zich enige Dames en Heeren te paard, als ter Jagt gaande met eenige Honden, mede als de vorige behandeld | *Mat:* op paneel *Size:* hoog 9, breed 12 duim	Herman ten Kate	(Sold) fl 60 Pruijssenaar
1801/06/10	AMSCH	0100	*Lingelbach. (J.)* | Een Landschap, ter linker zyde van een Sluis ziet men een beladen Kar afkomen, waarnevens een Man, die het Paard stuurt, verders een Reiziger en een Hond, krachtig van coloriet en een fraai penceel | *Mat:* op doek *Size:* hoog 14, breed 16 duim	Herman ten Kate	(Sold) fl 48 Taijs
1801/06/10	AMSCH	0101	*Lingelbach. (J.)* | In een Landschap, voor een Tent ziet Men eenige Paarden; waar by Officieren en andere Krygsknegten, meede als de voorgaande uitgevoerd | *Mat:* op paneel *Size:* hoog 9, breed 12 duim	Herman ten Kate	(Sold) fl 13 van Dijl
1801/06/13	LNDLS	0040	*J. Lingelbagh* | Een Italiaansche Zeehaven, met vaartuigen, op de voorgrond verscheiden kooplieden en werkende beelden, verder gebouwen en gebergten, op doek | *Mat:* op doek *Size:* hoog 17, breed 21 duimen	D van R	(Sold) fl 35 Spruyt
1801/06/13	LNDLS	0043	*J. Lingelbagh* | Een Duinachtig Landschap, daar een man, zittende op een wit paard, langs den weg gaat, nevens hem, een vrouw met een kind aan de hand, en een rustend man bij een heuvel, zeer uitvoerig, zoo goed als van Ph. Wouwerman, op paneel | *Mat:* op paneel *Size:* hoog 7 ¼, breed 10 ¼ duimen	D van R	(Sold) fl 50 Coclers
1801/08/19	AMSCH	0055	*J. Lingelbach* | Een Heuvelachtig Landschap, op de voorgrond ziet men een Heer op een wit Paard, waar by Jagers en Honden, verders ryk met Beelden en Beesjes gestoffeerd, en in de manier van Wouwerman, gepenceeld door J. Lingelbach	Pruyssen[r] [for] Q	(Sold) fl 80 Reeringh
1801/08/19	AMSCH	0056	*J. Lingelbach* | Twee stuks, zynde het eenen een Levantsche Zeehaaven en het andere een Zeeslag met de Turken, beide vol gewoel van Beelden; meesterlyk op Doek | *Mat:* op doek *Size:* hoog 41, breed 55 duim	Van Forreest	(Sold) fl 150 Vinkeles
1801/10/19	AMSCH	0037	*Lingelbach (J.)* | Dit Schildery vertoond een Italiaansch Huisgezin, houdende het middagmaal voor deszelfs wooning, een man op een Paard, neemt van een oud man een glas wyn aan, ter linkerzyde in 't verschiet ziet men een Herder rusten; dit stuk is zonächtig en zeer transparant geschilderd | *Mat:* op paneel *Size:* hoog 15 ½, breed 19 duim	Jonkheer Menno Baron van Coehoorn	(Sold) fl 180 W Reijers
1801/10/19	AMSCH	0038	*Lingelbach (J.)* | Een Italiaans Landschap met een steene Waterbak, waarby een rustend Man, verder een Man te Paard en een Vrouw op een Ezel, fraay geschildert | *Mat:* op paneel *Size:* hoog 14 ¾, breed 18 duim *Loc:* Rotterdam, Nederland. Museum Boymans-Van Beuningen. (1459)	Jonkheer Menno Baron van Coehoorn	(Sold) fl 215 C S Roos
1802/04/13	HAVIN	0001	*Lingelbach* | Een Italiaans plyn, met eenige Macarade, en een Wagen met Muzykanten; waarvoor een Man op stelten, die met een Hengel met aas de Kindren [sic] laat byten, Grappig, en uitmuntend helder en verstandig		(Unknown)
1802/04/13	HAVIN	0002	*J. Lingelbach* | Een Zee Battaille tegen de Turken, voor in leggen eenige Sloepen, waar in woedend gevogten word, zoo als ook door de in 't water leggende persoonen, konstig geordineert en geschildert		(Unknown)
1802/05/05	AMSCH	0103	*J. Lingelbach* | Een capitaal Italiaansch Marktgezicht, met prachtige Gebouwen, ryk gestoffeerd met Kooplieden en Kramers, zonachtig en breed gepenceeld | *Size:* hoog 28, breed 36 duim	C	(Bought In) fl 68
1802/05/05	AMSCH	0104	*J. Lingelbach* | Een Zee Bataille, tusschen de Turken en Hollanders, de woede van 't krygsvolk, en een fraai ligt en bruin, zyn in dit stuk wel geobserveerd, en meesterachtig geschilderd | *Size:* hoog 43, breed 62 duim	J	(Sold) fl 35 v d Vinne
1802/05/10	MGSAN	0014	*J. Lingelbach* | Een dito [fraai] dito [Landschap], daarop een geladen Wagen, met Paarden; voorts eenige Reizigers, rydende, daarby eenige Jachthonden, krachtig geschilderd, door J. Lingelbach: op Doek, in vergulde Lyst | *Mat:* op doek *Size:* hoog 21 duim, breed 26 duim	Johan Dirk Kruysse	(Sold) £ 28 H Meertens
1802/05/24	HGBAK	0048	*J. Lingelbach* | Een Landschap verbeeldende een Graanoogst, op de voorgrond eenige Landlieden, met vrugten, groentens en bloemen beladen, fraai van ordonnantie door J. Lingelbach, van zyn beste tyd, 1669, hoog 26 duim, breed 20 ½ duim, op doek, in zw. lyst met vergulde bies | *Mat:* op doek *Size:* hoog 26 duim, breed 20 ½ duim *Inscr:* 1669 (dated?) *Notes:* It is unclear whether the date is inscribed on the painting.	Mejuffrouw A van der Mieden	(Sold) fl 53 Kleijn
1802/07/21	HGKAN	0081	*Lingebeek* | Een Zeeslag met Europeesche Scheepen, tegen Barbaarsche Galeyen		(Unknown)

1802/07/21	HGKAN	0106	*Lingelback* | Eenige rustende figuuren, in een Landschap		(Unknown)
1802/07/27	AKHRK	0026	*Lingelbag* | Een Levantsche Zeehaven, een Jufvrouw en Heer staan bij twee Kolommen en een Standbeeld, nevens een Galeij; verders Kooplieden, en Slaaven, bezig met gepakte Goederen aan den oever der Haven, goed gepenseeld | *Mat:* op paneel *Size:* hoog 11 ¾, breed 14 duim	Maria Stategaart	(Sold) fl 6 Gruyter
1802/09/06	AMSCH	0063	*J. Lingelbach* | In 't midden van dit Schildery, ziet men een Galley, en van deszelfs boord, vaardt een Sloep, gestoffeerd met onderscheiden Beelden, op de voorgrond eenige Vreemdelingen by hunne Koopgoederen; meesterlyk en fix | *Mat:* op doek *Size:* hoog 25, breed 24 duim	J	(Sold) fl 8:15 van Iperen
1802/09/29	AMSCH	0032	*J. Lingelbach* | By eenige Italiaansehe [sic] Gebouwen ziet men een werkenden Hoefsmit, terwyl eenen knaap het vuur aanblaast; een Boerejongen vraagt na den weg, verders ziet men een goede gelukzegster een Ryziger iets voorzeggen; de penceelbehandeling is meesterlyk fraai; en de Ordenantie is aangenaam [Le sujet d'un marechal ferrand, devant des habitations Italiennes. Il paroit entierement occupé, de son Travail pendant qu'un apprentis entretient le feu ; un jeune campagnard, tenant un pagnier au bras demande des indications pour sa route ; derriere ce groupe setient [sic] debout une Bohemienne qui dit la bonne avanture [sic] à un voyageur. Lefond [sic] représente des Batimens & un pont prés de quelques figures dans une Barque. Ce Tableau est recommandable pour le charme du Pinceau de la Composition.] | *Mat:* op doek *Size:* hoog 18 ¾, breed 15 ½ duim	[Labouchere?]	(Sold) fl 51 v d Vinne
1802/12/13	AMSCH	0095	*J. Lingelbagh* | By een Levantsche Zeehaven, ziet men een Heer en Dame de Trap afkoomen van een treffelyk Gebouw by een verheeven Standbeeld en Galleijen, op de voorgrond diverse Kooplieden en Slaven, by hunne Koopmanschappen, ter zyden een Fontyn en een aangenaam verschiet; bevallig van Licht en meesterachtig geschilderd | *Mat:* op paneel *Size:* hoog 12, breed 14 ½ duim	Pruyssenaar [for] A	(Sold) fl 19:10 Yver
1803/07/18	AMSCH	0025	*Lingelbagh. (Jan)* | Dit capitaale Schildery verbeeld een Markt te Romen, ter regterzyde by een Gebouw staat een Obelisk, waarby een Quakzalver en een menigte toezienders, op de voorgrond is een Vrouw beezig een Vogel te kopen van een Vogelkoper, in het midden wandeld een Heer en een Dame, ter linkerzyde een Schoenlapper, een menigte andere Beelden, en andere stoffagie van Ezels, Honden, enz. Dit stuk is met regt in allen deelen, zoo van coloriet als groeping der Beelden, een der schoonste van deezen voortreffelyken Meester [Ce tableau capital est une representation d'une place publicque de Rome au bas du mont Capitolin, elle est ornée d'un Obelisque. Autour de cette vaste enceinte l'on voit les batimens tels qu'ils étoient au tems de l'auteur. Audevant du tableau est un marchand doviétan [sic] avec un second farceur, tous deux singulierement costumés, ils sont entourrés par des spectateurs en differentes attitudes ; une poulaliere [sic] est près de ce groupe, vendent [sic] des volailles. A droite du tableau est une maison de boutiquier devant la quelle sont trois hommes, dont un est à boire devant un tonneau. Un homme & une Dame à la promenade se distinguent vèrs le milieu, & à gauche est une femme remplissant ses vases de l'eau d'une fontaine. Audevant de cette partie est assis un savetier occupé à son travail dont deux geux [sic] attendent leurs chaussures. Ce détail ne regarde que les figures du premier plan, ce morceau étant enrichi à toutes les distences de personnages & d'animaux. Cette production marquante unit à une harmonie de couleur l'effet vaporeux & vrai, qualitées requises dans les meilleurs tableaux de ce peintre ingenieux. Il s'est appliqué à soigner celui-ci dans toutes ses parties, les figures en étant d'un dessin aisé & naturel, & la perspective variée ne laisse rien à désirer.] | *Mat:* op doek *Size:* hoog 30, breed 34 duim *Loc:* Bruxelles, Belgique. Musées Royaux des Beaux-Arts. (130)	Maria Theresia Andrioli	(Sold) fl 575 Isaak Smit
1803/07/18	AMSCH	0026	*Lingelbagh. (Jan)* | Op een Plein met Italiaansche Gebouwen ziet men op de voorgrond een Heer bezig zynde zyn Laarzen aan te trekken, ter zyde een ander staande, waarby een derde te Paard zittende, benevens een Piquer, ter linkerzyde een fraai wit Paard, waaragter een bruin door twee Stalknegts geleid wordende, niet minder behandeld als de voorgaande [Sur un marché d'Italie sont representés deux Cavaliers descendus de leurs chevaux, dont l'un rajuste sa chaussure ; le second en manteau rouge tourne le dos. Vèrs la gauche sont leurs chevaux tenus par deux valets, & en arriere est un autre Cavalier monté, auquel un piqueur fait faire le manège. Des figures vèrs le fond terminent la perspective. Ce tableau plein de charme tient de la maniere de Dujardin par l'éclât & la fraicheur de la couleur, un pinceau gras & un effet lumineux, harmonieux, designent amplement la meilleure manière de l'Artiste.] | *Mat:* op doek *Size:* hoog 20, breed 18 duim	Maria Theresia Andrioli	(Sold) fl 138 Hodges
1803/07/18	AMSCH	0027	*Lingelbagh. (Jan)* | Men ziet by het Vaticaan te Romen den H. Vader in een Draagstoel, verzeld van eenige Cardinaalen te Paard en eenige andere Geestelyken, voorts een groote menigte Beelden, in het verschiet den Tyber met eenige Vaartuigen gestoffeerd, alles meesterlyk behandeld [Au bas du Vatican l'on voit une sortie du St. Père, porté dans une chaise de velours rouge, avec un Cortége de Cardinaux. Il est précedé d'une haquenée blanche, & suivi par une voiture & une garde de Cuirassiers : un peuple nombreux environne le Cortége. Aux deux Côtés du tableau sont des groupes de figures majeures, qui attendent le passage Cérémonial : une femme montée sur un mulet, & des nobles Romains sont à droite. A la gauche l'on voit un Asiatique, un Pelerin assis, & plusieurs autres	Maria Theresia Andrioli	(Bought In) fl 75

			personnages. Le Tibre est garni de quelques galères & navires, il và s'aboutir à un pont & au Chateau St. Ange. Ce riche morceau, d'un ton de couleur claire & harmonieuse est éclairé par un beau ciel bien nuagé, produisant un bel effet de lumiere. On ne balancera pas de l'admettre pour un des morceaux capitaux produits par le genie fertile de son Auteur.] | *Mat:* op doek *Size:* hoog 48, breed 44 duim *Loc:* Amsterdam, Nederland. Rijksmuseum. (A 3973) (?)		
1803/08/24	HGKAN	0068	*Lingelbach* | Een Lantschap met een Fontein, waar by Rustende Landlieden en Vee, fraay van Coloriet, en Meesterlyk behandelt | *Mat:* op doek *Size:* hoog 25, breet 22 duim *Loc:* Mainz, Deutschland. Landesmuseum. (97)	[Teissier] [or others]	(Sold) fl 43 Kan
1803/08/24	HGKAN	0069	*Lingelbach* | Een Landschap, verbeeldende de Hooibouw, ryk gestoffeerd en fraay behandeld | *Size:* hoog 16, breet 23 duim	[Teissier] [or others]	(Sold) fl 20 Huybregt
1803/12/12	AMSCH	0050	*J. Lingelbach* | Dit Capitaale Schildery vertoont een Gezicht op den Dam te Amsterdam, ten tyde dat het Stadhuis nog onvolbouwd was, zynde met meer dan twee honderd Beeldjes gestoffeerd, van allerleije rang en staat, als mede Paarden en Sleeden met Koopmansgoederen; alles bevallig geördoneerd en geschilderd | *Mat:* op doek *Size:* hoog 48, br. 79 duim *Loc:* Amsterdam, Nederland. Historisch Museum. (A 3044)	C	(Sold) fl 1725 v d Schleij [for] S
1804/02/27	AMSCH	0065	*Lingelbach. (J.)* | Een Landschap, by een Fontein ziet men eenige Lieden, welke hun Vée te drinken geven, op den voorgrond een Vrouw te Paard, en eenige Bokjes en Schaapjes; meesterlyk gepenceeld | *Mat:* op doek *Size:* hoog 25, breed 19 duim *Loc:* Mainz, Deutschland. Landesmuseum. (97)	B	(Sold) fl 29 Theys
1804/02/27	AMSCH	0066	*Lingelbach. (J.)* | Een ryke Ordonantie, voorstellende een Carnavals vermakelykheid, op St. Marcus Plaats te Venetiën, zonachtig van behandeling | *Mat:* op doek *Size:* hoog 41, breed 54 duim	B	(Sold) fl 20 Thais
1804/08/08	AMSCH	0104	*J. Linglebach* | In een Heuvelachtig Landschap ziet men eenige Heeren en Dames te Paard, met hunne Jagers en Honden; verders een Jachtparty in het verschiet; helder op Paneel | *Mat:* op paneel *Size:* hoog 8, breed 10 duim	Roos a	(Bought In) fl 23 ½
1804/10/16	DLOND	0126	*J. Lingelbach* | Een Italiaansche Zeehaven met een Fontein en veel Gewoel. Port de Mer en Italie. On y voit une Fontaine & beaucoup de Figures | *Mat:* op doek *Size:* hoog 17, breed 15		(Unknown)
1805/07/03	AMSCH	0028	*Lingelbach. (J.)* | Voor en op de stoep van een huis binnen Romen, ziet men een Ryffelaar met verscheide omstanders, op de voorgrond zit een Schoenlapper, waar by een Jonge, op de stoep staat een galant Heer zyn lief welke uit het vengster kykt toe te lachen, verders, muziek makende, ter marktgaande en een ménigte andere Beelden; zynde dit stuk van de delicaatste van dezen voortreffelyken meester | *Mat:* op doek *Size:* hoog 25, breed 28 duim	R[oos]	(Sold) fl 720 Lafontaine
1805/07/03	AMSCH	0101	*J. Lingelbach* | Deze Capitaale Ordinantie vol gewoel, verbeeld een hévig gevecht op Zee, tusschen Christenen, en Turken, die met hun Schuiten en Manschap een Galey aanvallen, en moedig worden afgeslaagen; de Caracters der woeden zyn kennelyk verbeeld; en is meesterlyk fraay van Penceel behandeling | *Mat:* op doek *Size:* hoog 44, breed 63 duim	R[oos]	(Sold) fl 80 L Pakker
1805/07/10	AMSCH	0087	*J. Lingelbach* | Een Landgezicht aan een Rivier, alwaar eenige Lieden bezig zyn eenige Goederen intescheepen; breed en meesterlyk gepenceelt | *Size:* hoog 15, breed 17 duim	V[inkeles] [for] J	(Sold) fl 9:10 van Iperen
1805/07/10	AMSCH	0088	*J. Lingelbach* | Aan een Zeehaven ziet men een groote ménigte Krygslieden, schynende Eer-schoote te doen, aan een Vloot van verscheide Scheepen, welke in volle Zeylen binnenkoomen; zonachtig en delicaat gepenceeld | *Mat:* op doek *Size:* hoog 21, breed 28 duim	V[inkeles] [for] L	(Withdrawn)
1806/08/13	AMSCH	0094	*Lingelbach. (J.)* | Deeze Ordinantie vertoont een Italiaansche Markt, met verscheide Gebouwen en Fontyn, ryk gestoffeert met een ménigte Lieden, zoo wandelende Dames als Heeren en anander Mannen, Vrouwen en Kinderen, met hun Koopmanschappen, verder Rytuigen en andere Persoonen, bevallig van Coloriet en uitvoerig gepenceeld | *Mat:* op doek *Size:* hoog 22, breed 29 duim *Loc:* Minneapolis, MN, USA. Institute of Arts. (60.34)	van der Voort	(Sold) fl 110 Roos
1806/08/13	AMSCH	0095	*Lingelbach. (J.)* | Dit Voorwerp vertoont een Levantsche Zeehaven, op de voorgrond by een pragtig Gebouw, een Standbeeld op een Piedestal, waarby een wandelende Dame en Heer; op de voorgrond verscheide Kooplieden, Arbyders, Baalen en Pakgoederen; verder een Sloep met Zeevolk, Galyen en anderen Vaartuigen by een gedeelten van een Vestmuur; in alles als de vorige behandeld | *Mat:* op doek *Size:* hoog 24, breed 30 duim	van der Voort	(Sold) fl 100 Josi
1806/08/13	AMSCH	0096	*Lingelbach. (J.)* | Een Boom- en Heuvelachtig Landschap, gestoffeerd met een Heer en Dame te Paard, verzeld van eenige jagers met hun Honden. delicaat en bevallig van coloriet | *Mat:* op paneel *Size:* hoog 10, breed 13 duim	van der Voort	(Sold) fl 113 Haffner
1806/08/13	AMSCH	0097	*Lingelbach. (J.)* | Op een uitgestrekte vlakte vertoont zich een gecampeerd Leger, op de voorgrond in een Tent eenige vrolyke Militairen, terzyde eenige Officiers te paard, verders een Bergachtig verschiet; delicaat en uitmuntend geschilderd | *Mat:* op paneel *Size:* hoog 9 ½, breed 10 ½ duim	Vinkeles [for] G[ruyter]	(Sold) fl 34 Schumacher

1806/08/13	AMSCH	0098	*Lingelbach. (J.)* | Een Levantsche Zeehaven, met een ménigte Lieden te paard en te voet, enz.; fiks van schildering | *Mat:* op paneel *Size:* hoog 12, breed 19 duim	Vinkeles [for] F	(Sold) fl 8:5 Richters
1807/06/10	HGBSM	0087	*J. Lingelbach* | Voor een Italiaansch Buitenhuis, ziet men een menigte Boeren en Boerinnen zig vermaakende met danssen en differente vrolijkheden, helder en konstig geschilderd, en wel geconserveerd &c | *Mat:* op doek *Size:* hoog 25 ½, breed 28 ½ duim *Loc:* New York, NY, USA. Metropolitan Museum of Art. (1871.123)	Abraham Delfos [or others]	(Sold) fl 345 LaCourt
1807/08/26	AMSCH	0113	*J. Lingelbagh* | Een Levantsche Zeehaven, gestoffeerd met een menigte pragtig gekleede Beelden en Werklieden, Gebouwen en onderscheide Vaartuigen; zonachtig en bevallig gepenceeld | *Mat:* op doek *Size:* hoog 17, breed 21 duim	Roos	(Bought In or Withdrawn)
1807/08/26	AMSCH	0114	*J. lingelbagh* | Een gezelschap van Heeren en Dames te Paard met verscheide Jagers en Honden; behandeld als het voorgaande [zonachtig en bevallig gepenceeld] | *Mat:* op paneel *Size:* hoog 8, breed 10 duim	Roos	(Sold) fl 13:10 Gruiter
1808/04/26	GDAN	0089	*Lingelbach (J.)* | Dit uitmuntende Schiiderij [sic] is een hoog Geboomt Landschap, waar in het verschiet een groot Kasteel, voorts eenige Jagers te Paard met hunne Honden, fraai gedaan | *Size:* hoog 36, breed 42 duim	G H Fortuyn	(Unknown)
1808/05/18	LNAN	0040	*Lingebag* | 2 Stuks Italiaansche Groen-Markten met veel Volk | *This Lot:* Een Stuk Italiaansche Groen-Markt met veel Volk *Notes:* Lots 40 and 41 were printed in the catalogue as one item. The artist's name "Lingebag" was added in by hand in the RKDH copy of the catalogue.	Mr Cornelis Versluys	(Unknown)
1808/05/18	LNAN	0041	*Lingebag* | 2 Stuks Italiaansche Groen-Markten met veel Volk | *This Lot:* Een Stuk Italiaansche Groen-Markt met veel Volk *Notes:* Lots 40 and 41 were printed in the catalogue as one item. The artist's name "Lingebag" was added in by hand in the RKDH copy of the catalogue.	Mr Cornelis Versluys	(Unknown)
1808/06/06	RMRIJ	0071	*Lingelbach. (Johannes)* | Dit kloek stuk vertoont eene Italiaansche Zeehaven vol gewoel van Beelden van onderscheidene volken. Schepen, Galeijen, trotsche Gebouwen, Ruinen, een Standbeeld van Neptunus en een aangenaam verschiet maken te zamen een konstig geheel. Alles zeer uitvoerig, helder en dun geschilderd en een der beste stukken van dezen beroemden Meester [Cette riche Composition offre un Port de mer d'Italie. On y découvre une multitude de figures differemment costumées et occupées, et plusieurs galéres, et autres Bâtiments et Barques etc, à droite des Morceaux d'Architecture imposants, des Statues, des Colonnes etc. se presentent aux Regards. L'Ensemble sans confusion, la belle manière de faire, le ton vrai et l'Effet général de ce précieux Tableau, le font regarder comme un des meilleurs de ce cèlèbre Artiste] | *Annots:* van P Fouquet Jr te Amst 9 April 1783 (f 1200.-) (RMA I) *Mat:* op doek *Size:* Hoog 41 ½ en breed 47 ¼ duim	Gerrit van der Pot, Heer van Groeneveld	(Sold) fl 2050 Allard Paris
1808/06/06	RMRIJ	0072	*Lingelbach. (Johannes)* | Eene welgekozene Italiaansche Zeehaven, rijk gestoffeerd met Gebouwen, Galeijen, Beelden en verder bijwerk. Zilverachtig en fijn van toon, breed en meesterlijk in zijnen gewonen trant behandeld [Ce Tableau nous offre un autre Port de mer d'Italie, avec plusieurs Bâtiments, un Mouilage [sic], des Galéres, des Barques etc., et un superbe lointain. Des figures de differentes Nations, et plusieurs accessoires se presentent sur le devant. Ce Morceau d'un argentin et harmonieux est du plus beau fini et d'un mèrite supérieur] | *Mat:* op doek *Size:* Hoog 29 ¼, en breed 24 ½ duim *Loc:* Amsterdam, Nederland. Rijksmuseum. (A223)	Gerrit van der Pot, Heer van Groeneveld	(Sold) fl 785 Stratenus [for] le Roi
1808/06/06	RMRIJ	0073	*Lingelbach. (Johannes)* | In deze Schilderij, bekend onder den naam van het Hooiwagentje, ziet men een door verscheiden personen beladen wordenden Hooiwagen; twee ontspannen Paarden, waarvan een aan 't hooi knabbelt en 't andere daarneven staat, worden vergezeld van een derde Paard, waarop een Man en eene Vrouw gezeten zijn, welken, door een daarbij staand persoon, eene kruik wordt aangeboden: op den tweeden grond twee Visschers aan eene Rivier, en bij eene brug eene derde figuur met een hond. De zilverachtige toon, en de geestige toets en behandeling, doen eer aan dezen Meester [Ce Tableau connu sous le nom *Chariot à foin*, represente plusieurs personnes occupées à charger un Chariot de foin, à côté du quel on voit aussi deux Chevaux dételés. Un homme et une femme à qui une autre personne presente un pot de bière, sont montés sur un troisième Cheval. Sur le second plan, et prés d'un Rivière, on apperçoit deux Pêcheurs à la ligne et un autre homme qui passe sur un Pont. Un Paysage termine la vue. Une Composition variée, un beau Ciel, un ton argentin et un grand fini, forment un Tableau précieux dans le gout de Philippe Wouwerman] | *Annots:* vd Pot kocht op veiling P. Calkoen, Wz Amst 10 Sept 1781 J. Lingelback veldgezicht fl 201 (RKDH I) *Mat:* op paneel *Size:* Hoog 15, en breed 20 duim *Loc:* Den Haag, Nederland. Mauritshuis. (87)	Gerrit van der Pot, Heer van Groeneveld	(Sold) fl 780 Stratenus [for] le Roi
1808/06/13	AMSCH	0094	*Lingelbach (J.)* | Dit aangenaam Landschapje is gestoffeerd met eenige Jagers te paard en te voet, alle hunne oogen vestigende op een Valk, die in de lucht vliegt; verder eenige Honden. Keuriglijk gepenceeld | *Mat:* op doek *Size:* hoog 19, breed 21 duim	R[oos]	(Sold) fl 290 Th[S] Spaan
1808/08/23	AMSCH	0092	*Lingelbach. (J.)* | In een ruim Landgezigt, vertoont zig een rustend Huisman, zittende op een grasige Heuvel, ter zijde staat eene Vrouw,	C	(Sold) fl 195 Gruyter

			houdende een Hooi hark op de schouder, waar bij een Man op een Knie liggende, als iets verzoekende, ter zijde word een Wagen met Hooi belaaden, daar nevens een grazend Paard, verders eenige Arbeiders; het is bevallig van licht, en uitvoerig gepenceeld | *Mat:* op doek *Size:* hoog 14, breed 12 duim		
1808/10/28	AMVRS	0029	*Lingelbach (J.)* | Een Italiaansch Landschap, met een Steenen Waterbak, waarbij een rustend Man; verder een Man te Paard en eene Vrouw op een Ezel. Dit uitmuntend stukje is zeer teder en uitnemend bevallig geschilderd | *Mat:* op paneel *Size:* hoog 14 ¾, breed 18 duim *Loc:* Rotterdam, Nederland. Museum Boymans-Van Beuningen. (1459)	Marten Udink	(Sold) fl 700 Joukes en Oijens
1809/04/17	AMSCH	0053	*J. Lingelbach* | In een Italiaansch Bergachtig Landschap, ziet men voor een oud Cebouw [sic], eenige Landlieden zig met Speelen, Zingen en Dansen vermakenden, ter zijde bij een Fontijn eenige Reizigers, met beladen Wagens, en andere die hunnen Paarden laaten Drinken; zonachtig en delicaat gepenceeld | *Mat:* op doek *Size:* hoog 26, breed 30 duim	[Gruyter?]	(Sold) fl 16
1809/04/17	AMSCH	0122	*J. Lingelbach* | Een Boomrijk Landschap, ter zijde met een Rivier; fiks geschilderd en gestoffeerd | *Mat:* op doek	T	(Sold) fl 3:15
1809/06/13	AMSCH	0093	*J. Lingelbach* | Twee stuks Heuvelachtige Landschappen, gestoffeerd met Huislieden, die 't Koorn Maijen, en anderen hetzelve op Wagens Laden, waarbij Vrouwen en Kinderen; meesterlijk gepenceeld | *Mat:* op doek op paneel *Size:* hoog 12, breed 15 duim	M	(Sold) fl 52 T Spaan
1809/07/19	AMSCH	0030	*Lingelbach (J.)* | Dit uitmuntend Tafreel, zijnde eene rijke Ordonnantie van eene meenigte Beelden, vertoont in een Italiaansch Landschap, een Kermisvreugd; voor een hoog Gebouw of Herberg, onder een gespannen Zijl, ziet men verscheide Lieden, zoo Mannen als Vrouwen, zich met drinken, liefkozen en danzen vermaken, een Speelman staat op een Tafel, met de flagolet en trommeltje, verzeld van een ander, zittende op de Doedelzak te speelen, anderen danzen om een versierde Paal, op den voorgrond een Boeren-Wagen, waar op eene Vrouw met eene Rinkelbom in de hand, verder eenige Gebouwen en Bergachtig verschiet. Het zonlicht doet eene natuurlijke werking, het is van eene uitvoerige penceels-behandeling | *Mat:* op doek *Size:* hoog 34, breed 46 duim *Loc:* Nottingham, England, UK. Castle Art Gallery (04–92)	[Bicker]	(Sold) fl 376 T van Iperen
1809/07/19	AMSCH	0031	*Lingelbach (J.)* | In een Italiaansch Landzigt, voor de Ruïne van een groot Gebouw, bij een verwulfde Poort, zit een Boeren Smit ijzerwerk te smeeden, een Jongen schijnt bezig het Vuur aan te blaazen; verder staat eene Vrouw, Kind en twee Jongelingen, die zig bij het vuur warmen. Het is bevallig van licht en koloriet, en meesterlijk fraai gepenceeld | *Mat:* op doek *Size:* hoog 18, breed 15 duim	[Bicker]	(Sold) fl 96 Gruyter
1809/07/19	AMSCH	0032	*Lingelbach (J.)* | Een Romeinsch Gezicht, met eenige Gebouwen en Overblijfzelen der Oudheid, gestoffeerd met verscheide behoeftige en arme Lieden, dewelke aldaar schijnen gespijzigd te worden. Helder en uitvoerig van behandeling | *Mat:* op doek *Size:* hoog 20, breed 16 duim	C	(Sold) fl 64 Coclers
1809/09/06	AMSCH	0035	*Lingelbagh (J.)* | Deze kapitale rijke Ordinantie, vertoond binnen Romen een uitrijding van den Paus uit zijn Paleis, verzeld van Kardinaalen en andere Geestelijken, verders zijn Lijfwagten en statelijk gevolg, onder een toevloed van een meenigte Aanschouwers die deze plegtige statie verzellen; in 't verschiet het Kasteel St. Angelo en andere treffelijke Gebouwen aan de Rivier; dit stuk is bevallig van licht en koloriet en van een uitmuntende penceelbehandeling en een der fraaiste van deze Meester | *Mat:* op doek *Size:* hoog 45, breed 36 duim *Loc:* Amsterdam, Nederland. Rijksmuseum. (A 3973)	Johannes Caudri	(Sold) fl 114 van Iperen
1809/09/06	AMSCH	0036	*Lingelbagh (J.)* | Een kapitale Ordinantie, verbeeldende de Haven van Smirna, op de voorgrond ziet men bij een Vorstelijk Paleis een Levants Koopman, beveelen geven aan een Slaaf; verders een meenigte Kooplieden, benevens onderscheiden Koopmanschappen ter inschéping op de Vloot gereed liggende; veelerlei soorten van In- en Uitlandsche Vaartuigen, vertoonen zich aan de Wal; zijnde van een schoone en meesterlijke penceelbehandeling | *Mat:* op doek *Size:* hoog 60, breed 81 duim	Johannes Caudri	(Sold) fl 51 van Iperen
1809/09/06	AMSCH	0037	*Lingelbagh (J.)* | In een Italiaansch Bergachtig Landschap met een Rivier doorsneeden, vertoonen zig op de voorgrond twee Paarden, een wit en een bruin, op welk een Landman gezeeten is, en daar névens een staande Rijsiger, schijnende een teeken te geven aan Lieden op een beladen Schuit onder een Brug doorvaarende, waar na de Paarden gereed wagten, verders rustende en staande Rijsigers en een Zeehaven met andere Vaartuigen; alles helder en meesterlijk fraai gepenceeld, in de manier van K. du Jardin | *Mat:* op doek *Size:* hoog 41, breed 41 duim	Johannes Caudri	(Sold) fl 162 Gruyter
1809/09/06	AMSCH	0038	*Lingelbach (J.)* | Op het Voorplijn van een pragtige Hofstéden, ziet men eenige Dames en Heeren gereed om ter Jagt uit te reiden, verzeld van een meenigte Jagers met hunne Honden en andere stoffagie; zonagtig en van een bevallige schildering | *Mat:* op doek *Size:* hoog 20, breed 25 duim	Johannes Caudri	(Sold) fl 235 Bredius
1810/03/07	UTWLD	0031	*J. Lingelbach* | Eene Turksche Zeehaven, op de voorgrond een Tempel en Beelden fraay behandeld | *Size:* hoog 2 voet 4 duim, breed 2 voet 2 duim	J J Woertman	(Unknown) fl 59
1810/03/07	UTWLD	0053	*Lingelbag* | Een tempel, eenige Kooplieden &c. | *Size:* hoog 1 voet 2 duim, breed 2 voet 5 duim	J J Woertman	(Unknown) fl 200

1810/03/23	HAVIN	0005	*Lingelbach* | Een Zee-battaille tusschen Hollanders en Turken: verscheide zijn slaags met een Hollands Schip dat op zij legt; en vooraan word wreed gevogten, extra fraai | *Size:* hoog 4 voet, breet 5 voet 10 duim.	Rudolf Hendrik de Wetstein [or others]	(Unknown) fl 74
1810/05/22	AMSCH	0053	*Lingelbach. (J.)* | In een aangenaam Landschap, ziet men eenige Heeren en Dames te Paard en te Voet, schijnende ter Valkenjagt te gaan; ieder behandeld | *Mat:* op paneel *Size:* hoog 14, breed 17 duim	Johannes van de Putte Nicolaasz.	(Sold) fl 94 van Iperen
1810/05/22	AMSCH	0054	*Lingelbach. (J.)* | Eene Italiaansche Markt, op den voorgrond zijn eenige Landlieden en eene Vrouw die Groenten schijnt te koopen, verder een Fontein en eenige Reizigers, en voorts verscheide Gebouwen; fiks en krachtig gepenceeld | companion to lot 55 *Mat:* op doek *Size:* hoog 11, breed 14 duim	Ij[ver]	(Sold) fl 102 for lots 54 & 55. Gruyter
1810/05/22	AMSCH	0055	*Lingelbach. (J.)* | Een dito [Italiaansche Markt], zijnde de wederga, verbeeldende eene Vrouw op eene Markt, Groentens verkopende, waarbij andere Lieden en een Jongeling, ter linkerzijde ziet men eenige Reizigers bij een springende Fontein, verder Gebouwen en een bevallig verschiet; als de voorgaande behandeld | companion to lot 54	Ij[ver]	(Sold) fl 102 for lots 54 & 55. Gruyter
1810/06/06	RMMUY	0043	*J. Lingelbach* | Tullia het Ligchaam van haren vermoorden Vader, Servius Tullius, onder haar Rijtuig verplettende. Stout en meesterlijk geschilderd | *Mat:* op paneel		(Unknown) fl 24
1810/07/23	DOLGI	0033	*Lingelbach* | Een Italiaansche Zeehaven. Op den voorgrond een Heer en een Dame ter Valken-Jagt rijdende; voords Turksche en Armenische Kooplieden, met hunne Koopgoederen, Slaven, enz; op de Rivier Galeijen, en andere Vaartuigen. Alles los, en tevens uitvoerig van behandeling | *Mat:* op paneel *Size:* hoog 15 ½, breed 20 duim	Mr Pieter van den Santheuvel	(Sold) fl 305 Dansaert van Brussel
1810/07/26	AMSCH	0050	*Lingelbach* | Een Zeehaven met Gebouwen, gestoffeerd met Kooplieden en Vaartuigen | *Mat:* op doek *Size:* hoog 27, breed 34 duimen	Cassino	(Sold) fl 2:15 Spruyt
1810/08/01	AMSCH	0053	*Lingelbag (Johannes)* | Eene Legerplaats; op den voorgrond voor eene Zoetelaarstent ziet men eenige Krijgslieden, zoo te voet als te paard, zich ververschen [Le sujet d'un Campement au devant duquel se trouve une Tente de Vivendiers, devant laquelle s'arretent quelques Cavaliers, tant à pied qu'à Cheval pour se rafraichir] | *Annots:* Passable. (NGW) *Mat:* op paneel *Size:* hoog 17, breed 24 duimen	Mr Pieter de Smeth van Alphen	(Sold) fl 305 De Lelie d'Amsterdam
1810/08/06	AMSCH	0060	*Lingelbach (J.)* | In een heuvelagtig Landschap vertoont zig op den voorgrond een hevig gevegt tusschen Spaansche en andere Ruiterij, ter zijde liggen eenige doode en gekwetste; krachtig en meesterlijk geschilderd | *Mat:* op doek *Size:* hoog 39, breed 54 duimen	R[oos]	(Sold) fl 30 de Burtin
1810/08/06	AMSCH	0061	*Lingelbach (J.)* | Een hevig gevegt tusschen Turksche en andere Ruiterij; vol uitdrukking en stout geschilderd | *Mat:* op paneel *Size:* hoog 26, breed 34 duimen	Q	(Sold) fl 8:10 Dupre
1810/10/11	AMSCH	0045	*J. Lingelbach* | Een Italiaansch Landschap, bij aloude Gebouwen ziet men eenige Lieden zich met speelen en drinken vermaken, en op den voorgrond voor een open Stal anderen, die musiceeren en dansen; zonachtig en fraai behandeld | *Mat:* op doek *Size:* hoog 34, breed 40 duimen	[Gruyter?]	(Sold) fl 10 Spaan

Lingelbach, Johannes (and Asch, P.J. van)

1810/06/06	RMMUY	0045	*P. van As; Lingelbach* | Een Landschapje, waar in een kerk, op den weg een Postwagen en verdere Figuren, fiks geschilderd. Door P. van As, en gestoffeerd door Lingelbach | *Mat:* op paneel		(Unknown) fl 10

Lingelbach, Johannes (and Beck)

1804/10/16	DLOND	0127	*J. Lingelbach; Beck* | Een Schermutseling met de Turken. Une Escarmouche avec les Turcs | *Mat:* op doek *Size:* hoog 21, breed 15		(Sold) fl 25 Thijs

Lingelbach, Johannes (and Beerstraten, A.)

1808/06/13	AMSCH	0013	*Beerestraten (A.); J. Lingelbag* | Deze Ordonantie verbeeldt het Stadhuis en de Markt te Kampen; rijk gestoffeerd door J. Lingelbag. Is zonachtig en meesterlijk behandeld, en kan voor het beste van deze Meester gehouden worden | *Mat:* op doek *Size:* hoog 36, breed 50 duim	E M Engelberts	(Sold) fl 380 O W J Berg
1809/06/13	AMSCH	0006	*A. Beerstraten; J. Lingelbach* | In een kapitaale Winter, ziet men langs een sterk bevrozen Rivier, op een hoogte een Kerk en de ingang van een Dorp, verders een oud Adelijk Kasteel en andere Gebouwen, het IJs is rijk gestoffeerd met Schaatsenrijders, Kolvers, Wandelende Heeren en Dames en langs den Weg eenige na de Kerk gaande Dorpelingen, de voorgrond de Daken der Gebouwen en het Geboomten zijn alle als met Sneeuw bedekt; het is schoon van effect, konstig en natuurlijk gepenceeld, door A. Beerstraten en gestoffeerd door J. Lingelbach | *Mat:* op doek *Size:* hoog 36, breed 49 duim	[Gruyter?]	(Bought In) fl 125
1810/10/11	AMSCH	0005	*A. Beerstraten; J. Lingelbag* | Een kapitaal Wintergezigt, ziende over een Steenen Sluis, een Kerk, bij de ingang van een Dorp, benevens een sterk bevrozen Rivier, bij een Adelijk Slot, het is rijk gestoffeert met Schaatsenrijders, Wandelaars, en ter Kerk gaande Dorpelingen, de besneeuwde Daken en het Geboomte zijn natuurlijk, en de stoffagie uitvoerig geschilderd | *Mat:* op doek *Size:* hoog 33, breed 48 duimen	[Gruyter?]	(Bought In) fl 110

Lingelbach, Johannes (and Beerstraten, J.)

1809/04/17 AMSCH 0004

J. Beerstraaten; J. Lingelbach | Een kapitaal Wintergezicht, ziende over een bevrozen Rivier op een Dorp, met verscheide Wooningen, Kerk en Tooren, ter zijde een Slot of adelijk Huis, het IJs is rijk gestoffeerd met Schaatzenrijders, Wandelaars, Kolvers en Arresleeden: de voorgrond, het Geboomte en de Daken der Huizen zijn alle met Sneeuw bedekt; alles is zeer kunstig en natuurlijk door J. Beerstraaten en de stoffagie uitvoerig door J. Lingelbach, behandeld op Doek | *Mat:* op doek *Size:* hoog 36, breed 51 duim

C

(Sold) fl 275

Lingelbach, Johannes (and Esselens, Jacob)

1807/06/02 AMHUY 0017

Esselens; Lingelbach | Een Landschap, by een Boerewoning eenige Bomen, ter zyde een Brug, waar over een Man ligt, benevens een Heer en Dame met de Knecht daar agter, aan de andere zyde eenige Schapen, waarby de Herder ligt te rusten, meesterlijk geschilderd door Esselens, gestoffeerd door Lingelbach

(Unknown)

Lingelbach, Johannes (and Everdingen, A.)

1808/08/23 AMSCH 0048

Everdingen (A. van); J. Lingelbagh | Een Noords bergachtig Landschap, met hoog Geboomte en nederstortende Watervallen, gestoffeert op de voorgrond met twee beladen Muil-Ezels, op de eene zit een Huisman, nevens hem eene gaande Vrouw en Hond, en ter zijde drie Vissers; het bruischen van het Water is natuurlijk verbeeld, en meesterlijk schoon geschilderd | *Mat:* op doek *Size:* hoog 42, breed 45 duim

X

(Bought In) fl 50

Lingelbach, Johannes (and Hackaert, J.)

1802/09/06 AMSCH 0048

J. Hackaert; J. Lingelbach | Een Boschachtig Landschap, met een Rivier doorsneeden, waarin verbeeld een Hartejacht, op de voorgrond, en in 't verschiet, Heeren te Paard, en Jagers te voet, met verscheide Honden, die het wild vervolgen; het natuurlyk zonlicht, doet een fraaye werking, is kragtig van Coloriet, en meesterlyk gepenceeld, door J. Hackaert, en de Stoffagie door J. Lingelbach | *Mat:* op paneel *Size:* hoog 17, breed 12 ½ duim

H^{n} Smit

(Sold) fl 131 Izaac Smit

1802/09/06 AMSCH 0049

J. Hakkert; J. Lingelbach | Een Boom- en bergachtig Landschap, met een stille Rivier, gestoffeerd met danssende beelden; uitvoerig en zonachtig | *Mat:* op paneel *Size:* hoog 16, breed 21 duim

Mevrouw Achtienhoven

(Sold) fl 10:10 van Iperen

1802/12/13 AMSCH 0078

J. Hackaert; J. Lingelbagh | In een Italiaansch bevallig Landschap, met hoog Geboomten, by een Rivier, waar over een Steene Brug en aloude Poort, ziet men op de voorgrond een Heer te Paard, gevolgt van een Jager met Honden: in 't verschiet eenige Gebouwen en Gebergtens, dit voorwerp is natuurlyk warm en zonagtig gepenceelt | *Mat:* op paneel *Size:* hoog 13, breed 17 duim

Schley [for] Lauwers

(Sold) fl 24 J^{n} Yver

1809/04/22 AMYVR 0054

J. Hakkert; J. Lingelbach | Een fraai Boom- en Bergachtig Landschap, aan een Rivier, gestoffeerd met een Heer te Paard; het zonlicht doet een uitmuntende werking, en is meesterlijk gepenceelt door J. Hakkert en J. Lingelbach | *Mat:* op doek *Size:* hoog 50, breed 58 duim

van den Bracke

(Sold) fl 56 C S Roos

Lingelbach, Johannes (and Hagen, Joris)

1805/07/03 AMSCH 0025

Hagen (J. van der); J. Lingelbagh | Dit magnifique Schildery steld voor: het gezicht van de Rhynkant op de Stad Arnhem, den Rhyn met Vaartuigen, en de op de voorgrond geleegene Weg, met Huifkarren, Paarden en Reisigers gestoffeerd; het Geboomten, de Zandgronden en het dynzend verschiet, doen een uirmuntend [sic] effect; zynde van een kloeke penceels behandeling | *Mat:* op doek *Size:* hoog 46, breed 68 duim

G

(Sold) fl 50 C S Roos

Lingelbach, Johannes (and Heusch, Wm.)

1808/06/13 AMSCH 0069

Heusch (G. de); J. Lingelbach | Een Italiaansch bergachtig Landschap, waarin eenige Reizigers, zoo te voet als te paard, van een Brug komen; op den voorgrond twee Muilezels. Rijk uitgedoscht, zonachtig en uitmuntend gestoffeerd, door J. Lingelbach | *Mat:* op doek *Size:* hoog 37, breed 58 duim

E M Engelberts

(Sold) fl 60 Glad

Lingelbach, Johannes (and Kessel, J. (III))

1808/08/23 AMSCH 0086

Kessel (J. van); Lingelbag | Aan den ingang van een schilderachtig bosch, zit in de schaduwe van een Eiken Boom, eene rustende Landvrouw met een Jongen, verder ziet men over een heldere Waterplas een Heer te Paard, en een gaande Man bij een gedeelte Graanland; natuurlijk zonachtig en van een fraaije penceelbehandeling | *Mat:* op doek

J

(Sold) fl 230 Jan Spaan

Lingelbach, Johannes (and Koninck, P.)

1805/07/10 AMSCH 0086b

P. de Koning; J. Lingelbach | Een gezicht na het Leeven, zeer natuurlyk van lieht [sic] en bruin, en gestoffeerd met een uittogt ter Valken-Jagt, op Doek, door denzelven [P. de Koning] en J. Lingelbach | *Mat:* op doek *Size:* hoog 52, breed 62 duim

R[oos]

(Sold) fl 275 Hulswit

Lingelbach, Johannes (and Moucheron)

1801/04/08 HAVIN 0042

Moucheron; Lingelbach | Een Landschap, door Moucheron en door Lingelbach gestoff:

(Unknown)

Lingelbach, Johannes (and Moucheron, F.)

1802/02/23	AMREB	0036	*F. Moucheron; Lingelbach* | 1 Schoorsteenstuk, door F. Moucheron en Lingelbach | *Fmt:* schoorsteenstuk	Margaretha Maria van Laar	(Sold) fl 3 Royers
1804/05/07	AMSCH	0102	*Moucheron. (F. de); Lingelbach* | Een capitaal hoog Bergachtig Landschap met zwaar opgaand Geboomten, op de voorgrond gestoffeerd met en [sic] Vrouw op een Ezel, die door een Man geleid wodt [sic], terzyden een rustende reiziger, met een Jongen en een Hondt, op de hoogten tusschen 't Gebergten eenige Veedryvende Lieden, zonachtig en bevallig geschilderd | *Mat:* op doek *Size:* hoog 29, breed 37 duim	Vinkeles [for] G	(Sold) fl 30 Wed Achtienhoven
1804/05/07	AMSCH	0103	*Moucheron. (F. de); Lingelbach* | Een aangenaam Boom en Berachtig [sic] Landschap op de voorgrond ryk gestoffeerd met eenige Jaagers te voet en te paard, verzeldt van een ménigte van Honden, dewelken en Hert agterhalen, tusschen 't Geboomte op 't Gebergten eenigen capitalen sterk door den zon verligt werden Gebouwen, en eeu [sic] Bergachtig verschiet; meesterlyk geschilderd | *Mat:* op doek *Size:* hoog 35, breed 43 duim	Vinkeles [for] G	(Sold) fl 5 Gruyter
1804/07/25	AMSCH	0053	*Moucheron (F. de); J. Lingelbach* | In een dito [allerbevalligst capitaal Italiaansch Heuvelachtig] Landschap, verschillende van Ordinantie, vertoont zig ter linkerzyde, by een opgaande Weg, een Vrouw op een Ezel rydende, verzeld van een Hond, en agterwaarts een gaande Reiziger; hooger op een Huisman eenig Vee voortdryvende; ter andere zyde een stil Water en een bevallig verschiet; zonachtig, natuurlyk en uitvoerig door beide deeze Meesters gepenceeld | *Mat:* op doek *Size:* hoog 21, breed 25 duim *Notes:* It is unclear what "dito" refers to in the title.		(Sold) fl 200 Thais
1808/06/06	RMRIJ	0085	*Moucheron (Frederik de); Lingelbach. (Johannes)* | Een aangenaam bergachtig Landschap, rijk in allerhande hoog en laag geboomte, onder eene voortreffelijke Zomerlucht, gestoffeerd met reizende en rustende Beelden. Alles zeer schoon van kleur en uitvoerig behandeld [Paysage Italien richement orné de differentes sortes d'arbres distingués par leurs feuillages. Des Montagnes, des sites agréables, un beau lointain et un Ciel clair, tout cela joint aux figures soignées, forme un ensemble qui charme l'oeil. Ce Morceau d'un ton chaud et piquant et d'une touche spirituelle, est une Production savante de ces deux Artistes] | *Annots:* van Thys, Juli 1799 (f 270.-) Thijs berichtte 22 Juli 1798 het te Brussel gekocht te hebben (RMA I) *Mat:* op paneel *Size:* Hoog 12 ½, en breed 15 ¼ duim	Gerrit van der Pot, Heer van Groeneveld	(Sold) fl 450 van Leen
1810/08/01	AMSCH	0067	*Moucheron (Fredrik de); Johannes Lingelbag* | Een bergachtig Landschap met een Water, waar langs een opgaande Weg naar eene steenen Poort, verder Heeren en Vrouwen te paard, en Jagers met hunne Honden [Un Paysage coupé par des Collines, où l'on remarque un ruisseau le long d'une route qui mène à une porte batie en pierres ; il est orné de Seigneurs et de Dames, suivis de Chasseurs et de Chiens, allant à la chasse] | *Annots:* assez piquant, et bonnes figures mais les jours ij papillotent trop. (NGW) *Mat:* op doek *Size:* hoog 36, breed 50 duimen	Mr Pieter de Smeth van Alphen	(Sold) fl 910 T Spaan [for] Croese

Lingelbach, Johannes (and Moucheron, I.)

1809/09/06	AMSCH	0045	*Moucheron (J. de); J. Lingelbach* | Een Hofgezicht met fraaije Vijvers, springende Fontijnen en stoffagie van Beelden; zonagtig geschilderd | *Mat:* op doek *Size:* hoog 38, breed 45 duim	Johannes Caudri	(Sold) fl 6 L Pakker

Lingelbach, Johannes (and Roghman, R.)

1802/05/05	AMSCH	0181	*R. Rogman; J. Lingelbag* | Een hoog bergachtig Landschap, met Gebouwen en Geboomten, gestoffeerd met een optocht van geestelyke Persoonen te paard, en een Prelaat in een Draagstoel, alles meesterlyk | *Mat:* op doek *Size:* hoog 52, breed 82 duim	E	(Sold) fl 13:10 Cocler
1807/08/26	AMSCH	0183	*R. Roghman; J. Lingelbagh* | Een Italiaansch heuvelachtig Landschap, met eenig Geboomte, op den voorgrond ter zyde eene Vrouw, op een Ezel rydende, waarby een gaande Huisman en Hond, en een Pelgrim, by een stil Water, verders gestoffeerd met een rydende Wagen en eenig Vee by de Rivier; krachtig gepenceeld, door R. Roghman, en de stoffage door J. Lingelbagh | *Mat:* op doek *Size:* hoog 27, breed 34 duim	Yver [for] S	(Bought In) fl 18

Lingelbach, Johannes (and Ruisdael, J.)

1808/11/28	AMSCH	0053	*J. Ruijsdaal; J. Lingelbach* | Een Duinachtig Landschap, met opgaand Geboomte en dartel Kreupelgewas, ziende van de Duinen over de Linnebleekerijen op de Stad Haarlem, gestoffeerd op de voorgrond met een Jager met zijn Honden, verders gaande Arbeiders en rustende Reizigers, zonagtig en natuurlijk gepenceel, op Paneel, door J. Ruijsdaal en gestoffeerd door J. Lingelbach | *Mat:* op paneel *Size:* hoog 16, breed 14 duim	[Gruyter?]	(Bought In) fl 83
1810/03/26	RMMUY	0033	*Jacob Ruisdaal; J. Lingelbach* | Een Geldersch Landschap, verbeeldende eene uitgestrekte Vlakte, van een Hoogte te zien, doorsneden met water en verrijkt met Ruïnen, Dorpen en Gehuchten. Eene wolkrijke lucht, waar het zonlicht hier en daar doorstralende, aangename en piquante partijen van licht en schaduwen veroorzaakt; rijk gestoffeerd met Beelden en Beestjes door J. Lingelbach [Un Paysage après nature ; vue d'oiseaux d'une grande étenduë, plat pays, coupé par des eaux qui y serpentent ; plusieurs viilages [sic], ruïnes et chaumières, se découvrent de distance en distance, un beau ciel bien nuagé, et une distribution savante des clairs et	Daniel de Jongh Az	(Sold) fl 360 A van Beeftingh

des ombres, forment un ensemble piquant et agréable. Les figures sont peintes par Lingelbach.] | *Mat:* op doek *Size:* hoog 24 ½, breed 29 ½ duimen

Lingelbach, Johannes (and Schellinks, Daniel)

1808/06/13	AMSCH	0145	*Schellings (D.); J. Lingelbach* | Een bergachtig Landschap, ter zijde ziet men een Heer en eene Dame ter Valkenjagt uitrijden, op den voorgrond een Jager, welke met eenige Honden door het Water baadt; in 't verschiet eenige Landloopers en een Herberg. Dit Schilderij is in voorstelling der Natuur alleruitmuntendst behandeld | *Mat:* op doek *Size:* hoog 43, breed 57 duim	E M Engelberts	(Sold) fl 201 Reijers
1808/06/13	AMSCH	0146	*Schellings (D.); J. Lingelbach* | Een Geleerde in zijne Studeerkamer, omgeven van eene Globe, Landkaarten en eenige Boeken, ter zijde een Wenteltrap. Het invallend licht geeft eene schoone houding, en het is in de manier van Philip Koning meesterlijk gepenceeld | *Mat:* op doek *Size:* hoog 21, breed 19 duim	[Jan Tersteeg]	(Sold) fl 40 J du Pree

Lingelbach, Johannes (and Schellinks, W.)

1808/08/23	AMSCH	0145	*Schellings (W.); J. Lingelbag* | Een donker Bosch-gezigt, op de voorgrond tusschen Kreupelhout, Jagers, die met hunne Honden een Hart vervolgen, dieper in het Bosch, Heeren te Paard, verzeld van hunne Loopers en Honden; alles is bevallig en zeer natuurlijk voorgesteld | *Mat:* op doek *Size:* hoog 25, breed 27 duim	J	(Sold) fl 20 Spruit

Lingelbach, Johannes (and Swanevelt)

1808/11/12	HGSCR	0020	*H. Zwaneveld; J. Lingelbach* | Een heuvelagtig boschgezigt met hoog geboomte verbeeldende een morgenstond, zeer natuurlyk en zonagtig behandeld door H. Zwaneveld en gestoffeerd met een hertenjagt door J. Lingelbach, het zonligt is in dit stuk van een uitmuntende uitwerking | *Mat:* op doek	Mr J van Buren	(Unknown) fl 48

Lingelbach, Johannes (and Verboom, A.H.)

1801/04/13	AMSCH	0079	*A. Verboom; J. Lingelbach* | Een Italiaansch bergachtig Landschap met gebouwen, hoog geboomte en watervallen, op den voorgrond een man op een Ezel, waar nevens een vrouw met een kind; alles zonachtig en delicaat gepenceeld | *Mat:* op paneel *Size:* hoog 15, breed 19 duim	Pierre Fouquet, junior	(Sold) fl 100 Pruyssenaar
1801/04/13	AMSCH	0080	*A. Verboom; J. Lingelbach* | Een boomryk Landschap met gebouwen, ruïnen en stoffage van Jagers te paard en te voet, op den voorgrond een waterplas; alles behandeld als de voorgaande | *Mat:* op doek *Size:* hoog 20 ½, breed 24 ½ duim	Pierre Fouquet, junior	(Sold) fl 101 Pruyssenaar
1801/04/13	AMSCH	0081	*A. Verboom; J. Lingelbach* | Een boom- en bergachtig gestoffeerd Landschap; mede behandeld als de voorgaande | *Mat:* op paneel *Size:* hoog 19, breed 16 duim	Pierre Fouquet, junior	(Sold) fl 18:10 Lafontaine
1801/05/11	AMSCH	0096	*A. Verboom; J. Lingelbach* | Een aangenaam Landschap met verscheiden Geboomte, by een anticque Poort en een Waterplas, fraai gestoffeerd met verscheiden Beeldjes, zonachtig en bevallig gepenceeld | *Size:* hoog 19, breed 24 ½ duim	E[lias]	(Sold) fl 190 Allard
1801/06/10	AMSCH	0172	*Verboom. (A.); J. Lingelbach* | Een fraai Boomryk Landschap, met een stroomende Waterplas doorsneeden, gestoffeerd op de voorgrond met een Huifkar en een menigte verschillende Beelden, verder en aangenaam verschiet; delicaat en Zonachtig geschilderd | *Mat:* op doek *Size:* hoog 30, breed 39 duim	Herman ten Kate	(Sold) fl 565 J Yver
1801/06/10	AMSCH	0173	*Verboom. (A.); J. Lingelbach* | Een Landschap met hoog Geboomte, terzyde langs den weg, een Boerenwooning, waarby eenige Huislieden; natuurlyk van behandeling | *Mat:* op paneel *Size:* hoog 17, breed 15 duim	[Doublet]	(Sold) fl 6 Spruit van Gend
1803/08/01	AMSCH	0043	*Verboom (A.); J. Lingelbach* | Een Heuvelachtig en boomryk Landschap of Boschgezigt, met verscheide Kruiden op de voorgrond, beneevens een Water ter linkerzyde, zeer ryk gestoffeerd met eenige Jagers, een Heer en Dame te Paard, verzeld van hunne Honden, die een Hart vervolgen, zeer natuurlyk, uitvoerig en fraay behandeld | *Mat:* op doek *Size:* hoog 25 ½, breed 31 ½ duim	Ij[ver]	(Sold) fl 46 Hodges
1808/11/28	AMSCH	0064	*A. Verboom; J. Lingelbach* | Een hoog Bergachtig Landschap, ter zijde door een zwaar Bosch, een sterk nederstortende Waterval, gestoffeerd met een Landman, zittende op een Esel en voorts gaande en rustende Rijzigers, zonachtig en uitvoerig geschilderd, op Doek, door A. Verboom en gestoffeerd door J. Lingelbach | *Mat:* op doek *Size:* hoog 19, breed 20 duim	[Gruyter?]	(Bought In) fl 23 ½
1810/08/06	AMSCH	0105	*Verboom (A); J. Lingelbach* | Een Landschap met Geboomte, gestoffeerd met Reizigers en Huislieden; zeer natuurlijk verbeeld | *Mat:* op paneel *Size:* hoog 28, breed 41 duimen		(Withdrawn)
1810/10/11	AMSCH	0087	*A. Verboom; J. Lingelbach* | Een Boschachtig Landschap, met eenige Boerenwoningen op een Heuvel, achterwaards bij een sterk door de zon verlicht wordende zandige Weg ziet men een Houten Brug over eene stille Rivier, gestoffeert met eene overvarende Pontschuit, waarin Landlieden met hun Vee, verders gaande en rustende Reizigers en een aangenaam verschiet; zonachtig en uitvoerig geschilderd, door A. Verboom,	[Gruyter?]	(Sold) fl 100 H^{n} Pakker

			gestoffeerd door J. Lingelbach | *Mat:* op doek *Size:* hoog 26, breed 30 duimen		

Lingelbach, Johannes (and Vries, R.)

1801/05/11	AMSCH	0101	*R. de Vries; J. Lingelbach* | Gestoffeerd door J. Lingelbach. Een Landschap ter zyde een vervallen Gebouw, gestoffeerd met een Heer en Dame te Paard, by dezelve een Valkejager en Honden, alles meesterlyk van schildering en natuurlyk behandeld | *Mat:* op doek *Size:* hoog 26, breed 21 duim	E[lias]	(Sold) fl 39:10 Cocler
1804/05/07	AMSCH	0172	*Vries (A. de); J. Lingelbagh* | Een stille Rivier, langs oude Gebouwen en Geboomten, gestoffeerd met een Visscher in een Schuit en zwemmende Eenden, in 't verschiet een Weide met Beesten; natuurlyk en zonachtig behandeld | *Mat:* op paneel *Size:* hoog 19, breed 21 duim *Notes:* The artist's name was given as "Vries (A. de)" but we have assumed this is an error.	JJ [through] Y[ver]	(Sold) fl 26 T van Iperen
1810/10/11	AMSCH	0092	*R. De Vries; J. Lingelbach* | Een Landschap met Gebouwen en oude vervallen Muren bij Geboomte, gestoffeerd met een Heer te Paard en Reizigers met beladen Muil-Ezels; zonachtig en uitvoerig behandeld, door R. De Vries, gestoffeerd door J. Lingelbach | *Mat:* op paneel *Size:* hoog 13, breed 11 duimen	[Gruyter?]	(Sold) fl 10 T Spaan

Lingelbach, Johannes (and Wijnants)

1801/05/11	AMSCH	0114	*J. Wynands; Lingelbach* | Denzelven [J. Wynands] gestoffeerd, door Lingelbach. Een bevallig Landschap, doorsneede met een stil water, op de Voorgrond een Vrouw, nevens een Kind en een Hond, verders een Kar en een Jager, zonachtig en natuurlyk van behandeling | *Mat:* op doek op paneel *Size:* hoog 11, breed 16 duim	E[lias]	(Sold) fl 100 Pruijssenaar [for] R
1801/05/11	AMSCH	0115	*J. Wynands; Lingelbach* | Denzelven [J. Wynands] gestoffeerd, door Lingelbach. Een duinachtig Landschap, met hoog geboomte gestoffeerd, met een Man te Paard, nevens een Voetganger en een Hond, in 't verschiet een Herder by eenige Schaapen, alles zonachtig en natuurlyk behandeld | *Mat:* op paneel *Size:* hoog 15, breed 16 duim	P[ruyssenaar]	(Sold) fl 37 Yver
1801/06/10	AMSCH	0181	*Wynants. (J.); Lingelbach* | Een Heuvelachtig Landschap, op de Voorgrond ziet men een Man en Vrouw te Paard, achter dezelve een Voetganger, verders een Koornoogst, in het verschiet een Dorp en hoog Geboomte; zonachtig en natuurlyk behandeld | *Mat:* op doek op paneel *Size:* hoog 11, breed 14 duim	Herman ten Kate	(Sold) fl 130 Thaijs
1801/10/06	AMSCH	0078	*J. Wynands; J. Lingelbach* | Dit Stukje verbeeld een Aangenaam, Heuvelagtig Landschap, op de voorgrond op een Heuvel met eenig Geboomten, ziet men Huislieden, met Schaapen, ter andere zyde in een Valei, met een Rivier doorsneeden, een staand Man en rustende Vrouw; verders een bevallig verschiet, alles is Zonagtig en uitvoerig behandeld | *Mat:* op doek *Size:* hoog 11, breed 15 duim	L	(Bought In) fl 405
1802/06/16	AMSCH	0208	*J. Wynands; J. Lingelbach* | Een aangenaam Duinachtig Landschap met eenige laag Geboomten: op de voorgrond ziet men een Heer te Paard, en een Beedelaar een Almoes vragende; verder ter zyde by een opgaande zandweg, rust een Vrouw, verzelt van een Man en Jongeling, hooger een Véehoeder Ossendryvende; en een Kerktooren: in 't verschiet een Rytuig; alles is helder zonachtig en fraay gepenceeld door deeze Meesters | *Mat:* op doek *Size:* hoog 18 ½, breed 21 ½ duim	[Merrem]	(Sold) fl 135 I Smit Gz
1803/12/15	MGLAC	0013	*J. Weynands; Lingelbach* | Een heerlyk Landschap; zeer uitvoerig en fraai, zynde gestoffeerd met Figuuren, door Lingelbach | *Mat:* op doek *Size:* hoog duim 40, breed duim 34	Mr L H de Haze Bomme	(Unknown)
1804/05/07	AMSCH	0191	*Wynands. (J.); (gestoffeerd door Lingelbach)* | In een bevallig Duinachtig Landschap, ziet men by een Heyning ter zyde een Watertje, op de voorgrond een gaande Huisman, waarby een Hond, iets achterwaards een rustende Vrouw, waarby een Jongen, en verders twee gaande Lieden, in 't verschiet op eenig Gebergte en Geboomte een Kasteel, enz.; uitvoerig en piquant van licht en van de beste schildering van deeze Meesters | *Mat:* op paneel *Size:* hoog 13, breed 14 duim	Roos [for] A	(Sold) fl 200 Coclers
1804/05/07	AMSCH	0192	*Wynands. (J.); (gestoffeerd door Lingelbach)* | Dit stukje verbeelde een aangenaam Heuvelachtig Landschap, op de voorgrond op een Heuvel met eenig Geboomte, ziet men Huislieden met Schaapen, ter andere zyde in een Valey, met een Rivier doorsneeden, een staand Man en rustende Vrouw, verders een bevallig verschiet; alles is zonachtig en uitvoerig behandeld | *Mat:* op doek	Y[ver] [for] JJ	(Bought In) fl 200
1804/08/02	BDAN	0002	*J. Wynants; J. Lingelbacht* | Een zeer aangenaam en mooy bergachtig Landschap, den voorgrond verciert met eenige Boomen, Planten, enz:, zeer rykelyk gestoffeerd | *Mat:* op doek *Size:* b. 25 d. h. 19 d.	J G Calckberner	(Unknown)
1804/08/08	AMSCH	0218	*J. Wynands; J. Lingelbach* | Een capitaal Boom en Bergachtig Landschap, op de voorgrond eenige Distelen en Kreupelgewas, gestoffeerd met Beelden, te Paard en te voet; meesterlyk op Doek | *Mat:* op doek *Size:* hoog 65, breed 49 duim	Roos [for] K[=Gruyter?]	(Sold) fl 35 Gruiter
1806/08/13	AMSCH	0210	*Wynands (J.); J. Lingelbach* | Een Duin- en Boomryk Landschap, met een aangenaam verschiet, op de voorgrond by een Waterplas, ziet men	van der Voort	(Sold) fl 235 Thais

			een Heer en Dame te paard, verzeld van Jagers en Honden, delicaat geschilderd | *Mat:* op paneel *Size:* hoog 16, breed 21 duim		
1808/06/06	RMRIJ	0147	*Wijnants. (Jan); Lingelbach. (Johannes)* | Een Landschap, op den voorgrond rijk versierd met Geboomte en Gewassen, en een Valkenier, verzeld van twee Honden, den weg afkomende. Hooger op zit een Jager met zijne Honden te rusten. Verder ziet men Heeren en Dames te Paard den weg opkomen, en, bij eene afgeslotene schutting, een wit Paard en eene Koe. Ter zijden van den opgaanden weg eene ruime Vallei, doorsneden van eene Rivier, loopende langs Gebergte, Weg en Zaailanden, met Beelden, enz. gestoffeerd. Alles zeer schoon en uitvoerig door bovengemelde twee Meesters behandeld [Dans un riche Paysage décoré d'arbres, et agréablement varié par des plantes et des Brouissailles [sic], on apperçoit sur le penchant d'une colline, un fauconnier et deux Chiens ; plus loin repose un chasseur avec deux autres Chiens, et au sommet de cette Colline, on découvre un Cavalier et une Dame à cheval, accompagnés d'un Chasseur et de ses Chiens. A droite un Boeuf et un Cheval sont dans un enclos, et à gauche on voit un agréable vallon, où se trouvent un Carosse, des figures etc. Ce Morceau d'un ton vrai, d'une Composition riante, et d'un beau faire, mérite beaucoup d'èloge] | *Annots:* Van Jac. de Vos, 14 Aug. 1785 (f 650.-) (RMA I) *Mat:* op doek *Size:* Hoog 19 ¾, en breed 25 ¼ duim	Gerrit van der Pot, Heer van Groeneveld	(Sold) fl 905 P Roelszema
1808/06/13	AMSCH	0173	*Wijnands (J.); J. Lingelbach* | Deze rijke Ordonantie stelt voor een Nederlandsch Landschap, op den voorgrond een Herberg, alwaar een Heer op een Paard een Glas wordt ingeschonken, in 't verschiet eenige Reizigers. Allernatuurlijkst en zonachtig behandeld | *Mat:* op doek *Size:* hoog 40, breed 56 duim	E M Engelberts	(Sold) fl 175 T Boelen
1808/06/13	AMSCH	0174	*Wijnands (J.); J. Lingelbach* | Een boomrijk Landschap, gestoffeerd met eene Boerin op een Kar, ter zijde twee Reizigers, op den voorgrond een verdorde Boom en Kruiden. Als de voorgaande geschilderd | *Mat:* op doek *Size:* hoog 20, breed 25 duim	E M Engelberts	(Sold) fl 101 Engelberts
1810/06/20	AMSCH	0101	*J. Wijnands; J. Lingelbach* | In een aangenaam duinachtig Landschap, ziet men, ter regter zijde, eenen ouden bijna dooden Boom, nevens eenen ouden hollen Stam, met verschillende Struiken en Gewassen; verder omgehakte Boomstammen, achterwaards en in het verschiet fraai Geboomte. Het is gestoffeerd met Jagers te paard en te voet, met hunne Honden, gaande op de Valkenjagt. Dit kapitale Schilderij is van de beste en natuurlijkste schildering van J. Wijnands, en fraai en uitvoerig gestoffeerd door J. Lingelbach | *Mat:* op doek *Size:* hoog 45, breed 55 ½ duimen	D	(Sold) fl 250 de Vries
1810/06/20	AMSCH	0101a	*J. Wijnands; J. Lingelbach* | Dit fraaije Schilderij verbeeld een aangenaam Landschap, met Geboomte, verschillende Kruiden en Plantgewassen. Het is gestoffeerd in het midden, langs een zandige Weg, met een Heer te Paard, verzeld van een Jager en Honden; voorts een rustend Reiziger, benevens eene Vrouw met een Kind; achterwaards een helder spiegelend Water, grootsche Gebouwen en een bevallig verschiet. Dit stuk is warm van koloriet en van de beste schildering van J. Wijnands, gestoffeerd door J. Lingelbach | *Size:* hoog 43, breed 54 duimen	Y	(Sold) fl 161 T Spaan
1810/08/06	AMSCH	0130	*Wijnands (J.); Gestoffeerd door J. Lingelbag* | Twee stuks Duinachtige Landschappen, met opgaande Wegen en Geboomte, beide met Huislieden, Heeren te Paard, Jagers en andere Voorwerpen, zonachtig en natuurlijk behandeld | *Mat:* op paneel *Size:* ieder is hoog 9 ½, breed 11 ½ duimen	A	(Sold) fl 220 $\mathrm{J^{mo}}$ de Vries
1810/10/11	AMSCH	0103	*J. Wijnands; J. Lingelbach* | In een aangenaam duinachtig Landschap, ziet men, ter regter zyde, eenen ouden byna dooden Boom, nevens eenen ouden hollen Stam, met verschillende Struiken en Gewassen; verder omgehakte Boomstammen, achterwaards en in het verschiet fraai Geboomte. Het is gestoffeerd met Jagers te paard en te voet, met hunne Honden, gaande op de Valkenjagt. Dit voortreffelijken kapitale Schilderij is van de beste, uitvoerigsten en natuurlykste schildering van J. Wijnands, en fraai gestoffeerd door J. Lingelbach | *Mat:* op doek *Size:* hoog 45, breed 55 ½ duimen	V[ries]	(Sold or Bought In) fl 500 $\mathrm{J^{mo}}$ de Vries
1810/10/11	AMSCH	0104	*J. Wijnands; J. Lingelbach* | Een Heuvelachtig Landschap, voor aaan [sic] voor een Smits Winkel, Paarden die beslagen worden, verder Officieren te Paard, Vragtwagens en andere Stoffagie; zonachtig behandeld | *Mat:* op doek *Size:* hoog 28, breed 31 duimen	Y	(Sold) fl 21:10 Gruiter

Lingelbach, Johannes (and Wijnants and Velde, A.)

1802/06/16	AMSCH	0206	*J. Wynands; A. v. de Velde; J. Lingelbach* | Een Capitaal Boom- en Bergachtig Landschap met een stille Rivier en aangenaam verschiet, zynde gestoffeerd met eenige Landlieden, welken eenig Vée voortdryven; het frapante Zonlicht en de meesterlyke penceels-behandeling maken dit Schildery een der fraayste van deezen Meesters | *Mat:* op doek *Size:* hoog 65, breed 76 duim	[Merrem]	(Sold) fl 250 Coclers
1802/06/16	AMSCH	0207	*J. Wynands; A. v. de Velde; J. Lingelbach* | Ter regter zyde vertoont zich de ingang van een Bosch; op de voorgrond legt eene Boomstam; verder een Man te Paard, waarby een Jager met Honden, ter linker zyde een stil Water en Boeren Huis; verder hoog Gebergte in het verschiet; meesterlyk en zonachtig geschilderd | *Mat:* op doek *Size:* hoog 25, breed 29 duim	[Merrem]	(Sold) fl 190 H de Valk

Lingelbach, Johannes (and Withoos, M.)

1802/09/21	UTHDG	0056	*Withoos; Lingelbach* | Op den voorgrond zijn beladene Muilezels en verscheidene Beelden geplaatst; ter zijde gebergtens waarop gebouwen. Dit, met een Rivier doorsneede Landschap, is helder behandeld door Withoos, de stoffagie door Lingelbach | *Mat:* op doek *Size:* hoog 39, breed 47 duimen		(Bought In) fl 20

Lingelbach, Johannes (or Lingelbach, manner)

1806/05/05	AMSCH	0233	*Lingelbach* | Twee capitaale Bataljes op Zee, tusschen Turken, Hollanders en Russen; meesterlyk geschilderd door Lingelbach, of in de manier | *Mat:* op doek *Size:* hoog 24, breed 38 duim	V[inkeles]	(Sold) fl 4:10 van Laar

Lingelbach, Johannes (copy after)

1802/09/06	AMSCH	0210	*J. Lingelbach* | Eenige Beelden voor een Gebouw, na J. Lingelbach	Mevrouw Achtienhoven	(Sold) fl 0:16 Gruyter
1802/09/18	RMDRS	0075	*Lingelbach* | Een Zee Haven, na Lingelbach	Casper de Haas	(Unknown) fl 1:8
1808/06/11	RMRIJ	0047	*Na Lingelbach* | Een Valke Jagt | *Mat:* op doek		(Sold) fl 7:10 V
1808/06/11	RMRIJ	0048	*Na Lingelbach* | Een Venetiaansche Zeehaven, fraai en verdienstig geschilderd | *Mat:* op doek		(Sold) fl 30:10 Luchtmans

Lingelbach, Johannes (manner)

1801/04/13	AMSCH	0103	*J. Lingelbach* | Een Levantsche Stad en Zeehaven met trotsche Gebouwen en Vaartuigen, ryk gestoffeerd met een menigte Beelden; het zonlicht maakt dit stuk aangenaam, en is geschilderd op Doek, in de manier van J. Lingelbach | *Mat:* op doek *Size:* hoog 27, breed 38 duim	Pierre Fouquet, junior	(Sold) fl 49 Lafontaine
1802/12/13	AMSCH	0216	*Lingelbagh* | Een Heer te Paard rydende; fix geschiiderd [sic] op Paneel, in de manier van Lingelbagh | *Mat:* op paneel	Schley [for] Lauwers	(Sold) fl 1 van Dijl
1803/09/07	AMSCH	0245	*J. Lingelbach* | Een Italiaansche Zéehaven, by de Vestmuur van eene Stad en treffelyk Gebouw, vertoonen zig staande en rustende Lieden, by eenige Koopmans Goederen, verder beladen Muil-Ezels en Zéegezicht; bevallig geschilderd, in de manier van J. Lingelbach [Un port de mer d'Italie ; près de la muraille d'une ville, un bel édifice ; plusieurs ouvriers occupés à transporter et à rouler des marchandises ; plus loin des mulets chargés et en perspective la mer ; tableau d'une touche agréable dans la manière de Lingelbach] | *Mat:* op doek *Size:* hoog 42, breed 32 duim	Smidt	(Sold) fl 15:10 J Roelofs
1806/05/05	AMSCH	0232	*Lingelbach* | Een Levantsche Zeehaven, met een ménigte Gebouwen, Scheepen, vol gewoel van Beelden and andere stoffagie; als Lingelbach	V[inkeles]	(Sold) fl 1:5 Levy Pakker
1810/10/11	AMSCH	0237	*J. Lingelbach* | Eene Rijschool met Heeren te Paard; als J. Lingelbach	A	(Sold) fl 5 van Leen

Lingelbach, Johannes (manner; and Aalst)

1802/11/01	DOBRA	0149	*van Aalst; Lingelbach* | Een Boomrijk Landschap, door van Aalst. De stoffagie als van Lingelbach | *Mat:* op paneel *Size:* hoog 15, br. 18 ½ duim		(Unknown) fl 40:10 for lots 149 & 150
1802/11/01	DOBRA	0150	*van Aalst; Lingelbach* | Een dito [Boomrijk Landschap], als boven [De stoffagie als van Lingelbach]; door van Aalst | *Mat:* op paneel *Size:* hoog 15, br. 18 ½ duim		(Unknown) fl 40:10 for lots 149 & 150

Lint, Peter van

1808/09/13	HABRU	0058	*P. van Lindt* | Een Boere Werf, gestoffeerd met veel Bijwerk		(Unknown) fl 2:14

Linthorst, Jacobus

1807/08/26	AMSCH	0115	*J. Linthorst* | Dit fraai kunststuk steld voor een ryke Ordonnantie van verscheiden Bloemen en Vrugten, welken op een Marmeren Tafel geplaatst zyn; de Vrugten zyn transparand, en de Bloemen, van een dunne Penceelsbehandeling en is een der beste stukken | *Size:* hoog 41, breed 35 duim	Joseph Vallette	(Sold) fl 101 T van Iperen
1809/06/13	AMSCH	0095	*J. Linthorst* | Twee stuks, ovaal Formaat, op gecouleurde Marmere Tafels, ziet men in de eene verschillende zoort van bevallige Bloemen, waarop verscheide Vlinders aazen; den anderen vertoont diversche zoort van Smakelijke Vruchten, als Persiken, Druiven, Granaatappelen, enz.; beide zeer natuurlljk [sic] en uitvoerig gepenceeld | *Mat:* op doek *Fmt:* ovaal *Size:* ieder hoog 15, breed 12 duim	Q	(Bought In) fl 11
1809/06/13	AMSCH	0096	*J. Linthorst* | Twee stuks rijk geordoneerde Manden met Bloemen, als roode, witte en bonten Roosen, Hijacinten, Tulpen, Papavers en anderen, staande op Marmere Tafels, voor dezelven eenige smaakelijke Vruchten, als witte en blaauwe Druiven, Persiken, Abricoozen, Canteloupen en anderen, waarop Insectens azen; helder en delicaat gepenceeld | *Mat:* op doek *Size:* hoog 19, breed 16 duim	[Gruyter?]	(Bought In) fl 26

Liss, Johann (Pan)

1801/06/13	LNDLS	0032	*van der Lis* | Een bergagtig Landschap, op den voorgrond rustende Nimphen, delicaat, op paneel | *Mat:* op paneel *Size:* hoog 10, breed 13 duimen	D van R	(Sold) fl 15 Richter S [for] Stevens
1802/09/06	AMSCH	0064	*J. Lis* | Twee stuks bevallige Arcadische Landschappen, met Gebergten en Geboomten, en Waterval, beide gestoffeerd met naakte Beeldjes,	Wed Grave [or others]	(Sold) fl 28 Pruijssenaar

			zoo rustende, als danssende, en andere die zig in een Riviertje baaden; uitvoerig en zonagtig behandeld | *Mat:* op paneel *Size:* ieder hoog 14, breed 12 duim		
1802/12/13	AMSCH	0096	*Jan Lis* | In een hoog Bergachtig Landschap, ziet men eenige vrolyke Bachanten, ter zyden in 't Water eenige Badende Nimphen; uitvoerig geschilderd | *Mat:* op paneel *Size:* hoog 20, breed 21 duim	Pruyssenaar [for] A	(Sold) fl 0:14 L Pakker
1803/09/07	AMSCH	0099	*J. Lis* | In een Landschap met eenig Geboomten ziet men twee Nimphen elkander omhelzende, verzelt van een Minnewigt, by een stil Waterbeekje; uitvoerig op Paneel [Dans un paysage orné de quelques arbres, on voit deux Nymphes qui s'embrassent ; elles sont accompagnées d'un amour auprès d'un ruisseau limpide ; ce tableau est d'un fini agréable] | *Mat:* op paneel *Size:* hoog 10, breed 13 duim	Smidt	(Sold) fl 1:10 Toselli
1805/10/09	HGBSM	0124	*J. Lis* | Een landschap met eenige honden, op de voorgrond een mans figuur gedeeltelyk naakt en voor over bukkende om in 't water te zien | *Mat:* op paneel *Size:* hoog 13 breet 17 duim	T H van Willigen [or others]	(Sold) fl 10 De Gelder
1807/06/10	HGBSM	0076	*J. van der Lis* | Een heuvelagtig Landschap met geboomte, op de voorgrond een water met badende Nimphen, helder en konstig geschilderd | *Mat:* op doek *Size:* hoog 32, breed 38 duim	Abraham Delfos [or others]	(Sold) fl 44:15 de Gelder
			Liss, Johann (Pan) (and Keirincx, Alex.)		
1809/04/17	AMSCH	0048	*Keerings; Lis* | Een Boomrijk Landschap, ter zijde een stille Rivier, met verscheidene Badende Nimphen; fiks geschilderd | *Mat:* op paneel *Size:* hoog 21, breed 28 duim	T	(Sold) fl 6
			Locatelli, Andrea		
1808/06/13	AMSCH	0096	*Locatelli* | Twee stuks Gezichten in het Colliséum te Rome, fraai gestoffeerd met Beelden en Beesten. Het zonlicht doet eene schoone uitwerking in deze Tafereelen, welke van eene allezins [sic] meesterlijke penceelsbehandeling zijn | *Mat:* op doek *Size:* ieder is hoog 39, breed 29 duim	R[oos]	(Sold) fl 300 Reyers pour Allard
1809/06/13	AMSCH	0098	*J. Locatelli* | Een Land- en Watergezicht, met grootsche Gebouwen en Beeldjes, gestoffeerd | *Mat:* op doek *Fmt:* rond *Size:* 15 duim *Notes:* The artist's name was given as "J. Locatelli" but we have assumed this is an error.	E	(Sold) fl 3 du Pree
1810/07/26	AMSCH	0046	*Locatelli* | Een gezigt van het oude Paleis en Vatican te Rome: uitmuntend met Beeldjes gestoffeerd. Zijnde een der beste stukken van dezen Meester | *Mat:* op doek *Size:* hoog 43, breed 48 duimen	Cassino	(Bought In) fl 41
1810/07/26	AMSCH	0099	*Locatelli* | Een Italiaansch Gezigt, met Gebouwen en Beelden | *Mat:* op paneel	Cassino	(Bought In) fl 2
			Looten, Jan		
1802/05/24	HGBAK	0032	*Jan Louten* | Een boschachtig Landschap, op de voorgrond eenige rustende Reizigers, in 't verschiet eenige gebouwen en bergen, zeer fix en wel behandeld, door Jan Louten 1656, hoog 11 duim, breed 1 d, paneel, zwarte lyst en verg. bies | *Mat:* op paneel *Size:* hoog 11 duim, breed 1 duim *Inscr:* Jan Louten 1656 (signed and dated?) *Notes:* It is unclear whether the name and date are inscribed on the painting.	Mejuffrouw A van der Mieden	(Sold) fl 3:5 van Giezen
1805/07/10	AMSCH	0090	*J. Looten* | Twee stuks Boom en Duinachtige Landschappen, met helder Spiegelende Waters; zonachtig op Doek | *Mat:* op doek *Size:* hoog 36, breed 28 duim	V[inkeles] [for] N	(Sold) fl 13:10 LaFontaine
1805/12/16	AMSCH	0037	*J. Loten* | Een Boomryk Landschap, op de Voorgrond met Beelden gestoffeerd, gaande over een Brug, verders een aangenaam verschiet; meesterlyk op Doek | *Mat:* op doek *Size:* hoog 54, breed 70 duim	R[oos]	(Bought In) fl 5
1806/08/20	HGBSM	0209	*J. Looten* | Een Landschap zeer natuurlijk | *Mat:* op doek *Size:* hoog 33, breed 53 ½ duim	Macalester Loup [or others]	(Sold) fl 40 Ph Meij
1810/06/20	AMSCH	0041	*J. Looten* | Een bevallig boomrijk Landschap, ter zijde met eenen opgaanden Weg, gestoffeerd met een wandelende Heer, Dame en gaande Huislieden; verder eenige omgevallene Boomstammen en een Dorp-toren in het verschiet. Zeer natuurlijk behandeld | *Mat:* op doek *Size:* hoog 54, breed 70 duimen	R[oos]	(Sold) fl 13 Hodges
			Looten, Jan (and Wouwerman, P.)		
1809/04/17	AMSCH	0052	*J. Looten; P. Wouwerman* | Een Boschachtig Landschap, gestoffeerd met een Heer en Dame te Paard, waar bij Jagers met hunnen Honden, en een aangenaam verschiet; natuurlijk van schildering, door J. Looten, gestoffeerd, door P. Wouwerman | *Mat:* op doek *Size:* hoog 42, breed 32 duim	A	(Sold) fl 8:10
			Loren, S. [Unidentified]		
1809/07/25	HGBSM	0053	*S. Loren* | Een Vrouwtje by een Spinnewiel zittende, met een jakje met bont gevoert en een witte satyne rok aan | *Mat:* op paneel *Size:* hoog 9 en een half, breed 7 en een half duim	D van der Aa [or] E B ten Dall	(Sold) fl 54 Gruiter
			Lorme, Anthonie de		
1808/06/13	AMSCH	0221	*A. de Lorme* | Een Kerk van binnen te zien; fraai van licht en bruin	E M Engelberts	(Sold) fl 18 Glad

1809/06/13	AMSCH	0094	*A. de Lorme* | Een Protestansche Kerk, van binnen rijk gestoffeerd met Heeren en Dames, speelende Jongens, ter zijde een Doodgraaver, bézig een Graf te openen; fraai van licht en doorzicht, en kunstig geschilderd | *Mat:* op paneel *Size:* hoog 31, breed 40 duim	Y	(Sold) fl 13:5 du Pree
1810/03/26	RMMUY	0011	*A. de Lorme* | Een gedeelte van de Groote of Sint Laurens Kerk te Rotterdam. Men ziet nog daar verbeeld het kleine Orgel, zoo als het voorheen is gesteld geweest. De keurige uitvoering en verkiezing der lichten en schaduwen, geven eene ongemeene verdienste aan dit Schilderij [Vue intérieure de l'Eglise de Saint Laurent à Rotterdam. On y voit le petit orgue tel qu'il s'y trouvoit autrefois ; plusieurs figures s'y promênent, ce tableau fin et précieusement exécuté, est piquant et agréable.] | *Mat:* op doek *Size:* hoog 30, breed 24 ½ duimen	Daniel de Jongh Az	(Sold) fl 180 Ringeling S'Hage
1810/08/01	AMSCH	0054	*Lorme (A. de)* | Een gedeelte der Nieuwe-Kerk te Amsterdam, van binnen te zien, met het kleine Orgel, Wapenborden en verder bijwerk [Vue persective intérieure d'une partie de l'Eglise Neuve à Amsterdam, donnant sur la petitte Orgue, et sur des Blasons et Armories, étant ornée de plus de quelqu'autres accessoires] | *Annots:* très bon. (NGW) *Mat:* op doek *Size:* hoog 30, breed 25 duimen	Mr Pieter de Smeth van Alphen	(Sold) fl 170 Van Heekeren Van Brandsenburg te Utrecht

Lorme, Anthonie de (and Palamedesz., P. (I))

1802/02/16	AMSCH	0070	*de Lorne; P. Palanudes* | Een capitaal Binnegezigt van een trots Kerkgebouw, versiert met Orgel, Predikstoel en brandende Kerkkroon. ryk gestoffeerd met wandelende beelden, zoo Heeren als Dames, het kaarsligt geeft een natuurlyke werking, alles is kragtig gepenceeld, door de Lorne, en de stoffagie door P. Palanudes | *Notes:* The artist was presumably Anthonie Palamedesz. and not Palamedes Palamedesz (I).	C	(Bought In) fl 40
1803/06/20	AMSCH	0018	*J. de Lorme; P. Palamedes* | Een Protestande Kerk, van binnen te zien by Kaarslicht, het geen een byzondere werking van licht en bruin geeft, de ryke stoffagie door P. Palamedes, maakt te samen een geheel uit, zynde van de beste van J. de Lorme | *Mat:* op paneel *Size:* hoog 44, breed 62 duim *Notes:* The artist's name was given as "J. de Lorme" but we have assumed this is an error. The second artist was presumably Anthonie Palamedesz. and not Palamedes Palamedesz (I).	Roos [for] E	(Sold) fl 50 B Kooij

Lorme, Anthonie de (manner)

1810/06/06	RMMUY	0111	*de Lorme* | Een klein fraaij Kerkje van binnen te zien. Als door de Lorme | *Mat:* op paneel		(Unknown) fl 14:10

Loth, Johann Carl (Carlotto)

1803/04/27	AMSCH	000H	*C. Lotti* | Deux Pieces, la Chute d'Adam & d'Eve, & la mort d'Abel | *Size:* h. 47, l. 59 pouces	B	(Bought In) fl 50

Lourens, C. [Unidentified]

1809/10/20	UTWLD	0020	*C. Lourens* | Een Boeren gezelschap door C. Lourens	J J van Rhyn	(Unknown)

Loutherbourg, Philip James de

1803/12/12	AMSCH	0051	*J. Lautherbourg* | Twee stuks Bergachtige Landschappen, fraai gestoffeerd met Herders met hun Vée; meesterlyk op Paneel | *Mat:* op paneel *Size:* hoog 16, breed 19 duim	D	(Sold) fl 40 Coclers
1803/12/12	AMSCH	0052	*J. Lautherbourg* | Een dito [stuk] dito [Bergachtig Landschap] | *Mat:* op paneel *Size:* hoog 5, breed 7 duim *Notes:* It is unclear what "dito" refers to in the title.	D	(Sold) fl 4:5 Hijm Pakker

Louw, Pieter

1801/11/10	AMPOS	0028	*P. Louw* | 1 bevallige Dame, met een bloem, zeer uitvoerig door P. Louw, 1757 | *Inscr:* P. Louw, 1757 (signed and dated?) *Notes:* It is unclear whether the name and date are inscribed on the painting.		(Unknown)

Lubienietski, Christoffel

1802/05/05	AMSCH	0117	*Lubinitsky* | Twee stuks bevallige Ordonnantiën, de een verbeeld een Haringvrouwtje, schynende aan een Jongetje een Haring te verkoopen, en 't andere een Schoorsteenveeger met zyn Jongen, beiden zeer dun en delicaat geschilderd | *Mat:* op doek *Size:* hoog 22, breed 19 duim	A	(Sold) fl 35 Pruijssenaar [for] R
1802/06/28	AMSCH	0106	*C. Luberitski* | Het Pourtrait van den Dichter Willink, delicaat gepenceeld, door C. Luberitski, op Doek | *Mat:* op doek *Size:* hoog 17, breed 13 duim	Anna Elink	(Sold) fl 1 Taak
1804/05/07	AMSCH	0098	*Lubinitsky. (C.)* | In een Boere School zit den Schoolmeester bézig den Jongeling een plak te geven, agter deze een ander, en in 't verschiet eenige vegtende en andere Jongens, verders allerlei Schoolgereedschappen; natuurlyk behandeld | *Mat:* op doek *Size:* hoog 23, breed 20 duim	Roos [for] A	(Sold) fl 206 Tijs
1806/08/13	AMSCH	0099	*Lubinitsky. (C.)* | Twee stuks, 't eene een Vogelenkoper in een Landschap, en 't andere een bevallig Vischvrouwtje; beide delicaat van schildering | *Mat:* op doek *Size:* Ieder hoog 15, breed 12 duim	Vinkeles [for] F	(Sold) fl 7:10 de Meyer
1808/04/26	GDAN	0088	*Lebaniski* | Verbeeldende een Buitenverblijf, waar op een Heer en Dame wandelen | *Size:* hoog 21, breed 16 duim	G H Fortuyn	(Unknown)
1810/06/20	AMSCH	0044	*Lubinitzki* | Twee stuks; een Tuinman met een Mandje met Gevogelte en een bevallig Meisje, met een Emmer met Visch. Vrolijk | *Mat:* op doek *Size:* hoog 13, breed 11 duimen	A	(Sold) fl 13 Cassino

Lucas van Leyden

1808/08/23	AMSCH	0093	*Leijden. (Lucas van)* | Deeze rijke Ordonantie vertoont in een Landschap, bij de ruïne van een Gebouw, Maria met het Kindeken op haar schoot, verzelt van St. Joseph, voor dezelven leggen eerbiedig nedergeknield, de Koningen die den Heiland aanbidden en Geschenken offeren, verder een meenigte Lieden van hun gevolg, te paard en te voet; het is krachtig van koloriet en uitvoerig behandeld | *Mat:* op paneel	C	(Sold) fl 21 Spruit
1808/09/13	HABRU	0056	*L. van Lijden* | Een oud Pourtrait		(Sold) fl 1:2 V D W[illigen]
1808/11/12	HGSCR	0015	*Lucas van Leyden* | Vier stuks verbeeldende de Vier Euangelisten [sic], extra fraai en uitvoerig op koper geschildert door Lucas van Leyden en bekend door de vier prentjes, daar van door de schilder gegraveerd 1518. en welke hier agter gevoegt zyn, deze wel geconserveerde stukjes zyn zeer fraai en extra raar in vier antieke gebeeldhouwde zwaar vergulde lysten | *Mat:* op koper	Mr J van Buren	(Unknown) fl 41
1810/07/26	AMSCH	0049	*Leiden (Lucas van)* | Eene Lezende Vrouw in rijke kleeding. Krachtig en alleruitvoerigst van schildering | *Mat:* op paneel *Size:* hoog 25, breed 21 duimen	Cassino	(Sold) fl 32 de Vries

Lucas van Leyden (or Lucas van Leyden, manner)

1803/08/24	HGKAN	0082	*Lucas van Leyden* | Een Maria met het Kindje, fraay en uitvoerig geschilderd, door of in de trant van Lucas van Leyden	[Teissier] [or others]	(Unknown) fl 3:4

Lucas van Leyden (or Lucas van Leyden, manner; or Dürer, or Dürer, manner)

1810/06/06	RMMUY	0088	*Lucas van Leiden; Albert Durer* | Een doode Christus, Maria en een Heilige. Ongemeen uitvoerig en raar. Door of als Lucas van Leiden, of Albert Durer | *Mat:* op paneel		(Sold) fl 5 Luchtmans

Lucas van Leyden (copy after)

1803/09/07	AMSCH	0272	*L. van Lyden* | De Aanbidding der Koningen; zynde gevolgd na de Prent van L. van Lyden [L'adoration des trois rois ; imité d'une estampe de van Lyden] | *Mat:* op paneel *Size:* hoog 24, breed 19 duim	Smidt	(Sold) fl 7 Gruiter

Ludick, Lodewijk van

1803/08/01	AMSCH	0018	*Ludick. (J)* | Een Boschagtig Landschap, met twee lieden, en belaaden Muilezels, op de voorgrond een Herder, zittende te paard, waarby eenige Schaapen, natuurlyk behandeld | *Mat:* op doek *Size:* hoog 20, breed 24 duim *Notes:* The artist's name was given as "Ludick. (J)" but we have assumed this is an error.	J	(Sold) fl 13:10 Pruijssenaar

Lundens, Gerrit

1801/03/16	AMSCH	0018	*Lundens* | Vier stuks, alwaar een Bruid gevreid word, trouwd, bruiloft houd, en vervolgens naar Bed geleid word, geestig	K[ip]	(Sold) fl 12:10 Gruiter
1801/06/13	LNDLS	0042	*G. Lundens* | Een Binnenvertrek, waarin een Man bij het vuur zit, die zijn tabakspijp aan een brandhout aansteekt, nevens hem zit een bevallig vrouwtje, en verder een persoon, die bij een ton schijnt te slaapen, alles zeer uitvoerig, op paneel | *Mat:* op paneel *Size:* hoog 14, breed 12 duimen	D van R	(Sold) fl 30 A Delfos
1801/08/19	AMSCH	0057	*Lundens* | Twee vrolyke Boerenstukken, in het eene ziet men de Bruid na Bed brengen, en in het andere 't Kraambed van de zelven	Pruyssen[r]	(Sold) fl 7 Gruiter
1801/10/06	AMSCH	0042	*G. Lundens* | Voor een Buitenhuis vertoont zig een gezelschap van Dames en Heeren, op de voorgrond een Jager met dood Wilt, helder en fraay gepenceeld | *Mat:* op paneel *Size:* hoog 43, breed 33 duim	M	(Sold) fl 32 Theijs
1801/10/06	AMSCH	0043	*G. Lundens* | Twee stuks Binnehuyzen, byde gestoffeerd met verliefde Boeren en Boerinnen, geestig behandeld | *Mat:* op doek *Size:* yder hoog 12, breed 10 duim	M	(Sold) fl 36 van der Schley H [for] Hijnen
1801/11/10	AMPOS	0024	*G. Lunders* | Speelende en vrolyke Boeren, in een Binnenhuis, door G. Lunders, 1670 | *Inscr:* G. Lunders, 1670 (signed and dated?) *Notes:* It is unclear whether the name and date are inscribed on the painting.		(Unknown)
1801/11/10	AMPOS	0025	*G. Lunders* | 1 dito [speelende en vrolyke Boeren] dito [in een Binnenhuis], als door dito [G. Lunders]		(Unknown)
1802/02/16	AMSCH	0076	*J. Lundens* | In een dito [Binnehus] Vertrek, vertoonen zig vrolyke Huislieden, zig vermakende met het spel handjeplak, plaisant geschilderd | *Notes:* The artist's name was given as "J. Lundens" but we have assumed this is an error. It is unclear what "dito" refers to in the title.	C	(Sold) fl 35 Coclers
1802/05/05	AMSCH	0114	*G. Lundens* | Een Boere Binnenhuis, waarin verscheiden Boeren en Boerinnen zich met speelen als anderzints vermaaken, verders eenig Bywerk, zeer natuurlyk en fraai geschilderd | *Mat:* op paneel *Size:* hoog 23, breed 24 duim	A	(Sold) fl 77 Ackina
1802/05/05	AMSCH	0115	*G. Lundens* | Eenige Lieden op het Verkeerbord speelende, waarby een vrolyke Boer met een Kan in de hand; de karakters zyn geestig en uitvoerig gepenceeld | *Mat:* op paneel *Size:* hoog 13, breed 10 duim	A	(Sold) fl 21:10 Spruit
1802/05/05	AMSCH	0116	*G. Lundens* | Twee Boeren Binnenhuizen	J	(Sold) fl 1:10 A Schotte

1802/09/29	AMSCH	0033	*J. Lundens* | Twee Binnehuisjes, ieder hoog 10, breed 8 duim. Paneel. Verbeeldende twee Chirurgyns Winkels, de carakters der figuren zyn wel waargenoomen, en de penceelbehandeling is dun en natuurlyk [Deux Tableaux faisant pendans, offrant des Boutiques de Chirurgien. Les figures portent les vrais caractères analogues aux sujets. Plusieurs accessoires y sont placés avec Intelligence. Ces petits morceaux sont traités avec beaucoup d'art, d'un Pinceau délicat et d'un bel Effet.] | *Mat:* op paneel *Size:* ieder hoog 10, breed 8 duim *Notes:* The artist's name was given as "J. Lundens" but we have assumed this is an error.	[Labouchere?]	(Sold) fl 41 Coclers
1802/12/13	AMSCH	0097	*J. Lundens* | Twee stuks, verbeeldénde 't eene een Kerk, waar men een paar ziet Trouwen, en 't andere waar men bézig is, Bruilof te houden; beide geestig gecaracteriseerd, en meesterachtig gepenceeld | *Mat:* op doek *Size:* hoog 26, breed 21 duim *Notes:* The artist's name was given as "J. Lundens" but we have assumed this is an error.	Pruyssenaar [for] A	(Sold) fl 3:5 Gruiter
1802/12/13	AMSCH	0105	*J. Lundens* | Een Binnenhuis met vrolyke Boeren, en Boerinnen | *Size:* hoog 15, breed 12 duim *Notes:* The artist's name was given as "J. Lundens" but we have assumed this is an error.	Pruyssenaar [for] D	(Sold) fl 2:10 L Pakker
1803/06/20	AMSCH	0045	*J. Lundens* | In een Boere Binnenhuis ziet men een Boere Bruiloft van een ménigte Gasten, op de voorgrond danssen Bruid en Bruidegom, alles is geestig gepenceeld door J. Lundens, op Doek | *Mat:* op doek *Size:* hoog 20, breed 24 duim *Notes:* The artist's name was given as "J. Lundens" but we have assumed this is an error.	Roos [for] C	(Sold) fl 30:10 Gruiter
1803/06/20	AMSCH	0049	*G. Lundens* | Een Smits Winkel, van binnen te zien, zyn twee Smits bézig met Smeeden, een Boer staat 'er by te kyken, het licht is spreekend en de behandeling fix, door G. Lundens, op Paneel | *Mat:* op paneel *Size:* hoog 12, breed 9 duim	Roos [for] C	(Sold) fl 11:10 Gruiter
1803/12/12	AMSCH	0053	*Lundens* | Een ryke Ordenantie van verscheide Beelden, voorstellende een Boeren-Bruiloft, van een zeer uitvoerige schildering; door Lundens, op Paneel | *Mat:* op paneel *Size:* hoog 34, breed 44 duim	B	(Sold) fl 56 W^{l} Reijers
1804/08/08	AMSCH	0106	*J. Lundens* | Een Boeren Binnenhuis of Herberg, ryk gestoffeerd met vrolyke huislieden, zoo Mans als Vrouwen, die zich met danssen, zingen en drinken vermaaken, op de voorgrond speeld een bevallig Boerinnetje op de Phiool; de ordinantie is geestig en bevallig van schildering | *Mat:* op paneel *Size:* hoog 22, breed 25 duim *Notes:* The artist's name was given as "J. Lundens" but we have assumed this is an error.	Schley [for] A	(Sold) fl 30 Jan Spaan
1804/10/08	RMCNL	0009	*Lundens* | Gezigt van een Straat, waar in een Tamboer en Trompetter met verscheide omstanders	A t'Hooft	(Unknown)
1804/10/16	DLOND	0128	*J. Lundens* | Een Vrolyk Gezelschap. Une Compagnie joyeuse | *Mat:* op koper *Fmt:* ellipt *Size:* hoog 3, breed 3 ½ *Notes:* The artist's name was given as "J. Lundens" but we have assumed this is an error.		(Unknown)
1804/10/16	DLOND	0129	*J. Lundens* | Een Rokende Boer en verder Gezelschap. Un Paysan qui fume sa pipe &c. | *Mat:* op paneel *Size:* hoog 8, breed 5 *Notes:* The artist's name was given as "J. Lundens" but we have assumed this is an error.		(Unknown)
1805/07/03	AMSCH	0105	*G. Lundens* | Een vrolyk Gezelschap van diversche Figuuren, welken zich lustig vermaken, onder het gespeel van twee Musikanten; geestig geordineerd en geschilderd | *Mat:* op paneel *Size:* hoog 21, breed 28 duim	C	(Sold) fl 85 Gruyter
1805/07/03	AMSCH	0106	*G. Lundens* | In een Chirurgyns Winkel, ziet men den Meester bézig om een Patient een Accident op den rug te verbinden, waarby twee Vrouwen aandachtig staan te kyken; geestig behandeld op Paneel | *Mat:* op paneel *Size:* hoog 21, breed 30 duim	C	(Sold) fl 5:5 L Pakker
1806/08/13	AMSCH	0326	*Lundens. (G.)* | Twee vrolyke Boere Binnehuizen, in de eene ziet men 't na Bed brengen van een Bruid, en 't andere een Kraambed, beide delicaat en uitvoerig gepenceeld | *Mat:* op doek *Size:* hoog 25, breed 31 duim	Vinkeles [for] G[ruyter]	(Sold) fl 5 Schumacher
1807/08/26	AMSCH	0120	*J. Lundens* | Een Binnenhuis, verbeeldende een Chirurgyns Winkel, in dezelve ziet men het berugte Jantje van Emnes, die door den Meester het Brandmerk uit den Rug wordt gesnéden; nevens dezelve twee staande Vrouwen; krachtig behandeld | *Mat:* op paneel *Size:* hoog 31, breed 30 duim *Notes:* The artist's name was given as "J. Lundens" but we have assumed this is an error.	de Vries	(Sold) fl 9 Gruiter
1808/08/23	AMSCH	0223	*J. Lundens* | In een Binnehuis zitten vrolijke Boeren, een derzelve speelt op de Fiool, twee schijnen te luisteren, en een ander zit bij de haardstede; meesterlijk op Paneel geschilderd | *Mat:* op paneel *Notes:* The artist's name was given as "J. Lundens" but we have assumed this is an error.	Z	(Sold) fl 9 Spruit
1808/09/13	HABRU	0057	*J. Lundens* | Een Binnehuis, waarin een Varken op een Ladder hangt, welke door de Slagter schijnt afgespoeld te worden, met verder veel Beeldjes | *Notes:* The artist's name was given as "J. Lundens" but we have assumed this is an error.		(Unknown) fl 18:10
1808/11/28	AMSCH	0039	*Lundens* | Een Boeren Binnenhuis, gestoffeerd met verscheide Huislieden en een Varken op de Leder, ter zijde staat een Jongen met een Blaas in de Hand, geestig | *Mat:* op paneel	Z	(Sold) fl 130 A Kits
1809/04/22	AMYVR	0075	*H. Lundens* | Twee Boeren, bij een Vat hunne Pijp stoppende; krachtig | *Mat:* op paneel *Size:* hoog 9, breed 7 duim *Notes:* The artist's name was given as "H. Lundens" but we have assumed this is an error.	de Bruin	(Sold) fl 4:10 du Pree

1809/06/13	AMSCH	0223	*J. Lundens* | In een Binnenhuis zit een verliefde Huisman eene Boerinnetje te liefkoozen, terzijde staat een Vat, waarop een Bierkan geplaatst is; fiks op Paneel geschilderd | *Mat:* op paneel *Notes:* The artist's name was given as "J. Lundens" but we have assumed this is an error.	R[ijfsnijder]	(Sold) fl 5:10 Buck
1809/07/19	AMSCH	0033	*Lunders (G.)* | Voor een Buitenhuis, onder een Wijngaard, zit een Gezelschap van vrolijke Huislieden bij eene gedekte Tafel, op den voorgrond een Boer en Boerin, welke zig met danzen vermaken, terwijl andere op de viool en lier spelen. Dit stukje is bevallig, uitvoerig, en fraai behandeld | *Mat:* op paneel *Size:* hoog 23, breed 20 duim	[Wijkersloot?]	(Sold) fl 30 Reijdon
1810/06/20	AMSCH	0043	*J. Lundens* | Een Binnenhuis, met vrolijke, drinkende en liefkoozende Boeren en Boerinnen. Kloek geschilderd | *Mat:* op doek *Size:* hoog 20, breed 26 duimen *Notes:* The artist's name was given as "J. Lundens" but we have assumed this is an error.	S	(Sold) fl 1:15 T Spaan
1810/10/11	AMSCH	0047	*J. Lunduns* | Een Boeren Binnehuis of Herberg, op den voorgrond een Heer, staande nevens een bevallig Meisje, verder vrolijke Huislieden; geestig geschilderd | *Mat:* op paneel *Size:* hoog 29, breed 23 duimen *Notes:* The artist's name was given as "J. Lunduns" but we have assumed this is an error.	Y	(Sold) fl 14:10 van Leen
			Lundens, Gerrit (manner)		
1802/05/05	AMSCH	0250	*Lundens* | Een Boere Binnenhuis, met vrolyke Boeren en Boerinnen, zich met dansen en speelen vermakende, in de manier van Lundens | *Mat:* op paneel *Size:* hoog 23, breed 35 duim	G	(Sold) fl 1:15 L Pakker
1807/08/26	AMSCH	0307	*Lundens* | Een Binnenhuis, gestoffeerd met vrolyke Boeren en Boerinnen; in de manier van Lundens | *Mat:* op doek	Yver [for] S	(Bought In) fl 2
1809/04/22	AMYVR	0191	*Lundens* | Een vrolijk Gezelschap; als Lundens	de Bruin	(Sold) fl 11:10 du Pree
			Lust, Antoni de		
1804/10/29	HRBAU	0050	*Lust, (De)* | Een zeer fraaie Feston van keurige Bloemen, welken op eene uitmuntende wyze gegroept en geschakeerd zyn; allen zeer dun en uitvoerig behandeld, en kunnende de eer van dien Meester volkomen in wezen houden | *Mat:* op doek *Size:* hoog 26 ½, breed 46 duim	Simon Styl	(Unknown)
1810/10/10	MGCIT	0098	*Lust* | Een dito [Stuk] met Bloemen en Vruchten	Caspar van Citters	(Unknown)
			Lust, D. de [Unidentified]		
1809/07/25	HGBSM	0084	*D. de Lust* | Het Portret van den Burgemeester van der Werf, in het grauw Geschildert, verbeeldende een Basrelief, omringt met een Krans van differente Bloemen, waar op Insecten azen; uitvoerig en delicaat Geschildert, niet minder als Rachel Ruis, door D. de Lust, 1659 | *Mat:* op doek *Size:* hoog 37, breed 30 en een halve duim *Inscr:* D. de Lust, 1659 (signed and dated?) *Notes:* It is unclear whether the name and date are inscribed on the painting.	D van der Aa [or] E B ten Dall	(Sold) fl 40 Oosthuyzen [or] L Voerman
			Luyken, Jan		
1805/10/21	GRBOL	0021	*J. v Luiken* | Een Riviergezicht, waar by enige Visschers en andere Stoffagie, ryk geordonneerd, en stout geschilderd	Gerardus Nicolaus Heerkens	(Unknown)
			Maas, F. [Unidentified]		
1806/08/13	AMSCH	0116	*Maas. (F.)* | Een bevroozen Rivier- en Dorpgezicht, ryk gestoffeerd met Arresleeden enz.; plaisant geschilderd | *Mat:* op paneel *Size:* hoog 22, breed 27 duim	Roos	(Sold) fl 6 Hymans
			Maas, Jan (Johannes)		
1802/09/06	AMSCH	0159	*J. Maas* | Een Jongeling met een Hond; en een Vogel op zyn Vinger; meesterlyk | *Mat:* op paneel	Mevrouw Achtienhoven	(Sold) fl 2:5 Th^{s} Spaan
1806/08/20	HGBSM	0131	*Js. Maas* | Twee Stuks Portraiten, zijnde een Heer en eene Dame | *Mat:* op doek *Notes:* The artist was presumably Nicolaes Maes and not Jan (Johannes) Maas.	Macalester Loup [or others]	(Sold) fl 1:2 Ab Salomon
1808/11/28	AMSCH	0043	*J. Maas* | Een Hofgezicht, op de voorgrond een staande Jongeling, beneevens een zittend Meisje, houdende een Mandje met Vruchten op haar schoot, in het verschiet twee wandelende Heeren, fiks behandeld | *Mat:* op doek *Size:* hoog 33, breed 30 duim	S	(Sold) fl 0:14 L Pakker
1809/05/26	HADAA	0044	*J. Maas* | Een Landschap, gestoffeerd met beeldjes, paarden en honden, fraaij	Mejuffrouw de Wed David Heemskerk [or others]	(Unknown)
			Maas, P. [Unidentified] (manner)		
1801/04/23	AMYVR	0018	*P. Maas* | Een Landschap, gestoffeerd met Heeren en Dames die ter Jagt gaan, in de manier van P. Maas		(Sold) fl 1 ¾ Gruyter
1801/04/23	AMYVR	0019	*P. Maas* | Een Bergachtig Landschap, gestoffeerd met een Hartenjagt, dito [in de manier van] dito [P. Maas]		(Sold) fl 3 ¾ A Mayer
			Maat, N. [Unidentified]		
1807/08/26	AMSCH	0138	*N. Maat* | Het Afbeeldzel van eene Dame, halverlyf, in een deftige kleeding, staande in een Landschap; meesterlyk en fiks geschilderd | *Mat:* op paneel	v d Schley [for] L	(Sold) fl 0:12 Spruit

1807/08/26	AMSCH	0139	*N. Maat* | Een Mans Pourtrait	Roos	(Sold) fl 2 Coclair
1807/08/26	AMSCH	0140	*N. Maat* | Twee zeer fraaije Mans en Vrouwe Pourtraite	Roos	(Sold) fl 3:5 du Pree
1807/08/26	AMSCH	0141	*N. Maat* | Een Vrouwe en een Mans Pourtrait	Roos	(Sold) fl 1 du Pree
			Maddersteeg, Michiel		
1807/08/26	AMSCH	0131[b]	*Maddersteg* | Twee stuks stille Waters, by het opkomen der Zon, gestoffeerd met zylende en dryvende Vaartuigen, Visschers in hunne Schuiten, en ruime verschieten; zeer natuurlyk, de eene door L. Bakhuysen, en de ander door Maddersteg | *This Lot:* Een stil Water; lot 131[a] by Backhuysen *Mat:* op doek *Size:* hoog 16, breed 16 duim	de Vries	(Sold) fl 14 for lots 131[a] & 131[b]. Spruit
			Maes		
1803/12/15	MGLAC	0057	*Maas* | Een Turqsche Zeebattaille; breed en goed geschilderd | *Mat:* op doek *Size:* hoog duim 26, breed duim 35	Mr L H de Haze Bomme	(Unknown)
			Maes, Dirk		
1801/06/10	AMSCH	0123	*Maas. (D.)* | Twee stuks, met een Menigte Heeren en Militairen te paard en te voet, alles is in de manier van J. Hugtenburg, geschilderd | *Size:* yder hoog 20, breed 24 duim	Herman ten Kate	(Sold) fl 27:10 Taijs
1801/10/19	AMSCH	0002	*Maas. (D.)* | Een dito [Italiaansch] Landschap met een Ruïne, Beelden en Beesten; uitvoerig geschilderd, dienende tot een wederga van de vorige | companion to lot 1, by Asselyn *Mat:* op paneel *Size:* hoog 7, breed 10 ½ duim	Jonkheer Menno Baron van Coehoorn	(Sold) fl 19:10 Hulswit
1802/02/16	AMSCH	0026	*D. Maas* | Twee stuks een bevallig mans en vrouwe Portret; uitmuntend behandeld | *Notes:* The artist was presumably Nicolaes Maes and not Dirk Maes.	E	(Sold) fl 50 J Spaan
1802/02/16	AMSCH	0027	*D. Maas* | Twee klynder dito [stuks] dito [mans en vrouwe Portret] | *Notes:* The artist was presumably Nicolaes Maes and not Dirk Maes. It is unclear what "dito" refers to in the title.	E	(Sold) fl 11:10 Pruijssenaar
1802/05/11	GRGRW	0008	*D. Maas* | Een Jachtstuk [Schilderijen met Olie-Verf; In zwarte Lijsten] | *Mat:* in olyverf *Notes:* The bracketed information in the title appears above lot 1 and refers to lots 1 to 79a.	Arnold Sicco Werumeus	(Unknown)
1802/05/11	GRGRW	0017	*D. Maas* | Een Plundering en Wegvoering door Militie [Schilderijen met Olie-Verf; In zwarte Lijsten] | *Mat:* in olyverf *Notes:* The bracketed information in the title appears above lot 1 and refers to lots 1 to 79a.	Arnold Sicco Werumeus	(Unknown)
1802/05/11	GRGRW	0018	*D. Maas* | Een Picquet Cavallerie [Schilderijen met Olie-Verf; In zwarte Lijsten] | *Mat:* in olyverf *Notes:* The bracketed information in the title appears above lot 1 and refers to lots 1 to 79a.	Arnold Sicco Werumeus	(Unknown)
1802/05/11	GRGRW	0047	*D. Maas* | Een Marketenter [Schilderijen met Olie-Verf; In zwarte Lijsten] | *Mat:* in olyverf *Notes:* The bracketed information in the title appears above lot 1 and refers to lots 1 to 79a.	Arnold Sicco Werumeus	(Unknown) fl 1:12
1802/09/06	AMSCH	0197	*D. Maas* | Twee stuks Land-Batailjes	Spaan	(Sold) fl 2 Baur
1802/09/21	UTHDG	0065	*D. Maas* | Twee stuks Legerplaatzen, beiden met veele Beelden, Paarden, en menigerlei andere toepasselijke voorwerpen; rijk voorzien | *Mat:* op doek *Size:* hoog 21, breed 25 duimen		(Sold) fl 6 v der Mast Vismark
1803/09/07	AMSCH	0108	*D. Maas* | Een stormachtig Landschap, gestoffeerd met eenige Reizigers te Paard, welke voor het Onweder schynen te vlugten, kragtig en fix op Doek [Un orage ; quelques voyageurs à cheval traversent un site de campagne, et semblent fuir la tempète ; touche vigoureuse et d'un beau fini] | *Mat:* op doek *Size:* hoog 29, breed 38 duim	Smidt	(Sold) fl 25 C S Roos
1804/05/07	AMSCH	0110	*Maas. (D.)* | Een hevige Rencontre tusschen Ruitery, men ziet op de voorgrond eenige Doden en Gekwetsten, in het verschier [sic] een vegtende Armé; meesterlyk behandeld | *Mat:* op doek *Size:* hoog 35, breed 44 duim	Roos [for] A	(Sold) fl 10 Pruissenaar
1804/07/25	AMSCH	0054	*Maas. (D.)* | In een Heuvelagtig Landschap, ziet men Prins Willem de III. ter Jagt, verzeld van zyne Hovelingen en Jagers, op de voorgrond werd een Hart door de Honden aangevallen, en in 't verschiet vertoond zig een Kasteel en Gebergten; fraai en natuurlyk behandeld | companion to lot 55 *Mat:* op doek *Size:* hoog 25, breed 35 duim		(Sold) fl 25 for lots 54 & 55. Hulswit
1804/07/25	AMSCH	0055	*Maas. (D.)* | In een dito [Heuvelagtig] Landschap, ziet men op de voorgrond een Jager te Paard, verder een Hartenjagt, en in 't verschiet hoog Gebergten; dit stuk is niet minder van qualiteit dan het voorgaande, en kan tot een wederga van 't zelve verstrekken | companion to lot 54 *Mat:* op doek *Size:* hoog 25, breed 35 duim		(Sold) fl 25 for lots 54 & 55. Hulswit
1804/08/08	AMSCH	0120	*D. Maas* | In een Binnenhuis zit een Vrouw te spinnen, by haar hebbende drie Kinderen, waarvan een in de Kinderstoel, alles verlicht wordende door een helder brandende Lamp, welke by het Vuur onder de Schoorsteen hangt; kragtig en meesterlyk behandeld | *Mat:* op paneel *Size:* hoog 29, breed 23 duim *Notes:* The artist was presumably Nicolaes Maes and not Dirk Maes.	Roos [for] D	(Sold) fl 7 Pruizenaar
1804/10/29	HRBAU	0051	*Maas, (D.)* | Op den Voorgrond, die klipagtig is, ziet men 'een Veldoversten, op een moedig wit getygerd paard, zyn orders aan een Soldaat geeven, die met zyn' hoed in de hand by hem staat; hy is	Simon Styl	(Unknown)

			vergezeld van verscheidene Officiers, mede te paard gezeeten; waar agter een trein Artillerie en Paardenvolk voorby marcheert, tusschen de Rotsen, die met Kasteelen bebouwd zyn. Dit Stuk is in alle deelen zo fraai behandeld, als of het door Huchtenburg vervaardigd ware | *Mat:* op doek *Size:* hoog 20 ½, breed 24 duim		
1804/10/29	HRBAU	0052	*Maas, (D.)* | Voor aan, by eene Pleisterplaats, zit een Heer op een wit paard, welks Stegelreep door een' Knegt wordt vastgemaakt, vergezeld door nog twee Heeren, op een vos en bruin paard gezeeten: terwyl de Hospita, met een Kind op den arm, en aan de hand, voorby passeert. Zeer uitvoerig behandeld | *Mat:* op doek *Size:* hoog 11 ½, breed 14 duim	Simon Styl	(Unknown)
1805/07/03	AMSCH	0111	*D. Maas* | Eenige Jagers te paard en te voet, met hunne Honden, in een Boomryk Landschap; aangenaam van coloriet en penceels behandeling | *Mat:* op doek *Size:* hoog 22, breed 27 duim	G	(Sold) fl 40 Gruyter
1805/10/21	GRBOL	0005	*D. Maas* | Een Herberg, waar in een Officier te Paard een Glas Wyn drinkende, en verder Bywerk | companion to lot 6	Gerardus Nicolaus Heerkens	(Unknown)
1805/10/21	GRBOL	0006	*D. Maas* | Een dito [Herberg] door Denzelfden [D. Maas], zynde een Weêrga | companion to lot 5 *Notes:* It is unclear what "dito" refers to in the title.	Gerardus Nicolaus Heerkens	(Unknown)
1805/10/21	GRBOL	0027	*D. Maas* | Een Marquetenter, waar voor enig Krygsvolk	Gerardus Nicolaus Heerkens	(Unknown)
1805/12/16	AMSCH	0042	*D. Maas* | Een hevige Rencontre tusschen Ruitery, in een Boomryk Landschap; alles vol vuur en kragtig geschilderd | *Size:* hoog 20, breed 25 duim	R[oos]	(Sold) fl 2:10 T van Iperen
1806/08/20	HGBSM	0080	*D. Maas* | Koning William, gezeten op een wit Paard, de agtergrond verbeeld, eene belegerde stad, konstig, in den trant van Hugtenburg geschilderd | *Mat:* op doek *Size:* hoog 25, breed 22 duim	Macalester Loup [or others]	(Sold) fl 11 Vallette
1807/06/10	HGBSM	0095	*D. Maas* | Een buiten Manégie daar een Paard gedresseert word, waar bij eenige Heeren met hunne Paarden, fraaij geteekend en uitvoerig geschilderd | *Mat:* op doek *Size:* hoog 15 ½, breed 18 ½ duim	Abraham Delfos [or others]	(Sold) fl 16:10 Tessier
1807/06/10	HGBSM	0096	*D. Maas* | Een dito [buiten Manégie] zijnde een Landschap, met eenige Cavalliers te Paard, niet minder als de voorgaande | *Size:* hoog 15 ½, breed 18 ½ duim	Abraham Delfos [or others]	(Sold) fl 10:10 Uittenbogaart
1807/08/26	AMSCH	0135	*D. Maas* | Twee stuks, zynde boom- en bergachtige Landschappen, gestoffeerd met verscheiden Vorstelyke Personen, welke zich met jaagen,zoo te Paard als te voet, verlustigen, waarby een menigte Honden; geestig | *Mat:* op doek *Size:* hoog 15, breed 36 duim	Joseph Vallette	(Sold) fl 39 Coclair
1807/08/26	AMSCH	0136	*D. Maas* | Een hevige Bataille tusschen Ruitery | *Mat:* op doek *Size:* hoog 34, breed 42 duim	de Vries	(Sold) fl 4:10 du Pree
1807/08/26	AMSCH	0142	*D. Maas* | Prins Willem de Derden, zittenden te Paard; meesterlyk | *Mat:* op doek *Size:* hoog 25, breed 22 duim	Joseph Vallette	(Sold) fl 7:5 van Dijl
1808/04/26	GDAN	0103	*Maas (D)* | Een Gezigt van een prachtige Buitenplaats, met het gezigt op den Thuin en 't Fontein, waar men eenige Heeren te Paard ziet rijden, en bij de Fontein de Paarden te drinken geeft | *Size:* hoog 10 ½, breed 13 duim	G H Fortuyn	(Unknown)
1808/04/26	GDAN	0104	*Maas (D)* | Een Gezigt van een Buitenplaats onder Geboomte, waar in op het plein eenige Heeren te Paard rijden om een tourtje te doen, in het verschiet eenige Beelden, en een bergägtig Landschap | companion to lot 105	G H Fortuyn	(Unknown)
1808/04/26	GDAN	0105	*Maas (D)* | Een dito [Gezigt van een Buitenplaats] tot een wederga | companion to lot 104	G H Fortuyn	(Unknown)
1808/05/18	LNAN	0038	*Maas* | Vechtende Ruiters te Paard in een Landschap | *Notes:* The artist's name "Maas" was added in by hand in the RKDH copy of the catalogue.	Mr Cornelis Versluys	(Unknown)
1808/05/18	LNAN	0049	*Maas* | Een Heer te Paard, en anderen te Voet | *Notes:* The artist's name "Maas" was added in by hand in the RKDH copy of the catalogue.	Mr Cornelis Versluys	(Unknown)
1808/05/18	LNAN	0055	*Maas* | 2 Stuks Batailles van Ruiters te Paard, vol gewoel | *This Lot:* Een Stuk Bataille van Ruiters te Paard *Notes:* Lots 55 and 56 were printed in the catalogue as one item. The artist's name "Maas" was added in by hand in the RKDH copy of the catalogue.	Mr Cornelis Versluys	(Unknown)
1808/05/18	LNAN	0056	*Maas* | 2 Stuks Batailles van Ruiters te Paard, vol gewoel | *This Lot:* Een Stuk Bataille van Ruiters te Paard *Notes:* Lots 55 and 56 were printed in the catalogue as one item. The artist's name "Maas" was added in by hand in the RKDH copy of the catalogue.	Mr Cornelis Versluys	(Unknown)
1808/06/13	AMSCH	0104	*Maas (D.)* | Een Jagtpartij van verscheide Heeren en Dames te Paard, op den voorgrond een Hert, 't welk door de Honden wordt aangevallen. Goed geschilderd | *Mat:* op doek *Size:* hoog 22, breed 27 duim	E M Engelberts	(Sold) fl 28:10 Th Spaan
1810/03/23	HAVIN	0016	*D. Maas* | Een Campement uitmuntend uitvoerig | *Size:* hoog 24 breet 28 d.	Rudolf Hendrik de Wetstein [or others]	(Unknown) fl 53
1810/03/23	HAVIN	0043	*D. Maas* | Een Jagtpartij	Rudolf Hendrik de Wetstein [or others]	(Unknown)
1810/03/23	HAVIN	0044	*D. Maas* | Een dito [Jagtpartij]	Rudolf Hendrik de Wetstein [or others]	(Unknown)

1810/06/20	AMSCH	0050	*Maas* | Een Jagtpartij, met Heeren en Dames, verzeld van hunne Jagers en Honden. Goed geschilderd | *Size:* hoog 31, breed 37 duimen	A	(Sold) fl 2:5 du Pree
1810/08/06	AMSCH	0067	*Maas (D)* | Twee stuks, een Heer en eene Dame, beide in rijke Kleeding; uitvoerig van behandeling | *Size:* ieder hoog 25, breed 21 duimen *Notes:* The artist was presumably Nicolaes Maes and not Dirk Maes.	A	(Sold) fl 2 L Pakker
1810/10/11	AMSCH	0049	*D. Maas* | Een Terugkomst van de Harte Jagt | *Mat:* op doek *Size:* hoog 27, breed 34 duimen	C	(Sold) fl 8:15 Posthumus

Maes, Dirk (manner)

1801/04/23	AMYVR	0033	*D. Maas* | Een Hevige Bataille, in de manier van D. Maas | *Notes:* This lot was sold with lot 34 by J. Meyering.		(Sold) fl 1 ¾ for lots 33 & 34. Scheide
1803/08/24	HGKAN	A0009	*Maas* | Een Boomryk Landschap met Rustende Beelden, agter een Man te Paard, uitvoerig en fraai geschildert als door Maas | *Mat:* op doek *Size:* breet 30, hoog 26 duim		(Sold) fl 5 Giesen

Maes, Godfried

1803/07/18	AMSCH	0032	*Maes. (Godfried)* | Dit stuk steld voor de edelmoedigheid van Scipio, hy zit op een Troon, aan welkers voeten de Koning Massinissa hem de schoone Sophonisba aanbied, de Romeinsche Slaaf is verzeld van twee Pages en andere Krygsknegten te Paard; by den Troon zyn nog verscheide Beelden, en een Jongeling welke een Papegaay op zyn hand draagd; dit Schildery is ryk van ordonnantie en meesterlyk behandeld in de styl van Rubbens, waarvan hy een leerling was [Le Sujet de ce tableau est la continence de Scipion l'Africain. Ce Général Romain est assis sur un trone consulair, au pied duquel le Roi Massinissa lui presente la belle Sophonisbe, l'Esclave de Rome est accompagnée d'un viellard & suivie de deux pages & de quelques guerriers à cheval. Autour du Consul Romain sont differens personnages & un jeune homme tenant un peroquet. Ce tableau traité en maître, a de la vigeur [sic], la composition & la couleur y font connoître la belle Ecole de Rubbens.] | *Mat:* op doek [sur bois] *Size:* hoog 22, breed 29 duim *Notes:* The materials differ in the Dutch and French editions of the catalogue.	Maria Theresia Andrioli	(Sold) fl 14 Grimpen
1803/12/12	AMSCH	0059	*G. Maas* | Een Deftig Heer, rustende tegens een Colom; meesterlyk op Doek | *Mat:* op doek *Size:* hoog 26, breed 22 duim	F	(Sold) fl 1:5 Gruiter

Maes, Nicolaes

1801/03/16	AMSCH	0078	*Maas* | Twee Poutraitten [sic] | *Notes:* This lot was sold with lot 77 by Wm. Ferguson.	P[ruyssenaar]	(Sold) fl 4:5 for lots 77 & 78. Coclers
1801/04/13	AMSCH	0045	*N. Maas* | Een Dienstmaagd uit een kelder komende met een kan en glas, schynt een Heer en Dame te beluisteren, de ploijing der klederen, en het licht en bruin is zeer geestig in dit stuk waargenomen, en is voorts Meesterlyk behandeld | *Mat:* op doek *Size:* hoog 46, breed 36 duim	Pierre Fouquet, junior	(Sold) fl 49 Spruit van Gend
1801/05/11	AMSCH	0047	*N. Maas* | Een bevallig Kind in een cierlyke kleding, met een Rheetje en hondje nevens zich, alles is van een meesterlyke penceels behandeling | *Mat:* op doek *Size:* hoog 21, breed 19 duim	P[ruyssenaar]	(Sold) fl 42 Pruijssenaar [for] R
1802/05/05	AMSCH	0119	*N. Maas* | Op een Steene Sluis staat een Groenvrouw met verscheiden groentens, schynende te kyven met een andere Vrouw met een Kind, verders verscheiden Aanschouwers, alles krachtig | *Mat:* op doek *Size:* hoog 28, breed 35 duim *Loc:* Amsterdam, Nederland. Rijksmuseum. (A3254)	H	(Sold) fl 41 Spruit
1802/05/05	AMSCH	0120	*N. Maas* | In een Boomryk Landschap, by een Fontyn, ziet men eenige Heeren en Dames te voet en te paard, verders Jagers en Honden, natuurlyk geschilderd | *Size:* hoog 34, breed 44 duim *Notes:* The artist was presumably Dirk Maes and not Nicolaes Maes.	J	(Sold) fl 2:15 Mensard
1802/11/01	DOBRA	0118	*N. Maas* | Een fraai Mansportrait | *Mat:* op paneel *Size:* hoog 26, breed 19 duim	Paulus van der Spyk [or others]	(Unknown)
1802/12/13	AMSCH	0116	*N. Maas* | Ter zyden een Tafel, waarop een Mandje met Bloemen en Vrugten, ziet men een bevalligen Damen, nevens haar een Dienstmaagd, van agteren een Hofgezigt | *Mat:* op doek *Size:* hoog 22, breed 19 duim	Pruyssenaar [for] A	(Sold) fl 0:12 DuPree
1802/12/13	AMSCH	0117	*N. Maas* | Twee stuks bevallige Vrouwe Pourtraiten | *Mat:* op paneel *Size:* hoog 8, breed 6 duim	Pruyssenaar [for] A	(Sold) fl 0:12 DuPree
1802/12/13	AMSCH	0118	*N. Maas* | Een Hofgezigt met Heeren en Dames te Paard en verder Stoffagie; uitvoerig geschilderd | *Mat:* op doek *Size:* hoog 21, breed 27 duim *Notes:* The artist was presumably Dirk Maes and not Nicolaes Maes.	Pruyssenaar [for] A	(Sold) fl 0:18 Gruiter
1803/04/20	AMSCH	0048	*N. Maas* | Het Afbeeldzel van een bevallige Jonge Dame, in treffelyke kleeding, rustende met de Armen op een Steene Baluster, zeer uitvoerig van penceelsbehandeling [Le Portrait d'une jeune Dame distinguée, s'appuyant sur une balustrade, le bon choix des vetemens, la verité des carnations, & la franchise du pinceau que l'on distingue dans les bons ouvrages de peintre, est un reproche pour les amateurs, du trop peu d'estime que l'on a pour ses talens.] | *Mat:* op doek *Size:* hoog 19, breed 15 ½ duim	Maria Magdalena van Sluypwyk, gravinne van Moens	(Sold) fl 14 Theijs
1803/04/20	AMSCH	0049	*N. Maas* | Het dito [Afbeeldzel] van een bedaagde Dame, in deftige zatyne kleeding, zittende in een Landschap, als de vorige, meesterlyk behandeld [Autre Portrait de femme traité comme le précedent.] | *Mat:*	Maria Magdalena van Sluypwyk, gravinne van Moens	(Sold) fl 3:5 Gruiter

			[sur toile] *Size:* hoog 19, breed 15 ½ duim *Notes:* The material was given only in the French edition of the catalogue.		
1803/04/20	AMSCH	0050	*N. Maas* | Twee stuks: zynde Afbeeldzels van een Dame en Heer in deftige kleeding, staande in Hofgezichten, meesterlyk en uitvoerig gepenceeld [Deux Portraits pour pendans le premier est celui d'un Homme de marque, le second est une Dame ; ils sont du même mérite de premiers.] | *Mat:* op doek *Size:* [hauts 19, larges 15 pouces] *Notes:* The dimensions are given only in the French edition of the catalogue.	Maria Magdalena van Sluypwyk, gravinne van Moens	(Sold) fl 16:10 Hulswit
1803/04/20	AMSCH	0051	*N. Maas* | In een Boomryk Landschap ziet men een Meisje verzeld van een Jongeling, met eenige Honden en Jachtgeweer, als ter Jacht gaande, breed en fiks gepenceeld [Un sujet de famille étant une jeune fille & un jeune homme disposés pour aller à la chasse : se fond est un beau paysage. Ce tableau est traité avec la facilité & la verité propres à son auteur.] | *Mat:* op doek *Size:* hoog 25, breed 31 duim [haut 51, large 31 pouces] *Notes:* The artist was presumably Dirk Maes and not Nicolaes Maes. The dimensions differ in the Dutch and French editions of the catalogue.	Maria Magdalena van Sluypwyk, gravinne van Moens	(Sold) fl 1 W^{n} v d Schleij
1803/12/12	AMSCH	0060	*N. Maas* | Twee stuks, één Mans en een Vrouwen Pourtrait; van de beste qualiteit en schildering | *Mat:* op doek *Size:* hoog 52, breed 43 duim	B	(Sold) fl 22 Coclers
1804/05/07	AMSCH	0118	*Maas* | Een Mans Pourtraait [sic] | *Size:* hoog 45, breed 35 duim	Vinkeles [for] G	(Sold) fl 0:12 Gruyter
1804/10/16	DLOND	0130	*Nic. Maas* | Een Binnenwacht. Un Corps de Guarde | *Mat:* op doek *Size:* hoog 21, breed 27		(Unknown)
1804/10/16	DLOND	0131	*Nic. Maas* | Een Vrouwen Portrait. Un Portrait de Femme | *Mat:* op doek *Size:* hoog 16, breed 12		(Unknown)
1806/08/13	AMSCH	0327	*Maas. (C.)* | Een capitaal Hofgezicht; fiks geschilderd | *Size:* hoog 33, breed 30 duim *Notes:* The artist's name was given as "Maas. (C.)" but we have assumed this is an error.	Vinkeles [for] G[ruyter]	(Withdrawn)
1806/08/20	HGBSM	0129	*N. Maas* | Twee Stuks dito Portraiten | *Mat:* op paneel *Notes:* It is unclear what "dito" refers to in the title.	Macalester Loup [or others]	(Sold) fl 2 de Gelder
1808/04/26	GDAN	A0001	*Maas (Nicolaas)* | Een Mans Pourtret tot de Knoop, met een Mantel om, konstig en kragtig, geheel in de trant van Rembrand | *Size:* hoog 52, breed 42 duim *Notes:* This lot has been renumbered to distinguish it from another lot with the same number in a different section of the catalogue.	G H Fortuyn	(Unknown)
1808/04/26	GDAN	A0002	*Maas (Nicolaas)* | Een dito Mans Pourtret, schijnende een Geestelijk Persoon te wezen, zittende op een Stoel in een peinzende houding, bruin Hair op het Hoofd, los van Kleding, schoon van ligt en bruin, konstig en kragtig geschilderd, en is een der beste van dezen vermaarde Pourtretschilder | *Size:* hoog 52, breed 48 duim *Notes:* It is unclear what "dito" refers to in the title.	G H Fortuyn	(Unknown)
1808/04/26	GDAN	A0003	*Maas (Nicolaas)* | Een Kindje met een blozende kleur, een Hoed met Veder op het Hoofd, bij 't zelve een omkijkend blijvend Hondje, op de Vinger van de linkerhand een Vogeltje, de losse kleding is ongemeen van ligt en bruin en is mede een der beste van dezen Meester | *Size:* hoog 31, breed 28 duim *Notes:* This lot has been renumbered to distinguish it from another lot with the same number in a different section of the catalogue.	G H Fortuyn	(Unknown)
1808/06/06	RMRIJ	0074	*Maas. (Nicolaas)* | Eene Meid, van de markt komende en op een Pothuis rustende, benevens eene Vrouw uit een Venster liggende en bijwerk. Krachtig geschilderd. Eene wedergade. Eene Melkmeid voorstellende, die aan een huis aanschelt, benevens Melk-Emmers, een Hond, enz. Als boven behandeld [Une Laitière avec ses Seaux et un Chien, est devant une Maison, prête à sonner. D'un ton Vigoureux. Le Pendant. Une Servante retourne du Marché et s'entretient avec une personne qui est à une Croisée etc. Egal en mérite au Précédent] | *Annots:* uit de houd gekocht voor f 52.10 (RMA I) *Mat:* op paneel *Size:* Twee Stukken. Hoog 21 ¾ en breed 15 ¾ duim *Loc:* Den Haag, Nederland. Rijksdienst Beeldende Kunst (NK 3045) and London, England, UK. Harold Samuel Coll. (39)	Gerrit van der Pot, Heer van Groeneveld	(Sold) fl 600 Messing
1808/08/23	AMSCH	0109	*Maas. (N.)* | Voor de Ruïne van een groot Gebouw, zit een Man die door een daar nevens staand Meisje, om een aalmoes gevraagd word, waar bij zig een Heer te Paard en andere Lieden bevinden, ter zijde een Landman, die op een Instrument speeld, zittende op een Ezel; deeze Ordonantie is breed en meesterlijk behandeld | *Mat:* op doek *Size:* hoog 24, breed 29 duim *Notes:* The artist was presumably Dirk Maes and not Nicolaes Maes.	J	(Bought In) fl 21:10
1809/07/25	HGBSM	0180	*C. Maes* | Het Portret van een Heer en eene Dame, breed geschildert door C. Maes, op Doek, hoog 25 en een half, breed 20 en een half duim, twee Stuks | *Mat:* op doek *Size:* hoog 25 en een half, breed 20 en een half *Notes:* The artist's name was given as "C. Maes" but we have assumed this is an error.	D van der Aa [or] E B ten Dall	(Sold) fl 10:5 Nieuwenhuizen
1809/07/25	HGBSM	0231	*Maes* | Het Portret van een Dame, met een Krans met Bloemen | *Mat:* op doek *Size:* hoog 26 en een half, breed 21 en een half duim	D van der Aa [or] E B ten Dall	(Sold) fl 1:6 de Gelder
1810/06/20	AMSCH	0049	*Maas* | Twee stuks: een deftig Heer en eene Vrouw, beide in rijke kleeding. Zeer uitvoerig | *Mat:* op doek *Size:* hoog 16, breed 11 duimen	A	(Sold) fl 25 T Spaan
1810/06/20	AMSCH	0051	*Maas* | Eene bevallige Dame, in rijke kleeding, staande in een Landschap. Krachtig geschilderd | *Mat:* op doek *Size:* hoog 22, breed 18 duimen	A	(Sold) fl 3:10 Sardet

1810/07/23	DOLG1	0035	*Nikolaas Maas* | Een Oudhollandsch Burger-Vertrek, eigen aardig gestoffeerd, waar in eene oude Vrouw bij haar Spinnewiel zit te lezen. Ongemeen fraai van Ordonnantie, en van eene bevallige Penseelsbehandeling | *Mat:* op doek *Size:* hoog 18, breed 22 duim	Mr Pieter van den Santheuvel	(Sold) fl 90 P de Heere à Dordt
1810/07/23	DOLG2	000X	*N. Maes* | Op den voorgrond, op een steenen voet, vertoont zich een mande, vol met Perziken, Druiven, en meer andere Vruchten en Bladeren. In het verschiet is een Tuingezicht; breed geschilderd | *Mat:* op doek *Size:* hoog 23, breed 28 duim *Loc:* Oxford, England, UK. Ashmolean Museum. (A577)	Pieter Quinting	(Sold) fl 2 A v Strij
1810/07/23	DOLG2	00AA	*N. Maes* | Eenige Perziken en Pruimen | *Mat:* op paneel *Size:* hoog 12 ½, breed 11 ½ duim *Notes:* This lot was bought by the anonymous annotator of the FLNY copy of the catalogue.	Pieter Quinting	(Sold) fl 4:10
1810/10/11	AMSCH	0114	*Maas* | Eene bejaarde Vrouw, in oude Hollandsche Kleeding, zittende in een Leuningstoel; krachtig geschilderd | *Mat:* op doek	Y	(Sold) fl 1 Gruiter
1810/10/11	AMSCH	0195	*Maas* | Een deftig Heer, staande bij eene steenen Baluster | *Mat:* op doek	A	(Sold) fl 0:10 L Pakker
1810/12/03	DOBRA	0021	*Maas* | Een Meisje, zittende in een Landschap, met eenige Vruchten, geschilderd door Maas		(Unknown)
1810/12/03	DOBRA	0054	*Maas* | De wegzending van Hagar | *Size:* hoog 35, breed 26 duim *Loc:* New York, NY, USA. Metropolitan Museum of Art. (1971.73)		(Unknown)
			Maes, Nicolaes (and Nickelen)		
1804/10/16	DLOND	0132	*Nic. Maas; J.H. Nickelen* | Het Raadhuis te Amsterdam, met de Waag, en veel gewoel. L'Hôtel de Ville d'Amsterdam, avec beaucoup de figures | *Size:* hoog 40, breed 49 *Notes:* The lot was changed from "Nic. Maas en J.H. Nickelen, Het Raadhuis te Amsterdam, met de Waag, en veel gewoel," to "F. Bol," without giving a title, at the front of the catalogue.		(Withdrawn)
			Maes, Nicolaes (or Maes, N., manner)		
1802/05/05	AMSCH	0266	*N. Maas* | Een Landschap, met een Herder, Herderin en twee Kinderen, speelende met Bloemen, delicaat gepenceeld door of in de manier van N. Maas | *Notes:* The artist was presumably Dirk Maes and not Nicolaes Maes.	C	(Sold) fl 1 L Pakker
			Maes, Nicolaes (manner)		
1806/08/13	AMSCH	0257	*Maas* | Een jongeling voor een Nis, waterbellen blazende, op de Rand der Nis ligt een Tapyt, waarop een Hondje; in de manier van Maas	Roos	(Sold) fl 1 Graun
			Malo, Vincent (I)		
1803/07/18	AMSCH	0034	*Malo. (Vincent)* | De Sabynsche Maagdenroof op een Marktplein met treffelyke Gebouwen voorgesteld, ter zyde op een verhevenheid ziet men de Koning zyne bevelen geevende aan de Soldaaten welke dien roof uitvoeren; de aart van schilderen in de manier van Rubbens: doet eer aan deeze Meester [Le Rapt des Sabines. Au milieu d'un vaste emplacement l'on voit une foule innombrable & tumultueuse de Soldats Romains à ravir les Sabines. A la gauche est dressé un theâtre ou le Roi donne le Signal convenu, & au fond de la place, le peintre a trouvé bon de placer un arc triomphal. Cette composition a de l'effet malgré le grand nombre de figures, une touche facile, & une couleur qui laissent appercevoir qu'il étoit Eleve de Rubens.] | *Mat:* op paneel *Size:* hoog 23, breed 32 duim	Maria Theresia Andrioli	(Sold) fl 40 Thys
			Man		
1802/08/24	LNDLS	0109	*D. Man* | Een Binnenhuis, daar een Visboer visch aan twee Juffers aanbied | companion to lot 110 *Mat:* op doek	Leonardus Bouman [or others]	(Unknown) fl 1:16 for lots 109 & 110
1802/08/24	LNDLS	0110	*D. Man* | Een weêrga met speelende Kinderen bij een zittende Juffer, en een Heer bij zijn Lessenaar | companion to lot 109	Leonardus Bouman [or others]	(Unknown) fl 1:16 for lots 109 & 110
1804/04/28	LNDLS	0020	*de Man* | Een Binnenhuis, waarin een vrouw en kind, zittende by een wieg, benevens een man, die een tabakspyp aansteekt, door de Man, op doek | *Mat:* op doek *Size:* hoog 20, breed 15 duim	[Abraham Delfos] [or others]	(Sold) fl 12:5 Rigter [for] A
1809/04/17	AMSCH	0056a[H]	*V Man* | [Untitled] | *Notes:* This lot was added in by hand in the EBNP copy of the catalogue, but without giving a title.		(Sold) fl 19:10
			Man, Cornelis de		
1802/05/05	AMSCH	0147	*C. de Man* | Een Laboratorium van een Goudsmit, op de Voorgrond aan een Tafel, schynen eenige over de gehalte van het Goud te spreeken, verders toepasselyk bywerk | *Size:* hoog 31, breed 34 duim	J	(Sold) fl 8 B^{d} Kooij
1803/06/20	AMSCH	0034	*C. de Man* | Een Protestanten Kerk van binnen te zien, gestoffeerd met verscheide Beeldjes, Wapenborden en een Hond; zonachtig op Panneel | *Mat:* op paneel *Size:* hoog 15, breed 18 duim	Schley [for] G	(Sold) fl 18 Gruiter
1804/10/16	DLOND	0133	*C. de Man* | Een Kamer, waarin eene Vrouw die met haar Kind nevens de Wieg zit, terwyl de Man zyn pyp rookt. L'Intérieur d'une Chambre, on y voit une Mère avec son Enfant, à côté d'un Berceau, tandis que son Mari fume sa pipe | *Mat:* op doek *Size:* hoog 31, breed 25		(Unknown)
1809/06/13	AMSCH	0113	*C. de Man* | Twee stuks Binnekamers, rijk met Beelden en bijwerk gestoffeerd, en kloek geschilderd | *Mat:* op doek *Size:* ieder hoog 21, breed 26 duim	Y	(Sold) fl 12 Gruiter

1809/07/25	HGBSM	0015	*C. de Man* | Een Man voor een Lessenaar staande, aan een Vrouw een Stuk Geld presenteerende, konstig gepenseelt | *Mat:* op paneel *Size:* hoog 18 ½, breet 15 ½ duim	D van der Aa [or] E B ten Dall	(Sold) fl 10:5 van Eyk
			Man, Joost de		
1801/06/13	LNDLS	0025	*J. de Man* | Een modern Binnenvertrek, daar een Man en Vrouw aan een tafel zitten en op het Schaakspel speelen, met meer bijwerk, helder en plaizant, op doek geschilderd | *Mat:* op doek *Size:* hoog 38, breed 32 duimen	D van R	(Sold) fl 9:10 de Roy
1808/12/31	RMHSN	0024	*J. de Man* | Simeon in den Tempel | *Mat:* op doek	G Spanjaart [or] H de Haas [or] C van der Looy Lans	(Unknown)
1810/06/06	RMMUY	0038	*J. de Man* | Een Binnenkamer, waar eene Dame eene jonge Jufvrouw onderwijst, met aangenaam bijwerk | *Mat:* op doek		(Unknown) fl 14
			Man, L.D.		
1809/06/13	AMSCH	0114	*L.J. de Man* | Een stille Zee, met Oorlogscheepen, Jagten en Sloepen gestoffeerd, goed geschilderd | *Mat:* op doek *Size:* hoog 44, breed 52 duim	Y	(Sold) fl 3 T Spaan
			Mancadan, Jacobus Sibrandi		
1805/10/21	GRBOL	0049	*Mankendam* | Een Landschapje	Gerardus Nicolaus Heerkens	(Unknown)
1805/10/21	GRBOL	0054	*Mankendam* | Een dito [Landschapje]	Gerardus Nicolaus Heerkens	(Unknown)
			Mander, Karel van (I)		
1808/11/12	HGSCR	0013	*Karel van Mander* | De kruiziging van Christus ryk van ordonnantie, fraay en uitvoerig gepenseeld, rond formaat | *Mat:* op paneel *Fmt:* rond	Mr J van Buren	(Unknown) fl 29:5
1810/03/27	RMCNL	0018	*van Manderen* | Twee Koppen, voorstellende Heracliet en Democriet, levensgrootte, zeer natuurlijk, in volle uitdrukking geschilderd		(Unknown)
			Manes		
1802/07/09	AMSTO	0007	*de Manes* | In een Binnenhuys ziet men een Heer, zittenden aan een Tafel zyn Pyp aantesteeken, neevens hem een staande Vrouw, en ander bywerk		(Unknown)
			Manfredi, Bartolomeo		
1801/04/13	AMSCH	0049	*B. Manfrede* | David in zyn rechterhand een Zwaard, en in de linkerhand de kop van Goliath hebbende, Meesterlyk gepenceeld | *Mat:* op doek *Size:* hoog 30, breed 23 duim	Pierre Fouquet, junior	(Sold) fl 3 van Dijl
			Mansker [Unidentified]		
1809/04/22	AMYVR	0091	*Mansker* | Twee stuks Boschgezichten, met verscheidene Beeldjes gestoffeerd; warm en meesterlijk | *Mat:* op doek *Size:* hoog 15, breed 20 duim	de Bruin	(Sold) fl 6 C S Roos
			Maratti, Carlo		
1803/04/27	AMSCH	0042	*C. Maratte* | l'Adoration des Mages | *Size:* h. 4 ½, l. 3 ½ pieds	A	(Sold) fl 3 V d Brink
1806/05/05	AMSCH	0101	*C. Marat* | Twee Kluizenaars in een Hol; breed gepenceeld door C. Marat | *Mat:* op doek *Size:* hoog 16, breed 12 duim	L	(Sold) fl 4 Fortman
1806/08/20	HGBSM	0001	*Carlo Marat* | Christus in den Hof van Getzemanè. ondersteund door een Engel die den Kelk aanwijst; het Hoofd van den Zaligmaker, is vol uitdrukking, verders krachtig en breed geschilderd en uitmuntend geteekend door Carlo Marat | *Mat:* op doek *Size:* hoog 39, breed 45 duim	Macalester Loup [or others]	(Sold) fl 8:10 Praison
1810/08/06	AMSCH	0069	*Marratti (Carlo)* | Moses ontfangt de Wet op Sinai, hij is omgeven door verscheidene Engelen; meesterlijk en breed geschilderd | *Mat:* op doek *Size:* hoog 51, breed 37 duimen	R[oos]	(Bought In) fl 25
			Maratti, Carlo (or Maratti, manner)		
1806/08/13	AMSCH	0261	*C. Marat* | Deeze ryke Ordinantie van een ménigte Beelden, vertoont de Dooping Christi, door St. Jan, verzelt van verscheide andere Lieden, zig tot den ontfangst der Doop gereed makende; krachtig en meesterlyk gepenceeld op Doek, door of in de manier van C. Marat | *Mat:* op doek	van der Voort	(Sold) fl 37 Spruit van Gend
			Marcelis, Jan Claes		
1808/04/26	GDAN	0106	*Marcelis* | Een bergägtig Gezigt, waar op een Buitenplaats gelegen is, zeer Bosrijk, met diverse Beelden, wel geschildert | *Size:* hoog 18, breed 22 duim	G H Fortuyn	(Unknown)
			Marrel, Jacob		
1802/05/24	HGBAK	0073	*Jacobus Marcellus* | Een Vaas met bloemen in een nis, met insecten en hoorns gestoffeerd, door Jacobus Marcellus, 1640, hoog 52 ½ duim, breed 34 duim, op paneel, zwarte lyst | *Mat:* op paneel *Size:* hoog 52 ½ duim, breed 34 duim *Inscr:* Jacobus Marcellus, 1640 (signed and dated?) *Notes:* It is unclear whether the name and date are inscribed on the painting.	Mejuffrouw A van der Mieden	(Sold) fl 1:2 Kaijpets
1803/09/07	AMSCH	0111	*J. Marell* | Een capitaal stil Leeven, op een Tafel ziet men een ménigte zoorten van Vruchten, met Steel en Bladeren, waarby een gekookte	Smidt	(Bought In) fl 52

			Kreeft, een Roemer Wyn, en Annanas-plant. zeer Natuurlyk en uitvoerig gepenceeld [Un intérieur, représentant une table sur laquelle on voit différentes espèces de fruits avec leurs queues et leurs feuilles ; une écrevisse cuite, un verre à la romaine et une plante d'Ananas. Tableau capital, plein de vérité et d'un coloris naturel] | *Mat:* op doek *Size:* hoog 30, breed 42 duim		
1803/09/07	AMSCH	0112	*J. Marell* | Op een Tafel legt een schoone party zoo witte als blauwe Druiven, Canteloepen, Oranjeäppelen, en een geschilde Citroen, alles behandeld als de voorgaande [Une table chargée de raisins blancs et rouges, d'oranges, de citrons pelés ; même manière et d'un mérite semblable au précédent] | *Mat:* op paneel *Size:* hoog 25, breed 31 duim [Haut 30, large 42 pouces] *Notes:* The dimensions differ in the Dutch and French editions of the catalogue.	Smidt	(Bought In) fl 21
			Marseus van Schrieck, Otto		
1802/05/05	AMSCH	0144	*O. Marceus* | Een Vaas met verscheide Bloemen, waar op diversche Insecten aazen, aller uitvoerigst | *Mat:* op doek *Size:* hoog 22, breed 18 duim	C	(Sold) fl 13 Stevens
1802/05/11	GRGRW	0013	*Marceus* | Een dito [Bloemstuk], met een Beker van hoorn [Schilderijen met Olie-Verf; In zwarte Lijsten] | *Mat:* in olyverf *Notes:* The bracketed information in the title about the medium appears above lot 1 and refers to lots 1 to 79a.	Arnold Sicco Werumeus	(Unknown)
1802/06/28	AMSCH	0117	*O. Marseus* | In een Hofgezicht ziet men eenige rustende Kippen, Haan, Eendvogels enz., fiks gepenceeld, door O. Marseus. Doek | *Mat:* op doek *Size:* hoog 24, breed 21 duim	B	(Sold) fl 1 L Pakker
1802/07/27	AKHRK	0015	*Otto Marseus* | In een aangenaam Landschap beschouwt men, aan den voet van een Distel, een kronkelende verstoorde Slang uitschieten na een Hagedis; een IJsvogel neemt hier op de vlugt. Voorts ziet men Kapellen, Uilen en verdere Insecten, neffens Bladen en Kruidjes, en zijn zonderlinge manier van gronden, op de schoonste en uitvoerigste wijze behandeld | *Mat:* op doek *Size:* hoog 39 ½, breed 22 duim	Maria Stategaart	(Sold) fl 38 Bucerus
1802/09/06	AMSCH	0080	*Otto Marceus* | Eenige Distelen, Planten, Slangen, Hagedis en Capellen; zeer uitvoerig | *Mat:* op doek *Size:* hoog 29, breed 21 duim	Mevrouw Achtienhoven	(Sold) fl 13:5 de Meijer
1802/09/06	AMSCH	0081	*Otto Marceus* | Twee stuks dito met dito [Distelen, Planten, Slangen, Hagedis en Capellen]; door denzelven [Otto Marceus]	Mevrouw Achtienhoven	(Sold) fl 4 Gruiter
1803/06/20	AMSCH	0066	*O. Marseus* | By een Berkenstam, ziet men eenige Kruiden en Insecten, uitvoerig op Doek | *Mat:* op doek *Size:* hoog 22, breed 17 duim	Schley [for] K	(Sold) fl 1:5 Plux
1803/09/07	AMSCH	0113	*O. Marceus* | Twee stuks Landschappen, met Plantgewassen en Distelen, alwaar verscheide Insecten op aazen, uitvoerig op Paneel [Deux paysages, plein d'arbrisseaux et d'épines, avec des insectes ; d'une bonne ordonnance] | *Mat:* op paneel *Size:* hoog 14, breed 10 duim [Hauts 14, larges 19 pouces] *Notes:* The dimensions differ in the Dutch and French editions of the catalogue.	Smidt	(Sold) fl 5 de Lafontaine
1804/02/27	AMSCH	0077	*Marseus. (O.)* | Eenige Distels en Planten, waarop Insecten aazen; byzonder uitvoerig van schildering | *Mat:* op paneel *Size:* hoog 23, breed 20 duim	B	(Sold) fl 13 Coclers
1804/08/08	AMSCH	0129	*O. Marseus* | Twee stuks Landschappen, beiden gestoffeerd met verschillend Plantgewas, waarop eenige Capellen aazen, op de grond Slangen, een Hagedisch, en een Muisje; zeer natuurlyk en uitvoerig gepenceeld | *Mat:* op doek *Size:* yder hoog 24, breed 19 duim	Schley [for] A	(Sold) fl 23:10 Th Spaan
1804/10/08	RMCNL	0003	*Otto Marsaeus* | Twee stuks met Distels en Bloemen	A t'Hooft	(Unknown)
1805/12/16	AMSCH	0043	*O. Marceus* | Een Boomstam, met eenige Distelen en Insecten, uitvoerig op Doek | *Mat:* op doek *Size:* hoog 23, breed 17 duim	R[oos]	(Sold) fl 0:6 L Pakker
1807/04/13	AMSCH	0009	*O. Marceus* | Twee stuks Landschappen, met Geboomte, Bloemen en Bladen, waarop Insectens aazen, fraai van schildering | *Size:* Ieder hoog 11, breed 7 duim	Everard de Burlett	(Sold) fl 2 Levy Pakker
1808/05/18	LNAN	0009	*O. Marseus* | Een Fruit-Stuk, zeer uitvoerig geschilderd | *Notes:* The artist's name "O. Marseus" was added in by hand in the RKDH copy of the catalogue.	Mr Cornelis Versluys	(Unknown)
1808/05/18	LNAN	0010	*O. Marseus* | 2 Stuks Dito [Fruit-Stukken], zeer uitvoerig | *This Lot:* Een Fruit-Stuk *Notes:* Lots 10 and 11 were printed in the catalogue as one item. The artist's name "O. Marseus" was added in by hand in the RKDH copy of the catalogue.	Mr Cornelis Versluys	(Unknown)
1808/05/18	LNAN	0011	*O. Marseus* | 2 Stuks Dito [Fruit-Stukken], zeer uitvoerig | *This Lot:* Een Fruit-Stuk *Notes:* Lots 10 and 11 were printed in the catalogue as one item. The artist's name "O. Marseus" was added in by hand in the RKDH copy of the catalogue.	Mr Cornelis Versluys	(Unknown)
1808/11/28	AMSCH	0041	*Otto Marseus* | In een Landschap, ziet men bij de Stam van een Boom, eenige Kruijden en Plantgewas, waar op onderscheidene Capellen aasen, op de grond een Hagedis, uitvoerig | *Mat:* op doek *Size:* hoog 17, breed 15 duim	S	(Bought In) fl 14:10
1809/06/13	AMSCH	0115	*O. Marseus* | In een Landschap ziet men op de voorgrond eenige fraaije Bloemen, bij Kruiden en Plantgewas, waarop Capellen aazen; uitvoerig | *Mat:* op paneel *Size:* hoog 22, breed 16 duim	Q	(Sold) fl 0:12 v der Schley [for] A

1810/07/23	DOLG2	0029	*O. Marsenus* | Een dito Fruitstuk, niet minder behandeld dan het voorgaande | *Mat:* op doek *Size:* hoog 22, breed 19 duim *Notes:* It is unclear what "dito" refers to in the title.	Pieter Quinting	(Unknown) fl 1:10

Marseus van Schrieck, Otto (changed to Begeyn)

1809/04/17	AMSCH	0065	*O. Marseus; Begyn* | In een Landschap, ziet men bij de Stam van een Boom, eenige Kruijden en Plantgewas, waarop onderscheidene Capellen aazen, op de grond een Kikvorsch en ander Gedierten; uitvoerig geschilderd | *Mat:* op doek *Size:* hoog 41, breed 35 duim *Notes:* The artist's name was changed by hand from "O. Marseus" to "Begyn" in the EBNP copy of the catalogue.	H	(Sold) fl 6:10

Mart, van der [Unidentified]

1808/12/31	RMHSN	0035	*Vander Mart* | Een klein Landschapje | *Mat:* op paneel	G Spanjaart [or] H de Haas [or] C van der Looy Lans	(Unknown)

Martelli

1801/03/16	AMSCH	0059	*Martelli* | Een Italiaansche Vrouw, houdende een Spaansch Hondje in den arm, fraai geschilderd | companion to lot 60	P[ruyssenaar]	(Bought In) fl 5 ¼ for lots 59 & 60
1801/03/16	AMSCH	0060	*Martelli* | Een Italiaansche Boer, met een mand Appelen by zich, rustende met de hand onder 't hoofd | companion to lot 59	P[ruyssenaar]	(Bought In) fl 5 ¼ for lots 59 & 60

Martin

1804/10/16	DLOND	0134	*Martin* | Twee stukjens. Ene Zalmvisschery. Deux pièces. Une pêche de Saumon | *Mat:* op paneel *Size:* hoog 10, breed 16		(Unknown)

Martszen, Jan (the younger)

1801/03/16	AMSCH	0054	*Jan Marssen* | Een hevige Bataille tusschen Ruytery, op de voorgrond leggen eenige dooden, natuurlyk en breed geschilderd	P[ruyssenaar]	(Sold) fl 3:5 J v^{n} d^{n} Bergh
1801/12/22	AMOTT	0038	*J. Marse* | 1 Schermutseling te Paard	Bartholomeus Ruloffs	(Unknown) fl 1:10
1802/05/05	AMSCH	0140	*J. Marsse de Jonge* | Voor eenige Tenten ziet men een Dame te Paard, waarby eenige Militairen te Paard en te Voet, natuurlyk | *Mat:* op paneel *Size:* hoog 19, breed 24 duim	E	(Sold) fl 22 Spruit
1802/05/05	AMSCH	0141	*J. Marsse de Jonge* | Een Rencontre tusschen Ruiters, zeer natuurlyk | *Mat:* op paneel *Size:* hoog 11, breed 13 duim	G	(Sold) fl 1:10 L Pakker
1802/05/05	AMSCH	0142	*J. Marsse de Jonge* | Een dito [Rencontre tusschen Ruiters] als de voorgaande | *Mat:* op paneel *Size:* hoog 11, breed 14 duim	G	(Sold) fl 2:10 Mensard
1802/06/16	AMSCH	0116	*Jan Marsen, de Jonge* | Het inneemen van een Stad, met verscheiden Krygslieden, zo te voet als te Paard, die elkander hévig bevegten; dit stuk is vol Vuur; en fraai gepenceeld | *Mat:* op doek *Size:* hoog 26, breed 42 duim	[Merrem]	(Sold) fl 30 Coclers
1802/06/28	AMSCH	0116	*J. Marsen de Jongen* | Een Legerplaats, op de voorgrond een menigte Krygslieden te Voet en te Paard, verders verscheide Tenten; fiks door J. Marsen de Jongen, Panneel | *Mat:* op paneel *Size:* hoog 18, breed 24 duim	B	(Sold) fl 1:15 Mensart
1802/12/13	AMSCH	0124	*J. Marsen, de Jonge* | Een hevige Rencontre tusschen Ruitery, in een Landschap | *Mat:* op paneel *Size:* hoog 18, breed 24 duim	Pruyssenaar [for] D	(Sold) fl 19:10 B Boelen
1803/04/27	AMSCH	00BB[H]	*J Marsen* | Een Bataille door J Marsen | *Notes:* This lot was added in by hand in the LBDa copy of the catalogue.	C	(Sold) fl 4:5 Vermeulen
1803/09/07	AMSCH	0110	*J. Marssen de Jonge* | Een Rencontre tusschen verscheiden Ruiters, in een Landschap, de Paarden zyn stout geschilderd, zoo ook de Beelden, alles in een breede manier [Une rencontre de plusieurs cavaliers, dans une campagne ; le chevaux et les figures sont d'un dessin hardi. Ce tableau est largement peint] | *Mat:* op paneel *Size:* hoog 16, breed 25 duim	Smidt	(Sold) fl 10 La fontaine
1804/05/07	AMSCH	0117	*Marssen, de jonge. (J.)* | De beroemde Slag by Nieuwpoort in Vlaandederen [sic], tusschen Prins Maurits, en Albertus van Oostenryk, den 3 July, 1600. – met het welgelykend Pourtrait van Maurits; zynde dit een ryke ordonantie en van een fraaije schildering | *Mat:* op doek *Size:* hoog 47, breed 64 duim	R[oos]	(Bought In) fl 135
1804/08/08	AMSCH	0127	*J. Marssen de Jonge* | Een Musicant met zyn Phiool in de Hand, schynende uit een Musiekboek te zingen; geestig gepenceeld | *Mat:* op paneel *Size:* hoog 12, breed 8 duim	Roos [for] G	(Sold) fl 3:15 Gruyter
1804/08/08	AMSCH	0128	*J. Marssen de Jonge* | Een hévige Rencontre, tusschen Ruitery, vol gewoel; de hartstochten zyn fraai en meesterlyk geschilderd | *Mat:* op paneel *Size:* hoog 18, breed 24 duim	Vink[eles] [for] W	(Sold) fl 6 van Iperen
1805/07/03	AMSCH	0032	*Marssen de Jonge. (J.)* | In een Bergachtig Landschap, ziet men een hevige rencontre tusschen Cavallerie, eenige doode en gekweste zo wel Ruiters als Paarden ziet men op de voorgrond; zynde alles vol vuur, en de behandeling meesterlyk | *Mat:* op paneel *Size:* hoog 19, breed 32 duim	R[oos]	(Sold) fl 22:10 Reyers
1805/07/03	AMSCH	0033	*Marssen, de Jonge (J.)* | Dit verbeeld mede een dito [hevige] Rencontre en is als de voorgaande behandeld | *Mat:* op paneel *Size:* hoog 19, breed 25 duim	R[oos]	(Sold) fl 1 Menzart

1805/07/10	AMSCH	0106	*J. Marssen, de Jonge* | Een Hévige Battaille tusschen Ruitery en Voetvolk in een Bergachtig Landschap; fraai van Hartstochten en delicaat gepenceeld | *Mat:* op doek *Size:* hoog 21, breed 32 duim	V[inkeles] [for] H[affner]	(Sold) fl 18 Tozelli
1805/07/10	AMSCH	0107	*J. Marssen, de Jonge* | In een Bergachtig Landschap, ziet men de Bataille Roeroix, tusschen de Spaansche en Fransche Generaal Enghuin; meesterlyk in de manier van Wouwerman | *Mat:* op doek *Size:* hoog 40, breed 53 duim	V[inkeles] [for] P	(Sold) fl 14 L Pakker
1806/05/05	AMSCH	0186	*J. Marssen* | Een Batailje van Ruiters	R[oos]	(Sold) fl 1 L Pakker
1806/08/13	AMSCH	0287	*J. Marsen, de jonge* | Twee stuks hévige Rencontres tusschen Ruitery	Vinkeles [for] E	(Sold) fl 8:15 Gruiter
1806/08/13	AMSCH	0295	*J. Marsen* | Een hévige Rencontre tusschen Ruitery; als J. Marsen	Vinkeles [for] F	(Sold) fl 5:5 Nieuwenhuis
1808/10/28	AMVRS	0030	*Marse, (J) de Jonge* | Twee hevige Gevechten, vol gewoel van Krijgsvolk. De karakters zijn natuurlijk en alles is vol uitdrukking | *Mat:* op koper *Size:* beide hoog 18, breed 28 duim	Marten Udink	(Sold) fl 20:10 H Pakker
1809/04/17	AMSCH	0137	*J.M. de Jong* | Een hevige Bataille tusschen Ruiterij en Voetvolk | *Mat:* op paneel	[Gruyter?]	(Sold or Bought In) fl 0:8 Gruyter
1810/06/20	AMSCH	0119	*J. Marsse de Jonge* | Twee Batailles	N	(Sold) fl 0:6 L Pakker
1810/10/11	AMSCH	0194	*J. Marsen* | Een hevig Gevegt tusschen Ruiterij, vol uitdrukking | *Mat:* op doek	A	(Sold) fl 0:10 L Pakker
1810/10/11	AMSCH	0216	*J. Marsen Den Jonge* | Een hevig Gevecht tusschen Spaansche en andere Ruiterij; krachtig | *Mat:* op paneel *Notes:* This lot was sold with lot 200, which is in the manner of Rubens.	A	(Sold) fl 2 for lots 200 & 216. Yver

Martszen, Jan (the younger) (and Miereveld, M.)

1803/08/17	AMSCH	0062	*Marsse de Jonge. (J.); Miereveld* | Het Pourtrait van Fredrik Hendrik, Prins van Orange, zittende op een schoon bruin Paard, in het verschiet het beleg der Stad Grol, uitvoerig en kragtig behandeld | *Mat:* op paneel *Size:* hoog 14, breed 11 duim	Anna Catharina Putman	(Sold) fl 25 Gruyter

Martszen, Jan (the younger) (manner)

1803/09/07	AMSCH	0229	*J. Marsse* | Een hevige Schermutzeling van Ruitery; geestig in de manier van J. Marsse [Un escarmouche de cavalerie ; composition spirituelle, d'après J. Marsse] | *Mat:* op paneel *Size:* hoog 17, breed 28 duim	Smidt	(Sold) fl 2 Levie Pakker
1805/07/03	AMSCH	0203	*J. Marsen* | Twee stuks, verbeeldende den eene een Schermutseling tusschen Ruitery, en den andere een Campement; beide ovaal formaat, in de manier van J. Marsen | *Mat:* op paneel *Fmt:* ovaal	R[oos]	(Sold) fl 4:10 Menzart

Massys, Quentin

1803/04/20	AMSCH	0042	*Matzys. (Q)* | Dit Voorwerp verbeeld Maria in een bedrukte gestalte, het doode Lyk van Christus met beide Armen Omhelzende, zynde uitvoerig van penceelsbehandeling [J.C. mort dans les bras de la V.M. vû à mi-corps, peint sur fond doré . tableau fini ayant le merite de l'ancienté.] | *Mat:* op paneel *Size:* hoog 26, breed 20 duim	Maria Magdalena van Sluypwyk, gravinne van Moens	(Sold) fl 19 Gruiter

Massys, Quentin (manner)

1807/08/26	AMSCH	0302	*Quintin Matsys* | Een Regtsgeleerde in zyn Kamer, waarby verscheiden Boeren als met angst eetbare waren komende brengen; in de manier van Quintin Matsys	Joseph Vallette	(Sold) fl 6:5 Caré

Maton, Bartholomeus

1802/08/24	LNDLS	0004	*M. Matton* | Dit Stuk verbeeld een Wijnkelder, waar in een beschonken Dienstmaagd tegen een Wijuvat [sic] rustende, met een roemer in de hand, nevens haar staat een potsig mannetje, die haar, met een brandende kaars in de hand, lagchende beschouwd, en een Jongeling die dat aanwijst. Uitvoerig en kragtig, zoo goed als van G. Dou, door M. Matton, op paneel geschilderd | *Mat:* op paneel *Size:* hoog 18 ½, breed 14 ½ duimen *Notes:* The artist's name was given as "M. Matton" but we have assumed this is an error.	Leonardus Bouman [or others]	(Unknown) fl 117
1806/08/13	AMSCH	0105	*Matton. (B.)* | In een verwulft Vertrek ziet men een Schoenmaker bézig een schoen te maken, voor dezelve een Tafel en Stoel, waarop verscheide Schoenmakers gereedschap en verder bywerk; piquant van licht en alleruitvoerigst van penceelsbehandeling | *Mat:* op paneel *Size:* hoog 13, breed 10 duim	Coclers	(Withdrawn)
1810/08/01	AMSCH	0056	*Matton (J.)* | Voor een Buitenhuis zit een bedaagd Man tegen den Stam van eenen Boom op de Viool te spelen, wordende hem door eene oude Vrouw een Glas met Bier aangeboden; voor hem bij eene Tafel zit een vergenoegde Boer, die zijn Pijp rookt, daarnevens een Meisje, dat zingt, en een staand vrolijk Jongeling [Audevant d'une habitation de Campagne s'assit un Viellard, adossé contre un tronc-d'arbre, jouant du Violon, auquel une Vielle vient presenter un verre de bierre, et auprès d'une Table est assis un rustre jovial fumant sa pipe à côté d'une fille qui chante, et d'un jeune homme qui paroit prendre part à la joye] | *Annots:* Bien composé, dessiné et colorié. (NGW) *Mat:* op paneel *Size:* hoog 18, breed 14 duimen *Notes:* The artist's name was given as "Matton (J.)" but we have assumed this is an error.	Mr Pieter de Smeth van Alphen	(Sold) fl 710 T Spaan [for] Croese d'Amsterdam

Maton, Bartholomeus (manner)

1807/06/10	HGBSM	0186	*Matton* | Een Schilder in een Nis, in de trand van Matton | *Mat:* op paneel *Size:* hoog 12 ½, breed 9 ½ duim	Abraham Delfos [or others]	(Sold) fl 3 Van Dongen

Matthieu, Cornelis

1801/05/11	AMSCH	0057	*C. Mathieu* | Een bergachtig Landschap met een waterval, op de Voorgrond met beelden en beesten gestoffeerd, fix geschilderd | *Mat:* op doek *Size:* hoog 26, breed 21 duim	Pruisse [for] M	(Sold) fl 3:15 Mensart
1804/04/28	LNDLS	0039	*C. Mattheiu* | Een Landschap met gebergten, boomen, gebouwen en stoffagie, in de trant van Both, door C. Mattheiu 1654, op doek | companion to lot 40 *Mat:* op doek *Size:* hoog 24, breed 30 duim *Inscr:* C. Mattheiu 1654 (signed and dated?) *Notes:* It is unclear whether the name and date are inscribed on the painting.	[Abraham Delfos] [or others]	(Sold) fl 5:5 Rigter [for] A
1804/04/28	LNDLS	0040	*C. Mattheiu* | Een Weêrga, nier minder en uitvoerig, door denzelven [C. Mattheiu] | companion to lot 39 *Notes:* It is unclear whether the name and date are inscribed on the painting.	[Abraham Delfos] [or others]	(Sold) fl 5:5 Rigter [for] A
1807/08/26	AMSCH	0132	*Mathieu* | Een bevallig natuurlyk Landschap, met Woning en Geboomte, by een stil Water; op den voorgrond Visschers, bézig een Net op te halen, waarby een Schuitje in de Rivier; alles vertoont zich by opkomend Maanlicht, en is meesterlyk gepenceeld, op Paneel, door .... Mathieu | *Mat:* op paneel *Size:* hoog 17, breed 14 duim	Yver [for] S	(Sold) fl 9 T Spaan

Maurer, Jacob (I)

1801/02/18	AMBOS	0035	*Jac. Maurer* | Den Heiland in Gethsemané, door den Engel gesterkt	J Schonevelt	(Unknown)
1801/02/18	AMBOS	0036	*Jac. Maurer* | Den Heiland, daar dezelfde gevangen genoomen word	J Schonevelt	(Unknown)
1801/02/18	AMBOS	0037	*Jac. Maurer* | Een Basrelief met Kindertjes, in het graauw	J Schonevelt	(Unknown)
1805/12/16	AMSCH	0038	*J. Maurer* | Christus Dood aan het Kruis hangende, Maria ondersteund schynt in zwym te vallen, waar by verscheide Godvrugtige Vrouwen, op de Voorgrond zit een Romynsche Soldaat, en verder andere lieden; de Hartstogten zyn natuurlyk verbeeld, en uitvoerig van Penceel behandeling | *Mat:* op doek *Size:* hoog 44, breed 36 duim	R[oos]	(Bought In) fl 260

Mazyn, H. [Unidentified]

1801/04/23	AMYVR	0044	*H. Mazyn* | Twee stuks Zeegezichten met Scheepen en Schuiten gestoffeerd, op Doek geschilderd | *Mat:* op doek		(Unknown)

Meer, N. van der [Unidentified]

1802/09/06	AMSCH	0074	*N. van der Meer* | Een Boomryk Landschap, op de voorgrond gestoffeerd met Schaapjes en Bokjes, verder een Reiziger met een beladen Ezel, plaisant geschilderd | *Mat:* op paneel *Size:* hoog 14, breed 11 duim	Wed Grave [or others]	(Bought In) fl 5 ¼

Meer, N. van der [Unidentified] (manner)

1806/08/13	AMSCH	0272	*N. van der Meer* | Een Grazige Heuvel, gestoffeerd met verscheide Schaapen en Véehoeders; in de manier van N. van der Meer	Roos	(Sold) fl 2 du Pree

Meijer, Hendrik

1801/08/19	AMSCH	0062	*H. Meyer* | Twee Arcadische Landschappen, ryk gestoffeerd met Beelden en Vee	Pruyssen^{r} [for] Q	(Sold) fl 19:10 Le Dantú
1802/05/05	AMSCH	0121	*H. Meyer* | Voor de Ruïne van een Oud Gebouw ziet men eenige Huislieden te paard en te voet, met verscheiden Ossen en Schapen, alles delicaat en uitvoerig behandeld | companion to lot 122 *Size:* hoog 24, breed 30 duim	D	(Bought In) fl 120 for lots 121 & 122
1802/05/05	AMSCH	0122	*H. Meyer* | De Wedergade van de voorgaande, is mede een Ruïne met een Watermolen, en een menigte stoffagie van bevallige Vrouwen en verscheiden Veê, in alles als de voorgaande | companion to lot 121 *Size:* hoog 24, breed 30 duim	D	(Bought In) fl 120 for lots 121 & 122
1802/05/22	RMHSN	0024	*Meijer* | Een Zee-strand volgewoel, door Meijer	Lambertus Bicker	(Unknown)
1804/12/10	AMSCH	0062	*H. Meyer* | Een capitaale Ordinantie, zynde een gezicht naar Duin, op de voorgrond ryk gestoffeerd met verscheide Dames en Heeren die zig aan zee-strand lustig vermaaken, ter zyde vertoont zig een Rytuig met vier paarden bespannen, Heeren met Rypaarden, en een rustende Visser met zyn Vrouw, hoger op Duin een rydende Wagen, en verscheide Vissers by een vuurtooren, verder een Kerk, in 't verschiet, aan zee vissers Vaartuigen en diverse Zeelieden; alles is bevallig, natuurlyk en zeer uitvoerig gepenceeld | *Mat:* op doek *Size:* Hoog 22, breed 32 ½ duim	Jan De Groot	(Sold) fl 68 Numan
1806/05/05	AMSCH	0091	*de Meyer* | Aan het Strand ziet men een talryke Visverkooping, aankomende Pinken, eenige Viskarren, en eene meenigte van Aanschouwers, maken dit tot een ryk en verdienstig schildery | *Mat:* op paneel *Size:* hoog 32, breed 47 duim	V[inkeles]	(Sold) fl 2:15 Gruyter
1807/04/00	LNDLS	0013	*H. Meyer* | Een Landschapje, op den voorgrond een heuvel daar een man bij twee zittende vrouwtjes staat, verder een gebouw bij een vervallen muur en waterval, daar een vrouwtje met een kind op haar rug langs een water gaat, en verder meer stoffagie, alleruitvoerigst en fraai van couleur | *Mat:* op paneel *Size:* hoog 11 en een half, breed 13 en een half duim	[Abraham Delfos] [or others]	(Unknown)

1807/06/10	HGBSM	0013	*H. Meyer* | Een Landschapje, op den voorgrond een heuvel daar een man bij twee zittende vrouwtjes staat, verder een gebouw bij een vervallen muur en waterval, daar een vrouwtje men een kind op haar rug langs een water gaat, en verder meer stoffagie, alleruitvoerigst en fraai van couleur | *Mat:* op paneel *Size:* hoog 11 ½, breed 13 ½ duim	Abraham Delfos [or others]	(Sold) fl 19:5 Tessier
1808/08/23	AMSCH	0112	*Meijer. (H.)* | Een Duin en Boomrijk Landschap met Boeren Woningen, op de voorgrond staande en rustende Landlieden, benevens Jagers met hunne Honden, verder bij een Waterplas, een Herder met een kudde Schaapen, en een aangenaam verschiet; zonachtig en uitvoerig geschilderd | *Mat:* op doek *Size:* hoog 19, breed 26 duim	[Gruyter?]	(Sold) fl 42 Reijers
1808/11/28	AMSCH	0045	*H. Meijer* | Een aangenaam Gezicht buiten een der Stads Poorten te Leijden, rijk met Beeldjes gestoffeerd en uitvoerig op Doek behandeld | *Mat:* op doek	[Gruyter?]	(Sold) fl 4:5 du Pree
1809/04/17	AMSCH	0064	*H. Meijer* | Een aangenaam Landschap, ter zijde bij een Rivier een Molen en stoffagie van Beeldjes; zonagtig en plaisant geschilderd | *Mat:* op doek *Size:* hoog 13, breed 16 duim	[Gruyter?]	(Sold) fl 2:15
1810/05/22	AMSCH	0063	*Meijer (H.)* | Twee stuks aangenaame Heuvelachtige Landschappen, met Boeren Woningen, Watermolen en Geboomten, beide rijk gestoffeerd met Huislieden, Kinderen, Veehoeders en Schaapen, in 't verschiet een Kerktoren en Gebergte; beide zonachtig en uitvoerig gepenceeld | *Mat:* op paneel *Size:* Jeder hoog 17, breed 21 duim	Johannes van de Putte Nicolaasz.	(Sold) fl 70 van Iperen
1810/06/06	RMMUY	0049	*H. de Meyer* | Een kapitaal Duin, Strand en Zeegezigt, rijk gestoffeerd met Figuren, Paarden, Wagens enz. Meesterlijk geschilderd door H. de Meyer | *Mat:* op paneel		(Unknown) fl 6
1810/06/20	AMSCH	0063	*H. Meijer* | Een hoog bergachtig Landschap, gestoffeerd met Landlieden en hun Vee, gaande en rustende Reizigers en een aangenaam verschiet. Zonachtig en uitvoerig van schildering | *Mat:* op doek *Size:* hoog 18, breed 23 duimen	A	(Sold) fl 14:10 du Pree
			Meijer, Hendrik (II)		
1801/10/19	AMSCH	0039	*Meijer. (H.) 1778* | Een ryk gestoffeerd Landschap met rustende Reizigers, en in 't verschiet ziet men een Dorp | companion to lot 40 *Mat:* op paneel *Size:* hoog 13, breed 17 duim *Inscr:* 1778 (dated?) *Notes:* It is unclear whether the date is inscribed on the painting.	Jonkheer Menno Baron van Coehoorn	(Sold) fl 80 for lots 39 & 40. van der Schleij [for] A
1801/10/19	AMSCH	0040	*Meijer. (H.) 1778* | Een dito [Landschap] tot weederga, zynde mede een duinächtig Landschap; ryk gestoffeerd en beiden zeer fraay en uitvoerig gepenseeld | companion to lot 39 *Mat:* op paneel *Size:* hoog 13, breed 17 duim *Inscr:* 1778 (dated?) *Notes:* It is unclear whether the date is inscribed on the painting.	Jonkheer Menno Baron van Coehoorn	(Sold) fl 80 for lots 39 & 40. van der Schleij [for] A
			Meijer, Hendrik de (I)		
1805/10/09	HGBSM	0135	*H: de Meyer* | Een rencontre van cavallerie, door H. de Meyer 1647 | *Mat:* op paneel *Size:* hoog 22 ½ breet 31 ½ duim *Inscr:* H. de Meyer 1647 (signed and dated?) *Notes:* It is unclear whether the name and date are inscribed on the painting.	T H van Willigen [or others]	(Sold) fl 2:18 Van der Meer
1807/06/10	HGBSM	0100	*Meyer* | Een Rencontre van Cavallerie, op een brug | *Mat:* op paneel *Size:* hoog 14 ½, breed 19 duim	Abraham Delfos [or others]	(Sold) fl 3 Smeets
			Meincs, Gabriel [Unidentified]		
1810/08/06	AMSCH	0070	*Meincs (Gabriel)* | Maria Magdalena in berouw, aandagtig knielende voor een Crucifix; Kragtig en meesterlijk geschilderd | *Mat:* op doek *Size:* hoog 28, breed 23 duimen	A	(Sold) fl 8 T Spaan
			Melder, Gerard		
1810/10/11	AMSCH	0146	*G. Melder* | Een Badje van Diana, in miniatuur	C	(Sold) fl 6:15 Posthumus
			Metsu, Gabriel		
1801/03/16	AMSCH	0001	*G. Metzu* | Een bevallig Mans Pourtret ter halven lyven, meesterlyk en zeer fraai van penceel behandeling	P[ruyssenaar]	(Sold) fl 219 for lots 1 & 2. Cocler
1801/03/16	AMSCH	0002	*G. Metzu* | Een dito [Pourtret] zynde een Vrouwe Poutret, niet minder als de vorige	P[ruyssenaar]	(Sold) fl 219 for lots 1 & 2. Cocler
1801/04/13	AMSCH	0042	*G. Metzu* | In een gemeubileerd binnevertrek zit een bevallige Dame in 't rood zyd gekleed, aan een Tafel met een Tapytenkleed, waarop een Bas ligt, zy heeft een Muzykblad in haar hand, ter zyde de Tafel staat een Heer beezig zyn Viool te stellen, op de voorgrond een Patryshond, het bevallige licht aangenaame coloriet en delicaate penceels behandeling, maken dit stukje tot een der beste van deezen voortreflyken Meester | *Mat:* op doek *Size:* hoog 17, breed 15 duim *Loc:* London, England, UK. National Gallery. (838)	Pierre Fouquet, junior	(Sold) fl 670 C S Roos
1801/05/11	AMSCH	0046	*G. Metzu* | In een gemeubileert Vertrek, vertoont zig een oud Man, zittende voor een tafel, met een kleed bedekt, waar op een koffertje en eenig los goud en zilver geld geplaast is, hy schynt speetsie te weegen: ter zyde staat een Vrouw in treurige gestalten, met een gezeegeld [sic] papier in de hand, als met een bedrukt gelaat, hem toespreekende: de caracters zyn natuurlyk, het licht bevallig, en alles meesterlyk en fraay gepenceeld |	E[lias]	(Sold) fl 850 C Buijs

			Mat: op doek *Size:* hoog 28 ½, breed 25 duim *Loc:* Boston, MA, USA. Museum of Fine Arts. (1889.501)		
1801/06/10	AMSCH	0108	*Metzu. (G.)* | In een gemeubileerd Binnevertrek, zit een Heer aan een Tafel, waar over een Tapytenkleed ligt te schryven, dit Stuk is aller delicaatst en kloek behandeld | *Mat:* op doek *Size:* hoog 22, breed 17 duim	Herman ten Kate	(Sold) fl 135 Pruijssenaar
1801/06/10	AMSCH	0109	*Metzu. (G.)* | Op een Tafel, ziet men een Mand met groente nevens een met Eyeren, waar voor twee dooden Eenden, ter zyde hangt een dooden Haan, alles uitvoerig en krachtig geschilderd | *Mat:* op paneel *Size:* hoog 9, breed 8 duim	Herman ten Kate	(Sold) fl 145 Coclers
1802/06/16	AMSCH	0104	*G. Metzu* | Voor een open steene Nis, vertoont zich een Neegerin, in deftige kleeding, halver lyf; voor de Plint ziet men een Basrelief van speelende Kindertjes; uitvoerig en natuurlyk gepenceeld | *Mat:* op paneel *Size:* hoog 9, breed 7 duim	[Merrem]	(Sold) fl 25 v d Schley
1802/06/28	AMSCH	0118	*G. Metzu* | In een Binnenvertrek, zit een bevallig Vrouwtje beezig Kant te werken; voor een open vengster legt een oude Vrouw met een Kip in de hand, gestoffeert met verscheide Bywerk; meesterlyk geschilderd door G. Metzu | *Mat:* op paneel *Size:* hoog 14, breed 11 duim	Anna Elink	(Sold) fl 3:5 Vermeulen
1802/07/20	MGSAN	0048	*G. Metzu* | Een extra schoon Stuk, verbeeldende een Dame, aan haar Toilet, een Brief ontfangende, en een Knecht by haar, schynende antwoord te wachten, op Paneel: extra delicaat en schoon geschilderd | *Mat:* op paneel *Size:* hoog duim 20 ½, breed duim 15		(Unknown)
1802/07/21	HGKAN	0009	*Get. Metzu* | Een slapende Vrouw by de Wieg		(Unknown)
1804/05/07	AMSCH	0099	*Metzu. (G.)* | In een deftig Gemeubileerde Binnenkamer, zit een Dame met een bond Jakje, door de Doctor de pols gevoeld wordende, terwyl de Chirurgyn beezig is haar op haar voet te koppen [sic], verder een Dienstmaagd en een Kind; alles is bevallig en delicaat gepenceeld | *Mat:* op doek *Size:* hoog 21, breed 18 duim	Roos [for] A	(Bought In) fl 50
1804/07/25	AMSCH	0051	*Metzu. (G.)* | Dit capitaal zinryk geordineert Tafreel, vertoont de Gerechtigheid, als beschermster van Weduwe en Weezen; en werd door een vliegend Kindje een Kroon boven het hoofd gehouden; zy staat in een edele houding, in witte Zatyne Kleeding, met de eene hand de Schaal in evenwigt houdende, en in de andere het Zwaard, op de borst gezet van List, die, op den grond nedergeworpen, door haare voeten vertreeden word; nevens deeze legt geldbeurs en het Masque van bedrog; ter eener zyde vertoont zig een Vrouw met een klein Kind in den armen, beneevens een Jongeling, beide op de knien leggende, als om hulp en bystand smeekende; ter andere zyde staat een prachtige Rechterstoel; de onderscheide hartstogten zyn natuurlyk, het licht en Coloriet bevallig, en een der uitvoerigste van deeze Meester | *Mat:* op doek *Size:* hoog 59, breed 47 duim *Loc:* Den Haag, Nederland. Mauritshuis. (95)		(Sold) fl 200 Pruizenaar [for] J
1804/08/08	AMSCH	0107	*G. Metzu* | In een deftig Gemeubileerde Binnenkamer zit een Dame met een Bont Jakje aan, welke door een Doctor de Pols gevoeld wordt, terwyl de Heelmeester bézig is haar op haar voet te koppen, verders een Dienstmaagd en een Kind; alles is bevallig gepenceelt | *Size:* hoog 21, breed 18 duim	Roos [for] F	(Sold) fl 37 Moll
1804/08/08	AMSCH	0108	*G. Metzu* | In een Binnenkamer voor een Tafel, met een Tapyt Kleed gedekt, waarop een Inktkooker staat, ziet men een bevallige Dame, gekleed met een Rood Fluweel Jak, met een Bonte Rand, en een Geele Zyde Rok, houdende in de rechterhand een Pen, en met de linker een Papier, zy schynt in gedachten te zitten over 't geen zy voorneemens is te schryven; allerfraaist getéekend, en uitvoerig geschilderd | *Mat:* op paneel *Size:* hoog 12, br. 10 ¼ duim	Vink[eles] [for] K[=Gruyter?]	(Bought In) fl 30
1804/10/16	DLOND	0136	*G. Metzu* | Een Meisjen, liggende over de deur bij enige Wyngaardranken. Une Fille s'appuye sur une porte entourée de quelques Sarmans | *Size:* hoog 9, breed 7 *Notes:* The lot was changed from "G. Metzu, Een Meisjen, liggende over de deur bij enige Wyngaardranken," to "C. Polenburg en B. Breenburg," without giving a title, at the front of the catalogue.		(Withdrawn)
1804/12/10	AMSCH	0052	*G. Metzu* | In het Voorhuis van een gebouw, staat een bevallige Dame, gekleed in een rood zatyn jakje met bont gevoerd, en geel zatyne rok; houdende by de hand een jong aardig kindje, met een hond speelende; door de openstaande deur, komt een man, met zyn hoed in de hand, een Bennetje met vis brengen, op de stoep zyn twee speelende kindertjes, verder aan de overzyde der gragt een gebouw, alles is natuurlyk, het licht bevallig en van een uitvoerige penceel behandeling | *Mat:* op doek op paneel *Size:* Hoog 21 ½, breed 17 duim	Jan De Groot	(Sold) fl 351 van der Schley [and] C S Roos
1806/08/13	AMSCH	0102	*Metzu. (G.)* | In een gemeubileerd Binnenvertrek ziet men een bevallig Vrouwtje, zittende voor een Tafel, waarop een groen kleed ligt leezende in een Boek; delicaat en uitvoerig van penceelsbehandeling | *Mat:* op paneel *Size:* hoog 9, breed 8 duim	Vinkeles [for] D	(Sold) fl 203 Izaac Smit
1806/11/24	AMSCH	0041	*Metzu (G.)* | In een gemeubileerde Kamer zit een bedaagde Dame, in een Jakje met Bond gekleed, voor een Tafel, met een kleed gedekt, houdende een Hondje op de schoot, zy schynt een briefje aangenomen te hebben van een Dienstmaagd die ter zyde staat; natuurlyk fraai, en van eene uitvoerige penceelbehandeling | *Mat:* op paneel *Size:* hoog 13, breed 11 duim	Munnikhuizen	(Sold) fl 120 du Pree

1808/04/26	GDAN	0109	*Metzu (Gab.)* | In dit overheerlijk Schilderij ziet men een pragtig Gebouw, waar voor Geboomte, een reizig Heer in zeer deftige Kleding zijn bruin moedig Paard te bekijken, dat door een Jongeling aan den toom gehouden wordt | *Size:* hoog 42, breed 33 ½ duim	G H Fortuyn	(Unknown)
1808/04/26	GDAN	0110	*Metzu (Gab.)* | Een Vrouwtje zittende voor haar Toilet zich te tooijen, gekleed in een Jakje met een bonte rant, met bijwerk, zeer dun, kragtig en uitvoerig geschilderd | companion to lot 111 *Size:* hoog 9, breed 7 duim	G H Fortuyn	(Unknown)
1808/04/26	GDAN	0111	*Metzu (Gab.)* | Een dito tot een wederga, zijnde een Heer die met veel attentie op de Fluit speeld, 't Muziek legt voor hem op een tafel met een groen kleedje, mede zeer uitvoerig als het voorgaande | companion to lot 110 *Size:* hoog 9, breed 7 duim *Notes:* It is unclear what "dito" refers to in the title.	G H Fortuyn	(Unknown)
1808/06/13	AMSCH	0097	*Metzu (M.)* | Eene Haringvrouw, welke uit een Ton, die voor haar staat, een Haring aanbiedt, ter zijde een Tafel, waarop eenige Uijens en eene roode Schotel. Dit stuk verdient zoo in de voorstelling der Natuur, als in de penceelsbehandeling aller aanmerking | *Mat:* op doek *Size:* hoog 33, breed 27 duim *Notes:* The artist's name was given as "Metzu (M.)" but we have assumed this is an error.	E M Engelberts	(Sold) fl 281 vd Berghe de Gand
1809/04/22	AMYVR	0077	*G. Metzu* | In een Binnenkamer zit voor een Tafel eene bevallige Dame, gekleed in een Bont Jakje, zij ontvangt een Brief van eene Dienstmaagd, die achter haar staat; hetzelve is delicaat behandeld | *Mat:* op paneel *Size:* hoog 13, breed 11 duim	de Bruin	(Bought In) fl 85
1809/07/19	AMSCH	0034	*Metzu (G.)* | In een gemeubileerd Vertrek, zit een bevallig Vrouwtje, in aloude Hollandsche Kleeding, bij eene Tafel, waar op een Aarden Bierkan en Brood geplaatst zijn, zij houdt op den Schoot een Schotel, waar op een' stuk Vlees ligt, en in de regterhand een Mes. Dit fraai stukje is van eene uitvoerige penceelsbehandeling | *Mat:* op doek op paneel *Size:* hoog 8, breed 7 ½ duim	[Bicker]	(Sold) fl 50 Hendriks
1809/09/06	AMSCH	0046	*Metzu (G)* | Dit Voorwerp verbeeld de Dochter des Konings Herodes, houdende een Schotel in haare handen, waar op het Hoofd van Johannes den Dooper ligt, verder ziet men de Scherprechter; het is gloeijend en van een meesterlijke penceelbehandeling | *Mat:* op paneel *Fmt:* van boven toogsgewijs *Size:* hoog 8, breed 7 duim	Johannes Caudri	(Sold) fl 20:10 Gruyter
1809/09/06	AMSCH	0047	*Metzu (G)* | Een Schilder in zijn Kamer zittende, heeft voor zich op den Tafel, een Kan, Glas en Fiool leggen, hij schijnt door een Kijker naar eenig voorwerp te zien; het zelve is van een bevallige behandeling | *Mat:* op paneel *Size:* hoog 7 ½, breed 6 ½ duim	Johannes Caudri	(Sold) fl 16:10 Gruyter
1810/03/26	RMMUY	0029	*Gabriel Metzu* | Een Heer en Dame, gezeten aan eene met tapijt overdekte tafel, bezig met de kaart te spelen. Den Heer zijn kaart gespeeld hebbende, ziet men de verlegenheid der Dame, wat kaart zij spelen zal, natuurlijk uitgedrukt. Uitvoerig, breed en meesterlijk gepenceeld [Un Cavallier et sa Dame, assis à une table couverte d'un tapis, jouent aux cartes ; le cavallier paroit avoir joué, et on voit l'embarras de la Dame, ne sachant quelle carte elle jouera à son tour. Ce petit tableau, fin et rare de ce maître, est très précieux et d'un beau faire.] | *Mat:* op paneel *Fmt:* ovaal *Size:* hoog 7 ½, breed 6 ½ duimen	Daniel de Jongh Az	(Sold) fl 600 Le Brun Parys
1810/08/01	AMSCH	0058	*Metzu (Gabriel)* | Voor eene Boerenwoning staat eene Vrouw, met een Haringtobbetje onder haar arm; zij houdt in de regterhand eenen Haring, welken zij aan eene oude Boerin aanbiet [Devant une habitation de Village se presente une Marchande de Hareng, tenant une cuvette sous le bras, et un hareng à la main, elle offre cette denrée à une vielle Paysane, qui paroit la marchander] | *Annots:* médiocre. NB : il est de sa manière empâtée (NGW); 1729, 18 maart. Cat. van Philip Cosson, Amsterdam, no.7, 121 fl. aan G. Braancamp 1771, 13 Jul. Cat. van G. Braancamp, Amsterdam, no.128, 1610 fl. aan P Locquet (VAL I) *Mat:* op paneel *Size:* hoog 14 ½, breed 13 duimen *Loc:* Amsterdam, Nederland. Rijksmuseum. (A 2328)	Mr Pieter de Smeth van Alphen	(Bought In) fl 1650
1810/08/01	AMSCH	0059	*Metzu (Gabriel)* | In een Vertrek ziet men eene deftige Vrouw, in een rood fluweelen Jakje met bont, en met satijnen Rok gekleed, zittende te slapen, nevens haar bij een Ledikant staat eene Dienstmaagd, die het Bed warmt; op den voorgrond een Katje [Dans un apartement meublé se voit une Dame endormie ; elle est vétue d'un Casaquin de Velours rouge, doublé d'Ermine, et d'un Jupon de Satin blanc ; à son côté près d'un lit se trouve une Servante bassinant le lit. Sur le devant du tableau s'assit un Chat] | *Annots:* médiocre. (NGW) *Mat:* op paneel *Size:* hoog 16, breed 13 ½ duimen	Mr Pieter de Smeth van Alphen	(Sold) fl 2300 Cremer te Rotterdam
1810/08/01	AMSCH	0060	*Metzu (Gabriel)* | Een vergenoegd oud Man, rustende met zijnen arm op een Biervat, en houdende een Kan en Pijp in de handen [Un viellard Joyeux appuyant le bras sur un tonneau, et tenant une Pipe et sa Canette des deux mains] | *Annots:* fort bon, sauf la couleur de l'habit. NB : l'habit est d'un ton sale et sans effet. (NGW) *Mat:* op paneel *Size:* hoog 9, breed 7 ½ duimen *Loc:* Amsterdam, Nederland. Rijksmuseum. (A 250)	Mr Pieter de Smeth van Alphen	(Sold) fl 1560 T Spaan [for] Croese
			Metsu, Gabriel (or Metsu, manner)		
1804/02/27	AMSCH	0151	*G. Metzu* | In een gemeubileerde Kamer ziet men een Dame met een Kind op haar schoot zittende, op een Rustbank, waarby een Heer in aloude kleeding; fraai op Paneel, door of in de manier van G. Metzu | *Mat:* op paneel *Size:* hoog 19, breed 15 duim	D	(Sold) fl 2:5 van Iperen

<table>
<tr><td>1807/06/10</td><td>HGBSM</td><td>0071</td><td>*G. Metzu* | Een Smit, staande in zijn werkhuis op een aambeeld, een hoef ijzer te smeeden, met een Jongeling bij de Slijpsteen nevens hem, en veel gereedschap, terwijl een Heer neffens zijn Paard in 't travaille staat te wagten, door G. Metzu geördonneerd, door of in die trand geschilderd | *Mat:* op doek *Size:* hoog 24 breed 27 duim *Loc:* Den Haag, Nederland. Rijksdienst Beeldende Kunst. (1698) as copy after Metsu (?)</td><td>Abraham Delfos [or others]</td><td>(Sold or Bought In) fl 100 D</td></tr>
<tr><td>1808/06/11</td><td>RMRIJ</td><td>0127</td><td>*Door of in de manier van G: Metzu* | Eene Dame voor haar Toilettafel, met aangenaam Bywerk | *Mat:* op paneel</td><td></td><td>(Sold) fl 7 [or] 47 Rohan</td></tr>
<tr><td>1808/06/13</td><td>AMSCH</td><td>0098</td><td>*Metzu (M.), of in de manier* | Dit voorwerp verbeeld een Bordeel; in eene gemeubileerde Kamer vertoont zich eene galante Dame, op een Ledikant zittende, die door een Heer geliefkoosd wordt, daar nevens staat eene oude Matrone; verder gestoffeerd met onderscheiden bijwerk. Het is bevallig en meesterlijk gepenceeld | *Mat:* op paneel *Size:* hoog 22, breed 16 ½ duim *Notes:* The artist's name was given as "Metzu (M.)" but we have assumed this is an error.</td><td>[Jan Tersteeg]</td><td>(Sold) fl 46 van Drielst</td></tr>
<tr><td>1810/07/23</td><td>DOLGI</td><td>0069</td><td>*G. Metzu* | Door een Nis ziet men een Vrouwtje aan een Waschtobbe bezig met wasschen; op de Nis een roode aarden Kan, Zeep-Bak en Doek; uitmuntend van schikking en behandeling, en door, naar, of in de manier van, G. Metzu geschilderd | *Mat:* op paneel *Size:* hoog 10 ½, breed 8 ¼ duim</td><td>Mr Pieter van den Santheuvel</td><td>(Sold) fl 30:10 van Eijk à 's Hage</td></tr>
<tr><td>1810/10/11</td><td>AMSCH</td><td>0050</td><td>*G. Metzu* | Een Gezigt op de Groenmarkt te Leyden, met met verscheide Beelden, door of als G. Metzu | *Mat:* op paneel *Size:* hoog 14, breed 18 ½ duimen</td><td>C</td><td>(Sold) fl 6 Posthumus</td></tr>
</table>

Metsu, Gabriel (copy after)

<table>
<tr><td>1801/03/16</td><td>AMSCH</td><td>0145</td><td>*G. Metzu* | Een Dame in 't bond, naast haar een Heer met een roemer in de hand, naar G. Metzu</td><td>K[ip]</td><td>(Sold) fl 3 Koopman</td></tr>
<tr><td>1801/06/10</td><td>AMSCH</td><td>0124</td><td>*Metzu. (naar G.)* | Anna Maria Schuurman, zittende te Tekenen, naar een pleister Kop, aanhebbende een rood satyn Kleed, met een bonte Rand, alles is uitvoerig gevolgd | *Mat:* op paneel *Size:* hoog 14 ½, breed 11 ½ duim</td><td>Herman ten Kate</td><td>(Sold) fl 66 Reynders</td></tr>
<tr><td>1802/07/27</td><td>AKHRK</td><td>0062</td><td>*Metsu* | Een zeer uitvoerige Haringverkoopster; uitmuntend gevolgd na Metsu | *Mat:* op paneel *Size:* hoog 7, breed 5 ¼ duim</td><td>Maria Stategaart</td><td>(Sold) fl 7 for lots 62 & 63. Gruyter</td></tr>
<tr><td>1802/07/27</td><td>AKHRK</td><td>0063</td><td>*Metsu* | Een Botverkooper, stoppende zijn Pijp, behandeld als de voorige</td><td>Maria Stategaart</td><td>(Sold) fl 7 for lots 62 & 63. Gruyter</td></tr>
<tr><td>1802/09/06</td><td>AMSCH</td><td>0158</td><td>*G. Metzu* | Twee stuks, een Jongeling beezig zynde Vlees te snyden; en een Meisje met een Kan en Glas; na G. Metzu</td><td>Mevrouw Achtienhoven</td><td>(Sold) fl 11:10 Texier</td></tr>
<tr><td>1804/02/27</td><td>AMSCH</td><td>0064</td><td>*Lauwers. (J.); na G. Metzu* | Deze bevallige Ordonantie steld voor een Vrouwtje, bezig een Schelvis schoon te maken, nevens haar een Kopere Ketel, waarop een jong Katje; dit stukje is byzonder uitvoerig, zeer accuraat en meesterlyk gevolgd na het orgineel, berustende in het Kabinet van den Heer Hk. Muylman | copy by J.J. Lauwers after Metsu *Mat:* op doek *Size:* hoog 11, breed 10 duim</td><td>B</td><td>(Sold) fl 104 I^{c} Smit</td></tr>
<tr><td>1806/08/13</td><td>AMSCH</td><td>0162</td><td>*Regenmorter; na G. Metzu* | Door eene Steene Nis, met een Wyngaardrank en Vogelkooi, ziet men een bevallig Vrouwtje bézig zynde linnen te naaijen en verder bywerk; dun en delicaat en van de beste schildering van deeze Meester | copy by P. Regemorter after Metsu *Mat:* op paneel *Size:* hoog 12, breed 9 duim</td><td>Vinkeles [for] F</td><td>(Sold) fl 37 Schumacher</td></tr>
<tr><td>1808/06/06</td><td>RMRIJ</td><td>0023</td><td>*Coclers. (Bernard); naar Metzu* | Eene Vrouw aan eene Waschtobbe. Getrouw gevolgd en aangenaam geschilderd [Une Blanchisseuse occupée devant son Cuvier. Cette Copie est fidelle et bien traitée] | copy by B. Coclers after Metsu *Annots:* Verk. P. Spyk 23 Avril 1781 (f 50.-) Verk Drk Haak, Leiden, 8 April 1782 (f 17.-) (RMA I) *Mat:* op paneel *Size:* Hoog 8 ¾, en breed 7 ¾ duim</td><td>Gerrit van der Pot, Heer van Groeneveld</td><td>(Sold) fl 53 W van der Pot</td></tr>
</table>

Metsu, Gabriel (manner)

<table>
<tr><td>1802/12/13</td><td>AMSCH</td><td>0187</td><td>*Metzu* | Een Vrouw met een Kind op haar schoot, zittende by een Tafel, fix op Paneel als Metzu | *Mat:* op paneel</td><td>Yver</td><td>(Sold) fl 1 Van Iperen</td></tr>
<tr><td>1803/12/12</td><td>AMSCH</td><td>0140</td><td>*G. Metzu* | Een bevallig Meisje over een Nis leggende, met een Tinne Kan in haar hand; uitvoerig op Paneel, als G. Metzu | *Mat:* op paneel *Size:* hoog 11, breed 8 duim</td><td>Arnoud de Lange</td><td>(Sold) fl 49 Th^{s} Spaan</td></tr>
<tr><td>1804/04/28</td><td>LNDLS</td><td>0004</td><td>*G. Metzu* | Een Smit, staande in zyn werkhuis op een aambeeld een hoefyzer te smeden, met een Jonge by den slypsteen nevens hem, verders gereeschap, tot dien winkel behorende, terwyl een heer, nevens zyn paard (die in 't ravalje [sic] staat) daar na wagt. Dit stuk is door G. Metzu geordonneert, en geheel in die trant geschildert | *Mat:* op doek *Size:* hoog 24, breed 27 duim *Loc:* Den Haag, Nederland. Rijksdienst Beeldende Kunst. (1698) as copy after Metsu (?)</td><td>[Abraham Delfos] [or others]</td><td>(Bought In) fl 51</td></tr>
<tr><td>1806/08/13</td><td>AMSCH</td><td>0114</td><td>*Metzu. (als G.)* | In een Binnevertrek zit een Grysaard in een biddende gestalten; de schildering is breed en 't coloriet van een aangenaame couleur | *Mat:* op paneel *Size:* hoog 12, breed 9 duim</td><td>Roos</td><td>(Sold) fl 15:10 Th Spaan</td></tr>
<tr><td>1806/08/20</td><td>HGBSM</td><td>0083</td><td>*G. Metzu* | In een deftig Burger Binnevertrek, zit een jong Meisje met een groen Naaikussen op den schoot, bezig aan eenig linnen te verwerken, nevens haar een Mandtje met Linnen, uitvoerig geschilderd in de trant van G. Metzu | *Mat:* op doek *Size:* hoog 13, breed 11 duim</td><td>Macalester Loup [or others]</td><td>(Sold) fl 71 Lafontaine</td></tr>
</table>

<table>
<tr><td>1806/08/20</td><td>HGBSM</td><td>0084</td><td>G. Metzu | Een Boertje met een vergenoegd gelaat, voor hem een Schotel met Vleesch waar van hij een stuk schijnt te willen afsnijden, in de manier van het voorgaande [G. Metzu], geschilderd op paneel | Mat: op paneel Size: hoog 9 ½, breed 7 ½ duim</td><td>Macalester Loup [or others]</td><td>(Sold) fl 7 Gram</td></tr>
<tr><td>1808/06/11</td><td>RMRIJ</td><td>0106</td><td>Metzu | Een Vrouwtje zittende te Naaijen, heel fraai als door Metzu | Mat: op paneel Size: hoog 8, breed 6 ¾ duim</td><td></td><td>(Bought In) fl 2</td></tr>
</table>

Mettenleiter, Johann Jakob

<table>
<tr><td>1801/08/19</td><td>AMSCH</td><td>0058</td><td>Mettenleiter | In een Binnenhuis ziet men een Boer op een Stoel zitten, welke met aandacht naar een comique Landlooper luistert, die op een Lier speelt, waar by een Jongen met een Hond en een Aap, welke hy doet dansen, verders eenig Huisraad; alles delicaat en uitvoerig gepenceeld</td><td>Pruyssen^{r} [for] Q</td><td>(Bought In) fl 70 for lots 58 & 59</td></tr>
<tr><td>1801/08/19</td><td>AMSCH</td><td>0059</td><td>Mettenleiter | Men ziet een bedaagd Man yverig bezig Hout te kappen, ter zyde zit een aardig Boerinnetje dat bézig is Vlas te spinnen, zy ziet naar een Jongeling die van buiten door 't vengster kykt; in alles niet minder als de vorigen</td><td>Pruyssen^{r} [for] Q</td><td>(Bought In) fl 70 for lots 58 & 59</td></tr>
<tr><td>1802/06/28</td><td>AMSCH</td><td>0115</td><td>J. Mertenleiter | Een Comieke Zot met een Uil op zyn Schouder; bevallig geschilderd door J. Mertenleiter, op Koper | Mat: op koper Size: hoog 11, breed 9 duim</td><td>Anna Elink</td><td>(Sold) fl 20 Yver</td></tr>
<tr><td>1803/06/20</td><td>AMSCH</td><td>0032</td><td>Mettenleiter | Een Heremiet voor zyn Cluis, zittende met een Kruis in zyn Hand, in een mediteerende houding, agter hem een Boomstam, verders eenig bywerk, alles uitvoerig op Paneel geschilderd | Mat: op paneel Size: hoog 18, breed 14 duim</td><td>Schley [for] G</td><td>(Sold) fl 133 Hodges</td></tr>
<tr><td>1804/05/07</td><td>AMSCH</td><td>0111</td><td>Mettenleiter. (J.) | In een Boere Binnenhuis zit een oude Vrouw, bezig een Jongen welke voor haar tegen haar schoot ligt, te reinigen, agter dezelven een Jongen met een blaas, op de voorgrond een Biervat, Bierkan, een Kruiwagen met Groenten en verder bywerk, alles uitvoerig na G. Douw, geschilderd | Mat: op paneel Size: hoog 16, breed 13 duim</td><td>Roos [for] A</td><td>(Sold) fl 200 Coclers</td></tr>
<tr><td>1807/08/26</td><td>AMSCH</td><td>0130</td><td>Mettenlyter | Voor een Buitenhuis by een Kaarslicht ziet men eene oude Vrouw, die bézig is met Koeken te bakken, voor haar staat een bevallig Meisje, die met haar in gesprek schynt te zyn, en haar een stuk Geld aanbiedt, ter zyde een Jongen met een Rommelpot voor een Huis, op den voorgrond staat een Lamptaarn en ander bywerk; natuurlyk en fiks behandeld | Mat: op paneel Size: hoog 27, breed 22 duim</td><td>de Vries</td><td>(Sold) fl 5:5 T van Iperen</td></tr>
<tr><td>1808/08/23</td><td>AMSCH</td><td>0113</td><td>Mettenleiter. (J.) | Voor een Buitenhuis bij een Kaarslicht, zit eene oude Vrouw, bézig koeken te bakken, voor haar staat een bevallig Meisje, welke haar een stuk geld aanbied, ter zijde een Jongen met een rommelpot, en op voorgrond een Lantaarn en ander bijwerk; schoon van efect en delicaat gepenceeld | Mat: op paneel Size: hoog 27, breed 22 duim</td><td>C</td><td>(Sold) fl 20 Van Iperen</td></tr>
<tr><td>1809/04/22</td><td>AMYVR</td><td>0090</td><td>J. Mittenleiter | Eene Oude Dame, in 't Fluweel met Bond gekleed, zit aandachtig in een Boek te leezen, waarbij een Zandlooper enz.; delicaat gepenseeld | Mat: op doek Size: hoog 14, breed 12 duim</td><td>de Bruin</td><td>(Bought In) fl 75</td></tr>
</table>

Meuleman, P. [Unidentified]

<table>
<tr><td>1802/08/24</td><td>LNDLS</td><td>0112</td><td>P. Meuleman | Een dito [hevige Batailje van Ruiterij]</td><td>Leonardus Bouman [or others]</td><td>(Unknown) fl 11 [?]</td></tr>
</table>

Meulemans (copy by)

<table>
<tr><td>1807/09/28</td><td>DOHAA</td><td>00PP</td><td>Meulemans; A. Cuyp | Een Landschap, op den voorgrond gestoffeerd met Koebeesjes [sic], naar A. Cuyp, door Meulemans | copy by Meulemans after A. Cuyp</td><td>Mattheus Westerouen van Meeteren</td><td>(Unknown)</td></tr>
</table>

Meulen, Adam Frans van der

<table>
<tr><td>1801/08/19</td><td>AMSCH</td><td>0060</td><td>van der Meulen | Voor een beleegerde Vesting ziet men een ménigte van Krygslieden, zo te voet als te paard, en verdere Oorlogs toebereidsels; meesterlyk geschilderd</td><td>Pruyssen^{r} [for] Q</td><td>(Sold) fl 5:10 Pruijssenaar [for] R</td></tr>
<tr><td>1802/06/16</td><td>AMSCH</td><td>0117</td><td>A. F. van der Meulen | Twee stuks heevige schermutzelingen tusschen Ruitery in Landschapjes, in de eene ziet men twee Krygslieden te Paard, als woedende op elkander losbranden; in den andere een hoop vlugtende Ruiters, door hun vyanden vervolgt; de Caracters zyn natuurlyk, en beide meesterlyk fraai gepenceeld | Mat: op paneel Size: hoog 5, breed 7 ½ duim</td><td>[Merrem]</td><td>(Sold) fl 12:10 Kuypers</td></tr>
<tr><td>1803/04/27</td><td>AMSCH</td><td>000F</td><td>van der Meulen | la Bataille de St. Denis, le 14 Aout 1672 | Inscr. 14 Aout 1672 (dated?) Notes: It is unclear whether the date is inscribed on the painting.</td><td>B</td><td>(Bought In) fl 2:5</td></tr>
<tr><td>1803/08/01</td><td>AMSCH</td><td>0020</td><td>Meulen, (J. van der) | Op de voorgrond van dit Schildery is een stil Water, waarin twee Visschers in een Schuit, daar agter een Bosch, verders hoog Geboomte waarop een Kasteel, het frappante zonlicht het welk door dit Stukje straald, maakt het allerbehaaglykst voor 't oog van den beschouwer, en is van een meesterlyke behandeling | Mat: op doek Size: hoog 18, breed 25 duim Notes: The artist's name was given as "Meulen, (J. van der)" but we have assumed this is an error.</td><td>C</td><td>(Sold) fl 25 Hodges</td></tr>
<tr><td>1803/12/12</td><td>AMSCH</td><td>0063</td><td>van den Meulen | Een Italiaansch Boomryk Landschap, met een Rivier met Scheepen in het verschiet, gestoffeerd met een ménigte Beeldjes, te Paard en te voet; uitvoerig op Paneel | Mat: op paneel Size: hoog 10, breed 13 duim</td><td>D</td><td>(Sold) fl 24 Hodges</td></tr>
</table>

1804/08/08	AMSCH	0117	*A. F. van der Meulen* | Een Koets met Passagiers, door een bende Struikroovers aangevallen wordende, in een Boom- en Bergachtig Landschap; kragtig op Doek | *Mat:* op doek *Size:* hoog 28, breed 39 duim	Roos [for] C	(Sold) fl 3:5 Menzart
1804/08/08	AMSCH	0118	*A. F. van der Meulen* | Een Vorstelyk Personaadje, te Paard zittende, in een prachtig Gewaad; uitvoerig behandeld | *Mat:* op paneel *Size:* hoog 15, br. 14 duim	Roos [for] C	(Sold) fl 9:10 Coclers
1806/05/05	AMSCH	0094	*A. van der Meulen* | In een bergagtig Landschap vertoont zich een hévige schermutseling tusschen Ruitery van Christenen en Turken, vol gewoel; meesterlyk en fiks gepenceeld door A. van der Meulen | *Mat:* op doek *Size:* hoog 9, breed 12 duim	E	(Sold) fl 4 van Laar
1806/08/13	AMSCH	0115	*Meulen. (A. van der)* | In een Landschap vertoont zich een Rennend gezadeld Paard; fiks behandeld | *Mat:* op doek op paneel *Size:* hoog 11, breed 13 duim	Roos	(Sold) fl 1 T van Iperen
1808/06/11	RMRIJ	0087	*Vander Meulen* | Lodewyk de 14de, gezeten in eene Koets met Zes Paarden bespannen, en verder Gevolg, Cevennis in 't Verschiet, zeer verdienstig en meesterlyk geschilderd | *Mat:* op paneel *Size:* hoog 8, breed 10 ¾ duim		(Sold) fl 24 van Leen
1808/06/11	RMRIJ	0112	*Vander Meulen* | Het Beleg van Bon, Lodewyk de Veertiende met vele zyner Generaals op den voorgrond, de Stad en Werken in het verschiet, meesterlyk geschilderd | *Mat:* op doek *Size:* hoog 52, breed 39 ½ duim		(Bought In) fl 14
1810/06/06	RMMUY	0178	*van der Meulen* | Het Beleg van eene Vesting, onder Lodewijk de XIV. | *Mat:* op doek		(Sold) fl 6 Strikland
1810/07/26	AMSCH	0055	*Meulen (van der)* | In een Landschap ziet men eenige Ruiters, die Gevangenen geleiden | *Mat:* op doek *Size:* hoog 20, breed 24 duimen	Cassino	(Sold) fl 1:15 L Pakker
			Meulen, Adam Frans van der (or Meulen, A.F., manner)		
1803/08/24	HGKAN	A0015	*Vermeule* | Een Battaillie van Cavallerie, door of in de trant van Vermeule | *Mat:* op paneel *Size:* breet 34, hoog 22 duim		(Sold) fl 14 van Hoven
			Meulen, Adam Frans van der (manner)		
1806/08/13	AMSCH	0304	*van der Meulen* | Een hévige Rencontre tusschen Ruitery, vol gewoel en expressie; als van der Meulen	Vinkeles [for] F	(Sold) fl 5 Menzart
			Meulener, Pieter		
1802/09/06	AMSCH	0153	*P. Meulen* | Een heevig Gevegt tusschen Ruitery, vol gewoel; meesterlyk gepenceeld | *Mat:* op paneel *Size:* hoog 22, breed 28 duim	B	(Sold) fl 2 Royers
			Meyer		
1805/10/09	HGBSM	0145	*D. Meyer* | Twee stuks binne huisjes | *Mat:* op paneel *Size:* hoog 10 breet 13 duim	T H van Willigen [or others]	(Sold) £ 6:10 De Gelder
			Meyer, A. de [Unidentified]		
1808/04/26	GDAN	0096	*Meyer (A. de)* | Een Rivier Gezigt, bij een Herberg of Pleisterplaats, over de Rivier word een Pont gevoerd, waar in een Koets met Paarden, Beesten en Menschen, fiks en uitvoerig geschildert | *Size:* hoog 27, breed 40 duim	G H Fortuyn	(Unknown)
1808/04/26	GDAN	0097	*Meyer (A. de)* | Een Zee Gezigt, waar op eenige Vaartuigen, onder anderen, een vol Menschen, waar in zich een Vorst bevind die aan Land moet komen, en door een groot Corps Cavallerie schijnt te moeten worden ingehaald, dit stuk is uitmuntend geschildert met zijn bijwerk | *Size:* hoog 20, breed 29 duim	G H Fortuyn	(Unknown)
1808/04/26	GDAN	0098	*Meyer (A. de)* | Een dito Rivier met zeilende Schepen en Schuiten | *Size:* hoog 27, breed 40 duim *Notes:* It is unclear what "dito" refers to in the title.	G H Fortuyn	(Unknown)
			Meyering, Albert		
1802/05/05	AMSCH	0127	*A. Myering* | Een Boom- en Bergachtig Landschap, op de Voorgrond eenig grazend en leggend Vee | *Mat:* op doek *Size:* hoog 21, breed 27 duim	BB	(Sold) fl 15:10 Stevens
1802/05/05	AMSCH	0128	*A. Myering* | Een Boom- en Rotsachtig Landschap, met een Waterval, op de Voorgrond eenige Reizigers te Paard en te Voet, zeer natuurlyk | *Mat:* op paneel *Size:* hoog 18, breed 24 duim	BB	(Sold) fl 20 Pruijssenaar [for] R
1802/07/20	MGSAN	0030	*Meyering* | Een hevige Schermutseling van Ruitery, op Paneel | *Mat:* op paneel *Size:* hoog duim 14, breed duim 18 ½		(Unknown)
1802/07/27	AKHRK	0033	*A. Meijering* | Een zeer bevallig Landschapje in Arcadische smaak; op de voorgrond een speelende Herder met zijn Vee, zittende bij een Pedestal, waar op een Vaas; en een wandelend Vrouwtje met een Kind; zeer uitvoerig en net gepenseeld | companion to lot 34 *Mat:* op doek *Size:* hoog 8, breed 12 duim	Maria Stategaart	(Sold) fl 3:5 for lots 33 & 34. Gruyter
1802/07/27	AKHRK	0034	*A. Meijering* | Dito [A. Meijering] de weerga. Een Berg en Boschagtig Landschapje, een Herder met zijn Vee op de voorgrond, en een Hengelaar in het verschiet, Antieksche Gebouwen; zeer fraai | companion to lot 33	Maria Stategaart	(Sold) fl 3:5 for lots 33 & 34. Gruyter
1803/09/07	AMSCH	0103	*A. Meijering* | In dit bevallig Bergachtig Landschap, vertoond zig op de voorgrond, by een opgaande Weg eenig Geboomte en verscheide Veehoeders met Schaapen, hoger een Vragtkar, en stroomende Waterval	Smidt	(Sold) fl 111 for lots 103 & 104. C S Roos

			en eenige Gebouwen, ter zyde in een Vally, een Rivier met eenig Vaartuig; zonachtig en fraai gepenceeld [Dans cet agréable et montueux paysage, sont représentés sur le devant, à l'entrée d'un grand chemin quelques arbres et plusieurs pâtres avec des moutons ; plus loin une charrette, un ruisseau qui tombe en cascade, et quelques batimens. A coté, dans une vallée, une rivière avec quelques bateaux ; il règne dans ce tableau un beau soleil et un charmant fini] | companion to lot 104 *Mat:* op doek *Size:* hoog 37, breed 49 duim		
1803/09/07	AMSCH	0104	*A. Meijering* | Een capitaal Wintergezigt, langs een bevrosen Rivier, ziet men verscheide Arbeiders hout hakken en andere Schaatseryders, langs de Weg een Vragtkar en verscheide Woningen; alles is met besneeuwde Weegen en Daken, en zeer Natuurlyk behandeld, op Doek, door denzelven [A. Meijering], dito hoogte [37] en breedte [49 duim], zynde een wederga van de vorige [Une vue d'hiver, sur une rivière prise de glaces ; on voit divers ouvriers occupés à hacher du bois, et d'autres courant à pâtins ; le long d'un chemin une charette et plusieurs habitations. Partout se présentent des chemins et des toits chargés de neige ; tableau capital et d'une exécution très naturelle] | companion to lot 103 *Mat:* op doek *Size:* hoog 37, breed 49 duim	Smidt	(Sold) fl 111 for lots 103 & 104. C S Roos
1810/03/27	RMCNL	0081	*Meyering* | Een Bergachtig Landschap, op de tweede grond een rustend gezelschap, in 't verschiet tusschen de Bergen een Dorp, krachtig van coloriet		(Unknown)

Meyering, J. [Unidentified]

1801/04/23	AMYVR	0034	*J. Meyering* | Een gestoffeerd Hofgezicht | *Notes:* This lot was sold with lot 33, which is in the manner of D. Maes.		(Sold) fl 1 ¾ for lots 33 & 34. Scheide

Meyling, J. [Unidentified]

1802/02/16	AMSCH	0053	*J. Meyling* | Een aangenaam Landschap, op de voorgrond gestoffeert met een rustend Veehoeder, by een staande Os- en graasend Schaap, uitvoerig geschilderd	F	(Sold) fl 3:5 van Dijl

Michaelis, Gerrit Jan

1809/06/13	AMSCH	0109	*G. Michaëlis* | Een Besneeuwd Wintergezigt, met Boeren-Woningen, gestoffeerd met Arbeiders, Vrouwen en Kinderen; natuurlijk voorgesteld | *Mat:* op doek *Size:* hoog 16, breed 24 duim	A	(Sold) fl 14 van Iperen
1809/06/13	AMSCH	0110	*G. Michaëlis* | Eenige Boeren Woningen ter zijde een bevrozen Water, gestoffeerd met een Ijssleede en schaatsenrijders, bij een Brug; kloek van Penceel | *Mat:* op paneel *Size:* hoog 13, breed 17 duim	A	(Sold) fl 17 R[emmers] Bredius

Michau, Theobald

1803/07/14	MGKLY	0008	*Michou* | Twee fraaye Landschapjes vol gewoel	Mr Caspar Jacob van Citters	(Unknown)
1808/08/23	AMSCH	0110	*Michaud. (F.)* | Dit aangenaam bergachtig Landschap met Geboomte, vertoond op de voorgrond verscheide rustende en andere Reisigers, zoo te Paard als te Voet, benevens een rijdende Vragtwagen, verder een Kasteel, en een bevallig verschiet; alles zonachtig en meesterlijk fraai van penceel behandeling | *Mat:* op paneel *Size:* hoog 16, breed 21 duim *Notes:* The artist's name was given as "Michaud. (F.)" but we have assumed this is an error.	[Van Iperen?]	(Sold or Bought In) fl 4 Van Iperen
1810/10/10	MGCIT	0067	*Michau* | Een zeer aangenaam Schildery, zynde een Landschap met Gebergtens, voorzien van veelerhande Boomgewas,uit hetwelk zig hier en daar een Gebouw laat zien; vertonende zig wyders op hetzelve een soort van Caravane, aan een Water, met Paarden, Muil-Ezels, Rundvee, Schapen en Geiten, halte schynende te houden; zeer aartig en verdienstig op het Paneel gebragt | *Mat:* op paneel	Caspar van Citters	(Unknown)
1810/10/10	MGCIT	0085	*Michau* | Twee Stukjes, zynde Landschapjes, ryk in allen opzigte gestoffeerd, en van eene bevallige compositie	Caspar van Citters	(Unknown)

Michau, Theobald (and Neeffs, P. (I))

1804/10/16	DLOND	0156	*Pet. Neefs; Michau* | Een Roomsche Kerk, van binnen te zien, met zeer veel Beelden van den laatsten. L'intérieur d'une Eglise Romaine, avec beaucoup de Figures du dernier | *Mat:* op paneel *Size:* hoog 17, breed 26		(Sold) fl 102 v Giesen
810/10/10	MGCIT	0055	*P. Neefs; Michau* | Een kapitaal Stuk, zynde een Roomsche Kerk, schoon van Bouworde, met zeer veel beelden en ander bijwerk, door P. Neefs; rijk en fraai gestoffeerd door Michau, en door beide Meesters uitvoerig en kunstig behandeld	Caspar van Citters	(Unknown)

Michelangelo Buonarroti (or Italian)

810/08/06	AMSCH	0136	*M. Angelo; Italiaansch Meester* | Zeven stuks, voorstellende de Werken van Barmhartigheid, ieder stuk eigenaardig met Beelden en toepasselijk bijwerk gestoffeerd en alle meesterlijk en breed geschilderd, door M. Angelo of een ander voornaam Italiaansch Meester | *Mat:* op doek *Size:* ieder is hoog 28, breed 38 duimen	A	(Sold) fl 40 J Spaan

Michelangelo Buonarroti (manner)

803/09/07	AMSCH	0279	*M. Angelo* | Een Zinnebeeldige Ordonantie, zynde een Vrouw met eenige Kinderen; meesterlyk als M. Angelo, door een voornaam Meester	Smidt	(Sold) fl 22 Toselli

			[Tableau d'une belle ordonnance, représentant un femme entourée d'enfans ; d'après Michel-Ange, d'un bon maître] | *Mat:* op paneel *Size:* hoog 14, breed 21 duim		

Michelangelo Buonarroti (school)

1804/10/16	DLOND	0278	*Uit de School van Michael Angelo* | De Zaligmaker, na zyne Geboorte, door de Herders begroet. J.C. environné des Bergers dans l'Ecurie de Bethlehem | *Mat:* op paneel *Size:* hoog 21, breed 15		(Unknown) fl 17:10

Micker, Jan Christaensz.

1801/08/19	AMSCH	0066	*J. Mikker* | Een Bybelsche Ordenantie, verbeeldende de drie Jongelingen, in de Gloeijende Oven, fraai op paneel | *Mat:* op paneel *Size:* hoog 18, breed 25 duim	Van Forreest	(Sold) fl 3:5 Le Dantú
1807/08/26	AMSCH	0133	*den Micker* | Een geestlyke zinnebeeldige Ordonnantie op het verkiezen van de breede of smalle Weg naar het toekomende Leven, door verschillende figuren afgebeeld; op Paneel, door .... den Micker | *Mat:* op paneel *Size:* hoog 30, breed 41 duim	Helsdinge	(Sold) fl 11:10 H Jansen

Miel, Jan

1801/03/16	AMSCH	0116	*Bieke* | In een dito [Italiaansch heuvelagtig Landschap], by de ruïne van een Gebouw ziet men een staande en een rustende Landman; verzelt van verscheide Vee, zonagtig en meesterlyk gepenceeld | *Mat:* op doek	K[ip]	(Sold) fl 54 Pruissenaar [for] R
1801/04/13	AMSCH	0050	*J. Miël alias Bieke* | Een Italiaansch Landschap met fonteinen en gebouwen, op de voorgrond een Schoenmaker, alles breed behandeld | *Mat:* op doek *Size:* hoog 26, breed 21 duim	Pierre Fouquet, junior	(Sold) fl 14:10 Lafontaine
1801/10/06	AMSCH	0045	*J. Miel* | Een Landschap, gestoffeerd met de Geschiedenis van de verlooren Zoon, meesterlyk en uitvoerig behandeld | *Mat:* op doek *Size:* hoog 13, breed 16 duim	M	(Sold) fl 14 Wed Achtienhoven
1802/02/16	AMSCH	0084	*Bieke* | Voor een Plysterplaats zyn eenige Krygslieden bezig zich met danssen te vermaken; kragtig op doek | *Mat:* op doek	E	(Sold) fl 8:15 Th^{S} Spaan
1802/06/16	AMSCH	0118	*J. Miel* | In een Italiaansch Landschap, voor eene Steene Muur, zit een rustende Landlooper zig te reinigen; zeer natuurlyk, krachtig, en teffens uitvoerig van Penceel behandeling | *Mat:* op paneel *Size:* hoog 8 ½, breed 6 ½ duim	[Merrem]	(Sold) fl 15:10 Wed Achtienhoven
1803/12/12	AMSCH	0062	*Jan Miel* | Een Landschap, op de voorgrond ziet men verscheiden belaaden Muilezels, waarby eenige Reizigers; alles fraai behandeld | *Mat:* op doek *Size:* hoog 36, breed 50 duim	B	(Sold) fl 50 Hodges
1809/04/17	AMSCH	0066	*J. Miel* | Voor een Buitenhuis zitten zig vier Lieden bij een Vuur te warmen; fiks geschilderd | *Mat:* op doek *Size:* hoog 11, breed 10 duim	A	(Sold) fl 3

Miel, Jan (or Miel, manner)

1808/08/23	AMSCH	0117	*Miel. (J.) Of in de manier* | Twee stuks bevallig gestoffeerde Italiaansche Landschappen, met Woningen en Geboomte en Huislieden, eenige beladen een Muil-Ezel, een ander voerd een Paard, terwijl andere gerust slapen; op de voorgrond liggen verscheide Pakken, Vaten, en verder bijwerk; in den andere vertoont zig voor een Gebouw twee op de kaart speelende Lieden, waar bij Man en Vrouw, en een Jongeling bij een Vat, verder een Man op een Ezel zittende, speelende op een Cither, en een jong Kind met een Hond speelende; het is geestig geordoneert en van een meesterlijk penceel behandeling | *Mat:* op doek *Size:* Ieder hoog 19, breed 25 duim	C	(Sold) fl 60 Texier

Miel, Jan (manner)

1801/10/06	AMSCH	0089	*als door J. Miel* | Een Italiaansch Landschap met eenige Gebouwen, gestoffeerd met een Heer te Paard, een Almoes geevende aan arme Lieden, kragtig geschilderd | *Mat:* op paneel *Size:* hoog 14, breed 10 duim	L	(Sold) fl 7 Th Spaan

Miereveld, Jan van

1804/02/27	AMSCH	0070	*Miereveld. (J.)* | Een Mans Pourtrait; leunende met de Rechterhand op een Stoel, en met de linker op eenige Boeken, voor hem een Tafel met een Tapyt bedekt, waarop een Inktkoker, Cachet en ander Schryf gereedschap, dit Pourtrait is byzonder fraai geteekend en meesterlyk van coloriet en penceel behandeling | *Mat:* op doek *Size:* hoog 47, breed 36 duim	B	(Sold) fl 20 Gruiter
1804/02/27	AMSCH	0071	*Miereveld (J.)* | Het Afbeeldsel van Hugo de Groot, schynende te zullen Schryven in een Boek dat voor hem legt, delicaat geschilderd | *Mat:* op paneel *Size:* hoog 45, breed 32 duim	B	(Sold) fl 0:18 L Pakker
1804/08/08	AMSCH	0119	*J. Miereveld* | Een capitaal Manspourtrait, leunende met de rechterhand op een Stoel, en met de linker op eenige Boeken, voor hem een Tafel met een Tapyt Kleed bedekt, waarop een Inktkooker, Cachet en andere Schryfgereedschappen; dit Pourtrait is byzonder fraai geteekend, en meesterlyk van coloriet en penceelbehandeling, door J. Miereveld, op Doek | *Mat:* op doek *Size:* hoog 47, br. 36 duim	Vink[eles] [for] K[=Gruyter?]	(Bought In) fl 12
1810/08/06	AMSCH	0143	*J. Miereveld* | Het Pourtret van Fredrik Hendrik	F	(Sold) fl 8 W v d Schley

Miereveld, Michiel Jansz. van

1801/02/18	AMBOS	0019	*Mireveld* | Een mans Hoofd	J Schonevelt	(Unknown)

1802/05/05	AMSCH	0143	*M. van Miereveld* | Twee Stuks, zynde de Pourtraiten van Hugo Grootsius en deszelfs Huisvrouw | *Mat:* op koper *Size:* yder hoog 7, breed 5 duim	A	(Sold) fl 25 Pruyssenaar [for] J
1802/07/21	HGKAN	0028	*Miereveld* | Een extra fraay geschilderd Mans- en Vrouwe Pourtrait door Miereveld, in vergulde Lyst met ovaale binnen rand | *Mat:* op paneel *Fmt:* ovaal		(Unknown)
1802/07/21	HGKAN	0084	*Miervelt* | Een Vrouwen Pourtrait		(Unknown)
1804/10/16	DLOND	0137	*Miereveld* | Een Mans-Portrait met een Kraag. Portrait d'Homme avec un Collet | *Mat:* op paneel *Size:* hoog 14, breed 11		(Unknown)
1804/10/16	DLOND	0138	*Miereveld* | Portrait van Oldenbarneveld | *Mat:* op paneel *Size:* hoog 24, breed 20		(Unknown)
1804/10/29	HRBAU	0053	*Miereveld, (M.)* | Een Mans Pourtrait, zynde een Borststuk, hebbende een van Kanten gemaakte Spaansche Kraag om den hals, en is in zwart satyn gekleed. Byzonder natuurlyk en uitvoerig geschilderd | *Mat:* op paneel *Size:* hoog 19 ½, breed 14 ½ duim	Simon Styl	(Unknown)
1804/10/29	HRBAU	0054	*Miereveld, (M.)* | Een zeer bevallig Vrouwen Pourtrait, mede naar de Spaansche manier gehuld, hebbende een dubbelde Kanten Kraag, benevens een gouden Keten, om den hals; zynde in het zwart gekleed. Niet minder fraai en uitvoerig dan het voorige behandeld | *Mat:* op paneel *Size:* hoog 18, breed 15 duim	Simon Styl	(Unknown)
1805/10/21	GRBOL	0065	*Miereveld* | Het Origineel Pourtrait van den beroemden Dichter J. Cats	Gerardus Nicolaus Heerkens	(Unknown)
1805/10/21	GRBOL	0066	*Miereveld* | Deszelfs Vrouwe Elisabeth van Valkenburg	Gerardus Nicolaus Heerkens	(Unknown)
1806/05/05	AMSCH	0082	*M. Miereveld* | Twee stuks Pourtretten, van Willem den Eerste, en Maurits, Prinsen van Oranje; fraai en uitvoerig op Paneel | *Mat:* op paneel *Size:* hoog 10, breed 8 duim	O	(Sold) fl 4:5 J Yver
1806/05/05	AMSCH	0083	*M. Miereveld* | Een capitaal Mans Pourtret, voor hem een tafel met een tapyt Kleed bedekt, waarop een Inkkoker; meesterlyk van coloriet door denzelven [M. Miereveld] | *Mat:* op doek *Size:* hoog 47, breed 36 duim	V[inkeles]	(Sold) fl 29:10 Vinkeles [for] S
1806/06/07	RMHSN	0128	*Miereveld* | Twee stuks, Mans- en Vrouwe Pourtrait	A E K L	(Unknown)
1806/08/20	HGBSM	0100	*M. Miereveld* | Het Portrait van de Grootmoeder van beiden Heeren, gebroeders de Witt, door M. Miereveld 1631 | *Mat:* op paneel *Size:* hoog 43 ½, breed 33 ½ duim *Inscr:* M. Miereveld 1631 (signed and dated?) *Notes:* It is unclear whether the name and date are inscribed on the painting.	Macalester Loup [or others]	(Bought In) fl 10
1806/08/20	HGBSM	0106	*Miereveld* | Een oud mans Portrait met een grijze baard, en Kalottie op het hoofd | *Mat:* op paneel *Size:* hoog 28, breed 23 duim	Macalester Loup [or others]	(Sold) fl 11 for lots 106 & 107. Loef
1806/08/20	HGBSM	0107	*Miereveld* | Een vrouwe Portrait | *Mat:* op paneel *Size:* hoog 26 ½, breed 23 duim	Macalester Loup [or others]	(Sold) fl 11 for lots 106 & 107. Loef
1808/06/11	RMRIJ	0051	*Miereveld* | Een zeer fraai Mans Pourtrait | *Mat:* op paneel		(Sold) fl 3 [or] 13:10 Van Zanten [?]
1809/06/13	AMSCH	0238	*Miereveld* | Het Pourtrait van Prins Maurits	Y	(Sold) fl 0:18 J de Vries
1810/06/20	AMSCH	0048	*M. Van Miereveld* | Een Vrouwe Pourtrait, in oude Hollandsche kleeding | *Mat:* op paneel *Size:* hoog 23, breed 19 duimen	A	(Sold) fl 36 de Vries
1810/06/20	AMSCH	0048a	*M. Van Miereveld* | Eene deftige Vrouw in oude Hollandsche kleeding, met een Linnen Kraag om den hals en tot de knieën te zien. Meesterlijk geschilderd | *Mat:* op paneel *Size:* hoog 44, breed 33 duimen	K	(Sold) fl 10:10 Van Iperen
1810/08/01	AMSCH	0061	*Mierevelt (Michiel van)* | De Afbeelding van eenen Man in oude Hollandsche Kleeding, blootshoofds en van voren te zien, houdende zijne regterhand op de borst [Portrait d'Homme vetu à l'ancienne mode Hollandoise, vû de face, la tête decouverte, appuyant sa main droite sur sa poitrine] | *Annots:* Passable. (NGW) *Mat:* op paneel *Size:* hoog 29, breed 22 duimen	Mr Pieter de Smeth van Alphen	(Sold) fl 86 T Spaan [for] Croese
1810/08/06	AMSCH	0138	*M. Miereveld* | Het Afbeeldsel van Prins Maurits; meesterlijk geschilderd | *Mat:* op paneel	C	(Sold) fl 4 Stoopendaal [for] B
1810/10/11	AMSCH	0051	*M. Miereveld* | Twee stuks, het Portret van een oud Burgemeester en zijne Vrouw | *Mat:* op koper *Size:* hoog 5 ½, breed 4 ½ duimen	C	(Sold) fl 1:15 Posthumus
1810/10/11	AMSCH	0227	*Miereveld* | Een Vrouwe portret	A	(Sold) fl 1:15 Mensart

Miereveld, Michiel Jansz. van (and Martszen, J. (II))

1803/08/17	AMSCH	0062	*Marsse de Jonge. (J.); Miereveld* | Het Pourtrait van Fredrik Hendrik, Prins van Orange, zittende op een schoon bruin Paard, in het verschiet het beleg der Stad Grol, uitvoerig en kragtig behandeld | *Mat:* op paneel *Size:* hoog 14, breed 11 duim	Anna Catharina Putman	(Sold) fl 25 Gruyter

Miereveld, Michiel Jansz. van (manner)

1803/04/20	AMSCH	0123	*M. van Miereveld* | Een Dames Pourtrait, halver Lyf te zien, fraay in de manier van M. van Miereveld [Un Portrait de femme à mi-corps, peint dans la maniere de M. van Miereveld.] | *Mat:* op paneel *Size:* hoog 28, breed 22 duim	Maria Magdalena van Sluypwyk, gravinne van Moens	(Sold) fl 8:10 Theijs

1803/12/12	AMSCH	0130	*Miereveld* | Twee stuks Vorstelyke Pourtraiten, als Miereveld | *Mat:* op koper *Size:* hoog 10, breed 8 duim	W	(Sold) fl 2:5 v d Schley [for] R[ijfsnijder]
1805/12/16	AMSCH	0077	*Miereveld* | Prins Maurits, als door Miereveld	R[oos]	(Sold) fl 0:10 Heybroek
1807/08/26	AMSCH	0144	*Miereveld* | Het Pourtrait van een Vorstelyk Perzoon met een Kraag om den Hals en een Medailje op de Borst; in de manier van Miereveld | *Mat:* op paneel *Size:* hoog 13 ½, breed 11 duim	de Vries	(Sold) fl 2 A Rynders
1810/10/11	AMSCH	0108	*Miereveld* | Een fraai Manne en Vrouwe Portret; zeer goed geschilderd, als Miereveld | *Mat:* op paneel	V[ries]	(Sold) fl 9 Hodges
1810/10/11	AMSCH	0109	*Miereveld* | Het afbeeldsel van Willem den II., Prins van Orange; als Miereveld | *Mat:* op doek	V[ries]	(Sold) fl 0:6 Ijver

Miereveld, Pieter van (or Miereveld, P., manner)

1806/05/05	AMSCH	0204	*P. Miereveld* | Twee stuks, een bevallig Mans en Vrouwe Pourtrait, beide ten voeten uit, in ryke deftige Kleeding, staande in prachtige Paleisen met Gordynen omhangen; beide allermeesterlykst en fraai gepenceeld, door of als P. Miereveld	V[inkeles]	(Sold) fl 181 C S Roos

Mieris

1809/07/25	HGBSM	0008	*T. v. Mieris* | Dit uitvoerige Stukje verbeelt Ulisses en Cyrcée, konstig gepenseelt | *Mat:* op paneel *Size:* hoog 12 ½, breed 16 ½ duim	D van der Aa [or] E B ten Dall	(Sold) fl 40 van Eijk

Mieris (copy after)

1804/10/29	HRBAU	0155	*Mieris* | Een Vrouwtjen, zittende Koeken te bakken; en meer bywerk. Na Mieris | *Mat:* op doek *Size:* hoog 19, breed 14 duim	Simon Styl	(Unknown)

Mieris (manner)

1801/08/19	AMSCH	0061	*Mieris* | Een Man aan Tafel zittende te Bidden, voor hem een Haring, Brood en Kannetje; uitvoerig op Paneel, in de manier van Mieris | *Mat:* op paneel *Size:* hoog 10 ¼, breed 9 duim	Van Forreest	(Sold) fl 20:10 Hulswit
1802/05/05	AMSCH	0263	*Mieris* | Door een Nis ziet men eenige Lieden zig met Comptoirzaaken bezig houden, fraai behandeld als Mieris	J	(Sold) fl 9:10 Stevens
1808/05/17	LNAN	0033	*Mieris* | Een man met een glas in zijn hand, als van Mieris		(Unknown)

Mieris, Frans van (the elder)

1801/10/19	AMSCH	0041	*Mieris. (den Ouden F. van)* | Een Schilder in Spaansche kleeding een Pyp stoppende; staande op de rand van de Nis, een Rhynse Wynroemer en een keurig Tapyt is daar van afhangende: zeer kragtig en delicaat uitgevoerd | *Mat:* op paneel *Size:* hoog 7, breed 5 ¼ duim	Jonkheer Menno Baron van Coehoorn	(Sold) fl 305 Coclers
1802/06/16	AMSCH	0105	*F. Mieris, de Oude* | Een Dame in deftige kleeding, zittende voor een Tafel, waar op een Fles geplaats is: zy houd in de regterband een Roemer Wyn; meesterlyk, krachtig en bevallig gepenceeld | *Mat:* op paneel *Size:* hoog 8, breed 7 duim	[Merrem]	(Sold) fl 11:5 van Iperen
1802/06/16	AMSCH	0106	*F. Mieris, de Oude* | Het Afbeeldzel van een bedaagd Heer in aloude deftige Kleeding, krachtig en teffens uitvoerig van penceel-behandeling | *Mat:* op doek *Fmt:* ovaal *Size:* hoog 4, breed 3 ½ duim	[Merrem]	(Sold) fl 6 Cobel
1802/09/29	AMSCH	0034	*F. van Mieris, de Oude* | Een Mans Pourtrait, hoog 8 ½, breed 6 ½ duim. Koper. Zynde het afbeeldsel van een bevallig Jongheer staande voor de deur van een trosch Gebouw, tot de knien afgebeeld, gekleed met een deftige zwarte zyde Mantel, zyn regterhand uytstrekkende, terwyl zyn linkerhand met een Handschoen met Franjes pronkt, en waarin hy die van de regterhand houd, zyn ligt bruin Hair met een bevallige zwier over zyn Bef, en Schouderen, de ploijen der Mantel zyn breed, edel, en krachtig behandeld; in het verschiet, ziet men eenig Geboomten, de fraaye Teekening, en delicate Penseel behandeling, toont den beschouwer aan dat dit stukje van deze groote Meester in zyn beste tyd geschilderd is, (komt uit het Cabinet van den Heer Griffier Fagel.) [Cette representation nous offre simplement un homme gracieux vu à trois-quarts de face et jusqu'aux genoux, portant un rabat plat et un riche costume noir, ses cheveux chatains clairs flottent à grosses boucles sur ses epaules ; il avance sa main droite, et sa gauche est garnie de ses gands ornés de franges. Le fond presente un batiment et la vue sur une avenue. Tout plait dans cette charmante figure, la delicatesse du dessin, la force du coloris, la belle maniere de toucher dans le plus précieux fini, le Gôut de la draperie, enfin tout y concourt à la rendre digne d'être rangée parmi les meilleures productions de son auteur célébre. Il est d'une belle conservation ayant appartenu au Cabinet de Mr. le Gref. Fagel.] | *Mat:* op koper *Size:* hoog 8 ½, breed 6 ½ duim *Loc:* Ascott, Bucks., England, UK. National Trust. (53)	[Hendrik III, baron Fagel?]	(Sold) fl 480 Pruijssenaar
1802/09/29	AMSCH	0035	*F. van Mieris, de Oude* | Jacobs Droom, hoog 8 ½, breed 11 duim. Paneel. Hy is verbeeld Rustende teegens eene hoogte, gedeeltelyk bedekt met een linnen Kleed en bruine Mantel, by hem ligt een bevallig slapend Hondje, hoog Geboomten en Kruidgewas verreiken dit fraaye Cabinetstukje, en in 't verschiet ziet men de Ladder Jacobs met eenige Engelen; zynde edel, delicaat en uitvoerig behandeld, (komt uit het	[Hendrik III, baron Fagel?]	(Sold) fl 600 J Spaan

			Cabinet van den Heer Griffier Fagel.) [Le songe de Jacob : Ce Patriarche est representé couché et presque decouvert, quelque linge et une partie de son manteau ne couvrent que peu son corps ; un beau chien est couché près de lui, et le fond offre les Anges qui designent le sujet du Tableau. Cette figure dessinée avec caractère prouve aussi à quel point F. Mieris étoit grand coloriste ; la légereté du pinceau et la vérité de la carnation produisent l'illusion de la nature, les amateurs observeront qu'il est bien conservé. – Sortant du Cabinet de Mr. Le Grefr. Fagel.] | *Mat:* op paneel *Size:* hoog 8 ½, breed 11 duim [haut 8 ½, large 11 ½ pouces] *Notes:* The dimensions differ in the Dutch and French editions of the catalogue. *Loc:* Amsterdam, Nederland. Rijksmuseum. (A 704) as Ary de Vois		
1803/04/20	AMSCH	0036	*Mieris, de oude. (F. van)* | Het Afbeeldzel van een bevallige Dame, in witte zatyne kleeding, houdende een Hondje in den Arm, staande in een Hofgezicht; alles is delicaat en uitvoerig gepenceeld [Le Portrait d'une jeune Dame vetue de satin blanc, tenant un epagneul dans le bras ; elle est vue jusqu'aux genoux. Le fond est une Collonade ou vue de chateau. Ce morceau très précieux réunit au bon choix de la disposition l'éclat des draperies & le fini le plus précieux.] | companion to lot 37 *Mat:* op paneel *Size:* hoog 12, breed 10 duim	Maria Magdalena van Sluypwyk, gravinne van Moens	(Sold) fl 221 Th^s Spaan
1803/04/20	AMSCH	0037	*Mieris, de oude (F. van)* | Het dito [Afbeeldzel] van een bedaagd Heer in krygsmans kleeding, houdende een Rotting in de hand, leunende tegen een Baluster, ter zyde staat een Jachthond, verder een Hofgezicht; in alles als de voorige behandeld [Pour pendant c'est le portrait d'un guerrier armée d'un cuirasse polie, tenant un baton & s'appuyant sur une balustrade : un dogue est à son côté. Le fond presente une partie d'un batiment somptueux. Cette figure élégamment postée est du même précieux de la précedente, l'or des franges, lacier de l'armure, & en général tous le details ne laissent rien à désirer pour l'agrement du faire, & la verité de la representation.] | companion to lot 36 *Mat:* op paneel *Size:* hoog 12, breed 10 duim	Maria Magdalena van Sluypwyk, gravinne van Moens	(Sold) fl 699 Coclers
1803/12/12	AMSCH	0056	*F. van Mieris* | Een Bevallige Vrouw, houdende in haar regter Hand een Roemer met Wyn, die zy met genoegen schynt te beschouwen; delicaat gepenceeld | *Mat:* op paneel *Size:* hoog 8, breed 6 ½ duim	B	(Sold) fl 6:5 Gruiter
1805/07/03	AMSCH	0029	*Mieris De Oude. (F. van)* | Dit kabinetstukje vertoont een gemeubileerd Binnen-Vertrek met een Ledikant gestoffeerd, in 't zelve zit een jeugdige bevallige Dame, gekleed in een loshangende fluweele jakje met bont, en witte satyne Rok, zy heeft in de linkerhand een glas met wyn, en in de rechter een Oester, waarvan haar nog eenige op een zilver schenkbord aangeboden worden, – door een bedaagd Heer, die névens haar staat en haar vriendelyk toelacht; de tafel is overdekt met een turks tapyt kleed, waar op een witte porcelynen wynkan; zynde van een zeer uitvoerige penceelsbehandeling en van de besten van dezen Meester | *Mat:* op paneel *Size:* hoog 10, breed 8 duim	R[oos]	(Sold) fl 800 Cremer
1806/05/05	AMSCH	0084	*F. van Mieris* | Een Model in het grauw geschilderd, zynde het Pourtret van F. van Mieris, door hem zelve op paneel | *Mat:* op paneel *Size:* hoog 9, breed 7 duim	H	(Sold) fl 12 Roos
1806/08/13	AMSCH	0112	*Mieris. (F.)* | Een bevallige Vrouw, houdende een roemer wyn in de hand dewelke zy met genoegen schynt te beschouwen; delicaat gepenceeld | *Mat:* op paneel *Size:* hoog 8, breed 6 ½ duim	Vinkeles [for] G[ruyter]	(Sold) fl 2 Gruiter
1806/08/20	HGBSM	0189	*De oude Frans van Mieris* | Het Portrait van een Heer, zijnde uit de Famillie van Heemskerk, te Leijden staande te rusten tegen een gebroken Pijlaar schijnende ergens na te wijzen. Delicaat en uitvoerig geschilderd, door de oude Frans van Mieris, op paneel tooggewijs | *Mat:* op paneel *Fmt:* tooggewijs *Size:* hoog 9, breed 6 ¾ duim	Macalester Loup [or others]	(Sold) fl 34 Cocard
1806/08/20	HGBSM	0190	*De oude Frans van Mieris* | Een dito [Het Portrait van een Heer], door denzelven [de oude Frans van Mieris], denkelijk zijn eigen Portrait jong zijnde | *Mat:* op koper *Size:* hoog 3 ½, breed 2 ¾ duim	Macalester Loup [or others]	(Sold) fl 7 Spruyt
1808/06/06	RMRIJ	0076	*Mieris. (Frans van)* | Eene in het Satijn rijk gekleede Dame, zittende, voor eene met rood fluweel bedekte tafel, eenen brief te schrijven, waarnaar een bediende schijnt te wachten. Op de tafel ligt eene Luit, en op den voorgrond staat eene met groen fluweel bekleede Tabouret, waarop een slapend Spaansch Hondje ligt. De achtergrond vertoont eene deftige en verstandige Architectuur. Men mag van dit tafereel zeggen, dat hetzelve het Ultimatum is in dien trant van schilderen [Ce chef-d'oeuvre represente une Dame richement costumée en satin de couleur jaunâtre, assise devant une Table couverte d'un Tapis de velours cramoisi, et qui s'occupe à ècrire. Un Luth est auprés d'elle, et un Domestique semble attendre ses ordres. Devant la Table sur un Taboûret couvert de velours verd, est couché un bel Epagneul blanc tacheté de brun. Le fond offre une Architecture simple et noble. La Composition sage, le ton vrai et harmonieux, et le fini inconcevable font regarder ce Morceau comme le *nee plus ultra* de la Peinture en ce genre] | *Mat:* op paneel *Size:* Hoog 9 ¼, en breed 7 ¼ duim. *Loc:* Amsterdam, Nederland. Rijksmuseum. (A 261)	Gerrit van der Pot, Heer van Groeneveld	(Sold) fl 2025 J M Jorissen [for] le Roi
1808/08/23	AMSCH	0104	*Mieris. (F. van)* | In een gemeubileerde Kamer, zit eene bevallige Dame, in deftige Kleeding van rood en wit Satijn, rustende met de rechter Arm op een groen fluweel Kussen, liggende op een Tafel, daar neevens een	C	(Bought In) fl 230

			zilver Schenkbord, waar op een cristalle Bokaal met Wijn geplaatst is, verder bij den openstaande Deur, staat een bedaagde Man en Vrouw; dit fraaije stukje is schoon geteekent, aangenaam van koloriet, en van een uitvoerige penceelbehandeling | *Mat:* op paneel *Size:* hoog 9, breed 8 duim		
1808/08/23	AMSCH	0105	*Mieris. (F. van)* | In een Thuin-gezicht staat een bedaagt Heer in deftig Gewaad, rustende met de linker Arm op een steene Baluster, houdende in de hand een blauw Papier als een Teekening, en in de rechter hand een Zakdoek; het is als de vorige uitvoerig gepenceeld | *Mat:* op paneel *Size:* hoog 9, breed 7 duim	C	(Bought In) fl 135
1808/08/23	AMSCH	0183	*F. Mieris* | Eene bevallige Vrouw, houdende een Roemer Wijn in haar hand, dewelke zij met aandacht beschouwd, delicaat gepenceeld	[Gruyter?]	(Sold) fl 5:10 Van Iperen
1809/07/19	AMSCH	0035	*Mieris (F. van)* | In dit fraaije Kabinetstukje zit een bevallig Vrouwtje; zij is gekleed met een geel Wollen Jakje en blaauwe Rok, zij schijnt uit een Muziekboek iets voor te zingen, nevens haar staat een Muziekmeester, houdende een Viool in de eene, en de Strijkstok in de andere hand, waar mede hij haar iets schijnt aan te wijzen, voor hun staat een Tafel, waar op een Bierkan en Glazen Fluit geplaatst zijn. Dit stukje is zacht en uitvoerig van schildering, en kan voor een der beste van dezen voortreffelijken Meester gehouden worden | *Mat:* op paneel *Size:* hoog 12, breed 10 duim	[Bicker]	(Sold) fl 1625 T Spaan
1809/09/06	AMSCH	0048	*Mieris (F. van) de Oude* | Twee stuks, in het eene ziet men een bejaard Heer in een Fluweele Japon aan een Tafel zitten, waar op eenige Vrugten; de weerga eene Dame geheel in 't Satijn gekleed, zit aan een Tafel met een Tapijtje gedekt in een Boek te leezen, ter zijde een Hondje; alleruitvoerigst gepenceeld | *Mat:* op paneel *Size:* ieder hoog 14, breed 11 duim	Johannes Caudri	(Sold) fl 101 Swanenburg
1810/05/22	AMSCH	0061	*Mieris. (F. van) de oude* | Een deftig Heer, met een purpere Japon gekleed, Blootschoofd, houdende zijn regterhand op de Borst; uitvoerig en fraai geschilderd | *Mat:* op koper *Size:* hoog 9, breed 8 duim	T	(Bought In) fl 6
1810/06/06	RMMUY	0012	*Frans van Mieris den ouden* | Een Kabinet stukje, waar in men eene zittende Dame ziet men een Naaikussen op haar Schoot, aanhebbende een Paars Jakje met witte bonte randen, en een Geele Satijne Rok, zij geeft met de regterhand een amandel aan een Papegay die op een kruk bij haar staat, in de linkerhand heeft zij het linne Werk, wonderlijk uitvoerig en krachtig uitgewerkt | *Mat:* op paneel *Size:* hoog 8, breed 6 duimen		(Sold) fl 157 Vermeulen
1810/08/01	AMSCH	0062	*Mieris (Frans van) de Oude* | Eene bevallige Vrouw met een Muzijkboek in de hand, schijnende te zingen, nevens haar een Muzijkmeester met Viool en Strijkstok, voor hun op eene Tafel staat een Bierkan en Glas [Une Femme gentille tenant un Livre de Musique ; son expression indique qu'elle chante. Le Maitre de Musique qui est à son côté, tient un Violon et son archet. Sur une Table on voit une Canette et un verre] | *Annots:* fort médiocre. (NGW); [par] H Devoys (BPG) *Mat:* op paneel *Size:* hoog 12, breed 10 duimen	Mr Pieter de Smeth van Alphen	(Sold) fl 1320 J de Vries
1810/08/01	AMSCH	0063	*Mieris (Frans van) de Oude* | Een Binnenvertrekje, door eene brandende Kaars verlicht, gestoffeerd met vier lieden, en een Standbeeld [Un intérieur de Chambre éclairée à l'effet d'une Chandelle allumée : on y distingue quatre figures et une Statue] | *Annots:* fort médiocre et fort douteux (NGW) *Mat:* op paneel *Size:* hoog 7 ½, breed 6 duimen	Mr Pieter de Smeth van Alphen	(Sold) fl 185 C S Roos
1810/08/06	AMSCH	0071	*Mieris (F. van) de Oude* | In een gemeubileerde Kamer, zit eene bevallige Dame in satijnen Kleeding, rustende met den rechter Arm op een groen fluweel Kussen, liggende op eene Tafel, daar nevens een zilver Schenkbord, waar op een Pokaal met Wijn geplaats is, verder bij een openstaande Deur staat een bedaagd Man en Vrouw; dit stukje is aangenaam van koloriet, en van eene uitvoerige penceelsbehandeling | *Mat:* op paneel *Size:* hoog 9, breed 8 duimen	B	(Sold) fl 200 C S Roos
1810/08/06	AMSCH	0072	*Mieris (F. van) de Oude* | In een Tuingezigt staat een deftig Heer, rustende met den linker arm op een steenen Baluster, houdende een Teekening en Zakdoek in zijn handen; het is als de vorige uitvoerig gepenceeld | *Mat:* op paneel *Size:* hoog 9, breed 7 duimen	B	(Bought In) fl 41
1810/10/10	MGCIT	0033	*Frans Mieris, den ouden* | Een uitnemend fraai Kabinetstuk, waar in verbeeld word een oud afgeleefd en tevens blind Man, met wit grijs hair en baard, met een kruk, digt aan het lijf houdende, de eene hand in eene naar iets tastende richting, en de andere vast houdende aan de leuning van de stoel, waar op hij gezeten is; naast hem staat een zeer bevallige Vrouw in een antique en kunstig geplooide Kleeding; houdende een porceleine Kruik in haar hand, en voor haar een lang hairig wit Hondje staande; terwijl zoo dit, als 't overige Bijwerk eer doet aan het Penceel van den beroemden Frans Mieris, den ouden	Caspar van Citters	(Unknown)

Mieris, Frans van (the elder) (and Mieris, W.)

1808/06/06	RMRIJ	0077	*Mieris (Frans van); Mieris (Willem van)* | Eene Heilige Familie. Maria, zittende met aandacht in een boek te lezen; voor haar ligt op eene knie gebogen het kind Jezus, zijn kruis metende; in den achtergrond vertoont zich Jozef aan zijne werkbank. Verder rijk van bijwerk; het licht, dat tusschen de vensters op de voorwerpen valt, is heerlijk van uitwerking. Dit kunststuk is onvoltooid gebleven door F. van Mieris, en is door deszelfs Zoon, Willem van Mieris, voleind. Zie verder, over dit tafereel,	Gerrit van der Pot, Heer van Groeneveld	(Sold) fl 1000 Noortwyk

Houbraken Leven der Kunstschilders, 3 deel, pag. II. [Une sainte famille. Marie est assise occupée à lire dans un livre qu'elle tient sur ses genoux. On voit devant elle l'Enfant Jésus qui en se courbant, mesure sa croix, et dans le fond Joseph qui travaille à son Etabli. La lumiere piquante qui entre par une croisée, produit un superbe effet. D'autres accessoires enrichissent ce beau Tableau qui a été fini par Guillaume van Mieris, comme on peut le voir dans l'histoire des Peintres par Houbraken Edition Hollandaise vol. 3. pag.11] | *Mat:* op paneel *Size:* Hoog 13 ¼, en breed 16 ½ duim

Mieris, Frans van (the elder) (or Mieris, F. (I), manner)

1801/06/13	LNDLS	0012	*F. van Mieris, den Ouden* | Een Heer, staande voor een Landschap, deftig gekleed, met een kantekraag en mouwen, konstig en krachtig, op kooper, van of zoo goed als F. van Mieris, den Ouden | *Mat:* op koper *Size:* hoog 6, breed 5 duimen	D van R	(Sold) fl 23 Richter S [for] Stevens
1801/06/13	LNDLS	0046	*F. van Mieris* | Een zittend Mannetje, met een bonte muts op 't hooft, en een japon om zijn lijf, zittende een pijp tabak te rooken, zeer uitvoerig, door of in de trant van F. van Mieris | *Mat:* op paneel *Size:* hoog 6 ½, breed 5 duimen	D van R	(Sold) fl 6:15 Spruyt
1805/07/03	AMSCH	0113	*Frans van Mieris, de oude* | Het Afbeeldsel, halver lyf, van den vermaarde Kunstschilder, Frans van Mieris, de oude, in ovaal, houdende Palet en Penceelen in de hand; uitvoerig op Paneel geschilderd, door hem zelfs, of in zyn manier | *Mat:* op paneel *Fmt:* ovaal *Size:* hoog 6, breed 4 ½ duim	R[oos]	(Bought In) fl 44

Mieris, Frans van (the elder) (copy after)

1802/09/18	RMDRS	0036	*F. Mieris* | Een Dame, zittende te Speldewerken, terwyl een oude Vrouw door een raam een Hoen presenteert, na F. Mieris | *Annots:* Zeer Slegt (MB) *Size:* hoog 13 ½, breed 11 ½ duim	Casper de Haas	(Unknown) fl 21
1809/04/22	AMYVR	0092	*F. van Mieris* | Een drinkende Krijgsman; naar F. van Mieris | *Size:* hoog 8, breed 6 duim	de Bruin	(Bought In) fl 17
1810/07/23	DOLG1	0068	*Frans van Mieris, den oudsten* | Een zittende Dame, en een oud Heer agter dezelve, haar door een Moor eenige Vruchten aanbiedende; naar, of in de smaak van Frans van Mieris, den oudsten. Zeer goed van tekening, en van eene krachtige en delikate penseelsbehandeling | *Mat:* op paneel *Size:* hoog 13 ½, breed 10 ½ duim	Mr Pieter van den Santheuvel	(Sold) fl 14 [or] 86 A van Strij à Dordt

Mieris, Frans van (the elder) (manner)

1802/09/06	AMSCH	0253	*F. van Mieris* | Twee stuks Manspourtraiten, in deftige kleeding; als door F. van Mieris	Mevrouw Achtienhoven	(Sold) fl 0:10 L Pakker
1804/12/10	AMSCH	0104	*de oude Frans van Mieris* | Men ziet in dit stukje een bevallige jongvrouw, zy ligt op een rustbank en is halver lyve naakt, zy houd in de linkerhand een bundel geld en gezégelde papieren, terwyl haar rechter hand, op het kussen rust, waarin zy een snoer paarlen houd, nevens haar ziet men een bejaard man in zatyne kleeding met een hoed met veeren op het hoofd, hy schynt by haar op 't bed te wille koomen. – Dit stukje is fraai smeltend geschilderd, en zeer in de manier van de oude Frans van Mieris behandeld | *Mat:* op doek *Size:* hoog 18, breed 15 duim	Jan De Groot	(Sold) fl 100 Coclers
1805/07/03	AMSCH	0114	*Frans van Mieris, de oude* | In een Binnenvertrek zit een bevallige jonge Dame, in galante Negligé Kleeding, by een openstaande Vengster, waar voor een bekleede Tafel, alwaar een Kisje met kleinodien op geplaast is; uitvoerig van behandeling, als door denzelven [Frans van Mieris, de oude] | *Mat:* op paneel *Size:* hoog 9, breed 7 ½ duim	R[oos]	(Sold) fl 18 Zurmuklen
1809/04/22	AMYVR	0209	*F. van Mieris* | Een Vorstelijk Persoon; als F. van Mieris	de Bruin	(Sold) fl 1:15 du Pree

Mieris, Frans van (the younger)

1801/04/08	HAVIN	0008	*F. van Miers, de Jonge* | Een Mans Pourtrait in een Japon leunende met de hand op een Balustrade uitvoerig | companion to lot 9		(Unknown)
1801/04/08	HAVIN	0009	*F. van Miers, de Jonge* | Een Vrouwe Pourtrait in een pragtige kleeding tot een weerga niet minder | companion to lot 8		(Unknown)
1801/06/13	LNDLS	0013	*F. van Mieris* | Een Man, zittende voor een tafel, waarop boeken leggen, en een studeerlamp op staat, konstig en uitvoerig, op paneel geschilderd, door F. van Mieris 1740., zijnde het Portrait van zijn vader W. van Mieris | *Mat:* op paneel *Size:* hoog 11, breed 9 duimen *Inscr:* F. van Mieris 1740 (signed and dated?) *Notes:* It is unclear whether the name and date are inscribed on the painting.	D van R	(Sold) fl 17 A Delfos [for] W
1802/04/13	HAVIN	0063	*F. van Mieris, de Jonge* | Een Mans Hoofd, met een bonte muts, uitvoerig		(Unknown)
1802/06/28	AMSCH	0109	*F. van Mieris, de Jonge* | Een Binnenvertrek, voor en Lessenaar zit een bedaagd Heer, nevens hem een Boer met een mand met Eyeren | *Mat:* op paneel *Size:* hoog 14, breed 11 duim	Anna Elink	(Sold) fl 48:10 Roijers
1802/08/24	LNDLS	0013	*F. van Mieris* | In een Binnen – vertrek zit een bevallig Vrouwtje met een naaikussen op haar schoot, nevens haar een Jongetje met een hoepel in de hand, voor haar rust een Patrijshondje op een dwijl bij een mandje met linnen, voords een Tafel met een tinnen bord, een brood en een boek; aan de wand hangt een Schilderij, een Vogelkooi en eenig Huisraad. Alles helder, extra uitvoerig en delicaat, op paneel, door F. van Mieris, 1739 | *Mat:* op paneel *Size:* hoog 18 ½, breed 15 duimen *Inscr:* F. van Mieris,	Leonardus Bouman [or others]	(Unknown) fl 80

			1739 (signed and dated?) *Notes:* It is unclear whether the name and date are inscribed on the painting.		
1802/09/29	AMSCH	0037	*F. van Mieris. de Jonge.1735* | Een Binnenhuis, hoog 21, breed 18 duim. Paneel. Dit Tafreel vettoond [sic] een Keuken, in dewelke een Dienstmaagd by een Tafel staat, die met een Kleed gedekt is, en waarop veel keuken gereedschap geplaatst is; als een mand met Eyeren, Beslagpot, Kruiddoos, enz. zy is bézig Eyeren te klessen, terwyl de knegt een mand Appelen, een dood Hoen, en een schotel Carbonade haar schynt aantebieden; op de voorgrond een menigte Kool, Uyen, Keukengoed, en een blaffend Hondje, verder fraai gewerkt Tapyt en ander Bywerk, alles met een onvermoeid geduld naar de natuur bewerkt en alleruitvoerigst gepenceeld [Linterieur [sic] d'une cuisine ou une servante apprête quelque mêt ; un homme lui opporte [sic] differens commestibles de fruits et de la volaille : le nombre des meubles et la diversité des objets ne pourroient être detaillés sans confusion, nous nous bornerons donc d'observer que ce morceau est un des plus precieux de cet artiste, que le fini des legumes, des ustenciles de cuivre, ceux en bois, et surtout les objets de tapisserie est presque inconcevable, imitant parfaitement la nature. Il est frais et conservé.] | *Mat:* op paneel *Size:* hoog 21, breed 18 duim *Inscr:* F. van Mieris. de Jonge. 1735 (signed and dated?) *Notes:* It is unclear whether the name and date are inscribed on the painting.	C	(Sold) fl 495 Vinkeles
1802/09/29	AMSCH	0038	*F. van Mieris. de Jonge* | Twee stuks zynde het eene, een Bevallige en schoone Vrouw in ryke kleeding, speelende met een aartig bruin en wit gevlakt hondje, welke zy met de regterhand by 't oor trekt en met haar linkerhand ondersteunt; in het andere Stukje ziet men een zittende jongen Krygsman in ryke Kleeding als in overdenking, rustende met zyn linker arm over de Leuning van zyn Stoel, deeze twee bevallige Schilderytjes, zyn alleruitvoerigst en zeer zuiver behandelt [Deux sujets faisant pendant l'un offre une belle femme jouant avec un chien et l'autre un Officier appuyé du Coude sur sa chaise. Ils sont richement costumés et ce dernier porte un chapeau de velours à plumêts. Ces deux petits Tableaux sont d'une grande finesse de Pinceau & d'une couleur brillante.] | *Mat:* op paneel *Size:* ieder hoog 6 ¾, breed 5 ½ duim	[Labouchere?]	(Sold) fl 37 Gruiter
1804/08/08	AMSCH	0109	*F. van Mieris, de jonge* | Voor een Broodbakkers Winkel ziet men een bevallige Dienstmaagd, met een Mandje Broodjes in de Hand, schynende met de Bakker, welke uit zyn Raam ligt, met een Blaashoorn in de Hand, te praaten, voor hem een Plank, waarop gevlochte Teenen, waarop een ménigte van klein allerhande Brood, en ander toepasselyk Bywerk; dit stukje is fraai van licht en alleruitvoerigst gepenceeld | *Mat:* op paneel *Size:* hoog 12, breed 10 duim	Vink[eles] [for] S	(Bought In) fl 54
1804/10/16	DLOND	0140	*Frans van Mieris de jonge* | Een Jufvrouw, die een Brief schryft op een Lessenaartjen. Dit Stuk is slegts ten halven afgemaakt. Une Dame occupée à écrire une Lettre sur un petit Pupître. Pièce à moitié achevée | *Mat:* op paneel *Size:* hoog 9, breed 5		(Unknown)
1804/12/10	AMSCH	0054	*Frans v. Mieris de Jonge* | dit uitvoerig stukje, steld voor, een Keuken, welke men door een Nis ziet, achter dezelve een bevallige dienstmaagt in gesprek met een jongeling, welke een mand met vlees heeft, in zyn rechterhand houd hy twee patrysen, voor haar op de Nis leggen bloemkoolen en wortelen, ter zyde hangen Haasen en snippen, verders ziet men onderscheiden Keukengereedschap; dit Schilderytje is byzonder uitgewerkt en gunstig gepenceeld | *Mat:* op paneel *Size:* Hoog 15, breed 13 duim	Jan De Groot	(Sold) fl 200 Coclers
1808/06/13	AMSCH	0100	*Mieris (F. van) de Jonge* | Eene bevallige Dame, aan haar Toilet zittende, wordt door een Grijsaard een Beurs met geld aangeboden, welke zij met verachting van de hand wijst. Fraai uitgevoerd | *Mat:* op paneel *Size:* hoog 12, breed 10 duim	R[oos]	(Sold) fl 23 J Schuman
1808/10/28	AMVRS	0032	*Mieris, (F. van) de Jonge* | In een Binnehuis ziet men een Vrouw voor een Toonbank met Karstanjes, gedroogde Bokkens, Schol, Eieren, Koek, benevens Schaal en Gewicht, zij schijnt aan een Man, nevens haar staande, Eieren te verkopen, deze houdt een Mandje in de hand met Brood, Eieren, enz. Dit Kabinetstukje is uitvoerig en helder | *Mat:* op doek *Size:* hoog 8 ½, breed 7 duim	Marten Udink	(Sold) fl 130 J de Vries
1810/03/26	RMMUY	0036	*Frans van Mieris, den jongen* | In een aangenaam bergachtig Landschap, ligt op den voorgrond, den door het Zwijn gewonden Piramus. Thisbé, verzeld van den God der Liefde, beschreid het gewonde lijk. Alles is konstig en zeer uitvoerig behandeld [L'Histoire de Pirame et Thisbe, accompagnés de l'Amour. Dans un paysage soigné et fini.] | *Mat:* op paneel *Size:* hoog 6 ¼, breed 7 ½ duimen	Daniel de Jongh Az	(Sold) fl 26 Van Iperen Amsterdam voor Kobell

Mieris, Willem van

1801/06/10	AMSCH	0115	*Mieris. (W. van)* | Een Jongeling in zyn Schilderkamer, zittende voor een Tafel, waarop een vel blaauw Papier geplaatst is met een Pen, wit en zwart Kryt, nevens hem een Palet op een fluweel Kleet, alles is zeer uitvoerig en van eene delicaate penceels behandeling | *Mat:* op paneel *Size:* hoog 9, breed 7 duim	Herman ten Kate	(Sold) fl 102 C S Roos
1801/06/10	AMSCH	0116	*Mieris. (W. van)* | Voor een Tafel, ziet men een bejaard Man, met een Pyp in de hand, welke door een bevallig Meisje aangesprooken [sic] word, voor hem ziet men een Lier, nevens een Papier met Tabak, alles is	Herman ten Kate	(Sold) fl 150 van der Schley [for] Ter Smitten

			uitvoerig, krachtig en meesterlyk geschilderd | *Mat:* op paneel *Size:* hoog 13, breed 11 duim		
1801/06/13	LNDLS	0008	*W. van Mieris* | Een Mannetje, halverlijf te zien, met een hoed met pluimen op zijn hoofd, en een kante kraag om zijn hals, aartig gekleed, houdende een rhijnsche wijnromer in zijn hand, waarvan hij schijnt geproeft te hebben, zoo uitvoerig, konstig en kragtig van schildering als van zijn vader F. van Mieris, den Ouden, op paneel, ovaal formaat, door W. van Mieris, hoog 6, breed 4 ½ duimen. NB. Dit Stukje is geplaatst in een zwart ebben-houte lijst en kasje, kunnende gesloten worden | *Mat:* op paneel *Fmt:* ovaal *Size:* hoog 6, breed 4 ½ duimen	D van R	(Sold) fl 128 A Delfos [for] C
1801/06/13	LNDLS	0010	*W. van Mieris* | Een Visvrouw, halverlijf, met een borlflesje in de hand, extra uitvoerig en kragtig, op paneel, door W. van Mieris, boven toogsgewijs | *Mat:* on paneel *Fmt:* boven toogsgewijs *Size:* hoog 6, breed 4 ½ duimen	D van R	(Sold) fl 86 A Delfos [for] W
1801/06/13	LNDLS	0011	*W. van Mieris* | Pomona en Vertumnus, in een Landschap met geboomte, zeer uitvoerig, eél en krachtig, op paneel, door denzelven [W. van Mieris], 1693 | *Mat:* op paneel *Size:* hoog 17, breed 14 duimen *Inscr:* W. van Mieris, 1693 (signed and dated?) *Notes:* It is unclear whether the name and date are inscribed on the painting.	D van R	(Sold) fl 108 Thyes
1801/10/19	AMSCH	0042	*Mieris (W. van)* | Een Visvrouw met een Moot versche Zalm in de hand, en een mand of korfje by haar staande, waar in nog eenige andere Mooten Zalm gezien worden; zeer fraay en uitvoerig geschildert | *Mat:* op paneel *Size:* hoog 6 ¾ duim, breed 6 ⅜ *Notes:* The materials and dimensions were given in an errata sheet located at the end of the catalogue.	Jonkheer Menno Baron van Coehoorn	(Sold) fl 89 van der Schleij [for] A
1801/10/19	AMSCH	0043	*Mieris (W. van)* | Twee Jongelingen, waar van een speelende op een Guitard, staande by een steenen Tafel, waar van een prachtig Tapyt is afhangende; meede zeer uitvoerig gepenseeld | *Mat:* op paneel *Size:* hoog 10 ¼ duim, breed 8 ½ *Notes:* The material and dimensions were given in an errata sheet located at the end of the catalogue.	Jonkheer Menno Baron van Coehoorn	(Sold) fl 312 Coclers
1802/04/13	HAVIN	0064	*W. van Mieris* | Een Morin [sic], in de Hand een sluijer		(Unknown)
1802/04/13	HAVIN	0065	*W. van Mieris* | Een Hist:, uit Ovidius		(Unknown)
1802/05/05	AMSCH	0118	*W. van Mieris* | Dit uitmuntend Kabinetstukje verbeeld een bejaarde Visboer, houdende in zyn regterhand een keurige Schelvis, nevens hem een Ben met meerdere Schelvissen, een Tabaksdoos, Pyp en een Mes, delicaat en zeer uitvoerig behandeld | *Mat:* op paneel *Size:* hoog 9, breed 7 ½ duim	D	(Sold) fl 96 v d Schley [for] A[=Putte]
1802/06/28	AMSCH	0110	*W. Mieris* | In een Boomryk Landschap, ziet men Venus en Adonis, elkander liefkoozen; ter zyde staat een Minnewigt met een Jagthond, alles zeer delicaat en uitvoerig op Panneel | *Mat:* op paneel *Size:* hoog 16, breed 18 duim	Anna Elink	(Sold) fl 99 Geld
1802/06/28	AMSCH	0111	*W. Mieris* | Een zinryke Ordonnantie, van twee Vrouwenbeelden in een Landschap; gestoffeert met verscheide Bywerk, meesterlyk gepenceeld, door Denzelven [W. Mieris], hoog 32, breed 25 duim, op Doek | *Mat:* op doek *Size:* hoog 32, breed 25 duim	Anna Elink	(Sold) fl 98 Geld
1802/07/21	HGKAN	0064	*Wm. van Mieris* | Een overheerlyk fraay geschildert stuk, zynde de drie Gracien, nevens twee Kindertjes, dragende een Mandje met Bloemen, zeer natuurlyk en fraay behandeld, door Wm. van Mieris, in zwarte Lyst, op Doek | *Mat:* op doek		(Unknown)
1802/09/06	AMSCH	0187	*W. Mieris* | Een Historieele Ordenantie, met verscheide Beelden; meesterlyk geschilderd	Spaan	(Sold) fl 5:10 Jan Spaan
1802/09/18	RMDRS	0039	*W. Mieres* | Een Hoerhuisje, geteekend | *Size:* hoog 8 ½, breed 13 ½	Casper de Haas	(Unknown) fl 5:10
1802/09/29	AMSCH	0036	*W. van Mieris* | Een Krygsman in fraaije oude Kleeding, met een Hoed met Pluimen op het Hoofd, hond in de linkerhand een roemer Rynsche Wyn, en in de andere hand een pyp Tabak, terwyl hy met een vergenoegt en lachend gelaat Omziet; op een Tafel nevens hem staat een Wynfles en papier met Tabak, dit stukje is een Kunstjuweel en een meesterstuk van deezen konstenaar, zo van ongemeene uitvoerigheid, goed Caracter, als kragtig coloriet [Un militaire, en riche costume Hollandois, d'un caractere riant, dans le plus beau de l'age. Il porte un chapeau relevé à plumets, tenant de la main gauche un verre à vin du Rhin & de la droite une pipe allumée ; il se tient debout près d'une Table ou sont placées une Bouteille de vin une cornette de Papier ouverte, avec du Tabac ; ses vétemens sont des couleurs les plus Eclatantes, ce Bejoux [sic] de Tableau est d'un ton de couleur & d'une beauté de touche qui produisent l'Illusion.] | *Mat:* op koper *Fmt:* toog gewys *Size:* hoog 6, breed 4 ½ duim	[Labouchere?]	(Sold) fl 96 Pruijssenaar
1803/04/20	AMSCH	0038	*Mieris. (W.)* | Vertumnis in de gedaante van een oude Vrouw, by Pomona, hy is gekleed in een Fluweele kleeding, Pomona is half naakt en heeft in haar arm een korfje met Fruiten, agter haar een Boom- en Bergachtig Landschap; alles delicaat en zeer uitvoerig gepenceeld [Vertumne & Pomone font le sujet de cette piéce : l'amant deguisé est vétû de velours, sa nimphe est moité nue ; elle tient une corbeille remplie de fruits, au fond est un arbre & des collines. Ce tableau est eclattant & d'un pinceau très soigné.] | *Mat:* op paneel *Size:* hoog 10, breed 8 ½ duim	Maria Magdalena van Sluypwyk, gravinne van Moens	(Sold) fl 200 Pruijssenaar [for] R

1804/05/07	AMSCH	0100	*Mieris. (W. van)* | Een Dame in een bond Jakje aan een Tafel zittende, een kopje Koffy te drinken, agter haar een Dienstmaagd het Bed maakende, verders een uitmuntend gewerk Tapyt, eenig Gebak en bywerk; dit stukje is zeer bevallig, zynde zeer delicaat gepenceeld | *Mat:* op paneel *Size:* hoog 9, breed 7 ½ duim	Roos [for] A	(Sold) fl 125 Tijs
1804/05/07	AMSCH	0101	*Mieris. (W. van)* | In een Boomryk Landschap, vertoont zig den Heiland zittende by de Waterput, als redeneerende met de Samaritaansche Vrouw, welke in zeedige houding, aandachtig schynt te luisteren; alles is meesterlyk en uitvoerig van penceelbehandeling | *Mat:* op doek *Size:* hoog 32, breed 26 duim	Schley	(Sold) fl 21 Thys
1804/10/16	DLOND	0139	*Willem van Mieris* | Een Mans-Portrait, zeer uitvoerig. Portrait d'Homme, très fini | *Mat:* op doek *Size:* hoog 22, breed 19		(Unknown)
1804/12/10	AMSCH	0053	*W. Mieris* | In een binnenvertrek ziet men een bevallige Vrouw met een kind aan de borst, zy zit naast een tafel waarop een Papkom, kandedelaar [sic] en een stuk brood, ter andere zyde een wieg en een stoel; dit stukje is zeer uitvoerig, dun en tevens kragtig van schildering | *Mat:* op paneel *Size:* Hoog 14, breed 12 duim	Jan De Groot	(Sold) fl 126 Coclers
1805/07/03	AMSCH	0030	*Mieris. (W. van)* | Dit tafreel vertoont het Paleis van Circe, waar Ulisses in een toornige houding de Tovergodin met het zwaart dreigt te straffen wegens het ontaarden zyner gezellen; zy smeekt zyn Genade op haar knie geboogen; by haar staat op de vloer een gouden vaas met haar toverstok, vier Vrouwen van haar gevolg in een verschrikte houding, zoeken zig door de vlugt te redden. Verder ziet men aan de regter hand een marmere Tafel, met een alleruitvoerigst tapyt bedekt alsmeede een Toover-vaas; dit luisteryk tafreel is met veel zuiverheit, en alleruitvoerigst behandeld, de hartstochten zyn uitdruklyk, de kleeding fraai geploit, en het geheel doet een kragtige werking van licht en donker | *Mat:* op paneel *Size:* hoog 23 ½, breed 20 duim	R[oos]	(Sold) fl 430 W Ryers
1805/07/10	AMSCH	0095	*W. Mieris* | Pomona en Vertumnes [sic] in een Landschap, verzelt van een Paauw; delicaat op Paneel | *Mat:* op paneel *Size:* hoog 17, breed 15 duim	V[inkeles] [for] L	(Sold) fl 40 L Pakker
1806/08/13	AMSCH	0338	*Mieris. (W.)* | Een bevallig Boom- en Bergachtig Landschap met een Rivier doorsneeden, ryk gestoffeerd met Beeldjes; Schuiten, Vrachtgoederen, enz.; zonachtig en uitvoerig behandeld | *Mat:* op paneel *Size:* hoog 9, breed 12 duim	Vinkeles [for] J	(Sold) fl 3:15 Richters
1806/08/20	HGBSM	0186	*W. Mieris* | Het afbeeldsel van een deftig Heer met de regterhand op de borst en een Mantel over de linker schouder omhangen; delicaat en uitvoerig geschildert, door W. Mieris, op paneel, ovaal formaat | *Mat:* op paneel *Fmt:* ovaal *Size:* hoog 7 ½, breed 5 ¾ duim	Macalester Loup [or others]	(Withdrawn)
1806/08/20	HGBSM	0187	*W. Mieris* | Een dito [afbeeldsel], zijnde deszelfs Huisvrouw, in alles als de voorgaande behandelt | *Size:* hoog 7 ½, breed 5 ¾ duim	Macalester Loup [or others]	(Withdrawn)
1806/08/20	HGBSM	0188	*W. Mieris* | Een Portraitje van een Heer alleruitvoerigst Gepenseeld, door W. Mieris, op koper, ovaal formaat | *Mat:* op koper *Fmt:* ovaal *Size:* hoog 3 ¾, breed 3 duim	Macalester Loup [or others]	(Withdrawn)
1807/06/10	HGBSM	0156	*W. Mieris* | Het afbeeldsel van een deftig Heer, met de regterhand op de borst, en een mantel over de linker schouder omhangen, delicaat en uitvoerig geschilderd door W. Mieris, op paneel, ovaal formaat | *Mat:* op paneel *Fmt:* ovaal *Size:* hoog 7 ½, breed 5 ¾ duim	Abraham Delfos [or others]	(Sold) fl 25 Noordwyk
1807/06/10	HGBSM	0157	*W. Mieris* | Een dito [afbeeldsel], zijnde deszelfs Huisvrouw, in alles als de voorgaande behandelt [delicaat en uitvoerig geschilderd], door denzelfden [W. Mieris], eender grootte | *Mat:* op paneel *Fmt:* ovaal *Size:* hoog 7 ½, breed 5 ¾ duim	Abraham Delfos [or others]	(Sold) fl 24 Noordwyk
1807/06/10	HGBSM	0158	*W. Mieris* | Een Portretje van een Heer, alleruitvoerigst gepenceeld, door denzelven Meester, op koper, ovaal formaat | *Mat:* op koper *Fmt:* ovaal *Size:* hoog 3 ¾, breed 3 duim	Abraham Delfos [or others]	(Sold) fl 11:10 v Giese
1807/08/26	AMSCH	0123	*W. van Mieris* | Dit uitmuntend Stukje verbeeld een Visboer, halverlyf te zien, hebbende in zyn regterhand een Schelvis, terwyl hy in zyn linkerhand een Pyp houdt, en op een Visben rust; de schildering is zoo uitvoerig als 'er van dezen voortreffelyken Meester bekend is | *Mat:* op paneel *Fmt:* van boven rond *Size:* hoog 7, breed 5 duim	Helsdinge	(Sold) fl 120 Coclair
1808/04/26	GDAN	0092	*Mieres (Wm. van)* | Zijnde de Schakéring van Proserpina, waar na badende Nimphen, met verwondering en zigtbaare droefheid dezelve naöogen, zeer goed geschildert | *Size:* hoog 25 ½, breed 29 duim	G H Fortuyn	(Unknown)
1808/04/26	GDAN	0093	*Mieres (Wm. van)* | Een fraai Mans Pourtretje | *Size:* hoog 6 ½, breed 5 ½ duim	G H Fortuyn	(Unknown)
1808/06/06	RMRIJ	0078	*Mieris. (Willem van) 1733* | Een bejaard man met eene muts op het hoofd, rustende met zijn linkerarm op een Oestervaatje, een mes in de hand houdende; met de regterhand biedt hij eene opengemaakte Oester aan; op de tafel een bak met opengemaakte Oesters; in den achtergrond eenig bijwerk. Uitvoerig en fraai geschilderd [Devant une table se trouve un homme d'un certain âge en bonnet, qui appuyant son bras gauche sur un tonneau, tient un couteau à la main, et offre une huitre ouverte de la main droite. Il y a sur la table des huitres, et dans le fond quelques accessoires. D'un grand fini et éxécuté avec beaucoup de vérité] | *Annots:* verk. W. Kinckee, Leiden, 9 April 1782 (f 330.-) (RMA I) *Mat:* op paneel *Size:*	Gerrit van der Pot, Heer van Groeneveld	(Sold) fl 500 Coclers

			Hoog 8 ¼, en breed 7 duim *Inscr:* Willem van Mieris. 1733 (signed and dated?) *Notes:* It is unclear whether the name and date are inscribed on the painting.		
1808/06/06	RMRIJ	0079	*Mieris. (Willem van)* | Een biddende Hermiet, met de oogen op een Crucifix gevestigd. Een doodshoofd, boeken en schriften versieren dit uitvoerig konststukje [Un Hermite en meditation a ses regards fixés sur un Crucifix. Auprès de lui, on voit une tête de mort, des livres et des papiers. Ce Tableau d'un précieux fini, et d'un ton soutenu, est dans le stile de Gérard Dou] | *Mat:* op paneel *Size:* Hoog 5 ⅝, en breed 4 ⅞ duim *Loc:* Amsterdam, Nederland. Rijksmuseum. (A265) as F. van Mieris II.	Gerrit van der Pot, Heer van Groeneveld	(Sold) fl 165 van Lennep [for] le Roi
1808/06/13	AMSCH	0099	*Mieris (W. van)* | Voor een Gebouw zit een deftig Heer, in losse rijke kleeding, rustende met den linker arm op een Wijnvat, waarop zijn Muts met een Pluim geplaatst is, met een vergenoegd gelaat houdt hij in de linker hand een roemer Wijn, ter zijde eene Dame, met een Scharretje in de hand, verder een Hofgezicht. Bevallig van koloriet en uitvoerig | *Mat:* op paneel *Size:* hoog 11 ½, breed 10 duim	[Jan Tersteeg]	(Sold) fl 81 J Schuman
1808/10/28	AMVRS	0031	*Mieris, (W. van)* | Een Schilder in zijn Kamer, met teekenpen, wit en zwart krijt, palet, enz. voor en bij zich op een fluweel kleed. Dit kunststukje is uitnemend zacht, teder en bevallig | *Mat:* op paneel *Size:* hoog 9, breed 7 ½ duim	Marten Udink	(Sold) fl 199 Josi
1809/04/17	AMSCH	0057	*W. Mieris* | Voor een Herberg zit een Krijgsman, in 't Harnas, rustende met den regter Arm op een Tafel, waar op een Tabakscomvoir, een Fles, en drie Schollen geplaatst zijn, hij houdt met een vergenoegd gelaat een Roemer Wijn in de Hand, agterwaards een Vrouw die de Deur in gaat; bevallig van koloriet en uitvoerig behandeld | *Mat:* op doek *Size:* hoog 15, breed 12 duim	[Gruyter?]	(Sold or Bought In) fl 66
1809/09/06	AMSCH	0049	*Mieris (W. van)* | Deze konstige Ordinantie verbeeld in een pragtige Zaal Circe nedergeknield aan den Voeten van de in woeden zijnde Ullisis [sic], gereed zijn Zwaard te trekken, eene vlugtende Nimph vertoond zig bij den ingang, verder gestoffeerd met een fraai gewerkte Vaas op een Pedestal en een afhangend Tapijt op een Stoel en verder bijwerk; de Hartstogten zijn treffend verbeeld, het licht en koloriet bevallig en van een aller-uitvoerigste penceelbehandeling, en een der fraaiste van deze Meester | *Mat:* op paneel *Size:* hoog 13, breed 17 duim	Johannes Caudri	(Sold) fl 181 Tomassen
1809/09/06	AMSCH	0050	*Mieris (W. van)* | Dit bevallig Schilderstukje, verbeeld een staand Heer in een Hofgezicht, in deftige Kleeding, met Kanten, Das en Lubben, houdende in de regterhand een sierlijk gewerkte Deegen, rustende met de linker arm op een Baluster, waar over een gedeelten van een tapijt kleedje ligt. Het is bevallig van licht en coloriet, en zeer uitvoerig gepenceeld | *Mat:* op paneel *Size:* hoog 9, breed 7 duim	Johannes Caudri	(Sold) fl 100 Tomassen
1810/05/22	AMSCH	0060	*Mieris. (W. van)* | Dit uitmuntend Kabinetstukje verbeeld een bejaarde Vischboer, houdende in zijn regterhand een keurige Schelvisch, nevens hem een Ben met verscheide Visschen, een Tabaksdoos, Pijp en Mes; alles teeder en uitvoerig behandeld | *Mat:* op paneel *Size:* hoog 9, breed 7 ½ duim	Johannes van de Putte Nicolaasz.	(Sold) fl 150 T Spaan
1810/08/01	AMSCH	0064	*Mieris (Willem van)* | Een Officier met eenen lederen Kolder gekleed, zittende voor eene Herberg, rustende met zijnen regter arm op eene Ton, waarop gedroogde Schollen geplaatst zijn, houdende eene Bierkan en Trompet in de handen, neven hem een Hond [Audevant d'un Cabaret est representé un militaire Cuirassé ; il est assis et appuyé contre un tonneau, ou l'on voit des plies salées ; d'une main il tient une trompette, et de l'autre une Canette de Bierre ; un Chien se trouve à côté de lui] | *Annots:* assez bon. (NGW) *Mat:* op paneel *Size:* hoog 11, breed 9 ½ duimen *Loc:* Leiden, Nederland. Stedelijk Museum De Lakenhal. (1201)	Mr Pieter de Smeth van Alphen	(Bought In) fl 700
1810/08/01	AMSCH	0065	*Mieris (Willem van)* | Een deftig Heer, zittende nevens eene tafel, waarop een Komfoor, Fles en Pijp geplaatst zijn, en welke Tafel gedeeltelijk met een Tapijt gedekt is; hij houdt eenen Roemer in de regterhand [Un homme cossu assis auprès d'une Table couverte en partie d'un tapis, un rechaut, une pipe et une bouteille se trouvent devant lui, tandis qu'il tient son verre à la main] | *Annots:* assez bon. (NGW) *Mat:* op paneel *Size:* hoog 11, breed 9 ½ duimen *Loc:* Leiden, Nederland. Stedelijk Museum De Lakenhal. (1202)	Mr Pieter de Smeth van Alphen	(Sold) fl 620 J^mo de Vries

Mieris, Willem van (and Mieris, F. (I))

1808/06/06	RMRIJ	0077	*Mieris (Frans van), Mieris (Willem van)* | Eene Heilige Familie. Maria, zittende met aandacht in een boek te lezen; voor haar ligt op eene knie gebogen het kind Jezus, zijn kruis metende; in den achtergrond vertoont zich Jozef aan zijne werkbank. Verder rijk van bijwerk; het licht, dat tusschen de vensters op de voorwerpen valt, is heerlijk van uitwerking. Dit kunststuk is onvoltooid gebleven door F. van Mieris, en is door deszelfs Zoon, Willem van Mieris, voleind. Zie verder, over dit tafereel, Houbraken Leven der Kunstschilders, 3 deel, pag. II. [Une sainte famille. Marie est assise occupée à lire dans un livre qu'elle tient sur ses genoux. On voit devant elle l'Enfant Jésus qui en se courbant, mesure sa croix, et dans le fond Joseph qui travaille à son Etabli. La lumiere piquante qui entre par une croisée, produit un superbe effet. D'autres accessoires enrichissent ce beau Tableau qui a été fini par Guillaume van Mieris, comme on peut le voir dans l'histoire des Peintres par Houbraken Edition	Gerrit van der Pot, Heer van Groeneveld	(Sold) fl 1000 Noortwyk

Hollandaise vol. 3. pag.11] | *Mat:* op paneel *Size:* Hoog 13 ¼, en breed 16 ½ duim

Mieris, Willem van (or Mieris, W., copy after)

1805/07/10 AMSCH 0094 *W. Mieris* | Een Krygsman in 't Harnas met een Lederen Kolder, voor een Herberg zittende met een Roemer in zyn hand, leunende op een Tafel, waarop geplaatst is, een Fles, Tabaks-Comvoir en drie Schollen, achterwaarts een Vrouw het Huis ingaande; uitvoerig op Doek, hoog 15, breed 12 duim, door of na W. Mieris | *Mat:* op doek *Size:* hoog 15, breed 12 duim — R[oos] — (Sold) fl 105 Gruiter

Mieris, Willem van (or Mieris, W., manner)

1804/08/08 AMSCH 0258 *W. Mieris* | Twee stuks Fabel-Ordinantiën; uitvoerig op Paneel, door W. Mieris, of in zyn manier | *Mat:* op paneel — Roos [for] J — (Sold) fl 1:15 Kamphuizen

Mieris, Willem van (copy after)

1802/08/24 LNDLS 0142 *W. van Mieris* | Een Pouliers-winkel [sic], na W. van Mieris | *Mat:* op paneel — Leonardus Bouman [or others] — (Unknown) fl 0:11

1804/10/16 DLOND 0240a[f] *C. Vermeulen; W. v. Mieris* | [Een Stuk, bevattende 13 zeer schone Copiën van de volgende Meesters. Un Tableau, contenant 13 Copies très-belles des Peintres suivans.] 6. W. v. Mieris. Keukenstuk, une Cuisine | copy by Corn. Vermeulen (III) after W. Mieris *Mat:* op paneel *Size:* hoog 41, breed 55 *Notes:* The bracketed information in the title appears above lot 240a[a] and refers to lots 240a[a-m]. — (Sold) fl 150 for lots 240a[a-m]. Ond d Wyngaert

1804/10/16 DLOND 0240a[h] *C. Vermeulen; W. v. Mieris* | [Een Stuk, bevattende 13 zeer schone Copiën van de volgende Meesters. Un Tableau, contenant 13 Copies très-belles des Peintres suivans.] 8. W. v. Mieris. Een Bontwerker, un Pelletier | copy by Corn. Vermeulen (III) after W. Mieris *Mat:* op paneel *Size:* hoog 41, breed 55 *Notes:* The bracketed information in the title appears above lot 240a[a] and refers to lots 240a[a-m]. — (Sold) fl 150 for lots 240a[a-m]. Ond d Wyngaert

1805/06/24 DOBLU 0002 *W. Mieris* | Twee stuks, naar W. Mieris; verbeeldende het eene een Keuken, en het andere een Boutwinkel — Willem Snellen [or] F R E Nibbelinck [or] Gysbert Visser — (Unknown)

1807/06/10 HGBSM 0166 *W. Mieris* | Een Mannetje met een kan en glas in de handen, na W. Mieris | *Mat:* op paneel *Size:* hoog 6 ¼, breed 5 duim — Abraham Delfos [or others] — (Sold) fl 3 Vermeulen

1809/04/22 AMYVR 0164 *W. van Mieris* | Een galant Gezelschap; naar W. van Mieris — de Bruin — (Sold) fl 6:10 du Pree

Mieris, Willem van (manner)

1802/08/24 LNDLS 0153 *W. v. Mieris* | De liggende Nimph Danaë en den gouden Regen, als van W. v. Mieris — Leonardus Bouman [or others] — (Unknown) fl 2:2

1804/04/28 LNDLS 0057 *W. van Mieris* | Een Juffer, met een speldewerk-kussen op haar schoot, terwijl een vrouw haar een haan aanbied, in een binnenvertrek, met meer bywerk, als door W. van Mieris — [Abraham Delfos] [or others] — (Sold) fl 4:5 Richters [for] G

Mieris, Willem van (style)

1808/08/23 AMSCH 0255 *W, van Mieris* | Een Doctor in zijn Studeervertrek, waar bij eene staande Vrouw die met dezelven raadpleegt, geestig verbeeld in de stijl van W, van Mieris — J — (Sold) fl 3 L Pakker

Mignon, Abraham

1802/05/24 HGBAK 0042 *A. Mignon* | Een tros blauwe en witte Druiven, benevens twee Persiken op een tafel, door A. Mignon, hoog 13 ½ duim, breed 11 duim, op doek, zwarte lyst en vergulde binnenrand | *Mat:* op doek *Size:* hoog 13 ½ duim, breed 11 duim *Notes:* This lot was sold with lot 43 by an anonymous artist. — Mejuffrouw A van der Mieden — (Sold) fl 4:5 for lots 42 & 43. Kleijn

1802/09/18 RMDRS 0016 *J. Mignon* | Een Tafel, waar op verscheide Vrugten, en een drink Pocaal, in een heldere manier uitvoerig geschilderd | *Size:* hoog 27 ½, breed 35 ½ duim *Notes:* The artist's name was given as "J. Mignon" but we have assumed this is an error. — Casper de Haas — (Sold) fl 6 Verweij

1803/12/15 MGLAC 0029 *Mignon* | Een fraai stukje met Vrugten; zeer delicaat geschilderd | *Mat:* op doek *Size:* hoog duim 14, breed duim 13 — Mr L H de Haze Bomme — (Unknown)

1804/10/29 HRBAU 0058 *Mignon, (A.)* | Op een marmersteenen Voetstuk staat een glazen Vles, gevuld met keurige Bloemen als Roozen Papavers, Tulpen, Balroozen, en meer andere soorten, met hun lof, fraai gestoffeerd met diverse soorten van Capellen en Insecten. Dit Schildery is zeer bevallig gegroept, alleruitvoerigst en natuurlyk behandeld, zo dat men hetzelve met recht onder de beste werken van dien Schilder stellen kan | *Mat:* op paneel *Size:* hoog 23, breed 19 ½ duim — Simon Styl — (Unknown)

1805/07/03 AMSCH 0031 *Mignon, (A.)* | Op een steenen Tafel gedeeltelyk met een kleed gedekt, ziet men een zilvere Schotel met Oesters, Castangiën en opengesnéden Citroen, terzyde een Kom met Punsch, een Roemer, en een ménigte delicaaten Vrugten, Insecten enz.; zynde van een aangename en uitvoerige behandeling | *Mat:* op paneel *Size:* hoog 21 ½, breed 17 ½ duim — R[oos] — (Sold) fl 155 Coclers

1805/07/03 AMSCH 0107 *A. Mignon* | Dit Bevallig en Uitmuntend stuk vertoont, op een steene Barstweering, een omvallende cierlyk gewerkte Vaas, gevuld met een ménigte verschillende keurige Bloemen, als: Roosen van diversche — R[oos] — (Sold) fl 215 Reyers

			soorten, Tulpen, Papaver, Angelieren, Irias, Takken met Bloeisem en Bladeren, enz., ter zyde ziet men een schreeuwende Kat, by een Muizeval, die als door een stoot, dezelve Vaas omver werpt: alles evenaart de natuur, en is alleruitvoerigst van penceel behandeling | *Mat:* op doek *Size:* hoog 34, breed 28 duim		
1806/08/13	AMSCH	0110	*Mignon. (A.)* | Op de voorgrond in een Landschap by Plantgewas, ziet men eenige doode Vissen; en een Nesje met Vogel-Eyeren; natuurlyk en uitvoerig geschilderd | *Mat:* op paneel *Size:* hoog 15, breed 16 duim	Roos	(Sold) fl 6:5 Van Dijl
1808/05/18	LNAN	0015	*Mignon* | Een dito [Pot met verscheide soorten van Bloemen] door een voornaam Meester | *Notes:* The artist's name "Mignon" was added in by hand in the RKDH copy of the catalogue.	Mr Cornelis Versluys	(Unknown)
1808/06/06	RMRIJ	0080	*Mignon. (Abraham)* | Dit uitmuntend tafereel stelt voor eene Marmeren Tafel, waarop een groen fluweel kleed ligt. Wijders overheerlijke Vruchten, een Kreeft, Rijnwijnroemer en verder rijk bijwerk. In den achtergrond eene Zijden Gordijn en in een Kozijn, waar men doorziet, een Putter bezig met putten, enz. Alles is even delicaat, uitvoerig, warm en krachtig geschilderd [Un panier rempli de fruits Choisis, un Homar, un verre de vin du Rhin, et d'autres accessoires sont exposés sur une table de marbre couverte d'un tapis de velours verd brodé en or. Une draperie en soie, et auprés d'une croisée un Chardonneret qui puise son eau, ornent ce Tableau, qui est d'une Imitation parfaite jusques dans les moindres détails. Une couleur brilliante et vraie, et un beau faire rendent ce Morceau un chef-d'oeuvre capital de ce fameux Artiste] | *Mat:* op doek *Size:* Hoog 29 ½, en breed 25 ¼ duim *Loc:* Amsterdam, Nederland. Rijksmuseum. (A266)	Gerrit van der Pot, Heer van Groeneveld	(Sold) fl 790 Johs Eck en Zoon [for] le Roi
1808/06/11	RMRIJ	0008	*A: Mignon* | Eenig Dood Gevogelte en verder Bywerk; uitmuntend, uitvoerig en natuurlyk behandeld | *Mat:* op doek *Size:* hoog 22, breed 18 ½ duim		(Sold) fl 90 Coclers
1808/06/13	AMSCH	0103	*Mignon (A.)* | In een Landschap, bij de Stam van een ouden Boom, ziet men op den voorgrond verscheidene Vruchten liggen, als Kanteloep, Druiven, Abricosen, Pruimen, en andere Fruit, waarbij verschillende Bloemen en andere Plantgewassen, met Bladeren, waarop onderscheidene Kapellen azen, op den grond een Hagedisje, een Insekt vervolgende. Alles evenaart de Natuur, en van eene zeer uitvoerige penceelsbehandeling | *Mat:* op paneel *Size:* hoog 22, breed 17 duim	[Jan Tersteeg]	(Sold) fl 102 van Drielst
1808/06/13	AMSCH	0185	*A. Mignon* | Een Fruitstuk als voren [waarin uitmunten een Kweepeer en blaauwe Pruimen]; niet minder als het voorgaande	E M Engelberts	(Sold) fl 30 Glad
1809/09/06	AMSCH	0051	*Mignon (A)* | Dit kapitaal voorwerp verbeeld een rijk geordineerd Bloemstuk: voor een steenen Nis, staat op een steenen Plint, een sierlijke gewerkte Vaas, waarin verscheidene geurige Bloemen geplaatst zijn, als verschillende soorten van Roozen, Tulpen, Irias, Papaver en andere fraaije soorten, waarop verscheiden Insecten aazen, ter zijde vertoont zich een nederdalende Spin, en een Web met verscheidene kleinder. De bevallige schikking en het natuurlijk coloriet, bij een uitvoerige penceel-behandeling, geven alle verdiensten aan dit Tafereel | *Mat:* op doek *Size:* hoog 34, breed 26 duim	Johannes Caudri	(Sold) fl 200 van Iperen
1810/03/07	UTWLD	0032	*Mignon* | Een zeer uitvoerig bloemstuk met vrugten | *Size:* hoog 1 voet 2 duim, breed 1 voet 5 duim	J J Woertman	(Unknown) fl 62
1810/06/20	AMSCH	0047	*A. Mignon* | Voor de Stam van een oude Boom, liggen witte en blaauwe Druiven, Perziken, Abrikozen, Kweepeer en andere Vruchten, omgeven van Wijngaardranken en andere Planten, waarop Insekten azen. Aanlokkend en uitvoerig gepenceeld | *Mat:* op doek *Size:* hoog 23, breed 20 duimen	D	(Sold) fl 110 Gruyter
1810/08/06	AMSCH	0073	*Mignon (A.)* | Twee stuks met smakelijke Vrugten, als witte en blaauwe Druiven, Persiken, Abrikozen en anderen, waar op onderscheidene Insecten aazen; meesterlijk en teder gepenceeld | *Mat:* op doek *Size:* ieder hoog 22, breed 19 duimen	C	(Sold) fl 7 Stoopendaal [for] B

Mij, Hieronymus van der

1806/05/05	AMSCH	0086	*H. van der My* | De voornaame Muzikant Solniz; uitvoerig op Paneel | *Mat:* op paneel *Size:* hoog 7 ½, breed 6 ½ duim	H	(Sold) fl 1 L Pakker
1806/06/07	RMHSN	0115	*Van der My* | De Sabynsche Maagdenroof, in 't Graauw | *Mat:* op doek	A E K L	(Unknown)

Mijin, J. [Unidentified]

1802/05/05	AMSCH	0123	*J. Mijin* | Op een Boerewerf ziet men eenige Huislieden op een Wagen met twee Paarden, verders een menigte andere stoffagie van Beelden, Geboomte en Boerenwoningen, alles van een aangenaam Coloriet | *Mat:* op paneel *Size:* hoog 21, breed 30 duim	D	(Bought In) fl 139 for lots 123 & 124
1802/05/05	AMSCH	0124	*J. Mijin* | Voor een Boeren Herberg ziet men een menigte Wagens en Voerlieden beezig zich te Ververschen, in alles als de Voorgaande | *Size:* hoog 21, breed 30 duim	D	(Bought In) fl 139 for lots 123 & 124

Mijts, J. [Unidentified]

1810/06/20	AMSCH	0067	*J. Mijts* | Een boomrijk Landschap, met een Rivier doorsneden, en stoffage van Beelden | *Mat:* op paneel *Size:* hoog 20, breed 24 duimen	A	(Sold) fl 24:10 Hodges

Millet, Jean François (I) (Francisque Millet)

<table>
<tr><td>1803/08/24</td><td>HGKAN</td><td>0003</td><td>Fracisque | Een Italiaansch Landschap met een Waterval, verbeeldende een Gezicht by Tivoli, de voorgrond met figuuren gestoffeerd, fraay geschilderd | companion to lot 4</td><td>[Teissier] [or others]</td><td>(Unknown) fl 9:5</td></tr>
<tr><td>1803/08/24</td><td>HGKAN</td><td>0004</td><td>Fracisque | Een dito [Italiaansch Landschap] verbeeldende het Graf van Virgilius, zynde een weergaay [sic], van de voorgaande | companion to lot 3</td><td>[Teissier] [or others]</td><td>(Unknown) fl 5</td></tr>
<tr><td>1810/07/26</td><td>AMSCH</td><td>0051</td><td>Millet (F.) | De Feestviering van het Gouden Kalf, door een aantal Beelden, in allerlei houdingen afgebeeld. Zijnde een der beste stukken van dezen Meester | Mat: op doek Size: hoog 20, breed 30 duimen</td><td>Cassino</td><td>(Bought In) fl 71</td></tr>
</table>

Minderhout, Hendrik van

<table>
<tr><td>1801/08/19</td><td>AMSCH</td><td>0064</td><td>H. Minderhout | Een gezicht van de Vismarkt te Antwerpen, ryk gestoffeerd met een ménigte Beelden</td><td>Pruyssen^{r}</td><td>(Sold) fl 7:5 Le Dantú</td></tr>
<tr><td>1801/11/10</td><td>AMPOS</td><td>0046</td><td>J. Meerhout | 1 Land- en Watergezigt</td><td></td><td>(Unknown)</td></tr>
</table>

Moens, F. [Unidentified]

<table>
<tr><td>1802/05/22</td><td>RMHSN</td><td>0005</td><td>F. Mons | Twee, een Winter met Schaatze Ryders, en een Zomer</td><td>Lambertus Bicker</td><td>(Unknown)</td></tr>
<tr><td>1806/06/07</td><td>RMHSN</td><td>0052</td><td>F. Moens | Twee Stuks Zeestrandjes, met veel Gewoel | Mat: op paneel</td><td>A E K L</td><td>(Unknown)</td></tr>
</table>

Moesgever [Unidentified]

<table>
<tr><td>1808/12/30</td><td>HGIMM</td><td>[0071h]</td><td>Moesgever | Voorts een exquis kabinetje Schilderijen van voorname Nederlandsche Meesters, welke uit hoofde van de kortheid des tijds niet stuk voor stuk kunnen beschreven worden; doch waarvan de beschrijving op den Kijkdag zal voorhanden zijn. Dus wij hier alleen de namen van eenige dier Meesters laten volgen, als: A. Kuyp, Ruysdaal, Karel du Jardyn, Loqwi ('t beste dat hij schilderde) Hondekoeter, van Dyk, Janson, Moesgever, Kamphuyzen, van Gooijen, A. van der Neer, T. Wyk, Huchtenburgh, Zolemaker, van Hassel, A. Vermeulen, van Dongen, Scheffer, van Os enz. | This Lot: Een Schilderij, Moesgever Notes: Because this lot was not numbered in the catalogue, we have assigned the number.</td><td></td><td>(Unknown)</td></tr>
</table>

Moeyaert, Claes Cornelisz.

<table>
<tr><td>1802/05/05</td><td>AMSCH</td><td>0148</td><td>Claas Mooijaart | In een Landschap met Ruïnes, ziet men verscheide staand en leggend Vee, waarby de Herders, delicaat en uitvoerig | Size: hoog 14, breed 18 duim</td><td>B</td><td>(Sold) fl 12 Spruit</td></tr>
<tr><td>1803/04/20</td><td>AMSCH</td><td>0039</td><td>Moyaert. (J.) [Moyaert. (C.)] | Het Afbeeldzel van den R. P. Marius, zittende in zyn Studeerkamer aan een Tafel, met een Pen in zyn hand, als in overdenking, hy is gekleed in een zwart Fluweele Toga met Bond gevoerd: op de Tafel leggen verscheide Boeken, ter zyde staat een Kruisbeeld en ander bywerk, alles meesterlyk fraay behandeld [Le Portrait du P. Marius assis dans son etude devant une table garnie de livres ; son vetement est une robe de docteur en velours & fourrée, d'autres accessoires terminent ce tableau qui est touché en maître.] | Mat: op doek Size: hoog 48, breed 39 duim Notes: The artist's name differs in the Dutch and French editions of the catalogue.</td><td>Maria Magdalena van Sluypwyk, gravinne van Moens</td><td>(Sold) fl 19 Theijs</td></tr>
<tr><td>1803/04/20</td><td>AMSCH</td><td>0040</td><td>Moyaert. (C. J.) | Dit Voorwerp vertoont den Heiland, stervende aan het Kruis, in het verschiet een Bergagtig Landschap, de Hartstogt is natuurlyk, en meesterlyk gepenceeld [J.C. mourant sur la croix ; le fond est terminé par une vue montueuse : ce sujet est traité d'une maniere édifiante & naturelle.] | Mat: op doek Size: hoog 33, breed 21 duim</td><td>Maria Magdalena van Sluypwyk, gravinne van Moens</td><td>(Sold) fl 31 Theijs</td></tr>
<tr><td>1808/06/06</td><td>RMRIJ</td><td>0086</td><td>Moijaert (C.J.) 1629 | De Zaligmaker aan het kruis. Meesterlijk geschilderd [Un Christ en Croix. D'une touche belle et légére] | Annots: verk gravin. Moens, Amst. 20 April, 1803 (f.31-) (RMA I) Mat: op doek Size: Hoog 31 ¾, en breed 20 duim Inscr: C.J. Moijaert 1629 (signed and dated?) Notes: It is unclear whether the name and date are inscribed on the painting.</td><td>Gerrit van der Pot, Heer van Groeneveld</td><td>(Sold) fl 40 Dr Luchtmans</td></tr>
<tr><td>1808/11/28</td><td>AMSCH</td><td>0113</td><td>C. Moijaert | Een dito [Bergachtig] Landschap, gestoffeerd met drie Jongelingen, bij eenige Bokken en Schaapen</td><td>S</td><td>(Sold) fl 1 Coclers</td></tr>
<tr><td>1810/06/20</td><td>AMSCH</td><td>0151</td><td>K. Moijaert | Een Landschap, met staand en rustend Vee</td><td>B</td><td>(Sold) fl 1:5 Koopman</td></tr>
<tr><td>1810/10/11</td><td>AMSCH</td><td>0159</td><td>K. Moyaart | De aanbidding der Herders</td><td>S</td><td>(Sold) fl 5:15 Gruiter</td></tr>
<tr><td>1810/10/11</td><td>AMSCH</td><td>0185</td><td>K. Moyaart | Een Historiëele Ordonantie, verbeelende een Vorstelijk Persoon, welke wapens en vaandels werden aangeboden; meesterlijk</td><td>A</td><td>(Sold) fl 0:16 van der Voort</td></tr>
</table>

Moijelle, Ridder [Unidentified]

<table>
<tr><td>1808/06/13</td><td>AMSCH</td><td>0109</td><td>Moijelle (Ridder) | Een hoog bergachtig Landschap, op eene Rots staat een Kasteel, op den voorgrond Beelden, Schapen en Bokken, in het verschiet meerdere Stoffage. Dun en warm behandeld | Mat: op paneel Size: hoog 20, breed 29 duim</td><td></td><td>(Withdrawn)</td></tr>
</table>

Mola, Pier Francesco

<table>
<tr><td>1803/04/27</td><td>AMSCH</td><td>000K</td><td>F. Mola | St. Francois recevant les Stigmates dans le Desert | Size: h. 25, l. 37 pouces</td><td>B</td><td>(Sold) fl 57 Josi</td></tr>
</table>

1804/07/25	AMSCH	0057	*Mola. (F.)* | In een Bergachtig Landschap, ziet men den Martelaar St. Sebastiaan met twee Pylen gewond, aan een Boom gebonden; verder eenig Geboomte en een steene Piramide; zeer meesterlyk en breed behandeld | *Mat:* op doek *Size:* hoog 50, breed 37 duim		(Sold) fl 8 Thais
1810/07/26	AMSCH	0053	*Mola (F.)* | Een Italiaansch Landschap: in het midden van een Valei ziet men een knielend Heeremiet | *Mat:* op doek *Size:* hoog 19, breed 14 duimen	Cassino	(Bought In) fl 1:5

Mola, Pier Francesco (copy after)

1810/06/06	RMMUY	0099	*F. Mola* | Hagar en Ismaël. naar F. Mola | *Mat:* op paneel		(Unknown) fl 1:8

Molenaer

1802/11/01	DOBRA	0048	*S. Molenaar* | Twee galante Stukjes	Paulus van der Spyk [or others]	(Sold) fl 1 Meloen

Molenaer, Bartholomeus

1807/08/26	AMSCH	0290	*B. Molenaar* | Een Landgezicht met Geboomte, by een stil Water, op de voorgrond gestoffeerd met twee Hengelaars; plaisant geschilderd | *Mat:* op paneel	v d Schley [for] [Smits Wed]	(Sold) fl 8 Coclair

Molenaer, Cornelis

1804/10/29	HRBAU	0061	*Molenaar, (C.)* | Een aangenaam Duingezigt omtrent Scheveningen; gestoffeerd langs strand met verschillende groepen, waar men bezig is Visch te verkoopen en te verdraagen; waar by verscheiden Heeren en Dames, die zich aldaar schynen te vermaaken; wyders ziet men verscheiden Visschers-vaartuigen, en in het verschiet de Zee. Zeer bevallig en natuurlyk verbeeld | *Mat:* op doek *Size:* hoog 19 ½, breed 26 ½ duim	Simon Styl	(Unknown)

Molenaer, Jan Miense

1801/02/18	AMBOS	0004	*J.M. Molenaar* | Een Herberg, waarin een vrolyk Gezelschap, dat van de drank verzadigd schynt, de Vrouw om geld vragende, en een der Gasten betuigd het zelve met een lagchend weezen niet te hebben, het zyn Pourtraiten van Schilders in die tyd	J Schonevelt	(Unknown)
1801/02/18	AMBOS	0061	*J. Molenaar* | Twee stuks Boere Gezelschappen	J Schonevelt	(Unknown)
1801/02/24	AMOTT	0004	*Molenaar* | 1 Boeren Gezelschap, op koper | *Mat:* op koper		(Unknown)
1801/03/16	AMSCH	0023	*J.M. Moolenaar* | Een Binnehuis met Kaartspelende Huislieden, waarby een zingende Munnik uitvoerig	K[ip]	(Sold) fl 12 J Yver
1801/03/16	AMSCH	0182	*J. Molenaar* | Twee Boeren Binnenhuizen	P[ruyssenaar]	(Sold) fl 1 Wijland
1801/04/08	HAVIN	0068	*Molenaar* | Het Gebed voor den Eeten		(Unknown)
1801/04/08	HAVIN	0069	*Molenaar* | Twee met Eetende en Drinkende Boeren		(Unknown)
1801/05/11	AMSCH	0052	*Jan Miense Molenaar* | In een Binnenhuis, ziet men voor een tafel, waar op een koffertje, nevens eenig geld geplaatst is, een Vrouw zitten, schynende aan een jongeling geluk te zeggen, agter hem een meisje, alle de caracters zyn natuurlyk en meesterlyk uitgevoerd | *Mat:* op paneel *Size:* hoog 11, breed 9 duim	P[ruyssenaar]	(Sold) fl 6 Van der Vinne
1801/05/11	AMSCH	0053	*Jan Miense Molenaar* | Eenige biddende Huisluiden, zittende aan een tafel, waar op spys geplaast is, krachtig behandeld | *Mat:* op paneel *Size:* hoog 12, breed 10 duim	P[ruyssenaar]	(Sold) fl 13 Allard
1801/05/11	AMSCH	0054	*Jan Miense Molenaar* | In een Binnehuis, zitten verscheide Boeren met hunne Vrouwtjes zich te verlustigen met zingen, roken en drinken; uitvoerig gepenceeld | *Mat:* op paneel *Size:* hoog 14, breed 16 duim	E[lias]	(Sold) fl 15:10 C S Roos
1801/06/10	AMSCH	0122	*Molenaar. (J. M.)* | Een Meisje, welke een Boer liefkoost, fiks behandeld | *Mat:* op paneel *Size:* hoog 9, breed 7 duim	[Doublet]	(Sold) fl 1:5 Gruyter
1801/06/10	AMSCH	0216[H]	*Molenaer* | Twee gesildzhapies [sic] | *Notes:* This lot was added in by hand in the AA, BRB and RKDH copies of the catalogue.	Herman ten Kate	(Sold) fl 8 Spruyt
1801/06/13	LNDLS	0034	*J. Molenaar* | Een Boeren-Gezelschap, op paneel | *Mat:* op paneel *Size:* hoog 11, breed 9 duimen	D van R	(Sold) fl 5:5 Thyes
1801/08/19	AMSCH	0067	*J. Molenaar* | Een Binnebuis met Rokende, Drinkende en Galantiseerende Boeren, als door J. Molenaar, fix geschilderd op Doek | *Mat:* op doek *Size:* hoog 11, breed 14 duim	Van Forreest	(Sold) fl 3 Gruiter
1801/08/19	AMSCH	0069	*J.M. Molenaar* | Een Dorpgezicht alwaar een Bruid naar de Kerk geleid wordt, verzeld van een menigte Mannen en Vrouwen, natuurlyk behandeld	Pruyssen^{r} [for] Q	(Bought In) fl 52
1801/08/19	AMSCH	0071	*J. M. Molenaar* | Een Kaartspeelend Gezelschap	Pruyssen^{r} [for] Q	(Sold) fl 7:5 Le Dantú
1801/08/19	AMSCH	0072	*J. M. Molenaar* | En Man, die een Meisje omhelst	Van Forreest	(Sold) fl 1:5 Wolft
1801/08/19	AMSCH	0073	*J. M. Molenaar* | Twee stuks Boere Bruiloften, vol gewoel van Beelden, uitvoerig op paneel | *Mat:* op paneel *Size:* hoog 14, breed 12 duim	Van Forreest	(Sold) fl 14 Roos
1801/10/19	AMSCH	0047	*Moolenaar. (J.)* | In dit Capitaal Stuk, 't welk een Binnenhuis verbeeld, ziet men een maaltyd van verscheide Boeren en Boerinnen met veel bywerk, ryk gestoffeerd en uitvoerig geschildert | *Mat:* op doek *Size:* hoog 2 voet 4 duim, breed 3 voet 3 ½ duim	Jonkheer Menno Baron van Coehoorn	(Sold) fl 109 B^{d} Kooy

1801/11/10	AMPOS	0032	*Molenaar* | 1 Vioolspeelder voor een vrolyk boeren Gezelschap, delicaat geschilderd door Molenaar, 1643 | *Inscr:* Molenaar, 1643 (signed and dated?) *Notes:* It is unclear whether the name and date are inscribed on the painting.		(Unknown)
1801/11/21	RMVIS	0004	*Molenaar* | Een Vrouwtje halverlyf te zien	Gelinus van Spaan	(Unknown)
1801/12/22	AMOTT	0056	*J. Molenaar* | 2 stuks, Treurende en Verheugde, by Doodkisten, in Binnevertrekken	Bartholomeus Ruloffs	(Unknown) fl 2:10
1801/12/22	AMOTT	0104	*Molenaar* | 2 stuks, de Boeren Chirurgyn en een Binnenhuis	Bartholomeus Ruloffs	(Unknown) fl 4:10
1802/02/16	AMSCH	0075	*J. M. Molenaar* | In een Binnehus zit een huisman te rooken, verzelt van twee anderen, die met een hond speelen, verder twee vrouwen en een man over de deur leggende, fiks gepenceeld	C	(Bought In) fl 50
1802/04/13	HAVIN	0052	*Molenaar* | Een Boer en een Boerin		(Unknown)
1802/05/05	AMSCH	0129	*J. M. Molenaar* | In een Boerebinnehuis, ziet men een menigte Huislieden aan Tafel zich Vrolyk met eten en drinken vermakende, op de regterzyde staat een Jongen, Bier in een Kan te tappen, alles delicaat en van de beste schildering | *Mat:* op doek *Size:* hoog 48, breed 62 duim	H	(Sold) fl 65 Pruijssenaar [for] J
1802/05/05	AMSCH	0130	*J. Molenaar* | Een Boeren Bruiloft, met verscheiden vrolyke en danssende Boeren en Boerinnen, bevallig | *Mat:* op paneel *Size:* hoog 23, breed 33 duim	A	(Sold) fl 30:10 van Iperen
1802/05/05	AMSCH	0131	*J. Molenaar* | Een biddend Huisgezin | *Size:* hoog 13, breed 15 duim	J	(Sold) fl 7:10 v d Vinne
1802/05/05	AMSCH	0132	*J. Molenaar* | Een Boeren Binnenhuis	J	(Sold) fl 2:15 Rigters
1802/05/24	HGBAK	0028	*Molenaer* | Een stukje met vrolyke Boertjes en Boerin, door Molenaer, hoog 11 duim, breed 9 duim paneel, zwarte lyst en vergulde bies | companion to lot 29 *Mat:* op paneel *Size:* hoog 11 duim, breed 9 duim	Mejuffrouw A van der Mieden	(Unknown) fl 12 for lots 28 & 29
1802/05/24	HGBAK	0029	*Molenaer* | Een dito [stukje] tot een weerga, met musiceerende Boertjes, door denzelven Meester [Molenaer], hoog en breed als vooren [hoog 11 duim, breed 9 duim] en dito [zwarte] lyst | companion to lot 28 *Size:* hoog 11 duim, breed 9 duim *Notes:* It is unclear what "dito" refers to in the title.	Mejuffrouw A van der Mieden	(Unknown) fl 12 for lots 28 & 29
1802/06/16	AMSCH	0110	*Jan Miense Moolenaar* | Onder een Troep Heidenen, ziet men een bevallig Meisje, welke door een van hun geluk gezegt word; krachtig en breed gepenceeld | *Mat:* op paneel *Size:* hoog 16, breed 22 duim	[Merrem]	(Sold) fl 43 Wed Achtienhoven
1802/06/16	AMSCH	0111	*Jan Miense Moolenaar* | In een Binnenhuis zitten verscheiden vrolyke Boeren; zig met drinken, rooken en zingen vermaakende; verder vertoond zig den Haartsteeden; alles is natuurlyk en meesterlyk gepenceeld | *Mat:* op paneel *Size:* hoog 13, breed 11 duim	[Merrem]	(Sold) fl 20 Wed Achtienhoven
1802/06/28	AMSCH	0119	*J. M. Molenaar* | Een Boere Binnenhuis, met een aantal Beelden, zig vermaakende met muziek, verders eenig Huisraad; uitvoerig gepenceeld | *Mat:* op paneel *Size:* hoog 21, breed 18 duim	Anna Elink	(Sold) fl 20:10 van Iperen
1802/06/28	AMSCH	0121	*J. M. Molenaar* | Een Dame met een Glas Wyn, waarby een Heer met een Fiool; uitvoerig op Panneel | *Mat:* op paneel *Size:* hoog 11, breed 9 duim	Anna Elink	(Sold) fl 2:5 L Pakker
1802/06/28	AMSCH	0122	*J. M. Molenaar* | Voor een Boeren Herreberg ziet men een menigte Huislieden, zich met danssen als anderzints vermakende; in 't verschiet eenige Kwakzalvers, zynde een Boeren Kermis; zeer fiks en dun gepenceeld, door Denzelven [J. M. Molenaar], op Panneel | *Mat:* op paneel *Size:* hoog 25, breed 22 duim	Anna Elink	(Sold) fl 9:5 de Meyer
1802/07/20	MGSAN	0009	*J. M. Molenaar* | Een Binnenvertrekje met drinkende en rookende Boeren, zeer fraai geschilderd op Paneel | *Mat:* op paneel *Size:* hoog duim 11, breed duim 8 ½		(Unknown)
1802/07/21	HGKAN	0007	*J. M. Molenaar* | Een Conversatie		(Unknown)
1802/07/27	AKHRK	0017	*J. M. Molenaar* | Men ziet eene menigte van speelende, drinkende, en dansende Figuuren op het geluid van den Doedelzak, zich vermaaken; op de voorgrond staat een Kruik op een Bank, waar voor een groote Hond meesterlijk geschilderd | *Mat:* op paneel *Size:* hoog 15 ½, breed 20 ½ duim	Maria Stategaart	(Sold) fl 17 Deesing
1802/07/27	AKHRK	0018	*J. M. Molenaar* | Een gezelschap van jonge lieden. Een Meisje speelt op een Fluit, naast haar staat een zeer galant zingend Boertje met een Roemer Wijn in de hand; twee andere schijnen bezig met een Liefdensverklaaring, terwijl de laatste elkander liefkoozen, in het verschiet een Man, zich bij een Vuur warmende. Dit is een zeer fraai welgeteekend en uitvoerig geschilderd stukje | *Mat:* op paneel *Size:* hoog 10 ½, breed 13 ½ duim	Maria Stategaart	(Sold) fl 12 Gruyter
1802/08/24	LNDLS	0064	*Molenaar* | Een Binnen-huis met vrolijke Boeren en Boerinnen die danssen | *Mat:* op paneel *Size:* hoog 16, breed 19 duimen	Leonardus Bouman [or others]	(Unknown) fl 3
1802/09/06	AMSCH	0079	*J. Molenaar* | Langs een weg met Geboomte, by een boerewoning, ziet men eenig Lieden; fiks geschilderd	Wed Grave [or others]	(Sold) fl 9:10 M van Iperen
1802/09/06	AMSCH	0256	*Molenaar* | Een Boerestuk	J	(Sold) fl 4:15 van Iperen
1802/09/06	AMSCH	0257	*Molenaar* | Een dito dito [Boerestuk], door dito [Molenaar]	J	(Sold) fl 0:10 L Pakker

1802/09/21	UTHDG	0062	*J.M. Molenaar* | In een vrolijk Boeren gezelschap zit vooräan een Heer galantizeerende met een aardig Boerinnetje, zij houd fles en glas in de handen enz. Aangenaam geschildert | *Mat:* op paneel *Size:* hoog 15 ½, breed 13 ½ duimen		(Sold) fl 15:15 Gevaerts
1802/11/01	DOBRA	0052	*J.M. Molenaar* | Een vrolyk Gezelschap, zich vermaakende met het speelen van Handtje-Plak [sic] [beiden ryk met beelden gestoffeerd] | companion to lot 53 *Mat:* op paneel *Size:* breed 2 v. 8 d. hoog 2 v. 2 d. *Notes:* The bracketed information in the title appears in lot 53 and refers to lots 52 and 53.	Paulus van der Spyk [or others]	(Bought In) fl 30 for lots 52 & 53
1802/11/01	DOBRA	0053	*J.M. Molenaar* | Een dito [vrolyk Gezelschap], verbeeldende een ander Bruiloftspelletje, zynde een weerga, door denzelven [J.M. Molenaar]; beiden ryk met beelden gestoffeerd | companion to lot 52	Paulus van der Spyk [or others]	(Bought In) fl 30 for lots 52 & 53
1802/12/13	AMSCH	0111	*J. Molenaar* | Een aangenaam Dorpgezicht, gestoffeerd met Boere Woningen, hoog Geboomte en een menigte Beeldjes; kragtig | *Fmt:* ovaal *Size:* hoog 16, breed 21 duim	Yver	(Sold) fl 5:10 van Iperen
1802/12/13	AMSCH	0112	*J. M. Molenaar* | In een Boere Binnehuis, ziet men een vrolyke drie Koningen Maaltyd, geestig geordoneerd en Meesteragtig geschilderd | *Mat:* op paneel *Size:* hoog 19 ½, breed 25 duim	Pruyssenaar [for] A	(Sold) fl 0:12 L Pakker
1802/12/13	AMSCH	0113	*J. Molenaar* | Een Boere Binnenhuis | *Mat:* op paneel *Size:* hoog 9, breed 8 duim	Pruyssenaar [for] A	(Sold) fl 0:10 L Pakker
1802/12/13	AMSCH	0113a	*J. Molenaar* | Een Boeren Gezelschap | *Mat:* op paneel *Size:* hoog 16, breed 13 duim	Pruyssenaar [for] A	(Sold) fl 0:6 L Pakker
1803/04/18	HGBAK	0030	*Molenaar* | Een dito [Boerenvreugd] vol gewoel door Molenaar [Schilderyen in Olyverf] | *Mat:* in olyverf op doek *Size:* hoog 31, breed 34 duim *Notes:* The bracketed information in the title about the medium appears above lot 1 and refers to lots 1 to 48.	Johan Pieter Reigersman [or others]	(Unknown)
1803/04/20	AMSCH	0043	*Molenaer. (J.)* | Twee stuks Boere Binnenhuizen, waarin het ongelyke Huwlyk verbeeld word, door een oude Vrouw welke een Jong Man, en een ond [sic] Man welke een Jong Meisje door hun Geld begeerden, uitvoerig gepenceeld [Le mariage mal assorti representé dans ces deux pieces, dans la premiere est une vielle [sic] qui prend un jeune-homme pour epoux ; la seconde designe un viellard [sic] qui obtient une jeune femme avare. Ces sujets sont mieux choisis qu'executés.] | *Mat:* op paneel *Size:* ieder hoog 9, breed 7 duim	Maria Magdalena van Sluypwyk, gravinne van Moens	(Sold) fl 3:5 L Pakker
1803/04/20	AMSCH	0044	*Molenaar. (J. M.)* | Een Vrorwtje [sic] speelende op de Phiool, waarnevens een Boer zit te zingen; delicaat gepenceeld [Une femme racclant du violon pour accompagner un braillard rustique : cette representation est très bien rendue.] | *Mat:* op paneel *Size:* hoog 10, breed 8 duim	Maria Magdalena van Sluypwyk, gravinne van Moens	(Sold) fl 19:10 Petit
1803/04/20	AMSCH	0045	*Molenaar. (J. M.)* | Een Boer aan een Tafel zittende zyn pyp te rooken, nevens hem een Bierkan en Glas; alles behandeld als de voorgaande [Un villageois occupé à fumer & disposé pour boire, rendu avec verité comme le précedent.] | *Mat:* op paneel *Size:* hoog 6 ½, breed 5 ½ duim	Maria Magdalena van Sluypwyk, gravinne van Moens	(Sold) fl 2:5 Lesscher
1803/06/20	AMSCH	0053	*J. Molenaar* | Een Boere Binnenhuis met een ménigte van Beelden, geestig geordeneerd en geschilderd, door J. Molenaar, op Paneel | *Mat:* op paneel *Size:* hoog 16, breed 16 duim	Roos [for] E	(Sold) fl 3 Plux
1803/08/01	AMSCH	0022	*Molenaar. (J.)* | Een Herderin met eenige Bloemen, beneevens een speelende Herder en ander Bywerk, fix gepenceeld | *Mat:* op paneel *Size:* hoog 15, breed 13 duim	J	(Sold) fl 1:10 Hulswit
1803/08/01	AMSCH	0023	*Molenaar. (J.)* | Een Boere Binnenhuis, verbeeldende een Bruiloft, vol gewoel en krachtig geschilderd | *Mat:* op paneel *Size:* hoog 24, breed 21 duim	Thoen	(Sold) fl 0:10 Levy Pakker
1803/08/17	AMSCH	0056	*Molenaar. (J. M.)* | Een Boere Bruiloft, vol gewoel, op de Voorgrond de Bruidegom, welke de Bruid schynt te animeeren tot een dansje, een Vrouw op de Phiool speelende, word geacompagneerd van drie Muzikanten, op een Stellagie zittende; dit stuk is van een kragtige schildering | companion to lot 57 *Mat:* op paneel *Size:* hoog 27, breed 22 duim	Anna Catharina Putman	(Sold) fl 76 for lots 56 & 57. L Pakker
1803/08/17	AMSCH	0057	*Molenaar. (J. M.)* | De weerga van de voorgaande is een Boerendorp, Een vrolyke party Huislieden zyn bezig zich met Danssen en Galantiseeren te vermaken, ter zyde de Speelman, alles vol gewoel en van gelijke behandeling | companion to lot 56 *Size:* hoog 27, breed 22 duim	Anna Catharina Putman	(Sold) fl 76 for lots 56 & 57. L Pakker
1803/08/17	AMSCH	0058	*Molenaar. (J. M.)* | In een Binnevertrek zyn eenige Jonge Lieden bezig te speelen, het bekende spel: Stommetje, Stommetje onder de Deken, geestig verbeeld | *Mat:* op paneel *Size:* hoog 14 ½ breed 11 duim	Anna Catharina Putman	(Sold) fl 17:10 Pruijssenaar
1803/08/17	AMSCH	0059	*Molenaar. (J. M.)* | Twee stuks, het eene verbeeld een vrolyk, en het andere een vegtend Gezelschap, beide als de voorgaande uitgevoerd | *Mat:* op paneel *Size:* ieder hoog 9, breed 9 duim	Anna Catharina Putman	(Sold) fl 15 Teengs
1803/08/17	AMSCH	0060	*Molenaar. (J. M.)* | Een vrolyk Boere Gezelschap, alwaar om het Ey gedanst word, mede als de voorgaande | *Mat:* op paneel *Size:* hoog 20, breed 25 duim	Anna Catharina Putman	(Sold) fl 9:5 LaBouchere
1803/08/17	AMSCH	0061	*Molenaar. (J. M.)* | Een Chirurgyns Winkel, alwaar een Boer zyn Been verbonden word, verders een menigte Omstanders, behandeld als vooren | *Mat:* op paneel *Size:* hoog 26, breed 20 duim	Anna Catharina Putman	(Sold) fl 6:5 LaBouchere

1803/08/24	HGKAN	0028	*J. Molenaar* | Een Biddent Huisgezin | *Mat:* op paneel *Size:* hoog 10, breet 14 duim	[Teissier] [or others]	(Sold) fl 2:5 Huybregt
1803/08/24	HGKAN	0029	*J. Molenaar* | Een met vrolyke Boertjes | *Mat:* op paneel	[Teissier] [or others]	(Sold) fl 0:10 Ler...
1803/12/15	MGLAC	0035	*J. M. Molenaar* | Een schoon Schildery, zynde een Boere Kermis, vol met vrolyke Figuuren en Bywerk | *Mat:* op paneel *Size:* hoog duim 18, breed duim 27	Mr L H de Haze Bomme	(Unknown)
1804/02/27	AMSCH	0078	*Molenaar. (J. M.)* | In een Binnevertrek; ziet men eenige Lieden het Spel Speelen, Stommetje Stommetje onder de Deeken; zeer geestig verbeeld | *Mat:* op paneel *Size:* hoog 14, breed 11 duim	B	(Sold) fl 12 Vinkeles
1804/05/07	AMSCH	0113	*Molenaar* | In een Boere Binnenhuis ziet men een Boere Bruiloft; ryk gestoffeerd met een ménigte van dansende, etende, drinkende en speeiende [sic] Lieden, fiks en meesterlyk gepenceeld | *Mat:* op paneel *Size:* hoog 15, breed 18 duim	Vinkeles	(Sold) fl 20 Coclers
1804/05/07	AMSCH	0114	*Molenaar* | In een Boere Binnehuis ziet men eenige Lieden 't Spel speelen van Handjeklap [sic]; natuurlyk en fiks behandeld | *Mat:* op paneel *Size:* hoog 16, breed 22 duim	Roos [for] A	(Sold) fl 49 Coclers
1804/05/07	AMSCH	0115	*Molenaar* | In een Boere Binnenhuis ziet men eenige vrolyke Boeren en Boerinnen en by 't vuur eenige drinkende en rookende, ter zyde door een deur waarin een Boer koomt, een Boomryk Landschap, verders eenig Huisraad, uitvoerig en fraai gepenceeld | *Mat:* op paneel *Size:* hoog 22, breed 28 duim	Vinkeles [for] H[affner]	(Bought In) fl 9
1804/07/25	DLGRO	0059	*J. Molenaer* | Een Boere Bruiloft of een danssende Boer en Boerin, en verder vrolyk gezelschap | *Mat:* op paneel *Size:* hoog 15, breed 11 ½ duim	Mr Franc van der Burch Wz.	(Unknown)
1804/07/25	DLGRO	0060	*J. Molenaer* | Een vrolyk gezelschap of eenige Boeren en Boerinnen, die om een Tafel zitten en staan te stoeijen, door denzelfde [J. Molenaer] op Paneel | *Mat:* op paneel *Size:* hoog 15, breed 11 ½ duim	Mr Franc van der Burch Wz.	(Unknown)
1804/07/25	DLGRO	0071	*J. Molenaer* | Een Boeren gezelschap van vyf Persoonen onder een glaasje Bier zittende | *Mat:* op paneel *Size:* hoog 12, breed 9 duim	Mr Franc van der Burch Wz.	(Unknown)
1804/08/02	BDAN	0014	*J. Molenaer* | Een aangenaam Binnen-huis vol gewoel | *Mat:* op paneel *Size:* b. 30 d. h. 24 d.	J G Calckberner	(Unknown)
1804/08/02	BDAN	0035	*Moolenaer* | Een Binnen-huis | *Mat:* op paneel *Size:* breed 23 en een half d. h. 17 d.	J G Calckberner	(Unknown)
1804/08/08	AMSCH	0122	*J.M. Molenaar* | Aan een Tafel met Spyzen zit een Huisgezin van onderscheiden jaaren aandachtig te bidden; zynde dit van de fraaiste behandeling van J. M. Molenaar | *Mat:* op paneel *Size:* hoog 13 ½, br. 16 ½ duim	Roos a	(Bought In) fl 14 ½
1804/08/08	AMSCH	0123	*J.M. Molenaar* | In een Chirurgyns Winkel ziet men een Boer, welke door een Heelmeester een Tand getrokken wordt, op de grond staat een Mand met Eijeren en zynen Hoed, en op de Tafel en op de Planken eenig Chirurgyns Gereedschappen; fraai van hartstochten en kloek geschilderd | *Mat:* op doek *Size:* hoog 15, breed 13 duim	Vink[eles] [for] W	(Sold) fl 6:15 Graffelman
1804/08/08	AMSCH	0126	*J. Moolenaar* | In een Binnenvertrek ziet men een ménigte Militairen, welke bézig zyn Kleinodiën te rooven van een deftig Huisgezin; uitvoerig op Paneel | *Mat:* op paneel *Size:* hoog 20, breed 31 duim	Roos [for] H	(Sold) fl 23 Toselli
1804/10/16	DLOND	0148	*J. Molenaer* | Twee stukken, op ieder ene Heidin, bezig om ene Boerin waartezeggen. Deux pièces, chacune repr. une Paysane attentive aux divinations d'une Bohémienne | *Mat:* op paneel *Size:* hoog 13, breed 10		(Unknown)
1804/10/16	DLOND	0149	*J. Molenaer* | Een Huisgezin, biddende voor den Maaltyd. Une Famille faisant la prière avant le repas | *Mat:* op paneel *Size:* hoog 16, breed 20		(Unknown)
1804/10/16	DLOND	0150	*J. Molenaer* | Twee stukjens. Een zingende Man en Vrouw. Deux pièces. Homme & Femme qui chantent | *Mat:* op paneel *Size:* hoog 5, breed 5		(Unknown)
1804/10/16	DLOND	0151	*J. M. Molenaer* | Een Vrouwtjen, dat Koeken bakt voor enige Boeren. Une Femme, au milieu de quelques Paysans faisant des Omelettes | *Mat:* op paneel *Size:* hoog 11, breed 8		(Unknown)
1804/10/29	HRBAU	0059	*Molenaar, (J. M.)* | Dit Schildery vertoont een Boerenhuishouding, waar Vader, Moeder, en verscheiden Kinderen, by de tafel gezeten, zeer aandagtig het gebed verrigten; zynde zeer fraai geordineerd, de expressiën wel uitgedrukt, en zeer uitvoerig behandeld | *Mat:* op doek *Size:* hoog 31, breed 28 duim	Simon Styl	(Unknown)
1804/10/29	HRBAU	0060	*Molenaar, (J. M.)* | In een Binnenhuis ziet men twee Boeren en Boerinnetjes naar het geluid der viool dansen, terwyl andere zich met drinken en liefkoozen vermaaken: daar een Boertje, van buiten inkomende, dit alles komt beschouwen; voorts is de Schuur eigenaartig gestoffeerd, en alles zeer uitvoerig geschilderd | *Mat:* op paneel *Size:* hoog 18 ½, breed 24 ½ duim	Simon Styl	(Unknown)
1804/10/29	HRBAU	0062	*Molenaar, (J.)* | Twee Stuks vrolyke Boerengezelschappen, waar men zich op verschillende wyzen vermaakt, welke zeer uitvoerig behandeld zyn | *Mat:* op doek *Size:* hoog 16, breed 20 duim	Simon Styl	(Unknown)
1805/07/03	AMSCH	0119	*Molenaar* | Eenige vrolyke Boeren en Boerinnen, in een Binnenhuis, schynende zich met Kaartspeelen te vermaaken; fiks en meesterlyk op Doek | *Mat:* op doek *Size:* hoog 31, breed 35 duim	S	(Sold) fl 16:10 van Giesen

1805/07/10	AMSCH	0099	*Molenaar* | Twee stuks een vrolyke Boer en Boerin, de eene met een Rommelpot en de andere met een Kan; beide allernatuurlykst en breed geschilderd | *Mat:* op paneel *Size:* hoog 20, breed 15 duim	V[inkeles] [for] N	(Sold) fl 16 Sukerbekker
1805/07/10	AMSCH	0101	*J. Molenaar* | Een Boere Binnenhuis met galantiseerende en speelende Boeren en Boerinnen, gezeeten aan een tafel; uitvoerig op Paneel | *Mat:* op paneel *Size:* hoog 10, breed 8 ½ duim	V[inkeles] [for] M	(Sold) fl 25 Lafontaine
1805/07/10	AMSCH	0102	*J. Molenaar* | Twee stuks Dorpgezichten, met Rivieren, Geboomte, stoffagie van Beeldjes, Zylschuit enz.; zonachtig en piquant van licht | *Mat:* op paneel *Size:* hoog 13, breed 13 duim	V[inkeles] [for] P	(Sold) fl 14 Lafontaine
1805/07/10	AMSCH	0103	*J. Molenaar* | Twee stuks Binnenhuizen met Gezelschappen, schynen zich met Kaartspeelen, Rooken en Drinken te vermaken, beide meesterlyk en fraai gepenceeldschilderd | *Size:* hoog 20, breed 15 duim	V[inkeles] [for] J	(Sold) fl 21 Sukerbekker
1805/07/10	AMSCH	0199	*Molenaar* | Een Gezelschap	R[oos]	(Sold) fl 1 Lafontaine
1805/07/10	AMSCH	0244	*J. M. Molenaar* | In een Boere Woning ziet men verscheide vrolyke Huislieden; zig met drinken en rooken vermaken | *Mat:* op paneel	Wed Grave	(Sold) fl 5 van Iperen
1806/05/05	AMSCH	0097	*Molenaar* | Een Boeren Binnenhuis met rokende en drinkende Boeren, krachtig door Molenaar	V[inkeles]	(Sold) fl 3 Grauu
1806/06/07	RMHSN	0003	*J: M: Molenaar* | Een Vrolyk Boeren Gezelschap, in een Binnenhuis met ryk Binnewerk | *Mat:* op paneel	A E K L	(Unknown)
1806/06/07	RMHSN	0037	*J. Molenaar* | Twee Stuks Vrolyke Boere Gezelschappen | *Mat:* op paneel	A E K L	(Unknown)
1806/06/07	RMHSN	0038	*J. Molenaar* | Een met Zingende en Musicerende Boeren | *Mat:* op paneel	A E K L	(Unknown)
1806/08/13	AMSCH	0117	*Molenaar. (J. M.)* | Twee stuks, verbeeldende den eene galantiseerde Boeren en Boerinnen in een Binnenhuis by een Tafel, gestoffeerd met verscheide stoffagie; den andere vertoont een biddend Huisgezin by een gedekte Tafel met spys; beide geestig behandeld | *Mat:* op paneel *Size:* Ieder hoog 18, breed 13 duim	van der Voort	(Sold) fl 36 T Spaan
1806/08/13	AMSCH	0118	*Molenaar. (J. M.)* | Een biddend Huisgezin van Man, Vrouw en Kinderen, by een gedekte Tafel met Eeten; natuurlyk behandeld | *Mat:* op paneel *Size:* hoog 15, breed 14 duim	Roos	(Sold) fl 3:10 L Pakker
1806/08/13	AMSCH	0119	*Molenaar. (J. M.)* | Twee stuks, een drinkend Boertje en een zingend Boerinnetje; uitvoerig gepenceeld | *Mat:* op paneel *Size:* Ieder hoog 5, breed 4 duim	Roos	(Sold) fl 6 Rynbergh
1806/08/13	AMSCH	0120	*Molenaar. (J. M.)* | Twee stuks Binnehuizen met vrolyke Boeren en Boerinne en verder bywerk, fiks gepenceeld | *Mat:* op paneel *Size:* Ieder hoog 9, breed 8 duim	Daniel Mansveld	(Sold) fl 2:5 Wed Achtienhoven
1806/08/20	HGBSM	0015	*J. M. Molenaar* | Een binnen vertrek met een Vrolijk Boeren Gezelschap alles zeer geestig afgebeeld; verders op de voorgrond een Hond, en ander bijwerk | *Mat:* op paneel *Size:* hoog 15 ½, breed 17 duim	Macalester Loup [or others]	(Sold) fl 28 Λ Taixera
1806/08/20	HGBSM	0208	*J. Molenaar* | Een goede Geluksegster in een duin gezicht | *Mat:* op paneel *Size:* hoog 23, breed 27 ½ duim	Macalester Loup [or others]	(Sold) fl 6:15 Gram
1806/10/16	UTWLD	0008	*Molenaar* | Een Binnenhuis met een Boeren Chirurgyn die een Boer verbind	Mr P de Malapert [or] W Beeldsnyder	(Unknown)
1807/06/10	HGBSM	0191	*J.M. Molenaar* | Een vrolijk Gezelschap | *Mat:* op paneel *Size:* hoog 18, breed 26 ½ duim	Abraham Delfos [or others]	(Sold) fl 2:14 Dupré
1807/08/26	AMSCH	0145	*J. Moolenaar* | Twee stuks Binnenhuizen met Boerinnen die zig met roken en drinken vermaken | *Mat:* op paneel *Size:* hoog 6 ½, breed 5 ½ duim	de Vries	(Sold) fl 1 L Pakker
1807/08/26	AMSCH	0146	*J. Moolenaar* | Twee stuks Binnenhuizen, met vrolyke Landlieden, Musiceerende, en die zig met drinken vermaken | *Mat:* op paneel	Roos [for] A	(Sold) fl 2 Levy Pakker
1807/08/26	AMSCH	0147	*J. Moolenaar* | In een Binnenhuis, zitten Boeren en Boerinne met de Kaart te speelen, vergezelt van andere Huislieden | *Mat:* op paneel	Yver [for] S	(Sold) fl 2:5 Peeters
1807/08/26	AMSCH	0148	*J. Moolenaar* | Een dito [Binnenhuis] met Boeren in een Herberg met de Kaart speelende | *Mat:* op paneel	Yver [for] S	(Sold) fl 2 G Dykhost
1808/03/03	HAVIN	0023	*Molenaar* | Een Binnehuis met een vrolijk Gezelschap	Jacobus Spillebout	(Unknown) fl 2:10
1808/04/26	GDAN	0099	*Molenaar (J.M.)* | Een extra schoon geschilderd Binnenhuis, met een aantal vrolijke Boeren en Boerinnen | *Size:* hoog 16, breed 13 duim	G H Fortuyn	(Unknown)
1808/04/26	GDAN	0100	*Molenaar (J.M.)* | Een Binnenhuis, waar in zich eenige Boeren aan tafel zich vermaken met Speelen, Zingen en Drinken, in het verschiet eenige Persoonen die na 't Gezang en de verdere verrigtingen staan te luisteren, heel wel geschildert | *Size:* hoog 9 ½, breed 12 ½ duim	G H Fortuyn	(Unknown)
1808/05/17	LNAN	0008	*J.M. Molenaar* | Een ruim binnen vertrek, vol gewoel van kinderen, die bij hun meester ter school zijn, en allerhande bezigheden verrigten, zoo leerende, speelende, vegtende enz.; kunstig van schildering en helder van coloriet | *Mat:* op doek *Size:* hoog 31, breed 47 duim		(Sold) fl 36 Nieuwenhuis
1808/05/17	LNAN	0011	*J. Molenaar* | Een muziecerend gezelschap, van eenige personen bij een tafel zittende, uitvoerig behandeld | *Mat:* op paneel *Size:* hoog 12, breed 17 duim		(Sold) fl 5:5 Nieuwenhuis
1808/05/17	LNAN	0031	*J.M. Molenaar* | Een op de kaart speelend gezelschap		(Sold) fl 1:10 Nieuwenhuis

1808/06/06	RMRIJ	0081	*Molenaar. (Jan Miense) 1650* | Een Boerengezelschap vol gewoel, benevens een Man, die door zijne Vrouw met de pantoffel geslagen wordt. Zeer uitvoerig en aangenaam behandeld [L'Intérieur d'un Cabaret, où plusieurs personnes sont en ribote. Une femme en fureur frappe son Mari dans la figure avec sa pantouffle, et menace par son regard une femme qui se trouve auprés de lui etc. Composition gaie, de beaucoup d'expression, et d'un beau faire] | *Annots:* Verk J. Maul, Leiden, 28 Sept, 1782 (f 76.-) (RMA I) *Mat:* op paneel *Size:* Hoog 17 ½ en breed 13 ½ duim *Inscr:* Jan Miense Molenaar. 1650 (signed and dated?) *Notes:* It is unclear whether the name and date are inscribed on the painting.	Gerrit van der Pot, Heer van Groeneveld	(Sold) fl 100 Allard
1808/06/13	AMSCH	0105	*Molenaar (J.M.)* | In een Binnenvertrek ziet men eenige vrolijke Boeren, op den voorgrond eene Vrouw, welke een Kind de Borst geeft, ter zijde een Jongen, welke met een Hond speelt. Alles geestig en vol uitdrukking | *Mat:* op doek *Size:* hoog 42, breed 56 duim	E M Engelberts	(Sold) fl 58 Allard
1808/06/13	AMSCH	0106	*Molenaar (J.M.)* | Een vrolijk Gezelschap, waarin eenige Boeren danssen. Hetzelve is niet minder als de voorgaande van hartstochten en zacht in uitvoering | *Mat:* op paneel *Size:* hoog 30, breed 33 duim	E M Engelberts	(Sold) fl 203 van Drielst
1808/06/13	AMSCH	0107	*Molenaar (J.)* | In een Boerendorp ziet men een Kwakzalver, omgeven van eene menigte Menschen, verder een Heer en eene Dame, welken zich daarmede vermaken. Zijnde van de beste schildering | *Mat:* op doek *Size:* hoog 33, breed 48 duim	E M Engelberts	(Sold) fl 145 W Reijers pour Allard
1808/06/13	AMSCH	0206	*J. Molenaar* | Een zingend Boerengezelschap, alwaar een Jongen op een Varken zit; vol geest	E M Engelberts	(Sold) fl 30 Simons
1808/07/19	AMROU	0003	*J. Molenaar* | 1 Boeren Binnenvertrek, waar een Jonge met een Kat speelt, en een Vrouw met een Hond op de schoot zit, en de Man en Jonge zig over vermaaken		(Unknown)
1808/07/19	AMROU	0020	*Molenaar* | 1 Boere Kermisvreugd, vol gewoel		(Unknown)
1808/09/13	HABRU	0063	*J. Molenaar* | Een Binnehuis, de Koekebakster		(Unknown) fl 3:5
1808/10/28	AMVRS	0033	*Molenaar, (J.)* | Een Landschap, waarin men voor een Boerewoning eenige Huislieden met elkander in gesprek ziet | *Mat:* op paneel *Size:* hoog 14, breed 13 duim *Notes:* The artist was presumably Klaes Molenaer and not Jan Miense Molenaer.	Marten Udink	(Sold) fl 20 Vermeulen
1808/10/28	AMVRS	0034	*Molenaar, (J.)* | In een Binnenvertrek zitten vier Boeren en twee Boerinnen bij een Tafel zig met zingen, speelen en drinken vermakende, verder eenig Boeren Huisraad. Kloek geschilderd | *Mat:* op paneel *Size:* hoog 14, breed 16 duim	Marten Udink	(Sold) fl 9:10 Rijdon
1808/11/28	AMSCH	0042	*J. Molenaar* | In een Binnehuis zit een Gezelschap van vrolijke Lieden aan een Tafel, zig met musiceeren, eeten en drinken vermaakende, fiks gepenceeld | *Mat:* op paneel *Size:* hoog 17, breed 26 duim	S	(Sold) fl 5 Coclers
1808/11/28	AMSCH	0042a	*J.Miense Molenaar* | Een Binnehuis, met vrolijke Huislieden, welke zig met dansen, speelen, rooken en drinken vermaaken, bevallig en natuurlijk voorgesteld | *Mat:* op paneel *Size:* hoog 19, breed 15 duim	S	(Bought In) fl 26:10
1809/04/17	AMSCH	0060	*J.M. Molenaar* | Een Binnenhuis, in het zelve zitten verscheide Boeren en Boerinnen bij een Tafel, zig met rooken en drinken vermakende, op de voorgrond eenige die Handje Plak speelen; geestig behandeld | *Mat:* op paneel *Size:* hoog 15, breed 21 duim	T	(Sold or Bought In) fl 10
1809/04/17	AMSCH	0061	*J.M. Molenaar* | Een Binnenhuis met drie vrolijke Boeren; geestig en fiks | *Mat:* op paneel *Size:* hoog 10, breed 8 duim	A	(Sold) fl 5:15
1809/04/17	AMSCH	0165	*Molenaar* | In een Smederij ziet men eenige Werkende Lieden, fiks | *Mat:* op paneel	R	(Sold) fl 1
1809/04/22	AMYVR	0081	*J.M. Molenaar* | In een Boeren-Binnenvertrek ziet men eene menigte galantizeerende, speelende en rokende Landlieden, verder eenig bijwerk | *Mat:* op doek *Size:* hoog 34, breed 44 duim	de Bruin	(Bought In) fl 14
1809/04/22	AMYVR	0082	*J.M. Molenaar* | Een Biddend Gezelschap, aan een met Spijzen gevulde Tafel | *Mat:* op paneel *Size:* hoog 16, breed 14 duim	de Bruin	(Sold) fl 1:10 du Pree
1809/04/22	AMYVR	0083	*J.M. Molenaar* | Twee vrolijke Gezelschappen | *Mat:* op paneel *Size:* hoog 14, breed 11 duim	de Bruin	(Sold) fl 5:5 du Pree
1809/04/22	AMYVR	0084	*J.M. Molenaar* | Een liefkoozend Paar in een Binnenvertrek; geestig | *Mat:* op paneel *Size:* hoog 12, breed 9 duim	de Bruin	(Sold) fl 1:15 du Pree
1809/04/22	AMYVR	0156	*Molenaar* | Twee als vooren [stuks], divers	Juff^{r} Julikker	(Sold) fl 1 v d Schley
1809/05/26	HADAA	0040	*Jan Molenaar* | Een dito [Binnenvertrek], waarin een bedroefde Vrouw bij een doodkist weent, terwijl een Boer in rouwgewaad tegen de doodkist leunende na een andere Vrouw schijnt te vreijen, geestig geördonneerd en meesterachtig geschilderd	Mejuffrouw de Wed David Heemskerk [or others]	(Unknown)
1809/07/19	AMSCH	0036	*Molenaar (J.M.)* | Een Binnenvertrek, in het midden zitten twee Mannen en eene Vrouw aan een Tafel op de Kaart te spelen, waar bij eenige staande Lieden, het zelve met aandacht beschouwende, ter zijde eene Dienstmaagd, die de Deur inkomt, houdende een Schotel met gebak in de hand, agterwaards een haardsteede. Uitvoerig en fraai van schildering | *Mat:* op paneel *Size:* hoog 34, breed 44 duim	[Bicker]	(Sold) fl 30 Hendriks
1809/07/19	AMSCH	0037	*Molenaar (J.M.)* | In eene Schilderkamer, ziet men den Konstenaar, schijnende in gesprek met eene bevallige Vrouw; een Leerling is bezig	[Wijkersloot?]	(Sold) fl 13 T Spaan

			het Palet klaar te maken, terwijl een zittend oud Man op de Lier speelt en een Dwerg een Hond laat Danzen; op een Schilder-Ezel staat eene Schildering, deze Kamer aanduidende, voorts toepasselijk bijwerk. Geestig geordonneerd, meesterlijk en breed geschilderd | *Mat:* op doek *Size:* hoog 39, breed 58 duim *Loc:* Berlin, Deutschland. Gemäldegalerie. (873)		
1809/07/19	AMSCH	0038	*Molenaar (J.M.)* | In een Binnehuis, zit een bejaard Man, speelende met een Hond; twee Vrouwen en twee Jongens, schijnen zich hier mede te verlustigen, terwijl een Boer daarbij zijn Pijp zit te rooken, een oud Man, die de Deur inkomt, en eenig Huisraad stoffeeren verder dit Schilderij, het welk van de uitvoerige en beste penceelsbehandeling is van dezen Meester | *Mat:* op doek *Size:* hoog 37, breed 32 duim	[Wijkersloot?]	(Sold) fl 360 Jan Spaan
1809/07/19	AMSCH	0039	*Molenaar (J.M.)* | In een Boere Binnevertrek of Schuur, zit een Gezelschap van agt drinkende, rokende en spelende Boeren, eenige zitten te spelen, anderen zich aan de Haard te warmen, een derde liefkoost eene Boerin, ter linker en regter zijde heeft men eene Steenen Bank en Tafeltje, met Vaat- en Aardewerk. Alles is geestig, en het Vaat- en Aardewerk vooral natuurlijk | *Mat:* op doek *Size:* hoog 34, breed 44 duim	V	(Sold) fl 15 Dupré
1809/07/25	HGBSM	0196	*J. Molenaer* | Een Binnenhuis, waarin eenige Boeren en Boerinne schynende Vis te kopen | *Mat:* op paneel *Size:* hoog 24 en een half, breed 20 duim	D van der Aa [or] E B ten Dall	(Sold) fl 9:5 Schoon
1809/07/25	HGBSM	0260	*J. Molenaer* | Een musiceerend Gezelschap in een Binnenhuis | *Mat:* op paneel *Size:* hoog 18 en een half, breed 14 en een half duim	D van der Aa [or] E B ten Dall	(Sold) fl 5:5 ten Haaf
1810/03/07	UTWLD	0015	*J. Molenaar* | Een ruim Binnenvertrek, en eene menigte zingende en dansende menschen, behoorende onder de schoonste stukken | companion to lot 16 *Size:* hoog 2 voet 2 duim, breed 3 voet	J J Woertman	(Unknown) fl 37
1810/03/07	UTWLD	0016	*J. Molenaar* | Een dito [ruim] dito [Binnenvertrek], zynde het pendant | companion to lot 15 *Size:* hoog 2 voet 2 duim, breed 3 voet	J J Woertman	(Unknown) fl 34:10
1810/03/07	UTWLD	0017	*Molenaar* | Een Binnenhuis, met groente en vrugten op de voorgrond | *Size:* hoog 2 voet 5 duim, breed 3 voet 6 duim	J J Woertman	(Unknown) fl 22:10
1810/03/23	HAVIN	0061a	*J.M. Molenaar* | Een Drie Koningen feest, vrolijk en vol gewoel	Rudolf Hendrik de Wetstein [or others]	(Unknown)
1810/03/27	RMCNL	0056	*J. M. Molenaar* | Een Gezelschap van vrolijke Boeren, zeer snaaks geschilderd		(Unknown)
1810/03/27	RMCNL	0059	*J. Molenaar* | Twee Stuks Binnenhuisjes, waarin men op het eene, eene oude Vrouw hare Dochter ziet uithuwelijken, op het andere eenen Grijsaard, bezig geld te geven tot hetzelfde einde, fraai gepenceeld		(Unknown)
1810/03/27	RMCNL	0064	*J. Molenaar* | In een Binnenhuis ziet men eene meenigte Boeren en Boerinnen, op de aardigste wijze zich vermaken; alles is vrolijk en vol gewoel		(Unknown)
1810/05/22	AMSCH	0065	*Molenaar (J. Miense)* | Voor een Buitenhuis ziet men vrolijke Boeren en Boerinnen, die Handje-Plak speelen, terwijl andere het met vermaak aanzien, voorts Jongens met Honden en speelende Kinderen; van de beste schildering | *Mat:* op paneel *Size:* hoog 24, breed 32 duim	S	(Bought In) fl 32
1810/05/22	AMSCH	0066	*Molenaar (J. Miense)* | Twee stuks, een rookende Boer en eene zingende Boerin; fiks geschilderd | *Mat:* op paneel *Size:* Jeder hoog 5, breed 4 duim	R	(Sold) fl 4 Contant
1810/06/06	RMMUY	0232	*Molenaar* | Eene Zwangere Vrouw voor de Wichelaars | *Mat:* op paneel *Notes:* According to the MA copy of the catalogue, this lot was sold with lot 231 by an anonymous-modern artist for fl. 2:2.		(Unknown) fl 2
1810/06/20	AMSCH	0052	*J. M. Molenaar* | Een Boeren Binnenhaard: in het midden zitten twee Lieden bij eene Tafel, met de Kaart spelende, eenige zien hetzelve met vermaak aan, terwijl andere zich met rooken en drinken vermaken; verder eenig Huisraad en toepasselijk bijwerk. Uitvoerig en van de beste schildering van J. M. Molenaar | *Mat:* op paneel *Size:* hoog 23, breed 32 duimen	D	(Sold) fl 16:10 Boelhouwer
1810/06/20	AMSCH	0053	*J. M. Molenaar* | In een Binnenhuis, zitten drie Lieden bij eene Tafel hun Pijp te rooken; op den voorgrond een slapende Hond. Fiks gepenceeld | *Mat:* op paneel *Size:* hoog 17, breed 14 duimen	D	(Sold) fl 4 Pantijn
1810/06/20	AMSCH	0054	*J. M. Molenaar* | Een Binnenhuis, waarin drie vrolijke drinkende Boeren. Geestig en fiks | *Mat:* op paneel *Size:* hoog 10, breed 8 duimen	B	(Sold) fl 1:5 T Spaan
1810/06/20	AMSCH	0055	*J. M. Molenaar* | Eene rijke Ordonnantie, voorstellende een Driekoningenfeest. Delikaat behandeld | *Mat:* op doek *Size:* hoog 33, breed 36 duimen	X	(Sold) fl 16 T Spaan
1810/06/20	AMSCH	0056	*J. Molenaar* | Vier Boeren bezig zijnde met vegten, van achter komt een vijfde om hun te scheiden. Behandeld als voren | *Mat:* op paneel *Size:* hoog 12, breed 15 duimen *Notes:* The artist's name was changed by hand from "J. Molenaar" to "J. Steen" in the AA copy of the catalogue.	Q	(Sold) fl 55 Roos
1810/06/20	AMSCH	0057	*J. Molenaar* | Een Boeren Kermis, met eene menigte Huislielieden [sic], Kramers en Kinderen; op den voorgrond een danssende Boer en Boerin. Geestig verbeeld | *Mat:* op paneel *Size:* hoog 26, breed 23 duimen	A	(Sold) fl 4:15 Van Dijl
1810/06/20	AMSCH	0128	*J. Molenaar* | Een rookend Man en Vrouw	X	(Sold) fl 4 Pantijn

1810/08/01	AMSCH	0066	*Molenaar (Jan Miense)* | In een Binnenhuis zit een bejaard Man, spelende met eenen Hond, waar bij twee Vrouwen en twee Jongens benevens eenen Boer, die zijn Pijp rookt; achterwaarts een oud man, die de Deur inkomt; verder eenig Huisraad [Dans l'intérieur d'une habitation rustique est assis un Viellard caressant un Chien ; auprès de celui-ci sont deux Femmes et deux Jeunesgens ; il y a de plus un rustre fumant sa pipe, et un Homme qui entre par la porte, avec quelques assessoires] | *Annots:* très bon. (NGW) *Mat:* op doek *Size:* hoog 37, breed 32 duimen	Mr Pieter de Smeth van Alphen	(Sold) fl 330 R Pot te Rotterdam
1810/08/06	AMSCH	0076	*Molenaar (J.M.)* | Een Binnenhuis, waar in verscheiden vrolijke Boeren en Boerinnen, die handjeplak speelen, en anderen die het zelve met vermaak aanzien; zeer geestig behandeld | *Mat:* op paneel *Size:* hoog 19, breed 14 duimen	C	(Sold) fl 17 Stoopendaal [for] B
1810/08/06	AMSCH	0077	*Molenaar (J.)* | Twee stuks Binnenhuizen met vrolijke liefkozende Boeren en Boerinnen; fiks geschilderd | *Mat:* op paneel *Size:* ieder hoog 12, breed 10 duimen	C	(Sold) fl 10 Stoopendaal [for] B
1810/08/10	RMRIJ	0007	*Jan Miense Molenaar* | Een Binnenhuis, waar in veel Figuren zig vermaken, en handjeplak spelen. Konstig en plaisant geschilderd | *Mat:* op paneel *Size:* hoog 20, breed 25 duim		(Sold) fl 10 [or] 55 de Bruin
1810/10/11	AMSCH	0052	*J. M. Molenaar* | Een stuk met eene menigte Beelden en Bijwerk | *Mat:* op paneel *Size:* hoog 20 ½, breed 16 duimen	C	(Sold) fl 3 Posthumus
1810/10/11	AMSCH	0053	*J. M. Molenaar* | Het Binnengezigt van eene Woning, met Beelden en bijwerk | *Size:* hoog 25, breed 21 duimen	C	(Sold) fl 10:10 Posthumus
1810/10/11	AMSCH	0124	*J. M. Moolenaar* | Een Binnenhuis, met spelende en dansende Huislieden	[Gruyter?]	(Sold) fl 4:5 Mensart
1810/10/11	AMSCH	0234	*J. Molenaar* | Een Binnehuis met twee kaartspeelende Boeren en eene Boerin	A	(Sold) fl 1 L Pakker
1810/11/07	UTWLD	0023	*Molenaar* | Een zingende Vrouw, geaccompagneerd door eene andere op een Guitaar; een zingende Man met een glas in de hand, waar agter een op de viool speelend ventje – een Boer zijn pijp aanstekende, op de Tafel eenige ververschingen, alles zeer wel geordineerd, klaar en kragtig geschilderd door Molenaar op doek, 2 voet 1 en een half duim hoog, 2 voet 4 duim breed, zwarte Lijst | *Mat:* op doek *Size:* 2 voet 1 en een half duim hoog, 2 voet 4 duim breed		(Unknown) fl 18:5
1810/11/07	UTWLD	0025	*Molenaar* | Een vrolijk Boerengezelschap waar een meenigte beeltjes zig aanmuseeren [sic], in het volle licht een danzend Boertje met zijn Meisje – een oud Man een bij hem zittend vrouwtje te streelen, terwijl andere bezig zijn met rooken, zingen en zig te vermaken, 't licht in dit stuk is zeer bepaald genomen, vallende door een openstaande deur en vengster, de teekening, uitdrukking zeer geestig, door Molenaar op doek, 1 voet 9 duim hoog, zwarte Lijst | companion to lot 26 *Mat:* op doek *Size:* 1 voet 9 duim hoog		(Unknown) fl 7
1810/11/07	UTWLD	0026	*Molenaar* | Een pendant – Een Boeren gezelschap met speelen, drinken, etc. zig te vervrolijken, zeer geestig, op paneel, zwarte Lijst | companion to lot 25 *Mat:* op paneel		(Unknown) fl 7
			Molenaer, Jan Miense (manner)		
1801/03/16	AMSCH	0140	*Molenaar* | Een Vrouw zittende te lezen, in de manier van Molenaar	K[ip]	(Sold) fl 1:15 Mensart
1802/08/24	LNDLS	0113	*Molenaar* | Een vrolijk Boeren-gezelschap, als van Molenaar	Leonardus Bouman [or others]	(Unknown) fl 1:18
1802/08/24	LNDLS	0140	*Molenaar* | Een Binnen-vertrek met vrolijke Mannen en Vrouwen, als van Molenaar | *Mat:* op paneel	Leonardus Bouman [or others]	(Unknown) fl 1:5
1803/08/24	HGKAN	0030	*J. Molenaar* | Een vrolyk laggend Boertje op een Fluit Blasende, in de manier van denzelve [J. Molenaar]	[Teissier] [or others]	(Sold) fl 1:2 H
1804/10/29	HRBAU	0152	*Molenaar* | In een Binnenhuisjen zitten drie Boertjens op de Kaart te speelen. Zynde in de manier van Molenaar behandeld | *Mat:* op doek *Size:* hoog 13 ½, breed 11 ½ duim	Simon Styl	(Unknown)
1806/06/07	RMHSN	0067	*Molenaar* | Een Vrolyke Maaltyd, als door Molenaar | *Mat:* op paneel	A E K L	(Unknown)
1806/08/13	AMSCH	0274	*Molenaar* | Een Binnehuis met vegtende Boeren; als Molenaar | *Notes:* This lot was sold with lot 273, which is in the manner of G. ter Borch (II).	Vinkeles [for] D	(Sold) fl 3:5 for lots 273 & 274. Yver [for] G
1806/08/13	AMSCH	0279	*Molenaar* | Twee stuks, een slapende Man by een Tafel, en een Boerin met een Glas in de Hand; als Molenaar	Daniel Mansveld	(Sold) fl 3:15 L Pakker
1809/07/25	HGBSM	0159	*Molenaar* | Een Vertrek met vrolyke Boeren, in de trant van Molenaar | *Mat:* op paneel *Size:* hoog 11, breed 14 en een half duim	D van der Aa	(Sold) fl 1:2 van der Aa
			Molenaer, Klaes		
1801/02/18	AMBOS	0039	*C. Molenaar* | Een Stadgezicht met een Gragt doorsneeden, een Melkboer met zyn Schuitjen aanleggende, waar by eenige Vrouwen welke Melk koopen, zeer natuurlyk en fraay geschilderd	J Schonevelt	(Unknown)
1801/03/16	AMSCH	0047	*K. Molenaar* | Twee stuks Wintergezichten, ryk gestoffeerd met Beeldjes en Arresleede, natuurlyk behandeld	Z	(Sold) fl 14 Rijnders
1801/03/16	AMSCH	0086	*K. Molenaar* | Een Duinachtig Landschap | *Notes:* This lot was sold with lot 85 by Rietschoof.	P[ruyssenaar]	(Sold) fl 12:10 for lots 85 & 86. Gruiter

1801/05/11	AMSCH	0055	*K. Molenaar* | Een Dorp met verscheide boerewoningen en kerktoren, en dor geboomten, gestoffeerd met een wandelaar, alles verbeeld een besneeuwt winter gezicht, zeer natuurlyk gepenceeld | *Mat:* op paneel *Size:* hoog 27, breed 23 duim	E[lias]	(Sold) fl 41 Gruiter
1801/05/11	AMSCH	0056	*K. Molenaar* | Een wintergezigt, langs een weg met verscheiden gebouwen, ziet men een bevroozen rivier, met schaatseryders en wandelende beelden, krachtig en meesterlyk gepenceeld | *Mat:* op paneel *Size:* hoog 11, breed 21 duim	Pruisse [for] M	(Sold) fl 33:10 Rijnders
1801/06/10	AMSCH	0119	*Molenaar. (K.)* | Aan een Stadsmuur, ziet men op het Ys, eenige Schaatseryders en Arresleeden, natuurlyk geschilderd | *Mat:* op paneel *Size:* hoog 10, breed 14 duim	[Doublet]	(Sold) fl 10:10 Pruijssenaar
1801/06/10	AMSCH	0120	*Molenaar. (K.)* | Twee stuks, een Zomer en een Winter, beiden met Beeldjes en Beesten gestoffeerd, fraai en bevallig van penceels behandeling | *Mat:* op paneel *Size:* yder hoog 8, breed 10 duim	[Doublet]	(Sold) fl 23 Spruit van Gend
1801/06/10	AMSCH	0121	*Molenaar. (K.)* | Een Bergachtig en Boomryk Landschap, met een Waterval en stoffage, in de manier van J. Ruisdaal | *Mat:* op doek *Size:* hoog 40, breed 32 duim	[Doublet]	(Sold) fl 49 Teyler van Hall
1801/08/19	AMSCH	0068	*K. Molenaar* | Een Dorpgezicht, met een bevrozen Rivier, ryk met Beelden en Schaatzeryders gestoffeerd, meesterlyk op Doek | *Mat:* op doek *Size:* hoog 30, breed 42 duim	W Wynen	(Sold) fl 10 Coclers
1801/08/19	AMSCH	0070	*K. Molenaar* | Een natuurlyk Land en Watergezigt, met eenige Vissers, in hun Schuiten, op paneel geschilderd | *Mat:* op paneel *Size:* hoog 19, breed 16 duim	van der Schly [for] F	(Sold) fl 5:5 Wolft
1801/12/22	AMOTT	0002	*K. Molenaar* | 1 bevroose en besneeuwt boere Dorpgezigt op het Y, gestoffeerd door een Arresleede, Schaatseryders en verdere Beelden; zeer fraai	Bartholomeus Ruloffs	(Unknown) fl 14:10
1802/05/05	AMSCH	0133	*K. Molenaar* | Een Gezicht op een met Beelden gestoffeerde Bleekery, aan het Duin, zeer natuurlyk | *Mat:* op paneel *Size:* hoog 16, breed 22 duim	C	(Sold) fl 4:5 Th[s] Spaan
1802/05/11	GRGRW	0015	*Molenaar* | Een Zomerstuk [Schilderijen met Olie-Verf; In zwarte Lijsten] | *Mat:* in olyverf *Notes:* The bracketed information in the title appears above lot 1 and refers to lots 1 to 79a.	Arnold Sicco Werumeus	(Unknown)
1802/05/11	GRGRW	0016	*Molenaar* | Een Winterstuk [Schilderijen met Olie-Verf; In zwarte Lijsten] | *Mat:* in olyverf *Notes:* The bracketed information in the title appears above lot 1 and refers to lots 1 to 79a.	Arnold Sicco Werumeus	(Unknown)
1802/05/24	HGBAK	0030	*K. Molenaer* | Een binnen vertrek, alwaar een Kleermaker met een Knegt en Jonge op de Tafel zit te werken, terwyl hy tegen de Vrouw schynt te spreeken, en onder de Tafel een Jonge bezig om uit de Kleermakers-ton eenige lappen te bescharen, zittende in het agter vertrek twee Boertjes by den haard, alles zeer natuurlyk door K. Molenaer, hoog 13 ½ duim, breed 11 duim, op paneel, zwarte lyst en verg binnenrand | *Mat:* op paneel *Size:* hoog 13 ½ duim, breed 11 duim	Mejuffrouw A van der Mieden	(Sold) fl 16:10 Takséra
1802/05/24	HGBAK	0068	*K. Molenaer* | Een Strandgezicht, vol gewoel van Visschers die de Visch aanbrengen, en andere figuren, in 't verschiet het Dorp Scheveningen, heel uitvoerig door K. Molenaer, hoog 18 duim, breed 24 ½, paneel, zwarte lyst | *Mat:* op paneel *Size:* hoog 18 duim, breed 24 ½	Mejuffrouw A van der Mieden	(Sold) fl 22 Ondorp
1802/06/16	AMSCH	0112	*K. Molenaar* | Langs een opgaande Weg, vertoond zig by Geboomten een Boeren-Werf, gestoffeert met verscheiden gaande en rustende Huislieden; zonachtig en natuurlyk behandeld | *Mat:* op paneel *Size:* hoog 14, breed 12 ½ duim	[Merrem]	(Sold) fl 30 v d Schley
1802/06/16	AMSCH	0113	*K. Molenaar* | Een stil Water, aan de Vestmuur van een oude Stad, waar op eenige Wooningen en een Moolen, gestoffeert met twee Boeren in een Schuit; verder eenige Vaartuigen, zonachtig en bevallig gepenceeld | *Mat:* op paneel *Size:* hoog 16, breed 14 duim	[Merrem]	(Sold) fl 25 v d Schley
1802/06/16	AMSCH	0114	*K. Molenaar* | Een Duinachtig Landschap by een opgaande Weg met eenig Geboomten, zit een Boer, waar by een ander staande; verder een gaand Man en Vrouw, ter zyde een stil Water, waar in Visschers in een Schuit, en een aangenaam verschiet; zonachtig en bevallig van schildering | *Mat:* op paneel *Size:* hoog 15 ½, breed 14 ½ duim	[Merrem]	(Sold) fl 25 v d Schley
1802/06/16	AMSCH	0115	*K. Molenaar* | Voor een Boeren Woning, ziet men eenige Huislieden, nevens Paarden; ter zyden een stil Water met Vaartuigen, verders een aangenaam verschiet, krachtig van penceel behandeling | *Mat:* op paneel *Size:* hoog 15 ½, breed 21 ½ duim	[Merrem]	(Sold) fl 15 v d Schleij [for] Sneck
1802/06/28	AMSCH	0120	*K. Molenaar* | Een Landschap langs Boeren Wooningen en een Stil Water, ziet men een aantal Huislieden, speelende toffeltje klap, op de voorgrond eenige Kinderen; alles zeer natuurlyk behandeld, door K. Molenaar; hoog 20, breed 24 duim. Panneel | *Mat:* op paneel *Size:* hoog 20, breed 24 duim	Anna Elink	(Sold) fl 21 Coclaur
1802/06/28	AMSCH	0123	*K. Molenaar* | Twee stuks, ryk met Beelden gestoffeerde Land- en Watergezigten, zynde een Zomer en een Winter, natuurlyk op Panneel | *Mat:* op paneel *Size:* hoog 16, breed 22 duim	Anna Elink	(Sold) fl 14:10 Reijers
1802/06/28	AMSCH	0124	*K. Molenaar* | Een Dorpgezicht aan een bevrozen Rivier, ryk gestoffeerd met een menigte zich op het Ys vermakende Beeldjes; natuurlyk op Panneel behandeld | *Mat:* op paneel *Size:* hoog 14, breed 19 duim	Anna Elink	(Sold) fl 19:10 Jan Spaan

1802/06/28	AMSCH	0125	*K. Molenaar* | Twee stuks gestoffeerde Landschappen, met verscheiden Woningen en Huislieden, verbeeldende Zomer- en Wintergezigt, beide naar den aart der saisoennen [sic], natuurlijk gepenceeld | *Mat:* op paneel *Size:* ieder hoog 9, breed 10 duim	Anna Elink	(Sold) fl 4:10 Vermeulen
1802/07/20	MGSAN	0031	*K. Molenaar* | Een Winter | *Mat:* op paneel *Size:* hoog duim 15, breed duim 12		(Unknown)
1802/07/21	HGKAN	0036	*K. Molenaar* | Een Winter, zynde een Gezicht buiten een Stad, vol gewoel, zoo van Schaatzen rydende, Wandelende als andere met Werken bezich zynde Figuuren, zeer uitvoerig en krachtig geschildert, door K. Molenaar, paneel zwarte Lyst en vergulde binnen rand | *Mat:* op paneel		(Unknown)
1802/07/21	HGKAN	0066	*K. Molenaar* | Een Strand Gezicht vol gewoel van Visschers, die de Visch aanbrengen en andere figuuren, in het verschiet het Dorp Scheveningen, heel uitvoerig, door K. Molenaar, zwarte Lyst		(Unknown)
1802/07/21	HGKAN	0070	*K. Molenaar* | Een Winter, eenige Schaatze-ryders, in het verschiet een Dorp, zeer fraay geschildert, door K. Molenaar, zonder Lyst		(Unknown)
1802/08/24	LNDLS	0050	*K. Molenaar* | Een Capitaal Stuk, verbeeldende een Zeestrand met eene menigte Kooplieden in Visch, Wagens met Paarden en wandelende beelden, op eene hoogte, Gebouwen en een Kerk, benevens een Baaktoorn op het Duin, en op den Voorgrond een Boerenhuis met rustend Volk. Zeer konstig geschilderd op doek, door K. Molenaar, zoo goed als van dien Meester bekend is | *Mat:* op doek *Size:* hoog 39, breed 61 duimen	Leonardus Bouman [or others]	(Unknown) fl 34
1802/08/24	LNDLS	0083	*K. Molenaar* | Een Landschap met Gebouwen, op den voorgrond Vischers in een Schuit en op het Land | companion to lot 84 *Mat:* op paneel *Size:* hoog 17, breed 16 duimen	Leonardus Bouman [or others]	(Unknown) fl 27 for lots 83 & 84
1802/08/24	LNDLS	0084	*K. Molenaar* | Een Weêrga, vertoond een Winter met veel Volk en Sleden op 't Ys en op het Land. Door denzelven [K. Molenaar], mede op paneel en dito groote | companion to lot 83 *Mat:* op paneel *Size:* hoog 17, breed 16 duimen	Leonardus Bouman [or others]	(Unknown) fl 27 for lots 83 & 84
1802/08/24	LNDLS	0085	*K. Molenaar* | Een Gezelschap van Mannen en Vrouwen aan een tafel met eeten, zittende in een binnen-vertrek | *Mat:* op paneel *Size:* hoog 15, breed 11 ½ duimen *Notes:* The artist was presumably Jan Miense Molenaer and not Klaes Molenaer.	Leonardus Bouman [or others]	(Unknown) fl 7
1802/09/06	AMSCH	0076	*K. Molenaar* | Voor een Beestehuis, ziet men eenige landlieden, bézig zynde een Os te dollen, omringt van verscheide omstanders en kinderen; dit Schilderytje is allerbevalligst, en zo naauwkeurig als A. van Ostade | *Mat:* op paneel *Size:* hoog 14, breed 19 duim	J	(Sold) fl 42 Jan Spaan
1802/09/06	AMSCH	0077	*K. Molenaar* | Een besneeuwd Wintergezigt, gestoffeerd met een Yssleede met Ryzigers	B	(Sold) fl 3 van Iperen
1802/09/06	AMSCH	0078	*K. Molenaar* | Een zinnebeeldig voorwerp, op de verganckelykheid van het Leeven	Wed Grave [or others]	(Bought In) fl 0:8
1802/09/21	UTHDG	0063	*K. Molenaar* | Een Boerenwerf en woning, met geboomte, de stoffagie is een vrouw zittende en sprekende met iemand die over de onderdeur ligt. Zeer fraaij en natuurlijk | *Mat:* op doek *Size:* hoog 17, breed 15 duimen		(Sold) fl 15:10 Niekerk
1802/12/13	AMSCH	0114	*K. Molenaar* | In een aangenaam Landschap met Boeren Woningen, ziet men langs een zandige Weg een meenigte gaande en rustende Beeldjes, en een Boomryk verschiet, bevallig van Licht | *Mat:* op paneel *Size:* hoog 19, breed 24 ½ duim	Pruyssenaar [for] A	(Bought In) fl 10 ½
1802/12/13	AMSCH	0115	*K. Molenaar* | Een natuurlyk Wintergezicht, ryk gestoffeerd met gaande en rydende Beeldtjes; ter zyde een Besneeuwde Weg, Boere Wooningen en een Dorp in 't verschiet, bevallig van Licht en meesterachtig geschilderd | *Mat:* op doek *Size:* hoog 17, breed 15 duim	Pruyssenaar [for] A	(Sold) fl 2:15 Gruiter
1803/06/20	AMSCH	0003	*K. Molenaar* | Langs een Opgaande Weg, by hoog Geboomte en een Boeren Werf, ziet men verscheide Beeldjes, zonachtig en natuurlyk behandeld, door K. Molenaar, op Paneel | *Mat:* op paneel *Size:* hoog 14, breed 12 duim	Schley [for] B	(Sold) fl 41 for lots 3 & 4. Hodges
1803/06/20	AMSCH	0004	*K. Molenaar* | Een stil Water aan een Vestmuur, waarop eenige Woningen en een Molen, gestoffeerd met twee Boeren in een Schuit, zonachtig gepenceeld op Paneel | *Mat:* op paneel *Size:* hoog 16, breed 14 duim	Schley [for] B	(Sold) fl 41 for lots 3 & 4. Hodges
1803/08/01	AMSCH	0024	*Molenaar. (K.)* | Een Wintergezicht met Schaatzeryders, Arresleede, en verders een Molen, fix gepenceeld | *Mat:* op paneel *Size:* hoog 16, breed 19 duim	J	(Sold) fl 2:5 Teengs
1803/08/01	AMSCH	0025	*Molenaar. (K.)* | Een natuurlyk Land- en Watergezicht, gestoffeerd met Boeren in een Schuit, een Vrouw die goed spoelt, en een zittende Hengelaar, helder en bevallig gepenceeld | *Mat:* op paneel *Size:* hoog 9 ½, breed 12 ½ duim	J	(Sold) fl 5:10 Van Dijl
1803/08/24	HGKAN	0070	*Moolenaar* | Een Landschap	[Teissier] [or others]	(Sold) fl 2:18 Uytenbogerd
1803/09/07	AMSCH	0114	*K. Molenaar* | In een Winter ziet men een menigte Lieden, op 't Ys zich met Ryden en Wandelen vermaken, geestig op Paneel [Un hiver ; plusieurs figures s'amusant à glisser sur la glace et à se promener ; d'une ordonnance spirituelle] | *Mat:* op paneel *Size:* hoog 11, breed 15 duim	Smidt	(Sold) fl 3:5 Teengs

803/12/12	AMSCH	0064	*K. Molenaar* | Een Landschap met een Ruïne, Geboomten en stoffagie van Beeldjes; natuurlyk op Paneel | *Mat:* op paneel *Size:* hoog 16, breed 14 duim	D [?]	(Bought In) fl 12
803/12/15	MGLAC	0048	*K. Molenaar* | Een Winter, vol gewoel van Schaats- en Slederyders | *Mat:* op paneel *Size:* hoog duim 13, breed duim 18	Mr L H de Haze Bomme	(Unknown)
804/02/27	AMSCH	0079	*Molenaar. (K.)* | In een Boom en Duinachtig Landschap, ziet men in een Boerewoning, eenige Boeren en een Boerin | *Mat:* op paneel *Size:* hoog 14, breed 14 duim	D	(Sold) fl 3:10 Gruiter
804/04/28	LNDLS	0061	*K. Molenaar* | Een Landschap	[Abraham Delfos] [or others]	(Sold) fl 1 van Giesen
804/05/07	AMSCH	0116	*Molenaar* | Twee stuks, bevallige Landschapjes, zynde een Zomer en een Winter; byde natuurlyk gestoffeerd en van een uitvoerige penceelbehandeling | *Mat:* op paneel *Size:* ieder hoog 9, breed 8 duim	Vinkeles [for] J	(Sold) fl 36:10 van Iperen
804/08/08	AMSCH	0124	*Klaas Moolenaar* | Een natuurlyk Land- en Watergezicht, gestoffeerd met een Overhaalpond, eenige Lieden te Paard, en verdere Stoffagie | *Mat:* op doek *Size:* hoog 27, breed 40 duim	Vink[eles] [for] K[=Gruyter?]	(Sold) fl 5 Gruyter
804/08/08	AMSCH	0125	*Klaas Moolenaar* | In een Besneeuwd Wintergezicht ziet men op 't Ys, by een Muur, Kasteel, en andere Woninningen [sic], een ménigte Lieden, welke zich op 't Ys vermaaken; natuurlyk en fiks gepenceeld | *Mat:* op paneel *Size:* hoog 23, br. 33 duim	Vink[eles] [for] S	(Sold) fl 6 Coclers
804/10/08	RMCNL	0075	*Molenaar* | Een Winter	A t'Hooft	(Unknown)
804/10/16	DLOND	0141	*Klaas Molenaer* | Een Wintergezicht met verscheiden Sleden, Schaatsenryders en Wandelaars op het Ys. Tableau d'Hyver rempli de figures, Traineaux & Patineurs | *Mat:* op doek *Size:* hoog 45, breed 64		(Unknown)
804/10/16	DLOND	0142	*Klaas Molenaer* | Een Dorps-gewoel vol Menschen en Paarden. Vue d'un Village avec beaucoup d'Hommes & de Chevaux | *Mat:* op doek *Size:* hoog 48, breed 62		(Unknown)
804/10/16	DLOND	0143	*Klaas Molenaer* | Twee stukjens. Boeren-gezelschappen. Deux pièces. Compagnies de Paysans | *Mat:* op paneel *Size:* hoog 4, breed 5 *Notes:* The artist was presumably Jan Miense Molenaer and not Klaes Molenaer.		(Unknown)
804/10/16	DLOND	0144	*Klaas Molenaer* | Een Pleisterplaats, met een Heer en Dame te Paard, enz. Le devant d'une Auberge, un Monsieur & une Dame à Cheval | *Size:* hoog 18, breed 25		(Unknown)
804/10/16	DLOND	0145	*Klaas Molenaer* | Enige Schaatsenryders. Des Patineurs | *Size:* hoog 15, breed 21		(Unknown)
804/10/16	DLOND	0146	*Klaas Molenaer* | Een Wintergezicht. Tableau d'Hyver | *Mat:* op paneel *Size:* hoog 12, breed 14		(Sold) fl 3 Verlinden
804/10/16	DLOND	0147	*Klaas Molenaer* | Dezelve [Klaas Molenaer], als Ruysdaal. P. h. 16. b. 19. Een Landschap met Waterval. Paysage & une Cascade | *Mat:* op paneel *Size:* hoog 16, breed 19		(Unknown)
805/07/03	AMSCH	0118	*K. Molenaar* | Een bevrozen Rivier aan een Stads Muur, het Ys met Beeldjes gestoffeerd; geestig op Paneel | *Mat:* op paneel *Size:* hoog 9, breed 10 duim	G	(Sold) fl 11:10 Halingins
805/07/03	AMSCH	0213	*Molenaar* | Een Land- en Riviergezicht	V[inkeles]	(Sold) fl 0:12 Delprado
805/07/10	AMSCH	0098	*Molenaar* | Een Besneeuwd Wintergezicht, met een ménigte stoffagie van Beelden; en breed geschilderd | *Mat:* op paneel *Size:* hoog 12, breed 15 duim	V[inkeles] [for] L	(Bought In) fl 5
805/07/10	AMSCH	0100	*K. Molenaar* | Een Wintergezicht, op 't Ys, by oude Gebouwen eenige Lieden met hunne Paarden, Karren, enz.; dun en delicaat | *Mat:* op paneel *Size:* hoog 10, breed 10 duim	V[inkeles] [for] N	(Sold) fl 10 L Pakker
805/10/21	GRBOL	0018	*K. Molenaar* | Een Schoon Landschap	Gerardus Nicolaus Heerkens	(Unknown)
805/12/16	AMSCH	0041	*K. Molenaar* | Een geestig gestoffeerd Wintergezicht, fraay op Paneel | *Mat:* op paneel *Size:* hoog 7, breed 9 duim	R[oos]	(Sold) fl 2:10 Yver
805/12/16	AMSCH	0108	*K. Molenaar* | Een gestoffeerd Landschap	R[oos]	(Sold) fl 4 for lots 108 & 109. du Pree
805/12/16	AMSCH	0109	*K. Molenaar* | Een dito [gestoffeerd Landschap]	R[oos]	(Sold) fl 4 for lots 108 & 109. du Pree
806/05/05	AMSCH	0092	*K. Molenaar* | Twee stuks, zynde Zomer en Winter, beide verbeeldende, oude Vestmuuren van Steeden, gestoffeerd met Vissers en andere in Schuiten, en verscheide Lieden zig op het ys vermakende; natuurlyk en fiks gepenceeld door K. Molenaar | *Mat:* op paneel *Size:* hoog 12, breed 10 duim	E	(Sold) fl 6:5 Rynbergh
806/05/05	AMSCH	0098	*Molenaar* | Een Wintergezichtje met Geboomte, Gebouwen, stoffagie van Beeldjes enz.; meesterlyk door denzelven [Molenaar] | *Size:* hoog 12, breed 14 duim	V[inkeles]	(Sold) fl 5 A Reynders
806/08/13	AMSCH	0121	*Molenaar. (K.)* | Twee stuks, een Zomer- en Wintergezicht: met verschillende stoffagie, natuurlyk behandeld | *Mat:* op paneel *Size:* Ieder hoog 15, breed 12 duim	Roos [for] Ruel [?]	(Sold) fl 4:5 L Pakker

1806/08/13	AMSCH	0122	*Molenaar. (K.)* | Een Land- en Watergezicht langs een Weg, met Woningen, Molens en Vissers; als de vorige behandeld | *Mat:* op paneel *Size:* hoog 10, breed 9 duim	Roos	(Sold) fl 1 L Pakker
1806/08/13	AMSCH	0123	*Molenaar. (K.)* | Een Dorpgezicht, gestoffeerd met Postwagens en Ryzigers; meesterlyk van behandeling | *Mat:* op paneel *Size:* hoog 16, breed 21 duim	Vinkeles [for] G[ruyter]	(Sold) fl 5:5 T Spaan
1806/08/13	AMSCH	0124	*Molenaar. (K.)* | Een aangenaam Landschap, met Geboomten en Boerewoningen, gestoffeerd met gaande en rustende Landlieden; niet minder dan de voorgaande van behandeling | *Mat:* op paneel *Size:* hoog 31, breed 24 duim	Vinkeles [for] G[ruyter]	(Bought In) fl 8
1806/08/13	AMSCH	0125	*Molenaar. (K.)* | Een Binnenhuis met kaartspelende Boeren; breed en fiks gepenceeld | *Mat:* op paneel *Size:* hoog 10, breed 12 duim *Notes:* The artist was presumably Jan Miense Molenaer and not Klaes Molenaer.	Vinkeles [for] F	(Sold) fl 1 L Pakker
1806/08/13	AMSCH	0126	*Molenaar. (K.)* | Een bevallig Land- en Watergezicht met alaloude [sic] Gebouwen, Scheepen, Schuiten en Stoffagie van Beeldjes; delicaat en uitvoerig gepenceeld | *Mat:* op paneel *Size:* hoog 15, breed 14 duim	Roos	(Sold) fl 8:10 Richters
1806/08/13	AMSCH	0127	*Molenaar. (K.)* | Een besneeuwd Wintergezicht; ryk gestoffeerd met Schaatseryders, wandelende Persoonen, Arresleeden, enz.; en een alleraangenaamst verschiet; zonachtig en fiks van schildering | *Mat:* op doek *Size:* hoog 22, breed 26 duim	Vinkeles [for] J	(Sold) fl 18:10 Wed Achtienhoven
1806/08/13	AMSCH	0128	*Molenaar. (K.)* | Een Binnenhuis met vrolyke Boeren en Boerinnen; breed en fiks gepenceeld | *Mat:* op paneel *Size:* hoog 9 ½, breed 7 duim *Notes:* The artist was presumably Jan Miense Molenaer and not Klaes Molenaer.	Vinkeles [for] F	(Sold) fl 2:10 L Pakker
1806/08/13	AMSCH	0129	*Molenaar. (K.)* | Twee stuks gestoffeerde Duinachtige Landschap met Boerewoningen en bevallige verschieten | *Mat:* op paneel *Size:* hoog 5, breed 6 duim	Vinkeles [for] D	(Sold) fl 10 T Spaan
1806/11/24	AMSCH	0044	*Molenaar (K.)* | Een gehugt met Geboomten en Boerewoningen, by een stil water, waarin een Schuit met Menschen; in de manier van J. Ruisdaal gepenceeld | *Mat:* op paneel *Size:* hoog 16, breed 22 duim	Munnikhuizen	(Sold) fl 4 L Pakker
1807/06/02	AMHUY	0006	*K Moolenaar* | Een besneeuwd Wintergezicht, by een Boeren Dorp ziet men op het Ys eenige Schaatsenryders		(Unknown)
1807/06/02	AMHUY	0015	*Moolenaar* | Een Landschap met vervallen Gebouwen, op de voorgrond een Waterbeekje, waarby eenige rustende Landlieden, zonachtig geschilderd		(Unknown)
1807/08/26	AMSCH	0316a	*Molenaar* | Twee stuks Land- en Riviergezichten, met verscheiden Schuitjes en Beeldjes gestoffeerd | *Mat:* op paneel	Yver [for] S	(Sold) fl 2:5 T Spaan
1808/04/26	GDAN	0101	*Molenaar (Klaas)* | Een Dorp Gezigt bij den Winter, ziende op een bevroren Rivier of Water, op het zelve eenige Paarden voor Sleden trekkende, en een aantal Schaatserijders, in het verschiet een Molen, alles fiks en bijzonder uitmuntend geschildert | *Mat:* op paneel *Size:* hoog 15, breed 21 duim	G H Fortuyn	(Unknown)
1808/04/26	GDAN	0102	*Molenaar (Klaas)* | Een dito Binnenhuis, waar in een Heer die prachtig gekleed is, zich vertoond, met eenig bijwerk, ook zeer goed gehandeld | *Mat:* op koper *Size:* hoog 14, breed 10 duim *Notes:* The artist was presumably Jan Miense Molenaer and not Klaes Molenaer.	G H Fortuyn	(Unknown)
1808/05/18	LNAN	0047	*Molenaar* | Een Winter gezigt met Paarden en Sleeden | *Notes:* The artist's name "Molenaar" was added in by hand in the RKDH copy of the catalogue.	Mr Cornelis Versluys	(Unknown)
1808/05/18	LNAN	0057	*Molenaar* | Een Wintergezigt vol gewoel met Sleeden, Paarden en Schaatsen Rijders | *Notes:* The artist's name "Molenaar" was added in by hand in the RKDH copy of the catalogue.	Mr Cornelis Versluys	(Unknown)
1808/06/11	RMRIJ	0092	*K: Molenaar* | Een aardig Landschap, goed gestoffeerd | *Mat:* op paneel *Size:* hoog 15, breed 20 ¾ duim		(Unknown) fl 14
1808/06/13	AMSCH	0234	*K. Molenaar* | Een met Beelden en Paarden gestoffeerd Winter- en IJsgezicht	Z	(Sold) fl 5:10 Glad
1808/08/23	AMSCH	0114	*Molenaar. (K.)* | Een bevrozen Rivier, ter zijde Boeren Woningen, rijk gestoffeerd, met wandelende Heeren en Dames, Schaatserijders, Arre-, Prik- en Turfsleeden, en andere bijwerk; natuurlijk en fraai behandeld | *Mat:* op doek *Size:* hoog 35, breed 45 duim	C	(Sold) fl 57 Kerkhoven
1808/08/23	AMSCH	0115	*Molenaar. (K.)* | Een kapitaal Dorpgezicht met Woningen, bij Geboomte, rijk gestoffeert, met een meenigte Huislieden, verbeeldende een Kermisvreugd, Mans, Vrouwen en Kinderen vervrolijken zig bij een Herberg met drinken en roken, andere danzen naar het speelen der fiool, verscheide toehoorders bij Liedjes-zangers, een Heer en Dame wandelende, beschouwen deeze vermakelijkheden; het is geestig van Ordonantie en uitvoerig gepenceeld | *Mat:* op doek *Size:* hoog 31, breed 39 duim	Z	(Sold) fl 17 van Iperen [or] v d Sley [for] A
1808/08/23	AMSCH	0116	*Molenaar. (K.)* | Een natuurlijk Land- en Watergezicht, met versheiden Boeren Woningen, en gestoffeerd met gaande en rustende Huislieden, en Visschers in hunne Schuiten; warm en zonachtig behandeld | *Mat:* op paneel *Size:* hoog 19, breed 24 duim	Z	(Sold) fl 60 van Iperen
1808/08/23	AMSCH	0256	*K. Molenaar* | Een natuurlijk Land- en Watergezicht met stoffagie	J	(Sold) fl 5 Boelhouwer

1808/08/23	AMSCH	0269	*K. Molenaar* | Een besneeuwd Wintergezicht. gestoffeert met Schaatserijders en IJssleeden; natuurlijk	[Van Iperen?]	(Sold or Bought In) fl 5:5 Van Iperen
1808/09/13	HABRU	0062	*K. Molenaar* | Een Zeestrand, rijk gestoffeerd		(Unknown) fl 3:5
1809/04/22	AMYVR	0085	*K. Molenaar* | De Ruïne van een Kasteel aan een Watertje, drie Beeldjes stoffeeren het Landschap, hetwelk meesterlijk behandeld is | *Mat:* op paneel *Size:* hoog 16, breed 14 duim	de Bruin	(Sold) fl 1:15 du Pree
1809/04/22	AMYVR	0086	*K. Molenaar* | Een gestoffeerd Wintergezicht | *Mat:* op paneel *Size:* hoog 9, breed 8 duim	de Bruin	(Sold) fl 0:10 du Pree
1809/04/22	AMYVR	0087	*K. Molenaar* | Een gestoffeerd Land- en Riviergezicht; meesterlijk | *Mat:* op paneel *Size:* hoog 10, breed 13 duim	de Bruin	(Sold) fl 2 du Pree
1809/04/22	AMYVR	0088	*K. Molenaar* | Een Fluitspeeler | *Mat:* op paneel *Size:* hoog 6, breed 5 duim *Notes:* The artist was presumably Jan Miense Molenaer and not Klaes Molenaer.	de Bruin	(Sold) fl 0:14 du Pree
1809/04/22	AMYVR	0089	*K. Molenaar* | Twee stuks Duinachtige geestig gestoffeerde Landschappen | *Mat:* op paneel *Size:* hoog 19, breed 25 duim	Juff[r] Julikker	(Sold) fl 5 C S Roos
1809/06/13	AMSCH	0105	*K. Molenaar* | Een natuurlijk besneeuwd Wintergezicht, gestoffeerd met een Heer te Paard, Schaatsenrijders en Huislieden, in 't verschiet een Dorp, bij eenige Boere Woningen; kunstig in de stijl van Ruisdaal, door K. Molenaar | *Mat:* op paneel *Size:* hoog 22, breed 18 duim	E	(Sold) fl 7:10 Gruyter
1809/06/13	AMSCH	0106	*K. Molenaar* | Een vrolijke Kermis, vol gewoel van Dansende, Drinkende en Liefkoozende Boeren en Boerinnen, Kramers en andere Lieden, welke zich in Schuiten vermaken; grappig en natuurlijk verbeeld | *Mat:* op doek *Size:* hoog 25, breed 33 duim	Y	(Sold) fl 10:10 Keurvorst
1809/06/13	AMSCH	0107	*K. Molenaar* | Een natuurlijk Land- en Watergezigt, gestoffeerd met Visschers, zoo op de wal als in hunne schuiten, ter zijde een oude Ruïne en een Dorp-tooren in 't verschiet; fiks gepenceeld | *Mat:* op paneel *Size:* hoog 14, breed 22 duim	M	(Bought In) fl 9
1809/06/13	AMSCH	0242	*Molenaar* | Twee stuks, een woelend Zeetje, met Scheepen, en een kleintje	Y	(Sold) fl 1:10 van Iperen
1809/07/25	HGBSM	0051	*K. Molenaar* | Een Wintertje, zynde een Dorp-Gezigt met stoffage | *Mat:* op paneel *Size:* hoog 19, breed 14 en een half duim	D van der Aa [or] E B ten Dall	(Sold) fl 24:10 Ponse [or] Stees
1809/10/20	UTWLD	0022	*K. Molenaar* | Twee oude philosophen door K. Molenaar | *Notes:* The artist was presumably Jan Miense Molenaer and not Klaes Molenaer.	J J van Rhyn	(Unknown)
1810/03/27	RMCNL	0016	*K. Molenaar* | Twee Stuks Landschappen, Bergachtig, zeer fraai geschilderd		(Unknown)
1810/05/22	AMSCH	0067	*Molenaar. (K.)* | Twee stuks Duinachtige Landschappen, met Boeren-Woningen en Molen, beide met gaande en rustende Huislieden gestoffeerd, en natuurlijk behandeld | *Mat:* op paneel *Size:* Jeder hoog 19, breed 25 duim	R	(Sold) fl 15 Gruyter
1810/05/22	AMSCH	0068	*Molenaar. (K.)* | Twee stuks, een Zomer- en Wintergezicht, eigenaartig gestoffeerd en als de voorgaande van schildering | *Mat:* op paneel *Size:* Jeder hoog 14, breed 12 duim	R	(Sold) fl 10 du Pree
1810/06/06	RMMUY	0113	*K. Molenaar* | Een klein Landschapje | *Mat:* op paneel		(Unknown) fl 6
1810/06/06	RMMUY	0114	*K. Molenaar* | Twee stuks Boeren Vreugden | *Mat:* op paneel		(Unknown) fl 8:15
1810/06/06	RMMUY	0115	*K. Molenaar* | Twee stuks, een Winter en een Zomer | *Mat:* op paneel		(Unknown) fl 9:10
1810/06/06	RMMUY	0116	*K. Molenaar* | Een Wintertje met veele Figuren, zeer fraaij		(Unknown) fl 31:10 for lots 116 & 117
1810/06/06	RMMUY	0117	*K. Molenaar* | Een Landschap, waar in een Watertje met eenige Visschers | *Mat:* op paneel		(Unknown) fl 31:10 for lots 116 & 117
1810/06/20	AMSCH	0058	*K. Molenaar* | Een Dorpgezigt: voor eene Herberg zitten eenige vrolijke Huislieden bij eene welvoorziene Tafel, terwijl anderen zich met danssen en spelen vermaken. Natuurlijk voorgesteld | *Mat:* op doek *Size:* hoog 27, breed 35 duimen	A	(Sold) fl 2:10 Geld
1810/06/20	AMSCH	0058a	*K. Molenaar* | Een sterk bevrozen Water langs een Dorp, met besneeuwde Woningen; het is rijk gestoffeerd met wandelende Heeren en Dames, Huislieden, IJs- en Arresleden enz. Natuurlijk verbeeld en van de beste schildering van K. Molenaar | *Mat:* op doek *Size:* hoog 43, breed 59 duimen	Y	(Sold) fl 31 Hodges
1810/06/20	AMSCH	0059	*K. Molenaar* | Een Gezigt op een Bleekerij, boven Haarlem. Natuurlijk behandeld | *Mat:* op paneel *Size:* hoog 18, breed 26 duimen	N	(Sold) fl 3:15 Coclers
1810/06/20	AMSCH	0060	*K. Molenaar* | Een Duinachtig Landschap, met Boeren Woningen en Beeldjes | *Size:* hoog 11, breed 11 duimen	B	(Sold) fl 0:12 J de Vries
1810/06/20	AMSCH	0115	*K. Molenaar* | Een besneeuwde Winter	N	(Sold) fl 0:6 L Pakker
1810/07/23	DOLGI	0036	*Molenaar* | Een Landschap met Gebouwen, rijk gestoffeerd | *Mat:* op paneel *Size:* hoog 13, breed 10 duim	Mr Pieter van den Santheuvel	(Sold) fl 13 P de Heere à Dordt
1810/08/06	AMSCH	0078	*Molenaar (K.)* | Een Land- en Watergezigt met Boeren-woningen, Geboomte en stoffagie van Beeldjes; natuurlijk verbeeld | *Mat:* op paneel *Size:* hoog 15, breed 12 duimen	A	(Sold) fl 11 Texier Gerbet en Comp [for] Le Brun
1810/08/10	RMRIJ	0022	*Klaas Molenaar* | Een Boere Vreugd. Krachtig geschilderd en welgeordonneerd		(Sold) fl 2:10 [or] 2:8 Mulder [?]

1810/10/10	MGCIT	0082	*K. Molenaar* | Drie Stukken, alle Wintergezigten, vol van allerhande Voorwerpen, daartoe betrekkelijk; natuurlijk uitgevoerd.	Caspar van Citters	(Unknown)
1810/10/11	AMSCH	0054	*K. Molenaar* | Langs een bevroozen Rivier, ziet men op oude Ruïnen en Woningen, het IJs is rijk gestoffeerd met Vragtsleden, Schaatsenrijders en gaande Huislieden; natuurlijk en van de beste Schildering van K. Molenaar | *Mat:* op doek *Size:* hoog 27, breed 34 duimen	[Gruyter?]	(Sold) fl 20 H^n Pakker
1810/10/11	AMSCH	0232	*K. Molenaar* | Een Varkenmarkt	A	(Sold) fl 0:18 Yver
1810/11/07	UTWLD	0046	*Molenaar* | Een zeer aardig Landschapje tegen een boeren agterwooning met rijzend geboomte, 't verschiet over een rivier door Molenaar, op paneel, 2 voet hoog, 1 voet 5 en een half duim breed, zwarte Lijst | *Mat:* op paneel *Size:* 2 voet hoog, 1 voet 5 en een half duim breed		(Unknown) fl 7:5
1810/11/07	UTWLD	0047	*Molenaar* | Een zeer geestig en wel geordoneerd Wintergezigtje met een aantal woelende beeltjes, kar en paard door Molenaar op paneel, 1 en een half voet breed, 1 en een half voet hoog, zwarte Lijst | *Mat:* op paneel *Size:* 1 en een half voet breed, 1 en een half voet hoog		(Unknown) fl 26

Molenaer, Klaes (manner)

1801/11/10	AMPOS	0022	*Molenaar* | 1 Dorp- en Kerk-Gezigt, met een rivier en vrolyke Boeren, als door Molenaar		(Unknown)
1804/10/16	DLOND	0287	*In de manier van Kl. Molenaar* | Enige Soldaten, en een Boer, die met de Kaart spelen. Quelques Soldats jouants [sic] aux Cartes avec un Paysan | *Mat:* op paneel *Size:* hoog 14, breed 11		(Unknown)
1804/12/10	AMSCH	0114	*Moolenaar* | Twee stuks Landschappen, in de manier van Moolenaar | *Mat:* op paneel *Size:* hoog 17, br. 23 duim	Jan De Groot	(Sold) fl 10 Coclers
1809/05/26	HADAA	0012	*Molenaar* | Een Wintertje, als door Molenaar	Mejuffrouw de Wed David Heemskerk [or others]	(Unknown)
1809/10/20	UTWLD	0039	*Molenaar* | Een Landschap in de manier van Molenaar	J J van Rhyn	(Unknown)
1809/10/20	UTWLD	0040	*Molenaar* | Een dito [Landschap] dito [in de manier van Molenaar]	J J van Rhyn	(Unknown)
1810/06/04	DOBRA	0002	*Molenaar* | Een Wintertje, als door Molenaar	Hendrik de Haas	(Unknown)

Molijn, Pieter de

1801/03/16	AMSCH	0080	*P. Moulin* | Twee Landschappen	P[ruyssenaar]	(Sold) fl 1:10 Van Iperen
1802/02/16	AMSCH	0085	*P. Molyn* | Twee stuks diversche Landschappen op paneel | *Mat:* op paneel	E	(Sold) fl 14 Vermeulen
1802/04/13	HAVIN	0069	*P. Molyn* | Een Landschap		(Unknown)
1802/05/05	AMSCH	0134	*P. Molyn* | Een zeer natuurlyk Land- en Watergezicht | *Mat:* op paneel *Size:* hoog 16, breed 22 duim	G	(Sold) fl 5 Vermeulen
1802/05/05	AMSCH	0135	*P. Molyn* | Een Boom- en Bergachtig Landschap, op de voorgrond twee Reizigers met een Hond, fiks gepenceeld | *Mat:* op paneel *Size:* hoog 12, breed 14 duim	BB	(Sold) fl 9 Spruit
1802/09/21	UTHDG	0066	*P. Molijn* | Een Waterval tusschen Rotzen nederstortende | *Mat:* op paneel		(Sold) fl 8:5 La Maine
1802/12/13	AMSCH	0122	*P. Moulin* | Een Boomryk Landschap | *Mat:* op doek *Size:* hoog 25, breed 36 duim	Pruyssenaar [for] A	(Sold) fl 1:10 L Pakker
1802/12/13	AMSCH	0123	*P. Moulin* | Een Duinagtig Landschap, op de voorgrond, voor een Boere Herberg, staat een Kar met een Paard, benevens eenige Rysigers | *Mat:* op paneel *Size:* hoog 17 ½, breed 15 duim	Pruyssenaar [for] D	(Sold) fl 4:5 Van Iperen
1803/04/20	AMSCH	0046	*Molyn. (P.)* | Een Boerewerf met verscheide Boerewoningen aan een stil Water, waarin een Schuit met twee Vrouwen, verder hoog Geboomte en een aangenaam verschiet; warm van Coloriet, en natuurlyk gepenceeld [Le long d'un ruisseau sont quelques habitations entourrées de gros arbres ; des villageoises occupés & un joli lointain ajoutent à l'agrement de ce tableau plein d'effet & d'harmonie.] | *Mat:* op paneel *Size:* hoog 18, breed 26 duim	Maria Magdalena van Sluypwyk, gravinne van Moens	(Sold) fl 15 C S Roos
1803/04/20	AMSCH	0047	*Molyn. (P.)* | Een Heuvelachtig Landzicht, met een Boerewoning en Schuur by Geboomten, op de voorgrond een Waterbeekje, waarby een Veehoeder met Vee; verder een zittende Vrouw; bevallig en schilderagtig gepenceeld [La vue sur une colline legere plantée d'arbrisseaux ; l'on y distingue des habitations, & au bas un ruisseau qu'un pâtre cottoye avec des bestiaux ; la perspective d'une vaste etendue de pays termine ce joli tableau touché avec beaucoup de legereté.] | *Mat:* op paneel *Size:* hoog 19, breed 22 duim	Maria Magdalena van Sluypwyk, gravinne van Moens	(Sold) fl 62 Coclers
1803/06/20	AMSCH	0062	*P. Molyut* | Een Land- en Riviergezicht by een Dorp, met eenige Wooningen, gestoffeert met Vissers in een Schuit en verder bywerk, fix gepenceeld, door P. Molyut, op Paneel | *Mat:* op paneel *Size:* hoog 10, breed 14 duim	Schley [for] H	(Sold) fl 2 L Pakker
1803/06/20	AMSCH	0063	*P. Molyus* | Voor een Staketsel, waar agter een Boomstam, ziet men een Hond en Kat een Carrewy betwisten, verder een aangenaam verschiet, meesterlyk op Doek | *Mat:* op doek *Size:* hoog 44, breed 49 duim	Schley [for] K	(Sold) fl 1:15 Vermeulen
1803/09/07	AMSCH	0107	*P. Molyn* | Een Bevallig Boomryk Landschap, by eenige Boerewoningen ziet men een Wagen met Paarden, beneevens een ménigte Beeldjes enz.,	Smidt	(Bought In) fl 6

			zonagtig en fiks gepenceeld [Un paysage charmant et bocageux ; l'on voit, auprès de quelques habitations villagoises [sic], un charriot attelé de chevaux ; plusieurs figures etc. Les reflets de lumière répandent une belle harmonie et une clarté agréable sur l'ensemble] | *Mat:* op paneel *Size:* hoog 15, breed 19 duim [Haut 15, large 16 pouces] *Notes:* The dimensions differ in the Dutch and French editions of the catalogue.		
1804/05/07	AMSCH	0108	*Molyn. (P.)* | Een bevallig Boom en Bergachtig Landschap, met een ménigte Stoffagie, fiks en breed gepenceeld | *Mat:* op paneel *Size:* hoog 20, breed 30 duim	Vinkeles [for] J	(Sold) fl 2:5 van der Schley [for] R[ijfsnijder]
1804/05/07	AMSCH	0109	*Molyn. (P.)* | Een Duinachtig Landschap met Geboomten en Boere-woningen, gestoffeerd met rustende en gaande Huislieden, en twee Heeren te paard, benevens een Kerktooren in 't verschiet; natuurlyk en fiks behandeld | *Mat:* op paneel *Size:* hoog 17, breed 28 duim	Y[ver] [for] JJ	(Bought In) fl 17
1804/08/08	AMSCH	0130	*P. Molyn* | Een Heuvelachtig Landschap, op de voorgrond een Stroomend Waterbeekje, ter wederzyde Boerenwooningen by Geboomten, op de voorgrond gaande en rustende Huislieden, verders twee Heeren te Paard, by een Dorpgezicht; zonachtig en bevallig van coloriet, en meesterlyk geschilderd | *Mat:* op paneel *Size:* hoog 17, breed 27 duim	Schley [for] A	(Sold) fl 10:10 Van Iperen
1804/08/08	AMSCH	0131	*P. Molyn* | Twee stuks natuurlyke Landgezichten, beiden gestoffeerd met diversche Boerenwooningen, Hooischuur en Geboomte, op de voorgrond Reizigers en verder andere Huislieden en eenig Vée; beiden helder en bevallig van licht, coloriet, en meesterlyk gepenceeld | *Mat:* op paneel *Size:* hoog 17, breed 23 duim	Schley [for] A	(Bought In) fl 31
1804/10/29	HRBAU	0063	*Molyn, (P.)* | In een aangenaam Landschap heeft men voor aan een hoog opgaande zandige Weg, met boomen beplant, welke naar een' Molen gaat, die op de hoogte staat, waar op eenige Mannetjes zyn. Over een Watertjen, waar in verscheiden Hengelaars visschen is een Weiland met Beestjens, dat door Molenaarswerven wordt ingeslooten. Zeer plaisant en uitvoerig behandeld | *Mat:* op paneel *Size:* hoog 14, breed 22 duim	Simon Styl	(Unknown)
1805/07/10	AMSCH	0138	*P. Molyn* | Een Heuvelachtig Landschapje	V[inkeles] [for] K	(Sold) fl 3:5 Boelen
1805/12/16	AMSCH	0039	*P. Molyn* | Een Heuvelachtig Landgezicht, met Geboomte langs een Wegh, gestoffeerd met eenige Lieden, op Paneel geschilderd | *Mat:* op paneel *Size:* hoog 12, breed 15 duim	V	(Sold) fl 1 Roos
1805/12/16	AMSCH	0075	*P. Molyn* | Een Landschap	R[oos]	(Sold) fl 0:10 L Pakker
1805/12/16	AMSCH	0113	*P. Molyn* | Een Land- en Watergezicht	R[oos]	(Sold) fl 0:6 L Pakker
1806/05/05	AMSCH	0096	*P. Molyn* | Een boomryk Landschap, met onderscheiden stoffagie | *Mat:* op paneel *Size:* hoog 29, breed 29 duim	V[inkeles]	(Sold) fl 1:5 van Laar
1806/08/13	AMSCH	0130	*Molyn. (P.)* | Langs een Weg, met Woningen en Geboomten, by een stil Water vertoonen zich stilstaande en gaande Reizigers, verder een Dorpgezicht; fiks geschilderd | *Mat:* op paneel *Size:* hoog 18, breed 24 duim	Roos	(Sold) fl 6:5 Th Spaan
1806/11/24	AMSCH	0045	*Molyn (P.)* | Een heuvelachtig Landgezigt, met Geboomten, langs een weg, met eenige lieden; natuurlyk geschilderd | *Mat:* op paneel *Size:* hoog 12, breed 15 duim	Munnikhuizen	(Sold) fl 1 L Pakker
1807/04/00	LNDLS	0042	*P. Molyn* | Twee stuks dorpsgezigten, vol stoffagie | *Mat:* op paneel *Size:* hoog 12, breed 21 duim	[Abraham Delfos] [or others]	(Unknown)
1807/06/10	HGBSM	0042	*P. Molyn* | Twee stuks dorpsgezigten, vol stoffagie | *Mat:* op paneel *Size:* hoog 12, breed 21 duim	Abraham Delfos [or others]	(Sold) fl 3:5 Tessier
1807/08/26	AMSCH	0149	*P. Molyn* | Een gestoffeerd Duin en Boomryk Landschap | *Mat:* op paneel *Size:* hoog 13, breed 16 duim	Joseph Vallette	(Sold) fl 2:5 Yver
1807/08/26	AMSCH	0150	*P. Molyn* | Een Landschap met Boerenwoningen, Geboomten en Reizigers gestoffeerd | *Mat:* op paneel *Size:* hoog 16, breed 22 duim	de Vries	(Sold) fl 3:15 T van Iperen
1808/09/13	HABRU	0059	*P. Molijn* | Een Landschap, waarin Roovers een Postwagen overvallen		(Unknown) fl 5:10
1808/09/13	HABRU	0060	*P. Molijn* | Een Landschap, met Boere Woningen		(Unknown) fl 7:10
1808/09/13	HABRU	0061	*P. Molijn* | Een Watergezicht aan een Dijk, met Vissers Schuitjes		(Unknown) fl 3:6
1808/10/28	AMVRS	0035	*Molijn, (P.)* | Een natuurlijk Land- en Watergezicht, gestoffeerd met een wandelende Heer en Dame, gaande en rustende Huislieden, Schuiten en andere voorwerpen. Bevallig en fiks behandeld | *Mat:* op doek *Size:* hoog 27, breed 34 duim	Marten Udink	(Sold) fl 3:10 Spaan
1809/04/17	AMSCH	0062	*P. Molijn* | Een duinachtig Landschap, met Boeren Wooningen en Geboomten, gestoffeerd met rustende Landlieden en Vee; natuurlijk behandeld | *Mat:* op paneel	Y	(Sold or Bought In) fl 6
1809/04/17	AMSCH	0062a[H]	*P. Molijn* | 2 dito [Landschappen] | *Notes:* This lot was added in by hand in the EBNP copy of the catalogue.		(Sold) fl 7:15 Dupre [?]
1809/04/17	AMSCH	0063	*P. Molijn* | Een Land- en Watergezicht, ter zijde een Molen, bij eenige Wooningen, verder natuurlijk gestoffeerd | *Mat:* op paneel *Size:* hoog 19, breed 30 duim	R	(Sold) fl 5:5
1809/07/25	HGBSM	0065	*P. Molyn* | Een boomryk Landschap, met Figuuren gestoffeert | *Mat:* op paneel *Size:* hoog 11 en 1 half, breed 18 duim	D van der Aa	(Sold) fl 6:5 van der Aa [or] Mes

1809/07/25	HGBSM	0066	*P. Molyn* | Een dito [boomryk Landschap] | *Mat:* op paneel *Size:* hoog 13 en 1 half, breed 18 duim	D van der Aa	(Sold) fl 4:15 van der Aa [or] Mes
1809/07/25	HGBSM	0148	*P. Molyn* | Een Land- en Watergezigt, gestoffeert met een Pont en Koebeesten en Figuuren | *Mat:* op paneel *Size:* hoog 12, breed 15 en een half duim	D van der Aa	(Sold) fl 1:12 van der Aa
1809/07/25	HGBSM	0163	*P. Molyn* | Een Vogelmarkt in een Dorp | *Mat:* op paneel *Fmt:* rond *Size:* groot 6 duim in diameter	D van der Aa [or] E B ten Dall	(Sold) fl 12:5 A Taixeira
1809/07/25	HGBSM	0221	*P. Molyn* | Een Gezigt van Schevening, van 't Duin langs het Strand te zien, goed geschildert, door P. Molyn, 1663 | *Mat:* op paneel *Size:* hoog 18 en een half, breed 25 duim *Inscr:* P. Molyn, 1663 (signed and dated?) *Notes:* It is unclear whether the name and date are inscribed on the painting.	D van der Aa [or] E B ten Dall	(Sold) fl 1:18 Heymans [for] G
1810/03/07	UTWLD	0025	*Dumolyn* | Een Landschap	J J Woertman	(Unknown) fl 11
1810/03/27	RMCNL	0072	*Moulin* | Twee Stuks Landschappen, fix geschilderd | *This Lot:* Stuk Landschappen *Notes:* Lots 72 and 73 were printed in the catalogue as one item.		(Unknown)
1810/03/27	RMCNL	0073	*Molijn* | Twee Stuks Landschappen, fix geschilderd | *This Lot:* Stuk Landschappen *Notes:* Lots 72 and 73 were printed in the catalogue as one item.		(Unknown)
1810/03/27	RMCNL	0089	*Moulin* | Een Landschap, zeer aardig behandeld		(Unknown)
1810/03/27	RMCNL	0102	*Molijn* | Een Boschachtig Landschap		(Unknown)
1810/06/04	DOBRA	0023	*Moulin* | Een Strandgezicht, vol gewoel	Hendrik de Haas	(Unknown)
1810/06/20	AMSCH	0061	*P. Molijn* | Twee stuks; het eene verbeeldt een heuvelachtig Landschap, gestoffeerd met eenige Postwagens voor eene Herberg, en gaande Reizigers; het andere een bevallig Land- en Watergezigt, met Visschers en Huislieden. Zeer zonachtig en natuurlijk geschilderd | *Mat:* op paneel *Size:* Jeder hoog 17, breed 23 duimen	B	(Sold) fl 20:10 Reijers
1810/06/20	AMSCH	0062	*P. Molijn* | Een natuurlijk Land- en Watergezigt, eigenaartig gestoffeerd. Zonachtig en fiks behandeld | *Mat:* op paneel *Size:* hoog 18, breed 24 duimen	B	(Sold) fl 2:10 T Spaan
1810/07/23	DOLG1	0037	*P. Molijn* | Een Bergächtig en Boomrijk Landschap | *Mat:* op paneel *Size:* hoog 13, breed 22 duim	Mr Pieter van den Santheuvel	(Sold) fl 11 P de Heere à Dordt
1810/07/23	DOLG2	0083	*Molijn* | Een Land- en Watergezicht, gestoffeerd met Schuiten en Beeldtjes | *Mat:* op paneel *Size:* hoog 11, breed 15 duim	Pieter Quinting	(Sold) fl 5 Bogaard
1810/07/23	DOLG2	0092	*Molijn* | Een Landschap	Pieter Quinting	(Sold) fl 1:10 A van Strij [or] Visser
1810/10/10	MGCIT	0146	*Molijn* | Twee Stukken, verbeeldende Landschappen, rijk van Geboomte en andere Voorwerpen; zeer uitvoerig en goed behandeld	Caspar van Citters	(Unknown)
1810/10/11	AMSCH	0055	*P. Molyn* | Een aangenaam Duinachtig Landschap, met Boeren-Woningen en Geboomte, gestoffeerd met twee beladen Wagens voor eene Herberg, verder rustende Reizigers en een ruim verschiet; natuurlijk behandeld | *Mat:* op paneel *Size:* hoog 14, breed 19 duimen	[Levy Pakker?]	(Sold) fl 6:5 Vallée
1810/12/03	DOBRA	0043	*Moulin* | Een Strand-Gezicht, vol gewoel		(Unknown)
			Molijn, Pieter de (or Molijn, manner)		
1802/11/01	DOBRA	0113	*Molyn* | Een Landschap, door of in de manier van Molyn | *Mat:* op paneel *Size:* h. 14. breed 22 ½ duim	Paulus van der Spyk [or others]	(Unknown)
			Molijn, Pieter de (manner)		
1810/06/20	AMSCH	0138	*P. Molijn* | Een Landschap met stoffage, als P. Molijn	S	(Sold) fl 0:6 L Pakker
			Molyn, C. [Unidentified]		
1802/11/01	DOBRA	0105	*C. Molyn* | Een Bergagtig Landschap gemerkt C. Molyn | *Mat:* op doek *Inscr:* C. Molyn (signed)	Paulus van der Spyk [or others]	(Unknown)
			Momas, G.F. [Unidentified]		
1801/03/16	AMSCH	0118	*G.F. Momas* | In een Binnenvertrek voor een tafel, gedeeltelyk met een tapytkleed bedekt, staat een oude Philosooph, als mediteerend, beschouwende verscheide Antique Beeldwerken, op de voorgrond een Jongeling als op de Globe studeerende, terzyde een andere Jongeling, bezig te boetzeeren, op de grond leggen verscheide Kunstwerke en Gereedschappen, in 't verschiet Huislieden by een tafel, meesterlyk en uitvoerig op doek gepenceeld | *Mat:* op doek	K[ip]	(Sold) fl 20:10 Carli
			Mommers, C. [Unidentified]		
1801/12/22	AMOTT	0067	*C. Mommers* | 1 Binnekerk en Choor met een Verschiet	Bartholomeus Ruloffs	(Unknown) fl 8
			Mommers, Hendrik		
1801/03/16	AMSCH	0042	*Mommers* | Een Markt met aanzienlyke Gebouwen, op de voorgrond Kooplieden met belaaden Muyl-Ezels, fiks geschilderd	P[ruyssenaar]	(Sold) fl 49 Coclers
1801/03/16	AMSCH	0196	*Mommers* | Een Italiaansch Marktgezicht, gestoffeert met verscheide Lieden met Koopwaren, fiks geschilderd op doek | *Mat:* op doek	K[ip]	(Sold) fl 9 Wijland

1801/03/16	AMSCH	0197	*Mommers* | Een dito [Italiaansch Marktgezicht] verschillende van Ordonantie, zonagtig en meesterlyk behandeld	K[ip]	(Sold) fl 14:10 Cocler
1801/04/08	HAVIN	0023	*Mommers* | Twee Italiaansche Groenmarkten		(Unknown)
1801/04/08	HAVIN	0032	*Mommers* | Een Italiaansche Groenmarkt		(Unknown)
1801/06/13	LNDLS	0023	*H. Mommers* | Een kapitaal Landschap, met beelden en beesten, konstig op doek geschilderd | *Mat:* op doek *Size:* hoog 38, breed 50 duimen	D van R	(Sold) fl 125 Spaan
1801/11/10	AMPOS	0030	*Mommers* | 1 bevallig Mysje by een beladen Ezel, in 't verschiet een Herder met Schaapen		(Unknown)
1802/05/05	AMSCH	0146	*Mommers* | Een Italiaansche Markt met prachtige Gebouwen, ryk gestoffeert met een menigte Beelden, kragtig gepenceeld | *Size:* hoog 43, breed 65 duim	J	(Sold) fl 6:10 Hulswit
1802/05/11	GRGRW	0009	*Mommers* | Het Stadhuis, de Waag en N. Kerk van Amsterdam [Schilderijen met Olie-Verf; In zwarte Lijsten] | *Mat:* in olyverf *Notes:* The bracketed information in the title appears above lot 1 and refers to lots 1 to 79a.	Arnold Sicco Werumeus	(Unknown)
1802/05/11	GRGRW	0023	*Mommers* | Ene Herderin met Schapen en Beesten [Schilderijen met Olie-Verf; In zwarte Lijsten] | *Mat:* in olyverf *Notes:* The bracketed information in the title appears above lot 1 and refers to lots 1 to 79a.	Arnold Sicco Werumeus	(Unknown)
1802/07/27	AKHRK	0029	*Jacobus Mommers* | Een Italiaansche Markt, rijk gestoffeerd met menigte van Beelden, eetbaare waaren, Pluim en andere Gediertens, beladen Muilezels; als ook een Vragtwagen, met Ossen bespannen, en superbe gebouwen, en Fonteinwerk. Zeer bevallig geördonneerd en geschilderd | *Mat:* op doek *Size:* hoog 38, breed 50 duim *Notes:* The artist's name was given as "Jacobus Mommers" but we have assumed this is an error.	Maria Stategaart	(Sold) fl 32 V Iperen
1802/09/06	AMSCH	0225	*Mommers* | Een Italiaansche Markt, ryk gestoffeerd	J	(Sold) fl 2:5 A Vermeulen
1802/09/21	UTHDG	0060	*Mommers* | In een Landschap met Schapen, schijnt een Herder zijne Minnares te ontmoeten. zij omhelzen elkanderen, verder rustende Landlieden enz. Fiks geschildert, gemerkt Mommers | *Mat:* op paneel *Size:* hoog 20 ½, breed 27 ½ duimen *Inscr:* Mommers (signed)		(Bought In) fl 29
1802/09/21	UTHDG	0061	*Mommers* | Een Bergagtig Landschap met Ruine, Reizigers en Marktgangers gestoffeerd. Goed van licht, gem. als de voorgaande [Mommers] | *Mat:* op doek *Size:* hoog 31, breed 34 duimen *Inscr:* Mommers (signed)		(Bought In) fl 6
1802/12/13	AMSCH	0120	*Mommers* | Een Italiaansch Landschap, ryk gestoffeert, met Menschen en Beesten, en kloek gepenceeld | *Mat:* op doek *Size:* hoog 18, breed 27 duim	Pruyssenaar [for] A	(Sold) fl 1:15 Gruiter
1802/12/13	AMSCH	0121	*Mommers* | Een Markt, met Beelden gestoffeert	Pruyssenaar [for] B	(Sold) fl 5:15 Gruiter
1803/12/12	AMSCH	0065	*J. Mommers* | Een capitaale Italiaansche Mark, ryk gestoffeerd met een ménigte van Beelden, Eetbaaren Waaren. Pluim en andere Gediertens, beladen Muil-Ezels, Vragtkarren, met Ossen bespannen, capitaale Gebouwen, Fontein werken, en andere Ciraden; meesteragtig en bevallig van licht | *Mat:* op doek *Size:* hoog 38, breed 50 duim *Notes:* The artist's name was given as "J. Mommers" but we have assumed this is an error.	B	(Sold) fl 40 Theens
1803/12/12	AMSCH	0066	*J. Mommers* | Twee stuks, verbeeldende het eene een Romeinsche Groenmarkt, en het andere een Landschap, met Ryzigers, Ezels, Bokken en Schapen; helder en plaisant | *Size:* hoog 25, breed 33 duim *Notes:* The artist's name was given as "J. Mommers" but we have assumed this is an error.	H	(Sold) fl 57 Theengs
1803/12/12	AMSCH	0067	*J. Mommers* | Een Romeinsche Stad aan een Rivier, de voorgrond gestoffeerd met Beelden en Schapen, fix op Doek | *Mat:* op doek *Size:* hoog 25, breed 32 duim *Notes:* The artist's name was given as "J. Mommers" but we have assumed this is an error.	E	(Sold) fl 8:10 Th^{S} Spaan
1804/02/27	AMSCH	0074	*Mommers (J.)* | Een capitaale Italiaansche Mark, ryk gestoffeerd met een menigte van Beelden, Eetbaren waren, Pluim en anderen Gediertens, Muilezels, Vragtkarren, met Ossen bespannen, schoone Gebouwen, Fontynwerken, en andere cieraaden, meesterlyk en bevallig van licht | *Mat:* op doek *Size:* hoog 38, breed 50 duim *Notes:* The artist's name was given as "Mommers (J.)" but we have assumed this is an error.	C	(Bought In) fl 30
1804/02/27	AMSCH	0074a[H]	*Mommers (J.)* | Een dito [capitaale Italiaansche Mark] | *Notes:* This lot was added in by hand in the FLNY and RKDH copies of the catalogue. The artist's name was given as "Mommers (J.)" but we have assumed this is an error.	C	(Sold) fl 18:10 Theengs
1804/02/27	AMSCH	0075	*Mommers (J.)* | Twee stuks verbeeldende het eene een Groenmarkt, en 't andere een Landschap, byde ryk gestoffeerd met Ryzigers en differente zoorten van Vee; niet minder dan de voorgaande | *Size:* hoog 25, breed 33 duim *Notes:* The artist's name was given as "Mommers (J.)" but we have assumed this is an error.	C	(Sold) fl 5:5 Gruyter
1804/05/07	AMSCH	0104	*Mommers. (J.)* | Een capitalen Italiaansche Mark, ryk gestoffeerd met een ménigte van Eetbaarenwaaren, Beelden een Ezel, verders eenige prachtige Gebouwen en Ruïnen en andere cieraaden; bevallig van licht en meesterlyk geschilderd | *Mat:* op doek *Size:* hoog 32, breed 41 duim	Vinkeles [for] G	(Sold) fl 15 Pruissenaar

			Notes: The artist's name was given as "Mommers. (J.)" but we have assumed this is an error.		
1804/05/07	AMSCH	0105	*Mommers. (J.)* | Twee stuks Heuvelachtige Landgezichten, met met [sic] Geboomte en Woningen, geatoffeerd met vrolyke Huislieden en andere Werkende, verzeld van verschillende zoorten van Vee, plaisant geschilderd | *Mat:* op doek *Size:* hoog 19, breed 25 duim *Notes:* The artist's name was given as "Mommers. (J.)" but we have assumed this is an error.	Schley	(Bought In) fl 16
1804/08/08	AMSCH	0132	*Mommers* | In een Heuvelachtig Landschap ziet men op de voorgrond, by een Boerenschuur en eenig Geboomte, twee Boerinnen, waarnévens een ménigte van staand en rustend Vée, in het verschiet eenige Boerenwoningen en een Rivier; zonachtig en uitvoerig gepenceeld | *Mat:* op paneel *Size:* hoog 19, breed 28 duimen	Vink[eles] [for] S	(Sold) fl 42 Toselli
1804/08/08	AMSCH	0133	*Mommers* | In een Italiaansch Landschap ziet men by eenige Ruïnen en Groenvrouw, welke eenige Groentens aan een andere verkoopt, waar névens eenige andere Lieden en een belaaden Ezel; breed en zonachtig gepenceeld | *Mat:* op paneel *Size:* hoog 24, breed 31 duim	Vink[eles] [for] S	(Sold) fl 5 van Iperen
1804/08/08	AMSCH	0134	*Mommers* | Twee stuks capitaale Italiaansche Landschappen, beiden ryk gestofferd met prachtige Gebouwen en een ménigte van Beelden en Beesten; bevallig van licht en meesterlyk gepenceeld | *Mat:* op doek *Size:* hoog 25, breed 33 duim	Vink[eles] [for] K[=Gruyter?]	(Sold) fl 7 Texier
1804/08/08	AMSCH	0135	*Mommers* | Twee stuks, het ééne een Groenmarkt, en het andere een Vrouw op een Ezel | *Mat:* op doek *Size:* hoog 26, breed 24 ½ duim	Pruys[senaar]	(Bought In) fl 25
1804/10/16	DLOND	0152	*H. Mommers* | Enige Mannen en Vrouwen die Wild verkopen. Quelques Vendeurs de Gibier | *Mat:* op doek *Size:* hoog 24, breed 32		(Unknown) fl 23
1804/10/29	HRBAU	0064	*Mommers* | Een Italiaansche Groenmarkt, ryk gestofferd met Menschen, Groenten en Vee; welk alles zeer wel behandeld is | *Mat:* op doek *Size:* hoog 25, breed 36 duim	Simon Styl	(Unknown)
1804/10/29	HRBAU	0065	*Mommers* | Een Italiaansch Landschap, met Ruïnen: by dezelven zit een Herderin, en meer anderen, eene Kudde te hoeden; en een aardig verschiet | *Mat:* op doek *Size:* hoog 25, breed 36 duim	Simon Styl	(Unknown)
1804/12/10	AMSCH	0057	*J. Mommers* | Een Italiaansche Groenmarkt, gestofferd met diverse kooplieden, in 't verschiet de Ruine van een gebouw; krachtig en fix gepenceeld | *Mat:* op doek *Size:* Hoog 22, breed 18 duim *Notes:* The artist's name was given as "J. Mommers" but we have assumed this is an error.	Jan De Groot	(Sold) fl 2:10 Levie Pakker
1805/07/10	AMSCH	0104	*Mommers* | Een Italiaansche Groenmarkt, met een ménigte Beelden, Ezels enz; breed en meesterlyk | *Mat:* op doek *Size:* hoog 32, breed 38 duim	V[inkeles] [for] M	(Sold) fl 34 L Pakker
1805/10/21	GRBOL	0013	*Mommers* | Een Romeinsche Markt | companion to lot 14	Gerardus Nicolaus Heerkens	(Unknown)
1805/10/21	GRBOL	0014	*Mommers* | Een dito [Romeinsche Markt], door dito [Mommers], tot een Weêrga | companion to lot 13	Gerardus Nicolaus Heerkens	(Unknown)
1805/10/21	GRBOL	0017	*Mommers* | Een Vrouwtje, dat Groenten Verkoopt	Gerardus Nicolaus Heerkens	(Unknown)
1805/10/21	GRBOL	0029	*Mommers* | Een Landschap met Beelden en Beestjes	Gerardus Nicolaus Heerkens	(Unknown)
1805/10/21	GRBOL	0034	*Mommers* | Een Landschap met Beelden en Beestjes	Gerardus Nicolaus Heerkens	(Unknown)
1805/10/21	GRBOL	0036	*Mommers* | Een Gezelschap van de Jagt komende, in een schoon Landschap	Gerardus Nicolaus Heerkens	(Unknown)
1806/05/05	AMSCH	0088	*Mommers* | Een Italiaansche Markt, gestoffeert met een ménigte van eetbaaren Waaren, Beelden en Beesten, verders pragtige Gebouwen; meesterlyk geschildert door Mommers | *Mat:* op doek *Size:* hoog 32, breed 41 duim	V[inkeles]	(Bought In) fl 15
1806/05/05	AMSCH	0089	*Mommers* | Voor een Italiaans Gebouw zit een Musikant te speelen, waar voor eenige vrolyke Landlieden dansen; konstig verbeeld in de manier van du Jardyn	V[inkeles]	(Sold) fl 2 Hulswit
1806/08/13	AMSCH	0131	*Mommers. (H.)* | Een Italiaansche Groenmarkt, met Groenteverkoopsters, Ezel en verder bywerk en een bevallig Duinryk Landschap | *Mat:* op doek *Size:* hoog 27, breed 24 duim	Vinkeles [for] F	(Sold) fl 31 Thais
1808/03/03	HAVIN	0015	*Mommers* | Twee Italiaansche Groenmarkten	Jacobus Spillebout	(Unknown) fl 7
1808/06/13	AMSCH	0108	*Mommers (H.)* | Een kapitaal Marktgezicht te Rome, verbeeldende een Groen- en Beestenmarkt, op den voorgrond eene Dame, verzeld van een Dienstmeisje, schijnende iets te koopen van eene Landvrouw met jong Vee; achter dezelve vertoont zich een treffelijk Gebouw, met Steenen Trappen opgaande, waarop eene zittende Vrouw met Koopgoederen, ter zijde Marktlieden en beladen Ezels; verder een Fontijn met een Gedenkzuil en andere Gebouwen, bij Gebergten, en met verscheide Beeldjes gestoffeerd. Meesterlijk gepenceeld | *Mat:* op doek *Size:* hoog 47, breed 67 duim	Z	(Sold) fl 32 J^{n} Spaan
1808/06/13	AMSCH	0108a[H]	*Mommers (H.)* | 1 Landscap | *Notes:* This lot was added in by hand in the AA I, EBNP, FLNY and RKDH copies of the catalogue.	Z	(Sold) fl 81 van Iperen

<table>
<tr><td>1808/11/28</td><td>AMSCH</td><td>0077</td><td>*J. Mommers* | Een Landschap, met stoffage van Beelden en Beesten | *Notes:* The artist's name was given as "J. Mommers" but we have assumed this is an error.</td><td>[Gruyter?]</td><td>(Sold) fl 1 L Pakker</td></tr>
<tr><td>1810/10/11</td><td>AMSCH</td><td>0056</td><td>*J. Mommers* | Een groote Markt, met Gebouwen, Fonteinen, en Gedenkzuilen, gestoffeerd met Kooplieden, Vragtwagens, Muil-Ezels, enz., goed geschilderd | *Mat:* op doek *Size:* hoog 38, breed 50 duimen *Notes:* The artist's name was given as "J. Mommers" but we have assumed this is an error.</td><td>[Gruyter?]</td><td>(Bought In) fl 9</td></tr>
<tr><td>1810/10/11</td><td>AMSCH</td><td>0154</td><td>*Mommers* | Twee Landschappen, met dito [stoffagie]</td><td>S</td><td>(Sold) fl 5:5 Gruiter</td></tr>
<tr><td colspan="6">**Mommers, Hendrik (copy after)**</td></tr>
<tr><td>1802/08/24</td><td>LNDLS</td><td>0139</td><td>*H. Mommers* | Een Landschap met Mannen, Vrouwen en Beesten die door 't Water gaan na H. Mommers</td><td>Leonardus Bouman [or others]</td><td>(Unknown) fl 3:12</td></tr>
<tr><td colspan="6">**Mommers, Hendrik (manner)**</td></tr>
<tr><td>1801/03/16</td><td>AMSCH</td><td>0137</td><td>*Mommers* | Een Landschap met Beelden en Beesten, als Mommers</td><td>K[ip]</td><td>(Sold) fl 1 Wijland</td></tr>
<tr><td>1802/09/06</td><td>AMSCH</td><td>0251</td><td>*Mommers* | Twee stuks ryk met beelden gestoffeerde Italiaansche Zéehavens; op Doek als Mommers | *Mat:* op doek</td><td>Mevrouw Achtienhoven</td><td>(Sold) fl 6:15 T van Iperen</td></tr>
<tr><td colspan="6">**Momper, Joos de (II)**</td></tr>
<tr><td>1801/03/16</td><td>AMSCH</td><td>0176</td><td>*Momper* | Een dito [Wintergezicht] | *Notes:* This lot was sold with lot 175 by Pieter Santvoort.</td><td>P[ruyssenaar]</td><td>(Sold) fl 1 for lots 175 & 176. Gruiter</td></tr>
<tr><td>1802/09/06</td><td>AMSCH</td><td>0082</td><td>*J. Momper* | Een gestoffeerd bergagtig Landschap | *Mat:* op koper</td><td>B</td><td>(Sold) fl 1:15 Boelen</td></tr>
<tr><td>1802/09/06</td><td>AMSCH</td><td>0216</td><td>*J. Momper* | Twee stuks Brabandsche ryk gestoffeerde Landschappen</td><td>Mevrouw Achtienhoven</td><td>(Sold) fl 2:10 Gruiter</td></tr>
<tr><td>1802/12/13</td><td>AMSCH</td><td>0126</td><td>*J. Momper* | Een capitaal ryk gestoffeerd Landschap | *Mat:* op paneel *Size:* hoog 24, breed 31 duim</td><td>Pruyssenaar [for] A</td><td>(Sold) fl 0:12 Gruiter</td></tr>
<tr><td>1803/09/07</td><td>AMSCH</td><td>0106</td><td>*J. Momper* | Een capitaal Boomryk en Bergachtig Landschap met een Rievier doorsneeden, op de voorgrond, gestoffeerd met de Dooping van Christus, verzelt van twee Engelen. om hoog vertoont zig de Godheid, zonachtig en bevallig gepenceeld [Tableau capital, représentant un paysage, montueux et riche, il est entrecoupé d'une rivière ; sur le devant le baptème de Jésus-Christ, accompagné de deux anges et surmonté de la divinité qui apparoît au ciel. Il règne dans ce tableau un très beau serein, et toute l'exécution en est agréable] | *Mat:* op paneel *Size:* hoog 29, breed 32 duim</td><td>Smidt</td><td>(Sold) fl 5 de Lafontaine</td></tr>
<tr><td>1804/08/08</td><td>AMSCH</td><td>0136</td><td>*J. Momper* | Een ryk gestoffeerd Brabandsch Landschap; meesterlyk geschilderd | *Mat:* op paneel *Size:* hoog 28, breed 31 duim</td><td>Vink[eles] [for] K[=Gruyter?]</td><td>(Sold) fl 1:15 Toselli</td></tr>
<tr><td>1806/05/05</td><td>AMSCH</td><td>0099</td><td>*Momper* | Een berg en boomryk Landschap met prachtige Gebouwen, stoffagie van Beeldjes enz.; meesteriyk op Paneel | *Mat:* op paneel *Size:* hoog 20, breed 18 duim</td><td>V[inkeles]</td><td>(Sold) fl 2:5 A Reynders</td></tr>
<tr><td>1808/11/28</td><td>AMSCH</td><td>0105</td><td>*J. Momper* | Een Brabandsch Dorpgezicht, ter zijde een bevrozen Rivier, gestoffeerd met Schaatsenrijders en andere Figuuren, natuurlijk behandeld | *Mat:* op paneel</td><td>H</td><td>(Sold) fl 1 T Spaan</td></tr>
<tr><td>1810/08/06</td><td>AMSCH</td><td>0075</td><td>*Momper (J.)* | Twee stuks Brabandsche Landschappen met Lieden te Paard, Reizigers en andere stoffagie, kloek geschilderd | *Mat:* op paneel *Size:* ieder hoog 9, breed 14 duimen</td><td>C</td><td>(Sold) fl 4:10 Stoopendaal [for] B</td></tr>
<tr><td colspan="6">**Momper, Joos de (II) (and Brueghel, J. (I))**</td></tr>
<tr><td>1804/08/02</td><td>BDAN</td><td>0018</td><td>*J. Momper; Breughel* | Twee bergachtige Landschappen, vol gewoel, van de besten door deezen Meester gemaakt | *Mat:* op paneel *Size:* b. 24 en een half d. h. 17 d.</td><td>J G Calckberner</td><td>(Unknown)</td></tr>
<tr><td>1804/08/02</td><td>BDAN</td><td>0038</td><td>*Momper; Breugel* | Een schoon bergachtig Landschap, rykelyk gestoffeert | *Mat:* op paneel *Size:* b. 25 d. h. 17 en een half d.</td><td>J G Calckberner</td><td>(Unknown)</td></tr>
<tr><td>1805/07/10</td><td>AMSCH</td><td>0011</td><td>*Breugel; Momper* | Een besneeuwd Brabandsch Dorpgezicht, ryk gestoffeerd met Wagens, Paarden en Beelden; natuurlyk en fiks | *Size:* hoog 18, breed 29 duim</td><td>V[inkeles] [for] M</td><td>(Sold) fl 14 Lafontaine</td></tr>
<tr><td>1805/10/09</td><td>HGBSM</td><td>0092</td><td>*Momper; J. Breugel* | Een landschap door Momper, gestoffeerd, door J. Breugel | *Mat:* op paneel *Size:* hoog 18 breet 27 duim</td><td>T H van Willigen [or others]</td><td>(Sold) fl 3:8 Carré</td></tr>
<tr><td>1807/04/00</td><td>LNDLS</td><td>0028</td><td>*Momper; Breugel* | Een helder bergagtig Landschap met geboomte, ter regterzijde jagerspaarden, eu [sic] jagthonden, gevolgd van andere lieden, en beladen ezels, en heeren te paard | *Mat:* op paneel *Size:* hoog 30, breed 42 duim</td><td>[Abraham Delfos] [or others]</td><td>(Unknown)</td></tr>
<tr><td>1807/06/10</td><td>HGBSM</td><td>0028</td><td>*Momper; Breugel* | Een helder bergagtig Landschap met geboomte ter regterzijde jagerspaarden, en jagthonden, gevolgd van andere lieden, en beladen ezels en heeren te paard | *Mat:* op paneel *Size:* hoog 30, breed 42 duim</td><td>Abraham Delfos [or others]</td><td>(Sold) fl 2 de Gelder</td></tr>
<tr><td>1807/08/26</td><td>AMSCH</td><td>0128</td><td>*Momper; Breugel* | Twee stuks, verbeeldende Zomer en Winter. Den eene vertoont een Brabandsch Landschap, met Geboomte, op den voorgrond rydende Postwagens en vrolyke Huislieden, verders Graanlanden en een aangenaam verschiet. De wederga verbeeld een heuvelachtig Landgezigt, met besneeuwde Daken en Wegen, by dor en ander Geboomte; gestoffeerd met wandelende en rustende Lieden, op de bevrozen Rivier</td><td>v d Schley [for] L</td><td>(Sold) fl 7:5 du Pree</td></tr>
</table>

			verscheiden Schaatsenryders, in het verschiet en Stadzigt beide natuurlyk, en uitvoerig van penceelsbehandeling | *Mat:* op paneel *Size:* ieder hoog 9 ½, breed 13 ½ duim		
1808/08/23	AMSCH	0196	*Momper; Breägel* | Een natuurlijk Wintergezicht, met stoffagie van Beeldjes	[Gruyter?]	(Sold) fl 3 L Pakker
1809/06/13	AMSCH	0216	*Momper; Breugel* | Een Wintergezigt met Schaatserijders gestoffeerd, door Momper en Breugel	E	(Sold) fl 0:6 L Pakker

Momper, Joos de (II) (manner)

1801/08/19	AMSCH	0065	*Momper* | Een Bergachtig en Boomryk Zwitzers Landschap, gestoffeert met de Historieele Geschiedenis van William Tell, kragtig en teffens uitvoerig op paneel behandeld, in de manier van Momper | *Mat:* op paneel *Size:* hoog 29, breed 41 duim	F [through] van der Schly	(Withdrawn)

Monbellian [Unidentified]

1803/04/27	AMSCH	0037	*Monbellian* | Deux petits Tableaux ovales | *Fmt:* ovale	A	(Sold) fl 5:5 Stevens

Moni, Louis de

1801/10/19	AMSCH	0044	*Monie. (Louis de)* | Een oud Vrouwtje dat zit te haspelen, spreekende met een jong meisje die een mand met brood heeft in een Nis; zeer uitvoerig geschildert | *Mat:* op paneel *Size:* hoog 15, breed 12 duim	Jonkheer Menno Baron van Coehoorn	(Sold) fl 150 C S Roos
1801/10/19	AMSCH	0045	*Monie. (Louis de)* | Een Vrouw in nachtgewaad zittende en een kind de Borst geevende; aan de rechterzyde staat een wieg en ter linkerzyde een stoel, waar op een Tinne Waterpot; zeer schoon van schildering en uitvoerig behandeld | companion to lot 46 *Mat:* op paneel *Size:* hoog 12 ¼, breed 10 ¼ duim	Jonkheer Menno Baron van Coehoorn	(Sold) fl 46 Frantzen
1801/10/19	AMSCH	0046	*Monie. (Louis de)* | Een dito [Vrouw] tot weederga: een Binnekamer, waar in zich vertoond een bevallig Juffertje, zittende by een Tafel, bedekt met een Tapyt, waar op een Inktkoker, een Speldebakje en een geschreeven brief legt. In de hand houd zy een Pen, en in de andere een Brief: verders ziet men een knegt ten voeten uit, met een brandende kaars in de hand, en achter de Juffer een opgehaald Gordyn: In dit stukje zyn de twee Lichten van dag en kaars; zeer uitvoerig en konstig behandeld; en af komstig uit het Kabinet van wylen de Heer van der Mark | companion to lot 45 *Mat:* op paneel *Size:* hoog 13 ¼, breed 11 duim	Jonkheer Menno Baron van Coehoorn	(Sold) fl 40 van der Schley [for] B[=Putte]
1802/05/10	MGSAN	0036	*Mony* | Een zeer fraai Stukje, vertoonende een Man, met een oud Vrouwtje, houdende in haar hand een zoute Scholletje, voor hun een Bierkan, met een Glas, in een Nis, door Mony: op Paneel, in vergulde Lyst | *Mat:* op paneel *Size:* hoog 9 duim, breed 6 duim	Johan Dirk Kruysse	(Sold) £ 3:5 G Petersen
1802/06/16	AMSCH	0107	*L. de Moni* | Voor een open Steene Nis, vertoont zig een Vischboer, houdende een Roch in de handen, voor hem staat een Mand met verscheiden zoorten van Vissen; en een Bennetje met dito; alles natuurlyk, en zeer uitvoerig gepenceeld | *Mat:* op paneel *Size:* hoog 12 ½, breed 13 ½ duim	[Merrem]	(Sold) fl 43 v d Schley [for] R[ijfsnijder]
1802/06/16	AMSCH	0108	*L. de Moni* | Een Keukenmeisje voor een Steene Nis, in Oude Hollandsche Kleeding, zy schynt het Water uit een kopere Kookkeetel te gieten; op de rand der Nist [sic] legt Schuimspaan en Leepels, gestoffeerd met verder bywerk; meesterlyk fiks behandeld | *Mat:* op paneel *Size:* hoog 11, breed 8 ½ duim	[Merrem]	(Sold) fl 32 B^{d} Kooij
1802/06/28	AMSCH	0112	*L. de Monni* | Een Keuken, waarin een Meid die een Ketel schuurt, wordende door een oud Man gecarresseert; wyders onderscheide Bywerk | *Size:* hoog 21, breed 18 duim	Anna Elink	(Sold) fl 10 Geld
1802/08/24	LNDLS	0031	*L. de Moni* | Door een Nis ziet men een Jongetje, die een Mossen-pot in zijne eene en een Vogel in zijne andere hand heeft, benevens een Meisje met een Kat onder haar arm, agter haar een lagchende Jongeling die een Beurs houdt. Delicaat van schildering | *Mat:* op paneel *Size:* hoog 13, breed 10 ½ duimen	Leonardus Bouman [or others]	(Unknown) fl 18
1802/08/24	LNDLS	0070	*L. de Moni* | Een Juffer in 't wit satijn gekleed, staande voor een Tafel daar een Tapijt op ligt, met een spiegel en zilveren doos, terwijl een Dienstmaagd (zijnde een Moorin,) met een Lampet, Schotel en Kan aankomt, in een Binnen-vertrek. In de trant van Terburgh, door L. de Moni, delicaat op paneel | *Mat:* op paneel *Size:* hoog 15, breed 12 duimen	Leonardus Bouman [or others]	(Unknown) fl 47
1802/09/21	UTHDG	0058	*L. de Moni* | Een Teekenaar of Liefhebber bij zijne Konstboeken en Beeldwerk bezig, onsteekt zijn tabakspijp aan de Kaars, door welke dit uitvoerig en kragtig stukje fraaij verlicht wordt | *Mat:* op paneel *Size:* hoog 10, breed ½ duimen		(Sold) fl 43 Verhoude
1803/07/18	AMSCH	0033	*Moni. (L. de)* | In een Burgerkamer staat een Vrouw aan een Ton beezig Visch schoon te maaken, een Jongetje ter zyde haar wyst naar de Hond en de Kat, die in een vegtende houding zich vertoonen, een doode Haas en een menigte ander bywerk, maaken dit stukje van een schoonheid zoo als men weinig van deeze Meester ziet [Une femme occupée à depècer du poisson sur un tonneau, est distraite par un Jeune Garçon qui lui montre la querelle entre le chat & le chien pour obtenir la dépouille. Un cocq mort & un Panier sont à droite, & vèrs la gauche au devant est un Pot & des ustenciles de Mènage : la demeure est meublé avec d'autres objects	Maria Theresia Andrioli	(Sold) fl 124 C S Roos

			propres au lieu, qui se termine vèrs un Escalier courbé. Cette Representation éclairée par une fenêtre ouverte produit le plus charment [sic] effet de lumiere, elle est d'un [sic] verité singuliere. Un faire lèger, delicat ! une couleur lumineuse, joints aux expressions bien rendues lui assureront les suffrages des Amateurs.] | *Mat:* op paneel *Size:* hoog 19, breed 15 duim		
1803/12/12	AMSCH	0152	*Monie* | Een Stal met Paarden | *Size:* hoog 7, breed 9 duim	D	(Sold) fl 12 Hijman Pakker
1804/04/28	LNDLS	0044	*L. de Moni* | Een Vrouw met een lachend Man, die een uil op een kruk in zijn hand houd, door L. de Moni, op paneel | *Mat:* op paneel *Size:* hoog 10, breed 12 duim	[Abraham Delfos] [or others]	(Bought In) fl 10
1804/07/25	AMSCH	0056	*Moni. (L. de)* | In dit bevallig stukje zit een Jong Meisje een Brief te lézen, welke haar door een Oude Matrone van haar Minnaar schynt gebragt te zyn, zy is gekleed in een geel Jakje; dit stukje kan voor een der beste van dezen Meester in de eerste Cabinetten geplaatst worden, als zynde van een keurige schildering | *Mat:* op paneel *Size:* hoog 13 ½, breed 10 duim		(Sold) fl 91 Thais
1804/08/08	AMSCH	0112	*L. de Moni* | Twee stuks, de ééne verbeeld een bevallige Dame, welke een Roosje voor een Meisje plukt; en de andere door een Nis een Dienstmaagd, bézig Huisraad te schuuren, achter haar een Jongen met een Korf Gevogelte enz.; heiden uitvoerig gepenceeld | *Mat:* op paneel *Size:* hoog 9 ½, breed 7 ½ duim	Vink[eles] [for] S	(Sold) fl 20:10 Gruyter
1804/08/08	AMSCH	0113	*L. de Moni* | Een Man met een Bonte Rok en Muts, houdende een Vuurpot in zyn Handen; zeer natuurlyk behandeld | *Mat:* op paneel *Size:* hoog 14, breed 13 duim	Roos a	(Sold) fl 8 Graffelman
1804/12/10	AMSCH	0058	*L. de Moni* | Deeze bevallige Ordinantie verbeeld voor een open steenen Nis, een Vogelverkoopster, als met een koopvrouw handelende, die met een kopere markt-emmer aan den arm voor de Nis geplaast is, ter zyde op een tafel legt verscheide dood wilt en gevogelte, om hoog hangt een mand, en ter zyde een aarde kan, verder ziet men in een ander vertrek; alles natuurlyk en meesterlyk gepenceelt | *Mat:* op paneel *Size:* Hoog 17, breed 14 duim	Jan De Groot	(Sold) fl 96 van Iperen
1804/12/10	AMSCH	0059	*L. de Moni* | Voor een Nis waar op een tapyt legt, ziet men een bevallige Dame, welke door een Doctor de pols gevoeld word, hy heeft in de rechterhand een Urinaal, waar in men een kindje ziet, agter haar een jongeling met een klisteerspuit in potsige houding; alles is geestig van ordinantie en uitvoerig geschilderd | *Mat:* op paneel *Size:* Hoog 13, breed 10 duim	Jan De Groot	(Sold) fl 95 Gruyter
1804/12/10	AMSCH	0060	*L. de Moni* | Een Dienstmeisje rustende met haar rechter arm op een kopere kétel, nevens haar hangt een Haas, verder onderscheide manden en andere keukengereegschap [sic]; alles breed behandeld | *Mat:* op paneel *Size:* Hoog 17, breed 13 duim	Jan De Groot	(Sold) fl 40 Coclers
1804/12/10	AMSCH	0061	*L. de Moni* | Voor eeu Nis ziet men een bevallig Mysje men een blikke Emmer, en een Jongeling met een korfje of het hoofd, byde gevuld met St. Nicolaasgoed, hy heeft in zyn linkerhand een schoen, en schynen byde zeer vergenoegd; alles natuurlyk en krachtig behandeld | *Mat:* op paneel *Size:* Hoog 13, breed 10 duim	Jan De Groot	(Sold) fl 61 van Iperen
1805/07/03	AMSCH	0112	*L. de Moni* | Voor een Buitenhuis zit een Vogelverkoopster, houdende een Haan in de hand, schynende tegen een andere Vrouw, met een markt-Emmer aan den arm, in verschil over de pryzen, verders gestoffeert met dood Wilt, en Gevogelten; dit stuk is bevallig van coloriet en uitvoerig gepenceeld | *Mat:* op paneel *Size:* hoog 16, breed 13 duim	R[oos]	(Sold) fl 86 Hulswit
1806/05/05	AMSCH	0085	*L. de Moni* | Een Dame aan haar Toilet zittende een brief te lezen, daar agter een Dienstmaagd met een Pourtrait van haar Minnaar in de hand; delicaat op Paneel | *Mat:* op paneel *Size:* hoog 11, breed 9 duim	H	(Sold) fl 20 Menzart
807/04/00	LNDLS	0050	*L. de Moni* | Een lagchend man, met een dito vrouw, houdende een wijl op een kruk	[Abraham Delfos] [or others]	(Unknown)
807/06/10	HGBSM	0050	*L. de Moni* | Een lagchend man, met een dito vrouw, houdende een uil op een kruk	Abraham Delfos [or others]	(Sold) fl 3:12 v Iperen
807/08/26	AMSCH	0124	*L. de Moni* | Dit bevallig Stukje verbeeld eene Koopvrouw, staande voor een Tafel, waarop een Mand met Fruit, eenige Koek, gedroogde Schollen en andere Koopwaren geplaatst zyn: zy schynt iets te verkoopen aan een Jongeling, die voor haar staat, en het in zyn Hoed ontvangt; verder een aangenaam verschiet van Geboomte en Woningen, zynde alles van een uitvoerige penceelsbehandeling | *Mat:* op paneel *Size:* hoog 13, breed 11 duim	Helsdinge	(Sold) fl 99 Jozi
807/08/26	AMSCH	0125	*L. de Moni* | In een Keukenvertrek zit een Landman, rustende met den Arm op een Mand, gevuld met dood Wild en Gevogelten, verder staat eene Vrouw, als met hem sprekende, by een Tafel, waarop een doode Haas legt, daar nevens staat een Koperen Marktemmer met Uijen; gestoffeerd met verder bywerk, natuurlyk op Paneel, en als de vorige uitvoerig gepenceeld | *Mat:* op paneel *Size:* hoog 13, breed 11 duim	Helsdinge	(Sold) fl 89 T Spaan
807/08/26	AMSCH	0126	*L. de Moni* | In een dito [Keuken] Vertrek vertoont zich eene Vrouw, staande voor een Tafel, by een openstaand Vengster, schynende bezig Wortelen te schrapen, een Huisman daar nevens staande, met een Bierkan in de hand, schynt haar vriendelyk aan te spreken; gestoffeerd met verder	Helsdinge	(Sold) fl 58:10 van Iperen

			bywerk, als Koperen Ketel, Aarden Pot en Tobben, in alles als de voorgaande uitvoerig behandeld | *Size:* hoog 14, breed 11 duim		
1807/08/26	AMSCH	0127	*L. de Moni* | In een dito [Keuken] Vertrek staat een Huisman, bezig Water in een Emmer te pompen, op een Vat legt een dooden Haan en een bos Wortelen, verder by een Tafel staat eene Vrouw een Tobben te schuuren; gestoffeerd met divers Huisraad, mede als de vorige uitvoerig gepenceeld | *Mat:* op paneel *Size:* hoog 14, breed 11 duim	Helsdinge	(Sold) fl 89 T Spaan
1807/08/26	AMSCH	0127a[H]	*L. de Moni* | 1 Schilderij | *Notes:* This lot was added in by hand in the EBNP, FLNY and RKDH copies of the catalogue.	Yver [for] S	(Bought In) fl 36
1808/08/23	AMSCH	0118	*Moni. (L. de)* | Voor een open Nis staat een Jongeling met een brandende Kaars in de hand, op de rand van de Nis een Kat-Uil, en verder bijwerk; uitvoerig geschilderd | *Mat:* op paneel *Size:* hoog 11, breed 9 duim	[Van Iperen?]	(Sold or Bought In) fl 36 van Iperen
1808/10/28	AMVRS	0036	*Monie, (Louis de)* | Een oud Vrouwtje, zittende te haspelen, spreekt met een jong Meisje, die een Mand met Brood heeft. Zeer fraai en uitvoerig behandeld | *Mat:* op paneel *Size:* hoog 15, breed 12 duim	Marten Udink	(Sold) fl 192 Joukes en Oijens
1808/10/28	AMVRS	0037	*Monie, (Louis de)* | In een Binnenvertrek, staat een bevallig Vrouwtje bij een Ton, bezig Vis schoon te maken, ter zijde een Jongen, schijnende met haar in gesprek, op den voorgrond een vegtende Hond en Kat en verder bijwerk. Uitvoerig en fraai gepenceeld | *Mat:* op paneel *Size:* hoog 18, breed 15 duim	Marten Udink	(Sold) fl 109 J de Vries
1809/04/22	AMYVR	0079	*L. de Monie* | In een Binnenvertrek zit een Officier een Pijp te rooken, achter hem eene Vrouw met een Tinnen Kan, op de Tafel in het Vertrek eene menigte Huisraad; geestig als G. Ter Burg door L. de Monie | *Mat:* op paneel *Size:* hoog 14, breed 12 duim	de Bruin	(Sold) fl 4:15 du Pree
1809/04/22	AMYVR	0080	*L. de Monie* | Een Jongeling en een Meisje, speelende met een Musschenpot; geestig | *Mat:* op paneel *Size:* hoog 9, breed 7 duim	de Bruin	(Sold) fl 1:10 du Pree
1809/09/06	AMSCH	0052	*Moni (L. de)* | In een Vengsterbank ziet men eene Vrouw met een Glas in de eene en een Bord met eeten in de andere hand; zij schijnt te spreeken tegen een Man, welke achter haar staat met een Kan in de hand, en verder bijwerk; meesterlijk geschilderd | *Mat:* op paneel *Size:* hoog 13, breed 10 duim *Loc:* Den Haag, Nederland. Museum Bredius. (75–1946)	Johannes Caudri	(Sold) fl 70 Remmers [and] Bredius
1809/09/06	AMSCH	0053	*Moni (L. de)* | Dit natuurlijk Schilderij vertoont eene bedaagde Vrouw, zittende in een Keukenvertrek, houdende op den schoot een bak met Wortelen, welke zij schijnt te schrapen; verder op een Tafel een koperen Markt-Emmer en eenig Brood. Het is van een fraaije meesterlijke penceelbehandeling | *Mat:* op paneel *Size:* hoog 14, breed 11 duim	Johannes Caudri	(Sold) fl 39 Roos
1809/09/06	AMSCH	0054	*Moni (L. de)* | In een Nis ziet men eene bejaarde Vrouw, leunende met haar regterhand op een koperen Kan, ter zijde hangt een Lantaarn, Kooij en ander bijwerk, delicaat van schildering | *Mat:* op paneel *Size:* hoog 16, breed 13 duim *Loc:* Den Haag, Nederland. Museum Bredius. (75–1946)	Johannes Caudri	(Sold) fl 62 Bredius
1809/09/06	AMSCH	0055	*Moni (L. de)* | Een Jong Meisje in een Nis, is bézig een Bloem te plukken van een in een pot geplante Papaver; behandeld als de voorgaande | *Mat:* op paneel *Size:* hoog 10, breed 8 duim	Johannes Caudri	(Sold) fl 20 Tomassen
1810/05/22	AMSCH	0062	*Moni. (Louis de)* | In een gemeubileerde Kamer, vertoont zich eene bevallige Dame, zittende bij een Tafel met een Tapijtkleedje bedekt, waarop een Inktkoker, Speldebakje en Brief geplaatst is, in de hand houd zij een Pen en in de andere eenen Brief, verder een Knecht met een brandende Kaars in de Hand, achter de Dame een opgehaald Gordijn, in dit fraaije stukje zijn twee Lichten, van Dag en Kaars; zeer uitvoerig en kunstig behandeld, en afkomstig uit het Kabinet van Wijlen den Heer van der Mark | *Mat:* op paneel *Size:* hoog 13, breed 11 duim	Johannes van de Putte Nicolaasz.	(Sold) fl 31 T Spaan
1810/06/06	RMMUY	0013	*Louis de Monni* | Dit Fraaije Stukje vertoond eene Nis: voor dezelve ziet men een Vrouwtje zitten, met een kind voor zig, in de linkerhand houd zij een pot, en in de regterhand een lepel, achter haar een Jongeling die een Pannekoek van een Tinnen Bord neemd, en aan het kind een teken geeft dit geheim te houden. Op de kant der Nis een Bord met Brood, aan den Wand hangt een Kannetje en Lantaarn. Uitvoerig en van de beste soort van schildering | *Mat:* op paneel *Size:* hoog 14 ½, breed 11 ½ d.		(Unknown) fl 39
1810/10/13	HGDAW	0011	*L. de Monni* | Een Poelierster, zittende voor een Buitenhuis, waarby een Dienstmaagd met een Emmer aan den arm, in verwondering staande, verder gestoffeerd met gevogelte, zeer delicaat en uitvoerig behandeld | *Mat:* op paneel *Size:* hoog 16 ¼, breed 13 duim		(Unknown)
1810/12/03	DOBRA	0070	*L. de Monie* | Een afneming van 't Kruis		(Unknown)

Moni, Louis de (copy by)

1808/06/06	RMRIJ	0082	*Monni. (Louis de); naar Gerard Dou* | In een binnenvertrek zit, voor eene tafel, in een armstoel, eene slapende Vrouw, welke door eenen Krijgsman een rookende zwavelstok wordt onder den neus gehouden; op de tafel staat in eenen koperen kandelaar eene brandende Kaars, waaraan een ander Krijgsman zijne Pijp ontsteekt; in den achtergrond ziet men eene Vrouw het vertrek intreden, in de eene hand eene brandende lamp, in de andere eene kan houdende. Op den voorgrond staat eene licht inhoudende lantaarn, alles op eene aangename en verstandige wijze verlichtende. Eene roode Gordijn versiert het bovenste gedeelte van deze waarlijk uitvoerige, gloeijende en zeer natuurlijke schilderij [Dans l'Intérieur	Gerrit van der Pot, Heer van Groeneveld	(Sold) fl 200 la Coste

d'une Chambre, une femme est assise et endormie dans un fauteuil devant une table. Un Officier lui tient une allumette sous le nez, tandis que son amarade allume sa pipe à une chandelle, qui est sur la Table. Dans le fond on voit une jeune fille, qui entre, et qui tient d'une main un pot à bière, et de l'autre une Lampe. Une Lanterne, dont la lumière se répand sur le devant, est admirablement Imitée. Un Rideau artistement retroussé décore le haut de ce Tableau harmonieux et rempli de mérite] | copy by L. de Moni after Dou *Annots:* Verk coll B Kley, den Haag 10 Mei 1781 (RMA I) *Mat:* op koper *Size:* Hoog 11 en breed 8 ¾ duim

Moni, Louis de (or Moni, L. de, manner)

1806/05/05	AMSCH	0166	*L. de Moni* | Een Groenvrouw; zeer fraai door of in de manier van L. de Moni	R[oos]	(Sold) fl 6:5 van Dijl

Moni, Louis de (manner)

1802/06/28	AMSCH	0113	*L. de Monni* | In een Binnenkamer zit een Jonge Dame, ter zyde een Tafel, met een Tapyt bedekt, waar op een Musiekboek geplaatst is, ter zyde staat een verliefde Grysaart, met een geldbeurs in de hand, kragtig gepenceelt, in de manier van L. de Monni | *Mat:* op paneel *Size:* hoog 14, breed 11 duim	Anna Elink	(Sold) fl 4 T van Iperen
1808/06/11	RMRIJ	0103	*de Monni* | Een Keuken waar in een Vrouwtje Knollen zit te schillen, omringt van aartig Bywerk, in de manier van de Monni | *Mat:* op paneel *Size:* hoog 12, breed 11 duim		(Unknown) fl 10:10

Monogrammist A.A.

1803/12/15	MGLAC	0042	*Gemerkt A. A.* | Een woelende Zee met Schepen; stout en goed geschilderd | *Mat:* op paneel *Size:* hoog duim 24, breed duim 33 *Inscr:* A. A. (marked)	Mr L H de Haze Bomme	(Unknown)

Monogrammist A.B.

1802/06/28	AMSCH	0026	*A.B.* | Twee stuks Boeren Binnenhuizen, met verscheide Huisraad, Beelden, enz. zeer dun en delicaat behandeld | *Size:* hoog 9, breed 7 duim	Anna Elink	(Sold) fl 3:5 Jaak [?]
1803/12/15	MGLAC	0056	*A. B.* | Een stil Leven, waarop een Doodshoofd, Boek: Papieren enz.; zeer goed | *Mat:* op doek *Size:* hoog duim 25, breed duim 31	Mr L H de Haze Bomme	(Unknown)
1806/08/13	AMSCH	0270	*A. B.* | Eenige Krygslieden in een Corps de Garde	Roos	(Sold) fl 1:15 Boelen

Monogrammist A.B.S.

1810/07/23	DOLG1	0077	*A.B.S.* | Een woelend Water, A.B.S. 1664 | *Inscr:* A.B.S. 1664 (marked and dated)	Mr Pieter van den Santheuvel	(Sold) fl 2:12 Schouwman

Monogrammist A.D.

1809/10/16	ARNIJ	0005	*A.D.* | Een Bedelaar die een stuk Geld in de hand heeft, getekend A.D. | *Inscr:* A.D. (marked)	Wed N Nijhoff	(Sold) fl 5 v Leeuwen

Monogrammist A.L.

1809/10/20	UTWLD	0021	*A.L.* | Een Chirurgyns winkel door	J J van Rhyn	(Unknown)

Monogrammist A.S.

1802/11/01	DOBRA	0062	*A.S.* | Een Strandgezicht, met Pinkjes, vol gewoel van Visschers, enz. als van Goojen, door A.S. | *Mat:* op paneel *Size:* breed 24 d. hoog ruim 16 d.	Paulus van der Spyk [or others]	(Bought In) fl 4
1803/12/15	MGLAC	0024	*A. S.* | Een extra fraai en uitvoerig geschilderd Mans Kopje; als van A. de Vois: Ovaal Formaat | *Mat:* op koper *Fmt:* ovaal	Mr L H de Haze Bomme	(Unknown)
1810/07/23	DOLG2	0016	*A.S.* | Een Boeren Schuur, van binnen te zien. Op den voorgrond vertoont zich een aantal Koperen Ketels en Kannen, Potten, Vaten, Manden; een Vrouw is daar bij bezig met een Emmer te schuren; het zonnelicht, dat door de deur en scheuren invalt, is wel uitgedrukt. Dit Schilderij is geteekend A.S. 1648 | *Mat:* op paneel *Size:* hoog 23, breed 35 duim *Inscr:* A.S. 1648 (marked and dated)	Pieter Quinting	(Sold) fl 15:10 Blijk à Dordt

Monogrammist A.S.H.

1809/07/25	HGBSM	0052	*A S H.* | Een Binnen-Huis, waar in een Vrouwtje, staande Vleesch te hakken in een tobben, en verder Keuken-Gereedschap, gemerkt A S H | *Mat:* op paneel *Size:* hoog 18 en een half, breed 15 duim *Inscr:* A S H (marked)	D van der Aa [or] E B ten Dall	(Sold) fl 105 Oosthuyzen

Monogrammist A.S.H. (or Dou, manner)

1804/10/16	DLOND	0284	*Niet minder, zelfs geheel als G. Douw; A.S.H.* | Een Keukenmeid met een Tobbe en Hakmes voor zich, staande aan een Tafel voor een open Raam, nevens ene Pomp, omringd van Keukengereedschap enz. De tekening A. S. H. doet alleen twyffelen. Une Cuisinière occupée à hacher dans une Etuve sur une Table. Elle est debout devant une fenetre ouverte, à côté d'une Pompe, & entourée d'Ustensiles de Cuisine &c. Il n'y à que la seule marque A. S. H., laquelle fait douter | *Mat:* op paneel *Size:* hoog 19, breed 14 *Inscr:* A. S. H. (initialed)		(Sold) fl 104 Verbuyl [?]

Monogrammist A.V.

1802/09/06	AMSCH	0127	*A. V.* | Een Landschap met een Waterval; gemerkt A. V. | *Mat:* op paneel *Inscr:* A. V. (marked)	B	(Sold) fl 1:10 van Iperen

Monogrammist A.V.B.

1809/07/25	HGBSM	0186	*A.V.B.* | Een Stuk met Vrugten op een Tafel, waarby een Kan en Bokaal, natuurlyk | *Mat:* op doek *Size:* hoog 29 en een half, breed 32 duim	D van der Aa [or] E B ten Dall	(Sold) fl 2:2 A Vermeulen
1810/07/23	DOLG2	0008	*A.V.B.* | Op een tafel, of voetstuk, wordt verbeeld een Porselijnen Schotel met Vruchten; verder eenige Konijnen, een geplukt Hoen, Glas, Bokalen en verdere afbeeldingen. Welgepenseeld en geteekend A.V.B. | *Mat:* op doek *Size:* hoog 38, breed 34 duim *Inscr:* A.V.B. (marked)	Pieter Quinting	(Sold) fl 13 van Eyk 's Hage

Monogrammist A.V.D.

1803/07/14	MGKLY	0014	*Gemerked A.V.D.* | Een Woelende Zee met Scheepen in het verschiet eenig Gebergte fiks gepenseeld | *Inscr:* A. V. D. (marked)	Mr Caspar Jacob van Citters	(Unknown)

Monogrammist A.V.M.

1808/08/23	AMSCH	0260	*A. v. M.* | Een natuurlijk Landschap, geestig en fiks geschilderd	J	(Withdrawn)

Monogrammist A.V.O.

1801/12/22	AMOTT	0057	*A. V. O.* | 2 natuurlyk uitziende Grysaards met baarden	Bartholomeus Ruloffs	(Unknown) fl 6

Monogrammist A.V.R.

1802/09/18	RMDRS	0081	*A.V.R.* | De Domkerk tot Utrecht, waarin de eerste Protestanten Dienst in werd verrigt, gemerkt A.V.R. 1610, uitvoerig geschildert op doek | *Mat:* op doek *Size:* hoog 2 voet, breed 1 voet 9 ½ duim *Inscr:* A. V. R. 1610 (marked and dated)	Casper de Haas	(Unknown) fl 15:10

Monogrammist A.W.

1801/11/10	AMPOS	0027	*A. W. 1640* | 1 Zee- en Strand-Gezigt, met Schepen en Visschers | *Inscr:* A. W. 1640 (marked and dated)		(Unknown)
1802/05/24	HGBAK	0024	*A. W.* | Een Zeestrand, op de voorgrond een afslag van Vis, in 't verschiet een Oorlogschip &c., door A. W., hoog 17 d., breed 23 d. paneel, zwarte lyst, met verg. binnenrand | *Mat:* op paneel *Size:* hoog 17 duim, breed 23 duim	Mejuffrouw A van der Mieden	(Sold) fl 5:5 Ondorp
1802/07/21	HGKAN	0027	*A. W.* | Een Zeestrand, op de Voorgrond een afslag van Visch, in het verschiet een Oorlogschip, door A. W. hoog 7 duim, breed 23 duim, paneel zwarte Lyst met vergulde binnen rand | *Mat:* op paneel *Size:* hoog 7 duim, breed 23 duim		(Unknown)
1803/08/24	HGKAN	A0008	*A.W.* | Een dito [fraai Jagt Stuk] zeer natuurlyk en Meesterlyk gemerkt A.W. | *Mat:* op doek *Size:* breet 39, hoog 27 duim *Inscr:* A.W. (marked)		(Sold) fl 6:5 Valette

Monogrammist A.W.B.

1802/11/01	DOBRA	0167	*A.W.B.* | Twee stuks Watergezigtjes, met vaartuigen | *Mat:* op paneel		(Sold) fl 5:10 Lamme

Monogrammist AX

1806/11/24	AMSCH	0091	*AX* | Een Man met een Baard; gemerkt AX | *Inscr:* AX (marked)	Munnikhuizen	(Sold) fl 0:8 L Pakker

Monogrammist B.H.

1801/08/19	AMSCH	0148	*B. H.* | Een ryk gestoffeerd Strand gezicht, in Zee eenige Scheepen; natuurlyk | *Mat:* op paneel *Size:* hoog 17, breed 28 duim	Van Forreest	(Sold) fl 4:10 v d Vinne
1802/04/13	HAVIN	0055	*B. H.* | Een Binnenhuis met Boeren, als Molenaar, door B. H.		(Unknown)

Monogrammist B.R.

1802/09/29	AMSCH	0070	*B.R.* | Een uitgestrekt Arcadisch Landschap, met zwaar Geboomten en dansende Bacchanten en Nimphen; op de Wolken ziet men Bachus en Cères, en eenige Minnewigten; door een voornaam Fransch Meester, gemerkt B.R. [Un Beau Paysage d'Arcadie, orné de Bacchantes qui dansent au son de la musique, on voit Bacchus & Céres sur une nuée dans les Airs conduit par des génies. Ce Tableau d'un pinceau gracieux & Brillant est marqué B.R. & est attribué à un habile Peintre Francois.] | *Mat:* op doek *Size:* hoog 40 ½, breed 52 duim *Inscr:* B. R. (marked)	[Labouchere?]	(Sold) fl 9 J Spaan

Monogrammist B.V.S.

1808/06/11	RMRIJ	0039	*B: V: S:* | Een Boeren Binnehuis, waarin verscheide Lieden by een Haard bezig met Koken, stout geschilderd | *Mat:* op doek		(Sold) fl 4:5 v Giesen [?]

Monogrammist C.B.

1808/06/11	RMRIJ	0045	*C: B.* | Een aangenaam en boomryk Landschap met veel Stoffagie van Figuren, Os en Schapen, zonachtig en goed geschilderd | *Mat:* op doek *Size:* hoog 21 ½, breed 18 duim		(Sold) fl 10:5 Dupree

Monogrammist C.B. (or Brouwer, Adr.)

1802/08/24	LNDLS	0091	*C.B.; Brouwer* | Een Oud Man, zittende bij een kaars met Kan en Glas in de handen, en meer bijwerk. Gemerkt C.B. of Brouwer | *Mat:* op paneel *Size:* hoog 19, breed 15 duimen *Inscr:* C. B. (marked)	Leonardus Bouman [or others]	(Unknown) fl 20

Monogrammist C.D.

1804/03/27	MGSAN	0004	*C.D.* | Een extra fraai Landschap met een Boere Gehucht en verscheide Boere Wooningen, voor sommige derzelve Conversatie houdende Boertjes en Boerinnetjes, op de voorgrond eenige rustende en gaande		(Unknown)

Passagiers en ander Bywerk, zeer plaisant gepenseeld, door een zeer goed Meester, gemerkt C.D zonder Lyst | *Mat:* op paneel *Size:* hoog 24 duim x breed 33 ¼ duim *Inscr:* C.D. (marked)

Monogrammist C.H.

1801/02/18	AMBOS	0049	*C.H.* | Een dito [Landschap] met Vogels, ook natuurlyk, door C.H. in zyn vroege Tyd	J Schonevelt	(Unknown)

Monogrammist C.H. (1600)

1803/04/20	AMSCH	0103	*Gemerkt C. H. 1600* | De stervende Christus, hangende aan het Kruis, ter zyde in het verschiet de Stad Jerusalem, kragtig geschilderd [J.C. mourant sur la croix, la ville de Jerusalem est vers l'orison, expressivement rendu. Il porte la marque C.H. 1600.] | *Mat:* op paneel *Size:* hoog 38, breed 27 duim *Inscr:* C. H. 1600 (marked and dated)	Maria Magdalena van Sluypwyk, gravinne van Moens	(Sold) fl 1:10 Lesscher

Monogrammist cK.

1803/04/20	AMSCH	0104	*Gemerkt cK. 1593* | Een zinnebeeldige Ordenantie, alwaar te Tyd de Waarheid ten Hemel voerd, verder verscheide Engelen; meesterlyk gepenceeld [Une allegorie du Tems portant la verité au ciel ; des genies lui en ouvrent la route ; sujet qui est artistement rendu, marque cK. 1593.] | *Mat:* op doek *Size:* hoog 41, breed 70 duim *Inscr:* cK. 1593 (marked and dated)	Maria Magdalena van Sluypwyk, gravinne van Moens	(Sold) fl 0:12 Grimpen

Monogrammist C.P.S.

1804/10/16	DLOND	0318	*C.P.S.* | Een Rydschool met gedresseerd wordende Paerden. Uts^{a}. [Modern en zeer goed] get. C.P.S. Haag 1718. Un Manège avec des Chevaux. Uts^{a}. [Pièce moderne très belle] marqué C.P.S. Haag 1718 | *Mat:* op paneel *Size:* hoog 13, breed 16 *Inscr:* C. P. S. Haag 1718 (marked and dated)		(Unknown)

Monogrammist C.V.E.

1802/11/01	DOBRA	0098	*C.V.E.* | Twee stuks, zynde Pleisterplaatsen by boeren wooningen, gestoffeerd met Cavaliers enz. Doek. gemerkt. C.V.E. | *Mat:* op doek *Size:* breed 24 ½ hoog 18 ½ duim *Inscr:* C.V.E. (marked)	Paulus van der Spyk [or others]	(Sold) fl 7 Herweig [?]

Monogrammist C.V.M.

1810/05/22	AMSCH	0070	*C. V. M.* | Een Veldgezicht, gestoffeerd met Landlieden, bezig Hooi op een Wagen te laaden, ter zijde twee staande Paarden en een Hond; het is helder en natuurlijk verbeeld | *Mat:* op paneel *Size:* hoog 10, breed 12 duim	R	(Sold) fl 7 du Pree

Monogrammist C.W. (1686)

1801/11/10	AMPOS	0038	*C. W. 1686* | Veele koopmans Goederen in een Rhyngezigt | *Inscr:* C. W. 1686 (marked and dated)		(Unknown)

Monogrammist C.W.M.

1806/08/13	AMSCH	0309	*C.W.M.* | Een Boom en Duinryk Landschapje, met een ménigte van staand en rustende Vée, Herders en Herderinnen; als van de Velde, gemerkt C. W. M. | *Inscr:* C. W. M. (marked)	Vinkeles [for] F	(Sold) fl 5:5 Mettenbrink

Monogrammist C.W.V.D.B.

1809/07/25	HGBSM	0191	*C.W.V.D.B.* | Twee Stuks Land- en Watergezigten me [sic] stoffage, gemerkt C.W.V.D.B. | *Mat:* op doek *Size:* hoog 10, breed 13 en een half duim *Inscr:* C.W.V.D.B. (marked)	D van der Aa [or] E B ten Dall	(Sold) fl 4:2 Bakhuyzen

Monogrammist D.

1802/09/21	UTHDG	0021	*D.* | Een grijsaard leezende bij het licht der kaars, die hij in de hand houd, enz. goed van schildering, gem. D. Hoog, 9 breed, 6 ¾ duimen paneel | *Mat:* op paneel *Size:* hoog 9, breed 6 ¾ duimen *Inscr:* D. (marked) *Notes:* The artist was apparently intended to be Gerrit Dou.		(Sold) fl 4:10 La Maine

Monogrammist D.B.

1805/07/10	AMSCH	0280	*D. B.* | In een Italiaansch Landschap ziet men voor een oud vervallen Casteel, een Ezel met een Landman; zonachtig op Paneel, gem. D. B. | *Mat:* op paneel *Inscr:* D. B. (marked)	V[inkeles] [for] L	(Bought In) fl 3

Monogrammist D.T.

1804/02/27	AMSCH	0131	*D.T.* | In een Boom-, Duin- en Rotsachtig Landschap, ziet men ter eene zyde drie ryzende Lieden nevens hun een belaaden Ezel, ten andere zyde by een Water een Herder met een menigte Vee, verder een Bergachtig verschiet; meesterlyk en zonachtig gepenceeld, als de Heus, door D.T. op Paneel | *Mat:* op paneel *Size:* hoog 22, breed 29 duim	D	(Bought In) fl 5

Monogrammist D.V.B.

1801/11/10	AMPOS	0017	*D. v. B.* | 1 Bergachtig Landschap, met Geboomtens en Reizigers		(Unknown)
1802/07/27	AKHRK	000E	*D. v. B.* | Een Bergachtig Land- en Watergezicht aangenaam gestoffeert, en met oude Gebouwen en Dorpen in het verschiet; aangenaam geschilderd | companion to lot F *Mat:* op paneel *Size:* hoog 28, breed 41 ½ duim	Maria Stategaart	(Sold) fl 8:10 for lots E & F. L Veer

1802/07/27	AKHRK	000F	*D. v. B.* | Dito [een Bergachtig Land- en Watergezicht] van denzelven wederga. En op de zelve manier. Op de voorgrond een Fontein, waar bij Beelden te Paard en te Voet | companion to lot E	Maria Stategaart	(Sold) fl 8:10 for lots E & F. L Veer
1804/10/20	GRBOL	0010	*D.V.B.* | Een Landschap	Joannis Cannegieteri	(Unknown)
1804/10/20	GRBOL	0011	*D.V.B.* | Een dito [Landschap]	Joannis Cannegieteri	(Unknown)
1804/10/29	HRBAU	0129	*D. v. B.* | Een plaisant bergagtig Landschap, vol met Boomgewassen, Steden en Dorpen voorzien, en met een Rivier doorsneeden. Zynde ryk gestoffeerd en zonagtig behandeld. Gem: D. v. B. | *Mat:* op doek *Size:* hoog 25, breed 35 duim *Inscr:* D. v. B. (marked)	Simon Styl	(Unknown)
1806/05/05	AMSCH	0208	*D. v. B.* | Een Duin en boomryk Landschap, met Boeren Woningen, Beeldjes, staand en rustend Vee, enz.; meesterlyk op Doek gem., D. v. B. | *Mat:* op doek *Size:* hoog 44, breed 49 duim *Inscr:* D. v. B. (marked)	V[inkeles]	(Sold) fl 21 Van Laar
1808/09/13	HABRU	0010	*D.v.B.* | Een Rivier- en Dorpgezicht, met Scheepen		(Unknown) fl 2:6
1809/07/25	HGBSM	0147	*D.V.B.* | Een gezigt van een Buitenplaats, gestoffeert met Figuuren, gemerkt D.V.B. 1671 | *Mat:* op doek *Size:* hoog 28, breed 40 duim *Inscr:* D.V.B. 1671 (marked and dated)	D van der Aa [or] E B ten Dall	(Sold) fl 2:16 Carré
1809/07/27	AMYVR	0002	*D.V.B.* | Een Kabbelend Water met een Oorlogschip, en andere Vaartuigen, uitvoerig behandeld door D.V.B. | *Mat:* op paneel	H Munk [and] T van der Feen [and] G de Hoeft	(Sold) fl 0:12 H Bunt
1809/07/27	AMYVR	0003	*D.V.B.* | Twee Stuks Zeegezigten, rijk met diverse vaartuigen gestoffeerd, beiden op Paneel | *Mat:* op paneel	H Munk [and] T van der Feen [and] G de Hoeft	(Sold) fl 1 H Bunt

Monogrammist D.V.H.

1807/06/10	HGBSM	0122	*D.V.H.* | Een Stuk verbeeldende de aflaating van het Kruijs | *Mat:* op paneel *Size:* hoog 46 ½, breed 34 ½ duim	Abraham Delfos [or others]	(Sold) fl 10:10 Oosterwyk

Monogrammist D.W.

1805/10/21	GRBOL	0016	*D. W.* | Een Italiaansch Landschap, in de manier van Lastman, door D. W.	Gerardus Nicolaus Heerkens	(Unknown)
1809/04/22	AMYVR	0151	*D.W.* | Een Onstuimige Zee; geteekend D.W. | *Inscr:* D.W. (marked)	Juff^{r} Julikker	(Sold) fl 1:5 Andriessen

Monogrammist E.D.W.M.

1803/07/07	HGKAN	0023	*E.D.W.M.* | Een Kerk, door E. D. W. M. 1681 [Schilderyen in Olyverf] | *Mat:* in olyverf *Inscr:* E.D.W.M. 1681 (marked and dated) *Notes:* The bracketed information in the title appears above lot 1 and refers to lots 1 to 25.		(Unknown)

Monogrammist E.J.

1806/08/20	HGBSM	0114	*E.J.* | Een dito Mansportrait met eene hand | *Mat:* op doek *Notes:* It is unclear what "dito" refers to in the title.	Macalester Loup [or others]	(Sold) fl 1 for lots 114 & 115. Spruyt
1806/08/20	HGBSM	0115	*E.J.* | Een dito Vrouweportrait met twee handen | *Mat:* op doek *Notes:* It is unclear what "dito" refers to in the title.	Macalester Loup [or others]	(Sold) fl 1 for lots 114 & 115. Spruyt

Monogrammist E.M.

1801/11/10	AMPOS	0008	*E. M.* | 1 Boere Woning, Molen en Kerk, in een stil Landschap		(Unknown)

Monogrammist E.O.

1802/04/13	HAVIN	0059	*E. O.* | Een oud Man, met de handen over elkander		(Unknown)

Monogrammist E.V.N.

1810/10/11	AMSCH	0231	*E. V. N.* | Twee stuks Rijngezigten	A	(Sold) fl 5:15 H Pakker

Monogrammist F.A.O.

1802/07/27	AKHRK	0058	*F. A. O.* | Den H. Diaken Laurentius, daar men hem wil noodzaaken den Afgod te Eeren, met de toebereidselen tot zijn Marteling; in een edele manier geteekend en geschilderd | *Mat:* op paneel *Size:* hoog 11 ½, breed 8 ½ duim	Maria Stategaart	(Sold) fl 10:10 Backer

Monogrammist F.B.

1810/03/23	HAVIN	0029	*F.B.* | Twee, Een Man die een Meisje Oesters, en een andre die Wijn aanbied	Rudolf Hendrik de Wetstein [or others]	(Unknown)

Monogrammist F.B.A.

1801/11/10	AMPOS	0026	*F. B. A.* | 1 naturel Fruitstuk, met verscheiden insectens		(Unknown)

Monogrammist F.F.

1802/06/28	AMSCH	0244	*F. F.* | Het Afbeeldzel van een Geleerd Persoon, staande in Plegtgewaad, in een Tuingezigt | *Mat:* op koper *Size:* hoog 7, breed 5 duim	Anna Elink	(Sold) fl 2:15 Gruiter

Monogrammist F.M.

1810/03/23	HAVIN	0035	*F.M.* | Twee Landschappen	Rudolf Hendrik de Wetstein [or others]	(Unknown)

			Monogrammist F.S.		
1810/11/07	UTWLD	0052	*F. S.* | Een zeer aardig Landschapje, waarin in een bruine parthij eenige hooge geboomtens de hoofzaak uitmaken, wijders gestoffeerd met eenige wandelende beeltjes, zeer harmonieus geschilderd, gemerkt F. S., op paneel, 1 voet 2 duim hoog, 1 en een half voet breed, zwarte Lijst | *Mat:* op paneel *Size:* 1 voet 2 duim hoog, 1 en een half voet breed *Inscr:* F. S. (marked)		(Unknown) fl 3:10
			Monogrammist F.V.S.		
1810/12/03	DOBRA	0066	*F.v.S.* | Een groot Fruitstuk, door F.v.S., zeer fraai. In een zwarte Lyst | *Notes:* The artist was presumably Floris Gerritsz. van Schooten.		(Unknown)
			Monogrammist F.V.T.		
1802/05/22	RMHSN	0007	*F.V.T.* | Een Dorp Gezigt met Geboomten, als van As, selyn [sic] gemerkt F.V.T. | *Inscr:* F.V.T. (marked)	Lambertus Bicker	(Unknown)
			Monogrammist G.B.		
1802/06/28	AMSCH	0230	*G. B.* | Een Binnenhuis, in dezelve een blind oud Man, nevens hem een Vrouw, fiks gepenceeld door G. B. | *Mat:* op paneel *Size:* hoog 20, breed 15 duim	Anna Elink	(Sold) fl 14 Hulswit
			Monogrammist G.B.W.		
1810/10/10	MGCIT	0156	*G B W* | Een Stuk, waarop een hangende Roofvogel; natuurlijk gepenseeld, en gemerkt G B W | *Inscr:* G B W (marked)	Caspar van Citters	(Unknown)
			Monogrammist G.E.M.		
1805/07/10	AMSCH	0279	*G. E. M.* | Twee stuks Berg- en Rotsachtige Landschappen, met Rivieren, Geboomten, stoffagie van Beeldjes, gem. G. E. M. | *Mat:* op paneel *Inscr:* G. E. M. (marked)	V[inkeles] [for] L	(Bought In) fl 6
			Monogrammist G.G.F.		
1810/08/06	AMSCH	0032	*G. G. F. 1610* | Eene jonge bevallige Vrouw, halverlijf, gedeeltelijk met eene sluijer en een snoer Paarlen omhangen. Schoon geteekend en delicaat gepenceeld | *Annots:* [par] Goltius [i.e., Goltzius] (BPG) *Mat:* op paneel *Size:* hoog 23, breed 18 ½ duimen *Inscr:* G. G. F. 1610 (marked and dated)	A	(Sold) fl 31 Van Iperen
			Monogrammist G.K.R.B.		
1809/10/20	UTWLD	0042	*G.K.R.B.* | Twee stuks Zeegezigten met de pen gem. G.K.R.B. | *Inscr:* G.K.R.B (marked)	J J van Rhyn	(Unknown)
			Monogrammist G.V.H.		
1808/06/13	AMSCH	0226	*G. v. H.* | Twee stuks aangename Landschappen, met hoog Geboomte, Boerenwoningen en Stoffage van Beeldjes; zonachtig behandeld	R[oos]	(Sold) fl 295 van Os
			Monogrammist G.V.L.		
1801/03/16	AMSCH	0058	*G. v. L.* | Twee stuks Gezichten binnen Romen, zynde het eene de Brug en het Kasteel van St. Angelo, met de St. Pieters Kerk in 't verschiet, en de andere, de Kerk en 't Klooster van St. Carlino, met de Straat de vier Fontyne	P[ruyssenaar]	(Sold) fl 1:15 Van Iperen
			Monogrammist G.V.M.		
1809/05/26	HADAA	A0014	*G.V.M.* | Op een Tafel een Kreeft en eenige andere Spijs, zeer goed op Panel geschilderd | *Mat:* op paneel	Mejuffrouw de Wed David Heemskerk [or others]	(Unknown)
			Monogrammist H.		
1802/08/24	LNDLS	0043	*H.* | Een Boeren Binnen – huis, waar in een Man uit een put pompt, met eenig huisraad. Op paneel, gemerkt H. | *Mat:* op paneel *Inscr:* H. (marked)	Leonardus Bouman [or others]	(Unknown) fl 1:16
			Monogrammist H.B.		
1802/06/28	AMSCH	0248	*H. B.* | Een stormende Zee met Scheepen	Anna Elink	(Sold) fl 1:10 C Stants
1805/07/03	AMSCH	0092	*H: B:* | Twee stuks, hévige Schermutselingen tusschen Ruitery, vol gewoel; de Caracters zyn natuurlyk verbeeld, en fiks geteekend op Doek, gemerkt H: B: | *Mat:* op doek *Size:* yder hoog 12 ½, breed 15 duim *Inscr:* H: B: (marked)	C	(Sold) fl 3 Esser
			Monogrammist H.C.		
1801/12/22	AMOTT	0032	*H. C.* | 2 dito [stuks] Land- en Tuingezigten, met Beelden	Bartholomeus Ruloffs	(Unknown) fl 2:5
1802/11/01	DOBRA	0126	*H.C.* | Een Doctor die het water bezigtigt van eene zieke Vrouw, gemerkt H.C. | *Mat:* op koper *Size:* hoog 7, breed 6 duim *Inscr:* H.C. (marked) *Notes:* This lot was sold with lot 127.	Paulus van der Spyk [or others]	(Unknown)
1802/11/01	DOBRA	0127	*H.C.* | Een Heer en Dame, in eene vrolyke houding, door Denzelven [H.C.] | *Mat:* op koper *Size:* hoog 7, breed 6 duim *Notes:* This lot was sold with lot 126.	Paulus van der Spyk [or others]	(Unknown)

1802/11/01	DOBRA	0128	*H.C.* | Een jonge Juffrouw, die zig vermaakt met Bloemen, waar by een jong Heer, die haar dezelve aanbiedt, door Denzelven [H.C.] | *Mat:* op koper *Size:* hoog 7, breed 6 duim	Paulus van der Spyk [or others]	(Unknown)
1802/11/01	DOBRA	0129	*H.C.* | Een Boerin, met een Bierkan en Toebakspyp; nevens haar agter de taafel een vrolyk oud Man, door Denzelven [H.C.] | *Mat:* op koper *Size:* hoog 7, breed 6 duim	Paulus van der Spyk [or others]	(Unknown)
1802/11/01	DOBRA	0130	*H.C.* | Een vrolyk Man, die op de viool speelt, waar by een zingende Jonge en Meisje, door Denzelven [H.C.] | *Mat:* op koper *Size:* hoog 7, breed 6 duim	Paulus van der Spyk [or others]	(Unknown)

Monogrammist H.D.M.

1804/08/02	BDAN	0011	*H.D.M.* | Een Kalm Water vol Scheepen, in het verschiet de Stad Dordt, zeer aangenaam van Ordonnantie | *Mat:* op paneel *Size:* b. 31 d. h. 22 en 1 half d.	J G Calckberner	(Unknown)
1805/07/10	AMSCH	0184	*H D M* | Een Zeestrand met Scheepen en Beelden; gemerkt H D M | *Mat:* op paneel *Inscr:* H D M (marked)	R[oos]	(Sold) fl 0:6 L Pakker

Monogrammist H.F.W.

1807/08/26	AMSCH	0239	*H.F.W.* | In een Boeren Woning zit eene jonge Vrouw Appelen te schillen, in gesprek met haar Man, die aan een Tafel zit, waarop een roode Pan en verder bywerk; zonachtig en bevallig gepenceeld | *Mat:* op paneel *Size:* hoog 16, breed 13 duim	Roos	(Bought In) fl 41

Monogrammist H.J.

1810/03/07	UTWLD	0036	*H. J.* | Eene vrouw bezig by een Kaarslicht geld na te zien, geteekend H. J. | companion to lot 37 *Size:* hoog 2 voet 6 duim, breed 2 voet 3 duim *Inscr:* H. J. (marked)	J J Woertman	(Unknown) fl 11
1810/03/07	UTWLD	0037	*H.J.* | Een dito stuk zynde het pendant door dezelve Meester [H.J.] | companion to lot 36 *Size:* hoog 2 voet 6 duim, breed 2 voet 3 duim *Notes:* It is unclear what "dito" refers to in the title.	J J Woertman	(Unknown) fl 6

Monogrammist H.M. (1648)

1809/05/26	HADAA	0047	*H.M.* | Een Gezigt op het Noorden Spaarne door H.M. A^{O} 1648 | *Inscr:* H.M. A^{O} 1648 (marked and dated)	Mejuffrouw de Wed David Heemskerk [or others]	(Unknown)

Monogrammist H.P.

1810/03/23	HAVIN	0075	*H.P.* | Een Historiestuk [In Lysten met Glasen] | *Notes:* The bracketed information in the title appears above lot 63 and refers to lots 63 to 79.	Rudolf Hendrik de Wetstein [or others]	(Unknown)

Monogrammist H.R.

1802/11/01	DOBRA	0088	*H.R.* | Stilleeven, zynde een Taafel waarop een keulsche kan, een schaal met nooten, en een Oranjeappel | companion to lot 89, by Anonymous	Paulus van der Spyk [or others]	(Unknown) fl 6 ¾
1810/12/03	DOBRA	0049	*H. R.* | Een Boertje met een Kan, enz., get. H. R. | *Inscr:* H. R. (marked)		(Unknown)

Monogrammist H.T.

1802/11/01	DOBRA	0023	*H.T.* | Een Boeren-binnenhuis, met beeldjes, door H.T. in de manier van J. van Ostade	Paulus van der Spyk [or others]	(Sold) fl 4:5 J v Steeg

Monogrammist H.V.V.

1802/07/21	HGKAN	0034	*H. V. V.* | Een Kerkje van binnen te zien, door H. V. V. zwarte Lyst | *Mat:* op paneel		(Unknown)

Monogrammist I.A.H.

1804/12/10	AMSCH	0115	*I.A.H.* | Twee stuks, Roomsche Kerken, van binnen te zien, zeer ryk en uitvoerig gestoffeerd, met een menigte lieden; fraai van perspectief en meesterlyk geschilderd | *Mat:* op koper *Size:* hoog 8, breed 6 duim	Jan De Groot	(Sold) fl 41 J Yver

Monogrammist I.B.

1801/05/11	AMSCH	0129[a]	*I B* | Twee stuks, een kabbelend Water, getekend I B, en het ander eenig dood Wild | *This Lot:* Een kabbelend Water; lot 129[b] by Anonymous *Inscr:* IB (marked)	E[lias]	(Sold) fl 1 for lots 129[a] & 129[b]. Coclers

Monogrammist I.B. (1562)

1803/04/20	AMSCH	0102	*Gemerkt I B. 1562* | Deeze Ordenantie vol Gewoel van Beelden, vertoont Christus, zyn Kruis dragende naar den Berg Calvarien, op de voorgrond Maria als in zwym, waarby Johannes, en verscheide Godvrugtige Vrouwen; de Hartstogten zyn natuurlyk, en alles is kragtig gepenceeld [Le Portement de la croix ; composition nombreuse dont le groupe au devant du tableau est l'angoisse de la Vierge Marie entourrée de St. Jean & des femmes saintes. Ce morceau a du caractére & de la Vigeur [sic] ; il porte la marque IB. 1562.] | *Mat:* op paneel *Size:* hoog 38, breed 32 duim *Inscr:* I B. 1562 (marked and dated)	Maria Magdalena van Sluypwyk, gravinne van Moens	(Sold) fl 9 Coclers

Monogrammist I.B.I.R.

1803/04/20	AMSCH	0141	*IBIR* | Twee stuks groote Bybel-Ordenantiën, ryk gestoffeerd met Beelden; gemerkt IBIR [Deux Sujets de la Bible, avec une multitude de figures marqués IBIR.] | *Inscr:* IBIR (marked)	Maria Magdalena van Sluypwyk, gravinne van Moens	(Sold) fl 6 Th Spaan

Monogrammist I.P.

1807/09/28	AMWUR	0019	*I P* | Twee stuks, zynde woelende Zeeën, met zeilende en andere Vaartuigen, natuurlyk behandeld, door I P in zwarte Lyst		(Sold) fl 7:15 v Iperen

Monogrammist I.V.D.

1803/08/24	HGKAN	A0022	*I.V.D.* | Een Water Gezigt met Scheepen, op de agter grond een Stadt Gezigt gemerkt I.V.D. | *Mat:* op paneel *Size:* breet 30, hoog 19 duim *Inscr:* I.V.D. (marked)		(Sold) fl 5:5 van Hoven

Monogrammist I.W.

1804/07/25	DLGRO	0053	*I.W.* | Een fraai stuk vertonende een Battaille te Voet en te Paard, door I.W. | *Mat:* op paneel *Size:* hoog 14, breed 20 duim	Mr Franc van der Burch Wz.	(Unknown)

Monogrammist J.A.H.

1802/06/28	AMSCH	0080	*J. A. H.* | Twee stuks, voor Nissen ziet men een Jongen met een Toverlantaarn, en een ander met Muizevallen | *Mat:* op paneel *Size:* hoog 11, breed 9 duim	Anna Elink	(Sold) fl 16:10 Royers
1802/06/28	AMSCH	0081	*J. A. H.* | Twee stuks Boschgezichten, gestoffeerd met Reizigers en ander stoffagie, zynde vol gewoel van Beelden | *Mat:* op koper *Size:* hoog 11, breed 14 duim	Anna Elink	(Sold) fl 21 de Meyer
1802/06/28	AMSCH	0082	*J. A. H.* | Twee stuks, een Doktor in zyn Studeerkamer, en een Chirurgyn verbindende een Landman | *Mat:* op paneel *Size:* hoog 9, breed 11 duim	Anna Elink	(Sold) fl 20 Brouwer
1802/06/28	AMSCH	0083	*J. A. H.* | Twee stuks, een Boeren Kermis, en een Beestenmarkt; vol gewoel | *Mat:* op paneel *Size:* hoog 11, breed 14 duim	Anna Elink	(Sold) fl 30 Coclers
1802/06/28	AMSCH	0084	*J. A. H.* | Twee stuks met Heremieten in hun Kluizen; bevallig geordonneerd en delicaat gepenceeld | *Mat:* op paneel *Size:* hoog 10, breed 14 duim	Anna Elink	(Sold) fl 15 Boelen
1802/06/28	AMSCH	0085	*J. A. H.* | Twee stuks oude Grysaarts | *Size:* hoog 8, breed 7 duim	Anna Elink	(Sold) fl 4 Yver

Monogrammist J.B.

1802/11/01	DOBRA	0077	*J.B.* | Een Fruitstukje | *Notes:* This lot was sold with lot 78 by an anonymous artist.	Paulus van der Spyk [or others]	(Sold) fl 1 fot lots 77 & 78. Schalk
1810/11/07	UTWLD	0058	*J. B.* | Een boeren binnenhuisje, waar een vrouwtje zit koeken te bakken, een kind bij een tafel en een biddend boertje, getekend J. B. op paneel, 7 duim hoog, 9 duim breed, zwarte Lijst | *Mat:* op paneel *Size:* 7 duim hoog, 9 duim breed *Inscr:* J. B. (marked)		(Unknown) fl 7:15

Monogrammist J.B.S.

1810/06/04	DOBRA	0008	*J.B.S.* | Een Dame die een Oester aanbied, get. J.B.S. | *Inscr:* J.B.S. (marked)	Hendrik de Haas	(Unknown)

Monogrammist J.B.W.

1801/08/19	AMSCH	0018	*J. B. W.* | In een Landschap ziet men twee Vrouwen, by staande en rustende Schaapen, kragtig en fix geschilderd op Paneel, door J. B. W. in de manier van Cuyp | *Mat:* op paneel *Size:* hoog 14, breed 11 duim	W Wynen	(Sold) fl 7:10 Le Dantú

Monogrammist J.C.D.

1806/10/17	MGSAN	0024	*J. C. D.* | Een Dorpgezigt vol gewoel | *Mat:* op paneel	Gerardus Beljard	(Unknown)

Monogrammist J.D.

1802/09/29	AMSCH	0069	*J. D.* | Pourtraitten, ieder hoog 11 ½, breed 8 ¾ duim. Paneel. Twee Stuks, zynde het eene het Afbeeldzel van Willem den Eersten Prins van Oranjen; en 't andere dat van Elisabeth d'Yorck; zeer uitvoerig door een oud Meester gemerkt J. D. [Deux petits Tableaux, dont l'un offre de Portrait en Buste de Guilleaume Premier [sic], Prince d'Orange & l'autre celui d'Elisabeth de Yorck, peints avec finesse par un ancien maitre marqués J.D.] | *Mat:* op paneel *Size:* ieder hoog 11 ½, breed 8 ¾ duim *Inscr:* J. D. (marked)	[Labouchere?]	(Sold) fl 13 Van Dijl

Monogrammist J.D.B.

1802/04/13	HAVIN	0060	*J. D. B.* | Een Zee, met Scheepen		(Unknown)

Monogrammist J.D.S.

1804/02/27	AMSCH	0124	*J.D.S.* | In een Landschap, vertoonen zich eenige bynaar opgemetzelde Woningen, waar naar een Werkman schynt te wyzen, die een stuk Geld ontfangt van een Dame verzelt van een Heer, byden in aloude deftige Kleeding; zynde een zinspeelende Ordonantie, bevallig op Paneel, door J. D. S. 1640 | *Mat:* op paneel *Inscr:* J. D. S. 1640 (marked and dated)	B	(Sold) fl 1:10 V d^n Brink

Monogrammist J.G.

1804/07/25	DLGRO	0014	*J.G.* | Een Bergächtig Landschap, met een Water Kreek, waarïn twee gelaaden Schuiten, op den voorgrond eenige Boomen en Beeldjes, zeer fraai geschilderd door J.G. | *Size:* hoog 21, breed 13 duim	Mr Franc van der Burch Wz.	(Unknown)
1806/06/07	RMHSN	0077	*J.G.* | Een Italiaans Zonnig Landschap, gemerkt J.G. | *Mat:* op doek *Inscr:* J.G. (marked)	A E K L	(Unknown)

Monogrammist J.G.L.

1805/07/10	AMSCH	0258	*J. G. L.* | Een Storm op Zee, daar een Schip tégens een Rotsch verbryzeld word, verder andere zylende Scheepen | *Mat:* op paneel	Temmink	(Sold) fl 1:5 Lafontaine

Monogrammist J.K.

1801/12/22	AMOTT	0055	*J. K.* | 1 donker bosch en heuvel Landschap, door J. K., als de Vries	Bartholomeus Ruloffs	(Unknown) fl 11

Monogrammist J.L.

1806/06/07	RMHSN	0079	*J. L.* | Een Oud Man zittende in een Leunstoel met een Muts op 't Hoofd, gemerkt J. L. | *Mat:* op paneel *Inscr:* J. L. (marked)	A E K L	(Sold) fl 22 Thijs

Monogrammist J.M.

1802/07/27	AKHRK	000K	*J. M.* | Een Wintergezicht. Een bevroozen Water bij een Dorp, op 't IJs een menigte van Schaatsrijders en Arresleeden; zeer goed gepenceeld | *Mat:* op paneel *Size:* hoog 21, breed 37 ½ duim	Maria Stategaart	(Sold) fl 5:10 Vanderham

Monogrammist J.M.R.

1802/11/01	DOBRA	0030	*J.M.R.* | Twee Ovaaltjes, met wyn- en koffy-drinkers; enz. | *Fmt:* ovalen	Paulus van der Spyk [or others]	(Sold) fl 1 Vos v Rijswijk

Monogrammist J.P.

1801/11/21	RMVIS	0008	*J.P.* | Apollo en Daphne, getekend J.P. | *Inscr:* J.P. (marked)	Gelinus van Spaan	(Unknown)
1809/04/22	AMYVR	0181	*J.P.* | In een Slagers Winkel hangt een Varken op de Leer, verders de Slager, zijn Vrouw, en ander bijwerk	de Bruin	(Sold) fl 2:15 du Pree
1810/07/23	DOLG2	000Y	*J P* | Een Zeegezicht, met zeilende Schepen, helder en dun geschilderd, en gemerkt J P | *Mat:* op paneel *Size:* hoog 17, breed 21 duim *Inscr:* J P (marked)	Pieter Quinting	(Sold) fl 5 A v Strij

Monogrammist J.R.

1801/08/19	AMSCH	0145	*J. R.* | Een Jongeling, die een Vis Open snyd; krachtig en natuurlyk geschilderd | *Mat:* op paneel *Size:* hoog 13, breed 11 duim	Van Forreest	(Sold) fl 4:5 Roos [for] R
1801/12/22	AMOTT	0068	*J. R. 1654* | Krygslieden in een Boere Dorp, vol gewoel | *Inscr:* J. R. 1654 (marked and dated)	Bartholomeus Ruloffs	(Unknown) fl 1:10

Monogrammist J.R.W.

1804/10/22	MGWIN	0002	*J.R.W.* | Twee dito [extra fraaië Landschapjes], dito [met Beesten], door J.R.W. in vergulde Lysten | *Mat:* op glas	F Reytsma	(Sold) £ 0:17 Abr Buford

Monogrammist J.S.

1802/05/05	AMSCH	0249	*J. S.* | Een boom en bergachtig Landschap, op de voorgrond de vlugt na Egypten, zeer natuurlyk | *Mat:* op paneel *Size:* hoog 14, breed 20 duim	G	(Sold) fl 5 Stevens
1802/11/01	DOBRA	0125	*J.S.* | Een Boerengezelschap, get. J.S. | *Mat:* op paneel *Size:* h. 6 ½, br. 8 duim *Inscr:* J.S. (marked)	Paulus van der Spyk [or others]	(Sold) fl 20 Brandwyk
1803/07/14	MGKLY	0024	*Gemerkt J.S.* | Een Zee-Gevegt wel behandeld | *Inscr:* J.S. (marked)	Mr Caspar Jacob van Citters	(Unknown)

Monogrammist J.T.

1805/10/09	HGBSM	0021	*J. T.* | Een onstuimige zee met schepen | *Mat:* op paneel *Size:* hoog 14 breet 19 duim	T H van Willigen [or others]	(Sold) fl 2:5 Ph Mey

Monogrammist J.V.B.

1802/07/27	AKHRK	000G	*J. v. B.* | Democritus [beide zeer kunstig en krachtig geschilderd] | *Mat:* op doek *Size:* hoog 30 ½, breed 23 ½ duim *Notes:* The bracketed information in the title appears in lot H and refers to lots G and H.	Maria Stategaart	(Sold) fl 4:10 for lots G & H. J Winkel
1802/07/27	AKHRK	000H	*J. v. B.* | Heraclitus, beide zeer kunstig en krachtig geschilderd | *Notes:* The description in the title refers to lots G and H.	Maria Stategaart	(Sold) fl 4:10 for lots G & H. J Winkel
1809/07/25	HGBSM	0194	*J.V.B.* | Een Bergachtig Landschap, waarin een zittende Vrouw en Man, met een Koe, Schapen &c. | *Mat:* op doek *Size:* hoog 19, breed 25 en een half duim	D van der Aa [or] E B ten Dall	(Sold) fl 13:10 van Eyk

Monogrammist J.V.G.

1802/09/21	UTHDG	0031	*J. v. G.* | Boerewooningen en geboomte aan den oever eener Rivier, gestoffeerd met Vischers, gem. J. v. G. | *Size:* hoog 14, breed 18 duimen *Inscr:* J. v. G. (marked)		(Sold) fl 19 Niekerk
1804/05/07	AMSCH	0214	*J. v. G.* | Een stil Watertje met een Stadsgezicht, Vaartuigen, Vissers, enz.; gemerkt J. v. G. | *Mat:* op paneel *Size:* hoog 10, breed 17 duim *Inscr:* J. v. G. (marked)	Y[ver] [for] W	(Bought In) fl 1 ¾

Monogrammist J.V.H.

1801/03/16	AMSCH	0122	*J.v.H.* | twee stuks Landgezichten buiten Haarlem met verscheide stoffagie, bevallig op paneel geschilderd | *Mat:* op paneel	K[ip]	(Sold) fl 6 Roelofs
1801/03/31	HGCLF	0382	*J.V.H.* | Een rotsagtig Landschap, waar by eenige badende Nimphen door J. V. H. in een dito [zwarte] lyst	H van der Hoop	(Unknown) fl 3:15

Monogrammist J.V.M.

1801/12/22	AMOTT	0058	*J.V.M.* | 1 Naaister in een Binnevertrek	Bartholomeus Ruloffs	(Unknown) fl 1:10
1801/12/22	AMOTT	0077	*J. v. M.* | 2 dito [stuks] Gezigtjes buiten de stad Haarlem	Bartholomeus Ruloffs	(Unknown) fl 2:15
1809/10/20	UTWLD	0017	*J.v.M.* | Een Italiaansche pleisterplaats	J J van Rhyn	(Unknown)

Monogrammist J.W.

1806/08/13	AMSCH	0283	*J. W.* | Twee stuks Fruitstukken, dun en delicaat gepenceeld op Doek, gemerkt J. W. | *Mat:* op doek *Inscr:* J. W. (marked)	Roos	(Sold) fl 7:15 du Pree

Monogrammist J.W.B.

1806/06/07	RMHSN	0055	*J. W. B.* | Een Hevige Bataillie met Ruiters &c. gemerkt J.W.B. | *Mat:* op paneel *Inscr:* J. W. B. (marked)	A E K L	(Unknown)

Monogrammist L.

1809/07/25	HGBSM	0227	*L* | Twee Musiceerende Figuren, zeer oud, gemerkt L, 1527, op Paneel, hoog 19, breed 13 en een half duim. NB. Het origineele Plaatje is achter op het Stuk geplakt | *Mat:* op paneel *Size:* hoog 19, breed 13 en een half duim *Inscr:* L, 1527 (marked and dated)	D van der Aa [or] E B ten Dall	(Sold) fl 3 Boers
1809/07/25	HGBSM	0228	*L* | Een Man met een Doodshoofd, zeer oud, door denzelven [L], 1502. NB. Met een gravuur achter op geplakt | *Size:* hoog 7, breed 5 duim *Inscr:* 1502 (dated?) *Notes:* It is unclear whether the date is inscribed on the painting.	D van der Aa [or] E B ten Dall	(Sold) fl 5 Boers

Monogrammist L.B.

1804/07/25	DLGRO	0091	*L.B.* | Een Zee Haven, op de voorgrond een menigte Koopmans Goederen, en daar aan arbeidende Persoonen | *Mat:* op paneel *Size:* hoog 22, breed 31 duim	Mr Franc van der Burch Wz.	(Unknown)
1809/04/17	AMSCH	0014	*L.B.* | Een bergachtig Landschap, met een Rivier, op de voorgrond bij een Ruïne een Man met een beladen Muilezel, waar bij een Hond; krachtig geschilderd op Paneel, door L.B. 1670 | *Mat:* op paneel *Size:* hoog 7, breed 9 duim *Inscr:* L.B. 1670 (marked and dated)	A	(Sold) fl 5:10
1809/07/27	AMYVR	0004	*L.B.* | Een stil Water met drijvende en roeijende vaartuigen | *Mat:* op paneel	H Munk [and] T van der Feen [and] G de Hoeft	(Sold) fl 1:15 Jan Schneijders

Monogrammist L.I.B.

1806/06/07	RMHSN	0015	*L.I.B.* | Een Onstuimige Zee met Scheepjes, gemerkt L. I. B. Ovaal | *Mat:* op paneel *Fmt:* ovaal *Inscr:* L. I. B. (marked)	A E K L	(Unknown)

Monogrammist L.P.

1802/05/24	HGBAK	0013	*L. P.* | Een Landschap, op de voorgrond een gezadeld Paard &c., door L. P. 1647, hoog 19 duim, breed 17 ½ duim paneel, zwarte lyst en verg. binnenrand | *Mat:* op paneel *Size:* hoog 19 duim, breed 17 ½ duim *Inscr:* L. P. 1647 (marked and dated)	Mejuffrouw A van der Mieden	(Sold) fl 10:10 v Meulen

Monogrammist L.T.

1807/08/26	AMSCH	0216	*L.T.* | In een aangenaam Landzicht met Geboomte en Woningen, by een stil Water, ziet men op den voorgrond staande Ossen en rustende Schapen, verder een Veehoeder te Paard, eenige Beesten door een Beekje dryvende; uitvoerig behandeld op Paneel, gemerkt L.T. | *Mat:* op paneel *Size:* hoog 13, breed 22 duim *Inscr:* L.T. (marked)	Roos [for] A	(Sold) fl 1 L Pakker

Monogrammist M.

1802/09/06	AMSCH	0144	*M.* | Deeze capitaale Ordenantie, zinspeelende op de Onderdrukking der Nederlanden, door de Koning van Spanjen, en het moordadig ombrengen van veele Ingezeetenen, vol gewoel van Beelden; meesterlyk op Doek geschilderd, door M. 1620 | *Mat:* op doek *Size:* hoog 38, breed 63 duim *Inscr:* M. 1620 (marked and dated)	B	(Sold) fl 1:5 Vermeulen
1804/03/27	MGSAN	0012	*M.* | Een Zeestrandje vol gewoel van Menschen, Wagens, Paarden, in 't verschiet verscheide Scheepjes, gemerkt M. 1643. in zwarte met vergulde Binnenlyst | companion to lot 13 *Mat:* op paneel *Size:* hoog 9 ½ duim x breed 13 ½ duim *Inscr:* M. 1643 (marked and dated)		(Unknown)
1804/03/27	MGSAN	0013	*M.* | Een Landgezigtje tot weêrgaê, met Reizigers, en een Wagen met Stroo, door denzelven [M.], in dito [zwarte met vergulde Binnen-] Lyst | companion to lot 12 *Mat:* op paneel *Size:* hoog 9 ½ duim x breed 13 ½ duim		(Unknown)
1810/03/07	UTWLD	0012	*M.* | Een fraay Bloemstuk door M. | *Size:* hoog 3 voet 4 duim, breed 2 voet 8 duim	J J Woertman	(Unknown) fl 4

Monogrammist M.B.

1803/06/20	AMSCH	0065	*M.B.* | Een Binnehuis, waarin een Man, beévens een menigte Huisraad en een Kat, fix op Panneel, gemerkte M.B. | *Mat:* op paneel *Size:* hoog 24, breed 33 duim *Inscr:* M.B. (marked)	Schley [for] K	(Sold) fl 14 V d Vinnen
1810/03/23	HAVIN	0014	*M.B.* | Een Binnenhuis, met een Man bij veelerhande Huisraad ongemeen konstig en kragtig, door M.B. waarschijnlijk Matthys van den Bergh, dicipel van Rubbens | *Size:* hoog 24 d. breed 3 v.	Rudolf Hendrik de Wetstein [or others]	(Unknown)

Monogrammist M.C.

1807/06/10	HGBSM	0102	*M.C.* | Een Stukje waar in den Engel aan de Herders verschijnd, gemerkt M.C. | *Mat:* op paneel *Size:* hoog 18 ½, breed 17 duim *Inscr:* M.C. (marked)	Abraham Delfos [or others]	(Sold) fl 1:18 Carré

Monogrammist M.D.

1803/07/14	MGKLY	0032	*M.D.* | Een Italiaansch Landschapje, gemerkt M.D. | *Inscr:* M.D. (marked)	Mr Caspar Jacob van Citters	(Unknown)

Monogrammist M.L.

1805/10/21	GRBOL	0030	*M. L.* | Een Zeestrandje met enige Scheepen | companion to lot 31	Gerardus Nicolaus Heerkens	(Unknown)
1805/10/21	GRBOL	0031	*M. L.* | Een woelende Zee, door dito [M. L.], tot een Weerga | companion to lot 30	Gerardus Nicolaus Heerkens	(Unknown)

Monogrammist M.R.

1801/04/08	HAVIN	0050	*M. R.* | Jacobs droom, uitvoerig		(Unknown)

Monogrammist M.V.

1803/09/07	AMSCH	0257	*M.V.* | In een Boeren-Binnenhuis ziet men twee Boeren en twee Boerinen, zich met rooken als anderszints vermakende; op Koper, gemerkt M. V., op Paneel [L'intérieur d'une chaumière dans laquelle deux paysans et deux villageoises s'amusent à fumer et à folâtrer, sur cuivre, marqué M.V.] | *Mat:* op koper, op paneel *Size:* hoog 6, breed 9 duim *Inscr:* M. V. (marked)	Smidt	(Sold) fl 3 Gruiter

Monogrammist N.L.

1810/10/10	MGCIT	0144	*N.L.* | Een kalm Zeetje, waarop veelerlei Vaartuigen; verdienstelyk behandeld; gemerkt N. L. | *Inscr:* N. L. (marked)	Caspar van Citters	(Unknown)

Monogrammist NR

1804/10/08	RMCNL	0004	*NR* | Een Jongmans Pourtret fraay Geschilderd, gemerkt NR 1629 | *Inscr:* NR 1629 (marked and dated)	A t'Hooft	(Unknown)

Monogrammist P.

1802/12/13	AMSCH	0214	*P.* | Het dito [Afbeeldzel], van een bedaagd Heer in aloude Kleeding, met een geploide Kraag om den Hals; meesterlyk behandeld | *Mat:* op paneel	Schley [for] Lauwers	(Sold) fl 0:8 L Pakker
1803/08/24	HGKAN	A0004	*P* | Een dito [Landschap] met leggende en staande Vee, gemerk P | *Mat:* op paneel *Size:* breet 13, hoog 10 duim *Inscr:* P (marked)		(Sold) fl 4:5 Huybregts
1804/07/25	DLGRO	0049	*P.* | Een Jongeling ten halve lyve, fraai geschilderd door P. | *Mat:* op paneel *Size:* hoog 18, breed 14 duimen	Mr Franc van der Burch Wz.	(Unknown)
1808/04/26	GDAN	0219	*P.* | Een Pleisterplaats met eenige te Paard rijdende Personen, gem. P. | *Size:* hoog 13 ½, breed 18 duim *Inscr:* P. (marked)	G H Fortuyn	(Unknown)

Monogrammist P.A.V.H.

1804/10/16	DLOND	0319	*P.A.v.H.* | Een Slagters Binnenhuis, met een Put, waarby Kinders, Groentens en een Schapenkop. Get. P. A. v. H. 1642. L'intérieur d'une Maison de Boucher, on y voit un Puits, des Enfans, des Legumes & une tête de Mouton. Marqué P. A. v. H. | *Mat:* op paneel *Size:* hoog 18, breed 30 *Inscr:* P. A. v. H. 1642 (marked and dated)		(Unknown)

Monogrammist Pc.

1804/03/27	MGSAN	0005	*Pc.* | Een fraai Schildery, waarop een Tafel, op dezelve een Schotel met Vis, een dito met Brood, Citroen, Mes, Bocaal, en anders, krachtig geschilderd, door een goed Meester, gemerkt Pc. Ao. 1628. in vergulde Lyst | *Mat:* op paneel *Size:* hoog 19 ½ duim x breed 29 ½ duim *Inscr:* Pc. Ao. 1628 (marked and dated)		(Unknown)

Monogrammist P.L.

1802/05/05	AMSCH	0258	*P.L.* | Een Boeren Binnenhuis, met een Boer, zittende op een Mand, en verder bywerk | *Mat:* op paneel *Size:* hoog 10, breed 8 duim	BB	(Sold) fl 19 Spruit

Monogrammist P.M.

1806/11/24	AMSCH	0094	*PM* | Een storm op Zee, alwaar een Schip tegens de Rotzen verbryzeld wordt; gemerkt PM | *Inscr:* PM (marked)	Munnikhuizen	(Sold) fl 2:5 du Pree

Monogrammist P.S.

1802/06/28	AMSCH	0227	*P. S.* | Een Schoolmeester met een menigte Kinderen; meesterlyk op Panneel, door P. S. | *Size:* hoog 16, breed 20 duim	Anna Elink	(Sold) fl 5:5 Boelen
1810/03/26	RMMUY	0053	*PS* | Een Binnenhuis, waar verscheide Personen aan den haard bij het vuur zitten, verzeld van Honden, Katten en verder bijwerk. Gemerkt PS [L'intérieur d'un Ménage. Plusieurs personnes sont auprès du feu, entourées de chiens et de chats, et des ustensiles.] | *Inscr:* PS (marked)	Daniel de Jongh Az	(Sold) fl 12 LeBrun Parys

Monogrammist P.V.

1806/08/20	HGBSM	0226[H]	*P.V.* | Een sitzende Vrouwtie met 1 vivol [sic] in de hand | *Notes:* This lot was added in by hand in the JPGM copy of the catalogue.	Macalester Loup [or others]	(Sold) fl 14 Huybrechts

Monogrammist P.V.A.

1803/04/18	HGBAK	0039	*P. v. A.* | Een dito [Landschap] met een Ruïne, door P. v. A. op doek, hoog 18, breed 26 duim, zwarte lyst [Schilderyen in Olyverf] | *Mat:* in olyverf op doek *Size:* hoog 18, breed 26 duim *Notes:* The bracketed information in the title appears above lot 1 and refers to lots 1 to 48.	Johan Pieter Reigersman [or others]	(Unknown)

Monogrammist P.V.B.

1810/03/23	HAVIN	0020	*P. v. B.* | De Leeuwen Jagt, als van Rubbens, door P. v. B. | *Size:* hoog 34 breet 46 ½ d.	Rudolf Hendrik de Wetstein [or others]	(Unknown)

Monogrammist P.V.H.

1804/08/02	BDAN	0036	*P.V.H.* | Een aangenaam Landschap | *Mat:* op doek *Size:* b. 76 d. h. 26 d.	J G Calckberner	(Unknown)

Monogrammist P.V.S.

1810/12/03	DOBRA	0018	*P. V. S.* | Een Vrouwepourtret; uitvoerig geschilderd, gemerkt P. V. S. | *Inscr:* P. V. S. (marked)		(Unknown)

Monogrammist P.W.

1801/08/19	AMSCH	0085	*P. W.* | Gezicht binnen Amsterdam, uit het Y, ziende naer de Haringpakkers-Tooren, en verdere wooningen, gestoffeert met verscheide Scheepen, fix geschilderd | *Mat:* op doek *Size:* hoog 35, breed 26 duim	Wolf	(Sold) fl 3 Wijland
1802/04/13	HAVIN	0061	*P. W.* | Een Landschap met Paarden		(Unknown)
1804/10/08	RMCNL	0014	*P. W.* | Een Pleisterplaat [sic] gemerkt P. W. | *Inscr:* P. W. (marked)	A t'Hooft	(Unknown)
1807/06/10	HGBSM	0121	*P.W.* | Een Renconter van Cavallerie in een dorp, gemerkt P.W. | *Mat:* op paneel *Size:* hoog 16, breed 12 duim *Inscr:* P.W. (marked)	Abraham Delfos [or others]	(Sold) fl 5:5 v Giese

Monogrammist Q.B.

1802/09/21	UTHDG	0007	*Q.B.* | Een man zittende bij eene menigte huisraad, is bezig, een Deken te verstellen. Goed en natuurlijk gem. Q.B. | *Mat:* op paneel *Size:* hoog 15, breed 19 duimen *Inscr:* Q.B. (marked) *Notes:* The artist was presumably Quiringh Gerritsz. van Brekelencam.		(Bought In) fl 16:10
1810/06/04	DOBRA	0019	*Q.B.* | Een Groenvrouwtje; get. Q.B. | *Inscr:* Q.B. (marked)	Hendrik de Haas	(Unknown)

Monogrammist qR

1810/10/10	MGCIT	0060	*qR* | Een zeer bevallig Bloemstukje; zeer dun en natuurlyk uitgevoerd, en gemerkt qR | *Inscr:* qR (marked)	Caspar van Citters	(Unknown)

Monogrammist R.

1802/06/16	AMSCH	0243	*R.* | Een Land- en Water-Gezicht, op de voorgrond een Schutsluis; verder een Moolen, natuurlyk en meesterlyk geschilderd; gemerkt R. | *Mat:* op paneel *Size:* hoog 5, breed 9 duim *Inscr:* R. (marked)	[Merrem]	(Sold) fl 1:15 Boelen
1806/06/07	RMHSN	0132	*R.* | Een Oudmans Pourtrait, houdende in de hand een Boek, gemerkt R., zynde van een goed Meester | *Inscr:* R. (marked)	A E K L	(Unknown)

Monogrammist R.B.

1807/06/10	HGBSM	0142	*R.B.* | Een heuvelagtig Landschap met eenige figuurtjes, door een goed meester, gemerkt R.B. | *Mat:* op paneel *Size:* hoog 11, breed 13 ½ duim *Inscr:* R.B. (marked)	Abraham Delfos [or others]	(Sold) fl 2:10 Dupré

Monogrammist R.H.

1804/03/27	MGSAN	0009	*R.H.* | Een dito [fraai] Stuk, vertoonende een Landschap, waarin Joseph en maria zittende met het Kind Jesus op haar schoot, voor hun een Rei van dansende Kindertjes, in het verschiet vertoonen zich eenige Engeltjes in de Lucht met Bloemkransjes, door een oud goed Meester, gemerkt R.H. in vergulde Lyst | *Mat:* op paneel *Size:* hoog 16 duim x breed 25 duim *Inscr:* R.H. (marked)		(Unknown)

Monogrammist R.K.B.

1806/10/17	MGSAN	0043	*R.K.B.* | Een Vogelkooi met Vogels, waaronder een Weitasch met een Hoorn, door R.K.B. 1669 | *Mat:* op paneel *Inscr:* R.K.B. 1669 (marked and dated) *Notes:* This lot was sold with lots 44 and 45 by David Kleijne.	Gerardus Beljard	(Sold) £ 0.4.1 for lots 43–45

Monogrammist S.H.K.

1809/04/22	AMYVR	0204	*S.H.K.* | Twee stuks met Vee	de Bruin	(Sold) fl 5:5 du Pree

Monogrammist S.L.

1810/10/11	AMSCH	0048	*S. L.* | Op eene Tafel staat een zilvere Schaal, met Druiven, Wijnroemer, enz; zagt gepenceeld | *Mat:* op doek *Size:* hoog 23, breed 20 duimen	M	(Sold) fl 4:15 Gruiter

Monogrammist S.W.

1810/05/22	AMSCH	0125	*S. W.* | Een Landschap, gestoffeerd met een wit Paard met Hout beladen, waarbij Arbeiders; meesterlijk geschilderd | *Mat:* op paneel *Size:* hoog 9, breed 12 duim	Johannes van de Putte Nicolaasz.	(Sold) fl 8:10 van Iperen

Monogrammist T.D.K.B.

1804/02/27	AMSCH	0122	*TDKB* | In een Tuingezicht, met een Standbeeld vercierd, vertoont zich op den voorgrond een staand Heer, in deftig aloude Hollandsche Kleeding,	B	(Sold) fl 76 Jozi

			schynende een Pryshoek over te geeven, aan een bevallige Jongeling, meden in Kleeding van dien tydt, die het met blydschap schynt te ontfangen; het is bevallig van schildering op Doek en gemerkt TDKB 1660 | *Mat:* op doek *Inscr:* TDKB 1660 (marked and dated)		
			Monogrammist T.V.A.		
1810/10/10	MGCIT	0078	*T.V.A.* | Een Maria met het Kind Jezus, en voor dezelve Johannes, waar achter een Landschap geplaatst is; delicaat en teder geschilderd, gemerkt T.V.A. | *Inscr:* T.V.A. (marked)	Caspar van Citters	(Unknown)
			Monogrammist T.V.B.		
1801/12/22	AMOTT	0061	*T. v. B.* | 2 dito [stuks] boere Binnehuisjes	Bartholomeus Ruloffs	(Unknown) fl 12
			Monogrammist T.V.S.		
1805/07/10	AMSCH	0142	*T. v. S.* | In een Stadgezicht, ziet men twee Vrouwen, Groentens en Fruit verkoopen: waar by een Koopvrouw en twee Kinderen, staande by een Mand Appelen; meesterlyk op Paneel geschilderd | *Mat:* op paneel	Temmink	(Sold) fl 1 Spaan
			Monogrammist V.D.		
1805/07/10	AMSCH	0206	*V. D.* | Een aangenaam Land- en Riviergezicht, met zylende Schuiten, gemerkt V. D. | *Inscr:* V. D. (marked)	V[inkeles] [for] G	(Sold) fl 1 L Pakker
			Monogrammist V.D.H.		
1802/04/13	HAVIN	0022	*v: d: H:* | Een dito [steene Tafel] | *Notes:* It is unclear what "dito" refers to in the title.		(Unknown)
			Monogrammist V.H.		
1802/08/24	LNDLS	0044	*V.H.* | Een Jongeling halverlijf, houdende een schuln [sic] in zijne hand, terwijl hij bellen blaast. In de trant van C. Netscher, gemerkt V.H. 1665 | *Mat:* op doek *Size:* hoog 24, breed 18 duimen *Inscr:* V.H. 1665 (marked and dated)	Leonardus Bouman [or others]	(Unknown) fl 9:10
			Monogrammist V.Z.		
1804/07/25	DLGRO	0061	*V.Z.* | Het lachend Meisje, houdende een Haspel in de hand, naast haar een Jongeling of Manspersoon die haar in zyn arm heeft, door V.Z. | *Mat:* op doek *Size:* hoog 27, breed 28 duim	Mr Franc van der Burch Wz.	(Unknown)
			Monogrammist W.B.		
1808/11/12	HGSCR	0014	*W.B.* | Vyf stuks verbeeldende de vyf zinnen door drie vrouwen en twee mans voorgesteld by het kaarsligt, zeer uitvoerig en natuurlyk behandeld in de manier van Schalken door W.B. 1645 | *Inscr:* W.B. 1645 (marked and dated)	Mr J van Buren	(Unknown) fl 30
			Monogrammist W.G.		
1810/07/23	DOLG2	0028	*W.G.* | Een stuk met Vruchten, breed geschilderd; geteekend W.G. | *Mat:* op doek *Size:* hoog 22, breed 19 duim *Inscr:* W.G. (marked)	Pieter Quinting	(Unknown) fl 1
			Monogrammist W.K.		
1808/08/23	AMSCH	0091	*K. (W.)* | Een natuurlijk Land- en Watergezigt, met verscheiden Boeren Wooningen, op de voorgrond bij een opgaande Weg, staande en rustende Huislieden, ter zijde twee Vissers in een Schuit; bevallig en fiks behandeld | *Mat:* op doek *Size:* hoog 41, breed 55 duim	Y	(Sold) fl 10:10 Jan Spaan
			Monogrammist W.L.		
1807/08/26	AMSCH	0177	*W.L.* | Voor een Oud vervallen Gebouw ziet men op den voorgrond twee Vrouwtjes, die met elkander in gesprek schynen te zyn, ter zyde een Herder met Bokken en Schapen, en een aangenaam verschiet; helder en uitvoerig, geteekend W.L., in de manier van Poelenburg | *Mat:* op paneel *Size:* hoog 9, breed 11 duim *Inscr:* W.L. (marked)	de Vries	(Sold) fl 4:15 Coclair
			Monogrammist W.P.		
1806/05/05	AMSCH	0119	*W. P.* | In een Landschap met de Ruïnen van een prachtig Gebouw, ziet men twee Vrouwen, verzeld van verscheiden Bokjes en verder bywerk; zonachtig en meesterlyk gepenceeld door W. P. in de manier van Poelenburg | *Mat:* op paneel *Size:* hoog 9, breed 11 duim	E	(Sold) fl 6:15 van Iperen
			Monte (and Janson, J.)		
1810/03/27	RMCNL	0031	*J. Janssen; Monté* | Een Landschapje, geschilderd door J. Janssen, en gestoffeerd door Monté		(Unknown)
			Moor, Carel de		
1801/02/18	AMBOS	0064	*de Ridder de Moor* | Een fraay Pourtraitjen, fraay en delicaat geschilderd	J Schonevelt	(Unknown)
1801/04/13	AMSCH	0044	*C. de Moor* | Dit uitmundtend Schildery steld voor, het Sterfbed van Marcus Antonius, men ziet Cleopatra in een zeer droevige houding, verzeld van twee weenende Vrouwen, de hartstogten zyn treffend, wyders fraay van coloriet en schildering | *Annots:* [door] F. v. Mieris (OGA) *Mat:* op doek *Size:* hoog 75, breed 75 duim	Pierre Fouquet, junior	(Sold) fl 10 Spruit v Gent

1801/06/10	AMSCH	0117	*Moor. (C. de)* | Een Historieële Ordonantie, van vyf Beelden in een Landschap, krachtig en uitvoerig behandeld | *Mat:* op paneel *Size:* hoog 15, breed 18 duim	Herman ten Kate	(Sold) fl 26 Spruit van Gend
1802/08/24	LNDLS	0061	*Ridder Karel de Moor* | Het origineel Portrait van den Ridder Karel de Moor, in zijn hoogen ouderdom met zijn beroerde hand naar zich zelfs geschilderd. Ovaal formaat, doch op paneel | *Mat:* op doek op paneel *Fmt:* ovaal *Size:* hoog 30, breed 24 duimen	Leonardus Bouman [or others]	(Unknown) fl 3:10
1802/08/24	LNDLS	0062	*Ridder C. de Moor* | Een Juffertje halverlijf, fraai gekleed, houdende Bloemen in de hand | companion to lot 63 *Size:* hoog 8 ½, breed 6 ½ duimen	Leonardus Bouman [or others]	(Unknown) fl 26:10 for lots 62 & 63
1802/08/24	LNDLS	0063	*Ridder C. de Moor* | Een Weêrga, zijnde een Heertje, rustende op een piedestal met een wandelstok in de hand. Beide konstig en krachtig op paneel, boven toogsgewijs | companion to lot 62 *Mat:* op paneel *Fmt:* boven toogsgewijs *Size:* ieder hoog 8 ½, breed 6 ½ duimen	Leonardus Bouman [or others]	(Unknown) fl 26:10 for lots 62 & 63
1802/09/21	UTHDG	0059	*P. de Moor* | In een binnenhuis vermaken zich verscheiden Boeren met het spel, helder en breed behandeld | *Mat:* op doek *Size:* hoog 31, breed 38 duimen *Notes:* The artist's name was given as "P. de Moor" but we have assumed this is an error.		(Bought In) fl 19
1803/07/18	AMSCH	0028	*Moor. (Carel de)* | In een Binnenvertrek ziet men een Man aan een Tafel zittende de Courant te leezen, met een Pypje in zyn hand, agter de Tafel zit een andere zyn Glaasje te leegen, het caracter van den Leezer is zeer wel uitgedrukt, zynde van een delicaate penceelsbehandeling [Un homme lisant la gazette est assi [sic] devant une table, la pipe à la main ; son compagnon vuidant son verre est à l'autre bout. Le caractére attentif du lecteur est fort bien exprimé, & en général ce petit morceau est aussi soigné que la couleur en est vraye.] | *Mat:* op paneel *Size:* hoog 10, breed 8 duim	Maria Theresia Andrioli	(Sold) fl 40 Gruyter
1803/07/18	AMSCH	0029	*Moor. (Carel de)* | Het Pourtrait van een Meisje in het wit Satyn gekleed, houdende in haar schoot eenige Bloemen, alles van de beste schildering van deezen Meester [Le portrait d'une petitte fille marchent [sic] dans un appartement, tenant des fleurs ; son habillement de satin blanc est d'un beau fini & ajouté à l'agrement de la couleur & d'un fond intéressent [sic].] | *Mat:* op paneel *Size:* hoog 12, breed 9 duim	Maria Theresia Andrioli	(Sold) fl 39 Coclers
1803/09/07	AMSCH	0105	*De Ridder C. de Moor* | Door een Nis ziet men een jong Meisje, nevens haar eenig Vruchten, voor de Nis staat een Pot met Angelieren, uitvoerig en meesterlyk gepenceeld [A travers une niche, l'on apperçoit une jeune fille ; ayant à son côté quelques fruits ; sur le devant un pot d'oeillets. D'un fini agréable] | *Mat:* op paneel *Size:* hoog 12, breed 8 duim [Haut 11, large 8 pouces] *Notes:* The dimensions differ in the Dutch and French editions of the catalogue.	Smidt	(Sold) fl 12:10 Van Iperen
1803/12/12	AMSCH	0058	*C. de Moor* | In een Landschap ziet men Léda met de Zwaan, en ander bywerk; uitmuntend van schildering | *Mat:* op doek *Size:* hoog 25, breed 31 duim	B	(Bought In) fl 250
1804/10/16	DLOND	0153	*C. de Moor* | Een Binnenvertrek, waarin een Heer en Dame een glas Wyn drinken. Un Seigneur & une Dame dans une Chambre; ils prennent du Vin | *Size:* hoog 13, breed 11		(Unknown)
1806/08/13	AMSCH	0113	*Moor. (C. de)* | Een Boetvaardige Maria Magdaléna, in een Grot; met verscheide bywerk, krachtig behandeld | *Mat:* op paneel *Size:* hoog 9, breed 7 duim	Roos	(Sold) fl 4 Mettenbrink
1806/08/20	HGBSM	0069	*C. de Moor* | Een Familie Stuk | *Mat:* op doek *Size:* hoog 51, breed 70 duim	Macalester Loup [or others]	(Sold) fl 8:15 Gram
1808/04/26	GDAN	0108	*Moor Ridder (C de)* | Voor een Huis staat Hagar en Ismaël die afscheid nemen van Abraham, Hagar schynt zeer bedroeft en is schreijende, met een pakje onder haar arm, terwijl Izaak op de grond zit, en Sara om een hoekje kijkt, schoon geschilderd | *Mat:* op doek *Size:* hoog 19 ½, breed 23 duim	G H Fortuyn	(Unknown)
1808/06/06	RMRIJ	0083	*Moor. (Ridder Karel de)* | Op een ovaal koper plaatje de afbeelding van den Luit. Admiraal de Ruiter met zijne tweede Vrouw, twee Zonen, en eene Dochter; vertoonende zich zijne eerste Vrouw en twee Kinderen in de Wolken. Meesterlijk geschilderd en omvat van een zeer fraai gebeeldhouwd lijstje van bruin hout [Ce petit Tableau de forme ovale represente le Lieutenant Amiral M. A. de Ruyter entouré de sa seconde Epouse, de ses Deux fils et de sa fille. On voît sur un nuage sa première Epouse avec deux enfants. Cette Composition allégorique, riche et finie, est traitée en Maître. Encadré dans un bois brun et richement Sculpté] | *Annots:* [door] G. Hoet (RMA I) *Mat:* op koper *Fmt:* ovaal *Size:* Hoog 4 ¼, en breed 3 ½ duim *Loc:* Amsterdam, Nederland. Rijksmuseum. (A163) as G. Hoet	Gerrit van der Pot, Heer van Groeneveld	(Sold) fl 145 J J de Wit [for] le Roi
1808/06/13	AMSCH	0101	*Moor (C. de)* | Deze Ordonantie stelt voor Léda, met de Zwaan aan eene Vijver zittende, ter zijde haar een Mandje met Bloemen. Zeer zacht gepenceeld | *Mat:* op doek *Size:* hoog 24, breed 30 duim	E	(Sold) fl 31 J Schuman
1808/08/23	AMSCH	0108	*Moor. (C. de)* | In een Landschap zit op de voorgrond eene bevallig Herderinnetje, rustende met haar regter Arm op eene steene Balustrade, houdende een mandje met Vrugten op de schoot; natuurlijk en fraai gepenceeld | *Mat:* op doek *Size:* hoog 16, breed 14 duim	C	(Bought In) fl 17

1809/07/19	AMSCH	[A0007][H]	*C de Moor* | 1 Priames en Tisbe | *Notes:* This lot was added in by hand in the AA copy of the catalogue. Because it was not numbered, we have assigned the number.		(Unknown)
1810/07/23	DOLG1	0038	*Carel de Moor* | Een Dame, onder een Boom, zittende op eene Guitar te spelen. Zeer uitvoerig en kunstig behandeld | *Mat:* op paneel *Size:* hoog 9 ½, breed 12 duim	Mr Pieter van den Santheuvel	(Sold) fl 35 Spruijt van Gent
1810/08/06	AMSCH	0074	*Moor (C. de)* | Een bevallig Herderinnetje, houdende een Mandje met Vrugten op de schoot, zij rust met haaren arm op een steenen Baluster; fiks gepenceeld | *Mat:* op doek *Size:* hoog 16, breed 14 duimen	B	(Sold) fl 4 Texier Gerbet en Comp [for] Lebrun
1810/10/11	AMSCH	0057	*C. De Moor* | Een Mans Portret, halver Lijf, in het zwart gekleurd; meesterlijk | *Mat:* op paneel *Size:* hoog 16, breed 12 duimen	C	(Sold) fl 2:5 Posthumus
			Moor, Carel de (manner)		
1804/10/16	DLOND	0288	*Als van Carel de Moor* | Een Binnenvertrek, waarin een Heer en Dame aan een gedekte Tafel met Spyzen, alsmede ene Jufvrouw, die het Clavier speelt enz. L'intérieur d'une Chambre, dans laquelle un Monsieur & une Dame sont au Diner; une Demoiselle touche le Clavecin & c. | *Mat:* op paneel *Size:* hoog 14, breed 21		(Unknown)
1804/10/16	DLOND	0289	*Als van Carel de Moor* | Een Jongetjen in ene Nis, die bellen blaast. Un Enfant dans une Niche, faisant des bouteilles d'eau | *Mat:* op paneel *Size:* hoog 5, breed 5		(Unknown)
			Mooy, Cornelis Pietersz. de		
1802/09/18	RMDRS	0082	*P. Mooy* | Een groot Schildery, verbeeldende een stille Zee, met verscheide O. I. en andere Scheepen, op een Witte grond als met O. Inkt gewassen	Casper de Haas	(Unknown) fl 2:2
1802/09/18	RMDRS	0083	*P. Mooy* | Een Gezicht op een Stad, langs een Rivier geleegen, en gestoffeert met verscheide Scheepen, als vooren behandeld	Casper de Haas	(Unknown) fl 1:10
1808/12/31	RMHSN	0004	*C.P. Mooy* | Twee dito [stuks], de Haringvangst en Groenlandsche Visschery, op Witte Gronden met Zwart | *Mat:* op paneel	G Spanjaart [or] H de Haas [or] C van der Looy Lans	(Unknown)
			Moreelse, Paulus		
1803/04/20	AMSCH	0041	*Moreelse. (P.)* | Het Afbeeldzel van een bejaard Heer, in deftige zwarte kleeding, met een blaauw couleurde Kraag om den Hals, in een ovale Nis, met vier in 't graauw geschilderde Beeldjes in de vier Hoeken; kragtig en meesterlyk gepenceeld [Le Portrait d'un homme de Robe portant une fraise ; il est vû par une embrasure ovale. Les coins sont ornés avec des Basreliefs figurés. Ce morceau est traité avec force & intelligence.] | *Mat:* op paneel *Size:* hoog 25, breed 20 duim	Maria Magdalena van Sluypwyk, gravinne van Moens	(Sold) fl 50 Theijs
1810/03/26	RMMUY	0001	*Paulus Moreelse, A^{o} 1617* | De Maaltijd, van den Zaligmaker met de Discipelen te Emaus. Zijnde de beelden levensgrootte ten voeten uit. Van een uitmuntende omtrek, en de caracters zeer wel waargenomen, het coloriet, licht en bruin, zoo schoon als men weinig in een schilderij van deze tijd zal aantreffen, alles gaaf en zuiver geconserveerd [Jésus Christ à table avec les Pélerins d'Emmaüs. Le sujet est pris dans le moment de la fraction du pain ; on voit au second plan un autre personnage ; les figures sont de proportion de nature et vue à plein pieds. Ce morceau, exécuté avec beaucoup de sagesse, et offrant autant de variété que de noblesse dans les caractères, est, sans contredit, du meilleur choix parmi les productions de ce peintre, et peut tenir une place distinguée dans quelques musées ou belle collections.] | *Annots:* Heeft gekost f 362.13 (RMA II) *Mat:* op doek *Size:* hoog 62, breed 79 duimen *Inscr:* Paulus Moreelse, A^{o} 1617 (signed and dated?) *Notes:* It is unclear whether the name and date are inscribed on the painting.	Daniel de Jongh Az	(Sold) fl 110 de Jongh [for] A
1810/08/06	AMSCH	0079	*Moreelse (P.)* | Twee stuks, zijnde de afbeeldzels van Pieter Corneliszoon Hooft en deszelfs Huisvrouw; meesterlijk als A. van Dijk gepenceeld | *Mat:* op doek *Size:* ieder hoog 75, breed 52 duimen	R[oos]	(Bought In) fl 100
1810/11/07	UTWLD	0019	*P. Moreelse* | Een Vrouwen portrait zeer uitvoerig en meesteragtig geschilderd door P. Moreelse 1624, paneel, 1 voet 7 en een half duim breed, zwarte Lijst | *Mat:* op paneel *Size:* 1 voet 7 en een half duim breed *Inscr:* P. Moreelse 1624 (signed and dated?) *Notes:* It is unclear whether the name and date are inscribed on the painting.		(Unknown) fl 11:5
			Moreelse, Paulus (or Moreelse, P., copy after)		
1808/06/06	RMRIJ	0084	*Moreelse. (Door of naar Paul)* | Een Vrouwe Portret ten halven lijve uit [Une Jolie femme ornée de fleurs etc. vue à mi-corps] | *Annots:* Verk. 25 Nov. 1786 (3.8.8) (RMA I) *Mat:* op doek *Size:* Hoog 29 ½, en breed 23 ¾ duim	Gerrit van der Pot, Heer van Groeneveld	(Sold) fl 13 Levysohn
			Moreelse, Paulus (or Novelli, P.)		
1803/04/27	AMSCH	0039	*Morealése* | David avec la tête de Goliath, ce Tableau est d'un effêt très piquant, d'une bonne couleur & bien peint | *Size:* h. 4 ¼, l. 3 ½ pieds	A	(Sold) fl 70 Hodges
			Moreelse, Paulus (attributed; or Novelli, P., attributed)		
1803/04/27	AMSCH	0001	*Moréälese* | Ce magnifique Tableau attribué au Moréälese, représente l'aparition des anges aux bergers, & est peint d'une maniere large, le ton	A	(Sold) fl 151 D^{k} Versteegh

			de Couleur en est vigoureux, la Composition en est grande le dessin franc & de la plus grande maniere | *Size:* h. 8, l. 10 pieds		
			Moreelse, Paulus (manner)		
1806/08/13	AMSCH	0265	*P. Moreelsen* | Een staand Meisje met een Hond; als P. Moreelsen	Roos	(Sold) fl 1:10 L Pakker
			Morel, J.		
1802/05/05	AMSCH	0145	*Morel* | Twee bevallig geördonneerde Manden met Vrugten en Bloemen, schoon van ligt, en meesterlyk gepenceelt	J	(Sold) fl 1:5 Gruiter
1806/05/05	AMSCH	0093	*J. Morel* | Op een marmere Tafel ziet men eenige aangenaame Bloemen, als rooden en witten Roosen, Flosprinsipus, Auriculaas enz., waar op Insecten aassen; bevallig geordinneerd en delicaat gepenceeld door J. Morel | *Mat:* op paneel *Size:* hoog 10, breed 8 duim	V[inkeles]	(Bought In) fl 25
			Morel, Jan Evert		
1803/12/12	AMSCH	0061	*J. E. Morel* | Op een Egiptisch Marmere Tafel ziet men een Glas, gevuld met een ménigte van aangenaame Bloemen, als Roode en Bonte Roozen, Iriassen, Auriculaas, en andere welriekende Bloemen, ter zyde een Vogelnestje met Eijeren; delicaat en uitvoerig gepenceeld | *Mat:* op paneel *Size:* hoog 8, breed 11 ½ duim	B	(Sold) fl 11:10 C S Roos [for] N
1804/02/27	AMSCH	0076	*Morell. (J. E.)* | Op een Marmeren Tafel, ziet men eenige aangenaame Bloemen, als roode en witte Roosen, Flosprinsipius, Auriculaas en andere welriekende Bloemen, waarop Insectens aazen, bevallig geordoneert en delicaat gepenceeld | *Size:* hoog 10, breed 7 ½ duim	C	(Bought In) fl 30
1804/05/07	AMSCH	0112	*Morell. (J. E.)* | Op een Marmeren Tafel ziet men onderscheide smaakelyke Vrugten, als: blaauwe en witte Druiven, Pgrsiken [sic], Abricoosen en andere Vrugten, waarop Insectens Azen; allerbevalligst geordoneerd, dun en delicaat geschilderd | *Mat:* op paneel *Size:* hoog 14, breed 10 duim	Vinkeles [for] G	(Sold) fl 41 Frantze
1806/08/13	AMSCH	0111	*Morel. (J. E.)* | Op een steene Rand ziet men een cierlyke roode Pot, gevult met een ménigte van fraai geschakeerde Bloemen, als roode en witte Roozen, Hiacinten, Kroon-Imperiaal, Auriculaas en een ménigte van andere welriekende Bloemen, verders een aangenaam Boomryk verschiet; delicaat en uitvoerig van penceelsbehandeling | *Mat:* op paneel *Size:* hoog 25, breed 20	Vinkeles [for] J	(Bought In) fl 200
1807/08/26	AMSCH	0129	*J.E. Morel* | Op een Marmeren Tafel staat een Vaas, geschakeerd vol geurige Bloemen, waarop Insecten azen, ter zyde een Vogelnestje met Eijeren; dit Stukje is delicaat dun en bevallig gepenceeld | *Mat:* op paneel *Size:* hoog 20, breed 17 duim	Roos	(Sold) fl 101 T van Iperen
1808/08/23	AMSCH	0111	*Morel. (J. E.)* | Op een marmer Tafel, staat een Glas, gevuld met welriekende Bloemen als Roosen, Aüriculaas en anderen, voor en ter zijde dezelven leggen een menigte smakelijke Vrugten, als witte Druiven, Persiken, blauwe en witte Pruimen, enz., waar op Insectens aazen; zacht en teder gepenceeld | *Mat:* op doek *Size:* hoog 16, breed 13 ½ duim	[Gruyter?]	(Sold) fl 103 Van Iperen [or] Th Spaan
1809/04/22	AMYVR	0078	*J.E. Morel* | Op een Steenen Voetstuk staat een Vaas, gevuld met zeer dun en delicaat geschilderde Bloemen; met regt mag dit stukje als een der besten beschouwd worden | *Mat:* op paneel *Size:* hoog 25, breed 20 duim	de Bruin	(Bought In) fl 120
1810/08/06	AMSCH	0080	*Morel (J.E.)* | Een Glase fles gevuld met keurige Bloemen, staande op eene marmeren Tafel, bevallig van Ordonantie; teder en uitvoerig gepenceeld | *Mat:* op paneel *Size:* hoog 21, breed 19 duimen	S[paan]	(Bought In) fl 155
			Morgenstern, Johann Ludwig Ernst		
1802/06/28	AMSCH	0114	*J. E. Morgenstern* | Een Roomsche Kerk van binnen te zien, gestoffeerd met Beeldjes; fraay van perspectief en uitvoerig geschilderd. door J. E. Morgenstern, op Koper | *Mat:* op koper *Size:* hoog 12, breed 16 duim	Anna Elink	(Sold) fl 32 Gruiter
1803/09/07	AMSCH	0109	*J. Morgenstern* | Een Roomsche Kerk, van binnen te zien, gestoffeerd met een ménigte Autaren en Beeldjes, fraay van Perspectief, en zonachtig [L'intérieur d'une église romaine, orné de plusieurs autels et d'images ; belle perspective, la lumière qui y règne est d'un très bon effet] | *Mat:* op paneel *Size:* hoog 14, breed 15 duim	Smidt	(Sold) fl 91 Gruiter
1805/07/03	AMSCH	0185	*Morgenstern* | Een Roomsche Kerk van Binnen te zien gestoffeerd met een ménigte Beeldjes; zonachtig op Paneel | *Mat:* op paneel	R[oos]	(Sold) fl 31 Gruyter
1805/07/10	AMSCH	0108	*Morgenstern* | Een Roomsche Kerk van binnen te zien, ryk gestoffeerd met een ménigte Beelden, Schilderyen, Altaaren, enz; delicaat en uitvoerig gepenceeld | *Mat:* op paneel *Size:* hoog 20, breed 24 duim	V[inkeles] [for] L	(Bought In) fl 22
1808/10/28	AMVRS	0041	*Morgenstern* | Een Roomsche Kerk van binnen te zien, rijk gestoffeerd met Altaren en Beeldjes. Fraai van doorzicht en uitvoerig gepenceeld | *Mat:* op paneel *Size:* hoog 12, breed 9 duim	Marten Udink	(Sold) fl 40 Gruyter
			Morgenstern, Johann Ludwig Ernst (and Stöcklin, C.)		
1803/09/07	AMSCH	0169	*C. Stocklin; Morgenstern* | Een Roomsche Kerk van binnen te zien, gestoffeerd met een menigte Altaaren en Beeldjes, de perspectief is over fraay, zo ook de schildering op Panneel, door C. Stocklin en gestoffeerd door Morgenstern [L'intérieur d'une église, ornée d'autels et de figures ;	Smidt	(Bought In) fl 115

ce morceau joint à une exécution précieuse les règles de la perspective et de l'architecture] | *Mat:* op paneel *Size:* hoog 16, breed 21 duim

Moritz, Louis

1806/08/20	HGBSM	0032	*Moritz* | Een Pleijster plaats, alwaar zich eenige krijgslieden verversen, uitvoerig geschilderd | *Mat:* op paneel *Size:* hoog 14, breed 16 duim	Macalester Loup [or others]	(Sold) fl 14 Richters
1809/07/25	HGBSM	0027	*L. Moritz* | De Graflegging van Christus, omringt van een aantal toepasselyke Figuren, welke volgens het voorval vereischt werden; het dood Lichaam is zeer natuurlyk, en de verdere Figuren fraay van Coloriet en frisch Geschildert | *Mat:* op doek *Size:* hoog 38 ½, breed 51 ½ duim	D van der Aa	(Sold) fl 195 Oosthuyzen [or] L Voerman
1809/07/25	HGBSM	0028	*L. Moritz* | Een Christus aan 't Kruis, natuurlyk en fraay geschildert | *Mat:* op doek *Size:* hoog 47 ½, breed 33 ½ duim	D van der Aa	(Sold) fl 60 Ponse
1809/07/25	HGBSM	0029	*L. Moritz* | Jupiter onder de gedaante van een Zwaan by Leda, het Figuur is leevensgroote en kloek geschildert | *Mat:* op doek *Size:* hoog 38 ½, breed 52 duim	D van der Aa	(Sold) fl 95 Teissier
1809/07/25	HGBSM	0030	*L. Moritz* | Een Christus halverlyf verbeeld, het brood breekende, krachtig en fraay geschildert | companion to lot 31 *Size:* hoog 28, breed 21 ½ duim	D van der Aa	(Sold) fl 121 for lots 30 & 31. van Eyk
1809/07/25	HGBSM	0031	*L. Moritz* | Een weenende Magdalena, niet minder als de voorgaande, tot een weêrga | companion to lot 30	D van der Aa	(Sold) fl 121 for lots 30 & 31. van Eyk
1809/07/25	HGBSM	0032	*L. Moritz* | Een biddende Ermiet, knielende voor een Crucifix, de expressie is zeer aandagtig, en voorts zeer kragtig en uitvoerig geschildert | *Mat:* op paneel *Size:* hoog 14, breed 10 ½ duim	D van der Aa	(Sold) fl 160 Oosthuyzen [or] L Voerman
1809/07/25	HGBSM	0033	*L. Moritz* | Een Vrouwtje, zittende op de rand van een Nis, en speelende met een zogenaamde Joujou, de rand van de Nis is van onderen geschildert met een Basrelief speelende Kindertjes, uitvoerig en kragtig geschildert | *Mat:* op paneel *Size:* hoog 14 ½, breed 11 ½ duim	D van der Aa	(Sold) fl 36:10 van Eyk
1809/07/25	HGBSM	0034	*L. Moritz* | Een Balcon met een overhangend Tapyt, waar achter twee Kinderen, saamen musiceerende, door de nis ziet men een vertrek en een verder doorzigt in een Tuin, delicaat en uitvoerig geschildert | *Mat:* op paneel *Size:* hoog 15, breed 11 ½ duim	D van der Aa	(Sold) fl 110 Ponse [or] de Zwart
1809/07/25	HGBSM	0035	*L. Moritz* | Een Gezigt van een Buitenplaats, alwaar een Gezelschap van Heeren en Dames te Paard uitreiden, met meer figuren, helder en plaisant geschildert | *Mat:* op paneel *Size:* hoog 18, breed 24 ½ duim	D van der Aa	(Sold) fl 66 Ponse [or] de Zwart
1809/07/25	HGBSM	0036	*L. Moritz* | Een Stal waar in een wit en bruin Paart, en verdere Stalgereedschappen, met een Boer die water aanbrengt | *Mat:* op paneel *Size:* hoog 10, breed 11 ½ duim	D van der Aa	(Sold) fl 8 Ponse
1810/03/27	RMCNL	0038	*L. Morits* | In een Binnenhuis, ziet men eene menigte Bedelaars aan 't Vechten, Slaan, en alles in wanorder, geestig en aardig geschilderd		(Unknown)

Mortel, Jan

1801/05/11	AMSCH	0060	*J. Mortel* | In dit stuk ziet men verscheiden soorten van Vrugten, als druiven, abrikoozen, aardbesien, alles krachtig en uitvoerig geschilderd | *Mat:* op doek *Size:* hoog 21, breed 15 duim	Pruisse [for] M	(Sold) fl 18 Coclers
1801/06/13	LNDLS	0029	*Mortel* | Een Feston, met veelderlei Fruit, rustende op een tafel, daar een schotel met aardbezien en citroenen op leggen, op paneel geschilderd, door Mortel, 1697 | *Mat:* op paneel *Size:* hoog 24 ½, breed 17 ½ duimen *Inscr:* Mortel, 1697 (signed and dated?) *Notes:* It is unclear whether the name and date are inscribed on the painting.	D van R	(Sold) fl 20:5 A Delfos [for] W
1802/04/13	HAVIN	0021	*Mortel* | Een dito [steene Tafel], fraai | *Notes:* It is unclear what "dito" refers to in the title.		(Unknown)
1802/05/05	AMSCH	0136	*D. Mortel* | Twee Stuks, een Bloem- en Fruitstuk, zeer natuurlyk | *Mat:* op paneel *Size:* hoog 12, breed 10 duim *Notes:* The artist's name was given as "D. Mortel" but we have assumed this is an error.	BB	(Sold) fl 12 A Schotte
1804/07/25	DLGRO	0069	*J. Mortel* | Een stuk met Bloemen en Vruchte | *Mat:* op paneel *Size:* hoog 13, breed 11 duim	Mr Franc van der Burch Wz.	(Unknown)
1804/07/25	DLGRO	0070	*J. Mortel* | Een dito [stuk] met Vruchten, en een Pekelharing, door denzelfde [J. Mortel] | *Mat:* op paneel *Size:* hoog 13, breed 11 duim	Mr Franc van der Burch Wz.	(Unknown)
1806/06/07	RMHSN	0036	*Mortel* | Twee Stuks, waar in Haring, Brood, Fruiten &c. | *Mat:* op paneel	A E K L	(Unknown)
1807/06/10	HGBSM	0184	*J. Mortel* | Een konstig Fruitstukje met Persiken, &c. | *Mat:* op doek *Size:* hoog 15, breed 12 ½ duim	Abraham Delfos [or others]	(Sold) fl 2:18 Haag
1807/06/10	HGBSM	0185	*J. Mortel* | Een dito [konstig] Fruitstuk, waarop een porceleine schotel met Aardbeziën en andere vruchten, uitvoerig | *Mat:* op paneel *Size:* hoog 15, breed 18 ½ duim	Abraham Delfos [or others]	(Sold) fl 6 Tessiol [?]
1808/06/13	AMSCH	0184	*P. Mortel* | Een Fruitstuk, waarin uitmunten een Kweepeer en blaauwe Pruimen; zacht en teder | *Notes:* The artist's name was given as "P. Mortel" but we have assumed this is an error.	E M Engelberts	(Sold) fl 50 van Drielst

Moucheron

1801/03/31	HGCLF	0381	*Moucheron* | Een Thuyngezigt door Moucheron in een zwarte lyst	H van der Hoop	(Unknown) fl 1
1801/06/13	LNDLS	0093[H]	*Moucheron* | Een landschap d[oor?] Moucheron | *Notes:* This lot was added in by hand in the ESP and RKDH copies of the catalogue.	D van R	(Sold) fl 7:5 Spruyt

1802/08/24	LNDLS	0027	*Moucheron* | Een Boomrijk Landschap met een Waterval, een Brug daar een Man overgaat, benevens een Weg met Koeijen gevolgd van een Man | *Mat:* op doek *Size:* hoog 18, breed 15 ½ duimen	Leonardus Bouman [or others]	(Unknown) fl 30
1802/09/06	AMSCH	0069	*Moucheron* | Een Italiaansch Bergachtig Landschap, met verschillend Geboomten, ter zyde ziet men een Huisman met twee belaaden Muyl-Ezels, als van 't Gebergte afkomende; in 't verschiet eenige Reizigers, en een Rivier met Vaartuigen | *Mat:* op doek *Size:* hoog 20 ½, breed 26 duim	H^{n} Smit	(Sold) fl 30 van Iperen
1802/09/06	AMSCH	0070	*Moucheron* | Een Boomryk Landschap, aan een stil Water, gestoffeerd op de voorgrond met een Reiziger te Paard, verder langs een Wegh, een Ophaalbrug; natuurlyk gepenceeld | *Mat:* op paneel *Size:* hoog 19, breed 16 duim	H^{n} Smit	(Sold) fl 8 Texier
1809/04/17	AMSCH	0118	*Moucheron* | Een Italiaansch Landschap, met Beeldjes gestoffeerd | *Mat:* op paneel	A	(Sold) fl 0:16
1810/03/07	UTWLD	0024	*Moucheron* | Eene harte Jagt zeer konstig en breed behandeld | *Size:* hoog 5 voet 9 duim, breed 7 voet 8 duim	J J Woertman	(Unknown) fl 50
1810/03/23	HAVIN	0078	*Moucheron* | Een Landschap [In Lysten met Glasen] | *Notes:* The bracketed information in the title appears above lot 63 and refers to lots 63 to 79.	Rudolf Hendrik de Wetstein [or others]	(Unknown)
1810/07/23	DOLG2	000R	*Moucheron* | Een Berg- en Boomrijk Landschap, rijk gestoffeerd met Schapen, Paarden, Ezels, enz., krachtig, breed, het zonlicht wel uitgedrukt | *Mat:* op doek *Size:* hoog 45, breed 52 ½ duim	Pieter Quinting	(Sold) fl 31 Visser
1810/07/23	DOLG2	000S	*Moucheron* | Een dito [Berg- en Boomrijk Landschap], in denzelfden smaak, niet minder meesterlijk behandeld | *Mat:* op doek *Size:* hoog 45, breed 52 ½ duim	Pieter Quinting	(Sold) fl 31 Visser
1810/07/23	DOLG2	0031	*Moucheron* | Een Bergachtig Landschap, met oude gebouwen; aardig en zeer uitvoerig gestoffeerd | *Mat:* op doek *Size:* hoog 17, breed 22 duim	Pieter Quinting	(Sold) fl 4:15 Visser
1810/11/07	UTWLD	0013	*Moucheron* | Eene uitmuntende Schilderij, zijnde een bergachtig Landschap met een rivier doorsneden – men ziet een oude gothische brug aan de weg, tusschen twee hoogtens – gestoffeerd door paardrijders en wandelende beeldjes – eenige opgeschoten Bomen en Kreupelhout dat een gedeelte van de voorgrond uitmaakt, zeer geestig en zonagtig, en met de meeste harmonie geschilderd door Moucheron op doek, 2 voet 3 duim hoog, 3 voet 2 duim breed, vergulde Lijst | *Mat:* op doek *Size:* 2 voet 3 duim hoog, 3 voet 2 duim breed		(Unknown) fl 205
1810/12/03	DOBRA	0032	*Moucheron* | Een Landschap		(Unknown)

Moucheron (and Huysum, Jan)

1801/03/16	AMSCH	0069	*Moucheron; van Huysum* | Een Boomryk Landschap met Beeldjes gestoffeerd, door Moucheron en van Huysum	P[ruyssenaar]	(Sold) fl 8 Stevens

Moucheron (and Lingelbach)

1801/04/08	HAVIN	0042	*Moucheron; Lingelbach* | Een Landschap, door Moucheron en door Lingelbach gestoff:		(Unknown)

Moucheron (or Moucheron, manner)

1810/03/23	HAVIN	0027	*Moucheron* | Landschappen van of in de Manier van Moucheron	Rudolf Hendrik de Wetstein [or others]	(Unknown)

Moucheron (copy after)

1804/10/29	HRBAU	0144	*Moucheron* | Een gestoffeerd Arcadisch Landschap, met Watervallen. Na Moucheron | *Mat:* op doek *Size:* hoog 21, breed 26 duim	Simon Styl	(Unknown)

Moucheron (manner)

1802/09/06	AMSCH	0234	*Moucheron* | Een Boschagtig Landschap, met een Rivier doorsneeden; bevallig gestoffeerd in de manier van Moucheron	J	(Sold) fl 0:8 Coenraad Deppe
1808/06/13	AMSCH	0196	*Moucheron* | Een Landschap; in de manier van Moucheron	E M Engelberts	(Sold) fl 9 Engelberts
1810/10/11	AMSCH	0175	*Moucheron* | Een Landschap, in de manier van Moucheron	[Levy Pakker?]	(Sold or Bought In) fl 2:10 L Pakker

Moucheron, Frédéric de

1801/05/11	AMSCH	0049	*F. de Moucheron* | Twee stuks fraaye boom en bergachtige Landschappen, gestoffeerd met verscheide beelden en beesten, aangenaam van coloriet en meesterlyk behandeld | *Mat:* op doek *Size:* hoog 34, breed 43 duim	S[chley]	(Sold) fl 120 Coclers
1801/05/11	AMSCH	0050	*F. de Moucheron* | Een Landschap met beelden en beesten gestoffeerd, en een bergachtig verschiet, zonachtig behandeld | *Mat:* op doek *Size:* hoog 15, breed 18 duim	P[ruyssenaar]	(Sold) fl 20 van Iperen
1802/06/16	AMSCH	0109	*F. de Moucheron* | Een Bergachtig Landschap, gestoffeert met een Valkejager en zyn Honden, wyders een Heer te Paard, in 't verschiet een Gebouw; helder en zonachtig behandeld | *Mat:* op doek *Size:* hoog 26 ½, breed 21 duim	[Merrem]	(Sold) fl 32 Royers
1802/09/06	AMSCH	0071	*F. de Moucheron* | Een Boom- en Bergachtig Landschap, met Gebouwen, ter zyde een klaar Water, en een aangenaam verschiet; meesterachtig en fraay van licht | *Mat:* op doek *Size:* hoog 13, breed 11 duim	J	(Sold) fl 7 van Iperen

1802/09/06	AMSCH	0072	*F. de Moucheron* | In een aangenaam Boomryk Landschap, ziet men de ingang van een Bosschagie, gestoffeerd met een Hertejacht, ter zyde eenige Gebouwen, en een aangenaam verschiet | *Mat:* op paneel *Size:* hoog 17, breed 21 duim	J	(Sold) fl 2 Gruiter
1803/12/15	MGLAC	0036	*F. Moucheron* | Een Bergagtig Landschap, doorsneden met een Rivier, gestoffeerd met onderscheidene Figuuren; zeer fraai geordonneerd en geschilderd | *Mat:* op doek *Size:* hoog duim 23, breed duim 28	Mr L H de Haze Bomme	(Unknown)
1804/02/27	AMSCH	0073	*Moucheron (F.)* | Een Boschagtig Landschap, gestoffeerd met een Jagt en andere stoffage | *Size:* hoog 17, breed 22 duim	C	(Sold) fl 1:5 Van den Brink
1804/04/28	LNDLS	0059	*F. Moucheron* | Twee stuks Tuingezichten	[Abraham Delfos] [or others]	(Bought In) fl 2
1806/05/05	AMSCH	0087	*F. Moucheron* | Een aangenaam Landschap, op de voorgrond gestoffeerd met een Hartejagt, verders een bergagtig verschiet; zonagtig op Doek | *Mat:* op doek *Size:* hoog 35, breed 43 duim	V[inkeles]	(Sold) fl 10 Van Laar
1806/05/05	AMSCH	0095	*F. de Moucheron* | Een boom en bergagtig Landschap, ryk gestoffeerd en bevallig geschildert door F. de Moucheron | *Mat:* op doek *Size:* hoog 9, breed 12 duim	V[inkeles]	(Sold) fl 2 Gruiter
1806/08/13	AMSCH	0106	*Moucheron. (F. de)* | Een wyd uitgebreid Landgezicht, zynde een gezicht op 't binnenste van Ceylon; ryk gestoffeerd met Beelden en Beesten; en fiks van schildering | *Mat:* op doek *Size:* hoog 53, breed 65 duim	Vinkeles [for] J	(Sold) fl 0:18 Vinkeles
1806/08/13	AMSCH	0107	*Moucheron. (F. de)* | Een hoog Boom- en Bergachtig Landschap, met een Rivier doorsneeden, ryk met stoffagie van Beeldjes, Schuiten enz.; fraai van licht en zonachtig gepenceeld | *Mat:* op doek *Size:* hoog 23, breed 27 duim	Vinkeles [for] D	(Sold) fl 7:5 Swanenburg
1806/08/13	AMSCH	0108	*Moucheron. (F. de)* | Een bevallig Land- en Riviergezicht, met Scheepen, Schuiten en Beeldjes, zonachtig en bevallig gepenceeld | *Mat:* op doek *Size:* hoog 10, breed 13 duim	Daniel Mansveld	(Sold) fl 3 Nieuwenhuis
1806/08/13	AMSCH	0251	*F. de Moucheron* | Een Bergachtig Boomryk Landschap met Watervallen	Vinkeles [for] G[ruyter]	(Sold) fl 0:10 Gruiter
1806/08/20	HGBSM	0067	*De oude Moucheron* | Een Bergachtig Landschap met Gebouwen, rijk gestoffeerd met figuuren &c., door den ouden Moucheron | *Mat:* op doek *Size:* hoog 30, breed 25 duim	Macalester Loup [or others]	(Sold) fl 7 Praiston
1806/08/20	HGBSM	0212	*De oude Moucheron* | Een Italiaansch Landschap | *Mat:* op doek *Size:* hoog 22 ½, breed 29 ½ duim	Macalester Loup [or others]	(Sold) fl 18:10 Gram
1807/04/00	LNDLS	0039	*F. Moucheron* | Twee stuks hofgezigten met boomen, gebouwen en stoffagie | *Mat:* op doek *Size:* ieder hoog 24, breed 20 duim	[Abraham Delfos] [or others]	(Unknown)
1807/06/10	HGBSM	0039	*F. Moucheron* | Twee stuks hofgezigten met boomen, gebouwen en stoffagie | *Mat:* op doek *Size:* ieder hoog 24, breed 20 duim	Abraham Delfos [or others]	(Sold) fl 2:2 Tessier
1808/06/13	AMSCH	0102	*Moucheron (F. de)* | Een schoon boomrijk Italiaansch Landschap, met een troep Beesten. Zonachtig en fraai in uitvoering | *Mat:* op doek *Size:* hoog 39, breed 35 duim	E M Engelberts	(Sold) fl 92 J Schuman
1808/06/13	AMSCH	0220	*F. de Moucheron* | Een Graftombe, waarbij zich eenige Nimfen in het water baden; fraai	E M Engelberts	(Sold) fl 7:10 van Os
1808/10/28	AMVRS	0038	*Moucheron, (F. de)* | Een Bergachtig Landschap, met Geboomte, gestoffeerd met een Landman bij rustende Schapen, benevens eene Boerin, die eene Koe melkt, verder een Heer te Paard, ter regterzijde een Man bij een beladen Muilëzel en voorts een aangenaam verschiet. Zonachtig en fraai van Penceelsbehandeling | *Mat:* op doek *Size:* hoog 35, breed 31 duim	Marten Udink	(Sold) fl 15:10 Coclers
1808/10/28	AMVRS	0039	*Moucheron, (F. de)* | Een Italiaansch Landschap, ter zijde een stil Water, gestoffeerd met beladen Muilëzels, en gaande en rustende Reizigers. Warm van koloriet en meesterlijk gepenceeld | *Mat:* op paneel *Size:* hoog 17 ½, breed 27 ½ duim	Marten Udink	(Sold) fl 17 Rijdon
1809/06/13	AMSCH	0101	*F. Moucheron* | Dit Schilderij verbeeld een aangenaam Boom- en Bergachtig Landschap, op de voorgrond bij een opgaande Weg, een Heer te Paard, welke door een nevens hem gaande Knegt, door een Waterplas geleid word, verder ziet men rustende Reizigers en beladen Muilezels, het bevallige koloriet en de uitvoerige en zonachtige behandeling, maken dit stuk tot een der beste | *Mat:* op doek *Size:* hoog 25 ½, breed 22 duim	[Gruyter?]	(Bought In) fl 110
1809/06/13	AMSCH	0102	*F. Moucheron* | Een Italiaansch Bergachtig Landschap, met Gebouwen, ter zijde een Watertje, gestoffeerd met rijdende, gaande en rustende Landlieden, met hun Vee, warm van koloriet en meesterlijk behandeld | *Mat:* op doek *Size:* hoog 24, breed 30 duim	Y	(Sold) fl 14:10 T Spaan
1809/06/13	AMSCH	0103	*F. Moucheron* | Een Boomrijk Landschap, met Wooningen gestoffeerd, met Heeren en Dames te Paard, ter Jagt uitrijdende, verseld van Jagers en Honden; geschilderd | *Mat:* op doek *Size:* hoog 22, breed 26 duim	Y	(Sold) fl 2 Gruyter
1809/06/13	AMSCH	0104	*F. Moucheron* | Een Italiaansch Bergachtig Landschap, met beladen Muilezels en Rijzigers gestoffeerd, zonachtig behandeld | *Mat:* op paneel *Size:* hoog 18, breed 25 duim	Y [or] T	(Bought In) fl 26
1810/06/20	AMSCH	0045	*F. De Moucheron* | Een Italiaansch bergachtig Landschap, met Gebouwen, ter zijde een Watertje, waar door eenige Beesten gedreven worden; verder rijdende, gaande en rustende Landlieden, met hun Vee, en een bevallig	B	(Sold) fl 20 Roos

			verschiet. Warm van koloriet en meesterlijk geschilderd | *Mat:* op doek *Size:* hoog 24, breed 30 duimen		
1810/06/20	AMSCH	0046	*F. De Moucheron* | Een Italiaansch bergachtig Landschap, met Geboomte, en Water doorsneden, gestoffeerd met rustende en wandelende Reizigers. Meesterlijk | *Mat:* op doek *Size:* hoog 42, breed 56 duimen	S	(Sold) fl 1 L Pakker
1810/07/26	AMSCH	0054	*Moucheron (F.)* | Een aangenaam Landschap, met Gebouwen, Geboomte en Beeldjes. Uitvoerig en zonachtig behandeld | *Mat:* op doek *Size:* hoog 20, breed 15 duimen	Cassino	(Bought In) fl 2
1810/10/11	AMSCH	0058	*F. De Moucheron* | Een kapitaal Boschagtig Landschap, met hoog Geboomte, en Water doorsneeden, gestoffeerd met Heeren te Paard, gaande en rustende Reizigers; warm van koloriet, zonachtig en fraai geschilderd | *Mat:* op doek *Size:* hoog 42, breed 53 duimen	M	(Bought In) fl 41
1810/10/11	AMSCH	0059	*F. De Moucheron* | Een aangenaam Landschap, voor aan een Hofsteede, waarin een springend Fontijn, waarbij een Heer te Paard, benevens een Valkenier en een Jager met Honden, verder andere stoffagie en een Bergachtig verschiet, zonachtig en uitvoerig behandeld | *Mat:* op doek *Size:* hoog 30, breed 31 duimen	M	(Sold) fl 51 H Pakker
1810/10/11	AMSCH	0060	*F. De Moucheron* | Een Bergachtig Landschap, gestoffeerd met eene Vrouw zittende op een Ezel, waarbij een gaand Landman, verder eenige Koeijen en Schapen, zonachtig behandeld | *Mat:* op paneel *Size:* hoog 18, breed 16 duimen	[Levy Pakker?]	(Sold) fl 40 Gruiter
			Moucheron, Frédéric de (and Berchem, N.P.)		
1809/04/17	AMSCH	0054	*F. de Moucheron; N. Berchem* | Dit fraaije Schilderijtje verbeeld een Italiaansch Hoog Boschachtig Landschap, met een aanzienlijke Brug en Gebouwen, op de voorgrond een helder spiegelend Water, waar door eenige Beesten waaden, benevens een Landman zittende op een Ezel; voorts een aangenaam verschiet, het zonlicht doet een schoone werking, en is uitmuntend en van de beste behandeling, door F. de Moucheron, gestoffeerd door N. Berchem | *Mat:* op doek *Size:* hoog 15, breed 19 duim	C	(Sold or Bought In) fl 285
			Moucheron, Frédéric de (and Lingelbach)		
1802/02/23	AMREB	0036	*F. Moucheron; Lingelbach* | 1 Schoorsteenstuk, door F. Moucheron en Lingelbach | *Fmt:* schoorsteenstuk	Margaretha Maria van Laar	(Sold) fl 3 Royers
1804/05/07	AMSCH	0102	*Moucheron. (F. de); Lingelbach* | Een capitaal hoog Bergachtig Landschap met zwaar opgaand Geboomten, op de voorgrond gestoffeerd met en [sic] Vrouw op een Ezel, die door een Man geleid wodt [sic], terzyden een rustende reiziger, met een Jongen en een Hondt, op de hoogten tusschen 't Gebergten eenige Veedryvende Lieden, zonachtig en bevallig geschilderd | *Mat:* op doek *Size:* hoog 29, breed 37 duim	Vinkeles [for] G	(Sold) fl 30 Wed Achtienhoven
1804/05/07	AMSCH	0103	*Moucheron. (F. de); Lingelbach* | Een aangenaam Boom en Berachtig [sic] Landschap op de voorgrond ryk gestoffeerd met eenige Jaagers te voet en te paard, verzeldt van een ménigte van Honden, dewelken en Hert agterhalen, tusschen 't Geboomte op 't Gebergten eenigen capitalen sterk door den zon verligt werden Gebouwen, en eeu [sic] Bergachtig verschiet; meesterlyk geschilderd | *Mat:* op doek *Size:* hoog 35, breed 43 duim	Vinkeles [for] G	(Sold) fl 5 Gruyter
1804/07/25	AMSCH	0053	*Moucheron (F. de); J. Lingelbach* | In een dito [allerbevalligst capitaal Italiaansch Heuvelachtig] Landschap, verschillende van Ordinantie, vertoont zig ter linkerzyde, by een opgaande Weg, een Vrouw op een Ezel rydende, verzeld van een Hond, en agterwaarts een gaande Reiziger; hooger op een Huisman eenig Vee voortdryvende; ter andere zyde een stil Water en een bevallig verschiet; zonachtig, natuurlyk en uitvoerig door beide deeze Meesters gepenceeld | *Mat:* op doek *Size:* hoog 21, breed 25 duim *Notes:* It is unclear what "dito" refers to in the title.		(Sold) fl 200 Thais
1808/06/06	RMRIJ	0085	*Moucheron (Frederik de); Lingelbach. (Johannes)* | Een aangenaam bergachtig Landschap, rijk in allerhande hoog en laag geboomte, onder eene voortreffelijke Zomerlucht, gestoffeerd met reizende en rustende Beelden. Alles zeer schoon van kleur en uitvoerig behandeld [Paysage Italien richement orné de differentes sortes d'arbres distingués par leurs feuillages. Des Montagnes, des sites agréables, un beau lointain et un Ciel clair, tout cela joint aux figures soignées, forme un ensemble qui charme l'oeil. Ce Morceau d'un ton chaud et piquant et d'une touche spirituelle, est une Production savante de ces deux Artistes] | *Annots:* van Thys, Juli 1799 (f 270.-) Thijs berichtte 22 Juli 1798 het te Brussel gekocht te hebben (RMA I) *Mat:* op paneel *Size:* Hoog 12 ½, en breed 15 ¼ duim	Gerrit van der Pot, Heer van Groeneveld	(Sold) fl 450 van Leen
1810/08/01	AMSCH	0067	*Moucheron (Fredrik de); Johannes Lingelbag* | Een bergachtig Landschap met een Water, waar langs een opgaande Weg naar eene steenen Poort, verder Heeren en Vrouwen te paard, en Jagers met hunne Honden [Un Paysage coupé par des Collines, où l'on remarque un ruisseau le long d'une route qui mène à une porte batie en pierres ; il est orné de Seigneurs et de Dames, suivis de Chasseurs et de Chiens, allant à la chasse] | *Annots:* assez piquant, et bonnes figures mais les jours ij papillotent trop. (NGW) *Mat:* op doek *Size:* hoog 36, breed 50 duimen	Mr Pieter de Smeth van Alphen	(Sold) fl 910 T Spaan [for] Croese
			Moucheron, Frédéric de (and Schellinks)		
1803/12/12	AMSCH	0057	*F. de Moucheron; Schellinkx* | Een Landschap met hoog Geboomte, op de voorgrond een stil Water, waarby een Man met een Hond, aan de	B	(Sold) fl 50 Hodges

			overzyde van het Water ziet men een Heer en Dame op een Paard, waarby Jagers en Honden; krachtig en delicaat gepenceeld, door F. de Moucheron, gestoffeerd door Schellinkx | *Mat:* op doek *Size:* hoog 27, breed 31 duim		
1804/10/29	HRBAU	0066	*Moucheron (F. de); Schellings* | Een zeer bevallig bosch- en bergagtig Landschap; op den voorgrond ziet men eene Dame en een' Heer te paard, nevens eenige Jaagers en Honden, een Hert door een beek vervolgen; de tweede grond is klipagtig, met boomen en kreupelhout bewasschen, waar over men in een uitmuntend ver uitgestrekt bergagtig verschiet ziet, met Bosschen en Kasteelen voorzien, tot dat zig het blaauw Gebergte als in de lucht verliest. Zeer warm, zonagtig en uitvoerig behandeld | *Mat:* op doek *Size:* hoog 25, breed 33 duim	Simon Styl	(Unknown)
1804/10/29	HRBAU	0067	*Moucheron (F. de); Schellings* | Voor aan, op een' zandigen Weg, by hoog geboomte, zit eene Dame op een wit paard, benevens eenige Jaagers met Wild, welken schynen te rusten; waar agter een bosch- en bergagtig verschiet. Het coloriet is warm, en zeer uitvoerig behandeld | *Mat:* op doek *Size:* hoog 29, breed 37 duim	Simon Styl	(Unknown)

Moucheron, Frédéric de (and Schellinks, Daniel)

1803/08/17	AMSCH	0053	*Moncheron. (F. de); D Schellinks* | Een Italiaansch Landschap met Ruïnes, Geboomtens, en veruitgestrekt bergachtig Verschiet, de Voorgrond gestofeerd met een menigte Vee, een Herder, Herderin, en een ander op een Ezel, waarby een Hond, de beide Meesters hebben hierin ieder hun best gedaan, zynde voorts zonachtig behandeld | *Mat:* op doek op paneel *Size:* hoog 15, breed 19 duim	Anna Catharina Putman	(Bought In) fl 90
1803/08/17	AMSCH	0054	*Moncheron. (F. de); D Schellinks* | Een natuurlyk Landschap, op de Voorgrond met een Waterval, en hoog Gebergten in 't verschiet, ter zyde een Jager met zyn Honden, geschilderd als de voorgaande | *Mat:* op doek *Size:* hoog 19, breed 16 duim	Anna Catharina Putman	(Sold) fl 9:10 v^n Iperen

Moucheron, Frédéric de (and Velde, A.)

1801/04/13	AMSCH	0043	*F. de Moncheron; A. van de Velde* | Dit uitmundtend Taffereel [sic] verbeeld een aangenaam boom en bergachtig Landschap, met een heldere waterplas, gestoffeerd met een menigte Beeldjes, Paarden en Vee, een Jager is beezig op de voorgrond op eenige Eenden te schieten, het Geboomte is dun, het zonlicht frappant, en kan voor een der beste stukken van deeze voortreffelyke Meesters gehouden worden | *Mat:* op doek *Size:* hoog 21, breed 26 duim	Pierre Fouquet, junior	(Sold) fl 410 Coclers
1801/06/10	AMSCH	0110	*Moucheron. (F. de); stoffagie A. van de Velde* | Een Landschap, met hoog Geboomte en een Bergachtig verschiet, op de voorgrond ziet men een Jager met een Hond, verders een Man te paard, eenige Schaape dryvende, alles Zonachtig en delicaat behandeld | *Mat:* op doek *Size:* hoog 32, breed 27 duim *Notes:* Originally the artist's name was spelled "A. de Velde." This error was corrected in an errata sheet located at the end of the catalogue.	Herman ten Kate	(Sold) fl 405 J Yver
1801/06/10	AMSCH	0111	*Moucheron. (F. de); stoffagie A. van de Velde* | Een Zonachtig, Boom- en Bergachtig Landschap, met een aangenaam verschiet, gestoffeerd met Beelden en Vee, meesterlyk geschilderd | *Mat:* op doek *Size:* hoog 33, breed 44 duim *Notes:* Originally the artist's name was spelled "A. de Velde." This error was corrected in an errata sheet located at the end of the catalogue.	Herman ten Kate	(Sold) fl 39 Coclers
1801/06/10	AMSCH	0112	*Moucheron. (F. de); stoffagie A. van de Velde* | Een Landschap, doorsneden met een Rivier, op de voorgrond een staande en rustende Reiziger, Zonachtig en bevallig gepenceeld | *Mat:* op doek *Size:* hoog 26, breed 30 duim *Notes:* Originally the artist's name was spelled "A. de Velde." This error was corrected in an errata sheet located at the end of the catalogue.	Herman ten Kate	(Sold) fl 30 Taijs
1802/06/28	AMSCH	0107	*F. de Moucheron; A. van de Velde* | In dit alleraangenaamst Landschap, ziet men op een welig begroeiden Steenrots den Temple van Cybille te Tivoli, beneden ziet men een Herder met eenig Vee, verders over een Steene Brug twee Ezels met hun Dryver, en op de voorgrond by een stromende Beek een rustende Reiziger met een Hond; het heldere Zonlicht maakt dit stuk zeer bevallig; zynde delicaat gepenceeld, door F. de Moucheron en A. van de Velde | *Mat:* op doek *Size:* hoog 31, breed 25 duim	Anna Elink	(Bought In) fl 140
1802/09/06	AMSCH	0068	*F. de Moucheron; A. van de Velde* | Een hoog Bergachtig Landschap met een Waterval, op de voorgrond onder het Lommer van 't dartel Geboomte, staan en rusten eenige Schaapjes, beneevens een Gyt, verder een Véehoeder met Vée, en een aangenaam verschiet; natuurlyk gepenceeld | *Mat:* op doek *Size:* hoog 44, breed 35 duim	J	(Bought In) fl 18
1804/07/25	AMSCH	0052	*Moucheron (F. de); A. v. de Velde* | In dit allerbevalligst capitaal Italiaansch Heuvelachtig Landschap, met verschillend Geboomten, ziet men op de voorgrond by een opgaande Weg, ryk gestoffeert met een Drift Beesten, waarby een Huisman te Paard, daar nevens een gaande Vrouw met een Pak op het hoofd, en terzyde een ander Reiziger; in 't verschiet eenige Gebouwen op een Heuvel, en verders hoog Gebergten; het streelend zonlicht doet een aangenaame werking, en is van een fraaije en		(Sold) fl 315 Van der Schleij

			uitvoerige penceelbehandeling, door beide deeze vermaarde Meesters | *Mat:* op doek *Size:* hoog 36, breed 46 duim		
1809/09/06	AMSCH	0043	*Moucheron (F. de); A. van de Velde* | Een Gezicht op een Fontijn en Beek, waarbij twee Beeldjes; het water is helder, en alles word door een helder zonlicht bescheenen, en is delicaat gepenceeld | *Mat:* op doek *Size:* hoog 16, breed 18 duim	Johannes Caudri	(Sold) fl 59 van Iperen
1809/09/06	AMSCH	0044	*Moucheron (F. de); A. van de Velde* | Een Gezicht op een Hofstéden, in het midden ziet men een Fontijn, waarbij wandelende Beelden en in 't verschiet een Heer te Paard, waarbij eenige Honden; niet minder als de voorgaande | *Mat:* op paneel *Size:* hoog 20, breed 16 duim	Johannes Caudri	(Sold) fl 42 Coclers

Moucheron, Frédéric de (manner)

1809/06/13	AMSCH	0225	*F. Moucheron* | Een Bergachtig Landschap, met beladen Muil-Ezels, gestoffeerd; als F. Moucheron	S[chley]	(Sold) fl 0:6 L Pakker

Moucheron, Frédéric de (manner; and Bergen, D., manner)

1809/04/22	AMYVR	0178	*F. de Moucheron; D. van Bergen* | Een Landschap met Boerenwooningen en stoffagie van Beelden en Beesten, als door F. de Moucheron en D. van Bergen	de Bruin	(Sold) fl 2:5 du Pree

Moucheron, Isaac de (Ordonantie)

1801/06/10	AMSCH	0113	*Moucheron. (J.)* | Een Italiaansch Hofgezicht, met Geboomte en Gebouwen, gestoffeert met twee Heeren die te paard stygen, alles warm en Zonachtig uitgevoerd | *Mat:* op doek *Size:* hoog 24, breed 20 duim	[Doublet]	(Sold) fl 23 Stevens
1802/02/16	AMSCH	0029	*J. de Moncheron* | Een gezicht op Romen bevallig gestoffeerd en meesterlyk behandeld	E	(Sold) fl 60 Coclers
1802/02/16	AMSCH	0035	*J. de Moucheron* | een Capitaal, Boomryk, Heuvelagtig, Landschap, waar in verbeeld, Heeren te paard, met Jagers te voet. Een Harte-beest najaagende.zonagtig en fraay gepenceeld	H	(Sold) fl 4 van Iperen
1802/05/05	AMSCH	0125	*J. de Moucherron* | Een prachtig Hofgezicht, met een Bergachtig verschiet | *Mat:* op doek *Size:* hoog 29, breed 22 duim	BB	(Sold) fl 28 Pruijssenaar [for] R
1802/05/05	AMSCH	0126	*J. de Moucherron* | Een Bergachtig Landschap, met Ruïnes en hoog Geboomte | *Mat:* op doek *Size:* hoog 25, breed 32 duim	BB	(Sold) fl 17 Ackina
1802/05/24	HGBAK	0014	*J. Moucheron* | Een Italiaansch Gezicht met Gebouwen, op de voorgrond eenige badende Mannen, door J. Moucheron, hoog 15 duim, breed 21 duim, op doek, zwarte lyst en vergulde binnenrand | companion to lot 15 *Mat:* op doek *Size:* hoog 15 duim, breed 21 duim	Mejuffrouw A van der Mieden	(Sold) fl 38 for lots 14 & 15. Kleijn
1802/05/24	HGBAK	0015	*J. Moucheron* | Een dito [Italiaansch Gezicht met Gebouwen] tot een weerga, met figuren gestoffeerd, door denzelve Meester [J. Moucheron], hoog en breed als voren, dito [zwarte] lyst | companion to lot 14 *Size:* hoog 15 duim, breed 21 duim	Mejuffrouw A van der Mieden	(Sold) fl 38 for lots 14 & 15. Kleijn
1802/06/28	AMSCH	0108	*J. de Moucheron* | Twee stuks fraai gestoffeerde Arcadische Landschappen, met een menigte Beelden; beide dun en delicaat gepenceeld, door J. de Moucheron, op Doek | *Mat:* op doek *Size:* hoog 20, breed 25 duim	B	(Sold) fl 32 Coclers
1802/07/21	HGKAN	0112	*J. Moucheron* | Een Schildery op Doek, verbeeldende een Buyten-verblyf, versierd met dertien Beeldjes, zeer fraay geschildert | *Mat:* op doek *Size:* hoog 10 duym en breed 1 voet		(Unknown)
1803/08/01	AMSCH	0021	*Moucheron. (J.)* | Een zonachtig Landschap, in het midden met een Waterval en eenige Beelden gestoffeerd, natuurlyk behandeld | *Mat:* op doek *Size:* hoog 19, breed 14 duim	J	(Sold) fl 7:10 Hodges
1803/08/17	AMSCH	0055	*Moucheron, (J. de)* | Twee stuks Gezichten binnen Romen, gestoffeerd met verscheiden Beelden, en een Wagen met Ossen bespannen, delicaat, kragtig en zonachtig uitgevoerd | *Mat:* op paneel *Size:* ieder hoog 6 ½, breed 9 duim	Anna Catharina Putman	(Sold) fl 9:5 Camphuijsen
803/12/15	MGLAC	0004	*J. Moucheron* | Een Italiaansch Landschap, met een Rivier en verscheiden Figuuren; zeer fraai en natuurlyk geschilderd | companion to lot 5 *Mat:* op doek *Size:* hoog duim 16, breed duim 22	Mr L H de Haze Bomme	(Unknown)
803/12/15	MGLAC	0005	*J. Moucheron* | Een dito [Italiaansch Landschap, met een Rivier en verscheiden Figuuren], wêergaê; niet minder dan de voorgaande | companion to lot 4 *Mat:* op doek *Size:* hoog duim 16, breed duim 22 *Notes:* It is unclear what "dito" refers to in the title.	Mr L H de Haze Bomme	(Unknown)
804/08/08	AMSCH	0114	*J. de Moucheron* | In een Noordsch Berg- en Boomryk Landschap ziet men op de voorgrond, by eenige Rotsen, een Landman, met twee belaaden Ezels, verders langs een Weg twee belaaden dito en twee Lieden, verders in de Rivier verscheide Scheepen, waarby eenige Kooplieden, en over dezelve hooge Gebergtens; fraai van licht, en helder en uitvoerig gepenceeld | *Mat:* op doek *Size:* hoog 20, breed 24 duim	Vink[eles] [for] W	(Bought In) fl 29
804/08/08	AMSCH	0115	*J. de Moucheron* | Twee stuks Boom- Duin- en Bergachtige Landschappen, op de voorgrond helder spiegelende Waters, waardoor een ménigte Beesten waden, met hunne Hoeders, verders eenige wandelende en vrachtdraagende Beelden, en aangenaame Bergachtige verschieten, beiden zonachtig en fiks gepenceeld | *Mat:* op doek *Size:* hoog 27, breed 34, duim	Vink[eles] [for] S	(Sold) fl 2:15 Palmhoff

1804/08/08	AMSCH	0116	*J. de Moucheron* | Een Landschap met hoog Geboomte en een Fontyn, op de voorgrond gestoffeerd met een Teekenaar en wandelende Beeldjes, zonachtig op Paneel | *Mat:* op paneel *Size:* hoog 16, br. 13 duim	Roos [for] D	(Sold) fl 13 Hulswit
1804/10/16	DLOND	0154	*J. Moucheron* | Landschap met Ruïne en Watergezicht. Paysage, des Ruïnes &c. | *Mat:* op doek *Size:* hoog 22, breed 27		(Sold) fl 6:5 Mahy
1804/10/29	HRBAU	0068	*Moucheron, (J. de)* | Een fraai Arcadisch Landschap, met Geboomte, Kasteelen en Ruïnen voorzien, waar langs men in een ver uitgestrekt verschiet ziet. Dit Stukjen is van den grootsten smaak, en uitvoerig geschilderd | *Mat:* op doek *Size:* hoog 18, breed 19 duim	Simon Styl	(Unknown)
1804/12/10	AMSCH	0055	*J. de Moucheron* | Door een prachtig Gebouw ziet men een Haven met onderscheiden Scheepen, op de voorgrond gestoffeerd, met diverse figuuren, krachtig geschilderd | *Mat:* op doek *Size:* Hoog 35, breed 45 duim	Jan De Groot	(Sold) fl 3 Spaan
1804/12/10	AMSCH	0056	*J. de Moucheron* | Een fraai Landschap, met hoog geboomte, ryk gestoffeerd, met beelden; helder van coloriet, en fix gepenceeld | *Mat:* op doek *Size:* Hoog 23, breed 27 duim	Jan De Groot	(Sold) fl 3 Reyers
1805/07/03	AMSCH	0115	*J. de Moucheron* | Twee stuks Arcadische Landschappen, met hoog Geboomten, Gebouwen, Watervallen, en fraaije stoffagie van Beelden; het Landschap is zonachtig, en de Watervallen, als Ruisdaal behandeld | *Mat:* op doek *Size:* hoog 20, breed 24 duim	G	(Sold) fl 57 Agina
1805/07/03	AMSCH	0116	*J. de Moucheron* | Een Boom- en Bergachtig Landschap, met de Ruïne van een oude Temple, op de Voorgrond eenige badende Lieden; fiks en meesterlyk op Doek | *Mat:* op doek *Size:* hoog 12, breed 16 duim	V[inkeles]	(Sold) fl 5:10 Agina
1805/07/10	AMSCH	0092	*J. de Moucheron* | Twee stuks, Berg en Boomryke Italiaansche Landschappen met Fontynen, Statuën, prachtige Gebouwen en een ménigte stoffagie van Beelden en Beesten; beide deeze stukken zyn zonachtig en fraai gepenceeld | *Mat:* op doek *Size:* hoog 20, breed 25 duim	V[inkeles] [for] N	(Sold) fl 46 L Pakker
1805/07/10	AMSCH	0093	*J. de Moucheron* | Twee stuks Gezichten binne Rome; met een ménigte stoffagie; beide delicaat en zonachtig gepenceeld | *Size:* hoog 6 ½, breed 8 ½ duim	V[inkeles] [for] N	(Sold) fl 9:10 Agina
1805/07/10	AMSCH	A0001[a]	*J. de Moucheron* | Zes stuks Capitaale Kamerstukken, zynde fraai gestoffeerde Landschappen, met Gebouwen, Watervallen, enz. [Fraaije geschilderde Kamer-Behangsels] | *This Lot:* Vier stuks Capitaale Kamerstukken *Size:* hoog 11 voet, breed 9 voet *Notes:* The bracketed information in the title appears above lot A1 and refers to lots A1 to A8.	H	(Sold) fl 12 for lots A1[a] & A1[b]. T van Iperen
1805/07/10	AMSCH	A0001[b]	*J. de Moucheron* | Zes stuks Capitaale Kamerstukken, zynde fraai gestoffeerde Landschappen, met Gebouwen, Watervallen, enz. [Fraaije geschilderde Kamer-Behangsels] | *This Lot:* Twee stuks Capitaale Kamerstukken *Size:* hoog 11 voet, breed 3 voet, 8 duim *Notes:* The bracketed information in the title appears above lot A1 and refers to lots A1 to A8.	H	(Sold) fl 12 for lots A1[a] & A1[b]. T van Iperen
1806/08/13	AMSCH	0109	*Moucheron. (J. de)* | Een Italiaansch Bergachtig Landschap, op de voorgrond by een stil Water, ziet men ryzende Lieden te Paard, verders verscheide Gebouwen en Geboomten; warm en zonachtig van behandeling | *Mat:* op doek *Size:* hoog 24, breed 32 duim	van der Voort	(Sold) fl 53 Hafner
1808/06/11	RMRIJ	0097	*J: Moucheron* | Een Boomryk Landschap waar in een Man te Paard, Valbrug enz. | *Mat:* op paneel *Size:* hoog 19, breed 15 ½ duim		(Sold) fl 3 Van Giesen
1808/10/28	AMVRS	0040	*Moucheron, (J. de)* | Een Bergachtig Landschap, met Water en weelig Geboomte. Meesterlijk als de voorgaande behandeld | *Mat:* op doek *Size:* hoog 17, breed 22 duim	Marten Udink	(Sold) fl 11 T Spaan
1810/08/06	AMSCH	0149	*J. de Moucheron* | Een prachtig gestoffeerd Hofgezigt	G	(Sold) fl 5:5 Coclers [or] Dupre
1810/10/10	MGCIT	0026	*J. de Moucheron* | Een schoon en bekoorlijk Landschap, waar in veel Geboomte en een zeer aangenaam verschiet, zeer natuurlijk en fraai geschilderd; voorts is dit Stuk op den voorgrond gestoffeerd met verscheide te Paard rijdende en wandelende Figuren, als mede natuurlijke Gewassen &c.	Caspar van Citters	(Unknown)
1810/10/10	MGCIT	0027	*J. de Moucheron* | Nog één niet minder bevallig Landschap, op eene gelijke meesterlijke trant behandeld en schoon met vele verandering in de schikking en keuze der Voorwerpen, niet te min kragtig en tevens zeer zonägtig behandeld	Caspar van Citters	(Unknown)

Moucheron, Isaac de (Ordonantie) (and Berckheyde, G.)

1807/08/26	AMSCH	0014	*G. Berkheide; J. de Moucheron* | Op een Pleisterplaats ziet men verscheiden Reizigers te Paard, zich ververschende; by een Put staat eene Vrouw met een Koperen Kan, terwyl een andere eene Geit melkt, verders nog verscheiden Paarden, Honden, enz.; fraai geschilderd | *Mat:* op doek *Size:* hoog 22, breed 27 duim	de Vries	(Bought In or Withdrawn)

Moucheron, Isaac de (Ordonantie) (and Lingelbach)

1809/09/06	AMSCH	0045	*Moucheron (J. de); J. Lingelbach* | Een Hofgezicht met fraaije Vijvers, springende Fontijnen en stoffagie van Beelden; zonagtig geschilderd | *Mat:* op doek *Size:* hoog 38, breed 45 duim	Johannes Caudri	(Sold) fl 6 L Pakker

Moucheron, Isaac de (Ordonantie) (and Storck, Abr.)

1808/06/11	RMRIJ	0090	*J: de Moucheron; Gestoffeerd door Stork* | Een Italiaansch Hofgezicht, ryk gestoffeerd, geleerd en konstig geschilderd | *Mat:* op doek *Size:* hoog 20, breed 24 duim		(Sold) fl 40 Van Leen

Moyen, H. [Unidentified]

1802/05/10	MGSAN	0040	*H. Moyen: 1785* | Een Landschap, daarop een Boerenwooning; terzyden een Poort, waaruit een Man komt, met een Drift Koeiën en Schaapen; voorts een gelaaden Wagen, en een Man, een Paard den toom aandoende; voorts nog een Wagen, met een gezadeld Paard, aangenaam en zacht geschilderd, door H. Moyen: 1785. in vergulde Lyst | *Size:* hoog 11 ½ duim, breed 15 ½ duim *Inscr:* H. Moyen: 1785 (signed and dated?) *Notes:* It is unclear whether the name and date are inscribed on the painting.	Johan Dirk Kruysse	(Unknown) £ 5

Murant, Emanuel

1801/06/10	AMSCH	0114	*Murant. (E.)* | In het midden van dit Stukje, staat een vervallen Schuur, alwaar een Man over de deur ligt, zyn Kippen te voeren, verder enige Varkens en andere stoffage, zeer uitvoerig en natuurlyk gepenceeld | *Mat:* op doek *Size:* hoog 13, breed 16 duim	Herman ten Kate	(Sold) fl 131 Coclers
1802/05/05	AMSCH	0137	*E. Murant* | Een Landschap met eenige Boeren Woningen en verdere Huislieden | *Mat:* op paneel *Size:* hoog 7, breed 10 duim	G	(Sold) fl 10 van Iperen
1804/02/27	AMSCH	0072	*Murand. (E.)* | In een aangenaam Landschap, ter zyde eenige Boerenwoningen en een Moolen ziet men een belaaden Vragtkar en anderen stoffage, uitvoerig van penceel behandeling | *Mat:* op paneel *Size:* hoog 14, breed 19 duim	C	(Bought In) fl 18
1804/05/07	AMSCH	0107	*Murant. (E.)* | Twee stuks bevallige Landschappen met eenige Boerewoningen enz., uitvoerig en delicaat van behandeling | *Mat:* op paneel *Size:* hoog 12, breed 15 duim	Y[ver] [for] W	(Bought In) fl 33
1804/08/08	AMSCH	0121	*E. Murant* | Twee stuks, een Gezicht op eenige oude vervallen Gebouwen en een Pieramiede; en een andere een Boeren Dorpgezicht, aan een Rivier, waarin een Zeilschuit, verders beiden eigenaartig gestoffeerd, en uitvoerig gepenceeld | *Mat:* op paneel *Size:* hoog 13, breed 14 duim	Vink[eles] [for] W	(Bought In) fl 27
1804/10/16	DLOND	0155	*E. Murant* | Twee stukjens. Ruïnen met vele Beelden. Deux pièces. Ruïnes & des figures | *Size:* hoog 11, breed 14		(Unknown)
1805/07/10	AMSCH	0105	*E. Murant* | Twee stuks Boerendorpgezichten met stoffagie Beeldjes, zonachtig en piquant van licht | *Mat:* op doek *Size:* hoog 13, breed 14 ½ duim	V[inkeles] [for] G	(Sold) fl 9 Lafontaine
1806/05/05	AMSCH	0100	*E. Murant* | Een Stadgezicht met verscheide Beelden; meesterlyk door E. Murant	V[inkeles]	(Bought In) fl 3
1806/08/13	AMSCH	0104	*Murant. (E.)* | Een bevallig Landchapje met Boerewoningen, vervallen Schuur en Geboomten, gestoffeerd met een Boer en Boerin, leggende Varkens, Kippen en een aangenaam verschiet; delicaat gepenceeld | *Mat:* op doek *Size:* hoog 13, breed 16 duim	Coclers	(Withdrawn)
1808/06/11	RMRIJ	0117	*E: Murant* | Een aartig Landschapje met Gebouwen, zeer uitvoerig | *Mat:* op paneel		(Unknown) fl 4
1808/11/28	AMSCH	0044	*E. Murand* | Een Landschap, met vervallen Boeren Woningen, gestoffeerd met Huislieden bij eenig staand en leggend Vee, fiks | *Mat:* op paneel *Size:* hoog 14, breed 20 duim	[Gruyter?]	(Bought In) fl 5:5
1808/12/31	RMHSN	0025	*Muron* | Twee stuks Landschapjes | *Mat:* op paneel	G Spanjaart [or] H de Haas [or] C van der Looy Lans	(Unknown)
1809/04/17	AMSCH	0058	*E. Murand* | Een Landschap met vervalle Boere Woningen, gestoffeerd met een Landman, zittende op een Ezel, waar bij eene gaande Vrouw, en een roo [sic] bonte Koe; zeer natuurlijk behandeld | *Mat:* op paneel *Size:* hoog 15, breed 21 duim	T	(Sold) fl 85
1809/04/17	AMSCH	0059	*E. Murand* | Een Landschap met eenige Boere Woningen, gestoffeerd met verscheide Huislieden; bevallig geschilderd | *Mat:* op paneel *Size:* hoog 8 ½, breed 12 duim	Crajenschot	(Sold) fl 1

Murillo, Bartolomé Esteban

1801/06/13	LNDLS	0045	*Morelles* | Twee zittende Jongelingen die fruit eeten, daar nevens staat een met druiven, op paneel | *Mat:* op paneel *Size:* hoog 16, breed 12 duimen	D van R	(Sold) fl 7 A Delfos
1806/08/13	AMSCH	0103	*Morrillos. (F.)* | Deeze capitaale Ordinantie in een Landschap, verbeeld twee Italiaansche Landjongens met dobbelsteene speelende; de Caracters zyn natuurlyk, de voorwerpen levensgrooten, het coloriet aangenaam en van een meesterlyk stoute penceelbehandeling | *Mat:* op doek *Size:* hoog 55, breed 46 duim *Notes:* The artist's name was given as "Morrillos. (F.)" but we have assumed this is an error.	Roos	(Bought In) fl 50
1807/08/26	AMSCH	0122	*Morillos* | Twee stuks capitaale Voorwerpen, verbeeldende de eene een jong Meisje in galante Kleeding, levensgrootte, staande by een Tafel, waarop een Bennetje met Duiven geplaatst is, waarby een Hondje; zy houd in de regterhand een Duif by de Vlerken, en ter zyde leggen twee Hoenders. De andere vertoont een jong Meisje, die uit een Koperen Ketel	Joseph Vallette	(Sold) fl 10 Spruit

			Water in een dito Bekken giet, waarby een Gans, Hoenders, een Kat en twee O.I. Rotten; beide krachtig van koloriet, en van een meesterlyke fraaije penceelsbehandeling | *Mat:* op doek *Size:* ieder hoog 38, breed 50 duim		
1810/08/06	AMSCH	0081	*Morillos* | In een Landschap ziet men op den voorgrond, twee Jongelingen met Dobbelsteenen speelen; schoon geschilderd | *Mat:* op doek *Size:* hoog 55, breed 46 duimen	R[oos]	(Sold) fl 38 Cassano
			Murillo, Bartolomé Esteban (or Murillo, manner)		
1807/04/13	AMSCH	0001	*Door, of als Morillos* | Deeze Capitaale Ordinantie van twee Leevens-groote Beelden steld voor eene bejaarde Vrouw, bezig zijnde eenen Jongeling te reinigen, die een stuk brood in zijn hand heeft; verzeld van een Hond, en verder toepasselijk Bijwerk, fraai van Licht, en meesterlijk behandeld | *Mat:* op doek *Size:* hoog 53, breed 42 duimen	Everard de Burlett	(Sold) fl 900 for lots 1 & 2. Coclers
1807/04/13	AMSCH	0002	*Door, of als Morillos* | In dit stuk ziet men een jongen Fruitverkooper, schijnende wegens eenige Fruiten met een jong Meisje te handelen; verders eenige Vrugten enz., deeze Ordinantie is mede meesterlijk en fraai gepenseeld | *Mat:* op doek *Size:* hoog 53, breed 42 duimen	Everard de Burlett	(Sold) fl 900 for lots 1 & 2. Coclers
			Murillo, Bartolomé Esteban (manner)		
1805/10/09	HGBSM	0035	*Morillos* | Een jongman in 't bont gekleed, met een fluit in de hand, in de manier van Morillos | *Mat:* op paneel *Size:* hoog 19 ½ breet 16 duim	T H van Willigen [or others]	(Sold) fl 30 Valette
1807/08/26	AMSCH	0252	*Morillos* | Twee Italiaansche Landloopers Jongens, zittende in een Landschap, en schynen zig te vermaken met Fruit te eeten, kragtig gepenceeld, op Doek, in de manier van Morillos | *Mat:* op doek *Size:* hoog 45, breed 38 duim	Joseph Vallette	(Sold) fl 17 Jozi
1807/08/26	AMSCH	0287	*Morillos* | Een Jongeling met een Fluit in de hand; delicaat als Morillos	Joseph Vallette	(Sold) fl 3:15 Andriesse
1810/07/26	AMSCH	0052	*Morillos (als)* | Een vrolijk zingend Man, met een Muziekpapier in zijne hand en een Bril op de neus. Zeer schoon | *Mat:* op doek *Size:* hoog 28, breed 21 duimen	Cassino	(Sold) fl 6 Spruyt
			Musscher, Michiel van		
1803/07/18	AMSCH	0030	*Musscher (M. van)* | Een Medicus zittende in zyn Studeerkamer, met een Urinaal in zyn hand, verders een menigte bywerk, als Boeken, Vyzels, Potjes en andere schilderachtige geplaatste bywerken, het ligt is bevallig en de penceelsbehandeling in de manier van Ostads [Un Docteur assis dans sa Bibliotheque devant une table couverte d'un tapis, & entouré d'une multitude d'acçessoires, examine un Urinal. La Representation est eclairée par un fenêtre qui produit un très bel effet de lumiere. Ce joli tableau composé dans la maniere d'Ad. van Ostade, a le mérite d'être très soigné dans tous ses details & l'avantage d'un [sic] couleur vraye.] | *Mat:* op paneel *Size:* hoog 16, breed 14 duim	Maria Theresia Andrioli	(Sold) fl 63 C S Roos
1803/07/18	AMSCH	0031	*Musscher (M. van)* | Op een Brug van de Prinsegragt te Amsterdam, ziet men een Groenvrouw, dragende drie Manden met Groentens, zy word aangesproken door een Dienstmaagd die haar geld schynt te bieden, in het verschiet ziet men de Westertoren; dit door het zonligt zeer frappant stukje, is wel getoetst, en van een aangenaame couleur en penceels-behandeling [Sur un Pont du Canal du Prince à Amsterdam, l'on voit en face une verduriere chargée de trois Paniers de legumes & d'un vuide ; elle est accostée par une servante qui semble lui marchander des Haricôts. La perspective perce jusqu'á la Tour de l'eglise occidentale. Ce tableau agréable est expressif, & touché avec beaucoup d'intelligence ; les costumes bien rendus ajoutent au mérite de la couleur.] | *Mat:* op paneel *Size:* hoog 21, breed 16 duim [haut 12, large 16 pouces] *Notes:* The dimensions differ in the Dutch and French editions of the catalogue.	Maria Theresia Andrioli	(Sold) fl 95 van Iperen
1804/08/08	AMSCH	0110	*M. van Muscher* | In een Boeren Binnenhuis ziet men voor een Tafel, waarop een ménigte Huisraad, een Vrouw, welke Worst stopt, waarby een vrolyke Boer en een Jongen, welke een Blaas in de Hand houd, verders toepasselyk Huisraad; meesterlyk geschilderd | *Size:* hoog 18 ½, breed 16 ½ duim	Vink[eles] [for] W	(Bought In) fl 29 ½
1804/08/08	AMSCH	0111	*M. van Muscher* | In een Gemeubileerd Binnenvertrek zit een bejaarde Vrouw aan een Tafel, met een Tapyten Kleed gedekt, waarop een ménigte Schryfgereedschap, Kandelaar, Doos, en ander Bywerk, schynde te spreeken met een andere Vrouw, over een Brief welke zy in haar hand heeft; dit stuk is van een fraaije behandeling en couleur | *Mat:* op doek *Size:* hoog 40, breed 35 duim	Roos [for] H	(Sold) fl 21 Coclers
1805/07/10	AMSCH	0097	*M. Muscher* | Twee stuks een Mans en Vrouwe Pourtrait, beide in deftige Kleeding, zittende voor een Tafel brieven te schryven, en verder bywerk; uitvoerig op Paneel | *Mat:* op paneel *Size:* hoog 19, breed 22 duim	V[inkeles] [for] L	(Sold) fl 1 Mensaart
1810/08/06	AMSCH	0082	*Musscher (M. van)* | Een deftig Heer staande in een Landschap, houdende twee doode Vogels in zijn hand, nevens hem een Hond; uitvoerig geschilderd | *Mat:* op koper *Size:* hoog 14, breed 11 duimen	C	(Sold) fl 40 Stoopendaal [for] B
			Mutscher [Unidentified]		
1808/10/28	AMVRS	0037a[H]	*Mutscher* | [Untitled] | *Notes:* This lot was added in by hand in the AA and EBNP copies of the catalogue, but without giving a title.	Marten Udink	(Sold) fl 34:10 B Kooij

Mutscher, A. van [Unidentified]

1801/05/11	AMSCH	0058	*A. van Mutscher* | Een Landschap met hoog geboomte, ter linker zyde ziet men een rots, waar voor een zark ligt, uitvoerig geschilderd | *Mat:* op paneel *Size:* hoog 11, breed 11 duim	P[ruyssenaar]	(Sold) fl 4 Boelen

Muys, Nicolaes

1808/06/06	RMRIJ	0087	*Muijs. (Nicolaas)* | Op eene Publieke Markt, verrijkt met fraaije Gebouwen en Geboomte, vertoont zich op den voorgrond eene bevallige Juffrouw, twee Patrijzen in de hand houdende; achter haar eene Vrouw, bij eene tafel staande, waarop dood Wild en Gevogelte ligt. Een fraaije Paauw, gezeten op eene mande door eene muscovische mat bedekt, versiert den voorgrond. Verder een groot aantal figuren van beide sexe in verschillende bezigheden. Alles zeer konstig en alleruitvoerigst geschilderd [Un Marché public, où l'on voît de beaux Bâtiments, une riante verdure, et de belles figures. Une Dame, qui tient des Perdreaux à la main, semble quitter une Marchande qui a devant elle une Table chargée de toutes sortes de Volaille etc. Un Paon sur un Panier couvert de nattes, décore le devant de ce Tableau, qui est encore enrichi de plusieurs autres accessoires et dont le fini et l'imitation fidêle de la Nature, mérite les plus grands Eloges] | *Annots:* 1783 gekocht van Muys (f 525.-) (RMA I) *Mat:* op mahonie paneel *Size:* Hoog 27 ¾, en breed 23 ½ duim	Gerrit van der Pot, Heer van Groeneveld	(Sold) fl 310 J J Havelaar
1808/06/06	RMRIJ	0088	*Muijs. (Nicolaas)* | Een gezigt van Rotterdam; zijnde eene afbeelding van de Blaak naar de Beurs, van de Leuvenhaven af te zien. Uitvoerig behandeld. (N° 45, door G. Groenewegen, is de wedergade van deze) [Ce Tableau est le Pendant du N°. 45 par G. Groenewegen. Il represente un Canal nommé le *Blaak* prés de la Bourse, dans l'intérieur de la ville de Rotterdam, et est enrichi de quantité de Bateaux et de figures etc.] | companion to lot 45, by G. Groenewegen *Annots:* verk. Oct. 1802 (f 25 – 8) (RMA I) *Mat:* op paneel *Size:* Hoog 14 ½, en breed 18 ½ duim	Gerrit van der Pot, Heer van Groeneveld	(Sold) fl 130 Cremer

Myer, L. de [Unidentified]

1802/09/06	AMSCH	0083	*L. de Myer* | Een hévig Gevegt tusschen Ruitery, vol gewoel; fiks behandeld | *Mat:* op paneel	Wed Grave [or others]	(Sold) fl 2 Gruiter

Myin, Hendrik Aarnout

1809/06/13	AMSCH	0108	*H. Mayin* | In een kapitaal Bergachtig Landschap, ziet men op de voorgrond op een grasige vlakte, een rustende Landman bij grazende Bokken en Schaapen, verder op een hoogte een staande Ezel en een liggende Koe, agterwaards een stille Rivier met Vaartuigen en een bevallig verschiet; zonachtig en delicaat gepenceeld | *Mat:* op paneel *Size:* hoog 23, breed 29 duim	[Gruyter?]	(Bought In) fl 91

Myn, G. van der

1801/03/16	AMSCH	0035	*G. van der Meyn* | Twee stuks bevallige Meisjes, uitvoerig geschilderd	P[ruyssenaar]	(Sold) fl 3:10 v d Schley [for] S
1801/04/13	AMSCH	0048	*G. van der Myn* | Een bevallige Dame in galante kleeding beezig Oesters te eeten, haar satyne Rok is zeer fraay en glansryk, en voor het overige is hetzelve kloek geschilderd | *Mat:* op doek *Size:* hoog 33, breed 26 duim	Pierre Fouquet, junior	(Sold) fl 6:10 v Dijl
1804/08/08	AMSCH	0137	*G. v. d. Myn* | Het Afbeeldzel van Fredrik Koning van Pruissen; in 't graauw geschilderd	Schley [for] B	(Sold) fl 0:12 Bernard
1804/12/10	AMSCH	0063	*G. van der Myn* | Een bevallige Dame, in galante kleeding, staande in een hofgezicht, houdende met de eene hand vast het voorschoot met eenige Bloemen, en met de andere grypt ze een Angelierbloem, in een aarde pot staande, die voor haar geplaatst is; het natuurlyk coloriet, zoo van het naakt als onderscheide stoffen der kleederen zyn voortreffelyk behandeld | *Mat:* op doek *Size:* Hoog 31, breed 25 ½ duim	Jan De Groot	(Sold) fl 6:5 v Dijl
1809/05/26	HADAA	0022	*G. v.d. Myn* | Een Heer die een Teekening beziet bij kaarslicht	Mejuffrouw de Wed David Heemskerk [or others]	(Unknown)

Myn, Herman van der

1801/08/19	AMSCH	0063	*van der Myn* | In een Bosachtig Landschap ziet men een Dame, op de Guitar speelen, zonachtig geschilderd	Pruyssen[r] [for] Q	(Sold) fl 4:5 Boelen
1802/04/13	HAVIN	0066	*van der Myn* | Een dito [Hist:]		(Unknown)
1802/04/13	HAVIN	0068	*van der Myn* | Vertumnus en Pomona		(Unknown)
1802/05/05	AMSCH	0149	*van der Myn* | In een Boomryk Landschap staat een bevallige Herderin, nevens haar op de grond zit eene Slaapende Herder, uitvoerig gepenceeld	J	(Sold) fl 2:10 Hulk
1802/05/05	AMSCH	0150	*van der Myn* | Een bevallige Dame | *Size:* hoog 16, breed 14 duim	J	(Sold) fl 1:5 Pruijssenaar [for] R
1802/06/28	AMSCH	0126	*van der Myn* | Een Heer en een Dame in een Landschap | *Mat:* op doek *Size:* hoog 18, breed 14 ½ duim	Anna Elink	(Sold) fl 0:12 van Iperen
1802/12/13	AMSCH	0119	*van der Myn* | In een aangenaam Hofgezigt, ziet men een bevallige Dame, de Handen Wassen, by een loopende Fontyn, dun en bevallig gepenceeld | *Mat:* op paneel *Size:* hoog 17, breed 13 ½ duim	Pruyssenaar [for] A	(Sold) fl 1:10 L Pakker

1808/08/23	AMSCH	0106	*Mijn. (H. van der)* | Dit capitaal Schilderij verbeeld, alwaar Petrus uit het Scheepje getreeden, op de Zee wandeld, voor hem ziet men Christus, welke de hand naar hem toereikt; in het midden vertoond zig het Scheepje met de andere Apostelen; de karacters zyn treffend, en is krachtig en van een meesterlijk penceel. NB. Dit stuk is beschreven bij J. van Gool, 2de Deel, pag. 48 | *Mat:* op doek *Size:* hoog 49, breed 39 duim	C	(Bought In) fl 65
1808/12/31	RMHSN	0011	*Vander Myn* | Een Vrouwe Pourtrait, door Vander Myn, op Paneel, fiks behandeld | *Mat:* op paneel	G Spanjaart [or] H de Haas [or] C van der Looy Lans	(Unknown)
1810/08/06	AMSCH	0083	*Mijn (H. van der)* | Deze Ordonantie verbeelt, Petrus uit het Scheepje getreeden, op de Zee wandelende, voor hem ziet men den Zaligmaker, welke hem de hand toereikt, verder ziet men het Scheepje met de andere Apostelen, de karakters zijn treffend; het is meesterlijk geschilderd, en beschreeven bij J. van Gool, 2de Deel, bl. 47 en 48 | *Mat:* op doek *Size:* hoog 49, breed 39 duimen	B	(Bought In) fl 15

Myn, Herman van der (copy by)

1802/04/13	HAVIN	0067	*van der Myn; van Dyk* | Maria met het Kindje, na van Dyk | copy by H. Myn after Anth. van Dyck		(Unknown)

Mytens

1803/08/24	HGKAN	0081	*Mytens* | Een fraay Pourtraitje, tot aan de knien te zien, het verschiet is een fraay Landschap	[Teissier] [or others]	(Unknown) fl 2:10
1808/06/13	AMSCH	0246	*Mijtens* | Andromeda, staande aan een Rots gekluisterd; fiks op Doek geschilderd | *Mat:* op doek	Y[ver]	(Sold) fl 1:10 Gruyter
1810/06/06	RMMUY	0176	*Mytens* | Meleager en Atalante | *Mat:* op doek		(Sold) fl 3:15 Strikland
1810/10/10	MGCIT	0070	*Mytens* | Een Stuk, zynde het Pourtrait van Prins Frederik Hendrik in zyn jonge Jaren; ongemeen schoon geschilderd	Caspar van Citters	(Unknown)

Mytens, Aert

1806/08/20	HGBSM	0108	*A. Mytens* | Een Familliestuk van twee Kinderen in een aangenaam Landschap, gestoffeerd met een Schaapje en twee Hondjes &c., door A. Mytens, 1649 | companion to lot 109 *Mat:* op doek *Size:* hoog 31, breed 39 duim *Inscr:* A. Mytens, 1649 (signed and dated?) *Notes:* It is unclear whether the name and date are inscribed on the painting.	Macalester Loup [or others]	(Sold) fl 8:15 for lots 108 & 109. Gram
1806/08/20	HGBSM	0109	*A. Mytens* | Een dito [Familie] stuk met twee Kinderen, zijnde een wederga | companion to lot 108 *Mat:* op doek *Size:* hoog 31, breed 39 duim	Macalester Loup [or others]	(Sold) fl 8:15 for lots 108 & 109. Gram

Mytens, Daniel (the elder)

1801/04/13	AMSCH	0046	*D. Mytens* | Maria Magdalena in een weenende gestalte overleggende, fraay van Tekening, drappering, en van eene transperante behandeling | *Mat:* op doek *Size:* hoog 23, breed 29 duim	Pierre Fouquet, junior	(Sold) fl 8 V^{n} Dijl
1806/08/20	HGBSM	0111	*D. Mytens* | Een Mansportrait in het zwart gekleed | *Mat:* op paneel	Macalester Loup [or others]	(Sold) fl 8:5 for lots 111 & 112. Loef
1806/08/20	HGBSM	0112	*D. Mytens* | Een dito Vrouweportrait | *Mat:* op paneel *Notes:* It is unclear what "dito" refers to in the title.	Macalester Loup [or others]	(Sold) fl 8:5 for lots 111 & 112. Loef

Mytens, Jan

1808/06/11	RMRIJ	0109	*J. Mytens* | Melager enz. enz. schoon geschilderd | *Mat:* op doek *Size:* hoog 22, breed 35 duim		(Bought In) fl 7
1810/05/22	AMSCH	0069	*Mijtens. (J.)* | In een Bergachtig Landschap, zit op den voorgrond een Jager, verzeld van een Hond, ter zijde ligt eenig dood Wild; zeer uitvoerig behandeld | *Mat:* op doek *Size:* hoog 26, breed 22 duim	R	(Sold) fl 6 Otten

Naiveu, Matthys

1801/10/19	AMSCH	0050	*Neveu. (M.) 1673* | Een Binnenvertrek, waar in een oud Vrouwtje is zittende, zy snyd een Boterham voor een Jongetje dat bid, en in de eene hand een Boek en in de andere hand een Paternostre houd; in 't verschiet een Weever op zyn getouw met veel bywerk; zeer uitvoerig en delicaat geschildert in de manier van G. Douw | *Mat:* op paneel *Size:* hoog 14 ½, breed 11 ½ duim *Inscr:* 1673 (dated?) *Notes:* It is unclear whether the date is inscribed on the painting.	Jonkheer Menno Baron van Coehoorn	(Sold) fl 105 Jan Yver
1802/04/13	HAVIN	0027	*Naveu* | Een Vastenavond vreugd, met dansende en gemaskerde persoonen		(Unknown)
1802/05/05	AMSCH	0154	*Nepveu* | Een gratieuse Dame, in het Satyn gekleed, met een Bloem in de hand, agter dezelven een Vrouw en een Kind, fraai gepenceeld | *Size:* hoog 18, breed 15 duim	J	(Sold) fl 31 Stevens
1802/05/05	AMSCH	0155	*Nepveu* | Voor een Open Nits [sic] ziet men een Jongeling in prachtige Kleeding, in zyn hand een Roemer Wyn houdende, verders is de Rand van de Nits [sic] overdekt met een afhangend Tapyt, uitvoerig gepenceeld	J	(Sold) fl 14 Le Dantú
1802/06/28	AMSCH	0133	*Nepveu* | Een Doktor in zyn kamer bezig zynde een Urienaal [sic] te bekyken, waarby een huilende Vrouw, uitvoerig op Panneel | *Mat:* op paneel *Size:* hoog 10, breed 9 duim	Anna Elink	(Sold) fl 4:15 Van Iperen

1802/07/21	HGKAN	0103	*le Neven* | Een Binnenhuys met Heeren en Dames		(Unknown)
1802/08/24	LNDLS	0065	*M. Nacveu* | Een Juffer staande voor haar Toilet-tafel, terwijl zij zich opschikt, agter haar een Ledikant en meer bijwerk | *Mat:* op paneel *Size:* hoog 8, breed 6 duimen	Leonardus Bouman [or others]	(Unknown) fl 6:5
1802/09/21	UTHDG	0070	*M. Naiveu* | Een Heer en Dame met elkander spreekende, terwijl een Dame op een Orgel speeld, en een Heer zijn Viool stelt. Uitvoerig | *Mat:* op doek *Size:* hoog 23, breed 28 duimen		(Sold) fl 20:5 Verhoude
1803/09/07	AMSCH	0118	*M. Nepveu* | Twee stuks Binnenhuizen; in de eene ziet men een Rokende Boer, en in de andere een Oude Vrouw, zittende te spinnen, meesterlyk gepenceeld [Deux intérieurs, l'un représente un villageois fumant, et l'autre un vieille femme occupée à filer ; belle composition, touche excellente] | *Mat:* op paneel *Size:* hoog 13 ½, breed 16 duim	Smidt	(Sold) fl 62 van Iperen
1804/05/07	AMSCH	0123	*Naiveu. (M.)* | In een Prachtig Gemeubileerd Vertrek, ziet men een Heer welke een jonge Dame een ruiker Bloemen aanbiedt, waarachter een Meid en een ander Heer en Dame, enz; uitvoerig en delicaat gepenceeld | *Mat:* op doek *Size:* hoog 21, breed 23 duim	Vinkeles [for] H[affner]	(Bought In) fl 8
1804/08/08	AMSCH	0144	*M. Nepveu* | Voor een open Steenen Nis, van onder met een Basrelief van Kindertjes vercierd, rust op de Borstweering een Vrouwtje, in aloude Hollandsche Kleeding, houdende een Aarde Kan in de Handen, ter zyde staat een Pot met een Bloemplant, aan de anders zyde ziet men een Wyngaard, verders gestoffeerd met een Vogel-Kooi en Mossenpot; bevallig en uitvoerig gepenceeld | *Mat:* op paneel *Size:* hoog 14, breed 11 duim	Schley [for] A	(Sold) fl 25 van Iperen
1804/08/08	AMSCH	0145	*M. Nepveu* | Een Concert van een ménigte Dames en Heeren, in een prachtige Zaal; fraai | *Size:* hoog 30, breed 43 duim	Roos [for] E	(Sold) fl 5 Th Spaan
1804/10/29	HRBAU	0069	*Nepveu, (M.)* | Dit bevallig Schildery vertoont eene jonge Juffer, die door een' Doctor schynt adergelaaten te worden, welke haar naar een' comicquen Apothecar wyst, die met een Clisteer komt aanloopen, waar over zy schynt te glimlachgen [sic]; dit alles wordt door een Kaars, welke door een' Knegt, die voor de Juffer op de knie ligt, gehouden wordt, verlicht. Alles is uitmuntend, delicaat en uitvoerig, en het licht der Kaars zeer natuurlyk behandeld, in de manier van Schalken | *Mat:* op doek *Size:* hoog 13, breed 15 ½ duim	Simon Styl	(Unknown)
1805/07/03	AMSCH	0034	*Naiveu (M.)* | Op de stoep voor een Winkel-Huis, ziet men vier Kinderen, welken zich vermaken met Belleblazen; terzyde op een Bank legd een stuk Kaas en verder bywerk, in het verschiet over een gracht ziet men een Poort en verdere Gebouwen; dit stukje is zoo krachtig en delicaat van schildering, dat het voor A. van der Werf, niet behoeft te wyken | *Mat:* op paneel *Size:* hoog 11, breed 10 duim *Loc:* Innsbruck, Oesterreich. Ferdinandeum. (627)	R[oos]	(Sold) fl 160 Allard te Parys
1805/07/10	AMSCH	0114	*M. Naiveu* | In een Binnenkamer zit een bejaarde Vrouw, bézig een snee brood te snyden, waarnaast een bevallige Jongen, ter zyde voor een openstaand Raam een Tafel, waarop een aarde Kan, en op de voorgrond een Tlene Mand, een Tafel waarop Brood, Boter en Kaas ligt en verders een Hondje; Dit stukje is alerbevalligst [sic] van licht en delicaat gepenceeld | *Mat:* op paneel *Size:* hoog 15, breed 11 duim	Y[ver]	(Sold) fl 90 Reyers
1805/07/10	AMSCH	0115	*M. Naiveu* | In een Gemeubileerd Vertrek, ziet men een Heer welke een jonge Dame een Ruiker aanbied, agter hun eenige anderen Lieden en verder bywerk; uitvoerig op doek | *Mat:* op doek *Size:* hoog 20 ½, breed 24 ½ duim	V[inkeles] [for] H[affner]	(Sold) fl 4:10 Gruyter
1808/04/26	GDAN	0113	*Neveu (M)* | Een zeer uitvoerig Schilderij, en een pragtig gemeubileerde Kamer van 't Paleis, zijnde de Historie van de Koningin Ester en Ahasuëros, waar bij zij aan eene zeer pragtige gedekte Tafel zitten, terwijl Haman in tegenwoordigheid verschijnt, voorts in 't verschiet ziet men de Galg waar aan Haman moet gehangen worden, alles uitvoerig geschilderd | *Mat:* op doek *Size:* hoog 20, breed 16 duim	G H Fortuyn	(Unknown)
808/08/23	AMSCH	0200	*M. Nepveü* | In een prachtige Zaal, vertoond zich een Historiëele Ordonantie; schoon van licht en delicaat gepenceeld	[Gruyter?]	(Sold) fl 2:5 Dupré
809/04/17	AMSCH	0149	*Naiveu* | Een prachtige rijk gemeubileerde Zaal, gestoffeerd met Heeren en Dames; uitvoerig en krachtig | *Mat:* op doek	[Gruyter?]	(Sold) fl 3
810/06/20	AMSCH	0070	*M. Neveu* | Een Kwakzalver of Tandmeester, nevens hem staat zijn Knecht en een Jongen | *Mat:* op doek *Size:* hoog 19, breed 16 duimen	A	(Sold) fl 7:5 van Iperen
810/10/13	HGDAW	0012	*M. Neveu* | In een Nis ziet men een deftig gekleede Dame, met een Drinkschaal in de hand, waarin zy wyn schenkt, op de Balustrade leggen eenige Vrugten, extra schoon van ligt en bruin, Meesterlyk geschilderd | *Mat:* op doek op paneel *Size:* hoog 15, breed 12 ½ duim		(Unknown)

Naiveu, Matthys (manner)

803/09/07	AMSCH	0276	*Neveu* | Een Kok, bézig zynde Vis schoon te maken; alleruitvoerigst op Paneel, als Neveu, hoog 9, breed 7 duim. Eenige Boeren in een Herberg [Un cuisinier occupé à nettoyer des poissons ; quelques paysans dans une auberge : excellente composition, sur bois, d'après Neveu.] | *Mat:* op paneel *Size:* hoog 9, breed 7 duim *Notes:* This lot was misnumbered no. 176 in the French edition of the catalogue.	Smidt	(Sold) fl 3:5 Gruiter

1807/06/10	HGBSM	0140	*Neveu* | Een Binnevertrek waarin een zittend Vrouwtje met musiek op haar schoot, en een Viool in de hand, in de trant van Neveu | *Mat:* op doek *Size:* hoog 11 ½, breed 9 ½ duim	Abraham Delfos [or others]	(Sold) fl 14 Ten Haaf
			Nap, J. [Unidentified]		
1808/04/26	GDAN	0118	*Nap (J)* | Een zeer goed geschilderd Turks Pourtret | *Size:* hoog 7, breed 6 duim	G H Fortuyn	(Unknown)
			Nason, Pieter		
1807/08/26	AMSCH	0155	*P. Nazon* | Eene Dame in Satyne kleeding, voorstellende Diana; delicaat | *Mat:* op doek	Roos	(Sold) fl 2:5 du Pree
1807/08/26	AMSCH	0156	*P. Nazon* | Een Krygsheld in prachtige kleeding, meesterlyk	Roos	(Sold) fl 6 Coclair
1807/08/26	AMSCH	0157	*P. Nazon* | Een Staatsman in een Stoel zittende	Roos	(Sold) fl 2:5 du Pree
1807/08/26	AMSCH	0158	*P. Nazon* | Eene staande Dame	Roos	(Sold) fl 0:8 Yver
1807/08/26	AMSCH	0159	*P. Nazon* | Een staande Heer	Roos	(Sold) fl 1 Gruiter
1807/08/26	AMSCH	0160	*P. Nazon* | Eene deftige Dame	Roos	(Sold) fl 3 Coclair
			Neck, Jan van		
1802/09/06	AMSCH	0157	*J. van Nek* | Een bevallige Vrouwe Pourtrait	Mevrouw Achtienhoven	(Sold) fl 0:10 Frantszen
1803/07/07	HGKAN	0018	*Van Nek* | Een Slapende Vrouw, welke haar man, een Pot met Wyn op haar hoofd stort, door van Nek, 1673 [Schilderyen in Olyverf] | *Mat:* in olyverf *Inscr:* van Nek, 1673 (signed and dated?) *Notes:* It is unclear whether the date is inscribed on the painting. The bracketed information in the title appears above lot 1 and refers to lots 1 to 25.		(Unknown)
1808/04/26	GDAN	0117	*Neck (J. van)* | Een leggende naakte schoon geschilderde Nimph | *Size:* hoog 45, breed 62 duim	G H Fortuyn	(Unknown)
			Neeffs, Peeter (the elder)		
1801/04/13	AMSCH	0054	*P. Neefs* | Twee stuks Roomsche Kerken, het eene een Dag en het andere een Avondlicht, beide ryk gestoffeerd met een menigte Beeldjes; dezelve zyn alleruitvoerigst en natuurlyk gepenceeld | *Mat:* op koper *Size:* ieder hoog 7, breed 9 duim	Pierre Fouquet, junior	(Sold) fl 61 Lafontaine
1801/05/11	AMSCH	0062	*P. Neefs* | Een Roomsche Kerk van binnen te zien, gestoffeerd met een doop plechtigheid, fraay en meesterlyk gepenceeld | *Mat:* op paneel *Size:* hoog 12, breed 18 duim	Pruisse [for] M	(Sold) fl 17 Allard
1801/10/19	AMSCH	0049	*Neefs, (Pieter)* | Een fraay Perspectief, verbeeldende het binnenste van een Roomsche Kerk, daar de Missen [sic] geleezen word, ryk gestoffeerd met wandelende en anderen Persoonen op den voorgrond; zeer dun, helder en uitvoerig geschildert | *Mat:* op paneel *Size:* hoog 12 ½, breed 18 duim	Jonkheer Menno Baron van Coehoorn	(Sold) fl 143 Jan Yver
1801/12/22	AMOTT	0048	*Peeter Neeffs* | 1 Roomsche Binnekerk, met de Outaaren, Priesters en Beelden, in voldoende perspectief	Bartholomeus Ruloffs	(Unknown) fl 9:10
1802/06/28	AMSCH	0132	*P. Neefs* | Een Kerk, van binnen te zien, ryk met Beeldjes gestoffeerd, het Perspectief is zeer fraai waargenoomen, en uitvoerig gepenceeld door P. Neefs | *Mat:* op paneel *Size:* hoog 14, breed 20 duim	Anna Elink	(Sold) fl 60 Reyers
1802/07/20	MGSAN	0008	*P. Neefs* | Een extra fraai Kerkje, zeer uitvoerig op Paneel | *Mat:* op paneel *Size:* hoog duim 7 ½, breed duim 9 ½		(Unknown)
1802/07/20	MGSAN	0058	*P. Neefs* | Een fraai Kabinetstukje, zynde een Tempeltje met Figuuren, zeer uitvoerig op Paneel | *Mat:* op paneel *Size:* hoog duim 11, breed duim 9		(Unknown)
1802/07/27	AKHRK	0057	*P. Neefs* | Een zeer wel in de Perspectief gebragte en uitgevoerde Roomsche Kerk, van binnen naar het Choor te zien, met menigte van Outaaren en Beelden | *Mat:* op paneel *Size:* hoog 18 ¾, breed 24 ¼ duim	Maria Stategaart	(Sold) fl 10:5 Juffr Boersen
1803/08/01	AMSCH	0026	*Neefs. (P.)* | Een Roomsche Kerk van binnen te zien, gestoffeerd op de voorgrond met een Doopplegtigheid, waarby twee Jongelingen met brandende Flambouwen, verder eenige Altaaren, en een Gezicht op het Hooge Choor, uitvoerig en fraay behandeld | *Mat:* op paneel *Size:* hoog 10, breed 14 ½ duim	J	(Sold) fl 20 Levy Pakker
1803/09/07	AMSCH	0116	*P. Neefs* | In een Roomsche Kerk ziet men een ménigte stoffagie van Beeldjes, Priesters en Autaren, alles uitvoerig op Paneel [Une église décorée de statues de saints et d'autres ornemens, avec des prêtres à l'autel ; l'ensemble forme un beau tableau] | *Mat:* op paneel *Size:* hoog 17, breed 25 duim	Smidt	(Bought In) fl 75
1803/09/07	AMSCH	0117	*P. Neefs* | Een dito [Roomsche] Kerk, in alles als de voorgaande [Un autre église, même manière et même exécution que le précédent] | *Mat:* op paneel *Size:* hoog 12, breed 9 ½ duim	Smidt	(Sold) fl 21 Haffner
1804/04/28	LNDLS	0046	*P. Neefs* | Een Gezicht in een Kerk met een Altaar, uitvoerig, door P. Neefs; op paneel, rond | *Mat:* op paneel *Fmt:* rond *Size:* hoog 8 ½ duim	[Abraham Delfos] [or others]	(Sold or Bought In) fl 1:8 A Delfos
1804/05/07	AMSCH	0122	*Neefs. (P.)* | Een Protestante Kerk van binnen te zien, ziende na 't Choor ryk gestoffeerd met een ménigte van Aanschouwers en andere Lieden enz.; piquant van licht en allerfrayst gepenceeld | *Mat:* op paneel *Size:* hoog 12, breed 9 duim	Vinkeles [for] H[affner]	(Sold) fl 10:10 S Joseph

<table>
<tr><td>1805/07/10</td><td>AMSCH</td><td>0109</td><td>P. Neefs | Een Roomsche Kerk van binnen te zien, met verscheide Altaren voor sommige welke den dienst verrigt wordt, verders een ménigte Schilderyen en Kerkciraden; ryk met Beeldjes gestoffeerd | Mat: op paneel Size: hoog 13, breed 18 duim</td><td>Y[ver]</td><td>(Sold) fl 220 T Spaan</td></tr>
<tr><td>1805/10/09</td><td>HGBSM</td><td>0081</td><td>P. Neefs | Twee fraaije kerkjes van binnen te zien, zeer delicaat geschilderd, door P. Neefs, op koper, hoog 5 breet 6 ½ duim, twee stuks | Mat: op koper Size: hoog 5 breet 6 ½ duim</td><td>T H van Willigen [or others]</td><td>(Sold) fl 14:5 Teissier</td></tr>
<tr><td>1806/05/05</td><td>AMSCH</td><td>0102</td><td>P. Neefs | Een Roomsche Kerk met verscheiden Beelden gestoffeerd; uitvoerig op Paneel door P. Neefs | Mat: op paneel Size: hoog 14, breed 19 duim</td><td>R[oos]</td><td>(Sold) fl 8 Coclers</td></tr>
<tr><td>1806/08/13</td><td>AMSCH</td><td>0135</td><td>Neefs. (P.) | Een capitaale Kerk, ryk van Wapenborden voorzien, gestoffeerd met wandelende Heeren, Dames, brandende Toorsdragers, enz.; delicaat en uitvoerig behandeld | Mat: op paneel Size: hoog 12 ½, breed 17 duim</td><td>Vinkeles [for] G[ruyter]</td><td>(Sold) fl 27 Schumacher</td></tr>
<tr><td>1806/08/20</td><td>HGBSM</td><td>0206</td><td>P. Neefs | Een Roomsche Kerk van binne te zien, bij kaarslicht | Mat: op paneel Size: hoog 5 ¾, breed 7 ½ duim</td><td>Macalester Loup [or others]</td><td>(Sold) fl 8 Lafontaine</td></tr>
<tr><td>1808/04/26</td><td>GDAN</td><td>0114</td><td>Neefs (P) | Een fraaije Tempel, in de Nacht, bij een Fakkel licht te zien, het licht doet een zeer schoone uitwerking, gestoffeerd met Beelden | Size: hoog 22, breed 26 ½ duim</td><td>G H Fortuyn</td><td>(Unknown)</td></tr>
<tr><td>1808/04/26</td><td>GDAN</td><td>0115</td><td>Neefs (P) | Een fraaije Kerk van binnen te zien, gestoffeerd met Beelden en Bijwerk, schoon geschilderd | Size: hoog 14, breed 12 duim</td><td>G H Fortuyn</td><td>(Unknown)</td></tr>
<tr><td>1808/05/18</td><td>LNAN</td><td>0025</td><td>Neefs | Een Kerk, zeer uitvoerig geschilderd met Autaren | Notes: The artist's name "Neefs" was added in by hand in the RKDH copy of the catalogue.</td><td>Mr Cornelis Versluys</td><td>(Unknown)</td></tr>
<tr><td>1808/06/13</td><td>AMSCH</td><td>0187</td><td>Neefs | Een Kerk, van binnen te zien, fraai van doorzicht; uitvoerig</td><td>E M Engelberts</td><td>(Sold) fl 13:10 van Iperen</td></tr>
<tr><td>1808/08/23</td><td>AMSCH</td><td>0254</td><td>Neefs | Een Kerk van binnen te zien, fraai van doorzicht, uitvoerig gepenceeld</td><td>[Van Iperen?]</td><td>(Sold) fl 10:10 du Pree</td></tr>
<tr><td>1808/10/28</td><td>AMVRS</td><td>0042</td><td>Neefs, (P.) | Een Roomsche Kerk van binnen te zien, met verscheide Altaren. Fraai van doorzicht en zonachtig behandeld | Mat: op paneel Size: hoog 11, breed 15 duim</td><td>Marten Udink</td><td>(Sold) fl 7 Gruyter</td></tr>
<tr><td>1808/10/28</td><td>AMVRS</td><td>0043</td><td>Neefs, (P.) | Een fraai Binnengezicht van de groote Kerk te Antwerpen, rijk gestoffeerd met Beelden, Altaren, Predikstoel, enz. De bouw- en doorzichtkunde zijn meesterlijk, alles is zeer uitvoerig | Mat: op paneel Size: hoog 20, breed 26 duim</td><td>Marten Udink</td><td>(Sold) fl 72 Reijers</td></tr>
<tr><td>1810/07/23</td><td>DOLGI</td><td>0039</td><td>Pieter Neefs | Een Roomsche Kerk van binnen. Tusschen de Pilaren heen ziet men naar het Koor. Ter zijde een Predikstoel, en Altaren. Verder gestoffeerd met verscheiden biddende en wandelende figuren, Graftekens, Wapenborden, en ander bijwerk, zeer kunstig en uitvoerig geschilderd. Ongemeen helder en bevallig | Mat: op koper Size: hoog 6 ½, breed 9 duim</td><td>Mr Pieter van den Santheuvel</td><td>(Sold) fl 72 A van Strij</td></tr>
<tr><td>1810/10/11</td><td>AMSCH</td><td>0061</td><td>P. Neefs | Eene kapitale rijk geordonneerde Kerk, met Outaren en andere Sieraden, gestoffeerd met wandelende Beelden; zonachtig en uitvoerig | Mat: op paneel Size: hoog 15, breed 21 duimen</td><td>[Gruyter?]</td><td>(Bought In) fl 11:10</td></tr>
</table>

Neeffs, Peeter (the elder) (and Berckheyde, J.)

<table>
<tr><td>1806/11/24</td><td>AMSCH</td><td>0047</td><td>Neefs (P.); J. Berkheiden | Een gezigt in de groote Kerk te Rotterdam, gestoffeerd met verscheidene Wapenborden, Heeren en Dames, welke in dezelve wandelen; het zonligt is'er kragtig in werking, en is voorts delicaat geschildert | Mat: op doek Size: hoog 24, breed 24 duim</td><td>Munnikhuizen</td><td>(Sold) fl 70 Engelberts</td></tr>
</table>

Neeffs, Peeter (the elder) (and Michau)

<table>
<tr><td>1804/10/16</td><td>DLOND</td><td>0156</td><td>Pet. Neefs; Michau | Een Roomsche Kerk, van binnen te zien, met zeer veel Beelden van den laatsten. L'intérieur d'une Eglise Romaine, avec beaucoup de Figures du dernier | Mat: op paneel Size: hoog 17, breed 26</td><td></td><td>(Sold) fl 102 v Giesen</td></tr>
<tr><td>1810/10/10</td><td>MGCIT</td><td>0055</td><td>P. Neefs; Michau | Een kapitaal Stuk, zynde een Roomsche Kerk, schoon van Bouworde, met zeer veel beelden en ander bijwerk, door P. Neefs; rijk en fraai gestoffeerd door Michau, en door beide Meesters uitvoerig en kunstig behandeld</td><td>Caspar van Citters</td><td>(Unknown)</td></tr>
</table>

Neeffs, Peeter (the elder) (and Palamedesz., A.)

<table>
<tr><td>810/06/06</td><td>RMMUY</td><td>0041</td><td>P. Neefs; Palamedes | Eene kapitale en wel uitgevoerde Roomsche Kerk van binnen te zien. Door P. Neefs. Met stoffage door Palamedes | Mat: op paneel</td><td></td><td>(Unknown) fl 51</td></tr>
</table>

Neeffs, Peeter (the elder) (and Stalbemt)

<table>
<tr><td>804/08/02</td><td>BDAN</td><td>0003</td><td>P. Neefs; A. Stalbandt | Een binnen-gezigt van de Groote Kerk van Antwerpen, verlicht door een Fakkel, zeer delicaat behandeld en uitvoerig geschildert | Mat: op paneel Size: b. 21 d. h. 13 d.</td><td>J G Calckberner</td><td>(Unknown)</td></tr>
</table>

Neeffs, Peeter (the elder) (and Vinckeboons, D.)

<table>
<tr><td>803/07/18</td><td>AMSCH</td><td>0037</td><td>Neefs. (P.); Vinkebooms. (D.) | Een Gothische Roomsche Kerk van binnen tot aan het Choor te zien, 't welk een fraai perspectief opleverd; ter zyde ziet men een menigte Autaaren [sic]. De stoffagie door Vinkebooms steld voor, een processie van verscheide Mannen en Vrouwen, de onbegrypelyk uitvoerigheid en het zonligt, gepaard met een lieflyk coloriet, maaken dit</td><td>Maria Theresia Andrioli</td><td>(Sold) fl 180 Haffner</td></tr>
</table>

			stukje tot een aangenaam Schilderytje [Ce morceau nous offre le point de vue d'une eglise de construction gothique, percent [sic] par la nef de milieu jusqu'au fond du coeur. Les autels & les ornemens en sont traités avec finesse & d'un beau fini, ainsi que l'architecture. Vinkebooms a orné ce sujet d'une procession d'hommes & de femmes, sortant de l'eglise. L'effet de la degradation de lumiere bien observé & l'agrement des jolies figures lui assurent une distinction.] | *Mat:* op koper *Size:* hoog 13, breed 17 duim [haut 12, large 15 pouces] *Notes:* The dimensions differ in the Dutch and French editions of the catalogue.		
1805/07/10	AMSCH	0110	*P. Neefs; D. Vinkeboom* | Een Roomsche Kerk van binnen te zien, in de zelve ziet men een Professie van Nonnen, waarby Muzicanten enz., verders een ménigte stoffagie van Beeldjes; alleruitvoerigst en fraai gepenceeld, door denzelven [P. Neefs] en D. Vinkeboom | *Mat:* op koper *Size:* hoog 13, breed 17 ½ duim	V[inkeles] [for] H[affner]	(Sold) fl 60 Lafontaine

Neer

1809/04/17	AMSCH	0068a[H]	*v d Neer* | [Untitled] | *Notes:* This lot was added in by hand in the EBNP copy of the catalogue, but without giving a title.		(Sold) fl 6:15

Neer, Aert van der

1801/03/16	AMSCH	0030	*A. van der Neer* | Een Maanligt langs een stil Water by Boerenwoningen, op de voorgrond een Hengelaar, natuurlyk van schildering	P[ruyssenaar]	(Sold) fl 11 Gruiter
1801/04/08	HAVIN	0052	*A. van der Neer* | Een Watergezigt by Maanligt		(Unknown)
1801/04/08	HAVIN	0054	*A. van der Neer* | Een Rivier met Scheepen, zynde de Maan agter een Molen		(Unknown)
1801/04/13	AMSCH	0051	*A. van der Neer* | Een Dorpgezicht met een bevrozen Rivier doorsneeden, welke gestoffeerd is met Schaatzerydende en andere Beeldjes, den besneeuwden grond en de koude lucht zyn zeer wel in dit stukje waargenomen, en is voorts van eene Meesterlyke schildering | *Mat:* op paneel *Size:* hoog 10, breed 14 duim	Pierre Fouquet, junior	(Sold) fl 21 Yver
1801/04/13	AMSCH	0052	*A. van der Neer* | Een dito [Dorp-] gezicht met hoog geboomte aan een stille Rivier, waarin Vissers met hunne Netten, bezig zyn te vischen, alles verbeeld by helder Maanlicht; natuurlyk verbeeld, en uitvoerig geschilderd | *Mat:* op doek *Size:* hoog 22, breed 27 duim	Pierre Fouquet, junior	(Sold) fl 50 Lafontaine
1801/04/13	AMSCH	0053	*A. van der Neer* | Een bevrozen Rivier, ryk van stoffage, ter zyde een Dorp, en aangenaam verschiet, natuurlyk voorgesteld, en breed behandeld | *Mat:* op paneel *Size:* hoog 18, breed 27 duim	Pierre Fouquet, junior	(Sold) fl 31 Lafontaine
1801/05/11	AMSCH	0061	*A. van der Neer* | Een Riviergezicht, aan beider oevers, gestoffeerd met boerewoningen, moolen en geboomten, op de Voorgrond Visschers in een schuit, en verder zylende Scheepen, alles vertoont zig by helder maanlicht, natuurlyk gepenceeld | *Mat:* op doek *Size:* hoog 23, breed 32 duim	E[lias]	(Sold) fl 35 Allard
1801/06/10	AMSCH	0125	*Neer. (A. van der)* | Een Boomryk Landschap, met een stille Rivier, gestoffeerd met Beelden en Vaartuigen, alles by helder Maanlicht, aller natuurlykst en krachtig voorgesteld | *Mat:* op doek *Size:* hoog 31, breed 25 duim	Herman ten Kate	(Sold) fl 42 Taijs
1801/06/10	AMSCH	0126	*Neer. (A. van der)* | Een Bosh met zwaar Geboomte, en een Waterplas waaruit eenig Vee drinkt, op de voorgrond twee Houthakkers, verders andere stoffage en Boerewoningen: alles door een helder Zonlicht by een Morgenstond verlicht en meesterlyk gepenceeld | *Mat:* op doek *Size:* hoog 40, breed 36 duim	Herman ten Kate	(Sold) fl 170 Barent Kooij
1801/06/13	LNDLS	0056	*A. van der Neer* | En Gezicht langs een water met vaartuigen, benevens geboomten en wooningen, zijnde een maaneschijn, op paneel | *Mat:* op paneel *Size:* hoog 10, breed 16 duimen	D van R	(Sold) fl 23:10 Bryan
1801/10/19	AMSCH	0048	*Neer. (A. van der)* | Een Dorpgezicht langs een Rivier met eenige Vaartuigen, by een helder schynende Maan; zeer natuurlyk van Licht en bruin | *Mat:* op paneel *Size:* hoog 16, breed 17 ½ duim	Jonkheer Menno Baron van Coehoorn	(Sold) fl 51 B^{d} Kooy
1801/11/10	AMPOS	0020	*A. v. d. Neer* | 1 Maaneschein by een Rivier, waarin een Schuitje, en in 't verschiet eenige Boomen		(Unknown)
1802/02/16	AMSCH	0008	*A. van der Neer* | Een bevallig Dorpgezicht aan een Rivier, allernatuurlykst op paneel | *Mat:* op paneel	B[uys]	(Sold) fl 10:10 Coclers
1802/02/16	AMSCH	0039	*A. van der Neer* | Een Dorpgezigt, met Woningen, aan een Rivier zynde een Maanlicht, ter zyde vertoont zig een felle Brand, gestoffeerd met verder bywerk, natuurlyk behandeld	G	(Sold) fl 47 Jan Spaan
1802/02/16	AMSCH	0089	*A. v. der Neer* | Een Besneeuwt Wintergezigt, gestoffeerd met Schaatseryders, Arresleeden, Kolvers en Wandelaars, natuurlyk geschilderd	G	(Sold) fl 71 Gruiter
1802/05/05	AMSCH	0151	*A. van der Neer* | Een uitgestrekte bevrozen Rivier, met aan wederzyde een Dorp, op het Ys ziet men verscheide Schaatzeryders, Arreslede en andere stoffagie, alles met de natuur overeenkomende, gepenceeld | *Size:* hoog 26, breed 40 duim	H	(Sold) fl 161 Pruijssenaar [for] R
1802/05/05	AMSCH	0152	*A. van der Neer* | Een zwaare Brand in een Stad, op de Voorgrond een Schuit met verscheide Lieden en verder Bywerk, zeer natuurlyk | *Mat:* op paneel *Size:* hoog 18, breed 25 duim	G	(Sold) fl 7:15 Mensar

1802/05/05	AMSCH	0153	*A. van der Neer* | Een aangenaam gestoffeerd Dorpgezigt met hoog Geboomte, bevallig | *Mat:* op paneel *Size:* hoog 10, breed 14 duim	C	(Sold) fl 4 Spruit
1802/05/11	GRGRW	0031	*A. van der Neer* | Ene Ondergaande Zon [Schilderijen met Olie-Verf; In zwarte Lijsten] | *Mat:* in olyverf *Notes:* The bracketed information in the title appears above lot 1 and refers to lots 1 to 79a.	Arnold Sicco Werumeus	(Unknown)
1802/06/16	AMSCH	0120	*A. van der Neer* | Een zeer natuurlyk Land- en Water Gezicht, aan beider Oevers, gestoffeert met Kerktooren, Molens en Woningen, Landlieden en eenig Vée; op de voorgrond Visschers in 't Water staande, die de zeegen trekken, alles verbeeld by helder Maanlicht; en is bevallig en meesterlyk fraay behandelt | *Mat:* op doek *Size:* hoog 21, breed 22 duim	[Merrem]	(Sold) fl 205 B^{d} Kooij
1802/06/28	AMSCH	0128	*A. van der Neer* | Een aangenaam Wintergezicht, het Ys gestoffeerd met een menigte Beelden en Arresleeden; meesterlyk op Panneel | *Mat:* op paneel *Size:* hoog 33, breed 46 duim	Anna Elink	(Sold) fl 59 Coclers
1802/06/28	AMSCH	0129	*A. van der Neer* | Een Dorpgezicht aan een Rivier, gestoffeerd met Vaartuigen en Beeldjes; naaturlyk op Panneel behandeld | *Mat:* op paneel *Size:* hoog 9, breed 12 duim	Anna Elink	(Sold) fl 8:5 Royers
1802/08/24	LNDLS	0014	*A. van der Neer* | Een Landschap met Geboomte en Woningen, in het midden een Water langs een Weg en een Kerktoren; dit Stuk is gestoffeerd met beelden en beesten, en verbeeldt een vroege Morgenstond. Konstig en kragtig op doek | *Mat:* op doek *Size:* hoog 26, breed 41 duimen	Leonardus Bouman [or others]	(Unknown) fl 51
1802/08/24	LNDLS	0081	*A. van der Neer* | Een Land- en Water-Gezicht langs een Weg met Boomen en Woningen, en op den Voorgrond Koeijen, verbeeldende een Maaneschijn | *Mat:* op paneel *Size:* hoog 11, breed 13 duimen	Leonardus Bouman [or others]	(Unknown) fl 11
1802/09/06	AMSCH	0085	*A. v. d. Neer* | Twee stuks Levantsche Zéehavens, beide gestoffeerd met zylende en ten anker leggende Scheepen, en andere Vaartuygen, Sloepen, en Zeelieden, Vissers, die hun Netten ophaalen, Kooplieden, by vaaten en pakken, verders steene Wagttoorens en andere gebouwen; zeer natuurlyk behandeld | *Mat:* op doek *Size:* ieder hoog 11, breed 16 duim	Brave	(Sold) fl 3:5 Yver
1802/09/21	UTHDG	0068	*A. van der Neer* | Een Rivier welker oevers met een Kerk. Woningen, en Geboomte bezet zijn, de Maan door drijvende Wolken omringd, spiegeld zich in het zagt kabbelend water. Fraai en natuurlijk van uitwerking | *Mat:* op paneel *Size:* hoog 11, breed 13 ½ duimen		(Sold) fl 11:5 De Munnick
1802/09/21	UTHDG	0069	*A. van der Neer* | Een Landschap met een Boerenwoning en geboomte, bij Maaneschijn te zien. Als de voorgaande, behandelt door denzelven [A. van der Neer] | *Mat:* op paneel *Size:* hoog 15, breed 20 duimen		(Bought In) fl 28
1802/09/29	AMSCH	0040	*A. van der Neer* | Een Watergezigt by Maaneschyn, hoog 10 ¼, breed 14 ¼ duim. Paneel. Deezen Beroemde konstenaar in het verbeelden van Maan-Lichten, heeft door dit fraaije Schilderytje zyne groote vermogens aan den dag gelegd, zo omtrent uitvoerigheid, als bevallige verkiezinge, maar boven al in het verbeelden van het licht der Maan en de verlichte wolken, ieder na hunnen stand met de natuur overeenkomstig; het Water, de Woningen, de visschers Schuiten enz. alles is uitmuntend en delicaat behandelt [Le Riche point de vue, d'un Canal de la Hollande avec Barques & quelques Habitations, melées d'arbres. Ce Petit Tableau piquant, dont l'Effet de clair de Lune rend admirablement les details, est des plus précieux de de maître renommé dans ce genre.] | *Mat:* op paneel *Size:* hoog 10 ¼, breed 14 ¼ duim	[Labouchere?]	(Sold) fl 112 Roelofs
1802/11/01	DOBRA	0042	*van der Neer* | Een Maanlichtje, door van der Neer. item een Boertje	Paulus van der Spyk [or others]	(Sold) fl 2:5 Randwyk
1803/12/12	AMSCH	0068	*A. van de Neer* | Een Dorp gezigt, ter zyde een Rivier, gestoffeerd met differente soorten van vaarende en stil leggende Scheepjes en Schuiten, allernatuurlykst by maanligt verbeeld | *Mat:* op paneel *Size:* hoog 6, breed 9 ½ duim	B	(Sold) fl 2:5 Hijman Pakker
1804/02/27	AMSCH	0080	*Neer (A. van der)* | Een bevroosen Rivier, ryk gestoffeerd, met een meenigte Schaatseryders en wandelende Persoonen, op den voorgrond ziet men op het Ys Kolven, ter zyde by eenige Huizen, hoog opgaand Geboomte, en verder een aangenaam verschiet; zeer uitvoerig en meesterlyk gepenceeld | *Mat:* op paneel *Size:* hoog 46, breed 22 duim *Notes:* The dimensions are presumably reversed or otherwise erroneous.	B	(Sold) fl 82 van den Brink
1804/05/07	AMSCH	0119	*Neer. (A. van der)* | In een Land en Riviergezicht ziet men een opkomende Maneschyn; eigenaartig gestoffeerd en fraay van penceelbehandeling | *Mat:* op paneel *Size:* hoog 14, breed 21 duim	Vinkeles [for] H[affner]	(Bought In) fl 10
1804/05/07	AMSCH	0120	*Neer. (A. van der)* | Een ondergaande Zon, in een Land en Riviergezicht; allernatuurlykst voorgesteld, en eigenaartig gepenceeld | *Mat:* op paneel *Size:* hoog 11, breed 14 duim	Roos [for] A	(Bought In) fl 11
1804/05/07	AMSCH	0121	*Neer. (A. van der)* | Een opkomonde [sic] Maneschyn, in een Rivier en Landgezicht; piquant van licht en uitvoerig van behandeling | *Mat:* op paneel *Size:* hoog 14, breed 19 duim	Roos [for] A	(Sold) fl 3:15 van Iperen
1804/08/08	AMSCH	0141	*A. van der Neer* | Een aangenaam Dorpgezicht aan een Rivier, gestoffeerd met Geboomte, Schuiten, en Visschers met een Totebel; zeer natuurlyk verlicht door het schynsel der Maan | *Mat:* op paneel *Size:* hoog 16, br. 20 duim	Roos [for] D	(Sold) fl 6 van Iperen
804/08/08	AMSCH	0142	*A. van der Neer* | In een aangenaam Land- en Riviergezicht ziet men een opkomende Maan, het Water gestoffeerd met een Schuit met eenige	Vink[eles] [for] S	(Sold) fl 8 van Iperen [or] Jan Spaan

			Vissende Lieden; zeer natuurlyk van licht, en fraai geschilderd | *Mat:* op doek *Size:* hoog 11 ½, breed 14 duim		
1804/08/08	AMSCH	0143	*A. van der Neer* | Een ondergaande Zon, in een Land- en Riviergezicht; allernatuurlykst voorgesteld, en eigenaartig gepenceeld | *Size:* hoog 11, breed 14 duim	Roos [for] F	(Sold) fl 4:5 Reijers
1804/10/16	DLOND	0157	*A. van der Neer* | Een Dorpsgezicht, met een Water en Vaartuigen. Vue d'un Village, avec un Canal & des Vaisseaux | *Mat:* op doek *Size:* hoog 14, breed 20		(Unknown)
1804/10/29	HRBAU	0070	*Neer, (A. v. d.)* | By een' aangenaamen Avondstond, ziet men langs een Watertjen, welk aan weêrszyden met Boomen en Boerenwooningen bezet is, verscheidene Visschersschuitjens. 't Welk een bevallige vertooning maakt, en zeer uitvoerig behandeld is | *Mat:* op paneel *Size:* hoog 12, breed 14 ½ duim	Simon Styl	(Unknown)
1804/10/29	HRBAU	0071	*Neer, (A. v. d.)* | Op den voorgrond van dit Meirgezigt, by een stuk Land, liggen eenige Scheepen, welken een brand, die aan de overzyde in een Dorp onstaat, schynen te ontvlugten: waar men nog een menigte figuuren ondekt. Het licht der vlam, dat door de duisterheid van den Nagt alle voorwerpen verlicht, doet, benevens de spiegeling op het water, eene goede uitwerking. Dit Stukjen is niet minder dan het voorgaande behandeld | *Mat:* op paneel *Size:* hoog 12, breed 14 ½ duim	Simon Styl	(Unknown)
1804/10/29	HRBAU	0072	*Neer, (A. v. d.)* | Is mede een fraai Meirgezigt; voor aan, by eenig Paalwerk, liggen eenige Schuiten, waar by verscheiden Visschers in hun beroep bezig zyn, nevens eenige Heeren, welken daar naar zien; aan de overzyde van het water is een groot Dorp, met Molens voorzien; waar by eene menigte Vaartuigen en Driemasten, zo dryvende, als die gecalfaterd worden. Alles by een ondergaande Zon, welke zig in een nevelagtige lucht verbergt. Helder en uitvoerig behandeld | *Mat:* op paneel *Size:* hoog 12 ½, breed 17 ½ duim	Simon Styl	(Unknown)
1804/10/29	HRBAU	0073	*Neer, (A. v. d.)* | In een Boschgezigt, met Boerenwooningen bezet, met water doorsneeden, en fraaie doorzigten voorzien, en aardig gestoffeerd, doet de Maan, door heure straalschieting, eene bevallige werking, en spiegelt zig op den voorgrond in een klaare beek. Niet minder dan het voorige behandeld | *Mat:* op paneel *Size:* hoog 12 ½, breed 17 ½ duim	Simon Styl	(Unknown)
1805/07/03	AMSCH	0120	*A. van der Neer* | In een aangenaam Land- en Riviergezicht, ziet men langs een Weg by eenige Woningen, op de Voorgrond by een steene Brug een Boeren Herberg, een Kar met twee Paarden, waar in vier Heeren, waarby een ander Heer te paard en een te voet, verders eenige Landlieden en een bevallig Boomryk verschiet der Stad; aller natuurlykst van licht, fraai van schildering en uitvoerig gepenceeld | *Mat:* op paneel *Size:* hoog 34, breed 48 duim	V[inkeles]	(Bought In) fl 122
1805/07/03	AMSCH	0121	*A. van der Neer* | Een bevallig Wintergezicht, verbeeldende een Avondstond, 't Ys gestoffeerd met Schaatseryders, Wandelaars, Kolvers en andere Lieden, verders ziet men langs een Weg en Geboomte, eenige Boerewoningen, en een aangenaam verschiet; aller natuurlykst en niet minder dan de voorgaande | *Mat:* op paneel *Size:* hoog 24, breed 34 duim	V[inkeles]	(Sold) fl 100 Reyers
1805/07/10	AMSCH	0111	*A. van der Neer* | Een Maneschyn in een Land- en Riviergezicht, op de Voorgrond by een Brug eenige Vissers in een Schuit, enz.; meesterlyk op Paneel | *Mat:* op paneel *Size:* hoog 13 ½, breed 21 duim	V[inkeles] [for] H[affner]	(Sold) fl 2 Lafontaine
1805/07/10	AMSCH	0112	*A. van der Neer* | Twee stuks bevallige Land- en Watergezichten met onderscheidene stoffagien, by helder Maanlicht; natuurlyk op Paneel | *Mat:* op paneel *Size:* hoog 11, breed 16 duim	R[oos]	(Sold) fl 27 L Pakker
1806/05/05	AMSCH	0105	*A. van der Neer* | Een Maneschyntje | *Size:* hoog 18, breed 25 duim	V[inkeles]	(Sold) fl 25:10 W Reijers
1806/08/13	AMSCH	0132	*Neer. (A. van der)* | Dit fraaije stuk, vertoont een Land- en Watergezicht, op de voorgrond met Beelden en Schuiten, en op de tweede grond, met Beesten gestoffeert; aan de regter zyde staat een Molen by verscheide Boerewoningen en aan de linker zyde een Dorpgezicht met Kerk en Tooren; alles werd door een heldere Maan verlicht, en evenäart volkomen de natuur, en is van een uitvoerige penceelbehandeling en een der uitmunste voorwerpen van deze beroemde Meester | *Mat:* op paneel *Size:* hoog 13, breed 19 duim	van der Schley	(Bought In) fl 100
1806/08/13	AMSCH	0132a	*Neer. (A. van der)* | Een aangenaam Land- en Riviergezicht, zynde een Maneschyn, gestoffeerd met Schuiten, Vissers, Koebeesten en een bevallig verschiet; fraai en piquant van licht en meesterlyk gepenceeld | *Mat:* op paneel *Size:* hoog 18, breed 29 duim	Vinkeles [for] J	(Sold) fl 7:5 du Pre
1806/08/13	AMSCH	0133	*Neer. (A. van der)* | Een dito [aangenaam] Land- en Riviergezicht, meede een Maneschyn en in alles als de voorgaande behandeld | *Mat:* op paneel *Size:* hoog 9, breed 13 duim	Vinkeles [for] J	(Sold) fl 25 van Iperen
1806/08/13	AMSCH	0134	*Neer. (A. van der)* | Op een sterk bevroozen Rivier ziet men een groote ménigte van rydende, wandelende en kolvende Lieden; helder en schoon geschilderd | *Size:* hoog 11, breed 22 duim	Vinkeles [for] G[ruyter]	(Bought In) fl 32
1807/08/26	AMSCH	0151	*A. van der Neer* | Een Land en Riviergezigt, gestoffeerd met Reizigers te paard en te voet, by helder maanlicht; zynde van een zeer bevallige Penceelsbehandeling | *Mat:* op paneel *Size:* hoog 12, breed 19 duim	Roos	(Bought In) fl 60

1807/08/26	AMSCH	0152	*A. van der Neer* | Een Landschap met Woningen en Geboomte, gestoffeerd met een Landman met Schapen; alles verbeeld by helder maanlicht	Yver [for] S	(Sold) fl 3:5 Spaan
1807/08/26	AMSCH	0153	*A. van der Neer* | Een Wintergezigt, zynde een Dorp aan een bevroozen Rivier, gestoffeerd met verscheide Lieden op het Ys | *Mat:* op paneel	Yver [for] S	(Sold) fl 1:15 Coclair
1808/04/26	GDAN	0112	*Neer (A. van der)* | Een fraai Watergezigt, bij de opkomst der Maan ziet men hoog Geboomte, Gebouwen, Molens, een Hooijwagen, Schuit en verder gewoel, fiks geschilderd | *Size:* hoog 21 ½, breed 25 ½ duim	G H Fortuyn	(Unknown)
1808/06/11	RMRIJ	0031	*Aart van der Neer* | Een Wintergezich [sic] met veel Figuren, stout en meesterlyk geschilderd | *Mat:* op doek *Size:* hoog 41 ½, breed 51 duim		(Sold) fl 16 Rohen [?] [or] Van Geel
1808/06/13	AMSCH	0110	*Neer (A. van der)* | Een Dorpgezicht, met verscheide Woningen, aan een stil Water: op den voorgrond Lieden, die zich bij een aangestoken vuur warmen, verder Reizigers met een Paard, en een Postwagen voor eene Herberg; alles is verbeeld bij helder maanlicht. Zeer natuurlijk en meesterlijk gepenceeld | *Mat:* op paneel *Size:* hoog 9 ½, breed 11 ½ duim	[Jan Tersteeg]	(Bought In) fl 24
1808/06/13	AMSCH	0111	*Neer (A. van der)* | Een Land- en Riviergezicht, aan beide Oevers met Woningen, Dorpkerk, Molen en Geboomte, verder zeilende Schepen en andere Vaartuigen, gestoffeerd met Beeldjes en eenig Vee; alles vertoont zich bij helder maanlicht, en evenaart de Natuur. In alles als de voorgaande | *Mat:* op paneel *Size:* hoog 13, breed 19 duim	[Jan Tersteeg]	(Sold) fl 115 Thaijs
1808/06/13	AMSCH	0112	*Neer (A. van der)* | Een aangenaam Dorpgezicht, aan eene Rivier, met onderscheidene Stoffage van Beelden, Schuiten, enz; alles door een helder maanlicht beschenen wordende. Uitvoerig en natuurlijk behandeld | *Mat:* op paneel *Size:* hoog 16, breed 20 duim	R[oos]	(Sold) fl 152 Allard
1808/08/23	AMSCH	0120	*Neer. (A. van der)* | Een heldere Maaneschijn aan een Rivier, met zijlende en drijvende Scheepen en Vaartuigen; natuurlijk geschilderd | *Mat:* op paneel *Size:* hoog 13, breed 16 duim	J	(Sold) fl 19:10 T Spaan
1808/09/13	HABRU	0064	*A. v.d. Neer* | Een Wintergezicht, vol gewoel		(Unknown) fl 42:10
1808/10/28	AMVRS	0044	*Neer, (A. van der)* | Langs een Weg met Geboomte en Woningen bij een Rivier, waarover een Hout Bruggetje, ziet men eene Vrouw en Jongeling, verders een stilliggend Vaartuig en zeilende Schepen | *Mat:* op paneel *Size:* hoog 13, breed 10 duim	Marten Udink	(Sold) fl 17 Coclers
1808/10/28	AMVRS	0045	*Neer, (A. van der)* | Een Wintergezicht langs een bevrozen Rivier, aan den Oever Woningen, dor Geboomte en een Molen, op de Weg en op het IJs verscheide gaande en Schaatsenrijdende Lieden, Zeer natuurlijk behandeld | *Mat:* op paneel *Size:* hoog 15, breed 20 duim	Marten Udink	(Sold) fl 81 Engelberts
1808/12/30	HGIMM	[0071k]	*A. van der Neer* | Voorts een exquis kabinetje Schilderijen van voorname Nederlandsche Meesters, welke uit hoofde van de kortheid des tijds niet stuk voor stuk kunnen beschreven worden; doch waarvan de beschrijving op den Kijkdag zal voorhanden zijn. Dus wij hier alleen de namen van eenige dier Meesters laten volgen, als: A. Kuyp, Ruysdaal, Karel du Jardyn, Loqwi ('t beste dat hij schilderde) Hondekoeter, van Dyk, Janson, Moesgever, Kamphuyzen, van Gooijen, A. van der Neer, T. Wyk, Huchtenburgh, Zolemaker, van Hassel, A. Vermeulen, van Dongen, Scheffer, van Os enz. | *This Lot:* Een Schilderij, A. van der Neer *Notes:* Because this lot was not numbered in the catalogue, we have assigned the number.		(Unknown)
1808/12/31	RMHSN	0019	*Vander Neer* | Een Landschapje | *Mat:* op paneel	G Spanjaart [or] H de Haas [or] C van der Looy Lans	(Unknown)
1809/04/17	AMSCH	0068	*A. van der Neer* | In dit natuurlijk Schilderij ziet men aan den Oever van een stille Rivier een hevigen Brand op een Dorp, gestoffeerd met zijlende en stilleggende Scheepen en Schuijten; fraai van effect en goed geschilderd | *Mat:* op paneel *Size:* hoog 13, breed 15 duim	[Gruyter?]	(Sold or Bought In) fl 16:10 Spaan
1809/04/17	AMSCH	0069	*A. van der Neer* | Een besneeuwd Wintergezicht, gestoffeerd met Schaatsenrijders, Kolvers en Visschers, natuurlijk voorgesteld | *Mat:* op paneel *Size:* hoog 14, breed 18 duim	T	(Sold) fl 18:10
1809/04/17	AMSCH	0143	*A. v.d. Neer* | Een Maanlicht | *Mat:* op paneel	[Gruyter?]	(Sold) fl 6:10
1809/07/25	HGBSM	0020	*A. van der Neer* | Een Maneschyn, verbeeldende een Land en Watergezigt | *Mat:* op doek *Size:* hoog 14, breed 17 ½ duim	D van der Aa [or] E B ten Dall	(Sold) fl 15 van Eyk
1810/03/26	RMMUY	0004	*Aart van der Neer* | Een gezigt van eenige Dorpen langs een water, met eenige Vaartuigen. Men ziet in 't midden een Molen waar achter de maan schijnt 't welk daar door een krachtige uitwerking heeft [Un clair de lune, une rivière bordée de plusieurs maisons et villages ; au milieu du tableau se voit un moulin qui s'oppose en brun, contre la lumière répandue par la lune, qui produit une illusion et un effet admirable. Plusieurs bateaux et figures occupent les différens plans.] | *Mat:* op paneel *Size:* hoog 12 ½, breed 19 duimen	Daniel de Jongh Az	(Sold) fl 82 J van der Hoop Rott
1810/06/06	RMMUY	0032	*A. van der Neer* | Een Land en Watergezigt, zijnde een Maanlicht, op den Voorgrond ziet men eenige Boeren in een Schuitje, verder eenige Huizen onder geboomte, in 't verschiet twee torens, het licht en donker doet in dit stuk eene ongemeen schoone uitwerking, alles is natuurlijk en meesterlijk behandeld | *Mat:* op doek		(Sold) fl 27:5 Luchtmans

1810/06/20	AMSCH	0068	*A. Van Der Neer* | Een heldere Maneschijn aan een Rivier, met zeilende en drijvende Vaartuigen. Natuurlijk geschilderd | *Mat:* op paneel *Size:* hoog 13, breed 16 duimen	B	(Bought In) fl 7:5
1810/06/20	AMSCH	0069	*A. Van Der Neer* | Een Landschap, met Geboomte en eene Kerk, gestoffeerd met eenen Veedrijver, bij Maanlicht. Natuurlijk verbeeld | *Mat:* op paneel *Size:* hoog 23, breed 18 duimen	B	(Bought In) fl 3
1810/06/20	AMSCH	0147[a]	*van der Neer* | Twee stuks: een met Paarden, door van der Neer, en het andere met Beelden | *This Lot:* Een met Paarden; lot 147[b] by Jan Lairesse	B	(Sold) fl 0:16 for lots 147[a] & 147[b]. du Pree
1810/08/06	AMSCH	0084	*Neer (A. van der)* | Een Winter met Schaatzerijders, Kolvers, Visschers enz. op het IJs, verder een aangenaam verschiet en Dorpgezicht; alles is helder en natuurlijk | *Mat:* op paneel *Size:* hoog 14 ½, breed 18 duimen	V[ries]	(Sold) fl 15:10 F du Pree
1810/08/06	AMSCH	0140	*A. van der Neer* | Een Wintergezigt, vol stoffagie	F	(Sold) fl 20 Roelsma
1810/10/10	MGCIT	0019	*A. v.d. Neer* | Een Rivier en Dorpgezigt, vol gewoel van veelerhande Voorwerpen, alles verligt door een zeer fraaije Maneschijn, en in allen opzigten Natuurlijk behandeld	Caspar van Citters	(Unknown)
1810/10/11	AMSCH	0062	*A. Van Der Neer* | Een helder schijnende Maan, over een stille Rivier, aan den Oever ziet men de Bolwerken, en een gedeelte van de Stads Wal, gestoffeerd met Schepen, Schuiten en Visschers; fraai van uitdrukking en natuurlijk behandeld | *Mat:* op doek *Size:* hoog 21, breed 28 duimen	[Gruyter?]	(Bought In) fl 5:5
1810/10/11	AMSCH	0063	*A. Van Der Neer* | Twee stuks Land- en Watergezigten, met Woningen, Geboomten en Beeldjes; zeer natuurlijk bij maanlicht verbeeld | *Mat:* op paneel *Size:* hoog 11, breed 16 duimen	C	(Sold) fl 36 Posthumus
1810/11/07	UTWLD	0010	*v. d. Neer* | Een Riviergezigtje waarop zijlende en stilliggende Scheepjes en Schuitjes door de Maan omgeven van eenige wolken, verlicht wordende, zeer schoon behandeld door v. d. Neer, op Paneel, breed 4 duim hoog 10 en een half duim, zwarte Lijst | *Mat:* op paneel *Size:* breed 4 duim hoog 10 en een half duim		(Unknown) fl 26

Neer, Aert van der (and Ostade, I.)

1804/08/08	AMSCH	0146	*J. van Ostade; A. van der Neer* | In een Dorpgezicht ziet men op de voorgrond ter eene zyde een Kar, waarvoor een wit en een bruin Paard gespannen is, waarby eenige Kippen en een Haan, en ter andere zyde twee Huislieden, waarvan de eene is gezéeten op een Houten Bank, en houdende een Hond onder den Arm, en de andere op een Ton, houdende meede een Hond by de Halsband, schynende zylieden over dezelve te spreeken, iets achterwaards by eenige Boerenwoningen een Kerktooren, en een helder spiegelende Rivier, ziet men drie Boeren en een Boerin, verders eenige Wooningen en Geboomte, en een bevallig verschiet; dit stuk is piquant van licht, enuitmuntend [sic] gepenceeld, door J. van Ostade en A. van der Neer | *Mat:* op paneel *Size:* hoog 24, breed 18 duim	Vink[eles] [for] W	(Sold) fl 150 C S Roos

Neer, Aert van der (or Neer, A., manner)

1801/04/08	HAVIN	0065	*v. d. Neer* | Een dito [Landschap] van of in de manier van v. d. Neer | *Notes:* It is unclear what "dito" refers to in the title.		(Unknown)
1802/09/06	AMSCH	0084	*A. v. d. Neer* | Een capitaal Land- en Watergezigt, aan beider oevers gestoffeert met Boerewooningen en geboomten, ziende naar een Kerktooren; in 't midden der Rivier vertoond zig een strook Land waarop eenig Vée; op de voorgrond een staand Man en Jongeling, ziende naar Visschers die hun net inhaalen; alles is verbeeld by helder Maanlicht; dit voorwerp is zeer natuurlyk, en meesterlyk van penceel-behandeling, door A. v. d. Neer, of in de manier | *Mat:* op paneel *Size:* hoog 27, breed 33 duim	Brave	(Sold) fl 22:10 de Meijer
1805/07/03	AMSCH	0192	*A. van der Neer* | Een stil Water, met Vaartuigen en Beeldjes, door of in de manier van A. van der Neer	C	(Sold) fl 9:10 La Vallette
1805/07/10	AMSCH	0113	*A. van der Neer* | Een Land- en Watergezigt, aan byder Oevers met Dorpgezichten, op de Voorgrond twee Huislieden, en verder gestoffeert met verscheide Vaartuigen, Schuiten en eenig Vee; alles verbeeld by een opkomend Maanlicht, door of in de manier van A. van der Neer	Wed Grave	(Sold) fl 61 Teengs

Neer, Aert van der (copy after)

1802/12/13	AMSCH	0059	*Jan Eekels; A. van der Neer* | Op een Bevroozen Rivier in de nabyheid van een Stad, ziet men een meenigte van Lieden, die zig met Reyden en Kolven op het Ys vermaaken, uitvoerig geschilderd, door Jan Eekels, naar A. van der Neer | copy by Jan Ekels (I) after A. Neer *Mat:* op doek *Size:* hoog 19, breed 21 duim	Pruyssenaar [for] A	(Bought In) fl 8
1804/10/16	DLOND	0240a[e]	*C. Vermeulen; A. v. d. Neer* | [Een Stuk, bevattende 13 zeer schone Copiën van de volgende Meesters. Un Tableau, contenant 13 Copies très-belles des Peintres suivans.] 5. A. v. d. Neer. Maneschyn, clair de Lune | copy by Corn. Vermeulen (III) after A. Neer *Mat:* op paneel *Size:* hoog 41, breed 55 *Notes:* The bracketed information in the title appears above lot 240a[a] and refers to lots 240a[a-m].		(Sold) fl 150 for lots 240a[a-m]. Ond d Wyngaert

Neer, Aert van der (manner)

1801/03/16	AMSCH	0187	*A. van der Neer* | Een Landschap met Boerenwoningen, waar in een gaand Man, alles verbeeld by helder Maanlicht, op doek, in de manier van A. van der Neer | *Mat:* op doek	K[ip]	(Sold) fl 3 Pruissenaar [for] L

1801/05/11	AMSCH	0124[a]	*A. van der Neer* | Twee stuks, een in de manier van A. van der Neer, en een ander | *This Lot:* Een stuk; lot 124[b] by Anonymous *Notes:* This lot was sold with lot 123 by an anonymous artist.	E[lias]	(Sold) fl 4:15 for lots 123, 124[a] & 124[b]. Allard
1804/02/27	AMSCH	0176	*A. van der Neer* | Een Maaneschyn, als A. van der Neer	B	(Sold) fl 2:5 J Yver
1805/10/09	HGBSM	0125	*A. van der Neer* | Een landschapje met boerewoningen en kerktoren in 't verschiet, de voorgrond is gestoffeerd met eenige visschers in een schuit alles by heldere manenschyn, verbeeld konstig in de trand van A. van der Neer, door een goed Meester | *Mat:* op paneel *Size:* hoog 8 ½ breet 10 ½ duim	T H van Willigen [or others]	(Sold) fl 4:10 Schoon
1806/08/13	AMSCH	0228	*A. van der Neer* | Twee stuks Land- en Riviergezichten, gestoffeerd met verscheide Beeldjes en zylende Vaartuigen; alles verbeeld by helder maanlicht, in de manier van A. van der Neer | *Mat:* op paneel	Roos	(Sold) fl 9:10 Gruyter
1807/06/10	HGBSM	0138	*van der Neer* | Een Rhijn gezigt met veel Schepen, de voorgrond gestoffeerd met Koebeesten, alles fraai verbeeld bij helder maanligt, als van der Neer | *Mat:* op doek *Size:* hoog 18, breed 22 duim	Abraham Delfos [or others]	(Sold) fl 7 Tessier
1807/06/10	HGBSM	0189	*van der Neer* | Een Maneschijn met een uitgestrekt water, als van der Neer | *Mat:* op doek *Size:* hoog 14 ½, breed 23 duim	Abraham Delfos [or others]	(Sold) fl 3:2 Teixera
1808/08/23	AMSCH	0261	*A. van der Neer* | Een dito [natuurlijk] Landschap aan een Rivier; in de manier van A. van der Neer	J	(Sold) fl 2:5 Gruyter
1810/03/26	RMMUY	0077	*A. van der Neer* | Een stil Water met Schepen, als door A. van der Neer [Une Eau calme, dans le genre de Van der Neer.] | *Annots:* [par] van Goy[en] (BPG)	Daniel de Jongh Az	(Sold) fl 3 Le Brun Parys
1810/12/03	DOBRA	0022	*A. van der Neer* | Een Landschap, by Maanligt; in de trant van A. van der Neer		(Unknown)

Neer, C. van der [Unidentified]

1807/08/26	AMSCH	0154	*C. van der Neer* | Het Pourtrait van een geestelyke of Nonnetje in haar wolle kleding, met een koord om het lyf, en een Kapsel op het hoofd, zy rust met haar linker hand op een Doodshoofd dat nevens haar op een Tafel ligt, benevens een Crusifiks, ter zyde ziet men het Klooster in het verschiet; uitvoerig en kragtig van schildering | *Mat:* op doek *Size:* hoog 15 ½, breed 12 duim	de Vries	(Sold) fl 3:5 Sardet

Neer, Eglon Hendrik van der

1802/08/24	LNDLS	0007	*Eglon van der Neer* | In een Binnen-vertrek zit een Juffer, in een rood jakje met wit-bont gevoerd, en met een blaauwe satijne rok, met een Kind op haar schoot en een Patrijshondje nevens haar, voor haar staat een Tafel, welke met een Tapijt-kleed gedekt is, waar een Fles met bloemen, een Boek en Papkom op staan, agter haar een staande Dienstmaagd, benevens een Wieg en een Kinderstoel, en verder bijwerk. Delicaat op paneel geschilderd | *Mat:* op paneel *Size:* hoog 16 ½, breed 13 ½ duimen	Leonardus Bouman [or others]	(Unknown) fl 60
1803/07/18	AMSCH	0035	*Neer (Eglon van der)* | In een pragtig Binnenvertrek ziet men een Gezelschap van Dames en Heeren, alle ryk gekleed, op de voorgrond een staande Dame in het wit Satyn, wordende haar sleep gedragen door een Page, voorts een klein Moortje met een Fles in de handen, de fraaye Stoffen der Kleederen zyn delicaat en natuurlyk verbeeld, en delicaat gepenceeld [Dans un appartement orné, bâti en marbre, l'on voit entrer une Dame vétue d'une robe en satin blanc & d'un jupon rose d'etoffe semblable, garni d'un bord en galon d'argent. Elle est accompagnée d'un magistrat & d'un page portant la queue de sa robe. Un Cavalier & une Dame assis en vis-à-vis interrompent leur jeu de cartes pour recevoir la visite. De côté est un négre attendant les ordres, la bouteille à la main. La beauté des etoffes, la delicatesse de pinceau, l'agrément & le bel effet du sujet se réunissent en ce tableau, qui est d'une belle proportion de Cabinet.] | *Mat:* op doek *Size:* hoog 27, breed 29 duim	Maria Theresia Andrioli	(Sold) fl 200 Teissier
1804/08/08	AMSCH	0140	*E. van der Neer* | Een Heer in prachtige Turksche Kleeding, met een Tulband en Halscieraad, vol edele Gesteentens; de stoffe der Kleeding zoo wel als de uitvoerigheid van Schildering zyn in dit stukje te bewonderen | *Mat:* op paneel *Size:* hoog 8 ½, breed 7 duim	Roos a	(Sold) fl 41 Vinkeles [for] K
1806/11/24	AMSCH	0046	*Neer (Eglon van der)* | Dit fraai Cabinetstukje, vertoont een bevallige jeugdige Vrouw, staande in een Landschap voor een steene Tafel, houdende met de hand als eene glaase Waereld-Bol, waar in van binnen verbeeld: de ontmoeting van Elisabeth, de Vlugt naar Egypten, en de Kruisdraging door Christus, ter zyde staat een Engel, het als in verrukking te beschouwen; de caracters zyn fraai, het coloriet aangenaam en van eene alleruitvoerigste penceelbehandeling | *Mat:* op paneel *Size:* hoog 10, breed 8 duim	Munnikhuizen	(Sold) fl 80 Hulswit
1808/06/11	RMRIJ	0065	*Eglon van der Neer* | Een schoon Mans Pourtrait, deftig gekleed, Kniestuk rustende tegens een Pedestal en verdere Architecture, zeer uitvoerig en konstig geschilderd | *Mat:* op paneel *Size:* hoog 13, breed 10 duim		(Sold) fl 18:10 Luchtmans
1810/03/26	RMMUY	0015	*Eglon van der Neer* | Het Pourtrait van een Vrolijke Schilder. [Un Peintre en bonne humeur, faisant un signe de la main.] | companion to lot 16 *Mat:* op paneel *Fmt:* ovaal *Size:* hoog 4 ½, breed 3 ½ duimen	Daniel de Jongh Az	(Sold) fl 25:10 for lots 15 & 16. van Eyk s'Hage
1810/03/26	RMMUY	0016	*Eglon van der Neer* | Eene wedergade door denzelven [Eglon van der Neer], zijnde het Portrait van eene Vrolijke Dame, met een glas in de hand. Uitvoerig en delicaat behandeld [Un Pendant. Une Dame, tenant un	Daniel de Jongh Az	(Sold) fl 25:10 for lots 15 & 16. van Eyk s'Hage

			verre à la main, en [sic] qui paroit avoir une pointe de vin. Ces deux morceaux sont précieusement fini [sic] et d'un joli ton de couleur.] | companion to lot 15 *Mat:* op paneel *Fmt:* ovaal *Size:* hoog 4 ½, breed 3 ½ duimen		

Neer, Eglon Hendrik van der (manner)

1801/06/13	LNDLS	0065	*E. van der Neer* | Een Juffer, voor haar toilet, een Heer die een spiegel houd, en een dienstmeid die haar helpt, in de trant van E. van der Neer | *Size:* hoog 11, breed 9 duimen	D van R	(Sold) fl 30 van Iperen

Nellius, Martinus

1801/06/13	LNDLS	0076	*Nellius* | Een Stilleven, met een tafel met vruchten	D van R	(Sold) fl 3:18 Richter [for] S[tevens]
1807/06/10	HGBSM	0128	*Nelius* | Twee stukjes met Vrugten | *Mat:* op paneel *Size:* hoog 15, breed 13 duim	Abraham Delfos [or others]	(Sold) fl 1 Oosterwyk

Nepveu, Jacob

1801/06/10	AMSCH	0129	*Nepveu. (J.)* | In een Binnevertrek staat eene Vrouw, met een Hond dansende, achter dezelve zit een andere Vrouw met een Kind: alles in bevallige penceels behandeling | *Mat:* op doek *Size:* hoog 18, breed 15 duim *Notes:* The artist was presumably Matthys Naiveu and not Jacob Nepveu.	Herman ten Kate	(Sold) fl 47 Pruijssenaar
1802/02/16	AMSCH	0087	*J. Naipveu* | Verbeeld een Chirurgyns Winkel, waar in een Patient aan zyn arm verbonden word, ter zyde zit een schryende Vrouw, waar by een Juffrouw een kind; gestoffeert, met een ménigte bywerk, kragtig en uitvoerig gepenceeld | *Notes:* The artist was presumably Matthys Naiveu and not Jacob Nepveu.	Z	(Sold) fl 26 for lots 87 & 88. J^{b} Royers
1802/02/16	AMSCH	0088	*J. Naipveu* | In een dito Vertrek, word een Boer door den Heelmeester aan den arm, met een Lancet gesondeert, ter zyde een zittende Vrouw, en een staande Juffrouw: door een openstaande deur ziet men in de winkel; in alles als de vorige, uitvoerig behandeld | *Notes:* The artist was presumably Matthys Naiveu and not Jacob Nepveu. It is unclear what "dito" refers to in the title.	Z	(Sold) fl 26 for lots 87 & 88. J^{b} Royers
1802/09/06	AMSCH	0087	*J. Nepven* | Twee stuks, een Dame voor haar Toilet; en het andere een Dame welke door haar dienstmaagd wafelen aangeboden worden; heide delicaat gepenceeld | *Mat:* op doek *Size:* hoog 17, breed 14 duim *Notes:* The artist was presumably Matthys Naiveu and not Jacob Nepveu.	Mevrouw Achtienhoven	(Sold) fl 13:10 van Iperen
1808/06/13	AMSCH	0116	*Nepveu (J.)* | In eene Kraamkamer zit de Kraamvrouw op het Bed, eene Dame neemt het Kind van haar arm, om het in de Wieg te leggen, terzijde de Vader, met een Roemer Wijn, en ter andere zijde de Baker, met een Zilveren Papkom. Alles zacht en uitvoerig gepenceeld | *Mat:* op doek *Size:* hoog 28, breed 35 duim *Notes:* The artist was presumably Matthys Naiveu and not Jacob Nepveu.	Z	(Sold) fl 101 J Schuman
1808/06/13	AMSCH	0116a[H]	*Nepveu (J.)* | 1 dito dito [Kraamkamer?] [or] een fruitstuk[?] | *Notes:* This lot was added in by hand in the AA I, EBNP, FLNY and RKDH copies of the catalogue, with variations in the title as shown above. However, it is unclear what "dito" refers to in the first title. The artist was presumably M. Naiveu and not J. Nepveu.		(Sold) fl 27 J Spaan

Neranus, A.

1808/06/11	RMRIJ	0072	*A: Neranus* | Een Mans Pourtrait, in Oostersche Kleeding, als door Rembrand gecouleurd en geschilderd | *Mat:* op paneel *Size:* hoog 9, breed 7 duim		(Sold) fl 9 Luchtmans
1810/10/11	AMSCH	0211	*A. Neranus* | Een Ordonantie van eene menigte Beelden, op Paneel, door A. Neranus. Ao. 1635 | *Mat:* op paneel *Inscr:* A. Neranus. Ao. 1635 (signed and dated?) *Notes:* It is unclear whether the name and date are inscribed on the painting.	A	(Sold) fl 2:11 L Pakker

Neter, Laurentius de

1804/07/25	DLGRO	0064	*Laurence Neter* | Een Musicceerend gezelschap | *Mat:* op paneel *Size:* hoog 9, breed 13 duim	Mr Franc van der Burch Wz.	(Unknown)
1804/07/25	DLGRO	0065	*Laurence Neter* | Een dito [Musiceerend] dito [gezelschap], door denzelfde [Laurence Neter] | *Mat:* op paneel *Size:* hoog 9, breed 13 duim	Mr Franc van der Burch Wz.	(Unknown)

Netscher, Caspar

1801/04/08	HAVIN	0006	*Netscher* | Het Pourtrait van A. Paauw in een Japon, en wat agterwaarts het beeld der gerechtigheid extra uitvoerig en zeer fraai geschildert		(Unknown)
1801/04/08	HAVIN	0007	*Netscher* | Een Vrouwe Pourtrait by een Fontyn		(Unknown)
1801/06/13	LNDLS	0050	*C. Netscher* | Een Jongeling en een Meisje, die bellen blaazen, bij een tafel met fruit, in een Landschap, op doek | companion to lot 51 *Mat:* op doek *Size:* hoog 18, breed 15 duimen	D van R	(Sold) fl 15:5 for lots 50 & 51. Richter S [for] Stevens
1801/06/13	LNDLS	0051	*C. Netscher* | Een Weêrga, verbeeld een Juffertje, die een aartig hondje uit een schulp laat drinken, door denzelven [C. Netscher], en van dezelve groote | companion to lot 50 *Mat:* op doek *Size:* hoog 18, breed 15 duimen	D van R	(Sold) fl 15:5 for lots 50 & 51. Richter S [for] Stevens

1801/10/06	AMSCH	0047	*G. Netscher* | Het afbeeldsel van den beroemde Geleerden .... Hartzoeker, staande by een steene Baluster met een Basrelief versiert, in een zyde gebloemde Japon. wyzende met de regter hand naar een woelende Zee, waar in een Schip door storm geslingerd word, op de Baluster staat een Hemel-Globe en Microscoop, waar by verscheide andere Physische Instrumenten leggen, alles is meesterlyk, fraay behandeld en uitvoerig gepenceeld | *Mat:* op doek *Size:* hoog 19, breed 15 duim	S	(Sold) fl 71 v d Schley A [for] Merrem bectaals
1801/10/06	AMSCH	0048	*G. Netscher* | Een staand Krygsman of Bevelhebber, houdende de Staf van commande in de rechter hand, in 't verschiet vertoont zig een Schermutseliug [sic] tusschen eenige Ruiters, meesterlyk behandeld | *Mat:* op doek *Size:* hoog 28, breed 26 duim	M	(Sold) fl 5 Theijs
1802/02/16	AMSCH	0036	*G. Netscher* | Zynde het Afbeeldsel, van den beroemde Heer Hartzoeker, staande by een Tafel, waar op eene Globe en Physische Instrumenten geplaast zyn, uitvoerig geschilderd	Z	(Sold) fl 5 Coclers
1802/05/24	HGBAK	0074	*Netscher* | Een jonge Juffrouw ten halven lyf, door Netscher, hoog 18 duim, breed 15 duim, verg. lyst | *Size:* hoog 18 duim, breed 15 duim	Mejuffrouw A van der Mieden	(Unknown) fl 7
1802/06/16	AMSCH	0119	*G. Netscher* | Het Afbeeldsel van den beroemde Heer Hartzoeker; staande in deftige kleeding tot aan de kniën te zien; by een Steenvoetstuk, met een Basrelief, waar op geplaatst een Globe, en verscheiden Physische Instrumenten; zeer uitvoerig en meesterlyk gepenceeld | *Mat:* op doek *Size:* hoog 18 ½, breed 15 duim	[Merrem]	(Sold) fl 90 v d Schleij
1802/06/28	AMSCH	0130	*G. Netscher* | Een bevallig Vrouwe Pourtrait; delicaat op Zilver gepenceelt | *Mat:* op zilver *Size:* hoog 4, breed 3 duim	Anna Elink	(Sold) fl 8:15 Gruiter
1802/07/21	HGKAN	0059	*Netscher* | Een Kabinet stukje, verbeeldende een staande Dame, gekleed in wit Sautyn, Speelende op de Guitar, op een stoel ligt een Hondje, en op een Tafel door een Tapyt gedekt staat een Vles met Roosen, alles zeer uitvoerig en delicaat behandelt, door Netscher, hoog 11 3/4 duym breed en 9 1/4 duym, op paneel, vergulde Lyst | *Mat:* op paneel *Size:* hoog 11 ¾ duym breed en 9 ¼ duym		(Unknown)
1802/08/24	LNDLS	0036	*C. Netscher* | Een geopend Varken hangende aan een ladder, daar nevens de kop van dat dier in een Tobbe, terwijl een Jongeling de blaas opblaast. Zeer konstig de natuur gevolgd, en uitvoerig op paneel | *Mat:* op paneel *Size:* hoog 14, breed 11 duimen	Leonardus Bouman [or others]	(Unknown) fl 15:10
1802/09/06	AMSCH	0086	*G. Netscher* | In een Binnenkamer aan een tafel zit een Heer en Dame, zy schynen te spreeken over 't spel welke zy speelen, door een openstaande deur ziet men een dienstmaagd met een schotel met Vrugten binnenkoomen; bevallig van licht, en aangenaam gepenceeld | *Mat:* op doek *Size:* hoog 26, breed 22 duim	J	(Sold) fl 1:15 Hulswit
1802/09/21	UTHDG	0067	*Casp. Netscher* | Een zeer bevallige jonge Juffrouw, houdende een opene Brief in de hand, zij schijnt door den inhoud getroffen, en zit naa te denken; haare nette kleeding, is gedeeltelijk met wit bont omboord: ter zijde van haar een Mantje met Naaiwerk, het vertrek, is met Meubelen versierd, enz. Dit regt aangenaam schilderij is zeer natuurlijk en delicaat behandelt | *Mat:* op doek *Size:* hoog 13 ½, breed 11 duimen		(Bought In) fl 46
1802/09/30	HGBAK	0003	*Netscher* | Een zittende Dame, door Netscher, paneel, vergulde lyst. [Schilderyen in Olyverf] | *Mat:* in olyverf op paneel *Notes:* The bracketed information in the title appears above lot 1 and refers to lots 1 to 26.		(Unknown)
1802/12/13	AMSCH	0127	*G. Netscher* | Een Heer in een bevallige Kleeding, konstig gepenceeld | *Size:* hoog 19, breed 24 ½ duim	Pruyssenaar [for] A	(Sold) fl 3:10 Gruiter
1803/04/18	HGBAK	0017	*Netscher* | Een Damen verbeeldende de Wysheid, met bywerk door Netscher, hoog 29. breed 23 duym op doek, witte lyst [Schilderyen in Olyverf] | *Mat:* in olyverf op doek *Size:* hoog 29 breed 23 duym *Notes:* The bracketed information in the title appears above lot 1 and refers to lots 1 to 48.	Johan Pieter Reigersman [or others]	(Unknown)
1803/07/18	AMSCH	0036	*Netscher (G.)* | In een Corps du Garde zit aan een Tafel een Krygsman in 't Harnas en Ledere Kolder gekleed, met een Pyp in de hand, schynende zyn orders aan den Tamboer, die met de hoed in de hand ter zyde hem staat, te geeven, op de voorgrond een Trommel, Harnas en Casquet, alles zeer natuurlyk en van een malsch penceel [Le sujet du tableau est un guerrier cuirassé assis devant une table une pipe à la main [;] il se tourne vèrs un militaire qui reçoit ses ordres le chapeau à la main ; un grand tambour & des Armures sont à terre au devant du tableau, formant un Ensemble de bel effet. Ce morceau de mérite est peint d'une maniere delicate & Expressive.] | *Mat:* op paneel *Size:* hoog 14, breed 12 duim	Maria Theresia Andrioli	(Sold) fl 54 Theens
1803/08/24	HGKAN	0009	*C. Netscher* | Een Dame in het wit Satyn gekleed, speelende op een Guitar, met een Muziek Blad in de hand, een hond op Tafel zittende op een fraay Tapyt, uitvoerig geschilderd	[Teissier] [or others]	(Sold) fl 25 Taxera
1804/08/08	AMSCH	0138	*G. Netscher* | Door een Steene Nis, waar voor een opgeslagen groen Kleed, waarop een Tobben en Steene Pan met Linnen geplaatst is, ziet men een bevallige Jonge Dame, in ryke Kleeding, bézig te wasschen, achter haar voor een open Raam een Naaister, en verder toepasselyk Bywerk; alleruitvoerigst en fraai gepenceeld, op Paneel | *Mat:* op paneel *Size:* hoog 11, br. 10 duim	Vink[eles] [for] W	(Bought In) fl 63 for lots 138 & 139
1804/08/08	AMSCH	0139	*G. Netscher* | Door een dito [Steene] Nis en opgeslagen Gordyn ziet men een bevallige Dame, bézig Worst te stoppen, voor de Nis hangen eenige	Vink[eles] [for] W	(Bought In) fl 63 for lots 138 & 139

<table>
<tr><td></td><td></td><td></td><td>Ingewanden van Dieren, verders in een Vertrek ziet men de Meid een Kétel met Vleesch over 't Vuur hangen; alles is van een dito behandeling als de voorgaande | Mat: op paneel Size: hoog 11, breed 10 duim Notes: It is unclear what "dito" refers to in the title.</td><td></td><td></td></tr>
<tr><td>1808/06/06</td><td>RMRIJ</td><td>0089</td><td>Netscher. (Casparus) | Vertumne en Pomone ten voeten uit. De laatstgenoemde is gezeten in eenen fraaijen Hof op een prachtig tapijt bij een Term, versierd met Vruchten, Bloemen en Gewassen, staande Vertumne nevens haar. Op den voorgrond nog vele Vruchten. – Zie de Métamorphose van Ovidius. Zeer uitvoerig en konstig behandeld [Pomone, richement vétue est assise dans un beau Jardin auprés d'un Terme. Vertumne sous le Masque d'une Vieille s'entretient avec elle. De beaux fruits et d'autres accessoires embellissent ce Morceau, dont l'harmonie, le Coloris frais et brillant, les belles Etoffes, et le faire admirable charment l'oeil] | Annots: van Thys, Aug. 1806 als Constantyn Netscher (f 75.-) (RMA I); NB. c'est tout au plus l'ouvrage de Constantin Netscher, et nullement de gaspar (MA) Mat: op doek Size: Hoog 19 ¾, en breed 16 ¾ duim</td><td>Gerrit van der Pot, Heer van Groeneveld</td><td>(Sold) fl 310 Netscher</td></tr>
<tr><td>1808/08/23</td><td>AMSCH</td><td>0119</td><td>Netscher. (G.) | Dit kunstrijk Tafreel, vertoont in een binnenzicht van een Stal, een bedaagd Man, schijnende bézig Stroo tot haksel te kerven, daar nevens zit eene oude Vrouw bij een Spinnewiel, met de Gaarenklos in de handen, verders een Jongeling, staande bij een Ton, met een aarde Bierkan in de hand, op de grond liggen koper Ketel, ijzere Pot en Aardvrugten, en verder bijwerk, door de open Deur, ziet men in ander vertrekken, de Karacters zijn Natuurlijk, het Licht bevallig, en van een uitmuntende penceel behandeling; zijnde een zeldzaam voorwerp van deeze vermaarde Meester | Mat: op doek Size: hoog 26, breed 30 duim Loc: Philadelphia, PA, USA. Museum of Art. (Johnson Coll. 544)</td><td>E</td><td>(Sold) fl 1055 Van Iperen</td></tr>
<tr><td>1809/04/17</td><td>AMSCH</td><td>0067</td><td>C. Netscher | In een Keukenvertrek staat eene Dienstmaagd bij een Aanregtbank, Groenten te hakken, nevens haar op de voorgrond zit eene bevallige Vrouw Wortelen te Schraapen, ter zijde zit een Man bij de Haard, bézig het Spit te draaijen, verder ziet men verscheide Keukengereedschappen; fraai van Licht en uitvoerig gepenceeld | Mat: op doek Size: hoog 21 ½, breed 24 ½ duim</td><td>[Gruyter?]</td><td>(Sold) fl 15:10</td></tr>
<tr><td>1809/06/13</td><td>AMSCH</td><td>0116</td><td>G. Netscher | Eene bevallige Dame, in Satijn gekleed, zittende in een Landschap | Mat: op doek Size: hoog 21, breed 18 duim</td><td>Y</td><td>(Sold) fl 2 Gruyter</td></tr>
<tr><td>1809/07/19</td><td>AMSCH</td><td>0040</td><td>Netscher (G.) | Voor een open Steenen Nis met een open geschoven tapijt-Gordijn, staat een bedaagd Heer, in deftige oude Hollandsche Kleding, rustende met den arm op de Plint, welke van ondere met Kindertjes in Basrelief verzierd is, nevens hem staat een bevallig Jongeling, houdende met beide handen een ivoir Beeldje, ter zijde op de Plint ligt een gouden Uurwerk en een Roozetak. Het is van een uitmuntende penceelsbehandeling | Mat: op paneel Size: hoog 17 ½, breed 13 ½ duim</td><td>[Bicker]</td><td>(Sold) fl 51 Gruyter</td></tr>
<tr><td>1809/09/06</td><td>AMSCH</td><td>0056</td><td>Netscher (G) | In een gemeubileerde Kamer zit eene Zieken Dame in een Armstoel, in een satijn Onderkleed, met een Mantel met Bont gevoerd, voor een Tafel, met een Tapijt Kleedje bedekt, waarop een Urinaal en Inktkooker geplaatst is; ter zijde staat den Doctor, haar den Pols voelende, en tevens met de andere hand met aandagt het water bezienden, verder eene Dienstmaagd bij een Ledikant. De karakters zijn natuurlijk en uitvoerig van schildering | Mat: op paneel Size: hoog 11, breed 9 duim</td><td>Johannes Caudri</td><td>(Sold) fl 40
P Swanenburg</td></tr>
<tr><td>1810/06/20</td><td>AMSCH</td><td>0120</td><td>C. Netscher | Een Mans Pourtrait</td><td>N</td><td>(Sold) fl 5 Coclers</td></tr>
<tr><td>1810/08/01</td><td>AMSCH</td><td>0068</td><td>Netscher (Gasper) | In een Binnenvertrek zit een deftig Heer bij eene Tafel, voor hem staat zijne Vrouw in satijnen kleeding, hebbende een Kind aan de hand [Sujet de Famille, étant un intérieur d'apartement, où l'on voit un Seigneur assis devant une Table ; et à son côté sa Femme vétue en Satin, tenant un Enfant par la main] | Annots: très médiocre et fort inférieur à Netscher. (NGW) Mat: op doek Size: hoog 20, breed 18 duimen</td><td>Mr Pieter de Smeth van Alphen</td><td>(Sold) fl 290 Texier, Gerbet en Comp [for] LeBrun</td></tr>
<tr><td>1810/10/10</td><td>MGCIT</td><td>0086</td><td>Netscher | Twee Schilderyen, zynde een Heer, het andere een Dame; de eerste zittende aan een Tafel, waarop een Tapyt, terwyl naast Hem aan d'andere zyde een Tafeltje is, waarop een Koelvat en glazen, waarvan hy er ook één in de hand heeft; de tweede mede in eene zittende houding aan een Tafel, waarop insgelyks een Tapyt, en spelende op de Guitar, delicaat geschilderd</td><td>Caspar van Citters</td><td>(Unknown)</td></tr>
<tr><td>1810/12/03</td><td>DOBRA</td><td>0052</td><td>Netscher | Een Vrouwe Pourtrait</td><td></td><td>(Unknown)</td></tr>
<tr><td></td><td></td><td></td><td>Netscher, Caspar (or Netscher, Casp., manner)</td><td></td><td></td></tr>
<tr><td>1803/07/14</td><td>MGKLY</td><td>0027</td><td>Netscher of zyn manier | De Koningin van Scheba, komt met geschenken, voor Salomon, vol gewoel en extra fraay geschildert | Mat: op koper</td><td>Mr Caspar Jacob van Citters</td><td>(Unknown)</td></tr>
<tr><td>1803/08/24</td><td>HGKAN</td><td>0079</td><td>Netscher | Twee Portraitten op een stuk, door of in de manier van Netscher</td><td>[Teissier] [or others]</td><td>(Unknown) fl 1</td></tr>
<tr><td>1803/08/24</td><td>HGKAN</td><td>0080</td><td>Netscher | Een dito [Portrait], dito als vooren [door of in de manier van Netscher]</td><td>[Teissier] [or others]</td><td>(Unknown) fl 1:4</td></tr>
<tr><td></td><td></td><td></td><td>Netscher, Caspar (copy after)</td><td></td><td></td></tr>
<tr><td>1806/08/20</td><td>HGBSM</td><td>0193</td><td>C. Netscher | Lucretia in eene aandoenelijke houding, naar C. Netscher | Mat: op paneel Size: hoog 11 ½, breed 10 duim</td><td>Macalester Loup [or others]</td><td>(Sold) fl 23:5 Thys</td></tr>
</table>

Netscher, Caspar (manner)

1802/06/28	AMSCH	0131	*Netscher* | Twee stuks, een Jongeling en een Meisje met Vogelkoijen en Katten speelende, uitvoerig op Panneel, in de manier van Netscher | *Mat:* op paneel *Size:* hoog 11, breed 9 duim	Anna Elink	(Sold) fl 17 Coclers
1805/10/09	HGBSM	Z0025	*Netscher* | Een portret van een heer in zyn Japon, in de manier van Netscher, op doek, hoog 18 breed 15 duim, ovaal formaat | *Mat:* op doek *Fmt:* ovaal *Size:* hoog 18 breed 15 duim	T H van Willigen [or others]	(Sold) fl 6 van der Linden
1809/07/25	HGBSM	0235	*Netscher* | Het Portret van een Dame in een Tuin, in de manier van Netscher | *Mat:* op doek *Size:* hoog 21 en een half, breed 17 duim	D van der Aa [or] E B ten Dall	(Sold) fl 2:16 Hari
1810/06/06	RMMUY	0186	*C. Netscher* | Door eene Nis ziet men drie Kindertjes met Bloemen spelende. In de manier van C. Netscher | *Mat:* op paneel		(Unknown) fl 2:2

Netscher, Theodorus

1808/11/28	AMSCH	0046	*Th. Netscher* | Een zinnebeeldige Ordonantie, verbeeldende het Portrait van Henriëtta Maria, Koningin van Engeland, beneevens eenig bijwerk, kloek geschilderd | *Mat:* op doek *Size:* hoog 39, breed 30 duim	H	(Sold) fl 18 Cocler

Neustück, Maximilian

1803/09/07	AMSCH	0119	*M. Neustuk, 1788* | Twee stuks Bergachtige Landschappen, met Geboomte, Watervallen, en stoffagie van Beeldjes, by een Watermolen, geestig op Doek [Deux paysages riches en arbres, en colines, en cascades et en figures auprès d'un moulin ; composition spirituelle] | *Mat:* op doek *Size:* hoog 17, breed 22 duim *Inscr:* M. Neustuk, 1788 (signed and dated?) *Notes:* It is unclear whether the name and date are inscribed on the painting.	Smidt	(Sold) fl 10:5 Gruiter
1806/08/13	AMSCH	0136	*Neustuk. (M.)* | Twee capitaale hooge Bergachtige Landschappen met zwaar Geboomten, Watervallen en Watermolens, beide ryk gestoffeerd met Beelden en Beesten; schoon van licht; en meesterlyk geschilderd | *Mat:* op doek *Size:* hoog 17, breed 22 duim	Vinkeles [for] G[ruyter]	(Sold) fl 20 Swanenburg

Neyburgh, B.J. [Unidentified]

1808/04/26	GDAN	0116	*Neyburgh (B J)* | Verbeeldende in twee Kinderen, Herakliet en Democriet, met een Spaansch Hondje, zeer goed geschilderd | *Size:* hoog 34, breed 42 duim	G H Fortuyn	(Unknown)

Nickelen

1801/08/19	AMSCH	0075	*van Nikkelen* | Een capitaalen Kerk, schoon van Architectuur en ryk gestoffeerd met een ménigte Beeldjes	Pruyssen[r]	(Sold) fl 5 Gruiter
1802/05/05	AMSCH	0156	*van Nikkelen* | Een Protestante Kerk, van binnen ziende na 't Choor, gestoffeerd met wandelende en zittende Beelden, uitvoerig gepenceeld	J	(Sold) fl 14 v d Vinne
1803/04/20	AMSCH	0052	*Nikkelen (.... van)* | Een Binnengezicht van een Roomsche Kerk, ryk gestoffeert met verscheide Altaaren, in 't verschiet een Priester de dienst verrigtende, waarby eenige Lieden, bevallig van licht en uitvoerig behandeld [Perspective interieure d'une Eglise Catholique ornée d'autels & de quelques figures : ce sujet est traité avec verité & effet.] | *Mat:* op doek *Size:* hoog 20, breed 16 duim	Maria Magdalena van Sluypwyk, gravinne van Moens	(Sold) fl 31 Hodges
1803/04/20	AMSCH	0053	*Nikkelen (... van)* | Een Binnengezicht van een Protestantsche Kerk, ziende naar de Predikstoel, Orgel en Choor, in alles als de vorige behandeld [Une Eglise Protestante dont le point de vue part de la grande nef sur la chaire, les orgues & le choeur ; du même merite de l'article precedent.] | *Mat:* op doek *Size:* hoog 19, breed 16 duim	Maria Magdalena van Sluypwyk, gravinne van Moens	(Sold) fl 20 Hodges
1810/06/06	RMMUY	0109	*N. van Nikkelen* | Eene Protestantsche Kerk van binnen te zien, uitvoerig en aangenaam verbeeld en gestoffeerd | companion to lot 110, by Anonymous *Mat:* op doek *Notes:* This lot was sold with lot 110 by an anonymous artist.		(Sold) fl 68 for lots 109 & 110. V Eyk

Nickelen (and Hals)

1801/04/08	HAVIN	0002	*van Nikkelen; Hals* | Een gezigt in de Groote Kerk te Haarlem, na 't Choor te zien extra fraai door van Nikkelen en door Hals gestoff:		(Unknown)

Nickelen (and Maes, N.)

1804/10/16	DLOND	0132	*Nic. Maas; J.H. Nickelen* | Het Raadhuis te Amsterdam, met de Waag, en veel gewoel. L'Hôtel de Ville d'Amsterdam, avec beaucoup de figures | *Size:* hoog 40, breed 49 *Notes:* The lot was changed from "Nic. Maas en J.H. Nickelen, Het Raadhuis te Amsterdam, met de Waag, en veel gewoel," to "F. Bol," without giving a title, at the front of the catalogue.		(Withdrawn)

Nickelen (and Vinne, J.)

1808/03/03	HAVIN	0002	*van Nikkelen; J. van der Vinne* | De Groote Kerk te Haarlem, na 't Choor te zien, fraai, door van Nikkelen, en gestoffeerd door J. van der Vinne	Jacobus Spillebout	(Unknown) fl 8

Nickelen, Isaak van

1801/02/18	AMBOS	0017	*van Nickelen* | De groote Kerk van Haarlem, zonachtig en natuurlyk geschilderd	J Schonevelt	(Unknown)

Nickelen, Jacoba Maria van

1805/07/03	AMSCH	0122	*J. M. van Nikkelen* | Twee stuks Binnegezichten, van Protestanten Kerkjes, gestoffeerd met verscheide Beeldjes; fiks geschilderd op Doek | *Mat:* op doek *Size:* yder hoog 9, breed 7 duim	G	(Sold) fl 12:10 Lamb Jan Nieunwenhuys

Nickelen, Jan van

1801/03/16	AMSCH	0017	*J. van Nikkelen* | Een gestoffeerde Protestante Kerk; bevallig gepenceeld	K[ip]	(Sold) fl 5:5 Roelofs
1801/03/16	AMSCH	0045	*J. van Nikelen* | Een Protestansche Kerk van binnen te zien, 't Choor gestoffeerd met wandelende Beelden, fraai van perspectief	P[ruyssenaar]	(Sold) fl 2 Wijland
1801/04/08	HAVIN	0021	*J. van Nikkelen* | Twee Hofgezigten, uitvoerig		(Unknown)
1801/04/08	HAVIN	0022	*J. van Nikkelen* | Een dito [Hofgezigt] met een prachtig gebouw en Fontyn | *Notes:* It is unclear what "dito" refers to in the title.		(Unknown)
1802/06/16	AMSCH	0121	*J. van Nickelen* | Een Binnengezicht van een Roomsche Kerk, gestoffeert met prachtige Altaaren en Predikstoel, beneevens verscheiden wandelende Kerkelyke en andere Persoonen; helder, natuurlyk en uitvoerig behandeld | *Mat:* op paneel *Size:* hoog 10 ½, breed 9 duim	[Merrem]	(Sold) fl 16:10 Gruiter
1802/06/16	AMSCH	0122	*J. van Nickelen* | Een Protestansche Kerk van binnen te zien, gestoffeert met wandelende Beelden; het perspectief is wel in acht genoomen, en meesterlyk van Penceel behandeling | *Mat:* op doek *Size:* hoog 19, breed 16 duim	[Merrem]	(Sold) fl 25 Reijers
1804/10/29	HRBAU	0074	*Nikkelen, (J. van)* | Twee differente Gezigten van pragtige Hofsteden, met Fonteinen en Standbeelden versierd, zynde zeer ryk gestoffeerd met Heeren en Dames, welken zig op verschillende wyzen vermaaken. Plaisant behandeld | *Mat:* op doek *Size:* hoog 10, breed 12 duim	Simon Styl	(Unknown)
1806/05/05	AMSCH	0103	*J. van Nikkelen* | Een Protestantsche Kerk, van binnen met diversche stoffagie van Beeldjes; dun en zonachtig op Paneel | *Mat:* op paneel *Size:* hoog 14, breed 12 duim	R[oos]	(Sold) fl 7:15 van Iperen
1806/05/05	AMSCH	0104	*J. van Nikkelen* | Een Landschap met Gebouwen en Fonteinwerk, ryk gestoffeerd; uitvoerig en bevallig geschilderd door denzelven [J. van Nikkelen] | *Mat:* op doek *Size:* hoog 20 ½, breed 24 ½ duim	V[inkeles]	(Sold) fl 9:15 Schley [for] Ryfsnyder
1809/09/06	AMSCH	0057	*Nikkelen (J. van)* | Een Gezigt in de groote Kerk te Haarlem, gestoffeerd met Beeldjes; zonachtig en dun gepenceeld | *Mat:* op doek *Size:* hoog 21, breed 19 duim	Johannes Caudri	(Sold) fl 21 Reijers

Nicodemo, Augusto

1801/02/18	AMBOS	0031	*Nicodemi* | De Geboorte des Heilands, delicaat geschilderd	J Schonevelt	(Unknown)
1801/02/18	AMBOS	0032	*Nicodemi* | Den Heiland aan het Kruis	J Schonevelt	(Unknown)
1801/02/18	AMBOS	0033	*Nicodemi* | De Opstanding des Heeren	J Schonevelt	(Unknown)
1802/06/28	AMSCH	0135	*Aug. Nicodemo* | Een Graauwtje | *Notes:* This lot was sold with lot 51 by O. Elliger (II).	Anna Elink	(Sold) fl 0:6 for lots 51 & 135. L Pakker
1808/11/28	AMSCH	0047	*A. Nicodemo* | In een Boomrijk Landschap, bij een stille Rivier, ziet men onder zwaar Geboomte, een rustende Vénus, delicaat gepenceeld | *Mat:* op paneel *Size:* hoog 15, breed 21 duim	[Gruyter?]	(Sold) fl 12:10 van der Schley [for] E v Dyk

Nieulandt

1801/04/23	AMYVR	0011	*Nieuwland* | Een Landschap, op de voorgrond een Wagen met twee Ossen bespannen en andere Stoffagie		(Sold) fl 7 Coclaire
1808/03/03	HAVIN	0020	*van Nieuwland* | Twee Landschappen met Ruïnes	Jacobus Spillebout	(Unknown)
1808/06/13	AMSCH	0237	*Nieuwland* | Een rijk met Beelden gestoffeerd Gezicht binnen Rome; uitvoerig | *Mat:* op paneel	Z	(Sold) fl 3:10 Glad
1810/12/03	DOBRA	0033	*Nieuwland* | Een door Nieuwland		(Unknown)

Nieulandt, Adriaen van (I)

1802/05/24	HGBAK	0034	*A. v. Nieuwland* | De Boodschap aan Maria, met een Choor van Engelen, door A. v. Nieuwland 1651, hoog 13 d., breed 10 duim, paneel, zwarte lyst en vergulde binnenrand | *Mat:* op paneel *Size:* hoog 13 duim, breed 10 duim *Inscr:* A. v. Nieuwland 1651 (signed and dated?) *Notes:* It is unclear whether the name and date are inscribed on the painting.	Mejuffrouw A van der Mieden	(Sold) fl 5 Te Ché
1802/05/24	HGBAK	0053	*A. Nieuwland* | De verkondiging van de geboorte aan de Herders, ryk van ordonnantie, door A. Nieuwland, hoog 3 voet 7 ½ duim, breed 2 ½ voet, op paneel, zwarte lyst en vergulde bies | *Mat:* op paneel *Size:* hoog 3 voet 7 ½ duim, breed 2 ½ voet	Mejuffrouw A van der Mieden	(Sold) fl 14 Panse [?]
1802/05/24	HGBAK	0054	*A. Nieuwland* | Een Landschap, met een Jagtparty, zo te paard als te voet, door denzelven Meester [A. Nieuwland], hoog 3 voet, breed 3 ½ voet, op doek, zwarte lyst | *Mat:* op doek *Size:* hoog 3 voet, breed 3 ½ voet	Mejuffrouw A van der Mieden	(Sold) fl 9:5 v Giez[en]
1802/06/28	AMSCH	0134	*A. van Nieuwland* | Een Ordonnantie van een aantal Beelden, op de voorgrond ziet men de Triumphwagen van Bacchus | *Size:* hoog 39, breed 51 duim	Anna Elink	(Sold) fl 4:15 Bergveld
1805/07/03	AMSCH	0123	*A. van Nieuwland* | De Boodschap van den Engel aan Maria, om hoog ziet men den Heiligen Geest, in de gedaante eener duif, verder een glorie van Engelen; zynde een bevallige Ordinantie, warm van coloriet en delicaat behandeld | *Mat:* op paneel *Size:* hoog 25, breed 29 duim	C	(Sold) fl 5 Josi

Nieulandt, Willem van (II) (Guglielmo Terranova)

1802/07/27 AKHRK 0059 *G. van Nieuwland* | De Ruine van een oude Tempel. Met Beelden en Wolvee [sic]; goed geschilderd | *Mat:* op paneel *Size:* hoog 10, breed 12 ½ duim — Maria Stategaart — (Sold) fl 2:6 Goor

Nijmegen, Dionys van

1806/11/24 AMSCH 0050 *Nymegen (D.v.)* | Romulus en Rémus den Wolvin zuigende; natuurlyk Basrelief in 't graauw geschilderd | *Mat:* op doek *Size:* hoog 23, breed 32 duim — Munnikhuizen — (Sold) fl 3 Yver

1808/06/13 AMSCH 0115 *Nijmegen (D. van)* | Een Zinspeeling op de Liefde, zijnde eene bevallige Vrouw, welke drie Kinderen liefkoozen. Meesterlijk als door J. de Wit geschilderd | *Mat:* op doek *Size:* hoog 49, breed 38 duim — R[oos] — (Sold) fl 18 Hoogers

1810/06/06 RMMUY 0200 *D. van Nymegen* | Het Pourtrait van een Rabbijn | *Mat:* op paneel — (Unknown) fl 14:5

1810/06/06 RMMUY 0201 *D. van Nymegen* | Een Basrelief met spelende Kindertjes, in het graauw | *Mat:* op doek — (Unknown) fl 1:4

Nijmegen, Dionys van (copy by)

1810/06/06 RMMUY 0199 *D. van Nymegen; A. van Dyk* | Een Mans Pourtrait, zijnde het afbeeldsel van Q. Mathijs. Naar A. van Dyk, door D. van Nymegen | copy by D. Nijmegen after Anth. van Dyck *Mat:* op doek — (Sold) fl 7 Brunelli

Nijmegen, Gerard van

1801/06/10 AMSCH 0128 *Nymegen. (G. van)* | Een hoog Bergachtig Landschap: in het midden ligt een houten Brug, waarop een met hout beladen Wagen, verders een Waterval: natuurlyk en meesterlyk geschilderd | *Mat:* op doek *Size:* hoog 45, breed 34 duim — Herman ten Kate — (Sold) fl 100 Pruijssenaar

1802/09/18 RMDRS 0008 *G. van Nymegen* | Een Landschap met hoog Gebergte, en van het Gebergte een soort van Waterval, voorts gestoffeerd met een Kar met Paarden bespannen, die door een Voerman werden opgejaagd, voor op de Voorgrond een Herder met Schapen, kragtig en uitvoerig geschilderd | *Size:* hoog 23 ½, breed 18 ½ duim — Casper de Haas — (Sold) fl 48 Muis

1804/04/28 LNDLS 0016 *G van Nymegen* | Een bergagtig Landschap, met een waterval, benevens een man een vrouw, en eenige koebeesten op een heuvel, verder een herder, die schaapen langs den weg drijft; konstig en kragtig gepenceelt, in den trant van Pynaker, door G van Nymegen, op paneel | *Mat:* op paneel *Size:* hoog 18, breed 15 duim — [Abraham Delfos] [or others] — (Sold) fl 23:5 Gerrit Mulder

1805/07/10 AMSCH 0116 *G. van Nymegen* | Eenige Boerewoningen by hoog geboomte, aan een ruisend Beekje, waarin een zwemmende Hond, twee Zwaanen en drie Beeldjes; zeer zonachtig en meesterlyk | *Mat:* op doek *Size:* hoog 30, breed 24 duim — Y[ver] — (Bought In) fl 38

1806/11/24 AMSCH 0048 *Nymegen (G. van)* | Een Kapucyner Klooster, men ziet 'er eenige Munnikken, welke iets geven aan een arme Vrouw; het invallende zonlicht en de meesterachtige behandeling maken dit tot een der beste stukken in dien aard van dien bekwaamen Meester | *Mat:* op doek *Size:* hoog 32, breed 25 duim — Munnikhuizen — (Bought In) fl 15

1806/11/24 AMSCH 0049 *Nymegen (G. van)* | Dit frappante stukje verbeeld op de Voorgrond een steene Sluis, alwaar het water door komt ruisschen; met eenige trappen komt men op een weg met hoog Geboomte, daarby bevallige stoffagie van Paarden en Beelden; delicaat gepenceeld | *Mat:* op paneel *Size:* hoog 23, breed 18 duim — Munnikhuizen — (Bought In) fl 110

1808/06/06 RMRIJ 0090 *Nijmegen. (Gerard van)* | Een Landschap, waarin zich, in 't verschiet, vertoont het Vorstelijk Lusthuis te Hondsholredijk; op den voorgrond eenige Beelden en Beesten. Naar 't leven geschilderd [Vue d'après Nature du Château de *Honsholredyk* et de ses Environs. Sur le devant plusieurs animaux domestiques et quelques figures etc. le tout d'un ton brillant] | *Mat:* op mahonie paneel *Size:* Hoog 23, en breed 29 ½ duim — Gerrit van der Pot, Heer van Groeneveld — (Sold) fl 125 Hakoun

1808/06/06 RMRIJ 0091 *Nijmegen. (Gerard van)* | Een Boschgezigt, rijk gestoffeerd met Koeijen, Schapen, enz. Warm, fiks en Zonachtig geschilderd. Eene wedergade. Boschgezigt in alle opzigten als boven [Une Forêt et plusieurs animaux et figures. D'un ton chaud et piquant. Un Pendant au précédent et qui lui est égal en mérite] | *Annots:* van den schilder 1781 (f 150.-) (RMA I) *Mat:* op paneel *Size:* Twee Stukken. Hoog 12 ½, en breed 15 duim — Gerrit van der Pot, Heer van Groeneveld — (Sold) fl 127 Roelszema

1808/06/06 RMRIJ 0092 *Nijmegen. (Gerard van)* | Een gezigt op Schoonderloo, van den Lusthof Schoonenberg van Wijlen den Wel Edelen Geboren Heer G. van der Pot van Groeneveld, af te zien. Uitvoerig en fraai geschilderd [Vue de Schoonderloo prés de Rotterdam, prisc de Schooneberg, Maison de campagne de feu Monsieur van der Pot de Groeneveld] | *Mat:* op doek *Size:* Hoog 19 ½, en breed 23 ½ duim — Gerrit van der Pot, Heer van Groeneveld — (Sold) fl 52 G van der Pot

1808/06/06 RMRIJ 0093 *Nijmegen. (Gerard van)* | Een Landschapje met Beesten, benevens een gezigt op den Lusthof Schoonenberg. Eene wedergade, met Schapen en Lammeren, benevens een gezigt op Schoonenberg, van achteren te zien. Beiden aangenaam, fijn en Zonachtig geschilderd [Vue de la campagne de *Schooneberg* dans les environs de Rotterdam. D'un ton chaud et piquant, et d'une belle touche. Le Pendant represente une Prairie avec — Gerrit van der Pot, Heer van Groeneveld — (Sold) fl 100 Baars

			des Brebis et des Agneaux, et dans le lointain on découvre la grande Allée de la Campagne de *Schooneberg*. Egal en mérite au Précédent] | *Annots:* Geschenk van nicht.[?] Wed. J.C. Valck (RMA I) *Mat:* op paneel *Size:* Twee Stukken. Hoog 7, en breed 9 duim		
1808/06/13	AMSCH	0113	*Nijmegen (G. van)* | Een Italiaansch bergachtig Landschap, waarin eene voortreffelijke Waterval, ter zijde eenige rustende Jagers enz. Schoon van uitdrukking en schildering | *Size:* hoog 24, breed 30 duim	E M Engelberts	(Sold) fl 30 Thaijs
1808/06/13	AMSCH	0114	*Nijmegen (G. van)* | Twee stuks: het eene een Gezicht aan het einde van den Haarlemmer Hout, en het andere eene gepaste Wederga, beiden met Beelden en Beesten gestoffeerd. Natuurlijk en zonachtig behandeld | *Mat:* op paneel *Size:* ieder hoog 10, breed 13 duim	G	(Sold) fl 65 Allard
1810/06/06	RMMUY	0203	*G. van Nymegen* | Een Ovaal dito [Basrelief], met Kindertjes, 't zinnebeeld van de Herfst, linkschen dag | *Mat:* op doek *Fmt:* ovaal		(Unknown) fl 0:14
1810/06/06	RMMUY	0204	*G. van Nymegen* | Eene Schets voor een Zaalstuk, arcadisch Landschap		(Sold) fl 4:10 v Eijnden

Nijmegen, Tobias van

1802/09/18	RMDRS	0021	*T. van Nymegen* | Een fraay Gebouw, waarin het Krankbed van Hiskia verbeeld word | *Size:* hoog 7 ½, breed 9 ½ duim	Casper de Haas	(Unknown) fl 7

Nijmegen, Willem van

1806/05/05	AMSCH	0190	*W. van Nymegen* | Het Pourtrait van H. Goltius, als met de pen gearceerd	H	(Sold) fl 1:15 van Laar

Nisp, Nikolaus van

1810/10/10	MGCIT	0163	*van Nispen* | Een Stukje, zijnde een Herder en herderin naast elkander zittende, en de eerste op een Fluit spelende, geplaatst in een Landschap, de Voorgrond rijk van Bloemen; in de manier van Breugel, door van Nispen | *Notes:* This lot was misnumbered no. 164 and changed in an errata sheet located at the front of the catalogue.	Caspar van Citters	(Unknown)

Nollekens

1801/08/19	AMSCH	0074	*B. Nollekens* | Een Binnenhuis, met verscheide Boeren en Boerinnen, zoo zittende by een Tafeltje, als staande, natuurlyk en meesterlyk geschilderd op paneel | *Mat:* op paneel *Size:* hoog 13, breed 12 duim	W Wynen	(Sold) fl 1:15 A Meijer

Nollekens, Pieter

1803/12/15	MGLAC	0059	*P. Nollekens* | Twee vrolyke Gezelschapjes; zeer fraai geschilderd | *Mat:* op doek *Size:* hoog duim 12, breed duim 16	Mr L H de Haze Bomme	(Unknown)

Noorde, Cornelis van

1808/03/03	HAVIN	0027	*C. van Noorde* | Twee dito [Landschappen]	Jacobus Spillebout	(Unknown) fl 1:2
1808/03/03	HAVIN	0028	*C. van Noorde* | Twee Watergezichten	Jacobus Spillebout	(Unknown) fl 1:5
1808/03/03	HAVIN	0032	*C. van Noorde* | De Groote Markt, na de Groote Kerk en het Stadhuis te zien, uitvoerig met Coul.	Jacobus Spillebout	(Unknown) fl 7:5
1809/05/26	HADAA	0052	*C. van Noorden* | Twee bevallige Landschapjes met beesten	Mejuffrouw de Wed David Heemskerk [orothers]	(Unknown)
1809/05/26	HADAA	0072	*C. van Noorden* | Het Pourtret van den Schilder Jan Heemskerk, uitvoerig met Sapjes | *Notes:* This lot was sold with lot 71 by an anonymous artist.	Mejuffrouw de Wed David Heemskerk [or others]	(Unknown) fl 1:16 for lots 71 & 72

Noort, Joan van

1801/06/10	AMSCH	0127	*Noordt. (J. van.)* | Deeze Ordonantie stelt voor een Heilige Familie; men ziet Maria met het Kindje, nevens haar Joseph: alles meesterlyk en fyn van penceels behandeling | *Mat:* op doek *Size:* hoog 44, breed 32 duim	Herman ten Kate	(Sold) fl 11 W Reyers
1810/06/06	RMMUY	0084	*Jan van Oort* | Juda en Thamar, ongemeen krachtig en stout geschilderd | *Mat:* op doek		(Unknown) fl 8:10

Noort, Pieter van

1801/06/10	AMSCH	0133	*Oort. (P. van)* | Een Keuken; in dezelve ziet men een Meid, de Vischketel overhangende, verder een menigte Huisraad, natuurlyk voorgesteld | *Mat:* op paneel *Size:* hoog 12, breed 19 duim	Herman ten Kate	(Sold) fl 6:15 A Meyer

Noot, van der [Unidentified]

1804/08/02	BDAN	0051	*Van der Noot* | Een Vanitas | *Mat:* op doek *Size:* b. 74 d. h. 43 d.	J G Calckberner	(Unknown)

Noppe, N. [Unidentified]

1809/05/26	HADAA	0055	*N. Noppe* | Landschappen met Beesten, naar v.d. Meer de Jonge, door N. Noppe	Mejuffrouw de Wed David Heemskerk [or others]	(Unknown)
1809/05/26	HADAA	0056	*N. Noppe* | Landschappen met Beesten, naar v.d. Meer de Jonge, door N. Noppe	Mejuffrouw de Wed David Heemskerk [or others]	(Unknown)

Norblin, Jean Pierre (de la Gourdaine)

1803/12/12	AMSCH	0069	*Norblin* | Een aangenaam Boomryk Landschap, met galante Beeldjes gestoffeerd; geestig | *Mat:* op doek *Size:* hoog 10, breed 12 duim	D	(Sold) fl 1 Pruijsenaar

Novelli, Pietro (Monrealese) (or Moreelse, P.)

1803/04/27	AMSCH	0039	*Morealése* | David avec la tête de Goliath, ce Tableau est d'un effêt très piquant, d'une bonne couleur & bien peint | *Size:* h. 4 ¼, l. 3 ½ pieds	A	(Sold) fl 70 Hodges

Novelli, Pietro (Monrealese) (attributed; or Moreelse, P., attributed)

1803/04/27	AMSCH	0001	*Moréälese* | Ce magnifique Tableau attribué au Moréälese, représente l'aparition des anges aux bergers, & est peint d'une maniere large, le ton de Couleur en est vigoureux, la Composition en est grande le dessin franc & de la plus grande maniere | *Size:* h. 8, l. 10 pieds	A	(Sold) fl 151 D^k Versteegh

Ny, W. van [Unidentified]

1804/10/16	DLOND	0158	*W. van Ny* | De grote Straat te Zalt-Boemel. La grande Rue de Zalt-Boemel | *Mat:* op paneel *Size:* hoog 10, breed 9		(Unknown)

O., Jaques [Unidentified]

1804/07/25	DLGRO	0084	*Jaques O.* | Een Winter gezicht, verbeeldende twee tegen elkander overliggende Dorpen, met veel Beelden en verder bywerk | *Mat:* op paneel *Size:* hoog 17, breed 33 duim	Mr Franc van der Burch Wz.	(Unknown)

Ochtervelt, Jacob

1801/06/10	AMSCH	0165	*Uchterveld. (J. van)* | In een gemeubileerde Kamer zit by een Tafel met een Tapyt bedekt, een Dame in syden kleed met een wit satynen Rok, zy heeft op haar schoot een Hond, welke zy aan de ooren trekt, nevens haar een Dienstmaagd met een zilver Lampet; in alles als G. Terburg behandeld | *Mat:* op doek *Size:* hoog 37, breed 30 duim	Herman ten Kate	(Sold) fl 63 B^d Kooij
1802/06/28	AMSCH	0187	*J. Uchterveld* | In een gemeubeleerd Binnevertrek, ziet men een Dame, speelende met haar Hond; achter haar staat een Meid welke een Bed afhaald, zeer natuurlyk en delicaat gepenceeld, door J. Uchterveld, op Doek | *Mat:* op doek *Size:* hoog 28, breed 18 duim	Anna Elink	(Sold) fl 10:10 Gruiter
1802/06/28	AMSCH	0188	*J. Uchterveld* | Een Doctor by een zieke Vrouw, welke met haar hoofd in een Kussen legd; meesterlyk, op Doek | *Mat:* op doek *Size:* hoog 19, breed 16 duim	Anna Elink	(Sold) fl 23 Geld
1802/09/06	AMSCH	0119	*Uchterveld* | In een Binnenkamer ziet men een bevallig gekleede Vrouw, met haar arm en hooft op een kussen rustende, terwyl de Doctor aan de Pols voelt, agter haar schynt een oude vrouw haar 't hoofd vast te houden; delicaat gepenceeld | *Size:* hoog 37, breed 29 duim	J	(Sold) fl 3:5 Pruijssenaar
1803/08/24	HGKAN	0059	*Ochterveld* | Twee stuks Binnenhuisen met Musiccerende Beelden	[Teissier] [or others]	(Sold) fl 21 Kan
1803/12/12	AMSCH	0096	*J. Ugterveld* | In een ryk Gemeubileerde Kamer ziet men een vrolyk Gezelschap van Heeren en Dames, het Zatyn en de andere Kleedingen zyn als ter Burgh, delicaat geschilderd | *Mat:* op doek *Size:* hoog 33, breed 33 duim	B	(Sold) fl 5 Reijers
1803/12/12	AMSCH	0097	*J. Ugterveld* | In een Gemeubileerd Binnenvertrek zit een Dame met een Kan en Glas in heer handen, tegens over haar zit een Heer op de Guitar te speelen, terwyl de Dienstmaagd een Bak met Oesters op Tafel zet; in alles als de voorgaande | *Mat:* op doek *Size:* hoog 19, breed 16 duim *Loc:* Madrid, España. Thyssen Collection. (1930.82)	F	(Sold) fl 48 H^n Pakker
1804/02/27	AMSCH	0086	*Ochterveld. (J.)* | Twee stuks Gezelschappen, met Musiceerende Beelden; byden meesterlyk gepenceeld | *Mat:* op doek *Size:* hoog 32, breed 26 duim	B	(Sold) fl 58 Thais
1804/10/16	DLOND	0101	*Hochtervelde* | Ene Dame spelende op een Guitarre, met een Jongeling, die een Hondjen vast houdt. Une Dame pinçant la Guitarre, a son coté se fait voir un Jeune Homme avec un petit Chien | *Size:* hoog 20, breed 18		(Unknown) fl 7
1806/08/13	AMSCH	0185	*Uchterveld. (J. van)* | In een gemeubileerd Binnevertrek ziet men bevallige Dame met een wit satyn Jakje en roode satyne Rok, welke aan een Kindje een krakeling aanbied, waarby een Schoothondje en achter dezelve een Heer spélende op een Phiool, en terzyde by een Tafel met een Tapyt Kleed bedekt een Knegt met een Zilveren Drinkschaal in de hand; delicaat en uitvoerig en als G. Metzu van schildering | *Mat:* op paneel *Size:* hoog 26, breed 21 duim	Vinkeles [for] F	(Sold) fl 112 Lafontaine
1807/08/26	AMSCH	0218	*J. Uchterveld* | Aan een Tafel met een Tapyte Kleed gedekt zit eene Dame, in een rood Jakje met Bont gekleed, welke door een Heer een schyfje van een Citroen wordt aangeboden, op de Tafel staat een Aarden Kan en een Roemer Wyn; delicaat als G. Terburg | *Mat:* op paneel *Size:* hoog 19, breed 14 duim	Joseph Vallette	(Sold) fl 95 C S Roos
1807/08/26	AMSCH	0219	*J. Uchterveld* | Eene zittende Jufvrouw in een Voorhuis, vergezeld van een jong Meisje en eene Dienstmaagd, met een Schotel in de hand, schynende Garnaalen te koopen van een Vischboer, die aan de deur staat; zonachtig en meesterlyk behandeld | *Mat:* op doek *Size:* hoog 24, breed 19 duim	Helsdinge	(Sold) fl 6:5 du Pree
1808/06/06	RMRIJ	0094	*Ochtervelt. (J.)* | Eene Vrouw, leunende over een steenen Baluster, schijnt een koperen bekken met water uit te gieten. Achter haar staat een Heer in Spaansche kleeding, eene fluweele muts met pluimen op het hoofd	Gerrit van der Pot, Heer van Groeneveld	(Sold) fl 70 Roelszema

			hebbende, die zijne eene hand op haren schouder legt en met de andere haar een beker met Rijnwijn aanbiedt. Dit stuk is uitvoerig en schoon geschilderd en gaat in Zwartekonstprent uit, door J Verkolje geschraapt [Une femme sur son Balcon verse de l'eau, tandis qu'un Cavalier en Costume Espagnol ayant une main sur son Epaule, semble lui offrir un verre de vin de l'autre. Ce Tableau d'un bon genre, est connu par l'Estampe en noir, qu'en a faite J. Verkolje] | *Annots:* was verk. Coornhart[?] verk. W. Coole, Rotterdam, 6 Aug 1782 (f 70-) (RMA I) *Mat:* op doek *Size:* Hoog 11 ¾, en breed 10 duim		
1808/06/13	AMSCH	0159	*Uchterveld (J. van)* | Twee stuks Voorhuizen: in het eene ligt eene Dame over de Onderdeur, terwijl de Jonge Jufvrouw Kerssen koopt van eene Boerin, staande de Dienstmaagd daarbij met eene Schotel. In de tweede staat eene Dame met een Kind aan de hand, van een vrolijke Boer en Boerin Eendvogels te koopen, waarbij een Hond. Het invallend zonlicht doet in deze stukken eene uitmuntende werking, en kunnen bij P. de Hooge in schildering geplaatst worden | *Mat:* op doek *Size:* ieder hoog 30, breed 24 ½ duim *Loc:* Antwerpen, Belgique. Museum Mayer van den Bergh. (895) The Cherry Seller only	[Jan Tersteeg]	(Sold) fl 345 T Boelen pour Henry
1809/09/06	AMSCH	0070	*Uchterveld (J. van)* | Dit Kabinetstukje, verbeeld een slapende Officier in een gemeubileerde Kamer als in diepe rust gevallen, die door eene bevallige Vrouw met een Strootje onder den Neus geprikkeld wordt, ter andere zijde, blaast een Heer op de Trompet; verder eene Diensmaagd de Trap opgaande; dit geestig voorwerp is bevallig van licht en koloriet en van een uitmuntende uitvoerige penceelbehandeling | *Mat:* op paneel *Size:* hoog 19, breed 15 duim	Johannes Caudri	(Sold) fl 252 Roos
1810/05/22	AMSCH	0108	*Uchtervelt. (J.)* | Een Voorvertrek, in het zelve zit op den voorgrond een Heer in 't zwart gekleed, houdende een Glas met Wijn in zijne hand, het welk hij aan eene bevallige Vrouw, die voor hem zit, schijnt toe te brengen, verder een Heer en eene Dame met de Kaart spelende, waarbij een Knegt met een Kan in de hand; meesterlijk schoon geschilderd | *Mat:* op doek *Size:* hoog 26, breed 23 duim	T	(Sold) fl 100 van Iperen
1810/06/20	AMSCH	0085	*J. Uchterveld* | Twee stuks gemeubileerde Kamers: in de eene zit eene deftige Vrouw bij eene Tafel, waarop eenige Vruchten liggen; nevens haar eene Dienstmaagd, houdende een Kind aan den leiband: – in de andere eene jonge Dame schijnende in gesprek met een Heer, en bij de deur een Moor. Beide meesterlijk geschilderd | *Mat:* op doek *Size:* Jeder hoog 35, breed 28 duimen	B	(Sold) fl 14:10 Hodges
1810/06/20	AMSCH	0086	*J. Uchterveld* | In een gemeubileerde Kamer zit eene prachtig gekleede Vrouw, ziende haar eenen Heer, die op de Guitar speelt en tevens danst. Zacht geschilderd | *Mat:* op doek *Size:* hoog 23, breed 19 duimen	Q	(Sold) fl 3:5 van Dijl
1810/10/10	MGCIT	0116	*Ugterfeld* | Een Schildery, waarop verbeeld word een aan de Kleding kenlyk voornaam Personage, een Bezoek by eene Dame afgelegd hebbende; wel behandeld	Caspar van Citters	(Unknown)
			Oever, Hendrick ten		
1803/12/12	AMSCH	0149	*Overe* | Een Gevegt van Ruiters, in een grot | *Mat:* op koper *Size:* hoog 7, br. 9 duim	D	(Sold) fl 1:5 Gruiter
1804/10/29	HRBAU	0076	*Oever, (Jan ten)* | In een bergagtig Landschap zit, op den Voorgrond, een Vrouwtjen op een wit paard, met een' Man spreekende, welke eenige Koeijen, Schaapen en Geiten dryft; wat verder zit mede een Man op een Ezel zyne Kudden voort te dryven. Meesterlyk behandeld | *Mat:* op paneel *Size:* hoog 18 ½, breed 24 ½ duim *Notes:* The artist's name was given as "Oever, (Jan ten)" but we have assumed this is an error.	Simon Styl	(Unknown)
1810/10/10	MGCIT	0159	*ten Oever* | Een Stuk, waarop verbeeld word een Woning en voor hetzelve een staande Ladder, waar aan een geslacht Varken is gebonden; voorts een Vrouw, bij zich hebbende drie Kinderen, spelende met de blaas, en ander bijwerk; ongemeen natuurlijk en meesterlijk op doek gebragt | *Mat:* op doek *Notes:* This lot was misnumbered no. 160 and changed in an errata sheet located at the front of the catalogue.	Caspar van Citters	(Unknown)
			Olis, Jan		
1801/06/13	LNDLS	0039	*Olis, gen. van Battem* | Een Vrouwtje, zittende vis te schrappen in een keuken, nevens haar staat een Man, die haar een schaapenbout vertoond, en een tafel, daar dood gevogelte, vlees, fruit en eeten op leggen, op de voorgrond een schotel met vis, koperen ketel, groetens, en meer bijwerk, alles op het uitvoerigst op doek geschilderd | *Mat:* op doek *Size:* hoog 18 ½, breed 24 ½ duimen	D van R	(Sold) fl 21 Teissier
1804/07/25	DLGRO	0011	*Jan Olis* | Een Vrouwtje by de Lamp zittende Kant te werken, met drie vrolyke Knaapen by haar staande | *Mat:* op paneel *Size:* hoog 13, breed 10 duim	Mr Franc van der Burch Wz.	(Unknown)
1804/07/25	DLGRO	0105	*Jan Olis* | Een vrolyk Gezelschap, aan Tafel zittende | *Mat:* op paneel *Size:* hoog 13, breed 10 duim	Mr Franc van der Burch Wz.	(Unknown)
1804/10/16	DLOND	0159	*Jan Olis* | Een Man en Vrouw, met Visschen, Wild, Vruchten enz. Un Homme & une Femme entourés de Poissons, du Gibier, des Fruits &c. | *Mat:* op paneel *Size:* hoog 15, breed 19		(Unknown) fl 18
1804/10/16	DLOND	0160	*Jan Olis* | Potten, Ketels, Vruchten, Wild enz. Des Pots, Chodrons, Fruits, du Gibier &c. | *Mat:* op paneel *Fmt:* ellipt *Size:* hoog 11, à 13		(Unknown)

Olta, J. [Unidentified]

1804/10/29	HRBAU	0077	*Olta, (J.)* | Een geslagt Varken op de Leer, waarby eenige Menschen, welken het ingewand schoonmaaken, en zich verlustigen | *Mat:* op paneel *Size:* hoog 15, breed 21 duim	Simon Styl	(Unknown)

Ommeganck, Balthazar Paul

1801/08/19	AMSCH	0086	*Ommegang* | In een Brabands Landschap, ziet men een Adelyk Huis, Omcingeld [sic] met een Gragt waar eenige Lieden bézig zyn te Vissen, op de Voorgrond met een drift Beesten gestoffeert en bevallig geschilderd	Pruyssen^r [for] Q	(Sold) fl 15:10 P M Levy
1802/05/05	AMSCH	0161	*Ommegank* | Een zeer bevallig en zonachtig Landschap met eenige Beelden en verscheide grazende en leggende Beesten, zeer delicaat gepenceeld	A	(Sold) fl 72 V^n Iperen
1802/05/05	AMSCH	0162	*Ommegank* | Een dito [zeer bevallig en zonachtig] Landschap, niet minder als de Voorgaande	A	(Sold) fl 59 V^n Iperen
1802/05/05	AMSCH	0163	*Ommegank* | Een aangenaam Landschap, gestoffeert met een menigte staand en leggend Vee, waarby een Landman, die zig met zyn Hond vermaakt, bevallig en uitvoerig gepenceeld | *Size:* hoog 16, breed 22 duim	J	(Bought In) fl 30
1802/09/06	AMSCH	0091	*Ommegang* | In een alleraangenaamst Heuvelagtig Landschap, ziet men op een grafige hoogte, een Landman by eenige Schaapen, verzeld van zyn Hond, op de voorgrond by hoog opgaande geboomte, eenige grasende en leggende Bokken, en Schaapen; en van agteren een aangenaam verschiet; zonagtig, warm en delicaat geschiderd [sic] | *Size:* hoog 15, breed 20 duim	J	(Bought In) fl 45
1802/09/18	RMDRS	0053	*Ommegang* | Een Landschap, met badende Nimphen	Casper de Haas	(Sold) fl 7 Gruiters
1803/12/12	AMSCH	0070	*Ommegang* | In een aangenaam Landschap, ziet men op de voorgrond eenige graasende en leggende Schapen en Bokken, ter zyde op een grasige Heuvel, een Landman speelende met zyn Hond, verzeld van een menigte van Schapen, verders een duin en sonagtig verschiet; uitvoerig | *Mat:* op paneel *Size:* hoog 15 ½, breed 20 ½ duim	B	(Sold) fl 40 v d Schleij
1804/02/27	AMSCH	0085	*Ommegang* | In een aangenaam Landschap, ziet men op den voorgrond eenige graasende en leggende Schaapen en Bokken, ter zyden op een Graasigen hoogten, onder 't Geboomten een rustende Landman, speelende met zyn Hondt, verzeld van een meenigte Schaapen; van agter een bevallig verschiet zonachtig en bevallig geschilderd | *Size:* hoog 15, breed 20 ½ duim	C	(Bought In) fl 35
1804/05/07	AMSCH	0130	*Ommegang* | Twee aangenaame en bevallige Landschappen, de voorgrond van byde zyn ryk gestoffeerd met staand en leggend Vee; en van agteren aangenaamen verschieten; byde bevallig geordoneerd; zonachtig en uitvoerig geschilderd | *Mat:* op paneel *Size:* hoog 8, breed 9 duim	Vinkeles [for] G	(Sold) fl 13:10 de Meijer
1804/08/08	AMSCH	0149	*Ommegang* | In een aangenaam zonachtig Landschap ziet men op de voorgrond eenige grazende en leggende Schaapen en Bokken, ter zyde op een grazige hoogte onder 't Geboomte een rustend Landman, speelende met een Hond, nevens hem eenige Schaapen, van achteren een aangenaam en bevallig verschiet; frappant van licht en uitvoerig geschilderd | *Mat:* op paneel *Size:* hoog 15, breed 20 ½ duim	Vink[eles] [for] K[=Gruyter?]	(Bought In) fl 29
1806/05/05	AMSCH	0106	*Ommegang* | Twee stuks grasige heuvelachtige Landschappen, ryk gestoffeerd met staand en rustend Vee, als Ossen, Koeijen, Schapen, Bokken, verzeld van Herders, Boerinnen, Kinderen enz., verders Geboomte, Woningen en allerbevalligste verschieten; beide zonachtig van licht en delicaat gepenceeld door Ommegang | *Mat:* op paneel *Size:* hoog 20 ½, breed 28 duim	L	(Sold) fl 158 van Laar
1806/05/05	AMSCH	0107	*Ommegang* | Een dito [grasige heuvelachtige] Landschap, op de voorgrond eenige grazende en leggende Schapen en Bokken, ter zyden op een grasige heuvel een Landman, speelende met een Hond, verzeld met een menigte van Schapen, verders een Duinachtig verschiet, uitvoerig op Paneel | *Mat:* op paneel *Size:* hoog 15 ½, breed 20 ½ duim	V[inkeles]	(Sold) fl 24 Reyers
1806/11/24	AMSCH	0051	*Ommegang (P.P.)* | Twee stuks Brabandsche Land- en Dorpgezigtjes, met allerfraaist Geboomte en Stoffagie; doorsneeden met heldere waters, waarin alles spiegelt; zynde van een aangenaame penceelsbehandeling | *Mat:* op paneel *Size:* Yder hoog 12, breed 15 duim *Notes:* The artist's name was give as "Ommegang (P.P.)" but we have assumed this is an error.	Munnikhuizen	(Sold) fl 76 Gruiter
1808/06/06	RMRIJ	0095	*Ommegang. (B. P.)* | Een Landgezigt bij de Zaagmolens buiten Antwerpen, zijnde een Avondstond met eene ondergaande Zon, rijk gestoffeerd met beesten, enz. Gloeijend en aangenaam geschilderd [Ce Tableau charmant offre une vue des environs de la ville d'Anvers, il est enrichi d'animaux et de figures, et est d'un ton chaud et piquant, et grandement traité] | *Annots:* Van Jac de Vos, Amst. 14 Aug 1785 (f 102-) (RMA I) *Mat:* op paneel *Size:* Hoog 14, en breed 20 ½ duim	Gerrit van der Pot, Heer van Groeneveld	(Sold) fl 175 van Beefting
1808/06/13	AMSCH	0118	*Ommegang* | Een Brabandsch Landschap, waarin een Herder, een troep voortdrijvende, ter zijde zwaar Geboomte, op den voorgrond eene liggende Boom. Warm en natuurlijk gepenceeld | *Mat:* op doek *Size:* hoog 39, breed 49 duim	G	(Sold) fl 69 Du Pré
1810/05/22	AMSCH	0081	*Ommegang. (N.)* | Een bevallig Landgezicht, met eene menigte staand en liggend Vee, waarbij een Jongen met een Hond; helder geschilderd | *Mat:*	Johannes van de Putte Nicolaasz.	(Sold) fl 14:10 du Pree

			op paneel *Size:* Jeder hoog 16, breed 22 duim *Notes:* The artist's name was given as "Ommegang. (N.)" but we have assumed this is an error.		

Ommeganck, Maria Jacoba (Maria Jacoba Myin)

1808/06/13	AMSCH	0119	*Ommegang (Maria)* | Twee fraaije Veldgezichten, met grazend en staand Vee. Beiden zeer natuurlijk behandeld | *Mat:* op paneel *Size:* ieder hoog 14, breed 20 duim	V[inkeles]	(Sold) fl 50 Du Pré

Oncker, H. [Unidentified]

1802/05/05	AMSCH	0173	*H. Oncker* | Eenige Kinderen by een Beekje speelende, met Bloemen en Fruit, verder een aangenaam verschiet | *Mat:* op paneel *Size:* hoog 42, breed 58 duim	E	(Sold) fl 3:15 Pruijssenaar [for] R

Oolen, Adriaen van

1802/02/16	AMSCH	0016	*van Olen* | Twee stuks Hofgezichten met levend Gevogelten, breed geschilderd in de manier van M. de Hondekoeter op doek | *Mat:* op doek	B[uys]	(Sold) fl 9 Boelen
1802/05/05	AMSCH	0169	*A. van Olen* | Een Boom- en Bergachtig Landschap, op de Voorgrond gestoffeerd met een menigte staand en leggend Vee, in 't verschiet ziet men een Schuit met eenige Lieden, verders hoog Gebergte, zeer delicaat van Penceelbehandeling | *Size:* hoog 23, breed 32 duim	F	(Sold) fl 24 Ackina
1802/05/05	AMSCH	0170	*A. van Olen* | Een Menagerie van Hoenders en Eenden, in een Hofgezigt, alles meesterlyk | *Mat:* op doek *Size:* hoog 42, breed 51 duim	B	(Sold) fl 1:15 Pruijssenaar [for] R
1802/12/13	AMSCH	0090	*van Hoolen* | Een Hof Gezigt, met Gevogelten en Vrugten | *Size:* hoog 29, breed 24 duim	Pruyssenaar [for] A	(Sold) fl 1:10 L Pakker
1803/12/12	AMSCH	0071	*van Olen* | Een Landschap met Gevogelte, als Hondekoeter | *Mat:* op doek *Size:* hoog 34, breed 29 duim	B	(Sold) fl 2:10 v d Schley [for] R[ijfsnijder]
1804/05/07	AMSCH	0134	*Olen. (A. van)* | Een Haan, witte Hen en een Duif in een Landschap; geestig behandeld | *Mat:* op doek *Size:* hoog 19, breed 16 duim	Y[ver] [for] JJ	(Sold) fl 4 Spaan
1805/07/10	AMSCH	0117	*A. van Olen* | In een Landschap met geboomte, ziet men een Goudlakensche Haan, witte Hen en Duif; meesterlyk op Doek | *Mat:* op doek *Size:* hoog 19, breed 16 duim	V[inkeles] [for] M	(Sold) fl 4 Lafontaine
1806/05/05	AMSCH	0113	*van Oolen* | Een capitaal Landschap, ryk gestoffeerd met Paauwen, Haanen, Hoenders en andere Gevogelten; meesterlyk als Hondekoeter | *Mat:* op doek *Size:* hoog 45, breed 66 duim	V[inkeles]	(Sold) fl 3:5 Boelen

Oolen, Jan van [Unidentified]

1802/09/06	AMSCH	0220	*J. van Olen* | Een Landschap met gevogelte, als van Hondekoeter door J. van Olen | *Size:* hoog 24, breed 29 duim	J	(Sold) fl 2:10 for lots 220 & 221. Gruiter
1802/09/06	AMSCH	0221	*J. van Olen* | Een dito [Landschap] dito [met gevogelte], door dito [J. van Olen] | *Size:* hoog 34, breed 32 duim	J	(Sold) fl 2:10 for lots 220 & 221. Gruiter
1802/09/06	AMSCH	0250	*J. van Oolen* | Eenige hangende Vogels	Mevrouw Achtienhoven	(Sold) fl 2 Gruiter
1804/08/08	AMSCH	0147	*J. van Olen* | Twee stuks Hofgezichten, in de ééne ziet men op een Steenen Rand een Paauw, waarby in 't Water by eenig Riet drie Eenden en ander Gevogelte; en in de andere ziet men by een Gebouw, een Eetbak en een witte en Goud lakense Hen, waarby drie vliegende Vogels en een aangenaam Boomryk verschiet; fraai en uitvoerig gepenceeld, in de manier van M. de Hondekoeter | *Mat:* op doek *Size:* hoog 50, breed 42 duim	Vink[eles] [for] W	(Withdrawn)
1804/10/29	HRBAU	0075	*Oelen, (Jan)* | Op den Voorgrond staat een Pauw, een Haan, en eenige Hoenders, benevens hunne Kuikens, welke gedeeltelyk hun voedzel zoeken, waar agter een bergagtig verschiet. In de manier van Hondekoeter behandeld | *Mat:* op doek *Size:* hoog 47, breed 67 duim	Simon Styl	(Unknown)
1805/12/16	AMSCH	0044	*J. van Olen* | Op een Boere Werf, ziet men een kloeken Haan, Hen, diverse Eenden met hun Kiekens, en ander Gevogelten; kragtig op Doek | *Mat:* op doek *Size:* hoog 38, breed 30 duim	R[oos]	(Bought In) fl 8
1805/12/16	AMSCH	0045	*J. van Olen* | Een Menagerie met verscheide Gevogeltens, als de voorgaande | *Size:* hoog 35, breed 38 duim	R[oos]	(Sold) fl 1 du Pree
1806/08/13	AMSCH	0140	*Olen. (H. van)* | Een Ménagerie met een Pauw, Hanen, Hoenders; Eenden en Kiekens; meesterlyk als Hondekoeter behandeld | *Mat:* op doek *Size:* hoog 64, breed 73 duim	van der Voort	(Sold) fl 24 Hafner
1807/08/26	AMSCH	0168	*J. van Oolen* | Een Hofgezigt, gestoffeerd met diverse zoorten van Gevogelten, door J. van Oolen, in de manier van Hondekoeter | *Mat:* op doek *Size:* hoog 35, breed 37 duim	de Vries	(Sold) fl 3 Spruit
1810/06/20	AMSCH	0072	*J. Van Olen* | Een Landschap met onderscheidene Land- en Watergevogelte. Zijnde als door Hondekoeter geschilderd, op doek, door J. Van Olen. | *Mat:* op doek *Size:* hoog 38, breed 30 duimen	R[oos]	(Sold) fl 9:10 J Twisk

Oolen, Jan van [Unidentified] (manner)

1810/10/11	AMSCH	0066	*J. Van Olen* | Een stuk, met Hoenders, een Haan en verscheide Eenden, op Doek, als J. Van Olen | *Mat:* op doek *Size:* hoog 35 ½, breed 31 duimen	C	(Sold) fl 6:5 Posthumus

Oosterwijck, Maria van

1803/08/01	AMSCH	0053	*M. van Oosterwyck* | Eenige Bloemen en Insecten, uitvoerig op Paneel geschilderd | *Mat:* op paneel	Ij[ver]	(Sold) fl 1 Gruiter
1810/07/23	DOLGI	0040	*Maria van Oosterwijk* | Een fraai Bloemstukje | *Mat:* op doek *Size:* hoog 13, breed 11 duim	Mr Pieter van den Santheuvel	(Sold) fl 11 [or] 18 P de Heere a Dordt

Oostrum, C. van [Unidentified]

1804/10/16	DLOND	0161	*C. van Oostrum* | Een Indisch Landschap. Paysage Indien | *Mat:* op doek *Size:* hoog 23, breed 17		(Unknown)

Orient, Josef

1803/09/07	AMSCH	0124	*F. Orient* | Twee stuks Bergachtige Landschappen, aan een Rivier, ryk gestoffeerd met een ménigte Beelden en Vaartuigen; bevallig van Coloriet [Deux sites de paysages montagneux, artistement composé et orné de figures ; on y voit un rivière portant quelques nacelles ; d'un coloris chaud et agréable] | *Mat:* op paneel *Size:* hoog 13, breed 18 duim *Notes:* The artist's name was given as "F. Orient" but we have assumed this is an error.	Smidt	(Sold) fl 22 Lamme

Orley, Jan van

1802/11/01	DOBRA	0180	*J. van Orley* | Een Tempelgebouw, verbeeldende Christus, daar hy zegt: laat de kinderkens tot my komen | *Mat:* op koper *Size:* hoog 12, breed 15 duim		(Sold) fl 17:10 v d Enden

Os

1802/05/05	AMSCH	0164	*C. P. van Os* | Twee capitaale Duinächtige Landschappen, met staande en leggend Vee, uitvoerig behandeld | *Size:* hoog 19, breed 15 duim	J	(Sold) fl 20 Vermeulen
1808/08/23	AMSCH	0090a[H]	*v. Os* | Een dito [Landschap?], id. v. Os | *Notes:* This lot was added in by hand in the FLNY copy of the catalogue. It is unclear what "dito" refers to in the title.		(Sold) fl 24:10 Th Spaan
1808/12/30	HGIMM	[0071s]	*Van Os* | Voorts een exquis kabinetje Schilderijen van voorname Nederlandsche Meesters, welke uit hoofde van de kortheid des tijds niet stuk voor stuk kunnen beschreven worden; doch waarvan de beschrijving op den Kijkdag zal voorhanden zijn. Dus wij hier alleen de namen van eenige dier Meesters laten volgen, als: A. Kuyp, Ruysdaal, Karel du Jardyn, Loqwi ('t beste dat hij schilderde) Hondekoeter, van Dyk, Janson, Moesgever, Kamphuyzen, van Gooijen, A. van der Neer, T. Wyk, Huchtenburgh, Zolemaker, van Hassel, A. Vermeulen, van Dongen, Scheffer, van Os enz. | *This Lot:* Een Schilderij, Van Os *Notes:* Because this lot was not numbered in the catalogue, we have assigned the number.		(Unknown)
1809/05/26	HADAA	0008	*van Os* | Twee Ossen grazende in een weide, zeer natuurlijk | *Mat:* op paneel *Size:* hoog 10 breed 14 duimen	Mejuffrouw de Wed David Heemskerk [or others]	(Unknown)

Os, Georg Jakob Johann

1802/12/13	AMSCH	0129	*J.G. van Os* | In een aangenaam Boomryk Landschap, ziet men ter zyden een Hooiberg, een Boere Wooning, eenig graasend en rustend Vee, en verder over een stil spiegelend Waater een aangenaam Verschiet, zonachtig en meesterlyk geschilderd | *Mat:* op doek *Size:* hoog 14, breed 18 duim	Pruyssenaar [for] A	(Sold) fl 13:5 Van Iperen
1802/12/13	AMSCH	0130	*J. G. van Os* | Een bevallig Hollands Landschap, de de voorgrond in een Beekje, staan twee Koeijen, een Bok en een Schaap, alles zonachtig en uitvoerig gepenceeld | *Mat:* op doek *Size:* hoog 26, breed 33 duim	Pruyssenaar [for] B	(Sold) fl 20 Van Iperen
1804/05/07	AMSCH	0126	*Os. de jonge. (J. van)* | Een eenvoudige maar allerbevalligste Ordonantie; men ziet op een rood Schoteltje, twee capitale Hollandse Haringen leggen, waarvan de eene reets gesneeden is, een Mes, Uijen, Peperbos en Brood, alles op een Steenen Aanregtbank en verders een Keukenvertrek; dit Schildery is in alles de natuur gelyk, en uitmuntend geschilderd | *Size:* hoog 12, breed 15 ½ duim	Vinkeles [for] G	(Sold) fl 33:10 Salomon Joseph
1809/06/13	AMSCH	0119	*G. J. J. van Os* | Op een Steene Tafel, staat eene sierlijke Vaas, gevuld met uitmuntende Bloemen, van allerlei zoort, met Rank en Bladeren, ter zijde ligt een rode Roos, waarop Insectens, en Waterdroppen; dit stukje is schoon van kleur en Ordonantie, en uitvoerig en behaaglijk van Penceelbehandeling | *Mat:* op paneel *Size:* hoog 19 ½, breed 14 duim	A	(Bought In) fl 169
1809/06/13	AMSCH	0120	*G.J.J. van Os* | Op een Marmere Tafel ligt een menigte Fruit, als blaauwe Druiven, Canteloup; Pruimen, Mispelen, Quépeeren, en andere smakelijke vrugten, eenige Roozen, Violieren, Papavers en andere Bloemen, versieren voorts dit stukje, het geen in allen deelen als de voorgaande behandeld is | *Mat:* op paneel *Size:* hoog 19 ½, breed 14 duim	A	(Bought In) fl 169
1810/05/22	AMSCH	0080	*Os. (G. J. J. van)* | Een Vaas, staande op een steenen Tafel, gevuld met onderscheidene zoorten van Bloemen; als Roozen, Hijacinten en anderen met Steel en Bladeren; uitvoerig en bevallig behandeld | *Mat:* op paneel *Size:* hoog 11, breed 9 ½ duim	Johannes van de Putte Nicolaasz.	(Sold) fl 42 Cardet van Iperen

Os, Jan van

1801/06/10	AMSCH	0132	*Os. (J. van)* | Twee stuks Bloem en Fruitstukken; op de steene Randen ziet men diversche soorten van Vrugten, benevens fraije geschakeerde	Herman ten Kate	(Sold) fl 105 J Roelofs

			Bloemen: dun, uitvoerig en krachtig behandeld | *Mat:* op doek *Size:* yder hoog 17, breed 14 duim		
1801/06/13	LNDLS	0057	*J. van Os* | Een boeren Wooning, waarvoor eenige koeijen, met volk, benevens een water met zeilende schepen, op paneel | *Mat:* op paneel *Size:* hoog 12, breed 17 duimen	D van R	(Sold) fl 25 Reijers
1801/10/19	AMSCH	0054	*OS. (J. van)* | Een zeer fraay Bloem- en Fruitstuk, delicaat en uitvoerig gepenseeld, overschoon en ryk van Ordonantie en een der capitaalste van deeze Meester | *Mat:* op paneel *Size:* hoog 34 ¼, breed 27 ¼ duim	Jonkheer Menno Baron van Coehoorn	(Sold) fl 480 C S Roos
1801/10/19	AMSCH	0055	*Os. (J. van)* | Een stil Water, verbeeldende een Gezicht op de Zeeuwsche Stroomen, by 't opkomen der zon, met eenige Scheepen ryk gestoffeerd | companion to lot 56 *Mat:* op paneel *Size:* hoog 11, breed 13 ½ duim	Jonkheer Menno Baron van Coehoorn	(Sold) fl 61 for lots 55 & 56. Gruiter
1801/10/19	AMSCH	0056	*Os. (J. van)* | Een weederga, met groote en kleine Scheepen; beide uitvoerig geschildert en warm van Coloriet | companion to lot 55 *Mat:* op paneel *Size:* hoog 11, breed 13 ½ duim	Jonkheer Menno Baron van Coehoorn	(Sold) fl 61 for lots 55 & 56. Gruiter
1802/09/18	RMDRS	0007	*J. van Os* | Een aangenaam Land- en Rivier gezicht, gestoffeerd met Boere Woninge en Beeldjens, op de Rivier verscheiden Vaartuigen, ongemeen uitvoerig en warm van Coloriet, geschildert | *Size:* hoog 20 ½, breed 26 ½ duim	Casper de Haas	(Sold) fl 66 Gruiter
1804/02/27	AMSCH	0082	*Os. (J. van)* | In een capitaal Bloem en Fruitstuk, ziet men op een Marmeren Tafel een Barnsteenen Vaas, gevult met een meenigte van Bloemen, als roode, geele en witte Roosen, Iriaasen, Haane, Kamme, Papavers, Auriculaas en andere welriekende Bloemen, ter zyde derzelve eenigen smaakelyke Vrugten; als witte Druiven, Persikes, Pruimen, Canteloupen, Nooten en een Nesje met Eijeren; bevallig van licht en delicaat gepenceeld | *Mat:* op paneel *Size:* hoog 24 ½, breed 19 duim	B	(Bought In) fl 59
1804/02/27	AMSCH	0083	*Os. (J. van)* | By een opkomende Morgenstond, ziet men een stille Zee, eenigen Zeilende en ten Ankerleggende Vaartuigen, ter zyde een Hooft- en Paalwerk, eenigen Schuiten en Scheepen; alles overeenkomstig de natuur, uitvoerig geschilderd | *Mat:* op paneel *Size:* hoog 10, breed 13 duim	B	(Sold) fl 60 for lots 83 & 84. Coclers
1804/02/27	AMSCH	0084	*Os (J. van)* | In een aangenaam Cabbelend Water, vertoonen zig eenige Zylende en ten Ankerleggende Scheepen, op den voorgrond by een Strand en Paalwerk, een Visschers Vaartuig en verderen stoffage; niet minder dan de voorigen | *Size:* hoog 10, breed 13 duim	B	(Sold) fl 60 for lots 83 & 84. Coclers
1804/05/07	AMSCH	0125	*Os. de oude. (J. van)* | Op een Marmere Tafel vertoonen zig een ménigte van smaakelyke Vrugten, als: Cantelouppen, witte Druiven, Persikens, Abricoosen, blaauwe Pruimen, Mispelen, Nooten en andere Vrugten, terzyden dezelven is een Muis beezig aan een noot te knabbelen; bevallig geordoneerd delicaat en uitvoerig geschilderd | *Mat:* op paneel *Size:* hoog 16, breed 13 ½ duim	Vinkeles [for] G	(Sold) fl 30 Coclers
1804/12/10	AMSCH	0064	*J. van Os* | Een capitaal Bloemstuk, verbeeldende een cierlyke Vaas, gevult met onderscheiden zoort van keurige bloemen, als roode en witte Roosen, hyacinten, Pioenroosen, gekroonde imperiaale, Anémiaas, Auriculaas en andere, staande op een marmere tafel; ter zyde leid een vogelnesje, alles evenaart de natuur, en de bevallige losheid en coloriet geeven verdienste aan deeze meester; en is alles uitvoerig gepenceelt | companion to lot 65 *Mat:* op paneel *Size:* Hoog 30 ½, breed 22 ½ duim	Jan De Groot	(Sold) fl 605 for lots 64 & 65. Gruyter
1804/12/10	AMSCH	0065	*J. van Os* | Op een dito [marmere] Tafel vertoonen zig verscheide zoorten van smakelyke Vrugten, als blauwe en witte Druiven, Annanas, diversche pruimen, cantaloup en andere vrugten, beneevens eenige Bloemen; en een vogeltje op een tak; zynde de wederga van de vorige, uitvoerig gepenceelt | companion to lot 64 *Size:* Hoog 30 ½, breed 22 ½ duim	Jan De Groot	(Sold) fl 605 for lots 64 & 65. Gruyter
1804/12/10	AMSCH	0066	*J. van Os* | Een capitaal woelend Water, met een zylend Oorlogschip, Beurtlieden, Boeijer en Vissersvaartuigen, ter zyde aan strand een Baak by een Hooft, waar by een Man en Vrouw en rustende Visser; het water is dun en doorschynend, en het golven natuurlyk; alles zonagtig en uitvoerig behandeld | *Mat:* op paneel *Size:* Hoog 23, breed 32 ½ duim	Jan De Groot	(Sold) fl 75 Coclers
1804/12/10	AMSCH	0067	*J. van Os* | Een Gezicht aan het Strand van het Dorp Schévelingen, ryk gestoffeert met Pinken, zo op strand als in zee, op de voorgrond ziet men een Heer te Paard, verders een bevallig verschiet; krachtig van schildering | *Mat:* op doek *Size:* Hoog 27, breed 33 duim	Jan De Groot	(Sold) fl 119 Coclers
1804/12/10	AMSCH	0068	*J. van Os* | Deeze twee fraaije Schilderyen doen zien een stil en woelend Water, ryk gestoffeerd met onderscheide Vaartuigen, de dunheid van water in beide deeze stukken is voortreffelyk en van een meesterachtige behandeling | *Mat:* op doek *Size:* Hoog 24, breed 33 duim	Jan De Groot	(Sold) fl 151 T van Iperen
1804/12/10	AMSCH	0069	*J. van Os* | Twee stuks bevallige Voorwerpen, zynde een stil en een woelend Water, ryk gestoffeert met zeilende en dryvende Oorlog- en andere Scheepen, Jagten en andere Vaartuigen; natuurlyk en zonachtig gepenceeld | *Mat:* op paneel *Size:* Hoog 14, breed 18 duim	Jan De Groot	(Withdrawn)
1804/12/10	AMSCH	0070	*J. van Os* | Twee bevallige Landschappen, ter zyde een Moolen en Boeren Woningen, beide doorsneede met stille waters, gestoffeerd met vaartuigen en diverse beeldjes; uitvoerig en fiks gepenceeld | *Mat:* op paneel *Size:* Hoog 11, breed 14 duim	Jan De Groot	(Sold) fl 93 Josi
1805/07/03	AMSCH	0126	*J. van Os* | Een Capitaal Bloemstuk, zynde een Vaas, staande op een marmere Tafel, gevuld met onderscheidene zoorten van fraaije Bloemen,	R[oos]	(Sold) fl 90 Reijers

			als geele en witte Roosen, Hyacinten, Haanekammen, Papavers met Steele [sic] en Bladeren, en diversche andere, warop [sic] Insecten aazen, ter zyde vertoont zig een Vogelnesje met Eijertjes; de schakéring der Bloemen is bevallig, het coloriet kragtig en tevens uitvoerig van penceel behandeling | *Size:* hoog 27, breed 23 duim		
1805/07/03	AMSCH	0127	*J. van Os* | Twee stuks, het eene een stil Water, in het midden een Jagt, verders een ménigte groote en klynere Scheepen en Vaartuigen; de andere is een Rivier met diversse Vaartuigen, aan een Dyk waarop verscheide Woningen en stoffagie van Beeldjes, Koejen, Paarden, Kippen, enz.; helder en aangenaam gepenceeld | *Mat:* op doek *Size:* hoog 20, breed 24 duim	C	(Sold) fl 60 L Pakker
1805/07/03	AMSCH	0128	*J. van Os* | Twee stuks stille Waters, beiden ryk gestoffeerd met zylende, dryvende en stilleggende Scheepen, Vissers Schuiten en andere Vaartuigen; helder en plaisant geschilderd op Doek | *Mat:* op doek *Size:* yder hoog 20, breed 25 duim	R[oos]	(Sold) fl 160 L Pakker
1805/10/09	HGBSM	0045	*J. van Os* | Een kabbelend water met verscheide soorten van scheepen, in 't verschiet een dorp gezigt, natuurlyk en aangenaam geschildert | *Mat:* op paneel *Size:* hoog 10 ½ breet 13 ½ duim	T H van Willigen [or others]	(Sold) fl 26:10 Teissier
1805/10/09	HGBSM	0046	*J. van Os* | Een stormagtige zee, waarin een jagt, en meer andere scheepen, niet minder als de voorgaande | *Mat:* op paneel *Size:* hoog 10 ½ breet 14 ½ duim	T H van Willigen [or others]	(Sold) fl 20:5 Teissier
1806/05/05	AMSCH	0110	*J. van Os* | Twee stuks bevallige Land en Rivier gezichten, gestoffeerd met Schapen, het water met Scheepen, Schuiten en Beeldjes; natuurlyk en zonachtig behandeld J. van Os | *Mat:* op doek *Size:* yder hoog 20, breed 24 duim	E	(Sold) fl 51 Van Iperen
1806/08/13	AMSCH	0339	*Os. (J. van)* | Dit bevallig stukje stelt voor een stil Water, met verscheide zylende en stilleggende Scheepen en Schuiten, op 't Land twee Vissers, bézig hunne Netten in te haalen en verders een aangenaam verschiet, dit alles voorgesteld by een helder opkoomende zon, piquant van licht en meesterlyk van schildering | *Mat:* op paneel *Size:* hoog 12, breed 18 duim	Vinkeles [for] J	(Sold) fl 38 Van Iperen
1806/08/20	HGBSM	0025	*J. van Os* | Een woelend Water, waarin eene damloper en vissers Schuit, en verscheiden andere Schepen; meesterlijk geschilderd door J. van Os | *Mat:* op mahoniehout paneel *Size:* hoog 18 ½, breed 24 duim	Macalester Loup [or others]	(Sold) fl 40 van Iperen
1808/05/18	LNAN	0014	*J: van Os* | Een Pot met verscheide soorten van Bloemen, zeer konstig | *Notes:* The artist's name "J: van Os" was added in by hand in the RKDH copy of the catalogue.	Mr Cornelis Versluys	(Unknown)
1808/10/28	AMVRS	0046	*Os, (J. van)* | Een heerlijk Bloem- en Fruitstuk, zeer rijk van Ordonantie, zeer natuurlijk van voorstelling, zeer uitvoerig van Penceels behandeling, en teder geschilderd, met eene keurige mengeling en zachte overgang van kleuren; zoo dat dit als een Meesterstuk van deezen Schilder met recht mag aangemerkt worden | *Mat:* op paneel *Size:* hoog 34 ¾, breed 27 ¼ duim	Marten Udink	(Sold) fl 560 B Kooij
1809/06/13	AMSCH	0117	*J. van Os* | Een kapitaal Bloem- en Fruitstuk, fraai met keurige Bloemen, als roode, witte en bonte Roosen, Angelieren, Tulpen en anderen, benevens smaakelijke delicaate Vruchten; uitmuntend van Ordonantie en schildering | *Mat:* op paneel *Size:* hoog 27, breed 23 duim	Y [or] O	(Bought In) fl 70
1809/06/13	AMSCH	0118	*J. van Os* | Een Gezicht op 't Strand, bij het Dorp Scheveningen, gestoffeerd met Visschers, Wandelaars en andere Beeldjes, in 't verschiet de Noordzee, met zeilende en andere Vaartuigen; helder, bevallig en van de beste schildering | *Mat:* op doek *Size:* hoog 27, breed 33 duim	Y [or] O	(Bought In) fl 61
1809/07/19	AMSCH	0043	*Os (J. van)* | Een kapitaal Bloemstuk, verbeelende eene fraai gewerkte Vaas, staande op een Marmeren Tafel, gevuld met onderscheidene keurige Bloemen, als roode, witte, en geele Roozen, Angelieren, Hijacinten, Slaapbollen en anderen, ter zijde ligt een Vogelnesje. De bevallige losheid en de zachte overgang der kleuren geven veel verdiensten, het is van eene alleruitvoerigste penceelsbehandeling | companion to lot 44 *Mat:* op paneel *Size:* hoog 31, breed 23 duim	[Bicker]	(Sold) fl 800 for lots 43 & 44. T van Iperen
1809/07/19	AMSCH	0044	*Os (J. van)* | Dit stuk, het welk een gepaste wederga van het voorgaande is, verbeelt een kapitaal Fruitstuk; op een Steenen Plint liggen onderscheidene Vruchten, als blaauwe en witte Druiven, Kanteloepen, Persikken, Abrikozen, Noten en andere Vruchten, waar op Kapellen aazen. Dit stuk is fraai van Ordonnantie en van gelijke Schildering als het voorgaande | companion to lot 43 *Size:* hoog 31, breed 23 duim	[Bicker]	(Sold) fl 800 for lots 43 & 44. T van Iperen
1810/05/22	AMSCH	0073	*Os. (J. van)* | Een Glazen Fles, gevuld met witte en roode Roosen, Papavers, Auriculaas en andere keurige Bloemen, staande op een Marmeren Voetstuk; zeer uitvoerig tegen eenen ligten grond geschilderd | *Mat:* op paneel *Size:* hoog 14 ½, breed 11 duim	Johannes van de Putte Nicolaasz.	(Sold) fl 140 de Lelie
1810/05/22	AMSCH	0074	*Os. (J. van)* | Op een Marmeren Tafel liggen verscheide smakelijke Vrugten: als Persikken, blaauwe en andere Druiven, benevens eenige fraaije Bloemen, waar op Insekten azen; alleruitvoerigst en delikaat gepenceeld | *Mat:* op paneel *Size:* hoog 11, breed 9 ½ duim	Johannes van de Putte Nicolaasz.	(Sold) fl 130 de Lelie
1810/05/22	AMSCH	0075	*Os. (J. van)* | Een stil Water met drijvende en stilleggende Vaartuigen en eene Stad in 't verschiet; zonachtig en fraai geschilderd | *Mat:* op paneel *Size:* hoog 9 ½, breed 13 duim	Johannes van de Putte Nicolaasz.	(Sold) fl 24:10 Gruyter

1810/05/22	AMSCH	0076	*Os. (J. van)* | Eene woelende Zee, met zeilende Kaag- en Beurtschepen; als de voorgaande behandeld | *Mat:* op paneel *Size:* hoog 10, breed 13 duim	Johannes van de Putte Nicolaasz.	(Sold) fl 17:10 Gruyter
1810/06/06	RMMUY	0053	*Jan van Os* | Een stil Water, rijk gestoffeerd met Vaartuigen van verscheide grootte, waar van eenige zeilende, en andere stilliggende verbeeld zijn, alles uitvoerig en zonachtig behandeld | *Mat:* op doek		(Unknown) fl 18
1810/06/06	RMMUY	0054	*Jan van Os* | Op eene steene Tafel zijn eene menigte Bloemen en Vrugten afgebeeld, en alleruitvoerigst en krachtig geschilderd | *Annots:* 2 stuks (EBNP) *Mat:* op paneel		(Unknown) fl 114
			Os, Pieter Gerardus van		
1801/03/16	AMSCH	0013	*P.G. van Os* | Een Duinachtig Landschap, voor een Boerenwoning ziet men eenige Huislieden by een belaaden Hooiwagen, op de voorgrond by en in een Plas, eenig staand en leggend Vee, uitvoerig van penceel behandeling	P[ruyssenaar]	(Sold) fl 62 Rijnders
1801/08/19	AMSCH	0087	*P. G. van Os* | Een capitaal Duinachtig Landschap, de Voorgrond is ryk gestoffeert met staand en leggend Vee, op de tweede Grond, ziet men een Jager te Paard, Verders een duinachtig Verschiet, uitvoerig en meesterlyk van Schildering	Pruyssen[r] [for] Q	(Bought In) fl 25
1802/09/06	AMSCH	0092	*P. G. v. Os* | In een aangenaam Land- en Watergezigt, ziet men op de voorgrond een rood bonte Os in 't water staan, ter zyde een leggende dito, waar agter eenige Boerewooningen, ter andere zyde eenige Schaapen by een schuur; zonagtig en uitvoerig gepenceeld | *Mat:* op doek *Size:* hoog 12, breed 16 duim	J	(Sold) fl 11 van Iperen
1802/09/29	AMSCH	0043	*P. G. van Os* | Een Landschap, hoog 11 ½, breed 9 ¾ duim. Paneel. Dit bevallig Schilderytje, verbeeld in een uitgestrekte Landstreek een Schaapstal tusschen hoog en laag geboomten en riete Heggen, voor dezelve graazende en rustende Schaapen, en een Geitje met haar Jongen by eenen helderen Waterplas; zeer uitvoerig en delicaat behandelt, en van eene aangenaame natuurlyke couleur [Ce Joli petit Paysage offre une variété d'arbres près desquels paissent & se reposent des chêvres & des moutons, au bord d'une marre d'eau. Ce morceau est d'un grand fini et traité avec autant d'art que de Vérité.] | *Mat:* op paneel *Size:* hoog 11 ½, breed 9 ¾ duim	[Labouchere?]	(Sold) fl 16:10 J van Eijk
1802/09/29	AMSCH	0044	*P. G. van Os* | Een Landschap, hoog 13, breed 17 ¼ duim. Paneel. Een zoelen Zomerdag word in dit Schilderytje verbeeld staande en leggend Vee ziet men in en omtrent het doorschynend stromend Water op den Voorgrond; den tweeden grond meerder verheven, is met opgaande Boomen beplant, waar tusschen een gaande Landman en een Jongen; den agtergrond verbeeld een uitgestrekte Bergagtige Landstreek; dit Stukje is uitvoerig en delicaat behandelt, en het Coloriet is bevallig en natuurlyk [Un Point de Vue de Paysage la droite offre un Terrain élevé couvert d'un Bosquet d'arbres, qui se détachent harmonieusement sur un beau ciel vaporeux ; on y voit des vaches & des moutons. La gauche présente une eau trés etendue, dans laquelle se tient un jeune Taureau. Tout annonce dans ce Tableau une belle journée d'Eté, la Verité de la couleur y ajoute des attraits, ainsi que la maniere dont ce sujet agreable est exécuté.] | *Mat:* op paneel *Size:* hoog 13, breed 17 ¼ duim	[Labouchere?]	(Sold) fl 18 J van Eijk
1804/02/27	AMSCH	0081	*Os (P.G. van)* | In een aangenaam Duinachtig Landschap, ziet men op een Graazige Hoogten, een Boer een Koe Melken, nevens hem een Man te Paard met eenige Honden, den voorgrond ryk gestoffeerd, met een meenigte van staand en leggendt Vee, en een alleraangenaamst verschiet, zonachtig en aller uitmuntendst geschilderd | *Size:* hoog 22, breed 28 duim	C	(Sold) fl 38 de Meijer
1804/05/07	AMSCH	0127	*Os. (D. G. van)* | In een aangenaam Boomryk Landschap, ziet men men terzyde een Water, by de overblyfzels van een vervallen Gebouw, twee Vissende Beeldjes, op de voorgrond eenig staand een leggend Vee, verders een aangenaam en Duinachtig verschiet; zonachtig en bevallig gepenceeld | *Mat:* op paneel *Size:* hoog 11, breed 9 duim *Notes:* The artist's name was given as "Os. (D. G. van)" but we have assumed this is an error.	Vinkeles [for] G	(Sold) fl 4 Gruyter
1804/05/07	AMSCH	0128	*Os. (D. G. van)* | Een bevallig Landschap, gestoffeerd met twee staande Paarden, eenige leggende Schaapen en een grazende Koe; voorts een gaande Vrouw by een oude Poort en een aangenaam verschiet; bevallig en uitvoerig behandeld | *Mat:* op paneel *Size:* hoog 11, breed 13 duim *Notes:* The artist's name was given as "Os. (D. G. van)" but we have assumed this is an error.	Vinkeles [for] G	(Bought In) fl 20
1804/05/07	AMSCH	0129	*Os (D. G. van)* | In een vlak Hollands Landschap ziet men in een Grazige Wyde, eenig staand en leggend Vee, terzyde onder 't Geboomte eenige Boerewooningen en een aangenaam verschiet | *Mat:* op paneel *Size:* hoog 11 ½, breed 15 duim *Notes:* The artist's name was given as "Os (D. G. van)" but we have assumed this is an error.	Vinkeles [for] G	(Sold) fl 12:10 Salomon Joseph
1804/05/07	AMSCH	0129a[H]	*Os (D. G. van)* | 1 Schildery | *Notes:* This lot was added in by hand in the EBNP, LBDa and RKDH copies of the catalogue. The artist's name was given as "Os (D. G. van)" but we have assumed this is an error.	Vinkeles [for] J	(Sold) fl 12 Nieuwenhuisen
1804/08/08	AMSCH	0150	*P.G. van Os* | In dit aangenaam en bevallig Landschap ziet men ter zyde by een Moolen en Boerenwooning eenig staand en leggend Vée, en aan	Vink[eles] [for] K[=Gruyter?]	(Bought In) fl 19 ½ for lots 150 & 151

			de kant van een Sloot eenige drinkende Schaapen, en een Dorp in 't verschiet; helder en zonachtig geschilderd | *Mat:* op paneel *Size:* hoog 15 ½, breed 20 duim		
1804/08/08	AMSCH	0151	*P.G. van Os* | In dit eenvoudige doch natuurlyke Landschap ziet men eenig dartel opgaand Geboomte, op de voorgrond een staand een leggend Beest, ter zyde eenige Schaapen en Bokken, en een aangenaam verschiet; niet minder dan de voorige | *Mat:* op paneel *Size:* hoog 15 ½, breed 20 duim	Vink[eles] [for] K[=Gruyter?]	(Bought In) fl 19 ½ for lots 150 & 151
1805/07/10	AMSCH	0118	*P. G. van Os* | Op een grazige Heuvel, in een Landschap met Geboomten, ziet men verscheide staande en rustende Schapen; bevallig geschilderd | *Mat:* op paneel	S[chley] [for] Doralle	(Withdrawn)
1806/05/05	AMSCH	0108	*P. G. van Os* | In een bevallig Landschap, onder het lommer van een zwaar opgaande Boom, ziet men twee Paarden en eenige leggende en grazende Beesten, en een aangenaam verschiet; zonagtig en uitvoerig gepenceeld door P. G. van Os | *Mat:* op paneel *Size:* hoog 11, breed 14 duim	V[inkeles]	(Bought In) fl 6:10
1806/05/05	AMSCH	0109	*P. G. van Os* | In een boomryk Landschap, by een water en vervallen gebouw, zyn twee vissende Beeldjes, op de voorgrond eenig staand en leggend Vee, verders een aangenaam en Duinachtig verschiet; zonachtig en bevallig gepenceeld door denzelven [P. G. van Os] op Paneel | *Mat:* op paneel *Size:* hoog 11, breed 9 duim	V[inkeles]	(Sold) fl 4:10 Gruyter
1808/08/23	AMSCH	0124	*Os. (P. G. van)* | Een Drentisch Landschap, op de voorgrond een vaalbonte Stier, benevens een Schaap en een Lam, bij eenige Kruiden; schoon en meesterlijk behandeld | *Mat:* op doek *Size:* hoog 27, breed 37 duim	S	(Sold) fl 59 Dupré
1808/08/23	AMSCH	0125	*Os. (P. G. van)* | Een aangenaam Landschap, ter zijde bij oude Ruïne een stil Water, gestoffeerd met twee visschende Beeldjes, eenig staand en rustende Vée, en een Duinachtig verschiet; zonachtig en uitvoerig gepenceeld | *Mat:* op paneel *Size:* hoog 11, breed 9 duim	[Gruyter?]	(Sold) fl 7:10 P Swanenburg
1809/04/17	AMSCH	0072	*P.G. van Os* | Twee stuks duinachtige Landschappen, met stoffagie van Beelden en Beesten; fraai van schildering | *Mat:* op paneel *Size:* ieder hoog 8, breed 10 duim	A	(Sold) fl 19
1809/04/22	AMYVR	0094	*P.G. van Os* | In eene grazige Weide staat aan de stam van een Boom een Stier gebonden; waarbij twee liggende Schapen en een aangenaam verschiet; meesterlijk | *Mat:* op doek *Size:* hoog 27, breed 32 duim *Loc:* Den Haag, Nederland. Museum Bredius. (85–1946)	de Bruin	(Sold) fl 89 Remmers Bredius
1809/04/22	AMYVR	0095	*P.G. van Os* | Twee stuks bevallige Landschapjes, gestoffeerd met Beelden en Beesten; bevallig | *Mat:* op paneel *Size:* hoog 9, breed 11 duim	de Bruin	(Bought In) fl 71
1810/05/22	AMSCH	0077	*Os. (P. G. van)* | In een Veldgezicht, ziet men op den voorgrond bij een Willigeboom, twee staande Paarden, waarbij rustende en grazende Schapen en eene liggende Koe, in 't verschiet eene Ruïne; uitvoerig en bevallig van schildering | *Mat.* op paneel *Size:* hoog 11, breed 14 ½ duim	Johannes van de Putte Nicolaasz.	(Sold) fl 21 Rinkhuizen
1810/05/22	AMSCH	0078	*Os. (P. G. van)* | In een aangenaam Landzicht met Geboomte ziet men op den voorgrond eenen Huisman te Paard, verzeld van vier anderen aan een gekoppelde Paarden, ter zijde twee Vrouwen, in 't verschiet Hooiwerkers; zonachtig en uitvoerig gepenceeld | *Mat:* op paneel *Size:* hoog 11 ½, breed 15 duim	Johannes van de Putte Nicolaasz.	(Sold) fl 15:10 du Pree
1810/05/22	AMSCH	0079	*Os. (P. G. van)* | Een Bergachtig Landschap met een Rivier, gestoffeerd met een Landman te Paard, benevens een Meisje bij eenig Vee; helder en uitvoerig geschilderd | *Mat:* op paneel *Size:* hoog 9, breed 11 duim	Johannes van de Putte Nicolaasz.	(Sold) fl 11:10 Twisk

Os, Pieter Gerardus van (copy by)

1804/08/08	AMSCH	0152	*P. G. van Os; K. du Jardin* | In een Landschap ziet men een staande Vrouw, névens dezelve een witte Os, een rustend Ezel, en twee Schaapen; zonachtig en bevallig geschilderd, door denzelven [P. G. van Os], op Doek, naar een Schildery door K. du Jardin | copy by Pieter G. Os after K. Dujardin *Mat:* op doek *Size:* hoog 13, breed 16 duim	Schley [for] B	(Sold) fl 3:5 Graffelman

Ossenbeck, Jan van (manner)

1810/06/06	RMMUY	0228	*Ossenbeek* | Een paar Wadende Koeijen, als door Ossenbeek		(Unknown) fl 1

Ostade

1802/07/21	HGKAN	0100	*Ostade* | Een Boeren Kermis, ryk van Ordonnantie en vol gewoel		(Unknown)
1804/07/25	DLGRO	0032	*Ostade* | Twee Boertjes hun Pyp aansteekende | *Mat:* op paneel *Size:* hoog 7, breed 6 duim	Mr Franc van der Burch Wz.	(Unknown)
1804/07/25	DLGRO	0033	*Ostade* | Twee dito [Boertjes], houdende den Een een Bierkan in de eene, en een Bierglas in de andere hand, terwyl den andere zyn Pyp aansteekt | *Mat:* op paneel *Size:* hoog 7, breed 6 duim	Mr Franc van der Burch Wz.	(Unknown)
1808/05/18	LNAN	0026	*Ostade* | Een stuk met rookende Boeren | *Notes:* The artist's name "Ostade" was added in by hand in the RKDH copy of the catalogue.	Mr Cornelis Versluys	(Unknown)
1808/05/18	LNAN	0032	*Ostade* | Een Gezelschap van vrolijke Boeren in een Binnen-Huis | *Notes:* The artist's name "Ostade" was added in by hand in the RKDH copy of the catalogue.	Mr Cornelis Versluys	(Unknown)

1808/06/13	AMSCH	0220c[H]	*Ostade* | 1 van Ostade | *Notes:* This lot was added in by hand in the AA I, EBNP, FLNY and RKDH copies of the catalogue.	R[oos]	(Sold) fl 52 van Drielst
1810/07/23	DOLG2	00GG	*van Ostade* | Een lezende Boer, meesterlijk en fraai geschilderd	Pieter Quinting	(Sold) fl 10 Strij
			Ostade (or Ostade, copy after)		
1805/07/10	AMSCH	0194	*Ostade* | Twee stuks, met Boertjes, door of na Ostade	R[oos]	(Sold) fl 1:10 Mensart
			Ostade (or Ostade, manner)		
1807/06/02	AMHUY	0009	*Ostade* | In een Boeren Herberg zyn eenige Huislieden lustig aan het eeten en drinken, door of in de manier van Ostade		(Unknown)
			Ostade (copy after)		
1801/03/16	AMSCH	0141a	*Ostade* | Twee stuks Boeren Binnehuizen, na Ostade	K[ip]	(Sold) fl 1:5 Mensart
1801/04/08	HAVIN	0057	*Ostade* | Een Copy na Ostade		(Unknown)
1803/12/12	AMSCH	0144	*Ostade* | Een Marskramer; naar Ostade | *Mat:* op paneel *Size:* hoog 5, breed 7 duim	D	(Sold) fl 1 Pruijsenaar
1804/02/27	AMSCH	0164[a]	*Ostade* | Twee stuks, de Koekebakster, naar Ostade, en een Landschap | *This Lot:* De Koekebakster; lot 164[b] by Anonymous	C	(Sold) fl 1 for lots 164[a] & 164[b]. L Pakker
1806/06/07	RMHSN	0068	*Ostade* | Twee Rookende Boertjes, na Ostade | *Mat:* op paneel	A E K L	(Unknown)
1806/10/17	MGSAN	0028	*Ostade* | Een Boeren Conversatie, naar Ostade | *Mat:* op paneel	Gerardus Beljard	(Unknown)
1807/06/02	AMHUY	0044	*Ostade* | 1 dito [Schildery] Boerengezelschap naar Ostade		(Unknown)
1809/04/22	AMYVR	0168	*Ostade* | Een drinkende Boer; naar Ostade	de Bruin	(Sold) fl 0:6 van Iperen
1809/04/22	AMYVR	0174	*Ostade* | Een Liereman; naar Ostade	de Bruin	(Sold) fl 1 du Pree
1810/06/06	RMMUY	0183	*Ostade* | Een Boeren Binnenhuis. Naar Ostade | *Mat:* op paneel		(Unknown) fl 7:10
1810/06/06	RMMUY	0219	*van Ostade* | De Schelviskopers. Naar van Ostade | *Mat:* op doek		(Unknown) fl 7:5
			Ostade (manner)		
1801/04/08	HAVIN	0071	*Ostade* | Een Boerewoonieg [sic] met vrolyke Boeren als Ostade		(Unknown)
1801/12/22	AMOTT	0065	*Ostade* | 1 Haardsteede met rookende Boeren, als Ostade	Bartholomeus Ruloffs	(Unknown) fl 5:10
1802/09/06	AMSCH	0255	*Ostade* | Twee stuks ryk gestoffeerde boere Binnehuizen; in de manier van Ostade	Mevrouw Achtienhoven	(Sold) fl 4:15 Boelen
1803/12/12	AMSCH	0133	*Ostade* | Twee stuks Binnenhuizen met rokende Boeren, en ander bywerk; in de manier van Ostade | *Mat:* op doek *Size:* hoog 15, breed 12 duim	H	(Sold) fl 6:10 van Iperen
1804/05/07	AMSCH	0213	*Ostade* | Een Buitenhuis, voor hetzelve een Doedelzakspeeler, waarby verscheide Aanschouwers; fiks en natuurlyk behandeld; in de manier van Ostade | *Mat:* op paneel *Size:* hoog 12, breed 15 duim	Y[ver] [for] W	(Sold) fl 1:10 S Joseph
1804/08/08	AMSCH	0256	*Ostade* | Eenige Danssende Huislieden, Musicanten en Aanschouwers, in een Boerenschuur; geestig in de manier van Ostade	Roos [for] C	(Sold) fl 10 Van Iperen
1804/10/29	HRBAU	0142	*Ostade* | In een Binnenhuis zitten, voor aan, twee Boertjens zich met drinken en rooken te verlustigen, waar by een slaapende Hond; iets verder, by een glasraam, zyn drie Boertjens bezig met de Kaart te speelen. Zeer bevallig in den trant van Ostade behandeld | *Mat:* op paneel *Size:* hoog 12, breed 10 duim	Simon Styl	(Unknown)
1805/10/09	HGBSM	J0009	*Ostade* | Een binnen stalletje met twee figuurtjes, in de trant van Ostade | *Mat:* op paneel *Size:* hoog 10 ½ breet 8 duim	T H van Willigen [or others]	(Sold) fl 6:10 Hardenberg
1805/10/21	GRBOL	0040	*Ostade* | Een Boerengezelschap, in de manier van Ostade | companion to lot 41	Gerardus Nicolaus Heerkens	(Unknown)
1805/10/21	GRBOL	0041	*Ostade* | Een dito [Boerengezelschap], zynde een Weêrga, door Denzelfen [in de manier van Ostade] | companion to lot 40	Gerardus Nicolaus Heerkens	(Unknown)
1806/08/13	AMSCH	0306	*Ostade* | Vrolyke Boeren en Boerinnen voor een Herberg, en in 't verschiet een Kermisvreugd, in de manier van Ostade	Yver	(Sold) fl 5:10 Schumacher
1807/09/28	AMWUR	0023	*Ostade* | Twee stukjes, zynde Rookende en drinkende Boeren, in de manier van Ostade		(Unknown) fl 1
1808/04/26	GDAN	0280	*Ostade* | In de manier van Ostade, een Manspersoon met een Kan in de hand | *Size:* hoog 7, breed 7 duim	G H Fortuyn	(Unknown)
1809/06/13	AMSCH	0205	*Ostade* | Een Binnenhuis, gestoffeerd met een Huisman, Vrouw en Kind, zittende in een Binnenvertrek; bevallig op Doek, in de manier van Ostade | *Mat:* op doek	S[chley]	(Sold) fl 2:10 du Pree
1810/06/06	RMMUY	0214	*Ostade* | Een Mans Pourtrait, met een bef en hoed Als door Ostade | *Notes:* This lot was sold with lot 215 by an anonymous artist.		(Unknown) fl 1:4 for lots 214 & 215
1810/10/13	HGDAW	0002	*Ostade* | Een Boeren Binnenhuis, aan de linkerzyde ziet men een Vrouw die Koeken bakt, waarby een Jongen staat te eeten, op de Voorgrond twee Kinderen aan een Tafel, in 't verschiet een zittend oud Man, met zyn regter arm op een Ton leunende, zeer transpirand als Ostade | *Mat:* op paneel *Size:* hoog 10 ¾, breed 10 duim		(Unknown)

			Ostade (style)		
1810/07/23	DOLG2	0055	*Ostade* | Een Speelman, met zijn Jongen, bij een Boerenwoning, in den stijl van Ostade | *Mat:* op paneel *Size:* hoog 10, breed 9 duim	Pieter Quinting	(Sold) fl 3 Schalk
			Ostade, Adriaen van		
1801/04/13	AMSCH	0055	*A. van Ostade* | Voor een boerewooning legt een Boer over een Balustrade te kyken, dit stukje hoewel eenvoudig van onderwerp caractriseerd [sic] deezen voortreffelyke Meester door deszelfs behandeling | *Mat:* op paneel *Size:* hoog 10, breed 8 duim	Pierre Fouquet, junior	(Sold) fl 50 Pruyssenaar
1801/04/13	AMSCH	0056	*A. van Ostade* | Twee stuks, een Boer welke zyn Pyp opsteekt, en een Vrouwtje dat een kan en glas in de hand heeft, beide uitvoerig behandeld | *Mat:* op paneel *Size:* ieder hoog 7, breed 5 ½ duim	Pierre Fouquet, junior	(Sold) fl 50 Coclers
1801/04/13	AMSCH	0057	*A. van Ostade* | In een binnenhuis zit een Boer met de Courant in zyn hand, schynende te spreken met een andere, die zyn pyp op wil steken, behandeld als de voorgaande | *Mat:* op paneel *Size:* hoog 9, breed 8 duim	Pierre Fouquet, junior	(Sold) fl 85 Spruit v Gent
1801/05/11	AMSCH	0063	*A. van Ostade* | Een Boereschuur, gestoffeerd met verscheide beelden en huisraad, kloek behandeld | *Mat:* op paneel *Size:* hoog 14, breed 15 duim	P[ruyssenaar]	(Sold) fl 20 Pruijssenaar [for] R
1801/06/10	AMSCH	0130	*Ostade. (A. van)* | Een Boere Binnehuis, gestoffeerd met een menigte vrolyke en drinkende Huislieden: uitvoerig gepenceeld | *Mat:* op paneel *Size:* hoog 14, breed 17 duim	Herman ten Kate	(Sold) fl 225 Taijs
1801/06/10	AMSCH	0131	*Ostade. (A. van)* | Een Boer geeft een stuk Koek aan een Boerin, welke over de Deur ligt: fraai van Hartstochten en breed geschilderd | *Mat:* op paneel *Size:* hoog 12, breed 11 duim	Herman ten Kate	(Sold) fl 50 Gruyter
1801/06/13	LNDLS	0007	*Adriaan van Ostade* | Dit Stukje, vertoonende een Bakker, die in zijn hemd op den onderdeur van zijn huis leund, met een hoorn in zijn hand, schijnende te blaazen, terwijl het brood nevens hem in een mande legt, en wijngaard bladen hangen, op paneel | *Mat:* op paneel *Size:* hoog 10 ½, breed 8 ½ duimen	D van R	(Sold) fl 200 A Delfos [for] W
1801/10/06	AMSCH	0049	*A. van Ostade* | Dit Natuurlyk en fraay Tafreel vertoont een Boere-binnehuis, ryk gestoffeerd met verscheide Beelden, op de voorgrond ter linker zyde by een vengster voor een tafel, zitten drie Huislieden, en een vrouw scheinende zig met zingen te Vermaaken; een derzelve speelt op de Phiool, een ander met een pyp in de hand, staat als beschouwer; verder bij een Haardstede zitten verscheide Mans en een Vrouw met een Kind, en op de grond legt verscheide Boere Huisraad; dit stuk is geestig Geordoneert, de Caracters natuurlyk, het Coloriet bevallig, en zeer uitvoerig gepenceeld | *Mat:* op paneel *Size:* hoog 17, breed 20 duim *Loc:* London, England, UK. Royal Collection (Buckingham Palace) (1006)	S	(Sold) fl 2075 Makelaar A E Sterk
1801/10/19	AMSCH	0051	*Ostade. (A. van)* | Een gezelschap van drie rookende Boeren in een Binnenvertrek aan den haard, op den voorgrond een hond de Pot uitlekkenden; in 't verschiet andere Boeren aan een Tafel zittende; zynde in allen deelen een uitmuntend stukje | *Mat:* op paneel *Size:* hoog 9 ¾, breed 8 duim *Loc:* London, England, UK. Royal Collection (Buckingham Palace) (1008)	Jonkheer Menno Baron van Coehoorn	(Sold) fl 800 A E Sterk
1801/10/19	AMSCH	0052	*Ostade. (A. van)* | Een rookend Boertje achter over leunende en de rook uitblaazende, zittende in een Binnenvertrek met een Tafel voor zich, waar op een glas bier, een pyp en papier met Tabak; zeer delicaat en uitvoerig geschildert | *Mat:* op paneel *Size:* hoog 10 ¾, breed 8 ½ duim *Loc:* Antwerpen, Belgique. Koninklijk Museum voor Schone Kunsten. (466)	Jonkheer Menno Baron van Coehoorn	(Sold) fl 365 Frantzen (Spruit van Gend)
1801/10/19	AMSCH	0053	*Ostade. (A. van)* | Een oud lagchend Vrouwtje in ovaal, schoon geschildert | *Mat:* op paneel *Fmt:* ovaal *Size:* hoog 6, breed 4 ½ duim	Jonkheer Menno Baron van Coehoorn	(Sold) fl 16:10 van der Schley [for] M[errem]
1801/11/10	AMPOS	0009	*van Ostade* | Vrolyke Boeren by een Buitenhuis, door van Ostade, 1671 | *Inscr:* van Ostade, 1671 (signed and dated?) *Notes:* It is unclear whether the name and date are inscribed on the painting.		(Unknown)
1801/12/22	AMOTT	0008	*A. van Ostade* | De Liereman voor de boere Wooning, omringd door Kinderen	Bartholomeus Ruloffs	(Unknown) fl 11
1802/04/13	HAVIN	0008	*A. van Ostade* | Een Binnehuis met een Boer, zittende by een Tafel, beezig een Pen te snyden, fraai en uitvoerig		(Unknown)
1802/04/13	HAVIN	0009	*A. van Ostade* | Eenige Boeren op het Verkeerbord speelende		(Unknown)
1802/05/05	AMSCH	0157	*A. van Ostade* | In een Boeren Binnenhuis ziet men een Vrouw aan de Wastobbe, waarby een Man zit te haspelen, ter zyde een Jongen en een menigte Huisraad, bevallig en dun gepenceeld | *Size:* hoog 10, breed 13 duim	A	(Sold) fl 18:10 Spruit
1802/06/16	AMSCH	0123	*A. van Ostade* | Voor een Boere Herberg, onder een Afdak ziet men Huislieden by een Tafel, op het Verkeerbort speelen. Een ander schenkt een glas bier, en een Jongeling speelt met een Hond, verder een Dorpgezicht met Kerktooren, en andere Woningen; kloek en krachtig gepenceeld | *Mat:* op doek *Size:* hoog 42, breed 33 duim	[Merrem]	(Sold) fl 80 LaFontaine
1802/06/16	AMSCH	0124	*A. van Ostade* | Het Afbeeldzel van een bedaagde Vrouw in al oude Huismans kleeding, met een linne kraagje om den hals; zy vertoond een vriendelyk gelaat; meesterlyk fraai en uitvoerig gepenceeld | *Mat:* op paneel *Fmt:* ovaal *Size:* hoog 6 ½, breed 5 duim	[Merrem]	(Sold) fl 12 van der Vinne

1802/06/28	AMSCH	0136	*A. van Ostade* | Voor een Boerenbuitenhuis onder Wyngaartsranken ziet men eenige Boeren, bezig een Os te dollen, waarby verscheide Omstanders; alles bevallige van licht, en zonachtig behandeld, op Panneel | *Mat:* op paneel *Size:* hoog 15, breed 17 duim	Anna Elink	(Sold) fl 150 C S Roos
1802/07/21	HGKAN	0033	*A. van Ostade* | Een dito [Schildery?] Boeren Binnenhuys met rookende en zittende Boeren, door A. van Ostade, paneel vergulde Lyst | *Mat:* op paneel *Notes:* It is unclear what "dito" refers to in the title.		(Unknown)
1802/08/24	LNDLS	0082	*A. van Ostade* | Een Binnen – schuur met Boeren en Boerinnen, met eene menigte Huisraad. Vet en kragtig op paneel, gem. A. van Ostade | *Mat:* op paneel *Size:* hoog 14, breed 15 duimen *Inscr:* A. van Ostade (signed)	Leonardus Bouman [or others]	(Unknown) fl 17:10
1802/09/06	AMSCH	0088	*A. v. Ostade* | Vier stuks, rond formaat, verbeeldende 3 Boertjes en 1 Boerin, meesterlyk fraay | *Mat:* op paneel *Fmt:* rond *Size:* over de diameter 4 duim	W ten Houten	(Sold) fl 14 Isaac Smit
1802/09/29	AMSCH	0041	*A. van Ostade* | Een Boertje zittende by een Tafel, waarop geplaatst een Pyp, Tabak en een Test, houdende in zyn hand een groot Bierglas, en met een vergenoegd gelaat omziende, hy rust met zyn linker arm over de Leuning van zyn Stoel [Un petit Tableau de la bonne couleur de ce Peintre offrant un Paysan assis à une Table, tenant un grand verre à Bierre de la main droite & s'appuyant du bras gauche sur le dos de sa chaise en fixant le spectateur d'un visage riant & satisfait, du Tabac, une pipe à fumer & une terrine à feu sont devant lui. Ce petit morceau ainsi que le suivant qui lui sert de pendant sont d'un faire large & délicat.] | companion to lot 42 *Mat:* op paneel *Size:* hoog 6 ¾, breed 6 ½ duim	[Labouchere?]	(Sold) fl 20:10 J van Eijk
1802/09/29	AMSCH	0042	*A. van Ostade* | Een zittend Boertje, uitvoerig en meesterlyk behandeltr [sic] gelyk het voorgaande [Un paysan assis prés d'un grange, à coté de la quelle, quelques arbres.] | companion to lot 41 *Mat:* op paneel *Size:* hoog 6 ¾, breed 6 ½ duim	[Labouchere?]	(Sold) fl 40 Vinkeles
1803/04/20	AMSCH	0054	*Ostade. (A. van)* | Voor de Deur van een Boerewoning ziet men een oude Grysaard met een stok in zyn hand, uitvoerig behandeld [Au-devant d'une masure est assis un viellard [sic] ténant un baton : ce petit morceau d'effet est d'une touche ferme & empatée.] | *Mat:* op paneel *Size:* hoog 10, breed 8 duim	Maria Magdalena van Sluypwyk, gravinne van Moens	(Sold) fl 116 Hulswit
1803/07/07	HGKAN	0007	*A. van Ostade* | Een Drinkend Boertje, door A. van Ostade [Schilderyen in Olyverf] | *Mat:* in olyverf *Notes:* The bracketed information in the title appears above lot 1 and refers to lots 1 to 25.		(Unknown)
1803/07/18	AMSCH	0038	*Ostade (A. van)* | In een Boere Binnenhuis zit een Vrouw met een Kind op haar schoot by het Vuur, de Huisvader agter haar staande is beezig Brood te snyden voor twee Jongens aan een Tafel staande; een meenigte Huisraad en ander bywerk maken dit stukje zeer bevallig en natuurlyk, zynde van de uitvoerigste schildering van deezen grooten Meester [Dans l'intérieur d'une habitation rustique dans laquelle est assise une femme près du feu accomodant son enfant, le villageois est un pas en arriere coupant du pain pour deux jeunes garçons qui attendent leur dejeuné à une table. Cette chaumiere intêressante par le nombre de details & de meubles chetifs, tous également traités d'une maniere aussi vraye que naturelle, produit le plus charmant effet de lumiere ; une légereté de pinceau, une couleur excellente jointe à un fini achevé, attestent que ce morceau est peint dans le meilleur tems de l'auteur.] | *Mat:* op paneel *Size:* hoog 17, breed 14 duim	Maria Theresia Andrioli	(Sold) fl 565 C S Roos
1803/08/01	AMSCH	0027	*Ostade. (A. van)* | Voor een Buitenhuis, ziet men een speelende Liereman, nevens hem staat een Meisje, beneevens een Boer en Boerin, die met aandagt schynen te luisteren, geestig van Ordonantie en fraay van penceelsbehandeling | *Mat:* op paneel *Size:* hoog 13 ½, breed 15 ½ duim	J	(Sold) fl 50 Coclers
1803/08/24	HGKAN	0064	*A. van Ostade* | Een Boere Binnehuis, waar in verscheide lieden in onderscheide Caracters, Geestig verbeeld | *Mat:* op paneel	[Teissier] [or others]	(Sold) fl 90 C [?]
1803/12/12	AMSCH	0071a	*A. v. Ostade* | Een bevallig Vrouwtje halverlyf, uitvoerig op Paneel | *Mat:* op paneel *Notes:* There are two lots with the number 71; this lot has been changed to 71a.	W	(Sold) fl 6 Coclers
1804/05/07	AMSCH	0124	*Ostade (A. van)* | In een Boere Binnenhuis, ziet men by een Schoorsteen aan een Tafel zitten, eenige vrolyke Boeren en Boerinnen, op de voorgrond een Boer met een Kan in de hand, verders eenig toepastelyk [sic] bywerk, uitvoerig gepenceeld | *Mat:* op paneel *Size:* hoog 8, breed 6 duim	Vinkeles [for] H[affner]	(Sold) fl 14:10 Gruiter
1807/08/26	AMSCH	0161	*A. v. Ostade* | Dit capitaale voorwerp, zynde een ryke Ordonnantie, verbeeld een aangenaam Dorpgezigt, met Woningen, Kerk en Tooren, by Geboomten: waar in een menigte Huislieden zig vermaken; op de voorgrond ziet men twee Boeren beezig met Keegels te speelen, en twee andere als met elkander spreekende; ter zyde voor een Woning, alwaar eene Vrouw met een Kind op de Arm, in de Deur staat, zit een Man met een Bierkan in de Hand, en verder verscheide die aan een Tafel zitten te drinken, in 't verschiet een Vragtwagen en wandelende Lieden; de karacters zyn natuurlyk, het licht bevallig en van een meesterlyke fraaije Penceelsbehandeling | *Mat:* op paneel *Size:* hoog 25, breed 27 duim	Joseph Vallette	(Sold) fl 415 H Jansen
1807/08/26	AMSCH	0162	*A. v. Ostade* | Voor een Boeren Buitenhuis, waar in eene bedaagde Vrouw over de Deur legt, en een Jongeling zit met een Blaas; hangt een	Helsdinge	(Bought In) fl 86

			opengesneeden Varken aan de Leer, gestoffeerd met verder bywerk; zeer natuurlyk | *Size:* hoog 18, breed 15 duim		
807/08/26	AMSCH	0163	*A. v. Ostade* | Eene oude Vrouw over de Onderdeur leggende van een met Wyngaards Ranken begroeide Boerenwoning; fraai van schildering | *Mat:* op paneel *Size:* hoog 11, breed 9 duim *Loc:* Philadelphia, PA, USA. Museum of Art. (E1924-3-71)	Roos	(Sold) fl 33 du Pree
808/06/06	RMRIJ	0096	*Ostade. (Adriaan van)* | In eene Schilderkamer ziet men op den voorgrond eene Schilder, voor zijn Ezel gezeten, aan een daar staande Tafereel bezig schijnende te arbeiden. Ter zijde van dezelve ligt een bruine Hond; achter in het vertrek staat een Jongen Verw te wrijven; wat verder een ton, waarop eenige teekeningen liggen, en een daarbij staande leering, die Verw op het Palet tempert. Verrijkt met een aantal bijwerk. Het door een kozijn invallend licht doet een goed effect. Warm, overeenstemmend, uitvoerig en fiks geschilderd [Dans l'intérieur d'un Attelier rustique, est assis un Peintre devant son Chevalet, qui travaille, et qui a un chien couché auprés de lui. Sur le second plan, un Elève broie les couleurs, et un autre dans le fond arrange la Palette. Plusieurs accessoires Pittoresques enrichissent ce Tableau harmonieux et d'un ton piquant] | *Mat:* op paneel *Size:* Hoog 13 ¾, en breed 13 duim *Loc:* Amsterdam, Nederland. Rijksmuseum. (A298)	Gerrit van der Pot, Heer van Groeneveld	(Sold) fl 600 van Lennep [for] le Roi
808/06/13	AMSCH	0117	*Ostade (A. van)* | In een Boerenschuur ziet men op den voorgrond eenig Gereedschap, als Manden, een Vat, Steenen Doofpot, Koperen Ketel, enz. in het verschiet staat eene Vrouw eene Ketel te schuren. Bevallig van koloriet en fraai geschilderd | *Mat:* op paneel *Size:* hoog 18, breed 15 duim	R[oos]	(Bought In) fl 220
808/08/23	AMSCH	0121	*Ostade. (A. v.)* | In een Boeren Woning zitten twee Huislieden bij een Tafel, aan den Haarstede, waar bij een andere staande, zig met roken en drinken vermakende, de Karakters zijn natuurlijk; en van een bevallig penceel behandeling | *Annots:* egt maar geen beste soort (FLNY) *Mat:* op paneel *Size:* hoog 10, breed 9 duim	H	(Sold) fl 66 Spruit
808/09/13	HABRU	0065	*A. v. Ostade* | Een Boer, speelende op een Lier		(Unknown) fl 26
808/09/13	HABRU	0066	*A. v. Ostade* | Een Boer, houdende een Pijp in de hand		(Unknown) fl 3:5
809/04/17	AMSCH	0070	*A. van Ostade* | Een Boeren Binnenhuis met op de Kaartspeelende, rookende en drinkende Huislieden en verder Bijwerk; fiks | *Mat:* op paneel *Size:* hoog 14, breed 10 ½ duim	[Gruyter?]	(Sold) fl 14
809/04/22	AMYVR	0096	*A. van Ostade* | Eene Bejaarde Vrouw, over de Onderdeur liggende; krachtig | *Mat:* op paneel *Size:* hoog 11, breed 9 duim *Loc:* Philadelphia, PA, USA. Museum of Art. (E1924-3-71)	de Bruin	(Bought In) fl 59
809/04/22	AMYVR	0207	*A. van Ostade* | Twee stuks: een Boer en eene Boerin	de Bruin	(Sold) fl 2 Yver
809/07/19	AMSCH	0041	*Ostade (A van)* | In een Dorpgezicht voor eene Boeren Woning bij Geboomte, ziet men een Kwakzalver voor een Tent aan Huislieden en bij staande Kinderen zijn Geneesmiddelen aanprijzen. Dit stukje is geestig geordoneerd en van eene uitvoerige penceelsbehandeling | *Mat:* op paneel *Size:* hoog 10 ½, breed 8 ½ duim *Loc:* Amsterdam, Nederland. Rijksmuseum. (A 300)	[Bicker]	(Sold) fl 425 D Teengs
809/07/19	AMSCH	0042	*Ostade (A. van)* | Dit fraai Kabinetstukje, vertoont een Boeren Binnenhuis, in het midden zit een Huisman op een Bank, nevens hem zit eene Vrouw, houdende in de eene hand een Glas met Bier en in de andere een Tinnen Kan, die op een Vat geplaatst is, een Boer daar nevens schijnt zijn Viool te stellen en een ander zit bij een Haardstede. De karakters zijn natuurlijk, het koloriet is bevallig, alles is zeer uitvoerig gepenceeld | *Mat:* op paneel *Size:* hoog 12, breed 9 duim	[Bicker]	(Sold) fl 385 Josi
809/07/25	HGBSM	0002	*A. van Ostade* | Twee rookende Boertjes, waarvan een zyn Pyp aansteekt, in 't verschiet nog een paar Figuurtjes, op de voorgrond een Driestal waar op Tabak, Kan, &c; dit fraaije Cabinet Stukje is uitvoerig en delicaat Geschildert | *Mat:* op paneel *Size:* hoog 8 ½, breed 7 duim	D van der Aa [or] E B ten Dall	(Sold) fl 170 van Eijk
809/07/25	HGBSM	0003	*A. van Ostade* | Een diergelyk voorwerp als 't voorgaande, waarin een Mannetje met een Kan en Glas in handen, en een die zyn Pyp aansteekt, in 't verschiet schynt een Mannetje de deur in te komen; niet minder als de vorige, en hoog en breet als vooren, en kunnende dienen tot een weerga | *Size:* hoog 8 ½, breed 7 duim	D van der Aa [or] E B ten Dall	(Sold) fl 156 Teissier
809/09/06	AMSCH	0058	*Ostade (A. van)* | In een Huismans Woning zitten eenige Boeren zich met rooken en drinken te vermaken, voor aan zit eene Vrouw met een Kind, en verder eenige bijwerken; uitvoerig van penceelsbehandeling | *Mat:* op paneel *Size:* hoog 12 ½, breed 10 ½ duim	Johannes Caudri	(Sold) fl 405 Gruyter
809/09/06	AMSCH	0059	*Ostade (A. van)* | Een Boer die met smaak rookt, en een ander welke Tabak snijdt op een Tafel, waarbij een Glas Bier; niet minder als de voorgaande | *Mat:* op paneel *Size:* hoog 8, breed 6 ½ duim	Johannes Caudri	(Sold) fl 91 Hulswit
809/09/06	AMSCH	0060	*Ostade (A. van)* | In een Boere Woning ziet men mede een zoodanige Ordinantie van Beeldjes en bywerk | *Mat:* op paneel *Size:* hoog 14, breed 18 duim	Johannes Caudri	(Sold) fl 25 Roos
810/03/26	RMMUY	0014	*Adriaan van Ostade* | Door een open kozijn, ziet men een Boer, die een Pijp en de hand heeft, en schijnt te spreken. Van zijnen besten tijd. Krachtig breed en doorschijnend geschilderd [Un Paysan à la fenêtre	Daniel de Jongh Az	(Sold) fl 225 A van Beeftingh

			appuyant son coude, tenant une pipe á la main ; il paroit adresser la parole à quelqu'un. De son meilleur faire et d'un joli ton de couleur.] | *Mat:* op paneel *Size:* hoog 10, breed 8 ¼ duimen		
1810/05/22	AMSCH	0071	*Ostade. (A. van)* | Een vergenoegd Huisman in een Tuinhuis, zittende bij een Bank, houdende een Pijp in zijne Hand, nevens hem een ander met een Bierkan; uitvoerig behandeld | *Mat:* op paneel *Size:* hoog 7 ½, breed 6 ½ duim	Johannes van de Putte Nicolaasz.	(Sold) fl 11:10 van Iperen
1810/08/01	AMSCH	0069	*Ostade (Adriaan van)* | Het Binnengezigt van eene Boerenwoning. In het midden zit een vergenoegd Huisman, bij eene gedekte Tafel, nevens zijne Vrouw, welke een Kind op haren schoot houdt; op den voorgrond bij eene Bank staat een Jongen Pap te eeten, waar bij een Hond, verder eenig Huisraad, en achterwaarts drie andere lieden [Vue intérieure ou se trouve une Famille Villageoise. Au milieu se presente un Viellard joyeux auprès d'une Table couverte : sa Femme tenant un Enfant est à son coté. Sur le devant du Tableau est un jeune Garçon mangeant de la bouillie auprès d'un banc. D'autres figures vèrs le fond, et des ustenciles et accessoires terminent cet ensemble] | *Annots:* Bon et d'un agréable effet. (NGW) *Mat:* op paneel *Size:* hoog 18 ½, breed 16 duimen *Loc:* London, England, UK. Royal Collection (Buckingham Palace) Inv.1009.	Mr Pieter de Smeth van Alphen	(Sold) fl 5000 Lafontaine
1810/08/01	AMSCH	0070	*Ostade (Adriaan van)* | Eene bevallige Vischvrouw, staande voor hare Bank, waarop onderscheidene Visschen geplaatst zijn, voor dezelve een Jongen met eene Mand aan den arm, verder andere lieden, en een Dorp in het verschiet [Une gentille Poissoniere étalent de la marée sur le devant de sa Boutique ; un jeune Garçon ténant un panièr au bras se presente pour la marchander. D'autres figures et un Village dans la perspective achevent cette composition] | *Annots:* très bon et d'un admirable effet. acquis pour la Cabinet de DeWinter, par Mr. Roos. (NGW) *Mat:* op doek *Size:* hoog 13 ½, breed 15 ½ duimen *Loc:* Amsterdam, Nederland. Rijksmuseum. (A 3246)	Mr Pieter de Smeth van Alphen	(Sold) fl 3010 C S Roos
1810/08/01	AMSCH	0071	*Ostade (Adriaan van)* | Voor een Buitenhuis ziet men eenige staande en zittende Huislieden, waarbij eene Boerin met eene Kan in de hand, op den voorgrond eenige Hoenders [Audevant d'un Cabaret de Village sont rassemblés des Villageois, dont quelques uns sont assis ; la Hotesse s'y presente tenant une Canette de Bierre à la main ; l'avant plan étant garni de quelques Poules] | *Annots:* Bon et fort agréable. (NGW); Vente le Brun No. 107 fr 12001 (SMLN) *Mat:* op paneel *Size:* hoog 26, breed 23 duimen	Mr Pieter de Smeth van Alphen	(Sold) fl 4600 Texier, Gerbet en Comp [for] LeBrun
1810/08/01	AMSCH	0072	*Ostade (Adriaan van)* | Voor eene Herberg ziet men eene Kaatsbaan, waarop twee Boeren zich vermaken, en waar naar een ander ziet; op de voorgrond een zittende en rookende Boer en twee spelende Kinderen, op den tweeden grond een Bleekveld, en achterwaarts voor de Herberg vrolijke Huislieden [Vue sur l'extérieur d'un Cabaret de Village devant lequel se trouve un jeu de boule. On y voit deux Paysans occupés à jouer et un troisième comme spectateur. Sur l'avant scène est un rustre assis, et un autre fumant auprès de deux Enfans qui s'amusent. Devant la Maison on voit des Villageois qui se divertissent, et dans la perspective est une Blanchisserie] | *Annots:* très bon et capital. (NGW) *Mat:* op paneel *Size:* hoog 13, breed 18 duimen *Loc:* London, England, UK. Wellington Museum, Apsley House. (WM 1521–1948)	Mr Pieter de Smeth van Alphen	(Bought In) fl 1200
1810/08/10	RMRIJ	0010	*A. van Ostade* | In een Boeren Binnenhuis zijn eenige Vegtende Boeren en Boerinnen, de hartstogten zijn verwonderlijk, het licht en bruin, konstig en van eene uitvoerige en delicate behandeling | *Mat:* op paneel *Size:* hoog 14 ¾ duim, breed 20 ½ duim		(Sold) fl 8 [or] 35 v Dyk
1810/10/10	MGCIT	0056	*A. v. Ostade* | Een Stukje, zynde een Gezelschap van vrolijke en drinkende Boeren, alsmede spelende Kinderen; naïf geschilderd	Caspar van Citters	(Unknown)
1810/10/11	AMSCH	0064	*A. Van Ostade* | Een Boeren-Woning, waarin een Gezelschap van Mannen en Vrouwen, waarvan eenige dansen, waarbij een bevallig Meisje, houdende een Bierkan in de hand | *Mat:* op paneel *Size:* hoog 11, breed 19 duimen	C	(Bought In) fl 5:5

Ostade, Adriaen van (and Decker, C.)

1801/04/13	AMSCH	0018	*C. Decker; A. van Ostade* | In een Binnevertrek ziet men een Weefgetouw, ter zyde het zelve zit een Boer een pyp te roken, daar by een Vrouw met een Kind op de schoot, terwyl een ander aan de broodkast staat, een Hond en een menigte boere Meubelen maken dit tot een bevallig schildery; het geen zonachtig en meesterlyk behandeld is | *Mat:* op paneel *Size:* hoog 18, breed 22 duim *Loc:* Bruxelles, Belgique. Musées Royaux des Beaux Arts. (inv. 3061) as C.G. Decker	Pierre Fouquet, junior	(Sold) fl 860 Yver
1809/04/17	AMSCH	0024	*C. Dekker; A. van Ostade* | Een kapitaal boschagtig Landschap, op de voorgrond met een helder Spiegelend Water, gestoffeerd met gaande Reizigers en Visschers in hunne Schuiten; helder en zonagtig behandeld, door denzelven [C. Dekker], gestoffeerd door A. van Ostade | *Mat:* op paneel *Size:* hoog 21 ½, breed 17 duim	[Gruyter?]	(Sold) fl 18 Spaan

Ostade, Adriaen van (or Ostade, A., manner)

1801/03/16	AMSCH	0107	*A. van Ostade* | Een Wapensmedery in 't graaw [sic], door of in de manier van A. van Ostade	K[ip]	(Sold) fl 21 Koopmar

1801/05/11	AMSCH	0064	*A. van Ostade, of in de manier* | Een Buitenhuis voor dezelven, ziet men een Lierman, waar by een menigte Huislieden, krachtig en meesterlyk behandeld | *Mat:* op doek *Size:* hoog 14, breed 17 duim	P[ruyssenaar]	(Sold) fl 21 Schimmelpenning
1807/06/10	HGBSM	0181	*A. van Ostade* | Een Boer die over een onder deur legt met een brandende kaars in de hand, achter hem een ander, door of in de manier van A. van Ostade | *Mat:* op paneel *Size:* hoog 9, breed 9 ½ duim	Abraham Delfos [or others]	(Sold) fl 1:8 V Giese

Ostade, Adriaen van (copy after)

1801/03/16	AMSCH	0038	*A. van Ostade* | Een Boeren Buitenhuis, met verscheide Beelden na A. van Ostade	S[chley]	(Sold) fl 2:5 Van Iperen
1801/03/16	AMSCH	0048	*A. van Ostade* | Twee Boere op het Veerkerbord [sic] speelende, waarnaa [sic] een andere staat te kyken, krachtig behandeld, naar A. van Ostade | *Notes:* This lot was sold with lot 49 by an anonymous artist.	Z	(Sold) fl 23 for lots 48 & 49. Stevens
1801/03/16	AMSCH	0142	*A. van Ostade* | Een gestoffeerd Dorpgezicht, na A. van Ostade	K[ip]	(Sold) fl 0:6 van Iperen
1801/03/16	AMSCH	0165	*A. van Ostade* | Het Boere-bal, zynde een ryke Ordonantie, fraai geschilderd naar A. van Ostade	K[ip]	(Sold) fl 9 Koopman
1802/07/27	AKHRK	0080	*Na A. Ostade* | De bekende Liereman met zijn Jongen, speelende op de Fiöol, en de Aanschouwers &c. | *Mat:* op paneel *Size:* hoog 15 ½, breed 12 ½ duim	Maria Stategaart	(Sold) fl 5:10 Beer
1802/08/24	LNDLS	0150	*A. v. Ostade* | Een zittend Vrouwtje met een Kind op haar schoot, na A. v. Ostade	Leonardus Bouman [or others]	(Unknown) fl 3:2
1802/08/24	LNDLS	0151	*A. v. Ostade* | Een Boeren – kermis met veel Beeldjes, na A. v. Ostade	Leonardus Bouman [or others]	(Unknown) fl 3:15
1802/09/06	AMSCH	0238	*A. van Ostade* | In een Buitenhuis ziet men een ménigte Huislieden, zich met Dansen en zingen vermaken; natuurlyk na A. van Ostade | *Mat:* op doek *Size:* hoog 37, breed 34 duim	J	(Bought In) fl 15
1802/11/01	DOBRA	0027	*A. van Ostade* | Een Boeren-binnenhuisje, met verkeerbord-speelers, enz. naar A. van Ostade | *Notes:* This lot was sold with lot 41 by an anonymous artist.	Paulus van der Spyk [or others]	(Sold) fl 1:15 for lots 27 & 41. J v Steegh
1802/12/13	AMSCH	0098	*J. Lauwers; A. van Ostade* | Een zittend vergenoegd Boertje, in een Binnehuis, houdende in de regter Hand een Pyp, en met de linker, rustende op zyn Hoed, die op zyn Knie voor hem legt, het caracter is natuurlyk; de penceelbehandeling bevallig, naar een Schildery, van A. van Ostade, door J. Lauwers | copy by J.J. Lauwers after A. Ostade *Mat:* op paneel *Size:* hoog 6 ½, breed 15 [duim]	Schley [for] Lauwers	(Sold) fl 11:10 Frantze
1803/04/20	AMSCH	0106	*A. van Ostade* | Twee stuks, de eene verbeeld een Regtsgeleerde, in zyn Studeervertrek, hy schynt met aandagt een Brief te leezen, die hy in de hand houd, verder verscheide bywerk; den anderen vertoont een Doctor, zittende in zyn Kamer, houdende een Urinaal in de hand, ter zyde staat een Tafel met een Tapytkleedje bedekt, waarop Boeken en ander bywerk; bevallig en uitvoerig behandeld, naar A. van Ostade [Deux petits Sujets, l'un étant un Avocat dans son etudé [sic] ; l'autre est un Medecin examinant un urinal : tous deux sont ornés de beaucoup d'accessoires, & imitent très bien la maniere d'A. van Ostade.] | *Mat:* op paneel *Size:* ieder hoog 11 ½, breed 10 duim	Maria Magdalena van Sluypwyk, gravinne van Moens	(Sold) fl 20 Coclers
1804/04/28	LNDLS	0058	*A. van Ostade* | Een Doctor, zittende in zyn studeerkamer, by een tafel met boeken, hy beschouwd het water, dat hy in een urinaal in zyn hand houd. Een Weêrga, verbeeldende een lezende Philosoof, nevens een tafel met boeken en papieren, en meer bywerk, na A. van Ostade, twee stuks	[Abraham Delfos] [or others]	(Sold) fl 4:2 van Giesen
1804/10/16	DLOND	0240a[a]	*C. Vermeulen; Adrien v. Ostade* | Een Stuk, bevattende 13 zeer schone Copiën van de volgende Meesters. Un Tableau, contenant 13 Copies très-belles des Peintres suivans. 1. Adrien v. Ostade. Een Herberg, Auberge | copy by Corn. Vermeulen (III) after A. Ostade *Mat:* op paneel *Size:* hoog 41, breed 55 *Notes:* The description in the title refers to lots 240a[a-m].		(Sold) fl 150 for lots 240a[a-m]. Ond d Wyngaert
1805/12/16	AMSCH	0111	*A. van Ostade* | Een Boer, met een Pyp, en Kan door een Vengster ziende; op Paneel, naar A. van Ostade | *Mat:* op paneel	R[oos]	(Sold) fl 1:5 du Pree
1806/05/05	AMSCH	0047	*van Dorne de Oude; A. van Ostade* | Een bevallig Boere Binnenhuis met een zittende rookende Boer, en divers bywerk; meesterlyk na A. van Ostade | copy by M. Dorne after A. Ostade *Mat:* op doek *Size:* hoog 12 ½, breed 11 duim	L	(Sold) fl 6 van Iperen
1806/11/24	AMSCH	0036	*Jaght (M. van der); A. v. Ostade* | Een Boeren Binnenhuis, gestoffeert men Mans, Vrouw, en Kinderen, zich met eeten en drinken vermaakende; verders vertoont zig verscheide Huisraad; alles uitvoerig behandeld naar A. v. Ostade | copy by M. Jagt after A. Ostade *Mat:* op paneel *Size:* hoog 11, breed 9 duim	Munnikhuizen	(Sold) fl 14 du Pree
806/11/24	AMSCH	0090	*A. van Ostade* | Een Boere gezelschap; naar A. van Ostade	Munnikhuizen	(Sold) fl 0:14 L Pakker
807/08/26	AMSCH	0165	*A. v. Ostade* | In een Huismanswoning ziet men eenige Huislieden zich met drinken en rooken vermaken; geestig op Paneel, na A. v. Ostade | *Mat:* op paneel *Size:* hoog 13, breed 16 duim	Roos	(Sold) fl 41 C Sardet
808/08/23	AMSCH	0258	*A. van Ostade* | Een Boeren Binnenhuis, waar in verscheide Lieden zig met dansen, zingen en speelen vermaaken; zijnde een Copij naar een der beroemde Schilderije van A. van Ostade	J	(Sold) fl 12:10 Dupré

1809/04/17	AMSCH	0132	*A. van Ostade* | Een Boeren Binnenhuis, waar in verscheide Huislieden zig met danzen, zingen en speelen vermaaken; zijnde een Copij naar een der beroemde Schilderijen van A. van Ostade en geestig en fiks geschilderd	Y	(Sold or Bought In) fl 8:10
1809/04/22	AMYVR	0162	*A. van Ostade* | Een Boer en Boerin; naar A. van Ostade	de Bruin	(Sold) fl 0:12 du Pree
1809/04/22	AMYVR	0200	*A. van Ostade* | Twee met Beeldjes; naar A. van Ostade	de Bruin	(Sold) fl 4:5 du Pree
			Ostade, Adriaen van (manner)		
1801/03/16	AMSCH	0210	*A. van Ostade* | Een Boeren Binnenhuis, in de manier van A. van Ostade	P[ruyssenaar]	(Sold) fl 2:5 van Iperen
1801/12/22	AMOTT	0009	*A. van Ostade* | Het Boertje met de Pyp, voor een venster, als vooren [A. van Ostade]	Bartholomeus Ruloffs	(Unknown) fl 1
1802/12/13	AMSCH	0131	*A. van Ostade* | Voor een Boere Huis, ziet men eenige Boeren zich met speelen en drinken vermaken; ter zyden een Landschap en een Boomryk verschiet, schoon van effect en meesterachtig geschilderd; als A. van Ostade | *Size:* hoog 21, breed 17 duim	Pruyssenaar [for] A	(Sold) fl 3 Yver
1804/04/28	LNDLS	0056	*A. van Ostade* | Een Kwakzalver, staande by zyn tent, benevens eenige aanschouwers in een landschap als van A. van Ostade	[Abraham Delfos] [or others]	(Sold) fl 2:2 Richters [for] G
1805/07/03	AMSCH	0178	*A. van Ostade* | In een Huismans Gemeubileerde Woning, ziet men eenige Boeren zitten by een Haardsteede, zig met rooken en drinken vermakende, verder staan twee anderen by een oude Vrouw, het is bevallig van licht en schildering, in de manier van A. van Ostade | *Mat:* op doek	R[oos]	(Sold) fl 146 Gruyter
1805/10/09	HGBSM	0063	*A. van Ostade* | Een boertje in een landschap, in de manier van A. van Ostade | *Mat:* op paneel *Size:* hoog 6 ½ breet 5 ½ duim	T H van Willigen [or others]	(Sold) fl 1:2 Kerber
1809/04/17	AMSCH	0176	*A. van Ostade* | Een Binnenhuis, met twee Boeren en een Boerin, in de manier van A. van Ostade	H	(Sold) fl 3:5
1809/04/22	AMYVR	0097	*A. van Ostade* | Een Boer, met een Kan en Pijp in de handen, ligt uit een Venster te kijken; geestig in de manier van denzelven [A. van Ostade] | *Mat:* op paneel *Size:* hoog 9, breed 7 duim	de Bruin	(Sold) fl 0:14 du Pree
1809/04/22	AMYVR	0208	*A. van Ostade* | Een als voren [een Boer en eene Boerin]; als denzelven [A. van Ostade]	de Bruin	(Sold) fl 1:5 du Pree
1809/06/13	AMSCH	0183	*A. van Ostade* | Twee stuks, een Boer en Boerin, als A. van Ostade	Y	(Sold) fl 1:5 de Gruiter
1810/05/22	AMSCH	0132	*A. van Ostade* | In een Boeren Herberg, zitten twee Lieden met de Kaart te speelen, waarbij een vergenoegd Man, die zijn Pijp aansteekt en eene Vrouw met een Bierkan in de hand; op Paneel, als A. van Ostade | *Mat:* op paneel	R	(Sold) fl 4 T Spaan
1810/05/22	AMSCH	0154	*A. van Ostade* | Een Boertje halver lijf; fiks geschilderd, als door A. van Ostade | *Notes:* This lot was sold with lot 153 by J. Glauber.	F	(Sold) fl 1:5 for lots 153 & 154. Geld
1810/06/20	AMSCH	0190	*A. van Ostade* | Twee stuke Herbergen, met danssende en andere Boeren en Boerinnen; in de manier van A. van Ostade	A	(Sold) fl 1:15 du Pree
			Ostade, Isack van		
1801/02/18	AMBOS	0005	*J. Ostade* | Een Schuur, in dezelfde hangt een geslagt Varken, verder eenige Beeldjes en verder Bywerk, alles fraai en zeer natuurlyk geschilderd	J Schonevelt	(Unknown)
1801/02/18	AMBOS	0022	*J. Ostade* | Een Boeren Binnenhuis, fix geschilderd	J Schonevelt	(Unknown)
1801/03/16	AMSCH	0184	*J. van Ostade* | Een Binnenhuis, met vrolyke drinkende Boeren en een Boerin, fiks en meesterlyk geschilderd op paneel | *Mat:* op paneel	K[ip]	(Sold) fl 1:5 Veldwijk
1801/06/13	LNDLS	0002	*Izaak van Ostade* | Een capitaal Schilderij, verbeeldende een Landschap met geboomte en wooningen, bij een Herberg, daar een boeren wagen met paarden voor een kribbe staan, terwijl een vrouwtje door een man daar af geholpen wordt, en een heer die met een jongeling schijnt te spreeken; een die met een Kan in zijn hand nevens den Hospes en zijn vrouw zit; op den voorgrond een hoogte, daar een boerin met melk – emmers, en een jongetje nevens haar, over eene hoogte gaat, alles tegen een helder bewolkte lucht; voor hetzelve, een man die water uit een beek schept, en meer beelden en beesten. Dit Stuk is uitmuntend konstig, kragtig, helder van couleur en uitvoerig op paneel geschilderd, en een der beste van Izaak van Ostade 1645 | *Mat:* op paneel *Size:* hoog 33 ½, breed 31 duimen *Inscr:* Izaak van Ostade 1645 (signed and dated?) *Notes:* It is unclear whether the name and date are inscribed on the painting.	D van R	(Sold) fl 1725 A Delfos
1801/12/22	AMOTT	0036	*J. van Ostade* | Het Varken op de Leer, in de Boere Winkel	Bartholomeus Ruloffs	(Unknown) fl 21
1802/05/05	AMSCH	0158	*J. van Ostade* | Een Boere Schoolmeester, onderwyzende eenige Kinderen, zynde een bevallige Ordonnantie en meesterlyk gepenceeld | *Mat:* op doek *Size:* hoog 10, breed 12 duim	D	(Sold) fl 42 Rigters
1802/05/05	AMSCH	0160	*J. van Ostade* | Een Boeren Binnenhuis met eenige Huislieden, nevens toepasselyk Bywerk, fiks gepenceeld | *Mat:* op paneel *Size:* hoog 21, breed 25 duim	E	(Sold) fl 15:10 Mensard
1802/06/28	AMSCH	0137	*J. van Ostade* | Twee vegtende Boeren, in een binnehuis, waarby een Vrouw, die een derzelve tegen houd; fiks geschildert, door J. van Ostade | *Mat:* op paneel *Size:* hoog 8, breed 10 duim	Anna Elink	(Sold) fl 4:10 Texier

1802/08/24	LNDLS	0002	*J. van Ostade* | Voor een Buiten-huis ziet men een Boeren Kermis, met eene menigte vrolijke Boeren en Boerinnen, die dansen, spelen en verkopen, verder een Dorp, met Kramen en Kerktoren, uitvoerig op paneel geschilderd | *Mat:* op paneel *Size:* hoog 20, breed 30 duimen	Leonardus Bouman [or others]	(Unknown) fl 40
1802/09/06	AMSCH	0089	*J. van Ostade* | In een Dorpgezicht, met verscheide wooningen en geboomten, ziet men voor een Boeren Plysterplaats een wagen, waarop een Heer en Juffrouw zittende, die door den Hospes een kan bier ontfangt, terwyl de Voerman de paarden laat drinken; ter zyde op de voorgrond zyn rustende huislieden die hun pyp rooken, en andere ryzende; natuurlyk en plaisant geschilderd | *Mat:* op doek *Size:* hoog 24, breed 37 duim	Brave	(Sold) fl 54 W Reijers
1802/09/06	AMSCH	0090	*J. van Ostade* | In een Huismanswooning ziet men een bedaagde Vrouw bezig boter te karnen, verzelt van een Jongeling; op de voorgrond legt Kool, Wortelen, Raapen en andere Groentens, kopere Keetel, Potten en ander huisraat; natuurlyk geschilderd | *Mat:* op paneel *Size:* hoog 14, breed 12 duim	Brave	(Bought In) fl 12
1802/09/21	UTHDG	0071	*J. van Ostade* | Van den weg langs een Boerenwerf en Huizing, rijd een Voerman met Paard en Slede de bevroozen Rivier op, een Slede met een wit Paard bespannen, schijnt te zullen volgen, waarbij Boeren, zich gereed maakende tot Schaatsrijden; vooraan en in het verschiet anderen, op het ijs. Alles bij Maanlicht, excellent geschildert | *Mat:* op doek *Size:* hoog 19, breed 23 duimen		(Bought In) fl 49
1803/09/07	AMSCH	0120	*J. van Ostade* | Voor een Boere Herberg staat een Bedelaar op de Fluit te speelen voor eenige Boeren, ter zyde een Hond, en een menigte andere stoffagie, van Krebben, Manden en Tobbes, alles is zeer schoon en aangenaam van Coloriet [Un hotellerie de village, devant laquelle un mendiant joue de la flute au milieu d'un groupe de paysans ; on voit a côté un chien, des chreches [sic], des paniers, des cuves etc. ; l'ensemble est d'une belle ordonnance, les détails bien soignés et d'un coloris très agréable] | *Mat:* op paneel *Size:* hoog 23, breed 18 duim	Smidt	(Bought In) fl 250
1803/09/07	AMSCH	0121	*J. van Ostade* | Een Boeren Dorp, op de voorgrond gestoffeerd met een Boeren Wagen, waar voor een wit Paard; een ménigte Huislieden, Varkens, Bokjes en andere stoffagie, vercieren dit warm geschilderd stukje [Un village ; sur le devant une charette attelée d'un cheval blanc, plusieurs villageois, des cochons, des chevres et d'autres objets décorent la composition agréable de ce tableau. Le coloris en est d'ailleurs chaud et d'un bon effet] | *Mat:* op paneel *Size:* hoog 15, br.21 duim	Smidt	(Bought In) fl 45
1803/12/15	MGLAC	0019	*J. Ostade* | Een Boere Binnenvertrek, waar in een Vrouw zit te spinnen, met nog andere Figuuren en verder Bywerk; alles even kragtig en natuurlyk geschilderd | *Mat:* op paneel *Size:* hoog duim 16, breed duim 21	Mr L H de Haze Bomme	(Unknown)
1804/10/08	RMCNL	0067	*J. Ostade* | Een buite Huis	A t'Hooft	(Unknown)
1805/07/03	AMSCH	0124	*J. van Ostade* | Voor een Boerewoning staat een oud Man op de Lier te speelen, waarnaar eenige Huislieden en Kinderen schynen te luisteren; geestig gegroept en meesterlyk op Paneel geschilderd | *Mat:* op paneel *Size:* hoog 15, breed 19 duim	C	(Sold) fl 25 L Pakker
1805/07/03	AMSCH	0125	*J. van Ostade* | Een Ordinantie van gelyken Voorwerpen; niet minder als de voorgaande | *Mat:* op paneel *Size:* hoog 19, breed 25 duim	C	(Sold) fl 75 Agina
1806/08/13	AMSCH	0137	*Ostade. (J. van)* | In een Boeren Schuur, zitten eenige Huislieden, zoo Mans als Vrouwen en Kinderen, zich met rooken en drinken vermakende; gestoffeert met verder bywerk, meesterlyk behandeld | *Mat:* op paneel *Size:* hoog 17, breed 23 duim	Roos	(Sold) fl 8:15 Boelen
1806/08/13	AMSCH	0138	*Ostade. (J. van)* | In een Binnehuis zit een Boeren Schoolmeester, met verscheide Leerlingen, een derzelve krygt een plak; in alles als de vorige behandeld | *Mat:* op paneel *Size:* hoog 13, breed 16 duim	Roos	(Sold) fl 5:5 du Pre
1807/06/10	HGBSM	0089	*J. van Ostade* | Voor een Boeren Buitenhuis, staat een Kar met een wit Paard bespannen, daar twee Boeren een vat op laaden, verder meer bijwerk en figuren, helder en kragtig | *Mat:* op paneel *Size:* hoog 14 ½, breed 21 duim	Abraham Delfos [or others]	(Sold) fl 19 Tessier
1807/08/26	AMSCH	0164	*J. v. Ostade* | In een Boeren Binnenhuis ziet men vrolyken Landlieden, Mans, Vrouw en Kinderen, zig met zingen en drinken vermaken; geestig van Ordonnantie en fiks | *Mat:* op paneel *Size:* hoog 12, breed 17 duim	Helsdinge	(Sold) fl 4 C Metz
1808/04/26	GDAN	0119	*Ostade (J. van)* | Een Binnenhuis, waar in een Varken op een Ladder, voorts eenige Kinderen zich met het opblazen der Blaas vermakende | *Size:* hoog 15, breed 19 ½ duim	G H Fortuyn	(Unknown)
1808/04/26	GDAN	0120	*Ostade (J. van)* | Een Buitenhuis, verbeeldende een Boere Kermis, op de voorgrond een Liereman, spelende op de Lier, aan een band deszelfs Spaansch Hondje houdende, met een aantal Kinderen en oude Lieden, die na het speelen met veel oplettenheid luisteren, voorts een Man die op een verhevenheid staat, mogelijk een Kwakzalver, waar bij ook een groot aantal Menschen, voorts ziet men Kramen daar wat gebakken wordt en koek gehakt, in 't verschiet een Boere Dorp, alles pragtig en uitvoerig gedaan, tot eer van den maker | *Size:* hoog 14, breed 23 duim	G H Fortuyn	(Unknown)
808/04/26	GDAN	0121	*Ostade (J. van)* | Een Boomrijk Landschap, waar in een Boere Herberg, op de voorgrond een Vrouwspersoon Water puttende, voor Paarden die men te drinken geeft, op 't midden van 't stuk eenige Passagiers te Paard,	G H Fortuyn	(Unknown)

			die wat tot verversching schijnen te nemen, op de tweede grond ziet men een Boer op een Kar ryden, komende van de hoogte, voorts ziet men in 't verschiet eenige Boere Wooningen, en een Dorp, alles zonägtig en kragtig geschilderd | *Size:* hoog 18 ½, breed 39 duim		
1808/05/17	LNAN	0001	*J. van Ostade* | Een capitaal en vorstelijk Schilderij, verbeeldende een uitgestrekt-Winter gezigt; ter regterzijde op den voorgrond gaat eene vrouw en jongeling langs een' weg, nevens denzelven een bevrozen water daar een man zijn schaatsen aanbindt, een ander die daar naar schijnt te wachten, en een slee met een biervat, die door een' jonge voortgetrokken en door een ander voortgeduuwd [sic] wordt; daar achter een hooge weg, met een wagen met stroo, voortgetrokken door een wit en zwart paard, en die door een' man bestuurd wordt, langs boere woningen; ter linkerzijde een gezigt op een Dorp, met veel paarden, sleden en volk op het bevrozen water, en een aangenaam verschiet, alles uitmuntend en krachtig, op doek geschilderd, en een der beste stukken | *Mat:* op doek *Size:* hoog 48, breed 58 duim *Loc:* Paris, France. Musée du Louvre. (inv. 1689)		(Sold) fl 860 Nieuwenhuis
1808/06/06	RMRIJ	0097	*Ostade. (Isaac van)* | Een Boeren Binnenhuis, waarin verscheidene figuren. Aangenaam van licht, breed en meesterlijk geschilderd [L'Intérieur d'une Chaumière, où plusieurs Personnes sont occupées. D'un bon effet, et peint en Maître] | *Annots:* Verk in 1782 (f. 7.-) (RMA I); NB Copie (SMLN) *Mat:* op paneel *Size:* Hoog 11 ¼, en breed 10 ¼ duim	Gerrit van der Pot, Heer van Groeneveld	(Sold) fl 40 Dr Luchtmans
1808/06/06	RMRIJ	0098	*Ostade. (Isaac van)* | Een lagchenden Boer, eene aarden kan in de handen houdende. Breed en meesterlijk geschilderd [Un Paysan tient, d'un air content, une Cruche entre ses mains. D'une touche savante et hardie] | *Mat:* op paneel *Size:* Hoog 6 ¼, en breed 5 ¼ duim *Loc:* Amsterdam, Nederland. Rijksmuseum. (A302) as A. Ostade	Gerrit van der Pot, Heer van Groeneveld	(Sold) fl 36 J M Jorissen [for] le Roi
1808/08/23	AMSCH	0122	*Ostade. (J. v.)* | Voor een Huisman Woning staat een Lierman, verzelt van verscheide Boeren Kinderen, ter zijde een zittende Landman, en een ander ligt over zijn Deur; het is bevallig en natuurlijk gepenceeld | *Mat:* op paneel *Size:* hoog 12, breed 9 duim	Z	(Sold) fl 20 Spruit
1808/08/23	AMSCH	0123	*Ostade. (J. v.)* | In een Boeren Schuur, zit eene Vrouw met een Weverspoel in de hand, als sprekende tegens een bedaagd man, verder gestoffeerd met Boeren gereedschap; fiks op paneel behandeld | *Mat:* op paneel *Fmt:* rond	Z	(Sold) fl 3 J Spaan
1808/09/13	HABRU	0067	*J. v. Ostade* | Een Boere Schuur, van binnen en gestoffeerd		(Unknown) fl 15:10
1808/09/13	HABRU	0068	*J. v. Ostade* | Een Binnenhuis, met vrolijke, drinkende en rokende Boeren		(Unknown) fl 4
1808/09/13	HABRU	0069	*J. v. Ostade* | Een dito [Binnenhuis]		(Unknown) fl 3:15
1808/09/13	HABRU	0070	*J. v. Ostade* | Een dito [Binnenhuis]		(Unknown) fl 5
1808/09/13	HABRU	0071	*J. v. Ostade* | Een dito [Binnenhuis], met dito [vrolijke, drinkende en rokende Boeren]		(Unknown) fl 1:8
1808/12/31	RMHSN	0001	*Izaac van Ostade* | Een fraaije Winter met Schaatse Ryders, vol Gewoel, met Paarden en Sleden, uitvoerig door Izaac van Ostade, 1644 | *Mat:* op paneel *Inscr:* Izaac van Ostade, 1644 (signed and dated?) *Notes:* It is unclear whether the name and date are inscribed on the painting.	G Spanjaart [or] H de Haas [or] C van der Looy Lans	(Unknown)
1809/04/17	AMSCH	0071	*J. van Ostade* | In een Boeren Schuur ziet men eene bedaagde Vrouw bij een Waterpomp, verder eenige Gereedschappen; fiks geschilderd | *Mat:* op paneel *Size:* hoog 14, breed 11 duim	T	(Sold) fl 1:5 Gruyter
1809/04/22	AMYVR	0098	*J. van Ostade* | Een Slagers Winkel, alwaar een geslagte Os aan den Balk hangt; meesterlijk | *Mat:* op paneel *Size:* hoog 19, breed 14 duim	de Bruin	(Sold) fl 5 du Pree
1809/05/26	HADAA	0045	*J. van Ostade* | Een Binnenhuisje met Boeren	Mejuffrouw de Wed David Heemskerk [or others]	(Unknown)
1809/06/13	AMSCH	0121	*J. van Ostade* | Een Schoorsteenvéger in een Landschap | *Mat:* op paneel *Size:* hoog 6, breed 5 duim	E	(Sold) fl 1:15 Boelhouwer
1809/07/25	HGBSM	0144	*Isac v. Ostade* | Een Boerdery aan een Water, met een Houtebrug met Stoffage, gemerkt Isac v. Ostade | *Mat:* op doek *Size:* hoog 16 en een half, breed 23 en een half duim *Inscr:* Isac v. Ostade (signed)	D van der Aa [or] E B ten Dall	(Sold) fl 18:10 van Eyk
1809/07/25	HGBSM	0261	*J. van Ostade* | Een Boeren-Stulp van binnen, met zingende Boeren en Boerinnen | *Mat:* op paneel *Size:* hoog 11, breed 12 duim	D van der Aa [or] E B ten Dall	(Sold) fl 3 van der Burgh
1810/03/23	HAVIN	0009	*J. van Ostade* | Een Binnenhuis, alwaar eenige Boeren bij het Vuur zitten en een Vrouw bij een derzelve staat te praten, extra natuurlijk en fraai | *Size:* hoog 16 breet 14 d.	Rudolf Hendrik de Wetstein [or others]	(Unknown) fl 190
1810/05/22	AMSCH	0072	*Ostade. (J. van)* | Voor een Buitenhuis zitten vier vrolijke Boeren, zich met speelen en drinken vermakende; fiks gepenceeld | *Mat:* op paneel *Size:* hoog 15, breed 12 duim	T	(Sold) fl 1 Levy Pakker
1810/06/20	AMSCH	0071	*Izaak Ostade* | Een Boeren Binnenhuis, met op de Kaartspelende, rookende en drinkende Huislieden, en verder bijwerk; fiks op paneel | *Mat:* op paneel *Size:* hoog 14, breed 20 ½ duimen	B	(Sold) fl 4:5 van Iperen
1810/07/23	DOLG1	0041	*Isaäk van Ostade* | In een Boerenwoning vertoont zich een geslagt Varken aan een ladder; waar bij een Vrouw, bezig met het schoonmaken der Darmen. Voords een Kind, Hond, en verder bijwerk. Alles natuurlijk, kragtig en helder | *Mat:* op paneel *Size:* hoog 27, breed 21 duim	Mr Pieter van den Santheuvel	(Sold) fl 85 A van Strij

1810/08/01	AMSCH	0073	*Ostade (Izaak van)* | Op eene sterk bevrozene Rivier ziet men, langs eenen Dijk, Woningen en Geboomte; Schaatsrijders, Arresleden, Paarden en andere voorwerpen [Representation en Hyver d'une Riviere gelée, bordée d'une Digue garnie de Maisons et d'Arbres ; on y voit des Patineurs, des Traineaux, des Chevaux et d'autres figures et accessoires] | *Annots:* un peu trop maigre et usé. (NGW) *Mat:* op doek *Size:* hoog 42, breed 57 duimen	Mr Pieter de Smeth van Alphen	(Sold) fl 520 H Koopman te Utrecht
1810/08/01	AMSCH	0074	*Ostade (Izaak van)* | Een heuvelachtig Landschap, gestoffeerd met Boeren, Boerinnen en Kinderen, benevens Vrachtwagens, Paarden en Schapen, achterwaarts eene Herberg bij geboomte [Paysage dont le point de vue donne sur une eminance légere, orné de Paysans et de Paysanes avec leurs Enfants ; on y remarque des Chariots chargés, des Chevaux et des Moutons. Dans l'éloignement est un Cabaret auprès d'un massif d'arbres] | *Annots:* très bon, mais beaucoup trop cher. (NGW); Vente le Brun No. 109 fr 13000 (SMLN); Coll. M. LeBrun no. 109–1845, Rome. Galerie du Cardinal Fesch, no. 173, p. 181 (VAL I) *Mat:* op paneel *Size:* hoog 28, breed 36 duimen	Mr Pieter de Smeth van Alphen	(Sold) fl 5050 Texier, Gerbet en Comp [for] LeBrun
1810/08/06	AMSCH	0085	*Ostade (J. van)* | Een Boeren Binnenhaard, waar in verscheiden vrolijke Lieden, welke zich op onderscheidene wijze vermaken, verder een liggende Hond en eenige Huisraad; geestig geordoneerd en fiks behandeld | *Mat:* op paneel *Size:* hoog 18, breed 21 duimen	C	(Sold) fl 60 Pot
1810/10/10	MGCIT	0119	*J. Ostade* | Een Stuk met vrolyke Boertjes; aardig bewerkt	Caspar van Citters	(Unknown)
1810/10/11	AMSCH	0065	*J. V. Ostade* | In een Dorpgezigt, voor een Plijsterplaats, staat een Ledige Postwagen, waarbij twee ontspannen Paarden, de Voerman schijnt uit een Kan te drinken, waarbij de Hospes, verzeld van twee Kinderen, voor de Woning ter zijde twee Huislieden, die een Kar laden, daar nevens een te Paard, en op de grond rust eene Vrouw, met een Kind op den schoot, verder ter zijde een Dorpskerk en andere Woningen, gestoffeerd met verscheide bijwerk; de Ordonnantie is geestig, en van eene meesterlijke penseelbehandeling | *Mat:* op doek *Size:* hoog 34, breed 46 duimen	S	(Bought In) fl 130

Ostade, Isack van (and Neer, A.)

1804/08/08	AMSCH	0146	*J. van Ostade; A. van der Neer* | In een Dorpgezicht ziet men op de voorgrond ter eene zyde een Kar, waarvoor een wit en een bruin Paard gespannen is, waarby eenige Kippen en een Haan, en ter andere zyde twee Huislieden, waarvan de eene is gezéeten op een Houten Bank, en houdende een Hond onder den Arm, en de andere op een Ton, houdende meede een Hond by de Halsband, schynende zylieden over dezelve te spreeken, iets achterwaards by eenige Boerenwoningen een Kerktooren, en een helder spiegelende Rivier, ziet men drie Boeren en een Boerin, verders eenige Wooningen en Geboomte, en een bevallig verschiet; dit stuk is piquant van licht, enuitmuntend [sic] gepenceeld, door J. van Ostade en A. van der Neer | *Mat:* op paneel *Size:* hoog 24, breed 18 duim	Vink[eles] [for] W	(Sold) fl 150 C S Roos

Ostade, Isack van (or Ostade, I., copy after)

1803/09/07	AMSCH	0122	*J. van Ostade* | Een geslagte Os, aan een Balk hangende, in een Binnenhuis, voorts een Man op een Bank, en een Vrouw by het Vuur staande, alles na de Natuur gevolgd, door of na denzelven [J. van Ostade] [Un boeuf tué, suspendu dans l'intérieur d'une maison ; sur le devant un homme assis sur un banc et un femme debout près du feu ; le tout d'après nature] | *Mat:* op paneel *Size:* hoog 14, breed 12 duim	Smidt	(Sold) fl 16:10 Gruiter

Ostade, Isack van (or Ostade, I., manner)

1802/09/18	RMDRS	0015	*J. van Ostade* | Een vrolyk Gezelschap, vol gewoel van speelende en drinkende Boeren en Boerinnen, door of in de manier van J. van Ostade | *Size:* hoog 20, breed 28 ½ duim	Casper de Haas	(Sold) fl 41 Gruiter
1808/06/11	RMRIJ	0035	*J: van Ostade, of in zyn manier* | Een Boeren Vreugd, met een aantal Boeren en Boerinnen, verder veel Bywerk | *Mat:* op paneel *Size:* hoog 22 ½, breed 33 ½ duim		(Sold) fl 12:5 V Giesen

Ostade, Isack van (copy after)

1806/08/13	AMSCH	0268	*J. van Ostade* | Vyf stuks, verbeeldende de vyf Zinnen, zynde Gezelschappen van Boeren en Boerinen, in Binnehuizen; op Paneel geschilderd, naar J. van Ostade | *Mat:* op paneel	Roos	(Sold) fl 10 Rijnbergh

Ostade, Isack van (manner)

1801/08/19	AMSCH	0173	*Isaak van Ostade* | Vyf stuks Binnenhuizen met Boertjes, als Isaak van Ostade	Pruyssen[r] [for] Q	(Sold) fl 3:15 Wed Achtienhoven
1802/05/05	AMSCH	0159	*J. van Ostade* | Een Binnehuis met speelende en drinkende Boeren en Boerinnen, in de manier van J. van Ostade | *Mat:* op paneel *Size:* hoog 8, breed 11 duim	G	(Sold) fl 3 Rigters
1804/08/08	AMSCH	0250	*J. van Ostade* | Een Wintergezicht, ryk van Stoffagie van Beelden, Arren en Yssleeden; in de manier van J. van Ostade	Roos a	(Sold) fl 8:10 Gruiter
1804/10/16	DLOND	0290	*In de manier van J. van Ostade* | Twee stukjens. Boeren Huisgezinnen. Deux pièces. Des Familles de Paysan | *Mat:* op paneel *Size:* hoog 8, breed 12		(Unknown)
1806/06/07	RMHSN	0050	*J. v. Ostade* | Een Stukje met Dronke Boertjes in een Binnenhuis, als door J. v. Ostade, Ovaal | *Mat:* op paneel *Fmt:* ovaal	A E K L	(Sold) fl 15 Thijs

1806/06/07	RMHSN	0051	*J. Ostade* | Een Geslagt Varken op een Leer, mec [sic] Beeldjes, in de manier van J. Ostade | *Mat:* op paneel	A E K L	(Unknown)
1806/08/13	AMSCH	0302	*J. Ostade* | Een Binnehuisje met vrolyke Boeren en Boerinnen; als J. Ostade	Vinkeles [for] F	(Sold) fl 18 for lots 302 & 311. Schumacher
1806/08/13	AMSCH	0311	*J. van Ostade* | Een Boere Binnehuis met vrolyke Boeren; als J. van Ostade	Vinkeles [for] F	(Sold) fl 18 for lots 302 & 311. Schumacher
1810/06/06	RMMUY	0160	*J. van Ostade* | Een Boeren Binnenhuis, op den voorgrond eene Ton en Schotel met Mosselen. In de manier van J. van Ostade | *Mat:* op doek		(Unknown) fl 2:2
1810/07/23	DOLG2	0027	*J. van Ostade* | Een geslacht Varken, hangende aan een ladder; meesterlijk en fraai gepenseeld, als door J. van Ostade | *Mat:* op doek *Size:* hoog 26, breed 21 duim	Pieter Quinting	(Sold) fl 37 de Heere
1810/07/23	DOLG2	0034	*J. van Ostade* | Eenige vrolijke en drinkende Boeren en Boerinnen, binnen's huis; fix, dun en helder, van mannier als J. van Ostade | *Mat:* op paneel *Size:* hoog 18, breed 25 duim	Pieter Quinting	(Sold) fl 8:10 van Eijk 's Hage
			Otter [Unidentified]		
1809/04/17	AMSCH	0072a[H]	*Otter* | [Untitled] | *Notes:* This lot was added in by hand in the EBNP copy of the catalogue, but without giving a title.		(Sold) fl 4:5
			Oudendyck		
1802/05/05	AMSCH	0171	*Oudendyk* | Twee stuks, de eene verbeeld een wilde Zwynejacht, en 't andere een hevige schermutzeling tusschen Ruyters, beide zeer fiks behandeld | *Mat:* op doek *Size:* ieder hoog 25, breed 33 duim	K	(Sold) fl 20 V^{n} Iperen
1802/05/05	AMSCH	0172	*Oudendyk* | Een Bergachtig Landschap, op de Voorgrond legt eenig Vee, in 't verschiet ziet men eenige rustende Herders, verzeld van eenige Schepen, en een Os, fiks gepenceeld | *Mat:* op doek *Size:* hoog 10, breed 8 duim	K	(Sold) fl 10:10 Spruit
1806/08/13	AMSCH	0139	*Oudendyk. (P.)* | Een Italiaansch Landschap met Ruïnen en anderen Gebouwen; gestoffeerd met Jagers te paard die eenig Wild attaqueren; schoon van coloriet en breed geschilderd | *Mat:* op doek *Size:* hoog 35, breed [ ] duim	Vinkeles [for] G[ruyter]	(Sold) fl 6:10 Gruiter
1808/08/23	AMSCH	0251	*Oudendijk* | Twee stuks Landschappen met Koebeesten en Beelden gestoffeert; meesterlijk	[Van Iperen?]	(Bought In) fl 21
			Oudendyck, Adrian		
1802/02/16	AMSCH	0031	*A. Oudendyk* | Twee stuks Aangenaame Landzigten; beide ryk gestoffeert, met Huyslieden, en verschyden zoorten van Vee, meesterlyk geschilderd	H	(Sold) fl 8:10 Gruiter
1809/04/22	AMYVR	0093	*A. Oudendijk* | Twee kapitale Italiaansche Landschappen, met Gebergtens, Ruinen, en fraaije stoffagie van Beelden, zoo te Paard als rustende, waarbij verscheiden Vee; zijnde van de beste van deezen Meester | *Mat:* op doek *Size:* hoog 23, breed 27 duim	de Bruin	(Sold) fl 51 C S Roos
			Oudendyck, Evert		
1803/09/07	AMSCH	0123	*E. Oudendyk* | Een Italiaansch Landschap, met Ruïnen, gestoffeerd met eenige Jagers te Paard en te voet, met hunne Honden, bevallig op Doek [Un paysage d'Italie, orné de ruines et animé par quelques chasseurs à cheval et à pied avec leurs chiens. Composition très agréable et bien traitée] | *Mat:* op doek *Size:* hoog 35, breed 33 duim	Smidt	(Sold) fl 6 Gruiter
1809/04/17	AMSCH	0073	*E. van Oudendijk* | Twee stuks bevallige Landschappen, met rustende Landlieden en staande en liggende Beesten | *Size:* hoog 21, breed 25 duim	S	(Sold) fl 8
			Oudenrogge, Johannes Dircksz. van		
1801/04/13	AMSCH	0058	*J. Oudenrogge* | Een Weverswinkel, waar het weefgetouw, een spinnewiel en andere ingrediënten, daar toe behorende, een aangename variatie maken, aan den haard zitten eenige rookende Huislieden, daar agter een slapende Hond, het licht zo door het vengster als van het vuur maken dit stuk frappant, zynde van een breede schildering | *Mat:* op paneel *Size:* hoog 16, breed 22 duim	Pierre Fouquet, junior	(Sold) fl 56 van der Vinne
1802/05/11	GRGRW	0054	*R. Oudenrogge* | Een geslacht Varken aan de ladder, met de Schierschoonster [Schilderijen met Olie-Verf; In zwarte Lijsten] | *Mat:* in olyverf *Notes:* The artist's name was given as "R Oudenrogge" but we have assumed this is an error. The bracketed information in the title appears above lot 1 and refers to lots 1 to 79a.	Arnold Sicco Werumeus	(Unknown) fl 14
1807/08/26	AMSCH	0169	*Ouderoggen* | Voor een Buitenhuis ziet men een Heer, die afscheid neemt van eenen Grysaart, die in de deur van een Gebouw staat, op de voorgrond ziet men Hoenders en een Jagthond | *Mat:* op paneel *Size:* hoog 13 ½, breed 11 duim	de Vries	(Sold) fl 2 Levy Pakker
			Ous, S. [Unidentified]		
1804/07/25	DLGRO	0044	*S. Ous* | Een Oude Schoenlapper, met een Tafeltje waaröp zyn Gereedschap naast zig, voorts een jonge Meid die het Huis veegd, en een paar Knaapen by het Vuur staande, fraai geschilderd door S. Ous | *Mat:* op doek *Size:* hoog 20, breed 27 duim	Mr Franc van der Burch Wz.	(Unknown)

Ouwater, Isaak

1801/05/11	AMSCH	0065	*J. Ouwater* | Twee stuks Stadsgezichten, beiden zeer fraay met beeldjes gestoffeerd, en uitvoerig gepenceeld | *Mat:* op doek *Size:* hoog 19, breed 25 duim	V	(Sold) fl 61 B^{d} Kooij
1801/08/19	AMSCH	0076	*J. Ouwater* | Een fraai Gezicht binnen Amsterdam, ziende van den Pypemarkt langs de Achtergével van het Stadhuis, en Voorburgwal, naar het Generale Post-Comptoir, gestoffeerd met verscheiden wandelende Beeldjes en verder bywerk, zonagtig en uitvoerig behandeld | *Mat:* op doek *Size:* hoog 18, breed 23 duim	Pruyssen^{r}	(Withdrawn)
1801/08/19	AMSCH	0077	*J. Ouwater* | Een dito [fraai] Gezicht, ziende van de Halvemaansbrug, over de Binnen-Amstel, langs de Agtergeevels der Huizen van de Doelestraat, naar de Munt-Toren, Schapenplyn, en Cingel, gestoffeerd met diverse stoffagie, in alles als de vorige uitvoerig en kunstig geschilderd, door denzelven [J. Ouwater] | *Mat:* op doek *Size:* hoog 18, breed 23 duim	Pruyssen^{r}	(Withdrawn)
1801/08/19	AMSCH	0078	*J. Ouwater* | Een dito [fraai] Gezicht buiten Amsterdam op de Buitencingel, by de Raampoort, ziende naar een Houtzaagmolen, Heere-Huis, Lootzen, en andere Gebouwen, verder een bevallig verschiet, gestoffeert met verscheiden Beeldjes, zonagtig en uitvoerig behandeld | *Mat:* op doek *Size:* hoog 17, breed 22 duim	Pruyssen^{r}	(Withdrawn)
1801/08/19	AMSCH	0079	*J. Ouwater* | Een dito [Gezicht] binnen Amsterdam, ziende van de Jooden- Breestaat, naer de Zuider Kerk en Tooren; en verdere Gebouwen, gestoffeert met verscheiden Beeldjes zonagtig en bevallig gepenceeld | *Mat:* op doek *Size:* hoog 16, breed 19 duim	Pruyssen^{r}	(Withdrawn)
1801/08/19	AMSCH	0080	*J. Ouwater* | Een dito [fraai] Gezicht, binnen de Stad Delft, ziende naar verscheiden Woningen, en een Kerk-Tooren, gestoffeert met een Dame en Heer, een Fergon met Paarden, en verdere bedienden, alles uitvoerig gepenceeld | *Mat:* op doek *Size:* hoog 16, breed 19 duim	Pruyssen^{r}	(Withdrawn)
1801/08/19	AMSCH	0081	*J. Ouwater* | Gezicht binnen de Stad Haarlem, op het Binnespaarn, ziende langs de Ophaalbrug en Steene Wacht-Tooren naar het Diaconie Weeshuis, verbeeldende een besneeuwt Wintergezicht, alwaar verscheiden Lieden, zig met Paard en Slee, en met Schaatzeryden vermaken, zeer natuurlyk en uitvoerig behandeld, op Doek | *Mat:* op doek *Size:* hoog 13, breed 17 duim	Pruyssen^{r}	(Bought In) fl 36
1801/08/19	AMSCH	0082	*J. Ouwater* | Een Dorpgezicht, ziende langs een weg, met Wooning en Geboomten, naar de Kerk, op de Voorgrond, gestoffeert met staand en rustend Vee, Beeldjes en verder Bywerk, bevallig en uitvoerig geschilderd, op Doek | *Mat:* op doek *Size:* hoog 13, breed 15 duim	Pruyssen^{r}	(Bought In) fl 25
1801/08/19	AMSCH	0083	*J. Ouwater* | Een dito [Dorpgezicht] langs een weg, met Geboomten, by een Boerewooning, en werf: ziet men verscheide Huislieden, verder een Langezicht met eenig vee, en verder bywerk, zonachtig behandeld, op Doek | *Mat:* op doek *Size:* hoog 13, breed 15 duim	Pruyssen^{r}	(Bought In) fl 30
1802/05/05	AMSCH	0165	*J. Ouwater* | Een Gezigt op het Stadhuis, Nieuwe Kerk en Waag, te Amsterda [sic], zynde den Dam gestoffeert met een menigte Beelden en andere stoffagie, alles zonachtig behandeld | *Mat:* op doek *Size:* hoog 24, breed 30 duim	D	(Bought In) fl 64
1802/05/05	AMSCH	0166	*J. Ouwater* | Een Gezigt uit de Zylstraat, op de Groote Kerk te Haarlem, ryk gestoffeerd met een menigte Beeldjes, zonachtig | *Mat:* op doek *Size:* hoog 24, breed 30 duim	D	(Bought In) fl 50
1802/05/05	AMSCH	0167	*J. Ouwater* | Een Gezicht te Purmerend op de Markt te zien, in alles als de voorgaande | *Mat:* op doek *Size:* hoog 24, breed 30 duim	D	(Bought In) fl 60
1802/05/05	AMSCH	0168	*J. Ouwater* | Een Gezicht van een Buitencingel | *Size:* hoog 11, breed 16 duim	J	(Sold) fl 3 Stevens
1802/06/28	AMSCH	0138	*J. Ouwater* | Een gezicht op de groote Houtpoort te Haarlem, met Beelden en andere stoffagie, natuurlyk, op Doek | *Mat:* op doek *Size:* hoog 15, breed 18 duim	Anna Elink	(Sold) fl 7:10 van Iperen
1802/06/28	AMSCH	0139	*J. Ouwater* | Twee stuks, zynde het eene de Haarlemmerpoort te Amsterdam, en 't andere de Zylpoort te Haarlem, op Doek | *Mat:* op doek *Size:* hoog 14, breed 18 duim	Anna Elink	(Sold) fl 10:10 van der Schley [for] R[ijfsnijder]
1802/06/28	AMSCH	0141	*J. Ouwater* | Een gezicht op de Joebelspoort te Aarnhem; fiks behandeld, door Denzelven [J. Ouwater], op Panneel | *Mat:* op paneel *Size:* hoog 8, breed 10 duim	Anna Elink	(Sold) fl 3 Gruiter
1802/06/28	AMSCH	0142	*J. Ouwater* | Een gezicht op 't Dorp Dooren, in Gelderland; gestoffeerd met een menigte Beelden; door Denzelven [J. Ouwater], op Panneel | *Mat:* op paneel *Size:* hoog 9, breed 12 duim	Anna Elink	(Sold) fl 2:5 Geld
1802/06/28	AMSCH	0143	*J. Ouwater* | Een Gezicht op het Rechthuis in de Diemermeer, buiten Amsterdam, bevallig met Beeldjes en Beesjes gestoffeerd | companion to lot 144 *Mat:* op doek *Size:* hoog 18, breed 22 duim	Anna Elink	(Sold) fl 42:10 for lots 143 & 144. De Meyer
1802/06/28	AMSCH	0144	*J. Ouwater* | Een dito [Gezicht op het Rechthuis in de Diemermeer, buiten Amsterdam, bevallig met Beeldjes en Beesjes gestoffeerd], zynde de weerga van de voorgaande, verbeeldende het gezicht op de Muyderpoort | companion to lot 143 *Size:* hoog 18, breed 22 duim *Notes:* It is unclear what "dito" refers to in the title.	Anna Elink	(Sold) fl 42:10 for lots 143 & 144. De Meyer
1803/06/20	AMSCH	0033	*J. Ouwater* | Een Stadgezicht, zynde een Winter, het Ys gestoffeerd met een ménigte Schaatzenryders en wandelende Beeldjes, zeer uitvoerig en	Schley [for] G	(Sold) fl 19 Frantsen

			natuurlyk behandeld, door J. Ouwater, op Panneel | *Mat:* op paneel *Size:* hoog 12, breed 15 duim		
1804/02/27	AMSCH	0088	*Ouwater. (J.)* | Het Gezigt van de Joebelspoort te Aarnhem; ryk gestoffeerd, en natuurlyk gepenceeld | *Mat:* op paneel *Size:* hoog 8, breed 10 duim	C	(Sold) fl 3 Coclers
1804/05/07	AMSCH	0131	*Ouwater. (J.)* | Twee stuks Gezichten te Hoorn, ziende byde na 't Stadhuis, ryk gestoffeerd met gaande werde en vragtdoende Persoonen; byde zonachtig en uitvoerig gepenceeld | *Mat:* op doek *Size:* ieder hoog 14, breed 17 duim	Roos [for] A	(Sold) fl 41 Tijs
1804/05/07	AMSCH	0132	*Ouwater. (J.)* | Twee stuks Stadgezichten, te Amsterdam, zynde de eene een Gezicht aan de Raampoort en de andere een aan de Weesperpoort, ryk gestoffeerd met een ménigte Beelden, Schuyten Rytuigen enz; zynde deeze byde van dito schildering en niet minder dan de voorgaande | *Mat:* op doek *Size:* hoog 13, breed 21 duim	Roos [for] A	(Sold) fl 51 Tijs
1804/05/07	AMSCH	0133	*Ouwater. (J.)* | Een Gezicht op de Haarlemmerweg by Sloterdyk, zien de na eenige Buitenplaatsen, op den voorgrond twee Heeren te Paard, in de Vaart de Trekschuit, en aan de wal een Jacht waarby een Heer en Dame enz.; zonachtig en natuurlyk geschilderd | *Mat:* op doek *Size:* hoog 13, breed 21 duim	Roos [for] A	(Sold) fl 33 T van Iperen
1804/08/08	AMSCH	0148	*J. Ouwater* | Twee stuks Gezichten op de Haarlemmer Weg, ziende na eenige Buitenplaatzen, Boerenwoningen, enz., beiden ryk gestoffeerd met wandelende Heeren en Dames, Véehoeders en Vée, Rytuigen en andere Stoffagie; beiden zonachtig en van een uitvoerige penceelbehandeling | *Mat:* op doek *Size:* hoog 19, br. 25 duim	Vink[eles] [for] S	(Sold) fl 47 Gruyter
1804/12/10	AMSCH	0071	*J. Ouwater* | Een bevallig en capitaal Gezicht, naar het Dorp Ouderkerk aan den Amstel, ziende naar de Herberg de Prins; en Ophaalbrug; verder naar de Kerk, diversche Woningen en Coupéls [sic], ryk gestoffeert met verscheide beeldjes, zeilend schip, jaagschuit en andere vaartuigjes, zonachtig en uitvoerig van penceel behandeling | *Mat:* op doek *Size:* Hoog 22, breed 30 duim	Jan De Groot	(Sold) fl 98 B^{d} Kooy
1804/12/10	AMSCH	0072	*J. Ouwater* | Twee Gezichten der Stad Amsterdam, men ziet op het eene de overzyde der Keizersgragt van de Westermarkt, ter regterzyde op de voorgrond de Vleeshal; en het andere steld voor den Dam en het Stadhuis, in het verschiet de Nieuwe Kerk en Waag, beide ryk gestoffeerd; en zonachtig gepenceeld | *Mat:* op doek *Size:* Hoog 21, breed 30 duim	Jan De Groot	(Sold) fl 200 B^{d} Kooy
1804/12/10	AMSCH	0073	*J. Ouwater* | Twee stuks Gezichten te Amsterdam, het eene het Leidsche Plein met de Hollandsche Schouwburg; en het andere het Luthersche Besteedelinghuis, beide zeer ryk en bevallig gestoffeerd, met onderscheide wandelaars, Ry- en vaartuigen; en zonachtig behandeld | *Mat:* op doek *Size:* Hoog 17, breed 21 duim	Jan De Groot	(Sold) fl 71 Josi
1804/12/10	AMSCH	0074	*J. Ouwater* | Een Gezicht binnen Amsterdam, ziende langs de Prinsegragt naar de Wester Kerk en Tooren, en verders verscheide woningen, gestoffeerd met een rydende Wagen, Scheepen en andere Vaartuigen; zonachtig en uitvoerig behandeld | *Mat:* op doek *Size:* Hoog 15 ½, breed 20 duim	Jan De Groot	(Sold) fl 115 for lots 74 & 75. Josi
1804/12/10	AMSCH	0075	*J. Ouwater* | Een dito [Gezicht] te dito [Amsterdam], zynde een Gezicht naar de Munt en Tooren, van de Reguliers Breestraat af te zien, verders langs den Cingel en Kalverstraat, en verscheide woningen, gestoffeerd met Rytuig, wandelende Dames en Heeren; zonachtig en uitvoerig van penceelbehandeling | *Mat:* op doek *Size:* Hoog 15 ½, breed 20 duim	Jan De Groot	(Sold) fl 115 for lots 74 & 75. Josi
1804/12/10	AMSCH	0076	*J. Ouwater* | Een dito [Gezicht] dito [te Amsterdam], zynde een Gezicht van de Montalbaans Tooren; fraai gestoffeerd en uitvoerig en zonachtig geschilderd | *Mat:* op paneel *Size:* Hoog 13, breed 14 duim	Jan De Groot	(Sold) fl 10 Josi
1804/12/10	AMSCH	0077	*J. Ouwater* | Een Gezicht van de Wester Kerk en een gedeelte der Kyzersgragt, ryk gestoffeerd met beelden en vaartuigen; dit stukje is byzonder uitvoerig en zonachtig geschilderd | *Mat:* op paneel *Size:* Hoog 17, breed 22 duim	Jan De Groot	(Sold) fl 70 Coclers
1804/12/10	AMSCH	0078	*J. Ouwater* | Twee stuks, byden Gezichten te Amsterdam, het eene 't Diaconie Weeshuis, en het ander het Besjeshuis langs de Binnen-Amstel, welk gestoffeerd zyn met verscheide Vaartuigen, wandelende en rydende Perzoonen; krachtig gepenceeld | *Mat:* op doek *Size:* Hoog 17, breed 22 duim	Jan De Groot	(Sold) fl 80 Moll
1804/12/10	AMSCH	0079	*J. Ouwater* | Twee stuks, beide Gezichten van de Onvolmaakte Tooren, en het Stadhuis te Amsterdam, ryk gestoffeerd; uitvoerig en zonachtig van schildering | *Mat:* op doek *Size:* Hoog 17, breed 22 duim	Jan De Groot	(Sold) fl 40 van Iperen
1804/12/10	AMSCH	0080	*J. Ouwater* | Het Gezicht van de Binnen Amstel, langs de Cloveniers Burgwal; uitvoerig gestoffeerd, met diverse Beeldjes; en fraai gepenceeld | *Mat:* op paneel *Size:* Hoog 17, breed 22 duim	Jan De Groot	(Sold) fl 23:10 T van Iperen
1804/12/10	AMSCH	0081	*J. Ouwater* | Een Stadsgezicht, ter midden derzelve een Kerk, op de voorgrond een Veedryver, met Ossen, koeijen en eenige schaapen; zeer uitvoerig behandeld | *Mat:* op paneel *Size:* Hoog 16, breed 18 duim	Jan De Groot	(Sold) fl 25 Coclers
1804/12/10	AMSCH	0082	*J. Ouwater* | Een Gezicht buiten de Stad Weesp, gestoffeerd met onderscheide lieden; zonachtig en fraai geschilderd | *Mat:* op doek *Size:* Hoog 13, breed 15 duim	Jan De Groot	(Sold) fl 14:10 Coclers

1804/12/10	AMSCH	0083	*J. Ouwater* | Een capitaal Gezicht binnen de Stadt Delft, ziende langs de groote markt naar het stadhuis en de groote kerk, en andere woningen, gestoffeert met wandelende lieden, vragtkar en verder bywerk; zonachtig en meesterlyk fraay gepenceelt | *Mat:* op paneel *Size:* Hoog 18, breed 24 duim	Jan De Groot	(Sold) fl 31 Josi
1805/07/03	AMSCH	0129	*J. Ouwater* | Twee stuks Gezichtjes aan den Overtoom buiten Amsterdam, ryk gestoffeerd met Beeldjes, Rytuigen, Schuiten, enz.; natuurlyk van licht en uitvoerig gepenceeld | *Mat:* op paneel *Size:* hoog 9, breed 11 duim	Y	(Sold) fl 9:10 Vallet
1805/07/03	AMSCH	0130	*J. Ouwater* | Twee stuks Stadgezichten, verbeeldende twee Poorten, van binnen te zien; eigenaartig gestoffeerd en uitvoerig geschilderd | *Mat:* op doek *Size:* hoog 13, breed 11 ½ duim	Y	(Sold) fl 30 van Iperen
1806/05/05	AMSCH	0111	*J. Ouwater* | Twee stuks Landschappen, zynde beide gezigten in Vreeland, langs de Plaats en Fabriek Vreedenhorst, beiden ryk gestoffeerd met wandelende Heeren en Dames, Rytuigen en Landlieden die Vee dryven, en andere stoffagie; zonachtig en uitvoerig geschildert door J. Ouwater | *Mat:* op doek *Size:* hoog 12, breed 25 duim	V[inkeles]	(Sold) fl 79 Gruiter
1806/08/13	AMSCH	0141	*Ouwater. (J.)* | Twee stuks bevallige Dorpgezichten, zynde een Zomer en een Winter beide eigenaartig gestoffeerd met wandelende Mans- en Vrouwebeeldjes, Schaatseryders, Arresleeden, Paarden, enz.; beide zonachtig en delicaat van schildering | *Mat:* op paneel *Size:* Ieder hoog 11, breed 13 duim	Vinkeles [for] F	(Sold) fl 33 Schumacher
1806/08/13	AMSCH	0145	*Ouwater. (J.)* | Een Gezicht te halfweegen Haarlem en Amsterdam, ryk gestoffeerd met rydende en wandelende Heeren en Dames en anderen Persoonen; zonachtig en delicaat van schildering | *Mat:* op doek *Size:* hoog 17, breed 20 duim	Vinkeles [for] D	(Sold) fl 30 Th Spaan
1807/08/26	AMSCH	0166	*J. Ouwater* | Twee stuks: zynde het eene, een Gezigt aan den Overtoom, en het anderen den Overhaal aan de Weteringspoort; beide geestig gestoffeerd en uitvoerig behandeld | *Mat:* op paneel *Size:* hoog 9, breed 11 duim	Joseph Vallette	(Sold) fl 16:10 T Spaan
1808/08/23	AMSCH	0126	*Ouwater. (J.)* | Twee stuks, beide Gezichten van de onvolmaakte Tooren, en het Stadhuis te Amsterdam; rijk gestoffeerd met een menigte Beeldjes, Rijtuigen en verder bijwerk; uitvoerig en zonachtig van schildering | *Mat:* op paneel *Size:* Ieder hoog 17, breed 22 duim	[Van Iperen?]	(Sold) fl 105 Barend Koy
1809/07/19	AMSCH	0045	*Ouwater (J.)* | Een Gezicht binnen Amsterdam, ziende over de Nieuwmarkt, langs de Geldersche Kaai, op de Schreijerstooren, rijk gestoffeerd met wandelende Heeren en Dames, Kooplieden, Kramers, Vragtsleden en anderen Voorwerpen. Zonagtig en meesterlijk behandeld | *Mat:* op doek *Size:* hoog 21, breed 26 duim	[Bicker]	(Sold) fl 40 Bredius
1810/08/10	RMRIJ	0025	*Oudewater* | Het Huis Maurik bij Vugt. Uitvoerig en delicaat geschilderd		(Sold) fl 3 [or] 3:5 v Dyk

Ouwater, Isaak (and Buys, Jac.)

1808/10/28	AMVRS	0047	*Ouwater (J.); J. Buys* | Een Gezicht te Utrecht met den Dom en Kerk, ter linkerzijde een Smits Winkel. Zeer zonachtig en uitvoerig | *Size:* hoog 20, breed 22 ½ duim	Marten Udink	(Sold) fl 51 Stopendaal

Ouwater, J.

1801/08/19	AMSCH	0084	*J. Ouwater* | Een Land- en Watergezicht, aan beider Oevers, met Geboomten en Woningen, gestoffeert met zeilende en andere Schépen en Schuiten, zonagtig en bevalig behandeld, op Doek | *Mat:* op doek *Size:* hoog 13, breed 15 duim	Pruyssen[r]	(Withdrawn)
802/06/28	AMSCH	0140	*J. Ouwater* | Twee stuks stille Waters, met Vaartuigen en Beeldjes, als vooren, door Denzelven [J. Ouwater] | *Mat:* op doek *Size:* hoog 12, breed 16 duim	Anna Elink	(Sold) fl 4:10 Gruiter
802/06/28	AMSCH	0145	*J. Ouwater* | Een onstuimige Zee, met verscheiden Vaartuigen; fiks gepenceeld, door Denzelven [J. Ouwater], op Panneel | *Mat:* op paneel *Size:* hoog 6, breed 8 duim	Anna Elink	(Sold) fl 1 L Pakker
804/02/27	AMSCH	0087	*Ouwater (J.)* | Twee stille Waters, met differenten zylende en stilleggende Vaartuigen; bevallig van licht en uitvoerig van schildering | *Mat:* op doek *Size:* hoog 12, breed 16 duim	C	(Bought In) fl 11
806/05/05	AMSCH	0112	*J. Ouwater* | Twee aangenaame stille Water, met differente zeilende en stil leggende Scheepen en Vaartuigen, bevallig van Licht als voren | *Mat:* op doek *Size:* hoog 12, breed 16 duim	V[inkeles]	(Bought In) fl 10
806/08/13	AMSCH	0142	*Ouwater. (J.)* | Twee stuks stille Waters, met zeilende Scheepen en Schuiten, roeijende Booten, Jollen en verders aangenaame Strandgezichten; beide dun en uitvoerig behandeld | *Mat:* op paneel *Size:* Ieder hoog 9, breed 10 duim	Vinkeles [for] F	(Sold) fl 8 Du Pre
806/08/13	AMSCH	0143	*Ouwater. (J.)* | Een bevallig Land- en Riviergezichtje, aan een Dorp met Boere Woning, Kerktooren, Geboomten en Stoffagie van Beeldjes; zonachtig en uitvoerig gepenceeld | *Mat:* op paneel *Size:* hoog 9, breed 10 duim	Vinkeles [for] F	(Sold) fl 7:10 Mettenbrink
806/08/13	AMSCH	0144	*Ouwater. (J.)* | Een dito [bevallig] dito [Land- en Riviergezichtje], als de voorgaande; iets kleinder | *Mat:* op paneel *Size:* hoog 7 ½, breed 9 duim *Notes:* It is unclear what "dito" refers to in the title.	Vinkeles [for] F	(Sold) fl 10 Rynbergh

1809/04/22	AMYVR	0099	*J. Ouwater* | Twee stille Waters, met Schepen, Schuiten en Beelden | *Mat:* op paneel *Size:* hoog 8, breed 10 duim	de Bruin	(Sold) fl 2:15 du Pree

Ouwater, Jacobus

1806/08/20	HGBSM	0076	*Ouwater* | Voor eene Steene Nis, staat een Vaas met veelderhande soort van Bloemen, rijk geordonneerd | *Mat:* op doek *Size:* hoog 33, breed 26 duim	Macalester Loup [or others]	(Sold) fl 13:5 for lots 76 & 77. Zwartsman
1806/08/20	HGBSM	0077	*Ouwater* | Een dito [Steene Nis] met Vrugten en Bloemen, en veel Insecten, de agtergrond een Tuingezicht | *Size:* hoog 33, breed 26 duim *Notes:* It is unclear what "dito" refers to in the title.	Macalester Loup [or others]	(Sold) fl 13:5 for lots 76 & 77. Zwartsman
1807/08/26	AMSCH	0167	*J. Ouwater* | Een Pot met diverse soorten van Bloemen | *Mat:* op doek *Size:* hoog 26, breed 22 duim	de Vries	(Sold) fl 2:5 Andriesse
1810/10/10	MGCIT	0131	*Ouwater* | Een fraai Bloemstuk, zeer uitvoerig	Caspar van Citters	(Unknown)

Ovens, Jürgen

1802/12/13	AMSCH	0128	*J. Ovens* | Twee stuks bevallige Kinderen, verbeeldende den Heiland, en de anderen St. Jan, met een Lam speelende, kragtig en meesterlyk gepenceeld | *Mat:* op doek *Size:* yder is hoog 28, breed 22 duim	Schley [for] Lauwers	(Sold) fl 1:15 Gruiter
1808/11/28	AMSCH	0048	*J. Ovens* | Een Oud Mans Portret, zittende in een Armstoel, gekleed in een Bonte Rok en een zwart Kalotje op 't Hoofd, kragtig en meesterlijk, als door Rembrand geschilderd | *Mat:* op doek *Size:* hoog 49, breed 39 duim	Y	(Sold) fl 95:10 v d Schley [for] Barlet [?]

Overmeer, C. [Unidentified]

1802/09/30	HGBAK	0004	*C. Overmeer* | Een Juffertje dat zit te naayen, zeer fraay, door C. Overmeer, paneel, in vergulde lyst. [Schilderyen in Olyverf] | *Mat:* in olyverf op paneel *Notes:* The bracketed information in the title appears above lot 1 and refers to lots 1 to 26.		(Unknown)

Palamedesz. (and Asch, P.J. van)

1804/10/16	DLOND	0004	*P. van As; Palamedes* | Een Landschap vol geboomte en gestoffeerd door Palamedes en anderen. Paysage avec des figures de Palamedes & d'autres | *Mat:* op paneel *Size:* hoog 23, breed 35		(Unknown)

Palamedesz., Anthonie

1801/03/16	AMSCH	0053	*Palamedes* | Twee stuks, een Mans en een Vrouwe Pourtrait	P[ruyssenaar]	(Sold) fl 1:10 Gruiter
1801/04/08	HAVIN	0013	*Palamedes* | Een Musiseerend Gezelschap, fraai		(Unknown)
1801/06/10	AMSCH	0138	*Palamedes. (J.)* | In een Binnenhuis ziet men een gezelschap vanvier Beelden: fyn gepenceeld | *Mat:* op paneel *Size:* hoog 15, breed 13 duim *Notes:* The artist's name was given as "Palamedes. (J.)" but we have assumed this is an error.	[Doublet]	(Sold) fl 1:5 Taijs
1801/06/13	LNDLS	0027	*Palamedes* | Eenige Persoonen, die met dobbelsteenen speelen, daar bij twee staande mannen en een vrouw, op paneel | *Mat:* op paneel *Size:* hoog 13, breed 16 duimen	D van R	(Sold) fl 20 Theys
1801/08/19	AMSCH	0092	*Palamedes* | Een zingend Gezelschap van Heeren en Dames, fix op Paneel | *Mat:* op paneel *Size:* hoog 15, breed 23 duim	Van Forreest	(Sold) fl 8:5 V^n Iperen
1801/08/19	AMSCH	0093	*Palamedes* | Een Gezelschap van Heeren en Dames, aan een wel opgerichten Disch	Pruyssen^r [for] Q	(Sold) fl 1:10 Ottens
1802/06/28	AMSCH	0150	*Pallamedes* | Een ryk gestoffeerd Vertrek, van een aantal Heeren en Dames, door Pallamedes, hoog 24, breed 33 duim. Doek | *Mat:* op doek *Size:* hoog 24, breed 33 duim	Anna Elink	(Sold) fl 10:10 T Spaan
1802/06/28	AMSCH	0152	*Palamedes* | Een Binnenvertrek, waar in verscheiden musiceerende Dames en Heeren; gestoffeerd met verder bywerk, door Denzelven [Palamedes]. Panneel | *Mat:* op paneel	B	(Sold) fl 7:15 Roos [for] A
1802/06/28	AMSCH	0153	*Palamedes* | Drie stuks Vaderlandsche Historie Pourtraiten, zynde een Man en twee Vrouwen; delicaat op Panneel | *Mat:* op paneel *Size:* hoog 21, breed 16 duim	Anna Elink	(Sold) fl 12 Gruiter
1802/07/21	HGKAN	0035	*Palamedes* | Een extra fraay dito [Schildery?], zynde een Gezelschap, welke zich met het speelen in een Bord met Dobbelsteenen schynen te vermaaken, door Palamedes, op koper, vergulde Lyst | *Mat:* op koper *Notes:* It is unclear what "dito" refers to in the title.		(Unknown)
1802/07/27	AKHRK	0022	*Palamedes* | Een gezelschap van deftige Persoonen, die zich bij een gedekte Tafel in de Musiek vermaaken, fraai van schikking en goed geschilderd. Ovaal formaat | *Mat:* op paneel *Fmt:* ovaal *Size:* hoog 18, breed 24 duim	Maria Stategaart	(Sold) fl 17 Stroo
1802/07/27	AKHRK	0023	*Palamedes* | Een Corps de Garde, waarin twee staande en een zittend Officier aan een Tafel bezig zijn met Reekenen; voorts twee gemeenen, bij een Vuur hun warmende. Fraai gepenseelt | *Mat:* op paneel *Size:* hoog 13 ½, breed 18 duim	Maria Stategaart	(Sold) fl 12 Stroo
1802/08/24	LNDLS	0108	*A. Palamedes* | Een Corps de Garde met Soldaten, en een Trompetter die tegen eene Vrouw spreekt en meer persoonen. Door Palamedes, 1658. op paneel | *Mat:* op paneel *Inscr:* Palamedes, 1658 (signed and dated?) *Notes:* It is unclear whether the name and date are inscribed on the painting.	Leonardus Bouman [or others]	(Unknown) fl 13

1802/09/21	UTHDG	0074	*J. Palamedes* | Een Corps de Guarde, waarin rookende en drinkende Soldaaten, en een vrouw met een pijp in de hand. Vrolijk van voorstelling | *Mat:* op paneel *Size:* hoog 19, breed 25 duimen *Notes:* The artist's name was given as "J. Palamedes" but we have assumed this is an error.		(Bought In) fl 24
1802/09/21	UTHDG	0075	*A. Palamedes* | Een oud Man met een bonnet en een lange grijze baard. Meesterlijk geschildert | *Mat:* op paneel *Size:* hoog 12, breed 7 duimen		(Bought In) fl 7:15
1802/09/30	HGBAK	0009	*Palamedes* | Een Gezelschap met Heeren en Dames, door Palamedes, op paneel, zwarte lyst. [Schilderyen in Olyverf] | *Mat:* in olyverf op paneel *Notes:* The bracketed information in the title appears above lot 1 and refers to lots 1 to 26.		(Unknown)
1802/11/01	DOBRA	0123	*Palamedes* | Een vrolyk Gezelschap | *Mat:* op paneel *Size:* h. 13. br. 23 duim	Paulus van der Spyk [or others]	(Sold) fl ¾ [Illegible]
1803/08/24	HGKAN	A0019	*Palemedes* | Een Binnehuis, met een staande en zittende Officier voor den haart | *Mat:* op paneel *Size:* breet 17, hoog 11 duim		(Sold) fl 1:12 Carre
1804/02/27	AMSCH	0092	*Palamedes* | Een Musiceerend Gezelschap van Heeren en Dames | *Mat:* op paneel *Size:* hoog 17, breed 25 duim	R[oos]	(Sold) fl 4:10 Thais
1804/04/28	LNDLS	0010	*A. Palamedes* | Een Binnenwacht, met eenige krygslieden, in 't midden een zittende trompetter, met een vrouwtje, die een bierkan draagt, fraai van coloriet en konstig geschildert, door A. Palamedes, 1655. op paneel | *Mat:* op paneel *Size:* hoog 19, breed 24 duim *Inscr:* A. Palamedes, 1655 (signed and dated?) *Notes:* It is unclear whether the name and date are inscribed on the painting.	[Abraham Delfos] [or others]	(Sold) fl 57 Jan Landa
1804/07/25	DLGRO	0040	*Palamedes* | Een binnen Vertrek, met drie Militaire en twee Vrouwen | *Mat:* op paneel *Size:* hoog 14, breed 17 duim	Mr Franc van der Burch Wz.	(Unknown)
1804/07/25	DLGRO	0043	*Palamedes* | Een binnen Vertrek, met een Musiceerend Gezelschap uit verscheide Persoonen bestaande, zeer uitvoerig door Palamedes | *Mat:* op paneel *Size:* hoog 18, breed 24 duim	Mr Franc van der Burch Wz.	(Unknown)
1804/08/08	AMSCH	0155	*A. Palamedes* | In een prachtige Zaal ziet men een Gezelschap met Dames en Heeren, welken zich met gastereeren vermaaken; zynde van de fraaiste behandeling van A. Palamedes | *Mat:* op paneel *Size:* hoog 21, breed 26 duim	Roos a	(Sold) fl 24 Moll
1804/08/08	AMSCH	0156	*A. Palamedes* | In een Gemeubileerde Kamer ziet men eenige Heeren en Dames, zittende te Musiceeren, waar naar twee anderen staan te luisteren; krachtig op Paneel | *Mat:* op paneel *Size:* hoog 18, breed 25 duim	Roos [for] H	(Sold) fl 19:10 Gruyter
1804/10/16	DLOND	0162	*A. Palamedes* | Een Jonker met enige Manschappen. Un Seigneur & quelques Soldats | *Mat:* op paneel *Size:* hoog 9, breed 12		(Unknown)
1804/10/16	DLOND	0163	*A. Palamedes* | Een Mans- en een Vrouwen-Portrait. Portraits d'Homme & Femme | *Mat:* op doek *Size:* hoog 32, breed 24		(Unknown)
1804/10/16	DLOND	0164	*A. Palamedes* | Een Binnenwacht. Corps de Garde | *Mat:* op paneel *Size:* hoog 15, breed 20		(Sold) fl 10 Verlinden
1804/10/16	DLOND	0165	*A. Palamedes* | Uts[a] [Een Binnenwacht. Corps de Garde] | *Mat:* op paneel *Size:* hoog 16, breed 22		(Sold) fl 4:18 Verlinden
1804/10/16	DLOND	0166	*A. Palamedes* | Uts[a] [Een Binnenwacht. Corps de Garde] | *Mat:* op paneel *Size:* hoog 14, breed 20		(Sold) fl 8 Verlinden
1804/10/16	DLOND	0167	*A. Palamedes* | Twee Stukjens. Gezelschappen. Deux pièces. Des Compagnies | *Mat:* op paneel *Size:* hoog 6, breed 8		(Sold) fl 6:5 Thijs
1804/10/16	DLOND	0168	*A. Palamedes* | Vyf Stukjens. De vyf Zinnen. Cinq pièces. Les cinq Sens | *Mat:* op paneel *Size:* hoog 6, breed 4		(Unknown)
1804/10/29	HRBAU	0078	*Palamedes* | In een gemeubileerd Binnenvertrek zit eene Dame, met een Kind aan de borst, waar by een Heer, met zyn elleboog op een' stoel leunende, met haar schynt te spreeken, terwyl eene andere Dame iets leest. Alles zeer delicaat en kragtig behandeld | *Mat:* op paneel *Size:* hoog 8 ½, breed 10 duim	Simon Styl	(Unknown)
1805/07/10	AMSCH	0121	*Palamedes* | Een Binnenvertrek met een menigte Heeren en Dames, in deftige aloude Kleeding, en verder bywerk; meesterlyk en fiks gepenceeld | *Mat:* op paneel *Size:* hoog 17, breed 25 duim	V[inkeles] [for] N	(Sold) fl 2:10 Lafontaine
1805/07/10	AMSCH	0197	*Palamedes* | Een Gezelschap van twee Heeren en een Dame	R[oos]	(Sold) fl 4 Lafontaine
1805/10/09	HGBSM	0080	*Palamedes* | Een musiceerend, en een rookend gezelschap, door Palamedes, op paneel, hoog 8 ½ breet 7 duim, twee stuks | *Mat:* op paneel *Size:* hoog 8 ½ breet 7 duim	T H van Willigen [or others]	(Sold) fl 6:5 Van Giesen
1806/05/05	AMSCH	0183	*Palamedes* | Een Gezelschap van Dames en Heeren, op het Bord speelende, en drinkende; fraai op Paneel | *Mat:* op paneel	R[oos]	(Sold) fl 6 Mensart
1806/06/07	RMHSN	0042	*Palamedes* | Een Musicerend Gezelschap van Heeren en Dames | *Mat:* op paneel	A E K L	(Unknown)
1806/06/07	RMHSN	0043	*Palamedes* | Een Binnenvertrek, waar in een Officier, Juffrouw &c. | *Mat:* op paneel	A E K L	(Unknown)
1806/10/16	UTWLD	0020	*Palamedes* | Een vrolyk gezelschap door Palamedes	Mr P de Malapert [or] W Beeldsnyder	(Unknown)
1806/11/24	AMSCH	0054	*Palamedes* | Eenige Dames en Heeren aan een Tafel zittende, ziende naar een Heer die op een Guitar speeld en tevens danst; delicaat gepenceeld | *Mat:* op paneel *Size:* hoog 17, breed 21 duim	Munnikhuizen	(Sold) fl 8:15 Spaan

1807/06/02	AMHUY	0040	*Pallemedes* | In een Binnenvertrek ziet men Lieden op zyn Spaans gekleed, op de voorgrond eenige Vlaggen en Geweeren		(Unknown)
1807/06/10	HGBSM	0149	*Palamedes* | Een Corps de Garde vol militairen en andere bijwerken, zeer fraai van tekening en schildering, van de beste tijd van Palamedes | *Mat:* op paneel *Size:* hoog 19, breed 24 duim	Abraham Delfos [or others]	(Sold) fl 40 S T
1807/06/10	HGBSM	0150	*Palamedes* | Een dito Stuk [Corps de Garde], verbeeldende daar de militairen de buit deelen, in alles niet minder als het voorgaande | *Mat:* op paneel *Size:* hoog 21, breed 29 duim	Abraham Delfos [or others]	(Sold) fl 39:15 S T
1807/08/26	AMSCH	0180	*Palamedes* | Het Afbeeldzel van eene Kunstschilder, in aloude Kleeding, zittende in een Kamer met vergenoeging zyn Pyp rooken, ter zyde staat een Tafeltje, waar op een Drinkglas, een Test met Vuur en Pypen geplaatst zyn, daar nevens staat een Schilder-Ezel, waarop een Schilderstuk; het is meesterlyk gepenceeld | *Mat:* op paneel *Size:* hoog 12, breed 9 ½ duim	v d Schley [for] L	(Sold) fl 3:5 Jozi
1807/08/26	AMSCH	0181	*Palamedes* | In een Binnenvertrek vertoont zich een musiceerend Gezelschap van Heeren en Dames, een derzelve speelt op het Klavier, en anderen schynen te zingen; krachtig gepenceeld | *Mat:* op paneel	Yver [for] S	(Sold) fl 2:5 Spruit
1808/04/26	GDAN	0127	*Palamedes (A)* | Dit uitmuntenden Stuk van die Meester verbeeld een gemeubileerde Kraamkamer, waarin de Kraamvrouw in een Stoel is gezeten, naast en om haar eenige Dames, in een Bakermat, by 't Vuur zit de Baker met haar handen het Kind aannemende, dat haar door eene Dame word overgereikt, om te bakeren, voor de Spiegel, aan de andere zijde des Vertreks staat een Dame om haar Hair in orde te brengen, voorts eenige Persoonen die een Candeeltje schijnen te nuttigen met diverse andere Persoonen, by het Vuur, Wieg en Vuurmand staan mede in 't Vertrek, en een Hond die aan een been schijnt geknabbelt te hebben, fraai gepenseeld | companion to lot 128 *Size:* hoog 23, breed 35 duim	G H Fortuyn	(Unknown)
1808/04/26	GDAN	0128	*Palamedes (A)* | Een dito [Stuk] uitmuntend tot een weerga, zijnde de Kraam Maaltijd, meest al uit dezelve Persoonen bestaande, op eene gedekte Tafel ziet men een groot gedeelte gebraden Vleesch en Podding, &c., aan welke Tafel een aantal Gasten, die schijnen gegeten te hebben, de Kraamvrouw zit in dezelfde Stoel, en 't Kindje word aldaar gepresenteerd, terwijl sommigen der Gasten er een Glaasje opnemen, terwijl andere bezig zijn den koele Wijn weer in Kannen te doen, pragtig en fiks geschildert | companion to lot 127 *Size:* hoog 23, breed 35 duim	G H Fortuyn	(Unknown)
1808/04/26	GDAN	0129	*Palamedes (A)* | In een Binnenhuis eenige Musiceerende Heeren en Dames met derzelver Instrumenten, goed geschilderd | *Size:* hoog 11 ½, breed 51 duim	G H Fortuyn	(Unknown)
1808/07/19	AMROU	0010	*Palamedes* | 1 gemeubeleerd Binnenvertrek, ziet men aan een Tafel eenige zittenden Heeren en Dames, in ryke kleedinge, speelende op onderscheidene Muziek Instrumenten		(Unknown)
1808/11/28	AMSCH	0074a	*Palamedes* | Een Kamer waarin een musiceerend Gezelschap	[Gruyter?]	(Sold) fl 2:5 Tythoff
1808/12/31	RMHSN	0017	*Palamedes* | Een Vrolyk Musicerend Gezelschap | *Mat:* op paneel	G Spanjaart [or] H de Haas [or] C van der Looy Lans	(Unknown)
1809/04/17	AMSCH	0074	*Palamedes* | Een Corps de Garde, op de voorgrond zit eene Krijgsman op de Trompet te blaasen, ter zijde eene Vrouw met een Kind, waarbij een bedaagd Man en andere Lieden; uitvoerig en fraai gepenceeld | *Mat:* op paneel *Size:* hoog 10, breed 14 duim	S	(Sold) fl 8
1809/04/17	AMSCH	0125	*Palamedes* | Een Zaal, met verscheide rijk gekleede Heeren en Dames | *Mat:* op paneel	T	(Sold) fl 2:5
1809/04/22	AMYVR	0104	*Palamedes* | In een Binnenvertrek ziet men eenige Krijgslieden, waarbij eene Vrouw met een Kind; geestig en krachtig | *Mat:* op paneel *Size:* hoog 16, breed 19 duim	de Bruin	(Sold) fl 10:5 du Pree
1809/07/25	HGBSM	0010	*A. Palamedes* | Een deftig Binnenvertrek met Heeren en Dames, waar een Heer op de Guitaar speeld terwyl een ander een Glaasje schynt te willen drinken, helder van couleur, door A. Palamedes 1635 | *Mat:* op paneel *Size:* hoog 17 ½, breed 23 duim *Inscr:* A. Palamedes 1635 (signed and dated?) *Notes:* It is unclear whether the name and date are inscribed on the painting.	D van der Aa [or] E B ten Dall	(Sold) fl 29:10 van Eijk
1809/10/20	UTWLD	0010	*Palamedes* | Een vrolyk gezelschap door Palamedes	J J van Rhyn	(Unknown)
1810/03/07	UTWLD	0010	*A. Palamedes* | Een fraay mans Pourtrait	J J Woertman	(Unknown) fl 20:5
1810/03/27	RMCNL	0058	*Palamedes* | Een bij uitnemenheid netjes en fraai behandeld Stukje, waarop men eene oude Ridder schijndt te zien buigen; op den voorgrond een klein snaaks Knaapje		(Unknown)
1810/06/06	RMMUY	0103	*Palamedes* | Een lezend Vrouwtje, waar bij een staand Jongeling, aartig en piquant van Effect | *Mat:* op paneel		(Unknown) fl 2:2
1810/06/06	RMMUY	0105	*Palamedes* | Een Corps de Garde | *Mat:* op paneel		(Unknown) fl 3:10
1810/06/06	RMMUY	0112	*Palamedes* | Een groter dito [fraaij Kerkje van binnen te zien]. Gestoffeerd door Palamedes | *Mat:* op paneel *Notes:* It is unclear what "dito" refers to in the title.		(Unknown) fl 5:5
1810/10/11	AMSCH	0246	*A. Palamedes* | Twee stuks: een Landschap met Herders en een Strandgezigt | *Mat:* op paneel	A	(Sold) fl 4:10 van Leen

Palamedesz., Anthonie (and Decker)

1810/06/06	RMMUY	0149	*Dekker; Palamedes* | Een Boschrijk Landschap. Door Dekker, gestoffeerd met Figuren. Door Palamedes | *Mat:* op paneel		(Unknown) fl 5:10

Palamedesz., Anthonie (and Houckgeest, G.)

1808/11/28	AMSCH	0028	*G.J. Houckaerts; Palamedes* | Een pragtig Paleijs- en Hofgezicht, gestoffeerd met de Bijbel-ordonantie van Lazarus en de Rijke Man, dit stuk is fraai van perspectief en bouwkundig behandeld, op Paneel, door G.J. Houckaerts, 1646 en gestoffeerd door Palamedes | *Mat:* op paneel *Size:* hoog 31, breed 34 duim *Inscr:* G.J. Houckaerts, 1646 (signed and dated?) *Notes:* It is unclear whether the name and date are inscribed on the painting.	C	(Sold) fl 19 T Spaan

Palamedesz., Anthonie (and Neeffs, P. (I))

1810/06/06	RMMUY	0041	*P. Neefs; Palamedes* | Eene kapitale en wel uitgevoerde Roomsche Kerk van binnen te zien. Door P. Neefs. Met stoffage door Palamedes | *Mat:* op paneel		(Unknown) fl 51

Palamedesz., Anthonie (and Verboom, A.H.)

1808/06/11	RMRIJ	0111	*A: Verboom; Palamedes* | Een zeer schoon Boomryk Landschap, vrolyk en konstig gestoffeerd | *Mat:* op doek *Size:* hoog 29, breed 40 ½ duim		(Bought In) fl 5
1808/06/11	RMRIJ	0114	*A: Verboom; Palamedes* | Een Bosch- en Boomryk Landschap, alwaar eenige Jagers op de Valken Jagt schynen te gaan, krachtig en goed geschilderd | *Mat:* op paneel *Size:* hoog 31 ½, breed 36 ½ duim		(Bought In)

Palamedesz., Anthonie (manner)

1801/06/13	LNDLS	0074	*Palamedes* | Een Gezelschap van Heeren en Juffers, bij een tafel met eeten, op paneel, als Palamedes | *Mat:* op paneel	D van R	(Sold) fl 6:5 Swart
1802/06/28	AMSCH	0151	*Palamedes* | In een gevangenis ziet men Hugo de Groot, in de Kist gaande waarmede hy vervoerd word, als door Palamedes | *Size:* hoog 10, breed 14 duim	Anna Elink	(Sold) fl 9:10 Texier
1803/08/24	HGKAN	0034	*Palamedes* | In een Gevangenis ziet men Hugo de Groot in de kist gaande waarmeede hy vervoerd werd als door Palamedes | *Size:* hoog 10, breed 14 duim	[Teissier] [or others]	(Sold) fl 17 vander A
1804/04/28	LNDLS	0055	*Palamedes* | Een Man, die op de Dwarsfluit speelt, in een binnenvertrek, en een Juffer die op de guitair [sic] speelt, met meer bywerk, in den trant van Palamedes, twee stuks	[Abraham Delfos] [or others]	(Sold) fl 5 Rigter [for] G
1805/07/03	AMSCH	0199	*Palamedes* | Een musiceerend Gezelschap van Dames en Heeren, in een Binnevertrek by een Tafel, waarop Boeken en Speel-instrumenten leggen; meesterlyk behandeld, in de manier van Palamedes	R[oos]	(Sold) fl 13:10 L Pakker
1806/06/07	RMHSN	0061	*Palamedes* | Twee Stuks Gezelschapjes, in de manier van Palamedes	A E K L	(Unknown)
1807/06/10	HGBSM	0193	*Palamedes* | Een zittend Krijgsheld, als Palamedes | *Mat:* op paneel	Abraham Delfos [or others]	(Sold) fl 2:4 Smeets
1807/08/26	AMSCH	0317	*Palamedes* | In een Binnenhuis ziet men eenige Heeren op het Verkeerbord spelen; in de manier van Palamedes	Joseph Vallette	(Sold) fl 36 Coclair
1808/06/11	RMRIJ	0105	*Palamedes* | Drie Figuren, in de manier van Palamedes | *Mat:* op paneel		(Unknown) fl 1:10
1810/03/27	RMCNL	0075	*In de smaak doch beter als die van Palamedes* | Een gezelschap, drinkende; zeer uitvoerig en fraai behandeld		(Unknown)

Palamedesz., Palamedes (I)

1802/02/16	AMSCH	0049	*P. Palamedes* | Een hévige Schermutseling tusschen Ruytery, op de voorgrond leggen dooden en gekwetsten, fiks gepenceeld	G	(Sold) fl 8 Vink & Fitsing
1802/06/16	AMSCH	0132	*P. Palamedes* | In een Binnevertrek zitten twee Heeren by een Tafel met een Tapytkleed bedekt, verzelt van drie Musiecérende Dames; op de voorgrond en ter zyde leggen Muziek Instrumenten; alles is delicaat en Meesterlyk fraay gepenceeld | *Mat:* op paneel *Size:* hoog 12 ½, breed 17 duim *Notes:* The artist was presumably Anthonie Palamedesz. and not Palamedes Palamedesz (I).	[Merrem]	(Sold) fl 41 Gruiter
1802/06/16	AMSCH	0133	*P. Palamedes* | In een Binnevertrek zitten twee Officieren by een Tafel, zich met Dames, al Zingende en Drinkende vermaaken; de Caracters zyn natuurlyk, en van een uitvoerige penceel-behandeling | *Mat:* op paneel *Size:* hoog 13 ½, breed 14 ½ duim *Notes:* The artist was presumably Anthonie Palamedesz. and not Palamedes Palamedesz (I).	[Merrem]	(Sold) fl 29 Van Iperen
1802/06/16	AMSCH	0134	*P. Palamedes* | In de Wynkelder van een treffelyk Gebouw, vertoont zig een Heer, in deftige kleeding, als spreekende tegen de Kelderknegt, die een Roemer Rinsche [sic] Wyn in de hand houd; op de voorgrond legt een Voederstuk, Kooper Bekken en Kan, verder verscheiden Wynvaten; in 't verschiet een Gebouw; zeer natuurlyk en meesterlyk fraay gepenceeld | *Mat:* op paneel *Size:* hoog 13 ½, breed 9 ½ duim *Notes:* The artist was presumably Anthonie Palamedesz. and not Palamedes Palamedesz (I).	[Merrem]	(Sold) fl 6:5 P M Levy
1802/06/16	AMSCH	0135	*P. Palamedes* | Eenige Heeren en Dames in een Vertrek, men ziet een Bediende de Spooren aan de Laarsen van een Krygsheld vast maaken; ter zyde zitten twee die kaart speelen; breed van schildering | *Mat:* op paneel	[Merrem]	(Sold) fl 20 Cobel

			Size: hoog 12, breed 15 duim *Notes:* The artist was presumably Anthonie Palamedesz. and not Palamedes Palamedesz (I).		
1802/06/16	AMSCH	0136	*P. Palamedes* | In een Corps de Garde, ziet men Krygslieden op een Trommel met de Kaart speelen, naast een derzelve staat een Dame in galante kleeding; verder drie andere Heeren, als met elkander spreekende; krachtig van Coloriet en meesterlyk gepenceeld | *Mat:* op doek *Size:* hoog 50, breed 41 duim *Notes:* The artist was presumably Anthonie Palamedesz. and not Palamedes Palamedesz (I).	[Merrem]	(Sold) fl 16:10 B^d Kooij
1802/08/24	LNDLS	0111	*P. Palamedes* | Een hevige Batailje van Ruiterij	Leonardus Bouman [or others]	(Unknown)
1802/09/06	AMSCH	0093	*Palamedes* | Een hevige schermutseling tusschen ruitery, vol gewoel; fix gepenceelt | *Size:* hoog 12, breed 15 duim	X	(Sold) fl 4:10 van Cooth
1802/09/18	RMDRS	0113	*Palamedes* | Een Postwagen met Reizigers, rustende voor een Herberg, met verscheide andere Figuren | *Size:* hoog 13 ½, breed 18 ½ duim	Casper de Haas	(Sold) fl 16:10 v Giesen
1802/09/18	RMDRS	0114	*Palamedes* | Een aangenaam Landschap, waarin een Koets met twee Paarden bespannen, op de voorgrond eenige Jagers met Honden | *Size:* hoog 19, breed 23 duim	Casper de Haas	(Sold) fl 9 v Giesen
1803/04/20	AMSCH	0059	*Palamédes. (P.)* | In een Binnenvertrek by een Haardstéde, zitten twee Heeren, by een Tafel op het Verkeerbord speelende, een ander met een Roemer Wyn in de hand schynt het te beschouwen, verder andere Heeren en Dames zig vermakende; meesterlyk gepenceeld [Dans un appartement sont representés deux joueurs de tric-trac, qu'un troisieme Cavalier Salue un verre à la main ; des Dames & des Hommes s'amusant de leur côté forme de cet ensemble une jolie Composition qui est spirituellement touchée.] | *Mat:* op paneel *Size:* hoog 16, breed 22 duim *Notes:* The artist was presumably Anthonie Palamedesz. and not Palamedes Palamedesz (I).	Maria Magdalena van Sluypwyk, gravinne van Moens	(Sold) fl 29 Van Iperen
1803/09/07	AMSCH	0125a	*P. Palamedes* | In een pragtige Kamer zitten eenige Heeren en Dames aan een Tafel, waarop verscheide keurlyke Spyzen, één derzelven speelt op de Guitar, en een ander staat voor het vuur; alles delicaat gepenceeld [Plusieurs seigneurs et dames à table dans une salle superbe ; la table est pleine de mets exquis, une des dames joue de la guittare, une autre debout se chauffe au feu ; le tout d'une exécution delicate] | *Mat:* op paneel *Size:* hoog 19, breed 25 duim *Notes:* The artist was presumably Anthonie Palamedesz. and not Palamedes Palamedesz (I).	Smidt	(Sold) fl 8 C S Roos
1803/09/07	AMSCH	0126	*P. Palamedes* | Aan een Tafel zitten drie Heeren aan het Verkeerbord, wordende door een Dame een Glas Wyn aangeboden; uitvoerig gepenceeld [Trois seigneurs assis à une table et jouant au tric-trac, une dame leur présente un verre de vin ; composition agréable et bien traitée] | *Mat:* op paneel *Size:* hoog 13, breed 15 duim *Notes:* The artist was presumably Anthonie Palamedesz. and not Palamedes Palamedesz (I).	Smidt	(Sold) fl 10:10 Haffner
1803/12/12	AMSCH	0073	*P. Palamedes* | Een Gezelschap van Dames en Heeren, zich met musiceeren vermakende; delicaat op Paneel | *Mat:* op paneel *Size:* hoog 24, breed 31 duim *Notes:* The artist was presumably Anthonie Palamedesz. and not Palamedes Palamedesz (I).	W	(Sold) fl 31 Coclers
1804/02/27	AMSCH	0091	*Pallamedes* | Een Heevige Recontre [sic] tusschen Ruitery; de Hartstochten zyn aller natuurlykst, en uitvoerig gepenceeld | *Size:* hoog 20, breed 31 duim	B	(Sold) fl 6:10 Coclers
1804/05/07	AMSCH	0137	*Palamedes. (P.)* | In een Gemeubileerde Kamer, staat een Dame in aloude Hollandsche Kleeding, bézig op het Clavier te speelen; ter zyde staat een Minnewigt, verders gestoffeerd met verscheide bywerk; uitvoerig en bevallig behandeld | *Mat:* op paneel *Size:* hoog 13, breed 11 duim *Notes:* The artist was presumably Anthonie Palamedesz. and not Palamedes Palamedesz (I).	Schley	(Bought In) fl 2
1804/07/25	DLGRO	0090	*Palamedes* | Een Campement, op de voorgrond verscheide Ruiters te Paard, voor een Marketenters Tent een glaasje Bier drinkende, en een Bedelaar, fraai geschilderd door Palamedes | *Mat:* op paneel *Size:* hoog 17, breed 32 duim	Mr Franc van der Burch Wz.	(Unknown)
1804/08/02	BDAN	0005	*Palamedes Palamedesse* | Een Corps-de-garde met veele Figuuren, zeer schoon behandelt | *Mat:* op paneel *Size:* b. 25 en een half d. h. 20 d. *Notes:* The artist was presumably Anthonie Palamedesz. and not Palamedes Palamedesz (I).	J G Calckberner	(Unknown)
1805/07/03	AMSCH	0133	*P. Palamedes* | In een Binnevertrek ziet men een Gezelschap van Dames en Heeren, waarvan 'er een op de Guitar speelt; delicaat behandeld op Panneel | *Mat:* op paneel *Size:* hoog 15, breed 22 duim *Notes:* The artist was presumably Anthonie Palamedesz. and not Palamedes Palamedesz (I).	R[oos]	(Sold) fl 6 Coclers
1806/06/07	RMHSN	0057	*Palamedes* | Een Kamp te Paard &c. | *Mat:* op paneel	A E K L	(Unknown)
1808/06/13	AMSCH	0122	*Palamedes (P.)* | Een vrolijk Musiceerend Gezelschap, op den voorgrond ziet men een Heer, met zijn eene Been op een Stoel staande, met een Pijp in zijn Hand. Uitmuntend behandeld | *Mat:* op paneel *Size:* hoog 14, breed 17 duim *Notes:* The artist was presumably Anthonie Palamedesz. and not Palamedes Palamedesz (I).	G	(Sold) fl 35 Allard
1808/08/23	AMSCH	0129	*Palamedes. (P.)* | In een Binnenvertrek, vertoond zich een musiceerend gezelschap van Heeren en Dames, een derzelve speeld op de Guitar,	[Coclers]	(Sold) fl 13:10 Spaan

			terwijl een Officier met een pijp in de hand aandachtig staat te luisteren; krachtig gepenceeld | *Mat:* op paneel *Size:* hoog 24, breed 30 duim *Notes:* The artist was presumably Anthonie Palamedesz. and not Palamedes Palamedesz (I).		
1808/08/23	AMSCH	0222	*P. Palamedes* | In een gemeubileerd Vertrek staat een Krijgsbevelhebber, nevens hem zit zijne Vrouw met een Kind aan de Borst, en twee groote Kinderen staan agter dezelve, verder eene Knegt die Wijn schenkt; krachtig op Paneel geschilderd | *Mat:* op paneel *Notes:* The artist was presumably Anthonie Palamedesz. and not Palamedes Palamedesz (I).	Z	(Sold) fl 6 L Pakker
1808/08/23	AMSCH	0243	*P. Palamedes* | Een Kraamkamer met verscheiden Beelden | *Notes:* The artist was presumably Anthonie Palamedesz. and not Palamedes Palamedesz (I).	S	(Sold) fl 9:15 van Os
1808/12/12	UTWLD	0007	*Palamedes* | Een Veldslag [Alle in swarte Lysten en wel geconserveerd.] | *Mat:* op paneel *Size:* hoog 1 voet 8 duim, breed 2 voet 6 duim *Notes:* The bracketed information in the title appears above lot 1 and refers to lots 1 to 19.	Mr D Hoola van Nooten	(Unknown)
1809/06/13	AMSCH	0126	*P. Palamedes* | In een pragtige Zaal zit een vrolijk Gezelschap bij een welvoorziene Tafel, agterwaards verscheide Bediendens, verder eigenaartig Bijwerk; geestig | *Mat:* op paneel *Size:* hoog 21, breed 26 duim *Notes:* The artist was presumably Anthonie Palamedesz. and not Palamedes Palamedesz (I).	M	(Bought In) fl 15
1809/07/25	HGBSM	0240	*Palemedes* | Een Scharmutseling van Cavallerie | *Mat:* op paneel *Size:* hoog 10 en een half, breed 12 duim	D van der Aa [or] E B ten Dall	(Sold) fl 1:4 Heymans [for] G
1810/06/06	RMMUY	0104	*Palamedes* | Een Kampement | *Mat:* op paneel		(Unknown) fl 2:15
1810/06/20	AMSCH	0073	*P. Palamedes* | In eene Binnenkamer zitten drie Officieren bij eene Tafel, waarvan twee in het Verkeerdbord spelen, waarbij eene Vrouw, welke hun een glas wijn aanbiedt. Uitvoerig gepenceeld | *Mat:* op paneel *Size:* hoog 12, breed 16 duimen *Notes:* The artist was presumably Anthonie Palamedesz. and not Palamedes Palamedesz (I).	B	(Bought In) fl 10
1810/06/20	AMSCH	0074	*P. Palamedes* | Een zich met Muziek vermakend en Kaartspelend Gezelschap; fiks gepenceeld | *Mat:* op paneel *Size:* hoog 18, breed 31 duimen *Notes:* The artist was presumably Anthonie Palamedesz. and not Palamedes Palamedesz (I).	X	(Sold) fl 13:10 Pantijn
1810/10/11	AMSCH	0067	*P. Palamedes* | In een gemeubileerde Kamer, zit een geleerde bij eenen Tafel, houdende een Boek in de hand, op de Tafel staat een Globe, opengeslagen Boek and ander toepasselijk bijwerk; meesterlijk geschilderd | *Mat:* op paneel *Size:* hoog 19, breed 17 duimen *Notes:* The artist was presumably Anthonie Palamedesz. and not Palamedes Palamedesz (I).	[Gruyter?]	(Sold) fl 3 L Pakker

Palamedesz., Palamedes (I) (and Lorme, A.)

1802/02/16	AMSCH	0070	*de Lorne; P. Palanudes* | Een capitaal Binnegezigt van een trots Kerkgebouw, versiert met Orgel, Predikstoel en brandende Kerkkroon. ryk gestoffeerd met wandelende beelden, zoo Heeren als Dames, het kaarsligt geeft een natuurlyke werking, alles is kragtig gepenceeld, door de Lorne, en de stoffagie door P. Palanudes | *Notes:* The artist was presumably Anthonie Palamedesz. and not Palamedes Palamedesz (I).	C	(Bought In) fl 40
1803/06/20	AMSCH	0018	*J. de Lorme; P. Palamedes* | Een Protestande Kerk, van binnen te zien by Kaarslicht, het geen een byzondere werking van licht en bruin geeft, de ryke stoffagie door P. Palamedes, maakt te samen een geheel uit, zynde van de beste van J. de Lorme | *Mat:* op paneel *Size:* hoog 44, breed 62 duim *Notes:* The artist's name was given as "J. de Lorme" but we have assumed this is an error. The second artist was presumably Anthonie Palamedesz. and not Palamedes Palamedesz (I).	Roos [for] E	(Sold) fl 50 B Kooij

Palamedesz., Palamedes (I) (manner)

1803/08/24	HGKAN	A0018	*Palemedes* | Een Campement, ryk gestoffeert in de manier van Palemedes | *Size:* breet 23, hoog 15 duim		(Sold) fl 2 Carre

Paling, Isaack

1807/08/26	AMSCH	0174	*J. Paling* | In een Hofgezicht vertoont zich een musiceerend Gezelschap van Heeren en Dames, in treffelyke Kleeding; het verschillende Satyn is natuurlyk verbeeld, en van een meesterlyk fraaije penceelsbehandeling | *Mat:* op doek *Size:* hoog 48, breed 41 duim	Helsdinge	(Sold) fl 28 Spruit
1807/08/26	AMSCH	0175	*J. Paling* | Op het Balcon van een Hofstede zitten eenige Dames en Heeren zich met musiceeren te vermaken; de Draperyen, en byzonder het Satyn, is allervoortreffelykst geschilderd | *Mat:* op paneel *Size:* hoog 34, breed 27 duim	Helsdinge	(Sold) fl 32 van Iperen

Palm, J. [Unidentified]

1802/05/24	HGBAK	0039	*J. Palm* | Een binnen vertrek, waarin een Boertje, welke met de eene hand een brandende pyp van een kind aanneemt en met de andere een Vrouw omhelst in eene galante houding, agter hem eene oude Vrouw, door J. Palm, hoog 10 ¾ duim, breed 9 duim, zwarte lyst en vergulde bies | *Size:* hoog 10 ¾ duim, breed 9 duim	Mejuffrouw A van der Mieden	(Sold) fl 6:5 Heijmoens
1803/08/24	HGKAN	0043	*Palm* | Een Vrolyke Boer met een Glas in de hand, door Palm Dicipel van Dou	[Teissier] [or others]	(Sold) fl 17:10 Kan [for] Palthe[?]

Palma

1808/09/13	HABRU	0073	*Palma* | St. Johannes		(Unknown) fl 0:6

Palma (or Palma, manner)

1803/04/20	AMSCH	0060	*Palma. (J.) of in de Manier.* | St. Hieronymus, zittende en mediteerende voor een opengeslagen Boek; wyzende met de Regterhand naar een Kruisbeeld, ter zyde hem legt een Doodshoofd, en op de grond een rustende Leeuw, kragtig en meesterlyk gepenceeld [St. Jerome meditant sur les livres saints : ce petit tableau a beaucoup de mérite pour le dessin, la couleur, & la bonne maniere dont il est executé, Louis carrache à gravé ce sujet à peu près de même grandeur.] | *Mat:* op koper *Size:* hoog 13, breed 10 duim	Maria Magdalena van Sluypwyk, gravinne van Moens	(Sold) fl 13 Coclers

Palmer, Cornelis [Unidentified]

1809/06/13	AMSCH	0128	*C. Palmer* | In een Landschap vertoont zich de Jagtgodin, Diana, gepaleert wordende door haare Nimphen; het is bevallig en uitvoerig van schildering | *Mat:* op doek *Size:* hoog 16, breed 12 duim	R[ijfsnijder]	(Sold) fl 7:15 van Iperen

Palmer, L. [Unidentified]

1808/08/23	AMSCH	0184	*L. Palmer* | Twee stuks vergenoegde Grijsaards, waar van de eene zig met rooken, en de anderen met drinken vermaakt; uitvoerig op Doek | *Mat:* op doek	[Gruyter?]	(Bought In) fl 11

Palthe

1803/12/15	MGLAC	0018	*Palthe* | Een Kaarsligtje, zynde een Jongeling tekenende naar een Pleister Beeld; extra fraai en natuurlyk geschilderd | *Mat:* op paneel *Size:* hoog duim 20, breed duim 16	Mr L H de Haze Bomme	(Unknown)
1809/04/22	AMYVR	0102	*Palthe* | In een Binnenvertrek zitten een Heer en eene Dame aan een Tafel Wijn te drinken, bij eene brandende Kaars, waarbij eene oude Dame, in het verschiet ziet men eene Meid bij de Lamp aan de Wastobben; verstandig van licht en bruin | *Mat:* op paneel *Size:* hoog 20, breed 16 duim	de Bruin	(Sold) fl 35 Remmers Bredius

Palthe (manner)

1806/05/05	AMSCH	0181	*Palthe* | Een Man en Vrouw, speelende op een Verkeerbord; krachtig op Paneel in de manier van Palthe | *Mat:* op paneel	R[oos]	(Sold) fl 2 du Pree

Palthe, Gerard Jan

1801/04/08	HAVIN	0056	*de Oude Palthe* | Twee Vrouwe by de Kaars		(Unknown)
1801/05/11	AMSCH	0071	*G. J. Palthe* | Een bevallig Meisje, houdende haar regterhand voor een brandende kaars, schoon van effect en konstig behandeld | *Mat:* op paneel *Size:* hoog 17, breed 13 duim	Pruisse [for] M	(Sold) fl 16 Allard
1801/05/11	AMSCH	0072	*G. J. Palthe* | Een dito [bevallig Meisje], zittende voor een Tafel, waarop een koffykan geplaatst is, niet minder dan de voorige | *Mat:* op paneel *Size:* hoog 13, breed 10 duim	Pruisse [for] M	(Sold) fl 11:10 Schimmelpenning
1802/05/05	AMSCH	0175	*G. Palthe* | Een bevallige jonge Dame, in een paars fluweel Jakje, met wit bont gevoerd, en geelagtig satyne Rok, zittende, ter zyde een Tafel, waarop een kopere Blaaker met een brandende Kaars, en een Guitar geplaatst is, zy schynt, opwaarts ziende lustig te zingen; houdende in de regterhand een rol papier, als de maat slaande, op deszelfs schoot legt een open Musiekboek; het kaarslicht doet eene natuurlye [sic] werking, en is zeer uitvoerig gepenceelt | *Mat:* op paneel *Size:* hoog 13, breed 10 ½ duim	B	(Sold) fl 17:10 Schimmelpenning
1802/05/24	HGBAK	0059	*G.J. Balthe* | Een extra fraay natuurlyk Kaarslicht, staande op een blaker, op een Tafel, waar aan een jonge Schilder, tekenende na een Plysterbeeld dat voor hem staat, door G.J. Balthe 1735, op paneel, hoog 19 ½ duim, breed 15 ½ duim, zwarte lyst en vergulde bies | *Mat:* op paneel *Size:* hoog 19 ½ duim, breed 15 ½ duim *Inscr:* G.J. Balthe 1735 (signed and dated?) *Notes:* It is unclear whether the name and date are inscribed on the painting.	Mejuffrouw A van der Mieden	(Sold) fl 38 Kleijn
1804/05/07	AMSCH	0138	*Palthe. (G.)* | In een Gemeubileerde Kamer, ziet men een bevallige Dame, waarnaast een Heer, zittende aan een Tafel, houdende elk een wynglas in de hand, achter dezelve een oude Vrouw, door een deur ziet men een Meid bézig zynde aan een Wastobben; 't verschillende kaars en lamplicht en de uitvoerige schildering maken hetzelve tot een der beste van deeze Meester | *Mat:* op paneel *Size:* hoog 20, breed 16 duim	Vinkeles [for] H[affner]	(Sold) fl 29 Gruyter
1806/08/13	AMSCH	0340	*Palthe. (G.)* | In een Binnevertrek by kaarslicht, ziet men een jonge bevallige Dame by een Tafel zitten, bézig zynde te musiceeren; fraai van licht en delicaat van schildering | *Mat:* op paneel *Size:* hoog 13, breed 11 duim	Vinkeles [for] J	(Sold) fl 30:10 Verhoesen
1810/10/10	MGCIT	0020	*G.J. Palthe* | Een extra fraai en Natuurlijk Kaarsligt, staande met een blaker op de Tafel, waar aan een Vrouw en Jongen zig bevinden, de eene in een zittende en slapende, en de andere in een staande en eetende houding; terwijl het Ligt, zoo op deze als verdere Voorwerpen, van dit bevallig Schilderij, van eene ongemeene kragtige werking is	Caspar van Citters	(Unknown)

			Palthe, Jan		
1810/05/22	AMSCH	0084	*Palthe. (J)* | Door een open Nis ziet men een bevallig Meisje, houdende een brandende Kaars in de hand, zij schijnt zich van eenen Jongeling, die haar omarmt, te willen los rukken, verder eenig Huisraad; uitvoerig behandeld | *Mat:* op paneel *Size:* hoog 15, breed 21 duim	S	(Sold) fl 12:10 Koopman
1810/10/10	MGCIT	0105	*J. Palthe* | Twee Stukjes, zynde Huizen van Debauche: in een grappige trant uitgevoerd	Caspar van Citters	(Unknown)
			Panini, Giovanni Paolo		
1803/04/27	AMSCH	0136	*Panini* | Un Païsage avec des Ruïnes | *Size:* h. 50, l. 34 pouces	A	(Sold) fl 3:15 V d Brink
1804/07/25	AMSCH	0058	*Panini (J. P.)* | Twee stuks, Bybelsche ordinantien, zynde het eene, de Herders aanbidden het Kindeken, en het ander, de Koningen aanbidden het zelven, en offeren geschenken; ryk van Beelden en andere Voorwerpen, by oude Ruïnen van prachtige Gebouwen voorgesteld; fix en krachtig van schildering en van een schoone uitwerking | *Mat:* op doek *Size:* ieder hoog 39, breed 29 duim		(Sold) fl 61 C S Roos
1804/07/25	AMSCH	0059	*Panini (J. P.)* | Twee stuks, het eene verbeeld Alexander by het Graf van Darius, en het ander de Prediking van Johannes den Dooper; byde ryk gestoffeerd met Ruïnen en fix gepenceeld | *Mat:* op doek *Size:* Jeder hoog 9, breed 15 duim		(Sold) fl 8 C S Roos
1806/05/05	AMSCH	0117	*Panini* | Twee stuks Italiaansche Landschappen, met Paarden, Beelden en verder bywerk; meesterlyk en fraai gepenceeld door Panini | *Mat:* op doek *Size:* hoog 38, breed 29 duim	L	(Sold) fl 20 van Laar
1808/10/28	AMVRS	0048	*Panini. (G. P.)* | Twee stuks met oude Ruïnen, het eene gestoffeerd met de aanbidding der Herders; en het andere met de wijzen uit het Oosten, welke het Kind Jezus hunne geschenken brengen. Meesterlijk en breed geschilderd | *Mat:* op doek *Size:* ieder is hoog 28, breed 29 duim	Marten Udink	(Sold) fl 34 Reijers
1810/05/22	AMSCH	0085	*Panini (J. P.)* | Een Italiaansch Landgezicht, met aloude treffelijke Gebouwen met Kolommen en eenige Ruinen, op den voorgrond gestoffeerd met verscheide Beeldjes; zonachtig en meesterlijk gepenceeld | *Mat:* op doek *Size:* hoog 31, breed 38 duim	D	(Sold) fl 7 Yver
1810/07/26	AMSCH	0134	*Panini* | Een Gezigt te Rome, met grootsche Gebouwen, Ruïne en Beelden. Fraai geschilderd | *Mat:* op doek *Size:* hoog 28, breed 38 duimen	Cassino	(Bought In) fl 11
			Pape, Abraham de		
1802/06/28	AMSCH	0147	*A. de Pupe* | In een Binnenhuis zit een Oude Vrouw aan een gedekte Tafel, bezig een aarde Pan uit te schrapen; meesterlyk op Panneel | *Mat:* op paneel *Size:* hoog 17, breed 14 duim	Anna Elink	(Sold) fl 13:10 Jan Spaan
			Pardanus, Abraham		
1809/04/22	AMYVR	0105	*A. Perdan* | Een Musiceerende Heer en Dame | *Mat:* op paneel *Size:* hoog 12, breed 11 duim	de Bruin	(Sold) fl 1:5 du Pree
			Parenti [Unidentified] (copy by)		
1810/10/11	AMSCH	0068	*Parenti; Raphael* | De Maagd Maria, houdende het Kind Jezus op de schoot, nevens haar St. Jan; zeer uitvoerig en fraai geschilderd, op Doek, door Parenti, naar het schilderij van Raphael, bekend onder den naam van La Madona de La Sidia, hoog 28, breed 28 duimen. rond Formaat | copy by Parenti after Raffaello Santi *Mat:* op doek *Fmt:* rond *Size:* hoog 28, breed 28 duimen	M	(Sold) fl 21 du Pree
1810/10/11	AMSCH	0069	*Parenti; Guerchino* | Het Afbeeldsel van Sybilla Samia, halver Lijf, en in rijke kleeding, rustende met hare handen op een Boek; meesterlijk geschilderd, op Doek, door denzelven [Parenti], naar het schilderij van Guerchino | copy by Parenti after Guercino *Mat:* op doek *Size:* hoog 45, breed 37 duimen	M	(Bought In) fl 9
1810/10/11	AMSCH	0070	*Parenti; Guido* | Een stervende Cleopatra; schoon geschilderd op Doek, door denzelven [Parenti], naar het schilderij van Guido | copy by Parenti after Reni *Mat:* op doek *Size:* hoog 49, breed 37 duimen	M	(Bought In) fl 8:10
1810/10/11	AMSCH	0071	*Parenti; Michel Angelo de Caravachio* | De Kaartspeelers, op Doek, door denzelven [Parenti], naar Michel Angelo de Caravachio | copy by Parenti after Caravaggio *Mat:* op doek *Size:* hoog 29, breed 38 duimen	M	(Sold) fl 10 du Pree
			Parmigianino (Francesco Mazzola)		
1804/10/29	HRBAU	0082	*Permigianino* | Op dit Schildery ziet men Diana, in een gracelyke houding, by een stroomende Beek zittende, Calisto bestraffen, welke in een schaamagtige houding tegens haar over zit. Zy is vergezeld van verscheiden Nimphen, waar van sommigen verwonderd staan, en anderen over het wangedrag van Calisto schynen te redeneeren; in een zeer bevallig Landschap. Dit Stuk is grootsch geordineerd, schoon van licht en uitvoerig behandeld | *Mat:* op doek *Size:* hoog 25, breed 32 duim	Simon Styl	(Unknown)
1805/10/09	HGBSM	0076	*Pamesiano* | Twee badende vrouwtjes | *Mat:* op doek *Size:* hoog 11 breet 8 ½ duim	T H van Willigen [or others]	(Sold) fl 10 De Gelder

1808/08/23	AMSCH	0132	*Parmens. (F.)* | Eene jonge Vrouw, met verrukking Hemelwaards ziende, schoon van uitdrukking | *Mat:* op doek *Size:* hoog 30, breed 23 duim	J	(Sold) fl 14 Th Spaan

Parrocel

1801/08/19	AMSCH	0088	*Parosel* | Een Meenigte Krygslieden te paard en te voet, vegtende op een Brug en in het Water; meesterlyk op Doek | *Mat:* op doek *Size:* hoog 38, breed 46 duim	C S Roos [for] G	(Sold) fl 4 Pruijssenaar [for] R

Pasch

1804/10/29	HRBAU	0079	*Pasch* | Een Jongeling, zittende voor eene tafel, waar op hy met zyn elleboog leunt, en Kaarten en Dobbelsteenen liggen, Bellen te blaazen; hy ziet, met ongedekten hoofde, waar langs, op de bevalligste wyze, zyn blonde lokken zwieren, den aanschouwer met een vrolyk gelaat aan, als schynende zeer vergenoegd te zyn met een schoone Waterbel, waar op zeer natuurlyk het invallend licht spiegelt, voortgebragt te hebben. Zynde alles zo frappant behandeld, dat het schynt te leeven | *Mat:* op doek *Size:* hoog 30, breed 23 duim	Simon Styl	(Unknown)

Pee

1805/07/03	AMSCH	0198	*van Pee* | Twee stuks, verbeeldende een Fruitvrouw, en het andere een Vogelverkoopster; fiks door van Pee	C	(Sold) fl 19 L Pakker
1805/07/10	AMSCH	0119	*van Pee* | Een zinnebeeldige Ordinnantie in een Berg- en Duinryk Landschap met Geboomte; breed en Meesterlyk op Doek | *Mat:* op doek *Size:* hoog 44, breed 58 duim	V[inkeles] [for] P	(Sold) fl 1:5 A Zeeman

Pee (manner)

1809/04/22	AMYVR	0206	*van Pée* | Een Jongeling die Bellen blaast; als van Pée	de Bruin	(Sold) fl 0:6 Smit

Pee, A. van [Unidentified]

1809/06/13	AMSCH	0129	*A. van Pee* | Eene bevallig Vrouwtje, staande voor een Ton, houdende een Haring in de hand; krachtig en uitvoerig geschilderd | *Mat:* op paneel *Size:* hoog 9, breed 7 duim	A	(Sold) fl 36 van Iperen

Pee, F. van [Unidentified]

1802/09/30	HGBAK	0008	*F. van Pee* | De Schilder F. van Pee, door hem zelve gedaan, op doek, zwarte lyst. [Schilderyen in Olyverf] | *Mat:* in olyverf op doek *Notes:* The bracketed information in the title appears above lot 1 and refers to lots 1 to 26.		(Unknown)

Pee, Theodor van

1802/06/28	AMSCH	0154	*Th. v. Pee* | Een Visboer, houdende in de hand een Bot, voor hem een gekapte Cabbellauw, breed behandeld | *Mat:* op paneel *Size:* hoog 19, breed 14 duim	Anna Elink	(Sold) fl 10 Spaan
1804/02/27	AMSCH	0089	*Pee (Theod. van)* | In deeze geestige Ordonnantie, ziet men een bestruifd Meisje met het Hoofd op een Kussen rustende, en op een Stoel zit, haar Minnaar, welke door de Moeder overtuigd word staat in een bedrukte gestalten, men ziet ter zyde een Notaris, welke het Contract schryft; de caracters, zyn geestig en fraai gepenceeld, en dit stuk behoeft geenzints voor een Schildery van Jan Steen te wyken | *Mat:* op doek *Size:* hoog 23, breed 19 duim	B	(Sold) fl 200 Roelofs
1805/07/03	AMSCH	0135	*T. van Pee* | Een rustende Jager, in een Landschap met zyn Honden, hy houd in zyn regter hand een Haas, terwyl hy onder de linker-arm een Roer houd, terzyde eenig dood Gevogelte; bevallig behandeld op Panneel | *Mat:* op paneel *Size:* hoog 26, breed 20 duim	R[oos]	(Sold) fl 11 Hardenberg
1809/04/22	AMYVR	0103	*T. van Pee* | Een Vischboer, met zijne Vrouw spreekende over een keurig Botje, verders andere Visch enz,; delicaat | *Mat:* op paneel *Size:* hoog 19, breed 14 duim	de Bruin	(Bought In) fl 31

Peeters, Bonaventura (I)

1801/03/16	AMSCH	0099	*B. Peters* | Een onstuimige Zee met verscheide Scheepen, fix	K[ip]	(Sold) fl 7:10 Koopman
1801/04/08	HAVIN	0033	*B. Peters* | Een woelende Zee		(Unknown)
1801/08/19	AMSCH	0095	*B. Peeters* | Een woelend Water, met zylende en dryvende Scheepen en andere vaartuigen, by een Fort, op Doek geschilderd | *Mat:* op doek *Size:* hoog 26, breed 44 duim	van der Schly [for] F	(Sold) fl 11 Le Dantú
1801/10/06	AMSCH	0054	*B. Peeters* | Een sterk woelend Water, by een Stad, gestoffeert met zylende Vaartuigen, kragtig geschilderd | *Mat:* op paneel *Size:* hoog 19, breed 24 duim	M	(Sold) fl 12 Spruit van Gend
1802/06/28	AMSCH	0148	*B. Peeters* | Een woelend Water, gestoffeerd met zylende Scheepen, Sloepen, en andere Vaartuigen; natuurlyk behandeld | *Mat:* op paneel *Size:* hoog 11, breed 16 duim	Anna Elink	(Sold) fl 3:10 H Schotte
1802/06/28	AMSCH	0149	*B. Peeters* | Een Stil Water, op de voorgrond Vissers in een Schuit, verderszylende Scheepen, fiks geschilderd, door Denzelven [B. Peeters], op Panneel | *Mat:* op paneel	Anna Elink	(Sold) fl 0:8 Vermeulen
1802/09/15	HGKAN	0004	*Bonaventura* | Een Watergezicht, met Zee- en Scheepen, door Bonaventura, op Paneel en Vergulde Lyst [In Oly Verff] | *Mat:* in		(Unknown)

			olyverf op paneel *Notes:* The bracketed information in the title appears above lot 1 and refers to lots 1 to 8.		
1803/09/07	AMSCH	0127	*B. Peters* | Een woelend Water, met verscheide Schepen en Schuiten, geestig op Paneel [Vue d'une mer agitée, plusieurs navires et d'autres batimens lutent contre les flots ; le tout d'un effet piquant et spirituel] | *Mat:* op paneel *Size:* hoog 22, breed 34 duim	Smidt	(Sold) fl 10 C S Roos
1803/09/07	AMSCH	0128	*B. Peters* | In een zeer onstuimige Zee, by een Rots, ziet men een zeilend Oorlogschip; meesterlyk op Paneel [Une mer orageuse, sur laquelle on voit nn [sic] vaisseau de guerre près d'échouer contre un rocher ; excellente composition et d'un grand effet] | *Mat:* op paneel *Size:* hoog 9, breed 11 duim	Smidt	(Sold) fl 4:10 Tessier
1803/12/12	AMSCH	0076	*Bonaventura Peters* | Een woelende Zee met twee Oorlogschépen, ter zyde het Strand en een Bergachtig verschiet | *Mat:* op doek *Size:* hoog 46, breed 63 duim	B	(Sold) fl 28 Hulswit
1803/12/12	AMSCH	0077	*Bonaventura Peters* | Twee stuks, een woelend Water en een onstuimige Zee | *Mat:* op paneel *Size:* hoog 10, breed 16 duim	B	(Bought In) fl 11
1804/10/16	DLOND	0171	*Bon. Peters* | Maas Gezicht met Zeilende Schepen. Vue de la Meuse avec des Vaisseaux qui font voile | *Mat:* op paneel *Size:* hoog 23, breed 31		(Unknown)
1805/10/09	HGBSM	0137	*B. Peeters* | Een onstuimige zee, daar een groot schip benevens een galey tegen een rots schipbreuk leid, kragtig en natuurlyk, door B. Peeters 1651 | *Mat:* op doek *Size:* hoog 39 breet 58 duim *Inscr:* B. Peeters 1651 (signed and dated?) *Notes:* It is unclear whether the name and date are inscribed on the painting.	T H van Willigen [or others]	(Sold) fl 4:14 Ebbens
1806/05/05	AMSCH	0118	*Peeters* | Een woelende Zee by een klipachtig Strand, met zeilende Scheepen en verdere stoffagie; allernatuurlykst verbeeld en van een fraaije schildering door Peeters	V[inkeles]	(Bought In) fl 3
1806/05/05	AMSCH	0256	*B. Peters* | Een Storm op Zee	R[oos]	(Sold) fl 6:10 van Laar
1806/08/13	AMSCH	0146	*Peters. (B.)* | Een woedende Orkaan op Zee, men ziet by een Rots een Schip vergaan, waarvan veele Scheepelingen zich zoeken te bergen, stout gepenceeld | *Mat:* op paneel *Size:* hoog 29, breed 42 duim	Roos	(Sold) fl 3 Nieuwenhuis
1806/08/13	AMSCH	0341	*Peters. (B.)* | Een sterk woelende Zee met een strandend Schip; fiks geschilderd | *Mat:* op doek *Size:* hoog 15, breed 12 duim	Vinkeles [for] J	(Sold) fl 1:10 Van Dijl
1809/04/17	AMSCH	0075	*B. Peeters* | Een sterk woelende Zee, gestoffeerd met een Bijbel-Ordonantie; meesterlijk | *Size:* hoog 39, breed 49 duim	S	(Sold) fl 3:5
1809/07/25	HGBSM	0021	*B. Peeters* | Een woelend Water met Zylende Scheepjes, pikant geschildert | *Mat:* op paneel *Size:* hoog 9 en 1 half, breed 13 en 1 half duim	D van der Aa [or] E B ten Dall	(Sold) fl 9:5 van Eyk
1810/06/20	AMSCH	0121	*B. Peters* | Een onstuimige Zee	N	(Sold) fl 0:14 Andriessen
1810/07/26	AMSCH	0068	*Peters (B.)* | Een kabbelende Zee, met zeilende Oorlogschepen en andere Vaartuigen | *Mat:* op paneel *Size:* hoog 21, breed 23 duimen	Cassino	(Bought In) fl 7
			Peeters, Bonaventura (I) (or Peeters, B. (I), manner)		
1803/07/14	MGKLY	0023	*Peeters of zyn manier* | Een onstuymige Zee met Scheepen	Mr Caspar Jacob van Citters	(Unknown)
			Peeters, Bonaventura (I) (manner)		
1801/03/16	AMSCH	0125	*B. Peeters* | Een zwaare storm op Zee, by een Rotsagtig strand, waar in eenige Scheepen vergaan, op de voorgrond eenige geredde Scheepelingen, meesterlyk gepenceeld op paneel, als door B. Peeters | *Mat:* op paneel	K[ip]	(Sold) fl 2 Mensart
1802/05/10	MGSAN	0052	*Peters* | Een Storm, met een woelende Zee, met diverse Schepen; in 't verschiet een Kasteel en verscheide Gebouwen, en op de voorgrond eenige Beelden, in de manier van Peters: op Doek: in vergulde Lyst | *Mat:* op doek *Size:* hoog 15 duim, breed 23 duim	Johan Dirk Kruysse	(Unknown) £ 0:10
1805/07/03	AMSCH	0181	*B. Peters* | Een onstuimige Zee met Schepen, als B. Peters	R[oos]	(Sold) fl 1 L Pakker
1806/05/05	AMSCH	0221	*B. Peters* | Een onstuimige Zee, by een Kasteel, op een Rots; als door B. Peters	F	(Sold) fl 11:5 Riemsdijk
1809/04/22	AMYVR	0166	*B. Peters* | Een Onstuimige Zee; als B. Peters	de Bruin	(Sold) fl 1:15 du Pree
			Peeters, Catharina		
1801/03/16	AMSCH	0034	*C. Peters* | Een woelend Water, langs de Vest, gestoffeerd met een Sloep met Officieren, verders een ten Anker leggend Scheepje, alles dun behandeld	P[ruyssenaar]	(Sold) fl 5:5 J Spaan
			Peeters, Clara		
1805/10/09	HGBSM	0051	*Clara* | Twee stuks, verbeeldende het eene differente soorten van vis, benevens een kat, en het andere met kreeften fruit; een beker met wyn, brood een kruik &c., bizonder waar geschilderd, volgens de natuur | *Mat:* op paneel *Size:* hoog 13 breet 18 duim	T H van Willigen [or others]	(Sold) fl 12 Valette
			Peine [Unidentified]		
1804/07/25	AMSCH	0061	*Peine* | Een Mans Pourtrait, met gryze Haire [sic] en witte Baard, in een deftige Kleeding, met een goude Kéten omhangen; fraai van Coloriet en breed gepenceeld | *Mat:* op doek *Size:* hoog 26, breed 19 duim		(Sold) fl 14:10 Gruyter

Pel, A. van [Unidentified]

1801/04/13	AMSCH	0060	*A. van Pel* | Een Haringvrouwtje, Meesterlyk in de trant van G. Metzu geschilderd | *Mat:* op paneel *Size:* hoog 14, breed 12 duim	Pierre Fouquet, junior	(Sold) fl 12:10 Hulswit

Pellegrini

1807/04/00	LNDLS	0017	*Pellegrini* | Een Outvader met een lange witten baart, omhangen met een rode mantel, borstuk, extra konstig. dun en fix van schildering | companion to lot 18, by A. Bloemaert *Mat:* op doek *Size:* hoog 23 en een half, breed 19 en een half duim	[Abraham Delfos] [or others]	(Unknown)
1807/06/10	HGBSM	0017	*Pellegrini* | Een Oudvader met een lange witten baart, omhangen met een rode mantel, borststuk, extra konstig, dun en fix van schildering | companion to lot 18, by A. Bloemaert *Mat:* op doek *Size:* hoog 23 ½, breed 19 ½ duim	Abraham Delfos [or others]	(Sold or Bought In) fl 21 D

Penners [Unidentified]

1806/06/07	RMHSN	0126	*Penners* | Een Arkadisch Landschap en Watergezigt, met Beelden &c. door Penners, zonder Lyst	A E K L	(Unknown)

Penning, Nicolaas Lodewyk

1807/06/10	HGBSM	0161	*N.L. Penning* | Een Stal, waar in men ziet twee Koebeesten en een Geit, en verder bijwerk, zeer natuurlijk | *Mat:* op doek *Size:* hoog 14, breed 19 duim	Abraham Delfos [or others]	(Sold) fl 20 de Gelder
1807/06/10	HGBSM	0162	*N.L. Penning* | Een Landschap, waarin een bruin Bles Paard en twee leggende Koeijen, niet minder | *Mat:* op paneel *Size:* hoog 10 ½, breed 13 duim	Abraham Delfos [or others]	(Sold) fl 10 Heymans

Penninks, J.

1802/09/18	RMDRS	0069	*J. Pennits* | Een Landschap met hoog Geboomte en stoffagie van Beelden	Casper de Haas	(Sold) fl 3 Verweij
1804/10/16	DLOND	0169	*J. Pennik* | Twee Landschapjens. Deux Paysages | *Mat:* op doek *Size:* hoog 22, breed 27		(Unknown)
1810/10/10	MGCIT	0130	*Pennink* | Een uitvoerig Landschap, met een Ruïne en veelerlei andere voorwerpen; aangenaam behandeld	Caspar van Citters	(Unknown)

Pennus [Unidentified]

1806/11/24	AMSCH	0053	*Pennus* | Een Boschgezigt met een Rivier en bergachtig Verschiet, gestoffeerd met Herders en Reizigers; natuurlyk en kloek van schildering | *Mat:* op doek *Size:* hoog 52, breed 55 duim	Munnikhuizen	(Sold) fl 1 L Pakker

Pepyn, Martin

1808/04/26	GDAN	A0006	*Papyn (Maarten)* | Een extra fraai Italiaansch Landschap, met een Kasteel op hetzelven, en eenige beelden, meesterlijk geschilderd | *Size:* hoog 40, breed 60 duim *Notes:* This lot has been renumbered to distinguish it from another lot with the same number in a different section of the catalogue.	G H Fortuyn	(Unknown)

Perrini [Unidentified]

1810/07/26	AMSCH	0063	*Perrini* | Een Landschap, waarin den Zaligmaker aan Petrus verschijnt. Zeer fraai | *Mat:* op doek *Size:* hoog 19, breed 25 duimen	Cassino	(Sold) fl 2 Spaan

Perugino (Pietro di Cristoforo Vannucci)

1802/02/16	AMSCH	0021	*Perigiano* | Twee stuks Italiansche Boom- en Bergachtige Landschappen, met stoffagie van Beelden en Paarden; meesterlyk op doek | *Mat:* op doek	E	(Bought In) fl 54 for lots 21–23
1802/02/16	AMSCH	0022	*Perigiano* | Twee stuks dito [Italiansche Boom- en Bergachtige Landschappen] met biddende Heremieten; niet minder als de voorgaande	E	(Bought In) fl 54 for lots 21–23
1802/02/16	AMSCH	0023	*Perigiano* | Twee dito [stuks] dito [Italiansche Boom- en Bergachtige Landschappen], met verschillende stoffagie	E	(Bought In) fl 54 for lots 21–23
1803/04/27	AMSCH	0065	*Perugino* | La Sainte Vierge & l'Enfant Jésus, peinte sur bois | *Mat:* sur bois *Size:* h. 3 ¾, l. 2 ¼ pieds	A	(Sold) fl 3 Pruijssenaar [for] L

Petit

1804/10/16	DLOND	0172	*Petit* | Een Landschap met veel Geboomte. Paysage très ombragé | *Mat:* op paneel *Size:* hoog 12, breed 14		(Unknown) fl 3

Piazzetta, Giovanni Battista

1803/09/07	AMSCH	0129	*Piazetta* | Twee stuks Bevallige Meisjes, halver lyf; breed en meesterlyk op Doek [Deux charmantes filles, à demi corps ; largement peint] | *Mat:* op doek *Size:* hoog 17, breed 14 duim	Smidt	(Sold) fl 3 Scheffer
1803/09/07	AMSCH	0130	*Piazetta* | Twee stuks, een Capuziner Monnik en een Bevallig Meisje; beide meesterlyk op Doek [Deux tableaux, l'un un capucin et l'autre une jolie fille ; tous les deux d'une exécution excellente] | *Mat:* op doek *Size:* hoog 17, breed 14 duim	Smidt	(Sold) fl 5:10 Scheffer

Pichenelli [Unidentified]

1803/04/27	AMSCH	0040	*Pichenelli* | Un Chasseur avec du Gibier | *Size:* h. 4 ½, l. 6 pieds	A	(Sold) fl 3:5 Gruiter

			Piemont, Nicolaes		
1803/08/17	AMSCH	0068	*Piemont. (N.)* | Een boom en bergachtig Landschap met een Waterval, in het verschiet een Kasteel op een Berg, verders gestoffeerd met Beeldjes, warm en natuurlyk behandeld | *Mat:* op paneel *Size:* hoog 12, breed 14 duim	Anna Catharina Putman	(Sold) fl 9:10 Agina
1804/08/08	AMSCH	0154	*N. Piemont* | Twee stuks Italiaansche Landschappen, met Geboomte, Gebouwen en aangenaame Beekjes, geestig gestoffeerd met Beeldjes, Beesjes, Paarden, als andere voorwerpen; dun en aangenaam van penceel, door N. Piemont, op Doek | *Mat:* op doek *Size:* hoog 32, breed 38 duim	Roos [for] G	(Sold) fl 50 Theod Spaan
1808/06/13	AMSCH	0121	*Piemont (C.)* | Ter linkerzijde van een aangenaam boschachtig Landschap bevindt zich eene Watermolen, alwaar een Man, over de deur liggende, wordt aangesproken, ter zijde een opgaande Weg, langs welke een Jager met twee Paarden en een Valkenier. Zeer natuurlijk voorgesteld | *Mat:* op doek *Size:* ieder hoog 37, breed 45 duim	E M Engelberts	(Sold) fl 44 Glad
1808/06/13	AMSCH	0197	*Piemont* | Een Italiaansch Landschap; zonachtig	E M Engelberts	(Sold) fl 6:10 Th Spaan
			Piemont, Nicolaes (and Huchtenburgh, Jan)		
1807/08/26	AMSCH	0088	*J. van Hugtenburg; G. Piemont* | In een aangenaam Bergachtig en Boomryk Landschap, ziet men op den voorgrond een hevige schermutseling van Ruiters en Voetvolk, terwyl anderen een Convooy en beladene Muil-Ezels aanvallen; alles is met veel vuur en levendigheid verbeeld, door J. van Hugtenburg en G. Piemont, in hunnen besten tyd | *Mat:* op doek *Size:* hoog 25, breed 30 ½ duim *Notes:* The artist's name was given as "G. Piemont" but we have assumed this is an error.	Coclers	(Bought In) fl 140
			Piemont, Nicolaes (manner)		
1802/02/16	AMSCH	0092	*Piemont* | Een boomryk Landschap, waar in een Jager ter Valke Jagt gaande; in de manier van Piemont	G	(Sold) fl 3 van Dijl
			Pieneman, Jan Willem		
1805/07/10	AMSCH	0120	*Peuneman* | Sophonisba, de Kelk met Vergift aanneemende; krachtig op Doek | *Mat:* op doek *Size:* hoog 48, breed 60 duim	V[inkeles] [for] H[affner]	(Sold) fl 0:12 Spaan
			Pierson, A. [Unidentified]		
1808/04/26	GDAN	0122	*Pierson (A)* | Zijnde de Historie van Annanias en Saffira, waar Annanias dood word uitgedragen, zeer veel Beelden en wel geschilderd | *Size:* hoog 61, breed 82 duim	G H Fortuyn	(Unknown)
1808/04/26	GDAN	0123	*Pierson (A)* | Eenige Geweeren, Patroontassen, &c. in een Binnenvertrek ophangende | *Size:* hoog 39, breed 46 duim	G H Fortuyn	(Unknown)
			Pierson, Christoffel		
1807/06/10	HGBSM	0130	*Pierson* | Een stuk met Jagtgereedschap, hangende aan de muur, natuurlijk | *Mat:* op doek *Size:* hoog 28, breed 38 ½ duim	Abraham Delfos [or others]	(Sold) fl 1:14 Oosterwyk
			Pietro da Cortona		
1803/04/27	AMSCH	0011	*P. de Cortone* | Un Sacrifice, cette belle composition, est largement peinte | *Size:* h. 4 ½, l. 3 ½ pieds	A	(Sold) fl 4:10 V d Brink
			Pimont, Jan [Unidentified]		
1808/06/06	RMRIJ	0099	*Pimont (Jan)* | In een bergachtig en boomrijk Landschap ziet men eenen Waterval, eene Rots en Gebouwen. Op den voorgrond vertoonen zich eenige Visschers. Dit aangenaam en grootsch tafereel is in de manier van den grooten Vernet geordineerd en uitvoerig geschilderd [Paysage Montagneux, enrichi de beaux Arbres, de fabriques, d'un Rocher, et d'une Chûte d'eau. Des Pêcheurs à la ligne occupent le premier Plan. Ce Tableau harmonieux et d'une Composition agréable, tient du grand Vernet] | *Annots:* Verk P. Locquet, Amst. 22 Sept 1783 (f 70.-) (RMA I) *Mat:* op doek *Size:* Hoog 37 ½, en breed 31 duim	Gerrit van der Pot, Heer van Groeneveld	(Sold) fl 125 Coclers
			Plankman, J. [Unidentified]		
1804/05/07	AMSCH	0139	*Plankman (J.)* | In een Landschap met eenig Vee, ziet men de Verkondiging van 's Heilands Geboorte aan de Herders; natuurlyk en fraay gepenceeld | *Mat:* op doek *Size:* hoog 19, breed 24 duim	Schley	(Sold) fl 7:5 Thais
			Platzer, Johann Georg		
1803/09/07	AMSCH	0133	*G. Platzer* | De Batailje van Actium, tusschen Keizer Augustus en Marcus Antonius, zynde een ryke Ordonantie, vol gewoel, en van een delicaate behandeling [La bataille d'Actium entre Auguste et Marc Antoine. Ce tableau est d'une ordonnance riche ; plein de mouvement, et d'une exécution delicate] | companion to lot 134 *Mat:* op koper *Size:* hoog 21, breed 31, duim *Loc:* London, England, UK. Wellington Museum, Apsley House.	Smidt	(Bought In) fl 280 for lots 133 & 134
1803/09/07	AMSCH	0134	*G. Platzer* | De wederga van het voorgaande, steld voor, de Dood van Cleopatra, zynde mede van een voortreffelyke Ordonantie en Schildering; van denzelfden Meester [G. Platzer], in dito groote [Le pendant du	Smidt	(Bought In) fl 280 for lots 133 & 134

			précédent, il représente la mort de Cléopatre ; morceau d'une excellente ordonnance et traité avec soin.] | companion to lot 133 *Size:* hoog 21, breed 31 duim *Loc:* London, England, UK. Wellington Museum, Apsley House.		
			Poel, Egbert van der		
1801/04/13	AMSCH	0059	*E. van der Poel* | Het onderwerp van dit stukje steld voor, de ruïne der stad Delft, na het springen van het Kruitmagazyn 1654, zeer natuurlyk voorgesteld, geestig gestoffeerd, en fraay van schildering | *Mat:* op paneel *Size:* hoog 15, breed 19 duim	Pierre Fouquet, junior	(Sold) fl 27 C S Roos
1801/05/11	AMSCH	0067	*E. van der Poel* | Voor een Boerenwoning, ziet men een Vrouw bezig linnen te spoelen, wyders eenige tobbes, kannen en ander huisraad, alles natuurlyk behandeld | *Mat:* op paneel *Size:* hoog 18, breed 22 duim	E[lias]	(Sold) fl 12:10 Allard
1801/05/11	AMSCH	0068	*E. van der Poel* | Voor een Boerenwoning, ziet men een Jongeling met een hond speelen, krachtig gepenceeld | *Mat:* op paneel *Size:* hoog 17, breed 15 duim	P[ruyssenaar]	(Sold) fl 9 Pruijssenaar [for] R
1801/10/06	AMSCH	0052	*E. van der Poel* | In een Dorpgezigt, vertoont zig de Brand in een Boere Woning, op de voorgrond een meenigte Beeldjes, zeer natuurlyk behandeld | *Mat:* op paneel *Size:* hoog 24, breed 28 duim	M	(Sold) fl 67 Theijs
1802/04/13	HAVIN	0028	*van der Poel* | Een slapende Nimph, en verscheide Bachanten		(Unknown)
1802/04/13	HAVIN	0032	*van der Poel* | Een Boere Huishouden, met veelerhande Stoffagie en een Varke aan de Ladder		(Unknown)
1802/05/05	AMSCH	0177	*J. van der Poel* | Een Gezicht van eenige Boere Wooningen, by een stil Water, zeer natuurlyk | *Mat:* op paneel *Size:* hoog 19, breed 24 duim *Notes:* The artist's name was given as "J. van der Poel" but we have assumed this is an error.	G	(Sold) fl 4:10 van Iperen
1802/05/11	GRGRW	0061	*Van der Poel* | Een Brand [Schilderijen met Olie-Verf; In Vergulde Lijsten] | *Mat:* in olyverf *Notes:* The bracketed information in the title appears above lot 1 and refers to lots 1 to 79a.	Arnold Sicco Werumeus	(Unknown) fl 5
1802/09/06	AMSCH	0196	*E. van der Poel* | Twee stuks Binnenhuizen, gestoffeerd met verscheide Beelden en Boeren Gereedschap; natuurlyk en meesterlyk gepenceeld	Spaan	(Sold) fl 29:10 Jan Spaan
1802/11/01	DOBRA	0124	*van der Poel* | Een Boeren-Werf enz. | *Mat:* op paneel *Size:* h. 18 ½ br. 14 duim	Paulus van der Spyk [or others]	(Unknown) fl 30
1803/08/17	AMSCH	0065	*Poel. (E. van der)* | De ruïne van het gesprongen Kruitmagazyn te Delft, ter zyde ziet men noch een gedeelte van hetzelve in de Lugt springen, eenige verschrikte Beeldjes stoffeeren de Voorgrond, allernatuurlykst voorgesteld en geschilderd | *Mat:* op paneel *Size:* hoog 16, breed 20 duim	Anna Catharina Putman	(Sold) fl 38 Yver
1803/08/17	AMSCH	0066	*Poel. (E. van der)* | Het zelve Voorwerp even na het Springen, in alles als de voorgaande | *Mat:* op paneel *Size:* hoog 14, breed 19 duim	Anna Catharina Putman	(Sold) fl 12:10 Pruijssenaar
1803/08/17	AMSCH	0067	*Poel (E. van der)* | Twee stuks brandende Steeden, waaruit de Inwooners met Goederen en Vee schynen te vlugten, verligt wordende door de Vlammen, kragtig en zeer natuurlyk daargesteld | *Mat:* op koper *Size:* ieder hoog 5, breed 6 ½ duim	Anna Catharina Putman	(Sold) fl 10 Gruyter
1803/08/24	HGKAN	A0011	*v.d. Poel* | Dit fraaye Schildery verbeelt een Binne Boerehuis, ryk gestoffeert met een menigte Huysraad, met een bezig zynde Boer en Boerinne, fraay en uitvoerig geschildert | companion to lot A12 *Mat:* op paneel *Size:* breet 18, hoog 13 duim		(Sold) fl 32 for lots A11 & A12. van Hoven
1803/08/24	HGKAN	A0012	*v.d. Poel* | Een dito [fraaye Schildery] weerga zynde een Buitenhuys, niet minder | companion to lot A11		(Sold) fl 32 for lots A11 & A12. van Hoven
1803/12/12	AMSCH	0072	*E. van der Poel* | Een hévige Brand in een Dorp, alwaar een groote menigte Menschen bezig zyn dezelve te blusschen; kragtig op Paneel | *Mat:* op paneel *Size:* hoog 18, breed 14 ½ duim	W	(Sold) fl 22 V[n] Iperen
1804/02/27	AMSCH	0090	*Poel (E. van der)* | Voor eenige Tenten, ziet men een menigte Krygsvolk zo te Voet als te Paard, de Brand die in eenzer Tente zig opdoet, waardoor de uitslaande Vlam een krachtig effect doet; is evenredig de natuur gepenceeld, en zeer fraai behandeld | *Mat:* op paneel *Size:* hoog 15, breed 19 duim	B	(Sold) fl 36 Coclers
1804/07/25	DLGRO	0001	*Van der Poel* | Een Landschap, op de Voorgrond, een reizende Man en Vrouw, fraai en uitvoerig geschilderd door van der Poel | *Mat:* op paneel *Size:* hoog 12, breed 16 duim	Mr Franc van der Burch Wz.	(Unknown)
1804/07/25	DLGRO	0088	*Van der Poel* | Een Boeren binnen Huis, waarin een Boer zyn Hond zit te vlooijen, staande de Vrouw 'er by te kyken, met veel bywerk | *Mat:* op paneel *Size:* hoog 13, breed 16 duim	Mr Franc van der Burch Wz.	(Unknown)
1804/08/08	AMSCH	0157	*E. van der Poel* | Een Gezicht op de Stad Delft, na het springen van het Kruitmagazyn, 1654. met verscheide Beeldjes gestoffeerd, en zeer natuurlyk geschilderd | *Mat:* op paneel *Size:* hoog 15, breed 19 duim	Roos a	(Bought In) fl 10
1804/10/16	DLOND	0173	*Van der Poel* | Een brandende Molen by naeht. Un Moulin en feu dans la nuit | *Mat:* op paneel *Size:* hoog 18, breed 23		(Unknown)
1804/10/16	DLOND	0174	*Van der Poel* | Een Hooiberg Uts[a] [by naeht]. Un Grange à foin Uts[a] [la nuit] | *Mat:* op paneel *Size:* hoog 18, breed 23		(Unknown)

1804/10/16	DLOND	0175	*Van der Poel* | Een Winter Gezicht. Tableau d'Hyver | *Mat:* op paneel *Size:* hoog 9, breed 14		(Unknown)
1804/10/16	DLOND	0176	*Van der Poel* | Gezicht van het Springen van het Kruidmagazyn te Delft. Vue des effets facheux du Sauter du Magazin de Poudre à Delft | *Mat:* op paneel *Size:* hoog 15, breed 19		(Unknown)
1805/07/03	AMSCH	0132	*van der Poel* | Een hévige Brand van een Kasteel, schynende door Krygslieden aangestoken te zyn, welke op de Voorgrond de geroofden Buit schynen te deelen; krachtig en frapant | *Mat:* op paneel *Size:* hoog 16, breed 13 duim	R[oos]	(Sold) fl 23 Halingins
1805/10/09	HGBSM	0140	*van der Poel* | Een binnen huis, waar in een varken op de ladder en meer bywerk | *Mat:* op paneel *Size:* hoog 16 ½ breet 21 duim	T H van Willigen [or others]	(Sold) fl 4 Carré
1805/10/09	HGBSM	P0015	*van der Poel* | Een winter met schaatzen ryders, zeer natuurlyk | *Mat:* op doek *Size:* hoog 35 breet 44 duim	T H van Willigen [or others]	(Sold) fl 3 Voerman
1805/12/16	AMSCH	0046	*van der Poel* | Afbeelding van een zwaare Brand, in een Dorpgezicht, gestoffeerd met een ménigte Lieden, die Goederen bergen, en ter hulp komen | *Mat:* op paneel *Size:* hoog 14, breed 19 duim	V	(Sold) fl 1 L Pakker
1806/01/30	RMAN	0008	*Van der Poel* | Een Brandend Dorp	Dirk Langendyk	(Unknown)
1806/05/05	AMSCH	0116	*E. van der Poel* | De Ruïne na het springen van het Kruitmagazyn te Delft, met toepasselyke stoffagie; kragtig op paneel | *Mat:* op paneel *Size:* hoog 15, breed 19 duim	H	(Sold) fl 33 van Iperen
1806/06/07	RMHSN	0039	*Van der Poel* | Een Boeren Binnenhuis met veel Bywerk en twee Beelden, zynde van zyn beste tyd | *Mat:* op paneel	A E K L	(Unknown) fl 22
1806/08/20	HGBSM	0046	*E. van der Poel* | Eene Maaneschijn, verbeeldende een Strand gezicht, op de voorgrond een Wagen en Paarden en verders vol stoffagie | *Mat:* op paneel *Size:* hoog 17, breed 14 duim	Macalester Loup [or others]	(Sold) fl 17:5 Gram
1806/08/20	HGBSM	0148	*E. van der Poel* | Het Strand gezicht van Scheveningen, rijk gestoffeerd | companion to lot 149 *Mat:* op paneel *Size:* hoog 14 ½, breed 17 ½ duim	Macalester Loup [or others]	(Sold) fl 15:10 for lots 148 & 149. Gram
1806/08/20	HGBSM	0149	*E. van der Poel* | Een dito [Strand gezicht van Scheveningen] tot wederga | companion to lot 148	Macalester Loup [or others]	(Sold) fl 15:10 for lots 148 & 149. Gram
1806/08/20	HGBSM	0155	*E. van der Poel* | Eene Kerk in brand staande | *Mat:* op koper *Size:* hoog 3 ¼, breed 6 ¾ duim	Macalester Loup [or others]	(Sold) fl 4 Smeets
1806/11/24	AMSCH	0056	*Poel (C. van der)* | Een Binnenhuis, alwaar een Varken op een Ladder Hangt, terwyl een Vrouw Darmen schoon maakt, in 't verschiet eenige Kinderen, een katje en verder Huisraad; zeer fraai behandeld | *Mat:* op paneel *Size:* hoog 18, breed 17 duim *Notes:* The artist's name was given as "Poel (C. van der)" but we have assumed this is an error.	Munnikhuizen	(Sold) fl 5:5 Dusart [for] Spies
1807/06/02	AMHUY	0019	*van der Poel* | In een Boeren Dorp vertoond zich by nagt een Brand in verscheide Huizen, waarby eenige lieden het schijnen te blussen		(Unknown)
1807/06/02	AMHUY	0020	*van der Poel* | Een dito, de Brand van Sodoma, daar Loth met zyne Dochters uittrekt | *Notes:* It is unclear what "dito" refers to in the title.		(Unknown)
1807/06/10	HGBSM	0147	*E. van der Poel* | Een Strand gezigt bij maneschijn vol gewoel, met figuuren enz. | *Mat:* op paneel *Size:* hoog 15, breed 12 ½ duim *Notes:* This lot was misnumbered no. 149.	Abraham Delfos [or others]	(Sold) fl 1:18 Ten Haaf
1808/04/26	GDAN	0126	*Poel (E. van der)* | Een hevige Brand in de Stad, bij de Nacht, waar door men alle de Huizen in den omtrek kan onderscheiden, ziende daar door alle de werkzaamheden des Volks, zijnde de natuur nageboodst | *Size:* hoog 24, breed 29 duim	G H Fortuyn	(Unknown)
1808/06/06	RMRIJ	0100	*Poel. (E. van der)* | Een zware brand in een Dorp; met veel gewoel van vlugtende figuren en beesten. Natuurlijk voorgesteld [L'Incendie d'un Village. Une foule de Personnes sont occupées à Eteindre le feu, tandis qui d'autres se sauvent avec du Bétail etc. Ce Tableau est d'un Effet piquant, et a beaucoup de Mérite] | *Annots:* Schoorsteentuk uit syn huis (RMA I) *Mat:* op paneel *Size:* Hoog 20 ¾, en breed 26 duim	Gerrit van der Pot, Heer van Groeneveld	(Sold) fl 115 Allard
1808/06/13	AMSCH	0242	*van der Poel* | Een Brand in eene Dorpskerk, waarbij eene menigte Beeldjes, welke goed bergen en den brand blusschen; goed van uitwerking	R[oos]	(Sold) fl 14:10 van Bergen
1808/08/23	AMSCH	0130	*Poel. (van der)* | Een brand in een Boeren Woning, aan de kant van een Rivier, gestoffeerd met een menigte Beeldjes welke in een Overhaal Pont het Vée en Goed bergen, en anderen die den brand blusschen; goed van uitwerking en natuurlijk behandeld | *Mat:* op paneel *Size:* hoog 19, breed 25 duim	[Coclers]	(Sold) fl 41 David Maijkel
1808/08/23	AMSCH	0253	*E. van der Poel* | Een Brand bij nacht, waar in door verscheiden Krijgslieden geplunderd word; natuurlijk verbeeld	[Van Iperen?]	(Sold) fl 18 Dupré
1809/04/17	AMSCH	0180	*van der Poel* | Een Boerenhuis, waarin eene Vrouw bezig de pot te Kooken, krachtig | *Mat:* op doek	[Gruyter?]	(Sold) fl 2
1809/04/22	AMYVR	0106	*J. van der Poel* | In een Boerenwooning zit een Schoenmaker te werken, terwijl zijne Vrouw wascht, en met een Buurman door een Venster een praatje houdt, verders fraai bijwerk; zonachtig en geestig | *Mat:* op paneel *Size:* hoog 11, bred 15 duim *Notes:* The artist's name was given as "J. van der Poel" but we have assumed this is an error.	de Bruin	(Bought In) fl 20

1809/04/22	AMYVR	0107	*J. van der Poel* | Twee stuks Buitenhuizen, met stoffagie van Beeldjes; krachtig | *Size:* hoog 11, breed 14 duim *Notes:* The artist's name was given as "J. van der Poel" but we have assumed this is an error.	de Bruin	(Bought In) fl 25
1809/06/13	AMSCH	0127	*E. van der Poel* | Een Strand- en Zeegezigt, met Visschers en andere Beeldjes gestoffeerd | *Mat:* op paneel *Size:* hoog 9, breed 11 duim	Y	(Sold) fl 0:8 du Pree
1809/07/25	HGBSM	0074	*van der Poel* | Een Schildery, verbeeldende een Dorp in den brand | *Mat:* op paneel *Size:* hoog 10, breed 16 duim	D van der Aa [or] E B ten Dall	(Sold) fl 5 Hassevoord
1809/07/25	HGBSM	0088	*E. van der Poel* | Een Schildery, verbeeldende de brand van Londen, natuurlyk en kragtig geschildert en vol gewoel | *Mat:* op paneel *Size:* hoog 35, breed 58 en een half duim	D van der Aa	(Sold) fl 54 van der Aa [or] Mes
1809/07/25	HGBSM	0138	*E. van der Poel* | Een Strandgezigt by Maneschyn, en een dito zynde een Brand in een Dorp | *Mat:* op paneel *Size:* hoog 9, breed 10 duim	D van der Aa	(Sold) fl 1:2 van der Aa
1809/10/16	ARNIJ	0004	*Van der Poel* | Een Smits Winkel door van der Poel	Wed N Nijhoff	(Sold) fl 6 v Leeuwen
1810/03/27	RMCNL	0037	*van der Poel* | Men ziet op eene Groenmarkt eene Vrouw met eene Kaars in de hand, aan eene Groentewinkel, waarin eene Lantaarn hangt, groente koopen, de uitwerking van het ligt der Lantaarn op het gezigt van den Man, en dat van de Kaars op het gelaat der Vrouw is schoon		(Unknown)
1810/03/27	RMCNL	0098	*van der Poel* | Een Binnenhuisje, voorstellende eene Keuke, waar in men eene bejaarde Vrouw aan 't werk ziet, aardig geschildert		(Unknown)
1810/05/22	AMSCH	0145[b]	*van der Poel* | Een Bergachtig Landschap, op den voorgrond met Watervallen, verder eenige Beeldjes; natuurlijk behandeld, op Doek en een Brand in een Dorp met Woningen, door van der Poel, op Paneel, 2 stuks | *This Lot:* Een Brand in een Dorp met Woningen; lot 145[a] by Anonymous *Mat:* op paneel	D	(Sold) fl 2:5 for lots 145[a] & 145[b]. du Pree
1810/06/04	DOBRA	0021	*Van der Poel* | Een Boerenwerf met veel bywerk en beeldjes	Hendrik de Haas	(Unknown)
1810/06/06	RMMUY	0130	*E. van der Poel* | Twee stuks. Een Winter, en een Zeestrandje | *Mat:* op paneel		(Unknown) fl 21:5
1810/07/26	AMSCH	0066	*Poel (E. van der)* | Een Brand in een Dorp. Natuurlijk verbeeld | *Mat:* op paneel *Size:* hoog 15, breed 19 duimen	Cassino	(Bought In) fl 7:10
1810/08/06	AMSCH	0086	*Poel (E. van der)* | Een gezigt binnen de Stad Delft, waar in vreugde bedrijven bij gelegenheid van de Vrede, in den Jaren 1648, gevierd werden; alles bij den avond en zeer natuurlijk verbeeld | *Mat:* op paneel *Size:* hoog 22, breed 17 duimen	C	(Sold) fl 71 J Spaan
1810/10/10	MGCIT	0053	*E. v.d. Poel* | Een Schildery, verbeeldende een Boerenbedrijf met Figuuren, bezig in Werkzaamheden tot dien Stand betrekkelijk; voorts verscheiden Huisraad, levendig Gevogelte en Groentens; terwijl terzyde van het Huis een kribbe en ruif is opgeslagen, waaraan Rundvee en een Paard zijn vastgebonden, alles zeer fraai en wel uitgevoerd op het paneel gebragt | *Mat:* op paneel	Caspar van Citters	(Unknown)
1810/10/10	MGCIT	0083	*E. v.d. Poel* | Twee Schilderijen, zijnde Boeren Bedrijven, zeer rijk van stoffage, tot dien stand behoorende; in den besten trand van den Meester behandelt	Caspar van Citters	(Unknown)
1810/10/10	MGCIT	0084	*E. v.d. Poel* | Nog een dito [Schilderij] kleinder, houdende evengelijke Voorwerpen; niet minder als 't vorige [nr.83]	Caspar van Citters	(Unknown)
1810/10/10	MGCIT	0128	*v. d. Poel* | Een Stukje, zijnde een fellen Brand; zeer natuurlijk uitgevoerd	Caspar van Citters	(Unknown)
1810/12/03	DOBRA	0003	*van der Poel* | Een Buitenhuis, met eenige Keukengereedschappen		(Unknown)
			Poel, Egbert van der (manner)		
1801/03/16	AMSCH	0141	*van der Poel* | Een Brandend Dorp, als van der Poel	K[ip]	(Sold) fl 1 Croese
1803/09/07	AMSCH	0269	*van der Poel* | Een Brandende Stad; zeer fraai van effect, zoo goed als van der Poel [L'incendie d'une ville ; l'exécution de ce morceau est d'un grand effet et d'un mérite égal aux ouvrages de Van der Poel] | *Mat:* op paneel *Size:* hoog 14, breed 18 duim	Smidt	(Sold) fl 12:10 van den Brink
1809/07/25	HGBSM	0277	*van der Poel* | Een groot Gebouw dat in brand staat, in de manier van van der Poel | *Mat:* op paneel *Size:* hoog 33 en een half, breed 27 en een half duim	D van der Aa [or] E B ten Dall	(Sold) fl 2:10 Carrée
1810/07/26	AMSCH	0067	*Poel (als E. van der)* | Een Gezigt op een brandende Stad, waarin verscheide Beeldjes | *Mat:* op paneel *Size:* hoog 22, breed 32 duimen	Cassino	(Bought In) fl 4:15
			Poelenburgh, Cornelis van		
1801/06/10	AMSCH	0136	*Poelenburg. (C.)* | Een naakte Juno uit het Bad komende, waarby een oude Matrone: delicaat en uitvoerig gepenceeld | *Mat:* op paneel *Size:* hoog 17, breed 13 duim	Herman ten Kate	(Sold) fl 33 van der Schley [for] Rijfsnyder
1801/06/10	AMSCH	0137	*Poelenburg. (C.)* | By een Ruïne van een Italiaansch Gebouw, ziet men een menigte naakte Vrouwen zich gebaad hebbende: de Ordonantie is bevallig en alles delicaat behandeld | *Mat:* op doek *Size:* hoog 17, breed 13 duim	Herman ten Kate	(Sold) fl 46 W[l] Reijers
1801/08/19	AMSCH	0090	*C. Poelenburg* | In een Heuvelagtig Landschap met eenige Ruïnes, ziet men verscheide naakte Nimphen en eenig grazend Vee, uitvoerig op paneel geschilderd | *Mat:* op paneel *Size:* hoog 12, breed 10 duim	Van Forreest	(Sold) fl 25 v d Schleij [for] Merrem

1801/10/19	AMSCH	0057	*Poelenburg. (Cornelis)* | Een Bergächtig Landschap, waar in zich vertoont Adonis, die een slapende Vénus verrast, vergezeld van Cupido; in 't verschiet hoog gebergte en geboomte, aller uitvoerigst geschildert | *Mat:* op koper *Size:* hoog 10, breed 9 duim	Jonkheer Menno Baron van Coehoorn	(Sold) fl 54 Booijmans van Utrecht
1802/02/23	AMREB	0027[b]	*C. Poelenburg* | 2 stuks zynde het eene den jongen Tobias, door den Engel geleid wordende en het andere een Landschap, met Ruïnes, gestoffeerd met Nimphen, fraay op Koper | *This Lot:* Een Landschap, met Ruïnes, gestoffeerd met Nimphen; lot 27[a] by A. Elsheimer *Mat:* op koper	Margaretha Maria van Laar	(Sold) fl 31 for lots 27[a] & 27[b]. J Rooyers
1802/05/10	MGSAN	0030	*Poelenburg* | Een extra fraai Stukje, vertoonende Maria en Joseph met het Kindje, en een Bezoek van de Herders, zeet [sic] zacht gepenseeld, door Poelenburg: op Paneel, in vergulde Lyst | *Mat:* op paneel *Size:* hoog 11 duim, breed 15 duim	Johan Dirk Kruysse	(Unknown) £ 4:10
1802/05/10	MGSAN	0047	*C. Poelenburg* | Een fraai Historiestuk, daar Jupiter er een uit den Hemel slaat | *Size:* hoog 14 duim, breed 11 duim	Johan Dirk Kruysse	(Sold) £ 5 Schoolm[r] Priester
1802/06/16	AMSCH	0130	*C. Poelenburg* | In een Heuvelachtig Landschap met eenige Ruwiene, ziet men verscheide zittende naakte Nimphen, gestoffeerd met verder Bywerk; zeer bevallig en uitvoerig gepenceeld | *Mat:* op paneel *Size:* hoog 10, breed 12 ½ duim	[Merrem]	(Sold) fl 25:10 Wed Achtienhoven
1802/06/16	AMSCH	0131	*C. Poelenburg* | Door een Rots Gezicht, ziet men in een aangenaam Landschap met eenige Ruwiene; drie Vrouwen en een Man als met elkander spreekende, zonachtig, bevallig en uitvoerig van penceel-behandeling | *Mat:* op paneel *Size:* hoog 8, breed 10 ½ duim	[Merrem]	(Sold) fl 12 van Iperen
1802/06/28	AMSCH	0146	*C. Poelenburg* | Maria Magdalena in berouw, verzeld van eenige Engelen; uitvoerig op Panneel | *Mat:* op paneel *Size:* hoog 7, breed 8 duim	Anna Elink	(Sold) fl 2:5 Gruiter
1802/09/21	UTHDG	0073	*C. Poelenburg* | Vooraan een groep Beeldjes, schijnende gebaad of zich gewasschen te hebben. Verder fraaije Ruines andere Beelden, en een uitgestrekt verschiet langs Bergen en Valeiën. Helder en delicaat | *Mat:* op koper *Size:* hoog 8 ½, breed 11 ½ duimen		(Sold) fl 65 Niekerk
1803/04/20	AMSCH	0055	*Poelenburg. (C.)* | In een bevallig Landschap ziet men een Veehoeder, en vrouw, verzelt van twee Kinderen, zeer uitvoerig en fraay gepenceeld [Dans un joli paysage est assis un pâtre près d'une femme & de deux enfants, ce sujet est traité d'un pinceau moëlleux & soigné.] | *Mat:* op koper *Size:* hoog 6 ½, breed 8 ½ duim	Maria Magdalena van Sluypwyk, gravinne van Moens	(Sold) fl 126 Th[S] Spaan
1803/04/20	AMSCH	0056	*Poelenburg. (C.)* | Twee stuks ongemeene fraaye Landschappen, met Gebouwen, Ruine, en een Rivier, beide gestoffeerd met badende Vrouwen, en Veehoeders, delicaat en bevallig van penceelsbehandeling [Deux petits morceaux intéressans, l'on y voit des baigneuses, des pâtres & quelques ruines d'anciens batimens ; ils sont touchés de la maniere agréable & fondue que l'on distingue dans les meilleurs ouvrages de cet auteur.] | *Mat:* op koper *Size:* ieder hoog 7, breed 5 ½ duim	Maria Magdalena van Sluypwyk, gravinne van Moens	(Sold) fl 200 Cocler
1803/06/20	AMSCH	0078	*C. Poelenburg* | Een Grot met Nimphen, en verder stoffagie | *Size:* hoog 9, breed 11 duim	Roos [for] L	(Sold) fl 40:10 Hulswit
1803/08/17	AMSCH	0064	*Poelenburg. (C.)* | In een rotsachtig Landschap met Ruïnes en Watervallen, ziet men een menigte naakte en gekleede Beeldjes, verders een zonachtig verschiet, zynde alles uitvoerig gepenceeld | *Mat:* op paneel *Size:* hoog 13, breed 17 duim	Anna Catharina Putman	(Sold) fl 43 Gruyter
1803/12/12	AMSCH	0075	*C. Poelenburg* | Een Landschap, met naakte Beelden en vliegende Minnewigtjes; uitvoerig op Paneel | *Mat:* op paneel *Size:* hoog 11, breed 9 duim	D	(Sold) fl 1 L Pakker
1803/12/15	MGLAC	0022	*Poelenburg* | Een fraai en delicaat Landschapje met naakte badende Figuurtjes | *Mat:* op paneel *Size:* hoog duim 10, breed duim 13	Mr L H de Haze Bomme	(Unknown)
1804/07/25	DLGRO	0072	*Poelenburg* | Diana en Acteon, met verscheide badende Nimphen | *Mat:* op koper *Size:* hoog 14, breed 12 ½ duim	Mr Franc van der Burch Wz.	(Unknown)
1804/08/02	BDAN	0010	*C. Poelenburg* | Een Arcadisch Landschap om den voorgrond zyn eenige Figuurtjes | *Mat:* op paneel *Size:* b. 6 d. h. 5 d.	J G Calckberner	(Unknown)
1804/10/16	DLOND	0179	*C. Poelenburg* | De Heilige Familie, op de vlucht uitrustende. La Sainte Famille se reposant en chemin | *Mat:* op paneel *Size:* hoog 13, breed 20		(Sold) fl 20:5 v Yperen
1804/10/16	DLOND	0180	*C. Poelenburg* | De Emmausgangers. J. C. & ses Disciples en chemin à Emmaus | *Mat:* op paneel *Size:* hoog 12, breed 10		(Unknown)
1804/10/16	DLOND	0181	*C. Poelenburg* | Ene Naakte Vrouw op ene Rots, voorover bukkende, om iemand uit het water te redden. Une Femme nue sur un Rocher se baissant pour sauver quelqu'un de l'eau | *Mat:* op paneel *Size:* hoog 8, breed 6		(Unknown)
1805/07/03	AMSCH	0131	*C. Poelenburg* | Een Italiaansch Landschap, met stoffagie van Beelden, een Ezel en Koejen by een aloud Gebouw; delicaat op Koper | *Mat:* op koper *Size:* hoog 11, breed 11 duim	R[oos]	(Sold) fl 32 Coclers
1806/05/05	AMSCH	0236[b]	*Poelenburg* | Twee diversche Landschappen, door Breugel en Poelenburg | *This Lot:* Landschap; lot 236[a] by Brueghel	V[inkeles]	(Sold) fl 0:8 for lots 236[a] & 236[b]. Gruyter
1806/08/20	HGBSM	0035	*C. Poelenbrug* | Eenige badende Nijmphjes, in een aangenaam Landschap | companion to lot 36 *Mat:* op paneel *Size:* hoog 6 ½, breed 8 duim	Macalester Loup [or others]	(Sold) fl 79 for lots 35 & 36. Nieuwenhuys

1806/08/20	HGBSM	0036	*C. Poelenbrug* | Een dito [badende Nijmphjes] wederga, zijnde niet minder gestoffeerd | companion to lot 35 *Mat:* op paneel	Macalester Loup [or others]	(Sold) fl 79 for lots 35 & 36. Nieuwenhuys
1807/08/26	AMSCH	0176	*C. Poelenburg* | Badende Lieden, in een aangenaam Landschap, by een stille Rivier, waarby eenige Ruïnen van Gebouwen; zonachtig en uitvoerig behandeld | *Mat:* op paneel *Size:* hoog 5, breed 7 duim	Helsdinge	(Sold or Bought In) fl 1 v d Schley A [for] Helsdingen
1808/06/06	RMRIJ	0101	*Poelenburg. (Cornelis)* | In een aangenaam bergachtig Landschap vertoonen zich verscheidene naakte Nimfen, van welke eenige vlugten op 't gezigt van twee Faunen, die haar van achter eenig geboomte bespieden. Zeer aangenaam van koloriet en schildering [Charmant Paysage montagneux, où l'on apperçoit plusieurs Nymphes au sortir du bain, qui effrayées se sauvent à la vue de deux Satyres, qu'elles découvrent derrière les broussailles. Dans le fond, un lointain magnifique et un ciel d'azur indiquent une belle matinée, Le tout est d'une perfection achevée et d'une finesse de Couleur, qui a toujours disttngué [sic] cet Artiste] | *Mat:* op paneel *Size:* Hoog 14 ½, en breed 17 ½ duim *Loc:* Amsterdam, Nederland. Rijksmuseum. (A313)	Gerrit van der Pot, Heer van Groeneveld	(Sold) fl 660 Stratenus [for] le Roi
1808/06/06	RMRIJ	0102	*Poelenburg. (Cornelis)* | Een bergachtig Italiaansch Landschap met Gebouwen en Ruinen. Op den voorgrond eene zittende Vrouw met een Kind, die tot eenen daarbij staanden Ezeldrijver schijnt te spreken. Wat verder een Ezel. Op den grond een Man en eenig Hoornvee. Eene wedergade. Een heuvelachtig Landschap. Op den voorgrond Geboomte en drie Geiten; wat verder twee Herders. Schoon van koloriet en ongemeen precieus geschilderd [Vue Pittoresque d'Italie ; Paysage, sur le devant duquel, une femme assise auprès d'un enfant, cause avec un Muletier. Plus loin un Pâtre conduit des Boeufs. D'une belle couleur, et d'un prècieux fini. Le Pendant est un Paysage Montagneux. Sur une Colline ornée d'arbres, on découvre des Bergers et des Chévres etc. Ce Tableau fin et précieux, ne le cède en rien au Précédent] | *Annots:* Verk. Amst. 21 Aug 1799 (f. 135) (RMA I) *Mat:* op koper *Size:* Twee Stukken. Hoog 5, en breed 6 ½ duim	Gerrit van der Pot, Heer van Groeneveld	(Sold) fl 250 van den Berghe de Gand
1808/08/23	AMSCH	0131	*Poelenburg. (C.)* | Een aangenaam bergachtig Landschap, gestoffeerd met eenige naakte Beeldjes, en verder bijwerk; helder bevallig en dun geschilderd | *Mat:* op paneel *Size:* hoog 11, breed 13 duim	J	(Sold) fl 20 Van Iperen
1808/09/13	HABRU	0072	*Poelenburg* | Een Landschap, met badende Nimphen		(Unknown) fl 4
1808/11/28	AMSCH	0049	*C. Poelenburg* | In een Bergachtig Landschap met oude Ruïne, zit op de voorgrond de H. Maagd Maria, houdende het Kindje in haar Arm, nevens haar staat St. Joseph, verder eenige anderen, delicaat en uitvoerig gepenceeld | *Mat:* op paneel *Size:* hoog 13, breed 19 duim	[Gruyter?]	(Sold) fl 55 T Spaan
1809/04/22	AMYVR	0100	*C. Poelenburg* | Een Biddende Munnik in een Grot; delicaat | *Mat:* op paneel *Size:* hoog 9, breed 11 duim	Juff[r] Julikker	(Sold) fl 5:5 van Iperen
1809/04/22	AMYVR	0101	*C. Poelenburg* | Een dito [Biddende Munnik] met twee Beeldjes | *Mat:* op paneel *Size:* hoog 7, breed 6 duim	Juff[r] Julikker	(Sold) fl 1 van der Schleij
1809/05/26	HADAA	0016	*Poelenburg* | Diana met hare Nimphen door Acteön bespied	Mejuffrouw de Wed David Heemskerk [or others]	(Unknown)
1809/06/13	AMSCH	0122	*C. Poelenburg* | In een hoog bergagtig Landschap met Ruïnen, vertoond zig op de voorgrond de Maagd Maria, zittende op een Heuvel, houdende het Kind op haar schoot; nevens haar staat St. Joseph, en in de Lucht een glorie van Engelen, fraai van koloriet en alleruitvoerigst gepenceeld | *Mat:* op paneel *Size:* hoog 15, breed 12 duim	E	(Sold) fl 70 T Spaan
1809/06/13	AMSCH	0123	*C. Poelenburg* | De Heilige Familje, rustende in een Landschap; uitvoerig | *Mat:* op paneel *Size:* hoog 13, breed 18 duim	E	(Sold) fl 8:5 du Pree
1809/06/13	AMSCH	0124	*C. Poelenburg* | Een Boom- en bergagtig gestoffeerd Landschap, op de voorgrond met een dansende Sater bij eenige naakte Nimphen, verder op een grazige Weiden Landlieden en Vee; helder en uitvoerig geschilderd | *Mat:* op paneel *Size:* hoog 8, breed 10 duim,	[Gruyter?]	(Bought In) fl 4
1809/09/06	AMSCH	0061	*Poelenburg (C.)* | Een Mans Pourtret met een Juweel in zijn hand; zeer uitvoerig van schildering | *Mat:* op koper *Size:* hoog 6, breed 5 duim	Johannes Caudri	(Sold) fl 12:10 Gruyter
1810/03/07	UTWLD	0044	*Poelenburg* | Twee Landschappen	J J Woertman	(Unknown) fl 8:5
1810/03/27	RMCNL	0040	*Poelenburg* | Een Stukje, voorstellende Diana, badende met de Nijmphen, zeer fraai en delicaat gepenceeld		(Unknown)
1810/07/26	AMSCH	0064	*Poelenburg (C.)* | Een Landschap met Ruïne, gestoffeerd met badende Nimfen. Zacht en uitvoerig gepenceeld | *Mat:* op paneel *Size:* hoog 8, breed 9 duimen	Cassino	(Bought In) fl 5:5
1810/07/26	AMSCH	0065	*Poelenburg (C.)* | Een fraai stukje, met Ruïne, Beeldjes en Beesten. Teder geschilderd | *Mat:* op koper *Size:* hoog 6, breed 7 duimen	Cassino	(Sold) fl 13:10 Spruyt
1810/10/10	MGCIT	0047	*C. Poelenburg* | Een bevallig Landschap, vercierd met fraai Geboomte, eene zeer zagte en aangenaame Lucht, natuurlijk Gebergte, en een voorgrond met allerlei Gewassen; voorts zeer fraai gestoffeerd	Caspar van Citters	(Unknown)
			Poelenburgh, Cornelis van (and Both, J.)		
1808/08/23	AMSCH	0007	*Both (J); C. Poelenburg* | Een bergachtig Landschap met geboomte en dartel Kreupelgewas, ter zijde met een loopend water doorsneeden,	X	(Bought In) fl 760

			gestoffeerd op den voorgrond met drie Vrouwen benevens een Jongen, en in het verschiet drie andere Beeldjes; het Landschap is zonachtig en warm van Coloriet, en de Beeldjes zijn delicaat en uitvoerig gepenceeld | *Mat:* op doek *Size:* hoog 38, breed 46 duim *Loc:* Roma, Italia. Busiri-Vici collection.		

Poelenburgh, Cornelis van (and Breenbergh)

1804/10/16	DLOND	0136a	*C. Polenburg; B. Breenburg* | [Untitled] | *Notes:* The lot was changed from "G. Metzu, Een Meisjen, liggende over de deur bij enige Wyngaardranken," to "C. Polenburg en B. Breenburg," without giving a title, at the front of the catalogue.		(Unknown)

Poelenburgh, Cornelis van (and Griffier, J. (I))

1810/10/10	MGCIT	0010	*J. Griffier; C. Poelenburg* | Een schoon Stuk met Ruïnen, door J. Griffier, en gestoffeerd met Figuuren en Gewassen, door C. Poelenburg; zijnde deze Schilderij door beide Meesters keurig en in een geëmailleerde trant behandeld	Caspar van Citters	(Unknown)

Poelenburgh, Cornelis van (or Poelenburgh, C., manner)

1805/06/24	DOBLU	0026	*Poelenburg* | Een Fabelsche Historie, door of in de Manier van Poelenburg	Willem Snellen [or] F R E Nibbelinck [or] Gysbert Visser	(Unknown)
1805/10/09	HGBSM	0108	*C. Poelenburg* | Een landschap met eenige ruïnes van oude gebouwen, de voorgrond gestoffeerd met een heilige famillie, in de hoogte een groep met engeltjes, uitvoerig geschilderd door of in de manier van C. Poelenburg | *Mat:* op doek *Size:* hoog 15 ½ breet 18 ½ duim	T H van Willigen [or others]	(Sold) fl 8:10 Tomasse

Poelenburgh, Cornelis van (manner)

1802/07/27	AKHRK	0069	*Poelenburg* | Een rotsachtig Landschap en Waterval, op de voorgrond badende Nimphen, door een Sater bespied; als van Poelenburg | *Mat:* op paneel *Size:* hoog 14 ½, breed 19 ½ duim	Maria Stategaart	(Sold) fl 2:10 for lots 69 & 70. Vanderham
1802/07/27	AKHRK	0070	*Poelenburg* | Een Brug over een Rivier, met vier badende Nimphen, mede als de voorige en goed geschilderd [als van Poelenburg]	Maria Stategaart	(Sold) fl 2:10 for lots 69 & 70. Vanderham
1803/08/24	HGKAN	0026	*Poelenburg* | Een Lantschapje met hoog Geboomte, gestoffeerd met badende en rustende figuuren, uitvoerig geschildert in de Trant van Poelenburg | *Mat:* op paneel *Size:* hoog 10, breet 11 duim	[Teissier] [or others]	(Unknown) fl 5
1804/02/27	AMSCH	0132	*Pollenburg* | Een Boomryk Landschap, met een Boksvoet bespiedende een slaapende Nimph; bevallig geschilderd, als Pollenburg | *Mat:* op doek *Size:* hoog 19, breed 24 duim	C	(Sold) fl 0:10 Oostwijn
1804/10/16	DLOND	0291	*Zo goed als van C. Poelenburg* | Diana in het Bad. Diana au Bain | *Mat:* op doek *Size:* hoog 14, breed 11		(Unknown) fl 8:5
1805/07/03	AMSCH	0212	*Poelenburg* | In een Bergachtig Landschap, met een Rivier, ziet men op de Voorgrond een Grot, waarin eenige naakte rustende Nimphen, verders een Bergachtig verschiet; en als Poelenburg geschilderd | *Mat:* op paneel	V[inkeles]	(Sold) fl 15 Gruyter
1805/10/09	HGBSM	0144	*C. Poelenburg* | Een landschapje met badende nimphjes, in de trant van C. Poelenburg | *Mat:* op doek *Size:* hoog 8 ½ breet 12 duim	T H van Willigen [or others]	(Sold) fl 1 van den Broek
1807/06/10	HGBSM	0208	*Poelenburg* | Een Landschap in de trant van Poelenburg | *Mat:* op koper	Abraham Delfos [or others]	(Sold) fl 3 de Gelder

Polidoro da Caravaggio (Polidoro Caldara)

1803/04/27	AMSCH	0081[a]	*Polidore* | Deux Tableaux, Christ mort peint en Grisaille par le Polidore, & Pan & la Nimphe Syrinx | *This Lot:* Christ mort peint en Grisaille; lot 81[b] by Anonymous	A	(Sold) fl 1:5 for lots 81[a] & 81[b]. Stevens

Pompe, Gerrit

1801/08/19	AMSCH	0094	*G. Pompe* | Een Zee met Scheepen | *Size:* hoog 40, breed 49 duim	Van Forreest	(Sold) fl 2:5 Roos

Ponse, Joris

1810/07/23	DOLG2	000D	*Joris Ponsen* | Een Schoorsteenstuk, met Vogels. Op den voorgrond ziet men een witten pronkenden Kalkoen, een Oost-Indische Rave, Faisant, en meer andere Vogels; benevens eenige Vruchten. Het verschiet is een Tuingezicht, meesterlijk en schoon geschilderd, door den beroemden Bloemschilder | *Mat:* op doek *Fmt:* schoorsteenstuk *Size:* hoog 68, breed 41 duim	Pieter Quinting	(Sold) fl 14 A v Strij

Poorter, Willem de (copy by)

1806/11/24	AMSCH	0057	*Poorter (W. de); Corégio* | De Herders aanbidden het Kindeken Jesus en offeren geschenken, zynde een Navolging van de beroemde Nagt van Corégio; zeer bevallig en uitvoerig van penceel | copy by W. Poorter after Correggio *Mat:* op paneel *Size:* hoog 8 ½, breed 11 duim	Munnikhuizen	(Sold) fl 8:10 Van Iperen

Pooter, J. de [Unidentified]

1803/09/07	AMSCH	0132	*J. de Pooter* | Twee stuks Binnenhuizen, met eenige Dansende en Drinkende Huislieden; geestig als Teniers [Deux intérieurs, où l'on voit quelques villageois s'amusant à danser et à boire ; composition spirituelle dans le genre de Téniers] | *Mat:* op paneel *Size:* hoog 11, breed 15 duim	Smidt	(Bought In) fl 20

Porcellis, Jan

1801/04/08	HAVIN	0063	*Pereelles* | Den dito [Zeën]		(Unknown)
1801/05/11	AMSCH	0070	*J. Percelles* | Een onstuimige Zee, in dezelve ziet men een Schip vergaan, de branding in het water is wel waargenoomen, en krachtig geschilderd | *Mat:* op doek *Size:* hoog 39, breed 50 duim	Pruisse [for] M	(Sold) fl 50:10 Coclers
1801/10/06	AMSCH	0053	*J. Percelis* | Een woelend water met een zylend Beurtschip, en een Sloep met eenige Visschers die hun netten ophaalen, verders andere Scheepen, natuurlyk en bevallig gepenceeld | *Mat:* op paneel *Size:* hoog 18, breed 24 duim	M	(Sold) fl 21:10 V^{n} Leering [or] Van Leeuwen
1802/04/13	HAVIN	0012	*Percelles* | Een Zee met Zeilende Scheepen, extra uitvoerig		(Unknown)
1802/08/24	LNDLS	0090	*Percelles* | Een Zeetje met zeilende Schepen | *Mat:* op paneel *Size:* hoog 12, breed 19 duimen	Leonardus Bouman [or others]	(Unknown) fl 2:14
1802/09/06	AMSCH	0235	*Percelles* | Twee stuks woelende waters	J	(Sold) fl 4:5 H Bauer
1802/11/01	DOBRA	0111	*Percelles* | Een woelend watertje met scheepen, zeer uitvoerig | *Mat:* op paneel *Size:* h. 12 breed 10 duim	Paulus van der Spyk [or others]	(Sold) fl 3 Randwyk [?]
1802/12/13	AMSCH	0133	*J. Percellis* | Een onstuimig Water met verscheide Vaartuigen en Beeldjes, natuurlyk behandeld | *Mat:* op paneel *Size:* hoog 12, breed 15 duim	Yver	(Sold) fl 15:10 L Pakker
1803/04/20	AMSCH	0058	*Percellis* | Twee stuks woelende Waters, met verscheide zylende Scheepen, natuurlyk en fiks behandeld [Deux marines ornée de navires, bien traitées.] | *Mat:* op paneel *Fmt:* rond *Size:* hoog 21 duim	Maria Magdalena van Sluypwyk, gravinne van Moens	(Sold) fl 1 Gruiter
1803/08/17	AMSCH	0069	*Percelles (J.)* | Twee stuks, zynde een stil en een woelend Water, gestoffeerd met verscheide Vaartuigen, uitvoerig geschilderd | *Mat:* op paneel *Size:* ieder hoog 8, breed 10 duim	Anna Catharina Putman	(Sold) fl 3 Gruyter
1803/12/12	AMSCH	0074	*Percelles* | Een Onstuimige Zee, met een zeilende Boot; meesterlyk op Doek | *Mat:* op doek *Size:* hoog 11, breed 15 duim	W	(Sold) fl 1:10 Coclers
1804/07/25	DLGRO	0094	*Percelles* | Een onstuimige Zee, met verscheidene in 't gevaar zynde Scheepen | *Mat:* op paneel *Size:* hoog 15, breed 25 duim	Mr Franc van der Burch Wz.	(Unknown)
1804/10/16	DLOND	0170	*J. Percelles* | Ene Onstuimige Zee met Schepen tegen ene Rots stotende. Une Mer orageuse avec des Vaisseaux brisans contre un Rocher | *Mat:* op paneel *Size:* hoog 25, breed 39		(Unknown)
1804/10/29	HRBAU	0080	*Percellis* | Een onstuimige Zee; voor aan op het zonlicht ziet men een Buis by den wind zeilen, die eene sterke Branding verwekt; wyders een Oorlogschip en meer andere Vaartuigen. De lugt is buijig, en het stuiven der Zee is in dit Stukjen zeer wel waargenomen | *Mat:* op paneel *Size:* hoog 14, breed 19 duim	Simon Styl	(Unknown)
1804/10/29	HRBAU	0081	*Percellis* | In een sterke woelende Zee ziet men een Buis by, en een ander voor den wind zeilen, benevens nog eenige Vaartuigen in 't verschiet. Fiks behandeld | *Mat:* op paneel *Size:* hoog 15, breed 24 duim	Simon Styl	(Unknown)
1806/08/13	AMSCH	0148	*Percelles. (J.)* | Twee stuks, een stil en woelend Water, gestoffeerd met zeilende en stilleggende Vaartuigen; beide geestig uitgevoerd | *Mat:* op paneel *Size:* Ieder hoog 8, breed 10 duim	Vinkeles [for] G[ruyter]	(Sold) fl 2 T Spaan
1808/11/28	AMSCH	0050	*J. Percellis* | Een sterk woelende Zee, met zeilende Beurtscheepen en andere Vaartuigen, fiks | *Mat:* op paneel *Size:* hoog 19, breed 24 duim	H	(Sold) fl 0:10 du Pree
1808/12/31	RMHSN	0022	*Percelles* | Een Zeetje | *Mat:* op paneel	G Spanjaart [or] H de Haas [or] C van der Looy Lans	(Unknown)
1809/06/13	AMSCH	0217	*Percellis* | Een sterkwoelende Zee	E	(Sold) fl 0:6 L Pakker
1810/05/22	AMSCH	0086	*Percellis (J.)* | Eene woelende Zee, met twee zeilende Schepen, ter zijde een Schuitje bij Paalwerk, fiks van schildering | *Mat:* op paneel *Size:* hoog 15, breed 18 duim	R	(Sold) fl 4:5 Twisk
1810/05/22	AMSCH	0087	*Percellis (J.)* | Een woelend Water, gestoffeerd met zeilende Schepen en andere Vaartuigen; meesterlijk behandeld | *Mat:* op paneel *Size:* hoog 24, breed 32 duim	F	(Sold) fl 1 v der Schleij
1810/05/22	AMSCH	0146	*J. Percellis* | Twee stuks woelende Waters, met zeilende Scheepen | *Mat:* op paneel	D	(Sold) fl 1:10 Boelhouwer
1810/06/20	AMSCH	0075	*J. Percellis* | Eene woelende Zee met Schepen. Natuurlijk voorgesteld | *Mat:* op paneel *Size:* hoog 22, breed 34 duimen	Q	(Sold) fl 2:10 Sardet
1810/06/20	AMSCH	0076	*J. Percellis* | Eene onstuimigen Zee, alwaar een Schip tegen de Rotsen verbrijseld wordt. Meesterlijk gepenceeld | *Mat:* op paneel *Size:* hoog 29, breed 41 duimen	X	(Sold) fl 1:5 Andriessen
1810/07/23	DOLGI	0042	*Percelis* | Een Zeestrand bij het Dorp Scheveningen. In Zee, en aan het Strand, eenige Pinkjes, Visschers, en andere Beeldtjes | *Mat:* op paneel *Size:* hoog 8 ½, breed 14 duim	Mr Pieter van den Santheuvel	(Sold) fl 6 van Braam a Dordt
1810/10/11	AMSCH	0172	*Percellis* | Eene kabbelende Zee, met Schepen | *Notes:* This lot was sold with lot 171 by R. La Haye.	[Levy Pakker?]	(Sold or Bought In) fl 0:6 for lots 171 & 172. L Pakker

Porcellis, Jan (copy after)

1802/09/18	RMDRS	0076	*Percelles* | Een woelende Zee, na Percelles	Casper de Haas	(Unknown) fl 1

Porcellis, Jan (manner)

1802/09/18	RMDRS	0070	*Percellis* | Een onstuimige Zee met Scheepen, in de manier van Percellis	Casper de Haas	(Unknown) fl 1
1802/11/01	DOBRA	0043	*Percelles* | Een woelende Zee met Scheepjes, als door Percelles | *Mat:* op paneel *Size:* breed 19, hoog 14 ½ duim	Paulus van der Spyk [or others]	(Sold) fl 5:10 Schouman
1810/06/06	RMMUY	0148	*Percelles* | Een Zee Storm, meesterlijk. Als door Percelles | *Mat:* op paneel		(Sold) fl 7 Strikland

Portengen

1809/04/17	AMSCH	0076	*Portingen* | Een bergachtig Landschap, met een Rivier doorsneeden, gestoffeerd met een Man te Paard, een Landman met twee Muilëzels en een drift Beesten; zonagtig behandeld, door Portingen, in de manier van Both | *Mat:* op doek *Size:* hoog 39, breed 50 duim	H	(Sold) fl 5

Post, Frans Jansz.

1801/04/08	HAVIN	0020	*F. Post* | Twee Westindische Landschappen		(Unknown)
1802/02/16	AMSCH	0082	*F. Post* | Een gestoffeerd West-Indiesch Landschap	E	(Sold) fl 28 Jan Spaan
1803/08/24	HGKAN	A0030	*Poost* | Een West-Indisch Gezigt		(Unknown)
1803/09/07	AMSCH	0131	*F. Post* | Twee stuks Gezichten in de Indien, gestoffeerd met een ménigte Beeldjes, enz; Natuurlyk door F. Post, beide op Paneel [Deux vues des Indes, animées par differentes figures etc. tableaux d'une expression naturelle et belle] | *Mat:* op paneel *Size:* yder hoog 8, br.10 duim	Smidt	(Sold) fl 10:10 Gruiter
1808/03/03	HAVIN	0024	*F. Post* | Een Landschap	Jacobus Spillebout	(Unknown) fl 0:8
1810/03/23	HAVIN	0077	*F. Post* | Een W. I. Landschap [In Lysten met Glasen] | *Notes:* The bracketed information in the title appears above lot 63 and refers to lots 63 to 79.	Rudolf Hendrik de Wetstein [or others]	(Unknown)
1810/06/06	RMMUY	0169	*Post* | Eene Plantage in de West | *Mat:* op paneel		(Sold) fl 1:10 Strikland

Pot, Hendrik Gerritsz.

1809/10/20	UTWLD	0035	*H. Pot* | Een Schip door H. Pot	J J van Rhyn	(Unknown)

Pothoven, Hendrik

1801/12/22	AMOTT	0001	*J. Pothoven* | 2 stuks bevallige Landschappen met een Plysterplaats, Vissers, Rivieren, Brug, Beelden en Rytuigen, met aangename verschieten en bywerk; zeer uitvoerig | *Notes:* The artist's name was given as "J. Pothoven" but we have assumed this is an error.	Bartholomeus Ruloffs	(Unknown) fl 7
1802/12/13	AMSCH	0132	*H. Pothoven* | Twee stuks aangenaame Land- en Riviergezichten, gestoffeert met Gebouwen, Geboomten, Heere te Paard, Landlieden met Vée en verder Bywerk, plaisant op Paneel geschilderd | *Mat:* op paneel *Size:* yder is hoog 11, breed 14 duim	Florijn [?]	(Sold) fl 5:10 van Iperen
1804/12/10	AMSCH	0085	*H. Pothoven* | Twee stuks Gezichten binnen 's Hage, den eene verbeeld het Binnen-hof; en den andere een Gezicht langs de Groenmarkt; met de Kerk en Gebouwen; beide gestoffeerd met wandelende Dames en Heeren, rytuigen, militairen en verder bywerk; zonachtig en uitvoerig gepenceeld | *Mat:* op paneel *Size:* Ieder hoog 12, breed 16 ½ duim	Jan De Groot	(Sold) fl 25 Texera
1804/12/10	AMSCH	0086	*H. Pothoven* | Twee stuks, een Gezicht binne de Stad Delft, langs de groote Markt ziende naar het Stadhuis, groote Kerk en verdere Woningen, ryk gestoffeert met wandelende Dames en Heeren, rytuigen enz., de wederga een Gezicht in den Haag na het Binnenhof, beide zeer natuurlyk behandeld | *Mat:* op paneel *Size:* Hoog 12, breed 16 ½ duim	Jan De Groot	(Sold) fl 25:10 van Iperen
1804/12/10	AMSCH	0087	*H. Pothoven* | Een Gezicht op het Buitenhof in den Haag, verbeeld op de Haagsche Kermis, men ziet ter zyde eenige Meyboomen; dit stuk is zeer ryk van onderscheide figuuren, en plaisant geschilderd | *Mat:* op paneel *Size:* Hoog 33, breed 24 duim	Jan De Groot	(Sold) fl 121 Texera
804/12/10	AMSCH	0088	*H. Pothoven* | De Trekking der Lotery in den Haag, ryk met beelden gestoffeerd; fraay van perspectief en krachtig van schildering | *Mat:* op doek *Size:* Hoog 22, breed 25 duim	Jan De Groot	(Sold) fl 21 Numan
805/12/16	AMSCH	0047	*J. Pothoven* | Twee stuks, een Winter en een Maneschyn, geestig op Paneel | *Mat:* op paneel *Size:* hoog 10, breed 14 duim *Notes:* The artist's name was given as "J. Pothoven" but we have assumed this is an error.	R[oos]	(Bought In) fl 2:10
805/12/16	AMSCH	0063	*H. Pothoven* | Twee stuks Heuvelachtige Land- en Watergezichten, zynde by het eene een woelend en 't andere een stil Water, beide met Beeldjes en Beesten gestoffeerd, en bevallig geschilderd	R[oos]	(Sold) fl 6 T van Iperen
806/11/24	AMSCH	0058	*Pothoven (H.)* | Twee stuks, een Wintergezigt met Schaatzeryders; en een Maaneschyn; natuurlyk voorgesteld | *Mat:* op paneel *Size:* Yder hoog 10, breed 14 duim	van den Bosch	(Sold) fl 5:10 du Pree
810/06/20	AMSCH	0174	*J. Pothoff* | Een Duinachtig Landschap, met Huislieden gestoffeerd | *Notes:* The artist's name was given as "J. Pothoff" but we have assumed this is an error.	A	(Sold) fl 2 Coclers

Potter, Paulus

301/05/11	AMSCH	0066	*Paulus Potter* | Deeze ryke Ordonnantie, vol gewoel in een aangenaam Landschap, verbeeld de optogt van den Aartsvader Jacob, na Hebron,	E[lias]	(Sold) fl 99 Pruijssenaar [for] R

			verzelt van zyn geheele huisgezin, en gevolg van dienstknegten en vee, op de Voorgrond een waterval, en verder een bevallig verschiet, meesterlyk en krachtig gepenceeld | *Mat:* op doek *Size:* hoog 37, breed 49 duim		
1801/06/13	LNDLS	0049	*P. Potter* | Een bergagtig Landschap, met geboomten, op den voorgrond rust een bruin bont koetje, benevens een schaap, zeer uitvoerig, op paneel geschilderd, en meer stoffage | *Mat:* op paneel *Size:* hoog 10, breed 12 duimen	D van R	(Sold) fl 25 Ryers
1801/10/06	AMSCH	0050	*Paulus Potter* | In dit faaay [sic] Cabinetstukje ziet men ter linker zyde op een grasige heuvel by een Boom, staan twee Ossen, een Rosbonte en een Roscouleurde, waar by een ander rustende, ter zyde een Vaal couleurde bonte Os, gedeeltelijk van agteren en op zyde te zien, het verschiet vertoont een Dorpgezigt; dit Schildery is van een bevallige verkiesing en coloriet, alles évenaart de Natuur, en is van een uitvoerige penceel behandeling | *Mat:* op paneel *Size:* hoog 14, breed 12 duim	S	(Sold) fl 75 v d Schleij A [for] Ter Smitte
1802/06/16	AMSCH	0125	*P. Potter* | In een heuvelachtig Landschap, ziet men een Herder, dryvende eenige Koeijen, Kalveren, Schapen en Bokjes; alles van een zeer bevallige en meesterlyke Penceels Behandeling | *Mat:* op paneel *Size:* hoog 17, breed 19 ½ duim	[Merrem]	(Sold) fl 120 v[n] d Schleij
1802/06/16	AMSCH	0126	*P. Potter* | In een Landschap, op de voorgrond vertoond zig een rustende Os en Ram, by twee staande Schaapen; verder een Bergachtig verschiet met Véehoeders en Schaapen; meesterlyk fiks en natuurlyk gepenceeld | *Mat:* op doek *Size:* hoog 15 ½, breed 21 duim	[Merrem]	(Sold) fl 51 LaFontaine
1802/09/29	AMSCH	0045	*P. Potter, 1653* | Een Landschap, de Morgenstond voorstellende, hoog 22, breed 25 ½ duim. Doek. Op welkers voorgrond, (eene grazige Weide voorstellende,) men ziet ter regter zyde eene rustende Roscouleurige jonge Stier, beneevens een leggend Schaap, en ter linker zyde by eene Heining van planken gemaakt, een slapend Ram; in 't midden by eenige willige Boomen zyn twee leggende Koeijen en een bulkende staande Os, waar by men nog een leggende dito gewaar word; voor een Boeren Huis, meer agterwaards ter regter zyde, werd een Koe door een Boerin gemolken; verder een Jager van zyn Hond gevolgt, ziet men teegens een aangenaam verschiet uitkomen, zynde een Land- en Watergezigt; alles is uitvoerig en delicaat gepenceeld, doende het Zonlicht eene frapante uitwerking in dit Stuk, en kan voor een der capitaalste werken van deeze voortreffelyke Kunstenaar gehouden worden; (komt uit het Cabinet van den Heer Griffier Fagel.) [Dans un pré planté d'une rangée d'osiers, ce parfait imitateur de la nature a marqué le lever du soleil, deux vaches couchées sont adosseés contre les arbres ; derriere celles-ci est un boeuf gris sur pied et une vache rousse couche derriere lui ; à gauche près d'une maison et de quelques arbres l'on voit une femme occupée à traïre une autre vache, de la maison sort un chasseur avec son chien. Au premier plan est couché un gros torreau et une brebis ; la gauche en offre un chemin mènant à une cloison de bois ou l'Artiste à posé son nom et l'année, au bas de ce-ci couche un bellier. Il seroit inutile de faire un eloge detaillé de ce morceau des plus capitaux, nous dirons simplement que la verité repandue dans ce site vaporeux est admirable, que le dessin des animaux est des plus précis ; ajoutons qu'une touche delicate et une couleur harmonieuse caracterisent ce morceau qui est parfaitement conservé, il vient du cabinet de Mr. Le Greffier Fagel.] | *Mat:* op doek *Size:* hoog 22, breed 25 ½ duim *Inscr:* P. Potter, 1653 (signed and dated?) *Notes:* It is unclear whether the name and date are inscribed on the painting. *Loc:* Amsterdam, Nederland. Rijksmuseum. (A 711)	[Hendrik III, baron Fagel?]	(Sold) fl 2210 Th[s] Spaan
1803/04/27	AMSCH	000Q	*P. Potter* | Un Tableau de Famille, representant un Chaiseur [sic], qui presente un Lievre, a une Femme de qualité ; le site represente un Paisage, ou l'on voit des chiens de Classe, dans le fond, des Bergers, & Bergeres, qui dansent, environnés de quelques Animaux ; peint par P. Potter, Ao. 1641 | *Size:* h. 48, l. 65 pouces *Inscr:* P. Potter, Ao. 1641 (signed and dated?) *Notes:* It is unclear whether the name and date are inscribed on the painting.	B	(Bought In) 40
1804/10/16	DLOND	0177	*P. Potter* | Een Hond onder een zwaren Boom staande. Un Chien au pied d'un Arbre | *Mat:* op paneel *Size:* hoog 19, breed 16		(Sold) fl 50:10 van Cle
1804/10/16	DLOND	0178	*P. Potter* | Een Landschap met Koeien, getekend Potter. Un Paysage avec des Vaches, marqué Potter | *Mat:* op paneel *Size:* hoog 11, breed 13 *Inscr:* Potter (signed)		(Unknown)
1807/08/26	AMSCH	0170	*P. Potter* | Op een Heuvel by de stam van een willige Boom, ziet men twee staande Beesten, welken door een lieflyk zonlicht van ter zyden gedaagd worden, in het verschiet een grazige Weide met Vee; dit stukje is van een meesterlyke schildering | *Mat:* op paneel *Size:* hoog 11, breed 14 duim	Roos	(Bought In) fl 70
1807/08/26	AMSCH	0171	*P. Potter* | Dit fraaije stukje stelt voor een aangenaam Landgezigt, met twee staande roodbonte Beesten, welke door een zonlicht van agteren gedaagd worden, verders een aangenaam verschiet; fraai op Paneel geschilderd | *Mat:* op paneel *Size:* hoog 11, breed 14 duim	Roos	(Bought In) fl 90
1808/04/26	GDAN	0124	*Potter (P)* | Een uitmuntend bergägtig Landschap, waar in eenige Heeren te Paard ryden, in 't verschiet ziet men eenige Koeijen en Schapen grazen, bij hoog Geboomte, fraai geschildert | *Mat:* op paneel *Size:* hoog 17, breed 23 duim	G H Fortuyn	(Unknown)

1808/04/26	GDAN	0125	*Potter (P)* | Een Jongen die met een Emmer in een Tobbe Water giet, om een Stier, die vast gebonden is, te laten drinken, in 't verschiet een Persoon met een Kindje, alles fiks en konstig behandeld | *Mat:* op doek *Size:* hoog 27 ½, breed 26 ½ duim	G H Fortuyn	(Unknown)
1808/06/06	RMRIJ	0103	*Potter. (Paulus)* | In een grootsch heuvelachtig Landschap ziet men, in 't midden van eenen plantrijken voorgrond, eenen roodbonten Os, eenen zwartbonten Bok, eenen Ram, twee Schapen en een Lam. Wat verder een liggend roodgeelachtig Kalf of Pink. Aan de linkerzijde eenen ouden Eik, waarbij eene door een kind gezoogd wordende Vrouw en een groote zwartbruine Hond gezeten zijn. Nevens en tegen den boom staat een op den Doedelzak spelend man. Op den tweeden grond ziet men eenen vaal gekleurden Os, een bruin Paard en eenen graauwen Ezel. Ter regterzijde eenen hoogen heuvel met rijk Geboomte, en een aantal grazende Schapen en Bokken. In 't verschiet een Oud Gebouw, tusschen geboomte, uitkomende tegen een gedeelte der schoon en meesterlijk geschilderde Lucht. Het licht en bruin, de verstandige, rijke en bevallige ordinantie, de kleur en uitvoering maken dit Tafereel tot een der zeldzaamsten en heerlijksten van dezen met regt beroemden Meester [Beau Paysage Montagneux, (choix rare de ce Peîntre.) Sur le devant d'une Colline, un Boeuf rougeâtre à tête blanche est auprès d'une jeune Vache de Couleur jaunâtre, qui est couchée. Un Bouc blanc et noir, une Brebis et un Agneau blancs, et deux Beliers bruns ornent le premier Plan. Un Boeuf d'un gris clair, un Cheval brun et un Ane se trouvent près d'un Pâtre, qui appuyé contre le tronc d'un vieux Chêne, joue de la Corne-muse, tandis qu'une femme, qui allaite son enfant, et un beau Chien de garde sont au pied de l'arbre. C'est ce qui forme le second Plan, et ce qui s'unit parfaitement avec le Groupe principal. A la droite, est une haute Colline courronnée d'arbres touffus, où l'on apperçoit neuf Moutons et deux Chèvres qui broutent. Le lointain agréable offre une riche masse d'arbres, au milieu de laquelle s'Elève un Donjon. Le tout est éclairé par un Ciel qui produit un effet admirable. Ce Tableau, qu'on peut regarder comme une des Productions Capitales et rares de ce grand imitateur de la Nature, est d'une belle et agréable Composition, d'un ton vrai et de la plus grande harmonie. Le dessin correct des Animaux et le grand fini, jusqués dans les plus petits détails, laissent cependant appercevoir cette touche fière et mâle qui fait tant admirer les Productions de Potter] | *Annots:* Pour le Musée d'Amsterdam (NGW) *Mat:* op doek *Size:* Hoog 30 ½, en breed 36 ½ duim *Loc:* Amsterdam, Nederland. Rijksmuseum. (A318)	Gerrit van der Pot, Heer van Groeneveld	(Sold) fl 10,050 van Lennep
1808/08/23	AMSCH	0128	*Potter. (P.)* | In een grazige Weide, staat een rosbonte Os en eene Koei, als met de Hoornen tegens elkander vrijvende [sic], ter zijde een rustende bij een willige Boom, het verschiet vertoont een Landschap met verscheide Vée; het is zonachtig en bevallig geschilderd | *Mat:* op paneel *Size:* hoog 14, breed 18 duim	C	(Bought In) fl 14
1808/08/23	AMSCH	0128a[H]	*Potter. (P.)* | 1 dito [grazige Weide] dito [staat een rosbonte Os en een Koei] | *Notes:* This lot was added in by hand in the EBNP and FLNY copies of the catalogue. It is unclear what "dito" refers to in the title.	[Van Iperen?]	(Bought In) fl 14
1810/03/26	RMMUY	0045	*Paulus Potter* | Een staande Witte Os, op den voorgrond, bij eenige Kruiden, een Hek. In het verschiet, eenige Beekjes en een Dorp. Konstig en natuurlijk [Cette belle et savante étude présente sur le devant d'une prairie un beau Boeuf, blanc jaunatre – un lointain avec quelques bestiaux, et un village termine l'horizon.] | *Mat:* op doek op paneel *Size:* hoog 7, breed 8 ½ duimen	Daniel de Jongh Az	(Sold) fl 81 van Yperen Amsterdam [for] Wreesman
1810/03/27	RMCNL	0010	*Paulus Potter* | Een Landschap, waarop men eene staande en eene liggende Koe ziet, zeer Meesterachtig en fraai geschildert		(Unknown)
1810/03/27	RMCNL	0101	*Potter* | Een Veldzicht met twee Paarden		(Unknown)
1810/05/22	AMSCH	0082	*Potter. (P.)* | In een Veldgezicht ziet men op den voorgrond op een grazige Heuvel drie staande en een liggende Os; uitvoerig behandeld en aangenaam van licht en koloriet | *Mat:* op paneel *Size:* hoog 10, breed 11 ½ duim	Johannes van de Putte Nicolaasz.	(Sold) fl 19 Klemans
810/05/22	AMSCH	0083	*Potter. (P.)* | Een ruim Landgezicht, met verscheide Woningen bij Geboomte, op den voorgrond gestoffeerd met een Heer te Paard, waarbij eene staande Vrouw en Huisman, verder eene Vrouw Varkens drijvende en eene andere eene Koe melkende; natuurlijk en fiks gepenceeld | *Mat:* op paneel *Size:* hoog 16, breed 21 duim	F	(Sold) fl 12 Rinkhuyzen
810/07/23	DOLGI	0043	*Paulus Potter* | In een vlak Landschapje, bij een wilgen Boom, aan een hek, bevinden zich een staande, en twee liggende Runderbeestjes. Meesterlijk behandeld | *Mat:* op paneel *Size:* hoog 9 ½, breed 11 duim	Mr Pieter van den Santheuvel	(Sold) fl 13 van Eijk 's Hage
810/08/01	AMSCH	0075	*Potter (Paulus)* | In een Landgezigt op eenen grazigen Heuvel bij den Stam van eenen Wilgenboom en houten Hek, ziet men eene roodbonte Koe liggen, waar achter eene andere, staande nevens eenen jongen Stier [Dans un gras Paturage sur une eminance légere on voit une Vache couchée, tachée de roux fauve, derriere celle-ci se trouve une autre qui est dresséé sur ses jambes ; ainsi qu'un jeune Taureau : un tronc de saule et une partie de Cloison varient ce site] | *Annots:* roide et dur. (NGW) *Mat:* op paneel *Size:* hoog 19, breed 14 ½ duimen	Mr Pieter de Smeth van Alphen	(Bought In) fl 3600
810/08/01	AMSCH	0076	*Potter (Paulus)* | Een groote en staande Jagthond, met eenen Ketting vastgehecht aan zijn Hok; voor hem ligt een Paardenbout; in het verschiet een ruim Landschap [Representation d'un Chien de chasse, attaché par	Mr Pieter de Smeth van Alphen	(Sold) fl 685 Texier, Gerbet en Comp [for] LeBrun

<table>
<tr><td></td><td></td><td></td><td>une Chaine à son chenil : on voit de la depouille de Cheval sur le devant du tableau, le sujet étant detaché sur une large Paysage] | Annots: composition dégoutante. (NGW); Vente le Brun No. 127 fr 4700 (SMLN) Mat: op doek Size: hoog 39, breed 50 duimen Loc: Sankt Peterburg, Rossiya. Ermitazh. (Inv. 817)</td><td></td><td></td></tr>
<tr><td>1810/08/01</td><td>AMSCH</td><td>0077</td><td>Potter (Paulus) | Een ruim Veldgezigt; op den voorgrond, op eenen zandigen Heuvel, staat een wit geappeld Paard, van voren te zien, verder eene Koets met vier Paarden bespannen, en een bergachtig verschiet [Une vaste vue de Campagne donnant sur une partie sabloneuse : au premier plan se dintingue [sic] un Cheval pommelé, vu de face ; un peu en arriere on trouve une voiture attelée de quatre Chevaux, et une perspective montagneuse termine le fond] | Annots: dur et mauvais sujet. (NGW) Mat: op doek Size: hoog 18 ½, breed 17 duimen</td><td>Mr Pieter de Smeth van Alphen</td><td>(Bought In) fl 500</td></tr>
<tr><td>1810/08/01</td><td>AMSCH</td><td>0078</td><td>Potter (Paulus) | Een Veldgezigt mede, met een wit geappeld Paard, ter zijde en van achteren te zien; verder een Heer te paard, Jagers met Honden, en een Heerenhuis in het verschiet [Autre Sujet correspondant au précédent offrant également un Cheval pommelé, vu par le côté et en arriere. Au second plan ou trouve un Cavalier à Cheval, un Chasseur et des Chiens. Dans la perspective on apperçoit une Maison de Campagne] | Annots: dur et mauvais sujet. (NGW); Vente le Brun Karel duJardin No. 129 fr. 1801 (SMLN) Mat: op doek Size: hoog 18 ½, breed 17 duimen Loc: Malibu, CA, USA. J. Paul Getty Museum. (88.PA.87)</td><td>Mr Pieter de Smeth van Alphen</td><td>(Sold) fl 655 Texier, Gerbet en Comp [for] LeBrun</td></tr>
<tr><td>1810/08/10</td><td>RMRIJ</td><td>0008</td><td>Paulus Potter | Een Hollandsch Landschap. Waar in een drift Beesten. Helder, dun, en konstig geordonneerd en behandeld | Mat: op paneel Size: hoog 11 duim, breed 14 duim</td><td></td><td>(Sold) fl 3 [or] 34 v Dyk</td></tr>
<tr><td>1810/08/10</td><td>RMRIJ</td><td>0026</td><td>P. Potter | Een Landschap met Figuren, Paard en Honden, op den voorgrond</td><td></td><td>(Sold) fl 1 [or] 5:10 Werland</td></tr>
<tr><td>1810/10/11</td><td>AMSCH</td><td>0179</td><td>P. Potter | In een Landschap ziet men een Herder, die aan eene Vrouw een Haas aanbiedt, waarbij eenige Jagthonden, en in 't verschiet dansende Herders en Herderinnen, benevens eenige Beesten; op Doek, door P. Potter. Ao. 1641 | Mat: op doek Inscr: P. Potter. Ao. 1641 (signed and dated?) Notes: It is unclear whether the name and date are inscribed on the painting.</td><td>A</td><td>(Sold) fl 3 Yver</td></tr>
<tr><td>1810/11/07</td><td>UTWLD</td><td>0015</td><td>P. Potter | Een zeer aardig Landschapje met liggende Koeijen en Schapen, op de voorgrond een sloot, waarbij een knoestige stam, ailes zeer krachtig en klaar gepenseeld, getekend P. Potter, 1 voet een half duim hoog, 1 voet 2 en een half duim breed op paneel, zwarte Lijst | Mat: op paneel Size: 1 voet een half duim hoog, 1 voet 2 en een half duim breed Inscr: P. Potter (signed)</td><td></td><td>(Unknown) fl 41</td></tr>
</table>

Potter, Paulus (or Potter, Paulus, manner)

<table>
<tr><td>1802/06/16</td><td>AMSCH</td><td>0127</td><td>P. Potter. Of in de manier | In een Landschap by een Boeren Woning, ziet men een staande Koey, nevens Schaapen en Bokken, wyders een bevallig verschiet; zonachtig en meesterlyk geschilderd | Mat: op paneel Size: hoog 16 ½, breed 14 duim</td><td>[Merrem]</td><td>(Sold) fl 26 Gruiter</td></tr>
<tr><td>1802/06/16</td><td>AMSCH</td><td>0128</td><td>P. Potter. Of in de manier | Een Land- en Riviergezicht, op de voorgrond staat een wit Paard, en aan de overzyde der Oever zyn eenige Woningen en Geboomten; zeer natuurlyk en fiks gepenceeld | Mat: op paneel Size: hoog 7, breed 8 duim</td><td>[Merrem]</td><td>(Sold) fl 21 Coclers</td></tr>
</table>

Potter, Paulus (copy after)

<table>
<tr><td>1801/03/16</td><td>AMSCH</td><td>0157</td><td>P. Potter | Twee stuks, met Beesten na P. Potter</td><td>K[ip]</td><td>(Sold) fl 4 Koopman</td></tr>
<tr><td>1801/06/10</td><td>AMSCH</td><td>0139</td><td>Potter. (naar P.) | Een grazige Weide met een roode bonte Koei, voor een Boerenwoning; meesterlyk behandeld | Mat: op doek op paneel Size: hoog 10, breed 12 duim</td><td>[Doublet]</td><td>(Sold) fl 12 Spruit van Gend</td></tr>
<tr><td>1802/07/21</td><td>HGKAN</td><td>0045</td><td>Potter | Een Gezicht aan een Water, waar eenige Beesten Grasen, terwyl een Jongen bezig is een Koe te melken, door een zeer goed Meester, na Potter, zwarte Lyst, vergulde binnen rand</td><td></td><td>(Unknown)</td></tr>
<tr><td>1802/09/18</td><td>RMDRS</td><td>0001</td><td>J.B.H. Thier; P. Potter | Een Hollands Landgezicht, met willige en andere Geboomte, gestoffeerd met beelden en verscheide Beesten, waar van eenige op den Voorgrond in het Water staan, verder eenige zwemmende Jongens, in het verschiet een Rytuig met ses Paarden bespannen; dit aangenaam Schildery, is uitmuntend gevolgd na het beroemde stuk van P. Potter 1648. – Voorheen berust hebbende, in de Kunstgallery van den voormalige Stadhouder, en tegenswoordig in het Nationaal Museum te Parys | copy by B.H. Thier after Paulus Potter; companion to lot 2 Size: hoog 16 ½, breed 22 duim</td><td>Casper de Haas</td><td>(Sold) fl 90 v Pot</td></tr>
<tr><td>1802/09/18</td><td>RMDRS</td><td>0002</td><td>J.B.H. Thier; P. Potter | Een dito [Hollands] Landgezicht, waar in een Boere Schuur uit welke een Koe gedreeven word, en voor dezelve een Boerin die met een Kind speeld, waarby twee Varkens; verder nog twee stotende Ossen die een Boer tragt te scheiden, met nog een daarby staande Koe; mede uitmuntend gevold na P. Potter, door denzelven [J. B. H. Thier] en kunnende tot een voegzame Wederga dienen | copy by B.H. Thier after Paulus Potter; companion to lot 1</td><td>Casper de Haas</td><td>(Sold) fl 39:10 Nagtegaal</td></tr>
<tr><td>1802/11/01</td><td>DOBRA</td><td>0173</td><td>Jacobus Janson; Paulus Potter | Een bruinbonte Koe, grazende, benevens een roodbonte, rustende; wat verder een witte, die door een meisje gemolken word, by hoog geboomte; kunstig gevolgd naar het Schildery</td><td></td><td>(Unknown) fl 22 for lots 173 & 174</td></tr>
</table>

			van Paulus Potter, door Jacobus Janson | copy by J. Janson after Paulus Potter; companion to lot 174 *Mat:* op paneel *Size:* hoog 16 ½, breed 14 duim *Notes:* This lot was sold with lot 174 by J. Janson.		
1806/11/24	AMSCH	0013	*Carré (M.); P. Potter* | Dit stuk is een accurate Copy na de beroemde Ossendrift van P. Potter, voormaals toebehorende aan de Heer G. Braamkamp, en ook van dezelfde groote, zynde een Ordinnantie van tien Beesten, waar agter een Boer en aangenaam verschiet; fraai gepenceeld | copy by M. Carree after Paulus Potter *Mat:* op doek *Size:* hoog 54, breed 78 duim	Munnikhuizen	(Sold) fl 21 Sukerbekker
1807/08/26	AMSCH	0199	*H.W. Schweikhardt; P. Potter* | Een aangenaam Boomryk Landschap, met een Rivier, in welke eenige Jongens zwemmen, terwyl twee Koeijen en een Ram in en by dezelve staan, en daar helder in spiegelen. Op de tweede grond by een Boeren Woning ziet men nog verscheiden Vee, in het verschiet een Koets, met zes Paarden; zynde dit Sukje [sic] zonachtig en uitvoerig behandeld, naar het Schildery van P. Potter | copy by H. Schweickardt after Paulus Potter *Mat:* op paneel *Size:* hoog 17, breed 24 duim	Joseph Vallette	(Sold) fl 171 Jozi
1807/09/28	DOHAA	00TT	*Potter* | Een dito [Landschap] met drie dito [Koebeestjes], naar Potter	Mattheus Westerouen van Meeteren	(Unknown)
1808/06/06	RMRIJ	0127	*Thier. (J. B. H.); naar Paulus Potter* | Een aangenaam boom- en waterrijk Landgezigt. (bekend onder den naam der wadende Koe.) Rijk gestoffeerd met figuren, Koeijen, Schapen en Lammeren. In 't verschiet ziet men eene Prinselijke Koets met zes Paarden bespannen, vooraf gegaan door twee Hardloopers; meer in 't verschiet de lustplaats den Binkhorst, den Toren van 't Dorp Rijswijk en aan den horizont den Haag. Dit stuk is eene ongemeen getrouwe kopij naar de Schilderij van Paulus Potter, voorheen in 't Kabinet van den Prins van Oranje berustende, doch nu in het Museum te Parijs [Paysage Hollandais. Sur le devant, on découvre près d'une ferme plusieurs Personnes qui se baignent dans une eau transparente etc., des Vaches, et beaucoup d'autres Animaux domestiques. Dans le second plan on apperçoit un Carosse à six Chevaux, et dans le Lointain la Campagne de Binkhorst, le Village de Ryswyck, et la Haye à l'Horison. Ce Tableau est une Copie éxacte d'après l'original de Paul Potter, connu sous le nom de *la Vache à l'eau*, qui fut un ornement de la Collection du Prince d'Orange, et qui se trouve actuellement au Muséum Napoléon] | copy by B.H. Thier after Paulus Potter *Annots:* Verk. Casper de Haas, Rotterdam, 18 Sept. 1802 (RMA I) *Mat:* op paneel *Size:* Hoog 16 ¼, en breed 22 duim	Gerrit van der Pot, Heer van Groeneveld	(Sold) fl 160 P Roelfzema
1808/11/28	AMSCH	0038	*J. Laquij; P. Potter* | Langs een opgaande vlakte, ziet men een Landman, een drift van tien Beesten voortdrijvende, nevens hem een Hond, agterwaards grazige Weiden en een Dorp in 't verschiet, meesterlijk op Doek, door J. Laquij. Hoog 49, breed 76 duim, zijnde dit stuk een Copij na de beroemde Ossedrift van P. Potter | copy by W.J. Laquy after Paulus Potter *Mat:* op doek *Size:* hoog 49, breed 76 duim	[Gruyter?]	(Sold) fl 16:10 du Pree
1809/09/06	AMSCH	0030	*Janson (J.); P. Potter* | Een bevallige Copij naar een stukje van P. Potter, zijnde een Ordinantie van twee staande en een leggend Koebeest; uitvoerig en zonagtig gepenceeld | copy by J. Janson after Paulus Potter *Mat:* op doek *Size:* hoog 16, breed 14 duim	Johannes Caudri	(Sold) fl 41 Gruyter
1810/03/26	RMMUY	0067	*A. Schouman; naar Potter* | Op den voorgrond bij eenig geboomte en een hek, staan een wit, en een zwartbruin Paard. In het verschiet eenig Hoornvee, Dorp, &c. [Un Paysage hollandois : sur le devant, près d'un arbre, est un cheval blanc pommelé à coté d'un autre, brun noiratre ; dans le lointain quelque betail et un village, parfaitement imité.] | copy by A. Schouman after Paulus Potter *Mat:* op paneel *Size:* hoog 9, breed 11 duimen	Daniel de Jongh Az	(Sold) fl 30 Le Brun Parys
1810/06/04	DOBRA	0011	*Potter* | Een Landschapje met Beesten; naar Potter	Hendrik de Haas	(Unknown)
1810/06/06	RMMUY	0157	*van Dongen; Potter* | Een stuk met Beesten, zijnde eene Copij naar Potter. Door van Dongen | copy by Dionys Dongen after Paulus Potter *Mat:* op doek		(Unknown) fl 13:5

Potter, Paulus (manner)

1802/07/21	HGKAN	0004	*Potter* | Een Landschap met Koeijen, in de trant van Potter		(Unknown)
1802/07/21	HGKAN	0085	*Potter* | Drie Koeijen, tegen een vervallen Gebouw, manier van Potter		(Unknown)
802/09/06	AMSCH	0240	*P. Potter* | In een Landschap, ziet men eenige staande en leggende Varkens, verder op een Heuvel twee rustende Herders; fraay in de manier van P. Potter | *Mat:* op paneel *Size:* hoog 9, breed 12 duim	J	(Sold) fl 3 van Iperen
804/10/16	DLOND	0292	*Als van P. Potter* | Twee Honden by een Long enz. Deux Chiens avec une Proïe | *Size:* hoog 26, breed 41		(Unknown)
804/10/22	MGWIN	0001	*Potter* | Twee extra fraaië Landschapjes met Beesten, in de manier van Potter, in vergulde Lysten | *Mat:* op doek	F Reytsma	(Sold) £ 0:19 Geld
808/04/26	GDAN	0264	*Potter* | Een heuvelägtig Landschap met Koeijen en Schapen, in de manier van Potter, fiks geschilderd | *Size:* hoog 10 ½, breed 13 ½ duim	G H Fortuyn	(Unknown)
808/04/26	GDAN	0276	*Potter* | In de manier van Potter, zijnde een Veehoeder met eenig Vee, en een wit Paard, wel gedaan | *Mat:* op paneel *Size:* hoog 11, breed 14 ½ duim	G H Fortuyn	(Unknown)

1809/04/22	AMYVR	0203	*P. Potter* | Een staande Os aan een Hek; in de manier van P. Potter	de Bruin	(Sold) fl 2 du Pree
1809/05/26	HADAA	A0009	*P. Potter* | Twee Landschapjes, bevallig met Beestjes gestoffeerd, als van P. Potter	Mejuffrouw de Wed David Heemskerk [or others]	(Unknown)
1809/05/26	HADAA	A0010	*P. Potter* | Twee dito [Landschapjes], dito [als van P. Potter]	Mejuffrouw de Wed David Heemskerk [or others]	(Unknown)
1810/08/06	AMSCH	0087	*Potter (als P.)* | In een Grazige Weide staat een rosbonte Os en eene Koe, met de Hoornen tegens elkander wrijvende, ter zijde eene andere rustende bij eenen willigen Boom; zonachtig en vrolijk geschilderd | *Mat:* op paneel *Size:* hoog 14, breed 18 duimen	B	(Bought In) fl 21
1810/10/11	AMSCH	0073	*P. Potter* | Een staande Koe; zeer natuurlijk, als P. Potter | *Mat:* op doek op paneel *Size:* hoog 6, breed 8 duimen	C	(Sold) fl 2 Posthumus
1810/10/11	AMSCH	0111	*P. Potter* | Een staande Os; breed geschilderd, als P. Potter	Y	(Sold) fl 4 Ijver

Potter, Pieter de

1801/08/19	AMSCH	0091	*P. Potter* | Een Corps de Guarde met Officieren, Vrouwe en Krygstuig; uitvoerig op Panneel | *Mat:* op paneel *Size:* hoog 13, breed 16 duim	W Wynen	(Sold) fl 4:5 Gruiter
1808/06/06	RMRIJ	0104	*Potter. (Pieter)* | Eene deftige Vrouw in Oude Hollandsche kleeding, een boek in de hand houdende. Halverlijf te zien [Une femme en Costume noir et en fraise, qui tient un livre à la main, vue à mi-corps] | *Annots:* Van Thijs, 1 Mei 1803 (f 5.-) (RMA I) *Mat:* op koper *Fmt:* ovaal *Size:* Hoog 7, en breed 5 ¼ duim	Gerrit van der Pot, Heer van Groeneveld	(Sold) fl 42 Roelszema
1808/08/23	AMSCH	0226	*De oude P. Potter* | In een Landschap vertoonen zich verscheiden Krijglieden, zoo te paard als te voet, bij een Legertent zich verversende een ander wandeld met eene Dame, verder Marquetenters, waar bij dansende Huislieden; fiks gepenceeld door den oude P. Potter | *Mat:* op paneel	Z	(Sold) fl 1:15 Dupré
1810/03/27	RMCNL	0093	*P. Potter* | Een Binnenhuis, een Hoofdwagt voorstellende, met eene Vrouw, zeer netjes behandeld		(Unknown)

Potuyl, Henrik

1806/11/24	AMSCH	0055	*Potuyl (....)* | In een Binnenwoning zit een Boerin en Boer, met elkander op de kaart speelende; verders een ander een pyp rookende; natuurlyk en geestig van penceelbehandeling | *Mat:* op doek *Size:* hoog 15, breed 12 duim	Munnikhuizen	(Sold) fl 23 Coclers
1809/07/19	AMSCH	0046	*Potuijl (J.)* | Een leezend Vrouwtje, in een Binnevertrek, waar bij een zittende Boer en verder Bijwerk. Natuurlijk verbeeld | *Mat:* op paneel *Size:* hoog 8 ½, breed 8 duim *Notes:* The artist's name was given as "Potuijl (J.)" but we have assumed this is an error.	[Wijkersloot?]	(Sold) fl 9 Reijdon

Pourbus, Frans (the younger)

1801/05/11	AMSCH	0069	*Frans Pourbus* | Een Mans Pourtret, in Spaansche kleeding, krachtig en uitvoerig behandeld | *Mat:* op doek *Size:* hoog 20, breed 18 duim	P[ruyssenaar]	(Sold) fl 1 Pruijssenaar [for] R
1802/06/16	AMSCH	0138	*Pouribus* | Het Afbeeldzel van een bedaagd Heer, in aloude Spaansche Kleeding; meesterlyk fraay en Malsch gepenceeld | *Mat:* op paneel *Size:* hoog 9 ½, breed 8 duim	[Merrem]	(Sold) fl 9 Agina

Poussin, Nicolas

1803/09/07	AMSCH	0125	*Poussin* | Een Italiaansch Landschap, met Gebouwen, hoog Geboomte en Beelden, breed en meesterlyk gepenceeld [Un paysage d'Italie, richement distribué et orné d'arbres, de figures et de maisons ; tableau digne de ce maître] | *Mat:* op doek *Size:* hoog 22, breed 19 duim	Smidt	(Sold) fl 45 W Reijers
1807/08/26	AMSCH	0179	*Poussin* | Een Italiaansch Landschap met antique Gebouwen, zwaar Geboomte en stoffage van Beelden; schoon en bevallig | *Mat:* op doek *Size:* hoog 24, breed 18 duim	Roos	(Bought In) fl 1
1810/07/26	AMSCH	0056	*Poussin (N.)* | Een zeer schoon Boom- en Bergachtig Landschap, met Nimfen en andere Beelden gestoffeerd. Zijnde een Meesterstuk uit de Fransche School | *Mat:* op doek *Size:* hoog 42, breed 32 duimen	Cassino	(Bought In) fl 50
1810/07/26	AMSCH	0057	*Poussin (N.)* | Een aangenaam Boomrijk Landschap, gestoffeerd met eenige Lieden bij een Put, op de voorgrond Bokken en Schapen. Zeer fraai geschilderd | *Mat:* op doek *Size:* hoog 15, breed 17 duimen	Cassino	(Bought In) fl 19:10

Poussin, Nicolas (copy by)

1810/06/06	RMMUY	0003	*N. Pousijn; André del Sarto* | Een konstrijke Copij. Door N. Pousijn, naar André del Sarto. Verbeeldende eene heilige Familie, het origineel van dezelve grootte berust, in het Museum Napoléon te Parijs; en deze Copij besloeg wel eer eene aanzienlijke plaats in de eerste verzamelingen aldaar, en is gemonteerd in eene kostbare lijst | copy by N. Poussin after Andrea del Sarto *Mat:* op doek		(Sold) fl 200 Brunelli

Poussin, Nicolas (copy after)

1803/04/27	AMSCH	0091	*Poussin* | Une Copie d'après le Poussin, réprésentant la Crucfiction [sic] de J. C. | *Size:* h. 3 ½, l. 4 ½ pieds	A	(Sold) fl 3 de Meijer

1810/10/11	AMSCH	0120	*N. Poussin* | Het Sterfbed van Germanicus, zijnde eene rijke Ordonnantie, krachtig op Doek, naar N. Poussin | *Mat:* op doek *Size:* hoog 28, breed 37 duimen	M	(Sold) fl 10:5 du Pree

Poussin, Nicolas (manner)

1801/04/23	AMYVR	0031	*Poussin* | Een capitaal gestoffeerd Landschap, in de manier van Poussin		(Sold) fl 2 ½ A Mayer
1801/08/19	AMSCH	0089	*Poussin* | In een Bergachtig Landschap, met eenig geboomte en op de voorgrond een Waterval, gestoffeerd met de geschiedenis der Broeder moord van Cain; meesterlyk en kragtig geschilderd op Doek, in de manier van Poussin | *Mat:* op doek *Size:* hoog 29, breed 34 duim	W Wynen	(Sold) fl 6:5 Le Dantú
1802/11/01	DOBRA	0191	*Poussin* | Een grootsche ordonnantie van Antique Gebouwen. Ter regterzyde een pragtig gedenkteeken. Naar den voorgrond word een Krygsheld, die doodelyk gekwest schynt, door Soldaaten gedraagen. De meenigte, die hem van allerwegen verzeldt, vertoont zig droefgeestig over het geval; meesterlyk behandeld, als van Poussin | *Mat:* op doek		(Unknown) fl 7:15

Primaticcio, Francesco

1810/07/26	AMSCH	0061	*Primaticio* | Het Pourtrait van Diana van Portier, Hertogin van Valentina, Minnaresse van Hendrik den Tweeden, gekleed als een Jagtgodin, houdende een Hoorn en Boog in hare Handen, dragende op de Borst den Naam van Hendrik den Tweeden. Zeer schoon geschilderd | *Mat:* op paneel *Size:* hoog 33, breed 24 duimen	Cassino	(Bought In) fl 5

Prins, Johannes Huibert

1801/10/19	AMSCH	0058	*Prins. (J. H) 1786* | Een Stad-Gezicht, zeer uitvoerig geschildert in de manier van J. van der Heyden, zeer ryk gestoffeerd met diversche Gebouwen, Boomen en verschillende Figuren, extra fraay en zonächtig behandeld | companion to lot 59 *Mat:* op paneel *Size:* hoog 15 ¾, breed 19 duim *Inscr:* 1786 (dated?) *Notes:* It is unclear whether the date is inscribed on the painting.	Jonkheer Menno Baron van Coehoorn	(Sold) fl 140 Gruyter
1801/10/19	AMSCH	0059	*Prins. (J. H) 1786* | Een dito [Stad-Gezicht], zynde een weederga niet minder als het voorgaande, en in alle deelen van dezelve qualiteit | companion to lot 58 *Mat:* op paneel *Size:* hoog 15 ¾, breed 19 duim *Inscr:* 1786 (dated?) *Notes:* It is unclear whether the date is inscribed on the painting.	Jonkheer Menno Baron van Coehoorn	(Sold) fl 200 Gruiter
1802/05/05	AMSCH	0174	*J. H. Prins* | Een Gezicht in een oude Stad, met prachtige Hardsteene Kerk, ter linker zyde een oud Klooster en verdere Gebouwen, op de voorgrond eene Steene Brug, waarop een menigte Beeldjes; alles van de uitvoerigste en beste schildering | *Mat:* op doek *Size:* hoog 20, breed 23 duim	H	(Sold) fl 101 Gruiter
1802/06/16	AMSCH	0139	*H. Prins* | In Een aangenaam bevallig Land- en Riviergezicht met verschillend Geboomten; ziet men ter zyde een Herberg, en verscheide Lieden, zoo wandelende als rydende te Paard, en andere met Wagens: in de Rivier eenige Vaartuigen, en een bergachtig verschiet; alles zonachtig en ongemeen uitvoerig gepenceeld | *Mat:* op paneel *Size:* hoog 5, breed 6 ½ duim	[Merrem]	(Sold) fl 3:15 Wed Achtienhoven
1804/12/10	AMSCH	0084	*J. H. Prins* | Dit aangenaam voorwerp verbeeld een Gezicht van een Stad aan de Vestmuur langs een Rivier, waar by een aloud Kasteel en andere Woningen, gestoffeert met verscheide beeldjes, zeilschuiten, houtvlot en verder bywerk; het metzelwerk is verwonderlyk uitvoerig, alles is zonachtig en van een fraaye penceel behandeling | *Mat:* op paneel *Size:* Hoog 17 ½, breed 15 duim	Jan De Groot	(Sold) fl 101 Josi
1806/05/05	AMSCH	0115	*J. H. Prins* | Een capitaal Stadgezigt, met schoone Gebouwen en Geboomten, ryk gestoffeerd met differente stoffagie; zonachtig en uitvoerig geschildert door J. H. Prins | *Mat:* op paneel *Size:* hoog 15 ¾, breed 19 duim	V[inkeles]	(Sold) fl 137 Spaan
1806/08/13	AMSCH	0147	*Prins. (H.)* | Een aangenaam Land- en Watergezicht; ryk gestoffeerd en uitvoerig geschilderd | *Mat:* op koper *Size:* hoog 7 ½, breed 10 ½ duim	Vinkeles [for] G[ruyter]	(Sold) fl 1:15 L Pakker
1806/08/20	HGBSM	0026	*J.H. Prins* | Een Stads binnen gezicht, langs een breede gragt, met Sluis en Ophaalbrug en Boomen; dit stuk een der beste van dezen Meester, is bijzonder aangenaam van verkiezing, de uitvoerigheid der steenen en metzelwerk gaat alles te boven, de boomen vindt men zelden zo goed van hem; en een aantal figuuren die er in voorkomen zijn uitmuntend. Verders volmaakt in de manier van van der Heiden | *Mat:* op mahoniehout paneel *Size:* hoog 16, breed 19 duim	Macalester Loup [or others]	(Sold) fl 200 Teissier
1806/11/24	AMSCH	0052	*Prins (J.H.)* | In een Binnenhuis zit een Vrouw met een Vogel op haar schoot, welke zy schynt te plukken, naast haar een Kind in de Kinderstoel, waarmede een Jongeling speeld; verders een Wieg en verder bywerk; alles delicaat en uitvoerig gepenceeld | *Mat:* op doek *Size:* hoog 22, breed 19 duim	Munnikhuizen	(Sold) fl 16:10 Gruiter
1807/08/26	AMSCH	0172	*J.H. Prins* | Een Stadgezigt met Beelden gestoffeerd, vertoonende op de hoek van een Straat een Winkelhuis; zeer uitvoerig behandeld | *Mat:* op paneel *Size:* hoog 11, breed 9 duim	Joseph Vallette	(Sold) fl 7 Jozi
1807/08/26	AMSCH	0173	*J.H. Prins* | Een Stadgezicht met fraai gemetzelde Gebouwen, Kerk en Standbeeld, en aartige stoffage van Beeldjes; zonachtig op Paneel geschilderd | *Mat:* op paneel *Size:* hoog 15, breed 19 duim	Joseph Vallette	(Sold) fl 79 Jozi

1808/08/23	AMSCH	0127	*Prins. (H.)* | Een Stadgezicht, ziende over eene Sluis op een groot Plein, met verscheide Gebouwen, gestoffeert op de voorgrond, met een gaande Heer, waarbij een Man met een beladen Kruiwagen, welke door eene Vrouw ondersteund word, verder een Heer, welke aan eene arme Vrouw met twee Kinderen een Almoes geeft, en in 't verschiet verscheide andere Beeldjes; dit stuk is zonachtig, bevallig en zoo uitvoerig behandeld, als of het door J. van der Heiden geschilderd was | *Mat:* op doek *Size:* hoog 21, breed 25 duim	X	(Sold) fl 360 Jan Spaan
1809/04/17	AMSCH	0077	*H. Prins* | Een Rhijngezicht, met Vaartuigen en Beeldjes gestoffeerd; helder en zonagtig | *Mat:* op koper *Size:* hoog 7 ½, breed 10 duim	R	(Sold) fl 1:10
			Procaccini		
1810/07/26	AMSCH	0062	*Procacini* | David het afgehouwen Hoofd van Goliath in zijn Hand houdende | *Mat:* op doek *Size:* hoog 26, breed 12 duimen	Cassino	(Sold) fl 9 J^{mo} de Vries
			Procaccini, Camillo (or Procaccini, Cam., manner)		
1801/04/13	AMSCH	0108	*Camillo Procacino* | Een Martelaresse gebonden wordende, door, of in de manier van Camillo Procacino; meesterlyk | *Mat:* op doek *Size:* hoog 38, breed 30 duim	Pierre Fouquet, junior	(Sold) fl 14 B Wolft
			Puyster [Unidentified]		
1802/05/10	MGSAN	0038	*Puister* | Een fraai en zeer uitvoerig Stuk, vertoonende een Binnenkeuken, daarin een Vrouwtje, zittende Appels te schillen, voor haar een Spinnewiel; verder ander Bywerk en Huisraad, door Puister: op Paneel, in vergulde Lyst | *Mat:* op paneel *Size:* hoog 19 duim, breed 24 duim	Johan Dirk Kruysse	(Sold) £ 24 Van de Sande
1810/10/10	MGCIT	0046	*Puyster* | Een Binnenhuisje, waar in een Vrouwtje zit die Appelen schild, naast haar een Spinnewiel; verder agter haar eenig Huisraad, fraai en uitnemend geschilderd door .... Puyster	Caspar van Citters	(Unknown)
			Pynacker, Adam		
1801/06/10	AMSCH	0134	*Pynacker. (A.)* | Een Landschap, waar in de geboorte aan de Herders word aangekondigd: men ziet op de voorgrond een Koei, benevens een Herder in eene angsstige [sic] gestalte: krachtig en meesterlyk behandeld | *Mat:* op paneel *Size:* hoog 15, breed 19 duim *Notes:* Originally the artist's name was spelled "J. Pynacker." This error was corrected in an errata sheet located at the end of the catalogue. *Loc:* San Francisco, CA, USA. M.H. DeYoung Memorial Museum. (52.14)	Herman ten Kate	(Sold) fl 205 Coclers
1801/06/10	AMSCH	0135	*Pynacker. (A.)* | Een Zonachtig Landschap, op de voorgrond ziet men een Boerin verschrikt door het omvallen van een Melkemmer, welk door het achter uitschoppen van een Koei, veroorzaakt word, verders een Bergachtig verschiet: fraai en uitvoerig van schildering | *Mat:* op paneel *Size:* hoog 16, breed 19 duim *Notes:* Originally the artist's name was spelled "J. Pynacker." This error was corrected in an errata sheet located at the end of the catalogue.	Herman ten Kate	(Sold) fl 66 De Roy
1801/10/06	AMSCH	0051	*A. Pynaker* | In dit Aangenaam Landschap ter zyde by hoog Geboomten en Plantgewassen, ziet men een gaand Huisman, verzelt van een hond, verder een Visser in een schuit, Bevallig van coloriet en meesterlyk fraay gepenceeld | *Mat:* op doek *Size:* hoog 21, breed 19 duim	S	(Bought In) fl 40
1802/06/16	AMSCH	0129	*A. Pynacker* | Een Italiaansch Landschap met Geboomte, Ruïnes en fraije stoffagie van Beelden en Beesten, ter zyde een stil Water, waar in de spiegeling van het Geboomte zeer wel is waargenomen, zynde alles zonachtig en meesterlyk behandeld | *Mat:* op paneel *Size:* hoog 17, breed 18 ½ duim	[Merrem]	(Sold) fl 135 Gruiter
1802/09/29	AMSCH	0046	*A. Pynaker* | Een Landschap, hoog 15, breed 20 duim. Paneel. Tusschen Rotsen, zwaar Geboomten en kreupel Houtgewas, ziet men een Landman, benevens een Hond eenig Vee door het Water dryven, als twee Rosse Koebeesten, een Schaap en een Bokje; een der Koebeesten staat reeds op het drooge, terwyl de anderen, waartegen den Hond is blaffende, met Stokslagen door het Water vervolgd word; het invallend Zonnelicht tusschen het Geboomten, verlicht allerkunstigst deeze zeldzame Ordenantie; de delicaate Penceelbehandeling is ongemeen bevallig, zynde dit Schildery een der fraaiste van deezen Meester [Paysage, orné de Rochers & chûtes d'Eaux avec Figure & animaux ; sur le devant est un Pâtre qui fait traverser l'Eau à deux Boeufs une chévre & un mouton. Le Pâtre, son chien & les animaux sont supérieurement éclairés par un rayon de soleil qui perce à travers les arbres. Ce Tableau piquant d'Effet & d'une touche precieuse est une des plus belle compositions de ce Peintre dont les productions deviennent plus râres de jour en jour.] | *Mat:* op paneel *Size:* hoog 15, breed 20 duim	[Labouchere?]	(Sold) fl 190 Gruyter
1803/08/17	AMSCH	0063	*Pynacker. (A.)* | Een Italiaansch Landschap met hoog Geboomte en Gebergtens, op de voorgrond een Man en Vrouw met een Ezel en rustende Vrouw, in het verschiet noch eenige Stoffagie, alles warm transparant en zonachtig gepenceeld | *Mat:* op paneel *Size:* hoog 23, breed 19 duim	Anna Catharina Putman	(Sold) fl 135 Gruyter
1804/05/07	AMSCH	0135	*Pynaker. (A.)* | Een bevallig Boomryk Landschap, met een Rivier doorsneeden, waarin een Visscher in een Schuit, op de voorgrond gestoffeerd, met een gaande Huisman, verzeld van een Hond, verder een	Schley	(Sold) fl 14:10 den Achtienhoven

			Bergachtig verschiet; zonachtig en meesterlyk gepenceeld | *Mat:* op doek *Size:* hoog 21, breed 19 duim		
1804/05/07	AMSCH	0136	*Pynaker. (A.)* | In een Boomryk Landschap by eenig kreupel Gewas en een stil Watertje, ziet men een Herder en Herderin, verzeld van eenig staand en rustend Vee, verders eenig Geboomte Gebouwen en Gebergten; zonachtig fiks en van fraaije penceelbehandeling | *Mat:* op paneel *Size:* hoog 19, breed 16 duim	Vinkeles [for] X	(Sold) fl 90 Gruyter
1804/08/08	AMSCH	0153	*A. Pynakker* | In een Italiaansch Landschap, by de Overblyfzels van eenig alóude trotsche Gebouwen, ziet men een Landman by een klaar spiegelend Water eenige Beesten hoeden; het piquante invallende zonlicht, en de meesterlyke schilderwys, maaken dit tot een alleraangenaamst zonachtig en bevallig Schildery | *Size:* hoog 10, breed 9 duim	Vink[eles] [for] K[=Gruyter?]	(Bought In) fl 20
1804/10/16	DLOND	0182	*A. Pynacker* | Een Heuvelig Landschap met Geboomte, Herder, Herderin en Koeien, zeer schoon. Paysage Collineux avec des Arbres, Berger, Bergère & Vaches, très beau | *Mat:* op paneel *Size:* hoog 22, breed 26		(Sold) fl 333 Mahy
1804/10/16	DLOND	0183	*A. Pynacker* | Een Landschap met veel Geboomte, waarop een Os, die zich uit de Struiken tracht te redden, enz. Paysage. Sous quelques arbres on voit un boeuf se sauvant d'entre les broussailles | *Mat:* op doek *Size:* hoog 26, breed 22		(Unknown) fl 15:15
1806/08/20	HGBSM	0058	*A. Pijnaaker* | Een Bergachtig Landschap met twee Stammen van Boomen, gestoffeerd met diverse soorten van Dieren | *Mat:* op doek *Size:* hoog 29, breed 24 ½ duim	Macalester Loup [or others]	(Sold) fl 35 Gruijter
1808/05/18	LNAN	0044	*Pijnakker* | Een helder Heuvelachtig Landschap met Gebouwen, Beelden en Beesten | *Notes:* The artist's name "Pijnakker" was added in by hand in the RKDH copy of the catalogue.	Mr Cornelis Versluys	(Unknown)
1808/06/06	RMRIJ	0105	*Pijnacker. (Adam)* | Op een stout gekozen bergachtig Rijngezigt, ziet men eenige met koopmans goederen beladene Barken en Schuiten, waarop een aantal werkzaam zijnde figuren. Aan land zit, op den tweeden grond, eene Vrouw met haar Kind op den schoot, eenen bij haar staanden Herders Jongen aanziende. Meer voorwaarts staan een stootende kloeke roodbonte Os en een bruine Ezel. Voor aan op den voorgrond ligt een aangename bogtige Beukenstam; bij denzelven staan eenige Planten, Kruiden, Bloemen en kapitale Boomen. Dit stuk, eenen Morgenstond verbeeldende, is vlug en meesterlijk getoetst, schoon gekleurd, verstandig geschikt, en in alle deelen een der verdienstelijkste van dezen beroemden Meester [Ce Tableau magnifique offre le choix hardi d'un site montagneux aubord d'une Rivière. Plusieurs barques chargées de marchandises se presentent à la vue, et beaucoup de personnes sont occupées. Une femme qui est assise sur le Rivage, tient un enfant sur ses genoux, et s'entretient avec un jeune Garçon, qui est devant elle. Le premier Plan est occupé par un Boeuf rougeâtre, qui semble menacer de ses cornes un Ane, qui est près de lui. Un beau Hêtre renversé, des Plantes et des troncs de differents arbres, dont la touche spirituelle fait trés bien distinguer les espèces de feuillages, forment le devant. Le lointain agréable et pittoresque, un Ciel superbe, et quelques légères vapeurs, tout cela annonce une belle et fraiche matinée, au moment où le Soleil paroit sur l'horison. Le bel Ensemble, l'harmonie et le beau faire charment l'oeil dans ce Morceau, qui peut être consideré comme une des plus savantes Productions de ce grand Artiste] | *Annots:* Pour le Musée d'Amsterdam (NGW) *Mat:* op paneel [sur toile, collé sur bois] *Size:* Hoog 36 ½, en breed 32 ¼ duim *Notes:* The materials differ in the Dutch and French editions of the catalogue. *Loc:* Amsterdam, Nederland. Rijksmuseum. (A321)	Gerrit van der Pot, Heer van Groeneveld	(Sold) fl 1800 A A Stratenus [for] le roi
1808/06/06	RMRIJ	0106	*Pijnacker. (Adam)* | Een bergachtig Landschap met veel geboomte, door eenen Bliksemstraal verlicht. Op den voorgrond een, door eene Beek, vlugtende Os. In 't verschiet met hun Vee vlugtende Landlieden. Alles zeer krachtig en meesterlijk behandeld [Ce Paysage represente un Orage éclatant ; un Berger et plusieurs Animaux sont effrayés par la foudre. Sur le devant un Boeuf dans un Ruisseau etc. Une Imagination vive, et une Touche Savante caracterisent ce Tableau] | *Annots:* Deurstuk uit syn huis (RMA I) *Mat:* op doek *Size:* Hoog 26, en breed 26 ½ duim	Gerrit van der Pot, Heer van Groeneveld	(Sold) fl 250 Josi
1808/06/11	RMRIJ	0073	*A: Pynaker* | Een bergachtig Landschap, op den Voorgrond Boomstammen; een Koe en twee Kalven verryken dit krachtig en meesterlyk Schildery | *Mat:* op paneel *Size:* hoog 12 ¾, breed 12 duim		(Bought In) fl 43
1808/06/13	AMSCH	0120	*Pijnacker (A.)* | Een Ruïne, aan eene Rots zit eene Vrouw op de Trappen, op den voorgrond een Man, op eene Ezel, daarbij een staand Man, als naar den weg vragende, daarbij een Hond. Het invallend zonlicht maakt eene schoone uitwerking, en is van eene alleruitmuntendste penceelsbehandeling | *Mat:* op paneel *Size:* hoog 13, breed 10 duim	R[oos]	(Bought In) fl 75
1809/06/13	AMSCH	0125	*A. Pynaker* | Aan een stil Water, bij eenig Kreupelgewas, ziet men eenige Landlieden bij staand en rustend Vee; verder eenig dartel opgaand Geboomten, en een bergagtig Verschiet; zonagtig behandeld | *Mat:* op paneel *Size:* hoog 19, breed 16 duim	[Gruyter?]	(Bought In) fl 98
1810/06/06	RMMUY	0068	*A. Pijnacker* | Een Landschap met Beesten, krachtig en meesterlijk geschilderd | *Mat:* op paneel		(Unknown) fl 8
1810/06/06	RMMUY	0069	*A. Pijnacker* | Een liggende en een slapende Windhond | *Mat:* op paneel		(Unknown) fl 2

1810/07/23	DOLGI	0044	*Adam Pijnacker* | Een Boschrijk Landschap. Op den voorgrond een Jager, een Rêe ontweiënde. Verder eenig dood Wild; als een Rijger, Haas en wild Zwijn. In 't verschiet Jagers te Paard, met hunne Jagthonden. Natuurlijk, zonächtig en uitvoerig geschilderd | *Mat:* op doek op paneel *Size:* hoog 15 ½, breed 13 ½ duim	Mr Pieter van den Santheuvel	(Sold) fl 113 A van Strij
1810/07/26	AMSCH	0069	*Pynacker (Gemerkt A.)* | Een Boomrijk Landschap, gestoffeerd met Huislieden en Reizigers. Zonachtig en natuurlijk behandeld | *Mat:* op paneel *Size:* hoog 28, breed 20 duimen *Inscr:* A. Pynacker (signed)	Cassino	(Sold) fl 9 Boelhouwer
1810/08/01	AMSCH	0079	*Pijnacker (Adam)* | Een fraai boomrijk Landschap, op den voorgrond eene Landvrouw bij eene staande en rustende Koe, en eenige Bokken; verder een bergachtig verschiet [Un beau Site de Paysage : au devant de ce tableau on voit une Villageoise auprès d'une Vache couchée, et d'une séconde qui est debout ; il y a de plus quelques Chévres, et une prespective montueuse qui se detache vèrs l'horison] | *Annots:* mal composé : effet trop embrouillé. (NGW) *Mat:* op paneel *Size:* hoog 14 ½, breed 18 ½ duimen *Loc:* Amsterdam, Nederland. Rijksmuseum. (A 322)	Mr Pieter de Smeth van Alphen	(Bought In) fl 1400
1810/08/01	AMSCH	0080	*Pijnacker (Adam)* | Een hoog bergachtig Landschap, gestoffeerd met Bokken en Schapen; op den voorgrond bij Distelplanten en Kruiden liggen Stammen van oude Boomen [Un Site montueux orné de Chèvres et de Brebis, le premier plan étant garni de Plantes et de Troncs d'arbres renversés] | possibly companion to lot 81 *Annots:* ancienne pièce des cheminée. (NGW); Vente le Brun ce tableau et le pendant furent retirés, No.179. fr: 4000 (SMLN); 1811. Coll. M. LeBrun no. 79. 1845. Rome. Galerie du Cardinal Fesch, no. 186, p.195 (VAL I) *Mat:* op doek *Size:* hoog 46, breed 40 duimen *Loc:* Paris, France. Musée du Louvre. (RF 709)	Mr Pieter de Smeth van Alphen	(Sold) fl 910 Texier, Gerbet en Comp [for] LeBrun
1810/08/01	AMSCH	0081	*Pijnacker (Adam)* | Een Landschap, in alles als het hier boven omschrevenen. Kunnende strekken tot eene wederga van de voorgaande [Un Sujet composé comme le précédent ; dont il peut servir de pendant] | possibly companion to lot 80 *Annots:* comme le précédent [ancienne pièce des cheminée] (NGW); 1811. Coll. M. LeBrun no. 79. 1845. Rome. Galerie du Cardinal Fesch, no. 187, p.196 (VAL I) *Mat:* op doek *Size:* hoog 46, breed 40 duimen *Loc:* London, England, UK. Wallace Collection. (P57)	Mr Pieter de Smeth van Alphen	(Sold) fl 1010 Texier, Gerbet en Comp [for] LeBrun
1810/08/10	RMRIJ	0002	*Adam Pijnacker* | Een aangenaam Landschap, rijk gestoffeerd met Beelden, Schuiten &c. Warm zonachtig en krachtig geschilderd | *Mat:* op paneel *Size:* hoog 18 ½ duim, breed 23 duim		(Sold) fl 200 v Dongen

Pynacker, Adam (or Pynacker, manner)

1808/03/03	HAVIN	0018	*Pynacker* | Een Landschap, door of in de manier van Pynacker	Jacobus Spillebout	(Unknown) fl 4:5

Pynacker, Adam (manner)

1802/08/24	LNDLS	0147	*Pijnacker* | Een Bergagtig Landschap met een Waterval en Stoffage, als van Pijnacker | *Mat:* op doek	Leonardus Bouman [or others]	(Unknown) fl 16
1802/09/06	AMSCH	0165	*A. Pynaker* | In een Bergagtig Landschap met verscheide geboomten, ziet men een waterval, op de voorgrond een rustend en een staand huisman, als met elkander spreekende, verder een aangenaam verschiet; meesterlyk en uitvoerig geschilderd, als door A. Pynaker | *Size:* hoog 20, breed 27 duim	Brave	(Sold) fl 40 Van Iperen
1803/08/24	HGKAN	A0003	*Pynaker* | Een Landschap met Gebergte en Vee, in de trant van Pynaker, op paneel, 24 duim in 't Vierkant | *Mat:* op paneel *Fmt:* in 't Vierkant *Size:* 24 duim		(Sold) fl 3:10 van Giesen
1804/12/10	AMSCH	0125	*Pynaker* | Een Landschap met hoog geboomte, op de voorgrond met een jacht gestoffeerd, fraai en meesterlyk gepenceeld als Pynaker | *Mat:* op doek *Size:* hoog 30, breed 42 duim	Jan De Groot	(Sold) fl 3:5 van Iperen
1808/04/26	GDAN	0245	*Pynaker* | In de manier van Pynaker, een boomrijk Landschap, met een Vrouw en eenig Vee | *Size:* hoog 12 ½, breed 10 ½ duim	G H Fortuyn	(Unknown)
1810/06/20	AMSCH	0189	*Pijnacker* | Een Bergachtig Landschap met Beelden en Beesten, gestoffeerd. Zonachtig in de manier van Pijnacker geschilderd	A	(Sold) fl 1 L Pakker
1810/10/11	AMSCH	0072	*A. Pijnakker* | Een Landgezigt, ter zijde een Bosch met Stoffage; als A. Pijnakker | *Size:* hoog 16, breed 12 duimen	C	(Sold) fl 1 Posthumus

Pynas, J.

1802/02/16	AMSCH	0019	*Pinas* | Twee stuks Bybelsche Ordenantiën fraay geordoneerd en geschilderd op paneel | *Mat:* op paneel	B[uys]	(Sold) fl 11 Vink en Fitsing
1802/05/05	AMSCH	0176	*Pinas* | Marcias, aan een Boom gebonden, word gevild, meesterlyk | *Mat:* op doek *Size:* hoog 40, breed 30 duim	A	(Sold) fl 0:6 L Pakker
1803/04/20	AMSCH	0057	*Pinas. (A.)* | Dit Tafereel vertoont in het middenstuk de Geboorte Christi, alwaar de Herders het Kindeken aanbidden, en geschenken brengen, ryk gestoffeert met beelden, omhoog ziet men een glorie van musiceerende Engelen; op de eene Deur zyn verbeeld vier Mannen en een Jong Kind, in aloude deftige kleeding, en in 't verschiet de Kruisdood van den Heiland: op de andere Deur vier Vrouwen in aloud gewaad, en in 't verschiet de Opstanding Christi, alles is van een bevallig Coloriet en een uitvoerige penceelsbehandeling [Ce tableau traité à la maniere ancienne avec deux battans, a pour sujet principal la naissance de J.C. ; composition riche ou	Maria Magdalena van Sluypwyk, gravinne van Moens	(Sold) fl 80 Hodges

			les pasteurs viennent faire leur offrande & leur adoration. Le haut est orné d'une gloire d'Anges. Sur un des volets sont quatre portraits d'hommes & un enfant ; l'autre est orné par quatre portraits de femmes en costume du tems de cet oeuvre. Ce morceau méritant est soigné & d'un beau coloris.] | *Mat:* op paneel *Fmt:* van boven Toogsgewys met twee toestaande Deuren *Size:* hoog 35, breed 24 duim [haut 35, large 23 pouces] *Notes:* The artist's name was given as "Pinas. (A.)" but we have assumed this is an error.		
1807/08/26	AMSCH	0178	*Pinas* | Een Bybelsche Ordonnantie, vol van Beelden, voorstellende daar Jozeph door zyne Broeders herkend wordt | *Mat:* op paneel *Size:* hoog 34, breed 53 duim	de Vries	(Sold) fl 3:5 Joh^{s} Hooft
1809/04/17	AMSCH	0142	*Pinas* | Petrus op Zee Vissende, wordt van Christus geroepen | *Mat:* op doek	[Gruyter?]	(Sold or Bought In) fl 2 Gruyter

Quast, Pieter Jansz.

1801/04/08	HAVIN	0034	*Quast* | Een Corps de Garde, als van le Duc		(Unknown)
1802/06/16	AMSCH	0140	*P. Quast* | Op een Markt ziet men een Quakzalver, waar by eenige Aanschouwers, op de voorgrond ziet men een Boer die op een Potsige manier de kies getrokken word: breed van penceel-behandeling | *Mat:* op paneel *Size:* hoog 16 ½, breed 13 ½ duim	[Merrem]	(Sold) fl 20 J Spaan
1804/10/16	DLOND	0184	*N. Quast* | Twee Stukjes met Boeren, zeer uitdrukkend. Deux pièces avec des Paysans très expressifs | *Mat:* op zilver *Fmt:* ellipt *Size:* hoog 1 ½, breed 2 ½ *Notes:* The artist's name was given as "N. Quast" but we have assumed this is an error.		(Unknown) fl 50
1808/04/26	GDAN	0130	*Quast (D)* | Verbeeldende een Chirurgijns Winkel, waar in den Chirurgijn met de grootste oplettenheid een Boer triponeerd, die uit al zijn magt zit te schreeuwen, eenige omstanders die met medelijden behebt zijn, fraai en fiks behandeld | *Size:* hoog 10, breed 8 duim *Notes:* The artist's name was given as "Quast (D)" but we have assumed this is an error.	G H Fortuyn	(Unknown)
1808/04/26	GDAN	0131	*Quast (D)* | Een Binnenhuis, waar in eenige Boeren die vrolijk zijn, en zich met Drinken, &c vermaken, goed geschilderd | *Size:* hoog 16, breed 23 duim *Notes:* The artist's name was given as "Quast (D)" but we have assumed this is an error.	G H Fortuyn	(Unknown)
1809/07/25	HGBSM	0165	*P. Quast* | Twee stuks Portretten, in de trant van Rembrand, door P. Quast | *Mat:* op paneel *Size:* hoog 10 en een half, breed 8 duim	D van der Aa [or] E B ten Dall	(Sold) fl 3:2 Heijmans [for] G

Quast, Pieter Jansz. (manner)

1808/12/12	UTWLD	0016	*Quast* | Een Boere Binnenhuis in de manier van Quast [Alle in swarte Lysten en wel geconserveerd.] | *Mat:* op paneel *Notes:* The bracketed information in the title appears above lot 1 and refers to lots 1 to 19.	Mr D Hoola van Nooten	(Unknown)

Quellinus, Erasmus (II)

1804/08/02	BDAN	0023	*Quellinus den Ouden* | Een Maria-beeld met het Kindje en St: Jan, zeer schoon geschilderd | *Mat:* op doek *Size:* b. 38 d. h. 46 d.	J G Calckberner	(Unknown)
1804/08/08	AMSCH	0158	*E. Quellinus* | Deze capitaale Ordinantie, met leevensgroote Figuuren, verbeeld de Heilige Familjie, in een Binnenvertrek, Maria zit met het Kind Jezu op de Schoot, daar neevens St. Anna, het met aandacht beschouwende, voor dezelve staat den Jongeling St. Jan, een Lam vasthoudende, en ter linker zyde staat een Wieg, op het Dekentje ziet men een rustende Kat, achterwaards staat St. Joseph, in een Boek leezende, verzeld van een Engel; door een open Vengster vertoont zig een Landschap; de Teekening en coloriet zyn bevallig, en is meesterlyk en uitvoerig gepenceeld, op Doek | *Mat:* op doek *Size:* hoog 5 voet 9 duim, breed 7 voet duim	Schley [for] B	(Sold) fl 41 Ferguson
1805/07/03	AMSCH	0136	*E. Quellinus* | Deeze Ordinantie vol gewoel van Beelden vertoont de Geboorten Christi in de Stal te Bethlem, alwaar de Herders het Kindeken aanbidden, en Geschenken brengen; de caracters zyn natuurlyk en van een meesterlyke penceel behandeling | *Mat:* op koper *Size:* hoog 16, breed 21 duim	R[oos]	(Sold) fl 41 Josi
1808/06/13	AMSCH	0123	*Quellinus (E.)* | De Geschiedenis van Jozef, in 't midden verschijnt Jakob voor Farao, rondsom de lotgevallen van Jozefs leven. Uitvoerig behandeld | *Annots:* [door] Franckn (MB) *Mat:* op paneel *Size:* hoog 36, breed 48 duim	E M Engelberts	(Sold) fl 55 W Reijers

Querfurt, August

1805/07/03	AMSCH	0137	*Quertfurth* | Twee stuks hévige Schermutselingen, tusschen Paardevolk en Voetvolk; natuurlyk en fiks gepenceeld op Doek | *Mat:* op doek *Size:* yder hoog 9, breed 12 duim	G	(Sold) fl 8 Valette
1806/08/20	HGBSM	0176	*Querfurt* | Een hevige actie van Cavallerij | companion to lot 177 *Mat:* op doek *Size:* hoog 17, breed 29 duim	Macalester Loup [or others]	(Sold) fl 4 for lots 176 & 177. Praiston
1806/08/20	HGBSM	0177	*Querfurt* | Een dito [hevige actie van Cavallerij] wederga | companion to lot 176	Macalester Loup [or others]	(Sold) fl 4 for lots 176 & 177. Praiston

Querfurt, August (manner)

1805/07/03	AMSCH	0193	*Quertfurth* | Twee stuks, Bataljes vol gewoel van Parden en Beelden, als Quertfurth | *Mat:* op doek	C	(Sold) fl 15 Suykerbecker

Quinkhard, Jan Maurits

1801/03/16	AMSCH	0178	*Quinckhart* | Een Pons-gezelschap	P[ruyssenaar]	(Sold) fl 2:10 I^c Smit
1807/06/10	HGBSM	0177	*J.M. Quinkhard* | Het welgelijkend Portrait, van den Kunstschilder J. de Witt, meesterlijk geschilderd | *Mat:* op paneel *Size:* hoog 11, breed 9 duim	Abraham Delfos [or others]	(Sold) fl 2:2 Heymans
1808/06/13	AMSCH	0124	*Quinkhart (J.)* | In eene gemeubileerde Kamer zitten twee Heeren bij eene Tafel, met een Kleed bedekt, waarop Muzijkpapieren liggen, speelende de een op de Fiool, en de andere op de Dwarsfluit, op den voorgrond tegen een Stoel staat een Bas. Het is meesterlijk gepenceeld | *Mat:* op paneel *Size:* hoog 19 ½, breed 16 duim	[Jan Tersteeg]	(Sold) fl 21 Du Pré

Rademaker

1810/03/23	HAVIN	0070	*Rademaker* | Twee Rhijngezigten met Coul. [In Lysten met Glasen] | *Notes:* The bracketed information in the title appears above lot 63 and refers to lots 63 to 79.	Rudolf Hendrik de Wetstein [or others]	(Unknown)

Rademaker, Abraham

1810/06/06	RMMUY	0066	*A. Rademaker* | Een Gezigt van de Duinen om de Stad Haarlem, op de voorgrond gestoffeerd met een Heer te Paard en een Jager &c. van een aangenaam Coloriet | *Mat:* op doek		(Unknown) fl 26 for lots 66 & 67
1810/06/06	RMMUY	0067	*A. Rademaker* | Een Gezigt buiten Haarlem in de Duinen, met Stoffage, niet minder als het vorige | *Mat:* op paneel		(Unknown) fl 26 for lots 66 & 67

Raffaello Santi (or Raffaello Santi, copy after)

1803/09/07	AMSCH	0135	*Raphaël* | Dit capitaale stuk verbeeld St. Jan, zittende in een Landschap een Lam vasthoudende; allerheerlykst geteekend, en meesterlyk fraay gepenceeld, naar of door Raphaël [Ce tableau capital montre St. Jean dans un paysage, tenant un agneau ; admirablement bien dessiné, et de la plus belle exécution] | *Annots:* Guidorini [i.e., Guido Reni] (RKDH II) *Mat:* op doek *Size:* hoog 53, breed 40 duim	Smidt	(Bought In) fl 105

Raffaello Santi (copy after)

1803/04/27	AMSCH	0120[a]	*Rafaël* | Deux tableaux, la pentecôte d'après Rafaël, & la Chasteté | *This Lot:* La pentecôte; lot 120[b] by C. Cignani	A	(Sold) fl 2 for lots 120[a] & 120[b]. L Pakker
1803/09/07	AMSCH	0258	*Raphael* | De Heilige Familelje, Maria schynt met het Kindeken Jezu als te speelen, dewyl Joseph hetzelve beschouwd; de caracters zyn Natuurlyk, kragtig van Coloriet, en uitvoerig gepenceelt, op Paneel, naar Raphael, door een goed Meester [La sainte famille. La vierge paroit s'amuser avec l'enfant Jesus, tandis que St. Joseph les considère. Ce tableau est remarquable par la vérité de l'expression, la force de coloris, et la beauté de sa composition, d'après Raphael] | *Mat:* op paneel *Size:* hoog 41, breed 33 duim	Smidt	(Bought In) fl 20
1804/05/07	AMSCH	0202	*Raphael d'Urbino* | Petrus en Johannes, geneezen de Kreupelen aan den ingang van den Tempel; fraai en uitvoerig gepenceeld, door een Italiaans Meester, na Raphael d'Urbino | *Mat:* op koper *Size:* hoog 26, breed 38 duim	Y[ver]	(Sold) fl 22 Gruyter
1806/05/05	AMSCH	0043	*van Dorne; Raphael* | Raphael met zyn Schermmeester; alles meesterlyk en breed gepenceeld door van Dorne na Raphael | copy by F. Dorne after Raffaello Santi *Mat:* op doek *Size:* hoog 36, breed 31 duim	L	(Sold) fl 12 van Laar
1808/06/06	RMRIJ	0154	*naar Raphaël d'Urbino* | Een Kopij naar de beroemde Madona della Sedia uit de Gallerij van 't Paleis Pitti te Florence, doch thans in het Museum te Parijs [Savante Copie de la *Madona della Sedia*, de la galerie de Florence, maintenant au Musée de Paris] | *Annots:* Verk. Utrecht Sept. 1798 (f 42.-10) (RMA I) *Mat:* op doek *Size:* Hoog 22 ¼, en breed 16 ¾ duim	Gerrit van der Pot, Heer van Groeneveld	(Sold) fl 40 van Leen
1810/10/11	AMSCH	0068	*Parenti; Raphael* | De Maagd Maria, houdende het Kind Jezus op de schoot, nevens haar St. Jan; zeer uitvoerig en fraai geschilderd, op Doek, door Parenti, naar het schilderij van Raphael, bekend onder den naam van La Madona de La Sidia, hoog 28, breed 28 duimen. rond Formaat | copy by Parenti after Raffaello Santi *Mat:* op doek *Fmt:* rond *Size:* hoog 28, breed 28 duimen	M	(Sold) fl 21 du Pree

Rande, Abraham van de

1801/03/16	AMSCH	0076	*A. van Randen* | Twee dito [capitaale] dito [Landschappen]	P[ruyssenaar]	(Sold) fl 2:10 Boelen

Randhorst [Unidentified]

1808/05/18	LNAN	0008	*Randhorst* | Een Musicerend Gezelschap van Man en Vrouw, konstig behandeld | *Notes:* The artist's name "Randhorst" was added in by hand in the RKDH copy of the catalogue.	Mr Cornelis Versluys	(Unknown)

Raoux, Jean

1803/08/24	HGKAN	0007	*Raoux* | Een historieele Ordonnantie verbeeldende Alexander by Diogenes, brillant van Couleur, fraay van Teekening en Meesterlyk geschilderd	[Teissier] [or others]	(Sold) fl 15 for lots 7 & 8. Teissier
1803/08/24	HGKAN	0008	*Raoux* | Een dito [historieele Ordonnantie] verbeeldende Poliphemus en Galathea	[Teissier] [or others]	(Sold) fl 15 for lots 7 & 8. Teissier

Ravesteyn, Hubert van

1803/08/17	AMSCH	0073	*Ravestyn (H. van)* | Twee stuks zynde een Mans en een Vrouwe Pourtrait, meesterlyk behandeld | *Mat:* op paneel *Size:* ieder hoog 27, breed 24 duim	Anna Catharina Putman	(Sold) fl 11 Gruyter
1803/12/12	AMSCH	0079	*H. v. Ravensteyn* | Twee stuks, zynde capitaale Mans en Vrouwe Pourtretten,; meesterlyk behandeld | *Mat:* op paneel *Size:* hoog 27, breed 24 duim	B	(Sold) fl 9:10 Hodges
1806/08/13	AMSCH	0240	*H. van Ravestyn* | Twee stuks Mans- en Vrouwe Pourtraitten	Vinkeles [for] G[ruyter]	(Sold) fl 1:10 Yver [for] G

Ravesteyn, Jan Anthonisz. van

1801/10/19	AMSCH	0060	*Ravenstyn* | Twee mans- en twee vrouwen Pourtraitjes in eene Lyst, allerkeurigst gepenseeld en geteekend door gemelde Ravenstyn en andere beroemde miniatuur Schilders in Olyverf | *This Lot:* Twee mans- en twee vrouwen Pourtraitjes in eene Lyst *Mat:* op koper *Fmt:* ovaal	Jonkheer Menno Baron van Coehoorn	(Sold) fl 22 van Leijden
1803/04/20	AMSCH	0066	*Ravenstein* | Het Afbeeldzel van een bedaagd Heer in aloude deftige kleeding, met een geploide Kraag, om den Hals, en het Hoofd gedekt met een Calotje, meesterlyk fraay gepenceeld [Le Portrait de quelqu'homme célébre vu â trois-quarts de face, portant une robe noire fourrée & une fraise autour du col ; sa tête est couverte d'une calotte. Cette tête, traitée d'une maniere franche & vraye, est du premier merite, elle fait infiniment d'honneur à son auteur.] | *Mat:* op paneel *Size:* hoog 27, breed 23 duim	Maria Magdalena van Sluypwyk, gravinne van Moens	(Sold) fl 38 Hodges

Ravesteyn, Jan Anthonisz. van (manner)

1801/11/10	AMPOS	0029	*Ravenstyn* | 1 mans Pourtrait met pyp en kan, met een bonte muts, in vergenoegd voordoend gelaat, als door Ravenstyn		(Unknown)

Redeker [Unidentified]

1801/12/22	AMOTT	0103	*Redeker* | 1 stil Water om een adelyk Slot	Bartholomeus Ruloffs	(Unknown) fl 1:10

Redeker, J. [Unidentified]

1802/09/06	AMSCH	0170	*J. Redeker* | Een Altaarstuk, verbeeldende het Pinxterfeest; kragtig geschilderd | *Size:* hoog 93 ½, breed 60 ½ duim	Spaan	(Sold) fl 1:10 L Pakker

Regemorter, Peter van

1802/07/20	MGSAN	0010	*Regenmorter* | Een schoon Landschap, gestoffeerd met Figuuren en Beesten, extra fraai geschilderd op Paneel | *Mat:* op paneel *Size:* hoog duim 18 ½, breed duim 25 ½		(Unknown)
1802/07/20	MGSAN	0052	*P. Regenmortel* | Een Kaarslicht, op Paneel: door P. Regenmortel, van zyn beste | *Mat:* op paneel *Size:* hoog duim 12 ½, breed duim 10 ½		(Unknown)
1802/07/20	MGSAN	0059	*P. Regenmortel* | Een Land- en Watergezigt, op Paneel | *Mat:* op paneel *Size:* hoog duim 15, breed duim 18		(Unknown)
1802/12/13	AMSCH	0138	*Regelmorter* | In een aangenaam Land- en Watergezicht, ziet men eenige Lieden by een heldere Maan, met het Zège Vissen, op de voorgrond, ziet men eenige Landlieden, zig by een helder brandend Vuur vermaaken, 't helder schynen van de Maan, zowel als 't Licht van 't Vuur, zyn in dit Stuk zeer wel geopserveerd, en is van een uitvoerig penceelbehandeling | *Mat:* op paneel *Size:* hoog 11, breed 14 duim	Pruyssenaar [for] A	(Sold) fl 18:10 de Meijer
1806/11/24	AMSCH	0065	*Regenmorther (P. v.)* | Een aangenaam Brabandsch Landschap, met Boere Woningen en fraaije stoffagie van een ménigte vrolyke Gasten, welke zich met eeten, drinken en speelen vermaken, op de Voorgrond Kinderen met Vliegers enz. ; in 't verschiet in de weiden eenig Vee; de schildering is bevallig, en kan tot een wederga verstrekken van N.11. door Borrekens | possibly companion to lot 11, by J.P. Borrekens *Mat:* op doek *Size:* hoog 40, breed 49 duim	Munnikhuizen	(Sold) fl 53 Yver
1808/08/23	AMSCH	0138	*Regemorter. (P. van)* | Bij een helder schijnende Maan, ziet men in een aangenaam Land- en Watergezigt, Boeren Woningen en Geboomten, op de voorgrond bij een brandend Vuur, eenigen Visschers de wagt bij hun Viswand houdende, verder zeilenden en anderen Schepen en Vaartuigen; schoon van effect, uitvoerig en natuurlijk behandeld | *Mat:* op paneel *Size:* hoog 10 ½, breed 13 ½ duim	[Gruyter?]	(Sold) fl 21 for lots 138 & 139. David Maykel
1808/08/23	AMSCH	0139	*Regemorter. (P. van)* | Bij een opkomende Maan, ziet men voor een Boeren Woning eenige Visschers, welke bij een sterk brandend Vuur hunne Netten en Kleederen droogen, verder zeilende Schepen en Visschers Vaartuigen; uitvoerig als de voorgaande behandeld | *Mat:* op paneel *Size:* hoog 10 ½, breed 13 ½ duim	[Gruyter?]	(Sold) fl 21 for lots 138 & 139. David Maykel

Regemorter, Peter van (copy by)

1806/08/13	AMSCH	0162	*Regenmorter; na G. Metzu* | Door eene Steene Nis, met een Wyngaardrank en Vogelkooi, ziet men een bevallig Vrouwtje bézig zynde linnen te naaijen en verder bywerk; dun en delicaat en van de beste schildering van deeze Meester | copy by P. Regemorter after Metsu *Mat:* op paneel *Size:* hoog 12, breed 9 duim	Vinkeles [for] F	(Sold) fl 37 Schumacher

Reigenbach, J.

1801/03/16	AMSCH	0172	*Reychenbach* | Een Maanlicht | *Notes:* This lot was sold with lot 171 by Berckheyde.	P[ruyssenaar]	(Sold) fl 3:5 for lots 171 & 172. van Iperen

1806/05/05	AMSCH	0125	*J. Rygenbach* | In een Smedery; ziet men eenige Lieden bézig een Anker dat in 't vuur ligt, bewerken; fraai van effect door J. Rygenbach | *Mat:* op doek *Size:* hoog 18, breed 24 ½ duim	V[inkeles]	(Bought In) fl 8
1808/11/28	AMSCH	0054	*Rijchenbagh* | In eene Smederij, ziet men eenige Werklieden bezig een Anker uit het Vuur te ligten, ter zijde andere Lieden, welke zig tot het Smeeden gereed maken, schoon van effect | *Mat:* op doek *Size:* hoog 16, breed 23 duim	[Gruyter?]	(Sold) fl 7:15 Van Iperen
			Rembrandt Harmensz. van Rijn		
1801/04/13	AMSCH	0061	*Rembrand van Rhyn* | Dit uitmuntend Schildery verbeeld de Dochter van Herodes, benevens den Scherprechter welke het hoofd van Joannes op een schotel heeft liggende, verzeld van een menigte van haar gevolg, de caracters zyn spreekend, het licht frappant, en het coloriet allerbevalligst, zo ook de ordonantie en Meesterlyk schildering | *Mat:* op doek *Size:* hoog 55, breed 47 duim *Loc:* Amsterdam, Nederland. Rijksmuseum. (A 91) as C. Fabritius	Pierre Fouquet, junior	(Sold) fl 775 C S Roos voor het Muséum in den Haag
1801/04/13	AMSCH	0062	*Rembrand van Rhyn* | Een bedaagd Man met een Mantel om, en een fluweele Muts op het Hoofd, dit stuk is aller fraaist behandeld en krachtig gepenceeld | *Mat:* op doek *Size:* hoog 36, breed 29 duim	Pierre Fouquet, junior	(Sold) fl 395 Coclers
1801/06/10	AMSCH	0140	*Rembrand van Rhyn* | Een geslachte Os, waar achter een Vrouw bezig is de vloer te feilen, op de voorgrond ligt den Huid; het licht en bruin, zo ook het coloriet en stoute behandeling maken dit voorwerp aangenaam voor het oog | *Mat:* op paneel *Size:* hoog 29, breed 20 duim	Herman ten Kate	(Sold) fl 50 C S Roos
1801/10/06	AMSCH	0055	*Rembrant* | Het Afbeeldzel, van dien Beroemde Kunst-Schilder, Levensgroote halver Lyf, in deftige ryke Kleeding, het Hoofd gedekt met een Mezetyne Muts, hy houd de Linkerhand in de Borst, en als met een ernstig gelaat iets beschouwende: dit Kunststuk, is helder en bevallig van Coloriet, en van een zeer uitvoerige Penceelsbehandeling, zynde een der schoonste van deeze Meester | *Mat:* op paneel *Size:* hoog 27 ½, breed 21 ½ duim *Loc:* London, England, UK. Royal Collection (Buckingham Palace) (1156) as imitation of Rembrandt	S	(Sold) fl 1650 A E Sterk
1802/05/01	HGCLF	0050	*Rembrand* | Een oude Mans Kop op de naam van Rembrand	Mr B de Moor van Immerzeel	(Unknown)
1802/06/16	AMSCH	0143	*Rembrand van Ryn* | Dit stuk staat bekend onder de naam van de Man met de staande Pluim op de Muts (bekend door de Prent) en is gekleed met een Mantel met Goude en Zilverachtige franje, een Kéten en Medailje om den hals; alles als de natuur zelve, meesterlyk en uitvoerig van behandeling | *Mat:* op paneel *Size:* hoog 37, breed 29 duim	[Merrem]	(Sold) fl 190 H de Valk
1802/06/16	AMSCH	0144	*Rembrand van Ryn* | Een zittend Man in deftige zwarte Kleeding, leunende met de linkerhand op de Stoel, in welke hy een papier vast houd; terwyl de Regterhand in de borst gehouden wordt; alles krachtig van Coloriet en meesterlyk gepenceeld | *Mat:* op doek *Size:* hoog 44, breed 35 duim	[Merrem]	(Sold) fl 94 LaFontaine
1802/06/16	AMSCH	0145	*Rembrand van Ryn* | Een bedaagd Man in een Leuningstoel by een Tafel, waar op een Glas met Bier geplaats is, nevens een kopere Kandelaar; alles is fiks en meesterlyk gepenceeld | *Mat:* op paneel *Size:* hoog 15, breed 12 ½ duim	[Merrem]	(Sold) fl 23:10 Reijers
1803/04/20	AMSCH	0065	*Rembrand van Rhyn* | Twee stuks zynde het eene een Manspourtrait, met een gryzen Baard, en het andere een oude Vrouw, beide meesterlyk gepenceeld [Deux bustes, dont un est celui d'un viellard [sic] à barbe grise, l'autre est une vielle [sic] ridée. Ces deux morceaux sont d'un pinceau franc & empaté, elles ont le merite d'une excellente couleur jointe à un effet de lumiere large & vray.] | *Mat:* op paneel *Size:* ieder hoog 18, breed 14 duim [haut 18 ½, large 14 pouces] *Notes:* The dimensions differ in the Dutch and French editions of the catalogue.	Maria Magdalena van Sluypwyk, gravinne van Moens	(Sold) fl 70 Gruiter
1803/09/07	AMSCH	0139	*Rembrand* | Een Geestlyke Grysäard, gekleed in een pragtig geborduurd Kleed, staande voor een met een Fluweel Kleed bedekte Tafel, in een groot Boek te leezen; het ligt en bruin is frappant, en de schildering van een kloeke meesterlyke penceels-behandeling [Un vieillard ecclésiastique, portant un superbe habit brodé, debout devant une table couverte d'une draperie de velours et occupé à lire dans un gros livre ; le clair-brun qui regne dans ce tableau est frappant, et la touche et l'exécution le rendent un chef-d'oeuvre] | *Mat:* op paneel *Size:* hoog 20, breed 16 duim	Smidt	(Sold) fl 130 Scheffer
1803/09/07	AMSCH	0140	*Rembrand* | Een Grysaard, met een Tulband, Gouden Keten, met een Medaille om den Hals, beezig zynde in een Boek te leezen; dit Stukje is zeer fray van behandeling [Un vieillard, ayant un turban et une chaine d'or au col au bout de laquelle pend une médaille ; il paroît occupé à lire dans un livre ; beau morceau] | *Mat:* op paneel *Size:* hoog 10, breed 7 duim	Smidt	(Bought In) fl 70
1803/09/07	AMSCH	0141	*Rembrand* | Een Manspourtrait halverlyf; zynde van een meesterlyke penceels behandeling en van een schoone werking [Un portrait d'homme à mi-corps ; la composition, le fini des traits et le coloris de ce tableau sont d'un bel effet et digne de ce maître] | *Mat:* op paneel *Size:* hoog 20, breed 15 duim	Smidt	(Bought In) fl 5
1804/02/27	AMSCH	0125	*Rembrandt* | Een Mans Pourtrait, ter Halverlyf, gekleed in 't zwart en een kante Kraag, houdende de Linkerhand welke met een Handschoen bedekt	B	(Sold) fl 6 Gruiter

			is, op de Borst; dit stuk is meesterlyk en krachtig gepenceeld, en getekend Rembrandt | *Inscr:* Rembrandt (signed)		
1804/07/25	AMSCH	0065	*Rhyn (Rembrant van)* | In een aloud Gebouw, zit een bedaard Heer, in deftige Kleeding, ter zyde een Tafel met een Kleed bedekt, waaraan een Boekhouder geplaast is, de Rentmeester schynt met zynen Arbyders afreekening te houden, eenige weggaande hebben hun loon ontfangen, andere zyn nog bezig te Arbeiden; verders gestoffeert met Geldkist, Boeken en Papieren en ander Bywerk; het invallende Licht ter zyde door twee Glaasen Vengsters doed een schoone werking; het is kragtig, en teffens bevallig van coloriet, en meesterlyk gepenceeld, zo eigen aan deeze beroemde Kunstschilder | *Mat:* op paneel *Size:* hoog 20, breed 27 duim		(Sold) fl 350 C S Roos
1804/07/25	AMSCH	0066	*Rhyn (Rembrant van)* | Een Mans Pourtait [sic] in een Turks gewaad, zyn Handen over een Stoel leggende, zyn Hoofdt gedekt men een kostbare Tulband, met edele gesteentens omzet; zynde van een aller krachtigst coloriet en een uitmundtende behandeling | *Mat:* op doek *Size:* hoog 35, breed 29 duim		(Sold) fl 200 Pruissenaar
1804/10/16	DLOND	0185	*Rembrand van Rhyn* | Een Oud Mans Hoofd. Tête de Vieillard | *Mat:* op paneel *Size:* hoog 17, breed 13		(Sold) fl 1:6 Thijs
1804/10/16	DLOND	0186	*Rembrand van Rhyn* | Uts[a] [Een Oud Mans Hoofd. Tête de Vieillard] | *Mat:* op paneel *Size:* hoog 7, breed 6		(Unknown)
1804/10/16	DLOND	0187	*Rembrand van Rhyn* | De Aanbidding der Wyzen. L'Adoration des Mages | *Size:* hoog 35, breed 27		(Sold) fl 77 Huijbregts
1806/08/13	AMSCH	0152	*Rembrant. (van Rhyn)* | Een bevallig Mans pourtrait halverlyf, leunende met de eene arm op een armstoel, waarop dezelve gezeeten is, houdende een handschoen in de hand, gekleed met een zwarte rok, witte kraag en zwarte hoed; allerfrapantst [sic] van licht en meesterlyk gepenceeld | *Mat:* op doek *Size:* hoog 29, breed 24 duim	Coclers	(Sold) fl 176 Du Pré
1806/08/20	HGBSM	0095	*Rembrant* | Een uitmuntend mans Portrait in het zwart gekleed, houdende in de regterhand een Horlogie; dit stuk is krachtig, uitvoerig geschilderd en fraai van Coloriet, door den beroemden Rembrant, op paneel, ovaal formaat | *Mat:* op paneel *Fmt:* ovaal *Size:* hoog 36 ½, breed 29 duim	Macalester Loup [or others]	(Sold) fl 495 for lots 95 & 96. Lafontaine
1806/08/20	HGBSM	0096	*Rembrant* | Een dito [uitmuntend] vrouwe Portrait in het zwart gekleed, met een Waaier in de hand, niet minder als het voorgaande en zeer helder van Coloriet | *Size:* hoog 36 ½, breed 29 duim	Macalester Loup [or others]	(Sold) fl 495 for lots 95 & 96. Lafontaine
1806/08/20	HGBSM	0201	*Rembrand* | Een Oudemanshoofd | *Mat:* op paneel *Size:* hoog 7, breed 5 ½ duim	Macalester Loup [or others]	(Sold) fl 20 Lafontaine
1806/08/20	HGBSM	0202	*Rembrand* | Een dito Oudevrouwehoofd | *Mat:* op paneel *Size:* hoog 6 ½, breed 5 ½ duim *Notes:* It is unclear what "dito" refers to in the title.	Macalester Loup [or others]	(Sold) fl 21 Spruyt
1806/10/22	HGBAK	0012	*Rembrand* | Twee Pourtraiten		(Unknown)
1807/08/26	AMSCH	0182	*Rembrand van Rhyn* | Een Prachtig Boschgezicht, met een stille Waterplas, op een Heuvel zit eene Vrouw met een Kind op haar schoot, ter zyde eenige Kruidgewassen; dit Schildery is fraai van licht en bruin, en van een meesterlyke penceelsbehandeling | *Mat:* op doek op paneel *Size:* hoog 36, breed 54 duim	Roos	(Bought In) fl 50
1808/04/26	GDAN	0135	*Rembrand* | Een bergägtig Landschap met een Gebouw, op de voorgrond eenige Bokken en Schapen, en een Vrouwtje op een Ezel, zittende te praten met een Persoon naast haar staande, en men ziet op een hoogte Abraham en Lot, afspreekende waar zij elk voor hun zullen heen trekken, terwijl Abraham de keus aan Lot laat, op de tweede grond ziet men een aantal Vee die de Herders van Abraham en Lot deelen, verder een aangenaam verschiet, zonägtig en kragtig gepenseeld | *Size:* hoog 21, breed 24 duim	G H Fortuyn	(Unknown)
1808/04/26	GDAN	0136	*Rembrand* | Zijnde een uitmuntend geschilderde vrolyk uitziend Jong Heer, rijk gekleed met een Kraag, Harnas, en een Goude Ketting met een Medaille versierd, op hebbende een Hoed met Pluimen, zittende in eene Stoel, en leunende op een rood fluweele Kussen met Goude kwasten, kragtig behandeld | *Mat:* op doek *Size:* hoog 37 ½, breed 30 duim	G H Fortuyn	(Unknown)
1808/04/26	GDAN	0137	*Rembrand* | Een fraai geschilderd Pourtretje | *Size:* hoog 6 ½, breed 5 ½ duim	G H Fortuyn	(Unknown)
1808/09/13	HABRU	0112	*Rembrand* | Een Pourtraitje | *Notes:* This lot was sold with lot 113 by Anth. van Dyck.		(Unknown) fl 4 for lots 112 & 113
1808/10/28	AMVRS	0049	*Rembrand* | Een geslachte Os, waarachter eene Vrouw bezig de vloer te seilen, op den voorgrond ligt de Huid. Het is stout gepenceeld | *Mat:* op paneel *Size:* hoog 29, breed 20 duim	Marten Udink	(Sold) fl 62 Hulswit
1808/11/28	AMSCH	0051	*Rembrand* | Deeze capitaale Ordonantie, verbeeld de Uittogt van een Romeinsche Veldoversten, hij is gezeeten op een wit Paard, verzeld van verscheide Krijgslieden, ter zijde een Vesting waar een Leger uittrekt, meesterlijk en breed geschilderd | *Mat:* op doek *Size:* hoog 69, breed 73 duim	H	(Sold) fl 62 Coclers
1809/04/17	AMSCH	0138	*Rembrand* | Een Mans Beeld, in oude Hollandsche Kleeding, meesterlijk | *Mat:* op paneel	[Gruyter?]	(Sold) fl 5
1809/04/22	AMYVR	0108	*Rembrand* | Dit overheerlijk Schilderij steld voor de Historie van den Barmhartigen Samaritaan, welke, van zijn Paard gestegen zijnde, de	van den Bracke	(Sold) fl 100 C S Roos

			Gewondene schijnt te willen opbeuren; de Ordonantie is schoon, het coloriet van een brillante toon, en van de beste tijd, meesterlijk geschilderd | *Mat:* op doek *Size:* hoog 77, breed 64 duim		
1809/04/22	AMYVR	0109	*Rembrand* | Een deftig Heer, leunende met zijne hand over een Stoel; dit stuk is van een fraai coloriet, en van de beste penseelbehandeling | *Mat:* op doek *Size:* hoog 28, breed 23 duim	de Bruin	(Bought In) fl 179
1809/07/19	AMSCH	0048	*Rembrand* | Een Biddende Heeremiet, knielende, en houdende een Krucifix in zijne Handen, voor hem ligt een opengeslagen Boek en Doodshoofd. Fiks en meesterlijk behandeld | *Mat:* op paneel *Size:* hoog 23, breed 18 duim	C	(Sold) fl 80 Gruyter
1809/09/06	AMSCH	0062	*Rembrant van Rhijn* | Het Afbeeldsel van den Apostel Bartholoméus, halver lijf levens grooten, houdende in de regterhand een Mes, het teeken zijner Marteling; het is schoon geteekend, krachtig en gloeijend van coloriet en kunstig gepenceeld, door deze beroemde Meester | *Mat:* op paneel *Size:* hoog 24, breed 19 duim	Johannes Caudri	(Sold) fl 140 Coclers
1810/08/01	AMSCH	0082	*Rhijn (Rembrand van)* | Een Scheepsbouwmeester met zijne Vrouw, welke haren Man, zittende voor eene Tafel, met de eene hand eenen Brief toereikt, houdende met de andere de Klink van de Deur; voor den Scheepsbouwmeester liggen Boeken en Papieren; hij houdt eenen Passer in de hand [Les Portraits d'un Constructeur de Vaisseaux et de sa Femme : le Viellard est assis devant une Table recevant une Lettre que sa Femme lui remet d'une main, tandis qu'elle tient la porte de l'autre. Ce Tableau est gravé en maniere noire par Mr. Hodges, et à l'eau forte par Jean de Frey] | *Annots:* morceau précieux, mais assez mal traîté et rétouché et dont les glacis sont partis. (NGW); 1800, 11 Junii, Amsterdam. Coll. J Gildemeester, no.180, 8050 fl. (VAL I) *Mat:* op doek *Size:* hoog 43, breed 66 duimen *Loc:* London, England, UK. Royal Collection (Buckingham Palace) Inv.1158.	Mr Pieter de Smeth van Alphen	(Sold) fl 16,500 T Spaan voor LaFontaine
1810/10/11	AMSCH	0074	*Rembrand* | Eene Historiëele Ordonantie | *Mat:* op paneel *Size:* hoog 27, breed 35 duimen	C	(Sold) fl 0:6 L^{y} Pakker

Rembrandt Harmensz. van Rijn (or Anonymous)

1804/07/25	DLGRO	0022	*Rembrand; een ander beroemd Meester* | Een Oud Mans Hoofd of Borstbeeld, zeer fraai geschilderd, door Rembrand, of een ander beroemd Meester | *Mat:* op paneel *Size:* hoog 17, breed 14 duim	Mr Franc van der Burch Wz.	(Unknown)

Rembrandt Harmensz. van Rijn (or Rembrandt, manner)

1802/02/16	AMSCH	0056	*Rembrant* | Maria en Joseph, beneevens het Kindeken in de kribbe, door of in de manier van Rembrant	F	(Sold) fl 1:10 Hulswit
1804/10/16	DLOND	0293	*Van of in de manier van Rembrand van Ryn* | De dood van Seneca, met vele Beelden vol uitdrukking. (Dit Stuk, naar de bogtige lyst van een Schoorsteenstuk gesneden zynde, is groot genoeg om weder vierkant gemaakt te worden.) La mort de Seneque, avec beaucoup de Figures caractéristiques. (La Toile de cette Pièce, quoiqu'ayant été coupée pour que le Tableau serait ajusté dans le cadre d'une Cheminée, est néanmoins assez grande pour redevenir quarrée) | *Mat:* op doek *Fmt:* schoorsteenstuk *Size:* hoog 51, breed 72		(Sold) fl 150 O D Wyngaert
1806/08/13	AMSCH	0153	*Rembrant, of in zyn manier* | Het Dochtertje van Jaïrus door Christus van den doden verwekt, zynde een uitmuntende Ordinantie; het licht en bruin is in dit stukje zoo fraai als of het wezentlyk door Renbrand [sic] zelve geschilderd, is als een model voor een uitvoeriger stukje van dien Meester | *Mat:* op paneel *Size:* hoog 13, breed 17 duim	Roos	(Sold) fl 20 Swanenburg
1808/04/26	GDAN	0262	*Rembrand* | Een Mans Pourtretje, in de manier of van Rembrand, zeer fraai geschildert | *Size:* hoog 10, breed 8 duim	G H Fortuyn	(Unknown)
1808/06/13	AMSCH	0136	*Rembrand, of in zijn manier* | Een Mansportret, verbeeldende een Pen te versnijden. Zeer fiks en kragtig geschilderd | *Mat:* op doek *Size:* hoog 27, breed 23 duim	E M Engelberts	(Sold) fl 26 J Schuman
1809/07/25	HGBSM	0171	*Rembrand* | Een hoofd van een Krygsman, door of in de manier van Rembrand | *Mat:* op koper *Size:* hoog 6, breed 4 en een half duim	D van der Aa [or] E B ten Dall	(Sold) fl 1:8 A Teixeira

Rembrandt Harmensz. van Rijn (attributed)

1803/09/07	AMSCH	0242	*Rembrant* | Een capitaal Egyptisch bergagtig Landschap, met eenig Geboomten, waar in verbeeld, by een afkomende weg, de Vlugt naar Egypten; op een Heuvel, vertoond zig een Man en Vrouw en verder Ryzigers; ter zyde een Waterval, dit Schildery is bevallig van licht en meesterlyk fraay van Penceelbehandeling, op Paneel, zeer waarschynlyk door Rembrant [Un paysage égyptien, montagneux et parsemé de quelques arbres ; on voit sur le pente d'un chemin la fuite de la sainte famille en Egypte ; sur le sommet d'une colline paroissent un homme et une femme et dans le lointain des voyageurs ; à côté une cascade. Ce tableau est d'une belle composition, et il excelle surtout par la distribution et l'effet du jour qui y regne ; sur bois, apparemment de Rembrand.] | *Mat:* op paneel *Size:* hoog 36, breed 49 duim	Smidt	(Bought In) fl 50

Rembrandt Harmensz. van Rijn (copy after)

1801/03/16	AMSCH	0073	*Greenwood; Rembrand* | 'T Poutrait [sic] van een Jongeling na Rembrand | copy by Greenwood after Rembrandt	P[ruyssenaar]	(Withdrawn)

1802/06/16	AMSCH	0241	*Rembrand* | Een Vaandrager, zynde een fraaije Copy, naar het Origineel van Rembrand, te Cassel berustende; Meesterlyk gepenceeld | *Mat:* op paneel *Size:* hoog 22 ½, breed 17 duim	[Merrem]	(Sold) fl 16 LaFontaine
1802/09/06	AMSCH	0217	*Rembrant* | De Cynspenning aan Christus vertoond; uitvoerig op Koper geschilderd naar Rembrant | *Mat:* op koper *Size:* hoog 5, breed 6 duim	W ten Houten	(Sold) fl 1:10 Frantzen
1802/09/06	AMSCH	0218	*Rembrant* | Siméon houdende het Kindeken in de Armen, verzelt van verscheide aanschouwers; fix gepenceeld, naar dito [Rembrandt]	W ten Houten	(Sold) fl 1:10 Isaac Smit
1804/10/16	DLOND	0295	*Naar Rembrand van Ryn* | De Besnydenis van Jesus. La Circoncision de J. C. | *Mat:* op paneel *Size:* hoog 22, breed 18		(Unknown)
1806/05/05	AMSCH	0042	*van Dorne, Discipel van David; Rembrand* | Het afbeeldsel van den Kunstschilder Rembrand; meesterlyk na Rembrand door Denzelven [van Dorne, Discipel van David] | copy by F. Dorne after Rembrandt *Mat:* op doek *Size:* hoog 32, breed 24 duim	L	(Sold) fl 5 van Laar
			Rembrandt Harmensz. van Rijn (manner)		
1802/02/16	AMSCH	0018	*Rembrand* | Een Man aan een Tafel zittende te schryven; meesterlyk op doek als door Rembrand | *Mat:* op doek	B[uys]	(Sold) fl 255 Gruiter
1802/06/16	AMSCH	0253	*Rembrand* | Twee stuks, verbeeldende den eene een bedaagd Man, halver lyf, in aloude Kleeding, met eene Mezetyne Muts op 't hoofd; als iets aandachtig beschouwende: den andere zit in een Armstoel in Poolsche Kleeding met een Muts met Bond gevoerd, op 't hoofd; beide krachtig en meesterlyk geschilderd op Paneel, in de manier van Rembrand | *Mat:* op paneel *Size:* ieder hoog 9, breed 6 ½ duim	[Merrem]	(Sold) fl 2:10 Gruiter
1802/11/01	DOBRA	0164	*Rembrand* | Twee stuks Manshoofden in agtkantte lysten, fiks, in den trant van Rembrand		(Unknown) fl 1
1803/04/27	AMSCH	000P	*Rembrant* | Le Portrait d'un Guerrier, dans la maniere de Rembrant | *Size:* h. 46, l. 36 pouces	B	(Bought In) fl 10:10
1803/08/17	AMSCH	0096	*Rembrand* | Een Grysaard met een Baard, meesterlyk als Rembrand behandeld | *Mat:* op paneel *Size:* hoog 28, breed 18 duim	Anna Catharina Putman	(Sold) fl 3:10 Coclers
1803/09/07	AMSCH	0241	*Rembrandt* | Een Manspourtrait met een lange Baard, natuurlyk, door een goed Meester, in de manier van Rembrandt [Le portrait d'un homme à longue barbe, peint au naturel par un bon maître, dans la manière de Rembrand] | *Mat:* op paneel *Size:* hoog 12, breed 10 duim	Smidt	(Bought In) fl 1 ¼
1803/09/07	AMSCH	0247	*Rembrand* | Een Krygsman, met een Hoed met Pluimen op 't hoofd, en een Ringkraag om den Hals; zynde van een Meesterlyke schildering, als Rembrand [Un guerrier avec un chapeau à plumets et portant un haussecol ; d'une belle exécution, d'après Rembrand] | *Mat:* op paneel *Size:* hoog 20, breed 15 duim	Smidt	(Sold) fl 34 Reijers
1803/12/12	AMSCH	0117	*Rembrand* | Een oud Manspourtrait met een Baard, in de Manier van Rembrand	F	(Sold) fl 1:5 van Dijl
1803/12/12	AMSCH	0118	*Rembrand* | Een dito [Manspourtrait] met dito [een Baard], door denzelven [in de Manier van Rembrand]	F	(Bought In) fl 25
1804/10/16	DLOND	0294	*Als Rembrand van Ryn* | Een Manshoofd. Un tête d'Homme | *Mat:* op doek *Size:* hoog 14, breed 11		(Unknown)
1804/10/29	HRBAU	0125	*Rembrand* | Een Mans Pourtrait, zynde een Borststuk, levensgrootte: verbeeldende een' Heer, hebbende zyn Hoofd met een' Tulband gedekt en de schouders met een' Mantel omhangen. Dit Stuk is zeer natuurlyk, kragtig, en fiks, in de manier van den grooten Rembrand geschilderd | *Mat:* op doek *Size:* hoog 26, breed 21 duim	Simon Styl	(Unknown)
1805/07/10	AMSCH	0201	*Rembrand* | Een Mansportrait; in de manier van Rembrand	R[oos]	(Sold) fl 1 Gruyter
1805/07/10	AMSCH	0275	*Rembrant* | In een Binnevertrek, zit een oude Grysaart by een Tafel Goud te weegen; meesterlyk op Paneel, als Rembrant | *Mat:* op paneel	V[inkeles] [for] K	(Bought In) fl 10
1805/10/09	HGBSM	0027	*Rembrand* | Een fraay oude mans hoofd, met een gryze baard, extra uitvoerig en kragtig geschildert als door Rembrand | *Mat:* op paneel *Size:* hoog 28 breet 23 duim	T H van Willigen [or others]	(Sold) fl 40 Valette
1806/05/05	AMSCH	0171	*Rembrand* | Twee stuks oude Mannenhoofden in de manier van Rembrand	R[oos]	(Sold) fl 1:15 Gruyter
1807/06/10	HGBSM	0082	*Rembrand* | Een Jongeling met een Hoedt met Pluimen op zijn hoofd, in de trant van Rembrand	Abraham Delfos [or others]	(Sold) fl 2:12 Praine [?]
1807/06/10	HGBSM	0083	*Rembrand* | Een dito [Jongeling] met een Duif op zijn hand, door denselven [in de trant van Rembrand]	Abraham Delfos [or others]	(Sold) fl 0:12 v Giese
1807/08/26	AMSCH	0259	*Rembrant* | Een Mans Pourtrait in Oostersche kleding, met een Baart; zeer krachtig behandeld, in de manier van Rembrant | *Mat:* op paneel *Size:* hoog 28, breed 23 duim	de Vries	(Sold) fl 64 Spruit
1807/08/26	AMSCH	0262	*Rembrant* | Een Oud-Mans Hoofd, in Oostersche Kleeding; fiks geschilderd op Paneel, in de manier van Rembrant | *Mat:* op paneel	Helsdinge	(Sold) fl 0:6 L Pakker
1807/08/26	AMSCH	0289	*Rembrand* | Een Oud-Mans Hoofd met een Baard; meesterlyk als Rembrand | *Mat:* op paneel *Size:* hoog 26, breed 22 duim	Joseph Vallette	(Sold) fl 31 Coclair
1808/04/26	GDAN	0230	*Rembrand* | Een Boetvaardige voor 't Kruis van Jezus in de Lugt een Raaf met Brood, in de manier van Rembrand | *Size:* hoog 31, breed 29 duim	G H Fortuyn	(Unknown)
1808/07/19	AMROU	0013	*Rembrand* | 1 Mans Pourtrait, met een ronde Hoed op, in de manier van Rembrand		(Unknown)

1808/08/23	AMSCH	0237	*Rembrant* | Het afbeeldzel van een Jongman, met een Mezetijne Muts op het hoofd in deftige Kleeding; meesterlijk geschilderd in de manier van Rembrant | *Mat:* op doek	C	(Sold) fl 1:15 J Spaan
1809/04/22	AMYVR	0110	*Rembrand* | Een Jongeling met een Katje in de handen, bij een Aarden Pot; krachtig als door denzelven [Rembrand] geschilderd | *Mat:* op doek *Size:* hoog 28, breed 21 duim	de Bruin	(Bought In) fl 80
1809/06/13	AMSCH	0182	*Rembrand* | Een Jongeling in het Harnas, in de manier van Rembrand	Y	(Sold) fl 1:5 du Pree
1810/06/06	RMMUY	0004	*Rembrandt* | Een Philosoof, zittende voor eene Tafel, waar op eene Globe, Lessenaar, en Papieren, eenen Gottischen achtergrond en doorzigt, maken een schoon, krachtig en piquant effect. Als door Rembrandt | *Mat:* op paneel		(Sold) fl 67 v Leen
1810/06/06	RMMUY	0142	*Rembrant* | Een Vorst op zijn Ledikant, verzeld van een persoon zittende te schrijven aan eene Tafel, en een Moor met een Fakkel in de hand, Eenige Krijgswapenen, verrijke deze konstige en krachtig uitgevoerde ordonnantie. Door een oud meester, in de manier van Rembrant | *Mat:* op paneel		(Unknown) fl 3:10
1810/07/23	DOLG1	0073	*Rembrandt* | Twee stuks, een Sultan en Sultane, halver lijfs. Zeer uitvoerig en kunstig behandeld, in de manier, en als van Rembrandt | *This Lot:* Een Sultan, halver lijf *Mat:* op koper *Fmt:* ovaal *Size:* ieder hoog 6 duim, breed 4 duim *Notes:* Lots 73 and 74 were printed in the catalogue as one item.	Mr Pieter van den Santheuvel	(Sold) fl 3 for lots 73 & 74. Strij [or] H
1810/07/23	DOLG1	0074	*Rembrandt* | Twee stuks, een Sultan en Sultane, halver lijfs. Zeer uitvoerig en kunstig behandeld, in de manier, en als van Rembrandt | *This Lot:* Een Sultane, halver lijf *Mat:* op koper *Fmt:* ovaal *Size:* ieder hoog 6 duim, breed 4 duim *Notes:* Lots 73 and 74 were printed in the catalogue as one item.	Mr Pieter van den Santheuvel	(Sold) fl 3 for lots 73 & 74. Strij [or] H
1810/07/23	DOLG2	000Cc[H]	*Rymbrant* | Een and[ere?] Wyt als Rymbrant | *Notes:* This lot was added in by hand in the FLNY copy of the catalogue and purchased by the anonymous annotator.	Pieter Quinting	(Sold) fl 4
1810/07/23	DOLG2	00KK[H]	*Rembrand* | Een Mans pourtrait in de smaak van Rembrand | *Notes:* This lot was added in by hand in the RKDH copy of the catalogue.	Pieter Quinting	(Sold) fl 11 A van Strij
			Rembrandt Harmensz. van Rijn (school)		
1802/07/27	AKHRK	0011	*Uit de School van Rembrant* | De Offerhande van Abraham. – Men ziet het naakt en schoon welgetekend Lichaam van Izaäk liggen op den Altaar, de geloovigen Aartsvader houd met de linke hand het Hoofd van zijn Zoon vast, om met de opgeheeven rechte hand, waar in hij het Mes heeft, hem den vermeenden doodelijken slag toe te brengen, hier in belet wordende door den Engel, die uit een Wolklicht tot hem nadert, om hem den Ram aantewijzen, welke achter den Oudvader in de Doornen verward is. Over het geheel is in dit stuk een schoone Toon van Licht en Bruin. Men ontdekt wel een meer of min beschroomde verbaasdheid, doch tevens eerwaardigheid in de vaste gelaatstrekken van dien grooten Held, en het naakt is bijzonder teder en krachtig gepenseelt | *Mat:* op paneel *Size:* hoog 19 ½, breed 25 duim	Maria Stategaart	(Sold) fl 18:10 Brouwer
1802/07/27	AKHRK	0012	*Uit de School van Rembrand* | Men beschouwt in het midden van een Grot een Persoon van waardigheid, in een deftige gestalte, wachtende na de uitspraak van eenen Wijsgeer; hij is bezig in een Boek te leezen, voor zijne voeten ligt het Ingewand van een Hart, Long, Lever en de gevilde Kop en Pooten van een Schaap, nevens het Offermes, denklijk ter zijner beschouwing in de Wigchelaarij-kunst. Hij zit ter zijde een steene Tafel, waarop een Doodshoofd en Boeken, het licht komt zijdlings door een Vengster: diep aan den ingang van dit hol ziet men twee Krijgsknechten. Alles is krachtig en excellent geschilderd | *Mat:* op paneel *Size:* hoog 21 ½, breed 27 ½ duim	Maria Stategaart	(Sold) fl 20:10 Gruyter
1802/09/21	UTHDG	0076	*Rembrand* | De Afneeming van het Kruis, eene schoone Ordonnantie, krachtig en Meesterlijk geschildert uit de school van Rembrand | *Mat:* op paneel *Size:* hoog 36, breed 29 ½ duimen		(Bought In) fl 7
1803/09/07	AMSCH	0255	*Rembrand* | Een Oud-Mans Pourtrait; uit het school van Rembrand [Le portrait d'un vieillard ; de l'école de Rembrand] | *Mat:* op paneel *Size:* hoog 22, breed 16 duim	Smidt	(Sold) fl 1 C S Roos
1806/08/20	HGBSM	0008	*Rembrand* | Een Hoofd met eene fluweele muts, uit het school van Rembrand | *Mat:* op doek *Size:* hoog 18 ½, breed 16 duim	Macalester Loup [or others]	(Sold) fl 3:8 Zwartsman
1810/06/06	RMMUY	0097	*Rembrand* | Hiskias Krankbedde, meesterlijk geschilderd, uit de school van Rembrand | *Mat:* op doek		(Unknown) fl 6:5
			Renard		
1801/11/10	AMPOS	0039	*Renard* | 2 stuks Gezigten van de Hofsteede Sparenhout		(Unknown)
1801/12/22	AMOTT	0079	*V. Renard* | 2 dito [stuks] de Amstel en Persiaansche Kerken te Amsterdam	Bartholomeus Ruloffs	(Unknown) fl 3:5
1801/12/22	AMOTT	0127	*Renard* | 1 Maanschyn	Bartholomeus Ruloffs	(Unknown) fl 1:5
1802/08/24	LNDLS	0122	*Renard* | Twee stuks, het Dorp Hilversom en Laarden. Plaizant en uitvoerig op paneel | *Mat:* op paneel	Leonardus Bouman [or others]	(Unknown) fl 5:10

Renard (manner)

1801/11/10	AMPOS	0040	*Renard* | 2 dito [stuks] dito [Gezigten] als de voorgaande [Renard] | *Notes:* It is unclear what "dito" refers to in the title.		(Unknown)
1801/11/10	AMPOS	0041	*Renard* | 2 dito [stuks] dito [Gezigten] dito [als Renard] | *Notes:* It is unclear what "dito" refers to in the title.		(Unknown)

Renars [Unidentified]

1801/12/22	AMOTT	0112	*Renars* | 1 kabbelend Watertje, met veele zylende Scheepen	Bartholomeus Ruloffs	(Unknown) fl 0:16
1801/12/22	AMOTT	0113	*Renars* | 2 stuks Land- en Watergezigtjes	Bartholomeus Ruloffs	(Unknown) fl 1
1801/12/22	AMOTT	0114	*Renars* | 1 wel gestoffeerd Wintergezigt, vol Schaatsenryders, by de Haarlemmer Poort te Amsterdam	Bartholomeus Ruloffs	(Unknown) fl 2
1801/12/22	AMOTT	0115	*Renars* | 2 stuks, de Roomsche Kerk, by Maarssen en een Gezigt naby Utrecht	Bartholomeus Ruloffs	(Unknown) fl 1:5
1801/12/22	AMOTT	0116	*Renars* | 2 dito [stuks], Soelen van de Lingen en het zwarte Varken, by Maarssen	Bartholomeus Ruloffs	(Unknown) fl 1:10
1801/12/22	AMOTT	0117	*Renars* | 2 dito [stuks] aangenaame Gezigtjes aan de Vegt	Bartholomeus Ruloffs	(Unknown) fl 1

Reni, Guido

1801/04/13	AMSCH	0027	*Guido Rheni* | De heilige Sebastiaan aan een Boom gebonden, met pylen doorschoten; dit stuk is allerfraaist en meesterlyk geschilderd | *Mat:* op doek *Size:* hoog 34, breed 28 duim	Pierre Fouquet, junior	(Sold) fl 53 Carli
1801/04/13	AMSCH	0028	*Guido Rheni* | Twee stuks, Christus met de doorne Kroon, en Maria, beiden met de Ogen ten Hemel geslagen, niet minder behandeld als het voorgaande | *Mat:* op koper *Fmt:* ovaal *Size:* ieder hoog 4, breed 3 duim	Pierre Fouquet, junior	(Sold) fl 126 I^{c} Smit
1802/07/20	MGSAN	0062	*G. Reni* | Een Stuk, verbeeldende de Sterkte, op Doek: fiks gepenseeld | *Mat:* op doek *Size:* hoog duim 46, breed duim 43		(Unknown)
1803/04/27	AMSCH	0012	*le Quide* | Marie Medelaine [sic] penitente, ce Tableau est rempli d'expression & moëlleusement peint | *Size:* h. 4 ½, l. 3 ¾ pieds	A	(Sold) fl 22 Stevens
1808/08/23	AMSCH	0058	*Guido Rheni* | Twee stuks, Christus met de Doorne Kroon en Maria, beide met de oogen ten Hemel geslagen; allerfraaist en meesterlijk geschildert | *Mat:* op koper *Fmt:* ovaal *Size:* ieder hoog 4, breed 3 duim	H	(Bought In) fl 199
1810/07/26	AMSCH	0034	*Guido Reni* | Het Borstbeeld van Maria. Zijnde een meesterstuk van dezen Kunstenaar | *Mat:* op doek *Size:* hoog 24, breed 31 duimen	Cassino	(Sold) fl 20 Boelhouwer

Reni, Guido (copy after)

1803/04/27	AMSCH	0101	*le Guide* | Un enfant qui dort, d'après le Guide | *Size:* h. 2 ¾, l. 3 ¼ pieds	A	(Sold) fl 34:10 V^{n} Iperen
1803/12/12	AMSCH	0141	*Guido* | Een Kind, zittende op een Kussen, naar Guido | *Mat:* op paneel *Size:* hoog 10, br. 14 duim	D	(Sold) fl 1 Frantsen
1803/12/12	AMSCH	0142	*Guido* | Een dito [Kind] met een Lam, als denzelven [naar Guido], op dito [Paneel], ovaal | *Mat:* op paneel *Fmt:* ovaal *Notes:* It is unclear what "dito" refers to in the title.	D	(Sold) fl 7 Coclers
1810/10/11	AMSCH	0070	*Parenti; Guido* | Een stervende Cleopatra; schoon geschilderd op Doek, door denzelven [Parenti], naar het schilderij van Guido | copy by Parenti after Reni *Mat:* op doek *Size:* hoog 49, breed 37 duimen	M	(Bought In) fl 8:10

Rennel, S. [Unidentified]

1807/08/26	AMSCH	0192	*S. Rennel* | Een Italiaansch Landschap, met Gebouwen en Geboomten, met een Rivier doorsnéden, op den voorgrond ter zyde een Steenen Brug over een Water, gaande naar een sterke Vesting, gestoffeerd met Reizigers; zonachtig behandeld | *Mat:* op doek *Size:* hoog 31, breed 42 duim	Yver [for] S	(Sold) fl 9 T Spaan

Rennet [Unidentified]

1801/08/19	AMSCH	0107	*Rennet* | Twee stuks Land- en Watergezichten; op Doek | *Mat:* op doek *Size:* hoog 31, breed 42 duim	Van Forreest	(Sold) fl 12 Wolft

Rentinck, Arnout

1803/08/01	AMSCH	0031	*Rentinck. (A.)* | Op een Steene Tafel vertoonen zich verscheide smaakelyke vrugten, als Persikken, Pruymen, Cantaloup, Oranje Appel, blaauwe en witte Druiven, en andere Fruiten, met Steel en Bladeren, en eenige Bloemen, uitvoerig op Doek geschilderd | *Mat:* op doek *Size:* hoog 17, breed 13 ½ duim	de Wed [Thoen?]	(Bought In) fl 7:10
1803/08/01	AMSCH	0032	*Rentinck. (A.)* | Deeze Ordonantie uit de Fabelen van Ovidius, verbeeld Alpheus, Arethusa vervolgende, in een Landschap, wordende door de Godin Diana in een wolk verborgen, uitvoerig gepenceeld | *Mat:* op doek *Size:* hoog 19, breed 18 duim	de Wed [Thoen?]	(Bought In) fl 10 ½
1803/08/01	AMSCH	0033	*Rentinck (A.)* | Twee stuks zinspeelende Ordonantien van verscheide Kindertjes, verbeeldende de eene de vervolging der Kunsten en Weetenschappen, en de anderen daar dezelve weder worden opgebeurt, beide bevallig in 't graauw, als Basrelief geschilderd | *Mat:* op doek *Size:* ieder hoog 21, breed 17 ½ duim	de Wed [Thoen?]	(Sold) fl 5 Pruijssenaar

			Reyers		
1804/10/08	RMCNL	0030	*Reyers* | Een Bus relief	A t'Hooft	(Unknown)
			Reyers, R. [Unidentified]		
1802/08/24	LNDLS	0101	*R. Reyers* | Twee Schoorsteen- en Deurstukken, met Kinderen. In 't graauw geschilderd | *This Lot:* Een Schoorsteen- en Deurstuk, met Kinderen *Notes:* Lots 101 and 102 were printed in the catalogue as one item.	Leonardus Bouman [or others]	(Unknown) fl 2:4 for lots 101 & 102
1802/08/24	LNDLS	0102	*R. Reyers* | Twee Schoorsteen- en Deurstukken, met Kinderen. In 't graauw geschilderd | *This Lot:* Een Schoorsteen- en Deurstuk, met Kinderen *Notes:* Lots 101 and 102 were printed in the catalogue as one item.	Leonardus Bouman [or others]	(Unknown) fl 2:4 for lots 101 & 102
			Reygers		
1803/08/24	HGKAN	A0032	*V. Reygers* | Een Extra fraay Schildery met diverse Vogels, zeer uitvoerig geschildert | *Mat:* op doek		(Unknown)
			Ribera, Jusepe de (Lo Spagnoletto)		
1803/04/27	AMSCH	0032	*L'Espagnoletti* | Un Saint Jêrome, ce Tableau à beaucoup d'effêt & est vigoureusement peint | *Size:* h. 4 ¼, l. 3 ¼ pieds	A	(Sold) fl 16 Hodges
1803/07/18	AMSCH	0044	*Ribera, (G. de) alias Spanjolet* | St. Pieter door den Engel uit de Gevangenis verlost wordende, in een grootsche en meesterlyke trant geschilderd [St. Pierre tiré de la prison. L'Apôtre profondement endormi est penché en arriere ; il est appellé par l'ange son libérateur. Ces figures de grandeur naturelle sont traitées d'une maniere large & facile, elles indiquent la maniere du grand peintre.] | *Mat:* op doek *Size:* hoog 46, breed 36 duim	Maria Theresia Andrioli	(Sold) fl 30 Pruijssenaar
1804/07/25	DLGRO	0046	*Spanjolet* | Een Borstbeeld of Oud- Mans Hoofd, in Meditatie zittende | *Mat:* op doek *Size:* hoog 26, breed 21 duim	Mr Franc van der Burch Wz.	(Unknown)
1808/06/06	RMRIJ	0117	*Spagnoletto* | Mozes met de Wet. Krachtig en meesterlijk geschilderd – ten halven lijve uit [Moïse tenant la Loi, et vu à mi-corps. D'une Touche fière et Vigoureuse] | *Annots:* Verk Utrecht Sept. 1790 (f 65.-) (RMA I) *Mat:* op doek *Size:* Hoog 27 ¼, en breed 23 duim	Gerrit van der Pot, Heer van Groeneveld	(Sold) fl 20 Hendriks
1808/09/13	HABRU	0083	*Spanjolot* | Vegtende Krijgslieden over 't speelen		(Unknown) fl 6:15
1809/06/13	AMSCH	0141	*Spanjolet* | Een mediteerende St. Hieronimus, zittende in zijn kluis, voor hem op een steen leggen papieren, en terzijde eenige boeken en bijwerk; krachtig van coloriet en heerlijk van schildering | *Mat:* op doek *Size:* hoog 46, breed 35 duim	H[odges]	(Bought In) fl 24
			Ribera, Jusepe de (Lo Spagnoletto) (manner)		
1804/10/16	DLOND	0304	*In de Manier van Spanjolet* | Een Oud Man. Un Vieillard | *Mat:* op doek *Size:* hoog 24, breed 21		(Unknown)
			Ricci, Sebastiano		
1804/07/25	AMSCH	0069	*Richi (S.)* | In deeze capitaale Ordinantie ziet men in een Tempel, de Aanbidding der Koningen, welke het Kind Jesu Geschenken aanbieden, waarby een menigte andere Beelden; fraai van licht, krachtig van coloriet en meesterlyke penceel behandeling | *Mat:* op doek *Size:* hoog 38, breed 44 duim		(Sold) fl 8 for lots 69 & 70. van der Schleij
1804/07/25	AMSCH	0070	*Richi (S.)* | Deeze ryke ordinantie in een prachtige Tempel verbeeld, het Vrouwtje in Overspel bevonden, waarby eenige Wyzen, Krygslieden en andere Persoonen; zynde dezelve niet minder en van een dito [meesterlyke penceel] behandeling als de voorgaande | *Mat:* op doek *Size:* hoog 38, breed 44 duim		(Sold) fl 8 for lots 69 & 70. van der Schleij
			Ridinger, Johann Elias		
1802/06/16	AMSCH	0154	*J. E. Ridinger* | In een Boomryk Landschap, ziet men een Heer in deftige Jagt-Kleeding, rustende tegen de stam van een Boom, houdende met de eene hand een Snaphaan en in de andere doode Patrysen: verder een Jager met een doode Rêe op de schouders, op de voorgrond staat een Jagthond; meesterlyk fraay van penseel-behandeling | *Mat:* op doek *Size:* hoog 20, breed 15 duim	[Merrem]	(Sold) fl 3 J Yver
1803/08/01	AMSCH	0052	*Ridinger* | Een Jager, staande in een Landschap, verzeld van zyn Hond, op Doek geschilderd | *Mat:* op doek	Ij[ver]	(Sold) fl 0:10 Jansje Nieuwland
			Rietschoof		
1801/03/16	AMSCH	0041	*A. Rietschoof* | Een ruim Gezicht in 't Y van Amsterdam, ziende op 't Tolhuis, gestoffeerd met zylende Scheepen, Jachten en andere Vaartuigen; natuurlyk fraay behandeld	P[ruyssenaar]	(Sold) fl 30 Coclers
1801/03/16	AMSCH	0085	*Rietschoof* | Een Groenlandsche Vissery | *Notes:* This lot was sold with lot 86 by Klaes Molenaer.	P[ruyssenaar]	(Sold) fl 12:10 for lots 85 & 86. Gruiter
1810/12/03	DOBRA	0010	*Rietschoof* | Een woelend Water, waar in een zeilende Kaag, verder Oorlog- en andere Vaartuigen; uitvoerig geschilderd		(Unknown)

Rietschoof, Hendrik

1802/05/05	AMSCH	0182	*H. Rietschoof* | Een kabbelend Water langs de Stad Rotterdam te zien, gestoffeerd met een menigte Vaartuigen, als Beurtscheepen, Jagten, Oorlogscheepen en Roeischuiten, alles zonachtig helder, en meesterlyk van schildering | *Mat:* op doek *Size:* hoog 24, breed 28 duim	E	(Bought In) fl 108 for lots 182 & 183
1802/05/05	AMSCH	0183	*H. Rietschoof* | Een stil Water, mede zeer ryk gestoffeerd met Vaartuigen, ter zyden aan het hoofd legt een fraai Jagt, waarby een menigte Beelden, op de voorgrond een dryvend Beurtschip en Roeischuiten | *Size:* hoog 24, breed 28 duim	E	(Bought In) fl 108 for lots 182 & 183
1802/05/05	AMSCH	0184	*H. Rietschoof* | Een Woelend Water, met verscheiden zylende Vaartuigen, ter zyde een Kasteel, delicaat in de manier van L. Bakhuizen | *Mat:* op doek *Size:* hoog 20, breed 22 duim	E	(Bought In) fl 35
1802/05/05	AMSCH	0185	*H. Rietschoof* | Twee stuks onstuimige Zeeën, met eenige Oorlog en andere Schepen, meesterlyk | *Mat:* op doek *Size:* hoog 15, breed 18 duim	E	(Sold) fl 32 v d Vinne
1802/05/05	AMSCH	0186	*H. Rietschoof* | Een Land- en Watergezicht, gestoffeerd met Beelden en Vaartuigen, ter zyden een Molen, en een Dorp in 't verschiet, zonachtig gepenceeld | *Mat:* op doek *Size:* hoog 20, breed 22 duim	E	(Sold) fl 16:10 Le Dantú
1802/06/16	AMSCH	0157	*H. Rietschoof* | Een Strand, waar op eenige Bootslieden met Koopmans Goederen, wyders een stormende Zee met eene ontakeld Oorlogschip; in 't verschiet eenige Bergen, fraay en dun van Schildering | *Mat:* op doek *Size:* hoog 11 ½, breed 15 duim	[Merrem]	(Sold) fl 19 Teyssier
1805/07/03	AMSCH	0041	*Rietschoof. (H.)* | Een woedende Orcaan op Zee; alwaar een Oorlogschip in groot gevaar in de branding tegens de Rotzen schynt te vergaan; een Sloep met Volk is aan 't omslaan, terwyl men in het verschiet een Wrak van een ander Schip gewaar word; deeze voorstelling hoewel akëlig, is egter om deszelfs behandeling en de dunheid van het Water en de lucht, by de beste schilderyen, een plaats waardig | *Mat:* op doek *Size:* hoog 22 ½, breed 29 ½ duim	R[oos]	(Sold) fl 40 Tessier
1805/07/10	AMSCH	0124	*H. Rietschoof* | Een Land- en Riviergezicht, in de Rivier een ménigte zylende, roeijende en schietende Vaartuigen; verders eigenaartig gestoffeerd en delicaat gepenceeld | *Mat:* op doek *Size:* hoog 19, breed 22 duim	V[inkeles] [for] P	(Sold) fl 3 Agina
1806/08/20	HGBSM	0087	*H. Rietschoof* | Een woedende Orkaan op Zee; alwaar een Oorlog Schip in groot gevaar in de Branding tegens de Rotzen schijndt te vergaan; eene Sloep met volk is aan het omslaan, terwijl men in het verschiet een Wrak van een ander Schip gewaar wordt. Deze voorstelling hoewel akelig, is echter om deszelfs behandeling, en de dunheid van het water en van de lucht, bij de beste Schilderijen eene plaats waardig een der schoonste stukken van H. Rietschoof | *Mat:* op doek *Size:* hoog 22, breed 29 duim	[Teissier]	(Bought In) fl 179
1808/06/13	AMSCH	0137	*Rietschoof (H.)* | Twee stuks ontstuimige Zeeën, waarin verscheidene Schepen in groot gevaar zijn, om zich tegen de Rotzen te verbrijzelen. Zeer zacht gepenceeld | *Mat:* op doek *Size:* ieder hoog 25, breed 31 duim	R[oos]	(Sold) fl 24 Nieuwenhuisen
1808/06/13	AMSCH	0138	*Rietschoof (H.)* | Twee stuks Gezichten op Hoorn, het Water gestoffeerd met eene groote partij Schepen en kleinere Vaartuigen. Fraai uitgevoerd | *Size:* ieer hoog 19, breed 27 duim	R[oos]	(Bought In) fl 50
1808/06/13	AMSCH	0139	*Rietschoof (H.)* | Twee stuks Levantsche Zeehavens, vol gewoel. Meesterlijk fraai geschilderd | *Mat:* op doek *Size:* ieder hoog 32, breed 25 duim	R[oos]	(Sold) fl 10 O W J Berg
1809/04/22	AMYVR	0111	*H. Rietschoof* | Twee stuks Gezichten op Steden, uit de Rivier te zien, gestoffeerd met Schepen en Beelden | *Mat:* op paneel *Size:* hoog 11, breed 14 duim	Juff^{r} Julikker	(Sold) fl 7.15 van Iperen
1809/04/22	AMYVR	0112	*H. Rietschoof* | Een Gezicht op Amsterdam, uit het IJ te zien, gestoffeerd met Schepen; fraai | *Mat:* op paneel *Size:* hoog 21, breed 38 duim	Juff^{r} Julikker	(Sold) fl 3:10 C S Roos

Rietschoof, Jan Claes

1801/10/06	AMSCH	0061	*J. Rietschoof* | Twee Stuks, een Stil, en een Woelend Water, byde gestoffeert, met zylende en dryvende Scheepen, en andere Vaartuigen, helder en Meesterlyk behandeld | *Mat:* op paneel *Size:* yder hoog 11, breed 14 duim	M	(Sold) fl 40 Theijs

Rigulds [Unidentified]

1804/10/16	DLOND	0188	*Rigulds* | Een Bloemstuk. Des Fleurs | *Mat:* op doek *Size:* hoog 33, breed 23		(Unknown)

Rijck, Cornelia de

1801/06/10	AMSCH	0143	*Ryk. (C. de)* | Een Haan, Hen en drie Duiven, in een Landschap, meesterlyk behandeld | *Mat:* op doek *Size:* hoog 32, breed 26 duim	Herman ten Kate	(Sold) fl 8 Van Dijl

Rijnenburg, Nicolaas

1802/11/01	DOBRA	0189	*N. Rynenburgh* | Twee stuks, zynde het eene een Zeevischverkoopster, het ander een Riviervischverkooper | *Mat:* op paneel *Size:* hoog 13, breed 10 ½ duim		(Unknown) fl 7
1803/06/20	AMSCH	0080	*N. Ruytenbergh* | Dit voorwerp verbeeld een Grot, waarin een Gedenkteeken geplaast is, waarby voorby Ryzende Persoonen | *Size:* hoog 9 ½, breed 8 duim	Roos [for] L	(Sold) fl 3 Hodges

1804/07/25	DLGRO	0012	*Nic. Reynenburg* | Een Vrouwtje aan haar Spinnewiel, met een Kruik op haar Schoot | *Mat:* op paneel *Size:* hoog 8, breed 7 duim	Mr Franc van der Burch Wz.	(Unknown)
1804/07/25	DLGRO	0013	*Nic. Reynenberg* | Een Visch Boertje | *Size:* hoog 8, breed 7 duim	Mr Franc van der Burch Wz.	(Unknown)
1805/07/03	AMSCH	0200	*N. Rynenburg* | Twee stuks Binnehuizen, met bevallige moderne Voorwerpen, gestoffeert met verscheide zoorten van Eetbaaren waaren; plaisant geschilderd op Paneel | *Mat:* op paneel	R[oos]	(Sold) fl 31 Van Iperen
1806/06/07	RMHSN	0053	*Reinenberg* | Twee dito [Stuks] Beeldjes, halverlyf | *Mat:* op paneel	A E K L	(Unknown)
1810/06/06	RMMUY	0106	*N. Rynenburgh* | Een modern Binnenhuis, met drie Figuren, bevallig en uitvoerig geschilderd | *Mat:* op paneel		(Unknown) fl 10

Ring [Unidentified]

1810/10/10	MGCIT	0077	*Ring* | Een Stuk met allerlei Soort van Riviervisch, zynde benevens het Aardewerk en verdere Voorwerpen; zeer natuurlijk op doek gebragt | *Mat:* op doek	Caspar van Citters	(Unknown)

Ring, Pieter de

1802/09/06	AMSCH	0100	*Rinck* | Op een marmere Tafel, ziet men een Pot, met verscheide geschakeerde Bloemen, als Roozen, Tulpen, Hiacinten, Papaver, Renonkels en diverse andere Bloemen, terzyde de pot een vogelnesje; uitvoerig gepenceeld | *Mat:* op doek *Size:* hoog 30, breed 24 duim	J	(Sold) fl 31 de Meijer
1802/12/13	AMSCH	0140	*Rink* | Een Grysaart met een langen Baart en kaale Kruin, zittende aan een Tafel, waar op geplaast een Globe, Inktkoker en Boek, schynende zeer aandagtig een geschrift te Leezen, uitvoerig en meesterlyk gepenceeld | *Mat:* op doek *Size:* hoog 15 ½, breed 13 duim	Pruyssenaar [for] C	(Sold) fl 1:10 van der Schley [for] R[ijfsnijder]
1803/12/15	MGLAC	0031	*Ringh* | Een stukje met Vrugten; zeer fraai | *Mat:* op doek *Size:* hoog duim 12, breed duim 15	Mr L H de Haze Bomme	(Unknown)
1805/10/09	HGBSM	FF0031	*de Ring* | Een fruit stukje | *Mat:* op doek op paneel *Size:* hoog 6 breet 7 ½ duim	T H van Willigen [or others]	(Sold) fl 1 van der Linden
1806/08/13	AMSCH	0163	*Rinck* | Twee stuks, 't eene een capitaal Bloem- en 't andere een Fruitstuk, beide ryk geördineerd met fraai geschakeerde Bloemen en Vrugten, als roode en witte Roozen, Tulpen, Hiacinten, Auriculaas, Anjelieren, blaauwe en witte Druiven, Noten, enz.; deeze beide zyn delicaat en uitvoerig gepenceeld | *Mat:* op paneel *Size:* Ieder hoog 16, breed 14 duim	Vinkeles [for] J	(Bought In) fl 39
1808/05/17	LNAN	0021	*de Ring* | Een met bloemen en fruit		(Sold) fl 1:18 Thom[asse]

Rink, P.J.

1801/12/22	AMOTT	0044	*P.J. Rink* | 1 Tafel en als aarde voordoende Pot, met natuur nagebootste, en door droppels vogt besproeide, veelerhande Bloemen, een Nestje met Vogel Eyeren, Insectens en ander bywerk; in welgeschikte orden uitvoerig behandelt | *Notes:* The artist was presumably Pieter de Ring and not P.J. Rink.	Bartholomeus Ruloffs	(Unknown) fl 15:10
1801/12/22	AMOTT	0045	*P.J. Rink* | 1 Tafel met een Mandje vol Fruiten en Bloemen; in alles en door denzelve Konstmeester [P.J. Rink] niet minder behandelt als vooren, kleinder formaat | companion to lot 46 *Notes:* The artist was presumably Pieter de Ring and not P.J. Rink.	Bartholomeus Ruloffs	(Unknown) fl 40 for lots 45 & 46
1801/12/22	AMOTT	0046	*P.J. Rink* | 1 Pot met Bloemen, op een Tafel, als de voorgaande, om te dienen tot een weerga | companion to lot 45 *Notes:* The artist was presumably Pieter de Ring and not P.J. Rink.	Bartholomeus Ruloffs	(Unknown) fl 40 for lots 45 & 46

Rissel, J. van [Unidentified] (manner)

1807/08/26	AMSCH	0256	*J. van Rissel* | Een Hofgezigt met een wandelende Heer en Dame op den voorgrond, achterwaarts een Kasteel; zeer natuurlyk als van J. van Rissel | *Mat:* op doek *Size:* hoog 30, breed 50 duim	de Vries	(Sold) fl 13 du Pree

Robert, Hubert

1804/08/08	AMSCH	0167	*Robbert* | Een Gezicht op de Tempel der Sybillen, te Tivoli, met hoog Gebergte, Watervallen en ryke Stoffagie van Beeldjes; zeer dun en aangenaam van behandeling | *Mat:* op doek *Size:* hoog 16, breed 21 duim	Roos a	(Sold) fl 22:10 Reijers
1804/08/08	AMSCH	0168	*Robbert* | Een Italiaansch Bergachtig Landschap, met Watervallen, Geboomte en Stoffagie, in alles als de voorgaande | *Mat:* op paneel *Size:* hoog 11, breed 9 duim	Roos a	(Bought In) fl 3
1807/08/26	AMSCH	0194	*Robbert* | Een bevallig Landschapje met een Waterval en stoffage van eene Herderin met Schapen; geestig | *Mat:* op paneel *Size:* hoog 11, breed 9 duim	Roos	(Bought In) fl 7
1810/06/06	RMMUY	0166	*Robert van Parys* | Een Brandje | *Mat:* op paneel		(Unknown) fl 1:2
1810/07/26	AMSCH	0074	*Robert* | Een Landschap met Lieden te paard en te voet. Helder geschilderd | *Mat:* op paneel *Size:* hoog 14, breed 10 duimen	Cassino	(Sold) fl 6 Spaan

Rode

1809/07/25	HGBSM	0158	*Rode* | Een Kerkelyke Historie | *Mat:* op paneel *Size:* hoog 10 en een half, breed 9 en een half duim	D van der Aa [or] E B ten Dall	(Unknown)

			Roedig, Johannes Christianus		
1802/07/21	HGKAN	0032	*J. Roedig* | Een dito [Boeren Binnenhuys] op een Tafel, staat een Mandje, daar in eenige Vrugten, als Pruymen, groote Nooten en een Tros witte Druyven, en eenige Insecten, zittende op de Vrugten, zeer fraay behandeld, door J. Roedig, paneel vergulde Lyst | *Mat:* op paneel		(Unknown)
1804/05/07	AMSCH	0144	*Roedig. (J.C.)* | In deeze ryke Ordonantie ziet men op een marmere Tafel, een omgekeerde Mand, waarin eenige fraaye Vrugten en Fruiten, als Persiken, Druiven, Quanteloepen, Pruimen, Roozen en witten Roozen, en een menigte van anderen welriekende Bloemen, waarop eenige Insecten aazen, agter dezelve een Vaas en eenig Geboomte; dit stuk is allerzonachtigst en uitvoerig gepenceeld | *Mat:* op paneel *Size:* hoog 29, breed 24 duim	Roos [for] A	(Sold) fl 120 T van Iperen
1804/05/07	AMSCH	0145	*Roedig. (J.C.)* | Twee stuks capitaale Bloem- en Fruitstukken, de eene ziet men op een marmere Tafel, waarby een Vaas en een menigte van Vruchten, als blaauwe en witte Druiven, Persiken, Abricoozen, Quanteloupen, Nooten, en eenige welriekende Bloemen, en in de andere, ziet men in een Hofgezicht een omgevallige Pot, welke gevuld is met eenige welgeschakeerde Bloemen, als Roozen, Tulpen, Auriculaas enz. waarby een Vogelnestje, en agterwaards een jonge Kat; deeze twee zoo ryke Ordonantie zyn van een dito schildering en niet minder dan de voorgaande | *Mat:* op paneel *Size:* Ieder hoog 29, breed 22 duim *Notes:* It is unclear what "dito" refers to in the title.	Roos [for] A	(Sold) fl 475 Wreesman
1805/12/16	AMSCH	0049	*J. C. Roedig* | Twee stuks, zynde Marmere Tafels, op de eene staat een Vaas, met zeer fraaije Bloemen, ter zyde een Vogelnestje met Eijeren; op de andere staat een Schotel met Vrugten, als blauwe en witte Druiven, Persiken, Pruimen, Noten, enz. aller delicaatst en uitvoerig behandeld | *Mat:* op paneel *Size:* hoog 27, breed 21 duim	R[oos]	(Bought In) fl 180
1809/07/25	HGBSM	0060	*J.C. Roedig* | Een Capitaal Stuk met Bloemen en Vrugten, uitvoerig en delicaat geschildert door J.C. Roedig 1796, zynde een der beste van deze Meester | *Mat:* op mahoniehout paneel *Size:* hoog 28, breed 23 duim *Inscr:* J.C. Roedig 1796 (signed and dated?) *Notes:* It is unclear whether the name and date are inscribed on the painting.	D van der Aa	(Sold) fl 131 van Ijperen
1809/07/25	HGBSM	0061	*J.C. Roedig* | Een Vaas met Bloemen op een Steene Rand, waar op een Vogelnest met Eyeren, uitvoerig | companion to lot 62 *Mat:* op mahoniehout paneel *Size:* hoog 23, breed 19 duim	D van der Aa	(Sold) fl 71 for lots 61 & 62. van Ijperen
1809/07/25	HGBSM	0062	*J.C. Roedig* | Een Fruitstuk tot een weerga | companion to lot 61 *Mat:* op paneel *Size:* hoog 23, breed 19 duim	D van der Aa	(Sold) fl 71 for lots 61 & 62. van Ijperen
1810/10/13	HGDAW	0015	*Rhoedig* | Een Bloem en Fruitstuk, waarin men ziet een tros witte Druiven en een Stokroos, voor aan een opengesneden Meloen en Okkernoten, zeer uitvoerig en Meesterlyk behandeld door Rhoedig, van zyn beste tyd | *Mat:* op paneel *Size:* hoog 21, breed 17 ¾ duim		(Unknown)
			Roeliswaard, A. [Unidentified]		
1804/10/16	DLOND	0189	*A. Roeliswaard* | Narcissus | *Mat:* op doek *Size:* hoog 19, breed 17		(Unknown)
			Roepel, Coenraet		
1802/06/16	AMSCH	0156	*C. Roepel* | Een Vaas, gevuld met onderscheiden soorten van bevallig geschakeérde Bloemen op een steene Rand, nevens dezelve blauwe Pruimen, witte Bessen en Karsen; alles uitvoerig gepenceeld | *Mat:* op doek *Size:* hoog 20 ½, breed 17 duim	[Merrem]	(Sold) fl 12 Teyssier
1804/05/07	AMSCH	0143	*Roepel. (C.)* | Twee stuks capitaale Bloem- en Fruitstukken, in de eene ziet men op een Tafel eenige Fruiten, als blaauwe en witte Druiven, Persiken, Kersen, Abricoozen, Pruimen, Granaatappelen enz waarop eenige Insecten aazen, en in de andere ziet men roode en witte Roozen, Tulpen, Hiacinten, Auriculaas en eenige andere Bloemen; deeze beide ryke Ordonantie zyn van een delicaate en beste behandeling van deeze Meester | *Mat:* op doek *Size:* Ieder hoog 22, breed 18 duim	Roos [for] A	(Sold) fl 52 T van Iperen
1804/07/25	AMSCH	0068	*Roepel. (C.)* | Op een Marmere Tafel staat een Porcelyne Kom, gevuld met witte Druiven, Persiken en Pruimen, ter zyde leggen nog eenige Trossen Druiven, Persiken en andere Vrugten; alles delicaat en uitvoerig behandeld | *Mat:* op doek *Size:* hoog 18 ½, breed 23 duim		(Sold) fl 40 Vinkeles
1806/11/24	AMSCH	0066	*Roepel* | Op een Tafel staat een bewerkte Vaas, gevuld met een ménigte welriekende Bloemen; delicaat en uitvoerig gepenceeld | *Mat:* op paneel *Size:* hoog 19, breed 15 duim	Munnikhuizen	(Sold) fl 8:5 T Spaan
1809/07/25	HGBSM	0280	*C. Roepel* | Een Stuk met Druiven en andere Vrugten | *Mat:* op doek *Size:* hoog 20, breed 17 duim	D van der Aa [or] E B ten Dall	(Sold) fl 2:10 Heijmans
1810/10/10	MGCIT	0015	*C. Roepel* | Een extra fraai Bloemstuk, delicaat, natuurlijk en zeer uitvoerig behandeld [mogende beiden deze schoone Tafereelen gehouden worden voor twee der beste van C. Roepel] | *Notes:* The bracketed information in the title appears in lot 16 and refers to lots 15 and 16.	Caspar van Citters	(Unknown)
1810/10/10	MGCIT	0016	*C. Roepel* | Een dito [Bloemstuk], met Vruchten; mede voortreflijk uitgevoerd, mogende beiden deze schoone Tafereelen gehouden worden voor twee der beste van C. Roepel | *Notes:* The description in the title refers to lots 15 and 16.	Caspar van Citters	(Unknown)

1810/11/07	UTWLD	0063	*C. Roepel* | Een zeer uitmuntend fruitstuk, op een steene voetstuk ligt een persik, blauwe en witte druiven, pruimen, hazenooten enz. op den tweeden grond een doos, waarop een porcelijne kom met abricosen, moerbezien enz. agter dezelve een pijlaar, alles zeer uitvoerig geschilderd, kunstig gecomponeerd en helder bewerkt door C. Roepel, op doek, 1 voet 4 en een half duim hoog, 1 voet 7 duim breed, vergulde Lijst | *Mat:* op doek *Size:* 1 voet 4 en een half duim hoog, 1 voet 7 duim breed		(Unknown) fl 35
			Roestraeten, Pieter Gerritsz. van		
1806/11/24	AMSCH	0067	*Roestraaten (....)* | Een staand Jongeling, verbeeldende een Beeldhouder in Steen, in zyn werkplaats; natuurlyk en meesterlyk behandeld | *Mat:* op paneel *Size:* hoog 12, breed 11 duim	Munnikhuizen	(Sold) fl 2:5 v d Schley [for] Ryfsneyder
			Roghman, Roelant		
1801/02/18	AMBOS	0062	*Rogmans* | Een Landschap verbeeldende het Kasteel van Bentheim	J Schonevelt	(Unknown)
1801/06/10	AMSCH	0144	*Rochman. (R.)* | Een hoog Bergachtig Landschap, met een Waterval en stoffage van Beelden; krachtig behandeld | *Mat:* op paneel *Size:* hoog 34, breed 48 duim	Herman ten Kate	(Sold) fl 3:5 A Meyer
1801/08/19	AMSCH	0108	*R. Rogman* | Een hoog Bergachtig Landschap, meesterlyk gepenceeld	Pruyssen[r] [for] Q	(Sold) fl 2:10 Wolft
1802/09/06	AMSCH	0099	*R. Roghman* | Een Bosch- en bergagtig Landschap, gestoffeerd met een Man te Paard en een Herder met Schaapen; fix | *Size:* hoog 32, breed 46 duim	J	(Sold) fl 1 Gruiter
1804/05/07	AMSCH	0142	*Rochman. (R.)* | Een Bergachtig en Boomryk Landschap, op de voorgrond by een klaar Water, gestoffeerd met een Man te Paard, een rustend Reiziger en een Hond, hooger op het Gebergten een Herder met Schaapen, en een aangenaam verschiet; meesterlyk geschilderd | *Mat:* op doek *Size:* hoog 32, breed 31 duim	Vinkeles [for] G	(Sold) fl 0:10 L Pakker
1804/08/08	AMSCH	0166	*R. Roghman* | Een Gezicht op het Kasteel te Benthem; kragtig op Doek | *Mat:* op doek *Size:* hoog 40, breed 23 duim	Roos a	(Sold) fl 0:12 Gruyter
1806/08/13	AMSCH	0161	*Rochman. (R.)* | Een capitaal Boom- en Berg- en Duinachtig Landschap, gestoffeerd op de voorgrond met een Landman met een Ezel, verders een allerzonachtigst verschiet; delicaat en uitvoerig van schildering | *Mat:* op doek *Size:* hoog 46, breed 58 duim	Coclers	(Sold) fl 115 E M Engelberts
1808/06/13	AMSCH	0108b[H]	*Rogman* | 1 Landscap | *Notes:* This lot was added in by hand in the AA I, EBNP, FLNY, MB and RKDH copies of the catalogue. However, only in the MB copy is the artist given as "Rogman."	Z	(Sold) fl 43 Nieuwenhuys
1809/04/17	AMSCH	0141	*R. Rogman* | Een boschtig Landschap, met Boeren Woningen en andere stoffagie | *Mat:* op doek	[Gruyter?]	(Sold) fl 3:15
1810/06/20	AMSCH	0078	*R. Roghman* | Een Noordsch bergachtig Landschap, met Watervallen en Beeldjes. Meesterlijk geschilderd | *Mat:* op doek *Size:* hoog 35, breed 40 duimen	Q	(Sold) fl 1 Hodges
1810/06/20	AMSCH	0123	*Roghman* | Een fraai Landschap	N	(Sold) fl 1:15 Eversdijk
1810/10/11	AMSCH	0196	*R. Roghman* | Een Bergachtig Landschap, met een Waterval, gestoffeerd met Reisigers, Pelgrims, enz.; zonachtig | *Mat:* op doek	A	(Sold) fl 2:15 T Spaan
			Roghman, Roelant (and Asselyn)		
1810/10/10	MGCIT	0061	*Rogman; Asselyn* | Een Landschap, waarin het overblyfsel van een oud publiek Gebouw, door Rogman, en gestoffeerd door Asselyn: door beide Meesters wel behandeld	Caspar van Citters	(Unknown)
			Roghman, Roelant (and Lingelbach)		
1802/05/05	AMSCH	0181	*R. Rogman; J. Lingelbag* | Een hoog bergachtig Landschap, met Gebouwen en Geboomten, gestoffeerd met een optocht van geestelyke Persoonen te paard, en een Prelaat in een Draagstoel, alles meesterlyk | *Mat:* op doek *Size:* hoog 52, breed 82 duim	E	(Sold) fl 13:10 Cocler
1807/08/26	AMSCH	0183	*R. Roghman; J. Lingelbagh* | Een Italiaansch heuvelachtig Landschap, met eenig Geboomte, op den voorgrond ter zyde eene Vrouw, op een Ezel rydende, waarby een gaande Huisman en Hond, en een Pelgrim, by een stil Water, verders gestoffeerd met een rydende Wagen en eenig Vee by de Rivier; krachtig gepenceeld, door R. Roghman, en de stoffage door J. Lingelbagh | *Mat:* op doek *Size:* hoog 27, breed 34 duim	Yver [for] S	(Bought In) fl 18
			Roghman, Roelant (manner)		
1802/09/06	AMSCH	0229	*R. Roghman* | Een Bergachtig Landschap, op de voorgrond een man gaande over een bruggetje; natuurlyk als door R. Roghman	J	(Sold) fl 0:10 L Pakker
1806/05/05	AMSCH	0162	*Rogman* | Een boom en bergachtig Landschap, met stoffagie van Ezeldryvers; op Doek, in de manier van Rogman | *Mat:* op doek	R[oos]	(Sold) fl 2:5 Gruyter
1808/06/13	AMSCH	0199	*R. Rogman* | Een als voren [Italiaansch Landschap], als R. Rogman | *Notes:* This lot was sold with lot 200 by an anonymous artist.	E M Engelberts	(Sold) fl 25 for lots 199 & 200. O W J Berg

Rombold [Unidentified]

1810/11/07	UTWLD	0053	*Rombold* | Een boomrijk Landschap met eenige stoffagie door Rombold, op doek, 3 voet 3 duim hoog, 4 voet 9 duim breed, zwarte Lijst | *Mat:* op doek *Size:* 3 voet 3 duim hoog, 4 voet 9 duim breed		(Unknown) fl 16:10

Rombouts

1803/09/07	AMSCH	0154	*Rombouts* | Twee stuks Boomryke Landschappen, met verscheide Stoffagie van Beeldjes, kragtig op Doek [Deux paysages bocageux avec plusieurs figures et d'autres accessoires ; peints avec beaucoup de vigueur et au naturel] | *Mat:* op doek *Size:* hoog 15, breed 14 ½ duim	Smidt	(Sold) fl 1 Vinkeles
1804/10/20	GRBOL	0009	*Rombout* | Een Zeehaven en Straat	Joannis Cannegieteri	(Unknown)
1805/10/09	HGBSM	0114	*Rombout* | Een zeestrand met duinen, waar op een meenigte figuuren te voet en te paard, in differente bezigheeden | *Mat:* op paneel *Size:* hoog 14 breet 18 duim	T H van Willigen [or others]	(Sold) fl 3:15 De Gelder
1805/12/16	AMSCH	0050	*Rombouts* | Een Land- en Watergezicht, by een Kasteel; over een Rivier legt een Valbrug, waar over een Rysiger gaat, op de Voorgrond zwemmende Zwaanen, en verdere stoffagie, zeer natuurlyk op Doek behandeld, door .... Rombouts | *Mat:* op doek *Size:* hoog 36, breed 48 duim	Spaan	(Sold) fl 6:10 Levie Pakker
1807/08/26	AMSCH	0191	*Rombouts* | Een Landschap met een oude Boeren Woning, in welke een Vrouwtje in de Deur staat, en verdere stoffage, zeer natuurlyk | *Mat:* op paneel *Size:* hoog 12, breed 19 duim	de Vries	(Sold) fl 1:5 Joh[s] Hooft
1807/08/26	AMSCH	0195	*Rombouts* | Een bevallig Landschap, met Geboomte en Boeren Woningen, gestoffeerd met Huislieden en Reizigers; plaisant behandeld | *Mat:* op paneel	Yver [for] S	(Sold) fl 17 Hulswit
1808/06/13	AMSCH	0133	*Rombouts* | Een Boerenkermis, op den voorgrond een Kwakzalver, met eene menigte omstanders: zoo wel het Landschap als de karakters der Beeldjes zijn geestig en natuurlijk uitgedrukt | *Mat:* op paneel *Size:* hoog 27, breed 22 duim	E M Engelberts	(Sold) fl 60 van Os
1808/09/13	HABRU	0078	*Rombout* | Een Boomrijk Landschap		(Unknown) fl 5
1809/04/17	AMSCH	0084	*R. Rombouts* | Een boschagtig Landschap, op de voorgrond een Watertje, waarbij staande en rustende Beeldjes, en een helder verschiet; natuurlijk geschilderd | *Mat:* op paneel *Size:* hoog 23, breed 20 duim	A	(Sold) fl 26 Gruyter
1810/07/26	AMSCH	0138	*Rombout* | Een Landschap, met een Water doorsneden, op de voorgrond Lieden in een Schuit, ter zijde Reizigers. Goed geschilderd | *Mat:* op doek *Size:* hoog 31, breed 39 duimen	Cassino	(Bought In) fl 12

Rombouts (and Velde, A.)

1808/06/13	AMSCH	0132	*Rombouts; A. van de Velde* | Een aangenaam boomrijk Landschap aan eene Rivier, met een Pont, waarin zich reeds een Heer te Paard, twee Reizigers en eenig Vee bevinden, terwijl een Koets, voorgegaan door een Looper, bezig is in dezelve te rijden, op den voorgrond eenige Visschers. Allernatuurlijkst en zonachtig behandeld | *Mat:* op doek *Size:* hoog 36, breed 31 duim	E M Engelberts	(Sold) fl 150 Simons

Rombouts (changed from Bout, P.)

1810/07/23	DOLG2	0043	*P. Bout; Rombout* | Een Boomrijk Landschap, krachtig van coloriet, en wel geschilderd | *Mat:* op paneel *Size:* hoog 15, breed 19 duim *Notes:* The artist's name was changed by hand from "P. Bout" to "Rombout" in the FLNY copy of the catalogue.	Pieter Quinting	(Sold) fl 50:10 Blijk

Rombouts (manner)

1808/03/03	HAVIN	0010	*Rombout* | Een Gezicht van de Groote Houtstraat na de Anegang, natuurlijk in de Manier van Rombout	Jacobus Spillebout	(Unknown) fl 1:8

Rombouts, Johannes

1810/03/26	RMMUY	0021	*J. Rombouts* | Een Boere binne woning: vooraan eenige musiceerende personen, met aangenaam bijwerk en rijkvercierden achtergrond, in de manier van Teniers. Breed en meesterlijk geschilderd [L'intérieur d'une maison rustique, où plusieurs personnes assises s'amusent à chanter et à boire ; un chien, et autres accessoires pitoresques, forment un ensemble bien entendu, piquant et agréable.] | *Mat:* op doek *Size:* hoog 24, breed 32 ½ duimen	Daniel de Jongh Az	(Sold) fl 52 van Eyk s'Hage

Romeyn, Willem

1801/03/16	AMSCH	0021	*W. Romyn* | Een Landschap, gestoffeerd met verscheiden Koeijen en Schaapen, nevens rustende Herders, meesterlyk van penceelbehandeling	P[ruyssenaar]	(Sold) fl 48 Coclers
1801/03/16	AMSCH	0109	*W. Romyn* | Een Landchap met Schapen en Beesten, kragtig	K[ip]	(Sold) fl 8 Mensart
1801/05/11	AMSCH	0078	*W. Romyn* | Een Landschap met twee staande en een leggende Koeyen, verders verscheiden Schapen en een Bergachtig Verschiet, zonachtg behandeld | *Mat:* op doek *Size:* hoog 19, breed 18 duim	Pruisse [for] M	(Sold) fl 67 Allard
1801/10/06	AMSCH	0056	*W. Romyn* | In een Aangenaam Italiaansch Bergagtig Landschap, met verschillend Geboomten, ziet men eenige Huislieden by hun Vee, op de voorgrond, staat een Huisman, by twee ingespannen Stieren voor een	S	(Sold) fl 460 C S Roos

			Wagen, daar neevens legt 'er een rustende; verder een zittende Vrouw, en staand Man, een belaaden Ezel, en staande en leggende Schaapen, Gyten en Bokjes, aan den ingang van een open Berg, vertoont zig eenig Vee, en hooger een Gebouw; de Ordinantie is bevallig, het Licht en Coloriet Natuurlyk, en van een uitvoerige Penceelbehandeling | *Mat:* op doek *Size:* hoog 25, breed 29 duim		
1801/10/19	AMSCH	0061	*Romyn. (W)* | Een vrolyk Italiaans Landschap met Gebouwen, Boomen en Bergen, ryk gestoffeerd met Koeijen, Schapen en Bokken, uitmuntend van Penceel en Teekening | *Mat:* op paneel *Size:* hoog 13 ¼, breed 15 ¼ duim	Jonkheer Menno Baron van Coehoorn	(Sold) fl 278 van der Schley [for] B[=Putte]
1802/09/06	AMSCH	0097	*W. Romyn* | Een aangenaam bergagtig Landschap, gestoffeerd met een menigte staand en leggend Vee; fraay gepenceeld | *Mat:* op paneel *Size:* hoog 15, breed 13 duim	B	(Sold) fl 122 Pruijssenaar
1802/09/06	AMSCH	0098	*W. Romyn* | Een Bergagtig Landschap, met staand en leggend Vee; meesterlyk | *Mat:* op doek *Size:* hoog 27, breed 23 duim	J	(Sold) fl 1 Gruiter
1803/07/18	AMSCH	0041	*Romyn (Willem)* | Twee stuks. Op de voorgrond van het eerste stukje ziet men twee Koeyen, een Ezel, drie Schaapen en een Bokje, ter zyde by een Rots dryft een Herder eenige Schaapen, voorts een aangenaam bergachtig verschiet. De wedergade vertoond een grazige Heuvel, waarop een leggende Os, twee Kalveren, een staande Ezel en eenige Schaapen, op de tweede grond ziet men een Herder eenig Vee door het Water dryvende, voorts een bergachtig verschiet waarop eenige Gebouwen, de behandeling deezer beide stukjes zyn in den zilverachtigen toon van K. du Jardin geschilderd, de tekening der voorwerpen zyn zeer accuraat, en men kan deeze stukjes onder de eerste classe van deezen Meester tellen [Sur une terrasse au devant du tableau l'on voit deux vaches couchées, un bellier & trois moutons, avec une chêvre & un ane sur pieds, achevent ce groupe. Au bas d'un rocher clair, garni d'arbres & d'habitations est un pâtre conduisant d'autres animaux. Des montagnes bleuâtres vèrs l'orison se confondent avec un ciel léger. Une couleur claire, argentine, le dessin précis des animaux, & une delicatesse de touche digne de Dujardin, sont des qualitées non equivoques qui distinguent ce morceau. Le second offre sur un paturage verduré, un boeuf couché avec deux veaux, trois moutons, & un ane debout. Au second plan est un pâtre faisant passer l'eau à trois vaches, au bas d'un plateau elevé, garni de fabriques. La vaste perspective s'unit vaporeusement au ciel. L'on seroit embarrassé dans le choix de l'un ou de l'autre de ces jolis morceaux egalement frais & intéressans ; ils méritent une place dans un cabinet du meilleur choix.] | *Mat:* op doek *Size:* yder hoog 13, breed 15 duim	Maria Theresia Andrioli	(Sold) fl 285 Hulswit
1803/09/07	AMSCH	0146	*W. Romyn* | Een Heuvelachtig Landschap, op de voorgrond een leggende Herder met zyn Hond, verders een menigte staand en leggend Vee, bevallig van Coloriet [Un site de paysage parsemé de collines ; sur le devant un berger reposant par terre, et à côté de lui son chien ; plus loin un troupeau couché : d'un coloris agréable] | *Mat:* op doek *Size:* hoog 17 ½, breed 16 duim	Smidt	(Bought In) fl 61
1803/09/07	AMSCH	0147	*W. Romyn* | Twee stuks bevallige Landschapjes, gestoffeerd met eenige Herders en een meenigte Vee; fix [Deux jolis paysages dans lesquels des troupeaux de bétail gardés par des pâtres produisent un coup d'oeil agréable et varié] | *Mat:* op doek *Size:* hoog 8 ½, breed 12 duim	Smidt	(Sold) fl 6 Toselli
1805/07/03	AMSCH	0040	*Romyn (W.)* | Een Capitaal Boom- en Bergachtig Italiaansch Landschap, op de Voorgrond op een grazigen Heuvel, ziet men een staande en leggende Os, terzyde ziet men een Herder, welke nog twee Ossen en verscheiden Schapen door een Water dryft; de Kruiden op de Voorgrond, en de dunne behandeling in dit stuk zyn benevens het coloriet zeer fraai; en is voorts van een uitvoerige penceels behandeling | *Mat:* op doek *Size:* hoog 20, breed 24 duim	G	(Sold) fl 260 Coclers
1806/11/24	AMSCH	0064	*Romyn (W.)* | Een Italiaansch Landschap, op de Voorgrond ziet men verscheide staande en leggende Koeijen en Schapen, waarby een zittende Herder, zynde van een delicate penceelsbehandeling | *Mat:* op doek *Size:* hoog 16, breed 14 duim	Munnikhuizen	(Sold) fl 46 Van Iperen
1807/06/10	HGBSM	0097	*W. Romyn* | Een Landschapje met een Grot, waarin Geiten, Bokjes en Schaapen | *Mat:* op doek *Size:* hoog 15, breed 13 ½ duim	Abraham Delfos [or others]	(Sold) fl 25:10 Spruit
1807/08/26	AMSCH	0189	*W. Romyn* | Twee stuks bergachtige Landschappen, beiden gestoffeerd met rustende Huislieden, staande en rustende Koeijen, Bokken en Schaapen; plaisant geschilderd | *Mat:* op paneel *Size:* ieder hoog 8, breed 11 duim	Yver [for] S	(Sold) fl 1 Levij Pakker
1808/04/26	GDAN	0132	*Romyn (Wm)* | Zijnde een goed Landschap, met Koeijen en Schapen, wel geschilderd | *Size:* hoog 32, breed 39 duim	G H Fortuyn	(Unknown)
1808/04/26	GDAN	0133	*Romyn (Wm)* | Een Alleé, met zwaare Boomen, en goed gestoffeerd, met Jagers te Paard en Honden | *Size:* hoog 31, breed 38 duim	G H Fortuyn	(Unknown)
1808/04/26	GDAN	0134	*Romyn (Wm)* | Een zeer goed Landschap, met een Koe, en Schapen | *Size:* hoog 20, breed 15 duim	G H Fortuyn	(Unknown)
1808/06/06	RMRIJ	0107	*Romeijn. (Willem)* | Een Italiaansch bergachtig Landschap: waarin, op den voorgrond, een Herders Jongen en Hond. Hooger op vertoonen zich staande en liggende Ossen, benevens eene spinnende Herderin bij eenige liggende schapen, enz. Fiks behandeld [Paysage Montagneux. Sur le devant on voit un Pâtre assis, et un Chien à côté de lui. Un troupeau de Boeufs, quelques Moutons, et une Bergère qui file, occupent le second	Gerrit van der Pot, Heer van Groeneveld	(Sold) fl 280 Allard

			Plan. Un beau lointain, et un Ciel Nuageux terminent ce sujet peint dans le Style de Charles du Jardin] | *Annots:* Verk. Jan Tak, Leiden, 5 Sept. 1781 (f.55.-10) (RMA I) *Mat:* op doek *Size:* Hoog 16 ½, en breed 20 ¼ duim		
1808/06/11	RMRIJ	0044	*W: Romeyn* | Een Italiaansch bergachtig Landschap, met onderscheiden Hoornvee, Figuren en ander Bywerk | *Mat:* op paneel *Size:* hoog 28 ½, breed 24 ½ duim		(Sold) fl 14:10 v Zanten [?] [or] Coclairs
1808/09/13	HABRU	0074	*W. Romijn* | Een Landschap, op de voorgrond een bruine Koe, agter dezelve een Herder op een Ezel, nevens een Boerin		(Unknown) fl 17
1810/03/23	HAVIN	0051	*W. Romijn* | Een Landschap met Beesten op een Heuvel, fraai	Rudolf Hendrik de Wetstein [or others]	(Unknown)
1810/03/26	RMMUY	0046	*Willem Romeyn* | Op den voorgrond, twee liggende Ossen en een Bokje. Wat verder, een staande Os, Boomen, enz. Op de tweede grond, een Man op een Ezel. Een bevallig en dun verschiet en lucht. Uitvoerig en fraai geschilderd [Un paysage d'Italie, sur le devant sont couchés deux boeufs et une chêvre, derrière eux un boeuf debout : près d'un arbre, dans le lointain, un homme monté sur son ane. Ce petit tableau est piquant et plein de merites.] | *Mat:* op paneel *Size:* hoog 5, breed 6 ½ duimen	Daniel de Jongh Az	(Sold) fl 32 LeBrun te Parys
1810/05/22	AMSCH	0088	*Romijn. (W.)* | Op een Heuvel ziet men bij een Stal eenig staand en liggend Vee, met een aangenaam verschiet; alles is meesterlijk en uitvoerig van penceelsbehandeling | *Mat:* op paneel *Size:* hoog 13, breed 15 duim	Johannes van de Putte Nicolaasz.	(Sold) fl 180 Hulswit
1810/11/07	UTWLD	0035	*Romyn* | Eenige beestjes waarbij eene Boerin bij eenen Ezel staande voor een Schuur in een aardig boomrijk Landschap door Romyn, op paneel, 2 voet hoog, 1 voet 5 en een half duim breed, zwarte Lijst | companion to lot 36 *Mat:* op paneel *Size:* 2 voet hoog, 1 voet 5 en een half duim breed		(Unknown) fl 5
1810/11/07	UTWLD	0036	*Romyn* | Een pendant – een staande en een liggende Os met een zittend Vrouwtje in een boomrijk Landschap | companion to lot 35		(Unknown) fl 4:10
			Romeyn, Willem (or Romeyn, manner)		
1802/08/24	LNDLS	0105	*W. Romijn* | Een Landschap met Gebouwen, voor dezelve staande en rustende Koeijen, Bokken en Schapen. Van of in den trant van W. Romijn | *Mat:* op paneel *Size:* hoog 12, breed 15 duimen	Leonardus Bouman [or others]	(Unknown) fl 4:15
			Romeyn, Willem (copy after)		
1806/08/20	HGBSM	0041	*W. Romijn* | Een Italiaansch Landschap, met een rustende Herder en verschillend soort van Vee. Door een goed meester, naar W. Romijn | *Mat:* op paneel *Size:* hoog 14, breed 16 duim	Macalester Loup [or others]	(Sold) fl 40 Teissier
			Romeyn, Willem (manner)		
1802/05/22	RMHSN	0004	*Romein* | Een Landschap waar in een Ruine met Beesten, in de trant van Romein	Lambertus Bicker	(Unknown)
1804/10/16	DLOND	0296	*In de Manier van Willem Romyn* | Landschap met Koeien, Schapen, Herders; hebbende veel van N. Berghem. Paysage avec des Vaches, Moutons, Bergers; ayant beaucoup de N. Berghem | *Mat:* op doek *Size:* hoog 23, breed 28		(Sold) fl 20:5 Thijs
1807/08/26	AMSCH	0190	*W. Romyn* | Een bergachtig Landschap, met staande en liggende Beesten, benevens twee rustende Herders en een Hond; in de manier van denzelven [W. Romyn] | *Mat:* op doek *Size:* hoog 30, breed 39 duim	de Vries	(Sold) fl 1:5 Gruiter
1807/08/26	AMSCH	0265	*Romyn* | Een aangenaam Landzicht, met een Boeren Woning, gestoffeerd met een staande en twee rustende Ossen, Schapen en Bokken, geschilderd op Doek, in de manier van Romyn | *Mat:* op doek	Roos [for] A	(Sold) fl 5:5 Graffelman
1808/04/26	GDAN	0258	*Romijn* | In de manier van Romijn, een Landschap met een Brug over het Water, in het verschiet eenige Gebouwen, en een aantal Vee, wel geschilderd | companion to lot 259, by Anonymous *Size:* hoog 35, breed 41 duim	G H Fortuyn	(Unknown)
1808/06/13	AMSCH	0192	*W. Romijn* | Een Landschap met Beesten, als door W. Romijn	E M Engelberts	(Sold) fl 14:10 Glad
1809/07/25	HGBSM	0025	*Romyn* | Een dito [Landschap] in de trant van Romyn | *Mat:* op doek *Size:* hoog 10 en 1 half, breed 13 en 1 half duim	D van der Aa [or] E B ten Dall	(Sold) fl 7:5 van Eyck
			Romyn, A. [Unidentified]		
1802/11/01	DOBRA	0119	*A. Romyn* | Een Groenmarkt met Beeldjes enz. | *Mat:* op paneel *Size:* hoog 16, breed 20 duim	Paulus van der Spyk [or others]	(Unknown)
			Ron, M. [Unidentified]		
1804/10/29	HRBAU	0083	*Ron, (M.)* | Op den Voorgrond zyn twee Mannetjens bezig in eene Beek te visschen; waar agter Steenrotsen, die met Geboomte en Kasteelen bezet zyn, en een bergagtig verschiet | *Mat:* op paneel *Size:* hoog 9, breed 10 ½ duim	Simon Styl	(Unknown)
			Roo, J. de [Unidentified]		
1810/10/11	AMSCH	0076	*J. De Roo* | In een aangenaam Landschap ziet men op een grazige vlakte een roodbonte Koe, benevens eenig Rundvee en Schapen, ter zijde twee Lieden die een Hond laten opzitten; bevallig geschilderd | *Mat:* op doek *Size:* hoog 26, breed 31 duimen	[Gruyter?]	(Bought In) fl 6:5

Roore, Jacobus Ignatius de

1801/08/19	AMSCH	0109	*de Rore* | Een Boedvaardige Magdaléna	Pruyssen^{r} [for] Q	(Sold) fl 1:15 Gruiter
1802/06/28	AMSCH	0157	*J. de Roore* | Een Historiëele Ordonantie, in een vorstelyk Paleis, vol gewoel, meesterlyk fraai geschilderd | *Mat:* op paneel *Size:* hoog 12, breed 10 duim	Anna Elink	(Sold) fl 10 Texier
1803/08/01	AMSCH	0030	*Rore. (J. de)* | De Godin Venus, verzeld van Cupido en een ander Minne-wicht, zittende in een Landschap, bevallig en fraay van behandeling | *Mat:* op paneel *Size:* hoog 11, breed 8 ½ duim	J	(Sold) fl 8:10 van Dijl

Roos

1802/07/21	HGKAN	0107	*Roos* | Een Landschapje		(Unknown)
1802/12/13	AMSCH	0141	*Roos* | Een plaisant Dorp Gezigt, voor een Herberg zit een Heer, waar by den Hospes en Hospita, en Heer te Paard, en verdere Huislieden; natuurlyk geschilderd | *Mat:* op doek *Size:* hoog 18, breed 24 duim	Florijn [?]	(Sold) fl 0:10 L Pakker

Roos (manner)

1806/08/13	AMSCH	0296	*Roos* | Twee stuks grazige Weide, met een ménigte Beelden; als Roos	Vinkeles [for] F	(Sold) fl 5 L Pakker

Roos, Jan (I)

1803/09/07	AMSCH	0152	*G. da Rosa* | Twee stuks bevallige Landschappen, beide ryk gestoffeerd met een menigte staand en rustend Vee, een Herder en Herderin, fix gepenceeld, door G. da Rosa, byde op Doek [Deux paysages charmans, tous les deux riches en figures, bestiaux, bergers et bergères, bien traité] | *Mat:* op doek *Size:* ieder hoog 26, breed 35 duim	Smidt	(Sold) fl 15:10 Scheffer

Roos, Johann Heinrich

1802/05/05	AMSCH	0187	*H. Roos* | Een boom en bergachtig Landschap, op de voorgrond eenige Schaapen en Bokken, meesterlyk gepenceeld | *Mat:* op paneel *Size:* hoog 15, breed 19 duim	K	(Sold) fl 11:10 Ackina
1802/05/05	AMSCH	0188	*H. Roos* | Twee aangenaame Landschappen met Vee | *Size:* hoog 14, breed 17 duim	J	(Sold) fl 17 P M Levy
1803/09/07	AMSCH	0148	*J. H. Roos* | Een hoog Bergachtig Landschap met Geboomte en Stoffagie van Herders, met hun staand en leggend Vee, zoo Koeijen, Schaapen als Paarden; alles in den aard van Berchem [Un paysage terminé par des hautes montagnes ; celles-ci sont parsemées d'arbres, de bergers, de betail et de chevaux ; d'après van Berchem] | *Mat:* op doek *Size:* hoog 19, breed 25 duim	Smidt	(Bought In) fl 165
1803/09/07	AMSCH	0149	*J. H. Roos* | Een Heuvelachtig Landschap met Ruïnen, op de voorgrond een staand witte Os, een Bokje en eenige Schaapen, fix op Doek [Un paysage sabloneux avec des ruines ; sur le devant un boeuf blanc, un bouc et quelques brebis, belle composition] | *Mat:* op doek *Size:* hoog 18, breed 14 duim	Smidt	(Sold) fl 6:5 Gruiter

Roos, K. [Unidentified]

1808/06/13	AMSCH	0134	*Roos (K.)* | Een Dorpgezicht, met Kerk, Toren, en verscheidene Huizen, rijk gestoffeerd met Boeren en Boerinnen en een Smit, welke een Paard in de Travailje beslaat. Bevallig van ordonantie, en natuurlijk behandeld, in de manier van Victor | *Mat:* op doek *Size:* hoog 26, breed 32 duim	Y[ver]	(Sold or Bought In) fl 29:10 for lots 134 & 135. Jan Yver
1808/06/13	AMSCH	0135	*Roos (K.)* | Een andere dito [Dorpgezicht], verbeeldende een Jaarmarkt of Boerenkermis, mede rijk en bevallig van ordonantie. In de manier als de voorgaande | *Mat:* op doek *Size:* hoog 26, breed 32 duim	Y[ver]	(Sold or Bought In) fl 29:10 for lots 134 & 135. Jan Yver
1809/06/13	AMSCH	0133	*K. Roos* | Twee stuks bevallige Voorwerpen, verbeeldende Dorpgezigten, met vrolijke Huislieden, Boeren Jongens en Kinderen; geestig verbeeld in de manier van Victor, door K. Roos | *Mat:* op doek *Size:* ieder hoog 26, breed 33 duim	S[chley]	(Sold) fl 21 Buck

Roos, Philipp Peter (Rosa da Tivoli)

1802/06/16	AMSCH	0153	*Roos, di Tivoli* | Een Bergachtig Italiaansch Landschap, in het zelve vertoond zich een rustend Heer, waarby een staande Landvrouw, als met hem spreekende, verzelt van Schaapen en Bokjes, krachtig en meesterlyk fiks gepenceeld | *Mat:* op doek *Size:* hoog 15, breed 12 ½ duim	[Merrem]	(Sold) fl 6 de Lelie
1803/04/27	AMSCH	0162	*Rosa de Tivoli* | Deux Tableaux avec des animaux | *Size:* h. 14, l. 18 pouces	A	(Sold) fl 4 Stevens

Roos, Philipp Peter (Rosa da Tivoli) (or Rosa, S.)

1802/02/16	AMSCH	0061	*Italiaansche Roos* | Een Landschap, op de voorgrond gestoffeerd met verscheide rustende Schaapen en een staand Ezel, by een Veehoedershut	G	(Sold) fl 6 L Pakker
1802/09/06	AMSCH	0179	*de Romynsche Roos* | Twee stuks Italiaansche gestoffeerde Landschappen, met Gebouwen, en verder bywerk; fix gepenceeld	Spaan	(Sold) fl 4 Th^{S} Spaan
1803/09/07	AMSCH	0150	*De Italiaansche Roos [Roos (S.) l'Italien]* | Een Italiaans Bergachtig Landschap met Gebouwen, ryk gestoffeerd met een menigte Vee, Huislieden, enz; door de Italiaansche Roos [Un paysage d'Italie richement distribué et varié d'arbres, de villageois, d'habitations et de bestiaux] | *Mat:* op doek *Size:* hoog 33, breed 42 duim *Notes:* The artist's name differs in the Dutch and French editions of the catalogue.	Smidt	(Sold) fl 7:10 Lammen

1803/09/07	AMSCH	0151	*De Italiaansche Roos [Roos (S.) l'Italien]* | In een Landschap, ziet men op de voorgrond een Schaapendrift, nevens hun een Herder gezeeten op een Ezel, een andere dito en een jong Meisje; kragtig en natuurlyk gepenceeld, door denzelven [de Italiaansche Roos] [Sur le devant d'un joli paysage, on voit un troupeau de moutons ; à côté un berger monté sur un âne ; et un autre berger avec une jeune fille ; d'un coloris vigoureux et naturel] | *Mat:* op doek *Size:* hoog 29, breed 39 duim *Notes:* The artist's name differs in the Dutch and French editions of the catalogue.	Smidt	(Sold) fl 17 Spruit van Gend
1804/07/25	AMSCH	0067	*Roos. (De Romeinsche)* | In een Italiaansch Landschap, met Ruïne, Gebergten, Geboomten en een Rivier, waarover een Brug, ziet men op de Voorgrond een Herderin met een Kind, speelende met een Hond, ter zyden staat een Stier, waarby eenige rustende Schapen en een Bokje; dit stuk is aangenaam van zonlicht en bevallig van coloriet, en meesterlyk gepenceeld | *Mat:* op doek *Size:* hoog 43, breed 43 duim		(Sold) fl 105 C S Roos
1808/10/28	AMVRS	0050	*Roos. (De Romeinsche)* | Een Italiaansch Landschap mer Ruïne, Gebergte, Geboomte, Rivier, waarover een Brug, enz. Op den voorgrond eene Herderin met een Kind, spelende met een Hond, terzijde een Stier, Schapen en Bok. Het is bevallig van kleur en licht | *Mat:* op doek *Size:* hoog 43, breed 43 duim	Marten Udink	(Sold) fl 100 Reijers
1810/07/26	AMSCH	0072	*Roos (De Romeinsche)* | Een Bergachtig Landschap, met verscheide Schapen gestoffeerd | *Mat:* op doek *Size:* hoog 31, breed 25 duimen	Cassino	(Bought In) fl 11
			Roos, Philipp Peter (Rosa da Tivoli) (manner; or Rosa, S., manner)		
1802/02/16	AMSCH	0058	*de Romynsche Roos* | Twee stuks Landzigten, in een dezelve een Veehoeder Beesten voortdryvende: in den andere een vrouw die een Gyt melkt, gestoffeert met verder bywerk. kragtig gepenceeld, als door de Romynsche Roos	G	(Sold) fl 5 Boelen
			Rootius, Jan Albertsz.		
1801/08/19	AMSCH	0103	*J. Rotius* | Twee stuks zynde een fraay Bloem en Fruitstuk, uitvoerig en natuurlyk behandeld op Doek | *Mat:* op doek *Size:* hoog 25, breed 20 duim	Van Forreest	(Sold) fl 4:15 Roos
1809/04/17	AMSCH	0085	*F. Rotius* | Een fraaije Ordonnantie, van verscheide zoorten van keurige Bloemen en smakelijke vrugten, kunstig zaamen geschikt en uitvoerig gepenceeld | *Mat:* op doek *Size:* hoog 22, breed 28 duim *Notes:* The artist's name was given as "F. Rotius" but we have assumed this is an error.	Y	(Sold or Bought In) fl 25
1809/10/20	UTWLD	0024	*J. Rotius* | Een bloemfeston door J. Rotius	J J van Rhyn	(Unknown)
			Rosa, Francesco de (Pacecco de Rosa)		
1803/04/27	AMSCH	0036[a]	*Pachette de Rosa* | Trois Tableaux, Tête de Seraphins, par Pachette de Rosa & têtes de femmes | *This Lot:* Tête de Seraphins; lot 36[b] by Anonymous	A	(Sold) fl 0:6 for lots 36[a] & 36[b]. L Pakker
			Rosa, Salvator		
1802/06/16	AMSCH	0151	*S. Rosa* | Een aangenaam Italiaans Landschap met Geboomten, op de voorgrond eenige Brokken Steen, waar door een kleine Waterval vloeit, het onderscheide Geboomten is met de Natuur Overëenkomende behandeld; en zonachtig en breed gepenceeld | *Mat:* op doek *Size:* hoog 16, breed 22 duim	[Merrem]	(Sold) fl 35 H de Valk
1802/12/13	AMSCH	0139	*Salvater Rosa* | In een hoog Bergachtig Italiaansch Landschap, ziet men op de voorgrond by een Water, eenige Militairen, breed geschilderd | *Size:* hoog 34, breed 57 duim	Pruyssenaar [for] A	(Sold) fl 2 B Wolft
1803/04/27	AMSCH	0035[c]	*Salv. Rosa* | Trois morceaux differens, dont l'un est une ébauche par Serenasio, le Second une Copie de la Cingarella du Corrége, & le troisiéme Socrate avec ses Disciples | *This Lot:* Socrate avec ses Disciples; lot 35[a] by Serenacio & 35[b] is copy after Correggio	A	(Sold) fl 5 for lots 35[a-c]. Stevens
1803/04/27	AMSCH	0084	*Salvator Rosa* | Saint Jérome dans un Païsage | *Size:* h. 1 ¾, l. 1 pieds	A	(Sold) fl 41 Josi
1803/06/20	AMSCH	0072	*Salvater Rosa* | Twee stuks Italiaansche gestoffeerde Landschappen met hoog Geboomte, Gebergtens en Watervallen, kragtig en fix gepenceeld, door Salvater Rosa, op Doek | *Mat:* op doek *Size:* hoog 35, breed 42 duim	Schley [for] F	(Sold) fl 57 Pruijssenaar
1803/06/20	AMSCH	0073	*Salvator Rosa* | Twee dito [stuks] dito [Italiaansche gestoffeerde Landschappen], als de voorgaande	Schley [for] F	(Sold) fl 57 Pruijssenaar
1803/06/20	AMSCH	0074	*Salvator Rosa* | Twee dito [stuks] dito [Italiaansche gestoffeerde Landschappen], als de voorgaande	Schley [for] F	(Sold) fl 57 Pruijssenaar
1804/02/27	AMSCH	0093	*Rosa. (S.)* | Twee capitaale hooge Bergachtige Landschappen met Watervallen en differente stoffage, meesterlyk geschildert | *Mat:* op doek *Size:* hoog 53, breed 47 duim	C	(Bought In) fl 10
1806/05/05	AMSCH	0124	*S. Rosa* | Twee hooge bergagtige boomryke Landschappen, met Watervallen en andere stoffagie; meesterlyk geschildert door S. Rosa | *Mat:* op doek *Size:* hoog 53, breed 47 duim	V[inkeles]	(Sold) fl 1:10 Gruyter
1809/06/13	AMSCH	0227	*S. Rosa* | Twee kapitaale Landschappen, met hoog Gebergte en zwaar Geboomten, sterk na beneden stortende Watervallen; beide gestoffeerd met Reizigers en Landlieden en Vee; schoon van licht en breed geschilderd | *Mat:* op doek	[Gruyter?]	(Sold) fl 0:8 T Spaan

1810/06/06	RMMUY	0187	*Salvator Rosa* | Een Landschap | *Mat:* op paneel		(Unknown) fl 1
1810/07/26	AMSCH	0070	*Rosa (Salvator)* | Een Land- en Zeegezigt, op de voorgrond Officieren bij een groot Gebouw. Zeer fraai | *Mat:* op paneel *Size:* hoog 10, breed 14 duimen	Cassino	(Bought In) fl 5:10
1810/07/26	AMSCH	0071	*Rosa (Salvator)* | Een van de schoonste Landschappen, met stoffage, van dezen Meester | *Mat:* op doek *Size:* hoog 35, breed 27 duimen	Cassino	(Sold) fl 4:5 Boelhouwer
			Rosa, Salvator (or Roos, P.P.)		
1802/02/16	AMSCH	0061	*Italiaansche Roos* | Een Landschap, op de voorgrond gestoffeerd met verscheide rustende Schaapen en een staand Ezel, by een Veehoedershut	G	(Sold) fl 6 L Pakker
1802/09/06	AMSCH	0179	*de Romynsche Roos* | Twee stuks Italiaansche gestoffeerde Landschappen, met Gebouwen, en verder bywerk; fix gepenceeld	Spaan	(Sold) fl 4 Th^S Spaan
1803/09/07	AMSCH	0150	*De Italiaansche Roos [Roos (S.) l'Italien]* | Een Italiaans Bergachtig Landschap met Gebouwen, ryk gestoffeerd met een menigte Vee, Huislieden, enz; door de Italiaansche Roos [Un paysage d'Italie richement distribué et varié d'arbres, de villageois, d'habitations et de bestiaux] | *Mat:* op doek *Size:* hoog 33, breed 42 duim *Notes:* The artist's name differs in the Dutch and French editions of the catalogue.	Smidt	(Sold) fl 7:10 Lammen
1803/09/07	AMSCH	0151	*De Italiaansche Roos [Roos (S.) l'Italien]* | In een Landschap, ziet men op de voorgrond een Schaapendrift, nevens hun een Herder gezeeten op een Ezel, een andere dito en een jong Meisje; kragtig en natuurlyk gepenceeld, door denzelven [de Italiaansche Roos] [Sur le devant d'un joli paysage, on voit un troupeau de moutons ; à côté un berger monté sur un âne ; et un autre berger avec une jeune fille ; d'un coloris vigoureux et naturel] | *Mat:* op doek *Size:* hoog 29, breed 39 duim *Notes:* The artist's name differs in the Dutch and French editions of the catalogue.	Smidt	(Sold) fl 17 Spruit van Gend
1804/07/25	AMSCH	0067	*Roos. (De Romeinsche)* | In een Italiaansch Landschap, met Ruïne, Gebergten, Geboomten en een Rivier, waarover een Brug, ziet men op de Voorgrond een Herderin met een Kind, speelende met een Hond, ter zyden staat een Stier, waarby eenige rustende Schapen en een Bokje; dit stuk is aangenaam van zonlicht en bevallig van coloriet, en meesterlyk gepenceeld | *Mat:* op doek *Size:* hoog 43, breed 43 duim		(Sold) fl 105 C S Roos
1808/10/28	AMVRS	0050	*Roos. (De Romeinsche)* | Een Italiaansch Landschap mer Ruïne, Gebergte, Geboomte, Rivier, waarover een Brug, enz. Op den voorgrond eene Herderin met een Kind, spelende met een Hond, terzijde een Stier, Schapen en Bok. Het is bevallig van kleur en licht | *Mat:* op doek *Size:* hoog 43, breed 43 duim	Marten Udink	(Sold) fl 100 Reijers
1810/07/26	AMSCH	0072	*Roos (De Romeinsche)* | Een Bergachtig Landschap, met verscheide Schapen gestoffeerd | *Mat:* op doek *Size:* hoog 31, breed 25 duimen	Cassino	(Bought In) fl 11
			Rosa, Salvator (manner; or Roos, P.P., manner)		
1802/02/16	AMSCH	0058	*de Romynsche Roos* | Twee stuks Landzigten, in een dezelve een Veehoeder Beesten voortdryvende: in den andere een vrouw die een Gyt melkt, gestoffeert met verder bywerk. kragtig gepenceeld, als door de Romynsche Roos	G	(Sold) fl 5 Boelen
			Rosenberg, Friedrich		
1806/08/20	HGBSM	0029	*Roozenberg* | Een Zwitsersgezicht, gestoffeerd met figuren en vol met Bomen, die natuurlijk en meesterlijk zijn behandelt | *Mat:* op doek *Size:* hoog 27, breed 39 duim	Macalester Loup [or others]	(Sold) fl 21 Praiston
1806/08/20	HGBSM	0030	*Roozenberg* | Een dito [Zwitzersgezicht] bergachtig gezicht, aangenaam gestoffeerd en geschilderd | companion to lot 31 *Mat:* op mahoniehout paneel *Size:* hoog 14, breed 17 ½ duim	Macalester Loup [or others]	(Sold) fl 18 for lots 30 & 31. Zwartsman
1806/08/20	HGBSM	0031	*Roozenberg* | Een dito [Zwitzersgezicht] wederga niet minder | companion to lot 30 *Mat:* op mahoniehout paneel *Size:* hoog 14, breed 17 ½ duim	Macalester Loup [or others]	(Sold) fl 18 for lots 30 & 31. Zwartsman
1806/08/20	HGBSM	0055	*Rozenberg* | Een Zwitsersch Landschap, met eene rustique Brug, aangenaam gestoffeerd | companion to lot 56 *Mat:* op doek *Size:* hoog 21 ½, breed 27 duim	Macalester Loup [or others]	(Sold) fl 33:10 for lots 55 & 56. Heijmans
1806/08/20	HGBSM	0056	*Rozenberg* | Een dito [Zwitsersch Landschap] wederga, niet minder als de voorgaande, door denzelven [Rozenberg], op doek, eender groote | companion to lot 55 *Mat:* op doek *Size:* hoog 21 ½, breed 27 duim	Macalester Loup [or others]	(Sold) fl 33:10 for lots 55 & 56. Heijmans
			Roskam, H. [Unidentified]		
1806/10/17	MGSAN	0013	*H. Roskam* | Een woelende Zee met twee O. I. Schepen en een eenmast Hoeker | *Mat:* op doek	Gerardus Beljard	(Unknown)
1808/06/13	AMSCH	0183	*H. Roskam* | Een woelende Zee, met verschillende Vaartuigen; kloek	E M Engelberts	(Sold) fl 4:5 T Spaan
			Rossen, Dirk van [Unidentified]		
1802/08/24	LNDLS	0029	*Dirk van Rossen* | Een uitvoerig Landschap met different Geboomte en Tempels, op den Voorgrond de drie Engelen, die door Abram vergast worden, terwijl Sara aan de deur luistert; in het verschiet meer Stoffagie. Alles zeer uitvoerig | *Mat:* op doek *Size:* hoog 17, breed 22 duimen	Leonardus Bouman [or others]	(Unknown) fl 8:10
			Rottenhammer, Hans (I)		
1801/10/06	AMSCH	0057	*H. Rottenhamer* | Deeze fraaije Ordinantie vertoont, de Heilige Familje, rustende in een Landschap: Maria in een zeedige Gestalten, houd het	S	(Sold) fl 16 ter Smitten

<table>
<tr><td></td><td></td><td></td><td>Kindeken op de Schoot, welke door St. Jan een Korfje met Vrugten word aangebooden, daar agter staat St. Joseph, het met aandagt beschouwende, dit Stukje is schoon van Teekening; bevallig van Coloriet, en uitvoerig behandeld | Mat: op koper Size: hoog 7, breed 6 ½ duim</td><td></td><td></td></tr>
<tr><td>1801/10/06</td><td>AMSCH</td><td>0058</td><td>H. Rottenhamer | In een Binnenvertrek ziet men de Godin Vénus, zittende als op een Rustbedde, houdende in de Linkerhand een Pyl; voor dezelven staat Cupido, beezig zyn Voet te wassen in een Bekken: op de grond legt Pylkooker en Boog, door de open Nis, vertoont zig een Landzigt, waar in Enéas zyn Vader uit de Brand van Troijen redt, alles is fraai van Teekening, bevallig van Coloriet en zeer uitvoerig gepenceelt. NB. Agter op het Stukje staat met gegraveerde Letters: Ce Tableau at ete donné a son Excelence Monseign. Le Marquis de Westerloo, par Don Carlo-Albany, Neveu du Pape Clement XI a Rome 1713 | Mat: op koper Size: hoog 7, breed 5 duim Inscr: on the back: Ce Tableau at ete donné a son Excelence Monseign. Le Marquis de Westerloo, par Don Carlo-Albany, Neveu du Pape Clement XI a Rome 1713</td><td>S</td><td>(Sold) fl 63 Jan Spaan</td></tr>
<tr><td>1801/10/06</td><td>AMSCH</td><td>0059</td><td>H. Rottenhamer | Maria staande, houdende het Kindeken, met byder Armen, en het zelve de Borst geevende; alles is Meesterlyk, kragtig van Coloriet, en teffens uitvoerig van Penceelbehandeling | Mat: op paneel Size: hoog 7 ½, breed 5 ½ duim</td><td>S</td><td>(Sold) fl 27 ter Smitten</td></tr>
<tr><td>1801/10/06</td><td>AMSCH</td><td>0060</td><td>J. Rottenhamer | Dit Onderwerp verbeeld; het Oordeel van den Herder Paris, in een Landschap met Geboomten, zit den Herder, voor hem staan de drie Godinnen Vénus, Juno en Pallas, de Gulde Appel afwagtende, welke Prys, Vénus word aangebooden, die door een vliegend Minnenwigt gekroond word, verder ziet men Mercuur, alles bevallig van Coloriet, en uitvoerig gepenceelt | Mat: op koper Size: hoog 10, breed 7 ½ duim</td><td>S</td><td>(Sold) fl 58 Theijs</td></tr>
<tr><td>1802/07/20</td><td>MGSAN</td><td>0042</td><td>Rottenhamer | Susanna met de Boeren, op Koper | Mat: op koper Size: hoog duim 8, breed duim 10</td><td></td><td>(Unknown)</td></tr>
<tr><td>1802/12/13</td><td>AMSCH</td><td>0137</td><td>H. Rottenhamer | Deeze Ordonantie verbeeld, de Graflegging Christi, op de voorgrond legt Maria als in zwym, ondersteunt door verschyde Godvruchtige Manne en Vrouwen, verder zyn de Dicipelen bézig ter Begraving; om hoog een glorie van Engelen, de hartstogten zyn natuurlyk en uitvoerig van Penceelbehandeling | Mat: op koper Size: hoog 15, breed 12 duim</td><td>Yver</td><td>(Sold) fl 30 Jan Spaan</td></tr>
<tr><td>1803/09/07</td><td>AMSCH</td><td>0145</td><td>Hans Rottenhamer | Maria met het Kind Jesus op haar Schoot, waarby een menigte Engelen; zynde een bevallige Ordonnantie en delicaat geschilderd [La Ste. Vierge avec l'enfant Jesus sur son giron, auprès d'elle plusieurs anges ; d'une ordonnance agréable et d'une touche délicate.] | Size: hoog 14, breed 11 duim</td><td>Smidt</td><td>(Sold) fl 8:5 Gruiter</td></tr>
<tr><td>1808/08/23</td><td>AMSCH</td><td>0137</td><td>Rottenhamer. (H.) | In een Landschap, ziet men op de voorgrond eene bevallige Vrouw met twee Kinderen, welke door een Sater bespied word; fraai van tekening en delicaat gepenceeld | Mat: op paneel Size: hoog 8, breed 9 duim</td><td>C</td><td>(Sold) fl 8:5 Dupré</td></tr>
<tr><td>1808/08/23</td><td>AMSCH</td><td>0137a[II]</td><td>Rottenhamer. (H.) | H. familie | Notes: This lot was added in by hand in the EBNP and FLNY copies of the catalogue.</td><td>[Gruyter?]</td><td>(Sold) fl 13 Van Iperen</td></tr>
<tr><td>1808/11/28</td><td>AMSCH</td><td>0052</td><td>G. Rottenhamer | De Maagd Maria, houdende het Kindje in haar Armen, voor haar eenige Heilige Mannen en Vrouwen in eerbiedige houding, en verder bijwerk, kragtig en uitvoerig | Mat: op koper Size: hoog 13, breed 11 duim Notes: The artist's name was given as "G. Rottenhamer" but we have assumed this is an error.</td><td>H</td><td>(Bought In) fl 20</td></tr>
<tr><td>1810/07/26</td><td>AMSCH</td><td>0073</td><td>Rottenhamer | Eene Heilige Familje, omringd van verscheidene Engelen, rustende in een Landschap. Krachtig geschilderd | Mat: op doek Size: hoog 12, breed 16 duimen</td><td>Cassino</td><td>(Sold) fl 9 Spaan</td></tr>
</table>

Rottenhammer, Hans (I) (and Bril, P.)

<table>
<tr><td>1805/10/09</td><td>HGBSM</td><td>0094</td><td>H. Bottenhamer; P. Bril | Een landschap daar Christus een blinde aan de weg geneest, door H. Bottenhamer, en het landschap door P. Bril | Mat: op koper Size: hoog 13 breet 18 duim</td><td>T H van Willigen [or others]</td><td>(Sold) fl 7:15 Teissier</td></tr>
</table>

Rottenhammer, Hans (I) (and Brueghel, J. (I))

<table>
<tr><td>1801/08/19</td><td>AMSCH</td><td>0096</td><td>Rottenhamer; Breugel | Een zinryke Ordenantie, in een Boomryk Landschap, met een stille Rivier, op de voorgrond ziet men drie Nimphen, een Net met verschillende Visschen, uitschudden, verders op de voorgrond leggen viervoetige Dieren en verscheide Vogels, waar by eenige staande Jagthonden; meesterlyk en uitvoerig op Paneel geschilderd | Mat: op paneel Size: hoog 25, breed 32 duim</td><td>W Wynen</td><td>(Sold) fl 19 Gruiter</td></tr>
<tr><td>1803/07/18</td><td>AMSCH</td><td>0042</td><td>Rottenhamer. (J.); J. Breugel | Het Paradys alwaar God den Vader in zyn Glorie aan Adam en Eva zyn bevelen geeft, welke zy met veel aandagt aanhooren, ter linkerzyde ziet men hun van den verboden Boom plukken, in het verschiet worden zy door een Engel verjaagd: op de voorgrond twee Tygers en een groot aantal andere Gediertens, alles is zeer uitvoerig door deeze beide voortreffelyke Meesters gepenceeld [Ce tableau est le Paradis terrestre, ou le Pere éternel accompagné de sa gloire préscrit à Adam & à Eve sa volonté, qu'ils ecoutent en attitude de prosternation. Au devant & un peu vèrs la gauche est assi [sic] le Pere Adam prenant de la main de sa moitié une pomme de l'arbre fatal ! tandis qu'elle a le bras levé pour en ceuillir davantage. Dans l'eloignement sont representés d'autres épisodes de la génèse, mais par de petittes figures. Le paysage de</td><td>Maria Theresia Andrioli</td><td>(Sold) fl 125 Thys</td></tr>
</table>

			Breugel richement boisé & très varié, est surtout enrichi d'une multitude de quadrupédes & d'oiseaux d'une finesse d'execution admirable. Quant aux figures elles sont d'un excellent dessin, & d'une fonte de couleur si belle ! que l'Albane même ne les desavoueroit pas.] | *Mat:* op paneel *Size:* hoog 23, breed 37 duim		
1810/06/06	RMMUY	0059	*Rottenhamer; Breugel* | Eene heilige Familie, zeer uitvoerig | *Mat:* op koper		(Unknown) fl 16

Rottenhammer, Hans (I) (or Rottenhammer, H. (I), manner)

1801/06/13	LNDLS	0060	*Rottenhamer* | De ontmoeting van Maria en Elizabeth, verzelt van een menigte beelden en engelen, uitvoerig op kooper, van of in de trant van Rottenhamer | *Mat:* op koper *Size:* hoog 14, breed 11 duimen	D van R	(Sold) fl 17 Reyers

Roy, Jean-Baptiste de

1806/05/05	AMSCH	0123	*B. de Roy* | Twee stuks capitaale Ordinnantien, voorstellende beide grasige Weide met Rivieren, Geboomte, Gebouwen enz., ryk gestoffeerd met grasende en leggende Beesten, in den eene op de voorgrond een Jonge Bul, en in de andere een jonge Os; beide allerzonachtigst en piquant van licht, en fraai van schildering door B. de Roy | *Mat:* op doek *Size:* yder hoog 35, breed 33 duim	L	(Sold) fl 9 van Laar
1808/12/12	UTWLD	0018	*B. du Roy* | De groote Kaart van de Provintie Utrecht, door B. du Roy met de adelyke huizen rondom [Alle in swarte Lysten en wel geconserveerd.] | *Mat:* op doek *Notes:* The bracketed information in the title appears above lot 1 and refers to lots 1 to 19.	Mr D Hoola van Nooten	(Unknown)

Roy, N. de [Unidentified]

1802/06/16	AMSCH	0155	*N. de Roy* | Op een Heuvel by een Boomstam, ziet men twee staande en een leggende Os, drie Schapen en in het verschiet een Weyde met een menigte Vée, 't verschiet vertoond een Dorp; zynde alles fiks en zonachtig behandeld | *Mat:* op doek *Size:* hoog 24, breed 33 duim	[Merrem]	(Sold) fl 60 Van Iperen

Royen, Wilhelm Frederik van

1802/02/16	AMSCH	0071	*W. van Royen* | In een Landschap met Geboomten, vertoonen zig twee vegtende Haanen, verder een Hen en andere Vogels, kragtig en meesterlyk gepenceeld	C	(Sold) fl 112 Hulswit
1802/02/16	AMSCH	0072	*W. van Royen* | Een Hofgezigt, gestoffeerd op de voorgrond met dood Wilt en Gevogelten, waar by een Jagthond, verder een bevallig verschiet, als de voorige, natuurlyk en kragtig behandeld	C	(Bought In) fl 40
1802/04/13	HAVIN	0014	*van Rooijen* | Een Landschap, met een Pauw en Pauwin, en verscheide Vogels, als Cardinaal, Wihoop, Tortelduif en andere op de voorgrond, O: I:, Rotten, en een Papegai, by eenige vrugten, plaisant en meesterlyk, door van Rooijen als van Hondekoeter		(Unknown)
1802/09/06	AMSCH	0101	*van Royen* | Een Landschap met gevogelte; fix | *Mat:* op doek *Size:* hoog 26, breed 32 duim	J	(Sold) fl 1 Harbome
1802/09/06	AMSCH	0102	*van Royen* | Een witte Hen, in een Landschap	Mevrouw Achtienhoven	(Sold) fl 0:18 Gruyter
1808/06/13	AMSCH	0140	*Roijen (van)* | Een Warande van staande en liggende Kippen, een Haan en Eenden met haar Kiekens, een Pauw, enz. Kloek behandeld | *Size:* hoog 47, breed 55 duim	E M Engelberts	(Sold) fl 49 Allard
1808/06/13	AMSCH	0141	*Roijen (van)* | Eene Ordonantie als voren, en van gelijke schildering | *Size:* hoog 47, breed 55 duim	E M Engelberts	(Sold) fl 46 Allard
1808/08/23	AMSCH	0140	*Rooijen. (J. van)* | Twee stuks capitaalen Hofgezichten, beide rijk gestoffeerd, met een menigten smakelijke Vrugten en geurige Bloemen, benevens een Aap en eenig uitlandsche Vogelen; helder en uitvoerig geschilderd | *Mat:* op doek *Size:* Ieder hoog 34, breed 28 duim *Notes:* The artist's name was given as "Rooijen. (J. van)" but we have assumed this is an error.	[Gruyter?]	(Bought In) fl 5:5
1808/08/23	AMSCH	0210	*G. van Rooien* | In een gebronde Vaas, ziet men verscheide geurige Bloemen, ter zijde zit een O. I. Raaf; en verder bijwerk	[Gruyter?]	(Sold or Bought In) fl 0:12 Gruyter
1809/06/13	AMSCH	0134	*J. van Rooijen* | Twee stuks kapitale Hofgezigten, beide rijk gestoffeert met een menigte smakelijke Vrugten en keurige Bloemen, waarbij een Aap en eenig Uitlands Gevogelten; uitvoerig geschilderd | *Mat:* op doek *Size:* hoog 34, breed 28 duim *Notes:* The artist's name was given as "J. van Rooijen" but we have assumed this is an error.	[Gruyter?]	(Sold) fl 6:10 Spaan
1810/10/11	AMSCH	0075	*Van Roijen* | Bij de Stam van een Boom zit een Aapje, benevens een Vogel op een Tak, verder vliegend en kruipend Gedierte; fiks geschilderd | *Mat:* op doek *Size:* hoog 33, breed 28 duimen	Y	(Sold) fl 10:10 Gruiter

Rubens, Arnold Frans

1810/03/23	HAVIN	0013	*F. Rubens* | Twee Turksche Battailles, extra uitvoerig en fraai | *Size:* hoog 14 ¾ breet 17 d.	Rudolf Hendrik de Wetstein [or others]	(Unknown)

Rubens, Peter Paul

1801/05/11	AMSCH	0078a	*P: P: Rubbens* | Een Vrouwe Pourtret, in een deftige Hollandsche kleeding, fraai van coloriet, krachtig en meesterlyk geschilderd | *Mat:* op paneel *Size:* hoog 18, breed 16 duim	P[ruyssenaar]	(Sold) fl 12 Gruiter

1802/04/13	HAVIN	0035	*P. Rubbens* | Daar de Vader in de gevangenis gelaaft word, gemerkt P. Rubbens | *Inscr:* P. Rubbens (signed)		(Unknown)
1802/06/16	AMSCH	0141	*P.P. Rubbens* | Deeze Ryke Ordenantie van verscheide Beelden, vertoont Maria zittende met het Kindeken op de schoot, op een verheeven zeetel; voor dezelve legt een Bisschop in plegtgewaad, en Maria Magdaléna, eerbiedig nedergeboogen op hunne kniën: ter eener zyde staat een vorstlyke Persoon, een geördende Geestelyke en geharnast Krygsman: ter andere zyde een vorstelyke Vrouw met een Boek en Kroon in de hand, verzelt van de Martelaresse St. Catharina en Barbara; alles krachtig en meesterlyk fraay gepenceeld | *Mat:* op paneel *Size:* hoog 16, breed 22 duim	[Merrem]	(Sold) fl 155 van der Schley
1802/06/16	AMSCH	0142	*P. P. Rubbens* | Het Afbeeldzel van dien beroemde KunstSchilder met deszelfs Huisvrouw, in deftige Kleeding; hy schynt haar met by de handen te Omärmen: zynde beide tot aan de kniën te zien; het Coloriet is bevallig en van een fraaije penceel behandeling | *Mat:* op paneel *Fmt:* ovaal *Size:* hoog 10, breed 7 ½ duim	[Merrem]	(Sold) fl 47 Reijers
1802/06/29	HGDAW	0013	*Rubbens* | Twee uitvoerige Batailles door den Jongen Rubbens op doek | *Mat:* op doek		(Unknown)
1802/07/20	MGSAN	0039	*P. P. Rubbens* | Een extra schoon Stuk zynde een Oud Man, op Paneel | *Mat:* op paneel *Size:* hoog duim 30, breed duim 23		(Unknown)
1803/04/20	AMSCH	0061	*Rubbens (P. P.)* | Maria in een zédige houding, het Kind Jesu op beide handen dragende, die een Appel in de hand houd. De Teekening is fraay, het Coloriet bevallig, en van een uitvoerige penceelsbehandeling: zynde van zyn allereersten tyd, in de manier van O. Venius [La vierge Marie tenant l'enfant Jesus, qui tient une pomme à la main : Elle est vue à mi-corps dans une attitude qui respire la modestie. L'enfant gentil est plein de grace, à ces qualitées sont joints un excellent coloris, & une touche pateuse & soignée. Ce tableau du premier tems de l'Auteur, est entierement dans la maniere de son maitre Otto Voenius.] | *Mat:* op paneel *Size:* hoog 21 ½, breed 16 duim	Maria Magdalena van Sluypwyk, gravinne van Moens	(Sold) fl 54 Van Iperen
1803/04/27	AMSCH	000A	*P.P. Rubbens* | Un Magnifique Tableau, representent Venus & Mars, peint par P.P. Rubbens, ce morceau à apartenu, au feu Roi de Pologne, & a été vendu à un tres haut prix, a sa vente, a St. Petersbourg	A	(Sold) fl 129 Josi
1803/08/17	AMSCH	0070	*Rubens. (P. P.)* | Een uitvoerig Model van een der verbrande Schilderstukken uit de Jesuiten Kerk te Antwerpen, voorstellende de Triumph der Kerk, ryk van Ordonantie, kragtag en vast van schildering | *Mat:* op paneel *Size:* hoog 19, breed 27 duim	Anna Catharina Putman	(Bought In) fl 130
1803/08/17	AMSCH	0071	*Rubens (P. P.)* | Twee stuks zinnebeeldige Ordonnantien, zynde Modellen uit het Plafon der Eetzaal van het Paleis Whitehall te Westmunster, mesterlyk [sic] behandeld | *Mat:* op doek op paneel *Size:* ieder hoog 19, breed 12 duim	Anna Catharina Putman	(Sold) fl 43 Gruyter
1803/09/07	AMSCH	0136	*P. P. Rubbens* | Maria, staande in een zedige gestalte, voor een Steene Baluster, waarop het Kind Iezu staande, door de Moeder werd vastgehouden; het is schoon van Teekening, bevallig van Coloriet, en fraay van Penceel-behandeling [La Vierge dans une attitude modeste, devant un balustre de pierre, sur lequel elle tient l'enfant Jesus debout ; le dessin en est beau, le coloris très agréable et la touche excellente] | *Mat:* op paneel *Size:* hoog 41, breed 28 duim	Smidt	(Bought In) fl 125
1803/09/07	AMSCH	0137	*P.P. Rubbens* | Dit capitaal ryk gestoffeerd Landschap, met enig Geboomten, vertoont in een Weide diversche Huislieden, verzelt van verscheide Vée, waarvan eenige gemolken worden; het Natuurlyk zonlicht doet een schoone werking, het is kragtig van Coloriet, en uitneemend fraai gepenceeld [Tableau capital, offrant un site de paysage charmant ; richement varié d'arbres et de bestiaux paturant dans un près ; on y voit des villageois, dont quelqu'uns occupé à traire des vaches ; le soleil qui regne sur l'ensemble est d'un superbe effet ; on y voit la nature dans toute sa beauté ; le coloris en est vigoureux et la composition très soignée.] | *Size:* hoog 29, breed 41 duim	Smidt	(Bought In) fl 1750
1804/04/28	LNDLS	0001	*P.P. Rubbens* | Maria's Hemelvaart, verzelt van een menigte engelen; beneden eenige mannen en vrouwen by het graf, fix en konstig van tekening en schildering, door P. P. Rubbens, op paneel | *Mat:* op paneel *Size:* hoog 18, breed 12 duim	[Abraham Delfos] [or others]	(Sold) fl 70 Gruyter
1804/07/25	AMSCH	0062	*Rubbens (P. P.)* | Dit uitmuntend en bevallig voorwerp vertoont, Maria zittende, houdende het slaapend Kind Jesu op de Schoot, en rustende tegen de Borst, welke zy met de Hand ondersteunt; de zeedige en bevallige houding, het aangenaam coloriet, en de meesterlyke fraaije penceel behandeling, geeven alle luister aan dit Tafreel | *Mat:* op paneel *Size:* hoog 39, breed 29 duim		(Sold) fl 150 Van der Schley
1804/08/02	BDAN	0001	*P.P. Rubens* | Een extra fraay Vrouwe Portrait, zittende in een Leuning-Stoel, gekleed in het zwart, zeer kunstig geschildert, zoo schoon als van die Meester bekent is | *Mat:* op doek *Size:* Breed 29 duim, hoog 41 duim	J G Calckberner	(Unknown)
1804/10/16	DLOND	0193	*P.P. Rubbens* | Abrahams Offerhande. (Dit Stuk draagt, op verscheiden plaatsen, de kenmerken van's Meesters toetsen. Het Paneel, hoewel naderhand vergroot, en zeer goed bygewerkt, is, met weinig moeite, weder uit het vergrotende raam te nemen). L'Offrande d' Abraham. (Cette pièce porte les traits du Maitre en divers endroits. Quoique le Tableau a été fait		(Sold) fl 200 O D Wyngaert

			plus grand par le moyen d'un cadre & que ce cadre est joliment peint dans le même goût, on peut avec peu de peine l'en ôter, & le faire reprendre sa grandeur originelle | *Mat:* op paneel *Size:* hoog 48, breed 38		
1805/07/10	AMSCH	0123	*P. P. Rubbens* | Het Portrait van den grooten Kunstschilder, P. P. Rubbens; meesterlyk op Doek geschilderd | *Mat:* op doek *Size:* hoog 29, breed 23 duim	R[oos]	(Sold) fl 16:10 Gruyter
1805/12/16	AMSCH	0048	*P. P. Rubbens* | Androméda aan de Rotz gekluistert, door Perseus verlost; meesterlyk fiks gepenceeld | *Mat:* op paneel *Size:* hoog 17, breed 10 duim	R[oos]	(Sold) fl 7:5 Gruiter
1806/08/13	AMSCH	0149	*Rubbens. (P. P.)* | Deeze ryke Ordinantie steld voor: drie Boetelingen, smekende om genade aan Christus, welke is staande op een vierkante Steen, houdende 't kruis in de hand, verzeld van een Devote Vrouw, welke naast Christus geknield ligt, verders eenige Seraphynen; dit Schildery is allerfrapanst van licht, uitmuntend van teekening en van de beste penceelbehandeling van deeze Meester | *Mat:* op doek *Size:* hoog 44, breed 34 duim	Coclers	(Sold) fl 85 Nieuwenhuis
1808/06/13	AMSCH	0125	*Rubbens (P.P.)* | De voorstelling van de Fabel der Schaking van Deianira, door den Centaurus Nessus. Deze schets, meesterlijk van koloriet, behoeft geene beschrijving, als bekend zijnde door het werk van le Brun | *Mat:* op paneel *Size:* hoog 40, breed 32 duim	E M Engelberts	(Sold) fl 142 B Boelen
1808/08/23	AMSCH	0133	*Rubbens. (P. P.)* | Deeze Ordonantie verbeeld Maria, houdende het Kind Jezu in de armen, staande voor den ingang van een Tempel, voor dezelve ligt een Pelgrom [sic] en eene Vrouw, met zaamgevoude handen eerbiedigd nedergeknielt; het is meesterlijk en uitvoerig gepenceeld | *Mat:* op koper *Size:* hoog 10, breed 8 duim	C	(Bought In) fl 42
1808/08/23	AMSCH	0133a[H]	*Rubbens. (P. P.)* | 1 Schilderij | *Notes:* This lot was added in by hand in the EBNP copy of the catalogue.	Z	(Bought In) fl 60
1810/06/06	RMMUY	0002	*P. P. Rubens* | Eene Prophetesse, kloek en schoon geschilderd. Door P. P. Rubens, weleer geplaatst in de Jesuiten Kerk te Antwerpen | *Mat:* op paneel		(Sold) fl 100 v Leen
1810/08/01	AMSCH	0083	*Rubbens (Petrus Paulus)* | In een Landschap ziet men den Zaligmaker, in de gedaante van eenen Hovenier, zich aan Maria Magdalena vertoonen, welke voor hem in eene eerbiedige houding nederknielt [Jesus Christ apparoissant à la Magdaleine sous l'apparence d'un Jardinier ; on voit le Penitente se jetter aux genoux du Sauveur. Ce Sujet traité de grandeur naturelle presente un paysage pour fond] | *Annots:* Vrai ; mais fort ruiné, et fort lourdement repeint par Coclers. N.B. vrai ; mais tout ruiné et repeint. (NGW); DeVries a Coclers achete (MB) *Mat:* op doek *Size:* hoog 78, breed 69 duimen *Loc:* Amsterdam, Nederland. Rijksmuseum. (A2336) as school of Rubens, on loan to Etten-Leur, St. Lambertusparochie	Mr Pieter de Smeth van Alphen	(Sold) fl 2700 J^{mo} De Vries
1810/08/01	AMSCH	0084	*Rubbens (Petrus Paulus)* | Hebe, de Godinne der Jeugd en der Gezondheid, voedt Esculapius in de gedaante van eene Slang [Hébé Déesse de la jeunesse et de la santé, nourrissant Esculape sous l'emblême d'un Serpent. La figure est en partie nue, ayant le Serpent tourné autour du bras. De grandeur naturelle vû jusqu'aux genoux] | *Annots:* médiocre et fort lourd. (NGW) *Mat:* op paneel *Size:* hoog 40, breed 28 duimen *Loc:* Detroit, MI, USA. Institute of Arts. (44.266)	Mr Pieter de Smeth van Alphen	(Bought In) fl 800
1810/08/06	AMSCH	0088	*Rubbens (P.P.)* | Maria houdende het Kind Jesus in hare armen, staande voor den ingang van een Tempel, voor dezelve ligt een Pelgrim en eene Vrouw eerbiedig neder geknielt; het is meesterlijk en uitvoerig gepenceeld | *Mat:* op paneel *Size:* hoog 10, breed 8 duimen	B	(Bought In) fl 7
1810/10/10	MGCIT	0002	*P.P. Rubbens* | Een Panther of Tijger, zogende drie jongen, en liggende met dezelve in een steene Hok, natuurlijk en meesterächtig behandeld	Caspar van Citters	(Unknown)
1810/10/11	AMSCH	0077a[H]	*P.P. Rubbens* | Een dito | *Notes:* This lot was added in by hand in the EBNP copy of the catalogue. It is unclear what "dito" refers to in the title.	C	(Sold) fl 1 Posthumus

Rubens, Peter Paul (and Brueghel, J. (I))

1806/08/13	AMSCH	0150	*Rubbens. (P. P.); J. Breugel* | Dit kunstryk Tafreel steld voor: de drie Gratien, door drie bevallige naakte Vrouwen-beelden in een Landschap, welke een korf met bloemen omhoog ophouden; achter hun is een rood kleed aan de boomen vastgehegt, waartegen de voorwerpen helder uitkomen; het Landschap en de Bloemen, zyn door J. Breugel, de ordinantie en couleur der Vrouwen is uitmuntend schoon, en van een uitvoerige penceelbehandeling; dit heerlyk Cabinetstukje, is een der uitmuntendste, welke van beide deeze beroemden Meesters bekend zyn | *Mat:* op koper *Size:* hoog 18, breed 13 ½ duim	van der Schley	(Sold) fl 400 Jan Spaan
1806/08/13	AMSCH	0151	*Rubbens (P. P.); J. Breugel* | Een Boom- en Bergachtig Landschap, met een Rivier doorsneeden, gestoffeerd met Herders met hun Vee, kragtig van penceelsbehandeling | *Mat:* op doek *Size:* hoog 39, breed 52 duim	Roos	(Sold) fl 41 Du Pré

Rubens, Peter Paul (and Snyders, F.)

1804/07/25	AMSCH	0063	*Rubbens. (P. P.); F. Snyders* | Een Wild Zwyn, meer dan leevensgrooten, door verschyde Honden aangevallen, drie Jagers gaan het met Spiesen te keer, een derzelve blaast op de Jachthoorn, alles is vol drift, en op de Voorgrond leggen diversche gekwetste Honden; het is ongemeen kragtig		(Sold) fl 65 Van der Schley

			van coloriet en van een breede penceel behandeling, door byde deeze beroemden meesters | *Mat:* op doek *Size:* hoog 68, breed 111 duim		
1809/07/19	AMSCH	[A0005][H]	*Snyder; Rubens* | 1 Herte Jagt | *Notes:* This lot was added in by hand in the AA copy of the catalogue. Because it was not numbered, we have assigned the number.		(Unknown)
1810/10/11	AMSCH	0077	*P. P. Rubbens; F. Snijders* | Een wild Zwijn, levensgroot, door verscheiden Honden aangevallen; drie Jagers gaan het met Spieren te keer, terwijl een derzelven op een Jagthoorn blaast, op den voorgrond liggen verscheiden gekwetste Honden; ongemeen krachtig en van eene breede penseelbehandeling | *Mat:* op doek *Size:* hoog 68, breed 111 duimen	K	(Bought In) fl 82

Rubens, Peter Paul (or Rubens, copy after)

1810/06/06	RMMUY	0220	*Rubbens* | Samson, den Leeuw verslaande, kragtig en schoon geschilderd. Door of naar Rubbens | *Mat:* op doek		(Unknown) fl 1:6

Rubens, Peter Paul (or Rubens, manner)

1801/08/19	AMSCH	0104	*P. P. Rubbens* | Een slaapende naakte Nimph in een Landschap, waar by een oude verliefde Grysaard, die een linne Kleedje schynt weg te schuiven; kragtig door of in de manier van P. P. Rubbens | *Mat:* op doek *Size:* hoog 41, breed 48 duim	C S Roos [for] G	(Sold) fl 10:10 V^{n} Dijl
1803/04/20	AMSCH	0062	*P.P. Rubbens, of in zyn Manier* | Een Herder een Herderin liefkozende in een Landschap, in het verschiet een Landman welke eenig Vee wegdryft, de behandeling zoo wel van het Landschap als van de Beelden, doet in allen deelen het kloek penceel van dien meester kennen [Le sujet de cette pièce est un Berger amoureux près de sa Bergere ; le fond offre un paysage dans les quel se distingue un pâtre conduisant ses bestiaux. Ce tableau est traité en maitre : les possesseurs en faisoient très grand cas.] | *Mat:* op doek *Size:* hoog 44, breed 65 duim	Maria Magdalena van Sluypwyk, gravinne van Moens	(Sold) fl 430 Gruiter
1804/05/07	AMSCH	0146	*Rubbens (of in de manier)* | Deeze Ordonantie steld voor, Mercuur en Argus, waarby eenige Ossen; enz. meesterlyk en fraay van coloriet | *Mat:* op doek *Size:* hoog 33, breed 42 duim	Vinkeles [for] J	(Sold) fl 1:10 Harbome
1804/08/02	BDAN	0008	*P.P. Rubens of in zyne manieren* | Diana in 't Bad met veele Nimphen, op den voorgrond ziet met Acteön, zeer transparant en gemakkelyk behandelt | *Mat:* op paneel *Size:* b. 27 d. h. 20 d.	J G Calckberner	(Unknown)
1807/08/26	AMSCH	0193	*P.P. Rubbens* | Een Trouwplegtigheid van twee Vorstelyke Personadiën; met een menigte bywerk van Beelden en andere zaken; meesterlyk op Doek, door of in de manier van P.P. Rubbens | *Mat:* op doek	Roos	(Sold) fl 0:10 v d Schley Willem

Rubens, Peter Paul (or Rubens, school)

1803/09/07	AMSCH	0138	*Rubens* | Een Madona met het Kind op haar schoot; door of uit het School van Rubens [Une Madone, ayant l'enfant Jesus sur ses genoux ; si ce tableau n'est pas de Rubens, au-moins est-il de son école] | *Mat:* op paneel *Size:* hoog 23, breed 18 duim	Smidt	(Bought In) fl 4
1807/06/10	HGBSM	0067	*P.P. Rubbens* | Een konstig Schilderij met naakte Nimphen, houdende den hoorn des overvloed, gevuld met bloemen en fruiten, op de voorgrond een Aapje bij meer vrugten, door of uit het school van P.P. Rubbens | *Mat:* op doek *Size:* hoog 67, breed 57 ½ duim	Abraham Delfos [or others]	(Sold) fl 3:6 v Giese
1809/04/17	AMSCH	0131a	*Rubbens* | Een rijke Ordonantie, voorstellende Vénus aan haar Toilet; breed geschilderd, door of uit het School van Rubbens	C	(Sold) fl 1 Spaan

Rubens, Peter Paul (copy after)

1802/05/10	MGSAN	0016	*P.P. Rubbens* | Een dito [Stuk], waarop een Mariabeeld, met het Kindje Jesus op haar schoot, krachtig, doch does gepenseeld, naar P. P. Rubbens, door een zeer goed Meester: op Paneel, in vergulde Lyst | *Mat:* op paneel *Size:* hoog 26 ½ duim, breed 23 duim	Johan Dirk Kruysse	(Unknown) £ 3:10
1802/07/20	MGSAN	0029	*Rubbens* | Simson, door de Filistynen gebonden wordende, op Paneel: naar Rubbens | *Mat:* op paneel *Size:* hoog duim 36, breed duim 44		(Unknown)
803/04/20	AMSCH	0004	*Beschay. (J.); Rubens* | Christus aan het Volk vertoond wordende, staat op een Bordes met den purperen mantel omhangen, ter zyde ziet men Pilatus, benevens eenige krygsknegten en een der moordenaren, op de voorgrond een menigte Jooden: als roepende Kruist hem; de hartstogten zyn zeer wel waargenomen, en is voorts van een meesterlyke behandeling [Le sujet de ce tableau est J.C. exposé sur le perron du Juge Pilate devant une multitude de Juifs & de Romains : c'est une bonne imitation d'après Rubens dont la belle estempe [sic] par Bolswert est assez connue.] | copy by J. Beschey after Rubens; companion to lot 5, by J. Beschey *Mat:* op doek *Size:* hoog 23, breed 19 duim	Maria Magdalena van Sluypwyk, gravinne van Moens	(Sold) fl 31 Theijs
803/04/27	AMSCH	000E	*Rubbens* | l'Erection de la Croix, bonne Copie, d'apres Rubbens	B	(Sold) fl 5:5 V den Brink
803/04/27	AMSCH	000U[H]	*Rubben* | Een Maria met het Kindjes, na Rubben | *Notes:* This lot was added in by hand in the LBDa and RKDH copies of the catalogue.	G	(Sold) fl 2 Grimpen
803/04/27	AMSCH	0083	*Rubens* | Deux Tableaux, dont l'un répésente le Génie de la peinture, & l'autre une vielle à la lumiere de Nuit, d'après Rubens	A	(Sold) fl 6:5 Gruiter
803/09/07	AMSCH	0249	*Rubbens* | De Aanbidding der Koningen, zynde een ryke Ordonantie van verscheide Beelden; naar Rubbens [L'adoration des rois. Ce tableau est	Smidt	(Sold) fl 5 Toselli

			d'une ordonnance riche et d'une variété d'objets très agréable ; d'après Rubens] | *Mat:* op paneel *Size:* hoog 25, breed 21 duim		
1803/09/07	AMSCH	0263	*P. P. Rubbens* | Deze ryke Ordonantie, vol gewoel, verbeeld de oprechting Christi, aan het Kruis, waarby wéenende Vrouwen met Kinderen, en Krygslieden te Paard; kragtig en meesterlyk op Doek geschilderd, naar P. P. Rubbens [Ce tableau d'une belle ordonnance, représente le crucifiement de Jesus Christ ; au pied de la croix des femmes et des enfans en pleurs ; à l'entour des gens de guerre à cheval ; peint avec une vigueur de coloris et une touche admirables, sur toile, d'après Rubens.] | *Mat:* op doek *Size:* hoog 39, br. 76 duim	Smidt	(Sold) fl 26 C S Roos
1804/08/02	BDAN	0012	*J. van Hoek; Rubens* | Venus Lusthof na Rubens, schoon in Couleur | copy by J. Hoecke after Rubens *Mat:* op paneel *Size:* b. 52 d. h. 36 d.	J G Calckberner	(Unknown)
1804/08/02	BDAN	0025	*Na Rubens* | Een Graflegging, schoon van Ordonnantie | *Mat:* op koper *Size:* b. 18 d. h. 14 en een half d.	J G Calckberner	(Unknown)
1804/10/16	DLOND	0297	*Naar P. P. Rubbens* | Mars, alles dreigende te vernielen, doch door de liefde wordende tegengehouden; vol gewoel; zeer goed. Mars en fureur, appaisé par l'amour; rempli de figures; très bon | *Mat:* op doek *Size:* hoog 30, breed 42		(Unknown)
1804/10/16	DLOND	0298	*Naar P. P. Rubbens* | Achilles onder de Maagden Uts[a] [vol gewoel; zeer goed]. Achile entre les Vierges Uts[a] [rempli de figures; très bon] | *Mat:* op doek *Size:* hoog 44, breed 60		(Unknown)
1804/10/29	HRBAU	0175	*Rubbens* | Eene H. Familie, na Rubbens | *Mat:* op doek *Size:* hoog 54, breed 41 duim	Simon Styl	(Unknown)
1805/10/09	HGBSM	0129	*Beschaey; Rubbens* | Christus aan het kruis tusschen de moordenaars, naar het groote schildery van Rubbens | copy by B. Beschey after Rubens *Mat:* op koper *Size:* hoog 9 ½ breet 7 duim	T H van Willigen [or others]	(Sold) fl 50 De Gelder, R
1808/12/12	DOHAA	0066	*Rubens* | De Maagd Maria met het kindeken Jesus, gecopiëerd naar een Schildery van Rubens | *Mat:* op doek		(Unknown)
1809/07/25	HGBSM	0114	*D. van der Aa; P.P. Rubbens* | Een Heilige Famillie na P.P. Rubbens, door D. van der Aa | copy by Dirk Aa after Rubens *Mat:* op doek *Size:* hoog 36, breed 30 duim	D van der Aa	(Sold) fl 36 van der Aa
1810/03/07	UTWLD	0014	*Rubens* | Twee extra fraaye Koppen naar Rubens | *Size:* hoog 2 voet 6 duim, breed 2 voet	J J Woertman	(Unknown) fl 10
1810/06/06	RMMUY	0180	*Rubens* | Christus den Cijnspenning vertonende. Naar Rubens | *Mat:* op doek		(Unknown) fl 14
1810/10/10	MGCIT	0123	*Snijder; Rubbens* | Een zeer schoone Kopie naar een stuk van Rubbens, voormaals en mogelijk nog te Antwerpen, verbeeldende een Charitas; bijzonder goed nagevolgd, door Snijder | copy by F. Snyders after Rubens	Caspar van Citters	(Unknown)

Rubens, Peter Paul (manner)

1801/04/23	AMYVR	0047	*Rubbens* | 1 Historieele Ordonnantie, in de manier van Rubbens | *Notes:* This lot was sold with lot 48, which is in the manner of P. Bril.		(Unknown) fl 5 for lots 47 & 48
1801/11/10	AMPOS	0012	*P. Rubbens* | 2 stuks, een bedrukte Christus met het Kruis, als P. Rubbens, en een ander		(Unknown)
1802/08/24	LNDLS	0040	*Rubbens* | Petrus en Johannes de Kreupele geneezende aan de deure van den Tempel, verzeld van veele persoonen, en een glorie van Engelen daar boven. Zeer konstig op koper geschilderd, in den trant van Rubbens, door een voornaam Meester | *Mat:* op koper *Size:* hoog 17, breed 10 duimen	Leonardus Bouman [or others]	(Unknown) fl 9:5
1803/04/20	AMSCH	0063	*P. P. Rubbens [maniere]* | Geloof, Liefde en Hoop, met drie Kinderen, door den H. Geest met een Hémelsch Licht bestraald wordende; de behandeling is in alles als de voorgaande [La foi, l'Esperance, & la Charité representée avec trois enfans. Cette allegorie est éclairée par la gloire du St. Esprit. L'effet, la couleur & la touche de maitre se distringuent [sic] dans ce morceau.] | *Mat:* op doek *Size:* hoog 64, breed 45 duim *Notes:* The artist modifier "maniere" is given only in the French edition of the catalogue.	Maria Magdalena van Sluypwyk, gravinne van Moens	(Sold) fl 19 Hulswit
1803/04/20	AMSCH	0064	*P. P. Rubbens [maniere]* | Een Hofgezicht waarin eenige Heeren en Dames zich met Caresseeren en Drinken vermaken, waarby eenige Minnewigtjes, meesterlyk behandeld [Le jardin d'amour, ce sujet suffisamment connu est une des compositions les plus agréables de Rubens. Ce tableau quoiqu'imitation tient beaucoup de la franchise du pinceau de l'inventeur.] | *Mat:* op doek *Size:* hoog 58, breed 83 duim *Notes:* The artist modifier "maniere" is given only in the French edition of the catalogue.	Maria Magdalena van Sluypwyk, gravinne van Moens	(Sold) fl 121 Gruiter
1803/08/17	AMSCH	0097	*Rubens* | Het Pourtrait van Justus Lipsius, beroemd Regtsgeleerden, meesterlyk als Rubens | *Mat:* op doek op paneel *Size:* hoog 22, breed 21 ½ duim	Anna Catharina Putman	(Sold) fl 1 Ijver
1803/11/30	MGBEO	0001	*Rubbens* | Een Capitaale Schildery, verbeeldende de Handwassing van Pontius Pilatus, schoon gepenseeld, door een goed Meester, in de manier van Rubbens | *Mat:* op doek *Size:* hoog 85 duim, breed 48 duim	Samuel de Wind	(Sold or Bought In) £ 1:1 Dr de Wind
1803/12/12	AMSCH	0143	*Rubens* | Twee Schetzen, op Paneel, als Rubens | *Mat:* op paneel *Size:* hoog 4, breed 7 duim	D	(Sold) fl 1:15 Menzard
1804/02/27	AMSCH	0157	*Rubbens* | Een liefkoozende Krygsheld; meesterlyk geschilderd, als Rubbens | *Mat:* op doek *Size:* hoog 36, breed 30 duim	C	(Sold) fl 0:6 L Pakke

1804/05/07	AMSCH	0209	*Rubens* | In een aangenaam Boomryk Landschap, ziet men een ménigte van vrolyke Dansende Landlieden; meesterlyk op Doek geschilderd, als Rubens | *Mat:* op doek *Size:* hoog 33, breed 46 duim	Vinkeles [for] G	(Sold) fl 1:5 L Pakker
1804/07/25	AMSCH	0064	*In de manier van Rubbens* | In een Landschap voor een Woning by Geboomten, vertoont zig de Heilige Familie, Maria zit, en houd het Kind Jesu staande op haar Schoot, welke door het Kind St. Jan, by het Voetje word gegreepen, verders verzelt van St. Joseph en St. Anna; alles is leevens grooten, kragtig van coloriet en van een meesterlyke penceel behandeling | *Mat:* op doek *Size:* hoog 73, breed 55 duim		(Sold) fl 10:10 Van der Schleij
1805/07/10	AMSCH	0180	*P. P. Rubbens* | Een Vorstelyk Persoon in 't Harnas, om hebbende, een prachtige Mantel, met edele Gesteentes en bonte Rand; meesterlyk op Paneel, in de manier van P. P. Rubbens | *Mat:* op paneel *Size:* hoog 46, breed 35 duim	R[oos]	(Sold) fl 71 Gruyter
1805/07/10	AMSCH	0210	*Rubbens* | Een Heylige Familje, verzeld van St. Jan, met een Lam; fraai van coloriet, in de manier van Rubbens | *Mat:* op doek	V[inkeles] [for] H[affner]	(Bought In) fl 2 ½
1805/12/16	AMSCH	0098	*Rubens* | Een ryke Historieele Romeinsche Ordinantie, meesterlyk, in de manier van Rubens	R[oos]	(Sold) fl 1 L Pakker
1806/05/05	AMSCH	0225	*Rubbens* | Een ryk gekleedde Dame, met een halscieraad in haar hand; meesterlyk op Doek, als Rubbens | *Mat:* op doek	O	(Sold) fl 4 Alberti
1807/08/26	AMSCH	0249	*P.P. Rubbens* | Deeze Ordonnantie vol gewoel, verbeeldt den val der kwade Engelen, door den Engel Michael ter nedergeworpen in den Helschen poel; kragtig en meesterlyk gepenceeld, in de manier van P.P. Rubbens | *Mat:* op doek *Size:* hoog 44, breed 34 duim	Joseph Vallette	(Sold) fl 4:10 Spakler
1808/04/26	GDAN	0266	*Rubbens* | In de manier van Rubbens, zijnde de bezigtiging van den Keizerlijken Penning door Jezus, met eenige Beelden | *Size:* hoog 27, breed 38 duim	G H Fortuyn	(Unknown)
1808/11/28	AMSCH	0102	*Rubbens* | Een Bijbelordonantie, verbeeldende alwaar Saul van zijn Paard nedervalt, verzeld van verscheide Krijgsknegten, meesterlijk behandeld, op Doek, in de manier van Rubbens | *Mat:* op doek	H	(Sold) fl 3:10 L Pakker
1808/11/28	AMSCH	0106	*Rubbens* | Een Mans Portrait, op Paneel, in de manier van Rubbens | *Mat:* op paneel *Notes:* This lot was sold with lot 107 by an Italian artist.	H	(Sold) fl 0:14 for lots 106 & 107. Levie Pakker
1810/10/11	AMSCH	0078	*P. P. Rubbens* | Voor eene woning zit de Maagd Maria, houdende het Kind Jezus op hare schoot, ter zijde St. Jan, verder St. Josef en St. Anna, alle levensgroot en zeer schoon geschilderd, op Doek, in de manier van P. P. Rubbens | *Mat:* op doek *Size:* hoog 73, breed 55 duimen	K	(Sold) fl 27:10 du Pree
1810/10/11	AMSCH	0163	*Rubbens* | Eene Historiëele Ordonantie, uit Ovidius, in de manier van Rubbens	S	(Sold) fl 0:10 L^y Pakker
1810/10/11	AMSCH	0189	*Rubbens* | Eene Historiëele Ordonantie, van verscheide Beelden, verbeelende de onthoofding van Johannes; goed in de manier van Rubbens geschilderd	A	(Sold) fl 1 van der Kooij
1810/10/11	AMSCH	0191	*P. P. Rubbens* | Eenige Nimfen en Saters in een Landschap; in de manier van P. P. Rubbens	A	(Sold) fl 1 Gruiter
1810/10/11	AMSCH	0200	*P. P. Rubbens* | Een Historiëele Ordonantie, vol gewoel; in de manier van P. P. Rubbens | *Notes:* This lot was sold with lot 216 by J. Martszen (II).	A	(Sold) fl 2 for lots 200 & 216. Yver

Rubens, Peter Paul (school)

1802/09/06	AMSCH	0195	*P. P. Rubens* | Maria zittende met het Kindeken op de schoot; door een Dicipel van P. P. Rubens, fix gepenceeld	Spaan	(Sold) fl 5 Jan Spaan
1803/07/18	AMSCH	0043	*Rubens (uit het school van)* | Dit stuk steld voor de Tuin der Liefde, deeze ryke Ordonantie is bekend door de Prent die na hetzelve uitgaat, de maaker van dit stuk heeft in allen deelen den aart van Rubens zyn Meester zeer goed gevolgd [Le jardin d'amour. Cette riche composition est si généralement connue qu'elle nexige [sic] pas de description : il suffira d'observer que ce tableau est peint par un élêve distingué de Rubbens, qu'il a le Brillant coloris de cette Ecole, & qu'il est traité d'une maniere si libre, & si heurté qu'il ne sent en rien l'imitation.] | *Mat:* op koper *Size:* hoog 27, breed 38 duim	Maria Theresia Andrioli	(Sold) fl 59 Gruyter
1803/09/07	AMSCH	0237	*Rubbens* | De Hemelvaard van Maria, in een glorie van Wolken en Seraphynen, meesterlyk gepenceeld, door een bekwaam Meester, uit het School van Rubbens [L'assomption de la vierge, dans une gloire environnée de nuages et de séraphins ; très bien peint par un excellent maître de l'école de Rubens] | *Mat:* op koper *Size:* hoog 26, breed 19 duim	Smidt	(Sold) fl 11 Gruiter
1804/10/16	DLOND	0299	*Uit de School van P. P. Rubbens* | De Wyzen uit het Oosten. Les Mages de l'Orient | *Mat:* op paneel *Size:* hoog 31, breed 44		(Unknown)
1804/10/16	DLOND	0300	*Uit de School van P. P. Rubbens* | Salomons eerste Recht. La première Sentence de Salomon | *Mat:* op doek *Size:* hoog 56, breed 59		(Unknown)

Rubens, Peter Paul (style)

808/11/28	AMSCH	0104	*Rubbens* | Het Portrait van Maria de Medicis, meesterlijk in de stijl van Rubbens geschilderd	H	(Sold) fl 19:10 Coclers
809/04/17	AMSCH	0130	*P.P. Rubbens* | Een Ordonantie, voorstellende Meléager en Athalante; meesterlijk en breed in de stijl van P.P. Rubbens	T	(Sold) fl 2

1809/04/17	AMSCH	0154	*Rubbens* | De Wijzen aanbidden en brengen Geschenken aan het Kind Jezus; meesterlijk in de stijl van Rubbens | *Mat:* op doek	[Gruyter?]	(Sold or Bought In) fl 0:8 Gruyter

Rugendas, Georg Philipp (I)

1803/09/07	AMSCH	0155	*Rugendas* | Twee stuks Batailjes, teegen de Turken, by eene Battery, meesterlyk op Doek [Deux batailles contre des turcs auprès d'une batterie, d'une excellente composition] | *Mat:* op doek *Size:* hoog 19, breed 14 duim	Smidt	(Sold) fl 8 J Yver
1804/02/27	AMSCH	0097	*Rugendas* | In 't binnenste van een Smeedery, ziet men eenige Lieden bezig een Anker dat in het Vuur legt bewerken, de verlichting der Beelden en Bywerk is in dit stuk schoon waargenomen, en doen een volmaakt effect, en is meesterlyk geschilderd | *Mat:* op doek *Size:* hoog 18, breed 24 ½ duim	B	(Bought In) fl 18
1806/08/13	AMSCH	0159	*Rugendas* | Twee stuks hévige Schermutselingen tusschen Ruitery, in een Landschap met Gebouwen; alles is vol vuur en de hartstochten natuurlyk; en van een meesterlyke penceelbehandeling | *Mat:* op paneel *Size:* Ieder hoog 16, breed 14 duim	Roos	(Sold) fl 9:10 Verhoesen
1806/08/13	AMSCH	0160	*Rugendas* | Een niet minder Bataiilje als de voorgaande | *Mat:* op paneel *Size:* hoog 15, breed 20 duim	Roos	(Sold) fl 1:15 Gruiter

Rugendas, Georg Philipp (I) (manner)

1810/03/23	HAVIN	0045	*Rugendas* | Twee stukken met Paarden fraai als van Rugendas	Rudolf Hendrik de Wetstein [or others]	(Unknown)

Ruisdael

1802/08/24	LNDLS	0104	*Ruysdaal* | Een gezigt langs een Water in een Landschap op een Dorptooren, op den voorgrond Koeijen in 't Water staande. Gem. Ruysdaal | *Mat:* op paneel *Size:* hoog 11 ½, breed 10 ½ duimen *Inscr:* Ruysdaal (signed)	Leonardus Bouman [or others]	(Unknown) fl 1:10
1807/04/00	LNDLS	0044	*Ruysdael* | Een Land- en Watergezigt met vaartuigen en beesten | *Mat:* op paneel *Size:* hoog 11, breed 10 duim	[Abraham Delfos] [or others]	(Unknown)
1807/06/10	HGBSM	0044	*Ruysdael* | Een Land- en Watergezigt met vaartuigen en beesten | *Mat:* op paneel *Size:* hoog 11, breed 10 duim	Abraham Delfos [or others]	(Sold) fl 4:15 Smeets
1808/12/30	HGIMM	[0071b]	*Ruysdaal* | Voorts een exquis kabinetje Schilderijen van voorname Nederlandsche Meesters, welke uit hoofde van de kortheid des tijds niet stuk voor stuk kunnen beschreven worden; doch waarvan de beschrijving op den Kijkdag zal voorhanden zijn. Dus wij hier alleen de namen van eenige dier Meesters laten volgen, als: A. Kuyp, Ruysdaal, Karel du Jardyn, Loqwi ('t beste dat hij schilderde) Hondekoeter, van Dyk, Janson, Moesgever, Kamphuyzen, van Gooijen, A. van der Neer, T. Wyk, Huchtenburgh, Zolemaker, van Hassel, A. Vermeulen, van Dongen, Scheffer, van Os enz. | *This Lot:* Een Schilderij, Ruysdaal *Notes:* Because this lot was not numbered in the catalogue, we have assigned the number.		(Unknown)
1810/11/07	UTWLD	0051	*Ruisdael* | Een boomrijk Landschapje over een water, waar langs een wegje zeer aardig en kragtig geschilderd door Ruisdael op paneel, 11 duim hoog, en 13 duim breed, zwarte Lijst | *Mat:* op paneel *Size:* 11 duim hoog, en 13 duim breed		(Unknown) fl 34

Ruisdael (manner)

1801/12/22	AMOTT	0130	*Ruisdaal* | 2 fraaije Landschapjes, als Ruisdaal	Bartholomeus Ruloffs	(Unknown) fl 3 for lots 130 & 131
1801/12/22	AMOTT	0131	*Ruisdaal* | 3 dito [fraaije] dito [Landschapjes], als de voorgaande [Ruisdaal]	Bartholomeus Ruloffs	(Unknown) fl 3 for lots 130 & 131
1805/07/10	AMSCH	0274	*Ruisdaal* | Een Boomryk Landschap met Beeldjes; in de manier van Ruisdaal	V[inkeles] [for] K	(Bought In) fl 4
1810/06/06	RMMUY	0136	*Ruisdaal* | Eene Onstuimige Zee. Stout en meesterlijk, in de manier van Ruisdaal | *Mat:* op doek		(Unknown) fl 2:5

Ruisdael, Jacob van

1801/02/18	AMBOS	0006	*J. Ruysdaal* | Een uitvoerig en aangenaam Boschgezigt, waarin een Hartenjagt gehouden word, alles natuurlyk en uitvoerig geschilderd	J Schonevelt	(Unknown)
1801/04/13	AMSCH	0063	*J. Ruysdaal* | Een heuvelachtig Landschap met hoog geboomte en Boerenwooning, ter linker zyde een Watermolen, op de voorgrond een Man en Vrouw by de stam van een Berkeboom, alles is natuurlyk, fix en breed gepenceeld | *Mat:* op doek *Size:* hoog 24, breed 30 duim	Pierre Fouquet, junior	(Sold) fl 265 Van Leen
1801/04/13	AMSCH	0064	*J. Ruysdaal* | Een gezicht van het Duin over de blekeryen op de stad Haarlem, natuurlyk verbeeld | *Mat:* op doek *Size:* hoog 10, breed 14 duim	Pierre Fouquet, junior	(Sold) fl 36 v d Schley [for] M[errem]
1801/05/11	AMSCH	0073	*Jacob Ruysdaal* | Een Bergachtig Landschap, ter zyde met hoog Geboomte, waarby een Waterval, in 't verschiet de Tooren van een Kerk, alles zonachtig en krachtig behandeld | *Mat:* op doek *Size:* hoog 25, breed 20 duim	E[lias]	(Sold) fl 100 Allard
1801/05/11	AMSCH	0074	*Jacob Ruysdaal* | Een woelende Zee, met zylende Scheepen, op de voorgrond by een Baak ziet men twee Beeldjes, fraai en uitvoerig gepenceeld | *Mat:* op doek *Size:* hoog 36, breed 50 duim	Pruisse [for] M	(Sold) fl 160 Th^{s} Spaan

1801/05/11	AMSCH	0075	*Jacob Ruysdaal* | Een stormende Zee, met een Oorlogschip, ter zyde ziet men by een klip het vergaan van een Vaartuig, natuurlyk van penceel behandeling | *Mat:* op paneel *Size:* hoog 14, breed 21 duim	P[ruyssenaar]	(Sold) fl 2:5 Isac Smit
1801/05/11	AMSCH	0076	*Jacob Ruysdaal* | Een Boschgezigt met zwaar Geboomte en Stoffagie van Beelden en Schapen, krachtig behandeld | *Mat:* op paneel *Size:* hoog 19, breed 25 duim	P[ruyssenaar]	(Sold) fl 52 Gruiter
1801/06/10	AMSCH	0141	*Ruysdaal. (J.)* | Dit bevallig Stukje, verbeeld een besneeuwd Landschap, met hoog dor Geboomte, op een Sloot ziet men eenige Schaatseryders, alles is natuurlyk verbeeld en meesterlyk gepenceeld | *Mat:* op doek op paneel *Size:* hoog 12, breed 17 duim	Herman ten Kate	(Sold) fl 151 Stevens
1801/06/13	LNDLS	0003	*Jacob Ruysdael* | Een heuvelagtig Landschap, met geboomte en een man die schaapen langs den weg drijft, en in 't verschiet bergen, boomen en woningen, langs dezelve een Rivier, waarvan op den voorgrond een bruischende Waterval, tusschen kluiten en brokken, extra konstig, op doek | *Mat:* op doek *Size:* hoog 20, breed 22 ½ duimen	D van R	(Sold) fl 500 A Delfos
1801/08/19	AMSCH	0097	*J. Ruysdaal* | Een Gezigt op de stad Weesp, koomende van de Vechtzyde, zynde gestoffeerd met Beeldjes, en het Water met diverse Vaartuigen, fraay van zonlicht en meesterlyk gepenceeld op Paneel | *Mat:* op paneel *Size:* hoog 29, breed 53 duim	C S Roos [for] G	(Sold) fl 18:10 v d Vinne
1801/10/19	AMSCH	0064	*Ruisdaal. (J.)* | Een Bergächtig Landschap met Boere Woningen, in 't verschiet een Watermoolen, drie kleine Beeldjes; op de voorgrond een stroomend Water met een Brug, zeer natuurlyk, zonächtig, en ongemeen fraay geschildert | *Mat:* op doek *Size:* hoog 15 ¼, breed 17 ½ duim	Jonkheer Menno Baron van Coehoorn	(Sold) fl 645 Roeloffs (B[d] Kooy)
1801/11/10	AMPOS	0015	*J. Ruisdaal* | 1 Lommeryk Boschgezigt met Reizigers		(Unknown)
1802/04/13	HAVIN	0003	*J. Ruysdaal* | Een Gezigt op de Stad Haarlem, van 't Duyn over de Bleekeryen te zien, uitmuntend, uitvoerig en fraai gestoffeerd		(Unknown)
1802/04/13	HAVIN	0004	*J. Ruysdaal* | Een Landschap, voor in een oude Schuur, waar langs het gezigt op de hooge Sluis te Amsterdam; ongemeen natuurlyk een Winter met veel sneeuw verbeeldende, en fraai geschildert		(Unknown)
1802/04/13	HAVIN	0019	*J. Ruysdaal* | Een Stadgezigt, fraai en verstandig		(Unknown)
1802/05/05	AMSCH	0178	*J. Ruysdaal* | Een capitaal boom en bergachtig Landschap, met een Waterval, gestoffeerd met vissende, badende en wandelende beelden, meesterachtig geschilderd | *Size:* hoog 64, breed 52 duim	J	(Sold) fl 11 Stevens
1802/05/05	AMSCH	0179	*J. Ruysdaal* | In een aangenaam boomryk Landschap, ziet men van een hoog opgaande weg een Landman afkomen, verzelt van een drift beesten, verders een heuvelachtig verschiet | *Size:* hoog 20, breed 26 duim	J	(Sold) fl 18:10 Spruit
1802/05/05	AMSCH	0180	*J. Ruysdaal* | In een stil Water ziet men eenige Visschers in hunne Schuiten, verders eenige ander Vaartuigen, en een aangenaam verschiet | *Size:* hoog 22, breed 31 duim	J	(Sold) fl 7:15 Pruijssenaar [for] R
1802/06/16	AMSCH	0146	*J. Ruisdaal* | Een bevallig heuvelachtig Landschap met verschillend Geboomten, en doorsneeden met een stromende Rivier en Watervalletje, die op de voorgrond tusschen brokken Steenen neder valt: verder op een heuvel by een Woning zit een Veehoeder, en Vrouw, verzelt van eenige Schaapen; het Water is dun en natuurlyk, het Licht bevallig en van een fraaije penceel-behandeling | *Mat:* op doek *Size:* hoog 26, breed 32 duim	[Merrem]	(Sold) fl 500 I Smit Gz
1802/06/16	AMSCH	0147	*J. Ruisdaal* | Een Capitaal wyd uitgestrekt Landzicht; van Duin afziende naar de Stadt Haarlem; op de voorgrond gestoffeerd, langs een weg, met verscheide Vissers en andere Lieden: bevallig van Licht, en zeer natuurlyk fraay gepenceeld | *Mat:* op doek *Size:* hoog 30, breed 56 duim	[Merrem]	(Sold) fl 120 I Smit Gz
1802/06/16	AMSCH	0148	*J. Ruisdaal* | Een bevallig en uitgestrekt Landgezicht, ziende naar verscheide Bleekeryen, Woningen en Geboomten; in 't verschiet vertoont zich de de Stadt Haarlem: zeer natuurlyk, zonachtig en uitvoerig van penceel-behandeling | *Mat:* op doek *Size:* hoog 11, breed 14 duim	[Merrem]	(Sold) fl 40 v d Schleij
1802/06/16	AMSCH	0149	*J. Ruisdaal* | Een stormende Zee langs een Klip, waar by het Water sterk opstuift; op de voorgrond een Schuitje met twee Beelden, krachtig geschilderd | *Mat:* op doek *Size:* hoog 11, breed 17 ½ duim	[Merrem]	(Sold) fl 2:15 van Iperen
1802/06/28	AMSCH	0155	*J. Ruysdaal* | Een gezicht op den Damrak, ziende langs het Water, te Amsterdam, gestoffeerd met een menigte Beelden en Scheepen, zonagtig gepenceeld, op Doek | *Mat:* op doek *Size:* hoog 17, breed 16 duim *Loc:* Den Haag, Nederland. Mauritshuis. (803)	Anna Elink	(Sold) fl 105 Gruiter
1802/07/21	HGKAN	0023	*Ruysdaal* | Een dito [Schildery], zynde en Landschap en Waterval, door Ruysdaal, in zwarte Lyst		(Unknown)
1802/08/24	LNDLS	0058	*J. Ruysdael* | Langs een Duinächtigen weg, ziet men een Zee-Dorp met Kerk en Tooren en veele Huizen, verders rijdende Wagens, en wandelend Volk op den Voorgrond, in het verschiet een Zee met Schepen. Door denzelven [J. Ruysdael], 1667 | *Mat:* op doek *Size:* hoog 25, breed 30 duimen *Inscr:* 1667 (dated?) *Notes:* It is unclear whether the date is inscribed on the painting.	Leonardus Bouman [or others]	(Unknown) fl 12:10
802/09/06	AMSCH	0094	*J. Ruisdaal* | Een Boomryk Landschap langs een weg, op de voorgrond een stil water, by een gedeelte van een Vestmuur, waar by twee hengelaars; alles zeer natuurlyk en van een meesterlyke penceel-behandeling | *Mat:* op doek *Size:* hoog 15 ½, breed 18 duim	H[n] Smit	(Sold) fl 97 Gruiter

1802/09/29	AMSCH	0047	*J. Ruysdael* | Een Landschap met Waterval, hoog 41, breed 49 ½ duim. Doek. Men ziet in dit Capitaale Schildery, een der schoonste Schouwtooneelen der Natuur verbeeld, eenen Steerrots, waar tusschen Water vloeit, en waar over eenen houten Brug, daar Landlieden met een Hond over gaan, is met een menigte onderscheidene Boomen beplant; aan den linker zyde ziet men tusschen het gebergten eenen Weg, waar twee Landlieden op en af komen; in de laagte by een afgekapten Boom zyn eenige Schaapen; verders klein Houtgewas, het welk zig voor het grootst gedeelte in het Water spiegelt; dit alles beschouwt men tegen eenen schoon bewolkten helderen Lucht. De Penceelbehandling is van de beste van deezen beroemden Meester, en alles evenaart de natuur [Un Tableau capital de ce Peintre et de cette belle qualité qui le distingue. Il offre un des spectacles les plus majestueux de la nature, des Rocs escarpés & couverts d'arbres & d'arbrisseaux de diffétentes [sic] especes, une chûte d'Eau, en sont le sujet principal ; un pont pittoresque placé sur la roche est occupé d'un Homme & d'une Femme qui le passent avec un chien. Il conduit à gauche vers un chemin entre des arbres & taillé dans le Roc, ou l'on remarque deux villageois qui se rencontrent. Au bas du Rocher paissent quelques moutons près de l'eau et d'un arbre rompu & terrassé par la Tempète. Ces objets vraiment admirables, de la représentation desquels notre artiste faisoit son sort, se détachent d'un ciel clair & couvert des plus beaux nuages.] | *Mat:* op doek *Size:* hoog 41, breed 49 ½ duim	[Labouchere?]	(Sold) fl 300 Gruyter
1802/09/29	AMSCH	0048	*J. Ruysdael* | Een Landschap, hoog 14 ½, breed 12 ½ duim. Doek. Zynde een uitgestrekt Wintergezigt, over den Weg ter zyde derzelve afgekapte Boomen; Boere Wooningen, eenige Huislieden die Hout verzamelen en anderen; de qualityt is van het fynste penceel van deezen Meester; de ordenantie is zeer fraay, en van een bevallig Effect [Un petit Tableau, d'un Effet piquant & vrai offre un Hyver traité avec un art extraordinaire, des chaumieres une Treille, un reste de Chateau & des arbres, sont placés en decà & audela du grand chemin, ou l'on voit des Bucherons amasser du bois, près de quelques arbres renversés. Le ciel couvert laisse échapper une Lumiere qui éclaire agréablement cette charmante composition, le faire en est de cette belle qualité qui caractérise les plus précieux ouvrages de ce peintre célébre.] | *Mat:* op doek *Size:* hoog 14 ½, breed 12 ½ duim	[Labouchere?]	(Sold) fl 530 Th^{s} Spaan
1803/07/18	AMSCH	0039	*Ruysdaal. (Jacob)* | Een Boomryk Landschap met verscheide Gebouwen en een stille Rivier, waarby een Watermolen, zeer bevallig van ligt en bruin en van een aangenaame penceelsbehandeling [Auprès d'un ruisseau clair coulant aux pieds de gros arbres de differente espèce, d'une forme heureuse & pittoresque, l'on voit percer des habitations ; d'autres demeures se dintinguent [sic] à la gauche dans une partie eclairée & produisant un effet piquant. La force & la verité repandues dans ce paysage, la légereté des oppositions, une touche & une couleur excellentes le feront gouter au vrai connoisseur.] | *Mat:* op paneel *Size:* hoog 17, breed 21 duim	Maria Theresia Andrioli	(Sold) fl 242 Josi
1803/08/24	HGKAN	0045	*J. Ruisdaal* | Twee stuks Lantschappen met hoog Geboomte doorsneeden met een stil water gestoffeerd met staand en rustend Vee, Meesterlyk gepenseeld, en van de beste Schildering | *Mat:* op paneel *Size:* hoog 21, breet 16 duim	[Teissier] [or others]	(Sold) fl 38 Kan
1803/09/07	AMSCH	0142	*J. Ruisdaal* | Dit uitmuntend Schildery is een Noords Berg, en Boomryk Landschap, met een breede op de voorgrond nederstortende Waterval, op het Gebergte eenige stoffagie van Beeldjes en Schaapen; de Natuur kan niet beeter uitgedrukt worden, als in dit Stuk, 't welk meesterlyk door J. Ruisdaal geschilderd is [Ce tableau présente un riant paysage varié d'arbres et de collines, ayant sur le devant une cascade qui se précipite en torrent dans un vallon ; sur la pente et le sommet des montagnes bondissent des moutons, et différentes figures artistement distribuées ; c'est l'aspect vivant de la belle nature, la composition et le coloris en sont admirables] | *Mat:* op doek *Size:* hoog 24, breed 31 duim	Smidt	(Bought In) fl 700
1803/09/07	AMSCH	0143	*J. Ruisdaal* | Een Boom- en Bergachtig Landschap, gestoffeerd met een Jager, Houthakker en een Hond; Natuurlyk en fix behandeld [Un paysage avec des montagnes et des arbres, animé par quelques figures représentant un chasseur, un bucheron et un chien ; peint au naturel et d'un coloris frais] | *Mat:* op doek *Size:* hoog 22, breed 28 duim	Smidt	(Bought In) fl 165
1803/09/07	AMSCH	0144	*J. Ruisdaal* | Een Boomryk Landschap, op de Voorgrond een Waterval, verders eenige Beeldjes, benevens twee Ezels, een Hond, enz.; meesterlyk en fray van behandeling [Une vue de paysage, sur le devant une cascade ; dans le fond plusieurs figures, un âne, un chien etc. composition admirable, exécution soignée] | *Mat:* op doek *Size:* hoog 24, breed 23 duim	Smidt	(Sold) fl 54 Haffner
1803/12/12	AMSCH	0078	*Jacob Ruysdaal* | Een Landschap, ter linker zyde een opgaande Weg, met hoog Geboomten, waar by een Woning die kragtig door de Zon verlicht wordt, op de grond een stil Water, waar by een Huisman en een Hond; alles is fix en uitvoerig geschilderd, krachtig van coloriet, als Hobbema gepenceeld | *Mat:* op paneel *Size:* hoog 21, breed 26 duim	B	(Sold) fl 170 V^{n} Iperen
1804/05/07	AMSCH	0140	*Ruisdaal (J.)* | In dit zoo bevallig als aangenaam Boomryk Landschap, ziet men op de voorgrond by een Waterval, een omgevalle dikke Boom, verders in een Laan, onder hoog Geboomte, twee Hoeders met twee belaaden Ezels en een Hond, waarachter een Boerin, ter zyde een Weg	Vinkeles [for] H[affner]	(Sold) fl 28 wed Achtienhoven

			waar een Heer te Paard, ziende na eenige Huizen, dit Schildery is uitvoerig en zonachtig gepenceeld en van de beste schilderiag [sic] van deeze Meester | *Mat:* op doek *Size:* hoog 24, breed 23 duim		
1804/05/07	AMSCH	0140a[H]	*Ruisdaal (J.)* | 1 Schildery | *Notes:* This lot was added in by hand in the EBNP, LBDa and RKDH copies of the catalogue.	Vinkeles [for] G	(Sold) fl 25 Coclers
1804/07/25	DLGRO	0004	*J. Ruysdaal* | Een Winter gezicht langs de Vest, waarop een Molen geplaatst is ziet men een Poort, op den voorgrond eenige Beeldjes, meesterlyk gepenceeld door J. Ruysdaal | *Mat:* op doek *Size:* hoog 16, breed 19 duim	Mr Franc van der Burch Wz.	(Unknown)
1804/07/25	DLGRO	0092	*J. Ruisdaal* | Een Boomryk Landschap, verbeeldende een Harte Jagt, zeer natuurlyk en fraai geschilderd | *Mat:* op doek *Size:* hoog 17 ½, breed 22 ½ duim	Mr Franc van der Burch Wz.	(Unknown)
1804/08/08	AMSCH	0160	*J. Ruisdaal* | In een Boschachtig Landschap, ter zyde eenige Gebouwen, onder het Geboomte, ziet men een wandelende Heer en Dame, verders een Man te Paard, op de voorgrond langs de met Riet bewassen kant van een klaar spiegelend Water, zit een Man te visschen; zonachtig en uitvoerig geschilderd | *Mat:* op paneel *Size:* hoog 14 ½, breed 12 duim	Vink[eles] [for] K[=Gruyter?]	(Bought In) fl 6
1804/08/08	AMSCH	0161	*J. Ruisdaal* | Een Boomryk Dorpgezicht, met een stil Water, waarin het licht der Maan een aartige werking doet, gestoffeerd met Visschers; zeer natuurlyk op Doek | *Mat:* op doek *Size:* hoog 21, breed 24 duim	Roos a	(Bought In) fl 32
1804/10/16	DLOND	0191	*Jacob Ruysdaal* | Een Bosch, doorsneden met enen breden weg, een Man te Paerd en verder Bywerk. Un Chemin large dans un Bois, on y voit un Homme a Cheval & d'autres figures | *Size:* hoog 24, breed 24		(Unknown)
1804/10/16	DLOND	0192	*Jacob Ruysdaal* | Een Landschap (dus getekend). Paysage (marqué tel) | *Mat:* op paneel *Size:* hoog 18, breed 24 *Inscr:* Jacob Ruysdaal (signed)		(Unknown)
1804/10/29	HRBAU	0084	*Ruisdael, (J.)* | In dit capitaal Boschgezicht ziet men vooraan een Kudde Beesten, benevens een Vrouwtjen, die op een Ezel zit, welke door een' Man door een Beekjen gedreeven worden. De doorschietende zonlichten doen in dit Stuk een goed effect, en alles is meesterlyk behandeld | *Mat:* op paneel *Size:* hoog 34, breed 45 duim	Simon Styl	(Unknown)
1804/10/29	HRBAU	0085	*Ruisdael, (J.)* | Een fraai Meirgezigt, gestoffeerd met een' Visscher, welke bezig is te visschen, benevens nog eenige Vaartuigjens, en in het verschiet een Wal. Het licht doet eene goede uitwerking, en is uitvoerig behandeld | *Mat:* op doek *Size:* hoog 20, breed 26 duim	Simon Styl	(Unknown)
1804/10/29	HRBAU	0086	*Ruisdael, (J.)* | Een boschagtig Landschapjen, waar in, voor aan, in een Watertjen eenige Visschers in hun schuitjen bezig zyn met visschen; met een fraai verschiet. Uitvoerig behandeld | *Mat:* op paneel *Size:* hoog 9 ½, breed 12 duim	Simon Styl	(Unknown)
1804/10/29	HRBAU	0087	*Ruisdael, (J.)* | Is mede een boschagtig Landschapjen, waar voor aan eenige Beestjens door een Beekjen gedreven worden. Niet minder dan het voorige behandeld | *Mat:* op paneel *Size:* hoog 9 ½, breed 12 duim	Simon Styl	(Unknown)
1805/07/03	AMSCH	0035	*Ruisdaal. (J.)* | Een Capitaal Boom- en Bergachtig Landschap, met een Klooster op een Heuvel staande, waarby eenige Beeldjes, benéden deezen heuvel loopt een Rivier, welken zich op de Voorgrond tusschen Rotsen met geweld ontlast; en daardoor een schilderachtigen Waterval veroorzaakt, de dunheid van lucht en water in dit Tafreel is in alles zoo schoon als de behandeling zelve | *Mat:* op doek *Size:* hoog 27, breed 21 duim	R[oos]	(Sold) fl 750 Josi
1805/07/03	AMSCH	0036	*Ruisdaal. (J.)* | Dit Tafreel ryker van Geboomten, vertoond mede een niet minder fraai geval als het voorgaande, en is insgelyks op de Voorgrond met een uitmuntende Waterval voorzien; en in alles behandeld als de voorgaande | companion to lot 37 *Mat:* op doek *Size:* hoog 26, breed 21 duim	G	(Sold) fl 1500 for lots 36 & 37. Coclers
1805/07/03	AMSCH	0037	*Ruisdaal. (J.)* | De wederga van de voorgaande steld voor: een Bosch-gezigt met een Rivier doorsneeden, welke zich mede op de Voorgrond door Heuvels verspreid; zynde meede als de voorgaande zeer fraai gepenceeld | companion to lot 36 *Mat:* op doek *Size:* hoog 26, breed 21 duim	G	(Sold) fl 1500 for lots 36 & 37. Coclers
1805/07/03	AMSCH	0038	*Ruisdaal. (J.)* | Dit uitmuntend Tafreel steld voor: een groot Heuvelachtig Bosch, met een helder Water doorsneeden, waarover een Vonder van hout en paalwerk: geestig gestoffeerd met Reisigers te paard en te voet; dit schildery, alschoon 'er geen Waterval in zynde, behoefd in fraaiheid niet voor de voorige te wyken | *Mat:* op doek *Size:* hoog 24, breed 32 duim	C	(Sold) fl 600 C S Roos
1805/07/10	AMSCH	0122	*J. Ruisdaal* | Een gezicht van de Duinen te Overveen, ziende over Blékeryen op de Stad Haarlem, gestoffeerd met verscheide Beldjes [sic]; de lucht is dun, en de welgeplaatste Wolkschaduwen maken dit stuk tot een der beste van J. Ruisdaal | *Mat:* op doek *Size:* hoog 21, breed 29 duim	R[oos]	(Bought In) fl 322
1805/10/09	HGBSM	0054	*J. Ruisdaal* | Een boomryk landschap, met stoffagie, gemerk J. Ruisdaal | *Mat:* op doek *Size:* hoog 30 breet 37 duim *Inscr:* J. Ruisdaal (signed)	T H van Willigen [or others]	(Sold) fl 1:12 Van Giesen
1806/05/05	AMSCH	0120	*J. Ruisdaal* | Een boom en heuvelachtig Landschap aan een Sloot, met fraaije Geboomten, Boeren Woningen en stoffagie van Beelden; uitvoerig en zonachtig door J. Ruisdaal | *Mat:* op paneel *Size:* hoog 21, breed 26 duim	R[oos]	(Bought In) fl 102

1806/05/05	AMSCH	0121	*J. Ruisdaal* | Een capitaal gezicht buiten Haarlem, na Duin te zien, naar Linnen en Gaaren Bleekeryen en verscheiden Woningen, gestoffeerd met Beeldjes, in 't verschiet de Stad Haarlem; natuurlyk, bevallig en fraai gepenceeld door denzelven [J. Ruisdaal] | *Mat:* op doek *Size:* hoog 25, breed 39 duim	E	(Sold) fl 81 Josi
1806/05/05	AMSCH	0121a	*J. Ruysdaal* | In een heuvelachtig Landschap, met verscheiden Geboomten, by een Boeren Woning, vertoont zig op den voorgrond, een rustend Man en Vrouw; verders gaande Huislieden; meesterlyk en fiks van Penceel behandeling op Paneel | *Mat:* op paneel *Size:* hoog 24, breed 33 duim	S[chley]	(Bought In) fl 28
1806/06/07	RMHSN	0001	*J. Ruisdaal* | Een kapitaal Rhyngezicht, ryk van Gebouwen en Bywerk, helder en kragtig geschilderd, door J. Ruisdaal, op Doek, Vergulde Lyst | *Mat:* op doek	A E K L	(Unknown)
1806/11/24	AMSCH	0059	*Ruisdaal (J.)* | Een Landschap met wélig Geboomte, doorsneden van Water; een ryziger op een Ezel, Herders met Schapen enz. ; van een fyne penceelsbehandeling | *Mat:* op paneel *Size:* hoog 19, breed 25 duim	Munnikhuizen	(Sold) fl 20:10 Gruiter
1806/11/24	AMSCH	0060	*Ruisdaal (J.)* | Een Boschgezigt, op de Voorgrond een Waterval, gestoffeerd met Herders met hunne Schapen ; kragtig van licht, en bruin en kloek gepenceeld | *Mat:* op doek *Size:* hoog 26, breed 19 duim	Munnikhuizen	(Sold) fl 12:10 Gruiter
1807/06/02	AMHUY	0018	*J. Ruysdaal* | Een fraai Landschap met hoog Geboomte, gestoffeerd met verscheide gaande en leggende Beeldjes, uitvoerig geschilderd		(Unknown)
1807/08/26	AMSCH	0186	*J. Ruysdaal* | Een Dorpgezicht met hoog Geboomten, Boeren Woningen met stoffage van Beeldjes, aan een stil Water, waarin het schynsel der Maan een fraaije werking doet; zynde het eenigste bekende Maanlicht, en van de beste schildering | *Mat:* op doek *Size:* hoog 21, breed 24 duim	Roos	(Sold) fl 17 H Jansen
1807/08/26	AMSCH	0187	*J. Ruysdaal* | Een zeer natuurlyk Land- en Watergezicht, op den voorgrond met staande en leggende Beesten by een stil Water, voorts twee dryvende Schepen, en ter zyde op Gebergten een Postwagen en andere stoffage | *Mat:* op paneel *Size:* hoog 16, breed 24 duim	de Vries	(Sold) fl 3:10 A Rynders
1807/08/26	AMSCH	0188	*J. Ruysdaal* | Een Boschachtig Landschap, waar in Rovers naar eenige Heeren te Paard schieten, en verder een natuurlyk verschiet | *Mat:* op paneel *Size:* hoog 13, breed 20 duim	de Vries	(Sold) fl 1:15 Coclair
1808/04/26	GDAN	0140	*Ruisdaal (Jacob)* | Een Burgt en Ruïne, zeer fraai gestoffeerd, in 't land een pissend Bokje | *Mat:* op paneel *Size:* hoog 13 ½, breed 12 ½ duim	G H Fortuyn	(Unknown)
1808/04/26	GDAN	0141	*Ruisdaal, (Jacob)* | Een Bosägtig Landschap, met uitmuntend hoog Geboomte, wrar [sic] in eenige Jagers te Paard en eenige Honden | *Size:* hoog 17, breed 25 duim	G H Fortuyn	(Unknown)
1808/04/26	GDAN	A0004	*J Ruijsdaal* | Een Landschapje | *Size:* hoog 16, breed 21 duim *Notes:* This lot has been renumbered to distinguish it from another lot with the same number in a different section of the catalogue.	G H Fortuyn	(Unknown)
1808/06/06	RMRIJ	0108	*Ruijsdael. (Jacob)* | Een Zee- Strand- en Duingezigt met eenige Vaartuigen. Op den voorgrond ziet men verscheidene Heeren en Dames door en langs het water wandelen. Rijk van stoffagie, schoon van lucht, en uitmuntend van toon [Vue de la Mer du Nord, qui baigne la Hollande. On y voit plusieurs bateaux à la voile, et differents Groupes de figures qui se promenent dans l'eau. Le Rivage represente une partie des dunes décorée de plusieurs figures. Un Ciel où l'on voit les Nuages Savamment peints, un ton vrai et agréable, tout cela forme un Ensemble rare et précieux] | *Mat:* op doek *Size:* Hoog 19 ½, en breed 24 duim. *Loc:* Den Haag, Nederland. Mauritshuis. (154) as copy after J. van Ruisdael	Gerrit van der Pot, Heer van Groeneveld	(Sold) fl 1165 Johs Eck en Zoon [for] le Roi
1808/06/13	AMSCH	0128	*Ruisdaal (J.)* | Twee Gezichten binnen Amsterdam, verbeeldende de Waag, den Dam, Dammerak, het begin van de Vischmarkt, en het Water; vol Stoffage van Beelden, Heeren en Jufvrouwen, Koopvrouwen, Schepen, enz. Zonachtig en uitvoerig. Zijnde zulke Stadgezichten van dezen Meester zeldzaam | *Size:* ieder hoog 21, breed 26 duim *Loc:* Berlin, Deutschland. Gemäldegalerie. (885D) and Rotterdam, Nederland. Museum Boymans-Van Beuningen. (1744)	W	(Sold) fl 260 Nieuwenhuys pour Henry
1808/06/13	AMSCH	0129	*Ruisdaal (J.)* | Een besneeuwde Winter, ter zijde een Scheprad-Molen, en een Dorp in het verschiet. Geestig gestoffeerd, en van een meesterlijke penceelsbehandeling | *Mat:* op doek *Size:* hoog 21, breed 26 duim	R[oos]	(Sold) fl 285 Du Pre
1808/06/13	AMSCH	0130	*Ruisdaal (J.)* | In een bevallig boomrijk Landschap vertoonen zich bij een Valbrug eenige Werklieden, bezig een Steenen Huis te bouwen. Alles Natuurlijk en meesterlijk fraai gepenceelt | *Mat:* op paneel *Size:* hoog 12 ½, breed 13 ½ duim	[Jan Tersteeg]	(Sold) fl 30 Gruiter
1808/07/19	AMROU	0001	*Jacob Ruysdaal* | 1 Boomryk Landschap buiten Haarlem, op de voorgrond ziet men op een Bleekery en eenige vervalle Huisjes, rykgestoffeerd		(Unknown)
1808/08/23	AMSCH	0135	*Ruisdaal. (J.)* | In een boschachtig Landschap, ziet men onder het Geboomte een wandelende Heer en Dame, en een Man te Paard, op de voorgrond aan de kant van een spiegelend Water, zit een Man te visschen; zonachtig en fraai behandeld | *Mat:* op paneel *Size:* hoog 14, breed 12 duim	[Gruyter?]	(Sold) fl 20 D Maijkel
1808/08/23	AMSCH	0135a[H]	*Ruisdaal. (J.)* | Een land. door id. [Ruisdaal J.] panneel | *Mat:* op paneel *Notes:* This lot was added in by hand in the EBNP and FLNY copies of the catalogue.	[Van Iperen?]	(Sold) fl 75 Coclers

1808/08/23	AMSCH	0135b[H]	*Ruisdaal. (J.)* | Een land. als Verboom | *Notes:* This lot was added in by hand in the EBNP and FLNY copies of the catalogue.	[Van Iperen?]	(Sold) fl 50 Tiessier
1808/08/23	AMSCH	0136	*Ruisdaal. (J.)* | Twee stuks Boschgezichten, beide met verscheide Beeldjes gestoffeerd; natuurlijk geschilderd | *Mat:* op paneel *Size:* Ieder hoog 15, breed 12 duim	[Coclers]	(Sold) fl 50 Hulswit [or] Wistenberg
1808/08/23	AMSCH	0136a[H]	*Ruisdaal. (J.)* | 1 dito [stuk] dito [Boschgezichten] | *Notes:* This lot was added in by hand in the EBNP and FLNY copies of the catalogue. It is unclear what "dito" refers to in the title.	[Van Iperen?]	(Bought In) fl 19:10
1808/08/23	AMSCH	0136b[H]	*Ruisdaal. (J.)* | 1 dito [stuk] dito [Boschgezichten] | *Notes:* This lot was added in by hand in the EBNP copy of the catalogue. It is unclear what "dito" refers to in the title.	[Van Iperen?]	(Sold) fl 225 Gruiter
1808/10/28	AMVRS	0052	*Ruisdaal, (J.)* | In een Landschap met Geboomte, ziet men langs een weg eene rustende Vrouw, met een Kind op de Schoot, waarbij een staand Huisman, verders eenig Vee. Het licht doet in dit schilderij eene bevallige werking | *Mat:* op paneel *Size:* hoog 27, breed 21 duim	Marten Udink	(Sold) fl 30 T Spaan
1809/04/17	AMSCH	0078	*J. Ruisdaal* | Dit fraaije Cabinetstukje verbeeld een boomrijk Landschap, met een stil Water, gestoffeerd met twee Hengelaars en andere Voorwerpen en een bevallig verschiet; het verschillend Geboomte is allernatuurlijkst, het dun en spiegelend Water en de bewolkte Lucht, alles evenaart de Natuur en is van een uitvoerige Penceelbehandeling | *Mat:* op doek *Size:* hoog 16, breed 21 duim	C	(Sold) fl 275
1809/04/17	AMSCH	0080	*J. Ruisdaal* | Een besneeuwd Wintergezicht, met Boeren Woningen en Hoog Geboomte, gestoffeerd met gaande en rustende Landlieden, uitvoerig en fraai gepenceeld | *Mat:* op doek *Size:* hoog 15, breed 12 duim	[Gruyter?]	(Sold or Bought In) fl 43
1809/06/13	AMSCH	0130	*J. Ruisdaal* | Een Landschap met hoog opgaand Geboomten, Kreupelgewas en heldere Waterplassen, gestoffeerd met Herders bij Schaapen, Landlieden, op Ezels en verdere Figuuren; meesterlijk en natuurlijk gepenceeld | *Mat:* op paneel *Size:* hoog 18, breed 24 duim	[Gruyter?]	(Bought In) fl 21
1809/07/19	AMSCH	[A0006][H]	*J Ruysdaal* | 1 Land[schap] | *Notes:* This lot was added in by hand in the AA copy of the catalogue. Because it was not numbered, we have assigned the number.		(Unknown)
1809/07/19	AMSCH	0047	*Ruisdaal (J.)* | Dit uitmuntend Kabinetstukje vertoont een natuurlijk Land- en Watergezicht, op een Heuvel met Boere-Woning en Geboomten ziet men een Koorenmolen, en in het stil Water een Visser in zijn Schuit, verder een bevallig verschiet. Alles evenaart de natuur, het aangenaam zonlicht, het koloriet en de uitvoerige penceelsbehandeling maken dit voorwerp tot een der fraaiste van dezen beroemden Meester | *Mat:* op paneel *Size:* hoog 10, breed 14 duim	[Bicker]	(Sold) fl 630 J[c[?]] de Vos
1810/03/27	RMCNL	0050	*J. Ruisdaal* | Een Landschapje, zeer fraai en uitvoerig geschilderd		(Unknown)
1810/03/27	RMCNL	0088	*J. Ruisdaal* | Een Kapitaal Schilderij, voorstelleude [sic] een stil Water, waarin men kleine Schepen ziet, als mede een Pond, waarmede Koebeesten worden overgevoerd, zeer schoon behandeld, bij uitnemenheid fraaij van Penseel		(Unknown)
1810/07/26	AMSCH	0075	*Ruisdaal (J)* | Een Landschap, met Woningen, Geboomte en een Korenakker. Natuurlijk verbeeld | *Mat:* op doek *Size:* hoog 9, breed 13 duimen	Cassino	(Sold) fl 9 Spaan
1810/08/01	AMSCH	0085	*Ruisdaal (Jacob)* | Een heuvelachtig Landschap met eenen Korenakker bij eene Kerk en Geboomte; in het midden eene Rivier, welke op den voorgrond tusschen aarden Kluiten nederstort; het is verlevendigd door eenen Herder en eenige Schapen [Un Paysage coupé par des monticules, dans lequel on distingue un Champ de bled. Au milieu vient couler une Riviere qui se brise entre des mottes de terre sur le devant du Tableau. Il est orné par un Berger et quelques Moutons] | possibly companion to lot 86 *Annots:* Bon. (NGW); Vente du 4 avril 1811 a Paris chez lebrun no.91. fr: 3180 (SMLN) *Mat:* op doek *Size:* hoog 26, breed 21 duimen	Mr Pieter de Smeth van Alphen	(Sold) fl 710 Texier, Gerbet en Comp [for] LeBrun
1810/08/01	AMSCH	0086	*Ruisdaal (Jacob)* | Een bergachtig Landschap, met een Kasteel en Geboomte op eene Hoogte, op den voorgrond een omgevallen Boom en sterk stroomend Water; het is gestoffeerd met eenen Herder en Schapen. Kunnende strekken tot eene wederga van de voorgaande [Un Paysage montueux : On y trouve un Chateau sur une colline et des grands arbres. Au premier plan se voit une large cascade d'eau et un vieux tronc d'arbre renversé ; il est embelli de plus d'un Berger gardant des Moutons. Ce Tableau peut faire pendant au précédent] | possibly companion to lot 85 *Annots:* Bon. (NGW) *Mat:* op doek *Size:* hoog 26, breed 21 duimen *Loc:* Amsterdam, Nederland. Rijksmuseum. (A347) as Castle of Bentheim	Mr Pieter de Smeth van Alphen	(Sold) fl 740 Coclers
1810/08/01	AMSCH	0087	*Ruisdaal (Jacob)* | Een boomrijk en bergachtig Landschap, met een nederstortend Water op den voorgrond, ter zijde op eenen Heuvel een Herder met zijne Kudde [Paysage richement boisé, coupé par des monticules, au travers desquels vient se briser une large Cascade d'eau jusqu'au premier Plan ; sur une eminance de côté est une Pâtre menent son troupeau] | *Annots:* Bon. (NGW); Vente du 4 avril 1811 chez lebrun No.90 pour francs 2601 (SMLN) *Mat:* op doek *Size:* hoog 20, breed 24 duimen	Mr Pieter de Smeth van Alphen	(Sold) fl 710 Texier, Gerbet en Comp [for] LeBrun

1810/08/01	AMSCH	0088	*Ruisdaal (Jacob)* | Een besneeuwd Wintergezigt, met Boerenwoningen en een groot Gebouw bij Geboomte, voorzien van Houthakkers en andere voorwerpen [Paysage representé en Hyver, couvert de Neige ; il est garni de chaumieres et d'une grand batiment adossé à une masse d'arbres. Les figures sont des Bucherons et d'autres objets] | *Annots:* Passable. (NGW) *Mat:* op doek *Size:* hoog 14 ½, breed 12 ½ duimen	Mr Pieter de Smeth van Alphen	(Sold) fl 400 T Spaan [for] Croes
1810/08/01	AMSCH	0089	*Ruisdaal (Jacob)* | Een boschachtig Landschap, met een opgaanden Weg, gaande en rustende Huislieden en eene Boerenwoning in het verschiet [Un Paysage indiquant une entrée de foret, varié par une route et differentes figures : on y trouve une chaumiere vèrs le fond] | *Annots:* Bon. (NGW); Vente du 4 avril 1811 chez lebrun No.93 francs 800 (SMLN) *Mat:* op paneel *Size:* hoog 13, breed 12 duimen	Mr Pieter de Smeth van Alphen	(Sold) fl 330 Texier, Gerbet en Comp [for] LeBrun
1810/08/06	AMSCH	0089	*Ruisdaal (J)* | Een aangenaam Boomrijk Landschap, met een breed stroomend Water, het welk zig op den voorgrond ontlast, ter zijde bij een opgaande weg een staand en zittend Huisman; alles evenaart de natuur, het is uitvoerig van penceelsbehandeling | *Mat:* op doek *Size:* hoog 23, breed 26 duimen	A	(Sold) fl 700 Texier Gerbet en Comp
1810/08/06	AMSCH	0134	*J. Ruisdaal* | Een Boomrijk Landschap: op den voorgrond een Waterplas, waarbij een Boer met een Hond, ter zijde een Koornakker en Boeren Woningen. Fraai van licht, en bruin en delikaat behandeld | *Mat:* op doek *Size:* hoog 25, breed 33 duimen		(Withdrawn)
1810/08/10	RMRIJ	0005	*Jacob Ruisdaal* | Een Zeestrand, met een aantal Figuren. Dun, helder, en aangenaam van couleur | *Mat:* op doek *Size:* hoog 18 ½ duim, breed 24 ½ duim		(Sold) fl 20 [or] 108 de Kok
1810/10/10	MGCIT	0063	*J. Ruysdaal* | Een kapitaal Stuk, zynde een zeer fraai Boschgezigt, bestaande uit matig hoog alsmede laag Geboomte, gelyk ook eenige op de voorgrond liggende Stammen van Boomen, Heesters en Gewassen; wyders een uitgestrekt duinachtig Verschiet, Gebergten en twee malende Windmolens; voorts naar den aart en aanleg van het Stuk behoorlyk gestoffeerd, en in allen opzigte zeer schoon en uitvoerig behandeld	Caspar van Citters	(Unknown)
1810/10/11	AMSCH	0167	*J. Ruisdaal* | Een natuurlijk Wintergezigt, met Woningen, Geboomte en stoffagie van Beeldjes | *Mat:* op paneel	[Levy Pakker?]	(Sold) fl 10 van Leen
1810/10/13	HGDAW	0001	*J. Ruysdaal* | Een Bergachtig Landschap met Geboomte, in 't midden een Water, waar eenig Vee door een Herder werd gedreven, zeer helder en aangenaam behandeld | *Mat:* op koper *Size:* hoog 7 ¾, breed 11 duim		(Unknown)

Ruisdael, Jacob van (and Borch, G. ter (II))

1803/08/17	AMSCH	0072	*Ruysdaal (J.); G. Terburg* | Een gezicht van de Dam, op het Damrak en Water te Amsterdam, te zien, het Water vol Scheepen en den Dam ryk van Beeldjes, door G. Terburg gestoffeerd, het ligt en bruin is frappant, en is voorts van de beste behandeling van dezen Meester | *Mat:* op doek *Size:* hoog 21, breed 29 duim	Anna Catharina Putman	(Sold) fl 76 W Reijers

Ruisdael, Jacob van (and Lingelbach)

1808/11/28	AMSCH	0053	*J. Ruijsdaal; J. Lingelbach* | Een Duinachtig Landschap, met opgaand Geboomte en dartel Kreupelgewas, ziende van de Duinen over de Linnebleekerijen op de Stad Haarlem, gestoffeerd op de voorgrond met een Jager met zijn Honden, verders gaande Arbeiders en rustende Reizigers, zonagtig en natuurlijk gepenceel, op Paneel, door J. Ruijsdaal en gestoffeerd door J. Lingelbach | *Mat:* op paneel *Size:* hoog 16, breed 14 duim	[Gruyter?]	(Bought In) fl 83
1810/03/26	RMMUY	0033	*Jacob Ruisdaal; J. Lingelbach* | Een Geldersch Landschap, verbeeldende eene uitgestrekte Vlakte, van een Hoogte te zien, doorsneden met water en verrijkt met Ruïnen, Dorpen en Gehuchten. Eene wolkrijke lucht, waar het zonlicht hier en daar doorstralende, aangename en piquante partijen van licht en schaduwen veroorzaakt; rijk gestoffeerd met Beelden en Beestjes door J. Lingelbach [Un Paysage après nature ; vue d'oiseaux d'une grande étenduë, plat pays, coupé par des eaux qui y serpentent ; plusieurs viilages [sic], ruïnes et chaumières, se découvrent de distance en distance, un beau ciel bien nuagé, et une distribution savante des clairs et des ombres, forment un ensemble piquant et agréable. Les figures sont peintes par Lingelbach.] | *Mat:* op doek *Size:* hoog 24 ½, breed 29 ½ duimen	Daniel de Jongh Az	(Sold) fl 360 A van Beeftingh

Ruisdael, Jacob van (and Velde, A.)

1808/06/13	AMSCH	0126	*Ruisdaal (J.); A. van de Velde* | Een Gezicht op het Dorp Scheveningen, het Strand gestoffeerd met eene menigte Heeren, Dames, Visschers, Honden, enz., verder Pinken, en op Zee eenige zeilende Vaartuigen. De verbolgene lucht doet hier eene schoone uitwerking van licht en donker, zijnde voorts van eene uitmuntende penceelsbehandeling | *Mat:* op doek *Size:* hoog 40, breed 62 duim	R[oos]	(Bought In) fl 580
1808/06/13	AMSCH	0127	*Ruisdaal (J.); A. van de Velde* | Deze heerlijke Ordonantie verbeeld een bergachtig Landschap, waarin eene Waterval, waarbij een Herder en Herderin, en eenig liggend Vee. Zonachtig en natuurlijk van schildering | *Mat:* op doek *Size:* hoog 43, breed 59 duim	E M Engelberts	(Sold) fl 61 Nieuwenhuys pour Henry

Ruisdael, Jacob van (and Wouwerman, Ph.)

1804/08/08	AMSCH	0159	*J. Ruisdaal; Wouwerman* | In een Landschap met hoog Geboomte ziet men langs een Weg een heldere Rivier, waarin een Reiziger te Paard, waarby een Jongen en een Vrouw, met een Kind op de Rug, ter zyde een Huisman, en verders by eenig Geboomte eenige rustende Lieden, en een Duin- en Boomryk verschiet; zonachtig en uitvoerig gepenceeld | *Mat:* op doek *Size:* hoog 24, breed 31 duim	Vink[eles] [for] W	(Bought In) fl 275
1806/08/13	AMSCH	0154	*Ruysdaal (J.); Ph. Wouwerman* | Dit aangenaam Tafreel, verbeeld een Heuvelachtig Landschap, ter linker zyde een Boerenwoning, op de voorgrond in een Waterplas lopen twee Kinderen, een Man op een Paard gezéten, laat er hetzelve uit drinken, verders langs een opgaande Weg een Ryziger te paard verzeld van een Voetganger met een Hond; terzyde op een Berg ziet men verscheiden Korenschoven staan; welke door een frappant zonlicht beschenen worden; zynde dit fraaije stukje voorts van een delicaate penceelsbehandeling | *Mat:* op doek *Size:* hoog 20, breed 23 duim	Daniel Mansveld	(Sold) fl 505 Hulswit
1809/04/17	AMSCH	0079	*J. Ruisdaal; Ph. Wouwerman* | Dit uitmuntend Schilderij, verbeeld een aangenaam Boomrijk Landschap, in 't midden een heldere Waterplas over de Zandige Weg, waar bij een Man te Paard, eene Vrouw met een Kind en een Jongen, ter zijde een gaande Huisman, ver onder het Geboomte ziet men verscheide gaande en rustende Reizigers, en een Dorptooren in 't verschiet; het invallende zonlicht geeft een natuurlijke werking, het koloriet is krachtig, en voorts van een uitvoerige penceelbehandeling | *Mat:* op doek *Size:* hoog 24, breed 32 duim	T	(Sold) fl 355

Ruisdael, Jacob van (or Decker, C.)

1810/03/26	RMMUY	0019	*C. Dekker; J. Ruisdaal* | Een Heuvelachtig Landschap, met boerenwooningen en hoog geboomte. Op den voorgrond, Boom-stammen, Planten en Kruiden. Krachtig en piquant geschilderd [Un Paysage rustique, plusieurs masures et belles masses d'arbres, des plantes et herbes, forment le devant. Le lointain est agréable ; vigoureusement traîté, et d'une bonne pate, digne de Ruisdaal.] | *Mat:* op paneel *Size:* hoog 18, breed 24 duimen *Notes:* The French edition of the catalogue gives only "C. Dekker" as the artist.	Daniel de Jongh Az	(Sold) fl 50 van Eyk s'Hage

Ruisdael, Jacob van (or Ruisdael, J., manner)

1801/11/10	AMPOS	0004	*Ruisdaal* | 1 gestoffeerd Bosch- en Bergachtig Landschap, door of als Ruisdaal		(Unknown)
1802/06/16	AMSCH	0150	*J. Ruisdaal of in de manier* | Een Heuvelachtig Boomryk Landschap, gestoffeerd met Voetgangers; op de voorgrond eenig Water, helder en bevallig van Penceel | *Mat:* op doek *Size:* hoog 21, breed 24 duim	[Merrem]	(Sold) fl 8 van Iperen
1802/09/06	AMSCH	0239	*J. Ruisdaal* | Een Bergachtig Landschap, op de voorgrond een Waterval tusschen de afgebrokkelde Aardkluyten, omringd van onderscheide Houtegewas, verders een van Hout en Takken gemaakte Brug over het water, en een aangenaam verschiet; bevallig gestoffeerd, zonachtig en frapant van Licht, door of in de manier van J. Ruisdaal | *Mat:* op doek *Size:* hoog 35, breed 46 duim	J	(Sold) fl 43 van Iperen
1807/04/00	LNDLS	0056	*J. Ruysdael* | De woelende Zuiderzee, met verscheide zeilende schepen, de stad Enkhuizen in 't verschiet, konstig geschildert van of in de trant van J. Ruysdael | *Mat:* op doek *Size:* hoog 44, breed 64 duim	[Abraham Delfos] [or others]	(Unknown)
1807/06/10	HGBSM	0056	*J. Ruysdael* | De woelende Zuiderzee, met verscheide zeilende schepen, de stad Enkhuizen in 't verschiet, konstig geschilderd van of in de trant van J. Ruysdael | *Mat:* op doek *Size:* hoog 44, breed 64 duim	Abraham Delfos [or others]	(Sold) fl 6:15 van Breemen
1808/04/26	GDAN	0215	*J Ruysdaal* | Een mooij Landschap, door of in de manier van J Ruysdaal, wel gestoffeerd | *Size:* hoog 13, breed 24 duim	G H Fortuyn	(Unknown)
1808/06/11	RMRIJ	0121	*Jacob Ruisdaal, of in zyn manier* | Een fraai Landschap		(Sold) fl 1:2 V Giesen
1809/04/22	AMYVR	0184	*J. Ruisdaal* | Een Boschgezicht, met stoffagie van Beeldjes; op Doek, door of in de manier van J. Ruisdaal | *Mat:* op doek	de Bruin	(Sold) fl 1:15 du Pree
1810/08/10	RMRIJ	0021	*J. Ruisdaal, of in zijn manier* | Eene onstuimige Zee, Rotsen en Schipbreukelingen. Konstig en meesterlijk behandeld, en van een schoon effect | *Mat:* op doek *Size:* hoog 46 ½ duim, breed 62 ½ duim		(Sold) fl 2:10 [or] 20 v Ryp

Ruisdael, Jacob van (copy after)

1801/03/16	AMSCH	0134	*J. Ruisdaal* | Een Landschap met een Molen, na J. Ruisdaal	K[ip]	(Sold) fl 4:15 Stevens
1802/09/18	RMDRS	0037	*J.B.H. Thier; Ruisdaal* | Een Landschap met Gebergte, een Waterval, en daarby eenige Vissers, na Ruisdaal | copy by B.H. Thier after J. Ruisdael *Annots:* Slegt Copien van Printen (MB) *Size:* hoog 16 ½, breed 21 ½ duim	Casper de Haas	(Unknown) fl 9
1802/12/13	AMSCH	0165	*A. Vermeulen; J. Ruisdaal* | Langs een met Sneeuw bedekte Weg, ter zyde een Sloot en Boere Woning, ziet men eenige gaande en rydende Beeldjes; meesterlyk geschilderd, door A. Vermeulen, na J. Ruisdaal | copy by A. Vermeulen after J. Ruisdael *Mat:* op paneel *Size:* hoog 16, breed 19 duim	Pruyssenaar [for] A	(Sold) fl 35 Coclers
1804/02/27	AMSCH	0108	*Vermeulen (A.); na J. Ruysdaal* | In een natuurlyke Winter, langs een met Sneeuw bedekten Weg, ter zyden een Sloot en Boerewoning ziet men	C	(Sold) fl 36 van Iperen

			eenige gaande en rydende Beeltjes; en verdere stoffage, meesterlyk geschilderd | copy by A. Vermeulen after J. Ruisdael *Mat:* op paneel *Size:* hoog 12, breed 17 duim		
1806/05/05	AMSCH	0122	*A. Vermeulen; J. Ruisdaal* | Een boom en bergagtig Landschap, met een Herder met Schapen, by eene Waterval; na J. Ruisdaal | copy by A. Vermeulen after J. Ruisdael *Mat:* op paneel *Size:* hoog 10, breed 9 duim	V[inkeles]	(Bought In) fl 7
1810/03/23	HAVIN	0046	*Ruysdaal* | Een Landschap, met een Waterval, na Ruysdaal	Rudolf Hendrik de Wetstein [or others]	(Unknown)
1810/03/23	HAVIN	0047	*Ruysdaal* | Een dito [Landschap], met een Watermolen na denzelven [Ruysdaal]	Rudolf Hendrik de Wetstein [or others]	(Unknown)
1810/11/07	UTWLD	0028	*J. Kobell; Ruisdael* | Een Copie van een der Kapitaalste Schilderijen van Ruisdael, verbeeldende een met geweld afkomenden Waterval, welks kracht aangezet word door een stuk Rots dat op onderscheiden kanten doorklieft is, op een verdere afstand ziet men op een duinagtige grond een Kloostergebouw, waaragter eenig geboomt en bergagtig verschiet in een bruine parthij: op een overhellende Rots eenige boomen, alles zeer klaar en kragtig, het water zeer vloeiend en schoon geschilderd door J. Kobell op doek, 2 voet 2 duim hoog, 1 voet 8 duim breed, zwarte Lijst | copy by Jan Kobell (II) after J. Ruisdael *Mat:* op doek *Size:* 2 voet 2 duim hoog, 1 voet 8 duim breed		(Unknown) fl 31
			Ruisdael, Jacob van (manner)		
1801/08/19	AMSCH	0098	*J. Ruysdaal* | Een Boom en Bergachtig Landschap met een Waterval stoffagie; meesterlyk op Doek, in de manier van denzelven [J. Ruysdaal] | *Mat:* op doek *Size:* hoog 37, breed 47 duim	W Wynen	(Sold) fl 47 Hulswit
1801/11/10	AMPOS	0016	*J. Ruisdaal* | 1 dito [Lommeryk Boschgezigt met Reizigers], als door dezelven [J. Ruisdaal] | *Notes:* It is unclear what "dito" refers to in the title.		(Unknown)
1802/08/24	LNDLS	0056	*J. Ruysdael* | Een Boschächtig Landschap, met Gebergte, gestoffeerd met Jagers te paard, en Honden die door een Water het Wild vervolgen. Op paneel, hoog 30, breed 46 duimen, in de trant van J. Ruysdael | *Mat:* op paneel *Size:* hoog 30, breed 46 duimen	Leonardus Bouman [or others]	(Unknown) fl 2
1802/08/24	LNDLS	0057	*J. Ruysdael* | Een Bergächtig Landschap met Geboomte, en konstig gestoffeerd. In de manier van denzelven [J. Ruysdael] | *Mat:* op paneel *Size:* hoog 14 ½, breed 13 ½ duimen	Leonardus Bouman [or others]	(Unknown) fl 14:10
1802/09/21	UTHDG	0077	*J. Ruisdaal* | Een boomrijk Landschap, vooraan een opgaande zandweg, waarop een Wagen en een Reiziger te voet. Het snelle zonlicht doet op deeze partij een schoone werking tegens het lager leggend sombre Bosch, door welk de weg vervolgd; natuurlijk geschildert als van J. Ruisdaal | *Mat:* op paneel *Size:* hoog 31, breed 40 duimen		(Bought In) fl 70
1805/10/09	HGBSM	0022	*J. Ruysdael* | Een bergagtig landschap, met een rivier, gestoffeerd met eenig vee, in de manier van J. Ruysdaal | *Mat:* op paneel *Size:* hoog 33 breet 44 duim	T H van Willigen [or others]	(Sold) fl 3:5 van Giesen
1808/04/26	GDAN	0241	*Ruysdaal* | Een Zwitzersch Landschap, in de manier van Ruysdaal, met bijwerk, zeer goed geschildert | *Size:* hoog 36, breed 40 duim	G H Fortuyn	(Unknown)
			Ruisdael, Jacob van (manner; and Velde, A., manner)		
1802/08/24	LNDLS	0052	*A. van de Velde; J. Ruisdaal* | Een Landschap met different Geboomte, op den Voorgrond een Beekje, nevens hetzelve een weg, met een Man en een Vrouw te Paard, alsmeede veel Koeijen en Schaapen. De Stoffagie is in de manier van A. van de Velde, en het Landschap als door J. Ruisdaal, konstig en krachtig op paneel geschilderd | *Mat:* op paneel *Size:* hoog 31, breed 40 duimen	Leonardus Bouman [or others]	(Unknown) fl 41
			Ruthart, Carl Borromäus Andreas		
1802/11/01	DOBRA	0169	*Carel Roetaard* | Twee stuks, verbeeldende het eene een Beever- het andere een Vossen-Jagt, juist van tekening, kunstig en uitvoerig geschilderd | *Mat:* op doek *Size:* hoog 23, breed 32 duim		(Sold) fl 41 Huybrichts
			Ruysch, J.		
1802/07/27	AKHRK	0030	*J. Ruijs* | Een bergachtig Landschap, doorsneeden met een Water, waadende hier door Vrouwen en Mannen, met Ossen, Muilezel, Wolvee [sic] en Geiten: zeer mooi gegroept en geschilderd | companion to lot 31 *Mat:* op paneel *Size:* hoog 23 ½, breed 32 ½ duim	Maria Stategaart	(Sold) fl 7:5 for lots 30 & 31. Zanegeest
1802/07/27	AKHRK	0031	*J. Ruijs* | Dito [J. Ruijs] de weerga. Een dito [Landschap] met hoogstaande Gebouwen, op de voorgrond twee Vrouwen, met staande en liggend Vee | companion to lot 30 *Notes:* It is unclear what "dito" refers to in the title.	Maria Stategaart	(Sold) fl 7:5 for lots 30 & 31. Zanegeest
			Ruysch, Rachel		
1801/05/11	AMSCH	0077	*Rachel Ruys* | Op een steene rand ziet men diverse zoorten van fraai geschakeerde Bloemen, dun en uitvoerig geschilderd | *Mat:* op doek *Size:* hoog 21, breed 15 duim	V	(Sold) fl 100 Van Iperen
1801/06/10	AMSCH	0142	*Ruysch. (R.)* | Dit capitaal Schildery, stelt voor een Bloemglas, staande op een steenen Tafel, ryk gestoffeerd met diversche fraaije geschakeerde	Herman ten Kate	(Sold) fl 300 Jan Yver

			bloemen, waarop Insectens aasen, ter zyde een Vogelnestje met Eyeren, alles op eene heldere Grond en van de fraaiste en beste behandeling van deeze beroemde Schilderes | *Mat:* op doek *Size:* hoog 20, breed 16 duim		
1801/08/19	AMSCH	0105	*R. Ruysch* | Op een Steene Rand ziet men verscheide soorten van welgeschakeerde Bloemen en Fruit, op welke Insectens Aasen; alles van de uitvoerigste en beste Schildering van R. Ruysch	Pruyssen^{r} [for] Q	(Bought In) fl 90
1801/08/19	AMSCH	0106	*R. Ruysch* | In een Glas ziet men verscheide Bloemen geplaastst; welke alle zeer schoon en krachtig zyn gepenceeld	Pruyssen^{r} [for] Q	(Sold) fl 24:10 Th^{s} Spaan
1801/10/19	AMSCH	0062	*Ruisch. (Rachel)* | Een Glaase Fles, staande op een marmer Tafel, in dezelve ziet men geplaast verscheide zoorten van uitmuntende Bloemen zeer konstig door elkander geschikt, waar op eenige vliegende Insecten aasen. – Alles is met de uitterste naauwkeurigheid behandeld, en de natuur zo verwonderlyk en uitvoerig nagevolgd, dat het met regt voor een der fraaiste van deeze Meesteres mag beschouwd worden | companion to lot 63 *Mat:* op doek *Size:* hoog 18 ¾, breed 15 ½ duim	Jonkheer Menno Baron van Coehoorn	(Sold) fl 480 Jan Spaan
1801/10/19	AMSCH	0063	*Ruisch. (Rachel)* | Dit stuk verbeeld als het voorgaande een Fles op een dito [marmer] Tafel, meede gevuld met onderscheide zoorten van fraaije Bloemen, waar op verscheiden Torren en Vlindertjes; het is met dezelfde onvermoeide arbeid als de voorige behandeld, en beiden ongemeen delicaat gepenseeld, en een weederga van het voorige | companion to lot 62 *Mat:* op doek *Size:* hoog 18 ¾, breed 15 ½ duim	Jonkheer Menno Baron van Coehoorn	(Sold) fl 400 C S Roos
1802/06/16	AMSCH	0152	*R. Ruysch* | Een Bloemstuk met Tulp, Pioen, Roos en andere Bloemen, op de voorgrond een Hagedis, voorts eenig Geboomten in het verschiet; delicaat behandeld | *Mat:* op doek *Size:* hoog 25 ½, breed 20 duim	[Merrem]	(Sold) fl 5 Coclers
1802/06/28	AMSCH	0156	*R. Ruisch* | Op een Steene Rand ziet men eenige fraaije geschakeerde Bloemen, als Rosen, Hiacinten, en andere keurige Bloemen; bevallig gepenceeld, door R. Ruisch, op Panneel | *Mat:* op paneel *Size:* hoog 14, breed 11 duim	Anna Elink	(Sold) fl 37 Geld
1804/05/07	AMSCH	0141	*Ruysch. (R.)* | Op een Marmere Tafel staat een Glazen Fles, gevuld met een ménigte geurige Bloemen, als diverse soorten van Roozen, Tulpen, Renonculaas, Angelieren, Hyacinten en anderen, als mede legt terzyde de Fles eenige Turksche Tarwe; uitvoerig en met de natuur overëenkomende gepenceeld | *Mat:* op doek *Size:* hoog 20, breed 16 duim	R[oos]	(Bought In) fl 150
1804/10/16	DLOND	0190	*Rachel Ruysch 1748* | Een Tafel met Bloemen, een Stuk van waardy, als zynde dit het laatste van hare hand. Het is door haar geschildert op haar 84ste Jaar, ter gedachtenis voor ene harer vriendinnen. Une Table avec des Fleurs, pièce precieuse, étant la dernière faite de sa main, dans son 84 age. C'etait un souvenir pour une de ses Amies | *Mat:* op paneel *Size:* hoog 11, breed 9 *Inscr:* Rachel Ruysch 1748 (signed and dated?) *Notes:* It is unclear whether the name and date are inscribed on the painting.		(Unknown)
1805/07/03	AMSCH	0039	*Ruysch. (R.)* | Dit Kunstjuweel steld voor: een Fles op den steenen Tafel staande, gevuld met wel geschakeerde geurige Bloemen van de edelste soort; terzyde op de Tafelleggen eenige Pruimen; eenige Vlinders, Vliegen en Waterdroppen, vercieren wyders dit Tafreel, hetwelk van de delicaatste behandeling kan genaamd worden | *Mat:* op doek *Size:* hoog 36, breed 27 duim	R[oos]	(Sold) fl 500 Reyers
1805/10/09	HGBSM	0044	*Rachel Ruysch* | Een stuk met bloemen en insecten, gemerkt Rachel Ruysch | *Mat:* op doek *Size:* hoog 20 ½ breet 16 duim *Inscr:* Rachel Ruysch (signed)	T H van Willigen [or others]	(Sold) fl 5:10 Ph Mey
1807/08/26	AMSCH	0184	*R. Ruysch* | In een Landschap, by den stam van een ouden Boom, vertoonen zich verscheiden soorten van verschillende Bloemen en ander Plantgewas, waarop Insecten aazen; allerbevalligst en uitvoerig op Doek gepenceeld, door den beroemden R. Ruysch | *Mat:* op doek *Size:* hoog 24, breed 19 duim	Helsdinge	(Sold) fl 25 Jozi
1807/08/26	AMSCH	0185	*R. Ruysch* | Op een Marmeren Tafel leggen verscheiden keurige Bloemen, van verschillende soort, en Bloembollen; zeer natuurlyk en uitvoerig van penceelsbehandeling | *Mat:* op doek op paneel *Size:* hoog 13, breed 10 duim	Helsdinge	(Sold) fl 21 Coclair
1808/08/23	AMSCH	0134	*Rachel Ruijsch* | Op een steene Rand, liggen verschillende zoorten van keurige Bloemen, als roode en witte Roozen, Goudsbloemen en anderen; waar op onderscheide Insecten aazen; teder en uitvoerig gepenceeld | *Mat:* op paneel *Size:* hoog 15, breed 12 duim	H	(Sold) fl 106 Kerkhoven
1808/10/28	AMVRS	0051	*Ruisch (Rachel)* | Een Glazen Fles, op eene Marmeren Tafel, in denzelven ziet men verscheide soorten van uitmuntende fraaije Bloemen, waarop Rupsen, enz. Alles is zeer natuurlijk, naauwkeurig en kunstig geschilderd | *Mat:* op doek *Size:* hoog 18 ¾, breed 15 ½ duim	Marten Udink	(Sold) fl 424 Gruyter
1808/11/28	AMSCH	0055	*R. Ruijsch* | Op een Marmere Tafel, staat een Glaase Fles, gevuld met verscheide Bloemen, waar op Insecten aasen, zeer natuurlijk gepenceeld | *Mat:* op doek *Size:* hoog 22, breed 19 duim	F	(Sold) fl 1:15 Gruiter
1810/05/22	AMSCH	0089	*Ruijsch (R.)* | Twee stuks sierlijke Vazen, staande op Steenen Tafels, beide gevuld met aangename Bloemen, een Vogelnesje met Eijertjes en Insekten, die op de Bloemen azen; alles helder en uitvoerig op deszelfs 75^{fte} Jaar gepenceeld | *Mat:* op doek *Size:* hoog 17, breed 15 duim	Johannes van de Putte Nicolaasz.	(Sold) fl 350 Gruyter [for] Dirkse

			Ruysch, Rachel (copy after)		
1808/08/23	AMSCH	0266	*R. Ruijsch* | Een Bouquet keurlijke Bloemen, leggende op de Tafel; zacht en teder naar R. Ruijsch	[Van Iperen?]	(Sold or Bought In) fl 2:15 Van Iperen
			Ruysdael, Salomon van		
1801/03/16	AMSCH	0039	*S. Ruysdaal* | Een gezicht op de stad Nymegen, op de voorgrond gestoffeerd met vier grasende Koeijen, meesterlyk gepenceeld	P[ruyssenaar]	(Sold) fl 5:5 Van Iperen
1801/08/19	AMSCH	0099	*S. Ruisdaal* | Een bevallig Landschap met een stil Water, gestoffeerd met Boerewoningen, Schuur en Geboomten, verders op de voorgrond twee Hengelaars; zonachtig en uitvoerig behandeld op Paneel | *Mat:* op paneel *Size:* hoog 12, breed 16 duim	Mevr Hogguer	(Bought In) fl 24
1801/08/19	AMSCH	0100	*S. Ruisdaal* | Een capitaal Duin- en Boomryk Landschap, gestoffeerd met twee Vrouwen die een drift Schaapen door een plas Water dryven, verders een Man te Paard, en andere figuuren; zonachtig gepenceeld	Pruyssen[r]	(Sold) fl 39 Wolft
1801/08/19	AMSCH	0101	*S. Ruisdaal* | Een Boomryk Landschap, gestoffeerd met Beelden en Beesten; zonachtig op Paneel | *Mat:* op paneel *Size:* hoog 33, breed 44 duim	Van Forreest	(Sold) fl 60 Wed Achtienhoven
1801/08/19	AMSCH	0102	*S. Ruisdaal* | Een Natuurlyk Land en Water gezicht	Pruyssen[r] [for] Q	(Sold) fl 3:15 Le Dantú
1802/08/24	LNDLS	0012	*S. Ruysdael* | Een Zee-dorp, waar van een Kerk en eenige huizen op een hoogte staan, op den Voorgrond ziet men veele wandelende en te paard zittende persoonen, verder een Strand-gezigt met visschers-Schepen, Wagens met Paarden, en gewoel van Volk op den Voorgrond. Zeer plaisant van coloriet | *Mat:* op doek *Size:* hoog 27, breed 38 duimen	Leonardus Bouman [or others]	(Unknown) fl 46
1802/09/06	AMSCH	0095	*S. Ruisdaal* | Twee stuks Strand- en Dorpgezigten, aan zee, de hooge Duinen, ryk gestoffeerd met vis handeldryvende figuuren, verders aangenaame verschieten; bevallig van ligt en meesteragtig gepenceelt | *Mat:* op paneel *Size:* hoog 12, breed 10 duim	J	(Sold) fl 3:10 Gruiter
1802/09/06	AMSCH	0096	*S. Ruisdaal* | In een Duinagtig Landschap, by hoog geboomte ziet men een Postwagen, die door Struikrovers overvallen word; fix geschildert | *Mat:* op paneel *Size:* hoog 20, breed 34 duim	J	(Sold) fl 1 Gruiter
1802/12/13	AMSCH	0134	*Salomon Ruisdaal* | Langs de kant van een Dyk, by eenige Gebouwen ziet men in een stil Water, een meenigte van zylende en stil leggende Vaartuigen en een aangenaam verschiet; fix geschilderd | *Mat:* op doek *Size:* hoog 33, breed 40 duim	Pruyssenaar [for] A	(Sold) fl 2:5 Theens
1802/12/13	AMSCH	0135	*Salomon Ruisdaal* | Een aangenaam Boomryk Landschap by een klaar Water, gestoffeerd met staand en leggend Vée | *Mat:* op paneel *Size:* hoog 19, breed 24 duim	Pruyssenaar [for] A	(Sold) fl 2:10 Wolft
1803/09/07	AMSCH	0153	*S. Ruisdaal* | Een Boomryk Landschap, met een Rivier doorsneden, waarby een Visscher en andere Stoffagien; fray en natuurlyk op Paneel [Un paysage varié et agréable, entrecoupé de ruisseaux ; l'ensemble est relevé par des pêcheurs et d'autres figures, et d'un effet tout naturel] | *Mat:* op paneel *Size:* hoog 19, breed 26 duim	Smidt	(Sold) fl 11 de Lafontaine
1803/12/12	AMSCH	0080	*S. Ruysdaal* | Twee Landschappen	B	(Sold) fl 56 H Pakker
1804/02/27	AMSCH	0094	*Ruysdaal. (S.)* | Een Land- en Watergezigt, ryk gestoffeerd met Beelden, Wagens en een Overhaalpondt | *Mat:* op doek *Size:* hoog 33, breed 47 duim	C	(Sold) fl 1 van Iperen
1804/02/27	AMSCH	0095	*Ruysdaal. (S.)* | Een bevallig Land- en Watergezicht, gestoffeerd met Vaartuigen en eenige drinkende Beesten | *Mat:* op paneel *Size:* hoog 20, breed 35 duim	C	(Sold) fl 0:14 L Pakker
1804/02/27	AMSCH	0096	*Ruysdaal. (S.)* | Een Bosch- en Hvächtig [sic] Landschap, waar eenige Wagens en Ryzigers, door Struykrovers overvallen worden | *Mat:* op paneel *Size:* hoog 20, breed 35 duim	C	(Sold) fl 0:14 Gruiter
1804/08/08	AMSCH	0162	*S. Ruisdaal* | Een Heuvelachtig Bosch, beplant met zwaar Geboomte, op de voorgrond in een heldere Waterplas ziet men verscheide Beesjes zich verfrisschen, waarby een Herder; dit stuk is zonachtig en van een meesterlyke behandeling | *Mat:* op paneel *Size:* hoog 21, breed 27 duim	Roos a	(Sold) fl 54 van Iperen
1804/08/08	AMSCH	0163	*S. Ruisdaal* | In een Rivier by een Dorp ziet men een ménigte van zeilende en stil leggende Schuiten, waarin verscheide Persoonen, in 't Dorp by eenige Boerenwoningen twee Wagens met Paarden, verders een Kertooren en Geboomte; meesterlyk op Paneel | *Mat:* op paneel *Size:* hoog 14, breed 20 duim	Vink[eles] [for] W	(Sold) fl 11 Hulswit
1804/08/08	AMSCH	0164	*S. Ruisdaal* | Een aangenaam Riviergezicht, met verscheide Vaartuigen, ter zyde het Land, met hoog Geboomte en Stoffagie van Beeldjes, met de Natuur overëenkomstig geschilderd | *Mat:* op paneel *Size:* hoog 19, breed 33 duim	Vink[eles] [for] K[=Gruyter?]	(Bought In) fl 7
1804/08/08	AMSCH	0165	*S. Ruisdaal* | Een Hei- en Boomryk Landschap, gestoffeerd met een Postwagen en eenige Reizigers, die door Struikroovers overvallen worden; fiks en meesterlyk gepenceeld | *Mat:* op paneel *Size:* hoog 20, breed 35 duim	Vink[eles] [for] K[=Gruyter?]	(Sold) fl 1:10 Toselli
1804/12/10	AMSCH	0089	*Salomon Ruysdael* | Een Landschap, ter linkerzyde Duin, en in 't verschiet hoog geboomten, op de voorgrond gestoffeerd met een drift Beesten en	Jan De Groot	(Sold) fl 1:5 Levie Pakker

			een Ryziger te paard; meesterlyk gepenceeld | *Mat:* op paneel *Size:* Hoog 23, breed 40 duim		
1805/07/03	AMSCH	0138	*S. Ruisdaal* | Een Dorpgezicht aan een Rivier gestoffeerd met een Overvarende Pont, op het Land Rysigers te paard en te voet, in het verschiet een Kasteel; natuurlyk op Doek | *Mat:* op doek *Size:* hoog 46, breed 50 duim	G	(Sold) fl 22:10 Agina
1806/06/07	RMHSN	0008	*S: Ruisdaal* | Twee Stuks, zynde Kabbelende Watertjes met Zeilende Scheepjes, helder en plaisant geschilderd | *Mat:* op paneel	A E K L	(Unknown)
1806/08/13	AMSCH	0155	*Ruysdaal. (S.)* | Een Duinachtig Landschap met Geboomten, en Gebouwen, op de voorgrond gestoffeerd met een Boerenwagen, by een Tolhek; zeer zonachtig, fiks en natuurlyk behandeld | companion to lot 156 *Mat:* op paneel *Size:* hoog 21, breed 19 duim	Yver	(Sold) fl 37 for lots 155 & 156. Schumacher
1806/08/13	AMSCH	0156	*Ruysdaal. (S.)* | Een ander Boomryk en Heuvelachtig Landschap, gestoffeerd met een Postwagen, en eenige Rysigers; zynde een weerga van de voorgaande | companion to lot 155	Yver	(Sold) fl 37 for lots 155 & 156. Schumacher
1806/08/13	AMSCH	0157	*Ruysdaal. (S.)* | Twee stuks Dorpgezichten aan de Noord-Zee, de Duinen en 't Strand zyn beide gestoffeerd; fiks en meesterlyk gepenceeld | *Mat:* op paneel *Size:* hoog 12 ½, breed 11 duim	Vinkeles [for] G[ruyter]	(Sold) fl 7 Th Spaan
1806/11/24	AMSCH	0061	*Ruisdaal (S.)* | Een stil Water aan een boomryk Land, met Boere woningen, gestoffeerd met Vissers in hun Schuiten; verders een Jagt en andere Vaartuigen; natuurlyk voorgesteld en fiks behandeld | *Mat:* op doek *Size:* hoog 33, breed 48 duim	Munnikhuizen	(Sold) fl 6 L Pakker
1806/11/24	AMSCH	0062	*Ruisdaal (S.)* | Een Land- en Dorpgezigt aan een stille Rivier, met Roeischuiten en Beeldjes, op 't Land een Wagen met Volk; geschilderd als de voorgaande [natuurlyk voorgesteld en fiks behandeld] | *Mat:* op paneel *Size:* hoog 21, breed 33 duim	Munnikhuizen	(Sold) fl 9:10 Coclers
1806/11/24	AMSCH	0063	*Ruisdaal (S.)* | Een Land- en Riviergezicht, het Land met Geboomte en een oud Kasteel; het Water met een overvarende Pont, wdarin [sic] verscheiden Menschen en Vee, welke in het water spiegelen; zynde een bevallig gepenceeld schildery | *Mat:* op paneel *Size:* hoog 29, breed 34 duim	Munnikhuizen	(Sold) fl 13:10 Reyers
1807/04/13	AMSCH	0011	*S. Ruysdaal* | Een Landschap	Everard de Burlett	(Sold) fl 1 Levie Pakker
1808/03/03	HAVIN	0031	*S. van Ruysdaal* | Een Hangende Roerdomp	Jacobus Spillebout	(Unknown) fl 0:6
1808/04/26	GDAN	0138	*Ruysdaal (S.)* | Een Wintergezigtje met een aantal Schaatsenrijders, en meerder bywerk, fiks gepenseeld | *Size:* hoog 15 ½, breed 19 duim	G H Fortuyn	(Unknown)
1808/04/26	GDAN	0139	*Ruysdaal (S.)* | Een zonägtig Boomrijk Landschap, met een Boere Wagen in 't verschiet, en eenige Personen te Paard, goed geschilderd | *Size:* hoog 25, breed 42 duim	G H Fortuyn	(Unknown)
1808/06/06	RMRIJ	0109	*Ruijsdael. (Salomon)* | Een Land- en Riviergezigt met Schuiten, wadende Koeijen en eenen beplanten Heuvel. Eene groote Stad in het verschiet [Une Colline et des Touffes d'arbres au bord d'une Rivière, dans la quelle plusieurs Vaches marchent. Plus loin quelques bateaux et une Ville etc.] | *Annots:* Verk B. Kley, den Haag, 10 Mei 1781 (f 65.-) (RMA I) *Mat:* op paneel *Size:* Hoog 23 ½, en breed 35 ½ duim	Gerrit van der Pot, Heer van Groeneveld	(Sold) fl 45 De Rohan
1808/06/11	RMRIJ	0052	*Salomon Ruisdaal* | Het Valkenhof te Nymegen aan de Maas, met veele Schepen, Schuiten en verder bywerk, meesterlyk, warm en natuurlyk geschilderd | *Mat:* op doek *Size:* hoog 38 ½, breed 53 ½ duim		(Sold or Bought In) fl 80 Rohan
1808/06/11	RMRIJ	0055	*Salomon Ruisdaal* | Twee stuks kabbelende Watertjes, natuurlyk en dun geschilderd | *Mat:* op paneel *Size:* hoog 16, breed 14 duim		(Bought In) fl 6
1808/06/13	AMSCH	0131	*Ruijsdaal (S.)* | In een Nederlandsch Landschap ziet men eenige Krijgslieden het Vee der Boeren wegdrijven, en Gijzelaars medenemen; ter regterzijde eenige Zoetelaars and verdere Stoffage. Zonachtig | *Mat:* op doek *Size:* hoog 42, breed 58 duim	E M Engelberts	(Sold) fl 75 Reijers
1808/09/13	HABRU	0075	*S. Ruijsdaal* | De Stad Rotterdam, van de Maaskant te zien, natuurlijk		(Unknown) fl 5:10
1808/09/13	HABRU	0076	*S. Ruijsdaal* | Een dito, op de Stad Dortrecht | *Notes:* It is unclear what "dito" refers to in the title.		(Unknown) fl 8:3
1808/09/13	HABRU	0076	*S. Ruijsdaal* | Een Watergezicht		(Unknown) fl 5:5
1808/10/28	AMVRS	0053	*Ruisdaal. (S.)* | Een Landzicht aan den Oever van een Rivier, met Geboomte, overvarende Pontschuit, met Reizigers en Vee, verder een Dorpgezicht en andere Vaartuigen. Helder behandeld | *Mat:* op paneel *Size:* hoog 22, breed 33 duim	Marten Udink	(Sold) fl 31 Van Enst en Dijk [or] Eversdyk
1809/04/17	AMSCH	0081	*S. Ruysdaal* | Een natuurlijk Landschap, met Boeren Woningen en Geboomten, gestoffeerd op de voorgrond met twee Landlieden, eenig Vee door een Waterplas drijvende, verder een opgaande Weg na een Brug, waar bij twee Heeren te Paard en een Postwagen, in 't verschiet een Weide met rustende Beesten; zonachtig en meesterlijk gepenceeld | *Mat:* op doek *Size:* hoog 39, breed 53 duim	[Gruyter?]	(Sold or Bought In) fl 30
1809/04/17	AMSCH	0082	*S. Ruysdaal* | Een stille Rivier, met verschillende Vaartuigen, op de voorgrond een overvarende Pontschuit, met Reizigers en Vee, ter zijde een Dorpgezicht en een Wagen met Huislieden; natuurlijk en zonachtig geschilderd | *Mat:* op paneel *Size:* hoog 21, breed 42 duim	T	(Sold or Bought In) fl 80

1809/04/17	AMSCH	0083	*S. Ruysdaal* | Een Land- en Watergezicht, met zijlende en drijvende Scheepen en Visschers Vaartuigen; helder en natuurlijk verbeeld | *Mat:* op doek *Size:* hoog 33, breed 48 duim	[Gruyter?]	(Sold) fl 14:10
1809/04/17	AMSCH	0144	*S. Ruijsdaal* | Een aangenaam Land- en Watergezicht, met stoffagie | *Mat:* op paneel	[Gruyter?]	(Sold) fl 2:15
1809/04/17	AMSCH	0179	*S. Ruisdaal* | Een Boomrijk Landschap, met Landlieden en Vee gestoffeerd	[Gruyter?]	(Sold) fl 1:5
1809/04/22	AMYVR	0113	*S. Ruisdaal* | Een bevallig Rhijngezicht, met Beeldjes en Vaartuigen gestoffeerd; meesterlijk behandeld | *Mat:* op paneel *Size:* hoog 13, breed 19 duim	de Bruin	(Sold) fl 2:5 C S Roos
1809/06/13	AMSCH	0131	*S. Ruisdaal* | Een aangenaam Landschap, op de voorgrond in een Dorp met verscheide Woningen, is een Boeren Kermis, afgebeeld; voor de Herberg ziet men een menigte Huislieden zo Mannen als Vrouwen, welke zich met Danssen, Speelen en Drinken vermaken, verders Post- en andere Wagens, met vrolijke Gasten, Heeren te Paard en Landlieden bij hun Vee; dit stuk is rijk van Ordonantie, en van de beste schildering | *Mat:* op doek *Size:* hoog 37, breed 49 duim	[Gruyter?]	(Bought In) fl 21
1809/06/13	AMSCH	0132	*S. Ruisdaal* | Een Boschagtig Landschap, op den voorgrond een heldere Waterplas, waardoor eenige Beesten waaden, verder een Vrouw op een Ezel en een gaande Huisman; natuurlijk behandeld | *Mat:* op paneel *Size:* hoog 22, breed 30 duim	T	(Sold) fl 39 van Iperen
1810/03/26	RMMUY	0048	*Salomon Ruisdael* | Twee welverkozen Land- en Water Gezigten, rijk gestoffeerd met Schuiten, Schepen en Figuren. Zonachtig, uitvoerig, en meesterlijk geschilderd [Deux Paysages et Marines, ornés de plusieurs figures et barques, clair et piquant, de son beau faire.] | *This Lot:* Een welverkozen Land- en Water Gezigt *Mat:* op paneel *Size:* hoog 12 ¾, breed 15 ¼ duimen *Notes:* Lots 48 and 49 were printed in the catalogue as one item.	Daniel de Jongh Az	(Sold) fl 80 for lots 48 & 49. LeBrun te Parys
1810/03/26	RMMUY	0049	*Salomon Ruisdael* | Twee welverkozen Land- en Water Gezigten, rijk gestoffeerd met Schuiten, Schepen en Figuren. Zonachtig, uitvoerig, en meesterlijk geschilderd [Deux Paysages et Marines, ornés de plusieurs figures et barques, clair et piquant, de son beau faire.] | *This Lot:* Een welverkozen Land- en Water Gezigt *Mat:* op paneel *Size:* hoog 12 ¾, breed 15 ¼ duimen *Notes:* Lots 48 and 49 were printed in the catalogue as one item.	Daniel de Jongh Az	(Sold) fl 80 for lots 48 & 49. LeBrun te Parys
1810/05/22	AMSCH	0090	*Ruisdaal (S.)* | Een Boschachtig Landschap, op den voorgrond een heldere Waterplas, waardoor eenige Beesten waaden, verder eene Vrouw op een Ezel en gaande Huisman; natuurlijk behandeld | *Mat:* op paneel *Size:* hoog 22, breed 30 duim	T	(Bought In) fl 35
1810/06/06	RMMUY	0033	*Salomon van Ruisdaal* | Een rijk gestoffeerde Winter, en eene groote Stad; in het verschiet, piquant en natuurlijk | *Mat:* op doek		(Unknown) fl 14:10
1810/06/06	RMMUY	0034	*Salomon van Ruisdaal* | Twee Stuks stille Waters met Schepen &c. Helder en natuurlijk verbeeld | *Mat:* op paneel		(Unknown) fl 4:5
1810/06/06	RMMUY	0172	*S. Ruisdaal* | Een krachtig Landschap | *Mat:* op paneel		(Sold) fl 14 V Leen
1810/06/20	AMSCH	0077	*S. Ruisdaal* | Een alleraangenaamst boomrijk Landschap aan een Rivier, gestoffeerd met Herders en Vee. Warm van koloriet en meesterlijk behandeld | *Mat:* op doek *Size:* hoog 44, breed 58 duimen	N	(Sold) fl 79 Roos

Ruysdael, Salomon van (or Ruysdael, S., manner)

1803/06/20	AMSCH	0069	*S. Ruisdaal* | Een Riviergezicht met verscheide Vaartuigen, terzyde het Land met hoog Geboomte en stoffagie van Beeldjes, met de natuur overeenkomstig geschilderd, op Paneel, door of in de manier van S. Ruisdaal | *Mat:* op paneel *Size:* hoog 19, breed 33 duim	Schley [for] K	(Sold) fl 13:10 Gruiter
1810/05/22	AMSCH	0091	*Ruisdaal (S.) of in de manier* | Een Dorpgezicht met verscheide Woningen aan eene stille Rivier, gestoffeerd met een overvarende Pontschuit met Reizigers; natuurlijk gepenceeld | *Mat:* op paneel *Size:* hoog 13, breed 18 duim	F	(Sold) fl 5:5 Rutten

Ruysdael, Salomon van (or Vlieger, S.)

1808/06/11	RMRIJ	0120	*Simon de Vlieger; of S: Ruisdaal* | Een Winter- Stad- en Rivier Gezicht, vol Gewoel en Stoffagie | *Mat:* op doek		(Unknown) fl 10:10

Ruysdael, Salomon van (manner)

1802/12/13	AMSCH	0136	*Salomon Ruisdaal* | Een Landschap met een stil Water, waardoor eenige Beesten Waaden: als door denzelven [Salomon Ruisdaal] | *Mat:* op doek *Size:* hoog 18, breed 24 duim	Pruyssenaar [for] D	(Sold) fl 50 Jan Spaan
1805/07/10	AMSCH	0230	*S. Ruisdaal* | Twee Dorpgezigten, met een ménigte stoffagie van Beelden, Kameelen, Paarden, Koeijen, enz.; op Paneel, als S. Ruisdaal | *Mat:* op paneel	Y[ver]	(Sold) fl 9 L Pakker
1806/08/13	AMSCH	0288	*S. Ruysdaal* | Twee stuks Boomryke Landschappen met Rivieren doorsneden, ryk gestoffeerd; als S. Ruysdaal	Vinkeles [for] E	(Sold) fl 14:10 T Spaan

Ruytenbach

1802/05/11	GRGRW	0032	*Ruitenbach* | Ene Herberg waar voor veel Volks [Schilderijen met Olie-Verf; In zwarte Lijsten] | companion to lot 33 *Mat:* in olyverf *Notes:* The	Arnold Sicco Werumeus	(Unknown) fl 33:10 for lots 32 & 33

			bracketed information in the title appears above lot 1 and refers to lots 1 to 79a.		
1802/05/11	GRGRW	0033	*Ruitenbach* | Ene dito [Herberg waar voor veel Volks], tot ene weerga [Schilderijen met Olie-Verf; In zwarte Lijsten] | companion to lot 32 *Mat:* in olyverf *Notes:* The bracketed information in the title about the medium appears above lot 1 and refers to lots 1 to 79a.	Arnold Sicco Werumeus	(Unknown) fl 33:10 for lots 32 & 33

Ruytenschild, Leendert

1803/08/17	AMSCH	0074	*Ruytenschild. (L.)* | Een woelend Water met verscheiden Vaartuigen, het Water is transparant en van een dunne behandeling | *Mat:* op doek *Size:* hoog 15, breed 19 duim	Anna Catharina Putman	(Sold) fl 6 v^n Iperen

Ruyter, H. de [Unidentified]

1802/05/05	AMSCH	0189	*H. de Ruyter* | Een Strandgezicht met verscheiden rydende en andere Lieden, in 't verschiet ziet men een menigte zylende en ander Vaartuigen, fiks gepenceeld | *Mat:* op paneel *Size:* hoog 35, breed 57 duim	BB	(Sold) fl 28 Le Dantú

Ruyven, Pieter Jansz. van

1810/08/06	AMSCH	0090	*Ruijven (P. van)* | Eene Ordonantie van verscheiden Vrouwen en Kinderen, zinspeelende op den Vrede enz.; meesterlijk gepenceeld | *Mat:* op doek *Size:* hoog 59, breed 55 duimen	C	(Sold) fl 49 Stoopendaal [for] B

Ryckaert, David (III)

1801/04/13	AMSCH	0065	*D. Rykaart* | Een Boerebinnenhuis, waarin een aantal, Huislieden bezig zyn op de kaart te speelen, terwyl zich andere met roken en drinken vermaken, voorts een menigte Huisraad, alles is fraay geordoneerd, aangenaam van coloriet en Meesterlyk gepenceeld | *Mat:* op koper *Size:* hoog 28, breed 39 duim	Pierre Fouquet, junior	(Sold) fl 410 J^b Roeloffs
1803/07/18	AMSCH	0040	*Ryckaert. (David) 1649* | In het midden van een Boere Binnenvertrek zitten twee Boeren op de Kaart te speelen, waar naar twee anderen met attentie kyken, een weinig voorwaards zit een Vrouw met een Kind aan de Borst en een ander aan haar zyde staande; een Grysaard schynt haar een Glas Bier aan te bieden, aan 't vuur ziet men een Man en Vrouw stoeijende, en in het verschiet nog eenige andere Huislieden die roken en drinken. Het Huisraad, als: Kopere Ketels, Tinne Kan, Manden en Aardewerk is allernatuurlykst voorgesteld, de hartstogten zyn spreekend, en het coloriet en fixe behandeling doen zien dat deeze Meester onder de beste van zyn tyd gerekend kan worden [Vèrs le milieu d'un mènage rustique l'on distingue deux hommes à jouer aux cartes ; l'un en chemise blanche paroit très attentif ; son adversaire gros rejoui semble le narguer. Ils sont observés par deux villageois derriere leurs chaises. Au devant est assise une grosse Mêre tenant un enfant au sein & un second s'appuye sur son genou ; à ses pieds est un gros vase à bierre, dont un viellard lui presente un verre. Derriere la hotesse est un rustre cajolant la servante. Les accessoires de mènage, comme chaudron, mandes, pots & bouteilles y sont distribués & executés avec l'art généralement reconnu à l'Auteur. Ce morceau dans son ensemble peut passer pour un des meilleurs ouvrages de Ryckaert : une maniere franche & pleine d'expression, une couleur forte & un bel effet parlent suffisamment en sa faveur.] | *Mat:* op paneel *Size:* hoog 24, breed 36 duim *Inscr:* David Ryckaert. 1649 (signed and dated?) *Notes:* It is unclear whether the name and date are inscribed on the painting.	Maria Theresia Andrioli	(Sold) fl 201 van Iperen
1806/08/13	AMSCH	0158	*Rykaart. (D.)* | Voor een Gebouw ziet men eenige vrolyke Gasten zich met speelen en drinken vermaken, op de voorgrond legt een Hond met Jongen, benévens een slapende Kat, verder een Paard en Kar, naar het Dorp reidende; delicaat gepenceeld | *Mat:* op paneel *Size:* hoog 24, breed 34 duim	van der Voort	(Sold) fl 489 Jan Spaan

Rynenburg, C. [Unidentified]

1809/10/20	UTWLD	0002	*C. Rynenburg* | Een Zeegezicht met differente vaartuigen door C. Rynenburg	J J van Rhyn	(Unknown)
1809/10/20	UTWLD	0003	*C. Rynenburg* | Een dito [Zeegezicht] door dito [C. Rynenburg]	J J van Rhyn	(Unknown)
1809/10/20	UTWLD	0011	*C. Rynenburg* | Twee Zeegezichtjes door C. Rynenburg	J J van Rhyn	(Unknown)
1809/10/20	UTWLD	0012	*C. Rynenburg* | Een dito [Zeegezichtje] door dito [C. Rynenburg], 1703 | *Inscr:* C. Rynenburg, 1703 (signed and dated?) *Notes:* It is unclear whether the name and date are inscribed on the painting.	J J van Rhyn	(Unknown)
1809/10/20	UTWLD	0013	*C. Rynenburg* | Een strandgezichtje door dito [C. Rynenburg] | *Mat:* op doek	J J van Rhyn	(Unknown)
1809/10/20	UTWLD	0014	*C. Rynenburg* | Arlequin in kleding van een geestelyken &c.	J J van Rhyn	(Unknown)

Rynsoever, Gerrit

1803/09/07	AMSCH	0267	*G. van Rynsoever* | Een Kabbelende Zee, met verscheide Zeilende Scheepen; fiks gepenceeld, gemerkt G. van Rynsoever [Une mer orageuse et des navires se débattant contre les flots en fureur ; tableau peint avec beaucoup d'expression ; marqué G. van Rynsoever] | *Mat:* op paneel *Size:* hoog 22, breed 34 duim *Inscr:* G. van Rynsoever (signed)	Smidt	(Sold) fl 7 C S Roos

<table>
<tr><td>1810/10/11</td><td>AMSCH</td><td>0235</td><td>C.V. Rijnsoever | Eene Ordonantie van eenige Vrouwen | Notes: The artist's name was given as "C.V. Rijnsoever" but we have assumed this is an error.</td><td>A</td><td>(Sold) fl 0:14 Yver</td></tr>
</table>

Rysbrack

<table>
<tr><td>1810/07/26</td><td>AMSCH</td><td>0113</td><td>Rijsbracht | Een Landgezigt. Goed geschilderd</td><td>Cassino</td><td>(Sold) fl 0:6 Lohuis</td></tr>
</table>

Sabaar, P. [Unidentified]

<table>
<tr><td>1802/05/24</td><td>HGBAK</td><td>0067</td><td>P. Sabaar | Een onstuimige Zee met Schepen, door P. Sabaar, hoog 18 duim, breed 23 ½ duim, zwarte lyst | Size: hoog 18 duim, breed 23 ½ duim</td><td>Mejuffrouw A van der Mieden</td><td>(Unknown) fl 1</td></tr>
</table>

Saenredam

<table>
<tr><td>1804/07/25</td><td>DLGRO</td><td>0039</td><td>Zaanredam | Eene Heilige Familie | Mat: op koper Size: hoog 7, breed 5 duim</td><td>Mr Franc van der Burch Wz.</td><td>(Unknown)</td></tr>
</table>

Saenredam, Pieter Jansz.

<table>
<tr><td>1801/06/10</td><td>AMSCH</td><td>0202</td><td>Zaenredam. (P. J.) | Een Protestantsche Kerk, van binnen te zien, gestoffeerd met wandelende Beelden; fraai van Perspectief en uitvoerig geschilderd | Mat: op paneel Size: hoog 10, breed 8 duim</td><td>Herman ten Kate</td><td>(Sold) fl 12 Pruijssenaar</td></tr>
<tr><td>1802/06/16</td><td>AMSCH</td><td>0168</td><td>P. J. Saenredam | Een gedeelte van een Kerk van binnen te zien, gestoffeerd met twee Beelden, helder en uitvoerig geschilderd | Mat: op paneel Size: hoog 16, breed 19 duim</td><td>[Merrem]</td><td>(Sold) fl 8 Gruiter</td></tr>
<tr><td>1802/06/16</td><td>AMSCH</td><td>0169</td><td>P. J. Saenredam | Een Binnegezicht van een Protestante Kerk, gestoffeerd met verscheide wandelende Dames en Heeren; helder en bevallig van penceelbehandeling | Mat: op paneel Size: hoog 13, breed 12 duim</td><td>[Merrem]</td><td>(Sold) fl 15 J Yver</td></tr>
<tr><td>1802/08/24</td><td>LNDLS</td><td>0045</td><td>P. Saanredam | Een Kerk van binnen te zien, met wandelende beeldjes, Extra uitvoerig, en helder van coloriet | Mat: op paneel Size: hoog 15, breed 21 duimen</td><td>Leonardus Bouman [or others]</td><td>(Unknown) fl 25</td></tr>
<tr><td>1806/11/24</td><td>AMSCH</td><td>0072</td><td>Saenredam (J.) | Een Protestantsche Kerk van binnen, ziende na het Orgel, op de Voorgrond word een Graf gemaakt; verder verscheide Wandelaars; het zonlicht is spreekend, en de behandeling dun | Mat: op paneel Size: hoog 24, breed 19 duim Notes: The artist's name was given as "Saenredam (J.)" but we have assumed this is an error.</td><td>Munnikhuizen</td><td>(Sold) fl 25 Reijers</td></tr>
<tr><td>1810/03/26</td><td>RMMUY</td><td>0008</td><td>J. Saenredam | Een gedeelte van eene Oude Gottische Kerk, waar in eenige figuren. Helder en uitvoerig geschilderd. 1630 [L'intérieur d'une Eglise gothique, ornée de figures, d'un ton clair et d'une grande vérité.] | Mat: op paneel Size: hoog 18, breed 14 ½ duimen Inscr: 1630 (dated?) Notes: The artist's name was given as "J. Saenredam" but we have assumed this is an error. It is unclear whether the date is inscribed on the painting. Loc: Paris, France. Musée du Louvre. (?)</td><td>Daniel de Jongh Az</td><td>(Sold) fl 22 Verweij Rott^{m}</td></tr>
<tr><td>1810/08/01</td><td>AMSCH</td><td>0090</td><td>Saenredam (Pieter) | Een Gezigt op de Mariekerk te Utrecht met den daar bij staanden Toren, van voren te zien; verlevendigd door eenige Beeldjes, verder Geboomte [Vue Perspective sur l'Eglise et sur la Tour de Sainte Marie à Utrecht, le batiment étant vû de face ; embelli de figures et de quelques arbres] | Annots: Bon. (NGW) Mat: op paneel Size: hoog 25, breed 20 ½ duimen Loc: Madrid, España. Thyssen Collection. (1979.27)</td><td>Mr Pieter de Smeth van Alphen</td><td>(Sold) fl 110 J de Vries</td></tr>
<tr><td>1810/12/03</td><td>DOBRA</td><td>0007</td><td>Zaanredam | Een Kerk van binnen te zien, tegen over den Spreekstoel; uitvoerig geschilderd, door Zaanredam 1618 | Inscr: Zaanredam 1618 (signed and dated?) Notes: It is unclear whether the name and date are inscribed on the painting.</td><td></td><td>(Unknown)</td></tr>
</table>

Saftleven, Cornelis

<table>
<tr><td>1801/03/16</td><td>AMSCH</td><td>0004</td><td>C. Saftleven | Een uitmuntend Stuk, zynde volgens de daar by zynde sleutel, een der twee Origineele stukken van de Historie van Johan van Oldenbarneveld, zittende voor zyn 24 gediligeerde Rechters, meesterlyk geschilderd, door C. Saftleven, benevens het Prentje van zyn Pourtret | Loc: Amsterdam, Nederland. Rijksmuseum. (A 1588)</td><td>P[ruyssenaar]</td><td>(Sold) fl 68:10 J Yver</td></tr>
<tr><td>1801/03/16</td><td>AMSCH</td><td>0074</td><td>Saftleeven | Een Binnehuis met Groentens, dood Wild en bywerk</td><td>P[ruyssenaar]</td><td>(Withdrawn)</td></tr>
<tr><td>1801/04/08</td><td>HAVIN</td><td>0029</td><td>Sachtleeve | Een Boere Werf ryk gestoffeerd met Boeren, Twee Bokken en Huisraad</td><td></td><td>(Unknown)</td></tr>
<tr><td>1801/04/13</td><td>AMSCH</td><td>0070</td><td>C. Saftlven | Twee stuks Binnenhuizen, gestoffeerd met een menigte Groentens, Potten, Pannen, Vaatwerk en ander stil leeven, natuurlyk verbeeld en Meesterlyk geschilderd | Mat: op paneel Size: ieder hoog 16, breed 13 duim</td><td>Pierre Fouquet, junior</td><td>(Sold) fl 23 Texier</td></tr>
<tr><td>1801/04/13</td><td>AMSCH</td><td>0071</td><td>C. Saftlven | Een Boereschuur met diversche gereedschappen, een Pomp en Vaatwerken, zonachtig behandeld | Mat: op paneel Size: hoog 12, breed 12 duim</td><td>Pierre Fouquet, junior</td><td>(Sold) fl 35 Pruyssenaar</td></tr>
<tr><td>1801/08/19</td><td>AMSCH</td><td>0143</td><td>C. Zaftleeven | In een Landschap by een Boere Woning, ziet men een rustend Huisman, by verscheide staand en rustend Veé, natuurlyk en fix gepenceeld op Paneel | Mat: op paneel Size: hoog 19, breed 23 duim</td><td>W Wynen</td><td>(Sold) fl 5:10 V^{n} Dijl</td></tr>
<tr><td>1802/06/28</td><td>AMSCH</td><td>0162</td><td>C. Saftleven | In een Boere Schuur, by een Pomp, ziet men een menigte Huisraad, als Ketels, Vaat- en Aardewerk, in 't verschiet een Vrouw by het vuur; alles kragtig en zonachtig, op Panneel | Mat: op paneel Size: hoog 17, breed 15 duim</td><td>Anna Elink</td><td>(Sold) fl 45 Hulswit</td></tr>
</table>

1802/06/28	AMSCH	0163	*C. Saftleven* | Een Boere Binnenhuis, gestoffeerd met een Boer en twee Boerinnen, verders toepasselyk Huisraad, fiks behandeld, door Denzelven [C. Saftleven], op Panneel | *Mat:* op paneel *Size:* hoog 13, breed 10 duim	Anna Elink	(Sold) fl 6:10 de Meijer
1802/06/28	AMSCH	0164	*C. Saftleven* | In een Boere Vertrek ziet men een Vrouw het vuur opstoken, verder eenig Huisraad, door Denzelven [C. Saftleven], op Panneel | *Mat:* op paneel *Size:* hoog 12, breed 9 duim	Anna Elink	(Sold) fl 3:15 Boelen
1802/09/06	AMSCH	0105	*C. Saftleeven* | In een Keukenvertrek, zit een bedaagde Vrouw verzelt van een Kind, by een Haardsteede, bézig Raapen te schillen; daar nevens op de grond, legt kopere keetel, tinne borden, aarde potten, en vaatwerk; alles natuurlyk bevallig van ligt, en meesterlyk gepenceeld | *Mat:* op paneel *Size:* hoog 14, breed 18 duim	Brave	(Bought In) fl 12 ½
1802/09/29	AMSCH	0052	*C. Saftleven* | Levend Pluimgedierte, hoog 12 ¾, breed 15 ¼ duim. Paneel. Gansen en Eenden by een Water, in een Landschap, zyn in dit stukje zeer natuurlyk verbeeld by eenig Paalwerk, en fraai van Penceelbehandeling [Des Oyes & des Canards, près d'une grange et d'une Marre d'Eau, rendus avec Art, et d'un Pinceau fidéle.] | *Mat:* op paneel *Size:* hoog 12 ¾, breed 15 ¼ duim	[Labouchere?]	(Sold) fl 3 Yver
1802/12/13	AMSCH	0223	*C. Saftleeven* | Een rustend Hondje, zeer natuurlyk behandeld; en een Rams-kop	Schley [for] Lauwers	(Sold) fl 1:5 van Dijl
1803/06/20	AMSCH	0014	*C. Saftleven* | In een Boereschuur zit een Boer een Koe te Melken, ter zyde een Vrouw by een Wastobben, uitvoerig door C. Saftleven | *Size:* hoog 8, breed 10 duim	Schley [for] B	(Sold) fl 9:10 Gruiter
1803/07/07	HGKAN	0008	*Zagtleeven* | Een fraay geschilderd binnen Stal, op Paneel, door Zagtleeven [Schilderyen in Olyverf] | *Mat:* in olyverf op paneel *Notes:* The bracketed information in the title appears above lot 1 and refers to lots 1 to 25.		(Unknown)
1803/09/07	AMSCH	0161	*C. Saftleeven* | Een Boeren Binnenschuur, gestoffeerd met verscheide Huismans Gereedschappen, op de voorgrond een Boeren Jongen met een Hond speelende, zeer Natuurlyk behandeld [L'intérieur d'une grange, ornée d'instrumens aratoires et d'ustensiles analogues au sujet ; sur le devant un jeune villageois jouant avec un chien ; composition naturelle et finie] | *Mat:* op paneel *Size:* hoog 29, breed 35 duim [Haut 29, large 29 pouces] *Notes:* The dimensions differ in the Dutch and French editions of the catalogue.	Smidt	(Sold) fl 2 C S Roos
1803/09/07	AMSCH	0162	*C. Saftleeven* | Een Vrouw over de Deur leggende, voor dewelke een menigte Keukengereedschap; alles zeer Natuurlyk [Une femme penchée sur la porte d'une maison, devant laquelle on apperçoit quelques ustensiles de cuisine ; le tout peint d'après nature] | *Mat:* op paneel *Size:* hoog 13, breed 14 duim	Smidt	(Sold) fl 5:5 Haffner
1804/07/25	DLGRO	0016	*C. Sagtleven* | De Herders het Kind Jesus in de Kribbe liggende, aanbiddende met Moeder Maria, en verder bywerk | *Mat:* op paneel *Size:* hoog 19, breed 25 duim	Mr Franc van der Burch Wz.	(Unknown)
1804/07/25	DLGRO	0038	*C. Sagtleven* | Een Boeren binnen Huis, met een Man die met zyn Hoofd in de handen zit te slaapen; op den voorgrond een Bok en twee Geiten | *Mat:* op paneel *Size:* hoog 14, breed 18 duim	Mr Franc van der Burch Wz.	(Unknown)
1804/07/25	DLGRO	0085	*C. Sagtleven* | Een Landschap, met Koeijen, Paarden, en Geiten, een Boer die een Karre oplaad &c. uitvoerig en fraai geschilderd door C. Sagtleven | *Mat:* op paneel *Size:* hoog 19, breed 28 duim	Mr Franc van der Burch Wz.	(Unknown)
1804/08/02	BDAN	0021	*C. Sagtleeven* | Een Boeren Binnen-huis, op den voorgrond veel Huissieraad, als Keetels, &c., en eenige Figuuren, zeer mooy van behandeling | *Mat:* op paneel *Size:* b. 22 d. h. 15 d.	J G Calckberner	(Unknown)
1804/10/16	DLOND	0194	*C. Sagtleven* | Een Dorpsgezicht met veel gewoel van allerlei Vee. Un Paysage rempli de toutes sortes de Betail à l'entrée d'un Village | *Mat:* op paneel *Size:* hoog 17, breed 25		(Sold) fl 28 O D Wyngaert
1804/10/16	DLOND	0195	*C. Sagtleven* | Twee Schilderyen Verbeeldende Beestenmarkten, vol gewoel. Deux Tableaux. Des Marchés de Betail, rempli de figures | *Size:* hoog 14, breed 19 *Notes:* The lot was changed from "C. Sagtleven, Twee Schilderyen Verbeeldende Beestenmarkten, vol gewoel," to "E. de Witte" and "A. Stork," without giving titles, at the front of the catalogue. They have been numbered 195a and 195b.		(Withdrawn)
1804/10/16	DLOND	0196	*C. Sagtleven* | Koeien en Vee. Des Vaches & du Betail | *Mat:* op paneel *Size:* hoog 15, breed 22		(Unknown)
1805/07/03	AMSCH	0149	*C. Saftleven* | Een Stal van binnen, alwaar een Vrouw Eten geeft aan twee Bokjes, fraai behandeld op Paneel | *Mat:* op paneel *Size:* hoog 10, breed 14 duim	C	(Sold) fl 9:10 Agina
1805/10/09	HGBSM	0093	*C. Sagtleven* | De verkondiging aan de herders, ryk van ordonnantie en fraay | *Mat:* op paneel *Size:* hoog 29 breet 41 duim	T H van Willigen [or others]	(Sold) fl 10:10 Basemoine
1806/06/07	RMHSN	0005	*C: Saftleven* | Een aangenaam Landschap, met Geiten en andere Gedierten	A E K L	(Unknown)
1806/06/07	RMHSN	0030	*C. Zaftleven* | Een Koestal met Koeijen, Geiten, Paarden &c. met Bywerk	A E K L	(Unknown)
1806/06/07	RMHSN	0031	*C. Zaftleven* | Een Landschap met Koeijen, Paarden, Geiten &c. | *Mat:* op paneel	A E K L	(Unknown) fl 41
1806/06/07	RMHSN	0032	*C. Zaftleven* | De Geboorte te Bethlehem, met Beelden, Beesten &c. van zyn beste soort | *Mat:* op paneel	A E K L	(Sold) fl 40 Thijs

1806/06/07	RMHSN	0033	*C. Zaftleven* | Een Binnestal met Geiten &c. | *Mat:* op paneel	A E K L	(Sold) fl 17 Thijs
1807/08/26	AMSCH	0203	*C. Saftleven* | Dit natuurlyk voorwerp verbeeld in een oud Hollandsch Keukenvertrek, eene zittende bedaagde Vrouw, bezig Wortelen te schrapen, op de Tafel ter zyde legt een Bierkan, waar by een Brood en Aarden Pot, op den grond staat een Koperen Ketel, Straatbeezem en Mand en verder bywerk, meesterlyk gepenceeld | *Mat:* op paneel *Size:* hoog 28, breed 33 duim	Roos	(Sold) fl 53 Spruit
1807/08/26	AMSCH	0204	*C. Saftleven* | In een Boerenschuur ziet men eenige Huislieden zich vermaken, verders een menigte Gereedschappen; natuurlyk | *Mat:* op doek *Size:* hoog 33, breed 44 duim	Joseph Vallette	(Sold) fl 12:10 H Jansen
1808/06/06	RMRIJ	0150	*Zachtleven. (Cornelis)* | In eene Boeren Schuur ziet men, op den voorgrond, eene zingende Vrouw, spelende en slapende Boeren. Naast hen eene liggende Kat, staanden Hond en meerder schilderachtig bijwerk. In den achtergrond eene Koe, eenige Bokken en Schapen. Deze uitgevoerde, fraaije en verstandige Schilderij is in ordinantie, koloriet en houding in de manier van David Teniers [Dans l'intérieur d'une Ferme, une femme assise parôit chanter, pendant que plusieurs Paysans auprès d'elle, s'amusent de differentes manières. Divers Animaux et plusieurs autres accessoires enrichissent cette scène champêtre et agréable, qui, par sa Composition, et son éxécution, tient beaucoup de D. Teniers] | *Annots:* Verk. W. Coole, 6 Aug. 1782 (f.31.-) als D. Ryckaert (RMA I) *Mat:* op paneel *Size:* Hoog 14 ½, en breed 20 duim	Gerrit van der Pot, Heer van Groeneveld	(Sold) fl 129 van Leen
1810/06/20	AMSCH	0110	*C. Zagtleeven* | Een Binnenschuur, waarin eenige Aardvruchten en Boeren Huisraad | *Mat:* op paneel *Size:* hoog 16, breed 12 duimen	N	(Sold) fl 3 van Dijl

Saftleven, Cornelis (or Saftleven, C., copy after)

1806/10/16	UTWLD	0018	*Sagtleven* | Twee landschapjes van of na Sagtleven	Mr P de Malapert [or] W Beeldsnyder	(Unknown)

Saftleven, Cornelis (copy after)

1802/06/16	AMSCH	0086	*J.H. Jelgersma; na C. Saftleven* | Dit stuk stelt voor den Olden Barnevelt onder zyn Rechters voorgesteld; en verscheiden soorten van Gediertens, fiks en zeer natuurlyk na het Orgineel behandeld | copy by T.H. Jelgersma after C. Saftleven *Mat:* op doek *Size:* hoog 25, breed 31 ½ duim	[Merrem]	(Sold) fl 14 de Meijer

Saftleven, Cornelis (manner)

1803/09/07	AMSCH	0250	*C. Saftleven* | In een Boerenschuur ziet men een Meid, bézig een Kétel te schuuren, op de grond legt verscheide Keukengereedschap, als Kopere Kétel, Potten en Pannen; eenige Raapen en ander bywerk; op Paneel geschilderd, in de manier van C. Saftleven [Une grange dans laquelle une servante est occupée à écurer un chaudron ; dans le fond differens ustensiles de cuisine, tels que des chaudrons, des pots et des péles, des navets et d'autres accessoires ; sur bois, dans le goût de Saftleven.] | *Mat:* op paneel *Size:* hoog 13, breed 14 duim	Smidt	(Sold) fl 2 L Pakker
1808/06/11	RMRIJ	0049	*Als door Saftleven* | Een Zieke oude Vrouw | *Mat:* op paneel		(Bought In) fl 3 for lots 49 & 50
1808/06/11	RMRIJ	0050	*Als door Saftleven* | Een Temple | *Mat:* op paneel		(Bought In) fl 3 for lots 49 & 50
1808/06/11	RMRIJ	0098	*Onbekend, in de manier van Saftleven* | In eene Schuur ziet men een Man bezig 't Want te Mazen, omringt van een aantal Bywerk, als Visschen, Tobben, Kruiken, Vaatwerk enz. van een schoone uitwerking en warm coloriet | *Mat:* op paneel *Size:* hoog 17 ½, breed 23 duim		(Sold) fl 19:10 Van Giesen
1810/03/26	RMMUY	0060	*C. Saftleeven* | Eene rijk gestoffeerde Binneschuur, met figuren, veel Huisraad en Moesvruchten, in de manier van C. Saftleeven [L'intérieur d'une Etable, avec figures et nombres de legûmes et ustensiles de ménage, d'un bon effet.] | *Annots:* Copie de Zenir[?] et sa elev (BPG)	Daniel de Jongh Az	(Sold) fl 2:10 Molenyzer Amsterdam
1810/07/23	DOLG2	0040	*Sagtleven* | In een Binnenhuis ziet men Boeren en Boerinnen, en eenige Kinderen; geschilderd als Sagtleven | *Mat:* op doek *Size:* hoog 12, breed 13 duim	Pieter Quinting	(Unknown)

Saftleven, Herman

1801/03/16	AMSCH	0019	*H. Saftleven* | Een Rhyngezigt, ryk gestoffeerd en uitvoerig behandeld	K[ip]	(Sold) fl 5:5 Stevens
1801/04/23	AMYVR	0010	*Zagtleven* | Een Gezicht aan den Rhyn, gestoffeerd met Vaartuigen en Beelden		(Sold) fl 11 Coclaire
1801/05/11	AMSCH	0117	*H. Zaftleeven* | Een bergachtig Landschap, met Ryzigers en andere stoffagie | *Mat:* op paneel *Size:* hoog 11, breed 11 duim	V	(Bought In) fl 30
1801/06/10	AMSCH	0157	*Saftleven. (H.)* | Twee stuks Rhyngezichten, gestoffeerd met allerhande Vaartuigen, en een menigte Beeldjes; alles is uitmuntend gepenceeld | *Mat:* op paneel *Size:* hoog 8, breed 11 duim	Herman ten Kate	(Sold) fl 23 van Iperen
1801/06/10	AMSCH	0158	*Saftleven. (H.)* | Een Rhyngezicht, gestoffeerd verscheiden Aken en Beeldjes; natuurlyk en uitvoerig behandeld | *Mat:* op paneel *Size:* hoog 16, breed 20 duim	[Doublet]	(Sold) fl 25 J Yver
1802/02/23	AMREB	0028	*H. Saftleven* | 1 Rhyngezicht, met verscheide stoffagie uitvoerig op Panneel | *Mat:* op paneel	Margaretha Maria van Laar	(Sold) fl 5 J Rooyers

1802/06/16	AMSCH	0162	*H. Saftleeven* | Een Italiaanch [sic] bergachtig Landschap met een Rivier doorsneeden, op de voorgrond ziet men Lieden in een Schuit, en verder andere Wandelaars, by laag Houtgewas; zonachtig uitvoerig en meesterlyk fraay gepenceeld | *Mat:* op paneel *Size:* hoog 12, breed 15 duim	[Merrem]	(Sold) fl 36 H de Valk
1802/06/16	AMSCH	0163	*H. Saftleeven* | Een aangenaam Rhyngezicht, gestoffeerd met verscheiden gelaaden Vaartuigen, aan de eene zyde der Oever, Gebergten en Huislieden; bevallig en zonachtig behandeld | *Mat:* op paneel *Size:* hoog 6 ½, breed 7 ½ duim	[Merrem]	(Sold) fl 11:10 A Vermeulen
1802/06/16	AMSCH	0165	*H. Saftleeven* | In een Boeren Schuur ziet men een Boer een Koei melken: ter zyde staat een Vrouw by een Was-Tobben; gestoffeerd met eenig Vée en diversch Huisraad; bevallig gepenceeld | *Mat:* op paneel *Size:* hoog 8, breed 10 duim	[Merrem]	(Sold) fl 15 van der Schleij
1802/06/16	AMSCH	0166	*H. Saftleeven* | Een Boere Binnenvertrek, op de voorgrond een meenigte Huisraad, zoo Koper, Hout als Mandewerk, Groentens en Fruitten, en een Hen met zyn Kiekens; op de tweede grond een Vrouw by het Vuur; meesterlyk behandeld | *Mat:* op doek *Size:* hoog 25, breed 28 ½ duim	[Merrem]	(Sold) fl 28:10 Van Iperen
1802/09/18	RMDRS	0031	*H. Sagtleven* | Een Ryn gezicht, gestoffeerd met een menigte Figuuren en Scheepen | *Annots:* mooij maan de neaf bloot en Kaal (MB) *Size:* hoog 11 ½, breed 15 duim	Casper de Haas	(Sold) fl 40 Verweij
1802/09/21	UTHDG	0106	*H. Zagtleeven* | Het hoofd eener Koopstad aan den Rhijn, met Scheepen, Aken, menigte Koopwaren en Beeldjes gestoffeerd | *Mat:* op paneel *Size:* hoog 8, breed 10 ½ duimen		(Sold) fl 8:5 V den Hoven heere Straat
1802/11/01	DOBRA	0067	*H. Sagtleeven* | Een Rhyngezichtje, door H. Sagtleeven. 1674. met Scheepjes, Beeldjes, enz. zeer uitvoerig | *Mat:* op paneel *Size:* breed 11 hoog 8 duim *Inscr:* H. Sagtleeven. 1674 (signed and dated?) *Notes:* It is unclear whether the name and date are inscribed on the painting.	Paulus van der Spyk [or others]	(Sold) fl 11:10 Randwyk
1802/12/13	AMSCH	0144	*H. Sagtleeven* | Twee aangenaame Boom- en Bergagtigen Landschappen, ryk gestoffeerd met gaande en rustende Lieden; uitvoerig gepenceeld | *Mat:* op doek *Size:* hoog 10, breed 11 duim	Pruyssenaar [for] A	(Sold) fl 1:5 v^{n} Limmen
1802/12/13	AMSCH	0151	*H. Sagtleeven* | Twee stuks Capitaale Gezigten aan den Rhyn, ryk gestoffeerd met Beelden en Vaartuigen; uitvoerig en zonachtig geschilderd | *Mat:* op paneel *Size:* hoog 19, breed 20 duim	Pruyssenaar [for] A	(Sold) fl 5 Yver
1803/08/01	AMSCH	0051	*Zagtleeven (H.)* | Een ruim uitgestrekt bergagtig Land- en Rhyngezicht, ter linkerzyde met verscheide Vaartuigen gestoffeerd, ter regterzyde over een vlak veld ziet men Gebouwen, op de voorgrond voor Boerewooningen een menigte Beelden, dit stuk is helder en aangenaam van coloriet en uitvoerig behandeld, en een der besten van dezen Meester | *Mat:* op doek *Size:* hoog 26, breed 37 duim	J	(Sold) fl 285 Hodges
1803/08/17	AMSCH	0078	*Sastleven. (H.)* | Een Rhyngezicht, ter zyde tegens hoog Gebergten, ziet men eenige Huizen, Beeldjes en Boomgewas, in de Valeijen eenige Gebouwen, een Stad en een wyd uitgestrekt verschiet, warm van coloriet en zonachtig voorgesteld | *Mat:* op koper *Size:* hoog 14, breed 18 duim	Anna Catharina Putman	(Sold) fl 14 v^{n} Iperen
1803/09/07	AMSCH	0158	*H. Salftleeven* | Een Duin- en Bergachtig Landschap; gestoffeerd met eenige Lieden, Beestjes, enz., bevallig behandeld [Un paysage montagneux animé par des paysans, et differentes espèces de bétail ; composition agréable et finie] | *Mat:* op paneel *Size:* hoog 14, breed 20 duim	Smidt	(Sold) fl 5 Gruiter
1803/09/07	AMSCH	0159	*H. Salftleeven* | Een Gezicht aan den Rhyn met Geboomten, een Stad op een Berg, en het Water met verscheide Vaartuigen en Beeldjes gestoffeerd; kragtig op Doek [Une vue du Rhin, bornée par une montagne chargée d'arbres et sur laquelle se montre une ville ; le fleuve est couvert de bateaux et de figures, touche vigoureuse] | *Mat:* op doek *Size:* hoog 14, breed 19 duim	Smidt	(Sold) fl 5:10 Gruiter
1803/09/07	AMSCH	0160	*H. Salftleeven* | Een bevallig Heuvelachtig Landschap, met eenige Gebouwen en laag Houtgewas, gestoffeerd met berscheide Beeldjes, en aangenaam verschiet; uitvoerig op Paneel geschilderd [Ce tableau développe un beau paysage, dans lequel des colonnes, des habitations et des figures diverses offrent une agréable variété ; le coloris en est vigoureux] | *Mat:* op paneel [sur toile] *Size:* hoog 9, breed 12 duim *Notes:* The materials differ in the Dutch and French editions of the catalogue.	Smidt	(Sold) fl 4:5 Gruiter
1804/07/25	AMSCH	0074	*Saftleeven. (H.)* | Een Boom- en Bergachtig Landschap, verbeeldende een gezicht aan de Rhyn op de voorgrond eenig Geboomten verscheiden Lieden en verders by Gebergte en Geboomten een groot Casteel en een aangenaam Zonachtig, Bergachtig verschiet; dit Schilderytje is aller uitvoerigst en van de beste behandeling van deeze meester | *Mat:* op koper *Size:* hoog 9, breed 11 duim		(Sold) fl 25 Vinkeles
1804/07/25	AMSCH	0075	*Saftleeven (H.)* | Twee stuks, Boom- en Bergachtige Landschappen, zynde den eene een Boomryk Landschap, waaronder op de Voorgrond eenige Boere en Boerinnen en Kinderen, waarby eenige Koorenlanden en een Waterbeekje, verschyde Lieden te Paard, in Wagens en te Voet, en in 't verschiet hoog Gebergten; en 't andere verbeeld een Bergachtig Landschap aan den Rhyn, met een Rivier doorsneeden, mede ryk gestoffeerd, enz. deeze byde Ordinantien zyn aller zonachtigst, en		(Sold) fl 50 C S Roos

			uitvoerig en van de fynste schildering; en kunnen in een der beste Kabinetten geplaatst worden | *Mat:* op paneel *Size:* hoog 11 ½, breed 15 ½ duim		
1804/07/25	DLGRO	0003	*H. Sagtleven* | Een Boere binnen Huis, met eenige Boeren, die vrolyk onder een Pypje en Glaasje by malkanderen zitten en staan, op de voorgrond eenig Boeren gereij en Kippen, fraai geschilderd op Paneel | *Mat:* op paneel *Size:* hoog 19, breed 26 duim	Mr Franc van der Burch Wz.	(Unknown)
1804/08/08	AMSCH	0169	*H. Saftleven* | Een capitaal Rhyn- Gezicht, met Gebouwen, Wyngaarden, Schuuren en hoog Gebergte, het Land zoo wel als den Rhyn zyn gestoffeerd met een aantal Beeldjes, Vaartuigen, enz., verders Watervallen, en hoog ver uitgestrekt Gebergte in het verschiet, fraai van licht en uitvoerig op Doek gepenceeld | *Mat:* op doek *Size:* hoog 24, breed 29 duim	Roos [for] G	(Bought In) fl 20
1804/08/08	AMSCH	0170	*H. Saftleven* | Een Gezicht aan den Ryhn, met een Stad en zwaar Geboomte op het Gebergte, den Rhyn ryk gestoffeerd met een ménigte van Scheepen en Schuiten; aangenaam van couleur, en uitvoerig gepenceeld | *Mat:* op doek *Size:* hoog 14, breed 19, duim	Vink[eles] [for] K[=Gruyter?]	(Sold or Bought In) fl 4 Gruyter
1804/08/08	AMSCH	0171	*H. Saftleven* | Een Gezicht langs den Rhyn, ryk gestoffeerd en uitvoerig geschilderd | *Size:* hoog 6 ½, breed 9 ½ duim	Vink[eles] [for] K[=Gruyter?]	(Sold) fl 1:15 Pieterse
1804/10/16	DLOND	0197	*H. Sagtleven* | Riviergezicht tusschen Bergen. Vue de Rivière entre des Montagnes | *Mat:* op doek *Size:* hoog 7, breed 9		(Unknown)
1804/10/16	DLOND	0198	*H. Sagtleven* | Een Landschap. Un Paysage | *Mat:* op paneel *Size:* hoog 6, breed 7		(Unknown)
1804/12/10	AMSCH	0090	*Herm. Saftleeven* | Twee stuks Rhyngezichten, met diverse Schuiten en Beeldjes gestoffeerd, en bergachtig verschieten; uitvoerig en bevallig van schildering | *Mat:* op paneel *Size:* Hoog 9, breed 11 duim	Jan De Groot	(Sold) fl 32 Coclers
1805/07/03	AMSCH	0148	*H. Saftleven* | Twee stuks bevallige Rhyngezichten, het Water zoo wel als het Land zyn vol gewoel van Beeldjes, zynde delicaat behandeld | *Size:* hoog 8, breed 11 duim	C	(Sold) fl 40 L Pakker
1805/07/10	AMSCH	0134	*Saftleeven* | Twee stuks Bergachtige Landschappen, met Waters en Vaartuigen | *Mat:* op paneel	V[inkeles] [for] K	(Bought In) fl 4:10
1805/12/16	AMSCH	0100	*H. Saftleven* | Een fraay Gezicht op de Rhyn	R[oos]	(Sold) fl 0:6 L Pakker
1806/05/05	AMSCH	0135	*Saftleeven* | Een Rhyngezichtje met stoffagie van Beeldjes, Schuiten enz.; delicaat op Paneel | *Mat:* op paneel *Size:* hoog 7, breed 9 duim	V[inkeles]	(Sold) fl 4:15 van Laar
1806/08/20	HGBSM	0195	*H. Zagtleeven* | Twee stuks klijne Rhijngezichten, helder en uitvoerig geschilderd | *Mat:* op koper *Size:* hoog 4 ½, breed 5 ½ duim	Macalester Loup [or others]	(Sold) fl 14 Ph Mey
1808/04/26	GDAN	0212	*Zaftleven (H.)* | Een Rhijngezigtje waar op eenige Bootjes, en 't gezigt op een Ruïne | *Size:* hoog 10, breed 13 ½ duim	G H Fortuyn	(Unknown)
1808/04/26	GDAN	0213	*Zaftleven (H.)* | Een dito Rhijn en Bergägtig Gezigt, met bijwerk | *Size:* hoog 14 ½, breed 17 duim *Notes:* It is unclear what "dito" refers to in the title.	G H Fortuyn	(Unknown)
1808/04/26	GDAN	0214	*Zaftleven (H.)* | Een Zon- en Bergägtig Landschap, fraai gestoffeerd met Ezel, &c. | *Mat:* op koper *Size:* hoog 7 ½, breed 9 duim	G H Fortuyn	(Unknown)
1808/06/06	RMRIJ	0151	*Zachtleven. (Herman)* | Een aangenaam Rijngezigt, rijk gestoffeerd met Schuiten, Beelden en Beesten, allerliefelijkst van koloriet en zeer uitvoerig behandeld [Ce Bijou represente un beau Sîte au bord du Rhin, et est orné de bateaux et de plusieurs figures etc. Trés fini, d'un Coloris vrai, et d'un effet admirable] | *Mat:* op paneel *Size:* Hoog 6 ¾, en breed 8 ¾ duim *Loc:* Amsterdam, Nederland. Rijksmuseum. (A361)	Gerrit van der Pot, Heer van Groeneveld	(Sold) fl 66 J J de Wit [for] le Roi
1808/06/11	RMRIJ	0040	*Harman Saftleven* | In een Boeren Binnehuis ziet men by een Born-Put een aantal Meubilen en Gereedschappen, waar by twee Kindertjes, allerschoonst en natuurlyk geschilderd | *Mat:* op paneel *Size:* hoog 17, breed 18 duim		(Sold) fl 39 Koning
1808/06/13	AMSCH	0152	*Saftleven (H.)* | Een boom- en bergachtig Landschap, op den voorgrond een Waterplas en Stoffage van Beeldjes. Uitvoerig en zonachtig | *Mat:* op paneel *Size:* hoog 11, breed 15 duim	R[oos]	(Sold) fl 45 Van Iperen
1808/08/23	AMSCH	0193	*H. Zagtleven* | Een Rhijngezicht, rijk gestoffeerd, met Schepen, Vaartuigen en Beeldjes; uitvoerig	[Gruyter?]	(Sold or Bought In) fl 4:10 Gruyter
1808/11/28	AMSCH	0057	*H. Sagtleeven* | Een Gezicht aan den Rhijn, met een Stad op het Gebergten, rijk gestoffeerd met Beeldjes en verder een Bergachtig verschiet, uitvoerig geschilderd | *Mat:* op doek *Size:* hoog 14, breed 19 duim	[Gruyter?]	(Bought In) fl 4:15
1809/04/17	AMSCH	0116	*H. Zagtleven* | Een Rhijngezicht, rijk met Vaartuigen gestoffeerd, op den voorgrond een Herder met eenig Vee; helder en bevallig voorgesteld | *Mat:* op doek *Size:* hoog 46, breed 64 duim	A	(Sold) fl 2:15
1809/06/13	AMSCH	0173	*H. Zagtleeven* | Een Gezicht langs den Rhijn, met een Stad, op het Gebergten, het water met onderscheide Vaartuigen gestoffeerd; uitvoerig geschilderd | *Mat:* op doek *Size:* hoog 14, breed 19 duim	[Gruyter?]	(Sold or Bought In) fl 2:15 Gruiter
1809/06/13	AMSCH	0174	*H. Zagtleeven* | Een Rhijngezicht, met Vaartuigen en Beeldjes | *Mat:* op paneel *Size:* hoog 10, breed 14 duim	E	(Sold) fl 0:14 L Pakker

1809/07/25	HGBSM	0193	*H. Sagtleven* | Een Landschap, op de voorgrond een Kar, en voorts gestoffeert met Figuren, door H. Sagtleven 1656 | *Mat:* op paneel *Size:* hoog 19, breed 26 duim *Inscr:* H. Sagtleven 1656 (signed and dated?) *Notes:* It is unclear whether the name and date are inscribed on the painting.	D van der Aa [or] E B ten Dall	(Sold) fl 2:18 Schoon
1810/03/07	UTWLD	0006	*H. Zaftleven* | Een Schildery verbeeldende de Neude binnen Utrecht, alwaar het Regiment Waardgelders, afgedankt wordt, zeer uitvoerig, en helder van coloriet | *Size:* hoog 2 voet, 3 duim, breed 3 voet 2 duim	J J Woertman	(Unknown) fl 32
1810/03/07	UTWLD	0050	*Zaftleven* | Twee Landschappen	J J Woertman	(Unknown) fl 15
1810/03/23	HAVIN	0012	*H. Zachtleven* | Twee Gezigten aan den Rhijn, uitvoerig | *Size:* hoog 8 ¼ breet 11 ¼ d.	Rudolf Hendrik de Wetstein [or others]	(Unknown)
1810/06/06	RMMUY	0046	*H. Saftleeven* | Een Rhijngezigt, waar in hoog gebergte, gestoffeerd met verscheiden Gebouwen, Figuren, Vaartuigen, Houtvlotten &c. uitvoerig en aangenaam van ordonnantie | *Mat:* op paneel		(Unknown) fl 28:15
1810/06/06	RMMUY	0047	*H. Saftleeven* | Twee Stuks uitvoerige en rijk gestoffeerde Rhijngezigten | *Mat:* op paneel		(Unknown) fl 31
1810/06/06	RMMUY	0222	*H. Saftleven* | Een fraaij, uitvoerig Rhijngezigtje | *Mat:* op koper		(Unknown) fl 5:15
1810/06/20	AMSCH	0108	*H. Zagtleeven* | Twee stuks bevallige Rhijngezigten, rijk met Beeldjes en Vaartuigen. Uitvoerig behandeld | *Mat:* op paneel *Size:* Jeder hoog 6, breed 7 duimen	D	(Sold) fl 13 Coclers
1810/06/20	AMSCH	0109	*H. Zagtleeven* | Een Rhijngezigt, met stoffage van Beeldjes en Vaartuigen | *Mat:* op paneel *Size:* hoog 10, breed 13 duimen	B	(Sold) fl 1:10 Cassino
1810/10/11	AMSCH	0258[a]	*H. Zagtleven* | Drie stuks, twee Rijngezigten, door H. Zagtleven en een Landschapje door Everdingen | *This Lot:* Twee Rijngezigten; lot 258[b] by A. Everdingen	A	(Sold) fl 1:10 for lots 258[a] & 258[b]. L Pakker
			Saftleven, Herman (or Saftleven, H., manner)		
1801/03/16	AMSCH	0081	*Zagtleeven* | Twee Rhyngezichten, door of als Zagtleeven	P[ruyssenaar]	(Sold) fl 1:5 Gruiter
1802/06/16	AMSCH	0164	*H. Saftleeven, of in de manier* | Een Aangenaam bevallig Rhyngezicht, aan beider Oevers, met Woningen, Geboomten en Gebergte gestoffeerd, met verscheide Rysigers en werkende Lieden; zonachtig en uitvoerig van penceel-behandeling | *Mat:* op paneel *Size:* hoog 14, breed 21 duim	[Merrem]	(Sold) fl 12:10 Reijers
1807/06/10	HGBSM	0081	*H. Sagtleeven* | Twee stuks Rhijngezigten, langs bergen en gebouwen, met veel stoffagie, door of in de trant van H. Sagtleeven | *Mat:* op paneel *Size:* hoog 12 breed 15 duim	Abraham Delfos [or others]	(Sold) fl 6 Noordwyk
			Saftleven, Herman (copy after)		
1810/07/23	DOLG2	0087	*H. Sachtleeven* | Een Rhijngezicht; naar H. Sachtleeven | *Mat:* op paneel *Size:* hoog 8, breed 11 duim	Pieter Quinting	(Unknown)
			Saftleven, Herman (manner)		
1802/05/22	RMHSN	0025	*Saftleven* | Twee stuks op Koper, zynde Rhyngezigtjes, in de trant van Saftleven | *Mat:* op koper	Lambertus Bicker	(Unknown)
1802/08/24	LNDLS	0118	*Zagtleven* | Een uitvoerig gestoffeerd Landschap als van Zagtleven	Leonardus Bouman [or others]	(Unknown) fl 3:18
1802/09/18	RMDRS	0054	*H. Sachtleven* | Een Ryn gezicht, in de manier van H. Sachtleven	Casper de Haas	(Unknown) fl 4:5
1806/05/05	AMSCH	0184	*Saftleven* | Twee stuks Land en Rivier Gezichten, met Beeldjes gestoffeerd; als Saftleven	R[oos]	(Sold) fl 1 L Pakker
1808/04/26	GDAN	0217	*Zaftleven* | In de manier van Zaftleven, een Zonagtig Schilderij, zijnde een Waterputting, met Beelden, Schapen en Bijwerk | *Size:* hoog 21, breed 35 duim	G H Fortuyn	(Unknown)
			Sages, de [Unidentified]		
1806/11/24	AMSCH	0075	*Sages (de)* | Een Zeegezigt, met een Stad in het verschiet, gestoffeerd met zeilende Schepen, fiks geschilderd | *Mat:* op paneel *Size:* hoog 20, breed 26 duim	Munnikhuizen	(Sold) fl 2:15 du Pree
			Sala, Gabrielle [Unidentified]		
1809/07/19	AMSCH	0053	*Sala (Gabrielle)* | Twee stuks kapitale Ordonantiën, verbeeldende Landschappen, rijk gestoffeerd met een doode Haas, Egelvarken, Rijger, Ganzen, Vinken en ander Gevogelte, benevens verscheide Jagttuig. Kragtig en meesterlijk geschilderd | *Mat:* op doek *Size:* ieder is hoog 38, breed 49 duim	[Wijkersloot?]	(Sold) fl 13 Gruyter
			Salm		
1807/09/28	AMWUR	0012	*Salm* | Een stuk op Paneel, zynde een Groenlandsche Vissery | *Mat:* op paneel		(Unknown) fl 1:5
			Salm, Abraham van		
1806/08/13	AMSCH	0227	*Zalm. (A.)* | In een sterk woelende Zee, ziet men een ménigte van Scheepen en Haringbuizen bézig zynde te Vissen; uitvoerig gepenceeld | *Mat:* op paneel *Size:* hoog 29, breed 41 duim	Vinkeles [for] G[ruyter]	(Sold) fl 2:10 Du Pré

1809/07/27	AMYVR	0001	*A. Salm* | Een kapitaal stuk verbeeldende eenen Storm op Zee, waarin op den voorgrond eene Schipbreuk vertoond wordt, verder andere Schepen, een Boot met Volk enz., uitvoerig in het graauw geschilderd | *Mat:* op paneel	H Munk [and] T van der Feen [and] G de Hoeft	(Sold) fl 3:5 du Prée

Salviati, Francesco (Francesco de' Rossi)

1810/07/26	AMSCH	0141	*Salviati* | Een Gezigt op het Kapitool te Rome. Rijk met Beelden en fraai geschilderd | *Mat:* op doek *Size:* hoog 41, breed 54 duimen	Cassino	(Bought In) fl 30

Sam, Engel

1808/06/13	AMSCH	0150	*Sam (E.)* | Deze Ordonantie stelt voor de Vlucht van Egipte, zittende Maria op eene Ezel, en Jozef haar het Kind aanreikende. Zeer zacht en fraai als A. van der Werf gepenceeld | *Mat:* op doek *Size:* hoog 23, breed 26 duim	E M Engelberts	(Sold) fl 280 Boelen pour Henry

Sanders, Gerard

1801/03/31	HGCLF	0386	*Sanders* | Een Seraphyns stukje door Sanders 1752, in een vergulde lyst | *Inscr:* 1752 (dated?) *Notes:* It is unclear whether the date is inscribed on the painting.	H van der Hoop	(Sold) fl 2:4 Besançon
1809/06/13	AMSCH	0146	*G. Sanders* | Eene bevallig Meisje, speelende met een Hondje voor een open vengster; goed geschilderd | *Mat:* op paneel *Size:* hoog 11, breed 9 duim	E	(Sold) fl 4 Gruyter

Sanders, Gerard (or Sanders, G., manner)

1805/12/16	AMSCH	0062	*G. Sanders* | Een Meisje, spelende met een Hondje, leggende door een Raam; geestig op Paneel, door of in de manier van G. Sanders | *Mat:* op paneel	R[oos]	(Sold) fl 5:5 Spaan

Sandrart, Joachim von (I)

1801/05/11	AMSCH	0084	*J. Sandrart* | Een Italiaansch Landschap, op de voorgrond een waterplas by een anticque Fontyn, waarby verscheide stoffagie van Menschen en Muilëzels, zonachtig en delicaat gepenceeld, als J. Asselyn | *Mat:* op doek *Size:* hoog 19, breed 15 duim	E[lias]	(Sold) fl 62 v d Schleij [for] Z[=Putte]
1806/08/20	HGBSM	0006	*J. Sandrart* | Het Borstbeeld van den Wijsgeer Plato, met een rol papier in de hand, zeer doorschijnend en meesterlijk geschilderd, door J. Sandrart, Ann- 1648 | *Mat:* op paneel *Size:* hoog 26, breed 20 duim *Inscr:* J. Sandrart, Ann- 1648 (signed and dated?) *Notes:* It is unclear whether the name and date are inscribed on the painting.	Macalester Loup [or others]	(Sold) fl 10 Coclers

Sandrart, Susanne Maria von (Auer)

1810/05/22	AMSCH	0092	*Sandrart. (S.)* | In een aangenaam Italiaansch Landschap vertoont zig op den voorgrond een Waterplas, waar bij een antique Fontijn, gestoffeerd met een Heer te paard, een Huisman en beladen Ezel, verder eene Vrouw en eenige Gebouwen; zonachtig en uitvoerig behandeld, in de manier van J. Asselijn | *Mat:* op doek *Size:* hoog 17 ½, breed 15 ½ duim	Johannes van de Putte Nicolaasz.	(Sold) fl 60 van Iperen

Sant Acker, F.

1809/07/25	HGBSM	0281	*T. Sant Acker* | Een doode Patrys, aan een Lint hangende, zeer uitvoerig | *Mat:* op doek *Size:* hoog 22, breed 16 en een half duim *Notes:* The artist's name was given as "T. Sant Acker" but we have assumed this is an error.	D van der Aa [or] E B ten Dall	(Sold) fl 1:5 Hassevoord

Santafede, Fabrizio

1803/04/27	AMSCH	0019	*Santafede* | Une Sainte Famille & le pére Eternel, ce Tableau est d'un bon effêt & est vigoureusement peint | *Size:* h. 5 ½, l. 4 pieds	A	(Sold) fl 98 Gruiter

Santvoort, Dirck Dircksz.

1803/04/20	AMSCH	0071	*Santvoord. 1640. (D. D.)* | Twee stuks, een Mans en een Vrouwe Pourtrait, beide in aloude prachtige zwart Satyne kleeding afgebeeld, de Man met een Kante Kraag, en andere geborduurde Vercierzelen, de Vrouw mede met Kant, edele Gesteentens en Paerlen vercierd, hebbende in haar Regterhand een Wayer, en verder bywerk; alles delicaat en meesterlyk behandeld, zoo schoon als B. van der Helst [Deux magnifiques Portraits, homme & femme. Le Mari paroit un personnage distingué par son riche vetement en satin noir, portant des rabats en dentelle. Le costume de la Dame correspond à celui du Mari par la richesse de ses ornemens : de sa droite elle tient un evanteil [sic]. Ces deux piéces sont traitées avec beaucoup de delicatesse, & ne cedent point aux ouvrages excellens de Barth. van der Helst.] | *Mat:* op doek *Size:* ieder hoog 49, breed 38 duim *Inscr:* D.D. Santvoord. 1640 (signed and dated?) *Notes:* It is unclear whether the name and date are inscribed on the painting.	Maria Magdalena van Sluypwyk, gravinne van Moens	(Sold) fl 112 Hulswit
1803/04/20	AMSCH	0124	*D. D. Santvoord* | Een Vrouwe Pourtrait, als dito [halver Lyf] [Un Portrait de femme largement peint par D.D. Santvoord.] | *Mat:* op paneel *Size:* hoog 27, breed 23 duim	Maria Magdalena van Sluypwyk, gravinne van Moens	(Sold) fl 1 Hulswit

Santvoort, Philipp van

1804/08/08	AMSCH	0234	*P. van Zandvoort* | In een Studeerkamer zit een deftig oud Man, in alöude Hollandsche Kleeding, leunende met zyn Regterhand op de Leuning	Vink[eles] [for] K[=Gruyter?]	(Sold) fl 14 La Bouchere

van zyn Stoel, met de Linker schynt hy een Blad te willen omslaan van een Boek, dat by hem open op een Tafel legt; uitvoerig en meesterlyk geschilderd | *Mat:* op doek *Size:* hoog 42, breed 49 duim

Santvoort, Pieter Dircksz.

1801/03/16	AMSCH	0175	*van Zantvoord* | Een Wintergezicht | *Notes:* This lot was sold with lot 176 by J. Momper (II).	P[ruyssenaar]	(Sold) fl 1 for lots 175 & 176. Gruiter
1806/08/13	AMSCH	0170	*Santvoort. (P. van)* | Een Landschap met drie Kinderen by eenige Schaapen; delicaat gepenceeld | *Mat:* op doek *Size:* hoog 42, breed 37 duim	Vinkeles [for] G[ruyter]	(Sold) fl 0:18 L Pakker
1808/12/12	UTWLD	0005	*P. van Santvoord* | Een Wintergezicht [Alle in swarte Lysten en wel geconserveerd.] | *Mat:* op paneel *Size:* hoog 11 duim, breed 19 duim *Notes:* The bracketed information in the title appears above lot 1 and refers to lots 1 to 19.	Mr D Hoola van Nooten	(Unknown)

Sarazin, Jean-Baptiste

1803/12/12	AMSCH	0089	*Sarrazin* | Een uitgestrekt Boom en Bergachtig Landschap, in het midden een Brug vol stoffagie van Beelden en Beesten, waar onder een Waterval; alles van een aangenaame couleur en fix behandeld | *Mat:* op paneel *Size:* hoog 27, breed 34 duim	D	(Sold) fl 10:10 Pruysenaar

Savery, J.

1802/09/18	RMDRS	0041	*J. Savry* | Een Landschap met Koeyen, Schapen en Herders | *Annots:* slegte Copien, die v. Pals heeft zien Copieeren (MB) *Size:* hoog 11 ½, breed 13 ½ duim	Casper de Haas	(Unknown) fl 19:5 for lots 41 & 42
1802/09/18	RMDRS	0042	*J. Savry* | Een dito [Landschap met Koeyen, Schapen en Herders] | *Annots:* slegte Copien, die v. Pals heeft zien Copieeren (MB) *Size:* hoog 11 ½, breed 13 ½ duim	Casper de Haas	(Unknown) fl 19:5 for lots 41 & 42
1802/09/18	RMDRS	0052	*J. Savry* | Een Herder en Herderin, met Schapen, en verder bywerk | *Size:* hoog 12, breed 10 ½ duim	Casper de Haas	(Sold) fl 9:10 Verweij

Savery, Jacob (I)

1805/10/09	HGBSM	0091	*Oude Xavery* | Twee stuks, zynde bosch gezigten, het eene met leeuwen, en het andere met harten, door den oude Xavery | *Mat:* op paneel *Size:* hoog 12 ½ breet 15 ½ duim	T H van Willigen [or others]	(Sold) fl 3:15 Valette

Savery, Roelandt

1802/04/13	HAVIN	0016	*Xavry* | Een Landschap, verbeeldende het Paradys, uitvoerig		(Unknown)
1802/06/28	AMSCH	0213	*R. Xaveri* | Twee stuks ryke Ordonnantien, verbeeldende den eene Achilles onder de Maagden; en de andere de Offerhande van Ephigenia | *Mat:* op paneel *Size:* ieder hoog 14, breed 12 duim	B	(Sold) fl 5:10 Texier
1802/09/06	AMSCH	0134	*R. Xavery* | In een Boomryk Landschap, ziet men een rustend Huisman, verzelt van zyn Hond, en van verscheide staand, graazend en leggend Vée, in 't verschiet zyn eenige Boerewoningen; meesterlyk op Doek geschilderd | *Mat:* op doek *Size:* hoog 31, breed 38 duim	H^n Smit	(Sold) fl 0:14 C Deppe
1803/06/20	AMSCH	0026	*R. Xavery* | Een Landschap met verscheide zoorten van staande en leggende Gediertens, uitvoerig op Paneel | *Mat:* op paneel *Size:* hoog 7, breed 8 duim	Schley [for] G	(Sold) fl 3:15 Gruiter
1803/07/07	HGKAN	0006	*Xavery* | Een Landschap met Beesten, door Xavery [Schilderyen in Olyverf] | *Mat:* in olyverf *Notes:* The bracketed information in the title appears above lot 1 and refers to lots 1 to 25.		(Unknown)
1803/07/14	MGKLY	0015	*R. Xavery* | Een Bergagtig Landschap met een Rivier ryk gestoffeert met Beesten en kunstig gepenseelt	Mr Caspar Jacob van Citters	(Unknown)
1803/08/01	AMSCH	0050	*Xavery. (R.)* | In een Nis ziet men Pot, gevuld met diversche zoorten van keurige Bloemen, waarop Insecten aazen, alleruitvoerigst en fraay gepenceeld | *Mat:* op paneel *Size:* hoog 9, breed 7 duim	J	(Sold) fl 6:5 Gruiter
1803/08/24	HGKAN	0035	*Xavery* | Twee stuks ryke Ordonnantien verbeeldende den eene Achilles onder de Maagden, en de andere de Offerhande van Ephigenia | *Mat:* op paneel *Size:* hoog 14, breet 12 duim	[Teissier] [or others]	(Sold) fl 10:10 Plukkooy
1803/09/07	AMSCH	0221	*R. Xavary* | By eenige Plantgewassen en Heesters, ziet men een menigte verschillende Vogelen, uitvoerig [Tableau représentant une touffe d'arbustes et de plantes sur lesquels sont assis plusieurs oiseaux ; belle composition] | *Mat:* op paneel *Size:* hoog 14, br. 22 duim	Smidt	(Bought In) fl 8
1803/12/12	AMSCH	0091	*R. Savery* | Twee stuks Landschappen, vol diversche Gediertens; uitvoerig op Paneel | *Mat:* op paneel *Size:* hoog 11, breed 16 duim	D	(Sold) fl 4:15 Valet
1804/02/27	AMSCH	0120	*Xavery. (R.)* | Twee stuks Boomryke Landschappen, ryk gestoffeerd met een menigte van allerhande zoorten Gediertens en Gevogelten | *Mat:* op paneel *Size:* hoog 26, breed 48 duim	B	(Sold) fl 3 Gruiter
1804/08/02	BDAN	0015	*Xavrie* | Een Bergachtig Landschap gestoffeert met Koeijen, Figuren, enz:, van zynen besten tyd | *Mat:* op doek *Size:* b. 21 en 1 half d. h. 18 d.	J G Calckberner	(Unknown)
1804/08/08	AMSCH	0231	*R. Xavery* | In een Bosch- en Bergachtig Landschap ziet men op 't speelen van Orféus al 't Gedierten tot hem naderen; uitvoerig geschilderd | *Mat:* op paneel *Size:* hoog 25 ½, br. 48 duim	Vink[eles] [for] K[=Gruyter?]	(Sold) fl 0:6 L Pakker

1804/10/16	DLOND	0274	*Xavouri* | Een Landschap met Vee. Paysage & du Betail | *Mat:* op paneel *Size:* hoog 13, breed 25		(Unknown)
1804/12/10	AMSCH	0101	*Xavery* | Een Landschap, ter zyde, by een bergh en geboomten, ziet men een Herder by een bevallig Mysje, welke haar voeten in een stroomend beekje wast, ter zyde ziet men Koeijen, Schaapen en een Bok; alles is bevallig geordineerd en zonachtig van penceelbehandeling | *Mat:* op paneel *Size:* Hoog 15, breed 19 duim	Jan De Groot	(Sold) fl 15:10 Coclers
1805/06/24	DOBLU	0009	*Roelend Xavery* | Een Allegorie	Willem Snellen [or] F R E Nibbelinck [or] Gysbert Visser	(Unknown)
1805/07/10	AMSCH	0174	*R. Xavery* | Een Landschap, met verslindende Dieren; breed gepenceeld | *Size:* hoog 12, breed 16 duim	V[inkeles] [for] N	(Sold) fl 0:6 L Pakker
1806/05/05	AMSCH	0156	*Xavery* | Een Duin en boomryk Landschap, op de voorgrond by een helder spiegelend Water, eenig staand en rustend Vee, verzeld van een Herder en Herderin; zonachtig en meesterlyk op Paneel | *Mat:* op paneel *Size:* hoog 18, breed 21 duim	V[inkeles]	(Sold) fl 4:5 Scheurleer
1806/05/05	AMSCH	0157	*Xavery* | Een bevallig Landschap, met staand en leggend Vee, en andere stoffagie | *Mat:* op paneel *Size:* hoog 25, breed 33 duim	V[inkeles]	(Sold) fl 1:15 Van Stroom
1806/08/13	AMSCH	0177	*Savery. (R.)* | Een bevallig en natuurlyk Heuvelachtig Landzicht, met een Rivier en verscheide Geboomten, en Gebouwen; gestoffeerd met eenige rustende en gaande Ryzigers; meesterlyk fraai en van een uitvoerige penceelbehandeling | *Mat:* op paneel *Fmt:* ovaals gewys *Size:* hoog 17, breed 23 duim	Roos	(Sold) fl 2 L Pakker
1806/08/13	AMSCH	0226	*Xavery* | Een Berg- en Boomryk Landschap gestoffeerd met Landlieden en Vee, uitvoerig geschildert | *Mat:* op paneel *Size:* hoog 11, breed 14 duim	Vinkeles [for] G[ruyter]	(Sold) fl 12:10 Swanenburg
1807/06/02	AMHUY	0039	*Xaverie* | Een Landschap met staande en leggende Beesten		(Unknown)
1807/08/26	AMSCH	0246	*Xavery* | Twee stuks met Leeuwen en Harten, in uitvoerige Landschappen | *Mat:* op paneel *Size:* hoog 13, breed 16 duim	Joseph Vallette	(Sold) fl 3 Jozi
1809/07/19	AMSCH	0068	*Xaverij (R)* | Twee stuks Bergachtige Landschappen, met Geboomte en verscheide Beesten gestoffeerd | *Mat:* op paneel *Size:* ieder is hoog 14, breed 25 duim	[Wijkersloot?]	(Sold) fl 1 Gruyter
1809/07/25	HGBSM	0202	*Roeland Savery* | Twee Stukjes | *Mat:* op koper *Size:* hoog 8, breed 11 duim	D van der Aa [or] E B ten Dall	(Sold) fl 1:10 Schoon
1810/03/07	UTWLD	0030	*Savery* | Een grot met Leeuwen | *Size:* hoog 1 voet 3 duim, breed 2 voet 1 duim	J J Woertman	(Unknown) fl 4
1810/03/23	HAVIN	0032	*Xavrij* | Een dito [Landschap]	Rudolf Hendrik de Wetstein [or others]	(Unknown)
1810/06/06	RMMUY	0139	*R. Savery* | Eenige Wilde Dieren met elkander vechtende, een Aap en Gevogelte, op een boom, in een Landschap. Uitvoerig | *Mat:* op koper		(Unknown) fl 4:14
1810/06/20	AMSCH	0135	*R. Xavery* | Een Noordsch Landschap, met Herten, Reën en Gevogelte	S	(Sold) fl 2:15 Cassino
1810/07/23	DOLGI	0065	*Xavarij* | Een Landschap met Koeijen, Schapen, een Geit en Beeldtjes; goed van teekening | *Mat:* op paneel *Size:* hoog 8 ½, breed 11 duim	Mr Pieter van den Santheuvel	(Sold) fl 10 J de Visser
1810/07/26	AMSCH	0132	*R. Xaverij* | Een Noordsch Bergachtig Landschap, met Herten, Reeën en ander Gedierten	Cassino	(Bought In) fl 3
1810/10/10	MGCIT	0115	*Savery* | Een Noords Landgezigt, met een menigte van viervoetig en ander Gedierte, aan die Streek eigen; zeer uitvoerig behandeld	Caspar van Citters	(Unknown)
			Savery, Roelandt (and Cornelisz. van Haarlem)		
1803/12/12	AMSCH	0090	*R. Savery; C. van Haarlem* | Het Paradys waarin Adam en Eva gezeten zyn, met den Appel, omgeeven van een groot aantal viervoetige en vliegende Gediertens; alles zeer uitvoerig op Paneel, door R. Savery, en de Beelden door C. van Haarlem | *Mat:* op paneel *Size:* hoog 32, breed 54 duim	E	(Sold) fl 42 Salsedo
			Savery, Roelandt (or Savery, R., manner)		
1802/09/06	AMSCH	0260	*R. Xavery* | Eenige wilde Gediertens in een Landschap, met Ruïnes en eenige lieden die Offeren; door of in de manier van R. Xavery	Mevrouw Achtienhoven	(Sold) fl 1:15 Gruiter
1803/09/07	AMSCH	0271	*P. Xavery* | Een Brabands Dorpgezigt, vol gewoel van Beeldjes, Wagens en Vée; uitvoerig op Paneel, door of in de manier van P. Xavery [La vue d'un village Flamand ; grand mouvement de figures, de chevaux et de voitures ; parfaitement traite, sur bois, dans le goût de Xavary.] | *Mat:* op paneel *Size:* hoog 18, breed 25 duim *Notes:* The artist's name was given as "P. Xavery" but we have assumed this is an error. This lot was misnumbered no. 171 in the French edition of the catalogue.	Smidt	(Sold) fl 6 W Reijers
			Savoye, Daniel de		
1809/04/17	AMSCH	0093	*D. Savoij* | In een Landschap ziet men Vénus dansende met Pan, ter zijde rustende Nimphen en Saters; meesterlijk | *Mat:* op doek *Size:* hoog 28, breed 25 duim	A	(Sold) fl 3:5 Gruyter

Schaalje, C.J.

1802/08/24	LNDLS	0009	*C.J. Schaalje* | Op een Marmeren Tafel staat een gefigureerde Pot met veele soorten van Bloemen, als: roode en witte Roozen, Zonnenbloem, Bol- en Stok roozen, Krul-leliën, Iriassen met eenige Insecten enz., bij den voet liggen bossen Blaauwe en Witte Druiven, Meloen en Appelen, agter hetzelve ziet men een Hof-gezigt. Alles zeer delicaat, uitvoerig en konstig op paneel | *Mat:* op paneel *Size:* hoog 25, breed 20 duimen	Leonardus Bouman [or others]	(Unknown) fl 130
1804/05/07	AMSCH	0158	*Schaalje. (C. J.)* | Een marmere Tafel, waarop een gevlogte Mandje met verscheide soorten van Bloemen; fraay behandeld en bevallig van Ordonantie | *Size:* hoog 16, breed 14 duim	Pruysnaar	(Bought In) fl 10

Schaaven, van [Unidentified]

1802/07/27	AKHRK	0053	*Van Schaaven* | Een Tafel waarop groote Schelvisschen en Botjes liggen, natuurlijk gevolgd | *Mat:* op paneel *Size:* hoog 20 ½, breed 25 ½ duim	Maria Stategaart	(Sold) fl 10:10 Banning
1802/07/27	AKHRK	0054	*Van Schaaven* | Op de Tafel ligt Snoek en Baars, zeer goed gepenceeld | *Mat:* op doek *Size:* hoog 13 ½, breed 22 ½ duim	Maria Stategaart	(Sold) fl 7:15 Banning

Schalch, Johann Jakob

1803/07/07	HGKAN	0009	*J.J. Schalch* | Een Bataille, door J.J. Schalch [Schilderyen in Olyverf] | *Mat:* in olyverf *Notes:* The bracketed information in the title appears above lot 1 and refers to lots 1 to 25.		(Unknown)
1803/07/07	HGKAN	0010	*J.J. Schalch* | Een Landschap, verbeeldende een Morgenstond, door denzelve [Schilderyen in Olyverf] | *Mat:* in olyverf *Notes:* The bracketed information in the title appears above lot 1 and refers to lots 1 to 25.		(Unknown)
1803/07/07	HGKAN	0011	*J.J. Schalch* | Een Landschap, verbeeldende een Avondstond, door denzelve [Schilderyen in Olyverf] | *Mat:* in olyverf *Notes:* The bracketed information in the title appears above lot 1 and refers to lots 1 to 25.		(Unknown)
1803/07/07	HGKAN	0012	*J.J. Schalch* | Een Landschap met Paarden, door denzelve [Schilderyen in Olyverf] | *Mat:* in olyverf *Notes:* The bracketed information in the title appears above lot 1 and refers to lots 1 to 25.		(Unknown)
1803/07/07	HGKAN	0013	*J.J. Schalch* | Een Engelsch Bergagtig Landschap met Schaapen, door denzelve [Schilderyen in Olyverf] | *Mat:* in olyverf *Notes:* The bracketed information in the title appears above lot 1 and refers to lots 1 to 25.		(Unknown)
1803/07/07	HGKAN	0014	*J.J. Schalch* | Een Landschap met Paarden, door denzelve [Schilderyen in Olyverf] | *Mat:* in olyverf *Notes:* The bracketed information in the title appears above lot 1 and refers to lots 1 to 25.		(Unknown)

Schalcke, Cornelis Symonsz. van der

1808/04/26	GDAN	0158	*Schalke* | In een Kamer zit een Jongeling aan een tafel die een brandende Kaers in zijne hand houdt, naast hem zit een Uil, doende het licht eene overheerlijke werking, en 't stuk schoon geschilderd | *Mat:* op paneel *Size:* hoog 10 ½, breed 9 duim	G H Fortuyn	(Unknown)
1808/04/26	GDAN	0159	*Schalke* | Men ziet hier in dit Schildery, een parthij Jongens op Drie Koningen Avond, met de verlichte Star lopen, als 't vorige geschilderd | *Size:* hoog 9, breed 7 ½ duim	G H Fortuyn	(Unknown)
1810/03/27	RMCNL	0036	*C. v. Schalken* | Een Bergachtig Landschap zeer warm, fraai en meesterachtig gepenseeld		(Unknown)
1810/10/10	MGCIT	0038	*Schalke* | Een klein rond ovaal Schilderijtje, zijnde een Mannetje met een lagchende tronie, hebbende een vol geschonken Glas in de hand, zeer uitvoerig en delicaat | *Fmt:* ovaal	Caspar van Citters	(Unknown)

Schalcke, Cornelis Symonsz. van der (or Schalcke, C., manner)

1801/05/11	AMSCH	0086	*J. Schalke, of in de manier* | Een Jongeling in een Landschap met een sluyer omhangen, bevallig van penceel behandeling | *Mat:* op doek *Size:* hoog 29, breed 25 duim *Notes:* The artist's name was given as "J. Schalke" but we have assumed this is an error.	P[ruyssenaar]	(Sold) fl 1:15 Coclers

Schalcke, Cornelis Symonsz. van der (manner)

1801/12/22	AMOTT	0011	*Schalke* | 1 speelende Jongeling op de Guitar, als van Schalke	Bartholomeus Ruloffs	(Unknown) fl 5

Schalcken, Godfried

1801/10/19	AMSCH	0065	*Schalcken. (G.)* | Een biddende Munnik, houdende beiden handen te zamen en rustende op een Boek, zeer delicaat geschildert | *Mat:* op paneel *Size:* hoog 10 ¼, breed 8 duim	Jonkheer Menno Baron van Coehoorn	(Sold) fl 80 C S Roos
1802/07/20	MGSAN	0056	*G. Schalken* | Een fraai Schildery, een Vrouw by een Kaarslicht, by haar nog een Figuur; op Paneel: extra delicaat en malsch geschilderd | *Mat:* op paneel *Size:* hoog duim 11, breed duim 9		(Unknown)
1802/08/24	LNDLS	0066	*G. Schalken* | Twee stuks een Mans en een Vrouwen Pourtrait. Konstig en delicaat van schildering, beide op doek, ovaal formaat | *This Lot:* Een Mans Pourtrait *Mat:* op doek *Fmt:* ovaal *Size:* hoog 28, breed 24 duimen *Notes:* Lots 66 and 67 were printed in the catalogue as one item.	Leonardus Bouman [or others]	(Unknown) fl 7:5 for lots 66 & 67
1802/08/24	LNDLS	0067	*G. Schalken* | Twee stuks een Mans en een Vrouwen Pourtrait. Konstig en delicaat van schildering, beide op doek, ovaal formaat | *This Lot:* Een	Leonardus Bouman [or others]	(Unknown) fl 7:5 for lots 66 & 67

			Vrouwen Pourtrait *Mat:* op doek *Fmt:* ovaal *Size:* hoog 28, breed 24 duimen *Notes:* Lots 66 and 67 were printed in the catalogue as one item.		
1802/08/24	LNDLS	0094	*G. Schalken* | Een Mans Poutrait, Borststuk. Konstig en Kragtig op doek, door G. Schalken, ovaal | *Mat:* op doek *Fmt:* ovaal *Size:* hoog 11 ½, breed 9 ½ duimen	Leonardus Bouman [or others]	(Unknown) fl 8
1802/09/18	RMDRS	0061	*Schalken* | Een Meid met een Kaars	Casper de Haas	(Sold) fl 4:5 Gruiters
1802/11/01	DOBRA	0146	*Schalken* | Het Hoofd van een Jongeling, meesterlyk geschilderd | *Mat:* op paneel *Size:* hoog 14, br. 13 d.		(Unknown) fl 15:5 for lots 146 & 147
1802/11/01	DOBRA	0147	*Schalken* | Een dito [Hoofd], zynde een Jong Meisje | *Mat:* op paneel *Size:* hoog 14, br. 13 d.		(Unknown) fl 15:5 for lots 146 & 147
1802/11/01	DOBRA	0157	*G. Schalken* | Een Oud-Mans Hoofd | *Mat:* op paneel *Size:* hoog 16, br. 12 duim		(Unknown) fl 2:10
1802/11/01	DOBRA	0162	*G. Schalken* | Een Vrouwe Beeld, haar spiegelende in een Fontein | *Mat:* op doek		(Unknown) fl 3
1803/08/24	HGKAN	0021	*G. Schalken* | Twee stuks van boven toogs gewys voorstellende, een Heer en Dame, tot de knien te zien, zy zyn beide Ryk gekleed, uitvoerig en delicaat geschildert | *Mat:* op paneel *Fmt:* van boven toogs gewys *Size:* hoog 11, breet 8 duim	[Teissier] [or others]	(Sold) fl 18 Huybregts
1803/12/15	MGLAC	0016	*G. Schalken* | Het Pourtrait van Maria Anna, Gemalinne van Karel de IIde. Koning van Spanjen, geschilderd by gelegenheid dat die Vorstin zig uit hoofde der strenge Vorst in 1690 te Dordrecht moest ophouden, eer zy haare Reis naar Madrid kon voort zetten, zoo als blykt, uit het hier bygevoegt Tractaatje | *Mat:* op doek *Size:* hoog duim 19, breed duim 16	Mr L H de Haze Bomme	(Unknown)
1804/07/25	AMSCH	0076	*Schalken. (G.)* | In een Hofgezicht, ziet men een bevallig Meisje, in deftige Kleeding, rustende op een Balustrade, over welke een Tapyt hangt, en houdende in de eene Hand een Tros witte Druiven en streelende met de andere een Hondje welke by haar ligt, ter zyde een Hoedt met verscheide roode en witte Pluimen, enz. dit stukje is aller uitvoerigst en fraai gepenceeld | *Mat:* op doek *Size:* hoog 19, breed 15 ½ duim		(Sold) fl 40 Van der Schley
1804/10/16	DLOND	0199	*G. Schalken* | Ene Vrouw by Kaarslicht. Une Femme à côté de la flamme d'une Chandelle | *Mat:* op paneel *Size:* hoog 9, breed 7		(Unknown)
1805/07/03	AMSCH	0043	*Schalken. (G.)* | Een oude Vrouw met een Hond op haar schoot, zy is gekleed met een mantel en met een zwart hoedje op haar hoofd en een bevallig geplooide kraag om haar hals; aller delicaatst en uitvoerig geschilderd | *Mat:* op paneel *Size:* hoog 7 ½, breed 6 duim	R[oos]	(Sold) fl 90 Coclers
1805/10/09	HGBSM	0112	*G. Schalken* | Het portrait van een schoone jonge dame, uitvoerig geschildert door G. Schalken, hoog 27 breet 22 duim, ovaal formaat op doek | *Mat:* op doek *Fmt:* ovaal *Size:* hoog 27 breet 22 duim	T H van Willigen [or others]	(Sold) fl 3:5 van den Broek
1806/05/05	AMSCH	0126	*G. Schalken* | Een bevallige Jonge Juffer, bézig met een Mesje een Oester te keeren; delicaat gepenceelt op Paneel door G. Schalken, ovaal formaat | *Mat:* op paneel *Fmt:* ovaal *Size:* hoog 7, breed 5 ½ duim	H	(Sold) fl 7 Vinkeles [for] S
1806/06/07	RMHSN	0012	*Schalken* | Een Heer, staande in zyn Japon, waar agter een Landschap en verder Bywerk, door Schalken, op Doek, Vergulde Lyst | *Mat:* op doek	A E K L	(Unknown)
1806/08/13	AMSCH	0167	*Schalken. (G.)* | By een helder brandent kaarslicht ziet men een bevallige Dame, met een glas in haar hand, dewelke door een Heer die nevens haar zit; eenig geld en kleinoodien word aangeboden; schoon van effect en delicaat gepenceeld | *Mat:* op paneel *Size:* hoog 9 ½, breed 10 duim	Vinkeles [for] G[ruyter]	(Sold) fl 24 Haffner
1807/06/10	HGBSM	0160	*G. Schalken* | Een Portret van een Dame, delicaat gepenceeld | *Mat:* op doek *Size:* hoog 16, breed 13 duim	Abraham Delfos [or others]	(Sold) fl 2:2 v Giese
1808/06/06	RMRIJ	0110	*Schalke. (Gottfried)* | Een peinzend Manskopje. Verdienstelijk geschilderd [La Tête d'un homme avec un Bonnet. Ce Tableau quoique petit, n'est pas sans mérite] | *Mat:* op paneel *Size:* Hoog 3 ¾, en breed 3 ½ duim	Gerrit van der Pot, Heer van Groeneveld	(Sold) fl 2 Van der Hart
1808/06/11	RMRIJ	0067	*G: Schalken* | Een Mans Pourtrait in zyn Japon, zeer uitvoerig en schoon | *Mat:* op paneel *Size:* hoog 9, breed 7 ½ duim		(Sold) fl 9 Rohan
1808/09/13	HABRU	0084	*Schalken* | Een Kaarsligt		(Unknown) fl 2:5
1808/10/28	AMVRS	0054	*Schalken, (G.)* | Een biddende Munnik, met gevouwe handen, rustende op een Boek. Zeer teder en bevallig, vol uitdrukking en kunstig geschilderd | *Mat:* op paneel *Size:* hoog 10 ½, breed 8 duim	Marten Udink	(Sold) fl 300 Joukes en Oijens
1809/07/25	HGBSM	0177[a]	*G. Schalken* | Twee Mans-Hoofdjes, door G. Schalken, op Paneel, het eene ovaal en het andere vierkant | *This Lot:* Een Mans-Hoofdje *Mat:* op paneel *Fmt:* ovaal	D van der Aa [or] E B ten Dall	(Sold) fl 11:10 for lots 177[a] & 177[b]. van Eyk
1809/07/25	HGBSM	0177[b]	*G. Schalken* | Twee Mans-Hoofdjes, door G. Schalken, op Paneel, het eene ovaal en het andere vierkant | *This Lot:* Een Mans-Hoofdje *Mat:* op paneel *Fmt:* vierkant	D van der Aa [or] E B ten Dall	(Sold) fl 11:10 for lots 177[a] & 177[b]. van Eyk
1809/09/06	AMSCH	0065	*Schalken (G.)* | Een Jong Heer met een brandende Kaars in zijn linkerhand, welke een Pijp schijnt aangestoken te hebben, voor hem een Bierkan en Blaker; frappant van licht en delicaat van schildering | *Mat:* op paneel *Size:* hoog 11, breed 9 duim	Johannes Caudri	(Sold) fl 30 Tomassen

1810/03/26	RMMUY	0073	*Godfried Schalke* | Een rijk gedoscht [sic] Jongeling, ter jacht gaande, verzeld van een Hond. Vast en breed geschilderd [Un jeune Homme accompagné de son Chien, allant à la chasse ; peint en maitre.] | *Annots:* [par] Maas (BPG) *Mat:* op doek *Size:* hoog 16, breed 12 duimen *Notes:* This lot was printed in the French edition of the catalogue as lot 74.	Daniel de Jongh Az	(Sold) fl 9:10 de Jongh [for] A
1810/03/27	RMCNL	0062	*Schalken* | Een groot Stuk, voorstellende Judith, het Hoofd van Holofernus in den Zak stekende, terwijl eene oude Vrouw dien Zak met den mond en de hand vast houdt, de uitwerking van het Kaarslicht op het hoofd van Judith is uitnemend		(Unknown)
1810/03/27	RMCNL	0068	*Schalken* | Eene bejaarde Vrouw, welke bij eene Lantaarn eene Pijp stopt, het licht door de hoorne Lantaarn is uitnemend, krachtig van coloriet		(Unknown)
1810/06/20	AMSCH	0082	*G. Schalken* | Eene Dame met een Pagegaai [sic] op den vinger: zij is met loshangend haar en in een bevallige kleeding. Teder en fraai behandeld | *Mat:* op doek *Size:* hoog 32, breed 26 duimen	C	(Sold) fl 81 T Spaan
1810/07/23	DOLG2	0035	*G. Schalck* | Door een open Nis ziet men een Jonge Vrouw, blazende in een test op het vuur, dat terstond vlam maakt. Zeer wel verbeeld en geschilderd | *Mat:* op doek *Size:* hoog 18, breed 14 duim *Notes:* This lot was bought by the anonymous annotator of the FLNY copy of the catalogue.	Pieter Quinting	(Sold) fl 3:5
1810/08/01	AMSCH	0091	*Schalken (Godfried)* | Eene Vrouw, houdende in de regterhand eene Kaars, welke zij aan een brandend Hout opsteekt; in de linkerhand heeft zij den Kandelaar [Sujet à l'effet de la Lumiere ; étant une Femme tenant da sa main droite une Chandelle, qu'elle allume à un tison enflammé ; de sa gauche elle tient un Chandelier] | *Annots:* Mauvais. (NGW) *Mat:* op doek *Size:* hoog 24, breed 21 duimen	Mr Pieter de Smeth van Alphen	(Sold) fl 150 C S Roos
1810/08/01	AMSCH	0092	*Schalken (Godfried)* | Een jong bevallig Meisje in rijke kleeding, staande voor eene steenen Borstwering, waarop liggen een rood fluweel Kussen en zilveren Schotel met een gesneden Citroen, waar van zij een gedeelte op een Mes in hare hand houdt [Une jeune et gentille Fille richement vetue, se presentant audevant d'une Balustrade garnie d'un Coussin de Velours rouge et d'un Plat d'argent : elle montre une Tranche de Citron sur la pointe d'un Couteau, dont le reste se trouve sur le plat] | *Annots:* médiocre. (NGW) *Mat:* op paneel *Size:* hoog 9 ½, breed 7 ½ duimen *Loc:* Amsterdam, Nederland. Rijksmuseum. (A 2339)	Mr Pieter de Smeth van Alphen	(Sold) fl 400 J de Vries
1810/08/01	AMSCH	0093	*Schalken (Godfried)* | Eene jonge en deftige Vrouw, in satijnen kleeding, zittende bij eene Tafel en spelende op de Guitar [Representation d'une jeune Femme gracieuse, habillée en Satin : elle est assise devant une Table, pinceant [sic] de la Guitarre] | *Annots:* fort médiocre. (NGW) *Mat:* op paneel *Size:* hoog 9, breed 7 ½ duimen *Loc:* Den Haag, Nederland. Museum Bredius. (101-1946)	Mr Pieter de Smeth van Alphen	(Sold) fl 200 van Iperen
1810/08/10	RMRIJ	0006	*Godfried Schalken* | Eene Biddende Madonna. Kaarslicht. Natuurlijk en konstig geschilderd | *Mat:* op doek *Size:* hoog 16 duim, breed 13 duim		(Sold) fl 6 [or] 14:10 v Dyk
1810/10/10	MGCIT	0048	*G. Schalken* | Een Vrouwtje in een Nis geplaatst, hebbende in haar eene hand een brandende Kaars; terwijl zij de andere digt tegen het licht aan houd, delicaat en natuurlijk uitgevoerd en van eene ongemeene schoone reflectie	Caspar van Citters	(Unknown)
1810/10/11	AMSCH	0079	*G. Schalken* | De Geboorte van den Heiland | *Mat:* op paneel *Size:* hoog 14, breed 22 duimen	C	(Sold) fl 2:10 Posthumus
1810/12/03	DOBRA	0026	*Schalken* | Een Vrouw, met een brandende kaars in de hand		(Unknown)

Schalcken, Godfried (or Schalcken, manner)

1807/06/02	AMHUY	0023	*Schalken* | Een capitale Ordonnantie, zynde een Vrouw die over haar onderdeur legt, met een brandende kaars in de hand, terwyl een menigte jonge Musicanten speelen, door of in de manier van Schalken		(Unknown)

Schalcken, Godfried (copy after)

1802/05/05	AMSCH	0195	*A. Boonen; G. Schalken* | In een Binnenvertrek by een Kaarslicht, ziet men een bevallige Dame voor haar Toilet, verzeld van een Dienstmaagd, welke een Spiegel vast houd, beneevens een Jongeling die achter haar staat, zeer natuurlyk en warm van Coloriet, door A. Boonen na G. Schalken | copy by A. Boonen after Schalcken *Mat:* op paneel *Size:* hoog 16, breed 13 duim	C	(Sold) fl 8 Rigters
1802/11/01	DOBRA	0068	*Schalken* | Een Juffer, by Kaarslicht een Portrait beschouwende; naar Schalken | *Size:* hoog 13 breed 10 d.	Paulus van der Spyk [or others]	(Sold) fl 2:15 J v Steegh
1803/09/07	AMSCH	0176	*G. Schalken* | In een Nis ziet men een bevallig Meisje, bezig een brandende Kaars in een Lantaarn te zetten; het ligt is frappant en de schildering delicaat, op Doek op Paneel, naar G. Schalken [Une jolie fille, occupée à placer une chandelle dans une lanterne ; la lumière en est frappante et l'exécution délicate] | *Mat:* op doek op paneel *Size:* hoog 9, breed 7 duim	Smidt	(Sold) fl 6:5 Grimpen
1804/10/16	DLOND	0301	*Naar G. Schalken* | Twee Stukjens. Een Man en Vrouw by Kaerslicht. Deux pièces. Homme & Femme, lumière de Chandelle | *Mat:* op paneel *Size:* hoog 10, breed 9		(Unknown)

1804/10/16	DLOND	0302	*Naar G. Schalken* | Ene Vrouw Uts[a] [by Kaerslicht]. Une Femme Uts[a] [lumière de Chandelle] | *Mat:* op paneel *Size:* hoog 8, breed 7		(Unknown)
1806/08/20	HGBSM	0194	*G. Schalken* | Een Naakte Jongeling bij een Rivier zittende, met meer bijwerk, naar G. Schalken | *Mat:* op paneel *Size:* hoog 10 ½, breed 8 duim	Macalester Loup [or others]	(Sold) fl 9 A Texeira
			Schalcken, Godfried (manner)		
1801/04/23	AMYVR	0026	*van Schalken* | Een Vasten-Avondsvreugd met verscheiden Kinderen, zynde een Kaarslicht, uitvoerig gepenceeld, in de manier van van Schalken | *Notes:* This lot was sold with lot 27, which is in the manner of Hondecoeter.		(Sold) fl 27 for lots 26 & 27. Gruijter
1802/06/28	AMSCH	0165	*G. Schalken* | Een Heremiet in zyn Kluys, met een Boek, Doodshoofd, en ander bywerk, uitvoerig op Doek, als G. Schalken | *Mat:* op doek *Size:* hoog 17, breed 14 duim	Anna Elink	(Sold) fl 19:10 Royers
1802/06/28	AMSCH	0166	*G. Schalken* | Een bevallig Meidje, houdende een brandende Kaars, in de manier van G. Schalken | *Mat:* op paneel	B	(Sold) fl 2:5 Roos [for] A
1803/08/24	HGKAN	0025	*Schalken* | Dit stukje steld voor, een Oud Vrouwtje met een Bril in de eene, en met de andere hand op een Boek wyzende aan een Mannetje dat voor haar zit, en dat met attentie beschouwt, schynende hunne schatten na te zien, dit alles verbeelt by Kaarsligt, en uitvoerig geschildert, in de manier van Schalken | *Mat:* op paneel *Size:* hoog 11, breet 9 duim	[Teissier] [or others]	(Sold) fl 12:5 Pulver
1805/07/10	AMSCH	0137	*Schalken* | Een Kopje; op Paneel als door Schalken | *Mat:* op paneel	V[inkeles] [for] K	(Sold) fl 11 Teengs
1810/05/22	AMSCH	0099	*Schalken (als G.)* | In een Binnenhuis bij het Kaarslicht zit eene Vrouw, hebbende een Kind aan de Borst, waarbij een bevallig Meisje en een bejaard Man; meesterlijk geschilderd | *Mat:* op paneel *Size:* hoog 20, breed 16 duim	T	(Bought In) fl 6:15
1810/10/11	AMSCH	0149	*Schalken* | Twee stuks, met Bokken en Schapen, met vrolijke Speelers, bij kaarslicht; als Schalken	C	(Sold) fl 9:10 Posthumus
			Schedoni, Bartolomeo		
1803/04/27	AMSCH	0099	*Schidone* | Sainte Marie Madelaine, ce tableau à beaucoup d'effet & est d'une bonne couleur | *Size:* h. 3 ½, l. 2 ¾ pieds	A	(Sold) fl 33 Hodges
1803/09/07	AMSCH	0163	*Schidoni* | Een Maria met het Kind Jesus, waarby Johannes, zynde een allerdelicaatst geschilderd Stukje van Schidoni [La Ste.-Vierge, avec l'enfant Jésus, et à côté St.-Jean-Baptiste ; composition délicate et belle] | *Mat:* op koper *Size:* hoog 7, breed 5 ½ duim	Smidt	(Sold) fl 3 C S Roos
			Schedoni, Bartolomeo (attributed)		
1803/04/27	AMSCH	0111	*Schidone* | Berger & bestiaux, attribué au Schidone | *Size:* h. 5 ¼, l. 6 pieds	A	(Sold) fl 45 Th Spaan
			Schedoni, Bartolomeo (copy after)		
1803/04/27	AMSCH	0078[a]	*Schidone* | Deux morceaux, dont l'un est une Copie de fameux Tableau du Schidone, réprésentant la Charité, & l'autre l'abondance | *This Lot:* La Charité; lot 78[b] by Anonymous	A	(Sold) fl 4:5 for lots 78[a] & 78[b]. V[n] Iperen
			Scheffer		
1806/08/13	AMSCH	0344	*Scheffer* | Twee stuks met bevallige Beeldjes	Vinkeles [for] G[ruyter]	(Sold) fl 0:10 Yver
1808/12/30	HGIMM	[0071r]	*Scheffer* | Voorts een exquis kabinetje Schilderijen van voorname Nederlandsche Meesters, welke uit hoofde van de kortheid des tijds niet stuk voor stuk kunnen beschreven worden; doch waarvan de beschrijving op den Kijkdag zal voorhanden zijn. Dus wij hier alleen de namen van eenige dier Meesters laten volgen, als: A. Kuyp, Ruysdaal, Karel du Jardyn, Loqwi ('t beste dat hij schilderde) Hondekoeter, van Dyk, Janson, Moesgever, Kamphuyzen, van Gooijen, A. van der Neer, T. Wyk, Huchtenburgh, Zolemaker, van Hassel, A. Vermeulen, van Dongen, Scheffer, van Os enz. | *This Lot:* Een Schilderij, Scheffer *Notes:* Because this lot was not numbered in the catalogue, we have assigned the number.		(Unknown)
1809/07/25	HGBSM	0022	*Scheffer* | Christus aan het Kruis, uitvoerig geschildert | *Mat:* op paneel *Size:* hoog 20, breed 14 duim	D van der Aa [or] E B ten Dall	(Sold) fl 10 van Eyk
			Scheffer, J.		
1810/03/27	RMCNL	0063	*J. Scheffer* | Een Kapitaal Landschap, zeer delicaat en aardig gepenseeld, eene van de weinige Landschappen van dien grooten Meester		(Unknown)
			Scheffer, J.L. [Unidentified]		
1809/04/17	AMSCH	0090	*J.L. Scheffer* | Door een open Nis, ziet men in een een oud Gebouw een Comique Vergadering, een derzelve is bézig uit een Papier iets voor te leezen; geestig gecaracteriseerd en meesterlijk geschilderd | *Mat:* op paneel *Size:* hoog 10, breed 8 duim	Z	(Sold or Bought In) fl 10 Spaan
			Scheffer, Jean-Baptiste		
1810/06/06	RMMUY	0143	*J. B. Scheffer* | Een Jong bevallig Vrouwe Beeld in bespiegeling staande, verdienstelijk geschilderd | *Mat:* op doek		(Sold) fl 52 Teekengenootschap

1810/06/06	RMMUY	0144	*J.B. Scheffer* | Eene bevallige Jonge Dame, aan haar Toilet zittende. Fraaij geschilderd | *Mat:* op doek		(Sold) fl 21 Klint [?]
1810/07/23	DOLG2	00II	*J.B. Scheffer* | Een Grijsäard, door J.B. Scheffer, op Panneel, in een zwarte Lijst | *Mat:* op paneel *Size:* hoog 23, breed 17 duim	Pieter Quinting	(Sold) fl 5 A van Strij
			Schellinks		
1802/12/13	AMSCH	0150	*J. Schellinx* | Een Bosch- en Bergachtig Landschap, gestoffeerd met Landlieden en Ezels; schoon van Licht en meesterachtig geschilderd | *Mat:* op doek *Size:* hoog 26, breed 35 duim	Pruyssenaar [for] A	(Sold) fl 7 Yver
1810/07/23	DOLG2	0064	*Schillingh* | Een Landschap, gestoffeerd met Beestjes en Beelden | *Mat:* op paneel *Size:* hoog 14, breed 19 duim	Pieter Quinting	(Sold) fl 13 Schouwman Dordt
			Schellinks (and Moucheron, F.)		
1803/12/12	AMSCH	0057	*F. de Moucheron; Schellinkx* | Een Landschap met hoog Geboomte, op de voorgrond een stil Water, waarby een Man met een Hond, aan de overzyde van het Water ziet men een Heer en Dame op een Paard, waarby Jagers en Honden; krachtig en delicaat gepenceeld, door F. de Moucheron, gestoffeerd door Schellinkx | *Mat:* op doek *Size:* hoog 27, breed 31 duim	B	(Sold) fl 50 Hodges
1804/10/29	HRBAU	0066	*Moucheron (F. de); Schellings* | Een zeer bevallig bosch- en bergagtig Landschap; op den voorgrond ziet men eene Dame en een' Heer te paard, nevens eenige Jaagers en Honden, een Hert door een beek vervolgen; de tweede grond is klipagtig, met boomen en kreupelhout bewasschen, waar over men in een uitmuntend ver uitgestrekt bergagtig verschiet ziet, met Bosschen en Kasteelen voorzien, tot dat zig het blaauw Gebergte als in de lucht verliest. Zeer warm, zonagtig en uitvoerig behandeld | *Mat:* op doek *Size:* hoog 25, breed 33 duim	Simon Styl	(Unknown)
1804/10/29	HRBAU	0067	*Moucheron (F. de); Schellings* | Voor aan, op een' zandigen Weg, by hoog geboomte, zit eene Dame op een wit paard, benevens eenige Jaagers met Wild, welken schynen te rusten; waar agter een bosch- en bergagtig verschiet. Het coloriet is warm, en zeer uitvoerig behandeld | *Mat:* op doek *Size:* hoog 29, breed 37 duim	Simon Styl	(Unknown)
			Schellinks (or Schellinks, manner)		
1808/06/11	RMRIJ	0062	*Schellings, of in zyn manier* | Een Landschap, waar in op den Voorgrond eene ryke drift van Bokken, Schapen, Ossen, Paard en Figuren door eene Beek waden, zonachtig, krachtig en natuurlyk geschilderd | *Mat:* op paneel *Size:* hoog 24 ¾, breed 33 duim		(Sold or Bought In) fl 19 Luchtmans
1808/06/11	RMRIJ	0091	*Schellings, of in zyn manier* | Een Boomryk Landschap, waar in eenige Heeren en Dames, zeer aartig en zonachtig | *Mat:* op paneel *Size:* hoog 17 ½, breed 24 duim		(Unknown) fl 5:10
			Schellinks, Daniel		
1802/02/16	AMSCH	0012	*D. Schellings* | In een Bergachtig Landschap, ziet men op de voorgrond een Vrouw op een Ezel waarby twee mannen te voet; verders nog verscheide stoffagie in 't verschiet, meesterlyk op doek | *Mat:* op doek	B[uys]	(Sold) fl 5:10 T Spaan
1803/06/20	AMSCH	0064	*D. Schellinks* | Een Boschgezigt met een stille Rivier, waarover een Steen Brug, gestoffeerd met Beelden en Beesten, natuurlyk op Doek | *Mat:* op doek *Size:* hoog 29, breed 25 duim	Schley [for] K	(Sold) fl 49:10 J Spaan
1803/08/17	AMSCH	0077	*Schellinks (D.)* | Een bergachtig Landschap met Ruïnen, men ziet in een Waterplas drie beladen Muilëzels, eenige Bokjes, Schapen en een Hond; op een der Ezels zit een Jogeling [sic] op de Fluit te spelen, een Meisje gaat daar nevens met een Korfje onder den arm, verders een aangenaam verschiet, dun en bevallig gepenceeld | *Mat:* op paneel *Size:* hoog 13, breed 16 ½ duim	Anna Catharina Putman	(Sold) fl 17 Gruyter
1809/06/13	AMSCH	0142	*D. Schellinxs* | Een Boschgezigt met hoog geboomten, bij een stille Rivier, gestoffeerd met Jagers, wilde Zwijnen en Eenden, en Bergachtig verschiet; kunstig en fraai geschilderd | *Mat:* op paneel *Size:* hoog 14, breed 13 duim	Y	(Sold) fl 1 L Pakker
1810/11/07	UTWLD	0056	*D. Schellings* | Een duinagtig Landschap, met hoog opgeschoten boomgewas, waar door een weg loopt, waarop een Postwagen door struikrovers aangevallen, op de voorgrond, een boom en kreupelhout enz. alles zeer natuurlijk behandeld door D. Schellings, op doek, 3 voet 1 en een half duim hoog, 4 voet 7 duim breed, zwarte Lijst | *Mat:* op doek *Size:* 3 voet 1 en een half duim hoog, 4 voet 7 duim breed		(Unknown) fl 23
			Schellinks, Daniel (and Kessel, J. (III))		
1808/06/13	AMSCH	0090	*Kessel (J. van); D. Schellings* | Een boom- en heuvelachtig Landschap: op den voorgrond een dooden Boom aan een Watertje, gestoffeerd met Jagers te paard en te voet, welke een Hert vervolgen. Zonachtig en meesterlijk gepenceeld | *Mat:* op doek *Size:* hoog 29, breed 41 duim	Z	(Sold) fl 20 Glad [or] Carré
			Schellinks, Daniel (and Lingelbach)		
1808/06/13	AMSCH	0145	*Schellings (D.); J. Lingelbach* | Een bergachtig Landschap, ter zijde ziet men een Heer en eene Dame ter Valkenjagt uitrijden, op den voorgrond een Jager, welke met eenige Honden door het Water baadt; in 't verschiet	E M Engelberts	(Sold) fl 201 Reijers

			eenige Landloopers en een Herberg. Dit Schilderij is in voorstelling der Natuur alleruitmuntendst behandeld | *Mat:* op doek *Size:* hoog 43, breed 57 duim		
1808/06/13	AMSCH	0146	*Schellings (D.); J. Lingelbach* | Een Geleerde in zijne Studeerkamer, omgeven van eene Globe, Landkaarten en eenige Boeken, ter zijde een Wenteltrap. Het invallend licht geeft eene schoone houding, en het is in de manier van Philip Koning meesterlijk gepenceeld | *Mat:* op doek *Size:* hoog 21, breed 19 duim	[Jan Tersteeg]	(Sold) fl 40 J du Pree

Schellinks, Daniel (and Moucheron, F.)

1803/08/17	AMSCH	0053	*Moncheron. (F. de); D Schellinks* | Een Italiaansch Landschap met Ruïnes, Geboomtens, en veruitgestrekt bergachtig Verschiet, de Voorgrond gestofeerd met een menigte Vee, een Herder, Herderin, en een ander op een Ezel, waarby een Hond, de beide Meesters hebben hierin ieder hun best gedaan, zynde voorts zonachtig behandeld | *Mat:* op doek op paneel *Size:* hoog 15, breed 19 duim	Anna Catharina Putman	(Bought In) fl 90
1803/08/17	AMSCH	0054	*Moncheron. (F. de); D Schellinks* | Een natuurlyk Landschap, op de Voorgrond met een Waterval, en hoog Gebergten in 't verschiet, ter zyde een Jager met zyn Honden, geschilderd als de voorgaande | *Mat:* op doek *Size:* hoog 19, breed 16 duim	Anna Catharina Putman	(Sold) fl 9:10 v^{n} Iperen

Schellinks, Willem

1801/03/16	AMSCH	0212	*W. Schellings* | Twee stuks Hofgezichten, gestoffeerd met Heeren en Dames te Paard, en Jagers met Honden, fiks gepenceeld	S[chley]	(Sold) fl 30 Coclers
1802/06/16	AMSCH	0174	*W. Schellinx* | Een Bergachtig Landschap met hoog Geboomte, waarby eenig Vée nevens een rustende Herder; krachtig van schildering | *Mat:* op paneel *Size:* hoog 24, breed 20 duim	[Merrem]	(Sold) fl 21 v d Schley [for] S[neck]
1803/06/20	AMSCH	0016	*W. Schellinx* | Een bevallig boomryk Landschap, met een Rivier en aangenaam verschiet, op de voorgrond een Jager met Honden, door W. Schellinx, hoog 28, breed 24 duim Panneel | *Mat:* op paneel *Size:* hoog 28, breed 24 duim	Schley [for] B	(Sold) fl 49 Hodges
1804/08/08	AMSCH	0175	*W. Schellings* | In een Landschap by een ondergaande zon, ter zyde een klaar spiegelend Water, ziet men onder zwaar Geboomte een gaande Man en Vrouw, op de voorgrond een Herder met eenige Schaapen en Bokken, achterwaards tusschen het Geboomte een Kerktooren, en een aangenaam verschiet; warm, zonachtig en uitvoerig geschilderd | *Mat:* op doek *Size:* hoog 15 ½, breed 13 duim	Vink[eles] [for] K[=Gruyter?]	(Bought In) fl 25
1804/10/16	DLOND	0200	*Schellings* | Een Landschap by Maneschyn. Paysage clair de Lune | *Mat:* op paneel *Size:* hoog 13, breed 18		(Unknown)
1805/07/10	AMSCH	0125	*W. Schellinx* | Een Capitaal Bergachtig Italiaansch Land- en Riviergezicht, waarin een Overvaarende Pont-Schuit, met Rysigers, Paarden en belaaden Muil-Ezels, verder eenige Lieden, by een aloude Waght-Tooren; meesterlyk fraai van behandeling, en uitvoerig gepenceeld | *Mat:* op doek *Size:* hoog 48, breed 61 duim	Temmink	(Sold) fl 51 C S Roos
1805/07/10	AMSCH	0125a[H]	*W. Schellinx* | [Untitled] | *Notes:* This lot was added in by hand in the EBNP and RKDH copies of the catalogue, but without giving a title.	Y[ver]	(Bought In) fl 130
1806/08/13	AMSCH	0168	*Schellings. (W.)* | Een Rotsachtig Landschap met hoog Geboomten, op de voorgrond eenige Herders en Vrouwen, gezéten op Ezels, waarby eenig ander Vée; krachtig geschilderd | *Mat:* op doek *Size:* hoog 26, breed 26 duim	van der Voort	(Sold) fl 51 Thais
1806/08/13	AMSCH	0169	*Schellings. (W.)* | Een capitaal Boomryk Landschap, op de voorgrond gestoffeerd met Lieden te paard, waarby Jagers en Honden, agterwaards een Herder met Vée en een aangenaam verschiet; zonachtig en fiks behandeld | *Mat:* op paneel *Size:* hoog 29, breed 34 duim	Vinkeles [for] G[ruyter]	(Sold) fl 20 P Swanenburgh
1807/08/26	AMSCH	0201	*W. Schellings* | Een aangenaam Landschap, ter rechterzyde van hetzelve ziet men een gekleeden Heer en Dame, van een groote trap afkomen, welke door een Knegt met twee Paarden worden opgewagt, waar by nog een Heer te paard, ter zyde van de trap Jagers en Honden die zich ter Jagt gereed maken, verder op de voorgrond een Fontyn, waar by een Man en Paard, en achterwaarts een Koets met vier Paarden bespannen; alles is zeer helder uitvoerig en aangenaam van Penceelsbehandeling | *Mat:* op doek *Size:* hoog 17 ½, breed 21 duim	de Vries	(Sold) fl 110 van Iperen
1807/08/26	AMSCH	0202	*W. Schellings* | Een Wintergezigt aan de Vestmuur van een oude Stad; op het Ys vertoont zich een Wedloop van Paarden, waar by een ménigte aanschouwers, zoo te paard als te voet, meesterlyk fraai gepenceeld | *Mat:* op doek *Size:* hoog 20, breed 29 duim	Helsdinge	(Sold) fl 20 Coclair
1808/06/06	RMRIJ	0111	*Schellings. (Willem)* | Een boomrijk Landschap, waarin, op den voorgrond, eenige figuren, op Muil-Ezels gezeten, door 't water waden, en verder bijwerk. In de manier van Asselijn [Paysage riche en arbres, sur le devant duquel plusieurs figures et animaux passent une Riviére à gué etc. Dans le genre d'Asselin] | *Annots:* gekocht v. P.J. Thijs, Aug 1806 (f 90.-) (RMA I) *Mat:* op doek *Size:* Hoog 25, en breed 25 duim	Gerrit van der Pot, Heer van Groeneveld	(Sold) fl 140 Nieuwenhuys
1808/06/06	RMRIJ	0112	*Schellings. (Willem)* | In eene Italiaansche Grot wordt een wit gezadeld Paard uit de hand beslagen, met eenige daarbij staande figuren. Op den	Gerrit van der Pot, Heer van Groeneveld	(Sold) fl 180 Nieuwenhuys

			voorgrond een Waterput en verder bijwerk. In de manier van Bamboots. Uitvoerig en goed geschilderd [Sur le devant de ce Tableau, auprés d'une Grotte, un Marèchal ferre un Cheval blanc tout sellé. Plusieurs figures et autres accessoires terminent ce Morceau agréable et piquant] | *Annots:* [door] P Laar Gek. van Jan de Neufville, Sept 1782 als P. Laer f 120.- door de Neufville gekocht van A. va. Hemers[?] (f 250.-) (RMA I) *Mat:* op doek *Size:* Hoog 24 ¾, en breed 24 duim		
1808/08/23	AMSCH	0146	*Schellings. (W.)* | Een prachtige Hofsteeden met verschillend Geboomte, op de voorgrond eenige rijk gekleede Turken bij een wel voorziene Tafel, verder eenige musiceerende en andere Lieden; schoon en uitvoerig gepenceeld | *Mat:* op paneel *Size:* hoog 20, breed 24 duim	[Gruyter?]	(Sold) fl 8 Reijdon
1808/09/13	HABRU	0079	*W. Schellinks* | Een Bosch- en Bergachtig Landschap, aan een Water, natuurlijk		(Unknown) fl 2:10
1808/11/28	AMSCH	0082	*W. Schellings* | Een Land- en Watergezicht, met Rijzigers en andere stoffage	[Gruyter?]	(Sold) fl 1:5 Monnick
1810/06/20	AMSCH	0081	*W. Schellings* | Een Manege of Rijschool; in het midden zit een Officier op een wit springend Paard, waarbij een andere met de zweep in de hand; ter zijde twee Heeren, welker Paarden door Bedienden worden vastgehouden; achterwaarts eene Vrouw, zittend op een Ezel, en andere voorwerpen. Het is bevallig van licht en kleur, en uitvoerig als Ph. Wouwerman geschilderd, op doek, door W. Schellings | *Mat:* op doek *Size:* hoog 23, breed 22 duimen	D	(Sold) fl 200 Roos

Schellinks, Willem (and Asch, P.J. van)

1808/08/23	AMSCH	0003	*Asch (P. van); W. Schellings* | Een capitaal hoog bergachtig Landschap, met opgaand geboomten, ter zijde over een helderen Rivier een steene Sluis, gestoffeert met Heeren te Paard, rustende Reisigers, beladen Muil-Ezels en andere figuuren; zonachtig behandeld | *Mat:* op doek *Size:* hoog 28, breed 38 duim	[Gruyter?]	(Bought In) fl 19:10

Schellinks, Willem (and Ast)

1809/06/13	AMSCH	0001	*B. van Ast; Schellinx* | Een kapitaal hoog Bergachtig Landschap, met hoog opgaand Geboomten, ter zijde over een klaar spiegelend Water een Steene Sluis, gestoffeerd met Heeren te Paard en gaande en rustende Reizigers; zonagtig en uitvoerig geschilderd, door B. van Ast en gestoffeerd door Schellinx | *Mat:* op doek *Size:* hoog 28, breed 38 duim *Notes:* The artist was presumably Pieter Jansz van Asch and not Balthasar van der Ast.	[Gruyter?]	(Sold) fl 10:10 Spaan

Schellinks, Willem (and Lingelbach)

1808/08/23	AMSCH	0145	*Schellings (W.); J. Lingelbag* | Een donker Bosch-gezigt, op de voorgrond tusschen Kreupelhout, Jagers, die met hunne Honden een Hart vervolgen, dieper in het Bosch, Heeren te Paard, verzeld van hunne Loopers en Honden; alles is bevallig en zeer natuurlijk voorgesteld | *Mat:* op doek *Size:* hoog 25, breed 27 duim	J	(Sold) fl 20 Spruit

Schellinks, Willem (and Verboom, A.H.)

1810/06/20	AMSCH	0093a	*A. Verboom; W. Schellings* | Een boschachtig Landschap, gestoffeerd met een Heer te Paard, beladen Muilezels en Landlieden bij hun Vee. Schoon geschilderd op paneel, door A. Verboom, gestoffeerd door W. Schellings | *Mat:* op paneel *Size:* hoog 46, breed 64 duimen	Y	(Sold) fl 15 Yver

Schellinks, Willem (and Vlieger, S.)

1802/06/16	AMSCH	0192	*N. de Vlieger; W. Schellingx* | Een Boomryk Landschap met een Rivier, en aangenaam verschiet, op de voorgrond een Jager met Honden, door W. Schellingx, zynde de behandeling niet minder dan de voorgaande | *Mat:* op paneel *Size:* hoog 27 ½, breed 24 duim *Notes:* The artist's name was given as "N. de Vlieger" but we have assumed this is an error.	[Merrem]	(Sold) fl 40 van der Schleij

Schendel, Bernardus van

1802/05/11	GRGRW	0042	*Schijndel* | De Kaartspelers [Schilderijen met Olie-Verf; In zwarte Lijsten] | *Mat:* in olyverf *Notes:* The bracketed information in the title appears above lot 1 and refers to lots 1 to 79a.	Arnold Sicco Werumeus	(Unknown) fl 1:18
1802/07/20	MGSAN	0001	*B. Schyndel* | Een vermaakelyke Boerenkermis, vol figuuren, extra fraai, op Paneel | companion to lot 2 *Mat:* op paneel *Size:* hoog duim 18 ½, breed duim 25		(Unknown)
1802/07/20	MGSAN	0002	*B. Schyndel* | Een vermaakelyke Boerenkermis Pendent van 't voorgaande, verbeeldende een Boerenbruiloft, op Paneel | companion to lot 1 *Mat:* op paneel *Size:* hoog duim 18 ½, breed duim 25		(Unknown)
1802/07/27	AKHRK	0019	*B. v. Schijndel* | Een gezelschap Heeren en Dames, welke zich in een Binnenvertrek amuseeren, en drie Jongelingen. Helder en goed geschilderd | *Mat:* op paneel *Size:* hoog 11 ½, breed 12 ½ duim	Maria Stategaart	(Sold) fl 4:15 Meyer
1802/11/01	DOBRA	0059	*B. v. Schyndel* | Een Feest van Flora in een Arkadischs Landschap | companion to lot 60 *Mat:* op doek *Size:* breed 22 d. hoog ruim 16 duim	Paulus van der Spyk [or others]	(Sold) fl 12:5 for lots 59 & 60. M v Steeg
1802/11/01	DOBRA	0060	*B. v. Schyndel* | Een dito [Feest van Flora in een Arkadischs Landschap], zynde een weergade | companion to lot 59	Paulus van der Spyk [or others]	(Sold) fl 12:5 for lots 59 & 60. M v Steeg

1804/10/16	DLOND	0201	*Scheyndel* | Een Musicerend Vrouwtjen. Une Musicienne | *Mat:* op doek *Size:* hoog 14, breed 12		(Unknown)
1804/10/16	DLOND	0202	*Scheyndel* | Een Doctor met ene Dame. Un Médecin avec une Dame | *Mat:* op doek *Size:* hoog 14, breed 12		(Unknown)
1804/10/16	DLOND	0203	*Scheyndel* | Uts[a] [Een Doctor met ene Dame. Un Médecin avec une Dame] | *Mat:* op doek *Size:* hoog 10, breed 13		(Unknown)
1804/10/16	DLOND	0204	*Scheyndel* | Uts[a] [Een Doctor met ene Damen. Un Medecin avec une Dame] | *Mat:* op doek *Size:* hoog 10, breed 13		(Unknown)
1804/10/29	HRBAU	0088	*Schindel, (B.)* | Een Officier schynt met eene Dame op het Trocodillebord [sic] gespeeld te hebben, en zyn verlies te voldoen, terwyl zy een glas wyn uitdrinkt. Uitvoerig behandeld | *Mat:* op paneel *Size:* hoog 10, breed 13 duim	Simon Styl	(Unknown)
1804/10/29	HRBAU	0089	*Schindel, (B.)* | Eene Dame, voor een Balluster zittende, wordt door eene Dienstmaagd een Schotel met Vrugten aangebooden, uit welke zy een Kers neemt, die zy aan een Pappegaai wil geeven. Als het voorige behandeld | *Mat:* op paneel *Size:* hoog 10, breed 13 duim	Simon Styl	(Unknown)
1804/10/29	HRBAU	0090	*Schindel, (B.)* | Een Musiceerend Gezelschap. Aardig behandeld | *Mat:* op paneel *Size:* hoog 18, breed 17 duim	Simon Styl	(Unknown)
1807/06/02	AMHUY	0001	*van Scheydel* | In een gemeubileerd Binnenvertrek zitten eenige Heeren en Dames aan een tafel een Oestermaal te houden; uitvoerig gepenceeld		(Unknown)
1807/06/02	AMHUY	0002	*van Scheydel* | In een gemeubileerd Binnenvertrek zitten eenige Heeren en Dames aan tafel, zich vermakende met Kaartspelen; kragtig en uitvoerig gepenceeld		(Unknown)
1807/06/10	HGBSM	0196	*Schydel* | Twee stuks, een school met Kinderen, en een boeren Gezelschap | *Mat:* op paneel *Size:* hoog 10, breed 12 duim	Abraham Delfos [or others]	(Sold) fl 5 Kramer
1808/06/11	RMRIJ	0032	*B: van Schyndel* | Een aangenaam Wintergezicht met vele Figuren en Gebouwen | *Mat:* op paneel *Size:* hoog 21 ½, breed 26 ½ duim		(Sold) fl 4:15 v Geel [?]
1810/05/22	AMSCH	0097	*Schijndel (B. v.)* | Een Land- en Watergezicht, waarin drie Lieden in een Schuit; alles verbeeld bij helder Maanlicht en fiks behandeld | *Mat:* op paneel *Size:* Jeder hoog 7 ½, breed 10 duim	F	(Sold) fl 2 Masse
1810/06/20	AMSCH	0191	*Van Schijndel* | Een Binnenhuis met vrolijke Huislieden en Kinderen	A	(Sold) fl 1:10 L Pakker
1810/08/10	RMRIJ	0023	*B. V. Schijndel* | Een lezende Boer, en verder bijwerk		(Unknown) fl 3 [or] 7: 0
			Schenis, W. [Unidentified]		
1806/11/24	AMSCH	0076	*Schenis (W.)* | Een Strandgezigt, met Beelden, te paard en te voet; en een aangenaam verschiet | *Mat:* op paneel *Size:* hoog 19, breed 24 duim	Munnikhuizen	(Sold) fl 2 L Pakker
			Schepper [Unidentified]		
1810/10/11	AMSCH	0164	*Schepper* | Twee stuks Wintergezigten	S	(Sold) fl 7:5 Boelhouwer
			Scheyndel, Gillis van		
1808/11/28	AMSCH	0059	*G. van Schijndel* | Twee stuks met opkomende Maanlichten, over stille Rivieren, beide gestoffeerd met Visschers die hunne Netten droogen, verder zeilende en stilleggende Vaartuigen, schoon van effect en uitvoerig geschilderd | *Mat:* op paneel *Size:* ieder hoog 12, breed 15 duim	[Gruyter?]	(Bought In) fl 5:5
			Schinnagl		
1803/09/07	AMSCH	0170	*Scheinagel* | Twee stuks Landschappen met Geboomten, Gebergtens, Watervallen en Zwitzersche Bruggen, gestoffeerd met Ryzigers te Paard en te Voet; zeer aangenaam van schildering [Deux paysages, entrecoupés de montagnes et de rivières sur lesquels on voit des ponts et de voyageurs à pied et à cheval ; les détails de ces morceaux sont agréablement variés et d'une belle exécution] | *Mat:* op paneel *Size:* hoog 15, breed 23 duim	Smidt	(Sold) fl 12 Tessier
1803/09/07	AMSCH	0171	*Scheinagel* | Een alleraangenaamst Boom- en Bergachtig Landschapje met Ryzigers te Paard en te Voet, fraay op Paneel [Un joli paysage, agréable sur tout par la diversité et la composition des objets, tels que des figures et des chevaux parmi des montagnes et des bocages] | *Mat:* op paneel *Size:* hoog 7, br. 16 duim [Haut 7, large 14 pouces] *Notes:* The dimensions differ in the Dutch and French editions of the catalogue.	Smidt	(Sold) fl 1:10 de LaFontaine
1807/06/10	HGBSM	0136	*Scheinagel* | Twee stuks bergagtige Landschappen, met hoog geboomte, helder en uitvoerig gepenceelt en aangenaam gestoffeerd | *Mat:* op paneel *Size:* hoog 15, breed 22 duim	Abraham Delfos [or others]	(Sold) fl 7 Tessier
			Schmitt, J.C. [Unidentified]		
1803/09/07	AMSCH	0175	*J. C. Schmitt* | Een Roomsche Kerk, van binnen met verscheide Stoffagie, op Koper [Un temple catholique, dont l'intérieur est orné de figures et de décoratious [sic] analogues au sujet] | *Mat:* op koper *Size:* hoog 15, breed 12 ½ duim	Smidt	(Sold) fl 6:15 Frantszen
1809/04/22	AMYVR	0118	*J.C. Schmit* | Een Roomsche Kerk van binnen, met verscheide stoffagie | *Mat:* op koper *Size:* hoog 15, breed 12 duim	de Bruin	(Sold) fl 6:15 du Pree

Schoevaerdts, Mathys

1801/10/06	AMSCH	0064	*M. Schoovaardts* | Twee Stuks Brabandsche Dorp Gezigten, ryk gestoffeert, met Postwagens, Vaartuigen en Beeldjes, helder en uitvoerig gepenceelt | *Mat:* op koper *Size:* yder hoog 11, breed 14 duim	M	(Sold) fl 30:10 Wed Achtienhoven
1802/09/18	RMDRS	0119	*Schovaarts* | Twee Landschappen	Casper de Haas	(Unknown) fl 5:10

Schoevaerdts, Mathys (and Boudewyns)

1803/07/18	AMSCH	0006	*Boudewyns, (F.); M. Schoevaerts* | Twee stuks aangenaame Brabandsche Landschappen, met Rivieren doorsneeden, gestoffeerd met verscheide Beeldjes en Paarden, warm van coloriet en uitvoerig geschilderd [Deux Jolis paysages traversés par des rivieres : ils sont ornés de figures & animaux spirituellement touchés, de la meilleure maniere des deux peintres.] | *Mat:* [sur bois] *Size:* yder hoog 12, breed 16 duim *Notes:* The material was given only in the French edition of the catalogue.	Maria Theresia Andrioli	(Sold) fl 17 Teissier

Schonevelt, Jan J. (copy by)

1801/02/18	AMBOS	0056	*J. Schooneveld; J. van Goyen* | Een Stadt aan een groote Rivier, waarop zeilende Scheepen, naar J. van Goyen | copy by J.J. Schonevelt after Goyen	J Schonevelt	(Unknown)

Schotanus, Petrus

1802/05/11	GRGRW	0037	*P. Schot* | Een Stuk met Vrnchten [sic], en geslachte Vogels [Schilderijen met Olie-Verf; In zwarte Lijsten] | companion to lot 38 *Mat:* in olyverf *Notes:* The bracketed information in the title appears above lot 1 and refers to lots 1 to 79a.	Arnold Sicco Werumeus	(Unknown)
1802/05/11	GRGRW	0038	*P. Schot* | Een dito [Stuk met Vrnchten], tot ene weerga [Schilderijen met Olie-Verf; In zwarte Lijsten] | companion to lot 37 *Mat:* in olyverf *Notes:* The bracketed information in the title about the medium appears above lot 1 and refers to lots 1 to 79a.	Arnold Sicco Werumeus	(Unknown)

Schoubroeck, Pieter

1802/09/21	UTHDG	0085	*P. Schubruck* | Een Landschap met eene menigte figuuren, rijk en uitvoerig | *Mat:* op koper		(Sold) fl 5:10 Verhoude

Schouman, Aert

1803/10/24	HGDAW	0001	*Schouman* | Een stukje verbeeldende het portrait van Schouman, waarby een Vrouwtje met een hondje en een kat zeer fraay, door hem zelfs geschilderd op paneel, in een vergulde lyst [Schilderyen in Olyverw] | *Mat:* in olyverf op paneel *Notes:* The bracketed information in the title appears above lot 1 and refers to lots 1 to 16.	M van Daalen Wetters	(Unknown)
1803/10/24	HGDAW	0002	*Schouman* | Een dito stukje, verbeeldende Schouman, zittende een Vrouw te portraiteren fraay geschilderd op koper, in een vergulde lyst [Schilderyen in Olyverw] | *Mat:* in olyverf op koper *Notes:* It is unclear what "dito" refers to in the title. The bracketed information in the title appears above lot 1 and refers to lots 1 to 16.	M van Daalen Wetters	(Unknown)
1804/02/27	AMSCH	0103	*Schouman. (A.)* | Een oud Man zittende te leezen | *Mat:* op paneel *Size:* hoog 13, breed 10 duim	R[oos]	(Sold) fl 2:15 Coclers
1804/05/07	AMSCH	0156	*Schouman. (A.)* | In een Boomryk Landschap, by een Boerewooning, ziet men verscheide onderscheide soorten van Gevogelten; krachtig en fraay geschilderd | *Mat:* op doek *Size:* hoog 40, breed 28 duim	Roos [for] A	(Sold) fl 30 Coclers
1808/06/06	RMRIJ	0113	*Schouman. (Aart)* | Een Landschapje; zijnde een gezigt uit de Vliet naar Voorschoten te zien [Paysage representant un Canal, des Prairies, et une Perspective du Village de Voorschoten] | *Annots:* gekocht van den schilder f 40.- (RMA I) *Mat:* op paneel *Size:* Hoog 8 ¼, en breed 10 duim	Gerrit van der Pot, Heer van Groeneveld	(Sold) fl 3:10 Bogaart
1808/08/23	AMSCH	0208	*A. Schouman* | Een Hofgezicht met verschillend Land en Watergevogelte; meesterlijk geschildert	[Gruyter?]	(Sold or Bought In) fl 1 Gruyter
1808/12/12	DOHAA	0075	*Schouman* | Een Man en Vrouw geld wegende | *Mat:* op paneel		(Unknown)
1809/06/13	AMSCH	0229	*A. Schouman* | Een Hofgezicht, met uit- en Inlandsch Gevogelten | *Mat:* op doek	[Gruyter?]	(Sold) fl 0:16 Boelhouwer
1810/06/04	DOBRA	0007	*A. Schouman* | Een kindje met een Hond	Hendrik de Haas	(Unknown)
1810/06/06	RMMUY	0023	*Aart Schouman* | Eene Bonte Hen, met hare Kuikens bij een water waar in twee Eendvogels zwemmen, een witte Phaisant en vliegende Duif, in een Landschap; konstig en fiks | companion to lot 24 *Mat:* op doek		(Unknown) fl 10 for lots 23 & 24
1810/06/06	RMMUY	0024	*Aart Schouman* | Eene Wedergade, in dit Landschap zit een Bonte Phaisant bij een water daar Eenden bij staan, en een zittende Kwikstaart, niet minder van konst | companion to lot 23		(Unknown) fl 10 for lots 23 & 24
1810/07/23	DOLG2	000L	*A. Schouman* | Een Schoorsteenstuk, met Kindertjes, in 't grauw | *Mat:* op doek *Fmt:* schoorsteenstuk *Size:* hoog 66, breed 47 duim	Pieter Quinting	(Unknown) fl 2:15
1810/10/13	HGDAW	0006	*A. Schouman* | Door een Raam ziet men het Pourtrait van den Schilder A. Schouman, een Kat streelende, waarby een Meisje met een Hondje op haar schoot, op de Tafel eenig Naaiwerk, extra uitvoerig en zeer delicaat behandeld door hem zelfs, van zyn besten tyd | *Mat:* op paneel *Size:* hoog 10, breed 8 duim		(Unknown)

1810/12/03	DOBRA	0044	*A. Schouman* | Een Kindje met een Hondje		(Unknown)

Schouman, Aert (copy by)

1810/03/26	RMMUY	0067	*A. Schouman; naar Potter* | Op den voorgrond bij eenig geboomte en een hek, staan een wit, en een zwartbruin Paard. In het verschiet eenig Hoornvee, Dorp, &c. [Un Paysage hollandois : sur le devant, près d'un arbre, est un cheval blanc pommelé à coté d'un autre, brun noiratre ; dans le lointain quelque betail et un village, parfaitement imité.] | copy by A. Schouman after Paulus Potter *Mat:* op paneel *Size:* hoog 9, breed 11 duimen	Daniel de Jongh Az	(Sold) fl 30 Le Brun Parys

Schouman, Martinus

1810/05/22	AMSCH	0095	*Schouman (M.)* | Een kabbelend Water, vooraan twee Vaartuigen bij Paalwerk, achter zeilende Schepen en eene Stad in 't verschiet; helder geschilderd | *Mat:* op paneel *Size:* hoog 14 ½, breed 18 duim	Johannes van de Putte Nicolaasz.	(Sold) fl 8:10 Frantzen
1810/05/22	AMSCH	0096	*Schouman. (M.)* | Eene woelende Zee, met Oorlogschepen, Schuiten en andere Vaartuigen; als de voorgaande behandeld | *Mat:* op paneel *Size:* hoog 14, breed 17 duim	Johannes van de Putte Nicolaasz.	(Sold) fl 3 du Pree
1810/07/23	DOLGI	0045	*Martinus Schouwman* | Een woelige Zee; op dezelve een Oorlogschip en een Advijs-Jagt [sic]. Op den voorgrond, op den Wal, twee Beeldtjes, en in het verschiet eenige Zeilende Schepen. Fraai getekend. Lucht en Water van eene zeer goede behandeling | *Mat:* op doek *Size:* hoog 25 ½, breed 30 duim	Mr Pieter van den Santheuvel	(Sold) fl 27 Logger
1810/12/03	DOBRA	0013	*M. Schouman* | Een stil water, met dryvende en ten anker liggende Vaartuigen; uitvoerig geschilderd		(Unknown)

Schoute, Gilbert

1802/06/28	AMSCH	0173	*G. Schouten* | Een lezend oud Man, by een lessenaar, door G. Schouten, op Panneel | *Mat:* op paneel *Size:* hoog 13, breed 10 duim	B	(Sold) fl 2 Roos [for] A

Schumacher, N. [Unidentified]

1802/06/16	AMSCH	0178	*N. Schumacher* | Maria Magdaléna in Berouw, in Devotie aandagtig ziende op een Kruisifix, ter zyde legt een Doodshoofd, Aarvruchten, en een opengeslaagen Boek; alles krachtig geschilderd | *Mat:* op paneel *Size:* hoog 16 ½, breed 14 ½ duim	[Merrem]	(Sold) fl 6 v d Schley [for] R[ijfsnijder]
1802/06/16	AMSCH	0179	*N. Schumacher* | In een Italiaansch Landschap, met eenige Gebouwen, ziet men op de voorgrond by Geboomten, een Jagthond en verscheide soorten van dood Wilt en Gevogelten, en verschillende soort van Jagtgereedschappen; alles meesterlyk fraay en uitvoerig gepenceeld | *Mat:* op paneel *Size:* hoog 18 ½, breed 25 duim	[Merrem]	(Sold) fl 6 Agina

Schut, Cornelis (I)

1803/04/20	AMSCH	0070	*Schut (C.)* | In een Arcadisch Landschap zit onder het Lommer van Geboomten, een vrolyke Bachante, met een Schaaltje met Wyn in de hand, ter zyde staat een Boksvoet of Zater, bézig uit een cierlyke Kan de Wyn te schenken, op de voorgrond legt een Jonge Bachant, als speelende met een Bok, welk een tros Druiven in de Bek houd, alles is kragtig van Coloriét en meesterlyk gepenceeld [A l'ombre de quelques arbres est assise une bâchante tenant une tasse de vin, un satir versant la liqueur d'un beau vase est près d'elle ; au devant est couchêe une autre nimphe folatrant avec un bouc qui mâche une grappe de la treille : tableau d'un bon effet & d'une couleur vigoureuse.] | *Mat:* op doek *Size:* hoog 44, breed 34 duim	Maria Magdalena van Sluypwyk, gravinne van Moens	(Sold) fl 13:10 de Meijer
1803/08/01	AMSCH	0035	*Schut. (A.)* | Een Heilige Familje verzeld van devote Vrouwen, in de lucht een glorie van Engelen, meesterlyk behandeld | *Mat:* op doek *Size:* hoog 17, breed 13 ½ duim *Notes:* The artist's name was given as "Schut. (A.)" but we have assumed this is an error.	J	(Sold) fl 3 van Dijl
1810/07/26	AMSCH	0136	*Schut* | Juno en Pallas, rustende in een Landschap, ter zijde een Arend en ander bijwerk. Schoon en krachtig uitgevoerd | *Mat:* op paneel *Size:* hoog 28, breed 40 duimen	Cassino	(Sold) fl 10 Van Iperen

Schut, Cornelis (I) (and Heem, David)

1808/06/13	AMSCH	0149	*Heem (D. de); J. Schut* | Christus in de schoot van Maria, waarbij eenige Engelen: deze Ordonantie is omgeven met Guirlandes van Bloemen, allen toepasselijk op het Lijden. Dit Stuk is even grootsch van onderwerp als behandeling | *Mat:* op doek *Size:* hoog 53, breed 47 duim *Notes:* The second artist's name was given as "J. Schut" but we have assumed this is an error.	E M Engelberts	(Sold) fl 30 Engelberts
1808/08/23	AMSCH	0078	*Heem. (D. de); J. Schut* | Eene schoone en bevallige Ordonantie van onderscheidene soorten van Bloemen, kunstig en met smaak zamengeschikt, en in het midden een Bijbelsche Ordonantie, door de beroemde J. Schut geschilderd, versierd dit heerlijk schilderij | *Mat:* op doek *Size:* hoog 53, breed 47 duim *Notes:* The second artist's name was given as "J. Schut" but we have assumed this is an error.	J	(Sold) fl 11 Hulswit

Schütz

1806/08/20	HGBSM	0044	*Schuz* | Een Rhijn gezicht, rijk gestoffeerd en zeer uitvoerig | companion to lot 45 *Mat:* op koper *Size:* hoog 10 ½, breed 14 duim	Macalester Loup	(Sold) fl 36 for lots 44 & 45. Teissier

1806/08/20	HGBSM	0045	*Schuz* | Een dito [Rhijn gezicht] wederga, niet minder als de voorgaande, door denzelven [Schuz], op koper, van gelijke groote | companion to lot 44 *Mat:* op koper *Size:* hoog 10 ½, breed 14 duim	Macalester Loup	(Sold) fl 36 for lots 44 & 45. Teissier
1809/06/13	AMSCH	0207	*Schuts* | Twee stuks Rhijngezigten, rijk met Vaartuigen en Beeldjes gestoffeerd	E	(Sold) fl 1:15 Buck
1809/06/13	AMSCH	0208	*Schuts* | Twee stuks als de voorgaande [Rhijngezigten?]	E	(Sold) fl 1 Grimmond
1809/06/13	AMSCH	0209	*Schuts* | Twee dito [stuks] als de voorgaande [Rhijngezigten?]	E	(Sold) fl 0:12 L Pakker
1810/10/11	AMSCH	0188	*Schuts* | Eene bevallige Vrouw, hebbende een Kind aan de Borst, ter zijde andere Kindertjes, zinspeelende op de Liefde, fraai | *Mat:* op doek	A	(Sold) fl 3:5 Yver

Schütz, Franz

1802/09/06	AMSCH	0111	*F. Schutz* | Twee stuks boomryke Land- en Rhyngezigten, met beeldjes gestoffeerd	Mevrouw Achtienhoven	(Sold) fl 1:10 Yver
1803/09/07	AMSCH	0165	*F. Schutz* | Twee stuks Gezichten in Duitsland, zynde het eene een Bergagtig Landschap; en het ander een Rivier met een Brug, verder gestoffeerd met verscheide Beelden en Beesten, zeer uitvoerig gepenceeld, en bevallig van Coloriet [Deux vues d'Allemagne ; l'une représentant un paysage montueux, l'autre une rivière avec un pont ;[fj plus loin plusieurs figures et du bétail artistement variés ; d'une très belle composition, et d'un coloris agréable] | *Mat:* op paneel *Size:* yder is hoog 10, breed 13 duim	Smidt	(Sold) fl 21 J Yver
1803/09/07	AMSCH	0166	*F. Schutz* | Een dito Schuur met dito Gereedschappen, en een Vrouw aan een Ton, en verders een Kat; behandeld als de voorgaande [Une grange avec ses accessoires ; au fond, une femme occupee près d'une tonne, à côté un chat ; même manière et composition que les deux précédens] | *Mat:* op paneel *Size:* hoog 13 ½, breed 19 duim [Haut 13 ½ large 19 ½ pouces] *Notes:* It is unclear what "dito" refers to in the title. The dimensions differ in the Dutch and French editions of the catalogue.	Smidt	(Sold) fl 11 van Iperen

Schutz, J.F. [Unidentified]

1805/07/03	AMSCH	0150	*J. F. Schuz* | Twee stuks ryk gestoffeerde Rhyngezichten, met Postwagen, belaaden Vaartuigen en werkende Beelden; plaisant zonachtig en bevallig geschilderd op Paneel | *Mat:* op paneel *Size:* yder hoog 17, breed 20 duim	R[oos]	(Sold) fl 28 Zurmuklen

Schütz, Johann George

1802/06/28	AMSCH	0174	*J. Schutz* | Twee stuks bevallige gestoffeerde Rhyngezigten | *Mat:* op paneel *Size:* ieder hoog 10, breed 12 duim	Anna Elink	(Sold) fl 0:10 Jan Yver
1802/06/28	AMSCH	0176	*J. Schutz* | Twee Rhyngezigten	Anna Elink	(Sold) fl 1:5 Weeber

Schütz, Johann George (manner)

1802/06/28	AMSCH	0175	*J. Schutz* | Twee dito [stuks], dito [bevallige gestoffeerde Rhyngezigten], als de vorigen [J. Schutz] | *Mat:* op paneel *Notes:* It is unclear what "dito" refers to in the title.	Anna Elink	(Sold) fl 1 van Iperen

Schutz, S. [Unidentified]

1803/09/07	AMSCH	0167	*S. Schutz* | Twee stuks Bergachtige Land- en Riviergezichten, met verschillend Geboomten en Wooningen, gestoffeerd met Huislieden met Vee, rydende Postwagen; en aangename verschieten, verbeeldende de eene een Avondstond, en de andere een Maneschyn, byde uitvoerig [Deux paysages, offrant des vues pittoresques et variées par des plaines, des montagnes, des rivières, des habitans et des figures entremélées de bétail ; on y voit entre autres une voiture publique, l'une représente une soirée, l'autre un claire de lune ; toutes deux d'une excellente composition et d'un effet admirable] | *Mat:* [sur bois] *Size:* yder hoog 12, breed 14 duim *Notes:* This lot was misnumbered no. 157 in the French edition of the catalogue. In addition, the material was given only in the French edition of the catalogue.	Smidt	(Sold) fl 5:10 Lamme
1803/09/07	AMSCH	0168	*S. Schutz* | Twee stuks Boom- en Duinachtige Landschapjes, ryk gestoffeerd met Beeldjes en Beestjes; zonachtig en uitvoerig van behandeling [Deux charmans paysages, riches en figures et bétail de tous genres ; un beau soleil règne sur l'ensemble de la composition et rend ces deux tableaux très recommandables] | *Mat:* [sur bois] *Size:* yder hoog 9, breed 12 duim *Notes:* The material was given only in the French edition of the catalogue.	Smidt	(Sold) fl 15 Teengs

Schuylenburgh

1810/03/27	RMCNL	0090	*Schuilenburg* | Een Stuk, voorstellende eenig dood gevogelte, zeer uitvoerig, delicaat en natuurlijk geschildert		(Unknown)

Schwarzenbach, Jacob

1802/05/10	MGSAN	0034	*Zwartzenbach* | Een Kaarslichtje, waarby een leezend oud Man, met een Bril op de Neus, zeer levendig en zacht gepenseeld, door Zwartzenbach: op Paneel, in vergulde Lyst | *Mat:* op paneel *Size:* hoog 10 duim, breed 9 duim	Johan Dirk Kruysse	(Unknown) £ 1:4

Schweickardt, Heinrich Wilhelm

1802/05/24	HGBAK	0055	*Swykhard* | Een schoon Watergezicht met veelerhande Schepen, op de voorgrond eenige Mannen, uit al hun magt werkende om een Schuit, waar voor een Paard gespannen, op de Scheepswerf te haalen, zeer uitvoerig door Swykhard, hoog 17 ½ duim, breed 21 ½ duim, op doek, vergulde lyst | companion to lot 56 *Mat:* op doek *Size:* hoog 17 ½ duim, breed 21 ½ duim	Mejuffrouw A van der Mieden	(Unknown) fl 20 for lots 55 & 56
1802/05/24	HGBAK	0056	*Swykhard* | Een dito [schoon Watergezicht] tot een weerga, verbeeldende een kabbelend water met veele Schepen, op de voorgrond eenige Visschers enz., door denzelven [Swykhard], niet minder als 't voorige, hoog en breed als 't voorige [hoog 17 ½ duim, breed 21 ½ duim] | companion to lot 55 *Size:* hoog 17 ½ duim, breed 21 ½ duim	Mejuffrouw A van der Mieden	(Unknown) fl 20 for lots 55 & 56
1802/05/24	HGBAK	0057	*Swykhard* | Een plaisant stuk, verbeeldende een Dorp, leggende aan een Rivier, op de voorgrond een pont of veerschuit met eenige figuren en goederen, op de agtergrond zeilende Scheepjes, door denzelven [Swykhard]; hoog 15 duim, breed 18 ½ duim, op doek, in vergulde lyst | companion to lot 58 *Mat:* op doek *Size:* hoog 15 duim, breed 18 ½ duim	Mejuffrouw A van der Mieden	(Sold) fl 20 for lots 57 & 58. v d Velde
1802/05/24	HGBAK	0058	*Swykhard* | Een dito [plaisant stuk] tot een weerga, verbeeldende een gehugt, leggende aan een Rivier met Scheepjes, Schuitjes en figuuren, door denzelve [Swykhard], niet minder als het voorige, en hoog en breed als vooren [hoog 15 duim, breed 18 ½ duim], dito [vergulde] lyst | companion to lot 57 *Size:* hoog 15 duim, breed 18 ½ duim	Mejuffrouw A van der Mieden	(Sold) fl 20 for lots 57 & 58. v d Velde
1802/06/28	AMSCH	0167	*W. Schweikhard* | Een Zomer en een Winter, beiden zeer ryk gestoffeerd van een menigte Beelden en Beesten, verders aangenaame Verschieten, uitvoerig op Doek | *Mat:* op doek *Size:* hoog 29, breed 39 duim	Anna Elink	(Sold) fl 99 van Iperen
1802/09/18	RMDRS	0022	*Zweikhard* | Een Winter gezicht, waarin veel gewoel van Arresleeden, Schaatsryders, en andere Stoffagie, zeer uitvoerig en aangenaam geschilderd | *Size:* hoog 12 ½, breed 16 ½ duim	Casper de Haas	(Unknown) fl 28
1802/09/18	RMDRS	0040	*Zweikhard* | Een fraay Winter gezicht, met een menigte Schaatsryders | *Size:* hoog 9 ½, breed 12 ½ duim	Casper de Haas	(Sold) fl 19 Gruiter
1803/04/18	HGBAK	0001	*H.W. Schweickhard* | Een stuk verbeeldende een Veengravery in Rynland, met Boerderyen, Beelden en Beesten gestoffeerd, in het verschiet Dorpgezichten, &c. extra uitvoerig, kragtig en schoon van Ordonnantie, door H. W. Schweickhard, hoog 17, breed 24 d. Paneel, verg l[yst]. [Schilderyen in Olyverf] | companion to lot 2 *Mat:* in olyverf op paneel *Size:* hoog 17, breed 24 d. *Notes:* The bracketed information in the title about the medium appears above lot 1 and refers to lots 1 to 48.	Johan Pieter Reigersman [or others]	(Unknown)
1803/04/18	HGBAK	0002	*H.W. Schweickhard* | Een Pendant verbeeldende een Wintergezicht, aan de veste van een Stad, met veele Schaatsryders gestoffeerd, op de voorgrond een welbekend kunstlievend Heer, en vlug Schaatsreyder, een Marketenter Arresleeder, &c. niet minder uitvoerig en kragtig behandeld, door denzelve Meester [H. W. Schweickhard], hoog en breed als vooren [hoog 17, breed 24 d.], in dito [verg.] lyst [Schilderyen in Olyverf] | companion to lot 1 *Mat:* in olyverf *Size:* hoog 17, breed 24 d. *Notes:* The bracketed information in the title about the medium appears above lot 1 and refers to lots 1 to 48.	Johan Pieter Reigersman [or others]	(Unknown)
1803/04/18	HGBAK	0003	*H. W. Schweickhard* | Een Zomeragtig Landschap met Beesten gestoffeerd op de voorgrond een Ram, Schaap an Lam, en een Stal waar uit een Stier de kop steekt, extra fraay en kragtig gepenceelt, door H. W. Schweickhard op paneel, hoog 12, breed 15 duim, vergulde lyst [Schilderyen in Olyverf] | *Mat:* in olyverf op paneel *Size:* hoog 12, breed 15 duim *Notes:* The bracketed information in the title appears above lot 1 and refers to lots 1 to 48.	Johan Pieter Reigersman [or others]	(Unknown)
1803/04/18	HGBAK	0004	*H. W. Schweickhard* | Een fraay stukje verbeeldende een Fruitkoper, welken aan twee Dames zyn waaren bied, benevens eenige anderen figuren, door H. W. Schweickhard, op paneel, hoog 12, breed 15 ½ duim, vergulde lyst [Schilderyen in Olyverf] | *Mat:* in olyverf op paneel *Size:* hoog 12, breed 15 ½ duim *Notes:* The bracketed information in the title appears above lot 1 and refers to lots 1 to 48.	Johan Pieter Reigersman [or others]	(Unknown)
1803/04/18	HGBAK	0005	*H. W. Schweikhard* | Een extra schoon stuk verbeeldende een Boerdery, waar in een Boerin een Koe melkt, benevens een leggende, en drinkende Koe, Schaapen, Geiten, een graazend Paard, &c. alles zeer uitvoerig en delicaat behandeld, door H. W. Schweikhard, hoog 15 ½ breed 21 d. in vergulde lyst paneel [Schilderyen in Olyverf] | companion to lot 6 *Mat:* in olyverf op paneel *Size:* hoog 15 ½, breed 21 duim *Notes:* The bracketed information in the title appears above lot 1 and refers to lots 1 to 48.	Johan Pieter Reigersman [or others]	(Unknown)
1803/04/18	HGBAK	0006	*H.W. Schweikhard* | Een dito [extra schoon stuk verbeeldende een Boerdery] dienende tot een Pendant, verbeeldende een boomryk Landschap met Koebeesten, Paarden, Schaapen, een Boertje met melk Emmers, &c. niet minder als het voorgaande en door denzelve Meester [H. W. Schweikhard], hoog en breed als voren [hoog 15 ½ breed 21 d.], en dito [vergulde] lyst op paneel [Schilderyen in Olyverf] | companion to lot 5 *Mat:* in olyverf op paneel *Size:* hoog 15 ½ breed 21 duim *Notes:* It is unclear what "dito" refers to in the title. The bracketed information in the title about the medium appears above lot 1 and refers to lots 1 to 48.	Johan Pieter Reigersman [or others]	(Unknown)

1803/04/18	HGBAK	0007	*H.W. Schweikhard* | Een niet minder fraay stuk met Runderen Schaapen gestoffeerd, een Boertie en Boerinne staande te spreeken, &c. zeer kragtig en fix behandeld door H. W. Schweikhard hoog 15 breed 19 duim paneel [Schilderyen in Olyverf] | *Mat:* in olyverf op paneel *Size:* hoog 15 breed 19 duim *Notes:* The bracketed information in the title appears above lot 1 and refers to lots 1 to 48.	Johan Pieter Reigersman [or others]	(Unknown)
1803/04/18	HGBAK	0008	*H.W. Schweickhard* | Een plaisant stuk verbeeldende een straat in London, met een Koperslagers Winkel, in de ingang drie Dames, voor het Huys een Stoelenmaker een Vrouw, met een Kind en andere figuren, zeer uitvoerig en kragtig behandeld door H. W. Schweickhard, hoog en breed als vooren [hoog 15 breed 19 duim], paneel, vergulde lyst [Schilderyen in Olyverf] | *Mat:* in olyverf op paneel *Size:* hoog 15 breed 19 duim *Notes:* The bracketed information in the title appears above lot 1 and refers to lots 1 to 48.	Johan Pieter Reigersman [or others]	(Unknown)
1803/07/18	AMSCH	0051	*Schweikhardt. (H.)* | Twee stuks aangenaame heuvelachtige Landschapjes, gestoffeerd met Beelden en Beesten, zynde van een bevallige schildering [Deux charmans paysages ornés de figures & d'animaux bien dessinés. Le choix est en [sic] heureux par la variété des sites & la maniere spirituelle dont les animaux sont touchés ; une bonne couleur & une exécution très soignée achevent ces rians tableaux.] | *Mat:* op paneel *Size:* hoog 13, breed 18 duim	Maria Theresia Andrioli	(Sold) fl 30 van Iperen
1803/12/12	AMSCH	0092	*Sweichhart* | In een bevallige Winter ziet men 't Ys ryk gestoffeert met een menigte van Schaatzenryders en Marketenter, ter zyde eenige Boerenwoningen en een Brug, waar agter zig een Dorp gezigt vertoond; bevallig van licht en uitvoerig op Paneel geschilderd | *Mat:* op paneel *Size:* hoog 9 ½, breed 12 ½ duim	B	(Bought In) fl 20
1804/05/07	AMSCH	0199	*Zweickhart* | In een aangenaamen Winter, ziet men het Ys ryk gestoffeerd met Arresleeden, Schaatsenryders en wandelende Beeldjes, langs de weg voor een Hëreberg een plysterende Postwagen en een ménigte van andere Stoffagie, terzyde eenige Molens en een Dorp in 't verschiet; uitvoerig en bevallig geschilderd | *Mat:* op paneel *Size:* hoog 13, breed 17 duim	Vinkeles [for] G	(Sold) fl 30 Coclers
1804/12/10	AMSCH	0091	*H. W. Schweikhardt* | Een Landschap, op de voorgrond ziet men twee grazende Koeijen, ter zyde twee rustende Schaapen, in 't verschiet een stil Water; zonachtig en breed behandeld | companion to lot 92 *Mat:* op paneel *Size:* Hoog 16, breed 20 duim	Jan De Groot	(Sold) fl 151 for lots 91 & 92. Coclers
1804/12/10	AMSCH	0092	*H. W. Schweikhardt* | Een dito Landschap, waarop een grazende en leggende Koey; niet minder fraai als de vorige, zynde een weerga | companion to lot 91 *Size:* Hoog 16, breed 20 duim *Notes:* It is unclear what "dito" refers to in the title.	Jan De Groot	(Sold) fl 151 for lots 91 & 92. Coclers
1804/12/10	AMSCH	0093	*H. W. Schweikardt* | Twee stuks fraaije en zonachtige Landschappen, met hoog geboomten en bergachtig verschiet, gestoffeerd met onderscheiden Beeldjes en Beesjes; meesterlyk van behandeling | *Mat:* op paneel *Size:* Hoog 10, breed 13 duim	Jan De Groot	(Sold) fl 20 Coclers
1806/05/05	AMSCH	0129	*Swichards* | Een bevallige Winter, 't Ys ryk gestoffeerd met een meenigte van Schaatseryders en Marketenters, ter zyden eenige Boeren Wooningen, een Brug waar agter zig een Dorpgezigt vertoont; bevallig van licht en uitvoerig op Paneel | *Mat:* op paneel *Size:* hoog 9 ½, breed 12 ½ duim	V[inkeles]	(Sold) fl 20 van der Does
1806/08/20	HGBSM	0038	*H.W. Schweickhardt* | Een IJsgezicht, met Boerewoning en vol Schaatzenrijders. op de voorgrond een Man, Vrouw en Kind, die een slee op het land stoten, uitvoerig en natuurlijk door H. W. Schweickhardt, 1783 | *Mat:* op paneel *Size:* hoog 12, breed 18 duim *Inscr:* H. W. Schweickhardt, 1783 (signed and dated?) *Notes:* It is unclear whether the name and date are inscribed on the painting.	Macalester Loup	(Sold) fl 65 A Taixera
807/08/26	AMSCH	0198	*H.W. Schweikhardt* | Een Italiaansch bergachtig Landschap, met een Waterval, welke in een Rivier uitstort, waarover een vervallen Brug, op den voorgrond eenige Visschers, welke bézig zyn met visschen, en verdere stoffage; zonachtig, delicaat en uitvoerig behandeld | *Mat:* op doek *Size:* hoog 28, breed 39 duim	Joseph Vallette	(Sold) fl 81 van Iperen
807/08/26	AMSCH	0200	*H.W. Schweikhardt* | Een met Kindertjes, in 't graauw, als door J. de Wit	Joseph Vallette	(Sold) fl 1:15 H[k] Jansen
808/06/06	RMRIJ	0114	*Schweickhardt. (H. W.) 1772* | Een aangenaam Landschap, rijk en uitvoerig gestoffeerd met figuren en beesten. Eene wedergade, in alles als boven [Un Paysage dans le goût de Pillement, très fini. Un Pendant égal en mérite au précédent] | *Annots:* uit den boedel von den Solliciteur Militair Mierlo, den Haag, 1781 (f 120.-) (RMA I) *Mat:* op paneel *Size:* Twee Stukken. Hoog 14 ½, en breed 19 duim *Inscr:* H.W. Schweickhardt. 1772 (signed and dated?) *Notes:* It is unclear whether the name and date are inscribed on the painting.	Gerrit van der Pot, Heer van Groeneveld	(Sold) fl 62 Du Pré
809/07/25	HGBSM	0038	*H.W. Schweickhardt* | Twee stuks Boere Binnehuizen, verbeeldende het eene een Vrouw die koeke bakt, waar by een Man staat een glas bier te drinken &c. Het andere een dito Gezelschap, waar in een Jonge Visch schoon maakt | *Mat:* op paneel *Size:* hoog 10 ½, breed 13 ½ duim	D van der Aa	(Sold) fl 34:15 van Eyk

Schweickardt, Heinrich Wilhelm (copy by)

807/08/26	AMSCH	0199	*H.W. Schweikhardt; P. Potter* | Een aangenaam Boomryk Landschap, met een Rivier, in welke eenige Jongens zwemmen, terwyl twee Koeijen en	Joseph Vallette	(Sold) fl 171 Jozi

			een Ram in en by dezelve staan, en daar helder in spiegelen. Op de tweede grond by een Boeren Woning ziet men nog verscheiden Vee, in het verschiet een Koets, met zes Paarden; zynde dit Sukje [sic] zonachtig en uitvoerig behandeld, naar het Schildery van P. Potter | copy by H. Schweickardt after Paulus Potter *Mat:* op paneel *Size:* hoog 17, breed 24 duim		

Schyndel

1801/08/19	AMSCH	0116	*van Schyndel* | Een Natuurlyk Land en Watergezicht, ryk met Schuitjes en Beeldjes gestoffeerd	Pruyssen^{r} [for] Q	(Sold) fl 3 Gruiter
1802/05/11	GRGRW	0052	*Schijndel* | De Overspelige Zondares voor Christus [Schilderijen met Olie-Verf; In zwarte Lijsten] | companion to lot 53 *Mat:* in olyverf *Notes:* The bracketed information in the title appears above lot 1 and refers to lots 1 to 79a.	Arnold Sicco Werumeus	(Unknown) fl 5:5 for lots 52 & 53
1802/05/11	GRGRW	0053	*Schijndel* | De Voorstelling van Christus in den Tempel, tot ene weerga [Schilderijen met Olie-Verf; In zwarte Lijsten] | companion to lot 52 *Mat:* in olyverf *Notes:* The bracketed information in the title appears above lot 1 and refers to lots 1 to 79a.	Arnold Sicco Werumeus	(Unknown) fl 5:5 for lots 52 & 53
1803/08/01	AMSCH	0037	*Van Schyndel* | Een zinnebeeldige Ordonantie, gestoffeert met Gebouwen, Beelden en ander bywerk, fix gepenceeld | *Mat:* op doek	J	(Sold) fl 10 Pruijssenaar
1804/05/07	AMSCH	0157	*Schyndel (van)* | Twee stuks Maanlichten, by eenige Huizen en een oud Casteel, ziet men heldere spiegelende Rivieren, waarin eenige Schuiten, enz.; beide natuurlyk en uitvoerig gepenceeld | *Mat:* op doek *Size:* hoog 16, breed 19 duim	Roos [for] A	(Sold) fl 16 Reijers
1805/10/21	GRBOL	0033	*Schyndel* | De Vinding van Moses	Gerardus Nicolaus Heerkens	(Unknown)
1805/10/21	GRBOL	0037	*Schyndel* | Een Bacchus Feest	Gerardus Nicolaus Heerkens	(Unknown)
1805/10/21	GRBOL	0053	*Schyndel* | Een dito [Landschapje]	Gerardus Nicolaus Heerkens	(Unknown)
1805/10/21	GRBOL	0055	*Schyndel* | Een Landschap met een Rhyngezicht gestoffeerd, met Menschen en Beesten, goed Geschilderd	Gerardus Nicolaus Heerkens	(Unknown)
1808/08/23	AMSCH	0248	*van Schijndel* | Een Maneschijn over een stille Rivier; op Paneel geschilderd | *Mat:* op paneel	S	(Sold) fl 3:5 van Iperen
1810/06/20	AMSCH	0179	*Van Schyndel* | Een Binnenhuis, met een Kaartspelend Gezelschap	A	(Sold) fl 1:15 du Pree
1810/11/07	UTWLD	0008	*Schyndel* | Een door hooggeboomte bewassen Landschap, op de voorgrond eenige stoffagie in 't volle licht, verder 't verschiet over een Rivier, fiks geschilderd door Schyndel op doek, 1 voet 8 duim breed 1 voet 6 en een half duim hoog, in een zwarte Lijst | *Mat:* op doek *Size:* 1 voet 8 duim breed 1 voet 6 en een half duim hoog		(Unknown) fl 21

Schyndel (manner)

1803/09/07	AMSCH	0251	*Schyndel* | Een Land- en Riviergezicht, verbeeldende een Maaneschyn, op de voorgrond gestoffeerd met verscheide Vée; fiks geschilderd, Doek op Paneel, in de manier van Schyndel [La vue d'une campagne et d'une rivière, représentée au claire de lune ; le devant est animé par des bestiaux ; belle composition] | *Mat:* op doek op paneel *Size:* hoog 11, br. 15 duim *Notes:* The French edition of the catalogue does not include an artist for this lot.	Smidt	(Sold) fl 2:10 Gruiter

Schyndel, J. van

1801/03/16	AMSCH	0036	*J. van Schyndel* | Twee stuks Binnenhuizen, het eene een Chirurgyns Winkel, en het andere een Doctor by een Zieke, konstig behandeld	P[ruyssenaar]	(Sold) fl 4 Stevens
1802/09/21	UTHDG	0081	*J. Scheindel* | Een Rivier lopende tusschen strooken laag land, onder anderen gestoffeerd met Visschers, hunne Netten gereed makende | *Mat:* op doek *Size:* hoog 22, breed 28 duimen		(Bought In) fl 20
1803/06/20	AMSCH	0076	*J. Schyndel* | Twee stuks, verbeeldende Maneschynen; in de manier van A. van der Neer | *Size:* yder hoog 11, breed 16 duim	Roos [for] L	(Bought In) fl 29 ½
1803/08/24	HGKAN	A0001	*J.V. Schydel* | Een Berg en Boomryk Landschap, gestoffeerd met Ryzigers, en een Boer die twee Ossen dryft | companion to lot A2 *Mat:* op doek *Size:* breet 28, hoog 25 duim		(Sold) fl 6 Uytenbogerd
1803/08/24	HGKAN	A0002	*J.V. Schydel* | Een Weerga | companion to lot A1		(Unknown)
1805/10/09	HGBSM	0103	*J. van Schyndel* | Een kwakzalver op zyn theäter, met een meenigte omstanders &c. | *Mat:* op paneel *Size:* hoog 12 breet 15 duim	T H van Willigen [or others]	(Sold) fl 16:5 for lots 103 & 104. Carré (de Secretaris)
1805/10/09	HGBSM	0104	*J. van Schyndel* | Een dito, zynde een boeren kermis, vol gewoel, niet minder als de voorgaande | *Size:* hoog 12 breet 15 duim *Notes:* It is unclear what "dito" refers to in the title.	T H van Willigen [or others]	(Sold) fl 16:5 for lots 103 & 104. Carré (de Secretaris)
1806/08/13	AMSCH	0173	*Schyndel. (J. van)* | Een Land- en Riviergezigt, gestoffeerd met Vaartuigen en Beeldjes, zynde een Avondstond; natuurlyk voorgesteld | *Mat:* op paneel *Size:* hoog 13, breed 20 duim	Daniel Mansveld	(Sold) fl 1:5 Hulswit
1806/08/13	AMSCH	0174	*Schyndel. (J. van)* | Twee stuks vrolyke Bachanaalen, vol gewoel van Nimphen, Kindertjes en Zaters, in Boomryke Landschappen; plaisant en bevallig geschilderd | *Mat:* op paneel *Size:* Ieder hoog 10, breed 14 duim	Roos	(Sold) fl 4:5 Gruiter

1807/08/26	AMSCH	0206	*J. v. Schyndel* | Een Land en Watergezigt, aan beide zyde met Woningen en Geboomten, op den voorgrond Vissers; alles by helder maanlicht | *Mat:* op paneel	Yver [for] S	(Sold) fl 4:10 Spaan
1809/04/22	AMYVR	0121	*J. van Schijndel* | Een Ruine aan een Rivier, waarover een Steene Brug, met eenige Lieden welke iets branden, het geen met het Maanlicht een aartig effect maakt; meesterlijk | *Mat:* op doek *Size:* hoog 25, breed 20 duim	de Bruin	(Sold) fl 4:5 du Pree

Scorel, Jan van

1802/04/13	HAVIN	0054	*Schorel* | Een H. Famielie		(Unknown)

Seghers, Daniel

1802/05/05	AMSCH	0244	*Pater Zegers* | Een Feston van een menigte Bloemen en Vrugten, in het midden ziet men een mans en vrouwe Pourtrait, zeer natuurlyk behandeld | *Mat:* op doek *Size:* hoog 32, breed 24 duim	C	(Sold) fl 2:5 Ackina
1802/05/11	GRGRW	0058	*Pater Zegers* | De Wijzen uit het Oosten, aanbiddende het Kind Jesus, met ene Krans van Bloemen in 't rond; op Koper geschilderd [Schilderijen met Olie-Verf; In zwarte Lijsten] | *Mat:* in olyverf op koper *Fmt:* rond *Notes:* The bracketed information in the title appears above lot 1 and refers to lots 1 to 79a.	Arnold Sicco Werumeus	(Unknown) fl 1:12
1802/06/29	HGDAW	0020	*Pater Zegers* | Een Vaes [sic] met Bloemen door Pater Zegers		(Unknown)
1802/09/06	AMSCH	0136	*D. Zeegers* | Op een Tafel staat een Glaase Fles, gevuld met onderscheide Bloemen, als roode, geele, en witte Roosen, met Knoppen, Steel en Bladeren; bevallig en uitvoerig geschilderd | *Mat:* op paneel *Size:* hoog 10, breed 7 duim	Brave	(Sold) fl 2 van der Schley [for] G
1803/06/20	AMSCH	0043a	*Pater Zegers* | In een Krans van onderscheide geurige Bloemen, ziet men Maria met het Kind Jesus op haaren schoot, alle de Bloemen zyn van een fraaije couleur en zeer uitvoerig op Paneel geschilderd | *Mat:* op paneel *Size:* hoog 36, breed 29 duim	Schley [for] G	(Sold) fl 15 V d Vinne
1804/10/29	HRBAU	0091	*Seegers, (D.)* | Een capitaale Bloemfeston, hangende aan een Steenen Ornament, gemaakt van roode, witte en geele Roozen, Irias, Tulppioenen, Zonnebloem, Kattestaart, en meer andere soorten, met hun lof. Alles fraai verdeeld, uitvoerig, en zeer natuurlyk behandeld | *Mat:* op doek *Size:* hoog 26, breed 20 duim	Simon Styl	(Unknown)
1805/10/09	HGBSM	0039	*P. Seegers* | Een krans met differente bloemen, in de midden een borstbeeld, in 't grauw natuurlyk | *Mat:* op doek *Size:* hoog 38 breet 31 duim	T H van Willigen [or others]	(Sold) fl 3 Ph Mey
1808/04/26	GDAN	0211	*Zegers (Paters)* | Een uitmuntend Bloemstuk, waar in 't midden een Beeld met Zeijs, verbeeldende de tijd geschilderd is, extra fraai | *Size:* hoog 33, breed 25 duim	G H Fortuyn	(Unknown)
1808/06/13	AMSCH	0154	*Seegers (P.)* | In het midden van eene fraai geschilderde Bloemkrans ziet men het Kind met 't Lam | *Mat:* op doek *Size:* hoog 20, breed 24 duim	E M Engelberts	(Sold) fl 13:10 Engelberts
1809/07/25	HGBSM	0211	*Pater Segers* | Een Krans met Bloemen, om een Ornament geslingert, in 't midden van 't stuk is een Heilige Familllie, in 't graauw verbeeld, de Bloemen zyn konstig geschildert | *Mat:* op koper *Size:* hoog 31 en een half, breed 23 duim	D van der Aa [or] E B ten Dall	(Sold) fl 8 Teissier
1810/08/06	AMSCH	0133	*Zegers (Pater)* | Eene Zinnebeeldige Ordonantie, met een Bloemenkrans omgeven. Fraai van koloriet | *Mat:* op doek *Size:* hoog 26, breed 33 duimen		(Withdrawn)

Seghers, Daniel (and Balen, H. (I))

1802/08/24	LNDLS	0023	*van Balen; D. Seegers* | Een Krans van veele Bloemen, rustende tegen Steenwerk. Delicaat en zeer konstig van schildering, door D. Seegers. In 't midden een Vrouw met Kinderen, verbeeldende de Liefde | *Mat:* op doek *Size:* hoog 31, breed 25 duimen	Leonardus Bouman [or others]	(Unknown) fl 16

Seghers, Daniel (and Diepenbeeck, A.J.)

808/06/13	AMSCH	0155	*Seegers (P.); A. Diepenbeek* | Eene Buste in 't graauw, omgeven met Guirlandes van Bloemen. Fraai van koloriet en uitvoerig gepenceelt | *Mat:* op koper *Size:* hoog 34, breed 24 duim	E M Engelberts	(Sold) fl 26 Simons
809/06/13	AMSCH	0231	*P. Zeegers; A. Diepenbeek* | Maria met het Kind, in een Bloemkrans, uitvoerig door P. Zeegers en A. Diepenbeek | *Mat:* op paneel *Size:* hoog 12, breed 10 duim	[Gruyter?]	(Sold or Bought In) fl 3 de Gruiter

Seghers, Daniel (and Hals, F. (I) or Hals, F. (I), manner)

810/07/26	AMSCH	0091	*F. Hals; Zegers (P.)* | Een fraai geschakeerde Krans, van onderscheidene keurige en uitvoerig geschilderde Bloemen, in het midden een vrolijk Mans Pourtrait, door of als F. Hals geschilderd	Cassino	(Bought In) fl 16

Seghers, Daniel (manner)

302/06/28	AMSCH	0215	*Pater Zeegers* | Een steene Ornamentlyst met verscheide zinnebeeldige Cieraden van Bloemen, Koornairen en Vrugten, in de midden in een Schilt, zit Christus by de Discipelen van Emaus aan Tafel. Om hoog een glorie van Engelen; kragtig gepenceeld als door Pater Zeegers | *Mat:* op doek *Size:* hoog 20, breed 15 duim	B	(Sold) fl 5:5 Roos [for] A

1805/10/09	HGBSM	0040	*P. Seegers* | Een dito [krans] met guirlandes, in de manier van denzelven [P. Seegers] | *Mat:* op doek *Size:* hoog 40 ½ breet 32 ½ duim	T H van Willigen [or others]	(Sold) fl 2 Ph Mey

Seghers, Gerard

1802/12/13	AMSCH	0184	*J. Zeegers* | Een Binnenvertrek, voor een Tafel, met een Tapyt bedekt, ziet men een Dame, in oude Hollandsche Kleeding, bezig haar halsdoek vast te maaken; alles is krachtig en bevallig gepenceeld, in de manier van G. Metzu, door J. Zeegers | *Mat:* op doek *Size:* hoog 30, breed 24 duim	Pruyssenaar [for] B	(Sold) fl 21 Hulswit

Seldron, Elizabeth

1801/12/22	AMOTT	0049	*E. Seldram* | 1 uitvoerige Paardenmarkt, by een Hof en Markententer [sic], vol gewoel en konst | companion to lot 50	Bartholomeus Ruloffs	(Unknown) fl 18 for lots 49 & 50
1801/12/22	AMOTT	0050	*E. Seldram* | 1 Beestenmarkt, by een boeren Plysterplaats, als vooren, om te dienen tot een weerga | companion to lot 49	Bartholomeus Ruloffs	(Unknown) fl 18 for lots 49 & 50

Seppo [Unidentified]

1802/06/28	AMSCH	0177	*Seppo* | Een gezicht op een Boere Dorp, met verscheide Stoffagie, door Seppo, op Panneel | *Mat:* op paneel *Size:* hoog 8, breed 9 duim	Anna Elink	(Sold) fl 1 van Iperen
1802/06/28	AMSCH	0178	*Seppo* | Een gezicht in een Dorp naar de Stad Utrecht, in 't verschiet de Stads Dom, zeer natuurlyk, door Denzelven [Seppo], op Panneel | *Mat:* op paneel *Size:* hoog 9, breed 12 duim	Anna Elink	(Sold) fl 4:10 de Meijer
1802/06/28	AMSCH	0179	*Seppo* | Twee stuks, het eene verbeeld een gezicht op een Stads Poort, en 't andere een Ysgezicht, zeer natuurlyk, door Denzelven [Seppo], op Panneel | *Mat:* op paneel *Size:* hoog 9, breed 10 duim	Anna Elink	(Sold) fl 2:10 Vermeulen

Serenacio [Unidentified]

1803/04/27	AMSCH	0035[a]	*Serenasio* | Trois morceaux differens, dont l'un est une ébauche par Serenasio, le Second une Copie de la Cingarella du Corrége, & le troisiéme Socrate avec ses Disciples | *This Lot:* Une ébauche; lot 35[b] is copy after Correggio & 35[c] by S. Rosa	A	(Sold) fl 5 for lots 35[a-c]. Stevens
1803/04/27	AMSCH	0150	*Serenacio* | Une Sainte Famille par Serenacio, & quatre petites esquisses, du méme Maitre	A	(Sold) fl 18 Hodges

Serenado [Unidentified]

1803/04/27	AMSCH	0062[a]	*Serenado* | Deux morceaux, dont l'un est l'esquisse d'un Tableau d'Autel, par Serenado, & l'autre une Copie d'après le Chevaliér van Dyk, réprésentant St. Augustin présenté par deux Anges à Jesus Christ | *This Lot:* L'esquisse d'un Tableau d'Autel; lot 62[b] is copy after Anth. van Dyck	A	(Sold) fl 36 for lots 62[a] & 62[b]. V^{n} Iperen
1803/04/27	AMSCH	0063	*Serénado* | Deux esquisees [sic] de Tableaux, dont l'un a pour object le baptême l'autre la Flagellation de Jesus Christ | *Size:* h. 1 ½, l. 2 ¾ pieds	A	(Sold) fl 16 Stevens

Settefano, M. [Unidentified]

1803/04/27	AMSCH	0025	*M. Settefano* | L'Ascention de la Sainte Vierge ; cette riche composition est d'un bel effêt & peinte avec beaucoup de Franchise | *Size:* h. 3 ½, l. 1 ¾ pieds	A	(Sold) fl 35 Hodges

Siberechts, Jan

1808/08/23	AMSCH	0144	*Sieberechts. (J.) (Ao.1672)* | In een bergachtig Landschap met Geboomte, ziet men op de voorgrond in een Waterplas, eene Vrouw zittende op een geappeld Paard, nevens haar een ros couleurde Koe, een Lam en twee Bokken, ter zijde zit eene bevallig Meisje, bézig de voeten te wasschen; zonachtig en natuurlijk behandeld | *Mat:* op doek *Size:* hoog 28, breed 23 duim *Inscr:* J. Sieberechts. Ao.1672 (signed and dated?) *Notes:* It is unclear whether the name and date are inscribed on the painting.	C	(Sold) fl 30 Dupré

Siberechts, Jan (and Amers, Piters)

1809/04/22	AMYVR	0119	*Sibrechts; Amers* | In een Waterplas, omgeven met zwaar Geboomte, ziet men eene Boerin te Paard, met een Kopere Kan op haar schoot, eenig Vee voortdrijvende, schijnende te spreeken met eene andere Vrouw, welke haar voeten wascht, in de manier van A. Cuijp, door Sibrechts en Amers, 1672 | *Mat:* op doek *Size:* hoog 27, breed 23 duim *Inscr:* Sibrechts en Amers, 1672 (signed and dated?) *Notes:* It is unclear whether the names and date are inscribed on the painting.	de Bruin	(Sold) fl 14:10 du Pree

Sibilla, Gijsbert

1805/07/03	AMSCH	0147	*G. Sybilla* | Deze ryke Ordinantie, vol gewoel van Beelden, vertoont: den Heiland, zittende voor een prachtig Palys, en laat de Kindertjes tot hem komen; alles is krachtig en meesterlyk gepenceeld op Paneel | *Mat:* op paneel *Size:* hoog 35, breed 26 duim	G	(Sold) fl 22 L Pakker
1808/04/26	GDAN	0157	*Sybilla* | Verbeeldende den Heere Jesus aan de Tafel bij de Emmausgangeren, zeer goed geschildert | *Size:* hoog 17, breed 12 duim	G H Fortuyn	(Unknown)
1809/07/25	HGBSM	0072	*G.J. Sybilla* | Een Historieel Stuk, verbeeldende een Offerhande, ryk van ordonnantie, uitvoerig en Meesterlyk geschildert door G.J. Syvilla, 1641 | *Mat:* op doek *Size:* hoog 31, breed 42 duim *Inscr:* G.J. Syvilla, 1641 (signed and dated?) *Notes:* It is unclear whether the name and date are inscribed on the painting.	D van der Aa	(Sold) fl 28 van der Aa

Silo, Adam

1801/03/16	AMSCH	0102a	*A. Silo* | Twee stuks, een woelend en een stil Water met Oorlogen andere Vaartuigen, fraai	K[ip]	(Sold) fl 12 v d Schley [for] S
1802/09/06	AMSCH	0112	*A. Silo* | Twee stuks woelende Waters, met verscheide zeilende Oorlogscheepen, en andere vaartuigen en sloepen; natuurlyk en bevallig geschildert | *Mat:* op doek *Size:* ieder hoog 11, breed 15 duim	W ten Houten	(Sold) fl 3 van Iperen
1802/09/06	AMSCH	0113	*A. Silo* | Twee Stille Watertjes, beide gestoffeerd met diversche zylende Scheepen; zeer uitvoerig op Paneel geschilderd | *Mat:* op paneel *Size:* ieder hoog 5, breed 6 duim	W ten Houten	(Sold) fl 2:15 van der Schley
1802/09/06	AMSCH	0114	*A. Silo* | Twee stuks kabbelende Waters, met verscheide vaartuigen en beeldjes; | *Mat:* op doek *Size:* hoog 17, breed 24 duim	Mevrouw Achtienhoven	(Sold) fl 3 van Iperen
1802/09/21	UTHDG	0083	*A. Silo* | Oorlogs en andere Vaartuigen, in een Rivier met een ruin verschiet, accuraat geschildert		(Sold) fl 2:16 Verhoude
1803/06/20	AMSCH	0035	*A. Silo* | Twee stuks woelende Waters met een ménigte Oorlog en andere Schepen en Schuiten, ter zyde op de Wal eenige Huizen en Geboomten en andere Stoffagie, fix op Doek | *Mat:* op doek *Size:* hoog 21, breed 26 duim	Schley [for] G	(Sold) fl 10 Hafner
1803/06/20	AMSCH	0051	*A. Silo* | Twee stuks woelende Waters, met een ménigte Schépen en andere Vaarttuigen, terzyde Strandgezichten, met Beeldjes, de Waters zyn dun en zyn verder frappant van licht, van de beste van A. Silo, op Doek | *Mat:* op doek *Size:* hoog 19, breed 25 duim	Roos [for] E	(Sold) fl 32 B Kooij
1803/09/07	AMSCH	0174	*A. Silo* | Een Zeeslag vol gewoel [Un combat maritime, plein de tumulte et de mouvement] | *Mat:* op paneel *Size:* hoog 16, breed 20 duim [Haut 14, large 20 pouces] *Notes:* The dimensions differ in the Dutch and French editions of the catalogue.	Smidt	(Sold) fl 1:15 L Pakker
1803/12/12	AMSCH	0093	*A. Silo* | Een woelend Water met een ménigte zeilende Vaartuigen; uitvoerig op Doek | *Mat:* op doek *Size:* hoog 9, breed 16 duim	Arnoud de Lange	(Sold) fl 0:10 L Pakker
1803/12/12	AMSCH	0094	*A. Silo* | Een kabbelend Water met verscheide Vaartuigen; bevallig op Doek | *Mat:* op doek *Size:* hoog 14, breed 17 duim	F	(Sold) fl 3:5 Theengs
1804/05/07	AMSCH	0160	*Silo. (A.)* | Twee stuks kabbelende Waters, met een meenigte van zeilende en stilleggende Scheepen en Vaartuigen; fiks en natuurlyk gepenceeld | *Mat:* op doek *Size:* Ieder hoog 22, breed 27 duim	Vinkeles [for] H[affner]	(Bought In) fl 10
1804/05/07	AMSCH	0161	*Silo. (A.)* | Een kabbelende Zee, met een meenigte van zeilende en stilleggende Scheepen en Vaartuigen, enz.; fiks gepenceeld | *Mat:* op doek *Size:* hoog 22, breed 31 duim	Roos [for] A	(Sold) fl 0:6 L Pakker
1805/07/03	AMSCH	0044	*Silo. (A.)* | Een kabbelend Water, met verscheide zeilende Scheepen, op de Voorgrond eenige Visschers by hun Schuit; geestig van Ordinantie en penceels behandeling | *Mat:* op paneel *Size:* hoog 12, breed 14 duim	R[oos]	(Sold) fl 3:5 Nieuwenhuys
1805/07/10	AMSCH	0135	*A. Silo* | Twee stuks Hollandsche Zeehavens, ryk met Scheepen enz.; krachtig op Doek | *Mat:* op doek *Size:* hoog 32, breed 46 duim	V[inkeles] [for] H[affner]	(Sold) fl 9 Lafontaine
1805/07/10	AMSCH	0266	*A. Sils* | Twee stuks stille Watergezichten, gestoffeert met zylende Scheepen; helder en uitvoerig behandeld	Schley	(Sold) fl 1 L Pakker
1806/05/05	AMSCH	0137	*A. Silo* | Twee stuks, een stil en woelend Water, ziende op de Stad Amsterdam, ryk met Scheepen en Schuiten | *Mat:* op doek *Size:* hoog 20, breed 25 duim	E	(Sold) fl 10:10 Gruyter
1806/08/13	AMSCH	0301	*A. Silo* | Twee stuks Zeeën met zeilende Oorlogschepen	Vinkeles	(Sold) fl 2:10 L Pakker
1807/06/02	AMHUY	0005	*A. Zieloo* | Een Gezicht van het Y naar het Bothuisje te zien, met verscheide Schepen en Vaartuigen		(Unknown)
1807/08/26	AMSCH	0205	*A. Silo* | Twee stuks, een stil en een woelend Water, beide ryk gestoffeerd met zeilende Oorlogschepen, Boeijers, diversche Vaartuigen en Vissers Schuiten; natuurlyk en uitvoerig gepenceeld | *Mat:* op doek *Size:* ieder hoog 17, breed 23 duim	Roos [for] A	(Sold) fl 7:5 du Pree
1808/04/26	GDAN	0160	*Silou (A)* | Een Zeetje met zeilende Schepen | *Size:* hoog 13, breed 17 duim	G H Fortuyn	(Unknown)
1808/06/13	AMSCH	0153	*Silo (A.)* | In een kabbelende Zee vertoont zich een hevig Gevecht tusschen verscheidene Oorlogschepen, die op elkanderen vuuren, eenigen derzelven zijn in brand geschoten, anderen schijnen te zinken, verder Sloepen met Zeevolk. Alles is natuurlijk en meesterlijk gepenceeld | *Mat:* op doek *Size:* hoog 46, breed 64 duim	Z	(Sold) fl 22 Van der Schley R [for] Rijfsnyder
1808/08/23	AMSCH	0156	*Silo. (A.)* | Twee stuks kabbelende Zeeën, met zeilende Oorlog en andere Scheepen en Vaartuigen; fiks geschilderd | *Mat:* op doek *Size:* hoog 17, breed 24 duim	Y	(Sold) fl 8 Rijfsnyder [or] Spaan
1808/08/23	AMSCH	0157	*Silo. (A.)* | Twee dito [stuks] Zee-gezichten, in alles als de voorgaande behandeld | *Size:* hoog 17, breed 24 duim	Y	(Sold) fl 12 Dupré
1808/10/28	AMVRS	0059	*Silo, (A.)* | Twee stuks stille Waters, beide rijk gestoffeerd met zeilende, drijvende en ten anker liggende Schepen en andere Vaartuigen. Helder behandeld | *Mat:* op doek *Size:* ieder hoog 24, breed 28 duim	Marten Udink	(Sold) fl 22 M Kooij
1808/10/28	AMVRS	0060	*Silo, (A.)* | Twee stuks woelende Zeeën, beide met onderscheidene Vaartuigen gestoffeerd, en als de voorgaande behandeld | *Size:* ieder hoog 24, breed 28 duim	Marten Udink	(Sold) fl 22 B Kooij

1808/11/28	AMSCH	0058	*A. Silo* | Twee stuks bevallige Voorwerpen, verbeeldende beide Gezichten in het IJ voor Amsterdam, rijk gestoffeerd met zeilende en stilleggende Oorlogschepen, Jachten, Boeijers, Beurtschepen en Sloepen, helder, zonachtig en van de beste Schildering | *Mat:* op doek *Size:* ieder hoog 31, breed 44 duim	S	(Sold) fl 13 T Spaan
1808/12/31	RMHSN	0002	*A. Silo* | Twee stuks de Groenlandse Visschery en Haringvangst | *Mat:* op doek	G Spanjaart [or] H de Haas [or] C van der Looy Lans	(Unknown)
1809/04/17	AMSCH	0094	*A. Silo* | Twee stuks Gezichten in het Y voor Amsterdam, rijk gestoffeerd met zijlende en ten Anker leggende Oorlogscheepen, Jagten, Boeijers, Beurtscheepen en Sloepen; zonachtig en van de beste schildering | *Mat:* op doek *Size:* hoog 31, breed 44 duim	S	(Sold) fl 12
1809/04/22	AMYVR	0115	*A. Silo* | Twee stuks woelende Waters, met verscheiden Oorlog- en andere Scheepen; zijnde van de beste van A. Silo | *Mat:* op doek *Size:* hoog 17, breed 24 duim	de Bruin	(Sold) fl 28 Remmers Bredius
1809/04/22	AMYVR	0116	*A. Silo* | Twee stuks niet minder fraaije dito [woelende Waters] | *Mat:* op doek *Size:* hoog 13, breed 19 duim	de Bruin	(Bought In) fl 18
1809/06/13	AMSCH	0150	*A. Silo* | Een kabbelende Zee, met zeilende en ten Anker liggende Oorlogscheepen, Jagten, Boeijers en andere Vaartuigen; helder en bevallig | *Mat:* op doek *Size:* hoog 30, breed 44 duim	R[ijfsnijder]	(Sold) fl 6:5 du Pree
1810/08/06	AMSCH	0091	*Silo (A.)* | Twee stuks Gezigten in het IJ voor Amsterdam, beide rijk gestoffeerd met zijlende Beurtschepen, Jagten, Sloepen en andere Vaartuigen; bevallig en helder van schildering | *Size:* ieder hoog 31, breed 44 duimen	S[paan]	(Sold) fl 13 Texier Gerbet en Comp [for] Lebrun
			Silo, Adam (manner)		
1803/09/07	AMSCH	0173	*A. Silo* | Een Woelend Water, met zylende Scheepen en Vaartuigen; vrolyk van kleur als A. Silo [Une mer agitée, avec des navires et des batimens voguant à pleines voiles ; d'un coloris agréable et piquant] | *Mat:* op paneel *Size:* hoog 11, breed 16 duim *Notes:* This lot was not numbered in the French edition of the catalogue.	Smidt	(Sold) fl 3:10 de Lafontaine
			Simons, Michiel		
1802/12/13	AMSCH	0152	*Simons* | In een Landschap ziet men eenige Jagers, verzeld van hunnen Honden, op de voorgrond een meenigte van dood Wild; kloek geschilderd | *Mat:* op doek *Size:* hoog 34, breed 44 duim	Pruyssenaar [for] A	(Sold) fl 1:10 Gruiter
1804/08/08	AMSCH	0182	*J.M. Simons* | In een Boomryk Landschap zit een Jager op zyn Hoorn te blazen, verzeld van een ménigte Honden en Dood Wild; meesterlyk op Doek | *Mat:* op doek *Size:* hoog 57, breed 79 duim	Roos a	(Sold) fl 5:5 Graffelman
1806/05/05	AMSCH	0136	*M. Simons* | Een bergagtig Landschap met Jagers te Paard, verzeld van een ménigten van Honden, dood Wild en ander bywerk; meesterlyk geschildert door M. Simons | *Mat:* op doek *Size:* hoog 39, breed 44 duim	V[inkeles]	(Sold) fl 1:15 Boelen
			Sin, P. le [Unidentified]		
1806/08/20	HGBSM	0116	*P. le Sin* | Een Vrouweportrait in het zwart, met een kraag, door P. le Sin 1637 | *Mat:* op paneel *Inscr:* P. le Sin 1637 (signed and dated?) *Notes:* It is unclear whether the name and date are inscribed on the painting.	Macalester Loup [or others]	(Sold) fl 0:18 Spruyt
			Sing, Johann Kaspar		
1804/10/29	HRBAU	0092	*Sing (Casper)* | Dit Stuk vertoont ons David, levensgrootte, in een gracelyke houding, leunende mat zyn' linkerarm op het hoofd van Goliath, houdende zyn Herdersstaf in zyne regterhand, daar het zwaard van den Overwonnenen aan zyn voeten ligt; in een bergagtig Landschap. Dit Schildery is stout, meesterlyk en in een' zeer grootschen trant geschilderd | *Mat:* op doek *Size:* hoog 71, breed 42 duim	Simon Styl	(Unknown)
1804/10/29	HRBAU	0093	*Sing (Casper)* | De manmoedige Judith, staande met het Hoofd van den Veldöversten Holofernus in heure hand, 't welk zy in een' zak, die door heure Dienstmaagd gehouden wordt, laat glyden, terwyl zy in de andere hand het bebloede zwaard houdt; staande naast haar zyn Helm en Cuiras op den grond. In alles niet minder grootsch dan het voorige behandeld | *Mat:* op doek *Size:* hoog 71, breed 42 duim	Simon Styl	(Unknown)
			Singleton, Henry		
1803/10/25	HHNOM	0008	*H. Singleton* | The Child Restored [Prenten en Schilderijen, in extra schoone vergulde Lysten en Glazen] | *Notes:* The bracketed information in the title appears above lot 1 and refers to lots 1 to 24. It is uncertain whether this lot is a painting.	Mr Stephanies Roosendaal	(Unknown)
1803/10/25	HHNOM	0009	*H. Singleton* | Gepsey's [sic] Stealing a Child [Prenten en Schilderijen, in extra schoone vergulde Lysten en Glazen] | *Notes:* The bracketed information in the title appears above lot 1 and refers to lots 1 to 24. It is uncertain whether this lot is a painting.	Mr Stephanies Roosendaal	(Unknown)
			Six, Nicolaas		
1806/05/05	AMSCH	0165	*N. Six* | Een Man met een Pyp in zyn hand; meesterlyk door N. Six	R[oos]	(Sold) fl 0:12 Scheurleer

Slabbaert, Karel

1806/08/20	HGBSM	0082	*Karel Slabbaert* | Een Burger Binnehuis, waar men bezig is de slagt gereed te maaken, voor den schoorsteen is een Man met een Bierkan in de hand, en eene Vrouw bezig om eene Ketel over het vuur te hangen, nevens de Vrouw zit een Kind in den stoel, aan de andere zijde is een Kind in de wieg, benevens een kleine Jongen die met eene blaas speeld. Voor aan den ingang hangt een Varken aan de ladder, in het verschiet een openstaande deur, waar voor eenige Bedelaars eene aalmoes vragen; dit stuk is schoon, helder van couleur en konstig geschilderd door Karel Slabbaert | *Mat:* op paneel *Size:* hoog 22, breed 19 duim	Macalester Loup [or others]	(Sold) fl 60 Schouman

Sliehe, J.H. [Unidentified]

1802/09/06	AMSCH	0213	*J. H. Sliehe* | Een Kunstzaal met Schilderyen, Beelden enz; natuurlyk | *Mat:* op doek	Mevrouw Achtienhoven	(Sold) fl 4:10 Vermeulen

Slingeland, Pieter Cornelisz. van

1801/03/16	AMSCH	0022	*P. van Slingeland* | Een Man in een zeer devote gestalte op zyn kniën leggende voor een Kruisbeeld, uitvoerig	K[ip]	(Sold) fl 31 C S Roos
1801/04/13	AMSCH	0068	*P. van Slingeland* | Een bevallig Meisje met een Muzykboek in de hand, aller uitvoerigst gepenceeld | *Mat:* op koper *Fmt:* ovaal *Size:* hoog 4 ½, breed 4 duim	Pierre Fouquet, junior	(Sold) fl 20 Rijnders
1801/05/11	AMSCH	0079	*P. Slingeland* | Een Binnenhuis, zeer uitvoerig met verscheiden huisraad gestoffeerd, ter zyde ziet men een Jongeling by een Meisje, in 't verschiet een pomp, 't koperwerk, nevens 't andere bywerk, is van eene fraaije schildering | *Mat:* op paneel *Size:* hoog 12, breed 14 duim	P[ruyssenaar]	(Sold) fl 47:10 Coclers
1801/05/11	AMSCH	0080	*P. Slingeland* | Een goede Gelukzegster, men ziet dezelve by een Jong Meisje, welke een stuk geld in de hand heeft, kragtig en meesterlyk behandeld | *Mat:* op paneel *Size:* hoog 14, breed 12 duim	P[ruyssenaar]	(Sold) fl 9 van Iperen
1801/05/11	AMSCH	0081	*P. Slingeland* | Twee stuks, zynde een Hond, en een Kat, zeer uitvoerig gepenceeld | *Mat:* op paneel *Size:* hoog 5, breed 7 duim	P[ruyssenaar]	(Sold) fl 0:14 Gruiter
1801/06/13	LNDLS	0009	*P. van Slingelant* | Een bevallig Juffertje halverlijf, gekleed naar vroeger tijd, met een paarlsnoer om haar hals, extra eel en uitvoerig, op paneel geschilderd, ovaal formaat | *Mat:* op paneel *Fmt:* ovaal *Size:* hoog 3 ¾, breed 3 duimen	D van R	(Sold) fl 24 Spruyt
1802/04/13	HAVIN	0051	*Slingeland* | Een Jongen bezig zynde met een Vogelknip		(Unknown)
1802/11/01	DOBRA	0176	*Pieter van Slingeland* | Een vrouwtje eenen koperen ketel schuurende; by haar staan een Ton en Bezem. Op de steenen vloer ligt een roode aarden Kan | *Mat:* op paneel		(Unknown) fl 7:5
1803/12/12	AMSCH	0085	*P. van Slingeland* | Over een Steene Nis ziet men een bevallige Visvrouw, leunende met haar arm op een Emmer, in haar hand houd zy een Mes, voor haar een Mand met gesneden Schellevis, agter haar op een met Boomen beplante Gragt is een Visboer bézig, geld te rug te geven, aan een Man en Vrouw, die van hem schyne gekogt te hebben, uitvoerig en bevallig van licht | *Mat:* op paneel *Size:* hoog 9 ½, breed 8 duim	B	(Sold) fl 9 Hodges
1804/10/16	DLOND	0205	*P. van Slingeland* | Twee stukjens. Hond en Kat. Deux pièces. Chien & Chat | *Mat:* op paneel *Size:* hoog 5, breed 6		(Unknown)
1808/06/06	RMRIJ	0115	*Slingelandt. (Pieter van)* | In een Oud Hollandsch binnenvertrek zit eene Vrouw; bezijden haar een Spinnewiel, en voor haar eene Wieg; aan de linkerzijde ligt een Bierton, Marktemmer en verder bijwerk: in den achtergrond ziet men eene Bedstede en verder Huisraad. Alles is ongemeen uitvoerig, aangenaam en bevallig van teekening, kleur en effect [Dans l'Intérieur d'un ancien Ménage Hollandais, une femme assise et tenant une Ecuelle sur ses genoux, paroit souffler sur une Cuillerée, qu'elle porte à sa bouche. On voit à l'entour d'elle un Rouet à filer, un Berceau et plusieurs autres Ustensiles de Ménage, et dans le fond on découvre un lit etc. Ce Tableau, dont la Perspective est bien entendue et le Coloris agrèable, est d'un fini recherché jusques dans les plus petits détails] | *Annots:* gek. van Thijs, 15 Sept. 1800 (f.350.-) (RMA I) *Mat:* op paneel *Size:* Hoog 19 ¼, en breed 14 ¾ duim	Gerrit van der Pot, Heer van Groeneveld	(Sold) fl 365 Vervier de Gand
1809/07/19	AMSCH	0049	*Slingeland (P. van)* | Twee stuks stil-levens, zijnde Voorwerpen, zinspeelende op het vergankelijke van 's Menschen leven, het eene vertoont eene Tafel, waarop geplaast is een Globe, Doodshoofd, Zandlooper, Speeltuig en een Brandende Lamp; het andere eene Tafel, waarop staat een fraai Kabinetje, met Klijnodien, ter zijde een cierlijke Drinkbeker, Kandelaar, Kaars en verder bijwerk. Alles natuurlijk en aller-uitvoerigst gepenceeld | *Mat:* op paneel *Size:* ieder hoog 12, breed 11 duim	[Bicker]	(Sold) fl 23:10 Gruyter
1809/09/06	AMSCH	0064	*Slingeland (P. van)* | Eene bevallig oud Vrouwtje als in een Nis te zien; alleruitvoerigst behandeld | *Mat:* op paneel *Size:* ieder hoog 6, breed 5 duim	Johannes Caudri	(Sold) fl 10 Tomassen
1810/03/23	HAVIN	0010	*P. v. Slingeland* | Een bevallig Meisje, zittende te speldewerken, extra uitvoerig en fraai, door P. v. Slingeland, hoog 9 d. zijnde ovaal | *Fmt:* ovaal *Size:* hoog 9 d.	Rudolf Hendrik de Wetstein [or others]	(Unknown)
1810/03/26	RMMUY	0034	*Pieter van Slingelandt* | Eene bedaagde deftig gekleede zittende Vrouw, bezig met speldewerken. Bij haar eene tafel, waarop een pot met bloemen	Daniel de Jongh Az	(Sold) fl 105 Le Brun Parys

			en verder bijwerk. Zeer krachtig, natuurlijk en uitvoerig geschilderd [Une Dame assise, faisant de la dentelle ; près d'elle, une table couverte d'un tapis, sur laquelle est posé un vase avec des fleurs. Dans le fond, contre la muraille, est une carte géographique, et sur le devant quelques accessoires, d'une grande imitation de nature et très fini.] | *Mat:* op paneel *Size:* hoog 9 ½, breed 7 ¾ duimen		
1810/10/10	MGCIT	0092	*Slingelandt* | Een Vrouwtje, zittende by een Toonbank, waarop veelerhande Groentens te koop leggen; al het welk nevens het daarop zynde Aarde en Mandwerk zeer bevallig is behandeld	Caspar van Citters	(Unknown)

Slingeland, Pieter Cornelisz. van (or Slingeland, P.C., manner)

1804/10/16	DLOND	0303	*Van of in de Manier van P. v. Slingeland* | Ene Dame in een Bloemperk, in gesprek met een Heer. Une Dame dans un Jardin de Fleurs en discours avec un Monsieur | *Mat:* op paneel *Size:* hoog 14, breed 11		(Unknown) fl 20
1810/05/22	AMSCH	0093	*Slingelandt of in de manier* | In een Keukenvertrek staat een bevallig Meisje bij een Tafel, bezig een Tinnen Schotel te schuuren, daar nevens een Jongeling met een Rommelpot, op den voorgrond eenig Huisraad, als koperen Ketels, Tobben met Koperwerk, Blaasbalk enz, benevens een zittend Katje; uitvoerig en fraai gepenceeld | *Mat:* op paneel *Size:* hoog 11 ½, breed 10 ½ duim	Johannes van de Putte Nicolaasz.	(Sold) fl 56 Gruyter [for] Dirkse

Slingeland, Pieter Cornelisz. van (manner)

1810/10/11	AMSCH	0080	*Slingeland* | Eene jonge Dame, bezig Kant te werken; op Paneel, in de manier van Slingeland | *Mat:* op paneel *Size:* hoog 12, breed 8 ½ duimen	C	(Sold) fl 1 Posthumus

Sluis, Jacob van der

1802/08/24	LNDLS	0032	*J. van der Sluys* | Een Vrolijke Gast of Bootsgezel, houdende een Wijnroemer in zijn regter hand, en zijn Muts in de opgeheven linker hand, verder eenige dansende persoonen, zoo goed als van A. de Vois | *Mat:* op paneel *Size:* hoog 11, breed 8 duimen	Leonardus Bouman [or others]	(Unknown) fl 14
1805/07/10	AMSCH	0136	*J. van der Sluys* | Voor een Boerewoningen zit een vrolyke Boer, houdende in de eene hand een roemer wyn en in de andere een kan, verders op een Tafel een Haring, Comvoir en Bierkan; delicaat gepenceeld | *Mat:* op paneel *Size:* hoog 10, breed 9 duim	V[inkeles] [for] M	(Sold) fl 16 Spaan
1808/11/12	HGSCR	0008	*Jacobus van der Sluys* | Een vrolyk man zittende en houdende een romer met wyn in zyn hand, uitvoerig behandeld	Mr J van Buren	(Unknown) fl 3
1810/10/10	MGCIT	0112	*van der Sluys* | Een opgeslagen Tent, waarin en voor, verschei- [sic] Personen zig bevinden, vol gewoel | *Notes:* In the title probably a part of the word "verschei-" is missing. It must be the word "verscheidene."	Caspar van Citters	(Unknown)

Sluys, G. van der [Unidentified]

1804/10/16	DLOND	0206	*G. van der Sluys* | Een Heer en twee Dames in ene Tuin. 3 Familie-Portraitten. Un Monsieur avec deux Dames dans un Jardin. 3 Portraits de Famille | *Mat:* op doek *Size:* hoog 20, breed 25		(Unknown)
1807/04/00	LNDLS	0052	*G. v. d. Sluys* | Twee stuks Bacchus en Ceres, uitvoerig door G. v. d. Sluys	[Abraham Delfos] [or others]	(Unknown)
1807/06/10	HGBSM	0052	*G. v.d. Sluys* | Twee stuks Bacchus en Ceres, uitvoerig	Abraham Delfos [or others]	(Sold) fl 1:10 Noordwyk

Smak Gregoor, Gillis

1810/07/23	DOLGI	0046	*Gilles Smak Gregoor* | In een Hollandsch Landschap ziet men een roodbonten Stier, waar agter een Koe. Ter zijde is een willige Stronk, en andere Bomen. Krachtig en meesterlijk behandeld | *Mat:* op paneel *Size:* hoog 15 ½, breed 14 ½ duim	Mr Pieter van den Santheuvel	(Sold) fl 25 P de Heere à Dordt

Smeesters

1809/04/17	AMSCH	0091	*Smeijsters* | Bij een helder schijnende Maan, ziet men langs een stille Rivier op een Dorp, met verscheide Boeren Wooningen, gestoffeerd met zijlende Scheepen en Visschers Vaartuigen; fraai van Licht en uitvoerig geschilderd | *Mat:* op paneel *Size:* hoog 9 ½, breed 13 ½ duim	Z	(Sold or Bought In) fl 21 Spaan
1810/06/20	AMSCH	0083	*Smeijters* | Een Maneschijn over een stille Rivier, gestoffeerd met Visschers en Vaartuigen | *Mat:* op paneel *Size:* hoog 10, breed 12 duimen	A	(Sold) fl 15 T Spaan

Smets, Jacob

1802/11/01	DOBRA	0184	*Jacob Smets* | Een Heer die een Juffer oesters aanbied | *Mat:* op paneel *Size:* hoog 13, breed 9 ½ duim		(Unknown) fl 2

Smit, Aernout

1802/07/27	AKHRK	0020	*A. Smit* | Een woelend Tijgezicht met Buiten- en Binnenlandsche Vaartuigen, het Water zeer dun, en alles zeer kundig en natuurlijk geschilderd | *Mat:* op doek *Size:* hoog 24, breed 33 duim	Maria Stategaart	(Sold) fl 17:10 Gruyter
1803/06/20	AMSCH	0010	*L. Smith* | Een onstuimige Zee, met verscheide zeilende vaartuigen, in het verschiet hoog gebergte en kasteelen, het water is dun, en het licht zeer spreekend, door L. Smith, op Doek | *Mat:* op doek *Size:* hoog 30, breed 42 duim *Notes:* The artist's name was given as "L. Smith" but we have assumed this is an error.	Schley [for] B	(Sold) fl 52 Hodges

1804/05/07	AMSCH	0155	*Smit. (A.)* | Twee stuks, het eene verbeeld een stil Water met een zeilend Oorlogschip en andere Vaartuigen, op de voorgrond Visschers in hunnen Pinken, en een Heer en Dame op Strand; het andere een bevroozen Rivier lang een Dyk, waarop Wooningen en een Molen, de Rivier is gestoffeerd met Schaatzeryders en andere Figuuren; natuurlyk en plaisant behandeld | *Mat:* op paneel *Size:* yder hoog 10, breed 14 duim	Y[ver] [for] JJ	(Sold) fl 12 Coclers
1804/10/29	HRBAU	0095	*Smit, (A.)* | Op den Voorgrond van deze kabbelende Zee, welke strand is, zit een Kaag, die men bezig is te lossen; wat verder ziet men een Oorlogschip en Ligter by den wind zeilen, een Driemast in de wending, en meer andere Vaartuigen; en in het verschiet een Landgezigt. Helder, plaisant, uitvoerig, en het rollen der golven tegens het strand zeer natuurlyk verbeeld | *Mat:* op doek *Size:* hoog 30, breed 41 duim	Simon Styl	(Unknown)
1804/10/29	HRBAU	0096	*Smit. (A.)* | Een zeer bevallig Ygezigt; voor aan , by Paalwerk, is een Kaag en Visscher bezig om binnen te werken, waar by een Driemast de Laag komt uitzeilen; op de Rheê ligt een Driemastschip zeilree, terwyl een Sloep met Volk naar de Stad geroeid wordt, welk hy door het Canon den afscheidgroet schynt te geeven, wyders nog twee Driemasten en andere Vaartuigen, die agter de Laag omzeilen: daar zig in het verschiet de Zandhoek en eenige Dorpen over het Y opdoen. Dit capitaal Schildery is zeer uitvoerig, en verdient als een der beste werken van dezen Schilder aangemerkt te worden | *Mat:* op doek *Size:* hoog 41, breed 44 duim	Simon Styl	(Unknown)
1804/10/29	HRBAU	0097	*Smit, (A.)* | Een Storm op Zee; voor aan ziet men een Driemast alle pogingen doen, om niet op den laager wal, die klipagtig is, waar tegen eene zwaare Branding staat, en waar een Wrak in ligt, te vervallen; wyders nog eenige Vaartuigen, en een rotsagtig verschiet. De lucht is buijig, het water doorschynend, en alles in de manier van Bakhuisen behandeld | *Mat:* op doek *Size:* hoog 17, breed 19 duim	Simon Styl	(Unknown)
1804/10/29	HRBAU	0098	*Smit, (A.)* | Dit fraaije Schilderytjen vertoont een' aangenaamen Avondstond, by stil weder, in een rotsagtige Baai; gestoffeerd met verscheidene soorten van Vaartuigen en Beeldjens. Niet minder bevallig dan het voorige behandeld | *Mat:* op doek *Size:* hoog 17, breed 19 duim	Simon Styl	(Unknown)
1804/10/29	HRBAU	0099	*Smit, (A.)* | Een woelend Water; voor aan, in het zonlicht, zeilt een Jagt voor den wind, waar by een Sloep met Volk; iets verder een vloot Driemasten, die hun koers langs de Kust zetten, die in 't verschiet gezien wordt. Helder en fiks behandeld | *Mat:* op doek *Size:* hoog 25, breed 31 duim	Simon Styl	(Unknown)
1805/07/10	AMSCH	0141	*A. Smith* | In een stormächtige Zee, ziet men by 't Strand een tegen de Klippen geworpen Schip, verders zylende Oorlogschepen, enz.; vol expressie en meesterlyk | *Size:* hoog 27, breed 38 duim	V[inkeles] [for] M	(Bought In) fl 6
1805/12/16	AMSCH	0051	*A. Smit* | In een sterk woelend Water, ziet men een zylend Beurtschip, verder andere Scheepen, en diversche Vaartuigen; het Water is natuurlyk behandeld, en aller meesterlyk fiks gepenceeld op Doek | *Mat:* op doek *Size:* hoog 36, breed 45 duim	R[oos]	(Bought In) fl 50
1805/12/16	AMSCH	0052	*A. Smit* | Een Zeegezicht aan Strand, gestoffeerd met eenige Vissers; op de Voorgrond, een Schip schynt in gevaar in de branding by een Klip, verder een ruime Zee, met zylende Scheepen | *Mat:* op doek *Size:* hoog 29, breed 37 duim	Spaan	(Sold) fl 6 v der Schley [for] R[ijfsnijder]
1806/08/13	AMSCH	0176	*Smit. (A. D.)* | Een Gezichtje aan Strand, met een ménigte Lieden, zoo Mans- als Vrouwen, in Zee eenige zeilende en stilleggende Scheepen en Schuiten; 't water is dun en uitvoerig van schildering | *Mat:* op doek *Size:* hoog 13, breed 12 duim	Vinkeles [for] F	(Sold) fl 41 Gruiter
1808/08/23	AMSCH	0153	*Smit. (A. D.)* | Een kabbelende Zee met verscheiden Scheepen, op de voorgrond bij het Strand, twee Visschers Pinken, en in 't verschiet hoog Gebergten; het Water is dun en fraai van schildering | *Mat:* op doek *Size:* hoog 17, breed 19 duim	[Coclers]	(Sold) fl 20:10 Th Spaan
1809/06/13	AMSCH	0147	*A. Smit* | In een stormende Zee ziet men drie Scheepen, waarvan eene tegen de Rotsen verbrijseld word; meesterlijk geschilderd | *Mat:* op doek *Size:* hoog 31, breed 40 duim	Y	(Sold) fl 5:15 du Pree
1809/06/13	AMSCH	0148	*A. Smit* | Een woelende Zee met een zijlend Kaagschip en andere Vaartuigen; meesterlijk | *Mat:* op doek *Size:* hoog 13, breed 20 duim	Q	(Bought In) fl 6
1809/06/13	AMSCH	0149	*A. Smit* | Een kabbelend Water, in de manier van Bakhuysen, door A. Smit | *Mat:* op doek *Size:* hoog 13, breed 18 duim	Y	(Sold) fl 1 L Pakker
1810/06/20	AMSCH	0159[a]	*Smit* | Twee stuks, een Strandgezigt, door Smit, en een Vrouwtje bij het Kaarslicht | *This Lot:* Een Strandgezigt; lot 159[b] by Anonymous	B	(Sold) fl 0:14 for lots 159[a] & 159[b]. L Pakker

Smit, Jan Borritsz.

1801/08/19	AMSCH	0115	*J. Smit* | Een woelende Zee met een Oorlogschip en andere Vaartuigen; dun op Doek | *Mat:* op doek *Size:* hoog 16, breed 19 duim	W Wynen	(Sold) fl 61 Gruiter
1804/10/29	HRBAU	0094	*Smit, (J. B.)* | Op den Voorgrond, by een Klip en sterke Branding, zyn verscheiden Matroozen bezig hunne Kameraaden te redden, welke van het Wrak schynen afgeslaagen te zyn; en meer andere Vaartuigen in het verschiet. Uitvoerig behandeld | *Mat:* op paneel *Size:* hoog 13 ½, breed 26 duim	Simon Styl	(Unknown)

Snayers, Peeter

1803/09/07	AMSCH	0172	*P. Snaijers* | Twee stuks Brabandsche Landschappen, alwaar in de eene een Plundering, en in de anderen daar de Boeren de Soldaten attakeeren; alles fix en natuurlyk [Deux paysages flamands ; l'un représente un pillage et l'autres des villageois attaquant des soldats : peint au naturel, bonne composition] | *Mat:* op paneel *Size:* yder hoog 15, breed 20 duim	Smidt	(Bought In) fl 25

Snellinck

1803/08/24	HGKAN	0074	*Snelling* | Een Lantschap	[Teissier] [or others]	(Unknown) fl 0:8
1804/10/16	DLOND	0207	*Snellings* | Een Landschap en Jager. Paysage & un Chasseur | *Mat:* op paneel *Size:* hoog 16, breed 23		(Sold) fl 3:12 Thijs

Snellinck, Cornelis

1810/07/26	AMSCH	0079	*Snellinks (C)* | Een boschachtig Landschap met Woningen, gestoffeerd met Huislieden. Zonachtig en natuurlijk behandeld | *Mat:* op paneel *Size:* hoog 15, breed 19 duimen	Cassino	(Sold) fl 4:10 Spaan

Snellinck, Jan (III)

1802/09/21	UTHDG	0082	*J. Snellingh* | Een Landschap gestoffeerd met de ontmoeting van Jacob en Rebecca, nevens veel ander bijwerk. Kragtig | *Mat:* op paneel *Size:* hoog 24, breed 19 ½ duimen		(Sold) fl 7:10 Verhoude

Snyders, Frans

1802/05/05	AMSCH	0198	*F. Snyders* | Op een Tafel een doden Haas, Phaisant, en een menigte Groentens en Fruiten, waarby een Aap, meesterlyk | *Mat:* op doek *Size:* hoog 32, breed 46 duim	A	(Sold) fl 37 Cocler
1802/06/29	HGDAW	0024	*Snyders* | Een Fruitstuk door Snyders		(Unknown)
1803/06/20	AMSCH	0036	*F. Snyders* | Een Vos een Kuiken onder zyne Klaauwen hebbende word door twee Katten aangegrimt welken hem dien buit misgunnen; meesterlyk op Paneel | *Mat:* op paneel *Size:* hoog 20, breed 25 duim	Schley [for] G	(Sold) fl 7:5 Gruiter
1804/02/27	AMSCH	0102	*Snyders. (F.)* | Een Tafel, waarop een Mand met Vrugten en eenig Wild geplaatst is; meesterlyk van penceel behandeling | *Size:* hoog 29, breed 39 duim	R[oos]	(Sold) fl 5 Higgens
1804/07/25	AMSCH	0071	*Snyders. (F)* | In een Capitaal Landschap, vertoont zig een Wild Zwyn, door een meenigte Honden overmeestert, die het woedende aanvallen; eenige derzelve leggen op de Grond zwaar Gekwest, Andere beyveren zig 'er by te koomen; het is van coloriet en breede penceelbehandeling, één der capitaalste van deeze meester | *Mat:* op doek *Size:* hoog 80, breed 134 duim		(Sold) fl 225 Izaac Smit
1804/08/02	BDAN	0041	*Sneyders* | Een hangend Hart, Ryger en ander bywerk | *Mat:* op doek *Size:* b. 42 en een half d. h. 66 d.	J G Calckberner	(Unknown)
1804/10/16	DLOND	0055a	*F. Sneyders* | [Untitled] | *Notes:* The lot was changed from "A. Cuyp, Een Landschap met Schapen," to "F. Sneyders," without giving a title, at the front of the catalogue.		(Unknown)
1806/08/13	AMSCH	0164	*Snyders. (F.)* | In een Boomryk Landschap ziet men een Wolf, welke een Schaap onder zyn Pooten heeft, grynzende tegens een andere Wolf, welke hen dien prooi schynt te misgunnen, in 't verschiet een Herder met Schapen; allerfraaist en meesterlyk geschilderd | *Mat:* op doek *Size:* hoog 46, breed 73 duim	Roos	(Bought In) fl 20
1806/08/13	AMSCH	0165	*Snyders. (F.)* | Een groote Hond, voor zich hebbende een Karrewy dien hy aan twee andere op hem afkomende Honden, schynt te willen afbyten; mede behandeld als de vorige | *Mat:* op doek *Size:* hoog 45, breed 71 duim	Roos	(Sold) fl 40 Roos [or] de Vos
1806/08/13	AMSCH	0166	*Snyders. (F.)* | Een Landschap, op de voorgrond twee vegtende Hanen, waarby eenige Hennen en Kiekens; als de voorgaande | *Mat:* op doek *Size:* hoog 46, breed 71 duim	Roos	(Sold) fl 2 de Vries
1808/04/26	GDAN	0152	*Snyders (F.)* | Een fraaije Krans van Bladeren en Vruchten, waar in zich eenig Gevogelte, Vliegen, Eenkhoorn [sic], &c ophouden, in 't midden een allerschoonst Beeld van Rubbens, alleruitmuntents geschilderd | *Size:* hoog 72, breed 54 duim	G H Fortuyn	(Unknown)
1808/04/26	GDAN	0153	*Snyders (F.)* | Zijnde een Heer met zyn Jager, die aan zijn Heer een aantal geschoten Wild doet zien | *Size:* hoog 68, breed 96 duim	G H Fortuyn	(Unknown)
1808/04/26	GDAN	0154	*Snyders (F.)* | Verbeeldende een bergägtig Woutgezigt, waar in zich Leeuwen, Tijgers, &c. zich spelend onder elkander vermaken, dit stuk is allerbyzonderst fraai, of men dezelve levendig zag, en of die van Weenix geschildert waren | *Size:* hoog 62, breed 84 duim	G H Fortuyn	(Unknown)
1808/06/06	RMRIJ	0116	*Snijders. (Frans)* | Eene hangende Ree, benevens een Wilde Zwijnskop, Kreeft, Groenten, Vruchten en Bloemen, enz. op eene tafel liggende, en verder bijwerk. Alles natuurlijk, schoon en meesterlijk geschilderd [Une table chargée de gros Gibier. Un Homar, des fruits, des légumes et plusieurs accessoires interessants forment un bel Ensemble. Ce Tableau peint en maitre, dans un grand Style, fait honneur à l'Artiste] | *Mat:* op doek *Size:* Hoog 45, en breed 66 duim *Loc:* Amsterdam, Nederland. Rijksmuseum. (A379)	Gerrit van der Pot, Heer van Groeneveld	(Sold) fl 455 van Lennep [for] le Roi

1809/04/17	AMSCH	0092	*F. Snijders* | Een Vos, houdende een Kuiken in zijn Klauwen, waarbij twee Katten; meesterlijk geschilderd | *Mat:* op paneel *Size:* hoog 20, breed 25 duim	Z	(Sold) fl 1:15 Gruyter
1810/03/07	UTWLD	0042	*Snyders* | Een Leeuwen en Tygers gevegt, breed en fraay behandeld | *Size:* hoog 6 voet 6 duim, breed 10 voet	J J Woertman	(Unknown) fl 21:15
1810/08/06	AMSCH	0092	*Snijders (F.)* | Eenen Wolf, een Schaap onder zijne poten hebbende, wordt van eenen anderen Wolf de prooi misgund; fiks geschilderd | *Mat:* op doek *Size:* hoog 46, breed 73 duimen	R[oos]	(Bought In) fl 7

Snyders, Frans (and Balen, J. and Vinckeboons, D.)

1803/07/18	AMSCH	0004	*Balen, (J. van); F. Snyders; D. Vinkebooms* | Twee Nimphen van de Jagt komende met een menigte Wild, 't geen op de grond legt, schynende met elkander daarover te spreeken, een derde ter zyde hun in de schaduwe, voor dezelven verscheide Jagthonden; het Bosch door Vinkebooms, het Wild door Snyders, en de Beelden door van Balen, maaken een schoon geheel uit, en doen de talenten van deeze drie Meesters alle eer aan [Deux Nimphes, au retour d'une chasse abondante, s'entretiennent vèrs la droite, ayant cinq beaux chiens bracs auprès d'elles ; une troisieme Nimphe s'achemine vèrs la foret. A la gauche sont les animaux morts, couchés sur une légère élévation, c'est un sanglier, un loup, un liévre avec d'autres quadrupédes & de la volaille. Cette réunion de talens des trois artistes s'accorde parfaitement bien. Les figures sont belles & de couleur riche ; les animaux traités avec légereté & delicatesse, & le Paysage repond bien au sujet.] | *Mat:* op paneel *Size:* hoog 24, breed 33 duim	Maria Theresia Andrioli	(Sold) fl 52 Hulswit

Snyders, Frans (and Hals, F. (I))

1801/04/13	AMSCH	0072	*F. Snyders; F. Hals* | Een Fruit- en Vogelverkoopster, voor haar hangt een hart en ander gedierten, nevens haar een meid met druiven, verder musicant en andere zingende gasten; meesterlyk gepenceeld | *Mat:* op doek *Size:* hoog 59, breed 80 duim	Pierre Fouquet, junior	(Sold) fl 30 Spruit van Gend

Snyders, Frans (and Jordaens, J. (I))

1802/05/05	AMSCH	0199	*F. Snyders; Jordaans* | Een Tafel met diverse soorten van Vrugten en Groentens, agter dezelven een bevallige Vrouw, die door een Jongeling geliefkoosd word, meesterlyk geschilderd | *Size:* hoog 68, breed 77 duim	J	(Sold) fl 20 v d Vinne

Snyders, Frans (and Rubens)

1804/07/25	AMSCH	0063	*Rubbens. (P. P.); F. Snyders* | Een Wild Zwyn, meer dan leevensgrooten, door verschyde Honden aangevallen, drie Jagers gaan het met Spiesen te keer, een derzelve blaast op de Jachthoorn, alles is vol drift, en op de Voorgrond leggen diversche gekwetste Honden; het is ongemeen kragtig van coloriet en van een breede penceel behandeling, door byde deeze beroemden meesters | *Mat:* op doek *Size:* hoog 68, breed 111 duim		(Sold) fl 65 Van der Schley
1809/07/19	AMSCH	[A0005][H]	*Snyder; Rubens* | 1 Herte Jagt | *Notes:* This lot was added in by hand in the AA copy of the catalogue. Because it was not numbered, we have assigned the number.		(Unknown)
1810/10/11	AMSCH	0077	*P. P. Rubbens; F. Snijders* | Een wild Zwijn, levensgroot, door verscheiden Honden aangevallen; drie Jagers gaan het met Spieren te keer, terwijl een derzelven op een Jagthoorn blaast, op den voorgrond liggen verscheiden gekwetste Honden; ongemeen krachtig en van eene breede penseelbehandeling | *Mat:* op doek *Size:* hoog 68, breed 111 duimen	K	(Bought In) fl 82

Snyders, Frans (copy by)

1810/10/10	MGCIT	0123	*Snijder; Rubbens* | Een zeer schoone Kopie naar een stuk van Rubbens, voormaals en mogelijk nog te Antwerpen, verbeeldende een Charitas; bijzonder goed nagevolgd, door Snijder | copy by F. Snyders after Rubens	Caspar van Citters	(Unknown)

Snyders, Frans (manner)

1802/04/13	HAVIN	0040	*Snyders* | Een Zwyne Jagt, als van Snyders		(Unknown)
1802/06/28	AMSCH	0257	*Snyders* | Op een Tafel ziet men een Ben met schoone Vrugten, ter zyde legt dood Wild; als door Snyders | *Mat:* op paneel *Size:* hoog 29, breed 38 duim	B	(Sold) fl 4:5 Roos [for] A
1802/09/21	UTHDG	0084	*Snijders* | Twee stuks met Honden, jacht makende op een Gans, en op een Rijger, natuurlijk en breed als van Snijders | *Mat:* op paneel *Size:* ieder hoog 13, breed 10 duimen		(Sold) fl 2:15 Gevaerts
1803/08/24	HGKAN	0099	*Snyders* | Een Zwyne Jagt, als Snyders	[Teissier] [or others]	(Sold) fl 8:15 Eustein [?]
1804/10/16	DLOND	0305	*In de Manier van Snyders* | Gevegt van Honden en Wilde Zwynen. Combat entre des Chiens & Porcs sauvages | *Mat:* op doek *Size:* hoog 27, breed 32		(Unknown)
1806/05/05	AMSCH	0249	*Snyders* | Een welvoorziende Keuken, met een Jongeling, die een Meisje caresseert; meesterachtig als Snyders	V[inkeles]	(Sold) fl 2:15 A Reynders
1808/08/23	AMSCH	0257	*Snijders* | Een Vos, die bezig is een Haan te verscheuren; zeer natuurlijk verbeeld, in de manier van Snijders	J	(Sold) fl 4:10 Hulswit

Sondervan, J. [Unidentified]

1810/05/22	AMSCH	0098	*Sondervan (J.)* | Twee stuks met geurige Bloemen en delikate Vrugten; zacht gepenceeld | *Mat:* op doek *Fmt:* ovaal *Size:* Jeder hoog 15, breed 11 duim.	R	(Sold) fl 10:10 Rutten

Sonje, Jan Gabrielsz.

1801/03/16	AMSCH	0087	*Sonjé* | Een Boschachtig Landschap	P[ruyssenaar]	(Sold) fl 1 Mensart
1801/04/08	HAVIN	0011	*Sonje* | Een Battaille, fraai		(Unknown)
1802/04/13	HAVIN	0047	*Sonje* | Een Battaille tusschen Ruitery		(Unknown)
1802/05/05	AMSCH	0194	*J. Sonjé* | Een Landschap met hoog Geboomte en een Boeren Woning aan een stil Water, gestoffeerd met eenige Beeldjes, het fraaije Zonligt, en de Spiegeling in het Water is allerbevalligst, en is delicaat | *Mat:* op doek *Size:* hoog 18, breed 22 duim	E	(Sold) fl 53 Hulswit
1802/07/20	MGSAN	0049	*Sonje* | Een schoon Landschap, op Doek | *Mat:* op doek *Size:* hoog duim 19, breed duim 16		(Unknown)
1802/09/06	AMSCH	0107	*Sonjé* | Een Bergagtig Landschap, gestoffeert met een ryziger en beladen muylëzel; verder een huisman over een bruggetje gaande; zonagtig behandeld | *Mat:* op paneel *Size:* hoog 19, breed 25 duim	Wed Grave [or others]	(Sold) fl 9 van Iperen
1802/12/13	AMSCH	0148	*J. Sonjé* | In een Italiaansch Bergachtig Landschap, vertoond zig gedeeltelyk de Ruïnen van een Gebouw, by een Steene Poort, op de voorgrond ryk gestoffeerd met verscheide Huislieden en Vée, en andere Reizigers; alles evenaart de Natuur, het Zonlicht is bevallig en meesterlyk fraay gepenceeld | *Mat:* op doek op paneel *Size:* hoog 12, breed 15 duim	Schley [for] Lauwers	(Sold) fl 14:5 van Iperen
1804/10/16	DLOND	0208	*J. Sonjé* | Een Overvaar-plaats en Scheepmakers-hoeve. Endroit de transport & attelier d'un Charpentier de Vaisseaux | *Mat:* op paneel *Size:* hoog 30, breed 24		(Unknown)
1806/11/24	AMSCH	0073	*Sonje* | Een boomryk Landschap, aan 't Gebergte geleegen, terzyde een Rivier en Waterval, en stoffagie van Beeldjes; kragtig behandeld | *Mat:* op paneel *Size:* hoog 30, breed 24 duim	Munnikhuizen	(Sold) fl 5:5 L Pakker
1808/04/26	GDAN	0149	*Sonje (J.)* | Een bergägtig Boomrijk Landschap, met Beelden en bijwerk | *Size:* hoog 41, breed 51 duim	G H Fortuyn	(Unknown)
1808/04/26	GDAN	0150	*Sonje (J.)* | Een Rhijngezigtje | *Size:* hoog 22 ½, breed 31 duim	G H Fortuyn	(Unknown)
1808/04/26	GDAN	0151	*Sonje (J.)* | Een dito [Rhijngezigtje] | *Size:* hoog 22 ½, breed 61 duim	G H Fortuyn	(Unknown)
1809/04/17	AMSCH	0089	*J. Sonjé* | Een hoog bergachtig Landschap, met een Rivier doorsneeden, gestofferd met Landlieden en beladen Muilëzels, zonagtig en fiks van schildering | *Mat:* op doek *Size:* hoog 20, breed 27 duim	T	(Sold) fl 24:10
1810/06/06	RMMUY	0073	*J. Sonjé* | Een dito [bergachtig] Landschap, op de Voorgrond gestoffeerd met een Vaartuig, Koetjes, Schapen en andere Figuren, zonachtig geschilderd | *Mat:* op paneel		(Unknown) fl 5:5

Sonje, Jan Gabrielsz. (manner)

1801/06/10	AMSCH	0214	*P. Sonjé* | Een Italiaansch Landschap met een Waterval, met Beeldjes gestoffeerd, in de manier van P. Sonjé | *Mat:* op doek *Size:* hoog 34, breed 46 duim *Notes:* The artist's name was given as "P. Sonjé" but we have assumed this is an error.	[Doublet]	(Sold) fl 6 de Gruiter
1802/02/16	AMSCH	0059	*J. Sonjé* | Een Duinachtig Landschap, gestofferd met Ryzigers, Gebouwen en geboomten, plaisant behandeld, als door J. Sonjé	G	(Sold) fl 7 Gruiter

Soolmaker, Jan Frans

1801/03/16	AMSCH	0067	*Zolemaker* | Een Landschap met Beelden en Beestjes	P[ruyssenaar]	(Sold) fl 12:10 Gruiter
1802/02/16	AMSCH	0033	*J. Soolmaker* | Een Ryke Ordonantie, in een heuvelachtig Landschap op de voorgrond, by een afgaande weg, ziet men een Boerekar, de Voerman op het paard zittende dryft verscheide zoorten van Beesten, door een Waterbeekje: waar by een gaande vrouw met een kind op de arm, verder gestoffeerd met andere Lieden, meesterlyk gepenceeld	H	(Sold) fl 132 J^{b} Roelofs
1802/05/05	AMSCH	0200	*Soolemaker* | Twee stuks, bergachtige Landschappen, gestoffeerd met een menigte staand en rustend Vee, waarby Herders en Herderinnen, zeer natuurlyk en fiks gepenceeld | *Mat:* op paneel *Size:* hoog 12, breed 15 duim	F	(Sold) fl 17 Auber
1802/06/16	AMSCH	0173	*J. F. Soolmaker* | Een Bergachtig Italiaansch Landschap, gestoffeerd met een Véehoeder, en verscheide staand en rustend Vée; krachtig en uitvoerig van penceel-behandeling | *Mat:* op doek *Size:* hoog 15, breed 16 duim	[Merrem]	(Sold) fl 27 Achina
1802/07/21	HGKAN	0111	*Salemaker* | Een fraay Landschap, op Paneel, verbeeldende een ver-Boomryk Landschap, waarop een liggende Herder met deszelfs Vee, en nog eenige andere Groepjes, zeer fraay en kragtig geschildert, door Salemaker | *Mat:* op paneel *Size:* hoog 1 voet 8 duym, en breed 1 voet 5 duym		(Unknown)
1802/08/24	LNDLS	0026	*H. Solemaker* | Een Landschap met Boomen en Gebouwen op eene hoogte, op den Voorgrond een Water daar Ossen, Koeijen en Schaapen door waden, met meer Stoffage. Krachtig, op paneel | *Mat:* op paneel *Size:* hoog 14 ½, breed 19 duimen *Notes:* The artist's name was given as "H. Solemaker" but we have assumed this is an error.	Leonardus Bouman [or others]	(Unknown) fl 40

1802/12/13	AMSCH	0149	*Solemaker* | In een Italiaansch Landschap, ziet men over een stille Rivier, een Steene Sluis, waarover een Landman, een Ezel dryft, verders een aangenaam verschiet, de voorgrond ryk gestoffeerd met twee Landlieden, verzeld van hun Vée; fraay van Licht en meesteragtig geschilderd | *Mat:* op doek *Size:* hoog 18, breed 25 duim	Pruyssenaar [for] A	(Sold) fl 5:10 Yver
1803/09/07	AMSCH	0157	*J. Soolemaker* | Dit uitmuntend Schildery verbeeld een Bergachtig Italiaans Landschap, ryk gestoffeerd met een groote meenigte Ossen, Koeijen, Schaapen, Bokjes, en ander Vee, ter zyde by een Fontyn zyn eenige Herders bezig hun Vee te drenken; de behandeling van dit Stuk is zoo fraay als Berghem en van de beste van J. Soolemaker [Un paysage riant et montagneux d'Italie ; composition très riche et variée par une grotte, des boeufs, des vaches, des chévres et d'autres bestiaux ; on voit sur le côté une fontaine et des bergers qui y vont abreuver leur bétail ; l'ordonnance et la touche de ce tableau sont comparables à Berghem, et en font un des meilleurs morceaux de Soolemaker] | *Mat:* op doek *Size:* hoog 30, breed 38 duim	Smidt	(Bought In) fl 400
1805/07/03	AMSCH	0177	*J. F. Zolemaker* | Een Italiaansch Landschap, met Geboomten en een Waterplas, ziet men op de Voorgrond verscheid staand en leggend Vee, een Herder en Herderin op de Voorgrond; fraai geordineerd en meesterlyk op Paneel | *Mat:* op paneel *Size:* hoog 12, breed 15 duim	R[oos]	(Sold) fl 90 Gruyter
1806/08/13	AMSCH	0328	*Solemaker. (J. F.)* | Een capitaal Bergachtig Landschap, met staand en leggend Vée; fiks behandeld | *Mat:* op doek *Size:* hoog 27, breed 24 duim	Vinkeles [for] G[ruyter]	(Sold) fl 1:5 Gruiter
1808/12/30	HGIMM	[0071n]	*Zolemaker* | Voorts een exquis kabinetje Schilderijen van voorname Nederlandsche Meesters, welke uit hoofde van de kortheid des tijds niet stuk voor stuk kunnen beschreven worden; doch waarvan de beschrijving op den Kijkdag zal voorhanden zijn. Dus wij hier alleen de namen van eenige dier Meesters laten volgen, als: A. Kuyp, Ruysdaal, Karel du Jardyn, Loqwi ('t beste dat hij schilderde) Hondekoeter, van Dyk, Janson, Moesgever, Kamphuyzen, van Gooijen, A. van der Neer, T. Wyk, Huchtenburgh, Zolemaker, van Hassel, A. Vermeulen, van Dongen, Scheffer, van Os enz. | *This Lot:* Een Schilderij, Zolemaker *Notes:* Because this lot was not numbered in the catalogue, we have assigned the number.		(Unknown)
1809/04/17	AMSCH	0134	*Soolemaker* | Twee stuks duin- en boomrijke Landschappen, met staand en leggend Vee; meesterlijk | *Mat:* op doek	[Gruyter?]	(Sold or Bought In) fl 0:16 Gruyter
1809/04/22	AMYVR	0114	*Soolemaker* | Een Italiaansch Landschap, op de voorgrond ziet men vier zoo staande als liggende Koeijen, en verscheiden Schapen en Bokjes, benevens een Hond, waarbij een Herder en eene Herderin, in 't verschiet een Pont met Vee enz.; meesterlijk gepenseelt | *Mat:* op doek *Size:* hoog 30, breed 34 duim	de Bruin	(Sold) fl 14 C S Roos
1809/07/25	HGBSM	0145	*Solemaker* | Een Landschap met een Fontein waar by eenige Herders en Reizigers met hun Vee staan te drinken &c. | *Mat:* op paneel *Size:* hoog 21, breed 18 en een half duim	D van der Aa [or] E B ten Dall	(Sold) fl 23:10 van Eyk
1810/03/27	RMCNL	0076	*Zolemaker* | Een Bergachtig Landschapje, zeer aardig behandeld, geheel in de smaak van van Berghem		(Unknown)
1810/10/10	MGCIT	0057	*Soolmaker* | Een treflyk Landschap, van weerszyde met hoog opgaande Boomen, waar tusschen zig een fraai Verschiet doet zien; terwyl op eene weluitgevoerde Voorgrond eenig Rundvee is geplaatst; zeer verdienstig behandeld door .... Soolmaker	Caspar van Citters	(Unknown)

Soolmaker, Jan Frans (or Soolmaker, manner)

1809/07/25	HGBSM	0026	*Zolemaker* | Twee Stuks Landschappen met Koeyen en Schapen en Figuuren, door of in de manier van Zolemaker | *Mat:* op doek *Size:* hoog 19, breed 16 duim	D van der Aa [or] E B ten Dall	(Sold) fl 25 van Eyck

Soolmaker, Jan Frans (manner)

1803/08/24	HGKAN	A0013	*Solemaker* | Een Landschap met een menigte Vee, waar in een Koe gemelk [sic] word, in de manier van Solemaker | companion to lot A14 *Mat:* op paneel *Size:* breet 24, hoog 18 duim		(Sold) fl 23:5 for lots A13 & A14. van Hoven
1803/08/24	HGKAN	A0014	*Solemaker* | Een dito [Landschap] weerga | companion to lot A13		(Sold) fl 23:5 for lots A13 & A14. van Hoven

Sorgh (or Sorgh, manner)

1808/06/11	RMRIJ	0123	*Door of in de manier van den Ouden Zorg* | Een Rivier Gezicht met Zeilende en andere Vaartuigen, op den voorgrond een zittende Oude Vrouw, Visser en een Jager met zyn Wildt en Hond | *Mat:* op paneel		(Sold) fl 3:15 V Giesen

Sorgh, Hendrik Martensz.

1801/05/11	AMSCH	0121	*H. M. Zorg* | In een Binnenvertrek, ziet men een Vrouwtje, welke bezig is appelen te schillen, met verder bywerk, plaisant gepenceeld | *Mat:* op doek op paneel *Size:* hoog 18, breed 15 duim	P[ruyssenaar]	(Sold) fl 12:10 van Iperen
1801/06/10	AMSCH	0204	*Zorgh. (H. M.)* | Een Binnenhuis alwaar vyf Boeren aan een Tafel zitten te rooken en te drinken, terwyl een ander tabak kerft, verders andere Huislieden; natuurlyk behandeld | *Mat:* op paneel *Size:* hoog 17, breed 22 duim	[Doublet]	(Sold) fl 90 Coclers

1801/06/13	LNDLS	0058	*H. M. Zorgh* | Een Binnenhuis, met een spinnend vrouwtje, speelende kinderen, en meer bijwerk, op paneel | *Mat:* op paneel *Size:* hoog 15, breed 19 duimen	D van R	(Sold) fl 18:5 van Iperen
1801/08/19	AMSCH	0144	*Zorg* | Een Binnenhuis, in dezelven ziet men een bevallige Vrouw by een ménigte Huisraad; alles natuurlyk behandeld	Pruyssen[r] [for] Q	(Sold) fl 18 Le Dantú
1802/05/05	AMSCH	0243	*H. M. Zorgh* | Een Boere Binnenhuis, waarin verscheiden rokende en drinkende Boeren, ter zyde een Vrouw, welke een Ketel schuurt, verders eenig Bywerk, zeer natuurlyk | *Mat:* op paneel *Size:* hoog 20, breed 20 duim	K	(Sold) fl 10 Claasens
1802/06/16	AMSCH	0232	*H. M. Zorgh* | In een Huismans Wouing [sic] zit een Boerin te Spinnen; ter zyde zit een Jongeling; op de voorgrond gestoffeerd met verscheide Huisraad, als Kopere Ketel, Potten, Pannen en Roode Kool; alles natuurlyk en bevallig gepenceeld | *Mat:* op paneel *Size:* hoog 9 ½, breed 11 ½ duim *Notes:* This lot was misnumbered no. 332.	[Merrem]	(Sold) fl 17 v d Vinne
1802/06/16	AMSCH	0233	*H. M. Zorgh* | In een Binnehuis, vertoont zich een slaapende Boer, op de grond leggende, waar by een andere Jongeling, schynende hem wakker te wille maken: een oude Vrouw bespiet dezelve, kykende over een schutting, verder gestoffeerd met verscheide Huisraad; natuurlyk en uitvoerig gepenceeld | *Mat:* op paneel *Size:* hoog 10, breed 8 duim	[Merrem]	(Sold) fl 16 Wed Achtienhoven
1802/06/28	AMSCH	0216	*H. M. Zorg* | In een Keuken Vertrek, zit een bevallig Vrouwtje by een Tafel, ziende ter zyde naar een Boer, die een Ben met Vis heeft, en dezelve aanbied; verder een Dienstmaagd, en gestoffeert met verder bywerk; bevallig gepenceeld door H. M. Zorg, op Panneel | *Mat:* op paneel *Size:* hoog 14, breed 17 duim	B	(Sold) fl 43 Texier
1802/06/28	AMSCH	0217	*H. M. Zorg* | In een Boeren Binnenhuis ziet men een oude gryze Boer, speelende met zyn Hond, in 't verschiet een Trap, Bedsteede en verder Huisraad; zeer natuurlyk door Denzelven [H. M. Zorg], Doek | *Mat:* op doek *Size:* hoog 17, breed 14 duim	Anna Elink	(Sold) fl 11 van der Schley A [for] Coclers
1802/07/21	HGKAN	0079	*Sorg* | Een Stukje zynde twee Boertjes die een Pyp rooken		(Unknown)
1802/08/24	LNDLS	0016	*H. M. Zorgh* | Een vrolijk Gezelschap in een Binnen-vertrek, ter regter zijde eene dansende Man en Vrouw, ter linker zijde eenige die aan tafel zitten, terwijl een man voor de dansenden op de Viool speeld, en in 't verschiet meer personen. Op paneel geschilderd | *Mat:* op paneel *Size:* hoog 16, breed 2 ½ duimen	Leonardus Bouman [or others]	(Unknown) fl 110
1802/09/15	HGKAN	0006	*Sorg* | Twee Boeren die een Pyp rooken, door Sorg, op Paneel en Lyst, en Vergulde binne rand [In Oly Verff] | *Mat:* in olyverf op paneel *Notes:* The bracketed information in the title appears above lot 1 and refers to lots 1 to 8.		(Unknown)
1802/12/13	AMSCH	0143	*H. M. Sorg* | In een Binnehuis ziet men eenige Boeren aan een Tafel zitten, ter zyden een meenigte van Groentens en Keuken-Gereedschappen; uitvoerig gepenceeld | *Mat:* op paneel *Size:* hoog 18, breed 25 duim	Pruyssenaar [for] A	(Sold) fl 1:15 Yver
1803/07/07	HGKAN	0017	*Sorg* | Een zeer fraay Schildery, verbeeldende twee Boertjes een Pyp rookende, door Sorg, met Swarte Lyst, en Goude binnen randen [Schilderyen in Olyverf] | *Mat:* in olyverf *Notes:* The bracketed information in the title appears above lot 1 and refers to lots 1 to 25.		(Unknown)
1803/07/18	AMSCH	0064	*Zorgh (H. M.)* | De aanbidding der Herders in de Stal te Bethlehem, zy leggen op hunne Kniën in een devote gestalte, een Bokje, een Korf met Eyeren en eenige Vogelen, zyn de geschenken welke door hun medegebragt en aan de H. Maagd aangeboden worden; de ordonantie is bevallig zoo ook de penceelsbehandeling [L'Adoration des Bergers, la V.M. àgenouillée devant la crêche ou est l'Enfant Nouveau né paroit repondre aux pasteurs & aux femmes qui apportent les dons d'une chêvre, d'un Panier avec des poules, & une corbeille remplie de fruits ; d'autres personnages dessendent [sic] d'un Escalier. Un chien & un vase de cuivre sont les principeaux [sic] accessoires de cette composition. La simplicité des caractères, une bonne couleur, & un excellent effet de lumiere, le feront remarquer.] | *Mat:* op paneel *Size:* hoog 23, breed 32 duim	Maria Theresia Andrioli	(Sold) fl 49 Thys
1803/08/24	HGKAN	A0025	*Sorg* | Een fraay Schildery, verbeeldende twee Boertjes een Pyp Rokende		(Sold) fl 2 Kan
1803/09/07	AMSCH	0164	*H. M. Sorg* | In een Boeren Woning, zit een Huisman, bezig Mosselen schoon te maken; ter zyde op de grond, ziet men verscheide huisraat, als kopere Ketele, Vat en Tobben, Aarde Potten en Pannen, en verder bywerk, natuurlyk en meesterlyk gepenceeld [Un paysage, assis dans sa cuisine et occupé à nétoier [sic] des moulles [sic], à côté et dans le fond se voient diverses meubles et ustensiles de menage ; tels que des chaudrons de cuivre, des tonneaux etc. peint au naturel et avec goût] | *Mat:* op paneel *Size:* hoog 10, br. 14 duim	Smidt	(Sold) fl 57 I[c] Smit
1803/12/15	MGLAC	0026	*M. Zorg* | Een Binnenvertrek, waarin drie Figuuren en ander Bywerk; zeer delicaat en natuurlyk | *Mat:* op paneel *Size:* hoog duim 15, breed duim 13	Mr L H de Haze Bomme	(Unknown)
1804/08/08	AMSCH	0232	*H. M. Zorg* | In een Keuken ziet men een Dienstmaagd bézig het Vuur aan te stooken, op de voorgrond een Doofpot, Kopere Kétel, Gatepetiel met Visch, een Tobben met Kool, en ander Bywerk; allerdelicaatst en uitvoerig | *Mat:* op paneel *Size:* hoog 11, breed 12 duim	Roos a	(Bought In) fl 0:12
1804/08/08	AMSCH	0233	*H. M. Zorg* | In een Binnenhuis ziet men een Bejaard Man op een Stoel zittende, schynende zyn Pyp aan een Test met Vuur aan te steeken, voor hem een omgekeerd Vat, waarop een Glas met Bier, Pyp, en Papier met	Vink[eles] [for] S	(Sold) fl 7:5 Van Iperen

			Tabak; uitvoerig en fraai gepenceeld | *Mat:* op paneel *Size:* hoog 12, breed 13 duim		
1804/10/29	HRBAU	0103	*Sorg, (H. M.)* | Een vrolyke Gast ziet zeer vergenoegd naar een' Roemer Rhynschen Wyn, welken hy schynt te willen drinken, terwyl hy met de linkerhand, waar in hy een tinnen Wynkan heeft, zig tot weder-inschenken schynt gereed te houden. Byzonder levendig en natuurlyk behandeld | *Mat:* op paneel *Size:* hoog 11, breed 8 ½ duim	Simon Styl	(Unknown)
1805/07/03	AMSCH	0176	*H. M. Zorg* | In een gemeubileerd Keukenvertrek, zit een Vrouw, beesig Appelen te Schillen, verders een Mysje by den Haardstee, en gestoffeerd met Keukengereedschap, Gevogelten, Kool, Wortelen, en andere Vrugten; natuurlyk en bevallig gepenceeld | *Mat:* op paneel *Size:* hoog 16, breed 20 duim	R[oos]	(Sold) fl 112 Tessier
1805/07/10	AMSCH	0175	*H. M. Zorg* | Een Boere Binnehuis, met rokende en drinkende Boeren en verder bywerk; meesterlyk op Paneel | *Mat:* op paneel *Size:* hoog 14, breed 17 duim	V[inkeles] [for] P	(Sold) fl 1:15 Rookmans
1805/07/10	AMSCH	0176	*H. M. Zorg* | Een Stadgezicht, verbeeldende een Groenmarkt, met een ménigte Beelden, enz; fiks op Paneel | *Mat:* op paneel *Size:* hoog 14, breed 18 duim	V[inkeles] [for] M	(Sold) fl 10:10 T van Iperen
1805/07/10	AMSCH	0177	*H. M. Zorg* | Een Boer zyn Pyp aan een Test aanstekende; uitvoerig op Paneel | *Mat:* op paneel *Size:* hoog 6 ½, breed 4 ½ duim	R[oos]	(Sold) fl 1:5 T Spaan
1805/10/09	HGBSM	0004	*H. M. Zorg* | Eenige huislieden zittende te eeten, dewelken bezocht worden door den Landheer met zyne famille, helder en uitvoerig geschildert | *Mat:* op paneel *Size:* hoog 19 en breet 24 duim	T H van Willigen [or others]	(Sold) fl 85 Ph Meij
1805/10/09	HGBSM	0005	*H. M. Zorg* | Een vrolyk boeren gezelschap in een schuur | *Mat:* op paneel *Size:* hoog 16 ½ breet 18 ½ duim	T H van Willigen [or others]	(Sold) fl 16 Ph Meij
1805/10/09	HGBSM	0118	*H. M. Zorgh* | Een meisje voor op een bank uit een potje eetende, met een hondje nevens haar, uitvoerig op paneel | *Mat:* op paneel *Size:* hoog 6 ½ breet 5 duim	T H van Willigen [or others]	(Sold) fl 4:5 De Gelder
1805/10/09	HGBSM	L0011	*H. M. Zorg* | Een zittende man &c. | *Mat:* op paneel *Size:* hoog 15 breet 12 duim	T H van Willigen [or others]	(Sold) fl 3:12 Blommers
1806/06/07	RMHSN	0029	*Zorg* | Een Boeren Binnenhuis, met ryk Bywerk, waar in verscheide Beelden die Rooken en Drinken | *Mat:* op paneel	A E K L	(Sold) fl 60 v Sartin [?]
1806/08/20	HGBSM	0016	*H. M. Zorg* | Een Binnenhuis waar verscheide Boeren en Boerinnen aan Tafel zitten te eeten, terwijl de Boerin of Vrouw van het huis met een glimplach [sic] op haar nederziet en een Boer de hand geeft om de kamer te verlaaten; de hartstogten vol uitdrukking en geestig. Zijnde een bijzonder goed stuk van die beroemde meester | *Mat:* op paneel *Size:* hoog 14, breed 17 duim	Macalester Loup	(Sold) fl 220 Burggraf
1806/08/20	HGBSM	0017	*H. M. Zorg* | Een dito [Binnenhuis] alwaar een oud Vrouwtje met een haspel in de hand zit, achter haar staat een Boer met eene lachende tronie, hebbende eene bierkan in de hand; in het verschiet een open deur, alwaar eene Boeremeid aan eene kuip staat te wasschen, op de voorgrond verscheiden Potten, Pannen en Ketels, alles even keurlijk, uitvoerig en zeer schoon van Coloriet | *Mat:* op paneel *Size:* hoog 8 ¼, breed 10 ½ duim *Notes:* It is unclear what "dito" refers to in the title.	Macalester Loup [or others]	(Sold) fl 100 Teissier
1806/11/24	AMSCH	0068	*Sorgh (H.M.)* | In een Paleis, ziet men de Vreede, onder de gedaante van een bevallige Vrouw, in witte Kleederen, houdende een Palmtak in de handen, zittende op een verheeven zetel, voor haar zyn verscheiden Vissers en Landlieden, die nedergeknielt, de vrugten van hun Land- en Zee-Arbeid, als offerhanden aanbrengen; verder gestoffeert met verscheide aanschouwers; op de Voorgrond leggen Musiek en Krygsgereedschappen; alles is van een uitmuntende penceelbehandeling | *Mat:* op doek *Size:* hoog 25, breed 24 duim	Munnikhuizen	(Bought In) fl 55
1806/11/24	AMSCH	0069	*Sorgh (H.M.)* | In een Keukenvertrek vertoont zig op de Voorgrond verscheiden zoorten van Keuken- en andere Gereedschappen, verder een Vrouw by een Tafel, die Groenten schynt te hakken; het licht is natuurlyk, en uitvoerig gepenceeld | *Mat:* op paneel *Size:* hoog 10, breed 13 duim	Munnikhuizen	(Sold) fl 14:5 L Pakker
1807/06/02	AMHUY	0021	*Zorg* | Op een fraai Schildery ziet men een Vrouw die zit te spinnen en een Kind dat by haar staat te kyken, en verder bywerk, uitvoerig geschilderd		(Unknown)
1807/08/26	AMSCH	0247	*M.H. Zorgh* | In een Keukenvertrek vertoont zich eene bedaagde Vrouw in aloude Hollandsche Kleeding, staande by een Tafel, waarop dood Gevogelte, ter zyde is eene Dienstmaagd bezig Vich [sic] schoon te maken, en verder een Jongeling by een Pomp, bezig een Roemer te spoelen, gestoffeerd met een menigte bywerk, als Koperen Ketels, Potten, Pannen en ander Huisraad; uitvoerig gepenceeld | *Mat:* op paneel *Size:* hoog 19, breed 25 duim	Helsdinge	(Sold) fl 103 Jozi
1808/04/26	GDAN	0207	*Zorg (H.M.)* | Een Binnenhuis waar een Boertje aan Tafel zit te roken, met een brandend Pijpje in de hand, met een Vergiettest met eenige Vischjes, er op die schoon gemaakt zijn, zeer kragtig geschilderd als of het van Dou was | companion to lot 208 *Size:* hoog 11, breed 8 duim	G H Fortuyn	(Unknown)
1808/04/26	GDAN	0208	*Zorg (H.M.)* | Een dito [Binnenhuis] tot een wederga, zynde een Vrouwtje dat met een Bril op de Neus zit te haspelen, mede zeer fraai gedaan | companion to lot 207 *Size:* hoog 11, breed 8 duim	G H Fortuyn	(Unknown)

1808/04/26	GDAN	0209	*Zorg (H.M.)* | Een gemeubileerd Binnenvertrek, waar in een Mannetje en eenig Keukengereedschap | *Size:* hoog 9, breed 11 duim	G H Fortuyn	(Unknown)
1808/04/26	GDAN	0210	*Zorg (H.M.)* | Een stil Watertje, waar in verscheidene zeilende Schepen, cierlijk behandeld | *Size:* hoog 17, breed 26 duim	G H Fortuyn	(Unknown)
1808/06/06	RMRIJ	0152	*Zorg. (Hendrik Maartensz.)* | Een stukje met allerhande Visschen, door eenen Man schoon gemaakt wordende. Zeer uitvoerig behandeld. Eene wedergade. Rijk van verschillende soort van Gevogelte; waarbij een Vrouwtje een Vogel zit te plukken. Niet minder dan het voorgaande behandeld [La Première represente un Vieillard occupé à une Table chargée de poissons. D'un bon genre. La Seconde. Une Table chargée de Volaille, près de laquelle une femme plume un Oiseau etc. Du même mérite que la précédente] | *Annots:* verk. S[?] S Beyerman, Gouda, 22 April 1778 (f 325.-) (RMA I) *Mat:* op paneel *Size:* Twee Stukken. Hoog 9 ½, en breed 13 ¼ duim	Gerrit van der Pot, Heer van Groeneveld	(Sold) fl 100 P Roelszema
1808/08/23	AMSCH	0178	*Zorgh. (H. M.)* | Een Boeren Schuur, in dezelven zit een Huisman, bézig Mosselen schoon te maaken ter zijden een Bank, waar op een Kaars en twee Kannen geplaatst zijn, en verder bijwerk; geestig en fiks behandeld | *Mat:* op paneel *Size:* hoog 10, breed 13 duim	H	(Sold) fl 66 Gruyter
1808/09/13	HABRU	0100	*H.M. Zorg* | Een Binnenhuis, fraai geschilderd en gestoffeerd		(Unknown) fl 63
1808/10/28	AMVRS	0067	*Zorgh, (H. M.)* | In een Boeren Schuur zitten drie Huislieden bij een Tafel zig met roken en drinken te vermaken benevens een Jongen speelende met een Hond, op den voorgrond en ter zijde verschillend Huisraad. Bevallig en natuurlijk verbeeld | *Mat:* op paneel *Size:* hoog 19, breed 16 duim	Marten Udink	(Sold) fl 82 B Kooij
1809/04/22	AMYVR	0117	*H.M. Sorgh* | In een Binnenvertrek zit een Man bij 't Vuur zijne Pijp aan te steeken, de Vrouw schilt Appelen, en het Kind warmt zich; krachtig | *Mat:* op paneel *Size:* hoog 21, breed 15 duim	de Bruin	(Sold) fl 8:5 du Pree
1809/05/26	HADAA	0017	*M. Zorg* | Een rokend Boertje met een kan en glas, benevens een vuurtest	Mejuffrouw de Wed David Heemskerk [or others]	(Unknown)
1809/09/06	AMSCH	0093	*Zorgh (H.M.)* | In een Binnenvertrek vertoont zich Christus bij Maria, die aandagtig in een boek schijnt te lezen; verder bij een Tafel met spijs staat Martha, schijnende haare bézigheden den Heiland te kennen te geven; verder gestoffeerd met verscheidene Keuken-gereedschappen. De hartstogten zijn natuurlijk verbeeld, bevallig van licht en uitvoerig van penceelbehandeling | *Mat:* op paneel *Size:* hoog 15, breed 19 duim	Johannes Caudri	(Sold) fl 126 van der Schley
1810/03/23	HAVIN	0076	*M. Zorg* | Een Binnenhuis [In Lysten met Glasen] | *Notes:* The bracketed information in the title appears above lot 63 and refers to lots 63 to 79.	Rudolf Hendrik de Wetstein [or others]	(Unknown)
1810/03/26	RMMUY	0035	*Hendrik Maartenszoon Zorg* | Eene Hollandsche Visch markt. Op den voorgrond ziet men eene Vischstal, waarop verscheide soorten van Visschen en ander bijwerk. De Vischverkoopster daarbijstaande, heeft in de eene hand het mes, en legt met de andere hand eene moot Kabbeljaauw in een vischben, die door een bij haar staand Jongeling word opgehouden. Verscheide figuren, masten en zeilen, vertonen zich op den tweeden en derden grond. De aangename heldere lucht, de bevallige schikking, het natuurlijke en konstige in dit Schilderij, doet het een der besten van dezen Meester achten [Une Poissonnerie hollandaise. Sur le devant sont étalés, sur un banc plusieurs poissons et autres accessoires : la marchande, qui se trouve au milieu, tient de la droite un couteau, et de sa gauche pose une tranche de cabbeljou, dans un panier qu'un jeune homme présente, plusieurs personnes l'entourent[.] Dans le lointain on apperçoit des mats des bateaux et leurs voiles. Un beau fini, une couleur vraie et harmonieuse, jointe à une composition charmante, font regarder ce morceau comme un des meilleurs de ce maître.] | *Mat:* op paneel *Size:* hoog 11 ¼, breed 9 ½ duimen	Daniel de Jongh Az	(Sold) fl 90 Van Leen Delfshaven
1810/03/26	RMMUY	0069	*Hendrik Maartenszoon Zorg* | Twee Pourtraiten, verbeeldende Théophilus Reijkwaardt en Huisvrouw. Verdienstelijk en krachtig geschilderd [Deux Portraits, étant Theophile Reikwaardt, et son Epouse, d'un bon ton et bien traité.] | *This Lot:* Een pourtrait *Mat:* op paneel *Size:* hoog 12, breed 9 ¾ duimen *Notes:* Lots 69 and 70 were printed in the Dutch edition of the catalogue as one item. In the French edition they were printed as lots 70 and 71.	Daniel de Jongh Az	(Sold) fl 22 for lots 69 & 70. Spaan Amsterdam
1810/03/26	RMMUY	0070	*Hendrik Maartenszoon Zorg* | Twee Pourtraiten, verbeeldende Théophilus Reijkwaardt en Huisvrouw. Verdienstelijk en krachtig geschilderd [Deux Portraits, étant Theophile Reikwaardt, et son Epouse, d'un bon ton et bien traité.] | *This Lot:* Een pourtrait *Mat:* op paneel *Size:* hoog 12, breed 9 ¾ duimen *Notes:* Lots 69 and 70 were printed in the Dutch edition of the catalogue as one item. In the French edition they were printed as lots 70 and 71.	Daniel de Jongh Az	(Sold) fl 22 for lots 69 & 70. Spaan Amsterdam
1810/08/01	AMSCH	0128	*Zorgh (Hendrik Martensz.)* | Een gezigt op de Erasmusmarkt binnen Rotterdam, waar op eene Groenvrouw, bij welke Kooplieden, Kinderen en andere Lieden [Vue perspective sur la place d'Erasme à Rottordam [sic] ; sur ce Marché se trouve une Marchande de Verdures, et des chalans amassés autour de sa Boutique, avec d'autres figures] | *Annots:* Passable. (NGW) *Mat:* op paneel *Size:* hoog 20, breed 27 duimen	Mr Pieter de Smeth van Alphen	(Sold) fl 365 R Pott te Rotterdam
1810/08/01	AMSCH	0129	*Zorgh (Hendrik Martensz.)* | In eene Kamer voor een open venster zit een vrolijk Man op de Luit te spelen, nevens hem eene deftige Vrouw,	Mr Pieter de Smeth van Alphen	(Sold) fl 315 De Lelie

			rustende met haren linkerarm op eene Tafel, waarop een Schotel met Vruchten, op den voorgrond liggen een Hond en eene Kat [Dans un intérieur de Chambre se presente un Homme Jovial devant un Fenètre ouverte, jouant du Luth ; à son côté on trouve une Dame appuyant son bras droit sur une Table, sur laquelle on voit un plat rempli de fruit. Audevant de la pièce se couchent un Chat et un Chien] | *Annots:* Passable. (NGW) *Mat:* op paneel *Size:* hoog 19, breed 15 ½ duimen		
1810/10/10	MGCIT	0034	*H. Maartensz. Zorg* | Een zeer plaisant Binnenhuis, waar in twee Vrouwen, hebbende voor zich, een Tafel met veelsoortige Groenten, terwijl op de voorgrond een Manspersoon op eene knie zich voor haar bevind, schijnende eenige Visch ter koop aan te bieden; wijders ziet men eenig ongemeen keurig behandeld Huisraad, terwijl het geheel door een van buiten invallend licht zeer verfraaid word; delicaat en uitvoerig op het Paneel gebragt | *Mat:* op paneel	Caspar van Citters	(Unknown)
			Sorgh, Hendrik Martensz. (or Sorgh, H.M., manner)		
1804/05/07	AMSCH	0201	*Zorg. (H. M.) of in de Manier* | Een heilige Familie in een Binnenhuis, met veel bywerk; uitvoerig en fraay geschilderd | *Size:* hoog 25 ½, breed 33 duim	Vinkeles [for] G	(Sold) fl 6:5 Thais
1810/06/06	RMMUY	0159	*H. M. Sorg* | Een stal met Groenten, waar bij eene Vrouw zit, welke aan eene Jufvrouw eenige Groenten aanbied; van achteren op de tweede grond eene Vischmarkt, en in 't verschiet Visschers Schuiten. Door of in de manier van H. M. Sorg | *Mat:* op doek		(Sold) fl 5 V Dongen
			Sorgh, Hendrik Martensz. (manner)		
1802/09/06	AMSCH	0135	*H. M. Zorg* | In een Binnenhuis, zit een bedaagde Vrouw, met een Haspel op de schoot, agter dezelve staat een vrolyke Boer, houdende een Bierkan in de hand, verder in het Voorhuis staat een Vrouw by de Waschtobben, gestoffeert met verscheide Huisraad, als Kopere Keetels en eenig Aardewerk; uitvoerig van Penceelbehandeling, in de manier van H. M. Zorg | *Mat:* op paneel *Size:* hoog 9 ½, breed 13 duim	H^{n} Smit	(Sold) fl 1 Gruiter
1804/10/16	DLOND	0314	*Als M. Zorg* | Een Huisgezin, waarin een Doedelzakspeler. Un Homme jouant de la Cornemuse au Millieu d'une Famille | *Mat:* op paneel *Size:* hoog 15, breed 21		(Sold) fl 150 O D Wyngaert
1805/10/09	HGBSM	H0008	*H. M. Zorg* | Een boeren binnenhuis, waarin een vrouw een keetel staat te schuuren en meer bywerk, in de manier van H. M. Zorg | *Mat:* op paneel *Size:* hoog 18 ½ breet 25 duim	T H van Willigen [or others]	(Sold) fl 3 Blommers
			Soukens		
1810/06/06	RMMUY	0193	*Soukens* | Twee Bergachtige Landschapjes | *Mat:* op koper		(Unknown) fl 1
			Spaendonck, Gerard van		
1806/05/05	AMSCH	0127	*Spandonck* | Op een steene Tafel staan twee sierelyke gewerkten Vaassen, waarvan den eenen rykelyk is voorzien van onderscheiden zoorten van Bloemen, ter zyden derzelven ziet men een Oost-Indische Raaf; breed en bevallig geschildert door Spandonck | *Mat:* op doek *Size:* hoog 33 ½, breed 43 duim	V[inkeles]	(Sold) fl 1 Gruyter
1808/08/23	AMSCH	0147	*Spandonk. (J.)* | Dit capitaal Bloem- en Fruitstuk, vertoont op een steene Plint, een cierlijke gewerkte Vaas, met Basrelieven, gevult met verschillende fraaije Bloemen, aan de voet derzelve een meenigte smakelijke Vrugten, als Persikken, blauwe en andere Druiven, Pruimen, Nooten, Aardbesien, Bessen en Turksche Graan, waar op verscheiden Insecten aazen; Bloem en Vrugten evenaaren de Natuur, en van een uitvoerige penceelbehandeling | *Mat:* op paneel *Size:* hoog 34, breed 27 duim	[Coclers]	(Sold) fl 98 Dupré
1809/04/22	AMYVR	0122	*van Spaandonck* | Op een Steenen Baluster staat een Vaas met geurige Bloemen, waarbij op de voorgrond liggen eene menigte Druiven, Persiken, Pruimen, Nooten en andere Vruchten; zeer schoon van kleur, en van eene bevallige penseelbehandeling | *Mat:* op paneel *Size:* hoog 34, breed 27 duim	de Bruin	(Bought In) fl 105
			Spilman, Hendrik		
1809/05/26	HADAA	A0024	*H. Spilman* | Twee stuks	Mejuffrouw de Wed David Heemskerk [or others]	(Unknown)
1809/05/26	HADAA	A0025	*H. Spilman* | Twee dito [stuks], dito [door H. Spilman]	Mejuffrouw de Wed David Heemskerk [or others]	(Unknown)
			Spranger [Unidentified]		
1802/09/29	AMSCH	0075[H]	*Spranger* | Een Bloemstuk Een Schildery door Spranger | *Notes:* This lot was added in by hand in the BMB, EBNP, FLNY and RKDH copies of the catalogue.	Y[ver]	(Sold) fl 32 de Roij
			Spranger, Bartholomaeus		
1802/06/16	AMSCH	0158	*B. Spranger* | Deeze Ryke Ordenantie verbeeld in een Krans met Medaíljons versiert, het Portrait van Keizer Mathias, als een Borstbeeld,	[Merrem]	(Sold) fl 41 J Yver

			rondsom versiert van boven, ter zyde, en van onder met verscheide zinnebeeldige Figuuren en een menigte bywerk; dit stuk is krachtig en bevallig van Coloriet, zeer uitvoerig van penseel-behandeling, en bekend door de Prent, naar 't zelve gegraveert | *Mat:* op paneel *Size:* hoog 25 ½, breed 17 duim		
1804/02/27	AMSCH	0158	*Spranger* | St. Sebastiaan aan de Boom gebonden en met Pylen doorschoten; door Spranger. op Paneel | *Mat:* op paneel *Size:* hoog 17 ½, breed 14 duim	C	(Sold) fl 0:6 L Pakker
1808/09/13	HABRU	0087	*Spranger* | Adam en Eva		(Unknown) fl 4
			Spruyt, Johannes		
1802/05/05	AMSCH	0201	*J. Spruyt* | Op een Steene Rand legt een doode Haan, waarby eenig toepasselyk Bywerk, konstig behandeld | *Mat:* op doek *Size:* hoog 27, breed 24 duim	E	(Sold) fl 15:10 Stevens
			Spruyt, Philippe Lambert Joseph		
1810/03/23	HAVIN	0028	*Spruit* | Twee, Een oud Man bij een galant Meisje, en Kinderen die staan te Leezen	Rudolf Hendrik de Wetstein [or others]	(Unknown)
			Staats [Unidentified]		
1804/02/27	AMSCH	0101	*Staats* | Twee stuks, en Bloem- en Fruitstuk, delicaat en uitvoerig gepenceeld | *Mat:* op doek *Size:* hoog 27, breed 21 duim	D	(Sold) fl 10 I^{c} Smit
			Stalbemt, Adriaen van (and Neeffs, P. (I))		
1804/08/02	BDAN	0003	*P. Neefs; A. Stalbandt* | Een binnen-gezigt van de Groote Kerk van Antwerpen, verlicht door een Fakkel, zeer delicaat behandeld en uitvoerig geschildert | *Mat:* op paneel *Size:* b. 21 d. h. 13 d.	J G Calckberner	(Unknown)
			Starrenberg, Johan		
1803/12/12	AMSCH	0088	*Sterrenberg* | Twee stuks, zynde het Pourtrait van Willem de Derden, Koning van Engeland, en deszelfs Gemalinne; beide in hun Koninglyke Kléding, allerpragtigst voorgesteld, ten voeten uit; dezelve zyn meesterlyk geschilderd, door Sterrenberg, in de manier van A. van Dyk | *Mat:* op doek *Size:* hoog 88, breed 64 duim	B	(Bought In) fl 12
			Staveren, Jacob van		
1803/07/18	AMSCH	0047	*Staveren (Jacob van)* | Een Heremiet in zyn Kluis, in een biddende gestalte, voor hem legt een Bybel, een Zandloper en ander bywerk, een doode Boomstam, een Crucifix, een Doodshoofd enz. zyn de bevallige vercierselen van zyn verblyf; het invallende zonlight en de zeer uitvoerige behandeling doen dit stukje als of het van G. Douw geschilderd was voorkomen [Un St. Hermite à genoux en priere dans son hermitage. Ce petit morceau orné par une infinité de détails offre le St. viellard dans une attitude édifiante ; sa barbe & ses cheveux blancs impriment beaucoup de caractère sur sa figure. Devant lui est un tronc d'arbre sec & son crucifix ; une lanterne, un pannier & quantité d'objets faisant allusion à la vanité & au tems l'environnent ; un parasol est penché au dessus de son chef, & une plante de chardons croit derriere lui. Le fond de son antre étant percé donne sur un desert. Ce morceau est d'un fini exquis, il produit un effet charment [sic] de clair obscur, approchant de très près la maniere de G. Dou.] | *Mat:* op paneel *Size:* hoog 16, breed 11 duim *Notes:* The artist was presumably Jan Adriaensz. van Staveren and not Jacob van Staveren.	Maria Theresia Andrioli	(Sold) fl 81 Meijling
			Staveren, Jan Adriaensz. van		
1801/05/11	AMSCH	0082	*J. van Staveren* | In een Rots by de Stam van een oude Boom ziet men op een steen een witte Rot, alles uitvoerig gepenceeld | *Mat:* op paneel *Size:* hoog 10, breed 8 duim	P[ruyssenaar]	(Sold) fl 1:5 Gruiter
1802/05/05	AMSCH	0196	*van Staaveren* | Een biddende Heremiet, in een bouvallige Rots, waarin eenige anticque Beelden, helder en meesterlyk geschildert | *Mat:* op paneel *Size:* hoog 24, breed 19 duim	E	(Sold) fl 43 Cocler
1802/06/16	AMSCH	0167	*J. A. van Staveren* | Een Hermiet in een Rotsgezicht, als in Devotie mediteerende, voor hem op een Steene Muur staat een brandende Kaars, waar by eenige Boeken, Zandloper en Doodshoofd geplaats zyn: het Kaarslicht geeft een Natuurlyke en bevallige werking, en is zeer uitvoerig gepenceeld | *Mat:* op paneel *Size:* hoog 12, breed 9 ½ duim	[Merrem]	(Sold) fl 43 C S Roos
1803/04/20	AMSCH	0068	*Staveren. (J. van)* | Het Afbeeldzel van een Professor in zyn Studeerkamer, staande by een Tafel met een Kleed bedekt, waar op een Inktkoker en een Boek geplaatst is, hy rust met de regterhand op een doorgezaagd Doodshoofd, het is kragtig en teffens uitvoerig gepenceeld [Le Portrait d'un professeur : il est devant sa table couverte d'un tapis, & garnie d'accessoires propres à son étât. Ce petit morceau bien fini, a de la force & de l'effet.] | *Mat:* op paneel *Size:* hoog 9 ½, breed 9 duim	Maria Magdalena van Sluypwyk, gravinne van Moens	(Sold) fl 18:10 Gruiter
1804/08/08	AMSCH	0172	*J. van Staveren* | In een Grot ziet men een oude Heremiet, in een biddende gestalte, voor hem een Boek enz. eenige doode Boomstammen, Kruiden en Distelen, en een Bergachtig verschiet; allerbevalligst verlicht, en zoo uitvoerig als G. Douw, door J. van Staveren | *Mat:* op paneel *Size:* hoog 14 ½, breed 11 ½ duim	Roos a	(Bought In) fl 153

1804/10/16	DLOND	0209	*Van Staveren* | Een Hermiet met een Boek onder een Boom. Hermite avec un grand Livre devant lui sous un Arbre | *Mat:* op paneel *Size:* hoog 13, breed 10		(Sold) fl 12:10 Mahy
1804/10/16	DLOND	0210	*Van Staveren* | Een Hermiet met een Boek en Bril in de hand. Hermite avec un Livre & des Lunettes dans la Main | *Mat:* op paneel *Size:* hoog 9, breed 8		(Unknown) fl 26:5
1804/10/16	DLOND	0211	*Van Staveren* | De Euangelist [sic] Mattheus met den Engel. St. Matthieu avec l' Ange | *Mat:* op paneel *Size:* hoog 9, breed 8		(Unknown) fl 12:5
1806/08/13	AMSCH	0172	*Staveren. (J. van)* | Een biddende Heremiet in zyn Cluis, voor hem legt een Boek, Zandloper, Doodshoofd en andere zaken; fraai gepenceeld | *Mat:* op paneel *Size:* hoog 24, breed 20 duim	Roos	(Sold) fl 10:10 Th Spaan
1806/11/24	AMSCH	0071	*Staveren (J. van)* | Een Heremiet in zyn Kluis zittende te schryven by Kaarsligt; verders eenig bywerk, als een Doodshoofd, een Boek, enz.; uitvoerig gepenceeld | *Mat:* op paneel *Size:* hoog 10, breed 8 duim	Munnikhuizen	(Sold) fl 7:5 Gruiter
1808/06/13	AMSCH	0156	*Staveren (J. van)* | Een Jongeling in eene Nis, bezig zijnde een Vogelkooi op te hangen, voor hem een Boek en zijn Hoed. Bevallig van behandeling | *Mat:* op paneel *Size:* hoog 17, breed 14 duim *Loc:* Den Haag, Nederland. Museum Bredius. (107-1946)	Z	(Sold) fl 20 Jan Spaan
1809/04/17	AMSCH	0086	*J. van Staveren* | Deeze Ordonnantie steld voor eene devote Vrouw, knielende voor een oud Gebouw of Poort, door welke men heen ziet, zij is verbeeld in een aandachtige gestalten, met de oogen hemelwaards geslagen, voor haar ligt een groot opengeslagen Boek, rustende tegen de Stam van een Boom, in het verschiet ziet men verscheide andere Beelden en grootsche Gebouwen; dit stuk is fraai van Licht, kragtig en van een uitvoerige Penceelbehandeling | *Mat:* op paneel *Size:* hoog 33, breed 21 duim	[Gruyter?]	(Sold or Bought In) fl 111
1809/09/06	AMSCH	0066	*Staveren (van)* | Een School, men ziet de Meester, welke een Schrift voorschrijft voor een bevallig Meisje, agterwaards ziet men verscheide Kinderen aan een Tafel zitten, op de voorgrond zit een groote Jongen te Cijfferen, en ander bijwerk; mede als de voorgaande behandeld | *Mat:* op paneel *Size:* hoog 19, breed 16 duim	Johannes Caudri	(Sold) fl 144 Hulswit
1809/09/06	AMSCH	0067	*Staveren (van)* | Een Philosoof in zijn Studeerkamer, hebbende voor zich een Lei en een opengeslagen Boek en Globe, behandeld als de voorgaande | *Mat:* op paneel *Size:* hoog 16, breed 18 duim	Johannes Caudri	(Sold) fl 60 Th^{S} Spaan
1810/06/06	RMMUY	0040	*van Staveren* | Een biddende Hermiet in eene Rots, zeer fraaij en uitvoerig geschilderd | *Mat:* op paneel		(Unknown) fl 13

Staveren, Jan Adriaensz. van (or Staveren, J.A., manner)

1806/05/05	AMSCH	0168	*van Staveren* | Een Heremiet in zyn Cluis, met verscheiden bywerk; door of in de manier van van Staveren	R[oos]	(Sold) fl 10:10 T van Iperen
1809/04/17	AMSCH	0087	*J. van Staveren* | Deeze Ordonantie verbeeld in een vervallen Rots een Kluisenaar in zijn Devotie, hij knielt eerbiedig met zaamgevouwen handen, voor hem ligt een opengeslagen Boek en op de grond een Doodshoofd, ter regterzijde ziet men de gedaante van een Jeugdig Mensch, en een bedaagd Man, houdende met beide handen een volle Geldbeurs, verders eenige helsche Monsters; de karakters zijn natuurlijk en van een uitvoerige behandeling, op Paneel, door of in de manier van denzelven [J. van Staveren] | *Mat:* op paneel *Size:* hoog 22 ½, breed 29 duim	Crajenschot	(Sold) fl 8

Staveren, Jan Adriaensz. van (manner)

1810/06/06	RMMUY	0140	*van Staveren* | Een Hermiet voor een Kluis, zittende te schrijven; ter zijde een stam van een boom, Als door van Staveren | *Mat:* op paneel		(Unknown) fl 3:5

Steem, C. de [Unidentified]

1802/05/01	HGCLF	0051	*C. de Steem* | Twee Fruytstukken	Mr B de Moor van Immerzeel	(Unknown)

Steen, Antoon van den

1809/07/19	AMSCH	0052	*Steen (A. van der)* | Dit voorwerp vertoont een bulkende Ossekop, meer dan levensgroote. Meesterlijk en breed geschilderd | *Mat:* op doek *Size:* hoog 33, breed 27 duim	[Bicker]	(Sold) fl 5:10 Van Iperen

Steen, Jan

1801/04/13	AMSCH	0066	*Jan Steen* | Deeze bevallige Ordonantie verbeeld voor een Buitenhuis onder een Wyngaard, een Boere bruiloft, ter regter zyde zitten, aan een gedekte Tafel met spyzen, verscheiden Gasten zich met eeten en drinken te vermaken, in het midden van het stuk, danssen Bruid en Bruidegom, op de voorgrond zitten een Boer en Boerin te drinken, ter linker zyde op een hoogte zyn de Muzikanten geplaatst, in het verschiet nog een menigte Beelden en aangenaam Dorpgezicht, dit geestige Schildery is van de beste van deezen Meester | *Mat:* op paneel *Size:* hoog 22, breed 30 duim	Pierre Fouquet, junior	(Sold) fl 265 Lafontaine
1801/04/13	AMSCH	0067	*Jan Steen* | Dit aangenaam voorwerp verbeeld een Markt, op de voorgrond by de Poort van een gebouw zit een Boer, welke aan een bevallige Vrouw met een Marktemmer aan haar Arm, een Haan schynt te willen verkopen, ter zyde en in het verschiet ziet men nog een menigte Marktgangers, dit	Pierre Fouquet, junior	(Sold) fl 430 C S Roos

			stukje is zoo uitvoerig als of het van G. Metzu gepenceeld was | *Mat:* op koper *Size:* hoog 14, breed 10 duim		
1801/05/11	AMSCH	0083	*J. Steen* | Een Boeren Binnenhuis, ryk gestoffeerd met een menigte Huislieden en Munnikken, welke zich met zingen en drinken vermaaken, zynde deze comique Ordonnantie van de uitvoerigste schildering van dezen Meester | *Mat:* op paneel *Size:* hoog 14, breed 16 duim	E[lias]	(Sold) fl 79 Coclers
1801/06/10	AMSCH	0145	*Steen. (J.)* | Deeze geestige Ordonantie, steld voor een Jongeling en een jong Meisje, by eenige Duiven zittende, welke tekenen van liefde geeven, achter in het Schildery staat een oud Man met een Haan, de behandeling is van de beste van deezen Meester [Men zal deeze drie stukken met de keuze verkopen] | *Mat:* op doek *Size:* hoog 25, breed 31 duim *Notes:* The bracketed information in the title appears below lot 147 and refers to lots 145 to 147.	Herman ten Kate	(Bought In) fl 205
1801/06/10	AMSCH	0146	*Steen. (J.)* | Onder een Boom, tegens een Heuvel stoeit een jonge Boer met een bevallig Boerinnetje, daar nevens een Mandje met Groente, in alles als de voorgaande [Men zal deeze drie stukken met de keuze verkopen] | *Mat:* op doek *Size:* hoog 25, breed 31 duim *Notes:* The bracketed information in the title appears below lot 147 and refers to lots 145 to 147. *Loc:* Leiden, Nederland. Stedelijk Museum de Lakenhal. (405)	Herman ten Kate	(Bought In) fl 205
1801/06/10	AMSCH	0147	*Steen. (J.)* | Deeze niet mindere Ordonantie is een vervolg op de voorgaande en niet minder behandeld. NB. Men zal deeze drie stukken met de keuze verkopen | *Mat:* op doek *Size:* hoog 25, breed 31 duim *Notes:* The description in the title refers to lots 145 to 147.	Herman ten Kate	(Bought In) fl 205
1801/06/10	AMSCH	0148	*Steen. (J.)* | Twee stuks, zynde het eene, de Pastyeeters en het andere de drinkers, beide van de beste, en in de manier van Metzu, behandelde stukjes | *Mat:* op paneel *Size:* hoog 10, breed 8 duim *Notes:* In the original title the words "de Pastyeeters" were printed as "de party eeters." This error was corrected in an errata sheet located at the end of the catalogue.	Herman ten Kate	(Sold) fl 105 C S Roos
1801/06/10	AMSCH	0149	*Steen. (J.)* | In een Binnenvertrek, ziet men een Doctor welke een Dame de pols voelt, nevens hem een Dinstmaagd [sic], schynende met hem over de ziekte te spreeken, alles is meesterlyk van schildering | *Mat:* op paneel *Size:* hoog 13, breed 11 duim	Herman ten Kate	(Sold) fl 31 v d Schleij [for] Uylenburg
1801/06/10	AMSCH	0150	*Steen. (J.)* | Een Boeren Binnenhuis, gestoffeert met een menigte Beelden, twee derzelven schynen over het Kaartspeelen geschil te hebben, waar over een zyn Mes trekt, de karakters zyn geestig en alles breed van schildering | *Mat:* op doek *Size:* hoog 13, breed 17 duim *Loc:* Leipzig, Deutschland. Museum der bildenden Künste. (1564)	Herman ten Kate	(Sold) fl 51 J Yver
1801/06/10	AMSCH	0151	*Steen. (J.)* | Een bevallig Vrouwtje, met een tinne Schotel op haar Schoot, waarop een Wafel geplaast is, nevens haar een Man die haar een glas Wyn aanbied, fraai en delicaat behandeld | *Mat:* op paneel *Size:* hoog 12, breed 9 duim	Herman ten Kate	(Sold) fl 70 De Lelie
1801/06/13	LNDLS	0006	*Jan Steen* | Een Binnenhuis, in hetzelve hangt een geslachten Os, benevens twee staande kinderen, waarvan een de blaas opblaast, en den Slachter met een Kan in zijn hand, die met de andere hand een Beker met drank aan een man en vrouw aanbied, met meer bijwerk, konstig en kragtig, op doek | *Mat:* op doek *Size:* hoog 20 ½, breed 25 duimen	D van R	(Sold) fl 51 Teissier
1801/08/19	AMSCH	0110	*J. Steen* | Deeze Grappige Ordonnantie steld voor een Haanegevegt in een Boere Herberg, waar by een ménigte Huislieden zig met dit Spel vermaakende; geestig en meesterlyk geschilderd	Pruyssen[r] [for] Q	(Bought In) fl 71
1801/08/19	AMSCH	0111	*J. Steen* | In een Huismans Woning ziet men een boose Vrouw, met een Muil, een op de grond leggende Boer, fris op zyn bloote agterste kloppen, een kleine Jongen schynt haar te rug te trekken, verder by een Haartsteede zyn drie Boeren, dit geval beschouwende; gestoffeerd met verder bywerk geestig gepenceeld op Paneel | *Mat:* op paneel *Size:* hoog 13, breed 14 duim	Van Forreest	(Sold) fl 40 Gruiter
1801/08/19	AMSCH	0112	*J. Steen* | Een Zoldaat [sic] staande voor een Boerewooning of Herberg, een Vrouw legt uit een Vengster, beide ziende naar een dronken Boer, fix geschilderd op Doek | *Mat:* op doek *Size:* hoog 12, breed 11 duim	Van Forreest	(Sold) fl 6:5 Gruiter
1801/10/06	AMSCH	0063	*J. Steen* | In een Binnenhuis ziet men een Boer by den Haart, welke door een Meisje een Glas Wyn, werd aangebooden, verder een ander Huisman zyn Pyp rookende, gestoffeert met verder bywerk, Meesterlyk gepenceelt | *Mat:* op paneel *Size:* hoog 14, breed 12 duim	M	(Sold) fl 111 v d Schley A [for] Hijnen
1801/10/19	AMSCH	0067	*Steen. (Jan)* | Een vrolyke Boer, die by een Meisje, welk een borrelfles en een glas in de hand heeft, by een Tafel zit, waar op eenige Suikergebak legt; breed en Meesterachtig geschilderd | *Mat:* op doek *Size:* hoog 14, breed 12 duim	Jonkheer Menno Baron van Coehoorn	(Sold) fl 51 de Lely
1801/10/19	AMSCH	0068	*Steen. (Jan)* | Een Boere Chirurgyns winkel, waarin de Heelmeester het Been verbind van een Boer; waarby een Vrouw die hem een glas water toereikt, en in het verschiet, verder bywerk; uitneemend schilderachtig, uitvoerig en fraay behandeld | *Mat:* op paneel *Size:* hoog 15 ¼, breed 12 duim	Jonkheer Menno Baron van Coehoorn	(Sold) fl 300 van der Schleij [for] A
1801/12/22	AMOTT	0121	*Jan Steen* | 't Pourtrait (door Jan Steen) van deszelfs Huisvrouw	Bartholomeus Ruloffs	(Unknown) fl 3

1802/05/05	AMSCH	0190	*J. Steen* | In een Boere Binnehuis ziet men op een geestige wyze verbeeld, de Historie van de Heet en Koudblazer, de Boer zit aan Tafel te blazen in zyn lepel, de Zater staat op, en het overige gezelschap lacht om het geval, een Kind in een Kakstoel, door een ander eeten aangeboden wordende, maakt deeze Ordonnantie nog bevalliger, zynde van de beste schildering van J. Steen | *Mat:* op doek *Size:* hoog 40, breed 45 duim *Loc:* Eindhoven, Nederland. Philips collection.	A	(Sold) fl 400 Pruijssenaar [for] R
1802/05/05	AMSCH	0191	*J. Steen* | Deeze commicque Ordonnantie verbeeld een Vrolyke Gast, met een Wortel in zyn hand by eenige Vrouwen, waarover eenige by het Vuur staande en zittende Snaaken, hartelyk lagchen, het Bywerk zoo wel als de Beelden zyn van de Uitvoerigsten van deezen Meester | *Mat:* op doek *Size:* hoog 18, breed 21 duim	A	(Sold) fl 40 v d Vinne
1802/05/05	AMSCH	0192	*J. Steen* | In een Boere Binnenhuis ziet men een Boer een Boerin galantiseerende, verders nog een menigte andere Huislieden, fiks | *Mat:* op doek *Size:* hoog 17, breed 19 duim	E	(Sold) fl 39 W Reijers
1802/05/05	AMSCH	0193	*J. Steen* | Een Binnenhuis, gestoffeerd met twee Lieden, verder een Vrouw met een Glas op de Tafel, een Bierkan en Confoor, meesterlyk behandeld | *Mat:* op doek *Size:* hoog 14, breed 11 duim	A	(Sold) fl 22 Yver
1802/05/24	HGBAK	0023	*Jan Steen* | Een gezelschap aan den disch gezeten, verbeeldende een drie Koningen vreugd, zeer ryk van Ordonnantie, door Jan Steen van zyn beste tyd, hoog 15 duim, breed 20 ½ duim, op doek, zwarte lyst met vergulde binnenrand | *Mat:* op doek *Size:* hoog 15 duim, breed 20 ½ duim	Mejuffrouw A van der Mieden	(Sold) fl 300 La Bouchêre
1802/06/16	AMSCH	0159	*J. Steen* | In een Binnevertrek ziet met eenige beschonke Boeren, waarvan 'er een met een Mes een ander schynt te bedrygen, waarover de anderen lagchen; alles delicaat en uitvoerig geschilderd | *Mat:* op paneel *Size:* hoog 13, breed 17 duim	[Merrem]	(Sold) fl 72 v d Schley
1802/06/16	AMSCH	0160	*J. Steen* | In een Landschap voor een Boere Woning, ziet men twee vegtende Huislieden; een derzelve word door een Vrouw tegen gehouden, de tafel met Speelkaarten, en Bierkan valt om ver: de Caracters zyn geestig verbeeld en uitvoerig van penceel-behandeling | *Mat:* op paneel *Size:* hoog 13 ½, breed 11 duim	[Merrem]	(Sold) fl 33 Gruiter
1802/06/16	AMSCH	0161	*J. Steen* | Het Afbeeldzel van dien Kunstschilder; leggende uit een vengster: meesterlyk fiks geschilderd door hem zelfs | *Mat:* op paneel *Size:* hoog 11, breed 9 duim	[Merrem]	(Sold) fl 13 B^{d} Kooij
1802/06/28	AMSCH	0158	*J. Steen* | Deeze grappige Ordonnantie steld voor het Drie Koningsfeest, aan tafel ziet men verscheiden vrolyke Gasten, ter linker zyde ziet men twee Kinderen over kaarssen springen; zeer natuurlyk en fraai gepenceeld, door J. Steen, op Panneel | *Mat:* op paneel *Size:* hoog 18, breed 25 duim	Anna Elink	(Sold) fl 30 Geld
1802/06/28	AMSCH	0159	*J. Steen* | Een Binnenhuis, met verscheiden vrolyke Lieden, zich vermakende met speelen, drinken en zingen, op de voorgrond een Kind in een Kinderstoel; zeer natuurlyk en fiks gepenceeld, door Denzelven [J. Steen], op Doek | *Mat:* op doek *Size:* hoog 24, breed 28 duim	Anna Elink	(Sold) fl 15 Mensart
1802/06/28	AMSCH	0160	*J. Steen* | In een Binnevertrek ziet men een ziek Meisje, rustende met haar hoofd tegen een Kussen, waarby een Doctor bezig is haar pols te voelen; dun en delicaat gepenceeld, door Denzelven [J. Steen], op Panneel | *Mat:* op paneel *Size:* hoog 10, breed 8 duim	B	(Sold) fl 16 Royers
1802/07/21	HGKAN	0005	*Jan Steen* | Een slapende Vrouw		(Unknown)
1802/07/21	HGKAN	0021	*Jan Steen* | Een dito [Schildery], zynde een Boere Binnenhuys, met danzende Boer- en Boerin, nevens eenige drinkende, zittende en musiceerende Boeren		(Unknown)
1802/07/27	AKHRK	0001	*Jan Steen* | In dit uitmuntend Kunststuk beschouwt men den twaalf-jaarigen Heiland, leerende en ondervraagende de Wetgeleerden in den Tempel: alle schijnen opgetoogen en diepdenkenden, vol verwondering en verbaastheid over den jongen Leeraar: een der voornaamsten zit op een verheeven gestoelte; aan de andere zijde ziet men de bedrukte en nedrige Maria en Joseph naast haar zoon, die zijne Moeder aanspreekt. Wonderbaarlijk is het aangezicht, vol wijsheid in den jongen Jesus, uitgedrukt, alle de verschillende Characters zoo edel geteekend, het kunstig verkoozen licht, het contrast, de houding en uitvoerige behandeling van het Penceel, vol vuur en kracht, maaken dit overheerlijk Kunsttafreel tot een der fraaisten, die deezen grooten Kunstheld eer aandoen | *Annots:* zee cat 18 April 1803 Paillet et Delaroche No. 214! (RKDH) *Mat:* op doek *Size:* hoog 32, breed 39 duim *Loc:* Basel, Schweiz. Kunstmuseum.	Maria Stategaart	(Sold) fl 160 Gruijter
1802/07/27	AKHRK	0002	*Jan Steen* | Dit onderwerp schijnt een Vastenavonds vreugd te zijn, de dartele, koddige, en levendige gebaarden der verschillende persoonen van beide de Sexen, drukken ieder hun aart zeer schoon uit; terwijl de Huisman met een frissche Roemer de zorgen des levens afspoelt, heft men een schreeuw-partij aan, te geweldig voor de oude Vrouw, die met beide haare handen de ooren vast houd: Een bevallige Moeder, met een kind voor haar staande, zit zeer vergenoegd; terwijl de Knecht met een roode Luijer om zijn Hoofd, al knielende voor het Vat, de Kan vuld; op de voorgrond, staat een Driestal met Wafelen, en ter zijde op de Grond een gebraade Gans. Dit stuk is mede zeer goed van Penseel, bijzonder de uitdrukking der Wezenstrekken | *Mat:* op doek *Size:* hoog 35 ½, breed	Maria Stategaart	(Sold) fl 31 Gruyter

			45 duim *Loc:* Leipzig, Deutschland. Museum der bildenden Künste. (556) (?) as copy after Steen		
1802/07/27	AKHRK	0003	*Jan Steen* | In dit Binnenhuisje zit een oude zieke Vrouw, bij een Tafel, een Doctor voeld haar de Pols, de Man, achter haar, luistert met een nieuwsgierige houding en lachgende tronie na de uitspraak van den Medicus, leunende met zijn Arm over den Stoel der Vrouw, en met den Hoed in zijne hand. Alles is aartig geördineerd en goed geschilderd | *Mat:* op paneel *Size:* hoog 11 ½, breed 14 ½ duim	Maria Stategaart	(Sold) fl 35 J Groen
1802/07/27	AKHRK	0004	*Jan Steen* | Men ziet in dit bevallig Chirurgijns Winkeltje een Lijder zitten, welke een gezwel agter zijn Oor heeft, de Chirurgijn achter hem houd met de linke hand het Hoofd vast, en heeft een groot Mes in zijn rechte hand, waar mede hij in de Wond snijd; dat de Man door de pijn in een zeer geweldige beweeging brengt: een mededogende Vrouw voegt haare handen te zaamen, en kijkt aandachtig wat de Meester verrigt, terwijl een ander van achter de deur inkoomt. De hartstochten zijn Meesterlijk uitgedrukt en geschilderd | *Mat:* op paneel *Size:* hoog 12, breed 14 duim	Maria Stategaart	(Sold) fl 21 J Groen
1802/08/24	LNDLS	0060	*J. Steen* | In een Barbiers Winkel wordt een Man door den Meester een pleister op zijn been gelegd, terwijl hij door den Knecht wordt vastgehouden, daar agter een Grijsäart die een Vrouw liefkoost en een bundel geld aanbiedt. Grappig verbeeld | *Mat:* op paneel *Size:* hoog 11, breed 9 ½ duimen	Leonardus Bouman [or others]	(Unknown) fl 41
1802/09/06	AMSCH	0103	*J. Steen* | Deeze Commique Ordenantie verbeeld in een binnenhuis verscheide huislieden, waarvan 'er een, een biervat 't welk op zyn einde loopt, opligt, terwyl een Meisje het laatste drupje in een pot opvangt, en verder geestig bywerk; alles meesterlyk | *Mat:* op doek *Size:* hoog 34, breed 40 duim	D	(Sold) fl 230 Hodges
1802/09/06	AMSCH	0104	*J. Steen* | Een bevallig Vrouwtje op haar arm leggende te slaapen, terwyl een Heer agter haar zittende, tabaksrook toeblaasd; verder een Meisje met een roemer wyn, een hond, en verder bywerk; delicaat | *Mat:* op paneel *Size:* hoog 15, breed 12 duim	B	(Sold) fl 40 van Iperen
1802/09/18	RMDRS	0035	*J. Steen* | Een Krygsman by een galant Meisje, en verder Stoffagie | *Annots:* Slegte Copie (MB) *Size:* hoog 15 ½, breed 13 ½ duim	Casper de Haas	(Unknown) fl 13
1802/09/18	RMDRS	0047	*J. Steen* | Een Boere Binnehuis, waarin een Boerin een Pyp stopt, en nog eenige Boeren, gemerkt J. Steen | *Inscr:* J. Steen (signed)	Casper de Haas	(Unknown) fl 6:15
1802/09/21	UTHDG	0078	*J. Steen* | Een jeugdig Geneesheer beziet grimlagchende het Water van een zieke jonge Dame, welkers bejaarde Dienstmaagd het resultaat afwacht, fraaij van expressie, gem. J. Steen | *Size:* hoog 27 ½, breed 23 ½ duimen *Inscr:* J. Steen (signed)		(Bought In) fl 22
1802/09/21	UTHDG	0079	*J. Steen* | Een bejaard Doctor voelende de Pols eener zieke Dame, zittende in een vertrek met veel bijwerk. Helder geschildert en gemerkt als de voorgaande [J. Steen] | *Mat:* op doek *Size:* hoog 23, breed 19 duimen *Inscr:* J. Steen (signed)		(Sold) fl 35 Pruijsner Amst
1802/09/29	AMSCH	0049	*Jan Steen* | Een Visch-markt, hoog 17, breed 22 duim. Doek. Een Gezigt op de Visch-markt te Leyden, op het ogenblik van de grootste levendigheid; klugtig en geestig verbeeld, van een Aangenaam zonagtig Coloriet, en van het delicaatst en uitvoerigst Penceel van deezen Meester [Cet artiste ingenieux & fertile à rendre des scènes comiques n'a pas manqué dans ce Tableau de s'y exercer, d'un Pinceau aussi facile que délicat & vrai. Nous y voions la Poissonnerie de la Ville de Leyden en Hollande, ou l'on compte plus de soixante figures, occupées différemment. Nous pouvons assurer que ce Tableau est une des compositions les plus agréables de son Auteur, tels qu'on les désire de lui & qui sont râres surtout quand elles sont comme celle-ci d'une couleur Brillante.] | *Mat:* op doek *Size:* hoog 17, breed 22 duim	[Labouchere?]	(Sold) fl 90 van Iperen
1802/09/29	AMSCH	0050	*J. Steen* | Een Binnenhuis. Hoog 16 ½, breed 13 duim. Paneel. In een Gemeubileerde Kamer, zit een bevallige jonge Dame, in geel en blauw satyne kleeding, voor een Clavercimbaal, als op het zelve speelende; daar nevens staat de Leermeester, als met aandagt luisterende; verder door de openstaande Deur, ziet men een Bediende, met een Guitard in de handen, de Trap afkoomende uit een ander vertrek; de natuurlyke Caracters zyn geestig verbeeld, en het aangenaam coloriet, en uitvoerige Penceel-behandling, stellen dit stuk onder een der beste en verdienstigsten van deezen Meester [Vue dans un appartement, ou est representé une Femme gentille occupée devant son clavecin, son vetement est en satin jaune et bleu ; à son côté se tient le maitre de musique en attitude attentive, et vers le fond l'on voit descendre un valet avec une guitarre à la main. La verité de la representation, le charme de la couleur et la delicatesse de pinceau en forment un ensemble des plus meritans.] | *Mat:* op paneel *Size:* hoog 16 ½, breed 13 duim *Loc:* London, England, UK. National Gallery. (856)	D	(Sold) fl 676 I^{c} Smit
1803/04/18	HGBAK	0022	*Jan Steen* | Een origineel Stuk, verbeeldende een Schoolmeester met eenige Scholieren, zeer natuurlyk en kragtig door Jan Steen, hoog 26, breed 22 ½ duim, op doek, zwarte lyst [Schilderyen in Olyverf] | *Mat:* in olyverf op doek *Size:* hoog 26 breed 22 ½ duim *Notes:* The bracketed information in the title appears above lot 1 and refers to lots 1 to 48.	Johan Pieter Reigersman [or others]	(Unknown)

1803/04/20	AMSCH	0067	*Steen. (J.)* | Dit bevallig Schildery verbeeld een Boere Bruiloft, in het midden ziet men twee paar Huislieden luchtig danssen voor de Fiool, terwyl ter rechterzyde de Bruiloftsgasten zich met Eeten en Drinken vermaken, ter linkerzyde ziet men een Trap naar een Opkamer, schynende de Meid de Waterpot van een Spyker te lichten, om die op die Kamer te brengen, een slapende Jongen zit op de Trap, daar neevens staat een Man in Spaansche kleeding, met een zilvere Kan in zyn hand, op de voorgrond legt een slapend Hondje. Dit Stuk van meer als twintig beelden, is fraay van Hartstogten, het Coloriet overschoon, en de behandeling alleruitvoerigst [Ce charment tableau a pour sujet l'interieur d'une ferme ou l'on fêtoye une noce : plus de vingt figures animées sont occupées dans ce morceau de caractère. Vers la droite au devant du tableau est une table couverte, où s'amusent les convives les plus distingués. Le milieu est occupé par un rondeau de danseurs au son du violon. La gauche designe l'entrée d'une autre pièce, ou est assis un jeune homme ivre ; près de lui est une second, debout, tenant une aiguire d'argent, & une servante detachant un pot de nuit accroché : d'autres figures & un joli chien couché sur le devant terminent cette composition joviale. On peut mettre ce tableau au rang des meilleurs ouvrages de ce Peintre vraiment original : L'expression vraye de chaque acteur, la bonne disposition, l'effet, l'harmonie de sa couleur, & la meilleure maniere de toucher de J. Steen font regrètter qu'un morceau de ce mérite ait èu l'accident d'une fente, d'ailleurs susceptible d'etre mieux reparée.] | *Mat:* op paneel *Size:* hoog 18, breed 24 duim *Loc:* Antwerpen, Belgique. Koninklijk Museum voor Schone Kunsten. (339)	Maria Magdalena van Sluypwyk, gravinne van Moens	(Sold) fl 710 Hodges
1803/06/20	AMSCH	0048	*J. Steen* | Een Naaystertje, schynende door een teugje genomen te hebben in de slaap gevallen te zyn, op de Tafel legt haar Naaywerk, geestig behandeld door J. Steen, op Paneel | *Mat:* op paneel *Size:* hoog 14, breed 12 duim	Roos [for] C	(Sold) fl 6 V d Vinne
1803/07/18	AMSCH	0045	*Steen. (Jan)* | Dit uitmuntend Kunstjuweel kan voor een der beste van deezen Meester gehouden worden, in het midden van een Binnenvertrek zit een Musikant op de Phiool te speelen, een jong Vrouwtje spreekt hem laggende aan, leunende op een Tafel met een Kleed gedekt, waaraan een Dame en twee Heeren zitten op de Kaart te speelen, waarna een vierde staat te kyken, ter linkerzyde by de Schoorsteen zit den Schilder met zyn Vrouw, daar nevens een oude Vrouw bezig zynbe [sic] Koeken te bakken, in het verschiet nog twee Boeren, waarvan de eene beschonken is. Op de Tafel legt een wit Serviet [sic], op de voorgrond een Hond, Tinne Kan en Vuurtest; voorts een menigte ander Huisraad door het geheele Vertrek, welke dit stuk zeer ryk van Ordonantie maaken en verders vercieren; het ligt en bruin is allerbevalligst, en de behandeling als G. Metzu [Ce morceau capital peut être compté parmi les productions des plus intéressantes de ce maitre. Au milieu d'une chambre est assis un joueur de violon fixant d'un oeuil avide une jeune femme qui lui sourit : elle porte un joli costume à l'ancienne, ayant une coëffe blanche sur sa tête, & s'appuye sur la table couverte d'un tapis. A cette table sont assis deux hommes & une femme jouant aux cartes, & un quatrième est debout qui les examine. A la cheminée vèrs la gauche est un gros personnage qui est le peintre lui-même avec sa femme & une vielle cuisant des gateaux. Près des fenêtres en face, est un homme en joie qui paroit un peu enyvré tenant le pot à bierre en air tandis qu'un autre mecontent & jaloux tourne le dos pour s'en aller. Les accessoires ne contribuent pas moins à embellir cette scène véridique & expressive ; au fond de la chambre est un lit ; au devant un joli chien ; sur la table est un drap blanc, une assiette & plusieurs autres objets. Rien de plus caractérisé n'est sorti des mains de cet homme original, on lit distinctement sur la figure & dans le maintien de chacun des personnages les passions differentes dont ils sont animés. Ce tableau marquant, d'une composition bien entendue produit un bel effet de lumiere ; il est soigné & d'une conservation très parfaite.] | *Mat:* op doek *Size:* hoog 32, breed 27 duim *Loc:* London, England, UK. Royal Collection (Buckingham Palace) (1338)	Maria Theresia Andrioli	(Sold) fl 1000 Pruijssenaar
1803/07/18	AMSCH	0046	*Steen. (Jan)* | Op de Binnenplaats van een Boeren Dorp ziet men eenige Jongens en Meisjes bezig een St. Martens Vuurtje te stooken, een oude Vrouw met een Kind aan de hand, een Meisje met een klein Kind op de arm, en een Boer in een gemakkelyke houding op een Bank zittende, zien alles met vermaak aan, het ligt van het vuur is brillant, de hartstogten geestig, zoo ook de schildering [Audevant de quelques maisons communes l'on voit un grand feu allumé. Une troupe d'enfans du voisinage sont autour à se divertir à l'occasion de la St. Martin ; une vielle en fait approcher un qui semble peureux, & une servante en tient un autre sur le bras. A sa porte est assi [sic] un homme observant la joie & la femme rentre chez elle. Cette represention [sic] vraye est legerement traitée ; elle donne une nouvelle preuve de la variété & de l'originalité du génie de son auteur pour peindre des scènes semblables, & avec autant de caractère.] | *Mat:* op doek [sur bois] *Size:* hoog 24, breed 20 duim *Notes:* The materials differ in the Dutch and French editions of the catalogue.	Maria Theresia Andrioli	(Sold) fl 108 Coclers
1803/08/17	AMSCH	0075	*Steen. (J.)* | In een Huismans Wooning ziet men een Vegtparty tusschen twee Mannen en twee Vrouwen, de omstanders zyn alle aan 't schreeuwen, agterwaarts houd een Vrouw met kragt de Deur toe, terwyl een ander de Wafelen bergt, en een Boer met verwondering de trap	Anna Catharina Putman	(Bought In) fl 240

			afkomt en naar dat Schouwspel ziet, de Hartetogten [sic] zyn in dit stuk byzonder waargenomen, en is voorts van een uitvoerige behandeling en van zyne beste schildering | *Mat:* op paneel *Size:* hoog 15, breed 19 duim		
1803/08/17	AMSCH	0076	*Steen. (J.)* | In een Binnevertrek legt een Vrouw met een bond Jakje te slapen, op haar regter arm op een Tafel, agter haar zit een Heer met een Pyp in zyn Hand, schynende de Rook in haar Gezicht te blazen, daar een andere Vrouw naar staat te kyken, een Hond en verder Bywerk maken dit stukje bevallig, en is als het voorgaande uitgevoerd | *Mat:* op paneel *Size:* hoog 15, breed 12 ½ duim	Anna Catharina Putman	(Sold) fl 40:10 W Reijers
1803/08/24	HGKAN	0041	*J. Steen* | Een Binnehuis op de voorgrond ziet men twee lieden op het verkeerbord speelen, een derde schynt met hun in gesprek te zyn, terwyl een ander lugtig drinkt, in het verschiet ziet men een Vrouw by de haard die een Pyp in de mond heeft, dit stuk is fraay van Tekening, kragtig van Coloriet, en Meesterlyk gepenseelt | *Size:* hoog 16, breet 20 duim	[Teissier] [or others]	(Sold) fl 50 Kan
1803/12/12	AMSCH	0081	*J. Steen* | Dit capitaale Schildery verbeeld het bedorven Huishouden, in het midden van een gemeubileerde Kamer, staat een Tafel met een Tapyt en wit Kleed gedekt, waarop verscheiden Eten geplaatst is, nevens dezelve zit Jan Steen en zyn Vrouw rustig te slapen, terwyl de Hond van de Pasty eet; ter zyde een Kind dat in Moeders zak tast, een ander die met een stuk Geld weggaat, en een derde in de Kinderstoel zittende, staat met een Strykstok na een Glazen Fluit, terwyl de Kat na de Canary-Vogel springt, en een Aap Papieren verscheurt, de Meid en Knegt steelen de Wyn; alles geestig geordoneerd en delicaat gepenceeld | *Mat:* op doek *Size:* hoog 33, breed 39 duim	Arnoud de Lange	(Sold) fl 1405 W Reijers
1803/12/12	AMSCH	0082	*J. Steen* | Een Landschap ryk gestoffeerd, op de voorgrond ziet men Boeren Keegelen, waar bij een Quaker die dit spel zeer aandachtig beschouwd, ter linker zyde op een Heuvel ook eenige Landlieden, welke hun attentie op dit spel vestigen, en zig met roken en drinken vermaaken, verders Ryzigers en wandelende Persoonen; de caracters zyn geestig en de Ordonantie bevallig en meesterlyk gepenceeld | *Mat:* op paneel *Size:* hoog 26, breed 33 duim	Arnoud de Lange	(Bought In) fl 251
1803/12/12	AMSCH	0083	*J. Steen* | In een Boere Binnenhuis ziet men twee Boeren, en een Boerin zich met rooken en drinken verlustigen, voorts een menigte bywerk, behandeld als de voorgaande | *Mat:* op doek *Size:* hoog 14, breed 11 duim	V[inkeles?]	(Sold) fl 6:5 Gruiter
1803/12/12	AMSCH	0084	*J. Steen* | In een Binnenhuis ziet men eenige Huislieden in het Verkeerbord speelen; zeer geestig gepenceeld | *Mat:* op doek	B	(Sold) fl 65 Theengs
1804/02/27	AMSCH	0098	*Steen. (J.)* | Deeze ryke Ordonantie steld voor, de Edelmoedigheid van Scipio; deeze beruchten Veldheer staat op zyn Throon, verzeld van Lyfwacht en Hovelingen, voor hem ligt op een Knie de Minnaar welke de bevallige Bruid in prachtig wit Zatyne Kleeding by de Hand houd, en aan hem weder als Minnaar terug gegeeven wordt; verders ziet men Krygslieden te Paard en te Voet, en op den voorgrond een meenigte van Goude en Zilvere kostbaarheeden, enz. alles is verbeeld in een Landschap, by de ingang van een prachtig Paleis; en is krachtig en meesterlyk in de trant van Metzu, gepenceeld | *Mat:* op paneel *Size:* hoog 35, breed 57 duim	R[oos]	(Bought In) fl 285
1804/02/27	AMSCH	0098a	*Steen. (J.)* | In een Binnehuis, ziet men eenige Huislieden in 't Verkeerbord speelen; geestig geordoneerd en schoon gepenceeld	C	(Withdrawn)
1804/04/28	LNDLS	0018	*J. Steen* | Een Gezelschap van Kooplieden en Kleinodien, in een binnenvertrek, kragtig geschildert, gemerkt J. Steen, op doek | *Mat:* op doek *Size:* hoog 32, breed 37 duim *Inscr:* J. Steen (signed)	[Abraham Delfos] [or others]	(Bought In) fl 3:10
1804/05/07	AMSCH	0147	*Steen. (J.)* | In een Binnenhuis zitten eenige Huislieden te spelen en te roken, waarnaar een Boerin staat te kyken, op de voorgrond staat 'er een zyn pyp te stoppen; geestig behandeld | *Mat:* op paneel *Size:* hoog 17, breed 13 duim	Roos [for] A	(Sold) fl 99 Wed van Achtienhoven
1804/05/07	AMSCH	0148	*Steen. (J.)* | Een Strandgezicht, gestoffeerd met verscheide Visschers, die hunne Visschen aan twee Heeren en een Dame ter verkoop aanbieden, waarby eenige Kinderen, in 't verschiet een ruime Zee met verscheiden Scheepen; meesterlyk en fraay geschilderd | *Mat:* op doek *Size:* hoog 20, breed 28 duim	Y[ver] [for] JJ	(Sold) fl 82 Kooy
1804/05/07	AMSCH	0149	*Steen. (J.)* | Twee stuks, in het eene legt een bevallig Vrouwtje met een bond Jakje op de Tafel te slapen, terwyl een Heer agter haar de rook van zyn pyp in haar gezigt blaast, en ander bywerk, in de wederga word een Dame door een Heer een Oester aangeboden, die door een Man en Vrouw opgemaakt worden; beiden zyn ze van een delicate schildering | *Size:* Ieder hoog 16, breed 13 duim *Loc:* London, England, UK. National Gallery. (2559) (?) second painting only	R[oos]	(Sold) fl 39 Pruissenaar
1804/05/07	AMSCH	0150	*Steen. (J.)* | In een Dorp ziet men een Jonge met een Rommelpot, een Meisje met een Wafel, en agter dezelven een Zottin met een Mandje op haar hoofd, een Wafelyzer in de eene en een Koekepan in de andere hand; geestig en meesterlyk gepenceeld | *Mat:* op doek *Size:* hoog 25, breed 20 duim	Roos [for] A	(Sold) fl 85 Coclers
1804/05/07	AMSCH	0151	*Steen. (J.)* | Een Binnehuis met een vrolyke Gezelschap, alle in Comique Actien; meesterlyk geschilderd | *Mat:* op doek *Size:* hoog 23, breed 27 duim	Y[ver] [for] W	(Bought In) fl 6

1804/07/25	AMSCH	0072	*Steen. (J.)* | In een capitaal Dorpgezicht, met verscheide Woningen, vol gewoel van een meenigte Lieden zo Mans als Vrouwen en Kinderen, die vrolyk Kermis schynen te houden, ter rechter zyde voor een Herberg ziet men verschyden Boeren en Boerinnen zig met Dansen en Liefkoozen vermaken; twee Rysigers te Paard schynen zig te ververschen; ter linker zyde vertoont zig een Rivier, met verschillende Vaartuigen, verder ziet men Kerk en Tooren, Kraamen, Kwakzalvers, en een bevallig verschiet met Zylende Scheepen; de geestige caracters van deeze Kermis Gasten, zyn natuurlyk verbeeld, en meesterlyk van penceel behandeling | *Mat:* op doek *Size:* hoog 33, breed 38 duim		(Sold) fl 190 C S Roos
1804/07/25	AMSCH	0073	*Steen. (J.)* | In een Boeren Binnenhuis, of Chirugyns Winkel, ziet men een Huisman, die een Operatie aan zyn Been ondergaat, zyn Gelaat en houding geeft te kennen dat hy veele pynen lyd, zyn Vrouw staat nevens hem met gevouwen Handen, terwyl de Heelmeester dit werk zeer bedaard schynt te verrigten; alles is uitvoerig, fix en meesterlyk gepenceeld | *Mat:* op paneel *Size:* hoog 14 ½, breed 11 ½ duim		(Sold) fl 150 C S Roos
1804/07/25	DLGRO	0063	*Jan Steen* | Een Ovaal stukje, verbeeldende een Boere Herberg, waarvoor eenige Boeren en Boerinnen danssen, op de voorgrond staat 'er een op een Ton, op den Doedelzak te speelen, een ander zit zyn Pyp te rooken, fraai geschilderd | *Mat:* op paneel *Fmt:* ovaal *Size:* hoog 13, breed 10 ½ duim	Mr Franc van der Burch Wz.	(Unknown)
1804/08/08	AMSCH	0173	*J. Steen* | In een Boeren Binnenhuis ziet men een bevallig Vrouwtje op een Bank zitten, door een oud Huisman geannimeerd wordende tot drinken, in het verschiet een slapende Boer and ander Bywerk; van de Metzu-achtige behandeling, op Doek | *Mat:* op doek *Size:* hoog 14, br. 8 duim	Roos a	(Bought In) fl 50
1804/08/08	AMSCH	0174	*J. Steen* | Voor een Buitenhuis met een Wyngaardrank bewasschen, ziet men voor een Tafel zitten een Boer en een bevallige Vrouw, schynende een Roemer Wyn te drinken, verders eenig Geboomte; fraai en uitvoerig gepenceeld | *Mat:* op paneel *Size:* hoog 12 ½, br. 10 duim	Vink[eles] [for] W	(Bought In) fl 41
1804/10/16	DLOND	0212	*Jan Steen* | Een Binnenvertrek, waarin een groot Gezelschap zich vermaakt, ter gelegenheid van een Bruiloft, zynde de Bruid gekroond en veinzende bedroeft te zyn. L'intérieur, d'une Maison, dans laquelle une grande Compagnie se rejoit [sic] autour d'une Fiancée. Cette derniere brille avec une Couronne, tandis qu'elle feigne d'être contristée | *Mat:* op paneel *Size:* hoog 18, breed 16		(Sold) fl 245 Berkhaut [?]
1804/10/16	DLOND	0213	*Jan Steen* | Een Man die op de fluit speelt, een ander die zyne voeten wascht; ene Vrouw die slaapt, en ene andere die Wyn schenkt. Un Homme qui joue de la flute, un autre lave ses pieds; une Femme s'endort, & une autre verse du Vin | *Mat:* op paneel *Size:* hoog 17, breed 14		(Sold) fl 95 O D Wyngaert
1804/10/16	DLOND	0213a	*Jan Steen* | Een Boeren Schoolmeester, dronken zynde, die door verscheiden bespot wordt. Un Maitre d'Ecole de Village, duquel on se joue à cause de son yvresse, tandis qu'il est endormi | *Size:* hoog 14, breed 18		(Sold) fl 600 o d Wyngaert
1805/07/03	AMSCH	0042	*Steen. (J.)* | In een Boere Binnenhuis, ziet men twee Huislieden zich met het verkeerbord en drinken vermaken, een bevallige Vrouw ziet over de leuning van een stoel leggende dit spel aan; een Boer houd uit 't vengster leggende, aan 't einde van het Vertrek, een praatje met een Vrouw die op straat staat; alles geestig voorgesteld, en als Metzu behandeld | *Mat:* op paneel *Size:* hoog 15, breed 13 duim	R[oos]	(Sold) fl 111 Wed Achtienhoven
1805/07/03	AMSCH	0139	*J. Steen* | Deeze Comique Ordinantie verbeeld, voor een Buitenhuis een zittende vrolyke bedaagde Musicant, in aloude Kleeding, houdende een Fiool in de eene, en een Pyp in de andere hand, naast hem zit een jonge Vrouw, houden een Naaikussen, met een linne Doek op de Schoot, en verder een oude Matroone, die hy al lagchende beschouwd; dit stuk is geestig geordineert en bevallig gepenceeld | *Mat:* op paneel *Size:* hoog 15, breed 19 duim	R[oos]	(Sold) fl 150 Coclers
1805/07/03	AMSCH	0140	*J. Steen* | Op de Binneplaats van een Boeren Herberg ziet men eenige Boeren met den Bal door de Ring gooijen, en verdere Aanschouwers; zynde een een aangenaam onderwerp, geestig behandeld op Paneel | *Mat:* op paneel *Size:* hoog 19, breed 22 duim	R[oos]	(Sold) fl 95 L Pakker
1805/07/10	AMSCH	0126	*J. Steen* | In een verwulfde Kelder, ziet men een Jonge met een Eend en een Meisje met een Y in de hand, achter dezelve een oud Man, en in 't verschiet twee jonge Lieden die elkander kussen, terzyde ligt een doode Haan, Wortelen and ander Keukengereedschap; uitvoerig op Paneel | *Mat:* op paneel *Size:* hoog 22, breed 18 duim	Y[ver]	(Sold) fl 145 Lafontaine
1805/07/10	AMSCH	0127	*J. Steen* | Een Ziekekamer, alwaar een Notaris bézig is een Testament te schryven, voor een zieke Vrouw welke op 't Bed legt, en verder bywerk; lugtig doch meesterlyk op Doek | *Mat:* op doek *Size:* hoog 23, breed 32 duim	V[inkeles] [for] G	(Sold) fl 1:10 van Iperen
805/07/10	AMSCH	0128	*J. Steen* | In een Binnevertrek, ziet men een gezelschap van vrolyke Lieden, welke zich op verschillende wyzen vermaaken; meede als de voorgaande | *Mat:* op doek *Size:* hoog 22, breed 30 duim	V[inkeles] [for] G	(Sold) fl 3:15 van Iperen
805/07/10	AMSCH	0129	*J. Steen* | In een Boerewoning ziet men een oud Man, zittende aan een Tafel goud te weegen, en verder bywerk; breed en fiks op Paneel | *Mat:* op paneel *Size:* hoog 10, breed 18 duim	V[inkeles] [for] M	(Bought In) fl 9:10

1805/10/09	HGBSM	0003	*J. Steen* | Een stuk verbeeldende de historie van de afgezanten der Samniten, aan Dentatus burgemeester van Romen, die hun den vreede bezorgd had, ryk van ordonnantie en fraay geschildert | *Mat:* op paneel *Size:* hoog 23, breet 31 ½ duim	T H van Willigen [or others]	(Sold) fl 45 Ph Meij
1806/06/07	RMHSN	0041	*J. Steen* | Een Boeren Dansparty met Musikanten voor een Buitenhuis, door J. Steen, Ovaal op Paneel | *Mat:* op paneel *Fmt:* ovaal	A E K L	(Unknown) fl 34
1806/08/13	AMSCH	0171	*Steen. (J.)* | In een Binnehuis ziet men een oud Man, zittende voor een Tafel goud te weegen, en verder bywerk; caracteristiek en delicaat van schildering | *Mat:* op paneel *Size:* hoog 10, breed 8 duim	Vinkeles [for] D	(Sold) fl 31 Richters
1806/08/20	HGBSM	0004	*Jan Steen* | De twee Emausgangers aan een tafel zittende en Christus die als het waare in een schim verdwijnt; terwijl een Emausganger biddende en den anderen in een diepe peinzende houding zit, verders twee bediendens Eetwaaren aanbrengende, alle deze vier beelden schoon en aangenaam van Coloriet, maar vooral de twee Emausgangers die verrukkelijk zijn, en waar in de meester zich overtroffen heeft; te meer het een onderwerp was, geheel vreemd aan zijn vernuftig penceel en nimmer of zelden door hem behandelt. In dit stuk heerscht eene aangenaame harmonie die den aanschouwer wegvoert en eene waare christelijke nadenking opleverdt | *Mat:* op doek *Size:* hoog 52, breed 41 duim *Loc:* Amsterdam, Nederland. Rijksmuseum. (A 1932)	Macalester Loup [or others]	(Sold) fl 185 Schouman
1806/08/20	HGBSM	0018	*Jan Steen* | Een Boeren binnenhuis, alwaar eene oude vrouw zit een kind te ontkleden, verders veel bijwerk, gemerkt J. Steen | *Mat:* op paneel *Size:* hoog 15 ½, breed 13 ½ duim *Inscr:* J. Steen (signed)	Macalester Loup [or others]	(Sold) fl 54 Zwartsman
1806/08/20	HGBSM	0196	*J. Steen* | Een Wintergezicht daar zij zig vermaaken met Kolven op het IJs, en verder Schaatsrijders, &c. alles zeer fix en natuurlijk | *Mat:* op paneel *Size:* hoog 14, breed 13 duim	Macalester Loup [or others]	(Sold) fl 59 Lafontaine
1807/04/00	LNDLS	0046	*J. Steen* | Een gezelschap van Kooplieden, in een binnenvertrek gem. J. Steen | *Inscr:* J. Steen (signed)	[Abraham Delfos] [or others]	(Unknown)
1807/06/10	HGBSM	0046	*J. Steen* | Een gezelschap van Kooplieden, in een binnenvertrek gem. J. Steen | *Inscr:* J. Steen (signed)	Abraham Delfos [or others]	(Sold) fl 3 v Giese
1807/08/26	AMSCH	0196	*J. Steen* | Deze grappige Ordonnantie verbeeld in een Binnenvertrek een Driekonings-Avond Party: by een gedekte Tafel zit eene Boerin, met een Wynkan in de hand en andere vrolyke Lieden. De Koning zit op een Vat, leunende tegen de Tafel, en schynt lustig zyn Roemer te ledigen, verder een Musikant, op de Rooster spelende, en andere Gasten die zich vermaken; alles is geestig en meesterlyk geschilderd | *Mat:* op paneel *Size:* hoog 9, breed 12 duim *Loc:* Bruxelles, Belgique. Musées royaux des Beaux-Arts. (1458)	Roos [for] A	(Sold) fl 105 Spruit
1807/08/26	AMSCH	0197	*J. Steen* | Twee stuks Binnenhuizen met vrolyke Boeren, welke Caresseeren, danssen en smullen; geestig geordonneerd en delicaat gepenceeld | *Mat:* op paneel *Size:* hoog 8, breed 9 duim	Roos	(Sold) fl 71:10 van Iperen
1808/04/26	GDAN	0142	*Steen (Jan)* | Een uitmuntend Schilderij, zijnde de tentoonstelling van Christus, waar Pilatus op den Rechterstoel gezeten is, en zegt, geen schuld in hem te vinden, het Volk willende te vreden stellen, dan alles te vergeefs, terwijl eene der Dienstknegten hem voornemens is in 't gezigt te slaan, men ziet in alle de gezigten de uitdrukkingen der haat, zeer mooij geschilderd | *Size:* hoog 48, breed 47 ½ duim	G H Fortuyn	(Unknown)
1808/04/26	GDAN	0143	*Steen (Jan)* | Een Binnenhuisje met eenige Personen | *Mat:* op paneel *Size:* hoog 6 ½, breed 5 duim	G H Fortuyn	(Unknown)
1808/04/26	GDAN	0144	*Steen (Jan)* | Een dito Binnenhuisje met een vrolijk Gezelschap, wel geschilderd | *Size:* hoog 51, breed 25 ½ duim *Notes:* It is unclear what "dito" refers to in the title.	G H Fortuyn	(Unknown)
1808/04/26	GDAN	0145	*Steen (Jan)* | Een fraai Wintergezigt, met een meenigte Schaatsenrijders en Sleeden, in 't verschiet een Boeren Dorp en eenige Boere Wooningen, vol gewoel, en bijzonder voor dezen Meester, alles konstig en kragtig gepenseeld | *Size:* hoog 15 ½, breed 21 duim	G H Fortuyn	(Unknown)
1808/04/26	GDAN	0146	*Steen (Jan)* | Een vrolijk Boertje, houdende in de eene hand een brandende Pijp, en de andere eene Kan, waar uit hij schijnt te willen drinken, op een Tafel ziet men een test met Vuur staan om zijn Pyp aan op te steken, en in 't verschiet een brandend Vuur, met bijwerk | *Mat:* op paneel *Size:* hoog 11 ½, breed 10 duim	G H Fortuyn	(Unknown)
1808/04/26	GDAN	0147	*Steen (Jan)* | Een gemeubileerd Binnenhuis, waar in een Ledikant, voor hetzelve zit een rokende Heer die eene slapende Vrouw, op de Tafel leunende, de rook van agteren in de nek blaast, zijnde het Vrouwtje gekleed in een Jakje met een witbonte rant, terwijl komt eene oude Dienstmaagd met een Glas Brandewijn aandragen, om den Heer te presenteeren, voor 't opbreken der Oesters die hij schijnt genuttigd te hebben, daar men een bak met ledige Oesterschulpen op een tafel met een rood Kleed ziet staan, een mooije Hond is op de grond ruikende, alles meesteragtig en geestig geschilderd | companion to lot 148 *Size:* hoog 14, breed 11 ½ duim	G H Fortuyn	(Unknown)
1808/04/26	GDAN	0148	*Steen (Jan)* | Een dito [gemeubileerd Binnenhuis] tot een wederga, waar in Jan Steen zelve staat, die van agteren aan zijn Vrouw een ledige Oesterschelp aanbied, waar over zij onvergenoegd schijnt, en die refuseerd aan te nemen, terwyl eene der Personen bezig is de Oesters	G H Fortuyn	(Unknown)

open te maken, 't welk door een ander bezien wordt, voorts nog een Man en Vrouw die over een en ander discoureeren, alles fiks en geestig geschildert | companion to lot 147 *Size:* hoog 14, breed 11 ½ duim *Loc:* London, England, UK. National Gallery. (2559) (?) second painting only

1808/05/17 LNAN 0002

Jan Steen | Een voornaam Schilderij, op den voorgrond vol vrolijk en ander volk, te veel om dezelve te beschrijven, en waar van de kenner en beschouwer de uitlegging maken kan; de actien en passien der tronien, zijn zeer geestig verbeeldend en zinspeelende op woelige tijden, alles voor een Buitenhuis, waar voor een uithangbord met de woorden: Het Misverstand, enz.; vrolijk en helder van kleur, en een der voornaamste Schilderijen | *Mat:* op doek *Size:* hoog 41, breed 65 duim

(Sold) fl 510 Nieuwenhuis

1808/05/17 LNAN 0007

Jan Steen | In een binnen vertrek staat een Doctor, aan een tafel een recept te schrijven, voor een meisje die achter hem op een ledikant ligt; nevens de tafel staat een lagchende jonge met een klisteer spuit in zijne handen, benevens eene vrouw en man, die naar het recept schijnen te wachten; op den voorgrond ligt een papier waar op geschreven staat: *Hier baat geen Medicijn, Want het is Minnepijn.* van de beste soort van schildering en teekening | *Mat:* op paneel *Size:* hoog 22, breed 18 duim *Loc:* Rotterdam, Nederland. Museum Boymans-van Beuningen. (vdV 76)

(Sold) fl 310 MVN[oort]

1808/05/17 LNAN 0010

Jan Steen | Een historiëel Schilderij, vol beelden, verbeeldende den verradelijken Schoolmeester van Falerii, welke op bevel van den Romeinsche Veldheer Camillus, door zijne Scholieren met geesselslagen stadwaards wordt gedreven, vol gewoel | *Mat:* op doek *Size:* hoog 41, breed 56 duim

(Sold) fl 100 Thomasse

1808/06/06 RMRIJ 0118

Steen. (Jan) | In eene Boeren Herberg vertoonen zich vele drinkende en rookende Boeren. Op den voorgrond ziet men een gevallen Boer, die door eene Boerin wordt vastgehouden, terwijl hij, in eene woedende houding, zijne tegenpartij eene Bierkan naar het hoofd schijnt te willen werpen; deze trekt, in eene alderwoedendste houding, zijn Zijdgeweer, doch wordt door eene jonge Boerin met kracht tegengehouden. Bij de tafel staat een Speelman. Verder nog een paar vechtende Boeren. Op den voorgrond liggen Kaarten, Bierkan, Bezem, Vuurtest, Schijven uit een Verkeerbord, enz. In 't midden van 't vertrek hangt eene Kroon met Wijngaardbladeren. Op den rand leest men Prov. Cap. 20. vs. 1. Dit stuk uitmuntend in licht en bruin, in teekening en breede wijze van Schildering, en bijzonder door de schoone uitdrukking der hartstogten van de vechtende en vrolijke Boeren, maakt hetzelve tot een der kapitaalste van dezen met regt beroemden Meester [L'Intérieur d'un Cabaret de Village, où plusieurs Paysans sont en ribotte. Sur le devant, un d'eux renversé et retenu par une Paysanne paroit vonloir [sic] jetter avec fureur une Cruche à la tête de son adversaire, qui, mordant les lêvres et tout pâle de colère, veut tirer son Coutelas, une jeune Paysanne, l'en Empêche. Auprés d'une table, un Paysan dans une attitude grottesque et monté sur un Banc, joue du violon. Deux Rustres se battent à coups de poing à côté de lui. tandis que d'autres les regardent en fumant tranquillement leurs pipes, et s'amusent de toute cette farce. On voit pêle-mêle des cartes, un trictrac, une Cruche, un Pot à Bière, et d'autres accessoires. Une Couronne de bois entourée de feuilles de Vigne, décore le haute, et on lit on à L'Entour : Prov. Chap. 20. vs. I. Le dessin, les passions, l'harmonie, et la manière savante et hardie, joints au ton vrai et Vigoureux, font placer ce Morceau au rang des Meilleures Productions de ce Célébre Artiste] | *Annots:* verk J. v. Velden, Amst. 3 Dec 1781 (f 35.10) (RMA I) *Mat:* op doek *Size:* Hoog 25 ¾, en breed 33 duim

Gerrit van der Pot, Heer van Groeneveld

(Sold) fl 550 Coclers

1808/06/06 RMRIJ 0119

Steen. (Jan) | Een Bakker, tot den gordel in het hemd, legt zijn warm Brood en Koeken op het Pothuis neder; achter hem staat een bevallige op den Hoorn blazende Jongen. In 't kozijn vertoont zich eene Vrouw, een zoogenaamde Zottinnekoek in de hand houdende. Eenige Wijngaardsranken en Bladeren versieren het bovenste gedeelte van deze alleszins verdienstelijke en geestige Schilderij. De navolgende Particulariteiten van dit stuk zijn achter op hetzelve te vinden. "Dit is een familje stuckje de Backer is 't portret van Arend Oostwaard de Vrouw Catharina Keijserswaard de Jonge is gedaan naar een Jonge van Jan Steen deese Backer met zijn vrou hebben gewoond op den Rhijn 3 a 4 huijsen van de Vrouwebrugge, tussen de Vrouwe Steegh en Gasthuijs binnen Leijden. Is nu Januarij 1738 ruijm 70 Jaaren geleeden geschildert." Deze Schilderij is onlangs in Plaat gebragt door den verdienstelijken J. Bemme [Ce Tableau represente un Boulanger, qui sort de sa maison les bras nuds, et Etale des gateaux devant sa Boutique. Une jeune Garçon, qu est derrière lui, donne du Cor pour annoncer que le pain sort tout chaud du four, et une femme à le Croiseé montre un Biscuit Hollandais. Une Vigne qui couvre tout le devant de la maison jusqu'au premier Étage, ajoute à l'ensemble parfait de ce Morceau piquant et plein d'expression, dont il vient de paroitre une gravure par J. Bemme. N.B. On trouve les particularités de ce Tableau écrites sur le dos du Panneau] | *Annots:* Door vd Pot gezonden? P. Calkoen Wz. 10 Sept. 1781. Amst. J. Steen, de bakker en zijn vrouw fl 181 (RKDH I) *Mat:* op paneel *Size:* Hoog 14 ¼, en breed 11 ¾ duim *Inscr:* on the back: Dit is een familje stuckje de Backer is 't portret van Arend Oostwaard de Vrouw Catharina Keijferswaard de Jonge is gedaan naar een Jonge van Jan Steen deese Backer met zijn vrou hebben gewoond op den Rhijn 3 a 4 huijfen van de

Gerrit van der Pot, Heer van Groeneveld

(Sold) fl 703 Johs Eck en Zoon [for] le Roi

			Vrouwebrugge, tusfen de Vrouwe Steegh en Gasthuijs binnen Leijden. Is nu Januarij 1738 ruijm 70 Jaaren geleeden gefchildert *Loc:* Amsterdam, Nederland. Rijksmuseum. (A 390)		
1808/06/06	RMRIJ	0120	*Steen. (Jan)* | Eene zittende zwangere Vrouw met de handen op haren buik rustende en ziende met aandacht en vergenoegen op eenen Ring, die haar, door eenen daarbij staanden, bejaarden Man, vertoond wordt. Bezijden haar, eene Oude Matrone; komiek van kleeding en uitdrukking. Deze schoone en geestige Schilderij is breed, krachtig en meesterlijk uitgevoerd [Une femme assise, dont l'extérieur annonce la grossesse, fixe attentivement les yeux sur une Bague, qu'un vieux Barbon semble lui presenter. Auprès d'elle une vieille Matrone, dans un Costume grotesque, paroit, par sa mine, avoir, déviné le Mystére. Cette Scène comique est d'un effet piquant, et d'un ton soutenu] | *Annots:* Verk. Jac. v d Velden, Amst. 3 Dec 1781 (f 315.-) (RMA I) *Mat:* op paneel *Size:* Hoog 10, en breed 8 duim	Gerrit van der Pot, Heer van Groeneveld	(Sold) fl 91 van Yperen
1808/06/06	RMRIJ	0121	*Steen. (Jan)* | Eene bevallige Boeremeid, bezig met eene Tinnen Kan te schuren; omringd van verscheiden Huisraad, als Koperen Lantaarn, Schotels, enz. Uitvoerig en fraai geschilderd [L'Intérieur d'une Cuisine de Village, où une jeune Servante est occupée à Ecurer. On voit, auprès d'elle, un Pot d'étain, une Lanterne de cuivre, et d'autres ustensiles. Sa mine agaçante et expressive, et l'Ensemble fin et harmonieux de ce Tableau, le rendent très interessant] | *Mat:* op paneel *Size:* Hoog 9, en breed 7 ½ duim	Gerrit van der Pot, Heer van Groeneveld	(Sold) fl 255 A A Stratenus [for] le Roi
1808/06/11	RMRIJ	0002	*Jan Steen* | Een Binnenvertrek, verbeeldende een Kraamkamer, met dertien Figuren; geestig geordonneerd en geschilderd | *Mat:* op doek *Size:* hoog 24, breed 39 duim		(Bought In) fl 100
1808/06/13	AMSCH	0142	*Steen (J.)* | Deze eenvoudige maar tevens allernatuurlijkste Ordonantie verbeeld een Burgemester van Delft, op zijne Stoep zittende, acht slaande op eene bedelende Vrouw, welke met haar Kind een Aalmoes vraagt, terwijl zijne Dochter de Stoep aftreedt. Dit Schilderij, in de stijl van G. Metzu geschilderd, kan zoo in uitdrukking, karakters als penceelsbehandeling, als eene der uitmuntendste Schilderstukken van dezen grooten Meester worden beschouwd | *Mat:* op doek *Size:* hoog 33, breed 27 duim *Loc:* Penrhyn Castle, Gwynedd, Wales, UK. Pennant collection. (National Trust)	E M Engelberts	(Sold) fl 750 Nieuwenhuys pour Henry
1808/06/13	AMSCH	0143	*Steen (J.)* | Onder een Priëel van Wijngaardsranken zit een Boer een bevallig Boerenmeisje te liefkoozen, voor hun op een Ton staat een tinnen kan. Zacht en teder gepenceeld | *Mat:* op paneel *Size:* hoog 14, breed 11 duim	[Jan Tersteeg]	(Sold) fl 30 Th Spaan
1808/06/13	AMSCH	0144	*Steen (J.)* | In een gemeubileerde Kamer zit eene bevallige Dame, schijnende ziek te zijn, achter de Tafel staat eene oude Vrouw met een Klisteerspuit. Dit stukje is mede in de manier van G. Metzu geschilderd | *Mat:* op paneel *Size:* hoog 10, breed 8 duim *Loc:* Rotterdam, Nederland. Museum Boymans-Van Beuningen. (vdV 77)	R[oos]	(Sold) fl 160 v d Berghe de Gand
1808/07/19	AMROU	0006	*Jan Steen* | Het Portrait van Jan Steen, met zyn Zuster, het Klopje schynende tegen elkander te spreken, waarby zy een Roemer in de hand heeft, en hy haar een Ring aanbied, in een schoone houding fraay gepenseeld | *Loc:* Bremen, Deutschland. Kunsthalle. (lost after World War II)		(Unknown)
1808/08/23	AMSCH	0141	*Steen. (J.)* | Dit rijk en geestig geordoneert Tafreel, vertoont een vrolijke Vasten Avond vreugd, van onderscheiden Mans, Vrouwen en Kinderen, in een Binnenvertrek, bij een Tafel zitten verscheide Lieden, een derzelve leegt een frisse Roemer, onder het gejuigh van verscheide vrolijke Gasten, eene oude Vrouw hond beide handen voor de ooren, terwijl eene Moeder met een Kind voor dezelve staande, met een vergenoegd gelaat die vreugde beschouwt, een Knegt met een roode Luijer om zijn hoofd, knielt voor een Vat, om een kan te vullen, op de voorgrond ziet men een Driestal, waar op een Schotel met Wafelen, ter zijde op de grond een gebraade Gans, en verder Huisraat; de karakters zijn alle Natuurlijk, het Licht bevallig, en van een uitvoerig penceelbehandeling | *Mat:* op doek *Size:* hoog 35, breed 45 duim	[Gruyter?]	(Sold) fl 200 Barend Koy
1808/08/23	AMSCH	0142	*Steen. (J.)* | In deeze Ordonantie van verscheide Beelden, ziet men bij den ingang van een groot Gebouw, een bejaarde Grijsaard met een opgeheeven hand, ernstig ziende naar een ter aarde leggende als een dood Man, door drie Jongelingen ondersteunt, verder eenige Aanschouwers in verbaazende houding, in 't verschiet eene aankomende Vrouw, op de voorgrond ligt een gezegelde Brief en eenig Geld, en ander bijwerk; het is uitvoerig gepenceeld | *Annots:* Ananias en Saphira (FLNY) *Mat:* op paneel *Size:* hoog 18, breed 15 duim	C	(Bought In) fl 245
1808/08/23	AMSCH	0143	*Steen. (J.)* | Deeze rijke Ordonantie verbeeld in een pragtig Palijs. Den Koningin Ester ter maaltijd, bij Ahassueris, die op zijn Vorstelijke Zetel, als in woede op Haman neder ziet, die door zijn houding en angstig gelaat met schaamte, zijn wroeging te kennen geeft: verder gestoffeerd met verscheide bediende, zoo Mans als Vrouwen, en eenige Aanschouwers; de karacters zijn geestig, het koloriet bevallig en meesterlijk geschilderd | *Mat:* op doek *Size:* hoog 31, breed 38 duim	C	(Sold) fl 50 Spruit
1808/09/13	HABRU	0080	*Jan Steen* | Een Binnenhuis, de oude Vrouw bezig zijnde Koeken te bakken, de Man het beslag met de Lepel in de Pan doet, verder het Gezelschap vermakende met eten en drinken, uitvoerig		(Unknown) fl 69

1808/09/13	HABRU	0081	*Jan Steen* | Een vrolijke vette Boer een Meisje op de schoot hebbende		(Unknown) fl 7:15
1808/09/13	HABRU	0082	*Jan Steen* | Een Boer met de Kan in de hand, schijnende een Meisje nevens hem zittende, een Glas ophoud, willende inschenken		(Unknown) fl 8
1808/10/28	AMVRS	0055	*Steen (Jan)* | Een Markt, waar op den voorgrond bij een Poort een Boer zit, welke aan eene Vrouw met een Marktëmmer aan haar Hand, een Haan schijnt te willen verkopen; in het verschiet eene menigte Marktgangers. Onder de stukjes van J. Steen, welke in den trant van Metzu geschilderd, door eene betamelijke geestigheid en zachte penceelsbehandeling uitmunten, verdient dit kunststukje eene voorname plaats | *Mat:* op koper *Size:* hoog 14, breed 10 duim	Marten Udink	(Sold) fl 506 Hulswit
1808/10/28	AMVRS	0056	*Steen (Jan)* | In een Boere Binnehuis of Chirugijns Winkel, ziet men een Boer, die eene pijnlijke operatie aan zijn Been ondergaat, gelaad en houding zijn uitnemend uitgedrukt; eene Vrouw staat nevens hem, terwijl de Heelmeester zeer eigenaardig zijn werk verricht. Alles is zeer natuurlijk en uitvoerig | *Mat:* op paneel *Size:* hoog 14 ¼, breed 11 ½ duim	Marten Udink	(Sold) fl 75 Spaan
1808/10/28	AMVRS	0057	*Steen (Jan)* | In een kapitaal Dorpgezicht met verscheidene Woningen, vol gewoel van eene menigte Beelden, zoo Mannen als Vrouwen en Kinderen, houdt men Kermis. Boeren en Boerinnen danzen en liefkozen, verder Reizigers te Paard, een Rivier met Vaartuigen, Kerk en Toren. De karakters zijn geestig, de Penceelsbehandeling is uitvoerig | *Mat:* op doek *Size:* hoog 33, breed 38 duim *Loc:* Detroit, MI, USA. Institute of Arts. (39.673)	Marten Udink	(Sold) fl 86 Gruyter
1808/10/28	AMVRS	0058	*Steen (Jan)* | In een Binnevertrek zit een bedaagd Man bij een Tafel, waarop een Inktkoker en Papier geplaast is, hij is bezig een Pen te snijden. Natuurlijk en zeer fraai gepenceeld | *Mat:* op paneel *Size:* hoog 10, breed 8 duim	Marten Udink	(Sold) fl 111 Joukes en Oijens
1808/11/28	AMSCH	0056	*Jan Steen* | In dit Galant Onderwerp, ziet men een vrolijke Gast, leggende op een Ledikant, voor hem staat een bevallige Meid, gereed om in het Bed te stappen, geestig gecarateriseerd [SIC] en delicaat gepenceeld | *Mat:* op paneel *Size:* hoog 12, breed 10 duim	[Gruyter?]	(Sold) fl 38:10 T Spaan
1808/11/28	AMSCH	0056a[H]	*Jan Steen* | 1 Schildery | *Notes:* This lot was added in by hand in the EBNP copy of the catalogue.		(Bought In) fl 130
1808/11/28	AMSCH	0056b[H]	*Jan Steen* | 1 Schildery | *Notes:* This lot was added in by hand in the EBNP copy of the catalogue.		(Bought In) fl 240
1809/04/17	AMSCH	0088	*J. Steen* | In een Boerenwoning zitten eenige Huislieden bij een Ton, zich met Speelen en Drinken vermaken, op de voorgrond eene bevallige Vrouw, bezig de Brandewijnskom te roeren, verder eene oude Vrouw met een Fles in de Hand; geestig geordoneerd en delicaat gepenceeld | *Mat:* op doek *Size:* hoog 27 ¼, breed 21 ½ duim	[Gruyter?]	(Sold) fl 12
1809/06/13	AMSCH	0136	*Jan Steen* | Deeze comique en fraaije Ordonantie, verbeeld in een Binnenhuis verscheide vrolijke Huislieden, waarvan een het Biervat, het welke op zijn einde loopt opligt, terwijl eene bevallig Boeren Meisje het laatste drupje in een Pot opvangt, verder geestig Bijwerk en Huisraad; de caracters zijn natuurlijk verbeeld, en het is bevallig en meesterlijk geschilderd | *Mat:* op doek *Size:* hoog 34, breed 40 duim	H[odges]	(Sold) fl 313 de Lelij
1809/06/13	AMSCH	0137	*Jan Steen* | In een Binnenvertrek zit eene bevallig Vrouwtje, in Oude Hollandsche kleeding, een deftig Man, nevens haar staande, schijnt haar een Goude Ring aantebieden, terwijl een oude Vrouw met een vergenoegd gelaat hetzelve aanziet; dit stukje is zeer geestig en van een delicaate penceelbehandeling | *Size:* hoog 11, breed 9 duim	A	(Sold) fl 112 T Spaan
1809/06/13	AMSCH	0138	*Jan Steen* | Dit fraai Schilderij verbeeld een Herberg, in hetzelve ziet men Jan Steen en deszelfs Huisvrouw in een vrolijke houding afgebeeld; verder met geestig Bijwerk en verschillend Huisraad gestoffeerd; uitvoerig en van de beste behandeling | *Mat:* op paneel *Size:* hoog 21 ½, breed 26 duim	B	(Sold) fl 164 Hulswit
1809/06/13	AMSCH	0139	*Jan Steen* | In een Boeren Chirurgijns Winkel word een Man door de meester een plijster op het been gelegt, terwijl hij door een knecht word vastgehouden, agterwaarts eene Grijsaard die eene Vrouwtje liefkoost en haar een beurs met geld aanbied; grappig verbeeld en zuiver van schildering | *Mat:* op paneel *Size:* hoog 11, breed 9 ½ duim	H[odges]	(Sold) fl 30 Gruiter
1809/06/13	AMSCH	0140	*Jan Steen* | In een gemeubileerde Kamer, zit op de voorgrond, bij eene Tafel, eene bevallige Dame, rustende met haar arm op een kussen, voor haar staat een Doctor haar de pols voelende, verder andere Beelden en Bijwerk; geestig en bevallig verbeeld | *Size:* hoog 23, breed 20 duim	M	(Bought In) fl 25
1809/07/19	AMSCH	0050	*Steen (J.)* | In een grootsch Gebouw is afgebeeld de gelijkenis van Lazarus, op een verheven plaats met een Balustrade zit de rijke Man met zijn Geliefde Vrouwen, aan eene welvoorziene Tafel, met keurige Spijs, op den voorgrond rust op den grond de behoeftige Lazarus, als smeekende iets te mogen hebben, verders zijn andere Bedienden bezig Spijs aan te dragen, anderen dezelve gereed te maken, ook Kinderen die met Honden speelen, Potzemakers en verder bijwerk. De karakters zijn natuurlijk, het licht en koloriet bevallig, en het geheel van eene uitvoerige penceelsbehandeling | *Mat:* op doek op paneel *Size:* hoog 27, breed 34 duim	[Bicker]	(Sold) fl 405 Reijers

1809/07/19	AMSCH	0051	*Steen (J.)* | In een vrolijk Buitenhuis of Lustplaats, vertoont zich de Bruiloft te Kanaan in Galilea, vol gewoel van Beelden, eenige zitten aan gedekte Tafels, met verscheide Spijzen bereid, andere vermaken zig met drinken. Het is geestig geordonneerd, de karakters zijn natuurlijk; alles is van eene zeer uitvoerige penceelsbehandeling | *Mat:* op paneel *Size:* hoog 25, breed 32 duim *Loc:* Dublin, Eire. National Gallery of Ireland.	[Bicker]	(Sold) fl 1150 Th^s Spaan
1809/07/25	HGBSM	0268	*J. Steen* | Een deftig Binnen Vertrek, waar in een Huishouden met Man en Vrouw en Kinderen en een Hond, en een Meid uit een andere Kamer binnen komende, kunstig geschildert | *Mat:* op paneel *Size:* hoog 24 en een half, breed 18 duim	D van der Aa [or] E B ten Dall	(Sold) fl 34 L Voerman [for] Huijbregts
1809/09/06	AMSCH	0063	*Steen (Jan)* | Den Meester zelven, zittende op de Guitar te speelen, in een vrolijke luim, vol expressie gepenceeld | *Mat:* op doek *Size:* hoog 9, breed 7 ½ duim	Johannes Caudri	(Sold) fl 40 Th^s Spaan
1810/03/07	UTWLD	0007	*J. Steen* | Een binnen huis, waar in Kinderen met een kat speelen, het welk van een ouden man door een raam beloerd word meesterlyk behandeld | *Size:* breed 2 voet 2 duim, hoog 2 voet 4 duim *Loc:* Mainz, Deutschland. Landesmuseum. (94) (?) as copy after Steen	J J Woertman	(Unknown) fl 49
1810/03/23	HAVIN	0001	*J. Steen* | De Uitdeeling van St. Nicolaas giften. Een klein Meisje word door de Meid voortgezet na de Moeder, om dank te betuigen: aan een Tafel staat een Jongen, hartelijk bedroeft over zijn deel, waaronder een Roe in een schoen; het geen door een oud Man en Vrouw word aangezien. Wonder natuurlijk in de verschillende hartstogten uitgedrukt; en uitvoerig geschildert door J. Steen | *Size:* hoog 23 ½ breet 20 d. *Loc:* Rotterdam, Nederland. Museum Boymans-Van Beuningen. (1826)	Rudolf Hendrik de Wetstein [or others]	(Unknown) fl 315
1810/03/23	HAVIN	0002	*J. Steen* | Een waarzegster. Uit de hand van een Vrouw die voor haar zit, vergelijkt de Figuur in een boek, dat zij in hande heeft; om het oogmerk te verrigten, het geen door een bejaarde Vrouw met ernst word waargenoomen, vooraan zit een Kind in een kakstoel te slapen, voorzien van poppen; en hier bij een Boomwiel. Alles als de vorige, fraai van teekening en schildering | *Size:* hoog 32 breet 25 ½ d.	Rudolf Hendrik de Wetstein [or others]	(Unknown) fl 550
1810/03/23	HAVIN	0003	*J. Steen* | De Pinkster Bloem voor een huis. Waar een oude Vrouw een Kindje geld doed geeven, in de kom van de Pinkster Bloem, en eenige kinderen bij staan; als ook een Man die zit te leunen op een Baluster, een Jongen met een Vaandel, en een Meid die op het Kind schijnt te passen | *Size:* hoog 40 breet 33 d.	Rudolf Hendrik de Wetstein [or others]	(Unknown) fl 400
1810/03/26	RMMUY	0037	*Jan Steen* | Deze ongemeen rijke en uitvoerige Schilderij, verbeeld op eene burlesque wijze, daar Simson, in de Schoot van Delila van zijn Haarlok beroofd word. Men ziet er een aantal figuren, zoo van krijgsknegten, kinderen, draperijen, en cierlijk bijwerk. Krachtig en schoon geschilderd [Cette riche composition, nous offre d'une manière comique, l'instant ou Samson couché devant Délila, perd la tresse de ses cheveux : plusieurs personnes et guerriers guëttent le moment pour le saisir, des accessoires de toute espèce, se voyent par tout, et forment un ensemble savant, harmonieux, et très fini.] | *Mat:* op doek *Size:* hoog 25, breed 29 ½ duimen *Loc:* Los Angeles, CA, USA. Los Angeles County Museum of Art. (M.87.64)	Daniel de Jongh Az	(Sold) fl 370 van Eyk s'Hage
1810/03/26	RMMUY	0038	*Jan Steen* | Een Kroeg. Op den voorgrond eene grappige uitgedoschte rookende Vrouw zittende op een blok, nevens eene bank, waarop een Man tabak kerft. In den achtergrond, eenige figuren en bijwerk. Geestig geordonneerd en geschilderd [Une Tabagie. Sur le devant est une vieille matrone assise et fumant sa pipe ; prés d'elle est un homme qui coupe du tabac, sur un banc ; dans le fond sont d'autres figures comiques, composées et peintes avec esprit et facilité.] | *Mat:* op paneel *Size:* hoog 9, breed 7 ½ duimen	Daniel de Jongh Az	(Sold) fl 74 Van Iperen Amsterdam [for] Wreesman
1810/03/26	RMMUY	0039	*Jan Steen* | Bij een Ton, zit een Dronke Karel, vastgehouden wordende door eene Vrouw, comicq van uitdrukking, en breed geschilderd [Un Homme ivre, la tête appuiée sur un tonneau, et soutenu par une femme ; beaucoup d'expressions comiques regnent dans ce sujet artistement peint.] | companion to lot 40 *Mat:* op paneel *Size:* hoog 7, breed 6 ¾ duimen	Daniel de Jongh Az	(Sold) fl 73:10 for lots 39 & 40. van Iperen Amsterdam
1810/03/26	RMMUY	0040	*Jan Steen* | Eene wedergade. Aan een Ton zit een Jongen te schrijven, onderrigt wordende door eene Vrouw, die in de eene hand een Kan heeft, in alles als het voorgaande behandeld [Un Pendant, aupres d'un tonneau qui sert de table à un rustre qui s'occupe gauchement à écrire ; une femme qui est près de lui, paroit lui donner instruction – pareille faire du précédent tableau, et de la même grandeur.] | companion to lot 39 *Mat:* op paneel *Size:* hoog 7, breed 6 ¾ duimen *Loc:* Paris, France. Institut Néerlandais, Fondation Custodia. (169)	Daniel de Jongh Az	(Sold) fl 73:10 for lots 39 & 40. van Iperen Amsterdam
1810/03/27	RMCNL	0017	*J. Steen* | Een Binnenhuis, waarin men eene Meid onder haar werk in Slaap ziet gevallen, zeer geestig en aardig geschilderd		(Unknown)
1810/03/27	RMCNL	0019	*J. Steen* | In een Binnenhuis ziet men een bejaard Man Goud wegen, snaaks en fraai geschilderd		(Unknown)
1810/03/27	RMCNL	0054	*J. Steen* | Een Binnenvertrek waarin men eene jonge Dame ziet, ontvangende van eene oude Vrouw eenen Brief, aardig en snaaks geschilderd		(Unknown)
1810/03/27	RMCNL	0070	*J. Steen* | Een Binnenhuis, zeer geestig en meesterachtig		(Unknown)

1810/03/27	RMCNL	0078	*J. Steen* | Een aantal Joodsche geleerden, alles vol werking en krachtig geschilderd		(Unknown)
1810/06/06	RMMUY	0016	*Jan Steen* | Een Grappig Stukje, waar in men eene Vrouw ziet welke een Man met de Klomp dreigt te slaan, daar anderen om lagchen terwijl een kind schreit. Door Jan Steen, van de beste soort | *Mat:* op paneel *Size:* hoog 9 ½, breed 12 duimen		(Sold) fl 35 Vermeulen
1810/06/06	RMMUY	0017	*Jan Steen* | Een zittend Vrouwtje, met een Naaikussen op haar schoot, een man schijnt haat aan te spreken, daar een Jongeling om lacht, vrolijk behandeld | *Mat:* op paneel *Size:* hoog 15, breed 12 ½ duim		(Unknown) fl 18:10
1810/06/06	RMMUY	0018	*Jan Steen* | In een Binnenhuis zit op den voorgrond een Boer op een bank met eene Vrouw op zijn knie, de Waard met een kan in de hand staat in 't midden, achter hem een Boer zittende bij eene Tafel, deze figuren zijn grappig van uitdrukking, verder ziet men drie te samen sprekende bedaagde Lieden, en twee Boeren aan den haard, op den voorgrond keuken gereedschap, konstig en natuurlijk | *Mat:* op paneel		(Unknown) fl 56
1810/06/06	RMMUY	0019	*Jan Steen* | Eene Kraamkamer, met eene menigte Beelden het kandeel-maal vrolijk vierende, geestig en konstig behandeld | *Mat:* op doek		(Bought In) fl 40
1810/06/20	AMSCH	0079	*J. Steen* | Dit bevallig voorwerp verbeeldt, in een Stadgezigt, een Jongen en een Meisje, komende uit eenen Winkel: de Jongen heeft een Mandje met Bokkens aan den arm, en in de hand een Kom met Siroop, waaruit hij met den vinger schijnt te likken; het Meisje houdt eenige lekkernij in den schoot, waarmede zij zeer verheugt schijnt te zijn. De karakters zijn zeer natuurlijk; het is geestig en van eene uitvoerige penceelsbehandeling | *Mat:* op doek *Size:* hoog 24, breed 17 ½ duimen *Loc:* Hamburg, Deutschland. Kunsthalle.	N	(Bought In) fl 300
1810/06/20	AMSCH	0080	*J. Steen* | In een Boeren-Herberg zitten verscheidene vrolijke Lieden, zoo Mannen als Vrouwen, bij eene welvoorziene Tafel; een Man staat op een Bank, bezig op de Viool te spelen, waarvoor een Boer en Boerin danzen. Op den voorgrond, bij een open Vengster, zit een bejaard Man, die eene jonge Boerin liefkoost; hier nevens eene Vrouw met een Kind. Het is geestig geordonneerd en teder van penceelsbehandeling | *Mat:* op doek *Size:* hoog 41, breed 55 duimen	D	(Sold) fl 127 Van Iperen
1810/07/23	DOLG1	0047	*Jan Steen* | In een Tuin, bij een Fontein, en rustende tegen een oud gebouwtje, is in dit keurig Schilderijtje Jan Steen zelf, met zijne Huisvrouw, aan een tafel, slapende afgebeeld. Op de tafel ligt een Boek, en staat een omgekeerde Rhijnschewynroemer, nevens een geopenden Okkernoot en Notendoppen. Alles uitmuntend fraai, kunstig behandeld, en zeer zeker een der beste Kabinetstukjes van dezen beroemden meester | *Mat:* op koper *Size:* hoog 7, breed 9 ½ duim	Mr Pieter van den Santheuvel	(Sold) fl 365 Beekmans van Antwerpen
1810/07/23	DOLG1	0048	*Jan Steen* | Voor een Boerenhuis bevindt zich een biddend Boeren Huisgezin, de Man, de Vrouw met een Kindje op haar schoot, en een daar bij staande Jongen. Op een Biervat staat een platte Pan met Pap, en voor hetzelve een witte Hond, bezig een pot uit te lekken. De biddende karakters zijn ongemeen wel uitgedrukt, en alles is van eenen goeden toon, en edele penseelsbehandeling | *Mat:* op doek *Size:* hoog 23, breed 29 duim	Mr Pieter van den Santheuvel	(Sold) fl 160 Beekmans van Antwerpen
1810/07/23	DOLG2	0061[H]	*J Steen* | Yermaaltijd rouw geschilderd | *Annots:* Eyer citers (FLNY) *Mat:* op doek *Notes:* This lot was added in by hand in the RKDH and FLNY copies of the catalogue.	Pieter Quinting	(Sold) fl 152 Tomasse à Leide
1810/08/01	AMSCH	0095	*Steen (Jan)* | Eene Trouwplegtigheid; men ziet eene Bruid, voor wie een Meisje Bloemen strooit, terwijl dezelve door twee deftige Vrouwen tot den Bruidegom gebragt wordt; deze gaat haar van den ingang van een grootsch Huis tegemoet; in het verschiet een Dorptoren en verscheiden Boerenhuizen [Le Sujet d'une Nosce [sic], dans lequel on voit arriver la Marié accompagnée de deux Dames, et d'une jeune Fille jonchant des Fleurs sur ses pas. Au devant du portique d'une grande Maison vient se presenter le jeune Epoux pour la rencontrer. Dans la perspective on voit le Clocher et une partie du Village] | *Annots:* Passable. (NGW) *Mat:* op doek *Size:* hoog 25, breed 31 duimen *Loc:* Den Haag, Nederland. Rijksdienst Beeldende Kunst (NK 3050) on loan to Rotterdam	Mr Pieter de Smeth van Alphen	(Sold) fl 2250 J^mo de Vries
1810/08/01	AMSCH	0096	*Steen (Jan)* | Eene Binnenkamer met verscheiden bejaarde en jonge Lieden: voorstellende eene bedorvene Huishouding; op den voorgrond verschillend Huisraad en eene menigte bijwerk [Une Scène familiere representant les desordres du Ménage, composée de differents personnages de tout age, garnie d'une multitude d'ustenciles et d'accessoires] | *Annots:* Assez bon. (NGW) *Mat:* op paneel *Size:* hoog 30, breed 33 duimen *Loc:* London, England, UK. Wellington Museum, Apsley House.	Mr Pieter de Smeth van Alphen	(Sold) fl 1299 Reijers
1810/08/01	AMSCH	0097	*Steen (Jan)* | Voor een Buitenhuis onder eenen Wijngaard zit een Heer, lezende en rustende tegen eene Bank, waarop een Pot met Bloemen en eene Pijp geplaatst zijn, en waar onder een Hond; op den voorgrond eene Vrouw, slapende bij eene welvoorziene Tafel, achterwaarts eene Dienstmaagd [Sur le devant d'une Maison de Campagne est assis un Personnage sous l'ombrage d'une Vigne, il est occupé à la lecture, et appuyé contre un banc, sur lequel on voit un Pot à Fleurs et une Pipe. Audevant du Tableau est une Femme endormie auprès d'une Table garnie	Mr Pieter de Smeth van Alphen	(Sold) fl 605 Reijers

			de mets, et sur l'arrière on rencontre une Servante] | *Annots:* Assez bon. (NGW) *Mat:* op doek *Size:* hoog 22, breed 30 duimen		
1810/08/06	AMSCH	0093	*Steen (J.)* | Een Boeren School, in het zelve ziet men de Meester zittende voor eene Tafel, houdende de Plak in zijn linkerhand, terwijl hij met de regterhand, eenen Jongen, die in eene droevige houding voor hem staat, zijn les schijnt aan te wijzen; twee Kinderen, ter zijde staande, zien het zelve met vermaak aan, en voor de Tafel ziet men een ander Jongeling zittende te schrijven; het is geestig geordonneerd, de karakters zijn natuurlijk, het is van een uitvoerige penceelsbehandeling | *Annots:* maitre d'ecolle (BPG) *Mat:* op paneel *Size:* hoog 22 ½, breed 22 duimen	A	(Sold) fl 315 Bredius
1810/08/06	AMSCH	0094	*Steen (J.)* | Eene Historiëeele [sic] Ordonantie, verbeeldende den dood van Ananias en Saphira, op den voorgrond, bij den ingang van den Tempel, ziet men den Apostel met opgeheven handen ernstig ziende na de doode, die voor hem ligt, en welke door drie Jongelingen ondersteund wordt, verder eenige aanschouwers, alle in verbaazende houding; het is van de uitvoerigste behandeling | *Mat:* op paneel *Size:* hoog 18, breed 15 duimen	B	(Sold) fl 165 J Spaan
1810/08/06	AMSCH	0095	*Steen (J.)* | Dit fraaije stukje verbeeld een Bruiloftspartij, ter regterzijde ziet men de Bruid in eene droevige houding, een oud Man, die nevens haar staat, schijnt haar tot den Bruidegom te willen geleiden, die aan de andere zijde van het Vertrek op eene Steenen Trap staat en haar schijnt te wagten, eene Dienstmaagd en eenige andere Lieden zien het zelve met vermaak aan, verder vrolijke Lieden, die in het rond danzen en andere die op Instrumenten speelen; het is bevallig van koloriet en kunstig behandeld | *Mat:* op paneel *Size:* hoog 18 ½, breed 15 duimen	C	(Sold) fl 235 Van Iperen
1810/10/11	AMSCH	0081	*J. Steen* | Onder het Lommer van zwaar Geboomte zit een vrolijk Gezelschap bij eene welvoorziene Tafel, op den voorgrond musiceerende en liefkoozende Lieden; de karakters zijn geestig en het is krachtig geschilderd | *Mat:* op paneel *Size:* hoog 23, breed 18 duimen	[Gruyter?]	(Sold) fl 9:5 H Pakker
1810/10/11	AMSCH	0082	*J. Steen* | Een Boeren Huisgezin | *Mat:* op paneel *Size:* hoog 19, breed 24 duimen	C	(Sold) fl 0:6 Gruiter

Steen, Jan (or Steen, J., copy after)

1802/05/11	GRGRW	0043	*Jan Steen* | Een Boeren – binnenhuis, door of naar Jan Steen [Schilderijen met Olie-Verf; In zwarte Lijsten] | *Mat:* in olyverf *Notes:* The bracketed information in the title appears above lot 1 and refers to lots 1 to 79a.	Arnold Sicco Werumeus	(Unknown) fl 7:5 for lots 43 & 44
1802/05/11	GRGRW	0044	*Jan Steen* | Een Binnenkamer, met een Heer en Dame, door of naar denzelfden [Jan Steen] [Schilderijen met Olie-Verf; In zwarte Lijsten] | *Mat:* in olyverf *Notes:* The bracketed information in the title about the medium appears above lot 1 and refers to lots 1 to 79a.	Arnold Sicco Werumeus	(Unknown) fl 7:5 for lots 43 & 44
1808/06/11	RMRIJ	0003	*Door of na Jan Steen* | Een Binnenhuis, waar in een aantal zingende, spelende en drinkende Boeren | *Mat:* op doek		(Sold) fl 17:10 V Giesen
1808/06/11	RMRIJ	0113	*Door of na Jan Steen* | Een Pinxtervreugd met verscheide Figuren geestig geschilderd | *Mat:* op paneel *Size:* hoog 30, breed 24 duim		(Sold) fl 6:5 [or] 16: 10 V Giesen
1810/06/06	RMMUY	0101	*J. Steen* | Een Binnenvertrek waar vier kinderen zich vrolijk maken, en Koekebakken, geestig en fraaij. Door of naar denzelven [J. Steen] | *Mat:* op doek		(Unknown) fl 16:10

Steen, Jan (or Steen, J., manner)

1802/06/28	AMSCH	0219	*J. Steen* | Twee stuks gemeubeleerde Binnevertrekken, in de eene ziet men een Doctoor by een jong Meisje, en de andere verbeeld een diergelyk geval; zeer natuurlyk behandeld, door of in de manier van J. Steen | *Mat:* op doek *Size:* hoog 28, breed 24 duim	Anna Elink	(Sold) fl 15 Brouwer
1802/09/30	HGBAK	0007	*Jan Steen* | Een dito Boertje, welke aan een wond op de rug gesnede word, met andere figuuren, door of in de manier van Jan Steen, op doek, zwarte lyst. [Schilderyen in Olyverf] | *Mat:* in olyverf op doek *Notes:* The bracketed information in the title appears above lot 1 and refers to lots 1 to 26.		(Unknown)
1804/05/07	AMSCH	0152	*Steen. (J.) (door of in de manier)* | Een Binnekamer, waarin een zieke Vrouw te bed liggende. de Notaris is bezig haar Testament te maken; enz. is van een krachtige penceelsbehandeling | *Mat:* op doek *Size:* hoog 23, breed 32 duim	W [through] Y[ver]	(Bought In) fl 8

Steen, Jan (copy after)

1801/04/08	HAVIN	0028	*J. Steen* | Een Meid die van een Boer melk neemt, na J. Steen		(Unknown)
1802/06/28	AMSCH	0161	*J. Steen* | Een Binnehuis met vegtende Boeren, op Panneel, naar J. Steen | *Mat:* op paneel *Size:* hoog 12, breed 15 duim	Anna Elink	(Sold) fl 5:10 van Iperen
1803/04/27	AMSCH	00RR[H]	*J Steen* | Een binnehuijs na J Steen | *Notes:* This lot was added in by hand in the LBDa copy of the catalogue.	C	(Bought In) fl 13 ½
1804/10/16	DLOND	0240a[g]	*C. Vermeulen; J. Steen* | [Een Stuk, bevattende 13 zeer schone Copiën van de volgende Meesters. Un Tableau, contenant 13 Copies très-belles des Peintres suivans.] 7. J. Steen. De Schoolmeester, le Maitre d'Ecole. (No. 213a) | copy by Corn. Vermeulen (III) after J. Steen *Mat:* op paneel *Size:* hoog 41, breed 55 *Notes:* The bracketed information in the title appears above lot 240a[a] and refers to lots 240a[a-m].		(Sold) fl 150 for lots 240a[a-m]. Ond d Wyngaert

1804/10/16	DLOND	0240a[j]	*C. Vermeulen; J. Steen* | [Een Stuk, bevattende 13 zeer schone Copiën van de volgende Meesters. Un Tableau, contenant 13 Copies très-belles des Peintres suivans.] 10. J. Steen. Het Bruidjen, la Fiancée. (N°. 212) | copy by Corn. Vermeulen (III) after J. Steen *Mat:* op paneel *Size:* hoog 41, breed 55 *Notes:* The bracketed information in the title appears above lot 240a[a] and refers to lots 240a[a-m].		(Sold) fl 150 for lots 240a[a-m]. Ond d Wyngaert
1806/05/05	AMSCH	0185	*J. Steen* | Een ziek Vrouwtje; na J. Steen	R[oos]	(Sold) fl 2 L Pakker
1809/04/22	AMYVR	0152	*J. Steen* | Een vrolijke Ordonantie; naar J. Steen	Juff[r] Julikker	(Sold) fl 5:10 van Iperen
1809/07/25	HGBSM	0204	*J. Steen* | Een party Figuren, in gesprek over een Haane gevegt, dat schynt te hebben plaats gehad, na J. Steen | *Mat:* op doek *Size:* hoog 32 en een half, breed 44 en een half duim	D van der Aa [or] E B ten Dall	(Sold) fl 3:16 van der Burgh
1810/03/23	HAVIN	0041	*J. Steen* | Een bedurve [sic] Huishouden, geestig van Ordonnantie, na J. Steen	Rudolf Hendrik de Wetstein [or others]	(Unknown)
1810/06/06	RMMUY	0100	*J. Steen* | De vlugt van Joseph en Maria naar Egijpte, bij maan en lantaarn licht. Naar J. Steen | *Mat:* op paneel		(Unknown) fl 8:10
1810/06/06	RMMUY	0102	*J. Steen* | Eene zieke Bruid. Naar denzelven [J. Steen] | *Mat:* op doek		(Unknown) fl 5:5
1810/06/06	RMMUY	0174	*Jan Steen* | Eene grappige Copij. Naar Jan Steen | *Mat:* op doek		(Sold) fl 6:5 V Galen

Steen, Jan (manner)

1801/04/08	HAVIN	0046	*J. Steen* | Een Juffer die drinkt en een Heer met een Kan, als J. Steen		(Unknown)
1802/02/16	AMSCH	0014	*J. Steen* | Een vrolyk Boeregezelschap; op paneel in de manier van J. Steen | *Mat:* op paneel	B[uys]	(Sold) fl 10 Gruiter
1802/07/09	AMSTO	0010	*J. Steen* | Voor een Buitenhuys, ziet men een vrolyke Jongen met een Mandje met Haaringen aan zyn Arm, neevens hem een Meisje, in de manier van J. Steen		(Unknown)
1802/09/06	AMSCH	0149	*J. Steen* | Een vrolyke Waardin, door een oude Boer geliefkoost, verders eenige andere Huislieden; in de manier van J. Steen | *Mat:* op doek	B	(Sold) fl 2 van Iperen
1802/09/21	UTHDG	0080	*J. Steen* | Een Koekebakster dreigende een kind te slaan, het welk haar Bord gebroken heeft, de andere bijstaande kinderen zijn in differente Actien. Alles natuurlijk en fiks behandeld, in de verkiezing van denzelven [J. Steen] | *Mat:* op doek *Size:* hoog 13, breed 15 ½ duimen		(Sold) fl 19:5 De Munnick
1804/02/27	AMSCH	0177	*J. Steen* | Een bevallig Vrouwtje, zittende aan een Tafel, geestig gepenceeld, als door J. Steen	B	(Sold) fl 3 J Yver
1805/07/03	AMSCH	0186	*J. Steen* | Een Boere Binnenhuis, met verscheide Huislieden en Kinderen, en verder Huisraad; geestig als J. Steen	R[oos]	(Sold) fl 16:10 L Pakker
1805/12/16	AMSCH	0112	*J. Steen* | Een Bakker op zyn Hoorn Blazende; in de manier van J. Steen	R[oos]	(Sold) fl 18:10 Taxera
1807/06/10	HGBSM	0092	*J. Steen* | Een Binnenvertrek, met een Biddend Huisgezin voor de Maaltijd, en meer bijwerk, zeer goed geschilderd, in den trant van J. Steen | *Mat:* op doek *Size:* hoog 17, breed 16 duim	Abraham Delfos [or others]	(Sold) fl 11:5 Uittenbogaart
1807/08/26	AMSCH	0280	*J. Steen* | Voor een Boeren Herberg ziet men dansende, speelende en rustende Huislieden en een Landman te Paard; fiks behandeld op Paneel, in de manier van J. Steen | *Mat:* op paneel	Roos [for] A	(Sold) fl 8:10 Spruit
1809/04/22	AMYVR	0185	*J. Steen* | Een vrolijke Bruiloft, met eene menigte danssende en andere Beelden; in de manier van J. Steen	de Bruin	(Sold) fl 8:5 du Pree
1810/07/23	DOLG2	0060	*Jan Steen* | Een Boerengezelschap op het verkeerd bord spelende, als door Jan Steen | *Mat:* op paneel *Size:* hoog 14, breed 19 duim	Pieter Quinting	(Sold) fl 16:10 v d Eynde Dordt
1810/11/07	UTWLD	0067	*Jan Steen* | Een Meisje door een oud Man geliefkoost wordende, die haar een stuk geld in de hand geeft, zeer schoon van licht en uitdrukking, in de manier van Jan Steen, op koper 4 duim rond, verguld Lijsje | *Mat:* op koper *Fmt:* rond *Size:* 4 duim		(Unknown) fl 110

Steen, Jan (18th c.)

802/07/27	AKHRK	0005	*Jan Steen, de Alkmaarsche* | Een Keukenstuk, waar in allerhande Boeren Huisraad, Een Man schijnt Zout in een kopere Pot te doen, een Vrouw agter hem heeft een platte Tobbe in de handen. Het Kooper-, Vaat- en Bijwerk zeer goed geschilderd | *Mat:* op paneel *Size:* hoog 10 ½, breed 14 ½ duim	Maria Stategaart	(Sold) fl 14 Impink

Steenbach [Unidentificd]

804/10/16	DLOND	0214	*Steenbach* | Zeegevecht voor Gibraltar A. 1623. Bataille de Mer à Gibraltar A. 1623 | *Mat:* op doek *Size:* hoog 45, breed 77 *Inscr:* 1623 (dated?) *Notes:* It is unclear whether the date is inscribed on the painting.		(Unknown)

Steens, D. [Unidentified]

802/09/06	AMSCH	0115	*D. Steens* | Twee stuks bevallige Laud [sic]- en Dorpgezigten, gestoffeerd met beelden en beesten; uitvoerig en zonagtig geschilderd | *Mat:* op paneel *Size:* hoog 16, breed 23 duim	Mevrouw Achtienhoven	(Sold) fl 19 van Iperen

Steenwyck, Hendrik van

801/04/13	AMSCH	0069	*H. van Steenwyk* | Een Roomsche Kerk van binnen te zien, gestoffeerd met verscheide Beeldjes, fraay van perspectief, en uitvoerig behandeld | *Mat:* op koper *Size:* hoog 13 ½, breed 20 duim	Pierre Fouquet, junior	(Sold) fl 51 Lafontaine

1801/06/10	AMSCH	0152	*Steenwyck. (H. van)* | Een Protestantsche Kerk, van binnen te zien, gestoffeerd met diversche Beeldjes, helder en fraai van perspectief | *Mat:* op paneel *Size:* hoog 12, breed 16 duim	Herman ten Kate	(Sold) fl 99 Coclers
1801/10/19	AMSCH	0066	*Steeenwyk. (Hendrik van)* | In een Kerkenkamer; ziet men ter linkerzyde een bejaard man voor een tafel zittende te schryven, achter zich een kast, waar op eenige Boeken en Papieren, hoger een Schildery en ter zyden een Horologie, alles word door een bevallig licht van een Zyvengster gedaagd; in 't verschiet ziet men een binnen Gezicht van een Kerk en Altaren, uitvoerig en ongemeen konstig behandeld | *Mat:* op koper *Size:* hoog 4 ½, breed 6 duim	Jonkheer Menno Baron van Coehoorn	(Sold) fl 150 Coclers
1802/12/13	AMSCH	0142	*H. Steenwyk* | Op een Steene Tafel, legt een doode Gans, en ander Gevogelten, waar by een Aarde Doorslag met verscheide Visschen en Koopere Keetel, en Mand met Druiven, en andere Vrugten; natuurlyk op Doek geschilderd | *Mat:* op doek	Florijn [?]	(Sold) fl 1 L Pakker [and] T Spaan
1803/07/18	AMSCH	0049	*Steenwyk (H. van)* | Een Roomsche Kerk van binnen te zien, met een schoone perspectief, aan wiens einde men het Choor gewaar word, verders eenige Beeldjes, en door een Portaal ziet men op straat, hetzelve is zonachtig en uitvoerig gepenceeld [Un point de vue intérieur d'une eglise gothique, d'une vaste étendue, la perspective percent [sic] jusqu'au maitre autel ; elle est ornée de differens objets relatifs aux ornemens du culte. Par un grand portail ouvert l'on voit sur une place publique, garnie de jolies figures. Ce petit morceau est d'un fini râre & du plus grand agrément.] | *Mat:* op koper *Size:* hoog 6, breed 7 duim	Maria Theresia Andrioli	(Sold) fl 48 Thys
1803/09/07	AMSCH	0156	*Steenwyk* | Een Roomsche Kerk, van binnen te zien, met verscheide Geestelyken, Autaren, enz.; zonachtig en uitvoerig, op Koper [Une église vue dans son intérieur ; plusieurs prêtres, des autels et d'autres ornemens bien distribués ; le jeu et les réflets de la lumière naturellement adaptés le rendent un excellent tableau] | *Mat:* op koper *Size:* hoog 14 ½, breed 11 duim	Smidt	(Sold) fl 26:10 Gruiter
1804/07/25	DLGRO	0019	*Steenwyk* | Twee Tempeltjes of Kerken van binnen te zien | *Mat:* op paneel *Size:* hoog 6, breed 8 duim	Mr Franc van der Burch Wz.	(Unknown)
1804/10/16	DLOND	0215	*H. Steenwyck* | Een Tafel met Vruchten, Visschen enz. Une Table avec des Fruits, Poissons &c. | *Mat:* op paneel *Size:* hoog 26, breed 36		(Unknown)
1805/07/10	AMSCH	0133	*H. Steenwyk* | Een Historiëele Ordinantie van verschyde Beelden, voorstellende een Boekekamer, enz. Delicaat en uitvoerig op Doek | *Mat:* op doek	V[inkeles] [for] K	(Bought In) fl 35
1805/10/09	HGBSM	0136	*H. Steenwyk* | Een kerk van binnen te zien met een outaar en verder bywerk, zeer uitvoerig | *Mat:* op doek *Size:* hoog 22 breet 39 ½ duim	T H van Willigen [or others]	(Sold) fl 10:10 Van der Vin
1808/06/06	RMRIJ	0122	*Steenwijk (H.J. van)* | Een Binnenvertrek, waaarin [sic] Christus benevens twee personen bij kaarslicht gezeten zijn. Eene wedergade. Eene fraaije Gothische Tempel of Kerk van binnen te zien, met Beeldjes en Kaarslichten. Beiden zeer uitvoerig en met veel konst geschilderd [L'Intérieur d'une Eglise d'une Architecture Gothique, et d'une belle Perspective, dans laquelle se promènent plusieurs Personnes, qui tiennent un flambeau à la main. D'un fini précieux. Le Pendant. L'Intérieur d'une Sacristie. Jésus est assis devant une Table, où l'on voit une Lumière et deux Personnes auprès de lui. Egal en mérite au précédent] | *Annots:* Verk. Jac. v d Lely, Delft 5 April 1796 (f 21.-) (RMA I) *Mat:* op koper *Size:* Twee Stukjes. Hoog 3 ½, en breed 2 ½ duim	Gerrit van der Pot, Heer van Groeneveld	(Sold) fl 40 R Pott
1808/08/23	AMSCH	0154	*Steenwijk. (J.)* | Een Roomsche Kerk van binnen, alwaar een Lijkdienst gedaan word; helder en fraai van perspectief en meesterlijk behandeld | *Mat:* op doek *Size:* hoog 29, breed 24 duim *Notes:* The artist's name was given as "Steenwijk. (J.)" but we have assumed this is an error.	[Coclers]	(Bought In) fl 21
1808/08/23	AMSCH	0213	*H. Steenwijk* | In een prachtige Zaal zit een bedaagd Heer voor een Tafel, achter hem een bediende, welke betaaling doet aan eenigen Werklieden, meesterlijk op Doek | *Mat:* op doek	[Gruyter?]	(Sold) fl 18:10 D Maijkel
1809/04/22	AMYVR	0124	*H. van Steenwijk* | Een Roomsche Kerk van binnen, gestoffeerd met eene menigte Beeldjes; fraai van perspectief en licht | *Mat:* op paneel *Size:* hoog 20, breed 29 duim	Juff^r Julikker	(Sold) fl 3 C S Roos
1810/12/03	DOBRA	0059	*H. Steenwyk* | Een Kerkje van binnen te zien, op den voorgrond twee Beeldjes, in het verschiet ziet men de trappen van het Outaar; door H. Steenwyk, op Koper, in een zwart Lystje, met een verguld biesje | *Mat:* op koper		(Unknown)

Steenwyck, Hendrik van (and Brueghel, J. (I))

1802/09/29	AMSCH	0051	*H. van Steenwyk; Fluweele Breugel* | Een Roomsche Kerk in Braband, hoog 14, breed 21 duim. Koper. Dezelve is verbeeld uit het Middenruim te zien, naar het Choor en den Hoogen Altaar, ryk gestoffeerd met een ménigte Persoonen, zoo Vrouwen als Mannen, waar onder eenige Geestelyken; ter zyde op de Voorgrond vertoond zig een Dame, met een Kindje op by de handen dragende, welke plechtig ter Doop gebragt word; by het hooge Choor werd de Ceremonie verrigt voor een Overleedene; verders ziet men verscheiden Altaaren, Orgel en Schilderstukken; de Perspectief, de vermindering van Lichten, de zuivere omtrek van Lysten en Gewelven, zyn 'er kunstig in waargenomen, en alles is van een uitvoerige Penceelbehandeling, door beide deeze Meesters [Une Eglise Catholique. Dont le point de Vue est pris de la grande nef sur le maitre	D	(Sold) fl 212 Vinkeles

autel ou l'on fait l'office des morts, parmi le nombre de belles figures de tout étàt qui ornent ce morceau, l'on distingue sur le devant un groupe portant un enfant à baptiser ; des autels, les orgues et des peintures achevent ce joli morceau dont la perspective et la gradation de lumiere sont parfaitement observés.] | *Mat:* op koper *Size:* hoog 14, breed 21 duim

1810/11/07 UTWLD 0001 *H. v. Steenwijk; Breugel* | Een Kerk waarin het de perspectief wel geobserveerd is, en zeer geestig gestoffeerd zo met staande als zittende beeldjes, zijnde het licht zeer fraai genomen, en formeert een Capitale Schilderdij door H. v. Steenwijk en Breugel, op paneel, 2 voet 3 duim hoog, 3 voet 3 duim breed in een vergulde Lijst | *Mat:* op paneel *Size:* 2 voet 3 duim hoog, 3 voet 3 duim breed — (Unknown) fl 105

Steenwyck, Hendrik van (and Dubordieu, P.; copy by)

1808/06/06 RMRIJ 0017 *Bordieu. (du); Steenwijk. (H. J. van); A. Durer; Holbeijn* | Eene zeer getrouwe kopij naar de origineele Schilderij van A. Durer en H. Holbeijn, Desiderius Erasmus verbeeldende. Het bijwerk door H. J. van Steenwijk. Alles zeer uitvoerig behandeld [Copie fidelle du Portrait de Désiré Erasme d'aprés l'original d'Albert Durer et H. Holbeyn. Les accessoires sont peints par van Steenwyk] | copy by P. Dubordieu and Hend. Steenwyck after Dürer and H. Holbein (II) *Annots:* Geschenk Teding Berkhout (RMA I) *Mat:* op paneel *Size:* Hoog 9 ½, en breed 7 ½ duim — Gerrit van der Pot, Heer van Groeneveld — (Sold) fl 21 du Pré

Steenwyck, Hendrik van (and Vrancx)

1802/06/16 AMSCH 0175 *H. van Steenwyck; S. Franks* | Een Tempel van binnen te zien; waar in verscheide Krygsknegten en andere Beelden; het Kaarsligt en het Vuur doet een goed effect en is meesterachtig gepenceeld | *Mat:* op paneel *Size:* hoog 15 ½, breed 19 ½ duim — [Merrem] — (Sold) fl 61 Gruiter

1803/04/20 AMSCH 0069 *H. Steenwyk; Franx [S. Frankx]* | Een Binnengezicht van een Roomsche Kerk, gestoffeert met wandelende Beeldjes, in 't verschiet een Priester den Dienst verrigtende, zonagtig en uitvoerig van penceelsbehandeling [Point de vue dans une Eglise Catholique ou l'on fait l'office : orné de plus par d'autres jolies figures ; rendu avec effet & précision.] | *Mat:* op paneel *Size:* hoog 8 ½, breed 13 duim *Notes:* The second artist's name differs in the Dutch and French editions of the catalogue. — Maria Magdalena van Sluypwyk, gravinne van Moens — (Sold) fl 31 Theijs

Steenwyk, F. [Unidentified]

1805/12/16 AMSCH 0053 *F. Steenwyk* | In een Onderaardsche gewulfde Gevangenis, vertoont zich de Verlossing van Petrus, door den Engel, de onderscheide Lichten van Lantaarn, Flambouw en vuur, geven een natuurlyke en bevallige houding, aan dit Schilderstuk; en is uitvoerig gepenceeld op Paneel | *Mat:* op paneel *Size:* hoog 8, breed 10 duim — R[oos] — (Bought In) fl 10:10

Steenwyk, J. [Unidentified]

1801/10/06 AMSCH 0062 *J. Steenwyk* | In een Keuken Vertrek, zit een Bedaagde Vrouw, in Al-oude Hollandsche Kleeding, als in diepe gedagten by een Spinnewiel, het Vertrek is gestoffeert met verschillend Huisraad, als Kasjes, Koopere Keetel, Vaatwerk, Potten en Pannen; het Natuurlyk Licht, geeft een bevallige werking, en is zeer uitvoerig gepenceelt | *Mat:* op paneel *Size:* hoog 17, breed 15 duim — M — (Bought In) fl 380

1804/05/07 AMSCH 0153 *Steenwyk (J)* | In een Keukenvertrek zit een bedaagde Vrouw in al-oude hollandsche kleeding, als in diepen gedachten by een Spinnewiel, het Vertrek is gestoffeerd met verschillend Huisraad, als Kasjes, koopere Ketel, Vaatwerk, Potten en Pannen, het natuurlyk licht geeft een bevallige werking; en is zeer uitvoerig en delicaat gepenceeld | *Mat:* op doek *Size:* hoog 17, breed 15 duim — Y[ver] [for] JJ — (Sold) fl 105 Gruyter

Stekelin [Unidentified]

1802/02/16 AMSCH 0068 *Stekelin* | Een Italiaansche Zeehaven, met treffelyke Gebouwen, verders gestoffeerd met beeldjes, vaartuigen en een bevallig verschiet, uitvoerig op koper geschilderd | *Mat:* op koper — G — (Sold) fl 0:14 van der Schley [for] G

Stella, Jacques

1803/04/27 AMSCH 000L *Stella* | La Sainte Vierge, tenant l'Enfant Jesus, sur ses genoux, St. Francois embrasse les pieds du Sauveur, & derriere lui est Saint Jean Baptiste, peint sur Marbre | *Mat:* sur marbre *Size:* h. 14, l. 17 pouces — B — (Sold) fl 71 Pruijssenaar [for] R

1810/07/26 AMSCH 0076 *Stella (J.)* | De Verschyning van Maria aan St. Theresia. Zacht en zeer schoon geschilderd | *Mat:* op doek *Size:* hoog 35, breed 26 duimen — Cassino — (Bought In) fl 52

Steur, Gerrit van der

1802/05/05 AMSCH 0203 *G. v. Steur* | Twee stuks, zeer onstuimige Zeeën, met zeylende Oorlogschepen | *Size:* ieder hoog 16, breed 19 duim — G — (Sold) fl 2:10 A Schotte

Stevens, Pieter (II)

806/05/05 AMSCH 0159 *Stevens* | Een Vanitas — R[oos] — (Bought In) fl 1

Stöcklin, Christian (and Morgenstern, J.L.E.)

803/09/07 AMSCH 0169 *C. Stocklin; Morgenstern* | Een Roomsche Kerk van binnen te zien, gestoffeerd met een menigte Altaaren en Beeldjes, de perspectief is over — Smidt — (Bought In) fl 115

			fraay, zo ook de schildering op Panneel, door C. Stocklin en gestoffeerd door Morgenstern [L'intérieur d'une église, ornée d'autels et de figures ; ce morceau joint à une exécution précieuse les règles de la perspective et de l'architecture] | *Mat:* op paneel *Size:* hoog 16, breed 21 duim		
			Stoffe, Jan Jacobsz. van der		
1801/03/16	AMSCH	0100	*A. van Stoffe* | Een hevige Batailje tusschen Ruytery, meesterlyk | *Notes:* The artist's name was given as "A. van Stoffe" but we have assumed this is an error.	K[ip]	(Sold) fl 6 Koopman
1801/06/13	LNDLS	0031	*H. van der Staffe* | Eene hevige Batailje van ruiters en soldaaten, op paneel | *Mat:* op paneel *Size:* hoog 14, breed 19 duimen *Notes:* The artist's name was given as "H. van der Staffe" but we have assumed this is an error.	D van R	(Sold) fl 5:15 Richter [for] S[tevens]
1802/06/16	AMSCH	0177	*J. B. Stoffe* | Een heevige schermutseling tusschen Ruitery; op de voorgrond legt een doodgeschooten Ruiter met zyn Paard; zeer natuurlyk en fiks behandeld | *Mat:* op paneel *Size:* hoog 12 ½, breed 11 ½ duim	[Merrem]	(Sold) fl 11:10 Wed Achtienhoven
1804/02/27	AMSCH	0156	*Stoffen* | Een hevige Bataille tusschen Ruitery en Voetvolk; door Stoffen, op Paneel | *Mat:* op paneel *Size:* hoog 24, breed 33 duim	C	(Sold) fl 0:6 L Pakker
1805/07/10	AMSCH	0140	*van Stoffe* | Een Landschap met Rovers, Paarden, Postwagens enz.; fiks op Paneel | *Mat:* op paneel *Size:* hoog 12, breed 19 duim	V[inkeles] [for] N	(Sold) fl 0:6 L Pakker
1806/08/13	AMSCH	0289	*van Stoffen* | Een hévige Schermutzeling tusschen Ruitery	Vinkeles [for] E	(Sold) fl 3:5 L Pakker
1806/08/13	AMSCH	0292	*van Stoffen* | Twee stuks hévige Rencontres tusschen Ruitery	Vinkeles [for] E	(Sold) fl 2:10 Levie Pakker
1807/06/10	HGBSM	0183	*Stoffe* | Een Battaille van Cavallerie | *Mat:* op paneel *Size:* hoog 14, breed 18 ½ duim	Abraham Delfos [or others]	(Sold) fl 1:6 Temmink
			Stoffer, H. [Unidentified]		
1808/04/26	GDAN	0161	*Stoffer (H.)* | Het Duin- en Strangezigt [sic] te Scheveningen, met eenige Viskopers en een Paard, fiks geschilderd | *Size:* hoog 13, breed 11 ½ duim	G H Fortuyn	(Unknown)
			Stom, J.F.D. [Unidentified]		
1805/10/21	GRBOL	0002	*J. F. D. Stom* | Een Capitaal Stuk, zynde een Gezelschap op de Kaart spelende, meesterlyk Geschilderd	Gerardus Nicolaus Heerkens	(Unknown)
			Stoop		
1802/06/28	AMSCH	0168	*Stoop* | Een Italiaansche Zeehaven, met eenige oude Ruïnen, op de voorgrond gestoffeerd met een Dame te Paard, en Heeren te voet, verder eenige Schepen, delicaat gepenceeld, door Stoop, op Panneel | *Mat:* op paneel *Size:* hoog 11, breed 15 duim	Anna Elink	(Sold) fl 28:10 Royers
1802/09/15	HGKAN	0003	*Stoop* | Een Rencontre van eenige Heeren te Paard, door Stoop, op Paneel en Lyst [In Oly Verff] | *Mat:* in olyverf op paneel *Notes:* The bracketed information in the title appears above lot 1 and refers to lots 1 to 8.		(Unknown)
1807/06/10	HGBSM	0212	*Stoop* | Een Landschap, met een Man Koebeesten en Paarden | *Mat:* op paneel *Size:* hoog 12 ½, breed 14 duim	Abraham Delfos [or others]	(Sold) fl 6:10 Wiggers
1807/10/12	MGBEO	0002	*Stoop* | Een Bataille | *Mat:* op paneel	Hermannus Johannes Heyman	(Sold) £ 0:6 Hardegai
1808/08/23	AMSCH	0204	*Stoop* | In een Stal, staat een jong Paard, waar agter een Knegt met de zweep in de hand, verder een liggende Bok, en eenig Stalgereedschap; bevallig gepenceeld	[Gruyter?]	(Bought In) fl 8:10
1808/09/13	HABRU	0086	*Stoop* | In een Bergachtig Landschap, een Jagtpartij		(Unknown) fl 10
1808/11/28	AMSCH	0083	*Stoop* | In een Landschap ziet men ter zijde voor een Bosch een Rijtuig met Rijzigers, welke door Roovers overvallen werden, stout geschilderd | *Mat:* op paneel	[Gruyter?]	(Bought In) fl 4:5
1810/10/10	MGCIT	0054	*Stoop* | Een zeer hevig Gevegt van Ruiterij, waarin beide Partijen zig de kans des Oorlogs trachten ten nutte te maken, en elkanderen de overwinning te betwisten, in eene schoone trant geschilderd	Caspar van Citters	(Unknown)
1810/10/10	MGCIT	0152	*Stoop* | Een Stuk, waarop een hevige Bataille van Ruiterij; stout behandelt	Caspar van Citters	(Unknown)
			Stoop (or Stoop, manner)		
1803/07/14	MGKLY	0012	*Stoop of zyn manier* | Een heevige Battailje, wel behandeld	Mr Caspar Jacob van Citters	(Unknown)
			Stoop (manner)		
1809/07/25	HGBSM	0270	*Stoop* | Een Man te Paard, in de manier van Stoop | *Mat:* op paneel	D van der Aa [or] E B ten Dall	(Sold) fl 6 Bakhuyzen
			Stoop, Dirck		
1802/09/06	AMSCH	0106	*D. Stoop* | Een Italiaansch Bergagtig Landschap, waar in verbeeld, twee ryzigers te paard, een derzelve laat zyn paard drinken, aan een aloude fontyn; neevens hem zyn twee honden; het zonlicht geeft een kragtige werking, en is meesterlyk van penceel-behandeling | *Mat:* op paneel *Size:* hoog 18, breed 21 duim	H^n Smit	(Sold) fl 7 Jan Spaan
1804/08/08	AMSCH	0176	*D. Stoop* | Een Bergachtig Landschap, met een Fontyn, waarby een halte de Chasse, zynde een ryke Ordinantie van verscheide Beelden, Paarden	Roos a	(Sold) fl 90 Reijers

			en Honden, welken zich ververschen; de Schildering is delicaat, de ordinantie fraai, en het zonlicht frappant | *Mat:* op paneel *Size:* hoog 27, breed 35 duim		
1804/08/08	AMSCH	0177	*D. Stoop* | By de Ruïne van een oud Gebouw ziet men eenige Reizigers te Paard, verders een Postwagen en andere Stoffagie; in alles als de voorgaande | *Mat:* op paneel *Size:* hoog 16, breed 21 duim	Roos [for] C	(Sold) fl 26:10 Van Iperen

Stoop, Jan Pieter

1801/06/10	AMSCH	0159	*Stoop. (J.)* | Een Landschap, ter zyde ziet men een Marketenter, waarby zich een gezelschap Heeren en Dames te Paard ververschen, verders een menigte Beelden, Paarden en Honden, in een bergachtig verschiet; keurig en fiks geschilderd | *Mat:* op paneel *Size:* hoog 34, breed 41 duim	[Doublet]	(Sold) fl 35 Coclers
1801/06/10	AMSCH	0160	*Stoop. (J.)* | Een heuvelachtig Landschap, op de voorgrond ziet men een Dame te Paard, nevens haar een wit Paard, en twee Landlieden, verders verscheide Honden, schynende van de Jagt te komen; alles zonachtig behandeld | *Mat:* op paneel *Size:* hoog 23, breed 32 duim	Herman ten Kate	(Sold) fl 131 Coclers
1802/06/16	AMSCH	0176	*J. Stoop* | Een Landschap, op de voorgrond ziet men een pissend Paard, nevens een rustende Huisman; verders een Ryziger, schynende na de weg te vraagen; krachtig gepenceeld | *Mat:* op paneel *Size:* hoog 17 ½, breed 16 duim	[Merrem]	(Sold) fl 31 Wed Achtienhoven

Storck

1809/06/13	AMSCH	0222	*De Oude Stork* | Een dito, zijnde een aloud Gezigt aan den Overtoom, buiten Amsterdam, ziende naar den Overhaal; gestoffeerd met verscheide Beeldjes, wooningen en eenige Vaartuigen; het zonlicht werkt natuurlijk, en fiks gepenceeld | *Mat:* op paneel *Notes:* It is unclear what "dito" refers to in the title.	R[ijfsnijder]	(Sold) fl 1:10 du Pree

Storck, Abraham

1801/03/16	AMSCH	0037	*A. Stork* | Een gezicht op het Admiraliteits Werf te Amsterdam gestoffeerd met verscheide Beeldjes, Schepen en Schuiten, uitvoerig	S[chley]	(Sold) fl 6:15 Coclers
1801/04/08	HAVIN	0015	*Stork* | Een Gezigt op de Haringpakkers Tooren te Amsterdan [sic], door Stork. In de Tooren is een gaand Horologie		(Unknown)
1801/05/11	AMSCH	0085	*A. Stork* | Twee stuks kabbelende Waters, ryk met Scheepen, Schuiten en Beeldjes, gestoffeerd, ter zyde ziet men in de eene een Dorpgezicht; en in de andere een Vesting: bevallig van licht, en uitvoerig gepenceeld | *Mat:* op doek *Size:* yder hoog 15, breed 19 duim	E[lias]	(Sold) fl 34 Coclers
1801/06/10	AMSCH	0153	*Stork. (A.)* | Een gezicht uit het Y voor Amsterdam, ziende op de Admiraliteits werf, ryk gestoffeerd met een menigte Scheepen en Schuiten, het kabbelende Water is dun, en voorts uitvoerig behandeld | *Mat:* op doek *Size:* hoog 20, breed 24 duim	Herman ten Kate	(Sold) fl 57 Taijs
1801/06/10	AMSCH	0154	*Stork. (A.)* | Een stil Water, ryk met een menigte Oorlogs en andere Scheepen en Vaartuigen gestoffeerd: dun van behandeling als W. van de Velde | *Mat:* op doek *Size:* hoog 20, breed 26 duim	Herman ten Kate	(Sold) fl 151 Jan Yver
1801/06/10	AMSCH	0155	*Stork. (A.)* | Een stil Water, met zeylende Beurtscheepen, Oorlogscheepen en andere Vaartuigen: natuurlyk geschilderd | *Mat:* op paneel *Size:* hoog 6, breed 8 duim	Herman ten Kate	(Sold) fl 17:10 Reynders
1801/06/10	AMSCH	0156	*Stork. (A.)* | Een kabbelend Water, gestoffeerd met een menigte Vaartuigen en stoffage van Beelden, ter zyde een Hoofd, waarop een Baak: dun behandeld | *Mat:* op doek op paneel *Size:* hoog 18, breed 20 duim	Herman ten Kate	(Sold) fl 37 Verheijen
1801/06/13	LNDLS	0083	*Stork* | Een Gezicht op Gebouwen, langs een water	D van R	(Sold) fl 8 Ryers
1801/06/13	LNDLS	0084	*Stork* | Een Gezicht langs een water met Oorlog- en andere Schepen	D van R	(Sold) fl 8 Spaan
1801/08/19	AMSCH	0113	*A. Stork* | Twee stuks, een Strandje en een woelend Water, ryk gestoffeerd met Vaartuigen en Beeldjes; natuurlyk behandeld op Paneel | *Mat:* op paneel *Size:* hoog 8, breed 11 duim	Van Forreest	(Sold) fl 19:10 Wed Achtienhoven
1801/08/19	AMSCH	0114	*A. Stork* | Een stil Water, gestoffeerd met Zylende Scheepen en andere, verder ziet men een Hooft, waar op eenige Lieden Goederen Laaden, op Doek geschilderd | *Mat:* op doek *Size:* hoog 29, breed 40 duim	van der Schly [for] F	(Sold) fl 10 Pruijssenaar [for] R
1801/11/10	AMPOS	0031	*Stork* | 1 woelend Zeetje met Scheepen		(Unknown)
1802/02/16	AMSCH	0077	*A. Stork* | Een woelende Zee, waar in twee zylende Oorlogscheepen en verschyde andere zylende Vaartuigen, zeer natuurlyk en bevallig gepenceeld	C	(Sold) fl 7 van Dijl
1802/04/13	HAVIN	0018	*Stork* | Een gezigt op Amsterdam, met een menigte Zylende Scheepen, en een aangenaame stoffagie op de voorgrond		(Unknown)
1802/05/05	AMSCH	0202	*A. Stork* | Een kabbelend Water	J	(Sold) fl 3 Spruit
1802/05/11	GRGRW	0035	*A. Stork* | Ene Italiaansche Zeehaven [Schilderijen met Olie-Verf; In zwarte Lijsten] | companion to lot 36 *Mat:* in olyverf *Notes:* The bracketed information in the title appears above lot 1 and refers to lots 1 to 79a.	Arnold Sicco Werumeus	(Unknown) fl 13 for lots 35 & 36
1802/05/11	GRGRW	0036	*A. Stork* | Ene dito [Italiaansche Zeehaven], tot ene weerga [Schilderijen met Olie-Verf; In zwarte Lijsten] | companion to lot 35 *Mat:* in olyverf *Notes:* The bracketed information in the title about the medium appears above lot 1 and refers to lots 1 to 79a.	Arnold Sicco Werumeus	(Unknown) fl 13 for lots 35 & 36

1802/06/16	AMSCH	0171	*A. Stork* | Een kabbelend Water met een ménigte Oorlogschepen en andere Vaartuigen, ter linker zyde op een Hooft, ziet men een menigte Beeldjes; alles met de Natuur overeenkomende, behandeld | *Mat:* op doek *Size:* hoog 29, breed 39 duim	[Merrem]	(Sold) fl 48 LaFontaine
1802/06/16	AMSCH	0172	*A. Stork* | Twee stuks stille Waters, ryk gestoffeerd met onderscheiden soorten van Vaartuigen; beide deeze stukken zyn ryk van Ordenantie en van de beste Schildering | *Mat:* op doek *Size:* hoog 22 ½, breed 30 ½ duim	[Merrem]	(Sold) fl 22 Teyssier
1802/06/28	AMSCH	0169	*A. Storck* | Twee stuks, een gezicht in het Y, en een gezicht aan den Buiten-Amstel, beiden ryk gestoffeerd met zeilende Scheepen, Jachten, Boeijers, Sloepen, en andere Vaartuigen, en verscheide wandelende Lieden; zonachtig gepenceeld | *Mat:* op doek *Size:* ieder hoog 16, breed 20 duim	Anna Elink	(Sold) fl 48 Reyers
1802/06/28	AMSCH	0170	*A. Storck* | Een aangenaam kabbelend Water, met verscheide Oorlog Scheepen, Jachten en Schuiten, uitvoerig behandeld, op Doek | *Mat:* op doek *Size:* hoog 12, breed 15 duim	Anna Elink	(Sold) fl 16 Coclers
1802/06/28	AMSCH	0171	*A. Storck* | Twee stuks Venetiaansche Zeehavens, met verscheide Vaartuigen, en Beelden gestoffeerd; bevallig op Panneel | *Mat:* op paneel *Size:* hoog 19, breed 24 duim	Anna Elink	(Sold) fl 10 Vermeulen
1802/06/28	AMSCH	0172	*A. Storck* | Twee Zeetjes, met Scheepen, op Panneel | *Mat:* op paneel *Size:* hoog 10, breed 12 duim	Anna Elink	(Sold) fl 3 Vermeulen
1802/08/24	LNDLS	0152	*A. Stork* | Een Zeehaven met Schepen en Kooplieden	Leonardus Bouman [or others]	(Unknown) fl 4:8
1802/09/06	AMSCH	0108	*A. Stork* | Een gezicht op de Haringpakkers Tooren, met veel stoffagie van beelden en vaartuigen | *Mat:* op doek *Size:* hoog 29, breed 24 duim	Mevrouw Achtienhoven	(Sold) fl 15 Gruiter
1802/09/06	AMSCH	0109	*A. Stork* | Een kabbelend Water, met zeilende en ten anker leggende vaartuigen; meesterlyk | *Mat:* op doek *Size:* hoog 13, breed 12 duim	J	(Sold) fl 1:5 Vermeulen
1802/09/06	AMSCH	0110	*A. Stork* | Een Strandgezigt, met verscheide beeldjes en pinken gestoffeerd | *Mat:* op doek *Size:* hoog 15, breed 13 duim	Mevrouw Achtienhoven	(Sold) fl 15 Gruiter
1802/11/01	DOBRA	0019	*A. Stork* | Een Italiaansche Zeehaven met pragtige gebouwen, op de rede ziet men galeien, enz. de markt is vol gewoel van beelden; in 't verschiet een rookende vuurberg | companion to lot 20 *Mat:* op paneel *Size:* breed 14, hoog 10 duim	Paulus van der Spyk [or others]	(Sold) fl 55 for lots 19 & 20. Schouman
1802/11/01	DOBRA	0020	*A. Stork* | Een dito [Italiaansche Zeehaven], niet minder dan de voorgaande, tot wedergade | companion to lot 19 *Mat:* op paneel *Size:* breed 14, hoog 10 duim	Paulus van der Spyk [or others]	(Sold) fl 55 for lots 19 & 20. Schouman
1802/11/01	DOBRA	0021	*A. Stork* | Twee dito [Italiaansche Zeehavens], zynde het eene een woelend, het ander een stilwater, met allerlei zeilende of drijvende Scheepen, enz. | *Mat:* op doek *Size:* breed 15, hoog 13 duim	Paulus van der Spyk [or others]	(Sold) fl 31 Lamme
1802/11/01	DOBRA	0022	*A. Stork* | Twee dito [Italiaansche Zeehavens], door denzelven [A. Stork]. kleiner	Paulus van der Spyk [or others]	(Sold) fl 4:10 Randwyk
1802/12/13	AMSCH	0145	*A. Storck* | Twee aangenaame Water-Gezigten, ryk gestoffeerd met differenten soorten van Vaartuigen | *Mat:* op doek *Size:* hoog 21, breed 24 duim	Pruyssenaar [for] A	(Sold) fl 2:15 L Pakker
1802/12/13	AMSCH	0147	*A. Storck* | Een Gezigt van de Haringpakkers Tooren, binnen Amsterdam, ryk gestoffeerd met Beelden en Vaartuigen | *Mat:* op doek *Size:* hoog 29, breed 24 duim	Pruyssenaar [for] D	(Sold) fl 16:10 Th[s] Spaan
1803/06/20	AMSCH	0079	*A. Stork* | Een ryk gestoffeerde Italiaansche Zeehaven | *Size:* hoog 18 ½, breed 27 duim	Roos [for] L	(Sold) fl 20 Hodges
1803/07/18	AMSCH	0048	*Stork. (A.)* | Twee stuks, yder hoog 32, breed 43 duim, Doek. Twee stuks Gezigten te Amsterdam, de eene verbeeld een Gezigt op de Nieuwe Stads Herberg aan het Y, en de andere een Gezicht op de Luthersche Nieuwe Kerk en Haarlemmersluis, beide ryk gestoffeerd met een menigte Schepen en andere Vaartuigen, Beelden en Geboomte, beide zeer natuurlyk zo van perspectief als behandeling [Deux vues à Amsterdam. Le premier a son point de vue dans l'intérieur du port sur l'auberge de la ville, qui est sur le bord du fleuve ; à la gauche est la tour des harengers [sic] avec une partie d'un canal voisin. L'eau est embellie par nombre de navires marchands & autres de plaisir, garnis de jolies figures. Le second donne sur le [sic] coupolle de l'eglise luterienne, & sur le côté opposé du canal dit le single, se terminant par la perspective du port ; de jolies figures, une couleur claire & vraye & une exacte perspective ajoutent à leur mérite.] | *Mat:* op doek *Size:* yder hoog 32, breed 43 duim	Maria Theresia Andrioli	(Sold) fl 81 van Iperen
1803/08/01	AMSCH	0036	*Stork. (A.)* | Een woelende Zee met zeilende Scheepen en Boejers, in 't verschiet een Stadgezigt, natuurlyk behandeld | *Mat:* op paneel *Size:* hoog 10, breed 10 duim	J	(Sold) fl 4:10 Th[s] Spann
1803/08/17	AMSCH	0079	*Stork (A.)* | Twee stukt [sic] Levantsche Zeehavens, ryk gestoffeerd en behandeld, als T. Wyk | *Mat:* op paneel *Size:* ieder hoog 13, breed 16 duim	Anna Catharina Putman	(Sold) fl 10:10 Agina
1803/12/15	MGLAC	0025	*Stork* | Een extra fraai Zeetje met Schepen | *Mat:* op doek *Size:* hoog duim 14, breed duim 17	Mr L H de Haze Bomme	(Unknown)
1804/02/27	AMSCH	0099	*Stork. (A.)* | Een Gezicht te Maarsen, naar de Brug ziende waarby een Jacht met verscheide vrolyke Lieden; verders ryk gestoffeerd met een	D	(Bought In) fl 2

			menigte Beelden, uitvoerig van behandeling | *Mat:* op doek *Size:* hoog 31, breed 42 duim		
1804/02/27	AMSCH	0100	*Stork. (A.)* | Twee stuks, en stil en een woelend Water | *Size:* hoog 20, breed 16 ½ duim	C	(Sold) fl 1 Coclers
1804/05/07	AMSCH	0154	*Stork. (A)* | Twee stuks, ryk met Monumenten, Beelden, Scheepen en Vaartuigen, gestoffeerde Italiaansche Zeehavens; kloek van behandeling | *Mat:* op paneel *Size:* Ieder hoog 8, breed 10 duim	Roos [for] A	(Sold) fl 11:10 Wed Achtienhoven
1804/08/08	AMSCH	0178	*A. Stork* | Twee stuks Italiaansche Zéehavens, ryk gestoffeerd met Gebouwen, Schépen en een vreedlyk gewoel van Beeldjes, Kwakzalvers en anderen; meesterlyk op Doek | *Mat:* op doek *Size:* hoog 21, breed 18 duim	Roos [for] G	(Sold) fl 25 Coclers
1804/08/08	AMSCH	0179	*A. Stork* | Op 't Y voor Amsterdam ziet men een ménigte van zeilende Scheepen, Jachten, Boeijers, verbeeldende hetzelve 't Admiraalschap zeilen; dun en helder gepenceeld | *Mat:* op doek *Size:* hoog 33, breed 41 duim	Vink[eles] [for] S	(Sold) fl 51 Jan Spaan
1804/10/16	DLOND	0195b	*A. Stork* | [Untitled] | *Notes:* This lot was changed from "C. Sagtleven, Twee Schilderyen Verbeeldende Beestenmarkten, vol gewoel," to "E. de Witte" and "A. Stork," without giving titles, at the front of the printed catalogue. They have been numbered 195a and 195b.		(Unknown)
1804/10/16	DLOND	0216	*A. Stork* | Riviergezicht met Schepen voor het Hoofd te Rotterdam. Vue du Port de Rotterdam & des Vaisseaux | *Mat:* op doek *Size:* hoog 29, breed 42		(Unknown)
1804/10/16	DLOND	0217	*A. Stork* | Een Haven met verscheiden Schepen. Un Port & des Vaisseaux différens | *Mat:* op doek *Size:* hoog 29, breed 42		(Unknown)
1804/10/16	DLOND	0218	*A. Stork* | Uts[a] [Een Haven met verscheiden Schepen. Un Port & des Vaisseaux différens] | *Mat:* op doek *Size:* hoog 18, breed 22		(Unknown) fl 26:15
1804/10/16	DLOND	0219	*A. Stork* | Riviergezicht met zeilende Schepen. Vue d'une Rivière & des Vaisseaux qui font voile | *Mat:* op doek *Size:* hoog 26, breed 36		(Unknown)
1804/10/16	DLOND	0219a	*A. Stork* | Gezicht van Cleef. Vue de Clèves | *Mat:* op paneel *Size:* hoog 18, breed 23		(Unknown)
1804/10/16	DLOND	0220	*A. Stork* | Uts[a] [Gezicht van Cleef. Vue de Clèves] | *Mat:* op paneel *Size:* hoog 18, breed 23		(Unknown)
1804/10/29	HRBAU	0100	*Stork. (A.)* | Op den Voorgrond van deze Zeehaven, welke een Kaai verbeeldt, staat een Fontein, die met het beeld van Naptunus pronkt, en waar by een pragtige Galei ligt: ook ziet men 'er eene menigte handeldryvende Persoonen van verschillende Natiën; wat verder ligt een Hollandsch Esquader, dat bezig is zeil te maaken, en reeds door 't lossen van 't kanon deszelfs vertrek te kennen geeft; aan de overzyde ligt een pragtige Stad aan den voet van het Gebergte, welk mede met Paleizen en Forten bezet is. Dit Schildery is alleruitvoerigst en zeer zonagtig behandeld | *Mat:* op doek *Size:* hoog 41, breed 59 duim	Simon Styl	(Unknown)
1805/07/03	AMSCH	0142	*A. Stork* | Een stil Water, met verscheide zylende en stilleggende Vaartuigen; fiks op Doek | *Mat:* op doek *Size:* hoog 28, breed 36 duim	V[inkeles]	(Sold) fl 1:5 L Pakker
1805/07/03	AMSCH	0143	*A. Stork* | Twee stuks, een stil en woelend Water, beiden ryk gestoffeert met zylende en stilleggende Scheepen en Vissers; plaisant geschilderd op Doek | *Mat:* op doek *Size:* hoog 11, breed 11 duim	G	(Sold) fl 20:10 La Vallette
1805/07/03	AMSCH	0144	*A. Stork* | Een gezicht aan 't Strand, gestoffeerd met Vissers, Pinken, wandelende en rydende Dames en Heeren, in het verschiet verscheide Scheepen in Zee; bevallig op Doek | *Mat:* op doek *Size:* hoog 23, breed 28 duim	G	(Sold) fl 12:10 Nieuwenhuys
1805/07/03	AMSCH	0145	*A. Stork* | Een Rivier aan een Stad, waarin diverse groote en klyne Vaartuigen; natuurlyk op Doek | *Mat:* op doek *Size:* hoog 22, breed 28 duim	C	(Sold) fl 5:10 Nieuwenhuys
1805/07/03	AMSCH	0146	*A. Stork* | Een gezicht op het oude Stadhuis te Amsterdam, gestoffeerd met een ménigte Beeldjes; kragtig op Doek | *Mat:* op doek *Size:* hoog 23, breed 32 duim	C	(Sold) fl 40 Vinkeles [for] S
1805/07/10	AMSCH	0130	*A. Stork* | Twee stuks, Amsterdam uit het Y, en Rotterdam uit de Maas te zien, beide ryk met onderscheide Scheepen en Vaartuigen gestoffeerd, als ook diverse Beeldjes enz. | *Mat:* op doek *Size:* hoog 26, breed 32 duim	Y[ver]	(Bought In) fl 10:10
1805/07/10	AMSCH	0131	*A. Stork* | Een Levantsche Zeehaven; meesterlyk op Doek | *Mat:* op doek *Size:* hoog 32, breed 46 duim	V[inkeles] [for] H[affner]	(Sold) fl 0:10 L Pakker
1805/07/10	AMSCH	0132	*A. Stork* | Een Onstuimige Zee, ryk met Scheepen en Schuiten, in 't verschiet een Stad; dun en als Bakhuyzen, door denzelven [A. Stork] | *Mat:* op doek	V[inkeles] [for] K	(Sold) fl 32 L Pakker
1805/10/09	HGBSM	0107	*A. Storck* | Een Italiaansche zeehaven met pragtige gebouwen, het water is ryk gestoffeerd, met differente soort van vaartuigen en figuuren, helder van couleur en konstig behandelt | *Mat:* op doek *Size:* hoog 29 breet 35 duim	T H van Willigen [or others]	(Sold) fl 22:10 De Gelder
1805/12/16	AMSCH	0054	*A. Stork* | Een Gezicht op een der Dorpen, aan de Vecht, het Land met Beelden, en 't Water met een Trekschuit en Jagt gestoffeerd; geestig geschilderd op Doek | *Mat:* op doek *Size:* hoog 31, breed 42 duim	R[oos]	(Sold) fl 2 T van Iperen

1806/05/05	AMSCH	0130	*A. Storck* | Twee, Amstel en Y gezigten, beiden ryk gestoffeerd met zeilende Scheepen, Jagten en andere kleindere Vaartuigen, en de Stad in het verschiet | *Mat:* op doek *Size:* hoog 21, breed 28 duim	V[inkeles]	(Sold) fl 5:5 Levy Pakker
1806/05/05	AMSCH	0131	*A. Storck* | Een Levantsche Zeehaven, met pragtige Gebouwen, differente Scheepen en Galeyen, en andere stoffagie; meesterlyk geschildert door denzelven [A. Storck] | *Mat:* op doek *Size:* hoog 35, breed 46 duim	V[inkeles]	(Bought In) fl 9:10
1806/05/05	AMSCH	0132	*A. Storck* | Een gezigt langs de Vegt, gestoffeerd met wandelende Heeren en Dames, Boejers, Jaagschuiten en andere Vaartuigen | *Mat:* op paneel *Size:* hoog 30, breed 41 duim	V[inkeles]	(Sold) fl 1:15 L Pakker
1806/05/05	AMSCH	0133	*A. Storck* | Twee stuks woelende Zeegezigten, met zeilende Scheepen en andere Turksche Vaartuigen; uitvoerig geschildert door denzelven [A. Storck] | *Mat:* op paneel *Size:* hoog 5, breed 7 duim	V[inkeles]	(Sold) fl 1:10 Rookmans
1806/05/05	AMSCH	0134	*A. Storck* | Een woelend Zeetje, met zeilende Vaartuigen | *Size:* hoog 13, breed 14 duim	V[inkeles]	(Sold) fl 2:5 van Laar
1806/05/05	AMSCH	0257	*A. Stork* | Twee Zeehavens	R[oos]	(Sold) fl 1 L Pakker
1806/08/13	AMSCH	0175	*Stork. (A.)* | Twee stuks Zeeën, met een ménigte van zeilende en stilleggende Scheepen en Schuiten; zonachtig en meesterlyk geschilderd | *Mat:* op doek *Size:* Ieder hoog 22, breed 28 duim	Vinkeles [for] F	(Sold) fl 46 T Spaan
1807/06/10	HGBSM	0077	*A. Stork* | Een Gezicht langs het Water op de Stad Amsterdam met zeilende Jachten en andere Vaartuigen, helder en konstig behandeld | companion to lot 78 *Mat:* op doek *Size:* hoog 22 breed 30 duim	Abraham Delfos [or others]	(Sold) fl 6:10 Wiggers
1807/06/10	HGBSM	0078	*A. Stork* | Een weerga, niet minder van konst en dito [helder en konstig] behandeld | companion to lot 77 *Mat:* op doek *Size:* hoog 22 breed 30 duim	Abraham Delfos [or others]	(Sold) fl 4:15 Wiggers
1807/08/26	AMSCH	0207	*A. Stork* | Twee stuks Levantsche Zeehavens met een menigte Vaartuigen en Beelden | *Mat:* op doek *Size:* hoog 19, breed 25 duim	Joseph Vallette	(Sold) fl 6:10 Coclair
1807/08/26	AMSCH	0208	*A. Stork* | Een Gezigt uit het Spaaren op Haarlem te zien, gestoffeerd met onderscheidene Vaartuigen en Beeldjes; fiks | *Mat:* op doek *Size:* hoog 19, breed 27 duim	Roos	(Sold) fl 6:15 Gruiter
1807/09/28	AMWUR	0020	*A. Stork* | Een stuk verbeeldende de Haven van Venetiën, zonachtig en warm geschilderd door A. Stork, in zwarte Lyst		(Unknown) fl 7
1808/03/03	HAVIN	0004	*A. Stork* | Een Gezicht op de Stad Haarlem, van 't N. Spaarne te zien, langs de Scheepswerf, uitvoerig en fraai	Jacobus Spillebout	(Unknown) fl 27
1808/04/26	GDAN	0155	*Stork (A.)* | Een Italiaansche Zeehaven, vol gewoel, bij voornaame Gebouwen en Kerken, in 't verschiet ziet men verscheidene zeilende en andere Schepen, fiks geschildert | companion to lot 156 *Size:* hoog 28 ½, breed 42 duim	G H Fortuyn	(Unknown)
1808/04/26	GDAN	0156	*Stork (A.)* | Een dito [Italiaansche Zeehaven] tot een wederga | companion to lot 155	G H Fortuyn	(Unknown)
1808/06/11	RMRIJ	0009	*A: Stork* | Een Stil Water, met Paalwerk, Hoofden en Duin, waar in een menigte Vaartuigen en Figuren; zeer plaisant en konstig | *Mat:* op paneel *Size:* hoog 10 ¾, breed 12 ½ duim		(Sold) fl 64 Luchtmans
1808/06/11	RMRIJ	0010	*A: Stork* | Een Woelend Water, in alles als 't voorgaande		(Sold) Coclairs
1808/06/13	AMSCH	0147	*Storck (A.)* | Dit kapitale stuk verbeeld een Gezicht te Amsterdam, ziende van de Kalverstraat, langs den Dam, naar een gedeelte van de voorgevel van 't Stadhuis, naar de Nieuwe Kerk, Stads Waag, Nieuwendijk en Damrak, rijk gestoffeerd met eene menigte Beeldjes, van allerlei rang en staat, Rijtuigen, en verder bijwerk. Het zonlicht is natuurlijk, en de schildering bevallig | *Mat:* op doek *Size:* hoog 49, breed 65 duim	Z	(Sold) fl 55 J^{mo} de Vries
1808/06/13	AMSCH	0148	*Storck (A.)* | Een Gezicht op het IJ voor Amsterdam, waarop Czaar Peter de Groote in een Jagt is zeilende, verder andere Jagten en Boeijers, welke een Spiegelgevegt houden. Geestig van uitdrukking | *Mat:* op doek *Size:* hoog 27, breed 35 duim	E M Engelberts	(Sold) fl 26 O W J Berg
1808/06/13	AMSCH	0220b[H]	*Stork* | 2 Zeetjes van Stork | *Notes:* This lot was added in by hand in the AA I, EBNP, FLNY, MB and RKDH copies of the catalogue.	R[oos]	(Sold) fl 80 Reyers
1808/08/23	AMSCH	0148	*Storck. (A.)* | Twee stuks bevallige voorwerpen, vol gewoel van zeilende Scheepen en andere Vaartuigen; het eene verbeeld een kabbelend Water, zijnde een gezicht uit het IJ naar de Stad te zien, gestoffeert met zeilende Oorlogscheepen, Boeijers, Jachten, en Vissers in Schuiten; den anderen een stil Water, ziende naar de Hoogesluis, aan den Buiten-Amstel, als de vorige gestoffeert met zeilende Jachten, Tentschuitjes, Vissers en andere Vaartuigen; beide helder, zonachtig en uitvoerig gepenceeld | *Mat:* op doek *Size:* Ieder hoog 21, breed 27 duim	C	(Bought In) fl 90
1808/08/23	AMSCH	0149	*Storck. (A.)* | Dit bevallig Schilderij, vertoont een IJ-gezicht, naar de Stad Amsterdam te zien, rijk gestoffeert in een kabbelend Water, met Oorlogscheepen, fraaije Boeijer, en andere zeilende Scheepen, Tent-Jacht, en andere Vaartuigen; op de voorgrond zijn verscheide Aanschouwers; het is helder, zonachtig en van een uitvoerige penceelbehandeling | *Mat:* op doek *Size:* hoog 24, breed 29 duim	[Coclers]	(Sold) fl 50 van Iperen [or] Molder
1808/08/23	AMSCH	0150	*Storck. (A.)* | Twee stuks Gezichten in het IJ voor Amsterdam, van en na de Stad te zien, gestoffeerd met zeilende en ten anker leggende Scheepen,	Y	(Sold) fl 14:10 Jan Spaan

			Boeijers, en andere Vaartuigen; helder en plaisant geschilderd | *Mat:* op doek *Size:* Ieder hoog 21, breed 25 duim		
1808/08/23	AMSCH	0151	*Storck. (A.)* | Twee stuks Gezichten, het eene ziende in het IJ, en het andere op de Buiten-Amstel, rijk gestoffeert met Vaartuigen, Rijtuigen en Beeldjes; natuurlijk en fiks behandeld | *Mat:* op paneel *Size:* Ieder is hoog 10, breed 17 duim	Y	(Sold) fl 3 Dupré
1808/08/23	AMSCH	0152	*Storck. (A.)* | Twee stuks Dorp-gezichten aan de Vecht, beide vol stoffagie van Beeldjes en andere Figuuren; natuurlijk als de voorgaande behandeld | *Mat:* op paneel *Size:* hoog 10, breed 17 duim	Y	(Sold) fl 5:10 D Maijkel
1809/04/17	AMSCH	0095	*A. Stork* | Twee dito Ordonantien, fiks behandeld als de voorgaande | *Mat:* op doek *Size:* ieder hoog 22, breed 27 duim *Notes:* It is unclear what "dito" refers to in the title.	S	(Sold) fl 6:15
1809/04/17	AMSCH	0096	*A. Stork* | Een Gezigt binnen Amsterdam, ziende op de Haringpakkerij en Nieuwe Stads Herberg; rijk gestoffeerd, met onderscheidene Vaartuigen en Beeldjes; fiks behandeld | *Mat:* op paneel *Size:* hoog 33, breed 43 duim	T	(Sold) fl 8 Gruyter
1809/04/17	AMSCH	0097	*A. Stork* | Twee stuks Levantsche Zeehavens, met prachtige Gebouwen, Scheepen, Galleijen en andere Vaartuigen, verder gestoffeerd met wandelende Heeren en Dames, Kooplieden, Slaaven en Bootsgezellen; helder en kragtig geschilderd | *Mat:* op doek *Size:* hoog 31, breed 24 duim	[Gruyter?]	(Sold or Bought In) fl 1 Gruyter
1809/04/17	AMSCH	0146	*A. Stork* | Een Venetiaansche Zeehaven, met pragtige Gebouwen en Overblijfsels van oude Gedenktekens, rijk gestoffeerd met Beelden en Vaartuigen | *Mat:* op doek	[Gruyter?]	(Sold) fl 0:6
1809/04/17	AMSCH	0163	*A. Stork* | Twee stuks IJgezichten, met Vaartuigen gestoffeerd	R	(Sold) fl 3
1809/06/13	AMSCH	0143	*A. Stork* | Twee stuks Levantsche Zeehavens, met grootsche Gebouwen en Gedenkzuilen, rijk gestoffeerd met Heeren en Dames, Kooplieden, Vaartuigen en andere figuren; helder en bevallig geschilderd | *Mat:* op doek *Size:* ieder is hoog 26, breed 33 duim	E	(Sold) fl 2:10 T Spaan
1809/06/13	AMSCH	0144	*A. Stork* | Twee stuks, verbeeldende Y-Gezichten voor de stadt Amsterdam, rijk gestoffeert met zijlende Oorlog- en andere Scheepen, Jagten en andere Vaartuigen, met verscheide Beeldjes, beide plaisant geschilderd | *Mat:* op paneel *Size:* hoog 13, breed 15 duim	R[ijfsnijder]	(Sold) fl 1:15 Gruyter
1809/07/19	AMSCH	0054	*Stork (A.)* | Twee stuks kabbelende Waters, rijk gestoffeerd met Schepen, Jagten en andere Vaartuigen. Helder en natuurlijk verbeeld | *Mat:* op doek *Size:* ieder is hoog 18 ½, breed 27 duim	C	(Sold) fl 12:10 Nieuwenhuys
1809/07/25	HGBSM	0071	*A. Stonck* | Een Groenlands Gezigt, verbeeldende een Walvischvangst, vol Scheepen en Chaloupen, met een witte Beerejagt op de voorgrond, met veel Figuren | *Mat:* op doek *Size:* hoog 23, breed 29 duim	D van der Aa	(Sold) fl 7:10 van der Aa [or] Mes
1809/07/25	HGBSM	0282	*Stork* | Twee stuks Zeegezigten, verbeeldende een Walvisch vangst | *Mat:* op doek *Size:* hoog 15, breed 18 en een half duim	D van der Aa [or] E B ten Dall	(Sold) fl 4 De Gelder
1810/03/07	UTWLD	0021	*Stork* | Een Italiaansche Zeehaven met scheepen en beeldjes | *Size.* hoog 3 voet 5 duim, breed 4 voet	J J Woertman	(Unknown) fl 17
1810/03/27	RMCNL	0001	*Storken* | Een Kapitaal Landschap, verbeeldende een Stadgezigt langs eene Rivier, waarin zeilende en stilliggende Schepen, zeer warm, fix en te gelijk uitvoerig geschilderd		(Unknown)
1810/03/27	RMCNL	0009	*Storken* | Een Stad en Watergezigtje, netjes en fraai van Penseel, om zijne kleinheid onder de enkelde van dien Meester		(Unknown)
1810/05/22	AMSCH	0094	*Stork. (A.)* | Een Gezicht aan den Buitenkant te Amsterdam, ziende naar het IJ, rijk gestoffeerd met Oorlogschepen, Beurtlieden, zijlende Jagten, Roeischuiten en andere Vaartuigen, op den voorgrond wandelende Lieden, Kramers en Arbeiders; natuurlijk en zonachtig behandeld | *Mat:* op doek *Size:* hoog 15, breed 19 duim	F	(Sold) fl 10 Rutte
1810/06/06	RMMUY	0050	*A. Storck* | Een stil Water. Gestoffeerd met een Haringbuis; en verscheiden Visschers Vaartuigen, verder een Oorlogschip, Jacht en andere Schepen. Warm en fiks gepenceeld | *Mat:* op paneel		(Unknown) fl 30
1810/06/06	RMMUY	0051	*A. Storck* | Een dito [stil Water]. Rijk van Schepen, Booten en Figuren, konstig en natuurlijk | companion to lot 52 *Mat:* op paneel		(Unknown) fl 34 for lots 51 & 52
1810/06/06	RMMUY	0052	*A. Storck* | Eene Wedergade, zijnde een woelend water met niet minder stoffage van Schepen | companion to lot 51 *Mat:* op paneel		(Unknown) fl 34 for lots 51 & 52
1810/07/23	DOLG2	000Z	*A. Storck* | Twee stuks Zeegezichten, wel gestoffeerd met onderscheiden soorten van Vaartuigen | *Mat:* op doek *Size:* hoog 12 ½, breed 15 duim	Pieter Quinting	(Unknown) fl 8
1810/07/23	DOLG2	0012	*A. Storck* | De afbeelding eener Zeehaven, vol Schepen, zoo Galijen als andere Vaartuigen. De gebouwen zijn van eene prachtige Bouwörder. In rijkheid van Beelden, enz., een der beste Schilderijen van dien Meester. Door A. Storck. A° 1688 | *Mat:* op doek *Size:* hoog 30, breed 26 duim *Inscr:* A. Storck. A° 1688 (signed and dated?) *Notes:* It is unclear whether the name and date are inscribed on the painting.	Pieter Quinting	(Unknown)
1810/07/26	AMSCH	0077	*Stork (A.)* | Een Zeehaven met prachtige Gebouwen, gestoffeerd met Kooplieden, Vaartuigen enz. | *Mat:* op doek *Size:* hoog 24, breed 29 duimen	Cassino	(Bought In) fl 3

1810/07/26	AMSCH	0078	*Stork (A.)* | Een Zeegezigt met Schepen, verbeeldende de Beeren- en Walvischvangst. Helder geschilderd | *Mat:* op doek *Size:* hoog 25, breed 28 duimen	Cassino	(Bought In) fl 3:15
1810/08/06	AMSCH	0096	*Stork (A.)* | Twee stuks bevallige Voorwerpen, zijnde het eene een Gezigt in het IJ na de Stad, het andere de Buiten-Amstel na de Hoogesluis te zien, beide rijk gestoffeerd; helder en zonachtig geschilderd | *Mat:* op doek *Size:* ieder hoog 21, breed 27 duimen	B	(Bought In) fl 30
1810/08/06	AMSCH	0097	*Stork (A.)* | Dit kapitale stuk verbeelt een Gezigt te Amsterdam, ziende van de Kalverstraat langs den Dam naar het Stadhuis, de Waag, Nieuwendijk en Damrak, alles is rijk gestoffeerd met eene menigte Beeldjes van allerleien rang; alles is zeer natuurlijk en uitvoerig van schildering | *Mat:* op doek *Size:* hoog 49, breed 65 duimen	V[ries]	(Bought In) fl 55
1810/08/10	RMRIJ	0024a	*A. Stork* | Eene fraaije Levantsche Zeehaven, rijk gestoffeerd | *Notes:* There are two lots with the number 24; this lot has been changed to 24a.		(Sold) fl 2:10 [or] 7: 10 v Dyk
1810/10/11	AMSCH	0135	*A. Stork* | Een Italiaansche Zeehaven, met pragtige Gebouwen, onderscheidene Vaartuigen, wandelende en arbeidende Lieden | *Mat:* op doek	[Gruyter?]	(Sold) fl 1:15 Van Leen
1810/10/11	AMSCH	0224	*A. Stork* | Een Rhijn- en Dorpgezigt, met Beeldjes en Vaartuigen gestoffeerd | *Notes:* This lot was sold with lots 214 by N. Verkolje and 223 by Jan Lairesse.	A	(Sold) fl 8 for lots 214, 223 & 224. Yver
			Storck, Abraham (and Moucheron, I.)		
1808/06/11	RMRIJ	0090	*J: de Moucheron; Gestoffeerd door Stork* | Een Italiaansch Hofgezicht, ryk gestoffeerd, geleerd en konstig geschilderd | *Mat:* op doek *Size:* hoog 20, breed 24 duim		(Sold) fl 40 Van Leen
			Storck, Abraham (copy by)		
1802/12/13	AMSCH	0146	*A. Storck; Willem van de Velde* | Een Bataillje op Zée; na Willem van de Velde, door A. Storck | copy by Abr. Storck after W. Velde *Mat:* op doek *Size:* hoog 24, breed 34 duim	Pruyssenaar [for] A	(Sold) fl 0:10 L Pakker
			Storck, Abraham (copy after)		
1805/06/24	DOBLU	0019	*Storck* | Twee Watertjes, naar Storck	Willem Snellen [or] F R E Nibbelinck [or] Gysbert Visser	(Unknown)
1810/10/10	MGCIT	0140	*Stork* | Een Zeestukje, naar Stork	Caspar van Citters	(Unknown)
			Storck, Abraham (manner)		
1802/08/24	LNDLS	0114	*Stork* | Een Zee met Schepen en andere Vaartuigen als van Stork	Leonardus Bouman [or others]	(Unknown) fl 1:10
1804/10/20	GRBOL	0002	*Stork* | Een Strant Gezigt in manier van Stork	Joannis Cannegieteri	(Unknown)
1804/10/29	HRBAU	0134	*Stork* | Een Levantsche Zeehaven, ryk gestoffeerd. In de manier van Stork | *Mat:* op doek *Size:* hoog 18, breed 25 duim	Simon Styl	(Unknown)
1807/08/26	AMSCH	0271	*A. Stork* | Een Gezicht langs een stil Water, by een Hofstede, met Schepen en andere Vaartuigen gestoffeerd, op Paneel, in de manier van A. Stork | *Mat:* op paneel	Roos [for] A	(Sold) fl 1:10 Gruiter
1810/07/23	DOLG2	0090	*Storck* | Een Strandgezicht, als door Storck | *Mat:* op paneel *Size:* hoog 7, breed 9 duim	Pieter Quinting	(Unknown)
			Storck, Jacobus		
1801/03/16	AMSCH	0020	*J. Stork* | Een Dorpgezicht aan de Vecht, ryk gestoffeerd met Schuiten en Beeldjes, meesterlyk en natuurlyk	K[ip]	(Sold) fl 42 Coclers
1801/06/13	LNDLS	0067	*J. Storck* | Een Gezicht langs een water met schepen, op een Stad	D van R	(Sold) fl 6:5 Schoolenaar
1802/05/24	HGBAK	0071	*Jacobus Sturck* | Een plaisant Dorpgezicht, aan een Rivier gelegen, met zeilende Schepen, zeer uitvoerig en wel behandeld, door Jacobus Sturck, hoog 29 duim, breed 40 ½ duim, op doek, zwarte lyst met verg. binnenrand | companion to lot 72 *Mat:* op doek *Size:* hoog 29 duim, breed 40 ½ duim	Mejuffrouw A van der Mieden	(Sold) fl 19:10 for lots 71 & 72. Ondorp
1802/05/24	HGBAK	0072	*Jacobus Sturck* | Een dito [plaisant Dorpgezicht] tot een weerga, hoog en breed als vooren, dito [zwarte] lyst | companion to lot 71 *Size:* hoog 29 duim, breed 40 ½ duim *Notes:* It is unclear what "dito" refers to in the title.	Mejuffrouw A van der Mieden	(Sold) fl 19:10 for lots 71 & 72. Ondorp
1802/07/21	HGKAN	0067	*Jacobus Stork* | Een plaisant Dorp Gezicht aan een Rivier geleegen, met zeilende Scheepen, zeer uitvoerig en wel behandeld door Jacobus Stork, op Doek, zwarte Lyst, met vergulde binnen rand | companion to lot 68, by Anonymous *Mat:* op doek		(Unknown)
1804/08/08	AMSCH	0180	*J. Stork* | Een Gezicht aan de Overtoom, buiten Amsterdam, by de Amstelveensche Weg, vol gewoel van Beelden, zeilende en stil leggende Vaartuigen; fiks en natuurlyk behandeld | *Mat:* op paneel *Size:* hoog 25, breed 33 duim	Vink[eles] [for] S	(Sold) fl 3:15 van der Schley [for] R[ijfsnijder]
1804/10/29	HRBAU	0101	*Stork, (J.)* | Voor aan, ter linkerzyde, ziet men verscheiden Gondels, by een' trap, langs welken men naar een Plein gaat, waar een pragtig Paleis op staat, alwaar verscheiden Heeren en Dames afscheid van elkander	Simon Styl	(Unknown)

			neemen: en meer andere Figuuren; iets verder schynt een Poort der Vest te zyn, waar langs men op eene Stad en menigte Scheepen ziet. Zeer uitvoerig geschilderd | *Mat:* op paneel *Size:* hoog 24, breed 32 duim		
1805/10/21	GRBOL	0022	*J. Stork* | Een Rhyngezicht	Gerardus Nicolaus Heerkens	(Unknown)
1806/10/16	UTWLD	0011	*J. Storck* | Een Stad gezicht leggende aan 't Water, gestoffeerd met Gebouwen, Vaartuigen en Beelden door J. Storck	Mr P de Malapert [or] W Beeldsnyder	(Unknown)
1806/11/24	AMSCH	0074	*Stork (J.)* | Een gezigt op het Dorp Maarssen, gestoffeerd met een ménigte Beelden en Vaartuigen, warm van coloriet | *Mat:* op paneel *Size:* hoog 29, breed 41 duim	Munnikhuizen	(Sold) fl 5 L Pakker
1808/10/28	AMVRS	0061	*Stork, (J.)* | Een Dorpgezicht aan de Vecht, gestoffeerd met Vaartuigen en verschillende Beelden. Helder en natuurlijk geschilderd | *Mat:* op paneel *Size:* hoog 24, breed 33 duim	Marten Udink	(Sold) fl 8:10 B Kooij
1809/04/17	AMSCH	0172	*J. Stork* | Een Levantsche Zeehaven, met Stoffagie	H	(Sold) fl 1:10
1809/04/22	AMYVR	0120	*J. Stork* | Twee stuks Venetiaansche Zeehavens, rijk en vol gewoel van Scheepen en kleinere Vaartuigen, bevallige verschieten en dunne behandeling | *Mat:* op doek *Size:* hoog 21, breed 25 duim	de Bruin	(Sold) fl 10:10 du Pree
1809/06/13	AMSCH	0145	*J. Stork* | Twee stuks Dorpgezichten aan de Vecht, rijk gestoffeerd met zijlende Jagten, Trekschuiten en Beeldjes; zeer bevallig verbeeld | *Mat:* op paneel *Size:* hoog 19, breed 25 duim	M	(Sold) fl 52:10 Preijn
1810/06/20	AMSCH	0153	*J. Stork* | Een Dorpgezigt aan de Vecht, rijk met Beelden en Vaartuigen	B	(Sold) fl 7 Jan Ijver
1810/10/11	AMSCH	0215	*J. Stork* | Een Zeehaven, met grootsche Gebouwen, Kooplieden en Vaartuigen gestoffeerd, fiks | *Mat:* op doek	A	(Sold) fl 1 Mensart

Storck, Jacobus (manner)

1807/08/26	AMSCH	0209	*J. Stork* | Twee stuks, een woelend en een stil Water, zynde een Ygezigt, beide gestoffeerd met zeilende en stilleggende Schepen, Jachten en Vissers Schuiten; natuurlyk op Paneel geschilderd, in de manier van J. Stork | *Mat:* op paneel *Size:* ieder hoog 10, breed 13 duim	Roos	(Sold) fl 17:10 Jarman

Straaten, van der

1808/10/28	AMVRS	0069	*Verstraaten* | Een Land- en Watergezicht, met vervallen Boeren Woningen en Huislieden gestoffeerd	Marten Udink	(Sold) fl 14:10 Spaan [or] Van Jepren
1810/06/20	AMSCH	0099	*J. Verstraaten* | Een natuurlijk Land- en Watergezigt, met gaande en rustende Huislieden | *Mat:* op paneel *Size:* hoog 16, breed 13 duimen	B	(Sold) fl 1:10 L Pakker

Straaten, van der (manner)

1803/04/06	MGSAN	0003	*Verstraaten* | Een Fraai Landschap met een Ruïne, in de manier van Verstraaten	Mr Evert Clyver	(Unknown)

Straaten, Hendrik van der

1801/08/19	AMSCH	0122	*H. Verstraten* | Een warm Boom- en Bergachtig Landschap, met een Water doorsneeden; fix door H. Verstraten, op Doek | *Mat:* op doek *Size:* hoog 22, breed 25 duim	W Wynen	(Sold) fl 7:5 V^{n} Dijl

Straaten, Johannes Josephus Ignatius

1810/11/07	UTWLD	0006	*J. v. Straten* | Een pendant door J. v. Straten, een opziende Haan, agter denzelven een drinkenspot, liggende en staande Hennen in 't volle licht, op den achtergrond een schuur, strooibos, een stil verschiet, alles zeer kragtig, klaar en fraai op doek geschilderd, hoog en breed als voren in een vergulde Lijst | companion to lot 5, by M. Hondecoeter *Mat:* op doek *Size:* 3 voet 2 en een half duim breed, 2 en een half voet hoog		(Unknown) fl 140
1810/11/07	UTWLD	0007	*J. v. Straten* | Een Haas, liggende tegen een Jagtroer 't welk tegen een schutting rust, Patrijzen en Jagtgereedschappen, op de voorgrond eenige planten, op de agtergrond agter de schutting een eiken stam en ander groen, alles zeer uitvoerig en meesteragtig behandeld, zijnde een der beste stukken van J. v. Straten, op doek, breed 3 voet 3 duim hoog 2 voet 8 duim, in een vergulde Lijst | *Mat:* op doek *Size:* breed 3 voet 3 duim hoog 2 voet 8 duim		(Unknown) fl 215

Strating, Jaco. [Unidentified]

1807/06/10	HGBSM	0170	*Jaco. Strating* | Een Historieel stuk | *Mat:* op doek	Abraham Delfos [or others]	(Sold) fl 1 Carré

Streeck, Hendrik van

1809/04/22	AMYVR	0123	*A. van Streek* | Een Gezicht in de Oude Kerk, gestoffeerd met Beelden; zonachtig | *Mat:* op doek *Size:* hoog 32, breed 27 duim *Notes:* The artist's name was given as "A. van Streek" but we have assumed this is an error.	Juff^{r} Julikker	(Sold) fl 2 du Pree

Streeck, Juriaen van

1802/02/16	AMSCH	0017	*van Streek* | Op een Tafel ziet men een schotel met Perziken, en glas met Bloemen, zeer natuurlyk geschilderd op doek | *Mat:* op doek	B[uys]	(Sold) fl 0:14 van Iperen
1804/10/29	HRBAU	0102	*Streek, (J.)* | Op een' Steenen Tafel, met een paars Kleed met gouden Franjes overdekt, staat een porceleinen Pot en Schotel, als ook een	Simon Styl	(Unknown)

			Nautulus en een glas met wyn; in den Schotel liggen Oranje appels, Citroenen en Persiken, waarnevens een Wittebrood op de tafel ligt. Dit alles is zeer natuurlyk en uitvoerig gepenseeld | *Mat:* op doek *Size:* hoog 24, breed 20 ½ duim		
1808/06/11	RMRIJ	0037	*J: van Streek* | Een Vanitas, schoon en stout geschilderd | *Mat:* op doek		(Sold) fl 6 van Leen
1808/06/13	AMSCH	0157	*Streek (J.)* | Twee Fruitstukken: in het eene een blaauwe Porceleinen Kom met Perziken, enz.; in het andere een blaauwe Chinesche Pot, met Perzik, Chinaas-Appelen, enz. Natuurlijk en uitvoerig | *Mat:* op doek *Size:* hoog 29, breed 26 duim	L	(Sold) fl 5:5 Gruiter

Strij, Abraham van

1810/07/23	DOLG1	0049	*Abraham van Strij* | Een Dienstmeisje, bij een Waterpomp werkende, en bij hetzelve onderscheiden Koperen en andere Keukengereedschappen, alles zeer bevallig van schikking, en kunstig van behandeling | *Mat:* op paneel *Size:* hoog 12, breed 10 duim	Mr Pieter van den Santheuvel	(Sold) fl 120 de Hant à Dordt
1810/07/23	DOLG1	0050	*Abraham van Strij* | Een Schoothondtje, naar het leven geschilderd, staande op een rood kussen | *Mat:* op doek *Size:* hoog 20, breed 13 duim	Mr Pieter van den Santheuvel	(Sold) fl 6 Vrouw de Visser [or] H
1810/10/10	MGCIT	0037	*A. van Strij* | Een zeer bevallig Schilderij, waar op verbeeld word, een Dame, in 't Hair gekapt met een rood fluweele Kleed, met Bont gevoerd, zittende te lezen voor een tafel, gedekt met een groen Kleed, waar op een Inktpot en verder toebehooren is geplaatst, zijnde dit zoo wel als het verdere Bijwerk ongemeen naauwkeurig en delicaat gepenceeld	Caspar van Citters	(Unknown)

Strij, Abraham van (copy by)

1806/08/13	AMSCH	0178	*Stry (A. van); na A. van de Velden* | In een vlak Landschap voor een Schuur, ziet men een Landman bézig een Koe te melken, nevens hem een Heer te Paard, dewelke naar de weg schynt te vraagen, verders een Koets met zes Paarden, enz., delicaat van penceelsbehandeling | copy by A. Strij after A. Velde *Size:* hoog 11, breed 14 duim	Vinkeles [for] G[ruyter]	(Sold) fl 10:10 Rijnbergh

Strij, Jacob van

1802/05/05	AMSCH	0197	*J. van Stry* | In een aangenaam Landschap ziet men voor eenige Gebouwen en Geboomte een Waterplas, waaruit eenige Beesten drinken. Verder een Bergachtig verschiet op de Voorgrond ryk gestoffeerd met staand en leggend Vee, zonachtig en breed gepenceeld | *Size:* hoog 24, breed 32 duim	J	(Sold) fl 15 Ackina
1805/07/03	AMSCH	0141	*J. van Stry* | Op een Duinachtigen Heuvel, ziet men eenige Huislieden en Kinderen, by een wit beladen Paard, terzyde komt een beladen Kar het Duin op, alles meesterlyk in de manier van P. Wouwerman | *Mat:* op paneel *Size:* hoog 19, breed 16 duim *Notes:* In the title the name "P. Wouwerman" was crossed out by hand in the RKDH copy of the catalogue.	R[oos]	(Sold) fl 70 van Iperen
1806/05/05	AMSCH	0128	*van Stry* | By een helderschynende Maan, in een aangenaam Land en Watergezigt, vertoonen zig eenige zeilende en andere Vaartuigen en Vissers, bevallig van licht en meesterlyk geschildert door van Stry | *Mat:* op paneel *Size:* hoog 12, breed 16 duim	V[inkeles]	(Sold) fl 20:15 Scheurleer
1808/06/13	AMSCH	0151	*Strij (J. van)* | In dit aangenaam Land- en Rivier-gezicht ziet men op den voorgrond een Heer te Paard, als in gesprek met een staand Huisman, waar nevens een rustende en een staande Jongen, verder op eene grazige Heuvel, bij de Ruïne van een aloud Gebouw, vertoont zich verscheiden staand en rustend Vee. Het zonlicht verspreid zich natuurlijk, en is van eene meesterlijke penceelsbehandeling | *Mat:* op paneel *Size:* hoog 13, breed 16 duim	[Jan Tersteeg]	(Sold) fl 52 Coclers
1810/07/23	DOLG1	0051	*Jacob van Strij* | Een Bergächtig Landschap. Op den voorgrond een Heer te Paard, en eenige staande en liggende Runderbeesten, met verdere stoffagie. Krachtig en Helder. Het Zonlicht is zeer wel uitgedrukt | *Mat:* op paneel *Size:* hoog 26, breed 34 duim	Mr Pieter van den Santheuvel	(Sold) fl 165 M Schouwman à Dordt
1810/07/23	DOLG1	0052	*Jacob van Strij* | Een Hollandsch Landschap, nevens eene Rivier. Op den voorgrond een staande en twee liggende Runderbeesten, eenige Schapen en een Geit. In het verschiet, zeilende Schepen; in alles niet minder dan het vorige, dun en meesterlijk behandeld | *Mat:* op paneel *Size:* hoog 17, breed 24 duim	Mr Pieter van den Santheuvel	(Sold) fl 95 de Hant à Dordt
1810/07/23	DOLG1	0053	*Jacob van Strij* | Een Landschap, waarin een oud Gebouw, en een Brug liggende over een Stroom. Op den voorgrond eenige Reizigers te Paard, en andere te voet. Op den tweeden grond beladen Vaartuigen. Alles zeer juist van tekening, helder en zonnig gedaagd | *Mat:* op paneel *Size:* hoog 18 ½, breed 24 duim	Mr Pieter van den Santheuvel	(Sold) fl 90 de Hant à Dordt

Stube [Unidentified]

1808/09/13	HABRU	0085	*Stube* | Een Ordonnantie met bloemen, staande in een Fles		(Unknown) fl 4:4

Sturtzenbach, S. [Unidentified]

1803/08/01	AMSCH	0034	*Sturtzenbach. (S.)* | Twee stuks, het eene verbeeld een bevallige Dame in galante kleeding, zittende in een Boomryk Landschap, ter halver lyf, houdende in de eene hand een doode Vogel, en rust met de andere op een Bennetje met vruchten, en de andere vertoont een Heer in zyn Japon, in zyn Studeervertrek, zittende voor een Tafel met een Kleed bedekt,	de Wed [Thoen?]	(Bought In) fl 6

			schynende met aandagt te leezen, neevens hem legt Meniatuur [sic] Schilders Gereedschap, en verder bywerk, beide bevallig van Coloriet, en uitvoerig gepenceelt | *Mat:* op doek *Size:* ieder hoog 13 ½, breed 11 ½ duim		
1803/08/01	AMSCH	0034a[H]	*Sturzenbach (S.)* | Een Gezicht op de Heilige wegs poort door denselve [S. Sturzenbach] | *Notes:* This lot was added in by hand in the BMPL copy of the catalogue.	de Wed [Thoen?]	(Unknown)

Stuven, Ernst

1801/03/16	AMSCH	0079	*Stuven* | Twee met vruchten	P[ruyssenaar]	(Sold) fl 2:15 Boelen
1802/04/13	HAVIN	0030	*E. Stuven* | Een steene Tafel met Persike en Druyven, fraai uitvoerig		(Unknown)
1804/07/25	AMSCH	0077	*Stuven. (E.)* | In een Landschap ziet men verscheide Vruchten, als blaauwe en witte Druiven, Persiken Abricoosen, enz. waarby een Adder fiks en meesterlyk behandeld | *Mat:* op doek *Size:* hoog 24, breed 20 duim		(Sold) fl 2:15 v d Schley
1807/04/00	LNDLS	0034	*E. Stuven* | Een Bloemstuk	[Abraham Delfos] [or others]	(Unknown)
1807/06/10	HGBSM	0034	*E. Stuven* | Een Bloemstuk	Abraham Delfos [or others]	(Sold) fl 1:6 Carré
1808/06/13	AMSCH	0195	*E. Stuven* | Een Fruitstuk; zeer natuurlijk	E M Engelberts	(Sold) fl 3:5 Gruiter
1809/04/17	AMSCH	0182	*E. Stuve* | Twee kapitale Vaasen met Bloemen | *Mat:* op doek	[Gruyter?]	(Sold) fl 1:10
1810/10/11	AMSCH	0083	*E. Stuven* | Twee stuks met Vruchten en Bloemen, met fraaije Steelen en Bladeren; mals geschilderd | *Mat:* op paneel *Size:* hoog 15, breed 12 duimen	S	(Bought In) fl 7:10

Swagers, L. François

1802/09/21	UTHDG	0107	*Zwagers* | Een Landschapje, gestoffeerd met een Hengelaar | *Mat:* op paneel *Size:* hoog 9 ½, breed 6 ½ duimen		(Sold) fl 4:5 Verhoude
1805/10/09	HGBSM	0049	*Swaagers* | Een landschap met geboomte, en een rivier gestoffeerd met figuuren &c., uitvoerig | *Mat:* op paneel *Size:* hoog 14 breet 11 ½ duim	T H van Willigen [or others]	(Sold) fl 14 Apostool
1810/03/07	UTWLD	0001	*F. Swagers* | Twee plaisante Landschappen | *Size:* hoog 2 voet 4 duimen, breed 3 voet	J J Woertman	(Unknown) fl 36
1810/03/07	UTWLD	0013	*Swagers* | Twee zonachtige Rivier-gezichten met scheepen en beelden, meesterlyk behandeld | *Size:* hoog 1 voet 9 duim, breed 2 voet 5 duim	J J Woertman	(Unknown) fl 57
1810/11/07	UTWLD	0048	*Swagers* | Twee Landgezigtjes, met rijzend geboomte, welke door een stormwind hevig geschud worden, verders eenige beeltjes, alles zeer fiks bewerkt door Swagers, op paneel, 9 duim hoog, 1 voet breed, zwarte Lijst | *Mat:* op paneel *Size:* 9 duim hoog, 1 voet breed		(Unknown) fl 6

Swanevelt, Herman van

1801/06/10	AMSCH	0203	*Zwaneveld. (H. van)* | Eeen [sic] Bosch met zwaar Geboomte, ryk gestoffeerd met Herders by hun Vee; alles is zonachtig en krachtig geschilderd | *Mat:* op doek *Size:* hoog 29, breed 38 duim	Herman ten Kate	(Sold) fl 56 Coclers
1802/06/16	AMSCH	0231	*J. Zwaeneveld* | Een Landschap met hoog Geboomten, waar in een Harte Jacht verbeeld word; verders een bergachtig verschiet, krachtig en breed van Penceel behandeling | *Mat:* op koper *Size:* hoog 30, breed 36 duim *Notes:* The artist's name was given as "J. Zwaeneveld" but we have assumed this is an error.	[Merrem]	(Sold) fl 13 C S Roos
1802/08/24	LNDLS	0071	*Zwaneveld* | Een Heuvelächtig en Boomrijk Landschap, in het midden een weg met eenige persoonen die ter Jacht gaan, verzeld van hunne Honden, en een Man rustende bij den weg, nevens een Water | *Mat:* op paneel *Size:* hoog 33, breed 35 duimen	Leonardus Bouman [or others]	(Unknown) fl 27
1803/09/07	AMSCH	0222	*W. Zwaneveldt* | Een Boomryk Landschap, ter zyde een Zeehaaven, ryk gestoffeerd met Beelden, Beesten, Scheepen, enz.; natuurlyk en fix van behandeling [Un paysage bocageux ; d'un côté un port, plein de figures et différens objets] | *Mat:* op doek op paneel [sur toile] *Size:* hoog 29, breed 38 duim *Notes:* The artist's name was given as "W. Zwaneveldt" but we have assumed this is an error. The materials differ in the Dutch and French editions of the catalogue.	Smidt	(Sold) fl 580 Th^{s} Spaan
1804/08/08	AMSCH	0235	*W. Zwaneveld* | Een capitaal Boschgezicht, met Gebergtens in het verschiet, doorsneeden met een helder Water, gestoffeerd met een Harten-Jacht; krachtig en zonachtig op Koper | *Mat:* op koper *Size:* hoog 30, breed 40 duim *Notes:* The artist's name was given as "W. Zwaneveld" but we have assumed this is an error.	Roos a	(Sold) fl 9:10 L Pakker
1804/10/16	DLOND	0220a	*Hugo van Swanevelt* | Landschap met veel Geboomte en Beeldwerk. Paysage avec beaucoup d'Arbres & des Figures | *Mat:* op doek *Size:* hoog 32, breed 48 *Notes:* The artist's name was given as "Hugo van Swanevelt" but we have assumed this is an error.		(Unknown)
1804/10/16	DLOND	0221	*Hugo van Swanevelt* | Uts^{a} [Landschap met veel Geboomte en Beeldwerk. Paysage avec beaucoup d'Arbres & des Figures] | *Mat:* op doek *Size:* hoog 32, breed 48 *Notes:* The artist's name was given as "Hugo van Swanevelt" but we have assumed this is an error.		(Unknown)
1806/11/24	AMSCH	0070	*Swaaneveld (H.)* | In dit aangenaam Italiaansch Landschap, gestoffeert met Ruïnen van aloude Gebouwen, en Geboomten, vertoonen zig	Munnikhuizen	(Sold) fl 21 Coclers

			op de Voorgrond, Veehoeders met Schaapen; verder Huislieden Vee voortdryvende; en een zonagtig verschiet; het licht en coloriet is bevallig, en van een meesterlyke penceelbehandeling | *Mat:* op koper *Size:* hoog 16, breed 23 duim		
1809/05/26	HADAA	0053	*W. Swaneveld* | Een Landschap, fraaij gestoffeerd | *Notes:* The artist's name was given as "W. Swaneveld" but we have assumed this is an error.	Mejuffrouw de Wed David Heemskerk [or others]	(Unknown)
1810/07/26	AMSCH	0090	*Zwaneveldt* | Een schoon Bergachtig Landschap, met Geboomte, Beelden enz. | *Mat:* op doek *Size:* hoog 28, breed 35 duimen	Cassino	(Bought In) fl 15:10
1810/07/26	AMSCH	0110	*Zwanevelt* | Een Landschap, met onderscheidene Voorwerpen | *Mat:* op doek	Cassino	(Bought In) fl 11
			Swanevelt, Herman van (and Lingelbach)		
1808/11/12	HGSCR	0020	*H. Zwaneveld; J. Lingelbach* | Een heuvelagtig boschgezigt met hoog geboomte verbeeldende een morgenstond, zeer natuurlyk en zonagtig behandeld door H. Zwaneveld en gestoffeerd met een hertenjagt door J. Lingelbach, het zonligt is in dit stuk van een uitmuntende uitwerking | *Mat:* op doek	Mr J van Buren	(Unknown) fl 48
			Swebach, Jacques François Joseph		
1802/06/16	AMSCH	0170	*N. Schwebach* | Den een vertoond een bevallig Landzicht met laag Geboomten, op de voorgrond een Staand wit Paard met hout belaaden, ter zyde een zittende drinkende Vrouw, waar by een staand Man, verder een Paard, en een Man hout torsen, den andere verbeeld een Land- en Rlviergezicht [sic]; op de voorgrond twee Militaire te Paard, gevolgt van een Bagagiewagen en Véehoeder met Schaapen; zeer uitvoerig en fraay geschilderd | *Mat:* op paneel *Size:* ieder hoog 9 ½, breed 12 ½ duim *Notes:* The artist's name was given as "N. Schwebach" but we have assumed this is an error.	[Merrem]	(Sold) fl 40 I Smit Gz
1803/06/20	AMSCH	0012	*N. Schwebach* | Een Land en Riviergezicht, op de voorgrond twee Militairen te Paard gevolgd van eene Bagagiewagen en Veehoeder met Schapen; uitvoerig gepenceeld, door N. Schwebach, op Paneel | *Mat:* op paneel *Size:* hoog 9 ½, breed 12 ½ duim *Notes:* The artist's name was given as "N. Schwebach" but we have assumed this is an error.	Schley [for] B	(Sold) fl 19:10 Gruiter
			Swieten, Cornelis van		
1804/10/16	DLOND	0275	*Van Zwieten* | Agt Landschapjens divers. Huit Paysages differens | *Mat:* op paneel *Size:* hoog 3, breed 7		(Sold) fl 96 O D Wyngaert
1804/10/16	DLOND	0276	*Van Zwieten* | Twee dito [Landschapjens divers] Uts[a] [Paysages differens] | *Mat:* op paneel *Size:* hoog 16, breed 13		(Unknown)
1804/10/16	DLOND	0277	*Van Zwieten* | Een dito Uts[a] [Landschapjens divers. Paysages differens] | *Mat:* op paneel *Size:* hoog 9, breed 25		(Unknown)
			Tamm, Franz Werner von		
1807/04/00	LNDLS	0033	*Dapret* | Twee stuks met fruit en dood gevogelte, konstig kragtig en fix | *Mat:* op doek *Size:* hoog 27, breed 36 duim	[Abraham Delfos] [or others]	(Unknown)
1807/06/10	HGBSM	0033	*Dapret* | Twee stuks met fruit en dood gevogelte, konstig kragtig en fix | *Mat:* op doek *Size:* hoog 27, breed 36 duim	Abraham Delfos [or others]	(Sold) fl 3:2 v Giesen
			Tempel, Abraham Lambertsz. van den		
1801/06/13	LNDLS	0001	*A. van den Tempel* | Een konstig Stuk, verbeeldende ter rechter zijde twee Heeren met Jachtgereedschap, en ter endere zijde drie Juffers, deftig gekleed; een in 't wit satijn, die met een hondje speeld, de tweede met vruchten in haar hand, en een die op het cither speelt, levens groote, halverlijf, zittende voor een Balustrade, uitmuntend van schildering, op doek | *Mat:* op doek *Size:* hoog 49, breed 68 duimen	D van R	(Sold) fl 185 A Delfos [for] W
1803/04/20	AMSCH	0073	*Tempel. (A. van den)* | Een oud Mans Portrait, met een langen Baard, ter halver Lyf gekleed met een zwarte Mantel, met Bont gevoerd, en een groote Kraag om de hals, houdende in zyn hand een Handschoen, uitvoerig en delicaat gepenceeld, in de manier van Miereveld [Le Portrait d'un Viellard [sic] à longue barbe, il porte une fraise et un manteau doublé de martre, tenant un gand à la main, il este [sic] traité artistement.] | *Mat:* op paneel *Size:* hoog 28, breed 22 duim	Maria Magdalena van Sluypwyk, gravinne van Moens	(Sold) fl 60 Hodges
1803/04/20	AMSCH	0074	*Tempel (C. van den)* | Twee stuks Afbeeldzels van een Dame en Heer, beide in aloude deftige kleeding, halver lyf, meesterlyk geschilderd [Deux portraits, un Homme et le Second est une Dame, en Costume très ancien : ils sont traités en maitre.] | *Mat:* op paneel *Size:* ieder hoog 25, breed 23 duim *Notes:* The artist's name was given as "Tempel (C. van den)" but we have assumed this is an error.	Maria Magdalena van Sluypwyk, gravinne van Moens	(Sold) fl 91 Gruiter
1807/04/00	LNDLS	0058	*A. v. d. Tempel* | Den Zeekapitein van Amstel, met deszelfs vrouw, in 't klein geschilderd, A. v. d. Tempel, 2 st.	[Abraham Delfos] [or others]	(Unknown)
1807/06/10	HGBSM	0058	*A. v.d. Tempel* | Den Zeekapitein van Amstel, met deszelfs vrouw, in 't klein geschilderd, door A. v. d. Temple, 2 stuks	Abraham Delfos [or others]	(Sold) fl 1:12 v Giese
1809/07/19	AMSCH	[A0008][H]	*VD Temple* | 1 Vrouw Poertret [sic] | *Notes:* This lot was added in by hand in the AA copy of the catalogue. Because it was not numbered, we have assigned the number.		(Unknown)

			Tency, Jan-Baptiste		
1810/03/27	RMCNL	0013	*Tencij* | Een Landschap, Bergachtig, op den voorgrond Koeijen, Schapen, enz. in 't verschiet ziet men eene overgedrevene Regenbui, waardoor de Zon hare stralen schiet		(Unknown)
1810/03/27	RMCNL	0033	*Tencij* | Een Landschapje, Bergachtig, waarop men eene Herderin bij eenig Vee ziet, fraai en uitvoerig geschildert		(Unknown)
			Tengeler, W. [Unidentified]		
1809/07/25	HGBSM	0154	*W. Tengeler* | Een Fles met Bloemen op een Marmere Tafel, door W. Tengeler 1770 | *Mat:* op doek *Size:* hoog 18 en een half, breed 23 duim *Inscr:* W. Tengeler 1770 (signed and dated?) *Notes:* It is unclear whether the name and date are inscribed on the painting.	D van der Aa [or] E B ten Dall	(Sold) fl 1:2 Stees
			Teniers, David (the younger)		
1801/04/13	AMSCH	0073	*D. Teniers* | Een Grysaard met zyn Vrouw beezig met goudgeld te weegen; de characters zyn intressant [sic], en de behandeling meesterlyk | *Mat:* op paneel *Size:* hoog 8, breed 6 duim	Pierre Fouquet, junior	(Sold) fl 32 v d Schley [for] M[errem]
1801/05/11	AMSCH	0089	*D. Teniers* | Een Binnenhuis, in dezelve ziet men verscheiden Gediertens rontsom een vuur zitten, met verder bywerk gestoffeerd, krachtig geschilderd | *Mat:* op paneel *Size:* hoog 10, breed 10 duim	P[ruyssenaar]	(Sold) fl 16:10 Pruijssenaar [for] R
1801/05/11	AMSCH	0090	*D. Teniers* | Een Philosooph in zyn studeerkamer, zittende voor een tafel, waarop Boeken en een Inktkoker geplaatst is, meesterlyk behandeld | *Mat:* op paneel *Size:* hoog 15, breed 13 duim	P[ruyssenaar]	(Sold) fl 10 Allard
1801/06/13	LNDLS	0044	*D. Teniers* | Een Binnenvertrek, waarin eenige boertjes bij een tafel tabak zitten te rooken, andere die bij den haard staan, en een die met een kan in zijn hand de deur van dat vertrek uitgaat, en meer bijwerk zeer uitvoerig van tekening en schildering, op paneel | *Mat:* op paneel *Size:* hoog 11 ¾, breed 8 ½ duimen	D van R	(Sold) fl 41 de Roy
1801/10/06	AMSCH	0065	*D. Teniers* | In een Boeren Wooning, vertoont zig ter regter zyde by een Haardsteede, verscheide zittende en staande Huislieden, zig met drinken en rooken vermaakende: ter andere zyde, klimt een Boer een Trap op, verder ziet men een andere, by de open staande Deur, gestoffeert met verscheide Huisraad, alles is helder, Natuurlyk, en van een fraaije Penceelbehandeling | *Mat:* op paneel *Size:* hoog 17, breed 22 duim	M	(Bought In) fl 1180
1801/10/19	AMSCH	0069	*Teniers. (David)* | Een Binnenhuis, in het zelve ziet men twee Boeren met de kaart speelen, waar na vyf anderen met aandacht schynen te zien, ter rechter zyde komt een Vrouw met een kan en glas de deur in, op den voorgrond worden verbeeld een Ton, Beezems, Bank en Potten, zeer delicaat gepenseeld, in de manier van Adriaan Brouwer. Dit Schildery is uit het Cabinet van den Heer van der Mark gekomen | *Mat:* op koper *Size:* hoog 9, breed 12 duim	Jonkheer Menno Baron van Coehoorn	(Sold) fl 250 A E Sterk
1802/05/05	AMSCH	0205	*D. Teniers, de Oude* | Dit voorwerp verbeeld een oud Philosooph, het hoofd gedekt met een bonte muts, en in een overkleed met bont gevoerd, zittende voor een Tafel, met een kleed bedekt, waarop een Globe, open Boek, Zantloper en Doodshoofd geplaatst is; hy houd in de regterhand een Bril, in de andere een Papier, en schynt met aandagt iets te overwegen; het caracter is natuurlyk, het licht en coloriet bevallig, en van een meesterlyke, penceel-behandeling | *Mat:* op paneel *Size:* hoog 17, breed 15 duim	E	(Bought In) fl 31
1802/06/16	AMSCH	0182	*D. Teniers* | In een binnen Huis staat een bedaagd Man en Vrouw, by een Tafel, met een Kleed bedekt, waar op een zak met geld, bezig eenige spétie te weegen: meesterlyk en fraay gepenceeld | *Mat:* op paneel *Size:* hoog 8 ½, breed 6 ½ duim	[Merrem]	(Sold) fl 51 Pruijssenaar
1802/06/16	AMSCH	0183	*D. Teniers* | In een binnen Huis zit een Boer smakelyk zyn Pyp opsteekende, ter zyde staat een Ton waar op een Kan en Glas; twee Boeren en een Boerin, zitten in een ander vertrek by een Vuur; alles meesterlyk fraay behandeld | *Mat:* op paneel *Size:* hoog 9 ½, breed 13 duim	[Merrem]	(Sold) fl 38 Van der Schleij
1802/06/16	AMSCH	0184	*D. Teniers* | Twee stuks Binnehuizen, in den eene vertoond zich een werkende Schoenmaaker; en den andere een zittende Vrouw spinnende; beide gestoffeerd met verder bywerk: meesterlyk fraay en krachtig geschilderd | *Mat:* op paneel *Size:* ieder hoog 9, breed 10 duim	[Merrem]	(Sold) fl 16:10 Agina
1802/07/20	MGSAN	0051	*D. Tenier* | Een schoon Stuk zynde een Aapenspel, op Doek | *Mat:* op doek *Size:* hoog duim 12, breed duim 16		(Unknown)
1802/07/21	HGKAN	0038	*David Teniers* | Een Bataille tusschen eenige Krygslieden te paard, door David Teniers, 1625, paneel zwarte Lyst | *Mat:* op paneel *Inscr:* David Teniers, 1625 (signed and dated?) *Notes:* It is unclear whether the name and date are inscribed on the painting.		(Unknown)
1802/07/21	HGKAN	0097	*Teniers* | Een Binnenhuisje met zes figuuren, zig vermaakende met eeten en Drinken, Origineel		(Unknown)
1802/07/21	HGKAN	0098	*Teniers* | Een schoon Landschap, met op den Voorgrond, een Waterval, gestoffeerd met veel Beeldjes, zeer zuiver van Thoon		(Unknown)
1802/08/24	LNDLS	0001	*D. Teniers* | Voor Boeren Buiten-huizen zitten en staan eenige boeren, die rooken en drinken, met eenig huisraad op den voorgrond; verder een	Leonardus Bouman [or others]	(Unknown) fl 50

			Vrouw die de deur van 't huis in gaat, in het verschiet een Landschap, fiks geschilderd | *Mat:* op doek op paneel *Size:* hoog 27, breed 32 duimen		
1802/09/21	UTHDG	0086	*D. Teniers* | Een Krijgsman naast een Boer zittende, onsteekt zijn pijp aan een zwavel; by hun zijn op de vloer en aan den wand een menigte Wapentuig, Harnassen, Helmetten, Vaandel, Trom, enz. geplaatst. Verder in het vertrek Soldaaten en Boeren zich met spel, drinken, en rooken, vermakende. Dit, en noch veel bijwerk, is zeer natunrlijk [sic] en fiks, ook het staal en ijzerwerk glinsterend behandeld | *Mat:* op paneel *Size:* hoog 22 ½, breed 34 duimen		(Bought In) fl 65
1803/04/20	AMSCH	0072	*Teniers. (D.)* | Dit uitmuntend Schildery verbeeld in een Huismans Wooning twee Huislieden, bézig zynde om op de Kaart te speelen, waarby drie anderen met yver naar staan te kyken, agterwaards ziet men drie Boeren by het Vuur, en een andere welke met een Schootel de Deur uitgaat, verders eenig Huisraad; dit Stuk is van een bevallige Ordenantie, fixe Schildering, en aangenaam Coloriet, doende het licht en bruin een schoone werking [Ce morceau Capital represente l'interieur d'une maison villageoise, le groupe principal est de cinq figures autour d'une table, dont deux sont assises et jouent aux cartes : les trois autres observent attentivement les joueurs. Vers le fond sont trois autres paysans rangé autour de la cheminée et un quatrième sortant avec un plat à la main ; un chien et des accessoires terminent cet ensemble. L'opposition d'un joueur en chemise blanche avec les figures qui l'entourrent y produit un effet singulierement vray, ajoutons que les caractéres des têtes bien exprimés, une touche fine et la lumiere harmonieusement repandue sur le tout en font un morceau très consequent.] | *Mat:* op paneel *Size:* hoog 19 ½, breed 24 duim	Maria Magdalena van Sluypwyk, gravinne van Moens	(Sold) fl 1340 Gruiter
1803/04/27	AMSCH	000R	*D. Teniers* | Un Tableau Alegorique, dans le quel est representée une Conversasion [sic] de Singes, qui s'amusent à Jouer, Fumer, & Rotir de la viande, dans une Cuisine flamande, peint avec beaucoup de finesse, & d'un bon ton de Couleur | *Mat:* sur cuivre *Size:* h. 19, l. 25 pouces	B	(Bought In) fl 50
1803/07/18	AMSCH	0052	*Teniers. (D.)* | Twee stuks Boere Binnenhuisen, in de eerste ziet men een Huisman met een Pyp en Bierkan by de Schoorsteen staan, en twee andere rooken, in de tweede ziet men twee rookende Boeren by een Vat, beide geestig gepenceeld [Deux petittes tabagies, sur la premiere est un villageois ténant la pipe & le pot á bierre ; à la cheminée sont deux paysans à fumer. Le second est composé de deux figures auprès d'un tonneau & d'un trepied ou ils fument du tabac ; un troisième est vèrs le fond. Ces petits sujets sont traités avec l'esprit & le caractère toujours propres à l'auteur, même dans ses moindres productions.] | *Mat:* op paneel *Size:* yder hoog 9, breed 6 duim	Maria Theresia Andrioli	(Sold) fl 18:10 Haffner
1803/08/24	HGKAN	0024	*D. Teniers* | Een Lantschap met Geboomte, de voorgrond met een stromend Water doorsneeden, en met figuurtjes gestoffeerd | *Mat:* op paneel *Size:* hoog 15, breet 20 duim	[Teissier] [or others]	(Sold) fl 6:5 van Lit
1803/08/24	HGKAN	0063	*D. Teniers* | Een oude Vrouw Groente verleezende	[Teissier] [or others]	(Sold) fl 10:10 Kan
1803/09/07	AMSCH	0177	*D. Teniers* | Een Brabandsch Landschap, vol Geboomten, Boere Wooningen, en een Waterplas, gestoffeerd op de voorgrond met Goedergelukzegsters en andere Beeldjes; alles breed en meesterlyk op Paneel [Un paysage Flamand, offrant une variété agréable, d'arbres et de chaumières ; le devant est rempli de diseurs de bonne aventure et d'autres figures ; largement peint et d'une exécution précieuse et digne de ce maître] | *Mat:* op paneel *Size:* hoog 15, breed 19 duim	Smidt	(Bought In) fl 77
1803/09/07	AMSCH	0178	*D. Teniers* | Een Boer zittende aan Tafel zyn pyp te Rooken, zynde van een dito [meesterlyke] behandeling [Une composition semblable au précédent tableau, représentant un paysan assis à une table et fumant sa pipe] | *Mat:* op paneel *Size:* hoog 12, breed 8 duim [Haut 12, large 9 pouces] *Notes:* The dimensions differ in the Dutch and French editions of the catalogue.	Smidt	(Bought In) fl 57
1803/09/07	AMSCH	0179	*D. Teniers* | In een Dorpgezicht, voor eenige Boerewoningen, ziet men drie Huislieden, nevens hun een Hond, verders door een Hek een gaande Vrouw en Kind, in 't verschiet een Kerktoren en Geboomten; helder en natuurlyk behandeld [Vue d'un village, présentant quelques habitations, devant lesquelles trois paysans, accompagnés d'un chien, plus loin une femme et un enfant traversant une haie ; le fond est borné par des clochers, et des hauts arbres ; il regne dans ce tableau un bel effet de lumière ; l'exécution en est naturelle et précieuse] | *Mat:* op paneel *Size:* hoog 7, breed 10 duim	Smidt	(Sold) fl 6 Gruiter
1803/09/07	AMSCH	0181	*D. Teniers* | Eenige Boerewoningen, waarvoor eenige Huislieden zitten te Rooken, niet minder als de voorgaanden [Quelques habitations devant lesquelles plusieurs paysans assis s'amusent à fumer ; d'un mérite égal aux précédens.] | *Mat:* op koper *Size:* hoog 7, breed 11 duim	Smidt	(Sold) fl 18 C S Roos
1803/12/15	MGLAC	0037	*D. Teniers* | Een Binnenvertrek, waarin een Tandtrekker die een Jongen een Tand getrokken heeft, met Bywerk; zeer natuurlyk en fix geschilderd | *Mat:* op doek *Size:* hoog duim 14, breed duim 12	Mr L H de Haze Bomme	(Unknown)
1804/05/07	AMSCH	0162	*Teniers. (D.)* | Voor een Herberg, ziet men verscheide dansende Boeren en Boerinnen, &ct.; uitvoerig en meesterlyk gepenceeld | *Mat:* op paneel *Size:* hoog 16, breed 22 duim	Y[ver] [for] W	(Bought In) fl 22

1804/07/25	AMSCH	0079	*Teniers. (D.)* | In een Huismans Wooning zitten en staan vier Dorpelingen te Muciceeren, een Vrouw staat aan de Deur te luisteren, op Voorgrond legt een Vat op zyn Stelling; dit stukje is aangenaam van coloriet, en van een delicaten schildering | *Mat:* op paneel *Size:* hoog 13 ½, breed 10 duim		(Sold) fl 98 Jan Ijver
1804/07/25	AMSCH	0080	*Teniers (D.)* | In een Binnehuis zitten twee Huislieden te Drinken en te Roken, agter dezelve staat een Vrouw en in verschiet een staande Boer, verders ziet men meenigte Boeren Gereedschappen, Kopere Keetels en Vaatwerk; alles kloek en met de na tuur overeen komende gepenceeld | *Mat:* op doek op paneel *Size:* hoog 17, breed 22 duim		(Sold) fl 10:10 Tessier
1804/07/25	AMSCH	0081	*Teniers. (D.)* | In een Boere Herberg zitten twee Huislieden te Roken, houdende de eene een Bierkan in de Hand, de Waardin komt de Deur in met een Glas Bier, op de Voorgrond een Hond en eenig Huisraad; behandeld als de voorgaande | *Mat:* op doek *Size:* hoog 12, breed 15 ½ duim		(Sold) fl 7 Van der Schleij
1804/07/25	DLGRO	0074	*D. Teniers* | Een fraai stukje, verbeeldende een Schoenlapper | *Mat:* op paneel *Size:* hoog 13, breed 8 ½ duim	Mr Franc van der Burch Wz.	(Unknown)
1804/10/16	DLOND	0222	*David Teniers* | Een Binnenvertrek, waarin een Boer, die zyn pyp rookt, met een ander by zich; terwyl ene Vrouw in de Kamer komt. L'intérieur d'une Chambre; on y voit deux Paysans, l'un fumant une, tandis qu'une Femme entre dans la Chambre | *Mat:* op doek op paneel *Size:* hoog 10, breed 13		(Unknown)
1804/10/16	DLOND	0223	*David Teniers* | Een Binnenwacht van Apen, die op de Kaart spelen. Un Corps de Garde, dans lequel il y a quelques Singes, qui jouent aux Cartes | *Mat:* op doek op paneel *Size:* hoog 11, breed 14		(Unknown)
1804/10/29	HRBAU	0104	*Teniers, (David)* | Op den Voorgrond gaat een Mannetjen, welke in zyn regterhand een' Stok houdt, daar zyn linkerhand in een' doek gewonden is; waar agter een fraai verschiet van Boerenwooningen en Geboomte. Zeer helder en fiks behandeld | *Mat:* op paneel *Size:* hoog 7, breed 6 duim	Simon Styl	(Unknown)
1805/07/03	AMSCH	0047	*Teniers (D.)* | In een aangenaam Brabandsch Landschap, ziet men op de Voorgrond een bejaard Man, leunende op zyn stok en in de andere hand zyn hoed houdende, als schynende iemand te groeten; warm en van de beste schildering van dezen voortreffelyke Meester | *Size:* hoog 6 ½, breed 5 duim	R[oos]	(Bought In) fl 76
1805/07/03	AMSCH	0151	*D. Teniers, de oude* | In een Binnenvertrek zit een oud Man te slapen, terwyl in het verschiet twee jonge Lieden zitten te Caresseeren; geestig op Paneel | *Mat:* op paneel *Size:* hoog 15, breed 12 duim	G	(Sold) fl 40 H Pakker
1805/10/09	HGBSM	0014	*D. Teniers* | Een tabaksroker, benevens andere figuren, by een vuur | *Mat:* op paneel *Size:* hoog 8 ½ breet 11 duim	T H van Willigen [or others]	(Sold) fl 26:15 Ph Meij
1805/10/09	HGBSM	0015	*D. Teniers* | Een rookende boer, &c. | *Mat:* op koper *Size:* hoog 9 breet 6 ½ duim	T H van Willigen [or others]	(Sold) fl 6:5 Basemoine
1805/10/09	HGBSM	0061	*Oude Teniers* | Een oud man, die den tyd verbeeld, in een landschap door den oude Teniers | *Mat:* op doek op paneel *Size:* hoog 27 breet 18 duim	T H van Willigen [or others]	(Sold) fl 11:10 Ph Meij
1806/05/05	AMSCH	0138	*D. Teniers de oude* | In een Landgezicht met een oude Poort en Brug, over een stil water, ziet men op de voorgrond een Huisman en Vrouw, eenig Vee voordryvende, verder een gaande Reiziger; krachtig en natuurlyk gepenceeld door D. Teniers de oude | *Mat:* op doek *Size:* hoog 24 ¼, breed 30 duim	E	(Sold) fl 3:5 L Pakker
1806/08/13	AMSCH	0181	*Teniers. (D.)* | Een capitaal Boom- en Bergachtig Landschap, gestoffeerd met Huislieden en Vee; zynde van een breede schildering | *Mat:* op doek *Size:* hoog 63, breed 47 duim	Roos	(Sold) fl 5:10 Boelhouwer
1806/08/13	AMSCH	0182	*Teniers. (D.)* | Twee stuks Rotsachtige Landschappen, met hoog Geboomten en verscheide Huislieden; kloek en meesterlyk behandeld | *Mat:* op doek *Size:* Ieder hoog 32, breed 22 duim *Notes:* This lot was sold with lot 385[H] by an anonymous artist.	Roos	(Sold) fl 1 for lots 182 & 385[H]. Coclers
1807/04/00	LNDLS	0059	*D. Teniers* | Een man tot de knieën staande, met een stok in zijn hand	[Abraham Delfos] [or others]	(Unknown)
1807/06/10	HGBSM	0059	*D. Teniers* | Een man tot de knieën staande, met een stok in zijn hand	Abraham Delfos [or others]	(Sold) fl 2:2 v Giese
1808/04/26	GDAN	0162	*Teniers (D.)* | Twee vrolijke Boeren, met een Brandewijns Fles, zeer fraai geschilderd | *Size:* hoog 8, breed 7 duim	G H Fortuyn	(Unknown)
1808/04/26	GDAN	0163	*Teniers (D.)* | Het Paleis van den Koning Salomon. Een uitmuntend zeer uitvoerig Schilderij, verbeeldende de Koning Salomon op zijnen aller prachtigsten Throon, omringd wordende door zijne Lijftrauwanten, waar voor de Koninginne van Scheba verschijnt, om de wijsheid van Salomon te horen, wordende de slippen haarer Kleed van twee jonge Staat Dames gedragen, terwijl eenige Staat Dames agter haar staan, voorts eenige Slaven die meer en meer Geschenken aanbrengen van Goud en Edele Gesteentens, terwijl er reeds een groot gedeelte van dergelijke op de grond voor den Throon geplaatst is, voorts ziet men in 't verschiet een Tempel en Toren, alle de Beelden zyn in allerpragtigst Gewaad uitgedost, en bijzonder uitvoerig gedaan | *Size:* hoog 13 ½, breed 17 duim	G H Fortuyn	(Unknown)

1808/05/18	LNAN	0030	*D Teniers* | Een vrolijk gezelschap van Boeren en Boerinnen, konstig en krachtig van schildering | *Notes:* The artist's name "D Teniers" was added in by hand in the RKDH copy of the catalogue.	Mr Cornelis Versluys	(Unknown) fl 36
1808/06/06	RMRIJ	0125	*Teniers. (David)* | Een gezelschap van vier Vlaamsche Boeren, die, staande en zittende aan eene tafel, met veel opmerking dobbelen en rooken. In den tweeden grond doet zich een Vrouwtje voor, die, met een Schotel en eene Kan in de handen, het vertrek in komt, en verder bijwerk. Fraai, teekenachtig en helder geschilderd. NB. Kan tot wederga dienen van het volgende Nommer [Dans L'Intérieur d'une Pièce Flamande, quatre Paysans fument en jouant aux Dés, pendant qu'une femme entre, portant dans ses mains une Cruche et un Plat. Beaucoup d'accessoires enrichissent cette Composition agréable et d'un beau faire] | companion to lot 126 *Annots:* Coll. J. de Neufville verk. Amsterdam 5 Aug. 1783 (f 240.-) (RMA I) *Mat:* op koper *Size:* Hoog 9 ½, en breed 13 duim	Gerrit van der Pot, Heer van Groeneveld	(Sold) fl 515 P Roelszema
1808/06/06	RMRIJ	0126	*Teniers. (David)* | Op den voorgrond vertoont zich een Boer in eene Ton zittende op de Viool te spelen; benevens hem eene zingende Oude Vrouw: zij worden beiden van eenen derden persoon, door een venster ziende, bespied. In den achtergrond rookende en kaartspelende Boeren. Als het voorgaande behandeld, en kan als deszelfs wederga aangemerkt worden. – In Plaat gebragt [Ce Tableau qu'on peut considerer comme le Pendant du Précédent, represente l'Intérieur d'un Cabaret Flamand. Sur le devant auprés d'un tonneau, sont assis un Paysan qui joue du violon, et une femme qui chante. Ils sont épiés par une autre Personne qui passe sa tête à travers une fenêtre ouverte. Dans le fond, et auprès de la Cheminée, plusieurs Paysans jouent aux cartes etc. D'un ton fin, et d'une Composition Spirituelle] | companion to lot 125 *Annots:* Coll. J. de Neufville Verk Amsterdam 6 Aug. 1783 (f 200.-) (RMA I) *Mat:* op paneel *Size:* Hoog 9, en breed 12 ½ duim	Gerrit van der Pot, Heer van Groeneveld	(Sold) fl 195 F J Nortwyck
1808/08/23	AMSCH	0159	*Teniers. (D.)* | Deeze rijke Ordonantie vol gewoel, vertoont in een Dorp-gezicht een Boeren Kermis, op de voorgrond zitten verscheiden Lieden, zoo Mannen als Vrouwen bij Tafels, zig met eeten en drinken vermakende, andere dansen lustig naar het geluid der Doedelzak speeler, ter zijde eene Vrouw, die haar dronken Man naar huis brengd, verder een Kerk bij Geboomten; de karakters zijn geestig en meesterlijk fraai gepenceeld | *Mat:* op doek *Size:* hoog 25, breed 38 duim	[Coclers]	(Sold) fl 38 Texier
1808/08/23	AMSCH	0205	*D. Teniers* | Een Dorpgezicht met verscheide Boeren Woningen, gestoffeerd met drie Huislieden, schijnende met elkander in gesprek, verder door een Hek, een gaande Vrouw met een Kind, krachtig geschilderd op Doek | *Mat:* op doek	[Gruyter?]	(Bought In) fl 20
1808/12/31	RMHSN	0008	*D. Teniers* | Twee Drinkende Boeren, zittende voor een Test met Vuur | *Mat:* op paneel	G Spanjaart [or] H de Haas [or] C van der Looy Lans	(Unknown)
1809/04/17	AMSCH	0098	*D. Teniers* | Een Binnehuis, met twee Boeren, waarvan de eene een Fles en Kan in de hand heeft en de andere in een papier leest, fiks geschilderd | *Mat:* op paneel *Size:* hoog 9, breed 7 duim	A	(Sold) fl 5
1809/04/22	AMYVR	0127	*D. Teniers* | Een meesterlijk geschilderd gestoffeerd Landschapje | *Mat:* op paneel *Size:* hoog 9, breed 12 duim	de Bruin	(Sold) fl 4:10 A de Lely
1809/06/13	AMSCH	0152	*D. Teniers* | Het Binnegezicht van een Huismanswooning, in hetzelve zit een Man en Vrouw, op de Kaart Speelende, bij den Haardsteede twee andere Beelden, verder eenig Boeren Huisraad; natuurlijk en fiks geschilderd | *Mat:* op paneel *Size:* hoog 11, breed 15 duim	Y	(Sold) fl 12:10 Buck
1809/07/19	AMSCH	[A0010][H]	*D Teniers* | 1 Temtase [i.e. Temtatie] | *Notes:* This lot was added in by hand in the AA copy of the catalogue. Because it was not numbered, we have assigned the number.		(Unknown)
1809/07/19	AMSCH	0055	*Teniers (D.)* | In een Rotsgezicht vertoont zig een Kluisenaar, eerbiedig nedergeknield met zaamgevouwen handen, voor een opengeslagen Boek, tegen een Doodshoofd rustende, ter zijde staat een aarden Kan, op den voorgrond gestoffeerd met verscheide Helsche Monsters en om hoog vliegende Gedrogten. Het licht en koloriet is bevallig, het is alleruit-voerigst gepenceeld | *Mat:* op paneel *Size:* hoog 12, breed 9 duim *Loc:* Amsterdam, Nederland. Rijksmuseum. (A 401)	[Bicker]	(Sold) fl 150 Jan Yver voor Z H den Koning
1810/05/22	AMSCH	0100	*Teniers. (D.)* | In een Binnengezicht van een Corps de Garde, vertoont zich ter linkerzijde een staand Jongeling op een steenen Drempel, dragende op zijn Schouder een roode Officiers-Mantel, op den Grond liggen verscheide Harnassen, Handschoenen en Trommel, daar nevens op eene Tafel staat een yzeren Helmet, met Pluimen versierd, waarbij een Overrok, aan de Muur hangt een Schietgeweer en Degen, ter andere zijde op den voorgrond eenig Krijgstuig, in 't verschiet Soldaten die op de Kaart spelen en anderen zich bij het vuur warmen; dit uitmuntend Schilderij is helder en bevallig van koloriet, het invallend licht geeft een natuurlijke werking het is van een uitvoerige penceelbehandeling | *Mat:* op koper *Size:* hoog 15 ½, breed 18 duim	Johannes van de Putte Nicolaasz.	(Sold) fl 136 Gruyter
1810/05/22	AMSCH	0101	*Teniers. (D.)* | In eene Boeren Woning zit een vergenoegd Landman, met een Pijp in de eene en een Bierkan in de andere hand, nevens hem zit eene bedaagde Vrouw bij een Houten Tafeltje, verder een zijn Pijp te stoppen en een de Deur inkomende, gestoffeerd met verder bijwerk; dit stukje is	Johannes van de Putte Nicolaasz.	(Sold) fl 7:10 Dupré

			helder en meesterlijk fraai gepenceeld | *Mat:* op koper *Size:* hoog 9, breed 11 duim		
1810/07/23	DOLGI	0054	*David Teniers* | In een Boerenkeuken zit een Boer zijn Pijp te stoppen; voor hem staat een ledige Ton, op denzelven een test met Vuur, en een Kan. Op den achtergrond een andere Boer, tegen een muur leunende. Zeer natuurlijk en fix van behandeling | *Mat:* op paneel *Size:* hoog 11, breed 8 duim	Mr Pieter van den Santheuvel	(Sold) fl 52 van Eijk à 's Hage
1810/07/23	DOLGI	0055	*David Teniers* | Een klein Landschapje, gestoffeerd met vele etende, drinkende, en dansende Boeren en Boerinnen, voor een Herberg. Helder en zuiver van kleur | *Mat:* op koper *Size:* hoog 7, breed 9 duim	Mr Pieter van den Santheuvel	(Sold) fl 16 P de Heere à Dordt
1810/07/26	AMSCH	0081	*Teniers (D.)* | Dit stuk verbeeldt een Binnenhuis, in hetzelve ziet men eene bevallige Vrouw, bezig met een Kalfskop, die voor haar op een blok ligt, schoon te maken; ter zijde hangt het geslagt en opgemaakt Kalf; verder toepasselijk bijwerk. Het is uitvoerig en fraai geschilderd | *Mat:* op doek *Size:* hoog 21, breed 25 duimen	Cassino	(Bought In) fl 200
1810/07/26	AMSCH	0082	*Teniers (D.)* | Een bevallig Veldgezigt, gestoffeerd met Huislieden en Reizigers. Mede zeer goed geschilderd | *Mat:* op paneel *Size:* hoog 10, breed 12 duimen	Cassino	(Bought In) fl 13:10
1810/08/01	AMSCH	0098	*Teniers (David)* | In een Binnenhuis of Herberg ziet men op den voorgrond twee Boeren op de Kaart spelen, waar bij een ander met een Glas in de hand, verder eene oude Vrouw en drie andere Lieden bij eene Haardstede [Un intèrieur de Cabaret : on y voit deux Paysans jouant aux Cartes ; auprès de ceux-ci trouve un troisième tenant un verre à la main. En arriere il y a une vielle Femme et trois personnages au coin de la Cheminée] | *Annots:* fort médiocre. Vendu chez Pauwels en 1803 pour fl: 484. (NGW); 1822, 23 March. Sale at Christie's, London, no.52 £97.13 s Pacey (SMLN) *Mat:* op paneel *Size:* hoog 14, breed 11 ½ duimen	Mr Pieter de Smeth van Alphen	(Sold) fl 625 C Josi
1810/08/06	AMSCH	0098	*Teniers (D.)* | Dit kunstrijk Tafreel vertoont een ruim Vertrek of Chimistwinkel, op den voorgrond, voor een open Vengster, zit de Chimist in een wit linnen overhemd, bezig het Vuur aan te blazen, achter hem is een Knegt, staande bij eene Tafel, op den tweeden grond een bejaard Man, houdende een Urinaal, waarbij een Landman en twee Bediende, verder eene menigte toepasselijk bijwerk; het invallend licht doet eene schoone werking en alles is ongemeen uitvoerig en fraai gepenceeld | *Mat:* op doek *Size:* hoog 24, breed 29 duimen	A	(Sold) fl 610 R[emmers] Bredius
1810/10/10	MGCIT	0042	*D. Teniers* | Een Manspersoon in een binnen vertrek, in eene vrolijke houding, op een stoel zittende en op een Viöol spelende: achter hem een persoon met een Glas in de hand, en eene uit de deur gaande Vrouw, met verder toepaslijk Bijwerk; breed en uitvoerig geschilderd	Caspar van Citters	(Unknown)
1810/10/10	MGCIT	0043	*D. Teniers* | Nog een uitmuntend Kabinet Stuk, zijnde een Binnenhuis, waarin een Man en Vrouw opeen vergenoegde wijze aan een Tafel eeten en drinken, terwijl anderen eenige Huislijke bezigheden verrigten; voorts is dit Huis vervuld met veelerhande op en dooréénġestapeld en leggend Huisraad, en Paardenwand; alles treflijk en meesterlijk op het paneel gebragt | *Mat:* op paneel	Caspar van Citters	(Unknown)
1810/10/11	AMSCH	0085	*Den Ouden Teniers* | De Tentatie van St; Anthonius | *Mat:* op paneel *Size:* hoog 13, breed 17 duimen	C	(Sold) fl 1 Posthumus
1810/10/11	AMSCH	0148	*Teniers* | Vrolijk dansende Dorpelingen	C	(Sold) fl 1 Posthumus
1810/10/11	AMSCH	0180	*D. Teniers* | In een Binnenhuis of Keuken, ziet men verscheide Aapen, dewelke spelen, rooken en vleesch braden; uitvoerig | *Mat:* op koper	A	(Sold) fl 43 Gruiter

Teniers, David (the younger) (and Heem, J.D.)

1810/08/01	AMSCH	0099	*Teniers (David); Jan Davidszoon de Heem* | Een Boerenschuur, waarin onderscheiden voorraad van Aard- en Boomvruchten, Vaatwerk, koperen Ketels, Koornmaat en verdere voorwerpen, verlevendigd met eenen Landman, Jongeling en eene Vrouw [Vue intérieure d'une grange, dans laquelle on voit un nombre de differents Fruits et de Légumes, ainsi que des ustenciles et des Meubles de Ménage. Cet ensemble est embelli par trois figures, étant un Cultivateur, un Jeunehomme et une Femme sortant par la porte] | *Annots:* Passable. (NGW) *Mat:* op paneel *Size:* hoog 19, breed 24 duimen *Loc:* Los Angeles, CA, USA. Los Angeles County Museum of Art. (M.72.67.1)	Mr Pieter de Smeth van Alphen	(Bought In) fl 1000

Teniers, David (the younger) (and Uden, Lucas)

1809/05/26	HADAA	A0001	*van Uden; Teniers* | Twee bergachtige Landschappen, rijk gestoffeerd met Boeren en Boerinnen, fiks, breed en tevens uitvoerig gepenseeld, door van Uden, en gestoffeerd door Teniers | *Mat:* op koper *Size:* hoog 33 breed 40 duimen	Mejuffrouw de Wed David Heemskerk [or others]	(Unknown)

Teniers, David (the younger) (copy by)

1810/06/06	RMMUY	0167	*D. Teniers; Bassano* | Een Postishe. Door D. Teniers, naar Bassano | copy by Teniers after Bassano *Mat:* op paneel		(Sold) fl 4:10 Pot
1810/07/26	AMSCH	0094	*D. Teniers; Caracci* | De afneming van het Kruis, bestaande in acht Beeldjes. Zeer uitvoerig op agaat, door D. Teniers, naar Caracci | copy by Teniers after Carracci *Mat:* op agaat	Cassino	(Bought In) fl 6

			Teniers, David (the younger) (or Teniers, manner)		
1803/07/14	MGKLY	0020	*Teniers of zyn manier* | Een Boere binnenhuis ryk gestoffeert en goed gepenseeld	Mr Caspar Jacob van Citters	(Unknown)
1803/08/01	AMSCH	0038	*D. Teniers, of in zyn manier* | Een Chimist in zyn Binnenvertrek, hy staat met aandagt de Courant te leezen, achter hem ziet men twee Boeren die hunne pyp stoppen, en voor hem een andere die het vuur aanblaast, verders eenige Potten, Flessen, Distileerketels en andere Gereedschappen, natuurlyk en fix behandeld | *Mat:* op paneel *Size:* hoog 19, breed 17 duim	J	(Sold) fl 31 Hodges
1803/08/01	AMSCH	0039	*D. Teniers, of in zyn manier* | Een Brabandsch Landschap, op de voorgrond voor een Herberg zyn een menigte Huislieden, welke zich met danssen en drinken vermaken, in het verschiet een Kasteel op een Heuvel, waarby een Herder met Schaapen, aangenaam van behandeling | *Mat:* op paneel *Size:* hoog 19 ½, breed 27 duim	R	(Sold) fl 26 Hodges
1805/07/10	AMSCH	0143	*D. Teniers* | In een Duinryk Landschap ziet men voor een Boere Buitenhuis, eenige Boeren zich met Kegelen vermaaken i geestig geordineerd en delicaat van behandeling, door of in manier van D. Teniers | *Mat:* op doek *Size:* hoog 14, breed 22 duim	V[inkeles] [for] J	(Sold) fl 14 Lafontaine
1805/12/16	AMSCH	0055	*D. Teniers* | Een Vergenoegd Boertje, in een lagchende houding; bevallig op Kooper geschilderd, door of in de manier van D. Teniers | *Mat:* op koper *Size:* hoog 5 ½, breed 4 ½ duim	Spaan	(Sold) fl 1 Levy Pakker
1807/08/26	AMSCH	0210	*D. Teniers* | Een capitaale ryke Ordonnantie, verbeeldende een Binnegezigt van een Corps de Garde. Op de voorgrond Krygslieden, die met de Kaart speelen, verder door een open Deur anderen, die by een Haardstede zich met rooken en drinken vermaken; voorts gestoffeerd met een Mortier, Harnassen, Zadels, Trommels, Vaandels en ander Oorlogtuig, meesterlyk fraai en bevallig gepenceeld, op Doek, door of in de manier van D. Teniers | *Mat:* op doek *Size:* hoog 23, breed 32 duim	Helsdinge	(Sold) fl 72 Wm Ryers
1807/08/26	AMSCH	0211	*D. Teniers* | In een Binnenhuis ziet men een Boer en Boerinnetje Liefkoozen, het welk een ander met vermaak beschouwd, gestoffeerd met verder bywerk; fraai geschilderd op Paneel, door denzelven [of in de manier van D. Teniers] | *Mat:* op paneel *Size:* hoog 14, breed 10 duim	Helsdinge	(Sold) fl 49 Spruit
1810/10/11	AMSCH	0084	*D. Teniers* | Een Schilder in zijn Kamer, met zijn Leerling; op Paneel, door of als D. Teniers | *Mat:* op paneel *Size:* hoog 11, breed 9 duimen	C	(Sold) fl 14:10 Posthumus
			Teniers, David (the younger) (copy after)		
1801/03/16	AMSCH	0071	*Teniers* | Een Landschap met Beelden, naa Teniers	P[ruyssenaar]	(Sold) fl 0:16 Veldwijk
1804/04/28	LNDLS	0045	*D. Teniers* | Een Gezelschap met spelende Boeren, na D. Teniers	[Abraham Delfos] [or others]	(Sold) fl 1:5 Carrée
1804/10/08	RMCNL	0022	*Teniers* | Rokende Boere na Teniers	A t'Hooft	(Unknown)
1805/10/09	HGBSM	CC0028	*Teniers* | Een binne vertrek met drie figuuren, na Teniers | *Mat:* op doek op paneel *Size:* hoog 11 breed 14 duim	T H van Willigen [or others]	(Sold) fl 3 van der Linden
1805/12/16	AMSCH	0099	*D. Teniers* | Twee Boere Dorpgezichten, naar D. Teniers	R[oos]	(Sold) fl 4:5 Rookmans
1806/05/05	AMSCH	0203[b]	*Teniers* | Drie stuks, een Hondje, en twee na Teniers | *This Lot:* Twee na Teniers; lot 203[a] by Anonymous	H	(Sold) fl 3 for lots 203[a] & 203[b]. Mensart
1809/04/22	AMYVR	0155	*D. Teniers* | Twee stuks geestige Copijtjes; naar D. Teniers	Juff^r Julikker	(Sold) fl 5:10 du Pree
1809/04/22	AMYVR	0157	*D. Teniers* | Twee stuks met Boeren; naar D. Teniers	de Bruin	(Sold) fl 2:10 du Pree
1809/04/22	AMYVR	0202	*D. Teniers* | Twee stuks Binnenhuizen met Beeldjes; naar D. Teniers	de Bruin	(Sold) fl 1:10 v d Schley
1809/05/26	HADAA	A0004	*Teniers* | Een Landschap, na Teniers	Mejuffrouw de Wed David Heemskerk [or others]	(Unknown)
1810/06/20	AMSCH	0158	*Teniers* | Twee stuks Binnenhuizen, naar Teniers	B	(Sold) fl 0:6 L Pakker
			Teniers, David (the younger) (manner)		
1801/03/16	AMSCH	0162	*Teniers* | Een Binnehuis met rokende Boeren, in de manier van Teniers	K[ip]	(Sold) fl 2:10 Rijnders
1801/11/10	AMPOS	0045	*Teniers* | 2 dito [stuks] mans en vrouwe Pourtraiten, op koper, als Teniers | *Mat:* op koper		(Unknown)
1801/11/10	AMPOS	0051	*Teniers* | Eenige op de kaart speelende Boeren, als Teniers		(Unknown)
1802/02/16	AMSCH	0086[a]	*Teniers* | Een Boere Binnehuis, als Teniers, en 't afbeeldzel van een oude Philosooph | *This Lot:* Een Boere Binnehuis; lot 86[b] by Anonymous	E	(Sold) fl 30 for lots 86[a] & 86[b]. Coclers
1802/04/13	HAVIN	0062	*Teniers* | St. Anthony, als van Teniers		(Unknown)
1802/07/20	MGSAN	0028	*D. Teniers* | Een Boertje, zyn Geld naaziende: in de manier van D. Teniers | *Mat:* op doek *Size:* hoog duim 6 ½, breed duim 5		(Unknown)
1802/09/06	AMSCH	0139	*D. Teniers* | In een Boeren Herberg-Vertrek, ziet men op de voorgrond een zittende bedaagde Huisman, hy houd in de eene hand, een Aarde Bierkan, en in de andere een Pyp, daar neevens staat een omgekeert Vat, waar op een Vuur-test, waar by een zittend Heer, met een Glas in de hand, en twee	Brave	(Bought In) fl 16

			andere Lieden, verder by een Haardsteede staan en zitten vyf Boeren, zig met rooken en drinken vermaakende; natuurlyk en krachtig gepenceeld, hoog 15, breed 21 duim, in de manier van D. Teniers | *Size:* hoog 15, breed 21 duim		
1802/09/06	AMSCH	0140	*D. Teniers* | Twee stuks, den eene vertoond een lachende Boer, zittende by een Tafel, waar op een stuk Brook legt, hy houd in de eene hand een Kan, en in de andere een Roemer Wyn; den andere verbeeld een oude Vrouw, zittende voor een Tafel, yverig beezig Goude en Zilveren Spétien te weegen; beide krachtig en fix gepenceeld, als door D. Teniers | *Mat:* op paneel *Size:* ieder hoog 7, breed 5 duim	Brave	(Sold) fl 6 van der Schley [for] A
1802/09/06	AMSCH	0141	*D. Teniers* | Een Chimist in zyn Laboratorium, staande by een Tafel, schynende iets klaar te maaken, ter zyde ziet men Fournuizen, by een derzelve, staat een Knegt het vuur aan te blaazen, het Vertrek is gestoffeerd met een meenigte Gereedschappen, tot die Fabriek behoorende; geestig en fix gepenceeld als door denzelven [D. Teniers]	Brave	(Sold) fl 3 J Spaan [or] T Spaan
1802/09/18	RMDRS	0051	*Teniers* | Een Boere Gezelschap, in de manier van Teniers	Casper de Haas	(Sold) fl 7:5 Carree
1803/04/06	MGSAN	0001	*den ouden Teniers* | Een Landschap met een Rots, gestoffeerd met een wit Paard en ander bywerk, in de manier van den ouden Teniers	Mr Evert Clyver	(Unknown)
1803/04/06	MGSAN	0010	*Teniers* | Een dito [Stuk], verbeeldende een Philosooph, in de manier van Teniers	Mr Evert Clyver	(Unknown)
1803/04/20	AMSCH	0151	*D. Teniers* | Twee stuks, de eene vertoont een Chimist in zyn Laboratorium, gestoffeert met een menigte Bywerk, den anderen verbeeld een werkende Smit, verder een Knegt by het Fournuis op de Grond leggen Harnassen; beide plaisant van Coloriet en penceelbehandeling, in de manier van D. Teniers [Deux Pendans dont l'un est un chimiste occupé dans son laboratoire garni d'une multitude d'accessoires ; l'autre est un forgeron occupé avec son compagnon à forger des armures : Sujets agréables peints dans la maniere de Teniers.] | *Mat:* op paneel *Size:* hoog 11, breed 9 duim	Maria Magdalena van Sluypwyk, gravinne van Moens	(Sold) fl 9:10 Gruiter
1803/04/20	AMSCH	0152	*D. Teniers* | Twee stuks, den eene verbeeld een zittende Boer voor een Tafel, waarop een Wynkan en een Roemertje met Wyn geplaatst is, ter zyde staat een bedaagde Vrouw; den anderen vertoont een zittende Huisman voor een Tafel, waarop een Aardekan en Test geplaatst is, bezig zyn pyp op te steeken, verder zit een oude Boer; beide als de voorige bevallig gepenceelt in de manier van denzelven [D. Teniers] [Deux autres petits tableaux dans la même maniere [de Teniers] le premier est un paysan assis devant une table garnie d'une verre & d'une bouteille, le Second represente un autre Villageois se disposant à fumer avec son compagnon, très jotiment [sic] traités.] | *Mat:* op paneel *Size:* hoog 8 ½, breed 7 duim	Maria Magdalena van Sluypwyk, gravinne van Moens	(Sold) fl 16:10 van Iperen
1803/04/20	AMSCH	0155	*D. Teniers* | Eenige Rookende en drinkende Boeren. in een Binnenhuis, in de manier van D. Teniers [Une tabagie, dans la même maniere,] | *Mat:* op paneel *Size:* hoog 9, breed 7 duim	Maria Magdalena van Sluypwyk, gravinne van Moens	(Sold) fl 1:10 Grimpen
1803/06/20	AMSCH	0013	*D. Teniers* | Een Boer, bézig zynde zyn Pyp te rooken, in het verschiet in een ander Vertrek nog eenige Huislieden by het Vuur, meesterlyk op Paneel, als D. Teniers | *Mat:* op paneel *Size:* hoog 10, breed 14 duim	Schley [for] B	(Sold) fl 25 Hodges
1803/09/07	AMSCH	0180	*D. Teniers* | Een Landschap waarin een Boerin bezig is een Koe te Melken, waarby een staande Boer, verders eenige Varkens, Boerewoningen, enz., als dito [D. Teniers] [Dans un site champêtre, une paysanne occupée à traire une vache ; à côté d'elle un paysan, des cochons et plus loin des chaumières ; même composition que le précédent] | *Mat:* [sur bois] *Size:* hoog 6 ½, breed 9 duim *Notes:* The material was given only in the French edition of the catalogue.	Smidt	(Sold) fl 1:15 Grimpen
1803/09/07	AMSCH	0282	*D. Teniers* | Een Boeren Binnenhuis met drie Boeren; geestig op Paneel, als D. Teniers [L'intérieur d'une habitation champêtre avec trois paysans ; composition spirituelle, sur bois, dans le goût de Teniers.] | *Mat:* op paneel *Size:* hoog 7, breed 5 duim	Smidt	(Sold) fl 8:10 Toselli
1803/12/15	MGLAC	0046	*In de manier van Teniers* | Een Kaarslicht, met een vrolyk Gezelschap; zeer goed van effect | *Mat:* op doek *Size:* hoog duim 19, breed duim 23	Mr L H de Haze Bomme	(Unknown)
1804/02/27	AMSCH	0134	*Teniers* | Een oud Vrouwtje bezig Groente te verleeze; in de manier van Teniers	B	(Sold) fl 9:10 Gruiter
1804/10/16	DLOND	0306	*Als D. Teniers* | Een Kwakzalver op zyn Theater Kruiden verkopende. Un Charlatan vendant des Drogues de sur son Theatre | *Mat:* op doek op paneel *Size:* hoog 11, breed 9		(Unknown)
1804/10/16	DLOND	0307	*Als D. Teniers* | Een Boeren Binnenhuis. L'Interieur d'une Maison de Paysan | *Mat:* op doek op paneel *Size:* hoog 11, breed 9		(Unknown)
1806/05/05	AMSCH	0158	*D. Teniers* | Een Boeren Gezelschap in een Herberg; geestig op Paneel, als D. Teniers | *Mat:* op paneel	R[oos]	(Bought In) fl 8
1807/08/26	AMSCH	0212	*D. Teniers* | Een Chimist in zyn Laboratorium, nevens hem een Jongen by een brandend Fournuis, en ander bywerk; in de manier van denzelven [D. Teniers] | *Mat:* op doek *Size:* hoog 12, breed 16 duim	de Vries	(Sold) fl 0:10 L Pakker
1807/08/26	AMSCH	0253	*D. Teniers* | Twee stuks Boeren Binnehuizen, ryk gestoffeerd met Landlieden, die zig met Kaartspelen, rooken en drinken vermaken, verders verscheide bywerk; in de manier van D. Teniers | *Mat:* op paneel	Joseph Vallette	(Sold) fl 4:10 Levy Pakker

1808/10/28	AMVRS	0071	*Teniers* | Een Binnehuis met een Boeren Heelmeester. Geestig in de manier van Teniers geschilderd	Marten Udink	(Sold) fl 1:10 Pakker
1810/07/23	DOLGI	0070	*Teniers* | Een Brabandsch Dorp-Feest, waar op zich eenige Boeren en Boerinnen met drinken en dansen vermaken, en bij dezelve een Speelman, op de Zakpijp spelende. Zeer fraai van behandeling, in de manier van Teniers | *Mat:* op doek *Size:* hoog 10, breed 14 ½ duim	Mr Pieter van den Santheuvel	(Sold) fl 6:10 Blussé à Dordt [or] van Eyk
1810/08/06	AMSCH	0152	*Teniers* | Een Boeren Binnen- en een Boeren Buitenhuis, beiden in den trant van Teniers	V[ries]	(Sold) fl 6 Roelsma
			Terwesten (and Verbruggen, G. (II))		
1805/10/09	HGBSM	0096	*C. P. Verbruggen; Terwesten* | Een bloemstuk, door C. P. Verbruggen, en gestofeerd met kindertjes, door Terwesten | *Mat:* op doek *Size:* hoog 15 breet 19 duim	T H van Willigen [or others]	(Sold) fl 2:18 Heijmans
1805/10/09	HGBSM	0097	*C. P. Verbruggen; Terwesten* | Een dito [bloemstuk] als de voorgaande, en door denzelven Meester [C. P. Verbruggen, en gestofeerd met kindertjes, door Terwesten] | *Size:* hoog 15 breet 19 duim	T H van Willigen [or others]	(Sold) fl 4:4 Heijmans
			Terwesten, Augustin (I)		
1809/04/17	AMSCH	0114	*A. ter Westen* | In een Landschap, ziet men ter zijde een Anticq Gebouw, georneerd met Groepen, Basrelieven en Beelden; uitvoerig | *Mat:* op paneel	Y	(Sold or Bought In) fl 12
			Terwesten, Matthaus		
1802/11/01	DOBRA	0168	*Mathys Terwesten* | Een ordonnantie van veel Beelden, verbeeldende den dood van Dido | *Mat:* op doek *Size:* h. 29, br. 37 duim		(Unknown) fl 3
1802/12/13	AMSCH	0183	*M. ter Westen* | Deeze Ordenantie, verbeeld de Maaltyd van Marcus Anthonius en Cléopatra; krachtig en meesterlyk gepenceeld | *Size:* hoog 50, breed 48 duim	Yver	(Sold) fl 1:10 L Pakker
1806/08/20	HGBSM	0219	*M. Terwesten* | Een bovendeur stuk, met speelende Kinderen | *Mat:* op doek	Macalester Loup [or others]	(Sold) fl 1:2 for lots 219 & 220. A de Gelder
1806/08/20	HGBSM	0220	*M. Terwesten* | Een dito [bovendeur stuk] met dito [speelende Kinderen] | *Mat:* op doek	Macalester Loup [or others]	(Sold) fl 1:2 for lots 219 & 220. A de Gelder
1806/08/20	HGBSM	0221	*M. Terwesten* | Een dito [bovendeur stuk] zijnde Pan en Seringa [sic] | *Notes:* It is unclear what "dito" refers to in the title.	Macalester Loup [or others]	(Sold) fl 1:4 for lots 221 & 222. A de Gelder
1806/08/20	HGBSM	0222	*M. Terwesten* | Een dito [bovendeur stuk] Historieel | *Notes:* It is unclear what "dito" refers to in the title.	Macalester Loup [or others]	(Sold) fl 1:4 for lots 221 & 222. A de Gelder
1806/08/20	HGBSM	0223	*M. Terwesten* | Een dito [bovendeur stuk] | *Notes:* It is unclear what "dito" refers to in the title.	Macalester Loup [or others]	(Sold) fl 0:12 Vermeulen
			Testa, Pietro (Il Lucchesino)		
1810/07/26	AMSCH	0024	*Della Testa (P.)* | Een Gezigt van een Brand, in een Stad van Italien. Fraai geschilderd | *Mat:* op doek *Size:* hoog 25, breed 32 duimen	Cassino	(Bought In) fl 6
			Thier, Bernhard Heinrich		
1802/04/13	HAVIN	0029	*B. H. Thier* | Een Landschap met Koeyen en Schapen, zeer plaizant		(Unknown)
1802/09/18	RMDRS	0006	*J.B.H. Thier* | Een Capitaal Landgezicht, ryk gestoffeerd met een drift Beesten, en in de Voorgrond een Schaap met twee Lammeren, en een Geit in het verschiet, een gezicht op de Stad Delft; konstig en uitvoerig geschilderd | *Size:* hoog 19 ½, breed 25 ½ duim	Casper de Haas	(Sold) fl 53 Gruiter
1802/09/18	RMDRS	0009	*J.B.H. Thier* | Een zeer fraay Landgezicht, met Koeyen en Schapen, in de manier van A. Pynaker; helder en warm geschilderd | *Annots:* slegt (MB) *Size:* hoog 12, breed 15 duim	Casper de Haas	(Unknown) fl 45 for lots 9 & 10
1802/09/18	RMDRS	0010	*J.B.H. Thier* | Een dito [zeer fraay Landgezicht], van dezelve groote als 't voorgaande | *Annots:* slegt (MB)	Casper de Haas	(Unknown) fl 45 for lots 9 & 10
1802/09/18	RMDRS	0018	*J.B.H. Thier* | Een Landschapje met Koeyen, Schapen, en een Boer en Boerin | *Size:* hoog 9 ½, breed 11 ½ duim	Casper de Haas	(Sold) fl 28 for lots 18 & 19. Gruiter
1802/09/18	RMDRS	0019	*J.B.H. Thier* | Een dito [Landschapje met Koeyen], van dezelve groote | *Size:* hoog 9 ½, breed 11 ½ duim	Casper de Haas	(Sold) fl 28 for lots 18 & 19. Gruiter
1802/09/18	RMDRS	0025	*J.B.H. Thier* | Een Landgezicht, waarin een Boer over een Brug gaat, twee Paarden, waar van een staat te drinken; verder eenige Koeyen en Schapen | *Size:* hoog 14 ½, breed 18 ½ duim	Casper de Haas	(Sold) fl 47 for lots 25 & 26. Gruiter
1802/09/18	RMDRS	0026	*J.B.H. Thier* | Een dito [Landgezicht], van dezelve groote, waarin een Boerin, met de Melk-emmers zig gereed maakt om de Koeyen te Melken, verder nog eenig Hoorn vee | *Size:* hoog 14 ½, breed 18 ½ duim	Casper de Haas	(Sold) fl 47 for lots 25 & 26. Gruiter
1802/09/18	RMDRS	0029	*J.B.H. Thier* | Een Land gezicht, waarin een Stier, over een Brug gedreeven word, door een Boer die een Geit draagt | *Size:* hoog 11 ½, breed 15 ½ duim	Casper de Haas	(Unknown) fl 5
1802/09/18	RMDRS	0030	*J.B.H. Thier* | Een dito [Land gezicht], van dezelve groote, waarin een drinkende Koe, en verdere stoffagie van Beesten | *Size:* hoog 11 ½, breed 15 ½ duim	Casper de Haas	(Sold) fl 4:5 Gruiter

1802/09/18	RMDRS	0032	*J. B. H. Thier* | Een Land gezicht, waarin een Os voor een Vlonder, nog een leggende Koe en eenige Schapen | *Size:* hoog 14, breed 17 ½ duim	Casper de Haas	(Sold) fl 21:18 v Wallen
1802/09/18	RMDRS	0034	*J.B.H. Thier* | Een Land gezicht, waarin een loeyende Os, en een liggende Stier, waarby een slapende Jonge | *Size:* hoog 11 ½, breed 15 ½ duim	Casper de Haas	(Sold) fl 14 Muis
1802/09/18	RMDRS	0038	*J.B.H. Thier* | Een dito [Landschap], van dezelve groote | *Annots:* Slegt Copien van Printen (MB) *Size:* hoog 16 ½, breed 21 ½ duim	Casper de Haas	(Unknown) fl 13
1802/09/18	RMDRS	0043	*J.B.H. Thier* | Een Landschap met Koeyen en Schapen | *Size:* hoog 9 ½, breed 12 ½ duim	Casper de Haas	(Sold) fl 15:10 v Beefting
1802/09/18	RMDRS	0044	*J.B.H. Thier* | Een dito [Landschap met Koeyen en Schapen] | *Size:* hoog 9 ½, breed 12 ½ duim *Notes:* A ms. note in the MB copy of the catalogue indicates that the buyer, G. van der Pot, was acting on behalf of someone else.	Casper de Haas	(Sold) fl 6:10 v Pot
1802/09/18	RMDRS	0045	*J.B.H. Thier* | Een Gezicht in het Cleefsche, waarin een Kar met Paarden, helder en fiks behandeld | *Size:* hoog 10, breed 14 duim	Casper de Haas	(Sold) fl 26 for lots 45 & 46. Gruiters
1802/09/18	RMDRS	0046	*J.B.H. Thier* | Een dito [Gezicht in het Cleefsche], van dezelve groote [hoog 10, breed 14 duim], waarin een Brug, beneeden een Kar met Paarden, waar een van drinkt | *Size:* hoog 10, breed 14 duim	Casper de Haas	(Sold) fl 26 for lots 45 & 46. Gruiters
1802/09/18	RMDRS	0048	*J.B.H. Thier* | Een Land gezicht met Koeyen | *Size:* hoog 9, breed 11 ½ duim	Casper de Haas	(Sold) fl 7 Verweij
1802/09/18	RMDRS	0049	*J.B.H. Thier* | Een Landschap, waarin een leggende, en verscheide andere Koeyen | *Size:* hoog 11 ½, breed 14 ½ duim	Casper de Haas	(Sold) fl 8:5 Gruiters
1802/09/18	RMDRS	0067	*J.B.H. Thier* | Een Land gezicht, waarin een Stier, met een Halster om	Casper de Haas	(Unknown) fl 2
1802/12/13	AMSCH	0156	*H. Thier* | Een aangenaam Landschap, op de voorgrond by en in een Plas klaar spiegelend Water, eenig staand en leggend Vée, ter zyde een bevallige Landvrouw en een Jongen, die zich met 't speelen met Honden vermaakt, van agteren een Man te Paard met een drift Beesten, en een Dorp in 't verschiet; warm en zonachtig en uitvoerig gepenceeld | *Mat:* op paneel *Size:* hoog 12, breed 16 duim	Pruyssenaar [for] A	(Sold) fl 9:10 Gruiter
1804/12/10	AMSCH	0097	*B. H. Thier* | Een fraai bergachtig Landschap, ryk gestoffeerd met Beelden en Beesten; zonachtig en fixs gepenceeld | *Mat:* op doek *Size:* Hoog 25, breed 22 duim	Jan De Groot	(Sold) fl 6:15 Gruyter
1806/05/05	AMSCH	0139	*B. H. Thier* | Twee stuks bevallige heuvelachtige Landschappen, met hoog Geboomte, Boeren Woningen en zeer fraaije stoffagie van Beelden en Beesten, gepaard met een aangenaam zonlicht, maken dezen stukjes tot de besten van dezen meester, en zyn geschilderd op Paneel door B.H. Thier | *Mat:* op paneel *Size:* hoog 22, breed 15 duim	R[oos]	(Sold) fl 26 van Iperen
1806/05/05	AMSCH	0140	*B. H. Thier* | Een aangenaam boomryk Landschap, gestoffeerd met Heeren en Dames te Paard, en andere stoffagie | *Mat:* op paneel *Size:* hoog 19, breed 25 duim	V[inkeles]	(Sold) fl 3:5 Scheurleer
1806/08/13	AMSCH	0183	*Thier. (B. H.)* | Twee stuks grazige Weiden met helder spiegelende Waters doorsneeden, beide ryk gestoffeerd met staand en rustend Vée, Landlieden en verders alleraangenaamste verschieten; beide allerzonachtigst en uitvoerigst gepenceeld | *Mat:* op paneel *Size:* Ieder hoog 13, breed 16 duim	Vinkeles [for] F	(Sold) fl 74 Schumacher
1806/08/13	AMSCH	0329	*Thier. (J. H.)* | Een Boomryk Landschap, ryk gestoffeerd en bevallig geschilderd | *Size:* hoog 12, breed 15 duim	Vinkeles [for] G[ruyter]	(Withdrawn)
1807/04/00	LNDLS	0011	*B. H. Thier* | Een Landschap, een bruine grazende koe, benevens eenige liggende schapen bij een hek met geboomte, een bokje rust bij eenige kruiden, en in 't verschiet gebouwen, konstig behandelt op paneel | companion to lot 12, by Anonymous *Mat.* op paneel *Size:* hoog 11 en een half, breed 15 duim	[Abraham Delfos] [or others]	(Unknown)
1807/06/10	HGBSM	0011	*B.H. Thier* | Een Landschap, een bruine grazende koe, benevens eenige liggende schapen bij een hek met geboomte, een bokje rust bij eenige kruiden, en in 't verschiet gebouwen, konstig behandelt | companion to lot 12 *Mat:* op paneel *Size:* hoog 11 ½, breed 15 duim	Abraham Delfos [or others]	(Sold) fl 11:10 Wiggers
1808/11/12	HGSCR	0009	*B.H. Thier* | Een aangenaam veldzigt met geboomte en een water op de voorgrond, ryk gestoffeerd met staande en leggend vee, uitvoerig en fraai gepenseeld | *Mat:* op paneel	Mr J van Buren	(Unknown) fl 50
1808/11/12	HGSCR	0010	*B.H. Thier* | Een dito [aangenaam veldzigt] met dito [geboomte], verder een molen en woning niet minder als de voorgaande	Mr J van Buren	(Unknown)
1809/04/22	AMYVR	0128	*J.H. Thier* | Een grazige Weide, met staand en liggend Vee; geestig | *Mat:* op paneel *Size:* hoog 11, breed 12 duim	de Bruin	(Sold) fl 11 Remmers Bredius
1809/06/13	AMSCH	0153	*B. H. Thier* | Voor een Boeren Wooning, ziet men eene grazende en eene rustende Koe, waarbij een Landman, en andere Beesten in 't verschiet, uitvoerig geschilderd | *Mat:* op paneel *Size:* hoog 17, breed 14 duim	Q	(Bought In) fl 5:10
1810/03/27	RMCNL	0083	*B. H. Thier* | Twee Stuks Landschapjes, uitvoerig en netjes behandeld		(Unknown)
1810/03/27	RMCNL	0085	*B. H. Thier* | Twee Stuks Bergachtige Landschappen, op de eene een Os, op de andere een Stier, krachtig behandeld		(Unknown)
1810/05/22	AMSCH	0107	*Thier. (B. H.)* | Twee stuks grazige Landzichten, met Boeren Woningen en Geboomten, beide rijk gestoffeerd met staand en rustend Vee; zonachtig en bevallig voorgesteld | *Mat:* op paneel *Size:* Jeder hoog 11, breed 15 duim	Johannes van de Putte Nicolaasz.	(Sold) fl 26:10 Lemens

			Thier, Bernhard Heinrich (copy by)		
1802/09/18	RMDRS	0001	*J.B.H. Thier; P. Potter* | Een Hollands Landgezicht, met willige en andere Geboomte, gestoffeerd met beelden en verscheide Beesten, waar van eenige op den Voorgrond in het Water staan, verder eenige zwemmende Jongens, in het verschiet een Rytuig met ses Paarden bespannen; dit aangenaam Schildery, is uitmuntend gevolgd na het beroemde stuk van P. Potter 1648. – Voorheen berust hebbende, in de Kunstgallery van den voormalige Stadhouder, en tegenswoordig in het Nationaal Museum te Parys | copy by B.H. Thier after Paulus Potter; companion to lot 2 *Size:* hoog 16 ½, breed 22 duim	Casper de Haas	(Sold) fl 90 v Pot
1802/09/18	RMDRS	0002	*J.B.H. Thier; P. Potter* | Een dito [Hollands] Landgezicht, waar in een Boere Schuur uit welke een Koe gedreeven word, en voor dezelve een Boerin die met een Kind speeld, waarby twee Varkens; verder nog twee stotende Ossen die een Boer tragt te scheiden, met nog een daarby staande Koe; mede uitmuntend gevold na P. Potter, door denzelven [J. B. H. Thier] en kunnende tot een voegzame Wederga dienen | copy by B.H. Thier after Paulus Potter; companion to lot 1	Casper de Haas	(Sold) fl 39:10 Nagtegaal
1802/09/18	RMDRS	0037	*J.B.H. Thier; Ruisdaal* | Een Landschap met Gebergte, een Waterval, en daarby eenige Vissers, na Ruisdaal | copy by B.H. Thier after J. Ruisdael *Annots:* Slegt Copien van Printen (MB) *Size:* hoog 16 ½, breed 21 ½ duim	Casper de Haas	(Unknown) fl 9
1808/06/06	RMRIJ	0127	*Thier. (J. B. H.); naar Paulus Potter* | Een aangenaam boom- en waterrijk Landgezigt. (bekend onder den naam der wadende Koe.) Rijk gestoffeerd met figuren, Koeijen, Schapen en Lammeren. In 't verschiet ziet men eene Prinselijke Koets met zes Paarden bespannen, vooraf gegaan door twee Hardloopers; meer in 't verschiet de lustplaats den Binkhorst, den Toren van 't Dorp Rijswijk en aan den horizont den Haag. Dit stuk is eene ongemeen getrouwe kopij naar de Schilderij van Paulus Potter, voorheen in 't Kabinet van den Prins van Oranje berustende, doch nu in het Museum te Parijs [Paysage Hollandais. Sur le devant, on découvre près d'une ferme plusieurs Personnes qui se baignent dans une eau transparente etc., des Vaches, et beaucoup d'autres Animaux domestiques. Dans le second plan on apperçoit un Carosse à six Chevaux, et dans le Lointain la Campagne de Binkhorst, le Village de Ryswyck, et la Haye à l'Horison. Ce Tableau est une Copie éxacte d'après l'original de Paul Potter, connu sous le nom de *la Vache à l'eau*, qui fut un ornement de la Collection du Prince d'Orange, et qui se trouve actuellement au Muséum Napoléon] | copy by B.H. Thier after Paulus Potter *Annots:* Verk. Casper de Haas, Rotterdam, 18 Sept. 1802 (RMA I) *Mat:* op paneel *Size:* Hoog 16 ¼, en breed 22 duim	Gerrit van der Pot, Heer van Groeneveld	(Sold) fl 160 P Roelfzema
			Thomas, Jan		
1806/08/20	HGBSM	0204	*J. Thomas* | Een Historiëelstuk, meesterlyk en krachtig geschilderd | *Mat:* op paneel *Size:* hoog 26, breed 35 duim	Macalester Loup [or others]	(Sold) fl 8:5 Gram
			Thulden, Theodoor van		
1804/07/25	AMSCH	0078	*Tulden. Th. van* | Deeze capitaale Ordinantie van meer dan leevens groote Beelden, vertoont in een Landschap een Zee, Nephtunus zittende en rustende op een stroomende Waterkruik, neevens hem staat een bevallige Nimph, houdende de Hoorn van Overvloed, welke door een gevleugelde Nimph gekroont word, op de Voorgrond in 't Water ziet men een Triton op een Zeehoorn blaazende en twee jonger Nayaden; de meesterlyke fraaije Teekening, het licht, het krachtig coloriet en de fraaije penceel behandeling, geeven een luister aan dit tafreel, als of het door Rubbens vervaardigt was | *Mat:* op doek *Size:* hoog 88, breed 67 duim		(Sold) fl 56 Gruyter
1805/10/09	HGBSM	0134	*van Tulden* | Een zinnebeeldige schets, ryk van ordonnantie | *Mat:* op doek *Size:* hoog 43 breet 30 duim	T H van Willigen [or others]	(Sold) fl 2:4 Van der Aa
1808/06/13	AMSCH	0177b[H]	*van Thulden* | Een Nepthunes | *Notes:* This lot was added in by hand in the AA I, EBNP, FLNY and RKDH copies of the catalogue.	R[oos]	(Sold) fl 8:10 Gruiter
1809/07/25	HGBSM	0073	*van Tulden* | Een Historieele Schets, kloek Geschildert | *Mat:* op doek *Size:* hoog 17, breed 19 duim	D van der Aa [or] E B ten Dall	(Sold) fl 6 Zwartzman
1810/07/26	AMSCH	0083	*Tulden (T. van)* | Flora en Zephyr, zittende op de wolken, omringd van Kupido's. Meesterlijk schoon en breed geschilderd | *Mat:* op doek *Size:* hoog 52, breed 44 duimen	Cassino	(Bought In) fl 26
1810/08/06	AMSCH	0101	*Tulden (T. van)* | Twee stuks kapitale Historiëele Ordonnantien, met levensgroote Beelden, Kupidoos enz; meesterlijk breed en krachtig in den stijl van P.P. Rubbens geschilderd | *Mat:* op doek *Size:* ieder is hoog 77, breed 98 duimen	U	(Sold) fl 37 Hodges
			Thulden, Theodoor van (or Thulden, manner)		
1809/07/25	HGBSM	0082	*van Tulden* | Een Bachanaal, door Kinderen verbeeld, door of in de manier van van Tulden | *Mat:* op doek *Size:* hoog 30 en een half, breed 26 duim	D van der Aa [or] E B ten Dall	(Sold) fl 1:10 Heymans [for] G
			Thyssen, J. [Unidentified]		
1802/05/10	MGSAN	0048	*J. Thyssen* | Koning Willem III. te Paard | *Mat:* op doek *Size:* hoog 32 duim, breed 26 duim	Johan Dirk Kruysse	(Unknown) £ 0:3

			Tieling, C.		
1810/08/06	AMSCH	0146	*C. Tieling* | Een Hofstede waar een Vrouw en Man naar Gevogelte zitten te kijken	F	(Sold) fl 0:10 Boelhouwer
1810/10/11	AMSCH	0230	*C. Telling* | Eene Weide met staande en liggende Koeijen	A	(Sold) fl 0:6 Yver
			Tieling, Lodewyk		
1802/02/16	AMSCH	0057	*Tieling* | Een Landschap met staande en rustende Beesten, verzelt van een Veehoeder, by een waterplas, met twee honden en schietgeweer, bevallig geschilderd	G	(Sold) fl 2:10 L Pakker
			Tieling, N. [Unidentified]		
1809/04/17	AMSCH	0099	*N. Tieling* | Twee stuks Landschappen, met Geboomten, beide rijk gestoffeerd met verschillend Vee, zoo staande als rustende; natuurlijk en meesterlijk behandeld | *Mat:* op doek *Size:* ieder hoog 12, breed 15 duim	Crajenschot	(Sold) fl 4
			Tilius, Jan		
1807/09/28	AMWUR	0006	*J. Tielius* | Een stukje, zynde een Bellenblazer, door J. Tielius, in zwarte Lyst		(Unknown) fl 41
			Tintoretto, Jacopo (Jacopo Robusti)		
1802/12/13	AMSCH	0212	*Tintoretti* | Het Afbeeldzel, van een Heer en Dame in aloude Kleeding; uitvoerig van Penceelbehandeling | *Mat:* op paneel *Size:* hoog 6, breed 9 duim	Schley [for] Lauwers	(Sold) fl 0:6 L Pakker
			Tischbein		
1802/06/29	HGDAW	0032	*De oude Thisbein* | Princes Carolina, door den oude Thisbein		(Unknown)
1802/06/29	HGDAW	0033	*De oude Thisbein* | Een Gely [sic] Juffer van Haar door denzelven [den oude Thisbein] in mans gewaad		(Unknown)
1808/06/06	RMRIJ	0128	*Tischbein* | Eene Dame in eene Armstoel zittende, benevens een jong Heer aan het venster een kind vasthoudende. Aangenaam van koloriet en fraai geschilderd. Eene wedergade. In eene gemeubileerde kamer eene op een Sopha zittende Dame bezig met lezen. Een Jongman bij haar. In dezelfde manier behandeld als boven [Dans un Appartement fort Elégant, on voit un jeune Dame assise sur un Sopha, qui fait la lecture, et un jeune Cavalier qui est auprès d'elle. Composition agréable et d'une belle éxécution. Le Pendant. Une jeune Dame dans un fauteuil, et près d'elle un Cavalier qui tient un Enfant par les mains etc. Dans le même goût et le même genre que le précédent] | *Annots:* verk. Amst. 21 Aug. 1799 (f.10-) (RMA I) *Mat:* op paneel *Size:* Twee Stukken. Hoog 7, en breed 8 ½ duim	Gerrit van der Pot, Heer van Groeneveld	(Sold) fl 61 R Pott
1808/06/06	RMRIJ	0129	*Tischbein* | Een Man in een open kozijn liggende en iets voorlezende; benevens hem twee toeluisterende personen. Dit stukje is aangenaam van koloriet en naar waarheid behandeld [Un homme appuyé sur une Croisée, fait la lecture, et deux personnes à côte de lui, semblent l'écouter avec attention. Tableau de mérite] | *Annots:* Verk. Amst 21 Aug. 1799 (f.32-) (RMA I) *Mat:* op paneel *Size:* hoog 7 ½, en breed 6 duim	Gerrit van der Pot, Heer van Groeneveld	(Sold) fl 70 Texier
			Titsinger [Unidentified]		
1802/06/28	AMSCH	0186	*Titsinger* | Een aangenaam Landschap, met een Rivier doorsneeden, op de Voorgrond een menigte Reizende Landlieden met Vee, fiks behandeld, door Titsinger, op Doek | *Mat:* op doek *Size:* hoog 25, breed 34 duim	B	(Sold) fl 3:5 Bergveld
			Tiziano Vecellio		
1801/10/06	AMSCH	0066	*Titiaan* | Dit Stukje verbeeld een Kinderhoofd, opwaards ziende, Leevensgroote; met een gedeelte van den Arm, kragtig en Meesterlyk behandeld | *Mat:* op doek op paneel *Size:* hoog 9, breed 8 duim	S	(Sold) fl 12 Ter Smitten
1808/08/23	AMSCH	0158	*Titiaan* | Deeze Ordonantie vertoont Christus, aan Tafel met de Discipelen van Emaus het brood brekende en zegenende; een bediende brengt een Schotel met Vrugten en een Kan in de hand; de hartstochten zijn kennelijk en krachtig geschilderd | *Mat:* op paneel *Size:* hoog 24, breed 33 duim	C	(Bought In) fl 205
1808/11/12	HGSCR	0018	*Titiaan* | Een muciseerend gezelschap waar by een jongeling zingende uit een boek, werdende door een die op de bas en een die op de fluit speeld geaccompagneerd, zeer fraai, delicaat en uitvoerig gepenseeld door Titiaan. P., bekend door 't prentje hier na gegraveerd | *Mat:* op paneel	Mr J van Buren	(Unknown) fl 30
1810/07/26	AMSCH	0080	*Titiano Vecelli* | Venus houdt Adonis, die op de Jagt gaat, terug. Zijnde een fraai stuk uit de Venetiaansch School | *Mat:* op doek *Size:* hoog 48, breed 52 duimen	Cassino	(Bought In) fl 5:15
1810/08/06	AMSCH	0099	*Titiaan* | Christus aan Tafel met de Discipelen te Emaus, het Brood brekende en zegenende, een Bediende brengt een Schotel met Vruchten en houdt een Kan in de hand, de hartstochten zijn kennelijk; het is krachtig en van eene meesterlijke penceelsbehandeling | *Mat:* op paneel *Size:* hoog 24, breed 33 duimen	B	(Sold) fl 77 Pot
			Tiziano Vecellio (copy after)		
1803/04/27	AMSCH	0016	*P. d'Aquila; Titiën* | Une bonne Copie d'Après la Danäé du Titiën | copy by P. Aquila after Tiziano *Size:* h. 4 ½, l. 6 pieds	A	(Sold) fl 10:10 V d Brink

1803/04/27	AMSCH	0089	*Titien* | Venus couchée sur un Lid de repos, copie d'après le Titien | *Size:* h. 3, l. 4 pieds	A	(Sold) fl 11:10 Camphuysen
			Tiziano Vecellio (manner)		
1808/09/13	HABRU	0089	*Titiaan* | Een Vrouwe Hoofd, als van Titiaan		(Unknown) fl 4 [?]
			Tol, Domenicus van		
1801/06/10	AMSCH	0164	*Toll. (D. van)* | Een Haringvrouwtje; zy staat aan een Tafel, waarop een Tobben met Haring geplaatst is, nevens een steenen Kom en eenige Oesters; krachtig en uitvoerig van penceels-behandeling | *Mat:* op paneel *Fmt:* van boven ovaal *Size:* hoog 8, breed 6 duim	Herman ten Kate	(Sold) fl 64 Coclers
1801/10/19	AMSCH	0071	*Tol. (D. van)* | Een extra fraay stukje van dien Meester, verbeeldende een bevallig Meisje in een Nis, zy rust met haar rechterhand op de kant der Nis, en in haar linkerhand, die als buiten de Nis uitsteekt, houd zy een aartig Kannetje, agter haar een opgehaald Gordyn, en in het verschiet een gezelschap van vrolyke Personen; alles zo natuurlyk krachtig en uitvoerig geschilderd, of het van zyn Meester G. Douw was | companion to lot 72 *Mat:* op paneel *Size:* hoog 11 ¾, breed 9 ½ duim	Jonkheer Menno Baron van Coehoorn	(Sold) fl 335 for lots 71 & 72. van der Schley [for] A
1801/10/19	AMSCH	0072	*Tol. (D. van)* | Een wederga, vertoonende door een Nis, een Mannetje fraay gekleed, en speelende op een Viool, op de kant der Nis, ziet men een tinne Kan, een Tabakspyp, en een gevouwe Papier met Tabak, achter dezelve een gedekte Tafel met Spys, waar aan een gezelschap met vrolyke Personen; niet minder konstig als de voorige, en van gelyke groote | companion to lot 71 *Mat:* op paneel *Size:* hoog 11 ¾, breed 9 ½ duim	Jonkheer Menno Baron van Coehoorn	(Sold) fl 335 for lots 71 & 72. van der Schley [for] A
1802/05/05	AMSCH	0204	*D. van Tol* | Een leezend oud man, met een Bril op de neus, zittende voor een Tafel met eenige Boeken, uitvoerig en kragtig behandeld | *Mat:* op paneel *Size:* hoog 11, breed 9 duim	E	(Sold) fl 17 Cocler
1802/06/16	AMSCH	0180	*D. van Tol* | Dit fraay Cabinet stukje verbeeld voor een open steene Nis, een bevallig Meisje, houdende in de hand een doode Vogel; op de rand der Nis legt een Tapytkleedje, een kopere Emmer en eenige Wortelen; voor de Plint met een Basrelief versiert, staat een Pot met een Bloemplant en een glaase Fles, in 't vertrek verder zitten drie Lieden by een Tafel, gestoffeerd met verder bywerk; alles is ongemeen uitvoerig en fraay gepenceeld | *Mat:* op paneel *Size:* hoog 12, breed 8 ½ duim	[Merrem]	(Sold) fl 190 I Smit Gz
1802/06/16	AMSCH	0181	*D. van Tol* | Een bevallig Vrouwtje, schynende een brandende Kaars in een Lantaarn te wille plaatsen, zeer natuurlyk en uitvoerig van penseel-behandeling | *Mat:* op paneel *Size:* hoog 7, breed 5 ½ duim	[Merrem]	(Sold) fl 41 I Smit Gz
1802/06/28	AMSCH	0180	*D. van Toll* | Door eene steene Nis ziet men een Jongeling met een Vogelkooitje in de hand | *Mat:* op paneel *Size:* hoog 12, breed 10 duim	B	(Sold) fl 3:10 Texier
1802/08/24	LNDLS	0078	*D. van Tol* | Een Meisje in een Nis halverlijf, voor den kant der Nis rust een Vlootje met Haring, Brood en Uiën, aan den wand hangt gedroogde Schol, een mand en maten. Zeer uitvoerig op paneel | *Mat:* op paneel *Size:* hoog 7, breed 6 ½ duimen	Leonardus Bouman [or others]	(Unknown) fl 25
1802/08/24	LNDLS	0079	*D. van Tol* | Een Haspelend Vrouwtje in een Nis met Wijngaardranken, voor hetzelve een Pot met Bloemen. Gem. denzelven [D. van Tol] | *Mat:* op paneel *Size:* hoog 13 ½, breed 11 duimen *Inscr:* D. van Tol (signed)	Leonardus Bouman [or others]	(Unknown) fl 0:12
1803/06/20	AMSCH	0017	*D. van Tol* | Een bevallig Vrouwtje, schynende een brandende Kaars in een Lantaarn te willen plaatsen, uitvoerig geschilderd, door D. van Tol, op Paneel | *Mat:* op paneel *Size:* hoog 7, breed 5 duim	Schley [for] B	(Sold) fl 40 V d Schleij [for] F
1804/07/25	DLGRO	0020	*Van Tol* | En Doctor in zyn Studeerkamer met een Urinaal met Water 't welk hy beziet, naast hem staat een Juffrouw die daar over schynt te Consuleeren, met verder bywerk, uitvoerig en fraai geschildert | *Mat:* op doek *Size:* hoog 17, breed 21 duim	Mr Franc van der Burch Wz.	(Unknown)
1804/10/16	DLOND	0224	*Dom. van Tol* | Een studerend Man met een Globe voor zich. Hy snydt zyne Pen. Un Homme étudiant devant une Table, sur laquelle un Globe. Il retaille sa Plume | *Mat:* op paneel *Size:* hoog 9, breed 8		(Unknown)
1805/10/09	HGBSM	0109	*D. van Tol* | Voor een steene nis met een wyngaards rank, ziet men een jongeling met een vogelkooy, benevens een fles met bloemen, uitvoerig geschilderd, gemerkt D. van Tol | *Mat:* op paneel *Size:* hoog 11 ½ breet 9 ½ duim *Inscr:* D. van Tol (signed)	T H van Willigen [or others]	(Sold) fl 1:2 Carré
1806/08/13	AMSCH	0179	*Tol. (D. van)* | Voor een Huis ziet men een bejaarde Vrouw, houdende een Vuurpotje op de Schoot, bézig zynde Koeken te bakken, nevens haar een beslagpot, Mand met appelen en verder toepasselyk bywerk; zonachtig en meesterlyk gepenceeld | *Mat:* op paneel *Size:* hoog 13, breed 11 duim	Vinkeles [for] J	(Sold) fl 52 Schumacher
1806/08/13	AMSCH	0180	*Tol. (D. van)* | In een welvoorziene Keuken, is een oude Vrouw, bézig Koeken te bakken, névens haar twee Eetende Kinderen; verders door een openstaande deur ziet men voor een open vengster een Vrouw bézig aan een wastobben; bevallig van licht en uitvoerig van schildering | *Mat:* op doek *Size:* hoog 19, breed 14 duim	Vinkeles [for] G[ruyter]	(Sold) fl 18 Schumacher
1806/11/24	AMSCH	0077	*Tol (D. van)* | Een Vrouw, zittende te haspelen naast haar staat een Spinnewiel in een ouwerwetsche Kamer; verders een ménigte Huisraad, kunstig behandeld | *Mat:* op paneel *Size:* hoog 17, breed 13 duim	Munnikhuizen	(Sold) fl 10 du Pree
1808/05/17	LNAN	0006	*D. van Tol* | In een binnen vertrek zit een aardig gekleed vrouwtje op een stoel, met een mande voor haar, zij schijnt bezig te zijn een eendvogel		(Sold) fl 610 M V Noort

			te plukken, nevens dezelve zit een man, als omziende, terwijl hij zijn tabakspijp aan het vuur dat hij met een tang die hij in zijn regter hand houdt, aansteekt; aan de wand hangt een vogelkooi, en op den voorgrond staat een emmer, bezem en meer huisraad aan de wand; zeer kunstig van teekening en schildering | *Mat:* op paneel *Size:* hoog 17, breed 15 duim		
1809/04/22	AMYVR	0125	*D. van Tol* | In een Binnenvertrek zit eene oude Vrouw te haspelen, bij een Spinnewiel, het door de Deur invallend licht doet eene uitmuntende werking, en is kloek geschilderd | *Mat:* op paneel *Size:* hoog 16, breed 13 duim	de Bruin	(Sold) fl 37 C S Roos
1809/06/13	AMSCH	0151	*D. van Tol* | In een Binnevertrek zit eene bedaagde Vrouw, in oude Hollandsche Kleeding, bij een Spinnewiel, zij is bézig Vlas te Spinnen, nevens haar zit een Jongeling, bij het Vuur zich te Warmen, op een Stoel ligt een Garen-klos en ander Gereedschap; krachtig en uitvoerig | *Mat:* op paneel *Size:* hoog 18, breed 16 duim	E	(Sold) fl 32 Buck
1809/09/06	AMSCH	0068	*Tol (D. van)* | In een antique Kamer, zit een geleerde in zijn Japon te Studéren, bij hem op de Tafel ligt een opengeslagen Atlas en andere Boeken, op de Grond staat een Globe; aan de Zolder hangt een Tapijt en Gordijn, 't geen gedeeltelijk opengeslagen is, zijnde van de uitvoerigste van deze Meester | *Mat:* op paneel *Size:* hoog 25, breed 20 duim	Johannes Caudri	(Sold) fl 114 Tomassen
1809/09/06	AMSCH	0069	*Tol (D. van)* | In een dito [antique] Kamer zit eene bevallig Meisje te Speldewerken, naast een Tafel, met een Bijbel en Tapijt; alles is als de voorgaande behandeld | *Mat:* op paneel *Size:* hoog 20, breed 16 duim	Johannes Caudri	(Sold) fl 50 Roos
1810/03/26	RMMUY	0055	*D. van Tol* | Voor een open hardsteenen Nis, zit een deftig Man (Gerard Dou verbeeldende) zijn eene hand rustende op een Doodshoofd, en wijzende met de andere hand. In het verschiet een Schilderkamer en verder bijwerk. Krachtig en uitvoerig geschilderd [Devant une ouverture d'une croisée, est assis un Peintre (portrait de Dou) posant sa main droite sur une tête de Mort, et montrant de la main gauche quelques objets qui se presentent dans le fond d'un attelier de peintre, tres precieusement fini, d'un ton soutenu et vigoureux.] | *Mat:* op paneel *Size:* hoog 18 ½, breed 13 duimen	Daniel de Jongh Az	(Sold) fl 49 Thomasse te Leyden
1810/05/22	AMSCH	0102	*Toll. (D. van)* | In dit fraaije stukje ziet men een bevalig Meisje, staande voor eene open steenen Nis, welke gedeeltelijk met een Tapijt Kleed bedekt is, zij houdt eene Vogel in haar linker hand, voor haar op de Plint der Nis een Koperen Emmer en eenige Aardvruchten, benevens een Pot met Bloemen en Glazen Fles, agterwaards in een gemeubileerd Vertrek, ziet men eenige Lieden bij eene Tafel; het is zeer uitvoerig en teder van schildering | *Mat:* op paneel *Size:* hoog 12, breed 9 duim	Johannes van de Putte Nicolaasz.	(Sold) fl 46 Hulswit
1810/05/22	AMSCH	0103	*Toll. (D. van)* | Eene bedaagde biddende Vrouw, zittende voor eene Tafel, waarop Brood en een Aarden Kan geplaatst is; krachtig en meesterlijk geschilderd | *Mat:* op paneel *Size:* hoog 15, breed 12 duim	S	(Sold) fl 7 Valee
1810/08/01	AMSCH	0102	*Tol (Dominicus van)* | In een prachtig Binnenvertrek zit op den voorgrond een jong bevallig Meisje, bezig Kant te werken; nevens haar een Jongeling met eene Trommel bij eene Tafel, met Tapijt gedekt; achterwaarts eene verwulfde Kamer, waarin twee bejaarde Heeren, zittende aan eene Tafel [Dans un apartement meublé est assise sur le premier plan une jeune et gentille Fille faisant de la Dentelle sur son Careau ; à son côté se trouve un Jeunehomme tenant un Tambour. On y distingue une Table couverte d'une Tapis, et dans le fond la vue perce dans une second pièce qui est voutée, dans laquelle deux personnages sont assis devant une Table] | *Annots:* NB : composition très merquine. (NGW) *Mat:* op paneel *Size:* hoog 22 ½, breed 17 duimen	Mr Pieter de Smeth van Alphen	(Sold) fl 1510 Texier, Gerbet en Comp [for] LeBrun
1810/10/10	MGCIT	0118	*v. Tol* | Een Oud Man en Vrouw, de eene met een stok de andere met een Kan in de hand, goed geschilderd en geteekend	Caspar van Citters	(Unknown)
1810/10/11	AMSCH	0086	*D. Van Toll* | Voor eene open Nis ziet men een bevallig Meisje benevens een Jongeling | *Mat:* op paneel *Size:* hoog 9, breed 7 duimen	C	(Sold) fl 2 Posthumus
			Tol, Domenicus van (or Tol, D., manner)		
1802/09/06	AMSCH	0118	*van Tol* | Een Jonge Chirurgyn, een Meisje van de huig ligtende; uitvoerig op Kooper, door of in de manier van van Tol | *Mat:* op koper *Size:* hoog 15, breed 11 duim	B	(Sold) fl 9:10 Jan Spaan
1806/08/20	HGBSM	0019	*D. van Tol* | Eene Boerin met een kopere Ketel die zij uitgiet in een Waschtobbe, vol effect en zeer doorschijnend geschilderd, door of in de manier van D. van Tol | *Mat:* op paneel *Size:* hoog 14, breed 11 ½ duim	Macalester Loup [or others]	(Sold) fl 47 Zwartsman
			Tol, Domenicus van (copy after)		
1804/10/16	DLOND	0067	*Duigenberg; naar van Thol* | Een oud Vrouwtje uit een Vengster ene Waterpot uitgietende, toogsgewys. Une vieille Femme dans une fenetre. Elle vuide son pot de Chambre | copy by Duigenberg after D. Tol *Mat:* op doek op paneel *Size:* hoog 9, breed 7		(Unknown)
1804/10/16	DLOND	0240a[c]	*C. Vermeulen; D. van Tol* | [Een Stuk, bevattende 13 zeer schone Copiën van de volgende Meesters. Un Tableau, contenant 13 Copies très-belles des Peintres suivans.] 3. D. van Tol. Een Binnenvertrek, une Chambre | copy by Corn. Vermeulen (III) after D. Tol *Mat:* op paneel *Size:* hoog 41, breed 55 *Notes:* The bracketed information in the title appears above lot 240a[a] and refers to lots 240a[a-m].		(Sold) fl 150 for lots 240a[a-m]. Ond d Wyngaert

			Tol, Domenicus van (manner)		
1808/06/13	AMSCH	0231	*D. van Toll* | Een Heelmeester, bezig zijnde een Boer eene kies te trekken, verder eene menigte Heelkundige noodwendigheden; alleruitvoerigst in de manier van D. van Toll	R[oos]	(Bought In) fl 7
			Tol, Pieter van		
1808/06/11	RMRIJ	0125	*Pieter van Tol* | Een Binnenvertrek waar in een Vrouwtje Peen Schrapt, met aangenaam Bywerk, piquant van licht en zeer uitvoerig geschilderd | *Mat:* op paneel		(Sold) fl 20 Rohan
			Tonderen, P. van [Unidentified]		
1808/06/13	AMSCH	0212	*P. van Tonderen* | Een Italiaansch Landschap, met Schapen, Bokken en Kruiden; fraai	E M Engelberts	(Sold) fl 1:10 Glad
			Toorenburgh, Gerrit		
1802/06/28	AMSCH	0182	*G. Torenburg* | Een gezicht op den Overhaal aan den Overtoom, buiten Amsterdam, gestoffeerd met verscheide Beeldjes en Paarden, uitvoerig op Doek | *Mat:* op doek *Size:* hoog 16, breed 17 duim	Anna Elink	(Sold) fl 8 Coclers
1802/06/28	AMSCH	0183	*G. Torenburg* | Twee stuks gezichten binnen Amsterdam, het eene op het Diaconie Weeshuis van agtere, en het andere ter zyde | *Mat:* op doek *Size:* hoog 15, breed 19 duim	Anna Elink	(Sold) fl 21:10 Jan Spaan
1802/06/28	AMSCH	0184	*G. Torenburg* | Een vermakelyk Ysgezicht, gestoffeerd met een menigte Schaatseryders en Arresleeden, zeer natuurlyk gepenceeld, door Denzelven [G. Torenburg], op Doek | *Mat:* op doek *Size:* hoog 17, breed 19 duim	Anna Elink	(Sold) fl 14:10 Coclers
1802/06/28	AMSCH	0185	*G. Torenburg* | Twee stuks Bergachtige Landschappen, ryk gestoffeerd en zonachtig behandeld | *Mat:* op doek *Size:* hoog 14, breed 17 duim	Anna Elink	(Sold) fl 4:10 Dijkman
1804/05/07	AMSCH	0165	*Torenbur. (G.)* | Twee stuks, het eene voorstellende het Luthersche Diaconiehuis te Amsterdam by de Plantasie, en het andere een gezicht op een Poort te Delft, beiden met fraay Geboomten en Staffagie [sic] van Beeldjes, Vaartuigen en anderen; zonachtig en uitvoerig gepenceeld | *Mat:* op doek *Size:* Ieder hoog 17, breed 19 duim	Roos [for] A	(Sold) fl 90 J Spaan
1804/05/07	AMSCH	0166	*Torenbur. (G.)* | Een gezicht op het Huis Altona by Delft, liggende in het Water, gestoffeerd met Vissers in een Schuit; als de voorgaande behandeld | *Mat:* op paneel *Size:* hoog 13, breed 15 duim	R[oos]	(Sold) fl 25 Jan Spaan
1804/05/07	AMSCH	0167	*Torenbur. (G.)* | Een gezicht op het Huis te Heemsteden, mede bevallig gestoffeerd; en als de voorgaande behandeld | *Size:* hoog 13, breed 15 duim	R[oos]	(Sold) fl 20 Jan Spaan
1804/05/07	AMSCH	0168	*Torenbur. (G.)* | Een dito [gezicht] op een ander Adelyk Huis te zien, niet minder als den voorgaande behandeld | *Size:* hoog 13, breed 15 duim	R[oos]	(Sold) fl 23 Jan Spaan
1804/05/07	AMSCH	0169	*Torenbur. (G.)* | Een gezicht aan het Spaarn te Haarlem; mede van een aangenaame behandeling | *Mat:* op paneel *Size:* hoog 13, breed 15 duim	Roos [for] A	(Sold) fl 11:10 Roelofs
1804/05/07	AMSCH	0170	*Torenbur. (G.)* | Twee stuks Boom- en Bergachtige Landschappen met Rivieren doorsneeden, waarin eenige Schuiten, verders gestoffeerd met een meenigte Vee met hunne Herders; beide uitvoerig en piqant [sic] van licht | *Mat:* op doek *Size:* Ieder hoog 12, breed 14 duim	Roos [for] A	(Bought In) fl 10
1804/08/08	AMSCH	0186	*G. Torenburg* | Twee stuks Boom- en Bergachtige Landschappen, met Rivieren doorsneeden, waarin eenige Schuiten, verders gestoffeerd met een ménigte Vée, met hunne Herders; beiden uitvoerig en piquant van zonlicht | *Mat:* op doek *Size:* hoog 12, breed 11 duim	Roos [for] F	(Sold) fl 11:10 Van Iperen
1804/12/10	AMSCH	0094	*G. Toorenburg* | Twee stuks capitaale Gezichten; verbeeldende Zomer en Winter, byde ryk gestoffeerd; ziende de eene van de Buitencingel naar een stads Poort en Vestmuur, met varende Schuiten, Hengelaars en wandelende Lieden: den andere een besneeuwde Wegh, met Woningen langs een bevrozen Rivier, waarop Arresleede en Schaatzeryders; byde natuurlyk en zeer uitvoerig gepenceeld | *Mat:* op doek *Size:* Ieder hoog 17, breed 19 duim	Jan De Groot	(Sold) fl 42 Josi
1804/12/10	AMSCH	0095	*G. Toorenburg* | Twee stuks capitaale Gezichten, zynde een Zomer- en Wintergezicht, ziende van de Buitencingel naar de Stad en Vestmuur, byden ryk gestoffeerd met Beeldjes en Schuiten, Rytuigen, Arreslee en Schaatzeryders; natuurlyk, en van een uitvoerige penceelbehandeling | *Mat:* op doek *Size:* Ieder hoog 17, breed 19 duim	Jan De Groot	(Sold) fl 51 Roelofs
1804/12/10	AMSCH	0096	*G. Toorenburg* | Een Gezicht binnen Amsterdam, op de Binnen-Amstel, langs de Doodkistemakersgragt op het Diaconie Weeshuis, met verscheide Vaartuigen en Beeldjes gestoffeerd; en zonachtig behandeld | *Mat:* op doek *Size:* hoog 15, breed 19 duim	Jan De Groot	(Sold) fl 8 Lamme
1805/07/03	AMSCH	0152	*G. Torenburg* | Twee stuks Gezichten op de Ingestorten Muider-Poort; zonachtig op Doek | *Mat:* op doek *Size:* hoog 10, breed 13 duim	G	(Sold) fl 8:5 van Iperen
1805/07/10	AMSCH	0145	*G. Toorenburg* | Twee stuks Riviergezichten, ziende op de Stads Wallen, met een ménigte Schuiten en stoffagie van Beeldjes; uitvoerig gepenceeld | *Mat:* op doek *Size:* hoog 13, breed 13 duim	V[inkeles] [for] J	(Sold) fl 8:5 van Iperen
1806/05/05	AMSCH	0141	*G. Toorenburg* | Twee stuks Gezigten van de Muider Poort, zo als die zig buiten en binnen de Stad vertoonden in 't Jaar 1772; uitvoerig geschildert	V[inkeles]	(Sold) fl 7 C van der Does

			door G. Toorenburg | *Mat:* op doek *Size:* hoog 10, breed 13 duim *Inscr:* 1772 (dated?) *Notes:* It is unclear whether the date is inscribed on the painting.		
1807/08/26	AMSCH	0213	*G. Toorenburg* | Een Gezicht binnen Amsterdam, ziende uit de Plantage naar de Muiderpoort, gestoffeerd met Hengelaars, een Schip en andere Schuiten; alles verbeeld by Maanlicht | *Mat:* op doek *Size:* hoog 16, breed 19 duim	Roos	(Sold) fl 4:10 Coclair
1810/05/22	AMSCH	0105	*Toorenburg (G.)* | Een Gezicht op het Buitenspaarn, ter zijde Heeren Huizinge, gestoffeerd met een groot Jagt, Visschuit en andere Voorwerpen; zonachtig gepenceeld | *Mat:* op paneel *Size:* hoog 18, breed 22 duim	Johannes van de Putte Nicolaasz.	(Sold) fl 16 v der Schleij [for] Ryfsnyder
1810/05/22	AMSCH	0106	*Toorenburg. (G.)* | Een Gezichtje buiten Utrecht, met Gebouwen en Beeldjes gestoffeerd; natuurlijk behandeld | *Mat:* op paneel *Size:* hoog 10, breed 13 ½ duim	Ij[ver]	(Sold) fl 3:10 Gruyter

Toorenvliet, Abraham

1807/08/26	AMSCH	0217	*A. Torenvliet* | In dit Stukje ziet men een blazende Bakker, liggende over zyn Onderdeur, nevens hem ligt eenig Brood op het Vengster, en ander bywerk | *Mat:* op paneel *Size:* hoog 10, breed 7 ½ duim	de Vries	(Sold) fl 1:10 L Pakker
1809/06/13	AMSCH	0154	*A. Toornvliet* | Eene bevallig Vrouwtje, wordende door een nevens haar zittend Huisman geliefkoost; geestig verbeeld | *Mat:* op doek *Size:* hoog 13 ½, breed 11 ½ duim	E	(Sold) fl 8:10 Buck
1809/06/13	AMSCH	0155	*A. Toornvliet* | Twee stuks, een vrolijk Krijgsman, houdende een Glas en Pijp in de Hand, en eene Vrouw met een Mandje aan haar Arm; beide fiks geschilderd | *Mat:* op paneel *Size:* ieder is hoog 11, breed 9 duim	E	(Sold) fl 0:14 L Pakker
1810/06/20	AMSCH	0084	*A. Torenvliedt* | Twee stuks: een vergenoegd Man en Vrouw | *Mat:* op doek *Size:* hoog 10, breed 6 ¼ duimen	A	(Sold) fl 4 de Vries

Toorenvliet, Jacob

1801/08/19	AMSCH	0117	*J. Toorenvliet* | In een Gemeubileerd Binnenvertrek ziet men twee Heere op het Verkeerbord speelen, by dezelven zit een bejaard Man, welke onder 't rooken van zyn Pyp 't spel aanziet, verders eenig bywerk; fraai gepenceeld	Pruyssen^{r} [for] Q	(Bought In) fl 81
1801/11/10	AMPOS	0044	*J. Toorenvliet* | 2 stuks Vis- en Vogelverkoopsters		(Unknown)
1801/12/22	AMOTT	0003	*Toorenvliet* | Deftige Mannen in Spaansche Kleeding, by een Tafel, vol Boeken, in 't verschiet twee tegen elkander spreekende vrouwe Beelden, alle in naturelle houdingen	Bartholomeus Ruloffs	(Unknown) fl 6
1802/05/05	AMSCH	0206	*Toornvliet* | Voor een Buytenhuis staat een Lierman, met zyn Hond, een Meisje en een Man, speelende op de Citer | *Mat:* op doek *Size:* hoog 10, breed 8 duim	C	(Sold) fl 3:10 Th^{s} Spaan
1802/08/24	LNDLS	0087	*J. Toornvliet* | Twee stuks, als een Man met een blad in zijn hand die zingt, en een met een Man met een Wijn-roemer. Beide op paneel | *This Lot:* Een Man met een blad in zijn hand die zingt *Mat:* op paneel *Size:* hoog 9 ½, breed 5 ½ duimen *Notes:* Lots 87 and 88 were printed in the catalogue as one item.	Leonardus Bouman [or others]	(Unknown) fl 3 for lots 87 & 88
1802/08/24	LNDLS	0088	*J. Toornvliet* | Twee stuks, als een Man met een blad in zijn hand die zingt, en een met een Man met een Wijn-roemer. Beide op paneel | *This Lot:* Een met een Man met een Wijn-roemer *Mat:* op paneel *Size:* hoog 9 ½, breed 5 ½ duimen *Notes:* Lots 87 and 88 were printed in the catalogue as one item.	Leonardus Bouman [or others]	(Unknown) fl 3 for lots 87 & 88
1802/09/06	AMSCH	0116	*J. Toornvliet* | Een Boeremeisje, door een Boer geliefkoost; uitvoerig | *Mat:* op doek *Size:* hoog 14, breed 12 duim	B	(Sold) fl 2:10 Jan Spaan
1802/09/06	AMSCH	0117	*J. Toornvliet* | Een Boer, welke aan een nevens hem zittende Vrouw geld schynt te geeven; als dito [uitvoerig] | *Size:* hoog 10, breed 12 duim	B	(Sold) fl 2:5 van Dijl
1802/09/06	AMSCH	0176	*Toorenvliet* | Voor een Buitenhuis, staat een Lierman, waar by verscheide andere Lieden; plaisant geschilderd	Spaan	(Sold) fl 1 van Iperen
1802/09/06	AMSCH	0185	*Toorenvliet* | Twee stuks gestoffeerde Binnenhuizen	Spaan	(Sold) fl 3 Barteling
1802/09/29	AMSCH	0053	*J. Toornvliet* | Een bevallig Stukje, verbeeldende Straat-Musikanten, waarby een Hond; delicaat en breed van Penceelbehandeling [Deux musiciens de Guinguettte [sic] ; une Vielle [sic] qui chante & un jeune Homme qui joue du Violon. Tableau Intéressant & bien touché.] | *Mat:* op doek *Size:* hoog 13 ¼, breed 11 ¼ duim	[Labouchere?]	(Sold) fl 37 C S Roos
1803/07/18	AMSCH	0054	*Torenvliet. (J.)* | Twee stuks, zynde een Goudzoeker en een Visboer, beide delicaat behandeld [Deux jolis sujets, dont le premier est un alchimiste occupé à chercher la pierre philosophale. Le second répresente une fruitiere [;] ils sont ornés de differens accessoires relatifs aux sujets. Petits morceaux d'une touche facile & d'un bon effet.] | *Mat:* op koper *Size:* hoog 9, breed 7 duim	Maria Theresia Andrioli	(Sold) fl 11 Hodges
1803/07/18	AMSCH	0055	*Torenvliet. (J.)* | Twee stuks, een Visvrouw en een Vogelkoopster, behandeld als de voorgaande [Deux pendans. Le premier est un poullalier [sic], & sur le second l'on voit une marchande de poisson, avec les marchandises & les attributs de l'etât de chacun. Ils sont d'une couleur claire & agréable, & d'une exécution semblable aux deux précedents.] |	Maria Theresia Andrioli	(Sold) fl 11 Hodges

			Mat: [sur bois] *Size:* hoog 9, breed 7 duim *Notes:* The material was given only in the French edition of the catalogue.		
1805/06/24	DOBLU	0025	*Toornvliet* | Een Musiceerend Gezelschap, zeer goed	Willem Snellen [or] F R E Nibbelinck [or] Gysbert Visser	(Unknown)
1806/08/13	AMSCH	0184	*Torenvliet. (J.)* | Twee stuks Gezelschappen van Dames en Heeren met eenig bywerk; beide van een delicate penceelsbehandeling | *Mat:* op doek *Size:* Ieder hoog 15, breed 13 duim	Daniel Mansveld	(Sold) fl 37 Pieter Swanenburgh
1807/04/00	LNDLS	0051	*Toornvliet* | Twee vrijlijke mans borststukken	[Abraham Delfos] [or others]	(Unknown)
1807/06/10	HGBSM	0051	*Toornvliet* | Twee vrolijke mans borststukken	Abraham Delfos [or others]	(Sold) fl 5:16 Nieukoop
1808/04/26	GDAN	0164	*Toornvliet* | Een slapend Vrouwtje op een ton leunende, fiks behandeld | *Size:* hoog 19, breed 14 duim	G H Fortuyn	(Unknown)
1808/06/13	AMSCH	0158	*Toorenvliet (J.)* | Een Musiceerend Gezelschap, in een Binnenvertrek. Fiks gepenceeld	E M Engelberts	(Sold) fl 5:10 Nieuwenhuisen
1809/04/22	AMYVR	0126	*J. Toornvliet* | Twee stuks met Vrouwen en Kinderen, overeenkomstig de natuur behandeld | *Mat:* op paneel *Size:* hoog 13, breed 10 duim	de Bruin	(Sold) fl 9:15 du Pree
1810/03/27	RMCNL	0077	*Torenvliet* | Een drinkend Boertje, zeer geestig en aardig gepenseeld		(Unknown)
1810/06/20	AMSCH	0113	*Toorenvliet* | Een zingende Boer	N	(Sold) fl 0:10 van Dijl
1810/10/11	AMSCH	0131	*Torenvliet* | Een Italiaansche Groenmarkt, vol gewoel met Beelden | *Mat:* op doek	[Gruyter?]	(Sold or Bought In) fl 1 Gruiter
			Toorenvliet, Jacob (manner)		
1801/10/06	AMSCH	0088	*als door Toorenvliet* | Een Vrouwtje halverlyf voor een steene Baluster, waar op geplaats, Kool en andere Groentens, fiks behandeld | *Mat:* op paneel *Size:* hoog 9, breed 7 duim	L	(Sold) fl 14 A E Sterk
1805/07/10	AMSCH	0252	*Torenvliet* | Twee stuks studérende Lieden, Man en Vrouw, verzelt van Kinderen; op Paneel, in de manier van Torenvliet | *Mat:* op paneel	Wed Grave	(Sold) fl 1 Mensaart
1810/10/11	AMSCH	0152	*Toorenvliet* | Een liefkoosende Boer en Boerin, voor een Herberg; als Toorenvliet	S	(Sold) fl 0:8 Geld
			Torelli, Felice		
1804/07/25	AMSCH	0082	*Torelli* | De Triomph van Nepthunus, hy is verbeeld op zyn Zeewagen, verzeld van Tritons, Naijaden en vliegende Minnewigten, welken Zeegewassen aanbrengen; helder en bevallig van couleur en uitvoerig geschilderd | *Mat:* op doek *Size:* hoog 23, breed 34 duim		(Sold) fl 28 Thais
			Torunia, R. [Unidentified]		
1810/05/22	AMSCH	0104	*Torunia. (R.)* | Een bevallig Meisje, staande voor een Steenen Baluster, met een Wijngaard bewassen, zij houdt een trots Druiven in haar hand; delikaat gepenceeld | *Mat:* op paneel *Size:* hoog 16, breed 12 duim	R	(Sold) fl 4:10 Rinkhuizen
			Trautmann, Johann Georg		
1803/09/07	AMSCH	0186	*Trautman* | Een Grot van binnen te zien, alwaar eenige Heidenen de Pot koken; bevallig van ligt en fix behandeld [Une caverne dans laquelle on voit des Bohémiens occupés à cuire la soupe ; agréable par le jeu de la lumière et d'une belle exécution] | *Mat:* op paneel *Size:* hoog 9, breed 11 duim	Smidt	(Sold) fl 1:5 Van den Brink
			Treu		
1805/07/10	AMSCH	0144	*Trey* | Christus bespotting, fraai van coloriet en uitvoerig gepenceeld | *Mat:* op doek *Size:* hoog 39 ¼, breed 21 ½ duim	V[inkeles] [for] H[affner]	(Sold) fl 13:10 Gruyter
			Treu, Catharina		
1803/09/07	AMSCH	0185	*C. Trey* | Een Fruitstuk waar in een Canteloup en andere Fruiten; delicaat [Un assemblage de fruits de toutes espèces dans une soucoupe ; composition délicate] | *Mat:* op doek *Size:* hoog 16, breed 15 duim	Smidt	(Sold) fl 3 Jan Yver
			Treu, Nicolaus		
1803/09/07	AMSCH	0184	*N. Trey* | Christus gebonden wordende door de Krygsknegten, de hartstogten zyn sprekend en de behandeling meesterlyk, op Doek, door N. Trey, 1764 te Parys [Jesus Christ, garotté par les juifs ; les passions qui caractérisent les differentes figures de ce tableau sont expressives, et l'exécution en est excellente] | *Mat:* op doek *Inscr:* N. Trey, 1764 (signed and dated?) *Notes:* It is unclear whether the name and date are inscribed on the painting.	Smidt	(Sold) fl 30 Hafner
1804/05/07	AMSCH	0171	*Trey. (N.)* | Een bevallige Jongeling, zittende voor een Tafel, schynende aandachtig te luisteren na een ander, welke hem een Brief voorleest; uitvoerig en fraay gepenceeld | *Mat:* op doek *Size:* hoog 34, breed 28 duim	Vinkeles [for] H[affner]	(Sold) fl 20 Lelie
			Troost, Cornelis		
1801/06/10	AMSCH	0161	*Troost. (C.)* | In een aangenaam Hofgezicht ziet men de passage uit het verliefde Brechtje, zynde een ryke bevallige Ordonantie van achttien	Herman ten Kate	(Sold) fl 13 Spruit van Gend

			Beelden; zonachtig en meesterlyk behandeld | *Mat:* op doek *Size:* hoog 29, breed 46 duim		
1801/06/10	AMSCH	0162	*Troost. (C.)* | Een Koffihuis, ryk gestoffeerd met een menigte Heeren in differente actien; op de voorgrond ziet men eene Dienstmaagd, nevens een Heer, hem een kelk morgendrank aanbiedende; de karakters zyn geestig en fiks geschilderd | *Mat:* op doek *Size:* hoog 26, breed 39 duim	Herman ten Kate	(Sold) fl 21 Reynders
1801/06/10	AMSCH	0163	*Troost. (C.)* | Deeze ryke Ordonantie stelt voor, de Spilpenning, of de Verkwistende Vrouw, in een fraaije gemeubileerde Kamer, met een menigte zilveren, porceleinen en andere Cieraaden; kragtig van schildering en natuurlyk gekaractriseert | *Mat:* op paneel *Size:* hoog 28, breed 33 duim	Herman ten Kate	(Sold) fl 92 Jozi
1801/10/19	AMSCH	0070	*Troost. (Cornelis)* | Een Corps de Guarde van Officieren, ryk gestoffeerd, zynde dit Cabinetstuk zo van Ordonantie als van uitvoerigheid, een der fraayste stukken van deeze Meester | *Mat:* op paneel *Size:* hoog 17, breed 22 duim	Jonkheer Menno Baron van Coehoorn	(Sold) fl 35 J Ijver
1801/12/22	AMOTT	0109	*Troost* | 1 deftig mans Pourtrait, de Grootvader van den beroemden Zels	Bartholomeus Ruloffs	(Unknown) fl 2:10
1802/02/16	AMSCH	0007	*C. Troost* | Een stadgezicht, op de voorgrond een Apotheekers Winkel; en verdere stoffagie van Beelden; fix op Doek | *Mat:* op doek	B[uys]	(Sold) fl 0:6 van Iperen
1802/05/05	AMSCH	0207	*Troost* | Een Coffyhuis	J	(Sold) fl 24:10 C S Roos
1802/06/28	AMSCH	0181	*C. Troost* | Een bevallig gezicht op een Buitenplaats in de Haarlemmer Hout, fiks behandeld, door C. Troost, op Panneel | *Mat:* op paneel *Size:* hoog 21, breed 25 duim	Anna Elink	(Sold) fl 8:10 Brouwer
1803/07/18	AMSCH	0053	*Troost (C.)* | In een deftig gemeubileerde Zaal ziet men verbeeld een Bedryf uit het bekende Toneelspel de Ingebeelde Zieke, zynde een bevallige Ordonantie, zonachtig en geestig gepenceeld [Dans une chambre est representée une scène du malade imaginaire : une jeune fille & un jeune homme s'emblent [sic] en explication au sujet de deux lettres qu'ils se montrent reciproquement. Le Papa accompagné d'un Medecin & d'un troisième les examine attentivement. Ce tableau a du Caractère & de l'effet.] | *Mat:* op paneel *Size:* hoog 20, breed 27 duim	Maria Theresia Andrioli	(Sold) fl 21 Josi
1803/12/15	MGLAC	0055	*Troost* | Een vrolyk Musicerend Gezelschap met een aantal wel geordonneerde Figuuren; schoon van ligt en bruin | *Mat:* op paneel *Size:* hoog duim 18, breed duim 25	Mr L H de Haze Bomme	(Unknown)
1804/02/27	AMSCH	0104	*Troost. (C.)* | Twee zeer aangenaame Gezichten op en langs Buitenplaatsen aan de Vegt; ryk en bevallig gestoffeerd, en meesterlyk geschilderd | *Mat:* op doek *Size:* hoog 33, breed 45 duim	B	(Sold) fl 13 Theengs
1804/04/28	LNDLS	0034	*C. Troost* | Heeren en Juffers voor een buitenplaats, op eene aartige wys blindeman speelende, terwyl een jong juffertje een Oostindische vogel fruit aanbied, door C. Troost, op doek | *Mat:* op doek *Size:* hoog 21, breed 28 duim	[Abraham Delfos] [or others]	(Bought In) fl 16
1804/05/07	AMSCH	0163	*Troost (C.)* | Deeze ryke Ordonantie in een prachtige Zaal, gestoffeerd met een menigte Ornamenten, ziet men Ashueros de Zaal, op een gramstorige wyze verlaten, terwyl Mordechai in een spreekende gestalte zich voor Hester vernederd, verders een Knegt, een Moortje en een O.I. Raaf; meesterlyk van schildering | *Mat:* op doek *Size:* hoog 41, breed 48 duim	Roos [for] A	(Sold) fl 19 Ferguson
1804/05/07	AMSCH	0164	*Troost (C.)* | Deeze geestige Ordonantie steld voor de Hopman Ulrich; allernatuurlykst en uitvoerig behandeld | *Mat:* op paneel *Size:* hoog 19 ½, breed 15 ½ duim	Vinkeles	(Sold) fl 3 B[d] Kooy
1807/04/00	LNDLS	0004	*C. Troost* | Een Corps de Garde van verscheide Officieren, die een landkaart beschouwen, een Housaar staat daar nevens, een ander schrijft een brief en meer bijwerk. Een der beste stukken van die meester, uit het kabinet van Braamcamp no. 228 | *Size:* hoog 36, breed 47 duim	[Abraham Delfos] [or others]	(Unknown)
1807/04/00	LNDLS	0005	*C. Troost* | Dit verbeeld een pragtige zaal, alwaar de Koningin Esther, nevens een tafel gezeten, door Haman werd aangezogt om vergiffenis te smeken, terwijl den Koning Ahasveros in eene woedende gestalte zulks beschouwt, en Mordechai als lovende en dankende voortgaat, met meer bijwerk. Alles zeer rijk van ordonnantie en hartstogten, konstig en kragtig op doek geschildert | *Mat:* op doek *Size:* hoog 39, breed 48 duim	[Abraham Delfos] [or others]	(Unknown)
1807/04/00	LNDLS	0006	*C. Troost* | Een pragtige zaal, daar Damocles op de plaats van Dionilius aan tafel zit, en een zwaard dat aan een paardehaar boven zijn hoofd hangende gewaar word, en meer beelden op doek | *Mat:* op doek *Size:* hoog 30, breed 37 duim	[Abraham Delfos] [or others]	(Unknown)
1807/06/10	HGBSM	0004	*C. Troost* | Een Corps de Garde van verscheide Officieren, die een landkaart beschouwen, een Housaar staat daar nevens, een ander schrijft een brief en meer bijwerk. Een der beste stukken van die meester, uit het kabinet van de Heer Braamcamp, no 228. | *Size:* hoog 36, breed 47 duim	Abraham Delfos [or others]	(Sold) fl 40:10 Tomas
1807/06/10	HGBSM	0005	*C. Troost* | Dit verbeeld een pragtige zaal, alwaar de Koningin Esther, nevens een tafel gezeten, door Haman werd aangezogt om vergiffenis te smeken, terwijl den Koning Ahasveros in eene woedende gestalte zulks beschouwt, en Mordechai als lovende en dankende voortgaat, met meer bijwerk. Alles zeer rijk van ordonnantie en hartstogten, konstig en kragtig op doek geschildert | *Mat:* op doek *Size:* hoog 39, breed 48 duim	Abraham Delfos [or others]	(Sold) fl 16 Tomas

1807/06/10	HGBSM	0006	*C. Troost* | Een pragtige zaal, daar Damocles op de plaats van Dionisius aan tafel zit, en een zwaard dat aan een paardehaar boven zijn hoofd hangende gewaar word, en meer beelden | *Mat:* op doek *Size:* hoog 30, breed 37 duim	Abraham Delfos [or others]	(Sold) fl 12:5 Spruit
1807/06/10	HGBSM	0079	*C. Troost* | Heeren en Dames, speelende voor een buitenplaats, met meer persoonen en bijwerk | *Mat:* op doek *Size:* hoog 21 breed 28 duim	Abraham Delfos [or others]	(Sold) fl 6:15 v Iperen
1808/05/17	LNAN	0003	*Corn. Troost* | Eene Koninglijke Zaal daar de Koningin Hester nevens eene gedekte tafel zit, terwijl Haman om genade smeekt, en Koning Ahosveros [sic] met een woedend gezigt hem aanziet en weg gaat, verzeld van Mordechai en een ander die hem ter dood aanwijst; alles kunstig verbeeld en zeer krachtig | *Mat:* op doek *Size:* hoog 39, breed 48 duim	[Abraham Delfos]	(Sold) fl 50 Sluyter
1808/11/28	AMSCH	0060	*C. Troost* | In een prachtig Paleis, zit de Koninginne Ester bij een Tafel, met verversingen, ter zijde ligt Haman nedergebogen, die door zijn houding en gelaat met schaamte zijn wroeging te kennen geeft, op de voorgrond Ahassuëris als weggaande die als in woede op de misdadige neder ziet, ter zijde staat een jonge Moor bij een Vogel op een Kruk, de Hartstogten zijn natuurlijk en van een meesterlijke Penceelsbehandeling | *Mat:* op doek *Size:* hoog 39, breed 58 duim	F	(Sold) fl 8:15 van Dijl
1810/08/06	AMSCH	0100	*Troost (C.)* | Dit bevallig Schilderij stelt voor een in den tijd van dezen Meester rijk met Beelden gestoffeerd Koffijhuis, zonachtig en geestig behandeld | *Mat:* op doek *Size:* hoog 26, breed 39 duimen	F	(Sold) fl 6:10 F du Pré
1810/10/10	MGCIT	0108	*Troost* | Een Moriaan, digt aan een Tafel, waarop onderscheiden Porcelein en Zilverwerk	Caspar van Citters	(Unknown)

Troost, Cornelis (copy after)

1806/10/17	MGSAN	0018	*J. Horemans; Troost* | De Corps de Guarde van Hollandsche Officiers, naar Troost, door J. Horemans | copy by J.J. Horemans (I) after C. Troost *Mat:* op doek	Gerardus Beljard	(Unknown)
1806/10/17	MGSAN	0019	*Troost* | De Hollandsche Kraamkamer, naar Troost | *Mat:* op doek	Gerardus Beljard	(Unknown)

Troost, Jan Hendrik

1801/04/13	AMSCH	0074	*Troost van Groenendoelen* | Een aangenaam bergachtig Landschap met een rivier doorsneeden, gestoffeerd met een Herder, Herderin, en eenig Vee; zonachtig en dun gepenceeld | *Mat:* op paneel *Size:* hoog 11, breed 13 duim	Pierre Fouquet, junior	(Sold) fl 27 Reynders
1801/04/13	AMSCH	0075	*Troost van Groenendoelen* | Een oude Grysaard met een Boek in de hand; meesterlyk geschilderd | *Mat:* op doek *Size:* hoog 33, breed 35 duim	Pierre Fouquet, junior	(Sold) fl 1:10 D^{k} Nieuland
1802/12/13	AMSCH	0153	*J. Troost van Groenendoelen* | Een Capitaale Bloem- en Fruitstuk, op een Steene Baluster staat een cierlyke Vaas, gevult met een meenigte zoorten van fraaije Bloemen en Vruchten; alles is meesterlyk en krachtig van Coloriet gepenceeld | *Mat:* op doek *Size:* hoog 66, breed 48 duim	Florijn [?]	(Bought In) fl 10
1802/12/13	AMSCH	0154	*J. Troost van Groenendoelen* | Een Arcadisch Landschap met een Rivier, waar over een Brug, en verdere Ruïne van Gebouwen, op de voorgrond twee Vrouwen; fix en krachtig behandelt | *Mat:* op doek *Size:* hoog 26, breed 22 duim	Florijn [?]	(Sold) fl 1:5 v d Schleij
1802/12/13	AMSCH	0155	*J. Troost van Groenendoelen* | Een Basrelief van vier Kindertjes, zinspeelende op de vier Getyden van 't Jaar; meesterlyk in 't graauw geschilderd	Florijn [?]	(Sold) fl 2:5 Gruiter
1803/08/24	HGKAN	0023	*Troost van Groenendoele* | Een Boomryk Lantschap met different soort van Vee, gestoffeert | *Mat:* op doek *Size:* hoog 32, breet 42 duim	[Teissier] [or others]	(Sold) fl 4:5 Giesen
1805/07/10	AMSCH	0146	*J. Troost van Groenendoelen* | Twee stuks Land- en Watergezichten, met verscheide Geboomten, Huislieden met Vee, en Rysigers gestoffeerd; plaisant op Doek geschilderd | *Mat:* op doek	S[chley] [for] Bernard	(Sold) fl 34 L Pakker
1807/08/26	AMSCH	0214	*Troost van Groenendoelen* | Twee stuks Land- en Riviergezichten, met hoog Geboomte, Gebouwen en stoffage van Beelden en Vaartuigen, fraai | *Mat:* op paneel *Size:* hoog 16, breed 20 duim	Roos	(Sold) fl 2 L Pakker
1807/08/26	AMSCH	0215	*Troost van Groenendoelen* | Twee dito [stuks Land- en Riviergezichten] als de voorgaande | *Size:* ieder hoog 11, breed 13 duim	Roos	(Sold) fl 2:10 van Iperen
1809/07/25	HGBSM	0014	*J.H. Troost van Groenendoelen* | Een diergelyk voorwerp als 't voorgaande | *Mat:* op paneel *Size:* hoog 24 ½, breet 23 duim *Notes:* The preceding lot which the title refers to is described as follows: "Voor een Buitenhuis is een Kraam waarin een Poelierster die aan een Dame een Vogel aanbied, terwyl een Bedelaars jonge een aalmoes vraagt" by Wulfraet.	D van der Aa [or] E B ten Dall	(Sold) fl 43 van Eyk

Troyen, Rombout van

1802/02/16	AMSCH	0042	*R. van Troyen* | Een Stadt gezigt met verscheide Gebouwen langs een Rivier, gestoffeerd met Scheepen, en Schuiten in 't verschiet een felle Brand, alles verbeeld by Nacht licht, uitvoerig geschilderd	G	(Sold) fl 1:10 Boelen
1803/09/07	AMSCH	0183	*R. van Troijen* | Deeze Ordonnantie vol gewoel, verbeeld de Brand van Troijen, op de voorgrond vertoonen zig een meenigte Beelden, waar onder Enéas zyn Vader op de Schouder dragende, verders de Stad in volle Brand; alles is kragtig en meesterlyk geschilderd [Le sac de Troyes ; sur	Smidt	(Bought In) fl 25

le devant beaucoup de mouvement et de désordre ; on remarque parmi une multitude de figures, Enée portant son père sur ses épaules ; la flamme perce au travers l'architecture ; dans le fond l'incendie est complet ; la composition de ce tableau est riche et vigoureuse, la touche en est hardie et le tout du plus grand effet] | *Mat:* op paneel *Size:* hoog 23, breed 44 duim *Notes:* This lot was not numbered in the French edition of the catalogue.

Trytam, E. van [Unidentified]

1804/07/25	DLGRO	0021	*E. van Trytam* | Een Landschap, fraai en uitvoerig geschilderd | *Mat:* op paneel *Size:* hoog 16, breed 21 duim	Mr Franc van der Burch Wz.	(Unknown)

Tuijlen, Hermanus (copy by)

1808/09/13	HABRU	0088	*H. Tuijlen; C. Dekker* | Een Landschap, met Boere Woningen, naar C. Dekker, door H. Tuijlen | copy by H. Tuijlen after C. Decker		(Unknown) fl 13

Tuling [Unidentified]

1801/08/19	AMSCH	0118	*Tuling* | Een Landschap, gestoffeerd met een drift Beesten	Pruyssen[r] [for] Q	(Sold) fl 1:10 Wijland

Turchi, Alessandro (Orbetto)

1810/10/11	AMSCH	0088	*Alexander Veronese* | Een grotachtig Gezigt, waarin eene Vrouw bij twee Kinderen, benevens een Man, dragende een bos hout op zijne schouderen; meesterlijk breed geschilderd | *Mat:* op doek *Size:* hoog 31, breed 44 duimen		(Withdrawn)

Udemans, Willem

1803/07/14	MGKLY	0004	*W. Udemans* | Een Stil Water met Scheepen	Mr Caspar Jacob van Citters	(Unknown)

Uden, Lucas van

1803/12/12	AMSCH	0098	*L. van Uden* | Twee stuks Boom en Bergachtige Landschapjes, gestoffeerd met Beeldjes, Schapen, Ryzigers en verdere stoffagie; uitvoerig op Koper | *Mat:* op koper *Size:* hoog 11, breed 16 duim	D	(Sold) fl 10 Gruiter
1806/08/13	AMSCH	0187	*Uden (L. van)* | Een Boschgezigt met onderscheide Geboomten en stoffagie van Beeldjes, en een aangenaam verschiet; pikant van licht en meesterlyk gepenceeld | *Mat:* op doek *Size:* hoog 23, breed 35 duim *Notes:* The artist's name "Artois" was added in by hand in the JPGM copy of the catalogue.	Roos	(Bought In) fl 2
1806/08/13	AMSCH	0188	*Uden. (L. van)* | Een aangenaam Boom en Duinachtig Landschap, met een Rivier doorsneeden, stoffagie van Beeldjes en een bevallig verschiet; zonachtig en fiks gepenceeld | *Mat:* op doek *Size:* hoog 23, breed 30 duim	Roos	(Sold) fl 1:5 Gruyter
1809/04/22	AMYVR	0129	*L. van Uden* | Een natuurlijk gestoffeerd Landschap | *Mat:* op paneel *Size:* hoog 8, breed 12 duim	de Bruin	(Sold) fl 7 Coclers

Uden, Lucas van (and Teniers)

1809/05/26	HADAA	A0001	*van Uden; Teniers* | Twee bergachtige Landschappen, rijk gestoffeerd met Boeren en Boerinnen, fiks, breed en tevens uitvoerig gepenseeld, door van Uden, en gestoffeerd door Teniers | *Mat:* op koper *Size:* hoog 33 breed 40 duimen	Mejuffrouw de Wed David Heemskerk [or others]	(Unknown)

Uden, Lucas van (manner)

1803/12/12	AMSCH	0145	*van Uden* | Twee Boom- en Bergachtige Landschapjes, als van Uden | *Mat:* op paneel *Size:* hoog 6, br. 7 duim	D	(Sold) fl 1:10 Mensart

Uijlenbroek [Unidentified]

1808/09/13	HABRU	0090	*Uijlenbroek* | Een Kerk, van binnen, waarin Gepredikt werd, met veele Toehoorders		(Unknown) fl 16:15

Ulft, Jacob van der

801/12/22	AMOTT	0101	*van der Ulfft* | 2 deftige Landschappen	Bartholomeus Ruloffs	(Unknown) fl 1:5
803/08/24	HGKAN	0001	*van der Ulft* | Een Italiaansche Zeehaave, Ryk gestoffeerd met Gebouwen en eene meenigte figuuren en Scheepen, op de voorgroud [sic] helder van couleur, meesterlyk geschilderd, en een der beste	[Teissier] [or others]	(Sold) fl 110 Kan
809/07/25	HGBSM	0001	*J. van der Ulft* | Dit fraaije Schildery steld voor daar Alexander het Joodsche Volk verdelgen wil, maar door tusschenkomst der Voorzienigheid haar Redder word; dit meesterstuk waarvan de figuuren het Landschap en de Gebouwen uitmuntend zyn, Geschildert is door J. van der Ulft, op Doek, hoog 31, breed 51 duim. N.B. Dit zeltzame voorval vind men in het breede beschreven door J. van Hamelsveld, Historie des Bybels, eerste Deel, Pag. 522 tot 529. | *Mat:* op doek *Size:* hoog 31, breed 51 duim	D van der Aa [or] E B ten Dall	(Sold) fl 276 van Eijk
809/09/06	AMSCH	0071	*Ulft (J. van der)* | Een Gezicht binnen Romen, gestoffeerd met een groote menigten Beelden, Paarden, Ezels enz., zijnde rijk geordoneerd, bevallig en zonachtig gepenceeld | *Mat:* op paneel *Size:* hoog 11 ½, breed 15 duim	Johannes Caudri	(Sold) fl 50 van Iperen

1809/09/06	AMSCH	0072	*Ulft (J. van der)* | Twee stuks andere Gezichten te Romen aan den Tijber, meede vol gewoel van Beelden, Wagens, Paarden en aangenaam verschiet; in alles als de voorgaande | *Mat:* op doek *Size:* ieder hoog 15, breed 13 duim	Johannes Caudri	(Sold) fl 40 van Iperen
1810/03/26	RMMUY	0005	*Jacob van der Ulft* | Eene rijke Ordonnantie, verbeeldende het voorbij trekken eener Turksche Caravane, met ongemeen veel gewoel, en schoone groepen van beelden, paarden en andere stoffagie, waar achter grootsche gebouwen en tempels, uitvoerig en meesterlijk geschilderd. Een der beste stukken van dezen Meester [Un port de Mer, enrichi de plusieurs batimens magnifiques : sur le devant passe une Caravanne Turque, un grand nombre de figures, chevaux et chameaux, chargés de marchandises, forment un bel ensemble, et un tableau capital, qui passe pour un des meilleurs de ce maître.] | *Annots:* Heeft gekost f 400 (RMA II) *Mat:* op paneel *Size:* hoog 20, breed 30 ½ duimen	Daniel de Jongh Az	(Sold) fl 300 G van der Pals Rott[m]
1810/06/06	RMMUY	0030	*J. van der Ulft* | Eene Italiaansche Zeehaven, met grootsche Gebouwen en eene menigte Figuren, zoo te Paard als te Voet, an endere Stoffage, konstrijk en plaisant gepenceeld | companion to lot 31 *Mat:* op paneel		(Unknown) fl 147 for lots 30 & 31
1810/06/06	RMMUY	0031	*J. van der Ulft* | Eene Wedergade, in alles als het bovenstaande behandeld | companion to lot 30		(Unknown) fl 147 for lots 30 & 31
1810/08/01	AMSCH	0103	*Ulft (Jacob van der)* | Een Romeinsch Gezigt met grootsche Gebouwen en Ruïnen, voorzien van een menigte Krijgslieden, Paarden en Kameelen [Vue perspective sur des Batiments et sur des Ruines Romaines, embellie par une multitude de Guerriers, de Chevaux et de Chamaux] | *Annots:* trop brun. (NGW) *Mat:* op doek *Size:* hoog 31, breed 51 duimen	Mr Pieter de Smeth van Alphen	(Sold) fl 710 A Schouwman te Dorth
1810/08/06	AMSCH	0102	*Ulft (J. van der)* | Een Romeinsch Gezigt met grootsche Gebouwen en Ruïne, het is rijk gestoffeerd met Krijgslieden, zo te Voet als te Paard, Wagens, Kameelen en eene menigte andere Voorwerpen; het iseen der beste van dezen Meester | *Mat:* op doek *Size:* hoog 31, breed 51 duimen	C	(Sold) fl 200 Jan Spaan
1810/08/06	AMSCH	0103	*Ulft (J. van der)* | Een Romeinsch Gezigt met de Tempel van Constantin en andere Gebouwen; rijk gestoffeerd en alleruitvoerigst behandeld | *Mat:* op paneel *Size:* hoog 11, breed 13 duimen	C	(Sold) fl 37 Coclers
1810/10/10	MGCIT	0003	*J. van der Hulft* | Een uitmuntende rijke Ordonnantie, zijnde een grootsch Gezicht op een gedeelte van Rome, met een menigte van Persoonen te voet en te paard; extra schoon gestoffeerd en konstrijk geschilderd	Caspar van Citters	(Unknown)
			Uppink		
1810/06/20	AMSCH	0130	*Upping* | Een Hofgezigt, waarin drie Hennen. Fiks geschilderd | *Mat:* op doek	S	(Sold) fl 3:10 Meijer
			Urlaub		
1803/09/07	AMSCH	0190	*Urlaub* | Cupido zyn Pylen doorbreekende in een Rots, geestig verbeeld [L'amour rompant ses fleches contre un rocher ; composition ingénieuse et délicate] | *Mat:* op paneel *Size:* hoog 8, breed 6 duim	Smidt	(Sold) fl 2:5 Toselli
			Utrecht, Adriaen van		
1802/05/10	MGSAN	0009	*A. van Uitert* | Een Stuk, waarop divers dood Wild, natuurlyk geschllderd [sic], door A. van Uitert: op Doek, zwarte Lyst, met vergulde Binnenlyst | *Mat:* op doek *Size:* hoog 34 duim, breed 27 duim	Johan Dirk Kruysse	(Unknown) £ 4:7
1807/10/12	MGBEO	0001	*Adriaan van Utrecht* | Een Stuk met Vrugten, Vogels en ander bywerk | *Mat:* op doek	Hermannus Johannes Heyman	(Sold) £ 0:16 Haccon
1809/06/13	AMSCH	0156	*A. van Utrecht* | In dit stuk welke een Menagerie verbeeld, ziet men bij een Voerbak een Haan, en eenige Hennen, waarvan er een zit te Broeijen; krachtig en stout geschilderd | *Mat:* op doek *Size:* hoog 46, breed 60 duim	E	(Sold) fl 18:10 Preijer
1810/10/10	MGCIT	0024	*A. v. Utrecht* | Een Stuk houdende allerhande soort van Wild en ander Gevogelte, alsmede Vrugten, Groenten en verdere huislijke Noodwendigheden; schoon en natuurlijk behandeld | companion to lot 25	Caspar van Citters	(Unknown)
1810/10/10	MGCIT	0025	*A. v. Utrecht* | Een wederga insgelijk in gelijken trant, even fix geschilderd | companion to lot 24	Caspar van Citters	(Unknown)
			Utrecht, Adriaen van (and Diepenbeeck, A.J.)		
1803/04/20	AMSCH	0022	*Diepenbeek (A.); A. van Utrecht* | In een Krans en Feston van Bloemen en Vrugten, welke allernatuurlykst voorgesteld zyn, ziet men Maria met het Kind Jesu op haar schoot zittende, waarby drie Kinderen; de Drapperie, en het Coloriet zyn van de beste Schildering van die meester [Au milieu de quelques guirlandes de fruits & de fleurs l'artiste a place [sic] L.V.M. avec l'enfant Jesus, accompagnés de trois Anges, cette representation est très bien rendue avec franchise & de l'éclât.] | *Mat:* op doek *Size:* hoog 45, breed 61 duim	Maria Magdalena van Sluypwyk, gravinne van Moens	(Sold) fl 48 Hodges
			Utrecht, Adriaen van (and Jordaens, J. (I))		
1808/03/03	HAVIN	0001	*van Utrecht; Jordaans* | Een Tafel met Vrugten en Groentens, als ook dood Wild, waarbij een Man die een Meid tracht te liefkoozen, uitmuntend, door van Utrecht, en de Beelden waarschijnelijk [sic], door Jordaans	Jacobus Spillebout	(Unknown) fl 20

Uytenbogaart, Izaäk

1805/10/21	GRBOL	0009	*J. V. Uittenbogaart* | Een Boere Kermis, Ryk in Stoffagie en stout geschilderd | companion to lot 10	Gerardus Nicolaus Heerkens	(Unknown)
1805/10/21	GRBOL	0010	*J. V. Uittenbogaart* | Een dito [Boere Kermis], door dito [J. V. Uittenbogaart], zynde een Weêrga | companion to lot 9 *Notes:* It is unclear what "dito" refers to in the title.	Gerardus Nicolaus Heerkens	(Unknown)

Uyttenbroeck, Moyses Matheusz. van

1808/11/28	AMSCH	0112	*M.W. van Bronk* | Een Bergachtig Landschap, rijk met Beelden en Beesten gestoffeerd, door M.W. van Bronk, 1623 | *Inscr:* M.W. van Bronk, 1623 (signed and dated?) *Notes:* It is unclear whether the name and date are inscribed on the painting.	S	(Sold) fl 1:10 du Pree

Uytter-Limmege, Wouter

1808/12/12	DOHAA	0072	*W. Uiterlimmege* | Een drift met Runderbeesen | *Mat:* op doek		(Unknown)

Vaart, Jan van der

1808/04/26	GDAN	0175	*Vaert (J. v.d.)* | Een Dorpgezigt voor een Herberg, met eenige Heeren te Paard onder het Geboomte, zeer wel behandelt | *Size:* hoog 35, breed 31 duim	G H Fortuyn	(Unknown)

Valck (Valk)

1801/04/08	HAVIN	0049	*Valk* | Twee Binnenhuize met een meenigte eetende en drinkende Persoonen		(Unknown)
1804/10/16	DLOND	0225	*Valk* | Twee Stukken. Dood Gevogelte. Deux Tableaux. Des Oiseaux morts | *Mat:* op doek *Size:* hoog 23, breed 20		(Unknown)
1810/10/11	AMSCH	0170	*Valk* | Een Boeren Binnehuis, met Huislieden	[Levy Pakker?]	(Sold) fl 1:15 H Pakker

Valck, A.

1802/12/13	AMSCH	0170	*A. Valk* | Voor een Buitenhuis ziet men een meenigte vrolyke Boeren en Boerinnen | *Mat:* op doek *Size:* hoog 24, breed 26 duim	Pruyssenaar [for] D	(Sold) fl 1 Mensard

Valckenburg, Dirk

1802/05/05	AMSCH	0211	*Valkenburg* | Aan de Stam van een Boom hangt een doden Haas, daarnevens een koppel Patryzen, een Snaphaan en ander Jagttuig, alles zoo delicaat gepenceeld, als J. Wenix | *Mat:* op doek *Size:* hoog 39, breed 31 duim	D	(Sold) fl 400 for lots 211 & 212. B^{d} Kooij
1802/05/05	AMSCH	0212	*Valkenburg* | Een Hofgezicht, op de voorgrond leggen twee Patryzen, een Vink, en Snaphaan, en een menigte Jagttuig, verders een aangenaam verschiet, niet minder als de voorgaande | *Size:* hoog 39, breed 31 duim	D	(Sold) fl 400 for lots 211 & 212. B^{d} Kooij
1804/04/28	LNDLS	0005	*D. Valkenburg* | Een uitmuntend Stuk; voor een Hofgezicht met geboomte staat een bonte haan, benevens een rustende witte, en een bruine hen, op de voorgrond een water, daar een witte waard. benevens een bonte eend in zwemmen; twee andere vogels, die op de tak van een boom zitten, ter rechter zyde staat een vaas, met een bachanaal bewert [sic], daar een pagegaai [sic] op zit, en voor deszelfs voet, kruiden; alles uitmuntend eel en zo goed als van J. Weninx, op doek geschilderd | *Mat:* op doek *Size:* hoog 50, breed 38 duim	[Abraham Delfos] [or others]	(Bought In) fl 108
807/06/10	HGBSM	0072	*G. Valkenburg* | Dit uitmuntend Schilderij verbeeld, voor een Hofgezigt, een staande bonten Haan, beneven Hennen, zwemmende Eenden en meer differente gevogelte, en bijwerk, zo goed als van J. Weninx | *Mat:* op doek *Size:* hoog 50 breed 38 duim *Notes:* The artist's name was given as "G. Valkenburg" but we have assumed this is an error.	Abraham Delfos [or others]	(Sold) fl 24 Tomas
809/04/22	AMYVR	0132a	*D. Valkenburg* | Dit fraaije Schilderij verbeeld in een Hofgezicht een Siepersche Kat, welke een Haan onder zijne pooten heeft, blazende tegens een Hondje, verder op de voorgrond eenige Druiven, Persiken en andere Vruchten; delicaat gepenceelt | *Mat:* op doek *Size:* hoog 39, breed 32 duim	Smit	(Bought In) fl 160
810/10/10	MGCIT	0088	*Valkenburg* | Een Steene Tafel, waarop een aan ééne Poot hangende Zee-Meeuw, en veelerlei ander op een Tafel liggend klein Gevogelte: staande naast dezelve een Jagthond, op 't een en ander loerende; zeer uitvoerig	Caspar van Citters	(Unknown)

Valentin de Boulogne

805/07/10	AMSCH	0154	*Valentini* | Twee Mannen en twee Vrouwen zich vermakende met drinken en musiceeren; meesterlyk op Doek, in de manier van Hondhorst | *Mat:* op doek *Size:* hoog 37, breed 50 duim	R[oos]	(Sold) fl 2 Royers
805/10/09	HGBSM	0066	*Valentyn* | Een musiceerend gezelschap | *Mat:* op koper *Size:* hoog 6 ½ breet 9 duim	T H van Willigen [or others]	(Sold) fl 5:10 Basemoine
806/05/05	AMSCH	0148	*Valentini* | De Geesseling Christi; allermeesterlyk gepenceeld door Valentini | *Mat:* op koper *Size:* hoog 13, breed 10 ¼ duim	L	(Sold) fl 6 van Laar
808/06/06	RMRIJ	0131	*Valentino. (Francisco)* | Johannes de Dooper ten halven lijve uit, de handen zamen gevouwen. Schoon van teekening en uitdrukking; krachtig en meesterlijk geschilderd [Saint Jean-Baptiste les mains jointes, vu mi-corps. D'un dessin, correct, d'un beau Coloris, et dans le grand Style] |	Gerrit van der Pot, Heer van Groeneveld	(Sold) fl 245 R Pott

			Annots: Verk 17 Sept 1798 (f 107.-) (RMA I) *Mat:* op doek *Size:* Hoog 27 ½, en breed 22 ½ duim		

Valk, Hendrik de

1804/02/27	AMSCH	0113	*Valck. (H. de) Disciple van A. v. Ostade* | Een Boeren Binnenhuis, op den voorgrond ziet men een Boer en Boerin danzen, verders eenige Huislieden en Huisraad; krachtig van coloriet en meesterlyk van schildering | *Mat:* op doek *Size:* hoog 23, breed 19 duim	B	(Bought In) fl 32

Valken, H. van [Unidentified]

1806/08/20	HGBSM	0210	*H. van Valken* | Een buiten Manegie | *Mat:* op doek *Size:* hoog 16 ½, breed 19 duim	Macalester Loup [or others]	(Sold) fl 12:5 Poelman

Vallee, Louis

1803/04/20	AMSCH	0088	*Vallée, 1649. (Louis)* | Deeze capitaale Ordenantie in een Hofgezicht met Gebouwen, Geboomten en Standbeelden, vertoont zig een Famielje, van een Heer een Dame by de hand houdende, beide in treffelyke ryke kleeding, verzelt van vier Kinderen, en een oude Dame; het Coloriet is bevallig, en van een meesterlyke fraaye penceelsbehandeling [Dans un magnifique Jardin auprès d'un chateau est representée la famille d'un homme opulent ; il tient son Epouse par la main ; étant accompagnée par quatre Enfans & une Gouvernante. Ce morceau frappant est d'un beau coloris & il est traité en maitre.] | *Mat:* op doek *Size:* hoog 97, breed 90 duim *Inscr:* Louis Vallée, 1649 (signed and dated?) *Notes:* It is unclear whether the name and date are inscribed on the painting.	Maria Magdalena van Sluypwyk, gravinne van Moens	(Sold) fl 14 Jan Spaan
1807/06/10	HGBSM	0068	*Louis Vallée* | Een groot Historieel Stuk, verbeeldende, daar Graaf Willem te bedde leggende, het vonnis over den Bailliuw van Zuidholland velt, met levensgroote beelden, konstig geschilderd, door Louis Vallée, 1646, op doek, hoog 63 breed 63 duim. Zie over deeze afbeelding de beschrijving van Dordrecht, door M. van Balen, Jz. 1677, pag. 735 | *Mat:* op doek *Size:* hoog 63, breed 63 duim *Inscr:* Louis Vallée, 1646 (signed and dated?) *Notes:* It is unclear whether the name and date are inscribed on the painting.	Abraham Delfos [or others]	(Sold) fl 17 v Olden

Valois, Jean François

1809/07/25	HGBSM	0039	*J.F. Valois* | Twee stuks Stads-Gezigten met gebouwen en gestoffeert met Figuren &c., het messelwerk [sic] is in allen deelen zo uitvoerig als van J. van der Heiden, helder en zonachtig door J.F. Valois | *Mat:* op paneel *Size:* hoog 13 ½, breed 10 duim	D van der Aa	(Sold) fl 190 Ponse

Vanloo, Charles André (Carle Vanloo)

1810/07/26	AMSCH	0048	*Loo (C. van)* | Een boomrijk Landschap, met eene Ruïne, Water en Beeldjes | *Mat:* op doek *Size:* hoog 24, breed 29 duimen	Cassino	(Bought In) fl 9

Vanloo, J.

1801/06/10	AMSCH	0103	*Loo. (J. van)* | In een gemeubileerd Vertrek, zitten drie Dames en twee Heeren, zich met kaartspeelen als andersints vermaakende, een der Dames heeft een witte Satyne Rok aan, waarom men dit Stuk in den eerste opslag voor een Schildery van G. Terburg zoude aanzien, zynde in dien trant gepenceeld | *Mat:* op doek *Size:* hoog 30, breed 24 duim	Herman ten Kate	(Sold) fl 151 Yver
1803/09/07	AMSCH	0096	*J. van Loo* | In een Landschap, onder zwaar Geboomte ziet men twee Jagt Nimphen, waar van een is rustende, werdende door twee Satyrs bespied, waar by twee leggende honden, en eenig Jagt Tuyg; zynde fraai van Teekening, kragtig van Coloriet en uitvoerig behandeld [Un paysage, où l'on voit deux Nymphes, dont l'une reposant sous une touffe de gros arbres est guetée par des satires ; auprès d'elle sont couchés deux chiens et quelques attributs de chasse ; le dessin en est très beau, le coloris superbe et d'un excellent fini] | *Mat:* op doek *Size:* hoog 22, breed 32 duim	Smidt	(Sold) fl 50 C S Roos
1804/07/25	AMSCH	0047	*Loo (J. van)* | Deeze ryke en schoone Ordinantie, met meer dan leevensgroote Beelden, vertoont de Fabelgeschiedenis van Bachus en Ariadne, zy is zittende by een Boom, waaraan een Masque en Pylkooker gehegt is, in een treffelyke Kleeding, en rust met de Linkerhand op een cierlyk Kussen; Bachus schynt in een verliefde gestalten haar een Sterrekroon boven het hoofd te houden; op de grond ziet men een jongen Bachant, houdende en Cristalle Wynkom in de handen, en rust met de eene voet op een dito omgevallen cierlyke Wynkan, waar neevens eenige Druiven en andere Vrugten liggen – in het verschiet een Schip in Zee; alles is meesterlyk fraai van teekening, de Hartstogten kennelyk verbeeld, de Kleederen natuurlyk geplooit, en het bevallig Licht en Coloriet uitmuntend afgebeeld, en van een voortreffelyke penceelbehandeling | *Mat:* op doek *Size:* hoog 80, breed 56 duim		(Sold) fl 28 J^n Yver
1809/07/25	HGBSM	0012	*J. van Loo* | Andromeda verlost door Perseus, uitvoerig geschildert | *Mat:* op paneel *Size:* hoog 19 ½, breet 16 duim	D van der Aa [or] E B ten Dall	(Sold) fl 30:10 A Taxaira

Vanloo, Jules Cesar Denis

1810/08/06	AMSCH	0064	*Loo (Cesar van)* | Een Italiaansch Boomrijk Landschap met een groot Gebouw en ruïne, op den voorgrond vier Beeldjes bij een Graftombe; helder en uitvoerig behandeld | *Mat:* op doek *Size:* hoog 18, breed 26 duimen	A	(Sold) fl 10 Gruyter

Vas, P. [Unidentified]

1804/08/08	AMSCH	0247	*P. Vas* | Een Heer en Dame, verzeld van een Minnewichtje, zitten in een Landschap; helder op Doek | *Mat:* op doek	Roos [for] D	(Sold) fl 0:10 L Pakker

Veen, Otto van

1803/09/07	AMSCH	0202	*O. van Veen* | De Prediking van Johannes voor een groote schaare; van allerlye kleeding en houding; uitvoerig en meesterlyk behandeld [St. Jean Baptiste préchant devant une multitude de peuple ; ingénieuse diversité dans les habillemens et les figures : composition admirable] | *Mat:* op paneel *Size:* hoog 18, breed 25 duim	Smidt	(Bought In) fl 5 ½
1810/06/06	RMMUY	0177	*Octavio van Veen* | Het Ontzet der Stad Leiden. Door Octavio van Veen. Uitvoerig en konstig | *Mat:* op paneel		(Unknown) fl 11:10

Veen, P. [Unidentified]

1802/09/18	RMDRS	0072	*P. Veen* | Een zeer uitvoerig Pourtretje	Casper de Haas	(Unknown) fl 0:12
1809/09/06	AMSCH	0082	*Veen (P.) Dicipel van A. van der Werf* | Christus als spreekende teegens de Samaritaansche Vrouw bij den Waterput, verder vertoonen zig de Dicipelen; de Hartstogten zijn kennelijk, het koloriet kragtig, en uitvoerig geschilderd | *Mat:* op paneel *Size:* hoog 19, breed 15 duim	Johannes Caudri	(Sold) fl 15 P Swanenburg

Veer, Abraham

1802/08/24	LNDLS	0096	*A. Veer* | Een hevige Batailje te Paard, in 't verschiet anderen die door het Water vlugten. Op doek, door A. Veer 1681 [beide zonder Lijsten] | companion to lot 97 *Mat:* op doek *Size:* hoog 30, breed 38 duimen *Inscr:* A. Veer 1681 (signed and dated?) *Notes:* It is unclear whether the name and date are inscribed on the painting. The bracketed information in the title appears in lot 97 and refers to lots 96 and 97.	Leonardus Bouman [or others]	(Unknown) fl 1:16
1802/08/24	LNDLS	0097	*A. Veer* | Een weêrga met rustende Krijgsknegten bij een tent, en staande Officieren bij een Huis. Mede op doek en van dezelfde groote, door denzelven [A. Veer], beide zonder Lijsten | companion to lot 96 *Mat:* op doek *Size:* hoog 30, breed 38 duimen	Leonardus Bouman [or others]	(Unknown) fl 1

Veerendael, Nicolas van

1810/10/10	MGCIT	0039	*N. Veerendaal* | Een Vaas, rondöm het welke ongemeen teder en uitvoerig behandelde Bloemen, door veele Kenners en Liefhebbers genomen wordende voor een Stuk van Pater Zeegers, treflijk geschilderd	Caspar van Citters	(Unknown)

Velázquez, Diego Rodríguez de Silva y

1810/07/26	AMSCH	0084	*Velasquez* | Een Monnik, zittende in de Gevangenis, wordende door Engelen bezogt. Zijnde een der beste stukken uit de Spaansche School | *Mat:* op doek *Size:* hoog 14, breed 29 duimen	Cassino	(Bought In) fl 30

Velde

1802/07/21	HGKAN	0082	*van de Velde* | Een Landschap, gestoffeerd met Heeren en Dames		(Unknown)
1810/03/07	UTWLD	0045	*van der Velden* | Een Winter gezigt, buiten Utrecht	J J Woertman	(Unknown) fl 16

Velde (manner)

1802/07/21	HGKAN	0010	*van de Velde* | Een liggende Koe, in de manier van van de Velde		(Unknown)
1802/08/24	LNDLS	0154	*v. d. Velde* | Een rustende Koe en Schapen in een Landschap, als van v. d. Velde | *Mat:* op paneel	Leonardus Bouman [or others]	(Unknown) fl 2:2

Velde (manner; and Wijnants or Wijnants, manner)

1808/04/26	GDAN	0272	*J. Wijnands; van de Velde* | Een Landschap, door of in de manier van J. Wijnands, met fraaije stoffage of het van van de Velde was | *Size:* hoog 11 ½, breed 15 duim *Notes:* This lot was misnumbered no. 271.	G H Fortuyn	(Unknown)

Velde, Adriaen van de

1801/04/13	AMSCH	0076	*A. van de Velde* | Op den voorgrond van dit aangenaam Schildery ziet men een boerin een roodbonte Koe melken, daar nevens eenige staande, liggende, en graazende koeijen en schapen, voorts een aangenaam bergachtig met kreupelhout bewassen verschiet; de schildering is delicaat, en de teekening alleruitmuntendst | *Mat:* op doek *Size:* hoog 15, breed 18 ½ duim	Pierre Fouquet, junior	(Sold) fl 400 v d Schley [for] M[errem]
1801/10/19	AMSCH	0073	*Velde (A. van de)* | Een zeer schoon Landschap met een graazend Paard, Koeijen en Schaapen, mitsgaders Herders en Herderin, zeer fraay van Ordonantie en delicaat geschilderd | *Mat:* op paneel *Size:* hoog 8, breed 12 ½ duim	Jonkheer Menno Baron van Coehoorn	(Sold) fl 301 van der Schley [for] B[=Putte]
1802/06/16	AMSCH	0185	*A. van de Velde* | In een Heuvelachtig Landzicht, vertoont zich op de voorgrond een zittende Vrouw beezig een Roscouleurde Koe te Melken, ter zyde staat een vaal bonte Os, en een andere rustende, waar by eenige Schaapen, verder een Bokje, en grazende Koe: alles zonachtig, bevallig van Coloriet en uitvoerig gepenceeld | *Mat:* op doek *Size:* hoog 14 ½, breed 17 ½ duim	[Merrem]	(Sold) fl 575 I Smit G^z
1802/06/16	AMSCH	0186	*A. van de Velde* | Dit uitmuntend Schilderytje steld voor een Roodbonte Koe aan een Waterplas, waar achter een leggende Koe en twee Schaapen, voorts opgaand Boomwerk; alles delicaat behandeld | *Mat:* op doek op paneel *Size:* hoog 18, breed 16 duim	[Merrem]	(Sold) fl 132 Wed Achtienhoven

1802/07/20	MGSAN	0022	*A. V. D. Velde* | Een extra fraai somber Landschapje, gestoffeerd met Beelden en Beestjes, extra schoon en helder van coloriet | *Size:* hoog duim 9 ¼, breed duim 11		(Unknown)
1802/07/20	MGSAN	0043	*A. v. d. Velde* | Een fraai Stukje, met Beestjes: op Paneel | *Mat:* op paneel *Size:* hoog duim 8 ½, breed duim 11		(Unknown)
1802/09/29	AMSCH	0054	*A. van de Velde* | Een Aangenaam Landschap, hoog 13, breed 11 duim. Doek. In dit magnifiek Kunststukje ziet men in het midden, by pragtig opgaand Geboomten, een zittende Herder, aan den Oever van een stil Beekje, spreekende met een bevallige Herderin die ter regter zyde neevens hem staat, waar agter een rood bonte Koe, welke zich uit her [sic] Beekje drenkt, gezien word; ter regter en iinker zyde ziet men eenige Schaapen en Lammeren, en op de derde grond nog een staande Os, uitkomende teegens eenig kreupel Gewas, en in 't verschiet Ruïnen en Gebergten; de spiegeling in het Water, de Voorgrond, die met een menigte Kruiden en Biezen beplant, en de Lucht, die dun en warm gepenseeld is, maken dit stukje tot een der fraaiste van deeze voortreffelyke Meester, en is van zyn delicaatste Penceelsbehandeling, (Komt uit het Cabinet van den Heer Griffier Fagel [Dans un Paysage au pieds de quelques grands arbres se trouve un ruisseau au bord duquel est une Femme parlant à un pâtre qui se baigne, derriere elle est une vache rousse et un chien ; une brebis et deux moutons sont couchés à la droite, et un autre groupe semblable se voit vers la gauche ; le fond offre un taureau et un mouton, des broussailles et quelques ruines. Il est rare de trouver dans un aussi petit espace, une ordonnance qui pourroit remplir un des Tableaux capitaux de ce maitre ; il est de sa maniere la plus précieuse, plein de force et d'effet, et du beau Velouté de cet artiste excellent. Il a fait partie du Cabinet de Mr. le Griffier Fagel.] | *Mat:* op doek *Size:* hoog 13, breed 11 duim	[Hendrik III, baron Fagel?]	(Sold) fl 790 Yver
1802/12/13	AMSCH	0157	*A. van de Velde* | Een Landschap met een staande en een leggende Koey en twee Schaapen, ter zyde een rustende Herder en Herderin; zeer uitvoerig en delicaat behandelt | *Mat:* op paneel *Size:* hoog 11, breed 13 duim	Pruyssenaar [for] B	(Sold) fl 38 Jan Yver
1802/12/13	AMSCH	0219	*A. van de Velde* | Een model van twee rustende Koeijen, en drie Ossen-Hoofden; meesterlyk fraay behandeld	Schley [for] Lauwers	(Sold) fl 15:10 Hulswit
1803/04/20	AMSCH	0076	*Velde. (A. van de)* | Tusschen eenige Heuvelen, by de stam van een Boom, ziet men een Herder en Herderin, waarby eenige Koeyen, Schapen, Lammeren, en een Bokje, alles door een aangenaam zonlicht bescheenen wordende, delicaat en uitvoerig gepenceeld [Près d'un gros arbre est un Berger, une Bergere, quelques vaches, des moutons et un bouc. Le fond est terminé par des collines. Ce morceau traité avec la legereté et la delicatesse de pinceau qui élevent l'auteur au premier rang de Peintre en ce genre. Nous pourrions, ômettre que les animaux sont parfaitement dessinés puisque cette qualité est commune à tous les ouvrages de ce artiste excellent] | *Mat:* op doek op paneel *Size:* hoog 14 ½, breed 13 duim	Maria Magdalena van Sluypwyk, gravinne van Moens	(Sold) fl 1010 Coclers
1803/04/27	AMSCH	000C	*Adrien van de Velde* | Un petit Païsage, D'Adrien van de Velde avec des Vaches, & une Laveuse, de la plus grande Beauté	B	(Bought In) fl 1500
1803/08/17	AMSCH	0082	*Velde (A. van de)* | Twee stuks aangenaame Landschapjes, beide met Boomstammen en Heiningen, voor dewelke in de eene een Ram en in de andere een geschoren Schaap legt, verzeld van meer andere Schaapen en een slapende Boer, verders aangenaame Verschieten en lieflyke Lugtjes; zynde van de beste schildertrant van deezen voortreffelyken Meester | *Mat:* op paneel *Size:* ieder hoog 5 ½, breed 5 ½ duim	Anna Catharina Putman	(Bought In) fl 190
1805/07/03	AMSCH	0048	*Velde. (A. van de)* | Dit stil en bevallig Onderwerp vertoond: een ménigte staand en rustend Vee, in een aangenaame Grasweide, omringd van Gebergtens en Kreupelgewas, een Boerin is bézig een roode Koe te melken; voorts is dit stukje fraai geordineerd, en van een edel penceel | *Mat:* op doek *Size:* hoog 14, breed 17 duim	R[oos]	(Sold) fl 750 Thomas Cremer
1806/08/13	AMSCH	0190	*Velde. (A. van de)* | In een Boomryk en aangenaam Hofgezicht, vertoont zich Vertumnus by Pomona, verders gestoffeerd met Gevogelte en Vrugten; dit Tafreel is bevallig van coloriet en van een uitvoerige penceelbehandeling | *Mat:* op doek *Size:* hoog 30, breed 40 duim	van der Voort	(Sold) fl 455 Jan Smit
1806/08/20	HGBSM	0039	*A. van de Velde* | In dit Landschapje is op de voorgrond een roode Os, agter denzelven een Vrouwtje op een Ezel zittende, en een Boer die eenige Schaapen voordrijft | *Mat:* op paneel *Size:* hoog 8 ½, breed 10 duim	Macalester Loup	(Sold) fl 72 Spruyt
1808/06/06	RMRIJ	0132	*Velde. (Adriaan van den)* | Een bergachtig Landschap, waarin staande en liggende Koeijen, Bokken en Schapen. Van deze laatste een op den voorgrond, in 't water staande, welks vacht veel verloren heeft. Hierbij een bruin Vospaard drinkende uit het ondiep water, waarin ter zijde eenige Ossen, onder de schaduw van eenen ouden muur en hoog geboomte, waden. Verder twee Herders, van welke er een staande met eene liggende Vrouw schijnt te spreken. Alles zeer konstig, uitvoerig, helder en aangenaam behandeld [Paysage Montagneux. On y apperçoit de belles Vaches, des Brebis et une Chévre sous la garde d'un Pâtre, qui s'entretient avec une femme et une autre figure : sur le devant, un Cheval alezan boit dans une vieille Muraille, et d'une belle touffe d'arbres. Un agréable lointain artistement varié, et un beau Ciel forment cette Composition	Gerrit van der Pot, Heer van Groeneveld	(Sold) fl 3000 Cremer

			Savante, précieuse et Capitale, qu'on peut classer parmi les chefs-d'oeuvre de cet Artiste distingué] | *Annots:* van P Fouquet Jr, 11 Sept 1781 (f 1500.-) (RMA I); Cremer à moi (NGW) *Mat:* op doek *Size:* Hoog 17 ½, en breed 21 ¼ duim		
1808/06/13	AMSCH	0160	*Velde (A. van de)* | In een Landschap staat eene Koe tegen een Boom te wrijven, op den voorgrond staat een roodbont Beest in het Water, waar nevens eene Vrouw met een Kind aan de borst, en een Jongen met een Hond, ter zijde twee Schapen, en in het verschiet ligt een Man te slapen in eene Schuur, waarbij een Kat. Alles zeer zacht en zonachtig gepenceeld | *Annots:* [door] P. de Leeuw (MB) *Mat:* op doek *Size:* hoog 15, breed 18 duim *Notes:* The artist's name was changed by hand from "A. van de Velde" to "P. de Leeuw[?]" in the MB copy of the catalogue.	[Jan Tersteeg]	(Sold) fl 218 Nieuwenhuys pour Henry
1809/07/19	AMSCH	0057	*Velden (A. van den)* | Een stil Water, met twee zeilende Vaartuigen, benevens een Visschers Schuitje aan een Weg met Geboomte, ter linkerzijde vertoont zig eene grazige Weide, gestoffeerd met eene Vaalbonte rustende Koe, waar bij een roskleurde Os, welke aan den kant van een Rivier staat te drinken, voorts een bevallig verschiet. Het Water, de Lucht en het verschiet is dun, aangenaam van koloriet en uitvoerig van behandeling | *Mat:* op doek op paneel *Size:* hoog 11 ½, breed 13 duim	[Bicker]	(Sold) fl 220 J^{mo} de Vries
1809/09/06	AMSCH	0073	*Velde (A. van de)* | Een Plijsterplaats, alwaar eenige Herders met hun Vee zich schijnen te ververschen; zijnde een rijke Ordinantie en is voorts delicaat gepenceeld | *Mat:* op doek *Size:* hoog 19, breed 25 duim	Johannes Caudri	(Sold) fl 400 Coclers
1809/09/06	AMSCH	0074	*Velde (A. van de)* | Aan een Waterplas zit een Herder zijn Voeten te wassen, agter en ter zijde denzelven eenige Koeijen en een Schaap bij weelig Geboomten; alles als de voorgaande behandeld | *Mat:* op paneel *Size:* hoog 12, breed 16 ½ duim	Johannes Caudri	(Sold) fl 55 Gruyter
1809/09/06	AMSCH	0075[a]	*Velde (A. van de)* | Twee stuks grazige Weiden met Geboomten en fraaije stoffage van Beelden, Koeijen, Paarden en Schapen, het licht en bruin doet een schoone werking in beiden de stukjes, en zijn van een uitvoerige schildering | *This Lot:* Een stuk grazing Weiden met Geboomten en fraaije stoffage van Beelden, Koeijen, Paarden en Schapen *Mat:* op paneel *Size:* hoog 12, breed 14 duim	Johannes Caudri	(Sold) fl 162 for lots 75[a] & 75[b]. Coclers
1809/09/06	AMSCH	0075[b]	*Velde (A. van de)* | Twee stuks grazige Weiden met Geboomten en fraaije stoffage van Beelden, Koeijen, Paarden en Schapen, het licht en bruin doet een schoone werking in beiden de stukjes, en zijn van een uitvoerige schildering | *This Lot:* Een stuk grazing Weiden met Geboomten en fraaije stoffage van Beelden, Koeijen, Paarden en Schapen *Mat:* op doek *Size:* hoog 12, breed 14 duim	Johannes Caudri	(Sold) fl 162 for lots 75[a] & 75[b]. Coclers
1810/05/22	AMSCH	0110	*Velde. (A. van de)* | Een Heuvelachtig Landschap, met Geboomten, gestoffeerd met een Landman en Vrouw bij rustende Koeijen en een grazen Paard, verder een Herder met zijn Schapen; zonachtig en meesterlijk behandeld | *Mat:* op paneel *Size:* hoog 8, breed 12 duim	Johannes van de Putte Nicolaasz.	(Sold) fl 305 Gruyter [for] Dirkse
1810/07/23	DOLGI	0058	*Adriaan van de Velden* | Dit voortreffelijk Schilderijtje vertoont een Gehucht aan een Zeestrand. De Boomptjes, Beeldtjes, en verdere figuren, zijn onverbeterlijk schoon geteekend, en uitmuntend geschilderd. Water en lucht helder, en natuurlijk van coloriet | *Mat:* op paneel *Size:* hoog 10, breed 14 duim	Mr Pieter van den Santheuvel	(Sold) fl 200 Beekmans van Antwerpen
1810/08/01	AMSCH	0104	*Velde (Adriaan van de)* | Een bergachtig Oostersch Landschap, waar in de Optogt van eenen Oudvader met zijn Huisgezin; in het midden ziet men de Vrouw met een Kind aan de borst, zittende op een wit Paard, hetwelk door eenen Jongeling geleid wordt; nevens haar de Oudvader op een bruin Paard; ter linkerzijde een Herder welke Schapen voor zich heen drijft; verder eene Vrouw en een Kind, zittende op eenen Bok; ter regter zijde, op den voorgrond en achterwaarts, Hoorn- en ander Vee [Un Site montueux de l'Asie, dans lequel est representé l'emigration d'un Patriarche avec sa Famille et son Bêtail. Vérs le milieu on voit une Femme tenant un Enfant au Sein, montée sur un Cheval blanc qui est conduit par un jeune Homme ; à côté de la Femme est le Patriarche, monté sur un Cheval brun. Vèrs la gauche se trouve un Pâtre, conduisant un troupeau de Moutons, avec une Femme, et un Enfant monté sur un bouc. A la droite et vèrs le fond on trouve different Bêtail] | *Annots:* capital ; mais mauvais coloris et mauvais ciel. (NGW); Vente le Brun No. 123 24000 (SMLN) *Mat:* op doek *Size:* hoog 52, breed 72 duimen *Loc:* London, England, UK. Wallace Collection. (P80)	Mr Pieter de Smeth van Alphen	(Sold) fl 3000 Texier, Gerbet en Comp [for] LeBrun
1810/08/01	AMSCH	0105	*Velde (Adriaan van de)* | Een aangenaam boomrijk Landschap; op den voorgrond een heldere Waterplas, waaruit eene roodbonte Koe drinkt, nevens welke eene staande Vrouw en Hond; terzijde een zittend Herder bij twee rustende Koeijen; verder eenige Schapen, Bokken en Lammeren [Un Site de Paysage agréable, richement boisé, audevant duquel se trouve une marre d'eau limpide : on y voit une Vache tachée de brun s'y abreuver, une Femme et un Chien traversent également ce gué. Vèrs le côté s'assit un Pâtre gardant deux Vaches couchées, ainsi que des Chèvres, des Moutons et leurs agneaux] | *Annots:* capital et très bon. (NGW) *Mat:* op doek *Size:* hoog 24, breed 30 duimen *Loc:* London, England, UK. Royal Collection (Windsor Castle) Inv. 3217.	Mr Pieter de Smeth van Alphen	(Sold) fl 7650 Lafontaine
1810/08/01	AMSCH	0106	*Velde (Adriaan van de)* | Een Veldgezigt, gestoffeerd met eene Kar, met een wit Paard bespannen, waar op een Boer met Vrouw en Kind; verder	Mr Pieter de Smeth van Alphen	(Sold) fl 850 J Yver

			een Herder met zijne Kudde en eene grazige Weide in het verschiet [Vue sur la Campagne ornée d'une charette attelée d'un Cheval blanc, sur laquelle sont montés un Paysan une Femme et un Enfant. Plus en avant on rencontre un Berger conduisant son troupeau, un gras paturage terminant l'horison] | *Annots:* NB : petites figures. (NGW) *Mat:* op paneel *Size:* hoog 11, breed 15 duimen		
1810/08/01	AMSCH	0107	*Velde (Adriaan van de)* | Een Veld- en Boschgezigt, gestoffeerd met staande en rustende Paarden, Koeijen, Schapen en ander Vee [Paysage donnant vue sur une partie de foret orné de different Bétail, comme Chevaux, Vaches, Moutons, et autres espèces en differentes actions] | *Annots:* NB : petites figures. (NGW) *Mat:* op paneel *Size:* hoog 14, breed 12 ½ duimen	Mr Pieter de Smeth van Alphen	(Sold) fl 315 C S Roos
1810/08/06	AMSCH	0104	*Velde (A. van de)* | Dit voortreffelijk Kunstjuweel verbeelt een aangenaam Landschap met Geboomte, in het zelve ziet men Merkuur en Argus, zittende aan den kant van een helder Water, waaruit eene roode Koe drinkt, verder staande en liggende Koeien, grazende Schapen en een Bok; dit stuk is fraai van koloriet, helder en alleruitvoerigst behandeld en bekend door den Prent, die naar hetzelve gegraveerd is | *Mat:* op doek *Size:* hoog 27, breed 35 duimen	A	(Sold) fl 3125 Josi [for] Burtyn
1810/10/10	MGCIT	0013	*A. van de Velde* | Een uitmuntend bevallig Landschap met een Boere woning, en op den Voorgrond verrijkt met een staande Paard en Geit, alsmede een liggende Koe en agter dezelve eenige Schapen; aangenaam en uitvoerig behandeld	Caspar van Citters	(Unknown)
1810/12/03	DOBRA	0051	*A. van der Velden* | Een Landschap met Koeijen, Schapen en Geiten, benevens Boerinnen, waar van eene bezig is, een Geit te melken, get. A. van der Velden | *Inscr:* A. van der Velden (signed)		(Unknown)

Velde, Adriaen van de (and Beerstraten, A.)

1801/06/10	AMSCH	0013	*Beerestraten. (A.); A. v.d. Velde* | Een Venetiaansche Zeehaven, met hooge Gebouwen, waarby een Fontein, waaruit eenig Vee drinkt, verders een menigte Beeldjes, het water is ryk gestoffeerd met Scheepen en Schuiten, en is voorts van eene delicaate penseels behandeling | *Mat:* op doek *Size:* hoog 41, breed 34 duim	Herman ten Kate	(Sold) fl 255 C S Roos

Velde, Adriaen van de (and Hackaert, J.)

1801/04/13	AMSCH	0029	*J. Hackaert; A. van de Velde* | Een alleraangenaamst Italiaansch Landschap met hoog Geboomte, ter regter zyde de Ruïne van eene Collonnade, waar by een Fontein, een Jager met zyn Hond, verfrisschen zig aan dezelve, voorts nog een Heer en Dame te paard, verders Jagers, Honden, Koeijen en Schapen; over een Rivier ziet men een aangenaam bergachtig verschiet; alles is zonachtig en transperant behandeld | *Mat:* op doek *Size:* hoog 22, breed 31 duim	Pierre Fouquet, junior	(Sold) fl 200 Pruyssenaar
1804/05/07	AMSCH	0076	*Hakkert (J.); A. van de Velde* | Een aangenaam Landschap, met een Waterplas op de voorgrond, waar by een Vrouw, die een Beest voort dryft, verder een opgaande Weg met Geboomte en een drift Beesten en voorts een aangenaam verschiet, zonachtig en bevallig gepenceeld | *Mat:* op doek *Size:* hoog 19 ½, breed 23 duim	Y[ver]	(Sold) fl 13 Reijers
1804/05/07	AMSCH	0077	*Hakkert (J.); A. van de Velde* | Een aangenaam Boom en Bergächtig Landschap, op de voorgrond gestoffeerd, met rustende Landlieden, verders een Herder eenig Vee langs den weg dryvenden, hooger op ziet men een vlietend Watertje, de toppen van Ruigbegroeide Bergen en aengenaam verschiet, warm en zonachtig van penceelbehandeling | *Mat:* op doek *Size:* hoog 32, breed 43 duim	Vinkeles [for] G	(Sold) fl 89 Thys
1808/06/06	RMRIJ	0047	*Hakkert. (Jan); Velde. (Adriaan van de)* | Een zeer aangenaam Landschap, rijk in hoog opgaande verschillende soorten van boomen. Op den voorgrond van eenen weg, welke met eene bogt langs een water loopt, ziet men een Heer op een Bruin Vos-Paard, daarnevens eene rijk gekleede Dame op een Wit Paard; uit de poort van een Oud Slot trekken eenige Jagers en Bedienden, met een groot aantal Honden, ter jagt. Alles zeer natuurlijk en allerschoonst door beide deze groote Meesters behandeld. Is in Plaat te vinden in het Prentwerk van het Kabinet van Mr. Le Brun [Sur le devant d'un chemin courbé, enrichi de beaux hêtres de haute futaie, et qui borde un Canal, on voit un Cavalier, dont le Cheval Alezan se cabre ; une Dame richement costumée et montée sur un Cheval blanc, se trouve prés de lui : ils sont suivis par un fauconnier accompagné d'un Chasseur, avec une meute de Chiens. Dans le fond, auprés de la Porte d'un Enclos, un Cavalier prend congé d'un Seigneur, deux Chasseurs et des Chiens sont auprés d'eux ; vers la gauche et sur le devant au bord du Canal, on voit un Chien qui aboye des Cignes. De beaux arbres, l'Effet de la Réverberation du Soleil dans l'eau, la Perspective Aérienne, l'harmonie bien sentie, tout cela joint aux figures et aux Animaux supériéurement peints par le célébre van den Velde, forme un Ensemble gracieux et par fait. Nous pouvons dire de ce superbe morceau qu'on chercheroit en vain son pareil. On trouve dans le Cabinet de Mr. le Brun une gravure de ce Tableau par Daudet] | *Mat:* op doek *Size:* Hoog 25, en breed 20 ⅛ duim *Loc:* Amsterdam, Nederland. Rijksmuseum. (A 130)	Gerrit van der Pot, Heer van Groeneveld	(Sold) fl 3005 Johs Eck en Zoon [for] le Roi
1810/03/26	RMMUY	0020	*Jan Hakkert; gestoffeerd door Adriaan van de Velde* | Een Italiaansch Bergachtig Landschap, met hoog en laag Geboomte. Op den breeden weg	Daniel de Jongh Az	(Sold) fl 505 Van Iperen Amsterdam

			een Herder zijne Schapen drijvende, en op den voorgrond een Man te Paard, dat aan een Water staat te drinken. Krachtig, zonachtig en meesterlijk behandeld [Un Paysage, site de l'Italie, au milieu un large chemin, bordé de montagnes et de beaux arbres : occupé par un berger conduisant ses moutons, sur le devant un homme monté sur son cheval, qui s'abreuve à une mare d'eau, d'un ton chaud, d'un beau faire et d'un brillant effet.] | *Mat:* op doek *Size:* hoog 23 ½, breed 28 ½ duimen		
1810/07/26	AMSCH	0041	*Hakkaert (J.); A. van de Velde* | Een aangenaam boomrijk Landschap bij een opgaanden Weg, waarop een Heer te Paard, verzeld van Jagers en Honden. Zonachtig en uitvoerig behandeld | *Mat:* op doek *Size:* hoog 17, breed 22 duimen	Cassino	(Sold) fl 20 Dupré
1810/08/01	AMSCH	0034	*Hakkaert (Jan); Adriaan van de Velde* | Een hoog bergachtig Landschap, op den voorgrond met eene Rivier doorsneden, verder een Waterval bij eene Brug, en hoog opgaand Geboomte, voorzien van Hengelaars, gaande en rustende Reizigers [Un Site de Paysage montueux, coupé par une Riviere au premier plan ; on y observe une Chutte [sic] d'Eau auprès d'un Pont de Pierres, et une variété d'Arbres et de Broussailles, ainsi que des Pécheurs, et d'autres qui semblent faire route] | *Annots:* médiocre. (NGW) *Mat:* op doek *Size:* hoog 26 ½, breed 20 ½ duimen	Mr Pieter de Smeth van Alphen	(Sold) fl 400 Hulswit
1810/08/01	AMSCH	0035	*Hakkaert (Jan); Adriaan van de Velde* | Een aangenaam zonachtig Landschap, met Beeldjes en Schapen, ter zijde een Water [Un Site agréable doré des Rayons de la lumiere, orné de Figures et de Moutons. On y distingue une marre d'eau sur le côté] | *Annots:* médiocre. (NGW) *Mat:* op doek *Size:* hoog 20 ½, breed 26 duimen	Mr Pieter de Smeth van Alphen	(Sold) fl 315 Van Iperen [for] Wreesman
1810/10/10	MGCIT	0004	*Jan Hakkert; A. van de Velde* | Een overheerlijk boschächtig Gezigt, door Jan Hakkert, en met eene fraaije Hertenjagt gestoffeerd, door A. van de Velde; meesterlijk door beide Kunstenaars geschilderd en uitgevoerd; zijnde het Daglicht door het Geboomte heen, alsmede een Waterplas waarin een Hert door de Honden word aangevallen, van een ongemeene schoone werking: Nota: Dit voortreffelijk Stuk is met veel waarschijnlijkheid de Pendant van dat het welk word gevonden in de verkogte Verzameling van wijlen de Heer van der Pot. Pag. 21. No. 47.	Caspar van Citters	(Unknown)
			Velde, Adriaen van de (and Heyden, J.)		
1801/06/10	AMSCH	0075	*Heyden. (J. van der); A. v. Velde* | Een Stadgezicht gestoffeerd met hoog Geboomte, Schuiten en Beeldjes, Zonachtigen uitvoerig behandeld | *Mat:* op paneel *Size:* hoog 14, breed 18 duim	Herman ten Kate	(Sold) fl 390 W Reijers
1802/05/05	AMSCH	0070	*J. van der Heyden; A. van de Velde* | Een Binnegezicht in een Oude Stad, voorzien van een Prachtige Tempel en andere Grootsche Gebouwen, staande op een Markt; op de Voorgrond een steene Brug en Cappelletje, ryk gestoffeert met verscheide Werkende en Gaande Beeldjes. Uitmuntend fraai uitvoerig en zonachtig gepenceeld | *Mat:* op doek *Size:* hoog 20 ½, breed 25 ½ duim	J	(Bought In) fl 505
1804/02/27	AMSCH	0045	*Heide (J. van der); A. van de Velde* | Een zeer aangenaam Landschap, met hoog opgaand Geboomte, op den voorgrond een stil Water, waarby een Hengelaar, ter zyde een Huysmanswoning, verders een Heer en een Dame Wandelende, en een bevallig verschiet; zeer uitvoerig van schildering | *Mat:* op paneel *Size:* hoog 9, breed 12 duim	B	(Sold) fl 67 Jozi
1805/07/03	AMSCH	0021	*Heyden. (J. van der); A. van de Velde* | Een Landschap met Gebergtens en een Waterval ontwaard men op de voorgrond, op de tweede grond ziet men een Stads Poort en verdere Gebouwen, Geboomten en een ménigte Beeldjes; kragtig en zonachtig en tevens uitvoerig gepenceeld | *Mat:* op paneel *Size:* hoog 12, breed 11 duim	G	(Sold) fl 30 Wed Achtienhoven
1808/06/06	RMRIJ	0053	*Heijden. (Joan van der); Velde. (Adriaan van de)* | Eenige fraaije Gebouwen, eene Valbrug en Boomen, langs waterachtige grachten. Lezende, Visschende en werkende figuren beschouwt men op dit in alle opzigten konstig en verwonderlijk uitgevoerd tafereel. Eene wedergade. In dit tafereel ziet men prachtige Gebouwen, rijk Geboomte en aangename Figuren, waaronder eene Vrouw met een Emmer eenen trap afgaande, terwijl een Heer, vergezeld van een Hond, een Heer en Dame schijnt te groeten. In alles gelijk aan het voorgaande [L'Intérieur d'une Ville Hollandaise. Un Canal bordé par des quais, un Pont-levis, des Bâtiments d'un bon gout, et plusieurs Figures admirablement peintes et du plus grand fini, décorent ce charmant Tableau Pendant au Précédent. Un Canal bordé d'un quai et traversé par un Pont-vouté, des joli Bâtiments, de beaux arbres et plusieurs figures agréables ornent cette belle Production] | *Mat:* op koper *Size:* Twee stukken. Hoog 13 ½, en breed 16 ¾ duim. *Loc:* Amsterdam, Nederland. Rijksmuseum. (A 152 & A 153)	Gerrit van der Pot, Heer van Groeneveld	(Sold) fl 1045 Johs Eck en Zoon [for] le Roi
1809/07/19	AMSCH	0020	*Heijden (J. van der); Velde (A. v. de)* | Dit fraai kapitaal Tafreel vertoont in een Heuvelachtig Landschap met Geboomte het Gezigt naar een aloud Kasteel, op den voorgrond gestoffeerd met twee Heeren te Paard, verzeld van een Valkenier en Jagthonden; by een opgaande Weg eenige Jagers en op een grazig Heuveltje eenig rustend Vee, verder een Riviergezicht naar een Dorp met Woningen en een gaand Rijziger. Het natuurlijk zonlicht, het bevallige koloriet, en de uitvoerige Penceelsbehandeling geven lof aan beide deze Meesters | *Mat:* op paneel *Size:* hoog 19, breed 26 duim	[Bicker]	(Sold) fl 255 T Spaan

1809/09/06	AMSCH	0021	*Heijden (J vam der); A. van de Velde* | In een Binnengezigt van een voorname Stad, op een ruim Plijn of Markt, vertoont zich op een Heuvel een groote Kerk, en verder andere Gebouwen; het is uitmuntend gestoffeert met wandelende Beeldjes, Rijtuigen en eenig Vee. Alles is ongemeen helder, zonachtig en van een uitvoerige penceelbehandeling door beide deze beroemde Meesters vervaardigd | *Mat:* op paneel *Size:* hoog 15, breed 17 duim *Loc:* Nieuwersluis, Nederland. B. de Geus van den Heuvel collection.	Johannes Caudri	(Sold) fl 81 Gruyter
1810/05/22	AMSCH	0035	*Heiden (J. van der); A. van de Velde* | Een fraai Boomrijk Landschap, op den voorgrond bij een Water een opgaande Weg naar een Gebouw, gestoffeerd met een Landman, eenig Vee voortdrijvende, verder een Heer te Paard en Reizigers; uitvoerig en zuiver van schildering | *Mat:* op paneel *Size:* hoog 11, breed 13 duim	Johannes van de Putte Nicolaasz.	(Sold) fl 122 Gruyter
1810/05/22	AMSCH	0036	*Heiden. (J. van der); A. van de Velde* | Twee stuks Gezichten buiten den Haag, verbeeldende het eene het Huis in het Bosch; het andere de Koekamp; beide met Beeldjes gestoffeerd en zeer uitvoerig van penceelbehandeling | *Mat:* op paneel *Size:* hoog 8 ½, breed 11 duim *Loc:* London, England, UK. National Gallery. (1914) (?)	Johannes van de Putte Nicolaasz.	(Sold) fl 256 Gruyter
1810/08/01	AMSCH	0038	*Heiden (Jan van der); Adriaan van de Velde* | Een Stadsgezigt met eene Brug bij een grootsch Gebouw, versierd met een Meisje, dat linnen spoelt, en andere zoo gaande als staande lieden [Vue intérieure de Ville prise sur un Canal, auprès d'un grand Batiment, contre lequel se trouve un pont. On observe au bord de l'eau une Fille blanchissant du linge et plusieurs Figures cheminans dans la rue] | *Annots:* Bon, mais nullement éminent. (NGW) *Mat:* op paneel *Size:* hoog 19, breed 22 duimen *Loc:* Waddesdon Manor, Bucks., England, UK. National Trust. (WI/60/9)	Mr Pieter de Smeth van Alphen	(Sold) fl 2999 J Yver
1810/08/06	AMSCH	0043	*Heiden (J. van der); Gestoffeerd door A. van de Velde* | Een oud Gezigt binnen Amsterdam, zijnde een gedeelte van de Heeregragt naar de Leliegragt te zien, gestoffeerd met onderscheidene Beeldjes en Vaartuigen; het is zonachtig en zeer uitvoerig door beide Meesters behandeld | *Mat:* op paneel *Size:* hoog 14, breed 17 duimen *Loc:* Waddesdon Manor, Bucks., England, UK. National Trust. (WI/60/8)	A	(Sold) fl 300 de Vries
			Velde, Adriaen van de (and Koninck, P.)		
1802/05/05	AMSCH	0091	*P. Koning; A. van de Velde* | Een Bergachtig Landschap, op de Voorgrond Boeren Wooningen, een Heer te Paard en eenige Hoenders. Natuurlyk en fraai behandeld | *Mat:* op paneel *Size:* hoog 19, breed 16 duim	C	(Sold) fl 7 Spruit
1804/08/08	AMSCH	0096	*Ph. Koning; A. van de Velde* | In een vlak en wyduitgestrekt Landzicht, met eenige Wooningen en Geboomte, vertoont zich een Vorstelyk Lusthuis en Thuin, by een Riviergezicht, waarin een Plaisierschuitje geplaatst is, op de voorgrond, by een opgaande Weg, ryk gestoffeerd met een Landman, een Drift Beesten voortdryvende, ter linker zyde een grazende en een rustende Os en Schaap; alles zonachtig en helder, en bevallig van coloriet, door Ph. Koning, en de Stoffagie door A. van de Velde | *Mat:* op doek *Size:* hoog 36, breed 42 duim *Loc:* Bruxelles, Belgique. Musées royaux des Beaux-Arts. (54)	Schley [for] A	(Sold) fl 36 Reyers
1806/08/13	AMSCH	0089	*Koning. (Ph. de); A. van de Velden* | In een uitgestrekt Landschap, ziet men over een klaar spiegelend Water een Stad, op de voorgrond by opgaand Geboomten eenige Gebouwen, verders Landlieden die eenig Vée dryven en een bevallig verschiet; zonachtig en meesterlyk geschildert | *Mat:* op doek *Size:* hoog 17, breed 21 duim	Vinkeles [for] G[ruyter]	(Sold) fl 25:10 van Iperen
			Velde, Adriaen van de (and Moucheron, F.)		
1801/04/13	AMSCH	0043	*F. de Moncheron; A. van de Velde* | Dit uitmundtend Taffereel [sic] verbeeld een aangenaam boom en bergachtig Landschap, met een heldere waterplas, gestoffeerd met een menigte Beeldjes, Paarden en Vee, een Jager is beezig op de voorgrond op eenige Eenden te schieten, het Geboomte is dun, het zonlicht frappant, en kan voor een der beste stukken van deeze voortreffelyke Meesters gehouden worden | *Mat:* op doek *Size:* hoog 21, breed 26 duim	Pierre Fouquet, junior	(Sold) fl 410 Coclers
1801/06/10	AMSCH	0110	*Moucheron. (F. de); stoffagie A. van de Velde* | Een Landschap, met hoog Geboomte en een Bergachtig verschiet, op de voorgrond ziet men een Jager met een Hond, verders een Man te paard, eenige Schaape dryvende, alles Zonachtig en delicaat behandeld | *Mat:* op doek *Size:* hoog 32, breed 27 duim *Notes:* Originally the artist's name was spelled "A. de Velde." This error was corrected in an errata sheet located at the end of the catalogue.	Herman ten Kate	(Sold) fl 405 J Yver
1801/06/10	AMSCH	0111	*Moucheron. (F. de); stoffagie A. van de Velde* | Een Zonachtig, Boom- en Bergachtig Landschap, met een aangenaam verschiet, gestoffeerd met Beelden en Vee, meesterlyk geschilderd | *Mat:* op doek *Size:* hoog 33, breed 44 duim *Notes:* Originally the artist's name was spelled "A. de Velde." This error was corrected in an errata sheet located at the end of the catalogue.	Herman ten Kate	(Sold) fl 39 Coclers
1801/06/10	AMSCH	0112	*Moucheron. (F. de); stoffagie A. van de Velde* | Een Landschap, doorsneden met een Rivier, op de voorgrond een staande en rustende Reiziger, Zonachtig en bevallig gepenceeld | *Mat:* op doek *Size:* hoog 26, breed 30 duim *Notes:* Originally the artist's name was spelled "A. de Velde." This error was corrected in an errata sheet located at the end of the catalogue.	Herman ten Kate	(Sold) fl 30 Taijs

1802/06/28	AMSCH	0107	*F. de Moucheron; A. van de Velde* | In dit alleraangenaamst Landschap, ziet men op een welig begroeiden Steenrots den Temple van Cybille te Tivoli, beneden ziet men een Herder met eenig Vee, verders over een Steene Brug twee Ezels met hun Dryver, en op de voorgrond by een stromende Beek een rustende Reiziger met een Hond; het heldere Zonlicht maakt dit stuk zeer bevallig; zynde delicaat gepenceeld, door F. de Moucheron en A. van de Velde | *Mat:* op doek *Size:* hoog 31, breed 25 duim	Anna Elink	(Bought In) fl 140
1802/09/06	AMSCH	0068	*F. de Moucheron; A. van de Velde* | Een hoog Bergachtig Landschap met een Waterval, op de voorgrond onder het Lommer van 't dartel Geboomte, staan en rusten eenige Schaapjes, beneevens een Gyt, verder een Véehoeder met Vée, en een aangenaam verschiet; natuurlyk gepenceeld | *Mat:* op doek *Size:* hoog 44, breed 35 duim	J	(Bought In) fl 18
1804/07/25	AMSCH	0052	*Moucheron (F. de); A. v. de Velde* | In dit allerbevalligst capitaal Italiaansch Heuvelachtig Landschap, met verschillend Geboomten, ziet men op de voorgrond by een opgaande Weg, ryk gestoffeert met een Drift Beesten, waarby een Huisman te Paard, daar nevens een gaande Vrouw met een Pak op het hoofd, en terzyde een ander Reiziger; in 't verschiet eenige Gebouwen op een Heuvel, en verders hoog Gebergten; het streelend zonlicht doet een aangenaame werking, en is van een fraaije en uitvoerige penceelbehandeling, door beide deeze vermaarde Meesters | *Mat:* op doek *Size:* hoog 36, breed 46 duim		(Sold) fl 315 Van der Schleij
1809/09/06	AMSCH	0043	*Moucheron (F. de); A. van de Velde* | Een Gezicht op een Fontijn en Beek, waarbij twee Beeldjes; het water is helder, en alles word door een helder zonlicht bescheenen, en is delicaat gepenceeld | *Mat:* op doek *Size:* hoog 16, breed 18 duim	Johannes Caudri	(Sold) fl 59 van Iperen
1809/09/06	AMSCH	0044	*Moucheron (F. de); A. van de Velde* | Een Gezicht op een Hofstéden, in het midden ziet men een Fontijn, waarbij wandelende Beelden en in 't verschiet een Heer te Paard, waarbij eenige Honden; niet minder als de voorgaande | *Mat:* op paneel *Size:* hoog 20, breed 16 duim	Johannes Caudri	(Sold) fl 42 Coclers

Velde, Adriaen van de (and Rombouts)

1808/06/13	AMSCH	0132	*Rombouts; A. van de Velde* | Een aangenaam boomrijk Landschap aan eene Rivier, met een Pont, waarin zich reeds een Heer te Paard, twee Reizigers en eenig Vee bevinden, terwijl een Koets, voorgegaan door een Looper, bezig is in dezelve te rijden, op den voorgrond eenige Visschers. Allernatuurlijkst en zonachtig behandeld | *Mat:* op doek *Size:* hoog 36, breed 31 duim	E M Engelberts	(Sold) fl 150 Simons

Velde, Adriaen van de (and Ruisdael, J.)

1808/06/13	AMSCH	0126	*Ruisdaal (J.); A. van de Velde* | Een Gezicht op het Dorp Scheveningen, het Strand gestoffeerd met eene menigte Heeren, Dames, Visschers, Honden, enz., verder Pinken, en op Zee eenige zeilende Vaartuigen. De verbolgene lucht doet hier eene schoone uitwerking van licht en donker, zijnde voorts van eene uitmuntende penceelsbehandeling | *Mat:* op doek *Size:* hoog 40, breed 62 duim	R[oos]	(Bought In) fl 580
1808/06/13	AMSCH	0127	*Ruisdaal (J.); A. van de Velde* | Deze heerlijke Ordonantie verbeeld een bergachtig Landschap, waarin eene Waterval, waarbij een Herder en Herderin, en eenig liggend Vee. Zonachtig en natuurlijk van schildering | *Mat:* op doek *Size:* hoog 43, breed 59 duim	E M Engelberts	(Sold) fl 61 Nieuwenhuys pour Henry

Velde, Adriaen van de (and Wijnants)

1801/04/13	AMSCH	0093	*J. Wynadts; A. van de Velde* | Twee stuks Duin en boomryke Landschappen, gestoffeerd met Jagers te paard en te voet, met hunne honden, en een rustende marskramer; het zonlicht, en de klikachtige kluitjes der zandgronden maken deeze stukjes tot een paar der bevalligste van deezen Meester | *Mat:* op doek *Size:* ieder is hoog 16, breed 14 duim	Pierre Fouquet, junior	(Sold) fl 310 v d Schley [for] M[errem]
1801/05/11	AMSCH	0113	*J. Wynands; A. v.d. Velde* | J. Wynands, gestoffeerd door A. v. d. Velde. Een zonachtig Landschap, op de Voorgrond eenige Koeijen en Schaapen, waarby een Herder, ter rechter zyde een stam van een eikenboom, verders een bergachtig verschiet, alles is van de beste en fraaiste schildering | *Mat:* op doek *Size:* hoog 10, breed 13 duim *Loc:* Amsterdam, Nederland. Rijksmuseum. (A 493)	E[lias]	(Sold) fl 305 Bern de Bosch
1801/06/10	AMSCH	0179	*Wynants. (J.); stoffagie van A. v. d. Velde* | Deeze ryke Ordonnantie stelt voor een Heuvelachtig Landschap, gestoffeerd met een drift Beesten, verzelt van een Man met een Hond, schynende aan een ander, die nevens hem staat, den weg te vraagen, verder over een stil Water ziet men een bergachtig Verschiet; alles zeer natuurlyk en van eene krachtige behandeling | *Mat:* op doek *Size:* hoog 31, breed 36 duim	Herman ten Kate	(Sold) fl 1041 Th^{s} Spaan voor Muilman
1802/06/16	AMSCH	0203	*J. Wynands; A. v. de Velde* | Een Duinachtig Landzicht, ter zyde een stil Water, ziet men op een zandige brokkelagtige Heuvel, met een van hout gevlogte Schutting bezet, en Stamme van Boomen; een Heer by een afkomende weg met Snaphaan op schouder, verzelt van een Jagthond, verder Geboomten, gaande Huislieden en een bevallig verschiet; zeer fraay en natuurlyk gepenceeld | *Mat:* op doek *Size:* hoog 20, breed 17 duim	[Merrem]	(Sold) fl 580 H de Valk
1802/06/16	AMSCH	0204	*J. Wynands; A. v. de Velde* | Deeze twee Cabinetstukjes zyn Duinachtige Landschapjes met hoog Geboomte, Kreupelgewas en afkalverende	[Merrem]	(Sold) fl 380 Cobel

			Zandgronden, Waterplassen en aangename verschieten; beide bevallig gestoffeerd met Jagers en Reizigers te Paard en te voet; alles van de beste schildering van deeze Meesters | *Mat:* op doek *Size:* hoog 16, breed 13 ½ duim		
1802/06/16	AMSCH	0205	*J. Wynands; A. v. de Velde* | Een Duinachtig Landschap met hoog Geboomte en aangenaam verschiet, de voorgrond met verscheide Koejen en een Herder gestoffeerd; alles van een aangenaame behandeling | *Mat:* op paneel *Size:* hoog 17 ½, breed 14 ½ duim	[Merrem]	(Sold) fl 73 Wed Achtienhoven
1806/08/13	AMSCH	0207	*Wynands (J.); A. van de Velde* | Dit capitaale Schildery steld voor, een hoogen Zandheuvel, waarby een opgaande Boom, langs een afkomende Weg ziet men aan een Waterplas drie Koeijen en eenige Schapen met hunne Herders; het bevallig licht hetgeen zich in dit aangenaam voorwerp vertoond, maakt dit tot een der fraaiste Schilderyen van dezen Meester | *Mat:* op paneel *Size:* hoog 26, breed 31 duim	Daniel Mansveld	(Sold) fl 611 Royers
1806/08/13	AMSCH	0208	*Wynands (J.); A. van de Velde* | Dit uitmuntend Duinachtig Landschapje met hoog Geboomten, omgehakte Stammen en welige Kruiden, is op de voorgrond gestoffeerd met Jagers te voet en te paard met Honden enz.; alles van een uitmuntende penceelsbehandeling | *Mat:* op paneel *Size:* hoog 15, breed 19 duim	Daniel Mansveld	(Sold) fl 400 van Iperen
1806/08/13	AMSCH	0209	*Wynands (J.); A. van de Velde* | Twee stuks Duin- en Bergachtige Landschappen, met Geboomten; Watervallen en onderscheiden stoffagie van Beelden, fiks gepenceeld | *Mat:* op doek *Size:* hoog 16, breed 21 duim	Daniel Mansveld	(Sold) fl 180 Thais
1810/08/01	AMSCH	0126	*Wijnands (Jan); Adriaan van de Velde* | Een aangenaam heuvelachtig Landschap met eene Rivier, Geboomte en Gebouwen. Op eenen zandigen Weg ziet men eenen Landman met eene Drift van Beesten; ter zijde ligt een Boomstam bij eenige Kruiden [Vue pitoresque sur un Sol sabloneux, coupé par une Riviere ; et varié par des Batimens et par des plantis d'Arbres. Dans une route sabloneuse se trouve un Pâtre conduisant du Bêtail. Vèrs le côté est un Tronc-d'arbre abattu et quelques Plantes] | *Annots:* Bon. (NGW) *Mat:* op paneel *Size:* hoog 12, breed 16 duimen	Mr Pieter de Smeth van Alphen	(Sold) fl 750 Cremer te Rotterdam
1810/08/01	AMSCH	0127	*Wijnands (Jan); Adriaan van de Velde* | Een duinachtig Landschap met eenen krommen Weg, hebbende aan beide kanten Water; het is gestoffeerd met Jagers en Honden, eenen Heer te paard en eenen Veedrijver [Une Vue de Bruïére dans laquelle serpente un Chemin sabloneux garni d'eau aux côtés. Ce site est embelli par un Chasseur et des Chiens, un Cavalier à Cheval, et par un Pâtre menant du Bêtail] | *Annots:* Bon. (NGW) *Mat:* op doek *Size:* hoog 14, breed 16 duimen	Mr Pieter de Smeth van Alphen	(Sold) fl 600 Perignon de Paris
			Velde, Adriaen van de (and Wijnants and Lingelbach)		
1802/06/16	AMSCH	0206	*J. Wynands; A. v. de Velde; J. Lingelbach* | Een Capitaal Boom- en Bergachtig Landschap met een stille Rivier en aangenaam verschiet, zynde gestoffeerd met eenige Landlieden, welken eenig Vée voortdryven; het frapante Zonlicht en de meesterlyke penceels-behandeling maken dit Schildery een der fraayste van deezen Meesters | *Mat:* op doek *Size:* hoog 65, breed 76 duim	[Merrem]	(Sold) fl 250 Coclers
1802/06/16	AMSCH	0207	*J. Wynands; A. v. de Velde; J. Lingelbach* | Ter regter zyde vertoont zich de ingang van een Bosch; op de voorgrond legt eene Boomstam; verder een Man te Paard, waarby een Jager met Honden, ter linker zyde een stil Water en Boeren Huis; verder hoog Gebergte in het verschiet; meesterlyk en zonachtig geschilderd | *Mat:* op doek *Size:* hoog 25, breed 29 duim	[Merrem]	(Sold) fl 190 H de Valk
			Velde, Adriaen van de (copy after)		
1801/02/18	AMBOS	0070	*Adr. van der Velde* | Een Landschap, fraay geschilderd, naar Adr. van der Velde	J Schonevelt	(Unknown)
1802/09/06	AMSCH	0154	*A. van de Velde* | Voor een Boerewooning, by Geboomten, ziet men verscheide staand en rustend Vée; naar A. van de Velde | *Mat:* op doek	B	(Sold) fl 51 Pruijssenaar
1804/10/16	DLOND	0243	*C. Vermeulen; naar A. v. d. Velde* | Twee Landschapjens met Vee. Deux Paysages & du Betail | copy by Corn. Vermeulen (III) after A. Velde *Mat:* op paneel *Size:* hoog 8, breed 11		(Unknown)
1804/10/16	DLOND	0309	*Naar A. van de Velde* | Een Landschap met Beesten. Paysage avec du Betail | *Mat:* op paneel *Size:* hoog 12, breed 15		(Unknown)
1806/08/13	AMSCH	0178	*Stry (A. van); na A. van de Velden* | In een vlak Landschap voor een Schuur, ziet men een Landman bézig een Koe te melken, nevens hem een Heer te Paard, dewelke naar de weg schynt te vraagen, verders een Koets met zes Paarden, enz., delicaat van penceelsbehandeling | copy by A. Strij after A. Velde *Size:* hoog 11, breed 14 duim	Vinkeles [for] G[ruyter]	(Sold) fl 10:10 Rijnbergh
			Velde, Adriaen van de (manner)		
1801/06/10	AMSCH	0212	*A. van de Velde* | Een pissende Koey, in een Landschap, op Paneel geschilderd, in de manier van A. van de Velde | *Mat:* op paneel *Size:* hoog 13, breed 10 duim	[Doublet]	(Sold) fl 2 van der Schley A [for] Uylenburg
1802/08/24	LNDLS	0124	*A. d. d. Velde* | Twee stuks Landschapjes met Ossen, Koeijen en Schapen, als door A. d. d. Velde	Leonardus Bouman [or others]	(Unknown) fl 8
1802/09/15	HGKAN	0005	*Van der Velde* | Een liggende Koe, in de manier van Van der Velde, op Paneel en Lyst [In Oly Verff] | *Mat:* in olyverf op paneel *Notes:* The		(Unknown)

<table>
<tr><td></td><td></td><td></td><td>bracketed information in the title appears above lot 1 and refers to lots 1 to 8.</td><td></td><td></td></tr>
<tr><td>1804/05/07</td><td>AMSCH</td><td>0206</td><td>A. van de Velde | In een Boomryk Landschap by een Rivier, ziet men een Veehoeder bezig zyn voeten te wassen, waarnaast een Vrouw en drinkende Os, verders eenig staand en rustend Vee, enz.; natuurlyk en fraay gepenceeld, in de manier van A. van de Velde</td><td>Roos [for] A</td><td>(Bought In) fl 3 ½</td></tr>
<tr><td>1804/08/08</td><td>AMSCH</td><td>0238</td><td>A. van de Velde | Een Boomryk Landschapje, by een Rivier, gestoffeerd met een Véehoeder, zyne voeten wasschende, waar naast een Vrouw, drinkende Os, en verders staand en leggend Vée; natuurlyk gepenceeld, in de manier van A. van de Velde</td><td>Roos [for] F</td><td>(Sold) fl 12 Van Iperen</td></tr>
<tr><td>1804/10/16</td><td>DLOND</td><td>0308</td><td>In de Manier van A. van de Velde | Een Landschap met Koeien. Paysage & des Vaches | Mat: op paneel Size: hoog 15, breed 14</td><td></td><td>(Unknown)</td></tr>
<tr><td>1804/10/29</td><td>HRBAU</td><td>0132</td><td>A. v. d. Velde | Op den Voorgrond is een Vrouwtjen bezig een rood bonte Koe te melken, waar by nog twee liggende Koeijen zyn; benevens een' Ezel, en eenige Schaapen en Lammeren; wyders een boomagtig verschiet. Bevallig in den trant van A. v. d. Velde behandeld | Mat: op doek Size: hoog 21, breed 25 duim</td><td>Simon Styl</td><td>(Unknown)</td></tr>
<tr><td>1804/12/10</td><td>AMSCH</td><td>0121</td><td>A. v. de Velde | Een Landschap met hoog geboomte, met diverse Harten en Reën gestoffeert, an als A. v. de Velde behandeld | Mat: op doek Size: hoog 18, breed 20 duim</td><td>Jan De Groot</td><td>(Sold) fl 1:15 Hamer</td></tr>
<tr><td>1805/07/10</td><td>AMSCH</td><td>0282</td><td>A. van de Velde | Twee stuks bevallige Landschappen, verbeeldende een Graazige Weiden met rustende en staande Koeijen, Ossen, Bokken, verders aangenaame Verschieten; dun in de manier van A. van de Velde, door een voornaame Meesters</td><td>V[inkeles] [for] M</td><td>(Sold) fl 5:15 L Philip</td></tr>
</table>

Velde, Adriaen van de (manner; and Ruisdael, J., manner)

<table>
<tr><td>1802/08/24</td><td>LNDLS</td><td>0052</td><td>A. van de Velde; J. Ruisdaal | Een Landschap met different Geboomte, op den Voorgrond een Beekje, nevens hetzelve een weg, met een Man en een Vrouw te Paard, alsmeede veel Koeijen en Schaapen. De Stoffagie is in de manier van A. van de Velde, en het Landschap als door J. Ruisdaal, konstig en krachtig op paneel geschilderd | Mat: op paneel Size: hoog 31, breed 40 duimen</td><td>Leonardus Bouman [or others]</td><td>(Unknown) fl 41</td></tr>
</table>

Velde, Esaias van de (I)

<table>
<tr><td>1801/08/19</td><td>AMSCH</td><td>0132</td><td>E. van de Velde | Twee stuks capitaale Land- en Watergezichten, ryk gestoffeerd met verscheide Lieden, te paard en te voet, onder zwaar Geboomten; alles is meesterlyk en krachtig geschilderd op Doek | Mat: op doek Size: hoog 41, breed 74 duim</td><td>Van Forreest</td><td>(Sold) fl 6 V^{n} Dijl</td></tr>
<tr><td>1801/10/06</td><td>AMSCH</td><td>0069</td><td>E. van de Velde | Gezicht op de Groote Markt te Haarlem, alwaar een Oproer plaats heeft, by het Laaden van eenige Wagens met Koorn, ryk geordineert en Natuurlyk behandeld | Mat: op doek Size: hoog 26, breed 40 duim</td><td>M</td><td>(Sold) fl 48 Jan Spaan</td></tr>
<tr><td>1802/02/16</td><td>AMSCH</td><td>0043</td><td>E. v. de Velde | Een bevallig Landschap met geboomten, gestoffeert met diversche Heeren te Paard; meesterlyk behandeld</td><td>G</td><td>(Sold) fl 5:10 J^{n} Spaan</td></tr>
<tr><td>1802/02/16</td><td>AMSCH</td><td>0044</td><td>E. v. de Velde | Een Besneeuwt Winter gezigt, in een Boeren Dorp, met verschyde woningen by een Rivier, waarop verschyde schaatzeryders, en andere Huislieden, natuurlyk gepenceeld</td><td>G</td><td>(Sold) fl 5 Vink & Fitsing</td></tr>
<tr><td>1802/04/13</td><td>HAVIN</td><td>0049</td><td>E. v. d. Velde | Een dito [Landschap]</td><td></td><td>(Unknown)</td></tr>
<tr><td>1802/05/24</td><td>HGBAK</td><td>0044</td><td>Elias v. d. Velde | Twee stuks Landschapjes in 't ovaal, met beelden en beestjes, door Elias v. d. Velde, hoog en breed 4 1/3 duim, op paneel, vergulde lystjes | Mat: op paneel Fmt: ovaal Size: hoog en breed 4 ⅓ duim</td><td>Mejuffrouw A van der Mieden</td><td>(Sold) fl 2:15 Bosset</td></tr>
<tr><td>1802/06/28</td><td>AMSCH</td><td>0196</td><td>E. van de Velde | Een Boeren Gehugt, met Geboomte en Watergezigt, gestoffeerd met Beelden, door E. van de Velde, op Panneel | Mat: op paneel Size: hoog 15, breed 29 duim</td><td>Anna Elink</td><td>(Sold) fl 1:5 Texier</td></tr>
<tr><td>1802/09/06</td><td>AMSCH</td><td>0126</td><td>E. van de Velde | Een Hartejagt, in een Boom- en Bergagtig Landschap; fix | Mat: op paneel Size: hoog 31, breed 52 duim</td><td>D</td><td>(Sold) fl 5:15 Gruiter</td></tr>
<tr><td>1802/09/21</td><td>UTHDG</td><td>0094</td><td>E. van de Velde | Reizigers door Rovers aangevallen, in een Landschap</td><td></td><td>(Bought In) fl 1</td></tr>
<tr><td>1802/11/01</td><td>DOBRA</td><td>0114</td><td>E. van der Velde | Een Schermutseling van Ruitery | Mat: op paneel Size: hoog 8. breed 11 ½ duim</td><td>Paulus van der Spyk [or others]</td><td>(Unknown)</td></tr>
<tr><td>1802/11/01</td><td>DOBRA</td><td>0148</td><td>E. v. de Velde | Een Landschap, vol Stoffagie; goed geteekend en meesterlyk geschilderd | Mat: op paneel</td><td></td><td>(Unknown) fl 1:15</td></tr>
<tr><td>1802/11/01</td><td>DOBRA</td><td>0153</td><td>E. v. de Velde | Een Bergagtig Landschap; goed gestoffeerd en fix behandeld | Size: hoog 4 ½, br. 7 duim Notes: This lot was sold with lots 154 and 155 by anonymous artists.</td><td></td><td>(Unknown) fl 3 for lots 153–155</td></tr>
<tr><td>1802/12/13</td><td>AMSCH</td><td>0166</td><td>E. van de Velden | Een Boomryk Landschap, met Gebouwen by een stil Water, op de voorgrond verscheiden Heeren te Paard | Mat: op paneel Size: hoog 12, breed 21 duim</td><td>Pruyssenaar [for] D</td><td>(Sold) fl 7:5 van Iperen</td></tr>
<tr><td>1803/04/20</td><td>AMSCH</td><td>0077</td><td>Velde. (E. van de) | Twee stuks, een Campement van Ruitery, en een Boomryk Landschap met stoffagie van Beelden en Vaartuig, natuurlyk geschilderd [Ces deux Tableaux ont pour Sujet des Campemens de Cavalerie, dans un terrein coupé d'une riviere et ornés par d'autres accessoires, ils sont traités d'une maniere vraye.] | Mat: op paneel Size: ieder hoog 11, breed 18 duim</td><td>Maria Magdalena van Sluypwyk, gravinne van Moens</td><td>(Sold) fl 4:10 Theijs</td></tr>
</table>

1803/04/20	AMSCH	0078	*Velde. (E. van de)* | Een hévige Rencontre, tusschen Ruitery, zynde een vlugtend Leeger, fix gepenceeld [Choc de Cavaliers d'une arriere garde en fuite, très bien touché.] | *Mat:* op paneel *Size:* hoog 14, breed 14 duim	Maria Magdalena van Sluypwyk, gravinne van Moens	(Sold) fl 3:10 L Pakker
1803/04/20	AMSCH	0079	*Velde. (E. van de)* | In een uitgestrekt Landzigt, met Geboomten, ziet men op de voorgrond Postwagens, door Rovers overvallen, en geplunderd; meesterlyk fraay van Penceelsbehandeling [Un paysage etendu, coupé par des avenues et des routes : au premier plan se voit l'attaque d'une voiture par des brigands. Tableau d'éclât et très Spirituellement touché.] | *Mat:* op paneel *Size:* hoog 17, breed 28 duim	Maria Magdalena van Sluypwyk, gravinne van Moens	(Sold) fl 40 Hodges
1803/04/20	AMSCH	0080	*Velde. (E. van de)* | In een Dorpgezicht met een Kerk, Boerewooningen en Moolen, by een stil Water, gestoffeerd met Schuiten, op de voorgrond Reizigers te Paard en te voet, zeer natuurlyk en bevallig behandeld [Le perspective d'un Village à clocher, coupée d'une riviere, elle est ornée par de jolies figures, batteaux [sic] et accessoires. C'est un morceau agréable, varié et d'une touche aisée et naturelle.] | *Mat:* op paneel *Size:* hoog 15, breed 30 duim	Maria Magdalena van Sluypwyk, gravinne van Moens	(Sold) fl 3:5 L Pakker
1803/04/20	AMSCH	0081	*Velde. (E. van de)* | In een bevallig Italiaansch Landschap, met overblyfzels van prachtige Gebouwen, op de voorgrond vertoonen zich Reizigers door Roovers aangevallen; het invallend zonlicht doet een natuurlyke werking, en is van een uitvoerige penceelsbehandeling [Dans un site d'Italie ou sont eparses des ruïnes de batimens antiques est representé une attaque de Voyageurs par des voleurs. Un j'eu [sic] de lumiere bien repandue ajoute à l'agrement de ce morceau qui est Spirituellement touché.] | *Mat:* op paneel *Size:* hoog 17, breed 31 duim	Maria Magdalena van Sluypwyk, gravinne van Moens	(Sold) fl 41 Theijs
1803/09/07	AMSCH	0192	*E. van de Velde* | Twee stuks nederlandsche Landschappen met Geboomte, Boerewoningen, aan stille Rievieren, waarin Huislieden in hun Schuiten, op de Weg Heeren te Paard, anderen te Voet en op de Landeryen verscheide Vée; natuurlyk behandeld [Deux paysages hollandois, agréablement variés par des figures, des bocages et des rivieres portant des nacelles ; des voyageurs à cheval et des prairies avec des bestiaux : peint d'après nature et bien exécuté] | *Mat:* op paneel *Size:* hoog 11, breed 21 duim	Smidt	(Sold) fl 21 W Reijers
1803/09/07	AMSCH	0193	*E. van de Velde* | Twee stuks, een Zomer zynde een bevallig Boomryk Landschap met een Rivier doorsneden, en 't andere een Winter, zynde een bevroosen Rivier, gestoffeerd met een menigte rydende en wandelende Beeldjes en Arresleeden, fix en natuurlyk [Deux paysages, l'un adapté à l'été, avec des rians paturages et des arbres, et traversé par une rivière : l'autre, une vue d'hiver ; on y voit une rivière prise de glace, sur laquelle plusieurs figures se promenent et courent à patin ; composition très belle et d'un effet naturel] | *Mat:* op paneel *Size:* hoog 8, breed 10 ½ duim	Smidt	(Bought In) fl 9
1803/09/07	AMSCH	0194	*E. van de Velde* | Een Dorpgezicht met een menigte stoffagie; geestig [La vue d'un village avec plusieurs figures et d'autres accessoires ; ordonnance très spirituelle et d'une belle exécution] | *Mat:* op paneel *Size:* hoog 10, breed 15 duim	Smidt	(Sold) fl 1:15 Grimpen
1804/10/29	HRBAU	0107	*Velde (Esaijas van de)* | Onder hoog Geboomte zit een deftig Gezelschap, in zeer ryke Spaansche kleeding, aan eene welöpgedischte tafel te eeten, waar by een Heer en Dame. op den grond zittende, zig in den Wyn verlustigen: terwyl eenige gemaskerde Heeren en Dames het Gezelschap komen vermeerderen; terwyl de Bediendeh het Desert schynen te rangeeren op een tweede tafel, die geheel voor aan staat. Het verschiet vertoont eene pragtige Hofstede. Alles is zeer uitvoerig geschilderd; zynde dit één der capitaalste Stukken, welken men van dezen Meester vindt | *Mat:* op paneel *Size:* hoog 32, breed 50 duim	Simon Styl	(Unknown)
1804/10/29	HRBAU	0108	*Velde, (Esaijas van de)* | Op den Voorgrond, by Rietgewas, zyn twee Mannetjens bezig te visschen; aan de overzyde een Kerk en Dorp, alwaar men bezig is het Hooi te vervoeren. Zonagtig behandeld | *Mat:* op paneel *Fmt:* rond *Size:* hoog en breed 14 duim	Simon Styl	(Unknown)
1805/07/10	AMSCH	0163a	*E. van de Velde* | Twee Landschapjes | *Mat:* op paneel	V[inkeles] [for] K	(Bought In) fl 3
1806/05/05	AMSCH	0150	*E. van de Velde* | Een gezicht op een Stad	V[inkeles]	(Sold) fl 0:6 Driesseler
1806/05/05	AMSCH	0182	*E. van de Velde* | Twee stuks Boeren Binnenhuizen, alwaar door de Militairen gemoord en geplunderd word; meesterlyk door E. van de Velde | *Mat:* op paneel	R[oos]	(Sold) fl 5:10 Boelen
1806/05/05	AMSCH	0255	*E. v. d. Velde* | Een natuurlyk Land en Watergezigt	R[oos]	(Sold) fl 7:15 Scheurleer
1806/08/13	AMSCH	0200	*Velde. (E. van de)* | Een Boomryk Landschap, gestoffeerd met Heeren te paard, waarby Jagers en Honden, die een Hert vervolgen; uitvoerig van penceelsbehandeling | *Mat:* op paneel *Size:* hoog 31, breed 43 duim	Vinkeles [for] G[ruyter]	(Sold) fl 4 L Pakker
1806/08/13	AMSCH	0204	*Velde. (E. van de)* | Een bevallig Dorpgezichtje, zynde een Winter met stoffagie van Beeldjes, delicaat gepenceeld | *Annots:* Verkogt (MA) *Mat:* op paneel *Size:* hoog 10, breed 16 duim *Notes:* This lot was sold with lot 280 by an anonymous artist.	Daniel Mansveld	(Sold) fl 1:5 for lots 204 & 280. Boelen
1807/06/10	HGBSM	0176	*E. van de Velde* | Een Attacke van Cavallerie | *Mat:* op paneel *Size:* hoog 16, breed 23 duim	Abraham Delfos [or others]	(Sold) fl 6 Theben

808/08/23	AMSCH	0164	*Velde. (E. van de)* | Een Bosch-gezigt, ter zijde een stil Water, op de voorgrond een Heer en Dame te Paard, waar bij een arme Man om een Almoes vragende, verder Jagers met Honden, en in 't verschiet een Dorps-tooren; natuurlijk voorgesteld | *Mat:* op doek *Size:* hoog 46, breed 62 duim	[Coclers]	(Sold) fl 9:10 du Pree
809/04/22	AMYVR	0138	*E. van de Velde* | Een hevige Rencontre tusschen Cavallerie; vol vuur, en delicaat van uitvoering | *Mat:* op paneel *Size:* hoog 8, breed 10 duim	de Bruin	(Sold) fl 3:5 du Pree
809/05/26	HADAA	0062	*Esaias v.d. Velden* | Een Capitaal Landschap	Mejuffrouw de Wed David Heemskerk [or others]	(Unknown)
809/06/13	AMSCH	0185	*E van de Velde* | Een dito [Bosachtig] Landschap met Jagers, met hunne Honden, en Huislieden gestoffeerd	Y	(Sold) fl 4 du Pree
809/07/19	AMSCH	0059	*Velden (E. van den)* | Deze rijke zinspelende Ordonnantie vol gewoel, vertoont in een Landschap een Vorstelijk Persoon, zittende bij eene Tafel, als bezig een Kat de bel om den hals te binden, verder schijnt hij verzeld van Vorstelijken Staats en andere Lieden, ter zijde in 't verschiet ziet men het Binnenhof in s'Hage. Het is kragtig en meesterlijk fraai gepenceeld | *Mat:* op paneel *Size:* hoog 24, breed 39 ½ duim *Loc:* Amsterdam, Nederland. Rijksmuseum. (A 434) as manner of Adriaen Pietersz. van de Venne	[Bicker]	(Sold) fl 35 J Yver voor Z H den Koning
1810/05/22	AMSCH	0114	*Velde. (E. van de)* | Gezicht van een Dorp, met eenige Woningen aan een bevrozen Rivier, waarop wandelende Lieden en andere die Kolven, ter zijde eenige Vaartuigen; natuurlijk behandeld | *Mat:* op paneel *Size:* hoog 10, breed 14 duim	D	(Sold) fl 4 van Iperen
1810/06/20	AMSCH	0149	*E. van de Velde* | Een Land- en Watergezigt, met een overvarende Pontschuit	B	(Sold) fl 2 J de Vries
1810/06/20	AMSCH	0160	*E. van de Velde* | Twee stuks	B	(Sold) fl 0:14 Teerling
1810/07/23	DOLG1	0059	*Esaïas van de Velden* | Een Rencontre van eenig Paardevolk. Zeer goed van teekening | *Mat:* op paneel *Size:* hoog 13, breed 14 duim	Mr Pieter van den Santheuvel	(Sold) fl 8 van Eijk 's Hage
1810/07/23	DOLG2	0007	*E. van de Velde* | In een Boomrijk Landschap worden verbeeld Struikrovers, die eenige reizigers aanvallen. Meesterlijk gepenseeld | *Mat:* op doek *Size:* hoog 36, breed 47 duim	Pieter Quinting	(Sold or Bought In) fl 3 Quin van Dordt
1810/08/06	AMSCH	0139	*E. van de Velde* | Twee stuks, een Brabandsch Dorpgezigt, met onderscheidene stoffagie en een Landschap, met Heeren te Paard en een Koets op een Brug; beide kloek geschilderd	C	(Sold) fl 2:10 Stoopendaal [for] B
1810/12/03	DOBRA	0062	*E. van de Velde* | Een fraai Landschapje, door E. van de Velde, in een zwarten Lyst		(Unknown)

Velde, Esaias van de (I) (manner)

1802/06/28	AMSCH	0197	*E. van de Velde* | Een Land- en Watergezicht, in de manier van E. van de Velde	Anna Elink	(Sold) fl 1:5 Wennegers
1803/08/24	HGKAN	0037	*E. van de Velde* | Een dito [Lantschap] Ryk gestoffeerd met Dames, en Heeren te Paard met hunne lansen verbeeld een tournooy party als E. van de Velde | *Mat:* op doek	[Teissier] [or others]	(Sold) fl 0:16 van Kuyk
1805/10/09	HGBSM	0070	*E. van de Velde* | Een rencontre van cavallerie, in de trand van E. van de Velde | *Mat:* op paneel *Size:* hoog 18 ½ breet 24 ½ duim	T H van Willigen [or others]	(Sold) fl 1 Ph Mey

Velde, Jan van de (II)

1804/05/07	AMSCH	0186	*Velde. (J. van de)* | Een heevige Bataille tusschen de Ruitery; aller-natuurlykst en fraay gepenceeld | *Mat:* op paneel *Size:* hoog 9, breed 12 duim	Vinkeles [for] J	(Sold) fl 2:5 Mensart
1804/10/16	DLOND	0226	*J. van de Velde* | Een Landschap. Paysage | *Mat:* op paneel *Size:* hoog 16, breed 22		(Unknown)
1806/06/07	RMHSN	0083	*J. v. Velde* | Een goed Landschapje | *Mat:* op paneel	A E K L	(Unknown)
1806/10/22	HGBAK	0009	*J. van de Velde* | Twee Schilderytjen van J. van de Velde, verbeeldende de Zomer en Winter		(Unknown)
1810/03/27	RMCNL	0030	*J. van de Velde* | Een Zeehoorn, klein doch zeer aardig gepenceeld		(Unknown)

Velde, Jan van de (II) (or Velde, J. (II), manner)

1802/09/18	RMDRS	0071	*J. v. d. Velde* | Een Landschap, door of in de manier van J. v. d. Velde	Casper de Haas	(Unknown) fl 1:6

Velde, Peter van den

1803/07/07	HGKAN	0004	*P. van der Velde* | Twee Woelende Zeetjes, door P. van der Velde, op Paneel [Schilderyen in Olyverf] | *Mat:* in olyverf op paneel *Notes:* The bracketed information in the title appears above lot 1 and refers to lots 1 to 25.		(Unknown)
1803/08/17	AMSCH	0086	*Veldens (P. V.)* | Twee stuks woelende Waters, gestoffeerd met een menigte Vaartuigen, en stoffagie van Beeldjes, vol waarheid en uitvoerig behandeld | *Mat:* op paneel *Size:* ieder hoog 10, breed 16 duim	Anna Catharina Putman	(Sold) fl 6 Pruijssenaar

Velde, Willem van de

1801/04/08	HAVIN	0019	*van de Velden* | Twee woelende Waters, op een witte Grond extra uitvoerig		(Unknown)

1801/05/11	AMSCH	0091	*W. van de Velden* | Een angenaam [sic] stil Water gestoffeerd met verscheiden Oorlogscheepen, Roeyschuiten en andere Vaartuigen, alles dun en meesterlyk gepenceeld | *Mat:* op paneel *Size:* hoog 11, breed 13 duim	P[ruyssenaar]	(Sold) fl 225 Pruijssenaar [for] R
1801/05/11	AMSCH	0092	*W. van de Velden* | Een stil Water, op de voorgrond ziet men een ter anker leggend Beurtschip waar by een Roeyschuit, in 't verschiet een Oorlogschip en andere zeilende Vaartuigen, 't water is dun, en alles van de edelste penceelbehandeling | *Mat:* op paneel *Size:* hoog 14, breed 13 duim	E[lias]	(Sold) fl 305 Hulswit
1801/05/11	AMSCH	0093	*W. van de Velden* | Een stil Water met een zeylend Jacht, Oorlogschip en andere Vaartuigen: niet minder van schildering als de voorgaande | *Mat:* op paneel *Size:* hoog 15, breed 12 duim	E[lias]	(Sold) fl 42:10 Van Iperen
1801/05/11	AMSCH	0094	*W. van de Velden* | Een woelend Water, met een zeylend Beurtschip en andere Vaartuigen, meesterlyk behandeld | *Mat:* op paneel *Size:* hoog 10, breed 14 duim	P[ruyssenaar]	(Sold) fl 12:10 v der Vinne
1801/05/11	AMSCH	0095	*W. van de Velden* | Een stormende Zee met twee Oorlogscheepen, kragtig behandeld | *Mat:* op doek *Size:* hoog 14, breed 23 duim	P[ruyssenaar]	(Sold) fl 5:10 Wolft
1801/06/10	AMSCH	0166	*Velde. (W. van de)* | Een woelend Water, gestoffeerd met een menigte zeilende Oorlogschepen en andere Vaartuigen; dit Stuk is alleruitmuntendst van licht en dun van penceels behandeling | *Mat:* op doek *Size:* hoog 18, breed 23 duim	Herman ten Kate	(Sold) fl 306 de Roy
1801/06/10	AMSCH	0167	*Velde. (W. van de)* | Twee stuks, een stil en een woelend Water, beiden gestoffeerd met Oorlogschepen en andere Vaartuigen; alleruitvoerigst en delicaat gepenceeld | *Mat:* op paneel *Size:* yder hoog 9, breed 8 duim	Herman ten Kate	(Sold) fl 133 Pruyssenaar
1801/06/10	AMSCH	0168	*Velde. (W. van de)* | Een stormende Zee, ter rechter zyde ziet men een Oorlogschip, ter zyde een Beurtschip; de natuur, zo in water als in lucht zyn wel waargenomen en meesterlyk geschilderd | *Mat:* op paneel *Size:* hoog 33, breed 45 duim	Herman ten Kate	(Sold) fl 235 Coclers
1801/06/10	AMSCH	0169	*Velde. (W. van de)* | Een stil Water, met verscheide Schepen en Schuiten, de spiegeling in het Water maakt dit stukje helder en transpirent | *Mat:* op paneel *Size:* hoog 14, breed 17 duim	Herman ten Kate	(Sold) fl 600 Coclers
1801/06/10	AMSCH	0170	*Velde. (W. van de)* | Een stil Water, met zeilende en roeijende Vaartuigen; uitvoerig en meesterlyk behandeld | *Mat:* op doek op paneel *Size:* hoog 13, breed 16 duim	[Doublet]	(Sold) fl 18:10 Bauer
1801/08/19	AMSCH	0124	*W. van de Velde* | Een Zee-slag, ryk van Schepen; gearceerd door W. van de Velde | *Size:* hoog 24, breed 33 duim	Van Forreest	(Sold) fl 2:5 Roos
1801/08/19	AMSCH	0125	*W. van de Velde* | Een woelend Water met Oorlogschépen; krachtig en meesterlyk geschilderd	Pruyssen[r] [for] Q	(Bought In) fl 3
1801/10/19	AMSCH	0075	*Velde (W. van de) 1671* | Een kabbelend Watertje, ter rechter zyde twee Scheepen met Volk ten anker, die zig zeilree maken, ter linker zyde twee Mannen, die in het Water staan, om een Schuit vlot te krygen; in 't verschiet eenige zeilende Scheepen en een ten anker leggend Driemast-Schip; extra konstig, krachtig en natuurlyk behandeld | *Mat:* op doek *Size:* hoog 14 ½, breed 21 duim *Inscr:* 1671 (dated?) *Notes:* It is unclear whether the date is inscribed on the painting. *Loc:* London, England, UK. Royal Collection (Buckingham Palace) (1489)	Jonkheer Menno Baron van Coehoorn	(Sold) fl 500 A E Sterk
1801/10/19	AMSCH	0076	*Velde. (W. van de)* | Een aangenaam stil Water, met zeilende Oorlog- en andere Scheepen, op den voorgrond twee Visschers Schuiten met Volk, zeer dun en krachtig geschilderd | *Mat:* op paneel *Size:* hoog 8 ½, breed 11 ¾ duim	Jonkheer Menno Baron van Coehoorn	(Sold) fl 205 for lots 76 & 77. Pruijssenaar
1801/10/19	AMSCH	0077	*Velde. (W. van de)* | Een kabbelend Watertje, met Visschers in hunne Schuiten, een zeilend Jagt, en verder veele Vaartuigen; extra fraay van Effect en konst | *Mat:* op paneel *Size:* hoog 9, breed 12 ½ duim	Jonkheer Menno Baron van Coehoorn	(Sold) fl 205 for lots 76 & 77. Pruijssenaar
1801/10/19	AMSCH	0078	*Velden (W. van de)* | Een stil Water, met een twee Mast Engelsche Visschuit, in 't verschiet een Fregat en meer andere Vaartuigen, helder en aangenaam geschilderd | companion to lot 79 *Mat:* op paneel *Size:* hoog 8 ¾, breed 10 ½ duim	Jonkheer Menno Baron van Coehoorn	(Sold) fl 505 for lots 78 & 79. Coclers
1801/10/19	AMSCH	0079	*Velden (W. van de)* | Een dito [Water] tot een wederga, waar in men ziet twee Damloopers, benevens een Fregat en andere Vaartuigen; in 't verschiet; niet minder als de voorgaande | companion to lot 78 *Mat:* op paneel *Size:* hoog 8 ¾, breed 10 ½ duim	Jonkheer Menno Baron van Coehoorn	(Sold) fl 505 for lots 78 & 79. Coclers
1801/11/10	AMPOS	0019	*W. van de Velden* | 1 dito [Landschap], met een Reiziger te Paard, spreekende met een Vrouw, als door dezelven [W. van de Velden] | *Notes:* It is unclear what "dito" refers to in the title.		(Unknown)
1802/02/23	AMREB	0029	*W. van de Velde* | 1 kabbelend Water, met verscheide Vaartuigen in 't graauw	Margaretha Maria van Laar	(Sold) fl 2:10 L Pakker
1802/05/05	AMSCH	0209	*W. van de Velde* | Een stil Water, met een Koopvaarder en andere Scheepen en Schuiten, in het verschiet een Oorlogschip, alles spiegelende in het dunne heldere Water, en is van een aangenaame penceels-behandeling | *Mat:* op paneel *Size:* hoog 16, breed 19 duim	A	(Sold) fl 22 Auber
1803/07/18	AMSCH	0057	*Velde. (W. van de)* | Een Strandgezicht, ter regterzyde op de voorgrond zit een Visser op een Boomstam, met een ander praatende, waarby een Hond, wat verder een Sloep en eenige Beelden, verder eenige Pinken en andere	Maria Theresia Andrioli	(Sold) fl 400 Josi

			Schepen, zynde het kabbelende water dun en transparant, zoo ook de lugt die mede meesterlyk geschilderd is [Ce tableau excellent offre une côte de mer de la hollande ou des barques de pêcheurs viennent aborder. Un homme assis sur des blocs de bois est sur la côte, parlant à un autre accompagné d'un chien ; à sa droite est une chaloupe à sec, un homme à cheval & autres figures. De la barque qui est à peu distanée [sic] de terre l'on voit apporter des charges à gué sur la côté, les bateliers étant occupés sur le pont & autour du navire. A des distances plus ou moins reculées, la mer est garnie de barques poissonieres, jusques à l'horison ou le ciel s'unit. La mer agitée repond à l'air chargé de nuages épais au declin du jour, offrant un spectacle aussi naturel que bien exprimé. La delicatesse de pinceau, qui est repandue dans tout ce morceau est exime [sic], les figures surtout en sont admirables.] | *Mat:* op doek *Size:* hoog 17, breed 21 duim		
1803/08/01	AMSCH	0040	*Van de Velde. (W.)* | Een stil Water, men ziet op de voorgrond ter linkerzyde een Hooft van Paalwerk, waarby twee Vishoekers leggen, en ter regterzyde wat verder, vertoond zig een Hollands Oorlogschip ten anker, en in 't verschiet meerder Oorlogscheepen of Fregatten, voorts beschouwt men een Oorlogssloep, een Boot en andere Vaartuigen, dit capitaal stuk is zonachtig, helder en uitvoerig van qualiteit, en van eene delicate en uitvoerige penceelsbehandeling | *Mat:* op doek *Size:* hoog 28, breed 34 duim	H	(Sold) fl 1525 J Spaan
1803/08/01	AMSCH	0041	*Van de Velde. (W.)* | Een kabbelend Water, met eenige zeilende en ten Anker leggende Oorlog- en andere Scheepen, Pinken en Sloepen, ter linkerzyde een Strandgezicht, op het welke men een Wagen met twee Paarden en een menigte Beeldjes gewaar word, het is aangenaam van zonlicht, gepaard met een lieflyke penceelsbehandeling | *Mat:* op doek *Size:* hoog 21, breed 25 duim	C	(Bought In) fl 575
1803/08/01	AMSCH	0042	*Van de Velde. (W.)* | Een kabbelend Watertje, met een zeilend Jagt en eenige ten Anker leggende Oorlogscheepen, op de voorgrond een Sloep met eenige Bootslieden, uitvoerig en fraay gepenceeld | *Mat:* op paneel *Size:* hoog 8, breed 10 duim	J	(Sold) fl 17 Pruijssenaar [for] O
1803/08/17	AMSCH	0083	*Velde (W. van de)* | Een stil Water, met verscheide Oorlog en andere Schepen, gestoffeerd met Beeldjes, het Water is dun, en is wyders van een lieflyk coloriet en uitvoerige behandeling | *Mat:* op paneel *Size:* hoog 7, breed 9 ½ duim	Anna Catharina Putman	(Sold) fl 12 Agina
1803/08/24	HGKAN	0062	*W. V. Develden* | Twee stuks een Stil en een Woelend Water	[Teissier] [or others]	(Sold) fl 20 Uyttenbogerd
1803/09/07	AMSCH	0191	*W. v. d. Velde* | Twee stuks woelende Waters met verscheide zeilende Scheepen en andere Vaartuigen; uitvoerig en delicaat gepenceeld [Deux marines ; toutes deux représentant l'agitation des ondes, sur lesquelles voguent des navires de differentes espèces ; d'un fini et d'une délicatesse admirables] | *Mat:* op paneel *Size:* hoog 7 ½, breed 10 duim	Smidt	(Sold) fl 14 C S Roos
1803/12/12	AMSCH	0099	*W. van de Velde* | Een Zee-Gezigt, ter regter zyde op de voorgrond zyn twee Chaloepen op elkander vuurende, waar nevens een Oorlogschip in vollen brand, aan de linker zyde meer agterwaards ziet men nog een groot Oorlogschip en andere Oorlogsvaartuigen; alles van een meesterlyke en aangename penceelsbehandeling | *Mat:* op doek *Size:* hoog 19, breed 26 duim	Arnoud de Lange	(Sold) fl 235 Jozi
1803/12/12	AMSCH	0100	*W. van de Velde* | Een aangenaame woelende Zee, met een menigte van zeilende Scheepen; frapant van licht en bevallig geschilderd op Paneel | *Mat:* op paneel *Size:* hoog 15, breed 19 duim	B	(Sold) fl 25 for lots 100 & 101. W[l] Reijers
1803/12/12	AMSCH	0101	*W. van de Velde* | Een sterk stormende Zee, waarop zig eenige Scheepen in gevaar bevinden van tegen de Klippen verbryzelt te zullen worden; niet minder als de voorgaande	B	(Sold) fl 25 for lots 100 & 101. W[l] Reijers
1804/08/08	AMSCH	0188	*W. van de Velde* | Een Haven met Paalwerk, waarin een Schip in de Branding, verders eenige andere Scheepen, op de voorgrond een Jolletje met Roeijers, welke zich haasten voor het opkomend Onweder; verbazend is de lucht, en de behandeling meesterlyk | *Mat:* op doek *Size:* hoog 12, breed 18 duim	Roos a	(Sold) fl 32 Gruyter
1804/08/08	AMSCH	0189	*W. van de Velde* | In een stille Zée ziet men by eenig Land twee zeilende Vaartuigen, waar achter een Oorlogschip, welke het Geschut lost, verders eenige andere Scheepen en Schuiten; de spiegeling in 't Water is fraai, en hetzelve is uitmuntend van schildering | *Mat:* op paneel *Size:* hoog 13, breed 19 duim	Vink[eles] [for] S	(Sold) fl 47 Jan Spaan
1804/08/08	AMSCH	0190	*W. van de Velde* | Deze fraaije Ordinantie vertoond een stil Water, ryk gestoffeerd met dryvende Oorlogschéepen, Beurtlieden, Visschers in Schuiten, en andere Vaartuigen, in 't verschiet een Dorpgezicht; alles helder, zonachtig, en van een uitvoerig penceelbehandeling | *Mat:* op doek *Size:* hoog 20, breed 25 duim	Schley [for] A	(Sold) fl 300 Gruyter
1804/08/08	AMSCH	0191	*W. van de Velde* | Een aangenaam woelend Water, met zeilende Scheepen en andere Vaartuigen; het Water is dun en de behandeling zeer fraai | *Mat:* op doek *Size:* hoog 8 ½, breed 10 duim	Roos a	(Sold) fl 57 Gruyter
1804/08/08	AMSCH	0192	*W. van de Velde* | Een stil Water, mede met verscheide Vaartuigen, en behandeld als de voorgaande | *Mat:* op doek *Size:* hoog 13, breed 16 duim	Roos a	(Sold) fl 13 Gruyter

1804/10/29	HRBAU	0105	*Velde (Willem van de)* | Voor aan, op dit bevallig stil Watertjen, is een Jagt en Kaag, welke by elkander aan boord dryvende zyn; wat verder is een Zandbank, alwaar drie Visschers liggen, en in het verschiet Oorlogschepen en andere Vaartuigen. Zeer helder, delicaat en uitvoerig behandeld | *Mat:* op paneel *Size:* hoog 11, breed 14 ½ duim	Simon Styl	(Unknown)
1804/10/29	HRBAU	0106	*Velde, (Willem van de)* | Op den Voorgrond, tusschen de Steenklippen, waar eene zwaare Branding staat, ziet men twee Driemasten, in het uiterste gevaar, voor hun anker liggen; waar agter een rotsagtig verschiet. Alles als 't voorige behandeld | *Mat:* op paneel *Size:* hoog 11, breed 14 ½ duim	Simon Styl	(Unknown)
1805/07/10	AMSCH	0161	*W. van de Velde* | Een Strandgezicht, vol gewoel; en meesterlyk geordineert | *Mat:* op paneel *Size:* hoog 12, breed 10 duim	V[inkeles] [for] J	(Sold) fl 1:5 Gruyter
1806/08/13	AMSCH	0189	*Velde. (W. van de)* | Dit bevallig Schilderstuk, steld voor, een stil Zeegezicht, tusschen de Helder en Texel, voor aan zyn twee Visschers Vaartuigen en een kleinder Scheepje, alle in hunne zylen van onderschelden couleur [sic], welk de voornaamste groep uitmaken; verders ziet men verscheide driemast Scheepen, en anderen Vaartuigen, welke het verryken; het Water en de Lucht zyn uitmuntend geschilderd, en maken te zamen door de daar in heerschende helderheid het tot een der beste Schilderyen van deeze groote Meester | *Mat:* op paneel *Size:* hoog 12, breed 16 duim	van der Schley	(Sold) fl 200 Schumacher
1808/04/26	GDAN	0169	*Velde (Willem v. de)* | Een Zee gezigtje, met zeilende Oorlogschepen en bijwerk, in 't graauw, goed geschilderd | *Size:* hoog 20, breed 27 duim	G H Fortuyn	(Unknown)
1808/04/26	GDAN	0170	*Velde (Willem v. de)* | Een woelende Zee, met eenige zeilende Scheepjes, dun en eel geschilderd | *Mat:* op paneel *Size:* hoog 13 ½, breed 16 duim	G H Fortuyn	(Unknown)
1808/04/26	GDAN	0171	*Velde (Willem v. de)* | Zijnde een buiägtige Lucht, waar een Onweder schijnt op te komen, en een woelende Zee, waar op een Sysebom, die 't Zeil voor het weer gestreken wordt, in 't verschiet een zeilende Schoender, en eenige andere Vaartuigjes, zeer konstig en uitvoerig behandeld | *Size:* hoog 10, breed 13 duim	G H Fortuyn	(Unknown)
1808/04/26	GDAN	0172	*Velde (Willem v. de)* | Een buijägtige Lucht, waar door een woelige Zee, verbeeldende het Y voor Amsterdam, waar op men Oorlog en Koopvaardijschepen ziet zeilen en laveeren, in 't verschiet een aantal kleindere Vaartuigen, en de Stad Amsterdam in al deszelfs lengte, de Regen strepen in de lucht zijn schoon, en het geheele stuk meesterlijk | *Mat:* op doek	G H Fortuyn	(Unknown)
1808/05/18	LNAN	0021	*W: van der Velde* | Een extra konstig stil Watergezigt met Schepen | *Notes:* The artist's name "W: van der Velde" was added in by hand in the RKDH copy of the catalogue.	Mr Cornelis Versluys	(Unknown)
1808/06/06	RMRIJ	0133	*Velde. (Willem van den)* | Dit schoon Tafereel vertoont het strijken der Vlag, en de overgave van het Engelsch Admiraalschip the Royale Prince, gevoerd door den Ridder George Askue, Admiraal van het Esquader der Witte Vlag, en welk groot en schoon Schip gedurende het gevecht vast geraakte op de Zandbank genaamd de Galpert. Men ziet het Engelsch Scheepsvolk, schoon reeds gevangen, op verschillende plaatsen de Geschutpoorten van gemelde Schip inkruipen. Wijders Oorlogschepen, benevens een klein Vaartuig, waarin zich de beroemde Scheepsschilder, Willen van den Velde, op dien tijd in de Vloot liet rond voeren, om alles van nabij te zien, en naar waarheid te kunnen afteekenen. Het bovengemelde gebeurde op den 13 Junij 1666, zijnde de derde dag van den roemrijken Zeeslag tusschen den Luitenant Admiraal van Holland en Westvriesland, Hertog en Ridder Michiel Adriaansz. de Ruiter, en de Engelsche Vloot onder het opperbevel van den Generaal Monk, Hertog van Albemarle, voorgevallen. Eene wedergade, en vervolg van de voorgaande Schilderij, voorstellende het opbrengen der vier veroverde Engelsche Oorlogschepen, als the Swifture gevoerd geweest door Ridder William Barclay, Vice-Admiraal der Witte Vlag, de Zevenwolden, de Getrouwe George en de Convertine. Alle gevoerd wordende naar het zoogenaamde Goereesche gat. Verder ziet men eene menigte zeilende Schepen. – In beide deze Tafereelen is alles, wat tot de Schepen behoort, juist geteekend, de lucht en het water helder, uitvoerig en zoo schoon geschilderd, dat zij beide met regt genoemd kunnen worden als de allerbeste bekende stukken van dezen in dit vak zoo hoog geroemden Schilder. N.B. Men zie, wegens den Zeeslag en het opbrengen der Schepen in de Goede Reede, door de voorgemelde stukken vertoond, eene volledige beschrijving in de folio uitgave van het Leven van M. A. de Ruiter door Gerard Brandt op pag. 488 en 496 [Ce Magnifique Tableau represente la prise du Vaisseau Anglais the Royal Prince, commandé par le Chevalier George Askue, Amiral du Pavillon Blanc, au moment qu'il baisse son Pavillon, et que les matelots Hollandais en prennent possession. Ce beau Bâtiment avoit touché, pendant l'action, sur un banc de Sable appellé le Galpert. On apperçoit d'autres vaisseaux de guerre, et un petit Bâtiment, dans lequel le célébre Peintre Guillaume van den Velde se fit conduire, à cette Epoque, sur le lieu, afin d'y tracer ses Esquisses d'après nature. Cet Evénement eut lieu le 13 Juin 1666, le 3me jour de la Bataille mémorable et glorieuse, livrée par le Lieutenant Amiral de Hollande et Westfrise, Duc et Chevalier M.A. de Ruyter contre la flotte Anglaise commandée par l'Amiral Monk Duc d'Albemarle. Le	Gerrit van der Pot, Heer van Groeneveld	(Sold) fl 8000 J J de Wit [for] le Roi

			Pendant qui fait suite au précédent, represente quatre vaisseaux de guerre Anglais amenés au Port de Goeree, savoir : the Swifture commandé par le Chevalier William Barclay Vice Amiral du pavillon Blanc, de Zevenwolden, de Getrouwe George, et Convertine. Ces deux Morceaux si renommés sont considerés par les Connoisseurs, comme les Productions les plus interessantes de ce célèbre Artiste. N.B. On trouve les particularités de cette action Mémorable dans la Vie de l'Amiral de Ruyter par G. Brandt, Edition Hollandaise in folio pag. 488 et 496] | *Mat:* op doek *Size:* Twee Stukken. Hoog 21 ½, en breed 30 ¼ duim *Loc:* Amsterdam, Nederland. Rijksmuseum. (A438 & A439)		
1809/05/26	HADAA	0001	*W. van der Velden* | Een woelend Water met verscheide Schepen, op den voorgrond een Schuit, waarin men bezig is netten op te halen, breed van Licht en meesterachtig	Mejuffrouw de Wed David Heemskerk [or others]	(Unknown)
1809/07/19	AMSCH	0058	*Velden (Willem van den)* | Een stil Water, met verschillende Vaartuigen, waarvan 'er met volle en gestrekene Zeilen zich vertonen, in het midden ziet men eene Boot met Gezelschap, van of naar een der Schepen roeijende, en ter zijde een Hollandsch Jagt, met loshangende Zeilen; voorts zijn de Vaartuigen rijk gestoffeerd met Beelden. Dit stuk is zeer helder en zeer uitvoerig behandeld | *Size:* hoog 15 ¼, breed 21 ¼ duim	F	(Sold) fl 170 Bredius
1809/07/25	HGBSM	0249	*W. van de Velde* | Een Zee met Oorlogscheepen, in 't grauw | *Mat:* op paneel *Size:* hoog 13, breed 16 en een half duim	D van der Aa [or] E B ten Dall	(Sold) fl 1 De Gelder
1809/09/06	AMSCH	0076	*Velde (W. van de)* | Een alleraangenaamst stil Water, gestoffeerd op de voorgrond met verscheide Beeldjes, Scheepen en andere Vaartuigen; dun en uitvoerig van penceelsbehandeling | *Mat:* op doek *Size:* hoog 13, breed 14 duim	Johannes Caudri	(Sold) fl 101 Gruyter
1810/03/26	RMMUY	0032	*Willem van de velde* | Een onstuimig Water, bij het opkomen van een Omweersbuij. Op den voorgrond ziet men een Lootsboot, bezig haar fok te strijken; wat verder een Oorlogschip met volle zeilen aansnellen. Een dito legt ten anker. Aan den horizont ziet men nog eenige Schepen. Het stuiven en zwalpen van het water, de ontzettende lucht, en alle de voorwerpen zijn verstandig, natuurlijk, en zeer konstig verbeeld [Une Mer agitée à l'approche d'un orage ; à l'embouchure d'un port de Hollande on voit au milieu une barque de pilote, occupée à baisser une de ses voiles ; plus loin, un batiment de guerre en pleines voiles ; un second est à l'ancre et plusieurs autres se distinguent à l'horizon. L'effet de l'eau et du ciel contraste supérieurement, et forme un brillant effet. Le tout bien étudié et le plus artistement traité.] | *Mat:* op doek *Size:* hoog 12 ¾, breed 14 ¾ duimen *Loc:* London, England, UK. National Gallery. (876)	Daniel de Jongh Az	(Sold) fl 300 Le Brun Parys
1810/08/01	AMSCH	0108	*Velde (Willem van de)* | Eene ruime en stille Zee, waar op onderscheidene Schepen, Jagten, Boten, Sloepen en verdere Vaartuigen [Vue de la pleine Mer au grand calme, garnie de Vaisseaux de toute construction, et de differentes Chaloupes] | *Annots:* Passable. (NGW) *Mat:* op doek *Size:* hoog 27, breed 38 duimen *Loc:* London, England, UK. Royal Collection (Windsor Castle) Inv.3223. (?)	Mr Pieter de Smeth van Alphen	(Sold) fl 3000 Reyers voor La Fontaine
1810/08/01	AMSCH	0109	*Velde (Willem van)* | Een kabbelend Water, met twee zeilende Kagen en andere Vaartuigen [Une Mer agitée, où l'on voit deux Cagues sous voiles, et plusieurs autres Navires] | *Annots:* fort médiocre. (NGW) *Mat:* op paneel *Size:* hoog 11, breed 14 duimen	Mr Pieter de Smeth van Alphen	(Sold) fl 200 T Spaan voor LaFontaine
1810/10/10	MGCIT	0035	*W. van de Velde* | Een fraai Schilderij, zijnde een woelende Zee, met eenige Schepen en een afgelegen Stad in het verschiet, natuurlijk en helder behandeld	Caspar van Citters	(Unknown)
			Velde, Willem van de (or Velde, W., manner)		
1801/06/10	AMSCH	0171	*Velde. (W. van de), of in de manier* | Twee stuks onstuimige Waters, met Scheegestoffeerd [sic] | *Mat:* op doek op paneel *Size:* yder hoog 13, breed 18 duim	[Doublet]	(Sold) fl 20 Gruyter
1804/10/16	DLOND	0310	*Van, of geheel in de Manier van W. van de Velde* | Vyf Oorlogschepen voor Vlissingen, onder welken het Schip Delft van den Admiraal de Ruyter. Cincq [sic] Navires de Guerre devant Flessingue, entre elles le Vaisseau Delft de l'Amiral de Ruyter | *Mat:* op doek *Size:* hoog 41, breed 51		(Unknown)
1810/03/23	HAVIN	0011	*W. v. d. Velde* | Een stil en aangenaame Zee, in het verschiet eenige Scheepen, en op strand verscheide vissers Pinken, helder en plaisant van of in de manier van W. v. d. Velde | *Size:* hoog 15 breet 28 d.	Rudolf Hendrik de Wetstein [or others]	(Unknown) fl 10:5
			Velde, Willem van de (copy after)		
1802/12/13	AMSCH	0146	*A. Storck; Willem van de Velde* | Een Batailje op Zée; na Willem van de Velde, door A. Storck | copy by Abr. Storck after W. Velde *Mat:* op doek *Size:* hoog 24, breed 34 duim	Pruyssenaar [for] A	(Sold) fl 0:10 L Pakker
1803/07/14	MGKLY	0025	*Na W.V. de Velde* | Een stil en woelend Water ryk gestoffeert met Scheepen, en goed geschilderd	Mr Caspar Jacob van Citters	(Unknown)
1803/07/14	MGKLY	0026	*Na W.V. de Velde* | Een dito woelend Water met Scheepen | *Notes:* It is unclear what "dito" refers to in the title.	Mr Caspar Jacob van Citters	(Unknown)
1804/04/25	HGBES	0014	*W. van de Velde* | Een Watergezicht na W. van de Velde | *Notes:* It is uncertain whether this lot is a painting.		(Unknown)

1805/12/16	AMSCH	0021	*J. Ekels; W. van de Velde* | Twee stuks woelende Zeegezichten, met zylende Oorlogscheepen, en Vissers Vaartuigen; uitvoerig behandeld door J. Ekels, naar W. van de Velde | copy by Jan Ekels (I) after W. Velde *Size:* yder hoog 9, breed 13 duim	R[oos]	(Sold) fl 2:5 L Pakker
1805/12/16	AMSCH	0022	*J. Ekels; W. van de Velde* | Twee stuks stille Zeegezichten, aan Strand, gestoffeerd met verscheide Vissers Scheepen, en andere Vaartuigen; bevallig geschilderd, op paneel, door dito [J. Ekels], naar dito [W. van de Velde] | copy by Jan Ekels (I) after W. Velde *Mat:* op paneel *Size:* yder hoog 11, breed 15 duim	R[oos]	(Sold) fl 3 T van Iperen
1806/08/13	AMSCH	0282	*W. van de Velde* | Twee stuks, een woelend en een kabbelend Water met Scheepen en Schuiten, na W. van de Velde	Roos	(Sold) fl 3:5 Yver
1809/04/22	AMYVR	0196	*W. v.d. Velde* | Een stil Water met Schepen; naar W. v.d. Velde	de Bruin	(Sold) fl 1:10 van Iperen

Velde, Willem van de (manner)

1801/10/06	AMSCH	0098	*W. van de Velde* | Twee stuks, een stil en een woelend Water, gestoffeerd met verscheide Scheepen en Schuyten, op Doek, in de manier van W. van de Velde | *Mat:* op doek *Size:* yder hoog 13, breed 16 duim	M	(Sold) fl 14:10 Coclers
1801/11/10	AMPOS	0018	*W. van de Velden* | 1 vallende Waterstroom in een Bergachtig Landschap, gestoffeerd met rustende Reizigers, als door W. van de Velden		(Unknown)
1804/05/07	AMSCH	0207	*W. van de Velde* | Een Onstuimige Zee, met een ménigte van zylende en stilleggende Scheepen en Vaartuigen enz.; fiks, in de manier van W. van de Velde	Roos [for] A	(Sold) fl 7 Coclers
1804/12/10	AMSCH	0113	*W. v. de Velde* | Een dito [woelen Water], op de voorgrond een beurtschip en andere vaartuigen, in de manier van W. v. de Velde | *Mat:* op paneel *Size:* hoog 19, breed 25 duim	Jan De Groot	(Sold) fl 19 Coclers
1805/07/10	AMSCH	0276	*van de Velde* | Een stil Watertje, met Scheepjes; als van de Velde	V[inkeles] [for] K	(Bought In) fl 4
1805/07/10	AMSCH	0284	*W. van de Velde* | Een Onstuimige Zee, met een ménigte Scheepen, in de manier van W. van de Velde	V[inkeles] [for] L	(Bought In) fl 0:16
1807/08/26	AMSCH	0228	*W. van de Velden* | Eene onstuimige Zee met eenige Schepen, die in gevaar schynen te zyn; in de manier van W. van de Velden | *Mat:* op doek *Size:* hoog 18, breed 25 duim	de Vries	(Sold) fl 2:5 Coclair
1807/08/26	AMSCH	0340	*W. van de Velde* | Een woelende Zee; in de manier van W. van de Velde	de Vries	(Sold) fl 1:5 du Pree
1808/04/26	GDAN	0279	*van de Velde* | In de manier van van de Velde, een fraai Watergezigtje met zeilende en leggende Scheepjes | *Size:* hoog 12, breed 14 duim	G H Fortuyn	(Unknown)
1808/08/23	AMSCH	0264	*W. van de Velde* | Een stil Water met verscheide drijvende en stilleggende Vaartuigen, op de voorgrond een Hooft, en eenige Beeldjes; fiks in de manier van W. van de Velde	[Van Iperen?]	(Sold) fl 6:15 Boelen
1809/06/13	AMSCH	0202	*W. van de Velde* | Een Strandgezigt, op de voorgrond verscheide Beeldjes, Visschers Pinken en zeilende Vaartuigen in het verschiet; dun van behandeling, in de manier van W. van de Velde | *Mat:* op paneel	Q	(Bought In) fl 12

Velde, Willem van de (I)

1801/10/19	AMSCH	0074	*Velde (W. van de) 1644* | Een stil Water met een Jagt, op de voorgrond ryk gestoffeerd met diversche soorten van Scheepen, Sloepen en andere Vaartuigen, zonachtig, uitvoerig en aangenaam geschilderd | *Mat:* op doek *Size:* hoog 21, breed 24 duim *Inscr:* 1644 (dated?) *Notes:* It is unclear whether the date is inscribed on the painting.	Jonkheer Menno Baron van Coehoorn	(Sold) fl 530 A E Sterk
1802/07/21	HGKAN	0074	*van de Velde den Ouden* | Een Kabbelend Water twee extra fraay geteekende Oorlogscheepen, door van de Velde den Ouden, zwarte Lyst		(Unknown)

Venne, Adriaen Pietersz. van de

1802/09/21	UTHDG	0093	*A. van der Venne* | Een Landschap, gestoffeerd met een Wagen, omvallende in het water met alle de Passagiers, geestig geschildert | *Mat:* op paneel		(Sold) fl 2 De Munnick
1803/08/17	AMSCH	0087	*Venne (A. van der)* | Twee stuks Zinnebeelden, het eene op Arremoede en het andere op de Rykdom zinspelende, geestig en uitvoerig behandeld | *Mat:* op paneel *Size:* ieder hoog 25, breed 20 duim	Anna Catharina Putman	(Sold) fl 5:5 Yver
1803/12/12	AMSCH	0131	*van der Venne* | Twee stuks, zinspélende op de Weelde en Armoede; door van der Venus | *Mat:* op paneel *Size:* hoog 21, breed 17 duim	E	(Sold) fl 6 Salcedo
1805/07/03	AMSCH	0157	*J. van der Venne* | Twee stuks Zinnebeeldige Ordinantien, voorstellende Rykdom en Armoede; beide breed en meesterlyk op Paneel | *Mat:* op paneel *Size:* hoog 25, breed 20 ½ duim *Notes:* The artist's name was given as "J. van der Venne" but we have assumed this is an error.	S	(Sold) fl 4:5 L Pakker
1807/08/26	AMSCH	0221	*A. van der Vinne* | Dit voorwerp, zynde een ryke Ordonnantie, vol gewoel van een menigte Lieden, zoo te Paard als te voet, verbeeld de Ryswyker Kermis, waardoor de Koning en Koningin van Bohemen, vergezeld van Prins Maurits en Frederik Hendrik, op een prachtige Wagen, met zes Paarden bespannen, ryden, onder de toevloed van een menigte aanschouwers, verders het bevallig Dorpgezicht met de Kerk en verdere Woningen; ongemeen uitvoerig op Paneel geschilderd | *Mat:* op paneel *Size:* hoog 22, breed 52 duim	Helsdinge	(Bought In) fl 17

1810/07/23	DOLG2	0077	*A. van der Vinnen* | Een Schilderij, vertonende een dans van kreupele Bedelaars; in 't graauw geschilderd | *Mat:* op paneel *Size:* hoog 14, breed 11 duim	Pieter Quinting	(Unknown)
			Venne, Pieter van de		
1802/05/11	GRGRW	0025	*P. van der Venne* | Ene Onstuimige Zee [Schilderijen met Olie-Verf; In zwarte Lijsten] | companion to lot 26, by Anonymous *Mat:* in olyverf *Notes:* The bracketed information in the title appears above lot 1 and refers to lots 1 to 79a.	Arnold Sicco Werumeus	(Unknown)
			Verbeeck, Pieter Cornelisz.		
1801/03/16	AMSCH	0070	*P. Verbeek* | Een Landschap met Paarden gestoffeerd	P[ruyssenaar]	(Sold) fl 4 Valentijn
1801/08/19	AMSCH	0127	*P. Verbeek* | Twee Landschapjes, in het eene een Bruinen in het andere een Bont Paard	Pruyssen[r] [for] Q	(Sold) fl 10 V[n] Dijl
1801/08/19	AMSCH	0128	*P. Verbeek* | In een Landschap, onder Geboomte ziet men een Gezelschap van Dames en Heeren van de Jagt komende, zig by een Fontyn Verfrissen; fix geschilderd op Doek | *Mat:* op doek *Size:* hoog 34, breed 36 duim	W Wynen	(Sold) fl 15:10 Coclers
1801/08/19	AMSCH	0129	*P. Verbeek* | Een Landschap met een Paard en een Hond; fix behandeld	Pruyssen[r] [for] Q	(Sold) fl 5:5 Gruiter
1802/02/16	AMSCH	0040	*P. Verbeek* | Een Heevige Schermutzeling, tusschen Ruytery in een Heuvelachtig Landschap, meesterlyk gepenceeldt door P. Verbeek, in de manier van Ph: Wouwerman	G	(Sold) fl 10 Coclers
1802/05/05	AMSCH	0227	*P. Verbeek* | Twee Landschapjes, met een bruin en een bont Paard, fiks gepenceeld | *Size:* hoog 8 ½, breed 8 ½ duim	J	(Sold) fl 8 v d Schleij [for] Rijfsnijder
1802/06/16	AMSCH	0198	*P. Verbeek* | In een Rots-Gezicht, vertoond zich een Jager een wit gezadeld Paard by den toom vasthoudende, staande by een Waterput, op de voorgrond is een Hond; meesterlyk van penceel-behandeling | *Mat:* op paneel *Size:* hoog 13, breed 11 duim	[Merrem]	(Sold) fl 10 LaFontaine
1804/08/08	AMSCH	0211	*P. Verbeek* | In een Italiaansch Landschap ziet men by een Ruïne van een oude Poort een belaaden Ezel, Landman en Hond; zonachtig en fiks | *Mat:* op paneel *Size:* hoog 7, breed 9 ½ duim	Vink[eles] [for] W	(Sold) fl 2:10 Van Iperen
1805/12/16	AMSCH	0056	*P. Verbeek* | Aan een Strand, ziet men verscheide Vissers Paarden en Rytuigen; kragtig op Kooper | *Mat:* op koper *Size:* hoog en breed 10 duim	R[oos]	(Sold) fl 3:15 T van Iperen
1806/08/20	HGBSM	0207	*Verbeek* | Een drinkend Paard, waarop een man zit, benevens een hond, en verders een aangenaam Landschap, door Verbeek, meester van Ph. Wouwerman | *Mat:* op paneel *Size:* hoog 9 ¾, breed 9 duim	Macalester Loup [or others]	(Sold) fl 47 Nieuwenhuis
1806/11/24	AMSCH	0079	*Verbeek (P.)* | Een heevig gevecht van Ruitery, tusschen Turkea [sic] en Tartaaren; vol gewoel, en van eene uitvoerige behandeling | *Mat:* op paneel *Size:* hoog 13, breed 17 duim	Munnikhuizen	(Sold) fl 18 [or] 11 L Pakker
1807/08/26	AMSCH	0332	*P Verbeek* | Een heuvelachtig Landschap, waarin twee Huislieden te Paard, verder badende Lieden; fiks geschilderd | *Mat:* op paneel	v d Schley [for] L	(Sold) fl 11 Coclair
1808/06/06	RMRIJ	0134[a]	*Verbeek. (Pieter)* | Een wit Paard en rustend Ruiter in een bergachtig Landschap. Edel geschilderd. [La Première. Un Cheval blanc, et un Cavalier à terre. Peint avec finesse] | companion to lot 134[b] *Annots:* Verk. C. Groeninx[?] Rotterdam 25 Juni 1800 (14.-10)(als P. Wouwerman) (RMA I) *Mat:* op paneel *Size:* Hoog 5, en breed 4 ¼ duim	Gerrit van der Pot, Heer van Groeneveld	(Sold) fl 41 for lots 134[a] & 134[b]. van Yperen
1808/06/06	RMRIJ	0134[b]	*Verbeek. (Pieter)* | Eene wederga. Een zittend Man in eene slapende houding; naast hem twee liggende Honden in een Landschap. Vol verdiensten, als boven [La Seconde. Un Chasseur endormi, et deux chiens couchés auprès de lui. Du même mérite que la précédente] | companion to lot 134[a] *Annots:* Verk. C. Groeninx[?] Rotterdam 25 Juni 1800 (14.-10)(als P. Wouwerman) (RMA I) *Mat:* op paneel *Size:* Hoog 5 ½, en breed 4 ½ duim	Gerrit van der Pot, Heer van Groeneveld	(Sold) fl 41 for lots 134[a] & 134[b]. van Yperen
1809/06/13	AMSCH	0157	*P. Verbeek* | Twee stuks Duinachtige Landschapjes, het eene met een wit Paard en een rustend Ruiter, het andere met een zittend Man, in eene Slapende houding, naast hem twee liggende Honden; vol verdiensten en edel geschilderd | *Mat:* op paneel *Size:* hoog 5, breed 4 ½ duim	A	(Sold) fl 26:10 van Iperen
1809/06/13	AMSCH	0158	*P. Verbeek* | Voor een open Stal staat een Jongen, houdende een wit gezadeld Paard bij den Toom, ter zijde een ander Jongeling, welke een Paard laat Drinken; meesterlijk | *Mat:* op paneel *Size:* hoog 10, breed 15 duim	T	(Sold) fl 60 R[emmers] Bredius
1810/03/27	RMCNL	0029	*P. Verbeek* | Een Landschap, waarop men een wit Paard aan de hand geleid ziet, warm en fraai behandeld		(Unknown)
1810/03/27	RMCNL	0041	*Verbeek* | Een Bergachtig Landschap, met een aantal Paarden en Honden, zeer fraai behandeld		(Unknown)
1810/03/27	RMCNL	0052	*Verbeek* | Een Landschap waar op een wit Paard, fix geschilderd		(Unknown)
1810/03/27	RMCNL	0053	*Verbeek* | Een Kinderschooltje, waarin men eene meenigte Jongens onder elkander ziet lezende, speelende, enz. alles in vol gewoel		(Unknown)
1810/10/10	MGCIT	0066	*P. Verbeek* | Een Schildery, vertonende allerhande soort van Visch: als Kabellauw [sic], Tarbot, Rog, Zalm, Oesters, Mosselen, liggende op een steene Tafel, in een Nis geplaatst; terwyl boven dezelve aan een Touw een Karper hangd; alles natuurlyk en naar kunst uitgevoerd	Caspar van Citters	(Unknown)

			Verbeeck, Pieter Cornelisz. (manner)		
1807/08/26	AMSCH	0338	*P. Verbeek* | Twee gezadelde Paarden voor een Boeren Woning; als P. Verbeek	de Vries	(Sold) fl 0:14 Levij Pakker
			Verboom, Adriaen Hendricksz.		
1801/08/19	AMSCH	0126	*A. Verboom* | By een Opkoomende Morgen, ziet men de Ingang van een Boschachtig Dorp, gelegen aan een Rivier, gestoffeerd met twee Vissende Beeldjes; 't aanbreken van den Dag is in dit stuk zeer natuurlyk verbeeld	Pruyssen[r] [for] Q	(Sold) fl 14 V[n] Dijl
1802/05/05	AMSCH	0219	*J. Verboom* | Een bergachtig Landschap, ryk gestoffeerd | *Size:* hoog 30, breed 24 duim *Notes:* The artist's name was given as "J. Verboom" but we have assumed this is an error.	J	(Sold) fl 0:12 L[y] Pakker
1802/06/16	AMSCH	0190	*J. Verboom* | Een fraay Boschachtig Landschap, gestoffeerd met Reisigers te voet en te Paard, op de voorgrond is dit Schildery doorsneeden met een stil Water; alles uitvoerig en konstig behandeld | *Mat:* op paneel *Size:* hoog 14, breed 16 duim *Notes:* The artist's name was given as "J. Verboom" but we have assumed this is an error.	[Merrem]	(Sold) fl 36 Coclers
1802/09/06	AMSCH	0120	*A. Verboom* | Een eenvoudige en natuurlyke Ordenantie, zynde een Boerenstulp, omschaduwd van zwaar geboomte, op de voorgrond een vrouw met een kind by een stil watertje; fraay | *Mat:* op paneel *Size:* hoog 12, breed 16 duim	J	(Bought In) fl 10 ½
1803/08/01	AMSCH	0044	*Verboom (A.)* | Een Gezicht van de Koekamp by het Haagsche Bosch, gestoffeerd met Harten en Rheen [sic], ter linkerzyde by de Stam van een Boom, eenige Arbeiders, en een wandelende Heer en Dame, zeer uitvoerig en natuurlyk van behandeling | *Mat:* op doek *Size:* hoog 24, breed 29 duim	J	(Sold) fl 185 Hodges
1803/08/24	HGKAN	0054	*Verboom* | Een Landschap	[Teissier] [or others]	(Sold) fl 7 Kan
1803/08/24	HGKAN	A0031	*Verboom* | Een Watergezigtje		(Unknown)
1804/02/27	AMSCH	0107	*Verboom. (A.)* | Een Duin- en Boschachtig Landschap, bevallig van licht en uitvoerig van penceel behandeling | *Mat:* op paneel *Size:* hoog 22, breed 34 duim	C	(Sold) fl 1 Gruiter
1804/05/07	AMSCH	0174	*Verboom. (A.)* | Twee stuks, alleraangenaamste Landschappen met hoog Geboomte en stille Waters; piquant van licht en meesterlyk gepenceeld | *Mat:* op doek *Size:* Ieder hoog 37, breed 28 duim	Vinkeles [for] H[affner]	(Bought In) fl 30
1804/08/08	AMSCH	0193	*A. Verboom* | Dit aangenaam Boomryk Dorpgezicht vertoond een vroege Morgenstond, by het opgaan der Zon, eenige Beeldjes ziet men op de voorgrond; het licht en bruin doet in dit stukje een fraaije uitwerking, zynde geestig op Paneel geschilderd | *Mat:* op paneel *Size:* hoog 21, breed 24 duim	Roos a	(Sold) fl 22 Gruyter
1804/08/08	AMSCH	0194	*A. Verboom* | Een Boschgezicht, vol hoog opgaand Geboomte, en een Kasteel in het verschiet, 'er heerscht in dit stuk een aangenaame stilte, en is van een fraaije schildering | *Mat:* op doek *Size:* hoog 23, breed 29 duim	Roos [for] D	(Bought In) fl 126
1804/08/08	AMSCH	0195	*A. Verboom* | Een dito [Boschgezicht], meede met opgaand Geboomte, en aangenaam zonachtig verschiet, gestoffeerd met Herders en Schaapen aan een Beekje; zynde niet minder als het voorgaande | *Mat:* op doek *Size:* hoog 29, breed 32 duim	Roos [for] L	(Sold) fl 26 Menzart
1806/08/13	AMSCH	0194	*Verboom. (A.)* | In een Boomryk Landschap ziet men een Vos, overvallen wordende door een ménigte van Honden, terzyde een Jager en een Bergachtig verschiet, zonachtig en fiks gepenceeld | *Mat:* op doek *Size:* hoog 22, breed 28 duim	Vinkeles [for] F	(Sold) fl 52 Haffner
1808/06/13	AMSCH	0161	*Verboom (A.)* | Een bergachtig Landschap, op den voorgrond een rustend Herder, welke met eene Boerin spreekt, die een Ezel voordrijft, en verdere Stoffage. Zonachtig en uitvoerig | *Mat:* op paneel *Size:* hoog 20, breed 18 duim	E M Engelberts	(Sold) fl 39:10 Th Spaan
1808/06/13	AMSCH	0203	*A. Verboom* | Een Landschap, met een Ruïne en Stoffage van Beelden | companion to lot 204 *Mat:* op doek	E M Engelberts	(Sold) fl 30 for lots 203 & 204. Nieuwenhuisen
1808/06/13	AMSCH	0204	*A. Verboom* | Een als voren [Landschap met een Ruïne en Stoffage van Beelden]; zijnde een wederga | companion to lot 203	E M Engelberts	(Sold) fl 30 for lots 203 & 204. Nieuwenhuisen
1810/06/20	AMSCH	0093	*A. Verboom* | Een Landschap met Boeren-Woningen, staande en rustende Beelden gestoffeerd. Natuurlijk behandeld | *Mat:* op paneel *Size:* hoog 26, breed 31 duimen	X	(Sold) fl 46 Eversdyk
1810/06/20	AMSCH	0093b[H]	*A. Verboom* | Dito [boschachtig Landschap] dito [door A. Verboom] | *Notes:* This lot was added in by hand in the AA and EBNP copies of the catalogue.	N	(Sold) fl 2:10 Cassino
			Verboom, Adriaen Hendricksz. (and Lingelbach)		
1801/04/13	AMSCH	0079	*A. Verboom; J. Lingelbach* | Een Italiaansch bergachtig Landschap met gebouwen, hoog geboomte en watervallen, op den voorgrond een man op een Ezel, waar nevens een vrouw met een kind; alles zonachtig en delicaat gepenceeld | *Mat:* op paneel *Size:* hoog 15, breed 19 duim	Pierre Fouquet, junior	(Sold) fl 100 Pruyssenaar
1801/04/13	AMSCH	0080	*A. Verboom; J. Lingelbach* | Een boomryk Landschap met gebouwen, ruïnen en stoffage van Jagers te paard en te voet, op den voorgrond een	Pierre Fouquet, junior	(Sold) fl 101 Pruyssenaar

			waterplas; alles behandeld als de voorgaande | *Mat:* op doek *Size:* hoog 20 ½, breed 24 ½ duim		
1801/04/13	AMSCH	0081	*A. Verboom; J. Lingelbach* | Een boom- en bergachtig gestoffeerd Landschap; mede behandeld als de voorgaande | *Mat:* op paneel *Size:* hoog 19, breed 16 duim	Pierre Fouquet, junior	(Sold) fl 18:10 Lafontaine
1801/05/11	AMSCH	0096	*A. Verboom; J. Lingelbach* | Een aangenaam Landschap met verscheiden Geboomte, by een anticque Poort en een Waterplas, fraai gestoffeerd met verscheiden Beeldjes, zonachtig en bevallig gepenceeld | *Size:* hoog 19, breed 24 ½ duim	E[lias]	(Sold) fl 190 Allard
1801/06/10	AMSCH	0172	*Verboom. (A.); J. Lingelbach* | Een fraai Boomryk Landschap, met een stroomende Waterplas doorsneeden, gestoffeerd op de voorgrond met een Huifkar en een menigte verschillende Beelden, verder en aangenaam verschiet; delicaat en Zonachtig geschilderd | *Mat:* op doek *Size:* hoog 30, breed 39 duim	Herman ten Kate	(Sold) fl 565 J Yver
1801/06/10	AMSCH	0173	*Verboom. (A.); J. Lingelbach* | Een Landschap met hoog Geboomte, terzyde langs den weg, een Boerenwooning, waarby eenige Huislieden; natuurlyk van behandeling | *Mat:* op paneel *Size:* hoog 17, breed 15 duim	[Doublet]	(Sold) fl 6 Spruit van Gend
1803/08/01	AMSCH	0043	*Verboom (A.); J. Lingelbach* | Een Heuvelachtig en boomryk Landschap of Boschgezigt, met verscheide Kruiden op de voorgrond, beneevens een Water ter linkerzyde, zeer ryk gestoffeerd met eenige Jagers, een Heer en Dame te Paard, verzeld van hunne Honden, die een Hart vervolgen, zeer natuurlyk, uitvoerig en fraay behandeld | *Mat:* op doek *Size:* hoog 25 ½, breed 31 ½ duim	Ij[ver]	(Sold) fl 46 Hodges
1808/11/28	AMSCH	0064	*A. Verboom; J. Lingelbach* | Een hoog Bergachtig Landschap, ter zijde door een zwaar Bosch, een sterk nederstortende Waterval, gestoffeerd met een Landman, zittende op een Esel en voorts gaande en rustende Rijzigers, zonachtig en uitvoerig geschilderd, op Doek, door A. Verboom en gestoffeerd door J. Lingelbach | *Mat:* op doek *Size:* hoog 19, breed 20 duim	[Gruyter?]	(Bought In) fl 23 ½
1810/08/06	AMSCH	0105	*Verboom (A); J. Lingelbach* | Een Landschap met Geboomte, gestoffeerd met Reizigers en Huislieden; zeer natuurlijk verbeeld | *Mat:* op paneel *Size:* hoog 28, breed 41 duimen		(Withdrawn)
1810/10/11	AMSCH	0087	*A. Verboom; J. Lingelbach* | Een Boschachtig Landschap, met eenige Boerenwoningen op een Heuvel, achterwaards bij een sterk door de zon verlicht wordende zandige Weg ziet men een Houten Brug over eene stille Rivier, gestoffeert met eene overvarende Pontschuit, waarin Landlieden met hun Vee, verders gaande en rustende Reizigers en een aangenaam verschiet; zonachtig en uitvoerig geschilderd, door A. Verboom, gestoffeerd door J. Lingelbach | *Mat:* op doek *Size:* hoog 26, breed 30 duimen	[Gruyter?]	(Sold) fl 100 H^{n} Pakker

Verboom, Adriaen Hendricksz. (and Palamedesz., A.)

1808/06/11	RMRIJ	0111	*A: Verboom; Palamedes* | Een zeer schoon Boomryk Landschap, vrolyk en konstig gestoffeerd | *Mat:* op doek *Size:* hoog 29, breed 40 ½ duim		(Bought In) fl 5
1808/06/11	RMRIJ	0114	*A: Verboom; Palamedes* | Een Bosch- en Boomryk Landschap, alwaar eenige Jagers op de Valken Jagt schynen te gaan, krachtig en goed geschilderd | *Mat:* op paneel *Size:* hoog 31 ½, breed 36 ½ duim		(Bought In)

Verboom, Adriaen Hendricksz. (and Schellinks, W.)

1810/06/20	AMSCH	0093a	*A. Verboom; W. Schellings* | Een boschachtig Landschap, gestoffeerd met een Heer te Paard, beladen Muilezels en Landlieden bij hun Vee. Schoon geschilderd op paneel, door A. Verboom, gestoffeerd door W. Schellings | *Mat:* op paneel *Size:* hoog 46, breed 64 duimen	Y	(Sold) fl 15 Yver

Verboom, Adriaen Hendricksz. (and Vermeer, Jan (II))

1802/06/16	AMSCH	0187	*A. Verboom; J. v. der Meer* | Een Heuvelachtig Landschap met kloek Geboomten en alleraangenaamst verschiet, op de voorgrond gestoffeerd met een Herder, dryvende eenige Ossen en Schaapen; het Zonlicht doet in dit stuk een aangenaame gewaarwording, en is meesterlyk gepenceeld | *Mat:* op doek *Size:* hoog 35, breed 36 duim	[Merrem]	(Sold) fl 110 I Smit Gz
1802/06/16	AMSCH	0188	*A. Verboom; J. v. der Meer* | Een Boomryk Landschap met zandige Heuvelen en Boerewoningen, ryk gestoffeerd met Reizigers te Paard en te voet; alles dun en uitvoerig behandeld | *Mat:* op paneel *Size:* hoog 27 ½, breed 36 duim	[Merrem]	(Sold) fl 71 LaFontaine
1802/06/16	AMSCH	0189	*A. Verboom; J. v. der Meer* | Een heuvelachtig Boomryk Landchap, ter zyde op een Heuvel zit een Herder te speelen op een schalmy, waarby Schaapen en Bokken, wyders een uitgestrekt verschiet; uitvoerig geschilderd | *Mat:* op doek *Size:* hoog 32, breed 39 ½ duim	[Merrem]	(Sold) fl 47 Gruiter

Verboom, Adriaen Hendricksz. (and Wouwerman, Ph.)

1809/07/25	HGBSM	0004	*Ph. Wouwerman; Verboom* | Een Boomryk Lantschap, in 't midden de overblyfzels van een aloude Poort, de Weg is gestoffeerd met een Mannetje te Paard, Hond en meer Figuuren, door Ph. Wouwerman, en 't Landschap is konstig geschildert door Verboom | *Mat:* op doek *Size:* hoog 20, breed 24 duim	D van der Aa [or] E B ten Dall	(Sold) fl 66 van Eijk

			Verboom, Adriaen Hendricksz. (manner)		
1806/08/13	AMSCH	0293	*Verboom* | Een Boomryk Landschap, met een ménigte van staand en rustend Vée, als Verboom	Vinkeles [for] F	(Sold) fl 2 Van Iperen
1810/07/23	DOLG2	000Cb[H]	*Verboom* | Land[schap] als Verboom | *Notes:* This lot was added in by hand in the FLNY copy of the catalogue and purchased by the anonymous annotator.	Pieter Quinting	(Sold) fl 1
			Verboom, Willem Hendriksz.		
1801/11/21	RMVIS	0010	*W.L. Boom* | Een Wintergezicht, door W.L. Boom, 1677 | *Inscr:* W.L. Boom 1677 (signed and dated?) *Notes:* It is unclear whether the name and date are inscribed on the painting.	Gelinus van Spaan	(Unknown)
1803/12/12	AMSCH	0012	*W. v. Boom* | Een Land- en Riviergezicht, gestoffeerd met Vaartuigen, Beelden en Beesten | *Mat:* op doek *Size:* hoog 31, breed 42 duim	F	(Sold) fl 1 L Pakker
			Verbrugge, J.		
1806/06/07	RMHSN	0118	*J. Verbrugge* | Een Kerk, met Wandelende Beelden	A E K L	(Unknown)
			Verbruggen, Gaspar Peeter de (the younger)		
1802/05/05	AMSCH	0226	*G. Verbrugge* | Een Tafel, waarop een tinne Schotel, gevuld met Druyven en Persiken, agter dezelven een glaaze Roemer, fraai gepenceeld | *Mat:* op doek *Size:* hoog 15, breed 20 duim	E	(Sold) fl 19:10 Cocler
1803/08/01	AMSCH	0046	*Verbrugge. (K. P.)* | Een Bloemstuk, zynde van een meesterlyke behandeling, dienende tot een Schoorsteenstuk | *Mat:* op doek *Fmt:* schoorsteenstuk *Size:* hoog 58, breed 43 duim	C	(Sold) fl 1:5 Gruiter
1803/08/24	HGKAN	0084	*Caspar Petro Verbrugge* | Twee Bloemstukken fraay en uitvoerig geschilderd	[Teissier] [or others]	(Unknown) fl 2:12
1804/04/28	LNDLS	0060	*G. P. Verbruggen* | Twee Bloemstukjes	[Abraham Delfos] [or others]	(Bought In) fl 1
1804/10/16	DLOND	0227	*C. P. Verbruggen* | Twee Bloemstukken. Deux Tableaux. Des Fleurs | *Mat:* op doek *Size:* hoog 34, breed 25		(Unknown)
1804/10/16	DLOND	0228	*C. P. Verbruggen* | Twee dito [Bloemstukken]. Deux dito [Tableaux de Fleurs] | *Mat:* op doek *Size:* hoog 18, breed 23		(Unknown) fl 20
1806/08/20	HGBSM	0079	*C. P. Verbruggen* | Om een Kop, in Bas-relief, is eene Festoen van Bloemen, kransgewijs geschikt en konstig geschilderd | *Mat:* op doek *Size:* hoog 27, breed 21 duim	Macalester Loup [or others]	(Sold) fl 2:10 Teissier
1807/04/00	LNDLS	0047	*G.P. Verbruggen* | Twee Bloemstukken	[Abraham Delfos] [or others]	(Unknown)
1807/06/10	HGBSM	0047	*G P. Verbruggen* | Twee Bloemstukken	Abraham Delfos [or others]	(Sold) fl 0:10 Gelder
1808/06/13	AMSCH	0163	*Verbrugge (G.)* | Twee stuks Vazen, versierd met eene menigte Bloemen en Vruchten. Alleruitvoerigst behandeld | *Mat:* op doek *Size:* ieder hoog 18, breed 15 duim	R[oos]	(Sold) fl 11 Glad
1808/08/23	AMSCH	0216	*P. Verbruggen* | Twee stuks, verbeeldende Vaasen op Steene Tafels, gevuld en omslingert met verscheide soorten van fraaije Bloemen; meesterlijk gepenceeld op Doek | *Mat:* op doek	Z	(Sold) fl 1:5 P van der Schley
1809/07/25	HGBSM	0286	*C.P. Verbruggen* | Een Bloemstuk | *Mat:* op doek *Size:* hoog 40, breet 32 duim	D van der Aa [or] E B ten Dall	(Sold) fl 0:10 Carrée [or] van Eik
			Verbruggen, Gaspar Peeter de (the younger) (and Terwesten)		
1805/10/09	HGBSM	0096	*C. P. Verbruggen; Terwesten* | Een bloemstuk, door C. P. Verbruggen, en gestoffeerd met kindertjes, door Terwesten | *Mat:* op doek *Size:* hoog 15 breet 19 duim	T H van Willigen [or others]	(Sold) fl 2:18 Heijmans
1805/10/09	HGBSM	0097	*C. P. Verbruggen; Terwesten* | Een dito [bloemstuk] als de voorgaande, en door denzelven Meester [C. P. Verbruggen, en gestoffeerd met kindertjes, door Terwesten] | *Size:* hoog 15 breet 19 duim	T H van Willigen [or others]	(Sold) fl 4:4 Heijmans
			Verbruggen, Gaspar Peeter de (the younger) (manner)		
1806/06/07	RMHSN	0021	*Verbrugge* | Een Festoen met Bloemen, als van Verbrugge, op Doek, zonder Lyst | *Mat:* op doek	A E K L	(Unknown)
			Verburgh		
1804/05/07	AMSCH	0183	*Verburgh (A.)* | Een historiële Fabel Ordonantie, verbeeldende Vertumnus by Pomona, in een Landschap; krachtig van coloriet, en meesterlyk gepenceeld | *Mat:* op doek *Size:* hoog 47, breed 32 duim	Roos [for] K	(Sold) fl 4:5 Gruyter
1805/10/21	GRBOL	0038	*Verburg* | Een Rhyngezicht	Gerardus Nicolaus Heerkens	(Unknown)
1805/10/21	GRBOL	0057	*Verburg* | Een Landschap	Gerardus Nicolaus Heerkens	(Unknown)
1808/11/28	AMSCH	0063	*A. Verburg* | Een Landschap, gestoffeerd met de Fabel-Historie van Vertumnus en Pomona, kragtig van koloriet en meesterlijk gepenceeld | *Mat:* op paneel *Size:* hoog 47, breed 32 duim	[Gruyter?]	(Sold) fl 2:10 Sleeswyk
1810/03/27	RMCNL	0086	*Verburg* | Twee fraaije Bloemstukken		(Unknown)

Verburgh, Dionijs

1801/04/23 AMYVR 0030 *Denys Verburg* | Twee stuks gestoffeerde Landschappen — (Sold) fl 1 A Mayer

1801/04/23 AMYVR 0035 *Denys Verburg* | Een Rhyngezicht, met verscheiden Stoffagie | *Notes:* This lot was sold with lot 36, which is in the manner of J.J. Horemans (I). — (Sold) fl 1 ¼ for lots 35 & 36. A Maijer

1801/10/06 AMSCH 0070 *D. Verburg* | Twee Stuks Landschappen met verscheide Stoffagie, fiks behandeld | *Mat:* op paneel *Size:* yder hoog 13, breed 14 duim — M — (Sold) fl 0:10 Ijver [for] Nieuland

1804/02/27 AMSCH 0136 *Denys Verburg* | Twee Bosch- en Bergachtige Landschappen — B — (Sold) fl 0:10 Geld

1805/10/21 GRBOL 0019 *D. Verburg* | Het Inkomen van een Bosch, stout Geschilderd — Gerardus Nicolaus Heerkens — (Unknown)

1807/06/02 AMHUY 0034 *de Nys Verburg* | Een Land- en Riviergezicht met eenige Visschersschuiten en andere Vaartuigen — (Unknown)

Verburgh, H. [Unidentified]

1810/06/20 AMSCH 0142 *H. Verburgh* | Een Landschap met Beestjes — B — (Sold) fl 1:10 van der Schleij

Verburgh, Rutger

1802/07/27 AKHRK 0035 *R. Verburg, 1702* | Een bergachtig Rhijngezicht, op de voorgrond een vervallen Herberg, met Reizigers te Paard en te Voet, vrolijk geschilderd | companion to lot 36 *Mat:* op doek *Size:* hoog 12 ½, breed 15 ½ duim *Inscr:* R. Verburg, 1702 (signed and dated?) *Notes:* It is unclear whether the name and date are inscribed on the painting. — Maria Stategaart — (Sold) fl 8 for lots 35 & 36. Sonnevelt

1802/07/27 AKHRK 0036 *R. Verburg* | De weerga. Waarin een Waterval met figuuren te Paard en te Voet. Als de voorige | companion to lot 35 *Mat:* op doek *Size:* hoog 12 ½, breed 15 ½ duim — Maria Stategaart — (Sold) fl 8 for lots 35 & 36. Sonnevelt

1806/08/13 AMSCH 0203 *Verburg. (R.)* | Een bevrozen Rivier- en Dorpgezicht, vol van stoffagie, van op het Ys zich vermakende Lieden; meesterlyk geschilderd | *Mat:* op dock *Size:* hoog 36, breed 36 duim — Roos — (Sold) fl 2:5 Hymans

Verbuys, Arnold

1802/11/01 DOBRA 0065 *A. Verbuys* | Een zinnebeeldig stuk, verbeeldende de Geregtigheid, naar 't schynt zich verdeedigende tegen Verleiding | companion to lot 66 *Mat:* op doek *Size:* circa 4 voet hoog, en breed 2 v. 13 d. — Paulus van der Spyk [or others] — (Sold) fl 4 for lots 65 & 66. v d Blyk

1802/11/01 DOBRA 0066 *A. Verbuys* | Een wedergade, mede zinnebeeldig | companion to lot 65 — Paulus van der Spyk [or others] — (Sold) fl 4 for lots 65 & 66. v d Blyk

1803/07/14 MGKLY 0011 *A. Verbuys* | Een Slaapende Diana goed gepenseeld — Mr Caspar Jacob van Citters — (Unknown)

1804/03/27 MGSAN 0010 *A. Verbuys* | Een Historiëele, vertoonende een Landgezicht, waar op een Vrouwebeeld haar voor een Tent vertoond, boven haar een Cupido houdende met haar een snoer Paarlen vast, voorts een tweede Cupido een Gordyn opligtende, op de voorgrond een liggende Cupido, met een Clarinet nevens hem, door A. Verbuys, in vergulde Lyst | *Mat:* op doek *Size:* hoog 16 duim x breed 12 duim — (Unknown)

1804/03/27 MGSAN 0011 *A. Verbuys* | Een dito [Historiëele] tot een weêrgaê, verbeeldende een knielend Vrouwebeeld, boven haar drie Cupidoos met Bloemkranssen, nevens haar nog twee Cupidoos met Bloemen, door denzelven [A. Verbuys], in vergulde Lyst | *Mat:* op doek *Size:* hoog 16 duim x breed 12 duim — (Unknown)

1805/07/10 AMSCH 0239 *A. Verbuys* | Een Historieele Ordinantie — Y[ver] — (Bought In) fl 0:18

1807/06/10 HGBSM 0163 *A. Verbuys* | De historie van Danaë met Jupiter, verbeeldende de goude regen, meesterlijk geschilderd | *Mat:* op doek *Size:* hoog 12, breed 25 ½ duim — Abraham Delfos [or others] — (Unknown)

1810/10/10 MGCIT 0106 *Verbuys* | Een naakte Venus door Satyrs bespied wordende in een daarby vertoond Landschap; verdienstelyk geschilderd — Caspar van Citters — (Unknown)

Verdoel, Adriaen

1810/10/13 HGDAW 0005 *A. Verdoel* | Een Binnen Vertrek, waarin een zieke Vrouw, waarbij een Doctor welke haar de Pols voelt, en het water bezigtigt, in het verschiet een Dienstmaagd met een bak Water in de handen, en verder bywerk, zeer eigenäartig en schoon van Coloriet | *Mat:* op paneel *Size:* hoog 15 ½, breed 12 ½ duim — (Unknown)

Verdonck, Cornelis

1801/11/10 AMPOS 0023 *C. Verdonk* | 2 Kermis-Gezigten aan den Ryn, vol Vaartuigen — (Unknown)

1802/02/16 AMSCH 0051 *C. Verdonk* | Twee dito [stuks] bevallige Rhyngezigten, beide gestoffeert met Houtvlotten, bovenlandsche Aaken en andere vaartuigen; plaisant geschilderd — F — (Sold) fl 6:5 van Iperen

1804/05/07 AMSCH 0182 *Verdonk (K.)* | Twee stuks bevallige Rhyngezichten, ryk gestoffeerd met meenigte Beelden, Beesten, Gebouwen, Schuiten, enz.; uitvoerig gepenceeld, in de manier van Griffier | *Mat:* op paneel *Size:* Ieder hoog 12, breed 15 duim — Vinkeles [for] J — (Sold) fl 5:15 S^{n} Joseph

1804/07/25 DLGRO 0026 *C. Verdonck* | Een Rhyn gezicht tusschen de Bergen, met verscheiden Schuiten en Beelden | *Mat:* op paneel *Size:* hoog 13, breed 15 duim — Mr Franc van der Burch Wz. — (Unknown)

1804/07/25	DLGRO	0027	*C. Verdonck* | Een dito [Rhyn gezicht] dito [tusschen de Bergen], met een afdryvend Houtvlot, mede zeer uitvoerig door denzelfde [C. Verdonck] | *Mat:* op paneel *Size:* hoog 13, breed 15 duim *Notes:* It is unclear what "dito" refers to in the title.	Mr Franc van der Burch Wz.	(Unknown)
1804/10/16	DLOND	0229	*Verdonk, als Wenix* | Twee Jagers met een groten Hond, omringd van dood Wild, Gevogelte en zeer vele Jacht-tuigen. Zeer schoon. Deux Chasseurs, un grand Chien, du Gibier, Volaille & beaucoup d'Ustensiles de Chasse. Pièce très-belle | *Mat:* op doek *Size:* hoog 64, breed 85		(Unknown) fl 40:8
1804/10/16	DLOND	0230	*Verdonk* | Een dode Reiger, waar nevens een Geweer met dood Gevogelte behangen. Un Heron mort, & un Fusil auquel sont suspendus des Oiseaux morts | *Mat:* op doek *Size:* hoog 41, breed 33		(Unknown)
1806/06/07	RMHSN	0076	*Verdonk* | Twee Stuks Rhyngezigten met Scheepjes | *Mat:* op paneel	A E K L	(Unknown)
1806/08/13	AMSCH	0205	*Verdonck* | Een Land- en Riviergezicht met Scheepen en Schuiten en stoffagie van Beeldjes; fiks gepenceeld | *Mat:* op paneel *Size:* hoog 10, breed 13 ½ duim	Vinkeles [for] F	(Sold) fl 1:5 T Spaan

Verdonck, Cornelis (manner)

1801/11/10	AMPOS	0048	*Verdonk* | 2 dito [stuks] Rhyngezigtjes, als Verdonk		(Unknown)

Verelst

1806/11/24	AMSCH	0078	*Verrelst* | Een Italiaansche Stad, op de Voorgrond zitten drie Mannen te Dobbelen, op een Balustraden staan eenige Jongens Belle te blazen; kragtig van coloriet en malsch gepenceeld | *Mat:* op doek op paneel *Size:* hoog 18, breed 14 duim	Munnikhuizen	(Sold) fl 5:8 [or] 58 Reyers
1810/12/03	DOBRA	0040	*Verelst* | Een Stuk met Bloemen en Fruiten		(Unknown)
1810/12/03	DOBRA	0042	*Verelst* | Een Vrouwe Pourtrait, door Verelst; fraai		(Unknown)

Verelst, Johannes

1802/05/05	AMSCH	0220	*J. Verelst* | Een glaaze Fles, staande op een Tafel, gevuld met diverse soorten van Bloemen, zeer dun en delicaat behandeld | *Mat:* op doek *Size:* hoog 27, breed 22 duim	C	(Sold) fl 7:10 Pruijssenaar [for] R
1804/08/08	AMSCH	0200	*J. Verelst* | Twee Tafels met differente Vruchten, als Druiven, Persiken, en andere Vruchten en Bladeren, waarop Insectens aazen; delicaat geschilderd | *Mat:* op doek *Size:* hoog 9 ½, breed 12 ½ duim	Vink[eles] [for] K[=Gruyter?]	(Sold) fl 3 A de Lely
1809/07/25	HGBSM	0254	*J. Verelst* | Een Boeren Binnenvertrek, waar in een Gezelschap met drinkende Boeren en verder Huisraad, door J. Verelst, 1647 | *Mat:* op paneel *Size:* hoog 24 en een half, breed 28 duim *Inscr:* J. Verelst, 1647 (signed and dated?) *Notes:* It is unclear whether the name and date are inscribed on the painting.	D van der Aa [or] E B ten Dall	(Sold) fl 1:12 Stees M

Verelst, Pieter

1803/12/15	MGLAC	0021	*Verelst* | Een Binnen Vertrek, met vrolyke Boeren; zeer kragtig en fraai geschilderd | *Mat:* op paneel *Size:* hoog duim 19, breed duim 27	Mr L H de Haze Bomme	(Unknown)
1804/10/16	DLOND	0069	*P. van der Elst* | Een Bloemstuk. Des Fleurs | *Mat:* op doek *Size:* hoog 47, breed 33		(Unknown)
1804/10/16	DLOND	0231	*P. Verelst* | Een Boerenhuis met enige vrolyke Boeren. Des Paysans joyeux | *Mat:* op paneel *Size:* hoog 22, breed 26 *Notes:* This lot was misnumbered no. 230.		(Sold) fl 6 Mahy
1804/10/16	DLOND	0232	*P. Verelst* | Uts^{a} [Een Boerenhuis met enige vrolyke Boeren. Des Paysans joyeux] | *Mat:* op paneel *Size:* hoog 23, breed 29		(Unknown)
1804/10/16	DLOND	0233	*P. Verelst* | Uts^{a} [Een Boerenhuis met enige vrolyke Boeren. Des Paysans joyeux] | *Mat:* op paneel *Size:* hoog 22, breed 27		(Unknown) fl 25
1804/10/16	DLOND	0234	*P. Verelst* | Uts^{a} [Een Boerenhuis met enige vrolyke Boeren. Des Paysans joyeux] | *Mat:* op paneel *Size:* hoog 10, breed 15		(Unknown)
1804/10/16	DLOND	0235	*P. Verelst* | Ene Koekebakster. Une Femme faisant des Gateaux | *Mat:* op paneel *Size:* hoog 10, breed 13		(Unknown) fl 12:5
1804/10/16	DLOND	0236	*P. Verelst* | Een lezend Man. Un Homme lisant | *Mat:* op paneel *Size:* hoog 12, breed 9		(Unknown)
1805/10/09	HGBSM	0062	*P. Verelst* | Een boertje die een glas bier in de hand heeft | *Mat:* op doek op paneel *Size:* hoog 8 ½ breet 7 ½ duim	T H van Willigen [or others]	(Sold) fl 1:8 Kuller
1810/06/06	RMMUY	0035	*P. Varelst* | Dit aangenaam onderwerp verbeeld een Kinderschool bij dag. Op den voorgrond zit den Meester aan zijn Lessenaar, eene pen te versnijden, drie kinderen staan nevens hem, hunne les op te zeggen, achter hem eene Vrouw, met een kind op den arm, in 't verschiet eenige kinderen aan eene tafel, bezig met schrijven en lezen, alles zeer natuurlijk en uitvoerig geschilderd | *Mat:* op doek		(Unknown) fl 61

Verelst, Simon Pietersz.

1802/05/05	AMSCH	0222	*Simon Verhelst* | Twee stuks, op Steene Randen ziet men glaaze Flessen, gevuld met onderscheiden soorten van welgeschakeerde Bloemen, waarop eenige Insecten aasen, beiden zeer uitvoerig en fraai gepenceeld | *Mat:* op doek *Size:* hoog 36, breed 27 duim	E	(Sold) fl 21 Stevens

1802/07/27	AKHRK	0049	*S. Verelst* | Een Tafel waarop een Perzik, Druiven en aazende Insecten, natuurlijk en murw geschilderd | *Mat:* op doek *Size:* hoog 9 ½, breed 12 ½ duim	Maria Stategaart	(Sold) fl 9 for lots 49 & 50. Gruyter
1802/07/27	AKHRK	0050	*S. Verelst* | Een schoone Perzik en roode Druiven, met Bladeren, kunstig geschilderd	Maria Stategaart	(Sold) fl 9 for lots 49 & 50. Gruyter
1803/04/20	AMSCH	0083	*Verelst. (S.)* | Een Steene Ornament Lyst, waar in een Nis, in het zelven staat een Fles, gevult met diverse Bloemen, en rondsom de Lyst met hangende Festonnen van een meenigte soorten van fraaije Bloemen; Ongemeen uitvoerig gepenceeld [La representation d'un ornement Scupté en pierre aumilieu [sic] duquel est placée une Caraffe de verre garnie d'un bouquet de fleurs variées ; autour des ornemens sont Suspendus des festons du même agrément : morceau précieusement fini, et d'une couleur brillante et narurelle [sic].] | *Mat:* op doek *Size:* hoog 29, breed 24 duim	Maria Magdalena van Sluypwyk, gravinne van Moens	(Sold) fl 6:10 Brunis
1809/06/13	AMSCH	0163	*S. Verelst* | Op een Tafel staat een fles met keurige bloemen, waarop Insectens azen; mals gepenceeld | *Mat:* op doek *Size:* hoog 29, breed 23 duim	E	(Sold) fl 0:14 L Pakker
1809/09/06	AMSCH	0083	*Verelst (Simon)* | Een Steene Vaas, staande op een Marmere Tafel, omslingerd met Rankwerk van verscheide zoorten van Bloemen, met Steel en Bladeren, waar op Insecten azen, alles natuurlijk verbeeld en van een uitvoerige penceelbehandeling | *Mat:* op doek *Size:* hoog 19, breed 16 duim	Johannes Caudri	(Sold) fl 8 van Dijl
			Verhagen, A. [Unidentified]		
1804/10/16	DLOND	0237	*A. Verhagen* | De Vyverberg in 's Hage van de Plaats te zien. Le Vivier de la Haye vu du côté de la Place | *Mat:* op doek *Size:* hoog 29, breed 44		(Unknown)
			Verkolje		
1809/07/19	AMSCH	[A0001][H]	*Vercolien [?]* | Twee Historich [sic] | *Notes:* This lot was added in by hand in the AA copy of the catalogue. Because it was not numbered, we have assigned the number.		(Unknown)
			Verkolje (copy after)		
1804/10/08	RMCNL	0021	*Verkolje* | Een Heer en Dame na Verkolje	A t'Hooft	(Unknown)
			Verkolje (manner)		
1802/08/24	LNDLS	0143	*Verkolje* | Een Vanitas met Kinderen, als van Verkolje | *Mat:* op paneel	Leonardus Bouman [or others]	(Unknown) fl 0:17
1802/08/24	LNDLS	0149	*Verkolje* | Eene zich spiegelende Narcissus in een grot, als van Verkolje | *Mat:* op paneel	Leonardus Bouman [or others]	(Unknown) fl 1:4
1803/08/17	AMSCH	0102	*Verkolje* | In een Hofgezicht ziet men een Gezelschap van Dames en Heeren, zich met gastereeren vermakende, in de manier van Verkolje behandeld | *Mat:* op doek *Size:* hoog 24, breed 27 duim	Anna Catharina Putman	(Sold) fl 5:5 Gruyter
1806/06/07	RMHSN	0062	*Verkolje* | Een Juffrouw die een Brief Toelakt, in de manier van Verkolje | *Mat:* op doek	A E K L	(Unknown)
			Verkolje, Nicolaas		
1801/05/11	AMSCH	0102	*N. Verkolje* | Deze Bybel-Ordonnantie verbeeld de Rentmeester van zyn Dienstknegt Reekening Eyssende: Hy zit in een gemeubileerde zaal voor een tafel met een tapytkleed bedekt, waarop eenige boeken geplaast zyn, terwyl hem door de bediende een Reekening vertoond werd; alles is meesterlyk en uitvoerig gepenceeld | *Mat:* op doek *Size:* hoog 23, breed 17 duim	E[lias]	(Sold) fl 43 Van Iperen
1801/05/11	AMSCH	0103	*N. Verkolje* | Een dito [Bybel-Ordonnantie], verbeeldende Hagar in de Woestyne, door een Engel getroost, in alles als de vorige, fraay en uitvoerig geschilderd | *Mat:* op doek *Size:* hoog 23, breed 17 duim	E[lias]	(Sold) fl 50 Van Iperen
1801/05/11	AMSCH	0104	*N. Verkolje* | Twee stuks, het eene een musiceerend gezelschap; en een weerga, beide meesterlyk behandeld | *Mat:* op paneel *Size:* hoog 19, breed 16 duim	V	(Sold) fl 44 Allard
1801/10/19	AMSCH	0080	*Verkolje. (N)* | Een bevallig Meisje in haar hemd op een Ledikant, by een kaarsligt, ter zyde een tinne Waterpot, in 't verschiet een Manspersoon de Gordynen Openende; fraay en delicaat van penceel behandeling, en aller natuurlykst verbeeld | *Mat:* op paneel *Size:* hoog 13 ⅛, breed 10 ¾ duim	Jonkheer Menno Baron van Coehoorn	(Sold) fl 51 J^{b} Roeloffs (B^{d} Kooy)
1802/06/16	AMSCH	0200	*N. Verkolje* | Een Historiëele Ordenantie waarin een Vorst zich schynt te willen doorsteeken en door een Krygsknegt word terug gehouden, krachtig van schildering | *Mat:* op doek *Size:* hoog 20 ½, breed 17 duim	[Merrem]	(Sold) fl 16 V^{n} Iperen
1802/06/28	AMSCH	0190	*N. Verkolje* | Een zinspeelende Ordonnantie, van verscheide Beelden op de Koophandel en Zeevaart, zeer dun van Coloriet, door N. Verkolje, op Doek | *Mat:* op doek *Size:* hoog 28, breed 37 duim	Anna Elink	(Sold) fl 10 Balkenschooten
1802/06/28	AMSCH	0192	*N. Verkolje* | Een bevallige Dame, speelende op de Guitar, nevens haar een Jongeling en een Hondje, uitmuntend behandeld | *Mat:* op doek *Size:* hoog 20, breed 18 duim	Anna Elink	(Sold) fl 18 Coclers
1802/06/28	AMSCH	0193	*N. Verkolje* | Voor een open Nis vertoont zig een aardig Meisje, houdende in de eene hand een brandende Kaars, en in de andere een Muyzeval; een	Anna Elink	(Sold) fl 3:10 de Meijer

			Jongeling daar nevens staande, wyst met de eene hand naar dezelve; om hoog een opgeschoven Gordyn, en verder bywerk; alles natuurlyk en uitvoerig geschilderd, op Panneel | *Mat:* op paneel *Size:* hoog 10, breed 8 duim		
1804/12/10	AMSCH	0098	*N. Verkolje* | Deeze Ordinantie stelt voor Abrahams Offerhande; met ziet den Engel nederdaalen, welke Abraham by den hand grypt, die bereid is zyn Zoon Isaac te slagten: dit schildery is van een fraaije ordinantie, uitmuntend van tekening en krachtig gepenceeld | *Mat:* op paneel *Size:* Hoog 24, breed 19 duim	Jan De Groot	(Sold) fl 26 Numan
1807/08/26	AMSCH	0222	*N. Verkolje* | In een Binnenvertrek zit eene bedaagde Vrouw, slapende op een Stoel, voor eene Tafel, waarop een Aarden Lamp geplaatst is. Een vrolyk Jongman, met een brandende Kaars in de hand, die al de voorwerpen verlicht, schynt haar met een Strooitje onder den Neus te vryven; de karakters zyn natuurlyk, en van een uitvoerige penceels-behandeling | *Mat:* op paneel *Size:* hoog 14, breed 12 duim	Helsdinge	(Bought In) fl 13
1809/09/06	AMSCH	0080	*Verkolje (N)* | Deze fraaije Ordinantie, verbeeld in een Landschap, de Sunamitische Vrouw eerbiedig nedergeknield voor den Profeet Elisa, daar nevens een Jongeling, en ter regter zijde staat het Ezel, waar bij een Jongman, verders een aangenaam verschiet; alles is helder; bevallig van koloriet en zeer uitvoerig gepenceeld | *Mat:* op paneel *Size:* hoog 17, breed 20 duim	Johannes Caudri	(Sold) fl 33 Th^{S} Spaan
1809/09/06	AMSCH	0081	*Verkolje (N)* | Twee stuks met Boeren, welke Rooken en Drinken; geestig in de manier van Ostade behandeld | *Mat:* op doek *Size:* ieder hoog 8, breed 7 duim	Johannes Caudri	(Sold) fl 10:10 Gruyter
1810/10/11	AMSCH	0214	*N. Verkolje* | Eene Dame voor een Nis | *Notes:* This lot was sold with lots 223 by Jan Lairesse and 224 by Abr. Storck.	A	(Sold) fl 8 for lots 214, 223 & 224. Yver

Verkolje, Nicolaas (copy after)

1802/06/28	AMSCH	0191	*N. Verkolje* | Een dito [zinspeelende Ordonnantie], zynde de Copy van de voorgaande [N. Verkolje] | *Notes:* It is unclear what "dito" refers to in the title.	Anna Elink	(Sold) fl 4 Brouwer

Vermeer, Jan

1801/05/11	AMSCH	0048	*De Delfsche van der Meer* | In een Binnenvertrek, ziet men een Dame met een blaauw jakje met bonte rant, welke goud weegt, alles overeenkomstig, de waarheid, en bevallig gepenceeld | *Mat:* op doek *Size:* hoog 24, breed 19 duim *Loc:* Berlin, Deutschland. Gemäldegalerie. (1041B) as P. de Hooch	Pruisse [for] M	(Sold) fl 60 V der Schleij [for] Merrem
1801/06/10	AMSCH	0118	*Meer. (Delftsche van der)* | Een Dame in 't blauw Fluweel gekleed, staat voor een Tafel, een brief te leezen, tegen de muur hangt een Landkaart het licht in dit stukje geeft een goede uitwerking en is kloek gepenceeld | *Mat:* op doek *Size:* hoog 19, breed 16 duim *Loc:* Amsterdam, Nederland. Rijksmuseum. (C 251)	Herman ten Kate	(Sold) fl 110 Taijs
1802/06/16	AMSCH	0098	*Delfsche van der Meer* | In een gemeubilleerd Binnenvertrek ziet men een Heer in zyn Japon beezig een Laadje in een Lessenaar te schuiven, nevens dezelve legt een Boek, voorts een Fles met water, Urinaal Stoelkussen en Tafelkleed; achter hem een Stoel welke zoo naby de natuur als mogelyk, geschildett [sic] is, het licht dat door een vengster op de muur schynt, is allerfrapandst [sic], en is voorts van een meesterlyke uitvoerige Schildering | *Mat:* op doek *Size:* hoog 28 ½, breed 23 ½ duim	[Merrem]	(Sold) fl 480 I Smit Gz
1802/06/16	AMSCH	0099	*Delfsche van der Meer* | In een gemeubileerde Kamer staat een bevallige Dame, gekleed in een Blauw Satyn Jakje met Bond gevoerd, en een roodcouleurde Rok, het hoofd gedekt met een zwart Kapje, houdende in de Regterhand een goud Schaaltje, welke spétie zy schynt te weegen; welk op een Tafel voor haar geplaats, en gedeeltelyk met een Tapytkleed bedekt is; verder door een openstaande Deur ziet men in een ander vertrek, alles is volmaakt de Natuur evenaarende; het invallende Licht doet een schoone werking, en is uitmuntend schoon gepenceeld | *Mat:* op doek *Size:* hoog 24, breed 21 duim *Loc:* Berlin, Deutschland. Gemäldegalerie. (1041B) as P. de Hooch	[Merrem]	(Sold) fl 140 Gruiter
1803/12/12	AMSCH	0055	*De Delfsche van der Meer* | In een Gemeubileerd Binnenvertrek staat een Geleerden aan een Tafel, met een Tapyten Kleed gedekt, houdende een Passer in zyn Hand, waar mede hy een voor hem liggende Landkaart schynt af te meeten; het zonlicht, dat door het Vengster invalt, is frappant, en de schildering meesterlyk | *Mat:* op doek *Loc:* Frankfurt, Deutschland. Städelsches Kunstinstitut.	Arnoud de Lange	(Sold) fl 360 Coclers
1808/11/12	HGSCR	0022	*de Delfsche van der Meer* | Een bevallig vrouwtje in 't geel satyn met bond gekleed, zittende te schryven aan een tafel waar op een snoer paerlen in een kistje geplaast zyn, uitmuntend fraai, uitvoerig en meesterlyk gepenseeld door de Delfsche van der Meer. D. zeer raar | *Mat:* op doek *Loc:* Washington, D.C., USA. National Gallery of Art. (1942.9.97)	Mr J van Buren	(Unknown) fl 80
1809/06/13	AMSCH	0100	*De Delfsche van der Meer* | In een gemeubileerde Kamer, staat eene bevallige Dame, gekleed in een blaauw Satijn Jakje, met Bont gevoerd en een rood couleurde Rok, het Hoofd gedekt met een zwart Kapje, houdende in de regterhand een Goudschaaltje, welke Spétie zij schijnt te weegen, die voor haar op een Tafel met een Tapijtkleedje geplaast is, verder door een openstaande Deur ziet men in een ander Vertrek; alles is	[Gruyter?]	(Bought In) fl 126

			volmaakt de natuur evenaarende, het invallend zonlicht doet eene schoone werking, en is uitmuntend gepenceeld | *Mat:* op doek *Size:* hoog 24, breed 21 duim *Loc:* Berlin, Deutschland. Gemäldegalerie. (1041B) as P. de Hooch		
1809/09/06	AMSCH	0042	*Meer (de Delfsche van der)* | In een gemeubileerde Kamer staat eene bevallige jonge Dame voor een Tafel, waar boven een Spiegel geplaatst is, zij is gekleed in een geel Satijn Jakje met Bont gevoerd, en schijnt zig te Paleeren; het invallende zonlicht versprijdt zig tégen een witte Muur en doet alle de Voorwerpen met luister voorwaards koomen; dit bevallig tafreel is een der natuurlijkste en alleruitvoerigst gepenceelden van deze beroemde Meester | *Mat:* op doek *Size:* hoog 20, breed 17 duim *Loc:* Berlin, Deutschland. Gemäldegalerie. (912B)	Johannes Caudri	(Sold) fl 55 Th^{S} Spaan
1810/08/01	AMSCH	0057	*Meer (de Delfsche van der)* | In eene Binnenkamer zit eene bevallige Vrouw bij eene Tafel, nevens haar een staand Heer, welke haar in de Toonkunde onderwijst, aan den Wand eene Viool en ander bijwerk [Dans un intérieur de Chambre est assise une Femme de bonne mine ; devant elle est une Table, et à son côté se trouve Maître de Musique lui donnant leçon. Un Violon pendu au mûr et autres accessoires terminent cet ensemble] | *Annots:* fort bon. (NGW); fau (BPG) *Mat:* op doek *Size:* hoog 15 ½, breed 17 duimen *Loc:* New York, NY, USA. Frick Collection (01.1.125)	Mr Pieter de Smeth van Alphen	(Bought In) fl 610
			Vermeer, Jan (or Vermeer, Jan, manner)		
1810/03/26	RMMUY	0051	*De Delftsche Vermeer of in zijn manier* | Eene Dame, gezeten aan eene tafel, bezig met Speldewerken. Bevallig geschilderd [Une Dame assise à côté d'une table, et s'occupant à faire de la dentelle.] | *Annots:* Copie (BPG) *Mat:* op paneel *Size:* hoog 9 ½, breed 8 duimen	Daniel de Jongh Az	(Sold) fl 10:5 van Iperen Amsterdam
			Vermeer, Jan (manner)		
1803/06/20	AMSCH	0006	*de Delfsche van der Meer* | In een Gemeubileerde Kamer ziet men een Heer in zyn Japon aan een Lessenaar; een Urinaal Waterfles, Stoel en Tafelkleed zynde Bywerken van dit frapante Schildery, het geen voorts natuurlyk behandeld is, op Doek, zoo goed als de Delfsche van der Meer | *Mat:* op doek *Size:* hoog 28, breed 23 duim	Schley [for] B	(Sold) fl 200 V d Schleij [for] F
			Vermeer, Jan (II)		
1801/10/06	AMSCH	0046	*J. van der Meer* | Twee stuks Landschappen, byde gestoffeerd met staande en rustende Schaapen, Bokken en Lammeren, verder een rustende Veehoeder, en vrouw, zeer natuurlyk behandeld | *Mat:* op paneel *Size:* yder hoog 10, breed 12 duim	M	(Sold) fl 20:10 Wed Achtienhoven
1801/12/22	AMOTT	0084	*J. v. Veemer* | Vegtende Boeren in een groot Landschap, vol gewoel, door J. v. Veemer, 1646 | *Inscr:* F. v. Veemer, 1646 (signed and dated?) *Notes:* It is unclear whether the name and date are inscribed on the painting.	Bartholomeus Ruloffs	(Unknown) fl 4
1802/09/06	AMSCH	0075	*van der Meer* | Een ryke Ordenantie van een drift Beesten, eenige Schaapen met hunne Herders, in een aangenaam Landschap; fraay en natuurlyk | *Mat:* op doek *Size:* hoog 27, breed 33 duim	J	(Sold) fl 6:5 A Schotte
1802/09/29	AMSCH	0039	*J. van der Meer. Ao. 1600* | Een Landschap, hoog 11, breed 13 ¾ duim. op Doek. Zynde een uitgestrekt Gezigt op bebouwde Landen, Bossen en Bleekeryen van Duin af te zien: eenige wooningen, rustende Visschers, en andre figuurtjes, zetten aan dit alleruitvoerigst Schilderytje eene aangename levendigheid by, zeer bevallig helder en natuurlyk van coloriet [Ce joli sujet de Paysage, offre le point de vue d'une vaste étendue de Pays, de Champs semés de differens grains, de Bois, de Blancheries & d'habitations rustiques. Ce spectacle se remarque de la hauteur des dunes, ou se reposent des Pécheurs chargés. – Ce Petit Tableau est de la plus riche couleur & de la plus grande vérité, joint à une exécution délicate & précieuse.] | *Mat:* op doek *Size:* hoog 11, breed 13 ¾ duim *Inscr:* J. van der Meer. Ao. 1600 (signed and dated?) *Notes:* It is unclear whether the name and date are inscribed on the painting.	[Labouchere?]	(Sold) fl 49 Vinkeles
1804/10/29	HRBAU	0109	*Vermeer (J.)* | Op een' zandigen Voorgrond liggen twee afgekapte Boomen, en aan den Weg, tusschen zwaar geboomte, staan eenige Boerenwooningen, waar agter eene Kerk en aangenaam verschiet, gestoffeerd met Rytuigen en gaande en rustende Beeldjens. Uitvoerig en zonagtig behandeld | *Mat:* op doek *Size:* hoog 37, breed 58 duim	Simon Styl	(Unknown)
1805/12/16	AMSCH	0040	*J. van der Meer* | Een Heuvelachtig Landschap, waarin een Véehoeder en twee Vrouwen, die een drift Schaapen en Bokken voortdryven, verder een Bergachtig verschiet; natuurlyk behandeld op Paneel | *Mat:* op paneel *Size:* hoog 11, breed 14 duim	V	(Sold) fl 13:10 Spaan
1806/11/24	AMSCH	0042	*Meer (J. van der)* | Twee stuks aangenaame Landschappen, in de eene een Sluis over een stil water; de andere een dorpgezigt met veel Geboomte, en stoffagie van Beelden en Beesten, als J. Ruisdaal behandeld | *Mat:* op doek *Size:* Yder hoog 20, breed 26 duim	Munnikhuizen	(Sold) fl 24:10 Engelberts
1807/08/26	AMSCH	0137	*J. van der Meer* | Twee stuks Duingezigten, gestoffeerd met Reizigers; natuurlyk behandeld | *Mat:* op paneel *Size:* ieder hoog 16, breed 22 duim	Yver [for] S	(Sold) fl 35 Hulswit
1808/07/19	AMROU	0002	*van der Meer* | 1 Duin en Bergachtig Landschap met een Rivier doorsneeden, op de voorgrond een drift van Schaapjes, Koebeesten, waarby een Herder en Herderin, en andere Stoffagies		(Unknown)

1808/07/19	AMROU	0009	*J. van der Meer* | 2 stuks Bergachtige Landschappen, met hooge Geboomtens, op de voorgrond ziet men eenige staande en leggende Schaapjes, waarby zit een Herder en Herderin, en op den andere waarby een ander een Drift Schappen voortdryft, Sonagtig en Natuurlyk gepenseeld		(Unknown)
1809/07/25	HGBSM	0156	*van der Meer* | Twee Schaapjes en een Lammetje | *Mat:* op doek *Size:* hoog 6 en een half, breed 8 duim	D van der Aa [or] E B ten Dall	(Sold) fl 1:2 A Vermeulen
1810/05/22	AMSCH	0064	*Meer. (J. van der)* | Een Heuvelachtig Landschap, met Geboomte, gestoffeerd met rustende Landlieden, eene staande en eene liggende Os en grazende Schapen en Lammeren; meesterlijk geschilderd | *Mat:* op paneel *Size:* hoog 27, breed 33 duim	S	(Bought In) fl 40
			Vermeer, Jan (II) (and Verboom, A.H.)		
1802/06/16	AMSCH	0187	*A. Verboom; J. v. der Meer* | Een Heuvelachtig Landschap met kloek Geboomten en alleraangenaamst verschiet, op de voorgrond gestoffeerd met een Herder, dryvende eenige Ossen en Schaapen; het Zonlicht doet in dit stuk een aangenaame gewaarwording, en is meesterlyk gepenceeld | *Mat:* op doek *Size:* hoog 35, breed 36 duim	[Merrem]	(Sold) fl 110 I Smit Gz
1802/06/16	AMSCH	0188	*A. Verboom; J. v. der Meer* | Een Boomryk Landschap met zandige Heuvelen en Boerewoningen, ryk gestoffeerd met Reizigers te Paard en te voet; alles dun en uitvoerig behandeld | *Mat:* op paneel *Size:* hoog 27 ½, breed 36 duim	[Merrem]	(Sold) fl 71 LaFontaine
1802/06/16	AMSCH	0189	*A. Verboom; J. v. der Meer* | Een heuvelachtig Boomryk Landchap, ter zyde op een Heuvel zit een Herder te speelen op een schalmy, waarby Schaapen en Bokken, wyders een uitgestrekt verschiet; uitvoerig geschilderd | *Mat:* op doek *Size:* hoog 32, breed 39 ½ duim	[Merrem]	(Sold) fl 47 Gruiter
			Vermeer, Jan (III)		
1801/04/13	AMSCH	0047	*J. van der Meer, de Jonge* | Een duinachtig Landschap met Kreupelgewas, gestoffeerd met diversche Beeldjes, en een uitgestrekt verschiet, natuurlyk behandeld | *Mat:* op doek *Size:* hoog 10, breed 15 duim	Pierre Fouquet, junior	(Sold) fl 47 v d Schley [for] M[errem]
1801/05/11	AMSCH	0051	*J. v. d. Meer, de jonge* | Een Landschap voor een boeren schuur, ziet men een staande en een leggende koey, benevens eenige schaapen, verders een Jongeling met een lammetje speelende, dit stuk is meesterlyk behandeld, en een der fraaiste van deezen meester | *Size:* hoog 23, breed 25 duim	E[lias]	(Sold) fl 83 Franzen
1802/04/13	HAVIN	0034	*J. van der Meer, de Jonge* | Twee Landschappen, uitvoerig		(Unknown)
1802/05/05	AMSCH	0138	*J. van der Meer de Jonge* | Een Boom- en Bergachtig Landschap, gestoffeerd met Schaapen, uitvoerig | *Mat:* op paneel *Size:* hoog 9, breed 12 duim	C	(Sold) fl 6 Spruit
1802/06/16	AMSCH	0100	*J. van der Meer, de Jonge* | In een bevallig heuvelachtig Landschap met Geboomten en laag Houtgewas, vertoont zich op de voorgrond by een opkoomende weg, een Vrouw op een Ezel rydende, verzelt van een andere gaande, gevolgt door een Huisman, een beladen Ezel voortdryvende, op de voorgrond een troep Schaapen en een Bokje; verder in 't verschiet eenige Gebouwen; alles is zonachtig warm en uitvoerig gepenceeld | *Mat:* op paneel *Size:* hoog 15, breed 19 duim	[Merrem]	(Sold) fl 50 I Smit G[z]
1802/06/16	AMSCH	0101	*J. van der Meer, de Jonge* | Een bergachtig Landschap met hoog Geboomte en Gebouwen gestoffeerd met een Herderin op een Ezel, waarby eenige Schapen; alles uitvoerig en zonachtig behandeld | *Mat:* op doek *Size:* hoog 33, breed 16 ½ duim	[Merrem]	(Sold) fl 19:10 Coclers
1802/06/16	AMSCH	0102	*J. van der Meer, de Jonge* | Een aangenaam Natuurlyk en vlak Landgezicht, van Duin afziende na Zee; op de voorgrond gestoffeerd met gaande en rustende Dorpelingen, en twee Heeren te Paard; meesterlyk geschilderd | *Mat:* op doek *Size:* hoog 10 ½, breed 15 duim	[Merrem]	(Sold) fl 26 Pruijssenaar
1802/06/16	AMSCH	0103	*J. van der Meer, de Jonge* | Op een grazige Heuvel, rusten twee Schaapen en een Bok, waar by een andere staande, verder vertoont zich eenig Geboomten; alles is natuurlyk en meesterlyk fraay gepenceeld | *Mat:* op paneel *Size:* hoog 5 ½, breed 7 ½ duim	[Merrem]	(Sold) fl 2:10 Gruiter
1802/12/13	AMSCH	0110	*J. van der Meer de Jonge* | Een bevallig bergachtig Landschap met eenig Geboomte en Woningen, aan een Rivier, op de voorgrond eenige staande en rustende Beeldjes, uitvoerig van Penceel behandeling | *Mat:* op doek *Size:* hoog 11, breed 14 duim	Schley [for] Lauwers	(Sold) fl 1 van der Schley
1804/05/07	AMSCH	0106	*Meer, de jonge. (J. van der)* | In een Berachtig [sic] Landgezicht met Wooningen en Geboomte, aan een Rivier ziet men op de voorgrond aan den oever verscheide Vrouwen, verzelt van Jagthonden; zonachtig en uitvoerig van penceelbehandeling | *Mat:* op doek *Size:* hoog 12, breed 14 duim	Schley	(Sold) fl 12:10 Gruyter
1804/10/16	DLOND	0135	*J. van der Meer Jr.* | Een helder Landschap met Koeien, Schapen en Herder. Paysage clair, avec des Vaches, Moutons & un Berger | *Mat:* op paneel *Size:* hoog 28, breed 23		(Sold) fl 58 v Yperen
1804/10/16	DLOND	0238	*J. Vermeer. 1693* | Een helder Landschap met een wit Paerd. Paysage clair & un Cheval | *Mat:* op paneel *Size:* hoog 15, breed 11 *Inscr:* J. Vermeer. 1693 (signed and dated?) *Notes:* It is unclear whether the name and date are inscribed on the painting.		(Unknown)

1805/07/03	AMSCH	0108	*J. van der Meer, de jonge* | In een Landschap, by een Beestenstal, vertoont zig twee rustende en een staan Schaap; bevallig gepenceelt | *Mat:* op paneel *Size:* hoog 7, breed 7 ½ duim	G	(Sold) fl 30 Cremer
1805/07/03	AMSCH	0109	*J. van der Meer, de jonge* | Een aangenaam Berg- en Boomryk Landschap, met een Rivier doorsneeden, op de Voorgrond op een Heuvel, met Plantgewassen, een ménigte van staande en rustende Schaapen, verzeld van een Herder en Herderin; aller zonachtigst en uitvoerigst gepenceeld | *Mat:* op koper *Size:* hoog 10, breed 13 duim	V[inkeles]	(Bought In) fl 90
1805/07/03	AMSCH	0110	*J. van der Meer, de jonge* | Een Grazige Weide met verscheid staand en leggend Vee, verders hoog Geboomten; smeltend behandeld | *Mat:* op paneel *Size:* hoog 22, breed 20 duim	C	(Sold) fl 10 Agina
1805/07/10	AMSCH	0096	*J. van der Meer, de Jonge* | Een bevallig Boomryk Landschap, met een stil Water, op de Voorgrond eenige Schapen en Bokken; verder een Landman met een beladen Ezel; zonachtig en warm behandeld | *Mat:* op doek *Size:* hoog 14, breed 19 duim	Wed Grave	(Sold) fl 3:15 Gruyter
1806/05/05	AMSCH	0090	*van der Meer de Jongen* | Een boomryk Landschap, gestoffeerd met Landlieden en Vee; zonagtig en bevallig geschildert door van der Meer de Jongen | *Mat:* op doek *Size:* hoog 32, breed 39 duim	V[inkeles]	(Sold) fl 5:5 van Laar
1808/04/26	GDAN	0107	*Meer (J. van der) de Jonge* | Zijnde een uitmuntend Boomryk Landschap, met Koeijen en Schapen, een Vrouwtje zittende op een Ezel te praten, met een Vrouwtje naast haar staande | *Size:* hoog 14 ½, breed 17 duim	G H Fortuyn	(Unknown)
1808/06/06	RMRIJ	0075	*Meer (Johan van der) de Jonge* | Dit stuk stelt voor een Bergachtig Landschap, rijk in Geboomte en Gewassen; op den voorgrond liggen eenige Schapen met derzelver Lammeren, benevens een slapende jonge Herder met zijn Hond bij zich. Alles schoon van kleur en behandeling, zijnde dit een der kunstrijkste Schilderijen van dezen Meester [Un beau Paysage Montagneux et riche en Arbres, Plantes et verdure : des Moutons et des Agneaux de differentes couleurs reposent sur le devant ; auprés d'eux est un Berger endormi et un beau Chien de garde à côté de lui. Ce Tableau d'un mérite supérieur ne le cède en rien aux Productions si recherchées du fameux Simon van der Does] | *Mat:* op doek *Size:* Hoog 23 ¾, en breed 31 duim. *Loc:* Amsterdam, Nederland. Rijksmuseum. (A248) as J. van der Meer III	Gerrit van der Pot, Heer van Groeneveld	(Sold) fl 705 Johs Eck en Zoon [for] le Roi
1808/08/23	AMSCH	0107	*Meer. (J. van der) de jonge* | Langs een Weg, vertoont zig een steene Brug bij een stil Water, verder een boomrijk Landschap, gestoffeert met Boeren Woningen, Vée, en Rijzigers; dit voorwerp is natuurlijk verbeeld, zonachtig en meesterlijk fraai behandeld | *Mat:* op doek *Size:* hoog 20, breed 26 duim	[Coclers]	(Sold) fl 20 Th Spaan
1809/04/17	AMSCH	0055	*J. van der Meer de Jonge* | Een Bergachtig Landschap, met een Rivier doorsneeden, op de voorgrond rijk met Beeldjes en onderscheide Beesten gestoffeerd; bevallig van licht, fraai en uitvoerig gepenceeld | *Mat:* op doek *Size:* hoog 13, breed 18 duim	A	(Sold) fl 106
1809/04/17	AMSCH	0056	*J. van der Meer de Jonge* | Een alleraangenaamst Boomrijk Landschap, met bevalige Doorzichten, gestoffeerd met grasende en rustende Schapen en Lammeren; helder en zonachtig van penceel | *Mat:* op doek *Size:* hoog 20, breed 23 duim	C	(Sold or Bought In) fl 50
1809/04/17	AMSCH	0056a	*J. van der Meer de Jonge* | Een aangenaam Landschap, met verscheide Boere Woningen en rustende Huislieden; alles natuurlijk geschildert | *Mat:* op doek *Size:* hoog 10, breed 16 duim	T	(Sold) fl 19:10
1810/03/26	RMMUY	0041	*J. Vermeer, de jonge* | Twee uitvoerige, konstige en natuurlijke Rhijn Gezigten. Fraai gestoffeerd [Deux riantes Sites, faisant pendants, prises sur le bord du Rhin, orneés de plusieurs figures, barques et animaux – d'un beau fini, et pleines de mérites.] | *This Lot:* Een Rhijn Gezigt *Annots:* genre moux (BPG) *Mat:* op koper *Size:* hoog 7 ½, breed 9 duimen *Notes:* Lots 41 and 42 were printed in the catalogue as one item.	Daniel de Jongh Az	(Sold) fl 47 for lots 41 & 42. Spaan Amsterdam
1810/03/26	RMMUY	0042	*J. Vermeer, de jonge* | Twee uitvoerige, konstige en natuurlijke Rhijn Gezigten. Fraai gestoffeerd [Deux riantes Sites, faisant pendants, prises sur le bord du Rhin, orneés de plusieurs figures, barques et animaux – d'un beau fini, et pleines de mérites.] | *This Lot:* Een Rhijn Gezigt *Annots:* genre moux (BPG) *Mat:* op koper *Size:* hoog 7 ½, breed 9 duimen *Notes:* Lots 41 and 42 were printed in the catalogue as one item.	Daniel de Jongh Az	(Sold) fl 47 for lots 41 & 42. Spaan Amsterdam
			Vermeulen		
1802/09/21	UTHDG	0091	*Vermeulen* | Een vrolijk Boertje, zittende met een kan in de hand enz. Vet en stout geschildert | *Mat:* op paneel *Size:* hoog 11 ½, breed 9 ½ duimen		(Bought In) fl 13
1806/08/13	AMSCH	0206	*Vermeulen* | In een Winterzicht ziet men op 't Ys, een ménigte Schaatseryders, Arresleeden, Marketenters en verdere gaande Lieden; zonachtig en fiks gepenceeld | *Mat:* op paneel *Size:* hoog 13, breed 17 duim	Vinkeles [for] D	(Sold) fl 11 de Meyer
1810/03/27	RMCNL	0028	*Vermeulen* | Een Kapitaal Landschap, voorstellende eene Winter bij het vallen van den Avond; men ziet op een Dorp, zeer uitvoerig en meesterachtig		(Unknown)
			Vermeulen (copy after)		
1806/10/17	MGSAN	0017	*Vermeulen* | Een Dorpgezicht, verbeeldende een Maanlicht, naar Vermeulen | *Mat:* op paneel	Gerardus Beljard	(Unknown)

Vermeulen (manner)

1806/08/13	AMSCH	0255	*Vermeulen* | Een staand bruin gezadeld Paard, in een Landschap, kragtig geschilderd op Paneel; als door Vermeulen | *Mat:* op paneel	Roos	(Sold) fl 1:5 du Pree

Vermeulen, Andries

1801/03/16	AMSCH	0040	*A. Vermeulen* | Een aangenaam Dorpgezicht met een menigte Beelden, voor een Herberg ziet men een halve Kapwagen, nevens een Fourgon, alles vol gewoel, bevallig en meesterlyk geschilderd	P[ruyssenaar]	(Bought In) fl 36
1801/08/19	AMSCH	0130	*A. Vermeulen* | In een Stal ziet men een schoon Geappeld Paard by een Kreb, voor hetzelven een witte leggende Koey, verders eenig toepasselyk bywerk; krachtig geschildert	Pruyssen^{r}	(Sold) fl 15 P M Levy
1802/02/16	AMSCH	0050	*A. Vermeulen* | Twee stuks aangenaame Landschappen, de voorgrond gestoffeerd met Koeijen, Paarden en Schaapen, helder van coloriet, en uitvoerig gepenceeld	F	(Sold) fl 9 Frantszen
1802/05/05	AMSCH	0229	*A. Vermeulen* | Een aangenaam Landschap, met stoffagie als Cuyp	J	(Sold) fl 7 Cocler
1802/05/10	MGSAN	0024	*A. Vermeulen* | Een plaisant Land- en Dorpgezigt, daarop een Drift met Schaapen, daarby een Man te Paard, en diverse andere Beeldjes, met een Hond, malsch geschilderd, door A. Vermeulen: op Paneel, in vergulde Lyst | *Mat:* op paneel *Size:* hoog 9 ½ duim, breed 8 ½ duim	Johan Dirk Kruysse	(Unknown) £ 0:15
1802/09/06	AMSCH	0125	*A. Vermeulen* | In een Duin- en Boomryk Landschap, ziet men op een zandigen weg, een Man by een kar, met een Paard, agter dezelve een Visboer, Boerin en Hond, verders eenige Schapen; bevallig en meesterlyk gepenceeld | *Size:* hoog 16, breed 21 duim	J	(Sold) fl 21 van Iperen
1802/09/29	AMSCH	0056	*A. Vermeulen* | Een Wintertje, hoog 15 ½, breed 20 ¾ duim. Paneel. By vervallene Muuren ziet men op het Ys wandelende Lieden, zo Mannen als Vrouwen, anderen die Schaatsen Ryden en zig met Yssleden vermaken. Een Vrouwtje wast Linnen in een Byt; twee Reizigers van hunne Paarden gesteegen, waar van de een is zittende, zyn met elkanderen in gesprek; dit stukje is delicaat en uitvoerig behandeld, en van een schoon Coloriet [Cette agréable composition offre les divers amusemens dont on jouit sur la glace, que cet artiste à représentés ingenieusement près d'une masure & d'une echappée de terrein ou des Cavaliers sont descendus de leurs Chevaux ; ce Tableau est peint avec délicatesse & d'une belle couleur & Indique un Morceau de Choix parmi les productions de ce Peintre.] | *Mat:* op paneel *Size:* hoog 15 ½, breed 20 ¾ duim	[Labouchere?]	(Sold) fl 75 J^{n} Spaan
1804/02/27	AMSCH	0109	*Vermeulen. (A.)* | In een Boom- en Bergachtig Landschap, ziet men onder het Geboomten op een graazige Vlakte een Herder met Schaapen en verdere stoffage, op den voorgrond by een omgevallen Boom een sterk bruizende Waterval; en niet minder dan de voorgaande van Schildering | *Mat:* op paneel *Size:* hoog 10, breed 9 duim	C	(Bought In) fl 13
1804/05/07	AMSCH	0177	*Vermeulen. (A.)* | Twee stuks bevallige Landschappen, gestoffeerd met Reizigers, Boerewooningen en Geboomten; zonachtig en fraay behandeld | *Mat:* op paneel *Size:* Ieder hoog 16, breed 21 duim	Y[ver]	(Sold) fl 6 Coclers
1804/05/07	AMSCH	0178	*Vermeulen. (A.)* | Twee Landschappen, met staande en leggende Beesten en eenige Herders, by hunne Schaapen | *Mat:* op paneel *Size:* Ieder hoog 15, breed 12 duim	Y[ver]	(Sold or Bought In) fl 3:10 Yver
1804/05/07	AMSCH	0179	*Vermeulen. (A.)* | Twee stuks aangenaame Bergachtig Lanschappen, gestoffeerd met Plysterplaatsen, waarby eenige Officiers en anderen Persoonen, beneevens hunne Paarden gezien worden | *Mat:* op paneel *Size:* Ieder hoog 14, breed 16 duim	Y[ver]	(Sold) fl 10 Coclers
1804/05/07	AMSCH	0180	*Vermeulen. (A.)* | Twee stuks, zynde het eene een Strandgezicht; en het ander een Landschap met Ruïnen, met Beelden en Beesten; aartig gestoffeerd | *Size:* Ieder hoog 9, breed 11 duim	Y[ver]	(Sold) fl 6:10 Gruyter
1804/08/08	AMSCH	0208	*A. Vermeulen* | In een aangenaam Duin-en Strandgezicht ziet men de Zée, wel voorzien van een ménigte van zeilende Scheepen, aan het Strand een ménigte van Aanschouwers, op en tusschen de Duinen eenige rustende en wandelende Heeren en Dames, uitvoerig geschilderd | *Mat:* op paneel *Size:* hoog 9 ½, breed 11 ½ duim	Vink[eles] [for] K[=Gruyter?]	(Sold) fl 6:5 Van Iperen
1804/08/08	AMSCH	0209	*A. Vermeulen* | Een Natuurlyk Wintergezicht, ryk gestoffeerd, op de voorgrond ziet men een Heer en een Dame, en een Sleede, waar voor een wit Paard, ter zyde een Marquetenter; alles fiks en fraai gepenceeld | *Mat:* op doek *Size:* hoog 29, breed 39 duim	Pruys[senaar]	(Bought In) fl 61
1804/10/16	DLOND	0244	*A. Vermeulen* | Een Landschap. Paysage | *Mat:* op paneel *Size:* hoog 8, breed 11		(Unknown)
1804/10/16	DLOND	0245	*A. Vermeulen, als v.d. Neer* | Een Landschap by Maneschyn. Paysage clair de Lune | *Mat:* op paneel *Size:* hoog 16, breed 17		(Unknown)
1806/08/20	HGBSM	0027	*A. Vermeulen* | Een uitgestrekt IJsgezicht, met verscheide Boerewoningen, en Watermolen, gestoffeerd met een menigte figuren en Schaatscherijders [sic]; alles even geestig en aangenaam geschilderd. de harmonie die in dit stuk heerst, en de diepte van het verschiet zijn meesterlijk | *Mat:* op paneel *Size:* hoog 23, breed 30 ½ duim	Macalester Loup [or others]	(Sold) fl 53 Teissier
1807/06/10	HGBSM	0101	*A. Vermeulen* | Een uitgestrek [sic] ijs gezicht, bij een stadsmuur gestoffeerd met schaatseryders, en wandelende figuren, op de voorgrond een slee, benevens een wit Paard, die door moeite van een hoogte	Abraham Delfos [or others]	(Sold) fl 15:15 Vermeulen

			afgedreven word, &c. helder en fix geschilderd | *Mat:* op paneel *Size:* hoog 25, breed 31 ½ duim		
1807/06/10	HGBSM	0209	*A. Vermeulen* | Een Wintertje rijk gestoffeerd | *Mat:* op paneel	Abraham Delfos [or others]	(Unknown)
1807/06/10	HGBSM	0219	*A. Vermeulen* | Een Landschap met Boerewoningen, voorstellende een Winter, gestoffeerd met Schaatsenrijders en Arresleeden, fix en meesterlijk gepenseelt | *Mat:* op paneel *Size:* hoog 11 ¼, breed 14 ½ duim	Abraham Delfos [or others]	(Sold) fl 10:15 Guicherit
1807/09/28	AMWUR	0018	*A. Vermeulen* | Een dito [stuk] Wintergezichtje, gestoffeerd met een Boerenwooning, Schaatsenryders en wendelende Beeldjes, door A. Vermeulen, in zwarte Lyst, met vergulde Sponnings		(Sold) fl 25 du Pree
1808/06/11	RMRIJ	0028	*A: Vermeulen* | Een helder, zonachtig, aangenaam Landschap met Stoffagie, in de manier van Cuyp, fraai geschilderd | *Mat:* op paneel *Size:* hoog 15 ½, breed 20 ½ duim		(Sold) fl 52 V D Wall
1808/06/11	RMRIJ	0029	*A: Vermeulen* | Een aangenaam ryk en zeer uitvoerig Wintervermaak, met een meenigte Schaatsrydende en andere Figuren, helder en wel geschilderd | *Mat:* op paneel *Size:* hoog 22, breed 26 duim		(Sold) fl 95 Van Ryp
1808/06/11	RMRIJ	0042	*A: Vermeulen* | Een ongemeene, kapitaale en ryke Winter, vol aangenaame stoffagie, zeer verdienstig geschilderd | *Mat:* op doek *Size:* hoog 39, breed 48 ½ duim		(Sold) fl 55 v Yperen
1808/06/11	RMRIJ	0061	*A: Vermeulen* | Een aangenaam Winter- Land- en Rivier Gezigt, met eene Brug, Molen en Tent, geestig en vermakelyk gestoffeert, fraai van coleur en zeer verdienstig geschilderd | *Mat:* op doek *Size:* hoog 38 ½, breed 41 ½ duim		(Bought In) fl 26
1808/06/11	RMRIJ	0083	*A: Vermeulen* | Een Landschap met Koeijen, Paard enz. enz. in de manier van Cuyp | *Mat:* op paneel *Size:* hoog 12 ½, breed 18 ½ duim		(Sold) fl 15 Wigmoore [?]
1808/12/30	HGIMM	[0071p]	*A. Vermeulen* | Voorts een exquis kabinetje Schilderijen van voorname Nederlandsche Meesters, welke uit hoofde van de kortheid des tijds niet stuk voor stuk kunnen beschreven worden; doch waarvan de beschrijving op den Kijkdag zal voorhanden zijn. Dus wij hier alleen de namen van eenige dier Meesters laten volgen, als: A. Kuyp, Ruysdaal, Karel du Jardyn, Loqwi ('t beste dat hij schilderde) Hondekoeter, van Dyk, Janson, Moesgever, Kamphuyzen, van Gooijen, A. van der Neer, T. Wyk, Huchtenburgh, Zolemaker, van Hassel, A. Vermeulen, van Dongen, Scheffer, van Os enz. | *This Lot:* Een Schilderij, A. Vermeulen *Notes:* Because this lot was not numbered in the catalogue, we have assigned the number.		(Unknown)
1809/04/17	AMSCH	0105	*A. Vermeulen* | Een Wintergezicht, met Schaatsenrijders en andere figuuren; bevallig van Schildering | *Mat:* op paneel *Size:* hoog 15, breed 19 duim	A	(Sold) fl 10:10
1809/04/22	AMYVR	0134	*A. Vermeulen* | Een Bosch- en Bergachtig Landschap, aan eene Rivier, gestoffeerd met een Herder, welke Koeijen en Schapen voortdrijft; meesterlijk | *Mat:* op paneel *Size:* hoog 21, breed 28 duim	de Bruin	(Bought In) fl 20
1809/04/22	AMYVR	0135	*A. Vermeulen* | Een besneeuwd Wintergezicht, het IJs met Schaatsenrijders, IJssleeden en wandelende Beeldjes; zonachtig | *Mat:* op paneel *Size:* hoog 24, breed 31 duim	de Bruin	(Sold) fl 40 C S Roos
1809/04/22	AMYVR	0136	*A. Vermeulen* | Twee stuks geestig gestoffeerde stukjes, zijnde het eene een Zomer, en het andere een Winter, in Dorpgezichten voorgesteld | *Mat:* op paneel *Size:* hoog 13, breed 18 duim	de Bruin	(Bought In) fl 20
1809/06/13	AMSCH	0161	*A. Vermeulen* | Een Gezigt aan Duin, gestoffeerd met verscheide Beeldjes, in 't verschiet een Zee met Schepen | *Mat:* op paneel *Size:* hoog 9, breed 11 duim	T	(Sold) fl 3 Buck
1809/07/25	HGBSM	0017	*A. Vermeulen* | Een Winter, verbeeldende een gezigt op de Maas by de Stad Dordrecht, het ys is volgewoel van Sleeden, Paarden en Schaatzeryders en andere Figuuren, kragtig en fraay van couleur, en meesterlyk geschildert | *Mat:* op doek *Size:* hoog 38 ½, breed 49 duim	D van der Aa [or] E B ten Dall	(Sold) fl 97 van Eyk
1809/07/25	HGBSM	0124	*A. Vermeulen* | Een Capitaal Wintergezigt, gestoffeerd met veel Schaatseryders en andere stoffage, aan de voorgrond een Pont waar Vee ingeladen word, fraay geschildert | companion to lot 125 *Mat:* op doek *Size:* hoog 23, breed 28 en een half duim	D van der Aa [or] E B ten Dall	(Sold) fl 45 for lots 124 & 125. Zwartzman
1809/07/25	HGBSM	0125	*A. Vermeulen* | Een Dito [Capitaal gezigt] zynde een Zomer, niet minder als de voorgaande, door denzelven [A. Vermeulen], zynde een weerga | companion to lot 124 *Size:* hoog 23, breed 28 en een half duim	D van der Aa [or] E B ten Dall	(Sold) fl 45 for lots 124 & 125. Zwartzman
1809/07/25	HGBSM	0126	*A. Vermeulen* | Een Capitaal Ysvermaak met een Dorp in 't verschiet, extra vol gewoel met schaatseryders &c., zeer natuurlyk geschildert | *Mat:* op doek *Size:* hoog 29 en een half, breed 4 en een half duim	D van der Aa	(Sold) fl 19 Mes
1809/07/25	HGBSM	0127	*A. Vermeulen* | Een Rivier gezigt, op de tweede grond gestoffeert met Boerewoningen, de voorgrond een opgaande Weg over een Brug, met Figuren, uitvoerig | *Mat:* op doek *Size:* hoog 18, breed 24 en een half duim	D van der Aa	(Sold) fl 15 Mes
1809/07/25	HGBSM	0128	*A. Vermeulen* | Een Wintertje, op de voorgrond een postwaagen waarby eenige Paarden staan te eeten, en verders eenige Figuren op het Ys | *Mat:* op paneel *Size:* hoog 11, breed 13 en een half duim	D van der Aa [or] E B ten Dall	(Sold) fl 10:5 van Eyk

1809/07/25	HGBSM	0129	*A. Vermeulen* | Een Bergachtig Landschap gestoffeerd met Koebeesten en Schaapen en een Vrouw te Paard waarby een Man, uitvoerig | *Mat:* op doek *Size:* hoog 18 en een half, breed 24 en een half duim	D van der Aa [or] E B ten Dall	(Sold) fl 16:10 van Eyk
1809/07/25	HGBSM	0130	*A. Vermeulen* | Twee Stuks Landschapjes, gestoffeert, het een met Koebeesten en het andere met Schaapen | *Mat:* op paneel *Size:* hoog 12 en een half, breed 11 duim	D van der Aa	(Sold) fl 41 Van der Aa
1809/07/25	HGBSM	0131	*A. Vermeulen* | Twee Stuks, zynde het eene een Zomer en het andere een Winter, met Figuuren en Beesten gestoffeert | *Mat:* op paneel *Size:* hoog 8, breed 10 en een half duim	D van der Aa [or] E B ten Dall	(Sold) fl 25:5 van Eyk
1809/07/25	HGBSM	0132	*A. Vermeulen* | Een Ysgezigtje, gestoffeert met veel Schaatseryders, aangenaam en helder geschildert | *Mat:* op paneel *Size:* hoog 7, breed 10 duim	D van der Aa [or] E B ten Dall	(Sold) fl 17:5 L Voerman
1809/07/25	HGBSM	0133	*A. Vermeulen* | Een Watergezigt by Maaneschyn, met stoffage | *Mat:* op paneel *Size:* diameter 6 duim	D van der Aa [or] E B ten Dall	(Sold) fl 1:18 Temminck
1809/07/25	HGBSM	0136	*A. Vermeulen* | Een levensgroote Bonte Osse Kop, stout geschildert | *Mat:* op doek *Size:* hoog 43 en een half, breed 37 en een half duim	D van der Aa	(Sold) fl 31 Mes
1810/06/06	RMMUY	0121	*A. Vermeulen* | Een Kapitaal Winter Gezigt, fraaij en bevallig gestoffeerd, krachtig en meesterlijk geschilderd | *Mat:* op doek		(Unknown) fl 32
1810/06/06	RMMUY	0122	*A. Vermeulen* | Een warm zonachtig Landschap, op den voorgrond eenige stoffage door het water wadende, en een aangenaam verschiet. Uitvoerig en goed geschilderd | *Mat:* op paneel		(Unknown) fl 25
1810/06/20	AMSCH	0096	*A. Vermeulen* | Twee stuks; een Zomer- en Wintergezigt, met Boeren Woningen en Geboomte, beide met Huislieden, Paarden en andere stoffage. Fraai geschilderd | *Mat:* op paneel *Size:* Jeder hoog 19, breed 24 duimen	A	(Sold) fl 80 Eekhof
1810/06/20	AMSCH	0097	*A. Vermeulen* | Een bevrozen Water, ter zijde Boeren Woningen, gestoffeerd met een Arreslede, Schaatzerijders enz. | *Mat:* op paneel *Size:* hoog 12, breed 16 duimen	A	(Sold) fl 16 Eekhof
1810/06/20	AMSCH	0098	*A. Vermeulen* | In een Landschap ziet men op den voorgrond drie Jagers, voor eene Herberg zich ververschen | *Mat:* op doek *Size:* hoog 23, breed 19 duimen	A	(Sold) fl 32 Van Iperen
1810/07/23	DOLG2	00CC	*A. Vermeulen* | Voor eene Woning zit de Vrouw te slapen. Nevens haar spelen twee Jongens, verder eene Hen met Kiekens, zeer vrolijk en bevallig geschilderd | *Mat:* op paneel *Size:* hoog 13 ½, breed 11 duim	Pieter Quinting	(Sold) fl 25 Nieuwenhuys
			Vermeulen, Andries (copy by)		
1802/12/13	AMSCH	0165	*A. Vermeulen; J. Ruisdaal* | Langs een met Sneeuw bedekte Weg, ter zyde een Sloot en Boere Woning, ziet men eenige gaande en rydende Beeldjes; meesterlyk geschilderd, door A. Vermeulen, na J. Ruisdaal | copy by A. Vermeulen after J. Ruisdael *Mat:* op paneel *Size:* hoog 16, breed 19 duim	Pruyssenaar [for] A	(Sold) fl 35 Coclers
1804/02/27	AMSCH	0108	*Vermeulen (A.); na J. Ruysdaal* | In een natuurlyke Winter, langs een met Sneeuw bedekten Weg, ter zyden een Sloot en Boerewoning ziet men eenige gaande en rydende Beeltjes; en verdere stoffage, meesterlyk geschilderd | copy by A. Vermeulen after J. Ruisdael *Mat:* op paneel *Size:* hoog 12, breed 17 duim	C	(Sold) fl 36 van Iperen
1804/10/16	DLOND	0246	*A. Vermeulen; naar A. de Voys* | Een Krygsheld op de Jagt. Un Militaire à la Chasse | copy by A. Vermeulen after Ary de Vois *Mat:* op paneel *Size:* hoog 10, breed 14		(Unknown)
1806/05/05	AMSCH	0122	*A. Vermeulen; J. Ruisdaal* | Een boom en bergagtig Landschap, met een Herder met Schapen, by eene Waterval; na J. Ruisdaal | copy by A. Vermeulen after J. Ruisdael *Mat:* op paneel *Size:* hoog 10, breed 9 duim	V[inkeles]	(Bought In) fl 7
1808/06/11	RMRIJ	0084	*A: Vermeulen; A. Cuyp* | Een Copy na A. Cuyp | copy by A. Vermeulen after A. Cuyp *Mat:* op paneel		(Sold) fl 7:15 van Yperen
1809/04/17	AMSCH	0106	*A. Vermeulen; J. Wijnands* | Twee stuks Duinachtige Landschappen, met Geboomten, gestoffeerd met gaande en rustende Huislieden; natuurlijk en Bevallig, naar J. Wijnands, door A. Vermeulen | copy by A. Vermeulen after Wijnants *Mat:* op paneel *Size:* ieder hoog 10, breed 12 ½ duim	R	(Sold) fl 15:10 Gruyter
1809/04/22	AMYVR	0137	*A. Vermeulen; M. Hobbema* | Een Boomrijk Landschap, aan eene Waterplas; zonachtig behandeld, naar M. Hobbema, door A. Vermeulen | copy by A. Vermeulen after Hobbema *Size:* hoog 29, breed 41 duim	de Bruin	(Sold) fl 14:15 du Pree
1809/07/25	HGBSM	0134	*A. Vermeulen; A. Cuyp* | Een uitgestrekt Landschap, waar in Heeren te Paard, en voorts gestoffeert met leggende Koebeesten en Schaapen &c., na A. Cuyp, door A. Vermeulen | copy by A. Vermeulen after A. Cuyp *Mat:* op doek *Size:* hoog 38, breed 59 duim	D van der Aa [or] E B ten Dall	(Sold) fl 12:10 A Vermeulen
1810/07/23	DOLG1	0060	*Andries Vermeulen; naar A. Cuip* | Een Landschap, in het zelve een bruin Paard, met witte Manen, en drie liggende Runderbeesten. Goed van tekening en coloriet, en zeer wel dezen grooten meester gevolgd | copy by A. Vermeulen after A. Cuyp *Size:* hoog 11, breed 15 duim	Mr Pieter van den Santheuvel	(Sold) fl 14:10 van de Hegge
			Vermeulen, B. [Unidentified]		
1801/12/22	AMOTT	0054	*B. Vermeulen* | 1 aangenaam duin- en heuvelachtig boschryk Landschap, met een op den Ezel rydende Herderin, omringd door andere Beesten en bywerk; in bevallige smaak	Bartholomeus Ruloffs	(Unknown) fl 13:10

Vermeulen, Cornelis (III)

1804/10/16	DLOND	0241	*C. Vermeulen* | De Samaritaansche Vrouw. La Samaritaine | *Mat:* op paneel *Size:* hoog 14, breed 16	(Unknown)

Vermeulen, Cornelis (III) (copy by)

1804/10/16	DLOND	0239	*C. Vermeulen; naar Berghem* | Ene zeer schone en allernaauwkeurigste Copy naar N. Berghem, verbeeldende een Hertenjacht. Une Copie superbe & très-exacte d'après N. Berghem, repres. une Chasse de Cerf | copy by Corn. Vermeulen (III) after N.P. Berchem *Mat:* op paneel *Size:* hoog 15, breed 20	(Sold) fl 28 O D Wyngaert
1804/10/16	DLOND	0240	*C. Vermeulen; naar Versteeg* | Ene dito uts[a]. [zeer schone en allernaauwkeurigste Copy] van het bekende Schildery van Versteeg, verbeeldende eene Familie, Coffy drinkende in een Vertrek, door Vuur en Kaarssen verlicht, met een Glazen Spiegelbol aan de Zolder. Un dito uts[a]. [Copie superbe & très-exacte] d'après le Tableau connu de Versteeg, repres. une Famille prenant le Caffé dans une Chambre, eclairée tant par le feu que par des Chandelles, avec une Boulè de Cristal étamé suspendue au plancher | copy by Corn. Vermeulen (III) after Versteeg *Mat:* op doek *Size:* hoog 23, breed 28	(Sold) fl 47 v Walle
1804/10/16	DLOND	0240a[a]	*C. Vermeulen; Adrien v. Ostade* | Een Stuk, bevattende 13 zeer schone Copiën van de volgende Meesters. Un Tableau, contenant 13 Copies très-belles des Peintres suivans. 1. Adrien v. Ostade. Een Herberg, Auberge | copy by Corn. Vermeulen (III) after A. Ostade *Mat:* op paneel *Size:* hoog 41, breed 55 *Notes:* The description in the title refers to lots 240a[a-m].	(Sold) fl 150 for lots 240a[a-m]. Ond d Wyngaert
1804/10/16	DLOND	0240a[b]	*C. Vermeulen; C. Bega* | [Een Stuk, bevattende 13 zeer schone Copiën van de volgende Meesters. Un Tableau, contenant 13 Copies très-belles des Peintres suivans.] 2. C. Bega. Vrolyk Gezelschap, Compagnie joyeuse | copy by Corn. Vermeulen (III) after Bega *Mat:* op paneel *Size:* hoog 41, breed 55 *Notes:* The bracketed information in the title appears above lot 240a[a] and refers to lots 240a[a-m].	(Sold) fl 150 for lots 240a[a-m]. Ond d Wyngaert
1804/10/16	DLOND	0240a[c]	*C. Vermeulen; D. van Tol* | [Een Stuk, bevattende 13 zeer schone Copiën van de volgende Meesters. Un Tableau, contenant 13 Copies très-belles des Peintres suivans.] 3. D. van Tol. Een Binnenvertrek, une Chambre | copy by Corn. Vermeulen (III) after D. Tol *Mat:* op paneel *Size:* hoog 41, breed 55 *Notes:* The bracketed information in the title appears above lot 240a[a] and refers to lots 240a[a-m].	(Sold) fl 150 for lots 240a[a-m]. Ond d Wyngaert
1804/10/16	DLOND	0240a[d]	*C. Vermeulen; Versteeg* | [Een Stuk, bevattende 13 zeer schone Copiën van de volgende Meesters. Un Tableau, contenant 13 Copies très-belles des Peintres suivans.] 4. Versteeg. Lamplicht, Lumière de Lampe | copy by Corn. Vermeulen (III) after Versteeg *Mat:* op paneel *Size:* hoog 41, breed 55 *Notes:* The bracketed information in the title appears above lot 240a[a] and refers to lots 240a[a-m].	(Sold) fl 150 for lots 240a[a-m]. Ond d Wyngaert
1804/10/16	DLOND	0240a[e]	*C. Vermeulen; A. v. d. Neer* | [Een Stuk, bevattende 13 zeer schone Copiën van de volgende Meesters. Un Tableau, contenant 13 Copies très-belles des Peintres suivans.] 5. A. v. d. Neer. Maneschyn, clair de Lune | copy by Corn. Vermeulen (III) after A. Neer *Mat:* op paneel *Size:* hoog 41, breed 55 *Notes:* The bracketed information in the title appears above lot 240a[a] and refers to lots 240a[a-m].	(Sold) fl 150 for lots 240a[a-m]. Ond d Wyngaert
1804/10/16	DLOND	0240a[f]	*C. Vermeulen; W. v. Mieris* | [Een Stuk, bevattende 13 zeer schone Copiën van de volgende Meesters. Un Tableau, contenant 13 Copies très-belles des Peintres suivans.] 6. W. v. Mieris. Keukenstuk, une Cuisine | copy by Corn. Vermeulen (III) after W. Mieris *Mat:* op paneel *Size:* hoog 41, breed 55 *Notes:* The bracketed information in the title appears above lot 240a[a] and refers to lots 240a[a-m].	(Sold) fl 150 for lots 240a[a-m]. Ond d Wyngaert
1804/10/16	DLOND	0240a[g]	*C. Vermeulen; J. Steen* | [Een Stuk, bevattende 13 zeer schone Copiën van de volgende Meesters. Un Tableau, contenant 13 Copies très-belles des Peintres suivans.] 7. J. Steen. De Schoolmeester, le Maitre d'Ecole. (No. 213a) | copy by Corn. Vermeulen (III) after J. Steen *Mat:* op paneel *Size:* hoog 41, breed 55 *Notes:* The bracketed information in the title appears above lot 240a[a] and refers to lots 240a[a-m].	(Sold) fl 150 for lots 240a[a-m]. Ond d Wyngaert
1804/10/16	DLOND	0240a[h]	*C. Vermeulen; W. v. Mieris* | [Een Stuk, bevattende 13 zeer schone Copiën van de volgende Meesters. Un Tableau, contenant 13 Copies très-belles des Peintres suivans.] 8. W. v. Mieris. Een Bontwerker, un Pelletier | copy by Corn. Vermeulen (III) after W. Mieris *Mat:* op paneel *Size:* hoog 41, breed 55 *Notes:* The bracketed information in the title appears above lot 240a[a] and refers to lots 240a[a-m].	(Sold) fl 150 for lots 240a[a-m]. Ond d Wyngaert
1804/10/16	DLOND	0240a[i]	*C. Vermeulen; Le Duc* | [Een Stuk, bevattende 13 zeer schone Copiën van de volgende Meesters. Un Tableau, contenant 13 Copies très-belles des Peintres suivans.] 9. Le Duc. Een Binnenwacht, un Corps de Garde | copy by Corn. Vermeulen (III) after Johan le Ducq *Mat:* op paneel *Size:* hoog 41, breed 55 *Notes:* The bracketed information in the title appears above lot 240a[a] and refers to lots 240a[a-m].	(Sold) fl 150 for lots 240a[a-m]. Ond d Wyngaert
1804/10/16	DLOND	0240a[j]	*C. Vermeulen; J. Steen* | [Een Stuk, bevattende 13 zeer schone Copiën van de volgende Meesters. Un Tableau, contenant 13 Copies très-belles des Peintres suivans.] 10. J. Steen. Het Bruidjen, la Fiancée. (N°. 212) | copy by Corn. Vermeulen (III) after J. Steen *Mat:* op paneel *Size:* hoog 41,	(Sold) fl 150 for lots 240a[a-m]. Ond d Wyngaert

			breed 55 *Notes:* The bracketed information in the title appears above lot 240a[a] and refers to lots 240a[a-m].		
1804/10/16	DLOND	0240a[k]	*C. Vermeulen; Brekelenkamp* | [Een Stuk, bevattende 13 zeer schone Copiën van de volgende Meesters. Un Tableau, contenant 13 Copies très-belles des Peintres suivans.] 11. Brekelenkamp. Een Vertrek, une Chambre | copy by Corn. Vermeulen (III) after Q. Brekelencam *Mat:* op paneel *Size:* hoog 41, breed 55 *Notes:* The bracketed information in the title appears above lot 240a[a] and refers to lots 240a[a-m].		(Sold) fl 150 for lots 240a[a-m]. Ond d Wyngaert
1804/10/16	DLOND	0240a[l]	*C. Vermeulen; Brakenburg* | [Een Stuk, bevattende 13 zeer schone Copiën van de volgende Meesters. Un Tableau, contenant 13 Copies très-belles des Peintres suivans.] 12. Brakenburg. Enige Boeren, des Paysans | copy by Corn. Vermeulen (III) after Brakenburg *Mat:* op paneel *Size:* hoog 41, breed 55 *Notes:* The bracketed information in the title appears above lot 240a[a] and refers to lots 240a[a-m].		(Sold) fl 150 for lots 240a[a-m]. Ond d Wyngaert
1804/10/16	DLOND	0240a[m]	*C. Vermeulen; Verschuring* | [Een Stuk, bevattende 13 zeer schone Copiën van de volgende Meesters. Un Tableau, contenant 13 Copies très-belles des Peintres suivans.] 13. Verschuring. Ene Jachtparty, une partie de Chasse | copy by Corn. Vermeulen (III) after H. Verschuring *Mat:* op paneel *Size:* hoog 41, breed 55 *Notes:* The bracketed information in the title appears above lot 240a[a] and refers to lots 240a[a-m].		(Sold) fl 150 for lots 240a[a-m]. Ond d Wyngaert
1804/10/16	DLOND	0242	*C. Vermeulen; naar Cuyp* | Een Pleisterplaats. Le devant d'une Auberge | copy by Corn. Vermeulen (III) after A. Cuyp *Mat:* op paneel *Size:* hoog 15, breed 19		(Unknown)
1804/10/16	DLOND	0243	*C. Vermeulen; naar A. v. d. Velde* | Twee Landschapjens met Vee. Deux Paysages & du Betail | copy by Corn. Vermeulen (III) after A. Velde *Mat:* op paneel *Size:* hoog 8, breed 11		(Unknown)
1808/06/11	RMRIJ	0082	*C: Vermeulen; na A: Klomp* | Een aangenaam Landschap, met ryke Stoffagie van Vee enz., goed gedaan | copy by Corn. Vermeulen (III) after Klomp *Mat:* op paneel *Size:* hoog 5, breed 4 ½ duim		(Bought In) fl 9:10
1809/04/22	AMYVR	0139	*de oude Vermeulen; M. Versteegh* | Een Copij, naar een beroemd Kaarslicht, door M. Versteegh, geschilderd door de oude Vermeulen | copy by Corn. Vermeulen (III) after Versteeg *Mat:* op paneel *Size:* hoog 20, breed 24 duim	de Bruin	(Sold) fl 4:15 du Pree
			Vermeulen, E. [Unidentified]		
1810/07/23	DOLG2	0072	*E. Vermeulen* | Een Landschap met Schaapjes, Runderen en Beeldtjes; zinnelijk en netjes behandeld | *Mat:* op paneel *Size:* hoog 6, breed 7 duim	Pieter Quinting	(Unknown)
			Vernet, Claude Joseph		
1807/08/26	AMSCH	0220	*J. Vernet* | Een onstuimige Zee en Rotsgezicht, verbeeld by het opkomen van een Onweder: aan de linkerzyde ziet men eenige Visschers, die hunne Netten inhalen, en ter regterzyde zyn andere bezig een Boot op Strand te trekken; alles is fiks, fraai en krachtig geschilderd | *Mat:* op doek *Size:* hoog 29, breed 25 duim	Coclers	(Bought In) fl 212
1810/03/23	HAVIN	0063	*Vernet* | Twee Italiaansche Landschappen met een Waterval, uitmuntend fraai met coul. [In Lysten met Glasen] | *Notes:* The bracketed information in the title appears above lot 63 and refers to lots 63 to 79.	Rudolf Hendrik de Wetstein [or others]	(Unknown)
1810/08/06	AMSCH	0106	*Vernet (Joseph)* | Een hoog Bergachtig Landschap, met een breed Water doorsneden, gestoffeerd met verscheide Arbeiders, zo Mannen als Vrouwen, die bezig zijn Linnen te spoelen, op den voorgrond twee Visschers in een Schuit; dit stuk is zoo van schildering als Ordonnantie een der beste van dezen Meester | possibly companion to lot 107 *Mat:* op doek *Size:* hoog 26, breed 38 duimen	A	(Sold) fl 600 for lots 106 & 107. Texier Gerbet en Comp [for] Lebrun
1810/08/06	AMSCH	0107	*Vernet (Joseph)* | Eene Ruime en stille Zee, met zeilende Oorlogschepen, vooraan bij een Hoofd ziet men Visschers, die een Net ophalen en anderen, die een Visschuit ontladen, achterwaarts een Zeehaven en Gebergte in het verschiet, als de voorgaande behandeld, kunnende dienen tot een wederga | possibly companion to lot 106 *Mat:* op doek *Size:* hoog 26, breed 38 duimen	A	(Sold) fl 600 for lots 106 & 107. Texier Gerbet en Comp [for] Lebrun
1810/08/06	AMSCH	0108	*Vernet (Joseph)* | Een Zeehaven, rijk gestoffeerd met Kooplieden en Arbeiders, bezig Koopmanschappen als Balen, Vaten en andere Goederen in Vaartuigen te laden, op den voorgrond Reizigers bij eenen Put, die hunnen Paarden laten drinken; warm van koloriet; uitvoerig en fraai gepenceeld | possibly companion to lot 109 *Mat:* op doek *Size:* hoog 26, breed 33 duimen	A	(Sold) fl 400 for lots 108 & 109. Texier Gerbet en Comp
1810/08/06	AMSCH	0109	*Vernet (Joseph)* | Een Italiaansch Land- en Watergezicht, met Gebouwen en Ruïne, rijk met Reizigers, Muilezels, Visschers en Vaartuigen gestoffeerd, en een ruim verschiet, het is van gelijke schildering als de voorgaande, kunnende strekken tot de wederga | possibly companion to lot 108 *Size:* hoog 26, breed 33 duimen	A	(Sold) fl 400 for lots 108 & 109. Texier Gerbet en Comp
			Vernet, Claude Joseph (or Vernet, C.J., manner)		
1803/12/12	AMSCH	0103	*J. Vernet* | Twee stuks, het eene een onstuimige Zee met Scheepen, in grooten nood, waar van de Schépelingen elkander redden; het andere een maneschyn by een Fort, met Visschers in hun Schuiten gestoffeerd; beide meesterlyk op Doek, door J. Vernet, of in zyn manier | *Mat:* op doek *Size:* hoog 15, breed 18 duim	D	(Sold) fl 40 Valet

Vernet, Claude Joseph (manner)

1801/04/23	AMYVR	0016	*Vernet* | Twee stuks Italiaansch Land- en Watergezichten, gestoffeerd met Beelden en Beesten, in de manier van Vernet		(Sold) fl 40 Carle van Brent
1805/07/03	AMSCH	0196	*J. Vernet* | Een Italiaansch Bergachtig Landschap, met een Waterval en stromend Riviertje, op de Voorgrond een staande Vrouw, by rustende Vissers; bevallig op Doek geschilderd, in de manier van J. Vernet | *Mat:* op doek	G	(Sold) fl 4:10 Agina
1805/07/10	AMSCH	0259	*J. Vernet* | Twee stuks stille Zeehavens, gestoffeert met een gedeelte van een Vest-Muur, diversche Beeldjes aan Strand en zylende Scheepen; in de manier van J. Vernet; plaisant op Doek geschilderd | *Mat:* op doek	S[chley] [for] Doralle	(Sold) fl 3:5 Rookmans
1806/08/13	AMSCH	0252	*J. Vernet* | Twee stuks Berg en Boomryke Landschappen, met fraaije Watervallen, en stoffagie van Beelden; zonachtig en plaisant geschilderd als J. Vernet	Roos	(Sold) fl 81 Yver
1809/07/25	HGBSM	0187	*Vernet* | Een Onstuimige Zee, waar in een schip vergaat tegen de Rotzen, in de trant van Vernet | *Mat:* op doek *Size:* hoog 26, breed 37 duim	D van der Aa [or] E B ten Dall	(Sold) fl 2 Nieuwenhuis

Veronese (Paolo Caliari)

1802/06/16	AMSCH	0194	*P. Veronese* | Deeze Ryke Ordenantie, vertoond Maria zittende op een verheeven Zeetel, met het Kindeken op de schoot, waar by St. Catharina eerbiedig de hand aan het zelve toerykende, verzelt van Musiceerende, en om hoog in de Wolken verscheide Engelen; alles is krachtig en van een meesterlyke penceel-behandeling | *Mat:* op doek *Size:* hoog 38, breed 34 duim	[Merrem]	(Sold) fl 11:10 Agina
1803/04/20	AMSCH	0075	*Veronese (Paulo)* | Dit Capitaal en uitmuntend Tafreel, vertoont de Dooping van Christus, door St. Jan, den Heiland staat als in een alleröotmoedigste gestalten, houdende beide handen kruisling over elkander geslaagen op de Borst, en met beide Voeten gedeeltelyk in 't Water, daar nevens staat, en als op een Knie rustende, den Boetgezant, met de Regterhand opgeheven, den Heiligen Doop verrigtende, onder het nederdaalen der Heilige Geest, verzeld van een glorie Engelen; het verschiet vertoont een Landschap, alles is groots geordeneert, de Teekening, de Hartstogten, en het schoon Coloriet van het Naakt, geeven een Luister aan dit stuk, zoo wel als de meesterlyke uitvoerige penceels-behandeling. NB. Den beroemden Dichter J. van den Vondel, heeft op dit Kunststuk, een fraay Lofgedicht gemaakt, te zien in het tweede Deel van zyn Poëzy, bladz. 317 [Ce Tableau capital est une representation du baptême de J.C. par St. Jean Baptiste : figures de grandeur naturelle, le haut du Tableau offre une gloire dont descend le St. Esprit. J.C. dans une attitude respectueuse croise les bras sur sa poitrine ayant les pieds sous l'eau du Jourdain. Le Precurseur plie le genous sur une motte de terre élévée, etendant la main droite remplie d'eau qu'il verse sur la tête du Sauveur. Le Caractére du Christ est vraiment élevé, et les Carnations sont d'une vérité à faire illusion! les contours sont naturels et faciles, et quel qu'en soit l'auteur, c'est une production de très grend [sic] mérité. Le Célébre Poëte Hollandois, Vondel, frappé de cette representation en fit un eloge pompeux, aussi expressif que le Tàbleau même.] | *Mat:* op doek *Size:* hoog 94, breed 61 duim [haut 44, large 61 pouces] *Notes:* The dimensions differ in the Dutch and French editions of the catalogue.	Maria Magdalena van Sluypwyk, gravinne van Moens	(Sold) fl 285 Pruijssenaar
1803/08/17	AMSCH	0081	*Veronese. (P.)* | Christus het Pascha vierende met zyne Discipelen. De Ordonnantie is schoon, de schildering meesterlyk, het effect en de uitdrukking onverbeterlyk, en uitmuntend van behandeling | *Mat:* op doek *Size:* hoog 15, breed 12 duim	Anna Catharina Putman	(Sold) fl 39 Pruijssenaar
1804/02/27	AMSCH	0106	*Veronese. (P.)* | Jezus het Paaschfeest vierende met zyne Dicipelen, meesterlyk gepenceeld | *Mat:* op doek *Size:* hoog 14, breed 12 duim	B	(Sold) fl 20 Josi
1810/07/26	AMSCH	0086	*Veronese (P.)* | De Heilige Ignatius, knielende voor Maria. Schoon geschilderd | *Mat:* op doek *Size:* hoog 28, breed 23 duimen	Cassino	(Sold) fl 1 L Pakker

Verrocchio, Andrea del

1810/07/26	AMSCH	0085	*Verdochio* | Het Huwelijk van St. Catharina, bestaande in zes Voorwerpen. Zijnde een zeer oud stuk uit de Romeinsche School | *Mat:* op paneel *Size:* hoog 23, breed 20 duimen	Cassino	(Sold) fl 3 Yver

Verschuir, Lieve

1801/06/10	AMSCH	0174	*Verschuur. (L.)* | Een Rieviergezicht, by een Fortres [sic], liggen eenige Scheepen en Vaartuigen, op de voorgrond eenige Visschers, alles tegen een opgaande Zon te zien; zynde meesterlyk gepenceeld | *Mat:* op paneel *Size:* hoog 14, breed 18 duim *Notes:* Originally the artist's name was spelled "L. Verschuir." This error was corrected in an errata sheet located at the end of the catalogue.	Herman ten Kate	(Sold) fl 43 C S Roos
1804/08/08	AMSCH	0202	*L. Verschuur* | In een stille Zée ziet men by 't Strand eenige stil leggende Scheepen en Vaartuigen en eenige Visschers in Schuiten, bézig hunne Netten uit te gooijen, verders eenige zeilende Scheepen en Vaartuigen; fiks en meesterlyk geschilderd | *Mat:* op doek *Size:* hoog 18, br. 25 duim	Vink[eles] [for] S	(Sold) fl 2 de Meijer
1804/10/16	DLOND	0248	*L. Verschuur* | Een stil Water voor Helvoetsluis, met Oorlogschepen, onder welken het Admiraalschip van de Ruyter, de 7 Provinciën. Un Calme. Vue devant Helvoetsluys avec des Navires de Guerre, & entre		(Unknown)

			elles celle de l'Amiral de Ruyter, les 7 Provinces | *Mat:* op doek *Size:* hoog 45, breed 77		
1805/07/10	AMSCH	0164	*Lieve Verschuur* | Een stil Water, by Maneschyn, met verscheide Vischers in hunne Schuiten; natuurlyk en fiks gepenceeld | *Mat:* op paneel *Size:* hoog 14, breed 19 duim	V[inkeles] [for] L	(Withdrawn)
1808/04/26	GDAN	0178	*Verschuur (L.)* | Een Zee Bataille, die zeer uitmuntend geschildert is | *Size:* hoog 19, breed 29 duim	G H Fortuyn	(Unknown)
1809/04/17	AMSCH	0109	*Lieve Verschuur* | Een Maneschijn over een stille Rivier, gestoffeerd met Visschers en Vaartuigen; piquant geschildert | *Mat:* op paneel *Size:* hoog 14, breed 19 duim	T	(Sold) fl 0:6
1810/06/06	RMMUY	0074	*Lieve Verschuur* | De oude Hoofdpoort te Rotterdam, en een gedeelte van de Maas, bij Winter, rijk gestoffeerd, meesterlijk en konstig | *Mat:* op doek		(Unknown) fl 21
1810/06/20	AMSCH	0167	*L. Verschuur* | Een stil Water met Vaartuigen, en bij het Strand Visschers	A	(Sold) fl 1:5 Andriessen
1810/10/10	MGCIT	0012	*L. Verschuure* | Een Stille Zee met een menigte Zeeschepen, drijvende in het zagt kabbelende Water; voorts een Zeehaven en gestoffeerd met nog verscheide andere Vaartuigen en Figuuren, zilverachtig uitgevoerd, en een der voornaamste Stukken	Caspar van Citters	(Unknown)
1810/10/11	AMSCH	0089	*L. Verschuring* | Een kapitaal Gezigt langs de Maas aan de zijde van Dordrecht, gestoffeerd met een zeilend Jagt en eenige Schepen en Vaartuigen; schoon en in de manier van A. Cuip geschilderd | *Mat:* op doek *Size:* hoog 32, breed 42 duimen	[Gruyter?]	(Bought In) fl 5

Verschuring

1802/09/21	UTHDG	0092	*Verschuring* | Twee stuks: in het eerste, een aanzienlijke vrouw bezig in papieren, in de wederga de Man componeerende Musiecq, ieder met een hondje bij zig, enz. Krachtig geschildert | *Mat:* op paneel *Size:* hoog 17 ½, breed 21 duimen		(Bought In) fl 7:10

Verschuring, Hendrik

1801/06/10	AMSCH	0175	*Verschuuring. (H.)* | Eenige Heeren te paard, als ter jagt uitrydende, in 't verschiet hoog Geboomte, en een Poort van een Stad; meesterlyk van behandeling | *Mat:* op doek *Size:* hoog 27, breed 33 duim	Herman ten Kate	(Sold) fl 59 J Yver
1801/08/19	AMSCH	0123a	*H. Verschuuring* | Een Grot Gezicht met diversche speelende en dansende Beelden, beneevens een staand Paard en Ezel, door H. Verschuuring, op Paneel | *Mat:* op paneel *Size:* hoog 18 ½, breed 25 duim	van der Schly [for] F	(Sold) fl 5:5 Le Dantú
1802/02/16	AMSCH	0041	*J. Verschuring* | Een staand gezadeld Paard op stal, by een kreb; meesterlyk, en natuurlyk geschildert | *Notes:* The artist's name was given as "J. Verschuring" but we have assumed this is an error.	G	(Sold) fl 5:10 Gruiter
1802/02/16	AMSCH	0047	*J. Verschuring* | Voor een wooning ziet men Heeren te paard, ter zyde staat een knegt, bézig een paard te zadelen, fiks geschilderd | *Notes:* The artist's name was given as "J. Verschuring" but we have assumed this is an error.	G	(Sold) fl 2 van der Schley [for] G
1802/05/05	AMSCH	0210	*H. Verschuuring* | Een Landschap, ter zyde een Gebouw, op de voorgrond gestoffeerd met Paarden, Beelden en Honden, bevallig | *Mat:* op doek *Size:* hoog 15, breed 18 duim	A	(Bought In) fl 5
1802/06/16	AMSCH	0199	*H. Verschuuring* | In een Landschap ziet men een Dame en Heer te Paard, beneevens een Jager met Honden ter jagt gaande; natuurlyk en meesterlyk gepenceeld | *Mat:* op paneel *Size:* hoog 7 ½, breed 9 ¾ duim	[Merrem]	(Sold) fl 3 Wed Achtienhoven
1802/07/20	MGSAN	0035	*H. Verschuuring* | Een extra fraai Battailletje: helder en krachtig geschilderd, op Paneel | *Mat:* op paneel *Size:* hoog duim 12, breed duim 14		(Unknown)
1802/11/01	DOBRA	0112	*H. Verschuuring* | Een Veldbatailje kloek behandeld | *Mat:* op doek *Size:* h. 28. br. 34 d.	Paulus van der Spyk [or others]	(Sold or Bought In) fl 7 Braam [?]
1802/12/13	AMSCH	0224	*J. Verschuuring* | Een staand zwart gezadeld Paard; fiks en meesterlyk behandeld | *Notes:* The artist's name was given as "J. Verschuuring" but we have assumed this is an error.	Schley [for] Lauwers	(Sold) fl 0:10 van Dijl
1803/08/17	AMSCH	0084	*Verschuring (H.)* | In een Rots ziet men een hevige Rencontre tusschen Cavallerie, schoon van effect en kragtig gepenceeld | *Mat:* op doek *Size:* hoog 19, breed 16 duim	Anna Catharina Putman	(Sold) fl 2 Agina
1803/09/07	AMSCH	0203	*H. Verschuuring* | Een Bergachtig Landschap, op de voorgrond voor een Grot, ziet men twee Paarden, nevens hun een Man en drie Honden, kragtig en meesterlyk [Un paysage montagneux ; sur le devant à l'entrée d'une grotte deux chevaux, avec un homme à côté et trois chiens, tableau d'un coloris vigoureux et d'une belle exécution] | *Mat:* op paneel *Size:* hoog 13, breed 19 duim	Smidt	(Bought In) fl 10
1804/08/08	AMSCH	0201	*H. Verschuring* | Voor de Intrée van een prachtige Hofstéede ziet men een Heer by een wit gezadeld Paard, en twee speelende Honden, en verdere Stoffagie; bevallig van licht en meesterlyk geschilderd | *Mat:* op doek *Size:* hoog 16, breed 14 ½ duim	Vink[eles] [for] K[=Gruyter?]	(Sold) fl 7:15 Menzart
1804/08/08	AMSCH	0241	*H. Verschuring* | Een Landschap met een Fontyn, Beelden, Paarden en Honden; kragtig op Doek | *Mat:* op doek *Size:* hoog 16, breed 19 duim	Roos a	(Sold) fl 1 Scheepens

1804/10/16	DLOND	0247	*H. Verschuring. 1676* | Enige Soldaten die gesneuvelden ontkleden. Quelques Soldats depouillant des tués | *Mat:* op doek *Size:* hoog 25, breed 31 *Inscr:* H. Verschuring. 1676 (signed and dated?) *Notes:* It is unclear whether the name and date are inscribed on the painting.		(Unknown) fl 50
1805/07/10	AMSCH	0163	*Verschuuring* | Een Italiaansch gestoffeerd Landschap, met een Fontyn, in 't verschiet een ménigte Beelden; uitvoerig als Lingelbach	V[inkeles] [for] K	(Sold) fl 1:15 Boelen
1805/10/09	HGBSM	0008	*H. Verschuuring* | Een smits winkel, waar een paard werd beslagen in een italiaansch landschap | *Mat:* op paneel *Size:* hoog 14 ½ breet 17 duim	T H van Willigen [or others]	(Sold) fl 7:5 De Gelder
1805/10/09	HGBSM	0111	*H. Verschuring* | Een landschap, de voorgrond gestoffeerd met veel figuuren, paarden en honden | *Mat:* op paneel *Size:* hoog 18 breet 23 duim	T H van Willigen [or others]	(Sold) fl 7 Teissier
1806/06/07	RMHSN	0086	*H. Verschuring* | Een Mans Portrait in een Landschap	A E K L	(Unknown)
1806/06/07	RMHSN	0113	*Verschuring* | Een Paardje en Hondjes &c. door Verschuring, op Paneel, zonder Lyst | *Mat:* op paneel	A E K L	(Unknown)
1806/08/20	HGBSM	0211	*H. Verschuring* | Een Hof gezicht, daar Heeren en Dames op de jagt gaan | *Mat:* op paneel *Size:* hoog 8 ¾, breed 7 duim	Macalester Loup [or others]	(Sold) fl 6:15 Praiston
1808/04/26	GDAN	0165	*Verschuuring (H)* | Een Dame op een wit Paard zittende, schijnende iets te bevelen aan een Knegt die bij haar Paard staat, agter dezelve ziet men eenige Gebouwen en stoffage | *Size:* hoog 8 ¾, breed 7 ¾ duim	G H Fortuyn	(Unknown)
1808/04/26	GDAN	0166	*Verschuuring (H)* | Een Paardje door een Jongen bij den toom gehouden wordende, bij zich hebbende een Hond, wel gepenseeld | *Size:* hoog 6 ½, breed 8 ½ duim	G H Fortuyn	(Unknown)
1808/04/26	GDAN	0167	*Verschuuring (H)* | Een bergägtig Landschap met hoog Geboomte, op de voorgrond een Heer met een wit Paard, bij zig hebbende twee mooije Jagt Honden, schijnende met een Herder in gesprek te wezen, in 't verschiet een party Vee en Volk, uitvoerig en delicaat behandeld | *Size:* hoog 18, breed 24 duim	G H Fortuyn	(Unknown)
1808/04/26	GDAN	0168	*Verschuuring (H)* | Eene Jagtpartij, waar by verscheidene Menschen, Paarden en Honden | *Size:* hoog 14, breed 12 duim	G H Fortuyn	(Unknown)
1808/05/17	LNAN	0009	*H. Verschuring* | Een Hofgezigt met boomen en gebouwen, op den voorgrond Heeren en Dames te paard, en veel andere beelden, kunstig | *Mat:* op doek *Size:* hoog 32, breed 43 duim		(Unknown)
1808/08/23	AMSCH	0161	*Verschuring. (H.)* | Voor een Soetelaars Tent ziet men Heeren te Paard en te voet, welke zig ververschen, en elkander een Kan met drinken toebrengen, verder een rustend Man en een duinachtig verschiet; meesterlijk en breed geschilderd | *Mat:* op paneel *Size:* hoog 14, breed 18 duim	[Coclers]	(Sold) fl 9 Van Iperen
1808/08/23	AMSCH	0190	*H. Verschuring* | Een hevige schermutseling, tusschen Ruiterij en Voetvolk; meesterlijk geschildert	[Gruyter?]	(Sold) fl 2:10 L Pakker
1808/09/13	HABRU	0092	*Verschuuring* | Een Landschap, gestoffeerd met ter Jagt gaande Gezelschap		(Unknown) fl 1
1809/07/25	HGBSM	0139	*H. Verschuring* | Een Slagveld van Cavallerie | *Mat:* op doek *Size:* hoog 16, breed 22 duim	D van der Aa [or] E B ten Dall	(Sold) fl 2:10 van Dongen
1810/06/20	AMSCH	0092	*H. Verschuring* | Eenige Jagers, te paard en te voet, schijnende zich te ververschen. Meesterlijk gedaan | *Mat:* op doek *Size:* hoog 17, breed 15 duimen	Q	(Sold) fl 2:5 Hodges
1810/08/01	AMSCH	0110	*Verschuring (Hendrik)* | Een Boerenfeest in eene Legerplaats; waar Boeren, Boerinnen en Krijgslieden zich vermaken; in het verschiet een bergachtig Landschap [Representation d'une Fête au milieu d'un Camp Militaire, ou des Paysan et des Paysanes se divertissent parmi la Soldatesque ; la perspective presente une Campagne montueuse] | possibly companion to lot 111 *Annots:* mauvais. (NGW) *Mat:* op doek *Size:* hoog 30, breed 52 duimen	Mr Pieter de Smeth van Alphen	(Sold) fl 72 for lots 110 & 111. Reijers
1810/08/01	AMSCH	0111	*Verschuring (Hendrik)* | Een Slagveld, waarin verscheidene Dooden en Gekwetsten worden opgeruimd; ter zijde Bevelhebbers te paard, Geschut en Krijgstuig; in het verschiet eene Stad. Kunnende strekken tot eene wederga van de voorgaande [Un Champ de Bataille d'où on enlève les morts et les blessés : sur le côté se trouvent les Officiers Commandant à Cheval. Quelqu'artillerie et des armures avec une Ville pour perspective achevent ce Tableau. Il peut servir de pendant au précédent] | possibly companion to lot 110 *Annots:* mauvais. (NGW) *Mat:* op doek *Size:* hoog 30, breed 52 duimen	Mr Pieter de Smeth van Alphen	(Sold) fl 72 for lots 110 & 111. Reijers
1810/11/07	UTWLD	0045	*Verschuren* | Een beleg: op eenigen afstand ziet men een stad door een meenigte Krijgslieden omgeven, op de voorgrond eene Dame met een Vaandrig sprekende – verder een huisgezin met eenig werkbezig, alles breed behandeld door Verschuren 1676 op doek, 2 voet 9 duim hoog, 3 en een half voet breed, zwarte Lijst | *Mat:* op doek *Size:* 2 voet 9 duim hoog, 3 en een half voet breed *Inscr:* Verschuren 1676 (signed and dated?) *Notes:* It is unclear whether the name and date are inscribed on the painting.		(Unknown) fl 22

Verschuring, Hendrik (copy after)

1804/10/16	DLOND	0240a[m]	*C. Vermeulen; Verschuring* | [Een Stuk, bevattende 13 zeer schone Copiën van de volgende Meesters. Un Tableau, contenant 13 Copies très-belles des Peintres suivans.] 13. Verschuring. Ene Jachtparty, une partie de		(Sold) fl 150 for lots 240a[a-m]. Ond d Wyngaert

			Chasse | copy by Corn. Vermeulen (III) after H. Verschuring *Mat:* op paneel *Size:* hoog 41, breed 55 *Notes:* The bracketed information in the title appears above lot 240a[a] and refers to lots 240a[a-m].		
			Verschuring, Hendrik (manner)		
1802/09/06	AMSCH	0208	*H. Verschuuring* | Eenige ter Jagt gaande Jagers te Paard, by een Fontyn; in de manier van H. Verschuuring	Mevrouw Achtienhoven	(Sold) fl 2 van Iperen
1802/11/01	DOBRA	0055	*Verschuring* | Een rustplaats van Ruiters, die hunne spijs bereiden en zich vermaken, als door Verschuring | companion to lot 56 *Mat:* op doek op paneel *Size:* breed 2 v. 8 d. hoog 2 v. 2 d.	Paulus van der Spyk [or others]	(Sold) fl 18:15 for lots 55 & 56. Randwyk
1802/11/01	DOBRA	0056	*Verschuring* | Een wederga, verbeeldende 't berooven van eenen afgemaakten; mede met Paarden en Krygsvolk, niet minder, door denzelfden meester | companion to lot 55 *Mat:* op doek op paneel	Paulus van der Spyk [or others]	(Sold) fl 18:15 for lots 55 & 56. Randwyk
1806/05/05	AMSCH	0169	*Verschuring* | Een Heer te Paard by een Ruïne; als Verschuring	R[oos]	(Sold) fl 2 L Pakker
			Verschuring, Willem		
1804/08/08	AMSCH	0181	*W. Schuring* | Voor een Vorstelyk Gebouw zitten twee Heeren in het Veerkeerbord [sic] te speelen, een Dame met een witte Satyne Rok en blaauw Jakje schynt er, benévens nog een andere na te zien; alles in de manier van G. ter Burg, kunstig uitgevoerd | *Mat:* op doek *Size:* hoog 23, breed 20 duim	Roos [for] H	(Sold) fl 18:10 Gruiter
			Verspronck, Johannes Cornelisz.		
1804/05/07	AMSCH	0159	*Sprong (van)* | Het Pourtrait van een oude Vrouw, met een breeden kraag om den hals; krachtig en breed geschilderd | *Size:* hoog 26, breed 22 duim	Vinkeles [for] G	(Sold) fl 0:6 L Pakker
1805/10/21	GRBOL	0004	*J. v. Spronck* | Een Boeren Binnenhuis, waar in enige Soldaten bezig zyn te Plunderen, meesterlyk Geschilderd	Gerardus Nicolaus Heerkens	(Unknown)
1808/03/03	HAVIN	0016	*Versprong* | Twee Man en Vrouwe Pourtraitten, konstig	Jacobus Spillebout	(Unknown) fl 61
1808/08/23	AMSCH	0155	*Sprong. (G. van)* | Een Vrouwe Pourtret in deftige Kleeding en een witte Kraag om de Hals, houdende een Boek in de handen; breed geschilderd | *Mat:* op doek *Size:* hoog 34, breed 25 duim *Notes:* The artist's name was given as "Sprong. (G. van)" but we have assumed this is an error.	J	(Sold) fl 18 D Maijkel
1810/08/01	AMSCH	0094	*Sprong (J. van)* | Het afbeeldsel van eenen Heer ter halver lijf, in het zwart gekleed, met eenen ronden Hoed en kanten Kraag [Un Portrait d'Homme vu à mi-corps, vétu de noir, portant une fraise en dentelle] | *Annots:* insignifiant (NGW) *Mat:* op doek *Size:* hoog 31, breed 26 duimen	Mr Pieter de Smeth van Alphen	(Sold) fl 18 Dupré
			Versteeg, Michiel		
1801/10/19	AMSCH	0081	*Versteegh (N)* | Een leezend Vrouwtje by de kaars, zeer natuurlyk en kunstig geschilderd, in de manier van Schalken | *Mat:* op paneel *Size:* hoog 7, breed 5 ¼ duim *Notes:* The artist's name was given as "Versteegh (N)" but we have assumed this is an error.	Jonkheer Menno Baron van Coehoorn	(Sold) fl 195 Jan Ijver
1802/04/13	HAVIN	0007	*M. Versteegh* | Een Vrouw in een Nis, in de Regterhand heeft zy een Kaars, en in de Linkerhand een Vulnisblik, konstig en uitvoerig		(Unknown)
1804/05/07	AMSCH	0176	*Versteeg. (N.)* | In deeze fraaije Ordonantie, ziet men by kaarslicht in een Vertrek, alwaar een Schoolmeester bézich is een Jongeling te onderwyzen, waarnaast eenige Kinderen hunne lessen leeren, en een andere hun de kaars houd: verders by een vuur twee Jongens welke zich warmen, en eenig toepasselyk bywerk; deeze zoo ryke Ordonantie is allerfraayst van penceelsbehandeling en deszelfs onderscheide lichten maken het tot een piquant Schildery | *Mat:* op paneel *Size:* hoog 15, breed 20 duim *Notes:* The artist's name was given as "Versteeg. (N.)" but we have assumed this is an error.	Vinkeles [for] X	(Sold) fl 90 Gruyter
1805/10/09	HGBSM	0048	*Versteeg* | Een boomryk landschap, gestoffeerd met figuuren en beesten, extra uitvoerig geschildert | *Mat:* op mahoniehout paneel *Size:* hoog 19 breet 16 ½ duim	T H van Willigen [or others]	(Sold) fl 17:10 Valette
1806/08/20	HGBSM	0024	*Versteeg* | Voor eene steene Nis, zit eene Vrouw, voor zich hebbende eene Tafel, met een Blaker en brandende Kaars, die zij bezig is met een Snuijter wat uit te halen, Dit Kaarslicht, is bijzonder, uitvoerig en vol effect | *Mat:* op mahoniehout paneel *Size:* hoog 12 ½, breed 10 duim	Macalester Loup [or others]	(Sold) fl 81 A Taixera
1807/08/26	AMSCH	0230	*Versteegh* | Een Boomryk en bergachtig Landschap, gestoffeerd met Koeijen en Schapen met hunne Herders; zonachtig en uitvoerig | *Mat:* op paneel *Size:* hoog 20, breed 16 duim	Joseph Vallette	(Sold) fl 29:10 van Iperen
1810/06/06	RMMUY	0014	*M. Versteeg* | Door eene open Nis, ziet men een Heer aan eene Tafel zittende, Geld tellen, bij kaarslicht achter hem eene Jufvrouw met een Schoudermantel met bont, houdende hare regterhand voor eene brandende kaars die zij in de linkerhand heeft, aan de Wand hangt een Schilderij &c. konstig en krachtig geschilderd | *Mat:* op paneel *Size:* hoog 19, breed 14 ½ duim		(Sold) fl 61 V Leen
1810/07/23	DOLGI	0061	*Machiel Versteeg* | Een oude Vrouw in een Nis verbeeld, ten halven lijve; hebbende een Nachtkap en Bril op, en zittende bij een Lamplicht, dat tegen een knaap hangt, te spinnen. De tekening is juist, en de reflectie van 't Lamplicht zeer natuurlijk, uitvoerig geschilderd | *Mat:* op paneel *Size:* hoog 12 ½, breed 11 duim	Mr Pieter van den Santheuvel	(Sold) fl 180 A van Strij

			Versteeg, Michiel (and Leen, Willem van)		
1801/08/19	AMSCH	0131	*W. van Leen; M. Versteegh* | Een Italiaansch Landschap met een drift Beesten, waar by een Vrouw op een Ezel; helder en bevallig gepenceeld door W. van Leen, en gestoffeerd door M. Versteegh	Pruyssen[r]	(Sold) fl 2:10 Pruijssenaar [for] R
			Versteeg, Michiel (copy after)		
1804/10/16	DLOND	0240	*C. Vermeulen; naar Versteeg* | Ene dito uts[a]. [zeer schone en allernaauwkeurigste Copy] van het bekende Schildery van Versteeg, verbeeldende eene Familie, Coffy drinkende in een Vertrek, door Vuur en Kaarssen verlicht, met een Glazen Spiegelbol aan de Zolder. Un dito uts[a]. [Copie superbe & très-exacte] d'après le Tableau connu de Versteeg, repres. une Famille prenant le Caffé dans une Chambre, eclairée tant par le feu que par des Chandelles, avec une Boulè de Cristal étamé suspendue au plancher | copy by Corn. Vermeulen (III) after Versteeg *Mat:* op doek *Size:* hoog 23, breed 28		(Sold) fl 47 v Walle
1804/10/16	DLOND	0240a[d]	*C. Vermeulen; Versteeg* | [Een Stuk, bevattende 13 zeer schone Copiën van de volgende Meesters. Un Tableau, contenant 13 Copies très-belles des Peintres suivans.] 4. Versteeg. Lamplicht, Lumière de Lampe | copy by Corn. Vermeulen (III) after Versteeg *Mat:* op paneel *Size:* hoog 41, breed 55 *Notes:* The bracketed information in the title appears above lot 240a[a] and refers to lots 240a[a-m].		(Sold) fl 150 for lots 240a[a-m]. Ond d Wyngaert
1806/05/05	AMSCH	0252	*Versteegh* | Een Binnenhuis, met een Koffydrinkend Gezelschap, by het kaarslicht; na Versteegh	R[oos]	(Sold) fl 10:10 van Iperen
1809/04/22	AMYVR	0139	*de oude Vermeulen; M. Versteegh* | Een Copij, naar een beroemd Kaarslicht, door M. Versteegh, geschilderd door de oude Vermeulen | copy by Corn. Vermeulen (III) after Versteeg *Mat:* op paneel *Size:* hoog 20, breed 24 duim	de Bruin	(Sold) fl 4:15 du Pree
			Versteeg, Michiel (manner)		
1804/10/16	DLOND	0332	*Versteeg* | Een Gezelschap by Kaarslicht, als door Versteeg. Une Compagnie à la lumière de Chandelle, comme par Versteeg | *Mat:* op paneel *Size:* hoog 10, breed 9		(Unknown)
			Vertangen, Daniel		
1801/05/11	AMSCH	0098	*D. Verstangen* | In een Heuvelachtig Landschap met Geboomte, vertoont zig een vreugdemaal, vrolyke, drinkende en dansende Bachanten, zoo Mans als Vrouwen, om hoog vliegende Minnewichten met een bloemkrans, uitvoerig en bevallig van penceelbehandeling | *Mat:* op paneel *Size:* hoog 16, breed 22 duim	E[lias]	(Sold) fl 40 Allard
1801/08/19	AMSCH	0123	*D. Vertangen* | Europa op de Stier, verzeld van een ménigte Vrouwen en Minnewigten; delicaat gepenceeld door D. Vertangen, op Paneel | *Mat:* op paneel *Size:* hoog 12, breed 16 duim	W Wynen	(Sold) fl 16 Wed Achtienhoven
1802/05/05	AMSCH	0218	*Vertange* | Een bergachtig Landschap met een Ruïne, op de voorgrond ziet men Maria met het Kindeke, nevens Joseph, ter zyde een Ezel, in 't verschiet eenige Bergen, alles fraai en uitvoerig van schildering | *Mat:* op koper *Size:* hoog 8, breed 10 duim	E	(Sold) fl 27:10 Stevens
1802/06/28	AMSCH	0194	*D. Vertange* | Twee stuks Landschappen, met Rivieren, gestoffeerd met verscheiden Nimphen; krachtig geschilderd, door D. Vertange, op Panneel | *Mat:* op paneel *Size:* hoog 18, breed 12 duim	Anna Elink	(Sold) fl 5:10 Vermeulen
1802/08/24	LNDLS	0020	*D. Vertangen* | De Begroeting der Herders bij Maria, met het Kind op haar schoot, terwijl eenige geknield aanbidden, in een landschap met Boomen en Gebouwen, boven een glorie van Engelen op de wolken. Delicaat op koper geschilderd | companion to lot 21 *Mat:* op koper *Size:* hoog en breed 13 ½ duim	Leonardus Bouman [or others]	(Unknown) fl 27 for lots 20 & 21
1802/08/24	LNDLS	0021	*D. Vertangen* | Een Weêrga, verbeeldende den Doop van Johannes in de Jordaan, ter wederzijde veel aanschouwers te paard en te voet, en in de lucht, veele Engelen. Mede op koper van dezelfde grootte | companion to lot 20 *Mat:* op koper	Leonardus Bouman [or others]	(Unknown) fl 27 for lots 20 & 21
1802/09/06	AMSCH	0183	*D. Vertangen* | In een Landschap, vertoond zig Loth met zyn Dochters; plaisant behandeld	Spaan	(Sold) fl 1:10 Gruiter
1802/11/01	DOBRA	0177	*D. Vertange* | In een Boschagtig Landschap ziet men een Nimph, door een Sater gekastyd wordende, terwyl een ander haar vast houdt. Agter een Bok, en in 't verschiet vlugtende Nimphen | *Mat:* op paneel *Size:* hoog 10 ½, breed 14 duim		(Unknown) fl 8
1803/04/20	AMSCH	0084	*Vertangen. (D.)* | Een Bybel-Ordenantie, verbeeldende Abraham gereed zyn Zoon op te offeren, om hoog vertoond zig den Engel, verders een bevallig Landzicht; kragtig en uitvoerig behandeld [Abraham prêt à Sacrifier son fils Isac : du ciel descend un Ange pour interrompre le Sacrifice, le fond offre une Vue étendue. Tableau fini et éclattant.] | *Mat:* op paneel *Size:* hoog 11, breed 9 duim	Maria Magdalena van Sluypwyk, gravinne van Moens	(Sold) fl 13 Ijver
1803/09/07	AMSCH	0195	*D. Vertangen* | Een Grot waarin Lot met zyn Dogters, in het verschiet ziet men den Brand van Sodom; delicaat [Une grotte dans laquelle se sont refugiés Lot et ses filles ; dans le lointain l'incendie de Sodome ; composition délicate] | *Mat:* op paneel *Size:* hoog 12, breed 15 duim	Smidt	(Sold) fl 76 C S Roos
1803/09/07	AMSCH	0196	*D. Vertangen* | Een slapende Nimph in een Grot, benevens Cupido, in 't verschiet een Boom- en Bergachtig Landschap, uitvoerig gepenceeld [Une	Smidt	(Sold) fl 7 v d Schley [for] R[ijfsnijder]

			nymphe nonchalamment couchée dans une grotte ; auprès d'elle Cupidon et dans le fond un paysage montagneux et melé d'arbres en perspective ; belle composition et d'un bon goût] | *Mat:* op paneel *Size:* hoog 11, breed 13 duim		
1803/12/12	AMSCH	0106	*D. Vertangen* | Vénus op de Wolken, waarby Jupiter; kragtig op Paneel | *Mat:* op paneel *Size:* hoog 9, breed 11 duim	W	(Sold) fl 2:15 v^n Iperen
1804/05/07	AMSCH	0181	*Vertangen. (D.)* | In een aangenaam Boom en Duinachtig Landschap, ziet men eenige Nimphen, zich met baden als andersints vermaken, verders hoog Geboomten; uitvoerig en delicaat van penceelbehandeling | *Mat:* op doek *Size:* Ieder hoog 20, breed 24 duim	Vinkeles [for] J	(Sold) fl 43 Thais
1804/08/08	AMSCH	0199	*D. Vertangen* | In een Landschap zit een Nimph, haar voeten gewasschen wordende door een Négerin, terwyl haar Hoofd door twee blanke Vrouwen vercierd wordt, ter zyde Cupido met een Korfje met Bloemen op zyn Hoofd; extra uitvoerig op Doek | *Mat:* op doek *Size:* hoog 11, breed 13 duim	Roos [for] D	(Sold) fl 15 Vallet
1805/07/03	AMSCH	0158	*D. Vertangen* | Een Historiëele Ordinantie, in een Duin- en Boomryk Landschap, met een helder Spiegelende Rivier: uitvoerig op Paneel | *Mat:* op paneel *Size:* hoog 13, breed 16 duim	Y	(Sold) fl 10:10 Gruyter
1805/07/10	AMSCH	0166	*D. Vertangen* | Een Zinnebeeldige Ordinantie | *Mat:* op paneel *Size:* hoog 9, breed 11 duim	V[inkeles]	(Sold) fl 2 Gruyter
1806/08/13	AMSCH	0193	*Vertangen. (D.)* | In een Heuvelachtig Landschap, vertoont zich een Bachenaal, van verscheide Nimphen en Mannen, verzeld van danzende Saters; bevallig gepenceeld | *Mat:* op paneel *Size:* hoog 14, breed 20 duim	Roos	(Sold) fl 58 Van Iperen
1806/08/13	AMSCH	0201	*Vertangen. (D.)* | Een Berg- en Boomryk Landschap, gestoffeerd met een ménigte vrolyke Nimphen, Saters, Kinderen en Bokjes; delicaat behandeld | *Mat:* op doek *Size:* hoog 18, breed 34 duim	van der Voort	(Sold) fl 37 Thais
1806/10/16	UTWLD	0004	*D. Vertangen* | Een Landschap met een dansende Satyr en Nimph, eenige Bachanten en Cupido's door D. Vertangen	Mr P de Malapert [or] W Beeldsnyder	(Unknown)
1807/08/26	AMSCH	0231	*A. Vertangen* | Diana met hare Nimphen, zich badende in een Rivier, in een rotsachtig Landschap | *Mat:* op doek *Size:* hoog 17, breed 15 duim *Notes:* The artist's name was given as "A. Vertangen" but we have assumed this is an error.	Roos	(Sold) fl 8:10 Spruit
1808/04/26	GDAN	0179	*Vertange (D.)* | Een Naakt slapende Diana, wordende door twee Saters bespied, goed geschilderd | *Size:* hoog 10 ½, breed 14 duim	G H Fortuyn	(Unknown)
1808/08/23	AMSCH	0160	*Vertangen. (D.)* | In een Bergachtig Landschap ziet men ter zijde bij een spiegelend Water, Tobias met den Engel hunne reis vervorderen; zacht en uitvoerig gepenceeld | *Mat:* op paneel *Size:* hoog 13, breed 16 duim	[Gruyter?]	(Sold) fl 12:10 J Spaan
1808/11/28	AMSCH	0065	*D. Vertangen* | In een Landschap ziet men op de voorgrond het Bad van Diana, waar bij verscheide Nimphen, meesterlijk | *Mat:* op paneel *Size:* hoog 20, breed 24 duim	Z	(Sold) fl 18 Gruiter
1809/04/17	AMSCH	0136	*D. Vertangen* | In een Grot ziet men eenige Nimphen zich baaden; delicaat gepenceeld | *Mat:* op paneel	[Gruyter?]	(Sold) fl 3
1809/06/13	AMSCH	0162	*D. Vertangen* | Een Landschap, gestoffeerd met een Fabel-Geschiedenis, men ziet eene rustende Nimph, door een Jongeling bespied, delicaat en uitvoerig gepenceeld | *Mat:* op koper *Size:* hoog 10, breed 12 duim	E	(Sold) fl 4 T Spaan
1810/06/20	AMSCH	0094	*D. Vertange* | Twee stuks, met spelende Kinderen. Zacht geschilderd | *Mat:* op paneel *Size:* Jeder hoog 10, breed 9 duimen	Q	(Sold) fl 2:5 du Pree
1810/06/20	AMSCH	0125	*D. Vertange* | Een Grot met badende Nimfen	X	(Sold) fl 0:6 L Pakker
1810/06/20	AMSCH	0126	*D. Vertange* | Een dito [Grot] dito [met badende Nimfen]	X	(Sold) fl 1:15 Pantijn

Vertangen, Daniel (and Keirincx, Alex.)

1801/03/16	AMSCH	0032	*Keerings; Vertangen* | Een heuvelachtig Landschap, doorsneede met een stil Water, met badende Nimphen en Saters, alles krachtig behandeld, door Keerings en Vertangen	P[ruyssenaar]	(Sold) fl 1:15 Gruiter

Vertangen, Daniel (manner)

1803/12/12	AMSCH	0129	*Vertangen* | Twee stuks met naakte Beelden; in de manier van Vertangen | *Mat:* op paneel *Size:* hoog 13, breed 16 duim	W	(Sold) fl 3:5 Uselino
1803/12/12	AMSCH	0146	*Vertangen* | Twee stuks met naakte Beelden; als Vertangen | *Size:* hoog 11, breed 14 duim	D	(Sold) fl 4:10 Coclers
1808/08/23	AMSCH	0282	*Vertangen* | In een Landschap met Geboomten, ziet men op de voorgrond drie badende Nimphen; in de manier van Vertangen, ovaal formaat | *Mat:* op paneel *Fmt:* ovaal *Notes:* This lot was sold with lot 281 by B. Denner.	Z	(Sold) fl 2 for lots 281 & 282. L Pakker

Vervoort, Joseph

1805/07/10	AMSCH	0165	*J. Vervoort* | In een Boomryk Bergachtig Arcadisch Landschap, met een Fontyn, en Waterbeekje, vertoonen zich eenige Vrouwen, zig badende; uitvoerig geschilderd | *Mat:* op paneel *Size:* hoog 19, breed 23 duim	S[chley] [for] de Wed Landers	(Sold) fl 2:5 Reyers

Verwilt, François

1802/07/20	MGSAN	0026	*Verwilt* | Een Landschap met baadende Vrouwtjes, op Paneel | *Mat:* op paneel *Size:* hoog duim 10 ½, breed duim 13 ½		(Unknown)

1802/09/15 HGKAN 0002 *van der Wilt* | Een Slaapende Nimph, door een Jager verrast, met zeer fraay Bywerk, door van der Wilt, op Paneel en Lyst [In Oly Verff] | *Mat:* in olyverf op paneel *Notes:* The bracketed information in the title appears above lot 1 and refers to lots 1 to 8. (Unknown)

1804/10/16 DLOND 0261 *Van der Wilt* | Een Landschap. Paysage | *Mat:* op paneel *Size:* hoog 14, breed 10 (Unknown)

1810/10/10 MGCIT 0102 *Verwilt* | Een Stuk, zynde een ryk en uitvoerig Landschap; op de voorgrond een Slapend Vrouwtje door Satyrs bespied wordende; goed behandeld | companion to lot 103 Caspar van Citters (Unknown)

1810/10/10 MGCIT 0103 *Verwilt* | Een Wederga, als voren, met badende Vrouwtjes; niet minder als 't vorige | companion to lot 102 Caspar van Citters (Unknown)

Victors, Jacobus

1801/04/08 HAVIN 0012 *Victor* | Een Landschap met Vogels, konstig geschilderd (Unknown)

1802/07/20 MGSAN 0055 *J. Fictor* | Een Landschap, waarin een Hond, die eenige Patryzen uit een Graanveld dryft, levensgroote, op Doek | *Mat:* op doek *Size:* hoog duim 41, breed duim 52 (Unknown)

1803/08/17 AMSCH 0088 *Victor* | Twee stuks met Hanen, Hennen, Kiekens, Duiven, en een Conyn, meesterlyk geschilderd als door Hondekoeter | *Mat:* op doek *Size:* ieder hoog 36, breed 30 duim Anna Catharina Putman (Sold) fl 62 Pruijssenaar

1810/06/06 RMMUY 0146 *Victor* | Een stuk met Hoenders en verder bijwerk. Zeer verdienstelijk | *Mat:* op doek (Unknown) fl 5:5

1810/08/10 RMRIJ 0029 *Victor* | Hoenders en Duiven. Ongemeen natuurlijk en konstig (Sold) fl 1:10 [or] 24 v Ryp

1810/10/10 MGCIT 0032 *Victor* | Een kapitaal Landschap, voorzien met Ganzen, een Haan, Hennen en andere Gevogelte; voorts nog eenig ander Bijwerk tot de verkozene [sic] voorwerpen betrekkelijk, zijnde een schoone ordonnantie, natuurlijk en meesterlijk uitgevoerd Caspar van Citters (Unknown)

Victors, Jan

1801/03/16 AMSCH 0188 *J. Victor* | Twee stuks, voor een Boerenwoning vertoond zig een oude Man en Vrouw, waar by een jong Boerinnetje verzeld van 2 Koeijen; den andere een overvarende Pontschuit met een Koe, natuurlyk behandeld, op paneel | *Mat:* op paneel K[ip] (Sold) fl 33 Rijnders

1801/03/16 AMSCH 0199 *J. Victor* | Twee stuks Dorpgezichten, een verbeeldende een Kermis vol gewoel, en een Hoefsmit die een Paard beslaat, waar by andere vrolyke Huislleden [sic], beide plaisant geschilderd op doek | *Mat:* op doek K[ip] (Sold) fl 5:5 Koopman

1801/05/11 AMSCH 0097 *J. Victor* | Een Binnenhuis, in hetzelve ziet men een slagter bezig een Os schoonmaken, ter zyde ziet men een meid een doek uitvringen [sic], in 't verschiet twee vrouwen, schynende vlees te snyden, alles meesterlyk en breed van schildering | *Mat:* op paneel *Size:* hoog 33, breed 27 duim E[lias] (Sold) fl 133 Rijnders

1801/08/19 AMSCH 0119 *J. Victor* | Een Boere Bruiloft in een Binnehuis, ryk gestoffeerd met een meenigte Lieden, als: Mans, Vrouwe en Kinderen, zittende aan gedekte Tafels met Spys, die zig vermaaken, een vrolyken Gast is met een Boerrinnetje aan den Dans, waar by een Mucicant op een Ton staande; alles is geestig en kragtig geschilderd op doek | *Mat:* op doek *Size:* hoog 32, breed 43 duim C S Roos [for] G (Sold) fl 33 Parrach

1801/08/19 AMSCH 0120 *J. Victor* | Op een Boeren Kermis ziet men een Wagen voor een Herberg met vrolyke Huislieden, verders een meenigte zig op den Kermis vermaakende Persoonen Pruyssen[r] [for] Q (Sold) fl 5 Wijland

1801/08/19 AMSCH 0121 *J. Victor* | Een Grysaard zich boven een Vuurpot warmende, nevens hem een Vrouw; meesterlyk door denzelven [J. Victor] | *Mat:* op doek *Size:* hoog 41, breed 35 duim W Wynen (Sold) fl 0:10 Hulswit

1802/05/05 AMSCH 0221 *Victor* | In een Landschap ziet men een Meid met een Kan in de hand, die door een Heer gecarresseerd word, waarby een Heer te Paard, met een Glas, benevens een Hond, meesterachtig gepenceeld | *Size:* hoog 29, breed 20 duim J (Sold) fl 13 Ackina

1802/06/28 AMSCH 0198 *Victor* | Het afbeeldzel van malle Jantje, zynde een oude Burger Weesjongen, waarby een menigte omstanders, kragtig op Doek | *Mat:* op doek *Size:* hoog 19, breed 17 duim Anna Elink (Sold) fl 1:10 Taak

1802/09/06 AMSCH 0121 *J. Victor* | Een Veld met staande en leggende Koeijen, verders een Boer en Boerin met twee melkëmmers, en in 't verschiet een Dorpgezigt, natuurlyk en kragtig behandeld | *Mat:* op paneel *Size:* hoog 16, breed 21 duim J (Sold) fl 8 Gruiter

1802/09/06 AMSCH 0122 *J. Victor* | In een Landschap voor een Gebouw, ziet men twee Jagers welke hunne Honden aan elkander schynen vast te binden; verders een Man met een Paard, en een aangenaam verschiet; meesterlyk gepenceeld | *Mat:* op doek *Size:* hoog 29, breed 20 duim J (Sold) fl 5:5 de Meijer

1802/12/13 AMSCH 0167 *Victor* | Een Bybelsche Ordenantie, de Zoeking van Laban, na d'Theraphin in Rachels-Tent; meesterlyk gepenceeld | *Size:* hoog 66, breed 77 duim Pruyssenaar [for] B (Bought In) fl 12 ½

1803/08/01 AMSCH 0045 *Victor (J.)* | In een Binnenvertrek staat by een Ton, een Jongeling op de Fiool te speelen, waarby nog drie andere Kinderen met een Hond en een Thoen (Sold) fl 83 Pruijssenaar

			Kat, uit een Vengster kykt een oude Vrouw, en aan de Deur is nog een kleine Jongen, zy zyn alle in een lachgende houding, en van een bevallige penceelsbehandeling | *Mat:* op doek *Size:* hoog 22, breed 27 duim		
1804/05/07	AMSCH	0175	*Victors* | Twee stuks, een Mans en Vrouwe Pourtrait; krachtig en fraay geschilderd | *Mat:* op doek *Size:* hoog 20, breed 25 duim	W [through] Y[ver]	(Bought In) fl 26
1804/08/08	AMSCH	0196	*J. Victor* | Deeze capitaale Bybel-Ordinantie steld voor, alwaar Isaak zyn Bruid Rebecca ontmoet, die in eerbiedige gestalte, in witte Satyne Kleeding needer geknield, voor hem legt; hy is verzeld van Eliëzer, zyn Vaders Afgezant, die achterwaards by hem geplaatst is; de hartstochten zyn natuurlyk verbeeld, bevallig van coloriet, krachtig en uitvoerig van penceelbehandeling, door J. Victor, in de manier G. van de Eckhout | *Mat:* op doek *Size:* hoog 66, br. 62 duim	Schley [for] A	(Withdrawn)
1804/08/08	AMSCH	0197	*J. Victor* | Den veelvervigen bebloeden Rok van Joseph aan zyn Vader Jacob vertoond wordende, zynde een fraaije Ordinantie van vyf Beelden; kragtig en meesterlyk op Doek | *Mat:* op doek *Size:* hoog 55, breed 71 duim	Roos [for] M	(Bought In) fl 5 ¾
1804/08/08	AMSCH	0198	*J. Victor* | Voor een Buitenhuis met een Wyngaardrank bewasschen, zit een oud Man en Vrouw, waarby een witte Bok, Emmer, enz.; fraai gepenceeld | *Mat:* op paneel *Size:* hoog 17, breed 22 duim	Vink[eles] [for] W	(Sold) fl 6:5 Van Iperen
1805/07/03	AMSCH	0153	*J. Victor* | Deeze ryke Ordonantie van een ménigte Beelden, stelt voor: Joseph zynen Vader Jacob voor Pharao brengende, welke in prachtige Vorstelyke Kleeding op zyne Throon is gezéten; verders ziet men door 't Paleis een Boomryk Landgezicht, waarin een groote ménigte Krygs- en andere Lieden; fraai van Coloriet en Teekening, en meesterlyk gepenceeld | *Mat:* op doek *Size:* hoog 64, breed 77 duim	G	(Withdrawn)
1805/07/03	AMSCH	0154	*J. Victor* | Een Manspourtrait, in deftige aloude Kleeding houdende een stok in de hand, fraai en als de voorgaande behandeld | *Mat:* op doek *Size:* hoog 37, breed 30 duim	V[inkeles]	(Sold) fl 32 Lafontaine
1805/07/03	AMSCH	0155	*J. Victor* | Twee stuks bevallige Landschappen, ryk gestoffeerd met staand en rustend Vee, Boere en Boerinnen en Boomryke verschieten | *Mat:* op paneel *Size:* hoog 19, breed 16 duim	V[inkeles]	(Sold) fl 16:10 Lafontaine
1805/07/10	AMSCH	0156	*J. Victor* | In een aangenaam Landschap ziet men op een grazige Weide, voor een Boerewoning en Schuur een ménigte van staand en rustend Veé, een Koe die door een Meid gemolken wordt, verders een Jongeling in een Schuit, en lang een Boomryke Weg een Drift Beesten; zonachtig en meesterlyk op Doek | *Mat:* op doek *Size:* hoog 39, breed 58 duim	V[inkeles] [for] M	(Bought In) fl 47
1805/07/10	AMSCH	0157	*J. Victor* | Twee stuks, een Mans en Vrouwe Pourtrait, in deftige oude Hollandsche Kleeding; meesterlyk en fraai van behandeling | *Mat:* op doek *Size:* hoog 36, breed 25 duim	V[inkeles] [for] G	(Sold) fl 13:10 Gruyter
1805/07/10	AMSCH	0158	*J. Victor* | Een Mans Pourtrait, halverlyf, met een ronde Hoed op 't Hoofd, in deftige Kleeding, meesterlyk | *Size:* hoog 43, breed 33 duim	V[inkeles] [for] L	(Withdrawn)
1805/10/09	HGBSM	0023	*J. Victor* | Een vrolyke boeren kermis, vol gewoel | *Mat:* op doek *Size:* hoog 41 breet 64 duim	T H van Willigen [or others]	(Sold) fl 25 Valette
1806/05/05	AMSCH	0142	*J. Victor* | In 't midden van een Straat, ziet men twee Honden vegten, waar na verscheiden Boeren en Jongens kyken, die dezelven schynen aantehitzen, ter regter zyden is een Smit bézig een Paard te beslaan, en andere stoffagie; zeer natuurlyk gepenceeld door J. Victor | *Mat:* op doek *Size:* hoog 26, breed 32 duim	V[inkeles]	(Bought In) fl 11
1806/05/05	AMSCH	0231	*Victor* | Een Historieele Ordinantie van verscheiden Beelden en Kinderen; bevallig door Victor	V[inkeles]	(Sold) fl 1 L Pakker
1806/06/07	RMHSN	0006	*Victor* | Een Fruitvrouw, zittende by haar Stal, waar by een Meid die Vrugten koopt &c. | *Mat:* op doek	A E K L	(Unknown)
1806/08/13	AMSCH	0238	*Victor* | Een oud Man, zittende in een Leuningstoel, met een hond op zyn schoot	Vinkeles [for] G[ruyter]	(Sold) fl 1 L Pakker
1806/08/13	AMSCH	0345	*Victor* | Een Strandgezicht	Vinkeles [for] G[ruyter]	(Sold) fl 1 du Pree
1807/08/26	AMSCH	0223	*J. Victor* | Een Boeren Kermis, vol gewoel van Beelden die vrolyk zyn, op den voorgrond een Paard voor een Kar; de ordonnantie en schildering is meesterlyk | *Mat:* op doek *Size:* hoog 42, breed 65 duim	Joseph Vallette	(Sold) fl 36 T Spaan
1807/08/26	AMSCH	0224	*J. Victor* | Jacob, zynen Zoon zegenende, is gezeten op een Bed, zyn zoon ter zyde en de Moeder aan 't voeteneinde geplaatst; de hartstogten zyn zeer wel waargenomen, en is voorts van een kloeke behandeling | *Mat:* op doek *Size:* hoog 43, breed 65 duim	Joseph Vallette	(Sold) fl 40 H Jansen
1807/08/26	AMSCH	0225	*J. Victor* | Twee stuks, zynde een Mans en een Vrouwe Pourtret, met handen, in aloude Kleeding; fiks op Doek | *Mat:* op doek *Size:* hoog 31, breed 29 duim	Joseph Vallette	(Sold) fl 7:10 van Iperen
1807/08/26	AMSCH	0226	*J. Victor* | Een Stadgezicht alwaar een Gilden-Os word rondgeleid, voorgegaan door een Trommelslager; krachtig op Doek | *Mat:* op doek *Size:* hoog 15, breed 18 duim	Roos	(Sold) fl 7 Spruit
1808/06/11	RMRIJ	0056	*Victor* | Eene Brabandsche Keuken, waar in eene Vrouw by het vuur zittende, en Bywerk, zeer natuurlyk en meesterlyk geschilderd | *Mat:* op paneel *Size:* hoog 21, breed 26 duim		(Bought In) fl 8

1808/06/13	AMSCH	0162	*Victor* | Deze Ordonantie stelt voor de Geschiedenis van Haman voor Esther; de beschuldiging van Esther, en de ontsteltenis van Haman zijn 'er natuurlijk in uitgedrukt | *Mat:* op doek *Size:* hoog 48, breed 67 duim *Loc:* Köln, Deutschland. Wallraf-Richartz Museum. (1016)	E M Engelberts	(Sold) fl 11:10 Th Spaan
1808/06/13	AMSCH	0166	*Vietor (J.)* | In een Dorpgezicht, met Boerenwoningen, voor eene Herberg, ziet men eene Heidin goedergelukzeggen aan een vrolijk Boerinnetje, verzeld van andere Huislieden, daar nevens een Hospes, Brood snijdende voor twee Paarden, bij eene Kreb, verder eene Vrouw, Visch schoonmakende, waarbij twee Dorpelingen. Het is kloek en fiks gepenceeld | *Mat:* op doek *Size:* hoog 35, breed 43 duim	Z	(Sold) fl 72 Glad
1808/08/23	AMSCH	0162	*Victor (J.)* | In het midden van een Straat ziet men twee vegtende Honden, waar bij verscheiden Boeren en Jongens staan te kijken, ter zijde een Smit, welke een Paard beslaat, benevens eene Vrouw bij eenige Kippen; bevallig gepenceeld | *Mat:* op doek *Size:* hoog 26, breed 32 duim	[Gruyter?]	(Sold) fl 16 Th Spaan
1808/08/23	AMSCH	0187	*J. Victor* | Een Boeren Kermis in een Dorp, gestoffeerd met een Wagen met vrolijke Huislieden, voor een Herberg, ter zijde een Quakzalver, en op de voorgrond eene Vrouw, welke Fruit verkoopt aan eene Boerin, waarbij eenigen speelende Jongens; natuurlijk behandeld	[Gruyter?]	(Bought In) fl 19 for lots 187 & 188
1808/08/23	AMSCH	0188	*J. Victor* | In een Dorp ziet men voor een Smederij een Paard dat beslagen word, verder een Landman met een drift Beesten, op de voorgrond zit een Schoenmaker te arbeiden, en verder bijwerk; als de voorgaande behandeld	[Gruyter?]	(Bought In) fl 19 for lots 187 & 188
1808/09/13	HABRU	0093	*Victor* | Een Landschap, met Koejen, Schaapen, &c. waar bij een Boerin schijnende gemolken te hebben		(Unknown) fl 3
1808/11/28	AMSCH	0078	*J. Victor* | Een Binnenplaats, gestoffeerd met Duiven en andere Vogelen, natuurlijk | *Mat:* op doek	[Gruyter?]	(Sold) fl 1:10 L Pakker
1809/04/17	AMSCH	0100	*J. Victor* | Deeze capitaale Ordonantie, verbeeld het wegzenden van Hagar en Ismaël door Abraham, agterwaards ziet men Sara; meesterlijk en schoon geschilderd | *Size:* hoog 50, breed 62 duim	S	(Sold) fl 11
1809/04/22	AMYVR	0133	*J. Victor* | Twee stuks: een Slager en eene Fruitvrouw, welke hunne Waren verkoopen; krachtig | *Mat:* op doek *Size:* ieder hoog 27, breed 30 duim	de Bruin	(Sold) fl 13 Bonte
1809/06/13	AMSCH	0159	*J. Victor* | Twee stuks kapitaale Dorpgezichten, beide rijk gestoffeerd met een Kwakzalver en een menigte Aanschouwers, Boerenwagens met vrolijke Gasten, Landlieden die Beesten drijven, arbeidende Huislieden en verdere stoffagie; schoon geschilderd | *Mat:* op doek *Size:* ieder hoog 20, breed 25 duim	[Gruyter?]	(Bought In) fl 9
1810/03/07	UTWLD	0009	*J. Victor* | Een plaisant Landschap, vol gewoel | *Size:* hoog 3 voet 7 duim, breed 5 voet 8 duim	J J Woertman	(Unknown) fl 26
1810/06/20	AMSCH	0088	*J. Victor* | Deze Ordonnantie stelt voor het wegzenden van Hagar en Ismael door Abraham, achterwaarts ziet men Sara. Meesterlijk geschilderd | *Mat:* op doek *Size:* hoog 50, breed 62 duimen		(Withdrawn)
1810/06/20	AMSCH	0089	*J. Victor* | Een Dorpgezigt: op den voorgrond voor eene Herberg ziet men een Officier te Paard, welken door eene Boerin een glas wijn wordt aangeboden; nevens hun een Boer, die het Paard van een ander Officier vasthoudt; verder drie andere Beelden. Helder, bevallig en van de beste schildering | *Mat:* op doek *Size:* hoog 31, breed 34 duimen	D	(Sold) fl 86 S M Levie

Victors, Jan (or Victors, Jan, manner)

1802/08/24	LNDLS	0131	*Victor* | Een Kwakzalver bij zijn kraam met eenige Mannen, Vrouwen en Kinderen, terwijl hij een Meisje in haar mond helpt, door of zoo goet als van Victor | *Mat:* op doek	Leonardus Bouman [or others]	(Unknown) fl 34
1803/04/20	AMSCH	0087	*Victor (J.) of in de manier* | Deeze Ordenantie van zes Beelden, vertoont in een Binnenvertrek, daar den ouden Tobias van zyn Blindheid geneezen word, in het byzyn van den Engel; meesterlyk en kloek gepenceeld [Cette composition de six figures a pour sujet le vieux Tobie gueri de son aveuglement par son fils, en presence de l'ange. Tableau traité avec vigeur [sic] & d'une bonne couleur.] | *Mat:* op doek *Size:* hoog 35, breed 43 duim	Maria Magdalena van Sluypwyk, gravinne van Moens	(Sold) fl 20 Vermeulen

Victors, Jan (manner)

1801/03/16	AMSCH	0027	*Victor* | Een vrolyk Gezelschap in een Binnevertrek, fiks als door Victor	K[ip]	(Sold) fl 1 Mensart
1801/04/08	HAVIN	0024	*Victor* | Een Gezicht van de Visbrug te Leiden plaisant als van Victor		(Unknown)
1801/04/13	AMSCH	0097	*J. Victor* | Een dito [bejaarde Vrouw], mede op een stoel zittende, met een Bybel in de eene, en een Bril in de andere hand; geschilderd als door J. Victor | *Mat:* op doek *Size:* hoog 35, breed 26 duim	Pierre Fouquet, junior	(Sold) fl 22 Reynders
1801/04/23	AMYVR	0042	*Victor* | Een Dorpgezicht waarin een Paard door een Smit beslaagen word, verders eenige andere Figuuren, op Doek in de manier van Victor | *Mat:* op doek		(Sold) fl 1 ¼ Jourdany
1809/04/22	AMYVR	0176	*Victor* | Een vrolijke Fruitverkooper; als Victor	de Bruin	(Sold) fl 2:5 du Pree
1810/06/06	RMMUY	0090	*Victor* | Eene bedaagde Vrouw, met de eene hand op een stok leunende, met de andere iets aanwijzende. Als door Victor | *Mat:* op paneel		(Unknown) fl 6:5
1810/06/06	RMMUY	0195	*Victor* | Een Keuken met verscheiden Figuren. Als door Victor | *Mat:* op paneel		(Sold) fl 2 Strikland

Vinck, Cornelis

1804/04/28	LNDLS	0038	*C. Vinck* | Een Landschap met gebouwen, als van van Goyen, door C. Vinck, op paneel | *Mat:* op paneel *Size:* hoog 23, breed 32 duim	[Abraham Delfos] [or others]	(Sold) fl 2:12 Rigter [for] G

Vinck, J.

1804/10/16	DLOND	0249	*J. Vinck* | Een Landschap met Ezels. Paysage avec des Aness | *Mat:* op paneel *Size:* hoog 14, breed 18		(Unknown)
1810/10/11	AMSCH	0260	*J. Vinck* | Een Landschap	A	(Sold) fl 0:6 Menzart

Vinckeboons, David

1802/04/13	HAVIN	0056	*Vinkeboons* | Een Buijtenhuis met vrolyke Persoonen		(Unknown)
1802/05/11	GRGRW	0055	*David Vinkeboom* | Een Bosch-gezicht [Schilderijen met Olie-Verf; In zwarte Lijsten] | *Mat:* in olyverf *Notes:* The bracketed information in the title appears above lot 1 and refers to lots 1 to 79a.	Arnold Sicco Werumeus	(Unknown) fl 1:1
1802/11/01	DOBRA	0178	*David Vinkeboom* | Een Boschgezigt met Jagers te paard en te voet, die Harten vervolgen | *Mat:* op paneel *Size:* hoog 20, breed 32 duim		(Unknown) fl 2:15
1803/04/20	AMSCH	0085	*Vinkeboom (D.)* | Een Gezicht op het Huis Kroonenburg, ter zyde ziet men de Domstooren van Utrecht, gestoffeerd met Beelden, en Schuiten welke in de Rivier by het Huis zich vertoonen, meesterlyk gepenceeld [Vue d'un Chateau, dit Kroonenburg, près de la riviere, la perspective donnant sur le dome d'Utrecht. Ce sujet est orné de jolies figures & nacelles qui sont bien touchées.] | *Mat:* op doek *Size:* hoog 19, breed 26 duim	Maria Magdalena van Sluypwyk, gravinne van Moens	(Sold) fl 7 Gruiter
1803/07/18	AMSCH	0058	*Vinkebooms (D.)* | Een Dorpgezicht alwaar het Kermis is, gestoffeerd mer [sic] honderde Beeldjes, waarvan er eenige danssen en andere zich met drinken vermaaken, dit stuk is alleraangenaamst en ryk van ordonantie, en is van een uitvoerige behandeling [Une Dedicaçe ou Kermesse de Village. Ce sujet enrichi de quelque centaine de figures est d'une variété infinie. Des groupes amassés près des boutiques & autour des Charlatans, d'autres sont a dancer ou à la promenade ; une partie est en querelle, & les plus avisés sont autour des tables à manger & à Boire. On y distingue aussi des groupes d'Enfans à des divertissemens. Le fond est un Paysage riant donnant sur une Eglise & sur un village. Ce tableau très fini est dans son genre un des plus riches & des Mieux Composés.] | *Mat:* op koper *Size:* hoog 17, breed 27 duim	Maria Theresia Andrioli	(Sold) fl 30 J Ijver
1803/09/07	AMSCH	0197	*Vinkeboom* | Twee stuks bevallige Boomryke Landschapjes, met Rivieren doorsneeden, en met verscheide Beeldjes gestoffeerd en eenige Woningen, beide uit voerig behandeld [Deux paysages agréables et riches, entrecoupés de rivieres et melé de figures et d'habitations ; tous les deux d'une exécution précieuse] | *Mat:* op paneel *Size:* yder hoog 10, breed 11 duim	Smidt	(Sold) fl 3:5 Toselli
1803/09/07	AMSCH	0198	*Vinkeboom* | Een zeer uitvoerig Landschap, met hoog Geboomte, Boerewoningen en stoffagie van Beeldjes; delicaat op Koper [Un très beau paysage ; les arbres qui en font le principal mérite, sont d'un beau fini ; on y voit aussi quelques chaumières et des figures, composition très délicate] | *Mat:* op koper *Size:* hoog 11, br. 15 duim	Smidt	(Bought In) fl 8
1803/09/07	AMSCH	0199	*Vinkeboom* | In een Boom- en Bergachtig Landschap, ziet men een Valken Jacht; ryk gestoffeerd [Une chasse aux faucons dans un paysage riant et richement varié d'arbres et de montagnes] | *Mat:* op koper *Size:* hoog 18, breed 24 duim	Smidt	(Sold) fl 10 C S Roos
1803/09/07	AMSCH	0200	*Vinkeboom* | Twee stuks Bosch- en Bergachtige Landschappen, gestoffeerd met een menigte Beeldjes, Beestjes, enz.; natuurlyk en fix gepenceeld, door denzelven [Vinkeboom], beide op Koper [Deux paysages bocageux, dans le goût des précédens ; peint au naturel et d'un bel effet] | *Mat:* op koper *Size:* hoog 12, breed 16 duim	Smidt	(Sold) fl 14 C S Roos
1803/09/07	AMSCH	0201	*Vinkeboom* | Een Bergachtig Boschgezigt met Watervallen en stoffagie van Beeldjes en andere stoffagie; zonachtig en uitvoerig [La vue d'une forêt ; cette composition est enrichie de cascades et de differentes figures, qui en rendent la variété charmante] | *Mat:* op paneel *Size:* hoog 22, breed 33 duim	Smidt	(Sold) fl 15 C S Roos
1804/04/28	LNDLS	0035	*D. Vinkeboom* | In een Landschap verbeeld een boere kermis, met een meenigte vrolyk volk, door D. Vinkeboom, op paneel | *Mat:* op paneel *Size:* hoog 16 ½, breed 26 duim	[Abraham Delfos] [or others]	(Bought In) fl 7
1805/07/10	AMSCH	0159	*D. Vinkeboom* | Een Brabandsche Kermis, in een Dorp, vol gewoel van Beelden; kragtig op Paneel | *Mat:* op paneel *Size:* hoog 19, breed 37 duim	Y[ver]	(Sold) fl 6 Lafontaine
1805/07/10	AMSCH	0160	*D. Vinkeboom* | Een Boere Kermisvreugd, vol gewoel van Beeldjes, welke zich op verschillende wyzen vermaken; allernatuurlykst en fraai van behandeling | *Mat:* op paneel *Size:* hoog 13, breed 21 duim	V[inkeles] [for] J	(Sold) fl 4:5 Gruyter
1805/10/09	HGBSM	0031	*Vinkeboom* | Een bosch gezigt gestoffeerd met jagers &c. uitvoerig | *Mat:* op paneel *Size:* hoog 16 ½ breet 22 ½	T H van Willigen [or others]	(Sold) fl 3:6 Carré
1805/10/09	HGBSM	0053	*Vinkeboom* | Een landschap met geboomtens en gebouwen op de voorgrond ziet men Abram, Hagar en Ismael uitdryven | *Mat:* op paneel *Size:* hoog 19 ½ breet 30 duim	T H van Willigen [or others]	(Sold) fl 5 De Gelder

1805/10/09	HGBSM	0095	*D. Vinkeboom* | Een boomryk landschap, gestoffeerd, met een menigte figuuren, verbeeldende de historie van Jefta, uitvoerig | *Mat:* op koper *Size:* hoog 12 ½ breet 17 duim	T H van Willigen [or others]	(Sold) fl 6 Zwartsman
1805/10/21	GRBOL	0058	*Vinkeboom* | Een Vorstelyk Binnenhof	Gerardus Nicolaus Heerkens	(Unknown)
1806/06/07	RMHSN	0088	*Vinkeboom* | Een Winter | *Mat:* op paneel	A E K L	(Unknown)
1806/08/20	HGBSM	0071	*Vinkeboom* | Een Gezicht van eene Buitenplaats, daar eene partij aanzienlijke Persoonen zich vermaaken, zo met speelen als anderzints, zeer uitvoerig geschilderd | *Mat:* op koper *Size:* hoog 8, breed 10 duim	Macalester Loup [or others]	(Sold) fl 5:15 Gram
1806/10/22	HGBAK	0010	*Vinkeboon* | Een Landschapje door Vinkeboon | *Mat:* op koper		(Unknown)
1807/04/00	LNDLS	0023	*D. Vinkeboom* | Een boere kermis, vol gewoel van een menfgte [sic] mannen, vrouwen en kinderen, die vrolijk zijn, in een landschap met boomen, gebouwen, en een kerktoren in 't verschiet | *Size:* hoog 16, breed 26 duim	[Abraham Delfos] [or others]	(Unknown)
1807/06/10	HGBSM	0023	*D. Vinnkboom* | Een boere Kermis, vol gewoel van een menigte mannen, vrouwen en kinderen, die vrolijk zijn, in een landschap met boomen, gebouwen, en een kerktoren in 't verschiet | *Size:* hoog 16, breed 26 duim	Abraham Delfos [or others]	(Sold) fl 8:5 Tessier
1808/04/26	GDAN	0173	*Vinkeboom (D)* | Een op koper boomrijk Landschap, met eenige Figuuren | *Mat:* op koper *Size:* hoog 12, breed 14 ½ duim	G H Fortuyn	(Unknown)
1808/04/26	GDAN	0174	*Vinkeboom (D)* | Een extra fraai Thuingezigt, met eenige Beelden en Vogels, uitmundend [sic] behandeld | *Size:* hoog 16 ½, breed 24 duim	G H Fortuyn	(Unknown)
1809/06/13	AMSCH	0184	*Vinkebooms* | Een Bosachtig Landschap met een Heer te Paard en Reizigers; bevallig geschildert | *Mat:* op paneel	Y	(Sold) fl 2 L Pakker
1810/05/22	AMSCH	0144	*D. Vinkebooms* | Twee kapitale Boschgezichten, gestoffeerd met Struikrovers, die Reizigers aanvallen en beroven; meesterlijk op Doek geschilderd | *Mat:* op doek	D	(Sold) fl 5:10 Otte
			Vinckeboons, David (and Balen, J. and Snyders, F.)		
1803/07/18	AMSCH	0004	*Balen, (J. van); F. Snyders; D. Vinkebooms* | Twee Nimphen van de Jagt komende met een menigte Wild, 't geen op de grond legt, schynende met elkander daarover te spreeken, een derde ter zyde hun in de schaduwe, voor dezelven verscheide Jagthonden; het Bosch door Vinkebooms, het Wild door Snyders, en de Beelden door van Balen, maaken een schoon geheel uit, en doen de talenten van deeze drie Meesters alle eer aan [Deux Nimphes, au retour d'une chasse abondante, s'entretiennent vèrs la droite, ayant cinq beaux chiens bracs auprès d'elles ; une troisieme Nimphe s'achemine vèrs la foret. A la gauche sont les animaux morts, couchés sur une légère élévation, c'est un sanglier, un loup, un liévre avec d'autres quadrupédes & de la volaille. Cette réunion de talens des trois artistes s'accorde parfaitement bien. Les figures sont belles & de couleur riche ; les animaux traités avec légereté & delicatesse, & le Paysage repond bien au sujet.] | *Mat:* op paneel *Size:* hoog 24, breed 33 duim	Maria Theresia Andrioli	(Sold) fl 52 Hulswit
			Vinckeboons, David (and Neeffs, P. (I))		
1803/07/18	AMSCH	0037	*Neefs. (P.); Vinkebooms. (D.)* | Een Gothische Roomsche Kerk van binnen tot aan het Choor te zien, 't welk een fraai perspectief opleverd; ter zyde ziet men een menigte Autaaren [sic]. De stoffagie door Vinkebooms steld voor, een processie van verscheide Mannen en Vrouwen, de onbegrypelyk uitvoerigheid en het zonligt, gepaard met een lieflyk coloriet, maaken dit stukje tot een aangenaam Schilderytje [Ce morceau nous offre le point de vue d'une eglise de construction gothique, percent [sic] par la nef de milieu jusqu'au fond du coeur. Les autels & les ornemens en sont traités avec finesse & d'un beau fini, ainsi que l'architecture. Vinkebooms a orné ce sujet d'une procession d'hommes & de femmes, sortant de l'eglise. L'effet de la degradation de lumiere bien observé & l'agrement des jolies figures lui assurent une distinction.] | *Mat:* op koper *Size:* hoog 13, breed 17 duim [haut 12, large 15 pouces] *Notes:* The dimensions differ in the Dutch and French editions of the catalogue.	Maria Theresia Andrioli	(Sold) fl 180 Haffner
1805/07/10	AMSCH	0110	*P. Neefs; D. Vinkeboom* | Een Roomsche Kerk van binnen te zien, in de zelve ziet men een Professie van Nonnen, waarby Muzicanten enz., verders een ménigte stoffagie van Beeldjes; alleruitvoerigst en fraai gepenceeld, door denzelven [P. Neefs] en D. Vinkeboom | *Mat:* op koper *Size:* hoog 13, breed 17 ½ duim	V[inkeles] [for] H[affner]	(Sold) fl 60 Lafontaine
			Vinckeboons, David (or Vinckeboons, D., manner)		
1808/06/11	RMRIJ	0017	*Vinckeboom, of in zyn manier* | Een alleruitvoerigst boomryk Land- en Watergezicht, met Figuren | *Mat:* op paneel *Size:* hoog 15, breed 19 duim		(Sold) fl 11 Van Dongen
			Vinckeboons, David (manner)		
1804/08/02	BDAN	0039	*Manier van Vinkenboom* | Een aangenaam Land-gezigt | *Mat:* op paneel *Size:* b. 23 d. h. 33 en een half d.	J G Calckberner	(Unknown)
			Vinne, J. van der		
1809/04/17	AMSCH	0108	*J. van der Vinne* | Een Protestantsche Kerk, van binnen, ziende na de Predikstoel en Koor, rijk gestoffeerd met wandelende en rustende	T	(Sold) fl 0:10

			Beelden; fraai van doorzicht en zonachtig behandeld, door J. van der Vinne 1703 | *Mat:* op doek *Size:* hoog 44, breed 57 duim *Inscr:* J. van der Vinne 1703 (signed and dated?) *Notes:* It is unclear whether the name and date are inscribed on the painting.		
1810/03/23	HAVIN	0015	*J. van der Vinne* | Het Gezigt van het Buitenspaarne na de stad te zien, fraai met Schepen gestoffeerd en uitvoerig geschilderd | *Size:* hoog 17 breet 27 d.	Rudolf Hendrik de Wetstein [or others]	(Unknown)
1810/10/11	AMSCH	0090	*J. Van Der Vinne* | Een Gezigt in den Hout buiten Haarlem, gestoffeerd met wandelende Heeren en Dames, spelende Jongens en andere Stoffage; uitvoerig geschilderd | *Mat:* op doek *Size:* hoog 26, breed 32 duimen	[Gruyter?]	(Sold) fl 8:5 Van Leen

Vinne, J. van der (and Nickelen)

1808/03/03	HAVIN	0002	*van Nikkelen; J. van der Vinne* | De Groote Kerk te Haarlem, na 't Choor te zien, fraai, door van Nikkelen, en gestoffeerd door J. van der Vinne	Jacobus Spillebout	(Unknown) fl 8

Vinne, Jan van der (I)

1801/04/08	HAVIN	0003	*J. van der Vinne* | Twee, een Campement en Rencontre, plaisant en uitvoerig		(Unknown)
1802/04/13	HAVIN	0024	*J. van der Vinne* | Een Campement, plaisant en fraai		(Unknown)
1808/03/03	HAVIN	0005	*Jan van der Vinne* | Twee Plaisante Landschappen	Jacobus Spillebout	(Unknown) fl 54
1808/03/03	HAVIN	0006	*Jan van der Vinne* | Twee, een Campement en Rencontre	Jacobus Spillebout	(Unknown) fl 27:5
1808/07/19	AMROU	0011	*van der Vindre* | 1 hevige Rencontre van Ruiters te Paard		(Unknown)

Vinne, Jan van der (II)

1809/05/26	HADAA	0014	*Jan v.d. Vinne* | Twee stuks, zijnde een Gezicht op de Hofstede Elswout, en een dito op de toren van Bloemendaal	Mejuffrouw de Wed David Heemskerk [or others]	(Unknown)

Vinne, Vincent Laurentsz. van der (I)

1801/04/08	HAVIN	0037	*V. L. van der Vinne* | Een Binnenhuis met een Varke aan de ladder		(Unknown)
1802/06/16	AMSCH	0201	*V. van der Vinne* | In een Landschap met Geboomten, vertoont zich een Harte Jagt; verscheide Heeren en Dames te Paard, met Jagers en Honden, vervolgen het Wild; zeer bevallig en plaisant gepenceeld | *Mat:* op doek op paneel *Size:* hoog 16, breed 18 ½ duim	[Merrem]	(Sold) fl 6 A Schotte
1802/09/06	AMSCH	0202	*V. van der Vinne* | Een comique Ordenantie	Spaan	(Sold) fl 0:6 L Pakker
1802/12/13	AMSCH	0164	*V. van der Vinne* | Dit bevallig Stukje vertoond een Land- en Rivier-Gezicht, gestoffeerd met zeilende Scheepen en Vissers in Schuiten, verders Boere Schuuren en andere Gebouwen; alles verbeeld by helder Maanlicht, zeer natuurlyk en uitvoerig behandeld, in de manier van A. van der Neer, door V. van der Vinne | *Mat:* op paneel *Size:* hoog 5 ½, breed 6 ½ duim	Schley [for] Lauwers	(Sold) fl 8 van der Schley
1808/03/03	HAVIN	0025	*V.L. van der Vinne* | Een dito [Landschap]	Jacobus Spillebout	(Unknown) fl 0:15
1810/05/22	AMSCH	0112	*Vinne. (V. van der)* | Een Duinachtig Hollandsch Landschap, op den voorgrond aan een zandige Weg, gestoffeerd met gaande en rustende Huislieden en eenige Visdragers bij Boeren Woningen en hoog Geboomten; bevallig en uitvoerig van schildering | *Mat:* op paneel *Size:* hoog 10, breed 13 duim	Johannes van de Putte Nicolaasz.	(Sold) fl 14 B Kooij
1810/05/22	AMSCH	0113	*Vinne. (V. van der)* | Een Landschap als de voorgaande, met een opgaande Weg, Geboomten en stoffage van Beeldjes; zeer natuurlijk voorgesteld | *Mat:* op paneel *Size:* hoog 11, breed 14 duim	Johannes van de Putte Nicolaasz.	(Sold) fl 8:10 van Iperen
1810/10/11	AMSCH	0145	*Van Der Vinne* | Een vrolijke Masquerade | *Mat:* op doek	C	(Sold) fl 0:6 van Iperen

Vinne, Vincent Laurentsz. van der (I) (or Vinne, V.L. (I), manner)

1801/08/19	AMSCH	0169	*van der Vinne* | Zeeven Vrouwen Vechten om de Mans Broek, door of in de manier van van der Vinne	Van Forreest	(Sold) fl 3 Roos

Visscher, Cornelis (II) (copy after)

1801/02/18	AMBOS	0075	*C. Visscher* | Een Vrouw Koeken bakkende, daar nevens zit een oud Man zyn Pyp opsteekende aan een Kooltjen, na C. Visscher	J Schonevelt	(Unknown)
1802/07/27	AKHRK	0086	*Na C. Fisscher* | De bekende Koekebakster, na Visscher | *Mat:* op doek *Size:* hoog 15 ½, breed 18 ¼ duim *Notes:* This lot was sold with lot 87 by an anonymous artist.	Maria Stategaart	(Sold) fl 4 for lots 86 & 87. Sonnevelt
1805/07/03	AMSCH	0197	*C. de Visscher* | In dit Voorwerp vertoont zig de Koekebakster in een Binnehuis; naar C. de Visscher, op Doek, plaisant geschilderd | *Mat:* op doek	G	(Sold) fl 54 L Pakker
1806/06/07	RMHSN	0110	*Visser* | De Koekebakster, na Visser | *Mat:* op paneel	A E K L	(Unknown)

Vitringa, Wigerus

1801/04/08	HAVIN	0025	*W. Vitringa* | Twee Watergezigten		(Unknown)
1802/05/05	AMSCH	0228	*Vitringa* | Een Turkse Zeehaven, gestoffeerd met Kooplieden en Koopwaren | *Size:* hoog 13, breed 15 duim	J	(Sold) fl 3:15 Spruit

1802/05/24	HGBAK	0016	*W. Vitringa* | Een Kermis-vreugd, met dansende Boeren en Boerinnen, een Kwaksalver op het Theater, in 't verschiet een Kerkgebouw, zeer uitvoerig en fix behandeld, door W. Vitringa 1705, hoog 11 ½ d., breed 14 duim, op doek, zwarte lyst en vergulde binnenrand | companion to lot 17 *Mat:* op doek *Size:* hoog 11 ½ duim, breed 14 duim *Inscr:* W. Vitringa 1705 (dated?) *Notes:* It is unclear whether the name and date are inscribed on the painting.	Mejuffrouw A van der Mieden	(Sold) fl 27 for lots 16 & 17. Te Ché
1802/05/24	HGBAK	0017	*W. Vitringa* | Een dito [Kermis-vreugd] tot een weerga, mede met dansende Boeren en Boerinnen, niet minder als het voorige, hoog 11 duim, breed 13 ½ duim, dito [zwarte] lyst | companion to lot 16 *Size:* hoog 11 duim, breed 13 ½ duim	Mejuffrouw A van der Mieden	(Sold) fl 27 for lots 16 & 17. Te Ché
1802/06/16	AMSCH	0196	*W. Vitringa* | Een stil en een woelend Water, beide gestoffeerd met Beurtscheepen, Roeischuiten, Jachten en andere Vaartuigen, ryk van Ordenantie en meesterlyk geschilderd | *Mat:* op doek *Size:* hoog 22, breed 27 duim	[Merrem]	(Sold) fl 61 LaFontaine
1802/06/16	AMSCH	0197	*W. Vitringa* | Een woelend Water met een Oorlogschip, Beurtscheepen en andere Vaartuigen; op de voorgrond een Visscherschuit; het Water is zeer dun, krachtig van Coloriet en helder gepenceeld | *Mat:* op paneel *Size:* hoog 17, breed 21 ½ duim	[Merrem]	(Sold) fl 12 LaFontaine
1802/07/27	AKHRK	0027	*W. van Vitringa* | Het inkomen der Stad Alkmaar bij de hooge Brug en Accijnshuis, voor dezelve een Jacht en verdere Scheepen en Schuiten; bevallig van licht en schaduw | *Mat:* op doek *Size:* hoog 17, breed 24 duim	Maria Stategaart	(Sold) fl 6:10 Brouwer
1802/07/27	AKHRK	0028	*W. van Vitringa* | Een stil Water met verschillende Scheepen en Schuiten, en een Stad in het verschiet: goed van licht en bruin | *Mat:* op doek *Size:* hoog 31 ½, breed 28 duim	Maria Stategaart	(Sold) fl 6 Gruyter
1802/12/13	AMSCH	0168	*W. Vitringa* | In een Levandsche Zeehaven, ziet men een Gally en andere Vaartuigen, op de voorgrond eenige Kooplieden by hunne Goederen; uitvoerig gepenceeld | *Mat:* op paneel *Size:* hoog 12, breed 14 duim	Pruyssenaar [for] A	(Sold) fl 0:14 Gruiter
1802/12/13	AMSCH	0169	*W. Vitringa* | Twee woelende Zeën, met zeilende Scheepen en Vaartuigen; door denzelven [W. Vitringa], in de manier van Bakhuyzen | *Mat:* op paneel *Size:* hoog 12, breed 14 duim	Pruyssenaar [for] D	(Sold) fl 5 Van Iperen
1803/08/24	HGKAN	0050	*Vitringa* | Een woelende Zee met verscheide Scheepen | *Mat:* op doek *Size:* hoog 44, breet 66 duim	[Teissier] [or others]	(Sold) fl 3:10 Carre
1803/12/15	MGLAC	0061	*Vitringa* | Twee Plaisante Zeehavens | *Size:* hoog duim 14, breed duim 19	Mr L H de Haze Bomme	(Unknown)
1804/04/28	LNDLS	0012	*W. Vitringa* | Een Zeehaven met schepen en Kooplieden, op de voorgrond beelden en beesten, als van J. Lingelbach, door W. Vitringa, op doek | companion to lot 13 *Mat:* op doek *Size:* hoog 20, breed 16 ½ duim	[Abraham Delfos] [or others]	(Bought In) fl 5:15
1804/04/28	LNDLS	0013	*W. Vitringa* | Een Weêrga, met gebouwen op gebergten, en op den voorgrond beelden en beesten; door denzelven [W. Vitringa] | companion to lot 12 *Size:* hoog 20, breed 16 ½ duim	[Abraham Delfos] [or others]	(Bought In) fl 5:15
1805/07/10	AMSCH	0148	*W. Vitringa* | In een woelende Zee ziet men 't verbryselen van een Oorlogschip tegen een Klip, verders een Visschers Pink, met verscheide Lieden, en in 't verschiet nog andere Scheepen; de stuiving van 't Water, en de donkeren lucht maken een frapart [sic] effect; en is meesterlyk op Doek | *Mat:* op doek *Size:* hoog 19, breed 27 duim	V[inkeles] [for] M	(Sold) fl 24 L Pakker
1805/07/10	AMSCH	0149	*W. Vitringa* | Twee stuks, een Onstuimige en een Kabelende Zee, met een ménigte zylende en roeijende Vaartuigen; fraai van lucht en meesterlyk gepenceeld | *Mat:* op paneel *Size:* hoog 11 ½, breed 14 ½ duim	V[inkeles] [for] H[affner]	(Sold) fl 7:10 Lafontaine
1806/05/05	AMSCH	0146	*Vitringa* | Een Levantsche Zeehaven, op de voorgrond eenige Kooplieden by hunne goederen, verders eenige Gebouwen en Vaartuigen | *Mat:* op paneel *Size:* hoog 18, breed 14 duim	V[inkeles]	(Sold) fl 2:10 Boelen
1806/08/20	HGBSM	0059	*W. Vitringa* | Vrolijke Boeren, dansende voor een Herberg | *Mat:* op paneel *Size:* hoog 11 ½, breed 14 duim	Macalester Loup [or others]	(Sold) fl 11:5 Koopman
1807/04/00	LNDLS	0040	*W. Vietringa* | Twee stuks Zeehavens, met kooplieden op den voorgrond | *Mat:* op doek *Size:* ieder hoog 20, breed 16 en een half duim	[Abraham Delfos] [or others]	(Unknown)
1807/06/10	HGBSM	0040	*W. Vietringa* | Twee stuks Zeehavens, met kooplieden op den voorgrond | *Mat:* op doek *Size:* ieder hoog 20, breed 16 ½ duim	Abraham Delfos [or others]	(Sold) fl 9:5 v Giese
1808/06/13	AMSCH	0186	*W. Vitringa* | Een stil Water met Schepen, op den voorgrond eenige Visschers; zonachtig	E M Engelberts	(Sold) fl 9 Rosenkrans
1808/06/13	AMSCH	0205	*W. Vitringa* | Een woelend Water, met een Jagt en andere Vaartuigen; fiks	E M Engelberts	(Sold) fl 5:5 Th Spaan
1808/06/13	AMSCH	0232	*W. Vitringa* | Twee stuks Land- en Watergezichten, gestoffeerd met Beelden en Vaartuigen | *Mat:* op paneel	Z	(Sold) fl 20 Rozekrans
1808/11/28	AMSCH	0062	*W. Vitringa* | Een woelende Zee, met zeilende Jagten, Beurtschepen en andere Vaartuigen gestoffeerd, helder en plaisant | *Mat:* op paneel *Size:* hoog 17, breed 22 duim	C	(Sold) fl 2:10 F Spaan

Vitringa, Wigerus (manner)

1806/11/24	AMSCH	0096	*W. Vitringa* | Een dito [woelende Zee], aan 't Strand eenige Beeldjes, welke een Schuit in haalen, zonachtig als W. Vitringa	Munnikhuizen	(Sold) fl 2 L Pakker

Vleughels, Nicolas

1803/08/24	HGKAN	0005	*N. Vleughels* | De verscheining van Minerva aan Hercules, helder en fraay van Couleur en Meesterlyk geschilderd	[Teissier] [or others]	(Unknown) fl 21 for lots 5 & 6
1803/08/24	HGKAN	0006	*N. Vleughels* | Een fraay Schildery verbeeldende Lazarus en de Ryke Man, ryk gecomponeerd en brillant van Couleur, Meesterlyk geschilderd	[Teissier] [or others]	(Unknown) fl 21 for lots 5 & 6
1805/07/10	AMSCH	0167	*Vleughels* | Twee stuks, Apollo en de Musen; en een andere Zinnebeeldige Ordinantie; beide fraai van Teekening en uitvoerig op Paneel | *Mat:* op paneel *Size:* hoog 11, breed 9 duim	V[inkeles] [for] N	(Sold) fl 2:5 Isaac Smit

Vlieger, C. de [Unidentified]

1809/04/22	AMYVR	0142	*C. de Vlieger* | Een onstuimige Zee, vol Scheepen and andere Vaartuigen | *Mat:* op paneel *Size:* hoog 19, breed 28 duim	Juff[r] Julikker	(Sold) fl 2 C S Roos

Vlieger, J. de [Unidentified]

1802/06/16	AMSCH	0191	*J. de Vlieger* | Een Bosch vol zwaar Geboomten, ter zyde een aangenaam verschiet, de voorgrond gestoffeerd met Jagers en Honden; alles zonachtig en natuurlyk geschilderd | *Mat:* op doek *Size:* hoog 21, breed 25 duim	[Merrem]	(Sold) fl 38 I Smit Gz

Vlieger, Simon de

1801/05/11	AMSCH	0106	*S. de Vlieger* | Een Strandgezicht, ryk met beelden gestoffeerd, ter zyde ziet men eenige Vissers Pinken, meesterlyk gepenceeld | *Mat:* op doek *Size:* hoog 26, breed 35 duim	Pruisse [for] M	(Sold) fl 29 Coclers
1801/05/11	AMSCH	0107	*S. de Vlieger* | Een Strandgezicht met verscheiden beelden gestoffeerd, en een ruim verschiet, zonachtig en plaisant geschilderd | *Mat:* op paneel *Size:* hoog 17, breed 21 duim	E[lias]	(Sold) fl 17 Allard
1801/05/11	AMSCH	0108	*S. de Vlieger* | Een diergelyke Ordonnantie, niet minder behandeld | *Mat:* op paneel *Size:* hoog 14, breed 19 duim	E[lias]	(Sold) fl 9 Coclers
1801/06/10	AMSCH	0178	*Vlieger. (S. de.)* | Een woelende Zee, met verscheiden Oorlogscheepen, Beurtscheepen en andere Vaartuigen, terzyde eenige Visscherspinken; alles meeeterlyk [sic] en krachtig geschilderd | *Mat:* op doek *Size:* hoog 39, breed 72 duim	Herman ten Kate	(Sold) fl 115 T van Iperen
1801/10/06	AMSCH	0067	*S. de Vlieger* | Een Land en Watergezigt by Boeren Wooningen, gestoffeert met een Vrouw die Goed spoelt, zeer Natuurlyk geschilderd | *Mat:* op paneel *Size:* hoog 19, breed 27 duim	M	(Sold) fl 18 ter Smitten
1801/10/06	AMSCH	0068	*Simon de Vlieger* | Een woelend Water, gestoffeert met een zylend Oorlog Schip, en andere Vaartuigen, op de voorgrond Vissers in een Schuit, bézig hun Net in te haalen, fiks gepenceelt | *Mat:* op paneel *Size:* hoog 26, breed 21 duim	L	(Sold) fl 26 Theijs
1802/06/16	AMSCH	0193	*N. de Vlieger* | Een Strandgezicht, gestoffeerd met Visschers Pinken en een menigte Huislieden; op de voorgrond eenige Vissen, ter zyde een woelende Zee, meesterlyk behandeld | *Mat:* op paneel *Size:* hoog 23 ½, breed 32 ½ duim *Notes:* The artist's name was given as "N. de Vlieger" but we have assumed this is an error.	[Merrem]	(Sold) fl 31 Coclers
1802/07/21	HGKAN	0058	*de Vlieger* | Een onstuimige Zee met Scheepen, door de Vlieger, zwarte Lyst, vergulde binnen rand		(Unknown)
1802/08/24	LNDLS	0051	*S. de Vlieger* | Een stil Water, met ten anker liggende en zeilende Schepen; ter regter zijde visschers in hun huit. Helder van coloriet, en krachtig geschilderd | *Mat:* op paneel *Size:* hoog 34, breed 46 duimen	Leonardus Bouman [or others]	(Unknown) fl 76
1802/08/24	LNDLS	0093	*S. de Vlieger* | Een woelend Water met Zeilende Schepen en Schuiten | *Mat:* op paneel *Size:* hoog 10, breed 13 duimen	Leonardus Bouman [or others]	(Unknown) fl 2:12
1802/09/21	UTHDG	0090	*S. de Vlieger* | Een Bosch en Watergezigt, vooraan met Schapen en Herders; gestoffeerd in een Meesterlijke trant, geschildert door S. de Vlieger | *Mat:* op doek *Size:* hoog 25 ½, breed 29 duimen		(Bought In) fl 19
1802/09/29	AMSCH	0055	*S. de Vlieger* | Een Water Gezigt, hoog 14 ½, breed 20 ¼ duim. Paneel. Zynde een zeer Aangenaam uitgestrekt gezigt op een stil Water, met zeilende Beurtman en Visschers Schépen; helder, natuurlyk, en van eene delicate Penceelbehandeling [Le Point de Vue, d'une vaste étendue d'Eau, avec des Barques garnies de Voiles & autres, l'horison fait voir plusieurs détails ; la Touche de ce morceau est facile & aussi brillante que vraie.] | *Mat:* op paneel *Size:* hoog 14 ½, breed 20 ¼ duim	[Labouchere?]	(Sold) fl 71 Gruyter
1803/04/20	AMSCH	0082	*Vlieger (S. de)* | In een ruim Binnenwater vertoonen zig Vissers in een Schiut [sic], ter andere zyde een Hooft van Paalwerk en Zeebaak, verder een uitgestrekt Dorpgezicht, zeer natuurlyk en meesterlyk gepenceeld [Une large etendue d'un fleuve ou les pécheurs sont occupés avec leur navire ; d'autre part se presente une tête en pilotis, un fanal et un village. Ce morceau traité avec tout l'agrement et la verité possibles est également intêressant pour l'execution.] | *Mat:* op paneel *Size:* hoog 23, breed 48 duim	Maria Magdalena van Sluypwyk, gravinne van Moens	(Sold) fl 51 Hodges
1803/08/24	HGKAN	0027	*S. de Vlieger* | Een woelende Zee met Scheepen | *Mat:* op paneel *Size:* hoog 9, breet 13 duim	[Teissier] [or others]	(Sold) fl 4 Uytenbogert
1803/12/12	AMSCH	0104	*S. de Vlieger* | Een sterk woelende Zee met onderscheiden Scheepen; frapant van licht en meesterlyk gepenceeld | *Mat:* op paneel *Size:* hoog 9 ½, breed 12 ½ duim	B	(Sold) fl 15 Hodges

1803/12/15	MGLAC	0063	*Vlieger* | Een Zeetje | *Size:* hoog duim 16, breed duim 22	Mr L H de Haze Bomme	(Unknown)
1804/02/27	AMSCH	0110	*Vlieger. (S. de)* | In een sterk omstuimige Zee, ziet men een zylend Beurdschip, beneevens nog eenige andere, delicaat gepenceeld | *Mat:* op paneel *Size:* hoog 14, breed 18 duim	D	(Bought In) fl 1
1804/02/27	AMSCH	0111	*Vlieger. (S. de)* | Een woelende Zee, met diverse soorten van zeilende en ten Anker leggende Vaartuigen; meesterlyk geschilderd | *Mat:* op doek *Size:* hoog 29, breed 41 duim	C	(Sold) fl 1 Gruiter
1804/02/27	AMSCH	0112	*Vlieger. (S. de)* | Twee woelende Waters, met zeilende Vaartuigen; bevallig van licht en fiks gepenceeld | *Mat:* op paneel *Size:* ieder hoog en breed 16 ½ duim	C	(Sold) fl 1 Gruiter
1804/07/25	DLGRO	0028	*S. de Vlieger* | Een Water gezicht met een Hoofd, en daar aan liggende Visschuit | *Mat:* op paneel *Size:* hoog 13, breed 10 duim	Mr Franc van der Burch Wz.	(Unknown)
1804/08/08	AMSCH	0210	*S. de Vlieger* | Een cabbelende Zée, met zeilende en ten Anker leggende Scheepen; bevallig van licht, en uitvoerig geschilderd | *Mat:* op doek *Size:* hoog 28, breed 41 duim	Vink[eles] [for] K[=Gruyter?]	(Sold) fl 1 Gruyter
1804/10/16	DLOND	0250	*S. de Vlieger* | Zeegezicht met Schepen. Vue de Mer avec des Vaisseaux | *Mat:* op paneel *Size:* hoog 18, breed 20		(Unknown) fl 3:4
1804/10/16	DLOND	0251	*S. de Vlieger* | Een Onstuimige Zee. Une Mer orageuse | *Mat:* op doek *Size:* hoog 34, breed 47		(Unknown)
1804/10/16	DLOND	0252	*S. de Vlieger* | Een Woelende Zee met Schepen. Une Mer avec des Vaisseaux | *Size:* hoog 27, breed 32		(Sold) fl 20:5 Thijs
1805/07/03	AMSCH	0159	*S. de Vlieger* | Een Storm op Zée, by een Rotsachtig Strand, waarby verscheide Scheepen in Gevaar; natuurlyk en fiks gepenceeld | *Mat:* op paneel *Size:* hoog 20, breed 27 duim	R[oos]	(Sold) fl 9 H Zurmuklen
1805/07/03	AMSCH	0160	*S. de Vlieger* | Een Onstuimige Zée, met verscheiden Vaartuigen, op de Voorgrond een Sloep met Volk; fraai als W. van de Velde | *Mat:* op paneel *Size:* hoog 12, breed 15 duim	R[oos]	(Sold) fl 12 Hardenberg
1805/07/03	AMSCH	0161	*S. de Vlieger* | Een Strandgezicht, met een ménigte Vaartuigen in Zee, zeer natuurlyk op Paneel | *Mat:* op paneel *Size:* hoog 11, breed 17 duim	C	(Sold) fl 8:10 Esser
1805/07/10	AMSCH	0162	*S. de Vlieger* | Een Onstuimige Zee, met verscheiden Scheepen; krachtig op Paneel | *Mat:* op paneel *Size:* hoog 21, breed 37 duim	V[inkeles] [for] H[affner]	(Bought In) fl 2
1805/12/16	AMSCH	0072	*S. de Vlieger* | Een woelend Water	R[oos]	(Sold) fl 0:16 Hybroek
1805/12/16	AMSCH	0085	*S. de Vlieger* | Een Zee met differente Oorlog- en andere Schepen	R[oos]	(Sold) fl 1 L Pakker
1806/05/05	AMSCH	0143	*S. de Vlieger* | Een gezigt langs de Maas, naar Bergen op Zoom, met zeilende en andere Scheepen en Vaartuigen; uitvoerig geschildert door S. de Vlieger | *Mat:* op doek *Size:* hoog 29, breed 41 duim	V[inkeles]	(Sold) fl 4 Levy Pakker
1806/05/05	AMSCH	0144	*S. de Vlieger* | Een kabbelende Zee, met zeilende, en anderen ten anker leggende Scheepen en Vaartuigen | *Mat:* op doek *Size:* hoog 29, breed 41 duim	V[inkeles]	(Sold) fl 0:12 Levy Pakker
1806/06/07	RMHSN	0045	*S. de Vlieger* | Een Stil Water by een Hoofdje, met een Vischers Schuitje | *Mat:* op paneel	A E K L	(Unknown)
1806/08/13	AMSCH	0195	*Vlieger. (S. de)* | Een Strandgezicht met verscheide Vissers-Pinken enz.; natuurlyk geschilderd | *Mat:* op paneel *Size:* hoog 9, breed 11 duim	Roos	(Sold) fl 7 T Spaan
1806/08/13	AMSCH	0196	*Vlieger. (S. de)* | Een woelende Zee met Schapen, als dito [natuurlyk geschilderd] | *Size:* hoog 9, breed 11 duim *Notes:* It is unclear what "dito" refers to in the title.	Roos	(Sold) fl 0:6 L Pakker
1806/08/13	AMSCH	0197	*Vlieger. (S. de)* | Een Ordinantie, verbeeldende de Haringvissery, waarby eenige Oorlogscheepen; natuurlyk behandeld | *Mat:* op paneel *Size:* hoog 35, breed 48 duim	Roos	(Sold) fl 4:5 du Pre
1806/08/13	AMSCH	0198	*Vlieger. (S. de)* | Een sterk woelend Water; gestofleert [sic] met een zylend Schip, en een sloep met Zeelieden, meesterlyk geschilderd | *Mat:* op paneel *Size:* hoog 12, breed 18 duim	Roos	(Sold) fl 3 Schumacher
1806/08/13	AMSCH	0199	*Vlieger. (S. de)* | In een sterk woelende Zee, vertoonen zich eenige zeilende en ten anker leggende Scheepen, op de voorgrond by eenig Paalwerk, Vissers in een Schuit; fiks gepenceeld | *Mat:* op paneel *Size:* hoog 15, breed 17 duim	Vinkeles [for] G[ruyter]	(Sold) fl 12:10 V Rynbergh
1806/08/20	HGBSM	0183	*S. de Vlieger* | Eene woelende Zee met Scheepen | *Mat:* op paneel *Size:* hoog 10 ½, breed 14 duim	Macalester Loup [or others]	(Sold) fl 2 Gram
1806/08/20	HGBSM	0184	*S. de Vlieger* | Een dito [woelende] Zee met Scheepen | *Mat:* op paneel *Size:* hoog 16, breed 21 duim	Macalester Loup [or others]	(Sold) fl 0:14 Temminck
1808/04/26	GDAN	0176	*Vlieger (S. de)* | Een woelend Watertje met zeilende Schepen | *Size:* hoog 15, breed 23 duim	G H Fortuyn	(Unknown)
1808/04/26	GDAN	0177	*Vlieger (S. de)* | Een stil Watergezigtje, konstig behandeld | *Size:* hoog 15, breed 15 duim	G H Fortuyn	(Unknown)
1808/11/28	AMSCH	0081	*S. de Vlieger* | Een kabbelende Zee, met zeilende en ten Anker leggende Vaartuigen	[Gruyter?]	(Sold) fl 2:5 Ebersdyk
1809/04/17	AMSCH	0171	*S. de Vlieger* | Een Gezicht op de Zuider Zee, rijk met Vaartuigen gestoffeerd	H	(Sold) fl 0:12

1809/07/25	HGBSM	0190	*S. de Vlieger* | Twee Stuks stille Watergezigten met scheepen | *Mat:* op doek *Size:* hoog 15, breed 20 duim	D van der Aa [or] E B ten Dall	(Sold) fl 9:10 De Gruyter
1809/07/25	HGBSM	0264	*S. de Vlieger* | Een Onstuimige Zee, waar in een Schip vergaat | *Mat:* op paneel *Size:* hoog 14, breed 19 duim	D van der Aa [or] E B ten Dall	(Sold) fl 4:16 van Zanten
1810/03/23	HAVIN	0034	*S. de Vlieger* | Een dito [stille Zee]	Rudolf Hendrik de Wetstein [or others]	(Unknown)
1810/03/27	RMCNL	0066	*de Vlieger* | Een stille Zee, waarop men eenige groote Schepen ziet, zeer fraai behandeld		(Unknown)
1810/06/06	RMMUY	0026	*S. de Vlieger* | Een woelend Water met eenige Schepen, voor aan Visschers, ongemeen helder geschilderd | *Mat:* op paneel		(Sold) fl 20 v Eyk
1810/06/06	RMMUY	0027	*S. de Vlieger* | Een dito, woelend Water | *Notes:* It is unclear what "dito" refers to in the title.		(Sold) fl 19 v Eyk
1810/06/06	RMMUY	0028	*S. de Vlieger* | Een Zee en Palenhoofd, met Schuiten en Figuren, aangenaam en helder van kleur | *Mat:* op doek		(Bought In) fl 30
1810/06/06	RMMUY	0029	*S. de Vlieger* | Een Zeeslag, tusschen Hollandsche en Spaansche Vlooten, uitmuntend geschilderd | *Mat:* op doek		(Unknown) fl 8
1810/06/06	RMMUY	0147	*S. de Vlieger* | Een stil Water met Schepen		(Unknown) fl 14:5
1810/06/20	AMSCH	0090	*S. De Vlieger* | In een sterk woelend Water vertoont zich voor aan een zeilend Beurtschip, waarop verscheidene Lieden zijn, voor hetzelve een Kaag, beide voor de wind zeilende; ter zijde een Visschers Vaartuig en Oorlogschepen in het verschiet. Dit stuk is bevallig van schildering en een der beste van S. De Vlieger | *Size:* hoog 33, breed 31 duimen	T	(Sold) fl 105 Hodges
1810/06/20	AMSCH	0091	*S. De Vlieger* | Een stil Water, met zeilende Beurtschepen; vooraan bij het Strand Visschers in hunne Schuiten. Helder en natuurlijk geschilderd | *Mat:* op paneel *Size:* hoog 15, breed 19 duimen	B	(Sold) fl 13:10 Reijers
1810/08/06	AMSCH	0111	*Vlieger (S. de)* | Een kabbelende Zee, vooraan met een zeilend Jagt, verder Oorlog- en Beurtschepen en een Stad in het verschiet; helder en vrolijk geschilderd | *Mat:* op doek *Size:* hoog 41, breed 57 duimen	S[paan]	(Bought In) fl 31
1810/08/06	AMSCH	0112	*Vlieger (S. de)* | Een stil Water, met eene menigte onderscheidene Vaartuigen en Beeldjes; natuurlijk voorgesteld | *Mat:* op doek *Size:* hoog 29, breed 44 duimen	F	(Sold) fl 1:10 van Iperen
1810/08/06	AMSCH	0113	*Vlieger (S. de)* | Een kabbelend Water, gestoffeerd met eene menigte Vaartuigen en Beelden, kloek geschilderd | *Mat:* op paneel *Size:* hoog 24, breed 32 duimen	G	(Sold) fl 8 Texier Gerbet en Comp
1810/11/07	UTWLD	0068	*Vlieger* | Een Schip door een felle storm belopen op 't punt van te vergaan, terwijl andere door zig bij den wind te houden zig tragten te behouden, terwijl eenige Menschen zig zoeken te redden op een drijvend stuk hout | *Mat:* op doek *Size:* 10 duim hoog 1 voet 3 duim breed		(Unknown) fl 12
			Vlieger, Simon de (and Schellinks, W.)		
1802/06/16	AMSCH	0192	*N. de Vlieger; W. Schellingx* | Een Boomryk Landschap met een Rivier, en aangenaam verschiet, op de voorgrond een Jager met Honden, door W. Schellingx, zynde de behandeling niet minder dan de voorgaande | *Mat:* op paneel *Size:* hoog 27 ½, breed 24 duim *Notes:* The artist's name was given as "N. de Vlieger" but we have assumed this is an error.	[Merrem]	(Sold) fl 40 van der Schleij
			Vlieger, Simon de (or Ruysdael, S.)		
1808/06/11	RMRIJ	0120	*Simon de Vlieger; of S: Ruisdaal* | Een Winter- Stad- en Rivier Gezicht, vol Gewoel en Stoffagie | *Mat:* op doek		(Unknown) fl 10:10
			Vlieger, Simon de (or Vlieger, S., manner)		
1802/08/24	LNDLS	0092	*S. de Vlieger* | Een woelend Water met Zeilende en ten Anker leggende Schepen bij een hoofd met Paalwerk. Van of in den trant van S. de Vlieger | *Mat:* op paneel *Size:* hoog 12, breed 15 duimen	Leonardus Bouman [or others]	(Unknown) fl 3:10
1804/08/02	BDAN	0033	*S. de Vlieger of zyn Manier* | Een woelende Zee | *Mat:* op paneel *Size:* b. 26 d. h. 17 d.	J G Calckberner	(Unknown)
1804/10/29	HRBAU	0110	*Vlieger, (S. de) of in zyn Manier* | Een sterk woelende Zee, gestoffeerd met verscheiden zeilende en ten anker liggende Vaartuigen. Fraai van licht, en zeer natuurlyk behandeld | *Mat:* op paneel *Size:* hoog 16, breed 24 duim	Simon Styl	(Unknown)
1806/11/24	AMSCH	0093	*S. de Vlieger* | Twee stuks Zeetjes met Scheepen; door of in de manier van S. de Vlieger	Munnikhuizen	(Sold) fl 3 Yver
			Vlieger, Simon de (copy after)		
1804/10/16	DLOND	0311	*Naar De Vlieger* | Enige Zeilende Schepen. Des Vaisseaux qui font voile | *Mat:* op doek *Size:* hoog 25, breed 36		(Unknown)
			Vlieger, Simon de (manner)		
1801/03/16	AMSCH	0192	*S. de Vlieger* | Een woelende Zee, waar in een Schip in gevaar by een Rotzagtig strand, in de manier van S. de Vlieger | *Notes:* This lot was sold with lot 191 by an anonymous artist.	K[ip]	(Sold) fl 1:5 for lots 191 & 192. Roelofs
1801/04/23	AMYVR	0025	*de Vlieger* | Twee stuks zynde en Stil en Woelend Water, in de manier van de Vlieger		(Sold) fl 6 ½ A Mayer

1804/04/28	LNDLS	0009	*S. de Vlieger* | Een hobbelende Zee, met verscheide oorlog schepen, die slaags zyn, benevens varende booten, die volk redden van een schip, dat in brand is, konstig op doek, niet minder als van S. de Vlieger | *Mat:* op doek *Size:* hoog 31, breed 41 duim	[Abraham Delfos] [or others]	(Sold) fl 15:10 Rigters [for] A
1805/12/16	AMSCH	0067	*S. de Vlieger* | Een kabbelende Zee, met verscheide Vaartuigen, als door S. de Vlieger	R[oos]	(Sold) fl 0:6 L Pakker
1809/07/25	HGBSM	0283	*de Vlieger* | Een Woelend Zeetje met schepen, in de trant van de Vlieger | *Mat:* op paneel *Size:* hoog 13, breed 20 en een half duim	D van der Aa [or] E B ten Dall	(Sold) fl 1:6 Penning
1810/06/06	RMMUY	0135	*S. de Vlieger* | Een Zeetje, in de trant van S. de Vlieger | *Mat:* op paneel		(Unknown) fl 1:2
1810/07/23	DOLGI	0066	*de Vlieger* | Een woelige Zee, met eenige Schepen; in den smaak van, en zoo goed als door, de Vlieger | *Mat:* op doek *Size:* hoog 42 ½, breed 66 duim	Mr Pieter van den Santheuvel	(Sold) fl 14 de Hant
			Vlier, A. [Unidentified]		
1807/04/13	AMSCH	0007	*A. Vlier* | Een Protestante Kerk van binnen te zien, alwaar dienst gedaan word, beneevens eene meuigte [sic] Aanhoorders, zonachtig en fiks geschilderd | *Mat:* op doek *Size:* hoog 30, breed 32 duim	Everard de Burlett	(Sold) fl 15:10 Van den Nulft
			Vliet		
1802/07/21	HGKAN	0018	*van Vliet* | Een dito [Schildery] met eenige Scheepen en Beelden, in een zwarte Lyst		(Unknown)
1802/07/21	HGKAN	0088	*van Vliet* | Twee Vrouwen Koppen		(Unknown)
1804/10/16	DLOND	0253	*Van Vliet* | Een Philosooph met een Globe voor zich. Un Philosophe examinant un Globe | *Mat:* op paneel *Size:* hoog 9, breed 8		(Unknown)
			Vliet, Hendrik Cornelisz. van		
1801/04/13	AMSCH	0082	*H. van Vliet* | Een Protestantsche Kerk van binnen te zien, op den voorgrond een open graf, voorts een menigte Beeldjes; het zonlicht is natuurlyk, en de behandeling dun van penceel | *Mat:* op paneel *Size:* hoog 20, breed 17 duim	Pierre Fouquet, junior	(Sold) fl 21 C S Roos
1801/05/11	AMSCH	0105	*H. van Vliet* | De Kerk te Delft van binnen te zien, gestoffeerd met wandelende beelden, ter zyde ziet men het graf van Prins Willem den Iste, alles fraai van perspectief en zonachtig van schildering | *Size:* hoog 41, breed 33 duim	E[lias]	(Sold) fl 56 Rijnders
1802/05/05	AMSCH	0213	*H. van Vliet* | Een Gezicht in een Protestandsche Kerk, ryk gestoffeerd met een menigte Beelden, krachtig en zonachtig | *Mat:* op doek *Size:* hoog 30, breed 27 duim	D	(Sold) fl 100 Hulswit
1802/05/05	AMSCH	0214	*H. van Vliet* | Een Protestandsche Kerk, van binnen te zien, ryk gestoffeerd met Beeldjes, krachtig en bevallig van zonlicht | *Mat:* op doek *Size:* hoog 46, breed 42 duim	H	(Sold) fl 65 Delfos
1802/05/05	AMSCH	0215	*H. van Vliet* | Een Kerk, van binnen te zien, zeer fraai gepenceeld | *Size:* hoog 12, breed 9 duim	H	(Bought In) fl 33
1802/12/13	AMSCH	0158	*H. van Vliet* | Een Gezicht in een Protestantsche Kerk, men ziet den Leeraar op den Predikstoel, verders een meenigte Toehoorders; het zonlicht geeft een uitmuntende uitwerking in dit stuk, zynde van de beste Penceelsbehandeling van H. van Vliet | *Mat:* op paneel *Size:* hoog 24, breed 22 duim	Yver	(Sold) fl 170 Th^{s} Spaan
1803/08/17	AMSCH	0085	*Vliet. (H. van)* | Een Protestante Kerk van binnen te zien, gestoffeerd met Wapenborden, en een menigte Beelden, zonachtig behandeld | *Mat:* op paneel *Size:* hoog 14, breed 8 duim	Anna Catharina Putman	(Sold) fl 25 G^{t} Buys
1803/08/24	HGKAN	A0016	*van Vliet* | Een Protestansche Kerk | companion to lot A17 *Size:* breet 13, hoog 15 duim		(Sold) fl 30 for lots A16 & A17. van der A
1803/08/24	HGKAN	A0017	*van Vliet* | Een weerga | companion to lot A16, "Een Protestansche Kerk"		(Sold) fl 30 for lots A16 & A17. van der A
1804/04/28	LNDLS	0019	*H. van Vliet* | Een Kerk, van binnen met wandelende beelden, konstig van doorzigt, door H. van Vliet, op doek | *Mat:* op doek *Size:* hoog 30, breed 24 duim	[Abraham Delfos] [or others]	(Sold) fl 19 Gruyter
1804/10/16	DLOND	0254	*C. van Vliet* | Gezicht van het Choor der Nieuwe Kerk te Delft. Vue interieure du Choeur de l'Eglise Neuve à Delft | *Mat:* op doek *Size:* hoog 42, breed 34		(Unknown)
1804/10/16	DLOND	0255	*C. van Vliet* | Dito [Gezicht] van de Oude Kerk te Delft. Dito [Vue interieure] de l'Eglise Vielle à Delft | *Mat:* op doek *Size:* hoog 31, breed 25		(Unknown)
1804/12/10	AMSCH	0099	*van Vliet* | Een Protestantsche Kerk, van binnen te zien, op de voorgrond een Graft, waarby eenige persoonen, ter zyde een Gordyn; dit schildery is fraai van licht, en zonachtig van schildering | *Mat:* op paneel *Size:* Hoog 26, breed 23 duim	Jan De Groot	(Sold) fl 14 Hulswit
1806/08/13	AMSCH	0192	*Vliet. (C. van der)* | Een capitaal Kerkgebouw van Binnen te zien, ryk gestoffeerd met Beelden, uit het Ruim van de Kerk, vertoont zich in het verschiet het Choor, waarin een Graftombe; de Banken, Preekgestoelte	Yver	(Bought In) fl 170

			en Wapenborden zyn natuurlyk geplaatst, voorts doet het licht zoo op de colommen, als door het geheele stuk eene uitmuntende en treffende uitwerking; zynde een der beste stukken van dezen meester | *Mat:* op doek *Size:* hoog 36 ½, breed 43 duim		
1807/06/10	HGBSM	0123	*H. van der Vliet* | Een Protestante kerk van binnen te zien, fraaij van perspectief, gestoffeerd met beelden. 1653 | *Mat:* op paneel *Size:* hoog 32 ½, breed 27 duim *Inscr:* 1653 (dated?) *Notes:* It is unclear whether the date is inscribed on the painting.	Abraham Delfos [or others]	(Sold) fl 11 Spruit
1808/04/26	GDAN	0180	*Vliet (H. van)* | Eene Kerk van binnen te zien, met het Orgel, wandelende Beelden, &c | *Size:* hoog 18 ½, breed 14 duim	G H Fortuyn	(Unknown)
1808/06/13	AMSCH	0217	*van Vliet* | Een Binnengezicht van een Kerk; zonachtig	E M Engelberts	(Sold) fl 8 Engelberts
1808/08/23	AMSCH	0163	*Vliet. (H. van)* | Een Protestante Kerk van bidden te zien, rijk met Beeldjes gestoffeert, en natuurlijk geschilderd | *Mat:* op doek *Size:* hoog 30, breed 24 duim	J	(Sold) fl 14 Van Iperen
1808/10/28	AMVRS	0062	*Vliet, (H. van)* | Een Protestantsche Kerk, van binnen te zien, op den voorgrond een open Graf, en eene menigte Beeldjes. Het Zonlicht is natuurlijk | *Mat:* op paneel *Size:* hoog 20, breed 17 duim	Marten Udink	(Sold) fl 20:10 T Udink
1809/04/17	AMSCH	0104	*D. van Vliet* | Een Gezicht in de Groote Kerk te Delft, rijk met Beelden gestoffeerd, op de voorgrond ziet men een open Graf; zonachtig en Natuurlijk behandeld | *Mat:* op paneel *Size:* hoog 27, breed 24 duim *Notes:* The artist's name was given as "D. van Vliet" but we have assumed this is an error.	T	(Sold or Bought In) fl 18
1809/04/22	AMYVR	0141	*J. van Vliet* | Een Protestanten Kerk van binnen, gestoffeerd met Beeldjes; zonachtig | *Mat:* op doek *Size:* hoog 19, breed 15 duim *Notes:* The artist's name was given as "J. van Vliet" but we have assumed this is an error.	de Bruin	(Sold) fl 6 van Dijl
1809/05/26	HADAA	0005	*van Vliet* | Een fraai Kerkje met twee personen in gesprek | *Mat:* op paneel *Size:* hoog 12 breed 9 duimen	Mejuffrouw de Wed David Heemskerk [or others]	(Unknown)
1809/05/26	HADAA	0037	*van Vliet* | Een Gezigt in de Groote Kerk te Haarlem, uitmuntend gestoffeerd, helder en zonachtig gepenseeld	Mejuffrouw de Wed David Heemskerk [or others]	(Unknown)
1809/10/20	UTWLD	0019	*H. v. Vliet* | Een Kerk	J J van Rhyn	(Unknown)
1810/06/06	RMMUY	0042	*van Vliet* | Een klein fraaij Kerkje, zijnde het Choor der Kerk te Delft, waar in men een gedeelte der Graftombe ziet van Prins Willem den Eersten | *Mat:* op paneel		(Unknown) fl 10
1810/08/01	AMSCH	0112	*Vliet (Hendrik van)* | Eene protestantsche Kerk van binnen te zien, op den voorgrond een Doodgraver bij een open Graf, verder andere Beelden [Vue perspective intérieure d'une Eglise Protestante. Sur le devant du Tableau on remarque un Fossoyeur auprès d'un Tombeau ouvert, et quelqu'autres figures] | *Annots:* assez bon (NGW) *Mat:* op doek *Size:* hoog 29, breed 26 duimen	Mr Pieter de Smeth van Alphen	(Sold) fl 90 R Pot te Rotterdam
1810/08/06	AMSCH	0114	*Vliet (H. van)* | Een gedeelte der grote Kerk te Delft, van binnen met Beeldjes, Wapenborden en andere Sieraden gestoffeerd; zonachtig behandeld | *Mat:* op doek *Size:* hoog 17, breed 14 duimen	C	(Sold) fl 35 Roelsema
1810/10/11	AMSCH	0091	*H. Vliet* | Een Jongeling die zijn Pijp aansteekt | *Mat:* op paneel *Size:* hoog 25 ½, breed 21 duimen	C	(Sold) fl 2:15 Posthumus

Vliet, Hendrik Cornelisz. van (copy after)

1802/08/24	LNDLS	0146	*H. v. Vliet* | Een Kerk, van binnen met wandelende Beelden, na H. v. Vliet	Leonardus Bouman [or others]	(Unknown) fl 12:5

Vliet, Hendrik Cornelisz. van (manner)

1804/08/08	AMSCH	0259	*van Vliet* | Een Protestanten Kerk, van binnen gestoffeerd met Beelden en Honden; als van Vliet	Roos [for] O	(Sold) fl 2 L Pakker
1806/05/05	AMSCH	0223	*van Vliet* | Een Protestante Kerk; als door van Vliet	F	(Sold) fl 4 van Dyl
1808/12/31	RMHSN	0026	*Van Vliet* | Een Kerk, in de manier van Van Vliet | *Mat:* op paneel	G Spanjaart [or] H de Haas [or] C van der Looy Lans	(Unknown)

Vliet, Willem Willemsz. van der

1804/08/08	AMSCH	0203	*W. van Vliet* | In een Protestanten Kerk, van binnen te zien, ziet men ter zyde een prachtige Graftomde, waarby een Heer en Dame, verders eenige andere Beelden, Jongens, enz.; fiks en natuurlyk behandeld | *Mat:* op doek *Size:* hoog 33, breed 28 duim	Vink[eles] [for] S	(Sold) fl 6:5 Van Iperen
1804/08/08	AMSCH	0204	*W. van Vliet* | De Groote Kerk te Haarlem, van binnen te zien, gestoffeerd met wandelende Heeren en Dames, ryk vercierd met Wapenborden enz.; uitvoerig gepenceeld | *Mat:* op paneel *Size:* hoog 15, breed 16 duim	Vink[eles] [for] W	(Sold) fl 7:10 Van Iperen

Vogelsang, Isaac

1802/05/24	HGBAK	0004	*G. Vogelesangh* | Een bergachtig Landschap, aan de boorden eener Rivier, met beesten en figuuren gestoffeerd, door G. Vogelesangh, hoog 15 duim,	Mejuffrouw A van der Mieden	(Sold) fl 12:5 for lots 4 & 5. Kleijn

			breed 18 duim, op doek, zwarte lyst en vergulde bies | companion to lot 5 *Mat:* op doek *Size:* hoog 15 duim, breed 18 duim *Notes:* The artist's name was given as "G. Vogelesangh" but we have assumed this is an error.		
1802/05/24	HGBAK	0005	*G. Vogelesangh* | Een dito [bergachtig Landschap] tot een weerga, en gelyk het voorgaande geordonneerd, hoog en breed als vooren [hoog 15 duim, breed 18 duim], en dito [zwarte] lyst | companion to lot 4 *Size:* hoog 15 duim, breed 18 duim *Notes:* The artist's name was given as "G. Vogelesangh" but we have assumed this is an error. It is unclear what "dito" refers to in the title.	Mejuffrouw A van der Mieden	(Sold) fl 12:5 for lots 4 & 5. Kleijn
1802/07/27	AKHRK	000A	*J. Vogelesang* | Een Landschap, waar in een staande witte Koe, een liggende roode, en een Boerin zittende te melken een Grijs-bonte Koe, met Schaapen en verder aangenaame Stoffagie; vrolijk en helder gepenceeld | companion to lot B *Mat:* op doek *Size:* hoog 15 ½, breed 21 ¾ duim	Maria Stategaart	(Sold) fl 18 for lots A & B. L Veer
1802/07/27	AKHRK	000B	*J. Vogelesang* | Dito [een Landschap], de wedergaa van dezelfde en van groote. Een Boerin Melkende eene roode Koe, en een liggende witte, met Schaapen en Bokjes en verdere Beesten en Beelden | companion to lot A *Mat:* op doek *Size:* hoog 15 ½, breed 21 ¾ duim	Maria Stategaart	(Sold) fl 18 for lots A & B. L Veer
1803/12/15	MGLAC	0012	*Vogelsangh* | Een zeer Plaisant Landschap, met Figuuren en Beestjes; warm en aangenaam geschilderd | *Mat:* op doek *Size:* hoog duim 16, breed duim 19	Mr L H de Haze Bomme	(Unknown)

Vois, Ary de

1801/04/13	AMSCH	0077	*A. de Voys* | Een vrolyke Gast met een Roemer in de hand, welke hy schynt geledigd te hebben, zyn rood fluweele mantel is breed geplooid; alles is fraai geteekend en uitvoerig gepenceeld | *Mat:* op paneel *Size:* hoog 7, breed 5 duim	Pierre Fouquet, junior	(Sold) fl 42 C S Roos
1801/04/13	AMSCH	0078	*A. de Voys* | Een oude Vischvrouw met een Vlesje in de hand, het geen zy smaaklyk beschouwd; delicaat en uitvoerig gepenceeld | *Mat:* op paneel *Size:* hoog 7 ½, breed 6 duim	Pierre Fouquet, junior	(Sold) fl 59 Spruit van Gend
1802/06/28	AMSCH	0195	*A. de Vois* | Als op de wolken zittende, vertoont zig een Schilder voor den Ezel, waarop een stuk geplaatst is; hy ziet met aandagt naar St. Cicilia op het Orgel speelende, waarby drie Engelen een tafreel, verbeelende de Dankbaarheid, vast houdt, meesterlyk gepenceeld, op Panneel | *Mat:* op paneel *Size:* hoog 8, breed 11 duim	Anna Elink	(Sold) fl 16 Gruiter
1805/07/03	AMSCH	0049	*Vois (A. de)* | In dit Tafreeltje zier men een Heer, in pragtige fluweele en zyde kleeding, op het hoofd een zwarte-fluweele Muts en roode pluim, hy heeft in zyn hand een roemer wyn, welke hy met een vergenoegd gelaat aanschouwd, zynde hetzelve van de delicaatste schildering van dezen grooten Meester | *Mat:* op paneel *Size:* hoog 7 ½, breed 6 duim	R[oos]	(Bought In) fl 100
1806/08/13	AMSCH	0191	*Vois. (A. de)* | Twee stuks, verbeeldende de eene een Engelsche Matroos, houdende een pyp in de mond, en de andere een Russische Matroos, met een zwarte baard en open borst; beide eigenaartig van kleding; delicaat gepenceeld, en van de beste Schildering van deeze beroemde Meester | *Mat:* op paneel *Size:* Ieder hoog 5, breed 4 duim	Coclers	(Bought In) fl 220
1806/08/13	AMSCH	0342	*Vois. (A. de)* | Een jongeling in deftige Kleeding, met een Fluit in de hand; delicaat en fraai van penceelsbehandeling | *Mat:* op paneel *Size:* hoog 8, breed 6 duim	Vinkeles [for] J	(Sold) fl 1 Van Os
1806/08/20	HGBSM	0051	*A. de Vois* | Een Vrolijke Boer, met eene Flesch in de eene en eene Pijp in de andere hand | *Mat:* op koper *Size:* hoog 4 ¼, breed 3 ¾ duim	Macalester Loup [or others]	(Sold) fl 12:10 Spruyt
1809/09/06	AMSCH	0077	*Vois (A. de)* | Eene bevallige Vrouw, halver lijf te zien, gekleed in 't wit Satijn, hebbende een Roosje in haar hand; delicaat gepenceeld | *Mat:* op koper *Size:* hoog 7, breed 5 duim	Johannes Caudri	(Sold) fl 40 Coclers
1809/09/06	AMSCH	0078	*Vois (A. de)* | Eene andere Vrouw, verbeeldende Diana, in 't blaauw Zijd gekleed, en niet minder van schildering als de voorgaande | *Mat:* op paneel *Size:* hoog 6, breed 5 ½ duim	Johannes Caudri	(Sold) fl 30 Gruiter
1809/09/06	AMSCH	0079	*Vois (A. de)* | Een bevallig Juffertje, in rijke Kleeding; uitvoerig behandeld | *Mat:* op koper *Fmt:* ovaal *Size:* hoog 5, breed 4 duim	Johannes Caudri	(Sold) fl 4:5 Gruyter
1810/08/06	AMSCH	0110	*Vois (A. de)* | In een aangenaam Landschap, ziet men op den voorgrond Eneas, gaande nevens de Koningin Dido, nevens hun een Moor met twee Jagthonden en achterwaarts hun gevolg; uitvoerig behandeld | *Mat:* op koper *Size:* hoog 11, breed 14 duimen *Loc:* Den Haag, Nederland. Rijksdienst Beeldende Kunst. (NK 2932)	C	(Sold) fl 2 L^{y} Pakker
1810/10/10	MGCIT	0049	*A. de Vois* | Een Jager in een zittende houding, met het Jagtgeweer langs het Lijf geplaatst, en hebbende een Patrijs in de eene hand, terwijl een Hondje op de voorgrond staande, hetzelve met veel levendigheid bekijkt; zijnde dit Schilderijtje geen der minste Kunststukjes	Caspar van Citters	(Unknown)

Vois, Ary de (copy after)

1804/10/16	DLOND	0246	*A. Vermeulen; naar A. de Voys* | Een Krygsheld op de Jagt. Un Militaire à la Chasse | copy by A. Vermeulen after Ary de Vois *Mat:* op paneel *Size:* hoog 10, breed 14		(Unknown)

Vois, Ary de (manner)

1804/08/08	AMSCH	0237	*A. de Vois* | Het Afbeeldzel van een Vorstelyk Persoon; uitvoerig gepenceeld, in de manier van A. de Vois	Roos [for] F	(Sold) fl 2 Van der Schley [for] R[ijfsnijder]
1810/06/06	RMMUY	0184	*A. de Vois* | Een zittend Man met eene Pijp in de hand bij eene Tafel, waar op een Kan &c. In de manier van A. de Vois | *Mat:* op paneel		(Unknown) fl 4:12
1810/06/06	RMMUY	0185	*A. de Vois* | Een Vrouwtje voor een Toonbank met een Glas in de hand, en voor haar een Fles, In dezelve [A. de Vois] manier | *Mat:* op paneel		(Unknown) fl 0:16

Volaire, Pierre Jacques

1802/06/16	AMSCH	0202	*N. Volaire, Dicipel van J. Vernet* | Twee stuks woelende Zee-Gezichten, beide gestoffeerd met zeilende Scheepen, Galyen en Sloepen; verder vertoonen zich Zeehavens, uitvoerig en bevallig van penceel-behandeling | *Mat:* op paneel *Size:* ieder hoog 4 ½, breed 6 duim	[Merrem]	(Sold) fl 2:5 Gruiter

Vollerdt, Johann Christian

1809/04/17	AMSCH	0107	*Vollerdt* | Een natuurlijk Land- en Watergezicht, met onderscheidene Beeldjes gestoffeerd | *Mat:* op doek *Size:* hoog 24, breed 30 duim	R	(Sold) fl 12:10
1809/06/13	AMSCH	0160	*J. Vollerdt* | Twee stuks Bergachtige Landschappen, met Gebouwen, rijk met onderscheidene Beeldjes gestoffeerd; aartig uitgevoerd | *Mat:* op paneel *Size:* ieder is hoog 12, breed 11 duim	Y	(Sold) fl 6:10 Buck

Vonck

1801/12/22	AMOTT	0018	*Vonk* | 1 Trophé van dood Gevogelte en Jagttuig	Bartholomeus Ruloffs	(Unknown) fl 1:10
1803/04/20	AMSCH	0114	*Vonck* | Eenige doode Vogels, leggen op een Tafel, natuurlyk en meesterlyk gepenceeld [Un groupe d'oiseaux morts sur une table. Sujet bien traité d'apres nature par Vonck.] | *Mat:* op paneel *Size:* hoog 21, breed 26 duim	Maria Magdalena van Sluypwyk, gravinne van Moens	(Sold) fl 2 Coclers
1803/06/20	AMSCH	0070	*Vonk* | Een Haan, witte Hen en een Duif in een Landschap, geestig op Doek | *Mat:* op doek *Size:* hoog 19, breed 16 duim	Schley [for] K	(Sold) fl 1:10 Ths Spaan
1807/06/10	HGBSM	0112	*Vonk* | Een Tafel waarop een doode Haas en verder dood Gevogelte, extra natuurlijk en uitvoerig | *Mat:* op paneel *Size:* hoog 26, breed 23 duim	Abraham Delfos [or others]	(Sold) fl 2:15 Temmink
1807/06/10	HGBSM	0218	*Vonk* | Een Jager levens groote ten halver lijf, staande voor eene Balustrade en hebbende in zijn regterhand een Haas die hij opligt, zeer krachtig, brillant van Coloriet, en zo goed als Rembrant door Vonk | *Mat:* op paneel *Size:* hoog 31, breed 24 duim	Abraham Delfos [or others]	(Sold) fl 9:15 Tessier
1809/04/17	AMSCH	0157	*Vonk* | Een stuk met dood Wild en verdere Keukenbehoeftens | *Mat:* op doek	[Gruyter?]	(Sold or Bought In) fl 1 Gruyter

Vonck, Elias

1801/03/16	AMSCH	0055	*Elias Vonk* | Een Keukenstuk met dood Wild en Gevogelte, waar by eenige Groentens, een Schapenbout en ander Vleesch, en drie staande Beelden	E	(Sold) fl 1:15 J v^{n} d^{n} Bergh
1809/07/25	HGBSM	0189	*E. Vonck* | Een Stuk met dood Gevogelte, een Haas en een levendige Patryshond, zeer natuurlyk geschildert | *Mat:* op doek *Size:* hoog 45, breed 38 duim	D van der Aa [or] E B ten Dall	(Sold) fl 1 Carré

Vonck, Jan

1802/07/20	MGSAN	0023	*Jan Vonk* | Een Vaas met Vruchten, Vogels en Insecten, schoon geschilderd op Doek | *Mat:* op doek *Size:* hoog duim 34, breed duim 27		(Unknown)
1802/07/20	MGSAN	0024	*Jan Vonk* | Een dito [Vaas met Vruchten] als 't voorgaande, zynde de Pendent | *Size:* hoog duim 34, breed duim 27 *Notes:* It is unclear what "dito" refers to in the title.		(Unknown)
1802/12/13	AMSCH	0163	*J. Vonk* | Twee hangende doode Vogels; zeer natuurlyk en meesterlyk behandeld | *Size:* hoog 17, breed 13 duim	Schley [for] Lauwers	(Sold) fl 0:8 van der Schley
1803/04/27	AMSCH	00HH[H]	*J Vonk* | Een met dood Vogels door J Vonk | *Notes:* This lot was added in by hand in the LBDa copy of the catalogue.	C	(Sold) fl 2 L Pakker
1803/08/17	AMSCH	0089	*Vonck. (J.)* | Op een Tafel legt een doode Zwaan en ander Gevogelte, verder hangt een Haas en ander Gevogelte aan een Kroon, fix geschilderd | *Mat:* op doek *Size:* hoog 64, breed 74 duim	Anna Catharina Putman	(Sold) fl 3:15 Gruyter
1804/02/27	AMSCH	0115	*Vonk. (J.)* | Op een Bank leggen eenige Vissen en ander bywerk | *Mat:* op paneel *Size:* hoog 29, breed 19 duim	D	(Sold) fl 1:5 Theys

Voordt, Jan van

1804/05/07	AMSCH	0185	*Voort. (J. van der)* | Een bevallig Boomryk Arcadisch Landschap, met verscheiden aloude Gedenkteekens, Fontein en Waterval, in 't midden een stille Rivier, waarby de Jachtgodin Diana, en verscheiden Nimphen, die zig baden; meesterlyk gepenceeld | *Mat:* op doek *Size:* hoog 19, breed 23 duim	Schley	(Bought In) fl 3

Voorhout, Johannes (I)

1802/05/05	AMSCH	0223	*J. Voorhout* | Twee stuks Bybelsche Ordonnantiën, fraai gepenceeld | *Mat:* op paneel *Size:* ieder hoog 9, breed 12 duim	BB	(Sold) fl 13:10 Stevens

1802/05/05	AMSCH	0224	*J. Voorhout* | In een prachtig Hofgezicht ziet men drie Jongelingen, zich met speelen vermakende | *Mat:* op doek *Size:* hoog 16, breed 13 duim	BB	(Sold) fl 17 Pruijssenaar [for] R
1802/05/05	AMSCH	0225	*J. Voorhout* | Een dito [prachtig] Gezicht met drie Kindertjes, speelende met een Hond | *Mat:* op doek *Size:* hoog 16, breed 13 duim	BB	(Sold) fl 17 Auber
1802/06/28	AMSCH	0199	*J. Voorhout* | Twee stuks, met Kinderen, spelende met Honden, op Panneel | *Mat:* op paneel *Size:* hoog 10, breed 9 duim	Anna Elink	(Sold) fl 2:10 Gruiter
1802/09/06	AMSCH	0123	*J. Voorhout* | In een Boschagtig Landschap, vertoont zich de Engel aan Hagar, van agteren ziet men Ismaël; breed gepenceeld | *Mat:* op doek *Size:* hoog 24, breed 24 duim	J	(Sold) fl 4:15 A Schotte
1802/09/06	AMSCH	0124	*J. Voorhout* | Een Jongeling en een Meisje, zittende in een Landschap	Mevrouw Achtienhoven	(Sold) fl 0:6 van Iperen
1802/09/06	AMSCH	0169	*J. Voorhout* | Een Altaarstuk, verbeeldende Christus aan het Kruis hangende, aan de voet ziet men godvrugtige Vrouwen, waarby St. Johannes, kloek gepenceeld | *Size:* hoog 93 ½, breed 60 ½ duim	Spaan	(Sold) fl 2 Jan Spaan
1803/12/12	AMSCH	0102	*J. Voorhout* | Eneas zyn Vader op de schouder dragende uit de Brand van Troyen; meesterlyk op Doek | *Mat:* op doek *Size:* hoog 62, breed 54 duim	R[oos]	(Sold) fl 10:10 Roos [for] N
1804/05/07	AMSCH	0184	*Voorhoud. (J.)* | De stervende Christus, hangende aan het Kruis, de Lydende Harts togt [sic] is treffende verbeeld, beneeden ziet men Krygslieden te Paard en te voet; alles is meesterlyk en krachtig gepenceeld | *Mat:* op doek *Size:* hoog 58, breed 43 duim	Schley	(Sold) fl 5:5 van Yperen
1804/07/25	AMSCH	0086	*Voorhout. (J.)* | In dit stuk ziet men op de Voorgrond Enéas, in een wanhoopende houding, by het beschouwen der Stad Troijen, voor hem ligt geknield zyn Vrouw, welken met de jonge Ascaan hem schynen te weerhouden, en ter zyden staat zyn Vader in een peinzenden gestalte; alles is kragtig van coloriet, schoon van Teekening, en teevens [sic] uitvoerig behandeld | *Mat:* op doek *Size:* hoog 31, breed 36 duim		(Sold) fl 86 Vinkeles
1805/07/10	AMSCH	0229	*Voorhout* | Twee dito [stuks], een Jongeling met een Fluit, en een Meisje met een Glas met wyn	Y[ver]	(Bought In) fl 1
1806/05/05	AMSCH	0145	*Voorhout* | In een Hofgezigt, ter zyden een steenen Balluster, ziet men twee Kinderen zig met Bloemen vlegten vermaaken, voor haar een speelend Hondje; meesterlyk door Voorhout | *Mat:* op doek *Size:* hoog 23, breed 25 duim	V[inkeles]	(Sold) fl 1:5 Van Stroom
1806/05/05	AMSCH	0147	*J. Voorhout* | De Boodschap aan Maria; meesterlyk geschilderd door J. Voorhout | *Mat:* op doek *Size:* hoog 50, breed 29 duim	V[inkeles]	(Sold) fl 0:10 Gruyter
1806/08/13	AMSCH	0237	*Voorhout* | De Bootschap aan Maria	Vinkeles [for] G[ruyter]	(Sold) fl 0:16 Yver [for] G
1807/08/26	AMSCH	0229	*J. Voorhout* | De stervende Heiland aan het Kruis, vergezeld van eenige Krygsknechten te Paard | *Mat:* op doek *Size:* hoog 57, breed 43 duim	de Vries	(Sold) fl 9 Yver
1808/06/13	AMSCH	0236	*J. Voorhout* | De Romeinsche Historie, daar de Vader in de Gevangenis door de Borst zijner Dochter gevoed wordt; zacht en teder | *Mat:* op doek	Z	(Sold) fl 5 H Hoogers
1809/07/19	AMSCH	0060	*Voorhout (J.)* | Diana en Endimion, verzeld van verscheide Minnewigten. Meesterlijk behandeld | *Mat:* op doek *Size:* hoog 26, breed 20 duim	[Wijkersloot?]	(Sold) fl 4:5 Zonnenberg Galand
1809/07/19	AMSCH	0061	*Voorhout (J.)* | Bij een Steenen Baluster, met een Tapijt behangen, ziet men drie bevallige Dames en een Kind, verder een Hofgezicht. Uitvoerig behandeld | *Mat:* op doek *Size:* hoog 20, breed 25 duim	C	(Sold) fl 18:10 Gruyter
1809/07/25	HGBSM	0011	*J. Voorhout* | Een Gezelschapje van drie Figuuren daar ze met Dobbelsteenen speelen; 't verschied is een ryk Tuingezigt, helder geschildert | *Mat:* op doek *Size:* hoog 15, breed 12 ½ duim	D van der Aa [or] E B ten Dall	(Sold) fl 4 van Eijk
1810/06/06	RMMUY	0221	*Jan Voorhout* | Een Geestelijke in zijn Studeerkamer, met veel bijwerk. Uitvoerig en zeer verdienstelijk geschilderd | *Mat:* op doek		(Unknown) fl 5
1810/06/20	AMSCH	0100	*J. Voorhout* | Eene Fabel Ordonnantie in een Landschap Krachtig | *Mat:* op doek *Size:* hoog 22, breed 24 duimen	A	(Sold) fl 1 Geld
1810/07/26	AMSCH	0087	*Voorhout (J.)* | Twee stuks, met spelende Kinderen en bijwerk | *Mat:* op paneel *Size:* hoog 10, breed 9 duimen	Cassino	(Bought In) fl 1:10

Vorsterman, Johannes

1805/10/21	GRBOL	0020	*J. Vorstermans* | Een Schoon Zeestuk, zynde een Woelend Water, met grote en kleine Scheepen: in het Verschiet ziet men de Stad Rotterdam	Gerardus Nicolaus Heerkens	(Unknown)

Vos

1801/08/19	AMSCH	0163	*Vos* | Twee Landschappen met Beesten gestoffeerd op Parkement	Van Forreest	(Sold) fl 0:18 Wolft
1810/06/20	AMSCH	0095	*De Vos 1666* | Twee stuks: het eene verbeeldt het Dorp Katwijk aan Zee, het andere een Gezigt buiten Leyden, beiden met Beelden, Beesten en Vaartuigen gestoffeerd. Natuurlijk geschilderd op paneel, door De Vos 1666 | *Mat:* op paneel *Size:* Jeder hoog 12, breed 19 duimen *Inscr:* De Vos 1666 (signed and dated?) *Notes:* It is unclear whether the name and date are inscribed on the painting.	T	(Sold) fl 19 Tuffers

Vos, Marten de (or Vos, M., manner)

1802/11/01	DOBRA	0016	*M. de Vos* | Een zinnebeeldig vertoog van het vertrouwen op Christus onder den moedwil van plunderend en moordend Krygsvolk; in den smaak of door M. de Vos | *Size:* breed 25 hoog 18 duim	Paulus van der Spyk [or others]	(Bought In) fl 7:5

			Vos, Simon de		
1803/04/27	AMSCH	000G	*S. de Vos* | Jesus Christ, portant sa Croix, riche composition | *Size:* h. 88, l. 120 pouces	B	(Bought In) fl 40
1805/07/03	AMSCH	0050	*Vos. (S. de)* | De voorstelling van Christus; de Voorgrond gedeeldtelyk een Markt voorstellende, is vol gewoel van Joden, welke in luid geschreeuw zyn; zynde voorts Meesterlyk behandeld | *Mat:* op paneel *Size:* hoog 19, breed 25 duim	R[oos]	(Sold) fl 20 Agina
1806/06/07	RMHSN	0019	*S: de Vos* | Een Vrolyke Maaltyd | *Mat:* op koper	A E K L	(Unknown)
			Vosmaer, Daniel		
1809/07/19	AMSCH	0062	*Vosmaer (D.)* | Een Italiaansch Bergachtig Landschap, met Gebouwen en een Steenen Sluis, gestoffeerd met Rijzigers en Vee. Zonagtig behandeld | *Mat:* op paneel *Size:* hoog 20, breed 22 duim	C	(Sold) fl 6:15 Gruyter
			Vosmaer, Nicolaes		
1802/11/01	DOBRA	0084	*Vosmade* | Eenige Zeevisschen door Vosmade. 1655 | *Mat:* op paneel *Inscr:* Vosmade. 1655 (signed and dated?) *Notes:* It is unclear whether the name and date are inscribed on the painting.	Paulus van der Spyk [or others]	(Sold or Bought In) fl 2 v Baam
			Vrancx, Sebastian		
1801/06/10	AMSCH	0060	*Franx. (S.)* | De triumph van Bacchus, zynde een ryke Ordonantie van verscheide Beelden; meesterlyk en aangenaam van coloriet en behandeling | companion to lot 61 *Mat:* op paneel *Size:* hoog 27, breed 18 duim	Herman ten Kate	(Sold) fl 60 for lots 60 & 61. Taijs
1801/06/10	AMSCH	0061	*Franx. (S.)* | Alexander de Groote op een triumphwagen, zynde mede een niet minder ryke als bevallige Ordonantie | companion to lot 60 *Size:* hoog 27, breed 18 duim	Herman ten Kate	(Sold) fl 60 for lots 60 & 61. Taijs
1801/06/10	AMSCH	0062	*Franx. (S.)* | Een Bybelsche Ordonnantie, voorstellende de Besnydenis; ryk van Beelden gestoffeert en krachtig geschilderd | *Mat:* op koper *Size:* hoog 9, breed 7 duim	Herman ten Kate	(Sold) fl 13 Pruyssenaar
1802/05/05	AMSCH	0059	*S. Franks* | Christus, zittende by Maria en Martha in een Binnevertrek, in 't verschiet een Keuken, delicaat en uitvoerig gepenceeld | *Mat:* op koper *Size:* hoog 9, breed 12 duim	A	(Sold) fl 15 Stevens
1802/06/28	AMSCH	0052	*S. Franks* | Een St. Hieronimus, in een biddende gestalte, in een antique Kamer, op de Voorgrond legt een Leeuw; uitvoerig op koper | *Mat:* op koper *Size:* hoog 15, breed 12 duim		(Sold) fl 14 van der Schley A [for] Coclers
1802/06/28	AMSCH	0053	*S. Franks* | Een Maaltyd van verscheide Goden aan een Tafel, in een Rotsgezigt aan Zee; waar in Neptunus op zyn Zeewagen, verzelt van een menigte Waternimphen, Tritons en Zeepaarden; kragtig gepenceeld, door denzelven [S. Franks] | *Mat:* op paneel *Size:* hoog 14, breed 34 duim	Anna Elink	(Sold) fl 14:10 Gruiter
1802/06/28	AMSCH	0054	*S. Franks* | Een jong Meisje, met een Aardepot in de hand, waarby een oud Man, welke een Uil in de Pot wil steeken; door Denzelven [S. Franks], op Koper | *Mat:* op koper *Size:* hoog 9, breed 7 duim	B	(Sold) fl 2:15 Roos [for] A
1802/06/28	AMSCH	0055	*S. Franks* | In een gemeubileerde Kamer, zyn verscheide Dames en Heeren, die zig met Dansen, Speelen en Musiceeren vermaken; uitvoerig gepenceeld door Denzelven, hoog 5, breed 6 duim. Panneel | *Mat:* op paneel *Size:* hoog 5, breed 6 duim	Anna Elink	(Sold) fl 2 Boelen
1803/04/20	AMSCH	0024	*Francks (P.) [Franckx. (S)]* | De H. Maagd Maria zit met het Kind Jesus op haar schoot, de Wyzen uit het Oosten leggen eerbiedig op hun Kniën en Offeren hunne Geschenken aan den Heiland, zy zyn verzeld van verscheiden anderen Beelden, de Teekening en het Coloriet in dit stukjen, is allerbevalligst, en is delicaat gepenceeld [L'adoration des Mages à l'enfant Jesus, avec leur suite nombreuse, offrans leurs dons dans les attitudes de la plus profonde prosternation. Cette piece est spirituellement touchée & d'une trés bonne couleur.] | *Mat:* op koper *Size:* hoog 12, breed 9 duim *Notes:* The artist's name differs in the Dutch and French editions of the catalogue.	Maria Magdalena van Sluypwyk, gravinne van Moens	(Sold) fl 70 Pruijssenaar [for] R
1803/04/20	AMSCH	0025	*Francks (P.) [Franckx. (S)]* | Deeze ryke Ordenantie vol gewoel van Beelden, vertoond de prachtige Maaltyd van Belzazar [sic], in zyn Paleis; meesterlyk fraay, en uitvoerig gepenceeld [Le festin de Balthasar : composition riche & agréable, egalement bien traitée que le No. précedent.] | *Mat:* op paneel *Size:* hoog 15, breed 18 duim *Notes:* The artist's name differs in the Dutch and French editions of the catalogue.	Maria Magdalena van Sluypwyk, gravinne van Moens	(Sold) fl 20 Ijver
1803/04/20	AMSCH	0026	*Francks (P.) [Franckx. (S)]* | In een Binnevertrek ziet men Christus by de Pharisëen ter Maaltyd, ter zyde op haar Kniën leggende, zalft Maria Magdaléna de voeten Christi; kragtig en uitvoerig behandeld [J.C. assis au festin du Pharisé, tandis que la Magdaleine se prosterne pour oindre les pieds du Sauveur : Joli morceau d'une touche nette & finie.] | *Mat:* op koper [sur bois] *Size:* hoog 14, breed 11 duim [haut 14, large 18 pouces] *Notes:* The artist's name, materials and dimensions differ in the Dutch and French editions of the catalogue.	Maria Magdalena van Sluypwyk, gravinne van Moens	(Sold) fl 36 Hodges
1803/04/27	AMSCH	000S	*S. Francks* | Un Sujet Historique, representant, un Repas Somptueux, trouble par une attaque de Guerriers, richement Composé, & fierrement peint | *Size:* h. 29, l. 35 pouces	B	(Bought In) fl 35

1803/09/07	AMSCH	0054	*S. Frankx* | Een Kunstzaal, verciert met een ménigte Kunststukken, benevens drie Beelden, uitvoerig door S. Frankx en verscheide andere Meesters [Un musée, orné d'un infinité d'objets d'arts et de sciences, dans le fond duquel trois figures parfaitement exécutées par Frankx et d'autres maîtres] | *Mat:* op paneel *Size:* hoog 21, breed 29 duim	Smidt	(Bought In) fl 86
1803/09/07	AMSCH	0055	*S. Frankx* | De Heilige Famielje, in een Landschap, waar by St. Catharina, de Trouwring van het Kindeken ontfangende, verder een geördende Geestelyken, uitvoerig op Koper gepenceeldt [Un paysage dans lequel se trouve la Ste.-Famille, auprès d'elle Ste.-Cathérine recevant des mains de l'enfant Jésus l'anneau nuptial ; dans le fond un prêtre régulier ; d'une belle exécution] | *Mat:* op koper *Size:* hoog 4 ½, breed 7 ½ duim	Smidt	(Sold) fl 11:10 Spruit van Gend
1803/09/07	AMSCH	0056	*S. Frankx* | Deeze Ordenantie verbeeld de Terugkomst uit Egypten, om hoog vertoont zig de Godheid, verders een aangenaam Landschap; alles zeer bevallig van Coloriet en op Koper gepenceeldt [Le retour d'Egypte : dans la région supérieure apparoit la divinité ; dans le lointain un paysage agréable ; ce tableau est d'un beau coloris d'une ordonnance admirable] | *Mat:* op koper [sur bois] *Size:* hoog 14, breed 11 ½ duim *Notes:* The materials differ in the Dutch and French editions of the catalogue.	Smidt	(Sold) fl 8 de Lafontaine
1803/09/07	AMSCH	0057	*S. Frankx* | Een Bybelsche Ordenantie, verbeeldende Christus ontkleed wordende, om gekruist te worden, verders de twee Moordenaars, verscheide Krygsknegten, en de Heilige Vrouwen in 't verschiet, Natuurlyk en fraay van Coloriet [Jésus-Christ depouillé de ses habits, prêt à être crucifié ; plus loin les deux larrons, plusieurs gens de guerre, et les saintes femmes dans l'éloignement ; d'un coloris naturel, fraix [sic] et vif] | *Mat:* op koper *Size:* hoog 27, breed 34 duim	Smidt	(Sold) fl 15:10 v d Schley [for] R[ijfsnijder]
1803/09/07	AMSCH	0058	*S. Frankx* | Christus gekruist tusschen de twee Moordenaaren, waarby een ménigte Krygslieden, benévens de Heilige Vrouwen, niet minder dan de voorgaande [Jésus-Christ en croix entre les deux larrons ; à l'entour de le croix une foule de gens de guerre, et les saintes femmes. Tableau d'un mérite égal au précédent.] | *Mat:* op paneel *Size:* hoog 29, breed 40 duim	Smidt	(Sold) fl 10 C S Roos
1805/07/03	AMSCH	0017	*Franks. (S.)* | Een Zinspeelende Ordinantie van verscheiden Beelden in een Binnevertrek, zynde Meesterlyk gepenceeld | *Mat:* op koper *Size:* hoog 9, breed 12 duim	R[oos]	(Sold) fl 10 Josi
1805/07/03	AMSCH	0018	*Franks. (S.)* | Twee stuks, een Dame op de Guitar spelende, ziet men in het eene, en in het andere een Heer, schynende te zingen; beide behandeld als de voorgaande | *Mat:* op koper *Size:* yder hoog 6, breed 5 duim	R[oos]	(Sold) fl 4 Gruyter
1805/07/03	AMSCH	0082	*S. Franckx* | In een Prachtig aloud Vertrek, ryk gestoffeerd met drink-schaalen, bekers, schilden, caskette, gordels, musiek-instrumenten en diversche rariteiten, ziet men Achilles onder de Maagden; alleruitvoerigst gepenceeld | *Mat:* op paneel *Size:* hoog 22, breed 32 duim	S	(Bought In) fl 25
1805/07/10	AMSCH	0060	*S. Frankx* | De Aanbidding der Koningen, ryk geordineerd, fraay van licht en uitvoerig gepenceeld | *Mat:* op koper *Size:* hoog 14, breed 10 duim	V[inkeles] [for] M	(Bought In) fl 18:10
1805/10/09	HGBSM	0089	*S. Franks 1618* | Het camp by Ostende en Nieupoort, vol gewoel, door S. Franks 1618 | *Mat:* op paneel *Size:* hoog 22 ½ breet 39 duim *Inscr:* S. Franks 1618 (signed and dated?) *Notes:* It is unclear whether the name and date are inscribed on the painting.	T H van Willigen [or others]	(Sold) fl 9 Smeets
1806/08/13	AMSCH	0057	*Franks. (S.)* | De verlochening door Petrus, zynde een ryken Ordinnantie van meer als vyftig Beelden, kragtig behandeld | *Mat:* op paneel *Size:* hoog 19, breed 22 duim	Roos	(Sold) fl 15 Haffner
1806/08/13	AMSCH	0058	*Franks. (S.)* | Maria Joseph en 't Kind Jesu, verzeld van Seraphynen, delicaat gepenceeld en van de beste Schildering | *Mat:* op koper *Size:* hoog 9, breed 7 duim	Vinkeles [for] D	(Bought In) fl 3 [or] 31
1806/08/13	AMSCH	0320	*Francks. (S.)* | In een prachtig aloud Vertrek, ryk gestoffeerd met Drinkschaalen, Bekers, Schilden, Caskette, Musiek Instrumenten en divers, ziet men Achilles onder de Maagden; alleruitvoerigst en delicaat gepenceeld | *Mat:* op paneel *Size:* hoog 22, breed 32 duim	Vinkeles [for] J	(Bought In) fl 14
1806/08/20	HGBSM	0153	*S. Franck* | De Aanbidding der drie Koningen | *Mat:* op paneel *Size:* hoog 19, breed 24 duim	Macalester Loup [or others]	(Sold) fl 1:12 Gram
1806/11/24	AMSCH	0025	*Franx (S.)* | Maria Hémelvaard; zynde een ryke Ordinantie, van verscheide Beelden; meesterlyk van coloriet en penseelbehandeling | *Mat:* op koper *Size:* hoog 14, breed 11 duim	Munnikhuizen	(Sold) fl 3:5 L Pakker
1808/06/06	RMRIJ	0038	*Franks. (Sebastiaan)* | Een historieel onderwerp; Esther voor den troon van Assuherus; krachtig geschilderd [Sujet tiré de l'ancien testament. Esther devant l'trône d'Assuèrus. D'une touche mâle, et dans la manière de Rubens] | *Mat:* op koper *Size:* Hoog 10 ½, en breed 15 ¼ duim	Gerrit van der Pot, Heer van Groeneveld	(Sold) fl 20 Gebroeders Levy
1808/06/13	AMSCH	0056	*Franks* | De ontdekking van Achilles, door Ulysses, gestoffeert met fraaije en welgekleede Vrouwen; uitneemend vaat- en hoornwerk, muzijk-instrumenten en andere voorwerpen. Uitvoerig en naauwkeurig van penceelbehandeling, en schoon van kleuren | *Mat:* op paneel *Size:* hoog 22, breed 30 duim	K	(Sold) fl 20 van Drielst
1809/04/22	AMYVR	0043	*S. Franks* | Een Biddende Munnik | *Mat:* op koper *Size:* hoog 7, breed 6 duim	Juff[r] Julikker	(Sold) fl 2:15 J de Vries
1809/07/19	AMSCH	0014	*Franx (S.)* | Deze rijke Ordonantie, vertoont den verloren en wellustigen Zoon, zittende aan eene Tafel, met verscheidene spijs voorzien, verzeld	[Bicker]	(Sold) fl 60 van Iperen

			van ligtvaardige Vrouwen, Muzicanten en anderen, verder ziet men in de Keuken anderen spijzen berijden. Alles is bevallig van licht en koloriet en alleruitvoerigst behandeld. Rondsom dit Middenstuk zijn agt bijzondere Vakken, waar in de verdere lotgevallen van dezen Zoon in 't grauw zeer konstig verbeeld zijn | *Mat:* op paneel *Size:* hoog 24, breed 19 duim		
1809/07/19	AMSCH	0015	*Franx (S.)* | Judith in de Tent van Holofernes, haar gereed makende het Hoofd af te houden, in het verschiet ziet men verscheide legertenten en Krijgsknegten, bij maanlicht. Krachtig en van eene uitvoerige penceelsbehandeling | *Mat:* op koper *Size:* hoog 13, breed 19 ½ duim	C	(Sold) fl 35 de Vos
1810/07/26	AMSCH	0032	*Franks (S.)* | Eene rijke Ordonantie van verscheidene Beelden, voorstellende de Onthoofding van Joannes. Fraai geschilderd | *Mat:* op paneel *Size:* hoog 23, breed 30 duimen	Cassino	(Bought In) fl 7:5
1810/07/26	AMSCH	0033	*Franks (S.)* | Verbeeldende Carricaturen tegen eenige Schilders van zijnen tijd. Uitvoerig en geestig behandeld | *Mat:* op doek *Size:* hoog 20, breed 25 duimen	Cassino	(Bought In) fl 10
1810/08/06	AMSCH	0033	*Franks (S.)* | Een Munnik, met een Boek en Doodshoofd. Fiks bewerkt | *Mat:* op koper *Size:* hoog 8 ½, breed 6 duimen	V[ries]	(Sold or Bought In) fl 3 de Vries
1810/08/06	AMSCH	0034	*Franks (S.)* | Een biddende Munnik, voor een Kruisbeeld. Vol uitdrukking | *Mat:* op koper *Size:* hoog 6, breed 5 duimen	V[ries]	(Sold) fl 3 L Pakker
1810/10/11	AMSCH	0032	*S. Franks* | De Romeinsche Kinderliefde | *Mat:* op koper *Size:* hoog 9, breed 13 duimen	C	(Sold) fl 3:15 Posthumus
1810/10/11	AMSCH	0181	*S. Franks* | Eene Historiëele Ordonantie, verbeelende eene pragtige Maaltijd, dewelke door eenige Krijgslieden gestoord word; uitvoerig en krachtig	A	(Sold) fl 6 Ijver

Vrancx, Sebastian (and Steenwyck, Hend.)

1802/06/16	AMSCH	0175	*H. van Steenwyck; S. Franks* | Een Tempel van binnen te zien; waar in verscheide Krygsknegten en andere Beelden; het Kaarsligt en het Vuur doet een goed effect en is meesterachtig gepenceeld | *Mat:* op paneel *Size:* hoog 15 ½, breed 19 ½ duim	[Merrem]	(Sold) fl 61 Gruiter
1803/04/20	AMSCH	0069	*H. Steenwyk; Franx [S. Frankx]* | Een Binnengezicht van een Roomsche Kerk, gestoffeert met wandelende Beeldjes, in 't verschiet een Priester den Dienst verrigtende, zonagtig en uitvoerig van penceelsbehandeling [Point de vue dans une Eglise Catholique ou l'on fait l'office : orné de plus par d'autres jolies figures ; rendu avec effet & précision.] | *Mat:* op paneel *Size:* hoog 8 ½, breed 13 duim *Notes:* The second artist's name differs in the Dutch and French editions of the catalogue.	Maria Magdalena van Sluypwyk, gravinne van Moens	(Sold) fl 31 Theijs

Vrancx, Sebastian (or Francken)

1801/03/16	AMSCH	0084	*Franks* | Een capitaale Bybelsche Ordonnantie, stellende voor, daar Christus 12 jaaren oud zynde, zig in den Tempel bevond, uitvoerig geschilderd	P[ruyssenaar]	(Sold) fl 19 Coclers
1801/08/19	AMSCH	0028	*Franks* | Een Capitaal Boomryk Landschap, gestoffeert met Christus, daar hy de Blinde Ziende maakt, onder een ménigte Aanschouwers	W Wynen	(Sold) fl 6 Yver
1802/02/16	AMSCH	0010	*Franks* | Twee stuks Bybelsche Ordenantiën op koper | *Mat:* op koper	B[uys]	(Sold) fl 2:5 Coclers
1802/05/05	AMSCH	0060	*Franks* | Een afgelaaten Christus van 't Kruis en verdere Beelden | *Size:* hoog 12, breed 15 duim	J	(Sold) fl 14:10 Spruit
1802/07/09	AMSTO	0009	*Franck* | 2 dito [stuks] dito [Binnenhuyzen]		(Unknown)
1804/08/02	BDAN	0048	*Franc* | Maria met het Kind | *Mat:* op koper *Size:* b. 6 d. h. 8 en een half d.	J G Calckberner	(Unknown)
1806/05/05	AMSCH	0234	*Francks* | Een Muziseerend Gezelschap | *Mat:* op koper *Size:* hoog 5, breed 4 duim	V[inkeles]	(Sold) fl 0:14 van Iperen
1806/08/20	HGBSM	0154	*Frank* | Een Zee triumf | *Mat:* op paneel *Size:* hoog 18, breed 25 duim	Macalester Loup [or others]	(Sold) fl 5 Smeets
1808/04/26	GDAN	0045	*Frank* | Verbeeldende de Steeniging van Stephanus, met veele Beelden, wel geschilderd | *Mat:* op koper *Size:* hoog 14 ½, breed 11 ½ duim	G H Fortuyn	(Unknown)
1808/04/26	GDAN	0046	*Frank* | De Wetgeving op Sinaï, de veréering van 't Goude Kalf, waarom de Israeliten zijn dansende, dus een groot aantal Beelden, zeer uitvoerig en fraai geschilderd | *Size:* hoog 19, breed 28 duim	G H Fortuyn	(Unknown)
1808/04/26	GDAN	0047	*Frank* | Zijnde de allerprachtigste Roomsche lieve Vrouwe Kerk van Antwerpen, met een overheerlijk verschiet, aan de Pijlaren een aantal schoone Beelden, en Altaaren, waar in verscheidene Geestelijken in hun gewaad werkzaam zijn, brandende Kaarsen ziet men hier en daar in 't verschiet, en een Lamptaarn, waar in licht brand, door een Geestelijk Persoon gedragen wordende, alles zo uitvoerig en vol gewoel en overheerlijk geschilderd | *Size:* hoog 31, breed 43 duim	G H Fortuyn	(Unknown)
1808/04/26	GDAN	0048	*Frank* | Zijnde de Kruisiging van Christus, vol gewoel, uitvoerig geschildert | *Size:* hoog 24 ½, breed 29 duim	G H Fortuyn	(Unknown)
1809/07/25	HGBSM	0170	*Frank* | De Dood van Cleopatra | *Mat:* op koper *Size:* hoog 5 en een half, breed 7 en een half duim	D van der Aa [or] E B ten Dall	(Sold) fl 2 de Gruyter
1809/07/25	HGBSM	0208	*Franck* | Dit onderwerp vertoond de Verloren Zoon, in zyn wellustigen stand verbeeld, en omringt met verscheiden Gebeurtenissen uit diergelyk leven voordgevloeid; het middenvak is in 't Coloriet, en de omringende	D van der Aa [or] E B ten Dall	(Sold) fl 1:12 Bogaard

			vakjes zyn in 't grauw geschildert | *Mat:* op doek *Size:* hoog 26 en een half, breed 33 duim		
1809/07/25	HGBSM	0213	*Francks* | De Bataille van Lekkerbeetje | *Mat:* op paneel *Size:* hoog 21, breet 31 en een half duim	D van der Aa [or] E B ten Dall	(Sold) fl 1:4 A Vermeulen

Vrancx, Sebastian (or Francken and Delen)

1802/07/20	MGSAN	0007	*D. van Deelen; Francq* | In dit fraaije Stuk vertoont zich in een prachtige Zaal, een zeer aanzienlyk Gezelschap aan een Tafel te eeten; in het verschiet ziet men een Vorstelyk Collonade en Tuin, alles helder en krachtig geschilderd door D. van Deelen en Francqu | *Mat:* op paneel *Size:* hoog duim 25, breed duim 33		(Unknown)

Vrancx, Sebastian (or Vrancx, manner)

1801/10/19	AMSCH	0088	*S. Franks* | Een St. Catharina, in prachtige kleeding, leunende met haar linkerhand op een Swaard, en met de rechterhand op een Rad; door of in de manier van S. Franks | *Mat:* op paneel *Size:* hoog 9 ¾, breed 7 ⅞ duim	Jonkheer Menno Baron van Coehoorn	(Sold) fl 12:10 van Iperen (D[k] Versteeg)
1804/10/16	DLOND	0335	*Sebastiaan Franks* | Ene Romeinsche Geschiedenis, op Koper, door, of in den trant van, Sebastiaan Franks. Sujet de l'Histoire des Romains, peint sur cuivre par, ou comme par, Sebastien Francks | *Mat:* op koper		(Unknown)

Vrancx, Sebastian (or Vrancx, manner; or Francken, or Francken, manner)

1805/12/16	AMSCH	0135	*Francx* | Een Bybelsche Ordinantie, van een ménigte Beelden; op Doek, door of als Francx | *Mat:* op doek	Y	(Sold) fl 0:10 Yver

Vrancx, Sebastian (manner)

1805/12/16	AMSCH	0023	*S. Franx* | In een Keukenvertrek, ryk gestoffeert, op een gedekte Tafel, staat verscheide keurlyke Spys geplaast, op de Voorgrond ziet men verscheide Aapen, in verschillende actien, zig met eeten, drinken en roken vermaken, ter zyde leggen eenige Vissen en Fruiten; verder braad een stuk Vleesch aan 't spit, en voorts versiert met een ménigte bywerk; geestig en bevallig geschilderd, als door S. Franx | *Mat:* op paneel *Size:* hoog 19, breed 24 duim	V	(Sold) fl 6:15 Levy Pakker

Vrancx, Sebastian (manner; or Francken, manner)

1802/12/13	AMSCH	0200	*Franx* | Een ryke Ordenantie, zinspeelende op het Oude en Nieuwe Verbondt, in 't midden vertoond zig de Boodschap van den Engel aan Maria, en omhoog een glorie van een meenigte Musiceerende Engelen op de Wolken; uitvoerig op Koper geschilderd, in de manier van Franx | *Mat:* op koper	Florijn [?]	(Sold) fl 8 Jan Spaan

Vree, Nicolaes de

1804/08/08	AMSCH	0207	*K. de Vree* | Een aangenaam Duinachtig Landschap, met fraaije Boomstammen, Distelen, aartige Stoffagie, en een aangenaam Bergachtig verschiet, aan een Rivier; zynde behandeld in een meesterachtige trant, als J. Wynants, op Doek, door K. de Vree. (bekend by Houbraken.) | *Mat:* op doek *Size:* hoog 26, breed 31 duim	Roos a	(Sold) fl 32 Van Iperen
1805/07/10	AMSCH	0155	*K. de Vrée* | Langs een hoog opgaande Weg ziet men by Geboomten eenige Woningen, Schuur, enz.; waarby rustende Lieden; breed op Paneel | *Mat:* op paneel *Size:* hoog 18, breed 16 duim	V[inkeles] [for] M	(Sold) fl 8:10 T Spaan

Vries

1801/03/16	AMSCH	0211	*C. de Vries* | Een boomryk Landschap met Boerewoningen en bevallige stoffagie, meesterlyk en natuurlyk behandeld	S[chley]	(Sold) fl 22 B[d] Kooij
1802/04/13	HAVIN	0011	*de Vries* | Een Landschap met een Duingrond, natuurlyk in de manier van J. Ruysdaal		(Unknown)
1802/04/13	HAVIN	0071	*de Vries* | Een Zeehaven		(Unknown)
1805/10/09	HGBSM	G0007	*de Vries* | Een landschap met een brug | *Mat:* op paneel *Size:* hoog 15 ½ breet 20 duim	T H van Willigen [or others]	(Sold) fl 7:5 Blommers
1805/10/09	HGBSM	S0018	*de Vries* | Twee stuks landschappen | *Mat:* op paneel *Size:* beide hoog 15 breet 13 duim	T H van Willigen [or others]	(Sold) fl 11:10 van der Vin
1805/10/09	HGBSM	T0019	*de Vries* | Een fraay bosch gezigt met stoffagie | *Mat:* op doek *Size:* hoog 24 breet 24 duim	T H van Willigen [or others]	(Sold) fl 12 Basemoine
1809/04/17	AMSCH	0101a[H]	*de Vries* | [Untitled] | *Notes:* This lot was added in by hand in the EBNP copy of the catalogue, but without giving a title.		(Sold) fl 15
1810/12/03	DOBRA	0037	*de Vries* | Twee kleine Landschapjes		(Unknown)

Vries (manner)

1810/03/26	RMMUY	0082	*de Vries* | Een Landschap en stoffagie. Als van de Vries [Un Paysage hollandois, dans la manière de De Vries.] | *Annots:* paysage noire (BPG)	Daniel de Jongh Az	(Sold) fl 7 W van Leen Delftshaven
1810/06/06	RMMUY	0156	*de Vries* | Een Boschrijk Landschap, met stoffage. Als door de Vries | *Mat:* op doek		(Sold) fl 2:12 Strikland

Vries, Hans Vredeman de

1806/11/24	AMSCH	0024	*Fries (Hans Fredeman de)* | Een grootsch en fraay met Beelden gestoffeerd Gebouw, daaragter een Tuin; kragtig en zonachtig van schildering | *Mat:* op doek *Size:* hoog 46, breed 83 duim	Munnikhuizen	(Sold) fl 8:10 L Pakker

Vries, Michiel van

1810/11/07	UTWLD	0054	*M. de Vries* | Een boomrijk Landschap met eenige stoffagie door M. de Vries, op paneel, 1 voet 10 en een half duim hoog, 2 voet 7 en een half duim breed, zwarte Lijst | *Mat:* op paneel *Size:* 1 voet 10 en een half duim hoog, 2 voet 7 en een half duim b		(Unknown) fl 8:15

Vries, Paul Vredeman de

1805/10/09	HGBSM	0132	*P. Vreedeman* | Een pragtige tempel, waarin met ziet de weduwe die haar penning in de offerkist stort. waar by den Heiland met zyne Discipulen, fraay en helder door P. Vreedeman | *Mat:* op doek *Size:* hoog 22 breet 32 duim	T H van Willigen [or others]	(Sold) fl 3:4 Van der Meer

Vries, Roelof van

1801/05/11	AMSCH	0099	*R. de Vries* | Een Hollandsch Landschap, met hoog Geboomte en Boeren Woningen, gestoffeerd met een Voetganger, verders een Man te Paard en andere Beelden, fix en natuurlyk gepenceeld | *Mat:* op paneel *Size:* hoog 20, breed 27 duim	Pruisse [for] M	(Sold) fl 23:10 Jan Spaan
1801/05/11	AMSCH	0100	*R. de Vries* | Langs verscheiden Gebouwen en hoog Geboomte ziet men twee in gesprek zynde Persoonen met een kind by haar, verders Rysigers, meesterlyk behandeld | *Mat:* op paneel *Size:* hoog 25, breed 19 duim	P[ruyssenaar]	(Sold) fl 53 Rijnders
1801/06/10	AMSCH	0176	*Vries. (R. de)* | Een bevroosen Rivier, langs een Vestmuur, met verscheiden gebouwen, gestoffeert met diversche Schaatseryders, fyn geschilderd | *Size:* hoog 25, breed 33 duim	[Doublet]	(Sold) fl 20 Pruyssenaar
1801/06/10	AMSCH	0177	*Vries. (R. de)* | Een Landschap, op de voorgrond gestoffeert met een liggende en staande Koei, in het verschiet een Boerenwoning; kloek van penceel | *Mat:* op paneel *Size:* hoog 9, breed 12 duim	[Doublet]	(Sold) fl 12 Gruyter
1802/02/16	AMSCH	0013	*R. de Vries* | Een Heuvelachtig Landschap met een gebouw, geboomte, en verdere stoffagie; zonachtig gepenceeld op paneel | *Mat:* op paneel	B[uys]	(Sold) fl 19 Coclers
1802/05/05	AMSCH	0216	*R. de Vries* | Een duinachtig Landschap, op de voorgrond eenige Reysigers, zeer nrtuurlyk [sic] behandeld | *Mat:* op paneel *Size:* hoog 13, breed 17 duim	G	(Sold) fl 10:10 Gruiter
1802/05/05	AMSCH	0217	*R. de Vries* | Een Landschap met eenige leggende Beesjes, een Boeren Wooning, en in 't verschiet twee Reysigers | *Mat:* op paneel *Size:* hoog 7, breed 8 duim	G	(Sold) fl 6:15 Hulswit
1802/06/16	AMSCH	0195	*R. de Vries* | Twee stuks Boschgezichten met zonachtige passagien, in de eene een Jager met Honden en in de andere in een Watertje, twee Zwaanen en ander Gevogelten op de weg een Reiziger, beide meesterlyk gepenceeld | *Mat:* op doek *Size:* ieder hoog 23, breed 21 duim	[Merrem]	(Sold) fl 70 Coclers
1802/08/24	LNDLS	0089	*R. de Vries* | Een gestoffeerd Landschapje met Geboomte en een Watertje daar Beesten bij zijn | *Mat:* op paneel *Size:* hoog 13, breed 10 duimen	Leonardus Bouman [or others]	(Unknown) fl 19:10
1802/12/13	AMSCH	0159	*R. de Vries* | In een Landschap, vertoond zig by Geboomten een Oude vervallen Poort, en een gedeelte van een Vest Muur aan een stil Water; een beladen Huisman, ziet men op de voorgrond, en verder andere Reizigers; het invallende zonlicht, is bevallig en meesterlyk gepenceeld | *Mat:* op paneel *Size:* hoog 11, breed 13 duim	Schley [for] Lauwers	(Sold) fl 2:15 L Pakker
1802/12/13	AMSCH	0160	*R. de Vries* | Een bevallig Dorp-Gezicht, met veel Geboomten en Boere Woningen, aan een stille Rivier, op de voorgrond, twee gaande Lieden; zeer natuurlyk en zonachtig, en meesterlyk gepenceeld | *Mat:* op paneel	Schley [for] Lauwers	(Sold) fl 4:15 Van Iperen
1802/12/13	AMSCH	0161	*R. de Vries* | Een aangenaam Land- en Water-Gezicht, met verscheiden Oude Gebouwen en Muurwerk, clikachtig geschilderd | *Mat:* op paneel *Size:* hoog 16, breed 20 duim	Pruyssenaar [for] A	(Sold) fl 0:10 L Pakker
1802/12/13	AMSCH	0162	*R. de Vries* | Een Landschap met een stil Water, by een Kasteel | *Mat:* op paneel *Size:* hoog 22, breed 18 duim	Pruyssenaar [for] D	(Sold) fl 1 L Pakker
1803/09/07	AMSCH	0204	*R. de Vries* | Een Boschgezigt met zwaar Geboomte, gestoffeerd met eenige Jaagers, verzeld van hunne Honden, die een Hart vervolgen langs een opgaande Weg; zeer fraay, meesterlyk en natuurlyk, op Doek geschilderd [La vue d'une forêt pleine de gros arbres ; on voit le long d'un chemin montueux quelques chasseurs et leurs chiens poursuivant un cerf ; excellente composition et d'un effet naturel] | *Mat:* op doek *Size:* hoog 27, br. 31 duim	Smidt	(Sold) fl 115 W Reijers
1803/12/12	AMSCH	0105	*R. de Vries* | Een Duin- en Boomryk Landschap, gestoffeerd met Boerewoningen en Beeldjes; meesterlyk op Paneel, door R. de Vries, als Hobbema | *Mat:* op paneel *Size:* hoog 13, breed 17 duim	F	(Sold) fl 6:5 Gruiter
1804/05/07	AMSCH	0173	*Vries. (R. de)* | Een bevallig Landschap met Geboomte en Gebouwen, gestoffeerd met gaande en rustende Beelden, en een aangenaam verschiet; zonachtig en meesterlyk gepenceeld | *Mat:* op paneel *Size:* hoog 30, breed 23 duim	Vinkeles [for] G	(Sold) fl 9 Roelofs
1804/08/02	BDAN	0032	*R. de Vries* | Een Landschap met Koeyen, Schaapen, &c, schoon van Couleur | *Mat:* op paneel *Size:* b. 39 en 1 half d. h. 28 d.	J G Calckberner	(Unknown)
1804/08/08	AMSCH	0205	*R. de Vries* | In een Boom- en Duinachtig Landschapje ziet men langs een Weg een staande en zittende Boer, verders Gebouwen en Geboomte; fiks en breed gepenceeld | *Mat:* op paneel *Size:* hoog 13 ½, breed 13 duim	Vink[eles] [for] S	(Sold) fl 4:10 Texier
1804/08/08	AMSCH	0206	*R. de Vries* | Twee stuks Gezichten op aloude Gebouwen, de ééne aan een Rivier, waarin eenige Lieden bézig zyn te visschen; en de andere langs	Vink[eles] [for] S	(Bought In) fl 34

			een Weg, waar een Drift Beesten aankomt, met hun Hoeder; beiden fraai en breed gepenceeld | *Mat:* op paneel *Size:* hoog 11, br 9 duim		
1804/10/29	HRBAU	0111	*Vries, (R. de)* | Dit Schildery vertoont een oud vervallen Kasteel, met Geboomte voorzien, uit het water opgebouwd; in de Gragt liggen eenige Schuitjens met Visschers, en over dezelve ziet men een boomryk Kerkdorp. Zeer natuurlyk en klikkig behandeld | *Mat:* op paneel *Size:* hoog 25, breed 19 duim	Simon Styl	(Unknown)
1805/07/03	AMSCH	0156	*R. de Vries* | Een Boomryk Landschap, met een Rysiger te paard en eenige Landlieden; fiks door R. de Vries | *Mat:* op paneel *Size:* hoog 10, breed 9 duim	V[inkeles]	(Sold) fl 4 Lafontaine
1805/07/10	AMSCH	0150	*R. de Vries* | Langs een Weg ziet men by een Heuvel en Geboomten, eenige Woningen, Kerktooren, rustende en gaande Lieden, enz. fiks op Paneel | *Mat:* op paneel *Size:* hoog 16, breed 21 duim	V[inkeles] [for] M	(Sold) fl 30 Lafontaine
1805/07/10	AMSCH	0151	*R. de Vries* | Een Duinachtig Landschap, gestoffeerd met Rysigers, Boerewooninge en Geboomten; natuurlyk behandeld | *Mat:* op paneel *Size:* hoog 16, breed 22 duim	Tem[mink]	(Sold) fl 13 Lafontaine
1805/07/10	AMSCH	0152	*R. de Vries* | Een Boomryk en Duinachtig Landschapje, met een Rivier doorsneeden, Boerewoningen, Molens, Schuiten, stoffagie van Beeldjes enz.; zonachtig en fraai gepenceeld | *Mat:* op paneel *Size:* hoog 15 ½, breed 18 ½ duim	V[inkeles] [for] P	(Sold) fl 8:10 Lafontaine
1805/07/10	AMSCH	0153	*R. de Vries* | Een Berg- en Boomryk Landschap, met Boerewoningen, enz.; breed geschilderd | *Mat:* op paneel *Size:* hoog 14, breed 17 ½ duim	V[inkeles] [for] P	(Sold) fl 4:10 Agina
1806/08/13	AMSCH	0202	*Vries. (R. de)* | Een Duin- en Boomryk Landschap, met stoffagie van Beeldjes; zonachtig en meesterlyk gepenceeld | *Mat:* op paneel *Size:* hoog 14, breed 23 duim	Vinkeles [for] F	(Sold) fl 6:5 Richters
1808/06/13	AMSCH	0164	*Vries (R. de)* | Een aangenaam Dorpgezicht, waarin een Heer voor een Herberg van zijn Paard stapt, verder eenige Aanschouwers, in 't verschiet een Postwagen. Allernatuurlijkst | *Mat:* op doek *Size:* hoog 19, breed 22 duim	G	(Sold) fl 73 Moll
1808/06/13	AMSCH	0165	*Vries (R. de)* | In een aangenaam Boerendorp ziet men een Boer een drift Beesten voortdrijven, in 't verschiet eenige Boeren tusschen Koornlanden. Zeer zonachtig en kragtig van uitdrukking | *Mat:* op doek *Size:* hoog 15, breed 18 duim	G	(Sold) fl 55 Nieuwenhuisen
1808/08/23	AMSCH	0197	*R. de Vries* | Twee stuks Hollandsche Zee-Dorpen, beide rijk gestoffeerd met Heeren en Dames en Rijtuigen, Visschers en anderen Figuren; helder op Doek | *Mat:* op doek	[Gruyter?]	(Sold or Bought In) fl 2:15 Gruyter
1808/09/13	HABRU	0091	*R. de Vries* | Een Landschap; natuurlijk en fraai geschilderd		(Unknown) fl 31:10
1808/11/28	AMSCH	0061	*R. de Vries* | Een aangenaam Land- en Watergezicht, gestoffeerd met een Hengelaar bij een stille Rivier, in 't verschiet een gaande Huisman, natuurlijk en plaisant geschilderd | *Mat:* op paneel *Size:* hoog 18, breed 22 duim	C	(Bought In) fl 49
1809/04/17	AMSCH	0101	*R. de Vries* | Een Landschap met een opgaande Weg, bij een Boerenwooning, gestoffeerd met rustende Huislieden, en een Duinachtig verschiet; helder en natuurlijk verbeeld | *Mat:* op paneel *Size:* hoog 16, breed 21 duim	A	(Sold) fl 20:10 Gruyter
1809/04/17	AMSCH	0102	*R. de Vries* | Een Land- en Watergezigt, met verscheide Boerenwooningen, gestoffeerd met Visschers in Schuiten en andere figuuren; zonachtig en zeer natuurlijk verbeeld | *Mat:* op doek *Size:* hoog 26, breed 35 duim	[Gruyter?]	(Sold or Bought In) fl 8 Spaan
1809/04/17	AMSCH	0103	*R. de Vries* | Een bevallig Land- en Watergezigt, met verscheide Boerenwooningen en Huislieden gestoffeerd; natuurlijk voorgesteld | *Mat:* op paneel *Size:* hoog 16, breed 21 duim	R	(Sold) fl 3:10
1809/04/22	AMYVR	0131	*R. de Vries* | Bij een Stads Vest ziet men een Pont, geladen met Menschen en Vee, welken de Rivier overvaren; zonachtig | *Mat:* op paneel *Size:* hoog 13, breed 17 duim	de Bruin	(Sold) fl 2:5 du Pree
1809/04/22	AMYVR	0132	*R. de Vries* | Een Schuur en Geboomte aan een Water, waarover een Hout Bruggetje en twee Visschers; zonachtig | *Mat:* op paneel *Size:* hoog 14, breed 19 duim	de Bruin	(Sold) fl 20 C S Roos
1809/06/13	AMSCH	0210	*R. de Vries* | Een Boomrijk Landschap, met Reizigers gestoffeerd	E	(Sold) fl 1:10 T Spaan
1810/05/22	AMSCH	0111	*Vries. (R. de)* | Een natuurlijk Land- en Watergezicht, gestoffeerd met een Man in een Schuit en andere Lieden, ter zijde Boeren Woningen, eene Kerk en oude Toren, waarin een zeer akkuraat lopend Uurwerk | *Mat:* op paneel *Size:* hoog 21 ½, breed 17 ½ duim	T	(Bought In) fl 55
1810/06/06	RMMUY	0137	*R. de Vries* | Twee stuks fraaije gestoffeerde Landschappen | *Mat:* op paneel		(Unknown) fl 13
1810/08/06	AMSCH	0115	*Vries (R. de)* | Een vervallen Kasteel met Geboomte, ter zijde een Weg met eenige Reizigers. Fraai van licht en bruin | *Mat:* op doek *Size:* hoog 14, breed 16 duimen		(Withdrawn)
1810/08/06	AMSCH	0116	*Vries (R. de)* | Een oude Vestmuur, aan een stil Water, met zwaar Geboomte. Zonachtig en natuurlijk behandeld | *Mat:* op doek *Size:* hoog 16, breed 14 duimen		(Withdrawn)
1810/11/07	UTWLD	0027	*R. Vriesz* | Een Boeren achterwooning, waar een beek voorbij stroomt, waaruit een Boerenmeid water schijnt geschept te hebben, verders een		(Unknown) fl 431

			boertje die met een schuit 't stroomtje afzakt, alles zeer geestig, natuurlijk en kragtig geschilderd door R. Vriesz op doek, 2 voet hoog, 2 en een half voet breed, vergulde Lijst | *Mat:* op doek *Size:* 2 voet hoog, 2 en een half voet breed		

Vries, Roelof van (and Lingelbach)

1801/05/11	AMSCH	0101	*R. de Vries; J. Lingelbach* | Gestoffeerd door J. Lingelbach. Een Landschap ter zyde een vervallen Gebouw, gestoffeerd met een Heer en Dame te Paard, by dezelve een Valkejager en Honden, alles meesterlyk van schildering en natuurlyk behandeld | *Mat:* op doek *Size:* hoog 26, breed 21 duim	E[lias]	(Sold) fl 39:10 Cocler
1804/05/07	AMSCH	0172	*Vries (A. de); J. Lingelbagh* | Een stille Rivier, langs oude Gebouwen en Geboomten, gestoffeerd met een Visscher in een Schuit en zwemmende Eenden, in 't verschiet een Weide met Beesten; natuurlyk en zonachtig behandeld | *Mat:* op paneel *Size:* hoog 19, breed 21 duim *Notes:* The artist's name was given as "Vries (A. de)" but we have assumed this is an error.	JJ [through] Y[ver]	(Sold) fl 26 T van Iperen
1810/10/11	AMSCH	0092	*R. De Vries; J. Lingelbach* | Een Landschap met Gebouwen en oude vervallen Muren bij Geboomte, gestoffeerd met een Heer te Paard en Reizigers met beladen Muil-Ezels; zonachtig en uitvoerig behandeld, door R. De Vries, gestoffeerd door J. Lingelbach | *Mat:* op paneel *Size:* hoog 13, breed 11 duimen	[Gruyter?]	(Sold) fl 10 T Spaan

Vries, Roelof van (and Wouwerman, Ph.)

1809/04/22	AMYVR	0130	*R. de Vries; Ph. Wouwerman* | Een Boomrijk met Paarden en Jagers gestoffeerd Landschap; geestig, door R. de Vries en Ph. Wouwerman | *Mat:* op paneel *Size:* hoog 19, breed 25 duim	de Bruin	(Sold) fl 30 Remmers Bredius

Vries, Roelof van (manner)

1801/08/19	AMSCH	0133	*R. de Vries* | Een gestoffeerd Boschgezicht; meesterlyk als R. de Vries | *Mat:* op doek *Size:* hoog 19, breed 25 duim	W Wynen	(Sold) fl 2:10 Wed Achtienhoven
1806/08/13	AMSCH	0260	*R. de Vries* | Een Landschap, zynde een Boschgezicht, in 't verschiet, terzyde met bezaaide Landen, op de voorgrond staat een Huisman by een zittende Vrouw, aan een stil Waterbeekje; alles is krachtig op Paneel geschilderd, in de manier van R. de Vries | *Mat:* op paneel	van der Voort	(Sold) fl 14:10 van Iperen

Vries, Simon Wynhoutsz.

1802/09/21	UTHDG	0087	*S. de Vries* | Van den voorgrond loopt een weg, waarop een Reiziger, over de hoogte het Bosch in, dat men ter zijde langs eene Rivier na den zichteinder ziet voortduren: zeer natuurlijk en kragtig | *Mat:* op doek *Size:* hoog 29, breed 37 ½ duimen		(Bought In) fl 30
1802/09/21	UTHDG	0088	*S. de Vries* | In een Dorp vooraan een Boerewoning, verder de Kerk, en andere woningen, het verschiet op Duinen. Dit stuk dat met Beeldjes, Hoenders en andere voorwerpen gestoffeerd is, is als het voorgaande behandeld | *Mat:* op paneel *Size:* hoog 18 ½, breed 24 duimen		(Bought In) fl 39

Vries, Simon Wynhoutsz. (manner)

1802/09/21	UTHDG	0089	*S. de Vries* | Een boomrijk Landschap met een Waterval onder een Brug, gestoffeerd met Reizigers: fiks behandeld in de manier van denzelven [S. de Vries] | *Mat:* op doek *Size:* hoog 26, breed 21 duimen		(Bought In) fl 34:10
1805/12/16	AMSCH	0071	*S. de Vries* | Een dito [Landschap], als S. de Vries	R[oos]	(Sold) fl 0:12 Rookmans

Vrijmoet, Jacobus

1810/10/11	AMSCH	0113	*J. Vrymoet* | Een Land- en Watergezigt, met Beelden en Beesten	Y	(Sold) fl 3 du Pree
1810/10/11	AMSCH	0247	*J. Vrymoet* | Twee stuks bevallige Landschappen, met Stoffage	A	(Sold) fl 3 Gruiter

Vroom, Cornelis Hendricksz.

1802/06/28	AMSCH	0200	*Vroom* | Twee stuks, boomryke Landschappen, op Doek | *Mat:* op doek	B	(Sold) fl 2:15 Roos [for] A

Vroom, Hendrick Cornelisz.

1801/04/08	HAVIN	0045	*Vroom* | Een watergezigt		(Unknown)
1801/04/08	HAVIN	0070	*Vroom* | Een Zeehaven met scheepen		(Unknown)
1802/04/13	HAVIN	0058	*Vroom* | Een Zee met Scheepen		(Unknown)
1803/08/24	HGKAN	0077	*Vroom* | Een fraay Zee-Stuk	[Teissier] [or others]	(Unknown) fl 6
1804/02/27	AMSCH	0114	*Vroom. (H.)* | Twee stuks zeer fraaye Landschappen, met stoffage van Beeldjes; natuurlyk gepenceeld | *Mat:* op doek *Size:* hoog 15, breed 19 duim *Notes:* The artist was presumably Cornelis Hendricksz. Vroom and not Hendrick Cornelisz. Vroom.	R[oos]	(Sold) fl 6 Gruiter
1804/10/29	HRBAU	0112	*Vroom, (W.)* | Eene sterke woelende Zee, gestoffeerd met Oorlog- en andere Schepen, en in het verschiet eene Stad. Zonagtig behandeld | *Mat:* op doek *Size:* hoog 11, breed 16 duim *Notes:* The artist's name was given as "Vroom, (W.)" but we have assumed this is an error.	Simon Styl	(Unknown)

1806/05/05	AMSCH	0149	*Vroom* | Een kabbelende Zee, gestoffeerd met verscheiden zeilende Oorlogscheepen; krachtig gepenceeld door .... Vroom | *Mat:* op paneel *Size:* hoog 11, breed 13 duim	S[chley]	(Sold) fl 3:15 van Laar
1810/10/11	AMSCH	0093	*H.C. Vroom* | Twee Zeegezigten; op Paneel, door H. C. Vroom, 11 duimen, rond formaat | *Mat:* op paneel *Fmt:* rond *Size:* 11 duimen	C	(Sold) fl 3 Posthumus

Vucht, Jan van

1803/04/20	AMSCH	0086	*Vucht. (J. van)* | Twee stuks Roomsche Kerken van binnen te zien, gestoffeerd met een meenigte Beeldjes, fraay van perspectief, en delicaat behandeld [Deux perspectives d'Eglises Catholiques, ornées de jolies figures ; la degradation de la lumiere & une touche nette les feront distinguer.] | *Mat:* op paneel *Size:* ieder hoog 8, breed 9 ½ duim	Maria Magdalena van Sluypwyk, gravinne van Moens	(Sold) fl 52 Coclers

Waal, J. de [Unidentified]

1806/08/13	AMSCH	0220	*Waal. (J. de)* | Een hévige Schermutseling tusschen Ruitery en voetvolk, op elkander aanvallende; verder by een Water een ménigte vegtende Krygslieden en het belégeren van een Vesting; alles meesterlyk uitgevoerd | *Mat:* op paneel *Size:* hoog 18, breed 26 duim *Notes:* The artist was presumably Cornelis de Wael and not J. de Waal.	Roos	(Sold) fl 7:15 Hymans

Waanen, van [Unidentified]

1808/04/26	GDAN	0203	*Waanen (van)* | Een stil Water met eenige zeilende en stil leggende Scheepjes | *Size:* hoog 15, breed 21 duim	G H Fortuyn	(Unknown)
1808/04/26	GDAN	0204	*Waanen (van)* | Een dito [stil Water met eenige zeilende en stil leggende Scheepjes] | *Size:* hoog 17, breed 24 duim	G H Fortuyn	(Unknown)

Waard, H. de [Unidentified]

1802/09/30	HGBAK	0001	*H. de Waard* | Een Capitaal stuk, met eenige Honden, Papegaayen en andere Vogelen, in een Landschap, door H. de Waard, op doek, in een vergulde lyst. [Schilderyen in Olyverf] | *Mat:* in olyverf op doek *Notes:* The bracketed information in the title appears above lot 1 and refers to lots 1 to 26.		(Unknown)

Waerdigh

1802/06/28	AMSCH	0211	*Wardich* | Een gezicht op de Montelbaans Tooren te Amsterdam, met Schepen, Schuiten en Beelden, gestoffeert natuurlyk op Panneel | *Mat:* op paneel *Size:* hoog 18, breed 22 duim	Anna Elink	(Sold) fl 12:10 Gruiter
1805/10/09	HGBSM	0110	*Wardig* | Een stervende Cleöpatra met meer figuuren, in de trant van G. Lairesse | *Mat:* op doek *Size:* hoog 16 breet 13 duim	T H van Willigen [or others]	(Sold) fl 2 Van der Vin

Wagner, Johann Georg

1806/08/13	AMSCH	0224	*Wagner* | In een aangenaam Landschap vertoont zich een Boerenwoning by Geboomten, gestoffeert met Ryzigers te paard en te voet; zonachtig en uitvoerig behandeld | *Mat:* op paneel *Size:* hoog 6, breed 7 ½ duim	Roos	(Sold) fl 6:5 Th Spaan

Waldorp, Jan Gerard

1801/03/16	AMSCH	0031	*J.G. Waldorp* | De Opstanding van Christus in tegenwoordigheid van verscheide Romeinsche Wachten, een ryke Ordonantie, zeer fraai en uitvoerig geschilderd	P[ruyssenaar]	(Sold) fl 6:15 Boelen
1809/09/06	AMSCH	0092	*Waldorp (J.G.)* | Eene Dame in een Nis, speelende op de Guitar; zeer uitvoerig geschilderd | *Mat:* op paneel *Size:* hoog 13, breed 11 duim	Johannes Caudri	(Sold) fl 3 L.y Pakker

Wall, Willem Rutgaart van der

1810/11/07	UTWLD	0037	*W. v. d. Wall* | Eenige staande beesten wagtende op een Boerin die hun komt melken, verder een zeer vrolijk boomrijk Landgezicht, op den voorgrond eenige liggende Schapen door W. v. d. Wall op doek. 3 voet 1 en een half duim hoog, 4 voet 2 en een half duim breed, zwarte Lijst | *Mat:* op doek *Size:* 3 voet 1 en een half duim hoog, 4 voet 2 en een half duim br		(Unknown) fl 16
1810/11/07	UTWLD	0038	*W. v. d. Wall* | Eene liggende en eene staande Koe in een Weiland met opgeschoten boomgewas en kreupelhout door W. v. d. Wall op doek, 9 en een half duim hoog, 1 duim breed, zwarte Lijst | *Mat:* op doek *Size:* 9 en een half duim hoog, 1 duim breed		(Unknown) fl 12
1810/11/07	UTWLD	0039	*W. v. d. Wall* | Twee beesten in een Weiland, door denzelven [W. v. d. Wall], op paneel 9 en een half duim hoog, 13 duim breed, zwarte Lijst | *Mat:* op paneel *Size:* 9 en een half duim hoog, 13 duim breed		(Unknown) fl 16
1810/11/07	UTWLD	0040	*W. v. d. Wall* | Twee beesten met een grazend Schaapje, door denzelven [W. v. d. Wall] op paneel, 9 duim hoog, 7 duim breed zwarte Lijst | *Mat:* op paneel *Size:* 9 duim hoog, 7 duim breed		(Unknown) fl 30
1810/11/07	UTWLD	0041	*W. v. d. Wall* | Een witte Os staande in een Weiland met eenig boomgewas, op paneel door W. v. d. Wall, hoog 11 duim, breed 14 duim, zwarte Lijst | *Mat:* op paneel *Size:* hoog 11 duim, breed 14 duim		(Unknown) fl 7:10
1810/11/07	UTWLD	0049	*W. v. d. Wall* | Een Heijgezichtje, op een duin staan eenige opgeschoten Beuken en Eijke stammen, agter welken eenig kort hout, verder een vrolijk duinagtig verschiet, op de voorgrond een plas met een drinkenden hond, en een door Ossen getrokken wagen, waarop een vrouwtje, zeer fraai behandeld door W. v. d. Wall 1799, 1 en een half voet breed, 1 voet		(Unknown) fl 20:10

3 duim hoog, zwarte Lijst | *Size:* 1 en een half voet breed, 1 voet 3 duim hoog *Inscr:* W. v. d. Wall 1799 (signed and dated?) *Notes:* It is unclear whether the name and date are inscribed on the painting.

Walrave [Unidentified]

1805/10/21	GRBOL	0026	*Walrave* | Een Zee-Storm	Gerardus Nicolaus Heerkens	(Unknown)

Walscapelle, Jacob van

1802/05/05	AMSCH	0238	*J. Walskapelle* | Op een Steene Tafel ziet men een Glas, gevuld met eenige fraaije geschakeerde Bloemen | *Mat:* op paneel *Size:* hoog 12, breed 15 duim	BB	(Sold) fl 6:5 Stevens
1808/06/13	AMSCH	0222	*Walscappelle* | Eenige verschillende Fruiten, op eene Tafel liggende, in het midden een tros Druiven; zacht en teder	E M Engelberts	(Sold) fl 46 T Spaan
1810/05/22	AMSCH	0121	*Walscappelle. (J.)* | Eenige smakelijke Vrugten: als Persikken, Abrikosen en anderen, met Steel en Bladeren; mals gepenceeld | *Mat:* op paneel *Size:* hoog 13, breed 11 duim	S	(Sold) fl 2:15 du Pree

Wanum, Ary van

1810/07/23	DOLG2	0068	*A. van Wanum* | Een Land- en Watergezicht | *Mat:* op paneel *Size:* hoog 12, breed 16 duim	Pieter Quinting	(Sold) fl 4:10 Ganse Winkel

Ward, James

1803/10/25	HHNOM	0010	*J. Wards* | Selling Rabbits [Prenten en Schilderijen, in extra schoone vergulde Lysten en Glazen] | *Notes:* The bracketed information in the title appears above lot 1 and refers to lots 1 to 24. It is uncertain whether this lot is a painting.	Mr Stephanies Roosendaal	(Unknown)
1803/10/25	HHNOM	0011	*J. Wards* | The Citizens retreat [Prenten en Schilderijen, in extra schoone vergulde Lysten en Glazen] | *Notes:* The bracketed information in the title appears above lot 1 and refers to lots 1 to 24. It is uncertain whether this lot is a painting.	Mr Stephanies Roosendaal	(Unknown)

Wassenbergh, Jan Abel

1802/05/11	GRGRW	0063	*Wassenbergh* | Het Portrait van Wassenbergh, door hem zelven geschilderd, als een Mosselman [Schilderijen met Olie-Verf; In Vergulde Lijsten] | *Mat:* in olyverf *Notes:* The bracketed information in the title appears above lot 1 and refers to lots 1 to 79a.	Arnold Sicco Werumeus	(Unknown) fl 15

Waterloo, Anthonie

1808/04/26	GDAN	0205	*Waterlo* | Een Bosägtig Landschap met hoog Geboomte, waar in eenige Boere Wooningen staan, uitmuntend gepoffeerd met Menschen en eenig Vee, alles konstig en kragtig geschilderd | *Size:* hoog 39, breed 48 duim	G H Fortuyn	(Unknown)
1808/06/11	RMRIJ	0116	*A: Waterloo* | Een aangenaam Landschapje met Stoffagie | *Mat:* op paneel		(Unknown) fl 4:15
1808/09/13	HABRU	0099	*A. Waterlo* | Een Boomrijk Landschap		(Unknown) fl 7

Waterloo, Anthonie (and Weenix, J.B.)

1802/06/16	AMSCH	0211	*A. Waterlo; G. B. Wenix* | Dit uitmundtend en zeldzaam voorkomend Kunststuk, steld voor een Boschryk Landschap met hoog Geboomte beplant, in 't verschiet een Kasteel aan een Rivier, voorts met een meenigte Jagers met Paarden en Honden gestoffeerd; het Coloriet en licht en bruin is byzonder met de natuur overëenkomende; en kan voor het fraayste dat van deezen Meester bekend is, gehoudend worden | *Mat:* op doek *Size:* hoog 51, breed 16 duim	[Merrem]	(Sold) fl 210 H de Valk

Waterloo, Anthonie (or Waterloo, A., manner)

1802/09/06	AMSCH	0133	*A. Waterlo* | Een aangenaam gestoffeerd Boomryk Landschap met een stil Watertje, en aangenaam verschiet; fix gepenceeld door of in de manier van A. Waterlo | *Size:* hoog 20, breed 25 duim	Mevrouw Achtienhoven	(Sold) fl 14 v d Schley [for] A
1804/10/29	HRBAU	0113	*Waterloo, (A.) of in zyn Manier* | Een zeer bevallig doorzicht in een Bosch, naar een fraai verschiet, gestoffeerd met een' Man, op een' Ezel rydende; benevens eene Geit. Zeer zonagtig en klikkig behandeld | *Mat:* op doek *Size:* hoog 25, breed 19 duim	Simon Styl	(Unknown)
1804/10/29	HRBAU	0114	*Waterloo, (A.) of in zyn Manier* | Is mede een Boschgezigt, welk zig in verscheiden bevallige Groepen verdeelt; zeer zonagtig en niet minder fraai dan het voorgaande behandeld | *Mat:* op doek *Size:* hoog 25, breed 19 duim	Simon Styl	(Unknown)
1809/10/20	UTWLD	0009	*Waterlo* | Een fraai Landgezicht door of in de manier van Waterlo	J J van Rhyn	(Unknown)

Waterloo, Anthonie (manner)

1802/06/28	AMSCH	0212	*Waterlo* | Een landschap met hoog Geboomte als Waterlo, meesterlyk gepenceelt	Anna Elink	(Sold) fl 1:5 Gruiter

Watteau, Jean Antoine

1801/08/19	AMSCH	0142	*Wattau* | Een Hofgezicht met verscheiden galant gekleeden Beelden gestoffeerd	Pruyssen[r]	(Sold) fl 2:10 Vermeulen

1802/12/13	AMSCH	0176	*A. Watteau* | Een Landschap met verscheide Beelden, fiks | *Mat:* op doek *Size:* hoog 19, breed 25 duim	Yver	(Sold) fl 0:10 L Pakker
1802/12/13	AMSCH	0177	*A. Watteau* | Een gezelschap van Dames en Heeren, in een Landschap | *Mat:* op paneel *Size:* hoog 18, breed 14 duim	Yver	(Sold) fl 5 Coclers
1803/09/07	AMSCH	0216	*Watteau* | Twee stuks Conversatien van verscheide Dames en Heeren in Landschappen; beide van een galante schildering [Deux morceaux, représentant des assemblées de seigneurs et de dames ; tous les deux d'une composition élégante] | *Mat:* op doek *Size:* yder is hoog 12, breed 15 duim	Smidt	(Sold) fl 9 Teengs
1803/12/12	AMSCH	0115	*A. Watteau* | Twee stuks, in het eene ziet men een Dansparty en in het andere speelt met Blindeman, delicaat op Paneel | *Mat:* op paneel *Size:* hoog 15, breed 12 duim	D	(Sold) fl 22 Coclers
1803/12/15	MGLAC	0047	*Wattouw* | Een vrolyk Gezelschap in een Landschap; zeer fraai geschilderd | *Mat:* op doek *Size:* hoog duim 19, breed duim 26	Mr L H de Haze Bomme	(Unknown)
1804/10/16	DLOND	0256	*Watton* | Twee Gezelschappen. Deux Compagnies | *Mat:* op paneel *Size:* hoog 11, breed 16		(Unknown)
			Watteau, Jean Antoine (manner)		
1802/02/16	AMSCH	0015	*Wattau* | Een Gezelschap van Dames en Heeren op een Buitenplaats; in de manier van Wattau	B[uys]	(Sold) fl 0:8 Vink en Fitsing
1804/05/07	AMSCH	0211	*A. Watteau* | Twee stuks prachtige Gebouwen, waarin Gemuziceerd en Gedanst wordt; in de manier van A. Watteau | *Mat:* op doek	R[oos]	(Sold) fl 3 Mensart
			Weenix		
1801/04/13	AMSCH	0092	*J. Wenix* | Ter linker zyde van dit Schildery hangt aan een Vaas een Patrys en ander Gevogelte, op den voorgrond een doode Haan en Kiewiet, voorts eenige bloemen, en in het verschiet een aangenaam Hofgezicht; uitvoerig met de natuur overeenstemmend geschilderd | *Mat:* op doek *Size:* hoog 41, breed 37 duim	Pierre Fouquet, junior	(Sold) fl 190 Coclers
1801/06/10	AMSCH	0183	*Wenix. (J.)* | In deeze capitaale Ordonantie hangt, aan een Balustrade, een dooden Haas, daar nevens ligt een Kalcoen, Patryzen en ander Gevogelte, verder eenige vliegende Vogels, waar tegens een Hond staat te blaffen; alles is delicaat gepenceeld | *Mat:* op doek *Size:* hoog 48, breed 40 duim	Herman ten Kate	(Sold) fl 855 Jan Spaan voor Muilman
1801/06/10	AMSCH	0184	*Wenix. (J.)* | In deeze Ordonantie is mede een Haas, Patryzen, Phaisant en ander dood Gevogelte; niet minder behandeld als de voorgaande | *Mat:* op doek *Size:* hoog 35, breed 28 duim	Herman ten Kate	(Sold) fl 415 Barent Koy
1801/06/10	AMSCH	0185	*Wenix. (J.)* | Op de voorgrond van dit uitmuntend Tafereel, hangt een doode Haas aan de stam van een Boom, daar nevens twee Patryzen, verders een menigte Jachtgereedschap, en een aangenaam Hofgezicht in 't verschiet; zeer frai uitgevoerd en delicaat gepenceeld | *Mat:* op doek *Size:* hoog 47, breed 39 duim	Herman ten Kate	(Sold) fl 1055 J Yver
1801/06/10	AMSCH	0186	*Wenix. (J.)* | Deeze capitaale Ordonantie stelt voor op de voorgrond een dood wild Zwyn, nevens een Reiger en ander Wild, ter zyde ziet men een Dog, verder een Geweer en Kruithoorn; alles is meesterlyk en fiks geschilderd | *Mat:* op doek *Size:* hoog 42, breed 58 duim	Herman ten Kate	(Sold) fl 350 Coclers
1801/06/10	AMSCH	0187	*Wenix. (J.)* | Een duinachtig Landschap, in hetzelve ziet men een meer als levensgroote Jachthond, in een springende houding, tegens een party Duiven, welke in de lucht vliegen, op de voorgrond staat een schotel met afval van beesten; dit stuk is van een meesterachtige Schildering | *Mat:* op doek *Size:* hoog 61, breed 70 duim	Herman ten Kate	(Sold) fl 200 Yver
1801/06/10	AMSCH	0188	*Wenix. (J.)* | Op de voorgrond van dit stuk ligt een Phaisant en twee Patryzen, een menigte Jachtgereedschap, voorts een aangenaam verschiet; meesterlyk behandeld | *Mat:* op doek *Size:* hoog 38, breed 32 duim	Herman ten Kate	(Sold) fl 160 Coclers
1801/06/10	AMSCH	0189	*Wenix. (J.)* | In een Hofgezicht, ziet men een bevallig Meisje, schynende Bloemen gesneden te hebben, by haar ligt een Phaisant en twee Partryzen, verders eenige Vruchten; alles is meesterlyk gepenceeld | *Mat:* op doek *Size:* hoog 47, breed 40 duim	Herman ten Kate	(Sold) fl 65 Spruit van Gend
1801/06/13	LNDLS	0005	*J. Weninx* | Een Hofgezicht, langs een water, op den voorgrond eenig dood gevogelte, bij Jagttuig, en een dooden vogel, hangende een een boom, konstig en delicaat, op doek geschilderd, door J. Weninx 1711 | *Mat:* op doek *Size:* hoog 40, breed 35 duimen *Inscr:* J. Weninx 1711 (signed and dated?) *Notes:* It is unclear whether the name and date are inscribed on the painting.	D van R	(Sold) fl 160 A Delfos [for] W
1801/08/19	AMSCH	0141	*J. Weenix* | In een Hofgezicht ziet men een bevallige Vrouw die door een Cupido een trots Druiven word gegeeven, verders eenige Vruchten; schoon van Licht en meesterlyk geschilderd	Pruyssen[r]	(Sold) fl 17 Pruijssenaar [for] R
1801/10/06	AMSCH	0074	*J. Weenix* | Dit uitmuntend Kunstig Tafreel, vertoont in een Landschap, een cierlyk gewerkte Steene Vaas, op zyn Voetstuk, aan dezelve ziet men een doode Zwaan, hangende met een Poot aan dezelve, daar neevens twee doode Haasen, en op het Voetstuk eenig dood Gevogelte; ter linker zyde rust een Pauw, op de Tak van een Boom, alles is van een Ongemeene uitvoerige Penceelsbehandeling, en de Natuur volmaakt Evenaarende, en een der capitaalste van deeze Beroemden Meester | *Mat:* op doek *Size:* hoog 77, breed 77 duim	L	(Sold) fl 600 Corn Seb Roos

1801/12/01	HGDAW	0003	*Wenix* | Een dito [Schildery] met eenig Jagttuig door of in de smaak van Wenix	Jonkheer Menno Baron van Coehoorn	(Unknown)
1802/05/05	AMSCH	0233	*J. Weenix* | Twee stuks, een Krygsman en een bevallige Vrouw in een Landschap, op de voorgrond een Patryshond, in 't verschiet een Zeehaven, beide van de fraaiste en uitvoerigste penceelbehandeling | *Mat:* op doek *Size:* hoog 34, breed 28 duim	A	(Sold) fl 78 Le Dantú
1802/05/05	AMSCH	0234	*J. Weenix* | Eenige oude Ruïnes, waarby by een Grafnaald een Vrouwtje op een Ezel, en verdere stoffagie, krachtig gepenceeld | *Mat:* op doek *Size:* hoog 24, breed 21 duim	C	(Sold) fl 8:5 Ackina
1802/05/05	AMSCH	0235	*J. Weenix* | Een bergachtig Landschap, met de Ruïne van een oud Gebouw, waarby een Waterval, gestoffeerd met Beelden	J	(Sold) fl 0:10 L Pakker
1802/05/05	AMSCH	0236	*J. Weenix* | Een Italiaansche Zeehaven | *Size:* hoog 23, breed 19 duim	J	(Sold) fl 4:5 Spruit
1802/06/16	AMSCH	0224	*J. Wénix* | Een Bloemstuk, fraay en meesterlyk van penceels-behandeling | *Mat:* op doek *Size:* hoog 30 ½, breed 27 duim	[Merrem]	(Sold) fl 15 Pruijssenaar
1803/07/18	AMSCH	0060	*Weenix (Jan)* | Een Voorportaal van een magnifiek Gebouw naar de Dorische Order, aan de linkerzyde ziet men een Zeehaven met eenige Schepen; by een Fontyn, waarop een ryke groep van Beelden geplaatst is, ziet men een menigte Beeldjes, op de voorgrond zit een Vrouw welke aan een Persiaan eenig Wild schynt te verkoopen, agter haar een Kind en een Ezel, verders twee Honden en ander bywerk, en onder de Colonnade eenige wandelende figuuren; het soort van Schilderyen van deezen Meester, in deezen trant geschilderd, is zeldzaam, zynde hetzelve zonachtig en delicaat gepenceeld [Une masse imposante d'architecture Dorique, en marbre, formant l'avant corps d'un temple magnifique, dont la porte ouverte laisse appercevoir l'intérieur. Vèrs la gauche est un port de mer garni de vaisseaux, d'une fontaine surmontée d'un beau groupe, & d'une multitude de figures. Audevant du tableau, au bas de la collonade est assise une marchande de gibier, dont elle presente à vendre quelque pièce à un persan ; derriere la femme est un enfant, un ane & une grande mande avec d'autres objets. Entre les collonnes l'on voit différentes personnes allant ou revenant du temple. Deux beaux chiens & quelques accessoires deplus [sic] composent cette production consequente. Ce morceau capital, unissant à une couleur eclâtante & forte une grande delicatesse de pinceau, est intéressant jusques dans ses moindres parties. Jean Weeninx n'a composé qu'un petit nombre de tableaux en ce genre ; & nous avançons que le prèsent en est un dès plus heureux, dès mieux finis, & des plus conservés.] | *Mat:* op doek *Size:* hoog 36, breed 47 duim	Maria Theresia Andrioli	(Sold) fl 276 C S Roos
1803/08/01	AMSCH	0047	*Wenix. (J.)* | Deeze uitmuntende Ordonantie steld voor de verloren Zoon in een démoedige gestalte, door zyn Vader ontfangen wordende, twee Vrouwen en een Jongeling, met een Zonnescherm staan agter dezelven, op de Stoep van een pragtig Paleis, verders nog een Man, een Patryshond en Hofgezicht, in 't verschiet, alles delicaat en zonachtig behandeld | *Mat:* op doek *Size:* hoog 44, breed 39 duim	C	(Bought In) fl 375
1803/08/17	AMSCH	0093	*Wenix. (J.)* | In een Binnevertrek zit een Meisje, met een rood zyde Jakje, en witte satyne Rok gekleed, op een Taboretje, bezig zynde een Hond te laten danssen; agter de Tafel staat een Heer op de Guitar te spelen, om de Tuindeur komt een Jongeling kyken; het vertrek is ryk georneerd, zeer raar zyn diergelyke voorwerpen van deeze voortreffelyken Meester | *Mat:* op paneel *Size:* hoog 21, breed 16 duim	Anna Catharina Putman	(Sold) fl 30 Pruijssenaar
1804/07/25	AMSCH	0088	*Wenix. (J.)* | Op de Voorgrond van dit Tafreel legt een doden Haan, Phaisant en Eend; ter zyde op een Steene Voetstuk, met een Basrelief met Kindertjes versiert, leggen eenige Vrugten, aan een Boom hangt een Tros Druiven, verders een Meisje met eenige Bloemen in haar Schoot, het verschiet vertoond een prachtig Hofgezicht; alles is delicaat en van de beste schildering van dezen onvergelykelyken meester | *Mat:* op doek *Size:* hoog 48, breed 40 duim		(Sold) fl 370 van der Schleij
1804/08/08	AMSCH	0216	*J. Wenix* | Op een Steene Rand, met een Groen Kleed, ziet men een Doode hangende Haas, waarby een Doode Patrys, en een ander Vogeltje, en een gevlochten Tienen Mand, waarin Dood Gevogelte; uitvoerig en fraai geschilderd | *Mat:* op doek *Size:* hoog 29, breed 26 duim	Vink[eles] [for] W	(Bought In) fl 75
1804/08/08	AMSCH	0217	*J. Wenix* | Dit voorwerp vertoond de Vogel Phénix, staande op een brandende Houtstapel; het coloriet, de breede, meesterlyke, en tévens uitvoerige penceelbehandeling is fraai | *Mat:* op doek *Size:* hoog 52, breed 39 duim	Schley [for] A	(Sold) fl 26 La Bouchere
1805/07/03	AMSCH	0051	*Weenix, (J.)* | Dit Capitaale Schildery verbeeld voor een pragtig Gebouw; de verloorene Zoon afscheid nemende van zyn Vader en Famillie; op de tweede Grond ziet men Paarden en gevolg welke hem op zyn reis zullen vergezellen, verders een aangenaam Boom- en Bergachtig verschiet; de Ordinantie is grootsch, en de schildering van de besten aard van dezen voortreffelyken Meester | *Mat:* op doek *Size:* hoog 37, breed 47 duim	R[oos]	(Sold) fl 140 Lafontaine
1805/07/10	AMSCH	0253	*J. Wierix* | Een Land en Watergezicht, gestoffeert met verscheide Vaartuigen en Lieden; fiks geschilderd | *Mat:* op paneel *Notes:* The artist's name was given as "J. Wierix" but we have assumed this is an error.	Temmink	(Sold) fl 1 Yver
1806/08/13	AMSCH	0212	*Wenix. (J.)* | Op een Stoel in een Binnevertrek, legt een Patryshond, in een bevallige gestalte; zynde van een uitmuntende schildering | *Mat:* op doek *Size:* hoog 48, breed 36 duim	Roos	(Bought In) fl 29

1806/08/13	AMSCH	0332	*Weenix. (J.)* | Een capitaal stuk met dood Wild, waarby een Hond en divers; breed van schildering	Vinkeles [for] G[ruyter]	(Sold) fl 3:10 van Dijl
1806/10/16	UTWLD	0014	*J. Weenix* | Twee stuks, een Hofgezicht en een Landschap beiden gestoffeerd met Patrys en Jagthonden	Mr P de Malapert [or] W Beeldsnyder	(Unknown)
1806/11/24	AMSCH	0080	*Weenix (J.)* | In een bevallig Landschap vertoonen zig eenige Ruïnen van treffelyke Gebouwen, op de Voorgrond ziet men een staand Hondje, by eenig Jagtgereedschap; verder by een Rivier een Hartejagt; het zonlicht geeft een natuurlyke werking, en van een meesterlyk fraaije penceel-behandeling | *Mat:* op doek *Size:* hoog 30, breed 25 duim	Munnikhuizen	(Sold) fl 106 Josi
1807/06/02	AMHUY	0026	*Weenix* | Een heuvelachtig Landschap, gestoffeerd met Beelden en Beesten, meesterlyk geschilderd		(Unknown)
1808/03/03	HAVIN	0030	*Wenix* | Een doode Gans	Jacobus Spillebout	(Unknown) fl 2:2
1808/04/26	GDAN	0197	*Weenix (J)* | Een rosägtig Boschgezigt, waar in een Wolf is zittende, met een grijnzende houding zijne tanden latende zien, fiks en kragtig geschildert | *Size:* hoog 63, breed 48 duim	G H Fortuyn	(Unknown)
1808/04/26	GDAN	0198	*Weenix (J)* | Een schoon gekleeden Jager, levensgroot leggende met zijn knie op een begraasden heuvel, houdende een geschoten Hert in de hoogte, aan de eene Poot, om die alzo aan een mik van een Boom op te hangen, agter denzelve ziet men eene overschoone Zwaan leggen, op den voorgrond eenig dood Gevogelte, voorts een mooije zwarte Hond aan eenig Ingewand ruikende, en 't Geweer en Weitas by dezelve, dit stuk is konstig en zeer uitvoerig geschilderd | *Size:* hoog 77, breed 69 duim	G H Fortuyn	(Unknown)
1808/06/11	RMRIJ	0119	*Jan Weenix* | Een Schildery waar in Vliegende Duiven en een Eend op den voorgrond, stout en meesterlyk gepenceeld | *Mat:* op doek op paneel		(Sold) fl 2:2 V Giesen
1808/06/13	AMSCH	0220a[H]	*Wenix* | Landscap van Wenix | *Notes:* This lot was added in by hand in the AA I, EBNP, FLNY, MB and RKDH copies of the catalogue.	R[oos]	(Sold) fl 120 Reyers
1808/08/23	AMSCH	0167	*Weenix. (J.)* | In een Landschap vertoont zig een Heer in deftige Kleeding, benevens een Jager met Windhonden, ter zijde een zittende Patrijs Hond bij eenig dood Wild; helder en uitvoerig van Penceel | *Mat:* op doek *Size:* hoog 30, breed 26 duim	Y	(Sold) fl 31 Kerkhoven
1809/04/17	AMSCH	0135	*J. Wenix* | Op de kant van een Steen ligt een dooden Uil, Goudvink en verder Bijwerk, agterwaards een Hofgezicht; meesterlijk geschilderd | *Mat:* op doek	[Gruyter?]	(Sold) fl 3 de Vries
1809/07/19	AMSCH	0063	*Weeninx (J)* | Dit voortreffelijk Schilderij verbeelt een Hofgezicht, waar in een doode Haas, hangende aan zijn Poot; waar bij een Koppel Patrijzen, Vinken en ander dood Gevogelte, ter zijde bij Plantgewas ligt een Wijtas, Kruidhoorn, Geweer en ander Jagtgereedschap. Alles evenaart de natuur en is van eene uitmuntende penceelsbehandeling | *Mat:* op doek *Size:* hoog 48, breed 43 duim	[Wijkersloot?]	(Sold) fl 200 Engelberts
1809/09/06	AMSCH	0088	*Weenix (J.)* | In een prachtig Hofgezigt ziet men op den voorgrond, bij een Colonnade, een dooden Haas, een zwarte Hen en ander Gevogelten, achter dezelven een Korf met Vruchten; voorts een aangenaam Verschiet; alles evenarende de natuur, en zijnde van een uitmuntende schildering | *Mat:* op doek *Size:* hoog 47, breed 56 duim	Johannes Caudri	(Sold) fl 350 Teissier
1809/09/06	AMSCH	0089	*Weenix (J.)* | Deze Ordinantie stelt voor, in een Landschap, een dood Hart, hangende met zijn poot aan een Boom, waar tegen een Hond schijnt te blaffen; verder eenig dood Gevogelten en een aangenaam Verschiet; zijnde van een meesterlijke behandeling | *Mat:* op doek *Size:* hoog 47, breed 57 duim	Johannes Caudri	(Sold) fl 87 Coclers
1809/09/06	AMSCH	0090	*Weenix (J.)* | Op een Tafel, gedeeltelijk met een Tapijt gedekt, ziet men een Zilvere Schotel, waarop eenige Persiken, Druiven en andere Vruchten; delicaat en natuurlijk behandeld | *Mat:* op doek *Size:* hoog 26, breed 23 duim	Johannes Caudri	(Sold) fl 15 Gruyter
1810/05/22	AMSCH	0116	*Weenix. (J.)* | Voor een open Nis hangt een doode Haas aan zijn Loper, nevens denzelven hangen twee Patrijzen, ter zijde eenig dood Gevogelte en ander Jagttuig; alles overeenkomstig de natuur behandeld | *Mat:* op doek *Size:* hoog 44, breed 36 duim	Johannes van de Putte Nicolaasz.	(Sold) fl 300 van Iperen
1810/08/01	AMSCH	0113	*Weeninx (Jan)* | Een prachtig en beeldrijk Hofgezigt; aan den Stam van eenen Boom hangen twee doode Hazen [sic], nevens onderscheiden Gevogelte; op den voorgrond liggen twee doode Patrijzen en een Fazant; ter zijde staat een Waterhond levensgrootte [Vue magnifique sur l'intérieur d'un Chateau orné de Sculptures, servant de fond à un riche groupe de Gibier mort. On voit suspendus à un tronc d'arbre deux Lièvres morts et plusieurs espèces d'oiseaux. Un peu en avant on trouve deux Perdrix et un Phaisan tués. Un Chien de Chasse à longs poils vient épier cette Chasse par la droite. Ces objets sont rendus de grandeur naturelle] | *Annots:* NB : mauvaise composition. (NGW); Vente le Brun No. 103 fr: 7200 (SMLN) *Mat:* op doek *Size:* hoog 62, breed 82 duimen	Mr Pieter de Smeth van Alphen	(Sold) fl 1130 Texier, Gerbet en Comp [for] LeBrun
1810/08/01	AMSCH	0114	*Weeninx (Jan)* | Een Hofgezigt, waarin een doode Haas; ter zijde ligt een doode Haan, Duiven en ander Gevogelte; op den voorgrond eene Mand met Vruchten [Un Lièvre mort suspendu, groupé avec un Cocq, des Pigeons et autre Volaille ; au devant se trouve un Panier garni de fruit. Une perspective de Parc et un Chateau composent le fond du Tableau] | *Annots:* NB : très foible. (NGW) *Mat:* op doek *Size:* hoog 48, breed 40 duimen	Mr Pieter de Smeth van Alphen	(Sold) fl 590 C S Roos

1810/08/01	AMSCH	0115	*Weeninx (Jan)* | Een doode Haas, Patrijzen en ander Gevogelte tegen eenen Boom; waarachter een Jongen met eenen Jagthond; op den voorgrond ligt een Kruidhoorn en Jagttuig [Un groupe composé d'un Lievre, de Perdrix, et d'autre Gibier mort, appuyé contre un Arbre, derriere lequel on voit un Jeunehomme et un Chien de Chasse ; audevant du Tableau est posé un Cornet avec des ustenciles de Chasse] | *Annots:* NB : sans aucun effet. (NGW) *Mat:* op doek *Size:* hoog 47, breed 40 duimen	Mr Pieter de Smeth van Alphen	(Sold) fl 650 Cremer te Rotterdam
1810/08/01	AMSCH	0116	*Weeninx (Jan)* | Een Hofgezigt, waarin twee doode Hanen en een Kalkoen, op den voorgrond Perziken en andere Vruchten, ter zijde bij eenen boom Bloemen en Fruiten [Audevant de ce Tableau on voit deux Cocqs et un Dindon morts, ainsi que des Pêches et d'autres Fruits. Sur la coté, auprès d'un Arbre, il y a des Fleurs et des Fruits. La perspective d'un Chateau sert de fond à ce composé] | *Annots:* NB : sans effet. (NGW) *Mat:* op doek *Size:* hoog 47, breed 40 duimen	Mr Pieter de Smeth van Alphen	(Sold) fl 400 Beekmans te Antwerpe
1810/08/06	AMSCH	0117	*Weenix (J.)* | Dit fraaije Voorwerp verbeelt een Boschachtig Landschap, vooraan op een Steenen Balustrade ligt een doode Haas, rustende tegens een Vaas, waarbij een koppel Patrijsen en verschillend Jagttuig, in het midden ligt een dode Faisant, verder een Patrijshond, blaffende tegen een vliegende Duif; alles evenaart de natuur, het is krachtig en van eene uitmuntende penceelsbehandeling | *Mat:* op doek *Size:* hoog 34, breed 59 duimen	A	(Sold) fl 705 T Spaan
1810/08/06	AMSCH	0118	*Weenix (J.)* | Een doode Haas, met eenig Gevogelte. Fiks en schetsachtig behandeld | *Mat:* op doek *Size:* hoog 44, breed 36 duimen		(Withdrawn)
1810/08/10	RMRIJ	0013	*Jan Weenix* | Op den voorgrond een Haas, Patrijzen, Weijtas en verder bijwerk, in het verschiet een Hofgezicht. Konstig en meesterlijk geordonneerd en behandeld | *Mat:* op doek *Size:* hoog 37 ½ duim, breed 31 duim		(Sold) fl 30 [or] 151 Lugtmans
1810/08/10	RMRIJ	0014	*Jan Weenix* | Een Haas, en hangende Patrijs. Natuurlijk verbeeld | *Mat:* op doek *Size:* hoog 29 duim, breed 24 duim		(Sold) fl 25 [or] 28 v Dyk
1810/10/11	AMSCH	0094	*J. Wenix* | Een gewerkte Vaas, gevuld met eene menigte geurige Bloemen, als roode en witte Roozen, Afrikanen en anderen; meesterlijk geschilderd | *Mat:* op doek *Size:* hoog 18, breed 14 duimen	[Gruyter?]	(Bought In) fl 4:10
1810/10/11	AMSCH	0168	*J. Wenix* | Op een Bank ligt een geslagt en opgemaakt Speenvarken; kloek geschilderd	[Levy Pakker?]	(Sold) fl 1 Gruiter

Weenix (or Weenix, manner)

1805/12/16	AMSCH	0057	*J. Weenix* | Een Landschap, waar in verscheide Jagthonden die een Hartebeest vervolgen door het Water, ter zyde ziet men twee Jagers, meesterlyk behandeld op Doek, door of in de manier van J. Weenix | *Mat:* op doek *Size:* hoog 48, breed 54 duim	Spaan	(Sold) fl 3:5 L Pakker

Weenix (manner)

1802/08/24	LNDLS	0132	*Weninx* | Een Haas hangende aan zijn looper, benevens dood gevogelte in een Landschap, in de trant van Weninx | *Mat:* op doek	Leonardus Bouman [or others]	(Unknown) fl 8:5
1809/10/16	ARNIJ	0001	*Wenix* | Een stuk met een dooden Haas en Patrijs en verder bijwerk, in de manier van Wenix	Wed N Nijhoff	(Bought In) fl 18:10

Weenix, Jan Baptist (Ratel)

1801/04/13	AMSCH	0089	*G. B. Wenix* | Op den voorgrond van een prachtig gebouw aan een Levantsche Zeehaven, ligt een Jongeling tegens een koffer te slapen, waarby eenige harnassen, een vaandel en een aap, verders eenige beelden, vaartuigen, en een uitgestrekt verschiet; het zonlicht is frappant en de schildering meesterlyk | companion to lot 90 *Mat:* op doek *Size:* hoog 33, breed 43 duim	Pierre Fouquet, junior	(Sold) fl 140 Spruit van Gend
1801/04/13	AMSCH	0090	*G.B. Wenix* | Dit stuk in alles als de voorgaande, verbeeld mede een grootsch Gebouw, aan een Levantsche Haven, en is mede ryk gestoffeerd en niet minder van schildering, kunnende zeer gepast tot een wederga dienen | companion to lot 89 *Mat:* op doek *Size:* hoog 32, breed 42 duim	Pierre Fouquet, junior	(Sold) fl 145 Lafontaine
1801/04/13	AMSCH	0091	*G.B. Wenix* | En Italiaansch Landschap met Ruïnes, Fonteinen, en een aangenaam verschiet, de voorgrond gestoffeerd met een Jonge op een Bok, waarby nog een andere met een hond, verder een rustende Heer, Dame en verdere stoffagie; zonachtig en meesterlyk gepenceeld | *Mat:* op paneel *Size:* hoog 16, breed 19 duim	Pierre Fouquet, junior	(Sold) fl 69 Lafontaine
1801/06/10	AMSCH	0190	*Weenix. (G.B.)* | Een Levantsche Zeehaven, gestoffeerd met verscheiden Scheepen, op de voorgrond ziet men eenige Persoonen in een Schuit, in een bergachtig verschiet een menigte Scheepen; zonachtig en fiks behandeld | *Mat:* op doek *Size:* hoog 17, breed 21 duim	Herman ten Kate	(Sold) fl 41 Pruyssenaar
1802/05/05	AMSCH	0232	*G. B. Wenix* | Voor een pragtig Gebouw ziet men een Heer en twee Dames, waarby een springende Hond, en een Paauw op een Balustrade, in het verschiet by een grootsch Gedenkteken ziet men een Zeehaven, met een menigte stoffagie van Beelden, kragtig | *Mat:* op doek *Size:* hoog 33, breed 27 duim	D	(Bought In) fl 190
1802/09/29	AMSCH	0059	*G. B. Weenix* | Een Landschap, hoog 30 ¾, breed 25 ¾ duim. op Doek. In een Italiaansch uitgestrekt Landschap, by schoone overblyfselen der	[Labouchere?]	(Sold) fl 101 W Reijers

			Oudheid, ziet men rustende Landlieden eenige ververschingen gebruiken, een derzelven vermaakt zig met een Hond, verders een grazend Paard en eenig toepasselyk Bywerk; zynde dit eene zeer bevallige Ordenantie, en de Penceelbehandeling is zeer kunstig en meesterlyk fraai, alles is zonägtig en zeer natuurlyk verbeeld [Un Riche point de Vue de Paysage orné de restes Imposans de la haute antiquité sur un Terrein élevé ; pres desquels se reposent des Moissoneurs prenant un repas rustique ; le Premier plan à gauche offre les détails analoques au sujet. Plusieurs objets intéressans, enrichissent cette belle & sage composition, dont le faire est de cette touche et de cette grande Harmonie, de couleur egale à la nature.] | *Mat:* op doek *Size:* hoog 30 ¾, breed 25 ¾ duim		
1803/07/18	AMSCH	0059	*Weenix. (G. B.)* | Ter linkerzyde van dit Tafreel ziet men een prachtige Colonnade, voor dewelke op een Heuvel een Vrouw ligt te slaapen, wordende door een man in het aangezigt gekitteld, waarnevens een ander Man op een stok leunende staat te kyken, voor hun een menigte Vee, zoo Koeyen, Schaapen als Bokken, verders een aangenaam verschiet, dit stuk in den aart van Pynacker is van een schoone Ordonantie, aangenaame couleur en meesterlyke schildering [Près d'une collonade Toscane est un groupe de quatre figures : une femme endormie, que l'on veut éveiller en lui causant quelque chatouillement au visage, occupe les trois pâtres autour d'elle. Vèrs le milieu est un homme debout appuyé sur son baton ; il se tourne du côté de son nombreux troupeau de chêvres, de boeufs, de moutons & d'anes couchés ou paturans pèle-mele. A la gauche est un homme à cheval auquel une femme indique la route. Le fond orné de quelques figures donne sur des colines éloignées & sur des ruines d'antiques batimens. Un ciel lumineux repand harmonieusement ses raïons sur tous les objets de cette admirable composition. Ce tableau un des capiteaux ouvrages de ce maître, peut très bien souténir la comparaison avec les chef d'oeuvres des Berghem & des Pynacker : les figures savamment dessinées, une couleur brillante & forte, une manière large & précieusement soignée, ajoutons le plus bel effet de lumiere désirable, doivent lui assurer une place distinguée dans un cabinet du meilleur choix.] | *Mat:* op doek *Size:* hoog 37, breed 48 duim	Maria Theresia Andrioli	(Sold) fl 275 Pruijssenaar
1803/09/07	AMSCH	0214	*G. B. Wénix* | In een Boomryk Landschap zit een Vrouw met een Kind op de Schoot, waarby een man met een Ezel, ter zyde en in het verschiet een menigte Bokken en Schaapen; de schildering is van de beste van G. B. Wénix [Dans un paysage bocageux, est assise une femme avec un enfant sur son giron ; à côté un homme avec un âne, à l'entour et dans l'éloignement des chévres et des brébis ; ce tableau est un des meilleurs de ce maître] | *Mat:* op paneel *Size:* hoog 22, breed 32 duim	Smidt	(Sold) fl 81 Tessier
1803/12/15	MGLAC	0014	*J. B. Weninks* | In dit Schildery vertoond zich een dode Haas en klein gevogelte, benevens een Jagtroer en Weitas, in een aangenaam Landschap; alles zeer delicaat en uitvoerig geschilderd | *Mat:* op doek *Size:* hoog duim 34, breed duim 27	Mr L H de Haze Bomme	(Unknown)
1804/05/07	AMSCH	0190	*Wenix. (G.B.)* | In een Italiaansch Boom- en Bergachtig Landschap, ziet men op een heuvel en meenigte staand en leggend Vee, zoo ook in het verschiet, op de voorgrond by eenige Kruiden, zit een Herder met een Hond, alles van een meesterlyke schildering | *Mat:* op doek *Size:* hoog 27, breed 32 duim	Roos [for] A	(Sold) fl 235 Coclers
1804/10/16	DLOND	0257	*G. B. Wenix* | Een Landschap waarop een Vrouw te Paerd en meer voor ene Grot. Paysage, ou l'on voit une Femme a Cheval, avec d'autres figures, devant une Grotte | *Mat:* op paneel *Size:* hoog 17, breed 13		(Unknown)
1805/04/23	HOBEE	0003	*G.B. Wenix* | Twee stukken, met Antique Beelden en Ruines, meesterlyk met stoffagien geschilderd op Doek | *Mat:* op doek		(Unknown)
1806/08/13	AMSCH	0211	*Wenix. (G. B.)* | In een aangenaam Heuvelachtig Landschap, ziet men eenige staande en rustende Schapen en Bokken, benevens een wit bonte Koe, waarby een Boerin met twee Melkëmmers, verders een Duinachtig verschiet; dit stukje is aller delicaatst en uitvoerig van schildering | *Mat:* op paneel *Size:* hoog 13, breed 11 duim	Vinkeles [for] F	(Sold) fl 32 Teengs
1807/08/26	AMSCH	0232	*J.B. Weenix* | Een Italiaansch Landschap, op welks voorgrond men ter linkerzyde, by een Pedestal, waarop een Paard dat door een Leeuw verscheurd wordt, een bejaard Man ziet zitten, die een Brief leest, en naast hem een Jongeling, spelende met een Yzeren Solitaire. Aan de regterzyde een zwartbonte liggende Bok en drie Schapen, verder een Karavane, en in 't verschiet een Zeehaven; dit Stuk is schoon van koloriet; meesterlyk en krachtig gepenceeld | *Mat:* op doek *Size:* hoog 32, breed 38 duim	Roos	(Withdrawn)
1808/06/06	RMRIJ	0135	*Weenix. (Jan Baptist)* | Eene aan den tak van eenen boom, en aan zijnen achtersten looper hangende levensgroote Haas. Ter zijde derzelve twee Patrijzen en op den voorgrond een Groninger. Eene Weitas, een Kruidhoorn, Planten en Bloemen, benevens eene steenen Vaas ziet men op den tweeden grond; – een grootsch Hofgezigt in 't verschiet. Een beter Tafereel, van dezen Meester, zoo in konst, natuur als schoonheid, is ons niet bekend [Un beau Liévre attaché par sa patte de derrière à une branche d'arbre ; auprès de lui deux Perdreaux morts et une Linotte. Une Gibecière, un Cornet à poudre, des fleurs, des Plantes, et un Vase décorent le devant, et le lointain offre une Perspective de Jardin etc. Ce Morceau est un chef-d'oeuvre, et nous ne connoissons aucun Tableau de cet Artiste, qui soit supérieur en mérite à celui-ci] | *Annots:* NB le No.135 est	Gerrit van der Pot, Heer van Groeneveld	(Sold) fl 2510 Johs Eck en Zoon [for] le Roi

			peint par Jean Weenix, et il est très inferieur à celui de ma Collection, tant pour la capitalité que pour l'exécution (MA) *Mat:* op doek *Size:* Hoog 43, en breed 36 duim *Loc:* Amsterdam, Nederland. Rijksmuseum. (A464) as J. Weenix		
1808/06/06	RMRIJ	0136	*Weenix. (Jan Baptist)* | Op den voorgrond een liggend Jagtgeweer, Rotgans, Paauw, Patrijzen en Broekexter, benevens eene witte Gans aan één poot hangende; ter zijde eene ongemeen grootsche rijke marmeren Vaas. Een aangenaam Hofgezigt, rijk geboomte, lucht en verschiet maken een konstig geheel. Zijnde dit mede een der kapitale stukken van dezen beroemden Man [Sur le devant d'un beau terrain, et auprès d'un superbe vase de marbre orné d'un bas-relief, on apperçoit une Oie blanche qui a ses âiles étendues, et qui est attachée par une patte, un Morillon, un beau Paon, des Perdrix, des Canards et d'autres volailles. Le lontain [sic] annonce une belle et vaste Campagne. De beaux Arbres et un Ciel agréable ajoutent encore a la beauté de ce magnifique Tableau] | *Annots:* Van Jan de Bosch Jeronimusz, 14 Aug. 1785 (f 525.-) (RMA I) *Mat:* op doek *Size:* Hoog 56 ½, en breed 69 ½ duim	Gerrit van der Pot, Heer van Groeneveld	(Sold) fl 685 Allard
1808/08/23	AMSCH	0165	*Weenix. (G. B.)* | Een Italiaansch Landschap, op welks voorgrond met ter linkerzijde bij een Pedestal, waar op een Paard dat door een Leeuw verscheurd word, een bejaard man ziet zitten, die een brief leest, en naast hem een Jongeling, speelende met eene ijseren [sic] Solitaire, aan de regterzijde een zwart bonte leggende Bok en drie Schaapen, verder een Caravane, en in 't verschiet een Zeehaven; dit stuk is schoon van koloriet, meesterlijk en krachtig gepenceeld | *Mat:* op doek *Size:* hoog 32, breed 38 duim	[Coclers]	(Sold) fl 101 Ryfsnyder
1808/08/23	AMSCH	0166	*Weenix. (G. B.)* | In een Bergachtig Landschap vertoond zig ter regterzijde den optogt van een Ambassadeur, waar bij eenige Heeren te Paard, in onderscheiden rijke Kleeding, op de voorgrond eene meenigte Vrouwen en Kinderen, ter linkerzijde een woelende Zee met zeilende Scheepen, en in 't verschiet een rijk gestoffeerd Strand; zonachtig en van een uitmuntende penceelbehandeling | *Mat:* op doek *Size:* hoog 38, breed 68 duim	C	(Sold) fl 140 Coclers
1809/04/17	AMSCH	0148	*J.B. Weenix* | Een Italiaansch Landschap, met overblijfsels van aloude prachtige Gebouwen, gestoffeerd met Landlieden en Vee; zonachtig en krachtig geschilderd | *Mat:* op doek	[Gruyter?]	(Sold or Bought In) fl 1 Gruyter
1809/04/22	AMYVR	0145	*G.B. Weenix* | Een Historieele Ordonantie in eene Italiaansche Stad; krachtig en meesterlijk geschilderd | *Mat:* op doek *Size:* hoog 25, breed 35 duim	de Bruin	(Bought In) fl 29
1810/06/20	AMSCH	0106	*G. B. Weenix* | Een Zeehaven, rijk gestoffeerd met wandelende Heeren en Dames, Kooplieden, Paarden enz.; in het verschiet eene ruime Zee met Schepen. Meesterlijk geschilderd | *Mat:* op doek *Size:* hoog 62, breed 48 duimen	S	(Sold) fl 2 Boelhouwer
1810/08/01	AMSCH	0117	*Weeninx (Gio Baptista)* | Een Italiaansch Gezigt, met aloude Gedenkteekens; op den voorgrond een Bevelhebber te paard, in eene gebiedende houding, voor hem eene knielende Vrouw en smeekende Jongen; verder andere Lieden en eene menigte Vee; een Zeehaven in het verschiet [Un Site pris en Italie, varié par des Monuments de l'Antiquité. Sur le devant du Tableau se distingue un Guerrier à Cheval, dans une attitude de commandement, devant lequel une Femme et un jeune Garçon paroissent implorer sa pitié. Plus en arriere on rencontre d'autres personnages et une multitude de Bêtail, un Port de Mer formant la perspective] | *Annots:* NB : fort médiocre. (NGW); Copie le même au Musée (BPG) *Mat:* op doek *Size:* hoog 41, breed 57 duimen	Mr Pieter de Smeth van Alphen	(Bought In) fl 410
1810/08/01	AMSCH	0118	*Weeninx (Gio Baptista)* | Een Italiaansch bergachtig Landschap, met grootsche Gebouwen en Gedenkteekenen, verlevendigd door Reizigers en andere Lieden [Un Site montagneux pris en Italie, varié par des vastes Batiments et des Monuments de l'Antiquité, orné de Passagers et d'autres figures] | *Annots:* NB : frappant ; mais trop émaillé et papillotant. (NGW); Vente le Brun No. 101 fr: 6005 (SMLN) *Mat:* op paneel *Size:* hoog 30, breed 40 duimen	Mr Pieter de Smeth van Alphen	(Sold) fl 900 Texier, Gerbet en Comp [for] LeBrun
1810/08/06	AMSCH	0120	*Weenix (G.B.)* | Aan het Strand ziet men eenen Visscher, welke een Mand met Visch uitstort, verders eene menigte onderscheide Visschen en een aangenaam verschiet | *Mat:* op doek *Size:* hoog 70, breed 98 duimen	R[oos]	(Sold) fl 41 van Iperen
1810/10/11	AMSCH	0095	*J. B. Wenix* | De Ruïne van een oud Gebouw, waarbij eenige Beeldjes | *Mat:* op paneel *Size:* hoog 11, breed 14 duimen	C	(Sold) fl 2 Posthumus
			Weenix, Jan Baptist (Ratel) (and Berchem, N.P.)		
1810/08/06	AMSCH	0119	*Weenix (G.B.); Gestoffeerd door N. Berchem* | Dit fraaije kapitale Tafreel verbeelt eene ruime Plaats, met grootsche Gebouwen, ter regterzijde bij den opgang van eenen prachtigen Tempel ziet men den Zaligmaker, voor wien eenige Schriftgeleerde en andere Personen elkander de Cijnspenning vertoonende, op den voorgrond op een Steenen Trap een zittende Jongeling, houdende een Paauw, waarbij drie staande Honden, verder een Landman en Vrouw bij onderscheiden Vee en een Zeehaven in het verschiet; dit stuk is bevallig van schikking, krachtig en schoon geschilderd en zeldzaam zoo fraai voorkomende | *Mat:* op paneel *Size:* hoog 37, breed 45 duimen *Loc:* Den Haag, Nederland. Mauritshuis. (1058)	A	(Sold) fl 765 J Spaan

Weenix, Jan Baptist (Ratel) (and Waterloo, A.)

1802/06/16	AMSCH	0211	*A. Waterlo; G. B. Wenix* | Dit uitmundtend en zeldzaam voorkomend Kunststuk, steld voor een Boschryk Landschap met hoog Geboomte beplant, in 't verschiet een Kasteel aan een Rivier, voorts met een meenigte Jagers met Paarden en Honden gestoffeerd; het Coloriet en licht en bruin is byzonder met de natuur overëenkomende; en kan voor het fraayste dat van deezen Meester bekend is, gehoudend worden | *Mat:* op doek *Size:* hoog 51, breed 16 duim	[Merrem]	(Sold) fl 210 H de Valk

Weenix, Jan Baptist (Ratel) (or Weenix, J.B., manner)

1801/05/11	AMSCH	0110	*G.B. Wenix, of in de manier* | Een Levantsche Zeehaaven, met verscheiden beelden gestoffeerd, ter zyden ziet men eenige Scheepen alles delicaat behandeld | *Mat:* op paneel *Size:* hoog 48, breed 61 duim	Pruisse [for] M	(Sold) fl 50 Allard
1810/03/23	HAVIN	0061	*J.B. Wenix* | Een Watergezigt met een Pont, van of in de manier van J.B. Wenix	Rudolf Hendrik de Wetstein [or others]	(Unknown)

Weenix, Jan Baptist (Ratel) (manner)

1801/03/16	AMSCH	0151	*G.B. Weenix* | Een Bybelsche Ordonantie, ryk en bevallig gepenceeld, als G.B. Weenix	K[ip]	(Sold) fl 2 Stevens
1802/06/16	AMSCH	0235	*B. G. Wenix* | Een Jager met eenige Honden in een heuvelachtig Landschap met Geboomten, zynde van een meesterlyke en kloeke behandeling, in de manier van B. G. Wenix | *Mat:* op doek *Size:* hoog 35, breed 38 duim	[Merrem]	(Sold) fl 15 van Iperen
1802/09/06	AMSCH	0223	*J. G. Weeninx* | Een Italiaansche Zéehaven, gestoffeert op de voorgrond met een fontyn, en trots gebouw, verder in de Haven diversche Scheepen; zonagtig geschilderd op Doek, in de manier van J. G. Weeninx | *Mat:* op doek *Size:* hoog 20, breed 17 duim *Notes:* The artist's name was given as "J. G. Weeninx" but we have assumed this is an error.	X	(Sold) fl 0:10 L Pakker
1807/08/26	AMSCH	0297	*G.B. Wenix* | Een Italiaansch Gezicht met een Ruïne, met Jagers en Honden; als G.B. Wenix	Joseph Vallette	(Sold) fl 8 Coclair

Weenix, Juffrouw [Unidentified]

1810/05/22	AMSCH	0126	*Weenix (Jufvr.)* | Dit voorwerp verbeeldt een omgevallen Vaas, met verscheide Bloemen, waarbij een Eekhoorentje en verder bijwerk; meesterlijk fraai gepenceeld | *Mat:* op doek	Johannes van de Putte Nicolaasz.	(Sold) fl 11:10 Voet [through] T Spaan
1810/07/26	AMSCH	0143	*Weenix (Juff.)* | Voor een open Steenen Nis, liggen onderscheidene keurige Bloemen, met Steelen en Bladeren, achter een opgeschoven Gordijn, boven aan op een Wijngaard twee Papegaaien. Uitvoerig en zeer fraai geschilderd | *Mat:* op doek *Size:* hoog 51, breed 42 duimen	Cassino	(Bought In) fl 30

Weirother, N. [Unidentified]

1802/06/16	AMSCH	0227	*N. Weirother* | Een Boomryk Landschap, waar in een Boere Woning, gestoffeerd met een Wandelaar; het Zonlicht doet een natuurlyke werking, en is meesterlyk gepenceeld | *Mat:* op doek *Size:* hoog 9, breed 10 duim	[Merrem]	(Sold) fl 2:10 Vermeulen

Wel, W.V. [Unidentified]

1802/07/27	AKHRK	000C	*W. V. Wel* | Een genoeglijk Huisgezin aan een Tafel, waar op een Ham: Zingende een Lied, een staande speelt op een Blaasbalg, terwijl op de voorgrond een Vrouw geliefkoosd werd. Goed van licht en bruin | companion to lot D *Mat:* op paneel *Size:* hoog 13 ½, breed 19 duim	Maria Stategaart	(Sold) fl 12 for lots C & D. L Veer
1802/07/27	AKHRK	000D	*W. V. Wel* | Dito, de weerga van dezelve. Een ongenoeglijke Vegtpartij. Hier is de woede op het felst [sic]; twee Vrouwen houden een Man tegen, die zijne onderliggende Partij met een Schop naar het Hoofd wil bruijen, die een Mes in de Hand heeft. Verder een Man met een Bezem de Herberg uit komende, om dit Volkje te scheiden | companion to lot C *Notes:* It is unclear what "dito" refers to in the title.	Maria Stategaart	(Sold) fl 12 for lots C & D. L Veer

Werff, Adriaen van der

1801/04/13	AMSCH	0086	*A. van der Werf* | Deeze Ordonantie verbeeld Batzeba naakt zittende aan het bad, aangesproken wordende door een oude matrone, zy zit op een zeer uitvoerig gewerkt tapyte kleed, en word door een helder zonlicht beschenen; dit tafereel is van een delicaate penceelsbehandling | *Mat:* op doek *Size:* hoog 22, breed 15 duim	Pierre Fouquet, junior	(Sold) fl 110 Lafontaine
1801/04/13	AMSCH	0087	*A. van der Werf* | Een bevallige Hospita met een stuk geld in de eene, en een lei in de andere hand, waarop zy het gelach aangeteekend heeft, op de Tafel een roemer met een pyp; delicaat en uitvoerig geschilderd | *Mat:* op paneel *Size:* hoog 7, breed 5 ½ duim	Pierre Fouquet, junior	(Sold) fl 105 for lots 87 & 88. Lafontaine
1801/04/13	AMSCH	0088	*A. van der Werf* | Een Jongeling in wit satyne kleeding, met een medaille in de eene, en een roemer in de andere hand; mede van dezelve behandeling | *Size:* hoog 7, breed 5 ½ duim	Pierre Fouquet, junior	(Sold) fl 105 for lots 87 & 88. Lafontaine
1801/05/11	AMSCH	0109	*De Ridder van der Werf* | Twee stuks, een Mans en een Vrouwe Pourtret, beiden in deftige Hollandsche Kleeding, zeer uitvoerig en krachtig gepenceeld | *Mat:* op doek *Size:* hoog 19, breed 15 duim	P[ruyssenaar]	(Sold) fl 103 Pruijssenaar [and] R [for] Cocler
1801/10/19	AMSCH	0083	*Werff. (de Ridder A. van der)* | In dit keurig stuk, ziet men het Pourtrait van P. van der Werf, staande met 't Palet en Penceele in de hand, agter zig een Ballustrade gedekt door een Tapyt, waar op hy met de rechterhand	Jonkheer Menno Baron van Coehoorn	(Sold) fl 205 Booijmans

			Rust, verder een Schildery op den Schilders-Ezel, en een Borstbeeld op een Piedestal, beneeden de ballustrade een Basrelief; alles is zeer uitneemend vertoond, kunstig van coloriet, en uitvoerig geschilderd | *Mat:* op doek *Size:* hoog 19, breed 16 duim		
1803/07/18	AMSCH	0061	*Werf. (Adr. van der)* | Door een steene Nis ziet men een Jongeling met een Muizeval in zyn hand, nevees [sic] hem een Meisje, zy schynen zeer te vreden te zyn over de vangst, de Kat voor de Nis zittende schynt te verlangen naar dat Muisje, op een gewerkt Tapyt legt de Hoed met Pluimen van den Jongeling, bevallig aangenaam van couleur en uitvoerig geschilderd [Dans l'embrasure d'une niche se voit un jeune homme tenant une sourisiere ; une petitte fille à son côté paroit toute émerveillée de la prise, etendant les mains dans son ravissement. Le chat attentif attend la proie au bas de l'entablure de pierre. Devant le jeune homme est posé un tapis replié sur lequel est son chapeau à plumets. Au dessus des figures pend un rideau verd qui termine le fond. Ce joli morceau d'une touche précieuse & d'une fonte de couleur admirable à de l'expression & beaucoup de vérité.] | *Mat:* op paneel *Size:* hoog 14, breed 10 duim	Maria Theresia Andrioli	(Sold) fl 112 Coclers
1803/09/07	AMSCH	0213	*van der Werf* | In een Landschap ziet men Maria, zittende met het kind Jesus op haar schoot, waar by St. Jan en verder Joseph met een Boek op zyn schoot, zeer fraay en delicaat gepenceeld [La Ste. Vierge, ayant l'enfant Jesus sur ses genoux, assise dans un joli paysage ; à côté d'elle St. Jean et plus loin St. Joseph, lisant dans un livre : d'une exécution délicate et précieuse] | *Mat:* op paneel *Size:* hoog 11, breed 9 duim	Smidt	(Bought In) fl 30
1804/07/25	AMSCH	0087	*Werf (A. van der)* | In een Landschap, by het Standbeeld van de Veldgod Pan, ziet men Boréas die de schoone Orythia tragt te omhelzen en door haar met den eenen Hand werd afgekeerd, terwyl zy met de andere een Boom tot haar redding aanvat, in 't verschiet, schynen vier anderen Nimphen dit voorval met aandagt te aanschouwen; het naakt en kleederen, zyn in dit uitmuntend Cabinetstukje aller delicaats behandeld, het coloriet bevallig, en alles uitvoerig en fraai gepenceeld | *Mat:* op doek *Size:* hoog 19, breed 15 duim		(Sold) fl 200 van der Schleij
1804/10/29	HRBAU	0115	*Werf, (A. van der)* | Door een Nis ziet men een' Krygsman, met een zeer vergenoegd gelaat, zyn pypjen stoppen: hy ziet een ieder lachgend aan, als of hy iets aartigs wilde verhaalen; hy is gekleed in een geelen lederen Kolder, waar over hy een staalen Cuiras getrokken heeft, en eene roode Echarpe om het lyf. Dit alles is zeer kragtig, smeltend, en de lederen Kolder zoo uitmuntend natuurlyk behandeld, als men slegts zeer zelden zien zal | *Mat:* op paneel *Size:* hoog 5 ½, breed 4 ½ duim	Simon Styl	(Unknown)
1808/04/26	GDAN	0183	*Werf, Ridder (A. van d.)* | Een prachtige Vorstelijke Stal, waar in de Statie Koets te zien is, voorts twee uitmuntende blaauwe Paarden, die door den Vorst zelve bezien worden, in bijzijn van zijne lieve Kinderen, en een Neger, alles deftig en groots uitgedoscht, met eene lange of Windhond, zijnde dit Kabinetstukje allernaauwkeurigst geschilderd en extra fraai | *Size:* hoog 8, breed 10 duim	G H Fortuyn	(Unknown)
1808/04/26	GDAN	0184	*Werf, Ridder (A. van d.)* | Een schoone Jongeling, met een Fluit in de eene en een gevederde Hoed in de ander Hand | *Size:* hoog 16 ½, breed 12 duim	G H Fortuyn	(Unknown)
1808/04/26	GDAN	0185	*Werf, Ridder (A. van d.)* | Een dito [schoone] Herderin, met Schietboog Koker, en twee Honden aan een leijsel, cierlijk uitgedoscht in Kleding, en fiks en kragtig behandeld | *Size:* hoog 16 ½, breed 12 duim	G H Fortuyn	(Unknown)
1808/06/06	RMRIJ	0137	*Werff. (Ridder Adriaan van der)* | Eene Heilige Familie. Maria, (zijnde de afbeelding van wijle Mevrouwe van der Werff,) in eene rustende houding, heeft voor zich liggen, het kindje Jezus, dat, spelende, vrolijk grijpt naar een takje met rijpe Kersen, hem door Jozef aangeboden wordende. Teekening, koloriet, draperij, alles is in dit uitmuntend Tafereel even schoon, en het kan als een der meesterstukken van dien Ridder aangemerkt worden. Hetzelve versierde eertijds het beroemd kabinet van den Hertog van Choiseul, en is, in Plaat, in de daarvan bekende gegraveerde collectie te vinden [Ce chef-d'oeuvre de van der Werff represente une sainte famille. La Vierge (le portrait de Madame van der Werff) est assise, et tient l'enfant Jésus sur ses genoux, tandis que Saint Joseph offre une branche de cerisier, dont l'Enfant en souriant tâche de cueillir les fruits. La Composition Savante et gracieuse, le dessin pur, la Carnation la plus fraiche, l'ensemble harmonieux, et l'Éxécution parfaite, font considerer ce Morceau comme un des plus précieux de ce grand Peintre. Il a été longtems l'ornement du Cabinet du Duc de Choiseul. On en trouve une Gravure dans le recueil dudit Cabinet] | *Annots:* Pour le Musée d'Amsterdam (NGW) *Mat:* op paneel *Size:* Hoog 13 ½, en breed 10 ½ duim *Loc:* Amsterdam, Nederland. Rijksmuseum. (A468)	Gerrit van der Pot, Heer van Groeneveld	(Sold) fl 5225 Stratenus
1808/06/06	RMRIJ	0138	*Werff. (Ridder Adriaan van der) 1700* | Bij eene fraaije Architectuur, een aan een Pedestal staande, en in rijke kleeding gedost deftig man, met beide handen op een boek rustende. Krachtig, uitvoerig en delicaat behandeld. Kniestuk [Le Portrait d'un homme de distinction noblement vêtu, qui appuye les mains sur un livre posé sur un Piédestal. Une belle Architecture, et dans le lointain une Campagne etc. Un bel effet, un grand fini, et de la vigueur brillent dans ce Tableau] | *Annots:* Gerard Visch uit den boedel van groatmoeder de Lange (RMA I) *Mat:* op doek *Size:* Hoog 18, en breed 14 ½ duim *Inscr:* Adriaan van der Werff. 1700	Gerrit van der Pot, Heer van Groeneveld	(Sold) fl 242 R Pott

			(signed and dated?) *Notes:* It is unclear whether the name and date are inscribed on the painting.		
1808/06/06	RMRIJ	0139	*Werff. (Ridder Adriaan van der) 1690* | In een Hofgezigt ziet men, bij eene prachtige fontein, eenen Jongeling rijk gekleed aan eenen Parkiet een Amandel aanbiedende. Zeer uitvoerig en schoon geschilderd. Kniestuk [Dans un beau Jardin, et près d'une Fontaine, un jeune homme richement habillé presente de la main droite du Bonbon à un Perroquet, qu'il tient à sa main gauche. Un grand fini, un Coloris vrai et brillant, et beaucoup de force font distinguer ce joli Tableau] | *Annots:* Ubriens[?] teenirarum[?] de Lange als voren [lot 138] (RMA I) *Mat:* op doek *Size:* Hoog 18, en breed 14 ½ duim *Inscr:* Adriaan van der Werff. 1690 (signed and dated?) *Notes:* It is unclear whether the name and date are inscribed on the painting.	Gerrit van der Pot, Heer van Groeneveld	(Sold) fl 187 Coclers
1810/05/22	AMSCH	0115	*Werff. (de Ridder A. van der)* | Dit fraaije stukje verbeeldt eenen eerwaardigen Grijsaard, in Pelgrims gewaad, zittende in een Grot, lezende in een Boek dat voor hem ligt, waarbij een Inktkoker en Pen, benevens een Pot met Bloemen geplaatst zijn, ter zijde ligt een Rol Papier, waarop een Doodshoofd; het is van eene uitmuntende en uitvoerige penceel-behandeling | *Mat:* op paneel *Size:* hoog 15, breed 12 duim	T	(Bought In) fl 190
1810/08/01	AMSCH	0131[H]	*A VanderWerff* | Portrait d'homme | *Annots:* Een Heer ten halve legt rustende met de linker arm op een balustrade door C. van der Werff (FLNY) *Notes:* This lot was added in by hand in the FLNY and NGW I copies of the catalogue.	M[r] Pieter de Smeth van Alphen	(Sold) fl 100 J de Vries
1810/08/06	AMSCH	0121	*Werf (de Ridder A. van der)* | Twee stuks, een deftig Heer en eene Dame, beide in rijke kleeding en rustende op steenen Balustraden; teder en zeer uitvoerig geschilderd | *Mat:* op doek *Size:* ieder is hoog 18 ½, breed 15 duimen *Loc:* Glasgow, Scotland, UK. Art Gallery. (630) female portrait only	R[oos]	(Sold) fl 100 van Leen [or] de Lelie
1810/08/06	AMSCH	0122	*Werf (de Ridder A. van der)* | Twee stuks, als de voorgaande en van gelijke schildering | *Size:* ieder is hoog 18 ½, breed 15 duimen	R[oos]	(Sold) fl 45 Mensart
1810/10/10	MGCIT	0045	*Ridder A. van der Werff* | Een weenend Vroutje, met een Sluiër om het hoofd en met een gouden beker in de hand, zittende voor een marmere tafel, waar op een Kistje met veelerhande kostbaarheden, uitnemend delicaat gepenceeld	Caspar van Citters	(Unknown)
			Werff, Adriaen van der (copy after)		
1802/08/24	LNDLS	0137	*v. d. Werff* | Christus en de Samaritaansche Vrouw bij den Put, na v. d. Werff | *Mat:* op paneel	Leonardus Bouman [or others]	(Unknown) fl 3:2
			Werff, Adriaen van der (manner)		
1802/05/10	MGSAN	0028	*A. van der Werf* | Dit Konststuk vertoont daar Christus en Johannes elkander omhelzen in haare kindsche jaaren, waarby Elizabeth, zeer levendig en krachtig gepenseeld, in de manier van A. van der Werf: op Doek, in vergulde Lyst | *Mat:* op doek *Size:* hoog 29 duim, breed 27 duim	Johan Dirk Kruysse	(Unknown) £ 3
1802/09/21	UTHDG	0099	*den Ridder van der Werf* | Lot met zijne Dogters in de spelonk, et verschiet op Sodom. Een fraaije ordonnantie, uitvoerig en transpirant geschildert in de manier van den Ridder van der Werf | *Mat:* op doek *Size:* hoog 17, breed 22 ½ duimen		(Sold) fl 14 La Maine
1805/07/03	AMSCH	0202	*van der Werf* | Een Zinnebeeldig Voorwerp, zynde een rustende Vrouw, houdende een Hoorn van Overvloed in den arm, waar voor eenige Vrugten op haare Schoot legt: terzyde vertoont zig een bedaagd Man en Jongeling; het is bevallig van coloriet, en in de manier van van der Werf behandeld | *Mat:* op doek	R[oos]	(Sold) fl 3:10 Valkert van Giesen
1810/08/01	AMSCH	0132[H]	*Adrien Vanderwerff* | Petite figure de femme dans le goût de Adrien Vanderwerff | *Annots:* Een Vrouwtje aan een Tafel zittende op dezelve een roemer en nevens dezelve Einoesterschelp door van Toll (FLNY) *Notes:* This lot was added in by hand in the FLNY and NGW I copies of the catalogue. *Loc:* Amsterdam, Nederland. Rijksmuseum. (A2347) as follower of A. van der Werff	M[r] Pieter de Smeth van Alphen	(Sold) fl 50 J de Vries
			Werff, H.N. [Unidentified]		
1802/12/13	AMSCH	0175	*H. N. Werff* | In een gemeubileerd Vertrek, zit een Dame, voor een Tafel, waarop een Muzykboek, ter zyde staat een Heer, en zyn byde Musiceerende; kragtig en plaisant geschilderd | *Mat:* op paneel *Size:* hoog 15, breed 12 duim	Florijn [?]	(Sold) fl 2 Mensart
			Werff, Pieter van der		
1801/03/16	AMSCH	0130	*P. van der Werff* | Een biddend Man	P[ruyssenaar]	(Sold) fl 7 v d Schley [for] Ryfsnyder
1801/06/10	AMSCH	0196	*Werf. (P. van der)* | Deeze Ordonantie steld voor, de Historie van Vertumnus en Pomona, het naakt en de Drappereien, zyn aller fraaist hier in waargenomen, en is van een der delicaatsten van dezen Meester | *Annots:* E: JAM F [possibly a signature] (BRB) *Mat:* op paneel *Size:* hoog 22, breed 18 duim	Herman ten Kate	(Sold) fl 210 Gruyter
1801/10/19	AMSCH	0084	*Werff. (Pieter van der)* | En zeer fraaye Ordonantie, vertonende op den voorgrond een bevallig Jongetje en Meisje, speelende met een Vogeltje,	Jonkheer Menno Baron van Coehoorn	(Sold) fl 155 De Roy

			en agter dezelve twee Jongelingen, speelende met een Kat; verders eenige antique Beelden en Piedestal, en een bergachtig Landschap in 't verschiet; ongemeen uitvoerig, delicaat en krachtig geschilderd | *Mat:* op paneel *Size:* hoog 18, breed 14 duim		
1802/06/16	AMSCH	0226	*P. van der Werff* | In een Aangenaam Landschap zit een naakte bevallige Jagt Nimph, op een blauw Zyd Kleed, ter zyde staat een Koker met Pylen: alles natuurlyk en zeer uitvoerig behandeld | *Mat:* op paneel *Size:* hoog 11 ½, breed 10 ½ duim	[Merrem]	(Sold) fl 20 Van der Schley
1802/07/20	MGSAN	0041	*P. v. der Verf* | Een Figuurtje, en verder Bywerk, zeer schoon, op Koper | *Mat:* op koper *Size:* hoog duim 19, breed duim 16		(Unknown)
1802/09/18	RMDRS	0005	*P. van der Werff* | Een Jongen en een Meisje, hunnen aandacht houdende op een Vogeltje dat uit de Kooy ontvlogen is, met verder bywerk; uitvoerig en helder geschildert | *Size:* hoog 12, breed 9 duim	Casper de Haas	(Sold) fl 7:10 Verweij
1803/04/20	AMSCH	0090	*Werf. (P. van de)* | Voor een Steene Baluster, staat een jong Heer, schynende beezig Waterbellen te blaazen, uit een Schulp die hy in de hand houd, zyn Hoed met Linten omvlogten legt op de rand der Borstweering; uitvoerig gepenceeld [Au devant d'une embrasure de niche l'on voit un adolescent formant des boules de savon ; il prend le liquide hors d'une belle coquille ; près de lui est posé son chapeau orné de rubans. Ce sujet agréable est d'un pinceau très Soigné & d'un bel effet.] | *Mat:* op paneel *Size:* hoog 9, breed 7 duim	Maria Magdalena van Sluypwyk, gravinne van Moens	(Sold) fl 4:5 W Reijers
1803/04/20	AMSCH	0091	*Werf. (P. van de)* | Maria Magdaléna in Berouw, in een Woestyn op haar Kniën leggende, voor haar een Doodshoofd en ander bywerk; delicaat en uitvoerig geschilderd [La Magdaleine penitente, dans un desert meditant à genoux sur la mort, orné d'accessoires analogues. Ce morceau est rendu avec expression & d'une execution comme le precedent.] | *Mat:* op paneel *Size:* hoog 17, breed 14 duim	Maria Magdalena van Sluypwyk, gravinne van Moens	(Sold) fl 67 Van Iperen
1806/06/07	RMHSN	0020	*P: van der Werff* | Een Ovaal Mans Pourtrait, door P: van der Werff, op Doek, zonder Lyst | *Mat:* op doek *Fmt:* ovaal	A E K L	(Sold) fl 7 Thijs
1806/11/24	AMSCH	0086	*Werf (P. van der)* | Het Pourtrait van Willem Bosman; delicaat geschilderd, benevens de Prent in Lyst en Glas	Munnikhuizen	(Sold) fl 1 L Pakker
1808/06/13	AMSCH	0216	*P. van der Werf* | De Godin Diana, met eene Godin in gesprek; zacht	E M Engelberts	(Sold) fl 13 Engelberts
1809/09/06	AMSCH	0091	*Werff (P. van der)* | Dit fraaije Kabinetstukje verbeeld de Boetvaardige Maria Magdaléna in een Rotsgezigt nedergeknielt, in een eerbiedige gestalten, schijnt ze aandagtig het oog te houden op een geschreeven rol papier, die voor haar ligt, waarbij ter zijde op den grond een Zalf-bus en Doodshoofd geplaatst is. De hartstogt is kennelijk verbeeld, de teekening, het koloriet en bevallig licht, gepaard met een uitvoerige penceel-behandeling, geven een luister aan dit stuk, als of het door A. van der Werff vervaardigd was | *Mat:* op paneel *Size:* hoog 15, breed 12 duim	Johannes Caudri	(Sold) fl 103 Gruyter

Werff, Pieter van der (or Werff, P., manner)

1805/10/09	HGBSM	V0021	*P. van der Werf* | Het portret van den Konstschilder van Valkenburg, met twee handen, zeer fraay geschilderd, door of in de manier van P. van der Werf, op doek, hoog 13 breet 11 duim, ovaal formaat | *Mat:* op doek *Fmt:* ovaal *Size:* hoog 13 breet 11 duim	T H van Willigen [or others]	(Sold) fl 11:5 Voerman

Werters [Unidentified]

1803/04/20	AMSCH	0099	*Werters* | Twee stuks Historieele Ordenantien, in Antique Landschappen met Gebouwen en een Rivier, beide ryk gestoffeerd met verscheide Beeldjes; en van een meesterlyke uitvoerige penceelsbehandeling [Deux sujets historiques, representés dans des paysages antiques : Compositions abondantes, variées & touchées avec finesse & entendement.] | *Mat:* op koper *Size:* hoog 8, breed 10 duim	Maria Magdalena van Sluypwyk, gravinne van Moens	(Sold) fl 19:10 Pruijssenaar

Westall, Richard

1803/10/25	HHNOM	0001	*R. Westall* | Le jeune Convaincu par le General Paoli de la necessite de la Mort de son Oncle [Prenten en Schilderijen, in extra schoone vergulde Lysten en Glazen] | *Notes:* The bracketed information in the title appears above lot 1 and refers to lots 1 to 24. It is uncertain whether this lot is a painting.	Mr Stephanies Roosendaal	(Unknown)
1803/10/25	HHNOM	0002	*R. Westall* | Le Bienfaisant Cardinal [Prenten en Schilderijen, in extra schoone vergulde Lysten en Glazen] | *Notes:* The bracketed information in the title appears above lot 1 and refers to lots 1 to 24. It is uncertain whether this lot is a painting.	Mr Stephanies Roosendaal	(Unknown)
1803/10/25	HHNOM	0003	*R. Westall* | Rhynfault Confronte a Sapphiera en Presence de Charles Duc de Bourgondie [Prenten en Schilderijen, in extra schoone vergulde Lysten en Glazen] | *Notes:* The bracketed information in the title appears above lot 1 and refers to lots 1 to 24. It is uncertain whether this lot is a painting.	Mr Stephanies Roosendaal	(Unknown)
1803/10/25	HHNOM	0004	*R. Westall* | Le Cardinal Ximenes, Repondant aux Grand d'Espagne qui Revoquoient en Doute son autorité [Prenten en Schilderijen, in extra schoone vergulde Lysten en Glazen] | *Notes:* The bracketed information in the title appears above lot 1 and refers to lots 1 to 24. It is uncertain whether this lot is a painting.	Mr Stephanies Roosendaal	(Unknown)

1803/10/25	HHNOM	0014	*R. Westall* | Innocent Mischief [Prenten en Schilderijen, in extra schoone vergulde Lysten en Glazen] | *Notes:* The bracketed information in the title appears above lot 1 and refers to lots 1 to 24. It is uncertain whether this lot is a painting.	Mr Stephanies Roosendaal	(Unknown)
1803/10/25	HHNOM	0015	*R. Westall* | Innocent Rettenge [sic] [Prenten en Schilderijen, in extra schoone vergulde Lysten en Glazen] | *Notes:* The bracketed information in the title appears above lot 1 and refers to lots 1 to 24. It is uncertain whether this lot is a painting.	Mr Stephanies Roosendaal	(Unknown)
			Westhoven, Huybert van		
1802/05/05	AMSCH	0241	*van Westhoven* | Twee stuks, op twee marmere Tafels ziet men Porcelynen Schotels, Manden en Drinkschaalen, en een menigte Vrugten, fraai geschilderd | *Size:* hoog 47, breed 40 duim	J	(Sold) fl 10 Pruijssenaar [for] J
			Wet, Gerrit de		
1803/08/01	AMSCH	0049	*Weth (G. de)* | Een Bybelsche Ordonantie, met verscheide beelden, fix behandeld | *Mat:* op paneel *Size:* hoog 22, breed 26 duim	J	(Sold) fl 1 Levy Pakker
			Wet, Jacob Willemsz. de		
1802/05/11	GRGRW	0022	*J. de Wet* | Jesus, lerende in den Tempel [Schilderijen met Olie-Verf; In zwarte Lijsten] | *Mat:* in olyverf *Notes:* The bracketed information in the title appears above lot 1 and refers to lots 1 to 79a.	Arnold Sicco Werumeus	(Unknown)
1802/08/24	LNDLS	0115	*J. de Wett* | Een gestoffeerd Landschap	Leonardus Bouman [or others]	(Sold) fl 6:5 Tersien [?]
1802/09/06	AMSCH	0198	*J. de Weth* | Twee stuks Bybelsche Ordenantien	Spaan	(Sold) fl 1:10 van der Schley [for] Rijfsnyder
1802/12/13	AMSCH	0181	*de Weth* | In een Boomryk Landschap by een klaar spiegelend Water, ziet men verbeeld: de Prediking van Christus, voor een menigte van aanhoorders; uitvoerig gepenceeld | *Mat:* op paneel *Size:* hoog 19, breed 24 duim	Pruyssenaar [for] A	(Sold) fl 0:6 L Pakker
1803/04/20	AMSCH	0098	*Weth. (J. de)* | In een Bergachtig Landschap ziet men de Godin Diana, met haar Nimphen, Honden en Jachtgereedschap, meesterlyk geschilderd [La Déesse Diane accompagnée de ses Nimphes & de chiens, allant à la chasse, le fond est un paysage montueux. Tableau d'effet, bien touché.] | *Mat:* op doek *Size:* hoog 48, breed 60 duim	Maria Magdalena van Sluypwyk, gravinne van Moens	(Sold) fl 19:10 Pruijssenaar
1804/08/08	AMSCH	0229	*de Wet* | Een Bybelsche Ordinantie, vol gewoel van Beelden; zynde een der fraaiste Schilderyën van de Wet | *Mat:* op paneel *Size:* hoog 26, breed 35 duim	Roos [for] C	(Sold) fl 12:10 Van Iperen
1804/10/16	DLOND	0258	*J. de Wet* | Paulus en Elymas | *Mat:* op paneel *Size:* hoog 38, breed 23		(Unknown)
1805/07/10	AMSCH	0173	*J. de Weth* | Een Bybel-Ordinantie; Christus laat de Kindertjes tot hem koomen, verder gestoffeerd met verscheide Beelden | *Mat:* op paneel	Temmick	(Sold) fl 0:10 L Pakker
1806/05/05	AMSCH	0153	*de Weth* | De Kinderen Israëls het gevallen Manna verzamelende, schoon geordineerd, en meesterlyk geschildert door de Weth | *Mat:* op doek *Size:* hoog 33, breed 36 duim	V[inkeles]	(Sold) fl 1:10 Gruyter
1807/08/26	AMSCH	0240	*J. de Weth* | Een ryke Ordondantie van verscheiden Beelden, vertoonende Jozeph door zyne Broederen aan de Ismaëliten verkocht; krachtig en meesterlyk gepenceeld | *Mat:* op doek *Size:* hoog 40, breed 54 duim	Helsdinge	(Sold) fl 4:5 Hooft
1808/04/26	GDAN	0194	*De Wet* | Verbeeldende het vergaan van Sodom en Gomorra | *Size:* hoog 12, breed 25 ½ duim	G H Fortuyn	(Unknown)
1808/04/26	GDAN	0195	*De Wet* | Verbeeldende eene Heidensche Offerhande, waar bij een aantal Beelden, fraai en uitvoerig geschilderd | *Size:* hoog 15, breed 23 duim	G H Fortuyn	(Unknown)
1808/05/17	LNAN	0009a	*J. de Wet* | Een land en water Gezigt, daar Christus in een schip staat, leerende, aan vele personen die voor hem op 't land verzameld en aandachtig toe zien, krachtig | *Mat:* op paneel *Size:* hoog 24, breed 31 duim		(Unknown) fl 32
1808/06/11	RMRIJ	0036	*Jan de Weth* | De Opwekking van Lazarus, krachtig en meesterlyk geschilderd | *Mat:* op paneel *Size:* hoog 23, breed 34 ½ duim		(Bought In) fl 14
1808/08/23	AMSCH	0173	*Weth. (J. de)* | Dit zinrijk Tafereel, zijnde een rijke Ordonantie van verscheide Beelden, vertoont in een Landschap op de voorgrond een oud Man, verzelt van eene Vrouw, beide op hunne knieën leggende, en als in een eerbiedige verrukking, opwaards ziende naar een Engel met een boek in de hand, die in een wolk schijnt op te rijsen, verder verscheide andere Lieden, die hun verwondering te kennen geeven, op de grond leggen verscheiden goude en andere Cieraden, ter linker zijde ziet men een Landman bij een beladen Ezel, verder rustende Lieden, en aangenaam verschiet; het is bevallig van kleur en licht, en meesterlijk gepenceeld, in de manier van Rembrant | *Mat:* op paneel *Size:* hoog 19, breed 25 duim	[Coclers]	(Sold) fl 110 Van Iperen
1808/12/31	RMHSN	0013	*De Wet* | Een Grot met een Reiziger te Paard | *Mat:* op paneel	G Spanjaart [or] H de Haas [or] C van der Looy Lans	(Unknown)
1810/03/27	RMCNL	0095	*de Wet* | Een Kapitaal Stuk, waarin men eene Koningin aan eenen Koning en Veldheer, de voorraad nog in de Stad zien aanbieden, uitvoerig, schoon en vol werking geschildert		(Unknown)

Wet, Jacob Willemsz. de (manner)

1806/06/07	RMHSN	0131	*de Wet* | Een Grot, waar in een Reiziger te Paard en ander Bywerk, in de manier van de Wet	A E K L	(Unknown)
1807/08/26	AMSCH	0241	*J. de Weth* | Een Historiëele Ordonnantie, in een Landschap, verbeeldende de vinding van Mozes, ryk gestoffeerd met verscheiden Beelden en verder bywerk; meesterlyk behandeld als door denselven [J. de Weth] | *Mat:* op paneel	Yver [for] S	(Sold) fl 0:10 Levy Pakker

Wet, S. de [Unidentified]

1802/05/11	GRGRW	0039	*S. de Wet* | De Besnijdenis van den Zaligmaker [Schilderijen met Olie-Verf; In zwarte Lijsten] | *Mat:* in olyverf *Notes:* The bracketed information in the title appears above lot 1 and refers to lots 1 to 79a.	Arnold Sicco Werumeus	(Unknown) fl 8
1808/09/13	HABRU	0097	*S. de Wett* | Simsom en Delia; kragtig en schoon van Ligt en Ordonnantie		(Unknown) fl 2:4
1808/09/13	HABRU	0098	*S. de Wett* | Philippus de Moorman doopende		(Unknown) fl 3:5

Weyerman, Jacob Campo

1802/09/06	AMSCH	0162	*J. C. Weyerman* | Een cierlyke Vaas, gevult met onderscheide Bloemen; meesterlyk geschilderd | *Mat:* op doek	X	(Sold) fl 0:6 Vermeulen

Wiemond [Unidentified]

1806/10/22	HGBAK	0008	*Wiemond* | Een Italiaansche have [sic] door Wiemond, in het grauw, in een zwarte lyst | *Notes:* It is uncertain whether this lot is a painting.		(Unknown)

Wiertz, Henricus Franciscus

1810/10/11	AMSCH	0096	*H. F. Wierts* | In een duinachtig Landschap, liggen op den voorgrond eenige Hoorns, Schelpen en andere Zeegewassen; zeer uitvoerig geschilderd | *Mat:* op paneel *Size:* hoog 16, breed 18 ½ duimen	S	(Bought In) fl 19
1810/10/11	AMSCH	0097	*H. F. Wierts* | In een gemeubileerd Vertrek, zit een bevallig Vrouwtje, bij eene Tafel, bezig Appelen te schillen, zij schijnt in gesprek met een Huisman, die over haar zit, verder eenig Huisraad; bevallig geschilderd | *Mat:* op paneel *Size:* hoog 15 ½, breed 13 duimen	S	(Bought In) fl 16:10
1810/10/11	AMSCH	0098	*H. F. Wierts* | Voor een Buitenhuis zit eene Groenvrouw, welke aan een Landmeisje, die nevens haar staat, haar waar schijnt aantebieden; als de voorgaande geschilderd | *Size:* hoog 15, breed 12 duimen	S	(Bought In) fl 20
1810/10/11	AMSCH	0099	*H. F. Wierts* | Een Landschap, met Boeren-Woningen, Kerk-Toren en Beeldjes gestoffeerd; natuurlijk | *Mat:* op doek *Size:* hoog 12, breed 13 duimen	S	(Sold) fl 6 L Pakker

Wigmana, Gerard

1802/06/28	AMSCH	0208	*Wigmana* | Mars, Venus en Cupido, op een Rustbedde; zeer natuurlyk, door Wigmana, op Panneel | *Mat:* op paneel *Size:* hoog 19, breed 15 duim	Anna Elink	(Sold) fl 5 Royers
1802/06/28	AMSCH	0209	*Wigmana* | Deeze Ordonnantie verbeeld de ontdekking van Calisto in het badt van Diana, verzeld van verscheide Nimphen, zich badende; zeer uitvoerig gepenceelt door Denzelven [Wigmana] | *Mat:* op paneel *Size:* hoog 21, breed 16 duim	Anna Elink	(Sold) fl 10 Texier
1802/12/13	AMSCH	0178	*Wigmana* | Een Vénus op haar rustbedde leggende, uitvoerig | *Mat:* op doek *Size:* hoog 30, breed 21 duim	Yver	(Sold) fl 5:10 L Pakker
1803/04/20	AMSCH	0092	*G. Wigmana* | Voor een Open Nis staat een vrolyk Heer, voor een Steene Baluster van onder met een Basrelief verciert, hy houd in de regterhand een glas Wyn, en in de andere een Fles met Tien omvlogten, op de Rand legt een Phiool en Musicq-boek, hoger een opgeschooven Gordyn, alles is ongemeen fraay en uitvoerig gepenceeld, in de manier van F. van Mieris [Au devant de l'embrasure d'une forme de niche, ornée d'un basrelief, se montre un homme joyeux, il tient le verre et la bouteille des deux mains ; son Violon et le livre de musique sont auprès de lui, le fond est terminé par un rideau relevé. Ce joli tableau d'un pinceau très soigné imite de près la maniere de F. Mieris.] | *Mat:* op paneel *Size:* hoog 13, breed 10 duim	Maria Magdalena van Sluypwyk, gravinne van Moens	(Sold) fl 45 Petit
1803/04/20	AMSCH	0093	*G. Wigmana* | Voor een dito [Open Nis] als de voorgaande, ziet men een bevallig Keukenmeisje, uit een aarde Kan Melk in een Schotel gieten, ter zyde op de Rand legt een Kopere Keetel, Kool en Wortelen, en verder gereedschap, omhoog een opgeschoven Gordyn, in alles niet minder uitvoerig behandeld als de vorige, in de manier van G. Dou [Un Sujet dont le fond est à peu près Semblable au precedent ; la figure dans celui-ci est une cuisiniere versant le lait d'un vase de terre dans un plat, des accessoires tels qu'un chaudron de cuivre, des legumes & autres objets embellissent cette agréable production, du même merite de la précedente, en observant que l'Artiste a imité dans celle-ci la maniere de G. Dou.] | *Mat:* op paneel *Size:* hoog 12, breed 9 duim	Maria Magdalena van Sluypwyk, gravinne van Moens	(Sold) fl 100 Petit
1803/04/20	AMSCH	0094	*G. Wigmana* | Dit Voorwerp vertoont Maria met het Kindje en Joseph, verzeld van Elizabeth en St. Jan, en eenige Engelen; uitvoerig geschilderd [Ce sujet esr [sic] la Ste. Famille, composée de la Vierge Marie avec l'Enfant Jesus, St. Joseph, Elisabeth, St. Jean & des Seraphins. Tableau eclattant de couleur & d'un pinceau Soigné.] | *Mat:* op doek *Size:* hoog 19, breed 16 duim [haut 19, large 18 pouces] *Notes:* The dimensions differ in the Dutch and French editions of the catalogue.	Maria Magdalena van Sluypwyk, gravinne van Moens	(Sold) fl 36 Gruiter

1803/04/20 AMSCH 0095 *G. Wigmana* | Apollo, zittende in een Landschap, houdende de Lier in de hand, ter zyde legt een Koker met Pylen; delicaat en uitvoerig gepenceeld [Apollon tenant sa lire se voit assis dans un site agréable, à côte est son carquois, peint avec delicatesse.] | *Mat:* op paneel *Size:* hoog 17 ½, breed 13 duim — Maria Magdalena van Sluypwyk, gravinne van Moens — (Sold) fl 26 for lots 95 & 96. C S Roos

1803/04/20 AMSCH 0096 *G. Wigmana* | Een Rustende Diana, zittende in een Boomryk Landschap, houdende een Spiets in de hand, ter zyde legt een Pylkooker; zeer delicaat en uitvoerig gepenceeld [Dans une foret est assise Diane, se reposans de la chasse ; elle tient une lance & ses atrubuts sont à terre. Tableau d'une jolie couleur et très fini.] | *Mat:* op paneel *Size:* hoog 17, breed 13 duim — Maria Magdalena van Sluypwyk, gravinne van Moens — (Sold) fl 26 for lots 95 & 96. C S Roos

1803/04/20 AMSCH 0097 *G. Wigmana* | Door een Open Nis ziet men een slapende Nimph, op een blaauw Kleed, in alles als de vorige uitvoerig behandeld [Autre Sujet agréable étant une niche autravers de la quelle l'on voit une Nimphe endormie sur une draperie bleue, morceau traité avec autant d'agrement que le précedent.] | *Mat:* op paneel *Size:* hoog 15, breed 12 duim — Maria Magdalena van Sluypwyk, gravinne van Moens — (Sold) fl 0:12 Brunis

1803/12/12 AMSCH 0116 *Wigmana* | Mars, Vénus en Cupido op het Rustbed, delicaat op Paneel | *Mat:* op paneel *Size:* hoog 20, breed 15 duim — W — (Sold) fl 4:15 v[n] Iperen

1803/12/15 MGLAC 0017 *Wigmana* | Een Bad met baadende Nimphen; zeer delicaat en schoon behandeld | *Mat:* op paneel *Size:* hoog duim 22, breed duim 17 — Mr L H de Haze Bomme — (Unknown)

1805/07/03 AMSCH 0173 *Wigmana* | Dit stukje steld voor; twee Jongelingen speelende met een Vogelnesje; uitvoerig | *Mat:* op paneel *Size:* hoog 12, breed 10 duim — R[oos] — (Sold) fl 5 Halingins

1805/10/09 HGBSM 0074 *G. Wigmana* | De teeken en schilderkonst verbeeld, door een vrouw aan een tafel zittende, uitvoerig | *Mat:* op paneel *Size:* hoog 18 ½ breet 14 duim — T H van Willigen [or others] — (Sold) fl 7:5 Kuller

1806/08/13 AMSCH 0290 *Wigmana* | Een Man in een Grot, bézig zynde in een Boek te leezen; fiks door Wigmana — Vinkeles [for] E — (Sold) fl 0:8 du Pree

1808/08/23 AMSCH 0177 *Wigmana* | Christus met de Doorne Kroon,houdende een Rietstok in de hand, en de Oogen hemelwaards opheffende; meesterlijk gepenceeld | *Mat:* op paneel *Size:* hoog 15, breed 12 duim — C — (Sold) fl 14 Ocke

1810/06/06 RMMUY 0165 *Wigmana* | Een Vrouwtje met een Papegaays Kooi | *Mat:* op paneel — (Unknown) fl 1:12

1810/07/23 DOLG1 0062 *Wigmans* | Op den voorgrond van dit fraai Schilderijtje, ziet men een blazenden Trompetter, ten halven lijve, in eene Gallerij, of Balustrade, en bij dezelven een Viool en andere Muzijk-Instrumenten; op den agtergrond een Gezelschap, in eene Kamer aan een tafel spijzende. Zeer uitvoerig en kunstig; behandeld in de manier van Mieris | *Mat:* op paneel *Size:* hoog 14, breed 11 duim — Mr Pieter van den Santheuvel — (Sold) fl 25 van Eijk à 's Hage

Wigmana, Gerard (or Wigmana, G., copy after)

1806/11/24 AMSCH 0088 *Wigmana* | Sinte Cecilia, op het Orgel speelende; door of naar Wigmana — Munnikhuizen — (Sold) fl 3:15 Th Spaan

Wigmana, Gerard (manner)

1809/06/13 AMSCH 0221 *G. Wigmana* | In een Studeervertrek zit een bejaarde Philosooph met aandagt een brief leezende, rustende met de regterhand op een Tafel met een kleedje bedekt, waarop een Globe: het is uitvoerig gepenceelt op Doek, als door G. Wigmana | *Mat:* op doek *Size:* hoog 16, breed 13 duim — R[ijfsnijder] — (Sold) fl 1:10 L Pakker

Wigmana, Johannes

1801/10/06 AMSCH 0079 *J. Wigmana* | In een deftig Gemeubileerd Vertrek, aan een Tafel met een Tapytkleed bedekt, zitten drie jonge Dames in zatyne Kleeding te Musiceeren, een derzelve speelt op 't Clavier en een op de Guitar, terwyl de derde met een Musiekboek in de handen, scheint te zingen ter zyde zit een Heer met de Dwarsfluyt in handen, waar by een Jongeling houdende een zilver Schenkbord met een Glas Wyn; alles is bevallig van coloriet en zeer uitvoerig gepenceeld | *Mat:* op paneel *Size:* hoog 18, breed 14 duim — S — (Sold) fl 29 v d Schleij A [for] Putte

1801/10/06 AMSCH 0080 *J. Wigmana* | Dit Afbeeldzel vertoont de Koninglijke Propheet David, zittende in een Vorstelijke Zétel, als in verrukking Opwaards ziende naar een Hemelglans, en is rustende met de regter arm op de Harp; alles is als de vorige van een uitvoerige Penceel behandeling | *Mat:* op paneel — S — (Sold) fl 20 Ter Smitten

1810/05/22 AMSCH 0122 *Wigmana (J.)* | In een gemeubileerd Binnenvertrek zitten drie Dames en een Heer te musiceeren, ter zijde een Jongeling met een Schenkbord in de handen; uitvoerig geschilderd | *Mat:* op paneel *Size:* hoog 18, breed 14 duim — Johannes van de Putte Nicolaasz. — (Sold) fl 12:10 van Iperen

1810/05/22 AMSCH 0123 *Wigmana (J.)* | Een Wijsgeer in zijn Vertrek, zittende voor eene Tafel, agterwaards eene Vrouw; fiks gepenceeld | *Mat:* op paneel *Size:* hoog 16, breed 12 duim — Johannes van de Putte Nicolaasz. — (Sold) fl 4:5 Otten

Wijnants, Jan

1801/08/19 AMSCH 0140 *J. Wynands* | Een Landschap met hoog Geboomte, langs Duin, op de voorgrond ziet men eenige Beeldjes gestoffeerd — Pruyssen[r] [for] Q — (Bought In) fl 19

1801/10/06 AMSCH 0077 *J. Wynands* | Een Natuurlyk Boomryk Landschap, op de Voorgrond leggen eenige afgehakten Stammen van Boomen, by verscheide Plantgewassen; verder een gaande Vrouw en Jongeling, en een rustende Ryziger, zeer kloek en Meesterlyk gepenceeld | *Mat:* op doek *Size:* hoog 19, breed 17 duim — L — (Sold) fl 65 Spruijt van Gend

1802/06/16	AMSCH	0209	*J. Wynants* | Een Aangenaam en bevallig Duinachtig Landschap, met eenig Geboomten, op de voorgrond by een Waterbeekje staat een Knegt een gezadeld Paard vasthoudende, terwyl den Heer bézig is naar een Vogel te schieten; verders een gaande Huisman, gestoffeerd met verder bywerk; zonachtig en meesterlyk fraay van Penceel-behandeling | *Mat:* op paneel *Size:* hoog 20, breed 25 duim	[Merrem]	(Sold) fl 33 J Yver
1802/06/28	AMSCH	0201	*J. Wynands* | Twee stuks bevallige duinachtige Landschapjes; uitvoerig door J. Wynands, op Panneel | *Mat:* op paneel *Size:* hoog 7, breed 6 duim	Anna Elink	(Sold) fl 5:10 Boelen
1803/06/20	AMSCH	0055	*J. Wynants* | Twee stuks, bevallige Duinachtige Landschappen, met eenig Geboomten, gestoffeerd met gaande Huislieden en eenige Woningen. byde zonagtig en meesterlyk fraay van Penceelbehandeling | *Mat:* op paneel *Size:* hoog 10, breed 13 ½ duim	Schley [for] H	(Sold) fl 52 Gruiter
1803/06/20	AMSCH	0058	*J. Wynants* | Een Bevallig heuvelachtig Landschap, met onderscheiden soort van Geboomten, gestoffeerd met een Veehoeder met Schaapen, en een Gebouw; zonagtig, natuurlyk en meesterlyk gepenceelt, op Doek | *Mat:* op doek *Size:* hoog 15, breed 12 duim	Schley [for] H	(Sold) fl 43 V d Vinnen
1803/06/20	AMSCH	0059	*J. Wynants* | Een aangenaam heuvelagtig Landschap, met een Rivier doorsneeden, op de voorgrond een Huisman met eenige Schaapen, verders eenig Geboomten, zonachtig, helder en natuurlyk gepenceeld, door denzelven [J. Wynants], op Paneel | *Mat:* op paneel *Size:* hoog 8, breed 8 ½ duim	Schley [for] H	(Bought In) fl 6
1803/08/17	AMSCH	0091	*Wynands. (J.)* | Een Duinachtig Landschap met hoog Geboomte, en aangenaam Verschiet, gestoffeerd met een Jager en zyn Hond, verder een Man op een Ezel, bevallig en met de natuur overeenkomende gepenceeld | *Mat:* op paneel *Size:* hoog 22, breed 19 duim	Anna Catharina Putman	(Sold) fl 61 Gruyter
1803/12/12	AMSCH	0107	*W. Wynands* | Een aangenaam Duinagtig Landschap met hoog Geboomten, stoffagie van Beeldjes en een aangenaam verschiet; geestig op Paneel | *Mat:* op paneel *Size:* hoog 12, breed 15 duim *Notes:* The artist's name was given as "W. Wynands" but we have assumed this is an error.	W	(Sold) fl 19 v^{n} Iperen
1803/12/12	AMSCH	0108	*J. Wynands* | Twee stuks Boomryke Duinachtige Landschappen met Distelen en stoffagie van Beeldjes; kragtig op Doek | *Mat:* op doek *Size:* hoog 14, breed 11 duim	W	(Bought In) fl 106
1803/12/12	AMSCH	0109	*J. Wynands* | Een Landschap met een Rivier doorsneeden, op de voorgrond twee Beeldjes, welke een Paard opzadelen, verders hoog Gebergten; uitvoerig op Doek | *Mat:* op doek	W	(Bought In) fl 1:15
1804/08/08	AMSCH	0219	*J. Wynands* | Een Boomryk Landschap, op de voorgrond legt een extra fraaije doode Berkenstam, aan een stil Water, verders een ménigte delicaat geschilderde Kruiden en Distelen, in het verschiet hoog Gebergte, met Stoffagie van Kasteelen en Beeldjes; fraai van coloriet en uitmuntend behandeld | *Mat:* op doek *Size:* hoog 19, breed 25 duim	Roos a	(Sold) fl 161 Izaac Smit
1804/08/08	AMSCH	0220	*J. Wynands* | In een aangenaam Boom- en Duinachtig Landschap ziet men een ménigte Hoornvée, waarby hun Hoeder en Hond, op de voorgrond een rustende Reiziger, en verders een aangenaam Bergachtig verschiet; piquant van licht, en fraai van schildering | *Mat:* op doek *Size:* hoog 21, breed 27 duim	Vink[eles] [for] W	(Bought In) fl 25
1804/08/08	AMSCH	0221	*J. Wynands* | Een Gezicht langs een Duinachtige Weg, met eenig Geboomte, op de voorgrond een gaande Man, verzeld van een Hond, verder een Heer te Paard; zonachtig en bevallig | *Mat:* op doek op paneel *Size:* hoog 10, br. 12 duim	Schley [for] A	(Sold) fl 20 Jan Spaan
1804/10/16	DLOND	0272	*J. Wynands* | Een Landschap met veel Geboomte. Paysage très ombragé | *Mat:* op doek *Size:* hoog 36, breed 45		(Sold) fl 88 Mahy
1805/07/03	AMSCH	0172	*J. Wynands* | Een gestoffeerd Duin- en Boomryk Landschapje, geestig gestoffeerd met een Ezeldryver en wandelende Beeldjes; kragtig op Paneel | *Mat:* op paneel *Size:* hoog 12, breed 8 duim	R[oos]	(Sold) fl 31 Hardenberg
1805/10/21	GRBOL	0051	*Wynands* | Een dito [Landschapje] door dito [Wynands]	Gerardus Nicolaus Heerkens	(Unknown)
1805/10/21	GRBOL	0052	*Wynands* | Een dito [Landschapje] door dito [Wynands]	Gerardus Nicolaus Heerkens	(Unknown)
1806/08/20	HGBSM	0053	*Wijnants* | Een Landschapje met Stoffagie, gemerkt Wijnants | *Mat:* op doek op paneel *Size:* hoog 13 ½, breed 10 ¾ duim *Inscr:* Wijnants (signed)	Macalester Loup [or others]	(Sold) fl 11:10 Praiston
1807/06/02	AMHUY	0011	*Wijnans* | Een aangenaam Boom- en Bergachtig Landschap, op de voorgrond ziet men een Drift Koejen, waarby een Herder, krachtig en meesterlyk geschilderd		(Unknown)
1808/04/26	GDAN	0181	*Wynands (Jan)* | Een Duin- Land- Riviergezigtje, gestoffeerd met Koeijen en Schapen, &c | *Size:* hoog 24, breed 33 duim	G H Fortuyn	(Unknown)
1808/04/26	GDAN	0182	*Wynands (Jan)* | Een zonägtig Landschap, met fraaije stoffage, of het van van de Velde was | *Size:* hoog 11 ½, breed 15 duim	G H Fortuyn	(Unknown)
1808/05/18	LNAN	0001	*Wijnants* | 2 Plaisante Bergachtige Landschappen, gestoffeerd met Beelden | *This Lot:* Een Plaisant Bergachtig Landschap, gestoffeerd met Beelden *Notes:* Lots 1 and 2 were printed in the catalogue as one item.	Mr Cornelis Versluys	(Unknown)

			The artist's name "Wijnants" was added in by hand in the RKDH copy of the catalogue.		
1808/05/18	LNAN	0002	*Wijnants* | 2 Plaisante Bergachtige Landschappen, gestoffeerd met Beelden | *This Lot:* Een Plaisant Bergachtig Landschap, gestoffeerd met Beelden *Notes:* Lots 1 and 2 were printed in the catalogue as one item. The artist's name "Wijnants" was added in by hand in the RKDH copy of the catalogue.	Mr Cornelis Versluys	(Unknown)
1808/06/13	AMSCH	0175	*Wijnands (J.)* | In een boom- en heuvelachtig Landschap ziet men bij een afgeschilde Boomstam twee Vrouwen en een Hond in een Waterplas, verder een aangenaam verschiet. Hetzelve is van eene kloeke en aangename schildering | *Mat:* op doek *Size:* hoog 26, breed 31 duim	[Jan Tersteeg]	(Sold) fl 285 J^{mo} de Vries
1809/07/19	AMSCH	0065	*Wijnands (J)* | In een boomrijk Landschap, bij een opgaande Weg, vertoont zig eene Boere Woning van Steen gebouwd, een Huisman ligt over den Deur, verder gestoffeerd met eene gaande Vrouw en Kind. Het invallend zonlicht doet eene zeer natuurlijke werking op het Gebouw, het is van eene uitvoerige penceelsbehandeling | *Mat:* op paneel *Size:* hoog 12, breed 14 duim *Loc:* Amsterdam, Nederland. Rijksmuseum. (A 492)	[Bicker]	(Sold) fl 425 Jan Yver voor Z H den Koning
1810/03/07	UTWLD	0051	*Wynands* | Een zeer uitvoerig Landschapje | *Size:* hoog 10 duim, breed 8 duim	J J Woertman	(Unknown) fl 40
1810/05/22	AMSCH	0117	*Wijnands (J.)* | Een duinachtig Landschap, waarin een Heer te Paard, welke aan Landlieden naar den Weg vraagt, verder gaande Reizigers; helder en zonachtig gepenceeld | *Mat:* op doek *Size:* hoog 19, breed 23 duim	R	(Sold) fl 18:10 Boelhouwer
1810/05/22	AMSCH	0118	*Wijnands (J.)* | Een aangenaam Duinachtig Landschap, met Geboomte, op den voorgrond een Jager te paard en een te voet; zonachtig behandeld | *Mat:* op doek op paneel *Size:* hoog 10, breed 12 duim	Johannes van de Putte Nicolaasz.	(Sold) fl 221 Hulswit
1810/10/10	MGCIT	0011	*J. Wijnants* | Een bekoorlijk Landschap Boschrijk, met zeer hoog opgaande Boomen; alsmede op den Voorgrond met Distels en andere Gewassen, en Vlindels [sic]; in 't verschiet met een Kasteel in 't midden van het geboomte vercierd; in allen opzigten van een kapitale behandeling	Caspar van Citters	(Unknown)
1810/11/07	UTWLD	0030	*T. Wynands* | Dit fraaie Kabinetstukje, verbeeld een boerengehugtje, waarbij een Hooiberg en Schuurtje omgeven met hoogrijzend geboomte, op de voorgrond een duinagtig zand met heijstoppels bewassen, gestoffeerd met een het stuk ingaand boertje en een houd, dit alles is zeer zonagtig klaar en kragtig geschilderd door T. Wynands op doek, 13 duim breed, 12 duim hoog, zwarte Lijst | *Mat:* op doek *Size:* 13 duim breed, 12 duim hoog *Notes:* The artist's name was given as "T. Wynands" but we have assumed this is an error.		(Unknown) fl 42

Wijnants, Jan (and Lingelbach)

1801/05/11	AMSCH	0114	*J. Wynands; Lingelbach* | Denzelven [J. Wynands] gestoffeerd, door Lingelbach. Een bevallig Landschap, doorsneede met een stil water, op de Voorgrond een Vrouw, nevens een Kind en een Hond, verders een Kar en een Jager, zonachtig en natuurlyk van behandeling | *Mat:* op doek op paneel *Size:* hoog 11, breed 16 duim	E[lias]	(Sold) fl 100 Pruijssenaar [for] R
1801/05/11	AMSCH	0115	*J. Wynands; Lingelbach* | Denzelven [J. Wynands] gestoffeerd, door Lingelbach. Een duinachtig Landschap, met hoog geboomte gestoffeerd, met een Man te Paard, nevens een Voetganger en een Hond, in 't verschiet een Herder by eenige Schaapen, alles zonachtig en natuurlyk behandeld | *Mat:* op paneel *Size:* hoog 15, breed 16 duim	P[ruyssenaar]	(Sold) fl 37 Yver
1801/06/10	AMSCH	0181	*Wynants. (J.); Lingelbach* | Een Heuvelachtig Landschap, op de Voorgrond ziet men een Man en Vrouw te Paard, achter dezelve een Voetganger, verders een Koornoogst, in het verschiet een Dorp en hoog Geboomte; zonachtig en natuurlyk behandeld | *Mat:* op doek op paneel *Size:* hoog 11, breed 14 duim	Herman ten Kate	(Sold) fl 130 Thaijs
1801/10/06	AMSCH	0078	*J. Wynands; J. Lingelbach* | Dit Stukje verbeeld een Aangenaam, Heuvelagtig Landschap, op de voorgrond op een Heuvel met eenig Geboomten, ziet men Huislieden, met Schaapen, ter andere zyde in een Valei, met een Rivier doorsneeden, een staand Man en rustende Vrouw; verders een bevallig verschiet, alles is Zonagtig en uitvoerig behandeld | *Mat:* op doek *Size:* hoog 11, breed 15 duim	L	(Bought In) fl 405
1802/06/16	AMSCH	0208	*J. Wynands; J. Lingelbach* | Een aangenaam Duinachtig Landschap met eenige laag Geboomten: op de voorgrond ziet men een Heer te Paard, en een Bedelaar een Almoes vragende; verder ter zyde by een opgaande zandweg, rust een Vrouw, verzelt van een Man en Jongeling, hooger een Véehoeder Ossendryvende; en een Kerktooren: in 't verschiet een Rytuig; alles is helder zonachtig en fraay gepenceeld door deeze Meesters | *Mat:* op doek *Size:* hoog 18 ½, breed 21 ½ duim	[Merrem]	(Sold) fl 135 I Smit G^{z}
1803/12/15	MGLAC	0013	*J. Weynands; Lingelbach* | Een heerlyk Landschap; zeer uitvoerig en fraai, zynde gestoffeerd met Figuuren, door Lingelbach | *Mat:* op doek *Size:* hoog duim 40, breed duim 34	Mr L H de Haze Bomme	(Unknown)
1804/05/07	AMSCH	0191	*Wynands. (J.); (gestoffeerd door Lingelbach)* | In een bevallig Duinachtig Landschap, ziet men by een Heyning ter zyde een Watertje, op de voorgrond een gaande Huisman, waarby een Hond, iets achterwaards een rustende Vrouw, waarby een Jongen, en verders twee gaande Lieden, in 't	Roos [for] A	(Sold) fl 200 Coclers

			verschiet op eenig Gebergte en Geboomte een Kasteel, enz.; uitvoerig en piquant van licht en van de beste schildering van deeze Meesters | *Mat:* op paneel *Size:* hoog 13, breed 14 duim		
1804/05/07	AMSCH	0192	*Wynands. (J.); (gestoffeerd door Lingelbach)* | Dit stukje verbeelde een aangenaam Heuvelachtig Landschap, op de voorgrond op een Heuvel met eenig Geboomte, ziet men Huislieden met Schaapen, ter andere zyde in een Valey, met een Rivier doorsneeden, een staand Man en rustende Vrouw, verders een bevallig verschiet; alles is zonachtig en uitvoerig behandeld | *Mat:* op doek	Y[ver] [for] JJ	(Bought In) fl 200
1804/08/02	BDAN	0002	*J. Wynants; J. Lingelbacht* | Een zeer aangenaam en mooy bergachtig Landschap, den voorgrond verciert met eenige Boomen, Planten, enz:, zeer rykelyk gestoffeerd | *Mat:* op doek *Size:* b. 25 d. h. 19 d.	J G Calckberner	(Unknown)
1804/08/08	AMSCH	0218	*J. Wynands; J. Lingelbach* | Een capitaal Boom en Bergachtig Landschap, op de voorgrond eenige Distelen en Kreupelgewas, gestoffeerd met Beelden, te Paard en te voet; meesterlyk op Doek | *Mat:* op doek *Size:* hoog 65, breed 49 duim	Roos [for] K[=Gruyter?]	(Sold) fl 35 Gruiter
1806/08/13	AMSCH	0210	*Wynands (J.); J. Lingelbach* | Een Duin- en Boomryk Landschap, met een aangenaam verschiet, op de voorgrond by een Waterplas, ziet men een Heer en Dame te paard, verzeld van Jagers en Honden, delicaat geschilderd | *Mat:* op paneel *Size:* hoog 16, breed 21 duim	van der Voort	(Sold) fl 235 Thais
1808/06/06	RMRIJ	0147	*Wijnants. (Jan); Lingelbach. (Johannes)* | Een Landschap, op den voorgrond rijk versierd met Geboomte en Gewassen, en een Valkenier, verzeld van twee Honden, den weg afkomende. Hooger op zit een Jager met zijne Honden te rusten. Verder ziet men Heeren en Dames te Paard den weg opkomen, en, bij eene afgeslotene schutting, een wit Paard en eene Koe. Ter zijden van den opgaanden weg eene ruime Vallei, doorsneden van eene Rivier, loopende langs Gebergte, Weg en Zaailanden, met Beelden, enz. gestoffeerd. Alles zeer schoon en uitvoerig door bovengemelde twee Meesters behandeld [Dans un riche Paysage décoré d'arbres, et agréablement varié par des plantes et des Brouissailles [sic], on apperçoit sur le penchant d'une colline, un fauconnier et deux Chiens ; plus loin repose un chasseur avec deux autres Chiens, et au sommet de cette Colline, on découvre un Cavalier et une Dame à cheval, accompagnés d'un Chasseur et de ses Chiens. A droite un Boeuf et un Cheval sont dans un enclos, et à gauche on voit un agréable vallon, où se trouvent un Carosse, des figures etc. Ce Morceau d'un ton vrai, d'une Composition riante, et d'un beau faire, mérite beaucoup d'èloge] | *Annots:* Van Jac. de Vos, 14 Aug. 1785 (f 650.-) (RMA I) *Mat:* op doek *Size:* Hoog 19 ¾, en breed 25 ¼ duim	Gerrit van der Pot, Heer van Groeneveld	(Sold) fl 905 P Roelszema
1808/06/13	AMSCH	0173	*Wijnands (J.); J. Lingelbach* | Deze rijke Ordonantie stelt voor een Nederlandsch Landschap, op den voorgrond een Herberg, alwaar een Heer op een Paard een Glas wordt ingeschonken, in 't verschiet eenige Reizigers. Allernatuurlijkst en zonachtig behandeld | *Mat:* op doek *Size:* hoog 40, breed 56 duim	E M Engelberts	(Sold) fl 175 T Boelen
1808/06/13	AMSCH	0174	*Wijnands (J.); J. Lingelbach* | Een boomrijk Landschap, gestoffeerd met eene Boerin op een Kar, ter zijde twee Reizigers, op den voorgrond een verdorde Boom en Kruiden. Als de voorgaande geschilderd | *Mat:* op doek *Size:* hoog 20, breed 25 duim	E M Engelberts	(Sold) fl 101 Engelberts
1810/06/20	AMSCH	0101	*J. Wijnands; J. Lingelbach* | In een aangenaam duinachtig Landschap, ziet men, ter regter zijde, eenen ouden bijna dooden Boom, nevens eenen ouden hollen Stam, met verschillende Struiken en Gewassen; verder omgehakte Boomstammen, achterwaards en in het verschiet fraai Geboomte. Het is gestoffeerd met Jagers te paard en te voet, met hunne Honden, gaande op de Valkenjagt. Dit kapitale Schilderij is van de beste en natuurlijkste schildering van J. Wijnands, en fraai en uitvoerig gestoffeerd door J. Lingelbach | *Mat:* op doek *Size:* hoog 45, breed 55 ½ duimen	D	(Sold) fl 250 de Vries
1810/06/20	AMSCH	0101a	*J. Wijnands; J. Lingelbach* | Dit fraaije Schilderij verbeeld een aangenaam Landschap, met Geboomte, verschillende Kruiden en Plantgewassen. Het is gestoffeerd in het midden, langs een zandige Weg, met een Heer te Paard, verzeld van een Jager en Honden; voorts een rustend Reiziger, benevens eene Vrouw met een Kind; achterwaards een helder spiegelend Water, grootsche Gebouwen en een bevallig verschiet. Dit stuk is warm van koloriet en van de beste schildering van J. Wijnands, gestoffeerd door J. Lingelbach | *Size:* hoog 43, breed 54 duimen	Y	(Sold) fl 161 T Spaan
1810/08/06	AMSCH	0130	*Wijnands (J.); Gestoffeerd door J. Lingelbag* | Twee stuks Duinachtige Landschappen, met opgaande Wegen en Geboomte, beide met Huislieden, Heeren te Paard, Jagers en andere Voorwerpen, zonachtig en natuurlijk behandeld | *Mat:* op paneel *Size:* ieder is hoog 9 ½, breed 11 ½ duimen	A	(Sold) fl 220 J^{mo} de Vries
1810/10/11	AMSCH	0103	*J. Wijnands; J. Lingelbach* | In een aangenaam duinachtig Landschap, ziet men, ter regter zyde, eenen ouden byna dooden Boom, nevens eenen ouden hollen Stam, met verschillende Struiken en Gewassen; verder omgehakte Boomstammen, achterwaards en in het verschiet fraai Geboomte. Het is gestoffeerd met Jagers te paard en te voet, met hunne Honden, gaande op de Valkenjagt. Dit voortreffelijken kapitale Schilderij is van de beste, uitvoerigsten en natuurlykste schildering van J. Wijnands, en fraai gestoffeerd door J. Lingelbach | *Mat:* op doek *Size:* hoog 45, breed 55 ½ duimen	V[ries]	(Sold or Bought In) fl 500 J^{mo} de Vries

1810/10/11	AMSCH	0104	*J. Wijnands; J. Lingelbach* | Een Heuvelachtig Landschap, voor aaan [sic] voor een Smits Winkel, Paarden die beslagen worden, verder Officieren te Paard, Vragtwagens en andere Stoffagie; zonachtig behandeld | *Mat:* op doek *Size:* hoog 28, breed 31 duimen	Y	(Sold) fl 21:10 Gruiter

Wijnants, Jan (and Velde, A.)

1801/04/13	AMSCH	0093	*J. Wynadts; A. van de Velde* | Twee stuks Duin en boomryke Landschappen, gestoffeerd met Jagers te paard en te voet, met hunne honden, en een rustende marskramer; het zonlicht, en de klikachtige kluitjes der zandgronden maken deeze stukjes tot een paar der bevalligste van deezen Meester | *Mat:* op doek *Size:* ieder is hoog 16, breed 14 duim	Pierre Fouquet, junior	(Sold) fl 310 v d Schley [for] M[errem]
1801/05/11	AMSCH	0113	*J. Wynands; A. v.d. Velde* | J. Wynands, gestoffeerd door A. v. d. Velde. Een zonachtig Landschap, op de Voorgrond eenige Koeijen en Schaapen, waarby een Herder, ter rechter zyde een stam van een eikenboom, verders een bergachtig verschiet, alles is van de beste en fraaiste schildering | *Mat:* op doek *Size:* hoog 10, breed 13 duim *Loc:* Amsterdam, Nederland. Rijksmuseum. (A 493)	E[lias]	(Sold) fl 305 Bern de Bosch
1801/06/10	AMSCH	0179	*Wynants. (J.); stoffagie van A. v. d. Velde* | Deeze ryke Ordonnantie stelt voor een Heuvelachtig Landschap, gestoffeerd met een drift Beesten, verzelt van een Man met een Hond, schynende aan een ander, die nevens hem staat, den weg te vraagen, verder over een stil Water ziet men een bergachtig Verschiet; alles zeer natuurlyk en van eene krachtige behandeling | *Mat:* op doek *Size:* hoog 31, breed 36 duim	Herman ten Kate	(Sold) fl 1041 Th^{s} Spaan voor Muilman
1802/06/16	AMSCH	0203	*J. Wynands; A. v. de Velde* | Een Duinachtig Landzicht, ter zyde een stil Water, ziet men op een zandige brokkelagtige Heuvel, met een van hout gevlogte Schutting bezet, en Stamme van Boomen; een Heer by een afkomende weg met Snaphaan op schouder, verzelt van een Jagthond, verder Geboomten, gaande Huislieden en een bevallig verschiet; zeer fraay en natuurlyk gepenceeld | *Mat:* op doek *Size:* hoog 20, breed 17 duim	[Merrem]	(Sold) fl 580 H de Valk
1802/06/16	AMSCH	0204	*J. Wynands; A. v. de Velde* | Deeze twee Cabinetstukjes zyn Duinachtige Landschapjes met hoog Geboomte, Kreupelgewas en afkalverende Zandgronden, Waterplassen en aangename verschieten; beide bevallig gestoffeerd met Jagers en Reizigers te Paard en te voet; alles van de beste schildering van deeze Meesters | *Mat:* op doek *Size:* hoog 16, breed 13 ½ duim	[Merrem]	(Sold) fl 380 Cobel
1802/06/16	AMSCH	0205	*J. Wynands; A. v. de Velde* | Een Duinachtig Landschap met hoog Geboomte en aangenaam verschiet, de voorgrond met verscheide Koejen en een Herder gestoffeerd; alles van een aangenaame behandeling | *Mat:* op paneel *Size:* hoog 17 ½, breed 14 ½ duim	[Merrem]	(Sold) fl 73 Wed Achtienhoven
1806/08/13	AMSCH	0207	*Wynands (J.); A. van de Velde* | Dit capitaale Schildery steld voor, een hoogen Zandheuvel, waarby een opgaande Boom, langs een afkomende Weg ziet men aan een Waterplas drie Koeijen en eenige Schapen met hunne Herders; het bevallig licht hetgeen zich in dit aangenaam voorwerp vertoond, maakt dit tot een der fraaiste Schilderyen van dezen Meester | *Mat:* op paneel *Size:* hoog 26, breed 31 duim	Daniel Mansveld	(Sold) fl 611 Royers
1806/08/13	AMSCH	0208	*Wynands (J.); A. van de Velde* | Dit uitmuntend Duinachtig Landschapje met hoog Geboomten, omgehakte Stammen en welige Kruiden, is op de voorgrond gestoffeerd met Jagers te voet en te paard met Honden enz.; alles van een uitmuntende penceelsbehandeling | *Mat:* op paneel *Size:* hoog 15, breed 19 duim	Daniel Mansveld	(Sold) fl 400 van Iperen
1806/08/13	AMSCH	0209	*Wynands (J.); A. van de Velde* | Twee stuks Duin- en Bergachtige Landschappen, met Geboomten; Watervallen en onderscheiden stoffagie van Beelden, fiks gepenceeld | *Mat:* op doek *Size:* hoog 16, breed 21 duim	Daniel Mansveld	(Sold) fl 180 Thais
1810/08/01	AMSCH	0126	*Wijnands (Jan); Adriaan van de Velde* | Een aangenaam heuvelachtig Landschap met eene Rivier, Geboomte en Gebouwen. Op eenen zandigen Weg ziet men eenen Landman met eene Drift van Beesten; ter zijde ligt een Boomstam bij eenige Kruiden [Vue pitoresque sur un Sol sabloneux, coupé par une Riviere ; et varié par des Batimens et par des plantis d'Arbres. Dans une route sabloneuse se trouve un Pâtre conduisant du Bêtail. Vèrs le côté est un Tronc-d'arbre abattu et quelques Plantes] | *Annots:* Bon. (NGW) *Mat:* op paneel *Size:* hoog 12, breed 16 duimen	Mr Pieter de Smeth van Alphen	(Sold) fl 750 Cremer te Rotterdam
1810/08/01	AMSCH	0127	*Wijnands (Jan); Adriaan van de Velde* | Een duinachtig Landschap met eenen krommen Weg, hebbende aan beide kanten Water; het is gestoffeerd met Jagers en Honden, eenen Heer te paard en eenen Veedrijver [Une Vue de Bruïére dans laquelle serpente un Chemin sabloneux garni d'eau aux côtés. Ce site est embelli par un Chasseur et des Chiens, un Cavalier à Cheval, et par un Pâtre menant du Bêtail] | *Annots:* Bon. (NGW) *Mat:* op doek *Size:* hoog 14, breed 16 duimen	Mr Pieter de Smeth van Alphen	(Sold) fl 600 Perignon de Paris

Wijnants, Jan (and Velde, A. and Lingelbach)

1802/06/16	AMSCH	0206	*J. Wynands; A. v. de Velde; J. Lingelbach* | Een Capitaal Boom- en Bergachtig Landschap met een stille Rivier en aangenaam verschiet, zynde gestoffeerd met eenige Landlieden, welken eenig Vée voortdryven; het frapante Zonlicht en de meesterlyke penceels-behandeling maken dit Schildery een der fraayste van deezen Meesters | *Mat:* op doek *Size:* hoog 65, breed 76 duim	[Merrem]	(Sold) fl 250 Coclers

1802/06/16	AMSCH	0207	*J. Wynands; A. v. de Velde; J. Lingelbach* | Ter regter zyde vertoont zich de ingang van een Bosch; op de voorgrond legt eene Boomstam; verder een Man te Paard, waarby een Jager met Honden, ter linker zyde een stil Water en Boeren Huis; verder hoog Gebergte in het verschiet; meesterlyk en zonachtig geschilderd | *Mat:* op doek *Size:* hoog 25, breed 29 duim	[Merrem]	(Sold) fl 190 H de Valk
			Wijnants, Jan (and Wouwerman, Ph.)		
1801/06/10	AMSCH	0180	*Wynants. (J.); stoffage van Ph. Wouwerman* | Een Capitaal Landschap met hoog Geboomte, gestoffeerd met een Heer te Paard en andere Lieden, nevens Honden, schynende op de Hartejagt te zyn, in 't verschiet een Kasteel by Geboomte; fraai van Coloriet en fiks gepenceeld | *Mat:* op paneel *Size:* hoog 36, breed 32 duim	Herman ten Kate	(Sold) fl 158 Reynders
1801/06/10	AMSCH	0182	*Wynants. (J.); gestoffeerd door Ph. Wouwernan* | Een aangenaam en duinachtig Landschap, gestoffeerd met Heeren en Dames te Paard, ter zyde een Watertje, verders eenige Jagers met Honden, welke zich in het zelve ververschen; bevallig van licht, en van een der beste van deezen Meester | *Mat:* op doek *Size:* hoog 12 ½, breed 15 ½ duim	Herman ten Kate	(Sold) fl 205 Thaijs
1802/09/29	AMSCH	0058	*J. Wynants; Ph. Wouwerman* | Een Landschap, hoog 26 ½, breed 32 duim. Doek. Deeze Capitaale Ordenantie verbeeld een zeer uitgestrekt Landschap, welkers agtergrond met eenige Duinen eindigt. Voor aan ter regter zyde zyn eenige Boeren Wooningen, een Schuur, een Waterput en houte Heiningen; tegen de Schuur ziet men eenen Wyngaard; agter en naast dezelve schoon opgaand Geboomten van onderscheiden aart. Ter linker zyde ryd eenen Boerenknaap op een bruin Paard, (over den kluitägtigen Weg, gedeeltelyk begroeid met zooijen Gras en Planten,) nevens dezelve een Herder met twee Honden, waar van hy de eene in zyn loop wil terug houden. Eene beladene Vrouw en een Kind komen den Weg af, een paar oude Huislieden, van agter te zien, gaan denzelven op. Deeze twee beroemde Kunstenaars hebben hun kunstvermogen in dit Tafereel aan den dag gelegd. De Penceelbehandeling is uitmuntend fraai, zeer natuurlyk, zonägtig, en van een schoon Effect [Le Point de vüe d'un riche Paysage, offrant une variété d'arbres de belle Espéces & de grande proportion ; un vieux chêne tortueux s'y fait remarquer autant par sa Touche brillante que par des détails aussi vrais que la nature. La droite présente des chaumieres, des habitations villageoises de belle forme & un puid [sic], ou frappe la principale Lumiere. Philippe Wouwerman à enrichi ce magnifigue [sic] Tableau de nombre de Figures, d'un cheval & d'autres animaux, d'un beau choix ; l'on voit dans l'Eloignement un Pays immense traversé par différens chemins, un lointain admirable & montagneux perdu dans l'horison un ciel couvert des plus beaux nuages. Les Talens réunis de ces deux habiles Peintres, offrent ici aux amateurs un Tableau très précieux & d'une composition râre, digne d'occuper une place distinguée dans les premieres collections.] | *Mat:* op doek *Size:* hoog 26 ½, breed 32 duim	[Labouchere?]	(Sold) fl 450 Vinkeles
1808/08/23	AMSCH	0168	*Wijnands (J.); Ph. Wouwerman* | In een Duinachtig Landschap met eenig Geboomten, ziet men eenige Schaapen en Huislieden, welke van de hoogte nederwaards ziende, naar een aangenaam Land- en Watergezigt, gestoffeert met verscheiden Reisigers; alles zonachtig en van een uitvoerige penceelbehandeling | *Mat:* op doek *Size:* hoog 14, breed 12 duim	E	(Sold) fl 116 van Iperen
			Wijnants, Jan (or Wijnants, manner)		
1802/06/16	AMSCH	0210	*J. Wynants, of in de manier* | Een Boschagtig Landschap, op de voorgrond by zwaar Geboomte ziet men eenige Jagers met hunne Honden; verder een Reiziger te Paard, meesterlyk gepenceeld | *Mat:* op doek *Size:* hoog 52, breed 55 duim	[Merrem]	(Sold) fl 14 v d Schleij [for] R[ijfsnijder]
1804/02/27	AMSCH	0155	*Wynants* | Een Duin – en Boomryk Landschap, ryk gestoffeerd met Beelden en Beesten, verders een aangenaam verschiet, door of in de manier van Wynants | *Size:* hoog 20 ½, breed 15 ½ duim	D	(Bought In) fl 7
1807/06/10	HGBSM	0088	*J. Wynands* | Een Capitaal Duinagtig Landschap, waarop een heuvel eenige gebouwen, omringd met fraaij geboomte de opgaande weg met de zandige voorgronden, zijn uitmuntend geschildert aangenaam gestoffeerd met figuren, door of zo goed als J. Wynands | *Mat:* op doek *Size:* hoog 36 ½, breed 28 duim	Abraham Delfos [or others]	(Sold) fl 352 LaCourt
			Wijnants, Jan (or Wijnants, manner; and Velde, manner)		
1808/04/26	GDAN	0272	*J. Wijnands; van de Velde* | Een Landschap, door of in de manier van J. Wijnands, met fraaije stoffage of het van van de Velde was | *Size:* hoog 11 ½, breed 15 duim *Notes:* This lot was misnumbered no. 271.	G H Fortuyn	(Unknown)
			Wijnants, Jan (copy after)		
1801/10/06	AMSCH	0087	*J. Wynands* | Een Duinagtig Landschap met eenig geboomten, gestoffeerd met een Man, Vrouw en Jongen, eenig Vee voortdryvende, bevallig en uitvoerig geschilderd, naar J. Wynands | *Mat:* op paneel *Size:* hoog 10, breed 13 duim	L	(Sold) fl 13:10 Coclers
1805/10/21	GRBOL	0050	*Wynands* | Een Landschapje naar Wynands	Gerardus Nicolaus Heerkens	(Unknown)
1809/04/17	AMSCH	0106	*A. Vermeulen; J. Wijnands* | Twee stuks Duinachtige Landschappen, met Geboomten, gestoffeerd met gaande en rustende Huislieden; natuurlijk en	R	(Sold) fl 15:10 Gruyter

			Bevallig, naar J. Wijnands, door A. Vermeulen | copy by A. Vermeulen after Wijnants *Mat:* op paneel *Size:* ieder hoog 10, breed 12 ½ duim		
1809/04/22	AMYVR	0194	*J. Wijnands* | Twee stuks Duinachtige Landschappen; naar J. Wijnands	de Bruin	(Sold) fl 18:15 C S Roos
1809/04/22	AMYVR	0195	*J. Wijnands* | Een als voren [Duinachtig Landschap]; naar denzelven [J. Wijnands]	de Bruin	(Sold) fl 4 L Pakker
1809/06/13	AMSCH	0026	*H. Du Bois; J. Wijnands* | Een Heuvelagtig Landschap met Geboomten, Kruidgewas en Koornakker, gestoffeerd met rustende en staande Landlieden; bevallig en uitvoerig geschilderd, naar J. Wijnands, door H. Du Bois | copy by H. Dubois after Wijnants *Mat:* op paneel *Size:* hoog 14, breed 19 duim	M	(Sold) fl 16:5 van Iperen
			Wijnants, Jan (manner)		
1801/03/16	AMSCH	0064	*J. Wynands* | Een Duinagtig Landschap met Beelden gestoffeerd, in de manier van J. Wynands	P[ruyssenaar]	(Sold) fl 6 C S Roos
1802/09/06	AMSCH	0168	*J. Wynands* | Een Landzigt met eenig Geboomte, op de voorgrond by een zandige heuvel, twee huislieden, en een bevallig verschiet; in de manier van J. Wynands | *Size:* hoog 16, breed 13 duim	Wed Grave [or others]	(Sold) fl 35 Gruiter
1802/09/06	AMSCH	0247	*J. Wynands* | Een Duinagtig Landschap, op de voorgrond een Boer, staande by een paard, verder een gaande Vischboer; fix geschilderd in de manier van J. Wynands	Wed Grave [or others]	(Sold) fl 1:10 Bauer
1804/10/29	HRBAU	0137	*Wynands* | Een bevallig duinagtig Landschap, gestoffeerd met Jaagers en hunne Honden. In de manier van Wynands geschilderd | *Mat:* op doek *Size:* hoog 14, breed 18 duim	Simon Styl	(Unknown)
1805/07/10	AMSCH	0248	*J. Wynands* | Een Hevvelachtig [sic] Landschap met Geboomten, Boerewoningen en Rysigers gestoffeert, in de manier van J. Wynands | *Mat:* op paneel	Wed Grave	(Sold) fl 19 Lafontaine
1805/07/10	AMSCH	0277	*Wynands* | Een Land- en Riviergezicht, met stoffagie, als Wynands	V[inkeles] [for] L	(Sold) fl 0:6 L Pakker
1805/12/16	AMSCH	0084	*J. Wynands* | Een bevallig Land- en Dorpgezicht, aan een Rivier, met diversse stoffagie, als door J. Wynands	R[oos]	(Sold) fl 1 L Pakker
1806/05/05	AMSCH	0177[b]	*Wynands* | Drie stuks Landschappen; als Wynands en Berghem | *This Lot:* Landschap[pen]; lot 177[a] is manner of N.P. Berchem	R[oos]	(Sold) fl 4:10 for lots 177[a] & 177[b]. Scheurleer
1807/06/10	HGBSM	0165	*J. Wynands* | Een Duin gezigtje in de manier van J. Wynands | *Mat:* op paneel *Size:* hoog 6 ½, breed 9 duim	Abraham Delfos [or others]	(Sold) fl 4 Colonbon
1808/08/23	AMSCH	0220	*J. Wijnands* | Een Duinachtig Landschap met Geboomten, op de voorgrond een Reiziger te Paard, als spreekende tegen een Huisman; zonachtig behandeld, op Paneel, als door J. Wijnands | *Mat:* op paneel	R	(Sold) fl 33 Hulswit
1808/08/23	AMSCH	0244	*J. Wijnands* | Een duinachtig Landschap met Beeldjes en Beesten gestoffeert; als J. Wijnands	S	(Sold) fl 7:10 van Os
1809/06/13	AMSCH	0180	*J. Wynands* | Een Duinachtig Landschap, gestoffeerd met een Man te Prard [sic] en rustende Jagers; fiks geschilderd in de manier van J. Wynands	T	(Sold) fl 0:12 Gruiter
			Wild, T. [Unidentified]		
1809/07/25	HGBSM	0198	*T. Wild* | Diana met haare Nimphen &c., in de manier van Poelenburg, door T. Wild | *Mat:* op paneel *Size:* hoog 8, breed 7 en een half duim	D van der Aa [or] E B ten Dall	(Sold) fl 2:8 Schoon
			Willaerts		
1801/10/06	AMSCH	0083	*Willaarts* | Een Gezigt op de Schelde, voor de Stad Antwerpen, gestoffeerd met zylende Vaartuigen, meesterlyk behandeld | *Mat:* op paneel *Size:* hoog 18, breed 44 duim	M	(Sold) fl 2:10 Van Iperen
1801/10/06	AMSCH	0084	*Willaarts* | Een Onstuymige Zee, met sterke Branding tegens een klip, natuurlyk verbeeld | *Mat:* op paneel *Size:* hoog 15, breed 18 duim	M	(Sold) fl 8:5 Theijs
1801/10/06	AMSCH	0085	*Willaarts* | Een Woelend Water, met zylende Scheepen, op de voorgrond aan Strand eenige Visschers fiks gepenceeld | *Mat:* op doek *Size:* hoog 40, breed 66 duim	M	(Sold) fl 2 Vos
1802/05/05	AMSCH	0240	*Willaards* | Een Strand- en Zeegezicht, in 't zelven verbeeld een groot Schip, op een Bank gestrand, 't Strand is ryk gestoffeerd met eenige Menschen die het ongeluk met verbaazing aanschouwen, gepenceeld | *Size:* hoog 43, breed 52 duim *Notes:* This lot was sold with lot 242 by M. Withoos.	J	(Sold) fl 3 for lots 240 & 242. L Pakker
1802/06/28	AMSCH	0210	*Willaerts* | Een Strandgezigt, gestoffeert met Vissers Schuyten en gaande Lieden aan Strandt door Willaerts, op Koper geschilderd | *Mat:* op koper *Size:* hoog 5, breed 6 duim	Anna Elink	(Sold) fl 0:6 L Pakker
1803/09/07	AMSCH	0217	*Willaerts* | Twee stuks Zeetjes, met verschyde Scheepen en Schuiten, fix op Koper [Deux petites marines, avec plusieurs navires et des chaloupes ; bonne composition] | *Mat:* op koper *Size:* hoog 4 ½, breed 7 duim	Smidt	(Sold) fl 2 Jan Yver
1803/09/07	AMSCH	0218	*Willaerts* | Een Zeestrand, vol gewoel van Beeldjes, verders een ménigte zylende en andere Scheepen; natuurlyk [La vue d'un rivage de mer ; le devant est plein de mouvement parmi les figures, le fond fait voir des	Smidt	(Sold) fl 2:10 Toselli

			batimens de diverses espèces] | *Mat:* op paneel *Size:* hoog 23, breed 33 duim		
1805/07/10	AMSCH	0220	*Willaarts* | Een Zeestrand, met verscheide Beelden en Scheepen	Y[ver]	(Bought In) fl 8
1808/08/23	AMSCH	0174	*Willaerts* | Een woelende Zee, op de voorgrond bij het Strand een Visschers Pink, waar in een Apostel prekende, op het Strand een menigte Lieden, zoo Mans, Vrouwen en Kinderen, ter zijde hoog Gebergte; krachtig en meesterlijk gepenceeld | *Mat:* op doek *Size:* hoog 55, breed 87 duim	C	(Sold) fl 30 Jan Spaan
1808/12/12	UTWLD	0006	*Willers* | Een fraaij Zeegezicht [Alle in swarte Lysten en wel geconserveerd.] | *Mat:* op paneel *Size:* hoog 2 voet 8 duim, breed 3 voet 8 duim *Notes:* The bracketed information in the title appears above lot 1 and refers to lots 1 to 19.	Mr D Hoola van Nooten	(Unknown)
1810/03/07	UTWLD	0034	*Weillarts* | Een Zeegezigt	J J Woertman	(Unknown) fl 2:12
1810/11/07	UTWLD	0057	*Willards* | Een duingezichtje waar een visscher in gesprek met een vrouwtje, voor hem een groote Visch, verder eenige kleine Visschen en eenig bijwerk door Willards op paneel, 11 duim hoog, 1 voet 2 duim breed, zwarte Lijst | *Mat:* op paneel *Size:* 11 duim hoog, 1 voet 2 duim breed		(Unknown) fl 3
			Willaerts (manner)		
1802/12/13	AMSCH	0203	*Willaarts* | Een Zée-Gezicht, aan de Muuren van een Stad, gestoffeerd met zeilende Scheepen, en Galyen; krachtig behandeld op Paneel, als door Willaarts | *Mat:* op paneel	Florijn [?]	(Sold) fl 0:12 Gruiter
			Willaerts, A.		
1803/04/20	AMSCH	0144	*H. Willaerts [A. Willaerts]* | Eenige Oorlogscheepen, in een breede Rivier voor de Vestmuur van een Stad; fiks geschilderd [Un Port de mer garni de gros Vaisseaux bien rendu par A. Willaerts.] | *Notes:* The artist's name differs in the Dutch and French editions of the catalogue.	Maria Magdalena van Sluypwyk, gravinne van Moens	(Sold) fl 3:5 Palmhoff
1806/08/13	AMSCH	0221	*Willaerts. (A.)* | De Prediking van Christus aan het Strand, zynde een Ordinantie van verscheide Beelden; uitvoerig gepenceeld | *Mat:* op paneel *Size:* hoog 25, breed 39 duim	Roos	(Sold) fl 3 Hymans
			Willaerts, Adam		
1802/12/13	AMSCH	0180	*A. Willaerts* | Een Strandgezicht aan een Dorp, met verscheiden Stoffagie van Pinken en Beeldjes; natuurlyk | *Mat:* op paneel *Size:* hoog 26, breed 42 duim	Yver	(Sold) fl 1 L Pakker
1803/08/24	HGKAN	A0006	*A. Willaerds* | Een Capitaal Strand Gezigt, op de voorgrond Ryk gestoffeert met Visschers, verders met Scheepen vol gewoel, op de Regterhand een Rotz met Gebouwen, door A. Willaerds, van zyn besten tyd, op paneel van een Stuk | *Mat:* op paneel *Size:* breet 31 ½, hoog 20 ½ duim		(Sold) fl 7:10 Kan
1804/10/16	DLOND	0259	*A. Willaart* | Een Stads Gezicht binnen Amsterdam. Un endroit de la Ville d'Amsterdam | *Mat:* op paneel *Size:* hoog 27, breed 40		(Unknown)
1804/10/16	DLOND	0260	*A. Willaart* | Een Zee Gezicht met Schepen. Une Mer avec des Vaisseaux | *Mat:* op paneel *Size:* hoog 17, breed 27		(Unknown)
1805/10/09	HGBSM	0020	*A. Willaards* | Een gezigt in de middelandsche zee, met verscheide schepen en figuren | *Mat:* op paneel *Size:* hoog 20 breet 29 duim	T H van Willigen [or others]	(Sold) fl 6:15 Van Os
1805/10/09	HGBSM	0083	*A. Willaerds* | Een strandgezicht met visschuiten en andere scheepen | *Mat:* op paneel *Size:* hoog 12 ½ breet 18 ½ duim	T H van Willigen [or others]	(Sold) fl 8:5 Ten Haaf
1807/06/10	HGBSM	0141	*A. Willaard* | Een Strand gezigt met Schepen en Figuuren, 1624 | *Mat:* op paneel *Size:* hoog 12 ½, breed 18 duim *Inscr:* 1624 (dated?) *Notes:* It is unclear whether the date is inscribed on the painting.	Abraham Delfos [or others]	(Sold) fl 3 Ten Haaf
1809/04/22	AMYVR	0148	*A. Willaarts* | Een Strandgezicht, met Vaartuigen en Beelden | *Mat:* op paneel *Size:* hoog 7, breed 10 duim	Juff^{r} Julikker	(Sold) fl 0:10 van der Schley
1809/06/13	AMSCH	0168	*A. Willaarts* | Een Strandgezigt met Visschers, Kooplieden en Vaartuigen | *Mat:* op paneel *Size:* hoog 20, breed 29 duim	Y	(Sold) fl 1:5 Gruiter
1809/06/13	AMSCH	0214	*A. Willaarts* | Een Strandgezigt met Vaartuigen en Beeldjes	E	(Sold) fl 1:5 Eversdijk
1809/06/13	AMSCH	0215	*A. Willaarts* | Een dito [Strandgezigt] als het voorgaande	E	(Sold) fl 0:8 du Prée
			Willaerts, Cornelis		
1801/11/10	AMPOS	0005	*C. Willarts* | 1 dito [gestoffeerd] Landschap, vol deftige en arme Lieden | *Mat:* op paneel		(Unknown)
1802/05/24	HGBAK	0066	*C. Willards* | Diana met haar Nymphen, in een Landschap, door C. Willards 1647, hoog 18 duim, breed 25 duim, paneel, zwarte lyst | *Mat:* op paneel *Size:* hoog 18 duim, breed 25 duim *Inscr:* C. Willards 1647 (signed and dated?) *Notes:* It is unclear whether the name and date are inscribed on the painting.	Mejuffrouw A van der Mieden	(Sold) fl 7:15 Sluijter
1810/10/11	AMSCH	0100	*C. Willers* | Maria Magdalena, zittende in een Grot, met zaam gevouwene handen voor een Crusifix [sic] en opengeslagen Boek; fiks geschilderd | *Mat:* op doek *Size:* hoog 14, breed 13 duimen	[Levy Pakker?]	(Sold) fl 4:15 T Spaan

Willeboirts, Thomas

1804/08/02	BDAN	0037	*T. Willeborts* | Een Mans-portrait | *Mat:* op doek *Size:* breed 14 d. h. 18 en 1 half d.	J G Calckberner	(Unknown)

Willegen, D. [Unidentified]

1805/10/09	HGBSM	0138	*D. Willegen* | De brand van Troijen &c. | *Mat:* op paneel *Size:* hoog 18 breet 24 duim	T H van Willigen [or others]	(Sold) fl 7 van den Broek

Willekens, T. [Unidentified]

1803/09/07	AMSCH	0219	*T. Willekens* | Twee stuks Boom- en Bergachtige Landschapjes met Rivieren, Gebouwen en stoffagie, fraay op Doek [Deux jolis paysages relevés par des arbres et des montagnes, entrecoupés de rivières et ornés d'une agréable diversité d'objets] | *Mat:* op doek *Size:* hoog 14, br. 19 duim	Smidt	(Bought In) fl 8 ½

Wils, Jan

1801/10/06	AMSCH	0075	*J. Wils* | Een Italiaansch Bergagtig Landschap, op de voorgrond, en in 't verschiet eenig Geboomten; by een opgaande Weg, zit een Ryziger te Paard, waar by een gaande Huisman twee belaaden Ezels voort dryvende: alles is Natuurlyk afgebeeld; en van een uitvoerige Penceelbehandeling | *Mat:* op koper *Size:* hoog 13 ½, breed 16 duim	S	(Sold) fl 399 for lots 75 & 76. Corn Seb Roos
1801/10/06	AMSCH	0076	*J. Wils* | In een dito [Italiaansch] Aangenaam Landschap, vertoont zich op de voorgrond, een Vrouw op een Ezel zittende, waar by een gaande Huisman, ter regter zyde by hoog Gebergten, ziet men een hoog opgaande Weg, gestoffeert met verscheide Ryzigers, zoo te Paard als te Voet, en andere rustende Lieden, verder is een Bergagtig verschiet, alles is als de vorige, Zonagtig en uitvoerig gepenceelt | *Mat:* op koper *Size:* hoog 13 ½, breed 16 duim	S	(Sold) fl 399 for lots 75 & 76. Corn Seb Roos
1802/05/05	AMSCH	0237	*J. Wils* | Twee stuks bergachtige Landschappen, met hoog geboomte, gestoffeerd met Ryzigers en andere Beelden, zonachtig | *Mat:* op paneel *Size:* hoog 13, breed 17 duim	E	(Sold) fl 32 Cocler
1802/09/21	UTHDG	0101	*J. Wils* | Hoog geboomte, langs welk een weg loopt waarop een Reiziger te voet. In het verschiet Graanvelden en een stad, bevallig van coloriet, geschildert door J. Wils | *Mat:* op paneel *Size:* hoog 15 ½, breed 21 ½ duimen		(Sold) fl 8 Niekerk
1810/03/26	RMMUY	0023	*Jan Wils* | Een Bergachtig Landschap, met Ruïnen en verdere Stoffagie van Figuren [Un Paysage, au milieu passe une rivière, un pont, des sites et fabriques le décorent. Un lointain agréable termine la vue ; sur le devant un beau terrain. De belles masses d'arbres et figures en font un bel ensemble, d'un bon ton de couleur, et vigoureusement traîté.] | *Mat:* op doek op paneel *Size:* hoog 25 ½, breed 31 ½ duimen	Daniel de Jongh Az	(Sold) fl 20 Le Brun Paris

Wilt, J. van der [Unidentified]

1802/09/21	UTHDG	0104	*J. van der Wilt* | De Historie van Danaë en de Guldenregen, zij is verzeld van een oude Vrouw en drie Minnegoden | *Mat:* op paneel *Size:* hoog 13 ½, breed 19 duimen		(Bought In) fl 10:10

Wiltens, C. [Unidentified]

1810/05/22	AMSCH	0124	*Wiltens. (C.)* | Maria Magdalena in berouw, verbeeld in een rotsachtig Landschap; gestoffeerd met verder bijwerk; krachtig en meesterlijk gepenceeld | *Mat:* op doek *Size:* hoog 9, breed 12 duim	F	(Sold) fl 5 Valee

Wiltschier, J. [Unidentified]

1806/08/13	AMSCH	0222	*Wiltschier. (J.)* | Een Gezicht by een Molen aan een Water, op de voorgrond staand en leggend Vee, in het verschiet een Stad; zeer natuurlyk van licht en penceelsbehandeling | *Mat:* op paneel *Size:* hoog 34, breed 48 duim	Roos	(Sold) fl 16:10 Du Pré

Winghen, B. van [Unidentified]

1806/08/20	HGBSM	0078	*B. van Winghen* | Op eene Steene Tafel, staat eene Flesch gevuld met verschillende soorten van Roozen en andere fraaije Bloemen, waar op Insecten aasen. Extra dun en natuurlijk geschilderd | *Mat:* op doek *Size:* hoog 23, breed 16 duim	Macalester Loup [or others]	(Sold) fl 5:5 Gram

Winter, Gillis de

1801/10/06	AMSCH	0082	*G. de Winter* | Een Binnehuis met een Boere Chirurgyn, die een Vrouw haar voet verbind, gestoffeerd met verder bywerk, fiks behandeld | *Mat:* op doek *Size:* hoog 12 ½, breed 10 duim	M	(Sold) fl 3 Jan Spaan
1801/11/21	RMVIS	0006	*A. van Winter* | Een Binnehuis, met Figuren en Bywerk	Gelinus van Spaan	(Unknown)
1802/02/16	AMSCH	0090	*G. de Winter* | Een Kermisvreugd in een Boeredorp, daar zich verschyde Lieden vermaken, plaisant geschilderd	G	(Sold) fl 9:10 Th Spaan
1802/05/05	AMSCH	0239	*de Winter* | Twee stuks, de eene een Kermis en de andere een Vismarkt, beide vol gewoel | *Size:* hoog 16, breed 19 duim	J	(Sold) fl 7:10 Rigters
1804/10/29	HRBAU	0116	*Winter, (de)* | Een Gezelschap van agttien Persoonen der beide sexe, en van verschillende jaaren, vermaakt zich met eeten, drinken, dansen, en	Simon Styl	(Unknown)

			caresseeren, in een welgemeubileerde Kamer. Vrolyk en plaisant behandeld | *Mat:* op doek *Size:* hoog 33, breed 38 duim		
1809/04/22	AMYVR	0147	*G. Winter* | Een Mosselpartij in een Huismans Wooning, verders een Hond en ander bijwerk | *Mat:* op doek *Size:* hoog 22, breed 17 duim	de Bruin	(Sold) fl 4 Frantzen

Wit, de (copy by)

1804/10/16	DLOND	0263	*De With; naar Bega* | Twee Stukjens. Vuur-en Lamplichtjens. Deux pièces. Lumière de Feu & de Lampe | copy by Wit after Bega *Mat:* op paneel *Size:* hoog 10, breed 8		(Unknown)

Wit, Jacob de

1801/03/16	AMSCH	0065	*J. de Wit* | Een Basrelief met speelende Kindertjes in 't graau, kunstig en uitvoerig	P[ruyssenaar]	(Sold) fl 2:5 for lots 65 & 66. Stevens
1801/03/16	AMSCH	0066	*J. de Wit* | Een dito [Basrelief] als de voorgaande [J. de Wit]	P[ruyssenaar]	(Sold) fl 2:5 for lots 65 & 66. Stevens
1801/05/11	AMSCH	0111	*J. de Wit* | Een zinspeelende Ordonnantie van drie Kindertjes, welke Belle blaazen, zeer meesterlyk behandeld | *Mat:* op doek *Size:* hoog 48, breed 36 duim	R[oos]	(Bought In) fl 40
1801/08/19	AMSCH	0137	*J. de Wit* | De Sterre-Kunde, verbeeld door twee Kinderen, staande by een Globe in een Nis, een derzelve heeft een Graad-Boog in de hand, ter zyde ziet men een Zonnewyzer, Winkelhaak, Passer en Boeken; meesterlyk in 't graauw als Basrelief op Doek geschilderd | *Mat:* op doek *Size:* hoog 44, breed 32 duim	van der Schly [for] F	(Sold) fl 8:10 I^{c} Smit
1801/12/22	AMOTT	0013	*J. de Wit* | 1 Soldering of Blafonstuk, door J. de Wit, 1728 | *Inscr:* J. de Wit, 1728 (signed and dated?) *Notes:* It is unclear whether the name and date are inscribed on the painting.	Bartholomeus Ruloffs	(Unknown) fl 5:5
1801/12/22	AMOTT	0014	*J. de Wit* | Kindertjes voor een Muur, gedekt met een blaauw Kleed, door denzelve [J. de Wit], 1725 | *Inscr:* J. de Wit, 1725 (signed and dated?) *Notes:* It is unclear whether the name and date are inscribed on the painting.	Bartholomeus Ruloffs	(Unknown) fl 3:10
1802/02/16	AMSCH	0020	*J. de Wit* | Twee stuks Blassonnen, fix gepenceeld op doek | *Mat:* op doek	B[uys]	(Sold) fl 16 Hulswit
1802/02/16	AMSCH	0069	*J. de Wit* | Een capitaal Schoorsteenstuk, gestoffeerd met vyf bevallige kindertjes, houdende twee Jagthonden, verbeeldende een jagtparty; kragtig en aangenaam van coloriet | *Fmt:* schoorsteenstuk	C	(Sold) fl 60 Isaac Smit
1802/06/16	AMSCH	0212	*J. de Wit* | Dit bevallig Tafereel verbeeld een Zinnebeeldige Ordenantie op den Koophandel: in 't midden van dit stuk staat het Standbeeld van Mercurius, geplaast op een cierlyke gewerkte Voetstuk, waar op in Medailon, Basreliefgewyze, een Eckhoorntje op een plank in Zee dryvende; ter zyde op de voorgrond een zittende Vrouw en drie speelende Kindertjes met Bouw-Gereedschappen; verder vier andere zinryke afbeeldzels van Vrouwen en Kindertjes by een Bykorf; alles is bevallig van Licht en Coloriet, en uitmuntend gepenceeld | *Mat:* op paneel *Size:* hoog 25 ½, breed 19 duim	[Merrem]	(Sold) fl 200 I Smit G^{Z}
1802/06/16	AMSCH	0213	*J. de Wit* | Deeze Ordenantie stelt voor Mozes kiezende de Zeventig Oudste van Israël; verders ziet men de Tabernakelen; zynde dit stuk een der modelle van het Raadhuis te Amsterdam | *Mat:* op paneel *Size:* hoog 9 ½, breed 20 duim	[Merrem]	(Sold) fl 16 Agina
1802/07/20	MGSAN	0034	*de Wit* | Een extra fraai Stuk, waar de Moorman door Philippus gedoopt wordt: zeer krachtig geschilderd | *Size:* hoog duim 24, breed duim 30		(Unknown)
1802/09/06	AMSCH	0132	*J. de Wit* | Een ryk geordeneert Blafonstuk; bevallig | *Mat:* op doek *Size:* hoog 20, breed 22 duim	J	(Sold) fl 4:10 Hulswit
1802/12/13	AMSCH	0179	*J. de Wit* | Een Basrelief van drie Kindertjes, zinspeelende op Vrede en Vryheid; bevallig | *Mat:* op doek *Size:* hoog 50, breed 39 duim	Yver	(Sold) fl 7 v der Schley
1803/08/24	HGKAN	0073	*de Witt* | Een Historieele Ordonnantie	[Teissier] [or others]	(Unknown) fl 6
1803/12/12	AMSCH	0111	*J. de Wit* | De vier Saisoenen door Kinderen afgebeeld, in een Landschap; meesterlyk en fraai op Doek | *Mat:* op doek *Size:* hoog 53, breed 58 duim	H	(Bought In) fl 60
1803/12/12	AMSCH	0112	*J. de Wit* | Vier spelende Kinderen, bedrieglyk als basrelief, in 't grauw | *Size:* hoog 23, breed 47 duim	Arnoud de Lange	(Sold) fl 5 Yver
1803/12/12	AMSCH	0113	*J. de Wit* | De Godin Diana benevens een andere Jagtnimph, verzeld van eenige Kindertjes in een Landschap, fiks gepenceeld op Doek | *Mat:* op doek *Size:* hoog 46, breed 38 duim	B	(Sold) fl 1:10 Boelen
1804/02/27	AMSCH	0118	*Wit. (De)* | Een Historieel Voorwerp; schoon gecoloreert en breed geschilderd | *Size:* hoog 30, breed 23 duim	C	(Sold) fl 3 W Knoop
1804/02/27	AMSCH	0133	*J. de Wit* | De vier Waerelddeelen; meesterlyk in het graauw gepenceeld	B	(Sold) fl 5:5 Gruiter
1804/04/28	LNDLS	0028	*J. de Wit* | Vliegende Kupido's, kunnende dienen voor een Blaffon	[Abraham Delfos] [or others]	(Bought In) fl 5
1804/04/28	LNDLS	0029	*J. de Wit* | Een Plint, met verscheiden kinderen, zinspelende op verscheide kunsten en wetenschappen, in 't graauw verbeeld, basrelief, op paneel | *Mat:* op paneel	[Abraham Delfos] [or others]	(Sold) fl 11 Parker
1804/04/28	LNDLS	0041	*J. de Witt* | Een Bachenaal van vier Cupido's, die druiven perssen, fraai van couleur en konstig geschilderd | *Mat:* op doek *Size:* hoog 41, breed 38 duim	[Abraham Delfos] [or others]	(Bought In) fl 12

1804/04/28	LNDLS	0042	*J. de Wit* | Een konstig Basrelief, uit graauw, verbeeldende geloof, hoop, en liefde, door een vrouw met een kind op haar schoot, een staande jongen, die op een altaar rust, daar een boek op legt, en een anker agter hem, terwijl hij van een vliegende cupido gekroond wordt; konstig en natuurlijk verbeeld, op doek | *Mat:* op doek *Size:* hoog 33, breed 41 duim	[Abraham Delfos] [or others]	(Bought In) fl 46
1804/05/07	AMSCH	0197	*Wit. (J. de)* | Op een Tafel legt een Schaal, waarin het Hoofd van St. Jan, welke door eenige Seraphine met verwondering aanschouwd word; allernatuurlykst gepenceeld | *Mat:* op doek *Size:* hoog 12, breed 16 duim	Roos [for] A	(Sold) fl 1:15 L Pakker
1804/07/25	AMSCH	0091	*Wit. (J. de)* | Een capitaal Schoorsteenstuk, zynde een Basrelief, met 4 Kindertjes, verbeeldende de vier Getyden des Jaars, kennelyk aan hem byhebbende teekenen; zeer kunstig, bevallig, en natuurlyk in 't graauw geschilderd | *Mat:* op doek *Fmt:* schoorsteenstuk *Size:* hoog 62, breed 36 duim		(Sold) fl 25:10 C S Roos
1804/08/08	AMSCH	0222	*J. de Wit* | Een Vanitas, verbeeld door Drie Kinderen, bézig zynde Bellen te blaazen, een Globe, Doodshoofd, Kroon, Fluit, Muziek, een Palet met Verf, Penceelen en andere Voorwerpen maaken dit stuk behaaglyk | *Mat:* op doek *Size:* hoog 48, breed 35 duim	Roos a	(Sold) fl 100 La Bouchere
1804/08/08	AMSCH	0226	*J. de Wit* | Christus onder de Geleerden door Maria en Joseph gezocht; in de manier van Rembrand | *Mat:* op paneel *Size:* hoog 24, breed 34 duim *Notes:* The artist was presumably Jacob Willemsz. de Wet and not Jacob de Wit.	Vink[eles] [for] K[=Gruyter?]	(Sold) fl 0:10 L Pakker
1804/08/08	AMSCH	0227	*J. de Wit* | In de Woestyne ziet men op het Gebed van Moses, 't nédergedaalde Manna door de Kinderen Israëls met yver verzamelen; in de manier van Rembrand | *Mat:* op doek *Size:* hoog 33, breed 36 duim *Notes:* The artist was presumably Jacob Willemsz. de Wet and not Jacob de Wit.	Vink[eles] [for] K[=Gruyter?]	(Sold) fl 1:15 Gruyter
1805/07/10	AMSCH	A0002	*J. de Wit* | Twee Schoorsteen-Stukken in couleuren [Fraaije geschilderde Kamer-Behangsels] | *Notes:* The bracketed information in the title appears above lot A1 and refers to lots A1 to A8.	H	(Withdrawn)
1805/07/10	AMSCH	A0004	*J. de Wit* | Een Platfond, met verscheide Beelden en Kinderen, overheerlyk in couleuren geschilderd [Fraaije geschilderde Kamer-Behangsels] | *Size:* lang 8 voet, 2 duim en breed 12 voet 8 duim *Notes:* The bracketed information in the title appears above lot A1 and refers to lots A1 to A8.	R[oos]	(Sold) fl 6 Isaac Smit
1805/10/09	HGBSM	0126	*J. de Wit* | Een gekruiste Christus, verbeeldende het oogenblik van de geest te geeven, meesterlyk geschilderd | *Mat:* op doek *Size:* hoog 31 breet 26 ½ duim	T H van Willigen [or others]	(Sold) fl 30 De Gelder, R
1805/10/09	HGBSM	0127	*J. de Wit* | Het hoofd van den Heiland | *Mat:* op doek *Size:* hoog 20 ½ breet 16 duim	T H van Willigen [or others]	(Sold) fl 3:5 Valette
1805/10/09	HGBSM	0128	*J. de Wit* | Het hoofd van de moeder Gods, niet minder als de voorgaande, door denzelven [J. de Wit], eender grooten | *Size:* hoog 20 ½ breet 16 duim	T H van Willigen [or others]	(Sold) fl 3 Teissier
1806/05/05	AMSCH	0154	*J. de Wit* | Twee stuks, met speelende Kindertjes | *Mat:* op paneel *Size:* hoog 10 ½, breed 12 ½ duim	V[inkeles]	(Sold) fl 10:10 Izaac Smit
1806/05/05	AMSCH	0247	*J. de Wit* | Een Blason	V[inkeles]	(Sold) fl 2 van Dyl
1806/08/13	AMSCH	0219	*Wit. (J. de)* | Een uitvoerig geschilderd Plafon	Vinkeles [for] G[ruyter]	(Sold) fl 4 Gruiter
1806/08/13	AMSCH	0284	*J. de Wit* | Een Zinnebeeldige Ordinantie	Coclers	(Sold) fl 1:15 B Janzen
1806/08/13	AMSCH	0331	*Wit. (J. de)* | In een Landschap, ziet men Maria met het Kind Jezu aan de Borst, in de Wolken eenige Seraphynen; dun en fiks behandeld | *Mat:* op doek *Size:* hoog 53, breed 40 duim	Vinkeles [for] G[ruyter]	(Bought In) fl 10
1807/04/00	LNDLS	0038	*J. de Witt* | Een Bachinaal van kinderen, met vrugten en wijngaard ranken, op doek, door J. de Witt, 1731 | *Mat:* op doek *Size:* hoog 42, breed 40 duim *Inscr:* J. de Witt, 1731 (signed and dated?) *Notes:* It is unclear whether the name and date are inscribed on the painting.	[Abraham Delfos] [or others]	(Unknown)
1807/06/02	AMHUY	0038	*de Wit* | Eenige Kinderen in graauw, door de Wit, 1733 | *Inscr:* de Wit, 1733 (signed and dated?) *Notes:* It is unclear whether the name and date are inscribed on the painting.		(Unknown)
1807/06/10	HGBSM	0038	*J. de Witt* | Een Bachanaal van kinderen, met vrugten en wijngaard ranken, 1731 | *Mat:* op doek *Size:* hoog 42, breed 40 duim *Inscr:* 1731 (dated?) *Notes:* It is unclear whether the date is inscribed on the painting.	Abraham Delfos [or others]	(Sold) fl 6:5 Tomas
1807/06/10	HGBSM	0073	*J. de Witt* | Een Basrelief uit graauw, verbeeld, Geloof, Hoop en Liefde, konstig en voor een schoorsteenstuk dienende | *Mat:* op doek *Fmt:* schoorsteenstuk *Size:* hoog 33 breed 41 duim	Abraham Delfos [or others]	(Sold) fl 6:5 Guicherit
1807/06/10	HGBSM	0074	*J. de Witt* | Vliegende Cupido's, kunnende dienen voor een klijn blaffon. in couleuren | *Mat:* op doek	Abraham Delfos [or others]	(Sold) fl 5:4 Vermeulen
1807/08/26	AMSCH	0242	*J. de Wit* | Een achtbaar Christus-Hoofd; meesterlyk | *Mat:* op doek *Size:* hoog 21, breed 16 duim	Joseph Vallette	(Sold) fl 5:15 Gruiter
1807/08/26	AMSCH	0243	*J. de Wit* | Drie speelende Kindertjes in basrelief, in een Landschap, meesterlyk fiks in 't graauw geschilderd	Yver [for] S	(Sold) fl 3:15 H Jansen

1807/08/26	AMSCH	0244	*J. de Wit* | Een lange Plint, versiert met een Medaillon, waarby verscheidene Kindertjes, zinspeelende op de Teeken-, Schilder- en Beeldhouwkunst; in basrelief geschilderd	Yver [for] S	(Sold) fl 5:10 Sardet
1808/05/17	LNAN	0013	*Jacob de Wit* | Een bachonaal [sic] met kinderen, een met wijngaard ranken om 't hoofd, een ander met een beker in zijn hand en een staf, met druive trossen en vruchten op den voorgrond, kunstig op doek geschilderd | *Mat:* op doek *Size:* hoog 42, breed 40 duim	[Abraham Delfos]	(Unknown) fl 18
1808/06/06	RMRIJ	0140	*Wit. (Jacob de)* | Twee Landschappen met Bacchanalen. In het eene ziet men vijf Kinderen, die met trossen Druiven spelen; digt bij hen staat een Term, het borstbeeld van Bacchus. In de wedergade spelen verscheidene kinderen met een Bok. De uitwerking der kleuren in beiden is verrukkelijk [Cinq Enfans auprès d'un Terme, s'amusent avec des raisins et des branches de vigne. Composition gracieuse, d'un Coloris agréable. Le Pendant. Quatre Enfants qui jouent avec une Chêvre blanche. D'un beau Coloris, et d'une Composition agréable et variée. Ces deux Morceaux sont de beaux Modèles en couleur de ce fameux Peintre en bas-relief] | *Annots:* Verk. Braamcamp. 1771 (f 510.-) Verk. P. Calkoen wz. 10 Sept 1781 (f 400.-) (RMA I) *Mat:* op paneel *Size:* Twee Stukken. Hoog 14, en breed 9 ½ duim	Gerrit van der Pot, Heer van Groeneveld	(Sold) fl 110 T T Cremer
1808/10/28	AMVRS	0064	*Wit, (J. de)* | Een zinspeelende Ordonantie, van 3 Kindertjes. Meesterlijk in 't graauw geschilderd | *Mat:* op doek *Size:* hoog 59, breed 66 duim	Marten Udink	(Sold) fl 4:15 Van Dijl
1809/04/17	AMSCH	0112	*J. de Wit* | Een Zinnebeeldige Ordonantie van verscheide Kindertjes zittende op de Wolken; schoon geteekend en meesterlijk behandeld | *Mat:* op doek *Size:* hoog 64, breed 47 duim		(Sold) fl 5
1809/05/26	HADAA	0006	*Jacob de Wit* | Een zinspelende Ordonnantie van vier Kinderen, zinspelende op den Wijnoogst, van voren met Druiventros en Meloen, uitmuntend, bevallig en natuurlijk gegroept en fraai gekleurd | *Mat:* op doek *Size:* hoog 42 breed 39 duimen	Mejuffrouw de Wed David Heemskerk [or others]	(Unknown)
1809/05/26	HADAA	0020	*J. de Wit* | Een Kindje	Mejuffrouw de Wed David Heemskerk [or others]	(Unknown)
1809/07/19	AMSCH	0066	*Wit (J. de)* | In een Landschap ziet men op den voorgrond een bevallig Kind, verbeelende St. Jan, zittende op een Steen, nevens hem een rustend Lam. Krachtig en helder van koloriet, uitvoerig en fraai gepenceeld | *Mat:* op doek *Size:* hoog 38, breed 30 duim	C	(Sold) fl 33:10 Van Iperen
1809/07/19	AMSCH	0067	*Wit (J. de)* | Een ander bevallig Kindje, staande in een Landschap, mede St. Jan verbeeldende, en verzeld van een Lam, en als de voorgaande behandeld | *Mat:* op doek *Size:* hoog 39, breed 32 duim	[Wijkersloot?]	(Sold) fl 5:5 Dupré
1809/07/25	HGBSM	0089	*J. de Wit* | De Boodschap aan Maria door den Engel | *Mat:* op doek op paneel *Size:* hoog 10 en een half, breed 9 duim	D van der Aa	(Sold) fl 8:5 de Gruyter
1809/07/25	HGBSM	0090	*J. de Wit* | Eenige Speelende Kinders met een Bok | *Mat:* op koper *Size:* hoog 8, breed 10 en 1 half duim	D van der Aa	(Sold) fl 15 A Vermeulen
1809/07/25	HGBSM	0091	*J. de Wit* | Eenige Kindertjes die bellen blazen schetsgewys | *Mat:* op doek op paneel *Size:* hoog 10, breed 5 duim	D van der Aa	(Sold) fl 1:8 A Vermeulen
1809/07/25	HGBSM	0092	*J. de Wit* | Een schets van een Platfond | *Mat:* op doek *Size:* hoog 24, breed 17 en 1 half duim	D van der Aa	(Sold) fl 1:10 A Vermeulen
1809/07/25	HGBSM	0093	*J. de Wit* | Een dito [schets van een Platfond] | *Mat:* op doek *Size:* hoog 17 en 1 half, breed 24 duim	D van der Aa	(Sold) fl 1:10 A Vermeulen
1809/07/25	HGBSM	0094	*J. de Wit* | Een dito [schets van een Platfond] | *Mat:* op doek *Size:* hoog 20 en 1 half, breed 23 en 1 half duim	D van der Aa	(Sold) fl 1:10 A Vermeulen
1809/07/25	HGBSM	0095	*J. de Wit* | Twee Stuks dito [schetsen van een Platfond] | *Mat:* op doek *Size:* hoog 20 en 1 half, breed 23 en 1 half duim	D van der Aa	(Sold) fl 2 A Vermeulen
1809/07/25	HGBSM	0166	*J. de Wit* | De Boodschap aan Maria, schetsgewys | *Mat:* op doek op paneel *Size:* hoog 13 en een half, breed 10 en een half duim	D van der Aa	(Sold) fl 9:10 van der Aa
1809/07/25	HGBSM	0167	*J. de Wit* | De Emausgangers aan tafel zittende daar Christus verschynt, schetsgewyze | *Mat:* op doek op paneel *Size:* hoog 9, breed 11 duim	D van der Aa [or] E B ten Dall	(Sold) fl 5 de Gelder
1809/07/25	HGBSM	0168	*J. de Wit* | Een Schets, waar de Liefde zyne vleugels worden gekort, door denzelven [J. de Wit], als het voorgaande | *Mat:* op doek op paneel *Size:* hoog 9, breed 11 duim	D van der Aa [or] E B ten Dall	(Sold) fl 2 Heymans [for] G
1809/07/25	HGBSM	0169	*J. de Wit* | Drie stuks Historieele Schetzen | *Mat:* op doek op paneel	D van der Aa [or] E B ten Dall	(Sold) fl 3:8 Bogaard
1810/07/23	DOLG1	0063	*Jacob de Witt* | Een Zinnebeeldige Ordonnantie op den Godsdienst, door Kindertjes uitgedrukt; in kleuren, meesterlijk en groot van behandeling | *Mat:* op doek *Size:* hoog 48 ½, breed 36 duim	Mr Pieter van den Santheuvel	(Sold) fl 16 van Eijk à 's Hage
1810/08/06	AMSCH	0123	*Wit (J. de)* | De Waarheid en Wijsheid doen de Geschiedenis hare Gedenkschriften opteekenen, alles is versierd met bevallige Engeltjes, verder een Aardkloot, Penning van Ptolomaeus Philadelphus, Boeken en verder bijwerk; het is fraai met kleuren geschilderd en van de beste van dezen Meester | *Mat:* op doek *Size:* hoog 112, breed 40 duimen *Loc:* Amsterdam, Nederland. Museum Willet-Holthuysen.	[J de Bos?]	(Sold) fl 25 Yver

1810/08/06	AMSCH	0124	*Wit (J. de)* | Eene kapitale Heidensche Offerhande, met eene glorie van Engelen en verder Offerwerk, fraai in het graauw gewerkt | *Mat:* op doek *Size:* hoog 105, breed 66 duimen	[J de Bos?]	(Sold) fl 10 Stoopendaal [for] B
1810/10/11	AMSCH	0101	*J. De Wit* | Vier spelende Kindertjes, in een Landschap, fraai geschilderd | *Mat:* op doek *Size:* hoog 29, breed 23 duimen	[Levy Pakker?]	(Sold or Bought In) fl 0:6 L^y Pakker
1810/10/11	AMSCH	0225	*J. De Wit* | Een stuk met Engelen en andere Hoofden	A	(Sold) fl 1 du Pree

Wit, Jacob de (or Wit, Jacob de, copy after)

1810/03/23	HAVIN	0048	*de Wit* | Twee Basrelieve in 't grauw, fraai van of na de Wit	Rudolf Hendrik de Wetstein [or others]	(Unknown)

Wit, Jacob de (copy after)

1801/05/11	AMSCH	0112	*na J. de Wit* | Een bevallige Vrouw, welke door Cupido geliefkoost word | *Mat:* op doek *Size:* hoog 48, breed 36 duim	R[oos]	(Sold) fl 7:10 Gruiter
1807/06/10	HGBSM	0119	*J. de Witt* | De jonge Tobias door den Engel geleid wordende, na J. de Witt | *Mat:* op doek *Size:* hoog 37 ½, breed 27 ½ duim	Abraham Delfos [or others]	(Sold) fl 5:2 Nieukoop
1809/07/25	HGBSM	0115	*D. van der Aa; J. de Wit* | Een Groep van Naakte Kinderen na J. de Wit, door D. van der Aa | copy by Dirk Aa after Jacob de Wit *Mat:* op doek *Size:* hoog 29 en een half, breed 24 duim	D van der Aa	(Sold) fl 12 van Eyk

Wit, Jacob de (manner)

1801/12/22	AMOTT	0031	*de Wit* | 3 stuks Mans en Vrouwe Pourtraiten en 1 Graauwtje, als de Wit	Bartholomeus Ruloffs	(Unknown) fl 1:10
1801/12/22	AMOTT	0111	*de Witt* | 3 stuks Paneelen, als door de Witt | *Mat:* op paneel	Bartholomeus Ruloffs	(Unknown) fl 1:10
1806/05/05	AMSCH	0209	*de Wit* | Een Bachenaal; als de Wit	V[inkeles]	(Sold) fl 1 Mensart
1809/04/22	AMYVR	0167	*J. de Wit* | Een Vrouwe-Pourtrait; als J. de Wit	de Bruin	(Sold) fl 0:6 Yver

Withoos, Johannes

1804/02/27	AMSCH	0119	*Withoos. (J.)* | Een Vanitas, alles toepasselyk op de Verganglykheid; meesterlyk gepenceeld | *Mat:* op doek *Size:* hoog 34, breed 30 duim	B	(Sold) fl 6 V^n Dijl
1809/04/17	AMSCH	0115	*J. Withoos* | Twee stuks Landschappen, met onderscheiden Bloemen en Plantgewas, op de voorgrond een Hagedis, een Weesel en ander kruipend Gedierten, kloek geschilderd | *Size:* ieder hoog 41, breed 31 duim	H	(Sold) fl 1

Withoos, Matthias

1801/08/19	AMSCH	0138	*M. Withoos* | Op een Tafel legt dood Gevogelte en eenig Jagtgereedschap; op Doek | *Mat:* op doek *Size:* hoog 25, breed 19 duim	Van Forreest	(Sold) fl 3 Meijer
1802/05/05	AMSCH	0242	*Wethoos* | Een schoon Hofgezicht, uitvoerig geschilderd | *Size:* hoog 40, breed 54 duim *Notes:* This lot was sold with lot 240 by Willaerts.	J	(Sold) fl 3 for lots 240 & 242. L Pakker
1802/11/01	DOBRA	0074	*M. Withoos* | Een Hofgezicht met Beelden, Vaazen, enz. | possibly companion to lot 75 *Mat:* op doek *Size:* hoog 2 v. 3 d. en br. circa 20 duim	Paulus van der Spyk [or others]	(Bought In) fl 4:15 for lots 74 & 75
1802/11/01	DOBRA	0075	*M. Withoos* | Een Vanitas, door denzelven [M. Withoos]; mede met Vaazen, Planten, enz. kunnende dienen tot een wedergade | possibly companion to lot 74	Paulus van der Spyk [or others]	(Bought In) fl 4:15 for lots 74 & 75
1803/03/07	AMBAE	0133	*Withoos* | Twee Vogeltjes in kleuren, door Withoos		(Unknown)
1803/08/24	HGKAN	0060	*M. Withoos* | Een Vanitas toepasselyk op de vergankelykheid zeer uitvoerig en fraay behandeld	[Teissier] [or others]	(Sold) fl 5 Kan
1803/08/24	HGKAN	0061	*M. Withoos* | Aan de Stam van een Beukeboom, ziet men verscheide Distels en Planten, op de voorgrond leggen drie Vissen, waar by een Otter, dit stuk is zeer verdienstelyk en konstig geschildert | *Mat:* op doek *Size:* hoog 55, breet 40 duim	[Teissier] [or others]	(Sold) fl 15 E
1805/07/03	AMSCH	0189	*Withoos* | Twee stuks met Eenden	C	(Sold) fl 0:12 L Pakker
1805/07/10	AMSCH	0172	*M. Withoos* | Twee stuks, met Distelen, dood Gevogelte en Insectens; uitvoerig | *Size:* hoog 21, breed 18 duim	V[inkeles] [for] L	(Sold) fl 3:5 Gruyter
1808/06/13	AMSCH	0180	*Withoos (M.)* | In een Haven ziet men verscheide Buizen en andere Vaartuigen, ter zijde eenige Woningen, een Molen en aangenaam verschiet, op den voorgrond eenige Korven met en zonder Visch, en ander gereedschap. Uitvoerig behandeld | *Mat:* op doek *Size:* hoog 27, breed 40 duim	R[oos]	(Sold) fl 5:5 Du Pré
1808/06/13	AMSCH	0181	*Withoos (M.)* | Een Bloemstuk, waarin een witte Lelij en bonte Slaapbol bijzonder uitmunten, op den voorgrond een Egel. Uitvoerig behandeld | *Mat:* op paneel *Size:* hoog 33, breed 28 duim	E M Engelberts	(Sold) fl 7:10 T Spaan
1810/06/04	DOBRA	0024	*Wethoos* | Twee stuks Tuingezichten	Hendrik de Haas	(Unknown)
1810/06/20	AMSCH	0107	*M. Withoos* | Eenige doode Vogels en Jagtgereedschap, liggende op eene Steenen Tafel | *Mat:* op doek *Size:* hoog 23, breed 17 duimen	A	(Sold) fl 5:5 Coclers
1810/07/23	DOLG2	0075	*Withoos* | Een stukje met Vruchten, waar bij een muisje; zeer uitvoerig behandeld | *Mat:* op doek *Size:* hoog 12, breed 11 duim	Pieter Quinting	(Unknown) fl 5:12
1810/10/10	MGCIT	0021	*M. Withoos* | Een zeer aangenaam Landschapje, rijk van Geboomte, Gewassen, Kruiden, Planten en Bloemen, als mede eenige fraai	Caspar van Citters	(Unknown)

behandelde Capellen, Vlinders en andere Insecten, zeer verdienstig geschildert

Withoos, Matthias (and Lingelbach)

1802/09/21	UTHDG	0056	*Withoos; Lingelbach* | Op den voorgrond zijn beladene Muilezels en verscheidene Beelden geplaatst; ter zijde gebergtens waarop gebouwen. Dit, met een Rivier doorsneede Landschap, is helder behandeld door Withoos, de stoffagie door Lingelbach | *Mat:* op doek *Size:* hoog 39, breed 47 duimen		(Bought In) fl 20

Withoos, Pieter

1801/03/16	AMSCH	0095	*P. Withoos* | Twee stuks Landschappen met Gevogelte en Conynen, uitvoerig	K[ip]	(Sold) fl 1 Gruiter

Witmont, Heerman

1803/07/07	HGKAN	0001	*Witmond* | Een Onstuimige Zee, door Witmond, op Paneel [Schilderyen in Olyverf] | *Mat:* in olyverf op paneel *Notes:* The bracketed information in the title appears above lot 1 and refers to lots 1 to 25.		(Unknown)
1804/08/08	AMSCH	0244	*H. Witmond* | Twee stuks woelende Waters, met verscheide Vaartuigen; als met de Pen	Roos [for] D	(Sold) fl 2 van Iperen
1804/08/08	AMSCH	0245	*H. Witmond* | Twee dito [stuks woelende Waters], dito [met verscheide Vaartuigen] | *Notes:* It is unclear what "dito" refers to in the title.	Roos [for] D	(Sold) fl 0:10 L Pakker
1804/10/16	DLOND	0264	*Witmondt* | Twee Zee Gezichten. Deux vues de Mer | *Mat:* op paneel *Size:* hoog 13, breed 17		(Unknown)
1805/07/10	AMSCH	0186	*H. Witmont* | Een woelende Zee, met Scheepen, uitvoerig op Paneel | *Mat:* op paneel *Notes:* This lot was sold with lot 185, which is in the manner of Heem.	R[oos]	(Sold) fl 0:8 for lots 185 & 186. W^{m} v d Schley
1809/07/25	HGBSM	0258	*H. Witmond* | Een Zeehaven met Scheepen, in 't grauw	D van der Aa [or] E B ten Dall	(Sold) fl 1:4 A Vermeulen

Witt, M. de [Unidentified]

1809/10/20	UTWLD	0007	*M. de Witt* | Een vrolyk Boerengezelschap door M. de Witt	J J van Rhyn	(Unknown)
1809/10/20	UTWLD	0008	*M. de Witt* | Een dito [vrolyk Boerengezelschap] dito [door M. de Witt]	J J van Rhyn	(Unknown)

Witte, Emanuel de

1801/06/10	AMSCH	0200	*Wit. (E. de)* | Een Kerk, van binnen te zien, versierd met een fraaije Graftombe en andere Kerkcieraaden, benevens verscheiden Beeldjes, fraai van licht en bruin | *Mat:* op doek *Size:* hoog 54, breed 56 duim	[Doublet]	(Sold) fl 66 W^{l} Reijers
1801/06/10	AMSCH	0201	*Wit. (E. de)* | Een Protestantsche Kerk van binnen te zien, ter linkerzyde ziet men een Predikant op de Predikstoel, wyders verscheiden Beeldjes; Zonachtig van behandeling | *Size:* hoog 19, breed 17 duim	[Doublet]	(Sold) fl 22 Taijs
1801/08/19	AMSCH	0142a	*E. de Wit* | Een Protestante Kerk, van binnen te zien, gestoffeerd met wandelende Beeldjes, verders een Predikstoel en verder Bywerk, door E. de Wit, op Paneel | *Mat:* op paneel *Size:* hoog 12, breed 10 ½ duim	van der Schly [for] F	(Sold) fl 11 v d Schleij [for] Merrem
1801/10/06	AMSCH	0081	*E. de Witt* | Dit Onderwerp vertoont op een Marktgezigt by avond, een meenigte Lieden van verschillende staat, zig vermaaken met het branden van Pektonnen, en het afsteeken van verscheide Vuurwerken, zynde een daar staande Tooren, verlicht, geestig geordoneert, en meesterlyk gepenceeld | *Mat:* op paneel *Size:* hoog 22, breed 18 duim	S	(Sold) fl 4 Ter Smitten
1802/06/28	AMSCH	0207	*E. de Wit* | Een Binnegezigt van een Protestanten Kerk, gestoffeerd met verscheiden Beeldjes, zonagtig behandeld | *Mat:* op paneel *Size:* hoog 17, breed 14 duim	Anna Elink	(Sold) fl 5:10 Gruiter
1802/09/21	UTHDG	0103	*E. de Wit* | Een doorzigt onder een Brug op een Sluis en weg, gestoffeerd met verscheidene figuren. Dit stukje is fraaij van effect en zeer zonächtig geschildert door E. de Wit | *Mat:* op paneel *Size:* hoog 9, breed 7 duimen		(Bought In) fl 3:5
1802/11/01	DOBRA	0166	*E. Witt* | Twee stuks Mans en Vrouwen Portraiten | *Mat:* op koper		(Unknown) fl 7
1802/12/13	AMSCH	0174	*E. de Witt* | Een Binnengezight van een Protestante Kerk, waarin een Leeraar op Stoel, verzelt van verscheiden Toehoorders; en gestoffeerd met Orgel, Wapenborden en andere Gedenkteekens; het zonlicht doet een natuurlyke werking, en is fiks gepenceeld | *Mat:* op paneel *Size:* hoog 17 ½, breed 14 duim	Schley [for] Lauwers	(Sold) fl 9 Pruyssenaar [for] R
1803/08/01	AMSCH	0048	*Wit. (E. de)* | Een gedeelte van de groote Kerk te Haarlem, van binnen te zien, gestoffeerd met Wandelaars en ander Bywerk, fraay van perspectief | *Mat:* op paneel *Size:* hoog 19, breed 15 duim	J	(Sold) fl 7:10 Gruiter
1803/08/17	AMSCH	0092	*Wit (E. de)* | Een Gezicht in de Oude Kerk te Amsterdam, gestoffeerd op de Voorgrond met een Man, welke in een Graf staat, waarby een Grysaard, schynende met hem te spreken, frappant van zonligt en malsch van behandeling, bekend voor een der beste van dezen Meester | *Mat:* op koper *Size:* hoog 10, breed 8 duim	Anna Catharina Putman	(Sold) fl 64 Van Leijden
1803/12/12	AMSCH	0110	*E. de Wit* | Een Protestanten Kerk van binnen te zien, gestoffeerd met wandelende en andere Beelden; kragtig op Doek | *Mat:* op doek *Size:* hoog 15, breed 15 duim	H	(Sold) fl 2:5 V^{n} Iperen

1804/05/07	AMSCH	0194	*Wit. (E. de)* | Een Protestante Kerk van binnen te zien, gestoffeerd met de Lykstatie van een Kind en verdere aanschouwers; het zonlicht is allerfrappantst [sic], en doet een uitmuntende werking zo ook de penceelsbehandeling | *Mat:* op doek *Size:* hoog 32, breed 40 duim	Roos [for] A	(Sold) fl 110 Coclers
1804/05/07	AMSCH	0195	*Wit. (E. de)* | Een Protestante Kerk van binnen te zien, ziende na 't Orgel en het Choor, vercierd met Wapenborden, enz; en een menigte Stoffagie van Heeren, Dames en Doodgravers, enz.; zonachtig en piquant van licht en van een fraaye penceelsbehandeling van deeze Meester | *Mat:* op doek *Size:* hoog 77, breed 66 duim	Roos [for] K	(Sold) fl 21 Teengs
1804/05/07	AMSCH	0196	*Wit. (E. de)* | Een Protestante Kerk van binnen te zien, gestoffeerd met een menigte Beelden, op den voorgrond een Doodgraver, welke met een Heer over 't zelve schynt te spreeken, enz.; zonachtig en fiks gepenceeld | *Mat:* op doek *Size:* hoog 31, breed 41 duim	Vinkeles [for] H[affner]	(Sold) fl 11:10 Gruyter
1804/08/08	AMSCH	0223	*E. de Wit* | Een Gezicht in de Nieuwe Kerk te Amsterdam, gestoffeerd met een Doodgraver, waarby een Aanspreeker en andere Beeldjes; dit stuk is frapant verlicht en malsch gepenceeld | *Mat:* op doek *Size:* hoog 50, br. 45 duim *Loc:* Boston, MA, USA. Museum of Fine Arts. (49.7)	Roos [for] D	(Sold) fl 40 C S Roos
1804/08/08	AMSCH	0224	*E. de Wit* | Een Gezicht in de Oude Kerk; meede als de voorgaande van licht en behandeling | *Mat:* op paneel *Size:* hoog 17, breed 13 duim	Roos [for] D	(Sold) fl 9 Coclers
1804/08/08	AMSCH	0225	*E. de Wit* | Een Gezicht in de Oude Kerk te Amsterdam, vol Beeldjes gestoffeerd; krachtig en frapéerend van zonlicht, op Paneel | *Mat:* op paneel *Size:* hoog 19, breed 22 duim	Roos a	(Bought In) fl 20
1804/10/16	DLOND	0195a	*E. de Witte* | [Untitled] | *Notes:* This lot was changed from "C. Sagtleven, Twee Schilderyen Verbeeldende Beestenmarkten, vol gewoel," to "E. de Witte" and "A. Stork," without giving titles, at the front of the printed catalogue. They have been numbered 195a and 195b.		(Unknown)
1804/10/16	DLOND	0265	*E. de Witte* | Twee Stukjens. Een Vischmarkt en Polierwinkel. Deux pièces. Une Poissonnerie & une Boutique de Gibier | *Mat:* op doek *Size:* hoog 20, breed 23		(Sold) fl 10:15 Thijs
1804/10/29	HRBAU	0117	*Wit (Emanuel de)* | Een Binnengezigt van eene Roomsche Kerk, ziende men, uit den omgang, langs het Orgel naar het Choor, alwaar een Priester bezig is den Godsdienst te verrichten, waar by een menigte Menschen, welken aldaar in hunne aandagt zyn. Wyders is de omgang versierd met Graftombes, Wapens en Eeretekens, als mede met wandelende Persoonen van beide sexe en verschillenden staat, welken aldaar het Gebouw, als ook de Tombes enz., beschouwen. De ordinantie is grootsch, de werking van het zonlicht frappant, en in alle deelen zeer uitvoerig geschilderd | *Mat:* op doek *Size:* hoog 44, breed 36 duim	Simon Styl	(Unknown)
1804/12/10	AMSCH	0100	*Emanuel de Wit* | Een fraaije en ryk geordineerde Kerk, van binnen te zien, ter rechterzyde ziet men het Orgel, en in het verschiet een Altaar, verders een meenigte Beelden; de perspectief is zeer fraai, en alles krachtig, en tevens helder gepenceeld | *Mat:* op doek *Size:* Hoog 28, breed 26 duim	Jan De Groot	(Sold) fl 49 Coclers
1805/07/03	AMSCH	0162	*E. de With* | Een Capitaal Binnegezicht van een Protestante Kerk, gestoffeerd met wandelende Beeldjes, een Doodgraver by een Graft; Predikstoel, Orgel, Wapenborden en andere Gedenkteekens; het invallend zonlicht, geeft een bevallige werking, en is uitvoerig van penceel-behandeling | *Mat:* op paneel *Size:* hoog 27, breed 33 duim	G	(Sold) fl 70 Nieuwenhuys
1805/07/03	AMSCH	0163	*E. de With* | Twee stuks Gezichten in de Oude Kerk te Amsterdam; beide ryk van stoffagie en behandeld als de voorgaande | *Size:* hoog 19, breed 16 duim	G	(Sold) fl 25:10 Vallet
1805/07/03	AMSCH	0164	*E. de With* | Een Protestante Kerk van binnen te zien, gestoffeerd met een ménigte Beeldjes, en aller zonachtigst gepenceeld | *Mat:* op paneel *Size:* hoog 17, breed 13 duim	V[inkeles]	(Sold) fl 7 Gruyter
1805/07/10	AMSCH	0171	*E. de With* | Een Protestante Kerk van binnen, met verscheide stoffagie van Beelden; zonachtig | *Mat:* op doek *Size:* hoog 22, breed 17 duim	Y[ver]	(Sold) fl 15:10 Gruyter
1806/05/05	AMSCH	0155	*E. de Wit* | Een Protestante Kerk, van binnen te zien, met een ménigte Beelden; fiks op Paneel | *Mat:* op paneel *Size:* hoog 18, breed 16 duim	V[inkeles]	(Sold) fl 2:5 Boelhouwer
1806/06/07	RMHSN	0117	*E. de Wit* | Een Zonagtige Kerk, daar in Gepredikt word	A E K L	(Unknown)
1806/08/13	AMSCH	0217	*Wit. (E. de)* | Een protestante Kerk van binnen te zien, ryk gestoffeerd met wandelende en rustende Beeldjes, Honden, enz. zonachtig en meesterlyk van schildering | *Mat:* op paneel *Size:* hoog 21, breed 17 duim	Vinkeles [for] F	(Sold) fl 33 Schumacher
1806/08/13	AMSCH	0218	*Wit. (E. de)* | Een gedeelte van de groote Kerk te Haarlem van binnen te zien, gestoffeerd met Wandelaars, enz. fraai van licht en meesterlyk geschilderd | *Mat:* op paneel *Size:* hoog 19, breed 16 duim	Vinkeles [for] G[ruyter]	(Sold) fl 6 Reydon
1806/11/24	AMSCH	0084	*Wit (E. de)* | Een Gezigt, ln [sic] een bynaar geruïneerde Tempel, vol antique Beelden, en fraaije stoffagie; het zonlicht doet een schoone werking, en is in alles als de voorgaande [kragtig en fraai van penceelsbehandeling] | *Size:* hoog 37, breed 31 duim	Munnikhuizen	(Sold) fl 8 L Pakker
1806/11/24	AMSCH	0085	*Wit (E. de)* | Een Protestanten Kerk, van binnen te zien; gestoffeerd met Beeltjes; zonachtig en natuurlyk gepenceeld | *Mat:* op paneel *Size:* hoog 24, breed 21 duim	Munnikhuizen	(Sold) fl 8:5 Van Dyl

1807/08/26	AMSCH	0235	*E. de Witt* | Het Gezicht van een Protestantsche Kerk, van binnen te zien, naar het kleine Orgel en Koor, gestoffeerd met verscheiden wandelende Lieden en verder bywerk; zonachtig en bevallig van perspectief, en meesterlyk fraai gepenceeld | *Mat:* op doek *Size:* hoog 23, breed 29 duim	Helsdinge	(Bought In) fl 4
1807/08/26	AMSCH	0236	*E. de Witt* | Twee stuks Protestantsche Kerken, vol stoffage van Beelden, alwaar het zonlicht een frappante werking doet; krachtig | *Mat:* op paneel *Size:* hoog 19, breed 16 duim	Joseph Vallette	(Sold) fl 32 van Iperen
1807/08/26	AMSCH	0237	*E. de Witt* | Een Binnengezicht van een Protestantsche Kerk, ziende naar het Koor en groot Orgel, gestoffeerd met Beelden en verder bywerk | *Mat:* op paneel *Size:* hoog 16, breed 12 duim	Roos [for] A	(Sold) fl 9 Spruit
1808/04/26	GDAN	0196	*Wit (E. de)* | Een fraaije Kerk van binnen te zien	G H Fortuyn	(Unknown)
1808/06/06	RMRIJ	0141	*Witt. (Emanuel de)* | Een Protestansch Kerkje van binnen te zien, met eenige Beelden [L'Intérieur d'une Eglise Protestante etc.] | *Annots:* Geschenk van syn vader W v d Pot (RMA I) *Mat:* op paneel *Size:* Hoog 17 ¾, en breed 13 ¾ duim *Loc:* Amsterdam, Nederland. Rijksmuseum. (A474)	Gerrit van der Pot, Heer van Groeneveld	(Sold) fl 43 J J de Wit [for] le Roi
1808/06/13	AMSCH	0179	*Wit (E. de)* | In de Oude Kerk te Amsterdam staat een Aanspreker bij een Graf, verder eenige andere Beelden. Zonachtig verbeeld en meesterlijk behandeld | *Mat:* op paneel *Size:* hoog 16, breed 13 duim	R[oos]	(Sold) fl 51 van Bergen
1808/08/23	AMSCH	0175	*Wit. (De)* | Een Roomsche Kerk van binnen te zien, gestoffeert met verscheiden Altaaren en Beelden; helder en fraai van Perspectief | *Mat:* op doek *Size:* hoog 36, breed 44 duim	Y	(Sold) fl 30 B^d Kooij
1808/10/28	AMVRS	0063	*Witt, (Emanuel de)* | Een Gezicht binnen de Oude Kerk te Amsterdam, met een gedeelte van het Koor, met Wapenbord en stoffage van Beelden. Het Zonlicht is treffend en doet eene meesterlijke werking | *Mat:* op doek *Size:* hoog 25, breed 28 duim	Marten Udink	(Sold) fl 33:10 Reijers
1808/11/28	AMSCH	0066	*E. de Witt* | Een Binnengezicht van een Protestantsche Kerk, ziende naar het Koor een groot Orgel, gestoffeerd met de Predikant op de Predikstoel, beneevens een menigte Aanhoorderen, zonagtig en natuurlijk behandeld | *Mat:* op paneel *Size:* hoog 19, breed 17 duim	S	(Sold) fl 30 T Spaan
1808/11/28	AMSCH	0067	*E. de Witt* | Twee stuks Gezichten in de Oude Kerk te Amsterdam, rijk met Beelden gestoffeerd, het zonlicht doet een frappante werking en het is natuurlijk behandeld | *Mat:* op paneel *Size:* ieder is hoog 17, breed 14 duim	S	(Bought In) fl 100
1808/11/28	AMSCH	0068	*E. de Witt* | Een Protestantsche Kerk, van binnen ziende na de Predikstoel en het Koor, gestoffeerd met wandelende en rustende Beelden, zonachtig behandeld | *Mat:* op doek *Size:* hoog 22, breed 17 duim	[Gruyter?]	(Bought In) fl 18
1808/11/28	AMSCH	0069	*E. de Witt* | Een dito [Protestantsche] Kerk, mede van binnen te zien, gestoffeerd op de voorgrond met een Doodgraver, zijnde als met een Heer in gesprek, verder verscheide andere Beelden, Wapenborden en Kerkciraaden, kunstig en fraai van Penceel | *Mat:* op doek *Size:* hoog 31, breed 41 duim	[Gruyter?]	(Bought In) fl 9:10
1810/03/26	RMMUY	0009	*Emanuel de Wit* | Het Koor der Kerk te Delft, waar in men de Tombe ziet van Prins Willem den Eersten, fraai geschilderd, bevallig van licht en schaduwe, en een der besten van dezen Meester [L'intérieur d'une Eglise à Delft, où l'on voit le Mausolée de Guillaume premier, Prince d'Orange, enrichi de figures, d'un beau choix et d'un effet piquant.] | *Annots:* Copie du Musée (BPG) *Mat:* op doek *Size:* hoog 21, breed 14 ½ duimen	Daniel de Jongh Az	(Sold) fl 85 Spaan Amsterdam
1810/06/20	AMSCH	0102	*E. De Witt* | Eene Protestante Kerk van binnen te zien: vooraan een open Graf, waarbij een Doodgraver en Aanspreker. Het is fraai van doorzigt en zonachtig behandeld | *Mat:* op paneel *Size:* hoog 28, breed 22 duimen	D	(Sold) fl 31:10 Hodges
1810/06/20	AMSCH	0103	*E. De Witt* | Eene Kerk van binnen, ziende naar een groot Orgel en Predikstoel, gestoffeerd met verscheidene Beeldjes. Schoon van licht en uitvoerig geschilderd | *Mat:* op doek *Size:* hoog 17, breed 15 duimen	B	(Bought In) fl 6
1810/06/20	AMSCH	0104	*E. De Witt* | Het binnengezigt van eene Kerk: op den voorgrond een Doodgraver bij een Graf en andere Beelden. Als de voorgaande behandeld | *Mat:* op doek *Size:* hoog 24, breed 20 duimen	B	(Sold) fl 7:5 Hodges
1810/06/20	AMSCH	0105	*E. De Witt* | Een Protestantsche Kerk, gestoffeerd met eene menigte Beelden: het zonlicht doet eene sterke werking | *Mat:* op doek *Size:* hoog 23, breed 26 duimen	Q	(Sold) fl 12:10 Roos
1810/10/10	MGCIT	0071	*E. de Wit* | Een zeer schoon Schildery, zynde een Kerkgebouw van een uitmuntende Bouworder; in allen opzigte voortreflyk en kunstig uitgevoerd	Caspar van Citters	(Unknown)
			Wittel, Gaspar van		
1803/08/24	HGKAN	0002	*C. Vitalli* | Vier Stuks Gezichten in en omstreeks Romen en Venetien met Italiaansche Gebouwen en ryk gestoffeerd	[Teissier] [or others]	(Sold) fl 155 Kann
			Wittig, Bartholomaus		
1803/09/07	AMSCH	0220	*Wittig* | Op de Binneplaats van een Antiecq Gebouw, zit een Man welke verbonden word, waarby eenige omstanders, zonachtig op Doek [Dans l'intérieur d'un batiment antique, un personnage blessé et assis qui paroit avoir été pansé ; autour de lui plusieurs autres figures. Il règne sur tout ce tableau une belle lumière] | *Mat:* op doek *Size:* hoog 34, breed 28 duim	Smidt	(Bought In) fl 2

			Wolfaerts, Artus		
1802/06/28	AMSCH	0202	*A. Wolfers* | Een vorstelyke jonge Dame, staande in een Hofgezigt; op een steene Baluster staat een tiene Vogelkorf, meesterlyk en bevallig gepenceeld | *Mat:* op paneel *Size:* hoog 16, breed 13 duim	Anna Elink	(Sold) fl 3 Coclers
1802/09/21	UTHDG	0100	*A. Wolfart* | In een Italiaansch Landschap ziet men bij Ruines op de eerste grond halte houden, een Boerin, Boer, Schaapen, Bokken, Ezels, enz. Verder komt een Jagtpartij te Paard en te voet naar een Fontein. Dit, nevens meer Beelden en een goed verschiet, is helder en kloeck behandeld | *Mat:* op doek *Size:* hoog 39 ½, breed 45 ½ duimen		(Sold) fl 37 Pastoor van Bennekom heere Straat
1808/04/26	GDAN	0206	*Wolfart (A.)* | Zynde een zeer goed Landschap, gestoffeerd met Menschen, Schapen, Koeijen, &c, fiks behandeld | *Size:* hoog 34, breed 28 ½ duim	G H Fortuyn	(Unknown)
			Wolfaerts, Jan Baptist		
1804/10/16	DLOND	0266	*Wolfert* | Een Rots met een oud Gebouw, Herder en Herderin. Zeer schoon, zo goed als N. Berghem. Un vieux Batiment sur un Rocher, Berger & Bergère. Pièce aussi belle que de N. Berghem | *Mat:* op doek *Size:* hoog 39, breed 49		(Unknown)
1806/08/13	AMSCH	0223	*Wolfers* | Een aangenaam Boom- en Duinryk Landschap met een ménigte stoffagie van Schaapen, Herders en Honden; allerzonachtigst gepenceeld en fraai van schildering | *Mat:* op paneel *Size:* hoog 46, breed 59 duim	Vinkeles [for] D	(Sold) fl 4 L Pakker
1810/10/11	AMSCH	0126	*Wolfers* | Een Landschap, met Beesten	[Gruyter?]	(Sold) fl 1:5 Mensart
			Wolfsen, Aleijda		
1808/08/23	AMSCH	0176	*Wolfsen. (Aleijda)* | Eene bevallige Dame in rijke Kleeding, staande voor een Tafel, waar op een Vogelkorfje geplaatst is, zij houd een zwarte Hoed met Véderen, benevens een vergulde Staf in de hand; uitvoerig en delicaat gepenceeld | *Mat:* op paneel *Size:* hoog 16, breed 12 duim	[Coclers]	(Sold) fl 4:15 Th Spaan
			Wolters, Henriette (van Pee) (manner)		
1807/08/26	AMSCH	0245	*Mejuffr. H. Wolters* | Het Afbeeldzel van een Jongman; meesterlyk fraai van penceelsbehandeling, op Koper, ovaal formaat, als van Mejuffr. H. Wolters | *Mat:* op koper *Fmt:* ovaal	Helsdinge	(Bought In) fl 1
			Wouters, Frans		
1804/08/02	BDAN	0031	*F. Wouters* | Een aangenaam Landschap | *Mat:* op paneel *Size:* b. 17 d. h. 13 d.	J G Calckberner	(Unknown)
			Wouwerman		
1801/11/21	RMVIS	0002	*Wouwerman* | Een Maanlicht, waarin een Paard en Jager	Gelinus van Spaan	(Unknown)
1802/05/11	GRGRW	0062	*Wouwerman* | Een Paard, met een Man, die het vast houdt [Schilderijen met Olie-Verf; In Vergulde Lijsten] | *Mat:* in olyverf *Notes:* The bracketed information in the title appears above lot 1 and refers to lots 1 to 79a.	Arnold Sicco Werumeus	(Unknown) fl 17:10
1805/04/23	HOBEE	0002	*Wouwerman* | Een wit Paard, met verdere stoffagie, in eene Grotte, fraay geschilderd door Wouwerman		(Unknown)
1808/05/18	LNAN	0012	*Wouerman* | Een Man met twee Paarden, uitvoerig behandeld | *Notes:* The artist's name "Wouerman" was added in by hand in the RKDH copy of the catalogue.	Mr Cornelis Versluys	(Unknown)
1808/05/18	LNAN	0024	*Wouerman* | Een Stal met Paarden en Wagens | *Notes:* The artist's name "Wouerman" was added in by hand in the RKDH copy of the catalogue.	Mr Cornelis Versluys	(Unknown) fl 63
1808/05/18	LNAN	0043	*Wouerman* | Een konstig Landschap met Heeren en Dames te Paard | *Notes:* The artist's name "Wouerman" was added in by hand in the RKDH copy of the catalogue.	Mr Cornelis Versluys	(Unknown) fl 101
1808/05/18	LNAN	0048	*Wouerman* | Een Landschap met Mannen en Paarden | *Notes:* The artist's name "Wouerman" was added in by hand in the RKDH copy of the catalogue.	Mr Cornelis Versluys	(Unknown)
1809/07/19	AMSCH	[A0003][H]	*Wouwerman* | 1 Wouwerman | *Notes:* This lot was added in by hand in the AA copy of the catalogue. Because it was not numbered, we have assigned the number.		(Unknown)
1810/03/07	UTWLD	0052	*F. Wouwermans* | Een heuvelachtig Landschap, op de voorgrond een Heer te paard, en eenige honden, op de tweede grond, een staande en een liggende Os, zeer schoon | *Size:* hoog 2 voet 5 duim, breed 2 voet 2 duim	J J Woertman	(Unknown) fl 370
			Wouwerman (and Hagen, Joris)		
1808/04/26	GDAN	0077	*Hagen (J van der); Wouerman* | Een Bos- en Boomrijk Landschap, door Wouerman gestoffeerd, met eenige Jagers te Paard en te Voet met hunne Honden, schoon geschildert | *Size:* hoog 58, breed 54 duim	G H Fortuyn	(Unknown)
			Wouwerman (and Kessel, J. (III))		
1801/08/19	AMSCH	0051	*van Kessel; Wouwerman* | Een Gezigt langs de Vaart, voor 't huis Overmeer, ryk gestoffeerd met een ter Jagt reidend Gezelschap, verder wandelende Persoonen; bevallig van licht, en schoon gepenceeld, door van Kessel, gestoffeerd door Wouwerman	Pruyssen[r] [for] Q	(Sold) fl 10 v d Vinne

Wouwerman (or Wouwerman, manner)

<table>
<tr><td>1802/05/05</td><td>AMSCH</td><td>0261</td><td>Wouwerman | Een Landschap, waarin eenige Paarden en rustende Landlieden, ter zyde een Ezel, verders een aangenaam verschiet, krachtig en bevallig geschilderd, door of in de manier van Wouwerman | Mat: op doek Size: hoog 15, breed 16 duim</td><td>E</td><td>(Sold) fl 11:10 Hulswit</td></tr>
</table>

Wouwerman (copy after)

<table>
<tr><td>1803/12/12</td><td>AMSCH</td><td>0148</td><td>Blommen; Wouwerman | Twee ryk met Paarden en Beelden gestoffeerde Landschappen; als van Blommen, naar Wouwerman | copy in the manner of Bloemen after Wouwerman Mat: op paneel Size: hoog 13, breed 17 duim</td><td>D</td><td>(Sold) fl 30 Coclers</td></tr>
<tr><td>1804/10/08</td><td>RMCNL</td><td>0025</td><td>Wouwerman | Een groot Landschappje na Wouwerman</td><td>A t'Hooft</td><td>(Unknown)</td></tr>
<tr><td>1804/10/29</td><td>HRBAU</td><td>0169</td><td>Wouwerman | Eene Pleisterplaats. Na Wouwerman | Mat: op paneel Size: hoog 11, breed 16 duim</td><td>Simon Styl</td><td>(Unknown)</td></tr>
<tr><td>1806/05/05</td><td>AMSCH</td><td>0175</td><td>Wouwerman | Twee stuks met Paarden en Beelden, na Wouwerman</td><td>R[oos]</td><td>(Sold) fl 7:5 L Pakker</td></tr>
<tr><td>1809/05/26</td><td>HADAA</td><td>0066</td><td>Wouwerman | Twee stuks een na Wouwerman en een ander</td><td>Mejuffrouw de Wed David Heemskerk [or others]</td><td>(Unknown)</td></tr>
<tr><td>1810/03/23</td><td>HAVIN</td><td>0064</td><td>Wouwerman | Een Man bij een pissend paard, fraai na Wouwerman [In Lysten met Glasen] | Notes: The bracketed information in the title appears above lot 63 and refers to lots 63 to 79.</td><td>Rudolf Hendrik de Wetstein [or others]</td><td>(Unknown)</td></tr>
</table>

Wouwerman (manner)

<table>
<tr><td>1801/06/13</td><td>LNDLS</td><td>0054</td><td>Wouwerman | Een Paardenwet, met zwemmers, in de trant van Wouwerman | Mat: op paneel Size: hoog 13, breed 16 duimen</td><td>D van R</td><td>(Sold) fl 7:5 Ryers</td></tr>
<tr><td>1801/11/10</td><td>AMPOS</td><td>0052</td><td>Wouwerman | 1 met Paarden en Varkens, als Wouwerman</td><td></td><td>(Unknown)</td></tr>
<tr><td>1802/04/13</td><td>HAVIN</td><td>0033</td><td>Wouwerman | Een Landschap met Paarden, als van Wouwerman</td><td></td><td>(Unknown)</td></tr>
<tr><td>1802/05/11</td><td>GRGRW</td><td>0029</td><td>Wouwerman | Een deel Volks bij ene Herberg, in den smaak van Wouwerman [Schilderijen met Olie-Verf; In zwarte Lijsten | Mat: in olyverf Notes: The bracketed information in the title appears above lot 1 and refers to lots 1 to 79a.</td><td>Arnold Sicco Werumeus</td><td>(Unknown)</td></tr>
<tr><td>1804/05/07</td><td>AMSCH</td><td>0215</td><td>Wouwerman | Een Landschap met rustende Ryzigers, Paarden enz; fiks gepenceeld, in de manier van Wouwerman | Mat: op paneel Size: hoog 13, breed 15 duim</td><td>Y[ver] [for] W</td><td>(Sold) fl 5:5 Sal Joseph</td></tr>
<tr><td>1804/08/02</td><td>BDAN</td><td>0016</td><td>Manier van Wouwermans | Een Winter, op den voorgrond eenige Kinderen met Sleeden en bywerk | Mat: op doek Size: b. 18 en een half d. h. 14 d.</td><td>J G Calckberner</td><td>(Unknown)</td></tr>
<tr><td>1804/10/16</td><td>DLOND</td><td>0312</td><td>Als Wouwerman | Een zwart Paerd, wordende door enen Man vast gehouden. Un Homme qui tient un Cheval noir | Mat: op doek Size: hoog 8, breed 10</td><td></td><td>(Unknown)</td></tr>
<tr><td>1804/10/16</td><td>DLOND</td><td>0313</td><td>Als Wouwerman | Een bont Paard aan een Struik gebonden. Un Cheval tacheté, lie à un Tronc d' Arbre | Mat: op doek Size: hoog 8, breed 10</td><td></td><td>(Unknown)</td></tr>
<tr><td>1805/07/03</td><td>AMSCH</td><td>0214</td><td>Wouwerman | In een Duinryk Landschap ziet men eenige Hee[ren] en Dames te voet, schynende ter Jacht te gaan; fiks en meesterlyk gepenceeld, in de manier van Wouwerman</td><td>V[inkeles]</td><td>(Bought In) fl 5 ¼</td></tr>
<tr><td>1806/08/13</td><td>AMSCH</td><td>0310</td><td>Wouwerman | Een bevallig Landschapje, met een Water, waarin eenige Lieden te Paard, benevens eenige op 't Land; als Wouwerman</td><td>Vinkeles [for] F</td><td>(Withdrawn)</td></tr>
<tr><td>1807/09/28</td><td>DOHAA</td><td>000D</td><td>Wouwerman | Een dito [Schilderstukje], met Paardjes, als Wouwerman | Size: hoog 14 ½ d. breed 12 d.</td><td>Mattheus Westerouen van Meeteren</td><td>(Unknown)</td></tr>
<tr><td>1808/12/12</td><td>UTWLD</td><td>0013</td><td>Wouwerman | Een Landschap met paarden enz. in de smaak van Wouwerman [Alle in swarte Lysten en wel geconserveerd.] | Mat: op paneel Size: hoog 2 voet, breed 2 voet 9 duim Notes: The bracketed information in the title appears above lot 1 and refers to lots 1 to 19.</td><td>Mr D Hoola van Nooten</td><td>(Unknown)</td></tr>
<tr><td>1808/12/12</td><td>UTWLD</td><td>0014</td><td>Wouwerman | Een dito [Landschap met paarden enz.], als voren [in de smaak van Wouwerman] [Alle in swarte Lysten en wel geconserveerd.] | Notes: The bracketed information in the title about the frame appears above lot 1 and refers to lots 1 to 19.</td><td>Mr D Hoola van Nooten</td><td>(Unknown)</td></tr>
<tr><td>1809/05/26</td><td>HADAA</td><td>A0017</td><td>Wouwerman | Het aanranden van een Postwagen, fiks op Paneel geschilderd, als door Wouwerman | Mat: op paneel</td><td>Mejuffrouw de Wed David Heemskerk [or others]</td><td>(Unknown)</td></tr>
</table>

Wouwerman, Jan

<table>
<tr><td>1801/06/10</td><td>AMSCH</td><td>0195</td><td>Wouwerman. (J.) | Een Wintergezicht, het Ys gestoffeerd met drie Mannen welke Hout verwerken, natuurlyk behandeld | Mat: op paneel Size: hoog 14, breed 19 duim</td><td>Herman ten Kate</td><td>(Sold) fl 36 Van Dijl</td></tr>
<tr><td>1801/08/19</td><td>AMSCH</td><td>0135</td><td>J. Wouwerman | Een Heuvelachtig Landschapje, met eenige Stoffagie | Size: hoog 9/12, breed 7 duim</td><td>Van Forreest</td><td>(Sold) fl 35 Coclers</td></tr>
<tr><td>1801/10/19</td><td>AMSCH</td><td>0087</td><td>Wouwerman. (Jan) | Een Wintergezicht, ter rechterzyde ziet men op het Ys, een Paard dat aan een Vragtslee staat te eeten, en ter linkerzyde een Stadsmuur, langs welke een Man, een Yssleede voorschuift, verder een zeer aangenaam verschiet, uitvoerig en helder behandeld | Mat: op doek Size: hoog 12 ½, breed 15 ½ duim</td><td>Jonkheer Menno Baron van Coehoorn</td><td>(Sold) fl 21:10 B^{d} Kooij</td></tr>
</table>

1802/06/16	AMSCH	0219	*J. Wouwerman* | In een Heuvelachtig Landschap met Geboomten, ziet men ter zyde een Vrouw over een Hout Bruggetje gaande, waar onder een Watervalletje, verder een Man te Paard, on een Voetganger, op een Heuvel staat een Visserswoning: natuurlyk, zonachtig en bevallig gepenceeld | *Mat:* op doek op paneel *Size:* hoog 15 ½, breed 20 duim	[Merrem]	(Sold) fl 24 Cobel
1802/06/16	AMSCH	0220	*J. Wouwerman* | In een Duinachtig Landzicht, vertoont zich een rydende Vragtkar; verder gestoffeerd met gaande Reizigers; zeer natuurlyk en bevallig behandeld | *Mat:* op paneel *Size:* hoog 13 ½, breed 18 ½ duim	[Merrem]	(Sold) fl 7:10 v d Vinne
1804/02/27	AMSCH	0117	*Wouwerman (J.)* | In een Duinachtig Landschap ziet men op de voorgrond een Dame te Paard, waarby eenige rustende Jagers met hunne Honden, op den tweede grondt een van de Jagt terugkomend Gezelschap, agterwaarts een Bergächtig verschiet | *Size:* hoog 27, breed 34 duim	C	(Bought In) fl 16
1805/07/03	AMSCH	0171	*J. Wouwerman* | Een Gezicht op 't oude Stadhuis te Amsterdam, van vooren te zien, ryk gestoffeerd met Beeldjes, Vrachtgoederen, enz.; krachtig en meesterlyk gepenceeld | *Mat:* op doek	S	(Bought In) fl 7
1807/06/02	AMHUY	0016	*Jan Wouwerman* | Een fraai Landschap, verbeeldende een Valkejacht, krachtig gepenceeld		(Unknown)
1810/03/07	UTWLD	0056	*J. Wouwermans* | Een Kantonnement, op de voorgrond Ruitery | *Size:* hoog 3 voet 7 duim, breed 5 voet 9 duim	J J Woertman	(Unknown) fl 199
1810/05/22	AMSCH	0120	*Wouwerman. (J.)* | Een Bergachtig Landschap met een Water, ter zijde een Boeren Woning; uitvoerig met Beeldjes gestoffeerd | *Mat:* op paneel *Size:* hoog 16, breed 22 duim	Johannes van de Putte Nicolaasz.	(Sold) fl 27 Ijver

Wouwerman, Jan (and Kessel, J. (III))

1808/03/03	HAVIN	0017	*van Kessel; J. Wouwerman* | Een Gezicht op de Buitenplaats Overmeer aan den Amstel, door van Kessel gestoffeerd	Jacobus Spillebout	(Unknown) fl 5

Wouwerman, P.

1801/03/16	AMSCH	0194	*P. Wouwerman* | Een Pleisterplaats in een Landschap, waar voor een Dame en Heer te Paard, verder een Huisman met een beladen Ezel, fiks geschilderd op doek | *Mat:* op doek	K[ip]	(Sold) fl 1 Gruiter
1801/06/13	LNDLS	0041	*P. Wouwerman* | Een Landschap, op de voorgrond een wit paard, die uit een water drinkt, benevens andere staande paarden, en een jongeling die bij een boom rust, verder geboomten bij een kerk en tooren, op doek | *Mat:* op doek *Size:* hoog 16, breed 20 ½ duimen	D van R	(Sold) fl 32 A Delfos [for] W
1802/05/24	HGBAK	0019	*P. Wouwerman* | Een Capitaal stuk, zynde de uittogt der Jagers, zo te paard als te voet, zeer fraay van ordonnantie, door P. Wouwerman, hoog 3 voet 4 duim, breed 4 voet 1 duim, op doek, zwarte lyst en vergulde binnenrand | *Mat:* op doek *Size:* hoog 3 voet 4 duim, breed 4 voet 1 duim	Mejuffrouw A van der Mieden	(Sold) fl 36 Laar [?]
1802/05/24	HGBAK	0065	*P. Wouwerman* | Een Bataille, door P. Wouwerman, hoog 9 ½ d., op doek, zwarte lyst | *Mat:* op doek *Size:* hoog 9 ½ duim	Mejuffrouw A van der Mieden	(Sold) fl 7:5 H Carré
1802/06/16	AMSCH	0215	*P. Wouwerman* | Deeze Ordenantie vol gewoel van Krygslieden, die een Dorp uitplunderen; ziet men een Overste, een Voerman te Paard zittende voor een Vragtkar dood schieten; terwyl andere bézig zyn de ongelukkige Dorplieden te vervolgen, te vermoorden, en vastbinden; op de grond legt verscheide Huisraad; verder by een Kerk waar van de Tooren gedeeltelyk geruineert is; ziet men Woningen in brand; de Caracters zyn Natuurlyk, en Meesterlyk van penceel-behandeling | *Mat:* op doek *Size:* hoog 26, breed 24 duim	[Merrem]	(Sold) fl 101 Van Iperen
1802/06/16	AMSCH	0216	*P. Wouwerman* | Voor de Ruïne van een oud Gebouw, ziet men wit gezadeld Paard waar by een Heer en twee Honden, ter zyde een rustende Jongeling; krachtig en uitvoerig gepenceeld | *Mat:* op paneel *Size:* hoog 13, breed 16 ½ duim	[Merrem]	(Sold) fl 24 Wed Achtienhoven
1802/06/16	AMSCH	0218	*P. Wouwerman* | Voor een Plysterplaats ververschen zich twee Heeren te Paard; terwyl de Knegt een ander los by den toom houd, verders Geboomten en andere Reizigers; plaisant geschilderd | *Mat:* op paneel *Size:* hoog 6, breed 5 duim	[Merrem]	(Sold) fl 3:10 Gruiter
1802/07/09	AMSTO	0068	*P. Wouwerman* | 1 fraay schildery verbeeldende een Plysterplaats met verscheiden Stoffagie, door P. Wouwerman, in vergulde Lyst		(Unknown)
1802/07/20	MGSAN	0046	*P. Wouwerman* | Een zeer uitvoerige Battaille, extra schoon en krachtig: op Doek | *Mat:* op doek *Size:* hoog duim 20, breed duim 29		(Unknown)
1802/07/21	HGKAN	0092	*P. Wouwerman* | Een Bataille tusschen Cavallerie		(Unknown)
1802/09/06	AMSCH	0129	*P. Wouwerman* | In een Landschap voor een Boeren Herberg, vertoond zig een Dame op een bruin Paard gezéten, terwyl den Hospes, een wit gezadelt Paard, schynt te laaten drinken, ter zyde rust den Ruiter, die door den Hospita een glas Wyn word ingeschonken, gestoffeert met verdere Reizigers; bevallig gepenceeld | companion to lot 130 *Mat:* op doek *Size:* hoog 13, breed 16 duim	Brave	(Bought In) fl 10 for lots 129 & 130
1802/09/06	AMSCH	0130	*P. Wouwerman* | In een dito [voor een Boeren Herberg] Landschap, vertoond zig een rydende Leeger-Wagen met zes Paarden bespannen, een Heer schynt een Aalmoes te geeven, aan een Boere Jongen, ter zyde volgt een Vrouw en Kind, en Militairen te Paard, die door een Beekje waden, ter andere zyde een Vrouw met Groentens, en een Huisman met een beladen Ezel; fix gepenceeld, door denzelven [P. Wouwerman], zynde de wederga | companion to lot 129	Brave	(Bought In) fl 10 for lots 129 & 130

1802/09/06	AMSCH	0131	*P. Wouwerman* | Een Manége, met verscheide Paarden, by een Anticq Gebouw; uitvoerig | *Mat:* op paneel *Size:* hoog 14, breed 17 duim	Mevrouw Achtienhoven	(Sold) fl 1:5 L Pakker
1802/09/21	UTHDG	0097	*P. Wouwerman* | Voor een Smits wooning wordt een Paard de Hoef voorzien, en een ander gecureerd, waarbij veele aanschouwers. Op den voorgrond speelen kinderen met een wagentje, getrokken door een Bok, verder het stuk in, zijn noch verscheiden Beelden en andere voorwerpen. Alles helder geschildert | *Mat:* op doek *Size:* hoog 15 ½, breed 17 duimen		(Bought In) fl 76
1802/09/21	UTHDG	0098	*P. Wouwerman* | Een wit paard uit een krib eetende, waarbij een zittend man en hond voor een Boerewooning, natuurlijk behandeld | *Mat:* op paneel *Size:* hoog 9, breed 7 ½ duimen		(Sold) fl 15 De Munnick
1802/12/13	AMSCH	0182	*P. Wouwerman* | Een Landschap, gestoffeerd met een Heer en Dame te Paard, en een Smit die een Paard beslaat | *Mat:* op paneel *Size:* hoog 19, breed 16 duim	Pruyssenaar [for] D	(Sold) fl 9:10 Van der Schley [for] R[ijfsnijder]
1803/07/18	AMSCH	0062	*Wouwerman (P.)* | In een heuvelachtig Landschap ziet men een schermutzeling van eenige Ruiters welke een Convooy geleiden, en uit een hinderlaag vreeslyk beschoten worden, in het verschiet ziet men een Kasteel; een fraaye Lugt, een schoone compositie en een vrye behandeling maaken dit stuk van veel waardy van deezen Meester [Sur une légére Eminence se passe un choc meurtrier entre un parti de cavallerie & des fantassins postés en Embuscade ; des hommes & des chevaux mis hors de combat sont épars sur le Champ de Bataille. Un Convoy passant vèrs la droite du tableau tombe dans une autre embuscade faisant feu. Le fond est un Paysage terminé par un fort & un beau ciel. Il y a beaucoup d'action & de feu dans cette representation, elle est traitée d'une maniere facile & légère formant un ensemble bien composé & de bon effet.] | *Mat:* op doek *Size:* hoog 27, breed 38 duim	Maria Theresia Andrioli	(Sold) fl 170 Thys
1803/09/07	AMSCH	0210	*P. Wouwerman* | Een Stal van binnen te zien, met verscheide Paarden, beneevens een Heer te Paard gezéten en een Paard drinkende uit een Emmer, door de open deur ziet men een bevallig Landschap; uitvoerig behandeld [L'intérieur d'une écurie avec plusieurs chevaux ; à côté un cavalier à cheval et un autre cheval buvant hors d'un seau ; l'on apperçoit par la porte ouverte de l'écurie un paysage agréable et parfaitement peint] | *Mat:* op doek *Size:* hoog 15, breed 15 duim	Smidt	(Bought In) fl 55
1803/09/07	AMSCH	0211	*P. Wouwerman* | In een Stal ziet men een wit Paard, een Knegt met een mand Hooy en in 't verschiet een Heer te Paard; bevallig op Paneel [Un cheval blanc dans une écurie, un valet s'en approche avec un panier de foin ; dans le fond un cavalier à cheval ; d'une charmante composition] | *Mat:* op paneel *Size:* hoog 7, breed 9 duim	Smidt	(Sold) fl 5:10 Gruyter
1803/09/07	AMSCH	0212	*P. Wouwerman* | Twee stuks Landschappen met Geboomte, gestoffeerd met rustende Ryzigers met hun Paarden en andere te Voet, kragtig op Paneel [Deux paysages, variés par des arbres, de voyageurs à pied et à cheval ; d'un coloris vigoureux] | *Mat:* op paneel *Size:* yder is hoog 12, breed 9 duim [Hauts 11, larges 9 pouces] *Notes:* The dimensions differ in the Dutch and French editions of the catalogue.	Smidt	(Sold) fl 16:10 W Reijers
1804/04/28	LNDLS	0007	*P. Wouwermans* | Een Gezelschap van heeren en juffers te paard en te voet, in een landschap uitvoerig, door P. Wouwerman, op doek | *Mat:* op doek *Size:* hoog 16, breed 19 duim	[Abraham Delfos] [or others]	(Sold) fl 22 Rigters [for] A
1804/05/07	AMSCH	0189	*Wouwerman (P.)* | In een wyd uitgestrekt Landschap, ziet men ter zyden in een klaaren Rivier eenige Mannen en Kinderen zig baaden, voor en ter zyden eenige Gebouwen, gaande en rustende Landlieden en Vee, op de voorgrond eenige Reizigers te Paard en anderen Stoffagie, van agteren een aangenaam en Bergachtig verschiet; allerbevalligst en zonachtig geschilderd | *Mat:* op doek *Size:* hoog 27 ½, breed 34 duim	Vinkeles [for] G	(Sold) fl 27 Den Achtienhoven
1804/08/08	AMSCH	0214	*P. Wouwerman* | In een Stal, van binnen te zien, ziet men drie Paarden, waar van er één uit een Emmer drenkt, waarby een Heer op een ander Paard, en by een Ruif staan 'er verscheiden te eeten, door een openstaande Deur ziet men een aangenaam Landschapje; dit stuk is delicaat en van een uitvoerige penceelsbehandeling, door P. Wouwerman, Doek op Paneel | *Mat:* op doek op paneel *Size:* hoog 14, br.18 duim	Vink[eles] [for] S	(Sold) fl 74 van Iperer
1804/08/08	AMSCH	0215	*P. Wouwerman* | In een Landschap met eenig Geboomte, ziet men op de voorgrond een hévig Gevecht, tusschen Ruitery, die elkander woedende aanvallen, op de Grond legt een Gesneuvelden; alles is natuurlyk, krachtig van coloriet, en meesterlyk gepenceeld | *Mat:* op paneel *Size:* hoog 22, breed 27 duim	Schley [for] A	(Sold) fl 87 Coclers
1805/07/03	AMSCH	0168	*P. Wouwerman* | Dit bevallig stuk steld voor, een Duin- en Boomryk Landschap, met een Waterval op de Voorgrond een Heer te paard, verzeld van een Hond en een Vrouw en achter hun een Kar met een Paard bespannen, waarop een Landman gezeeten is, verders op de Brug een Man, en een alleraangenaamst verschiet; helder en piquant van licht en meesterlyk gepenceeld | *Mat:* op doek *Size:* hoog 23, breed 27 ½ duim	Y	(Sold) fl 40 Gruyter
1805/07/03	AMSCH	0169	*P. Wouwerman* | In een Verwulfde Stal, ziet men eenige Krygslieden met Vrouw en Kinderen, verscheiden Paarden en verder bywerk; natuurlyk en fiks gepenceeld | *Mat:* op paneel *Size:* hoog 14, breed 17 duim	G	(Sold) fl 140 Gruyter
1805/07/03	AMSCH	0170	*P. Wouwerman* | Twee stuks Pleisterplaatsen, gestoffeerd met Heeren en Dames te Paard en verdere Beelden; de behandeling is van de besten | *Mat:* op paneel *Size:* hoog 14, breed 12 duim	C	(Sold) fl 91 Gruyter

1805/07/10	AMSCH	0170	*P. Wouwerman* | Eenige Ruiters te paard en te voet, by een Soetelaarstent, zich ververschende, in het verschiet nog andere Paarden en Beeldjes | *Mat:* op paneel *Size:* hoog 13, breed 14 duim	R[oos]	(Sold) fl 10 van Iperen
1806/05/05	AMSCH	0178	*P. Wouwerman* | Een heuvelachtig Landschapje, op de voorgrond by Kreupelgewas, aan een Beekje, ziet men een Man te Paard, en verdere stoffagie; fraai op Paneel | *Mat:* op paneel	R[oos]	(Sold) fl 17:10 Jan Smit
1806/08/13	AMSCH	0213	*Wouwerman. (P.)* | Op een Grazige Vlakte, ziet men een Knegt een wit Paard vast houden, terzyde een bevallige Landvrouw by eenige Schaapen en Gyten, dewelke door een Heer schynt geliefkoost te worden; achterwaards eenige Lieden te Paard en een aangenaam verschiet; bevallig van licht en meesterlyk gepenceeld | *Mat:* op paneel *Size:* hoog 11, breed 13 ½ duim	Vinkeles [for] G[ruyter]	(Sold) fl 41 Van Iperen
1806/08/13	AMSCH	0214	*Wouwerman. (P.)* | In een Landschap, by de Stam van een Boom staat een gezadeld Paard; terzyde ziet men de Ruiter bézig om er op te stygen, verders een Jagthond; meesterlyk gepenceeld | *Mat:* op paneel *Size:* hoog 8, breed 10 duim	van der Voort	(Sold) fl 9 du Pre
1806/08/13	AMSCH	0215	*Wouwerman. (P.)* | In een bevallig Boom- en Duinryk Landschap, met een Rivier doorsneeden, ziet men op de voorgrond een ter Jacht rydend Gezelschap te paard en voet, verders door 't Water eenige rydende Heeren en Dames in een aangenaam verschiet; zonachtig en dun uitgevoerd | *Mat:* op paneel *Size:* hoog 16, breed 21 duim	Vinkeles [for] J	(Sold) fl 17 Spruit
1806/08/13	AMSCH	0216	*Wouwerman. (P.)* | In een Heuvelachtig Landschapje, met Geboomten en Gebouwen, ziet men op de voorgrond een rustende Jager met Honden en dood wild waarby een wit pissend Paard en Jager en een aangenaam verschiet; fiks gepenceeld | *Mat:* op paneel *Size:* hoog 9, breed 12 duim	Vinkeles [for] F	(Sold) fl 31 Van Iperen
1806/08/13	AMSCH	0291	*P. Wouwerman* | Twee stuks Landschapjes met Landlieden, bézig zynde hooy op wagens te laden; verzeld van Vrouwen met Kinderen en aangenaame verschieten; fiks en breed gepenceeld	Vinkeles [for] E	(Sold) fl 15 Schumacher
1806/08/13	AMSCH	0330	*Wouwerman. (P.)* | Een Gezicht op 't oude Stadhuis te Amsterdam, van vooren te zien, ryk gestoffeerd met Beelden, Vrachtgoederen, enz.; krachtig en meesterlyk geschilderd	Vinkeles [for] J	(Sold) fl 9:10 Schumacher
1806/10/16	UTWLD	0001	*P. Wouwerman* | Een Land en Water gezigt, op de Voorgrond met staande Paarden door P. Wouwerman	Mr P de Malapert [or] W Beeldsnyder	(Unknown)
1806/11/24	AMSCH	0081	*Wouwerman (P.)* | Een Pleisterplaats, waarby een Dame en Heer met hunne Paarden; op de Voorgrond eenige Bedelaars; verders in de deur der Herberg de Hospes; zo goed als men van dezen Meester zien kan | *Mat:* op paneel *Size:* hoog 9, breed 10 duim	Munnikhuizen	(Sold) fl 10 Coclers
1806/11/24	AMSCH	0082	*Wouwerman (P.)* | Een Heer op een wit Paard, nevens hem een Vrouw, by het Huis een Vrouw met een Kind; delicaat van penceel | *Mat:* op paneel *Size:* hoog 10, breed 14 duim	Munnikhuizen	(Sold) fl 1:15 v d Schley [for] Ryfsneyder
1807/08/26	AMSCH	0227	*P. Wouwerman* | In een heiachtig Landzicht ziet men Heeren te Paard en Jagers met Honden zich met de Rygerjagt vermaken; bevallig behandeld | *Mat:* op paneel *Size:* hoog 9, breed 11 duim	Roos [for] A	(Sold) fl 2:10 du Pree
1807/08/26	AMSCH	0238	*P. Wouwerman* | Een Stal, van binnen te zien, ter regterzyde een Heer op een wit Paard; hy schynt van de Jagt te komen. Op den voorgrond een ander by eene Dame, achterwaarts drie gezadelde Paarden; uitvoerig behandeld | *Mat:* op doek *Size:* hoog 18, breed 22 duim	de Vries	(Sold) fl 3:15 du Pree
1808/04/26	GDAN	0186	*Wouerman (P)* | Zijnde een Duin- en Strandgezigt, waar men een Heer ziet te Paard rijden, nevens hem een Visser, en bijwerk | companion to lot 187 *Size:* hoog 10, breed 12 duim	G H Fortuyn	(Unknown)
1808/04/26	GDAN	0187	*Wouerman (P)* | Een dito [Duin- en Strandgezigt] tot een wederga, zijnde een Legertent met een Zoetelaar, en eenige Heesen [sic] te Paard, in 't verschiet, vol gewoel, wel gedaan | companion to lot 186 *Size:* hoog 10, breed 12 ½ duim	G H Fortuyn	(Unknown)
1808/04/26	GDAN	0188	*Wouerman (P)* | Een Zandheuvel, met fraai hoog Geboomte, waar in Heeren en Dames te Paard, en eene Jagtpartij, en wat er toe behoord, fiks geschilderd | *Size:* hoog 51, breed 20 duim	G H Fortuyn	(Unknown)
1808/04/26	GDAN	0189	*Wouerman (P)* | Een fraaije Paardenmarkt, verbeeldende vol gewoel, uitmuntend gepenceeld | *Size:* hoog 30 ½, breed 38 duim	G H Fortuyn	(Unknown)
1808/04/26	GDAN	0190	*Wouerman (P)* | Een Paardewedde, met twee schoone Paarden, &c | *Size:* hoog 10 ½, breed 13 duim	G H Fortuyn	(Unknown)
1808/04/26	GDAN	0191	*Wouerman (P)* | Een plaisant Landschapje, waar in een Heer en een Dame te Paard zitten, bij hun staat een Palfrenier, die een wit Paard bij den toom houdt; &c. | *Size:* hoog 15 ½, breed 19 duim	G H Fortuyn	(Unknown)
1808/08/23	AMSCH	0169	*P. Wouwerman* | Een Landschap, op de voorgrond een wit gezadeld Paard, dat door een Smit beslagen word, daar nevens een Heer te Paard, die door eene arme Vrouw met twee Kinderen om een Almoes gevraagt word, verder een Duinachtig verschiet; kloek en meesterlijk behandeld | *Mat:* op paneel *Size:* hoog 15, breed 19 duim	H	(Sold) fl 41 Coclers
1808/08/23	AMSCH	0170	*P. Wouwerman* | Een Bergachtig Landschap, met grootsche Gebouwen en Fonteinwerken, gestoffeert met Heeren en Dames te Paard, benevens Jagers, die met hunne Honden een Hart vervolgen; meesterlijk gepenceeld | *Mat:* op doek *Size:* hoog 20, breed 27 duim	[Gruyter?]	(Sold) fl 2:10 Spruit

1808/11/28	AMSCH	0071	*P. Wouwerman* | Voor het Plijn van een grootsch Gebouw, ziet men eenige Heeren en Dames, verzeld van hunne Jagers en Honden, zig tot de Jagt gereed maken, uitvoerig | *Mat:* op doek *Size:* hoog 13 ½, breed 15 duim	[Gruyter?]	(Sold) fl 16 T Spaan
1808/11/28	AMSCH	0072	*P. Wouwerman* | Een hevige Schermutseling tusschen Ruiterij en Voetvolk, meesterlijk | *Mat:* op doek *Size:* hoog 13, breed 15 duim	[Gruyter?]	(Sold or Bought In) fl 2 Gruyter
1809/05/26	HADAA	0002	*P. Wouwerman* | Een fraai Schilderijtje verbeeldende een Man houdende een paard aan den toom, natuurlijk en bevallig | *Mat:* op paneel *Size:* breed 9 hoog 6 ½ duimen	Mejuffrouw de Wed David Heemskerk [or others]	(Unknown)
1809/06/13	AMSCH	0167	*P. Wouwerman* | Een hevig Gevegt in een Landschap, tusschen Ruiterij en Voetvolk, vol uitdrukking | *Mat:* op paneel *Size:* hoog 15, breed 20 duim	E	(Sold) fl 11:10 Buck
1809/09/06	AMSCH	0086	*Wouwerman (P.)* | Een Grot, waarin rustende Jagers, met hun Paard en Hond; kragtig behandeld | *Mat:* op paneel *Size:* hoog 15, breed 11 duim	Johannes Caudri	(Sold) fl 23 van Iperen
1810/03/07	UTWLD	0033	*P. Wouwermans* | Eenige Ruiters zittende voor een tent te dobbelen op de voorgrond, springende Paarden door P. Wouwermans, zeer schoon behandeld | *Size:* hoog 1 voet 3 duim, breed 1 voet 6 duim	J J Woertman	(Unknown) fl 66
1810/03/27	RMCNL	0027	*P. Wouwerman* | Een Attacque van Voet en Paardenvolk, bij een klein Watertje; alles vol gewoel en uitdrukking, meesterachtig geschilderd		(Unknown)
1810/05/22	AMSCH	0119	*Wouwerman. (P.)* | In een Veldgezicht staan op den voorgrond twee Paarden bij een beladen Hooiwagen, verder twee Vrouwen met een Kind, Arbeiders en andere Lieden; helder en uitvoerig behandeld | *Mat:* op paneel *Size:* hoog 14, breed 15 duim	Johannes van de Putte Nicolaasz.	(Sold) fl 165 Engelberts
1810/06/20	AMSCH	0155	*P. Wouwerman* | Een Pleisterplaats, met Lieden te paard en te voet, die zich ververschen	B	(Sold) fl 2 du Pree
1810/08/06	AMSCH	0125	*Wouwerman (P.)* | In een Stal ziet men eenen Heer, schijnende een Paard te kopen, verder verscheide Paarden en een Jongen met een Bokje; bevallig geschilderd | *Mat:* op doek *Size:* hoog 14, breed 16 duimen	G	(Sold) fl 22:10 van Leen [and] Vallee
1810/10/11	AMSCH	0102	*P. Wouwerman* | Dit natuurlijk Schilderij verbeelt een Veldgezigt, gestoffeerd met Lieden, bezig Koorn te Maaijen, terwijl andere hetzelve inzamelen, op den voorgrond een beladen Wagen, benevens een ontspannen Kar, waarop eene Vrouw zit, met een Kind aan de Borst, verder een wit grazend Paard, Hond, enz.; fraai en uitvoerig geschilderd | *Mat:* op doek *Size:* hoog 26, breed 32 duimen	[Gruyter?]	(Bought In) fl 31
			Wouwerman, P. (and Looten, J.)		
1809/04/17	AMSCH	0052	*J. Looten; P. Wouwerman* | Een Boschachtig Landschap, gestoffeerd met een Heer en Dame te Paard, waar bij Jagers met hunnen Honden, en een aangenaam verschiet; natuurlijk van schildering, door J. Looten, gestoffeerd, door P. Wouwerman | *Mat:* op doek *Size:* hoog 42, breed 32 duim	A	(Sold) fl 8:10
			Wouwerman, P. (or Wouwerman, P., manner)		
1809/09/06	AMSCH	0087	*Wouwerman (P.), of in de manier* | Twee stuks Landschappen, met stoffagie van Paarden en Beelden; bevallig gepenceeld | *Mat:* op koper *Size:* ieder hoog 16, breed 20 duim	Johannes Caudri	(Sold) fl 23 Dupré
			Wouwerman, P. (copy after)		
1810/12/03	DOBRA	0046	*Drillenburg; P. Wouerman* | Een Landschap, door Drillenburg, naar P. Wouerman | copy by W. Drielenburch after P. Wouwerman		(Unknown)
			Wouwerman, P. (manner)		
1804/08/08	AMSCH	0243	*P. Wouwerman* | Eenige Militairen te Paard en te voet, schynen zich te ververschen, voor een Tent, verders in en by een Rivier zwemmende Jongens, een Pont, en verscheide andere Beeldjes; op Doek, als P. Wouwerman | *Mat:* op doek	Roos [for] C	(Sold) fl 5:10 Pruizenaar
1807/06/10	HGBSM	0164	*P. Wouwerman* | Het retour van een Jagtpartij van groote persoonagien met veel bijwerk, in de trant van P. Wouwerman | *Mat:* op paneel *Size:* hoog 16 ½, breed 21 duim	Abraham Delfos [or others]	(Sold) fl 6 Vermeulen
			Wouwerman, Philips		
1801/04/13	AMSCH	0083	*Ph. Wouwerman* | Dit uitmuntend Tafereel verbeeld een Groentemarkt in een Italiaansche plaats, men ziet in het midden een Vrouw met verscheide groentens, daarby een bruin paard voor een slee, welke met manden met groente beladen word, ter linker zyde eenige vogelkopers, een ander met kaas, een menigte Beeldjes, welke alle zeer fraaije groepen uitmaken versieren wyders dit stuk, ter regter zyde in een rivier, waarover een steenen brug ligt, ziet men verscheide vaartuigen, en verder een aangenaam verschiet; dit Schildery is van den zilverachtigen toon van deezen voortreflyken Meester, en delicaat bewerkt | *Mat:* op doek *Size:* hoog 29, breed 42 duim	Pierre Fouquet, junior	(Sold) fl 400 Pruyssenaar
1801/04/13	AMSCH	0084	*Ph. Wouwerman* | Voor een Soetelaars Tent ziet men eenige krygslieden met hunne paarden zich ververschen, en zich met de kastelynesse vermaken, voorts een ryk gestoffeerd verschiet; uitvoerig gepenceeld | *Mat:* op paneel *Size:* hoog 14, breed 16 duim	Pierre Fouquet, junior	(Sold) fl 110 Huijgen
1801/04/13	AMSCH	0085	*Ph. Wouwerman* | Een Gevangene voor eenige krygslieden gebragt wordende, behandeld als de voorgaande | *Mat:* op doek *Size:* hoog 9, breed 11 duim	Pierre Fouquet, junior	(Sold) fl 22 Rijnders

1801/06/10	AMSCH	0191	*Wouwerman. (Philip)* | Een Wintergezicht, het Ys gestoffeerd met een Heer en Dame in een Arreslede, verder een beladen Slee, waar nevens twee Kinderen met een Yssleede, verders Boere Wooningen, en een aangenaam verschiet; delicaat en meesterlyk behandeld | *Mat:* op paneel *Size:* hoog 20, breed 27 duim	Herman ten Kate	(Sold) fl 268 J Roelofs
1801/10/06	AMSCH	0071	*Ph. Wouwerman* | Dit fraai en Bevallig Tafreel, vertoont een Heuvelagtig Italiaansch Landschap, ryk gestoffeert met verscheide Beelden, op de voorgrond staat een Landloopster met twee Kinderen, waar by een Dame, die zy goeder geluk schynt te zeggen, daar neevens een Heer, op een bruin Paard, en een ander staande, een Jongen schynt een Almoes te vraagen, verder twee Knegts, beezig een Paard te Zadelen, en op een Heuvel staan, zitten en rusten, verscheide Landloopers, ter regter zyde ziet men de Ruwiene van een Gebouw, waar in een Gewulft, alwaar zig verscheide Mans, Vrouw en Kinderen van het Bédel-rot zig by het Vuur warmen, alles is Kunstig en van een uitvoerig Penceelbehandeling | *Mat:* op paneel *Size:* hoog 15, breed 13 ½ duim	S	(Sold) fl 1000 Coclers
1801/10/06	AMSCH	0072	*Ph. Wouwerman* | In een Landzigt, by een Boeren Wooning en Geboomten, zit een rustende Ryziger en Vrouw, waar by een staande Vrouw in deftige Kleeding, als met hun spreekende; ter zyde staat een wit Paard, welke door een Boer te drinken word gegeeven, en in 't verschiet een gaande Huisman, alles zeer Natuurlyk, Bevallig en van een fraai Penceelbehandeling | *Mat:* op paneel *Size:* hoog 12, breed 11 duim	S	(Sold) fl 420 Ter Smitten
1801/10/06	AMSCH	0073	*Ph. Wouwerman* | In een Hei-agtig Landschap met eenig Geboomten ter zyde, vertoont zig belaaden Rys-wagens, door Struikrovers te Paard aangevallen, en geplunderd, verder een andere Wagen het ontvlugtende, alles van een Meesterlyke en fikse Penceelbehandeling | *Mat:* op doek *Size:* hoog 25, breed 32 duim	L	(Sold) fl 300 C S Roos
1801/10/19	AMSCH	0085	*Wouwerman. (Philip)* | Dit uitmuntend Schildery, vertoont het binnengezicht van een Stal, men ziet te midden een appelgrys gezadeld Paard, door een Stalknegt gehouden wordende, terwyl de Ruiter bezig is zyne laarsen aantetrekken, waarby een Dame die zig gereed maakt een bruin Paard te bestygen, gehouden wordende door een Stalknegt; ter linkerzyde ziet men drie Paarden, Eetende aan de Ruif, en ter rechter vertoont zig een Ruiter op een grys Paard, schynende met de Stalmeester te spreeken, aan de deur vertoond zig een Dame te Paard, dragende een Valk op de hand; verzeld van een Jager en een Hond, verder ziet men twee Paarden aan een Eetensbak of krib, en buiten de Stal een aangenaam verschiet, dit Schilderstuk is in allen deelen uitmuntend schoon uitgewerkt, en men kan na waarheid getuigen dat het niets toegeefd aan een der beste werken van deeze voortreffelyke Meester | *Mat:* op paneel *Size:* hoog 19, breed 25 duim *Loc:* Amsterdam, Nederland. Rijksmuseum. (A 2348)	Jonkheer Menno Baron van Coehoorn	(Sold) fl 1810 J^b Roeloffs (B^d Kooy)
1801/10/19	AMSCH	0086	*Wouwerman. (Philip)* | Een Landgezicht by een ruïne, waar in een wit Paard grasende is, daar naast een Man, welke een Zadel draagt, verder een Heer te Paard, beneevens twee Jagers met eenig Jachtgereedschap, zeer dun en delicaat geschilderd | *Mat:* op paneel *Size:* hoog 10 ½, breed 12 duim	Jonkheer Menno Baron van Coehoorn	(Sold) fl 161 Frantzen (Spruit van Gend)
1802/02/16	AMSCH	0006	*Ph. Wouwerman* | By een steene Brug ziet men een man by een wit Paard, verders Jongens in een Rivier zich met baden verlustigende; delicaat op paneel geschilderd | *Mat:* op paneel	B[uys]	(Sold) fl 49 Coclers
1802/05/05	AMSCH	0230	*Philip Wouwerman* | Op een Heuvel, voor een Water, ziet men een Man op een Paard, waarby een ander graauw pissende, en een zwaar beladen bruin Paard, voor dezelven ziet men een ander de Heuvel afryden, en eenig Vee dat door het Water gedreeven word, op de overzyde op een Berg ligt een Gebouw, waarby eenige Voetgangers, verders een aangenaam verschiet, alles van een zilveragtige en uitvoerige behandeling | *Size:* hoog 14, breed 19 duim	J	(Sold) fl 680 I^c Smit
1802/05/05	AMSCH	0231	*Philip Wouwerman* | Een Dorpgezicht, gestoffeerd met een Ryziger, bezig zynde zyn Paard te zadelen, nevens hem de Hospes met een glas met bier in de hand; verders een Man met een Hond, in de Tooren van de Kerk is een Orlogie geplaatst, loopt 24 uuren, en is met een vergulde Wyzerplaat, fraai gepenceeld | *Mat:* op paneel *Size:* hoog 33, breed 28 duim	A	(Sold) fl 41 Spruit
1802/06/16	AMSCH	0214	*Ph Wouwerman* | In een Heuvelachtig Landschap met hoog Geboomte, ziet men eenige beladen Vragtwagens tegens een hoogte opryden, eenige Voerlieden doen moeite om een Paard door een Beekje te leiden; alles delicaat gepenceeld | *Mat:* op doek *Size:* hoog 18, breed 15 ½ duim	[Merrem]	(Sold) fl 37 Agina
1802/08/24	LNDLS	0003	*Ph. Wouwerman* | Voor een Gebouw staat een Heer die een Juffer caresseert, bij een gezadelt wit paard, voorts een ander te paard en een te voet, benevens een Vrouwtje met een Kind, en een Jongeling met eenige Jagt-honden op den voorgrond | *Mat:* op paneel *Size:* hoog 18, breed 15 duimen	Leonardus Bouman [or others]	(Unknown) fl 41
1802/09/21	UTHDG	0095	*Philip Wouwerman* | Uit uitmuntend Kabinetstuk, vertoond in een Landschap, bij een Vorstelijk gebouw, twee Paarden in het volle licht geplaatst, zijnde een wit en een bruin, waarbij een Heer gereed staat om de Dame, die van het Bordes word geleid, te ontvangen. Ter linkerzijde iemand werpende eeten uit zijn hoed, voor de Honden, waarbij een Dwerg en een Jaager. Op het Bordes veele bedienden, andere maaken zich gereed, of gaan reeds op weg. Vooraan blaast een te Paard zittend Heer,		(Bought In) fl 1450

			den Hoorn, nevens hem zijn Valkenier en Honden. Het verschiet is aangenaam en bergagtig; deeze rijke welgegroepte ordonn. zijnde den aanvang eener aanzienelijke Jagtparthij, is in couleur en houding voortreffelijk en van de beste penceelsbehandeling | *Mat:* op doek *Size:* hoog 20, breed 31 duimen		
1802/09/21	UTHDG	0096	*Philip Wouwerman* | Een Heer bij zijn wit paard staande, geeft aan een met haare kinderen Beedelende vrouw, aalmoessen [sic]; verder Jaagers, Honden, en een fraaij Duingezigt. Op de voorgrond gevelde boomstammen, kruiden, enz. Alles helder, zeer natuurlijk en met een los penceel behandeld | *Mat:* op doek *Size:* hoog 13, breed 16 ½ duimen		(Sold) fl 120 Cobell
1802/09/29	AMSCH	0057	*Ph. Wouwerman* | Een Zee-strand, hoog 21, breed 30 ½ duim. Doek. Word in dit bevallige Schildery verbeeld by het aankomen der Visch, die in zoorten ter aarde verspreid legt. Een wit Paard word door twee Visschers met Netren [sic] beladen, terwyl een Visch-Boerinnetje en een Meisje, door een jong Heer (met een Hoed met Pluimen, en in ryke kleeding zynde, op een bruin Paard gezeten) worden aangesprooken [sic]. Verders ziet men verscheiden rustende Visschers, in verwagting van meerdere Visch; wandelende Lieden, Visschers Hutten, Wooningen op Duin, een Vuurbaak en eenige Pinken aan Strand, verryken dit kunstig Tafreel, daar men de Eenvoudige en schoone Natuur in ziet voorgesteld; deeze gelukkige Ordenantie, zonagtig behandeld, is van eene delicate Penceel uitvoerigheid, en door een helder Licht gedaagd, zynde een de Capitaalste Stukken van deezen beroemden Meester [Un site de Paysage pittoresque, orné de dunes & Habitations de Pecheurs : la droite est enrichie de diverses Figures, dont un jeune Cavalier à cheval richement costumé & à chapeau à Plumets, s'arréte pour faire la causette avec une Femme & une Fille du village ; au milieu du Tableau se voit un cheval blanc que deux Pécheurs chargent de filets ; la scene représente, le Retour de la Pêche, des Poissons de plusieurs Espéces sont étalés sur le rivage, ou des Pécheurs dans des actions differentes : un seigneur & une Dame fixent leurs regards vers la mer, ou l'on remarque des Barques occupés de figures ; Les divers objets que l'on voit contre un ciel argentin & heureusement nuagé, en paroissent détachés à produire l'Illusion ; le soleil produit partout des Effets de clair, obscur admirables : Ce Tableau d'une beauté d'Exécution surprenante, réunit à un sujet des plus agréables, toutes les parties de la Peinture, surtout cette Harmonie de couleur qui à assigné à Philippe Wouwerman, le premier Rang, parmi les Peintres de son genre.] | *Mat:* op doek *Size:* hoog 21, breed 30 ½ duim	[Labouchere?]	(Sold) fl 1020 W Reijers
1803/04/20	AMSCH	0089	*Wouwerman (Ph.)* | Een Duinachtig Landschap met Geboomte, Kreupelgewas en een spiegelende Waterplas, op de voorgrond ziet men een Kar beladen met Zand, waarvoor een bruin Paard, benevens de Voerman, daarachter en verder in het verschiet een menigte Jagers te Paard en te voet; het licht en bruin en de kloeke penceelsbehandeling, maken dit Stukje tot een der bevalligste van deeze grooten Meester [Cet agréable tableau offre un site dans les Dunes de mêr, entrecoupé par des parties cultivées & une marre d'eau. Au premier plan est une charette attelée d'un cheval brun ; un autre cheval & des conducteurs. Une quantité de chasseurs à pied et à cheval orne lés [sic] plans reculés. Le ton clair, argentin, une touche large mais précieuse, & l'effet le plus brillant de cet ensemble vraiment pittoresque, le feront gouter aux artistes, comme aux amateurs.] | *Mat:* op paneel *Size:* hoog 14, breed 12 ½ duim	Maria Magdalena van Sluypwyk, gravinne van Moens	(Sold) fl 705 J Spaan
1803/08/17	AMSCH	0090	*Wouwerman (PH.)* | Op een grazigen Heuvel, by de Stam van een doden Boom, ziet men een Jongeling, welke een fraai wit gezadeld Paard by het bit hout, terwyl de Ruiter agter den heuvel zich vertoond; op den met kruiden bewassen Voorgrond legt een Hond: dit stukje is van de beste tyd van deezen groten Meester, en verdiend een plaats in een der beste Cabinetten | *Mat:* op paneel *Size:* hoog 17, breed 15 duim	Anna Catharina Putman	(Bought In) fl 650
1803/08/24	HGKAN	0049	*Ps. Wouwerman* | Voor een Rotz ziet men een Man op een oud wit Paard, en op de voorgrond twee honden, alles zeer uitvoerig en zilveragtig behandelt | *Mat:* op paneel *Size:* hoog 10, breet 11 duim	[Teissier] [or others]	(Sold) fl 101 Huybregts
1803/09/07	AMSCH	0205	*Ph. Wouwerman* | Dit uitmuntend Konststukje verbeeld een aangenaam Landschap, op de voorgrond staat een wit Paard, waarop een deftig Officier, voor een Tent, waarin verscheide Krygslieden, een derzelven stoeyt met een Meisje, op de tweede grond nog een Ruyter by zyn Paard en eenige andere in het verschiet, alles van een delicate behandeling [Ce chef-d'oeuvre représente un paysage riant ; sur le devant, un officier à cheval à l'entrée d'une tente remplie de gens de guerre, dont l'un folâtre avec une jeune fille ; plus loin un autre cavalier auprès de son cheval, le fond est rempli de differents sujets et de figures analogues ; composition précieuse et bien exécutée] | *Mat:* op paneel *Size:* hoog 14, br. 15 duim	Smidt	(Bought In) fl 700
1803/09/07	AMSCH	0206	*Ph. Wouwerman* | Op een grazigen Heuvel staat een beladen Hooywagen, waar op men bezig is Hooy te laden, een wit en een graauw Paard, op de voorgrond zitten twee Vrouwen en een Kind, waar by een staand Man en aangenaam verschiet, behandeld als de voorgaande, door denzelven [Ph. Wouwerman], en van een gelyke grooten [L'on voit dans une belle prairie une charrette de foin, qu'on est occupé de charger ; elle est attelée de deux chevaux dont l'un blanc et l'autre gris ; sur le devant deux femmes et un enfant auprès desquels un homme debout ; le fond offre une perspective agréable dans le même goût que le précédent tableau.] | *Size:* [Haut 14,	Smidt	(Sold) fl 255 v d Schley [for] Putti

			large 15 pouces] *Notes:* The dimensions are given only in the French edition of the catalogue.		
1803/09/07	AMSCH	0207	*Ph. Wouwerman* | Het atakeere van een Convoy, door eenige Cavallerie; welke door een bende Ruiters overvallen worden, de ordonnantie is schoon, het verschiet aangenaam, en de behandeling over fraay [Un convoi attaqué par un détachement de cavalerie ; l'ordonnance de ce tableau est belle et la perspective agréable ; l'exécution de l'ensemble et des détails d'une excellent fini] | *Mat:* op doek *Size:* hoog 21, breed 25 duim	Smidt	(Bought In) fl 70
1803/09/07	AMSCH	0208	*Ph. Wouwerman* | Een bevallig Landschap op de voorgrond eenige vrolyke Boeren en Boerinnen, benevens twee Paarden en een Hooywagen, verders een Rivier en eenige Bergen in 't verschiet; fraay van tekening en delicaat gepenceeld [Un paysage riant, dont le devant présente quelques villageois des deux sexes en gaïté ; à côté deux chevaux et une charrette de foin ; plus loin une rivière et dans le fond des montagnes qui bornent la perspective. Ce tableau se distingue par la beauté du dessin et la délicatesse de l'exécution] | *Mat:* op doek *Size:* hoog 14, breed 16 duim	Smidt	(Bought In) fl 61
1803/09/07	AMSCH	0209	*Ph. Wouwerman* | Een Land- en Watergezigt, met Jagers te paard en te voet, verders een aangenaam verschiet, bevallig [Une vue champêtre, donnant sur l'eau avec des chasseurs à pied et à cheval ; dans le fond une perspective agréable, belle exécution] | *Mat:* op paneel *Size:* hoog 10, breed 12 duim	Smidt	(Bought In) fl 43 ½
1803/12/15	MGLAC	0006	*Ph. Wouwerman* | Een extra schoon Ruitergevegt; zeer helder en kragtig geschilderd | *Mat:* op doek *Size:* hoog duim 20, breed duim 30	Mr L H de Haze Bomme	(Unknown)
1804/02/27	AMSCH	0116	*Wouwerman (Ph.)* | Een Landschap, met een Valkenjacht, ter rechterzyde van dit fraaye Landschap ziet men eene vlakte, waarby eenige hoog opgaande Boomen, op de voorgrond vertoonen zich de Jagers met hunne Paarden, welke bezig zyn de Valken die in de Lucht vliegen, te lokken; de onderscheidene Actien en Caracters zyn allerfraaist behandeld, ter linkerzyde ontdekt men een stil Watertje of Beekje, waarby een rustende Reiziger en een Hond, verders is dit Landschap verreikt met een alleruitmuntendst verschiet, waarin verscheide Bouw- en Weilanden, Boerenwooningen, Molens, een Dorp, en verders een Duin- en Bergächtig verschiet; de reflectie van de Lucht in het Water en de uitvoerigheid, en tevens de meesterlyke behandeling van dit Schildery, geven aan deeze meester de grootste lof, alles is van een bevallige Zilverachtige toon, en byzonder fraai van penceelsbehandeling | *Mat:* op doek *Size:* hoog 17, breed 23 duim	B	(Sold) fl 700 Burggraff
1804/05/07	AMSCH	0187	*Wouwerman (Ph.)* | Deeze ryke Ordonantie, vertoond zig in een Duinachtig Landschap, op de voorgrond ziet men Jagers met hunne Honden, waarby eenig dood Wild, als een doode Rhee en een Tyger, nevens hetzelve ligt eenig Jachtgereedchap, een weinig verder ziet men een Jongeling by een Ezel, waarby verscheide andere Persoonen en Honden, ter linkerzyde ziet men twee Heeren te Paard, en een ander die een Paard vast houd, verder een aangenaam verschied; alles zeer uitvoerig en krachtig van schildering | *Mat:* op doek *Size:* hoog 24, breed 31 duim	Pruysnaar	(Bought In) fl 1000
1804/07/25	AMSCH	0089	*Wouverman. (PH.)* | In een aangenaam Land- en Riviergezicht, waar over een Hout Bruggetje gelegt is, gaat een Huisman, op de Voorgrond legt een Vaartuig met Turf, welke door Arbyders op een Wagen geladen word, voor dezelve staat een wit en een bruin Paard en eenige Kinderen die zig by een Vuurtje Warmen; dit Cabinetstukje is zeer uitvoerig en fraai van penceel behandeling | *Mat:* op paneel *Size:* hoog 14 ½, breed 14 ½ duim		(Sold) fl 135 Jan Ijver
1804/08/08	AMSCH	0212	*Philip Wouwerman* | In en Duinachtig Landschap ziet men een belaaden Boerenwagen en Passagiers te Paard, welke door een Bende Roovers, uit een Bosch komende, overvallen worden, een der Passagiers legt reeds dood op de voorgrond, terwyl anderen zich door de vlucht of smeeken schynen te willen redden; dit stuk is van een fraaije en meesterlyke behandeling door Philip Wouwerman | *Mat:* op doek *Size:* hoog 26, breed 32 duim	Roos a	(Bought In) fl 480
1804/08/08	AMSCH	0213	*Philip Wouwerman* | In een Heuvelachtig Landschap ziet men de Bekeering van Paulus, hy legt van zyn Paard gevallen op de voorgrond, verders vluchtende Paarden, met hunne Ruiters, als verschrikt door den Blixem; dit stukje is van een uitvoerige en aangenaame schildering | *Mat:* op paneel *Size:* hoog 13, breed 14 duim	Roos a	(Bought In) fl 90
1804/10/16	DLOND	0267	*Philip Wouwerman* | Een open Stal, waarin ene Vrouw op een bruin Paerd, terwijl een Heer zich gereed maakt, om een wit Paerd te beklimmen. Voorts ziet men nog meer Paerden aan de ruif staan, met verder Bywerk. Zeer schoon. Vue interieure d'une ecurie de Campagne ouverte; on y voit une Femme montée en Cheval brun, tandis qu'un Cavallier se prepare à monter un Cheval blanc. On distingue d'autres Chevaux au ratelier. Pièce très-belle | *Mat:* op paneel *Size:* hoog 15, breed 19		(Sold) fl 140 O D Wyngaert
1805/07/03	AMSCH	0052	*Wouwerman. (Philip)* | Dit Onderwerp steld voor: een Heuvelachtig Landschap, alwaar eenige Krygslieden te paard, schynen te vlugten voor een zwaar Onweder, twee derzelven leggen reeds als door den blixem gestroffen op den grond, terwyl hun Paarden wegvlieden; het coloriet is aangenaam, en de schildering zeer uitvoerig | *Mat:* op paneel *Size:* hoog 11, breed 14 duim	R[oos]	(Bought In) fl 260

1806/08/20	HGBSM	0086	*Ph. Wouwerman* | Een Binnestalling, in het midden vertoond zich een wit gezadelt Paard, door een Stalknegt vastgehouden wordende, benevens eene Dame, en Jager, met Honden, verders Heeren te Paard en andere figuuren, rijk gestoffeerd. Dit fraaije Stuk is helder en uitvoerig geschilderd, door Ph. Wouwerman, op paneel uit een stuk | *Mat:* op paneel *Size:* hoog 17 ½, breed 24 ¾ duim	Macalester Loup [or others]	(Bought In) fl 210
1807/06/10	HGBSM	0175	*Ph. Wouwerman* | Eenige Soetelaars tenten, waar bij Krijgsvolk, zo te voet als te paard die zich ververschе, zeer aangenaam van ordonnantie, gemerkt Ph. Wouwerman | *Mat:* op doek *Size:* hoog 12 ½, breed 17 duim *Inscr:* Ph. Wouwerman (signed)	Abraham Delfos [or others]	(Sold) fl 30:10 Noordwyk
1808/04/26	GDAN	0192	*Wouerman (Philip)* | Een Rivier- en Duinägtig Landschap, waar op de voorgrond eenige Paarden en rustende pakdragende Menschen, op de tweede grond, eenige Vissers die een Zeege trekken, en eenige Zwemmers, voorts nog een Boere Woning met Beelden en Schapen, verder in 't verschiet, eenige Zandägtige Bergen, zonägtig en fraai geschilderd | *Mat:* op paneel *Size:* hoog 19, breed 24 duim	G H Fortuyn	(Unknown)
1808/04/26	GDAN	0193	*Wouerman (Philip)* | Een bergägtig Landschap, waar een Heer en een Dame te Paard rijden, aan de linkerzijde ziet men een Herberg, waar een wit Paard staat, dat te drinken word gegeven, aan de regterzijde eenige zittende en staande Petsonen [sic], in 't verschiet een Hooijwagen, &c alles fiks zonägtig en fraai gepenseeld | *Size:* hoog 15 ½, breed 13 duim	G H Fortuyn	(Unknown)
1808/06/06	RMRIJ	0142	*Wouwerman. (Philip)* | Dit is een der twee bekende en beroemde stukken van dezen grooten Meester. Het stelt voor de Overrompeling en Plundering van een Dorp, doch in 't welke de Boeren meester zijn en zegepralen over de Militairen. Ingevolge hiervan vertoont zich op den voorgrond een Officier halverlijf geheel uitgekleed, en de handen op den rug gebonden, terwijl een Boer in eene bespottende houding des Officiers Montering aan heeft; benevens hem nog twee snaaksche Boeren. Eenen dood liggenden Officier worden de kleederen uitgetrokken. Hierbij staat een gezadeld wit Paard, en eenige vale en bruine Paarden, van welke laatste kleur er een dood op den grond ligt. Ter zijde van dit alles wordt een Militair, door eenige Boeren, met geweld weggevoerd, en een tweede nog te Paard zittende overmeesterd, enz. Op den tweeden grond, in 't verschiet ziet men vechtende partijen, en veel bijwerk. Alles uitvoerig, schoon en meesterlijk behandeld. De wedergade van dit tafereel, waarin de Militairen meester zijn, is, zoo wij ons wel herinneren, in 't Kabinet van den Heere van Lankeren te Antwerpen [Ce Tableau (dont le Pendant se trouvoit, il y a quelques années, dans le Cabinet de M[r]. van Lankeren à Anvers) represente des Marodeurs vivement repoussés par des Paysans, qu'ils avoient attaqués dans leur village situé au milieu d'un terrein Montagneux. Sur le premier Plan, on voit un Officier moitié nud, et les bras liés, qui montre sur sa figure le dédain et la colère, à l'aspect de quatre Rustres, qui s'amusent à se décorer de son uniforme et de ses armes, pendant qu'un autre enlève les vetements d'un Officier étendu sur le carreau. Un Cheval blanc pommelé, plusieurs autres Chevaux de differentes coleurs [sic], et un Cheval bai mort, composent cette avant scène. Vers la droite, deux militaires sont saisis et entrâinés par des Paysans qui se sont emparé de leurs armes. Le Second Plan offre plusieurs attaques. Partout les Militaires poursuivis, fuyent au grand galop. Des scènes variées dans le même genre, se découvrent dans le lointain, qui, se reunissant agréablement avec un beau Ciel Savamment nuagé, forme par l'ensemble une des meilleures et des plus riches Compositions de ce célébre Artiste] | *Mat:* op doek *Size:* Hoog 22 ⅜, en breed 29 ⅜ duim *Loc:* Amsterdam, Nederland. Rijksmuseum. (A482)	Gerrit van der Pot, Heer van Groeneveld	(Sold) fl 3625 J M Jorissen [for] le Roi
1808/06/06	RMRIJ	0143	*Wouwerman. (Philip)* | Dit stuk is bekend onder den naam der Reigerjagt. Op den voorgrond ziet men drie Heeren en eene Dame te Paard, vergezeld van een Bediende en Honden. De tweede grond is mede verrijkt met het verder gevolg tot eene Reigerjagt behoorende. Een verschiet, doorsneden met eene Rivier, eindigt in aangenaam Gebergte, dat zich aan den horizont met de rijk bewolkte lucht vereenigt. Dit heerlijk tafereel is een der uitvoerigste en kunstigste van dezen weergadeloozen Meester. Daar hetzelve mede tot het Kabinet van den Hertog van Choiseul behoord heeft, zoo is de gegraveerde Kunstplaat daarvan in die bekende collectie te vinden [Ce Morceau est connu sous le nom de *la Chasse au vol.* Dans un vaste Paysage découvert, on voit une troupe de Chasseurs à cheval, parmi lesquels se trouve une femme, qui suivent au grand galop un Cavalier monté sur un Cheval isabelle. Diverses petites figures répandues avec art sur differents Plans, contribuent à la richesse de cette Composition. De beaux lointains terminés par des hautes Montagnes, se lient de la manière la plus piquante et la plus harmonieuse à un Ciel admirablement nuagé. La perfection de la touche et la vivacité du Coloris ajoutent encore a la beauté de ce Tableau, qui provient de la précieuse Collection du Duc de Choiseul. On en trouve la gravure dans le recueil de son Cabinet] | *Mat:* op koper *Size:* Hoog 9 ½, en breed 11 duim *Loc:* Amsterdam, Nederland. Rijksmuseum. (A481)	Gerrit van der Pot, Heer van Groeneveld	(Sold) fl 3030 J J de Wit [for] le Roi
1808/06/06	RMRIJ	0144	*Wouwerman. (Philip)* | In een bergachtig Landschap ziet men op den tweeden grond eene beladen Kar met eene figuur. Voor de Kar een wit ontspannen Paard; daarnevens een bruin Paard, aan den kop vastgehouden wordende door een Smids-Jongen, terwijl een ander een achterbeen bij	Gerrit van der Pot, Heer van Groeneveld	(Sold) fl 1055 Johs Eck en Zoon [for] le Roi

<table>
<tr><td></td><td></td><td></td><td>den schoen opligt, om hetzelve te beslaan. Wat verder ziet men den Smid bezig het hoefijzer te warmen; eene zittende Vrouw daarneven en verder veel bijwerk. Op den rijk versierden voorgrond ligt een rustende Hond. Ter regterzijde op den tweeden grond ziet men eenen Man gezeten op een beladen Paard, vergezeld van twee figuren en een hond. Een rond Gebouw, eene kloeke Rots, eene Brug en Boomen, doen zig liefelijk op, tegen eene meesterlijke lucht. Alles natuurlijk, uitvoerig en schoon geschilderd [Paysage d'un beau choix, où l'on découvre une grande Charette chargée, à laquelle une figure est occupée. Un Garçon tient un Cheval blanc par la bride, et un Maréchal lui ferre un pied de derrière. Plus loin, sous une espèce de voûte, on voit une forge, un forgeron et une femme assise, et auprés d'eux plusieurs accessoires artistement representés. Sur le devant du Tableau un Chien repose, plus loin à droite, un homme est à Cheval, et à côté de lui il y a deux personnes. Une Vieille Tour située sur un rocher, de beaux arbres, et un Pont suspendu, se detachent agréablement contre un Ciel clair. Ce Morceau d'une belle Composition, et d'un grand fini, est touché avec cette finesse qu'on admire tant dans les productions de ce grand Peintre] | Mat: op doek Size: Hoog 23, en breed 20 ½ duim Loc: Amsterdam, Nederland. Rijksmuseum. (A478)</td><td></td><td></td></tr>
<tr><td>1808/06/06</td><td>RMRIJ</td><td>0145</td><td>Wouwerman. (Philip) | Een Boeren Gehucht, voor 't welke een hevig gevecht van eene menigte Boeren en Boerinnen. Zijnde de hartstogten der vechtende personen zeer schoon uitgedrukt. Verdere stoffering en bijwerk, alles meesterlijk geschilderd [Ce Tableau d'un genre rare, represente plusieurs Paysans et Paysannes, qui se battent avec acharnement devant une Maison de campagne etc. Les figures sont savamment groupées, et les passions parfaitement exprimées. Un beau Coloris, et un beau faire distinguent cette production interessante] | Mat: op doek Size: Hoog 24 ¼, en breed 32 ¾ duim Loc: Amsterdam, Nederland. Rijksmuseum. (A476)</td><td>Gerrit van der Pot, Heer van Groeneveld</td><td>(Sold) fl 600 J J de Wit [for] le Roi</td></tr>
<tr><td>1808/06/13</td><td>AMSCH</td><td>0167</td><td>Wouwerman (Philip) | Een rijk gestoffeerd Landschap, op welks voorgrond men eenig dood Wild ziet liggen, verzeld van Jagers met Honden, terugkomende van de Jagt, ter linkerzijde Heeren te Paard, benevens een Valkenier te Paard in het verschiet. Fraai en uitvoerig | Size: hoog 24, breed 31 duim</td><td>W</td><td>(Sold) fl 455 Allard</td></tr>
<tr><td>1808/06/13</td><td>AMSCH</td><td>0168</td><td>Wouwerman (Philip) | In een doorgang van eene Grot ziet men een schoon wit Paard, het geen gezadeld wordt, daar achter eene Vrouw met een Kind, zittende op een bruin Paard, verder twee Honden, in het verschiet komt eene Vrouw met een Jongen van eene Berg. Kragtig en van schoon koloriet | Mat: op paneel Size: hoog 15, breed 19 duim</td><td>R[oos]</td><td>(Bought In) fl 70</td></tr>
<tr><td>1809/04/17</td><td>AMSCH</td><td>0110</td><td>Ph. Wouwerman | Voor een Buitenhuis, ziet men een staand en een rustend Krijgsman, waar bij een Hond, in 't verschiet een Landschap; uitvoerig en zuiver van penceelsbehandeling | Mat: op paneel Size: hoog 15, breed 13 duim</td><td>A</td><td>(Sold) fl 47</td></tr>
<tr><td>1809/04/17</td><td>AMSCH</td><td>0111</td><td>Ph. Wouwerman | Een Duinachtig Landschap met Geboomte, op de voorgrond een Man te Paard, schijnende een Water te willen door Waden, ter zijde zit een Visscher, in 't verschiet bij een afgaande weg een Man met twee Ezels; meesterlijk geschilderd | Mat: op paneel Size: hoog 13, breed 12 duim</td><td>A</td><td>(Sold) fl 4</td></tr>
<tr><td>1809/04/22</td><td>AMYVR</td><td>0146</td><td>Ph. Wouwerman | Een Heer, bezig zijnde een Paard te bestijgen, agterwaards een Hond, bij een Boom, en een aangenaam verschiet; fraai | Mat: op paneel Size: hoog 8, breed 11 duim</td><td>de Bruin</td><td>(Sold) fl 1:5 du Pree</td></tr>
<tr><td>1809/05/26</td><td>HADAA</td><td>0003</td><td>Philip Wouwerman | Een fraai Landschap waarin twee Ruiters met hunne Paarden, de een op hetzelve zittende, de andere daarbij staande, de Beelden en Paarden zijn fraai en helder | Mat: op paneel Size: hoog 11 ½ breed 15 ½ duim</td><td>Mejuffrouw de Wed David Heemskerk [or others]</td><td>(Unknown)</td></tr>
<tr><td>1809/07/19</td><td>AMSCH</td><td>0064</td><td>Wouwerman (Ph.) | Dit fraaije Schilderij verbeelt het Binnegezigt van een Stal, aan den ingang ziet men eenen Heer te Paard, spreekende met eene nevens hem staande Vrouw, twee beladen wagens, ieder met drie paarden bespannen, ziet men de stal inrijden, verder drie losse paarden bij een Voerbak, een Jonge met een Hond, en andere Voorwerpen. Dit stuk is fraai van Ordonnantie en van de beste en uitvoerigste penceelsbehandeling | Mat: op paneel Size: hoog 18, breed 24 duim</td><td>[Bicker]</td><td>(Sold) fl 1103 Izaac Smit</td></tr>
<tr><td>1809/07/25</td><td>HGBSM</td><td>0142</td><td>Ph. Wouwerman | Een dito Defect | Mat: op doek op paneel Size: hoog 11, breed 13 en een half duim</td><td>D van der Aa [or] E B ten Dall</td><td>(Sold) fl 4 de Gelder</td></tr>
<tr><td>1809/09/06</td><td>AMSCH</td><td>0084</td><td>Wouwerman (Ph.) | Dit uitmuntend Schilderij steld voor een Aftrekkend Leeger-corps, zittende de Veldoversten op een wit Paard, gevolgd wordende door een aantal Ruiters en Voetvolk, Marketenters en Bagagiewagens, ter zijde een Rivier waaruit eenige Paarden drinken, voorts een Stad in het verschiet; dit stuk is een der rijkste van Ordinantie van dezen Meester en is van een delicaate schildering | Mat: op doek op paneel Size: hoog 31, breed 40 duim</td><td>Johannes Caudri</td><td>(Sold) fl 2225 Th^{s} Spaan</td></tr>
<tr><td>1809/09/06</td><td>AMSCH</td><td>0085</td><td>Wouwerman (Ph.) | Een Duingrond, waarop een doode Boom; een Jager en veruitgestrekt verschiet; zonachtig gepenceeld | Mat: op paneel Size: hoog 10, breed 8 duim</td><td>Johannes Caudri</td><td>(Sold) fl 60 Gruyter</td></tr>
<tr><td>1810/03/26</td><td>RMMUY</td><td>0030</td><td>Philip Wouwerman | Een Duin- Water- en Land Gezigt, rijk en bevallig gestoffeerd met paarden en figuren. Piquant van effect; uitvoerig,</td><td>Daniel de Jongh Az</td><td>(Sold) fl 701 Le Brun Parys</td></tr>
</table>

<table>
<tr><td></td><td></td><td></td><td>natuurlijk en zeer schoon geschilderd. Van zijn beste tijd [Un Paysage formé par des terrains inégales [sic] et sablonneux, traversés par une rivière qui forme sur le devant une chute d'eau, où se trouvent deux chevaux, un chien, et trois cavalliers, qui paraissent vouloir le passer à un détroit : plus loin, sur une éminence plus élevée, un village, des arbres, plusieurs fabriques, figures et bestiaux ; un lointain léger et vaporeux, un ciël fin et bien nuagé, font le plus heureux ensemble, d'un effet piquant, très fini, de la plus belle touche, et de son meilleur temps.] | *Mat:* op paneel *Size:* hoog 9, breed 8 duimen</td><td></td><td></td></tr>
<tr><td>1810/03/26</td><td>RMMUY</td><td>0031</td><td>*Philip Wouwerman* | Een Heuvelachtig Landschap en Geboomte. Op den voorgrond, eenige Heeren te paard, die zich ververschen, verzeld van honden en schapen, en wat verder zwemmende figuren. Fraaij, uitvoerig en konstig behandeld. Van zijn vroege tijd [Un Paysage montagneux ; sur le devant quelques figures, chiens et chevaux, faisant halte et se rafraichissant devant une auberge : plus loin, un berger veillant ses moutons ; dans le lointain, plusieurs figures à la nage, d'un bon ton de couleur, et très étudié, de son jeune temps.] | *Mat:* op paneel *Size:* hoog 18, breed 25 duimen</td><td>Daniel de Jongh Az</td><td>(Sold) fl 200 Le Brun Parys</td></tr>
<tr><td>1810/03/27</td><td>RMCNL</td><td>0003</td><td>*Philip Wouwerman* | Een groot Bergachtig Landschap, zeer fraai en fix gepenseeld</td><td></td><td>(Unknown)</td></tr>
<tr><td>1810/06/06</td><td>RMMUY</td><td>0008</td><td>*Philip Wouwerman* | Een Winter Gezigt bij eene Stads Muur, op den voorgrond is het Ys; rijk gestoffeerd met verscheide Kinderen, die zig met Glijen, Tollen, en Sleetjes vermaken, andere die zich ter linker zijde aan de voet der muur verwarmen, ter regter zijde een Man die zijn Paard voert; verder een Brug en Stads Poort, benevens een besneeuwd Landschap met Boeren Huizen; alles natuurlijk behandeld en konstig gepenceeld | *Mat:* op paneel *Size:* hoog 13, breed 19 duimen</td><td></td><td>(Sold) fl 440 Pot</td></tr>
<tr><td>1810/06/06</td><td>RMMUY</td><td>0009</td><td>*Philip Wouwerman* | Eene Pleister Plaats, vooraan een Man op een wit Paard die hetzelve uit een Fontein laat drinken, benevens een bruin Paard het welk hij in de regterhand met de toom vast houd; van achteren eene Woning waar een Heer eene Dame de trap afleid, en ander bijwerk; verder in 't verschiet een vertrekkende, en een aankomende Reiziger te Paard; verstandig en meesterlijk behandeld | *Mat:* op paneel *Size:* hoog 13 ¼, breed 11 ¾ duimen</td><td></td><td>(Sold) fl 26 v Dongen</td></tr>
<tr><td>1810/06/06</td><td>RMMUY</td><td>0188</td><td>*Ph. Wouwerman* | Een Pissend Paardje | *Mat:* op paneel</td><td></td><td>(Unknown) fl 1:14</td></tr>
<tr><td>1810/08/01</td><td>AMSCH</td><td>0119</td><td>*Wouwerman (Philip)* | Een heuvelachtig Veldgezigt, met een Water op den voorgrond; het stelt voor den Hooibouw, en is versierd met staande, rustende en grazende Paarden, verscheidene Arbeiders, Jagers met hunne Honden, en twee beladene Hooiwagens; in het verschiet Boerenwoningen en Geboomte [Un Paysage varié par de légeres collines, ayant une marre d'eau sur le premier plan. Il offre la recolte du foin et les travaux de la saison. On y remarque six Chevaux en differentes attitudes et plusieurs travailleurs, ainsi que des Chasseurs suivis de leurs Chiens ; plus en avant il y a deux Chariots chargés de Foin, et dans la perspective on voit des habitations et quelques Plantis] | *Annots:* NB : argentin en très capital. (NGW); 1845. Rome. Galerie du Cardinal Fesch, no.254, p.300 (VAL I) *Mat:* op doek *Size:* hoog 25, breed 30 duimen *Notes:* The handwritten annotation from the VAL I copy of the catalogue probably does not refer to this lot, but to lot 120. *Loc:* London, England, UK. Royal Collection (Buckingham Palace) Inv.1563.</td><td>Mr Pieter de Smeth van Alphen</td><td>(Sold) fl 4200 Lafontaine</td></tr>
<tr><td>1810/08/01</td><td>AMSCH</td><td>0120</td><td>*Wouwerman (Philip)* | Een heuvelachtig Landschap, gestoffeerd met twee Heeren en eene Vrouw te paard, komende van de Valkejagt, met Jagers en Honden [Un Paysage coupé par des Collines, embelli par deux Cavaliers et par une Dame à Cheval, au retour d'une Chasse au Faucon, suivis de Chasseurs et de Chiens] | *Annots:* Bon. (NGW); Vente le Brun No.117. fr. 10200 (SMLN) *Mat:* op doek *Size:* hoog 25, breed 32 duimen</td><td>Mr Pieter de Smeth van Alphen</td><td>(Sold) fl 2500 Texier, Gerbet en Comp [for] LeBrun</td></tr>
<tr><td>1810/08/01</td><td>AMSCH</td><td>0121</td><td>*Wouwerman (Philip)* | Op een Land ziet men een wit Paard, gespannen voor een beladen Hooiwagen; verder vrolijke en in het Hooi werkende Landlieden [Au milieu d'un Paturage on voit un Cheval blanc attelé devant un Chariot chargé de Foin, et les Villageois travaillant gayement à cette recolte] | *Annots:* Bon. (NGW) *Mat:* op paneel *Size:* hoog 15, breed 13 duimen</td><td>Mr Pieter de Smeth van Alphen</td><td>(Sold) fl 1550 J de Vries [for] De Bosch d'Amsterdam</td></tr>
<tr><td>1810/08/01</td><td>AMSCH</td><td>0122</td><td>*Wouwerman (Philip)* | Aan den kant van een stil Water zijn eenige Lieden bezig Koopmanschappen op eenen Wagen te laden; ter zijde een wit Paard, waar achter eene Boerenkar, met een bruin Paard bespannen; voorts een slapende Jongen [Aux bords d'une Riviere on voit quelques Travailleurs occupés à charger des Marchandises sur un Chariot. Vèrs le côté se trouve un Cheval blanc, et derriere celui-ci il y a une Charette attelée d'un Cheval brun, ainsi qu'un Garçon endormi] | *Annots:* Bon. (NGW) *Mat:* op paneel *Size:* hoog 16, breed 14 duimen</td><td>Mr Pieter de Smeth van Alphen</td><td>(Sold) fl 1300 Cremer te Rotterdam</td></tr>
<tr><td>1810/08/01</td><td>AMSCH</td><td>0123</td><td>*Wouwerman (Philip)* | Aan den Oever van eene Rivier ziet men Arbeiders, bezig Goederen op Paarden en Sleden te laden; verder op eene hoogte een beladen Muilezel bij een Wagthuis [Sur le quai le long d'une Riviere se trouvent des Ouvriers occupés à charger des Marchandises sur le dos des Chevaux, et sur des Traineaux : on y voit sur une éminance un Mulet chargé, marchant vèrs une gueritte] | *Annots:* Bon. Vendu fl:2100 chez Verhulst en 1779. (NGW) *Mat:* op paneel *Size:* hoog 15, breed 19 duimen</td><td>Mr Pieter de Smeth van Alphen</td><td>(Sold) fl 2250 Reijers [for] Lafontaine</td></tr>
</table>

1810/08/01	AMSCH	0124	*Wouwerman (Philip)* | In een Landschap ziet men op den voorgrond twee Lieden, waar bij een ander, zittende op een graauw Paard, en ziende naar een wit springend Paard, waarop een Man gezeten is, ter zijde andere Paarden en Krijgslieden bij eene Herberg [Dans un Site ouvert on voit au premier plan deux Voyageurs assis ; et un troisième monté sur un Chaval [sic] gris, portant ses regards vèrs un Cheval fringuant, monté par un Cavalier. Vèrs le côté on trouve des Militaires et des Chevaux arretés devant un Cabaret] | *Annots:* Bon. (NGW) *Mat:* op paneel *Size:* hoog 16, breed 20 duimen	Mr Pieter de Smeth van Alphen	(Sold) fl 1850 De Lelie
1810/08/01	AMSCH	0125	*Wouwerman (Philip)* | Een ruim heuvelachtig Landschap, met een Water langs eenen opgaanden Weg, gestoffeerd met eenen Heer en Vrouw te paard, Reizigers en Landlieden; verder een bergachtig verschiet [Vue perspective sur une vaste étendue : on y voit sur une eminance coupée par une route un Seigneur et une Dame à Cheval, ainsi que des Voyageurs et des Villageois. Un Ruisseau coupant le Site contribue à le varier] | *Annots:* Bon. (NGW); Vente le Brun No.118 fr. 1760 (SMLN) *Mat:* op paneel *Size:* hoog 14, breed 12 ½ duimen	Mr Pieter de Smeth van Alphen	(Sold) fl 600 Texier, Gerbet en Comp [for] LeBrun
1810/10/10	MGCIT	0005	*Philip Wouwerman* | Een Zeestrand, rijk met Figuuren, te voet en te paard, gestoffeerd, onder anderen ook met een Kar en Wagen, waarop Visch word geladen en een op 't Strand opgeslagen Tent, vol van voorwerpen zo binnen als daar buiten; ongemeen aangenaam bewerkt	Caspar van Citters	(Unknown)
1810/10/10	MGCIT	0006	*Philip Wouwerman* | Nog een Zeestrandje, en in het verschiet een Gebouw op een Berg; niet minder lieflijk geschilderd	Caspar van Citters	(Unknown)
1810/11/07	UTWLD	0004	*Ph. Wouwerman* | Een stal waarin een Jagtgezelschap aangekomen, een Dame in gesprek met een Cavalier bezig zijnde zijnen Laars in order te schikken, waarbij een jonge een wit paard houdende, verder onderscheide paarden en beeltjes, alles meesteragtig geschilderd door Ph. Wouwerman, 1 voet 5 duim hoog, 2 voet breed op doek, zwarte Lijst | *Mat:* op doek *Size:* 1 voet 5 duim hoog, 2 voet breed		(Unknown) fl 45
			Wouwerman, Philips (and Ruisdael, J.)		
1804/08/08	AMSCH	0159	*J. Ruisdaal; Wouwerman* | In een Landschap met hoog Geboomte ziet men langs een Weg een heldere Rivier, waarin een Reiziger te Paard, waarby een Jongen en een Vrouw, met een Kind op de Rug, ter zyde een Huisman, en verders by eenig Geboomte eenige rustende Lieden, en een Duin- en Boomryk verschiet; zonachtig en uitvoerig gepenceeld | *Mat:* op doek *Size:* hoog 24, breed 31 duim	Vink[eles] [for] W	(Bought In) fl 275
1806/08/13	AMSCH	0154	*Ruysdaal (J.); Ph. Wouwerman* | Dit aangenaam Tafreel, verbeeld een Heuvelachtig Landschap, ter linker zyde een Boerenwoning, op de voorgrond in een Waterplas lopen twee Kinderen, een Man op een Paard gezéten, laat er hetzelve uit drinken, verders langs een opgaande Weg een Ryziger te paard verzeld van een Voetganger met een Hond; terzyde op een Berg ziet men verscheiden Korenschoven staan; welke door een frappant zonlicht beschenen worden; zynde dit fraaije stukje voorts van een delicaate penceelsbehandeling | *Mat:* op doek *Size:* hoog 20, breed 23 duim	Daniel Mansveld	(Sold) fl 505 Hulswit
1809/04/17	AMSCH	0079	*J. Ruisdaal; Ph. Wouwerman* | Dit uitmuntend Schilderij, verbeeld een aangenaam Boomrijk Landschap, in 't midden een heldere Waterplas over de Zandige Weg, waar bij een Man te Paard, eene Vrouw met een Kind en een Jongen, ter zijde een gaande Huisman, ver onder het Geboomte ziet men verscheide gaande en rustende Reizigers, en een Dorptooren in 't verschiet; het invallende zonlicht geeft een natuurlijke werking, het koloriet is krachtig, en voorts van een uitvoerige penceelbehandeling | *Mat:* op doek *Size:* hoog 24, breed 32 duim	T	(Sold) fl 355
			Wouwerman, Philips (and Verboom, A.H.)		
1809/07/25	HGBSM	0004	*Ph. Wouwerman; Verboom* | Een Boomryk Lantschap, in 't midden de overblyfzels van een aloude Poort, de Weg is gestoffeerd met een Mannetje te Paard, Hond en meer Figuuren, door Ph. Wouwerman, en 't Landschap is konstig geschildert door Verboom | *Mat:* op doek *Size:* hoog 20, breed 24 duim	D van der Aa [or] E B ten Dall	(Sold) fl 66 van Eijk
			Wouwerman, Philips (and Vries, R.)		
1809/04/22	AMYVR	0130	*R. de Vries; Ph. Wouwerman* | Een Boomrijk met Paarden en Jagers gestoffeerd Landschap; geestig, door R. de Vries en Ph. Wouwerman | *Mat:* op paneel *Size:* hoog 19, breed 25 duim	de Bruin	(Sold) fl 30 Remmers Bredius
			Wouwerman, Philips (and Wijnants)		
1801/06/10	AMSCH	0180	*Wynants. (J.); stoffage van Ph. Wouwerman* | Een Capitaal Landschap met hoog Geboomte, gestoffeerd met een Heer te Paard en andere Lieden, nevens Honden, schynende op de Hartejagt te zyn, in 't verschiet een Kasteel by Geboomte; fraai van Coloriet en fiks gepenceeld | *Mat:* op paneel *Size:* hoog 36, breed 32 duim	Herman ten Kate	(Sold) fl 158 Reynders
1801/06/10	AMSCH	0182	*Wynants. (J.); gestoffeerd door Ph. Wouwernan* | Een aangenaam en duinachtig Landschap, gestoffeerd met Heeren en Dames te Paard, ter zyde een Watertje, verders eenige Jagers met Honden, welke zich in het zelve ververschen; bevallig van licht, en van een der beste van deezen Meester | *Mat:* op doek *Size:* hoog 12 ½, breed 15 ½ duim	Herman ten Kate	(Sold) fl 205 Thaijs

1802/09/29	AMSCH	0058	*J. Wynants; Ph. Wouwerman* | Een Landschap, hoog 26 ½, breed 32 duim. Doek. Deeze Capitaale Ordenantie verbeeld een zeer uitgestrekt Landschap, welkers agtergrond met eenige Duinen eindigt. Voor aan ter regter zyde zyn eenige Boeren Wooningen, een Schuur, een Waterput en houte Heiningen; tegen de Schuur ziet men eenen Wyngaard; agter en naast dezelve schoon opgaand Geboomten van onderscheiden aart. Ter linker zyde ryd eenen Boerenknaap op een bruin Paard, (over den kluitägtigen Weg, gedeeltelyk begroeid met zooijen Gras en Planten,) nevens dezelve een Herder met twee Honden, waar van hy de eene in zyn loop wil terug houden. Eene beladene Vrouw en een Kind komen den Weg af, een paar oude Huislieden, van agter te zien, gaan denzelven op. Deeze twee beroemde Kunstenaars hebben hun kunstvermogen in dit Tafereel aan den dag gelegd. De Penceelbehandeling is uitmuntend fraai, zeer natuurlyk, zonägtig, en van een schoon Effect [Le Point de vüe d'un riche Paysage, offrant une variété d'arbres de belle Espéces & de grande proportion ; un vieux chêne tortueux s'y fait remarquer autant par sa Touche brillante que par des détails aussi vrais que la nature. La droite présente des chaumieres, des habitations villageoises de belle forme & un puid [sic], ou frappe la principale Lumiere. Philippe Wouwerman à enrichi ce magnifigue [sic] Tableau de nombre de Figures, d'un cheval & d'autres animaux, d'un beau choix ; l'on voit dans l'Eloignement un Pays immense traversé par différens chemins, un lointain admirable & montagneux perdu dans l'horison un ciel couvert des plus beaux nuages. Les Talens réunis de ces deux habiles Peintres, offrent ici aux amateurs un Tableau très précieux & d'une composition râre, digne d'occuper une place distinguée dans les premieres collections.] | *Mat:* op doek *Size:* hoog 26 ½, breed 32 duim	[Labouchere?]	(Sold) fl 450 Vinkeles
1808/08/23	AMSCH	0168	*Wijnands (J.); Ph. Wouwerman* | In een Duinachtig Landschap met eenig Geboomten, ziet men eenige Schaapen en Huislieden, welke van de hoogte nederwaards ziende, naar een aangenaam Land- en Watergezigt, gestoffeert met verscheiden Reisigers; alles zonachtig en van een uitvoerige penceelbehandeling | *Mat:* op doek *Size:* hoog 14, breed 12 duim	E	(Sold) fl 116 van Iperen

Wouwerman, Philips (or Wouwerman, Ph., manner)

1804/04/28	LNDLS	0008	*Ph. Wouwermans* | Voor een Buitenhuis met geboomte zit een Juffer op een wit paard, die 'er van een officier afgeholpen wordt, benevens een staande Dame, die van een Heer, te paard zittende, gegroet wordt, en meer bywerk, konstig door, of in den trand van Ph. Wouwerman | *Mat:* op paneel *Size:* hoog 17, breed 21 duim	[Abraham Delfos] [or others]	(Sold) fl 27 Rigters
1804/05/07	AMSCH	0188	*Wouwerman. (Ph.), of in de manier.)* | In een aangenaam Duinachtig Landschap by eenig Geboomte, ziet men op de voorgrond en Ruiter, welke met een bevallige Melkboerin stoeit, waarby een wit Paard en Hond, iets verder een Heer te Paard, waar naast een Huisman, ter zyde over een Waterbeekje een Brug, waarover een Visboer gaat, verders eenige rustende en gaande Lieden, en een allerbevalligst verschiet; dit stukje is zonachtig en alleruitvoerigst van behandeling | *Mat:* op paneel *Size:* hoog 16, breed 20 duim	Vinkeles [for] H[affner]	(Sold) fl 24:10 Coclers
1804/10/29	HRBAU	0118	*Wouwerman, (Philip) of in zyn Manier* | Ter regterzyde, by eene Smedery, staat een Paard, het welk men bezig is Medicynen in te geeven, waar by een Vrouwtjen met twee Kinderen. Voor hetzelve staat een wit Paard, dat uit de hand beslagen wordt, waar naar een Heer, die by een' rooden Schimmel staat, nevens nog een, die op een bruin Paard zit, zeer oplettend ziet. Op den tweeden grond is een Kasteel, waar by eenige Jaagers; waar agter een duinagtig verschiet. Dit Stukjen is schoon van licht en bruin, zeer smeltend en uitvoerig behandeld | *Mat:* op paneel *Size:* hoog 14, breed 18 duim	Simon Styl	(Unknown)

Wouwerman, Philips (copy after)

1801/03/16	AMSCH	0154	*Ph. Woumerman* | Een Heuvel, waarop een Paard voor een sleede, fix na Ph. Woumerman	K[ip]	(Sold) fl 21:10 C S Roos
1802/06/16	AMSCH	0217	*P. Wouwerman; Philip Wouwerman* | Een Manêgie ryk van Paarden en Beelden, Gebouwen en aangenaam verschiet, zynde een fraaye Copy naar de beroemde Manêge van zyn Broeder Philip Wouwerman | copy by Pieter Wouwerman after Ph. Wouwerman *Mat:* op doek op paneel *Size:* hoog 23, breed 27 duim	[Merrem]	(Sold) fl 55 Gruiter
1808/06/13	AMSCH	0172	*P^r. Wouwerman (in de manier); Ph. Wouwerman* | Een Manege, waarbij een Koets met zes Paarden en verscheidene Beeldjes, zijnde een fraaije Kopij naar Ph. Wouwerman | copy in the manner of Pieter Wouwerman after Ph. Wouwerman *Size:* hoog 21, breed 24 duim	E M Engelberts	(Sold) fl 69 J Schuman
1809/04/22	AMYVR	0159	*Ph. Wouwerman* | Een Heer met een Paard; naar Ph. Wouwerman	de Bruin	(Sold) fl 2:10 J^n de Vries
1809/04/22	AMYVR	0192	*Ph. Wouwerman* | Een bevallige Copij met Paarden en Beeldjes; naar Ph. Wouwerman	de Bruin	(Sold) fl 7:5 du Pree
1809/04/22	AMYVR	0197	*Ph. Wouwerman* | Een Landschap met Paard, Kar en Beelden; naar Ph. Wouwerman	de Bruin	(Sold) fl 4 van Iperen
1810/06/06	RMMUY	0138	*Ph. Wouwerman* | Een Kampement, waar in twee Ruiters en een Trompetter, bij eene Zoetelaars Tent. Naar Ph. Wouwerman | *Mat:* op doek		(Unknown) fl 3

Wouwerman, Philips (manner)

1807/08/26	AMSCH	0274	*Ph. Wouwerman* | In een Land- en Watergezicht ziet men op den voorgrond een staand Man, by een gezadeld Paard; verder Vrouwen die Linnen wassen; geestig geschilderd op Doek, in de manier van Ph. Wouwerman | *Mat:* op doek	Roos [for] A	(Sold) fl 2:5 du Pree
1810/08/06	AMSCH	0151	*Ph. Wouwerman* | Voor een Tent ziet men onderscheidene Krijgslieden op en bij hunne Paarden; natuurlijk in den trant van Ph. Wouwerman	V[ries]	(Sold) fl 14 Coclers [for] T

Wouwerman, Pieter

1801/06/10	AMSCH	0192	*Wouwerman. (Pieter)* | Een hevige Rencontre tusschen de Voorposten der Cavallerie, ter zyde ziet men Tenten, verders een bergachtig Verschiet; meesterlyk en fraai behandeld | *Mat:* op paneel *Size:* hoog 14, breed 18 duim	Herman ten Kate	(Sold) fl 165 Coclers
1801/06/10	AMSCH	0193	*Wouwerman. (Pieter)* | Voor een Smits Winkel word een wit Paard beslagen, daar by een Ruiter, op de voorgrond een Kind in een Wagen met een Bok, verders nog een menigte Paarden en Beelden; in alles als de voorgaande | *Annots:* dit was Een Copy (MA) *Mat:* op doek *Size:* hoog 18, breed 21 duim	Herman ten Kate	(Sold) fl 115 Coclers
1801/06/10	AMSCH	0194	*Wouwerman. (Pieter)* | Een heuvelachtig Landschap, gestoffeerd met verscheide speelende Kinderen; meesterlyk van schildering en krachtig van Coloriet | *Mat:* op paneel *Size:* hoog 12, breed 10 duim	Herman ten Kate	(Sold) fl 161 Stevens
1801/08/19	AMSCH	0136	*Pieter Wouwerman* | Een Landschap, voor een Herberg ziet men een Heer, nevens hem een Jongeling, houdende een wit Paard, verders een ander Ruiter bézig zyn Paard te Zadelen	Pruyssen^{r} [for] Q	(Bought In) fl 21
1802/11/01	DOBRA	0063	*Pieter Wouwerman* | Een Bergachtig Landschap gestoffeerd met Heeren en Damens te paard | *Mat:* op doek *Size:* hoog en breed circa 16 duim	Paulus van der Spyk [or others]	(Sold) fl 19 Hinbregts
1804/10/16	DLOND	0268	*Pieter Wouwerman* | Een Landschap met Lieden te Paard. Paysage & des gens a Cheval | *Mat:* op doek *Size:* hoog 43, breed 34		(Unknown) fl 2:5
1804/10/16	DLOND	0269	*Pieter Wouwerman* | Uts^{a} [Een Landschap met Lieden te Paard. Paysage & des gens a Cheval] | *Mat:* op paneel *Size:* hoog 6, breed 8		(Unknown)
1804/10/16	DLOND	0270	*Pieter Wouwerman* | Uts^{a} [Een Landschap met Lieden te Paard. Paysage & des gens a Cheval] | *Mat:* op paneel *Size:* hoog 9, breed 12		(Unknown)
1804/10/16	DLOND	0271	*Pieter Wouwerman* | Uts^{a} [Een Landschap met Lieden te Paard. Paysage & des gens a Cheval] | *Mat:* op paneel *Size:* hoog 9, breed 7		(Unknown)
1804/10/29	HRBAU	0119	*Wouwerman, (Pieter)* | Een Paardenmarkt in een Kerkdorp, ryk gestoffeerd met Koopers en Verkoopers, een Kwakzalver op zyn theater, en een menigte Aanschouwers. Fiks behandeld | *Mat:* op doek *Size:* hoog 25, breed 30 duim	Simon Styl	(Unknown)
1804/10/29	HRBAU	0120	*Wouwerman, (Pieter)* | Eene hevige Rencontre tusschen Paarden- en Voetvolk, op een' Heuvel, by geboomte; waar agter Boerenhuizen, en een bergagtig verschiet. Als het voorige behandeld | *Mat:* op doek	Simon Styl	(Unknown)
1808/06/06	RMRIJ	0146	*Wouwerman. (Pieter)* | Eene bovenlandsche Kar, bespannen met drie Paarden, door eene Poort rijdende; met bijwerk. Aangenaam geschilderd [Une grosse Charette attelée de trois Chevaux qui traverse l'ouverture ceintrée d'une Porte etc. D'un beau faire] | *Annots:* Verk. J. Maul, Leiden, 28 Sept 1782 (f 30.-) (RMA I) *Mat:* op paneel *Size:* Hoog 10, en breed 12 ¾ duim	Gerrit van der Pot, Heer van Groeneveld	(Sold) fl 69 Hakoun
1808/06/13	AMSCH	0169	*P^{r}. Wouwerman* | In een Stal met elf Paarden ziet men eenige Heeren en Stalknegten bezig met te Paard te stijgen en anderen te zadelen, terwijl ander volk bezig is in 't Hooi te werken, verder komt er ter linkerzijde een beladen Hooiwagen met twee Paarden aanrijden, twee Kinderen, een Bok, Kippen, enz. Dit stukje is zeer fraai van schildering | *Mat:* op doek *Size:* hoog 18, breed 19 duim	R[oos]	(Sold) fl 275 J Schuman
1808/06/13	AMSCH	0170	*P^{r}. Wouwerman* | Een Paardenmarkt, rijk met Paarden enz. gestoffeerd, op den voorgrond ziet men eenige Kinderen en Honden, en een Dorp in het verschiet. Zeer uitvoerig gepenceeld | *Mat:* op paneel *Size:* hoog 12 ½, breed 17 duim	[Jan Tersteeg]	(Sold) fl 25 Du Pré
1808/06/13	AMSCH	0171	*P^{r}. Wouwerman* | Een Stal van binnen, alwaar een Heer bezig is den Waard te betalen, terwijl de Knegt de Paarden gereed maakt, op den voorgrond een Jongen met een Bok. Mede als de voorgaande | *Mat:* op doek *Size:* hoog 14, breed 16 duim	E M Engelberts	(Sold) fl 36 Simons
1810/07/23	DOLG1	0064	*Pieter Wouwerman* | Een Landschap met Paardtjes | *Mat:* op paneel *Size:* hoog 8, breed 12 duim	Mr Pieter van den Santheuvel	(Sold) fl 41 J de Visser
1810/10/10	MGCIT	0009	*Pieter Wouwerman* | Een zeer bevallig Stukje, zijnde twee Heeren en een Bediende, alle drie te Paard, halte houdende aan een Pomp of Waterput, ziende men door de opening van een oud Gebouw, op een Landschap; fraai geschilderd	Caspar van Citters	(Unknown)

Wouwerman, Pieter (copy by)

1802/06/16	AMSCH	0217	*P. Wouwerman; Philip Wouwerman* | Een Manêgie ryk van Paarden en Beelden, Gebouwen en aangenaam verschiet, zynde een fraaye Copy naar de beroemde Manêge van zyn Broeder Philip Wouwerman | copy by Pieter Wouwerman after Ph. Wouwerman *Mat:* op doek op paneel *Size:* hoog 23, breed 27 duim	[Merrem]	(Sold) fl 55 Gruiter

Wouwerman, Pieter (manner)

1804/10/29	HRBAU	0131	*Pieter Wouwerman* | Vóór eene Pleisterplaats zyn eenige Krygslieden met hunne paarden, welken daar verversching neemen: waar by twee Jongens zyn; nevens een bergagtig verschiet. Fiks in de manier van Pieter Wouwerman behandeld | *Mat:* op doek *Size:* hoog 23, breed 27 duim	Simon Styl	(Unknown)

Wouwerman, Pieter (manner; copy by)

1808/06/13	AMSCH	0172	*Pr. Wouwerman (in de manier); Ph. Wouwerman* | Een Manege, waarbij een Koets met zes Paarden en verscheidene Beeldjes, zijnde een fraaije Kopij naar Ph. Wouwerman | copy in the manner of Pieter Wouwerman after Ph. Wouwerman *Size:* hoog 21, breed 24 duim	E M Engelberts	(Sold) fl 69 J Schuman

Wst, G.D. [Unidentified]

1809/07/25	HGBSM	0081	*G.D. Wst* | Een Historieel Stuk met veel Figuren, gemerkt G.D. Wst. | *Mat:* op doek *Size:* hoog 40 en een half, breed 57 duim *Inscr:* G.D. Wst. (marked)	D van der Aa [or] E B ten Dall	(Sold) fl 0:18 van Eyk

Wtewael, Joachim Antonisz.

1801/10/19	AMSCH	0082	*Uitewaal. (J.)* | Een Badje van Diana, waar by Actéon, zeer kunstig, uitvoerig en krachtig geschilderd | *Mat:* op koper *Size:* hoog 6, breed 8 ¼ duim	Jonkheer Menno Baron van Coehoorn	(Sold) fl 23 Spruit van Gend
1802/06/28	AMSCH	0189	*J. Uitewaal* | Deeze Ordonnantie vol gewoel van Beelden, vertoond de algemeene Zondvloed, zeer uitvoerig op Panneel geschilderd, door J. Uitewaal, ovaal formaat | *Mat:* op paneel *Fmt:* ovaal *Size:* hoog 7, breed 9 duim	Anna Elink	(Sold) fl 7 van der Schley A [for] Coclers
1803/07/18	AMSCH	0056	*Uitewaal. (J.)* | In een boomryk Landschap is verbeeld het Oordeel van Paris, op de voorgrond ziet men de Watergoden en de Overvloed, meer agterwaarts ziet men Paris met de drie Schoonheden, in de lugt vliegt Mercurius, fraai van coloriet en uitvoerig behandeld [Le jugement du berger Paris dans un paysage. Au devant sont âssis sur une motte de terre, des Dieux fleuves & l'abondance de la terre. Un peu en arrière est le Berger ayant les trois Déesies [sic] devant lui, & Mercure voltigeant audessus. Ce petit morceau est d'un grand fini, d'un bon dessin, & d'une couleur brillante.] | *Mat:* op koper *Size:* hoog 7, breed 8 duim	Maria Theresia Andrioli	(Sold) fl 9:10 Gruyter
1803/09/07	AMSCH	0187	*J. Uitewaal* | Andromeda door Perceus gered wordende, uitvoerig en delicaat gepenceeld [Andromède sauvée par Persée ; tableau d'une composition délicate, et exécuté avec soin] | *Mat:* op koper *Size:* hoog 9, breed 11 duim	Smidt	(Sold) fl 5:5 Gruiter
1803/09/07	AMSCH	0188	*J. Uitewaal* | Twee stuks, het eene een Badje van Diana en het andere spelende Kinderen met Vrugten, enz; als de voorgaande [Deux tableaux, l'un représentant Diane au bain, et l'autre des enfans jouant avec des fruits etc.] | *Size:* h. 8, br. 10 duim	Smidt	(Sold) fl 10:15 W Reijers
1803/09/07	AMSCH	0189	*J. Uitewaal* | Venus en Cupido op de Waters, mede als de voorgaande [Venus et Cupidon voguant sur les ondes ; même mérite que les précédens] | *Mat:* op paneel *Size:* hoog 9, breed 7 duim	Smidt	(Sold) fl 4:10 Gruiter
1804/02/27	AMSCH	0105	*Uitewael. (J.)* | Een bevallig Vrouwe Pourtrait, halverlyf; uitvoerig van penceel behandeling | *Mat:* op paneel	D	(Sold) fl 29 Theys
1804/07/25	AMSCH	0083	*Uytewaal (J.)* | De stryd der Reuzen, of Titans teegens Jupiter; en de andere Goden; zeer fraai en uitvoerig gepenceeld en kragtig van coloriet | *Mat:* op koper *Size:* hoog 9, breed 11 duim		(Sold) fl 35 C S Roos
1804/07/25	AMSCH	0084	*Uytewaal (J.)* | Het Bad van Diana, zy is verzelt van haare Nimphen. waarby Actéon, dewelke door de Jachtgodin in een Hart herschept word, mede uitvoerig en delicaat geschilderd | possibly companion to lot 85 *Size:* hoog 9, breed 11 duim		(Sold) fl 195 Jan Spaan
1804/07/25	AMSCH	0085	*Uytewaal. (J.)* | Het Oordeel van Paris, als de voorgaande behandeld kan tot eene geschikte wedergade verstrekken, en is als de vorigen uitvoerig gepenceeld | possibly companion to lot 84 *Size:* hoog 9, breed 11 duim		(Sold) Jan Spaan
1804/08/08	AMSCH	0187	*J. Uyttewaal* | Voor een Belégerde Stad ziet men de Aantocht van een ménigte van Krygslieden, achterwaards eenige Leegertenten en verdere Stoffagie; breed geschilderd | *Mat:* op doek *Size:* hoog 30, breed 59 duim	Vink[eles] [for] K[=Gruyter?]	(Sold) fl 0:10 L Pakker
1806/08/13	AMSCH	0186	*Uitewael. (J.)* | Vénus en Cupido, zittende op Zee in een Paerl d'Amoure Schulp, dewelke door twee Dolphynen werden getrokken; bevallig en uitvoerig geschilderd | *Mat:* op paneel *Size:* hoog 9 ½, breed 7 ½ duim	Vinkeles [for] G[ruyter]	(Sold) fl 6 Verhoesen
1808/06/06	RMRIJ	0130	*Uitenwaal. (Joachim)* | Mars en Venus, op een prachtig Rustbed, in eene wellustige houding liggende. Ter zijde ziet men Vulkaan in de houding, om het gesmede net over hen heen te werpen. In het bovenste gedeelte van dit tafereel vertoont zich de gansche Olympus hen verrasschende. Op den voorgrond ligt Amor op eene knie zijne Pijlen ter verdediging naar boven schietende. Ter zijde van denzelven de Wapenrusting van Mars en 't Toilet van Venus. Zeer allegorisch voorgesteld, schoon geteekend, gekleurd en alleruitvoerigst behandeld [Ce Bijou represente Mars et Vénus surpris par les artifices de Vulcain, et livrés dans un état honteux regards de l'Olympe. l'Amour tendant son arc, paroit vouloir les défendre. l'Armure de Mars, la Toilette de Vénus, et plusieurs autres accessoires décorent ce Morceau bien dessiné, et précieusement fini] | *Annots:* Verk. Jas. v d Lely, Delft, 5 April 1796 (f.13.-) (RMA I) *Mat:* op koper *Size:* Hoog 6 ⅞, en breed 5 ⅛ duim	Gerrit van der Pot, Heer van Groeneveld	(Sold) fl 57 le Medecin Vervier

1809/07/19	AMSCH	0056	*Uijtewaal (J.)* | Eene Vrouw zittende met een Kind op haar Schoot, waar bij twee andere Jongens, die het zelve eenige Vrugten aanbieden. Zeer uitvoerig en fraai geschilderd | *Mat:* op paneel *Size:* hoog 15, breed 23 duim	C	(Sold) fl 4:10 Jan Ijver
1810/05/22	AMSCH	0109	*Uijtewaal (J.)* | Eene Vrouw zittende met een Kind op haar Schoot, waarbij twee Jongens, die hetzelve eenige Vrugten aanbieden; uitvoerig en fraai gepenceeld | *Mat:* op paneel *Size:* hoog 15, breed 23 duim	Ij[ver]	(Sold) fl 10:15 Otten
1810/06/20	AMSCH	0087	*J. Uitewaal* | Eenige vrolijke danssende Kindertjes. Uitvoerig | *Mat:* op paneel *Size:* hoog 27, breed 36 duimen	S	(Sold) fl 8 Sardet
1810/06/20	AMSCH	0140	*J. Uitewaal* | Twee stuks: een met badende Nimfen, door J. Uitewaal, en een Landschapje	D	(Sold) fl 1:10 Cassino
			Wtewael, Joachim Antonisz. (manner)		
1802/04/13	HAVIN	0046	*Uitewaal* | Een zinnebeeldig stuk, op de vergankelykheid, als van Uitewaal		(Unknown)
			Wubbels, Jan		
1809/06/13	AMSCH	0165	*J. Wubbels* | Een aangenaam stil Water met eenige drijvende en ten anker leggende Vaartuigen, terzijde op een droogte ziet men eenige Visschers bij hunne Schuiten; zonachtig en fraai behandeld, in de manier van W. van de Velde, door J. Wubbels | *Mat:* op paneel *Size:* hoog 13, breed 18 duim	E	(Sold) fl 13 Buck
1809/06/13	AMSCH	0166	*J. Wubbels* | Een Gezigt in de Zuider Zee, op de voorgrond ziet men een Beurtman, bij een stijve koelte, voor de wind heenzeilenden, verder een zeilend Jagt en andere Vaartuigen, en in het verschiet de stad Enkhuizen; helder en bevallig geschilderd | *Mat:* op paneel *Size:* hoog 18, breed 23 duim	E	(Sold) fl 19:10 Buck
			Wüest, Johann Heinrich		
1801/02/18	AMBOS	0008	*H. Wüst* | Een fraai stads Gezigt, verbeeldende de stadt Zürich, zeer natuurlyk en fraai gepenseeld	J Schonevelt	(Unknown)
1801/02/18	AMBOS	0009	*H. Wüst* | Een Landschap, verbeeldende een fraai Boschgezigt met een Molen door het water gedreeven, zeer uitvoerig en fraai gepenseeld | companion to lot 10	J Schonevelt	(Unknown)
1801/02/18	AMBOS	0010	*H. Wüst* | Een dito [Landschap], zynde een weerga, in allen deelen fraai en schoon | companion to lot 9	J Schonevelt	(Unknown)
1801/02/18	AMBOS	0011	*H. Wüst* | Een Landschap, verbeeldende een Zwitzers Landgezigt, in allen opzigten fraai behandeld | companion to lot 12	J Schonevelt	(Unknown)
1801/02/18	AMBOS	0012	*H. Wüst* | Een dito [Landschap], zynde een weerga, niet minder als de voorgaande | companion to lot 11	J Schonevelt	(Unknown)
1801/02/18	AMBOS	0013	*H. Wüst* | Een bergagtig Landschap, zynde naar de Natuur, aan de St. Gotthardsberg in Zwitserland, extra schoon en natuurlyk geschilderd | companion to lot 14	J Schonevelt	(Unknown)
1801/02/18	AMBOS	0014	*H. Wüst* | Een dito [Landschap], zynde een weerga, ook naar de Natuur, aan de Gotthardsberg | companion to lot 13	J Schonevelt	(Unknown)
1801/02/18	AMBOS	0015	*H. Wüst* | Twee stuks fraaije Landschappen, naar de Natuur, in Zwitserland, gestoffeerd met Beesten, zeer fraai geschilderd	J Schonevelt	(Unknown)
1801/02/18	AMBOS	0016	*H. Wüst* | Een Riviergezigt, verbeeldende de groote Waterval des Ryns, ter hoogte van 70 voet, by Schafhausen, natuurlyk en fraai geschilderd	J Schonevelt	(Unknown)
1801/02/18	AMBOS	0024	*H. Wüst* | Een Landschap, zeer uitvoerig en natuurlyk, en fraai van ordonnantie | companion to lot 25	J Schonevelt	(Unknown)
1801/02/18	AMBOS	0025	*H. Wüst* | Een dito [Landschap], zynde een weerga, niet minder in allen opzigten | companion to lot 24	J Schonevelt	(Unknown)
1801/02/18	AMBOS	0026	*H. Wüst* | Een Landschap, zeer fraai en schoon geschilderd en geordonneerd	J Schonevelt	(Unknown)
1801/02/18	AMBOS	0027	*H. Wüst* | Een dito [Landschap], aangenaam en fraai van ordonnantie, en uitvoerig geschilderd	J Schonevelt	(Unknown)
1801/02/18	AMBOS	0028	*H. Wüst* | Een Landschap, niet minder als het voorgaande	J Schonevelt	(Unknown)
1801/02/18	AMBOS	0029	*H. Wüst* | Een Landschap, zeer schoon en fraay van Ordonnantie en Schildering	J Schonevelt	(Unknown)
1801/02/18	AMBOS	0034	*H. Wüst* | Een Landschap, zynde een Prospect na de Natuur	J Schonevelt	(Unknown)
1801/02/18	AMBOS	0034a	*H. Wüst* | Verbeeldende Diana en Endimion	J Schonevelt	(Unknown)
1801/02/18	AMBOS	0040	*H. Wust* | Een fraay en aangenaam Landgezigt, naar de Natuur, in Zwitserland	J Schonevelt	(Unknown)
1801/02/18	AMBOS	0041	*H. Wust* | Een dito [fraay en aangenaam] Landgezigt, niet minder als het voorgaande	J Schonevelt	(Unknown)
1801/02/18	AMBOS	0042	*H. Wust* | Een zeer aangenaam en fraay Landschap	J Schonevelt	(Unknown)
1801/02/18	AMBOS	0043	*H. Wust* | Twee stuks aangenaame en fraaije Landgezigten	J Schonevelt	(Unknown)
1801/02/18	AMBOS	0044	*H. Wust* | Twee stuks niet minder aangenaam en fraay	J Schonevelt	(Unknown)
1801/02/18	AMBOS	0045	*H. Wust* | Twee stuks zeer fraaije en aangenaame Landgezigten	J Schonevelt	(Unknown)

1801/02/18	AMBOS	0046	*H. Wust* | Een fraay Landschap, naar de Natuur, in Zwitserland	J Schonevelt	(Unknown)
1801/02/18	AMBOS	0047	*H. Wüst* | Twee stuks Landschappen, zeer fraay van Ordonnantie en Schildering	J Schonevelt	(Unknown)
1801/02/18	AMBOS	0052	*H. Wüst* | Twee stuks Landschappen, verbeeldende fraaije Zwitserse Gezigten	J Schonevelt	(Unknown)
1801/02/18	AMBOS	0053	*H. Wüst* | Twee stuks, mede voorstellende twee zeer aangename Gezigten in Zwitserland, fraay geschilderd	J Schonevelt	(Unknown)
1801/02/18	AMBOS	0054	*H. Wüst* | Een dito [Gezigt in Zwitserland], niet minder als de voorgaande	J Schonevelt	(Unknown)
1801/02/18	AMBOS	0058	*H. Wüst* | Twee stuks Landschappen, fraay en natuurlyk	J Schonevelt	(Unknown)
1801/02/18	AMBOS	0059	*H. Wüst* | Twee stuks, niet minder als de voorgaande	J Schonevelt	(Unknown)
1801/02/18	AMBOS	0060	*H. Wüst* | Een Landschap	J Schonevelt	(Unknown)
1808/09/13	HABRU	0095	*J. Wust* | Een Zwitschers Landschap, na de natuur verbeeldende de Duijvelsbrug en St.Godhars Berg		(Sold) fl 9:5 V D W[illigen]
1810/08/06	AMSCH	0126	*Wuest van Zurich* | Twee stuks Zwitsersche Landschappen, met Water doorsneden, rijk met Beelden en Beesten gestoffeerd en fiks behandeld | *Mat:* op koper *Size:* ieder hoog 15, breed 21 duimen	A	(Sold) fl 20:10 Dupre
			Wulde, T. [Unidentified]		
1810/11/07	UTWLD	0018	*T. Wulde* | Maria Magdalena in rouw haar hand op een voor haar liggend doodshoofd houdende, zeer expressief en kunstig getekend, Coloriet en plaatsing zeer fraai (getekend T. Wulde) op doek, 2 voet 2 duim breed, 2 voet 10 en een half duim hoog, zwarte Lijst | *Mat:* op doek *Size:* 2 voet 2 duim breed, 2 voet 10 en een half duim hoog *Inscr:* T Wulde (signed)		(Unknown) fl 10:10
			Wulfraet		
1801/08/19	AMSCH	0139	*M. Wulfraat* | Een Heer in een Zyde Japon in zyn Studeerkamer; delicaat geschilderd, door M. Wulfraat, op Koper | *Mat:* op koper *Size:* hoog 19, breed 15 duim	W Wynen	(Sold) fl 7:15 Gruiter
1802/06/28	AMSCH	0203	*M. Wulfraat* | Een Regtsgeleerde in zyn kamer, zittende in zyn japon, voor een tafel, met een tapyt kleed bedekt, waarop Lessenaar, Parkementen, Brieven en Boeken geplaatst zyn; ter zyde staat een Landman, houdende een geldbeurs in de hand, gestoffeerd met verder bywerk, natuurlyk en bevallig gepenceeld | *Mat:* op paneel *Size:* hoog 18, breed 15 duim	Anna Elink	(Sold) fl 6 van der Schley [for] R[ijfsnijder]
1802/06/28	AMSCH	0204	*M. Wulfraat* | In een prachtig Hofgezicht, ter zyde ziet men Susanna zich baadende, en de Boeven haar bespiedende; zeer natuurlyk, door Denzelven [M. Wulfraat], op Doek op panneel | *Mat:* op doek op paneel *Size:* hoog 23, breed 19 duim	Anna Elink	(Sold) fl 5 Hulk
1802/06/28	AMSCH	0205	*M. Wulfraat* | Een Gezelschap van rokende en drinkende Heeren, aan een tafel zittende, fraai op Panneel | *Mat:* op paneel *Size:* hoog 17, breed 13 duim	Anna Elink	(Sold) fl 5 Gruiter
1802/06/28	AMSCH	0206	*M. Wulfraat* | Een zinspelende Ordonnantie van verscheiden Beelden, uitvoerig op Panneel | *Mat:* op paneel *Size:* hoog 10, breed 9 duim	Anna Elink	(Sold) fl 12 Royers
1802/09/06	AMSCH	0152	*Wulfraat* | Een Binnehuis met rookende en drinkende Boeren by een Tafel; plaisant geschilderd | *Mat:* op doek op paneel *Size:* hoog 16, breed 13 duim	B	(Sold) fl 1:5 L Pakker
1803/07/18	AMSCH	0063	*Wulfraat. (M.)* | Voor een Vogelkopers Winkel staat een deftige Dame in het Satyn gekleed, schynende met de Vrouw te spreeken, terwyl een Jongen nevens haar staat te bedelen, verder een Schoorsteenveeger en een Stadtsgezigt in het verschiet, het zonligt doet een goede werking, het coloriet is schoon en de schildering bevallig [Au devant de la Boutique d'une Poulaliere [sic] est une Dame en Jupon de Soye à franges d'or, se garantissent [sic] du soleil par son Evanteil [sic] ; un Enfant demandent [sic] l'aumone lui tend le chapeau, tandis qu'une verduriere lui presente des choux fleurs ; un Petit Chien, un Ramoneur [de] Cheminée & des autres Personages à la boutique, forment ce tableau dont la perspective aboutit à une rue. Un coup de Soleil donnant sur les figures marquantes y fait Briller le coloris naturel & bien entendu ; le sujet étant traité d'un pinceau net & produisant un bel Effet.] | *Mat:* op doek *Size:* hoog 25, breed 21 duim	Maria Theresia Andrioli	(Sold) fl 20 Pruijssenaar
1803/12/12	AMSCH	0114	*Wulfraadt* | In een Binnenkamer ziet men eenige Heeren zig met Musiceeren en drinken vermaaken; fraai en delicaat op Paneel | *Mat:* op paneel *Size:* hoog 17, breed 13 ½ duim	B	(Sold) fl 5 Gruiter
1804/08/08	AMSCH	0230	*M. Wulfraat* | Twee stuks, een Man met een Phiöol in de ééne, en een Roemer Wyn in de andere Hand, en een leezende Vrouw; kragtig en uitvoerig op Doek | *Mat:* op doek	Roos [for] C	(Sold) fl 5 Coclers
1807/08/26	AMSCH	0234	*M. Wulfraat* | Twee stuks gemeubileerde Kamers, in een derzelve zit eene Dame aan een Tafeltje, bezig eenen Brief te vouwen, na welke een kleine Dienstknegt, zynde een Moortje, schynt te wachten. De wederga verbeeld eene musiceerende Dame, en een Heer by een Tafel, verder in een ander Vertrek jonge Lieden, by elkander zittende; het is bevallig geschilderd | *Mat:* op doek *Size:* ieder hoog 16, breed 13 duim	v d Schley [for] Smits Wed	(Sold) fl 5:10 T Spaan
1807/09/28	AMWUR	0028	*Wolfrath* | Een dito [stuk] op dito [Paneel], verbeeldende een Gezelschap, door Wolfrath, in ryk vergulde Lyst | *Mat:* op paneel		(Unknown) fl 12:10

1808/07/19	AMROU	0004	*Wutsrat* | In een Nis, ziet men een bejaard Heer, houdende in de eene hand een Glas met Wyn, en in de andere een Matteﬂes, uitvoerig geschildert		(Unknown)
1808/07/19	AMROU	0005	*Wutsrat* | 1 dito Dames Portrait, mede zittende in een Nis, speelende op een Guitar | *Notes:* It is unclear what "dito" refers to in the title.		(Unknown)
1809/06/13	AMSCH	0164	*M. Wulfraat* | Bij een Gebouw zit een arm Man om een aalmoes vragende, terzijde eenig Bijwerk; uitvoerig | *Mat:* op paneel *Size:* hoog 16, breed 12 duim	T	(Sold) fl 9 Buck
1809/07/25	HGBSM	0013	*M. Wulfraet* | Voor een Buitenhuis is een Kraam waarin een Poelierster die aan een Dame een Vogel aanbied, terwyl een Bedelaars jonge een aalmoes vraagt, helder geschildert | *Mat:* op doek *Size:* hoog 24, breet 20 duim	D van der Aa [or] E B ten Dall	(Sold) fl 16:10 van Eyk
1810/03/23	HAVIN	0018	*M. Wulfraat* | Een Gezelschap, met een Vrouw en een Kind op de schoot, en mannen die met de Viool en Rooken zig vermaken | *Size:* hoog 15 ¾ breed 13 d.	Rudolf Hendrik de Wetstein [or others]	(Unknown)
1810/03/23	HAVIN	0019	*M. Wulfraat* | Een Kind voor een Baluster met een Kat onder den arm, en een Hond voor de Baluster | *Size:* hoog 12 ¼ breed 10 d.	Rudolf Hendrik de Wetstein [or others]	(Unknown)
1810/03/23	HAVIN	0021	*Wulfraat* | Een Schilder, waarschijnlijk Mulfraat [sic] en een Juffer die een Pourtrait vertoond, door Wulfraat | *Size:* hoog 17 ½ breet 13 d.	Rudolf Hendrik de Wetstein [or others]	(Unknown)
1810/03/23	HAVIN	0022	*Wulfraat* | Twee Diana en .... door denz. [Wulfraat] | *Size:* h. 13 b. 12 d.	Rudolf Hendrik de Wetstein [or others]	(Unknown)
1810/03/23	HAVIN	0023	*Wulfraat* | Cleopatra, door denz. [Wulfraat] | *Size:* hoog 20 ½ breet 17 d.	Rudolf Hendrik de Wetstein [or others]	(Unknown)
1810/03/23	HAVIN	0024	*Wulfraat* | Twee, Een Heer die zit te rooken en een Dame speelende op de Viool de Gambe | *Size:* hoog 13 breet 11 ½ d.	Rudolf Hendrik de Wetstein [or others]	(Unknown)
1810/08/06	AMSCH	0127	*Wulfraat (M.)* | Batzeba zich badende, terwijl David haar bespiedt. Zij is gezeten in eene aangename Tuin en heeft achter haar eene Dienstmaagd, verder een Hondje; alles is teder van behandeling | *Mat:* op doek *Size:* hoog 18, breed 16 duimen	V[ries]	(Sold) fl 13 Stoopendaal [for] B
			Wulfraet (or Wulfraet, manner)		
1809/07/25	HGBSM	0263	*Wulfraet* | Een Mannetje over eene Steene Plint, met een Trompet en een Matte Fles in de Hand, door of in de manier van Wulfraet | *Mat:* op doek *Size:* hoog 15, breed 12 en een half duim	D van der Aa [or] E B ten Dall	(Sold) fl 1:12 Dupré
			Wulfraet, Margaretha		
1810/03/23	HAVIN	0025	*Marg. Mulfraat* | Twee, Een Juffer speelende op de Luit en een met een Hond, door Marg. Mulfraat [sic]	Rudolf Hendrik de Wetstein [or others]	(Unknown)
			Wyck		
1801/11/10	AMPOS	0021	*van Wyk* | 1 woedende Brand, agter een berg		(Unknown)
			Wyck, Jan		
1801/06/10	AMSCH	0197	*Wyk. (J.)* | Een Levantsche Zeehaven, by de ruïen van een treffelyk Gebouw, ziet men een Heer en Dame, Kooplieden en rustende Vrouwen en Kinderen, verders eenige Koopmansgoederen; alles bevallig en meesterlyk geschilderd | *Mat:* op doek *Size:* hoog 66, breed 75 duim *Notes:* The artist was presumably Thomas Wyck and not Jan Wyck.	[Doublet]	(Sold) fl 21 Coclers
1801/06/10	AMSCH	0198	*Wyk. (J.)* | In een verwulfd Binnevertrek zit een Vrouw te stryken, verder een Kind, een Kat by een menigte Huisraad; alles zeer uitvoerig en delicaat gepenceeld | *Annots:* [door] Le Ducq (BRB) *Size:* hoog 17, breed 13 duim *Notes:* The artist was presumably Thomas Wyck and not Jan Wyck.	Herman ten Kate	(Sold) fl 64 C S Roos
1801/06/10	AMSCH	0199	*Wyk. (J.)* | In een anticq Gebouw ziet men een Vrouw, nevens haar een Kind, op de voorgrond, diversche Groentens en huisraad; alles is zeer natuurlyk en krachtig behandeld | *Mat:* op paneel *Size:* hoog 18, breed 15 duim *Notes:* The artist was presumably Thomas Wyck and not Jan Wyck.	Herman ten Kate	(Sold) fl 86 Corn Seb Roos
1802/02/16	AMSCH	0079	*J. Wyk* | In een dito [Italiaansch] Landzigt, ziet men in een oude Poort, een Hoefsmit, een gezadeld Paard beslaan, ter zyde staat een vrouw by een waterput; zonachtig en kragtig gepenceeld | *Notes:* The artist was presumably Thomas Wyck and not Jan Wyck.	C	(Sold) fl 37 Coclers
1803/09/07	AMSCH	0215	*J.H. Wyck* | Een hevige Rencontre tusschen verscheide Ruiters waarvan 'er eenige dood ter aarde leggen; de hartstogten zyn fraay en de Schildering meesterlyk [Une rencontre de cavalerie ; l'action paroit très vive et plusieurs cavaliers sont étendus morts sur le carreau ; l'effet des passions est bien exprimé dans ce tableau et l'exécution parfaite] | *Mat:* op doek *Size:* hoog 25, br. 32 duim	Smidt	(Sold) fl 35 Lamme
1808/10/28	AMVRS	0065	*Wijk, (J.)* | In een verwulft Binnenvertrek zit eene Vrouw te strijken, verders een Kind, ook een Kast en veel Huisraad. Uitvoerig en geestig geschilderd | *Size:* hoog 17, breed 13 duim *Notes:* The artist was presumably Thomas Wyck and not Jan Wyck.	Marten Udink	(Sold) fl 90 B Kooij
			Wyck, Thomas		
1801/03/16	AMSCH	0168	*Thomas Wyck* | Een Landschap | *Notes:* This lot was sold with lot 169 by an anonymous artist.	P[ruyssenaar]	(Sold) fl 0:12 for lots 168 & 169. Gruiter

1801/04/13	AMSCH	0094	*T. Wyck* | Een Alchimist in zyn Laboratorium, het welk ryk gestoffeerd is, met daartoe betrekkelyke zaaken, geestig geschilderd | *Mat:* op paneel *Size:* hoog 18, breed 16 duim	Pierre Fouquet, junior	(Sold) fl 21 Coclers
1801/06/13	LNDLS	0021	*T. Wyck* | Bij het verwulft van een groot gebouw veele kooplieden, werkende en rustende persoonen en koopgoederen, en in 't verschiet meer stoffage, konstig en krachtig, op doek | *Mat:* op doek *Size:* hoog 32, breed 39 duimen	D van R	(Sold) fl 52 Versteeg
1801/08/19	AMSCH	0134	*T. Wyk* | Een Bergachtig Landschap op een Heuvel aan Strand, ziet men een Wagt-Tooren an andere Gebouwen, op de voorgrond eenige Beeldjes, ter linker zyde eenige Vaartuigen; fix geschilderd op Doek | *Mat:* op doek	Van Forreest	(Sold) fl 2:15 Gruiter
1801/12/22	AMOTT	0042	*Thomas Wyk* | 1 Chimist in het Labarotorium [sic]	Bartholomeus Ruloffs	(Unknown) fl 44:10
1802/04/13	HAVIN	0023	*T. Wyck* | Een Studioses [sic] in zijn Boekvertrek, schoon geschildert		(Unknown)
1802/05/11	GRGRW	0060	*Thomas Wijk* | De zo genaamde Waterputter [Schilderijen met Olie-Verf; In Vergulde Lijsten] | *Mat:* in olyverf *Notes:* The bracketed information in the title appears above lot 1 and refers to lots 1 to 79a.	Arnold Sicco Werumeus	(Unknown) fl 10
1802/05/24	HGBAK	0006	*T. Wyk* | Een Alchemiste Stookhuis, met veelerhande soorten van Gereedschappen en Boeken gestoffeerd door T. Wyk, hoog 15 ½ duim, breed 13 ½ duim, paneel, zwarte lyst en vergulde binnenrand | *Mat:* op paneel *Size:* hoog 15 ½ duim, breed 13 ½ duim	Mejuffrouw A van der Mieden	(Sold) fl 20 ver Meule[n]
1802/06/16	AMSCH	0221	*T. Wyck* | Deeze Ordenantie verbeeld een Levantsche Zeehaven; op de voorgrond staat een Koopman by een Baal en Koffer met Goederen, als bevelgeevende aan Slaaven en anderea [sic] Arbeiders; verder ziet men een Haven met Scheepen, alles is Meesterlyk fraay en uitvoerig gepenceeld | *Mat:* op doek *Size:* hoog 14, breed 18 duim	[Merrem]	(Sold) fl 105 de Lelie
1802/06/16	AMSCH	0222	*T. Wyck* | Twee Italiaansche Zeehavens, in de eene ziet men op de voorgrond eenige Koopmans Goederen waar by twee Lieden; verders verscheide Scheepen en Schuiten, in 't verschiet een Stad; de weêrga steld voor een gedeelte van een afgebrooke Sluis aan de Haven; ter zyde op het gebergte ziet men een Stad; beide deezen Schilderyen zyn zonachtig en meesterlyk van schildering | *Mat:* op doek op paneel *Size:* ieder hoog 20 ½, breed 24 ½ duim	[Merrem]	(Sold) fl 130 LaFontaine
1802/06/16	AMSCH	0223	*T. Wyck* | Een zonachtig Landschap, op de voorgrond by een stil Water ziet men een Visser, wyders een aloud Gebouw en een bergachtig verschiet, fraay van schildering | *Mat:* op paneel *Size:* hoog 9 ½, breed 6 duim	[Merrem]	(Sold) fl 8 Cobel
1802/08/24	LNDLS	0015	*T. Wyck* | Een Italiaansche Zee-Haven; op den Voorgrond door een boog ziet men eenige Mannen en Vrouwen te paard en te voet, en een Jongen met Jachthonden; verder Kooplieden bij Vaartuigen in 't verschiet | *Mat:* op doek *Size:* hoog 23 ½, breed 19 duimen	Leonardus Bouman [or others]	(Unknown) fl 41
1802/09/06	AMSCH	0128	*T. Wyck* | In een hoog Bergagtig Landschap, ziet men over een water aan een Steene Brug, een Landman, welke eenig Vée dryft, op de voorgrond twee rustende Lieden; zonagtig gepenceeld | *Mat:* op paneel *Size:* hoog 14, breed 12 duim	J	(Sold) fl 7 Hodges
1802/09/18	RMDRS	0011	*Th. Wyck* | Een Vrouwtje, zittende te Naaijen, waarby een Jongman staat, verder eenig bywerk, en in de Agtergrond een gedeelte van een Stads Muur | *Annots:* Copie (MB) *Size:* hoog 12, breed 10 ½ duim	Casper de Haas	(Sold) fl 22 v Beefting
1802/09/21	UTHDG	0102	*Th. Wijk* | Een Italiaansche gebouw, in een Landschap: vooraan een kleine Waterval, waarbij een rustend man enz. Zonägtig geschildert | *Mat:* op paneel *Size:* hoog 9, breed 16 duimen		(Bought In) fl 13:10
1802/12/13	AMSCH	0171	*Thomas Wyk* | Een Bergachtig Landschap, men ziet over een stil Water een Steene Sluis, over welke een Man te Paard, verzeld van twee andere Ryzigers, op de voorgrond, twee rustende Landlieden, zonachtig gepenceeld | *Size:* hoog 15 ½, breed 12 ½ duim	Pruyssenaar [for] A	(Sold) fl 2:5 Gruiter
1802/12/13	AMSCH	0172	*Thomas Wyk* | Een Chimist in zyn Laboratorium, ryk gestoffeerd met toepasselyk Bywerk, uitvoerig en krachtig van schildering | *Mat:* op doek *Size:* hoog 14, breed 12 duim	Pruyssenaar [for] B	(Sold) fl 28 Coclers
1802/12/13	AMSCH	0173	*Thomas Wyk* | In een Rotgezight, vertoonen zich eenige rustende Landlieden, waar by een Man op een Ezel zittende, verder een Huisman eenig Vée voortdryvende; alles is fiks en meesterlyk van Penceel-behandeling | *Mat:* op paneel *Size:* hoog 16, breed 12 duim	Schley [for] Lauwers	(Sold) fl 11:10 Gruiter
1803/07/14	MGKLY	0010	*T. Wyk* | Een Italiaansche Zeehaven fiks geschilderd	Mr Caspar Jacob van Citters	(Unknown)
1803/08/17	AMSCH	0094	*Wyck. (T.)* | Een Astrologist in zyn Studeerkamer, omgeven van een menigte Bywerk, als Globe, Boeken, enz. alles kragtig geschilderd | *Mat:* op paneel *Size:* hoog 10, breed 8 duim	Anna Catharina Putman	(Sold) fl 9 Pruijssenaar
1803/12/15	MGLAC	0015	*T. Wyk* | Een Pleisterplaats met Figuuren en Paarden; zeer kragtig en fraai | *Mat:* op doek *Size:* hoog duim 24, breed duim 19	Mr L H de Haze Bomme	(Unknown)
1804/02/27	AMSCH	0143	*T. Wyk* | Een Grot van binnen; bevallig van schildering	B	(Sold) fl 0:4 L Pakker
1804/05/07	AMSCH	0193	*Wyk. (T.)* | Door een open Nies, ziet men in een Studeervertrek een Man met een Pen in den hand voor een Tafel zitten, hy schynt sterk in gedagten over 't geen hy schryft, verders is het Vertrek ryk gestoffeerd, met een Globen en een meenigten van Boeken en Papieren; bevallig geordoneert en uitvoerig geschildert | *Mat:* op paneel *Size:* hoog 12, breed 10 duim	Vinkeles [for] G	(Bought In) fl 30

1804/07/25	AMSCH	0090	*Wyck. (T.)* | In een Stookhuis zit een Alchimist, bézig Goud te Smelten, verzelt van een Jongeling den Blaasbalg trekkende, op de Voorgrond staan verschyde Potten en Pannen, Flessen, Boeken en andere Gereedschappen; het licht ter zyde door een Vengster invallende, werkt natuurlyk en is meesterlyk gepenceeld | *Mat:* op paneel *Size:* hoog 12, breed 11 duim		(Sold) fl 51 C S Roos
1804/08/08	AMSCH	0228	*T. Wyk* | In een Italiaansche Zéehaven, by eenige hooge Gebouwen, zyn eenige zwaar gelaaden Vaartuigen, op de voorgrond eenige Kooplieden en andere Stoffagie; meesterlyk geschilderd | *Mat:* op paneel *Size:* hoog 7, breed 6 duim	Vink[eles] [for] K[=Gruyter?]	(Sold) fl 1 Texier
1804/10/29	HRBAU	0121	*Wyk, (Thomas)* | Een Levantsche Zeehaven; op den Voorgrond is een Kaai, waar op een Turk by eenige Pakgoederen zyn bevelen geeft, nevens eenige Jongens, welken zig baaden. Aan de overzyde, waar men hooge, en met Kasteelen bebouwde Klippen ziet, worden Schepen gekalfaterd; nevens een ruim verschiet. Zeer warm en uitvoerig behandeld | *Mat:* op doek *Size:* hoog 17, breed 24 duim	Simon Styl	(Unknown)
1804/10/29	HRBAU	0122	*Wyk (Thomas)* | Deze gepaste weêrgaê vertoont méde een Levantsche Zeehaven; voor aan is een Plein, op welk een Fontein staat, alwaar twee Vrouwtjens bezig zyn te wasschen; nevens hen staat een Turk by eenige Pakgoederen. Op den tweeden grond ligt eene Stad aan den voet van eene steile Rots; waar agter een bergagtig verschiet. Niet minder uitvoerig dan het voorige behandeld | *Mat:* op doek *Size:* hoog 17, breed 24 duim	Simon Styl	(Unknown)
1805/07/03	AMSCH	0053	*Wyck. (T.)* | Een Italiaansche Zeehaven, met onderscheide Vaartuigen en Bergachtig verschiet; de Voorgrond ryk met werkende Beelden en Pakgoederen gestoffeerd, en Meesterlyk behandeld | *Mat:* op doek *Size:* hoog 22, breed 24 duim	R[oos]	(Sold) fl 100 Agina
1805/07/03	AMSCH	0054	*Wyck. (T.)* | In een Boeren Schuur is een Moeder bézig haar Kind te reinigen, waarby de Vader en twee andere Kinderen, verders een ménigte Huisraad; zonachtig behandeld | *Mat:* op paneel *Size:* hoog 11 ½, breed 14 ½ duim	R[oos]	(Sold) fl 42 H Pakker
1805/07/03	AMSCH	0165	*T. Wyk* | Een Levantsche Zeehaven, by Rotschachtig Strand, waarop Wagttoorens en andere Gebouwen; op de Voorgrond een staande Vrouw met een pak onder den arm, verzeld van rustende Kinderen, verders een zittend Man, by Boeken en Papieren, waar agter een staand Koopman; zonagtig en meesterlyk gepenceeld | *Mat:* op doek *Size:* hoog 32, breed 25 duim	R[oos]	(Sold) fl 31 Tozelli
1805/07/03	AMSCH	0166	*T. Wyk* | In een Verwulft Binnevertrek, zit een studeerende Alchimist, in zyn Laboratorium by een Tafel, waarop verscheide Boeken, een Globe en Flessen geplaatst zyn, verders ryk gestoffeerd met stook-kundige Werktuigen, en een opgeschooven Gordyn; geestig en natuurlyk van penceelbehandeling | *Mat:* op paneel *Size:* hoog 17, breed 14 duim	G	(Sold) fl 57 Gruyter
1805/07/03	AMSCH	0167	*T. Wyk* | Twee stuks Italiaansche Zeehavens, met verscheide Gebouwen, Fontynen; een ménigte stoffagie van Beeldjes, Scheepen en Schuiten; breed en natuurlyk | *Mat:* op doek *Size:* hoog 15, breed 21 duim	V[inkeles]	(Sold) fl 80 L Pakker
1805/07/10	AMSCH	0168	*T. Wyk* | Een Alchimist in zyn Laboratorium, vol met bywerk van allerhanden aart daar toe behorende; kragtig op Paneel | *Mat:* op paneel *Size:* hoog 16, breed 14 duim	R[oos]	(Sold) fl 34:10 Gruiter
1805/07/10	AMSCH	0169	*T. Wyk* | Een Koperslager in zyn Werkplaats, bézig een Bekken te maken; en verder bywerk | *Mat:* op paneel *Size:* hoog 15, breed 12 duim	R[oos]	(Sold) fl 24:10 Spaan
1805/10/09	HGBSM	0120	*T. Wyk* | Een Italiaansche plaats, aan de overzyde van het water eenige gebouwen, en de voorgrond gestoffeerd met eenige figuuren en vaartuig | *Mat:* op doek op paneel *Size:* hoog 7 breet 6 duim	T H van Willigen [or others]	(Sold) fl 1:12 Kerber
1806/05/05	AMSCH	0151	*T. Wyk* | Voor een oud vervallen Gebouw ziet men een Paard, welke door een Smit beslagen wordt, verders eenige andere Beeldjes, en een aangenaam verschiet; meesterlyk en krachtig op Paneel | *Mat:* op paneel *Size:* hoog 19, breed 16 duim	V[inkeles]	(Sold) fl 3:10 Boelen
1806/05/05	AMSCH	0152	*T. Wyk* | Een Turksche Zeehaven, met Galleien en andere Vaartuigen, Kooplieden, en andere stoffagie | *Mat:* op doek *Size:* hoog 18, breed 26 duim	V[inkeles]	(Sold) fl 0:6 L Pakker
1806/08/13	AMSCH	0225	*Wyck. (T.)* | Twee stuks, een Italiaansch Landschap, met aloude Gebouwen en stoffagie; en een ander Landschap met Geboomten | *Mat:* op paneel *Size:* hoog 5, breed 8 duim	Vinkeles [for] D	(Sold) fl 3:15 Gruyter
1806/08/13	AMSCH	0248	*T. Wyk* | Een aloud Cebouw van binnen te zien	Vinkeles [for] G[ruyter]	(Sold) fl 1:10 L Pakker
1806/11/24	AMSCH	0083	*Wyck (T.)* | Een Italiaansche Zeehaven, vol gewoel van Beelden te paard en te voet; ter zyden eenige Scheepen; kragtig en fraai van penceelsbehandeling | *Mat:* op doek *Size:* hoog 16, breed 19 duim	Munnikhuizen	(Bought In) fl 14
1807/04/13	AMSCH	0003	*Thomas Wijk* | In een Binnenvertrek ziet men een Alchimist, zittende voor een Tafel, waarop een Lessenaar en Boek geplaatst is, leezen, in zijn Laboratorium verders toepasselijk Bijwerk, als Flessen, Potten, Smeltkroesen, Boeken, Papieren &c. meesterlijk en fiks van behandeling | companion to lot 4 *Mat:* op doek op paneel *Size:* hoog 12 ½, breed 10 duim	Everard de Burlett	(Sold) fl 20 for lots 3 & 4. Joh[S] Reus
1807/04/13	AMSCH	0004	*Thomas Wijk* | Deeze Ordinantie zijnde een wederga van de voorgaande, steld voor een aloude Kamer met een rood Gordijn omhangen, waarin een	Everard de Burlett	(Sold) fl 20 for lots 3 & 4. Joh[S] Reus

			Geleerde, zittende te studeeren voor een Lessenaar, waar bij verscheide Boeken en Papieren geplaatst zijn, verders Globes, Inktkoker en divers; in alles van behandeling als de voorgaande | companion to lot 3 *Mat:* op doek op paneel *Size:* hoog 12 ½, breed 10 duim		
1807/04/13	AMSCH	0005	*Thomas Wijk* | In een Italiaansch berg en heuvelachtig Landschap, met aloude Gebouwen bij een Rivier, ziet men op de Voorgrond eenige staande werkende en rustende Landlieden, zoo Mannen als Vrouwen, verders Ezels, Scheepen &c. zonachtig en fraai geschilderd | *Mat:* op paneel *Size:* hoog 20, breed 21 duim	Everard de Burlett	(Sold) fl 51 Coclers
1807/08/26	AMSCH	0233	*T. Wyk* | Dit bevallig Schildery vertoont de Werk- en Stookplaats van een Chimist: hy zit voor een Tafel, met een Kleed bedekt, bezig te schryven, waarop een Globe, Boeken, Parkemente Brieven en andere zaken geplaatst zyn; achter hem staat een Jongeling by een open Vengster, waardoor het licht valt, en een natuurlyke werking doet, verders de Grond en de Wand ryk gestoffeerd met Glase Flessen, Boeken, Kroezen, Potten en andere Gereedschappen; uitvoerig en meesterlyk gepenceeld | *Mat:* op doek *Size:* hoog 22, breed 19 duim	Roos	(Bought In) fl 26
1808/04/26	GDAN	0200	*Wyk (Th.)* | Voor een pragtig Gebouw ziet men eenige Kooplieden hunne Koopwaaren aanbieden, en Verkopen, als mede een Kwakzalver te Paard, verder vol gewoel van Beelden, konstig en kragtig geschilderd, zijnde eene der beste van dezen Meester | *Size:* hoog 31, breed 23 duim	G H Fortuyn	(Unknown)
1808/04/26	GDAN	0201	*Wyk (Th.)* | Een Italiaansche Zeehaven, op welker Strand men eenige Kooplieden ziet, bezig over een bij hunne Pakgoederen te handelen en te bezorgen, hebbende op de voorgrond eenige hooge Gebouwen, goed geschilderd | *Size:* hoog 41, breed 50 duim	G H Fortuyn	(Unknown)
1808/04/26	GDAN	0202	*Wyk (Th.)* | Een fraaije Italiaansche Zeehaven, waar men op de voorgrond eenige Kooplieden, met hunne Waaren en Pakgoederen ziet, op de tweede grond, eenige Vrouwen haare Vruchten aanbiedende, in 't verschiet een fraai bergägtig Gezigt op een Kasteel, vol gewoel, zonagtig en eel behandeld | *Size:* hoog 20 ½, breed 26 duim	G H Fortuyn	(Unknown)
1808/06/06	RMRIJ	0148	*Wijk. (Thomas)* | Onder de gewulfde boog van eene trotsche Brug, ziet men eenige Italiaansche Gebouwen en eene Zeehaven in 't verschiet. Op den voorgrond verscheidene figuren van verschillende natiën, verzeld van een aantal differente koop- en andere goederen. Waarlijk schoon en verstandig geschilderd [A travers une Arche, et près d'un Port de mer qu'on apperçoit à l'horison, on découvre plusieurs édifices, ce qui offre un coup d'oeil pittoresque. Le devant du Tableau est riche en personnages de differentes Nations, et en divers objects de Marchandises. Le Génie et la pénétration brillent dans cette belle Composition] | *Annots:* Coll. Lublink. Verk. Jan de Neufville, 6 Aug. 1783 (f 180-) (RMA I) *Mat:* op doek *Size:* Hoog 24, en breed 28 ¼ duim	Gerrit van der Pot, Heer van Groeneveld	(Sold) fl 251 Allard
1808/06/06	RMRIJ	0149	*Wijk. (Thomas)* | Een Buitenmuur bij Rome. Op den voorgrond zit eene Vrouw; bezijden haar ziet men eene Melkkan en Groenten; voor haar eenen staanden Man; achter denzelven eenen liggenden Hond. Op den tweeden grond eene Vrouw en eenen Jongen aan eene Bronput; in 't verschiet eenige Gebouwen. Dun, helder en uitvoerig geschilderd [Ce Tableau represente un Mur, et l'Extrémité d'une Arcade dans l'enceinte de Rome. Sur le devant est assise une Laitière, qui a son pot au lait et des légumes à côté d'elle, et qui s'entretient avec un garçon, qui a un Chien auprès de lui. Une femme et un enfant s'occupent à puiser de l'eau. Ce Morceau est très bien éxécuté] | *Annots:* Verk. Pictura, den Haag, 17 Sept. 1781 (f 14.-) (RMA I) *Mat:* op paneel *Size:* Hoog 11 ¾, en breed 9 ¾ duim	Gerrit van der Pot, Heer van Groeneveld	(Sold) fl 30:10 Allard
1808/06/11	RMRIJ	0095	*Thomas Wyk* | Een Italiaansche Grot en Gebergte, verrykt met verscheide Dieren en Figuren | *Mat:* op paneel *Size:* hoog 17, breed 12 ¾ duim		(Sold) fl 35 Coclers
1808/06/13	AMSCH	0176	*Wijck (T.)* | In een Keukenvertrek zit een Schoenmaker bij een Tafeltje te arbeiden, ter zijde bij een openstaand Venster eene Vrouw met een Schoen in de hand, op den grond zit een jong Meisje, en verder eene Vrouw bij de Haardstede, gestoffeerd met onderscheiden gereedschap en huisraad. Het invallend zonlicht door het venster geeft eene natuurlijke werking en is bevallig en uitvoerig gepenceeld | *Mat:* op paneel *Size:* hoog 15 ½, breed 11 ½ duim	[Jan Tersteeg]	(Sold) fl 131 T Boelen
1808/06/13	AMSCH	0177	*Wijck (T.)* | In een Binnenhuis aan de deur zit eene Vrouw bij den ingang naar eene Plaats, bezig linnen te naaijen, achter dezelve staat een Jongeling, verder gestoffeerd met verscheide Keukengereedschappen. Het invallende licht doet eene natuurlijke werking, en is als de voorige van een meesterlijk fraaije penceelsbehandeling | *Mat:* op paneel *Size:* hoog 14, breed 12 duim	[Jan Tersteeg]	(Sold) fl 84 Hulswit
1808/06/13	AMSCH	0177a[H]	*Wijck (T.)* | 1 dito dito [Binnenhuis?] | *Notes:* This lot was added in by hand in the EBNP, FLNY and RKDH copies of the catalogue. It is unclear what "dito" refers to in the title.	R[oos]	(Sold) fl 41 Du Pré
1808/06/13	AMSCH	0178	*Wijck (T.)* | Een Binnenhuis, waarin eenige Werklieden en twee Heeren, die door een Bedelaar aangesproken worden. Fraai van licht en bruin | *Mat:* op paneel *Size:* hoog 22, breed 16 duim	E M Engelberts	(Sold) fl 36 Allard
1808/08/23	AMSCH	0172	*Wijk. (Th)* | In een welgeordoneerde Studeerkamer zit een Philosoof voor een Tafel in een Boek te leezen, voor hem staat een Globe, eenige boeken	[Gruyter?]	(Sold) fl 22 Dupré

			Papier en Schrijfgereedschap, achterwaards een Boekenkast en ander toepasselijk bijwerk; uitvoerig behandeld | *Mat:* op paneel *Size:* hoog 10, breed 8 duim		
1808/08/23	AMSCH	0199	*Th. Wijk* | Een Venetiaansche Zeehaven, met capitaale Gebouwen, op de voorgrond bij eenigen Vaartuigen Turksche Kooplieden; warm van koloriet	[Gruyter?]	(Sold) fl 9 van Iperen
1808/08/23	AMSCH	0199a[H]	*Th. Wijk* | 1 dito [Venetiaansche] dito [Zeehaven] | *Notes:* This lot was added in by hand in the EBNP copy of the catalogue. It is unclear what "dito" refers to in the title.	[Gruyter?]	(Sold) fl 8 Van Iperen
1808/09/13	HABRU	0096	*T. Wijck* | Een Italiaansch Landschap, gestoffeerd met Beelden en Beesten		(Unknown) fl 2:10
1808/10/28	AMVRS	0066	*Wijk, (Th.)* | In een oud Gebouw, zit eene Vrouw bezig groente schoon te maaken, nevens haar een Kind, agterwaards twee andere Beelden, op den voorgrond bij een Waterput ziet men eenige Aardvruchten en verder Huisraad. Meesterlijk behandeld | *Mat:* op paneel *Size:* hoog 18, breed 15 ½ duim	Marten Udink	(Sold) fl 60 Van Iperen
1808/11/28	AMSCH	0070	*Th. Wijk* | Een Italiaansch Landschap, met hoog Gebergte en Gebouwen, gestoffeerd met Rijzigers en Vee, fiks geschilderd | *Mat:* op doek *Size:* hoog 14, breed 19 duim	[Gruyter?]	(Bought In) fl 5:10
1808/12/30	HGIMM	[00711]	*T. Wyk* | Voorts een exquis kabinetje Schilderijen van voorname Nederlandsche Meesters, welke uit hoofde van de kortheid des tijds niet stuk voor stuk kunnen beschreven worden; doch waarvan de beschrijving op den Kijkdag zal voorhanden zijn. Dus wij hier alleen de namen van eenige dier Meesters laten volgen, als: A. Kuyp, Ruysdaal, Karel du Jardyn, Loqwi ('t beste dat hij schilderde) Hondekoeter, van Dyk, Janson, Moesgever, Kamphuyzen, van Gooijen, A. van der Neer, T. Wyk, Huchtenburgh, Zolemaker, van Hassel, A. Vermeulen, van Dongen, Scheffer, van Os enz. | *This Lot:* Een Schilderij, T. Wyk *Notes:* Because this lot was not numbered in the catalogue, we have assigned the number.		(Unknown)
1809/04/17	AMSCH	0113	*T. Wijk* | Een Levantsche Zeehaven, rijk gestoffeerd met verschillende Beelden, op de voorgrond ter linker zijde voor een groot Gebouw, liggen verscheide Vaatwerk, Koffers en diversche Koopmans Goederen, waar bij Arbijders, verder beladen Vaartuigen, waar bij werkende Lieden, in 't verschiet Gebergten en Schepen in Zee; fiks en meesterlijk gepenceeld | *Mat:* op doek *Size:* hoog 22, breed 28 duim	Crajenschot	(Sold) fl 15:10
1809/04/22	AMYVR	0144	*T. Wijck* | Een Geleerde in zijn Studeervertrek; krachtig | *Mat:* op paneel *Size:* hoog 10, breed 8 duim	de Bruin	(Sold) fl 21 J^{mo} de Vries
1809/06/13	AMSCH	0191	*Th. Wyk* | Een Landschap met Reizigers, en Jagers met Honden gestoffeerd	Y	(Sold) fl 0:6 L Pakker
1810/03/26	RMMUY	0050	*Thomas Wyk* | Eenige rustende Figuren, verzeld van eene Vrouw op een wit Paard. Een Bergachtig, Zonachtig en warm Verschiet [Paysage d'Italie : sur le devant sont des voyageurs assis et debout, accompagnés d'une Dame à cheval, d'un ton chaud et piquant.] | *Mat:* op paneel *Size:* hoog 10, breed 7 ½ duimen	Daniel de Jongh Az	(Sold) fl 12:5 L B van der Hoop
1810/07/26	AMSCH	0142	*Wijck (T.)* | Een Zeehaven, rijk gestoffeerd met Kooplieden, Slaven, Vaartuigen enz. Goed geschilderd | *Mat:* op doek *Size:* hoog 44, breed 63 duimen	Cassino	(Sold) fl 10 Hulswit
1810/08/06	AMSCH	0128	*Wijk (Th.)* | In een Boekvertrek zit een Wijsgeer in een Boek te lezen, voor zich hebbende andere Boeken en Inktkoker, nevens hem een Aardglobe en verder bijwerk; meesterlijk behandeld | *Mat:* op paneel *Size:* hoog 10, breed 8 duimen	V[ries]	(Sold or Bought In) fl 14 de Vries
1810/08/06	AMSCH	0129	*Wijk (Th.)* | Een Italiaansche Brug, verder een Man op een Ezel, Visschers het Net trekkende, een Man in een Schuit en een Heer bij zijn Paard; natuurlijk en treffend geschilderd | *Mat:* op paneel *Size:* hoog 11, breed 10 duimen	V[ries]	(Sold) fl 27 J Spaan
1810/10/10	MGCIT	0062	*T. Wyk* | Een oud Kasteel, gebouwd aan een Water; alsmede een Brug annex aan dat Gestigt, waaronder door een Schip vaart; voorts een geen onaartig Verschiet; alles in een goeden smaak geschilderd | *Notes:* Originally the artist's name was spelled "F. Wyk." This error was corrected in an errata sheet located at the front of the catalogue.	Caspar van Citters	(Unknown)
1810/10/11	AMSCH	0105	*T. Wyk* | Een Binnenhuis, in hetzelve ziet men een Boer, houdende een stuk Brood en een Glas in zijn hand, hij schijnt in gesprek met eene nevens hem zittende Boerin, verder eenig Huisraad, geestig verbeeld | *Size:* hoog 13, breed 17 duimen	[Gruyter?]	(Bought In) fl 6:10

Wyck, Thomas (and Bergen, D.)

1802/09/21	UTHDG	0009	*Th. Wijk; Th. van Bergen* | Een Voerman laat de hoef van zijn paard voorzien, dit geschied bij een Herberg, uit welke de vrouw langs een steene trap, met een kan in de hand nederklimt, verder een Valkenier, komende door een poort: op de voorgrond Schapen, Ploeg en Planten, zeer zonägtig en fiks behandeld | *Mat:* op paneel *Size:* hoog 20, breed 15 ½ duimen		(Sold) fl 80 Cobell

Wyck, Thomas (and Both, J.)

1808/08/23	AMSCH	0171	*Wijk (Th.); J. Both* | Een kapitaal Heuvel en Bergachtig Landschap, ter rechterzijde van hetzelven ziet men voor een groot Gebouw eene Vrouw	[Coclers]	(Sold) fl 61 Dupré

			van eene Trap afkomende, onder aan dezelven zit eene Vrouw, waar bij een oud Man en twee staande Kinderen, meerder op den voorgrond eenige grasende Bokken en Schaapen, ter linker zijde op een Heuvel, een staande en een leggende Koe, benevens een Ram bij de stam van een Boom, en eenig Plantgewas; dit stuk is schoon van koloriet, en van een meesterlijke penceelbehandeling | *Mat:* op doek *Size:* hoog 36, breed 43 duim		
1809/04/22	AMYVR	0143	*T. Wijk; J. Both* | Een kapitaal Heuvelachtig Landschap: van de Trap van een groot Gebouw komt eene Vrouw nederwaarts, onder aan dezelve zit eene andere Vrouw, daarbij een oud Man en twee Kinderen, verders eenige Koeijen en Schapen; meesterlijk fraai gepenseeld, door T. Wijk en J. Both | *Mat:* op doek *Size:* hoog 36, breed 43 duim	de Bruin	(Sold) fl 51 C S Roos
			Wyck, Thomas (or Wyck, T., manner)		
1807/04/13	AMSCH	0008	*Door, of als T. Wijk* | Twee stuks bevallige boom en bergachtige landschappen, met Geboomte, Rivieren, stoffagie van Beelden enz., beide fiks gepenseeld | *Mat:* op doek *Size:* hoog 10, breed 12 duimen	Everard de Burlett	(Sold) fl 3 Levy Pakker
			Wyck, Thomas (copy after)		
1806/06/07	RMHSN	0071	*F. Wyk* | Een Turkse Zeehaven, na F. Wyk | *Mat:* op paneel *Notes:* The artist's name was given as "F. Wyk" but we have assumed this is an error.	A E K L	(Unknown)
			Wyck, Thomas (manner)		
1801/04/23	AMYVR	0037[a]	*T. Wyck* | Een Alchimist in de manier van T. Wyck, en een Spinnend Vrouwtje | *This Lot:* Een Alchimist; lot 37[b] by Anonymous		(Unknown)
1801/06/10	AMSCH	0213	*Thomas Wyk* | Een Chimist in zyn Laboratorium, in de manier van Thomas Wyk | *Mat:* op paneel *Size:* hoog 14, breed 12 duim	[Doublet]	(Sold) fl 3 Pruijssenaar [for] L
1802/08/24	LNDLS	0134	*T. Wijck* | Langs veele Gebouwen ziet men reizende en handeldrijvende Kooplieden; in 't verschiet gebergte. In de trant van T. Wijck | *Mat:* op paneel	Leonardus Bouman [or others]	(Unknown) fl 9:15
1802/08/24	LNDLS	0138	*T. Wijck* | In een Binnen-vertrek zit een Man bij een Lessenaar daar een brandende Kaars en een Globe opstaat bij eenige Vrouwen en een Kind, met bijwerk als van T. Wijck | *Mat:* op paneel	Leonardus Bouman [or others]	(Unknown) fl 6:15
1806/05/05	AMSCH	0218	*T. Wyck* | Twee stuks, Chimisten; als T. Wyck	V[inkeles]	(Sold) fl 1 Gruyter
1806/06/07	RMHSN	0009	*T: Wyk* | Een kloek Stuk, zynde een Binnenplaats met Ruïne en Fonteinwerken, voor dezelven verscheide Reizigers met hun byhebbend Vee, kragtig, helder en plaisant geschilderd, in de manier van T: Wyk	A E K L	(Unknown)
1809/04/22	AMYVR	0160	*T. Wijk* | Een Smids Winkel; als T. Wijk	de Bruin	(Sold) fl 2 C S Roos
			Wyckenburch [Unidentified]		
1802/05/24	HGBAK	0069	*Wyckenburch* | Een Boomryk Landschap, waarin op de voorgrond een zittend Juffertje, wordende door een Heer in Jagers kleeding een Trouwring gepresenteerd, verbeeldende de Historie van het Spaansch Heidinnetje, zeer fraay, door Wyckenburch, hoog 23 duim, breed 28 duim, op doek, zwarte lyst | *Mat:* op doek *Size:* hoog 23 duim, breed 28 duim	Mejuffrouw A van der Mieden	(Sold) fl 11 Kleijn
			Wyntrack, Dirck		
1802/06/16	AMSCH	0225	*J. Wyntrack* | By een Boerengemak ziet men een Willige Boom, waarby eenige Eenden aan een Waterplas; verders Boere Woningen en Geboomten; alles zeer natuurlyk gepenceeld | *Mat:* op paneel *Size:* hoog 28, breed 22 ½ duim *Notes:* The artist's name was given as "J. Wyntrack" but we have assumed this is an error.	[Merrem]	(Sold) fl 51 Pruijssenaar [for] R
1802/07/21	HGKAN	0042	*Wyntrak* | Een Boeren Binnenhuys, vol met musiceerende, dansende en drinkende Boeren, door Wyntrak, zwarte Lyst, vergulde binnen rand		(Unknown)
1802/07/21	HGKAN	0043	*Wyntrak* | Een dito [Schildery?], zynde een Koekebakster, door denzelven [Wyntrak], zwarte Lyst, vergulde binnen rand | *Notes:* It is unclear what "dito" refers to in the title.		(Unknown)
1804/10/16	DLOND	0273	*Wyntrak* | Ene Vrouw water puttende, met Groente rondom zich. Une Femme environnée des legumes, puisant de l'Eau | *Mat:* op paneel *Size:* hoog 18, breed 25		(Unknown)
1807/06/10	HGBSM	0091	*Wyntrak* | Een boeren binnen vertrek gestoffeerd met boeren huijsraad als tobbes, ketels, potten, pannen, kruywagen &c. in de agtergrond by de schoorsteen eenige figuuren, helder en transparant geschilderd | *Mat:* op paneel *Size:* hoog 18 ½, breed 24 ½ duim	Abraham Delfos [or others]	(Sold) fl 9:5 Tessier
1808/04/26	GDAN	0199	*Wynstrak* | Verbeeldende eenige Wafelëeters en Bierdrinkers, goed geschilderd | *Size:* hoog 24, breed 17 duim	G H Fortuyn	(Unknown)
1810/08/06	AMSCH	0131	*Wijntrak* | Op een Boeren-Werf ziet men een Huisman, komende van een Houten Trap, houdende een Vogel in zijn hand, op de voorgrond een Water, waarbij verscheide Eenden, Hoenders, vegtende Hanen en vliegende Duiven, verder eenig Huisraad en Boeren Gereedschappen; helder en bevallig van schildering | *Mat:* op doek *Size:* hoog 57, breed 73 duimen	Q	(Sold) fl 10 Texier Gerbet en Comp
1810/08/10	RMRIJ	0011	*J. Wijntrax* | Op den voorgrond in eene Boeren Schuur, vertoonen zig veel Huis- en Keukengereedschappen; Hoenders, Figuren en meer bijwerk. Uitvoerig en natuurlijk verbeeldt | *Mat:* op paneel *Size:* hoog 21 duim,		(Sold) fl 30 [or] 24 de Bruyn

			breed 17 duim *Notes:* The artist's name was given as "J. Wijntrax" but we have assumed this is an error.		
			Wyntrack, Dirck (manner)		
1809/07/25	HGBSM	0262	*Wyntrak* | Een Binnenhuis met allerhande Boeren Keuken Gereedschap, waarby een Boer en een Hond, fiks geschildert in de trant van Wyntrak | *Mat:* op paneel *Size:* hoog 14, breed 17 duim	D van der Aa [or] E B ten Dall	(Sold) fl 3 Hassevoord
			Xavery, Frans		
1801/03/16	AMSCH	0115	*F. Xaverij* | Een Italiaansch heuvelagtig Landschap, gestoffeerd met staand en rustend Vee, waar by een vrouw die een Gyt melkt, plaisant geschilderd op paneel door F. Xaverij, in de manier van Berghem | *Mat:* op paneel	K[ip]	(Sold) fl 16 Valentijn
1801/03/16	AMSCH	0121	*F. Xaverij* | In een heuvelagtig Landschap met geboomte, vertoont zig op de voorgrond staand en rustend Vee, terzyde zit een vrouw waar by een jongeling, Meesterlyk gepenceeld | *Mat:* op doek	K[ip]	(Sold) fl 9:5 Valentijn
1801/05/11	AMSCH	0116	*F. Xavery* | Een Landschap gestoffeerd, met Koeijen en Schaapen, nevens een Herder en Herderin, en een aangenaam verschiet, uitvoerig gepenceeld | *Mat:* op paneel *Size:* hoog 12, breed 15 duim	V	(Sold) fl 91 v d Schley [for] Z[=Putte]
1802/06/28	AMSCH	0214	*F. Xavery* | Een Bloem- en Fruitstuk, uitvoerig gepenceeld door F. Xavery | *Mat:* op paneel *Size:* hoog 17, breed 13 duim	Anna Elink	(Sold) fl 10 Geld
1805/07/03	AMSCH	0174	*F. Xavery* | Twee stuks Landschappen, met een ménigte Vee met hun Herders; Jongens, enz.; geestig gepenceeld op Paneel | *Mat:* op paneel *Size:* hoog 11, breed 15 duim	R[oos]	(Sold) fl 14 Halingins
1810/05/22	AMSCH	0127	*Xaverij. (T.)* | Een bergachtig Landschap, gestoffeerd met gaande en rustende Koeijen en Schapen, benevens een zittend Herder, waarbij eene staande Vrouw en Kind en een aangenaam verschiet; uitvoerig van schildering | *Mat:* op paneel *Size:* hoog 11 ½, breed 15 duim *Notes:* The artist's name was given as "Xaverij. (T.)" but we have assumed this is an error.	Johannes van de Putte Nicolaasz.	(Sold) fl 24:10 du Pree
			Yong, de [Unidentified]		
1803/11/30	MGBEO	0002	*De Yong* | De Stad Vlissingen van de Rheede te zien, ryk gestoffeerd met Zee- en andere Scheepen, door de Yong, op Paneel, zw. lyst | *Mat:* op paneel *Size:* hoog 32 duim, breed 58 duim	Samuel de Wind	(Sold) £ 0:11 Philipse
			Zeemann, Reinier		
1801/05/11	AMSCH	0120	*R. Zeeman* | Een stil water met verscheide Scheepen en Schuiten, ter zyde een zandbank met Vissers, zonachtig behandeld | *Mat:* op doek *Size:* hoog 15, breed 13 duim	E[lias]	(Sold) fl 30:10 van Iperen
1802/02/16	AMSCH	0025	*R. Zeeman* | Een woelend water ryk gestoffeerd met Oorlog en andere Schépen, en Schuiten; meesterlyk fix en natuurlyk behandeld op doek | *Mat:* op doek	E	(Sold) fl 12 Jan Spaan
1802/05/11	GRGRW	0048	*Reindert Zeeman* | Een schoon Zee-gezicht [Schilderijen met Olie-Verf; In zwarte Lijsten] | *Mat:* in olyverf *Notes:* The bracketed information in the title appears above lot 1 and refers to lots 1 to 79a.	Arnold Sicco Werumeus	(Unknown) fl 25:10
1802/06/16	AMSCH	0228	*R. Zeeman* | Een sterk woelende Zee met verscheiden zeilende Scheepen, en op de voorgrond een Sloep met eenige Lieden; verder een Haven met Gebouwen, Wagt-tooren en een bergachtig verschiet; het Water is natuurlyk golvende, dun en doorschynend, en van een fraaye penceel-behandeling | *Mat:* op doek *Size:* hoog 30, breed 41 duim	[Merrem]	(Sold) fl 40 H de Valk
1802/06/16	AMSCH	0229	*R. Zeeman* | Twee stuks Gezichten aan de Ykant te Amsterdam, ryk gestoffeerd met een meenigte Oorlogscheepen en andere Vaartuigen, zwemmende Jongens enz. alles uitvoerig behandeld | *Mat:* op doek *Size:* Ieder hoog 14 ½, breed 16 ½ duim	[Merrem]	(Sold) fl 75 H de Valk
1802/06/16	AMSCH	0230	*R. Zeeman* | In een Italiaansche Zeehaven ziet men een menigte Oorlog- en andere Scheepen; op de voorgrond een menigte Beeldjes, anderen welk een der Scheepen calfateren; alles uitvoerig gepenceeld | *Mat:* op doek *Size:* hoog 21, breed 42 duim	[Merrem]	(Sold) fl 30 Cobel
1802/06/29	HGDAW	0014	*Zeeman* | Twee Zeetjes door Zeeman		(Unknown)
1802/07/21	HGKAN	0051	*Zeeman* | Een Turksche Zeehaven, door Zeeman, 1664, in zwarte Lysten | *Inscr:* Zeeman, 1664 (signed and dated?) *Notes:* It is unclear whether the name and date are inscribed on the painting.		(Unknown)
1802/09/06	AMSCH	0137	*R. Zeeman* | Twee stille Waters met een ménigte van zeilende en andere Vaartuigen; meesterlyk behandeld | *Size:* hoog 7, breed 19 duim	J	(Sold) fl 6 I^{c} Smit
1802/09/21	UTHDG	0105	*R. Zeeman* | In een Baai of Haven liggen veele Oorlogschepen, van welke een gecalfaterd wordt. De voorgrond is met meenigerlei Beeldjes van allerlei rang gestoffeerd, en het verschiet is op de zee, langs hoog gebergte, alles uitvoerig geschildert | *Mat:* op doek *Size:* hoog 21, breed 24 ½ duimen		(Bought In) fl 34
1803/09/07	AMSCH	0223	*R. Zeeman* | Een Woelend Water met diversche Zylende Schépen en Sloepen, dun op Paneel [Une mer agitée, chargée d'un grand nombre de batimens qui lutent contre les flots ; d'un bonne composition, exécuté au naturel] | *Mat:* op paneel *Size:* hoog 9, breed 11 duim	Smidt	(Sold) fl 5:15 Texier

1803/09/07	AMSCH	0224	*R. Zeeman* | Een dito [Woelend] dito [Water], niet minder als het voorgaande [Un semblable sujet, du même mérite] | *Mat:* op paneel *Size:* hoog 15, br. 20 duim	Smidt	(Sold) fl 1:15 Crabbendam
1804/04/28	LNDLS	0054	*R. Zeeman* | Een woelend Water, met zeilende en ten anker leggende schepen, en een steenen hoofd met volk	[Abraham Delfos] [or others]	(Sold) fl 2:10 Rigter [for] A
1804/05/07	AMSCH	0198	*Zeeman. (R.)* | Een stil Water met een ménigte van zylende en stilleggende Scheepen en Schuiten; uitvoetig [sic] gepenceeld | *Size:* hoog 16, breed 18 duim	Vinkeles [for] J	(Sold) fl 2:5 T van Iperen
1804/07/25	AMSCH	0092	*Zeeman (R.)* | Een Italiaansche Zeehaven, ryk gestoffeert, met verscheide zylende en leggende Scheepen, waar van 'er twee Gekalfaatert worden, by het Strand op de Voorgrond ziet men twee Sloepen beneevens eenige Matroosen en ander Scheepsvolk; alles is helder van coloriet, bevallig en uitvoerig gepenceeld | *Mat:* op doek *Size:* hoog 25 ½, breed 28 duim		(Sold) fl 40 Tessier
1804/07/25	DLGRO	0005	*Rainier Zeemans* | Een Zee Inham of Haven, met eenige ten Anker leggende Scheepen, en verder bywerk, zeer natuurlyk en fraai geschilderd door Rainier Zeemans | *Mat:* op doek *Size:* hoog 19, breed 25 duim	Mr Franc van der Burch Wz.	(Unknown)
1804/08/08	AMSCH	0236	*R. Zeeman* | Een stil Water, gestoffeerd met Scheepen, Vlotten Balken en andere Stoffagie | *Mat:* op doek *Size:* hoog 14, breed 20 duim	Vink[eles] [for] K[=Gruyter?]	(Sold) fl 0:18 Texier
1804/10/29	HRBAU	0123	*Zeeman, (R.)* | Een Levantsche Zeehaven; op den Voorgrond van dezelve, welke zandagtig is, zyn eenige Kooplieden by hunne Goederen, waar by drie Galeien liggen. Aan de overzyde van het water is eene met Wagttorens voorziene Stadsmuur, over welken men pragtige Gebouwen ziet, en by den hoek deszelfs ziet men nog eene Galei; wyders Oorlog-schepen en Gebergte in 't verschiet. Dit Stuk is bevallig, zonagtig, en zo fraai behandeld, als men zelden van dezen Meester vindt | *Mat:* op doek *Size:* hoog 26, breed 35 duim	Simon Styl	(Unknown)
1804/10/29	HRBAU	0124	*Zeeman, (R.)* | Op eene stille Zee wordt een Oorlogschip gekalfaterd, waar by een ander ten anker ligt, nevens meer andere Vaartuigen. Uitvoerig behandeld | *Mat:* op doek *Size:* hoog 17, breed 20 duim	Simon Styl	(Unknown)
1805/07/03	AMSCH	0175	*R. Zeeman* | Een Gezicht op de Sint Anthoniessluis, van de Oude Schans af te zien, gestoffeerd met Vaartuigen en Beeldjes; kragtig op Doek | *Mat:* op doek	G	(Sold) fl 16 C van Hardenberg
1805/07/10	AMSCH	0182	*Zeeman* | Een Gezicht op de Stad Amsterdam, uit het Y te zien, gestoffeerd met diversse groote en klyne Scheepen en andere Vaartuigen, fraai op Paneel | *Mat:* op paneel	R[oos]	(Sold) fl 0:10 L Pakker
1805/10/09	HGBSM	D0004	*R. Zeeman* | Een 't Y gezicht met veel scheepen, waar van twee scheepen gekalfaterd worden, uitvoerig | *Mat:* op doek *Size:* hoog 16 ½ breet 20 ½ duim	T H van Willigen [or others]	(Sold) fl 9:15 Blommers
1805/10/21	GRBOL	0043	*R. Zeeman* | Een Zeestuk	Gerardus Nicolaus Heerkens	(Unknown)
1806/06/07	RMHSN	0046	*R. Zeeman* | Een Italiaansche Zeehaven met Schepen en Beelden | *Mat:* op doek	A E K L	(Sold) fl 19 Thijs
1806/06/07	RMHSN	0065	*Zeeman* | Een Onstuimige Zee | *Mat:* op paneel	A E K L	(Unknown)
1808/05/18	LNAN	0020	*Zeeman* | Een stil Water met Schepen en een Stad in 't verschiet | *Notes:* The artist's name "Zeeman" was added in by hand in the RKDH copy of the catalogue.	Mr Cornelis Versluys	(Unknown)
1808/08/23	AMSCH	0195	*R. Zeeman* | Een Stilwater, met zeilende Scheepen en Vaartuigen, kloek geschilderd	[Gruyter?]	(Sold) fl 5:10 Spruit
1809/06/13	AMSCH	0204	*R. Zeeman* | Een stormende Zee met een zeilend Schip dat door de golven geslingerd word	Q	(Sold) fl 1:5 Boldoot
1810/03/23	HAVIN	0040	*Leeman* | Een woelende Zee met Scheepen, door Leeman | *Notes:* The artist's name was given as "Leeman" but we have assumed this is an error.	Rudolf Hendrik de Wetstein [or others]	(Unknown)
1810/05/22	AMSCH	0128	*Zeeman (R.)* | Een stil Zeegezicht aan Strand, op den voorgrond verscheide Visschers en andere in Schuiten, verder vertoonen zich zeilende en andere Schepen; natuurlijk behandeld | *Mat:* op paneel *Size:* hoog 17, breed 11 duim	F	(Sold) fl 9:5 Gruyter
1810/08/06	AMSCH	0132	*Zeeman (R.)* | Een Zeegezigt met verscheide Oorlogschepen, vooraan en ter zijde op het strand Schepen die gekalvaterd worden; bevallig en zuiver van schildering | *Mat:* op doek *Size:* hoog 20, breed 25 duimen	A	(Sold) fl 35 T Spaan
1810/08/06	AMSCH	0141	*R. Zeeman* | Een stil Water, met onderscheidene Vaartuigen; natuurlijk	F	(Sold) fl 21 Roelsma
1810/10/11	AMSCH	0106	*R. Zeeman* | Een gezigt in het Y, voor de Stad Amsterdam | *Mat:* op paneel *Size:* hoog 23, breed 37 duimen	C	(Sold) fl 3:10 J Spaan
1810/12/03	DOBRA	0020	*R. Zeeman* | Een Scheepstimmerwerf, te Amsterdam; krachtig		(Unknown)

Zeemann, Reinier (or Zeemann, manner)

1806/08/13	AMSCH	0230	*R. Zeeman* | Een Stadgezicht aan een Rivier, dewelke met een ménigte Beelden, in onderscheiden Vaartuigen gestoffeerd; is door of in de manier, van R. Zeeman	Roos	(Sold) fl 9 Haffner

Zeemann, Reinier (manner)

1803/09/07	AMSCH	0265	*R. Zeeman* | Een Zee-Batailje; kragtig op Paneel, als door R. Zeeman [Un combat maritime ; excellente composition, peint avec vigueur] | *Mat:* op	Smidt	(Sold) fl 1:15 Gruiter

			paneel *Size:* hoog 22, breed 38 duim *Notes:* The French edition of the catalogue does not include an artist for this lot.		
1805/07/10	AMSCH	0195	*Zeeman* | Een Gevecht tusschen Oorlogscheepen op Zee; als door Zeeman | *Notes:* This lot was sold with lot 196 by an anonymous artist.	R[oos]	(Sold) fl 0:10 for lots 195 & 196. L Pakker
1806/08/13	AMSCH	0235	*Zeeman* | Een Zeegezicht met verscheide zeilende Oorlog- en andere Scheepen; krachtig geschilderd in de manier van Zeeman | *Mat:* op paneel	Roos	(Sold) fl 2:10 L Pakker
			Zegelaar, Gerrit		
1801/04/13	AMSCH	0095	*G. Zeegelaar* | Een Schoenlapper voor een Wynhuis staande, met een paar muilen in de hand; zeer uitvoerig gepenceeld | *Mat:* op paneel *Size:* hoog 10, breed 8 duim	Pierre Fouquet, junior	(Sold) fl 21 Reynders
1801/05/11	AMSCH	0118	*G. Zegelaar* | Op een Binnenplaats, ziet men een Kok, welke een steene schotel, waar Baars op geplaast is, in zyn hand heeft, nevens hem ziet men door een openstaande deur een ketel over 't vuur hangen, verders ziet men een pomp, waarop een vyzel, kandelaar en een kan geplaast is, nevens hem een komvoir, waarop een sous-pan, verders een menigte bywerk, alles zeer uitvoerig en van de fraaiste behandeling | *Mat:* op dun koper *Size:* hoog 10, breed 8 duim	V	(Sold) fl 43 Yver
1801/05/11	AMSCH	0119	*G. Zegelaar* | Voor een opgeschoven Raam, ziet men een Heer zyn pen versnyden, in alles niet minder als de vorige | *Mat:* op paneel *Size:* hoog 10, breed 9 duim	V	(Sold) fl 21 Gruiter
1802/05/05	AMSCH	0245	*Zeegelaar* | Twee stuks, het eene een Visboer, en het andere een Vrouwtje welke Uyens schoon maakt | *Mat:* op paneel *Size:* hoog 12, breed 10 duim	BB	(Sold) fl 30:10 Gruiter
1802/05/05	AMSCH	0246	*Zeegelaar* | Twee stuks, het eene verbeeld een vrolyke Boer met een Kan, en 't andere een Meisje met een Konyn in de hand, fiks gepenceeld | *Mat:* op paneel *Size:* hoog 11, breed 9 duim	BB	(Sold) fl 18:10 Gruiter
1802/05/05	AMSCH	0247	*Zeegelaar* | Een bevallige Vrouw	J	(Sold) fl 3:5 Schimmelpenning
1802/09/06	AMSCH	0138	*Zégelaar* | Een Historiëele Ordenantie; uitvoerig | *Mat:* op paneel *Size:* hoog 32, breed 29 duim	J	(Sold) fl 0:6 van Iperen
1803/12/12	AMSCH	0086	*G. Seegelaar* | Voor de deur van een Herberg staat een Hoy-Boer gereed zyn Pyp aantesteeken, houdende het Comvoirtje in de hand, en eenig Hooy onder den Arm, agter hem staat een Hooyvork tegen het Venster, daar nevens een Tafel waarop de Courant legt, en een Bierkan en Glas geplaast is; geestig geordoneerd, en alleruitvoerigst geschilderd | *Mat:* op paneel *Size:* hoog 9 ½, breed 8 duim	B	(Sold) fl 77 for lots 86 & 87. J Fokke
1803/12/12	AMSCH	0087	*G. Seegelaar* | Een bevallige Hooy-Boerin, staande meede voor de Muur van een Huis, dragende een Hooyvork op haar Schouder en een Net met Spek in haar andere hand; niet minder dan de voorige | *Mat:* op paneel *Size:* hoog 9 ½, breed 8 duim	B	(Sold) fl 77 for lots 86 & 87. J Fokke
1804/05/07	AMSCH	0200	*Zegelaar, (G.)* | Door een ryk geordoneerde Nis, ziet men in een Keuken een bevallige Meid. met twee dooden Vogels in haar hand, voor haar, op de kant van de Nis legt een dooden witte Haan, eenige Bloemkool en Wortelen, terzyde haar een Kok met een bak met Carbonaden in zyn handen, agter denzelven een Aanregtsbank met Keukengereedschappen, dit stukje is allerbevalligst en uitvoerig geschilderd | *Mat:* op paneel *Size:* hoog 16, breed 13 duim	Vinkeles [for] G	(Sold) fl 20 Salomon Joseph
1804/12/10	AMSCH	0102	*G. Zegelaar* | In een Modern vertrek ziet men een Dame kant werken, door een openstaande deur ziet men in de keuken, een dienstmaagd is bézig chocolaad gereed te maaken; alles is uitvoerig behandeld | *Mat:* op paneel *Size:* Hoog 16, breed 14 duim	Jan De Groot	(Sold) fl 10 Numan
1804/12/10	AMSCH	0103	*G. Zegelaar* | Voor een Opgeschooven raam ziet men een Heer met een blaauwe japon, hy is bézig een krytpen te scherpen, voor hem een portefuille, passer en tekenhaak, alles zeer fraai en krachtig gepenceeld | *Mat:* op paneel *Size:* Hoog 13, breed 11 duim	Jan De Groot	(Sold) fl 31 J Spaan
1809/06/13	AMSCH	0169	*G. Zegelaar* | Op de Stoep van een groot Gebouw, staat eene bevallig Meisje, houdende een Doos onder haar Arm, zij schijnd Mussen thuis te brengen; van de uitvoerigste schildering | *Mat:* op paneel *Size:* hoog 10, breed 8 duim	E	(Bought In) fl 21
1809/06/13	AMSCH	0170	*G. Zegelaar* | Voor een open Nis, staat eene Vrouwtje bij een Ton, bézig een Haring schoon te maken, voor haar op de rand ligt een groot Mes, eenige Haringen, benevens een Pot met Bloemen; als de voorgaande behandeld | *Mat:* op paneel *Size:* hoog 11, breed 8 ½ duim	E	(Sold) fl 50 Buck
1810/10/11	AMSCH	0107	*Zeegelaar* | Twee stuks, een vrolijke Man en Vrouw; geestig	V[ries]	(Sold) fl 1:15 van Dijl
			Zepp, Christian		
1809/04/22	AMYVR	0149	*C. Zepp* | Een Dorpgezicht; aartig gestoffeerd en uitvoerig gepenseelt | *Mat:* op doek *Size:* hoog 11, breed 14 duim	de Bruin	(Sold) fl 6:10 du Pree
1809/06/13	AMSCH	0171	*C. Zepp* | Twee stuks Hollandsche Landschappen, met Huismans Wooningen en Ruïnen, gestoffeerd met Boerenwagens, gaande Landlieden, met hun Vee, rustende Reisigers en bevallige verschieten; helder en zonachtig behandeld | *Mat:* op doek *Size:* ieder is hoog 19, breed 22 duim	R[ijfsnijder]	(Sold) fl 29 R[emmers] Bredius

1809/06/13	AMSCH	0172	*C. Zepp* | Een Duinachtig Landschap, ter zijde een groot Kasteel, gestoffeerd met gaande Huislieden, zonachtig | *Mat:* op doek *Size:* hoog 9, breed 11 duim	R[ijfsnijder]	(Sold) fl 1:15 Valee
1810/05/22	AMSCH	0129	*Zepp. (C.)* | Een aangenaam Landschap, met Woningen en Geboomten, gestoffeerd met Huislieden en verscheiden Vee, in 't verschiet eene grazige Weide; zonachtig behandeld | *Mat:* op paneel *Size:* hoog 11, breed 15 duim	Johannes van de Putte Nicolaasz.	(Sold) fl 7:15 Rinkhuizen
1810/05/22	AMSCH	0130	*Zepp. (C.)* | Een bevallig Landgezicht, op den voorgrond voor eene Herberg rustende en andere Lieden, ter zijde staande en rustende Beesten; als de voorgaande gepenceeld | *Mat:* op paneel *Size:* hoog 12, breed 16 duim	Johannes van de Putte Nicolaasz.	(Sold) fl 5 Grutte
			Zick, Januarius		
1803/09/07	AMSCH	0225	*J. Zieck* | In een Binnevertrek zitten eenige Boeren by een Ton te Rooken en te Drinken, kloek gepenceeld op Paneel [L'intérieur d'une chambre dans laquelle plusieurs paysans assis près d'une tonne, s'amusant à fumer et à boire ; peint avec beaucoup de vérité et au naturel] | *Mat:* op paneel *Size:* hoog 17, br 15 duim	Smidt	(Sold) fl 3:5 Vinkeles
1810/06/06	RMMUY	0080	*J. Zick* | Een Binnenhuis, waar in men eene Vrouw ziet koekenbakken, een staande Jongen met een koek in de hand daar bij, en een oud man op zijn stok leunende; in de manier van Rembrandt, meesterlijk behandeld | *Mat:* op paneel		(Unknown) fl 3
			Ziepe, A. van [Unidentified]		
1803/07/14	MGKLY	0021	*A. van Ziepe* | Twee Stuks, het een verbeeld, Arnenemuiden aan de Rivier, het ander Middelburg aan de Landzyde te van een oude datum	Mr Caspar Jacob van Citters	(Unknown)
			Zuccari, Federico		
1803/04/20	AMSCH	0100	*Zuccaro (F.)* | Deeze ryke Ordenantie vol gewoel, verbeeld geestelyke zinryke Voorwerpen, toepasselyk op het Oude en Nieuw Verbond, omhoog vertoont zig een Glorie van musiceerende Engelen, uitvoerig en fraay gepenceeld [Cette composition abondante est une allegorie sur l'ancien & le nouveau Testament : dans le haut est la gloire Celeste. Ce morceau de chevalet est très riche par la multitude de figures, il est d'une bonne couleur & très soigné pour l'execution.] | *Mat:* op koper *Size:* hoog 19, breed 27 duim	Maria Magdalena van Sluypwyk, gravinne van Moens	(Sold) fl 18 Pruijssenaar [for] R
			Zyl, Gerard Pietersz. van (changed from Gérard, M.)		
1806/08/13	AMSCH	0059	*Gerards. (M.); G P Zijl* | Dit bevallig Voorwerp, verbeeld een Musiceerend Gezelschap, voor een Buitenwoning, waar in twee Dames en vier Heeren, zig met Speel-Instrumenten en zingen vermaaken, zeer uitvoerig gepenceeld | *Mat:* op doek *Size:* hoog 16, breed 15 duim *Notes:* The artist's name was changed by hand from "Gerards. (M.)" to "G P Zijl" in the RKDH copy of the catalogue.	van der Voort	(Sold) fl 70 T Spaan
			Anonymous		
1801/02/18	AMBOS	0023	*[Anonymous]* | Een Basrelief met Kindertjes, in het grau geschilderd	J Schonevelt	(Unknown)
1801/02/18	AMBOS	0055	*[Anonymous]* | Een modern Vertrek, met een Gezelschap in hetzelve, aangenaam geschilderd	J Schonevelt	(Unknown)
1801/02/18	AMBOS	0057	*[Anonymous]* | Een stil Leven, verbeeldende een Citroen op een Tinne Bord en verder Bywerk, zeer natuurlyk geschilderd	J Schonevelt	(Unknown)
1801/02/18	AMBOS	0063	*[Anonymous]* | Een Bachinaal, fraay geschilderd	J Schonevelt	(Unknown)
1801/02/18	AMBOS	0065	*[Anonymous]* | Een Vrouw Koeken bakkende	J Schonevelt	(Unknown)
1801/02/18	AMBOS	0066	*[Anonymous]* | Een Ordonnantie met Bloemen in een Pot, staande op een Steene Voet	J Schonevelt	(Unknown)
1801/02/18	AMBOS	0067	*[Anonymous]* | Twee stuks, Laurens Koster benevens zyn Vrouw, zeer raar	J Schonevelt	(Unknown)
1801/02/18	AMBOS	0069	*[Anonymous]* | Een Hoofd met een Tulband, verbeeldende een Turk	J Schonevelt	(Unknown)
1801/02/18	AMBOS	0071	*[Anonymous]* | Twee stuks Vrouwen-Pourtraiten	J Schonevelt	(Unknown)
1801/02/18	AMBOS	0072	*[Anonymous]* | Twee stuks dito [Vrouwen Pourtraiten]	J Schonevelt	(Unknown)
1801/02/18	AMBOS	0073	*[Anonymous]* | Een Mans Hoofd	J Schonevelt	(Unknown)
1801/02/18	AMBOS	0076	*[Anonymous]* | Een Zeegezicht, zonder Lyst	J Schonevelt	(Unknown)
1801/02/18	AMBOS	0081	*[Anonymous]* | Drie stuks fyn geschilderde Landschapjes, in dito [in Lysten] met dito [met Glazen]	J Schonevelt	(Unknown)
1801/02/18	AMBOS	0082	*[Anonymous]* | Zeven stuks, divers	J Schonevelt	(Unknown)
1801/02/24	AMOTT	0001	*[Anonymous]* | 1 uitvoerig en plaisant geschilderd, Duël met Pistoolen, te Paard, by een Dorp, vol bywerk, in modieus gesneede vergulde Lyst		(Unknown)
1801/02/24	AMOTT	0002	*[Anonymous]* | Struikroovers op een heuvelachtige Heyden, als vooren [in modieus gesneede vergulde Lyst]		(Unknown)
1801/02/24	AMOTT	0003	*[Anonymous]* | 1 groot dito [Schildery?] van Krygslieden in wreede actie, by een Brug en Dorp, in dito [vergulde] Lyst		(Unknown)
1801/02/24	AMOTT	0008	*[Anonymous]* | 1 uitvoerig Zeetje		(Unknown)

1801/02/24	AMOTT	0009	*[Anonymous]* | Het gezigt op de oude Muiderpoort te Amsterdam		(Unknown)
1801/02/24	AMOTT	0010	*[Anonymous]* | 1 Stal van binnen te zien		(Unknown)
1801/02/24	AMOTT	0011	*[Anonymous]* | 1 mans Hoofd, in 't graauw, en een ander, 2 stuks		(Unknown)
1801/02/24	AMOTT	0012	*[Anonymous]* | 1 Leeman met zyn Voet		(Unknown)
1801/02/24	AMOTT	0013	*[Anonymous]* | 1 dito dito [Leeman] en dito [met zyn Voet]		(Unknown)
1801/02/24	AMOTT	0014	*[Anonymous]* | 3 diverse Schilderyen		(Unknown)
1801/02/24	AMOTT	0015	*[Anonymous]* | 3 dito [diverse] dito [Schilderyen]		(Unknown)
1801/02/24	AMOTT	0016	*[Anonymous]* | 1 modieus met papier beplakt Schoorsteenst.		(Unknown)
1801/02/24	AMOTT	0017	*[Anonymous]* | 't Pourtrait van Professor Curtenius, in Lyst met Glas		(Unknown)
1801/02/24	AMOTT	0018	*[Anonymous]* | 2 stuks, de verlooren Zoon op Glas | *Mat:* op glas		(Unknown)
1801/02/24	AMOTT	0019	*[Anonymous]* | 2 dito [stuks], van O.I. Riet gevlogten		(Unknown)
1801/03/16	AMSCH	0049	*[Anonymous]* | Een Mans Pourtraitje | *Notes:* This lot was sold with lot 48, which is a copy after A. Ostade.	Z	(Sold) fl 23 for lots 48 & 49. Stevens
1801/03/16	AMSCH	0063	*[Anonymous]* | Twee stuks bevallige Vrouw-Poutraite | *Notes:* This lot was sold with lot 62, which is in the manner of Balen.	P[ruyssenaar]	(Sold) fl 1:10 for lots 62 & 63. Gruiter
1801/03/16	AMSCH	0068	*Een goed Meester* | Een zinnebeeldige Ordonnantie op de geschille tusschen Gomarus en Arminus in den Jaare [1]619 bekend, door de prent naar 't stuk vervaardigd, onder den titil [sic] van de Politique Weegschaal door een goed Meester	P[ruyssenaar]	(Sold) fl 1:10 Roelofs
1801/03/16	AMSCH	0082	*Een oud Meester* | De Geboorte van Christus, door een oud Meester	P[ruyssenaar]	(Sold) fl 0:10 I^{c} Salomons
1801/03/16	AMSCH	0089	*[Anonymous]* | Twee diverse Poutraitten | *Notes:* This lot was sold with lot 88 by G. Grypmoed.	P[ruyssenaar]	(Sold) fl 1 for lots 88 & 89. Gruiter
1801/03/16	AMSCH	0090	*Een oud Meester* | Een capitaal Landschap, door een oud Meester	P[ruyssenaar]	(Sold) fl 0:10 Wijland
1801/03/16	AMSCH	0091	*[Anonymous]* | Twee stuks divers	P[ruyssenaar]	(Sold) fl 2 for lots 91 & 92. Wijland
1801/03/16	AMSCH	0092	*[Anonymous]* | Twee stuks dito [divers]	P[ruyssenaar]	(Sold) fl 2 for lots 91 & 92. Wijland
1801/03/16	AMSCH	0093	*[Anonymous]* | Twee stuks dito [divers]	P[ruyssenaar]	(Sold) fl 1 Van Iperen
1801/03/16	AMSCH	0124	*[Anonymous]* | Dartele Krygslieden in een Boere Woning zig met speelen en drinken vermakende, vol gewoel, en plaisant op doek geschilderd | *Mat:* op doek	K[ip]	(Sold) fl 9:10 Mensart
1801/03/16	AMSCH	0128	*Een goed Meester* | Een Krijgsheld in 't Harnas, uitvoerig op zilver geschilderd, door een goed Meester | *Mat:* op zilver	K[ip]	(Sold) fl 3:5 I^{c} Salomon
1801/03/16	AMSCH	0136	*[Anonymous]* | Een Binnehuis met Boeren	K[ip]	(Sold) fl 4:10 Roelofs
1801/03/16	AMSCH	0139	*Een goed Meester* | Een Landschap met Beesten, door een goed Meester	K[ip]	(Sold) fl 5:15 Stevens
1801/03/16	AMSCH	0144	*[Anonymous]* | Twee stuks, natuurlyke stille Leevens	K[ip]	(Sold) fl 1:10 Van Iperen
1801/03/16	AMSCH	0146	*Een oud Meester* | Twee stuks Bybelsche Ordonantien, door een oud Meester	K[ip]	(Sold) fl 1:10 Gruiter
1801/03/16	AMSCH	0148	*Een goed Meester* | Een Landschap met stoffagie van Paarden en Beelden, door een goed Meester	K[ip]	(Sold) fl 1 Valentijn
1801/03/16	AMSCH	0149	*Een goed Meester* | Een dito [Landschap] met Paarden, als voren [door een goed Meester]	K[ip]	(Sold) fl 2:5 Koopman
1801/03/16	AMSCH	0155	*Een goed Meester* | Een Gezelschap met Krygslieden en Vrouwen, door een goed Meester	K[ip]	(Sold) fl 12 J Yver
1801/03/16	AMSCH	0156	*[Anonymous]* | Twee stuks, gestoffeerde binnehuizen, fix behandeld	K[ip]	(Sold) fl 1:5 Wijland
1801/03/16	AMSCH	0158	*[Anonymous]* | Twee stuks, met Beelden en Beesten	K[ip]	(Sold) fl 8:5 Boelen
1801/03/16	AMSCH	0159	*[Anonymous]* | Twee stuks met Boeren	K[ip]	(Sold) fl 5:5 Koopman
1801/03/16	AMSCH	0160	*[Anonymous]* | Twee stuks, een Landschap, en een Watertje	K[ip]	(Sold) fl 1:5 Valentijn
1801/03/16	AMSCH	0169	*Een goed Meester* | Een Zee, door een goed Meester | *Notes:* This lot was sold with lot 168 by T. Wyck.	P[ruyssenaar]	(Sold) fl 0:12 for lots 168 & 169. Gruiter
1801/03/16	AMSCH	0189	*[Anonymous]* | Twee stuks oude Manshoofden met baarden: als in Oostersche kleeding, fiks geschilderd, op paneel | *Mat:* op paneel	K[ip]	(Sold) fl 1:5 Roelofs
1801/03/16	AMSCH	0191	*[Anonymous]* | Een zittende naakte Vrouw, by een Rotz gezigt, en Waterval, fiks op paneel geschilderd | *Mat:* op paneel *Notes:* This lot was sold with lot 192, which is in the manner of S. Vlieger.	K[ip]	(Sold) fl 1:5 for lots 191 & 192. Roelofs
1801/03/16	AMSCH	0193	*[Anonymous]* | By een Boerenwoning, zit een Bedelaar en een Jongen, waar by een staand Landman, fiks op paneel geschilderd | *Mat:* op paneel	K[ip]	(Sold) fl 25 Rijnders
1801/03/16	AMSCH	0195	*[Anonymous]* | Twee stuks gestoffeerde Landschappen, plaisant geschilderd, op paneel | *Mat:* op paneel	K[ip]	(Sold) fl 1:5 Boelen
1801/03/16	AMSCH	0198	*[Anonymous]* | Een woelend Water, gestoffeerd met verscheide zeilende Scheepen, en andere Vaartuigen, meesterlyk geschilderd op doek | *Mat:* op doek	K[ip]	(Sold) fl 2:5 Roelofs

1801/03/16	AMSCH	0201	*[Anonymous]* | Twee stuks Binnenhuizen met verscheide Landlieden, plaisant geschilderd	K[ip]	(Sold) fl 1 van Iperen
1801/03/16	AMSCH	0205	*Een goed Meester* | Eenige vrolyke drinkende en rokende Boeren, door een goed Meester	K[ip]	(Sold) fl 3:10 Koopman
1801/03/16	AMSCH	0206	*[Anonymous]* | Een Landschap met Beelden en Beesten	K[ip]	(Sold) fl 5:10 for lots 206 & 207. Wijland
1801/03/16	AMSCH	0207	*[Anonymous]* | Een stil water met Schepen en Schuiten	K[ip]	(Sold) fl 5:10 for lots 206 & 207. Wijland
1801/03/16	AMSCH	0208	*[Anonymous]* | Een naakte Venus, en een Binnehuis	K[ip]	(Sold) fl 1:10 Veldwijk
1801/03/16	AMSCH	0213	*[Anonymous]* | Een gestoffeerd Landschap, en een Binnenhuis	S[chley]	(Sold) fl 4:5 Stevens
1801/03/16	AMSCH	0214	*[Anonymous]* | Twee dito [gestoffeerde] dito [Landschappen], en een met Vogels	S[chley]	(Sold) fl 2:10 Coclers
1801/03/16	AMSCH	0215	*[Anonymous]* | Twee stuks klyne gestoffeerde Landschapjes	S[chley]	(Sold) fl 2:10 Stevens
1801/03/16	AMSCH	0216	*[Anonymous]* | Vyf stuks gestoffeerde Binnehuizen	S[chley]	(Sold) fl 1:10 Gruiter
1801/03/16	AMSCH	0217[H]	*[Anonymous]* | [Untitled] | *Notes:* This lot was added in by hand in the EBNP, LBDa and RKDH copies of the catalogue, but without giving an artist or title.	S[chley]	(Sold) fl 5 Pruijsenaar [for] L
1801/03/16	AMSCH	0218[H]	*[Anonymous]* | [Untitled] | *Notes:* This lot was added in by hand in the EBNP, LBDa and RKDH copies of the catalogue, but without giving an artist or title.	S[chley]	(Sold) fl 2:5 v d Berg
1801/03/16	AMSCH	0219[H]	*[Anonymous]* | [Untitled] | *Notes:* This lot was added in by hand in the EBNP, LBDa and RKDH copies of the catalogue, but without giving an artist or title.	S[chley]	(Sold) fl 18 Cocler
1801/03/16	AMSCH	0219a[H]	*[Anonymous]* | [Untitled] | *Notes:* This lot was added in by hand in the EBNP, LBDa and RKDH copies of the catalogue, but without giving an artist or title.	P[ruyssenaar]	(Sold) fl 2:5 Stevens
1801/03/16	AMSCH	0220[H]	*[Anonymous]* | [Untitled] | *Notes:* This lot was added in by hand in the EBNP, LBDa and RKDH copies of the catalogue, but without giving an artist or title.	R[oos]	(Sold) fl 1:10 Clement
1801/03/16	AMSCH	0221[H]	*[Anonymous]* | [Untitled] | *Notes:* This lot was added in by hand in the EBNP, LBDa and RKDH copies of the catalogue, but without giving an artist or title.	R[oos]	(Sold) fl 59 Cocler
1801/03/16	AMSCH	0222[H]	*[Anonymous]* | [Untitled] | *Notes:* This lot was added in by hand in the EBNP, LBDa and RKDH copies of the catalogue, but without giving an artist or title.	R[oos]	(Sold) fl 21 Pruijsenaar [for] R
1801/03/16	AMSCH	0223[H]	*[Anonymous]* | [Untitled] | *Notes:* This lot was added in by hand in the EBNP, LBDa and RKDH copies of the catalogue, but without giving an artist or title.	R[oos]	(Sold) fl 15:10 Gruiter
1801/03/16	AMSCH	0224[H]	*[Anonymous]* | [Untitled] | *Notes:* This lot was added in by hand in the EBNP, LBDa and RKDH copies of the catalogue, but without giving an artist or title.	R[oos]	(Sold or Bought In) fl 6:10 Roos
1801/03/16	AMSCH	0225[H]	*[Anonymous]* | [Untitled] | *Notes:* This lot was added in by hand in the EBNP, LBDa and RKDH copies of the catalogue, but without giving an artist or title.	R[oos]	(Sold) fl 1:10 Gruiter
1801/03/16	AMSCH	0226[H]	*[Anonymous]* | [Untitled] | *Notes:* This lot was added in by hand in the EBNP, LBDa and RKDH copies of the catalogue, but without giving an artist or title.	R[oos]	(Sold) fl 1:5 Boelen
1801/03/16	AMSCH	0227[H]	*[Anonymous]* | [Untitled] | *Notes:* This lot was added in by hand in the EBNP, LBDa and RKDH copies of the catalogue, but without giving an artist or title.	P[ruyssenaar]	(Sold) fl 11 v d Schley [for] S
1801/03/16	AMSCH	0228[H]	*[Anonymous]* | [Untitled] | *Notes:* This lot was added in by hand in the EBNP, LBDa and RKDH copies of the catalogue, but without giving an artist or title.	P[ruyssenaar]	(Bought In) fl 15
1801/03/16	AMSCH	0229[H]	*[Anonymous]* | [Untitled] | *Notes:* This lot was added in by hand in the EBNP, LBDa and RKDH copies of the catalogue, but without giving an artist or title.	P[ruyssenaar]	(Bought In) fl 10 ½
1801/03/16	AMSCH	0230[H]	*[Anonymous]* | [Untitled] | *Notes:* This lot was added in by hand in the EBNP, LBDa and RKDH copies of the catalogue, but without giving an artist or title.	P[ruyssenaar]	(Sold) fl 1:10 Wijland
1801/03/16	AMSCH	0231[H]	*[Anonymous]* | [Untitled] | *Notes:* This lot was added in by hand in the EBNP, LBDa and RKDH copies of the catalogue, but without giving an artist or title.	S[chley]	(Sold) fl 41 v d Schley [for] A
1801/03/31	HGCLF	0378	*[Anonymous]* | Een stuk in Oliverf, verbeeldende een mande met bloemen in een swarte lyst | *Mat:* in olyverf	H van der Hoop	(Unknown) fl 0:6
1801/03/31	HGCLF	0379	*[Anonymous]* | Een dito [stuk] met eenige danssende Boeren en Boerinnen, in een dito [swarte] lyst	H van der Hoop	(Unknown) fl 1:12
1801/03/31	HGCLF	0380	*[Anonymous]* | Twee dito [stuks] zynde Watertjes met Scheepen &c. in dito [swarte] lyste met vergulde binne randen	H van der Hoop	(Unknown) fl 2:14

1801/03/31	HGCLF	0383	*[Anonymous]* | Een Linnewever met verder bywerk in een swarte lyst en vergulde binne rand	H van der Hoop	(Sold) fl 5:10 La Bolichere
1801/03/31	HGCLF	0389	*[Anonymous]* | Twee Pourtraiten in 't ovaal, op koper in dito [swarte] lysten | *Mat:* op koper *Fmt:* ovaal	H van der Hoop	(Sold) fl 1:8 Brender [?]
1801/03/31	HGCLF	0390	*[Anonymous]* | Een Boerestukje, en twee Pourtraitten in 't koper, in swarte lysten | *Mat:* op koper	H van der Hoop	(Sold) fl 3:5 Leenhof
1801/04/08	HAVIN	0005	*[Anonymous]* | Een buitenhuis alwaar door een Vrouw eenige Hoenders en Duiven gevoert worden, uitvoerig door		(Unknown)
1801/04/08	HAVIN	0040	*[Anonymous]* | Een Tafel met vrugten en een Kat, door		(Unknown)
1801/04/08	HAVIN	0047	*[Anonymous]* | Twee met Bloemen fraai en uitvoerig door		(Unknown)
1801/04/08	HAVIN	0048	*[Anonymous]* | Twee de eene met een Roemer in de Hand de andere met een Lier by een Jongen meesterlyk door		(Unknown)
1801/04/08	HAVIN	0058	*[Anonymous]* | Een Manshoofd met een lange Baard fix geschilderd		(Unknown)
1801/04/08	HAVIN	0066	*[Anonymous]* | Een Bloemstuk		(Unknown)
1801/04/08	HAVIN	0067	*[Anonymous]* | N. Bodding en Vrouw. Zyn Pourrrait gaat in prent uit, door Suiderhoef		(Unknown)
1801/04/08	HAVIN	0072	*[Anonymous]* | Een Landsch. met Antieque [sic] gebouwen		(Unknown)
1801/04/08	HAVIN	0074	*[Anonymous]* | Een Landsch. met een Man die een Meisje Liefkoost, door		(Unknown)
1801/04/08	HAVIN	0075	*[Anonymous]* | Twee Zingende en Speelende Gezelschappen		(Unknown)
1801/04/08	HAVIN	0076	*[Anonymous]* | Een gezigt in 't Gyn, fraai met Goud op Glas | *Mat:* goud op glas		(Unknown)
1801/04/08	HAVIN	0077	*[Anonymous]* | Een dito [gezigt] zynde een Landsch. op de voorgrond een Jager | *Notes:* It is unclear what "dito" refers to in the title.		(Unknown)
1801/04/13	AMSCH	0098	*Onbekend Meester* | Een jonger dito [Vrouw], op een stoel zittende, met een kraag om den hals; mede kragtig behandeld | *Mat:* op doek *Size:* hoog 39, breed 31 duim	Pierre Fouquet, junior	(Sold) fl 24:10 C S Roos
1801/04/13	AMSCH	0099	*Onbekend Meester* | Twee geestelyke Personen; meesterlyk, op Paneel | *Mat:* op paneel *Size:* hoog 24, breed 19 duim	Pierre Fouquet, junior	(Sold) fl 5 Mensard
1801/04/13	AMSCH	0101	*Onbekend Meester* | De Verleiding van Adam en Eva in het Paradys; meesterlyk geschilderd, op Doek | companion to lot 102 *Mat:* op doek *Size:* hoog 46, breed 59 duim	Pierre Fouquet, junior	(Sold) fl 24:10 for lots 101 & 102. C S Roos
1801/04/13	AMSCH	0102	*Onbekend Meester* | Abel dood ter aarde liggende; zynde een wederga van de voorgaande, door denzelven Meester, en van gelyke groote | companion to lot 101 *Mat:* op doek *Size:* hoog 46, breed 59 duim	Pierre Fouquet, junior	(Sold) fl 24:10 for lots 101 & 102. C S Roos
1801/04/13	AMSCH	0105	*Onbekend Meester* | De Graflegging van Christus by toortslicht, verzeld van een menigte beelden, uitvoerig op Koper, door een goed Meester | *Mat:* op koper *Size:* hoog 10, breed 8 duim	Pierre Fouquet, junior	(Sold) fl 37 Coclers
1801/04/22	HGDAW	0001	*[Anonymous]* | Un Tableau Represant un Cordonnier peint sur verre avec un beau cadre d'or | *Mat:* sur verre		(Unknown)
1801/04/22	HGDAW	0002	*[Anonymous]* | Un Tableau Representant un remouleur peint sur Verre avec un beau cadre d'or | *Mat:* sur verre		(Unknown)
1801/04/22	HGDAW	0003	*[Anonymous]* | Dix Paysages Italiens Encadrés sous Verre		(Unknown)
1801/04/22	HGDAW	0010	*[Anonymous]* | Tableau Representant une Vache Couchée tres beau morceau		(Unknown)
1801/04/23	AMYVR	0037[b]	*[Anonymous]* | Een Alchimist in de manier van T. Wyck, en een Spinnend Vrouwtje | *This Lot:* Een Spinnend Vrouwtje; lot 37[a] is manner of T. Wyck		(Unknown)
1801/04/23	AMYVR	0038	*[Anonymous]* | Twee stuks, een Man met een Haan, op Koper geschilderd, en een Vrouwenpourtrait | *Mat:* op koper		(Sold) fl 6 ¼ van Hemert [?]
1801/04/23	AMYVR	0041	*[Anonymous]* | Twee stuks, een Kermisvreugd en een Landschapje, uitvoerig geschilderd		(Sold) fl 1 ¼ [?] Iver
1801/04/23	AMYVR	0043	*[Anonymous]* | Twee stuks Binnevertrekken in het eene zit een Vrouwtje Kant te werken en in het ander te naaijen, verseld van hunne Hondjes, op Paneel | *Mat:* op paneel		(Sold) fl 3 Jourdany
1801/04/23	AMYVR	0045	*[Anonymous]* | Twee stuks, een Zeegezicht, met Scheepen, met een Stad in het verschiet en een Landschap op Doek | *Mat:* op doek		(Unknown) fl 1 for lots 45 & 46
1801/04/23	AMYVR	0046	*[Anonymous]* | Twee stuks Bloemstukken en een zittend Kindje, te samen 3 stuks		(Unknown) fl 1 for lots 45 & 46
1801/04/23	AMYVR	0049	*[Anonymous]* | 6 diverse Schilderyën		(Unknown) fl 1 for lots 49 & 50
1801/04/23	AMYVR	0050	*[Anonymous]* | Eenige dito [diverse] dito [Schilderyën]		(Unknown) fl 1 for lots 49 & 50
1801/04/23	AMYVR	0051	*[Anonymous]* | Eenige dito [diverse] dito [Schilderyën]		(Withdrawn [?])
1801/04/23	AMYVR	0052	*[Anonymous]* | Eenige dito [diverse] dito [Schilderyën]		(Withdrawn [?])
1801/04/23	AMYVR	0053	*[Anonymous]* | 8 stuks Schilderyën		(Unknown) fl 1 for lots 53 & 54

1801/04/23	AMYVR	0054	*[Anonymous]* | 1 Pourtret en eenige Lysten met Glazen		(Unknown) fl 1 for lots 53 & 54
1801/04/23	AMYVR	0058	*[Anonymous]* | 't Pourtret van Kapt. Bentinck		(Unknown)
1801/04/23	AMYVR	0059	*[Anonymous]* | 1 dito [Pourtret] van den Ridder Kingsbergen		(Unknown)
1801/04/23	AMYVR	0060	*[Anonymous]* | 1 dito [Pourtret] van Do. [Ridder] Noordbeek en van Do. [Ridder] van den Broek		(Sold) fl 11 Gruyter
1801/05/11	AMSCH	0122	*Onbekend* | In een Boere binnewoning, zit een huisgezin van Mannen, Vrouw en Kind by een gedekte tafel met spys, als biddende; bevallig geschilderd | *Mat:* op paneel *Size:* hoog 12 ½, breed 9 ½ duim	E[lias]	(Sold) fl 6 Allard
1801/05/11	AMSCH	0123	*Onbekend* | Een heuvelachtig Landschap, gestoffeerd met verscheide Landhuizen en Vee, fix geschildert, op Paneel | *Mat:* op paneel *Size:* hoog 13, breed 17 duim *Notes:* This lot was sold with lot 124[a], which is in the manner of A. Neer.	E[lias]	(Sold) fl 4:15 for lots 123, 124[a] & 124[b]. Allard
1801/05/11	AMSCH	0124[b]	*Onbekend* | Twee stuks, een in de manier van A. van der Neer, en een ander | *This Lot:* Een ander stuk; lot 124[a] is manner of A. Neer	E[lias]	(Sold) fl 4:15 for lots 123, 124[a] & 124[b]. Allard
1801/05/11	AMSCH	0125	*[Anonymous]* | Een Landschap met hoog geboomte, doorsneede van een stil water, en met beeldjes gestoffeerd	E[lias]	(Sold) fl 3 Bendiks
1801/05/11	AMSCH	0126	*[Anonymous]* | Een Vanitas, toepasselyk op de vergankelykheid, meesterlyk en fix geschilderd	E[lias]	(Sold) fl 0:18 Coclers
1801/05/11	AMSCH	0127[b]	*Onbekend* | Twee stuks Landschappen, een in de manier van van Gooyen, en een ander | *This Lot:* Een Landschap; lot 127[a] is manner of Goyen	E[lias]	(Sold) fl 2:15 for lots 127[a] & 127[b]. Coclers
1801/05/11	AMSCH	0128	*[Anonymous]* | Twee stuks dito [Landschappen], het eene verbeeld de Wynoogst, en het ander een Noords Landschap	E[lias]	(Sold) fl 4:10 Boelen
1801/05/11	AMSCH	0129[b]	*Onbekend* | Twee stuks, een kabbelend Water, getekend I B, en het ander eenig dood Wild | *This Lot:* Eenig dood Wild; lot 129[a] by Monogrammist I.B.	E[lias]	(Sold) fl 1 for lots 129[a] & 129[b]. Coclers
1801/05/11	AMSCH	0130[H]	*[Anonymous]* | 1 Schiderij | *Notes:* This lot was added in by hand in the EBNP, FLNY and RKDH copies of the catalogue.	E[lias]	(Sold) fl 6 Allard
1801/05/11	AMSCH	0131[H]	*[Anonymous]* | 1 dito [Schiderij] | *Notes:* This lot was added in by hand in the EBNP, FLNY and RKDH copies of the catalogue.	P[ruyssenaar]	(Sold) fl 1:10 Gruiter
1801/05/11	AMSCH	0132[H]	*[Anonymous]* | 1 dito [Schiderij] | *Notes:* This lot was added in by hand in the EBNP, FLNY and RKDH copies of the catalogue.	S[chley]	(Sold) fl 34 Rijnders [and] v d Vinne
1801/05/11	AMSCH	0133[H]	*[Anonymous]* | 1 dito [Schiderij] | *Notes:* This lot was added in by hand in the EBNP, FLNY and RKDH copies of the catalogue.	S[chley]	(Bought In) fl 15
1801/05/11	AMSCH	0134[H]	*[Anonymous]* | 1 dito [Schiderij] | *Notes:* This lot was added in by hand in the EBNP, FLNY and RKDH copies of the catalogue.	S[chley]	(Bought In) fl 30
1801/05/11	AMSCH	0135[H]	*[Anonymous]* | 1 dito [Schiderij] | *Notes:* This lot was added in by hand in the EBNP, FLNY and RKDH copies of the catalogue.	P[ruyssenaar]	(Sold) fl 0:10 Cocler
1801/05/11	AMSCH	0136[H]	*[Anonymous]* | 1 dito [Schiderij] | *Notes:* This lot was added in by hand in the EBNP, FLNY and RKDH copies of the catalogue.	R[oos]	(Sold) fl 7:10 Allard
1801/05/11	AMSCH	0137[H]	*[Anonymous]* | 1 dito [Schiderij] | *Notes:* This lot was added in by hand in the EBNP, FLNY and RKDH copies of the catalogue.	R[oos]	(Sold) fl 0:8 Gruiter
1801/05/11	AMSCH	0138[H]	*[Anonymous]* | 1 dito [Schiderij] | *Notes:* This lot was added in by hand in the EBNP, FLNY and RKDH copies of the catalogue.	R[oos]	(Sold) fl 13:10 J Spaan
1801/05/11	AMSCH	0139[H]	*[Anonymous]* | 1 dito [Schiderij] | *Notes:* This lot was added in by hand in the EBNP, FLNY and RKDH copies of the catalogue.	R[oos]	(Sold) fl 3:15 Cocler
1801/05/11	AMSCH	0140[H]	*[Anonymous]* | 2 dito [Schilderijen] | *Notes:* This lot was added in by hand in the EBNP, FLNY and RKDH copies of the catalogue.	R[oos]	(Sold) fl 0:18 Boelen
1801/05/11	AMSCH	0141[H]	*[Anonymous]* | 1 dito [Schilderij] | *Notes:* This lot was added in by hand in the EBNP, FLNY and RKDH copies of the catalogue.	R[oos]	(Sold) fl 20 Allard
1801/05/11	AMSCH	0142[H]	*[Anonymous]* | 1 dito [Schilderij] | *Notes:* This lot was added in by hand in the EBNP, FLNY and RKDH copies of the catalogue.	R[oos]	(Sold) fl 10:10 van Iperen
1801/05/11	AMSCH	0143[H]	*[Anonymous]* | 2 dito [Schilderijen] | *Notes:* This lot was added in by hand in the EBNP, FLNY and RKDH copies of the catalogue.	R[oos]	(Sold) fl 26 v d Schley [for] M[errem]
1801/05/11	AMSCH	0144[H]	*[Anonymous]* | 1 dito [Schilderij] | *Notes:* This lot was added in by hand in the EBNP, FLNY and RKDH copies of the catalogue.	R[oos]	(Sold) fl 2:15 Allard
1801/05/11	AMSCH	0145[H]	*[Anonymous]* | 1 dito [Schilderij] | *Notes:* This lot was added in by hand in the EBNP, FLNY and RKDH copies of the catalogue.	R[oos]	(Sold) fl 1:10 P M Levij
1801/05/11	AMSCH	0146[H]	*[Anonymous]* | 2 dito [Schilderijen] | *Notes:* This lot was added in by hand in the EBNP, FLNY and RKDH copies of the catalogue.	R[oos]	(Sold) fl 28 Allard
1801/05/11	AMSCH	0147[H]	*[Anonymous]* | 1 dito [Schilderij] | *Notes:* This lot was added in by hand in the EBNP, FLNY and RKDH copies of the catalogue.	R[oos]	(Sold) fl 34:10 Th[s] Spaan
1801/05/11	AMSCH	0148[H]	*[Anonymous]* | 1 dito [Schilderij] | *Notes:* This lot was added in by hand in the EBNP, FLNY and RKDH copies of the catalogue.	R[oos]	(Sold) fl 1:15 Boelen
1801/05/11	AMSCH	0149[H]	*[Anonymous]* | 1 dito [Schilderij] | *Notes:* This lot was added in by hand in the EBNP, FLNY and RKDH copies of the catalogue.	R[oos]	(Sold) fl 92 Van Iperen

1801/05/11	AMSCH	0150[H]	*[Anonymous]* | 1 dito [Schilderij] | *Notes:* This lot was added in by hand in the EBNP, FLNY and RKDH copies of the catalogue.	R[oos]	(Sold) fl 41 Allard
1801/05/11	AMSCH	0151[H]	*[Anonymous]* | 1 dito [Schilderij] | *Notes:* This lot was added in by hand in the EBNP, FLNY and RKDH copies of the catalogue.	R[oos]	(Sold) fl 11:10 Jan Spaan
1801/05/11	AMSCH	0152[H]	*[Anonymous]* | 1 dito [Schilderij] | *Notes:* This lot was added in by hand in the EBNP, FLNY and RKDH copies of the catalogue.	R[oos]	(Sold) fl 1 Ipé
1801/05/11	AMSCH	0153[H]	*[Anonymous]* | 2 Schilderijen | *Notes:* This lot was added in by hand in the EBNP, FLNY and RKDH copies of the catalogue.	R[oos]	(Sold) fl 53 Josi
1801/05/11	AMSCH	0154[H]	*[Anonymous]* | 1 dito [Schilderij] | *Notes:* This lot was added in by hand in the EBNP, FLNY and RKDH copies of the catalogue.	R[oos]	(Sold) fl 42:10 J Spaan
1801/05/11	AMSCH	0155[H]	*[Anonymous]* | 2 dito [Schilderijen] | *Notes:* This lot was added in by hand in the EBNP, FLNY and RKDH copies of the catalogue.	R[oos]	(Sold) fl 6:15 Bendiks
1801/05/11	AMSCH	0156[H]	*[Anonymous]* | 2 dito [Schilderijen] | *Notes:* This lot was added in by hand in the EBNP, FLNY and RKDH copies of the catalogue.	R[oos]	(Sold) fl 6:10 v der Vinne
1801/05/11	AMSCH	0157[H]	*[Anonymous]* | 1 dito [Schilderij] | *Notes:* This lot was added in by hand in the EBNP, FLNY and RKDH copies of the catalogue.	R[oos]	(Sold) fl 19 Allard
1801/05/11	AMSCH	0158[H]	*[Anonymous]* | 1 dito [Schilderij] | *Notes:* This lot was added in by hand in the EBNP, FLNY and RKDH copies of the catalogue.	R[oos]	(Sold) fl 42:10 Rijnders
1801/05/11	AMSCH	0159[H]	*[Anonymous]* | 1 dito [Schilderij] | *Notes:* This lot was added in by hand in the EBNP, FLNY and RKDH copies of the catalogue.	R[oos]	(Sold) fl 40 Allard
1801/05/11	AMSCH	0160[H]	*[Anonymous]* | 1 dito [Schilderij] | *Notes:* This lot was added in by hand in the EBNP, FLNY and RKDH copies of the catalogue.	S[chley]	(Sold) fl 1:5 Bendiks
1801/05/11	AMSCH	0161[H]	*[Anonymous]* | 1 dito [Schilderij] | *Notes:* This lot was added in by hand in the EBNP, FLNY and RKDH copies of the catalogue.	S[chley]	(Sold) fl 3 Mensard
1801/05/11	AMSCH	0162[H]	*[Anonymous]* | 1 dito [Schilderij] | *Notes:* This lot was added in by hand in the EBNP, FLNY and RKDH copies of the catalogue.	S[chley]	(Sold) fl 2:5 Bendiks
1801/05/11	AMSCH	0163[H]	*[Anonymous]* | 1 dito [Schilderij] | *Notes:* This lot was added in by hand in the EBNP, FLNY and RKDH copies of the catalogue.	S[chley]	(Sold) fl 17:10 Pruijssenaar [for] R
1801/05/11	AMSCH	0164[H]	*[Anonymous]* | 1 dito [Schilderij] | *Notes:* This lot was added in by hand in the EBNP, FLNY and RKDH copies of the catalogue.	S[chley]	(Sold) fl 1:10 van Iperen
1801/05/11	AMSCH	0165[H]	*[Anonymous]* | 1 dito [Schilderij] | *Notes:* This lot was added in by hand in the EBNP, FLNY and RKDH copies of the catalogue.	S[chley]	(Sold) fl 1:10 Pruijssenaar [for] R
1801/05/11	AMSCH	0166[H]	*[Anonymous]* | 1 dito [Schilderij] | *Notes:* This lot was added in by hand in the EBNP, FLNY and RKDH copies of the catalogue.		(Sold) fl 0:8 van Iperen
1801/05/11	AMSCH	0167[H]	*[Anonymous]* | 1 dito [Schilderij] | *Notes:* This lot was added in by hand in the EBNP, FLNY and RKDH copies of the catalogue.		(Sold) fl 0:2 van Iperen
1801/06/10	AMSCH	0205	*Onbekend* | Een peinsende Vrouw op haar arm rustende, meesterlyk op Doek | *Annots:* [door] Jan Bronkhorst (BRB) *Mat:* op doek *Size:* hoog 30, breed 25 duim	Herman ten Kate	(Sold) fl 5:5 Camphuysen
1801/06/10	AMSCH	0206	*Onbekend* | Een zinspelende Ordonantie, meesterlyk op Paneel | *Mat:* op paneel *Size:* hoog 20, breed 16 duim	Herman ten Kate	(Sold) fl 8:10 Stevens
1801/06/10	AMSCH	0208	*Onbekend* | Meleager en Athelanthe, in een Landschap, meesterlyk op Koper | *Mat:* op koper *Size:* hoog 9, breed 11 duim	Herman ten Kate	(Sold) fl 27:10 Spruit van Gend
1801/06/10	AMSCH	0209	*Onbekend* | Een Mans Pourtrait, meesterlyk gepenceeld	Herman ten Kate	(Sold) fl 14:10 Hulswit
1801/06/10	AMSCH	0210	*Onbekend* | Een Zeestrand, op de voorgrond drie Visschers met een menigte Visschen, natuurlyk bewerkt, op Doek | *Mat:* op doek *Size:* hoog 70, breed 112 duim	Herman ten Kate	(Sold) fl 10:10 C S Roos
1801/06/10	AMSCH	0211	*Onbekend* | Een Dorpgezicht alwaar men Kermis houd, gestoffeerd met dansende en drinkende Beelden; fiks en bevallig gepenceeld op Paneel | *Mat:* op paneel *Size:* hoog 9, breed 13 duim	[Doublet]	(Sold) fl 25 Reynders
1801/06/13	LNDLS	0015	*[Anonymous]* | Een dito [Gezicht langs een Vaarwater], ter rechterzijde een menigte aanschouwers, bij een Kwakzalver, ter linkerzijde een bergagtig gezicht, en water met vaartuigen, niet minder uitvoerig en konstig | *Mat:* op paneel *Size:* hoog 14, breed 19 duimen	D van R	(Sold) fl 50 Versteeg
1801/06/13	LNDLS	0035	*[Anonymous]* | Een woelend Water, met zeilende Schepen, op paneel | *Mat:* op paneel *Size:* hoog 8, breed 9 duimen	D van R	(Sold) fl 9:5 Richter S [for] Stevens
1801/06/13	LNDLS	0036	*[Anonymous]* | Een Portrait van J. Secundus	D van R	(Sold) fl 1 for lots 36 & 37. A Delfos
1801/06/13	LNDLS	0036a[H]	*[Anonymous]* | [Untitled] | *Notes:* This lot was added in by hand in the RKDH copy of the catalogue, but without giving an artist or title.	D van R	(Sold) fl 2:6 for lots 36a[H] & 36b[H]. Beck
1801/06/13	LNDLS	0036b[H]	*[Anonymous]* | [Untitled] | *Notes:* This lot was added in by hand in the RKDH copy of the catalogue, but without giving an artist or title.	D van R	(Sold) fl 2:6 for lots 36a[H] & 36b[H]. Beck
1801/06/13	LNDLS	0036c[H]	*[Anonymous]* | [Untitled] | *Notes:* This lot was added in by hand in the RKDH copy of the catalogue, but without giving an artist or title.	D van R	(Sold) fl 1:12 A Delfos
1801/06/13	LNDLS	0037	*[Anonymous]* | Een Portrait van J. Lipsius	D van R	(Sold) fl 1 for lots 36 & 37. A Delfos

1801/06/13	LNDLS	0038	*Een Oud Meester* | Een Heremiet, op paneel, door een Oud Meester | *Mat:* op paneel	D van R	(Sold) fl 0:14 Bryan
1801/06/13	LNDLS	0052	*[Anonymous]* | Een Gezicht in 's Hage, daar speellieden met honden en aapen voor een deftig huis, bij eene dame met haar kinderen speelen, zeer plaizant, op paneel | *Mat:* op paneel *Size:* hoog 13, breed 16 duimen	D van R	(Sold) fl 10 Reyers
1801/06/13	LNDLS	0059	*Een voornaam Meester* | Een biddende Magdalena, voor een boek en kruis, konstig en krachtig op doek, door een voornaam Meester | *Mat:* op doek *Size:* hoog 27, breed 20 duimen	D van R	(Sold) fl 13:10 de Marree
1801/06/13	LNDLS	0061	*[Anonymous]* | Twee Stuks, een Buiten- en een Binnenhuis, met aartige beeldjes, uitvoerig behandelt, op paneel | *Mat:* op paneel *Size:* hoog 12, breed 9 ½ duimen	D van R	(Sold) fl 9 Reyers
1801/06/13	LNDLS	0063	*[Anonymous]* | Twee Stuks Landschappen, met gaande en rustende beelden en beesten, uitvoerig, op paneel | *Mat:* op paneel *Size:* hoog 11, breed 13 duimen	D van R	(Sold) fl 13:10 Richter G [for] v Giezen
1801/06/13	LNDLS	0064	*Een voornaam Meester* | Simpson, voor de schoot van Delila, konstig, op paneel, door een voornaam Meester | *Mat:* op paneel *Size:* hoog 14, breed 11 duimen	D van R	(Sold) fl 9:5 Thyes
1801/06/13	LNDLS	0066	*[Anonymous]* | Een met Gebouwen op een hoogte, en andere langs een water met schepen	D van R	(Sold) fl 3:2 Rigter
1801/06/13	LNDLS	0069	*Een voornaam Meester* | Maria met het Kind staande op haar Schoot, verzeld van eenige Engelen in een Landschap, op doek, door een voornaam Meester | *Mat:* op doek	D van R	(Sold) fl 10:10 A Delfos
1801/06/13	LNDLS	0070	*[Anonymous]* | Een Man, die een brief leest, levensgroote, halverlijf	D van R	(Sold) fl 5:5 Swart
1801/06/13	LNDLS	0071	*[Anonymous]* | Prins Willem den Eersten, zijnde een kniestuk	D van R	(Sold) fl 0:5 Thomasse
1801/06/13	LNDLS	0072	*[Anonymous]* | Een Historieele, met levensgroote beelden	D van R	(Sold) fl 4:2 de Marree
1801/06/13	LNDLS	0075	*Een goed Meester* | Zeilende Jagten en Schepen, door een goed Meester	D van R	(Sold) fl 0:14 Richter [for] G[iezen]
1801/06/13	LNDLS	0079	*[Anonymous]* | Octavus Angelia Rex | *Notes:* This lot was sold with lot 80, which is in the manner of Goyen.	D van R	(Sold) fl 0:8 for lots 79 & 80. Richter
1801/06/13	LNDLS	0081	*[Anonymous]* | Een Geestelijke, halverlijf, door een vooanaam [sic] Meester	D van R	(Sold) fl 24 Spruyt
1801/06/13	LNDLS	0082	*[Anonymous]* | Een Jufvrouw, die op de Luit speelt	D van R	(Sold) fl 0:16 Richter [for] G[iezen]
1801/06/13	LNDLS	0087	*Een oud Meester* | Maria, met het Kind, op paneel, door een oud Meester | *Mat:* op paneel	D van R	(Sold) fl 1:10 Swart
1801/06/13	LNDLS	0088	*[Anonymous]* | Een Vrouw met een Portrait in haar hand, en een kind aan haar schoot, op doek | *Mat:* op doek	D van R	(Sold) fl 7:10 J van Stepraan
1801/06/13	LNDLS	0089	*[Anonymous]* | Een uitvoerig Bloemstukje	D van R	(Sold) fl 5 Spruyt
1801/06/13	LNDLS	0090	*[Anonymous]* | Een Mans-Portrait, op koper | *Mat:* op koper	D van R	(Sold) fl 1:5 Richter G [for] v Giezen
1801/06/13	LNDLS	0091	*[Anonymous]* | Het Portrait van Erasmus	D van R	(Sold) fl 4:2 for lots 91 & 92. Thyes
1801/06/13	LNDLS	0092	*[Anonymous]* | Een Vrouwe-Portrait	D van R	(Sold) fl 4:2 for lots 91 & 92. Thyes
1801/06/13	LNDLS	0094[H]	*[Anonymous]* | [Untitled] | *Notes:* This lot was added in by hand in the RKDH copy of the catalogue, but without giving an artist or title.	D van R	(Sold) fl 2:6 J van Stepraan
1801/06/23	HGBAK	0001	*[Anonymous]* | Een ysvermaak [Schilderyen in Olyverf] | *Mat:* in olyverf *Notes:* The bracketed information in the title appears above lot 1 and refers to lots 1 to 163.	T Tamé [or others]	(Unknown)
1801/06/23	HGBAK	0002	*[Anonymous]* | Eenige geschilderde Bloemen in een fles op een steene Tafel [Schilderyen in Olyverf] | *Mat:* in olyverf *Notes:* The bracketed information in the title appears above lot 1 and refers to lots 1 to 163.	T Tamé [or others]	(Unknown)
1801/06/23	HGBAK	0003	*[Anonymous]* | Een Jongen Fioolspeelder nevens een oude Vrouw [Schilderyen in Olyverf] | *Mat:* in olyverf *Notes:* The bracketed information in the title appears above lot 1 and refers to lots 1 to 163.	T Tamé [or others]	(Unknown)
1801/06/23	HGBAK	0004	*[Anonymous]* | Twee Vrugtstukjes [Schilderyen in Olyverf] | *Mat:* in olyverf *Notes:* The bracketed information in the title appears above lot 1 and refers to lots 1 to 163.	T Tamé [or others]	(Unknown)
1801/06/23	HGBAK	0005	*[Anonymous]* | Een Historieel vol gewoel [Schilderyen in Olyverf] | *Mat:* in olyverf *Notes:* The bracketed information in the title appears above lot 1 and refers to lots 1 to 163.	T Tamé [or others]	(Unknown)
1801/06/23	HGBAK	0006	*[Anonymous]* | Een dito [Historieel] van zeven Beelden [Schilderyen in Olyverf] | *Mat:* in olyverf *Notes:* The bracketed information in the title about the medium appears above lot 1 and refers to lots 1 to 163.	T Tamé [or others]	(Unknown)
1801/06/23	HGBAK	0007	*[Anonymous]* | Een Boere Kermisvreugd [Schilderyen in Olyverf] | *Mat:* in olyverf *Notes:* The bracketed information in the title appears above lot 1 and refers to lots 1 to 163.	T Tamé [or others]	(Unknown)

1801/06/23	HGBAK	0008	*[Anonymous]* | Doode Vogelen [Schilderyen in Olyverf] | *Mat:* in olyverf *Notes:* The bracketed information in the title appears above lot 1 and refers to lots 1 to 163.	T Tamé [or others]	(Unknown)
1801/06/23	HGBAK	0009	*[Anonymous]* | Badende Vrouwtjes in een Landschap [Schilderyen in Olyverf] | *Mat:* in olyverf *Notes:* The bracketed information in the title appears above lot 1 and refers to lots 1 to 163.	T Tamé [or others]	(Unknown)
1801/06/23	HGBAK	0010	*[Anonymous]* | Een Watergezigt met zeilende Scheepjes [Schilderyen in Olyverf] | *Mat:* in olyverf *Notes:* The bracketed information in the title appears above lot 1 and refers to lots 1 to 163.	T Tamé [or others]	(Unknown)
1801/06/23	HGBAK	0011	*[Anonymous]* | Twee stuks met rokende & drinkende Boeren [Schilderyen in Olyverf] | *Mat:* in olyverf *Notes:* The bracketed information in the title appears above lot 1 and refers to lots 1 to 163.	T Tamé [or others]	(Unknown)
1801/06/23	HGBAK	0012	*[Anonymous]* | Een Jongeling in Spaansche Kleding [Schilderyen in Olyverf] | *Mat:* in olyverf *Notes:* The bracketed information in the title appears above lot 1 and refers to lots 1 to 163.	T Tamé [or others]	(Unknown)
1801/06/23	HGBAK	0013	*[Anonymous]* | Boerewoonigen langs het Waater [Schilderyen in Olyverf] | *Mat:* in olyverf *Notes:* The bracketed information in the title appears above lot 1 and refers to lots 1 to 163.	T Tamé [or others]	(Unknown)
1801/06/23	HGBAK	0014	*[Anonymous]* | Het Afbeeldsel van een Man in oude Hollandsche Kleding [Schilderyen in Olyverf] | *Mat:* in olyverf *Notes:* The bracketed information in the title appears above lot 1 and refers to lots 1 to 163.	T Tamé [or others]	(Unknown)
1801/06/23	HGBAK	0015	*[Anonymous]* | Koejen en Schaapjes in een Landschap [Schilderyen in Olyverf] | *Mat:* in olyverf *Notes:* The bracketed information in the title appears above lot 1 and refers to lots 1 to 163.	T Tamé [or others]	(Unknown)
1801/06/23	HGBAK	0016	*[Anonymous]* | Twee stuks met overblyfselen der Oudheid [Schilderyen in Olyverf] | *Mat:* in olyverf *Notes:* The bracketed information in the title appears above lot 1 and refers to lots 1 to 163.	T Tamé [or others]	(Unknown)
1801/06/23	HGBAK	0017	*[Anonymous]* | Een Linne Wever [Schilderyen in Olyverf] | *Mat:* in olyverf *Notes:* The bracketed information in the title appears above lot 1 and refers to lots 1 to 163.	T Tamé [or others]	(Unknown)
1801/06/23	HGBAK	0018	*[Anonymous]* | Een Landschap met Koebeesten & Schaapen, op een heuvel [Schilderyen in Olyverf] | *Mat:* in olyverf *Notes:* The bracketed information in the title appears above lot 1 and refers to lots 1 to 163.	T Tamé [or others]	(Unknown)
1801/06/23	HGBAK	0019	*[Anonymous]* | Een Nagtstukje [Schilderyen in Olyverf] | *Mat:* in olyverf *Notes:* The bracketed information in the title appears above lot 1 and refers to lots 1 to 163.	T Tamé [or others]	(Unknown)
1801/06/23	HGBAK	0020	*[Anonymous]* | Een oud Mans Hoofd [Schilderyen in Olyverf] | *Mat:* in olyverf *Notes:* The bracketed information in the title appears above lot 1 and refers to lots 1 to 163.	T Tamé [or others]	(Unknown)
1801/06/23	HGBAK	0021	*[Anonymous]* | Een byeenkomst van Geleerden [Schilderyen in Olyverf] | *Mat:* in olyverf *Notes:* The bracketed information in the title appears above lot 1 and refers to lots 1 to 163.	T Tamé [or others]	(Unknown)
1801/06/23	HGBAK	0022	*[Anonymous]* | Ryzigers te Paard by een Herberg [Schilderyen in Olyverf] | *Mat:* in olyverf *Notes:* The bracketed information in the title appears above lot 1 and refers to lots 1 to 163.	T Tamé [or others]	(Unknown)
1801/06/23	HGBAK	0023	*[Anonymous]* | Een Arbeider voor zynen Land Heer [Schilderyen in Olyverf] | *Mat:* in olyverf *Notes:* The bracketed information in the title appears above lot 1 and refers to lots 1 to 163.	T Tamé [or others]	(Unknown)
1801/06/23	HGBAK	0024	*[Anonymous]* | Twee stuks met Marketenters en Rysigers te Paard [Schilderyen in Olyverf] | *Mat:* in olyverf *Notes:* The bracketed information in the title appears above lot 1 and refers to lots 1 to 163.	T Tamé [or others]	(Unknown)
1801/06/23	HGBAK	0025	*[Anonymous]* | Een Historieel [Schilderyen in Olyverf] | *Mat:* in olyverf *Notes:* The bracketed information in the title appears above lot 1 and refers to lots 1 to 163.	T Tamé [or others]	(Unknown)
1801/06/23	HGBAK	0026	*[Anonymous]* | Rokende Boeren [Schilderyen in Olyverf] | *Mat:* in olyverf *Notes:* The bracketed information in the title appears above lot 1 and refers to lots 1 to 163.	T Tamé [or others]	(Unknown)
1801/06/23	HGBAK	0027	*[Anonymous]* | Een bevallige Vrouw [Schilderyen in Olyverf] | *Mat:* in olyverf *Notes:* The bracketed information in the title appears above lot 1 and refers to lots 1 to 163.	T Tamé [or others]	(Unknown)
1801/06/23	HGBAK	0028	*[Anonymous]* | Een stuk met allerhande Vrugten [Schilderyen in Olyverf] | *Mat:* in olyverf *Notes:* The bracketed information in the title appears above lot 1 and refers to lots 1 to 163.	T Tamé [or others]	(Unknown)
1801/06/23	HGBAK	0029	*[Anonymous]* | Hoorn Vee, in een Landschap by stil Water [Schilderyen in Olyverf] | *Mat:* in olyverf *Notes:* The bracketed information in the title appears above lot 1 and refers to lots 1 to 163.	T Tamé [or others]	(Unknown)
1801/06/23	HGBAK	0030	*[Anonymous]* | Een bevallige Vrouw by een Fontyn [Schilderyen in Olyverf] | *Mat:* in olyverf *Notes:* The bracketed information in the title appears above lot 1 and refers to lots 1 to 163.	T Tamé [or others]	(Unknown)
1801/06/23	HGBAK	0031	*[Anonymous]* | Een Landschap met Bergen, Geboomte en Waterval [Schilderyen in Olyverf] | *Mat:* in olyverf *Notes:* The bracketed information in the title appears above lot 1 and refers to lots 1 to 163.	T Tamé [or others]	(Unknown)

1801/06/23	HGBAK	0032	*[Anonymous]* | Het afbeeldsel van een aanzienlyk Persoon [Schilderyen in Olyverf] | *Mat:* in olyverf *Notes:* The bracketed information in the title appears above lot 1 and refers to lots 1 to 163.	T Tamé [or others]	(Unknown)
1801/06/23	HGBAK	0033	*[Anonymous]* | Twee stuks Historieele [Schilderyen in Olyverf] | *Mat:* in olyverf *Notes:* The bracketed information in the title appears above lot 1 and refers to lots 1 to 163.	T Tamé [or others]	(Unknown)
1801/06/23	HGBAK	0034	*[Anonymous]* | Vrolyke Boeren en Boerinnen [Schilderyen in Olyverf] | *Mat:* in olyverf *Notes:* The bracketed information in the title appears above lot 1 and refers to lots 1 to 163.	T Tamé [or others]	(Unknown)
1801/06/23	HGBAK	0035	*[Anonymous]* | Een uitzigt door een rots en overblyfselen der oudheid [Schilderyen in Olyverf] | *Mat:* in olyverf *Notes:* The bracketed information in the title appears above lot 1 and refers to lots 1 to 163.	T Tamé [or others]	(Unknown)
1801/06/23	HGBAK	0036	*[Anonymous]* | Een Schermutseling [Schilderyen in Olyverf] | *Mat:* in olyverf *Notes:* The bracketed information in the title appears above lot 1 and refers to lots 1 to 163.	T Tamé [or others]	(Unknown)
1801/06/23	HGBAK	0037	*[Anonymous]* | Een Watergezigt met Scheepen by een hoofd met geboomte [Schilderyen in Olyverf] | *Mat:* in olyverf *Notes:* The bracketed information in the title appears above lot 1 and refers to lots 1 to 163.	T Tamé [or others]	(Unknown)
1801/06/23	HGBAK	0038	*[Anonymous]* | Een oud Man en Jonge Vrouw by den haard zittende [Schilderyen in Olyverf] | *Mat:* in olyverf *Notes:* The bracketed information in the title appears above lot 1 and refers to lots 1 to 163.	T Tamé [or others]	(Unknown)
1801/06/23	HGBAK	0039	*[Anonymous]* | Een Bloemstuk [Schilderyen in Olyverf] | *Mat:* in olyverf *Notes:* The bracketed information in the title appears above lot 1 and refers to lots 1 to 163.	T Tamé [or others]	(Unknown)
1801/06/23	HGBAK	0040	*[Anonymous]* | Een Jonge Vrouw de Oogen Hemelwaards kerende [Schilderyen in Olyverf] | *Mat:* in olyverf *Notes:* The bracketed information in the title appears above lot 1 and refers to lots 1 to 163.	T Tamé [or others]	(Unknown)
1801/06/23	HGBAK	0041	*[Anonymous]* | Een Jong Mans Afbeeldsel met los Hair in oude Kleeding [Schilderyen in Olyverf] | *Mat:* in olyverf *Notes:* The bracketed information in the title appears above lot 1 and refers to lots 1 to 163.	T Tamé [or others]	(Unknown)
1801/06/23	HGBAK	0042	*[Anonymous]* | Een Chimist [Schilderyen in Olyverf] | *Mat:* in olyverf *Notes:* The bracketed information in the title appears above lot 1 and refers to lots 1 to 163.	T Tamé [or others]	(Unknown)
1801/06/23	HGBAK	0043	*[Anonymous]* | Twee stuks met grappige Snaaken [Schilderyen in Olyverf] | *Mat:* in olyverf *Notes:* The bracketed information in the title appears above lot 1 and refers to lots 1 to 163.	T Tamé [or others]	(Unknown)
1801/06/23	HGBAK	0044	*[Anonymous]* | Drinkende en rokende Boeren [Schilderyen in Olyverf] | *Mat:* in olyverf *Notes:* The bracketed information in the title appears above lot 1 and refers to lots 1 to 163.	T Tamé [or others]	(Unknown)
1801/06/23	HGBAK	0045	*[Anonymous]* | Eene Comique Ordonnantie [Schilderyen in Olyverf] | *Mat:* in olyverf *Notes:* The bracketed information in the title appears above lot 1 and refers to lots 1 to 163.	T Tamé [or others]	(Unknown)
1801/06/23	HGBAK	0046	*[Anonymous]* | Een Marktgezigt [Schilderyen in Olyverf] | *Mat:* in olyverf *Notes:* The bracketed information in the title appears above lot 1 and refers to lots 1 to 163.	T Tamé [or others]	(Unknown)
1801/06/23	HGBAK	0047	*[Anonymous]* | Een door den brand verwoeste Stad [Schilderyen in Olyverf] | *Mat:* in olyverf *Notes:* The bracketed information in the title appears above lot 1 and refers to lots 1 to 163.	T Tamé [or others]	(Unknown)
1801/06/23	HGBAK	0048	*[Anonymous]* | Een Nagtstuk [Schilderyen in Olyverf] | *Mat:* in olyverf *Notes:* The bracketed information in the title appears above lot 1 and refers to lots 1 to 163.	T Tamé [or others]	(Unknown)
1801/06/23	HGBAK	0049	*[Anonymous]* | Dit stuk zinspeelende op de Geestrykste Hollandsche Spreekwoorden [Schilderyen in Olyverf] | *Mat:* in olyverf *Notes:* The bracketed information in the title appears above lot 1 and refers to lots 1 to 163.	T Tamé [or others]	(Unknown)
1801/06/23	HGBAK	0050	*[Anonymous]* | Een Nagtstukje [Schilderyen in Olyverf] | *Mat:* in olyverf *Notes:* The bracketed information in the title appears above lot 1 and refers to lots 1 to 163.	T Tamé [or others]	(Unknown)
1801/06/23	HGBAK	0051	*[Anonymous]* | Paarden in een Landschap [Schilderyen in Olyverf] | *Mat:* in olyverf *Notes:* The bracketed information in the title appears above lot 1 and refers to lots 1 to 163.	T Tamé [or others]	(Unknown)
1801/06/23	HGBAK	0052	*[Anonymous]* | Een Musicerend Gezelschap van drie Beelden [Schilderyen in Olyverf] | *Mat:* in olyverf *Notes:* The bracketed information in the title appears above lot 1 and refers to lots 1 to 163.	T Tamé [or others]	(Unknown)
1801/06/23	HGBAK	0053	*[Anonymous]* | Een Vrouwe Borstbeeld met bloemen gecierd [Schilderyen in Olyverf] | *Mat:* in olyverf *Notes:* The bracketed information in the title appears above lot 1 and refers to lots 1 to 163.	T Tamé [or others]	(Unknown)
1801/06/23	HGBAK	0054	*[Anonymous]* | Een stil Water met zylende Schepen [Schilderyen in Olyverf] | *Mat:* in olyverf *Notes:* The bracketed information in the title appears above lot 1 and refers to lots 1 to 163.	T Tamé [or others]	(Unknown)

1801/06/23	HGBAK	0055	*[Anonymous]* | Een Schoolmeester met een Jongeling in vreemde Kledingen [Schilderyen in Olyverf] | *Mat:* in olyverf *Notes:* The bracketed information in the title appears above lot 1 and refers to lots 1 to 163.	T Tamé [or others]	(Unknown)
1801/06/23	HGBAK	0056	*[Anonymous]* | Doode Vogelen in een Landschap [Schilderyen in Olyverf] | *Mat:* in olyverf *Notes:* The bracketed information in the title appears above lot 1 and refers to lots 1 to 163.	T Tamé [or others]	(Unknown)
1801/06/23	HGBAK	0057	*[Anonymous]* | Rokende, speelende en zingende Boeren [Schilderyen in Olyverf] | *Mat:* in olyverf *Notes:* The bracketed information in the title appears above lot 1 and refers to lots 1 to 163.	T Tamé [or others]	(Unknown)
1801/06/23	HGBAK	0058	*[Anonymous]* | Twee Bedelaars Jongens die Vrugten Eeten [Schilderyen in Olyverf] | *Mat:* in olyverf *Notes:* The bracketed information in the title appears above lot 1 and refers to lots 1 to 163.	T Tamé [or others]	(Unknown)
1801/06/23	HGBAK	0059	*[Anonymous]* | Een Historieel met menigte Beelden [Schilderyen in Olyverf] | *Mat:* in olyverf *Notes:* The bracketed information in the title appears above lot 1 and refers to lots 1 to 163.	T Tamé [or others]	(Unknown)
1801/06/23	HGBAK	0060	*[Anonymous]* | Twee stuks de Borstbeelden van Prins Willem de Derde en deszelfs Gemalin in nissen konstig met bloemen gecierd [Schilderyen in Olyverf] | *Mat:* in olyverf *Notes:* The bracketed information in the title appears above lot 1 and refers to lots 1 to 163.	T Tamé [or others]	(Unknown)
1801/06/23	HGBAK	0061	*[Anonymous]* | Menigte naakte Kindertjes spelende met een Bok [Schilderyen in Olyverf] | *Mat:* in olyverf *Notes:* The bracketed information in the title appears above lot 1 and refers to lots 1 to 163.	T Tamé [or others]	(Unknown)
1801/06/23	HGBAK	0062	*[Anonymous]* | Allerley Keuken Gereedschap, Vissen en Brood op een Tafel [Schilderyen in Olyverf] | *Mat:* in olyverf *Notes:* The bracketed information in the title appears above lot 1 and refers to lots 1 to 163.	T Tamé [or others]	(Unknown)
1801/06/23	HGBAK	0063	*[Anonymous]* | Twee stuks een Mans en een Vrouwe Beelde [Schilderyen in Olyverf] | *Mat:* in olyverf *Notes:* The bracketed information in the title appears above lot 1 and refers to lots 1 to 163.	T Tamé [or others]	(Unknown)
1801/06/23	HGBAK	0064	*[Anonymous]* | Boerewoningen langs het Water [Schilderyen in Olyverf] | *Mat:* in olyverf *Notes:* The bracketed information in the title appears above lot 1 and refers to lots 1 to 163.	T Tamé [or others]	(Unknown)
1801/06/23	HGBAK	0065	*[Anonymous]* | Een bevallig Jongeling een Papegaay met Vrugten voedende [Schilderyen in Olyverf] | *Mat:* in olyverf *Notes:* The bracketed information in the title appears above lot 1 and refers to lots 1 to 163.	T Tamé [or others]	(Unknown)
1801/06/23	HGBAK	0066	*[Anonymous]* | Het opkomen van den dageraad [Schilderyen in Olyverf] | *Mat:* in olyverf *Notes:* The bracketed information in the title appears above lot 1 and refers to lots 1 to 163.	T Tamé [or others]	(Unknown)
1801/06/23	HGBAK	0067	*[Anonymous]* | Een oude Vrouw in gesprek met een bevallig Meisje [Schilderyen in Olyverf] | *Mat:* in olyverf *Notes:* The bracketed information in the title appears above lot 1 and refers to lots 1 to 163.	T Tamé [or others]	(Unknown)
1801/06/23	HGBAK	0068	*[Anonymous]* | Een Boomryk Landschap met stromend Water, rustende beeldjes by dorre boomen en Boerewoningen [Schilderyen in Olyverf] | *Mat:* in olyverf *Notes:* The bracketed information in the title appears above lot 1 and refers to lots 1 to 163.	T Tamé [or others]	(Unknown)
1801/06/23	HGBAK	0069	*[Anonymous]* | Hoorns, Metaal en Bloemen voor een steene gewerkte Nis [Schilderyen in Olyverf] | *Mat:* in olyverf *Notes:* The bracketed information in the title appears above lot 1 and refers to lots 1 to 163.	T Tamé [or others]	(Unknown)
1801/06/23	HGBAK	0070	*[Anonymous]* | Een Land en Watergezigt met een Pontschuit, verders grasende Koebeesten [Schilderyen in Olyverf] | *Mat:* in olyverf *Notes:* The bracketed information in the title appears above lot 1 and refers to lots 1 to 163.	T Tamé [or others]	(Unknown)
1801/06/23	HGBAK	0071	*[Anonymous]* | Den Heyland zyn Kruys dragende [Schilderyen in Olyverf] | *Mat:* in olyverf *Notes:* The bracketed information in the title appears above lot 1 and refers to lots 1 to 163.	T Tamé [or others]	(Unknown)
1801/06/23	HGBAK	0072	*[Anonymous]* | Overblyfselen der Oudheid in een Landschap met wandelende beeldjes [Schilderyen in Olyverf] | *Mat:* in olyverf *Notes:* The bracketed information in the title appears above lot 1 and refers to lots 1 to 163.	T Tamé [or others]	(Unknown)
1801/06/23	HGBAK	0073	*[Anonymous]* | Een vlugtende Krygsman [Schilderyen in Olyverf] | *Mat:* in olyverf *Notes:* The bracketed information in the title appears above lot 1 and refers to lots 1 to 163.	T Tamé [or others]	(Unknown)
1801/06/23	HGBAK	0074	*[Anonymous]* | Een bergagtig Landschap met Waterval en figuuren [Schilderyen in Olyverf] | *Mat:* in olyverf *Notes:* The bracketed information in the title appears above lot 1 and refers to lots 1 to 163.	T Tamé [or others]	(Unknown)
1801/06/23	HGBAK	0075	*[Anonymous]* | Op een Heuvel by het Water ziet men twee rustende Beelden, Koeyen en een Schaapje [Schilderyen in Olyverf] | *Mat:* in olyverf *Notes:* The bracketed information in the title appears above lot 1 and refers to lots 1 to 163.	T Tamé [or others]	(Unknown)
1801/06/23	HGBAK	0076	*[Anonymous]* | Een Gezelschap van elf Beelden, zo Mans als Vrouwen in Spaansche Kleding zig met spelen en drinken vermakende [Schilderyen in Olyverf] | *Mat:* in olyverf *Notes:* The bracketed information in the title appears above lot 1 and refers to lots 1 to 163.	T Tamé [or others]	(Unknown)

1801/06/23	HGBAK	0077	*[Anonymous]* | Twee oude Goudwegers [Schilderyen in Olyverf] | *Mat:* in olyverf *Notes:* The bracketed information in the title appears above lot 1 and refers to lots 1 to 163.	T Tamé [or others]	(Unknown)
1801/06/23	HGBAK	0078	*[Anonymous]* | Verscheide soorten van Honden in een Landschap [Schilderyen in Olyverf] | *Mat:* in olyverf *Notes:* The bracketed information in the title appears above lot 1 and refers to lots 1 to 163.	T Tamé [or others]	(Unknown)
1801/06/23	HGBAK	0079	*[Anonymous]* | Een Heer in Spaansche Kleding, van zyn Paard gestegen zynde, verliefd op een bevallig Boerinnetje dien hy by het intreden van zyn Huis ontmoet [Schilderyen in Olyverf] | *Mat:* in olyverf *Notes:* The bracketed information in the title appears above lot 1 and refers to lots 1 to 163.	T Tamé [or others]	(Unknown)
1801/06/23	HGBAK	0080	*[Anonymous]* | Een Jongeling by kaarsligt lesende [Schilderyen in Olyverf] | *Mat:* in olyverf *Notes:* The bracketed information in the title appears above lot 1 and refers to lots 1 to 163.	T Tamé [or others]	(Unknown)
1801/06/23	HGBAK	0081	*[Anonymous]* | Een Magdalena in berouw [Schilderyen in Olyverf] | *Mat:* in olyverf *Notes:* The bracketed information in the title appears above lot 1 and refers to lots 1 to 163.	T Tamé [or others]	(Unknown)
1801/06/23	HGBAK	0082	*[Anonymous]* | Een Schilder in gedagten voor zyn Ezel [Schilderyen in Olyverf] | *Mat:* in olyverf *Notes:* The bracketed information in the title appears above lot 1 and refers to lots 1 to 163.	T Tamé [or others]	(Unknown)
1801/06/23	HGBAK	0083	*[Anonymous]* | Een bergagtig Landschap met Wateren doorsneden en verscheidene figuren [Schilderyen in Olyverf] | *Mat:* in olyverf *Notes:* The bracketed information in the title appears above lot 1 and refers to lots 1 to 163.	T Tamé [or others]	(Unknown)
1801/06/23	HGBAK	0084	*[Anonymous]* | Voor een steene gebeeldhoude Nis ziet men onderscheide Vrugten waarop Insecten azen, in het midden der Nis Maria met het Kindeken [Schilderyen in Olyverf] | *Mat:* in olyverf *Notes:* The bracketed information in the title appears above lot 1 and refers to lots 1 to 163.	T Tamé [or others]	(Unknown)
1801/06/23	HGBAK	0085	*[Anonymous]* | Een studie Schildery van Schaapen, Bokken en Honden, Koppen & Pooten [Schilderyen in Olyverf] | *Mat:* in olyverf *Notes:* The bracketed information in the title appears above lot 1 and refers to lots 1 to 163.	T Tamé [or others]	(Unknown)
1801/06/23	HGBAK	0086	*[Anonymous]* | Een bergagtig Landschap (by 't opgaan der Zonne verbeeld) met Jaagers te voet en te paard [Schilderyen in Olyverf] | *Mat:* in olyverf *Notes:* The bracketed information in the title appears above lot 1 and refers to lots 1 to 163.	T Tamé [or others]	(Unknown)
1801/06/23	HGBAK	0087	*[Anonymous]* | Een Spaans Krygsman, zittende by een Tafel zig met rooken en drinken vermakende [Schilderyen in Olyverf] | *Mat:* in olyverf *Notes:* The bracketed information in the title appears above lot 1 and refers to lots 1 to 163.	T Tamé [or others]	(Unknown)
1801/06/23	HGBAK	0088	*[Anonymous]* | Eenige Vissers by de Vestmuuren van een Stad [Schilderyen in Olyverf] | *Mat:* in olyverf *Notes:* The bracketed information in the title appears above lot 1 and refers to lots 1 to 163.	T Tamé [or others]	(Unknown)
1801/06/23	HGBAK	0089	*[Anonymous]* | Eene Optogt ter Valke Jagt [Schilderyen in Olyverf] | *Mat:* in olyverf *Notes:* The bracketed information in the title appears above lot 1 and refers to lots 1 to 163.	T Tamé [or others]	(Unknown)
1801/06/23	HGBAK	0090	*[Anonymous]* | Een Jongeling met een hoed op het hoofd voor een Tafel by Lampligt [Schilderyen in Olyverf] | *Mat:* in olyverf *Notes:* The bracketed information in the title appears above lot 1 and refers to lots 1 to 163.	T Tamé [or others]	(Unknown)
1801/06/23	HGBAK	0091	*[Anonymous]* | Een Bloemstuk [Schilderyen in Olyverf] | *Mat:* in olyverf *Notes:* The bracketed information in the title appears above lot 1 and refers to lots 1 to 163.	T Tamé [or others]	(Unknown)
1801/06/23	HGBAK	0092	*[Anonymous]* | Twee stuks Kraamkamer, en een Thee Gezelschap [Schilderyen in Olyverf] | *Mat:* in olyverf *Notes:* The bracketed information in the title appears above lot 1 and refers to lots 1 to 163.	T Tamé [or others]	(Unknown)
1801/06/23	HGBAK	0093	*[Anonymous]* | Eene Zinspeling op Kunsten en Wetenschappen [Schilderyen in Olyverf] | *Mat:* in olyverf *Notes:* The bracketed information in the title appears above lot 1 and refers to lots 1 to 163.	T Tamé [or others]	(Unknown)
1801/06/23	HGBAK	0094	*[Anonymous]* | Een Zeetje met diverse Scheepen by een Vuurbaak [Schilderyen in Olyverf] | *Mat:* in olyverf *Notes:* The bracketed information in the title appears above lot 1 and refers to lots 1 to 163.	T Tamé [or others]	(Unknown)
1801/06/23	HGBAK	0095	*[Anonymous]* | Een stuk met Vrugten, Groentens, dood en levend Gevogelte [Schilderyen in Olyverf] | *Mat:* in olyverf *Notes:* The bracketed information in the title appears above lot 1 and refers to lots 1 to 163.	T Tamé [or others]	(Unknown)
1801/06/23	HGBAK	0096	*[Anonymous]* | Een heuvelagtig Landschap met Geboomte en Dorpgezigt [Schilderyen in Olyverf] | *Mat:* in olyverf *Notes:* The bracketed information in the title appears above lot 1 and refers to lots 1 to 163.	T Tamé [or others]	(Unknown)
1801/06/23	HGBAK	0097	*[Anonymous]* | Twee stuks met Groente en Vrugt verkoopsters [Schilderyen in Olyverf] | *Mat:* in olyverf *Notes:* The bracketed information in the title appears above lot 1 and refers to lots 1 to 163.	T Tamé [or others]	(Unknown)

1801/06/23	HGBAK	0098	*[Anonymous]* | Een bergagtig Landschap met Postwagen en te paard reyzende lieden [Schilderyen in Olyverf] | *Mat:* in olyverf *Notes:* The bracketed information in the title appears above lot 1 and refers to lots 1 to 163.	T Tamé [or others]	(Unknown)
1801/06/23	HGBAK	0099	*[Anonymous]* | Een Veldslag ten tyde der Spanjaarden zonder lyst [Schilderyen in Olyverf] | *Mat:* in olyverf *Notes:* The bracketed information in the title appears above lot 1 and refers to lots 1 to 163.	T Tamé [or others]	(Unknown)
1801/06/23	HGBAK	0100	*[Anonymous]* | Vrolyke Boeren en een Boerin in een binnehuis, meede zonder lyst [Schilderyen in Olyverf] | *Mat:* in olyverf *Notes:* The bracketed information in the title appears above lot 1 and refers to lots 1 to 163.	T Tamé [or others]	(Unknown)
1801/06/23	HGBAK	0101	*[Anonymous]* | Een uitgestrekt Watergezigt met zeylende Scheepen langs Boerewoningen [Schilderyen in Olyverf] | *Mat:* in olyverf *Notes:* The bracketed information in the title appears above lot 1 and refers to lots 1 to 163.	T Tamé [or others]	(Unknown)
1801/06/23	HGBAK	0102	*[Anonymous]* | Een bergagtig Landschap en geboomte met Jaagers te voet en te paard, en hoornvee dat voortgedreven word [Schilderyen in Olyverf] | *Mat:* in olyverf *Notes:* The bracketed information in the title appears above lot 1 and refers to lots 1 to 163.	T Tamé [or others]	(Unknown)
1801/06/23	HGBAK	0103	*[Anonymous]* | Een stil leven [Schilderyen in Olyverf] | *Mat:* in olyverf *Notes:* The bracketed information in the title appears above lot 1 and refers to lots 1 to 163.	T Tamé [or others]	(Unknown)
1801/06/23	HGBAK	0104	*[Anonymous]* | Gedenktekenen der Oudheid in een uitgestrekt Landschap met Beelden en Beesten [Schilderyen in Olyverf] | *Mat:* in olyverf *Notes:* The bracketed information in the title appears above lot 1 and refers to lots 1 to 163.	T Tamé [or others]	(Unknown)
1801/06/23	HGBAK	0105	*[Anonymous]* | Een Boere Schuur nevens geboomte waarby rustende Landlieden by hun Vee [Schilderyen in Olyverf] | *Mat:* in olyverf *Notes:* The bracketed information in the title appears above lot 1 and refers to lots 1 to 163.	T Tamé [or others]	(Unknown)
1801/06/23	HGBAK	0106	*[Anonymous]* | Een boomryk Landschap met Koorn – Velden, een gaande Jonge en een Vrouw [Schilderyen in Olyverf] | *Mat:* in olyverf *Notes:* The bracketed information in the title appears above lot 1 and refers to lots 1 to 163.	T Tamé [or others]	(Unknown)
1801/06/23	HGBAK	0107	*[Anonymous]* | Twee stuks een Landschap met Beelden en Beesten en een Zeehaven, waar goederen op sleede en wagen geladen worden [Schilderyen in Olyverf] | *Mat:* in olyverf *Notes:* The bracketed information in the title appears above lot 1 and refers to lots 1 to 163.	T Tamé [or others]	(Unknown)
1801/06/23	HGBAK	0108	*[Anonymous]* | Vier stuks diverse met en zonder Lysten [Schilderyen in Olyverf] | *Mat:* in olyverf *Notes:* The bracketed information in the title appears above lot 1 and refers to lots 1 to 163.	T Tamé [or others]	(Unknown)
1801/06/23	HGBAK	0115	*[Anonymous]* | Een Zee-Gezigt [Schideryen in Olyverf] | *Mat:* in olyverf *Notes:* The bracketed information in the title appears above lot 1 and refers to lots 1 to 163.	T Tamé [or others]	(Unknown)
1801/06/23	HGBAK	0116	*[Anonymous]* | Een Capitaal stuk, verbeeldende een tafel met geregten, dood gevogelte &c. in een ebbehoute lyst met vergulde binne rand op doek [Schilderyen in Olyverf] | *Mat:* in olyverf op doek *Notes:* The bracketed information in the title appears above lot 1 and refers to lots 1 to 163.	T Tamé [or others]	(Unknown)
1801/06/23	HGBAK	0117	*Een goed meester* | Saulus op de weg na Damascus, door een goed meester op paneel in dito [ebbehoute] lyst [Schilderyen in Olyverf] | *Mat:* in olyverf op paneel *Notes:* The bracketed information in the title about the medium appears above lot 1 and refers to lots 1 to 163.	T Tamé [or others]	(Unknown)
1801/06/23	HGBAK	0118	*Een goed meester* | Een Landschap, met hoog opgaand geboomte, badende figuren &c. door een goed meester, op doek in dito [ebbehoute] lyst [Schilderyen in Olyverf] | *Mat:* in olyverf op doek *Notes:* The bracketed information in the title about the medium appears above lot 1 and refers to lots 1 to 163.	T Tamé [or others]	(Unknown)
1801/06/23	HGBAK	0119	*Een voornaam meester* | Een bergagtig Landschap, door een voornaam meester op doek in dito [ebbehoute] lyst [Schilderyen in Olyverf] | *Mat:* in olyverf op doek *Notes:* The bracketed information in the title about the medium appears above lot 1 and refers to lots 1 to 163.	T Tamé [or others]	(Unknown)
1801/06/23	HGBAK	0120	*[Anonymous]* | Een dito [bergagtig] Landschap, met Beesten gestoffeerd niet minder, op paneel, dito [ebbehoute] lyst [Schilderyen in Olyverf] | *Mat:* in olyverf op paneel *Notes:* The bracketed information in the title about the medium appears above lot 1 and refers to lots 1 to 163.	T Tamé [or others]	(Unknown)
1801/06/23	HGBAK	0121	*[Anonymous]* | Een Land en Zeegezicht, op paneel, dito [ebbehoute] lyst [Schilderyen in Olyverf] | *Mat:* in olyverf op paneel *Notes:* The bracketed information in the title about the medium appears above lot 1 and refers to lots 1 to 163.	T Tamé [or others]	(Unknown)
1801/06/23	HGBAK	0122	*[Anonymous]* | Een Wintertje vol gewoel van Schaatsryders, &c. op paneel [Schilderyen in Olyverf] | *Mat:* in olyverf op paneel *Notes:* The bracketed information in the title appears above lot 1 and refers to lots 1 to 163.	T Tamé [or others]	(Unknown)

1801/06/23	HGBAK	0123	*Een goed meester* | De Offerhande Abrahams, door een goed meester op paneel, in dito [ebbehoute] lyst [Schilderyen in Olyverf] | *Mat:* in olyverf op paneel *Notes:* It is unclear what "dito" refers to in the title. The bracketed information in the title about the medium appears above lot 1 and refers to lots 1 to 163.	T Tamé [or others]	(Unknown)
1801/06/23	HGBAK	0124	*[Anonymous]* | Een Bachanaal, op paneel, in dito [ebbehoute] lyst [Schilderyen in Olyverf] | *Mat:* in olyverf op paneel *Notes:* It is unclear what "dito" refers to in the title. The bracketed information in the title about the medium appears above lot 1 and refers to lots 1 to 163.	T Tamé [or others]	(Unknown)
1801/06/23	HGBAK	0125	*[Anonymous]* | Een met Paarden, op doek, in vergulde lyst [Schilderyen in Olyverf] | *Mat:* in olyverf op doek *Notes:* The bracketed information in the title appears above lot 1 and refers to lots 1 to 163.	T Tamé [or others]	(Unknown)
1801/06/23	HGBAK	0126	*Een voornaam meester* | Een fraay stuk verbeeldende een Schilder in zyn Schilder vertrek, met bywerk, door een voornaam meester [Schilderyen in Olyverf] | *Mat:* in olyverf *Notes:* The bracketed information in the title appears above lot 1 and refers to lots 1 to 163.	T Tamé [or others]	(Unknown)
1801/06/23	HGBAK	0127	*[Anonymous]* | Een Land-Gezicht [Schilderyen in Olyverf] | *Mat:* in olyverf *Notes:* The bracketed information in the title appears above lot 1 and refers to lots 1 to 163.	T Tamé [or others]	(Unknown)
1801/06/23	HGBAK	0128	*[Anonymous]* | Een twistende Scharremoes [Schilderyen in Olyverf] | *Mat:* in olyverf *Notes:* The bracketed information in the title appears above lot 1 and refers to lots 1 to 163.	T Tamé [or others]	(Unknown)
1801/06/23	HGBAK	0129	*[Anonymous]* | Een Land en Water-Gezicht [Schilderyen in Olyverf] | *Mat:* in olyverf *Notes:* The bracketed information in the title appears above lot 1 and refers to lots 1 to 163.	T Tamé [or others]	(Unknown)
1801/06/23	HGBAK	0130	*[Anonymous]* | Een Zee-Gezicht [Schilderyen in Olyverf] | *Mat:* in olyverf *Notes:* The bracketed information in the title appears above lot 1 and refers to lots 1 to 163.	T Tamé [or others]	(Unknown)
1801/06/23	HGBAK	0132	*[Anonymous]* | Het Stadhuis van Schiedam, in vergulde lyst [Schilderyen in Olyverf] | *Mat:* in olyverf *Notes:* The bracketed information in the title appears above lot 1 and refers to lots 1 to 163.	T Tamé [or others]	(Unknown)
1801/06/23	HGBAK	0133	*[Anonymous]* | Seven stuks Kaarten en een Schildery in lysten [Schilderyen in Olyverf] | *Mat:* in olyverf *Notes:* The bracketed information in the title appears above lot 1 and refers to lots 1 to 163.	T Tamé [or others]	(Unknown)
1801/06/23	HGBAK	0134	*[Anonymous]* | Twee stuks Schilderyen [Schilderyen in Olyverf] | *Mat:* in olyverf *Notes:* The bracketed information in the title appears above lot 1 and refers to lots 1 to 163.	T Tamé [or others]	(Unknown)
1801/06/23	HGBAK	0135	*[Anonymous]* | W. C. Hendrik Friso, in vergulde lyst en glas [Schilderyen in Olyverf] | *Mat:* in olyverf *Notes:* The bracketed information in the title appears above lot 1 and refers to lots 1 to 163.	T Tamé [or others]	(Unknown)
1801/06/23	HGBAK	0136	*[Anonymous]* | Rauwers, Velse, Beukelman, en drie kleyne [Schilderyen in Olyverf] | *Mat:* in olyverf *Notes:* The bracketed information in the title appears above lot 1 and refers to lots 1 to 163.	T Tamé [or others]	(Unknown)
1801/06/23	HGBAK	0137	*[Anonymous]* | Een Zeegezicht met Scheepen in vergulde lyst en glas [Schilderyen in Olyverf] | *Mat:* in olyverf *Notes:* The bracketed information in the title appears above lot 1 and refers to lots 1 to 163.	T Tamé [or others]	(Unknown)
1801/06/23	HGBAK	0138	*[Anonymous]* | Een Heer op koper geschildert [Schilderyen in Olyverf] | *Mat:* in olyverf op koper *Notes:* The bracketed information in the title appears above lot 1 and refers to lots 1 to 163.	T Tamé [or others]	(Unknown)
1801/08/14	HGKAN	0132	*[Anonymous]* | Negen stuks Schilderyen zo op Paneel als op Linnen geschildert, welke by koopjes zullen verkogt worden | *Mat:* op paneel en linnen		(Unknown)
1801/08/19	AMSCH	0146	*Onbekende* | Een Schynbedrieger met een afhangend Gordyn, met ziet gedeeltelyk een Landschap; natuurlyk op Doek | *Mat:* op doek	van der Schly [for] F	(Sold) fl 0:10 V^n Iperen
1801/08/19	AMSCH	0147	*Een goed Meester* | Voor een oud Gebouw ziet men Maria met 't Kind, die door de Wysen Geschenken word gebracht; door een goed Meester	Pruyssen^r	(Sold) fl 3 Yver
1801/08/19	AMSCH	0151	*[Anonymous]* | De Steeniging van St. Stéphanus, vol gewoel	Van Forreest	(Sold) fl 3:10 Yver
1801/08/19	AMSCH	0153	*[Anonymous]* | Een Keukenstuk, meesterlyk gepenceeld	Van Forreest	(Sold) fl 4:5 V^n Dijl
1801/08/19	AMSCH	0154	*[Anonymous]* | Een hévige Bataille	Van Forreest	(Sold) fl 0:16 Wolft
1801/08/19	AMSCH	0155	*[Anonymous]* | Een Rotsachtig Landschapje	Van Forreest	(Withdrawn)
1801/08/19	AMSCH	0156	*[Anonymous]* | Een Keukenstuk	Van Forreest	(Sold) fl 5 Roos
1801/08/19	AMSCH	0157	*[Anonymous]* | Een Bordeeltje	Van Forreest	(Sold) fl 0:8 V^n Iperen
1801/08/19	AMSCH	0158	*[Anonymous]* | Een Bloemstukje	Van Forreest	(Sold) fl 2 C S Roos
1801/08/19	AMSCH	0159	*[Anonymous]* | Een stuk met Vissen	Van Forreest	(Sold) fl 0:8 V^n Dr Schley [for] R[ijfsnijder]
1801/08/19	AMSCH	0160	*[Anonymous]* | Een Strandgezicht	Van Forreest	(Sold) fl 1:10 V^n Dijl
1801/08/19	AMSCH	0161	*[Anonymous]* | Een Gestoffeerd Bergachtig Landschap	Van Forreest	(Sold) fl 1:15 Wijland

1801/08/19	AMSCH	0162	*[Anonymous]* | Een Vanitas door een Vrouw verbeeld	Van Forreest	(Sold) fl 0:8 J [?] Honstee
1801/08/19	AMSCH	0164	*[Anonymous]* | Een Zee met Scheepen	Van Forreest	(Sold) fl 0:12 Vermeulen
1801/08/19	AMSCH	0165	*[Anonymous]* | Een Jager met zyn Honden in een Landschap	Van Forreest	(Sold) fl 1:5 Gruiter
1801/08/19	AMSCH	0166	*[Anonymous]* | Een oud Mans Hoofd	Van Forreest	(Sold) fl 0:2 Wijland
1801/08/19	AMSCH	0167	*[Anonymous]* | Een stil Leeven, op een Tafel met een Kleed, legt Brood, Chinaas-Appel, waar by een Roemer en Glas Wyn, op Doek | *Mat:* op doek	Van Forreest	(Sold) fl 2:5 for lots 167 & 170. V[n] Dijl
1801/08/19	AMSCH	0168	*[Anonymous]* | Eenige naakte Nimphen in een Landschap, fix behandeld	Van Forreest	(Sold) fl 2:15 V[n] Dijl
1801/08/19	AMSCH	0170	*[Anonymous]* | Twee stuks, een Grysaard, en een Goudsmit	Van Forreest	(Sold) fl 2:5 for lots 167 & 170. V[n] Dijl
1801/08/19	AMSCH	0171	*[Anonymous]* | Een oude Grysaard	Van Forreest	(Sold) fl 1:5 V[n] d Schleij [for] R[ijfsnijder]
1801/08/19	AMSCH	0172	*[Anonymous]* | Een Zeehaven met Oorlogscheepen, ter zyde langs het Strand ziet men een Kasteel; alles word door de Maan verlicht	Pruyssen[r] [for] Q	(Bought In) fl 4
1801/08/19	AMSCH	0173a	*[Anonymous]* | Twee stuks Mans-Pourtraitten	Pruyssen[r] [for] Q	(Sold) fl 3 Wijland
1801/08/19	AMSCH	0174	*[Anonymous]* | Twee diverse Landschappen	Pruyssen[r] [for] Q	(Sold) fl 1 Croesen
1801/08/19	AMSCH	0175	*[Anonymous]* | Twee dito [diverse Landschappen] | *Notes:* It is unclear what "dito" refers to in the title.	Pruyssen[r] [for] Q	(Sold) fl 1 Wijland
1801/08/19	AMSCH	0176	*[Anonymous]* | Twee dito [diverse Landschappen] | *Notes:* It is unclear what "dito" refers to in the title.	Pruyssen[r] [for] Q	(Sold) fl 0:8 v d Schleij [for] Neyt [?]
1801/08/19	AMSCH	0177[H]	*[Anonymous]* | 4 Stuks [Extra Schilderijen] | *Notes:* This lot was added in by hand in the LBDa and RKDH copies of the catalogue. The bracketed information in the title appears above lot 177[H] and refers to lots 177[H] to 228[H].	Pruyssen[r]	(Sold) fl 8:10 Gruiter
1801/08/19	AMSCH	0178[H]	*[Anonymous]* | 1 Stuk [Extra Schilderijen] | *Notes:* This lot was added in by hand in the LBDa and RKDH copies of the catalogue. The bracketed information in the title appears above lot 177[H] and refers to lots 177[H] to 228[H].	Pruyssen[r]	(Sold) fl 1:5 Geld
1801/08/19	AMSCH	0179[H]	*[Anonymous]* | 1 Stuk [Extra Schilderijen] | *Notes:* This lot was added in by hand in the LBDa and RKDH copies of the catalogue. The bracketed information in the title appears above lot 177[H] and refers to lots 177[H] to 228[H].	Pruyssen[r]	(Bought In) fl 1 ¼
1801/08/19	AMSCH	0180[H]	*[Anonymous]* | 1 Stuk [Extra Schilderijen] | *Notes:* This lot was added in by hand in the LBDa and RKDH copies of the catalogue. The bracketed information in the title appears above lot 177[H] and refers to lots 177[H] to 228[H].	Pruyssen[r]	(Sold) fl 6:15 Gruiter
1801/08/19	AMSCH	0181[H]	*[Anonymous]* | 1 Stuk [Extra Schilderijen] | *Notes:* This lot was added in by hand in the LBDa and RKDH copies of the catalogue. The bracketed information in the title appears above lot 177[H] and refers to lots 177[H] to 228[H].	Pruyssen[r]	(Sold) fl 1:5 Carli
1801/08/19	AMSCH	0182[H]	*[Anonymous]* | 1 Stuk [Extra Schilderijen] | *Notes:* This lot was added in by hand in the LBDa and RKDH copies of the catalogue. The bracketed information in the title appears above lot 177[H] and refers to lots 177[H] to 228[H].	Pruyssen[r]	(Sold) fl 1 Wijland
1801/08/19	AMSCH	0183[H]	*[Anonymous]* | 1 Stuk [Extra Schilderijen] | *Notes:* This lot was added in by hand in the LBDa and RKDH copies of the catalogue. The bracketed information in the title appears above lot 177[H] and refers to lots 177[H] to 228[H].	Pruyssen[r]	(Sold) fl 0:8 Ijver
1801/08/19	AMSCH	0184[H]	*[Anonymous]* | 1 Stuk [Extra Schilderijen] | *Notes:* This lot was added in by hand in the LBDa and RKDH copies of the catalogue. The bracketed information in the title appears above lot 177[H] and refers to lots 177[H] to 228[H].	Pruyssen[r]	(Sold) fl 4:10 Achtienhoven
1801/08/19	AMSCH	0185[H]	*[Anonymous]* | 1 Stuk [Extra Schilderijen] | *Notes:* This lot was added in by hand in the LBDa and RKDH copies of the catalogue. The bracketed information in the title appears above lot 177[H] and refers to lots 177[H] to 228[H].	Pruyssen[r]	(Sold) fl 3:10 Gruiter
1801/08/19	AMSCH	0186[H]	*[Anonymous]* | 1 Stuk [Extra Schilderijen] | *Notes:* This lot was added in by hand in the LBDa and RKDH copies of the catalogue. The bracketed information in the title appears above lot 177[H] and refers to lots 177[H] to 228[H].	Pruyssen[r]	(Sold) fl 1:15 V[n] Dijl
1801/08/19	AMSCH	0187[H]	*[Anonymous]* | 5 Stuks [Extra Schilderijen] | *Notes:* This lot was added in by hand in the LBDa and RKDH copies of the catalogue. The bracketed information in the title appears above lot 177[H] and refers to lots 177[H] to 228[H].	Pruyssen[r]	(Sold) fl 7:10 for lots 187[H] & 188[H]. Carli
1801/08/19	AMSCH	0188[H]	*[Anonymous]* | 5 Stuks [Extra Schilderijen] | *Notes:* This lot was added in by hand in the LBDa and RKDH copies of the catalogue. The bracketed information in the title appears above lot 177[H] and refers to lots 177[H] to 228[H].	Pruyssen[r]	(Sold) fl 7:10 for lots 187[H] & 188[H]. Carli

1801/08/19	AMSCH	0189[H]	*[Anonymous]* | 5 Stuks [Extra Schilderijen] | *Notes:* This lot was added in by hand in the LBDa and RKDH copies of the catalogue. The bracketed information in the title appears above lot 177[H] and refers to lots 177[H] to 228[H].	Pruyssen^{r}	(Sold) fl 0:16 V^{n} Dijl
1801/08/19	AMSCH	0190[H]	*[Anonymous]* | 2 Stuks [Extra Schilderijen] | *Notes:* This lot was added in by hand in the LBDa and RKDH copies of the catalogue. The bracketed information in the title appears above lot 177[H] and refers to lots 177[H] to 228[H].	W Wynen	(Sold) fl 2 Gruiter
1801/08/19	AMSCH	0191[H]	*[Anonymous]* | 2 Stuks [Extra Schilderijen] | *Notes:* This lot was added in by hand in the LBDa and RKDH copies of the catalogue. The bracketed information in the title appears above lot 177[H] and refers to lots 177[H] to 228[H].	W Wynen	(Sold) fl 0:10 Wijland
1801/08/19	AMSCH	0192[H]	*[Anonymous]* | 2 Stuks [Extra Schilderijen] | *Notes:* This lot was added in by hand in the LBDa and RKDH copies of the catalogue. The bracketed information in the title appears above lot 177[H] and refers to lots 177[H] to 228[H].	W Wynen	(Sold) fl 3:15 Boelen
1801/08/19	AMSCH	0193[H]	*[Anonymous]* | 2 Stuks [Extra Schilderijen] | *Notes:* This lot was added in by hand in the LBDa and RKDH copies of the catalogue. The bracketed information in the title appears above lot 177[H] and refers to lots 177[H] to 228[H].	W Wynen	(Sold) fl 1:10 V^{n} Dijl
1801/08/19	AMSCH	0194[H]	*[Anonymous]* | 2 Stuks [Extra Schilderijen] | *Notes:* This lot was added in by hand in the LBDa and RKDH copies of the catalogue. The bracketed information in the title appears above lot 177[H] and refers to lots 177[H] to 228[H].	W Wynen	(Sold) fl 1 Van Iperen
1801/08/19	AMSCH	0195[H]	*[Anonymous]* | 2 Stuks [Extra Schilderijen] | *Notes:* This lot was added in by hand in the LBDa and RKDH copies of the catalogue. The bracketed information in the title appears above lot 177[H] and refers to lots 177[H] to 228[H].	W Wynen	(Sold) fl 7:5 Gruiter
1801/08/19	AMSCH	0196[H]	*[Anonymous]* | 2 Stuks [Extra Schilderijen] | *Notes:* This lot was added in by hand in the LBDa and RKDH copies of the catalogue. The bracketed information in the title appears above lot 177[H] and refers to lots 177[H] to 228[H].	W Wynen	(Sold) fl 0:14 Wijland
1801/08/19	AMSCH	0197[H]	*[Anonymous]* | 2 Stuks [Extra Schilderijen] | *Notes:* This lot was added in by hand in the LBDa and RKDH copies of the catalogue. The bracketed information in the title appears above lot 177[H] and refers to lots 177[H] to 228[H].	W Wynen	(Sold) fl 3:15 Wijland
1801/08/19	AMSCH	0198[H]	*[Anonymous]* | 2 Stuks [Extra Schilderijen] | *Notes:* This lot was added in by hand in the LBDa and RKDH copies of the catalogue. The bracketed information in the title appears above lot 177[H] and refers to lots 177[H] to 228[H].	W Wynen	(Sold) fl 3:5 Vermeulen
1801/08/19	AMSCH	0199[H]	*[Anonymous]* | 2 Stuks [Extra Schilderijen] | *Notes:* This lot was added in by hand in the LBDa and RKDH copies of the catalogue. The bracketed information in the title appears above lot 177[H] and refers to lots 177[H] to 228[H].	W Wynen	(Sold) fl 1:15 Boelen
1801/08/19	AMSCH	0200[H]	*[Anonymous]* | 2 Stuks [Extra Schilderijen] | *Notes:* This lot was added in by hand in the LBDa and RKDH copies of the catalogue. The bracketed information in the title appears above lot 177[H] and refers to lots 177[H] to 228[H].	W Wynen	(Sold) fl 0:16 V^{n} Dijl
1801/08/19	AMSCH	0201[H]	*[Anonymous]* | 2 Stuks [Extra Schilderijen] | *Notes:* This lot was added in by hand in the LBDa and RKDH copies of the catalogue. The bracketed information in the title appears above lot 177[H] and refers to lots 177[H] to 228[H].	W Wynen	(Sold) fl 0:6 A Meijer
1801/08/19	AMSCH	0202[H]	*[Anonymous]* | 2 Stuks [Extra Schilderijen] | *Notes:* This lot was added in by hand in the LBDa and RKDH copies of the catalogue. The bracketed information in the title appears above lot 177[H] and refers to lots 177[H] to 228[H].	W Wynen	(Sold) fl 1:10 for lots 202[H] & 203[H]. Frantszen
1801/08/19	AMSCH	0203[H]	*[Anonymous]* | 1 Stuk [Extra Schilderijen] | *Notes:* This lot was added in by hand in the LBDa and RKDH copies of the catalogue. The bracketed information in the title appears above lot 177[H] and refers to lots 177[H] to 228[H].	W Wynen	(Sold) fl 1:10 for lots 202[H] & 203[H]. Frantszen
1801/08/19	AMSCH	0204[H]	*[Anonymous]* | 2 Stuks [Extra Schilderijen] | *Notes:* This lot was added in by hand in the LBDa and RKDH copies of the catalogue. The bracketed information in the title appears above lot 177[H] and refers to lots 177[H] to 228[H].	W Wynen	(Sold) fl 5:10 Th^{s} Spaan
1801/08/19	AMSCH	0205[H]	*[Anonymous]* | 2 Stuks [Extra Schilderijen] | *Notes:* This lot was added in by hand in the LBDa and RKDH copies of the catalogue. The bracketed information in the title appears above lot 177[H] and refers to lots 177[H] to 228[H].	W Wynen	(Sold) fl 13:10 for lots 205[H] & 206[H]. V^{n} Iperen
1801/08/19	AMSCH	0206[H]	*[Anonymous]* | 2 Stuks [Extra Schilderijen] | *Notes:* This lot was added in by hand in the LBDa and RKDH copies of the catalogue. The bracketed information in the title appears above lot 177[H] and refers to lots 177[H] to 228[H].	W Wynen	(Sold) fl 13:10 for lots 205[H] & 206[H]. V^{n} Iperen
1801/08/19	AMSCH	0207[H]	*[Anonymous]* | 2 Stuks [Extra Schilderijen] | *Notes:* This lot was added in by hand in the LBDa and RKDH copies of the catalogue. The bracketed	W Wynen	(Sold) fl 2 for lots 207[H] & 208[H]. Wijland

			information in the title appears above lot 177[H] and refers to lots 177[H] to 228[H].		
1801/08/19	AMSCH	0208[H]	*[Anonymous]* | 2 Stuks [Extra Schilderijen] | *Notes:* This lot was added in by hand in the LBDa and RKDH copies of the catalogue. The bracketed information in the title appears above lot 177[H] and refers to lots 177[H] to 228[H].	W Wynen	(Sold) fl 2 for lots 207[H] & 208[H]. Wijland
1801/08/19	AMSCH	0209[H]	*[Anonymous]* | 2 Stuks [Extra Schilderijen] | *Notes:* This lot was added in by hand in the LBDa and RKDH copies of the catalogue. The bracketed information in the title appears above lot 177[H] and refers to lots 177[H] to 228[H].	W Wynen	(Sold) fl 2 for lots 209[H] & 210[H]. Wijland
1801/08/19	AMSCH	0210[H]	*[Anonymous]* | 2 Stuks [Extra Schilderijen] | *Notes:* This lot was added in by hand in the LBDa and RKDH copies of the catalogue. The bracketed information in the title appears above lot 177[H] and refers to lots 177[H] to 228[H].	W Wynen	(Sold) fl 2 for lots 209[H] & 210[H]. Wijland
1801/08/19	AMSCH	0211[H]	*[Anonymous]* | 2 Stuks [Extra Schilderijen] | *Notes:* This lot was added in by hand in the LBDa and RKDH copies of the catalogue. The bracketed information in the title appears above lot 177[H] and refers to lots 177[H] to 228[H].	W Wynen	(Sold) fl 5:5 for lots 211[H] & 212[H]. Wed Achtienhoven
1801/08/19	AMSCH	0212[H]	*[Anonymous]* | 3 Stuks [Extra Schilderijen] | *Notes:* This lot was added in by hand in the LBDa and RKDH copies of the catalogue. The bracketed information in the title appears above lot 177[H] and refers to lots 177[H] to 228[H].	W Wynen	(Sold) fl 5:5 for lots 211[H] & 212[H]. Wed Achtienhoven
1801/08/19	AMSCH	0213[H]	*[Anonymous]* | 2 Stuks [Extra Schilderijen] | *Notes:* This lot was added in by hand in the LBDa and RKDH copies of the catalogue. The bracketed information in the title appears above lot 177[H] and refers to lots 177[H] to 228[H].	W Wynen	(Sold) fl 7 Wed Achtienhoven
1801/08/19	AMSCH	0214[H]	*[Anonymous]* | 2 Stuks [Extra Schilderijen] | *Notes:* This lot was added in by hand in the LBDa and RKDH copies of the catalogue. The bracketed information in the title appears above lot 177[H] and refers to lots 177[H] to 228[H].	W Wynen	(Sold) fl 1:10 Wijland
1801/08/19	AMSCH	0215[H]	*[Anonymous]* | 2 Stuks [Extra Schilderijen] | *Notes:* This lot was added in by hand in the LBDa and RKDH copies of the catalogue. The bracketed information in the title appears above lot 177[H] and refers to lots 177[H] to 228[H].	W Wynen	(Sold) fl 1 V^n Iperen
1801/08/19	AMSCH	0216[H]	*[Anonymous]* | 2 Stuks [Extra Schilderijen] | *Notes:* This lot was added in by hand in the LBDa and RKDH copies of the catalogue. The bracketed information in the title appears above lot 177[H] and refers to lots 177[H] to 228[H].	W Wynen	(Sold) fl 3 V^n Dijl
1801/08/19	AMSCH	0217[H]	*[Anonymous]* | 2 Stuks [Extra Schilderijen] | *Notes:* This lot was added in by hand in the LBDa and RKDH copies of the catalogue. The bracketed information in the title appears above lot 177[H] and refers to lots 177[H] to 228[H].	W Wynen	(Sold) fl 8:10 Boelen
1801/08/19	AMSCH	0218[H]	*[Anonymous]* | 4 Stuks [Extra Schilderijen] | *Notes:* This lot was added in by hand in the LBDa and RKDH copies of the catalogue. The bracketed information in the title appears above lot 177[H] and refers to lots 177[H] to 228[H].	W Wynen	(Sold) fl 3 Wijland
1801/08/19	AMSCH	0219[H]	*[Anonymous]* | 4 Stuks [Extra Schilderijen] | *Notes:* This lot was added in by hand in the LBDa and RKDH copies of the catalogue. The bracketed information in the title appears above lot 177[H] and refers to lots 177[H] to 228[H].	W Wynen	(Sold) fl 3 Gruiter
1801/08/19	AMSCH	0220[H]	*[Anonymous]* | 4 Stuks [Extra Schilderijen] | *Notes:* This lot was added in by hand in the LBDa and RKDH copies of the catalogue. The bracketed information in the title appears above lot 177[H] and refers to lots 177[H] to 228[H].	W Wynen	(Sold) fl 3:15 Gruiter
1801/08/19	AMSCH	0221[H]	*[Anonymous]* | 2 Stuks [Extra Schilderijen] | *Notes:* This lot was added in by hand in the LBDa and RKDH copies of the catalogue. The bracketed information in the title appears above lot 177[H] and refers to lots 177[H] to 228[H].	W Wynen	(Sold) fl 1 Wijland
1801/08/19	AMSCH	0222[H]	*[Anonymous]* | 2 Stuks [Extra Schilderijen] | *Notes:* This lot was added in by hand in the LBDa and RKDH copies of the catalogue. The bracketed information in the title appears above lot 177[H] and refers to lots 177[H] to 228[H].	W Wynen	(Sold) fl 1 Wijland
1801/08/19	AMSCH	0223[H]	*[Anonymous]* | 2 Stuks [Extra Schilderijen] | *Notes:* This lot was added in by hand in the LBDa and RKDH copies of the catalogue. The bracketed information in the title appears above lot 177[H] and refers to lots 177[H] to 228[H].	W Wynen	(Sold) fl 5:15 Wolft
1801/08/19	AMSCH	0224[H]	*[Anonymous]* | 1 Stuk [Extra Schilderijen] | *Notes:* This lot was added in by hand in the LBDa and RKDH copies of the catalogue. The bracketed information in the title appears above lot 177[H] and refers to lots 177[H] to 228[H].	C S Roos [for] G	(Bought In) fl 3
1801/08/19	AMSCH	0225[H]	*[Anonymous]* | 1 Stuk [Extra Schilderijen] | *Notes:* This lot was added in by hand in the LBDa and RKDH copies of the catalogue. The bracketed information in the title appears above lot 177[H] and refers to lots 177[H] to 228[H].	C S Roos [for] G	(Sold) fl 7 T Spaan [or] J Spaan

1801/08/19	AMSCH	0226[H]	*[Anonymous]* | 1 Stuk [Extra Schilderijen] | *Notes:* This lot was added in by hand in the LBDa and RKDH copies of the catalogue. The bracketed information in the title appears above lot 177[H] and refers to lots 177[H] to 228[H].	van der Schly [for] F	(Sold) fl 0:6 Van der Schley [for] R[ijfsnijder]
1801/08/19	AMSCH	0227[H]	*[Anonymous]* | 1 Stuk [Extra Schilderijen] | *Notes:* This lot was added in by hand in the LBDa and RKDH copies of the catalogue. The bracketed information in the title appears above lot 177[H] and refers to lots 177[H] to 228[H].	van der Schly [for] F	(Bought In) fl 2
1801/08/19	AMSCH	0228[H]	*[Anonymous]* | 3 Stuks [Extra Schilderijen] | *Notes:* This lot was added in by hand in the LBDa and RKDH copies of the catalogue. The bracketed information in the title appears above lot 177[H] and refers to lots 177[H] to 228[H].	Pruyssen[r]	(Sold) fl 1:5 Gruiter
1801/09/04	MGWIN	0003	*[Anonymous]* | Een dito [Fruit- en Bloemen?] Keukenstuk | *Mat:* op doek *Size:* hoog 22 ½ en breed 32 ½ duim	Pieter Gillissen	(Unknown)
1801/09/04	MGWIN	0005	*[Anonymous]* | Twee Stuks met Vogels, in vergulde Lysten | *Size:* hoog 29 ½ en breed 30 ½ duim	Pieter Gillissen	(Unknown)
1801/09/04	MGWIN	0007	*[Anonymous]* | Twee Stuks Boere Conversatien, in vergulde Lysten	Pieter Gillissen	(Unknown)
1801/09/04	MGWIN	0008	*[Anonymous]* | Twee Stuks Landschapjes, in dito [vergulde] dito [Lysten]	Pieter Gillissen	(Unknown)
1801/09/04	MGWIN	0009	*[Anonymous]* | Twee Stuks Schilderyen, in een vergulde en zwarte Lyst	Pieter Gillissen	(Unknown)
1801/09/04	MGWIN	0010	*[Anonymous]* | Vier Plaaten van het Schip Woestduin, in vergulde Lysten met Glazen	Pieter Gillissen	(Unknown)
1801/09/04	MGWIN	0011	*[Anonymous]* | Het Portrait van Prof. J. Willemsen, in een vergulde Lyst en Glas	Pieter Gillissen	(Unknown)
1801/09/04	MGWIN	0012	*[Anonymous]* | Het Portrait van Prins Frederik Hendrik, Willem de II. en Willem de III. in zwarte Lysten met Glazen	Pieter Gillissen	(Unknown)
1801/09/04	MGWIN	0013	*[Anonymous]* | Het Portrait van Jonker Jan van Borselen, in dito [zwarte] Lyst en Glas	Pieter Gillissen	(Unknown)
1801/10/06	AMSCH	0044	*[Anonymous]* | Voor een open steene Nis, gedeeltelyk met een Wijngaard-Rank belegt, vertoont zich het afbeeldsel van een Kunstschilder, staande halverlijf in deftige kleeding, houdende in de regter hand een stuk Teekenkryt, en in de andere hand een Palet, Schilderstok en Penceelen; nevens denzelven staat een doek op een Schilder Ezel, op de rand der Nis staat en legt verscheide Schilder- en Teeken-Gereedschappen, een Gegoote Plysterhoofd, een bakje en afhangende Prent; zynde alles van een uitmuntende fraaye en uitvoerige penceel behandeling | *Mat:* op paneel *Size:* hoog 15, breed 12 duim *Notes:* Although this lot is found in the catalogue under the letter "M.," the artist's name was omitted; it was supposed to be "G. Metzu." *Loc:* London, England, UK. Royal Collection (Buckingham Palace) (901) as Metsu	S	(Sold) fl 1000 Aug[s] Elink Sterk
1801/10/06	AMSCH	0086	*Onbekend Meester* | Deze Ordinantie in een Landschap met geboomten, verbeeld een zittende Vrouw, gedeeltelyk met een Schaapsvacht bekleed, houdende een kindje aan de borst, nevens dezelve een Man in zoortgelyke kleeding, als ziende naar twee jonge Kinderen, waar van een op de Fluyt blaast, alles kragtig en meesterlyk gepenceeld | *Mat:* op doek	S	(Sold) fl 25 ter Smitten
1801/10/06	AMSCH	0090	*Onbekend Meester* | Het Afbeeldzel van een bejaard Man in oude Hollandsche Kleeding, met een Linne Kraag om den hals, en het hoofd met een bruine Muts gedekt, het Caracter is natuurlyk, en van een meesterlyke penceel behandeling, ovaal Formaat | *Fmt:* ovaal	S	(Sold) fl 34 Gruyter
1801/10/06	AMSCH	0091	*Onbekend Meester* | Het Afbeeldzel van een Leeraar met een Bef om den hals, en het hoofd met een Calotje bedekt, zeer uitvoerig in miniatuur behandeld, ovaal formaat, in een vergulde Lyst met een Glas | *Fmt:* ovaal *Notes:* This lot was sold with lot 92, which is a drawing.	S	(Sold) fl 8 for lots 91 & 92. ter Smitten
1801/10/06	AMSCH	0093	*Onbekend Meester* | Maria rustende in een Landschap, nevens dezelve rust op haar arm het slaapend Kindje, zynde van een meesterlyke penceel behandeling | *Mat:* op doek	S	(Sold) fl 0:10 Van Iperen
1801/10/06	AMSCH	0095	*Onbekend Meester* | Deze Ordinantie verbeeld een stil Léven, op een Tafel gedeeltelyk met een Kleed bedekt, staat een mandje met een Zilvere Schotel, waar op verschillende Vrugten leggen, verders een Schotel met een opgesneede Ham, Kreeft en andere Spys, gedreeven Bokaal en andere Glaazen met Wijn, alles is kragtig en meesterlyk gepenceeld	S	(Sold) fl 8:10 Coclers
1801/10/06	AMSCH	0096	*Onbekend Meester* | Voor een steene Nis, legt op de rand een Doodshoofd, brandende Lont, Speelkaarten, steene Lamp, en andere Voorwerpen, alles zinspeelende op het vergangelyke des Lévens, zeer natuurlyke en kragtig geschilderd	S	(Sold) fl 1:5 ter Smitten
1801/10/06	AMSCH	0097	*Onbekend Meester* | Maria houdende het kind Jesu in de armen, hetzelven eerbiedig beschouwende, ter wederzyde ziet men Cherubyns Hoofden, kragtig en van een meesterlyke penceel behandeling	S	(Sold) fl 8:10 Coclers
1801/10/06	AMSCH	0099	*Onbekend Meester* | Twee stuks, verschillende Vrouwe Portraitten	M	(Sold) fl 0:12 L Pakker
1801/10/06	AMSCH	0100	*Onbekend Meester* | Twee stuks met diversche zoorten van Fruiten op Glas geschilderd | *Mat:* op glas	M	(Withdrawn)
1801/10/06	AMSCH	0101	*Onbekend Meester* | Twee stuks fraay in 't koper gewerkt, verbeeldende Historieele Ordinantiën | *Mat:* op koper	M	(Sold) fl 6:5 Van Iperen

1801/10/06	AMSCH	0103[H]	*[Anonymous]* | 1 Schilderij | *Notes:* This lot was added in by hand in the EBNP, LBDa and RKDH copies of the catalogue.		(Bought In) fl 200
1801/10/06	AMSCH	0104[H]	*[Anonymous]* | 1 do [Schilderij] | *Notes:* This lot was added in by hand in the EBNP, LBDa and RKDH copies of the catalogue.		(Bought In) fl 60
1801/10/06	AMSCH	0105[H]	*[Anonymous]* | 1 do [Schilderij] | *Notes:* This lot was added in by hand in the EBNP, LBDa and RKDH copies of the catalogue.	Z	(Sold) fl 12:10 Theijs
1801/10/06	AMSCH	0106[H]	*[Anonymous]* | 1 do [Schilderij] | *Notes:* This lot was added in by hand in the EBNP, LBDa and RKDH copies of the catalogue.	Y[ver]	(Bought In) fl 11
1801/10/06	AMSCH	0107[H]	*[Anonymous]* | 1 do [Schilderij] | *Notes:* This lot was added in by hand in the EBNP, LBDa and RKDH copies of the catalogue.	Y[ver]	(Sold) fl 8 Bron
1801/10/06	AMSCH	0108[H]	*[Anonymous]* | 1 do [Schilderij] | *Notes:* This lot was added in by hand in the EBNP, LBDa and RKDH copies of the catalogue.	Y[ver]	(Bought In) fl 18
1801/10/06	AMSCH	0109[H]	*[Anonymous]* | 1 do [Schilderij] | *Notes:* This lot was added in by hand in the EBNP, LBDa and RKDH copies of the catalogue.	Y[ver]	(Sold) fl 8 Theijs
1801/10/06	AMSCH	0110[H]	*[Anonymous]* | 1 do [Schilderij] | *Notes:* This lot was added in by hand in the EBNP, LBDa and RKDH copies of the catalogue.	Y[ver]	(Sold) fl 46 T v^{n} Iperen
1801/10/06	AMSCH	0111[H]	*[Anonymous]* | 1 do [Schilderij] | *Notes:* This lot was added in by hand in the EBNP, LBDa and RKDH copies of the catalogue.	S	(Sold) fl 15:10 Gruiter
1801/10/06	AMSCH	0112[H]	*[Anonymous]* | 1 do [Schilderij] | *Notes:* This lot was added in by hand in the EBNP, LBDa and RKDH copies of the catalogue.	S	(Bought In) fl 25
1801/10/06	AMSCH	0113[H]	*[Anonymous]* | 1 do [Schilderij] | *Notes:* This lot was added in by hand in the EBNP, LBDa and RKDH copies of the catalogue.	S	(Sold) fl 3 Frantsz
1801/10/06	AMSCH	0114[H]	*[Anonymous]* | 2 do [Schilderijen] | *Notes:* This lot was added in by hand in the EBNP, LBDa and RKDH copies of the catalogue.	S	(Sold) fl 1:10 Van Houten
1801/10/06	AMSCH	0115[H]	*[Anonymous]* | 2 do [Schilderijen] | *Notes:* This lot was added in by hand in the EBNP, LBDa and RKDH copies of the catalogue.	S	(Sold) fl 1:10 T Van Ijperen
1801/10/06	AMSCH	0116[H]	*[Anonymous]* | 1 do [Schilderij] | *Notes:* This lot was added in by hand in the EBNP, LBDa and RKDH copies of the catalogue.	S	(Sold) fl 5 Theijs
1801/10/06	AMSCH	0117[H]	*[Anonymous]* | 1 do [Schilderij] | *Notes:* This lot was added in by hand in the EBNP, LBDa and RKDH copies of the catalogue.	S	(Sold) fl 1 L Pakker
1801/10/06	AMSCH	0118[H]	*[Anonymous]* | 1 do [Schilderij] | *Notes:* This lot was added in by hand in the EBNP, LBDa and RKDH copies of the catalogue.	S	(Sold) fl 0:18 Veldwijk
1801/10/06	AMSCH	0119[H]	*[Anonymous]* | 2 do [Schilderijen] | *Notes:* This lot was added in by hand in the EBNP, LBDa and RKDH copies of the catalogue.	S	(Sold) fl 3:10 Van Iperen
1801/10/06	AMSCH	0120[H]	*[Anonymous]* | 1 do [Schilderij] | *Notes:* This lot was added in by hand in the EBNP, LBDa and RKDH copies of the catalogue.	Y[ver]	(Sold) fl 1:10 Gruyter
1801/10/06	AMSCH	0121[H]	*[Anonymous]* | 2 do [Schilderijen] | *Notes:* This lot was added in by hand in the EBNP, LBDa and RKDH copies of the catalogue.	Y[ver]	(Sold) fl 8:10 Ter Smitten
1801/10/19	AMSCH	0089	*Onbekend* | Een leezende Dame, prachtig gekleed, zittende by een Tafel, waar op een Boek, een Inktkoker, en verder bywerk; uitvoerig en fraay geschilderd | *Mat:* op paneel *Size:* hoog 6 ¼, breed 7 ¼ duim	Jonkheer Menno Baron van Coehoorn	(Sold) fl 14:10 Texier
1801/11/10	AMPOS	0003	*[Anonymous]* | Beelden op en by een Bordes en springende Fontyn, in een gestoffeerd Landschap met Beesten, zeer uitvoerig		(Unknown)
1801/11/10	AMPOS	0006	*[Anonymous]* | 1 Brug over een vallend Water, in een bergachtig Landschap, op doek | *Mat:* op doek		(Unknown)
1801/11/10	AMPOS	0013	*[Anonymous]* | 1 Brug over een vallend Water, in een stil Landschap		(Unknown)
1801/11/10	AMPOS	0014	*[Anonymous]* | 4 diverse Pourtraiten		(Unknown)
1801/11/10	AMPOS	0033	*[Anonymous]* | De Oude Kerk in Amsterdam, fraai in perspectief, van binnen te zien		(Unknown)
1801/11/10	AMPOS	0034	*Een goed Meester, 1654* | Natuurlyk Gevogelte, door een goed Meester, 1654 | *Inscr:* 1654 (dated) *Notes:* It is unclear whether the date is inscribed on the painting.		(Unknown)
1801/11/10	AMPOS	0035	*[Anonymous]* | 1 extra wel gepenceeld mans Hoofd		(Unknown)
1801/11/10	AMPOS	0036	*[Anonymous]* | 1 dito [extra wel gepenceeld] Grysaard met een baard		(Unknown)
1801/11/10	AMPOS	0037	*Een goed Meester* | Maria met Joseph en het Kindeken, door een goed Meester		(Unknown)
1801/11/10	AMPOS	0042	*[Anonymous]* | 2 dito [stuks] Gezigten by Utrecht en het zwarte Varken by Maarzen		(Unknown)
1801/11/10	AMPOS	0043	*[Anonymous]* | 3 dito [stuks] diverse Gezigten		(Unknown)
1801/11/10	AMPOS	0047	*[Anonymous]* | 2 stuks, 1 Landschap en 1 Vioolspeelder		(Unknown)
1801/11/10	AMPOS	0049	*[Anonymous]* | 2 dito [stuks] divers		(Unknown)
1801/11/10	AMPOS	0050	*[Anonymous]* | 2 dito [stuks], een vrouwe Pourtrait en vrolyke Boer en Boerin		(Unknown)
1801/11/10	AMPOS	0053	*[Anonymous]* | 1 Philosooph, onderwyzende 2 Jongelingen		(Unknown)
1801/11/10	AMPOS	0054	*[Anonymous]* | 1 oude Vrouw, welke een Meisje de voeten reinigd		(Unknown)

1801/11/10	AMPOS	0055	*[Anonymous]* | 1 zeer uitvoerig klein Historieel van de Besnydenis		(Unknown)
1801/11/10	AMPOS	0056	*[Anonymous]* | 12 stuks, de onderscheidene Apostelen		(Unknown)
1801/11/10	AMPOS	0057	*[Anonymous]* | 2 Historie Stukken		(Unknown)
1801/11/10	AMPOS	0058	*[Anonymous]* | 2 Landschappen		(Unknown)
1801/11/10	AMPOS	0059	*[Anonymous]* | 1 Stuk met Glas		(Unknown)
1801/11/21	RMVIS	0003	*[Anonymous]* | Een Binnehuis, waarin een lezend Vrouwtje en een Jonge die op de Fluit speelt	Gelinus van Spaan	(Unknown)
1801/11/21	RMVIS	0007	*[Anonymous]* | Twee Stuks Arkadische Landschappen	Gelinus van Spaan	(Unknown)
1801/11/21	RMVIS	0009	*[Anonymous]* | Een Koopvrouw	Gelinus van Spaan	(Unknown)
1801/11/21	RMVIS	0011	*[Anonymous]* | Een Boere Gezelschap	Gelinus van Spaan	(Unknown)
1801/12/01	HGDAW	0001	*[Anonymous]* | Een extra groot Schildery verbeeldende de Dood van Cirus	Jonkheer Menno Baron van Coehoorn	(Unknown)
1801/12/01	HGDAW	0004	*[Anonymous]* | Een groot Schildery zynde een Vischstuk	Jonkheer Menno Baron van Coehoorn	(Unknown)
1801/12/01	HGDAW	0005	*[Anonymous]* | Twee Schilderyen met diverse beelden	Jonkheer Menno Baron van Coehoorn	(Unknown)
1801/12/01	HGDAW	0006	*[Anonymous]* | Een Schoorsten [sic] stuk met Chineesche Beelden van papier | *Mat:* van papier *Size:* schoorsteenstuk	Jonkheer Menno Baron van Coehoorn	(Unknown)
1801/12/22	AMOTT	0010	*[Anonymous]* | 1 bergachtig Landschap, met zeer net klyne stoffeeringe van Beelden, Beesten, Brug en Rivier	Bartholomeus Ruloffs	(Unknown) fl 33
1801/12/22	AMOTT	0016	*[Anonymous]* | De Geschenken der Wyzen uit het Oosten, aan het Kindeken, in devote Bybelorden	Bartholomeus Ruloffs	(Unknown) fl 1:10
1801/12/22	AMOTT	0020	*[Anonymous]* | 1 devote Vrouw, met twee bevallige Kindertjes, by een Tafel met Vrugten	Bartholomeus Ruloffs	(Unknown) fl 2
1801/12/22	AMOTT	0021	*[Anonymous]* | 2 stuks oude Grysaarts, met lange Baarden	Bartholomeus Ruloffs	(Unknown) fl 1:5
1801/12/22	AMOTT	0022	*[Anonymous]* | 3 dito [stuks] dito [oude Grysaarts] dito [met lange Baarden]	Bartholomeus Ruloffs	(Unknown) fl 2
1801/12/22	AMOTT	0023	*[Anonymous]* | 2 leezende Monnikken, als vooren [met lange Baarden]	Bartholomeus Ruloffs	(Unknown) fl 1:10
1801/12/22	AMOTT	0024	*[Anonymous]* | Maria Theresia in Rouwgewaad, in deftige houding	Bartholomeus Ruloffs	(Unknown) fl 2
1801/12/22	AMOTT	0025	*[Anonymous]* | 1 leezend Meisje, in Weeskleeding	Bartholomeus Ruloffs	(Unknown) fl 6
1801/12/22	AMOTT	0029	*[Anonymous]* | 1 playsant Landschapje, met Beesten	Bartholomeus Ruloffs	(Unknown) fl 0:16
1801/12/22	AMOTT	0035	*[Anonymous]* | 2 stuks, een mans Pourtrait en gezadelde staande Paardjes	Bartholomeus Ruloffs	(Unknown) fl 2:10
1801/12/22	AMOTT	0052	*[Anonymous]* | 1 Schoenmakers Winkel, in een, met de daar toe vereistens gestoffeerd Binnevertrek, in fraaije schikking	Bartholomeus Ruloffs	(Unknown) fl 6
1801/12/22	AMOTT	0059	*[Anonymous]* | 1 Minne of zuigende Vrouw, met een gebakert Kindeke, voor een Nis	Bartholomeus Ruloffs	(Unknown) fl 1
1801/12/22	AMOTT	0060	*[Anonymous]* | 2 stuks met bespied wordende Nimphen	Bartholomeus Ruloffs	(Unknown) fl 0:16
1801/12/22	AMOTT	0062	*[Anonymous]* | Gezadelde Paarden met een rustende Ryziger en Knegt, en leggende Koebeesten by een Fontyn	Bartholomeus Ruloffs	(Unknown) fl 7
1801/12/22	AMOTT	0064	*[Anonymous]* | 1 Gastmaal op Driekoningenfeest, in vrolyke Ordonnantie	Bartholomeus Ruloffs	(Unknown) fl 11
1801/12/22	AMOTT	0070	*[Anonymous]* | 1 Wynroemer, Zakhorlogie, en Schotel met Vruchten op een overdekte Tafel	Bartholomeus Ruloffs	(Unknown) fl 9
1801/12/22	AMOTT	0071	*[Anonymous]* | De Weegschaal van Holland of hollandsche Transformatie, zeer uitvoerig	Bartholomeus Ruloffs	(Unknown) fl 1
1801/12/22	AMOTT	0073	*[Anonymous]* | 2 stuks Man en Vrouwe Pourtraiten, div.	Bartholomeus Ruloffs	(Unknown) fl 3
1801/12/22	AMOTT	0076	*[Anonymous]* | 2 stuks, 1 Smit en 1 boere Schoolmeester	Bartholomeus Ruloffs	(Unknown) fl 1:5
1801/12/22	AMOTT	0078	*[Anonymous]* | 2 dito [stuks] liefkozende Boeren en Boerinnen in Binnen en Buitenhuisjes, in comicque actie	Bartholomeus Ruloffs	(Unknown) fl 3
1801/12/22	AMOTT	0080	*[Anonymous]* | 2 oude Mans Pourtraiten, met lange Baarden	Bartholomeus Ruloffs	(Unknown) fl 1:5
1801/12/22	AMOTT	0081	*[Anonymous]* | 3 stuks kleine Landschapjes, in 2 zoorten	Bartholomeus Ruloffs	(Unknown) fl 0:18
1801/12/22	AMOTT	0082	*[Anonymous]* | 2 dito [stuks], 1 Dame met een Guitar en 1 gezadeld Paardje	Bartholomeus Ruloffs	(Unknown) fl 2:10
1801/12/22	AMOTT	0083	*[Anonymous]* | 2 dito [stuks], 1 stil Watertje en 1 mans Pourtrait	Bartholomeus Ruloffs	(Unknown) fl 12
1801/12/22	AMOTT	0085	*[Anonymous]* | 6 kleine Pourtraitjes van verschillende Voorwerpen	Bartholomeus Ruloffs	(Unknown) fl 1:5
1801/12/22	AMOTT	0086	*[Anonymous]* | 5 dito [kleine] Landschapjes en Pourtraiten	Bartholomeus Ruloffs	(Unknown) fl 0:12
1801/12/22	AMOTT	0087	*[Anonymous]* | 2 diverse Pourtraiten	Bartholomeus Ruloffs	(Unknown) fl 0:10
1801/12/22	AMOTT	0088	*[Anonymous]* | 4 stuks kleine Pourtraitjes	Bartholomeus Ruloffs	(Unknown) fl 22:10
1801/12/22	AMOTT	0089	*[Anonymous]* | 4 dito [stuks] dito [kleine Pourtraitjes]	Bartholomeus Ruloffs	(Unknown) fl 0:18
1801/12/22	AMOTT	0091	*[Anonymous]* | 4 stuks kleine Pourtraiten	Bartholomeus Ruloffs	(Unknown) fl 0:10
1801/12/22	AMOTT	0092	*[Anonymous]* | 5 dito [stuks] Landschapjes en anderen	Bartholomeus Ruloffs	(Unknown) fl 0:16
1801/12/22	AMOTT	0093	*[Anonymous]* | 4 dito [stuks] Pourtraitjes	Bartholomeus Ruloffs	(Unknown) fl 1

1801/12/22	AMOTT	0094	*[Anonymous]* | 4 dito [stuks] dito [Pourtraitjes]	Bartholomeus Ruloffs	(Unknown) fl 0:12
1801/12/22	AMOTT	0095	*[Anonymous]* | 4 dito [stuks] Landschapjes	Bartholomeus Ruloffs	(Unknown) fl 1
1801/12/22	AMOTT	0096	*[Anonymous]* | 3 fraaie dito [Landschapjes]	Bartholomeus Ruloffs	(Unknown) fl 3
1801/12/22	AMOTT	0100[b]	*[Anonymous]* | 2 stuks, een Landschapje, door denzelven [Challon], en een Binnenvertrek | *This Lot:* Een Binnenvertrek; lot 100[a] by L. Chalon	Bartholomeus Ruloffs	(Unknown) fl 7:10 for lots 100[a] & 100[b]
1801/12/22	AMOTT	0102	*[Anonymous]* | 2 stuks, een Landschap en een Dorpgezigt	Bartholomeus Ruloffs	(Unknown) fl 1
1801/12/22	AMOTT	0105	*[Anonymous]* | 2 dito [stuks], een Schilderesse en Gevogelte op een Boom	Bartholomeus Ruloffs	(Unknown) fl 0:14
1801/12/22	AMOTT	0106	*[Anonymous]* | Cupidootjes die bellen blaazen, met Schilder- en Musicqtuig	Bartholomeus Ruloffs	(Unknown) fl 1:10
1801/12/22	AMOTT	0107	*[Anonymous]* | 2 diverse Fruitstukken	Bartholomeus Ruloffs	(Unknown) fl 0:16
1801/12/22	AMOTT	0108	*[Anonymous]* | 3 stuks dito [diverse] Landschappen	Bartholomeus Ruloffs	(Unknown) fl 21
1801/12/22	AMOTT	0110	*[Anonymous]* | 't Pourtrait van Keizer Joseph	Bartholomeus Ruloffs	(Unknown) fl 0:4
1801/12/22	AMOTT	0118	*[Anonymous]* | 2 stuks, de Geboorte Christi en de weerga	Bartholomeus Ruloffs	(Unknown) fl 1
1801/12/22	AMOTT	0119	*[Anonymous]* | 3 dito [stuks] plaisante Land- en Stadgezigten	Bartholomeus Ruloffs	(Unknown) fl 1
1801/12/22	AMOTT	0120	*[Anonymous]* | 2 stuks, met musiceerende Beelden, by kaarslicht	Bartholomeus Ruloffs	(Unknown) fl 1
1801/12/22	AMOTT	0123	*[Anonymous]* | 1 dito [mans Pourtrait], de beroemde Pater Smit	Bartholomeus Ruloffs	(Unknown) fl 0:6
1801/12/22	AMOTT	0124	*[Anonymous]* | 2 stuks Pourtraiten van Heiligen	Bartholomeus Ruloffs	(Unknown) fl 1
1801/12/22	AMOTT	0125	*[Anonymous]* | 1 dito [stuk] dito [Pourtrait] | *Mat:* op koper	Bartholomeus Ruloffs	(Unknown) fl 1 for lots 125 & 126
1801/12/22	AMOTT	0126	*[Anonymous]* | 2 stuks, een Grysaard met een bonte muts en een Boeren Vrolykheid	Bartholomeus Ruloffs	(Unknown) fl 1 for lots 125 & 126
1801/12/22	AMOTT	0128	*[Anonymous]* | 1 Landschap, met een rustende en leezende Venus	Bartholomeus Ruloffs	(Unknown) fl 2
1801/12/22	AMOTT	0129	*[Anonymous]* | 1 rol, met drie oude mans Pourtraiten	Bartholomeus Ruloffs	(Unknown) fl 0:14
1802/02/16	AMSCH	0030	*[Anonymous]* | Drie stuks diverse Pourtraitten	E	(Sold) fl 5:10 van Iperen
1802/02/16	AMSCH	0074[b]	*[Anonymous]* | Twee stuks Arcadische Landschapjes, gestoffeerd met Beeldjes, Gebouwen en Geboomten, uitvoerig op koper geschilderd, door N. van Bloemen, en een Trouwverbond, op koper, ovaal formaat, 3 stuk | *This Lot:* Een Trouwverbond; lot 74[a] by Nor. Bloemen *Mat:* op koper *Fmt:* ovaal	C	(Sold) fl 1:15 for lots 74[a] & 74[b]. L Pakker
1802/02/16	AMSCH	0080	*[Anonymous]* | Drie stuks diverse Pourtraitten	E	(Sold) fl 30 Jan Spaan
1802/02/16	AMSCH	0083	*Een oud Meester* | Een Vrouw, zinspeelende op de Studie; fiks op doek, door een oud Meester | *Mat:* op doek	E	(Bought In) fl 10
1802/02/16	AMSCH	0086[b]	*[Anonymous]* | Een Boere Binnehuis, als Teniers, en 't afbeeldzel van een oude Philosooph | *This Lot:* Een afbeeldzel van een oude Philosooph; lot 86[a] is manner of Teniers	E	(Sold) fl 30 for lots 86[a] & 86[b]. Coclers
1802/02/16	AMSCH	0091	*[Anonymous]* | Twee stuks een Gezigt in Italien, en een Binnehuis waar in een rookende Boer, gestoffeert met verder bywerk, fiks gepenceeld	G	(Sold) fl 1:5 Gruiter
1802/02/16	AMSCH	0093	*[Anonymous]* | Een Vrouwehoofd, halverlyf, houdende de hand op de borst, meesterlyk geschilderd	G	(Withdrawn)
1802/02/16	AMSCH	0095	*[Anonymous]* | Het afbeeldzel van Maria Stuart, Koningin van Schotland in 't verschiet het uitvoeren van haar Doodvonnis	Z	(Sold) fl 2:15 van der Schleij
1802/02/16	AMSCH	0096	*[Anonymous]* | Twee stuks Pourtraitten, Man en Vrouw, in deftige kleeding, meesterlyk gepenceeld, ovaal formaat | *Fmt:* ovaal	Z	(Sold) fl 0:10 van der Schleij
1802/02/16	AMSCH	0097	*[Anonymous]* | Twee stuks Schilderyen, een Slagter en een Fruyt-Vrouw	Z	(Sold) fl 0:12 van der Schleij
1802/02/16	AMSCH	0098	*[Anonymous]* | Het Afbeeldsel van H. G. van Gameren, Bisschop van Antwerpen, Overleeden 26 January 1775	Z	(Sold) fl 1 van der Schleij
1802/02/16	AMSCH	0114[H]	*[Anonymous]* | 1 Schildery | *Notes:* This lot was added in by hand in the LBDa and RKDH copies of the catalogue. It follows lot 98, but is numbered 114, the reasons for which are not clear.	C	(Sold) fl 10 Coclers
1802/02/23	AMREB	0032	*[Anonymous]* | 1 Haringvissery op Doek | *Mat:* op doek	Margaretha Maria van Laar	(Sold) fl 2 Ch Beÿer
1802/02/23	AMREB	0033	*[Anonymous]* | 1 Dame aan het Clavier zittende, waar agter een staand Heer	Margaretha Maria van Laar	(Sold) fl 5:15 A van Houten
1802/02/23	AMREB	0034	*[Anonymous]* | 2 stuks Pourtretten	Margaretha Maria van Laar	(Withdrawn)
1802/02/23	AMREB	0035	*[Anonymous]* | 2 dito [stuks] dito [Pourtretten]	Margaretha Maria van Laar	(Sold) fl 1:5 L Pakker
1802/02/23	AMREB	0037	*[Anonymous]* | 2 stuks, een gesigt op halfweg Haarlem en een Landschap	Margaretha Maria van Laar	(Sold) fl 2:5 ter Hoeve
1802/02/23	AMREB	0038	*[Anonymous]* | R. Perizonius, in lyst en glas	Margaretha Maria van Laar	(Sold) fl 1:5 for lots 38 & 39. van Lingen
1802/02/23	AMREB	0039	*[Anonymous]* | J. Temmink, dito [in lyst en glas]	Margaretha Maria van Laar	(Sold) fl 1:5 for lots 38 & 39. van Lingen

1802/02/23	AMREB	0040	*[Anonymous]* | J. Boskoop, dito [in lyst en glas]	Margaretha Maria van Laar	(Sold) fl 1:5 for lots 40 & 41. Bout
1802/02/23	AMREB	0041	*[Anonymous]* | P. Broes	Margaretha Maria van Laar	(Sold) fl 1:5 for lots 40 & 41. Bout
1802/02/23	AMREB	0042	*[Anonymous]* | A.F. van der Scheer	Margaretha Maria van Laar	(Sold) fl 2 Van Lingen
1802/02/23	AMREB	0043	*[Anonymous]* | R.A. ten Brink	Margaretha Maria van Laar	(Sold) fl 1:5 for lots 43 & 44. L Pakker
1802/02/23	AMREB	0044	*[Anonymous]* | A. Hellenbroek	Margaretha Maria van Laar	(Sold) fl 1:5 for lots 43 & 44. L Pakker
1802/02/23	AMREB	0045[H]	*[Anonymous]* | 1 Schilderij | *Notes:* This lot was added in by hand in the RKDH I copy of the catalogue.	Margaretha Maria van Laar	(Sold) fl 1 A van Houten
1802/02/23	AMREB	0046[H]	*[Anonymous]* | 1 dito [Schilderij] | *Notes:* This lot was added in by hand in the RKDH I copy of the catalogue.	Margaretha Maria van Laar	(Sold) fl 3:15 for lots 46[H], 47[H] & 48[H]. A van Houten
1802/02/23	AMREB	0047[H]	*[Anonymous]* | 1 dito [Schilderij] | *Notes:* This lot was added in by hand in the RKDH I copy of the catalogue.	Margaretha Maria van Laar	(Sold) fl 3:15 for lots 46[H], 47[H] & 48[H]. A van Houten
1802/02/23	AMREB	0048[H]	*[Anonymous]* | 1 dito [Schilderij] | *Notes:* This lot was added in by hand in the RKDH I copy of the catalogue.	Margaretha Maria van Laar	(Sold) fl 3:15 for lots 46[H], 47[H] & 48[H]. A van Houten
1802/04/13	HAVIN	0013	*[Anonymous]* | Een oude Gryze Blindeman, waarby een Man met de Hoed in de hand, een Aelmoes verzoekende, schoon geschildert		(Unknown)
1802/04/13	HAVIN	0025	*[Anonymous]* | Twee, verbeeldende een Kraamkamer en Kandeelmaal, zeer fraai		(Unknown)
1802/04/13	HAVIN	0041	*[Anonymous]* | Twee Historien, in 't Grauw, door		(Unknown)
1802/04/13	HAVIN	0042	*[Anonymous]* | Adam en Eva, schoon geschildert, door		(Unknown)
1802/04/13	HAVIN	0043	*[Anonymous]* | Een Landschap met een Campement, door		(Unknown)
1802/04/13	HAVIN	0076	*[Anonymous]* | Twee Manshoofden, door		(Unknown)
1802/04/13	HAVIN	0077	*[Anonymous]* | Twee Vrouwe, door dezelve		(Unknown)
1802/04/13	HAVIN	0078	*[Anonymous]* | Een Bachus		(Unknown)
1802/04/14	HGKAN	0004	*[Anonymous]* | Twee Schilderyen in Oly Verff | *Mat:* in olyverf		(Unknown)
1802/04/14	HGKAN	0005	*[Anonymous]* | Een Schildery		(Unknown)
1802/04/14	HGKAN	0006	*[Anonymous]* | Twee dito [Schilderyen]		(Unknown)
1802/04/14	HGKAN	0007	*[Anonymous]* | Een dito [Schildery] met het Portret van den Generaal Daendels		(Unknown)
1802/05/01	HGCLF	0046	*[Anonymous]* | Een Borstbeeld in Oliverf op paneel geschildert | *Mat:* in olyverf op paneel	Mr B de Moor van Immerzeel	(Unknown)
1802/05/01	HGCLF	0052	*[Anonymous]* | Een Blindemannetje	Mr B de Moor van Immerzeel	(Unknown)
1802/05/01	HGCLF	0053	*[Anonymous]* | Een Apen gezelschap, zynde een Negotie in Tulpen	Mr B de Moor van Immerzeel	(Unknown)
1802/05/01	HGCLF	0054	*[Anonymous]* | De Tempel der Vryheid met zyn byschrift, in Lyst en glas	Mr B de Moor van Immerzeel	(Unknown)
1802/05/01	HGCLF	0055	*[Anonymous]* | Twee Schilderytjes zynde Yvoore Scheepjes op een Zee van Wasch	Mr B de Moor van Immerzeel	(Unknown)
1802/05/05	AMSCH	0251	*Een goed Meester* | Een zinspeelende Ordonnantie van eenige Beelden, by een Kaarslicht, door een goed Meester | *Mat:* op paneel *Size:* hoog 21, breed 17 duim	G	(Sold) fl 3:15 Mensard
1802/05/05	AMSCH	0252	*Een goed Meester* | Een Mans Pourtrait, halverlyf, in ryke Kleeding, door een goed Meester | *Mat:* op doek *Size:* hoog 26, breed 21 duim	G	(Sold) fl 1 Cocler
1802/05/05	AMSCH	0253	*Een goed Meester* | Een Binnehuis, met eenige vegtende Krygslieden, welke een Boer plunderen, door een goed Meester | *Mat:* op doek *Size:* hoog 29, breed 34 duim	G	(Sold) fl 1 L Pakker
1802/05/05	AMSCH	0254	*[Anonymous]* | Een Duinachtig Landschap, op de Voorgrond een Man met een Paard, in het verschiet een Herder, by eenige grazende Schapen | *Mat:* op paneel *Size:* hoog 12, breed 14 duim	G	(Sold) fl 9:10 Rigters
1802/05/05	AMSCH	0257	*Een Voornaam Meester* | Door een open Vengster, ziet men by een Maanlicht op straat een Man, welke een Meisje, die een brandende Lamptaarn draagt, carresseeren; in 't verschiet eenige Boeren Wooningen, zeer dun en delicaat gepenceeld door een Voornaam Meester | *Mat:* op paneel *Size:* hoog 18, breed 14 duim	BB	(Sold) fl 30 v d Vinne
1802/05/05	AMSCH	0259	*Een goed Meester* | Een Zeeslag tusschen Hollandsche en Engelsche Scheepen, fiks gepenceeld door een goed Meester | *Size:* hoog 24, breed 35 duim	BB	(Sold) fl 0:10 L Pakker
1802/05/05	AMSCH	0260	*[Anonymous]* | Een Bloemstuk, meesterlyk | *Mat:* op doek *Size:* hoog 30, breed 27 duim	B	(Sold) fl 0:14 Ackina

1802/05/05	AMSCH	0262	*Een oud Meester* | In een Bosch ziet men een hevige Bataille tusschen Ruitery en Voetvolk, door een oud Meester	J	(Sold) fl 3 Rigters
1802/05/05	AMSCH	0264	*[Anonymous]* | Twee stuks diverse	J	(Sold) fl 1 L Pakker
1802/05/05	AMSCH	0265	*[Anonymous]* | Twee dito [stuks] dito [diverse]	J	(Sold) fl 0:6 V^{n} Iperen
1802/05/05	AMSCH	0267	*[Anonymous]* | Twee stuks divers	C	(Withdrawn)
1802/05/05	AMSCH	0268	*[Anonymous]* | Twee dito [stuks] dito [divers]	C	(Withdrawn)
1802/05/05	AMSCH	0269[H]	*[Anonymous]* | 1 [Schilderij] | *Notes:* This lot was added in by hand in the EBNP, LBDa and RKDH copies of the catalogue.	CC	(Sold) fl 39 I^{c} Smit
1802/05/05	AMSCH	0270[H]	*[Anonymous]* | 2 [Schilderijen] | *Notes:* This lot was added in by hand in the EBNP, LBDa and RKDH copies of the catalogue.	CC	(Sold) fl 23 Pruijssenaar [for] R
1802/05/05	AMSCH	0271[H]	*[Anonymous]* | 1 [Schilderij] | *Notes:* This lot was added in by hand in the EBNP, LBDa and RKDH copies of the catalogue.	CC	(Sold) fl 8:15 van Iperen
1802/05/05	AMSCH	0272[H]	*[Anonymous]* | 2 [Schilderijen] | *Notes:* This lot was added in by hand in the EBNP, LBDa and RKDH copies of the catalogue.	CC	(Sold) fl 20:10 Stevens
1802/05/05	AMSCH	0273[H]	*[Anonymous]* | 2 [Schilderijen] | *Notes:* This lot was added in by hand in the EBNP, LBDa and RKDH copies of the catalogue.	CC	(Sold) fl 10 Th Spaan
1802/05/05	AMSCH	0274[H]	*[Anonymous]* | 1 [Schilderij] | *Notes:* This lot was added in by hand in the EBNP, LBDa and RKDH copies of the catalogue.	CC	(Sold) fl 5:10 Rigters
1802/05/05	AMSCH	0275[H]	*[Anonymous]* | 1 [Schilderij] | *Notes:* This lot was added in by hand in the EBNP, LBDa and RKDH copies of the catalogue.	CC	(Sold) fl 12 Pruijssenaar [for] R
1802/05/05	AMSCH	0276[H]	*[Anonymous]* | 1 [Schilderij] | *Notes:* This lot was added in by hand in the EBNP, LBDa and RKDH copies of the catalogue.	CC	(Sold) fl 5:5 Rigters
1802/05/05	AMSCH	0277[H]	*[Anonymous]* | 1 [Schilderij] | *Notes:* This lot was added in by hand in the EBNP, LBDa and RKDH copies of the catalogue.	CC	(Sold) fl 4:10 van Dijl
1802/05/05	AMSCH	0278[H]	*[Anonymous]* | 1 [Schilderij] | *Notes:* This lot was added in by hand in the EBNP, LBDa and RKDH copies of the catalogue.	CC	(Sold) fl 3:10 Cocler
1802/05/05	AMSCH	0279[H]	*[Anonymous]* | 1 [Schilderij] | *Notes:* This lot was added in by hand in the EBNP, LBDa and RKDH copies of the catalogue.	CC	(Sold) fl 0:10 Gruiter
1802/05/05	AMSCH	0280[H]	*[Anonymous]* | 1 [Schilderij] | *Notes:* This lot was added in by hand in the EBNP, LBDa and RKDH copies of the catalogue.	CC	(Sold) fl 2:10 V^{n} Iperen
1802/05/05	AMSCH	0281[H]	*[Anonymous]* | 1 [Schilderij] | *Notes:* This lot was added in by hand in the EBNP, LBDa and RKDH copies of the catalogue.	CC	(Sold) fl 3 Cocler
1802/05/05	AMSCH	0282[H]	*[Anonymous]* | 1 [Schilderij] | *Notes:* This lot was added in by hand in the EBNP, LBDa and RKDH copies of the catalogue.	CC	(Sold) fl 29 Spruit
1802/05/05	AMSCH	0283[H]	*[Anonymous]* | 1 [Schilderij] | *Notes:* This lot was added in by hand in the EBNP, LBDa and RKDH copies of the catalogue.	CC	(Sold) fl 1:15 Stevens
1802/05/05	AMSCH	0284[H]	*[Anonymous]* | 1 [Schilderij] | *Notes:* This lot was added in by hand in the EBNP, LBDa and RKDH copies of the catalogue.	A	(Sold) fl 3 Gruiter
1802/05/05	AMSCH	0285[H]	*[Anonymous]* | 1 [Schilderij] | *Notes:* This lot was added in by hand in the EBNP, LBDa and RKDH copies of the catalogue.	A	(Sold) fl 1:15 Gruiter
1802/05/05	AMSCH	0286[H]	*[Anonymous]* | 1 [Schilderij] | *Notes:* This lot was added in by hand in the EBNP, LBDa and RKDH copies of the catalogue.	A	(Sold) fl 1:15 Gruiter
1802/05/05	AMSCH	0287[H]	*[Anonymous]* | 4 [Schilderijen] | *Notes:* This lot was added in by hand in the EBNP, LBDa and RKDH copies of the catalogue.	A	(Sold) fl 0:12 for lots 287[H] & 288[H]. Vermeulen
1802/05/05	AMSCH	0288[H]	*[Anonymous]* | 4 [Schilderijen] | *Notes:* This lot was added in by hand in the EBNP, LBDa and RKDH copies of the catalogue.	A	(Sold) fl 0:12 for lots 287[H] & 288[H]. Vermeulen
1802/05/05	AMSCH	0289[H]	*[Anonymous]* | 2 [Schilderijen] | *Notes:* This lot was added in by hand in the EBNP, LBDa and RKDH copies of the catalogue.	A	(Sold) fl 0:14 Gruiter
1802/05/05	AMSCH	0290[H]	*[Anonymous]* | 1 [Schilderij] | *Notes:* This lot was added in by hand in the EBNP, LBDa and RKDH copies of the catalogue.	A	(Sold) fl 1 van Iperen
1802/05/05	AMSCH	0291[H]	*[Anonymous]* | 5 [Schilderijen] | *Notes:* This lot was added in by hand in the EBNP, LBDa and RKDH copies of the catalogue.	BB	(Sold) fl 3:5 Spruit
1802/05/05	AMSCH	0292[H]	*[Anonymous]* | 5 [Schilderijen] | *Notes:* This lot was added in by hand in the EBNP, LBDa and RKDH copies of the catalogue.	BB	(Sold) fl 4 Spruit
1802/05/05	AMSCH	0293[H]	*[Anonymous]* | 5 [Schilderijen] | *Notes:* This lot was added in by hand in the EBNP, LBDa and RKDH copies of the catalogue.	BB	(Sold) fl 0:6 Gruiter
1802/05/05	AMSCH	0294[H]	*[Anonymous]* | 2 [Schilderijen] | *Notes:* This lot was added in by hand in the EBNP, LBDa and RKDH copies of the catalogue.	BB	(Sold) fl 2:15 A Schotte
1802/05/05	AMSCH	0295[H]	*[Anonymous]* | 3 [Schilderijen] | *Notes:* This lot was added in by hand in the EBNP, LBDa and RKDH copies of the catalogue.	BB	(Sold) fl 1 Spruit
1802/05/05	AMSCH	0296[H]	*[Anonymous]* | 2 [Schilderijen] | *Notes:* This lot was added in by hand in the EBNP, LBDa and RKDH copies of the catalogue.	BB	(Sold) fl 8 Stevens
1802/05/05	AMSCH	0297[H]	*[Anonymous]* | 3 [Schilderijen] | *Notes:* This lot was added in by hand in the EBNP, LBDa and RKDH copies of the catalogue.	BB	(Sold) fl 2:15 Stevens

1802/05/05	AMSCH	0298[H]	*[Anonymous]* | 3 [Schilderijen] | *Notes:* This lot was added in by hand in the EBNP, LBDa and RKDH copies of the catalogue.	BB	(Sold) fl 1:5 D^{k} Langenberg
1802/05/05	AMSCH	0299[H]	*[Anonymous]* | 2 [Schilderijen] | *Notes:* This lot was added in by hand in the EBNP, LBDa and RKDH copies of the catalogue.	BB	(Sold) fl 1 L^{y} Pakker
1802/05/05	AMSCH	0300[H]	*[Anonymous]* | 1 [Schilderij] | *Notes:* This lot was added in by hand in the EBNP, LBDa and RKDH copies of the catalogue.	BB	(Sold) fl 4:10 Gruiter
1802/05/05	AMSCH	0301[H]	*[Anonymous]* | 4 [Schilderijen] | *Notes:* This lot was added in by hand in the EBNP, LBDa and RKDH copies of the catalogue.	BB	(Sold) fl 5 J^{n} Spaan
1802/05/05	AMSCH	0304[H]	*[Anonymous]* | 1 [Schilderij] | *Notes:* This lot was added in by hand in the EBNP, LBDa and RKDH copies of the catalogue.	J	(Sold) fl 4:15 Gruiter
1802/05/05	AMSCH	0305[H]	*[Anonymous]* | 1 [Schilderij] | *Notes:* This lot was added in by hand in the EBNP, LBDa and RKDH copies of the catalogue.	J	(Sold) fl 2:5 Gruiter
1802/05/05	AMSCH	0306[H]	*[Anonymous]* | 1 [Schilderij] | *Notes:* This lot was added in by hand in the EBNP, LBDa and RKDH copies of the catalogue.	J	(Sold) fl 8:10 Cocler
1802/05/05	AMSCH	0307[H]	*[Anonymous]* | 1 [Schilderij] | *Notes:* This lot was added in by hand in the EBNP, LBDa and RKDH copies of the catalogue.	J	(Sold) fl 1 V^{n} Iperen
1802/05/05	AMSCH	0308[H]	*[Anonymous]* | 1 [Schilderij] | *Notes:* This lot was added in by hand in the EBNP, LBDa and RKDH copies of the catalogue.	CC	(Sold) fl 1:15 V^{n} Iperen
1802/05/05	AMSCH	0314[H]	*[Anonymous]* | 1 [Schilderij] | *Notes:* This lot was added in by hand in the EBNP, LBDa and RKDH copies of the catalogue.	CC	(Sold) fl 18 Stevens
1802/05/05	AMSCH	0314a[H]	*[Anonymous]* | 1 [Schilderij] | *Notes:* This lot was added in by hand in the EBNP, LBDa and RKDH copies of the catalogue.	CC	(Sold) fl 1:5 Mensard
1802/05/05	AMSCH	0315[H]	*[Anonymous]* | 1 [Schilderij] | *Notes:* This lot was added in by hand in the EBNP, LBDa and RKDH copies of the catalogue.	CC	(Sold) fl 1 Pruyssenaar [for] R
1802/05/05	AMSCH	0316[H]	*[Anonymous]* | 1 [Schilderij] | *Notes:* This lot was added in by hand in the EBNP, LBDa and RKDH copies of the catalogue.	CC	(Sold) fl 3:5 Stevens
1802/05/05	AMSCH	0317[H]	*[Anonymous]* | 1 [Schilderij] | *Notes:* This lot was added in by hand in the EBNP, LBDa and RKDH copies of the catalogue.	J	(Sold) fl 30 Stevens
1802/05/05	AMSCH	0318[H]	*[Anonymous]* | 1 [Schilderij] | *Notes:* This lot was added in by hand in the EBNP, LBDa and RKDH copies of the catalogue.	J	(Sold) fl 6:5 Cocler
1802/05/05	AMSCH	0319[H]	*[Anonymous]* | 1 [Schilderij] | *Notes:* This lot was added in by hand in the EBNP, LBDa and RKDH copies of the catalogue.	J	(Sold) fl 5 L Pakker
1802/05/05	AMSCH	0320[H]	*[Anonymous]* | 1 [Schilderij] | *Notes:* This lot was added in by hand in the EBNP, LBDa and RKDH copies of the catalogue.	A	(Sold) fl 0:10 L Pakker
1802/05/05	AMSCH	0321[H]	*[Anonymous]* | 1 [Schilderij] | *Notes:* This lot was added in by hand in the EBNP, LBDa and RKDH copies of the catalogue.	A	(Sold) fl 0:10 L Pakker
1802/05/05	AMSCH	0322[H]	*[Anonymous]* | 1 [Schilderij] | *Notes:* This lot was added in by hand in the EBNP, LBDa and RKDH copies of the catalogue.	A	(Sold) fl 0:6 V^{n} Iperen
1802/05/05	AMSCH	0323[H]	*[Anonymous]* | 2 [Schilderijen] | *Notes:* This lot was added in by hand in the EBNP, LBDa and RKDH copies of the catalogue.	A	(Sold) fl 1 J Spaan
1802/05/05	AMSCH	0324[H]	*[Anonymous]* | 2 [Schilderijen] | *Notes:* This lot was added in by hand in the EBNP, LBDa and RKDH copies of the catalogue.	A	(Sold) fl 0:12 Gruiter
1802/05/10	MGSAN	0001	*[Anonymous]* | Een capitaal Stuk, waarop de Tyd Cupido de vleugels snoeiënde; op de voorgrond een Doodshoofd, stout geschilderd, door een goed Meester: op Paneel, in zwarte Lyst | *Mat:* op paneel *Size:* hoog 68 duim, breed 44 duim	Johan Dirk Kruysse	(Unknown)
1802/05/10	MGSAN	0002	*[Anonymous]* | Een dito [capitaal] Historiestuk, vertoonende het uitdeelen van Brood en Wyn, en het aanschouwen van een Vorst, in Romeinsche Kleeding, zeer stout geschilderd, door een goed Meester: op Doek, in zwarte Lyst | *Mat:* op doek *Size:* hoog 42 duim, breed 64 duim	Johan Dirk Kruysse	(Unknown)
1802/05/10	MGSAN	0003	*[Anonymous]* | Een Boomryk Landschap, waarop een Dans van naakte Kinderen, levendig geschilderd, door een oud Meester: op Doek, zwarte Lyst, met vergulde Binnenlyst | *Mat:* op doek *Size:* hoog 36 duim, breed 47 duim	Johan Dirk Kruysse	(Unknown)
1802/05/10	MGSAN	0005	*[Anonymous]* | Een fraai Boschgezigt, waarin een Herder, met verscheide Schaapen, daarby een Man, met een Hond; in 't verschiet een Dorpgezigt, krachtig geschilderd: op Doek, in vergulde Lyst | *Mat:* op doek *Size:* hoog 38 duim, breed 50 duim	Johan Dirk Kruysse	(Unknown) £ 3:7
1802/05/10	MGSAN	0006	*[Anonymous]* | Een dito [fraai] Historiestuk, vertoonende een Landschap, daarop de drie Gratien, waarby Mercuur, en een Herder met Schaapen en eenige speelende Kindertjes; benevens een Paauw, door een zeer goed Meester: op Doek, in een vergulde Lyst | *Mat:* op doek *Size:* hoog 31 duim, breed 46 duim	Johan Dirk Kruysse	(Unknown) £ 11:01
1802/05/10	MGSAN	0010	*Een zeer goed Meester* | Een capitaal Stuk, vertoonende een prachtigen Tempel, daarby de Vlucht van Eneas met zyn Vader, uit den Brand van Troiën; verder eenig onderscheidene Beelden en ander Bywerk, stout en meesterachtig geschilderd, door een zeer goed Meester: op Doek, vergulde Lyst | *Mat:* op doek *Size:* hoog 34 duim, breed 46 duim	Johan Dirk Kruysse	(Unknown) £ 1:3
1802/05/10	MGSAN	0011	*[Anonymous]* | Een stille Zee, met verscheide Schepen en Schuiten, zeer uitvoerig, door een goed Meester: op Doek, in vergulde Lyst | *Mat:* op doek *Size:* hoog 37 duim, breed 59 duim	Johan Dirk Kruysse	(Unknown) £ 0:15

1802/05/10	MGSAN	0012	*[Anonymous]* | Een dito [stille Zee] aan een Kasteel, daarby een hooge Molen, op een Landschap, zeer uitvoerig als boven: op Doek, in vergulde Lyst | *Mat:* op doek *Size:* hoog 37 duim, breed 59 duim *Notes:* It is unclear what "dito" refers to in the title.	Johan Dirk Kruysse	(Unknown) £ 0:17
1802/05/10	MGSAN	0013	*[Anonymous]* | Een fraai Landschap, waarop een Drift met Beesten, zeer uitvoerig, door als boven: op Doek, in zwarte, met vergulde Binnenlyst | *Mat:* op doek *Size:* hoog 22 duim, breed 19 duim	Johan Dirk Kruysse	(Unknown) £ 2:6
1802/05/10	MGSAN	0015	*[Anonymous]* | Een Stuk, waarop twee naakte speelende Kindertjes, met Bloemptjes, op een Tafel zittende, extra levendig geschilderd, door een goed Meester: op Doek, in vergulde Lyst | *Mat:* op doek *Size:* hoog 29 duim, breed 49 duim	Johan Dirk Kruysse	(Unknown) £ 1:1
1802/05/10	MGSAN	0020	*[Anonymous]* | Een fraai Land- en Boschgezigt, met eenige Persoonen te Paard, verbeeldende een Valkenjacht, krachtig geschilderd, door een goed Meester: op Paneel, in vergulde Lyst | *Mat:* op paneel *Size:* hoog 13 duim, breed 20 duim	Johan Dirk Kruysse	(Unknown) £ 0:9
1802/05/10	MGSAN	0035	*[Anonymous]* | Een extra fraai Vrouwenbeeldje, op een zilveren plaat, extra malsch gepenseeld, door een oud Meester: in een zwarte Lyst, is geconserveerd in een met caret ingelegd kasje	Johan Dirk Kruysse	(Unknown) £ 3
1802/05/10	MGSAN	0037	*[Anonymous]* | Een dito [zeer fraai] Landschap, met Schaapen, daarby een zittende naakte Vrouw, met een fraaije zyde Sluiër omhangen; in 't verschiet eenig Gebergte, met een Ruïne, en een Brug over Water, als voren | *Size:* hoog 15 ½ duim, breed 20 duim *Notes:* It is unclear what "dito" refers to in the title.	Johan Dirk Kruysse	(Withdrawn)
1802/05/10	MGSAN	0039	*Een goed Meester* | Een Landschap, waarop een Man, houdende een Paard by den toom, op de voorgrond een Jachthond; in 't verschiet een Berg. en anders, door een goed Meester: op Paneel, in vergulde Lyst | *Mat:* op paneel *Size:* hoog 18 ½ duim, breed 15 duim	Johan Dirk Kruysse	(Unknown) £ 1:10
1802/05/10	MGSAN	0042	*Een goed Meester* | Een zittende Dame, leunende met haar arm tegen een Boom, hebbende een Jachthond vóór haar, fiks en zacht geschilderd, door een goed Meester: op Paneel, in vergulde Lyst | *Mat:* op paneel *Size:* hoog 19 duim, breed 14 duim	Johan Dirk Kruysse	(Unknown) £ 1:3
1802/05/10	MGSAN	0044	*[Anonymous]* | Een dito [Mansportrait], met een blaauwe Mantel: op Paneel. in zwarte Lyst, met vergulde Binnenlyst | *Mat:* op paneel *Size:* hoog 16 duim, breed 12 duim	Johan Dirk Kruysse	(Unknown) £ 0:4
1802/05/10	MGSAN	0045	*Een goed Meester* | Een Vrouwe Portrait, zeer fraai geschilderd, door een goed Meester: op Doek, in vergulde Lyst | *Mat:* op doek *Size:* hoog 18 duim, breed 13 ½ duim	Johan Dirk Kruysse	(Unknown) £ 0:5
1802/05/10	MGSAN	0050	*[Anonymous]* | Twee Land- en Zeegezigtjes, fraai geschilderd: op Paneel, in vergulde Lyst | *Mat:* op paneel *Size:* hoog 9 duim, breed 11 duim	Johan Dirk Kruysse	(Unknown) £ 1:9
1802/05/11	GRGRW	0001	*[Anonymous]* | Een Mans Portrait, Levensgrootte. Van ene goede hand [Schilderijen met Olie-Verf; In zwarte Lijsten] | *Mat:* in olyverf *Notes:* The bracketed information in the title appears above lot 1 and refers to lots 1 to 79a.	Arnold Sicco Werumeus	(Unknown)
1802/05/11	GRGRW	0002	*[Anonymous]* | Een dito [Portrait] Vrouwe [Schilderijen met Olie-Verf; In zwarte Lijsten] | *Mat:* in olyverf *Notes:* The bracketed information in the title about the medium appears above lot 1 and refers to lots 1 to 79a.	Arnold Sicco Werumeus	(Unknown)
1802/05/11	GRGRW	0003	*[Anonymous]* | Het welgelijkend Portrait van Menno Simons [Schilderijen met Olie-Verf; In zwarte Lijsten] | *Mat:* in olyverf *Fmt:* ovaal *Notes:* The bracketed information in the title appears above lot 1 and refers to lots 1 to 79a. The format appears in lot 4 and refers to lots 3 and 4.	Arnold Sicco Werumeus	(Unknown)
1802/05/11	GRGRW	0004	*[Anonymous]* | Een dito [welgelijkend Portrait] van Ubbo Emmius. Beiden in Ovaal, en wel geschilderd [Schilderijen met Olie-Verf; In zwarte Lijsten] | *Mat:* in olyverf *Fmt:* ovaal *Notes:* The bracketed information in the title appears above lot 1 and refers to lots 1 to 79a. The format mentioned in the title refers to lots 3 and 4.	Arnold Sicco Werumeus	(Unknown)
1802/05/11	GRGRW	0005	*[Anonymous]* | Een Mans portrait [Schilderijen met Olie-Verf; In zwarte Lijsten] | *Mat:* in olyverf *Notes:* The bracketed information in the title appears above lot 1 and refers to lots 1 to 79a.	Arnold Sicco Werumeus	(Unknown)
1802/05/11	GRGRW	0006	*[Anonymous]* | Een Vrouwe Portrait [Schilderijen met Olie-Verf; In zwarte Lijsten] | *Mat:* in olyverf *Notes:* The bracketed information in the title appears above lot 1 and refers to lots 1 to 79a.	Arnold Sicco Werumeus	(Unknown)
1802/05/11	GRGRW	0007	*[Anonymous]* | Een dito [Vrouwe Portrait] [Schilderijen met Olie-Verf; In zwarte Lijsten] | *Mat:* in olyverf *Notes:* The bracketed information in the title about the medium appears above lot 1 and refers to lots 1 to 79a.	Arnold Sicco Werumeus	(Unknown)
1802/05/11	GRGRW	0010	*[Anonymous]* | De slag voor Nieuwpoort [Schilderijen met Olie-Verf; In zwarte Lijsten] | *Mat:* in olyverf *Notes:* The bracketed information in the title appears above lot 1 and refers to lots 1 to 79a.	Arnold Sicco Werumeus	(Unknown)
1802/05/11	GRGRW	0020	*[Anonymous]* | Een dito [Landschap] [Schilderijen met Olie-Verf; In zwarte Lijsten] | *Mat:* in olyverf *Notes:* The bracketed information in the title about the medium appears above lot 1 and refers to lots 1 to 79a.	Arnold Sicco Werumeus	(Unknown)
1802/05/11	GRGRW	0021	*Een Goed Meester* | Een Vogelstuk. Van enen Goeden Meester [Schilderijen met Olie-Verf; In zwarte Lijsten] | *Mat:* in olyverf *Notes:*	Arnold Sicco Werumeus	(Unknown)

			The bracketed information in the title appears above lot 1 and refers to lots 1 to 79a.		
1802/05/11	GRGRW	0026	*[Anonymous]* | Ene dito [Omstuimige Zee], tot ene Weerga [Schilderijen met Olie-Verf; In zwarte Lijsten] | companion to lot 25, by P. van de Venne *Mat:* in olyverf *Notes:* The bracketed information in the title about the medium appears above lot 1 and refers to lots 1 to 79a.	Arnold Sicco Werumeus	(Unknown)
1802/05/11	GRGRW	0048a	*[Anonymous]* | Een dito [schoon Zee-gezicht], van enen anderen Meester [Schilderijen met Olie-Verf; In zwarte Lijsten] | *Mat:* in olyverf *Notes:* The bracketed information in the title about the medium appears above lot 1 and refers to lots 1 to 79a.	Arnold Sicco Werumeus	(Unknown) fl 2:14
1802/05/11	GRGRW	0049	*[Anonymous]* | Een Herder-Stukje [Schilderijen met Olie-Verf; In zwarte Lijsten] | *Mat:* in olyverf *Notes:* The bracketed information in the title appears above lot 1 and refers to lots 1 to 79a.	Arnold Sicco Werumeus	(Unknown) fl 0:16
1802/05/11	GRGRW	0059	*[Anonymous]* | De Vier Euangelisten [sic], zonder Lijsten [Schilderijen met Olie-Verf] | *Mat:* in olyverf *Notes:* The bracketed information in the title appears above lot 1 and refers to lots 1 to 79a.	Arnold Sicco Werumeus	(Unknown) fl 1
1802/05/11	GRGRW	0071	*Een goede hand* | Twee Stukjes, zijnde het Hoofd van enen lachenden jonge en Meisje; door ene goede hand [Schilderijen met Olie-Verf; In Vergulde Lijsten] | *Mat:* in olyverf *Notes:* The bracketed information in the title appears above lot 1 and refers to lots 1 to 79a.	Arnold Sicco Werumeus	(Unknown) fl 5:15 for lots 71 & 72
1802/05/11	GRGRW	0072	*[Anonymous]* | Twee dito [Stukjes] [Schilderijen met Olie-Verf; In Vergulde Lijsten] | *Mat:* in olyverf *Notes:* It is unclear what "dito" refers to in the title. The bracketed information in the title about the medium appears above lot 1 and refers to lots 1 to 79a.	Arnold Sicco Werumeus	(Unknown) fl 5:15 for lots 71 & 72
1802/05/11	GRGRW	0073	*[Anonymous]* | Een boucquet [sic] Bloemen, in een Vlesje, zeer fraai op koper geschilderd [Schilderijen met Olie-Verf; In Vergulde Lijsten] | *Mat:* in olyverf op koper *Notes:* The bracketed information in the title appears above lot 1 and refers to lots 1 to 79a.	Arnold Sicco Werumeus	(Unknown) fl 3
1802/05/11	GRGRW	0074	*[Anonymous]* | Zijdewormen, en andere Insecten, Visschen en Vogels; ad idem. [op koper] [Schilderijen met Olie-Verf; In Vergulde Lijsten] | *Mat:* in olyverf op koper *Notes:* The second bracketed information in the title appears above lot 1 and refers to lots 1 to 79a.	Arnold Sicco Werumeus	(Unknown) fl 1:18
1802/05/11	GRGRW	0075	*[Anonymous]* | Hendrik de IV. in koper gedreven, verguld, in ene bruine Lijst [Schilderijen met Olie-Verf] | *Mat:* in olyverf op koper *Notes:* The bracketed information in the title appears above lot 1 and refers to lots 1 to 79a.	Arnold Sicco Werumeus	(Unknown) fl 1:4
1802/05/11	GRGRW	0076	*[Anonymous]* | Hendrik de IV. en M. Augusta, in dito [koper gedreven], in vergulde Lijst [Schilderijen met Olie-Verf] | *Mat:* in olyverf op koper *Notes:* The second bracketed information in the title appears above lot 1 and refers to lots 1 to 79a.	Arnold Sicco Werumeus	(Unknown) fl 2
1802/05/11	GRGRW	0077	*[Anonymous]* | J. Caesar I. en Tiberius Caesar III. op koper geemailleerd, in dito [vergulde Lijst] [Schilderijen met Olie-Verf] | *Mat:* in olyverf op koper *Notes:* The bracketed information in the title about the medium appears above lot 1 and refers to lots 1 to 79a.	Arnold Sicco Werumeus	(Unknown) fl 4:15 for lots 77–79
1802/05/11	GRGRW	0078	*[Anonymous]* | Caligula Ceasar IV en Flav. Vespasianus X. in dito [vergulde Lijst] [Schilderijen met Olie-Verf] | *Mat:* in olyverf *Notes:* The bracketed information in the title about the medium appears above lot 1 and refers to lots 1 to 79a.	Arnold Sicco Werumeus	(Unknown) fl 4:15 for lots 77–79
1802/05/11	GRGRW	0079	*[Anonymous]* | Vespasianus XII. en C. T. Augustus. in dito [vergulde Lijst] [Schilderijen met Olie-Verf] | *Mat:* in olyverf *Notes:* The bracketed information in the title about the medium appears above lot 1 and refers to lots 1 to 79a.	Arnold Sicco Werumeus	(Unknown) fl 4:15 for lots 77–79
1802/05/11	GRGRW	0079a	*[Anonymous]* | De Slag op Doggersbank, in 3 platen [Schilderijen met Olie-Verf; In Vergulde Lijsten] | *Mat:* in olyverf *Notes:* The bracketed information in the title appears above lot 1 and refers to lots 1 to 79a.	Arnold Sicco Werumeus	(Unknown) fl 8:5
1802/05/22	RMHSN	0002	*[Anonymous]* | Een Geldtel ende [sic] Mannetje by een Vrouwtje die Naaid by Lampligt	Lambertus Bicker	(Unknown)
1802/05/22	RMHSN	0010	*[Anonymous]* | Een stil Leven met Vruchten, &c.	Lambertus Bicker	(Unknown)
1802/05/22	RMHSN	0011	*[Anonymous]* | Een dito [stil Leven] met Visch	Lambertus Bicker	(Unknown)
1802/05/22	RMHSN	0012	*[Anonymous]* | Een Maneschyn	Lambertus Bicker	(Unknown)
1802/05/22	RMHSN	0013	*[Anonymous]* | Twee stuks Landschapjes	Lambertus Bicker	(Unknown)
1802/05/22	RMHSN	0015	*[Anonymous]* | Een stuk met dood Wild en een Kat	Lambertus Bicker	(Unknown)
1802/05/22	RMHSN	0016	*[Anonymous]* | Een Keuken stuk met Vrugten, &c.	Lambertus Bicker	(Unknown)
1802/05/22	RMHSN	0019	*[Anonymous]* | Een Landschapje waarin een Kar met Paard en eenige Beeldjes	Lambertus Bicker	(Unknown)
1802/05/22	RMHSN	0020	*[Anonymous]* | Een St. Pieters Scheepje	Lambertus Bicker	(Unknown)
1802/05/22	RMHSN	0022	*[Anonymous]* | Een Zeehaven met Schepen	Lambertus Bicker	(Unknown)
1802/05/22	RMHSN	0023	*[Anonymous]* | De Historie van Cano in de gevangenis	Lambertus Bicker	(Unknown)
1802/05/22	RMHSN	0026	*[Anonymous]* | Een Zinnebeeldige schilderkonst	Lambertus Bicker	(Unknown)

1802/05/22	RMHSN	0027	*[Anonymous]* | Twee Vrouwebeelden, met een Moortje aan wien Paerle &c. worden overhandigd	Lambertus Bicker	(Unknown)
1802/05/22	RMHSN	0029	*[Anonymous]* | Een stil Leven met Fruiten, Visch &c. op Doek | *Mat:* op doek	Lambertus Bicker	(Unknown)
1802/05/22	RMHSN	0030	*[Anonymous]* | Een dito [stil Leven] dito [met Fruiten, Visch &c.]	Lambertus Bicker	(Unknown)
1802/05/24	HGBAK	0003	*[Anonymous]* | Een Italiaansch stukje, op de voorgrond eenige Slepers en Werklieden met hunne Paarden, op de agtergrond een bergachtig Landschap, door eene meesterlyke hand, hoog 14 duim, breed 12 ½ duim paneel, zwarte lyst en vergulde bies | *Mat:* op paneel *Size:* hoog 14 duim, breed 12 ½ duim	Mejuffrouw A van der Mieden	(Sold) fl 7 te ché
1802/05/24	HGBAK	0008	*[Anonymous]* | Een Bosch en bergachtig Landschap, met eenige Beelden gestoffeerd, zeer fraay behandeld, door een goed Meester, hoog 21 duim, breed 27 duim, op doek, zwarte lyst en vergulde binnenrand | *Mat:* op doek *Size:* hoog 21 duim, breed 27 duim	Mejuffrouw A van der Mieden	(Sold) fl 6:5 Sluijter
1802/05/24	HGBAK	0010	*[Anonymous]* | Willem de tweede, geharnast, hoog 18 duim, breed 15 duim, op doek | *Mat:* op doek *Size:* hoog 15 duim, breed 18 duim	Mejuffrouw A van der Mieden	(Sold) fl 6:5 for lots 10–12. Ondorp
1802/05/24	HGBAK	0011	*[Anonymous]* | Een Kwaksalver, bezig om een Boer te tand te trekken, hoog 22 duim, breed 16 ½ duim, vergulde lyst | companion to lot 12 *Size:* hoog 22 duim, breed 16 ½ duim	Mejuffrouw A van der Mieden	(Sold) fl 6:5 for lots 10–12. Ondorp
1802/05/24	HGBAK	0012	*[Anonymous]* | Een tot een weerga, daar een Boer de kop geslepen word, hoog en breed als boven | companion to lot 11 *Size:* hoog 22 duim, breed 16 ½ duim	Mejuffrouw A van der Mieden	(Sold) fl 6:5 for lots 10–12. Ondorp
1802/05/24	HGBAK	0018	*[Anonymous]* | Koningin Maria, houdende het pourtrait van Willem de derde, Prins van Orange en Koning van Engeland, hoog 3 voet 11 duim, breed 3 voet ½ duim, op doek, vergulde lyst | *Mat:* op doek *Size:* hoog 3 voet 11 duim, breed 3 voet ½ duim	Mejuffrouw A van der Mieden	(Sold) fl 1 Kleijn
1802/05/24	HGBAK	0020	*[Anonymous]* | Christus met de doorne Kroon, en de Rietstaf met de purpere Mantel omhangen, zeer fraay, hoog 2 voet 4 duim, breed 2 voet, op doek, zwarte ebbe lyst en vergulde binnenrand | *Mat:* op doek *Size:* hoog 2 voet 4 duim, breed 2 voet	Mejuffrouw A van der Mieden	(Sold) fl 15:5 for lots 20 & 21. Ondorp
1802/05/24	HGBAK	0021	*[Anonymous]* | Een weenende Maria, door denzelven Meester, hoog en breed als vooren [hoog 2 voet 4 duim, breed 2 voet] en dito [zwarte ebbe] lyst | *Size:* hoog 2 voet 4 duim, breed 2 voet	Mejuffrouw A van der Mieden	(Sold) fl 15:5 for lots 20 & 21. Ondorp
1802/05/24	HGBAK	0025	*[Anonymous]* | Een onstuimige Zee met Schepen, door een zeer goed Meester, hoog 18 ½ duim, breed 25 ½ duim paneel, zwarte lyst en vergulde binnenrand | *Mat:* op paneel *Size:* hoog 18 ½ duim, breed 25 ½ duim	Mejuffrouw A van der Mieden	(Sold) fl 5:15 Ondorp
1802/05/24	HGBAK	0031	*[Anonymous]* | Een Landschap, met twee Ruiters en andere figuren gestoffeerd, hoog 13 ½ duim, breed 16 ¾ duim, op doek, zwarte lyst en vergulde bies | *Mat:* op doek *Size:* hoog 13 ½ duim, breed 16 ¾ duim	Mejuffrouw A van der Mieden	(Unknown) fl 3
1802/05/24	HGBAK	0035	*[Anonymous]* | Een fraay Cabinet-stukje, zynde een Maneschyn, op de middelgrond vertoond zich een Slot daar eenige lieden voor op de brug een vuur stooken, zeer fix behandeld, hoog 8 ¾ duim, breed 10 duim, paneel, zwarte lyst en vergulde binnenrand | companion to lot 36 *Mat:* op paneel *Size:* hoog 8 ¾ duim, breed 10 duim	Mejuffrouw A van der Mieden	(Sold) fl 8 for lots 35 & 36. Boscet [?]
1802/05/24	HGBAK	0036	*[Anonymous]* | Een dito [fraay Cabinet-stukje] tot een weerga, hoog als vooren en dito [zwarte] lyst | companion to lot 35 *Mat:* op paneel *Size:* hoog 8 ¾ duim, breed 10 duim *Notes:* It is unclear what "dito" refers to in the title.	Mejuffrouw A van der Mieden	(Sold) fl 8 for lots 35 & 36. Boscet [?]
1802/05/24	HGBAK	0037	*[Anonymous]* | Een Bosch en Duinachtig Landschap, benevens eenige Jagers ter Valkenjagt, op de voorgrond eene van die welke zich door een Heidin in de hand laat zien, hoog 12 ½ duim, breed 16 ¼ duim, op doek, zwarte lyst en vergulde binnenrand | *Mat:* op doek *Size:* hoog 12 ½ duim, breed 16 ¼ duim	Mejuffrouw A van der Mieden	(Sold) fl 36 ver Meulen
1802/05/24	HGBAK	0038	*[Anonymous]* | Een schoon Cabinet-stukje, verbeeldende een staande Dame, gekleed in wit Satyn, speelende op de Guitar, op een Stoel ligt een Hondje, en op een Tafel, door een Tapyt gedekt, staat een fles met Roozen, alles zeer uitvoerig en delicaat behandeld, hoog 11 ½ duim, breed 9 ¼ duim, op paneel, vergulde lyst | *Mat:* op paneel *Size:* hoog 11 ½ duim, breed 9 ¼ duim	Mejuffrouw A van der Mieden	(Sold) fl 5:5 Ondorp
1802/05/24	HGBAK	0043	*[Anonymous]* | Een pourtrait van een Generaal, hoog 7 ½ duim, breed 6 duim, op doek, vergulde lyst | *Mat:* op doek *Size:* hoog 7 ½ duim, breed 6 duim *Notes:* This lot was sold with lot 42 by A. Mignon.	Mejuffrouw A van der Mieden	(Sold) fl 4:5 for lots 42 & 43. Kleijn
1802/05/24	HGBAK	0049	*[Anonymous]* | Een stuk, verbeeldende een plegtige optogt naar een Vorstelyk Paleis, vol beelden, hoog 2 voet 10 duim, breed 19 duim, op paneel, en zwarte lyst | *Mat:* op paneel *Size:* hoog 2 voet 10 duim, breed 19 duim	Mejuffrouw A van der Mieden	(Unknown) fl 6:5
1802/05/24	HGBAK	0050	*[Anonymous]* | Gezicht van Constantinopolen, hoog 1 voet 12 duim, breed 6 voet, op doek, zwarte lyst | *Mat:* op doek *Size:* hoog 1 voet 12 duim, breed 6 voet	Mejuffrouw A van der Mieden	(Sold) fl 1:2 Brendel
1802/05/24	HGBAK	0060	*[Anonymous]* | Een Fruitstukje, met Druiven, Abricoosen &c., hoog 14 duim, breed 10 duim, op doek, zwarte lyst | *Mat:* op doek *Size:* hoog 14 duim, breed 10 duim	Mejuffrouw A van der Mieden	(Sold) fl 3:15 Bosset

1802/05/24	HGBAK	0061	*[Anonymous]* | Twee Pourtraiten in ovale zwarte lysten | *Fmt:* ovaal	Mejuffrouw A van der Mieden	(Sold) fl 1:10 Ondorp
1802/05/24	HGBAK	0062	*[Anonymous]* | Een Kerkje van binnen met beeldjes, hoog 8 duim, breed 11 duim, zwarte lyst, paneel | *Mat:* op paneel *Size:* hoog 8 duim, breed 11 duim	Mejuffrouw A van der Mieden	(Sold) fl 6 v Meulen [?]
1802/05/24	HGBAK	0063	*[Anonymous]* | Een binnenhuis, met een Boertje, Boerinnetje en verder bywerk gestoffeerd, hoog 9 ½ duim, breed 11 ¼ duim, op paneel, zwarte lyst | *Mat:* op paneel *Size:* hoog 9 ½ duim, breed 11 ¼ duim	Mejuffrouw A van der Mieden	(Sold) fl 3:10 Lugtmans
1802/05/24	HGBAK	0064	*[Anonymous]* | Een Boschachtig Landschap, waarin Diana, hoog 17 duim, breed 21 duim, op paneel, zwarte lyst | *Mat:* op paneel *Size:* hoog 17 duim, breed 21 duim	Mejuffrouw A van der Mieden	(Unknown) fl 8
1802/06/16	AMSCH	0234	*Onbekend Meester* | Twee stuks fraaye Boschgezichte met hoog Geboomten, zynde dezelve beiden gestoffeerd met Jagers te paard en te voet, benevens hunne Honden; deeze Schilderyen zyn zeer zonachtig en meesterlyk behandeld | *Mat:* op paneel *Size:* yder is hoog 30, breed 24 duim	[Merrem]	(Sold) fl 115 Pruijssenaar [for] R
1802/06/16	AMSCH	0236	*Onbekend Meester* | Dit bevallig Voorwerp verbeeld, op een Marmer Steene Tafel en cierlyke Vaas, gevult met verscheide keurige Bloemen, als roode en witte Roozen en Knopjes, Angelieren, Tuberoosen, Orangebloeisem met Steel en Bladeren, Africaanen en andere zoorten; waar op Insecten aasen; de Groeping der Bloemen, de Harmonie der couleuren en de bevallige Loheid [sic], zyn zeer natuurlyk, en als door een krachtig Licht bescheenen en meesterlyk fraay gepenceeld | *Mat:* op paneel *Size:* hoog 24, breed 28 duim	[Merrem]	(Bought In) fl 100
1802/06/16	AMSCH	0237	*Onbekend Meester* | By de Ruwiene van een Gebouw, vertoont zich een Knielende en Biddende Bramine, in een Vorstinne gewaad, voor een brandend Altaar; verder een Landschap met Geboomten; het Caracter is fraay en natuurlyk, krachtig van Coloriet en van een uitvoerige penceel-behandeling | *Mat:* op paneel *Size:* hoog 13, breed 11 duim	[Merrem]	(Sold) fl 2 v d Schleij
1802/06/16	AMSCH	0238	*Onbekend Meester* | In een aangenaam Landschap met Geboomten, by een Beeste Stal ziet men een Boer een Koe melken, waar by rustende en staande Schaapen, op de voorgrond legt een Roscouleurde Koe; verder vertoonen zich twee Heeren te Paard en een Rytuig; uitvoerig en plaisant geschilderd | *Mat:* op paneel *Size:* hoog 11, breed 13 duim	[Merrem]	(Sold) fl 5 Gruiter
1802/06/16	AMSCH	0239	*Onbekend Meester* | Een Landzicht gestoffeerd, met verscheide vrolyke Huislieden, die zich vermaken; ter zyde staan twee losse Paarden, en een Boer by een Hooi-Wagen; natuurlyk behandeld | *Mat:* op paneel *Size:* hoog 12, breed 14 duim	[Merrem]	(Sold) fl 4:10 Agina
1802/06/16	AMSCH	0244	*Onbekend Meester* | Een Landschap met hoog Geboomten, gestoffeerd met een Kar en twee Paarden en eenige Voetgangers; verders een bergachtig verschiet, zonachtig behandeld	[Merrem]	(Sold) fl 4:5 Agina
1802/06/16	AMSCH	0246	*Onbekend Meester* | Een woelende Zee met verscheide zeilende Oorlogscheepen, ter zyde vertoont zich de Vestmuur, en gedeelte van een Stad; meesterlyk fiks geschilderd | *Mat:* op paneel *Size:* hoog 13, breed 16 duim	[Merrem]	(Sold) fl 1:10 L Pakker
1802/06/16	AMSCH	0247	*Onbekend Meester* | Een Bergachtig Landschap met Geboomten; by een opgaande weg zyn Reizigers met een beladen Ezel, en een Heer te Paard, waar by een gaande Huisman; verder een Rivier en eenige Gebouwen, fiks geschilderd | *Mat:* op paneel *Size:* hoog 13 ½, breed 17 ½ duim	[Merrem]	(Sold) fl 6:5 Cobel
1802/06/16	AMSCH	0249	*Onbekend Meester* | Twee stuks oude Mans Hoofden met gryze Baarden, in deftige Kleeding; krachtig van Coloriet, en is meesterlyk gepenceeld | *Mat:* op doek *Size:* ieder hoog 23, breed 19 duim	[Merrem]	(Sold) fl 2 Gruiter
1802/06/16	AMSCH	0250	*Onbekend Meester* | In een Keuken Vertrek staat ter een zyde een Ton, waar aan een kopere Leepel hangt, eenige Tinne Borden, Beezem en andere Huisraad; zeer uitvoerig op Paneel geschilderd | *Mat:* op paneel *Size:* hoog 5 ½, breed 4 ½ duim	[Merrem]	(Sold) fl 1:15 Gruiter
1802/06/16	AMSCH	0251	*Onbekend Meester* | Een Krygsheld, halver lyf, gedeeltelyk in het Harnas, op het Hoofd een Muts met Pluimen, krachtig geschilderd | *Mat:* op paneel *Size:* hoog 6, breed 4 ½ duim	[Merrem]	(Sold) fl 1:10 Takel
1802/06/16	AMSCH	0252	*Onbekend Meester* | Twee stuks stil Leevens, op Steene Tafels, gedeeltelyk met een Kleed bedekt; ziet men verscheide vruchten, bruine Aarde Kan; een Schootel met Vlees, doode Visch en Gevogelte; alles ongemeen krachtig en uitvoerig gepenceeld | *Mat:* op paneel *Size:* hoog 7 ½, breed 8 duim	[Merrem]	(Sold) fl 5 L Pakker
1802/06/28	AMSCH	0220	*[Anonymous]* | Twee stuks Fruitstukken, met verscheiden fraaije Bloemen en Fruiten, als blaauwe en witte Druiven, Canteloepen en Persiken, beide zeer natuurlyk gepenceeld, door een goed Meester, hoog 23, breed 27 duim, op Doek | *Mat:* op doek *Size:* hoog 23, breed 27 duim	Anna Elink	(Sold) fl 2 Dijkman
1802/06/28	AMSCH	0222	*[Anonymous]* | Twee stuks Historieele Ordonnantie, uit Ovidius; fiks gepenceeld door een goed Meester, hoog 20, breed 27 duim, op Doek | *Mat:* op doek *Size:* hoog 20, breed 27 duim	Anna Elink	(Sold) fl 5 Yver
1802/06/28	AMSCH	0223	*[Anonymous]* | Twee stuks gestoffeerde Landschappen, met aloude Kasteele, zynde een Zomer- en een Wintergezigt; natuurlyk gepenceelt op Panneel | *Mat:* op paneel *Size:* hoog 11, breed 13 duim	Anna Elink	(Sold) fl 1:10 Gruiter

1802/06/28	AMSCH	0224	*[Anonymous]* | Maria met het Kindje op de schoot, waar by Joseph, en verscheide Engelen; door een goed Meester, hoog 46, breed 40 duim, op doek | *Mat:* op doek *Size:* hoog 46, breed 40 duim	Anna Elink	(Sold) fl 6 Spaan
1802/06/28	AMSCH	0226	*[Anonymous]* | Zes stuks bevallige Bosch-, Dorp en Riviergezichten, alle uitvoerig op Doek | *Mat:* op doek *Size:* hoog 8, breed 12 duim	Anna Elink	(Sold) fl 6:5 Geld
1802/06/28	AMSCH	0228	*[Anonymous]* | Twee stuks Savoyaards; fiks door een goed Meester | *Size:* hoog 14, breed 11 duim	Anna Elink	(Sold) fl 3 v d Schleij A [for] Coclers
1802/06/28	AMSCH	0229	*[Anonymous]* | Een Kind in de Kinderstoel, waarby een ander huilende; fiks behandeld	Anna Elink	(Sold) fl 2:10 Coclers
1802/06/28	AMSCH	0231	*[Anonymous]* | Een Binnenhuis, waarin een Huisman en Vrouw, waarby een Kind in een Wieg; kragtig geschildert op Doek | *Mat:* op doek	Anna Elink	(Sold) fl 0:15 Taak
1802/06/28	AMSCH	0232	*[Anonymous]* | Een zittend rokend Boertje; fiks gepenceeld door een goed Meester	Anna Elink	(Sold) fl 1 van der Schley A [for] Coclers
1802/06/28	AMSCH	0233	*[Anonymous]* | Twee stuks, een Boom- en Duinachtig Landschap en een ander; beide fiks gepenceeld	Anna Elink	(Sold) fl 1:5 Coclaier
1802/06/28	AMSCH	0237	*[Anonymous]* | Een Bergachtig Landschap, op de Voorgrond eenige Lieden te Paard en te Voet, verders eenig Vee, ter zyde de Ruine van een oud Paleis; natuurlyk door een goed Meester, op Doek | *Mat:* op doek	Anna Elink	(Sold) fl 3 Mensart
1802/06/28	AMSCH	0239	*[Anonymous]* | Een Vrouwtje, zittende te Haspelen, zeer natuurlyk door een goed Meester, Panneel | *Mat:* op paneel *Size:* hoog 15, breed 12 duim	Anna Elink	(Sold) fl 13 Gruiter
1802/06/28	AMSCH	0240	*Een goed Meester* | Een Boom- en Bergachtig Landschap; fiks behandeld door een goed Meester, op Panneel | *Mat:* op paneel *Size:* hoog 5, breed 6 duim	Anna Elink	(Sold) fl 1 A Schotte
1802/06/28	AMSCH	0241	*[Anonymous]* | Twee stuks Landschappen met Beesten; door een goed Meester	Anna Elink	(Sold) fl 4 Yver
1802/06/28	AMSCH	0242	*[Anonymous]* | Een Boeren Buitenhuis met een Varken op de Leer, waar over twee Boeren handelen, door een goed Meester	Anna Elink	(Sold) fl 1:10 van der Schleij [for] Mars
1802/06/28	AMSCH	0243	*[Anonymous]* | Een Oud Vrouwe Pourtrait, uitvoerig gepenceeld	Anna Elink	(Sold) fl 2 Gruiter
1802/06/28	AMSCH	0245	*[Anonymous]* | Twee stuks, een Man en Vrouwen Pourtrait, in aloude Kleeding; meesterlyk geschilderd door een goed Meester, Panneel | *Mat:* op paneel	Anna Elink	(Sold) fl 1:5 Mensart
1802/06/28	AMSCH	0246	*[Anonymous]* | Een Heer en Dame, in een Hofgezicht	Anna Elink	(Sold) fl 0:12 Gruiter
1802/06/28	AMSCH	0246a	*[Anonymous]* | Een lezend Boertje, door een goed Meester | *Notes:* There are two lots with the number 246; this lot has been changed to 246a.	Anna Elink	(Sold) fl 2:10 Taak
1802/06/28	AMSCH	0249	*[Anonymous]* | Twee stuks met Paarden en Beeldjes	Anna Elink	(Sold) fl 2 Vermeulen
1802/06/28	AMSCH	0251	*[Anonymous]* | In een Binnenhuis ziet men een Drinkende en een Fioolspeelende Boer, in 't verschiet een Boerin; door een goed Meester. Doek | *Mat:* op doek *Size:* hoog 25, breed 22 duim	B	(Sold) fl 20 van der Schleij A [for] Coclers
1802/06/28	AMSCH	0252	*[Anonymous]* | De Geboorte Christi, door den Engel, aan den Herders verkondigt; kragtig op Panneel geschildert | *Mat:* op paneel	B	(Sold) fl 1 L Pakker
1802/06/28	AMSCH	0253	*[Anonymous]* | Eenige vegtende Mannen en Vrouwen, in 't graauw geschilderd	B	(Sold) fl 0:6 L Pakker
1802/06/28	AMSCH	0255	*[Anonymous]* | Een Boom en Bergachtig Landschap, met verscheide Reizigers; door een goed Meester. Doek | *Mat:* op doek *Size:* hoog 13, breed 9 duim	B	(Sold) fl 0:10 van Iperen
1802/06/28	AMSCH	0260	*[Anonymous]* | Een gestoffeerd Landschapp met een Jachtparty, door een goed Meester, op Doek | *Mat:* op doek	B	(Sold) fl 0:6 L Pakker
1802/06/28	AMSCH	0261	*[Anonymous]* | Een stil Leeven; door een goed Meester, op Doek | *Mat:* op doek	B	(Sold) fl 0:10 L Pakker
1802/06/28	AMSCH	0262[H]	*[Anonymous]* | 2 Schilderijen | *Notes:* This lot was added in by hand in the LBDa and RKDH copies of the catalogue.	Anna Elink	(Bought In)
1802/06/28	AMSCH	0263[H]	*[Anonymous]* | 1 dito [Schilderij] | *Notes:* This lot was added in by hand in the LBDa and RKDH copies of the catalogue.	Anna Elink	(Bought In)
1802/06/28	AMSCH	0264[H]	*[Anonymous]* | 1 Pourtrait | *Notes:* This lot was added in by hand in the LBDa and RKDH copies of the catalogue.	Anna Elink	(Bought In)
1802/06/28	AMSCH	0265[H]	*[Anonymous]* | 1 dito [Pourtrait] | *Notes:* This lot was added in by hand in the LBDa and RKDH copies of the catalogue.	Anna Elink	(Bought In)
1802/06/28	AMSCH	0266[H]	*[Anonymous]* | 1 dito [Pourtrait] | *Notes:* This lot was added in by hand in the LBDa and RKDH copies of the catalogue.	Anna Elink	(Bought In)
1802/06/29	HGDAW	0009	*[Anonymous]* | Twee Spelonkjes in Oliverf in Lyste | *Mat:* in olyverf		(Unknown)
1802/06/29	HGDAW	0010	*[Anonymous]* | De brand van Sodom in Oliverf | *Mat:* in olyverf		(Unknown)
1802/06/29	HGDAW	0012	*[Anonymous]* | David en Abigael op paneel | *Mat:* op paneel		(Unknown)
1802/06/29	HGDAW	0015	*[Anonymous]* | Een Tafel en Fruitstukje 2 stuks		(Unknown)
1802/06/29	HGDAW	0016	*[Anonymous]* | Een Chirurgyns Winkel, grappig geschilderd		(Unknown)
1802/06/29	HGDAW	0017	*[Anonymous]* | Twee Landschapjes op koper in lysten | *Mat:* op koper		(Unknown)
1802/06/29	HGDAW	0018	*[Anonymous]* | Een Fruitstukje		(Unknown)

1802/06/29	HGDAW	0019	*[Anonymous]* | Een Keukenstukje, uitvoerig	(Unknown)
1802/06/29	HGDAW	0021	*[Anonymous]* | Diana op de Jagt gaande een stuk van verscheide beelden op paneel | *Mat:* op paneel	(Unknown)
1802/06/29	HGDAW	0022	*[Anonymous]* | Twee Zeehavens op Doek | *Mat:* op doek	(Unknown)
1802/06/29	HGDAW	0023	*[Anonymous]* | Een Landschapje, op doek | *Mat:* op doek	(Unknown)
1802/06/29	HGDAW	0029	*[Anonymous]* | Een groot Fruytstuk	(Unknown)
1802/06/29	HGDAW	0030	*[Anonymous]* | Een Historieele	(Unknown)
1802/06/29	HGDAW	0034	*[Anonymous]* | Het gezigt van de Theems waar op de Beroemde Brug van Londen 2 groote stukken	(Unknown)
1802/07/09	AMSTO	0004	*Een goed Meester* | 1 Hylige Famille, door een goed Meester	(Unknown)
1802/07/09	AMSTO	0006	*Een goed meester* | 1 Dorpgezigt met diverse Menschen te Paard, Kwakzalvers, in het verschiet een Kerk, waarin de Toorn een loopend Uurwerk, zeer fraay geschildert, door een goed meester	(Unknown)
1802/07/09	AMSTO	0011	*Een nieuw Meester* | 1 Historiele Ordonantie, alwaar de Dochter haar Vader zynde een Gryzaard, door de Borst laaft, door een nieuw Meester	(Unknown)
1802/07/09	AMSTO	0013	*[Anonymous]* | 1 vrolyke Boer met een Pyp in de Hand	(Unknown)
1802/07/09	AMSTO	0036	*[Anonymous]* | 2 Schilderyen in zwarte Lysten	(Unknown)
1802/07/09	AMSTO	0038	*[Anonymous]* | 2 fraaye op Glas geschilderde Bybelsche Ordonantie verbeeldende het Lyden van den Heyland | *Mat:* op glas	(Unknown)
1802/07/09	AMSTO	0040	*[Anonymous]* | 2 ovale Schilderyen verbelende het monument van Nederland, in fraay gesneeden en vergulde Lysten | *Fmt:* ovaal	(Unknown)
1802/07/09	AMSTO	0042	*[Anonymous]* | 4 diverse Schilderyen	(Unknown)
1802/07/09	AMSTO	0043	*[Anonymous]* | 2 diverse Schilderyen, zynde 2 mans Potraiten, en 1 Landschap	(Unknown)
1802/07/09	AMSTO	0044	*[Anonymous]* | 1 dito [Schildery] verbeelende Diana aan het Bad, met de Maagden	(Unknown)
1802/07/09	AMSTO	0045	*[Anonymous]* | 1 dito [Schildery] verbelende de Tyd	(Unknown)
1802/07/09	AMSTO	0046	*[Anonymous]* | 1 dito [Schildery] verbeelende 1 Bybelse Ordonnantie, door een goed Meester	(Unknown)
1802/07/09	AMSTO	0047	*[Anonymous]* | 2 Landschappen	(Unknown)
1802/07/09	AMSTO	0048	*[Anonymous]* | 2 dito [Landschappen] verbeelende 2 vrouwe Beelden in Nissen	(Unknown)
1802/07/09	AMSTO	0049	*[Anonymous]* | 3 diverse dito [Landschappen]	(Unknown)
1802/07/09	AMSTO	0050	*[Anonymous]* | 1 geschildert Schoorsteenstuk | *Fmt:* schoorsteenstuk	(Unknown)
1802/07/09	AMSTO	0051	*[Anonymous]* | 1 zeer konstig en uitvoerig geschildert Famielliestuk, met 5 Beelden, in een bevallig Landschap, door een goed Meester	(Unknown)
1802/07/09	AMSTO	0052	*[Anonymous]* | 2 dito [Schilderyen?] met Beelden en Beesten | *Notes:* It is unclear what "dito" refers to in the title.	(Unknown)
1802/07/09	AMSTO	0056	*[Anonymous]* | 2 stuks Schilderyen en 1 Printbord | *This Lot:* 2 stuks Schilderyen	(Unknown)
1802/07/09	AMSTO	0060	*[Anonymous]* | 2 stuks Schilderyen	(Unknown)
1802/07/09	AMSTO	0061	*[Anonymous]* | 1 Schoorsteenstuk | *Fmt:* schoorsteenstuk	(Unknown)
1802/07/09	AMSTO	0063	*[Anonymous]* | 2 dito [Potraiten] Zeeslag en 1 Zeegezigt	(Unknown)
1802/07/09	AMSTO	0064	*[Anonymous]* | 2 dito [Potraiten] mans Koppen	(Unknown)
1802/07/09	AMSTO	0065	*[Anonymous]* | 2 stuks Schilderyen met bruine Lysten	(Unknown)
1802/07/09	AMSTO	0066	*[Anonymous]* | 3 stuks Schilderyen met bruine Lysten	(Unknown)
1802/07/09	AMSTO	0070	*[Anonymous]* | 2 Schilderyen in Lysten	(Unknown)
1802/07/09	AMSTO	0071	*[Anonymous]* | 1 Bosgezigt	(Unknown)
1802/07/09	AMSTO	0072	*[Anonymous]* | 1 Bloemstuk in zwarte Lyst	(Unknown)
1802/07/20	MGSAN	0012	*[Anonymous]* | Een Italiaansche Zeehaven: extra uitvoerig geschilderd op Doek | companion to lot 13 *Mat:* op doek *Size:* hoog duim 24, breed duim 35	(Unknown)
1802/07/20	MGSAN	0013	*[Anonymous]* | Een dito [Italiaansche Zeehaven] tot een Wederga | companion to lot 12 *Mat:* op doek *Size:* hoog duim 24, breed duim 35	(Unknown)
1802/07/20	MGSAN	0014	*Een voornaam Meester* | Een Capitaal Stuk, zynde een Waarzegster by twee Jonge Lieden, achter haar ziet men een Cupido, alles krachtig en schoon geschilderd, door een voornaam Meester: op Doek | *Mat:* op doek *Size:* hoog duim 43, breed duim 51	(Unknown)
1802/07/20	MGSAN	0019	*[Anonymous]* | De Rheede van de Caab de Goede Hoop, met Schepen: op Paneel | *Mat:* op paneel *Size:* hoog duim 18 ½, breed duim 26	(Unknown)
1802/07/20	MGSAN	0053	*[Anonymous]* | Een schoon Stuk, met doode Visch, waarby twee Figuuren: op Doek | *Mat:* op doek *Size:* hoog duim 39, breed duim 52	(Unknown)
1802/07/21	HGKAN	0001	*[Anonymous]* | De Onthoofding van Joännes, op Doek | *Mat:* op doek	(Unknown)

1802/07/21	HGKAN	0002	*[Anonymous]* | Ecce Homo, op Paneel | *Mat:* op paneel	(Unknown)
1802/07/21	HGKAN	0003	*[Anonymous]* | De stervende Franciscus, Italiaans stuk zeer fraay geschildert, op Doek | *Mat:* op doek	(Unknown)
1802/07/21	HGKAN	0008	*[Anonymous]* | Een Binnen-vertrek, met rookende Boeren	(Unknown)
1802/07/21	HGKAN	0015	*[Anonymous]* | Vier stuks different	(Unknown)
1802/07/21	HGKAN	0017	*[Anonymous]* | Een extra fraay dito [Schildery], zynde een Mans pourtrait van I. W. AEtatis A° 1644, in leven Bode der Stad Alkmaar, zeer fraay geschildert, door een goed Meester, vergulde Lyst | *Inscr:* I. W. AEtatis A° 1644 (dated)	(Unknown)
1802/07/21	HGKAN	0020	*[Anonymous]* | Twee dito [Schilderyen] extra fraaye Bosch-Gezichten, met wandelende Beeldjes, in zwarte Lysten, door een goed Meester	(Unknown)
1802/07/21	HGKAN	0022	*Een zeer goed Meester* | Twee dito [Schilderyen] Winter Gezichten, vol met Schaatzenrydende en andere Beeldjes, in fraaye vergulde Lysten, door een zeer goed Meester	(Unknown)
1802/07/21	HGKAN	0025	*Een zeer goed Meester* | Twee dito [Schilderyen], zynde het eene een Fruit-Verkoopster, en het ander een Visch-Boer, door een zeer goed Meester	(Unknown)
1802/07/21	HGKAN	0029	*Een goed Meester* | Een Fruit stuk zynde eenige Druyven en Persiken, leggende op een Tafel, door een goed Meester	(Unknown)
1802/07/21	HGKAN	0039	*Een zeer goed Meester* | Een Mande met Vrugten, staande op een Tafel en ander Bywerk, door een zeer goed Meester, zwarte Lyst	(Unknown)
1802/07/21	HGKAN	0041	*Een goed Meester* | Een Kerk van binnen te zien, de Gemeente is vergadert, terwyl de Leeraar op de Kansel staande een Leerreeden schynt te houden, door een goed Meester, paneel vergulde Lyst | *Mat:* op paneel	(Unknown)
1802/07/21	HGKAN	0049	*[Anonymous]* | Twee stuks, zynde een Mans en Vrouwe Pourtrait in Geestelyk gewaad, in zwarte Lysten	(Unknown)
1802/07/21	HGKAN	0052	*[Anonymous]* | Willem de II, geharnast, hoog 18 en breed 15 duym, op Doek | *Mat:* op doek *Size:* hoog 18 en breed 15 duym	(Unknown)
1802/07/21	HGKAN	0055	*[Anonymous]* | Christus met de Doorne Kroon, met de Purpere Mantel omhangen en de Riet-Staff, zeer fraay, hoog 2 voet 4 duym en breed 2 voet, op Doek, zwarte Lyst, vergulde binnen rand | *Mat:* op doek *Size:* hoog 2 voet 4 duym en breed 2 voet	(Unknown)
1802/07/21	HGKAN	0056	*[Anonymous]* | Een Weenende Maria, door denzelven Meester | *Size:* hoog 2 voet 4 duym en breed 2 voet	(Unknown)
1802/07/21	HGKAN	0063	*[Anonymous]* | Een Boschagtig Landschap, waar in Diana, op paneel zwarte Lyst | *Mat:* op paneel	(Unknown)
1802/07/21	HGKAN	0068	*[Anonymous]* | Een dito [plaisant Dorp Gezicht] tot een weerga, in dito [zwarte] Lyst | companion to lot 67, by J. Stork *Notes:* It is unclear what "dito" refers to in the title.	(Unknown)
1802/07/21	HGKAN	0069	*[Anonymous]* | Een oude Mans Pourtrait, in zwarte Lyst	(Unknown)
1802/07/21	HGKAN	0072	*[Anonymous]* | Twee stuks met Beelden en Beesten, in zwarte Lysten	(Unknown)
1802/07/21	HGKAN	0073	*[Anonymous]* | Twee stuks met drinkende Boeren, in vergulde Lysten	(Unknown)
1802/07/21	HGKAN	0076	*[Anonymous]* | Een Landschap, zynde een Maaneschyn	(Unknown)
1802/07/21	HGKAN	0077	*[Anonymous]* | Een Vrouwtje, zynde een Kaarsligt	(Unknown)
1802/07/21	HGKAN	0080	*[Anonymous]* | Twee kleyne stoeijende Boertjes en Boerinnen	(Unknown)
1802/07/21	HGKAN	0086	*[Anonymous]* | Twee Landschapjes met Koeijen	(Unknown)
1802/07/21	HGKAN	0093	*[Anonymous]* | Het Pourtrait van Oldenbarneveld	(Unknown)
1802/07/21	HGKAN	0104	*[Anonymous]* | Een fraay Landschap, met ryke Stoffagie, onbekend	(Unknown)
1802/07/21	HGKAN	0109	*[Anonymous]* | Een Landschap met Koeijen	(Unknown)
1802/07/21	HGKAN	0113	*Een goed Meester* | Een Schilderstuk, op paneel, zynde een Schets, waarop een Paard met twee Jagers, door een goed Meester | *Mat:* op paneel *Size:* hoog 9 à 10 duym, en breed 1 voet	(Unknown)
1802/07/21	HGKAN	0114	*Een zeer goed Meester* | Een Italiaansch Landschap op Doek, waarop een reyzende Vrouw op een Ezel zittende, en door een Man geleyd wordende, in het verschiet een Klooster, waar heen eenige Bedevaarden zich begeeven, door een zeer goed Meester | *Mat:* op doek *Size:* hoog 3 voet 2 duym en breed 3 ½ voet	(Unknown)
1802/07/21	HGKAN	0115	*Een goed Meester* | Een Binnenvertrek op paneel, waarin een Boerinnetje by een Tafel staande te Werken, en een Boertje zich by het Vuur zittende te Warmen, zeer fix geschildert, door een goed Meester | *Mat:* op paneel *Size:* hoog 10 duym en breed 1 voet	(Unknown)
1802/07/21	HGKAN	0117	*[Anonymous]* | Een Schildery op paneel, verbeeldende een Grot, waarin eenige Beeltjes, in het verschiet een Bergachtig Landschap, door een goed Meester | *Mat:* op paneel *Size:* hoog 1 voet 1 duym, en breed 10 duym	(Unknown)
1802/07/21	HGKAN	0118	*[Anonymous]* | Een Portefeuille met Academie Beelden, welke by Koopjes zullen verzogt worden	(Unknown)
1802/07/21	HGKAN	0119	*[Anonymous]* | Een Portefeuille	(Unknown)

1802/07/27	AKHRK	000I	*[Anonymous]* | Een Schermutseling van gewapende Manschappen te Paard, waar in een groote wanorde heerscht; en de Furie zeer wel uitgedrukt is; met schoone Paarden: en goed geschilderd | *Mat:* op doek *Size:* hoog 20 ½, breed 24 ½ duim	Maria Stategaart	(Sold) fl 3:10 J Kleyn
1802/07/27	AKHRK	000L	*[Anonymous]* | Een zittende Vrouw met drie Kinderen, en een staande Man, met een Pijp in de eene en een Kan in de andere Hand, voor een Huis; fix geschilderd | *Mat:* op paneel *Size:* hoog 23 ½, breed 32 duim	Maria Stategaart	(Sold) fl 4 Gruyter
1802/07/27	AKHRK	000N	*[Anonymous]* | De Prediking van Joannes den Dooper in de Woestijne, met menigte van Beelden, Vrouwen en Mannen, in verschillende Actien in ouderwetsche Kleeding; door een kundig oud Meester | *Mat:* op doek *Size:* hoog 44 ½, breed 55 ½ duim	Maria Stategaart	(Sold) fl 6:10 for lots N & O. Kleynefelden
1802/07/27	AKHRK	000O	*[Anonymous]* | De Dogter Pera bij haar ellendige Vader in de Gevangenis, hem lavende met haar Boesem; in een zeer goede trant, en het naakt schoon geschilderd | *Mat:* op doek *Size:* hoog 42 ½, breed 59 duim	Maria Stategaart	(Sold) fl 6:10 for lots N & O. Kleynefelden
1802/07/27	AKHRK	0064	*[Anonymous]* | De Wijzen uit het Oosten, brengende Gaven en Geschenken, aan den jonggebooren Heiland, zeer goed geschilderd. In deszelfs breede Lijst zijn nog agt Schilderstukjes op de Hoeken – de vier Evangelisten. op de Zijde – het Bezoek van Maria aan Elisabeth – en de Doop van Christus. Boven – de Samaritaansche Vrouw. En Onder – Magdalena in den Hof | *Mat:* op paneel *Size:* hoog 8 ¾, breed 14 ¼ duim	Maria Stategaart	(Sold) fl 10:5 Maas
1802/07/27	AKHRK	0065	*[Anonymous]* | Het Kind Jesus met Maria en Joseph in Egijpten, goed gepenceeld | *Mat:* op paneel *Size:* hoog 14, breed 16 duim	Maria Stategaart	(Sold) fl 4 Sprink
1802/07/27	AKHRK	0066	*[Anonymous]* | De Moeder Maagd met het Kindeken Jesus. Extra goed geschilderd, om dezelve een Feston van Bloemen | *Mat:* op paneel *Size:* hoog 12, breed 9 ¼ duim	Maria Stategaart	(Sold) fl 5 Gruyter
1802/07/27	AKHRK	0067	*[Anonymous]* | Een bevallig Rotsachtig Landschap, met een kronkelend Water, en op de voorgrond een Waterval, door een zeer bekwaame hand geschilderd, met verscheide Figuuren te Paard en te Voet | *Mat:* op doek *Size:* hoog 18, breed 21 ½ duim	Maria Stategaart	(Sold) fl 10 for lots 67 & 68. De Meyer
1802/07/27	AKHRK	0068	*[Anonymous]* | Als de voorige, goed gepenseeld	Maria Stategaart	(Sold) fl 10 for lots 67 & 68. De Meyer
1802/07/27	AKHRK	0071	*[Anonymous]* | Een zeer rijk geördineert Persiesch Hofgezicht met dito Figuuren, zeer fraai en goed geschilderd | *Mat:* op doek *Size:* hoog 12, breed 16 duim	Maria Stategaart	(Sold) fl 5:5 for lots 71 & 72. Vanderham
1802/07/27	AKHRK	0072	*[Anonymous]* | Als de voorige, Heeren en Dames te Paard en te Voet | *Mat:* op doek *Size:* hoog 12, breed 16 duim	Maria Stategaart	(Sold) fl 5:5 for lots 71 & 72. Vanderham
1802/07/27	AKHRK	0073	*[Anonymous]* | Een Maaneschijn, ziende over een Gragt op een Slot of Kasteel. Natuurlijk verbeeld | *Mat:* op koper *Size:* hoog 9 ½, breed 13 ¾ duim	Maria Stategaart	(Sold) fl 4:15 Backer
1802/07/27	AKHRK	0074	*[Anonymous]* | Een rijke Ordonnantie met menigte van Beelden in aloude Kleederdragt, op een Markt in een der Brabandsche Steden; op de voorgrond ziet men een Kwakzalver, in 't rood gekleed op een wit Paard, bezig met zwetsen; agter hem hangt een breed Schilderij, met de Lijders door zijn Ed. gecureert en met Zegels en Brieven bevestigd; als mede zijn Pourtrait, oud 39 jaar 1617. Onder de Omstanders een Beursenlichter en verder Liedjeszangers. Dit stuk is zeer raar | *Mat:* op paneel *Size:* hoog 26, breed 35 duim *Inscr:* oud 39 jaar 1617 (dated?) *Notes:* It is unclear whether the date is inscribed on the painting.	Maria Stategaart	(Sold) fl 6:10 Dreesen
1802/07/27	AKHRK	0075	*Een oud goed Meester* | Een bergachtig Land-en Watergezicht; op de voorgrond een Brug, en voor dezelve de Parabel van de twee Blinden; door een oud goed Meester | *Mat:* op doek *Size:* hoog 25 ½, breed 38 duim	Maria Stategaart	(Sold) fl 5:15 Meyer
1802/07/27	AKHRK	0078	*[Anonymous]* | Dit schijnt een Waterberoering te Sparendam te zijn, naar Haarlem te zien, met veel Scheepen bij de Sluis, het meest in gevaar; door een oud goed Meester | *Mat:* op paneel *Size:* hoog 13 ½, breed 16 duim	Maria Stategaart	(Sold) fl 3:5 for lots 78 & 79. Juffr Boerson
1802/07/27	AKHRK	0079	*[Anonymous]* | Op dezelve plaats naar de Duynkant te zien, met Scheepen onder Hollansche en Spaansche Vlag	Maria Stategaart	(Sold) fl 3:5 for lots 78 & 79. Juffr Boerson
1802/07/27	AKHRK	0081	*[Anonymous]* | Den Heiland zijn Kruis dragende; met menigte Beelden, te Paard en te Voet; goed gepenseeld | *Mat:* op koper *Fmt:* ovaal *Size:* hoog 7 ½, breed 9 duim *Notes:* This lot was misnumbered no. 25.	Maria Stategaart	(Sold) fl 2:15 Backer
1802/07/27	AKHRK	0082	*[Anonymous]* | De Emausgangers, en | *Mat:* op koper *Size:* hoog 8 ¼, breed 6 ¾ duim	Maria Stategaart	(Sold) fl 2:10 for lots 82 & 83. Beer
1802/07/27	AKHRK	0083	*[Anonymous]* | Het laatste Avondmaal, en boven dezelve de Voetwassing | *Mat:* op koper	Maria Stategaart	(Sold) fl 2:10 for lots 82 & 83. Beer
1802/07/27	AKHRK	0084	*[Anonymous]* | Een Pourtrait-stuk van deftige Persoonen | *Mat:* op doek *Size:* hoog 22 ½, breed 19 duim	Maria Stategaart	(Sold) fl 8:15 Gruyter
1802/07/27	AKHRK	0085	*[Anonymous]* | De Martelaar Dionysius van Ariopagita, met zijn Hoofd in de Hand, en de verschrikking onder de Omstanders; goed geschilderd | *Mat:* op doek *Size:* hoog 23 ¾, breed 31 duim	Maria Stategaart	(Sold) fl 3:15 Vandenheuvel
1802/07/27	AKHRK	0087	*[Anonymous]* | Zinnebeelden op de Rampen van den Oorlog | *Mat:* op paneel *Size:* hoog 10, breed 13 duim *Notes:* This lot was sold with lot 86, which is a copy after C. Visscher (II).	Maria Stategaart	(Sold) fl 4 for lots 86 & 87. Sonnevelt

1802/07/27	AKHRK	0091	*[Anonymous]* | De Zomer | *Notes:* This lot was sold with lot 90, which is a drawing.	Maria Stategaart	(Sold) fl 3:15 for lots 90–94. 8 Segaar
1802/07/27	AKHRK	0092	*[Anonymous]* | De Herfst | *Notes:* This lot was sold with lot 90, which is a drawing.	Maria Stategaart	(Sold) fl 3:15 for lots 90–94. 8 Segaar
1802/07/27	AKHRK	0093	*[Anonymous]* | De Winter, alle met Couleuren | *Notes:* This lot was sold with lot 90, which is a drawing.	Maria Stategaart	(Sold) fl 3:15 for lots 90–94. 8 Segaar
1802/07/27	AKHRK	0094	*[Anonymous]* | Een Pot met Bloemen op een Tafel, gecouleurd | *Notes:* This lot was sold with lot 90, which is a drawing.	Maria Stategaart	(Sold) fl 3:15 for lots 90–94. 8 Segaar
1802/08/24	LNDLS	0039	*Een voornaam Meester* | Een bedaagde Vrouw halverlijf, zittende voor een Tafel, waar een lantaarn op staat, zij schijnt een pijp te stoppen uit een doos die zij in haare handen houdt. Konstig en zeer uitvoerig op paneel geschilderd, door een voornaam Meester, niet minder dan van Honthorst | *Mat:* op paneel *Size:* hoog 21, breed 25 duimen	Leonardus Bouman [or others]	(Unknown) fl 20:10
1802/08/24	LNDLS	0041	*Een voornaam Meester* | Maria met het Kind Jesus op haar schoot, terwijl Joseph eerbiedig de hand van het Kind aanvat, boven twee Seraphynen op de wolken. Zeer konstig en delicaat op doek geschilderd, door een voornaam Meester | *Mat:* op doek *Size:* hoog 24, breed 27 duimen	Leonardus Bouman [or others]	(Unknown) fl 14
1802/08/24	LNDLS	0042	*Een voornaam Meester* | Een Schilderij verbeeldende Christus die de Kinderen tot zich laat komen. Helder van Coloriet, en konstig van Tekening en Schildering, op doek, door een voornaam Meester | *Mat:* op doek *Size:* hoog 28, breed 32 duimen	Leonardus Bouman [or others]	(Unknown) fl 5:5
1802/08/24	LNDLS	0072	*Een goed Meester* | Een Stads-Gezicht langs een Weg en Vaart met Schepen en Schuiten, gestoffeerd met wandelende Beelden. Helder van coloriet en konstig op doek, door een goed Meester | *Mat:* op doek *Size:* hoog 28, breed 36 duimen	Leonardus Bouman [or others]	(Unknown) fl 18
1802/08/24	LNDLS	0098	*[Anonymous]* | In een Nis op een Tafel staat een Flesch met veele Bloemen, voor dezelve Zeegewassen, alles onder een hangend Gordijn | *Mat:* op doek *Size:* hoog 48, breed 39 duimen	Leonardus Bouman [or others]	(Unknown) fl 7:5
1802/08/24	LNDLS	0099	*Een goed Meester* | Een boomrijk Landschap met een Water, daar met den Zegen gevist word en meer Beelden. Op doek, door een goed Meester | *Mat:* op doek	Leonardus Bouman [or others]	(Unknown) fl 3:4
1802/08/24	LNDLS	0100	*[Anonymous]* | Een Fles met veele Bloemen, staande op een steenen Tafel. Excellent teder en konstig geschildert door .... | *Mat:* op doek *Size:* hoog 19, breed 26 duimen	Leonardus Bouman [or others]	(Unknown) fl 8:15
1802/08/24	LNDLS	0103	*[Anonymous]* | Een biddende Petrus, halverlijf	Leonardus Bouman [or others]	(Unknown) fl 0:18
1802/08/24	LNDLS	0117	*[Anonymous]* | Een Zeestrand met Schepen, wandelende en rijdende persoonen	Leonardus Bouman [or others]	(Unknown) fl 3:10
1802/08/24	LNDLS	0119	*[Anonymous]* | Op een Tafel staat een pot met Bloemen en Fruit	Leonardus Bouman [or others]	(Unknown) fl 0:13
1802/08/24	LNDLS	0120	*[Anonymous]* | Een Gezelschap van gekleeden Aapen, daar den Meester Kinderschool houdt. Grappig verbeeld, op paneel geschilderd | *Mat:* op paneel	Leonardus Bouman [or others]	(Unknown) fl 7
1802/08/24	LNDLS	0125[a]	*[Anonymous]* | Twee stuks; zynde een Man bij een staand Paard, en een rond Landschap | *This Lot:* Man bij een staand Paard	Leonardus Bouman [or others]	(Unknown) fl 0:10 for lots 125[a] & 125[b]
1802/08/24	LNDLS	0125[b]	*[Anonymous]* | Twee stuks; zynde een Man bij een staand Paard, en een rond Landschap | *This Lot:* Een rond Landschap *Fmt:* rond	Leonardus Bouman [or others]	(Unknown) fl 0:10 for lots 125[a] & 125[b]
1802/08/24	LNDLS	0126	*[Anonymous]* | Twee stuks Gestoffeerde Landschappen	Leonardus Bouman [or others]	(Unknown) fl 0:14
1802/08/24	LNDLS	0128	*[Anonymous]* | Een Vanitas, verbeeld door een slapend Kindje bij een Tafel daar eenige toepaslijkheden op rusten, rond formaat, uitvoerig en konstig op paneel geschildert | *Mat:* op paneel *Fmt:* rond	Leonardus Bouman [or others]	(Unknown) fl 5:5
1802/08/24	LNDLS	0129	*[Anonymous]* | Een staand Meisje die aan twee aartige hondjes te eeten geeft, bevallig en uitvoerig op doek | *Mat:* op doek	Leonardus Bouman [or others]	(Unknown) fl 1:6
1802/08/24	LNDLS	0130	*[Anonymous]* | Een Nimph liggende op een rustbed, met een Vrouw nevens haar, uitvoerig op koper geschildert | *Mat:* op koper	Leonardus Bouman [or others]	(Unknown) fl 1:10
1802/08/24	LNDLS	0135	*[Anonymous]* | De Schilder en zijn Vrouw voor hem, grappig met meer bijwerk. Fix behandelt | companion to lot 136 *Mat:* op doek	Leonardus Bouman [or others]	(Unknown) fl 5:15 for lots 135 & 136
1802/08/24	LNDLS	0136	*[Anonymous]* | De Weerga niet minder koddig en kloek behandelt, door denzelven | companion to lot 135 *Notes:* It is unclear to whom "denzelven" refers to in the title, since the previous lot was by an anonymous artist.	Leonardus Bouman [or others]	(Unknown) fl 5:15 for lots 135 & 136
1802/08/24	LNDLS	0141	*Een goed Meester* | Een Historieel met Beelden, door een goed Meester | *Mat:* op paneel	Leonardus Bouman [or others]	(Unknown) fl 2:6
1802/08/24	LNDLS	0145	*[Anonymous]* | Twee stuks, een Winter en een Zomer met Beelden, op den voorgrond. Plaizant	Leonardus Bouman [or others]	(Unknown) fl 2:18
1802/08/24	LNDLS	0148	*[Anonymous]* | Een Man en Vrouw bij een tafel met drank, fraai geschildert	Leonardus Bouman [or others]	(Unknown) fl 2:6
1802/08/24	LNDLS	0155	*[Anonymous]* | Een Ossenkop, zeer uitvoerig, op paneel | *Mat:* op paneel	Leonardus Bouman [or others]	(Unknown)

1802/09/06	AMSCH	0142	*[Anonymous]* | Een Italiaansch Heuvelachtig Landschap, gestoffeerd met Huislieden en Vée; krachtig geschilderd | *Mat:* op paneel	B	(Sold) fl 0:10 Gruiter
1802/09/06	AMSCH	0143	*[Anonymous]* | Deeze ryke Ordenantie, verbeeld het laatste Oordeel; krachtig en meesterlyk gepenceeld | *Mat:* op doek *Size:* hoog 40, breed 38 duim	B	(Sold) fl 2:5 Gruiter
1802/09/06	AMSCH	0148	*[Anonymous]* | Een Binnehuis met vrolyke Boeren en Boerinen, en andere op de Harp speelende | *Mat:* op doek	B	(Sold) fl 1:10 A Schotte
1802/09/06	AMSCH	0150	*[Anonymous]* | Twee stuks oude Mans Hoofden | *Mat:* op paneel	B	(Sold) fl 0:10 L Pakker
1802/09/06	AMSCH	0161	*Een oud Meester* | Deeze ryke Ordenantie vol gewoel van beelden, vertoont: Maria met het Kindje, waar voor de wyzen uit het Oosten néderknielen, en geschenken offeren; de caracters zyn natuurlyk, en van een fraaye penceel-behandeling, door een oud Meester | *Mat:* op paneel *Size:* hoog 25, breed 21 duim	X	(Sold) fl 1:15 L Pakker
1802/09/06	AMSCH	0166	*[Anonymous]* | In een Boschagtig Landschap, ziet men Jagers te paard, en te voet, met verscheide honden, een Hartebeest vervolgen, verder een bergagtig verschiet; meesterlyk gepenceeld | *Mat:* op doek *Size:* hoog 22, breed 26 duim	H[n] Smit	(Sold) fl 2:5 Jan Spaan
1802/09/06	AMSCH	0171	*Een oud Meester* | De afbeelding van den Heiland gekruist, tusschen de Moordenaaren, waarby verscheide aanschouwers; door een oud Meester	Spaan	(Sold) fl 0:10 L Pakker
1802/09/06	AMSCH	0173	*Goed Meester* | Den Heiland zyn Kruis dragende, vertoond zig aan de H. Ignatius	Spaan	(Sold) fl 1:10 Th[s] Spaan
1802/09/06	AMSCH	0174	*[Anonymous]* | Een staande Bisschop, verbeeldende St. Willebrordus	Spaan	(Sold) fl 1:5 van der Schley
1802/09/06	AMSCH	0175	*[Anonymous]* | Een dito [staande Bisschop] Afbeeldzel	Spaan	(Sold) fl 0:12 L Pakker
1802/09/06	AMSCH	0177	*[Anonymous]* | Het Afbeeldzel van een Jongeling; fix gepenceeld	Spaan	(Sold) fl 0:10 L Pakker
1802/09/06	AMSCH	0178	*[Anonymous]* | Voor een open Steene Nis, ziet men een Jongeling en een Meisje, met een Vogelkooy, gestoffeerd met verder bywerk; plaisant geschilderd	Spaan	(Sold) fl 2:15 Yver
1802/09/06	AMSCH	0186	*Een goed Meester* | Twee stuks, een leezend oud Man, en een Meisje die Kool snydt; door een goed Meester	Spaan	(Sold) fl 1 L Pakker
1802/09/06	AMSCH	0189	*[Anonymous]* | Twee stuks, verbeeldende de Temptatie van St. Anthonius, en het ander een Landschap	Spaan	(Sold) fl 2:15 L Pakker
1802/09/06	AMSCH	0190	*Een goed Meester* | Een stil Leeven; door een goed Meester	Spaan	(Sold) fl 2 Baur
1802/09/06	AMSCH	0192	*[Anonymous]* | Twee stuks, verbeeldende St. Pétrus en St. Paulus; krachtig geschilderd	Spaan	(Sold) fl 0:10 for lots 192 & 194. L Pakker
1802/09/06	AMSCH	0193	*[Anonymous]* | De Afbeelding van den Heiland, op de Wolken zittende; meesterlyk gepenceeld	Spaan	(Sold) fl 0:10 van der Schley [for] mijn
1802/09/06	AMSCH	0194	*Een goed Meester* | Twee stuks diversche Historieele Ordenantiën; door een goed Meester	Spaan	(Sold) fl 0:10 for lots 192 & 194. L Pakker
1802/09/06	AMSCH	0209	*[Anonymous]* | Twee gestoffeerde Arcadische Landschapjes	Mevrouw Achtienhoven	(Sold) fl 1:10 Jan Yver
1802/09/06	AMSCH	0211	*[Anonymous]* | Twee Bloemstukjes; plaisant geschilderd	Mevrouw Achtienhoven	(Sold) fl 2 van der Schley (Zonnenbergh)
1802/09/06	AMSCH	0212	*Een voornaam Meester* | Een zittende Dame in een aloude kleeding, met twee Kinderen levensgroote; kragtig | *Mat:* op doek	Mevrouw Achtienhoven	(Sold) fl 5:5 Th[s] Spaan
1802/09/06	AMSCH	0214	*Een goed Meester* | Een Landschap met geboomte en stoffagie; door een goed Meester	Mevrouw Achtienhoven	(Sold) fl 0:6 L Pakker
1802/09/06	AMSCH	0224	*[Anonymous]* | Twee stuks Italiaansche Landschappen, gestoffeerd met ryzigers, landlieden en Vée, kragtig gepenceeld | *Mat:* op doek	X	(Sold) fl 1:10 L Pakker
1802/09/06	AMSCH	0228	*[Anonymous]* | Twee stuks gezichten op Haarlem; gestoffeerd met beelden en beesten	J	(Sold) fl 2:5 L Pakker
1802/09/06	AMSCH	0230	*[Anonymous]* | Een ryke Ordenantie, zynde een stil leeven	J	(Sold) fl 0:10 H Bauer
1802/09/06	AMSCH	0231	*Een goed Meester* | Eenige Goudlakensche Hennen en een staande Haan, by eenig Plantgewas; door een goed Meester	J	(Sold) fl 0:15 H Bauer
1802/09/06	AMSCH	0236	*Een goed Meester* | Een stil Leeven, en een Bloemstuk; natuurlyk geschilderd door een goed Meester		(Sold) fl 1 L Pakker
1802/09/06	AMSCH	0249	*Een voornaam Meester* | Een aangenaam Boomryk Landschap, met boerewooning en fraaye stoffagie; meesterlyk geschilderd, door een voornaam Meester | *Mat:* op doek	Mevrouw Achtienhoven	(Sold) fl 30 Hulswit
1802/09/06	AMSCH	0258	*[Anonymous]* | Twee stuks diverse	J	(Sold) fl 0:10 C Deppe
1802/09/06	AMSCH	0259	*[Anonymous]* | Een bevallig Vrouwen Portrait | *Mat:* op koper	Mevrouw Achtienhoven	(Sold) fl 0:18 Isaac Smit
1802/09/06	AMSCH	0261[H]	*[Anonymous]* | 1 [Schilderij] | *Notes:* This lot was added in by hand in the BMB, EBNP, LBDa and RKDH copies of the catalogue.	Spaan	(Sold) fl 228 Hodges

1802/09/06	AMSCH	0262[H]	*[Anonymous]* | 3 [Schilderijen] | *Notes:* This lot was added in by hand in the BMB, EBNP, LBDa and RKDH copies of the catalogue.	Spaan	(Sold) fl 4 Vermeulen
1802/09/06	AMSCH	0263[H]	*[Anonymous]* | 1 [Schilderij] | *Notes:* This lot was added in by hand in the BMB, EBNP, LBDa and RKDH copies of the catalogue.	Spaan	(Sold) fl 4 Jan Spaan
1802/09/06	AMSCH	0264[H]	*[Anonymous]* | 1 [Schilderij] | *Notes:* This lot was added in by hand in the BMB, EBNP, LBDa and RKDH copies of the catalogue.	Spaan	(Sold) fl 16:10 W Ryers
1802/09/06	AMSCH	0265[H]	*[Anonymous]* | 1 [Schilderij] | *Notes:* This lot was added in by hand in the BMB, EBNP, LBDa and RKDH copies of the catalogue.	Spaan	(Sold) fl 4:5 Jan Spaan
1802/09/06	AMSCH	0266[H]	*[Anonymous]* | 1 [Schilderij] | *Notes:* This lot was added in by hand in the BMB, EBNP, LBDa and RKDH copies of the catalogue.	Spaan	(Sold) fl 2:5 Groeneveld
1802/09/06	AMSCH	0267[H]	*[Anonymous]* | 1 [Schilderij] | *Notes:* This lot was added in by hand in the BMB, EBNP, LBDa and RKDH copies of the catalogue.	Spaan	(Sold) fl 2:5 Groeneveld
1802/09/06	AMSCH	0268[H]	*[Anonymous]* | 1 [Schilderij] | *Notes:* This lot was added in by hand in the BMB, EBNP, LBDa and RKDH copies of the catalogue.	Spaan	(Sold) fl 1 L Pakker
1802/09/06	AMSCH	0269[H]	*[Anonymous]* | 1 [Schilderij] | *Notes:* This lot was added in by hand in the BMB, EBNP, LBDa and RKDH copies of the catalogue.	Spaan	(Sold) fl 1 Pruijssenaar
1802/09/06	AMSCH	0270[H]	*[Anonymous]* | 1 [Schilderij] | *Notes:* This lot was added in by hand in the BMB, EBNP, LBDa and RKDH copies of the catalogue.	Spaan	(Sold) fl 51 van Iperen
1802/09/06	AMSCH	0271[H]	*[Anonymous]* | 1 [Schilderij] | *Notes:* This lot was added in by hand in the BMB, EBNP, LBDa and RKDH copies of the catalogue.	Spaan	(Sold) fl 10 Hodges
1802/09/06	AMSCH	0272[H]	*[Anonymous]* | 1 [Schilderij] | *Notes:* This lot was added in by hand in the BMB, EBNP, LBDa and RKDH copies of the catalogue.	B	(Sold) fl 0:6 Coenraad Depper
1802/09/06	AMSCH	0273[H]	*[Anonymous]* | 1 [Schilderij] | *Notes:* This lot was added in by hand in the BMB, EBNP, LBDa and RKDH copies of the catalogue.	X	(Sold) fl 1 Gruiter
1802/09/06	AMSCH	0274[H]	*[Anonymous]* | 2 [Schilderijen] | *Notes:* This lot was added in by hand in the BMB, EBNP, LBDa and RKDH copies of the catalogue.	X	(Withdrawn)
1802/09/06	AMSCH	0275[H]	*[Anonymous]* | 2 [Schilderijen] | *Notes:* This lot was added in by hand in the BMB, EBNP, LBDa and RKDH copies of the catalogue.	X	(Withdrawn)
1802/09/06	AMSCH	0276[H]	*[Anonymous]* | 2 [Schilderijen] | *Notes:* This lot was added in by hand in the BMB, EBNP, LBDa and RKDH copies of the catalogue.	X	(Withdrawn)
1802/09/06	AMSCH	0277[H]	*[Anonymous]* | 2 [Schilderijen] | *Notes:* This lot was added in by hand in the BMB, EBNP, LBDa and RKDH copies of the catalogue.	Mevrouw Achtienhoven	(Sold) fl 1:10 Vermeulen
1802/09/06	AMSCH	0278[H]	*[Anonymous]* | 1 [Schilderij] | *Notes:* This lot was added in by hand in the BMB, EBNP, LBDa and RKDH copies of the catalogue.	Mevrouw Achtienhoven	(Sold) fl 1 van Eyk
1802/09/06	AMSCH	0279[H]	*[Anonymous]* | 2 [Schilderijen] | *Notes:* This lot was added in by hand in the BMB, EBNP, LBDa and RKDH copies of the catalogue.	Mevrouw Achtienhoven	(Sold) fl 1 L Pakker
1802/09/06	AMSCH	0280[H]	*[Anonymous]* | 2 [Schilderijen] | *Notes:* This lot was added in by hand in the BMB, EBNP, LBDa and RKDH copies of the catalogue.	Mevrouw Achtienhoven	(Sold) fl 3 L Pakker
1802/09/06	AMSCH	0281[H]	*[Anonymous]* | 2 [Schilderijen] | *Notes:* This lot was added in by hand in the BMB, EBNP, LBDa and RKDH copies of the catalogue.	Mevrouw Achtienhoven	(Sold) fl 0:10 L Pakker
1802/09/06	AMSCH	0282[H]	*[Anonymous]* | 2 [Schilderijen] | *Notes:* This lot was added in by hand in the BMB, EBNP, LBDa and RKDH copies of the catalogue.	Mevrouw Achtienhoven	(Sold) fl 5:10 Jan Spaan
1802/09/06	AMSCH	0283[H]	*[Anonymous]* | 2 [Schilderijen] | *Notes:* This lot was added in by hand in the BMB, EBNP, LBDa and RKDH copies of the catalogue.	Mevrouw Achtienhoven	(Sold) fl 2 Vermeulen
1802/09/06	AMSCH	0284[H]	*[Anonymous]* | 2 [Schilderijen] | *Notes:* This lot was added in by hand in the BMB, EBNP, LBDa and RKDH copies of the catalogue.	Mevrouw Achtienhoven	(Sold) fl 1:15 Gruiter
1802/09/06	AMSCH	0285[H]	*[Anonymous]* | 2 [Schilderijen] | *Notes:* This lot was added in by hand in the BMB, EBNP, LBDa and RKDH copies of the catalogue.	Mevrouw Achtienhoven	(Sold) fl 1:10 L Pakker
1802/09/06	AMSCH	0286[H]	*[Anonymous]* | 1 [Schilderij] | *Notes:* This lot was added in by hand in the BMB, EBNP, LBDa and RKDH copies of the catalogue.	Mevrouw Achtienhoven	(Sold) fl 1 Jan Spaan
1802/09/06	AMSCH	0287[H]	*[Anonymous]* | 2 [Schilderijen] | *Notes:* This lot was added in by hand in the BMB, EBNP, LBDa and RKDH copies of the catalogue.	Mevrouw Achtienhoven	(Sold) fl 4:5 Boelen
1802/09/06	AMSCH	0288[H]	*[Anonymous]* | 2 [Schilderijen] | *Notes:* This lot was added in by hand in the BMB, EBNP, LBDa and RKDH copies of the catalogue.	Mevrouw Achtienhoven	(Sold) fl 0:10 Vermeulen
1802/09/06	AMSCH	0289[H]	*[Anonymous]* | 4 [Schilderijen] | *Annots:* portrayt mijn (EBNP) *Notes:* This lot was added in by hand in the BMB, EBNP, LBDa and RKDH copies of the catalogue.	Mevrouw Achtienhoven	(Sold) fl 0:10 van der Schley
1802/09/06	AMSCH	0290[H]	*[Anonymous]* | 3 [Schilderijen] | *Notes:* This lot was added in by hand in the BMB, EBNP, LBDa and RKDH copies of the catalogue.	Mevrouw Achtienhoven	(Sold) fl 0:10 Roijers
1802/09/06	AMSCH	0291[H]	*[Anonymous]* | 1 [Schilderij] | *Notes:* This lot was added in by hand in the BMB, EBNP, LBDa and RKDH copies of the catalogue.	J	(Sold) fl 30 C S Roos
1802/09/06	AMSCH	0292[H]	*[Anonymous]* | 1 [Schilderij] | *Annots:* bernard (EBNP) *Notes:* This lot was added in by hand in the BMB, EBNP, LBDa and RKDH copies of the catalogue.	Wed Grave [or others]	(Sold) fl 0:10 Frantsen
1802/09/06	AMSCH	0293[H]	*[Anonymous]* | 1 [Schilderij] | *Notes:* This lot was added in by hand in the BMB, EBNP, LBDa and RKDH copies of the catalogue.	X	(Sold) fl 52 C S Roos
1802/09/06	AMSCH	0294[H]	*[Anonymous]* | 1 [Schilderij] | *Notes:* This lot was added in by hand in the BMB, EBNP, LBDa and RKDH copies of the catalogue.	X	(Sold) fl 41 Pruijssenaar

1802/09/06	AMSCH	0295[H]	*[Anonymous]* | 1 [Schilderij] | *Notes:* This lot was added in by hand in the BMB, EBNP, LBDa and RKDH copies of the catalogue.	X	(Sold) fl 5:10 Frantsen
1802/09/06	AMSCH	0296[H]	*[Anonymous]* | 1 [Schilderij] | *Notes:* This lot was added in by hand in the BMB, EBNP, LBDa and RKDH copies of the catalogue.	X	(Sold) fl 1 Gruiter
1802/09/06	AMSCH	0297[H]	*[Anonymous]* | 1 [Schilderij] | *Notes:* This lot was added in by hand in the BMB, EBNP, LBDa and RKDH copies of the catalogue.	Spaan	(Sold) fl 10:10 van Iperen
1802/09/15	HGKAN	0001	*[Anonymous]* | Het Spaansche Heydinnetje, op Paneel en Lyst [In Oly Verff] | *Mat:* in olyverf op paneel *Notes:* The bracketed information in the title appears above lot 1 and refers to lots 1 to 8.		(Unknown)
1802/09/15	HGKAN	0007	*[Anonymous]* | Een Jager, met zeer fraay Bywerk, op Paneel en Lyst [In Oly Verff] | *Mat:* in olyverf op paneel *Notes:* The bracketed information in the title appears above lot 1 and refers to lots 1 to 8.		(Unknown)
1802/09/15	HGKAN	0008	*[Anonymous]* | Een Ouden-Mans-Hoofd, op Doek en Lyst. [In Oly Verff] | *Mat:* in olyverf op doek *Notes:* The bracketed information in the title appears above lot 1 and refers to lots 1 to 8.		(Unknown)
1802/09/18	RMDRS	0056	*[Anonymous]* | Een Landschap, waarin een Herder en Herderin	Casper de Haas	(Unknown) fl 2:10
1802/09/18	RMDRS	0057	*[Anonymous]* | Een dito [Landschap], met Koetjens en Schapen	Casper de Haas	(Sold) fl 5:5 Verweij
1802/09/18	RMDRS	0058	*[Anonymous]* | Een dito [Landschap], waarin eenige Vissers, en een Dorp in 't verschiet	Casper de Haas	(Sold) fl 8 Verweij
1802/09/18	RMDRS	0059	*[Anonymous]* | Een galante Boer en Boerin	Casper de Haas	(Unknown) fl 4:15
1802/09/18	RMDRS	0062	*[Anonymous]* | Een Landschap, waarin de vinding van Moses	Casper de Haas	(Sold) fl 7 Verweij
1802/09/18	RMDRS	0063	*[Anonymous]* | Een Landschap met Herders	Casper de Haas	(Sold) fl 3 Verweij
1802/09/18	RMDRS	0073	*Een oud Meester* | Twee stuks, het eene Salomons eerste Regt, en het andere de aanbidding der drie Koningen, door een oud Meester, op koper | *Mat:* op koper	Casper de Haas	(Unknown) fl 2:12
1802/09/18	RMDRS	0074	*[Anonymous]* | Een en twintig stuks Pourtrette, van de Gouverneurs van India, van den jare 1614 tot 1733, welke by paare of in eene koop zullen verkogt werden	Casper de Haas	(Sold) fl 13:10 Carrée
1802/09/18	RMDRS	0077	*[Anonymous]* | Een Vrouwe Pourtret	Casper de Haas	(Unknown) fl 0:12
1802/09/18	RMDRS	0078	*[Anonymous]* | Een Gecrayonneerd oud Manshoofd, in lyst en glas	Casper de Haas	(Sold) fl 1:10 v Giesen
1802/09/18	RMDRS	0084	*[Anonymous]* | Een dito [Gezicht op een Stad], als de voorgaande	Casper de Haas	(Unknown) fl 1:10
1802/09/18	RMDRS	0085	*[Anonymous]* | Een dito [Gezicht op een Stad], zynde een gezicht op de Stad Rotterdam	Casper de Haas	(Unknown) fl 3
1802/09/18	RMDRS	0088	*[Anonymous]* | Een dito [groot stuk], Cleopatra door den Adder gebeeten	Casper de Haas	(Unknown) fl 0:12
1802/09/18	RMDRS	0090	*[Anonymous]* | Een Gezelschap van muciceerende en dansende Heere en Damens, uitvoerig geschildert	Casper de Haas	(Unknown) fl 1
1802/09/18	RMDRS	0091	*[Anonymous]* | Twee kleine Landschappen	Casper de Haas	(Sold) fl 1:2 v[an] G[iesen]
1802/09/18	RMDRS	0092	*[Anonymous]* | Twee dito [kleine Landschappen], met Boeren en Boerinnen	Casper de Haas	(Unknown) fl 2
1802/09/18	RMDRS	0093	*[Anonymous]* | Een stil Waaterje met Scheepjes	Casper de Haas	(Unknown) fl 0:11
1802/09/18	RMDRS	0094	*[Anonymous]* | Een Landschap met Paarden	Casper de Haas	(Unknown) fl 1:10
1802/09/18	RMDRS	0095	*[Anonymous]* | Een dito Landschap, met Paarden en een Hond | *Notes:* It is unclear what "dito" refers to in the title.	Casper de Haas	(Unknown) fl 1:10
1802/09/18	RMDRS	0096	*[Anonymous]* | Een Vrouwtje dat zit te Haspelen	Casper de Haas	(Sold) fl 1:6 v[an] G[iesen]
1802/09/18	RMDRS	0097	*[Anonymous]* | Een Boere Kermis, vol Beelden	Casper de Haas	(Unknown) fl 2:4
1802/09/18	RMDRS	0098	*[Anonymous]* | Een Landschap met Koeyen	Casper de Haas	(Unknown) fl 1:12
1802/09/18	RMDRS	0099	*[Anonymous]* | Een Ryn gezicht met Scheepjes en Beelden	Casper de Haas	(Unknown) fl 5:5
1802/09/18	RMDRS	0100	*[Anonymous]* | Een Italiaanse Zeehaven	Casper de Haas	(Unknown) fl 1:14
1802/09/18	RMDRS	0101	*[Anonymous]* | Een Romeinse Triumph	Casper de Haas	(Sold) fl 0:15 v[an] G[iesen]
1802/09/18	RMDRS	0102	*[Anonymous]* | Twee vrolyk drinkende Boertjes	Casper de Haas	(Unknown) fl 1:10
1802/09/18	RMDRS	0103	*[Anonymous]* | Een Landschap met een Naakte Venus	Casper de Haas	(Sold) fl 1 v[an] G[iesen]
1802/09/18	RMDRS	0104	*[Anonymous]* | Een fraay Landschap	Casper de Haas	(Sold) fl 2 v[an] G[iesen]
1802/09/18	RMDRS	0105	*[Anonymous]* | Een stil Water met een Stad gezigt	Casper de Haas	(Unknown) fl 2:2
1802/09/18	RMDRS	0106	*[Anonymous]* | Een mooy Landschap met Koeyen	Casper de Haas	(Unknown) fl 2:14
1802/09/18	RMDRS	0107	*[Anonymous]* | Een Wintertje	Casper de Haas	(Sold) fl 7:10 Gruiters
1802/09/18	RMDRS	0108	*[Anonymous]* | Een dito Winter | *Notes:* It is unclear what "dito" refers to in the title.	Casper de Haas	(Unknown) fl 1:2
1802/09/18	RMDRS	0109	*[Anonymous]* | Een Landschap	Casper de Haas	(Unknown) fl 1

1802/09/18	RMDRS	0110	*[Anonymous]* | Een dito Landschap | *Notes:* It is unclear what "dito" refers to in the title.	Casper de Haas	(Unknown) fl 0:12
1802/09/18	RMDRS	0111	*[Anonymous]* | Een Alchimist in zyn Labatorium	Casper de Haas	(Sold) fl 2 Gruiter
1802/09/18	RMDRS	0112	*[Anonymous]* | Een stil Watertje met Scheepjes	Casper de Haas	(Sold) fl 0:12 V Wallen
1802/09/18	RMDRS	0116	*[Anonymous]* | Een dito [Ordonnantie] met danzende kinderen	Casper de Haas	(Unknown) fl 10:10
1802/09/18	RMDRS	0120	*[Anonymous]* | Twee dito [Landschappen], onbekend	Casper de Haas	(Unknown) fl 1:10
1802/09/18	RMDRS	0121	*[Anonymous]* | Twee Boere binnen huizen	Casper de Haas	(Unknown) fl 3:10
1802/09/18	RMDRS	0123	*[Anonymous]* | Een Batailje	Casper de Haas	(Unknown) fl 0:8
1802/09/21	UTHDG	000A[H]	*[Anonymous]* | Rustende Jagers in een Landschap | *Notes:* This lot was added in by hand in the OGA copy of the catalogue.		(Bought In) fl 3
1802/09/21	UTHDG	000B[H]	*[Anonymous]* | Eene magdalena in Devotie | *Notes:* This lot was added in by hand in the OGA copy of the catalogue.		(Bought In) fl 11
1802/09/21	UTHDG	000C[H]	*[Anonymous]* | Gezicht van Hellevoet | *Notes:* This lot was added in by hand in the OGA copy of the catalogue.		(Bought In) fl 3:10
1802/09/21	UTHDG	000D[H]	*[Anonymous]* | Een oud Kasteel bij een Rivier | *Notes:* This lot was added in by hand in the OGA copy of the catalogue.		(Bought In) fl 5:5
1802/09/21	UTHDG	000G[H]	*[Anonymous]* | Twee stuks Landschapjes Ovaal | *Fmt:* ovaal *Notes:* This lot was added in by hand in the OGA copy of the catalogue.		(Bought In) fl 3:10
1802/09/21	UTHDG	000I[H]	*[Anonymous]* | Een Kloek mans pourtrait | *Notes:* This lot was added in by hand in the OGA copy of the catalogue.		(Bought In) fl 3
1802/09/21	UTHDG	000K[H]	*[Anonymous]* | Twee Stuks boeregezelschappen | *Notes:* This lot was added in by hand in the OGA copy of the catalogue.		(Sold) fl 2:6 Gevaerts agter dem Dom
1802/09/21	UTHDG	000L[H]	*[Anonymous]* | Een Rokend boertje | *Notes:* This lot was added in by hand in the OGA copy of the catalogue.		(Sold) fl 1:16 J La Maine
1802/09/21	UTHDG	000M[H]	*[Anonymous]* | Bloemen in een pot | *Notes:* This lot was added in by hand in the OGA copy of the catalogue.		(Bought In) fl 1
1802/09/21	UTHDG	000N[H]	*[Anonymous]* | Een Heilige Familje | *Notes:* This lot was added in by hand in the OGA copy of the catalogue.		(Sold) fl 1:2 Ostie
1802/09/21	UTHDG	000O[H]	*[Anonymous]* | Een boere Kermis in een Landschap | *Notes:* This lot was added in by hand in the OGA copy of the catalogue.		(Sold) fl 0:11 J La Maine
1802/09/21	UTHDG	000R[H]	*[Anonymous]* | Een Historieel | *Notes:* This lot was added in by hand in the OGA copy of the catalogue.		(Sold) fl 0:8 Ostie
1802/09/21	UTHDG	000S[H]	*[Anonymous]* | Joseph uit de put komende | *Notes:* This lot was added in by hand in the OGA copy of the catalogue.		(Sold) fl 0:8 De Meyer
1802/09/21	UTHDG	000T[H]	*[Anonymous]* | Een boere binnehuis met Stilleven | *Notes:* This lot was added in by hand in the OGA copy of the catalogue.		(Bought In) fl 0:12
1802/09/21	UTHDG	000U[H]	*[Anonymous]* | Een Rivier met Scheepen | *Notes:* This lot was added in by hand in the OGA copy of the catalogue.		(Bought In) fl 0:6
1802/09/21	UTHDG	000V[H]	*[Anonymous]* | Een Landschapje | *Notes:* This lot was added in by hand in the OGA copy of the catalogue.		(Bought In) fl 0:6
1802/09/21	UTHDG	000W[H]	*[Anonymous]* | Twee Stuks met vrolyke boere | *Notes:* This lot was added in by hand in the OGA copy of the catalogue.		(Sold) fl 0:11 Cobell
1802/09/21	UTHDG	000X[H]	*[Anonymous]* | Twee Stuks met galantizeerende boeren | *Notes:* This lot was added in by hand in the OGA copy of the catalogue.		(Sold) fl 1:4 De Meijer metselaar
1802/09/21	UTHDG	0072	*[Anonymous]* | Een Man staande bij een wit paard, dat uit een Tobbe, die door een jongen word vastgehouden, eet. | *Mat:* op doek *Size:* hoog 13, breed 11 duimen		(Sold) fl 4:15 De Munnick
1802/09/29	AMSCH	0060	*Onbekend Meester* | Een Landschap. hoog 19, breed 21 ½ duim. Paneel. Deeze bevallige Ordenantie steld voor, een Italiaansch Bergagtig Landschap met fraai Geboomten en dartel Houtgewas; op den Voorgrond een stromend Water, waar uit een Landman Water geschept heeft, om eenen beladenen Ezel te laten drinken; terwyl een Reiziger met een Ezel de Weg schynt als op te gaan. Verders een Herder eenig Vee voortdryvende; dit Stuk is kunstig en delicaat van Penceelbehandeling [Un beau site de Paysage, offrant à gauche une etendue d'Eau qui se termine par une chaine de montagnes, le milieu du Tableau est occupé par un chemin éclairé avec Art, ou un Paysan fait boire un Mulet, tandis qu'un autre continue sa route ; on remarque plus loin un Pâtre, qui conduit quelques boeufs : La droite est enrichie de Rochers chargés d'Arbres & de broussailles. Un Ton Chaud & brillant soutenu de l'Effet le plus Harmonieux sont assigner cette Peinture à un Artiste Habile.] | *Mat:* op paneel *Size:* hoog 19, breed 21 ½ duim	[Labouchere?]	(Sold) fl 27 V^{n} Iperen
1802/09/29	AMSCH	0061	*Een goed Meester* | Twee Stuks, ieder hoog 9 ¾, breed 7 ½ duim. Paneel. Zynde twee Boeren Jongens, met los hair en ronde Hoeden, halverlyf; van den jaare 1649. Stout gepenceeld door een goed Meester [Deux petits Tableaux, offrans les Portraits en buste d'Enfans de Village à Chapeaux ronds ; traités d'une touche large & facile.] | *Mat:* op paneel *Size:* ieder hoog 9 ¾, breed 7 ½ duim *Inscr:* 1649 (dated?) *Notes:* It is unclear whether the date is inscribed on the painting.	[Labouchere?]	(Sold) fl 28 J van Eijk

1802/09/29	AMSCH	0062	*Zeer bekwamen Meester* | Een Stil Water-gezicht, hoog 21, breed 24 ½ duim. Doek. Een alleräangenaamst Watergezigt, waarin gezien worden een fraai Jagt met witte Zeilen, Visschers Pinken, een pontvaarder, Boten vol Volk, en ménigte andere Scheepen met onderscheide couleur van Zeilen. Dit Stuk is fraai geördeneerd, delicaat behandelt, warm, zonägtig en natuurlyk van Coloriet; de doorschynende bewolkte Lucht is zeer schoon, het Water is dun, en de spiegeling der Voorwerpen is meede kunstig waargenomen, alles kondigt aan in dit Stuk eenen zeer bekwamen Meester [Une mer calme, chargée de differens Batimens & Barques ; La gauche offre un jacht Hollandois garni d'une grande voile avec ses Pavillons que vient aborder une chaloupe dirigée par six Rameurs, à droite se remarquent des Barques de Pecheurs & un Bac avec des figures & des animaux. Ces divers objets se détachent admirablement sur un beau ciel nuageux. Ce Tableau est executé jusques dans les détails avec autant d'art que de finesse et la couleur en est d'une vérité étonnante. Il peut être mis de niveau aux plus belle productions dans ce genre, des celébres artistes, de la grande Ecole Hollandoise.] | *Mat:* op doek *Size:* hoog 21, breed 24 ½ duim	[Labouchere?]	(Sold) fl 180 Vinkeles
1802/09/29	AMSCH	0063	*Onbekend Meester* | Een Musiceerend Gezelschap, hoog 19, breed 16 ¼ duim. Doek. In een gemeubileerd Binnenvertrek, door de Zon bescheenen, ziet men aan een Tafel zitten (gedeeltelyk met een groenagtig geborduurd Kleed bedekt) eenige Heeren en Dames in oude Hollandsche en Spaansche Kleeding, welke met musiceeren, drinken en andere bezighéden zig Vermaken; op een Stoel leggen onderscheide couleuren van Kleederen, een Wynkan en meerder Bywerk leggen op den Voorgrond. Dit Stuk is zeer fraai en meesterlyk gepenceeld [Un sujet de quelques Figures, Hommes & Femmes dans l'ancien costume Hollandois & Espagnol, assis à une Table couverte en partie d'un tapis verd [sic] Brodé, dans un appartement meublé éclairé du soleil ; occupés à faire de la musique. Leurs Habillemens sont riches & des couleurs les plus éclatantes, des accessoires analogues au sujet y produisent les Effets les plus marquans. Ce Tableau est d'une touche moëlleuse & soignée.] | *Mat:* op doek *Size:* hoog 19, breed 16 ¼ duim [haut de 19, large 16 ½ pouces] *Notes:* The dimensions differ in the Dutch and French editions of the catalogue.	[Labouchere?]	(Sold) fl 88 Vermeulen
1802/09/29	AMSCH	0064	*Onbekend Meester* | Een Binnehuisje, hoog 13 ½, breed 11 duim. Paneel. In een Huismans Woning ziet men een Biddend Huisgezin voor het Eeten, aan Tafel zitten, kunstig verbeeld en bevallig Behandelt [L'Interieur d'une chambre rustique, ou des campagnards, prennent leur repas, les caractères des têtes sont plein d'Expression.] | *Mat:* op paneel *Size:* hoog 13 ½, breed 11 duim	[Labouchere?]	(Sold) fl 17 Coclers
1802/09/29	AMSCH	0065	*Onbekend Meester* | Een Stil-Leven, Hoog 30, breed 26 duim. Doek. Op een Tafel met een rood Fluweel Kleed bedekt, zyn geplaatst Globe, oude Boeken en Papieren, Zandloper, een naakt Kindje van Plyster; enz. zeer goed, kragtig en meesterlyk geschildert [Des sujets inanimés, placés sur une Table couverte d'un tapis de Velours Ecarlate, comme globe, vieux Livres & Papiers, Enfant de Plâtre &c. traité avec beaucoup d'art & d'Intelligence de clair obscur.] | *Mat:* op doek *Size:* hoog 30, breed 26 duim	[Labouchere?]	(Sold) fl 2:5 L Pakker
1802/09/29	AMSCH	0066	*Onbekend Meester* | Op eenen Heuvelagtigen grond onder Geboomten, ziet men eene bevallige Herderin, als nedergezeten, welke door eenen jeugdigen Herder word geliefkoost; de Caracters zyn byzonder wel uitgedrukt. Verders ziet men twee Bokjes op den Heuvel, de Beelden zyn leevensgroote halverlyf, het Coloriet is schoon en kragtig, en van eene meesterlyke fraaye Penceelbehandeling [Declaration, d'amour d'un jeune Berger à une belle Bergere a chevelure blonde, assise près d'un Bosquet. Elle paroit résister avec douceur à ses empressemens, leurs caracteres sont de la plus grande expression ces Figures sont vües à mi-corps de grandeur naturelle : ce sujet est traitê par un des meilleurs artistes dans ce genre, d'un dessein correct d'une fonte de couleurs pure & vigoureuse & d'une Harmonie bien entendue.] | *Mat:* op doek *Size:* hoog 38, breed 50 duim	[Labouchere?]	(Sold) fl 4 Hulswit
1802/09/29	AMSCH	0067	*Onbekend Meester* | Een Landschap, hoog 18 ½, breed 24 ½ duim. Doek, Paneel. In dit fraaye Schildery ziet men in het midden van zwaar opgaand Geboomten, onderscheiden van aart, een helder en transparant Waater, waarby Boeren Woningen en een werkende Watermolen, welke zig in het Water spiegelen; en voor aan eenige dryvende Waterbiezen, verders laat zig bevallige Stoffagie in dit Stuk bemerken, en eenige dorre afgekapte Boomen leggen op de Voorgrond; het geval is aangenaam en de Penceelbehandeling is meesterlyk [Un des plus Heureux sites de Paysages offrant le point de vüe d'un Terrein richement boisé avec divers chemins qui le traversent, quelques Habitations près d'une Eau claire & transparante & des figures naturellement distribuées, ajoutent à la richesse et à la vérité de l'Illusion, ainsi qu'un moulin à Eau en pleine activité y produit un Effet agréable. Ce Tableau est touché avec cette intelligence digne d'un grand artiste.] | *Mat:* op doek op paneel *Size:* hoog 18 ½, breed 24 ½ duim	[Labouchere?]	(Sold) fl 228 Hulswit
1802/09/29	AMSCH	0068	*Onbekend Meester* | Een Land- en Watergezigt, hoog 16, breed 14 duim. Paneel. Een ruim uitgestrekt Landschap is het voorwerp van dit Stukje, zynde met Wateren doorsneeden, Steeden, Dorpen, Figuren en fraai Geboomten worden 'er als van Duin af ingezien, alles is uitvoerig en zonagtig behandelt [Un joli Tableau de Paysage qu'une Eau traverse en	[Labouchere?]	(Sold) fl 30 L Pakker

			serpentant, des Figures & des Habitations y produisent des Variétés agréables. Les premiers plans sont eclairés ; la touche fine, la belle entente de la couleur, prouvent en faveur d'un maitre éclairé.] | *Mat:* op paneel *Size:* hoog 16, breed 14 duim		
1802/09/29	AMSCH	0071	*Een zeer goed Meester* | Een Kinder Hoofdje, zeer fraai Ao. 1585; door een zeer goed Meester [Le Portrait d'un joli petit Garçon agé de cinq Ans de l'Année 1585, très bien exécuté & d'une belle carnation.] | *Mat:* op paneel *Size:* hoog 7 ½, breed 6 ¼ duim *Inscr:* Ao. 1585 (dated)	[Labouchere?]	(Sold) fl 2:10 Ijver
1802/09/30	HGBAK	0002	*[Anonymous]* | Een oude Vrouw over een Stoof de handen warmende, op doek, in vergulde lyst. [Schilderyen in Olyverf] | *Mat:* in olyverf op doek *Notes:* The bracketed information in the title appears above lot 1 and refers to lots 1 to 26.		(Unknown)
1802/09/30	HGBAK	0006	*[Anonymous]* | Een Boertje, schynende zig zelve aan de Arm te verbinde, paneel, zwarte lyst. [Schilderyen in Olyverf] | *Mat:* in olyverf op paneel *Notes:* The bracketed information in the title appears above lot 1 and refers to lots 1 to 26.		(Unknown)
1802/09/30	HGBAK	0010	*[Anonymous]* | Een Oud Man en Vrouw, zwarte lyst. [Schilderyen in Olyverf] | *Mat:* in olyverf *Notes:* The bracketed information in the title appears above lot 1 and refers to lots 1 to 26.		(Unknown)
1802/09/30	HGBAK	0011	*[Anonymous]* | Twee stuks stil Water gezichten, met Scheepen gestoffeerd, paneel, zwarte lysten. [Schilderyen in Olyverf] | *Mat:* in olyverf op paneel *Notes:* The bracketed information in the title appears above lot 1 and refers to lots 1 to 26.		(Unknown)
1802/09/30	HGBAK	0012	*[Anonymous]* | Vier stuks met Honden en Schapen, paneel, zwarte lysten. [Schilderyen in Olyverf] | *Mat:* in olyverf op paneel *Notes:* The bracketed information in the title appears above lot 1 and refers to lots 1 to 26.		(Unknown)
1802/09/30	HGBAK	0013	*[Anonymous]* | Vier dito met Jagten en Boeren gezelschap, dito [zwarte] lyst. [Schilderyen in Olyverf] | *Mat:* in olyverf *Notes:* The bracketed information in the title about the medium appears above lot 1 and refers to lots 1 to 26.		(Unknown)
1802/09/30	HGBAK	0014	*[Anonymous]* | Ses stuks met oude Mans koppen, kwarte [sic] lystjes. [Schilderyen in Olyverf] | *Mat:* in olyverf *Notes:* The bracketed information in the title appears above lot 1 and refers to lots 1 to 26.		(Unknown)
1802/09/30	HGBAK	0015	*[Anonymous]* | Pourtrait van Sultan Solyman, zwarte lyst. [Schilderyen in Olyverf] | *Mat:* in olyverf *Notes:* The bracketed information in the title appears above lot 1 and refers to lots 1 to 26.		(Unknown)
1802/09/30	HGBAK	0016	*[Anonymous]* | Een Vrouwe Kop, en een Krygsman in 't harnas, twee stuks. [Schilderyen in Olyverf] | *Mat:* in olyverf *Notes:* The bracketed information in the title appears above lot 1 and refers to lots 1 to 26.		(Unknown)
1802/09/30	HGBAK	0017	*[Anonymous]* | Mercurius en Argus, in een Landschap, op doek. [Schilderyen in Olyverf] | *Mat:* in olyverf op doek *Notes:* The bracketed information in the title appears above lot 1 and refers to lots 1 to 26.		(Unknown)
1802/09/30	HGBAK	0018	*[Anonymous]* | Een zittende Dame, houdende een Brief in de hand, op doek. [Schilderyen in Olyverf] | *Mat:* in olyverf op doek *Notes:* The bracketed information in the title appears above lot 1 and refers to lots 1 to 26.		(Unknown)
1802/09/30	HGBAK	0019	*[Anonymous]* | Een dito [zittende] Dame, op doek. [Schilderyen in Olyverf] | *Mat:* in olyverf op doek *Notes:* The bracketed information in the title about the medium appears above lot 1 and refers to lots 1 to 26.		(Unknown)
1802/09/30	HGBAK	0020	*[Anonymous]* | Venus en Cupido, Capitaal, op doek. [Schilderyen in Olyverf] | *Mat:* in olyverf op doek *Notes:* The bracketed information in the title appears above lot 1 and refers to lots 1 to 26.		(Unknown)
1802/09/30	HGBAK	0021	*[Anonymous]* | Vier stuks met Dames, op doek. [Schilderyen in Olyverf] | *Mat:* in olyverf op doek *Notes:* The bracketed information in the title appears above lot 1 and refers to lots 1 to 26.		(Unknown)
1802/09/30	HGBAK	0022	*[Anonymous]* | Een stuks met Honden. [Schilderyen in Olyverf] | *Mat:* in olyverf *Notes:* The bracketed information in the title appears above lot 1 and refers to lots 1 to 26.		(Unknown)
1802/09/30	HGBAK	0023	*[Anonymous]* | Een fraay Landschap met Figuren gestoffeerd, in een zwarte lyst en vergulde bies. [Schilderyen in Olyverf] | *Mat:* in olyverf *Notes:* The bracketed information in the title appears above lot 1 and refers to lots 1 to 26.		(Unknown)
1802/09/30	HGBAK	0024	*[Anonymous]* | Een geforceerde Jagt, op koper, in dito [vergulde] lyst. [Schilderyen in Olyverf] | *Mat:* in olyverf op koper *Notes:* The bracketed information in the title about the medium appears above lot 1 and refers to lots 1 to 26.		(Unknown)
1802/09/30	HGBAK	0025	*[Anonymous]* | Een oud stukje met Vrouwebeelden &c. mede op koper, in dito [vergulde] lyst. [Schilderyen in Olyverf] | *Mat:* in olyverf op koper *Notes:* The bracketed information in the title about the medium appears above lot 1 and refers to lots 1 to 26.		(Unknown)
1802/09/30	HGBAK	0026	*[Anonymous]* | Een Pourtrait van een Generaal, in een vergulde lyst. [Schilderyen in Olyverf] | *Mat:* in olyverf *Notes:* The bracketed information in the title appears above lot 1 and refers to lots 1 to 26.		(Unknown)

1802/10/18	MGBEO	0001	*[Anonymous]* | [Untitled] | *Notes:* The only extant copy of this catalogue is annotated with the buyers and prices, but it does not include a printed list of the paintings.	(Bought In) £ 12
1802/10/18	MGBEO	0002	*[Anonymous]* | [Untitled] | *Notes:* The only extant copy of this catalogue is annotated with the buyers and prices, but it does not include a printed list of the paintings.	(Sold) £ 0:8 Klittenberg
1802/10/18	MGBEO	0003	*[Anonymous]* | [Untitled] | *Notes:* The only extant copy of this catalogue is annotated with the buyers and prices, but it does not include a printed list of the paintings.	(Sold) £ 0:18 Modera
1802/10/18	MGBEO	0004	*[Anonymous]* | [Untitled] | *Notes:* The only extant copy of this catalogue is annotated with the buyers and prices, but it does not include a printed list of the paintings.	(Sold) £ 1:1 Modera
1802/10/18	MGBEO	0005	*[Anonymous]* | [Untitled] | *Notes:* The only extant copy of this catalogue is annotated with the buyers and prices, but it does not include a printed list of the paintings.	(Sold) £ 1:10 v d Andel
1802/10/18	MGBEO	0006	*[Anonymous]* | [Untitled] | *Notes:* The only extant copy of this catalogue is annotated with the buyers and prices, but it does not include a printed list of the paintings.	(Sold) £ 1:1 v d Andel
1802/10/18	MGBEO	0007	*[Anonymous]* | [Untitled] | *Notes:* The only extant copy of this catalogue is annotated with the buyers and prices, but it does not include a printed list of the paintings.	(Sold) £ 0:6 Klittenberg
1802/10/18	MGBEO	0008	*[Anonymous]* | [Untitled] | *Notes:* The only extant copy of this catalogue is annotated with the buyers and prices, but it does not include a printed list of the paintings.	(Sold) £ 0:12 Ooms
1802/10/18	MGBEO	0009	*[Anonymous]* | [Untitled] | *Notes:* The only extant copy of this catalogue is annotated with the buyers and prices, but it does not include a printed list of the paintings.	(Sold) £ 0:11 Beljaart
1802/10/18	MGBEO	0010	*[Anonymous]* | [Untitled] | *Notes:* The only extant copy of this catalogue is annotated with the buyers and prices, but it does not include a printed list of the paintings.	(Sold) £ 0:5 P d Meijer
1802/10/18	MGBEO	0011	*[Anonymous]* | [Untitled] | *Notes:* The only extant copy of this catalogue is annotated with the buyers and prices, but it does not include a printed list of the paintings.	(Sold) £ 0:5 Vlamink
1802/10/18	MGBEO	0012	*[Anonymous]* | [Untitled] | *Notes:* The only extant copy of this catalogue is annotated with the buyers and prices, but it does not include a printed list of the paintings.	(Sold) £ 0:4 de Schinkel
1802/10/18	MGBEO	0013	*[Anonymous]* | [Untitled] | *Notes:* The only extant copy of this catalogue is annotated with the buyers and prices, but it does not include a printed list of the paintings.	(Sold) £ 0:6 de Schinkel
1802/10/18	MGBEO	0014	*[Anonymous]* | [Untitled] | *Notes:* The only extant copy of this catalogue is annotated with the buyers and prices, but it does not include a printed list of the paintings.	(Sold) £ 0:5 A Meertens
1802/10/18	MGBEO	0015	*[Anonymous]* | [Untitled] | *Notes:* The only extant copy of this catalogue is annotated with the buyers and prices, but it does not include a printed list of the paintings.	(Sold) £ 0:2 v d Andel
1802/10/18	MGBEO	0016	*[Anonymous]* | [Untitled] | *Notes:* The only extant copy of this catalogue is annotated with the buyers and prices, but it does not include a printed list of the paintings.	(Sold) £ 0:5 Vlamink
1802/10/18	MGBEO	0017	*[Anonymous]* | [Untitled] | *Notes:* The only extant copy of this catalogue is annotated with the buyers and prices, but it does not include a printed list of the paintings.	(Sold) £ 0:8 Hooghuis
1802/10/18	MGBEO	0018	*[Anonymous]* | [Untitled] | *Notes:* The only extant copy of this catalogue is annotated with the buyers and prices, but it does not include a printed list of the paintings.	(Sold) £ 1:7 Vlamink
1802/10/18	MGBEO	0019	*[Anonymous]* | [Untitled] | *Notes:* The only extant copy of this catalogue is annotated with the buyers and prices, but it does not include a printed list of the paintings.	(Sold) £ 0:2 Vlamink
1802/10/18	MGBEO	0020	*[Anonymous]* | [Untitled] | *Notes:* The only extant copy of this catalogue is annotated with the buyers and prices, but it does not include a printed list of the paintings.	(Sold) £ 1:1 v d Andel
1802/10/18	MGBEO	0021	*[Anonymous]* | [Untitled] | *Notes:* The only extant copy of this catalogue is annotated with the buyers and prices, but it does not include a printed list of the paintings.	(Bought In)
1802/10/18	MGBEO	0022	*[Anonymous]* | [Untitled] | *Notes:* The only extant copy of this catalogue is annotated with the buyers and prices, but it does not include a printed list of the paintings.	(Bought In)
1802/10/18	MGBEO	0023	*[Anonymous]* | [Untitled] | *Notes:* The only extant copy of this catalogue is annotated with the buyers and prices, but it does not include a printed list of the paintings.	(Sold) £ 1:8 Sande
1802/10/18	MGBEO	0024	*[Anonymous]* | [Untitled] | *Notes:* The only extant copy of this catalogue is annotated with the buyers and prices, but it does not include a printed list of the paintings.	(Bought In)

1802/10/18	MGBEO	0025	*[Anonymous]* | [Untitled] | *Notes:* The only extant copy of this catalogue is annotated with the buyers and prices, but it does not include a printed list of the paintings.		(Sold) £ 0:17 Klittenberg
1802/10/18	MGBEO	0026	*[Anonymous]* | [Untitled] | *Notes:* The only extant copy of this catalogue is annotated with the buyers and prices, but it does not include a printed list of the paintings.		(Sold) £ 0:4 Vlamink
1802/10/18	MGBEO	0027	*[Anonymous]* | [Untitled] | *Notes:* The only extant copy of this catalogue is annotated with the buyers and prices, but it does not include a printed list of the paintings.		(Sold) £ 0:4 A Koster
1802/10/18	MGBEO	0028	*[Anonymous]* | [Untitled] | *Notes:* The only extant copy of this catalogue is annotated with the buyers and prices, but it does not include a printed list of the paintings.		(Sold) £ 0:2 Beljaart
1802/10/18	MGBEO	0029	*[Anonymous]* | [Untitled] | *Notes:* The only extant copy of this catalogue is annotated with the buyers and prices, but it does not include a printed list of the paintings.		(Sold) £ 0:5 Beljaart
1802/10/18	MGBEO	0030	*[Anonymous]* | [Untitled] | *Notes:* The only extant copy of this catalogue is annotated with the buyers and prices, but it does not include a printed list of the paintings.		(Sold) £ 0:5 Vlamink
1802/10/18	MGBEO	0031	*[Anonymous]* | [Untitled] | *Notes:* The only extant copy of this catalogue is annotated with the buyers and prices, but it does not include a printed list of the paintings.		(Sold) £ 0:2 Vlamink
1802/10/18	MGBEO	0032	*[Anonymous]* | [Untitled] | *Notes:* The only extant copy of this catalogue is annotated with the buyers and prices, but it does not include a printed list of the paintings.		(Sold) £ 1:1 v Benthem
1802/10/18	MGBEO	0033	*[Anonymous]* | [Untitled] | *Notes:* The only extant copy of this catalogue is annotated with the buyers and prices, but it does not include a printed list of the paintings.		(Sold) £ 0:4 Ooms
1802/10/18	MGBEO	0034	*[Anonymous]* | [Untitled] | *Notes:* The only extant copy of this catalogue is annotated with the buyers and prices, but it does not include a printed list of the paintings.		(Sold) £ 0:1 v Dongen
1802/10/18	MGBEO	0035	*[Anonymous]* | [Untitled] | *Notes:* The only extant copy of this catalogue is annotated with the buyers and prices, but it does not include a printed list of the paintings.		(Sold) £ 2:18 Ooms
1802/10/18	MGBEO	0036	*[Anonymous]* | [Untitled] | *Notes:* The only extant copy of this catalogue is annotated with the buyers and prices, but it does not include a printed list of the paintings.		(Sold) £ 0:1 v Dongen
1802/10/18	MGBEO	0037	*[Anonymous]* | [Untitled] | *Notes:* The only extant copy of this catalogue is annotated with the buyers and prices, but it does not include a printed list of the paintings.		(Sold) £ 0:1 Hicken
1802/10/18	MGBEO	0038	*[Anonymous]* | [Untitled] | *Notes:* The only extant copy of this catalogue is annotated with the buyers and prices, but it does not include a printed list of the paintings.		(Sold) £ 0:2 v Dongen
1802/10/18	MGBEO	0039	*[Anonymous]* | [Untitled] | *Notes:* The only extant copy of this catalogue is annotated with the buyers and prices, but it does not include a printed list of the paintings.		(Sold) £ 0:1 A Meertens
1802/10/18	MGBEO	0040	*[Anonymous]* | [Untitled] | *Notes:* The only extant copy of this catalogue is annotated with the buyers and prices, but it does not include a printed list of the paintings.		(Sold) £ 0:3 Ooms
1802/10/18	MGBEO	0041	*[Anonymous]* | [Untitled] | *Notes:* The only extant copy of this catalogue is annotated with the buyers and prices, but it does not include a printed list of the paintings.		(Sold) £ 0:7 Wed Bijdals
1802/10/18	MGBEO	0042	*[Anonymous]* | [Untitled] | *Notes:* The only extant copy of this catalogue is annotated with the buyers and prices, but it does not include a printed list of the paintings.		(Sold) £ 0:1 Hooghuis
1802/10/18	MGBEO	0043	*[Anonymous]* | [Untitled] | *Notes:* The only extant copy of this catalogue is annotated with the buyers and prices, but it does not include a printed list of the paintings.		(Sold) £ 0:1 for lots 43 & 43a. Hicken
1802/10/18	MGBEO	0043a	*[Anonymous]* | [Untitled] | *Notes:* The only extant copy of this catalogue is annotated with the buyers and prices, but it does not include a printed list of the paintings.		(Sold) £ 0:1 for lots 43 & 43a. Hicken
1802/11/01	DOBRA	0035	*[Anonymous]* | De Maaltyd van Belsazar [sic] | *Mat:* op paneel	Paulus van der Spyk [or others]	(Sold) fl 1:4 de Keser
1802/11/01	DOBRA	0041	*[Anonymous]* | Een Strandgezigtje | *Mat:* op paneel *Notes:* This lot was sold with lot 27, which is a copy after A. Ostade.	Paulus van der Spyk [or others]	(Sold) fl 1:15 for lots 27 & 41. v Steegh
1802/11/01	DOBRA	0043a	*[Anonymous]* | Een Bergagtig Landschap met een ruïne, beeltjes enz. | *Mat:* op doek	Paulus van der Spyk [or others]	(Sold) fl 2:5 Randwyk
1802/11/01	DOBRA	0047	*[Anonymous]* | Twee dito [stukjes met Boertjes]	Paulus van der Spyk [or others]	(Sold) fl 2 v Leen
1802/11/01	DOBRA	0057	*[Anonymous]* | Een Boeren-Binnenhuis | *Mat:* op paneel	Paulus van der Spyk [or others]	(Sold) fl 2:5 A v Well

1802/11/01	DOBRA	0072	*[Anonymous]* | Een stilleeven met verscheidenerlij Vogels | *Mat:* op paneel *Size:* breed 21, hoog 16 duim *Notes:* This lot was sold with lot 71 by Abr. Droochsloot.	Paulus van der Spyk [or others]	(Bought In) fl 4:5 for lots 71 & 72
1802/11/01	DOBRA	0073	*[Anonymous]* | Een Landschapje | *Mat:* op paneel	Paulus van der Spyk [or others]	(Sold) fl 0:10 Randwyk
1802/11/01	DOBRA	0078	*[Anonymous]* | Een Landschap, met ruïnen; op den voorgrond een Hoppe en andere vogels | *Mat:* op doek *Notes:* This lot was sold with lot 77 by Monogrammist J.B.	Paulus van der Spyk [or others]	(Sold) fl 1 for lots 77 & 78. Schalk
1802/11/01	DOBRA	0079	*[Anonymous]* | Een Landschap met Boomen, Boeren, enz. | *Mat:* op paneel	Paulus van der Spyk [or others]	(Sold) fl 1:2 Lamme
1802/11/01	DOBRA	0080	*[Anonymous]* | Een Bloemstukje | *Mat:* op paneel	Paulus van der Spyk [or others]	(Sold) fl 0:14 for lots 80 & 81. v d Weiden
1802/11/01	DOBRA	0081	*[Anonymous]* | Een stukje verbeeldende de Samaritaansche Vrouw by de put Jacobs | *Mat:* op paneel	Paulus van der Spyk [or others]	(Sold) fl 0:14 for lots 80 & 81. v d Weiden
1802/11/01	DOBRA	0082	*[Anonymous]* | Salomons eerste regt; en twee stuks diverse	Paulus van der Spyk [or others]	(Sold) fl 1 Roe
1802/11/01	DOBRA	0083	*[Anonymous]* | Een Taafel, waarop een Haas, Patryzen, en ander gevoogelte, vrugten, groentens, enz. Meesterlyk geschilderd | *Mat:* op doek *Size:* hoog 5 ½ en breed circa 4 voet	Paulus van der Spyk [or others]	(Sold or Bought In) fl ¾ v Baam
1802/11/01	DOBRA	0085	*[Anonymous]* | Een Vleesch en Vogelstal | *Mat:* op paneel	Paulus van der Spyk [or others]	(Sold) fl 16 [Illegible]
1802/11/01	DOBRA	0086	*[Anonymous]* | Portrait van Prins Willem den II. ten halverlyf byna Levensgrootte | *Mat:* op doek	Paulus van der Spyk [or others]	(Unknown) fl 10
1802/11/01	DOBRA	0089	*[Anonymous]* | Een dito [stilleeven] tot een wedergade | companion to lot 88, by Monogrammist H.R.	Paulus van der Spyk [or others]	(Unknown)
1802/11/01	DOBRA	0090	*[Anonymous]* | Een vinkeslag en vinkekooytjes, enz.	Paulus van der Spyk [or others]	(Unknown)
1802/11/01	DOBRA	0091	*[Anonymous]* | Een Stilleeven | *Mat:* op doek op paneel	Paulus van der Spyk [or others]	(Unknown)
1802/11/01	DOBRA	0092	*[Anonymous]* | Een Vrouwe Portrait | *Mat:* op paneel	Paulus van der Spyk [or others]	(Unknown)
1802/11/01	DOBRA	0099	*[Anonymous]* | Een gaandery van een pragtig Hofgebouw | *Mat:* op doek	Paulus van der Spyk [or others]	(Sold) fl 26 [Illegible]
1802/11/01	DOBRA	0100	*[Anonymous]* | Een Jaager gewaapend met pyl en boog | *Mat:* op doek	Paulus van der Spyk [or others]	(Unknown) fl 20
1802/11/01	DOBRA	0101	*[Anonymous]* | Twee Landschapjes met ruïnen, op koper | *Mat:* op koper	Paulus van der Spyk [or others]	(Unknown)
1802/11/01	DOBRA	0102	*[Anonymous]* | Een Binnenhuis waar in een vroolyk [sic] Gezelschap | companion to lot 103 *Mat:* op paneel *Size:* hoog 8 duim, breed 7 duim	Paulus van der Spyk [or others]	(Unknown)
1802/11/01	DOBRA	0103	*[Anonymous]* | Een dito [Binnenhuis] tot een wederga, hoog als de voorgaande | companion to lot 102 *Size:* hoog 8 duim	Paulus van der Spyk [or others]	(Unknown)
1802/11/01	DOBRA	0104	*[Anonymous]* | Een Oudenmans hoofd, met een langen baard | *Mat:* op paneel	Paulus van der Spyk [or others]	(Unknown)
1802/11/01	DOBRA	0106	*[Anonymous]* | Jupiter by Semelé	Paulus van der Spyk [or others]	(Unknown)
1802/11/01	DOBRA	0107	*[Anonymous]* | Een Dorpsgezigt	Paulus van der Spyk [or others]	(Unknown)
1802/11/01	DOBRA	0108	*[Anonymous]* | Twee Landschappen	Paulus van der Spyk [or others]	(Unknown)
1802/11/01	DOBRA	0115	*[Anonymous]* | Een Landschapje met Schaapjes, enz. fraai geschilderd | *Mat:* op paneel *Size:* hoog 15 breed 12 duim	Paulus van der Spyk [or others]	(Unknown)
1802/11/01	DOBRA	0121	*[Anonymous]* | Twee met Boeren | *Mat:* op paneel *Size:* hoog 6 ½ duim, breed 11 duim	Paulus van der Spyk [or others]	(Unknown)
1802/11/01	DOBRA	0131	*[Anonymous]* | Een Landschap, meesterlyk gepenseeld | *Mat:* op paneel	Paulus van der Spyk [or others]	(Unknown)
1802/11/01	DOBRA	0132	*[Anonymous]* | De Koninginne Esther, den gouden Scepter aanraakende	Paulus van der Spyk [or others]	(Unknown)
1802/11/01	DOBRA	0133	*[Anonymous]* | Geboorte en Opstanding van Jezus Christus	Paulus van der Spyk [or others]	(Unknown)
1802/11/01	DOBRA	0134	*[Anonymous]* | De Samaritaansche vrouw by den Waterput	Paulus van der Spyk [or others]	(Unknown)
1802/11/01	DOBRA	0135	*[Anonymous]* | Een Kerkje van binnen, zynde een kaarslicht	Paulus van der Spyk [or others]	(Unknown)
1802/11/01	DOBRA	0136	*[Anonymous]* | Een vrolyk gezelschap van 4 beelden, zig in den Wyn, met Zang en Spel vermaakende | *Mat:* op doek *Size:* hoog 27 ½, breed 52 duim	Paulus van der Spyk [or others]	(Unknown)
1802/11/01	DOBRA	0137	*[Anonymous]* | Een Fruitstuk, in de hoogte | *Mat:* op paneel *Fmt:* in de hoogte	Paulus van der Spyk [or others]	(Unknown)

1802/11/01	DOBRA	0138	*[Anonymous]* | Een Fruit- en Bloemstuk, in de breette [sic] | *Mat:* op doek *Fmt:* in de breette	Paulus van der Spyk [or others]	(Unknown)
1802/11/01	DOBRA	0139	*[Anonymous]* | Een Boertje, op de Viool di Gamba speelende | *Mat:* op paneel	Paulus van der Spyk [or others]	(Unknown)
1802/11/01	DOBRA	0141	*[Anonymous]* | Een onderaardsche Spelonk, of Kluizenaars celle; in het bruin, agter glas	Paulus van der Spyk [or others]	(Unknown)
1802/11/01	DOBRA	0151	*[Anonymous]* | Een Landschap, waarop Boeren en Boerinnen zig vermaaken met drinken		(Unknown) fl 1:2
1802/11/01	DOBRA	0152	*[Anonymous]* | Twee stuks Waters, met vaarende Schepen		(Unknown) fl 1
1802/11/01	DOBRA	0154	*[Anonymous]* | Een dito [Bergagtig Landschap], als het voorgaande [goed gestoffeerd en fix behandeld] | *Notes:* This lot was sold with lot 153 by E. Velde (I).		(Unknown) fl 3 for lots 153–155
1802/11/01	DOBRA	0155	*[Anonymous]* | Een dito [Bergagtig Landschap] niet minder; in alles dezelfde smaak | *Mat:* op paneel *Notes:* This lot was sold with lot 153 by E. Velde (I).		(Unknown) fl 3 for lots 153–155
1802/11/01	DOBRA	0158	*[Anonymous]* | Een Landschap | *Mat:* op paneel		(Unknown)
1802/11/01	DOBRA	0159	*[Anonymous]* | Een dito [Landschap] | *Mat:* op paneel		(Unknown) fl 0:10
1802/11/01	DOBRA	0160	*[Anonymous]* | Het Pourtrait van Erasmus | *Size:* hoog 12, br. 8 duim		(Unknown)
1802/11/01	DOBRA	0161	*[Anonymous]* | Een dito Pourtrait [van Erasmus], geschilderd 1533 | *Inscr:* 1533 (dated?) *Notes:* It is unclear whether the date is inscribed on the painting.		(Unknown) fl 1:12
1802/11/01	DOBRA	0171	*[Anonymous]* | Een Rivier-Gezigt, met een Visschers-Schuitje; op den voorgrond, aan de overzyde, eenige boeren huizen en geboomte | *Mat:* op paneel		(Unknown) fl 4:10
1802/11/01	DOBRA	0194	*[Anonymous]* | Een wit gevlekt Paard; wijders Mannen te voet en te paard, in Oostersche kleding | *Mat:* op paneel		(Unknown) fl 4
1802/11/01	DOBRA	0196	*[Anonymous]* | Een Mans-Portrait | *Mat:* op koper *Fmt:* ovaal		(Unknown) fl 8
1802/12/13	AMSCH	0190	*Een Oud Meester* | Een Manspourtret, houdende een Papier in zyn hand; door een Oud Meester	Yver	(Sold) fl 1 J Spaan
1802/12/13	AMSCH	0191	*Een Goed Meester* | Een Vrouwenbeeld, bynaar naakt in een Paleis; door een Goed Meester	Yver	(Sold) fl 1:15 Th[s] Spaan
1802/12/13	AMSCH	0192	*[Anonymous]* | Twee Stillevens, met verschillend Schryftuig; meesterlyk behandeld	Yver	(Sold) fl 0:10 L Pakker
1802/12/13	AMSCH	0193	*[Anonymous]* | Het Pourtret van Willem de Derde geharnast, in het verschiet ziet men een Bataille	Yver	(Sold) fl 0:6 L Pakker
1802/12/13	AMSCH	0198	*[Anonymous]* | Een Levantsche Zéehaven, ryk gestoffeerd met Handeldryvende Kooplieden | *Mat:* op doek *Size:* hoog 14, breed 17 duim	Pruyssenaar [for] A	(Sold) fl 1 Theens
1802/12/13	AMSCH	0199	*Een goed Meester* | Een zinryke Geestelyke Ordenantie van drie Beelden; krachtig op Paneel geschilderd, door een goed Meester | *Mat:* op paneel	Florijn [?]	(Sold) fl 1 L Pakker
1802/12/13	AMSCH	0201	*[Anonymous]* | Een Mans Hoofd, halver Lyf, in Spaansche Kleeding; krachtig en meesterlyk geschilderd | *Mat:* op doek	Florijn [?]	(Sold) fl 5 Coclers
1802/12/13	AMSCH	0202	*[Anonymous]* | Een dito [Mans Hoofd], verbeeldende een weenende Pétrus; kloek behandeld | *Mat:* op doek	Florijn [?]	(Sold) fl 1:10 Van Iperen
1802/12/13	AMSCH	0204	*[Anonymous]* | En Jongeling voor een Open Nis, houdende een Vogeltje op een Krukje, waar naar een Kat schynt te zien, gestoffeerd met verder Bywerk; plaisant geschilderd | *Mat:* op paneel	Florijn [?]	(Sold) fl 2:10 Theens [or] Stevens
1802/12/13	AMSCH	0205	*[Anonymous]* | Een Oude Grysaard een Jonge Dame liefkoozende, in een gestoffeerd Binnenvertrek; fix geschilderd | *Mat:* op paneel	Florijn [?]	(Sold) fl 0:10 L Pakker
1802/12/13	AMSCH	0206	*[Anonymous]* | Een Smits Winkel, met werkende Arbeidslieden; natuurlyk behandeld | *Mat:* op paneel	Florijn [?]	(Sold) fl 0:14 L Pakker
1802/12/13	AMSCH	0207	*[Anonymous]* | Een Weever voor zyn Getouw, verzelt van Vrouw en Kinderen, met verder Bywerk; fix op Paneel behandeld | *Mat:* op paneel	Florijn [?]	(Sold) fl 4 Gruiter
1802/12/13	AMSCH	0209	*[Anonymous]* | Een bevallig Mysje, voor een Steene Nis, by een Mand met verscheide Bloemen, hoger hangt een Bierkan en Vogelkooy; plaisant geschilderd | *Mat:* op paneel	Florijn [?]	(Sold) fl 5 van der Schley [for] R[ijfsnijder]
1802/12/13	AMSCH	0210	*[Anonymous]* | Een Joodsch Mans Hoofd met een Muts gedekt; krachtig op Paneel geschilderd | *Mat:* op paneel	Florijn [?]	(Sold) fl 1:5 Gruiter
1802/12/13	AMSCH	0211	*[Anonymous]* | Twee stuks, gewerkte Vaasen, gevult met onderscheide zoorten van Bloemen, staande op Steene Voetstukken; fix en bevallig behandeld | *Mat:* op paneel	Florijn [?]	(Sold) fl 0:10 L Pakker
802/12/13	AMSCH	0215	*[Anonymous]* | Twee stuks, een geleerd Persoon met een Boek in de Hand, en een studeerend Jongeling; beide meesterlyk fix gepenceeld | *Mat:* op doek op paneel	Schley [for] Lauwers	(Sold) fl 0:6 L Pakker
802/12/13	AMSCH	0217a[H]	*[Anonymous]* | 1 Schildery | *Notes:* This lot was added in by hand in the EBNP copy of the catalogue.	Schley [for] Lauwers	(Sold) fl 3:5 van Dijl
1802/12/13	AMSCH	0221	*[Anonymous]* | Een dito [Ossekop] opwaards ziende; meesterlyk, fraay als de voorige behandeld	Schley [for] Lauwers	(Sold) fl 5 Hulswit

1802/12/13	AMSCH	0227	*[Anonymous]* | In een Landschap ziet men een Slaapende Jongeling, rustende tegens een Heuvel, waarop een rustende Hond, ter zyde op de grond staande een Mandje met Aardvruchten; alles is meesterlyk en konstig gepenceeld	Schley [for] Lauwers	(Sold) fl 7 de Meijer
1802/12/13	AMSCH	0228	*[Anonymous]* | Drie stuks uitvoerig op Koper geschilderde Portretten | *Mat:* op koper	Pruyssenaar [for] A	(Sold) fl 1 L Pakker
1802/12/13	AMSCH	0229	*[Anonymous]* | Drie stuks op Paneel geschilderde dito [Portretten] | *Mat:* op paneel	Pruyssenaar [for] A	(Sold) fl 0:16 Gruiter
1802/12/13	AMSCH	0231	*[Anonymous]* | Twee diverse Landschappen	Pruyssenaar [for] A	(Sold) fl 2:10 Vermeulen
1802/12/13	AMSCH	0232	*[Anonymous]* | Twee dito [diverse] dito [Landschappen]	Pruyssenaar [for] A	(Sold) fl 1 Levij Pakker
1802/12/13	AMSCH	0233	*[Anonymous]* | Twee dito [diverse] dito [Landschappen]	Pruyssenaar [for] A	(Sold) fl 0:14 L Pakker
1802/12/13	AMSCH	0234	*[Anonymous]* | Twee dito [diverse] dito [Landschappen]	Pruyssenaar [for] A	(Sold) fl 1 L Pakker
1802/12/13	AMSCH	0238[H]	*[Anonymous]* | Een [Schilderij] | *Notes:* This lot was added in by hand in the EBNP, LBDa and RKDH copies of the catalogue.	Stech [?]	(Sold) fl 3 J Spaan
1802/12/13	AMSCH	0239[H]	*[Anonymous]* | Een [Schilderij] | *Notes:* This lot was added in by hand in the EBNP, LBDa and RKDH copies of the catalogue.	Stech [?]	(Bought In) fl 2 ¼
1802/12/13	AMSCH	0240[H]	*[Anonymous]* | Twee [Schilderijen] | *Notes:* This lot was added in by hand in the EBNP, LBDa and RKDH copies of the catalogue.	de Neufville	(Sold) fl 4:5 L Pakker
1802/12/13	AMSCH	0241[H]	*[Anonymous]* | Een [Schilderij] | *Notes:* This lot was added in by hand in the EBNP, LBDa and RKDH copies of the catalogue.	de Neufville	(Sold) fl 1:10 Mensard
1802/12/13	AMSCH	0242[H]	*[Anonymous]* | Twee [Schilderijen] | *Notes:* This lot was added in by hand in the EBNP, LBDa and RKDH copies of the catalogue.	Stech [?]	(Sold) fl 0:8 Dupree
1802/12/13	AMSCH	0243[H]	*[Anonymous]* | Twee [Schilderijen] | *Notes:* This lot was added in by hand in the EBNP, LBDa and RKDH copies of the catalogue.	Stech [?]	(Sold) fl 0:6 L Pakker
1802/12/13	AMSCH	0244[H]	*[Anonymous]* | Twee [Schilderijen] | *Notes:* This lot was added in by hand in the EBNP, LBDa and RKDH copies of the catalogue.	Stech [?]	(Sold) fl 0:6 L Pakker
1802/12/13	AMSCH	0245[H]	*[Anonymous]* | Twee [Schilderijen] | *Notes:* This lot was added in by hand in the EBNP, LBDa and RKDH copies of the catalogue.	Stech [?]	(Sold) fl 4:5 J Spaan
1802/12/13	AMSCH	0246[H]	*[Anonymous]* | Twee [Schilderijen] | *Notes:* This lot was added in by hand in the EBNP, LBDa and RKDH copies of the catalogue.	Stech [?]	(Sold) fl 4 Cocler
1802/12/13	AMSCH	0247[H]	*[Anonymous]* | Drie [Schilderijen] | *Notes:* This lot was added in by hand in the EBNP, LBDa and RKDH copies of the catalogue.	Stech [?]	(Sold) fl 0:10 L Pakker
1802/12/13	AMSCH	0248[H]	*[Anonymous]* | Drie [Schilderijen] | *Notes:* This lot was added in by hand in the EBNP, LBDa and RKDH copies of the catalogue.	Stech [?]	(Sold) fl 2 L Pakker
1802/12/13	AMSCH	0249[H]	*[Anonymous]* | Een [Schilderij] | *Notes:* This lot was added in by hand in the EBNP, LBDa and RKDH copies of the catalogue.	Stech [?]	(Sold) fl 1 L Pakker
1802/12/13	AMSCH	0250[H]	*[Anonymous]* | Een [Schilderij] | *Notes:* This lot was added in by hand in the EBNP, LBDa and RKDH copies of the catalogue.	Stech [?]	(Sold) fl 0:10 L Pakker
1802/12/13	AMSCH	0251[H]	*[Anonymous]* | Een [Schilderij] | *Notes:* This lot was added in by hand in the EBNP, LBDa and RKDH copies of the catalogue.	Vermeulen	(Sold) fl 3:5 Gruiter
1802/12/13	AMSCH	0252[H]	*[Anonymous]* | Een [Schilderij] | *Notes:* This lot was added in by hand in the EBNP, LBDa and RKDH copies of the catalogue.	Vermeulen	(Sold) fl 1 van Iperen
1802/12/13	AMSCH	0253[H]	*[Anonymous]* | Twee [Schilderijen] | *Notes:* This lot was added in by hand in the EBNP, LBDa and RKDH copies of the catalogue.	Vermeulen	(Sold) fl 3 van Iperen
1802/12/13	AMSCH	0254[H]	*[Anonymous]* | Een [Schilderij] | *Notes:* This lot was added in by hand in the EBNP, LBDa and RKDH copies of the catalogue.	Vermeulen	(Sold) fl 4 L Pakker
1802/12/13	AMSCH	0255[H]	*[Anonymous]* | Een [Schilderij] | *Notes:* This lot was added in by hand in the EBNP, LBDa and RKDH copies of the catalogue.	Vermeulen	(Sold) fl 9 Coclers
1802/12/13	AMSCH	0256[H]	*[Anonymous]* | Een [Schilderij] | *Notes:* This lot was added in by hand in the EBNP, LBDa and RKDH copies of the catalogue.	Vermeulen	(Sold) fl 4:15 Van Iperen
1802/12/13	AMSCH	0257[H]	*[Anonymous]* | Twee [Schilderijen] | *Notes:* This lot was added in by hand in the EBNP, LBDa and RKDH copies of the catalogue.	Vermeulen	(Sold) fl 3 Gruiter
1802/12/13	AMSCH	0258[H]	*[Anonymous]* | Twee [Schilderijen] | *Notes:* This lot was added in by hand in the EBNP, LBDa and RKDH copies of the catalogue.	Vermeulen	(Sold) fl 3:5 Dupré
1802/12/13	AMSCH	0259[H]	*[Anonymous]* | Een [Schilderij] | *Notes:* This lot was added in by hand in the EBNP, LBDa and RKDH copies of the catalogue.	Vermeulen	(Sold) fl 3:5 Coclers
1802/12/13	AMSCH	0260[H]	*[Anonymous]* | Twee [Schilderijen] | *Notes:* This lot was added in by hand in the EBNP, LBDa and RKDH copies of the catalogue.	Vermeulen	(Sold) fl 1:15 Gruiter
1802/12/13	AMSCH	0261[H]	*[Anonymous]* | Twee [Schilderijen] | *Notes:* This lot was added in by hand in the EBNP, LBDa and RKDH copies of the catalogue.	Vermeulen	(Sold) fl 1 Duprée
1802/12/13	AMSCH	0261a[H]	*[Anonymous]* | Twee [Schilderijen] | *Notes:* This lot was added in by hand in the EBNP, LBDa and RKDH copies of the catalogue.	Vermeulen	(Sold) fl 1 L Pakker
1802/12/13	AMSCH	0262[H]	*[Anonymous]* | Een [Schilderij] | *Notes:* This lot was added in by hand in the EBNP, LBDa and RKDH copies of the catalogue.	Vermeulen	(Sold) fl 1:5 J Spaan

1802/12/13	AMSCH	0263[H]	*[Anonymous]* | Een [Schilderij] | *Notes:* This lot was added in by hand in the EBNP, LBDa and RKDH copies of the catalogue.	Vermeulen	(Sold) fl 0:6 L Pakker
1802/12/13	AMSCH	0264[H]	*[Anonymous]* | Twee [Schilderijen] | *Notes:* This lot was added in by hand in the EBNP, LBDa and RKDH copies of the catalogue.	Pruyssenaar [for] A	(Sold) fl 5:10 van Dijl
1802/12/13	AMSCH	0267[H]	*[Anonymous]* | Twee [Schilderijen] | *Notes:* This lot was added in by hand in the LBDa and RKDH copies of the catalogue.	Pruyssenaar [for] A	(Sold) fl 8:10 Gruiter
1802/12/13	AMSCH	0268[H]	*[Anonymous]* | Twee [Schilderijen] | *Notes:* This lot was added in by hand in the LBDa and RKDH copies of the catalogue.	Pruyssenaar [for] A	(Sold) fl 2:5 L Pakker
1802/12/13	AMSCH	0269[H]	*[Anonymous]* | Twee [Schilderijen] | *Notes:* This lot was added in by hand in the LBDa and RKDH copies of the catalogue.	Pruyssenaar [for] A	(Sold) fl 1:5 L Pakker
1803/03/07	AMBAE	0130	*[Anonymous]* | Pourtret van Albertus Eggius, in Olyverw, op paneel | *Mat:* in olyverf op paneel		(Unknown)
1803/03/07	AMBAE	0131	*[Anonymous]* | Een Binnenvertrek met drinkende en rookende Boeren, meesterlyk in Olywerf, op paneel | *Mat:* in olyverf op paneel		(Unknown)
1803/03/07	AMBAE	0132	*[Anonymous]* | Twee Bloemstukken met Insecten, fix getekend		(Unknown)
1803/04/06	MGSAN	0004	*Een oud Meester* | Een Stuk, verbeeldende Scheveningen, vol gewoel, door een oud Meester	Mr Evert Clyver	(Unknown)
1803/04/06	MGSAN	0008	*Een oud Meester* | Een Stuk, verbeeldende den Brand van Trooijen, goed geschilderd, door een oud Meester	Mr Evert Clyver	(Unknown)
1803/04/06	MGSAN	0009	*Een oud Meester* | Een dito [Stuk], verbeeldende het Gevangen neemen van Christus, door een oud Meester	Mr Evert Clyver	(Unknown)
1803/04/06	MGSAN	0011	*[Anonymous]* | Een Zeehaven	Mr Evert Clyver	(Unknown)
1803/04/06	MGSAN	0012	*[Anonymous]* | Gezicht van Amsterdam en Rotterdam	Mr Evert Clyver	(Unknown)
1803/04/06	MGSAN	0013	*[Anonymous]* | Een Watermolen en Kasteel, in 't ovaal | *Fmt:* ovaal	Mr Evert Clyver	(Unknown)
1803/04/06	MGSAN	0014	*[Anonymous]* | Een Stuk, met Hoorns en Vruchten, goed gepenceeld	Mr Evert Clyver	(Unknown)
1803/04/06	MGSAN	0020	*[Anonymous]* | Een Landschapje, op koper | *Mat:* op koper	Mr Evert Clyver	(Unknown)
1803/04/06	MGSAN	0021	*[Anonymous]* | Een Bloem en Kapel, op koper | *Mat:* op koper	Mr Evert Clyver	(Unknown)
1803/04/18	HGBAK	0010	*[Anonymous]* | Twee stuks de Geboorten van Christus en de Aanbidding der Wyzen, op Paneel in vergulde lysten [Schilderyen in Olyverf] | *Mat:* in olyverf op paneel *Size:* hoog 4 breed 17 duim *Notes:* The bracketed information in the title appears above lot 1 and refers to lots 1 to 48.	Johan Pieter Reigersman [or others]	(Unknown)
1803/04/18	HGBAK	0011	*[Anonymous]* | Een Vrouw en Kind, en een Boertje, 2 stuks [Schilderyen in Olyverf] | *Mat:* in olyverf *Notes:* The bracketed information in the title appears above lot 1 and refers to lots 1 to 48.	Johan Pieter Reigersman [or others]	(Unknown)
1803/04/18	HGBAK	0012	*[Anonymous]* | Een Dame spelende op de Guitar, hoog en breed 3 voet 4 d. op Paneel, zwarte lyst [Schilderyen in Olyverf] | *Mat:* in olyverf op paneel *Size:* hoog en breed 3 voet 4 duim *Notes:* The bracketed information in the title appears above lot 1 and refers to lots 1 to 48.	Johan Pieter Reigersman [or others]	(Unknown)
1803/04/18	HGBAK	0013	*[Anonymous]* | Een oud Man, biedende een Damen een Snoer met Paarlen op doek, hoog 2 v. 2 duim. breed 4 voet, zw. lyst [Schilderyen in Olyverf] | *Mat:* in olyverf op doek *Size:* hoog 2 voet 2 duim. breed 4 voet *Notes:* The bracketed information in the title appears above lot 1 and refers to lots 1 to 48.	Johan Pieter Reigersman [or others]	(Unknown)
1803/04/18	HGBAK	0014	*[Anonymous]* | Een heilige Famillie, Paneel, h. 27 b. 25 d. zw. l. [Schilderyen in Olyverf] | *Mat:* in olyverf op paneel *Size:* hoog 27 breed 25 duim *Notes:* The bracketed information in the title appears above lot 1 and refers to lots 1 to 48.	Johan Pieter Reigersman [or others]	(Unknown)
1803/04/18	HGBAK	0015	*[Anonymous]* | Een dronk Wyf op een Kruywagen, met eenige Jongens, Paneel hoog 19. breed 28 d. zw. lyst [Schilderyen in Olyverf] | *Mat:* in olyverf op paneel *Size:* hoog 19 breed 28 d. *Notes:* The bracketed information in the title appears above lot 1 and refers to lots 1 to 48.	Johan Pieter Reigersman [or others]	(Unknown)
1803/04/18	HGBAK	0016	*[Anonymous]* | Pourtraiten van zyn Doorlugtige Hoogheid, Willem de Vyfde en Gemalin, op Paneel, hoog 19 ½ br. 15 d. in vergulde lysten [Schilderyen in Olyverf] | *Mat:* in olyverf op paneel *Size:* hoog 19 ½ breed 15 d. *Notes:* The bracketed information in the title appears above lot 1 and refers to lots 1 to 48.	Johan Pieter Reigersman [or others]	(Unknown)
1803/04/18	HGBAK	0018	*[Anonymous]* | Een fraay stuk, zynde een Damen in een zittende houding met Bloemen, &c. zeer kragtig op doek, hoog en breed als voren [hoog 29. breed 23. duym], dito [witte] lyst [Schilderyen in Olyverf] | *Mat:* in olyverf op doek *Size:* hoog 29 breed 23 duym *Notes:* The bracketed information in the title about the medium appears above lot 1 and refers to lots 1 to 48.	Johan Pieter Reigersman [or others]	(Unknown)
1803/04/18	HGBAK	0019	*[Anonymous]* | Een dito Dame in 't wit Zatyn, houdende onder de linker Arm de Hoorn des Overvloeds, en rustende met de Regterhand om gekluysterde Kryksknegten [sic], aan de Voeten Wapenrustingen, ongemeen delikaat behandeld, hoog 28. breed 22. duym op doek, dito [witte] lyst [Schilderyen in Olyverf] | *Mat:* in olyverf op doek *Size:* hoog 28 breed 22 duym *Notes:* It is unclear what "dito" refers to in the title. The bracketed information in the title about the medium appears above lot 1 and refers to lots 1 to 48.	Johan Pieter Reigersman [or others]	(Unknown)

1803/04/18	HGBAK	0020	*[Anonymous]* | Een staande Damen in een Landschap, hoog 26. breed 21. duym op doek, dito [witte] lyst [Schilderyen in Olyverf] | *Mat:* in olyverf op doek *Size:* hoog 26 breed 21 duym *Notes:* The bracketed information in the title about the medium appears above lot 1 and refers to lots 1 to 48.	Johan Pieter Reigersman [or others]	(Unknown)
1803/04/18	HGBAK	0021	*[Anonymous]* | Een zittende dito [Damen] met Bloemen, op paneel hoog 12. breed 9. duym, vergulde lyst [Schilderyen in Olyverf] | *Mat:* in olyverf op paneel *Size:* hoog 12 breed 9 duym *Notes:* The bracketed information in the title about the medium appears above lot 1 and refers to lots 1 to 48.	Johan Pieter Reigersman [or others]	(Unknown)
1803/04/18	HGBAK	0024	*[Anonymous]* | Een Capitaale, verbeeldende de Stad en Kasteel van Heydelberg, zeer uitvoerig op doek, hoog 5 voet 3 duim, breed 7 voet 4 duim, zwarte lyst [Schilderyen in Olyverf] | *Mat:* in olyverf op doek *Size:* hoog 5 voet 3 duim breed 7 voet 4 duim *Notes:* The bracketed information in the title appears above lot 1 and refers to lots 1 to 48.	Johan Pieter Reigersman [or others]	(Unknown)
1803/04/18	HGBAK	0025	*[Anonymous]* | Een groot stuk met veelerhande soorten van Vrugten, Drinkschaalen &c. staande op een Tafel gedekt door een groen kleed, op doek, hoog 4 voet 4 duim, breed 4 voet 9 duim, bruine lyst [Schilderyen in Olyverf] | *Mat:* in olyverf op doek *Size:* hoog 4 voet 4 duim, breed 4 voet 9 duim *Notes:* The bracketed information in the title appears above lot 1 and refers to lots 1 to 48.	Johan Pieter Reigersman [or others]	(Unknown)
1803/04/18	HGBAK	0026	*[Anonymous]* | Een Landschap met een Herderin en Schaapen, op paneel, hoog 3 voet, breed 3 voet 4 duim, zwarte lyst [Schilderyen in Olyverf] | *Mat:* in olyverf op paneel *Size:* hoog 3 voet, breed 3 voet 4 duim *Notes:* The bracketed information in the title appears above lot 1 and refers to lots 1 to 48.	Johan Pieter Reigersman [or others]	(Unknown)
1803/04/18	HGBAK	0027	*[Anonymous]* | Een Landschap met een Harten Jagt, op paneel, hoog 3 voet, breed 3 voet 2 duim, zwarte lyst [Schilderyen in Olyverf] | *Mat:* in olyverf op paneel *Size:* hoog 3 voet, breed 3 voet 2 duim *Notes:* The bracketed information in the title appears above lot 1 and refers to lots 1 to 48.	Johan Pieter Reigersman [or others]	(Unknown)
1803/04/18	HGBAK	0028	*[Anonymous]* | Een Boomryk Landschap, met beesten en beeltjes gestoffeerd, op paneel, hoog 2 voet 7 duim, breed 4 voet 4 duim, zwarte lyst [Schilderyen in Olyverf] | *Mat:* in olyverf op paneel *Size:* hoog 2 voet 7 duim, breed 4 voet 4 duim *Notes:* The bracketed information in the title appears above lot 1 and refers to lots 1 to 48.	Johan Pieter Reigersman [or others]	(Unknown)
1803/04/18	HGBAK	0029	*[Anonymous]* | Een Boerenvreugd, op paneel, hoog 2 voet 3 duim, breed 3 voet 5 duim, zwarte lyst [Schilderyen in Olyverf] | *Mat:* in olyverf op paneel *Size:* hoog 2 voet 3 duim, breed 3 voet 5 duim *Notes:* The bracketed information in the title appears above lot 1 and refers to lots 1 to 48.	Johan Pieter Reigersman [or others]	(Unknown)
1803/04/18	HGBAK	0031	*[Anonymous]* | Een verbeeldende de Torenbouw van Babel door een oud Meester, hoog 30, breed 38 duim, zw. lyst [Schilderyen in Olyverf] | *Mat:* in olyverf *Size:* hoog 30, breed 38 duim *Notes:* The bracketed information in the title appears above lot 1 and refers to lots 1 to 48.	Johan Pieter Reigersman [or others]	(Unknown)
1803/04/18	HGBAK	0032	*[Anonymous]* | Een Boomryk Landschap, op paneel, hoog 22, breed 35 duim, zwarte lyst [Schilderyen in Olyverf] | *Mat:* in olyverf op paneel *Size:* hoog 22, breed 35 duim *Notes:* The bracketed information in the title appears above lot 1 and refers to lots 1 to 48.	Johan Pieter Reigersman [or others]	(Unknown)
1803/04/18	HGBAK	0034	*[Anonymous]* | Een Zee met Scheepen, op paneel, hoog 23, breed 31 duim, bruine lyst [Schilderyen in Olyverf] | *Mat:* in olyverf op paneel *Size:* hoog 23, breed 31 duim *Notes:* The bracketed information in the title appears above lot 1 and refers to lots 1 to 48.	Johan Pieter Reigersman [or others]	(Unknown)
1803/04/18	HGBAK	0035	*[Anonymous]* | Een Landschap met Figuuren, hoog 19, breed 28 duim, zwarte lyst [Schilderyen in Olyverf] | *Mat:* in olyverf *Size:* hoog 19, breed 28 duim *Notes:* The bracketed information in the title appears above lot 1 and refers to lots 1 to 48.	Johan Pieter Reigersman [or others]	(Unknown)
1803/04/18	HGBAK	0036	*[Anonymous]* | Een Dorpgezicht, op paneel, hoog 22, breed 33 d. zwarte lyst [Schilderyen in Olyverf] | *Mat:* in olyverf op paneel *Size:* hoog 22, breed 33 duim *Notes:* The bracketed information in the title appears above lot 1 and refers to lots 1 to 48.	Johan Pieter Reigersman [or others]	(Unknown)
1803/04/18	HGBAK	0037	*[Anonymous]* | Een Bergagtig Landschap, hoog 15, breed 22 duim, zwarte lyst [Schilderyen in Olyverf] | *Mat:* in olyverf *Size:* hoog 15, breed 22 duim *Notes:* The bracketed information in the title appears above lot 1 and refers to lots 1 to 48.	Johan Pieter Reigersman [or others]	(Unknown)
1803/04/18	HGBAK	0038[a]	*[Anonymous]* | Twee Landschappen, op paneel en doek, hoog 19, breed 22 duim, zwarte lyst [Schilderyen in Olyverf] | *This Lot:* Een Landschap *Mat:* in olyverf op paneel *Size:* hoog 19, breed 22 duim *Notes:* The bracketed information in the title appears above lot 1 and refers to lots 1 to 48.	Johan Pieter Reigersman [or others]	(Unknown)
1803/04/18	HGBAK	0038[b]	*[Anonymous]* | Twee Landschappen, op paneel en doek, hoog 19, breed 22 duim, zwarte lyst [Schilderyen in Olyverf] | *This Lot:* Een Landschap *Mat:* in olyverf op doek *Size:* hoog 19, breed 22 duim *Notes:* The bracketed information in the title appears above lot 1 and refers to lots 1 to 48.	Johan Pieter Reigersman [or others]	(Unknown)

1803/04/18	HGBAK	0040	*[Anonymous]* | Een Stadsgezicht, hoog 18, breed 25 duim, zwarte lyst [Schilderyen in Olyverf] | *Mat:* in olyverf *Size:* hoog 18, breed 25 duim *Notes:* The bracketed information in the title appears above lot 1 and refers to lots 1 to 48.	Johan Pieter Reigersman [or others]	(Unknown)
1803/04/18	HGBAK	0041	*[Anonymous]* | Een Stuk, verbeeldende een Kraamkamer met veele beelden, hoog 23, breed 28 duim, zwarte lyst [Schilderyen in Olyverf] | *Mat:* in olyverf *Size:* hoog 23, breed 28 duim *Notes:* The bracketed information in the title appears above lot 1 and refers to lots 1 to 48.	Johan Pieter Reigersman [or others]	(Unknown)
1803/04/18	HGBAK	0042	*[Anonymous]* | Een stuk in de ronten, verbeeldende een Boeren Herberg, zwarte lyst [Schilderyen in Olyverf] | *Mat:* in olyverf *Notes:* The bracketed information in the title appears above lot 1 and refers to lots 1 to 48.	Johan Pieter Reigersman [or others]	(Unknown)
1803/04/18	HGBAK	0043	*[Anonymous]* | Een Landschap en Vissery, paneel, hoog 23, breed 36 duim, zwarte lyst [Schilderyen in Olyverf] | *Mat:* in olyverf op paneel *Size:* hoog 23, breed 36 duim *Notes:* The bracketed information in the title appears above lot 1 and refers to lots 1 to 48.	Johan Pieter Reigersman [or others]	(Unknown)
1803/04/18	HGBAK	0044	*[Anonymous]* | Een stukje in 't ovaal met een ruïne, paneel, zwarte lyst [Schilderyen in Olyverf] | *Mat:* in olyverf op paneel *Fmt:* ovaal *Notes:* The bracketed information in the title appears above lot 1 and refers to lots 1 to 48.	Johan Pieter Reigersman [or others]	(Unknown)
1803/04/18	HGBAK	0045	*[Anonymous]* | Een Guitarspeeler, en een Spinner, 2 stuks, op paneel [Schilderyen in Olyverf] | *Mat:* in olyverf op paneel *Notes:* The bracketed information in the title appears above lot 1 and refers to lots 1 to 48.	Johan Pieter Reigersman [or others]	(Unknown)
1803/04/18	HGBAK	0046	*[Anonymous]* | Drie stuks met Scheepjes, op paneel, bruine lyst [Schilderyen in Olyverf] | *Mat:* in olyverf op paneel *Notes:* The bracketed information in the title appears above lot 1 and refers to lots 1 to 48.	Johan Pieter Reigersman [or others]	(Unknown)
1803/04/18	HGBAK	0047	*[Anonymous]* | Een stukje met Riviervis door Vosmaar, paneel [Schilderyen in Olyverf] | *Mat:* in olyverf op paneel *Size:* hoog 16, breed 20 duim *Notes:* The bracketed information in the title appears above lot 1 and refers to lots 1 to 48.	Johan Pieter Reigersman [or others]	(Unknown)
1803/04/18	HGBAK	0048	*[Anonymous]* | Een Musicerend Gezelschap, 2 met pourtraiten en een met een Haan, 4 stuks [Schilderyen in Olyverf] | *Mat:* in olyverf *Notes:* The bracketed information in the title appears above lot 1 and refers to lots 1 to 48.	Johan Pieter Reigersman [or others]	(Unknown)
1803/04/20	AMSCH	0107	*[Anonymous]* | Maria Magdaléna in Berouw, staande in een Rotsgezicht, voor haar legt een Boek en Doodshoofd, en ter zyde een Zalfbusch, meesterlyk behandeld [La Magdaleine penitente, vue dans une grotte avec les accessoires ordinaires de ce sujet, bien rendu.] | *Mat:* op doek [sur cuivre] *Size:* hoog 9, breed 7 duim *Notes:* The materials differ in the Dutch and French editions of the catalogue.	Maria Magdalena van Sluypwyk, gravinne van Moens	(Sold) fl 1:10 Grimpen
1803/04/20	AMSCH	0109	*[Anonymous]* | Twee stuks, een Geestelyke Ordenantie; en een Landschap [Deux piéces : un Sujet Saint & un paysage.]	Maria Magdalena van Sluypwyk, gravinne van Moens	(Sold) fl 0:6 Yver
1803/04/20	AMSCH	0110	*[Anonymous]* | Twee stuks, Afbeeldzels van een Dame en Heer, beide in aloude deftige kleeding, kragtig van Coloriet, en meesterlyk gepenceeld [Deux Portraits d'un homme & d'une Dame costumés à l'espagnolle, ils sont d'un pinceau decidé & d'une bonne couleur.] | *Mat:* op paneel *Size:* ieder hoog 28, breed 21 duim	Maria Magdalena van Sluypwyk, gravinne van Moens	(Sold) fl 13:10 Hodges
1803/04/20	AMSCH	0116	*[Anonymous]* | In een Binnenvertrek, staat een Jong bevallig Kind, in deftige Kleeding, met een Paerelsnoer omhangen, houdende met beide Handjes een Stokje, waaraan een Goude Kindere Bel hangt, meesterlyk fraay gepenceeld [Dans un appartement est vu un joli enfant richement vetu, tenant des deux mains son hocquet d'or, artistement peint & collorié.] | *Mat:* op doek *Size:* hoog 46, breed 34 duim	Maria Magdalena van Sluypwyk, gravinne van Moens	(Sold) fl 2 Coclers
1803/04/20	AMSCH	0120	*Een oud Meester* | Twee stuks Afbeeldingen van Kindertjes, beide door een oud Meester [Deux pieces, sur chacune est peint un Enfant.] | *Mat:* op paneel	Maria Magdalena van Sluypwyk, gravinne van Moens	(Sold) fl 1 L Pakker
1803/04/20	AMSCH	0121	*Een oud Meester* | Twee stuks Bybel-Ordenantiën, op Paneel, door een oud Meester [Deux Sujets historiques.] | *Mat:* op paneel	Maria Magdalena van Sluypwyk, gravinne van Moens	(Sold) fl 9:10 Gruiter
1803/04/20	AMSCH	0122	*Een oud Meester* | Een bevallig Mans Pourtrait ter Halver Lyf, in aloude Kleeding, houdende in de eene hand een Handschoen, en rustende met de andere tegen zyn Mantel; door een oud Meester [Un Portrait de merite, vu à mi corps & a deux mains, en costume très ancien.] | *Mat:* op paneel *Size:* hoog 30, breed 24 duim [haut 30, large 22 pouces] *Notes:* The dimensions differ in the Dutch and French editions of the catalogue.	Maria Magdalena van Sluypwyk, gravinne van Moens	(Sold) fl 2 Yver
1803/04/20	AMSCH	0125	*[Anonymous]* | Het Toilet van Vénus, verzeld van een ménigte Cupidootjes en ander Bywerk, kragtig geschilderd [La toilette de Venus, entourrée des Graces & d'Amours, peint dans le Stile Italiën.] | *Mat:* op paneel *Size:* hoog 23, breed 31 duim	Maria Magdalena van Sluypwyk, gravinne van Moens	(Sold) fl 2 Hulswit
1803/04/20	AMSCH	0126	*Een oud Meester* | Maria met het Kindje, rustende in een Landschap, door een oud Meester [Le repos de la Sainte famille en Egypte, tableau fort ancien.] | *Mat:* op paneel *Size:* hoog 19, breed 13 duim	Maria Magdalena van Sluypwyk, gravinne van Moens	(Sold) fl 7:10 Hodges

1803/04/20	AMSCH	0127	*Een oud Meester* | De Aanbidding der Koningen, door een oud Meester [l'Adoration des mages.] | *Mat:* op paneel *Size:* hoog 22, breed 16 duim	Maria Magdalena van Sluypwyk, gravinne van Moens	(Sold) fl 2 Lesscher
1803/04/20	AMSCH	0128	*[Anonymous]* | Twee diverse, een gestoffeerd Landschapje, en een Vaderlandsche Historie, beide in 't Graauw [Deux Paysages dans lesquels sont representés des trait [sic] d'histoire, peints en grisille [sic].]	Maria Magdalena van Sluypwyk, gravinne van Moens	(Sold) fl 0:14 Hodges
1803/04/20	AMSCH	0129	*[Anonymous]* | Twee stuks, Geestelyke Ordenantiën, de eene de aanbidding der Koningen, en de andere Tobias by den Engel [Deux tableaux : l'adoration des mages, & l'autre Tobie avec l'Ange.]	Maria Magdalena van Sluypwyk, gravinne van Moens	(Sold) fl 3 A Bruning
1803/04/20	AMSCH	0130	*[Anonymous]* | Twee stuks, een Binnenhuis met Eetende Boeren, en de andere, een Biddend Vrouwtje, by een gedekte Tafel [Une femme faisant sa priere avant son repas, & une autre tableau de Paysans occupés à manger.]	Maria Magdalena van Sluypwyk, gravinne van Moens	(Sold) fl 3:5 Brunis
1803/04/20	AMSCH	0131	*[Anonymous]* | Twee stuks Manspourtraiten, een in aloude en de andere in moderne kleeding [Deux differens portraits d'homme.]	Maria Magdalena van Sluypwyk, gravinne van Moens	(Sold) fl 0:6 Mensard
1803/04/20	AMSCH	0132	*[Anonymous]* | Twee stuks, een bevallig Man- en Vrouwe Pourtrait, beide halver Lyf, in aloude kleeding, beide uitvoerig gepenceeld [Deux portraits, homme & femme à mi corps bien finis.]	Maria Magdalena van Sluypwyk, gravinne van Moens	(Sold) fl 13 Gruiter
1803/04/20	AMSCH	0133	*[Anonymous]* | Twee diverse Mans Pourtraiten, met Kraagen om de Hals, beide fiks gepenceeld [Deux portraits portant des fraises au col peints d'une bonne maniete [sic].]	Maria Magdalena van Sluypwyk, gravinne van Moens	(Sold) fl 1:5 Mensard
1803/04/20	AMSCH	0134	*[Anonymous]* | Twee dito [Pourtraiten], zynde een Mans- en Vrouwe Pourtrait [Deux Portraits, homme & femme.]	Maria Magdalena van Sluypwyk, gravinne van Moens	(Sold) fl 2 Gruiter
1803/04/20	AMSCH	0135	*[Anonymous]* | Twee diverse Mans Pourtraiten [Deux Portraits d'hommes.]	Maria Magdalena van Sluypwyk, gravinne van Moens	(Sold) fl 25 L Pakker
1803/04/20	AMSCH	0136	*[Anonymous]* | Twee dito [diverse] dito [Mans Pourtraiten] [Deux Sujets de même [Portraits d'hommes].]	Maria Magdalena van Sluypwyk, gravinne van Moens	(Sold) fl 1:10 L Pakker
1803/04/20	AMSCH	0137	*[Anonymous]* | Twee stuks, een Storm aan Strand, en een ander [Deux pieces : une tempête sur la côte & une autre.]	Maria Magdalena van Sluypwyk, gravinne van Moens	(Sold) fl 1:5 Overhorst
1803/04/20	AMSCH	0138	*[Anonymous]* | Twee stuks diversche Landschappen [Deux paysages.]	Maria Magdalena van Sluypwyk, gravinne van Moens	(Sold) fl 1:10 Van Dijk
1803/04/20	AMSCH	0139	*[Anonymous]* | Twee stuks, een Zeestrand en een Landschap [La Vue sur une côte maritime, & un paysage.]	Maria Magdalena van Sluypwyk, gravinne van Moens	(Sold) fl 2:10 Geld
1803/04/20	AMSCH	0140	*Een oud Meester* | Een Famieljestuk, van zeven Beelden; fraay gepenceeld door een oud Meester [Un tableau de famille avec sept personnages, bien traité par un peintre ancien.]	Maria Magdalena van Sluypwyk, gravinne van Moens	(Sold) fl 1 Grimpen
1803/04/20	AMSCH	0142	*[Anonymous]* | Een Schoorsteenstuk, verbeeldende een Pot gevuld met verscheide fraaye Bloemen [Un tableau pour Cheminée, le Sujet est un vase avec les plus Belles fleurs.] | *Fmt:* schoorsteenstuk	Maria Magdalena van Sluypwyk, gravinne van Moens	(Sold) fl 5 Van Iperen
1803/04/20	AMSCH	0143	*Een oud Meester* | Een Binnehuis, met verscheide vrolyke Boeren en Boerinnen, fiks gepenceeld door een oud Meester [Un tabagie ou des paysans & des paysanes se divertissent, bien touchée.]	Maria Magdalena van Sluypwyk, gravinne van Moens	(Sold) fl 3 C S Roos
1803/04/20	AMSCH	0145	*[Anonymous]* | Twee stuks het Pourtrait van een Dame en Heer in deftige Kleeding, beide fiks geschilderd [Deux portraits, Homme & Femme en costume très ancien, bien peints, sur Cuivre.] | *Mat:* op koper	Maria Magdalena van Sluypwyk, gravinne van Moens	(Sold) fl 0:14 L Pakker
1803/04/20	AMSCH	0147	*Een oud Meester* | Twee stuks Geestelyke Ordenantiën, zinspeelende op de Passie Christus, kragtig op Doek geschilderd, door een oud Meester [Deux allegories sur les Souffrances de J.C. rendues avec expression.] | *Mat:* op doek	Maria Magdalena van Sluypwyk, gravinne van Moens	(Sold) fl 9:10 Gruiter
1803/04/20	AMSCH	0148	*[Anonymous]* | Vyf stuks capitaale Ordenantiën, verbeeldende de vyf Zinnen, meer dan leevensgroote Beelden, in ieder derzelve ziet men een Bybel Historie, toepasselyk op deeze Voorwerpen; zynde meesterlyk en kloek gepenceeld [Cinq tableaux allegoriques des sens : les figures sont de proportion naturelle, & dans chacune des piéces est representée une episode des ecritures Saintes, appliquée aux cinq sens. Peints avec entendement & Vigeur [sic]] | *Mat:* op doek *Size:* ieder hoog 77, breed 68 duim	Maria Magdalena van Sluypwyk, gravinne van Moens	(Sold) fl 6:10 Schonnenberg
1803/04/20	AMSCH	0149	*[Anonymous]* | Twee stuks capitaale gestoffeerde Italiaansche Landschappen, met Geboomten, Gebouwen en Beelden, meesterlyk en kloek gepenceeld [Deux sites d'Italie grandement composés, avec figures, peints d'une maniere ferme & decidée.] | *Mat:* [sur toile] *Size:* ieder hoog 72, breed 68 duim [hauts 72, larges 98 pouces] *Notes:* The material was given only in the French edition of the catalogue. The dimensions differ in the Dutch and French editions of the catalogue.	Maria Magdalena van Sluypwyk, gravinne van Moens	(Sold) fl 14 Van Leen
1803/04/20	AMSCH	0150	*[Anonymous]* | Twee stuks stille Leevens, men ziet op Tafels diversche Visschen en Fruiten, zeer natuurlyk afgebeeld [Ces deux Sujets sont des tables remplies de poisson [sic] & de fruits ; très naturellement representés.] | *Size:* ieder hoog 5 ½, breed 7 duim	Maria Magdalena van Sluypwyk, gravinne van Moens	(Sold) fl 5 Josi

1803/04/20	AMSCH	0153	*[Anonymous]* | Een vergenoegt Boertje, in een Binnehuis zittende by een Tafel, houdende een Glas met Bier in de hand, daar nevens staat een Aardekan, Vuurtest en Pyp, fiks behandeld [Un Villageois le verre à la main, ayant sur sa table de quoi fumer, peint avec esprit & caractére.] | *Mat:* op paneel *Size:* hoog 10, breed 9 duim	Maria Magdalena van Sluypwyk, gravinne van Moens	(Sold) fl 1:10 L Pakker
1803/04/20	AMSCH	0154	*[Anonymous]* | Een Boere Huisgezin [Un menage Rustique.] | *Mat:* op paneel *Size:* hoog 9, breed 8 duim	Maria Magdalena van Sluypwyk, gravinne van Moens	(Sold) fl 2 Grimpen
1803/04/27	AMSCH	0002	*[Anonymous]* | Hercule & Anthée, les figures plus grandes que nature sont fiérement dessinées, ce Tableau est d'un grand effet | *Size:* h. 8 ½, l. 5 pieds	A	(Sold) fl 39 V d Brink
1803/04/27	AMSCH	0005	*[Anonymous]* | Un Tableau répresentant la Sainte Vierge avec l'Enfant Jësus sur les Nuages, distribuante des Chapelést [sic] à Sainte Therése, Sainte Chaterine [sic], Sainte Maria Madeleine & Sainte Dominique ; ce sujêst [sic] est entouré d'une bordure de fleurs qu, environne quinze petits sujêst rélatifs à la Vie de Jesus Christ & de la Sainte Vierge ; ce petit Tableau peint sur cuivre est d'un fini extrémement précieux & de la plus belle conservation | *Mat:* sur cuivre *Size:* h. 1 ¼, l. 1 pieds	A	(Sold) fl 30 Th^s Spaan
1803/04/27	AMSCH	0006	*Un bon Maitre* | La nativité de Jesus Christ ; cette riche composition est peinte avec beaucoup de Franchise par un bon Maitre, sur bois | *Mat:* sur bois *Size:* h. 1 ¾, l. 1 ¼ pieds	A	(Sold) fl 39 Stevens
1803/04/27	AMSCH	0007	*Un ancien Maitre* | Saint Jérome en dévotion, peint sur bois par un ancien Maitre | *Mat:* sur bois *Size:* h. 1 ½, l. 1 ¼ pieds	A	(Sold) fl 3:10 Gruiter
1803/04/27	AMSCH	0008	*[Anonymous]* | Judith avec la tête de Holopherne, ce Tableau est d'un effêt piquant & d'un bon ton de couleur | *Annots:* School v[an] Caravaggo (MB) *Size:* h. 4 ½, l. 3 ½ pieds	A	(Sold) fl 70 Hulswit
1803/04/27	AMSCH	0009	*Un bon Maitre* | Jacob trompant son pere Isaac, par un bon Maitre | *Annots:* [door] Calabrese (MB) *Size:* h. 3 ½, l. 4 ½ pieds	A	(Sold) fl 37:10 Th^s Spaan
1803/04/27	AMSCH	000V[H]	*[Anonymous]* | Twee stuks Man & Vrouw, portrat [sic] | *Notes:* This lot was added in by hand in the LBDa and RKDH copies of the catalogue.	G	(Bought In) fl 24
1803/04/27	AMSCH	000X[H]	*[Anonymous]* | Twee stuks Bijbels ordonantien | *Notes:* This lot was added in by hand in the LBDa and RKDH copies of the catalogue.	G	(Sold) fl 1 Gruiter
1803/04/27	AMSCH	000Y[H]	*[Anonymous]* | Twee dito [stuks] dito [Bijbels ordonantien] | *Notes:* This lot was added in by hand in the LBDa and RKDH copies of the catalogue.	G	(Sold) fl 1 L Pakker
1803/04/27	AMSCH	0010	*[Anonymous]* | Susanne avec les Anciens, bien composê & largement peint | *Size:* h. 3 ¾, l. 4 ½ pieds	A	(Sold) fl 8:5 Th^s Spaan
1803/04/27	AMSCH	0013	*Un bon Maitre* | Le même sujet [Marie Medelaine [sic] penitente], par un bon Maitre | *Size:* h. 4, l. 3 pieds	A	(Sold) fl 23 Van Dijl
1803/04/27	AMSCH	0014	*[Anonymous]* | David avec la tête de Goliath, ce morceau est rempli d'expression, est d'un bon effêt & est vigoureusement peint | *Size:* h. 4, l. 5 pieds	A	(Sold) fl 1:5 Hulswit
1803/04/27	AMSCH	0015	*Un ancien Maitre* | Sainte Ursule avec les onze mille Vierges | *Size:* h. 3 ½, l. 5 pieds	A	(Sold) fl 1 Grimpen
1803/04/27	AMSCH	0020[a]	*Un bon Maitre* | Deux Tableaux, représentant l'age d'or | *This Lot:* Un Tableau, représentant l'age d'or *Size:* h. 4 ½, l. 3 ¾ pieds	A	(Sold) fl 18:10 for lots 20[a] & 20[b]. Pruijssenaar [for] R
1803/04/27	AMSCH	0020[b]	*Un bon Maitre* | Deux Tableaux, représentant l'age d'or | *This Lot:* Un Tableau, représentant l'age d'or *Size:* h. 4, l. 3 pieds	A	(Sold) fl 18:10 for lots 20[a] & 20[b]. Pruijssenaar [for] R
1803/04/27	AMSCH	0024[b]	*Un bon Maitre* | Deux Tableaux, dont l'un réprésente l'ascention de la Sainte Vierge, par Seb: Conca, & l'autre une Sainte, entre deux Anges | *This Lot:* Une Saint, entre deux Anges; lot 24[a] by S. Conca *Mat:* sur bois	A	(Sold) fl 11 for lots 24[a] & 24[b]. Stevens
1803/04/27	AMSCH	0027	*Un bon Maitre* | Deux esquisses de Plafonds, dont l'une réprésente Moïse & Avon, & l'Autre un Saint présenté à la trés Sainte Trinité, par la Sainte Vierge	A	(Sold) fl 14:10 Th Spaan
1803/04/27	AMSCH	0030	*[Anonymous]* | Une Sainte recueillante [sic] dans un Vase le Sang des Martirs ; ce Tableau est largement peint, la tête de la Sainte est remplie d'expression, & le dessin en est fort corret | *Size:* h. 4 ½, l. 3 ½ pieds	A	(Sold) fl 23:10 Stevens
1803/04/27	AMSCH	0031	*Un bon Maitre* | Le Mariage de Jesus Christ avec Sainte Cathérine ; rise [sic] composition peinte, par un bon Maitre | *Size:* h. 4 ¾, l. 3 ½ pieds	A	(Sold) fl 2:15 Hulswit
1803/04/27	AMSCH	0033[a]	*[Anonymous]* | Deux Tableaux avec des bordures d'écaille dont l'un peint sur cuivre, représente Salomon & la Reine de Saba & l'autre sur Marbre, une Sainte Cicile | *This Lot:* Salomon & la Reine de Saba *Mat:* sur cuivre	A	(Sold) fl 23:10 for lots 33[a] & 33[b]. Stevens
1803/04/27	AMSCH	0033[b]	*[Anonymous]* | Deux Tableaux avec des bordures d'écaille dont l'un peint sur cuivre, représente Salomon & la Reine de Saba & l'autre sur Marbre, une Sainte Cicile | *This Lot:* Une Sainte Cicile *Mat:* sur marbre	A	(Sold) fl 23:10 for lots 33[a] & 33[b]. Stevens
1803/04/27	AMSCH	0034	*[Anonymous]* | Deux Tableaux dont l'un réprésente St. Jérome & l'autre St. Joseph	A	(Sold) fl 1:5 Stevens
1803/04/27	AMSCH	0036[b]	*[Anonymous]* | Trois Tableaux, Tête de Seraphins, par Pachette de Rosa & têtes de femmes | *This Lot:* Têtes de femmes; lot 36[a] by Fr. Rosa	A	(Sold) fl 0:6 for lots 36[a] & 36[b]. L Pakker

1803/04/27	AMSCH	0041	*Un bon Maitre* | La Sainte Vierge tenant l'Enfant Jésus sur les genoux, dans une Guirlande de Fleurs, par un bon Maitre | *Size:* h. 5, l. 4 ¾ pieds	A	(Sold) fl 2:10 V d Brink
1803/04/27	AMSCH	0043	*Un bon Maitre* | Adam en Eva, Chassez du Paradis, par un bon Maitre | *Size:* h. 3 ¼, l. 4 ¼ pieds	A	(Sold) fl 5 Esser
1803/04/27	AMSCH	0044	*Un bon Maitre* | Deux Enfans avec des Fleurs, par dito [un bon Maitre] | *Size:* h. 4 ½, l. 3 ¾ pieds	A	(Sold) fl 1:15 V d Brink
1803/04/27	AMSCH	0047	*[Anonymous]* | La Conversion de St. Paul, riche composition, remplie de Mouvement | *Size:* h. 4 ½, l. 6 ½ pieds	A	(Sold) fl 3:15 L Pakker
1803/04/27	AMSCH	0049	*Un bon Maitre* | l'Annonciation de la Sainte Vierge, par un bon Maitre | *Size:* h. 6, l. 4 ¼ pieds	A	(Sold) fl 21:10 Hulswit
1803/04/27	AMSCH	0051	*Un bon Maitre* | Orphée tué par les Bacchantes, par un bon Maitre | *Size:* h. 6 ½, l. 5 pieds	A	(Sold) fl 1 Hulswit
1803/04/27	AMSCH	0052	*Un bon Maitre* | Tancréde pansé par Clorinde sur le Champ de Bataille, par un dito [bon Maitre] | *Size:* h. 6 ½, l. 9 ½ pieds	A	(Sold) fl 0:10 Vinkeles
1803/04/27	AMSCH	0053	*[Anonymous]* | Adam & Eva pleurant la mort d'Abel ce Tableau est d'un grand effêt & est fort bien peint | *Size:* h. 7, l. 8 pieds	A	(Sold) fl 2:5 Gruiter
1803/04/27	AMSCH	0057	*Un bon Maitre* | Samson & Dalila, par un bon Maitre | *Size:* h. 3 ¾, l. 5 ½ pieds	A	(Sold) fl 6 Grimpen
1803/04/27	AMSCH	0058	*Un bon Maitre* | Un Tableau représentant du Gibier, par un bon Maitre | *Size:* h. 4 ¼, l. 6 ¼ pieds	A	(Sold) fl 1:10 Esser
1803/04/27	AMSCH	0059	*Un bon Maitre* | Un dito [Tableau], avec du Gibier & des Fruits, par un dito [bon Maitre] | *Size:* h. 4 ½, l. 5 pieds	A	(Sold) fl 7 Pruijssenaar [for] L
1803/04/27	AMSCH	0060	*Un bon Maitre* | Une Bataille, peinte par un bon Maitre | *Size:* h. 4 ½, l. 6 pieds	A	(Sold) fl 12 Grimpen
1803/04/27	AMSCH	0061	*[Anonymous]* | Saint Jérome, ce morceau à beaucoup d'effêt & d'expression & est tres bien peint | *Size:* h. 4 ½, l. 3 ¼ pieds	A	(Sold) fl 5:5 V d Brink
1803/04/27	AMSCH	0064[b]	*Un bon Maitre* | Deux Esquisses de Tableaux dont l'une réprésente le Saveur Nourissant la Multitude, par P. d'Anne, & l'autre un Sujét historique | *This Lot:* Un Sujét historique; lot 64[a] by P. Anne	A	(Sold) fl 2 for lots 64[a] & 64[b]. Stevens
1803/04/27	AMSCH	0067	*Un bon Maitre* | Une Bacchanale, par un bon Maitre | *Size:* h. 6, l. 8 ½ pieds	A	(Sold) fl 3 Mensard
1803/04/27	AMSCH	0068	*[Anonymous]* | St. Sebastien, ce Morceau a beaucoup d'effêt | *Size:* h. 7, l. 5 pieds	A	(Sold) fl 19:10 Th Spaan
1803/04/27	AMSCH	0069	*[Anonymous]* | Quatre Tableaux, représentant Icare & Dédale, Hercule combattant l'Hydre de Lerne, la mort de Meléagre, & Narcisse, amoureux de soi même | *Size:* h. 8, l. 5 pieds	A	(Sold) fl 1:15 L Pakker
1803/04/27	AMSCH	0071	*Un bon Maitre* | Cette belle composition représente le Martire de St. Etienne & est peinte, par un bon Maitre | *Size:* h. 6, l. 5 pieds	A	(Sold) fl 9:5 Th Spaan
1803/04/27	AMSCH	0072	*[Anonymous]* | Le Martire d'une Sainte, ce Tableau est très bien composé & moëlleusement peint | *Size:* h. 5 ½, l. 4 ½ pieds	A	(Sold) fl 30 Hodges
1803/04/27	AMSCH	0076	*Un bon Maitre* | Quatre Sujets de Batailles, par un bon Maitre	A	(Sold) fl 7:10 Gruiter
1803/04/27	AMSCH	0078[b]	*Un bon Maitre* | Deux morceaux, dont l'un est une Copie de fameux Tableau du Schidone, réprésentant la Charité, & l'autre l'abondance | *This Lot:* L'abondance; lot 78[a] is copy after Schedoni	A	(Sold) fl 4:5 for lots 78[a] & 78[b]. V^{n} Iperen
1803/04/27	AMSCH	0079	*Un bon Maitre* | Le Sauveur mort adoré par les Anges ; ce Tableau a beaucoup d'effêt & est largement peint sur bois par un bon Maitre | *Mat:* sur bois *Size:* h. 1 ½, l. 1 pied	A	(Sold) fl 16 V d Brink
1803/04/27	AMSCH	0081[b]	*Un bon Maitre* | Deux Tableaux, Christ mort peint en Grisaille par le Polidore, & Pan & la Nimphe Syrinx | *This Lot:* Pan & la Nimphe Syrinx; lot 81[a] by Polidoro da Caravaggio	A	(Sold) fl 1:5 for lots 81[a] & 81[b]. Stevens
1803/04/27	AMSCH	0082	*Un bon Maitre* | Narcisse se mirant dans une Fontaine, par un bon Maitre | *Size:* h. 2 ¼, l. 2 ¾ pieds	A	(Sold) fl 29 Pruijssenaar
1803/04/27	AMSCH	0086	*[Anonymous]* | Trois anciens Tableaux, dont le premier réprésente La St. Vierge & l'Enfant, le second le même sujet avec Sainte Thérese & le troisieme Saint Jérome, sur Bois | *Mat:* sur bois	A	(Sold) fl 6 Gruiter
1803/04/27	AMSCH	0087	*[Anonymous]* | Diana au Bain, peint avec beaucoup de naïveté | *Size:* h. 1 ¼, l. 1 ½ pieds	A	(Sold) fl 79 Th Spaan
1803/04/27	AMSCH	0088	*[Anonymous]* | Un Saint Hérémite en méditation, ce petit Tableau est d'un grand fini, l'effet de la lumiére de chandelle est rendu avec beaucoup de vérité ; peint sur bois | *Mat:* sur bois *Size:* h. 1, l. 1 ¾ pieds	A	(Sold) fl 36 Van Iperen
1803/04/27	AMSCH	0090	*Un bon Maitre* | Quatre Tableaux de la Passion de Jesus Christ, par un bon Maitre | *Size:* h. 2 ½, l. 5 ¼ pieds	A	(Sold) fl 69 Pruijssenaar [for] L
1803/04/27	AMSCH	0092	*Un bon Maitre* | La Nimphe Calisto, par un bon Maitre | *Size:* h. 3 ½, l. 4 ½ pieds	A	(Sold) fl 6:10 Stevens
1803/04/27	AMSCH	0094	*Un bon Maitre* | Sainte Jérome, par un bon Maitre | *Size:* h. 3 ½, l. 2 ½ pieds	A	(Sold) fl 0:6 Camphuysen
1803/04/27	AMSCH	0095	*Un bon Maitre* | St. Joseph tenant l'Enfant Jésus sur ses genoux, par un dito [bon Maitre] | *Size:* h. 3 ½, l. 2 ½ pieds	A	(Sold) fl 2:15 Gruiter

1803/04/27	AMSCH	00AA[H]	*[Anonymous]* | Twee Stuks Een Mans & Vrouw portrait | *Notes:* This lot was added in by hand in the LBDa copy of the catalogue.	C	(Sold) fl 1:5 Vermeulen
1803/04/27	AMSCH	00DD[H]	*[Anonymous]* | Twee Stuks een Mans & Vrouw portrait | *Notes:* This lot was added in by hand in the LBDa copy of the catalogue.	C	(Sold) fl 3:5 Hodges
1803/04/27	AMSCH	00EE[H]	*[Anonymous]* | Twee dito [stuks] Vrouwen portraits | *Notes:* This lot was added in by hand in the LBDa copy of the catalogue.	C	(Sold) fl 0:14 for lots EE & FF. Fredriks
1803/04/27	AMSCH	00FF[H]	*[Anonymous]* | Twee dito [stuks] Mans & vrouwen dito [portraits] | *Notes:* This lot was added in by hand in the LBDa copy of the catalogue.	C	(Sold) fl 0:14 for lots EE & FF. Fredriks
1803/04/27	AMSCH	00JJ[H]	*[Anonymous]* | Een pleijster plaats | *Notes:* This lot was added in by hand in the LBDa copy of the catalogue.	C	(Sold) fl 2:5 van Iperen
1803/04/27	AMSCH	00KK[H]	*[Anonymous]* | Een Mans portrait | *Notes:* This lot was added in by hand in the LBDa copy of the catalogue.	C	(Sold) fl 0:6 L Pakker
1803/04/27	AMSCH	00LL[H]	*[Anonymous]* | Twee Landschappen met beelden [?] | *Notes:* This lot was added in by hand in the LBDa copy of the catalogue.	C	(Bought In) fl 10
1803/04/27	AMSCH	00MM[H]	*[Anonymous]* | Twee dito [Landschappen] dito [met beelden?] | *Notes:* This lot was added in by hand in the LBDa copy of the catalogue.	C	(Bought In) fl 11
1803/04/27	AMSCH	00NN[H]	*[Anonymous]* | Twee Stuks V Winter & binnehuys | *Notes:* This lot was added in by hand in the LBDa copy of the catalogue.	C	(Sold) fl 6 Vinkeles
1803/04/27	AMSCH	00OO[H]	*[Anonymous]* | Twee dito [Stuks] .... Mertis/ey[?] & Mans portrait | *Notes:* This lot was added in by hand in the LBDa copy of the catalogue.	C	(Sold) fl 1 Gruiter
1803/04/27	AMSCH	00PP[H]	*[Anonymous]* | Twee Stuks Mans hoofden [?] | *Notes:* This lot was added in by hand in the LBDa copy of the catalogue.	C	(Sold) fl 0:14 Westhoff
1803/04/27	AMSCH	00QQ[H]	*[Anonymous]* | Vier Stuks divers | *Notes:* This lot was added in by hand in the LBDa copy of the catalogue.	C	(Sold) fl 1:15 Vermeulen
1803/04/27	AMSCH	00SS[H]	*[Anonymous]* | Een Landschap met Beelden | *Notes:* This lot was added in by hand in the LBDa copy of the catalogue.	C	(Bought In) fl 5 ½
1803/04/27	AMSCH	00TT[H]	*[Anonymous]* | Een Bybelsche ordonantie | *Notes:* This lot was added in by hand in the LBDa copy of the catalogue.	C	(Sold) fl 1 Vinkeles
1803/04/27	AMSCH	00UU[H]	*[Anonymous]* | Een dito [Bybelsche ordonantie] | *Notes:* This lot was added in by hand in the LBDa copy of the catalogue.	C	(Sold) fl 2 Hodges
1803/04/27	AMSCH	0102	*Un bon Maitre* | Une Sybille, ce tableau est d'un bel effet & est fiérement peint, par un bon Maitre | *Size:* h. 4 ½, l. 3 pieds	A	(Sold) fl 16 V^n Iperen
1803/04/27	AMSCH	0103	*[Anonymous]* | David avec la tête de Goliath | *Size:* h. 3 ¾, l. 3 ¼ pieds	A	(Sold) fl 4 Pruijssenaar [for] L
1803/04/27	AMSCH	0104	*[Anonymous]* | Sainte Cicile | *Size:* h. 4, l. 2 ¾ pieds	A	(Sold) fl 1 Grimpen
1803/04/27	AMSCH	0106	*Un bon Maitre* | Un Saint François en devotion, par un bon Maitre | *Size:* h. 5 ¼, l. 3 ¼ pieds	A	(Sold) fl 4:15 V d Brink
1803/04/27	AMSCH	0107	*[Anonymous]* | Neptune & Amphitrite, ce tableau a beaucoup d'effet, le Colosis en est fraix [sic] & l'expression en est fort belles | *Size:* h. 7, l. 9 pieds	A	(Sold) fl 41 Pruijssenaar
1803/04/27	AMSCH	0108	*[Anonymous]* | Le Martire de St. Laurent, ce tableau a beaucoup d'effet | *Size:* h. 9, l. 7 pieds	A	(Sold) fl 15:10 Gruiter
1803/04/27	AMSCH	0109	*[Anonymous]* | Rénaud & Armide, ce morceau a un bel effêt & les figures ont beaucoup d'expression | *Size:* h. 6, l. 7 pieds	A	(Sold) fl 15:10 Hodges
1803/04/27	AMSCH	0112	*Un bon Maitre* | L'Adoration des berges, par un bon Maitre | *Size:* h. 4 ½, l. 5 ½ pieds	A	(Sold) fl 14:10 Th Spaan
1803/04/27	AMSCH	0113	*Un bon Maitre* | Le Samaritain charitable, par un dito [bon Maitre] | *Size:* h. 4 ¼, l. 6 pieds	A	(Sold) fl 2:15 Gruiter
1803/04/27	AMSCH	0114	*Un bon Maitre* | Une Jeune Fille richement parée & occupée à filer, par un dito [bon Maitre] | *Size:* h. 2 ½, l. 2 pieds	A	(Sold) fl 18 J Vinkeles
1803/04/27	AMSCH	0115	*[Anonymous]* | Deux Morceaux avec de fruits	A	(Sold) fl 0:10 V^n Iperen
1803/04/27	AMSCH	0116	*[Anonymous]* | Le portrait de Louis quatorze	A	(Sold) fl 1 Grimpen
1803/04/27	AMSCH	0117	*[Anonymous]* | Sept études de têtes	A	(Sold) fl 6:10 Gruyter
1803/04/27	AMSCH	0118	*[Anonymous]* | Trois tableaux répresentans St. Antoine, Héraclite & Démocrite	A	(Sold) fl 1:15 Levy Pakker
1803/04/27	AMSCH	0119	*[Anonymous]* | Quatre tableaux de fleurs & de fruits	A	(Sold) fl 2:10 Gruiter
1803/04/27	AMSCH	0121	*[Anonymous]* | Quatre petits Tableaux Historiques peints sur Cuivre | *Mat:* sur cuivre	A	(Sold) fl 16 Gruiter
1803/04/27	AMSCH	0123	*[Anonymous]* | Trois Tableaux historiques & un paisage peint sur cuivre | *Mat:* sur cuivre	A	(Sold) fl 6:5 Pruyssenaar [for] L
1803/04/27	AMSCH	0124	*[Anonymous]* | La Sainte Vierge, peinte sur bois | *Mat:* sur bois	A	(Sold) fl 5 Stevens
1803/04/27	AMSCH	0125	*[Anonymous]* | Six Tableaux différens	A	(Sold) fl 2:10 L Pakker
1803/04/27	AMSCH	0126	*[Anonymous]* | Deux petites Batailles, & une Diane	A	(Sold) fl 2 Stevens

1803/04/27	AMSCH	0127	*[Anonymous]* | Deux pieces, une Sainte Thérése morte & la Chasteté de Susanne	A	(Sold) fl 1:10 L Pakker
1803/04/27	AMSCH	0128	*[Anonymous]* | Une Sainte Vierge avec l'enfant Jésus accompagnée de Sainte Elisabeth | *Size:* h. 37, l. 30 pouces	A	(Sold) fl 1 Grimpen
1803/04/27	AMSCH	0130	*[Anonymous]* | L'Ascensíon de la Sainte Vierge | *Size:* h. 56, l. 49 pouces	A	(Sold) fl 4:10 Gruiter
1803/04/27	AMSCH	0131	*Un bon Maitre* | Saint Pierre, par un bon Maitre | *Size:* h. 46, l. 37 pouces	A	(Sold) fl 2 Hulswit
1803/04/27	AMSCH	0132	*Un bon Maitre* | Une Sainte Madelaine, accompagnée d'autres figures, par un dito [bon Maitre] | *Size:* h. 52, l. 39 pouces	A	(Sold) fl 3 V^{n} Dyl
1803/04/27	AMSCH	0133	*Un bon Maitre* | Saint Jérome, par un dito [bon Maitre] | *Size:* h. 39, l. 28 pouces	A	(Sold) fl 3 Gruiter
1803/04/27	AMSCH	0134	*[Anonymous]* | Deux piéces, le songe de Joseph, & l'adoration des bergers	A	(Sold) fl 1:15 Stevens
1803/04/27	AMSCH	0135	*[Anonymous]* | La Conversion de Saint Paul | *Size:* h. 38, l. 48 pouces	A	(Sold) fl 1 Grimpen
1803/04/27	AMSCH	0138	*[Anonymous]* | Une frise répresentant une bachanale avec des Eufans [sic] | *Size:* h. 20, l. 57 pouces	A	(Sold) fl 6:5 Stevens
1803/04/27	AMSCH	0139	*[Anonymous]* | Un Saint Francois, & sept têtes differentes	A	(Sold) fl 5:15 Hulswit
1803/04/27	AMSCH	0141	*[Anonymous]* | Plusieurs Tableaux differens qui seront vendus par Lots	A	(Sold) fl 0:8 V^{n} Iperen
1803/04/27	AMSCH	0141a[H]	*[Anonymous]* | [Untitled] | *Notes:* This lot was added in by hand in the LBDa copy of the catalogue, but without giving an artist or title.	A	(Sold) fl 0:10 L Pakker
1803/04/27	AMSCH	0141b[H]	*[Anonymous]* | [Untitled] | *Notes:* This lot was added in by hand in the LBDa copy of the catalogue, but without giving an artist or title.	A	(Sold) fl 1:15 Vinkeles
1803/04/27	AMSCH	0141c[H]	*[Anonymous]* | [Untitled] | *Notes:* This lot was added in by hand in the LBDa copy of the catalogue, but without giving an artist or title.	A	(Sold) fl 1 Vinkeles
1803/04/27	AMSCH	0141d[H]	*[Anonymous]* | [Untitled] | *Notes:* This lot was added in by hand in the LBDa copy of the catalogue, but without giving an artist or title.	A	(Sold) fl 1 Vinkeles
1803/04/27	AMSCH	0141e[H]	*[Anonymous]* | [Untitled] | *Notes:* This lot was added in by hand in the LBDa copy of the catalogue, but without giving an artist or title.	A	(Sold) fl 2:5 Vinkeles
1803/04/27	AMSCH	0142	*[Anonymous]* | Une Marine & deux Païsages, trois piéces	A	(Sold) fl 2:10 V d Brink
1803/04/27	AMSCH	0143	*[Anonymous]* | Deux Païsages ornés de figures	A	(Sold) fl 1:5 Pruijssenaar [for] L
1803/04/27	AMSCH	0144	*[Anonymous]* | Quatre sujets de Marines	A	(Sold) fl 1:5 Gruiter
1803/04/27	AMSCH	0145	*[Anonymous]* | Trois Païsages	A	(Sold) fl 1:10 Stevens
1803/04/27	AMSCH	0146	*[Anonymous]* | Trois petits dito [Païsages]	A	(Sold) fl 5:10 Th Spaan
1803/04/27	AMSCH	0147	*[Anonymous]* | Un petit Païsage, & un morceau avec des fruits	A	(Sold) fl 1 Gruiter
1803/04/27	AMSCH	0148	*[Anonymous]* | Deux Garcons qui rient | *Size:* h. 13, l. 18 pouces	A	(Sold) fl 6:10 I^{c} Moses
1803/04/27	AMSCH	0149	*[Anonymous]* | Une Sainte Famille, peinte sur bois | *Mat:* sur bois	A	(Sold) fl 1 Stevens
1803/04/27	AMSCH	0151	*Un bon Maitre* | Une Sainte Famille, par un bon maitre | *Size:* h. 50, l. 39 pouces	A	(Sold) fl 4:10 V d Brink
1803/04/27	AMSCH	0152	*Un bon Maitre* | L'Enlevement de Ganiméde, par un dito [bon maitre] | *Size:* h. 37, l. 50 pouces	A	(Sold) fl 3 Stevens
1803/04/27	AMSCH	0153	*[Anonymous]* | Saint Pierre pénitent | *Size:* h. 52, l. 39 pouces	A	(Sold) fl 1 L Pakker
1803/04/27	AMSCH	0154	*[Anonymous]* | Deux Tableaux répresentans des Saints Apôtres	A	(Sold) fl 16 J Vinkeles
1803/04/27	AMSCH	0155	*[Anonymous]* | Deux Tableaux avec des fruits | *Size:* h. 48, l. 58 pouces	A	(Sold) fl 1:5 V d Maasen
1803/04/27	AMSCH	0156	*[Anonymous]* | Deux dito [Tableaux] dito [avec des fruits]	A	(Sold) fl 0:8 Grimpen
1803/04/27	AMSCH	0157	*[Anonymous]* | Deux dito [Tableaux] dito [avec des fruits] | *Size:* h. 46, l. 36 pouces	A	(Sold) fl 1:5 Gruiter
1803/04/27	AMSCH	0158	*[Anonymous]* | Deux dito [Tableaux] dito [avec des fruits] | *Size:* h. 25, l. 48 pouces	A	(Sold) fl 1:5 Insinger
1803/04/27	AMSCH	0159	*[Anonymous]* | Deux dito [Tableaux] dito [avec des fruits]	A	(Sold) fl 0:12 Gruiter
1803/04/27	AMSCH	0160	*[Anonymous]* | Cinq dito [Tableaux] dito [avec des fruits]	A	(Sold) fl 0:6 I^{c} Levy
1803/04/27	AMSCH	0161	*Un bon Maitre* | Un Chimiste dans son Labortoire, par un bon maitre | *Size:* h. 27, l. 37 pouces	A	(Sold) fl 0:6 L Pakker
1803/04/27	AMSCH	0163	*Un bon Maitre* | Deux dito [Tableaux], répresentans [sic] Narcisse, & Ganiméde, par un bon maitre | *Size:* h. 29, l. 34 pouces	A	(Sold) fl 0:10 Grimpen
1803/04/27	AMSCH	0164	*Un bon Maitre* | Quatre Tableaux, avec des fleurs, des Poules & des Canards, par un dito [bon maitre]	A	(Sold) fl 1:5 Esser
1803/04/27	AMSCH	0165	*Un bon Maitre* | Un Viellard cueilland [sic] des fruits, par un dito [bon maitre] | *Size:* h. 36, l. 47 pouces	A	(Sold) fl 0:10 Grimpen
1803/04/27	AMSCH	0166	*[Anonymous]* | Une Bataille | *Size:* h. 17, l. 24 pouces	A	(Sold) fl 1 V d Brink

1803/06/07	MGBEO	0001	*[Anonymous]* | Een Land- en Dorpgezicht, op den voorgrond eenige Beelden, in een Zwarte lyst	A Wagenaar	(Sold) £ 0:7 Beljaart
1803/06/07	MGBEO	0002	*[Anonymous]* | Twee stuks, verbeeldende den Brand in een Boere Wooning, in vergulde lysten	A Wagenaar	(Sold) £ 0:2 Beljaart
1803/06/07	MGBEO	0003	*[Anonymous]* | Een Landschap, op den voorgrond twee Venussen en een Sater, in vergulde lyst	A Wagenaar	(Sold) £ 0:2 Beljaart
1803/06/07	MGBEO	0004	*[Anonymous]* | Een Vrouw, waar by een Man zit in een boek te lezen, in vergulde lyst	A Wagenaar	(Sold) £ 0:1 Koning
1803/06/07	MGBEO	0005	*[Anonymous]* | Een Portrait van G.J. Nahuis, in lyst en glas	A Wagenaar	(Sold) £ 0:3 v Benthem
1803/06/20	AMSCH	0030	*[Anonymous]* | Abraham zyn Zoon Isaak willende Offeren. meesterlyk op Doek, door een zeer bekwaam Schilder vervaardigd | *Mat:* op doek *Size:* hoog 17, breed 14 duim	Schley [for] G	(Sold) fl 7:10 Gruiter
1803/06/20	AMSCH	0031	*[Anonymous]* | Een Jongeling, zittende aan een Lessenaar te Tekenen, naar het Handekykertje, by een Lamplicht; zeer natuurlyk van licht en bevallig gepenceeld op Paneel, door denzelven | *Mat:* op paneel *Size:* hoog 18, breed 16 duim	Schley [for] G	(Sold) fl 6:10 Hafner
1803/06/20	AMSCH	0038	*Een goed Meester* | Twee stuks gestoffeerde Boom en Bergagtige Landschappen met Watervallen, meesterlyk op Doek, door een goed Meester | *Mat:* op doek *Size:* hoog 52, breed 48 duim	Schley [for] G	(Sold) fl 10:10 Gruiter
1803/06/20	AMSCH	0057	*Een braaf Meester* | Een Italiaansch Landschap, met Ruïne van verschyde Gebouwen, gestoffeerd op de voorgrond met een Heer te Paard, schynende teegens eenige Landlieden te spreeken; het is fix en zonachtig gepenceelt op Koper, door een braaf Meester; Ovaal Formaat | *Mat:* op koper *Fmt:* ovaal	Schley [for] H	(Sold) fl 3 V Dijl
1803/06/20	AMSCH	0061	*[Anonymous]* | Een bergagtig Italiaansch Landschap, met eenig Geboomte op de Voorgrond by een Rivier zyn Huislieden, met verscheide Vée, eenige derzelven Waden in de Rivier; natuurlyk gepenceelt, op Doek | *Mat:* op doek *Size:* hoog 15, breed 19 duim	Schley [for] H	(Bought In) fl 10
1803/06/20	AMSCH	0071	*[Anonymous]* | Twee stuks geschilderde Modellen	Schley [for] K	(Sold) fl 6 Plux
1803/06/20	AMSCH	0081	*[Anonymous]* | Asbeeldsel van een geleerd Persoon | *Size:* hoog 10 ½, breed 9 ½ duim	Roos [for] L	(Sold) fl 1 Grimpen
1803/06/20	AMSCH	0082[H]	*[Anonymous]* | 4 [Schilderijen] | *Notes:* This lot was added in by hand in the LBDa and RKDH copies of the catalogue.		(Sold) fl 19 Claasens
1803/06/20	AMSCH	0083[H]	*[Anonymous]* | 1 [Schilderij] | *Notes:* This lot was added in by hand in the LBDa and RKDH copies of the catalogue.		(Sold) fl 1:10 Grimpen
1803/06/20	AMSCH	0084[H]	*[Anonymous]* | 2 [Schilderijen] | *Notes:* This lot was added in by hand in the LBDa and RKDH copies of the catalogue.		(Sold) fl 1:10 J Spaan
1803/06/20	AMSCH	0085[H]	*[Anonymous]* | 2 [Schilderijen] | *Notes:* This lot was added in by hand in the LBDa and RKDH copies of the catalogue.		(Sold) fl 1:5 V^{n} Iperen
1803/06/20	AMSCH	0086[H]	*[Anonymous]* | 2 [Schilderijen] | *Notes:* This lot was added in by hand in the LBDa and RKDH copies of the catalogue.		(Sold) fl 3 Gruiter
1803/06/20	AMSCH	0087[H]	*[Anonymous]* | 4 [Schilderijen] | *Notes:* This lot was added in by hand in the LBDa and RKDH copies of the catalogue.		(Sold) fl 0:14 V^{n} Iperen
1803/06/20	AMSCH	0088[H]	*[Anonymous]* | 2 [Schilderijen] | *Notes:* This lot was added in by hand in the LBDa and RKDH copies of the catalogue.		(Bought In) fl 1
1803/06/20	AMSCH	0089[H]	*[Anonymous]* | 2 [Schilderijen] | *Notes:* This lot was added in by hand in the LBDa and RKDH copies of the catalogue.		(Sold) fl 1 Gruiter
1803/06/20	AMSCH	0090[H]	*[Anonymous]* | 2 [Schilderijen] | *Notes:* This lot was added in by hand in the LBDa and RKDH copies of the catalogue.		(Sold) fl 0:8 Gruiter
1803/06/20	AMSCH	0091[H]	*[Anonymous]* | 2 [Schilderijen] | *Notes:* This lot was added in by hand in the LBDa and RKDH copies of the catalogue.		(Sold) fl 1 L Pakker
1803/06/20	AMSCH	0092[H]	*[Anonymous]* | 1 [Schilderij] | *Notes:* This lot was added in by hand in the LBDa and RKDH copies of the catalogue.		(Bought In) fl 1:5
1803/06/20	AMSCH	0093[H]	*[Anonymous]* | 3 [Schilderijen] | *Notes:* This lot was added in by hand in the LBDa and RKDH copies of the catalogue.		(Sold) fl 1:15 Gruiter
1803/06/20	AMSCH	0094[H]	*[Anonymous]* | 3 [Schilderijen] | *Notes:* This lot was added in by hand in the LBDa and RKDH copies of the catalogue.		(Sold) fl 1 L Pakker
1803/06/20	AMSCH	0095[H]	*[Anonymous]* | 2 [Schilderijen] | *Notes:* This lot was added in by hand in the LBDa and RKDH copies of the catalogue.		(Sold) fl 2 Th^{s} Spaan
1803/06/20	AMSCH	0096[H]	*[Anonymous]* | 3 [Schilderijen] | *Notes:* This lot was added in by hand in the LBDa and RKDH copies of the catalogue.		(Sold) fl 1:15 for lots 96[H] & 97[H]. L Pakker
1803/06/20	AMSCH	0097[H]	*[Anonymous]* | 3 [Schilderijen] | *Notes:* This lot was added in by hand in the LBDa and RKDH copies of the catalogue.		(Sold) fl 1:15 for lots 96[H] & 97[H]. L Pakker
1803/06/20	AMSCH	0098[H]	*[Anonymous]* | 3 [Schilderijen] | *Notes:* This lot was added in by hand in the LBDa and RKDH copies of the catalogue.		(Sold) fl 1 Geld

1803/06/20	AMSCH	0099[H]	*[Anonymous]* | 4 [Schilderijen] | *Notes:* This lot was added in by hand in the LBDa and RKDH copies of the catalogue.	(Sold) fl 2 Leyster
1803/06/20	AMSCH	0100[H]	*[Anonymous]* | 4 [Schilderijen] | *Notes:* This lot was added in by hand in the LBDa and RKDH copies of the catalogue.	(Sold) fl 0:6 L Pakker
1803/06/20	AMSCH	0101[H]	*[Anonymous]* | 4 [Schilderijen] | *Notes:* This lot was added in by hand in the LBDa and RKDH copies of the catalogue.	(Sold) fl 4:5 L Pakker
1803/06/20	AMSCH	0102[H]	*[Anonymous]* | 6 [Schilderijen] | *Notes:* This lot was added in by hand in the LBDa and RKDH copies of the catalogue.	(Sold) fl 5:10 Frantszen
1803/06/20	AMSCH	0103[H]	*[Anonymous]* | 4 [Schilderijen] | *Notes:* This lot was added in by hand in the LBDa and RKDH copies of the catalogue.	(Bought In) fl 1
1803/06/20	AMSCH	0104[H]	*[Anonymous]* | 6 [Schilderijen] | *Notes:* This lot was added in by hand in the LBDa and RKDH copies of the catalogue.	(Sold) fl 2:5 for lots 104[H] & 105[H]. L Pakker
1803/06/20	AMSCH	0105[H]	*[Anonymous]* | 6 [Schilderijen] | *Notes:* This lot was added in by hand in the LBDa and RKDH copies of the catalogue.	(Sold) fl 2:5 for lots 104[H] & 105[H]. L Pakker
1803/06/20	AMSCH	0106[H]	*[Anonymous]* | 6 [Schilderijen] | *Notes:* This lot was added in by hand in the LBDa and RKDH copies of the catalogue.	(Sold) fl 1:15 Rabe
1803/06/20	AMSCH	0107[H]	*[Anonymous]* | 6 [Schilderijen] | *Notes:* This lot was added in by hand in the LBDa and RKDH copies of the catalogue.	(Sold) fl 1:10 L Pakker [or] Vinkeles
1803/06/27	MGBEO	0001	*[Anonymous]* | [Untitled] | *Notes:* The only extant copy of this catalogue is annotated with the buyers and prices, but it does not include a printed list of the paintings.	(Sold) £ 0:13 Dubach
1803/06/27	MGBEO	0002	*[Anonymous]* | [Untitled] | *Notes:* The only extant copy of this catalogue is annotated with the buyers and prices, but it does not include a printed list of the paintings.	(Sold) £ 0:4 Beljaart
1803/06/27	MGBEO	0003	*[Anonymous]* | [Untitled] | *Notes:* The only extant copy of this catalogue is annotated with the buyers and prices, but it does not include a printed list of the paintings.	(Sold) £ 0:4 Hicken
1803/06/27	MGBEO	0004	*[Anonymous]* | [Untitled] | *Notes:* The only extant copy of this catalogue is annotated with the buyers and prices, but it does not include a printed list of the paintings.	(Bought In) £ 0:3
1803/06/27	MGBEO	0005	*[Anonymous]* | [Untitled] | *Notes:* The only extant copy of this catalogue is annotated with the buyers and prices, but it does not include a printed list of the paintings.	(Bought In)
1803/06/27	MGBEO	0006	*[Anonymous]* | [Untitled] | *Notes:* The only extant copy of this catalogue is annotated with the buyers and prices, but it does not include a printed list of the paintings.	(Bought In) £ 0:1
1803/06/27	MGBEO	0007	*[Anonymous]* | [Untitled] | *Notes:* The only extant copy of this catalogue is annotated with the buyers and prices, but it does not include a printed list of the paintings.	(Sold) £ 0:1 Specht
1803/06/27	MGBEO	0008	*[Anonymous]* | [Untitled] | *Notes:* The only extant copy of this catalogue is annotated with the buyers and prices, but it does not include a printed list of the paintings.	(Sold) £ 0:9 Dubach
1803/06/27	MGBEO	0009	*[Anonymous]* | [Untitled] | *Notes:* The only extant copy of this catalogue is annotated with the buyers and prices, but it does not include a printed list of the paintings.	(Sold) £ 0:6 Warem (Bleksl)[?]
1803/06/27	MGBEO	0010	*[Anonymous]* | [Untitled] | *Notes:* The only extant copy of this catalogue is annotated with the buyers and prices, but it does not include a printed list of the paintings.	(Bought In)
1803/06/27	MGBEO	0011	*[Anonymous]* | [Untitled] | *Notes:* The only extant copy of this catalogue is annotated with the buyers and prices, but it does not include a printed list of the paintings.	(Sold) £ 0:13 Haze Bomme
1803/06/27	MGBEO	0012	*[Anonymous]* | [Untitled] | *Notes:* The only extant copy of this catalogue is annotated with the buyers and prices, but it does not include a printed list of the paintings.	(Sold) £ 0:8 Warem (Blecks Vlasm) [?]
1803/06/27	MGBEO	0013	*[Anonymous]* | [Untitled] | *Notes:* The only extant copy of this catalogue is annotated with the buyers and prices, but it does not include a printed list of the paintings.	(Sold) £ 0:15 Specht
1803/06/27	MGBEO	0014	*[Anonymous]* | [Untitled] | *Notes:* The only extant copy of this catalogue is annotated with the buyers and prices, but it does not include a printed list of the paintings.	(Bought In)
1803/06/27	MGBEO	0015	*[Anonymous]* | [Untitled] | *Notes:* The only extant copy of this catalogue is annotated with the buyers and prices, but it does not include a printed list of the paintings.	(Sold) £ 0:14 Specht
1803/06/27	MGBEO	0016	*[Anonymous]* | [Untitled] | *Notes:* The only extant copy of this catalogue is annotated with the buyers and prices, but it does not include a printed list of the paintings.	(Sold) £ 0:15 Versonne
1803/07/07	HGKAN	0015	*Een zeer goed Meester* | Een Italiaansch Landschap op doek, waar op een reyzende Vrouw op een Ezel zittende, door een Man geleid word, door	(Unknown)

			een zeer goed Meester [Schilderyen in Olyverf] | *Mat:* in olyverf op doek *Size:* hoog 3 Voet 2 duym en breed 3 en een half Voet *Notes:* The bracketed information in the title appears above lot 1 and refers to lots 1 to 25.		
1803/07/07	HGKAN	0016	*Een zeer goedmeester* | Een zeer fraay en uitvoerig Schildery op doek verbeelde een Vrouw, die Groentens en Fruyt verkoopt, door een zeer goedmeester, met een fraaye Swarte Lyst [Schilderyen in Olyverf] | *Mat:* in olyverf op doek *Notes:* The bracketed information in the title appears above lot 1 and refers to lots 1 to 25.		(Unknown)
1803/07/07	HGKAN	0019	*Een Goedmeester* | Twee stuks Schilderyen op Doek, door een Goedmeester [Schilderyen in Olyverf] | *Mat:* in olyverf op doek *Notes:* The bracketed information in the title appears above lot 1 and refers to lots 1 to 25.		(Unknown)
1803/07/07	HGKAN	0020	*Een Goedmeester* | Twee Stuks dito [Schilderyen] op doek, mede door een Goedmeester [Schilderyen in Olyverf] | *Mat:* in olyverf op doek *Notes:* The bracketed information in the title about the medium appears above lot 1 and refers to lots 1 to 25.		(Unknown)
1803/07/07	HGKAN	0021	*[Anonymous]* | Een dito [stuk] dito [Schildery] op Paneel [Schilderyen in Olyverf] | *Mat:* in olyverf op paneel *Notes:* The bracketed information in the title about the medium appears above lot 1 and refers to lots 1 to 25.		(Unknown)
1803/07/07	HGKAN	0022	*Een zeer goed Meester* | Een fraay stuk, verbeeldende Maria met het Kind, Jezus en Joseph, door een zeer goed Meester [Schilderyen in Olyverf] | *Mat:* in olyverf *Notes:* The bracketed information in the title appears above lot 1 and refers to lots 1 to 25.		(Unknown)
1803/07/07	HGKAN	0025	*Een zeer Goedmeester* | Een Turkin, door een zeer Goedmeester [Schilderyen in Olyverf] | *Mat:* in olyverf *Notes:* The bracketed information in the title appears above lot 1 and refers to lots 1 to 25.		(Unknown)
1803/07/07	HGKAN	A0070	*[Anonymous]* | Een Schilderytje met een Verguld Lystje		(Unknown)
1803/07/14	MGKLY	0016	*[Anonymous]* | Twee Landschapjes op Koper | *Mat:* op koper	Mr Caspar Jacob van Citters	(Unknown)
1803/07/14	MGKLY	0017	*[Anonymous]* | Twee dito [Landschapjes] | *Mat:* op koper	Mr Caspar Jacob van Citters	(Unknown)
1803/07/14	MGKLY	0018	*[Anonymous]* | Twee dito [Landschapjes] op Koper | *Mat:* op koper	Mr Caspar Jacob van Citters	(Unknown)
1803/07/14	MGKLY	0019	*[Anonymous]* | Twee dito [Landschapjes] | *Mat:* op koper	Mr Caspar Jacob van Citters	(Unknown)
1803/07/14	MGKLY	0028	*[Anonymous]* | De Verloore Zoon, fiks gepenseeld	Mr Caspar Jacob van Citters	(Unknown)
1803/07/14	MGKLY	0030	*[Anonymous]* | Een Historie Stukje	Mr Caspar Jacob van Citters	(Unknown)
1803/07/14	MGKLY	0031	*[Anonymous]* | Een Architectuur	Mr Caspar Jacob van Citters	(Unknown)
1803/07/14	MGKLY	0033	*[Anonymous]* | Een hevige Schermutseling	Mr Caspar Jacob van Citters	(Unknown)
1803/07/14	MGKLY	0034	*[Anonymous]* | Een Landschapje	Mr Caspar Jacob van Citters	(Unknown)
1803/07/14	MGKLY	0035	*[Anonymous]* | Twee stille Waters, zonder Lysten	Mr Caspar Jacob van Citters	(Unknown)
1803/07/14	MGKLY	0036	*[Anonymous]* | Twee stuks op Glas geschildert | *Mat:* op glas	Mr Caspar Jacob van Citters	(Unknown)
1803/07/14	MGKLY	0037	*[Anonymous]* | Twee dito [stuks] dito [op Glas geschilderd] | *Mat:* op glas	Mr Caspar Jacob van Citters	(Unknown)
1803/07/14	MGKLY	0039	*[Anonymous]* | Een Landschap fraay met Beelden en Paarden gestoffeert	Mr Caspar Jacob van Citters	(Unknown)
1803/08/01	AMSCH	0055[H]	*[Anonymous]* | 1 Stuk [Extra Schilderijen] | *Notes:* This lot was added in by hand in the EBNP, LBDa and RKDH copies of the catalogue. The bracketed information in the title appears above lot 55[H] and refers to lots 55[H] to 93[H].	Y[ver]	(Sold) fl 1:5 Gruiter
1803/08/01	AMSCH	0056[H]	*[Anonymous]* | 1 Stuk [Extra Schilderijen] | *Notes:* This lot was added in by hand in the EBNP, LBDa and RKDH copies of the catalogue. The bracketed information in the title appears above lot 55[H] and refers to lots 55[H] to 93[H].	Y[ver]	(Sold) fl 0:6 L Pakker
1803/08/01	AMSCH	0057[H]	*[Anonymous]* | 1 Stuk [Extra Schilderijen] | *Notes:* This lot was added in by hand in the EBNP, LBDa and RKDH copies of the catalogue. The bracketed information in the title appears above lot 55[H] and refers to lots 55[H] to 93[H].	Y[ver]	(Sold) fl 0:10 L Pakker
1803/08/01	AMSCH	0058[H]	*[Anonymous]* | 1 Stuk [Extra Schilderijen] | *Notes:* This lot was added in by hand in the EBNP, LBDa and RKDH copies of the catalogue. The bracketed information in the title appears above lot 55[H] and refers to lots 55[H] to 93[H].	Y[ver]	(Sold) fl 0:10 Niermeijer

1803/08/01	AMSCH	0059[H]	*[Anonymous]* | 1 Stuk [Extra Schilderijen] | *Notes:* This lot was added in by hand in the EBNP, LBDa and RKDH copies of the catalogue. The bracketed information in the title appears above lot 55[H] and refers to lots 55[H] to 93[H].	Y[ver]	(Sold) fl 0:12 Vermeulen
1803/08/01	AMSCH	0060[H]	*[Anonymous]* | 1 Stuk [Extra Schilderijen] | *Notes:* This lot was added in by hand in the EBNP, LBDa and RKDH copies of the catalogue. The bracketed information in the title appears above lot 55[H] and refers to lots 55[H] to 93[H].	R[oos]	(Sold) fl 0:14 v[n] Dijl
1803/08/01	AMSCH	0061[H]	*[Anonymous]* | 1 Stuk [Extra Schilderijen] | *Notes:* This lot was added in by hand in the EBNP, LBDa and RKDH copies of the catalogue. The bracketed information in the title appears above lot 55[H] and refers to lots 55[H] to 93[H].	R[oos]	(Sold) fl 0:12 D[k] Nieuland
1803/08/01	AMSCH	0062[H]	*[Anonymous]* | 1 Stuk [Extra Schilderijen] | *Notes:* This lot was added in by hand in the EBNP, LBDa and RKDH copies of the catalogue. The bracketed information in the title appears above lot 55[H] and refers to lots 55[H] to 93[H].	R[oos]	(Sold) fl 3:10 Vermeulen
1803/08/01	AMSCH	0063[H]	*[Anonymous]* | 1 Stuk [Extra Schilderijen] | *Notes:* This lot was added in by hand in the EBNP, LBDa and RKDH copies of the catalogue. The bracketed information in the title appears above lot 55[H] and refers to lots 55[H] to 93[H].	R[oos]	(Sold) fl 1 Pruijssenaar
1803/08/01	AMSCH	0064[H]	*[Anonymous]* | 1 Stuk [Extra Schilderijen] | *Notes:* This lot was added in by hand in the EBNP, LBDa and RKDH copies of the catalogue. The bracketed information in the title appears above lot 55[H] and refers to lots 55[H] to 93[H].	R[oos]	(Sold) fl 1:15 Mensard
1803/08/01	AMSCH	0065[H]	*[Anonymous]* | 2 Stuks [Extra Schilderijen] | *Notes:* This lot was added in by hand in the EBNP, LBDa and RKDH copies of the catalogue. The bracketed information in the title appears above lot 55[H] and refers to lots 55[H] to 93[H].	R[oos]	(Sold) fl 19:10 Jozi
1803/08/01	AMSCH	0066[H]	*[Anonymous]* | 1 Stuk [Extra Schilderijen] | *Notes:* This lot was added in by hand in the EBNP, LBDa and RKDH copies of the catalogue. The bracketed information in the title appears above lot 55[H] and refers to lots 55[H] to 93[H].	R[oos]	(Sold) fl 1:10 L Pakker
1803/08/01	AMSCH	0067[H]	*[Anonymous]* | 1 Stuk [Extra Schilderijen] | *Notes:* This lot was added in by hand in the EBNP, LBDa and RKDH copies of the catalogue. The bracketed information in the title appears above lot 55[H] and refers to lots 55[H] to 93[H].	R[oos]	(Sold) fl 24:10 Hulswit
1803/08/01	AMSCH	0068[H]	*[Anonymous]* | 1 Stuk [Extra Schilderijen] | *Notes:* This lot was added in by hand in the EBNP, LBDa and RKDH copies of the catalogue. The bracketed information in the title appears above lot 55[H] and refers to lots 55[H] to 93[H].	R[oos]	(Sold) fl 16:10 Gruiter
1803/08/01	AMSCH	0069[H]	*[Anonymous]* | 1 Stuk [Extra Schilderijen] | *Notes:* This lot was added in by hand in the EBNP, LBDa and RKDH copies of the catalogue. The bracketed information in the title appears above lot 55[H] and refers to lots 55[H] to 93[H].	R[oos]	(Sold) fl 5:5 Th Spann
1803/08/01	AMSCH	0070[H]	*[Anonymous]* | 1 Stuk [Extra Schilderijen] | *Notes:* This lot was added in by hand in the EBNP, LBDa and RKDH copies of the catalogue. The bracketed information in the title appears above lot 55[H] and refers to lots 55[H] to 93[H].	R[oos]	(Sold) fl 1 L Pakker
1803/08/01	AMSCH	0071[H]	*[Anonymous]* | 1 Stuk [Extra Schilderijen] | *Notes:* This lot was added in by hand in the EBNP, LBDa and RKDH copies of the catalogue. The bracketed information in the title appears above lot 55[H] and refers to lots 55[H] to 93[H].	R[oos]	(Sold) fl 1 V[n] Iperen
1803/08/01	AMSCH	0072[H]	*[Anonymous]* | 2 Stuks [Extra Schilderijen] | *Notes:* This lot was added in by hand in the EBNP, LBDa and RKDH copies of the catalogue. The bracketed information in the title appears above lot 55[H] and refers to lots 55[H] to 93[H].	R[oos]	(Sold) fl 9:10 Coclers
1803/08/01	AMSCH	0073[H]	*[Anonymous]* | 2 Stuks [Extra Schilderijen] | *Notes:* This lot was added in by hand in the EBNP, LBDa and RKDH copies of the catalogue. The bracketed information in the title appears above lot 55[H] and refers to lots 55[H] to 93[H].	R[oos]	(Sold) fl 1:10 L Pakker
1803/08/01	AMSCH	0074[H]	*[Anonymous]* | 2 Stuks [Extra Schilderijen] | *Notes:* This lot was added in by hand in the EBNP, LBDa and RKDH copies of the catalogue. The bracketed information in the title appears above lot 55[H] and refers to lots 55[H] to 93[H].	R[oos]	(Sold) fl 1:10 L Pakker
1803/08/01	AMSCH	0075[H]	*[Anonymous]* | 1 Stuk [Extra Schilderijen] | *Notes:* This lot was added in by hand in the EBNP, LBDa and RKDH copies of the catalogue. The bracketed information in the title appears above lot 55[H] and refers to lots 55[H] to 93[H].	R[oos]	(Sold) fl 2:5 Gruiter
1803/08/01	AMSCH	0076[H]	*[Anonymous]* | 1 Stuk [Extra Schilderijen] | *Notes:* This lot was added in by hand in the EBNP, LBDa and RKDH copies of the catalogue. The bracketed information in the title appears above lot 55[H] and refers to lots 55[H] to 93[H].	R[oos]	(Sold) fl 1:10 Haffner
1803/08/01	AMSCH	0077[H]	*[Anonymous]* | 2 Stuks [Extra Schilderijen] | *Notes:* This lot was added in by hand in the EBNP, LBDa and RKDH copies of the catalogue. The	R[oos]	(Sold) fl 1 L Pakker

			bracketed information in the title appears above lot 55[H] and refers to lots 55[H] to 93[H].		
1803/08/01	AMSCH	0078[H]	*[Anonymous]* | 2 Stuks [Extra Schilderijen] | *Notes:* This lot was added in by hand in the EBNP, LBDa and RKDH copies of the catalogue. The bracketed information in the title appears above lot 55[H] and refers to lots 55[H] to 93[H].	R[oos]	(Sold) fl 1 v^{n} Iperen
1803/08/01	AMSCH	0079[H]	*[Anonymous]* | 1 Stuk [Extra Schilderijen] | *Notes:* This lot was added in by hand in the EBNP, LBDa and RKDH copies of the catalogue. The bracketed information in the title appears above lot 55[H] and refers to lots 55[H] to 93[H].	R[oos]	(Sold) fl 3:10 Boelen
1803/08/01	AMSCH	0080[H]	*[Anonymous]* | 1 Stuk [Extra Schilderijen] | *Notes:* This lot was added in by hand in the EBNP, LBDa and RKDH copies of the catalogue. The bracketed information in the title appears above lot 55[H] and refers to lots 55[H] to 93[H].	R[oos]	(Sold) fl 16 Gruiter
1803/08/01	AMSCH	0081[H]	*[Anonymous]* | 1 Stuk [Extra Schilderijen] | *Notes:* This lot was added in by hand in the EBNP, LBDa and RKDH copies of the catalogue. The bracketed information in the title appears above lot 55[H] and refers to lots 55[H] to 93[H].	R[oos]	(Sold) fl 3:10 Pruijssenaar
1803/08/01	AMSCH	0082[H]	*[Anonymous]* | 1 Stuk [Extra Schilderijen] | *Notes:* This lot was added in by hand in the EBNP, LBDa and RKDH copies of the catalogue. The bracketed information in the title appears above lot 55[H] and refers to lots 55[H] to 93[H].	R[oos]	(Sold) fl 0:10 L Pakker
1803/08/01	AMSCH	0083[H]	*[Anonymous]* | 1 Stuk [Extra Schilderijen] | *Notes:* This lot was added in by hand in the EBNP, LBDa and RKDH copies of the catalogue. The bracketed information in the title appears above lot 55[H] and refers to lots 55[H] to 93[H].	R[oos]	(Sold) fl 0:10 v^{n} Iperen
1803/08/01	AMSCH	0084[H]	*[Anonymous]* | 1 Stuk [Extra Schilderijen] | *Notes:* This lot was added in by hand in the EBNP, LBDa and RKDH copies of the catalogue. The bracketed information in the title appears above lot 55[H] and refers to lots 55[H] to 93[H].	R[oos]	(Sold) fl 0:10 L Pakker
1803/08/01	AMSCH	0085[H]	*[Anonymous]* | 1 Stuk [Extra Schilderijen] | *Notes:* This lot was added in by hand in the EBNP, LBDa and RKDH copies of the catalogue. The bracketed information in the title appears above lot 55[H] and refers to lots 55[H] to 93[H].	R[oos]	(Sold) fl 0:10 L Pakker
1803/08/01	AMSCH	0086[H]	*[Anonymous]* | 1 Stuk [Extra Schilderijen] | *Notes:* This lot was added in by hand in the EBNP, LBDa and RKDH copies of the catalogue. The bracketed information in the title appears above lot 55[H] and refers to lots 55[H] to 93[H].	R[oos]	(Sold) fl 0:6 L Pakker
1803/08/01	AMSCH	0087[H]	*[Anonymous]* | 2 Stuks [Extra Schilderijen] | *Notes:* This lot was added in by hand in the EBNP, LBDa and RKDH copies of the catalogue. The bracketed information in the title appears above lot 55[H] and refers to lots 55[H] to 93[H].	R[oos]	(Sold) fl 4:5 de Meijer
1803/08/01	AMSCH	0088[H]	*[Anonymous]* | 2 Stuks [Extra Schilderijen] | *Notes:* This lot was added in by hand in the EBNP, LBDa and RKDH copies of the catalogue. The bracketed information in the title appears above lot 55[H] and refers to lots 55[H] to 93[H].	R[oos]	(Sold) fl 11 Gruiter
1803/08/01	AMSCH	0089[H]	*[Anonymous]* | 1 Stuk [Extra Schilderijen] | *Notes:* This lot was added in by hand in the EBNP, LBDa and RKDH copies of the catalogue. The bracketed information in the title appears above lot 55[H] and refers to lots 55[H] to 93[H].	R[oos]	(Sold) fl 8:5 Teengs
1803/08/01	AMSCH	0090[H]	*[Anonymous]* | 1 Stuk [Extra Schilderijen] | *Notes:* This lot was added in by hand in the EBNP, LBDa and RKDH copies of the catalogue. The bracketed information in the title appears above lot 55[H] and refers to lots 55[H] to 93[H].	R[oos]	(Sold) fl 20:10 Hulswit
1803/08/01	AMSCH	0091[H]	*[Anonymous]* | 1 Stuk [Extra Schilderijen] | *Notes:* This lot was added in by hand in the EBNP, LBDa and RKDH copies of the catalogue. The bracketed information in the title appears above lot 55[H] and refers to lots 55[H] to 93[H].	R[oos]	(Sold) fl 8:5 Theengs
1803/08/01	AMSCH	0092[H]	*[Anonymous]* | 1 Stuk [Extra Schilderijen] | *Notes:* This lot was added in by hand in the EBNP, LBDa and RKDH copies of the catalogue. The bracketed information in the title appears above lot 55[H] and refers to lots 55[H] to 93[H].	R[oos]	(Sold) fl 5 Pruijssenaar
1803/08/01	AMSCH	0093[H]	*[Anonymous]* | 1 extra – Een dorp gezigt. [Extra Schilderijen] | *Notes:* This lot was added in by hand in the EBNP, FLNY, LBDa and RKDH copies of the catalogue. The bracketed information in the title appears above lot 55[H] and refers to lots 55[H] to 93[H].	Thoen	(Sold) fl 8 Th Spaan [or] J Spaan
1803/08/17	AMSCH	0095	*[Anonymous]* | Een Jongeling, in oude Hollandsche kleeding, uitvoerig op Koper | *Mat:* op koper *Size:* hoog 9, breed 6 ½ duim	Anna Catharina Putman	(Sold) fl 0:12 L Pakker
1803/08/17	AMSCH	0098	*[Anonymous]* | Een Mans Pourtrait, met een witte Kraag, uitvoerig op Panneel | *Mat:* op paneel *Size:* hoog 22, breed 16 duim	Anna Catharina Putman	(Sold) fl 0:6 L Pakker
1803/08/17	AMSCH	0104	*[Anonymous]* | Een Christus en Maria Beeld, konstig in Yvoor gewerkt	Anna Catharina Putman	(Sold) fl 5:5 V^{n} Leijden

1803/08/17	AMSCH	0105[H]	*[Anonymous]* | 2 Stuks | *Notes:* This lot was added in by hand in the EBNP, LBDa, NGW and RKDH copies of the catalogue.	Anna Catharina Putman	(Sold) fl 0:6 L Pakker
1803/08/17	AMSCH	0106[H]	*[Anonymous]* | 2 dito [Stuks] | *Notes:* This lot was added in by hand in the EBNP, LBDa, NGW and RKDH copies of the catalogue.	Anna Catharina Putman	(Sold) fl 0:10 L Pakker
1803/08/17	AMSCH	0107[H]	*[Anonymous]* | 2 dito [Stuks] | *Notes:* This lot was added in by hand in the EBNP, LBDa, NGW and RKDH copies of the catalogue.	Anna Catharina Putman	(Sold) fl 1 Agina
1803/08/17	AMSCH	0108[H]	*[Anonymous]* | 2 dito [Stuks] | *Notes:* This lot was added in by hand in the EBNP, LBDa, NGW and RKDH copies of the catalogue.	Anna Catharina Putman	(Sold) fl 3:5 Teissier
1803/08/24	HGKAN	0032	*[Anonymous]* | Een Lantschap steld voor, een Zeehaven 't verschiet is met Scheepen gestoffeerd, de tweede en voorgrond is met differente Groepen van figuuren in allerhande vrolyke bezigheeden verbeeld | *Mat:* op doek	[Teissier] [or others]	(Sold) fl 3:5 van Leeuwen
1803/08/24	HGKAN	0036	*Een voornaam Meester* | Een groot Boomryk Lantschap met figuuren en Vee gestoffeerd, konstig geschildert door een voornaam Meester | *Mat:* op doek	[Teissier] [or others]	(Sold) fl 0:10 van Kuyk
1803/08/24	HGKAN	0039	*Een groot Meester* | Een Schets verbeeldt een Gevegt, stout geschildert, door een groot Meester | *Mat:* op doek	[Teissier] [or others]	(Sold) fl 1:6 van der A
1803/08/24	HGKAN	0040	*[Anonymous]* | Een Lantschap | *Mat:* op paneel	[Teissier] [or others]	(Sold) fl 1 van Leeuwen
1803/08/24	HGKAN	0044	*[Anonymous]* | Een Vanitas, op paneel, zonder Lyst | *Mat:* op paneel	[Teissier] [or others]	(Sold) fl 1:18 Giesen
1803/08/24	HGKAN	0048	*[Anonymous]* | Een Lantschap	[Teissier] [or others]	(Unknown)
1803/08/24	HGKAN	0052	*[Anonymous]* | Het Gezicht op het Diaconie Weeshuis te Amsterdam | *Mat:* op doek *Size:* hoog 19, breet 20 duim	[Teissier] [or others]	(Sold) fl 8 Kan
1803/08/24	HGKAN	0067	*[Anonymous]* | Een Mans Portrait	[Teissier] [or others]	(Sold) fl 7 Kan
1803/08/24	HGKAN	0075	*[Anonymous]* | Twee Boere Gezelschapjes	[Teissier] [or others]	(Unknown) fl 7
1803/08/24	HGKAN	0076	*Een voornaam Meester* | Een Doode Christus met Maria en andere figuuren, door een voornaam Meester	[Teissier] [or others]	(Unknown) fl 15
1803/08/24	HGKAN	0078	*Een oud voornaam Meester* | Twee Heeren op het Schaak-bord speelende, door een oud voornaam Meester	[Teissier] [or others]	(Unknown) fl 6
1803/08/24	HGKAN	0089	*Een goed Meester* | De Aanbidding der Herders, door een goed Meester	[Teissier] [or others]	(Unknown) fl 1:2
1803/08/24	HGKAN	0090	*Een goed Meester* | Suzanna met de Boeven, mede door een goed Meester	[Teissier] [or others]	(Sold) fl 0:10 Burger
1803/08/24	HGKAN	0093	*Een zeer goed Meester* | Het Kind Jesus met de Wereld Globe en de geheele Passie verbeelde, door een zeer goed Meester	[Teissier] [or others]	(Sold) fl 2 E
1803/08/24	HGKAN	0094	*Een zeer goed Meester* | Maria, Jesus en Johannes, door een zeer goed Meester	[Teissier] [or others]	(Sold) fl 1:12 Carre
1803/08/24	HGKAN	0095	*Een goed Meester* | Een Famille Stukje met drie Poutraitjes, door een goed Meester	[Teissier] [or others]	(Sold) fl 1 Carre
1803/08/24	HGKAN	0100	*Een goed Meester* | Een Heilige in Devotie, door een goed Meester	[Teissier] [or others]	(Sold) fl 0:10 Carre
1803/08/24	HGKAN	0102	*[Anonymous]* | Een Schildery met drie figuuren	[Teissier] [or others]	(Sold) fl 0:7 Giesen
1803/08/24	HGKAN	0103	*[Anonymous]* | Het Kasteel van Duplessis Mornay	[Teissier] [or others]	(Sold) fl 0:7 Royer
1803/08/24	HGKAN	0104	*Een zeer goed Meester* | Een Magdalena, door een zeer goed Meester	[Teissier] [or others]	(Sold) fl 1:6 Giesen
1803/08/24	HGKAN	0105	*[Anonymous]* | Maria, Jesus en Johannes met een Glorie van Engelen, door &c.	[Teissier] [or others]	(Sold) fl 2:16 Grundel
1803/08/24	HGKAN	0106	*[Anonymous]* | Twee stuk Waayer Bladen, in Lysten met Glazen	[Teissier] [or others]	(Sold) fl 0:8 [Illegible]
1803/08/24	HGKAN	0107	*[Anonymous]* | Philippus de 2de Koning van Spanje en deszelfs Gemallin, 2 stuks	[Teissier] [or others]	(Sold) fl 1:4 Carre
1803/08/24	HGKAN	0108	*[Anonymous]* | Het Pourtrait van Cats & du Plessis Mornay	[Teissier] [or others]	(Sold) fl 10:10 Huybregt
1803/08/24	HGKAN	0109	*[Anonymous]* | Een dito [Pourtrait] van Cats zonder Lyst	[Teissier] [or others]	(Sold) fl 1:6 Huybregt
1803/08/24	HGKAN	0110	*Een goed Meester* | Het Pourtrait van een Hondje, door een goed Meester	[Teissier] [or others]	(Sold) fl 0:6 Kan
1803/08/24	HGKAN	0111	*[Anonymous]* | Drie en Twintig stuks Pourtraitten, welke by het paar zullen verkogt worden	[Teissier] [or others]	(Unknown) fl 5:15
1803/08/24	HGKAN	0112[H]	*[Anonymous]* | [Untitled] | *Notes:* This lot was added in by hand in the RKDH copy of the catalogue, but without giving an artist or title.	[Teissier] [or others]	(Sold) fl 4:5 Van de A
1803/08/24	HGKAN	0113[H]	*[Anonymous]* | [Untitled] | *Notes:* This lot was added in by hand in the RKDH copy of the catalogue, but without giving an artist or title.	[Teissier] [or others]	(Sold) fl 1:10 Kan
1803/08/24	HGKAN	0114[H]	*[Anonymous]* | Schet | *Notes:* This lot was added in by hand in the RKDH copy of the catalogue, but without giving an artist or complete title.	[Teissier] [or others]	(Sold) fl 25 Kan
1803/08/24	HGKAN	0115[H]	*[Anonymous]* | Silver | *Notes:* This lot was added in by hand in the RKDH copy of the catalogue, but it is uncertain whether it is a painting.	[Teissier] [or others]	(Sold) fl 21 Kan
1803/08/24	HGKAN	0116[H]	*[Anonymous]* | Dito [Silver] | *Notes:* This lot was added in by hand in the RKDH copy of the catalogue, but it is uncertain whether it is a painting.	[Teissier] [or others]	(Sold) fl 84 Kan
1803/08/24	HGKAN	A0020	*Een oud Meester* | Een in Meditatie zittende Oud Man, met de pen in de hand, verder een menigte Boeken en meer, door een oud Meester | *Size:* breet 12, hoog 13 ½ duim		(Sold) fl 2:5 Giesen

1803/08/24	HGKAN	A0021	*[Anonymous]* | Een Binnekamer, met een zittende Heer en Twee staande Boeren, verders een Tuyn Gezigt | *Size:* [breet] 24, hoog 18 duim		(Sold) fl 1:8 Giesen
1803/08/24	HGKAN	A0023	*[Anonymous]* | Een Berg Gezigt met eenig Vee | *Mat:* op paneel *Size:* breet 34, hoog 22 duim		(Sold) fl 0:15 van Giesen
1803/08/24	HGKAN	A0024	*[Anonymous]* | Een Extra fraay Stuk, verbeeldende een Vrouw die Groentens en Fruit verkoopt, door een zeer goed Meester | *Mat:* op doek		(Sold) fl 8 Kan
1803/08/24	HGKAN	A0026	*[Anonymous]* | Een Slapende Vrouw, welke de Man een Pot met Water op haar Hooft stort, in 1673 | *Inscr:* 1673 (dated?) *Notes:* It is unclear whether the date is inscribed on the painting.		(Sold) fl 3:5 Giesen
1803/09/07	AMSCH	0016	*Inconnu* | Twee stuks Brabandsche Dorpgezichten, met Geboomte en stoffagie van Beeldjes en Schaapen, zeer uitvoerig [Deux vues de villages Flamands ; ils sont ornés d'arbres, de figures et de moutons ; d'un très beau fini] | *Mat:* op paneel *Size:* hoog 9, breed 12 duim	Smidt	(Sold) fl 14:10 Gruiter
1803/09/07	AMSCH	0231	*[Anonymous]* | Een staande Maria, met een Bloemkrans in de hand, houdende met de andere het Kind Jezu, die naar dezelve schynt te grypen; alles is meesterlyk en kragtig gepenceeld [Une Ste.-Vierge debout, tenant une couronne de fleurs dans une main et l'enfant Jésus par l'autre ; ce dernier paroit vouloir s'attacher à sa mère ; l'ensemble est d'une composition précieuse et peint avec vigueur] | *Mat:* op doek *Size:* hoog 47, breed 37 duim	Smidt	(Sold) fl 16:10 C S Roos
1803/09/07	AMSCH	0232	*[Anonymous]* | In een Boeren Schuur, ziet men een menigte vrolyke Huislieden, zig met danssen, eeten en drinken vermaaken; alles plaisant verbeeld en kragtig geschilderd [L'intérieur d'une grange, où plusieurs paysans se livrent à la gaïté etc. et s'amusent à boire, à manger et à danser ; composition joviale et d'une touche vigoureuse] | *Mat:* op paneel *Size:* hoog 23, breed 34 duim	Smidt	(Bought In) fl 25
1803/09/07	AMSCH	0235	*Een goed Meester* | Twee stuks, een Mans en Vrouwe Pourtrait in al oude kleeding, door een goed Meester [Deux tableaux représentant les portraits d'un homme et d'une femme, vétus d'une manière antique ; par un bon maître] | *Mat:* op paneel *Size:* hoog 10, breed 8 duim	Smidt	(Bought In) fl 2
1803/09/07	AMSCH	0240	*Een goed Meester* | Een Boom- en Bergachtig Landschap met een Waterval, verbeeldende een zwaare Storm; fix geschilderd, door een goed Meester [Un paysage plein de rochers et d'arbres avec une cascade formant un gros torrent ; excellent tableau dont la touche et la composition décelent un bon maître] | *Mat:* op doek *Size:* hoog 26, breed 32 duim	Smidt	(Sold) fl 2:10 Van den Brink
1803/09/07	AMSCH	0246	*[Anonymous]* | Een Minnewigt, zittende op een Steen, met een Zéehoorn in de hand; meesterlyk en bevallig geschilderd [Un amour assis sur une pierre et tenant à la main une coquille ; composition de maitre et d'une touche agréable] | *Mat:* op doek *Size:* hoog 35, breed 21 duim	Smidt	(Sold) fl 2 Scheffer
1803/09/07	AMSCH	0248	*[Anonymous]* | Een Meisje met een Kaars in de hand, schynt een Gevangenen te willen bezoeken; het Kaarslicht doet een goede werking, en is voorts alleruitvoerigst geschilderd [Une jeune fille, une chandelle à la main, semble aller visiter un prisonnier ; la lumière de la chandelle est d'un très bel effet. L'exécution du tableau est parfaitement bien soignée] | *Mat:* op paneel *Size:* hoog 10, breed 8 duim	Smidt	(Bought In) fl 13
1803/09/07	AMSCH	0252	*[Anonymous]* | Twee stuks Italiaansche Landschappen, gestoffeerd met Ruïnen en verscheide Beelden; uitvoerig en bevallig gepenceeld [Deux paysages Italiens, entremelé de ruines et de beaucoup de figures ; parfaitement bien peint] | *Mat:* op doek *Size:* ieder hoog 13, breed 19 duim	Smidt	(Sold) fl 16:10 Tessier
1803/09/07	AMSCH	0259	*[Anonymous]* | Een Oud Man, van vooren te zien, ten halver lyf; kragtig op Paneel geschilderd [Un vieillard, vu de face et à demi-corps ; d'un coloris vigoureux] | *Mat:* op paneel *Size:* hoog 20, breed 14 duim	Smidt	(Sold) fl 3:10 Gruiter
1803/09/07	AMSCH	0261	*[Anonymous]* | Twee stuks Bachanalen Feesten, waarin Sileenus en verscheide Bachanten gezien worden; ryk van Ordonantie, bevallig van Coloriet, en uitvoerig geschilderd [Deux Baccanales, dans lesquelles figurent Silène et plusieurs baccantes ; d'une ordonnance riche et d'un coloris agréable] | *Mat:* op koper *Size:* ieder hoog 13, br. 16 duim	Smidt	(Sold) fl 30 C S Roos
1803/09/07	AMSCH	0262	*[Anonymous]* | Een Oude Vrouw, zittende in een Stoel, van vooren te zien, rustende met haar handen op een Boek; zeer fraai en Natuurlyk behandeld [Une vieille femme assise dans un siége, vue en face et reposant ses mains sur un livre ; composition régulière et naturelle] | *Mat:* op doek *Size:* hoog 30, breed 25 duim	Smidt	(Bought In) fl 15
1803/09/07	AMSCH	0266	*[Anonymous]* | In een Rotsachtig Landschap ziet men de boetvaardige Maria Magdaléna, in een meditéerende gestalte, rustende op een Matras; het is meesterlyk geschilderd op Doek [Ste.-Marie-Madelaine, au milieu d'un paysage aride et plein de rochers, et dans l'attitude d'une pénitente, reposant sur un grabat ; d'une composition excellente] | *Mat:* op doek *Size:* hoog 38, breed 34 duim	Smidt	(Bought In) fl 5
1803/09/07	AMSCH	0268	*[Anonymous]* | Een Rhyngezicht, gestoffeerd met een ménigte Beeldjes en Vaartuigen [Une vue du Rhin, enrichie d'une agréable variété de figures et d'objets] | *Mat:* op doek *Size:* hoog 32, breed 44 duim [Haut 14, large 18 pouces] *Notes:* The dimensions differ in the Dutch and French editions of the catalogue.	Smidt	(Sold) fl 30 W Reijers

1803/09/07	AMSCH	0270	*[Anonymous]* | Twee stuks met dood Gevogelte en Distelplanten; kragtig en uitvoerig op Doek [Deux tableaux réprésentant de la volaille tuée, et une touffe de plantes et de chardons ; morceaux d'une belle expression et d'un coloris vigoureux] | *Mat:* op doek *Size:* ieder hoog 17, breed 24 duim	Smidt	(Sold) fl 8 Gruiter
1803/09/07	AMSCH	0275	*[Anonymous]* | Eenige Danssende Boeren, in een Binnenhuis [Une danse de paysans et de paysannes dans l'intérieur d'une maison] | *Mat:* op paneel *Size:* hoog 13, breed 15 duim	Smidt	(Sold) fl 1 W^{m} v der Schley
1803/09/07	AMSCH	0277	*Een goed Meester* | Twee stuks Italiaansche Zeehavens, ryk gestoffeerd; door een goed Meester [Deux ports de mer d'Italie ; composition riche ; par un excellent maître] | *Mat:* op doek *Size:* hoog 21, breed 30 duim	Smidt	(Sold) fl 14 C S Roos
1803/09/07	AMSCH	0278	*Een Braaf Meester* | In een Boom- en Bergachtig Landschap ziet men eenige ter Jacht gaande Lieden; fiks gepenceeld, door een Braaf Meester [Plusieurs personnes se livrant au plaisir de la chasse dans un paysage montagneux et plein de bois ; belle exécution sur toile, par un bon maître.] | *Mat:* op doek *Size:* hoog 29, breed 46 duim	Smidt	(Sold) fl 8:10 Toselli
1803/09/07	AMSCH	0281	*[Anonymous]* | Een Berg- en Boomryk Landschap, alwaar eenige Struikrovers bézig zyn eenige Wagens en Passagiers te plunderen; kragtig en zonachtig op Paneel [Un paysage montueux, dans lequel des voleurs de grand chemin son occupés à dépouiller une voiture publique et des passagers ; il règne un beau jour sur l'ensemble de ce tableau] | *Mat:* op paneel *Size:* hoog 20, breed 26 duim *Notes:* The dimensions are given in the French edition as "Haut 20, large 25 pouces"; the width has been changed by hand to "26" in the RKDH copy of the catalogue.	Smidt	(Bought In) fl 5
1803/09/07	AMSCH	0283	*[Anonymous]* | De Vinding van Mozes [La découverte de Moïse] | *Mat:* op paneel *Size:* hoog 12, breed 9 duim	Smidt	(Sold) fl 1:5 van den Brink
1803/09/07	AMSCH	0284	*[Anonymous]* | Een Bloemstukje [Un assemblage de fleurs] | *Mat:* op paneel *Size:* hoog 12, breed 9 duim *Notes:* This lot was misnumbered no. 184 in the French edition of the catalogue.	Smidt	(Sold) fl 0:10 L Pakker
1803/09/07	AMSCH	0285	*[Anonymous]* | Een stil Leeven [Un intérieur] | *Mat:* op paneel *Size:* hoog 8, breed 12 duim	Smidt	(Sold) fl 1 Scheffer
1803/09/07	AMSCH	0286	*[Anonymous]* | Een dito [stil Leeven] [Un semblable [intérieur] ; même grandeur] | *Mat:* op paneel *Size:* hoog 8, breed 12 ½ duim [Haut 8, large 12 pouces] *Notes:* The dimensions differ in the Dutch and French editions of the catalogue.	Smidt	(Sold) fl 0:12 v d Schley
1803/09/07	AMSCH	0287	*[Anonymous]* | Twee dito [stil Leevens] [Deux intérieurs] | *Mat:* op doek *Size:* hoog 13, breed 25 duim	Smidt	(Sold) fl 1:15 L Pakker
1803/09/07	AMSCH	0288	*[Anonymous]* | Een Maria met het Kindje [La Ste.-Vierge avec l'enfant Jésus] | *Mat:* op paneel *Size:* hoog 14, breed 11 duim *Notes:* The dimensions are given in the French edition as "Haut 14, large 14 pouces"; the width has been changed by hand to "11" in the RKDH copy of the catalogue.	Smidt	(Sold) fl 1:10 L Pakker
1803/09/07	AMSCH	0289	*[Anonymous]* | Een Landschap [Un paysage] | *Mat:* op paneel *Size:* hoog 9, breed 11 duim	Smidt	(Sold) fl 0:2 L Pakker
1803/09/07	AMSCH	0290	*[Anonymous]* | Een Man met een Kat [Un homme avec un chat.] | *Size:* hoog 10, breed 7 ½	Smidt	(Sold) fl 1 de Meijer
1803/10/10	MGBEO	0001	*[Anonymous]* | [Untitled] | *Notes:* The only extant copy of this catalogue is annotated with the buyers and prices, but it does not include a printed list of the paintings.		(Sold) £ 0:1 Ooms
1803/10/10	MGBEO	0002	*[Anonymous]* | [Untitled] | *Notes:* The only extant copy of this catalogue is annotated with the buyers and prices, but it does not include a printed list of the paintings.		(Sold) £ 0:1 Ooms
1803/10/10	MGBEO	0003	*[Anonymous]* | [Untitled] | *Notes:* The only extant copy of this catalogue is annotated with the buyers and prices, but it does not include a printed list of the paintings.		(Sold) £ 0:1 Manul
1803/10/10	MGBEO	0004	*[Anonymous]* | [Untitled] | *Notes:* The only extant copy of this catalogue is annotated with the buyers and prices, but it does not include a printed list of the paintings.		(Sold) £ 0:4 Buike
1803/10/10	MGBEO	0005	*[Anonymous]* | [Untitled] | *Notes:* The only extant copy of this catalogue is annotated with the buyers and prices, but it does not include a printed list of the paintings.		(Sold) £ 0:1 Meertens
1803/10/10	MGBEO	0006	*[Anonymous]* | [Untitled] | *Notes:* The only extant copy of this catalogue is annotated with the buyers and prices, but it does not include a printed list of the paintings.		(Sold) £ 0:3 for lots 6 & 7. Lepelaar
1803/10/10	MGBEO	0007	*[Anonymous]* | [Untitled] | *Notes:* The only extant copy of this catalogue is annotated with the buyers and prices, but it does not include a printed list of the paintings.		(Sold) £ 0:3 for lots 6 & 7. Lepelaar
1803/10/10	MGBEO	0008	*[Anonymous]* | [Untitled] | *Notes:* The only extant copy of this catalogue is annotated with the buyers and prices, but it does not include a printed list of the paintings.		(Sold) £ 0:2 Meijer
1803/10/10	MGBEO	0009	*[Anonymous]* | [Untitled] | *Notes:* The only extant copy of this catalogue is annotated with the buyers and prices, but it does not include a printed list of the paintings.		(Sold) £ 0:4 Ooms

1803/10/10	MGBEO	0010	*[Anonymous]* | [Untitled] | *Notes:* The only extant copy of this catalogue is annotated with the buyers and prices, but it does not include a printed list of the paintings.	(Sold) £ 0:1 Ooms
1803/10/10	MGBEO	0011	*[Anonymous]* | [Untitled] | *Notes:* The only extant copy of this catalogue is annotated with the buyers and prices, but it does not include a printed list of the paintings.	(Sold) £ 0:2 G M Petersen
1803/10/10	MGBEO	0012	*[Anonymous]* | [Untitled] | *Notes:* The only extant copy of this catalogue is annotated with the buyers and prices, but it does not include a printed list of the paintings.	(Sold) £ 1:1 G M Petersen
1803/10/10	MGBEO	0013	*[Anonymous]* | [Untitled] | *Notes:* The only extant copy of this catalogue is annotated with the buyers and prices, but it does not include a printed list of the paintings.	(Sold) £ 0:1 for lots 13 & 14. v d Wiere
1803/10/10	MGBEO	0014	*[Anonymous]* | [Untitled] | *Notes:* The only extant copy of this catalogue is annotated with the buyers and prices, but it does not include a printed list of the paintings.	(Sold) £ 0:1 for lots 13 & 14. v d Wiere
1803/10/10	MGBEO	0015	*[Anonymous]* | [Untitled] | *Notes:* The only extant copy of this catalogue is annotated with the buyers and prices, but it does not include a printed list of the paintings.	(Sold) £ 0:1 Buiker
1803/10/10	MGBEO	0016	*[Anonymous]* | [Untitled] | *Notes:* The only extant copy of this catalogue is annotated with the buyers and prices, but it does not include a printed list of the paintings.	(Sold) £ 0:6 Doct Boom
1803/10/10	MGBEO	0017	*[Anonymous]* | [Untitled] | *Notes:* The only extant copy of this catalogue is annotated with the buyers and prices, but it does not include a printed list of the paintings.	(Sold) £ 0:1 van Uije
1803/10/10	MGBEO	0018	*[Anonymous]* | [Untitled] | *Notes:* The only extant copy of this catalogue is annotated with the buyers and prices, but it does not include a printed list of the paintings.	(Sold) £ 0:8 Andel
1803/10/10	MGBEO	0019	*[Anonymous]* | [Untitled] | *Notes:* The only extant copy of this catalogue is annotated with the buyers and prices, but it does not include a printed list of the paintings.	(Sold) £ 0:1 for lots 19 & 20. van Eps
1803/10/10	MGBEO	0020	*[Anonymous]* | [Untitled] | *Notes:* The only extant copy of this catalogue is annotated with the buyers and prices, but it does not include a printed list of the paintings.	(Sold) £ 0:1 for lots 19 & 20. van Eps
1803/10/10	MGBEO	0021	*[Anonymous]* | [Untitled] | *Notes:* The only extant copy of this catalogue is annotated with the buyers and prices, but it does not include a printed list of the paintings.	(Sold) £ 0:3 Schipperl
1803/10/10	MGBEO	0022	*[Anonymous]* | [Untitled] | *Notes:* The only extant copy of this catalogue is annotated with the buyers and prices, but it does not include a printed list of the paintings.	(Sold) £ 0:12 Doct Boom
1803/10/10	MGBEO	0023	*[Anonymous]* | [Untitled] | *Notes:* The only extant copy of this catalogue is annotated with the buyers and prices, but it does not include a printed list of the paintings.	(Sold) £ 0:2 for lots 23 & 24. Pels
1803/10/10	MGBEO	0024	*[Anonymous]* | [Untitled] | *Notes:* The only extant copy of this catalogue is annotated with the buyers and prices, but it does not include a printed list of the paintings.	(Sold) £ 0:2 for lots 23 & 24. Pels
1803/10/10	MGBEO	0025	*[Anonymous]* | [Untitled] | *Notes:* The only extant copy of this catalogue is annotated with the buyers and prices, but it does not include a printed list of the paintings.	(Sold) £ 0:2 A Meertens
1803/10/10	MGBEO	0026	*[Anonymous]* | [Untitled] | *Notes:* The only extant copy of this catalogue is annotated with the buyers and prices, but it does not include a printed list of the paintings.	(Sold) £ 0:2 Weksteen
1803/10/10	MGBEO	0027	*[Anonymous]* | [Untitled] | *Notes:* The only extant copy of this catalogue is annotated with the buyers and prices, but it does not include a printed list of the paintings.	(Sold) £ 0:6 A v d Wiere
1803/10/10	MGBEO	0028	*[Anonymous]* | [Untitled] | *Notes:* The only extant copy of this catalogue is annotated with the buyers and prices, but it does not include a printed list of the paintings.	(Sold) £ 0:1 Schippers
1803/10/10	MGBEO	0029	*[Anonymous]* | [Untitled] | *Notes:* The only extant copy of this catalogue is annotated with the buyers and prices, but it does not include a printed list of the paintings.	(Sold) £ 0:1 Meertens
1803/10/10	MGBEO	0030	*[Anonymous]* | [Untitled] | *Notes:* The only extant copy of this catalogue is annotated with the buyers and prices, but it does not include a printed list of the paintings.	(Sold) £ 0:1 for lots 30 & 31. Ooms
1803/10/10	MGBEO	0031	*[Anonymous]* | [Untitled] | *Notes:* The only extant copy of this catalogue is annotated with the buyers and prices, but it does not include a printed list of the paintings.	(Sold) £ 0:1 for lots 30 & 31. Ooms
1803/10/10	MGBEO	0032	*[Anonymous]* | [Untitled] | *Notes:* The only extant copy of this catalogue is annotated with the buyers and prices, but it does not include a printed list of the paintings.	(Sold) £ 1:6 de Maagd
1803/10/10	MGBEO	0034	*[Anonymous]* | [Untitled] | *Notes:* The only extant copy of this catalogue is annotated with the buyers and prices, but it does not include a printed list of the paintings.	(Sold) £ 0:1 Bosse

1803/10/10	MGBEO	0035	*[Anonymous]* | [Untitled] | *Notes:* The only extant copy of this catalogue is annotated with the buyers and prices, but it does not include a printed list of the paintings.		(Sold) £ 0:1 W Ingelse
1803/10/10	MGBEO	0036	*[Anonymous]* | [Untitled] | *Notes:* The only extant copy of this catalogue is annotated with the buyers and prices, but it does not include a printed list of the paintings.		(Sold) £ 0:3 for lots 36 & 37. Meertens
1803/10/10	MGBEO	0037	*[Anonymous]* | [Untitled] | *Notes:* The only extant copy of this catalogue is annotated with the buyers and prices, but it does not include a printed list of the paintings.		(Sold) £ 0:3 for lots 36 & 37. Meertens
1803/10/24	HGDAW	0005	*[Anonymous]* | Een stukje, verbeeldende Simeon in de Gevangenis met zyn Dochter, in een vergulde lyst [Schilderyen in Olyverw] | *Mat:* in olyverf *Notes:* The bracketed information in the title appears above lot 1 and refers to lots 1 to 16.	M van Daalen Wetters	(Unknown)
1803/10/24	HGDAW	0006	*[Anonymous]* | Een groot stuk met Visschen, in een zwarte lyst [Schilderyen in Olyverw] | *Mat:* in olyverf *Notes:* The bracketed information in the title appears above lot 1 and refers to lots 1 to 16.	M van Daalen Wetters	(Unknown)
1803/10/24	HGDAW	0007	*[Anonymous]* | Een groot schoorsteen stuk verbeeldende de Vrouw in overspel [Schilderyen in Olyverw] | *Mat:* in olyverf *Notes:* The bracketed information in the title appears above lot 1 and refers to lots 1 to 16.	M van Daalen Wetters	(Unknown)
1803/10/24	HGDAW	0008	*[Anonymous]* | Een stil leeven in een zwarte lyst [Schilderyen in Olyverw] | *Mat:* in olyverf *Notes:* The bracketed information in the title appears above lot 1 and refers to lots 1 to 16.	M van Daalen Wetters	(Unknown)
1803/10/24	HGDAW	0009	*[Anonymous]* | Twee Familie stukken in zwarte lysten [Schilderyen in Olyverw] | *Mat:* in olyverf *Notes:* The bracketed information in the title appears above lot 1 and refers to lots 1 to 16.	M van Daalen Wetters	(Unknown)
1803/10/24	HGDAW	0010	*[Anonymous]* | Een dito [stuk] met een Vroubeeld in dito [zwarte] lyst [Schilderyen in Olyverw] | *Mat:* in olyverf *Notes:* The bracketed information in the title about the medium appears above lot 1 and refers to lots 1 to 16.	M van Daalen Wetters	(Unknown)
1803/10/24	HGDAW	0011	*[Anonymous]* | Een Landschap in een dito [zwarte] lyst [Schilderyen in Olyverw] | *Mat:* in olyverf *Notes:* The bracketed information in the title about the medium appears above lot 1 and refers to lots 1 to 16.	M van Daalen Wetters	(Unknown)
1803/10/24	HGDAW	0012	*[Anonymous]* | Een Historieel op papier in vergulde lyst [Schilderyen in Olyverw] | *Mat:* in olyverf op papier *Notes:* The bracketed information in the title appears above lot 1 and refers to lots 1 to 16.	M van Daalen Wetters	(Unknown)
1803/10/24	HGDAW	0013	*[Anonymous]* | Een dito [Historieel] op paneel in een zwarte lyst [Schilderyen in Olyverw] | *Mat:* in olyverf op paneel *Notes:* The bracketed information in the title about the medium appears above lot 1 and refers to lots 1 to 16.	M van Daalen Wetters	(Unknown)
1803/10/24	HGDAW	0014	*[Anonymous]* | Een Musiceerend Man in 't rond in dito [zwarte] lyst [Schilderyen in Olyverw] | *Mat:* in olyverf *Fmt:* rond *Notes:* The bracketed information in the title about the medium appears above lot 1 and refers to lots 1 to 16.	M van Daalen Wetters	(Unknown)
1803/10/24	HGDAW	0015	*[Anonymous]* | Een stukje met dood wild in een verguld lystje [Schilderyen in Olyverw] | *Mat:* in olyverf *Notes:* The bracketed information in the title appears above lot 1 and refers to lots 1 to 16.	M van Daalen Wetters	(Unknown)
1803/10/24	HGDAW	0016	*[Anonymous]* | Een grappige met Boertjes [Schilderyen in Olyverw] | *Mat:* in olyverf *Notes:* The bracketed information in the title appears above lot 1 and refers to lots 1 to 16.	M van Daalen Wetters	(Unknown)
1803/11/30	MGBEO	0005	*Een goed Meester* | Een Chimist in zyn Laboratorium, met veel Bywerk, door een goed Meester | *Mat:* op doek *Size:* hoog 24 duim, breed 18 ½ duim	Samuel de Wind	(Sold) £ 0:13 Geld
1803/11/30	MGBEO	0006	*Een oud goed Meester* | De Kruisdraging van Christus, ryk gestoffeerd met figuuren, door een oud goed Meester | *Mat:* op paneel *Size:* hoog 14 duim, breed 28 ½ duim	Samuel de Wind	(Sold) £ 0:4 G M Petersen
1803/11/30	MGBEO	0013	*[Anonymous]* | De Kop van Seneca | *Mat:* op paneel *Size:* hoog 10 duim, breed 9 duim *Notes:* This lot was sold with lot 12 by C. Holsteijn.	Samuel de Wind	(Sold) £ 0:4 for lots 12 & 13. van Benthem
1803/11/30	MGBEO	0014	*[Anonymous]* | Het Portrait van H. Boerhaave | *Mat:* op paneel *Size:* hoog 10 duim, breed 9 duim	Samuel de Wind	(Sold) £ 0:5 van Benthem
1803/11/30	MGBEO	0017	*[Anonymous]* | Een Bloemstukje, fraai gepenseeld op een ovaal Paneel | *Mat:* op paneel *Fmt:* ovaal *Size:* hoog 13 duim, breed 10 duim	Samuel de Wind	(Sold) £ 0:1 Van den Andel
1803/12/12	AMSCH	0120	*Een goed Meester* | De Brand van het Oude Stadhuis van Amsterdam; natuurlyk afgebeeld door een goed Meester | *Mat:* op paneel *Size:* hoog 9, br. 12 ½ duim	W	(Sold) fl 7 Gruiter
1803/12/12	AMSCH	0123	*Een goed Meester* | Een Boom en Bergachtig Italiaansch Landschap, met een Rivier en stoffagie, natuurlyk op Doek, door een goed Meester | *Mat:* op doek *Size:* hoog 27, breed 37 duim	V[inkeles?]	(Sold) fl 14:10 La Bouchere
1803/12/12	AMSCH	0125	*[Anonymous]* | Een ryk met Beelden en Altaren gestoffeerde Roomsche Kerk; kragtig op Doek | *Mat:* op doek *Size:* hoog 33, breed 23 duim	W	(Sold) fl 13 Th^{S} Spaan
1803/12/12	AMSCH	0126	*[Anonymous]* | Een Christus Hoofd | *Size:* hoog 32, breed 24 duim	W	(Sold) fl 5:5 Gruiter

1803/12/12	AMSCH	0127	*[Anonymous]* | Een Meisjes Hoofd | *Size:* hoog 14, br 14 duim	W	(Sold) fl 10 Chalome
1803/12/12	AMSCH	0128	*[Anonymous]* | Een Landschap met Jagers te paard en te voet | *Mat:* op doek *Size:* hoog 14, breed 16 duim	W	(Sold) fl 3 Coclers
1803/12/12	AMSCH	0132	*[Anonymous]* | Een Zeegezigt met Scheepen | *Mat:* op paneel *Size:* hoog 14, breed 19 duim	E	(Sold) fl 3:10 Salsedo
1803/12/12	AMSCH	0134	*Een goed Meester* | Een Historieele Ordonantie van verscheide Beelden; door een goed Meester | *Size:* hoog 16, breed 14 duim	H	(Sold) fl 1 Th Spaan
1803/12/12	AMSCH	0139	*Een goed Meester* | Een magnifiek Mans-pourtrait; meesterlyk op Doek, door een goed Meester | *Mat:* op doek *Size:* hoog 34, breed 25 duim	Arnoud de Lange	(Sold) fl 4 Mensard
1803/12/12	AMSCH	0150	*[Anonymous]* | Een bevallig gestoffeerd Landschapje | *Mat:* op paneel *Size:* hoog 6, breed 8 duim	D	(Sold) fl 0:16 Scheffers
1803/12/12	AMSCH	0151	*[Anonymous]* | Een dito [Landschapje] met Gebouwen | *Mat:* op paneel *Size:* hoog 7, breed 9 duim *Notes:* It is unclear what "dito" refers to in the title.	D	(Sold) fl 0:12 Coclers
1803/12/12	AMSCH	0156	*[Anonymous]* | Twee Landschapjes met stoffagie van Beeldjes en Beestjes | *Mat:* op paneel *Size:* hoog 8, breed 10 duim	D	(Sold) fl 1:15 Coclers
1803/12/12	AMSCH	0157	*[Anonymous]* | Twee dito [Landschapjes] dito [met stoffagie van Beeldjes en Beestjes] | *Size:* hoog 11, breed 9 duim *Notes:* It is unclear what "dito" refers to in the title.	D	(Sold) fl 2 Gruiter
1803/12/12	AMSCH	0158	*[Anonymous]* | Een Jongeling in een Nis met een Vogelkooy | *Mat:* op doek *Size:* hoog 10, breed 8 duim	D	(Sold) fl 3 Hijm Pakker
1803/12/12	AMSCH	0160	*[Anonymous]* | Een Speldewerkster | *Mat:* op paneel *Size:* hoog 10, breed 8 duim	D	(Sold) fl 4 Uselino
1803/12/12	AMSCH	0161	*[Anonymous]* | Twee bevallige gestoffeerde Landschapjes | *Mat:* op paneel *Size:* hoog 10, breed 9 duim	D	(Sold) fl 5 Coclers
1803/12/12	AMSCH	0162[H]	*[Anonymous]* | 1 Schilderij | *Notes:* This lot was added in by hand in the LBDa and RKDH copies of the catalogue.	V[inkeles?]	(Sold) fl 0:10 L Pakker
1803/12/12	AMSCH	0163[H]	*[Anonymous]* | 1 Schilderij | *Notes:* This lot was added in by hand in the LBDa and RKDH copies of the catalogue.	V[inkeles?]	(Sold) fl 1:5 Gruiter
1803/12/12	AMSCH	0164[H]	*[Anonymous]* | 1 Schilderij | *Notes:* This lot was added in by hand in the LBDa and RKDH copies of the catalogue.	V[inkeles?]	(Sold) fl 1:5 Coclers
1803/12/12	AMSCH	0165[H]	*[Anonymous]* | 1 Schilderij | *Notes:* This lot was added in by hand in the LBDa and RKDH copies of the catalogue.	V[inkeles?]	(Sold) fl 0:6 L Pakker
1803/12/12	AMSCH	0166[H]	*[Anonymous]* | 1 Schilderij | *Notes:* This lot was added in by hand in the LBDa and RKDH copies of the catalogue.	V[inkeles?]	(Sold) fl 1:10 Coclers
1803/12/12	AMSCH	0167[H]	*[Anonymous]* | 4 Schilderijen | *Notes:* This lot was added in by hand in the LBDa and RKDH copies of the catalogue.	V[inkeles?]	(Sold) fl 8 Mensard
1803/12/12	AMSCH	0168[H]	*[Anonymous]* | 1 Schilderij | *Notes:* This lot was added in by hand in the LBDa and RKDH copies of the catalogue.	V[inkeles?]	(Sold) fl 1 L Pakker
1803/12/12	AMSCH	0169[H]	*[Anonymous]* | 1 Schilderij | *Notes:* This lot was added in by hand in the LBDa and RKDH copies of the catalogue.	V[inkeles?]	(Sold) fl 2:5 for lots 169[H]-171[H]. Hafner
1803/12/12	AMSCH	0170[H]	*[Anonymous]* | 1 Schilderij | *Notes:* This lot was added in by hand in the LBDa and RKDH copies of the catalogue.	V[inkeles?]	(Sold) fl 2:5 for lots 169[H]-171[H]. Hafner
1803/12/12	AMSCH	0171[H]	*[Anonymous]* | 1 Schilderij | *Notes:* This lot was added in by hand in the LBDa and RKDH copies of the catalogue.	V[inkeles?]	(Sold) fl 2:5 for lots 169[H]-171[H]. Hafner
1803/12/12	AMSCH	0172[H]	*[Anonymous]* | 1 Schilderij | *Notes:* This lot was added in by hand in the LBDa and RKDH copies of the catalogue.	V[inkeles?]	(Sold) fl 0:18 Hodges
1803/12/12	AMSCH	0173[H]	*[Anonymous]* | 1 Schilderij | *Notes:* This lot was added in by hand in the LBDa and RKDH copies of the catalogue.	V[inkeles?]	(Sold) fl 1:5 Mensard
1803/12/12	AMSCH	0174[H]	*[Anonymous]* | 1 Schilderij | *Notes:* This lot was added in by hand in the LBDa and RKDH copies of the catalogue.	V[inkeles?]	(Sold) fl 3:15 for lots 174[H] & 175[H]. Gruiter
1803/12/12	AMSCH	0175[H]	*[Anonymous]* | 1 Schilderij | *Notes:* This lot was added in by hand in the LBDa and RKDH copies of the catalogue.	V[inkeles?]	(Sold) fl 3:15 for lots 174[H] & 175[H]. Gruiter
1803/12/12	AMSCH	0176[H]	*[Anonymous]* | 1 Schilderij | *Notes:* This lot was added in by hand in the LBDa and RKDH copies of the catalogue.	V[inkeles?]	(Sold) fl 1:5 Mensard
1803/12/12	AMSCH	0177[H]	*[Anonymous]* | 1 Schilderij | *Notes:* This lot was added in by hand in the LBDa and RKDH copies of the catalogue.	V[inkeles?]	(Sold) fl 2:5 Coclers
1803/12/12	AMSCH	0178[H]	*[Anonymous]* | 2 Schilderijen | *Notes:* This lot was added in by hand in the LBDa and RKDH copies of the catalogue.	V[inkeles?]	(Sold) fl 2:15 for lots 178[H] & 179[H]. Hafner
1803/12/12	AMSCH	0179[H]	*[Anonymous]* | 1 Schilderij | *Notes:* This lot was added in by hand in the LBDa and RKDH copies of the catalogue.	V[inkeles?]	(Sold) fl 2:15 for lots 178[H] & 179[H]. Hafner

1803/12/12	AMSCH	0180[H]	*[Anonymous]* | 1 Schilderij | *Notes:* This lot was added in by hand in the LBDa and RKDH copies of the catalogue.	V[inkeles?]	(Sold) fl 1:5 Mensard
1803/12/12	AMSCH	0181[H]	*[Anonymous]* | 2 Schilderijen | *Notes:* This lot was added in by hand in the LBDa and RKDH copies of the catalogue.	V[inkeles?]	(Sold) fl 1:10 Gruiter
1803/12/12	AMSCH	0182[H]	*[Anonymous]* | 1 Schilderij | *Notes:* This lot was added in by hand in the LBDa and RKDH copies of the catalogue.	V[inkeles?]	(Sold) fl 2:5 for lots 182[H] & 183[H]. Gruiter
1803/12/12	AMSCH	0183[H]	*[Anonymous]* | 1 Schilderij | *Notes:* This lot was added in by hand in the LBDa and RKDH copies of the catalogue.	V[inkeles?]	(Sold) fl 2:5 for lots 182[H] & 183[H]. Gruiter
1803/12/12	AMSCH	0184[H]	*[Anonymous]* | 1 Schilderij | *Notes:* This lot was added in by hand in the LBDa and RKDH copies of the catalogue.	V[inkeles?]	(Sold) fl 2:5 Gruiter
1803/12/12	AMSCH	0185[H]	*[Anonymous]* | 1 Schilderij | *Notes:* This lot was added in by hand in the LBDa and RKDH copies of the catalogue.	V[inkeles?]	(Sold) fl 2:5 for lots 185[H] & 186[H]. Gruiter
1803/12/12	AMSCH	0186[H]	*[Anonymous]* | 1 Schilderij | *Notes:* This lot was added in by hand in the LBDa and RKDH copies of the catalogue.	V[inkeles?]	(Sold) fl 2:5 for lots 185[H] & 186[H]. Gruiter
1803/12/12	AMSCH	0187[H]	*[Anonymous]* | 1 Schilderij | *Notes:* This lot was added in by hand in the LBDa and RKDH copies of the catalogue.	V[inkeles?]	(Sold) fl 0:14 for lots 187[H] & 188[H]. Gruiter
1803/12/12	AMSCH	0188[H]	*[Anonymous]* | 1 Schilderij | *Notes:* This lot was added in by hand in the LBDa and RKDH copies of the catalogue.	V[inkeles?]	(Sold) fl 0:14 for lots 187[H] & 188[H]. Gruiter
1803/12/12	AMSCH	0189[H]	*[Anonymous]* | 1 Schilderij | *Notes:* This lot was added in by hand in the LBDa and RKDH copies of the catalogue.	V[inkeles?]	(Sold) fl 6:15 La Boucher
1803/12/12	AMSCH	0190[H]	*[Anonymous]* | 1 Schilderij | *Notes:* This lot was added in by hand in the LBDa and RKDH copies of the catalogue.	V[inkeles?]	(Sold) fl 1:10 Mensard
1803/12/12	AMSCH	0191[H]	*[Anonymous]* | 2 Schilderijen | *Notes:* This lot was added in by hand in the LBDa and RKDH copies of the catalogue.	V[inkeles?]	(Sold) fl 1:5 Gruiter
1803/12/12	AMSCH	0192[H]	*[Anonymous]* | 2 Schilderijen | *Notes:* This lot was added in by hand in the LBDa and RKDH copies of the catalogue.	V[inkeles?]	(Sold) fl 4 Coclers
1803/12/12	AMSCH	0193[H]	*[Anonymous]* | 3 Schilderijen | *Notes:* This lot was added in by hand in the LBDa and RKDH copies of the catalogue.	V[inkeles?]	(Sold) fl 6:5 Gruiter
1803/12/12	AMSCH	0194[H]	*[Anonymous]* | 1 Schilderij | *Notes:* This lot was added in by hand in the LBDa and RKDH copies of the catalogue.	V[inkeles?]	(Sold) fl 2:5 Gruiter
1803/12/12	AMSCH	0195[H]	*[Anonymous]* | 1 Schilderij | *Notes:* This lot was added in by hand in the LBDa and RKDH copies of the catalogue.	V[inkeles?]	(Sold) fl 1:5 for lots 195[H] & 196[H]. Boelen
1803/12/12	AMSCH	0196[H]	*[Anonymous]* | 1 Schilderij | *Notes:* This lot was added in by hand in the LBDa and RKDH copies of the catalogue.	V[inkeles?]	(Sold) fl 1:5 for lots 195[H] & 196[H]. Boelen
1803/12/12	AMSCH	0197[H]	*[Anonymous]* | 1 Schilderij | *Notes:* This lot was added in by hand in the LBDa and RKDH copies of the catalogue.	H	(Sold) fl 4:5 Versteegh
1803/12/12	AMSCH	0198[H]	*[Anonymous]* | 1 Schilderij | *Notes:* This lot was added in by hand in the LBDa and RKDH copies of the catalogue.	H	(Sold) fl 20 Coclers
1803/12/12	AMSCH	0199[H]	*[Anonymous]* | 1 Schilderij | *Notes:* This lot was added in by hand in the LBDa and RKDH copies of the catalogue.	H	(Sold) fl 1:5 for lots 199[H] & 200[H]. Gruiter
1803/12/12	AMSCH	0200[H]	*[Anonymous]* | 1 Schilderij | *Notes:* This lot was added in by hand in the LBDa and RKDH copies of the catalogue.	H	(Sold) fl 1:5 for lots 199[H] & 200[H]. Gruiter
1803/12/12	AMSCH	0201[H]	*[Anonymous]* | 2 Schilderijen | *Notes:* This lot was added in by hand in the LBDa and RKDH copies of the catalogue.	H	(Sold) fl 1:5 Bergh
1803/12/12	AMSCH	0202[H]	*[Anonymous]* | 4 Schilderijen | *Notes:* This lot was added in by hand in the LBDa and RKDH copies of the catalogue.	H	(Sold) fl 0:10 L Pakker
1803/12/12	AMSCH	0203[H]	*[Anonymous]* | 1 Schilderij | *Notes:* This lot was added in by hand in the LBDa and RKDH copies of the catalogue.	W	(Bought In) fl 35
1803/12/12	AMSCH	0204[H]	*[Anonymous]* | 2 Schilderijen | *Notes:* This lot was added in by hand in the LBDa and RKDH copies of the catalogue.	W	(Sold) fl 0:10 L Pakker
1803/12/12	AMSCH	0205[H]	*[Anonymous]* | 2 Schilderijen | *Notes:* This lot was added in by hand in the LBDa and RKDH copies of the catalogue.	W	(Sold) fl 1:5 Mensard
1803/12/12	AMSCH	0206[H]	*[Anonymous]* | 1 Schilderij | *Notes:* This lot was added in by hand in the LBDa and RKDH copies of the catalogue.	W	(Sold) fl 1 Boelen
1803/12/12	AMSCH	0207[H]	*[Anonymous]* | 1 Schilderij | *Notes:* This lot was added in by hand in the LBDa and RKDH copies of the catalogue.	W	(Sold) fl 0:10 v^n Iperen
1803/12/12	AMSCH	0208[H]	*[Anonymous]* | 1 Schilderij | *Notes:* This lot was added in by hand in the LBDa and RKDH copies of the catalogue.	W	(Sold) fl 0:10 v^n Iperen

1803/12/12	AMSCH	0209[H]	*[Anonymous]* | 1 Schilderij | *Notes:* This lot was added in by hand in the LBDa and RKDH copies of the catalogue.	W	(Sold) fl 1:5 Mensart
1803/12/12	AMSCH	0210[H]	*[Anonymous]* | 1 Schilderij | *Notes:* This lot was added in by hand in the LBDa and RKDH copies of the catalogue.	F	(Sold) fl 1 Bergh
1803/12/12	AMSCH	0211[H]	*[Anonymous]* | 1 Schilderij | *Notes:* This lot was added in by hand in the LBDa and RKDH copies of the catalogue.	F	(Sold) fl 4:10 Gruiter
1803/12/12	AMSCH	0212[H]	*[Anonymous]* | 1 Schilderij | *Notes:* This lot was added in by hand in the LBDa and RKDH copies of the catalogue.	F	(Sold) fl 1:5 Gruiter
1803/12/12	AMSCH	0213[H]	*[Anonymous]* | 1 Schilderij | *Notes:* This lot was added in by hand in the LBDa and RKDH copies of the catalogue.	F	(Sold) fl 1:10 for lots 213[H] & 214[H]. L Pakker
1803/12/12	AMSCH	0214[H]	*[Anonymous]* | 2 Schilderijen | *Notes:* This lot was added in by hand in the LBDa and RKDH copies of the catalogue.	F	(Sold) fl 1:10 for lots 213[H] & 214[H]. L Pakker
1803/12/12	AMSCH	0215[H]	*[Anonymous]* | 2 Schilderijen | *Notes:* This lot was added in by hand in the LBDa and RKDH copies of the catalogue.	F	(Sold) fl 3:15 Hafner
803/12/12	AMSCH	0216[H]	*[Anonymous]* | 1 Schilderij | *Notes:* This lot was added in by hand in the LBDa and RKDH copies of the catalogue.	F	(Sold) fl 1:10 Bergh
803/12/12	AMSCH	0217[H]	*[Anonymous]* | 1 Schilderij | *Notes:* This lot was added in by hand in the LBDa and RKDH copies of the catalogue.	F	(Sold) fl 0:16 Bergh
803/12/12	AMSCH	0218[H]	*[Anonymous]* | 1 Schilderij | *Notes:* This lot was added in by hand in the LBDa and RKDH copies of the catalogue.	F	(Sold) fl 0:16 Bergh
803/12/12	AMSCH	0219[H]	*[Anonymous]* | 2 Schilderijen | *Notes:* This lot was added in by hand in the LBDa and RKDH copies of the catalogue.	F	(Sold) fl 1 V Iperen
803/12/12	AMSCH	0220[H]	*[Anonymous]* | 2 Schilderijen | *Notes:* This lot was added in by hand in the LBDa and RKDH copies of the catalogue.	F	(Sold) fl 5:5 Scheffer
803/12/12	AMSCH	0221[H]	*[Anonymous]* | 1 Schilderij | *Notes:* This lot was added in by hand in the LBDa and RKDH copies of the catalogue.	F	(Sold) fl 0:10 L Pakker
803/12/12	AMSCH	0222[H]	*[Anonymous]* | 1 Schilderij | *Notes:* This lot was added in by hand in the LBDa and RKDH copies of the catalogue.	F	(Sold) fl 1:10 L Pakker
803/12/12	AMSCH	0223[H]	*[Anonymous]* | 2 Schilderijen | *Notes:* This lot was added in by hand in the LBDa and RKDH copies of the catalogue.	F	(Sold) fl 2:5 Gruiter [or] Bergh
803/12/12	AMSCH	0224[H]	*[Anonymous]* | 1 Schilderij | *Notes:* This lot was added in by hand in the LBDa and RKDH copies of the catalogue.	F	(Sold) fl 5:15 Gruiter
803/12/12	AMSCH	0225[H]	*[Anonymous]* | 1 Schilderij | *Notes:* This lot was added in by hand in the LBDa and RKDH copies of the catalogue.	Arnoud de Lange	(Sold) fl 1 Gruiter
803/12/12	AMSCH	0226[H]	*[Anonymous]* | 2 Schilderijen | *Notes:* This lot was added in by hand in the LBDa and RKDH copies of the catalogue.	Arnoud de Lange	(Sold) fl 1:10 Gruiter
803/12/12	AMSCH	0227[H]	*[Anonymous]* | 2 Schilderijen | *Notes:* This lot was added in by hand in the LBDa and RKDH copies of the catalogue.	Arnoud de Lange	(Sold) fl 0:10 L Pakker
803/12/12	AMSCH	0228[H]	*[Anonymous]* | 3 Schilderijen | *Notes:* This lot was added in by hand in the LBDa and RKDH copies of the catalogue.	Arnoud de Lange	(Sold) fl 2 Gruiter
803/12/12	AMSCH	0229[H]	*[Anonymous]* | 1 Schilderij | *Notes:* This lot was added in by hand in the LBDa and RKDH copies of the catalogue.	B	(Sold) fl 5:10 Coclers
803/12/12	AMSCH	0230[H]	*[Anonymous]* | 1 Schilderij | *Notes:* This lot was added in by hand in the LBDa and RKDH copies of the catalogue.	B	(Sold) fl 27 Coclers
803/12/12	AMSCH	0231[H]	*[Anonymous]* | 1 Schilderij | *Notes:* This lot was added in by hand in the LBDa and RKDH copies of the catalogue.	V[inkeles?]	(Sold) fl 5:5 Coclers
803/12/12	AMSCH	0232[H]	*[Anonymous]* | 1 Schilderij | *Notes:* This lot was added in by hand in the LBDa and RKDH copies of the catalogue.	V[inkeles?]	(Sold) fl 6 Coclers
803/12/12	AMSCH	0233[H]	*[Anonymous]* | 1 Schilderij | *Notes:* This lot was added in by hand in the LBDa and RKDH copies of the catalogue.	V[inkeles?]	(Sold) fl 6:10 Coclers
803/12/12	AMSCH	0234[H]	*[Anonymous]* | 1 Schilderij | *Notes:* This lot was added in by hand in the LBDa and RKDH copies of the catalogue.	V[inkeles?]	(Sold) fl 7:5 V^n Iperen
803/12/12	AMSCH	0235[H]	*[Anonymous]* | 1 Schilderij | *Notes:* This lot was added in by hand in the LBDa and RKDH copies of the catalogue.	V[inkeles?]	(Sold) fl 8 V^n Iperen
803/12/12	AMSCH	0236[H]	*[Anonymous]* | 1 Schilderij | *Notes:* This lot was added in by hand in the LBDa and RKDH copies of the catalogue.	W	(Sold) fl 1:5 Coclers
803/12/12	AMSCH	0237[H]	*[Anonymous]* | 1 Schilderij | *Notes:* This lot was added in by hand in the LBDa and RKDH copies of the catalogue.	W	(Sold) fl 1 Weddelink
803/12/12	AMSCH	0238[H]	*[Anonymous]* | 1 Schilderij | *Notes:* This lot was added in by hand in the LBDa and RKDH copies of the catalogue.	W	(Sold) fl 13 Hafner
803/12/12	AMSCH	0239[H]	*[Anonymous]* | 1 Schilderij | *Notes:* This lot was added in by hand in the LBDa and RKDH copies of the catalogue.	W	(Sold) fl 1 v d Schley [for] R[ijfsnijder]
803/12/12	AMSCH	0240[H]	*[Anonymous]* | 1 Schilderij | *Notes:* This lot was added in by hand in the LBDa and RKDH copies of the catalogue.	W	(Sold) fl 0:6 L Pakker
803/12/12	AMSCH	0241[H]	*[Anonymous]* | 1 Schilderij | *Notes:* This lot was added in by hand in the LBDa and RKDH copies of the catalogue.	W	(Sold) fl 0:6 L Pakker

1803/12/12	AMSCH	0242[H]	*[Anonymous]* | 1 Schilderij | *Notes:* This lot was added in by hand in the LBDa and RKDH copies of the catalogue.	W	(Sold) fl 12:10 Blauwpot
1803/12/12	AMSCH	0243[H]	*[Anonymous]* | 2 Schilderijen | *Notes:* This lot was added in by hand in the LBDa and RKDH copies of the catalogue.	W	(Bought In) fl 7
1803/12/12	AMSCH	0244[H]	*[Anonymous]* | 4 Schilderijen | *Notes:* This lot was added in by hand in the LBDa and RKDH copies of the catalogue.	W	(Bought In) fl 35
1803/12/12	AMSCH	0245[H]	*[Anonymous]* | 2 Schilderijen | *Notes:* This lot was added in by hand in the LBDa and RKDH copies of the catalogue.	W	(Bought In) fl 14 ½
1803/12/12	AMSCH	0246[H]	*[Anonymous]* | 1 Schilderij | *Notes:* This lot was added in by hand in the LBDa and RKDH copies of the catalogue.	R[oos]	(Sold) fl 19 Hodges
1803/12/15	MGLAC	0032	*Een goed Meester* | Een Oud Man met een gryzen Baard; kragtig en fix geschilderd | *Mat:* op paneel *Size:* hoog duim 12, breed duim 10	Mr L H de Haze Bomme	(Unknown)
1804/02/27	AMSCH	0123	*[Anonymous]* | Een Levantsche Zeehaven, ryk gestoffeerd met een prachtig Fontyn en Standbeeld, waar nevens een rustende Dame en Heer en een Levants Koopman te Paard, verder een Vaartuig, met een Tent, waarin Lieden die zich ververschen aan Strand, en verder in Zee eenige verschillende Schepen; fiks gepenceeld op Doek | *Mat:* op doek *Size:* hoog 39; breed 52 duim	B	(Sold) fl 7 Th[S] Spaan
1804/02/27	AMSCH	0126	*Een oud meester* | Le Duc d'Alba op zyn Throon, verscheurt de Privilegies van de Nederlanden, de 17 Provincien zinnebeeldig verbeeld, leggen voor hem geknield, in 't verschiet de Executie verrigting aan de Graave van Egmont en Hoorn; door een oud meester	B	(Bought In) fl 1:10
1804/02/27	AMSCH	0128	*[Anonymous]* | Op een Aanregtbank, ziet men eenig dood Wild, en ander bywerk, achter dezelven een Man met een Geweer in zyn Hand, meesterlyk geschilderd	B	(Sold) fl 1:5 for lots 128 & 129. Gruiter
1804/02/27	AMSCH	0129	*[Anonymous]* | Twee stuks met diverse zoorten van smaakelyke Vrugten, meesterlyk behandeld	B	(Sold) fl 1:5 for lots 128 & 129. Gruiter
1804/02/27	AMSCH	0130	*[Anonymous]* | Twee capitaale Italiaansche Gezichten, met prachtigen Gebouwen en Historien gestoffeerd; breed en zonachtig geschilderd	B	(Sold) fl 5 Gruiter
1804/02/27	AMSCH	0141	*[Anonymous]* | Twee stuks Binnenhuizen met Beelden	B	(Sold) fl 0:10 L Pakker
1804/02/27	AMSCH	0142	*[Anonymous]* | Een dito [stuk] met speelende Beelden	B	(Sold) fl 0:6 L Pakker
1804/02/27	AMSCH	0146	*[Anonymous]* | Twee stuks, een Wintergezigt en een Landschap	B	(Sold) fl 0:10 L Pakker
1804/02/27	AMSCH	0149	*[Anonymous]* | Een Historieele Ordonantie, en een Manspourtrait	B	(Sold) fl 1:10 van Iperen
1804/02/27	AMSCH	0150	*[Anonymous]* | Een bevallig Landschap	B	(Sold) fl 0:12 Theys
1804/02/27	AMSCH	0153	*Een goed Meester* | Twee stuks Arcadische Landschappen, ryk gestoffeerd met Beelden en Beesten; fraai op Doek, door een goed Meester | *Mat:* op doek	D	(Sold) fl 1:15 de Veer
1804/02/27	AMSCH	0154	*Een goed Meester* | Het Pourtrait van C. Drakenburg, in den hogen ouderdom van 143 Jaaren, door een goed meester | *Size:* hoog 11, breed 8 duim	R[oos]	(Sold) fl 1 v[n] d Schleij [for] R[ijfsnijder]
1804/02/27	AMSCH	0159	*Een goed Meester* | Een Christus Hoofd, door een goed Meester, op Doek | *Mat:* op doek *Size:* hoog 35, breed 27 duim	C	(Sold) fl 0:10 W v d Schleij
1804/02/27	AMSCH	0160	*Een goed Meester* | Een slapend Vrouwtje met een bont Jakje; fiks op Doek, door een goed Meester | *Mat:* op doek	B	(Sold) fl 3:5 v[n] Dijl
1804/02/27	AMSCH	0162	*Een oud meester* | In een Landschap ziet men vyf differente zoorren [sic] van Hoofden, door een oud meester	B	(Sold) fl 4 de Lelij
1804/02/27	AMSCH	0163	*Een oud Meester* | Maria, Joseph en 't Kind Jesu, door een oud Meester	B	(Sold) fl 1:5 Coclers
1804/02/27	AMSCH	0164[b]	*[Anonymous]* | Twee stuks, de Koekebakster, naar Ostade, en een Landschap | *This Lot:* Een Landschap; lot 164[a] is copy after Ostade	C	(Sold) fl 1 for lots 164[a] & 164[b]. L Pakker
1804/02/27	AMSCH	0165	*[Anonymous]* | Twee diverschen Landschappen	C	(Sold) fl 0:14 Gruiter
1804/02/27	AMSCH	0166	*[Anonymous]* | Twee dito [diverschen] dito [Landschappen]	C	(Sold) fl 1 J Yver
1804/02/27	AMSCH	0167	*[Anonymous]* | Twee stuks divers	C	(Sold) fl 10 La Bouchere
1804/02/27	AMSCH	0168	*[Anonymous]* | Twee dito [stuks] dito [divers]	C	(Sold) fl 1:5 La Bouchere
1804/02/27	AMSCH	0169	*[Anonymous]* | Twee dito [stuks] dito [divers]	C	(Sold) fl 0:14 L Pakker
1804/02/27	AMSCH	0170	*[Anonymous]* | Twee stuks Pourtraiten	C	(Sold) fl 7 de Lelij
1804/02/27	AMSCH	0171	*[Anonymous]* | Twee dito [stuks] dito [Pourtraiten]	C	(Sold) fl 6 Coclers
1804/02/27	AMSCH	0172	*[Anonymous]* | Twee dito [stuks] dito [Pourtraiten]	C	(Sold) fl 1 Gruiter
1804/02/27	AMSCH	0173	*[Anonymous]* | Twee dito [stuks] dito [Pourtraiten]	C	(Sold) fl 0:2 L Pakker
1804/02/27	AMSCH	0174	*[Anonymous]* | Drie stuks, divers	C	(Sold) fl 0:10 Hafner

1804/02/27	AMSCH	0175	*[Anonymous]* | Drie dito [stuks] dito [divers]	C	(Sold) fl 1 L Pakker
1804/02/27	AMSCH	0179[H]	*[Anonymous]* | [Untitled] | *Notes:* This lot was added in by hand in the FLNY, LBDa and RKDH copies of the catalogue, but without giving an artist or title.	R[oos]	(Sold) fl 2 Coclers
1804/02/27	AMSCH	0180[H]	*[Anonymous]* | [Untitled] | *Notes:* This lot was added in by hand in the FLNY, LBDa and RKDH copies of the catalogue, but without giving an artist or title.	R[oos]	(Sold) fl 1:5 Oostwijn
1804/02/27	AMSCH	0181[H]	*[Anonymous]* | [Untitled] | *Notes:* This lot was added in by hand in the FLNY, LBDa and RKDH copies of the catalogue, but without giving an artist or title.	R[oos]	(Sold) fl 1:15 de Veer
1804/02/27	AMSCH	0182[H]	*[Anonymous]* | [Untitled] | *Notes:* This lot was added in by hand in the FLNY, LBDa and RKDH copies of the catalogue, but without giving an artist or title.	R[oos]	(Sold) fl 3 Jozi
1804/02/27	AMSCH	0183[H]	*[Anonymous]* | [Untitled] | *Notes:* This lot was added in by hand in the FLNY, LBDa and RKDH copies of the catalogue, but without giving an artist or title.	R[oos]	(Sold) fl 0:4 W v d Schley
1804/02/27	AMSCH	0184[H]	*[Anonymous]* | [Untitled] | *Notes:* This lot was added in by hand in the FLNY, LBDa and RKDH copies of the catalogue, but without giving an artist or title.	R[oos]	(Sold) fl 1:10 Coclers
1804/02/27	AMSCH	0185[H]	*[Anonymous]* | [Untitled] | *Notes:* This lot was added in by hand in the FLNY, LBDa and RKDH copies of the catalogue, but without giving an artist or title.	R[oos]	(Sold) fl 1:5 du Pree
1804/02/27	AMSCH	0186[H]	*[Anonymous]* | [Untitled] | *Notes:* This lot was added in by hand in the FLNY, LBDa and RKDH copies of the catalogue, but without giving an artist or title.	R[oos]	(Sold) fl 35 Theys
1804/02/27	AMSCH	0187[H]	*[Anonymous]* | [Untitled] | *Notes:* This lot was added in by hand in the FLNY, LBDa and RKDH copies of the catalogue, but without giving an artist or title.	R[oos]	(Sold) fl 12 Jozi
1804/03/27	MGSAN	0001	*[Anonymous]* | Twee Stuks fraaije Tuingezigten met onderscheide Tuincieraden en Gebouwen, op de voorgrond een Groep van Haanen, Faisanten en andere Gedierte, levendig en krachtig geschilderd, in vergulde Lysten | *Mat:* op doek *Size:* hoog 27 duim x breed 23 ½ duim		(Unknown)
1804/03/27	MGSAN	0003	*[Anonymous]* | Een extra uitvoerig Bergachtig Landschap met een stil Watertje, op de voorgrond eenige rustende en gaande Reizigers, in het Landschap een hoogen Heuvel op welkers top een Kasteel, alles zeer plaisant en aangenaam gepenseeld, door een zeer goed Meester, in vergulde Lyst | *Mat:* op paneel *Size:* hoog 20 duim x breed 26 ½ duim		(Unknown)
1804/03/27	MGSAN	0006	*Een oud goed Meester* | Een extra fraai Bosch- en Landgezigt, waarop eenige Molens, op de voorgrond een Hek aan het Bosch, waarby een Man met een Pot met Bloemen, verder eenig Gedierte, stout en krachtig geschilderd, door een oud goed Meester, in vergulde Lyst | *Mat:* op paneel *Size:* hoog 27 duim x breed 30 duim		(Unknown)
1804/04/25	HGBES	0011	*[Anonymous]* | Depart pour les Peche | *Notes:* It is uncertain whether this lot is a painting.		(Unknown)
1804/04/28	LNDLS	0047	*[Anonymous]* | Een Lagchend Mannetje, halverlyf, houdende een glas bier in zyn hand, van boven togsgewys [sic] | *Fmt:* van boven toogsgewys	[Abraham Delfos] [or others]	(Sold) fl 2:12 Jan Landa
1804/04/28	LNDLS	0062	*[Anonymous]* | Een Fruitstuk	[Abraham Delfos] [or others]	(Sold) fl 1:10 Rigter
1804/05/07	AMSCH	0203	*[Anonymous]* | Twee stuks Schoorsteenstukken, op Doek, zynde een Bloemstuk en een Landschap | *Mat:* op doek	Y[ver]	(Sold or Bought In) fl 0:10 J[n] Yver
1804/05/07	AMSCH	0204	*[Anonymous]* | Een oud Manshoofd met een lange Baard; breed en meesterlyk gepenceeld	Roos [for] A	(Sold) fl 6 Pruissenaar
1804/05/07	AMSCH	0208	*Een goed Meester* | 't Afbeeldzel van een Vorstelyk Persoon, in aloude Kleeding; uitvoerig gepenceeld door een goed Meestet [sic]	Roos [for] A	(Bought In) fl 2 ¾
1804/05/07	AMSCH	0210	*Een oud Meester* | In een Binnenkamer zit een bevallige Vrouw met twee Kinderen, aandachtig in een Boek te leezen, agter haar zit een Grysaart by 't Vuur; 't brandend kaarslicht en 't Vuur doet een natuurlyk effect, meesterlyk op Doek geschilderd door een oud Meester | *Mat:* op doek *Size:* hoog 30, breed 39 duim	Vinkeles [for] G	(Sold) fl 0:12 Gruiter
1804/05/07	AMSCH	0212	*[Anonymous]* | Mars en Vénus, in een prachtige zaal te Bed leggende, waar by twee Cupidoos; fraay van Teekening en delicaat gepenceeld, op Koper | *Mat:* op koper	R[oos]	(Sold) fl 44 Jan Spaan
1804/05/07	AMSCH	0216	*[Anonymous]* | Zes stuks Mans Hoofden, in diversche Kleeding, fiks gepenceeld, op Paneel | *Mat:* op paneel	Roos [for] K	(Sold) fl 3:5 Yver
1804/05/07	AMSCH	0217	*[Anonymous]* | Twee stuks stille Waters, gestoffeerd met verscheide Vissers Scheepen en diversche andere Vaartuigen; plaisant geschilderd, op Paneel | *Mat:* op paneel	Roos [for] K	(Sold) fl 1:5 Yver
1804/05/07	AMSCH	0218	*[Anonymous]* | Een Schuur waarin een Huisman zyn Pyp rookt, gestoffeerd met verscheide Boere Huisraad, fiks geschilderd	Roos [for] K	(Sold) fl 2:15 Gruiter
1804/05/07	AMSCH	0220	*[Anonymous]* | Vier stuks comique Mans Hoofden; geestig en meesterlyk behandeld, op Paneel | *Mat:* op paneel	Roos [for] K	(Sold) fl 0:12 L Pakker

1804/05/07	AMSCH	0221	*[Anonymous]* | Een Schilder in zyn Studeervertrek, zittende voor zyn Schilderëzel, ter zyde een Jongeling, bézig zyn Palet te schikken; fiks gepenceeld, op Paneel | *Mat:* op paneel	Roos [for] K	(Sold) fl 1:15 Pruissenaar
1804/05/07	AMSCH	0222	*[Anonymous]* | Een zittende Dame, in een witte Satyne Kleeding, in een Thuingezicht; fiks en krachtig geschilderd, op Doek | *Mat:* op doek	Schley	(Sold) fl 0:10 Van der Schley [for] A[=Putte]
1804/05/07	AMSCH	0224	*[Anonymous]* | Een Schoorsteenstuk, verbeeldende de Vreede door een staande Vrouw in een Nis, leevens groot, en houdende in de Regterhand een Olyftak, en met den Linker den Hoorn van Overvloed; krachtig en meesterlxk [sic] in 't graauw geschilderd | *Fmt:* schoorsteenstuk	Schley	(Bought In) fl 0:10
1804/05/07	AMSCH	0225	*Een goed Meester* | Een Historieele Ordonantie van verscheiden Beelden, meesterachtig geschilderd door een goed Meester | *Size:* hoog 23, breed 21 duim	Vinkeles [for] G	(Sold) fl 0:12 Hulswit
1804/05/07	AMSCH	0226	*[Anonymous]* | Twee stuks Boom en Bergachtige Landschappen, met verscheide Stoffagie; fiks geschilderd	Roos [for] K	(Sold) fl 1 L Pakker
1804/05/07	AMSCH	0228	*Een goed Meester* | Een Zinnebeeldige Ordonantie met verscheiden Beelden, Kinderen, enz.; fraay van coloriet en uitvoerig, door een goed Meester	Vinkeles [for] H[affner]	(Bought In) fl 1
1804/05/07	AMSCH	0229	*Een goed Meester* | In een Land- en Watergezicht, ziet men langs een Weg een oud Casteel, in 't welke een Horlogie, loopende zeer accuraat, 8 dagen lang, verders eenige wandelende, vaarende en andere Persoonen, en een alleraangenaamst verschiet; fiks door een goed Meester	Vinkeles [for] J	(Sold) fl 51 Josi
1804/05/07	AMSCH	0230	*Een voornaam Meester* | Twee capitaale rykgekleeden Mans en Vrouwen Pourtretten; konstig op doek geschilderd, door een voornaam Meester | *Mat:* op doek *Size:* hoog 43, breed 32 duim	Vinkeles [for] G	(Sold) fl 1 Gruiter
1804/05/07	AMSCH	0231	*[Anonymous]* | Twee diversen Pourtretten	Vinkeles [for] G	(Sold) fl 1 Harbome
1804/05/07	AMSCH	0232	*[Anonymous]* | Twee capitalen dito [Pourtretten]	Vinkeles [for] G	(Sold) fl 3:15 Pluks
1804/05/07	AMSCH	0233	*[Anonymous]* | Twee diversen Landschappen	Vinkeles [for] G	(Sold) fl 2:15 Verlem
1804/05/07	AMSCH	0234	*[Anonymous]* | Twee dito [diversen] dito [Landschappen]	Vinkeles [for] G	(Sold) fl 0:8 Gruiter
1804/05/07	AMSCH	0235	*[Anonymous]* | Twee dito [diversen] dito [Landschappen]	Vinkeles [for] G	(Sold) fl 0:8 L Pakker
1804/05/07	AMSCH	0236	*[Anonymous]* | Twee stuks divers	Vinkeles [for] G	(Sold) fl 1:5 Gruyter
1804/05/07	AMSCH	0237	*[Anonymous]* | Twee dito [stuks] dito [divers]	Vinkeles [for] G	(Sold) fl 4:15 Gruyter
1804/05/07	AMSCH	0238[H]	*[Anonymous]* | 1 Schilderij | *Notes:* This lot was added in by hand in the EBNP, LBDa and RKDH copies of the catalogue.	Vinkeles [for] J	(Sold) fl 19:10 Thais
1804/05/07	AMSCH	0239[H]	*[Anonymous]* | 1 dito [schilderij] | *Notes:* This lot was added in by hand in the EBNP, LBDa and RKDH copies of the catalogue.	Vinkeles [for] J	(Sold) fl 12:5 Sal Joseph
1804/05/07	AMSCH	0240[H]	*[Anonymous]* | 1 dito [schilderij] | *Notes:* This lot was added in by hand in the EBNP, LBDa and RKDH copies of the catalogue.	Vinkeles [for] J	(Sold) fl 6:5 Coclers
1804/05/07	AMSCH	0241[H]	*[Anonymous]* | 1 dito [schilderij] | *Notes:* This lot was added in by hand in the EBNP, LBDa and RKDH copies of the catalogue.	Vinkeles [for] J	(Bought In) fl 24
1804/05/07	AMSCH	0242[H]	*[Anonymous]* | 1 dito [schilderij] | *Notes:* This lot was added in by hand in the EBNP, LBDa and RKDH copies of the catalogue.	Vinkeles [for] J	(Sold) fl 0:6 L Pakker
1804/05/07	AMSCH	0243[H]	*[Anonymous]* | 1 dito [schilderij] | *Notes:* This lot was added in by hand in the EBNP, LBDa and RKDH copies of the catalogue.	Vinkeles [for] J	(Sold) fl 17:10 Wed Achtienhoven
1804/05/07	AMSCH	0244[H]	*[Anonymous]* | 1 dito [schilderij] | *Notes:* This lot was added in by hand in the EBNP, LBDa and RKDH copies of the catalogue.	Vinkeles [for] J	(Bought In) fl 10
1804/05/07	AMSCH	0245[H]	*[Anonymous]* | 1 dito [schilderij] | *Notes:* This lot was added in by hand in the EBNP, LBDa and RKDH copies of the catalogue.	Y[ver] [for] JJ	(Sold) fl 5 Ferguson [or] Wilkensohn
1804/05/07	AMSCH	0246[H]	*[Anonymous]* | 1 dito [schilderij] | *Notes:* This lot was added in by hand in the EBNP, LBDa and RKDH copies of the catalogue.	Y[ver] [for] JJ	(Sold) fl 5:10 Jan Spaan
1804/05/07	AMSCH	0247[H]	*[Anonymous]* | 1 dito [schilderij] | *Notes:* This lot was added in by hand in the EBNP, LBDa and RKDH copies of the catalogue.	Vinkeles [for] J	(Bought In) fl 29
1804/05/07	AMSCH	0248[H]	*[Anonymous]* | 1 dito [schilderij] | *Notes:* This lot was added in by hand in the EBNP, LBDa and RKDH copies of the catalogue.	Vinkeles [for] J	(Sold) fl 12:5 S Joseph
1804/05/07	AMSCH	0249[H]	*[Anonymous]* | 1 dito [schilderij] | *Notes:* This lot was added in by hand in the EBNP, LBDa and RKDH copies of the catalogue.	Roos [for] K	(Sold) fl 0:6 L Pakker
1804/06/18	MGBEO	0001	*[Anonymous]* | [Untitled] | *Notes:* The only extant copy of this catalogue is annotated with the buyers and prices, but it does not include a printed list of the paintings.		(Sold) £ 0.3 Ledrach
1804/06/18	MGBEO	0002	*[Anonymous]* | [Untitled] | *Notes:* The only extant copy of this catalogue is annotated with the buyers and prices, but it does not include a printed list of the paintings.		(Sold) £ 1.7 Ooms
1804/06/18	MGBEO	0003	*[Anonymous]* | [Untitled] | *Notes:* The only extant copy of this catalogue is annotated with the buyers and prices, but it does not include a printed list of the paintings.		(Sold) £ 0.10 Andel
1804/06/18	MGBEO	0004	*[Anonymous]* | [Untitled] | *Notes:* The only extant copy of this catalogue is annotated with the buyers and prices, but it does not include a printed list of the paintings.		(Sold) £ 0.2 Fraaienhove [?]

1804/06/18	MGBEO	0005	*[Anonymous]* | [Untitled] | *Notes:* The only extant copy of this catalogue is annotated with the buyers and prices, but it does not include a printed list of the paintings.	(Sold) £ 0.5 Andel
1804/06/18	MGBEO	0006	*[Anonymous]* | [Untitled] | *Notes:* The only extant copy of this catalogue is annotated with the buyers and prices, but it does not include a printed list of the paintings.	(Sold) £ 0.4 Modera
1804/06/18	MGBEO	0007	*[Anonymous]* | [Untitled] | *Notes:* The only extant copy of this catalogue is annotated with the buyers and prices, but it does not include a printed list of the paintings.	(Sold) £ 0.1 Lepelaar
1804/06/18	MGBEO	0008	*[Anonymous]* | [Untitled] | *Notes:* The only extant copy of this catalogue is annotated with the buyers and prices, but it does not include a printed list of the paintings.	(Sold) £ 0.2 Haccon
1804/06/18	MGBEO	0009	*[Anonymous]* | [Untitled] | *Annots:* 2 stuks (ZBM) *Notes:* The only extant copy of this catalogue is annotated with the buyers and prices, but it does not include a printed list of the paintings.	(Sold) £ 0.4 Ooms
1804/06/18	MGBEO	0010	*[Anonymous]* | [Untitled] | *Notes:* The only extant copy of this catalogue is annotated with the buyers and prices, but it does not include a printed list of the paintings.	(Sold) £ 0.2 Meertens
1804/06/18	MGBEO	0011	*[Anonymous]* | [Untitled] | *Notes:* The only extant copy of this catalogue is annotated with the buyers and prices, but it does not include a printed list of the paintings.	(Sold) £ 0.3 Haccon
1804/06/18	MGBEO	0012	*[Anonymous]* | [Untitled] | *Notes:* The only extant copy of this catalogue is annotated with the buyers and prices, but it does not include a printed list of the paintings.	(Sold) £ 0.1 Meertens
1804/06/18	MGBEO	0013	*[Anonymous]* | [Untitled] | *Notes:* The only extant copy of this catalogue is annotated with the buyers and prices, but it does not include a printed list of the paintings.	(Sold) £ 0.7 Haccon
1804/06/18	MGBEO	0014	*[Anonymous]* | [Untitled] | *Notes:* The only extant copy of this catalogue is annotated with the buyers and prices, but it does not include a printed list of the paintings.	(Sold) £ 0.2 Haccon
1804/06/18	MGBEO	0015	*[Anonymous]* | [Untitled] | *Notes:* The only extant copy of this catalogue is annotated with the buyers and prices, but it does not include a printed list of the paintings.	(Sold) £ 0.9 Andel
1804/06/18	MGBEO	0016	*[Anonymous]* | [Untitled] | *Notes:* The only extant copy of this catalogue is annotated with the buyers and prices, but it does not include a printed list of the paintings.	(Sold) £ 0.8 de Ryke
1804/06/18	MGBEO	0017	*[Anonymous]* | [Untitled] | *Notes:* The only extant copy of this catalogue is annotated with the buyers and prices, but it does not include a printed list of the paintings.	(Sold) £ 0.10 Petersen
1804/06/18	MGBEO	0018	*[Anonymous]* | [Untitled] | *Notes:* The only extant copy of this catalogue is annotated with the buyers and prices, but it does not include a printed list of the paintings.	(Sold) £ 0.8 Frederiksen
1804/06/18	MGBEO	0019	*[Anonymous]* | [Untitled] | *Notes:* The only extant copy of this catalogue is annotated with the buyers and prices, but it does not include a printed list of the paintings.	(Sold) £ 0.19 Benthem
1804/06/18	MGBEO	0020	*[Anonymous]* | [Untitled] | *Notes:* The only extant copy of this catalogue is annotated with the buyers and prices, but it does not include a printed list of the paintings.	(Sold) £ 0.5 Ooms
1804/06/18	MGBEO	0021	*[Anonymous]* | [Untitled] | *Notes:* The only extant copy of this catalogue is annotated with the buyers and prices, but it does not include a printed list of the paintings.	(Sold) £ 0.13 Modera
1804/06/18	MGBEO	0022	*[Anonymous]* | [Untitled] | *Notes:* The only extant copy of this catalogue is annotated with the buyers and prices, but it does not include a printed list of the paintings.	(Sold) £ 0.9 Andel
1804/06/18	MGBEO	0023	*[Anonymous]* | [Untitled] | *Notes:* The only extant copy of this catalogue is annotated with the buyers and prices, but it does not include a printed list of the paintings.	(Sold) £ 0.7 Ledragh
1804/06/18	MGBEO	0024	*[Anonymous]* | [Untitled] | *Notes:* The only extant copy of this catalogue is annotated with the buyers and prices, but it does not include a printed list of the paintings.	(Sold) £ 0.6 Petersen
1804/06/18	MGBEO	0025	*[Anonymous]* | [Untitled] | *Notes:* The only extant copy of this catalogue is annotated with the buyers and prices, but it does not include a printed list of the paintings.	(Sold) £ 0.3 Modera
1804/06/18	MGBEO	0026	*[Anonymous]* | [Untitled] | *Notes:* The only extant copy of this catalogue is annotated with the buyers and prices, but it does not include a printed list of the paintings.	(Bought In)
1804/06/18	MGBEO	0027	*[Anonymous]* | [Untitled] | *Notes:* The only extant copy of this catalogue is annotated with the buyers and prices, but it does not include a printed list of the paintings.	(Sold) £ 0.4 Ooms
1804/06/18	MGBEO	0028	*[Anonymous]* | [Untitled] | *Notes:* The only extant copy of this catalogue is annotated with the buyers and prices, but it does not include a printed list of the paintings.	(Sold) £ 0.2 for lots 28 & 29. Reygers

1804/06/18	MGBEO	0029	*[Anonymous]* | [Untitled] | *Notes:* The only extant copy of this catalogue is annotated with the buyers and prices, but it does not include a printed list of the paintings.		(Sold) £ 0.2 for lots 28 & 29. Reygers
1804/06/18	MGBEO	0030	*[Anonymous]* | [Untitled] | *Notes:* The only extant copy of this catalogue is annotated with the buyers and prices, but it does not include a printed list of the paintings.		(Sold) £ 0.9 Reygers
1804/06/18	MGBEO	0031	*[Anonymous]* | [Untitled] | *Notes:* The only extant copy of this catalogue is annotated with the buyers and prices, but it does not include a printed list of the paintings.		(Sold) £ 0.1 Schenkel (Vader)
1804/06/18	MGBEO	0032	*[Anonymous]* | [Untitled] | *Notes:* The only extant copy of this catalogue is annotated with the buyers and prices, but it does not include a printed list of the paintings.		(Bought In)
1804/06/18	MGBEO	0033	*[Anonymous]* | [Untitled] | *Notes:* The only extant copy of this catalogue is annotated with the buyers and prices, but it does not include a printed list of the paintings.		(Sold) £ 0.18 Schenkel
1804/06/18	MGBEO	0034	*[Anonymous]* | [Untitled] | *Notes:* The only extant copy of this catalogue is annotated with the buyers and prices, but it does not include a printed list of the paintings.		(Sold) £ 0.1 for lots 34 & 35. Heron
1804/06/18	MGBEO	0035	*[Anonymous]* | [Untitled] | *Notes:* The only extant copy of this catalogue is annotated with the buyers and prices, but it does not include a printed list of the paintings.		(Sold) £ 0.1 for lots 34 & 35. Heron
1804/06/18	MGBEO	0036	*[Anonymous]* | [Untitled] | *Notes:* The only extant copy of this catalogue is annotated with the buyers and prices, but it does not include a printed list of the paintings.		(Sold) £ 0.1 Ooms
1804/07/25	AMSCH	0060	*[Anonymous]* | Twee stuks Allegorische, of Fabel ordinantien, ryk met Beelden, en kragtig op Doek geschilderd | *Mat:* op doek *Size:* Jeder hoog 14, breed 19 duim		(Sold) fl 5 Van der Schley
1804/07/25	DLGRO	0008	*Een voornaam Meester* | Een Boerer binnen Huis, waarin een Oude Boer Mosselen zit open te maaken, in het agterste van 't Vertrek de Vrouw, die een Ketel over het Vuur haagt, door een voornaam Meester | *Mat:* op paneel *Size:* hoog 12, breed 10 duim	Mr Franc van der Burch Wz.	(Unknown)
1804/07/25	DLGRO	0025	*Een goed Meester* | Adam en Eva onder den verboden Boom in 't Paradys, fraai geschilderd door een goed Meester op Paneel, Rond | *Mat:* op paneel *Fmt:* rond *Size:* hoog 13, breed 13 duim	Mr Franc van der Burch Wz.	(Unknown)
1804/07/25	DLGRO	0030	*Een voornaam Meester* | Een Boomryk Landschapje, met verder bywerk, door een voornaam Meester | *Mat:* op paneel *Size:* hoog 12, breed 11 duim	Mr Franc van der Burch Wz.	(Unknown)
1804/07/25	DLGRO	0031	*Een voornaam Meester* | Een Oud Mans Hoofd of Borstbeeld, fraai geschilderd, door een voornaam Meester | *Mat:* op paneel *Size:* hoog 10 ½, breed 9 duim	Mr Franc van der Burch Wz.	(Unknown)
1804/07/25	DLGRO	0035	*Een goed Meester* | Een Vrouwen Beeld of Juffrouw, die een Brief toelakt, staande een brandende Kaars voor haar, met verder bywerk, op Doek door een goed Meester | *Mat:* op doek *Size:* hoog 16, breed 14 duim	Mr Franc van der Burch Wz.	(Unknown)
1804/07/25	DLGRO	0037	*Een voornaam Meester* | Een Oud Man, die zyne handen over een Test met Vuur warmt, naast denzelve zyn Vrouwtje, welke hem vriendelyk aanziet, fraai geschilderd door een voornaam Meester | *Mat:* op doek *Size:* hoog 16, breed 14 duim	Mr Franc van der Burch Wz.	(Unknown)
1804/07/25	DLGRO	0047	*Een goed Meester* | Een dito [Borstbeeld] dito [of Oud- Mans Hoofd] met omhoog geslagene Oogen, op Paneel, door een goed Meester | *Mat:* op paneel *Size:* hoog 19, breed 14 duim	Mr Franc van der Burch Wz.	(Unknown)
1804/07/25	DLGRO	0048	*Een voornaam Meester* | Een binnen Huis of Keuken, met een Vrouwtje dat Koeken zit te bakken, zittende haar Man in het hoekje van den Haard zyn Pyp aan te steeken, aan de andere zyde een Jongetje met een Koek in zyn hand, agter haar een jonge Meid en een Persoon die door het Vengster kykt, fraai en uitvoerig geschilderd door een voornaam Meester | *Size:* hoog 20, breed 15 duim	Mr Franc van der Burch Wz.	(Unknown)
1804/07/25	DLGRO	0051	*Een goed Meester* | Een Jongeling die op de Fiool speelt, door een goed Meester | *Size:* hoog 7, breed 6 duim	Mr Franc van der Burch Wz.	(Unknown)
1804/07/25	DLGRO	0062	*Een voornaam Meester* | Maria met het Kindje, zeer keurig en fraai op Koper, door een voornaam Meester | *Mat:* op koper *Size:* hoog 14, breed 10 duim	Mr Franc van der Burch Wz.	(Unknown)
1804/07/25	DLGRO	0066	*Een voornaam Meester* | Een fraai stukje, verbeeldende een geslagt Varken op de Leer, met eenige Boeren en Kinderen, die met de Blaas speelen, door een voornaam Meester op Paneel | *Mat:* op paneel *Size:* hoog 8, breed 10 duim	Mr Franc van der Burch Wz.	(Unknown)
1804/07/25	DLGRO	0067	*Een voornaam Meester* | Een fraai stukje, verbeeldende een Boer en Boerin aan een Tafel zittende te Vryën, in het verschiet een oude Vrouw die eenig Eeten op een Bord binnen brengt, door een voornaam Meester op Paneel | *Mat:* op paneel *Size:* hoog 10, breed 8 duim	Mr Franc van der Burch Wz.	(Unknown)
1804/07/25	DLGRO	0078	*Een goed Meester* | Een Juffrouw, hebbende een Guithare op haar schoot, en een Papegaai voor zich door een goed Meester | *Mat:* op paneel *Size:* hoog 9, breed 7 duim	Mr Franc van der Burch Wz.	(Unknown)

1804/07/25	DLGRO	0079	*Een goed Meester* | Een Fiool Speelder, door een goed Meester | *Mat:* op paneel *Size:* hoog 10, breed 9 duim	Mr Franc van der Burch Wz.	(Unknown)
1804/07/25	DLGRO	0087	*Een goed Meester* | Een Bergächtig Landschap met Boomen en verder bywerk, op den voorgrond twee rustende Reizigers of Boeren, fraai geschilderd door een goed Meester op Paneel | *Mat:* op paneel *Size:* hoog 22, breed 26 duim	Mr Franc van der Burch Wz.	(Unknown)
1804/07/25	DLGRO	0093	*Een goed Meester* | Een Ruïne of Tempel, verbeeldende de Begraafplaats der Ouden, zeer uitvoerig en fraai geschilderd door een goed Meester | *Mat:* op paneel *Size:* hoog 23, breed 32 duim	Mr Franc van der Burch Wz.	(Unknown)
1804/07/25	DLGRO	0095	*Een goed Meester* | Een helder Landschap, met een oude Ruïne, op den voorgrond een Man die zyn Paard laat drinken, en verder bywerk door een goed Meester op Paneel | *Mat:* op paneel *Size:* hoog 22, breed 26 duim	Mr Franc van der Burch Wz.	(Unknown)
1804/07/25	DLGRO	0098	*Een goed Meester* | Twee Mans Hoofden, fraai geschilderd door een goed Meester op Paneel | *Mat:* op paneel *Size:* hoog 6, breed 5 duim	Mr Franc van der Burch Wz.	(Unknown)
1804/07/25	DLGRO	0099	*Een goed Meester* | Twee stukjes, zynde heilige Zinnebeelden, door een goed Meester | *Mat:* op koper	Mr Franc van der Burch Wz.	(Unknown)
1804/07/25	DLGRO	0100	*Een goed Meester* | Een Mans en een Vrouwe Pourtrait, fraai op Paneel geschilderd door een goed Meester | *Mat:* op paneel	Mr Franc van der Burch Wz.	(Unknown)
1804/07/25	DLGRO	0102	*Een goed Meester* | Een Italiaansch Landschap, met eenige oude Ruïnen, door een goed Meester | *Mat:* op doek *Size:* hoog 32, breed 29 duim	Mr Franc van der Burch Wz.	(Unknown)
1804/07/25	DLGRO	0106	*[Anonymous]* | Een Mans Pourtrait	Mr Franc van der Burch Wz.	(Unknown)
1804/07/25	DLGRO	0107	*[Anonymous]* | Een dito [Mans Pourtrait]	Mr Franc van der Burch Wz.	(Unknown)
1804/08/02	BDAN	0020	*[Anonymous]* | Het gezicht van Scheeveling, den voorgrond gestoffeerd met vissers en een deel andere Figuren | *Mat:* op paneel *Size:* b. 48 d. h. 34 en een half d.	J G Calckberner	(Unknown)
1804/08/02	BDAN	0030	*[Anonymous]* | Twee bergachtige Landschappen met Figuren | *Mat:* op paneel *Size:* b. 20 en een half d. h. 14 en een half d.	J G Calckberner	(Unknown)
1804/08/02	BDAN	0040	*[Anonymous]* | Twee stukken met Vrugten | *Mat:* op paneel *Size:* b. 20 en een half d. h. 14 en een half d.	J G Calckberner	(Unknown)
1804/08/02	BDAN	0043	*[Anonymous]* | Twee dito [Landschappen] | *Mat:* op doek *Size:* hoog 10 en 1 half d. b. 10 en 1 half d.	J G Calckberner	(Unknown)
1804/08/02	BDAN	0044	*[Anonymous]* | Twee dito [Landschappen] | *Mat:* op doek *Size:* hoog 10 en 1 half d. b. 10 en 1 half d.	J G Calckberner	(Unknown)
1804/08/02	BDAN	0045	*[Anonymous]* | Een Advocaat zittende voor een Tafel | *Mat:* op doek *Size:* b. 50 d. h. 39 en een half d.	J G Calckberner	(Unknown)
1804/08/02	BDAN	0046	*[Anonymous]* | Een Mans-portrait | *Mat:* op doek *Size:* b. 31 en 1 half d. h. 40 d.	J G Calckberner	(Unknown)
1804/08/02	BDAN	0047	*[Anonymous]* | Een Oude Vrouw met een Kaars in de hand | *Mat:* op doek *Size:* b. 15 d. h. 17 en een half duim	J G Calckberner	(Unknown)
1804/08/02	BDAN	0050	*[Anonymous]* | Een woelende Zee | *Mat:* op doek *Size:* b. 98 d. h. 48 d.	J G Calckberner	(Unknown)
1804/08/02	BDAN	0052	*[Anonymous]* | Een Boeren-Kermis	J G Calckberner	(Unknown)
1804/08/02	BDAN	0053	*[Anonymous]* | Een Portrait | *Mat:* op paneel *Size:* breed 28 en een half d. h. 39 d.	J G Calckberner	(Unknown)
1804/08/02	BDAN	0054	*[Anonymous]* | Een Maria-beeld | *Mat:* op koper *Size:* b. 11 en 1 half d. h. 15 en 1 half d.	J G Calckberner	(Unknown)
1804/08/02	BDAN	0055	*[Anonymous]* | Een stuk met Jagt	J G Calckberner	(Unknown)
1804/08/02	BDAN	0056	*[Anonymous]* | Een Tafel met een Haring en Wyn-romer	J G Calckberner	(Unknown)
1804/08/02	BDAN	0057	*[Anonymous]* | Een Vrouwe Kopje	J G Calckberner	(Unknown)
1804/08/02	BDAN	0058	*[Anonymous]* | Een Bloemstuk	J G Calckberner	(Unknown)
1804/08/02	BDAN	0059	*[Anonymous]* | Een met Vrugten en Vis	J G Calckberner	(Unknown)
1804/08/02	BDAN	0060	*[Anonymous]* | Twee Portraiten	J G Calckberner	(Unknown)
1804/08/02	BDAN	0061	*[Anonymous]* | De Dooping van Johannes	J G Calckberner	(Unknown)
1804/08/02	BDAN	0062	*[Anonymous]* | Een Landschapje	J G Calckberner	(Unknown)
1804/08/02	BDAN	0063	*[Anonymous]* | Drie Studie Koppen	J G Calckberner	(Unknown)
1804/08/02	BDAN	0064	*[Anonymous]* | Een Doode Entvogel met ander bywerk	J G Calckberner	(Unknown)
1804/08/02	BDAN	0065	*[Anonymous]* | Een Mans Kop	J G Calckberner	(Unknown)
1804/08/02	BDAN	0066	*[Anonymous]* | Een Rookende Boer	J G Calckberner	(Unknown)
1804/08/02	BDAN	0067	*[Anonymous]* | Een Kop	J G Calckberner	(Unknown)
1804/08/02	BDAN	0068	*[Anonymous]* | Een stuk met Jagt-tuig	J G Calckberner	(Unknown)
1804/08/02	BDAN	0069	*[Anonymous]* | Een Vrugt stuk	J G Calckberner	(Unknown)
1804/08/02	BDAN	0070	*[Anonymous]* | Een Bloem-stuk	J G Calckberner	(Unknown)
1804/08/02	BDAN	0071	*[Anonymous]* | Twee Binnen-huisen	J G Calckberner	(Unknown)

1804/08/02	BDAN	0072	*[Anonymous]* | Een Liedjes-zanger	J G Calckberner	(Unknown)
1804/08/02	BDAN	0073	*[Anonymous]* | Een Mans-portrait	J G Calckberner	(Unknown)
1804/08/02	BDAN	0074	*[Anonymous]* | Een dito [Mans-portrait] op zyn Turks gekleedt	J G Calckberner	(Unknown)
1804/08/02	BDAN	0076	*[Anonymous]* | Twee Landschappen, den voorgrond verciert met Koeyen, Schaapen, &c.	J G Calckberner	(Unknown)
1804/08/02	BDAN	0077	*[Anonymous]* | Twee idem [Landschappen]	J G Calckberner	(Unknown)
1804/08/02	BDAN	0078	*[Anonymous]* | Een Boschachtig Landschap	J G Calckberner	(Unknown)
1804/08/08	AMSCH	0246	*Een oud Meester* | De Graflegging Christi, zynde een ryke Ordinantie van verscheide Beelden; schoon van coloriet, en fiks op Doek geschilderd, door een oud Meester | *Mat:* op doek	Roos [for] D	(Sold) fl 2:10 Cramer
1804/08/08	AMSCH	0248	*Een oud Meester* | Een geestige Ordinantie; door een oud Meester	Roos [for] D	(Sold) fl 0:6 Pieterse
1804/08/08	AMSCH	0257	*Een oud Meester* | In een Binnenkamer zit een bevallige Vrouw, met een Kind op haar Schoot, ter zyde haar een oud Man, op de voorgrond een Kind met een Hond speelende; zeer natuurlyk by kaarslicht verbeeld, door een oud Meester, op Doek | *Mat:* op doek *Size:* hoog 30, breed 39 duim	Vink[eles] [for] K[=Gruyter?]	(Sold) fl 0:12 Gruiter
1804/08/08	AMSCH	0261	*[Anonymous]* | Een Grysaard by een Jong Vrouwtje, dat hy Geld aanbied; meesterlyk gepenceeld	Roos [for] E	(Sold) fl 0:14 L Pakker
1804/08/08	AMSCH	0262	*Een allervoornaamst Meester* | Christus aan Tafel zittende met de Emausgangers; zynde kragtig en meesterlyk gepenceeld, door een allervoornaamst Meester	Roos a	(Sold) fl 1:5 Van Iperen
1804/08/08	AMSCH	0265	*[Anonymous]* | Een stil Leeven, zinspeelende op de Verganglykheid; ryk van Ordinantie, en breed en meesterlyk gepenceeld | *Mat:* op doek *Size:* hoog 34, breed 44 duim	Vink[eles] [for] S	(Sold) fl 10:10 Vinkeles [for] K
1804/08/08	AMSCH	0266	*[Anonymous]* | Een diverse Landschappen | *Notes:* In the original title "Twee diverse Landschappen," the word "Twee" was changed by hand to "Een" in the RKDH copy of the catalogue.	Vink[eles] [for] K[=Gruyter?]	(Sold) fl 0:8 Pieterse
1804/08/08	AMSCH	0267	*[Anonymous]* | Twee dito [diverse] dito [Landschappen]	Vink[eles] [for] K[=Gruyter?]	(Sold) fl 1 Pieterse
1804/08/08	AMSCH	0268	*[Anonymous]* | Twee dito [diverse] dito [Landschappen]	Vink[eles] [for] K[=Gruyter?]	(Sold) fl 0:10 L Pakker
1804/08/08	AMSCH	0269	*[Anonymous]* | Twee diverse Schilderyën	Vink[eles] [for] K[=Gruyter?]	(Sold) fl 1 L Pakker
1804/08/08	AMSCH	0270	*[Anonymous]* | Twee dito [diverse] dito [Schilderyën]	Vink[eles] [for] K[=Gruyter?]	(Sold) fl 0:10 L Pakker
1804/08/08	AMSCH	0271[H]	*[Anonymous]* | 1 Schilderij | *Notes:* This lot was added in by hand in the EBNP and LBDa copies of the catalogue.	Roos	(Sold) fl 0:10 L Pakker
1804/08/08	AMSCH	0272[H]	*[Anonymous]* | 2 Schilderijen | *Notes:* This lot was added in by hand in the EBNP and LBDa copies of the catalogue.	Roos	(Sold) fl 8 Coclers
1804/08/08	AMSCH	0273[H]	*[Anonymous]* | 1 Schilderij | *Notes:* This lot was added in by hand in the EBNP and LBDa copies of the catalogue.	Roos	(Sold) fl 0:6 Pieterse
1804/08/08	AMSCH	0274[H]	*[Anonymous]* | 2 Schilderijen | *Notes:* This lot was added in by hand in the EBNP and LBDa copies of the catalogue.	Pruys[senaar]	(Sold) fl 4:10 Gruiter
1804/08/08	AMSCH	0275[H]	*[Anonymous]* | 2 Schilderijen | *Notes:* This lot was added in by hand in the EBNP and LBDa copies of the catalogue.	Pruys[senaar]	(Sold) fl 12 Gruiter
1804/08/08	AMSCH	0276[H]	*[Anonymous]* | 2 Schilderijen | *Notes:* This lot was added in by hand in the EBNP and LBDa copies of the catalogue.	Pruys[senaar]	(Sold) fl 8:10 Gruiter
1804/08/08	AMSCH	0277[H]	*[Anonymous]* | 4 Schilderijen | *Notes:* This lot was added in by hand in the EBNP and LBDa copies of the catalogue.	Roos [for] M	(Sold) fl 1 L Pakker
1804/08/08	AMSCH	0278[H]	*[Anonymous]* | 2 Schilderijen | *Notes:* This lot was added in by hand in the EBNP and LBDa copies of the catalogue.	Roos [for] M	(Sold) fl 0:14 L Pakker
1804/08/08	AMSCH	0279[H]	*[Anonymous]* | 1 Schilderij | *Notes:* This lot was added in by hand in the EBNP and LBDa copies of the catalogue.	Roos [for] M	(Sold) fl 2 L Pakker
1804/08/08	AMSCH	0280[H]	*[Anonymous]* | 1 Schilderij | *Notes:* This lot was added in by hand in the EBNP and LBDa copies of the catalogue.	Roos [for] M	(Sold) fl 1:5 L Pakker
1804/08/08	AMSCH	0281[H]	*[Anonymous]* | 1 Schilderij | *Notes:* This lot was added in by hand in the EBNP and LBDa copies of the catalogue.	Roos [for] M	(Sold) fl 0:6 Pieterse
1804/08/08	AMSCH	0282[H]	*[Anonymous]* | 2 Schilderijen | *Notes:* This lot was added in by hand in the EBNP and LBDa copies of the catalogue.	Roos [for] M	(Sold) fl 0:10 L Pakker
1804/08/08	AMSCH	0283[H]	*[Anonymous]* | 2 Schilderijen | *Notes:* This lot was added in by hand in the EBNP and LBDa copies of the catalogue.	Roos [for] M	(Sold) fl 10:5 Gruiter
1804/08/08	AMSCH	0284[H]	*[Anonymous]* | 1 Schilderij | *Notes:* This lot was added in by hand in the EBNP and LBDa copies of the catalogue.	Roos [for] M	(Sold) fl 0:8 Pieterse
1804/08/08	AMSCH	0285[H]	*[Anonymous]* | 2 Schilderijen | *Notes:* This lot was added in by hand in the EBNP and LBDa copies of the catalogue.	Roos [for] M	(Sold) fl 1 Pieterse
1804/08/08	AMSCH	0287[H]	*[Anonymous]* | 1 Schilderij | *Notes:* This lot was added in by hand in the EBNP and LBDa copies of the catalogue.	Schley [for] B	(Sold) fl 0:2 Pieterse

1804/08/08	AMSCH	0288[H]	*[Anonymous]* | 1 Schilderij | *Notes:* This lot was added in by hand in the EBNP and LBDa copies of the catalogue.	Vink[eles] [for] S	(Sold) fl 0:14 L Pakker
1804/08/08	AMSCH	0289[H]	*[Anonymous]* | 1 Schilderij | *Notes:* This lot was added in by hand in the EBNP and LBDa copies of the catalogue.	Vink[eles] [for] K[=Gruyter?]	(Sold) fl 1 L Pakker
1804/08/08	AMSCH	0290[H]	*[Anonymous]* | 1 Schilderij | *Notes:* This lot was added in by hand in the EBNP and LBDa copies of the catalogue.	Vink[eles] [for] S	(Sold) fl 3:15 Hijbrock
1804/10/08	RMCNL	0001	*[Anonymous]* | Een Watergezigt met verscheide Scheepe en een Voorgrond met geboomte en andere stoffagie	A t'Hooft	(Unknown)
1804/10/08	RMCNL	0002	*[Anonymous]* | Een Badseba	A t'Hooft	(Unknown)
1804/10/08	RMCNL	0005	*[Anonymous]* | Twee dito [fraay Geschilderd] Mans en Vrouwe Pourtrette | *Notes:* It is unclear what "dito" refers to in the title.	A t'Hooft	(Unknown)
1804/10/08	RMCNL	0006	*[Anonymous]* | Een dito [Pourtret]	A t'Hooft	(Unknown)
1804/10/08	RMCNL	0007	*[Anonymous]* | Een Gottique Tempel gestoffert met Beelden verbeeldende Christus de Koopers en Verkoopers uit den Tempel dryvende, uitvoerig geschilderd	A t'Hooft	(Unknown)
1804/10/08	RMCNL	0008	*[Anonymous]* | Lot met zyn Dogters	A t'Hooft	(Unknown)
1804/10/08	RMCNL	0010	*[Anonymous]* | Een stil Leven waar in een Henne groentens, &c.	A t'Hooft	(Unknown)
1804/10/08	RMCNL	0012	*[Anonymous]* | Een Boere Gezelschap	A t'Hooft	(Unknown)
1804/10/08	RMCNL	0015	*[Anonymous]* | Een raad van Goden en Godinne	A t'Hooft	(Unknown)
1804/10/08	RMCNL	0017	*[Anonymous]* | Een Ruwine met eenige Kintjes	A t'Hooft	(Unknown)
1804/10/08	RMCNL	0018	*[Anonymous]* | Een vrolyk Gezelschap in een Goot	A t'Hooft	(Unknown)
1804/10/08	RMCNL	0019	*[Anonymous]* | Een Herder en Herderin	A t'Hooft	(Unknown)
1804/10/08	RMCNL	0023	*[Anonymous]* | Drie stuks Landschappen	A t'Hooft	(Unknown)
1804/10/08	RMCNL	0024	*[Anonymous]* | Een rokend Boertje	A t'Hooft	(Unknown)
1804/10/08	RMCNL	0026	*[Anonymous]* | Een met dood Wilt	A t'Hooft	(Unknown)
1804/10/08	RMCNL	0027	*[Anonymous]* | Een Strand gezigt	A t'Hooft	(Unknown)
1804/10/08	RMCNL	0028	*[Anonymous]* | Een Landschap met stoffagie	A t'Hooft	(Unknown)
1804/10/08	RMCNL	0029	*[Anonymous]* | Drie Lysten	A t'Hooft	(Unknown)
1804/10/08	RMCNL	0031	*[Anonymous]* | Een Kaart van Engeland	A t'Hooft	(Unknown)
1804/10/08	RMCNL	0032	*Een voornaam Meester* | Een schoone Battalje, door en voornaam Meester op paneel | *Mat:* op paneel	A t'Hooft	(Unknown)
1804/10/08	RMCNL	0033	*Een voornaam Meester* | Een Zee gezigt met Scheepen, door dito [een voornaam Meester] | *Mat:* op paneel *Notes:* It is unclear what "dito" refers to in the title.	A t'Hooft	(Unknown)
1804/10/08	RMCNL	0034	*Een voornaam Meester* | Admiraal Schip, door dito [een voornaam Meester] op dito [panneel] | *Mat:* op paneel *Notes:* It is unclear what "dito" refers to in the title.	A t'Hooft	(Unknown)
1804/10/08	RMCNL	0035	*[Anonymous]* | Een fraay Getekent Jagt op Papier en Panneel | *Mat:* op papier op paneel	A t'Hooft	(Unknown)
1804/10/08	RMCNL	0036	*Een goet Meester* | Een schoon gezigt van Rotterdam buiten by Krooswyk, door een goet [sic] Meester | *Mat:* op paneel	A t'Hooft	(Unknown)
1804/10/08	RMCNL	0037	*Een goet Meester* | Twee fraaye Landschappen met Beesten, door dito [een goet [sic] Meester] | *Mat:* op paneel	A t'Hooft	(Unknown)
1804/10/08	RMCNL	0038	*Een goet Meester* | Twee dito [fraaye] Landschappen, door dito [een goet [sic] Meester] | *Mat:* op paneel	A t'Hooft	(Unknown)
1804/10/08	RMCNL	0039	*Een goet Meester* | Twee Maan gezigten, door dito [een goet Meester] | *Mat:* op paneel	A t'Hooft	(Unknown)
1804/10/08	RMCNL	0040	*Een goet Meester* | Een Bloemstuk en een Vrouw en Kint, door dito [een goet [sic] Meester] | *Mat:* op paneel	A t'Hooft	(Unknown)
1804/10/08	RMCNL	0041	*[Anonymous]* | De uitwerping van Hagar | *Mat:* op paneel	A t'Hooft	(Unknown)
1804/10/08	RMCNL	0042	*Een goet Meester* | Een fraay Geschildert oude Vrouwe Kop en een Jong Meisje, door dito [een goet [sic] Meester] | *Mat:* op paneel	A t'Hooft	(Unknown)
1804/10/08	RMCNL	0043	*Een goed Meester* | De vinding van Mosis en een dito [fraay Geschildert?] Bybelsche Historie op Doek, door een goed Meester | *Mat:* op doek *Notes:* It is unclear what "dito" refers to in the title.	A t'Hooft	(Unknown)
1804/10/08	RMCNL	0044	*[Anonymous]* | Een Landschap	A t'Hooft	(Unknown)
1804/10/08	RMCNL	0045	*[Anonymous]* | Een dito Landschap | *Notes:* It is unclear what "dito" refers to in the title.	A t'Hooft	(Unknown)
1804/10/08	RMCNL	0046	*[Anonymous]* | Een dito [Landschap]	A t'Hooft	(Unknown)
1804/10/08	RMCNL	0047	*[Anonymous]* | Een dito [Landschap]	A t'Hooft	(Unknown)
1804/10/08	RMCNL	0048	*[Anonymous]* | Een Zee	A t'Hooft	(Unknown)
1804/10/08	RMCNL	0049	*[Anonymous]* | Een Mans Kop	A t'Hooft	(Unknown)
1804/10/08	RMCNL	0050	*[Anonymous]* | Een Landschap	A t'Hooft	(Unknown)

1804/10/08	RMCNL	0051	*[Anonymous]* | Een dito [Landschap]	A t'Hooft	(Unknown)
1804/10/08	RMCNL	0052	*[Anonymous]* | Een Vrouw met een Spinwiel	A t'Hooft	(Unknown)
1804/10/08	RMCNL	0053	*[Anonymous]* | Een Landschap	A t'Hooft	(Unknown)
1804/10/08	RMCNL	0054	*[Anonymous]* | Een dito [Landschap]	A t'Hooft	(Unknown)
1804/10/08	RMCNL	0055	*[Anonymous]* | Een Batalje	A t'Hooft	(Unknown)
1804/10/08	RMCNL	0056	*[Anonymous]* | Een Meysje met een Mandtje Eyeren	A t'Hooft	(Unknown)
1804/10/08	RMCNL	0057	*[Anonymous]* | Een Landschap	A t'Hooft	(Unknown)
1804/10/08	RMCNL	0058	*[Anonymous]* | Een spelende Vrouw	A t'Hooft	(Unknown)
1804/10/08	RMCNL	0059	*[Anonymous]* | Een Landschap met Koejen | *Notes:* This lot was misnumbered no. 69.	A t'Hooft	(Unknown)
1804/10/08	RMCNL	0060	*[Anonymous]* | Een dito [Landschap met Koejen]	A t'Hooft	(Unknown)
1804/10/08	RMCNL	0061	*[Anonymous]* | Een dito [Landschap] met Koejen	A t'Hooft	(Unknown)
1804/10/08	RMCNL	0062	*[Anonymous]* | Een Vrouwe Pourtret	A t'Hooft	(Unknown)
1804/10/08	RMCNL	0063	*[Anonymous]* | Een Landschap	A t'Hooft	(Unknown)
1804/10/08	RMCNL	0064	*[Anonymous]* | Een Vrouw met Fruit	A t'Hooft	(Unknown)
1804/10/08	RMCNL	0065	*[Anonymous]* | Maria met het Kind	A t'Hooft	(Unknown)
1804/10/08	RMCNL	0066	*[Anonymous]* | Een Kersnagt	A t'Hooft	(Unknown)
1804/10/08	RMCNL	0069	*[Anonymous]* | Een Gezelschap	A t'Hooft	(Unknown)
1804/10/08	RMCNL	0070	*[Anonymous]* | Een Landschapje	A t'Hooft	(Unknown)
1804/10/08	RMCNL	0071	*[Anonymous]* | Een dito Landschap | *Notes:* It is unclear what "dito" refers to in the title.	A t'Hooft	(Unknown)
1804/10/08	RMCNL	0072	*[Anonymous]* | Een drinkend Man	A t'Hooft	(Unknown)
1804/10/08	RMCNL	0073	*[Anonymous]* | Een Varken op de Leer	A t'Hooft	(Unknown)
1804/10/08	RMCNL	0074	*[Anonymous]* | 't Verkeerde Huishouden, 2 stuks	A t'Hooft	(Unknown)
1804/10/16	DLOND	0315	*[Anonymous]* | Een bergagtig helder Landschap, met Paerden, Manschappen en Boeren Woning. Dit Stuk, gemerkt met een Cyffer, heeft veel van Wouwerman, ook van Stoop, ook van van Lin, en is zeer schoon. Paysage clair & montagneux, avec des Hommes & Chevaux, dans le lointain une Maison de Paysan. Dans cette très-belle pièce, marquée d'un Chiffre, on distingue les goûts de Wouwerman, Stoop & van Lin | *Mat:* op doek *Size:* hoog 32, breed 41		(Sold) fl 68 Thijs
1804/10/16	DLOND	0316	*[Anonymous]* | Een oud Man, slapende, met het hoofd in den arm, voor ene Tafel, waarop een glas Wyn, Tabaks-pyp enz.; zeer uitvoerig. Un Vieillard, appuyé avec la main sur une Table, la tête couchée dans son bras; très fini | *Mat:* op doek *Size:* hoog 12, breed 11		(Unknown)
1804/10/16	DLOND	0320	*[Anonymous]* | Een Landschap met een Fontein, waar voor ene Herderin met enig Vee. Paysage avec une Bergère & quelques Animaux devant une Fontaine | *Mat:* op doek *Size:* hoog 13, breed 17		(Unknown)
1804/10/16	DLOND	0321	*[Anonymous]* | Twee stukjens. Vrolyke Boeren en een Scharenslyper. Deux pièces. Des Paysans joyeux & un Gagnepetit | *Mat:* op paneel *Size:* hoog 8, breed 6		(Unknown)
1804/10/16	DLOND	0322	*[Anonymous]* | Twee stukjens. Rokende Boeren. Deux pièces. Des Paysans fumans du Tabac | *Mat:* op paneel *Size:* hoog 7, breed 6		(Unknown)
1804/10/16	DLOND	0323	*[Anonymous]* | Een Vrouwen Hoofd. Tête de Femme | *Mat:* op doek *Size:* hoog 16, breed 13		(Unknown)
1804/10/16	DLOND	0324	*[Anonymous]* | De uitoeffening der Wet van Zaleucus tegen het Overspel, in zyn eigen persoon en dien van zynen Zoon. L'exécution de l'Edit de Zaleucus contre les Adultères, & dans sa propre personne, & dans celle de son Fils | *Mat:* op doek op paneel *Size:* hoog 54, breed 85		(Unknown)
1804/10/16	DLOND	0325	*[Anonymous]* | Sebastiaan met pylen doorschoten. Sebastien percé des flêches | *Mat:* op doek *Size:* hoog 66, breed 51		(Unknown)
1804/10/16	DLOND	0326	*[Anonymous]* | Een Italiaansche Markt, met Gebouwen, Beelden, Naald enz. Vue d'un Marché Italien, avec des Batimens, divers Figures, un Monument &c. | *Mat:* op doek *Size:* hoog 33, breed 71		(Unknown)
1804/10/16	DLOND	0327	*[Anonymous]* | Democritus en Heraclitus | *Size:* hoog 28, breed 22 *Notes:* This lot consisted of two paintings.		(Unknown)
1804/10/16	DLOND	0328	*Een zeer goed Meester* | Een Historie-stuk, door een zeer goed Meester. Pièce Historique très-belle | *Mat:* op doek *Size:* hoog 19, breed 15		(Unknown)
1804/10/16	DLOND	0329	*Een oud Meester* | Uts[a]. [Een Historie-stuk] door een oud Meester. Uts[a]. [Pièce Historique] d'un ancien Maitre | *Mat:* op doek *Size:* hoog 39, breed 29		(Unknown)
1804/10/16	DLOND	0330	*[Anonymous]* | Uts[a] [Een Historie-stuk. Pièce Historique] | *Mat:* op doek *Size:* hoog 29, breed 22		(Unknown)
1804/10/16	DLOND	0333	*[Anonymous]* | Een Schildery met verscheiden Beeldjens. Zeer goed. Tableau avec beaucoup de Figures. Très-bon | *Mat:* op paneel *Size:* hoog 9, breed 7		(Unknown)

1804/10/16	DLOND	0334	*[Anonymous]* | Een oud stuk, met veel gewoel, zynde een Pasquil op Hertog Alva enz. Zeer aartig. Une pièce ancienne, représent. le Duc d' Alva & autres personnes. Pasquinade intéressante | *Mat:* op doek *Size:* hoog 26, breed 42		(Unknown)
1804/10/16	DLOND	0336	*[Anonymous]* | Een Landschap op Doek, volkomen als geëtst. Zeer aartig en fraai. Paysage sur Toile, comme à l'eau forte. Pièce très-intéressante | *Mat:* op doek		(Unknown)
1804/10/16	DLOND	0337	*[Anonymous]* | De overige Schilderyen, waar onder zeer goede Stukken, die op de Catalogus niet konden gebragt worden, zal men, op hunne Nummers, verkopen. On vendra le reste des Tableaux, entre lesquels on distingue de très bonnes pièces, suivant leurs Numéros. Ils ne pouvaient étre placés dans Catalogue		(Sold) fl 53 Oghtersell [?]
1804/10/20	GRBOL	0005	*[Anonymous]* | Een Landschap met Harten	Joannis Cannegieteri	(Unknown)
1804/10/20	GRBOL	0012	*[Anonymous]* | Een Bybelsche Historie	Joannis Cannegieteri	(Unknown)
1804/10/20	GRBOL	0014	*[Anonymous]* | Willem de Eerste Prins van Oranje [Met Lysten en Glazen] | *Notes:* The bracketed information in the title appears above lot 14 and refers to lots 14 to 52.	Joannis Cannegieteri	(Unknown)
1804/10/20	GRBOL	0015	*[Anonymous]* | Maurits Prins van Oranje [Met Lysten en Glazen] | *Notes:* The bracketed information in the title appears above lot 14 and refers to lots 14 to 52.	Joannis Cannegieteri	(Unknown)
1804/10/20	GRBOL	0016	*[Anonymous]* | Fredrik Hendrik [Met Lysten en Glazen] | *Notes:* The bracketed information in the title appears above lot 14 and refers to lots 14 to 52.	Joannis Cannegieteri	(Unknown)
1804/10/20	GRBOL	0017	*[Anonymous]* | Willem de Tweede [Met Lysten en Glazen] | *Notes:* The bracketed information in the title appears above lot 14 and refers to lots 14 to 52.	Joannis Cannegieteri	(Unknown)
1804/10/20	GRBOL	0018	*[Anonymous]* | Willem de derde en deszelfs Gemalinne, 2 stuk [Met Lysten en Glazen] | *Notes:* The bracketed information in the title appears above lot 14 and refers to lots 14 to 52.	Joannis Cannegieteri	(Unknown)
1804/10/20	GRBOL	0019	*[Anonymous]* | Johan Willem Friso en deszelfs Gemalinne, 2 stuk [Met Lysten en Glazen] | *Notes:* The bracketed information in the title appears above lot 14 and refers to lots 14 to 52.	Joannis Cannegieteri	(Unknown)
1804/10/20	GRBOL	0020	*[Anonymous]* | Willem de vierde en deszelfs Gemalinne, 2 stuk [Met Lysten en Glazen] | *Notes:* The bracketed information in the title appears above lot 14 and refers to lots 14 to 52.	Joannis Cannegieteri	(Unknown)
1804/10/20	GRBOL	0021	*[Anonymous]* | Willem de vyfde en Carolyna deszelfs Zuster [Met Lysten en Glazen] | *Notes:* The bracketed information in the title appears above lot 14 and refers to lots 14 to 52.	Joannis Cannegieteri	(Unknown)
1804/10/20	GRBOL	0022	*[Anonymous]* | J.A. Zoutman, Schout by Nacht [Met Lysten en Glazen] | *Notes:* The bracketed information in the title appears above lot 14 and refers to lots 14 to 52.	Joannis Cannegieteri	(Unknown)
1804/10/20	GRBOL	0023	*[Anonymous]* | Zee Capitein van Kinsbergen [Met Lysten en Glazen] | *Notes:* The bracketed information in the title appears above lot 14 and refers to lots 14 to 52.	Joannis Cannegieteri	(Unknown)
1804/10/20	GRBOL	0024	*[Anonymous]* | Zee Capitein Salomon Dedel [Met Lysten en Glazen] | *Notes:* The bracketed information in the title appears above lot 14 and refers to lots 14 to 52.	Joannis Cannegieteri	(Unknown)
1804/10/20	GRBOL	0025	*[Anonymous]* | Zee Capitein Willem van Braam [Met Lysten en Glazen] | *Notes:* The bracketed information in the title appears above lot 14 and refers to lots 14 to 52.	Joannis Cannegieteri	(Unknown)
1804/10/20	GRBOL	0026	*[Anonymous]* | Zee Capitein E.C. Staringh [Met Lysten en Glazen] | *Notes:* The bracketed information in the title appears above lot 14 and refers to lots 14 to 52.	Joannis Cannegieteri	(Unknown)
1804/10/20	GRBOL	0027	*[Anonymous]* | Zee Capitein Bentinck [Met Lysten en Glazen] | *Notes:* The bracketed information in the title appears above lot 14 and refers to lots 14 to 52.	Joannis Cannegieteri	(Unknown)
1804/10/20	GRBOL	0028	*[Anonymous]* | Zee Capitein A. Braak [Met Lysten en Glazen] | *Notes:* The bracketed information in the title appears above lot 14 and refers to lots 14 to 52.	Joannis Cannegieteri	(Unknown)
1804/10/20	GRBOL	0029	*[Anonymous]* | T. Paine [Met Lysten en Glazen] | *Notes:* The bracketed information in the title appears above lot 14 and refers to lots 14 to 52.	Joannis Cannegieteri	(Unknown)
1804/10/20	GRBOL	0030	*[Anonymous]* | Van Jr. D. van der Capellen tot del Pol., 2 stuk [Met Lysten en Glazen] | *Notes:* The bracketed information in the title appears above lot 14 and refers to lots 14 to 52.	Joannis Cannegieteri	(Unknown)
1804/10/20	GRBOL	0031	*[Anonymous]* | Necker [Met Lysten en Glazen] | *Notes:* The bracketed information in the title appears above lot 14 and refers to lots 14 to 52.	Joannis Cannegieteri	(Unknown)
1804/10/20	GRBOL	0032	*[Anonymous]* | Du Mourier [Met Lysten en Glazen] | *Notes:* The bracketed information in the title appears above lot 14 and refers to lots 14 to 52.	Joannis Cannegieteri	(Unknown)
1804/10/20	GRBOL	0033	*[Anonymous]* | G. Noodt [Met Lysten en Glazen] | *Notes:* The bracketed information in the title appears above lot 14 and refers to lots 14 to 52.	Joannis Cannegieteri	(Unknown)

1804/10/20	GRBOL	0034	*[Anonymous]* | Een Schildery met glas en lyst [Met Lysten en Glazen] | *Notes:* The bracketed information in the title appears above lot 14 and refers to lots 14 to 52.	Joannis Cannegieteri	(Unknown)
1804/10/22	MGWIN	0004[H]	*[Anonymous]* | Een koper lak telescoop in an Seg[ ]ein[ ] koke | *Notes:* This lot was added in by hand in the ZBM copy of the catalogue under the heading "Schilderyen," but it is uncertain whether it is a painting.	F Reytsma	(Bought In) £ 1
1804/10/22	MGWIN	0005[H]	*[Anonymous]* | 2 kaffe n st kapellen | *Notes:* This lot was added in by hand in the ZBM copy of the catalogue under the heading "Schilderyen," but it is uncertain whether it is a painting.	F Reytsma	(Sold) £ 0.5 Geld
1804/10/29	HRBAU	0126	*[Anonymous]* | Eene Vrouw, zittende by eene Tafel, waar op zy met den elleboog rust, schynende den Aanschouwer hartelyk toe te lachgen. Dit Schildery doet, op eenen afstand, eene schoone werking; wyders is het in eene byzondere manier, doch teffens zeer meesterlyk, uitgevoerd | *Mat:* op doek *Size:* hoog 30, breed 26 duim	Simon Styl	(Unknown)
1804/10/29	HRBAU	0127	*[Anonymous]* | Eene zeer bevallige Dame, welker hoofd gedekt is met een blauw satynen Herderinnen Hoed, met Pluimen versierd, schynende zeer natuurlyk op de Bas te speelen. Bevallig en meesterlyk geschilderd | *Mat:* op doek *Size:* hoog 32, breed 24 duim	Simon Styl	(Unknown)
1804/10/29	HRBAU	0128	*[Anonymous]* | Het Pourtrait van een Hindeloper Zee-Kapitein. Fiks en smeltend behandeld | *Mat:* op doek *Size:* hoog 30, breed 25 duim	Simon Styl	(Unknown)
1804/10/29	HRBAU	0130	*[Anonymous]* | Voor aan, op een' hoek Lands, zyn eenige Heeren en Dames, welken zig met visschen vermaaken. Aan de overzyde van het water is een boschagtig en met Hofsteden versierd Landschap; het water is gestoffeerd met Schuiten en andere Vaartuigen. De deinzigheid der lucht, als in den morgenstond, is in dit Stuk zeer wel waargenomen, en is zeer bevallig en uitvoerig behandeld | *Mat:* op doek *Size:* hoog 20, breed 25 duim	Simon Styl	(Unknown)
1804/10/29	HRBAU	0133	*Een oud Meester* | Twee stuks sterk woelende Zeeën, gestoffeerd met verschillende Schepen. Door een oud Meester | *Mat:* op paneel *Size:* hoog 17, breed 24 duim	Simon Styl	(Unknown)
1804/10/29	HRBAU	0135	*[Anonymous]* | Het Gezigt van het inzeilen van een Haven, ryk met Schepen versierd en plaisant behandeld | *Mat:* op doek *Size:* hoog 17, breed 22 duim	Simon Styl	(Unknown)
1804/10/29	HRBAU	0136	*[Anonymous]* | Op den Voorgrond zit eene Herderin met een Hondjen, welke door heur galant gestreeld wordt; hier by zyn eenige staande en liggende Koeijen en Schaapen; met een bergagtig verschiet. Fiks behandeld | *Mat:* op doek *Size:* hoog 20, breed 15 ½ duim	Simon Styl	(Unknown)
1804/10/29	HRBAU	0139	*[Anonymous]* | De Zomer, door Kindertjens, die Koorn oogsten, verbeeld | *Mat:* op doek *Size:* hoog 24, breed 29 duim	Simon Styl	(Unknown)
1804/10/29	HRBAU	0140	*Een goed Meester* | Maria Magdalena in overdenking zynde, schynende door een' Engel vertroost te worden. Breed en kragtig behandeld door een goed Meester | *Mat:* op doek *Size:* hoog 48, breed 32 duim	Simon Styl	(Unknown)
1804/10/29	HRBAU	0141	*[Anonymous]* | Een Ruiter zit in volle Equipagie op een wit paard, nevens een' rustenden Hond by eene Ruïne; waar agter een Gebouw en bergagtig verschiet. Fiks en uitvoerig geschilderd | *Mat:* op paneel *Size:* hoog 16 ½, breed 13 duim	Simon Styl	(Unknown)
1804/10/29	HRBAU	0143	*[Anonymous]* | Een Heremiet in zyn Kluis, zittende in eene opgetoogene houding: hy heeft een Boek op zyn' schoot, terwyl naast hem op eene tafel nog eenige andere, benevens een Doodshoofd, liggen. Zeer zonagtig behandeld | *Mat:* op paneel *Size:* hoog 16, breed 14 duim	Simon Styl	(Unknown)
1804/10/29	HRBAU	0145	*Een groot Meester* | Een Mans Hoofd in profil, hebbende een' zwarten Baard. Helder en fiks behandeld door een groot Meester | *Mat:* op paneel *Size:* hoog 10, breed 8 duim	Simon Styl	(Unknown)
1804/10/29	HRBAU	0147	*[Anonymous]* | Een rood bont Koetjen staat op den Voorgrond, waar by een roode Koe, benevens eenig klein Vee, is liggende, welke door een spinnende Herderin schynen gehoed te worden. Iets verder is een Ruïn van een Colom, en een bergagtig verschiet | *Mat:* op doek *Size:* hoog 18, breed 32 duim	Simon Styl	(Unknown)
1804/10/29	HRBAU	0148	*[Anonymous]* | In een' Stal ziet men twee Geiten by hunne Jongen, welke door een' Knegt schynen gevoerd te zullen worden. Zeer fraai en meesterlyk behandeld | *Mat:* op paneel *Size:* hoog 12 ½, breed 15 duim	Simon Styl	(Unknown)
1804/10/29	HRBAU	0149	*[Anonymous]* | Een bevallig stil Water, ryk gestoffeerd met diverse Vaartuigen; aan de overzyde zyn brandende Kalkövens, en in 't verschiet eene Stad. Dit alles wordt door de Maan, welke zig gedeeltelyk agter de wolken verschuilt verlicht; 't welk eene fraaije verdeeling van lichten maakt, zo op de voorwerpen als op het water, dat zeer dunnetjes behandeld is | *Mat:* op paneel *Size:* hoog 9, breed 11 duim	Simon Styl	(Unknown)
1804/10/29	HRBAU	0150	*[Anonymous]* | Een hoog bergagtig Landschap, met eene Rivier doorsneeden, en met veel Geboomte beplant. Hetzelve is aartig gestoffeerd en uitvoerig geschilderd | *Mat:* op paneel *Size:* hoog 20, breed 27 duim	Simon Styl	(Unknown)
1804/10/29	HRBAU	0151	*[Anonymous]* | Door een Nis, waar voor eene Tafel met Meloenen, Comcommers en Wortelen staat, ziet men een Vrouwtjen bezig Kool	Simon Styl	(Unknown)

			te snyden; terwyl een Man haar onder de kin streelt. Zeer uitvoerig geschilderd | *Mat:* op paneel *Size:* hoog 10, breed 10 duim		
1804/10/29	HRBAU	0154	*[Anonymous]* | Een Oud Mans Hoofd met gryze hairen en baard, welken hy in zyne handen vasthoudt. Zeer kloek en meesterlyk behandeld | *Mat:* op paneel *Size:* hoog 30, breed 23 duim	Simon Styl	(Unknown)
1804/10/29	HRBAU	0156	*[Anonymous]* | De Geboorte Christi in den stal van Bethlehem. Fiks en meesterlyk behandeld | *Mat:* op paneel *Size:* hoog 20, breed 14 duim	Simon Styl	(Unknown)
1804/10/29	HRBAU	0157	*[Anonymous]* | Een bevallig Landschapjen, met Schaapjens en Bokjens gestoffeerd; waar agter een aangenaam verschiet. Helder en zeer plaisant behandeld | *Mat:* op paneel *Size:* hoog 11 ½, breed 14 duim	Simon Styl	(Unknown)
1804/10/29	HRBAU	0158	*[Anonymous]* | Een zittend Boertjen, met een Pypjen in zyn hand, wordende door een Vrouwtjen op eene aartige wyze gecaresseerd waar over hy hartelyk schynt te lachgen; waar by nog twee Boertjens. Fiks behandeld | *Mat:* op doek *Size:* hoog 13, breed 16 duim	Simon Styl	(Unknown)
1804/10/29	HRBAU	0161	*[Anonymous]* | Een zeer bevallig Jongetjen, houdende met zyn linkerhand een Geit by zyn kopjen, terwyl hy in zyn regterhand de Koorde houdt: zyn hoofd is gedekt door een' ronden Hoed; hy is in het zwart gekleed, met een' linnen Kraag om den hals, ziende naar den Aanschouwer met een zeer vergenoegd gelaat. Alles is spreekend, zeer smeltend, en meesterlyk behandeld | *Mat:* op paneel *Size:* hoog 22, breed 17 duim	Simon Styl	(Unknown)
1804/10/29	HRBAU	0162	*[Anonymous]* | In een Landschap wordt aan de Herders, omtrent Bethlehem, de Geboorte des Heilands, door de Engelen, welken zig in gloirie vertoonen, aangekondigd. Het licht werkt fraai, en is klikkig geschilderd | *Mat:* op paneel *Size:* hoog 22, breed 18 ½ duim	Simon Styl	(Unknown)
1804/10/29	HRBAU	0163	*[Anonymous]* | Een Mannetjen, met een ruige muts op het hoofd, staande te rooken. Fiks behandeld | *Mat:* op paneel *Size:* hoog 7, breed 6 duim	Simon Styl	(Unknown)
1804/10/29	HRBAU	0165	*[Anonymous]* | Joseph, den Beeker in den Koornzak van Benjamin vindende, waar over alle de aanwezenden verwonderd schynen. Fiks en in eene grootsche manier behandeld | *Mat:* op doek *Size:* hoog 44, breed 66 duim	Simon Styl	(Unknown)
1804/10/29	HRBAU	0166	*Een oud Meester* | Een Gevegt tusschen Ruitery en Voetvolk. Door een oud Meester | *Mat:* op paneel *Size:* hoog 16, breed 20 duim	Simon Styl	(Unknown)
1804/10/29	HRBAU	0167	*[Anonymous]* | Een Gevegt in een Grot. Door een goed Meester | *Mat:* op paneel *Size:* hoog 16, breed 23 duim	Simon Styl	(Unknown)
1804/10/29	HRBAU	0168	*[Anonymous]* | Een Riviergezigt aan welker oever eene Stad, waarschynlyk Antwerpen, ligt; zynde het water ryk met Schepen en Schuiten gestoffeerd | *Mat:* op doek *Size:* hoog 24, breed 32 duim	Simon Styl	(Unknown)
1804/10/29	HRBAU	0170	*[Anonymous]* | Drie stuks, een Landschapjen, een leezend Man en een Kop	Simon Styl	(Unknown)
1804/10/29	HRBAU	0171	*[Anonymous]* | Twee dito [stuks], een leezend en een rookend Vrouwtjen	Simon Styl	(Unknown)
1804/10/29	HRBAU	0172	*[Anonymous]* | Drie dito [stuks], een Landschap, een Paardenstuk en een Slaapende Venus	Simon Styl	(Unknown)
1804/10/29	HRBAU	0173	*[Anonymous]* | Twee stuks, het vertrekken van Willem den V. van Scheveningen, en het gevangen neemen van den Russischen Generaal Herman, in fraaie Lysten en Glaazen	Simon Styl	(Unknown)
1804/10/29	HRBAU	0174	*[Anonymous]* | Twee dito [stuks], Vrede en Vryheid, en Liefde en Eendragt, als boven in Lysten en Glaazen	Simon Styl	(Unknown)
1804/12/10	AMSCH	0105	*[Anonymous]* | Een Historieele Ordinantie, fix en krachtig van schildering | *Mat:* op doek *Size:* hoog 45, breed 38 duim	Jan De Groot	(Sold) fl 2 J Spaan
1804/12/10	AMSCH	0106	*[Anonymous]* | Een Gezicht langs de Vaart op de Stad Delft, ryk gestoffeerd met vaartuigen en fix behandeld | *Mat:* op doek *Size:* hoog 23, breed 32 duim	Jan De Groot	(Sold) fl 1 Coclers
1804/12/10	AMSCH	0107	*[Anonymous]* | Een Stads Gezicht, op de voorgrond ziet men een Brug, door welk men een gedeelte der Stad ziet, fraai en plaisant behandeld | *Mat:* op paneel *Size:* hoog 11, breed 15 duim	Jan De Groot	(Sold) fl 10 Coclers
1804/12/10	AMSCH	0108	*[Anonymous]* | Een zinnebeeldige Fabel-ordinantie, gestoffeerd met verscheide beelden en verder bywerk, kloek en meesterlyk geschilderd | *Mat:* op doek *Size:* hoog 21, breed 26 duim	Jan De Groot	(Sold) fl 1:15 Scheepens
1804/12/10	AMSCH	0109	*[Anonymous]* | In een Landschap vertoont zich een slaapende Nimph, gedeeltelyk met een linnen kleed omhangen en is van een meesterlyke penceel behandeling | *Mat:* op doek *Size:* hoog 24, breed 35 duim	Jan De Groot	(Sold) fl 2:10 Coclers
1804/12/10	AMSCH	0110	*[Anonymous]* | De Marteldood van St. Laurentius; op een ruime markt met verscheide gebouwen, vertoonen zig krygslieden te paard en een meenigte aanschouders [sic], vol gewoel; het is krachtig, geschilderd op Doek | *Mat:* op doek *Size:* hoog 29, breed 38 duim	Jan De Groot	(Sold) fl 3:5 W v d Schley
1804/12/10	AMSCH	0116	*[Anonymous]* | Een Gezicht buiten Utrecht na de Maliebaan, frai en bevallig gestoffeerd, en fix behandeld | *Mat:* op paneel *Size:* hoog 11, breed 15 duim	Jan De Groot	(Sold) fl 8:10 van Iperen
1804/12/10	AMSCH	0118	*[Anonymous]* | Een Gezicht van een Klooster, men ziet op de voorgrond twee monniken en andere wandelende persoonen; zeer fraai en meesterlyk gepenceeld | *Mat:* op paneel *Size:* hoog 17, breed 20 duim	Jan De Groot	(Sold) fl 6 Coclers

1804/12/10	AMSCH	0119	*[Anonymous]* | Een boere Kermis, fiks van schildering | *Mat:* op doek *Size:* hoog 21, breed 33 duim	Jan De Groot	(Sold) fl 1 Levy Pakker
1804/12/10	AMSCH	0120	*[Anonymous]* | Een Landschap met Beelden en beesjes gestoffeerd, en een bergachtig verschiet; fraai gepenceeld op Doek | *Mat:* op doek *Size:* hoog 14, breed 24 duim	Jan De Groot	(Sold) fl 4 Yver
1804/12/10	AMSCH	0122	*[Anonymous]* | Een capitaal Strand-Gezicht aan Zee, gestoffeerd met wandelende lieden, rydende postwagen, vissers in hunne vaartuigen, ter zyde aan duin vertoont zig een kerktooren, zonagtig en meesterlyk behandeld | *Mat:* op doek *Size:* hoog 21, breed 27 duim	Jan De Groot	(Sold) fl 43 Valette
1804/12/10	AMSCH	0123	*[Anonymous]* | Een Landschap, verbeeldende de zondvloet, men ziet verscheide persoonen die zig zoeken te redden, dit stuk is zeer ryk van ordinantie en krachtig gepenceeld | *Mat:* op paneel *Size:* hoog 29, breed 49 duim	Jan De Groot	(Sold) fl 2 van Iperen
1804/12/10	AMSCH	0124	*[Anonymous]* | op een steene tafel ziet men verscheide jachtgereedschap, waarby een doode Haan en ander dood wild, meesterlyk geschilderd op Doek | *Mat:* op doek *Size:* hoog 37, breed 38 duim	Jan De Groot	(Sold) fl 5 Gruiter
1804/12/10	AMSCH	0126	*[Anonymous]* | Twee stuks een jongeling met een grens en een meisje in een landschap, fraai gepenceeld | *Mat:* op paneel *Size:* hoog 10, breed 8 duim	Jan De Groot	(Sold) fl 3 Yver
1805/02/09	HGBES	0002	*[Anonymous]* | Een Klein ovaal [P]ourtrait, op Paneel in een vergulde Lyst en Glas | *Mat:* op paneel *Fmt:* ovaal		(Unknown)
1805/02/09	HGBES	0003	*[Anonymous]* | Een dito [Klein ovaal Pourtrait] verbeeldenbe [sic] een gekweste Krygsman, dito [vergulde] Lyst en Glas | *Fmt:* ovaal		(Unknown)
1805/02/09	HGBES	0004	*[Anonymous]* | Een Staande Pourtret in een zwarte Lyst, item Man en Vrouw in een vergulde Lyst en Glas, zamen 3 stukken		(Unknown)
1805/04/23	HOBEE	0005	*[Anonymous]* | Een Watergezichtje		(Unknown)
1805/06/24	DOBLU	0003	*[Anonymous]* | Twee Fabelsche Historiën	Willem Snellen [or] F R E Nibbelinck [or] Gysbert Visser	(Unknown)
1805/06/24	DOBLU	0004	*[Anonymous]* | Een Oudmans Portrait, Konstig Geschildert	Willem Snellen [or] F R E Nibbelinck [or] Gysbert Visser	(Unknown)
1805/06/24	DOBLU	0005	*[Anonymous]* | Een dito [Oudmans Portrait]	Willem Snellen [or] F R E Nibbelinck [or] Gysbert Visser	(Unknown)
1805/06/24	DOBLU	0006	*[Anonymous]* | Een Woelend Zeetje	Willem Snellen [or] F R E Nibbelinck [or] Gysbert Visser	(Unknown)
1805/06/24	DOBLU	0007	*[Anonymous]* | Een Boere Binnenhuis	Willem Snellen [or] F R E Nibbelinck [or] Gysbert Visser	(Unknown)
1805/06/24	DOBLU	0010	*[Anonymous]* | Een met Vruchten	Willem Snellen [or] F R E Nibbelinck [or] Gysbert Visser	(Unknown)
1805/06/24	DOBLU	0011	*[Anonymous]* | Een Landschap	Willem Snellen [or] F R E Nibbelinck [or] Gysbert Visser	(Unknown)
1805/06/24	DOBLU	0012	*[Anonymous]* | Een Rookende Man	Willem Snellen [or] F R E Nibbelinck [or] Gysbert Visser	(Unknown)
1805/06/24	DOBLU	0013	*[Anonymous]* | Een Landschap	Willem Snellen [or] F R E Nibbelinck [or] Gysbert Visser	(Unknown)
1805/06/24	DOBLU	0014	*[Anonymous]* | Een dito [Landschap]	Willem Snellen [or] F R E Nibbelinck [or] Gysbert Visser	(Unknown)
1805/06/24	DOBLU	0016	*[Anonymous]* | Een Landschap	Willem Snellen [or] F R E Nibbelinck [or] Gysbert Visser	(Unknown)
1805/06/24	DOBLU	0018	*[Anonymous]* | Een Ruïne	Willem Snellen [or] F R E Nibbelinck [or] Gysbert Visser	(Unknown)
1805/06/24	DOBLU	0020	*[Anonymous]* | Een Rookend Boertje	Willem Snellen [or] F R E Nibbelinck [or] Gysbert Visser	(Unknown)
1805/06/24	DOBLU	0022	*[Anonymous]* | Twee dito [kleine Stukjes]	Willem Snellen [or] F R E Nibbelinck [or] Gysbert Visser	(Unknown)
1805/06/24	DOBLU	0027	*Een Voornaam Meester* | Een Romeinsch Stuk met veel Beelden en Paarden, door een Voornaam Meester	Willem Snellen [or] F R E Nibbelinck [or] Gysbert Visser	(Unknown)

1805/06/24	DOBLU	0030	*Een voornaam Meester* | De Opwekking van Lazarus, door een voornaam Meester | *Mat:* op doek	Willem Snellen [or] F R E Nibbelinck [or] Gysbert Visser	(Unknown)
1805/06/29	GDBRK	[0001]	*[Anonymous]* | Twintig stuks Schilderyen, door differente Meesters, by het paar, of stuk te verkoopen | *Notes:* Because this lot was not numbered in the catalogue, we have assigned the number.		(Unknown)
1805/07/01	MGBEO	0001	*[Anonymous]* | [Untitled] | *Notes:* The only extant copy of this catalogue is annotated with the buyers and prices, but it does not include a printed list of the paintings.		(Sold) £ 0.4 Valkenar [?]
1805/07/01	MGBEO	0002	*[Anonymous]* | [Untitled] | *Notes:* The only extant copy of this catalogue is annotated with the buyers and prices, but it does not include a printed list of the paintings.		(Sold) £ 0.5 Ooms
1805/07/01	MGBEO	0003	*[Anonymous]* | [Untitled] | *Notes:* The only extant copy of this catalogue is annotated with the buyers and prices, but it does not include a printed list of the paintings.		(Sold) £ 0.2 Ooms
1805/07/01	MGBEO	0004	*[Anonymous]* | [Untitled] | *Notes:* The only extant copy of this catalogue is annotated with the buyers and prices, but it does not include a printed list of the paintings.		(Sold) £ 0.1 Ooms
1805/07/01	MGBEO	0005	*[Anonymous]* | [Untitled] | *Notes:* The only extant copy of this catalogue is annotated with the buyers and prices, but it does not include a printed list of the paintings.		(Sold) £ 0.1 Geld
1805/07/01	MGBEO	0006	*[Anonymous]* | [Untitled] | *Notes:* The only extant copy of this catalogue is annotated with the buyers and prices, but it does not include a printed list of the paintings.		(Bought In)
1805/07/03	AMSCH	0179	*[Anonymous]* | Twee stuks differente Zeetjes, met verscheiden zoorten van Vaartuigen	R[oos]	(Sold) fl 29 L Pakker
1805/07/03	AMSCH	0180[b]	*[Anonymous]* | Een Bloemstuk, door P. van den Heuvel, en een ander dito | *This Lot:* Een ander Bloemstuk; lot 180[a] by P. Heuvel	R[oos]	(Sold) fl 1:5 for lots 180[a] & 180[b]. Agina
1805/07/03	AMSCH	0187	*[Anonymous]* | Een vrolyke Boer met een Kan op zyn Knie en een Roemer in de Hand, by een Tafel met spyzen; kragtig en uitvoerig op Paneel | *Mat:* op paneel	C	(Sold) fl 3:10 H Pakker
1805/07/03	AMSCH	0190	*[Anonymous]* | Twee stuks, een Jonge met een Mossepot en een Vrouw die een Pen versnyd; kragtig op Doek | *Mat:* op doek	C	(Sold) fl 62 van Iperen
1805/07/03	AMSCH	0194[H]	*[Anonymous]* | Een Schildery | *Notes:* This lot was added in by hand in the FLNY copy of the catalogue.	C	(Sold) fl 2:5 Esser
1805/07/03	AMSCH	0204	*Een goed Meester* | Een Hert overvallen wordende door eenige Honden in een Water; breed en meesterlyk gepenceeld op Doek, door een goed Meester | *Mat:* op doek	V[inkeles]	(Sold) fl 4 Coclers
1805/07/03	AMSCH	0205	*[Anonymous]* | De Kruisdraging Christi, verzeld van een ménigte Krygslieden te paard en te voet, op de Voorgrond eenige Vrouwen; uitvoerig behandeld op Paneel, gem. Anno 1562 | *Mat:* op paneel *Size:* hoog 29, breed 32 duim *Inscr:* Anno 1562 (dated)	V[inkeles]	(Sold) fl 3 Levy Pakker
1805/07/03	AMSCH	0206	*Een geed Meester* | Een Boomryk Landschap met een Rivier doorsneeden, gestoffeerd met een Heer en Dame te paard; aller natuurlykst en meesterlyk op Paneel, door een geed [sic] Meester | *Mat:* op paneel	V[inkeles]	(Sold) fl 2 Agina
1805/07/03	AMSCH	0208	*[Anonymous]* | Twee stuks bevallige Boom- en Duinachtige Landschapjes, zynde een Winter en Zomer; fiks op Paneel | *Mat:* op paneel	V[inkeles]	(Sold) fl 5:10 Tessier
1805/07/03	AMSCH	0210	*[Anonymous]* | Een Binnehuis, waarin een Vrouw, verzelt van eenige Kinderen, bézig Koeken te bakken | *Mat:* op paneel	G	(Sold) fl 3 Agina
1805/07/03	AMSCH	0211	*[Anonymous]* | Twee stuks Binnenhuizen, beide gestoffeerd met vrolyke Huislieden en verder bywerk; alles als by brandend kaarslicht, fiks gepenceeld op Doek | *Mat:* op doek	G	(Sold) fl 4:15 Van Giesen
1805/07/03	AMSCH	0215	*[Anonymous]* | Eenige Boeren zittende te rooken by een Schoorsteen; fiks gepenceeld	V[inkeles]	(Sold) fl 0:6 L Pakker
1805/07/10	AMSCH	0157a[H]	*[Anonymous]* | [Untitled] | *Notes:* This lot was added in by hand in the EBNP copy of the catalogue, but without giving an artist or title.	V[inkeles]	(Bought In) fl 10
1805/07/10	AMSCH	0178	*Een voornaam Meester* | Joseph ontvlugt Potifars Huisvrouw, welk bynaar naakt op een Bed zit; meesterlyk getékend en geschilderd, door een voornaam Meester | *Mat:* op doek *Size:* hoog 48, breed 67 duim	R[oos]	(Sold) fl 1 Jan Yver
1805/07/10	AMSCH	0179	*Een voortreffelyk Meester* | Een Man, welke met een vrolyk gelaat, Vrugten aan een Dame verkoopt, agterwaarts een Grysaard met een Bos Zeldry [sic]; kragtig op Doek, door een voortreffelyk Meester | *Mat:* op doek *Size:* hoog 38, breed 52 duim	R[oos]	(Sold) fl 4 Gruyter
1805/07/10	AMSCH	0183	*Een goed Meester* | Een vervallen Steene Brug, over een Rivier leggende, gestoffeerd met Beelden; bevallig op Doek, door een goed Meester | *Mat:* op doek	R[oos]	(Sold) fl 16 Lafontaine
1805/07/10	AMSCH	0187	*[Anonymous]* | Een oud Man in een Nis, met een Haring en Uijen; geestig op Paneel | *Mat:* op paneel	R[oos]	(Sold) fl 0:10 Mensaart

1805/07/10	AMSCH	0196	*[Anonymous]* | Het verbranden van een Oorlogschip op Zee | *Notes:* This lot was sold with lot 195, which is in the manner of Zeemann.	R[oos]	(Sold) fl 0:10 for lots 195 & 196. L Pakker
1805/07/10	AMSCH	0202	*Een goed Meester* | Mercuur en Argus, in een Landschap; krachtig en breed geschilderd, door een goed Meester	V[inkeles] [for] P	(Sold) fl 0:10 L Pakker
1805/07/10	AMSCH	0203	*Een goed Meester* | Twee stuks Gezichten binnen Amsterdam, het eene een Gezicht op 't Kweekschool, en 't andere na de Munt-Tooren; zonachtig door een goed Meester	V[inkeles] [for] J	(Sold) fl 7 L Pakker
1805/07/10	AMSCH	0207	*Een goed Meester* | Een rustend Krygsman; door een goed Meester	V[inkeles] [for] G	(Sold) fl 1 Gruyter
1805/07/10	AMSCH	0212	*Een goed Meester* | In een hoog en steyl Bergachtig Landschap, ziet men een Postwagen, Reysigers, enz.; fiks op Doek, door een goed Meester | *Mat:* op doek	V[inkeles] [for] H[affner]	(Bought In) fl 2
1805/07/10	AMSCH	0216	*[Anonymous]* | Een Onstuimige Zee, met twee zylende Scheepen; fraai van licht en meesterlyk geschildert	V[inkeles] [for] H[affner]	(Bought In) fl 3:5
1805/07/10	AMSCH	0221	*[Anonymous]* | Twee stuks, met Boeren in Binnehuizen	Y[ver]	(Sold) fl 0:6 L Pakker
1805/07/10	AMSCH	0222	*[Anonymous]* | Twee dito [stuks], met dito [Boeren in Binnehuizen] | *Notes:* It is unclear what "dito" refers to in the title.	Y[ver]	(Sold) fl 0:6 for lots 222 & 223. L Pakker
1805/07/10	AMSCH	0223	*[Anonymous]* | Twee Landschapjes, divers	Y[ver]	(Sold) fl 0:6 for lots 222 & 223. L Pakker
1805/07/10	AMSCH	0224	*[Anonymous]* | Vier stuks dito [Landschapjes] dito [divers] | *Notes:* It is unclear what "dito" refers to in the title. This lot was sold with lot 225, which contained drawings.	Y[ver]	(Sold) fl 0:6 for lots 224 & 225. L Pakker
1805/07/10	AMSCH	0226	*[Anonymous]* | Twaalf stuks Portraiten, der Famillie van de Princen van Oranje, welke in één Koop, of by Paren Verkogt zullen worden	Spaan [for] H	(Sold) fl 9:10 Vallet
1805/07/10	AMSCH	0227	*[Anonymous]* | Twee stuks Portraiten | *Mat:* op koper	Y[ver]	(Sold) fl 1 for lots 227 & 228. Gruyter
1805/07/10	AMSCH	0228	*[Anonymous]* | Twee dito [stuks] musiceerende Gezelschappen	Y[ver]	(Sold) fl 1 for lots 227 & 228. Gruyter
1805/07/10	AMSCH	0233	*[Anonymous]* | Een Bergachtig Landschap, met een Ruïne | *Notes:* This lot was sold with lot 232 by L. Doomer.	Y[ver]	(Bought In) fl 10 for lots 232 & 233
1805/07/10	AMSCH	0236	*[Anonymous]* | Een Grysaard met gevouwe Handen	Y[ver]	(Sold) fl 0:6 L Pakker
1805/07/10	AMSCH	0237	*[Anonymous]* | Een ryk gestoffeerd Zeestrand	Y[ver]	(Bought In) fl 0:10
1805/07/10	AMSCH	0238	*[Anonymous]* | Een Tafel, waarop diversch dood Gevogelten	Y[ver]	(Sold) fl 1 Agina
1805/07/10	AMSCH	0240	*[Anonymous]* | Eenige zittende Beelden in een Landschap	Y[ver]	(Sold) fl 1 Gruyter
1805/07/10	AMSCH	0241	*[Anonymous]* | De Bekeering van Paulus in een Landschap	Y[ver]	(Bought In) fl 0:6
1805/07/10	AMSCH	0245	*[Anonymous]* | In een Heuvelachtig Landschap, met eenig Geboomten en stroomend Watertje, ziet men eenige Huislieden met hun Vee; bevallig op Doek geschilderd | *Mat:* op doek	Wed Grave	(Sold) fl 9 Lafontaine
1805/07/10	AMSCH	0246	*Een goed Meester* | Een Heuvelachtig Landzigt met Geboomten, op de Voorgrond een Boerin die een Koe melkt, daar neevens een rustende, en een Schaap en Bokje; uitvoerig op Paneel, door een goed Meester | *Mat:* op paneel	Wed Grave	(Sold) fl 1:10 Isaac Smit
1805/07/10	AMSCH	0247	*[Anonymous]* | Langs een Wegh met Geboomten, ziet men Boere Woninge en eenige Huislieden; fiks behandeld op Paneel | *Mat:* op paneel	Wed Grave	(Sold) fl 3:5 Gruyter
1805/07/10	AMSCH	0249	*[Anonymous]* | Twee stuks Binnehuizen, gestoffeert met Boeren, Boerinnen en Kinderen, en verder bywerk | *Mat:* op doek	Wed Grave	(Sold) fl 6 T van Iperen
1805/07/10	AMSCH	0250	*[Anonymous]* | Een Woelend Watertje, gestoffeert met zylende en andere Vaartuigen; fiks geschilderd op Paneel | *Mat:* op paneel	Wed Grave	(Sold) fl 0:10 L Pakker
1805/07/10	AMSCH	0255	*[Anonymous]* | Een Woelend Water, met zylende Oologschepen [sic], op de Voorgrond een Jaght en een Sloep met Dames en Heeren, naar hetzelve roeijende; fiks op Paneel behandeld | *Mat:* op paneel	Temmink	(Sold) fl 3:5 Gruyter
1805/07/10	AMSCH	0256	*[Anonymous]* | In een Bergachtig Landschap; by een Water-Beekje, ziet met verscheide Nimphen, en Saters, die zig Baaden; kragtig geschilderd op Doek | *Mat:* op doek	Temmink	(Sold) fl 6:5 L Pakker
1805/07/10	AMSCH	0257	*[Anonymous]* | Een Heuvelachtig Boomryk Landschap, gestoffeerd met eenige Rysigers, bevallig behandeld | *Mat:* op paneel	Temmink	(Sold) fl 1 L Pakker
1805/07/10	AMSCH	0260	*[Anonymous]* | Een Heuvelachtig Landschap met Geboomten, gestoffeerd met staand en rustend Vee, en twee Huislieden; fiks op Doek geschilderd | *Mat:* op doek	S[chley] [for] Doralle	(Sold) fl 3 Tozelli
1805/07/10	AMSCH	0261	*[Anonymous]* | Twee stuks, een Land- en Watergezicht, met eenige Vaartuigen en een Waterval, verders Landlieden en eenig Vee: den ander een Pot met verscheide zoorten van Bloemen; plaisant behandeld	S[chley] [for] Doralle	(Sold) fl 1 Isaac Smit
1805/07/10	AMSCH	0262	*[Anonymous]* | Twee stuks, het eene verbeeld een Wintergezicht; op een bevroosen Rivier, aan de Vest-Muur van een Stadt, vermaken zich verscheide Lieden; den ander een bevallig Land- en Watergezicht, met verscheide stoffagie	S[chley] [for] Doralle	(Sold) fl 0:6 L Pakker
1805/07/10	AMSCH	0263	*[Anonymous]* | Voor een Boeren Slagter zyn Woning, hangen twee Varkens op de Leer, gestoffeerd met Beeldjes en verder bywerk, fiks geschilderd	S[chley] [for] Doralle	(Sold) fl 2 for lots 263 & 264. Rookmans

1805/07/10	AMSCH	0264	*[Anonymous]* | Twee stuks Boeren Kinderen-Schoolen, met verscheide stoffagie	S[chley] [for] Doralle	(Sold) fl 2 for lots 263 & 264. Rookmans
1805/07/10	AMSCH	0265	*[Anonymous]* | Het Afbeeldsel van een Kunstschilder, houdende Palet en Penceelen in de hand; uitvoerig op Paneel geschilderd | *Mat:* op paneel	Schley	(Bought In) fl 0:16
1805/07/10	AMSCH	0267	*[Anonymous]* | Op een Steene Piedestal, staat een Vaas, met verscheide zoorten van Bloemen, plaisant geschilderd | *Mat:* op doek	Schley	(Sold) fl 1:5 Isaac Smit
1805/07/10	AMSCH	0269	*[Anonymous]* | Een Onstuimige Zee, met verscheide Scheepen	S[chley] [for] Bernard	(Sold) fl 0:6 v d Schley [for] R[ijfsnijder]
1805/07/10	AMSCH	0270	*[Anonymous]* | Twee stuks, een Manshoofd; fiks behandeld, en een gestoffeert Landschap	S[chley] [for] Bernard	(Sold) fl 0:6 L Pakker
1805/07/10	AMSCH	0271	*[Anonymous]* | Twee dito [stuks], een stil Leeven, en een dito [gestoffeert] Landschap	S[chley] [for] Bernard	(Sold) fl 0:6 for lots 271 & 272. L Pakker
1805/07/10	AMSCH	0272	*[Anonymous]* | Drie stuks diversche Schilderyen	S[chley] [for] Bernard	(Sold) fl 0:6 for lots 271 & 272. L Pakker
1805/07/10	AMSCH	0286	*[Anonymous]* | Een Ruïne met eenige Landlopers; dun op Paneel | *Mat:* op paneel *Notes:* This lot was sold with lot 285, which is in the manner of O. Elliger (II).	V[inkeles]	(Sold) fl 0:14 for lots 285 & 286. Agina
1805/07/10	AMSCH	0287[H]	*[Anonymous]* | 2 Landschappen met beesten | *Notes:* This lot was added in by hand in the AA, EBNP and RKDH copies of the catalogue.	V[inkeles]	(Bought In) fl 3
1805/07/10	AMSCH	0289[H]	*[Anonymous]* | Een Stilwater en een Hystorich | *Notes:* This lot was added in by hand in the AA, EBNP and RKDH copies of the catalogue.	V[inkeles]	(Sold) fl 1 Rooyers
1805/07/10	AMSCH	0290[H]	*[Anonymous]* | Een Stilleeven en dood Wild | *Notes:* This lot was added in by hand in the AA, EBNP and RKDH copies of the catalogue.	V[inkeles]	(Sold) fl 1:5 Boelen
1805/07/10	AMSCH	0292[H]	*[Anonymous]* | 2 dito [Landschappen] 1 Landscap & Stilwater | *Notes:* This lot was added in by hand in the AA, EBNP and RKDH copies of the catalogue. It is unclear what "dito" refers to in the title.	V[inkeles]	(Sold) fl 1:5 Boelen
1805/07/10	AMSCH	0294[H]	*[Anonymous]* | 1 dito [Landschappen] Historieele Ordonnantie | *Notes:* This lot was added in by hand in the AA, EBNP and RKDH copies of the catalogue. It is unclear what "dito" refers to in the title.	V[inkeles] [for] Menzard	(Sold or Bought In) fl 1 Mensart
1805/07/10	AMSCH	0295[H]	*[Anonymous]* | 1 dito [Landschappen] Groote Zee | *Notes:* This lot was added in by hand in the AA, EBNP and RKDH copies of the catalogue. It is unclear what "dito" refers to in the title.	V[inkeles] [or] Ipen	(Withdrawn)
1805/07/10	AMSCH	0296[H]	*[Anonymous]* | Een Zeestrand | *Notes:* This lot was added in by hand in the AA, EBNP and RKDH copies of the catalogue.	V[inkeles] [or] Ipen	(Withdrawn)
1805/07/10	AMSCH	A0003	*Een voornaam Meester* | Vyf stuks Kamerstukken; mede zeer fraai behandeld door een voornaam Meester [Fraaije geschilderde Kamer-Behangsels] | *Size:* yder hoog 9 voet, 7 duim, breed 7 voet en 8 duim *Notes:* The bracketed information in the title appears above lot A1 and refers to lots A1 to A8.	R[oos]	(Sold) fl 7 Spaan
1805/07/10	AMSCH	A0005	*[Anonymous]* | Een Schoorsteen-Stuk, in 't grauw, zinspeelende op de Godsdienst [Fraaije geschilderde Kamer-Behangsels] | *Size:* hoog 4 voet, 7 duim, breed 3 voet, 5 duim *Notes:* The bracketed information in the title appears above lot A1 and refers to lots A1 to A8	R[oos]	(Sold) fl 12:10 Isaac Smit
1805/07/10	AMSCH	A0006	*[Anonymous]* | Een Schoorsteen-Stuk, met Kindertjes [Fraaije geschilderde Kamer-Behangsels] | *Size:* hoog 4 voet, 4 duim, breed 3 voet *Notes:* The bracketed information in the title appears above lot A1 and refers to lots A1 to A8.	R[oos]	(Sold) fl 16:10 Isaac Smit
1805/07/10	AMSCH	A0008	*[Anonymous]* | Drie stuks Schoorsteen-Stukken; in 't graauw [Fraaije geschilderde Kamer-Behangsels] | *Size:* yder hoog 7 voet, 5 duim, breed 3 voet, 2 duim *Notes:* The bracketed information in the title appears above lot A1 and refers to lots A1 to A8.	R[oos]	(Sold) fl 3 Hyman Pakker
1805/09/23	MGBEO	0002	*[Anonymous]* | Een extra fraaië Bachus-kop, op Paneel, zw. Lyst | *Mat:* op paneel		(Withdrawn)
1805/09/23	MGBEO	0005	*[Anonymous]* | [Untitled] | *Notes:* The only extant copy of this catalogue is annotated with the buyers and prices for lots 5–9, but it does not include a printed list of the paintings.		(Sold) £ 0.1 Ooms
1805/09/23	MGBEO	0006	*[Anonymous]* | [Untitled] | *Notes:* The only extant copy of this catalogue is annotated with the buyers and prices for lots 5–9, but it does not include a printed list of the paintings.		(Sold) £ 0.3 Meertense
1805/09/23	MGBEO	0007	*[Anonymous]* | [Untitled] | *Notes:* The only extant copy of this catalogue is annotated with the buyers and prices for lots 5–9, but it does not include a printed list of the paintings.		(Unknown) £ 0.3
1805/09/23	MGBEO	0008	*[Anonymous]* | [Untitled] | *Notes:* The only extant copy of this catalogue is annotated with the buyers and prices for lots 5–9, but it does not include a printed list of the paintings.		(Unknown) £ 0.7
1805/09/23	MGBEO	0009	*[Anonymous]* | [Untitled] | *Notes:* The only extant copy of this catalogue is annotated with the buyers and prices for lots 5–9, but it does not include a printed list of the paintings.		(Unknown) £ 0.6
1805/09/24	FKROM	[0013]	*[Anonymous]* | Eenige Schilderyen | *Notes:* Because this lot was not numbered in the catalogue, we have assigned the number.	Hermannus Cannegieter	(Unknown)

1805/10/09	HGBSM	0025	*[Anonymous]* | St. Pieters kerk te Romen, gestoffeerd met figuren | *Mat:* op doek *Size:* hoog 39 breet 52 duim	T H van Willigen [or others]	(Sold) fl 10:5 Ebbens
1805/10/09	HGBSM	0028	*Een oud goed Meester* | Een biddende munnik voor een krucifix, fraay geschildert, en getekend door een oud goed Meester | *Mat:* op doek *Size:* hoog 34 breet 30 duim	T H van Willigen [or others]	(Sold) fl 20:10 Ebbens
1805/10/09	HGBSM	0029	*[Anonymous]* | Een herderinne met een fluit in de hand, en een muziek boek op haar schoot | *Mat:* op doek op paneel *Size:* hoog 38 breet 30 duim	T H van Willigen [or others]	(Sold) fl 3 Carré
1805/10/09	HGBSM	0038	*[Anonymous]* | Door een venster, ziet men een maneschyn met drie figuuren, voor de opening van het venster een gordyn, in een Italiaansche trand geschildert | *Mat:* op paneel *Size:* hoog 20 ½ breet 16 duim	T H van Willigen [or others]	(Sold) fl 3:12 Van Giesen
1805/10/09	HGBSM	0064	*[Anonymous]* | Een boer met een kan en glas in de handen op paneel | *Mat:* op paneel *Size:* hoog 7 breet 5 ½ duim	T H van Willigen [or others]	(Sold) fl 3:5 Kuller
1805/10/09	HGBSM	0067	*Een goed Meester* | Een oud man, die een vrouw caresseert, in de eene hand houd hy een zak met geld door een goed Meester | *Mat:* op paneel *Size:* hoog 10 breet 7 ½ duim	T H van Willigen [or others]	(Sold) fl 11 De Gelder
1805/10/09	HGBSM	0068	*Een oud Meester* | De verlochenis van Petrus, door een oud Meester | *Mat:* op paneel *Size:* hoog 11 ½ breet 13 duim	T H van Willigen [or others]	(Sold) fl 3:10 Basemoine
1805/10/09	HGBSM	0141	*Een goed Meester* | Een landschap met beesten en figuuren, door een goed Meester | *Mat:* op paneel *Size:* hoog 19 breet 23 duim	T H van Willigen [or others]	(Sold) fl 9 van den Broek
1805/10/09	HGBSM	0142	*[Anonymous]* | Een valkenier te paard met nog twee jagers &c., kragtig geschilderd op doek | *Mat:* op doek *Size:* hoog 20 ½ breet 29 duim	T H van Willigen [or others]	(Sold) fl 3:15 van den Broek
1805/10/09	HGBSM	0147	*[Anonymous]* | Drie slaapende beeldjes in de maneschyn | *Mat:* op paneel *Size:* hoog 5 ½ breet 6 ½ duim	T H van Willigen [or others]	(Sold) fl 3:15 van den Broek
1805/10/09	HGBSM	0148	*[Anonymous]* | Een gezigt van een buitenplaats tusschen het geboomte | *Mat:* op paneel *Size:* hoog 7 breet 9 duim	T H van Willigen [or others]	(Sold) fl 2 van den Broek
1805/10/09	HGBSM	AA0026	*[Anonymous]* | Een mans portret met een kraagom [sic] | *Mat:* op paneel *Size:* hoog 16 ½ breed 15 duim	T H van Willigen [or others]	(Sold) fl 3:6 van der Linden
1805/10/09	HGBSM	DD0029	*[Anonymous]* | Een rokend boertje met meer bywerk, in een binne vertrek | *Mat:* op paneel *Size:* hoog 13 breed 10 duim	T H van Willigen [or others]	(Sold) fl 2 van der Linden
1805/10/09	HGBSM	EE0030	*[Anonymous]* | Een vrouwtje zittende te slaapen, by kaarslicht | *Mat:* op paneel *Size:* hoog 15 ½ breed 13 duim	T H van Willigen [or others]	(Sold) fl 4 van der Linden
1805/10/09	HGBSM	GG0032	*[Anonymous]* | Het gezicht op de Rotterdamschevaart langs het kruidmagezyn van Delft | *Mat:* op paneel *Size:* hoog 6 breed 8 ½ duim	T H van Willigen [or others]	(Sold) fl 4:4 van der Linden
1805/10/09	HGBSM	II0034	*[Anonymous]* | Een man en vrouw halverlyf | *Mat:* op doek	T H van Willigen [or others]	(Sold) fl 3 van der Linden
1805/10/09	HGBSM	KK0035	*[Anonymous]* | Een kleeremaakers winkel | *Mat:* op paneel	T H van Willigen [or others]	(Sold) fl 2:6 Basemoine
1805/10/09	HGBSM	LL0036	*[Anonymous]* | Eenige dansende boeren en boerinnen, in een binnen huis | *Mat:* op doek	T H van Willigen [or others]	(Sold) fl 2:4 van der Linden
1805/10/09	HGBSM	M0012	*[Anonymous]* | Twee leggende schaapjes | *Mat:* op paneel *Size:* hoog 11 breet 14 ½ duim	T H van Willigen [or others]	(Sold) fl 3:12 Blommers
1805/10/09	HGBSM	MM0037	*[Anonymous]* | Een rokend boertje | *Mat:* op paneel	T H van Willigen [or others]	(Sold) fl 5 van der Linden
1805/10/09	HGBSM	NN0038	*[Anonymous]* | Een boeren gezelschap | *Mat:* op paneel	T H van Willigen [or others]	(Sold) fl 1 van der Linden
1805/10/09	HGBSM	O0014	*[Anonymous]* | Een Satyr met Nimphen in een bosch | *Mat:* op doek *Size:* hoog 25 breet 29 ½ duim	T H van Willigen [or others]	(Sold) fl 3:5 Blommers [or] Huybregts
1805/10/09	HGBSM	OO0039	*[Anonymous]* | Een landschap met ruïne en stoffagie | *Mat:* op paneel	T H van Willigen [or others]	(Sold) fl 2 van der Linden
1805/10/09	HGBSM	PP0040	*[Anonymous]* | Twee boeren kinderen met een kat speelende voor een buitenhuis | *Mat:* op paneel	T H van Willigen [or others]	(Sold) fl 1:18 De Gelder
1805/10/09	HGBSM	QQ0041	*[Anonymous]* | Twee stukjes | *Mat:* op paneel	T H van Willigen [or others]	(Sold) fl 1:10 van der Linden
1805/10/09	HGBSM	U0020	*[Anonymous]* | Een heer en een dame te paard, met meer bywerk in een landschap | *Mat:* op paneel *Size:* hoog 13 breet 15 ½ duim	T H van Willigen [or others]	(Sold) fl 2 Voerman
1805/10/09	HGBSM	W0022	*Een goed Meester* | Maria met het kind, en Joseph in de stal verbeeld, kragtig geschildert, door een goed Meester | *Mat:* op doek *Size:* hoog 49 breet 48 duim	T H van Willigen [or others]	(Sold) fl 6:10 De Gelder
1805/10/09	HGBSM	Y0024	*[Anonymous]* | Een Venetiaansch gezicht | *Mat:* op paneel *Size:* hoog 25 breet 21 duim	T H van Willigen [or others]	(Sold) fl 3:16 De Gelder
1805/10/21	GRBOL	0025	*[Anonymous]* | Een Schildery, waar in een bejaard Man enig geld aan ene jonge Dochter aanbied, en verder Bywerk, goed Geschilderd	Gerardus Nicolaus Heerkens	(Unknown)
1805/10/21	GRBOL	0039	*Een goed Meester* | Een Stuk, waar in een Mosselman, and andere Beelden, door een goed Meester geschilderd	Gerardus Nicolaus Heerkens	(Unknown)
1805/10/21	GRBOL	0042	*Een goed Meester* | Een Stuk, verbeeldende een Vismarkt, door een goed Meester	Gerardus Nicolaus Heerkens	(Unknown)

1805/10/21	GRBOL	0047	*Een goed Meester* | Een Monnik in een Biddende Houding, door een Goed Meester	Gerardus Nicolaus Heerkens	(Unknown)
1805/10/21	GRBOL	0048	*[Anonymous]* | De Vlucht van Maria en Joseph met haar Kindje, goed Geschilderd	Gerardus Nicolaus Heerkens	(Unknown)
1805/10/21	GRBOL	0056	*Een goed Meester* | Een Stuk, zynde een Vrolyk Gezelschap, door een goed Meester	Gerardus Nicolaus Heerkens	(Unknown)
1805/10/21	GRBOL	0060	*Een Oud Meester* | De Dooping van Christus, door een Oud Meester, schoon geschilderd	Gerardus Nicolaus Heerkens	(Unknown)
1805/10/21	GRBOL	0061	*[Anonymous]* | Een Kaarslichtje, goed Geschilderd	Gerardus Nicolaus Heerkens	(Unknown)
1805/10/21	GRBOL	0062	*[Anonymous]* | Een Vrouwen Pourtrait	Gerardus Nicolaus Heerkens	(Unknown)
1805/10/21	GRBOL	0063	*[Anonymous]* | Een Mans dito [Pourtrait]	Gerardus Nicolaus Heerkens	(Unknown)
1805/10/21	GRBOL	0064	*[Anonymous]* | Een dito [Mans Pourtrait]	Gerardus Nicolaus Heerkens	(Unknown)
1805/10/21	GRBOL	0067	*[Anonymous]* | Een gapend Turksch Pourtrait	Gerardus Nicolaus Heerkens	(Unknown)
1805/10/21	GRBOL	0068	*[Anonymous]* | Een Biddende Monnik, op Koper geschilderd | *Mat:* op koper	Gerardus Nicolaus Heerkens	(Unknown)
1805/12/16	AMSCH	0036	*Een goed Meester* | Een bevallig Vrouwe Pourtrait, door een goed Meester	O	(Bought In) fl 1
1805/12/16	AMSCH	0058	*Een oud Meester* | In een Huismans Woning, vertoont zich een gestoorde Boeren Vreugd, waar by verscheide geestelyke zoo Mannen als Vrouwen, die elkander schynen afterossen, de gedekte Tafel met Spys, raakt het onderste boven; alles is grappig geordineert, en plaisant geschilderd op Paneel, door een oud Meester | *Mat:* op paneel *Size:* hoog 23, breed 32 duim	V	(Sold) fl 7:10 T van Iperen
1805/12/16	AMSCH	0076	*[Anonymous]* | Een Mans Pourtrait	R[oos]	(Sold) fl 1:10 Kamphuisen
1805/12/16	AMSCH	0078	*[Anonymous]* | Een gestoffeerd Landschap	R[oos]	(Sold) fl 0:16 Pieterse
1805/12/16	AMSCH	0082	*[Anonymous]* | Een Christusbeeld, fiks geschilded [sic]	R[oos]	(Sold) fl 0:6 L Pakker
1805/12/16	AMSCH	0087	*[Anonymous]* | Een krachtig geschilderd Boschgezicht, meesterlyk behandeld	R[oos]	(Sold) fl 1 L Pakker
1805/12/16	AMSCH	0088	*Een goed Meester* | Een aangenaam Italiaansch Landschap, met fraay Geboomte, Watervallen, en stoffagie, warm en uitvoerig behandeld, door een goed Meester	R[oos]	(Sold) fl 3 du Pree
1805/12/16	AMSCH	0092	*[Anonymous]* | Een Musiceerende Dame en een Heer, fiks op Doek geschilderd | *Mat:* op doek	R[oos]	(Sold) fl 0:8 du Pree
1805/12/16	AMSCH	0093	*[Anonymous]* | Een bevallige Vrouw, houdende een Kindje op de schoot, waar neevens een andere Vrouw; krachtig behandeld	R[oos]	(Sold) fl 4 T van Iperen
1805/12/16	AMSCH	0094	*Een oud Meester* | Een Historieele Ordonantie, door een oud Meester	R[oos]	(Sold) fl 0:6 L Pakker
1805/12/16	AMSCH	0095	*[Anonymous]* | Een uitgeplunderd brandend Dorpgezicht	R[oos]	(Sold) fl 1:5 Rookmans
1805/12/16	AMSCH	0096	*Een goed Meester* | Een staande Krygsheld in 't Harnas, door een goed Meester	R[oos]	(Sold) fl 2:15 Jozi
1805/12/16	AMSCH	0097	*[Anonymous]* | Joseph ontvlugt Potifars Huisvrouw	R[oos]	(Sold) fl 0:6 Boelen
1805/12/16	AMSCH	0101	*Een oud Meester* | Twee stuks Comique Ordinantien, door een oud Meester, rond format | *Mat:* op paneel *Fmt:* rond	V	(Sold) fl 0:6 L Pakker
1805/12/16	AMSCH	0102	*[Anonymous]* | Het afbeeldsel van Dr. M. Lutherus | *Mat:* op paneel	V	(Sold) fl 0:6 Geld
1805/12/16	AMSCH	0103	*[Anonymous]* | Het afbeeldsel van Hugo Grotius, in 't grauw geschilderd, en twee anderen, verbeeldende een Vorstelyk Persoon, en zyn Gemalinne, in ovaal formaat, 3 stuks | *Fmt:* ovaal	V	(Sold) fl 1:10 Yver
1805/12/16	AMSCH	0107	*[Anonymous]* | Twee stuks diversche Pourtretten | *Notes:* This lot was sold with lot 106, which is in the manner of Brakenburg.	V	(Sold) fl 0:6 for lots 106 & 107. L Pakker
1805/12/16	AMSCH	0110	*[Anonymous]* | Een Bergachtig Landschapje, met Vée, en een woelend Zeetje	R[oos]	(Sold) fl 1 du Pree
1805/12/16	AMSCH	0114	*[Anonymous]* | Een Dames Pourtret en vier andere, divers	R[oos]	(Sold) fl 0:10 L Pakker
1805/12/16	AMSCH	0115	*[Anonymous]* | Drie stuks, een Held, en de weerga; en een Fluitspeeler	R[oos]	(Bought In) fl 2
1805/12/16	AMSCH	0116	*[Anonymous]* | Twee Zeetjes, met Scheepen	R[oos]	(Bought In) fl 7
1805/12/16	AMSCH	0117	*Een oud Meester* | Een Romynsche Geschiedenis voor een Paleis; door een oud Meester	R[oos]	(Bought In) fl 1
1805/12/16	AMSCH	0118	*[Anonymous]* | Een Landschap met een Ruïne; fiks op Paneel | *Mat:* op paneel	Y	(Sold) fl 0:6 for lots 118 & 119. L Pakker
1805/12/16	AMSCH	0119	*[Anonymous]* | Twee stuks, een Landschap met een Haan, en een ander	Y	(Sold) fl 0:6 for lots 118 & 119. L Pakker

1805/12/16	AMSCH	0120	*[Anonymous]* | Een Mans Pourtret	Y	(Sold) fl 0:6 for lots 120 & 121. L Pakker
1805/12/16	AMSCH	0121	*[Anonymous]* | Een Strandgezicht	Y	(Sold) fl 0:6 for lots 120 & 121. L Pakker
1805/12/16	AMSCH	0122	*[Anonymous]* | Een Italiaansch Landschap, met een Quakzalver, en andere Beelden	Y	(Sold) fl 1 for lots 122 & 123. L Pakker
1805/12/16	AMSCH	0123	*[Anonymous]* | Een Winterje [sic], met Schaatseryders	Y	(Sold) fl 1 for lots 122 & 123. L Pakker
1805/12/16	AMSCH	0125	*[Anonymous]* | Een hevige Rencontre tussen Ruitery | *Notes:* This lot was sold with lot 124 by an Italian artist.	Y	(Sold) fl 0:10 for lots 124 & 125. L Pakker
1805/12/16	AMSCH	0126	*[Anonymous]* | Een Landschap, met naakte Beelden, en Geboomte	Y	(Sold) fl 1 du Pree
1805/12/16	AMSCH	0127	*[Anonymous]* | Een zinnebeeldige Ordinantie, van drie Beelden	Y	(Sold) fl 2:15 for lots 127–129. L Pakker
1805/12/16	AMSCH	0128	*[Anonymous]* | Een Landschap, met vervallen Gebouwen	Y	(Sold) fl 2:15 for lots 127–129. L Pakker
1805/12/16	AMSCH	0129	*[Anonymous]* | Twee stuks, een bevallig Meisje en Jongen, halver lyf; delicaat op Doek | *Mat:* op doek	Y	(Sold) fl 2:15 for lots 127–129. L Pakker
1805/12/16	AMSCH	0130	*[Anonymous]* | Een Zeestrand | *Mat:* op paneel	Y	(Sold) fl 0:6 for lots 130 & 131. L Pakker
1805/12/16	AMSCH	0131	*[Anonymous]* | Een capitaal Bloemstuk | *Mat:* op doek	Y	(Sold) fl 0:6 for lots 130 & 131. L Pakker
1805/12/16	AMSCH	0132	*[Anonymous]* | Joseph en Pothifars Huisvrouw; meesterlyk op Doek | *Mat:* op doek	Y	(Sold) fl 0:12 T van Iperen
1805/12/16	AMSCH	0134	*[Anonymous]* | Pomona en Vértumnus, delicaat op Doek | *Mat:* op doek	Y	(Sold) fl 1:5 Yver
1805/12/16	AMSCH	0136	*[Anonymous]* | Een Bloemstuk voor een Schoorsteenstuk | *Fmt:* schoorsteenstuk	R[oos]	(Sold) fl 0:6 L[e] Pakker
1805/12/16	AMSCH	0137	*[Anonymous]* | Een Vuurschutje, met verscheide Cieraden	R[oos]	(Bought In) fl 3
1805/12/16	AMSCH	0138[H]	*[Anonymous]* | 1 Schilderij | *Notes:* This lot was added in by hand in the EBNP, LBDa and RKDH copies of the catalogue.	R[oos]	(Sold) fl 2:5 Heybroek
1805/12/16	AMSCH	0139[H]	*[Anonymous]* | 2 dito [Schilderijen] | *Notes:* This lot was added in by hand in the LBDa and RKDH copies of the catalogue.	R[oos]	(Sold) fl 0:6 for lots 139[H], 140[H] & 141[H]. L Pakker
1805/12/16	AMSCH	0140[H]	*[Anonymous]* | 2 dito [Schilderijen] | *Notes:* This lot was added in by hand in the LBDa and RKDH copies of the catalogue.	R[oos]	(Sold) fl 0:6 for lots 139[H], 140[H] & 141[H]. L Pakker
1805/12/16	AMSCH	0141[H]	*[Anonymous]* | 2 dito [Schilderijen] | *Notes:* This lot was added in by hand in the LBDa and RKDH copies of the catalogue.	R[oos]	(Sold) fl 0:6 for lots 139[H], 140[H] & 141[H]. L Pakker
1805/12/16	AMSCH	0142[H]	*[Anonymous]* | 2 dito [Schilderijen] | *Notes:* This lot was added in by hand in the LBDa and RKDH copies of the catalogue.	R[oos]	(Sold) fl 0:6 for lots 142[H] & 143[H]. L Pakker
1805/12/16	AMSCH	0143[H]	*[Anonymous]* | 2 dito [Schilderijen] | *Notes:* This lot was added in by hand in the LBDa and RKDH copies of the catalogue.	R[oos]	(Sold) fl 0:6 for lots 142[H] & 143[H]. L Pakker
1805/12/16	AMSCH	0144[H]	*[Anonymous]* | 4 dito [Schilderijen] | *Notes:* This lot was added in by hand in the LBDa and RKDH copies of the catalogue.	R[oos]	(Sold) fl 1:5 for lots 144[H] & 145[H]. L Pakker
1805/12/16	AMSCH	0145[H]	*[Anonymous]* | 4 dito [Schilderijen] | *Notes:* This lot was added in by hand in the LBDa and RKDH copies of the catalogue.	R[oos]	(Sold) fl 1:5 for lots 144[H] & 145[H]. L Pakker
1805/12/16	AMSCH	0146[H]	*[Anonymous]* | 2 dito [Schilderijen] | *Notes:* This lot was added in by hand in the LBDa and RKDH copies of the catalogue.	R[oos]	(Sold) fl 1 Rookmans
1805/12/16	AMSCH	0147[H]	*[Anonymous]* | 3 dito [Schilderijen] | *Notes:* This lot was added in by hand in the LBDa and RKDH copies of the catalogue.	R[oos]	(Sold) fl 0:18 L Pakker
1805/12/16	AMSCH	0148[H]	*[Anonymous]* | 3 dito [Schilderijen] | *Notes:* This lot was added in by hand in the LBDa and RKDH copies of the catalogue.	R[oos]	(Sold) fl 0:6 L Pakker
1805/12/16	AMSCH	0149[H]	*[Anonymous]* | 2 Schilderijen | *Notes:* This lot was added in by hand in the LBDa and RKDH copies of the catalogue.	R[oos]	(Unknown) fl 1
1805/12/16	AMSCH	0153[H]	*[Anonymous]* | 2 dito [Schilderyen] | *Notes:* This lot was added in by hand in the EBNP, LBDa and RKDH copies of the catalogue.	Z	(Sold) fl 0:8 L Pakker
1806/01/30	RMAN	0001	*[Anonymous]* | Een Zeehaven	Dirk Langendyk	(Unknown)
1806/01/30	RMAN	0006	*[Anonymous]* | Een Platfond met Kindertjes	Dirk Langendyk	(Unknown)
1806/01/30	RMAN	0007	*[Anonymous]* | Een Schynbedrieger	Dirk Langendyk	(Unknown)
1806/01/30	RMAN	0009	*[Anonymous]* | Een Drinkende Saters Hoofd	Dirk Langendyk	(Unknown)
1806/05/05	AMSCH	0163	*Een goed Meester* | Czaar Peter de Groote; door een goed Meester	R[oos]	(Bought In) fl 1:10
1806/05/05	AMSCH	0167	*[Anonymous]* | De aanbidding der Herders; fiks gepenceeld	R[oos]	(Sold) fl 2:15 L Pakker

1806/05/05	AMSCH	0170	*Een goed Meester* | Een Manspourtrait, met een Kraag; door een goed Meester	R[oos]	(Sold) fl 4 L Pakker
1806/05/05	AMSCH	0173	*Een goed Meester* | Een Maria Magdaléna en Petrus; door een goed Meester	R[oos]	(Sold) fl 0:6 L Pakker
1806/05/05	AMSCH	0174a	*[Anonymous]* | Een Bordeel met vier Beelden	R[oos]	(Sold) fl 7:10 van Iperen
1806/05/05	AMSCH	0187	*[Anonymous]* | Twee stuks Landschapjes, de eene met Beelden	R[oos]	(Sold) fl 1 L Pakker
1806/05/05	AMSCH	0188	*[Anonymous]* | Twee stuks met Bloemen	R[oos]	(Sold) fl 4 Coclers
1806/05/05	AMSCH	0189	*Een goed Meester* | Het Pourtrait van Hendrik de Vierden; door een goed Meester	H	(Sold) fl 0:6 Gruyter
1806/05/05	AMSCH	0191	*Een oud Meester* | Een Vanitas; door een oud Meester	H	(Sold) fl 2:5 J Yver
1806/05/05	AMSCH	0194	*Een goed Meester* | Een bevallig Vrouwe Pourtrait; door een goed Meester	H	(Sold) fl 2:15 J Yver
1806/05/05	AMSCH	0195	*Een goed Meester* | Een fraai Mans Pourtrait, door een dito [goed Meester]	H	(Sold) fl 0:16 Gruyter
1806/05/05	AMSCH	0196	*Een goed Meester* | Een dito [fraai Mans Pourtrait] dito [door een goed Meester]	H	(Sold) fl 0:12 van Iperen
1806/05/05	AMSCH	0197	*Een goed Meester* | Een dito [fraai Mans Pourtrait] dito [door een goed Meester]	H	(Sold) fl 0:10 L Pakker
1806/05/05	AMSCH	0198	*Een goed Meester* | Een dito [fraai Mans Pourtrait] dito [door een goed Meester] | *Notes:* It is unclear what "dito" refers to in the title.	H	(Sold) fl 0:12 Riemsdijk
1806/05/05	AMSCH	0199	*Een goed Meester* | Een dito [fraai Mans Pourtrait] dito [door een goed Meester] | *Notes:* It is unclear what "dito" refers to in the title.	H	(Sold) fl 3 van Dijl
1806/05/05	AMSCH	0200	*Een goed Meester* | Een dito [fraai Mans Pourtrait] dito [door een goed Meester] | *Notes:* It is unclear what "dito" refers to in the title.	H	(Sold) fl 2 Riemsdijk
1806/05/05	AMSCH	0201	*Een goed Meester* | Dirk Volkertze Koornhaard, mede als dito [door een oud Meester]	H	(Sold) fl 8 van Dijl
1806/05/05	AMSCH	0202	*[Anonymous]* | Twee Landschapjes divers	H	(Sold) fl 4:5 L Pakker
1806/05/05	AMSCH	0203[a]	*[Anonymous]* | Drie stuks, een Hondje, en twee na Teniers | *This Lot:* Een Hondje; lot 203[b] is copy after Teniers	H	(Sold) fl 3 for lots 203[a] & 203[b]. Mensart
1806/05/05	AMSCH	0205	*[Anonymous]* | Twee dito [stuks] dito [een bevallig Mans en Vrouwe Pourtrait], in alles als de voorgaande | *Mat:* op doek *Size:* hoog 85, breed 59 duim *Notes:* It is unclear what "dito" refers to in the title.	V[inkeles]	(Sold) fl 7 Gruyter
1806/05/05	AMSCH	0206	*[Anonymous]* | Een aangenaam boom en duinachtig Landschap, met een ménigte van staande en rustende Schapen, Herders, Honden, enz.; fiks en meesterlyk gepenceeld | *Mat:* op doek *Size:* hoog 46, breed 59 duim	V[inkeles]	(Sold) fl 5:15 Spaan
1806/05/05	AMSCH	0210	*[Anonymous]* | Een bejaard Man, zittende in een Armstoel, verzeld van een klein Hondje enz; delicaat gepenceeld	V[inkeles]	(Sold) fl 1:15 Gruyter
1806/05/05	AMSCH	0211	*Een oud Meester* | Hagar door Sara aan Abraham voorgesteld; krachtig op Doek, door een oud Meester | *Mat:* op doek	V[inkeles]	(Sold) fl 5:15 Gruyter
1806/05/05	AMSCH	0212	*[Anonymous]* | Diversche soorten van Vruchten; fiks gepenceeld	V[inkeles]	(Sold) fl 1:5 L Pakker
1806/05/05	AMSCH	0213	*[Anonymous]* | Een deftig oud Mans Pourtrait	V[inkeles]	(Sold) fl 0:6 L Pakker
1806/05/05	AMSCH	0214	*Een voornaam Meester* | Twee stuks, een bevallig Mans en Vrouwen Pourtrait, in deftige aloude Kleeding; allerdelicaatst gepenceelt, door een voornaam Meester	V[inkeles]	(Sold) fl 1 L Pakker
1806/05/05	AMSCH	0215	*[Anonymous]* | Een oud Mans Pourtrait, in aloude Kleeding	V[inkeles]	(Sold) fl 1 Coclers
1806/05/05	AMSCH	0216	*[Anonymous]* | Twee stuks, een bevallig Mans en Vrouwen Pourtrait, in aloude deftige Kleeding	V[inkeles]	(Sold) fl 0:12 Boelhouwer
1806/05/05	AMSCH	0217	*[Anonymous]* | Twee stuks, een Jongens en Meisjes Pourtrait	V[inkeles]	(Sold) fl 13 Spaan
1806/05/05	AMSCH	0219	*Een oud Meester* | Maria met het Kindje; door een oud Meester	V[inkeles]	(Sold) fl 0:6 Levy Pakker
1806/05/05	AMSCH	0220	*[Anonymous]* | Drie stuks, divers met Glazen	V[inkeles]	(Sold) fl 1:10 Levy Pakker
1806/05/05	AMSCH	0222	*Een goed Meester* | Een Strandgezicht, met een ménigte Beelden; door een goed Meester	F	(Sold) fl 3:15 T van Iperen
1806/05/05	AMSCH	0224	*[Anonymous]* | Een meesterlyk geschilderde Heiligen	F	(Sold) fl 8:10 Riemsdijk
1806/05/05	AMSCH	0227	*Een voornaam Meester* | Pomona en Vertumnus, in een Landschap; door een voornaam Meester	Y	(Sold) fl 2 L Pakker
1806/05/05	AMSCH	0228a	*[Anonymous]* | 't Afbeeldsel van P.P. Rubbens	Y	(Sold) fl 0:10 Riemsdyk
1806/05/05	AMSCH	0235	*[Anonymous]* | Drie diversche kleine Pourtraitjes	V[inkeles]	(Sold) fl 4 van Iperen
1806/05/05	AMSCH	0237	*Een oud Meester* | In een Binnenkamer zit een Vrouw met een Kind op haar schoot, ter zyde haar een oud Man, op de voorgrond een Kind met	V[inkeles]	(Sold) fl 0:10 van der Schley

			een Hond speelende; natuurlyk by kaarslicht verbeeld, door een oud Meester | *Mat:* op doek *Size:* hoog 30, breed 39 duim		
1806/05/05	AMSCH	0238	*Een oud Meester* | Twee capitaale Italiaansche Gezigten, met prachtige Gebouwen en Historien gestoffeerd; door een oud Meester | *Mat:* op doek	V[inkeles]	(Sold) fl 4 Vermeulen
1806/05/05	AMSCH	0239	*[Anonymous]* | Twee diversche Landschappen	V[inkeles]	(Sold) fl 1 L Pakker
1806/05/05	AMSCH	0240	*[Anonymous]* | Twee dito [diversche] dito [Landschappen]	V[inkeles]	(Sold) fl 1:15 Boelen
1806/05/05	AMSCH	0241	*Een oud Meester* | David met het hoofd van Goliath; door een oud Meester	V[inkeles]	(Sold) fl 0:6 L Pakker
1806/05/05	AMSCH	0246	*[Anonymous]* | Twee stuks, een oud Mans Hoofd, met een gryse Baard, en een Historieele Ordinantie	V[inkeles]	(Sold) fl 1:5 van Laar
1806/05/05	AMSCH	0248	*[Anonymous]* | Kaartspeelende Soldaaten, in een Binnenhuis; krachtig gepenceeld	V[inkeles]	(Withdrawn)
1806/05/05	AMSCH	0254	*[Anonymous]* | Twee stuks Nissen met Beelden	R[oos]	(Sold) fl 1 van der Schley
1806/05/05	AMSCH	0259[b]	*[Anonymous]* | Een Kaarslicht; na A. Bloemaert en een Bloemstukje | *This Lot:* Een Bloemstukje; lot 259[a] is copy after A. Bloemaert	R[oos]	(Sold) fl 1:10 for lots 259[a] & 259[b]. L Pakker
1806/05/05	AMSCH	0260[H]	*[Anonymous]* | 1 Schilderij | *Notes:* This lot was added in by hand in the RKDH copy of the catalogue.	Y	(Sold) fl 3 L Pakker
1806/05/05	AMSCH	0261[H]	*[Anonymous]* | 2 dito [Schilderijen] | *Notes:* This lot was added in by hand in the RKDH copy of the catalogue, but it was subsequently crossed out and apparently withdrawn.	V[inkeles]	(Withdrawn)
1806/05/05	AMSCH	0263[H]	*[Anonymous]* | 2 Schilderijen | *Notes:* This lot was added in by hand in the RKDH copy of the catalogue.	V[inkeles]	(Sold) fl 0:14 Groend [?]
1806/05/05	AMSCH	0264[H]	*[Anonymous]* | 1 dito [Schilderij] | *Notes:* This lot was added in by hand in the RKDH copy of the catalogue.	V[inkeles]	(Sold) fl 1:10 L Pakker
1806/05/05	AMSCH	0265[H]	*[Anonymous]* | 1 dito [Schilderij] | *Notes:* This lot was added in by hand in the RKDH copy of the catalogue.	V[inkeles]	(Sold) fl 4:5 van Iperen
1806/05/05	AMSCH	0266[H]	*[Anonymous]* | 1 dito [Schilderij] | *Notes:* This lot was added in by hand in the RKDH copy of the catalogue.	V[inkeles]	(Sold) fl 4:5 Gruiter
1806/05/05	AMSCH	0267[H]	*[Anonymous]* | 1 dito [Schilderij] | *Notes:* This lot was added in by hand in the RKDH copy of the catalogue.	V[inkeles]	(Sold) fl 1:10 L Pakker
1806/05/05	AMSCH	0268[H]	*[Anonymous]* | 1 dito [Schilderij] | *Notes:* This lot was added in by hand in the RKDH copy of the catalogue.	V[inkeles]	(Sold) fl 0:10 Mensart
1806/05/05	AMSCH	0269[H]	*[Anonymous]* | 3 dito [Schilderijen] | *Notes:* This lot was added in by hand in the RKDH copy of the catalogue.	R[oos]	(Sold) fl 1 for lots 269[H] & 270[H]. L Pakker
1806/05/05	AMSCH	0270[H]	*[Anonymous]* | [Untitled] | *Notes:* This lot was added in by hand in the RKDH copy of the catalogue, but without giving an artist or title.	R[oos]	(Sold) fl 1 for lots 269[H] & 270[H]. L Pakker
1806/05/05	AMSCH	0271[H]	*[Anonymous]* | 2 dito [Schilderijen] | *Notes:* This lot was added in by hand in the RKDH copy of the catalogue.	R[oos]	(Sold) fl 0:10 L Pakker
1806/05/05	AMSCH	0272[H]	*[Anonymous]* | 1 dito [Schilderij] | *Notes:* This lot was added in by hand in the RKDH copy of the catalogue.	R[oos]	(Sold) fl 1:15 van Laar
1806/05/05	AMSCH	0273[H]	*[Anonymous]* | 1 dito [Schilderij] | *Notes:* This lot was added in by hand in the RKDH copy of the catalogue.	R[oos]	(Sold) fl 2 L Pakker
1806/05/05	AMSCH	0274[H]	*[Anonymous]* | 4 dito [Schilderijen] | *Notes:* This lot was added in by hand in the RKDH copy of the catalogue.	R[oos]	(Sold) fl 10 Jozi
1806/05/19	MGBEO	0001	*[Anonymous]* | [Untitled] | *Notes:* The only extant copy of this catalogue is annotated with the buyers and prices, but it does not include a printed list of the paintings.		(Withdrawn)
1806/05/19	MGBEO	0002	*[Anonymous]* | [Untitled] | *Notes:* The only extant copy of this catalogue is annotated with the buyers and prices, but it does not include a printed list of the paintings.		(Withdrawn)
1806/05/19	MGBEO	0003	*[Anonymous]* | [Untitled] | *Notes:* The only extant copy of this catalogue is annotated with the buyers and prices, but it does not include a printed list of the paintings.		(Withdrawn)
1806/05/19	MGBEO	0004	*[Anonymous]* | [Untitled] | *Notes:* The only extant copy of this catalogue is annotated with the buyers and prices, but it does not include a printed list of the paintings.		(Withdrawn)
1806/05/19	MGBEO	0005	*[Anonymous]* | [Untitled] | *Notes:* The only extant copy of this catalogue is annotated with the buyers and prices, but it does not include a printed list of the paintings.		(Withdrawn)
1806/05/19	MGBEO	0006	*[Anonymous]* | [Untitled] | *Notes:* The only extant copy of this catalogue is annotated with the buyers and prices, but it does not include a printed list of the paintings.		(Withdrawn)
1806/06/07	RMHSN	0010	*Een voornaam Meester* | Een kapitaal Stuk met byna levensgroote Beelden, zynde de Genezing van den Blinden Tobias, schoon van	A E K L	(Unknown)

			Couleur, Schildering en Teekening, door een voornaam Meester | *Mat:* op doek		
1806/06/07	RMHSN	0013	*Een goed Meester* | Een Arkadisch Landschapje, met ryk Geboomten en Waterval, helder en plaisant geschilderd, door een goed Meester | *Mat:* op paneel	A E K L	(Unknown)
1806/06/07	RMHSN	0016	*Een goed Meester* | Een Vrouwe Pourtrait met een groote Kraag over de Schouders, door een goed Meester, op Paneel, zonder Lyst | *Mat:* op paneel	A E K L	(Unknown)
1806/06/07	RMHSN	0063	*Een goed Meester* | Een Kantewerkster by de Lamp, door een goed Meester | *Mat:* op paneel	A E K L	(Unknown)
1806/06/07	RMHSN	0064	*Een goed Meester* | Een Mossel Eter, door een goed Meester, op Paneel | *Mat:* op paneel	A E K L	(Unknown)
1806/06/07	RMHSN	0069	*Een goed Meester* | Een Doctor in zyn Studeerkamer, waar by een Vrouw &c. door een goed Meester | *Mat:* op doek	A E K L	(Unknown)
1806/06/07	RMHSN	0070	*Een goed Meester* | Een Schoenmakers Winkel met verder Bywerk, door een goed Meester | *Mat:* op doek	A E K L	(Unknown)
1806/06/07	RMHSN	0075	*Een goed Meester* | Twee Stuks Landschapjes, uitvoerig geschilderd door een goed Meester | *Mat:* op paneel	A E K L	(Unknown)
1806/06/07	RMHSN	0081	*Een goed Meester* | Twee Stuks Oude Mans Hoofden, door een goed Meester | *Mat:* op paneel	A E K L	(Unknown)
1806/06/07	RMHSN	0082	*Een goed Meester* | Twee dito [Stuks] dito [Oude Mans Hoofden] kleinder dito [door een goed Meester] | *Notes:* It is unclear what "dito" refers to in the title.	A E K L	(Unknown)
1806/06/07	RMHSN	0084	*Een goed Meester* | Een Jongeling spelende op een Guitar, door een goed Meester | *Mat:* op paneel	A E K L	(Unknown)
1806/06/07	RMHSN	0085	*[Anonymous]* | Twee Stuks Kerkjes, van binnen te zien | *Mat:* op paneel	A E K L	(Unknown)
1806/06/07	RMHSN	0089	*Een Oud Meester* | Een dito [Winter], door een Oud Meester | *Mat:* op paneel	A E K L	(Unknown)
1806/06/07	RMHSN	0090	*Een goed Meester* | Een Aangenaam Landschapje, door een goed Meester | *Mat:* op paneel	A E K L	(Unknown)
1806/06/07	RMHSN	0091	*[Anonymous]* | Twee Stuks Boertjes | *Mat:* op paneel	A E K L	(Unknown)
1806/06/07	RMHSN	0094	*Een goed Meester* | Een Oude Vrouw die Ongedierte zoekt op 't Hoofd van haar Man, door een goed Meester	A E K L	(Unknown)
1806/06/07	RMHSN	0095	*Een goed Meester* | Een Boer die een Boerin Karesseert, door een goed Meester | *Mat:* op paneel	A E K L	(Unknown)
1806/06/07	RMHSN	0096	*Een goed Meester* | Een Landschap met Beestjes, door een goed Meester | *Mat:* op paneel	A E K L	(Unknown)
1806/06/07	RMHSN	0098	*[Anonymous]* | Een Stil Leven met Visschen | *Mat:* op doek	A E K L	(Unknown)
1806/06/07	RMHSN	0099	*Een goed Meester* | Een Vrouw die een Papegaai te Eten geeft, door een goed Meester | *Mat:* op paneel	A E K L	(Unknown)
1806/06/07	RMHSN	0100	*[Anonymous]* | Een jonge die op de Viool speeld | *Mat:* op paneel	A E K L	(Unknown)
1806/06/07	RMHSN	0101	*[Anonymous]* | Een Man dito dito [die op de Viool speeld] | *Mat:* op paneel *Notes:* It is unclear what "dito" refers to in the title.	A E K L	(Unknown)
1806/06/07	RMHSN	0103	*Een goed Meester* | Een Landschapje, door een goed Meester | *Mat:* op paneel	A E K L	(Unknown)
1806/06/07	RMHSN	0104	*[Anonymous]* | Een dito [Landschapje] | *Mat:* op paneel	A E K L	(Unknown)
1806/06/07	RMHSN	0107	*[Anonymous]* | Een Kopstuk, verbeeldende een Gekroonde Koning | *Mat:* op paneel	A E K L	(Unknown)
1806/06/07	RMHSN	0108	*[Anonymous]* | Een dito [Kopstuk], zynde een Jongeling | *Mat:* op paneel	A E K L	(Unknown)
1806/06/07	RMHSN	0109	*[Anonymous]* | Het Pourtrait van Oldenbarneveld | *Mat:* op paneel	A E K L	(Unknown)
1806/06/07	RMHSN	0111	*[Anonymous]* | Eenige Beeldjes in een aangenaam Landschap | *Mat:* op doek	A E K L	(Unknown)
1806/06/07	RMHSN	0112	*[Anonymous]* | Eenige Beeldjes in een Binnenvertrek	A E K L	(Unknown)
1806/06/07	RMHSN	0114	*[Anonymous]* | Een Landschap | *Mat:* op koper	A E K L	(Unknown)
1806/06/07	RMHSN	0116	*[Anonymous]* | De Graftombe van Tromp, Prent &c.	A E K L	(Unknown)
1806/06/07	RMHSN	0125	*Een goed Meester* | Een met Drinkende en Rookende Boeren, door een goed Meester	A E K L	(Unknown)
1806/08/13	AMSCH	0229	*[Anonymous]* | Een Fluitspeelder; in aloude Kleeding, staande by een Ton waarop een fles wyn en glas geplaatst is; fiks geschilderd op Paneel | *Mat:* op paneel	Roos	(Sold) fl 1 Coclers
1806/08/13	AMSCH	0232	*[Anonymous]* | Eenige speelende Kinderen, twee jongelingen en een meisje; in een Landschap; fiks geschilderd op Doek | *Mat:* op doek	Roos	(Sold) fl 10:10 Schumacher
1806/08/13	AMSCH	0233	*[Anonymous]* | Een Vrouw in deftige kleeding, met een lykbusch in de handen; krachtig gepenceeld | *Mat:* op doek	Roos	(Sold) fl 0:10 Royers
1806/08/13	AMSCH	0253	*[Anonymous]* | Twee stuks Landschappen met Vissers, Schuiten, enz.; in alles als de voorgaande behandeld	Roos	(Sold) fl 81 Yver

1806/08/13	AMSCH	0254	*[Anonymous]* | Verscheide Engelen, als op de Wolken zweevende, omhoog een glorie van Cherubynen; meesterlyk op Paneel geschilderd | *Mat:* op paneel	Roos	(Sold) fl 1 Gruiter
1806/08/13	AMSCH	0258	*[Anonymous]* | Een zittend jong Mysje in een Landschap, in deftige Kleeding, houdende een Vogeltje op de eene en een tak kersse in de andere hand; meesterlyk geschilderd	Roos	(Sold) fl 1:5 L Pakker
1806/08/13	AMSCH	0262	*Een voornaam Meester* | Een fraaije Ordinantie van vier Beelden, zinspelende op de vier Elementen; door een voornaam Meester	Roos	(Sold) fl 3 L Pakker
1806/08/13	AMSCH	0263	*[Anonymous]* | Eenige onderscheide fraai geschilderde Duiven in hun Hok	Roos	(Sold) fl 2 Nieuwenhuis
1806/08/13	AMSCH	0264	*Een beroemd Meester* | Een naakte Vénus in een Landschap; zynde van een beroemd Meester; krachtig geschilderd	Roos	(Sold) fl 2:15 L Pakker
1806/08/13	AMSCH	0266	*[Anonymous]* | Eenige vrolyke Boeren in een Dorp; geestig geschilderd	Roos	(Sold) fl 1 L Pakker
1806/08/13	AMSCH	0275	*[Anonymous]* | Drie stuks diversche Pourtraiten	Vinkeles [for] D	(Sold) fl 1:15 Yver
1806/08/13	AMSCH	0276	*[Anonymous]* | Twee stuks, een Boer een Boerin liefkoozende en een Strandgezichtje	Vinkeles [for] D	(Sold) fl 1 du Pree
1806/08/13	AMSCH	0278	*[Anonymous]* | Een Binnehuis met vrolyke Boeren en Boerinnen en verder bywerk	Daniel Mansveld	(Sold) fl 0:6 L Pakker
1806/08/13	AMSCH	0280	*[Anonymous]* | Een deftig Mans Pourtrait, halverlyf, staande by een Tafel | *Notes:* This lot was sold with lot 204 by E. Velde (I).	Daniel Mansveld	(Sold) fl 1:5 for lots 204 & 280. Boelen
1806/08/13	AMSCH	0285	*[Anonymous]* | Een stille Zee, met een groote ménigte van Oorlogschepen, in 't verschiet een stad; meesterlyk gepenceeld	Coclers	(Sold) fl 3:15 Jan Spaan
1806/08/13	AMSCH	0298	*[Anonymous]* | Een stil Leven met een Pot, Schenkbord, Kom, en diversche Vrugten	Vinkeles [for] F	(Sold) fl 4:5 Coclers
1806/08/13	AMSCH	0303	*[Anonymous]* | Twee stuks Tuingezichten met Menageriën van Gevogelte en Fontynwerk	Vinkeles [for] F	(Sold) fl 12:10 Zwanenburgh
1806/08/13	AMSCH	0305	*[Anonymous]* | Twee stuks Landschappen, met staand en leggend Vee, Boerenwoningen en Geboomten, bevallig geschilderd | *Mat:* op paneel	Yver	(Sold) fl 7 van Iperen
1806/08/13	AMSCH	0307	*[Anonymous]* | Een Protestante Kerk van binnen te zien; fiks en natuurlyk op Paneel geschilderd | *Mat:* op paneel	Yver	(Sold) fl 4:5 du Pree
1806/08/13	AMSCH	0313	*[Anonymous]* | Een Vrouwe Portrait, levens groote, in 't wit satyn gekleed; krachtig op Doek geschilderd | *Mat:* op doek	Yver	(Sold) fl 1 L Pakker
1806/08/13	AMSCH	0315	*[Anonymous]* | Een Binnehuis, waarin eenige Vrouwen zitten te spinnen en te weeven, by kaarslicht; meesterlyk behandeld | *Notes:* The artist's name "Basano" was added in by hand in the JPGM copy of the catalogue.	Roos	(Sold) fl 4 Jozi
1806/08/13	AMSCH	0343	*Een oud Meester* | Twee stuks Apostelen, door een oud Meester	Vinkeles [for] G[ruyter]	(Sold) fl 4 Spruit van Gend
1806/08/13	AMSCH	0346	*[Anonymous]* | Twee diversche Landschappen	Vinkeles [for] G[ruyter]	(Sold) fl 2 Yver [for] G
1806/08/13	AMSCH	0347	*[Anonymous]* | Twee dito [diversche] dito [Landschappen]	Vinkeles [for] G[ruyter]	(Sold) fl 1:5 du Pree
1806/08/13	AMSCH	0348[H]	*[Anonymous]* | Eenige Stuks | *Notes:* This lot was added in by hand in the EBNP, LBDa and RKDH copies of the catalogue.	Roos [for] g	(Sold) fl 35 for lots 348[H] & 349[H]. Coclers
1806/08/13	AMSCH	0349[H]	*[Anonymous]* | Eenige d^{o} [Stuks] | *Notes:* This lot was added in by hand in the EBNP, LBDa and RKDH copies of the catalogue.	Roos [for] g	(Sold) fl 35 for lots 348[H] & 349[H]. Coclers
1806/08/13	AMSCH	0350[H]	*[Anonymous]* | 12 d^{o} [Stuks] | *Notes:* This lot was added in by hand in the LBDa and RKDH copies of the catalogue.	Roos [for] g	(Sold) fl 1:10 L Pakker
1806/08/13	AMSCH	0351[H]	*[Anonymous]* | Eenige d^{o} [Stuks] | *Notes:* This lot was added in by hand in the LBDa and RKDH copies of the catalogue.	Roos [for] g	(Sold) fl 0:16 for lots 351[H] & 352[H]. Royers
1806/08/13	AMSCH	0352[H]	*[Anonymous]* | d^{o} [Eenige] d^{o} [Stuks] | *Notes:* This lot was added in by hand in the LBDa and RKDH copies of the catalogue.	Roos [for] g	(Sold) fl 0:16 for lots 351[H] & 352[H]. Royers
1806/08/13	AMSCH	0353[H]	*[Anonymous]* | 3 d^{o} [Stuks] | *Notes:* This lot was added in by hand in the LBDa and RKDH copies of the catalogue.	Roos [for] g	(Sold) fl 3:15 for lots 353[H] & 354[H]. L Pakker
1806/08/13	AMSCH	0354[H]	*[Anonymous]* | 12 d^{o} [Stuks] | *Notes:* This lot was added in by hand in the LBDa and RKDH copies of the catalogue.	Roos [for] g	(Sold) fl 3:15 for lots 353[H] & 354[H]. L Pakker
1806/08/13	AMSCH	0355[H]	*[Anonymous]* | 3 d^{o} [Stuks] | *Notes:* This lot was added in by hand in the LBDa and RKDH copies of the catalogue.	Roos [for] g	(Sold) fl 1:10 L Pakker
1806/08/13	AMSCH	0356[H]	*[Anonymous]* | Eenige d^{o} [Stuks] | *Notes:* This lot was added in by hand in the LBDa and RKDH copies of the catalogue.	Roos [for] R[uel?]	(Sold) fl 8:10 for lots 356[H] & 357[H]. Levie Pakker
1806/08/13	AMSCH	0357[H]	*[Anonymous]* | d^{o} [Eenige] d^{o} [Stuks] | *Notes:* This lot was added in by hand in the LBDa and RKDH copies of the catalogue.	Roos [for] R[uel?]	(Sold) fl 8:10 for lots 356[H] & 357[H]. Levie Pakker

1806/08/13	AMSCH	0358[H]	*[Anonymous]* | 2 d° [Stuks] | *Notes:* This lot was added in by hand in the LBDa and RKDH copies of the catalogue.	Roos [for] R[uel?]	(Sold) fl 1 for lots 358[H] & 359[H]. L Pakker
1806/08/13	AMSCH	0359[H]	*[Anonymous]* | 3 d° [Stuks] | *Notes:* This lot was added in by hand in the LBDa and RKDH copies of the catalogue.	Roos [for] R[uel?]	(Sold) fl 1 for lots 358[H] & 359[H]. L Pakker
1806/08/13	AMSCH	0360[H]	*[Anonymous]* | 2 d° [Stuks] | *Notes:* This lot was added in by hand in the LBDa and RKDH copies of the catalogue.	Roos [for] R[uel?]	(Sold) fl 0:14 L^{vie} Pakker
1806/08/13	AMSCH	0361[H]	*[Anonymous]* | 3 d° [Stuks] | *Notes:* This lot was added in by hand in the LBDa and RKDH copies of the catalogue.	Roos [for] R[uel?]	(Sold) fl 1:15 L Pakker
1806/08/13	AMSCH	0362[H]	*[Anonymous]* | 3 d° [Stuks] | *Notes:* This lot was added in by hand in the LBDa and RKDH copies of the catalogue.	Roos [for] R[uel?]	(Sold) fl 3 Vermeulen
1806/08/13	AMSCH	0363[H]	*[Anonymous]* | 4 d° [Stuks] | *Notes:* This lot was added in by hand in the LBDa and RKDH copies of the catalogue.	Roos [for] R[uel?]	(Sold) fl 2:5 L Pakker
1806/08/13	AMSCH	0364[H]	*[Anonymous]* | 2 d° [Stuks] | *Notes:* This lot was added in by hand in the LBDa and RKDH copies of the catalogue.	Roos [for] R[uel?]	(Sold) fl 1:15 du Pree
1806/08/13	AMSCH	0365[H]	*[Anonymous]* | 3 d° [Stuks] | *Notes:* This lot was added in by hand in the LBDa and RKDH copies of the catalogue.	Roos [for] R[uel?]	(Sold) fl 4 Vermeulen
1806/08/13	AMSCH	0366[H]	*[Anonymous]* | 1 d° [Stuks] | *Notes:* This lot was added in by hand in the LBDa and RKDH copies of the catalogue.	Roos [for] R[uel?]	(Sold) fl 10 Gruiter
1806/08/13	AMSCH	0367[H]	*[Anonymous]* | 1 d° [Stuks] | *Notes:* This lot was added in by hand in the LBDa and RKDH copies of the catalogue.	Roos [for] R[uel?]	(Sold) fl 6 Vermeulen
1806/08/13	AMSCH	0368[H]	*[Anonymous]* | 1 d° [Stuks] | *Notes:* This lot was added in by hand in the LBDa and RKDH copies of the catalogue.	Roos [for] R[uel?]	(Sold) fl 33 Gruiter
1806/08/13	AMSCH	0369[H]	*[Anonymous]* | 1 d° [Stuks] | *Notes:* This lot was added in by hand in the LBDa and RKDH copies of the catalogue.	Roos [for] R[uel?]	(Sold) fl 0:10 Levie Pakker
1806/08/13	AMSCH	0370[H]	*[Anonymous]* | 1 d° [Stuks] | *Notes:* This lot was added in by hand in the LBDa and RKDH copies of the catalogue.	Roos [for] R[uel?]	(Sold) fl 3:15 Gruiter
1806/08/13	AMSCH	0371[H]	*[Anonymous]* | 1 d° [Stuks] | *Notes:* This lot was added in by hand in the LBDa and RKDH copies of the catalogue.	Roos [for] R[uel?]	(Sold) fl 2 Vermeulen
1806/08/13	AMSCH	0372[H]	*[Anonymous]* | 3 d° [Stuks] | *Notes:* This lot was added in by hand in the LBDa and RKDH copies of the catalogue.	Roos [for] R[uel?]	(Sold) fl 3:15 Coclers [for] C Rens
1806/08/13	AMSCH	0373[H]	*[Anonymous]* | 4 Stuks | *Notes:* This lot was added in by hand in the LBDa and RKDH copies of the catalogue.	Roos	(Sold) fl 6 Vermeulen
1806/08/13	AMSCH	0374[H]	*[Anonymous]* | 4 d° [Stuks] | *Notes:* This lot was added in by hand in the LBDa and RKDH copies of the catalogue.	Roos	(Sold) fl 1:5 Gruiter
1806/08/13	AMSCH	0375[H]	*[Anonymous]* | 3 d° [Stuks] | *Notes:* This lot was added in by hand in the LBDa and RKDH copies of the catalogue.	Roos	(Sold) fl 3:5 du Pree
1806/08/13	AMSCH	0376[H]	*[Anonymous]* | 4 d° [Stuks] | *Notes:* This lot was added in by hand in the LBDa and RKDH copies of the catalogue.	Roos	(Sold) fl 1:10 L Pakker
1806/08/13	AMSCH	0377[H]	*[Anonymous]* | 4 d° [Stuks] | *Notes:* This lot was added in by hand in the LBDa and RKDH copies of the catalogue.	Roos	(Sold) fl 2 L Pakker
1806/08/13	AMSCH	0378[H]	*[Anonymous]* | 4 d° [Stuks] | *Notes:* This lot was added in by hand in the LBDa and RKDH copies of the catalogue.	Roos	(Sold) fl 6 for lots 378[H] & 379[H]. L Pakker
1806/08/13	AMSCH	0379[H]	*[Anonymous]* | 2 d° [Stuks] | *Notes:* This lot was added in by hand in the LBDa and RKDH copies of the catalogue.	Roos	(Sold) fl 6 for lots 378[H] & 379[H]. L Pakker
1806/08/13	AMSCH	0380[H]	*[Anonymous]* | 4 d° [Stuks] | *Notes:* This lot was added in by hand in the LBDa and RKDH copies of the catalogue.	Roos	(Sold) fl 8 L Pakker
1806/08/13	AMSCH	0381[H]	*[Anonymous]* | 12 d° [Stuks] | *Notes:* This lot was added in by hand in the LBDa and RKDH copies of the catalogue.	Roos	(Sold) fl 1:5 du Pree
1806/08/13	AMSCH	0382[H]	*[Anonymous]* | 5 d° [Stuks] | *Notes:* This lot was added in by hand in the LBDa and RKDH copies of the catalogue.	Roos	(Sold) fl 1 L Pakker
1806/08/13	AMSCH	0383[H]	*[Anonymous]* | 2 d° [Stuks] | *Notes:* This lot was added in by hand in the LBDa and RKDH copies of the catalogue.	Roos	(Sold) fl 0:12 L Pakker
1806/08/13	AMSCH	0384[H]	*[Anonymous]* | 2 d° [Stuks] | *Notes:* This lot was added in by hand in the LBDa and RKDH copies of the catalogue.	Roos	(Sold) fl 0:14 T van Iperen
1806/08/13	AMSCH	0385[H]	*[Anonymous]* | Zie | *Notes:* This lot was added in by hand in the LBDa and RKDH copies of the catalogue. It was sold with lot 182 by Teniers.	Vinkeles [for] J	(Sold) fl 1 for lots 182 & 385[H]. Coclers
1806/08/13	AMSCH	0386[H]	*[Anonymous]* | 1 d° [Stuks] | *Notes:* This lot was added in by hand in the LBDa and RKDH copies of the catalogue.	Vinkeles [for] J	(Bought In) fl 1
1806/08/13	AMSCH	0387[H]	*[Anonymous]* | 1 d° [Stuks] | *Notes:* This lot was added in by hand in the LBDa and RKDH copies of the catalogue.	Vinkeles [for] J	(Bought In) fl 3
1806/08/13	AMSCH	0388[H]	*[Anonymous]* | 1 d° [Stuks] | *Notes:* This lot was added in by hand in the LBDa and RKDH copies of the catalogue.	Vinkeles [for] J	(Sold) fl 2:10 Lafontaine
1806/08/13	AMSCH	0389[H]	*[Anonymous]* | 1 d° [Stuks] | *Notes:* This lot was added in by hand in the LBDa and RKDH copies of the catalogue.	Vinkeles [for] J	(Sold) fl 3:5 Boelen

1806/08/13	AMSCH	0390[H]	*[Anonymous]* | 1 d^o^ [Stuks] | *Notes:* This lot was added in by hand in the LBDa and RKDH copies of the catalogue.	Daniel Mansveld	(Sold) fl 0:10 for lots 390[a], 391[H] & 392[H]. L Pakker
1806/08/13	AMSCH	0391[H]	*[Anonymous]* | 1 d^o^ [Stuks] | *Notes:* This lot was added in by hand in the LBDa and RKDH copies of the catalogue.	Daniel Mansveld	(Sold) fl 0:10 for lots 390[a], 391[H] & 392[H]. L Pakker
1806/08/13	AMSCH	0392[H]	*[Anonymous]* | 1 d^o^ [Stuks] | *Notes:* This lot was added in by hand in the LBDa and RKDH copies of the catalogue.	Daniel Mansveld	(Sold) fl 0:10 for lots 390[a], 391[H] & 392[H]. L Pakker
1806/08/13	AMSCH	0393[H]	*[Anonymous]* | 1 d^o^ [Stuks] | *Notes:* This lot was added in by hand in the LBDa and RKDH copies of the catalogue.	Vinkeles [for] F	(Sold) fl 8 Lafontaine
1806/08/20	HGBSM	0007	*Een goed meester* | Het Hoofd van een Grijsaard met een langen Baard, fiks geschilderd door een goed meester | *Mat:* op paneel *Size:* hoog 24, breed 19 ½ duim	Macalester Loup [or others]	(Sold) fl 14:5 Zwartsman
1806/08/20	HGBSM	0009	*[Anonymous]* | Het Borstbeeld eener Galante Vrouw meer dan levensgroote; breed geschilderd door een goed fransch meester, in ovaal formaat | *Mat:* op doek *Fmt:* ovaal *Size:* hoog 30 ½, breed 25 duim	Macalester Loup [or others]	(Sold) fl 10 Gram
1806/08/20	HGBSM	0050	*Een goed Meester* | Het Portrait van G. Brandt, door een goed meester | *Mat:* op paneel *Size:* hoog 6, breed 4 duim	Macalester Loup [or others]	(Sold) fl 7:5 Hardenberg
1806/08/20	HGBSM	0054	*Een oud meester* | De Besnijdenis van Christus door een oud meester | *Mat:* op koper *Size:* hoog 8, breed 9 duim	Macalester Loup [or others]	(Sold) fl 1:4 Praiston
1806/08/20	HGBSM	0060	*[Anonymous]* | Een Kwakzalver, die zijne Waar aan eenige Boeren uitvent | *Mat:* op paneel *Size:* hoog 21, breed 16 duim	Macalester Loup [or others]	(Sold) fl 4 Praiston
1806/08/20	HGBSM	0061	*Een goed meester* | Een Historieel Stuk, op doek, door een goed meester | *Mat:* op doek	Macalester Loup [or others]	(Sold) fl 31 for lots 61 & 62. Spruyt
1806/08/20	HGBSM	0062	*Een goed meester* | Een Bachanaal, op doek, door een goed meester | *Mat:* op doek	Macalester Loup [or others]	(Sold) fl 31 for lots 61 & 62. Spruyt
1806/08/20	HGBSM	0070	*[Anonymous]* | Eene Heilige Famillie | *Mat:* op doek *Size:* hoog 19, breed 15 duim	Macalester Loup [or others]	(Sold) fl 2 Baake
1806/08/20	HGBSM	0110	*Een goed meester* | Een groot Familliestuk, bestaande uit Man, Vrouw en drie Kinderen, ten voeten uit; krachtig en meesterlijk geschilderd, door een goed meester | *Mat:* op doek	Macalester Loup [or others]	(Sold) fl 5:10 Spruyt
1806/08/20	HGBSM	0118	*Een oud Meester* | Een knielende Ridder met zijne famillie in devotie, en verder bijwerk, door een oud Meester | companion to lot 119 *Mat:* op doek	Macalester Loup [or others]	(Sold) fl 25:5 for lots 118 & 119. Gram
1806/08/20	HGBSM	0119	*Een oud Meester* | Een dito [knielende Ridder] tot een wederga, met twee biddende figuuren | companion to lot 118 *Notes:* It is unclear what "dito" refers to in the title.	Macalester Loup [or others]	(Sold) fl 25:5 for lots 118 & 119. Gram
1806/08/20	HGBSM	0120	*[Anonymous]* | Twee stuks Portraiten, van Kinderen met hondjes | *Mat:* op paneel	Macalester Loup [or others]	(Sold) fl 2:8 Heijmans
1806/08/20	HGBSM	0121	*[Anonymous]* | Twee dito [stuks] Portraiten met bloemen | *Mat:* op paneel	Macalester Loup [or others]	(Sold) fl 0:16 Ab Salomons
1806/08/20	HGBSM	0122	*[Anonymous]* | Twee dito [stuks] Portraiten | *Mat:* op paneel	Macalester Loup [or others]	(Sold) fl 1:6 Praiston
1806/08/20	HGBSM	0123	*[Anonymous]* | Twee dito [stuks] Portraiten, met hondjes | *Mat:* op paneel	Macalester Loup [or others]	(Sold) fl 1:2 Praiston
1806/08/20	HGBSM	0124	*[Anonymous]* | Twee dito [stuks] portraiten, met dito [hondjes] | *Mat:* op paneel	Macalester Loup [or others]	(Sold) fl 1:6 Zwartsman
1806/08/20	HGBSM	0125	*[Anonymous]* | Een Portrait van eenen jongen Heer met pijl en boog | *Mat:* op paneel	Macalester Loup [or others]	(Sold) fl 1 Guicherit
1806/08/20	HGBSM	0126	*[Anonymous]* | Twee stuks Portraiten, zijnde een Heer en eene Dame | *Mat:* op paneel	Macalester Loup [or others]	(Sold) fl 1:2 Praiston
1806/08/20	HGBSM	0127	*[Anonymous]* | Twee stuks dito Portraiten | *Mat:* op paneel *Notes:* It is unclear what "dito" refers to in the title.	Macalester Loup [or others]	(Sold) fl 2 Praiston
1806/08/20	HGBSM	0130	*[Anonymous]* | Twee Stuks dito [Portraiten] kleinder	Macalester Loup [or others]	(Sold) fl 9 Gram
1806/08/20	HGBSM	0132	*[Anonymous]* | Twee Stuks kleine Portraitjes | *Mat:* op koper	Macalester Loup [or others]	(Sold) fl 2:2 L Voerman voor Huibrechts
1806/08/20	HGBSM	0133	*[Anonymous]* | Twee Stuks Mans en Vrouwe Portraiten, zijnde kniestukken | *Mat:* op doek	Macalester Loup [or others]	(Sold) fl 1:18 Zwartsman
1806/08/20	HGBSM	0135	*[Anonymous]* | Twee dito [Stuks Mans en Vrouwe Portraiten] | *Mat:* op paneel	Macalester Loup [or others]	(Sold) fl 1:10 Scheltema
1806/08/20	HGBSM	0136	*[Anonymous]* | Twee dito [Stuks Mans en Vrouwe Portraiten] | *Mat:* op paneel	Macalester Loup [or others]	(Sold) fl 1:2 Zwartsman
1806/08/20	HGBSM	0137	*[Anonymous]* | Twee dito [Stuks Mans en Vrouwe Portraiten] | *Mat:* op paneel	Macalester Loup [or others]	(Sold) fl 0:12 Praiston
1806/08/20	HGBSM	0138	*[Anonymous]* | Twee dito [Stuks Mans en Vrouwe Portraiten] | *Mat:* op doek op paneel	Macalester Loup [or others]	(Sold) fl 0:9 van Leeuwen

1806/08/20	HGBSM	0139	*[Anonymous]* | Twee dito [Stuks Mans en Vrouwe Portraiten] | *Mat:* op doek	Macalester Loup [or others]	(Sold) fl 1:8 Zwartsman
1806/08/20	HGBSM	0140	*[Anonymous]* | Twee dito [Stuks Mans en Vrouwe Portraiten] | *Mat:* op paneel	Macalester Loup [or others]	(Sold) fl 1:2 Vermeulen
1806/08/20	HGBSM	0141	*[Anonymous]* | Een Mans Portrait | *Mat:* op doek	Macalester Loup [or others]	(Sold) fl 0:6 Vermeulen
1806/08/20	HGBSM	0142	*[Anonymous]* | Een dito [Mans Portrait] | *Mat:* op doek *Notes:* It is unclear what "dito" refers to in the title.	Macalester Loup [or others]	(Sold) fl 0:6 Carré
1806/08/20	HGBSM	0143	*[Anonymous]* | Een Vrouwe Portrait	Macalester Loup [or others]	(Sold) fl 0:10 J Heymans
1806/08/20	HGBSM	0144	*[Anonymous]* | Drie Kindertjes met Bokjes speelende	Macalester Loup [or others]	(Sold) fl 1:6 L Voerman voor Huibrechts
1806/08/20	HGBSM	0145	*[Anonymous]* | Twee Stuks Portraiten Man en Vrouw	Macalester Loup [or others]	(Sold) fl 0:14 Praiston
1806/08/20	HGBSM	0146	*[Anonymous]* | Drie Stuks Portraiten	Macalester Loup [or others]	(Sold) fl 1:4 Van Westreenen
1806/08/20	HGBSM	0161	*Een oud Meester* | De Evangelist Marcus, door een oud Meester	Macalester Loup [or others]	(Sold) fl 1 Coclers
1806/08/20	HGBSM	0162	*Een oud Meester* | De Evangelist Lucas, door denzelven [een oud Meester]	Macalester Loup [or others]	(Sold) fl 0:12 Ab Salomons
1806/08/20	HGBSM	0163	*Een oud Meester* | De Evangelist Johannes, door denzelven [een oud Meester]	Macalester Loup [or others]	(Sold) fl 1 Spruyt
1806/08/20	HGBSM	0164	*[Anonymous]* | Een Boere binnehuis en stal | *Mat:* op doek	Macalester Loup [or others]	(Sold) fl 1:2 Praiston
1806/08/20	HGBSM	0165	*[Anonymous]* | Eene Bataille | *Mat:* op doek	Macalester Loup [or others]	(Sold) fl 0:10 Harmeyer
1806/08/20	HGBSM	0166	*[Anonymous]* | Twee stuks, vrolijke Boere gezelschappen | *Mat:* op paneel	Macalester Loup [or others]	(Sold) fl 2:2 Praiston
1806/08/20	HGBSM	0168	*[Anonymous]* | Een zingende Boer | *Mat:* op paneel	Macalester Loup [or others]	(Sold) fl 16 Zwartsman
1806/08/20	HGBSM	0169	*[Anonymous]* | Een Portrait met een doodshoofd | *Mat:* op koper	Macalester Loup [or others]	(Sold) fl 1:6 Richter
1806/08/20	HGBSM	0170	*[Anonymous]* | Eene Ruïne | *Mat:* op paneel	Macalester Loup [or others]	(Sold) fl 0:6 Abr Salomons
1806/08/20	HGBSM	0171	*[Anonymous]* | Een Herder en Herderin, met Schapen &c. | *Mat:* op paneel	Macalester Loup [or others]	(Sold) fl 1:16 Praiston
1806/08/20	HGBSM	0172	*[Anonymous]* | Dansende Boeren | *Mat:* op paneel	Macalester Loup [or others]	(Sold) fl 0:14 Gram
1806/08/20	HGBSM	0173	*[Anonymous]* | Een Kiezetrekker | *Mat:* op paneel	Macalester Loup [or others]	(Sold) fl 5 for lots 173 & 174. Gram
1806/08/20	HGBSM	0174	*[Anonymous]* | Een Boere gezelschap | *Mat:* op paneel	Macalester Loup [or others]	(Sold) fl 5 for lots 173 & 174. Gram
1806/08/20	HGBSM	0200[b]	*Anonymous* | Twee stuks agthoekige Lijsjes, waarin elk negen stuks aardige ovaale Landschapjes, op koper en in de midden Fruitstukjes, op paneel, de Landschapjes door Asselijn | *This Lot:* Fruitstukjes; lot 200[a] by Asselyn *Mat:* op paneel	Macalester Loup [or others]	(Sold) fl 20:10 for lots 220[a] & 200[b]. Cocard
1806/08/20	HGBSM	0216	*[Anonymous]* | Twee stukjes zijnde zinnebeelden, op paneel, in 't rond | *Mat:* op paneel *Fmt:* rond *Size:* 3 ½ duim diameter	Macalester Loup [or others]	(Sold) fl 4 Praiston
1806/08/20	HGBSM	0224	*[Anonymous]* | Een Schoorsteen stuk	Macalester Loup [or others]	(Sold) fl 2 for lots 224 & 225. de Gelder
1806/08/20	HGBSM	0225	*[Anonymous]* | Een dito [Schoorsteen stuk]	Macalester Loup [or others]	(Sold) fl 2 for lots 224 & 225. de Gelder
1806/08/20	HGBSM	0228[H]	*[Anonymous]* | Een Coertze [?] be een Ton Zittende te Leezen | *Notes:* This lot was added in by hand in the JPGM copy of the catalogue.	Macalester Loup [or others]	(Sold) fl 4:2 Praiston
1806/09/24	HGBES	0005	*[Anonymous]* | 4 stuks op glas Geschilderde Vrouwe Beelde iu [sic] zwarte lyste met verg. biesjes		(Unknown)
1806/09/24	HGBES	0006	*[Anonymous]* | Le bonne Peche & le mauvais Peche 2 st. zwarte Lyste en Glaze		(Unknown)
1806/09/24	HGBES	0007	*[Anonymous]* | L'Eté & 'l hyver als voore [sic] [2 st. zwarte Lyste en Glaze]		(Unknown)
1806/09/24	HGBES	0008	*[Anonymous]* | 3 stuks diverse in Lyste en Glaze		(Unknown)
1806/10/16	UTWLD	0021	*[Anonymous]* | Een biddend oudman, zittende op een stoeltje, levensgroote, extra schoon	Mr P de Malapert [or] W Beeldsnyder	(Unknown)
1806/10/16	UTWLD	0022	*[Anonymous]* | Een stil leven	Mr P de Malapert [or] W Beeldsnyder	(Unknown)

1806/10/16	UTWLD	0023	*[Anonymous]* | Twee landschapjes	Mr P de Malapert [or] W Beeldsnyder	(Unknown)
1806/10/16	UTWLD	0024	*[Anonymous]* | Een fraei [sic] vrouwe portraitje, speelende op 't Clavier	Mr P de Malapert [or] W Beeldsnyder	(Unknown)
1806/10/16	UTWLD	0025	*[Anonymous]* | De portraitten van Columbus en Bastet Greten, op hout geschildert | *Mat:* op hout	Mr P de Malapert [or] W Beeldsnyder	(Unknown)
1806/10/17	MGSAN	0001	*[Anonymous]* | De Kruisdraaging van Christus | *Mat:* op doek	Gerardus Beljard	(Unknown)
1806/10/17	MGSAN	0002	*[Anonymous]* | De Geboorte van Christus | *Mat:* op paneel	Gerardus Beljard	(Unknown)
1806/10/17	MGSAN	0003	*[Anonymous]* | Een Bergachtig Landschap, op de voorgrond staande en leggende Beestjes, in 't verschiet een Dorpgezigt | *Mat:* op paneel	Gerardus Beljard	(Unknown)
1806/10/17	MGSAN	0004	*Een goed Meester* | Een steene Tafel, waarop een Schotel met Aardbezien, een Wynglas omslingert met een Lauwertak, door een goed Meester | *Mat:* op paneel	Gerardus Beljard	(Unknown)
1806/10/17	MGSAN	0005	*[Anonymous]* | Een Nymph, spelende op een Trom de Bas, waarby een danzende groep van Cupidoos | *Mat:* op doek	Gerardus Beljard	(Unknown)
1806/10/17	MGSAN	0007	*[Anonymous]* | Een Tafel met Fruit, waarby een Papegaay op een Druiventak | *Mat:* op doek	Gerardus Beljard	(Unknown)
1806/10/17	MGSAN	0011	*Een goed Meester* | Een Rotsachtig Landschap, op de voorgrond een Brug, ryk gestoffeerd met Figuuren en Beesten, door een goed Meester | *Mat:* op paneel	Gerardus Beljard	(Unknown)
1806/10/17	MGSAN	0012	*Een goed Meester* | Het Oordeel van Paris over de III Bevalligheden, door een goed Meester | *Mat:* op paneel	Gerardus Beljard	(Unknown)
1806/10/17	MGSAN	0016	*[Anonymous]* | Twee Watergezigtjes met Schepen, in 't verschiet een Stad- en Dorpgezigt | *Mat:* op paneel	Gerardus Beljard	(Unknown)
1806/10/17	MGSAN	0020	*[Anonymous]* | De Huwelyksche Voorstelling aan de Ouders van Saartje Jansz | *Mat:* op doek	Gerardus Beljard	(Unknown)
1806/10/17	MGSAN	0021	*[Anonymous]* | Jan Klaassen by Saartje Jansz, als voren [op Doek] | *Mat:* op doek *Notes:* It is unclear what "als voren" refers to in the title.	Gerardus Beljard	(Unknown)
1806/10/17	MGSAN	0025	*[Anonymous]* | Een Grot, waarin op de voorgrond twee worstelende Figuuren | *Mat:* op paneel	Gerardus Beljard	(Unknown)
1806/10/17	MGSAN	0026	*[Anonymous]* | Een Binnenvertrek, waarin een zittende Vrouw in eene neêrslachtige houding, achter haar een Manspersoon met een Brief | *Mat:* op paneel	Gerardus Beljard	(Unknown)
1806/10/17	MGSAN	0027	*Een goed Meester* | Een zwaare Storm, op de voorgrond een strandend Schip op een Rots, door een goed Meester | *Mat:* op paneel	Gerardus Beljard	(Unknown)
1806/10/17	MGSAN	0029	*[Anonymous]* | Een Legerplaats, gestoffeerd met Figuuren, Wagens en Paarden | *Mat:* op paneel	Gerardus Beljard	(Unknown)
1806/10/17	MGSAN	0030	*[Anonymous]* | Een Landschap met een Marketenter, op de voorgrond zittende Figuuren | *Mat:* op paneel	Gerardus Beljard	(Unknown)
1806/10/17	MGSAN	0031	*Een goed Meester* | 5 Stuks met Fruit en Vruchten, en ander bywerk, door een goed Meester | *Mat:* op paneel	Gerardus Beljard	(Unknown)
1806/10/17	MGSAN	0033	*[Anonymous]* | Een Rhyngezigt aan den voet van een Berg, de voorgrond ryk gestoffeerd met Figuuren en Schuiten | *Mat:* op paneel *Notes:* This lot was sold with lot 34, which is a copy after Backhuysen.	Gerardus Beljard	(Sold) £ 0.4.7 for lots 33 & 34. de Onde
1806/10/17	MGSAN	0035	*[Anonymous]* | Een Rekbank, waarop een Schotel met Schelvisch, Snoek en anders | *Mat:* op paneel	Gerardus Beljard	(Sold) £ 1.7 Ooms
1806/10/17	MGSAN	0039	*[Anonymous]* | 2 Dorpgezigtjes, vol gewoel met Wagens en Paarden | *Mat:* op paneel	Gerardus Beljard	(Sold) £ 0.7.1
1806/10/17	MGSAN	0040	*[Anonymous]* | Een Tafel, waarop een Schotel met Haring by een aarde Kan, en ander bywerk | *Mat:* op paneel	Gerardus Beljard	(Sold) £ 0.2.7 for lots 40 & 41
1806/10/17	MGSAN	0041	*[Anonymous]* | 2 Batailles met schermutselende Cavallery | *Mat:* op doek	Gerardus Beljard	(Sold) £ 0.2.7 for lots 40 & 41
1806/10/17	MGSAN	0046	*[Anonymous]* | 2 Boomryke Landschapjes | *Mat:* op koper	Gerardus Beljard	(Sold) £ 0.2.2
1806/10/17	MGSAN	0049	*[Anonymous]* | Een Stad- en Dorpgezigtje | *Mat:* op paneel	Gerardus Beljard	(Sold) £ 0.3.1
1806/10/17	MGSAN	0050	*Een goed Meester* | Een Geruïneerde Tempel van binnen te zien, op de voorgrond een Romeinsch Figuur met Houden, in 't ovaal, door een goed Meester | *Mat:* op paneel *Fmt:* ovaal	Gerardus Beljard	(Sold) £ 0.4.1
1806/10/17	MGSAN	0051	*[Anonymous]* | Een Landschap, op de voorgrond een Fuik, vol Figuuren | *Mat:* op paneel	Gerardus Beljard	(Sold) £ 0.2.1 for lots 51–53
1806/10/17	MGSAN	0052	*[Anonymous]* | Een Pedestal, waarop een Man met Vruchten | *Mat:* op koper	Gerardus Beljard	(Sold) £ 0.2.1 for lots 51–53
1806/10/17	MGSAN	0053	*[Anonymous]* | 2 Boomryke Landschapjes, op de voorgrond een Drift met Beestjes | *Mat:* op koper	Gerardus Beljard	(Sold) £ 0.2.1 for lots 51–53
1806/10/17	MGSAN	0054	*[Anonymous]* | 6 Landschapjes | *Mat:* op koper	Gerardus Beljard	(Sold) £ 0.4.1
1806/10/17	MGSAN	0056	*[Anonymous]* | 2 Bergachtige Landschapjes, zonder Lysten | *Mat:* op doek *Notes:* This lot was sold with lot 55, which is a copy after Goyen.	Gerardus Beljard	(Sold) £ 0.6.7 for lots 55 & 56
1806/10/17	MGSAN	0057	*[Anonymous]* | 3 Stuks Landschapjes | *Mat:* op paneel	Gerardus Beljard	(Sold) £ 0.2 Ooms

1806/10/17	MGSAN	0058	*[Anonymous]* | 2 knielende Monniken in devotie in hunne Cellen | *Mat:* op paneel	Gerardus Beljard	(Unknown)
1806/10/17	MGSAN	0059	*[Anonymous]* | Het Portrait van Rolardus Boghaert, 1544 | *Mat:* op paneel *Inscr:* 1544 (dated?) *Notes:* It is unclear whether the date is inscribed on the painting.	Gerardus Beljard	(Unknown)
1806/10/17	MGSAN	0060	*[Anonymous]* | Een onstuimig Reegezigt met Schepen by een Rots | *Mat:* op paneel	Gerardus Beljard	(Unknown)
1806/10/17	MGSAN	0061	*[Anonymous]* | Een Bergachtig Landschap, de voorgrond gestoffeerd met te Paard zittende Figuuren | *Mat:* op paneel	Gerardus Beljard	(Unknown)
1806/10/17	MGSAN	0062	*[Anonymous]* | Een Dorpgezigt aan de Vaart met Schepen | *Mat:* op paneel	Gerardus Beljard	(Unknown)
1806/10/17	MGSAN	0063	*[Anonymous]* | Een party Schilderyen welke volgens hun Nommer [lots 63–131] zullen verkocht worden | *Notes:* The catalogue indicates that lots 63 to 131 were to contain a number of undescribed paintings. We have not listed them separately.	Gerardus Beljard	(Unknown)
1806/10/22	HGBAK	0001	*[Anonymous]* | Le Mariage Rompu la Gaiëté & bonheur du menage conjugale, 3 stuks in bruine Lysten met glasen | *Notes:* It is uncertain whether this lot consists of paintings.		(Unknown)
1806/10/22	HGBAK	0002	*[Anonymous]* | Het Pourtrait van Kinsbergen, in een zwarte lyst en glas | *Notes:* It is uncertain whether this lot is a painting.		(Unknown)
1806/10/22	HGBAK	0003	*[Anonymous]* | Een Zeetje met Schepen, in een dito [zwarte] lyst en glasen		(Unknown)
1806/10/22	HGBAK	0004	*[Anonymous]* | Twee stuks, een jonge met de rommel pot, en met vogeltjes, in dito [zwarte] lysten en glas		(Unknown)
1806/10/22	HGBAK	0005	*[Anonymous]* | Le Savoyard in een bruine lyst en glas		(Unknown)
1806/10/22	HGBAK	0006	*[Anonymous]* | Twee stuks, een Zeegezicht en een Landschap met een Waterval, in zwarte lysten met glasen		(Unknown)
1806/10/22	HGBAK	0007	*[Anonymous]* | Gezicht van Berg op Zoom, getekend, in dito [zwarte] lyst en glas | *Notes:* It is uncertain whether this lot is a painting.		(Unknown)
1806/10/22	HGBAK	0011	*[Anonymous]* | Een Studie		(Unknown)
1806/11/24	AMSCH	0092	*[Anonymous]* | Physche met een Lamp by Cupido	Munnikhuizen	(Sold) fl 0:10 L Pakker
1806/11/24	AMSCH	0095	*[Anonymous]* | Een woelende Zee, met een meenigte Scheepen en Beelden; in 't graauw, als met de pen gearceerd	Munnikhuizen	(Sold) fl 0:10 L Pakker
1806/11/24	AMSCH	0098[H]	*[Anonymous]* | 1 Schilderij | *Notes:* This lot was added in by hand in the RKDH I copy of the catalogue.	Roos [for] Ferguson	(Sold) fl 13 van Iperen
1806/11/24	AMSCH	0099[H]	*[Anonymous]* | 1 Schilderij | *Notes:* This lot was added in by hand in the RKDH I copy of the catalogue.	Roos [for] Ferguson	(Sold) fl 3:15 L Pakker
1806/11/24	AMSCH	0100[H]	*[Anonymous]* | 1 Schilderij | *Notes:* This lot was added in by hand in the RKDH I copy of the catalogue.	Roos [for] Ferguson	(Sold) fl 7 T Spaan
1806/11/24	AMSCH	0101[H]	*[Anonymous]* | 1 Schilderij | *Notes:* This lot was added in by hand in the RKDH I copy of the catalogue.	Roos [for] de Flines	(Sold) fl 3 Coclers
1806/11/24	AMSCH	0102[H]	*[Anonymous]* | 1 Schilderij | *Notes:* This lot was added in by hand in the RKDH I copy of the catalogue.	Roos [for] de Flines	(Sold) fl 2 Van Iperen
1806/11/24	AMSCH	0103[H]	*[Anonymous]* | 1 Schilderij | *Notes:* This lot was added in by hand in the RKDH I copy of the catalogue.	Roos [for] de Flines	(Sold) fl 0:10 L Pakker
1806/11/24	AMSCH	0104[H]	*[Anonymous]* | 1 Schilderij | *Notes:* This lot was added in by hand in the RKDH I copy of the catalogue.	Roos [for] de Flines	(Sold) fl 2:10 L Pakker
1806/11/24	AMSCH	0105[H]	*[Anonymous]* | 1 Schilderij | *Notes:* This lot was added in by hand in the RKDH I copy of the catalogue.	Roos [for] de Flines	(Sold) fl 3:5 Van Dyl
1807/04/00	LNDLS	0010a	*[Anonymous]* | Een duinagtig Landschapje, op de voorgrond twee mannetjes die visschen bij een water, en verder een herder met schapen op paneel | *Mat:* op paneel *Size:* hoog 6, breed 7 duim	[Abraham Delfos] [or others]	(Unknown)
1807/04/00	LNDLS	0012	*[Anonymous]* | Een weerga, op de voorgrond staat een rood bonte os op een heuvel bij een watertje, verder meer rustende koeijen bij geboomte, en aangenaam verschiet, meesterlijk van ligt en bruin, en niet minder konstig op Paneel | companion to lot 11, by B.H. Thier *Mat:* op paneel	[Abraham Delfos] [or others]	(Unknown)
1807/04/00	LNDLS	0035	*Een voornaam Meester* | Twee stuks met vrouwen en Kinderen, konstig van teken en schilderkonst, door een voornaam Meester	[Abraham Delfos] [or others]	(Unknown)
1807/04/00	LNDLS	0048	*[Anonymous]* | Een verbeeld het vlugten der Spanjaarden, van de schans Lamme bij de Stad Leyden	[Abraham Delfos] [or others]	(Unknown)
1807/04/00	LNDLS	0060	*[Anonymous]* | Christus hangende aan het kruis, op steen gedrukt in een gevlamde lijst | *Mat:* op steen *Size:* hoog 11, breed 7 duim	[Abraham Delfos] [or others]	(Unknown)
1807/04/13	AMSCH	0010	*[Anonymous]* | Een Ordinantie van zes Beelden, voorstellende een Regentenstuk, fraai van behandeling	Everard de Burlett	(Sold) fl 3:5 de Burlett
1807/04/13	AMSCH	0012[H]	*[Anonymous]* | Een Schilderij | *Notes:* This lot was added in by hand in the RKDH I and RKDH II copies of the catalogue.	Everard de Burlett	(Sold) fl 4 Gruiter

1807/06/02	AMHUY	0022	*Een goed Meester* | Een oude Vrouwe Pourtrait, door een goed Meester		(Unknown)
1807/06/02	AMHUY	0030	*Een goed Meester* | Sebastiaan aan een Steenrots gekluisterd, door een goed Meester		(Unknown)
1807/06/02	AMHUY	0035	*[Anonymous]* | Vyf stuks Schilderijen		(Unknown)
1807/06/02	AMHUY	0037	*Een goed Meester* | Een besneeuwd Wintergezicht, by een Poort ziet men een beladen Kar, waarby een Heer en een jonge Dame en verder bywerk, door een goed Meester		(Unknown)
1807/06/02	AMHUY	0041	*[Anonymous]* | 1 Schildery verbeeldende eenige groote Schepen in Brandings		(Unknown)
1807/06/02	AMHUY	0042	*[Anonymous]* | 1 dito [Schildery] verbeeldende het Y, waarvan men in het verschiet Kattenburg en Oostenburg ziet		(Unknown)
1807/06/02	AMHUY	0043	*[Anonymous]* | 1 klein dito [Schildery] van een Boer met eenig Vee, in vergulde Lyst		(Unknown)
1807/06/10	HGBSM	0010a	*[Anonymous]* | Een duinagtig Landschapje, op de voorgrond twee mannetjes die visschen bij een water, en verder een herder met schapen | *Mat:* op paneel *Size:* hoog 6, breed 7 duim	Abraham Delfos [or others]	(Unknown)
1807/06/10	HGBSM	0012	*[Anonymous]* | Een weerga, op de voorgrond staat een rood bonte os op een heuvel bij een watertje, verder meer rustende koeijen bij geboomte, en aangenaam verschiet, meesterlijk van ligt en bruin, en niet minder konstig | companion to lot 11 *Mat:* op paneel	Abraham Delfos [or others]	(Sold) fl 11:10 Wiggers
1807/06/10	HGBSM	0035	*Een voornaam meester* | Twee stuks met vrouwen en kinderen, konstig van teken en schilderkonst, door een voornaam meester	Abraham Delfos [or others]	(Sold) fl 28 v Giese
1807/06/10	HGBSM	0048	*[Anonymous]* | Een verbeeld het vlugten der Spanjaarden van de schans Lamme bij de Stad Leijden	Abraham Delfos [or others]	(Sold) fl 1:2 Tomas
1807/06/10	HGBSM	0060	*[Anonymous]* | Cristus hangende aan het kruis, op steen gedrukt in een gevlamde lijst | *Mat:* op steen *Size:* hoog 11, breed 7 duim	Abraham Delfos [or others]	(Sold) fl 1:4 Carré
1807/06/10	HGBSM	0075	*[Anonymous]* | De Nieuwe Kerk te Delft van binnen te zien, op het monument van Prins Willem den Eerste, met stoffagie en wandelende personen, konstig geschildert | *Mat:* op doek *Size:* hoog 40 breed 33 duim	Abraham Delfos [or others]	(Sold) fl 32 Tomas
1807/06/10	HGBSM	0076a	*Een voornaam Meester* | Een klein Mans borststuk, door een voornaam Meester | *Mat:* op paneel *Size:* hoog 5 breed 4 ½ duim	Abraham Delfos [or others]	(Sold) fl 4:2 Spruit
1807/06/10	HGBSM	0080	*[Anonymous]* | Een Capitaal Schilderij, vertoonende daar Pilatus zijn handen wascht in 't bijzijn zijner Dienaars | *Mat:* op doek *Size:* hoog 43 ½ breed 50 duim	Abraham Delfos [or others]	(Sold) fl 5:10 Margadont
1807/06/10	HGBSM	0085	*Een Oud Meester* | Een Zee met Scheepen en Rotzen uitvoerig van Papier gemaakt, door een Oud Meester in een lijst agter glas | *Mat:* van papier *Notes:* It is uncertain whether this lot is a painting.	Abraham Delfos [or others]	(Sold) fl 3:8 Theben
1807/06/10	HGBSM	0086	*[Anonymous]* | Een Onstuimige Zee met Scheepen, &c	Abraham Delfos [or others]	(Sold) fl 1:10 Temmink
1807/06/10	HGBSM	0094	*Een goed Meester* | Een Bergagtig Landschapje, met een Man te Paard, en een zittend vrouwtje, &c. door een goed Meester | *Mat:* op paneel *Size:* hoog 15, breed 13 duim	Abraham Delfos [or others]	(Sold) fl 2:10 v Giese
1807/06/10	HGBSM	0103	*Een goed Meester* | Een Bergagtig Landschap met Watervallen, door een goed Meester | *Mat:* op doek *Size:* hoog 30 ½, breed 37 ½ duim	Abraham Delfos [or others]	(Sold) fl 3:2 Bogard [or] van Giezen
1807/06/10	HGBSM	0115	*[Anonymous]* | Maria Magdalena weenende | *Mat:* op doek *Size:* hoog 20, breed 14 ½ duim	Abraham Delfos [or others]	(Sold) fl 5:2 v Zante
1807/06/10	HGBSM	0116	*[Anonymous]* | Maria met het Kind | *Mat:* op doek *Size:* hoog 26, breed 21 ½ duim	Abraham Delfos [or others]	(Sold) fl 56 Nieukoop
1807/06/10	HGBSM	0118	*[Anonymous]* | Het portret van J. de Witt | *Mat:* op doek *Size:* hoog 26, breed 23 duim	Abraham Delfos [or others]	(Sold) fl 3:6 Spruit
1807/06/10	HGBSM	0120	*Een goed Meester* | Een portret van een Heer in zijn japon, door een goed Meester | *Mat:* op paneel *Size:* hoog 11, breed 9 duim	Abraham Delfos [or others]	(Sold) fl 1:10 Temmink
1807/06/10	HGBSM	0124	*Een oud Meester* | Een extra oud stukje verbeeldende daar de Sijspenning gegeeven word, zeer uitvoerig door een oud Meester 1529 | *Mat:* op paneel *Inscr:* 1529 (dated?) *Notes:* It is unclear whether the date is inscribed on the painting.	Abraham Delfos [or others]	(Sold) fl 11 Oosterwyk
1807/06/10	HGBSM	0129	*[Anonymous]* | Een borststuk zijnde een oud Man met een grijze baard | *Mat:* op doek *Size:* hoog 22, breed 18 duim	Abraham Delfos [or others]	(Sold) fl 1:4 Vermeulen
1807/06/10	HGBSM	0143	*Een goed Meester* | Een dito [heuvelagtig] Landschapje met stoffagie, door een goed meester | *Mat:* op doek op paneel *Size:* hoog 13 ½, breed 10 ½ duim	Abraham Delfos [or others]	(Sold) fl 6:5 Colonbon
1807/06/10	HGBSM	0145	*Een goed meester* | Een Binnevertrek, waarin een vrolijk gezelschap, door een goed meester | *Mat:* op doek *Size:* hoog 22, breed 17 duim	Abraham Delfos [or others]	(Sold) fl 1 Carré
1807/06/10	HGBSM	0148	*[Anonymous]* | De Brand van Sodom | *Mat:* op paneel *Size:* hoog 10 ½, breed 13 ½ duim	Abraham Delfos [or others]	(Sold) fl 1:16 Ten Haaf
1807/06/10	HGBSM	0159	*[Anonymous]* | Een bergagtig Landschap, waar op de voorgrond eenige lieden zig bezig houden met visschen en meer bijwerk, kragtig en uitvoerig geschildert | *Mat:* op paneel *Size:* hoog 14 ½, breed 19 duim	Abraham Delfos [or others]	(Sold) fl 3:10 Noordwyk

1807/06/10	HGBSM	0168	*[Anonymous]* | Twee stuks, het eene zijnde een Schoenmaker, en het andere een vrouw die een brief leest | *Mat:* op doek	Abraham Delfos [or others]	(Sold) fl 1:2 Vermeulen
1807/06/10	HGBSM	0169	*Een goed Meester* | Een groot Bachanaal Feest, rijk van Ordonnancie, door een goed Meester | *Mat:* op doek	Abraham Delfos [or others]	(Sold) fl 1:2 Vermeulen
1807/06/10	HGBSM	0172	*[Anonymous]* | Een stil leven van verscheiden instrumenten, en andere gereedschappen | *Mat:* op doek	Abraham Delfos [or others]	(Sold) fl 2 Oosterwyk
1807/06/10	HGBSM	0174	*[Anonymous]* | Een witte Rijger, met een Hond onder zijn poot | *Mat:* op doek	Abraham Delfos [or others]	(Sold) fl 1:10 de Gelder
1807/06/10	HGBSM	0188	*Een goed Meester* | Twee stuks uitvoerige Landschapjes, door een goed Meester | *Mat:* op paneel *Size:* hoog 12, breed 9 ½ duim	Abraham Delfos [or others]	(Sold) fl 3:18 v Giese
1807/06/10	HGBSM	0192	*[Anonymous]* | Paulus met een Zwaart in de handen | *Mat:* op paneel	Abraham Delfos [or others]	(Sold) fl 0:14 Van Zante
1807/06/10	HGBSM	0194	*[Anonymous]* | Twee stuks, een Man die Tabak rook en een Vrouw, &c. | *Mat:* op paneel	Abraham Delfos [or others]	(Sold) fl 6:10 v Giese
1807/06/10	HGBSM	0195	*[Anonymous]* | Een Man met een kan in zijn hand | *Mat:* op paneel	Abraham Delfos [or others]	(Sold) fl 1:12 v Giese
1807/06/10	HGBSM	0197	*[Anonymous]* | Een Vrouwtje in een Nis | *Mat:* op paneel	Abraham Delfos [or others]	(Sold) fl 0:16 Dupré
1807/06/10	HGBSM	0198	*[Anonymous]* | Jagers met Honden &c. | *Mat:* op paneel	Abraham Delfos [or others]	(Sold) fl 2 Noordwyk
1807/06/10	HGBSM	0199	*[Anonymous]* | Een Man met een Zwaart voor hem | *Mat:* op paneel	Abraham Delfos [or others]	(Sold) fl 1 de Gelder
1807/06/10	HGBSM	0200	*[Anonymous]* | Een Landschap met Koeijen en Schaapen, helder | *Mat:* op paneel	Abraham Delfos [or others]	(Sold) fl 1:6 Carré
1807/06/10	HGBSM	0201	*[Anonymous]* | Twee stuks met Vogelen | *Mat:* op doek	Abraham Delfos [or others]	(Sold) fl 3 de Gelder
1807/06/10	HGBSM	0202	*[Anonymous]* | Twee stuks Watervallen | *Mat:* op doek	Abraham Delfos [or others]	(Sold) fl 2:14 Heymans
1807/06/10	HGBSM	0203	*[Anonymous]* | Een stuk met speelende Boertjes, en een dito [stuk] met het portret van Willem den 3[de] | *Mat:* op koper	Abraham Delfos [or others]	(Sold) fl 5 Ocke
1807/06/10	HGBSM	0204	*[Anonymous]* | Drie stuks op glas geschilderd, waaronder de portretten van Direk en Wouter Crabeth | *Mat:* op glas	Abraham Delfos [or others]	(Sold) fl 5:14 v Giese
1807/06/10	HGBSM	0205	*[Anonymous]* | Een gestampte kopere plaat met figuuren | *Mat:* op koper	Abraham Delfos [or others]	(Sold) fl 0:16 v Zante
1807/06/10	HGBSM	0206	*[Anonymous]* | Een Kinder portret in Jagers gewaad | *Mat:* op paneel	Abraham Delfos [or others]	(Sold) fl 1 Carré
1807/06/10	HGBSM	0207	*[Anonymous]* | Eene Dame met een Hondje speelende | *Mat:* op paneel	Abraham Delfos [or others]	(Sold) fl 2:2 Noordwyk
1807/06/10	HGBSM	0214	*Een Goed Meester* | Een woelend Water met Scheepen door een goed Meester | *Mat:* op paneel *Size:* hoog 14, breed 19 duim	Abraham Delfos [or others]	(Sold) fl 1:2 Dupré
1807/06/10	HGBSM	0215	*Een goed Meester* | Een stil Water met Scheepjes, door een goed Meester | *Mat:* op paneel *Size:* hoog 7 ½, breed 9 ½ duim	Abraham Delfos [or others]	(Sold) fl 1 de Gelder
1807/06/10	HGBSM	0216	*[Anonymous]* | Een Landschap, rijk met Koebeesten gestoffeerd, waar bij eene Vrouw zit te melken, in het Verschiet de Stad Dordrecht | *Mat:* op paneel *Size:* hoog 22, breed 30 ½ duim	Abraham Delfos [or others]	(Sold) fl 3:12 Ten Haaf
1807/06/10	HGBSM	0220[H]	*[Anonymous]* | [Schilderij] | *Notes:* This lot was added in by hand in the MWH copy of the catalogue.	Abraham Delfos [or others]	(Sold) fl 1:8 Nieuwkoop
1807/06/10	HGBSM	0221[H]	*[Anonymous]* | [Schilderij] | *Notes:* This lot was added in by hand in the MWH copy of the catalogue.	Abraham Delfos [or others]	(Sold) fl 1:12 Ten Haaf
1807/06/10	HGBSM	0222[H]	*[Anonymous]* | [Schilderij] | *Notes:* This lot was added in by hand in the MWH copy of the catalogue.	Abraham Delfos [or others]	(Sold) fl 290 de Gelder
1807/06/10	HGBSM	0223[H]	*[Anonymous]* | [Schilderij] | *Notes:* This lot was added in by hand in the MWH copy of the catalogue.	Abraham Delfos [or others]	(Sold) fl 290 de Gelder
1807/07/20	MGSAN	0002	*[Anonymous]* | Een fraai Historiestuk, verbeeldende het vertrek van Willem III. van Scheveningen naar Engeland, vol gewoel | *Mat:* op paneel	C J van den Helm Boddaert [or others]	(Unknown)
1807/07/20	MGSAN	0003	*[Anonymous]* | Een Boeren Binnenhuis, met Vruchten, Schapen en anders | *Mat:* op paneel	C J van den Helm Boddaert [or others]	(Unknown)
1807/07/20	MGSAN	0004	*[Anonymous]* | Zinnebeeldige Schildery op de Begraafnis-Societeit van 1776. met alle de daarop toepasselyke Afbeeldingen, in Kouleuren, zeer raar | *Inscr:* 1776 (dated?) *Notes:* It is unclear whether the date is inscribed on the painting.	C J van den Helm Boddaert [or others]	(Unknown)
1807/08/26	AMSCH	0248	*Een oud Meester* | Joannes de Dooper, zittende in een Landschap, ter zyde ligt een Lam, op welk hy met de linker hand, waar in hy een Kruisje houdt, schynt te rusten; het is bevallig van Teekening en koloriet, en uitvoerig van Penceelsbehandeling, door een oud Meester | *Mat:* op doek *Size:* hoog 19, breed 14 duim	v d Schley [for] L	(Sold) fl 18:10 Jozi
1807/08/26	AMSCH	0251	*[Anonymous]* | In een Landschap, ziet men een bedaagd Man op de Dwarsfluit speelende, vergezelt van een zingend Meisje, met een blad	Joseph Vallette	(Sold) fl 8:15 for lots 250 & 251. Hulswit

			papier in de hand; breed en meesterlvk [sic] gepenceeld | *Mat:* op doek *Size:* hoog 38, breed 41 duim *Notes:* This lot was sold with lot 250 by an Italian artist.		
1807/08/26	AMSCH	0254	*[Anonymous]* | Een Landschap met een Heer te paard, verder een wit gezadelt Paard, dat door een Knegt wordt vastgehouden, voorts een Heer en Dame, by een springende Fontyn, en ander bywerk | *Mat:* op paneel *Size:* hoog 9 ½, breed 12 duim	de Vries	(Sold) fl 2 Levy Pakker
1807/08/26	AMSCH	0255	*[Anonymous]* | Twee stuks aangenaame Land en Watergezigten, het eene gestoffeerd met een rustende Herder by Koeijen en Schapen, en het ander met een Vrouwtje, houdende een Jongen by de hand, benevens een Hond | *Mat:* op paneel *Size:* ieder hoog 12 ½, breed 14 duim	de Vries	(Sold) fl 16 T Spaan
1807/08/26	AMSCH	0257	*[Anonymous]* | Een staand jong Meisje, in deftige kleeding, verzelt van een Kindje; meesterlyk gepenceeld	de Vries	(Sold) fl 2:15 du Pree
1807/08/26	AMSCH	0260	*[Anonymous]* | Twee diverse Mans Pourtraiten, kleinder	de Vries	(Sold) fl 0:6 Levij Pakker
1807/08/26	AMSCH	0261	*Een oud Meester* | In een Italiaansch Landschap vertoont zich een Jachtparty van eene Dame en een Heer te Paard, gevolgt van Jagers met Honden, verder over een Rivier een Steenen Brug, waarover eenig Vee gedreven wordt; op Doek geschilderd, door een oud Meester | *Mat:* op doek *Size:* hoog 36, breed 45 duim	Helsdinge	(Sold) fl 2:10 L Pakker
1807/08/26	AMSCH	0263	*[Anonymous]* | In een Landschap staan twee Kinderen Waterbellen te blazen; meesterlyk | *Mat:* op doek *Size:* hoog 34, breed 26 duim	Helsdinge	(Sold) fl 0:10 L Pakker
1807/08/26	AMSCH	0264	*[Anonymous]* | Een Italiaansch Landschap: by een aloud Gebouw ziet men een Jongeling by een jong Meisje, welk eenig Fruit in een Korfje en een Haas in haar hand heeft, ter zyde eenig dood Wild, eenige Honden, en verders op den tweeden grond eenig Vee; bevallig op Doek geschilderd | *Mat:* op doek *Size:* hoog 23, breed 26 duim	Helsdinge	(Sold) fl 11:10 van Iperen
1807/08/26	AMSCH	0266	*Een goed Meester* | Een Schaapekop, by een Waterbeekje, fiks en meesterlyk gepenceeld, op Paneel, door een goed Meester | *Mat:* op paneel	Roos [for] A	(Sold) fl 0:6 Spruit
1807/08/26	AMSCH	0267	*[Anonymous]* | Twee stuks gestoffeerde Landgezichten, verbeeldende de Zomer en de Winter, met verschillende stoffage | *Mat:* op paneel	Roos [for] A	(Sold) fl 1 L Pakker
1807/08/26	AMSCH	0269	*[Anonymous]* | Twee stuks: een Binnenhuis met Landlieden en een Riviergezigt, met verscheiden stoffage | *Mat:* op paneel	Roos [for] A	(Sold) fl 4:5 v d Schley A [for] Helsdingen
1807/08/26	AMSCH	0270	*[Anonymous]* | Twee stuks Binnengezichten in Woningen, zynde het eene een Schoenmaker, en de andere drie Lieden by Kaarslicht | *Mat:* op paneel	Roos [for] A	(Sold) fl 2:15 T Spaan
1807/08/26	AMSCH	0271a	*[Anonymous]* | Twee stuks, een Binnenhuis, en een Afbeeldzel van een Bisschop	Roos [for] A	(Sold) fl 2:5 van der Schley Willem
1807/08/26	AMSCH	0272	*[Anonymous]* | Twee stuks bergachtige gestoffeerde Landschappen, met Watervallen en verscheide Reizigers | *Mat:* op doek	Roos [for] A	(Sold) fl 1:5 du Pree
1807/08/26	AMSCH	0273	*[Anonymous]* | Een Haring Visschery, gestoffeerd met verscheiden Schepen en Sloepen | *Mat:* op doek	Roos [for] A	(Sold) fl 1 Levy Pakker
1807/08/26	AMSCH	0275	*[Anonymous]* | Twee stuks, een Land- en Watergezicht, met Woningen en Geboomte, op den voorgrond een Schuit met eenige Lieden, en een ander Landschap | *Mat:* op doek op paneel	Roos [for] A	(Sold) fl 1 Levij Pakker
1807/08/26	AMSCH	0276	*[Anonymous]* | Een Campement, waar by verscheiden Militairen te Paard, en gestoffeerd met verder bywerk; fiks op Doek geschilderd | *Mat:* op doek	Roos [for] A	(Sold) fl 9:10 Hooft
1807/08/26	AMSCH	0277	*[Anonymous]* | Een Familiestuk, verbeeldende twee Jufvrouwen, zittende by een Tafel, bezig Koffy te drinken, ter zyde staat een Heer | *Mat:* op doek	Roos [for] A	(Sold) fl 0:10 van Iperen
1807/08/26	AMSCH	0278	*[Anonymous]* | Twee stuks hevige Gevechten tusschen Ruitery, vol gewoel; krachtig gepenceeld	Roos [for] A	(Sold) fl 1 C Metz
1807/08/26	AMSCH	0281	*[Anonymous]* | Twee stuks Binnenhuizen, met vrolyke musiceerende Boeren en Boerinnen, en andere zingende; beide fiks op Paneel geschilderd | *Mat:* op paneel	Roos [for] A	(Sold) fl 1:5 Levij Pakker
1807/08/26	AMSCH	0282	*[Anonymous]* | Twee stuks, een Wintergezicht, daar Lieden zich op het Ys vermaken, by de Vestmuur van een Stad, en een zittende Boer | *Mat:* op paneel	Roos [for] A	(Sold) fl 1:15 A Rynders
1807/08/26	AMSCH	0283	*[Anonymous]* | Twee stuks Afbeeldzels van jonge Vrouwen, in Landschappen | *Mat:* op paneel	Roos [for] A	(Sold) fl 1:15 du Pree
1807/08/26	AMSCH	0285	*Een goed Meester* | Christus door Judas verraden wordende, in den Nacht, by Fakkellicht; zynde fraai geordonneerd en uitvoerig geschilderd, door een goed Meester	Joseph Vallette	(Sold) fl 15 Peeterse
1807/08/26	AMSCH	0288	*[Anonymous]* | De Heilige Familie, zittende in een Landschap, verbeeldende Maria met het Kindje op de schoot, waar nevens St. Joseph, in een Boek lezende; krachtig op Paneel geschilderd | *Mat:* op paneel	Joseph Vallette	(Sold) fl 4:15 du Pree
1807/08/26	AMSCH	0292	*[Anonymous]* | In een Binnenhuis zitten agt Boeren by een Tafel te spyzigen; krachtig geschilderd | *Mat:* op doek	v d Schley [for] [Smits Wed]	(Sold) fl 7 H^k Jansen

1807/08/26	AMSCH	0293	*[Anonymous]* | Een bevallig Italiaansch Landschap, fiks geschilderd	Joseph Vallette	(Sold) fl 0:6 Geld
1807/08/26	AMSCH	0294	*[Anonymous]* | Eene Vrouw met vyf Kindertjes, verbeeldende de Liefde; door een oud Meester	Joseph Vallette	(Sold) fl 0:10 du Pree
1807/08/26	AMSCH	0295	*[Anonymous]* | Vier stuks Gezichten in Italië; zynde van een meesterlyke penceelsbehandeling	Joseph Vallette	(Sold) fl 1:10 Gruiter
1807/08/26	AMSCH	0298	*[Anonymous]* | Een boomryk Landschap, gestoffeerd met Beelden en Beesten die door een Water gaan; kloek gepenceeld	Joseph Vallette	(Sold) fl 2:15 A Rynders
1807/08/26	AMSCH	0299	*[Anonymous]* | Een Oud-Mans Hoofd; als denzelven | *Notes:* It is unclear to whom "denzelven" refers to in the title, since the previous lot was by an anonymous artist.	Joseph Vallette	(Sold) fl 0:6 L Pakker
1807/08/26	AMSCH	0300	*[Anonymous]* | Een Stuk met verscheiden Visschen in een Mand, op een Tafel staande; natuurlyk behandeld	Joseph Vallette	(Sold) fl 5 Gruiter
1807/08/26	AMSCH	0301	*[Anonymous]* | Een deftig Heer, met een Papier in zyn hand; krachtig behandeld	Joseph Vallette	(Sold) fl 4:5 Gruiter
1807/08/26	AMSCH	0305	*[Anonymous]* | Twee stuks Pourtretten van Prinsen | *Mat:* op paneel	Yver [for] S	(Sold) fl 5:10 Frantzen
1807/08/26	AMSCH	0309	*Een oud Meester* | Een mediterende Philosooph, aandachtig in een Boek lezende, voor een Tafel, waarop geplaatst een Doodshoofd, Boeken en andere Papieren; krachtig op Doek geschilderd, door een oud Meester | *Mat:* op doek	Yver [for] S	(Sold) fl 1:10 du Pree
1807/08/26	AMSCH	0310	*[Anonymous]* | Twee stuks: het eene een boomryk heuvelachtig Landschap, met rustende Reizigers. De wederga een dito Landschap, daar badende Lieden elkander naloopen; fiks geschilderd	Yver [for] S	(Sold) fl 8 van Iperen
1807/08/26	AMSCH	0313	*[Anonymous]* | Drie stuks: een Landschap, een Zeegezicht en eene Meid met dood Wild	Yver [for] S	(Sold) fl 2:5 Gruiter
1807/08/26	AMSCH	0314	*[Anonymous]* | Twee stuks diversche Pourtretten	Yver [for] S	(Sold) fl 0:6 L Pakker
1807/08/26	AMSCH	0315	*[Anonymous]* | Twee dito [stuks] dito [diversche Pourtretten]	Yver [for] S	(Sold) fl 0:6 L Pakker
1807/08/26	AMSCH	0316	*[Anonymous]* | Een woelende Zee, met verscheiden Scheepen | *Mat:* op doek	Yver [for] S	(Sold) fl 6 Zonnenbergh
1807/08/26	AMSCH	0320	*Een goed Meester* | Een Italiaansch Gezicht; door een goed Meester	Joseph Vallette	(Sold) fl 1 Coclair
1807/08/26	AMSCH	0321	*[Anonymous]* | Twee stuks Stillevens; natuurlyk verbeeld	Joseph Vallette	(Sold) fl 2:5 du Pree
1807/08/26	AMSCH	0322	*[Anonymous]* | Een Herder met een Fluit; als dito [natuurlyk verbeeld]	Joseph Vallette	(Sold) fl 0:6 Levy Pakker
1807/08/26	AMSCH	0323	*[Anonymous]* | Twee stuks Italiaansche Landschapjes	Joseph Vallette	(Sold) fl 0:12 Jacobs
1807/08/26	AMSCH	0324	*Een goed Meester* | Een Landschapje; door een goed Meester	Joseph Vallette	(Sold) fl 0:6 Levy Pakker
1807/08/26	AMSCH	0325	*Een goed Meester* | Zes stuks, zynde de Historie van den verloren Zoon; geestig behandeld door een goed Meester	Roos	(Sold) fl 14 Coclair
1807/08/26	AMSCH	0326	*Een goed Meester* | Vier stuks vrolyke Voorwerpen; door een goed Meester	Roos	(Sold) fl 10:10 Levy Pakker
1807/08/26	AMSCH	0327	*Een goed Meester* | Een Mans Pourtret, als voren [door een goed Meester]	Roos	(Sold) fl 4:10 Coclair
1807/08/26	AMSCH	0328	*Een goed Meester* | Twee dito [Mans] dito [Pourtretten]; als voren [door een goed Meester]	Roos	(Sold) fl 3:5 du Pree
1807/08/26	AMSCH	0329	*Een goed Meester* | Een Vrouw met een Hondje; als voren [door een goed Meester]	Roos	(Sold) fl 0:6 Levij Pakker
1807/08/26	AMSCH	0330	*Een goed Meester* | Twee capitaale Mans en Vrouwe Pourtretten, als voren [door een goed Meester]	Roos	(Sold) fl 3 Gruiter
1807/08/26	AMSCH	0335	*[Anonymous]* | Drie stuks: twee Italiaansche Landschapjes en een ander	Schott	(Sold) fl 1 Coclair
1807/08/26	AMSCH	0336	*[Anonymous]* | Drie stuks: een Zeegezicht en twee Hoofden	Schott	(Sold) fl 0:6 Levij Pakker
1807/08/26	AMSCH	0337	*[Anonymous]* | Twee Stillevens, met Vruchten op Porceleine Schotels	Schott	(Sold) fl 1 Levij Pakker
1807/08/26	AMSCH	0339	*[Anonymous]* | Een Triumf van eenige Cupido's	de Vries	(Sold) fl 0:6 Levij Pakker
1807/08/26	AMSCH	0341[H]	*[Anonymous]* | 2 Schilderijen | *Notes:* This lot was added in by hand in the EBNP and RKDH copies of the catalogue.	Roos	(Sold) fl 0:8 L Pakker
1807/08/26	AMSCH	0342[H]	*[Anonymous]* | 2 dito [Schilderijen] | *Notes:* This lot was added in by hand in the EBNP and RKDH copies of the catalogue.	Roos	(Sold) fl 1 du Pree
1807/08/26	AMSCH	0343[H]	*[Anonymous]* | 1 dito [Schilderij] | *Notes:* This lot was added in by hand in the EBNP and RKDH copies of the catalogue.	Roos	(Sold) fl 1:5 Coclair
1807/08/26	AMSCH	0344[H]	*[Anonymous]* | 2 dito [Schilderijen] | *Notes:* This lot was added in by hand in the EBNP and RKDH copies of the catalogue.	Roos	(Sold) fl 4:5 du Pree
1807/08/26	AMSCH	0345[H]	*[Anonymous]* | 2 dito [Schilderijen] | *Notes:* This lot was added in by hand in the EBNP and RKDH copies of the catalogue.	Roos	(Sold) fl 0:6 for lots 345[H] & 346[H]. L Pakker
1807/08/26	AMSCH	0346[H]	*[Anonymous]* | 3 dito [Schilderijen] | *Notes:* This lot was added in by hand in the EBNP and RKDH copies of the catalogue.	Roos	(Sold) fl 0:6 for lots 345[H] & 346[H]. L Pakker

1807/08/26	AMSCH	0347[H]	*[Anonymous]* | 2 dito [Schilderijen] | *Notes:* This lot was added in by hand in the EBNP and RKDH copies of the catalogue.	Roos	(Sold) fl 0:6 van Iperen
1807/08/26	AMSCH	0348[H]	*[Anonymous]* | 2 dito [Schilderijen] | *Notes:* This lot was added in by hand in the EBNP and RKDH copies of the catalogue.	Roos	(Sold) fl 2 van Iperen
1807/08/26	AMSCH	0349[H]	*[Anonymous]* | 1 dito [Schilderij] | *Notes:* This lot was added in by hand in the EBNP and RKDH copies of the catalogue.	Roos	(Sold) fl 1:15 Gruiter
1807/08/26	AMSCH	0350[H]	*[Anonymous]* | 1 dito [Schilderij] | *Notes:* This lot was added in by hand in the EBNP and RKDH copies of the catalogue.	Roos	(Sold) fl 3 du Pree
1807/08/26	AMSCH	0351[H]	*[Anonymous]* | 2 dito [Schilderijen] | *Notes:* This lot was added in by hand in the EBNP and RKDH copies of the catalogue.	Roos	(Sold) fl 1 du Pree
1807/08/26	AMSCH	0352[H]	*[Anonymous]* | 1 dito [Schilderij] | *Notes:* This lot was added in by hand in the EBNP and RKDH copies of the catalogue.	Roos	(Sold) fl 1:15 L Pakker
1807/08/26	AMSCH	0353[H]	*[Anonymous]* | 1 dito [Schilderij] | *Notes:* This lot was added in by hand in the EBNP and RKDH copies of the catalogue.	Roos	(Sold) fl 2:15 Coclair
1807/08/26	AMSCH	0354[H]	*[Anonymous]* | 1 dito [Schilderij] | *Notes:* This lot was added in by hand in the EBNP and RKDH copies of the catalogue.	Roos	(Sold) fl 6 Coclair
1807/08/26	AMSCH	0355[H]	*[Anonymous]* | 1 dito [Schilderij] | *Notes:* This lot was added in by hand in the EBNP and RKDH copies of the catalogue.	Roos	(Sold) fl 33:10 Coclair
1807/08/26	AMSCH	0356[H]	*[Anonymous]* | 1 dito [Schilderij] | *Notes:* This lot was added in by hand in the EBNP and RKDH copies of the catalogue.	Roos	(Sold) fl 6:10 du Pree
1807/08/26	AMSCH	0357[H]	*[Anonymous]* | 1 dito [Schilderij] | *Notes:* This lot was added in by hand in the EBNP and RKDH copies of the catalogue.	Roos	(Sold) fl 1 L Pakker
1807/08/26	AMSCH	0358[H]	*[Anonymous]* | 2 dito [Schilderijen] | *Notes:* This lot was added in by hand in the EBNP and RKDH copies of the catalogue.	Roos	(Sold) fl 0:6 L Pakker
1807/08/26	AMSCH	0359[H]	*[Anonymous]* | 2 dito [Schilderijen] | *Notes:* This lot was added in by hand in the EBNP and RKDH copies of the catalogue.	Roos	(Sold) fl 10:10 van Iperen
1807/08/26	AMSCH	0360[H]	*[Anonymous]* | 2 dito [Schilderijen] | *Notes:* This lot was added in by hand in the EBNP and RKDH copies of the catalogue.	Roos	(Sold) fl 2:5 du Sart
1807/08/26	AMSCH	0361[H]	*[Anonymous]* | 2 dito [Schilderijen] | *Notes:* This lot was added in by hand in the EBNP and RKDH copies of the catalogue.	Roos	(Sold) fl 2:5 Gruiter
1807/08/26	AMSCH	0362[H]	*[Anonymous]* | 2 dito [Schilderijen] | *Notes:* This lot was added in by hand in the EBNP and RKDH copies of the catalogue.	Roos	(Sold) fl 7 H Jansen
1807/08/26	AMSCH	0363[H]	*[Anonymous]* | 2 dito [Schilderijen] | *Notes:* This lot was added in by hand in the EBNP and RKDH copies of the catalogue.	Roos	(Sold) fl 2:5 du Pree
1807/08/27	AMSCH	0364[H]	*[Anonymous]* | 1 Schilderij | *Notes:* This lot was added in by hand in the EBNP and RKDH copies of the catalogue.	Yver [for] S	(Sold) fl 0:8 v Iperen
1807/08/27	AMSCH	0365[H]	*[Anonymous]* | 1 dito [Schilderij] | *Notes:* This lot was added in by hand in the EBNP and RKDH copies of the catalogue.	Yver [for] S	(Sold) fl 2 Gruiter
1807/08/27	AMSCH	0366[H]	*[Anonymous]* | 1 dito [Schilderij] | *Notes:* This lot was added in by hand in the EBNP and RKDH copies of the catalogue.	Yver [for] S	(Sold) fl 4:10 du Pree
1807/08/27	AMSCH	0367[H]	*[Anonymous]* | 1 dito [Schilderij] | *Notes:* This lot was added in by hand in the EBNP and RKDH copies of the catalogue.	Yver [for] S	(Sold) fl 3:10 Gruyter
1807/08/27	AMSCH	0368[H]	*[Anonymous]* | 1 dito [Schilderij] | *Notes:* This lot was added in by hand in the EBNP and RKDH copies of the catalogue.	Yver [for] S	(Sold) fl 3:15 A Rynders
1807/08/27	AMSCH	0369[H]	*[Anonymous]* | 1 dito [Schilderij] | *Notes:* This lot was added in by hand in the EBNP and RKDH copies of the catalogue.	Yver [for] S	(Sold) fl 0:14 L Pakker
1807/08/27	AMSCH	0370[H]	*[Anonymous]* | 1 dito [Schilderij] | *Notes:* This lot was added in by hand in the EBNP and RKDH copies of the catalogue.	Yver [for] S	(Sold) fl 5:15 Caree
1807/08/27	AMSCH	0371[H]	*[Anonymous]* | 1 dito [Schilderij] | *Notes:* This lot was added in by hand in the EBNP and RKDH copies of the catalogue.	Yver [for] S	(Sold) fl 11 Nieuwenhuis
1807/08/27	AMSCH	0372[H]	*[Anonymous]* | 1 dito [Schilderij] | *Notes:* This lot was added in by hand in the EBNP and RKDH copies of the catalogue.	Yver [for] S	(Sold) fl 2:15 du Pree
1807/09/28	AMWUR	0001	*Een goed Meester* | Een aangenaam Landschap, met hoog geboomte en rivieren doorsneeden, op den voorgrond vertoond zich een Herder met zyne kudde, en wandelende Beelden; zonachtig en warm gepenceeld, door een goed Meester		(Unknown) fl 1:6
1807/09/28	AMWUR	0001	*Een goed Meester* | Een dito [aangenaam] dito [Landschap], waarin zich vertoond een Heer te Paard voor een Herberg als drinkende, op den voorgrond een wandelende Boer met zyn Hond, door een goed Meester		(Unknown) fl 0:6
1807/09/28	AMWUR	0003	*[Anonymous]* | Een Dorpgezichtje, alwaar aan 't strand eenige Visschers Pinken leggen		(Unknown) fl 0:6
1807/09/28	AMWUR	0004	*[Anonymous]* | Een Zeegezichtje, met zeilende en andere Scheepen, Vaartuigen, in zwarte Lyst		(Unknown) fl 9:10
1807/09/28	AMWUR	0005	*[Anonymous]* | Een Landschap, waarin zich een Boer met eenig grazend Vee vertoond, in zwarte Lyst		(Unknown) fl 2:10
1807/09/28	AMWUR	0007	*[Anonymous]* | Een dito [stukje] verbeeldende het Pourtrait van den Kunstschilder F. Mieris, in vergulde Lyst		(Unknown) fl 9:10

1807/09/28	AMWUR	0008	*[Anonymous]* | Een dito [stukje] op Marmer geschilderde Zeehaaven in Turkyen [sic], in zwarte Lyst		(Unknown) fl 4
1807/09/28	AMWUR	0009	*[Anonymous]* | Twee dito [stukjes] op Doek, verbeeldende onstuimige Zeeën, met in nood zynde Scheepen, in zwarte Lysten | *Mat:* op doek		(Unknown) fl 1:10
1807/09/28	AMWUR	0010	*[Anonymous]* | Twee stuks zynde Historieele Ordonnantien, in vergulde Lysten		(Unknown) fl 3:15
1807/09/28	AMWUR	0016	*[Anonymous]* | Een Spaansch Hondje op Doek | *Mat:* op doek		(Unknown) fl 3
1807/09/28	AMWUR	0017	*[Anonymous]* | Een stuk zynde een Zeetje, met een Scheepje zich van Bakboordzyde vertoonende, in zwarte Lyst		(Unknown) fl 1:5
1807/09/28	AMWUR	0022	*[Anonymous]* | Een dito [stuk] op Paneel, verbeeldende 1 Smitswinkel | *Mat:* op paneel		(Unknown) fl 20
1807/09/28	AMWUR	0024	*Een voornaam Meester* | Twee stuks op Doek, zynde twee fraaije en weluitgevoerde Bloemstukken, door een voornaam Meester, in zwarte Lyst, met vergulde sponning | *Mat:* op doek		(Unknown) fl 0:10
1807/09/28	AMWUR	0025	*Een voornaam Meester* | Een dito [stuk], verbeeldende Eenige Landlieden by den Haard, mede door een voornaam Meester, in dito [zwarte] Lyst		(Unknown) fl 8:10
1807/09/28	AMWUR	0026	*Een voornaam Meester* | Een dito [stuk] verbeeldende de Brand in 's Lands Magazyn 1793, door een voornaam Meester, origineel in vergulde Lyst		(Unknown) fl 7:10
1807/09/28	AMWUR	0027	*[Anonymous]* | Een dito [stuk] op Paneel, verbeeldende 't Leidsche Haringvrouwtje | *Mat:* op paneel		(Unknown) fl 15
1807/09/28	AMWUR	0030	*[Anonymous]* | Een dito [stuk] dito [op Doek] als 't voorgaande | *Mat:* op doek *Notes:* This lot was sold with lot 29 by B. Gael.		(Unknown) fl 30 for lots 29 & 30
1807/09/28	AMWUR	0032	*[Anonymous]* | Een dito [stuk] dito [op Paneel] als vooren | *Mat:* op paneel		(Unknown) fl 8:5
1807/09/28	AMWUR	0033	*[Anonymous]* | Een dito [stuk] dito [op Paneel] dito [als vooren] | *Mat:* op paneel		(Unknown) fl 8
1807/09/28	AMWUR	0034	*[Anonymous]* | Twee stuks onstuimige Zeeën		(Unknown) fl 0:8
1807/09/28	AMWUR	0035[H]	*[Anonymous]* | [Illegible] | *Notes:* This lot was added in by hand in the AA copy of the catalogue, but the title is illegible.		(Unknown) fl 10:10
1807/09/28	DOHAA	000V	*[Anonymous]* | Een Schildery, zynde eeu [sic] Boeren Werf, met Hoenderen en Eenden | *Mat:* op doek	Mattheus Westerouen van Meeteren	(Unknown)
1807/09/28	DOHAA	000W	*[Anonymous]* | Een Italiaansche Zeehaven | *Mat:* op doek	Mattheus Westerouen van Meeteren	(Unknown)
1807/09/28	DOHAA	000X	*[Anonymous]* | Een Expeditie van de Ruiter, op Chatham | companion to lot Y *Mat:* op paneel	Mattheus Westerouen van Meeteren	(Unknown)
1807/09/28	DOHAA	000Y	*[Anonymous]* | Een dito [Expeditie] tot een wederga | companion to lot X *Mat:* op paneel	Mattheus Westerouen van Meeteren	(Unknown)
1807/09/28	DOHAA	000Z	*[Anonymous]* | Een Zeeslag, vry stout behandeld | *Mat:* op paneel	Mattheus Westerouen van Meeteren	(Unknown)
1807/09/28	DOHAA	00BB	*[Anonymous]* | Gezigt van 't Y voor Amsterdam | *Mat:* op paneel	Mattheus Westerouen van Meeteren	(Unknown)
1807/09/28	DOHAA	00II	*[Anonymous]* | Pamona en Vertumnus	Mattheus Westerouen van Meeteren	(Unknown)
1807/09/28	DOHAA	00KK	*[Anonymous]* | Een Landschap	Mattheus Westerouen van Meeteren	(Unknown)
1807/09/28	DOHAA	00LL	*[Anonymous]* | Een Koekbakster	Mattheus Westerouen van Meeteren	(Unknown)
1807/09/28	DOHAA	00MM	*Een goed Meester* | Een Winter Gezigt, door een goed Meester	Mattheus Westerouen van Meeteren	(Unknown)
1807/09/28	DOHAA	00NN	*[Anonymous]* | Twee stuks met Beeldjes	Mattheus Westerouen van Meeteren	(Unknown)
1807/09/28	DOHAA	00OO	*[Anonymous]* | Venus en Adonis	Mattheus Westerouen van Meeteren	(Unknown)
1807/09/28	DOHAA	00UU	*[Anonymous]* | Een dito [Landschap] met lastdragende Ezels, en Beeldjes	Mattheus Westerouen van Meeteren	(Unknown)
1807/09/28	DOHAA	00WW	*[Anonymous]* | Een dito [Landschap] zynde een weerga van de voorgaande	Mattheus Westerouen van Meeteren	(Unknown)
1807/10/12	MGBEO	0003	*[Anonymous]* | Een Landschap met eenige Figuuren | *Mat:* op paneel	Hermannus Johannes Heyman	(Sold) £ 0:2 Andriessen
1807/10/12	MGBEO	0006	*[Anonymous]* | Een Mans Potrait [sic], in vergulde Lyst	Hermannus Johannes Heyman	(Sold) £ 0:2 Benthem
1807/10/12	MGBEO	0007	*[Anonymous]* | Een Mans en Vrouwe Potrait [sic], in verg. Lyst	Hermannus Johannes Heyman	(Sold) £ 0:19 Priester
1807/10/12	MGBEO	0010	*[Anonymous]* | Vier Portraiten | *Mat:* op koper	Hermannus Johannes Heyman	(Sold) £ 0:1 Benthem

1807/10/29	RMDRS	0069[H]	*[Anonymous]* | Schoorsteenstuk | *Fmt:* schoorsteenstuk *Notes:* This lot was added in by hand in the AMR copy of the catalogue. In the inventory of Van der Pot's collection, the painting is described as "Abr. Hondius, Buitenplaats, gestoffeerd met jagers te paard, die van de jacht terugkomen (uit den schoorsteen van de benedenzaal." (See E. Wiersum in *Oud Holland*, 48, 1931, p.205)	Gerrit van der Pot, Heer van Groeneveld	(Unknown) fl 30:15
1807/11/26	HGBES	0015	*Een Voornaam Meester* | Een Keurlyk Portrait van een Turks Keiz-rin [sic] Oliverf op Koper door een Voornaam Meester | *Mat:* in olyverf op koper		(Unknown)
1807/12/00	ARNIJ	0003	*Een voornaam Meester* | Een Brand, zeer fraaij en kunstig geschildert, door een voornaam Meester	Meinsmaa [or] Engelan	(Sold) fl 2 Kieboon
1807/12/00	ARNIJ	0005	*[Anonymous]* | Heraklit en Democrit, twee stuks met fraaije Lijsten	Meinsmaa [or] Engelan	(Unknown) fl 0:14
1807/12/00	ARNIJ	0006	*[Anonymous]* | Twee Famille Pourtraiten	Meinsmaa [or] Engelan	(Unknown) fl 0:2
1808/03/03	HAVIN	0009	*[Anonymous]* | Het laatste Avondmaal, konstig, door	Jacobus Spillebout	(Unknown) fl 1:16
1808/04/26	GDAN	0094	*[Anonymous]* | Een zonägtig Landscap [sic], waar in eenige Boere Wooningen, en daar bij eenige Werklieden | *Size:* hoog 14, breed 22 duim *Notes:* The artist's name has been accidentally omitted, although the last line of the previous page indicates it began with "Mo."	G H Fortuyn	(Unknown)
1808/04/26	GDAN	0095	*[Anonymous]* | Een zon- en duinägtig Landschap, met Boere Wooningen | *Size:* hoog 15, breed 23 duim *Notes:* The artist's name has been accidently omitted, although the last line of the previous page indicates it began with "Mo."	G H Fortuyn	(Unknown)
1808/04/26	GDAN	0216	*[Anonymous]* | Een Binnenhuis | *Size:* hoog 17 ½, breed 23 ½ duim	G H Fortuyn	(Unknown)
1808/04/26	GDAN	0218	*[Anonymous]* | Een Italiaansch Stuk, konstig en kragtig geschilderd, verbeeldende eenige hoge Personagien die eene vreemde jonge Dame les geven in hun Muziek, alle deftig gekleed, met bijwerk | *Size:* hoog 38, breed 46 duim	G H Fortuyn	(Unknown)
1808/04/26	GDAN	0220	*[Anonymous]* | Een dito, zijnde een Valke Jagt | *Notes:* It is unclear what "dito" refers to in the title.	G H Fortuyn	(Unknown)
1808/04/26	GDAN	0221	*[Anonymous]* | Een Binnenhuis, zynde een School, waar men den Schoolmeester met zijne Kinderen ziet | *Size:* hoog 13, breed 18 duim	G H Fortuyn	(Unknown)
1808/04/26	GDAN	0222	*[Anonymous]* | Een Rhijngezigtje, wel geschilderd | *Size:* hoog 3 ½, breed 6 duim	G H Fortuyn	(Unknown)
1808/04/26	GDAN	0223	*[Anonymous]* | Een dito [Rhijngezigtje] | *Size:* hoog 3 ½, breed 6 duim	G H Fortuyn	(Unknown)
1808/04/26	GDAN	0224	*[Anonymous]* | Een op Koper geschilderde Romeinsche Bataille, goed geschilderd | *Mat:* op koper *Size:* hoog 6, breed 10 duim	G H Fortuyn	(Unknown)
1808/04/26	GDAN	0225	*[Anonymous]* | Een uitmuntend fraai ovaal Mans Pourtretje, konstig en kragtig geschilderd | *Fmt:* ovaal *Size:* hoog 5, breed 3 ½ duim	G H Fortuyn	(Unknown)
1808/04/26	GDAN	0226	*[Anonymous]* | Een Boomryk Bos met een Jager | *Size:* hoog 5 ½, breed 7 ½ duim	G H Fortuyn	(Unknown)
1808/04/26	GDAN	0227	*[Anonymous]* | Een Boertje kijkende in een Kan of die ledig is, wel geschilderd | *Size:* hoog 11 ½, breed 10 duim	G H Fortuyn	(Unknown)
1808/04/26	GDAN	0228	*[Anonymous]* | Een Boere Binnenhuis, waar in aan een Tafel een Vrouwtje zit te slapen, en verder nog eenige Boertjes | *Size:* hoog 12, breed 13 ½ duim	G H Fortuyn	(Unknown)
1808/04/26	GDAN	0229	*[Anonymous]* | Een Zonägtig Landschap, bij een Boere Woning, met een Melkboer, eenige Koeijen en Schapen, zeer fiks geschilderd | *Size:* hoog 22, breed 30 ½ duim	G H Fortuyn	(Unknown)
1808/04/26	GDAN	0231	*Een goed Meester* | Een duinägtig Landschap, door een goed Meester | *Size:* hoog 4 ½, breed 5 duim	G H Fortuyn	(Unknown)
1808/04/26	GDAN	0232	*[Anonymous]* | Een biddend Mans Pourtretje, fiks geschildert | *Size:* hoog 17, breed 13 duim	G H Fortuyn	(Unknown)
1808/04/26	GDAN	0233	*[Anonymous]* | Suzanna met de boeven, wel geschilderd | *Size:* hoog 37, breed 30 duim	G H Fortuyn	(Unknown)
1808/04/26	GDAN	0234	*[Anonymous]* | Een Vrouwe Pourtret | *Size:* hoog 29, breed 23 duim	G H Fortuyn	(Unknown)
1808/04/26	GDAN	0235	*[Anonymous]* | Een dito [Vrouwe Pourtret] | *Size:* hoog 16, breed 12 duim	G H Fortuyn	(Unknown)
1808/04/26	GDAN	0236	*[Anonymous]* | Adam en Eva wordende uit het Paradijs gejaagt | *Size:* hoog 11, breed 13 ½ duim	G H Fortuyn	(Unknown)
1808/04/26	GDAN	0237	*[Anonymous]* | Twee Paarden op een Heuvel | *Size:* hoog 11 ½, breed 19 duim	G H Fortuyn	(Unknown)
1808/04/26	GDAN	0238	*[Anonymous]* | Een ten toonstelling van een fraai Meisje, goed geschilderd | *Size:* hoog 52, breed 63 duim	G H Fortuyn	(Unknown)
1808/04/26	GDAN	0240	*[Anonymous]* | Een zeer fraai Pourtret, verbeeldende den Ambassadeur Bevening | *Size:* hoog 48, breed 37 duim	G H Fortuyn	(Unknown)
1808/04/26	GDAN	0242	*[Anonymous]* | Een Pourtret van een goed Meester | *Size:* hoog 20, breed 16 duim	G H Fortuyn	(Unknown)

1808/04/26	GDAN	0243	*[Anonymous]* | Een Italiaansche Schilderij, Europa met de Stier verbeeldende, fiks gepenseeld | *Size:* hoog 19, breed 24 duim	G H Fortuyn	(Unknown)
1808/04/26	GDAN	0244	*[Anonymous]* | Een stormägtig Zeetje, met Schepen | *Size:* hoog 21, breed 32 duim	G H Fortuyn	(Unknown)
1808/04/26	GDAN	0247	*[Anonymous]* | Maria met het Kind Jezus | *Size:* hoog 6, breed 5 duim	G H Fortuyn	(Unknown)
1808/04/26	GDAN	0248	*[Anonymous]* | Een Rivier Gezigtje bij een overvaards plaats, met eenige Schepen | *Size:* hoog 19, breed 34 duim	G H Fortuyn	(Unknown)
1808/04/26	GDAN	0249	*Een goed Meester* | Een Italiaansch Bosgezigt, door een goed Meester | *Size:* hoog 30, breed 26 duim	G H Fortuyn	(Unknown)
1808/04/26	GDAN	0250	*Een goed Meester* | Een zonagtig Duingezigt, door een goed Meester, gestoffeerd met Schapen en Beelden | *Size:* hoog 19, breed 26 duim	G H Fortuyn	(Unknown)
1808/04/26	GDAN	0251	*[Anonymous]* | Een Landschap met Gebouwen en Beelden | *Size:* hoog 11, breed 16 duim	G H Fortuyn	(Unknown)
1808/04/26	GDAN	0252	*[Anonymous]* | Een Grotgezigt | *Size:* hoog 16 ½, breed 17 duim	G H Fortuyn	(Unknown)
1808/04/26	GDAN	0253	*[Anonymous]* | Een Boere Gezelschap | *Size:* hoog 22, breed 31 duim	G H Fortuyn	(Unknown)
1808/04/26	GDAN	0254	*[Anonymous]* | Een fraai stil Leven | *Size:* hoog 23, breed 19 duim	G H Fortuyn	(Unknown)
1808/04/26	GDAN	0259	*[Anonymous]* | Een dito [Landschap] tot een wederga | companion to lot 258, manner of Romeyn	G H Fortuyn	(Unknown)
1808/04/26	GDAN	0261	*[Anonymous]* | Een fraai Schilderijtje, verbeeldende Petrus uit de Gevangenis verlost | *Size:* hoog 16, breed 13 duim	G H Fortuyn	(Unknown)
1808/04/26	GDAN	0263	*[Anonymous]* | Een dito [Mans Pourtretje], uitmuntend geschilderd | *Size:* hoog 9, breed 7 duim	G H Fortuyn	(Unknown)
1808/04/26	GDAN	0265	*[Anonymous]* | Een zonägtig boomrijk Landschap, waar in een Boer een koppel Koeijen voorddrijft, fraai geschildert | *Size:* hoog 13 ½, breed 18 duim	G H Fortuyn	(Unknown)
1808/04/26	GDAN	0267	*[Anonymous]* | Een Binnenhuis met vrolijke Boeren en Boerinnen, fiks geschilderd | *Size:* hoog 26, breed 20 duim	G H Fortuyn	(Unknown)
1808/04/26	GDAN	0269	*[Anonymous]* | Door een Italiaansch Meester, zynde de Aanbidding van den Geboren Zaligmaker, met Engelen, Menschen en Beesten, goed geschilderd | *Size:* hoog 52, breed 45 duim	G H Fortuyn	(Unknown)
1808/04/26	GDAN	0270	*[Anonymous]* | Een goed Italiaansch Schildery, zijnde eene Heilige Familie | *Size:* hoog 50, breed 40 duim	G H Fortuyn	(Unknown)
1808/04/26	GDAN	0271	*[Anonymous]* | Een Pourtret | *Size:* hoog 27, breed 24 duim	G H Fortuyn	(Unknown)
1808/04/26	GDAN	0273	*[Anonymous]* | Een Mans Pourtret, verbeeldende Prins Maurits | *Size:* hoog 16, breed 14 duim	G H Fortuyn	(Unknown)
1808/04/26	GDAN	0274	*[Anonymous]* | Een jonge Juffrouw, die een Kommetje in haar hand heeft en daar uit schijnt te eeten, en een fraai Hondje bij zich hebbende, wel geschilderd | *Size:* hoog 13, breed 10 duim	G H Fortuyn	(Unknown)
1808/04/26	GDAN	0275	*[Anonymous]* | Een duinägtig Landschapje, met goed Geboomte, en wandelende Beeldjes | *Mat:* op paneel *Size:* hoog 10, breed 13 duim	G H Fortuyn	(Unknown)
1808/04/26	GDAN	0277	*[Anonymous]* | Een zeer goed geschilderd Poutret | *Mat:* op paneel *Size:* hoog 12 ½, breed 10 duim	G H Fortuyn	(Unknown)
1808/04/26	GDAN	0281	*[Anonymous]* | Een zeer goed Pourtret, zijnde Jan Graaf van Nassau	G H Fortuyn	(Unknown)
1808/04/26	GDAN	0282	*[Anonymous]* | Een dito [Pourtret], Prins Maurits	G H Fortuyn	(Unknown)
1808/04/26	GDAN	0283	*[Anonymous]* | Karel den I, Koning van Engeland	G H Fortuyn	(Unknown)
1808/04/26	GDAN	0284	*[Anonymous]* | Fredrik Hendrik, Prins van Oranje	G H Fortuyn	(Unknown)
1808/04/26	GDAN	0285	*[Anonymous]* | Jan, Graaf van Nassau	G H Fortuyn	(Unknown)
1808/04/26	GDAN	0286	*[Anonymous]* | Philip, Graaf van Buuren	G H Fortuyn	(Unknown)
1808/04/26	GDAN	0287	*[Anonymous]* | Willem Lodewijk, oudste Zoon van Jan van Nassau	G H Fortuyn	(Unknown)
1808/04/26	GDAN	0288	*[Anonymous]* | Willem den I	G H Fortuyn	(Unknown)
1808/04/26	GDAN	0289	*[Anonymous]* | Philip, Graaf van Nassau	G H Fortuyn	(Unknown)
1808/04/26	GDAN	0290	*[Anonymous]* | Hendrik Casimir, Stadhouder van Vriesland	G H Fortuyn	(Unknown)
1808/04/26	GDAN	0291	*[Anonymous]* | George, Graaf van Nassau	G H Fortuyn	(Unknown)
1808/04/26	GDAN	0292	*[Anonymous]* | Hendrik Casimir, 5de Zoon van Jan van Nassau	G H Fortuyn	(Unknown)
1808/04/26	GDAN	0293	*[Anonymous]* | Een plaisante Varkenmarkt, vol gewoel, wel geschilderd | *Size:* hoog 18, breed 23 duim	G H Fortuyn	(Unknown)
1808/04/26	GDAN	0294	*[Anonymous]* | Eene Italiaansche Zeehaven, met eenige Ruïne | *Size:* hoog 26, breed 22 duim	G H Fortuyn	(Unknown)
1808/04/26	GDAN	0295	*[Anonymous]* | Een Binnenvertrek, waar in een Eend en lagchend persoon zijn pijp zit te roken, goed behaud [sic] | *Size:* hoog 16, breed 10 duim	G H Fortuyn	(Unknown)
1808/04/26	GDAN	A0005	*Een voornaam Meester* | Door een voornaam Meester het origineele Pourtret van Hironimus Beverning, na 't leven geschildert, met alle zijne Ambassades, te vinden, Wagenaars Vad. Historie, 16 deel, bladz 130 | *Size:* hoog 46, breed 34 duim *Notes:* This lot has been renumbered to	G H Fortuyn	(Unknown)

			distinguish it from another lot with the same number in a different section of the catalogue.		
1808/05/17	LNAN	0014	*[Anonymous]* | Een heuvelachtig Landschap met beelden, koeijen, bokken en schapen | *Mat:* op doek *Size:* hoog 33, breed 43 duim		(Sold) fl 20 Thomasse
1808/05/17	LNAN	0017	*[Anonymous]* | Een Gezigt langs het water op de stad Leyden, met vele schepen, vol met vlugtende Spanjaarden van de Lammenschans bij Leyden		(Unknown)
1808/05/17	LNAN	0018	*[Anonymous]* | Een stil leven met veel huisraad		(Unknown)
1808/05/17	LNAN	0019	*[Anonymous]* | Een Jagthond met dood gevogelte		(Unknown)
1808/05/17	LNAN	0024	*[Anonymous]* | Een woelende zee		(Unknown)
1808/05/17	LNAN	0025	*[Anonymous]* | Een water met schepen		(Unknown)
1808/05/17	LNAN	0026	*[Anonymous]* | Een landschap met beelden		(Unknown) fl 0:9
1808/05/17	LNAN	0027	*[Anonymous]* | Een gezelschap met vrolijke boeren		(Unknown)
1808/05/17	LNAN	0028	*[Anonymous]* | Maria met het kind		(Unknown) fl 0:6
1808/05/17	LNAN	0029	*[Anonymous]* | Een mans pourtrait		(Unknown)
1808/05/17	LNAN	0032	*[Anonymous]* | Een op de kaart speelend gezelschap		(Sold) fl 2 Thomasse
1808/05/17	LNAN	0034	*[Anonymous]* | Een groot Schilderij, verbeeldende Schipio's bruid		(Unknown)
1808/05/17	LNAN	0035	*[Anonymous]* | Een dito [groot Schilderij] met slapende Nimphen		(Unknown)
1808/05/17	LNAN	0036	*[Anonymous]* | Vijf stuks schoorsteen en deurstukken met bloemen en fruit | *This Lot:* Een stuk schoorsteen of deurstuk met bloemen en fruit *Notes:* Lots 36 to 40 were printed in the catalogue as one item.		(Unknown)
1808/05/17	LNAN	0037	*[Anonymous]* | Vijf stuks schoorsteen en deurstukken met bloemen en fruit | *This Lot:* Een stuk schoorsteen of deurstuk met bloemen en fruit *Notes:* Lots 36 to 40 were printed in the catalogue as one item.		(Unknown)
1808/05/17	LNAN	0038	*[Anonymous]* | Vijf stuks schoorsteen en deurstukken met bloemen en fruit | *This Lot:* Een stuk schoorsteen of deurstuk met bloemen en fruit *Notes:* Lots 36 to 40 were printed in the catalogue as one item.		(Unknown)
1808/05/17	LNAN	0039	*[Anonymous]* | Vijf stuks schoorsteen en deurstukken met bloemen en fruit | *This Lot:* Een stuk schoorsteen of deurstuk met bloemen en fruit *Notes:* Lots 36 to 40 were printed in the catalogue as one item.		(Unknown)
1808/05/17	LNAN	0040	*[Anonymous]* | Vijf stuks schoorsteen en deurstukken met bloemen en fruit | *This Lot:* Een stuk schoorsteen of deurstuk met bloemen en fruit *Notes:* Lots 36 to 40 were printed in the catalogue as one item.		(Unknown)
1808/05/18	LNAN	0016	*[Anonymous]* | Een stil Water met differente Schepen | companion to lot 17	Mr Cornelis Versluys	(Unknown)
1808/05/18	LNAN	0017	*[Anonymous]* | Een dito [stil Water met differente Schepen] Weêrga | companion to lot 16	Mr Cornelis Versluys	(Unknown)
1808/05/18	LNAN	0018	*[Anonymous]* | Een Historieele Zee-Triumph	Mr Cornelis Versluys	(Unknown)
1808/05/18	LNAN	0019	*[Anonymous]* | Een stil Water met differente zeilende Schepen	Mr Cornelis Versluys	(Unknown)
1808/05/18	LNAN	0022	*[Anonymous]* | Een woelend Water met Schepen, konstig van Papier gesneden | companion to lot 23 *Mat:* van papier	Mr Cornelis Versluys	(Unknown)
1808/05/18	LNAN	0023	*[Anonymous]* | Een weerga door denzelven | companion to lot 22	Mr Cornelis Versluys	(Unknown)
1808/05/18	LNAN	0027	*[Anonymous]* | Een Biddende Maria	Mr Cornelis Versluys	(Unknown)
1808/05/18	LNAN	0029	*[Anonymous]* | Eene stervende Cleopatra met hare Nymphen	Mr Cornelis Versluys	(Unknown)
1808/05/18	LNAN	0036	*[Anonymous]* | Een Tafel met een Schotel met Visch en meer bijwerk	Mr Cornelis Versluys	(Unknown)
1808/05/18	LNAN	0045	*[Anonymous]* | Een Buitenhuis, met Beelden op den Voorgrond	Mr Cornelis Versluys	(Unknown)
1808/05/18	LNAN	0051	*[Anonymous]* | Een Gezigt op een Stad, en op den Voorgrond veel gewoel	Mr Cornelis Versluys	(Unknown)
1808/05/18	LNAN	0052	*[Anonymous]* | Een dito [Gezigt op een Stad], mede met veel gewoel	Mr Cornelis Versluys	(Unknown)
1808/05/18	LNAN	0053	*[Anonymous]* | Een Schaal met allerhande Fruit	Mr Cornelis Versluys	(Unknown)
1808/05/18	LNAN	0054	*[Anonymous]* | Een Historieel Schilderij	Mr Cornelis Versluys	(Unknown)
1808/05/18	LNAN	0058	*[Anonymous]* | Een Schaal met allerhande Fruit	Mr Cornelis Versluys	(Unknown)
1808/05/18	LNAN	0059	*[Anonymous]* | Een Mans Pourtrait halverlijf	Mr Cornelis Versluys	(Unknown)
1808/05/18	LNAN	0060	*[Anonymous]* | Een Familie Stuk ten voeten uit	Mr Cornelis Versluys	(Unknown)
1808/05/18	LNAN	0061	*[Anonymous]* | Een Vrouwen Pourtrait	Mr Cornelis Versluys	(Unknown)
1808/05/18	LNAN	0062	*[Anonymous]* | Een Historieel	Mr Cornelis Versluys	(Unknown)
1808/05/18	LNAN	0063	*[Anonymous]* | 2 Stuks met Zeeën	Mr Cornelis Versluys	(Unknown)
1808/06/06	RMRIJ	0153	*Onbekend* | Philemon en Baucis door Jupiter en Mercurius geleid wordende [Philémon et Baucis accompagnés par Jupiter et Mercure] | *Mat:* op doek *Size:* Hoog 28, en breed 36 ¼ duim	Gerrit van der Pot, Heer van Groeneveld	(Sold) fl 3 van Leen
1808/06/06	RMRIJ	0156	*Onbekend* | Het Portret van eenen Dichter of Schilder. Fiks behandeld [Le Portrait d'un Poëte, où d'un Peintre] | *Mat:* op doek *Size:* Hoog 30 ½, en breed 25 ¼ duim	Gerrit van der Pot, Heer van Groeneveld	(Sold) fl 10 R Pott

1808/06/06	RMRIJ	0157	*Onbekend* | Een zeer schoon Vrouwe Portret in Oud Hollandsche Kleeding en Witten Kraag. Uitvoerig en konstig geschilderd; ook in Plaat gebragt [Le Portrait en ovale, d'une Dame Hollandaise costumée en fraise. D'un beau fini, et de beauVerbatim mérite] | *Mat:* op koper *Fmt:* ovaal *Size:* Hoog 4 ½, en breed 3 ½ duim	Gerrit van der Pot, Heer van Groeneveld	(Sold) fl 65 R Pott
1808/06/06	RMRIJ	0158	*Onbekend* | De Dochter van Herodes met het Hoofd van Johannes den Dooper, op een Schotel, enz. [Hérodiade tenant la tête de Saint Jean-Baptiste etc.] | *Annots:* Verk. Utrecht 17 Sept 1798 als Guido Reni (f 28.-) (RMA I) *Mat:* op toetssteen *Size:* Hoog 10 ½, en breed 7 ⅕ duim	Gerrit van der Pot, Heer van Groeneveld	(Sold) fl 9:10 Nieuwenhuys
1808/06/06	RMRIJ	0159	*Onbekend* | Een woelend water met Schepen. Eene wedergade, zijnde een stil water met Schepen [Une Eau calme, où l'on voit plusieurs Bâtiments et Chaloupes. Le Pendant. Une Eau agitée sur laquelle se trouvent plusieurs Bateaux à la voile etc.] | *Mat:* op paneel *Size:* Twee Stukken. Hoog 10 ¾, en breed 15 ¼ duim	Gerrit van der Pot, Heer van Groeneveld	(Sold) fl 54 Hakoun
1808/06/11	RMRIJ	0019	*Onbekend* | Een bergachtig Landschap, met veel Stoffagie, zeer verdienstelijk geschilderd | *Mat:* op paneel *Size:* hoog 34 ½, breed 46 ½ duim		(Sold) fl 5:5 van Giesen
1808/06/11	RMRIJ	0022	*Onbekend* | Een Stilleven, natuurlyk en meesterlyk geschilderd | *Mat:* op paneel		(Sold) fl 2:10 Du Pree
1808/06/11	RMRIJ	0038	*Onbekend* | Een Woelend Water, fraai geschilderd | *Mat:* op paneel		(Sold) fl 16:10 V Der Wall
1808/06/11	RMRIJ	0046	*Onbekend* | Het gezicht van een Hollands Zeestrand en Dorp, ryk gestoffeerd | *Mat:* op paneel		(Sold) fl 6 van Dongen
1808/06/11	RMRIJ	0068	*Onbekend* | Twee Geestelyke Personen, d'eene een Schotel in de handen houdende, waar op een afgeslagen Hoofd ligt, uitvoerig en zeer verdienstig, getekend en geschilderd | *Mat:* op paneel *Size:* hoog 9 ½, breed 6 duim		(Sold) fl 15:10 Luchtmans
1808/06/11	RMRIJ	0069	*[Anonymous]* | Een Vrouwe Pourtraitje | *Mat:* op paneel		(Sold) fl 1:5 Van Leen
1808/06/11	RMRIJ	0071	*Onbekend* | Twee Stuks, een Mans en Vrouwe Pourtrait, goed behandeld		(Sold) fl 9 Luchtmans
1808/06/11	RMRIJ	0074	*Onbekend* | Een Onstuimige Zee met Schepen | *Mat:* op paneel		(Sold) fl 1:2 van Giesen
1808/06/11	RMRIJ	0076	*Onbekend* | Twee Stuks Winter Gezichten | *Mat:* op paneel		(Sold) fl 5 [or] 52 Van Giesen
1808/06/11	RMRIJ	0077	*Onbekend* | Op den Voorgrond zit een Man, op de Lier Spelende, waar by eenige Krygslieden, in 't Verschiet een Stad enz., vol verdiensten | *Mat:* op koper *Size:* hoog 9 ½, breed 14 duim		(Bought In) fl 8
1808/06/11	RMRIJ	0086	*Onbekend* | Een Heuvelachtig Landschap, eenige Schapen en Schaapskooy, natuurlyk en konstig | *Mat:* op paneel *Size:* hoog 6, breed 7 ¼ duim		(Sold) fl 15 Rohan
1808/06/11	RMRIJ	0094	*Onbekend* | Een Verdienstig Gelders Landschap, waar in een Rad en Watervalletje, aangenaam gestoffeerd, piquant van Licht | *Mat:* op paneel *Size:* hoog 18, breed 24 duim		(Sold) fl 47 Noortwyck
1808/06/11	RMRIJ	0100	*Onbekend* | Samson en Delila | *Mat:* op paneel		(Unknown) fl 1
1808/06/11	RMRIJ	0101	*[Anonymous]* | Een Landschap met Figuren, Bokken, Hond en Schaap | *Mat:* op doek		(Unknown) fl 1
1808/06/11	RMRIJ	0104	*[Anonymous]* | Een Stal met Paarden en Figuren | *Mat:* op paneel		(Unknown) fl 1:10
1808/06/11	RMRIJ	0107	*[Anonymous]* | Twee Landschappen | *Mat:* op paneel		(Unknown) fl 5
1808/06/11	RMRIJ	0108	*[Anonymous]* | Drie stuks, een Historie, een Bok, een Mossel Eeter		(Unknown) fl 1:10
1808/06/11	RMRIJ	0115[a]	*[Anonymous]* | Drie Doeken zonder Ramen en een Paneel, welke in eens zullen verkogt worden | *This Lot:* Drie Doeken *Mat:* op doek		(Sold) fl 10:5 for lots 115[a] & 115[b]. V Giesen
1808/06/11	RMRIJ	0115[b]	*[Anonymous]* | Drie Doeken zonder Ramen en een Paneel, welke in eens zullen verkogt worden | *This Lot:* Een Paneel *Mat:* op paneel		(Sold) fl 10:5 for lots 115[a] & 115[b]. V Giesen
1808/06/11	RMRIJ	0122	*Onbekend* | Eenige Schutters ten voeten uit | *Mat:* op doek op paneel		(Unknown) fl 2:12
1808/06/13	AMSCH	0192a[H]	*[Anonymous]* | 1 schilderij | *Notes:* This lot was added in by hand in the EBNP, FLNY and RKDH copies of the catalogue.	E M Engelberts	(Sold) fl 2:10 Glad
1808/06/13	AMSCH	0200	*[Anonymous]* | Een als voren [Italiaansch Landschap], zijnde de ontmoeting van Jakob en Esau | *Notes:* It is unclear to what "een als voren" refers to in the title. This lot was sold with lot 199, which is in the manner of R. Roghman.	E M Engelberts	(Sold) fl 25 for lots 199 & 200. O W J Berg
1808/06/13	AMSCH	0207	*[Anonymous]* | Petrus de Kreupelen genezende, ter zijde eene Vrouw, die zijn Kleed aanraakt, verder eenige Aanschouwers; fraai van uitdrukking en penceelsbehandeling	E M Engelberts	(Sold) fl 100 van Bergen
1808/06/13	AMSCH	0224	*[Anonymous]* | Het Afbeeldsel van den Kunstschilder C. Netscher, 1659 | *Mat:* op koper *Fmt:* ovaal *Inscr:* 1659 (dated?) *Notes:* It is unclear whether the date is inscribed on the painting.	[Jan Tersteeg]	(Sold) fl 2:15 C S Roos [or] Versteeg
1808/06/13	AMSCH	0228	*[Anonymous]* | Een fraai gestoffeerd Italiaansch Landschap, met verscheide Beelden	R[oos]	(Sold) fl 2:10 L Pakker

1808/06/13	AMSCH	0229	*[Anonymous]* | Op eene Tafel staat een Mandje met Bloemen, verder eenige Vruchten, Hoorns en Insekten; allerfraaist en uitvoerig op Koper geschilderd | *Mat:* op koper	R[oos]	(Bought In) fl 10
1808/06/13	AMSCH	0230	*[Anonymous]* | Een aangenaam boomrijk Landschap, met Beelden en Beesten; uitvoerig en tevens natuurlijk	R[oos]	(Sold) fl 5:15 Gruiter
1808/06/13	AMSCH	0238	*[Anonymous]* | Een kapitaal boomrijk Landschap, met eene menigte Stoffage van Jagers te Paard en te voet; meesterlijk behandeld	R[oos]	(Sold) fl 1:15 Th Spaan
1808/06/13	AMSCH	0248	*[Anonymous]* | Het Afbeeldsel van Dirck Volkertzoon Coornhert, Secretaris van Prins Willem den Eersten; krachtig en fraai op Paneel geschilderd | *Mat:* op paneel	Y[ver]	(Sold) fl 1:5 O W J Berg
1808/06/13	AMSCH	0249	*[Anonymous]* | Het Portret van een Krijgsman, van voren te zien; op Paneel geschilderd | *Mat:* op paneel	Y[ver]	(Sold) fl 0:10 Engelberts [or] Simons
1808/06/13	AMSCH	0250	*[Anonymous]* | Twee stuks Marktgezichten, met Gebouwen en onderscheidene Beeldjes gestoffeerd | *Mat:* op paneel	Y[ver]	(Sold) fl 1:5 Geld
1808/06/13	AMSCH	0251[H]	*[Anonymous]* | 2 stuks | *Notes:* This lot was added in by hand in the EBNP, FLNY and RKDH copies of the catalogue.	Z	(Sold) fl 1 L Pakker
1808/06/13	AMSCH	0252[H]	*[Anonymous]* | 2 Stuks | *Notes:* This lot was added in by hand in the EBNP, FLNY and RKDH copies of the catalogue.	Z	(Sold) fl 2:10 Gruiter
1808/06/13	AMSCH	0253[H]	*[Anonymous]* | 2 stuks | *Notes:* This lot was added in by hand in the EBNP, FLNY and RKDH copies of the catalogue.	Z	(Sold) fl 3 J Spaan
1808/06/13	AMSCH	0254[H]	*[Anonymous]* | 2 stuks | *Notes:* This lot was added in by hand in the EBNP, FLNY and RKDH copies of the catalogue.	Z	(Sold) fl 1:10 L Pakker
1808/06/13	AMSCH	0255[H]	*[Anonymous]* | 2 stuks | *Notes:* This lot was added in by hand in the EBNP, FLNY and RKDH copies of the catalogue.	Z	(Sold) fl 2:10 de Vries
1808/06/13	AMSCH	0256[H]	*[Anonymous]* | 2 stuks | *Notes:* This lot was added in by hand in the EBNP, FLNY and RKDH copies of the catalogue.	Z	(Sold) fl 2 Coclers
1808/06/13	AMSCH	0257[H]	*[Anonymous]* | 2 stuks | *Notes:* This lot was added in by hand in the EBNP, FLNY and RKDH copies of the catalogue.	Z	(Sold) fl 5:10 Levie Pakker
1808/06/13	AMSCH	0258[H]	*[Anonymous]* | 3 stuks | *Notes:* This lot was added in by hand in the EBNP, FLNY and RKDH copies of the catalogue.	Z	(Sold) fl 1 Coclers
1808/06/13	AMSCH	0259[H]	*[Anonymous]* | 1 stuk | *Notes:* This lot was added in by hand in the EBNP, FLNY and RKDH copies of the catalogue.	Z	(Sold) fl 0:10 L Pakker
1808/06/13	AMSCH	0260[H]	*[Anonymous]* | 2 stuks | *Notes:* This lot was added in by hand in the EBNP, FLNY and RKDH copies of the catalogue.	Z	(Sold) fl 10 Allard
1808/06/13	AMSCH	0261[H]	*[Anonymous]* | 2 stuks | *Notes:* This lot was added in by hand in the EBNP, FLNY and RKDH copies of the catalogue.	Z	(Sold) fl 20:10 J Spaan
1808/06/13	AMSCH	0262[H]	*[Anonymous]* | 1 stuk | *Notes:* This lot was added in by hand in the EBNP, FLNY and RKDH copies of the catalogue.	Z	(Sold) fl 1:10 Coclers
1808/06/13	AMSCH	0263[H]	*[Anonymous]* | 1 stuk | *Notes:* This lot was added in by hand in the EBNP, FLNY and RKDH copies of the catalogue.	Z	(Sold) fl 1 Coclers
1808/06/13	AMSCH	0264[H]	*[Anonymous]* | 1 stuk | *Notes:* This lot was added in by hand in the EBNP, FLNY and RKDH copies of the catalogue.	E M Engelberts	(Sold) fl 3:10 Glad
1808/06/13	AMSCH	0265[H]	*[Anonymous]* | 2 stuks | *Notes:* This lot was added in by hand in the EBNP, FLNY and RKDH copies of the catalogue.	E M Engelberts	(Sold) fl 8:5 Gruiter
1808/06/13	AMSCH	0266[H]	*[Anonymous]* | 2 stuks | *Notes:* This lot was added in by hand in the EBNP, FLNY and RKDH copies of the catalogue.	E M Engelberts	(Sold) fl 1:15 Gruiter
1808/06/13	AMSCH	0267[H]	*[Anonymous]* | 2 stuks | *Notes:* This lot was added in by hand in the EBNP, FLNY and RKDH copies of the catalogue.	E M Engelberts	(Sold) fl 5:5 Th Spaan
1808/06/13	AMSCH	0268[H]	*[Anonymous]* | 2 stuks | *Notes:* This lot was added in by hand in the EBNP, FLNY and RKDH copies of the catalogue.	E M Engelberts	(Sold) fl 8 Glad
1808/06/13	AMSCH	0269[H]	*[Anonymous]* | 2 stuks | *Notes:* This lot was added in by hand in the EBNP, FLNY and RKDH copies of the catalogue.	E M Engelberts	(Sold) fl 2:15 Glad
1808/06/13	AMSCH	0270[H]	*[Anonymous]* | 2 stuks | *Notes:* This lot was added in by hand in the EBNP, FLNY and RKDH copies of the catalogue.	E M Engelberts	(Sold) fl 10 Coclers
1808/06/13	AMSCH	0271[H]	*[Anonymous]* | 2 stuks | *Notes:* This lot was added in by hand in the EBNP, FLNY and RKDH copies of the catalogue.	E M Engelberts	(Sold) fl 4:15 Th^{s} Spaan
1808/06/13	AMSCH	0272[H]	*[Anonymous]* | 1 stuk | *Notes:* This lot was added in by hand in the EBNP, FLNY and RKDH copies of the catalogue.	E M Engelberts	(Sold) fl 18:10 Coclers
1808/06/13	AMSCH	0273[H]	*[Anonymous]* | 2 stuks | *Notes:* This lot was added in by hand in the EBNP, FLNY and RKDH copies of the catalogue.	E M Engelberts	(Sold) fl 8:10 Glad
1808/06/13	AMSCH	0274[H]	*[Anonymous]* | 1 stuk | *Notes:* This lot was added in by hand in the EBNP, FLNY and RKDH copies of the catalogue.	E M Engelberts	(Sold) fl 1:10 L Pakker
1808/06/13	AMSCH	0275[H]	*[Anonymous]* | 1 stuk | *Notes:* This lot was added in by hand in the EBNP, FLNY and RKDH copies of the catalogue.	E M Engelberts	(Sold) fl 6:15 L Pakker
1808/06/13	AMSCH	0276[H]	*[Anonymous]* | 2 stuks | *Notes:* This lot was added in by hand in the EBNP, FLNY and RKDH copies of the catalogue.	E M Engelberts	(Sold) fl 1:10 Glad

1808/06/13	AMSCH	0277[H]	*[Anonymous]* | 2 stuks | *Notes:* This lot was added in by hand in the EBNP, FLNY and RKDH copies of the catalogue.	E M Engelberts	(Sold) fl 12:10 Glad
1808/06/13	AMSCH	0278[H]	*[Anonymous]* | 2 stuks | *Notes:* This lot was added in by hand in the EBNP, FLNY and RKDH copies of the catalogue.	E M Engelberts	(Sold) fl 3 L Pakker
1808/06/13	AMSCH	0279[H]	*[Anonymous]* | 4 stuks | *Notes:* This lot was added in by hand in the EBNP, FLNY and RKDH copies of the catalogue.	E M Engelberts	(Sold) fl 2 Glad
1808/06/13	AMSCH	0280[H]	*[Anonymous]* | 5 stuks | *Notes:* This lot was added in by hand in the EBNP, FLNY and RKDH copies of the catalogue.	E M Engelberts	(Sold) fl 0:10 Engelberts
1808/06/13	AMSCH	0281[H]	*[Anonymous]* | 2 stuks | *Notes:* This lot was added in by hand in the EBNP, FLNY and RKDH copies of the catalogue.	R[oos]	(Sold) fl 3:15 Th Spaan
1808/06/13	AMSCH	0282[H]	*[Anonymous]* | 2 stuks | *Notes:* This lot was added in by hand in the EBNP, FLNY and RKDH copies of the catalogue.	R[oos]	(Sold) fl 0:10 L Pakker
1808/06/13	AMSCH	0283[H]	*[Anonymous]* | 2 stuks | *Notes:* This lot was added in by hand in the EBNP, FLNY and RKDH copies of the catalogue.	R[oos]	(Sold) fl 2:15 du Pree
1808/06/13	AMSCH	0284[H]	*[Anonymous]* | 2 stuks | *Notes:* This lot was added in by hand in the EBNP, FLNY and RKDH copies of the catalogue.	R[oos]	(Sold) fl 1:15 L Pakker
1808/06/13	AMSCH	0285[H]	*[Anonymous]* | 5 stuks | *Notes:* This lot was added in by hand in the EBNP, FLNY and RKDH copies of the catalogue.	R[oos]	(Sold) fl 1 L Pakker
1808/06/13	AMSCH	0286[H]	*[Anonymous]* | 1 stuk | *Notes:* This lot was added in by hand in the EBNP, FLNY and RKDH copies of the catalogue.	L	(Sold) fl 4 Boelhouwer
1808/06/13	AMSCH	0287[H]	*[Anonymous]* | 1 stuk | *Notes:* This lot was added in by hand in the EBNP, FLNY and RKDH copies of the catalogue.	L	(Sold) fl 1 du Pree
1808/06/13	AMSCH	0288[H]	*[Anonymous]* | 1 stuk | *Notes:* This lot was added in by hand in the EBNP, FLNY and RKDH copies of the catalogue.	L	(Sold) fl 2:5 van Drielst
1808/06/13	AMSCH	0289[H]	*[Anonymous]* | 1 stuk | *Notes:* This lot was added in by hand in the EBNP, FLNY and RKDH copies of the catalogue.	Z	(Sold) fl 6 Boelhouwer
1808/06/13	AMSCH	0290[H]	*[Anonymous]* | 1 stuk | *Notes:* This lot was added in by hand in the EBNP, FLNY and RKDH copies of the catalogue.	Z	(Sold) fl 6:5 de Vries
1808/06/13	AMSCH	0291[H]	*[Anonymous]* | 1 stuk | *Notes:* This lot was added in by hand in the EBNP, FLNY and RKDH copies of the catalogue.	Z	(Sold) fl 8:5 Jan Spaan
1808/06/13	AMSCH	0292[H]	*[Anonymous]* | 2 stuks | *Notes:* This lot was added in by hand in the EBNP, FLNY and RKDH copies of the catalogue.	Z	(Sold) fl 5:10 for lots 292[H] & 293[H]. Gruiter
1808/06/13	AMSCH	0293[H]	*[Anonymous]* | 2 stuks | *Notes:* This lot was added in by hand in the EBNP, FLNY and RKDH copies of the catalogue.	Z	(Sold) fl 5:10 for lots 292[H] & 293[H]. Gruiter
1808/06/13	AMSCH	0294[H]	*[Anonymous]* | 2 stuks | *Notes:* This lot was added in by hand in the EBNP, FLNY and RKDH copies of the catalogue.	Z	(Sold) fl 2 for lots 294[H] & 295[H]. L Pakker
1808/06/13	AMSCH	0295[H]	*[Anonymous]* | 2 stuks | *Notes:* This lot was added in by hand in the EBNP, FLNY and RKDH copies of the catalogue.	Z	(Sold) fl 2 for lots 294[H] & 295[h]. L Pakker
1808/06/13	AMSCH	0296[H]	*[Anonymous]* | 2 stuks | *Notes:* This lot was added in by hand in the EBNP, FLNY and RKDH copies of the catalogue.	Z	(Sold) fl 24 van Drielst
1808/06/13	AMSCH	0297[H]	*[Anonymous]* | 1 stuk | *Notes:* This lot was added in by hand in the EBNP, FLNY and RKDH copies of the catalogue.	Z	(Sold) fl 2:10 Gruiter
1808/06/13	AMSCH	0298[H]	*[Anonymous]* | 2 stuks | *Notes:* This lot was added in by hand in the EBNP, FLNY and RKDH copies of the catalogue.	Z	(Sold) fl 1:10 L Pakker
1808/06/13	AMSCH	0299[H]	*[Anonymous]* | 1 stuk | *Notes:* This lot was added in by hand in the EBNP, FLNY and RKDH copies of the catalogue.	Z	(Sold) fl 3:5 Gruiter
1808/06/13	AMSCH	0300[H]	*[Anonymous]* | 2 stuks | *Notes:* This lot was added in by hand in the EBNP, FLNY and RKDH copies of the catalogue.	Z	(Sold) fl 2 van Iperen
1808/06/13	AMSCH	0301[H]	*[Anonymous]* | 2 stuks | *Notes:* This lot was added in by hand in the EBNP, FLNY and RKDH copies of the catalogue.	Z	(Sold) fl 1 Gruiter
1808/06/13	AMSCH	0302[H]	*[Anonymous]* | 2 stuks | *Notes:* This lot was added in by hand in the EBNP, FLNY and RKDH copies of the catalogue.	Z	(Sold) fl 1 L Pakker
1808/06/13	AMSCH	0303[H]	*[Anonymous]* | 1 stuk | *Notes:* This lot was added in by hand in the EBNP, FLNY and RKDH copies of the catalogue.	Z	(Sold) fl 0:10 L Pakker
1808/06/13	AMSCH	0304[H]	*[Anonymous]* | 1 stuk | *Notes:* This lot was added in by hand in the EBNP, FLNY and RKDH copies of the catalogue.	Z	(Sold) fl 9 van Iperen
1808/06/13	AMSCH	0305[H]	*[Anonymous]* | 1 stuk | *Notes:* This lot was added in by hand in the EBNP, FLNY and RKDH copies of the catalogue.	Z	(Sold) fl 3:10 J Spaan
1808/06/13	AMSCH	0306[H]	*[Anonymous]* | 1 stuk | *Notes:* This lot was added in by hand in the EBNP, FLNY and RKDH copies of the catalogue.	Z	(Sold) fl 6:10 van Iperen
1808/06/13	AMSCH	0307[H]	*[Anonymous]* | 1 stuk | *Notes:* This lot was added in by hand in the EBNP, FLNY and RKDH copies of the catalogue.	Z	(Sold) fl 10 du Pree
1808/06/13	AMSCH	0308[H]	*[Anonymous]* | 1 stuk | *Notes:* This lot was added in by hand in the EBNP, FLNY and RKDH copies of the catalogue.	Z	(Withdrawn)

1808/06/13	AMSCH	0309[H]	*[Anonymous]* | 4 stuks | *Notes:* This lot was added in by hand in the EBNP, FLNY and RKDH copies of the catalogue.	Z	(Sold) fl 2:5 for lots 309[H] & 310[H]. Gruiter
1808/06/13	AMSCH	0310[H]	*[Anonymous]* | 1 stuk | *Notes:* This lot was added in by hand in the EBNP, FLNY and RKDH copies of the catalogue.	Z	(Sold) fl 2:5 for lots 309[H] & 310[H]. Gruiter
1808/06/13	AMSCH	0311[H]	*[Anonymous]* | 1 stuk | *Notes:* This lot was added in by hand in the EBNP, FLNY and RKDH copies of the catalogue.	Z	(Sold) fl 3:15 van Iperen
1808/06/13	AMSCH	0312[H]	*[Anonymous]* | 1 stuk | *Notes:* This lot was added in by hand in the EBNP, FLNY and RKDH copies of the catalogue.	Z	(Sold) fl 15:10 Allard
1808/06/13	AMSCH	0313[H]	*[Anonymous]* | 2 stuks | *Notes:* This lot was added in by hand in the EBNP, FLNY and RKDH copies of the catalogue.	Z	(Sold) fl 5:15 Jan Smit
1808/06/13	AMSCH	0314[H]	*[Anonymous]* | 1 stuk | *Notes:* This lot was added in by hand in the EBNP, FLNY and RKDH copies of the catalogue.	Z	(Sold) fl 0:10 Th Spaan
1808/06/13	AMSCH	0315[H]	*[Anonymous]* | 1 stuk | *Notes:* This lot was added in by hand in the EBNP, FLNY and RKDH copies of the catalogue.	Z	(Sold) fl 8 L Pakker
1808/06/13	AMSCH	0317[H]	*[Anonymous]* | 1 Schilderij | *Notes:* This lot was added in by hand in the EBNP, FLNY and RKDH copies of the catalogue.	Y[ver]	(Sold) fl 97 B Roelofs
1808/06/13	AMSCH	0318[H]	*[Anonymous]* | 1 Schilderij | *Notes:* This lot was added in by hand in the EBNP, FLNY and RKDH copies of the catalogue.	Y[ver]	(Sold) fl 43 Moll
1808/07/19	AMROU	0007	*Een goed meester* | 1 grappig gezelschap van comique houding, zittende aan een Tafel waarop een Ham, fix gepenseeld, door een goed meester		(Unknown)
1808/07/19	AMROU	0012	*Een goed meester* | 1 Bergachtig Landschap, door een goed meester		(Unknown)
1808/07/19	AMROU	0014	*Een oud meester* | 1 dito Mans Pourtrait, door een oud meester | *Notes:* It is unclear what "dito" refers to in the title.		(Unknown)
1808/07/19	AMROU	0016	*Een voornaam Meester* | 1 Mans Pourtrait, in een aloude en deftige kleeding, houdende in de eene hand een Passer en in de andere een tekening van een Huis, door een voornaam Meester		(Unknown)
1808/07/19	AMROU	0021	*[Anonymous]* | 2 differente Schilderyen		(Unknown)
1808/07/19	AMROU	0022	*[Anonymous]* | 2 Pourtraitten		(Unknown)
1808/07/19	AMROU	0023	*[Anonymous]* | 2 dito [Pourtraitten]		(Unknown)
1808/07/19	AMROU	0024	*[Anonymous]* | 1 Vrouwe Beeld, staande in een Nis, verbelende de Lente, in 't grauw		(Unknown)
1808/07/19	AMROU	0025	*Een goed meester* | 2 Bybelse Ordonanties, door een goed meester		(Unknown)
1808/07/19	AMROU	0026	*Een goed meester* | 2 Bergachtige Landschappen, meede door een goed meester | *Notes:* This lot was misnumbered no. 27.		(Unknown)
1808/07/19	AMROU	0042	*[Anonymous]* | 1 Schildery Salomons Gebed en 1 Spion Spiegel | *This Lot:* 1 Schildery Salomons Gebed		(Unknown)
1808/08/23	AMSCH	0180	*Een goed Meester* | Twee stuks plaisante Arcadische Landschappen, met verschillende Geboomten, beide gestoffeerd met Ruwiene en aloude Gedenktekens, en verscheide Beeldjes, meesterlijk fraai en zonachtig behandeld, op Paneel, door een goed Meester | *Mat:* op paneel		(Withdrawn)
1808/08/23	AMSCH	0181	*Een bekwaam Meester* | Een Voorportaal van een prachtige Tempel, met verscheide Colommen, gestoffeerd op de voorgrond met eene wandelende Dame, en een Kind, verder gaande en rustende Beeldjes, en in 't verschiet grootsche Gebouwen; kunstuig door een bekwaam Meester geschilderd	[Van Iperen?]	(Sold) fl 16:10 Coclers
1808/08/23	AMSCH	0215	*Een goed Meester* | Het Afbeeldsel van een bejaarde Dame, in deftig gewaad, houdende een Orlogie in de hand; het is uitvoerig op koper geschilderd, door een goed Meester | *Mat:* op koper	Z	(Sold) fl 6 D Maijkel
1808/08/23	AMSCH	0217	*[Anonymous]* | In een Binnehuis zitten twee Boeren bij een Haarstede en een staande, zig met drinken vermakende, verder drie andere bij een Tafel, op de Kaart speelende; het is geestig en natuurlijk op Paneel geschilderd | *Mat:* op paneel	R	(Sold) fl 18 J Spaan
1808/08/23	AMSCH	0218	*[Anonymous]* | Twee woelende Zeën, met verscheide zeilende Scheepen; fiks geschilderd op Paneelen | *Mat:* op paneelen	R	(Sold) fl 1 L Pakker
1808/08/23	AMSCH	0221	*[Anonymous]* | Een staand bruin Paard in een Landschap, op de grond een slapend Huisman, natuurlijk behandeld op Paneel | *Mat:* op paneel	R	(Sold) fl 0:6 Boelen
1808/08/23	AMSCH	0224	*[Anonymous]* | Twee stuks met aloude Gezichten binnen Romen, gestoffeert met verscheide Beeldjes en Reisigers over een steene Brug; fiks en krachtig gepenceeld op Paneel | *Mat:* op paneel	Z	(Sold) fl 2 du Prée
1808/08/23	AMSCH	0225	*[Anonymous]* | Twee stuks Landschappen met Boeren Wooningen, gestoffeert met Huislieden en verscheiden Huismans Gereedschappen; meesterlijk op Paneel geschildert | *Annots:* [door] A V. Pach[?] (FLNY) *Mat:* op paneel	Z	(Sold) fl 0:6 W van der Schley
1808/08/23	AMSCH	0227	*[Anonymous]* | Een Boeren Binnenhuis, waar in een bedaagd Huisman zittende, met een Pijp en Bierkan in de handen, waar bij een Jongeling, wijzende op eene oude Vrouw die over de Onderdeur ligt, op de voorgrond gestoffeert met een meenigte Huisraad, als kopere Ketels, Potten, Pannen, Tobbens, Mandewerk met Fruit, dood Gevogelte, en verder bijwerk; zeer natuurlijk behandeld op Paneel | *Mat:* op paneel	Z	(Sold) fl 3 L Pakker

1808/08/23	AMSCH	0228	*[Anonymous]* | In een Boeren Wooning met eenige Huislieden, zittende bij een gedekte Tafel met spijs, vertoont zig een Zater, zinspeelende op de heet en koud blaaser; fiks geschilderd op Doek | *Mat:* op doek	Z	(Sold) fl 1 Spruit
1808/08/23	AMSCH	0229	*[Anonymous]* | Een bergachtig Landschap met hoog Geboomte en Waterval, op de voorgrond gestoffeert met Huislieden en eenig Vee, in 't verschiet een Gebouw; kloek geschilderd op Doek | *Mat:* op doek	Z	(Sold) fl 3:5 van Iperen
1808/08/23	AMSCH	0230	*[Anonymous]* | Langs een Weg met Geboomten, aan een stil Water, waar in Vissers in een Schuit, ziet men Boere Woningen, en Dorp-kerk, op Paneel geschilderd | *Annots:* rood[?] (FLNY) *Mat:* op paneel	Z	(Sold) fl 1:5 Reydon
1808/08/23	AMSCH	0231	*[Anonymous]* | In een Landschap, bij de ruïne van een Gebouw en Waterval, een Véehoeder met Schaapen; krachtig op Paneel geschilderd | *Mat:* op paneel	Z	(Sold) fl 0:6 for lots 231 & 232. Dupré
1808/08/23	AMSCH	0232	*[Anonymous]* | Een stuk met Bloemen en Fruit, op Paneel geschilderd | *Mat:* op paneel	Z	(Sold) fl 0:6 for lots 231 & 232. Dupré
1808/08/23	AMSCH	0233	*[Anonymous]* | Een boere Binnenhuis, waar in een zittende Huisman, verzelt van eene Vrouw, op de voorgrond ziet men verscheide Huisraat, als kopere Ketels, Melkkan, verscheide Vaatwerk, Tobbens, divers Aardewerk en Vruchten; zeer natuurlijk behandeld op Paneel | *Mat:* op paneel	Z	(Sold) fl 1 Spruit
1808/08/23	AMSCH	0234	*[Anonymous]* | Een Gezicht aan Strand bij Schéveningen, rijk gestoffeert met Vissers, en Vrouwen met hunne Koopwaren, waar bij een Heer te Paard, verder eenige Lieden bij een afvarende Vissers Pink; meesterlijk op Paneel geschilderd | *Mat:* op paneel	Z	(Sold) fl 0:12 L Pakker
1808/08/23	AMSCH	0238	*[Anonymous]* | In een Stad-gezicht vertoont zig een Kermisvreugd van Jonge Kinderen, die als een Compagnie optrekken, eene oude Vrouw ligt over de Deur het beschouwende; het is plaisant van schildering | *Mat:* op paneel	C	(Sold) fl 8 Van Iperen
1808/08/23	AMSCH	0239	*[Anonymous]* | Een Bybelsche Ordonantie, verbeeldende de drie Wijzen, welke het Kind Jesus hun geschenken opdraagen; meesterlijk en breed gepenceeld	C	(Sold) fl 10 D Maijkel
1808/08/23	AMSCH	0240	*[Anonymous]* | In deze Ordonantie zit op de voorgrond eene bevallige Jonge Vrouw, welke door een jong Krijgsheld geliefkoosd werd; de hartstochten zijn natuurlijk, en van eene meesterlijke penceelbehandeling	C	(Sold) fl 20 Boelhouwer
1808/08/23	AMSCH	0241	*[Anonymous]* | Een Dorp-gezicht, vol gewoeld van een menigte Beelden; natuurlijk en fiks behandeld	C	(Sold) fl 2 Bonvoije
1808/08/23	AMSCH	0245	*[Anonymous]* | Een Dorp-gezicht met vervallen Boeren Woeningen [sic]; natuurlijk behandeld	S	(Sold) fl 5 van Os
1808/08/23	AMSCH	0249	*[Anonymous]* | Een Galant Vrouwtje, geestig verbeeld	S	(Sold) fl 0:8 van Iperen
1808/08/23	AMSCH	0250	*Een oud Meester* | Twee stuks met Ruïnen, door een oud Meester	S	(Sold) fl 1:15 Spruit
1808/08/23	AMSCH	0252	*[Anonymous]* | Een kabbelende Zee met een menigte Schepen en Vaartuigen; kloek geschilderd	[Van Iperen?]	(Sold) fl 1:5 L Pakker
1808/08/23	AMSCH	0263	*Een goed Meester* | Twee Schilderijen door een goed Meester	J	(Sold) fl 2:5 Spruit
1808/08/23	AMSCH	0265	*[Anonymous]* | Een Heilige Famielie, verbeeldende Maria met het Kind op haar schoot; meesterlijk behandeld	[Van Iperen?]	(Sold or Bought In) fl 3:10 van Iperen
1808/08/23	AMSCH	0271	*[Anonymous]* | Een Historieele Ordonantie, voorstellende Diogenes op de Markt van Athenen, waar bij een menigte Beelden; krachtig en meesterlijk behandeld	Y	(Sold) fl 2:10 Bonvoije
1808/08/23	AMSCH	0273	*[Anonymous]* | Twee stuks woelende Zeeën, beide gestoffeert met zeilende Scheepen en andere Vaartuigen; fiks behandeld	Y	(Sold) fl 3:5 du Prée
1808/08/23	AMSCH	0274	*[Anonymous]* | Twee stuks bevallige Landschappen met Beelden en Beesten gestoffeert; natuurlijk behandeld	Y	(Sold) fl 0:10 van Iperen
1808/08/23	AMSCH	0276	*[Anonymous]* | Een dooden Christus in de schoot van Maria; kloek geschilderd	Y	(Sold) fl 1 L Pakker
1808/08/23	AMSCH	0277	*[Anonymous]* | Een boetvaardige Magdalena; meesterlijk op Doek geschilderd | *Mat:* op doek	Y	(Sold) fl 9 Spruit
1808/08/23	AMSCH	0278	*[Anonymous]* | Twee stuks, Maria met het Kindje, en een oud Mans Hoofd	Y	(Sold) fl 1 L Pakker
1808/08/23	AMSCH	0279	*[Anonymous]* | Een Landschap gestoffeert met twee gaande Jongelingen; uitvoerig gepenceeld	Y	(Sold) fl 2:10 Reydon
1808/08/23	AMSCH	0280	*[Anonymous]* | Twee stuks, een Mans Pourtret en een zittend Vrouwtje	Y	(Sold) fl 2:10 van Iperen
1808/08/23	AMSCH	0283	*[Anonymous]* | Eenige Druiven en Persikken liggen op een Tafel met een kleed; meesterlijk behandeld op Paneel | *Mat:* op paneel	Z	(Sold) fl 0:10 Th Spaan
1808/08/23	AMSCH	0284	*[Anonymous]* | Twee stuks, een gestoffeert Landschap, en eee [sic] woelende Zee met Scheepen	Z	(Sold) fl 0:12 for lots 284 & 285. W V D Schley
1808/08/23	AMSCH	0285	*[Anonymous]* | Twee stuks gestoffeerde Italiaansche Landschappen, met Huislieden en Vee	Z	(Sold) fl 0:12 for lots 284 & 285. W V D Schley

1808/08/23	AMSCH	0286	*[Anonymous]* | Een Heuvelachtig Landschap met verscheiden Boeren Woningen, bij Geboomten, langs een opgaande Weg, gestoffeert met gaande en andere Huislieden; zonachtig en fiks gepenceeld | *Mat:* op paneel	Z	(Sold) fl 2:15 L Pakker
1808/08/23	AMSCH	0288	*[Anonymous]* | Twee stuks verschillende gestoffeerde Landschappen	Z	(Sold) fl 3 for lots 288 & 289. Spruit
1808/08/23	AMSCH	0289	*[Anonymous]* | Twee stuks diversche dito [gestoffeerde] dito [Landschappen]	Z	(Sold) fl 3 for lots 288 & 289. Spruit
1808/08/23	AMSCH	0290[H]	*[Anonymous]* | 1 Stuk | *Notes:* This lot was added in by hand in the EBNP copy of the catalogue.	Z	(Sold) fl 6:5 Boelhouwer
1808/08/23	AMSCH	0291[H]	*[Anonymous]* | 1 Stuk | *Notes:* This lot was added in by hand in the EBNP copy of the catalogue.	[Coclers]	(Sold) fl 1 L Pakker
1808/08/23	AMSCH	0292[H]	*[Anonymous]* | 1 Stuk | *Notes:* This lot was added in by hand in the EBNP copy of the catalogue.	[Van Iperen?]	(Sold or Bought In) fl 1 van Iperen
1808/08/23	AMSCH	0293[H]	*[Anonymous]* | 1 Stuk | *Notes:* This lot was added in by hand in the EBNP copy of the catalogue.	[Van Iperen?]	(Sold or Bought In) fl 5 van Iperen
1808/08/23	AMSCH	0294[H]	*[Anonymous]* | 2 Stuks | *Notes:* This lot was added in by hand in the EBNP copy of the catalogue.	[Van Iperen?]	(Sold) fl 0:18 L Pakker
1808/08/23	AMSCH	0295[H]	*[Anonymous]* | 1 Stuk | *Notes:* This lot was added in by hand in the EBNP copy of the catalogue.	[Van Iperen?]	(Sold) fl 0:12 for lots 295[H] & 296[H]. Harbomé
1808/08/23	AMSCH	0296[H]	*[Anonymous]* | 1 Stuk | *Notes:* This lot was added in by hand in the EBNP copy of the catalogue.	[Van Iperen?]	(Sold) fl 0:12 for lots 295[H] & 296[H]. Harbomé
1808/08/23	AMSCH	0297[H]	*[Anonymous]* | 2 Stuks | *Notes:* This lot was added in by hand in the EBNP copy of the catalogue.	[Van Iperen?]	(Sold) fl 0:8 du Pree
1808/08/23	AMSCH	0298[H]	*[Anonymous]* | 2 Stuks | *Notes:* This lot was added in by hand in the EBNP copy of the catalogue.	[Van Iperen?]	(Sold) fl 1 L Pakker
1808/08/23	AMSCH	0299[H]	*[Anonymous]* | 1 Stuk | *Notes:* This lot was added in by hand in the EBNP copy of the catalogue.	[Van Iperen?]	(Sold) fl 1:5 du Pree
1808/08/23	AMSCH	0300[H]	*[Anonymous]* | 1 Stuk | *Notes:* This lot was added in by hand in the EBNP copy of the catalogue.	[Van Iperen?]	(Sold) fl 4 Spaan
1808/08/23	AMSCH	0301[H]	*[Anonymous]* | 1 Stuk | *Notes:* This lot was added in by hand in the EBNP copy of the catalogue.	[Van Iperen?]	(Sold) fl 0:10 du Pree
1808/08/23	AMSCH	0302[H]	*[Anonymous]* | 1 Stuk | *Notes:* This lot was added in by hand in the EBNP copy of the catalogue.	[Van Iperen?]	(Sold) fl 8:5 du Pree
1808/08/23	AMSCH	0303[H]	*[Anonymous]* | 1 Stuk | *Notes:* This lot was added in by hand in the EBNP copy of the catalogue.	[Van Iperen?]	(Sold) fl 0:8 W v d Schley
1808/08/23	AMSCH	0304[H]	*[Anonymous]* | 1 Stuk | *Notes:* This lot was added in by hand in the EBNP copy of the catalogue.	[Van Iperen?]	(Sold) fl 1:10 L Pakker
1808/08/23	AMSCH	0305[H]	*[Anonymous]* | 1 Stuk | *Notes:* This lot was added in by hand in the EBNP copy of the catalogue.	[Van Iperen?]	(Sold) fl 0:10 L Pakker
1808/08/23	AMSCH	0306[H]	*[Anonymous]* | 1 Stuk | *Notes:* This lot was added in by hand in the EBNP copy of the catalogue.	[Van Iperen?]	(Sold) fl 4 L Pakker
1808/08/23	AMSCH	0307[H]	*[Anonymous]* | 2 Stuks | *Notes:* This lot was added in by hand in the EBNP copy of the catalogue.	[Van Iperen?]	(Sold) fl 100 Hulswit
1808/08/23	AMSCH	0308[H]	*[Anonymous]* | 2 Stuks | *Notes:* This lot was added in by hand in the EBNP copy of the catalogue.	[Van Iperen?]	(Sold) fl 9 D Maykel
1808/08/23	AMSCH	0309[H]	*[Anonymous]* | 1 Stuk | *Notes:* This lot was added in by hand in the EBNP copy of the catalogue.	[Gruyter?]	(Sold) fl 0:10 W v d Schley
1808/08/23	AMSCH	0310[H]	*[Anonymous]* | 2 Stuks | *Notes:* This lot was added in by hand in the EBNP copy of the catalogue.	[Gruyter?]	(Sold) fl 0:6 L Pakker
1808/08/23	AMSCH	0311[H]	*[Anonymous]* | 1 Stuk | *Notes:* This lot was added in by hand in the EBNP copy of the catalogue.	[Gruyter?]	(Sold) fl 1:15 Spruit
1808/08/23	AMSCH	0312[H]	*[Anonymous]* | 1 Stuk | *Notes:* This lot was added in by hand in the EBNP copy of the catalogue.	[Gruyter?]	(Sold) fl 2:10 Spaan
1808/08/23	AMSCH	0313[H]	*[Anonymous]* | 1 Stuk | *Notes:* This lot was added in by hand in the EBNP copy of the catalogue.	[Gruyter?]	(Sold or Bought In) fl 2 Gruiter
1808/08/23	AMSCH	0314[H]	*[Anonymous]* | 1 Stuk | *Notes:* This lot was added in by hand in the EBNP copy of the catalogue.	[Gruyter?]	(Sold) fl 2 du Pree
1808/08/23	AMSCH	0315[H]	*[Anonymous]* | 1 Stuk | *Notes:* This lot was added in by hand in the EBNP copy of the catalogue.	[Gruyter?]	(Sold) fl 3:10 Spruit
1808/08/23	AMSCH	0316[H]	*[Anonymous]* | 1 Stuk | *Notes:* This lot was added in by hand in the EBNP copy of the catalogue.	[Gruyter?]	(Sold) fl 4:10 van Iperen
1808/08/23	AMSCH	0317[H]	*[Anonymous]* | 1 Stuk | *Notes:* This lot was added in by hand in the EBNP copy of the catalogue.	[Gruyter?]	(Sold or Bought In) fl 1:5 Gruiter
1808/08/23	AMSCH	0318[H]	*[Anonymous]* | 1 Stuk | *Notes:* This lot was added in by hand in the EBNP copy of the catalogue.	[Gruyter?]	(Sold or Bought In) fl 1:15 Gruiter

1808/08/23	AMSCH	0319[H]	*[Anonymous]* | 1 Stuk | *Notes:* This lot was added in by hand in the EBNP copy of the catalogue.	[Gruyter?]	(Sold) fl 4 du Pree
1808/08/23	AMSCH	0320[H]	*[Anonymous]* | 1 Stuk | *Notes:* This lot was added in by hand in the EBNP copy of the catalogue.	[Gruyter?]	(Sold) fl 5:5 A Kempe
1808/08/23	AMSCH	0321[H]	*[Anonymous]* | 1 Stuk | *Notes:* This lot was added in by hand in the EBNP copy of the catalogue.	[Gruyter?]	(Sold or Bought In) fl 1:10 Gruiter
1808/08/23	AMSCH	0322[H]	*[Anonymous]* | 1 Stuk | *Notes:* This lot was added in by hand in the EBNP copy of the catalogue.	[Gruyter?]	(Sold) fl 8:10 Spaan
1808/08/23	AMSCH	0323[H]	*[Anonymous]* | 1 Stuk | *Notes:* This lot was added in by hand in the EBNP copy of the catalogue.	[Gruyter?]	(Sold) fl 6:10 Coclers
1808/08/23	AMSCH	0324[H]	*[Anonymous]* | 1 Stuk | *Notes:* This lot was added in by hand in the EBNP copy of the catalogue.	[Gruyter?]	(Bought In) fl 12
1808/08/23	AMSCH	0325[H]	*[Anonymous]* | 2 Stuks | *Notes:* This lot was added in by hand in the EBNP copy of the catalogue.	[Gruyter?]	(Sold) fl 13:10 van Iperen
1808/08/23	AMSCH	0326[H]	*[Anonymous]* | 2 Stuks | *Notes:* This lot was added in by hand in the EBNP copy of the catalogue.	[Van Iperen?]	(Sold or Bought In) fl 13 van Iperen
1808/08/23	AMSCH	0327[H]	*[Anonymous]* | 1 Stuk | *Notes:* This lot was added in by hand in the EBNP copy of the catalogue.	[Van Iperen?]	(Sold or Bought In) fl 7:10 van Iperen
1808/08/23	AMSCH	0328[H]	*[Anonymous]* | 1 Stuk | *Notes:* This lot was added in by hand in the EBNP copy of the catalogue.	[Van Iperen?]	(Sold) fl 5:10 Gruiter
1808/08/23	AMSCH	0329[H]	*[Anonymous]* | 1 Stuk | *Notes:* This lot was added in by hand in the EBNP copy of the catalogue.	[Van Iperen?]	(Sold or Bought In) fl 3:15 van Iperen
1808/08/23	AMSCH	0330[H]	*[Anonymous]* | 1 Stuk | *Notes:* This lot was added in by hand in the EBNP copy of the catalogue.	[Van Iperen?]	(Sold) fl 4:5 L Pakker
1808/08/23	AMSCH	0331[H]	*[Anonymous]* | 1 Stuk | *Notes:* This lot was added in by hand in the EBNP copy of the catalogue.	[Van Iperen?]	(Sold) fl 4:10 L Pakker
1808/08/23	AMSCH	0332[H]	*[Anonymous]* | 1 Stuk | *Notes:* This lot was added in by hand in the EBNP copy of the catalogue.	[Van Iperen?]	(Sold) fl 5:10 Spruit
1808/08/23	AMSCH	0333[H]	*[Anonymous]* | 1 Stuk | *Notes:* This lot was added in by hand in the EBNP copy of the catalogue.	[Van Iperen?]	(Sold) fl 1:5 du Prée
1808/08/23	AMSCH	0334[H]	*[Anonymous]* | 1 Stuk | *Notes:* This lot was added in by hand in the EBNP copy of the catalogue.	[Van Iperen?]	(Sold or Bought In) fl 14 van Iperen
1808/08/23	AMSCH	0335[H]	*[Anonymous]* | 1 Stuk | *Notes:* This lot was added in by hand in the EBNP copy of the catalogue.	[Gruyter?]	(Sold) fl 4:5 van Iperen
1808/08/23	AMSCH	0336[H]	*[Anonymous]* | 1 Stuk | *Notes:* This lot was added in by hand in the EBNP copy of the catalogue.	[Van Iperen?]	(Sold) fl 3:5 du Pree
1808/09/13	HABRU	0055	*[Anonymous]* | Een Watergezicht bij Geboomte en gestoffeerd met Beesten, &c.		(Unknown) fl 6:5
1808/09/13	HABRU	0101	*[Anonymous]* | Een Bergachtig Landschap, op de voorgrond een Koe door een Vrouw word gemolken, nevens haar een andere vrouw bij haar staande, door | *Notes:* In the printed catalogue, there is a space following the word "door," presumably for the later insertion of the artist's name.		(Unknown) fl 2.10
1808/09/13	HABRU	0102	*[Anonymous]* | Een Hartejagt en een verversing op de Jagt; uitvoerig, twee stuks		(Unknown) fl 0:6
1808/09/13	HABRU	0104	*[Anonymous]* | Twee stuks Rhijngezichten		(Unknown) fl 1:14
1808/09/13	HABRU	0105	*[Anonymous]* | Een Watergezicht aan een Dorp		(Unknown) fl 1:10
1808/09/13	HABRU	0110	*[Anonymous]* | Twee Bloemstukken		(Unknown) fl 1:4
1808/09/13	HABRU	0114	*[Anonymous]* | Twee stuks dito [Pourtraitjes]		(Unknown) fl 2:6
1808/09/13	HABRU	0115	*[Anonymous]* | Twee dito [stuks] dito [Pourtraitjes]		(Unknown) fl 0:12 for lots 115 & 116
1808/09/13	HABRU	0116	*[Anonymous]* | Een St. Johannes		(Unknown) fl 0:12 for lots 115 & 116
1808/09/13	HABRU	0117	*[Anonymous]* | Een zinspeelende Ordonnantie op de Reformatie, voorstellende de droom van de Keurvorst van Saxen, raar		(Unknown) fl 1:2
1808/10/28	AMVRS	0068	*[Anonymous]* | Een Strandgezicht, gestoffeerd met beladen Vragtwagens, Arbeiders, Vaartuigen en andere Voorwerpen	Marten Udink	(Sold) fl 14 B Kooij
1808/10/28	AMVRS	0070	*[Anonymous]* | Een Maneschijn over een stille Rivier, op den voorgrond Visschers bij eenig Paalwerk. Fiks behandeld op Doek | *Mat:* op doek	Marten Udink	(Sold) fl 2:5 Gruyter
1808/10/28	AMVRS	0072	*Een goed Meester* | Een Gezicht op de Blokhuijzen aan de Buitenamstel alhier, gestoffeerd met Vaartuigen en Beeldjes, door een goed Meester	Marten Udink	(Sold) fl 3:5 Rosekrans
1808/10/28	AMVRS	0073	*[Anonymous]* | Twee stuks Landschappen, met Beelden en Beesten gestoffeerd. Kloek geschilderd	Marten Udink	(Sold) fl 3 Spaan
1808/10/28	AMVRS	0074	*[Anonymous]* | Een Landschap, gestoffeerd met de Bijbel-Ordonantie van den Barmhartigen Samaritaan	Marten Udink	(Sold) fl 1:5 Bakkering
1808/10/28	AMVRS	0075	*[Anonymous]* | Een vrolijk Man met een Glas in de hand. Geestig verbeeld	Marten Udink	(Sold) fl 2 Van Iperen

1808/10/28	AMVRS	0077	*[Anonymous]* | Een Landgezicht met twee Paarden, staande bij een Hek. Meesterlijk behandeld	Marten Udink	(Sold) fl 2 Pakker
1808/10/28	AMVRS	0078	*[Anonymous]* | Drie diversche Landschappen	Marten Udink	(Sold) fl 1 Pakker
1808/10/28	AMVRS	0079[H]	*[Anonymous]* | [Untitled] | *Notes:* This lot was added in by hand in the EBNP copy of the catalogue, but without giving an artist or title.	Marten Udink	(Sold) fl 15 Josi
1808/11/10	AMAN	0026	*[Anonymous]* | 4 Schilderyen		(Unknown)
1808/11/10	AMAN	0028	*[Anonymous]* | 3 Schilderyen		(Unknown)
1808/11/10	AMAN	0029	*[Anonymous]* | 2 dito [Schilderyen] en 2 Prenteborden		(Unknown)
1808/11/10	AMAN	0031	*[Anonymous]* | 3 Schilderytjes		(Unknown)
1808/11/10	AMAN	0053	*[Anonymous]* | 2 dito [Prentenborden] en 3 Schilderyen		(Unknown)
1808/11/12	HGSCR	0001	*Een goed meester* | Een hevige rencontre of schermutseling van Turksche en Christen krygsknegten in een beragtig landschap, kragtig behandeld door een goed meester | *Mat:* op paneel	Mr J van Buren	(Unknown) fl 5:5
1808/11/12	HGSCR	0005	*Een goed meester* | Een dorp gezigt waar in men ziet voor een herberg of pleysterplaats verscheide lieden en kinderen in diversche actien, benevens een wit paard dat aan een ruyf staat, de caracters zyn geestig uitgedrukt en alles fix en meesterlyk behandeld door een goed meester | *Mat:* op paneel	Mr J van Buren	(Unknown) fl 10:10
1808/11/12	HGSCR	0011	*[Anonymous]* | Twee stuks gestoffeerde landschappen met paarden, geboomte en ruine op marmersteene-plaaten zeer konstig geschildert | *Mat:* op marmersteene-plaaten	Mr J van Buren	(Unknown) fl 2
1808/11/28	AMSCH	0073	*[Anonymous]* | Een aangenaam Landschap, met Boeren Woningen en Geboomte, ter zijde voor een Wooning ziet men Huislieden bezig een Wagen met Kooren te beladen, en voorts een bevallig verschiet, natuurlijk op Doek behandeld | *Mat:* op doek	C	(Sold) fl 4 Cocler
1808/11/28	AMSCH	0074	*[Anonymous]* | Een hoog Noordsch Bergachtig Landschap, met Steenklippen, bij eenige Houte Hutten, op de voorgrond een sterk nederstortende Waterval, gestoffeerd met een Herder bij eenige Schaapen, natuurlijk op Paneel behandeld | *Mat:* op paneel	[Gruyter?]	(Sold) fl 30 T Spaan
1808/11/28	AMSCH	0097a[H]	*[Anonymous]* | Een dito [Boeren kermis] | *Notes:* This lot was added in by hand in the EBNP copy of the catalogue.	[Gruyter?]	(Sold or Bought In) fl 3:10 Gruiter
1808/11/28	AMSCH	0099	*[Anonymous]* | Een Landschap, ter zijde een groot Kasteel, gestoffeerd met twee Heeren te Paard, natuurlijk op Paneel geschilderd | *Mat:* op paneel	Z	(Sold) fl 0:18 Klijnveld
1808/11/28	AMSCH	0101	*[Anonymous]* | Twee stuks, een stil Leeven en een Liedjeszanger	Z	(Sold) fl 0:14 L Pakker
1808/11/28	AMSCH	0103	*[Anonymous]* | De Koningen Aanbidden het Kind Jesus en Offeren Geschenken, krachtig op Doek behandeld | *Mat:* op doek	H	(Sold) fl 2:5 Gruiter
1808/11/28	AMSCH	0110	*[Anonymous]* | Twee stuks Mans Portraitten, halver lijf, in deftige Kleeding, meesterlijk op Doek geschilderd | *Mat:* op doek	S	(Sold) fl 1:5 du Pree
1808/11/28	AMSCH	0114	*[Anonymous]* | Negen diversche Schilderijen | *Notes:* In the original title "Twee diversche Schilderijen," the word "Twee" was crossed out by hand and replaced with "Negen" in the AA and EBNP copies of the catalogue.	H	(Sold) fl 5:15 T Spaan
1808/11/28	AMSCH	0114a[H]	*[Anonymous]* | Een dito [Schilderij] | *Notes:* This lot was added in by hand in the EBNP copy of the catalogue.	S	(Sold) fl 1 Gruiter
1808/11/28	AMSCH	0115[H]	*[Anonymous]* | [Untitled] | *Notes:* This lot was added in by hand in the EBNP copy of the catalogue, but without giving an artist or title.	S	(Sold) fl 4:5 van Dijl
1808/11/28	AMSCH	0116[H]	*[Anonymous]* | [Untitled] | *Notes:* This lot was added in by hand in the EBNP copy of the catalogue, but without giving an artist or title.	P	(Sold) fl 12:10 T Spaan
1808/11/28	AMSCH	0117[H]	*[Anonymous]* | [Untitled] | *Notes:* This lot was added in by hand in the EBNP copy of the catalogue, but without giving an artist or title.	P	(Sold) fl 5:15 T Spaan
1808/11/28	AMSCH	0118[H]	*[Anonymous]* | [Untitled] | *Notes:* This lot was added in by hand in the EBNP copy of the catalogue, but without giving an artist or title.	P	(Sold) fl 3 Van Iperen
1808/11/28	AMSCH	0119[H]	*[Anonymous]* | [Untitled] | *Notes:* This lot was added in by hand in the EBNP copy of the catalogue, but without giving an artist or title.	P	(Sold) fl 1 de Gruiter
1808/11/28	AMSCH	0120[H]	*[Anonymous]* | [Untitled] | *Notes:* This lot was added in by hand in the EBNP copy of the catalogue, but without giving an artist or title.	P	(Sold) fl 12 T Spaan
1808/11/28	AMSCH	0121[H]	*[Anonymous]* | [Untitled] | *Notes:* This lot was added in by hand in the EBNP copy of the catalogue, but without giving an artist or title.	P	(Sold) fl 10:10 van Iperen
1808/11/28	AMSCH	0122[H]	*[Anonymous]* | [Untitled] | *Notes:* This lot was added in by hand in the EBNP copy of the catalogue, but without giving an artist or title.	P	(Sold) fl 16 T Spaan
1808/11/28	AMSCH	0123[H]	*[Anonymous]* | [Untitled] | *Notes:* This lot was added in by hand in the EBNP copy of the catalogue, but without giving an artist or title.	P	(Sold) fl 1:5 W v d Schleij
1808/11/28	AMSCH	0124[H]	*[Anonymous]* | [Untitled] | *Notes:* This lot was added in by hand in the EBNP copy of the catalogue, but without giving an artist or title.	P	(Sold) fl 8:5 du Pree
1808/11/28	AMSCH	0125[H]	*[Anonymous]* | [Untitled] | *Notes:* This lot was added in by hand in the EBNP copy of the catalogue, but without giving an artist or title.	P	(Unknown)

1808/11/28	AMSCH	0126[H]	*[Anonymous]* | [Untitled] | *Notes:* This lot was added in by hand in the EBNP copy of the catalogue, but without giving an artist or title.	P	(Sold) fl 0:10 L Pakker
1808/11/28	AMSCH	0127[H]	*[Anonymous]* | [Untitled] | *Notes:* This lot was added in by hand in the EBNP copy of the catalogue, but without giving an artist or title.	P	(Sold) fl 0:8 P Oosterman
1808/11/28	AMSCH	0128[H]	*[Anonymous]* | [Untitled] | *Notes:* This lot was added in by hand in the EBNP copy of the catalogue, but without giving an artist or title.	P	(Sold) fl 1 du Pree
1808/11/28	AMSCH	0129[H]	*[Anonymous]* | [Untitled] | *Notes:* This lot was added in by hand in the EBNP copy of the catalogue, but without giving an artist or title.	P	(Sold) fl 0:12 P Oosterman
1808/11/28	AMSCH	0130[H]	*[Anonymous]* | [Untitled] | *Notes:* This lot was added in by hand in the EBNP copy of the catalogue, but without giving an artist or title.	P	(Unknown)
1808/11/28	AMSCH	0131[H]	*[Anonymous]* | [Untitled] | *Notes:* This lot was added in by hand in the EBNP copy of the catalogue, but without giving an artist or title.	P	(Sold) fl 6 Coclers
1808/11/28	AMSCH	0132[H]	*[Anonymous]* | [Untitled] | *Notes:* This lot was added in by hand in the EBNP copy of the catalogue, but without giving an artist or title.	P	(Sold) fl 1 du Pree
1808/11/28	AMSCH	0133[H]	*[Anonymous]* | [Untitled] | *Notes:* This lot was added in by hand in the EBNP copy of the catalogue, but without giving an artist or title.	P	(Sold) fl 1 Van Iperen
1808/11/28	AMSCH	0134[H]	*[Anonymous]* | [Untitled] | *Notes:* This lot was added in by hand in the EBNP copy of the catalogue, but without giving an artist or title.	P	(Sold) fl 1 Wm van der Schley
1808/11/28	AMSCH	0135[H]	*[Anonymous]* | [Untitled] | *Notes:* This lot was added in by hand in the EBNP copy of the catalogue, but without giving an artist or title.	P	(Sold) fl 1:10 van Iperen
1808/11/28	AMSCH	0136[H]	*[Anonymous]* | [Untitled] | *Notes:* This lot was added in by hand in the EBNP copy of the catalogue, but without giving an artist or title.	S	(Sold) fl 0:12 L Pakker
1808/11/28	AMSCH	0137[H]	*[Anonymous]* | [Untitled] | *Notes:* This lot was added in by hand in the EBNP copy of the catalogue, but without giving an artist or title.	S	(Sold) fl 1 L Pakker
1808/11/28	AMSCH	0138[H]	*[Anonymous]* | [Untitled] | *Notes:* This lot was added in by hand in the EBNP copy of the catalogue, but without giving an artist or title.	S	(Sold) fl 20 van Os
1808/11/28	AMSCH	0139[H]	*[Anonymous]* | [Untitled] | *Notes:* This lot was added in by hand in the EBNP copy of the catalogue, but without giving an artist or title.	S	(Sold) fl 2:5 Gruiter
1808/11/28	AMSCH	0140[H]	*[Anonymous]* | [Untitled] | *Notes:* This lot was added in by hand in the EBNP copy of the catalogue, but without giving an artist or title.	S	(Sold) fl 1:5 L Pakker
1808/11/28	AMSCH	0141[H]	*[Anonymous]* | [Untitled] | *Notes:* This lot was added in by hand in the EBNP copy of the catalogue, but without giving an artist or title.	S	(Sold) fl 0:10 van Iperen
1808/11/28	AMSCH	0142[H]	*[Anonymous]* | [Untitled] | *Notes:* This lot was added in by hand in the EBNP copy of the catalogue, but without giving an artist or title.	S	(Sold) fl 1 W van der Schley
1808/12/12	DOHAA	0068	*[Anonymous]* | Een Zeegezicht met Schepen, verbeeldende de Zyp, tusschen Oostduiveland en Philipsland | *Mat:* op paneel		(Unknown)
1808/12/12	DOHAA	0069	*[Anonymous]* | De Engel Raphaël en Tobias, met den Visch in zyne hand | *Mat:* op paneel		(Unknown)
1808/12/12	DOHAA	0070	*[Anonymous]* | Een Doodshoofd, op eene Tafel, en gedeeltelyk op den Bybel leggende, met een brandend licht er nevens | *Mat:* op paneel		(Unknown)
1808/12/12	DOHAA	0074	*[Anonymous]* | Een smaakelyk Man in zyn japon, by zyn flesch en viool | *Mat:* op paneel		(Unknown)
1808/12/12	UTWLD	0002	*[Anonymous]* | Een ruine met een fontein daar een paard uit drinkt [Alle in swarte Lysten en wel geconserveerd.] | *Mat:* op doek *Size:* hoog 12 duim, breed 10 duim *Notes:* The bracketed information in the title appears above lot 1 and refers to lots 1 to 19.	Mr D Hoola van Nooten	(Unknown)
1808/12/12	UTWLD	0003	*Een goed meester* | Een fraai Landschap met bergen, geboomte enz. door een goed meester [Alle in swarte Lysten en wel geconserveerd) | *Mat:* op paneel *Size:* hoog 2 voet 5 duim, breed 3 voet 8 duim *Notes:* The bracketed information in the title appears above lot 1 and refers to lots 1 to 19.	Mr D Hoola van Nooten	(Unknown)
1808/12/12	UTWLD	0004	*[Anonymous]* | Een dito [fraai Landschap] [Alle in swarte Lysten en wel geconserveerd.] | *Mat:* op paneel *Size:* hoog 16 duim, breed 23 duim *Notes:* The bracketed information in the title about the frame appears above lot 1 and refers to lots 1 to 19.	Mr D Hoola van Nooten	(Unknown)
1808/12/12	UTWLD	0008	*[Anonymous]* | Een Landschap met St. Augustinus, 1562 [Alle in swarte Lysten en wel geconserveerd.] | *Mat:* op paneel *Size:* hoog 18 duim, breed 22 duim *Inscr:* 1562 (dated?) *Notes:* It is unclear whether the date is inscribed on the painting. The bracketed information in the title appears above lot 1 and refers to lots 1 to 19.	Mr D Hoola van Nooten	(Unknown)
1808/12/12	UTWLD	0009	*[Anonymous]* | Een Fruitstuk [Alle in swarte Lysten en wel geconserveerd.] | *Mat:* op paneel *Notes:* The bracketed information in the title appears above lot 1 and refers to lots 1 to 19.	Mr D Hoola van Nooten	(Unknown)
1808/12/12	UTWLD	0010	*[Anonymous]* | Een Vischstuk 1561 [Alle in swarte Lysten en wel geconserveerd.] | *Mat:* op paneel *Inscr:* 1561 (dated?) *Notes:* It is unclear whether the date is inscribed on the painting. The bracketed information in the title appears above lot 1 and refers to lots 1 to 19.	Mr D Hoola van Nooten	(Unknown)
1808/12/12	UTWLD	0011	*[Anonymous]* | De Weg des Hemels [Alle in swarte Lysten en wel geconserveerd.] | *Mat:* op paneel *Notes:* The bracketed information in the title appears above lot 1 and refers to lots 1 to 19.	Mr D Hoola van Nooten	(Unknown)

1808/12/12	UTWLD	0012	*[Anonymous]* | Twee kleine Landschapjes [Alle in swarte Lysten en wel geconserveerd.] | *Mat:* op paneel *Notes:* The bracketed information in the title appears above lot 1 and refers to lots 1 to 19.	Mr D Hoola van Nooten	(Unknown)
1808/12/12	UTWLD	0015	*[Anonymous]* | Een Landschap, waar in een Kwakzalver enz. [Alle in swarte Lysten en wel geconserveerd.] | *Mat:* op paneel *Notes:* The bracketed information in the title appears above lot 1 and refers to lots 1 to 19.	Mr D Hoola van Nooten	(Unknown)
1808/12/12	UTWLD	0017	*[Anonymous]* | Een Gezelchap Kaartspeelers [Alle in swarte Lysten en wel geconserveerd.] | *Mat:* op paneel *Notes:* The bracketed information in the title appears above lot 1 and refers to lots 1 to 19.	Mr D Hoola van Nooten	(Unknown)
1808/12/12	UTWLD	0019	*[Anonymous]* | Plan van de Stad Utrecht [Alle in swarte Lysten en wel geconserveerd.] | *Mat:* op bordpapier *Notes:* The bracketed information in the title appears above lot 1 and refers to lots 1 to 19.	Mr D Hoola van Nooten	(Unknown)
1808/12/31	RMHSN	0003	*Een goed Meester* | Een de Walvisvangst, door een goed Meester | *Mat:* op doek	G Spanjaart [or] H de Haas [or] C van der Looy Lans	(Unknown)
1808/12/31	RMHSN	0005	*[Anonymous]* | Een Mans Portrait, ovaal | *Fmt:* ovaal	G Spanjaart [or] H de Haas [or] C van der Looy Lans	(Unknown)
1808/12/31	RMHSN	0006	*[Anonymous]* | Een Kind zittende op een Kussen enz.	G Spanjaart [or] H de Haas [or] C van der Looy Lans	(Unknown)
1808/12/31	RMHSN	0007	*[Anonymous]* | Een Oud Man met een Eijer Korf aan zyn Arm | *Mat:* op paneel	G Spanjaart [or] H de Haas [or] C van der Looy Lans	(Unknown)
1808/12/31	RMHSN	0009	*Een goed Meester* | Een Wintertje met Schaatze Ryders, door een goed Meester | *Mat:* op doek	G Spanjaart [or] H de Haas [or] C van der Looy Lans	(Unknown)
1808/12/31	RMHSN	0012	*Een goed Meester* | Twee stuks Landschappen met Koejen en Paarden, door een goed Meester | *Mat:* op paneel	G Spanjaart [or] H de Haas [or] C van der Looy Lans	(Unknown)
1808/12/31	RMHSN	0014	*[Anonymous]* | Een Stil Leven, Patrys en End | *Mat:* op doek	G Spanjaart [or] H de Haas [or] C van der Looy Lans	(Unknown)
1808/12/31	RMHSN	0015	*[Anonymous]* | De Vier Getyden des Jaars | *Mat:* op doek	G Spanjaart [or] H de Haas [or] C van der Looy Lans	(Unknown)
1808/12/31	RMHSN	0016	*[Anonymous]* | Twee stuks Landschappen met Ruïnen | *Mat:* op doek	G Spanjaart [or] H de Haas [or] C van der Looy Lans	(Unknown)
1808/12/31	RMHSN	0027	*Een goed Meester* | De Kruiciging van Petrus, door een goed Meester | *Mat:* op paneel	G Spanjaart [or] H de Haas [or] C van der Looy Lans	(Unknown)
1808/12/31	RMHSN	0029	*[Anonymous]* | Het Verdrinken van Pharao in de Roode Zee | *Mat:* op paneel	G Spanjaart [or] H de Haas [or] C van der Looy Lans	(Unknown)
1808/12/31	RMHSN	0030	*Een goed Meester* | Een Italiaansche Ruïne, door een goed Meester | *Mat:* op doek	G Spanjaart [or] H de Haas [or] C van der Looy Lans	(Unknown)
1808/12/31	RMHSN	0031	*Een goed Meester* | De Prediking van Johannes, door een goed Meester | *Mat:* op paneel	G Spanjaart [or] H de Haas [or] C van der Looy Lans	(Unknown)
1808/12/31	RMHSN	0032	*[Anonymous]* | Een Schynbedrieger | *Mat:* op doek	G Spanjaart [or] H de Haas [or] C van der Looy Lans	(Unknown)
1808/12/31	RMHSN	0033	*[Anonymous]* | Een Bloemstuk | *Mat:* op doek	G Spanjaart [or] H de Haas [or] C van der Looy Lans	(Unknown)
1808/12/31	RMHSN	0034	*[Anonymous]* | Een dito [Bloemstuk] | *Mat:* op doek	G Spanjaart [or] H de Haas [or] C van der Looy Lans	(Unknown)
1808/12/31	RMHSN	0036	*[Anonymous]* | Twee Bloemstukken, op Paneel &c. | *Mat:* op paneel	G Spanjaart [or] H de Haas [or] C van der Looy Lans	(Unknown)
1808/12/31	RMHSN	0037	*[Anonymous]* | Twee stuks, een Mans- en Vrouwe Pourtrait | *Mat:* op doek	G Spanjaart [or] H de Haas [or] C van der Looy Lans	(Unknown)
1808/12/31	RMHSN	0038	*[Anonymous]* | Een Mans Pourtrait | *Mat:* op paneel	G Spanjaart [or] H de Haas [or] C van der Looy Lans	(Unknown)
1808/12/31	RMHSN	0039	*[Anonymous]* | Agt stuks diverse	G Spanjaart [or] H de Haas [or] C van der Looy Lans	(Unknown)

1809/04/17	AMSCH	0117	*[Anonymous]* | Een Drentisch Landschap, op de voorgrond een Boeren Schuur, waar bij grasende en rustende Schaapjes, zonagtig behandeld | *Mat:* op doek	A	(Sold) fl 12:10 Gruyter
1809/04/17	AMSCH	0119	*[Anonymous]* | Een vrolijk Man, houdende een Roemer in de eene en een Pijp in de andere hand, nevens hem staat een Wijnkan; geestig | *Mat:* op paneel	A	(Sold) fl 3:8
1809/04/17	AMSCH	0120	*Een voornaam Meester* | Een Historiëele Ordonantie, voorstellende de Offerhande van den Propheet Elia, tegens die van den Propheeten Baals, op de voorgrond ziet men de Koning Achab met een talrijk gevolg; meesterlijk en breed geschilderd, op Paneel, door een voornaam Meester | *Mat:* op paneel	A	(Sold) fl 0:8
1809/04/17	AMSCH	0123	*[Anonymous]* | Een Veldgezicht, gestoffeerd met een Boerin, twee rustende Koeijen en eenige Schaapen | *Mat:* op doek	T	(Sold) fl 0:6 Gruyter
1809/04/17	AMSCH	0124	*[Anonymous]* | Een natuurlijk Landschap, met rustende Huislieden en Rijzigers gestoffeerd | *Mat:* op doek	T	(Sold) fl 1
1809/04/17	AMSCH	0126	*[Anonymous]* | Twee stuks Landschappen, met Beelden en Beesten gestoffeerd	T	(Sold) fl 2:10
1809/04/17	AMSCH	0127	*Een goed Meester* | Een rijke Ordonantie; meesterlijk en breed geschilderd, op Doek, door een goed Meester | *Mat:* op doek	T	(Sold) fl 0:8 Gruyter
1809/04/17	AMSCH	0128	*[Anonymous]* | Een woelende Zee, met zijlende Scheepen; kloek op Paneel geschilderd | *Mat:* op paneel	T	(Sold) fl 1:10 Gruyter
1809/04/17	AMSCH	0129	*[Anonymous]* | Een Kerk van binnen te zien, gestoffeerd met wandelende Heeren en Dames en andere figuuren; zonagtig op Paneel geschilderd | *Mat:* op paneel	T	(Sold) fl 2:10
1809/04/17	AMSCH	0131	*Een goed Meester* | In een Landschap zit een bevallig Meisje, waar bij een Jongeling met een Valk op de hand; meesterlijk op Doek, door een goed Meester | *Mat:* op doek	C	(Sold) fl 3 Tomasse [?]
1809/04/17	AMSCH	0133	*[Anonymous]* | Een Mans Hoofd, met een grijse Baard; meesterlijk en breed geschilderd	Y	(Sold or Bought In) fl 1
1809/04/17	AMSCH	0133a	*[Anonymous]* | Een Wintergezicht, gestoffeerd met verscheide Aapen, welke zich met Schaatserijden en speelen vermaaken; geestig | *Mat:* op paneel	Y	(Sold or Bought In)
1809/04/17	AMSCH	0160	*[Anonymous]* | In een Gang of Voorportaal van een groot Gebouw, ziet men eene Vrouw, staande voor een Vengster, fraai van doorzicht | *Mat:* op doek	R	(Sold) fl 0:12
1809/04/17	AMSCH	0161	*[Anonymous]* | Een bevallig Landschap, met een Adelijk Huis, en Beelden gestoffeerd, fiks geschilderd | *Mat:* op doek	R	(Sold) fl 3
1809/04/17	AMSCH	0162	*[Anonymous]* | Een kabbelend Water, met zeilende en drijvende Vaartuigen | *Mat:* op paneel	R	(Sold) fl 0:6
1809/04/17	AMSCH	0166	*[Anonymous]* | Twee Jongelingen met een Vogelnesje in een Landschap | *Mat:* op paneel	R	(Sold) fl 0:14
1809/04/17	AMSCH	0167	*[Anonymous]* | Een Geestelijke Ordonantie, fiks geschilderd | *Mat:* op doek	R	(Sold) fl 2:5
1809/04/17	AMSCH	0168	*[Anonymous]* | Twee stuks een Kerk van Binnen, en een Landschap met Paarden	R	(Sold) fl 4
1809/04/17	AMSCH	0170	*[Anonymous]* | Op een Tafel liggen verscheide zoorten van Vruchten, kloek op Paneel geschilderd | *Mat:* op paneel	H	(Sold) Gruyter
1809/04/17	AMSCH	0173	*Een goed Meester* | Een kabbelend Water, met Zeilende Beurtschepen en Schuiten, door een goed Meester	H	(Sold) fl 1:15
1809/04/17	AMSCH	0183	*[Anonymous]* | Twee diversche Landschappen	[Gruyter?]	(Sold) fl 0:6
1809/04/17	AMSCH	0184	*[Anonymous]* | Twee dito [diversche] dito [Landschappen]	[Gruyter?]	(Sold) fl 1:10
1809/04/17	AMSCH	0184a[H]	*[Anonymous]* | [Untitled] | *Notes:* This lot was added in by hand in the EBNP copy of the catalogue, but without giving an artist or title.	[Gruyter?]	(Sold) fl 0:10
1809/04/17	AMSCH	0184b[H]	*[Anonymous]* | [Untitled] | *Notes:* This lot was added in by hand in the EBNP copy of the catalogue, but without giving an artist or title.		(Bought In) fl 8:10
1809/04/17	AMSCH	0187[H]	*[Anonymous]* | [Untitled] | *Notes:* This lot was added in by hand in the EBNP copy of the catalogue, but without giving an artist or title.	S	(Sold) fl 11:10
1809/04/17	AMSCH	0188[H]	*[Anonymous]* | [Untitled] | *Notes:* This lot was added in by hand in the EBNP copy of the catalogue, but without giving an artist or title.	S	(Sold) fl 0.8
1809/04/17	AMSCH	0189[H]	*[Anonymous]* | [Untitled] | *Notes:* This lot was added in by hand in the EBNP copy of the catalogue, but without giving an artist or title.	S	(Unknown) fl 1:10
1809/04/17	AMSCH	0190[H]	*[Anonymous]* | [Untitled] | *Notes:* This lot was added in by hand in the EBNP copy of the catalogue, but without giving an artist or title.	A	(Sold) fl 1:10
1809/04/17	AMSCH	0191[H]	*[Anonymous]* | [Untitled] | *Notes:* This lot was added in by hand in the EBNP copy of the catalogue, but without giving an artist or title.	A	(Sold) fl 4
1809/04/17	AMSCH	0192[H]	*[Anonymous]* | [Untitled] | *Notes:* This lot was added in by hand in the EBNP copy of the catalogue, but without giving an artist or title.	A	(Sold) fl 2:15
1809/04/17	AMSCH	0193[H]	*[Anonymous]* | [Untitled] | *Notes:* This lot was added in by hand in the EBNP copy of the catalogue, but without giving an artist or title.	A	(Sold) fl 2:5

1809/04/17	AMSCH	0194[H]	*[Anonymous]* | [Untitled] | *Notes:* This lot was added in by hand in the EBNP copy of the catalogue, but without giving an artist or title.	A	(Sold) fl 1
1809/04/17	AMSCH	0195[H]	*[Anonymous]* | [Untitled] | *Notes:* This lot was added in by hand in the EBNP copy of the catalogue, but without giving an artist or title.	A	(Sold) fl 3:5
1809/04/17	AMSCH	0196[H]	*[Anonymous]* | [Untitled] | *Notes:* This lot was added in by hand in the EBNP copy of the catalogue, but without giving an artist or title.	A	(Sold) fl 1:5
1809/04/17	AMSCH	0197[H]	*[Anonymous]* | [Untitled] | *Notes:* This lot was added in by hand in the EBNP copy of the catalogue, but without giving an artist or title.	A	(Sold) fl 1
1809/04/17	AMSCH	0198[H]	*[Anonymous]* | [Untitled] | *Notes:* This lot was added in by hand in the EBNP copy of the catalogue, but without giving an artist or title.	A	(Sold) fl 2
1809/04/22	AMYVR	0140	*[Anonymous]* | Een Riviergezicht, met differente Vaartuigen | *Mat:* op paneel *Size:* hoog 11, breed 13 duim	de Bruin	(Sold) fl 2:5 du Pree
1809/04/22	AMYVR	0150	*Een Goed Meester* | Een gekruiste Christus; door een Goed Meester	Juff[r] Julikker	(Sold) fl 1:5 Rijfsnijder
1809/04/22	AMYVR	0154	*[Anonymous]* | Een Munnik; fraai | *Mat:* op koper	Juff[r] Julikker	(Sold) fl 1:5 de Vries
1809/04/22	AMYVR	0158	*Een Goed Meester* | Twee met Scheepen en Vaartuigen geschilderde Tafereeltjes; door een Goed Meester	de Bruin	(Sold) fl 2 L Pakker
1809/04/22	AMYVR	0163	*[Anonymous]* | Eene Appelschilster; zeer uitvoerig	de Bruin	(Sold) fl 1:15 du Pree
1809/04/22	AMYVR	0169	*[Anonymous]* | Een Kom met Vruchten; fraai geschilderd	de Bruin	(Sold) fl 1:5 du Pree
1809/04/22	AMYVR	0170	*[Anonymous]* | Een galantiseerende Boer en Boerin	de Bruin	(Sold) fl 1 Coclers
1809/04/22	AMYVR	0171	*[Anonymous]* | Een Schilder voor zijn Ezel	de Bruin	(Sold) fl 0:6 v d Schley
1809/04/22	AMYVR	0173	*[Anonymous]* | Een Gevangenis, waarin een Bejaarde Man	de Bruin	(Sold) fl 2:5 du Pree
1809/04/22	AMYVR	0179	*[Anonymous]* | Op een Tafel liggen eenige Vruchten, welken delicaat geschilderd zijn	de Bruin	(Sold) fl 1 C S Roos
1809/04/22	AMYVR	0180	*Een Goed Meester* | Den Heiligen Johannes in de Woestijnen; door een Goed Meester	de Bruin	(Sold) fl 1 du Pree
1809/04/22	AMYVR	0182	*[Anonymous]* | Een Schoenmakers Winkel; geestig behandeld	de Bruin	(Sold) fl 6:5 du Pree
1809/04/22	AMYVR	0183	*Een Goed Meester* | Twee stuks onderscheidene Ordonantiën; door een Goed Meester	de Bruin	(Sold) fl 2:15 du Pree
1809/04/22	AMYVR	0186	*[Anonymous]* | Een Historieele Ordonantie, in een prachtige Zaal; meesterlijk | *Mat:* op paneel	de Bruin	(Sold) fl 3:5 du Pree
1809/04/22	AMYVR	0187	*[Anonymous]* | Een Chirurgijn, welke een Boer zijn Voet verbind	de Bruin	(Sold) fl 2 du Pree
1809/04/22	AMYVR	0189	*Een Goed Meester* | Een Boeren-Gezelschap; door een Goed Meester	de Bruin	(Sold) fl 11:10 van Iperen
1809/04/22	AMYVR	0193	*[Anonymous]* | Een Landschap met Vee en een slapende Boer	de Bruin	(Sold) fl 3 du Pree
1809/04/22	AMYVR	0198	*[Anonymous]* | Een Vrouwe-Pourtrait; uitvoerig geschilderd	de Bruin	(Sold) fl 3:15 du Pree
1809/04/22	AMYVR	0201	*[Anonymous]* | Twee stuks: een Heer en eene Dame; meesterlijk behandeld	de Bruin	(Sold) fl 2:15 du Pree
1809/04/22	AMYVR	0210[H]	*[Anonymous]* | 1 Schilderij | *Notes:* This lot was added in by hand in the RKDH copy of the catalogue.	V	(Sold) fl 96 Remmers Bredius
1809/04/22	AMYVR	0211[H]	*[Anonymous]* | 1 dito [Schilderij] | *Notes:* This lot was added in by hand in the RKDH copy of the catalogue.	van den Bracke	(Bought In) fl 8
1809/04/22	AMYVR	0212[H]	*[Anonymous]* | 1 dito [Schilderij] | *Notes:* This lot was added in by hand in the RKDH copy of the catalogue.	van den Bracke	(Sold) fl 0:6 van Iperen
1809/04/22	AMYVR	0213[H]	*[Anonymous]* | 1 dito [Schilderij] | *Notes:* This lot was added in by hand in the RKDH copy of the catalogue.	van den Bracke	(Sold) fl 2 for lots 213 & 214. C S Roos
1809/04/22	AMYVR	0214[H]	*[Anonymous]* | 2 dito [Schilderijen] | *Notes:* This lot was added in by hand in the RKDH copy of the catalogue.	van den Bracke	(Sold) fl 2 for lots 213 & 214. C S Roos
1809/04/22	AMYVR	0215[H]	*[Anonymous]* | 6 dito [Schilderijen] | *Notes:* This lot was added in by hand in the RKDH copy of the catalogue.	van den Bracke	(Sold) fl 0:6 Martins
1809/04/22	AMYVR	0216[H]	*[Anonymous]* | 2 dito [Schilderijen] | *Notes:* This lot was added in by hand in the RKDH copy of the catalogue.	Juff[r] Julikker	(Sold) fl 1:5 du Pree
1809/04/22	AMYVR	0217[H]	*[Anonymous]* | 2 schilderijen | *Notes:* This lot was added in by hand in the RKDH copy of the catalogue.	Juff[r] Julikker	(Sold) fl 1:15 du Pree
1809/05/26	HADAA	0004	*Een goed Meester* | Twee Kinderen, spelende in een Landschap met een Mossenestje, bevallig door een goed Meester | *Mat:* op paneel *Size:* hoog 10 breed 8 duimen	Mejuffrouw de Wed David Heemskerk [or others]	(Unknown)
1809/05/26	HADAA	0011	*[Anonymous]* | Een Lagchende Vrouw, door	Mejuffrouw de Wed David Heemskerk [or others]	(Unknown)
1809/05/26	HADAA	0024	*[Anonymous]* | Een Gezigt in het Dorp Heemstede	Mejuffrouw de Wed David Heemskerk [or others]	(Unknown)
1809/05/26	HADAA	0025	*[Anonymous]* | Een Landschap	Mejuffrouw de Wed David Heemskerk [or others]	(Unknown)

1809/05/26	HADAA	0026	*[Anonymous]* | Een dito [Landschap]	Mejuffrouw de Wed David Heemskerk [or others]	(Unknown)
1809/05/26	HADAA	0027	*[Anonymous]* | Bacchus en Ariadne met eenige dansende kindertjes in een Landschap	Mejuffrouw de Wed David Heemskerk [or others]	(Unknown)
1809/05/26	HADAA	0028	*[Anonymous]* | Een heilige Familje	Mejuffrouw de Wed David Heemskerk [or others]	(Unknown) fl 5:10
1809/05/26	HADAA	0029	*[Anonymous]* | Een Italiaansche Zeehaven, met veel stoffagie | companion to lot 30	Mejuffrouw de Wed David Heemskerk [or others]	(Unknown)
1809/05/26	HADAA	0030	*[Anonymous]* | Een dito [Italiaansche Zeehaven], zijnde een wederga van de voorgaande | companion to lot 29	Mejuffrouw de Wed David Heemskerk [or others]	(Unknown)
1809/05/26	HADAA	0031	*[Anonymous]* | Een Heer die een Jagtroer laadt	Mejuffrouw de Wed David Heemskerk [or others]	(Unknown)
1809/05/26	HADAA	0032	*[Anonymous]* | Een stuk met dood wild	Mejuffrouw de Wed David Heemskerk [or others]	(Unknown)
1809/05/26	HADAA	0033	*[Anonymous]* | Een Autaar [sic] stuk in een kast met geschilderde deuren | *Fmt:* een altaarstuk met deuren	Mejuffrouw de Wed David Heemskerk [or others]	(Unknown)
1809/05/26	HADAA	0034	*[Anonymous]* | Twee Pourtraiten	Mejuffrouw de Wed David Heemskerk [or others]	(Unknown)
1809/05/26	HADAA	0038	*[Anonymous]* | In een Binnenvertrek ziet men een Wever aan zijn getouw bezig, terwijl een ander met hem praat, op den voorgrond eene Vrouw die koeken bakt, fiks op Paneel geschilderd door .... Zijnde dit stuk volgens overlevering de Voorouders van een zeer bekende Holl. Familje | *Mat:* op paneel	Mejuffrouw de Wed David Heemskerk [or others]	(Unknown)
1809/05/26	HADAA	0039	*[Anonymous]* | Een dito [Binnenvertrek], waarin eenige lieden bezig zijn toebereidselen tot den maaltijd te maken; ter zijde een Koestal met eenig Vee, fraai van licht en kloek behandeld door	Mejuffrouw de Wed David Heemskerk [or others]	(Unknown)
1809/05/26	HADAA	0043	*[Anonymous]* | Een capitaal Boomrijk Landschap met een waterplas en stoffage kloek geschilderd door	Mejuffrouw de Wed David Heemskerk [or others]	(Unknown)
1809/05/26	HADAA	0048	*[Anonymous]* | Een Landschap en Watertje zeer goed gestoffeerd door .... | *Mat:* op doek	Mejuffrouw de Wed David Heemskerk [or others]	(Unknown)
1809/05/26	HADAA	0051	*[Anonymous]* | Een Strandgezigt, rijk gestoffeerd door	Mejuffrouw de Wed David Heemskerk [or others]	(Unknown)
1809/05/26	HADAA	0054	*[Anonymous]* | Een dito [Landschap], fraaij door	Mejuffrouw de Wed David Heemskerk [or others]	(Unknown)
1809/05/26	HADAA	0057	*[Anonymous]* | De Steeniging van Stefanus door	Mejuffrouw de Wed David Heemskerk [or others]	(Unknown)
1809/05/26	HADAA	0063	*[Anonymous]* | Drie stuks, zijnde een Binnenhuisje en twee Landschappen	Mejuffrouw de Wed David Heemskerk [or others]	(Unknown)
1809/05/26	HADAA	0065	*[Anonymous]* | Een boomrijk Landschap met een Jagtpartij door	Mejuffrouw de Wed David Heemskerk [or others]	(Unknown)
1809/05/26	HADAA	0068	*[Anonymous]* | Een Strandgezigt door	Mejuffrouw de Wed David Heemskerk [or others]	(Unknown)
1809/05/26	HADAA	0069	*[Anonymous]* | Twee diverse	Mejuffrouw de Wed David Heemskerk [or others]	(Unknown)
1809/05/26	HADAA	0071	*[Anonymous]* | Het Pourtret van Tako Jelgersma, uitvoerig met Sapverwen | *Notes:* This lot was sold with lot 72 by Corn. Noorde.	Mejuffrouw de Wed David Heemskerk [or others]	(Unknown) fl 1:16 for lots 71 & 72
1809/05/26	HADAA	0073	*[Anonymous]* | Een Mans Pourtret	Mejuffrouw de Wed David Heemskerk [or others]	(Unknown)
1809/05/26	HADAA	0074	*[Anonymous]* | Een dito [Mans Pourtret]	Mejuffrouw de Wed David Heemskerk [or others]	(Unknown)

1809/05/26	HADAA	0075	*[Anonymous]* | Een Vrouwe Pourtret	Mejuffrouw de Wed David Heemskerk [or others]	(Unknown)
1809/05/26	HADAA	0076	*[Anonymous]* | Een Schoorsteenstuk, verbeeldende Atalante met het Zwijnshoofd | *Fmt:* schoorsteenstuk	Mejuffrouw de Wed David Heemskerk [or others]	(Unknown)
1809/05/26	HADAA	0077	*[Anonymous]* | Een Landschap met dansende kindertjes | *Mat:* op paneel	Mejuffrouw de Wed David Heemskerk [or others]	(Unknown)
1809/05/26	HADAA	0078	*[Anonymous]* | Een Kop, zijnde Mercuur	Mejuffrouw de Wed David Heemskerk [or others]	(Unknown)
1809/05/26	HADAA	0079	*[Anonymous]* | Een dito [Kop], zijnde Faëton	Mejuffrouw de Wed David Heemskerk [or others]	(Unknown)
1809/05/26	HADAA	0080	*[Anonymous]* | Een dito [Kop], zijnde Diana	Mejuffrouw de Wed David Heemskerk [or others]	(Unknown)
1809/05/26	HADAA	0081	*[Anonymous]* | Een dito [Kop], zijnde Flora	Mejuffrouw de Wed David Heemskerk [or others]	(Unknown)
1809/05/26	HADAA	0082	*[Anonymous]* | Een dito [Kop], zijnde Saturnus	Mejuffrouw de Wed David Heemskerk [or others]	(Unknown)
1809/05/26	HADAA	0084	*[Anonymous]* | Twee dito [ten voeten uit], Jupiter en Diana	Mejuffrouw de Wed David Heemskerk [or others]	(Unknown)
1809/05/26	HADAA	0085	*[Anonymous]* | Twee dito [ten voeten uit], Merkuur en Ceres	Mejuffrouw de Wed David Heemskerk [or others]	(Unknown)
1809/05/26	HADAA	0086	*[Anonymous]* | Twee dito [ten voeten uit], Apollo en Juno	Mejuffrouw de Wed David Heemskerk [or others]	(Unknown)
1809/05/26	HADAA	A0005	*[Anonymous]* | Een Corps de Garde, door	Mejuffrouw de Wed David Heemskerk [or others]	(Unknown)
1809/05/26	HADAA	A0008	*[Anonymous]* | Twee kleine Mans Pourtretjes	Mejuffrouw de Wed David Heemskerk [or others]	(Unknown)
1809/05/26	HADAA	A0018	*[Anonymous]* | Een Historiëele, op Paneel geschilderd, door .... | *Mat:* op paneel	Mejuffrouw de Wed David Heemskerk [or others]	(Unknown)
1809/05/26	HADAA	A0020	*[Anonymous]* | Een Land- en Watergezigtje, met zeilende Schepen	Mejuffrouw de Wed David Heemskerk [or others]	(Unknown)
1809/05/26	HADAA	A0021	*[Anonymous]* | Een woelend Water, met zeilende Vaartuigen, fiks geschilderd door	Mejuffrouw de Wed David Heemskerk [or others]	(Unknown)
1809/05/26	HADAA	A0022	*[Anonymous]* | Een Landschap met Boertjes, door	Mejuffrouw de Wed David Heemskerk [or others]	(Unknown)
1809/05/26	HADAA	A0023	*[Anonymous]* | Een dito [Landschap], dito [met Boertjes]	Mejuffrouw de Wed David Heemskerk [or others]	(Unknown)
1809/05/26	HADAA	A0026	*[Anonymous]* | Twee Boere Kermissen, door	Mejuffrouw de Wed David Heemskerk [or others]	(Unknown)
1809/06/13	AMSCH	0175	*[Anonymous]* | Een Bijbel-Ordonantie, voorstellende de Wijze welke het Kind Jesus aanbidden, en geschenken brengen; krachtig en uitvoerig geschilderd, op Paneel, A°. 1500 | *Mat:* op paneel *Size:* hoog 18, breed 16 duim *Inscr:* A°. 1500 (dated?) *Notes:* It is unclear whether the date is inscribed on the painting.	E	(Sold) fl 4:15 du Pree
1809/06/13	AMSCH	0176	*Een zeer ond Meester* | Een Bédevaart van verscheide devote Mannen en Vrouwen bij de Kapel te Heyloo; kragtig op Paneel, door een zeer ond [sic] Meester, A°. 1540 | *Mat:* op paneel *Inscr:* A°. 1540 (dated?) *Notes:* It is unclear whether the date is inscribed on the painting.	E	(Sold) fl 8 L Pakker
1809/06/13	AMSCH	0177	*Een heel oud Meester* | Een Bijbel-Ordonantie, de Kruisiging Christus op Kalvarie; kragtig door een heel oud Meester, 1580 | *Inscr:* 1580 (dated?) *Notes:* It is unclear whether the date is inscribed on the painting.	S[chley]	(Sold) fl 35:15 T Spaan
1809/06/13	AMSCH	0181	*[Anonymous]* | Een Heilige Familje in een Landschap; uitvoerig geschilderd	Y	(Sold) fl 3:5 du Pree

1809/06/13	AMSCH	0186	*[Anonymous]* | Op een plaats met pragtige Gebouwen ziet men verscheiden Persoonen en Rijtuigen, zijnde alles verlicht door fakkels en flambouwen; meesterlijk en breed geschilderd	Y	(Sold) fl 16:10 du Pree
1809/06/13	AMSCH	0187	*Een oud Meester* | Een zinnebeeldige Ordonantie op de vergankelijkheid van 't menschelijke leven, verbeeldende eene jonge Vrouw, leggende dood op 't stroo, waarbij toepasselijk Bijwerk, breed geschilderd door een oud Meester	Y	(Sold) fl 0:10 Gruiter
1809/06/13	AMSCH	0188	*[Anonymous]* | Een Bergachtig Landschap, met stoffagie van Beelden en Beesten, goed op Paneel geschilderd | *Mat:* op paneel	Y	(Sold) fl 1:10 du Pree
1809/06/13	AMSCH	0190	*[Anonymous]* | Een Bergachtig Landschap, met Gebouwen, Beelden en Beesten, kloek op Paneel geschilderd | *Mat:* op paneel	Y	(Sold) fl 2:15 Gruiter
1809/06/13	AMSCH	0194	*[Anonymous]* | Een Landschap met Beesten, kloek op Paneel geschilderd | *Mat:* op paneel	Y	(Sold) fl 0:12 Gruiter
1809/06/13	AMSCH	0197	*[Anonymous]* | Een Zeegezigt met zeilende Scheepen; fiks | *Mat:* op paneel	Y	(Sold) fl 0:8 Grimmond
1809/06/13	AMSCH	0198	*[Anonymous]* | In een Landschap ziet men de Godin Diana, verzeld van verscheide Jagt-Nimphen en Honden; uitvoerig op Koper geschilderd | *Mat:* op koper	Y	(Sold) fl 4:5 Gruyter
1809/06/13	AMSCH	0200	*[Anonymous]* | Een Jongeling in een Nis, met een Vogelnesje, fiks geschilderd	Y	(Sold) fl 3:5 for lots 200 & 201. van Iperen
1809/06/13	AMSCH	0201	*Een goed Meester* | Een Mans Hoofd, breed geschilderd, door een goed Meester	Y	(Sold) fl 3:5 for lots 200 & 201. van Iperen
1809/06/13	AMSCH	0206	*[Anonymous]* | Een Ordonantie van verscheide Beelden | *Mat:* op paneel	S[chley]	(Sold) fl 1 L Pakker
1809/06/13	AMSCH	0213	*[Anonymous]* | Twee stuks, verbeeldende een Herder en Herderin	E	(Sold) fl 0:6 L Pakker
1809/06/13	AMSCH	0219	*[Anonymous]* | Een Oudmans Hoofd met een baard, meesterlijk fiks op Paneel geschilderd | *Mat:* op paneel	R[ijfsnijder]	(Sold) fl 1:5 T Spaan
1809/06/13	AMSCH	0220	*[Anonymous]* | Een dito [Oudmans] dito [Hoofd], met een Mezetijne Muts op 't hoofd | *Mat:* op paneel	R[ijfsnijder]	(Sold) fl 0:10 J de Vries
1809/06/13	AMSCH	0224	*[Anonymous]* | Een Mans Beeld, halver lijf, gedeeltelijk naakt en half gekleed, als in een smeekende gestalten krachtig op Paneel geschilderd | *Mat:* op paneel	R[ijfsnijder]	(Sold) fl 5:5 Buck
1809/06/13	AMSCH	0228	*Een oud Meester* | De Kinderliefde aan de Vader in de Gevangenis bewezen; krachtig geschilderd door een oud Meester | *Mat:* op doek	[Gruyter?]	(Sold) fl 0:12 Royers
1809/06/13	AMSCH	0239	*[Anonymous]* | Twee stuks woelende Zeën, met zeilende en stilleggende Vaartuigen; bevallig geschilderd | *Mat:* op doek	Y	(Sold) fl 0:10 L Pakker
1809/06/13	AMSCH	0240	*[Anonymous]* | Twee stuks Landschappen, met stoffagie	Y	(Sold) fl 0:10 L Pakker
1809/06/13	AMSCH	0241	*[Anonymous]* | Een vergenoegd Huisman, staande voor een Ton, houdende een Bierkan in de Hand; natuurlijk | *Mat:* op paneel	Y	(Sold) fl 0:6 L Pakker
1809/06/13	AMSCH	0243	*[Anonymous]* | Vijf stuks, met Beelden, divers	Y	(Sold) fl 1:15 du Pree
1809/06/13	AMSCH	0245	*[Anonymous]* | Twee diversche Schilderijen | *Notes:* This lot was misnumbered no. 145. It was sold with lot 233 by P. La Croix.	Y	(Sold) fl 0:6 for lots 233 & 245. L Pakker
1809/06/13	AMSCH	0246[H]	*[Anonymous]* | 1 Stuk | *Notes:* This lot was added in by hand in the EBNP copy of the catalogue.	[Gruyter?]	(Sold) fl 0:6 van Iperen
1809/06/13	AMSCH	0247[H]	*[Anonymous]* | 1 Stuk | *Notes:* This lot was added in by hand in the EBNP copy of the catalogue.	[Gruyter?]	(Sold) fl 0:14 for lots 247[H] & 248[H]. L Pakker
1809/06/13	AMSCH	0248[H]	*[Anonymous]* | 1 Stuk | *Notes:* This lot was added in by hand in the EBNP copy of the catalogue.	[Gruyter?]	(Sold) fl 0:14 for lots 247[H] & 248[H]. L Pakker
1809/06/13	AMSCH	0249[H]	*[Anonymous]* | 1 Stuk | *Notes:* This lot was added in by hand in the EBNP copy of the catalogue.	[Gruyter?]	(Sold) fl 1 Eversdyk
1809/06/13	AMSCH	0250[H]	*[Anonymous]* | 1 Stuk | *Notes:* This lot was added in by hand in the EBNP copy of the catalogue.	S[chley]	(Sold) fl 0:6 L Pakker
1809/06/13	AMSCH	0251[H]	*[Anonymous]* | 1 Stuk | *Notes:* This lot was added in by hand in the EBNP copy of the catalogue.	S[chley]	(Sold) fl 0:6 W v d Schley
1809/07/13	RMIMM	0103	*Een onbekend Meester* | Een Schilderytje, verbeeldende een oud Ruiter te Paard door een onbekend Meester		(Unknown)
1809/07/13	RMIMM	0104	*[Anonymous]* | Een Bloemstuk met Lyst		(Unknown)
1809/07/13	RMIMM	0105	*[Anonymous]* | Een dito [Bloemstuk] dito [met Lyst]		(Unknown)
1809/07/13	RMIMM	0106	*[Anonymous]* | Een Schildery met eenige Vogels		(Unknown)
1809/07/13	RMIMM	0107	*[Anonymous]* | Een dito [Schildery] dito [met eenige Vogels] iets kleiner		(Unknown)
1809/07/13	RMIMM	0108	*[Anonymous]* | Een Schilderytje met eenige Kindertjes		(Unknown)
1809/07/13	RMIMM	0109	*[Anonymous]* | Een Academiebeeld, fiks geschilderd		(Unknown)
1809/07/19	AMSCH	0026a[H]	*[Anonymous]* | Een Schildery | *Notes:* This lot was added in by hand in the FLNY copy of the catalogue.	E	(Sold) Gruiter

1809/07/19	AMSCH	0070	*Een oud Meester* | Een Binnehuis, verbeelende een Herberg, met verscheide vrolijke, drinkende en speelende Lieden, krachtig en uitvoerig geschilderd, op Paneel, door een oud Meester | *Mat:* op paneel *Size:* hoog 12, breed 15 duim	C	(Sold) fl 7:5 Gruyter
1809/07/19	AMSCH	0071	*Een goed Meester* | Het Afbeeldsel van eenen Beeldhouwer, ten halve Lijve, levens groote, en van voren te zien, rustende met zijn Linkerhand op een Marmer Borstbeeld. Krachtig op Doek geschilderd door een goed Meester | *Mat:* op doek	C	(Sold) fl 1:15 Gruyter
1809/07/19	AMSCH	0072	*[Anonymous]* | Een deftig gekleed Heer, zittende in een Leuningstoel, houdende een Papier in zijne Handen. Meesterlijk op Doek geschilderd | *Mat:* op doek	C	(Sold) fl 1:5 Gruyter
1809/07/19	AMSCH	0073	*[Anonymous]* | Twee stuks, een Mans en Vrouwe Portrait, in oude Hollandsche Kleeding. Beide uitvoerig op Paneel geschilderd. Anno 1548 | *Mat:* op paneel *Inscr:* Anno 1548 (dated?) *Notes:* It is unclear whether the date is inscribed on the painting.	C	(Sold) fl 1:10 Gruyter
1809/07/19	AMSCH	0074	*[Anonymous]* | Twee stuks Pourtraiten van geestelijke Persoonen, beide op Doek geschilderd | *Mat:* op doek	C	(Sold) fl 2:5 T Spaan
1809/07/19	AMSCH	0075[H]	*[Anonymous]* | Een Schilderij | *Notes:* This lot was added in by hand in the EBNP I and FLNY copies of the catalogue.	Y	(Sold) fl 4:10 Levie Pakker
1809/07/19	AMSCH	0076[H]	*[Anonymous]* | Een Dito [Schilderij] | *Notes:* This lot was added in by hand in the EBNP I and FLNY copies of the catalogue.	Y	(Sold) fl 3:5 Gruiter
1809/07/19	AMSCH	0077[H]	*[Anonymous]* | Een dito [Schilderij] | *Notes:* This lot was added in by hand in the EBNP I and FLNY copies of the catalogue.	Y	(Sold) fl 2:10 T Spaan
1809/07/19	AMSCH	0078[H]	*[Anonymous]* | Een dito [Schilderij] | *Notes:* This lot was added in by hand in the EBNP I and FLNY copies of the catalogue.	Y	(Sold) fl 1:15 Levie Pakker
1809/07/19	AMSCH	0079[H]	*[Anonymous]* | Twee dito [Schilderijen] | *Notes:* This lot was added in by hand in the EBNP I and FLNY copies of the catalogue.	Y	(Sold) fl 2 Levie Pakker
1809/07/25	HGBSM	0079	*Een goed Meester* | Een Vrouw, half naakt, met een Boek voor haar &c., door een goed Meester | *Mat:* op doek *Size:* hoog 25 en een half, breed 22 en 1 half duim	D van der Aa [or] E B ten Dall	(Sold) fl 1:10 van der Burgh
1809/07/25	HGBSM	0087	*Een goed Meester* | Een weenende Vrouw in devotie, met een Boek, Doodshooft enz., door een goed Meester | *Mat:* op paneel *Size:* hoog 25, breed 21 en een half duim	D van der Aa [or] E B ten Dall	(Sold) fl 2 de Gelder
1809/07/25	HGBSM	0135	*[Anonymous]* | Een Dito [uitgestrekt Landschap], met een leggende Koey en een staand Paard | *Mat:* op paneel *Size:* hoog 12 en een half, breed 16 duim	D van der Aa [or] E B ten Dall	(Sold) fl 12:5 Bogaard
1809/07/25	HGBSM	0152	*Een goed meester* | Eenige overblyfzels van een antiek gebouw tegen een Rots, met stoffage, door een goed meester | *Mat:* op doek *Size:* hoog 19 en een half, breed 24 duim	D van der Aa [or] E B ten Dall	(Sold) fl 1:6 Bakhuyzen
1809/07/25	HGBSM	0153	*[Anonymous]* | Een Mande met Fruit | *Mat:* op doek *Size:* hoog 20 en een half, breed 25 duim	D van der Aa	(Sold) fl 4:10 van der Aa
1809/07/25	HGBSM	0157	*Een braaf Meester* | Een staande Koe met twee Schaapen in een Landschap, door een braaf Meester | *Mat:* op paneel *Size:* hoog 12 en een half, breed 10 duim	D van der Aa [or] E B ten Dall	(Sold) fl 14:10 van Dongen
1809/07/25	HGBSM	0161	*[Anonymous]* | Twee stuks Landschapjes met stoffage | *Mat:* op paneel *Size:* hoog 5, breed 8 en een half duim	D van der Aa	(Sold) fl 2 van der Aa
1809/07/25	HGBSM	0164	*[Anonymous]* | Een Goden Maaltyd | *Mat:* op paneel *Size:* hoog 13, breed 11 duim	D van der Aa [or] E B ten Dall	(Sold) fl 1:6 Heijmans [for] G
1809/07/25	HGBSM	0174	*[Anonymous]* | Een Stukje, verbeeldende waar Hugo de Groot in de Boeke Kist word gelegt | *Mat:* op paneel *Size:* hoog 9, breed 13 en een half duim	D van der Aa [or] E B ten Dall	(Sold) fl 0:10 de Gelder
1809/07/25	HGBSM	0175	*[Anonymous]* | Een Mans-Hooft | *Mat:* op doek op paneel	D van der Aa [or] E B ten Dall	(Sold) fl 0:14 Heymans [for] G
1809/07/25	HGBSM	0176	*[Anonymous]* | Een Schets, verbeeldende Jupiter	D van der Aa [or] E B ten Dall	(Sold) fl 0:7 van Eyk
1809/07/25	HGBSM	0178	*[Anonymous]* | Twee dito Keizers hoofden in 't rond | *Mat:* op paneel *Fmt:* rond *Notes:* It is unclear what "dito" refers to in the title.	D van der Aa [or] E B ten Dall	(Sold) fl 0:10 ten Haaf
1809/07/25	HGBSM	0179	*[Anonymous]* | Een gegeesselde Christus aan de kolom | *Mat:* op doek	D van der Aa	(Sold) fl 1:4 van der Aa
1809/07/25	HGBSM	0182[a]	*[Anonymous]* | Het Portret van Willem den eersten en Prins Maurits, op Koper in 't rond, en twee Boertjes in 't vierkant, op Paneel, vier stuks | *This Lot:* Het Portret van Willem den eersten en Prins Maurits *Mat:* op koper *Fmt:* rond	D van der Aa [or] E B ten Dall	(Sold) fl 0:12 for lots 182[a] & 182[b]. Bosboom
1809/07/25	HGBSM	0182[b]	*[Anonymous]* | Het Portret van Willem den eersten en Prins Maurits, op Koper in 't rond, en twee Boertjes in 't vierkant, op Paneel, vier stuks | *This Lot:* Twee Boertjes in 't vierkant *Mat:* op paneel *Fmt:* vierkant	D van der Aa [or] E B ten Dall	(Sold) fl 0:12 for lots 182[a] & 182[b]. Bosboom
1809/07/25	HGBSM	0183	*[Anonymous]* | Een Boeregezelschap buiten's Huis | *Mat:* op paneel *Size:* hoog 16, breed 21 duim	D van der Aa	(Sold) fl 1:2 van der Aa
1809/07/25	HGBSM	0197	*[Anonymous]* | Twee Stuks met Zwitzersche Boeren in hunne Landskleding, fix en natuurlyk geschildert | *Mat:* op doek *Size:* hoog 14, breed 10 en een half duim	D van der Aa [or] E B ten Dall	(Sold) fl 5:5 Heymans [for] G

1809/07/25	HGBSM	0201	*[Anonymous]* | Een Landschap met Koeyen en een Herder | *Mat:* op doek *Size:* hoog 20, breed 24 en een half duim	D van der Aa [or] E B ten Dall	(Sold) fl 7:5 Nieuwenhuizen
1809/07/25	HGBSM	0205	*Een voornaam Meester* | Een Vrouw, levensgroote tot de Knien, waar van de Borst voor 't grootste gedeelte naakt is, een Brief in de Regterhand hebbende, breed en konstig geschildert door een voornaam Meester | *Mat:* op doek *Size:* hoog 39, breed 33 duim	D van der Aa [or] E B ten Dall	(Sold) fl 38 L Voerman
1809/07/25	HGBSM	0210	*Een goed Meester* | Een oud Man met een groote Baard, een Doodshoofd in zyn handen hebbende, door een goed Meester | *Mat:* op doek *Size:* hoog 27 en een half, breed 22 en een half duim	D van der Aa [or] E B ten Dall	(Sold) fl 1:6 Heijmans
1809/07/25	HGBSM	0214	*Een goed Meester* | Een troup Krygslieden te paard, door een goed Meester | *Mat:* op doek *Size:* hoog 28, breed 25 duim	D van der Aa [or] E B ten Dall	(Sold) fl 6:5 van Zanten
1809/07/25	HGBSM	0217	*Een goed Meester* | Een menigte Antiquiteiten, konstig geschildert door een goed Meester | *Mat:* op koper *Size:* hoog 17 en een half, breed 22 en een half duim	D van der Aa [or] E B ten Dall	(Sold) fl 4:2 van Voorden
1809/07/25	HGBSM	0220	*Een goed Meester* | Een Buiten-Stadsgezigt, langs het water te zien, in 't midden een Moolen, verder goed gestoffeerd, door een goed Meester | *Mat:* op paneel *Size:* hoog 18, breed 24 duim	D van der Aa [or] E B ten Dall	(Sold) fl 1 Zwarts
1809/07/25	HGBSM	0224	*Een oud Meester* | Een Vrouw en twee Oude Mans Borststukken, Susanna met de Boeven voorstellende, door een oud Meester | *Mat:* op paneel *Size:* hoog 20, breed 25 en een half duim	D van der Aa [or] E B ten Dall	(Sold) fl 1:8 van Zanten
1809/07/25	HGBSM	0225	*Een zeer oud Meester* | Een oud Man, zittende in overdenking voor een tafel, waar op een Boek, Doodshoofd en Kandelaar, en verder bywerk, verbeeldende de Vergankelykheid, door een zeer oud Meester, op paneel geschildert | *Mat:* op paneel *Size:* hoog 25, breed 18 duim	D van der Aa [or] E B ten Dall	(Sold) fl 2 de Gelder
1809/07/25	HGBSM	0226	*[Anonymous]* | Een Heilige Familie, ook zeer oud | *Mat:* op paneel *Size:* hoog 18, breed 14 en een half duim	D van der Aa [or] E B ten Dall	(Sold) fl 1:8 Boers
1809/07/25	HGBSM	0229	*Een oud Meester* | Christus met de Doorne Kroon en de Riedstaf &c, halverlyf, door een oud Meester | *Mat:* op paneel *Size:* hoog 12 en een half, breed 16 en een half duim	D van der Aa [or] E B ten Dall	(Sold) fl 3:18 L Voerman
1809/07/25	HGBSM	0236	*[Anonymous]* | Twee Stuks verbeeldende drinkende Boeren | *Mat:* op doek *Size:* hoog 15 en een half, breed 12 en een half	D van der Aa [or] E B ten Dall	(Sold) fl 1:6 Dupré
1809/07/25	HGBSM	0237	*[Anonymous]* | Twee Stuks, verbeeldende het eene de Aanbidding der Herders, en het andere der Koningen van den Heiland | *Mat:* op koper *Fmt:* ovaal *Size:* hoog 10, breed 13 en een half duim	D van der Aa [or] E B ten Dall	(Sold) fl 0:18 van Zanten
1809/07/25	HGBSM	0238	*Een goed Meester* | Een Dame voor een Tafel musiceerende en verders met Figuuren, door een goed Meester | *Mat:* op paneel *Size:* hoog 12, breed 16 duim	D van der Aa [or] E B ten Dall	(Sold) fl 10:10 De Gruyter
1809/07/25	HGBSM	0241	*[Anonymous]* | Een grauw Paard met een Hond, fraai geschildert | *Mat:* op paneel *Size:* hoog 8 en een half, breed 10 duim	D van der Aa [or] E B ten Dall	(Sold) fl 31 De Gruijter
1809/07/25	HGBSM	0242	*[Anonymous]* | Een Kerk, van binnen te zien | *Mat:* op paneel *Size:* hoog 7 en een half, breed 9 duim	D van der Aa [or] E B ten Dall	(Sold) fl 5 Nieuwenhuis
1809/07/25	HGBSM	0244	*[Anonymous]* | De Aanbidding van Christus door de Wyzen uit het Oosten | *Mat:* op koper *Size:* hoog 9, breed 6 en een half duim	D van der Aa [or] E B ten Dall	(Sold) fl 1 Heymans [for] G
1809/07/25	HGBSM	0245	*[Anonymous]* | Een dito [Aanbidding van Christus door de Wyzen?] | *Mat:* op koper *Size:* hoog 8 en een half, breed 10 en een half duim *Notes:* It is unclear what "dito" refers to in the title.	D van der Aa [or] E B ten Dall	(Sold) fl 0:10 Landa
1809/07/25	HGBSM	0248	*[Anonymous]* | Een Riviergezigt langs een Vest, met vaartuigen | *Mat:* op doek *Size:* hoog 12, breed 17 duim	D van der Aa [or] E B ten Dall	(Sold) fl 1 Carrée
1809/07/25	HGBSM	0250	*[Anonymous]* | Een Boschgezigt met stoffage | *Mat:* op paneel *Size:* hoog 8, breed 11 duim	D van der Aa [or] E B ten Dall	(Sold) fl 19 L Voerman
1809/07/25	HGBSM	0251	*[Anonymous]* | Een Landschap, waarin een Ruine, gestoffeert met Figuurtjes en Gyten | *Mat:* op paneel *Size:* hoog 10, breed 14 duim	D van der Aa [or] E B ten Dall	(Sold) fl 5:5 Pulver
1809/07/25	HGBSM	0252	*Een goed Meester* | Een Landschapje met een Rivier, waar over een Brug, op de voorgrond een Man die twee Ossen voortdryft, door een goed Meester | *Mat:* op paneel *Size:* hoog 9, breed 12 en een half duim	D van der Aa [or] E B ten Dall	(Sold) fl 6:10 van Eyk
1809/07/25	HGBSM	0253	*Een zeer oud Meester* | Een Portret, door een zeer oud Meester, van het jaar 1547 | *Inscr:* 1547 (dated?) *Notes:* It is unclear whether the date is inscribed on the painting.	D van der Aa [or] E B ten Dall	(Sold) fl 1 Zwarts
1809/07/25	HGBSM	0256	*Een goed Meester* | Een Rots, waarin een Doorzigt, met verder stoffage, door een goed Meester | *Mat:* op doek op paneel *Size:* hoog 24, breed 19 duim	D van der Aa [or] E B ten Dall	(Sold) fl 4.10 Zwartzman
1809/07/25	HGBSM	0257	*Een oud Meester* | Een rencontre van Cavallery, door een oud Meester | *Mat:* op paneel *Size:* hoog 18, breed 22 en een half duim	D van der Aa [or] E B ten Dall	(Sold) fl 2:8 van Ijperen [or] Stees
1809/07/25	HGBSM	0265	*Een goed Meester* | Rustende Jagers met Jagthonden en een doode Haas, fraay geschildert door een goed Meester | *Mat:* op doek op paneel *Size:* hoog 15, breed 18 duim	D van der Aa [or] E B ten Dall	(Sold) fl 1:14 van Zanten
1809/07/25	HGBSM	0267	*[Anonymous]* | Een Geharnast Vorst te Paard, fraai geschildert | *Mat:* op doek *Size:* hoog 35, breed 30 duim	D van der Aa [or] E B ten Dall	(Sold) fl 6:15 Bakhuyzen
1809/07/25	HGBSM	0271	*Een goed Meester* | Een Land- en Watergezigt, door een goed Meester | *Mat:* op paneel	D van der Aa [or] E B ten Dall	(Sold) fl 1:6 Bakhuyzen

1809/07/25	HGBSM	0273	*[Anonymous]* | Een Landschap daar een Stier vervolgd word | *Mat:* op paneel	D van der Aa [or] E B ten Dall	(Sold) fl 3:12 Bakhuyzen [or] Huisrand
1809/07/25	HGBSM	0275	*[Anonymous]* | Twee Landschapjes | *Mat:* op paneel	D van der Aa [or] E B ten Dall	(Sold) fl 1:18 Bakhuyzen
1809/07/25	HGBSM	0276	*[Anonymous]* | Een klein Landschapje | *Mat:* op koper	D van der Aa [or] E B ten Dall	(Sold) fl 1 Bogaard
1809/07/25	HGBSM	0284	*Een goed Meester* | Een Zomer- en Wintergezigt, door een goed Meester, op doek, twee stuks | *Mat:* op doek	D van der Aa [or] E B ten Dall	(Sold) fl 1:8 Zwarts
1809/07/25	HGBSM	0287	*[Anonymous]* | Twee dito Schoorsteen-Stukken, waar op een Papegaay | *Mat:* op doek *Notes:* It is unclear what "dito" refers to in the title.	D van der Aa [or] E B ten Dall	(Sold) fl 0:5 Rosier
1809/07/25	HGBSM	A0001[H]	*[Anonymous]* | [Untitled] | *Notes:* This lot was added in by hand in the NGW and RKDH copies of the catalogue, but without giving an artist or title. It has been renumbered to distinguish it from lot 1 in the printed section of the catalogue.	D van der Aa [or] E B ten Dall	(Sold) fl 1 De Gelder
1809/07/25	HGBSM	A0002[H]	*[Anonymous]* | [Untitled] | *Notes:* This lot was added in by hand in the NGW and RKDH copies of the catalogue, but without giving an artist or title. It has been renumbered to distinguish it from lot 2 in the printed section of the catalogue.	D van der Aa [or] E B ten Dall	(Sold) fl 6 De Gelder
1809/07/25	HGBSM	A0003[H]	*[Anonymous]* | [Untitled] | *Notes:* This lot was added in by hand in the NGW and RKDH copies of the catalogue, but without giving an artist or title. It has been renumbered to distinguish it from lot 3 in the printed section of the catalogue.	D van der Aa [or] E B ten Dall	(Sold) fl 1 De Gelder
1809/07/25	HGBSM	A0004[H]	*[Anonymous]* | [Untitled] | *Notes:* This lot was added in by hand in the NGW and RKDH copies of the catalogue, but without giving an artist or title. It has been renumbered to distinguish it from lot 4 in the printed section of the catalogue.	D van der Aa [or] E B ten Dall	(Sold) fl 0:12 Zwarts
1809/07/25	HGBSM	A0005[H]	*[Anonymous]* | [Untitled] | *Notes:* This lot was added in by hand in the NGW and RKDH copies of the catalogue, but without giving an artist or title. It has been renumbered to distinguish it from lot 5 in the printed section of the catalogue.	D van der Aa [or] E B ten Dall	(Sold) fl 3 De Gelder
1809/07/25	HGBSM	A0006[H]	*[Anonymous]* | [Untitled] | *Notes:* This lot was added in by hand in the NGW and RKDH copies of the catalogue, but without giving an artist or title. It has been renumbered to distinguish it from lot 6 in the printed section of the catalogue.	D van der Aa [or] E B ten Dall	(Sold) fl 2 van der Burgh
1809/07/25	HGBSM	A0007[H]	*[Anonymous]* | [Untitled] | *Notes:* This lot was added in by hand in the NGW and RKDH copies of the catalogue, but without giving an artist or title. It has been renumbered to distinguish it from lot 7 in the printed section of the catalogue.	D van der Aa [or] E B ten Dall	(Sold) fl 0:10 Zwarts
1809/07/25	HGBSM	A0008[H]	*[Anonymous]* | [Untitled] | *Notes:* This lot was added in by hand in the NGW and RKDH copies of the catalogue, but without giving an artist or title. It has been renumbered to distinguish it from lot 8 in the printed section of the catalogue.	D van der Aa [or] E B ten Dall	(Sold) fl 1:6 Stees
1809/07/25	HGBSM	A0009[H]	*[Anonymous]* | [Untitled] | *Notes:* This lot was added in by hand in the NGW and RKDH copies of the catalogue, but without giving an artist or title. It has been renumbered to distinguish it from lot 9 in the printed section of the catalogue.	D van der Aa [or] E B ten Dall	(Sold) fl 0:4 De Gelder
1809/07/25	HGBSM	A0010[H]	*[Anonymous]* | [Untitled] | *Notes:* This lot was added in by hand in the NGW and RKDH copies of the catalogue, but without giving an artist or title. It has been renumbered to distinguish it from lot 10 in the printed section of the catalogue.	D van der Aa [or] E B ten Dall	(Sold) fl 0:6 De Gelder
1809/07/25	HGBSM	A0011[H]	*[Anonymous]* | [Untitled] | *Notes:* This lot was added in by hand in the NGW and RKDH copies of the catalogue, but without giving an artist or title. It has been renumbered to distinguish it from lot 11 in the printed section of the catalogue.	D van der Aa [or] E B ten Dall	(Sold) fl 0:14 Stees
1809/07/25	HGBSM	A0012[H]	*[Anonymous]* | [Untitled] | *Notes:* This lot was added in by hand in the NGW and RKDH copies of the catalogue, but without giving an artist or title. It has been renumbered to distinguish it from lot 12 in the printed section of the catalogue.	D van der Aa [or] E B ten Dall	(Sold) fl 0:14 A Vermeulen
1809/07/25	HGBSM	A0013[H]	*[Anonymous]* | [Untitled] | *Notes:* This lot was added in by hand in the NGW and RKDH copies of the catalogue, but without giving an artist or title. It has been renumbered to distinguish it from lot 13 in the printed section of the catalogue.	D van der Aa [or] E B ten Dall	(Sold) fl 0:12 Pulver
1809/07/25	HGBSM	A0014[H]	*[Anonymous]* | [Untitled] | *Notes:* This lot was added in by hand in the NGW and RKDH copies of the catalogue, but without giving an artist or title. It has been renumbered to distinguish it from lot 14 in the printed section of the catalogue.	D van der Aa [or] E B ten Dall	(Sold) fl 1:14 van Dongen
1809/07/25	HGBSM	A0015[H]	*[Anonymous]* | [Untitled] | *Notes:* This lot was added in by hand in the NGW and RKDH copies of the catalogue, but without giving an artist or title. It has been renumbered to distinguish it from lot 15 in the printed section of the catalogue.	D van der Aa [or] E B ten Dall	(Sold) fl 1:2 van der Burgh
1809/07/25	HGBSM	A0016[H]	*[Anonymous]* | [Untitled] | *Notes:* This lot was added in by hand in the NGW and RKDH copies of the catalogue, but without giving an artist or	D van der Aa [or] E B ten Dall	(Sold) fl 10 De Gelder

			title. It has been renumbered to distinguish it from lot 16 in the printed section of the catalogue.		
1809/07/25	HGBSM	A0017[H]	*[Anonymous]* | [Untitled] | *Notes:* This lot was added in by hand in the NGW and RKDH copies of the catalogue, but without giving an artist or title. It has been renumbered to distinguish it from lot 17 in the printed section of the catalogue.	D van der Aa [or] E B ten Dall	(Sold) fl 0:4 Stees
1809/07/25	HGBSM	A0018[H]	*[Anonymous]* | [Untitled] | *Notes:* This lot was added in by hand in the NGW and RKDH copies of the catalogue, but without giving an artist or title. It has been renumbered to distinguish it from lot 18 in the printed section of the catalogue.	D van der Aa [or] E B ten Dall	(Sold) fl 0:2 Rosier
1809/07/25	HGBSM	A0019[H]	*[Anonymous]* | [Untitled] | *Notes:* This lot was added in by hand in the NGW and RKDH copies of the catalogue, but without giving an artist or title. It has been renumbered to distinguish it from lot 19 in the printed section of the catalogue.	D van der Aa [or] E B ten Dall	(Sold) fl 2:4 van Zanten
1809/10/16	ARNIJ	0002	*Een goed Meester* | Een Boeren binnen Huis met veel bijwerk door een goed Meester	Wed N Nijhoff	(Sold) fl 4:15 Daman
1809/10/16	ARNIJ	0003	*[Anonymous]* | Een fraaij Landschap met Beesten	Wed N Nijhoff	(Sold) fl 5:5 Daman
1809/10/16	ARNIJ	0006	*[Anonymous]* | Een vrolijke Wijndrinker met zijn pijp	Wed N Nijhoff	(Unknown) fl 2:10
1809/10/16	ARNIJ	0008a	*Een goed Meester* | Een Landschap van een goed Meester	Wed N Nijhoff	(Sold) fl 1 Enschut
1809/10/16	ARNIJ	0010	*Een goed Meester* | Een Landschap van een goed Meester	Wed N Nijhoff	(Sold) fl 1:15 Verniker
1809/10/16	ARNIJ	0011	*[Anonymous]* | Een dito [Landschap]	Wed N Nijhoff	(Sold) fl 0:8 Verniker
1809/10/16	ARNIJ	0014[H]	*[Anonymous]* | [Untitled] | *Notes:* This lot was added in by hand in the VBBA copy of the catalogue, but without giving an artist or title.	Wed N Nijhoff	(Sold) fl 0:7 for lots 14[H] & 15[H]. Daman
1809/10/16	ARNIJ	0015[H]	*[Anonymous]* | [Untitled] | *Notes:* This lot was added in by hand in the VBBA copy of the catalogue, but without giving an artist or title.	Wed N Nijhoff	(Sold) fl 0:7 for lots 14[H] & 15[H]. Daman
1809/10/16	ARNIJ	0016[H]	*[Anonymous]* | [Untitled] | *Notes:* This lot was added in by hand in the VBBA copy of the catalogue, but without giving an artist or title.	Wed N Nijhoff	(Sold) fl 0:3 for lots 16[H]-21[H]. Daman
1809/10/16	ARNIJ	0017[H]	*[Anonymous]* | [Untitled] | *Notes:* This lot was added in by hand in the VBBA copy of the catalogue, but without giving an artist or title.	Wed N Nijhoff	(Sold) fl 0:3 for lots 16[H]-21[H]. Daman
1809/10/16	ARNIJ	0018[H]	*[Anonymous]* | [Untitled] | *Notes:* This lot was added in by hand in the VBBA copy of the catalogue, but without giving an artist or title.	Wed N Nijhoff	(Sold) fl 0:3 for lots 16[H]-21[H]. Daman
1809/10/16	ARNIJ	0019[H]	*[Anonymous]* | [Untitled] | *Notes:* This lot was added in by hand in the VBBA copy of the catalogue, but without giving an artist or title.	Wed N Nijhoff	(Sold) fl 0:3 for lots 16[H]-21[H]. Daman
1809/10/16	ARNIJ	0020[H]	*[Anonymous]* | [Untitled] | *Notes:* This lot was added in by hand in the VBBA copy of the catalogue, but without giving an artist or title.	Wed N Nijhoff	(Sold) fl 0:3 for lots 16[H]-21[H]. Daman
1809/10/16	ARNIJ	0021[H]	*[Anonymous]* | [Untitled] | *Notes:* This lot was added in by hand in the VBBA copy of the catalogue, but without giving an artist or title.	Wed N Nijhoff	(Sold) fl 0:3 for lots 16[H]-21[H]. Daman
1809/10/16	ARNIJ	0023[H]	*[Anonymous]* | 6 Schilder[ijen] | *Notes:* This lot was added in by hand in the VBBA copy of the catalogue.	Wed N Nijhoff	(Sold or Bought In) fl 0:14
1809/10/16	ARNIJ	0024[H]	*[Anonymous]* | 6 d [Schilderijen] | *Notes:* This lot was added in by hand in the VBBA copy of the catalogue.	Wed N Nijhoff	(Sold or Bought In) fl 0:12
1809/10/16	ARNIJ	0025[H]	*[Anonymous]* | 6 d [Schilderijen] | *Notes:* This lot was added in by hand in the VBBA copy of the catalogue.	Wed N Nijhoff	(Sold or Bought In) fl 0:6
1809/10/19	HGBAK	0175	*[Anonymous]* | Twee Landschapjes	D van der Aa [or] P v d Heuvell	(Unknown)
1809/10/19	HGBAK	0176	*[Anonymous]* | Twee dito [Landschapjes]	D van der Aa [or] P v d Heuvell	(Unknown)
1809/10/19	HGBAK	0177	*[Anonymous]* | Ruïne van een Anticq Gebouw	D van der Aa [or] P v d Heuvell	(Unknown)
1809/10/19	HGBAK	0178	*[Anonymous]* | Een met Hoenderen	D van der Aa [or] P v d Heuvell	(Unknown)
1809/10/19	HGBAK	0180	*[Anonymous]* | Een Stieren gevegd	D van der Aa [or] P v d Heuvell	(Unknown)
1809/10/19	HGBAK	0181	*[Anonymous]* | Twee faaaye [sic] Bloemstukken in Glaase kassjes [sic]	D van der Aa [or] P v d Heuvell	(Unknown)
1809/10/20	UTWLD	0006	*[Anonymous]* | Een Keuken met een Keukenmeid en allerlei bywerk	J J van Rhyn	(Unknown)
1809/10/20	UTWLD	0018	*[Anonymous]* | Batseba, een brief bekomende, etc.	J J van Rhyn	(Unknown)
1809/10/20	UTWLD	0023	*[Anonymous]* | Een Heer de pyp aansteekende	J J van Rhyn	(Unknown)
1809/10/20	UTWLD	0025	*[Anonymous]* | Pourtrait van Petrus Hogerbeets	J J van Rhyn	(Unknown)
1809/10/20	UTWLD	0026	*[Anonymous]* | Een heilige familie	J J van Rhyn	(Unknown)
1809/10/20	UTWLD	0027	*[Anonymous]* | Een Mariabeeltje	J J van Rhyn	(Unknown)
1809/10/20	UTWLD	0028	*[Anonymous]* | Pourtrait van B. Bekker | *Mat:* op koper	J J van Rhyn	(Unknown)
1809/10/20	UTWLD	0029	*[Anonymous]* | Een Levantsche Zeehaven	J J van Rhyn	(Unknown)
1809/10/20	UTWLD	0034	*[Anonymous]* | Drie stuks met vogels	J J van Rhyn	(Unknown)

1809/10/20	UTWLD	0037	*[Anonymous]* | Pourtrait van G. de Vries en G. Voetius	J J van Rhyn	(Unknown)
1809/10/20	UTWLD	0038	*[Anonymous]* | Twee Pourtraitjes in lyst en glas	J J van Rhyn	(Unknown)
1809/10/20	UTWLD	0041	*[Anonymous]* | Twee dito [Landschappen]	J J van Rhyn	(Unknown)
1809/10/20	UTWLD	0043	*[Anonymous]* | Een Landschap met Olyverf op papier | *Mat:* in olyverf op papier	J J van Rhyn	(Unknown)
1809/10/20	UTWLD	0044	*[Anonymous]* | Een Scherm voor een Schoorsteen | *Notes:* It is uncertain whether this lot is a painting.	J J van Rhyn	(Unknown)
1810/02/28	RMBAA	0028	*[Anonymous]* | Een Schildery van de Molen de Valk, met de beschryving		(Unknown)
1810/03/07	UTWLD	0038	*[Anonymous]* | Een bloemstuk | *Size:* hoog 2 voet 6 duim, breed 2 voet 1 duim	J J Woertman	(Unknown) fl 2:4
1810/03/07	UTWLD	0046	*[Anonymous]* | Een zeer fraay Landschap, op de voorgrond een wit paard, en eenige rustende beelden | *Size:* hoog 1 voet 9 duim, breed 2 voet 1 duim	J J Woertman	(Unknown) fl 51
1810/03/07	UTWLD	0057	*[Anonymous]* | Een Bloemstuk	J J Woertman	(Unknown) fl 3
1810/03/07	UTWLD	0058	*[Anonymous]* | Zeven Pourtraiten, verbeeldende de Prinsen van Orange	J J Woertman	(Unknown) fl 28:10
1810/03/23	HAVIN	0030	*[Anonymous]* | De H. Famielie, door	Rudolf Hendrik de Wetstein [or others]	(Unknown)
1810/03/23	HAVIN	0031	*[Anonymous]* | Een Landschap, met een Hond en dood Wild, door	Rudolf Hendrik de Wetstein [or others]	(Unknown)
1810/03/23	HAVIN	0033	*[Anonymous]* | Een stille Zee, door	Rudolf Hendrik de Wetstein [or others]	(Unknown)
1810/03/23	HAVIN	0036	*[Anonymous]* | Een Stadgezigt, door	Rudolf Hendrik de Wetstein [or others]	(Unknown)
1810/03/23	HAVIN	0037	*[Anonymous]* | Een Juffer voor een Baluster, bij eenig geld, door	Rudolf Hendrik de Wetstein [or others]	(Unknown)
1810/03/23	HAVIN	0038	*[Anonymous]* | Een oud Man op 't Ledikant leggende een Naakt Meisje te verwagten, door	Rudolf Hendrik de Wetstein [or others]	(Unknown)
1810/03/23	HAVIN	0050	*[Anonymous]* | Twee met een doode Haas en Gevogelte, door	Rudolf Hendrik de Wetstein [or others]	(Unknown)
1810/03/23	HAVIN	0053	*[Anonymous]* | Twee Landschappen, door	Rudolf Hendrik de Wetstein [or others]	(Unknown)
1810/03/23	HAVIN	0054	*[Anonymous]* | Twee dito [Landschappen]	Rudolf Hendrik de Wetstein [or others]	(Unknown)
1810/03/23	HAVIN	0055	*[Anonymous]* | De Vrouw die haar dode Zoon aan de Propheet vertoond, door	Rudolf Hendrik de Wetstein [or others]	(Unknown)
1810/03/23	HAVIN	0056	*[Anonymous]* | Een Mans Pourtrait, leevensgroote, ten voeten uit	Rudolf Hendrik de Wetstein [or others]	(Unknown)
1810/03/23	HAVIN	0057	*[Anonymous]* | Twee stukken met dood Gevogelte	Rudolf Hendrik de Wetstein [or others]	(Unknown)
1810/03/23	HAVIN	0058	*[Anonymous]* | Een dito [stuk met dood Gevogelte]	Rudolf Hendrik de Wetstein [or others]	(Unknown)
1810/03/23	HAVIN	0059	*[Anonymous]* | Een Bergachtig Landschap	Rudolf Hendrik de Wetstein [or others]	(Unknown)
1810/03/23	HAVIN	0060	*[Anonymous]* | Een Binnenhuis, met een Gezelschap	Rudolf Hendrik de Wetstein [or others]	(Unknown)
1810/03/23	HAVIN	0067	*[Anonymous]* | Twee Landschappen [In Lysten met Glasen] | *Notes:* The bracketed information in the title appears above lot 63 and refers to lots 63 to 79.	Rudolf Hendrik de Wetstein [or others]	(Unknown)
1810/03/23	HAVIN	0068	*[Anonymous]* | Zeventien Pourtraiten uit den huize van Nassau [In Lysten met Glasen] | *Notes:* The bracketed information in the title appears above lot 63 and refers to lots 63 to 79.	Rudolf Hendrik de Wetstein [or others]	(Unknown)
1810/03/23	HAVIN	0069	*[Anonymous]* | Twee Geestelijke Geslagtlijsten [In Lysten met Glasen] | *Notes:* The bracketed information in the title appears above lot 63 and refers to lots 63 to 79.	Rudolf Hendrik de Wetstein [or others]	(Unknown)
1810/03/23	HAVIN	0071	*[Anonymous]* | Een Mans Pourtrait, levensgroote, ten voeten uit [In Lysten met Glasen] | *Notes:* The bracketed information in the title appears above lot 63 and refers to lots 63 to 79.	Rudolf Hendrik de Wetstein [or others]	(Unknown)
1810/03/23	HAVIN	0074	*[Anonymous]* | Een Meisje in een Venster [In Lysten met Glasen] | *Notes:* The bracketed information in the title appears above lot 63 and refers to lots 63 to 79.	Rudolf Hendrik de Wetstein [or others]	(Unknown)
1810/03/23	HAVIN	0079	*[Anonymous]* | Een dito [Landschap], door .... [In Lysten met Glasen] | *Notes:* The bracketed information in the title about the frame appears above lot 63 and refers to lots 63 to 79.	Rudolf Hendrik de Wetstein [or others]	(Unknown)
1810/03/26	RMMUY	0018	*Een onbekend Meester* | Een Landschap met Boomen, Struiken en Gebergte: op den voorgrond een waterval; stout en meesterlijk geschilderd [Un Paysage montagneux, une belle chute d'eau passe au travers ; d'un bon effet, et peint en maître.] | *Mat:* op doek *Size:* hoog 35, breed 49 duimen	Daniel de Jongh Az	(Sold) fl 15:5 L B van der Hoop

1810/03/26	RMMUY	0054	*[Anonymous]* | Een Sloot of Binnevliet aan een Dorp, en Ophaalbrug, met Schuiten en Figuren [La vue d'un Village, un pont-levis, un canal et quelques barques.] | *Annots:* Exp[?]... vanderner [i.e., Van der Neer] (BPG)	Daniel de Jongh Az	(Sold) fl 3:10 Doctor Luchtmans
1810/03/26	RMMUY	0057	*[Anonymous]* | In eenen Tempel of Kerker ziet men op den voorgrond een historieel onderwerp, verbeeldende de Gevangenis van Paulus; &c. Verdienstelijk geschilderd op koper [L'intérieur d'un Temple ; sur le devant quelques figures : sujet historique et representant l'emprisonnement de Saint Paul] | *Annots:* [par] Stenwyck [i.e., Steenwyck] (BPG) *Mat:* op koper	Daniel de Jongh Az	(Sold) fl 36 R Pott a Rott[m]
1810/03/26	RMMUY	0063	*[Anonymous]* | Eene Vrouw die haar gelaat met de handen dekt [Une Tête de Femme, se couvrant le visage de sa main.]	Daniel de Jongh Az	(Sold) fl 1 for lots 63 & 64. van der Giesen
1810/03/26	RMMUY	0064	*[Anonymous]* | Een Mans Pourtrait in Oud Hollandsch gewaad [Un Portrait d'Homme, costumé à la maniere ancienne d'Hollande.]	Daniel de Jongh Az	(Sold) fl 1 for lots 63 & 64. van der Giesen
1810/03/26	RMMUY	0065	*[Anonymous]* | Een Vrouwtje bij eenen Lantaarn, met eene brandende Kaars in de hand [Une Femme, avec une lanterne, tenant une chandelle à la main.]	Daniel de Jongh Az	(Sold) fl 1:6 for lots 65 & 66. van der Giesen
1810/03/26	RMMUY	0066	*[Anonymous]* | Een klein Mans Pourtraitje [Un petit Portrait] | *Annots:* drogue (BPG) *Mat:* op koper *Fmt:* ovaal	Daniel de Jongh Az	(Sold) fl 1:6 for lots 65 & 66. van der Giesen
1810/03/26	RMMUY	0071	*[Anonymous]* | Een Land- en Water Gezigt, met een menigte Watervogels, en in het verschiet een Eendekooi [Un Paysage, avec plusieurs oiseaux aquatiques ; dans le lointain un filet à canards.] | *Annots:* ... van Goyen (BPG) *Notes:* This lot was printed in the French edition of the catalogue as lot 72.	Daniel de Jongh Az	(Sold) fl 6:5 van Eyk s'Hage
1810/03/26	RMMUY	0075	*[Anonymous]* | Een klein Vrouwe Pourtraitje, hare handen te zamen houdende [Le Portrait d'une Femme, les mains jointes.] | *Annots:* tete de femme Brekelancamp (BPG) *Notes:* This lot was printed in the French edition of the catalogue as lot 76.	Daniel de Jongh Az	(Sold) fl 2 Le Brun Parys
1810/03/26	RMMUY	0078	*[Anonymous]* | Een Biddende Heilige. In het grauw [Un Saint en devotion, en camaieux.]	Daniel de Jongh Az	(Sold) fl 0:12 G C van Ryp
1810/03/26	RMMUY	0083	*[Anonymous]* | Een Italiaansch Hofgezigt en Gebouwen. In het midden eene springende Fontein en stoffagie [Plusieurs Batiments somptueux, formant une cour, au milieu une riche fontaine, avec figures.] | *Annots:* architecture blanche (BPG)	Daniel de Jongh Az	(Sold) fl 3:15 van der Giesen
1810/03/26	RMMUY	0088	*[Anonymous]* | Een bedaagd oud Man. Knie stukje [La Tête d'un Viellard, bien fini.] | *Annots:* Rickart [i.e., Ryckaert] un viellard (BPG)	Daniel de Jongh Az	(Sold) fl 6:15 van Eyk s'Hage
1810/03/27	RMCNL	0043	*[Anonymous]* | Eene Jagtpartij, met ziet een aanzienlijk gezelschap gereed ter Jagt te gaan, alles is in beweging en vol werking, zeer net en fraai van Penceel | *Mat:* op koper		(Unknown)
1810/03/27	RMCNL	0044	*[Anonymous]* | Een Landschapje, waarop men een wit Paardje ziet, aan eene Boomstronk bij eene Muur, bij uitnemenheid netjes gepenceeld		(Unknown)
1810/03/27	RMCNL	0061	*[Anonymous]* | Een Kapitaal Stuk, verbeeldende het doode Ligchaam van Christus in de armen van Maria, het gelaat van Maria, zeer kwijnend en vol uitdrukking, schoon geschilderd		(Unknown)
1810/03/27	RMCNL	0080	*[Anonymous]* | Een Binnenhuisje, waarin men een Boertje met eene Boerin vrolijk ziet stoeien		(Unknown)
1810/03/27	RMCNL	0094	*[Anonymous]* | Men ziet een Schilder in zijn Binnevertrek aan 't werk, op de Tafel het vermaarde Handekijkertje, mooi en fix geschildert		(Unknown)
1810/03/27	RMCNL	0097	*[Anonymous]* | Een Stukje, van de soorte bekend onder de naam van Vanitas		(Unknown)
1810/03/27	RMCNL	0099	*[Anonymous]* | Een Binnenhuisje, waarin men een Jongen aan zijne Moeder eten ziet vragen, zeer fix geschild		(Unknown)
1810/03/27	RMCNL	0103	*Een goed Meester* | Een dito [Boschachtig Landschap], door een goed Meester		(Unknown)
1810/03/27	RMCNL	0104	*Een goed Meester* | Een groot Paleis, door dito [een goed Meester]		(Unknown)
1810/03/27	RMCNL	0105	*Een goed Meester* | Een Batalje, door dito [een goed Meester]		(Unknown)
1810/03/27	RMCNL	0106	*Een goed Meester* | Twee Boere Huishoudens, door dito [een goed Meester]		(Unknown)
1810/04/17	MGBEO	0001	*Een goed Meester* | Een fraai Wintergezicht op doek, door een goed Meester | *Mat:* op doek	Mr J H Milet	(Sold) £ 0:1 van Benthem
1810/04/17	MGBEO	0002	*Een goed Meester* | Een fraai Dorpgezicht vol gewoel op paneel, door een goed Meester | *Mat:* op paneel	Mr J H Milet	(Sold) £ 0:1 van Benthem
1810/05/16	AMPOS	0001	*[Anonymous]* | 2 Landschapjes, in zwarte Lyst, met vergulde randen		(Unknown)
1810/05/16	AMPOS	0002	*[Anonymous]* | 2 stille Levens, met dito [vergulde randen]		(Unknown)
1810/05/16	AMPOS	0003	*Een goed Meester* | 1 Schilderstuk op Doek, door een goed Meester | *Mat:* op doek		(Unknown)
1810/05/16	AMPOS	0008	*[Anonymous]* | 5 stuks op Paneel, met vrolyke boeren, in zwarte Lysten met Glazen | *Mat:* op paneel		(Unknown)

1810/05/16	AMPOS	0040	*Een goed Meester* | 1 Schildery, zynde een Bergagtig Landschap, door een goed Meester		(Unknown)
1810/05/16	AMPOS	0046	*[Anonymous]* | 3 Bloemstukken | *Mat:* op doek		(Unknown)
1810/05/16	AMPOS	0047	*[Anonymous]* | 2 ovale Schilderytjes | *Fmt:* ovaal		(Unknown)
1810/05/16	AMPOS	0051	*[Anonymous]* | 6 diverse Schilderyen		(Unknown)
1810/05/22	AMSCH	0111a[H]	*[Anonymous]* | 1 dito [Schildery] | *Notes:* This lot was added in by hand in the EBNP copy of the catalogue.	S	(Sold) fl 24:10 T Spaan
1810/05/22	AMSCH	0133	*[Anonymous]* | Een bevrozen Rivier, ter zijde Boeren Woningen, Hooiberg en Geboomte, gestoffeerd met Schaatsenrijders; natuurlijk behandeld op Paneel | *Mat:* op paneel	R	(Sold) fl 14:10 Yver
1810/05/22	AMSCH	0134	*[Anonymous]* | Een aangenaam Landschap, rijk gestoffeerd met twee Heeren te paard, een Koets men zes Paarden bespannen en grazende Bokken en Schaapen; zonachtig en uitvoerig op Paneel geschilderd | *Mat:* op paneel	R	(Sold) fl 6:5 du Pree
1810/05/22	AMSCH	0138	*[Anonymous]* | Een Landschap met Ruïne, gestoffeerd met eene Vrouw, zittende op een Ezel; fiks op Koper geschilderd | *Mat:* op koper	Johannes van de Putte Nicolaasz.	(Sold) fl 1:5 Levij Pakker
1810/05/22	AMSCH	0139	*[Anonymous]* | Een Duitsch Landschap, gestoffeerd met een beladen Wagen met vier Paarden bespannen, Reizigers enz.; fiks geschilderd	Johannes van de Putte Nicolaasz.	(Sold) fl 10 Boelhouwer
1810/05/22	AMSCH	0140	*[Anonymous]* | Een stil Water; met Schepen en Sloepen gestoffeerd	Johannes van de Putte Nicolaasz.	(Sold) fl 1:10 Topher
1810/05/22	AMSCH	0142	*[Anonymous]* | Twee stuks met Bloemen | *Mat:* op doek	Johannes van de Putte Nicolaasz.	(Sold) fl 3:15 du Pree
1810/05/22	AMSCH	0145[a]	*[Anonymous]* | Een Bergachtig Landschap, op den voorgrond met Watervallen, verder eenige Beeldjes; natuurlijk behandeld, op Doek en een Brand in een Dorp met Woningen, door van der Poel, op Paneel, 2 stuks | *This Lot:* Een Bergachtig Landschap, op den voorgrond met Watervallen, verder eenige Beeldjes; lot 145[b] by E. Poel *Mat:* op doek	D	(Sold) fl 2:5 for lots 145[a] & 145[b]. du Pree
1810/05/22	AMSCH	0147	*[Anonymous]* | Twee stuks diversche Landschappen; met verschillende stoffagie | *Notes:* This lot was sold with lot 148, which is in the manner of Backhuysen.	D	(Sold) fl 1:10 for lots 147 & 148. Topher
1810/05/22	AMSCH	0149	*[Anonymous]* | Een Boomrijk Landschap bij een opgaande Weg, in 't verschiet eenige Gebouwen; meesterlijk behandeld | *Mat:* op paneel	D	(Sold) fl 4:5 Rinkhuyzen
1810/05/22	AMSCH	0150	*Een goed Meester* | Twee stuks Stil-levens; door een goed Meester | *Mat:* op paneel	R	(Sold) fl 1 Geld
1810/05/22	AMSCH	0156	*[Anonymous]* | Twee stuks, Zomer en Winter, beide eigenaartig gestoffeerd en fiks geschilderd	F	(Sold) fl 2 Yver
1810/05/22	AMSCH	0157[a]	*[Anonymous]* | Drie stuks, zijnde het eene een Boeren-Barbier, op Paneel, en de twee anderen Binnenkamers met drinkende en liefkozende Heeren en Dames, op Doek | *This Lot:* Een Boeren-Barbier *Mat:* op paneel	Y[ver]	(Sold) fl 2 for lots 157[a] & 157[b]. Geld
1810/05/22	AMSCH	0157[b]	*[Anonymous]* | Drie stuks, zijnde het eene een Boeren-Barbier, op Paneel, en de twee anderen Binnenkamers met drinkende en liefkozende Heeren en Dames, op Doek | *This Lot:* Binnenkamers met drinkende en liefkozende Heeren en Dames *Mat:* op doek	Y[ver]	(Sold) fl 2 for lots 157[a] & 157[b]. Geld
1810/05/22	AMSCH	0158	*[Anonymous]* | Een proper van Maghonyhout gewerkt Kasje, met twee Deurtjes, tot berging van een Schilderij | *Notes:* This lot was sold with lot 7 by P. Brussel.	Johannes van de Putte Nicolaasz.	(Sold) fl 41 for lots 7 & 158. Twisk [?]
1810/05/22	AMSCH	0159[H]	*[Anonymous]* | [Untitled] | *Notes:* This lot was added in by hand in the EBNP copy of the catalogue, but without giving an artist or title.	S	(Sold) fl 1 Levij Pakker
1810/05/22	AMSCH	0160[H]	*[Anonymous]* | [Untitled] | *Notes:* This lot was added in by hand in the EBNP copy of the catalogue, but without giving an artist or title.	S	(Sold) fl 1 Claus Scholten
1810/05/22	AMSCH	0161[H]	*[Anonymous]* | [Untitled] | *Notes:* This lot was added in by hand in the EBNP copy of the catalogue, but without giving an artist or title.	Johannes van de Putte Nicolaasz.	(Bought In) fl 32
1810/05/22	AMSCH	0162[H]	*[Anonymous]* | [Untitled] | *Notes:* This lot was added in by hand in the EBNP copy of the catalogue, but without giving an artist or title.	Johannes van de Putte Nicolaasz.	(Sold) fl 1:15 T Spaan
1810/05/22	AMSCH	0163[H]	*[Anonymous]* | [Untitled] | *Notes:* This lot was added in by hand in the EBNP copy of the catalogue, but without giving an artist or title.	D	(Sold) fl 9:5 Gruiter
1810/05/22	AMSCH	0164[H]	*[Anonymous]* | [Untitled] | *Notes:* This lot was added in by hand in the EBNP copy of the catalogue, but without giving an artist or title.	S	(Sold) fl 3 Gruiter
1810/05/22	AMSCH	0165[H]	*[Anonymous]* | [Untitled] | *Notes:* This lot was added in by hand in the EBNP copy of the catalogue, but without giving an artist or title.	S	(Sold) fl 2:5 Gruiter
1810/05/22	AMSCH	0166[H]	*[Anonymous]* | [Untitled] | *Notes:* This lot was added in by hand in the EBNP copy of the catalogue, but without giving an artist or title.	S	(Sold) fl 6:10 Gruiter
1810/05/22	AMSCH	0167[H]	*[Anonymous]* | [Untitled] | *Notes:* This lot was added in by hand in the EBNP copy of the catalogue, but without giving an artist or title.	S	(Sold) fl 4 Gruiter
1810/05/22	AMSCH	0168[H]	*[Anonymous]* | [Untitled] | *Notes:* This lot was added in by hand in the EBNP copy of the catalogue, but without giving an artist or title.	S	(Sold) fl 6 Gruiter
1810/05/22	AMSCH	0169[H]	*[Anonymous]* | [Untitled] | *Notes:* This lot was added in by hand in the EBNP copy of the catalogue, but without giving an artist or title.	S	(Sold) fl 6 Gruiter

1810/05/22	AMSCH	0170[H]	*[Anonymous]* | [Untitled] | *Notes:* This lot was added in by hand in the EBNP copy of the catalogue, but without giving an artist or title.	S	(Sold) fl 2:15 Gruiter
1810/05/22	AMSCH	0171[H]	*[Anonymous]* | [Untitled] | *Notes:* This lot was added in by hand in the EBNP copy of the catalogue, but without giving an artist or title.	S	(Sold) fl 3 du Pree
1810/05/22	AMSCH	0172[H]	*[Anonymous]* | [Untitled] | *Notes:* This lot was added in by hand in the EBNP copy of the catalogue, but without giving an artist or title.	S	(Sold) fl 2:5 du Pree
1810/05/22	AMSCH	0173[H]	*[Anonymous]* | [Untitled] | *Notes:* This lot was added in by hand in the EBNP copy of the catalogue, but without giving an artist or title.	Johannes van de Putte Nicolaasz.	(Sold) fl 1:10 Gruiter
1810/06/04	DOBRA	0005	*[Anonymous]* | Een Wintergezigt met Schaatsryders	Hendrik de Haas	(Unknown)
1810/06/04	DOBRA	0012	*[Anonymous]* | Een Italiaansch Landschap, met Beesten en Visschers	Hendrik de Haas	(Unknown)
1810/06/04	DOBRA	0015	*[Anonymous]* | Een Kermis met een Kwakzalver	Hendrik de Haas	(Unknown)
1810/06/04	DOBRA	0018	*[Anonymous]* | Een Watertje	Hendrik de Haas	(Unknown)
1810/06/06	RMMUY	0061	*[Anonymous]* | Eene Wedergade, in alles als de voorgaande | companion to lot 60 *Mat:* op paneel *Notes:* This lot was sold with lot 60 by Bredael or Brueghel.		(Unknown) fl 14:10 for lots 60 & 61
1810/06/06	RMMUY	0063	*[Anonymous]* | Eene Wedergade, in alles als de voorgaande | companion to lot 62 *Mat:* op paneel *Notes:* This lot was sold with lot 62 by Bredael.		(Unknown) fl 29:5 for lots 62 & 63
1810/06/06	RMMUY	0077	*Een goed Meester* | Een boschrijk Landschap, fraaij gestoffeerd met eene drift Koebeesten. Door een goed Meester | *Mat:* op doek		(Unknown) fl 16
1810/06/06	RMMUY	0085	*Een oud meester* | Loth met zijne Dochters, levensgroote beelden ten voeten uit. Door een oud meester | *Mat:* op doek		(Sold) fl 7:5 Luchtmans
1810/06/06	RMMUY	0091	*[Anonymous]* | Maria, het Kindje, en Joseph. Bevallig geschilderd | *Mat:* op doek		(Unknown) fl 2
1810/06/06	RMMUY	0093	*[Anonymous]* | Eene Vrouw in Boetvaardige houding, goed van uitdrukking en behandeling | *Mat:* op doek		(Unknown) fl 3
1810/06/06	RMMUY	0108	*[Anonymous]* | Een Man met een Rommelpot en verdere Figuren aan de deur, verzeld van een Hond, uitvoerig en natuurlijk | *Mat:* op paneel		(Unknown) fl 9
1810/06/06	RMMUY	0110	*[Anonymous]* | Eene Wedergade, in alles als de vorige behandeld | companion to lot 109, by Nickelen *Mat:* op doek *Notes:* This lot was sold with lot 109 by Nickelen.		(Sold) fl 68 for lots 109 & 110. V Eyk
1810/06/06	RMMUY	0120	*[Anonymous]* | In een Binnenhuis zit eene Vrouw, een kind drinken gevende, verder eenig bijwerk. Meesterlijk behandeld | *Mat:* op paneel		(Unknown) fl 2
1810/06/06	RMMUY	0131	*[Anonymous]* | Twee stuks met Bloemen | *Mat:* op doek		(Unknown) fl 3:2
1810/06/06	RMMUY	0132	*[Anonymous]* | Twee kloeke Bloem en Fruitstukken. Meesterlijk behandeld | *Mat:* op doek		(Unknown) fl 2:5
1810/06/06	RMMUY	0141	*[Anonymous]* | Een Aanbidding der Herders. Meesterlijk geschilderd | *Mat:* op doek		(Sold) fl 11:5 Brunelli
1810/06/06	RMMUY	0153	*[Anonymous]* | Een Landschap, op den voorgrond eene zittende Dame die een Citroen aanbied, aan een voor haar staand Jager, verzeld door Honden, Wild &c. goed en meesterlijk geschilderd | *Mat:* op doek		(Unknown) fl 1:6
1810/06/06	RMMUY	0155	*Een oud meester* | Een Kampement, eene Stad in 't verschiet; op den voorgrond een man op de Lier spelende, waar bij eenig Krijgsvolk. Op Koper. Door een oud meester | *Mat:* op koper		(Unknown) fl 4:2
1810/06/06	RMMUY	0163	*[Anonymous]* | Een Boertje met een Pijp in de hand. Rond formaat | *Mat:* op paneel *Fmt:* rond		(Unknown) fl 1
1810/06/06	RMMUY	0181	*[Anonymous]* | Eenige Bloemen in een Fles | companion to lot 182 *Mat:* op doek		(Unknown) fl 1 for lots 181 & 182
1810/06/06	RMMUY	0182	*[Anonymous]* | Een dito [Bloemen in een Fles] Wedergade | companion to lot 181 *Mat:* op doek		(Unknown) fl 1 for lots 181 & 182
1810/06/06	RMMUY	0189	*[Anonymous]* | Het Pourtrait van Leo de X. | *Mat:* op paneel		(Unknown) fl 0:10
1810/06/06	RMMUY	0191	*[Anonymous]* | Eene Woelende Zee | *Mat:* op paneel		(Unknown) fl 1:4
1810/06/06	RMMUY	0192	*[Anonymous]* | Een Jongetje met een koek in de hand | *Mat:* op paneel		(Unknown) fl 0:8
1810/06/06	RMMUY	0202	*[Anonymous]* | Een dito [Basrelief], zijnde een Zinnebeeld van Vrede en Vrijheid, regtschen dag | *Mat:* op doek *Size:* hoog 4 voet 5 duim, breed 3 voet 9 duim		(Unknown) fl 3
1810/06/06	RMMUY	0211	*[Anonymous]* | Een fraaij Landschap met Koeijen, Schapen &c. | *Mat:* op paneel		(Unknown) fl 1:10
1810/06/06	RMMUY	0215	*[Anonymous]* | Een Landschap | *Mat:* op paneel *Notes:* This lot was sold with lot 214, which is in the manner of Ostade.		(Unknown) fl 1:4 for lots 214 & 215
1810/06/06	RMMUY	0216	*[Anonymous]* | Een Mans Pourtrait | *Notes:* This lot was sold with lot 217, which is a watercolor copy after Wouwerman.		(Unknown) fl 1:10 for lots 216 & 217
1810/06/06	RMMUY	0218	*Een Oud Meester* | Het pourtrait van Erasmus, zeer fraaij. Door een oud Meester, op Paneel, rond format | *Mat:* op paneel *Fmt:* rond		(Unknown) fl 8:10
1810/06/06	RMMUY	0223	*Een goed Meester* | Een stuk met dood gevogelte. Door een goed Meester | *Mat:* op doek		(Unknown) fl 4:15

1810/06/06	RMMUY	0224	*[Anonymous]* | Eene Polierster met meer bijwerk, fraaij geschilderd | *Mat:* op doek		(Unknown) fl 1:4
1810/06/06	RMMUY	0225	*[Anonymous]* | Twee Stil Levens | *Mat:* op paneel		(Unknown) fl 1:4
1810/06/06	RMMUY	0229	*[Anonymous]* | Een Boere Kermis | *Mat:* op doek		(Unknown) fl 3:10
1810/06/06	RMMUY	0234	*[Anonymous]* | Drie opgerolde Schilderijen		(Unknown) fl 1:2
1810/06/20	AMSCH	0112	*Een oud Meester* | Eene Geestelijke Ordonnantie, voorstellende Maria met het Kindje, waarbij twee Godvruchtige Vrouwen. Krachtig op paneel, door een oud Meester | *Mat:* op paneel	N	(Sold) fl 51 Coclers
1810/06/20	AMSCH	0118	*[Anonymous]* | Een gezigt op de Montalbaans Toren te Amsterdam, natuurlijk geschilderd	N	(Sold) fl 2:10 T Spaan
1810/06/20	AMSCH	0122	*Een goed Meester* | Eene Vischvrouw, door een goed Meester	N	(Sold) fl 1 L Pakker
1810/06/20	AMSCH	0124	*[Anonymous]* | Eene Zee met Schepen	N	(Sold) fl 0:6 L Pakker
1810/06/20	AMSCH	0124a[H]	*[Anonymous]* | 1 Schilderij | *Notes:* This lot was added in by hand in the AA and EBNP copies of the catalogue.	N	(Sold) fl 1 L Pakker
1810/06/20	AMSCH	0127	*[Anonymous]* | Een Vischboer, met een Kan in de hand	X	(Sold) fl 1 Pantijn
1810/06/20	AMSCH	0129	*[Anonymous]* | De Wijzen uit het Oosten, hunne Geschenken brengende aan het Kind Jezus; zijnde alleruitmuntendst geschilderd in den Jare 1517 | *Inscr:* 1517 (dated)	X	(Sold) fl 42 Pantijn
1810/06/20	AMSCH	0132	*[Anonymous]* | Het Pourtrait van Maria de Medicis; goed geschilderd	S	(Sold) fl 1 L Pakker
1810/06/20	AMSCH	0136	*[Anonymous]* | Een Dorp, vol gewoel van vrolijke Lieden, zoo Mannen als Vrouwen. Geestig geschilderd | *Mat:* op doek	S	(Sold) fl 2:5 Van Dijl
1810/06/20	AMSCH	0139	*[Anonymous]* | Twee stuks Schoorsteenstukken	S	(Sold) fl 0:12 W v d Schleij
1810/06/20	AMSCH	0144	*[Anonymous]* | Twee stuks met Beelden, geestig | *Mat:* op doek	B	(Sold) fl 0:16 Focken
1810/06/20	AMSCH	0145	*[Anonymous]* | Twee stuks Landschappen, met stoffage	B	(Sold) fl 0:6 L Pakker
1810/06/20	AMSCH	0148	*Een goed Meester* | Een Mans Pourtraitje, door een goed Meester	B	(Sold) fl 0:6 L Pakker
1810/06/20	AMSCH	0152	*[Anonymous]* | Een Porceleinen Schaal met uitmuntende Vruchten, fiks behandeld | *Mat:* op paneel	B	(Sold) fl 0:12 Andriessen
1810/06/20	AMSCH	0154	*Een goed Meester* | Twee stuks, een Oud Mans en een Vrouwepourtrait, door een goed Meester	B	(Sold) fl 0:6 de Vries
1810/06/20	AMSCH	0159[b]	*[Anonymous]* | Twee stuks, een Strandgezigt, door Smit, en een Vrouwtje bij het Kaarslicht | *This Lot:* Een Vrouwtje bij het Kaarslicht; lot 159[a] by Aernout Smit	B	(Sold) fl 0:14 for lots 159[a] & 159[b]. L Pakker
1810/06/20	AMSCH	0161	*[Anonymous]* | Een Wintergezigt, rijk gestoffeerd met Schaatzerijders, Kolvers en Arresleden; fiks geschilderd	A	(Sold) fl 2 Yver
1810/06/20	AMSCH	0162	*[Anonymous]* | In eene Herberg zitten eenige Lieden zich bij een Kagchel te warmen, achterwaards andere bij eene Tafel. Kloek op doek geschilderd | *Mat:* op doek	A	(Sold) fl 4 van Iperen
1810/06/20	AMSCH	0165	*[Anonymous]* | Voor een Buitenhuis ziet men twee Jagers met hunne Honden; verder een Huisman met een Paard	A	(Sold) fl 1:15 J Stam
1810/06/20	AMSCH	0171	*[Anonymous]* | Vier verschillende Schilderijen en twee ledige Lijsten	A	(Sold) fl 0:10 L Pakker
1810/06/20	AMSCH	0172	*[Anonymous]* | Een Landschap met Gebouwen, Beelden enz.	A	(Sold) fl 2 Geld
1810/06/20	AMSCH	0176	*[Anonymous]* | Een Landschap met Ruine en stoffagie van Beelden	A	(Sold) fl 2 L Pakker
1810/06/20	AMSCH	0177	*[Anonymous]* | Een Landschap met Beelden en Beesten gestoffeerd	A	(Sold) fl 2:5 Gruiter
1810/06/20	AMSCH	0178	*Een Oud Meester* | Eene Ordonantie van drie Beelden, door een Oud Meester	A	(Sold) fl 0:10 L Pakker
1810/06/20	AMSCH	0181	*[Anonymous]* | Een Duitsch Landschap, met Woningen, Geboomte en stoffage van Beeldjes	A	(Sold) fl 2:15 Yver
1810/06/20	AMSCH	0182	*[Anonymous]* | Een Binnenhuis met twee Boeren	A	(Sold) fl 1:15 J Stam
1810/06/20	AMSCH	0183	*[Anonymous]* | Een Binnenvertrek, waarin een Vrouwtje bezig Kant te werken	A	(Sold) fl 2:15 Eekhof
1810/06/20	AMSCH	0185	*[Anonymous]* | Een Strandgezigt, met Visschers en Vaartuigen gestoffeerd	A	(Sold) fl 3:5 Koopman
1810/06/20	AMSCH	0186	*[Anonymous]* | Een Binnenhuis, waarin een Boeren Huisgezin, zittende bij eene Tafel	A	(Sold) fl 3:10 J Stam
1810/07/23	DOLGI	0067	*[Anonymous]* | De Bekering van Paulus. Krachtig en stout van behandeling | *Mat:* op doek *Size:* hoog 61, breed 83 duim	Mr Pieter van den Santheuvel	(Sold) fl 12 van Eijk 's Hage
1810/07/23	DOLGI	0071	*[Anonymous]* | De Zondvloed; goed geschilderd | *Mat:* op paneel *Size:* hoog 11 ½, breed 20 duim	Mr Pieter van den Santheuvel	(Sold) fl 6:10 J de Visser
1810/07/23	DOLGI	0072	*[Anonymous]* | Een Boomrijk Landschapje, met Beesten en Beeldtjes | *Mat:* op paneel *Size:* hoog 13, breed 16 ½ duim	Mr Pieter van den Santheuvel	(Sold) fl 3 Spruijt van Gent
1810/07/23	DOLGI	0075	*[Anonymous]* | Een Bloemstukje	Mr Pieter van den Santheuvel	(Sold) fl 0:10 Hey Dordt
1810/07/23	DOLGI	0076	*[Anonymous]* | Een dito [Bloemstukje]	Mr Pieter van den Santheuvel	(Sold) fl 2 [or] 8 v d Einden

1810/07/23	DOLG1	0078	*[Anonymous]* | Een Bosch met Harten	Mr Pieter van den Santheuvel	(Sold) fl 1:10 Spruijt v Gent
1810/07/23	DOLG1	0079	*[Anonymous]* | Een Fruitstuk	Mr Pieter van den Santheuvel	(Sold) fl 1:10 [or] 0:10 A v Stry
1810/07/23	DOLG1	0080	*[Anonymous]* | Een Schaking	Mr Pieter van den Santheuvel	(Sold) fl 1:10 Nieuwenhuisen
1810/07/23	DOLG1	0081	*[Anonymous]* | Een Rhijngezicht	Mr Pieter van den Santheuvel	(Sold) fl 1:10 A v Stry
1810/07/23	DOLG1	0082	*[Anonymous]* | De Afbeelding van een Eendekooi	Mr Pieter van den Santheuvel	(Sold) fl 1:6 J de Gelder
1810/07/23	DOLG2	0002	*Een goed Meester* | Een zinnebeeldige ordonnantie, door verscheiden Beelden uitgedrukt; door een goed Meester | *Mat:* op doek *Size:* hoog 44, breed 66 duim	Pieter Quinting	(Unknown) fl 2:12
1810/07/23	DOLG2	0003	*[Anonymous]* | De Schaking van Europa; stout en goed geschilderd | *Mat:* op doek *Size:* hoog 48, breed 66 duim	Pieter Quinting	(Unknown) fl 2
1810/07/23	DOLG2	0004	*[Anonymous]* | Bij een Tafel, waar op eenige bijzondere soorten van Vruchten, vertoont zich een Vrouw, met haar arm leunende op een koperen Marktëmmer. Benevens haar staat een Jongen. Meesterlijk geschilderd | *Mat:* op doek *Size:* hoog 42, breed 61 duim	Pieter Quinting	(Unknown) fl 1:16
1810/07/23	DOLG2	0005	*[Anonymous]* | De Historie van Esau en Jakob; meesterlijk en krachtig geteekend en geschilderd | *Mat:* op doek *Size:* hoog 35, breed 58 duim	Pieter Quinting	(Sold) fl 3 A v Stry
1810/07/23	DOLG2	000A	*[Anonymous]* | Een Riviergezicht langs de Stad Dordrecht, met verscheiden Vaartuigen | *Mat:* op doek *Size:* hoog 33, breed 39 duim	Pieter Quinting	(Unknown) fl 2:14
1810/07/23	DOLG2	000C	*[Anonymous]* | Een deur stuk, met Chineesche Beelden | *Mat:* op doek *Size:* hoog 29, breed 72 duim	Pieter Quinting	(Unknown)
1810/07/23	DOLG2	000E	*Een goed meester* | Een Basrelief, door een goed meester | *Mat:* op doek *Size:* Hoog 55, breed 40 duim	Pieter Quinting	(Unknown)
1810/07/23	DOLG2	000H	*[Anonymous]* | Een Bloemstuk | *Mat:* op doek *Size:* hoog 39, breed 58 duim	Pieter Quinting	(Unknown) fl 0:6
1810/07/23	DOLG2	000I	*[Anonymous]* | Een Zinnebeeldige Ordonnantie; in het verschiet ziet men den Haag	Pieter Quinting	(Sold) fl 1:10 Visser
1810/07/23	DOLG2	000K	*[Anonymous]* | Een Landschap met Beesten en Beelden	Pieter Quinting	(Unknown) fl 1:10
1810/07/23	DOLG2	000M	*[Anonymous]* | Een Schoorsteenstuk, met Chineesche Beelden | *Mat:* op doek *Fmt:* schoorsteenstuk *Size:* hoog 77, breed 46 duim	Pieter Quinting	(Unknown)
1810/07/23	DOLG2	000N	*[Anonymous]* | Twee deur Stukken, in 't grauw	Pieter Quinting	(Sold) fl 0:6 A v Strij
1810/07/23	DOLG2	000O	*[Anonymous]* | Een Wijnkelder, van binnen te zien, waar in een Man bezig is flesschen te stoppen	Pieter Quinting	(Unknown) fl 3
1810/07/23	DOLG2	000P	*[Anonymous]* | Een Gevecht van Paardevolk	Pieter Quinting	(Unknown) fl 1
1810/07/23	DOLG2	000Q	*[Anonymous]* | Een Jongen met een Rommel Pot	Pieter Quinting	(Unknown)
1810/07/23	DOLG2	000T	*[Anonymous]* | De vier Euangelisten [sic], zittende, aan een tafel, in hunne boeken te schrijven. Men ziet den Engel, den Leeuw, enz., en verdere verbeeldingen, eigen aan deze Personaadjen. Alles meesterlijk en stout uitgebeeld. Hoog 57, Breed 84 Duim. Om de grootte kan het Raam toegeslagen, en de Lijst uit elkander genomen worden | *Size:* hoog 57, breed 84 duim	Pieter Quinting	(Sold) fl 8 A v Strij
1810/07/23	DOLG2	0014	*[Anonymous]* | Een Doctor, zittende voor eene tafel, bezig zijnde Pis te bekijken. Nevens en rondom hem vertonen zich een menigte Beelden, en Werktuigen, aan deze konst eigen. Fix geschilderd | *Mat:* op doek	Pieter Quinting	(Sold) fl 2 Makai a Dordt
1810/07/23	DOLG2	0015	*[Anonymous]* | In denzelfden smaak en ordonnantie, wordt er verbeeld een Barrebiers [sic] Winkel. Niet minder behandeld dan het voorgaande | *Mat:* op doek *Size:* hoog 26, breed 32 duim	Pieter Quinting	(Sold) fl 2:10 Makai
1810/07/23	DOLG2	0019	*[Anonymous]* | Twee witte Eenden, bij een water, levens grootte | *Mat:* op doek *Size:* hoog 23, breed 31 duim	Pieter Quinting	(Unknown) fl 1:12
1810/07/23	DOLG2	0023	*[Anonymous]* | Een Schoolvrouw, met een aantal Kinderen; aardig verbeeld | *Mat:* op paneel *Size:* hoog 16, breed 19 duim	Pieter Quinting	(Unknown)
1810/07/23	DOLG2	0024	*[Anonymous]* | Een Grot, van binnen te zien, waar in zich vertonen eenige oude gedenkstukken; krachtig geschilderd | *Mat:* op paneel *Size:* hoog 21, breed 29 duim	Pieter Quinting	(Sold) fl 2:15 Visser
1810/07/23	DOLG2	0025	*[Anonymous]* | Een Bergachtig Landschap, gestoffeerd met Beeldtjes en Beestjes; krachtig en zonnig gedaagd | *Mat:* op doek *Size:* hoog 19, breed 22 duim	Pieter Quinting	(Sold) fl 10 Spruyt van Gent
1810/07/23	DOLG2	0026	*[Anonymous]* | Een Slapende Venus | *Mat:* op doek *Size:* hoog 22, breed 48 duim	Pieter Quinting	(Unknown)
1810/07/23	DOLG2	0030	*[Anonymous]* | Op een steenen voet ligt een doode Patrijs, een Putter en Ijsvogel. Breed behandeld | *Mat:* op doek *Size:* hoog 18, breed 19 duim	Pieter Quinting	(Unknown)
1810/07/23	DOLG2	0032	*[Anonymous]* | Een woelend water met eenige Schepen; lustig gepenseeld | *Mat:* op paneel *Size:* hoog 18, breed 24 duim	Pieter Quinting	(Unknown) fl 1:5

1810/07/23	DOLG2	0033	*[Anonymous]* | Een oude geleerde, in zijn Boekenkamer; krachtig geschilderd | *Mat:* op paneel *Size:* hoog 21, breed 18 duim	Pieter Quinting	(Unknown)
1810/07/23	DOLG2	0037	*[Anonymous]* | Een Schilder voor zijn Ezel, krachtig geschilderd | *Mat:* op paneel *Size:* hoog 16, breed 14 duim	Pieter Quinting	(Sold) fl 1:4 J Meurrens
1810/07/23	DOLG2	0039	*[Anonymous]* | Een Bloem- en Fruit Stuk, met veel Insekten versierd; goed geschilderd | *Mat:* op doek *Size:* hoog 16, breed 15 duim	Pieter Quinting	(Unknown) fl 1
1810/07/23	DOLG2	0041	*[Anonymous]* | Eenige Beeldtjens, drinkende, rookende en spelende | *Mat:* op paneel *Size:* hoog 14, breed 10 duim	Pieter Quinting	(Unknown)
1810/07/23	DOLG2	0042	*[Anonymous]* | Een Boeren Binnenhuis, vrolijk behandeld | *Mat:* op paneel *Size:* hoog 17, breed 25 duim	Pieter Quinting	(Sold) fl 4:5 van der Hegge
1810/07/23	DOLG2	0045	*[Anonymous]* | Een Wintergezicht met Schepen, verlicht door de Maan | *Mat:* op paneel *Size:* hoog 17, breed 23 duim	Pieter Quinting	(Unknown) fl 1:10
1810/07/23	DOLG2	0047	*[Anonymous]* | Twee Zeegezichten, met zeer veele Schepen | *This Lot:* Een Zeegezicht, met zeer vele Schepen *Notes:* Lots 47 and 48 were printed in the catalogue as one item.	Pieter Quinting	(Unknown)
1810/07/23	DOLG2	0048	*[Anonymous]* | Twee Zeegezichten, met zeer veele Schepen | *This Lot:* Een Zeegezicht, met zeer veele Schepen *Notes:* Lots 47 and 48 were printed in the catalogue as one item.	Pieter Quinting	(Unknown)
1810/07/23	DOLG2	0058	*[Anonymous]* | Een zeer wel uitgevoerd Schilderij, met Bloemen | *Mat:* op paneel *Size:* hoog 18, breed 15 duim	Pieter Quinting	(Sold) fl 3 Schalk
1810/07/23	DOLG2	0061	*[Anonymous]* | Een Kwakzalver en verscheiden Beeldtjes | *Mat:* op paneel *Size:* hoog 15, breed 18 duim	Pieter Quinting	(Unknown)
1810/07/23	DOLG2	0062	*[Anonymous]* | Een vrolijk Gezelschap, koddig verbeeld | *Mat:* op paneel	Pieter Quinting	(Unknown) fl 1:15
1810/07/23	DOLG2	0066	*[Anonymous]* | Een Binnenvertrek met Beeldtjes | *Mat:* op paneel *Size:* hoog 12, breed 13 duim	Pieter Quinting	(Unknown)
1810/07/23	DOLG2	0069	*[Anonymous]* | Een Boomrijk Landschap, fix gepenseeld | *Mat:* op paneel *Size:* hoog 12, breed 17 duim	Pieter Quinting	(Unknown) fl 3:10
1810/07/23	DOLG2	0070	*[Anonymous]* | Een Wintergezicht | *Mat:* op paneel *Size:* hoog 11, breed 13 duim	Pieter Quinting	(Unknown) fl 2
1810/07/23	DOLG2	0071	*[Anonymous]* | Een dito [Wintergezicht]	Pieter Quinting	(Unknown)
1810/07/23	DOLG2	0073	*[Anonymous]* | Een Zeeslag; stout behandeld | *Mat:* op paneel *Size:* hoog 12, breed 17 duim	Pieter Quinting	(Unknown)
1810/07/23	DOLG2	0074	*[Anonymous]* | Een Kwakzalver,bezig een man zijn tant uit den mond te trekken; breed en wel geschilderd | *Mat:* op paneel *Size:* hoog 12, breed 11 duim	Pieter Quinting	(Sold) fl 1:15 A van Strij
1810/07/23	DOLG2	0078	*[Anonymous]* | Een oude Vrouw die Pap zit te eten | *Mat:* op paneel *Size:* hoog 12, breed 10 duim	Pieter Quinting	(Unknown)
1810/07/23	DOLG2	0082	*[Anonymous]* | Een Doctor in zijn kamer | *Mat:* op paneel *Size:* hoog 10, breed 8 duim	Pieter Quinting	(Unknown)
1810/07/23	DOLG2	0084	*[Anonymous]* | Een woelend Water; ovaal formaat | *Mat:* op paneel *Fmt:* ovaal *Size:* hoog 11, breed 16 duim	Pieter Quinting	(Unknown) fl 8
1810/07/23	DOLG2	0085	*[Anonymous]* | Een oude Vrouw, met een Jongen | *Mat:* op paneel *Size:* hoog 8, breed 6 duim	Pieter Quinting	(Unknown)
1810/07/23	DOLG2	0086	*[Anonymous]* | Een Boer, wien een Heelmeester een pleister op het been legt | *Mat:* op paneel *Size:* hoog 12, breed 11 duim	Pieter Quinting	(Unknown)
1810/07/23	DOLG2	0088	*[Anonymous]* | Een Landschap, door een Brabandsch Meester | *Mat:* op paneel *Size:* hoog 9, breed 11 duim	Pieter Quinting	(Unknown) fl 0:16
1810/07/23	DOLG2	0089	*[Anonymous]* | Een Wintergezicht | *Mat:* op paneel *Size:* hoog 9, breed 11 duim	Pieter Quinting	(Unknown) fl 16
1810/07/23	DOLG2	0093	*[Anonymous]* | Een Jongen, met een Vogelnestje | *Mat:* op paneel *Size:* hoog 10, breed 9 duim	Pieter Quinting	(Unknown)
1810/07/23	DOLG2	0094	*[Anonymous]* | Een Landschapje | *Mat:* op paneel *Size:* hoog 7, breed 8 duim	Pieter Quinting	(Unknown)
1810/07/23	DOLG2	0096	*[Anonymous]* | Een Landschapje | *Mat:* op paneel	Pieter Quinting	(Unknown)
1810/07/23	DOLG2	0097	*[Anonymous]* | Een Maneschijn	Pieter Quinting	(Unknown)
1810/07/23	DOLG2	0098	*[Anonymous]* | Een doode Geestelijke; zeer uitvoerig; op Koper geschilderd | *Mat:* op koper	Pieter Quinting	(Unknown)
1810/07/23	DOLG2	0099	*[Anonymous]* | Een Oudenmans-Hoofdtje	Pieter Quinting	(Unknown)
1810/07/23	DOLG2	00MM[H]	*[Anonymous]* | Een varken op de Leer | *Notes:* This lot was added in by hand in the RKDH copy of the catalogue.	Pieter Quinting	(Sold) fl 37 P de Heere
1810/07/23	DOLG2	0102	*[Anonymous]* | Ganymedes op den Arend	Pieter Quinting	(Unknown)
1810/07/26	AMSCH	0095	*[Anonymous]* | De Heilige Famielje. Fraai op albast geschilderd | *Mat:* op albast	Cassino	(Sold) fl 5:5 Spaan
1810/07/26	AMSCH	0097	*[Anonymous]* | Een Italiaansch Landschap | *Mat:* op doek	Cassino	(Sold) fl 2:15 van Dijl
1810/07/26	AMSCH	0098	*[Anonymous]* | Twee kleine Landschapjes, door een onbekend Meester	Cassino	(Sold) fl 2 Dupré

1810/07/26	AMSCH	0100	*[Anonymous]* | Susanna in den Hof, waarbij de twee Grijsaards. Krachtig | *Mat:* op paneel	Cassino	(Sold) fl 1 Haring
1810/07/26	AMSCH	0102	*[Anonymous]* | Een Landschap, met Beelden enz. Zeer fraai geschilderd	Cassino	(Bought In) fl 1:5
1810/07/26	AMSCH	0103	*[Anonymous]* | Een Landschap, met Gebouwen, Geboomte enz.	Cassino	(Bought In) fl 0:16
1810/07/26	AMSCH	0104	*[Anonymous]* | De maagd Maria, houdende het Kind Jesus in hare armen. Meesterlijk geschilderd	Cassino	(Sold) fl 7:10 Spaan
1810/07/26	AMSCH	0106	*[Anonymous]* | Eene kabbelende Zee, met een brandend Schip. Kloek geschilderd	Cassino	(Sold) fl 4:10 van Iperen
1810/07/26	AMSCH	0107	*[Anonymous]* | Drie Persoonen, die Muziceeren. Zijnde een zeer schoon stuk	Cassino	(Bought In) fl 1:10
1810/07/26	AMSCH	0108	*[Anonymous]* | Een Boomrijk Landschap, met een Herder en Schapen gestoffeerd	Cassino	(Sold) fl 0:6 Lohuijs
1810/07/26	AMSCH	0109	*[Anonymous]* | Twee kleine Landschapjes	Cassino	(Sold) fl 0:6 Yver
1810/07/26	AMSCH	0115	*[Anonymous]* | Een Groep van drie Ruiters	Cassino	(Sold) fl 1:5 L Pakker
1810/07/26	AMSCH	0117	*Een goed Meester* | Een dito [Landschap], door een goed Meester	Cassino	(Sold) fl 0:12 Yver
1810/07/26	AMSCH	0118	*[Anonymous]* | Een klein Landschapje	Cassino	(Sold) fl 1:5 L Pakker
1810/07/26	AMSCH	0119	*[Anonymous]* | Een Landschap, met Figuren	Cassino	(Sold) fl 0:12 van Iperen
1810/07/26	AMSCH	0120[a]	*[Anonymous]* | Twee kleine stukjes, een op Koper, en een op Paneel | *This Lot:* Een kleine stukje *Mat:* op koper	Cassino	(Sold) fl 2:10 for lots 120[a] & 120[b]. Dupree
1810/07/26	AMSCH	0120[b]	*[Anonymous]* | Twee kleine stukjes, een op Koper, en een op Paneel | *This Lot:* Een kleine stukje *Mat:* op paneel	Cassino	(Sold) fl 2:10 for lots 120[a] & 120[b]. Dupree
1810/07/26	AMSCH	0121	*[Anonymous]* | Een Landschap, gestoffeerd met een hevig Gevegt. Zynde schoon zamengesteld	Cassino	(Sold) fl 5:10 Dupré
1810/07/26	AMSCH	0123	*[Anonymous]* | Een hevige Storm in een Landschap. Schoon geschilderd	Cassino	(Bought In) fl 0:10
1810/07/26	AMSCH	0124	*[Anonymous]* | Twee kleine Landschapjes	Cassino	(Bought In) fl 1:5
1810/07/26	AMSCH	0125	*[Anonymous]* | Drie kleine Schilderijtjes, met Beelden. Zeer uitvoerig en fraai op Koper geschilderd | *Mat:* op koper	Cassino	(Sold) fl 5:5 Geld
1810/07/26	AMSCH	0126	*[Anonymous]* | Een stuk met Vrugten en Vogels	Cassino	(Sold) fl 0:16 Geld
1810/07/26	AMSCH	0128	*[Anonymous]* | Een klein Landschapje | *Mat:* op paneel	Cassino	(Sold) fl 0:8 Geld
1810/07/26	AMSCH	0129	*[Anonymous]* | Eene Historieele Ordonantie | *Annots:* Jeronimo (EBNP)	Cassino	(Sold) fl 0:10 L Pakker
1810/07/26	AMSCH	0131	*[Anonymous]* | Christus aan het Kruis. Goed geschilderd | *Mat:* op paneel	Cassino	(Bought In) fl 2
1810/07/26	AMSCH	0147	*[Anonymous]* | Een Landschap, gestoffeerd met de Fabel-Historie van Angelika en Medor, verder een vliegende Kupido. Zeer fraai geschilderd | *Mat:* op doek *Size:* hoog 17, breed 24 duim	Cassino	(Bought In) fl 4:15
1810/07/26	AMSCH	0148	*[Anonymous]* | Joseph vlugtende van Potiphars Huisvrouw. Fraai geschilderd | *Mat:* op doek *Size:* hoog 25, breed 16 duim	Cassino	(Bought In) fl 6
1810/07/26	AMSCH	0149	*[Anonymous]* | Narsissus, zittende aan de kant van een helder Water. Goed geschilderd	Cassino	(Sold) fl 2 T Spaan
1810/08/01	AMSCH	0130	*[Anonymous]* | Een Wolf, verscheurende eenen Haan; ter zijde een blaffende Hond [Representation d'un Loup, devorant un Agneau ; un Chien aboyant est vû sur le côté] | *Mat:* op doek *Size:* hoog 25, breed 66 duimen	Mr Pieter de Smeth van Alphen	(Sold) fl 20 Dupré
1810/08/06	AMSCH	0137	*[Anonymous]* | Een heuvelachtig Landschap, met verscheide Officieren te Paard, bij Soetelaars-Tenten en op den voorgrond speelende Kinderen; bevallig op Paneel geschilderd | *Mat:* op paneel	C	(Sold) fl 20 Texier Gerbet en Comp [for] Lebrun
1810/08/06	AMSCH	0144	*[Anonymous]* | Het dito [Pourtret] van Willem den Tweeden	F	(Sold) fl 0:10 de Vries
1810/08/06	AMSCH	0145	*[Anonymous]* | Een Paus met zijn Kroon op het Hoofd	F	(Sold) fl 6 Josi
1810/08/06	AMSCH	0148	*Een goed Meester* | Een Land- en Watergezigt, door een goed Meester	G	(Sold) fl 1 L Pakker
1810/08/06	AMSCH	0150	*Een oud Meester* | De Voorstelling van het laatste Oordeel, vol hartstocht en uitdrukking, door een oud Meester	V[ries]	(Sold) fl 7:10 L Pakker
1810/08/06	AMSCH	0153	*[Anonymous]* | Twee kleine Beestendrifjes; natuurlijk geschilderd	V[ries]	(Sold) fl 2:5 Stoopendaal
1810/08/06	AMSCH	0154	*[Anonymous]* | Een Jood aan eenige Jongelieden Eijeren en Zuur verkopende, bij Kaarslicht	V[ries]	(Sold) fl 2:5 van Iperen
1810/08/06	AMSCH	0156[H]	*[Anonymous]* | Een stuk | *Notes:* This lot was added in by hand in the EBNP copy of the catalogue.	S[paan]	(Sold) fl 15 Coclers
1810/08/06	AMSCH	0157[H]	*[Anonymous]* | Een stuk | *Notes:* This lot was added in by hand in the EBNP copy of the catalogue.	V[ries]	(Sold) fl 15 M Maas
1810/08/06	AMSCH	0158[H]	*[Anonymous]* | Twee stuks | *Notes:* This lot was added in by hand in the EBNP copy of the catalogue.	V[ries]	(Bought In) fl 3

1810/08/06	AMSCH	0159[H]	*[Anonymous]* | Een stuk | *Notes:* This lot was added in by hand in the EBNP copy of the catalogue.	V[ries]	(Sold) fl 5:10 Roelsma
1810/08/06	AMSCH	0160[H]	*[Anonymous]* | Een stuk | *Notes:* This lot was added in by hand in the EBNP copy of the catalogue.	S[paan]	(Bought In) fl 36
1810/08/06	AMSCH	0161[H]	*[Anonymous]* | Een stuk | *Notes:* This lot was added in by hand in the EBNP copy of the catalogue.	J	(Sold) fl 42 Cassano
1810/08/06	AMSCH	0162[H]	*[Anonymous]* | Een stuk | *Notes:* This lot was added in by hand in the EBNP copy of the catalogue.	J	(Sold) fl 22:10 Burtin
1810/08/06	AMSCH	0163[H]	*[Anonymous]* | Een stuk | *Notes:* This lot was added in by hand in the EBNP copy of the catalogue.	J	(Sold) fl 90 Texier
1810/08/06	AMSCH	0164[H]	*[Anonymous]* | Twee stuks | *Annots:* 2 Italien (BPG) *Notes:* This lot was added in by hand in the EBNP copy of the catalogue.	J	(Sold) fl 1 Hulswit
1810/08/06	AMSCH	0165[H]	*[Anonymous]* | Drie Stuks | *Annots:* 3 Portraits (BPG) *Notes:* This lot was added in by hand in the EBNP copy of the catalogue.	J	(Sold) fl 25 T Spaan
1810/08/06	AMSCH	0166[H]	*[Anonymous]* | Een stuk | *Notes:* This lot was added in by hand in the EBNP copy of the catalogue.	J	(Sold) fl 0:10 L Pakker
1810/08/06	AMSCH	0167[H]	*[Anonymous]* | Een stuk | *Notes:* This lot was added in by hand in the EBNP copy of the catalogue.	J	(Sold) fl 3 L Pakker
1810/08/06	AMSCH	0168[H]	*[Anonymous]* | Een stuk | *Annots:* deschat Renard (BPG) *Notes:* This lot was added in by hand in the EBNP copy of the catalogue.	J	(Sold) fl 3:15 Royers
1810/08/06	AMSCH	0169[H]	*[Anonymous]* | Een stuk | *Notes:* This lot was added in by hand in the EBNP copy of the catalogue.	J	(Withdrawn)
1810/08/06	AMSCH	0170[H]	*[Anonymous]* | Een Stuk | *Annots:* Maas [i.e., Maes] Portrait 8 ½ (BPG) *Notes:* This lot was added in by hand in the EBNP copy of the catalogue.	J	(Sold) fl 19:10 Gruiter
1810/08/06	AMSCH	0171[H]	*[Anonymous]* | Een stuk | *Notes:* This lot was added in by hand in the EBNP copy of the catalogue.	J	(Sold) fl 22 Hulswit
1810/08/06	AMSCH	0172[H]	*[Anonymous]* | Een stuk | *Notes:* This lot was added in by hand in the EBNP copy of the catalogue.	J	(Sold) fl 16 van Iperen
1810/08/06	AMSCH	0173[H]	*[Anonymous]* | Een stuk | *Notes:* This lot was added in by hand in the EBNP copy of the catalogue.	D	(Bought In) fl 8:10
1810/08/06	AMSCH	0174[H]	*[Anonymous]* | Een stuk | *Notes:* This lot was added in by hand in the EBNP copy of the catalogue.	D	(Sold) fl 41 van Leen
1810/08/06	AMSCH	0175[H]	*[Anonymous]* | Een stuk | *Notes:* This lot was added in by hand in the EBNP copy of the catalogue.	D	(Sold) fl 40 Texier
1810/08/06	AMSCH	0176[H]	*[Anonymous]* | Een stuk | *Notes:* This lot was added in by hand in the EBNP copy of the catalogue.	D	(Bought In) fl 14:10
1810/08/06	AMSCH	0177[H]	*[Anonymous]* | Een stuk | *Annots:* portrait (BPG) *Notes:* This lot was added in by hand in the EBNP copy of the catalogue.	D	(Sold) fl 0:14 L Pakker
1810/08/06	AMSCH	0178[H]	*[Anonymous]* | Een stuk | *Annots:* Lepn[?] (BPG) *Notes:* This lot was added in by hand in the EBNP copy of the catalogue.	D	(Sold) fl 0:6 L Pakker
1810/08/06	AMSCH	0179[H]	*[Anonymous]* | Een stuk | *Notes:* This lot was added in by hand in the EBNP copy of the catalogue.	S[paan]	(Bought In) fl 2
1810/08/06	AMSCH	0180[H]	*[Anonymous]* | Een stuk | *Notes:* This lot was added in by hand in the EBNP copy of the catalogue.	S[paan]	(Sold) fl 0:6 Westenberg
1810/08/06	AMSCH	0181[H]	*[Anonymous]* | Een stuk | *Notes:* This lot was added in by hand in the EBNP copy of the catalogue.	J	(Sold) fl 60 Roelsma
1810/08/06	AMSCH	0182[H]	*[Anonymous]* | Een stuk | *Notes:* This lot was added in by hand in the EBNP copy of the catalogue.	J	(Sold) fl 110 Texier
1810/08/06	AMSCH	0183[H]	*[Anonymous]* | Een stuk | *Notes:* This lot was added in by hand in the EBNP copy of the catalogue.	D	(Bought In) fl 91
1810/08/06	AMSCH	0184[H]	*[Anonymous]* | Een stuk | *Notes:* This lot was added in by hand in the EBNP copy of the catalogue.	D	(Unknown)
1810/08/06	AMSCH	0185[H]	*[Anonymous]* | Een stuk | *Annots:* Copie Bool [i.e., Boel?] (BPG) *Notes:* This lot was added in by hand in the EBNP copy of the catalogue.	D	(Sold) fl 10 Coclers
1810/08/06	AMSCH	0186[H]	*[Anonymous]* | Een stuk | *Notes:* This lot was added in by hand in the EBNP copy of the catalogue.	D	(Sold) fl 6:15 L^y Pakker
1810/08/06	AMSCH	0187[H]	*[Anonymous]* | Een stuk | *Notes:* This lot was added in by hand in the EBNP copy of the catalogue.	D	(Sold) fl 6 T Spaan
1810/08/06	AMSCH	0188[H]	*[Anonymous]* | Een stuk | *Notes:* This lot was added in by hand in the EBNP copy of the catalogue.	D	(Bought In) fl 25
1810/08/06	AMSCH	0189[H]	*[Anonymous]* | Twee stuks | *Notes:* This lot was added in by hand in the EBNP copy of the catalogue.	S[paan]	(Sold) fl 2:5 Texier [for] LeBrn
1810/08/06	AMSCH	0190[H]	*[Anonymous]* | Een stuk | *Annots:* Cop[ie] Salome (BPG) *Notes:* This lot was added in by hand in the EBNP copy of the catalogue.	S[paan]	(Sold) fl 1 du Pree
1810/08/06	AMSCH	0191[H]	*[Anonymous]* | Een stuk | *Annots:* Vierge (BPG) *Notes:* This lot was added in by hand in the EBNP copy of the catalogue.	D	(Bought In) fl 5

1810/08/06	AMSCH	0192[H]	*[Anonymous]* | Een stuk | *Notes:* This lot was added in by hand in the EBNP copy of the catalogue.	S[paan]	(Sold or Bought In) fl 10 T Spaan
1810/08/06	AMSCH	0193[H]	*[Anonymous]* | Een stuk | *Notes:* This lot was added in by hand in the EBNP copy of the catalogue.	S[paan]	(Sold or Bought In) fl 12:10 T Spaan
1810/08/06	AMSCH	0194[H]	*[Anonymous]* | Een stuk | *Notes:* This lot was added in by hand in the EBNP copy of the catalogue.	S[paan]	(Sold or Bought In) fl 15:10 Spaan T
1810/08/06	AMSCH	0195[H]	*[Anonymous]* | Een stuk | *Notes:* This lot was added in by hand in the EBNP copy of the catalogue.	R[oos]	(Sold) fl 18 Dupré
1810/08/06	AMSCH	0196[H]	*[Anonymous]* | Een stuk | *Notes:* This lot was added in by hand in the EBNP copy of the catalogue.	S[paan]	(Sold) fl 2:15 van Iperen
1810/08/06	AMSCH	0197[H]	*[Anonymous]* | Twee stuks | *Notes:* This lot was added in by hand in the EBNP copy of the catalogue.	V[ries]	(Sold) fl 1 L^{y} Pakker
1810/08/06	AMSCH	0197a[H]	*[Anonymous]* | Een stuk | *Notes:* This lot was added in by hand in the EBNP copy of the catalogue.	S[paan]	(Sold) fl 15 Jozi [for] Bertin
1810/08/06	AMSCH	0198[H]	*[Anonymous]* | Een stuk | *Notes:* This lot was added in by hand in the EBNP copy of the catalogue.	Q	(Sold) fl 21 T Spaan
1810/08/06	AMSCH	0199[H]	*[Anonymous]* | Een stuk | *Notes:* This lot was added in by hand in the EBNP copy of the catalogue.	Q	(Sold) fl 1:15 L Pakker
1810/08/06	AMSCH	0200[H]	*[Anonymous]* | Een stuk | *Notes:* This lot was added in by hand in the EBNP copy of the catalogue.	Q	(Sold) fl 15:10 Roelsma
1810/08/06	AMSCH	0201[H]	*[Anonymous]* | Een stuk | *Notes:* This lot was added in by hand in the EBNP copy of the catalogue.	Q	(Sold) fl 12 Gruiter
1810/08/06	AMSCH	0202[H]	*[Anonymous]* | Een stuk | *Notes:* This lot was added in by hand in the EBNP copy of the catalogue.	Q	(Sold) fl 7 Coclers
1810/08/06	AMSCH	0203[H]	*[Anonymous]* | Een stuk | *Notes:* This lot was added in by hand in the EBNP copy of the catalogue.	Q	(Sold) fl 4:10 Fokke
1810/08/06	AMSCH	0204[H]	*[Anonymous]* | Een stuk | *Notes:* This lot was added in by hand in the EBNP copy of the catalogue.	Q	(Sold) fl 6 van Leen
1810/08/06	AMSCH	0205[H]	*[Anonymous]* | Een stuk | *Notes:* This lot was added in by hand in the EBNP copy of the catalogue.	Q	(Sold) fl 19:10 van Iperen
1810/08/06	AMSCH	0206[H]	*[Anonymous]* | Een stuk | *Notes:* This lot was added in by hand in the EBNP copy of the catalogue.	Q	(Sold) fl 8 Texier
1810/08/06	AMSCH	0207[H]	*[Anonymous]* | Een stuk | *Notes:* This lot was added in by hand in the EBNP copy of the catalogue.	Q	(Sold) fl 4:15 Dupré
1810/08/06	AMSCH	0208[H]	*[Anonymous]* | Een stuk | *Notes:* This lot was added in by hand in the EBNP copy of the catalogue.	Q	(Sold) fl 1:5 van Vlymen [or] Coclers
1810/08/06	AMSCH	0209[H]	*[Anonymous]* | Een stuk | *Notes:* This lot was added in by hand in the EBNP copy of the catalogue.	Q	(Sold) fl 28 van Leen
1810/08/06	AMSCH	0210[H]	*[Anonymous]* | Een stuk | *Notes:* This lot was added in by hand in the EBNP copy of the catalogue.	Q	(Sold) fl 2 L Pakker
1810/08/06	AMSCH	0211[H]	*[Anonymous]* | Een stuk | *Notes:* This lot was added in by hand in the EBNP copy of the catalogue.	Q	(Bought In) fl 6
1810/08/06	AMSCH	0212[H]	*[Anonymous]* | Een stuk | *Notes:* This lot was added in by hand in the EBNP copy of the catalogue.	Q	(Sold) fl 1 J Spaan
1810/08/06	AMSCH	0213[H]	*[Anonymous]* | Een stuk | *Notes:* This lot was added in by hand in the EBNP copy of the catalogue.	Q	(Sold) fl 4:15 Fokke
1810/08/06	AMSCH	0214[H]	*[Anonymous]* | Een stuk | *Notes:* This lot was added in by hand in the EBNP copy of the catalogue.	Q	(Sold) fl 1:10 L Pakker
1810/08/06	AMSCH	0215[H]	*[Anonymous]* | Een stuk | *Notes:* This lot was added in by hand in the EBNP copy of the catalogue.	Q	(Sold) fl 21 Coclers
1810/08/06	AMSCH	0216[H]	*[Anonymous]* | Een stuk | *Notes:* This lot was added in by hand in the EBNP copy of the catalogue.	J	(Sold) fl 4 L Pakker
1810/08/06	AMSCH	0217[H]	*[Anonymous]* | Een stuk | *Notes:* This lot was added in by hand in the EBNP copy of the catalogue.	J	(Sold) fl 12:10 Pot
1810/08/06	AMSCH	0218[H]	*[Anonymous]* | Een stuk | *Notes:* This lot was added in by hand in the EBNP copy of the catalogue.	J	(Sold) fl 8:10 van Leen
1810/08/06	AMSCH	0219[H]	*[Anonymous]* | Een stuk | *Notes:* This lot was added in by hand in the EBNP copy of the catalogue.	J	(Bought In) fl 14
1810/08/06	AMSCH	0220[H]	*[Anonymous]* | Een stuk | *Notes:* This lot was added in by hand in the EBNP copy of the catalogue.	J	(Bought In) fl 10
1810/08/06	AMSCH	0221[H]	*[Anonymous]* | Een stuk | *Notes:* This lot was added in by hand in the EBNP copy of the catalogue.	J	(Sold) fl 30 Texier
1810/08/06	AMSCH	0222[H]	*[Anonymous]* | Een stuk | *Notes:* This lot was added in by hand in the EBNP copy of the catalogue.	J	(Sold) fl 30 Roelsma
1810/08/06	AMSCH	0223[H]	*[Anonymous]* | Een stuk | *Notes:* This lot was added in by hand in the EBNP copy of the catalogue.	D	(Sold) fl 10 Roelsma

1810/08/06	AMSCH	0224[H]	*[Anonymous]* | Een stuk | *Notes:* This lot was added in by hand in the EBNP copy of the catalogue.	D	(Bought In) fl 14
1810/08/06	AMSCH	0225[H]	*[Anonymous]* | Een stuk | *Notes:* This lot was added in by hand in the EBNP copy of the catalogue.	D	(Sold) fl 0:14 L Pakker
1810/08/06	AMSCH	0226[H]	*[Anonymous]* | Een stuk | *Notes:* This lot was added in by hand in the EBNP copy of the catalogue.	D	(Sold) fl 0:10 L Pakker
1810/08/06	AMSCH	0227[H]	*[Anonymous]* | Een stuk | *Notes:* This lot was added in by hand in the EBNP copy of the catalogue.	D	(Sold) fl 1:10 Gruiter
1810/08/06	AMSCH	0228[H]	*[Anonymous]* | Een stuk | *Notes:* This lot was added in by hand in the EBNP copy of the catalogue.	D	(Sold) fl 2:5 Pakker
1810/08/06	AMSCH	0229[H]	*[Anonymous]* | Een stuk | *Notes:* This lot was added in by hand in the EBNP copy of the catalogue.	D	(Sold) fl 7 Hodges
1810/08/06	AMSCH	0230[H]	*[Anonymous]* | Een stuk | *Notes:* This lot was added in by hand in the EBNP copy of the catalogue.	D	(Sold) fl 6:10 L Pakker
1810/08/06	AMSCH	0231[H]	*[Anonymous]* | Een stuk | *Notes:* This lot was added in by hand in the EBNP copy of the catalogue.	D	(Sold) fl 2:15 Dupré
1810/08/06	AMSCH	0232[H]	*[Anonymous]* | Twee stuks | *Notes:* This lot was added in by hand in the EBNP copy of the catalogue.	S[paan]	(Sold) fl 0:8 van Iperen
1810/08/06	AMSCH	0233[H]	*[Anonymous]* | Een stuk | *Notes:* This lot was added in by hand in the EBNP copy of the catalogue.	S[paan]	(Sold) fl 2 Texier
1810/08/06	AMSCH	0234[H]	*[Anonymous]* | Een stuk | *Notes:* This lot was added in by hand in the EBNP copy of the catalogue.	S[paan]	(Sold) fl 0:6 L Pakker
1810/08/06	AMSCH	0235[H]	*[Anonymous]* | Een stuk | *Notes:* This lot was added in by hand in the EBNP copy of the catalogue.	S[paan]	(Sold) fl 1:15 Dupré
1810/08/06	AMSCH	0236[H]	*[Anonymous]* | Een stuk | *Notes:* This lot was added in by hand in the EBNP copy of the catalogue.	D	(Sold) fl 0:6 for lots 236[H] & 237[H]. L Pakker
1810/08/06	AMSCH	0237[H]	*[Anonymous]* | Een stuk | *Notes:* This lot was added in by hand in the EBNP copy of the catalogue.	D	(Sold) fl 0:6 for lots 236[H] & 237[H]. L Pakker
1810/08/06	AMSCH	0238[H]	*[Anonymous]* | Een stuk | *Notes:* This lot was added in by hand in the EBNP copy of the catalogue.	D	(Sold) fl 50 Pot
1810/08/06	AMSCH	0239[H]	*[Anonymous]* | Een stuk | *Notes:* This lot was added in by hand in the EBNP copy of the catalogue.	D	(Sold) fl 20 Texier
1810/08/06	AMSCH	0240[H]	*[Anonymous]* | Een stuk | *Notes:* This lot was added in by hand in the EBNP copy of the catalogue.	D	(Bought In) fl 48
1810/08/06	AMSCH	0241[H]	*[Anonymous]* | Een stuk | *Notes:* This lot was added in by hand in the EBNP copy of the catalogue.	D	(Bought In) fl 9:10
1810/08/06	AMSCH	0242[H]	*[Anonymous]* | Een stuk | *Notes:* This lot was added in by hand in the EBNP copy of the catalogue.	D	(Sold) fl 20 Roelsma
1810/08/06	AMSCH	0243[H]	*[Anonymous]* | Een stuk | *Notes:* This lot was added in by hand in the EBNP copy of the catalogue.	D	(Sold) fl 0:12 Gruiter
1810/08/06	AMSCH	0244[H]	*[Anonymous]* | Vier stuks | *Notes:* This lot was added in by hand in the EBNP copy of the catalogue.	S[paan]	(Sold) fl 3:5 Fokke
1810/08/06	AMSCH	0245[H]	*[Anonymous]* | Twee stuks | *Notes:* This lot was added in by hand in the EBNP copy of the catalogue.	S[paan]	(Sold) fl 12 Texier
1810/08/06	AMSCH	0246[H]	*[Anonymous]* | Een stuk | *Notes:* This lot was added in by hand in the EBNP copy of the catalogue.	S[paan]	(Sold) fl 8:10 Texier
1810/08/06	AMSCH	0247[H]	*[Anonymous]* | Een stuk | *Notes:* This lot was added in by hand in the EBNP copy of the catalogue.	S[paan]	(Sold) fl 5 Burtin
1810/08/06	AMSCH	0248[H]	*[Anonymous]* | Een stuk | *Notes:* This lot was added in by hand in the EBNP copy of the catalogue.	S[paan]	(Sold) fl 1:10 Burtin
1810/08/06	AMSCH	0249[H]	*[Anonymous]* | Een stuk | *Notes:* This lot was added in by hand in the EBNP copy of the catalogue.	S[paan]	(Sold) van Iperen
1810/08/06	AMSCH	0250[H]	*[Anonymous]* | Een stuk | *Notes:* This lot was added in by hand in the EBNP copy of the catalogue.	S[paan]	(Sold) fl 3:15 Maas
1810/08/06	AMSCH	0251[H]	*[Anonymous]* | Een stuk | *Notes:* This lot was added in by hand in the EBNP copy of the catalogue.	S[paan]	(Sold) fl 3:10 J Spaan
1810/08/06	AMSCH	0252[H]	*[Anonymous]* | Een stuk | *Notes:* This lot was added in by hand in the EBNP copy of the catalogue.	S[paan]	(Sold) fl 14:10 Cramer
1810/08/06	AMSCH	0253[H]	*[Anonymous]* | Een stuk | *Notes:* This lot was added in by hand in the EBNP copy of the catalogue.	S[paan]	(Bought In) fl 12
1810/08/06	AMSCH	0254[H]	*[Anonymous]* | Twee stuks | *Notes:* This lot was added in by hand in the EBNP copy of the catalogue.	S[paan]	(Sold) van Iperen
1810/08/06	AMSCH	0255[H]	*[Anonymous]* | Een stuk | *Notes:* This lot was added in by hand in the EBNP copy of the catalogue.	S[paan]	(Sold) fl 5 Cassano

1810/08/06	AMSCH	0256[H]	*[Anonymous]* | Twee stuks | *Notes:* This lot was added in by hand in the EBNP copy of the catalogue.	S[paan]	(Sold) fl 18:10 Roelsma
1810/08/06	AMSCH	0257[H]	*[Anonymous]* | Een stuk | *Notes:* This lot was added in by hand in the EBNP copy of the catalogue.	S[paan]	(Sold) fl 0:10 L^y Pakker
1810/08/06	AMSCH	0258[H]	*[Anonymous]* | Een stuk | *Notes:* This lot was added in by hand in the EBNP copy of the catalogue.	S[paan]	(Sold) fl 1:10 L Pakker
1810/08/06	AMSCH	0259[H]	*[Anonymous]* | Een stuk | *Notes:* This lot was added in by hand in the EBNP copy of the catalogue.	S[paan]	(Withdrawn)
1810/08/06	AMSCH	0260[H]	*[Anonymous]* | Een stuk | *Notes:* This lot was added in by hand in the EBNP copy of the catalogue.	S[paan]	(Sold) fl 0:6 Gruiter
1810/08/06	AMSCH	0261[H]	*[Anonymous]* | Een stuk | *Notes:* This lot was added in by hand in the EBNP copy of the catalogue.	S[paan]	(Sold) fl 28 Texier
1810/08/06	AMSCH	0262[H]	*[Anonymous]* | Een stuk | *Notes:* This lot was added in by hand in the EBNP copy of the catalogue.	S[paan]	(Sold) fl 6 Stoopendaal
1810/08/06	AMSCH	0263[H]	*[Anonymous]* | Een stuk | *Notes:* This lot was added in by hand in the EBNP copy of the catalogue.	S[paan]	(Sold) fl 17:10 Dupré
1810/08/06	AMSCH	0264[H]	*[Anonymous]* | Een stuk | *Notes:* This lot was added in by hand in the EBNP copy of the catalogue.	S[paan]	(Sold) fl 2 Royers
1810/09/17	MGBEO	0001	*[Anonymous]* | [Untitled] | *Notes:* The only extant copy of this catalogue is annotated with the buyers and prices, but it does not include a printed list of the paintings.	R Engelberts [or others]	(Sold) £ 0.5 for lots 1 & 2. A de Koster
1810/09/17	MGBEO	0002	*[Anonymous]* | [Untitled] | *Notes:* The only extant copy of this catalogue is annotated with the buyers and prices, but it does not include a printed list of the paintings.	R Engelberts [or others]	(Sold) £ 0.5 for lots 1 & 2. A de Koster
1810/09/17	MGBEO	0003	*[Anonymous]* | [Untitled] | *Notes:* The only extant copy of this catalogue is annotated with the buyers and prices, but it does not include a printed list of the paintings.	R Engelberts [or others]	(Sold) £ 0.2 Benthem (grand)
1810/09/17	MGBEO	0004	*[Anonymous]* | [Untitled] | *Notes:* The only extant copy of this catalogue is annotated with the buyers and prices, but it does not include a printed list of the paintings.	R Engelberts [or others]	(Sold) £ 0.2 v d Sande
1810/09/17	MGBEO	0005	*[Anonymous]* | [Untitled] | *Notes:* The only extant copy of this catalogue is annotated with the buyers and prices, but it does not include a printed list of the paintings.	R Engelberts [or others]	(Sold) £ 0.1 v Benthem
1810/09/17	MGBEO	0006	*[Anonymous]* | [Untitled] | *Notes:* The only extant copy of this catalogue is annotated with the buyers and prices, but it does not include a printed list of the paintings.	R Engelberts [or others]	(Sold) £ 0.3 Benthem (grand)
1810/09/17	MGBEO	0007	*[Anonymous]* | [Untitled] | *Notes:* The only extant copy of this catalogue is annotated with the buyers and prices, but it does not include a printed list of the paintings.	R Engelberts [or others]	(Sold) £ 0.1 for lots 7 & 8. Benthem (grand)
1810/09/17	MGBEO	0008	*[Anonymous]* | [Untitled] | *Notes:* The only extant copy of this catalogue is annotated with the buyers and prices, but it does not include a printed list of the paintings.	R Engelberts [or others]	(Sold) £ 0.1 for lots 7 & 8. Benthem (grand)
1810/09/17	MGBEO	0009	*[Anonymous]* | [Untitled] | *Notes:* The only extant copy of this catalogue is annotated with the buyers and prices, but it does not include a printed list of the paintings.	R Engelberts [or others]	(Sold) £ 1.15 v d Meer
1810/09/17	MGBEO	0010	*[Anonymous]* | [Untitled] | *Notes:* The only extant copy of this catalogue is annotated with the buyers and prices, but it does not include a printed list of the paintings.	R Engelberts [or others]	(Sold) £ 0.1 Benthem
1810/09/17	MGBEO	0011	*[Anonymous]* | [Untitled] | *Notes:* The only extant copy of this catalogue is annotated with the buyers and prices, but it does not include a printed list of the paintings.	R Engelberts [or others]	(Sold) £ 0.4 for lots 11, 13 & 14. Ooms
1810/09/17	MGBEO	0012	*[Anonymous]* | [Untitled] | *Notes:* The only extant copy of this catalogue is annotated with the buyers and prices, but it does not include a printed list of the paintings.	R Engelberts [or others]	(Bought In)
1810/09/17	MGBEO	0013	*[Anonymous]* | [Untitled] | *Notes:* The only extant copy of this catalogue is annotated with the buyers and prices, but it does not include a printed list of the paintings.	R Engelberts [or others]	(Sold) £ 0.4 for lots 11, 13 & 14. Ooms
1810/09/17	MGBEO	0014	*[Anonymous]* | [Untitled] | *Notes:* The only extant copy of this catalogue is annotated with the buyers and prices, but it does not include a printed list of the paintings.	R Engelberts [or others]	(Sold) £ 0.4 for lots 11, 13 & 14. Ooms
1810/09/17	MGBEO	0015	*[Anonymous]* | [Untitled] | *Notes:* The only extant copy of this catalogue is annotated with the buyers and prices, but it does not include a printed list of the paintings.	R Engelberts [or others]	(Sold) £ 0.2 Benthem (Hackleij)
1810/09/17	MGBEO	0016	*[Anonymous]* | [Untitled] | *Annots:* Brandspiegel (ZBM) *Notes:* The only extant copy of this catalogue is annotated with the buyers and prices, but it does not include a printed list of the paintings.	R Engelberts [or others]	(Sold) £ 0.5 Ooms
1810/09/17	MGBEO	0017	*[Anonymous]* | [Untitled] | *Notes:* The only extant copy of this catalogue is annotated with the buyers and prices, but it does not include a printed list of the paintings.	R Engelberts [or others]	(Sold) £ 2 Ardesch

1810/10/10	MGCIT	0050	*[Anonymous]* | Een ovaal rond Schilderijtje op Zilver, zijnde een aanzienlijke Vrouw, in een rijke en pragtige kleeding, zeer uitvoerig, kloek en tevens zeer malsch behandeld, door een onbekend Meester. Achter het Plaatje staat gegraveerd God gaav God naam met welbehagen | *Mat:* op zilver *Fmt:* ovaal	Caspar van Citters	(Unknown)
1810/10/10	MGCIT	0090	*Een voornaam Meester* | Een schoon Mans Figuur, halver Lyf, met grys Hair en Baard, en in roode kleeding, leunende met de hand op een stok, in een Italiaansche trant; zeer fix geschilderd door een voornaam Meester	Caspar van Citters	(Unknown)
1810/10/10	MGCIT	0091	*Een onbekend Meester* | Een dito [schoon] mede kapitaal Mans Figuur, in een lezende Houding; schoon behandeld, door een onbekend Meester	Caspar van Citters	(Unknown)
1810/10/10	MGCIT	0099	*[Anonymous]* | Een dito [Stuk] met dito [Bloemen en Vruchten]: de Meester onbekend	Caspar van Citters	(Unknown)
1810/10/10	MGCIT	0100	*[Anonymous]* | Een dito [Stuk], als voren | *Mat:* op koper	Caspar van Citters	(Unknown)
1810/10/10	MGCIT	0107	*Een onbekend Meester* | Een klein Mans Figuur, in eene lezende houding; door een onbekend Meester	Caspar van Citters	(Unknown)
1810/10/10	MGCIT	0109	*Een onbekend Meester* | Een deftig Manspersoon, zittende in een Kamer, waarin Boeken en ander Bywerk, door een onbekend Meester	Caspar van Citters	(Unknown)
1810/10/10	MGCIT	0132	*[Anonymous]* | Twee bevallige Stukjes, zijnde het eene een Landschapje, het andere een Zeetje; de Meester onbekend	Caspar van Citters	(Unknown)
1810/10/10	MGCIT	0135	*[Anonymous]* | Twee Schilderijen met Bloemen	Caspar van Citters	(Unknown)
1810/10/10	MGCIT	0136	*[Anonymous]* | Een Landschapje met Beestjes	Caspar van Citters	(Unknown)
1810/10/10	MGCIT	0138	*Een onbekend Meester* | Een slapend Mannetje; wel behandeld, door een onbekend Meester	Caspar van Citters	(Unknown)
1810/10/10	MGCIT	0141	*Een onbekend Meester* | Een Schildery, zynde een naakte Vrouw, in eene liggende houding; natuurlyk behandeld, door een onbekend Meester	Caspar van Citters	(Unknown)
1810/10/10	MGCIT	0142	*Een goed Meester* | Een Stukje met Groentens en Huisraad, naar een goed Meester	Caspar van Citters	(Unknown)
1810/10/10	MGCIT	0145	*Een onbekend Meester* | Een Stuk, zynde een Land-, Water- en verafgelegen Bergachtig Gezigt, door een onbekend Meester	Caspar van Citters	(Unknown)
1810/10/10	MGCIT	0147	*Een onbekend Meester* | Twee Landschapjes, gestoffeerd met Figuuren, genomen uit de Fabelkunde; aardig bewerkt door een onbekend Meester	Caspar van Citters	(Unknown)
1810/10/10	MGCIT	0148	*Een onbekend Meester* | Een Stuk, zijnde een Wintertje, vol van wandelende, en op schaatsen rijdende Figuuren; aardig behandeld, door een onbekend Meester	Caspar van Citters	(Unknown)
1810/10/10	MGCIT	0149	*Een goed Meester* | Een zittende Zwaan, wel gevolgd naar een goed Meester	Caspar van Citters	(Unknown)
1810/10/10	MGCIT	0161	*Een onbekend Meester* | Een Stuk, waarop verscheide doode Vogels, onderanderen een wel uitgevoerd Patrijs, leggende alle op een steene Tafel; wel behandeld door een onbekend Meester | *Notes:* This lot was misnumbered no. 162 and changed in an errata sheet located at the front of the catalogue.	Caspar van Citters	(Unknown)
1810/10/10	MGCIT	0164	*Een onbekend Meester* | Een klein Mansfiguurtje, met een lachgende tronie; vrolijk behandeld, door een onbekend Meester | *Notes:* This lot was misnumbered no. 165 and changed in an errata sheet located at the front of the catalogue.	Caspar van Citters	(Unknown)
1810/10/10	MGCIT	0165	*Een onbekend Meester* | Nog een Stukje, zijnde een Man in zwarte kleeding met een bef, en een papier in de Hand; door een onbekend Meester | *Notes:* This lot was misnumbered no. 166 and changed in an errata sheet located at the front of the catalogue.	Caspar van Citters	(Unknown)
1810/10/10	MGCIT	0166	*Een onbekend Meester* | Een Stuk, waarop Maria met het Kind Jezus, als mede verscheide Voorwerpen daarbij gevoegd, alles geplaast in een zeer goed bewerkt Landschap; door een onbekend Meester, zonder Lijst | *Notes:* This lot was misnumbered no. 197 and changed in an errata sheet located at the front of the catalogue.	Caspar van Citters	(Unknown)
1810/10/11	AMSCH	0110	*[Anonymous]* | Twee Portretjes. zijnde Jacob Arminius en Huisvrouw | *Mat:* op paneel	V[ries]	(Sold) fl 0:6 L^{y} Pakker
1810/10/11	AMSCH	0115	*Een goed Meester* | Een Land-en Watergezigt, met stoffagie, door een goed Meester	Y	(Sold) fl 1 L Pakker
1810/10/11	AMSCH	0121	*[Anonymous]* | De dood van Lucretia, zeer schoon geschilderd | *Mat:* op doek *Size:* hoog 34, breed 29 duimen	M	(Sold) fl 10:5 H Pakker
1810/10/11	AMSCH	0127	*[Anonymous]* | Een Italiaansch Landschap | *Mat:* op doek	[Gruyter?]	(Sold or Bought In) fl 0:6 Gruiter
1810/10/11	AMSCH	0128	*[Anonymous]* | Een Landschap, met Beelden | *Mat:* op doek	[Gruyter?]	(Sold or Bought In) fl 0:6 Gruiter
1810/10/11	AMSCH	0138	*[Anonymous]* | Een Man en Vrouw in eene Binnenkamer	C	(Sold) fl 0:6 L Pakker
1810/10/11	AMSCH	0139	*[Anonymous]* | Een slapend Man, zittende nevens een Ton; fiks | *Mat:* op paneel	C	(Sold) fl 1:5 Posthumus
1810/10/11	AMSCH	0140	*[Anonymous]* | Een Landschap met een Waterplas, waaruit een Jager zijn Paard laat drinken | *Mat:* op paneel	C	(Sold) fl 13 Posthumus

1810/10/11	AMSCH	0141	*[Anonymous]* | Twee stuks Portretten van eenen Turkschen Man en Vrouw	C	(Sold) fl 6 Posthumus
1810/10/11	AMSCH	0142	*[Anonymous]* | Een gezigt met Woningen en Beeldjes | *Mat:* op paneel	C	(Sold) fl 22:10 Posthumus
1810/10/11	AMSCH	0143	*[Anonymous]* | Een marmeren Tafel, waarop eenige doode Vogels	C	(Sold) fl 0:10 L Pakker
1810/10/11	AMSCH	0144	*Een goed Meester* | Een Stil-leven; op Doek, door een goed Meester | *Mat:* op doek	C	(Sold) fl 1 Posthumus
1810/10/11	AMSCH	0149a[H]	*[Anonymous]* | 1 dito [stuk] | *Notes:* This lot was added in by hand in the EBNP copy of the catalogue. It is unclear what "dito" refers to in the title.	C	(Sold) fl 1:15 Posthumus
1810/10/11	AMSCH	0155	*[Anonymous]* | Twee stuks, een Mans- en een Vrouwe Portret	S	(Sold) fl 1:10 du Pree
1810/10/11	AMSCH	0156	*[Anonymous]* | Twee dito [stuks] als de voorgaande [Een Mans- en een Vrouwe Portret]	S	(Sold) fl 1:5 L Pakker
1810/10/11	AMSCH	0160	*[Anonymous]* | Twee stuks, een Wintergezigt en een hangende Patrijs	S	(Sold) fl 0:12 Gruiter
1810/10/11	AMSCH	0161	*[Anonymous]* | Twee stuks, een Mans Portret en een zittend Hondje	S	(Sold) fl 1:5 Gruiter
1810/10/11	AMSCH	0162	*Een oud Meester* | Een Kindje dat bellen blaast, zinspeelende op de Vergankelijkheid; door een oud Meester	S	(Sold) fl 2:5 van Dijl
1810/10/11	AMSCH	0173	*[Anonymous]* | Een Mediteerend Heilige	[Levy Pakker?]	(Sold) fl 1 Gruiter
1810/10/11	AMSCH	0174	*[Anonymous]* | Een Jongeling met een Blaas in de hand	[Levy Pakker?]	(Sold) fl 3 Gruiter
1810/10/11	AMSCH	0178	*[Anonymous]* | Twee stuks, een Jongelings en een Oud-Mans Hoofd	[Levy Pakker?]	(Sold) fl 0:6 van Iperen
1810/10/11	AMSCH	0186	*[Anonymous]* | Het Portret van R. Villers, Gravinne van Castlemay; fraai en uitvoerig geschilderd | *Mat:* op doek	A	(Sold) fl 1:5 Yver
1810/10/11	AMSCH	0197	*Een oud Meester* | Een Landschap met een Water, in 't verschiet eene Stad, op Paneel, door een oud Meester | *Mat:* op paneel	A	(Sold) fl 1 Boelhouwer
1810/10/11	AMSCH	0201	*[Anonymous]* | Eene naakte Vrouw, staande voor een Ledikant	A	(Sold) fl 2:10 Yver
1810/10/11	AMSCH	0202	*[Anonymous]* | Een besneeuwd Wintergezigt | *Mat:* op paneel	A	(Sold) fl 0:14 Yver
1810/10/11	AMSCH	0203	*[Anonymous]* | Eene Kerk van binnen te zien, rijk met Beelden gestoffeerd en goed op Doek geschilderd | *Mat:* op doek	A	(Sold) fl 0:6 L Pakker
1810/10/11	AMSCH	0206	*[Anonymous]* | Een Hofgezigt, met eene menigte vrolijke Lieden, zoo Mannen als Vrouwen; kloek geschilderd | *Mat:* op paneel	A	(Sold) fl 0:6 Ijver
1810/10/11	AMSCH	0212	*[Anonymous]* | Susanna door de Ouden verrast, fiks | *Mat:* op doek *Notes:* This lot was sold with lot 226, which is in the manner of D. Bergen.	A	(Sold) fl 0:6 for lots 212 & 226. T Spaan
1810/10/11	AMSCH	0213	*Een oud Meester* | Een Vrouwe Portret, door een oud Meester | *Notes:* This lot was sold with lot 222 by Alex. Keirincx.	A	(Sold) fl 0:8 for lots 213 & 222. Gruiter
1810/10/11	AMSCH	0218	*[Anonymous]* | De Hemelvaart van Maria, fiks | *Mat:* op paneel	A	(Sold) fl 0:8 T Spaan
1810/10/11	AMSCH	0219	*[Anonymous]* | Een Zeehaven, met groote Gebouwen en stoffagie	A	(Sold) fl 0:10 L Pakker
1810/10/11	AMSCH	0220	*Een oud Meester* | De opwekking van Lazarus, door een oud Meester	A	(Sold) fl 0:8 T Spaan
1810/10/11	AMSCH	0221	*[Anonymous]* | Een Land- en Zeegezigt, eigenaartig gestoffeerd	A	(Sold) fl 1 du Pree
1810/10/11	AMSCH	0233	*[Anonymous]* | Een Land- en Watergezigt, gestoffeerd met eenen Hengelaar; natuurlijk geschilderd	A	(Sold) fl 1 van Leen
1810/10/11	AMSCH	0236	*[Anonymous]* | Een Strand- en Zeegezigt, met Visschers en Vaartuigen	A	(Sold) fl 1 Yver
1810/10/11	AMSCH	0239	*[Anonymous]* | Een Meisje, zittende in een Landschap, voor twee Honden	A	(Sold) fl 0:6 L Pakker
1810/10/11	AMSCH	0240	*Een goed Meester* | Een Fabel-Ordonantie, door een goed Meester	A	(Sold) fl 0:8 Yver
1810/10/11	AMSCH	0241	*[Anonymous]* | Een Zinger met de Star, voor een Buitenhuis	A	(Sold) fl 2:5 Royere
1810/10/11	AMSCH	0243	*[Anonymous]* | Een Land- en Watergezigt	A	(Sold) fl 0:6 Ijver
1810/10/11	AMSCH	0244	*[Anonymous]* | Twee stuks Historiëele Ordonantien	A	(Sold) fl 1:5 for lots 244 & 255. L Pakker
1810/10/11	AMSCH	0245	*[Anonymous]* | Twee diverse Landschappen	A	(Sold) fl 0:6 L Pakker
1810/10/11	AMSCH	0248	*[Anonymous]* | Twee stuks, een lezend oud Man en Vrouw	A	(Sold) fl 1 L Pakker
1810/10/11	AMSCH	0249	*[Anonymous]* | Drie stuks, twee stille Levens en een met Vogels	A	(Sold) fl 1 L Pakker
1810/10/11	AMSCH	0252	*[Anonymous]* | Twee stuks, Loth met zijne Dochters, en Susanna in den Hof	A	(Sold) fl 0:6 L Pakker
1810/10/11	AMSCH	0254	*[Anonymous]* | Twee stuks, een Landschap en een Zeegezigt	A	(Sold) fl 0:14 van der Schley
1810/10/11	AMSCH	0255	*[Anonymous]* | Twee Paarden in een Landschap	A	(Sold) fl 1:5 for lots 244 & 255. L Pakker
1810/10/11	AMSCH	0256	*[Anonymous]* | Twee stuks, met Vrugten	A	(Sold) fl 0:10 Gruiter
1810/10/11	AMSCH	0257	*[Anonymous]* | Twee Binnenhuizen	A	(Sold) fl 1 L Pakker
1810/10/11	AMSCH	0259	*Een Oud Meester* | Eene Historiëele Ordonantie, door een Oud Meester	A	(Sold) fl 0:10 Yver

1810/10/11	AMSCH	0261	*[Anonymous]* | Twee stuks Historiëele Ordonantien	A	(Sold) fl 0:6 L Pakker
1810/10/11	AMSCH	0262	*[Anonymous]* | Twee stuks ovaal, Een Vrouwe-Portret en een met Kindertjes | *Fmt:* ovaal	A	(Sold) fl 0:10 Ijver
1810/10/11	AMSCH	0263	*[Anonymous]* | Vijf stuks, verschillende Voorwerpen. ovaal formaat | *Fmt:* ovaal	A	(Sold) fl 1 Roijere
1810/10/11	AMSCH	0264	*[Anonymous]* | Twee stuks Portretten, zijnde Willem de derde en een ander	A	(Sold) fl 0:6 L Pakker
1810/10/11	AMSCH	0265	*[Anonymous]* | Een naakt Vrouwe Beeld en een Mans Portret	A	(Sold) fl 0:12 Yver
1810/10/11	AMSCH	0266	*[Anonymous]* | Drie stuks, twee Zeegezigten en een Historieele	A	(Sold) fl 0:10 Yver
1810/10/11	AMSCH	0267	*[Anonymous]* | Vier diversche Landschappen	A	(Sold) fl 0:10 L Pakker
1810/10/11	AMSCH	0268	*[Anonymous]* | Vijf kleine Schilderijen, met Bloemen	A	(Sold) fl 0:12 Roijere
1810/10/11	AMSCH	0269	*[Anonymous]* | Zeven stuks, Historiëele Ordonantiën	A	(Sold) fl 3 Roijere
1810/10/11	AMSCH	0270	*[Anonymous]* | Vier kleine diversche Landschapjes	A	(Sold) fl 0:10 L Pakker
1810/10/11	AMSCH	0271	*[Anonymous]* | Vier ovale Portretjes | *Fmt:* ovaal	A	(Sold) fl 0:14 L Pakker
1810/10/11	AMSCH	0272	*[Anonymous]* | Eene Heilige Familie, op albast geschilderd | *Mat:* op albast	A	(Sold) fl 0:6 van Dijl
1810/10/11	AMSCH	0273[H]	*[Anonymous]* | Een Stuk | *Notes:* This lot was added in by hand in the EBNP copy of the catalogue.	R[oos]	(Sold) fl 44 Gruiter
1810/10/11	AMSCH	0274[H]	*[Anonymous]* | Twee Stuks | *Notes:* This lot was added in by hand in the EBNP copy of the catalogue.	R[oos]	(Sold) fl 33 Gruiter
1810/10/11	AMSCH	0275[H]	*[Anonymous]* | Een Stuk | *Notes:* This lot was added in by hand in the EBNP copy of the catalogue.	R[oos]	(Sold) fl 7 J Spaan
1810/10/11	AMSCH	0276[H]	*[Anonymous]* | Een Stuk | *Notes:* This lot was added in by hand in the EBNP copy of the catalogue.	R[oos]	(Sold) fl 13 Mensart
1810/10/11	AMSCH	0277[H]	*[Anonymous]* | Een Stuk | *Notes:* This lot was added in by hand in the EBNP copy of the catalogue.	R[oos]	(Bought In) fl 5 ½
1810/10/11	AMSCH	0278[H]	*[Anonymous]* | Een Stuk | *Notes:* This lot was added in by hand in the EBNP copy of the catalogue.	S	(Sold) fl 9 van Dijl
1810/10/11	AMSCH	0279[H]	*[Anonymous]* | Een Stuk | *Notes:* This lot was added in by hand in the EBNP copy of the catalogue.	S	(Sold) fl 2:10 J Spaan
1810/10/11	AMSCH	0280[H]	*[Anonymous]* | Een Stuk | *Notes:* This lot was added in by hand in the EBNP copy of the catalogue.	S	(Sold) fl 2:10 Boelhouwer
1810/10/13	HGDAW	0016	*Een goed Meester* | Een Historiëele, verbeeldende een Vorst te Paard, met zyn gevolg, door een goed Meester, hoog 50, breed 62 duimen, doek | *Mat:* op doek *Size:* hoog 50, breed 62 duimen		(Unknown)
1810/11/07	UTWLD	0011	*[Anonymous]* | Een door hoog Boomgewas omgeven Klooster ingang – verder een stil bergagtig verschiet, op den voorgrond een knotzige boom in een bruine parthij, verders een Priester die met een paar voorbijgangers in gesprek schijnt te zijn, alles zeer geestig en fraai behandeld, hoog 1 voet 5 duim, breed 2 voet, zwarte Lijst | *Size:* 1 voet 5 duim, breed 2 voet		(Unknown) fl 6
1810/11/07	UTWLD	0016	*[Anonymous]* | Een aardig Watervalletje – uit een berg, met een Kasteel en Brug, en eenige stoffagie, zeer geestig, op paneel, 6 duim hoog, 8 en een half duim breed, zwarte Lijst | *Mat:* op paneel *Size:* 6 duim hoog, 8 en een half duim breed		(Unknown) fl 5:5
1810/11/07	UTWLD	0043	*[Anonymous]* | Een Landschap, waarin een moedig Paard teugelloos galoppeerd, op paneel, 8 duim hoog, 9 en een half duim breed, zwarte Lijst | *Mat:* op paneel *Size:* 8 duim hoog, 9 en een half duim breed		(Unknown) fl 1
1810/11/07	UTWLD	0050	*[Anonymous]* | Een Landgezichtje bij een Klooster, waarbij eenig door een hevige wind geschokt geboomt, op den voorgrond een Hooiwagen, door den blixem aangestoken, waarbij Paarden en Menschen, alles vol effect klaar en kragtig geschilderd, op paneel 1 voet 3 duim breed, 11 duim hoog, zwarte Lijst | *Mat:* op paneel *Size:* 1 voet 3 duim breed, 11 duim hoog		(Unknown) fl 7:5
1810/11/07	UTWLD	0059	*[Anonymous]* | Een aardig Arcadisch Landgezichtje, ovaal, op paneel, 1 en een half voet breed, 1 voet 1 en een half duim hoog, zwarte Lijst | *Mat:* op paneel *Fmt:* ovaal *Size:* 1 en een half voet breed, 1 voet 1 en een half duim hoog		(Unknown) fl 1:4
1810/11/07	UTWLD	0060	*[Anonymous]* | Een vrolijk boerengezelschap zingende en speelende, zeer geestig geordoneerd, op paneel, 8 en een half duim hoog, 10 en een half duim breed, zwarte Lijst | *Mat:* op paneel *Size:* 8 en een half duim hoog, 10 en een half duim breed		(Unknown) fl 3:5
1810/11/07	UTWLD	0061	*[Anonymous]* | Twee Riviergezichten, ziende op een Haven en Stadspoort, met eenig verder bijwerk, zeer warm van Coloriet, op paneel, 1 voet 5 duim hoog, 1 voet 11 duim breed, zwarte Lijst | *Mat:* op paneel *Size:* 1 voet 5 duim hoog, 1 voet 11 duim breed		(Unknown) fl 7
1810/11/07	UTWLD	0064	*[Anonymous]* | Een zeer aardig bloemstukje met eenige Vlinders, Slakken, enz. 't verschiet een boomrijk uitzigt, op doek, 1 voet 2 en een half duim		(Unknown) fl 2

			hoog, 1 voet breed, zwarte Lijst 1671 | *Mat:* op doek *Size:* 1 voet 2 en een half duim hoog, 1 voet breed *Inscr:* 1671 (dated?) *Notes:* It is unclear whether the date is inscribed on the painting.		
1810/11/14	HGBAK	0001	*[Anonymous]* | De Bruiloft in Canaän | *Notes:* It is uncertain whether this lot is a painting.	J N Chanfleurij [or] L Swanenburg	(Unknown)
1810/11/14	HGBAK	0002	*[Anonymous]* | Het laatste Avondmaal | *Notes:* It is uncertain whether this lot is a painting.	J N Chanfleurij [or] L Swanenburg	(Unknown)
1810/11/14	HGBAK	0003	*[Anonymous]* | De Schatting Penning | *Notes:* It is uncertain whether this lot is a painting.	J N Chanfleurij [or] L Swanenburg	(Unknown)
1810/11/14	HGBAK	0004	*[Anonymous]* | De Overspeelige Vrouw | *Notes:* It is uncertain whether this lot is a painting.	J N Chanfleurij [or] L Swanenburg	(Unknown)
1810/11/14	HGBAK	0005	*[Anonymous]* | De Engelsche Boem- [sic] en Kers-Verkoopster, 2 stuks | *Notes:* It is uncertain whether this lot is a painting.	J N Chanfleurij [or] L Swanenburg	(Unknown)
1810/11/14	HGBAK	0050	*[Anonymous]* | Drie groote Schildereijen	J N Chanfleurij [or] L Swanenburg	(Unknown)
1810/11/29	HALOO	0006	*[Anonymous]* | Portrait van Jacobus Tyken, in Lyst en Glas | *Notes:* It is uncertain whether this lot is a painting.	Abraham Rutgers	(Unknown)
1810/11/29	HALOO	0007	*[Anonymous]* | Het Portrait van Oldenbarneveld op Doek, in een Lyst | *Mat:* op doek	Abraham Rutgers	(Unknown)
1810/11/29	HALOO	0008	*[Anonymous]* | Twee Fruitstukken op Doek, in Lysten | *Mat:* op doek	Abraham Rutgers	(Unknown)
1810/12/03	DOBRA	0004	*[Anonymous]* | Een Bergachtig Landschap; uitvoerig geschilderd		(Unknown)
1810/12/03	DOBRA	0005	*[Anonymous]* | Een Vrouwe Pourtretje; uitvoerig op Koper geschilderd | *Mat:* op koper		(Unknown)
1810/12/03	DOBRA	0006	*[Anonymous]* | Twee stuks Boerengezelschappen		(Unknown)
1810/12/03	DOBRA	0019	*[Anonymous]* | Een Man met een pyp in de hand, zittende by een brandende kaars		(Unknown)
1810/12/03	DOBRA	0024	*[Anonymous]* | Een dito [Historie]		(Unknown)
1810/12/03	DOBRA	0027	*[Anonymous]* | Een Vrouw met vier Kinderen, in een Landschap		(Unknown)
1810/12/03	DOBRA	0028	*[Anonymous]* | Een Historie		(Unknown)
1810/12/03	DOBRA	0029	*[Anonymous]* | Een dito [Historie]		(Unknown)
1810/12/03	DOBRA	0030	*[Anonymous]* | Een Boerengezelschap		(Unknown)
1810/12/03	DOBRA	0031	*[Anonymous]* | Een Boomryk Landschap, met Koeijen en Schapen; in 't grauw		(Unknown)
1810/12/03	DOBRA	0034	*[Anonymous]* | Drie stuks divers		(Unknown)
1810/12/03	DOBRA	0036	*Een goed Meester* | Een kloek Landschap met Geboomte en Gebouwen, door een goed Meester		(Unknown)
1810/12/03	DOBRA	0045	*[Anonymous]* | Drie stuks Zinnebeelden, Geloof, Hoop en Liefde		(Unknown)
1810/12/03	DOBRA	0061	*[Anonymous]* | Twee Zegezigtjes, ieder in een zwarte Lyst		(Unknown)
1810/12/03	DOBRA	0063	*[Anonymous]* | Een Pourtretje, zeer fraai geschilderd, in een verguld Lystje		(Unknown)
1810/12/03	DOBRA	0064	*[Anonymous]* | Een Pourtret, fraai geschilderd, op Koper, in een zwarten Lyst | *Mat:* op koper		(Unknown)
1810/12/03	DOBRA	0065	*[Anonymous]* | Een dito [Pourtret]		(Unknown)
1810/12/03	DOBRA	0071	*[Anonymous]* | Een Landschap		(Unknown)
1810/12/03	DOBRA	0072	*[Anonymous]* | Een Kop		(Unknown)
1810/12/03	DOBRA	0073	*[Anonymous]* | Een Historie		(Unknown)
1810/12/03	DOBRA	0074	*[Anonymous]* | Een Boer		(Unknown)
1810/12/03	DOBRA	0075	*[Anonymous]* | Een klein Landschap		(Unknown)
1810/12/03	DOBRA	0076	*[Anonymous]* | Een met drie Koeijen		(Unknown)

Anonymous (or Lievens, J. (I))

1804/07/25	DLGRO	0101	*Jan Lievens; een ander oud Meester* | Een oude Boertje, zittende met een Bierkan in de eene, en een Glas in de ander hand, door Jan Lievens, of een ander oud Meester | *Mat:* op paneel *Size:* hoog 7 ½, breed 6 ½ duim	Mr Franc van der Burch Wz.	(Unknown)

Anonymous (or Rembrandt)

1804/07/25	DLGRO	0022	*Rembrand; een ander beroemd Meester* | Een Oud Mans Hoofd of Borstbeeld, zeer fraai geschilderd, door Rembrand, of een ander beroemd Meester | *Mat:* op paneel *Size:* hoog 17, breed 14 duim	Mr Franc van der Burch Wz.	(Unknown)

Anonymous - Antique

1803/04/20	AMSCH	0101	*Een aloud Kunstschilder* | Dit fraay en ryk geordeneert Tafreel, door een aloud Kunstschilder vervaardigt, stelt voor het leeven van den wellustigen Zoon, zynde het Stuk met twee Deurtjes geslooten, op de eene ziet men verbeeld het Vertrek van dien Jongeling, in de andere Deur, den zelve in Armoede gedompeld by de Varkens; het Middenvak vertoont de	Maria Magdalena van Sluypwyk, gravinne van Moens	(Sold) fl 15 Josi

			Vaderlyke Liefde, zyn Zoon in Genade weder ontfangende, verder in een prachtig Gebouw ziet men een gedekte Tafel; waaraan verscheide Genoodigden, terwyl Musicanten zig op een Balcon laaten hooren, op welker Steene Rand men gemerkt vind: 1526. fact sum Hant, de Hartstogten zyn kennelyk uitgedrukt, en alles is van een meesterlyke en uitvoerige penceelsbehandeling [Un Tableau Gothique. Cette piéce est a deux battans, maniere ordinaire du tems de sa date, il a pour sujet principal le retour de l'Enfant prodigue acceuilli par son pere. Sur la porte à droite est son depart de la maison paternelle, et la gauche presente le comble de sa misere après ses debauches. Sur une partie de batiment est cette inscription 1526. fact. sum Hant. Il est bien conservé & fini avec Soin.] | *Mat:* op paneel *Fmt:* [deux battans] *Size:* hoog 36, breed 28 duim *Inscr:* 1526 fact sum Hant (signed and dated)		
1803/04/27	AMSCH	0066	*Un ancien Maitre* | Deux Batailles | *Size:* h. 5 ½, l. 8 pieds	A	(Sold) fl 2 Esser
1803/04/27	AMSCH	0070	*Un ancien Maitre* | Un berger & des Animaux | *Size:* h. 5 ¼, l. 7 pieds	A	(Sold) fl 0:16 Westhoff
1803/04/27	AMSCH	0075	*Un ancien Maitre* | Le Sauveur Soutenant sa Croix | *Mat:* sur bois *Size:* h. 3 ¼, l. 2 ¼ pieds	A	(Sold) fl 3:5 V d Schley [for] R[ijfsnijder]
1803/07/18	AMSCH	0065	*Gottisch* | Een Gottisch Schildery, met twee Deuren. hoog 35, breed 29 duim, Paneel. In het Middenstuk de Kruissiging van den Heiland tusschen de Moordenaaren, op de eene Deur de oprichting van den Kopere Slang, en op de andere daar Moses het water uit de steenrotze slaat [Il est d'une forme ancienne avec deux battans peints aux deux Côtés ; le sujet principal est le crucifiement de J.C. entre les Larrons. Audevant est la Vierge Marie avec les femmes saintes : nombre de Soldats & autres personnages en font une composition nombreuse. Sur l'intérieur des volets est representé l'erection du serpent d'airain par Moïse, & sur l'autre est le même législateur faisant jaillir l'eau d'un rocher, par un coup de sa baguette. Aux revers sont des figures emblêmatiques de la loi hebraïque, & du Christianisme. Nous le laissons anonime n'en connoissant pas l'auteur.] | *Mat:* op paneel *Fmt:* met twee deuren *Size:* hoog 35, breed 29 duim	Maria Theresia Andrioli	(Sold) fl 11:10 Th^{s} Spaan
1804/10/16	DLOND	0331	*Anticq* | De Abtdy van Egmond, zo als die bevorens met het Slot geweest is. Anticq en fraai. L'Abbaye d'Egmond, comme elle était ci-devant. Pièce antigue & belle | *Mat:* op doek *Size:* hoog 40, breed 72		(Unknown)

Anonymous – Modern

1802/05/10	MGSAN	0027	*Modern Meester* | Een fraai Landschap, daarop een Drift met Schaapen, geleid wordende door eene in sierlyk gewaad gekleede Herderinne; in 't verschiet een Berggezigt, daarby nog een Drift met Schaapen, door een modern Meester: op Paneel: in zwarte Lyst, met vergulde Binnenlyst | *Mat:* op paneel *Size:* hoog 19 ½ duim, breed 24 duim	Johan Dirk Kruysse	(Withdrawn)
1802/05/22	RMHSN	0008	*Moderne* | Twee stuks Moderne Landschapjes	Lambertus Bicker	(Unknown)
1802/05/22	RMHSN	0009	*Modern* | Een dito [stuk] dito [Modern Landschapje]	Lambertus Bicker	(Unknown)
1802/05/22	RMHSN	0017	*Modern* | Een Modern Landschap met Danssende Boeren, &c.	Lambertus Bicker	(Unknown)
1802/05/22	RMHSN	0018	*Modern* | Een dito [Modern Landschap] een Arkadiesch Landschap	Lambertus Bicker	(Unknown)
1802/09/21	UTHDG	000E[H]	*Modern* | Een Modern Historieel | *Notes:* This lot was added in by hand in the OGA copy of the catalogue.		(Sold) fl 22:10 J Niekerk
1803/04/27	AMSCH	0028	*Un peintre Moderne* | La continence de Scipion, par un peintre Moderne | *Size:* h. 4 ¼, l. 5 ½ pieds	A	(Sold) fl 7:10 Hijm Pakker
1803/04/27	AMSCH	0046	*Un peintre Moderne* | Le même Sujet, par un peintre Moderne | *Size:* h. 3 ½, l. 4 ½ pieds	A	(Sold) fl 8:10 L Pakker
1803/09/07	AMSCH	0234	*Een Modern Meester* | Twee stuks een wilde Zwyne Jacht, en een Gevecht tusschen Harten, byde door een Modern Meester [Deux tableaux représentant des chasses, et un combat de cerf ; tous les deux d'un maître moderne] | *Mat:* op doek *Size:* hoog 9, breed 12 duim	Smidt	(Sold) fl 1:5 Gruiter
1804/03/27	MGSAN	0002	*Een modern Meester* | Twee Stuks fraaije Land- en Zeegezigten met zwemmend en ander Gedierte, door een modern Meester, in vergulde Lysten | *Mat:* op doek *Size:* hoog 14 duim x breed 19 duim		(Unknown)
1804/10/16	DLOND	0317	*Modern* | Een Meisjen in een Vengsterraam, spelende met de Jou Jou de Normandie. Modern en zeer goed. Une Fille assise dans une croisée. Elle s'amuse avec le Jou Jou de Normandie. Pièce moderne très belle | *Mat:* op paneel *Size:* hoog 14, breed 11		(Unknown) fl 25
1805/07/10	AMSCH	0211	*een modern meester* | Een Maneschyn, in een Land- en Riviergezicht; in de manier van A. van der Neer, door een modern meester	V[inkeles] [for] H[affner]	(Sold) fl 1:10 Mook
1806/06/07	RMHSN	0097	*Een modern Meester* | Twee Stuks Landschappen, door een modern Meester | *Mat:* op doek	A E K L	(Unknown)
1806/08/20	HGBSM	0175	*Moderne* | Twee moderne stukjes | *Mat:* op paneel	Macalester Loup [or others]	(Sold) fl 1 Zwarts
1807/06/10	HGBSM	0213	*Een modern Meester* | Een Landschap, zeer zonachtig met figuren, door een modern Meester | *Mat:* op paneel *Size:* hoog 17 ½, breed 20 ½ duim	Abraham Delfos [or others]	(Sold) fl 5 de Gelder

1808/11/28	AMSCH	0100	*Een modern Meester* | Twee stuks Landschappen, met wandelende en rustende Heeren en Dames, kloek behandeld, door een modern Meester	Z	(Sold) fl 2:15 Gruyter
1809/07/25	HGBSM	0184	*Een modern Meester* | Een aangenaam Landschap | *Mat:* op paneel *Size:* hoog 9, breed 14 en een half duim	D van der Aa [or] E B ten Dall	(Sold) fl 6 Zwartsman
1810/03/07	UTWLD	0048	*Modern* | Een modern Landschap | *Size:* hoog 9 duim, breed 1 voet 1 duim	J J Woertman	(Unknown) fl 34
1810/06/06	RMMUY	0231	*Moderne* | Twee Moderne Stukjes met Vrouwe Beeldjes | *Mat:* op paneel *Notes:* According to the MA copy of the catalogue, this lot was sold with lot 232 by J.M. Molenaer for fl. 2:2.		(Unknown) fl 4

British

1807/06/02	AMHUY	0027	*Een Engelsch Meester* | De Opstanding van den Heiland, waarby de Engel de Zark vasthoud, ter zyde leggen de Wakers te slapen, door een Engelsch Meester		(Unknown)
1807/06/02	AMHUY	0028	*Een Engelsch Meester* | De Tentatie van Anthonius, door denzelven [een Engelsch Meester]		(Unknown)
1807/06/02	AMHUY	0029	*Een Engelsch Meester* | Christus onder de Leeraars toen hy twaalf jaren oud was, door denselven [een Engelsch Meester]		(Unknown)

Dutch

1806/08/20	HGBSM	0158	*Een oud Hollandsch Meester* | Het gezicht van eene Groente en Varkenmarkt, door een oud Hollandsch Meester | *Mat:* op paneel *Size:* hoog 18, breed 28 duim	Macalester Loup [or others]	(Sold) fl 1:2 Teissier
1808/06/11	RMRIJ	0102	*Hollandsch* | Een Hollandsch Hofgezicht met Figuren, goed gedaan | *Mat:* op paneel		(Unknown) fl 1:5
1810/07/26	AMSCH	0127	*Een oud Hollandsch Meester* | Een Maneschijn, door een oud Hollandsch Meester	Cassino	(Sold) fl 0:12 Lohuijs

Flemish – Brabant

1801/08/19	AMSCH	0152	*Brabands Meester* | Een Venétiaansche Groenmarkt, door een Brabands Meester	Van Forreest	(Sold) fl 7:5 V^{n} Dijl
1801/11/21	RMVIS	0005	*Een Brabands Meester* | Een Vrouwtje halverlyf te zien	Gelinus van Spaan	(Unknown)
1802/06/28	AMSCH	0238	*Brabandsch Meester* | Twee stuks Bybelsche Ordonnantien, ryk van Beelden; zeer natuurlyk en krachtig gepenceeld, door een Brabandsch Meester, op Doek | *Mat:* op doek *Size:* hoog 35, breed 27 duim	Anna Elink	(Sold) fl 7 J Spaan
1802/06/28	AMSCH	0247	*Brabands Meester* | Twee stuks oude Philosophen, door een Brabands Meester	Anna Elink	(Sold) fl 1 Dykman
1803/06/20	AMSCH	0042	*Brabands Meester* | Een Heilige Famiellie, door een Brabands Meester, op Doek | *Mat:* op doek *Size:* hoog 21, breed 18 duim	Schley [for] G	(Sold) fl 1 Yver
1803/09/07	AMSCH	0230	*Een voornaam Brabands Meester* | Het Stefbed [sic] van Maria Magdaléna met het Kruis in handen, waarby twee Engelen met een fakkel in de hand, het geen een kragtige werking doet, op Doek, door een voornaam Brabands Meester [Le lit de mort de Ste.-Marie-Madélaine : elle tient la croix dans ses mains, à côté deux anges avec des flambeaux. La composition et le coloris de ce tableau sont vigoureux et d'un grand effet, sur toile ; par un maître distingué de l'école flamande.] | *Mat:* op doek *Size:* hoog 32, breed 25 duim	Smidt	(Sold) fl 7:10 C S Roos
1805/10/09	HGBSM	0011	*Een goed Brabands Meester* | Een gezelschap van heeren en dames, die gastereeren, door een goed Brabands Meester | *Mat:* op koper *Size:* hoog 7 ½ breet 10 duim	T H van Willigen [or others]	(Sold) fl 5 Carré
1805/10/09	HGBSM	0065	*Een oud Brabandsch Meester* | Een boeren vreugd voor een buitenhuis, door een oud Brabandsch Meester | *Mat:* op paneel *Size:* hoog 12 breet 15 duim	T H van Willigen [or others]	(Sold) fl 1:14 Kerber
1806/08/20	HGBSM	0011	*Een goed Brabansch meester* | Een Amazone Strijd, deze rijke ordonnantie met figuuren, geeft eene levendige zielsverbeelding te kennen, alle beelden zijn vol actie, aangenaam van Coloriet en drukken het onderwerp ten hoogsten uit, door een goed Brabansch meester | *Mat:* op paneel *Size:* hoog 27, breed 38 duim	Macalester Loup [or others]	(Sold) fl 40 Spruyt
1809/07/25	HGBSM	0075	*Een Brabands Meester* | Twee stuks Landschappen met Rivieren, en verder met veel stoffagie, door een Brabands Meester | *Mat:* op doek *Size:* hoog 12 en breed 15 duim	D van der Aa [or] E B ten Dall	(Sold) fl 3:15 Bakhuyzen
1809/07/25	HGBSM	0143	*Een Brabands Meester* | Een Carnaval in een Stadt, met veel vermakelykheden en gewoel, door een Brabands Meester | *Mat:* op paneel *Size:* hoog 21, breed 27 en een half duim	D van der Aa	(Sold) fl 7 van der Aa
1810/06/06	RMMUY	0095	*De Brabantsche school* | Eene Boetvaardige Magdalena, uit de Brabantsche school | *Mat:* op doek		(Unknown) fl 2

French

1802/04/13	HAVIN	0044	*Een frans Meester* | Een comicq Gezelschap, door een frans Meester		(Unknown)
1802/05/05	AMSCH	0255	*Een Fransch Meester* | Een Meisje op de grond zittende, met een Bos Koornäaren op haar schoot, delicaat op Doek, door een Fransch Meester | *Mat:* op doek *Size:* hoog 10, breed 9 duim	C	(Sold) fl 4:15 Van Dijl

1802/09/06	AMSCH	0156	*Een Fransch Meester* | Twee stuks, een Schoolmeester en een spinnende Vrouw; door een Fransch Meester, fix behandeld	Mevrouw Achtienhoven	(Sold) fl 18 Delfos
1802/09/18	RMDRS	0087	*Een Fransch Meester* | Een dito [groot stuk], Ariadne vertroost over het verlaten van Theseus, door een Fransch Meester	Casper de Haas	(Unknown) fl 1:10
1802/12/13	AMSCH	0185	*Een Fransch Meester* | In een Arcadisch Landschap, zit een Nimph de Jonge Bachus op de schoot houdende, waar by een Bachant een tros druiven boven hem uitdrukkende, verder een Minnewigt met een Bok speelende, en andere dansende Nimphen; meesterlyk en kragtig gepenceeld, door een Fransch Meester | *Mat:* op doek *Size:* hoog 28, breed 38 duim	Yver	(Sold) fl 4 Coclers
1803/08/17	AMSCH	0099	*Een goed Fransch Meester* | Maria met het Kind Jesus, in een glorie van Engelen, helder van Coloriet, door een goed Fransch Meester | *Mat:* op doek *Size:* hoog 17, breed 14 duim	Anna Catharina Putman	(Sold) fl 9:10 Agina
1803/09/07	AMSCH	0253	*Een voornaam Fransch Meester* | Twee stuks Historiëele Ordonantien, verbeeldende Mars en Vénus, en Vénus en Adonis; kragtig van Coloriet, en meesterlyk behandeld, door een voornaam Fransch Meester [Deux tableaux historiques, représentant Mars et Venus et Adonis et Venus ; d'un coloris vigoureux ; belle composition d'un maître de l'école française] | *Mat:* op doek *Size:* ieder hoog 25, breed 31 duim	Smidt	(Bought In) fl 10:10
1806/05/05	AMSCH	0161	*Een Fransch Meester* | Een Dame een haar ontbyt, met een bevallig Kind, en fraai bywerk, een Meisje nevens haar; zeer fraai door een Fransch Meester	R[oos]	(Bought In) fl 12
1809/04/17	AMSCH	0177	*Een Fransch Meester* | Voor een Gebouw ziet men eene slaapende Vrouw, waar bij een Jongen met een Hond, door een Fransch Meester	H	(Sold) fl 1:15 Gruyter
1809/05/26	HADAA	0019	*Een Fransch Meester* | Eene Vrouw met een zuigend kind, door een Fransch Meester	Mejuffrouw de Wed David Heemskerk [or others]	(Unknown)
1809/07/25	HGBSM	0181	*Een goed Frans Meester* | Een levensgroot Portret van een Schilder, rustende met de hand op een Doodshoofd, waar by een Palet met Penseelen, kragtig en breed geschildert door een goed Frans Meester | *Mat:* op doek *Size:* hoog 45 en een half, breed 38 en een half duim	D van der Aa [or] E B ten Dall	(Sold) fl 41 Teissier
			German		
1802/06/28	AMSCH	0225	*Duitsch Meester* | Twee stuks galante Voorwerpen, tusschen geestelyke en waereldlyke Persoonen; op Panneel, door een Duitsch Meester | *Mat:* op paneel *Size:* hoog 13, breed 12 duim	Anna Elink	(Sold) fl 12 Coclers
1802/06/28	AMSCH	0236	*Duitsch Meester* | Twee stuks Ryngezichten, door een Duitsch Meester	Anna Elink	(Sold) fl 1:5 Yver
1802/06/28	AMSCH	0259	*Duitsch Meester* | Twee stuks, met eenig dood Wild; door een Duitsch Meester, Panneel | *Mat:* op paneel *Size:* hoog 10, breed 10 duim	B	(Sold) fl 1:10 H Schotte
1807/08/26	AMSCH	0319	*Een Duitsch Meester* | Twee stuks Rencontres van Militairen te Paard en te voet; geestig geschilderd door een Duitsch Meester	Joseph Vallette	(Sold) fl 5:5 Gruiter
1810/05/22	AMSCH	0137	*Een Duitsch Meester* | Een Boomrijk Landschap, met stoffagie van Beelden en Beesten; door een Duitsch Meester	Johannes van de Putte Nicolaasz.	(Sold) fl 1 Levij Pakker
1810/05/22	AMSCH	0155	*Een Duitsch Meester* | Het Afbeeldsel van eenen Turk, halver lijf, in deftige Kleding; uitvoerig behandeld, door een Duitsch Meester	F	(Sold) fl 3 Jeronimo de Vries
1810/07/26	AMSCH	0122	*Een Duitsch Meester* | Een Landschap, met Beelden, door een Duitsch Meester	Cassino	(Sold) fl 2:5 Spaan
			Italian		
1801/04/13	AMSCH	0100	*Een Italiaansche Meester* | Een heilige Familie, kloek door een Italiaansche Meester | *Mat:* op doek *Size:* hoog 29, breed 26 duim	Pierre Fouquet, junior	(Sold) fl 1 Gruyter
1801/06/13	LNDLS	0077	*Een Italiaansch Meester* | Een Petrus, halverlijf, door een Italiaansch Meester	D van R	(Sold) fl 2:2 for lots 77 & 78. Richter [for] G[iezen]
1801/06/13	LNDLS	0078	*Een Italiaansch Meester* | Een Bouwkundige, halverlijf, door Italiaansch Meester	D van R	(Sold) fl 2:2 for lots 77 & 78. Richter [for] G[iezen]
1802/02/16	AMSCH	0024	*Een Italiaansch meester* | Een boetvaardige Maria Magdaléna meesterlyk door een Italiaansch meester	E	(Sold) fl 41 Jan Spaan
1802/05/05	AMSCH	0256	*Een Italiaansch Meester* | Een Historiëele Ordonnantie van verscheiden Beelden, voorstellende de Pest, meesterlyk op Paneel, door een Italiaansch Meester | *Mat:* op paneel *Size:* hoog 15, breed 20 duim	C	(Sold) fl 3:5 Stevens
1802/05/10	MGSAN	0029	*Een goed Italiaans Meester* | Een Maria met het Kindje op haar schoot, door een goed Italiaans Meester: op Paneel, in vergulde Lyst | *Mat:* op paneel *Size:* hoog 28 duim, breed 24 duim	Johan Dirk Kruysse	(Withdrawn)
1802/05/10	MGSAN	0046	*Een Italiaan* | Een galant Stukje, krachtig geschilderd, zynde Mars en Venus, door een Italiaan: op Koper, in vergulde Lyst | *Mat:* op koper *Size:* hoog 7 ½ duim, breed 6 duim	Johan Dirk Kruysse	(Unknown) £ 0:4
1802/06/16	AMSCH	0245	*Een Italiaansch Meester* | Deeze Ordenantie van verscheide Beelden en Zaters, vertoont het Oordeel van Midas; het is krachtig en meesterlyk op Paneel geschilderd, door een Italiaansch Meester | *Mat:* op paneel *Size:* hoog 11, breed 14 duim	[Merrem]	(Sold) fl 10 de Lelie

<table>
<tr><td>1802/06/28</td><td>AMSCH</td><td>0256</td><td>*Een Italiaans Meester* | Een Bybelsche Ordonnantie, verbeeldende de aanbidding der Herders, fiks gepenceeld als door een Italiaans Meester, op Doek | *Mat:* op doek</td><td>B</td><td>(Sold) fl 11:10 Geld</td></tr>
<tr><td>1802/07/09</td><td>AMSTO</td><td>0041</td><td>*Een Italiaans Meester* | 1 historie van Surinamen, door een Italiaans Meester</td><td></td><td>(Unknown)</td></tr>
<tr><td>1802/07/21</td><td>HGKAN</td><td>0047</td><td>*Een voornaam Italiaans Meester* | Een overheerlyk fraay geschildert stuk, verbeeldende Maria met het Kind en den ouden Simeon, zeer natuurlyk en na het leven geschildert, zwarte Lyst, op Doek, door een voornaam Italiaans Meester | *Mat:* op doek</td><td></td><td>(Unknown)</td></tr>
<tr><td>1802/07/21</td><td>HGKAN</td><td>0087</td><td>*Italiaans* | La Charite Romaine, Italiaans</td><td></td><td>(Unknown)</td></tr>
<tr><td>1802/07/21</td><td>HGKAN</td><td>0095</td><td>*Italiaansch* | Het Pourtrait van Cibille, Italiaansch</td><td></td><td>(Unknown)</td></tr>
<tr><td>1802/07/21</td><td>HGKAN</td><td>0108</td><td>*Een Italiaansch Meester* | Een Historieel, door een Italiaansch Meester</td><td></td><td>(Unknown)</td></tr>
<tr><td>1802/08/24</td><td>LNDLS</td><td>0116</td><td>*Een Italiaansch Meester* | Een dito [gestoffeerd Landschap] door een Italiaansch Meester | *Notes:* It is unclear what “dito” refers to in the title.</td><td>Leonardus Bouman [or others]</td><td>(Unknown) fl 1:10</td></tr>
<tr><td>1802/09/06</td><td>AMSCH</td><td>0182</td><td>*Een Italiaansch Meester* | De doode Christus, werdende door een Engel, ondersteund; fix gepenceeld als door een Italiaansch Meester</td><td>Spaan</td><td>(Sold) fl 1 Jan Spaan [or] Th^{S} Spaan</td></tr>
<tr><td>1802/09/06</td><td>AMSCH</td><td>0227</td><td>*Een Italiaansch Meester* | Twee stuks; fraay gepenceeld door een Italiaansch Meester</td><td>J</td><td>(Sold) fl 1:5 van Dijl</td></tr>
<tr><td>1802/09/18</td><td>RMDRS</td><td>0086</td><td>*Een Italiaans Meester* | Een groot stuk, verbeeldende de Koning David met de Propheet Nathan, levens groote figuuren, door een Italiaans Meester</td><td>Casper de Haas</td><td>(Unknown) fl 3:5</td></tr>
<tr><td>1802/09/18</td><td>RMDRS</td><td>0117</td><td>*Een Italiaans Meester* | Een pourtret, door een Italiaans Meester</td><td>Casper de Haas</td><td>(Unknown) fl 2:6</td></tr>
<tr><td>1802/09/29</td><td>AMSCH</td><td>0072</td><td>*Een goed Italiaansch Meester* | Een Kluizenaar, Levens groote, zynde een Kniestuk; hy is verbeeld met eenen witten gryzen Baard en een kaal Hoofd, als in eerbiedige beschouwinge van een Crucifix; die hy in zyn linker hand houd, de oogen nedergeslaagen; voor hem zyn geplaatst eenige Boeken, Zandlooper, enz. het Caracter is schoon, de Teekening is accuraat, de Penceelbehandeling is meesterlyk, en van een breed en kragtig Coloriet; door een goed Italiaansch Meester [Le sujet d’un Hermite en dévotion vu à mi-corps de Grandeur naturelle, sa Tête presque chauve est de la plus grande Vérité, la méditation & les macérations semblent l’avoir Silloné ; ce Tableau est d’un dessein Correct d’un beau Pinceau & d’une couleur Vigoureuse & l’Ouvrage d’un bon Peintre Italien.] | *Mat:* op doek *Size:* hoog 42, breed 41 ½ duim [haut de 42, large 31 ½ pouces] *Notes:* The dimensions differ in the Dutch and French editions of the catalogue.</td><td>[Labouchere?]</td><td>(Sold) fl 37 van Dijl</td></tr>
<tr><td>1802/09/29</td><td>AMSCH</td><td>0073</td><td>*Een voornaam Italiaans Meester* | De Romeinsche Kinderliefde, levensgroote, een Kniestuk; schoon en breed van Penceelbehandeling, door een voornaam Italiaans Meester [Ce Tableau offre le sujet intéressant de la Charité romaine, les figures sont vues à mi corps de Grandeur naturelle, traité en grand Maitre, on peut hardiment l’attribuer au Pinceau, d’un des plus savans artistes que la Haute Ecole d’Italie ait produite ; Toutes les parties de la Peinture y sont observés, à un dégré éminent. On y remarque clairement que le Peintre étoit pénétré parfaitement de son sujet en le traitant. Les Caractères sont d’une expression sûblime et l’Effet de cette Piece capitale est de la plus grande beauté.] | *Mat:* op dock *Size:* hoog 45 ½, breed 35 duim</td><td>[Labouchere?]</td><td>(Sold) fl 0:10 L Pakker</td></tr>
<tr><td>1802/09/30</td><td>HGBAK</td><td>0005</td><td>*Een Italiaansch Meester* | Maria met het Kindeke, en Elisabeth, door een Italiaansch Meester, op doek. [Schilderyen in Olyverf] | *Mat:* in olyverf op doek *Notes:* The bracketed information in the title appears above lot 1 and refers to lots 1 to 26.</td><td></td><td>(Unknown)</td></tr>
<tr><td>1802/12/13</td><td>AMSCH</td><td>0186</td><td>*Een Italiaanseh Meester* | Deeze Ordenantie in een Lanschap vertoond verscheiden Musiceerende Lieden; kragtig geschilderd, door een Italiaanseh [sic] Meester | *Mat:* op doek</td><td>Yver</td><td>(Sold) fl 9 J Spaan</td></tr>
<tr><td>1802/12/13</td><td>AMSCH</td><td>0188</td><td>*Een Italiaansch Meester* | Een Bybelsche Ordenantie van drie Beelden, op Steen, door een Italiaansch Meester | *Mat:* op steen</td><td>Yver</td><td>(Sold) fl 10 Vallet</td></tr>
<tr><td>1802/12/13</td><td>AMSCH</td><td>0189</td><td>*Een Italiaansch Meester* | Een oud Man een jong Meisje omhelzende; door een Italiaansch Meester</td><td>Yver</td><td>(Sold) fl 1 Van Dijl</td></tr>
<tr><td>1802/12/13</td><td>AMSCH</td><td>0194</td><td>*Een Italiaansch Meester* | Twee Oude Filosophen by hun Globe en Boeken; stout gepenceeld, door een Italiaansch Meester | *Mat:* op doek *Size:* hoog 48, breed 36 duim</td><td>Pruyssenaar [for] A</td><td>(Sold) fl 2:5 Gruiter</td></tr>
<tr><td>1802/12/13</td><td>AMSCH</td><td>0195</td><td>*Een Italiaansch Meester* | In een Binnen Kamer voor een Tafel met een groen Kleed bedekt, ziet men een bevallige Vrouw, met een Kind op haar Schoot en een Boek in de hand, ter zyden dezelven een oud Man by ’t Vuur zittende, op de voorgrond een Kind met een Hond, by Kaarslicht; schoon geschilderd, door een dito [Italiaansch] Meester | *Mat:* op doek *Size:* hoog 30, breed 39 duim</td><td>Pruyssenaar [for] A</td><td>(Sold) fl 1:5 Gruiter</td></tr>
<tr><td>1802/12/13</td><td>AMSCH</td><td>0196</td><td>*Een Italiaansch Meester* | Christus in ’t Hof van Getzemané. door den Engel de Beeker aangebooden, terwyl zyn Discipelen slaapen; door een dito [Italiaansch] Meester | *Mat:* op doek *Size:* hoog 59, breed 43 duim</td><td>Pruyssenaar [for] A</td><td>(Sold) fl 0:6 L Pakker</td></tr>
<tr><td>1802/12/13</td><td>AMSCH</td><td>0197</td><td>*Een Italiaansch Meester* | Christus by Maria; meesterachtig geschilderd, door een dito [Italiaansch] Meester | *Mat:* op doek *Size:* hoog 68, breed 47 duim</td><td>Pruyssenaar [for] A</td><td>(Sold) fl 0:12 Gruiter</td></tr>
</table>

1802/12/13	AMSCH	0225	*Een Italiaansch Meester* | Deeze bevallige Ordenantie in een Landschap verbeeld Maria in een zedige gestalten, houdende het Kind Jezu op de schoot, voor dezelve knielende Herders, Eerbiedig het Kindeken beschouwende, verder St. Joseph, en rustend Vée; om hoog een glorie van Engelen; alles is kragtig van Coloriet, en van een Meesterlyke fraaije Penceelbehandeling, door een Italiaansch Meester | *Mat:* op doek *Size:* hoog 21, breed 22 duim	Schley [for] Lauwers	(Sold) fl 19 W Reijers
1802/12/13	AMSCH	0226	*Een Italiaansch Meester* | Een staand Studiebeeld, vertoonende een Italiaansch Landman; Meesterlyk fiks gepenceeld door een dito [Italiaansch Meester] | *Mat:* op doek op paneel *Size:* hoog 20, breed 12 duim	Schley [for] Lauwers	(Sold) fl 3:10 Van Dijl
1802/12/13	AMSCH	0230	*Een Italiaansch Meester* | Twee stuks Bosch- en Bergachtige Landschappen; door een Italiaansch Meester | *Mat:* op paneel *Size:* hoog 12, breed 19 duim	Pruyssenaar [for] A	(Sold) fl 0:10 L Pakker
1803/04/06	MGSAN	0007	*Een Italiaansch Meester* | Een Historiestuk, extra stout geschilderd en konstig behandeld, door een Italiaansch Meester	Mr Evert Clyver	(Unknown)
1803/04/20	AMSCH	0105	*Een Italiaansch Meester* | Maria het Kind Jesu op de Schoot houdende, speelende met St. Jan, ter zyde twee Engelen en Joseph, in de lugt eenige Cerafynen, behaaglyk van Coloriet, door een Italiaansch Meester [La Vierge tenant l'Enfant Jesus qui caresse le petit St. Jean ; deux Anges, St. Joseph & une gloire Seraphique forment cette composition, par un Maitre Italien.] | *Mat:* op koper *Size:* hoog 17, breed 12 ½ duim	Maria Magdalena van Sluypwyk, gravinne van Moens	(Sold) fl 20 Coclers
1803/06/20	AMSCH	0075	*Een Italiaansch Meester* | Een zinspeelende Ordennantie op de Kunsten en Wetenschappen, door een Italiaansch Meester, op Doek | *Mat:* op doek *Size:* hoog 30, breed 18 duim	Schley [for] F	(Sold) fl 4:5 Gruiter
1803/08/24	HGKAN	0085	*Een voornaam Italiaansch Meester* | De Kruissing van St. Pieter, door een voornaam Italiaansch Meester	[Teissier] [or others]	(Unknown) fl 5:5
1803/08/24	HGKAN	0086	*Een voornaam Italiaansch Meester* | Een Heilige in Devotie, mede door een voornaam Italiaansch Meester	[Teissier] [or others]	(Unknown) fl 2:10
1803/08/24	HGKAN	0096	*Een Italiaans Meester* | Een Vergadering der Heidensche Goden, door een Italiaans Meester	[Teissier] [or others]	(Sold) fl 0:10 Carre
1803/08/24	HGKAN	0097	*Een Italiaans Meester* | Twee historieele Italiaansche Schilderyen, door een Italiaans Meester	[Teissier] [or others]	(Sold) fl 3 Carre
1803/09/07	AMSCH	0274	*Een Italiaansch Meester* | St. Sebastiaan, met Pylen doorschooten, word door een Vrouw de Pylen uitgetogen, voorts een glorie van Engelen; meesterlyk behandeld, door een Italiaansch Meester [St.-Sébastien percé de flèches ; une femme lui arrache les flèches et des anges l'entourent au milieu d'une gloire ; d'une exécution parfaite, par un maître Italien] | *Mat:* op doek *Size:* hoog 21, breed 16 duim [Haut 21, large 15 pouces] *Notes:* The dimensions differ in the Dutch and French editions of the catalogue.	Smidt	(Sold) fl 1:10 Gruiter
1803/09/07	AMSCH	0280	*Een goed Italiaansch Meester* | Christus, de Kreupelen genéezende, zynde een ryke Ordonantie; fiks en meesterlyk op Doek geschilderd, door een goed Italiaansch Meester [Jésus-Christ guèrissant des boiteux ; d'une ordonnance riche : peint par un excellent maître Italien] | *Mat:* op doek *Size:* hoog 25, breed 29 duim *Notes:* The dimensions are given in the French edition as "Haut 25, large 19 pouces"; the width has been changed by hand to "29" in the RKDH copy of the catalogue.	Smidt	(Sold) fl 19 Tessier
1803/12/12	AMSCH	0136	*Een Italiaansch Meester* | Twee stuks, de Heilige Petrus en Paulus; op Doek, door een Italiaansch Meester | *Mat:* op doek *Size:* hoog 73, breed 43 duim	V[inkeles?]	(Sold) fl 2:5 Gruiter
1804/02/27	AMSCH	0127	*Een Italiaansche meester* | In een hoog Bergachtig Landschap, ziet men een optogt van eenige Krygslieden; fiks gepenceeld, door een Italiaansche meester	B	(Sold) fl 0:8 Geld
1804/02/27	AMSCH	0178	*Een Italiaansche meester* | Een groote Historiele Ordonantie; meesterlyk geschilderd, door een Italiaansche meester	B	(Sold) fl 0:6 Pruijssenaar [for] R
1804/05/07	AMSCH	0205	*Een Italiaans Meester* | Een Italiaans Boomryk Landschap, met eenige Gebouwen en een Rivier doorsneeden waarin een Schuit, op de voorgrond eenige Reizigers frapant van licht; door een Italiaans Meester	Roos [for] A	(Sold) fl 0:6 L Pakker
1804/05/07	AMSCH	0227	*Een Italiaansch Meester* | Een St. Fransiscus in de Woestyn, stout en meesterlyk behandeld, door een Italiaansch Meester, op Koper | *Mat:* op koper *Size:* hoog 8, breed 6 duim	Y[ver] [for] JJ	(Sold) fl 15:10 Lelie
1804/08/08	AMSCH	0252	*Een Italiaansch Meester* | Christus op den Berg, in een Biddende Gestalte, op de voorgrond leggen de Discipelen te slapen; fraai van Teekening en Coloriet, door een Italiaansch Meester | *Mat:* op koper	Roos a	(Sold) fl 5:10 Coclers
1804/08/08	AMSCH	0255	*Een voornaam Italiaansch Meester* | Een Herder en Herderin, bézig zynde uit een Rots te drinken; de behandeling is krachtig, en het coloriet toont dat het van een voornaam Italiaansch Meester geschilderd is, op Doek | *Mat:* op doek	Roos [for] C	(Sold) fl 6:10 Reijers
1804/08/08	AMSCH	0263	*Een Italiaansch Meester* | Een doode Christus, ondersteund wordende door een Engel, waarby een oud Man, verders een Landschap, op Koper, hoog 14, breed 10 duim, door een Italiaansch Meester | *Mat:* op koper *Size:* hoog 14, breed 10 duim	Vink[eles] [for] S	(Sold) fl 4 Gruyter

1804/08/08	AMSCH	0264	*Een Italiaansch Meester* | Twee oude Philosoophen, by hunne Globens en Boeken, geschilderd door een Italiaansch Meester | *Mat:* op doek *Size:* hoog 48, breed 36 duim	Vink[eles] [for] K[=Gruyter?]	(Sold) fl 0:10 L Pakker
1805/07/03	AMSCH	0209	*Een Italiaansch Meester* | Twee stuks Italiaansche Rots- en Boomryke Landschappen; breed op Doek, door een Italiaansch Meester | *Mat:* op doek	V[inkeles]	(Sold) fl 0:10 Yver
1805/07/03	AMSCH	0217	*Een Italiaansch Meester* | Een bevallig jong Vrouwepourtrait, schynende Vlas te winden, in ryke Kleeding; breed en meesterlyk gepenceeld op Doek, door een Italiaansch Meester | *Mat:* op doek	C	(Sold) fl 1 Agina
1805/07/10	AMSCH	0205	*Een Italiaansch Meester* | Een Zinnebeeldige Ordinantie; op Doek, door een Italiaansch Meester | *Mat:* op doek	V[inkeles] [for] G	(Sold) fl 1:5 Rookmans
1805/07/10	AMSCH	0208	*Een Italiaansch Meester* | Het Bruidje van Scipio; fraai van Hartstogten en meesterlyk gepenceeld, door een Italiaansch Meester | *Mat:* op doek *Size:* hoog 46, breed 59 duim	V[inkeles] [for] H[affner]	(Bought In) fl 3
1805/07/10	AMSCH	0209	*Een Italiaansch Meester* | Loth met zyn Dochters; fraai van coloriet en meesterlyk gepenceeld, door een Italiaansch Meester	V[inkeles] [for] H[affner]	(Bought In) fl 9:10
1805/07/10	AMSCH	0213	*Een Italiaansch Meester* | Een Boom- en Duinryk Landschap, met een Rivier doorsneeden; op Doek, door een Italiaansch Meester | *Mat:* op doek	V[inkeles] [for] H[affner]	(Bought In) fl 12
1805/07/10	AMSCH	0219	*Een Italiaansch Meester* | Christus aan 't Kruys, waarby Maria en Johannes; als door dito [een Italiaansch Meester]	Y[ver]	(Sold) fl 15 Kellerman
1805/07/10	AMSCH	0283	*Een Italiaansch Meester* | 't Afbeeldsel van een Apostel, halverlyf, houdende een Schulp in de Handen; breed en meesterlyk op Doek, door een Italiaansch Meester | *Mat:* op doek	V[inkeles] [for] L	(Sold) fl 3 Gruyter
1805/10/09	HGBSM	0037	*Een Italiaansch Meester* | Een ecce homo, door een Italiaansch Meester | *Mat:* op doek *Size:* hoog 28 breet 24 duim	T H van Willigen [or others]	(Sold) fl 5:5 Smeets
1805/12/16	AMSCH	0059	*Een beroemd Italiaansch Meester* | Twee stuks Italiaansche Boomryke Landschappen, met Rivieren doorsneeden, ryk gestoffeerd met Beelden, als Man, Vrouw en eenige naakte Kindertjes, beide deeze Schilderyen zyn aller delicaatst en uitvoerig gepenceeld, door een beroemd Italiaansch Meester | *Mat:* op doek *Size:* yder hoog 24, breed 28 duim	O	(Bought In) fl 35
1805/12/16	AMSCH	0124	*Een Italiaansch Meesters* | Twee stuks Bergachtige Landschappen; door een Italiaansch Meesters | *Notes:* This lot was sold with lot 125 by an anonymous artist.	Y	(Sold) fl 0:10 for lots 124 & 125. L Pakker
1806/05/05	AMSCH	0179	*Een Italiaansch Meester* | Een Historiele Ordinantie; meesterlyk op Paneel, door een Italiaansch Meester | *Mat:* op paneel	R[oos]	(Sold) fl 1:10 Alberti
1806/05/05	AMSCH	0229	*Een Italiaansch Meester* | Een Romeinsch Landschap, met antique Tempels en Gebouwen; meesterlyk door een Italiaansch Meester | *Mat:* op doek *Size:* hoog 44, breed 42 duim	L	(Sold) fl 6 van Laar
1806/05/05	AMSCH	0230	*Een Italiaansch Meester* | Een bevallig Vrouwen Pourtrait; door een Italiaansch Meester | *Mat:* op koper	L	(Sold) fl 2:5 Yver
1806/05/05	AMSCH	0243	*Een Italiaansch Meester* | Een Historieele Ordinantie; door een Italiaansch Meester	V[inkeles]	(Withdrawn)
1806/08/20	HGBSM	0147	*Italiaansche school* | Een Ecce Homo, levensgroote, natuurlijk en krachtig uit het Italiaansche school | *Mat:* op doek *Size:* hoog 42, breed 31 ½ duim	Macalester Loup [or others]	(Sold) fl 21 Zwartsman
1807/08/26	AMSCH	0250	*Een Italiaansch Meester* | Dit stuk vertoont, eene Vrouw met een pynelyk [sic] gelaat, half naakt, houdende de linker hand tegen de Borst, die gekwest schynt, en door een bejaard Heelmeester geholpen word; de hartstogten zyn natuurlyk, en van een meesterlyke breede Penceels-behandeling, op Doek, door een Italiaansch Meester | *Mat:* op doek *Size:* hoog 37, breed 45 duim *Notes:* This lot was sold with lot 251 by an anonymous artist.	Joseph Vallette	(Sold) fl 8:15 for lots 250 & 251. Hulswit
1807/08/26	AMSCH	0312	*Een Italiaansch Meester* | Een Italiaansch Landschap, gestoffeerd met verscheide Huislieden en verschillend Vee; krachtig geschilderd op Doek, door een Italiaansch Meester | *Mat:* op doek	Yver [for] S	(Sold) fl 0:10 L Pakker
1808/06/13	AMSCH	0241	*Een Italiaansch Meester* | Eene Venus, uit het Bad komende; meesterlijk fraai geschilderd, door een Italiaansch Meester	R[oos]	(Sold) fl 80 W Reijers
1808/08/23	AMSCH	0179a	*Een Italiaans Meester* | In een Landschap, vertoond zig Maria, zittende met Kindje aan de Borst, nevens haar staat Joseph, en in de Wolke een glorie van Engelen; bevallig en breed behandeld, op Koper, door een Italiaans Meester | *Mat:* op koper		(Withdrawn)
1808/08/23	AMSCH	0214	*Een Italiaans Meester* | Een jongen Bachus, houdende een Zilveren Lampet in de eene, en een Glasen Schaal in de anderen hand; meesterlijk en breed van penceelbehandeling, door een Italiaans Meester	[Coclers]	(Sold) fl 24:10 de Lelie
1808/11/28	AMSCH	0107	*Een Italiaansch Meester* | Het Copij naar een groot Blason, meesterlijk door een Italiaansch Meester | *Notes:* This lot was sold with lot 106, which is in the manner of Rubens.	H	(Sold) fl 0:14 for lots 106 & 107. Levie Pakker
1808/11/28	AMSCH	0108	*Een Italiaansch Meester* | Een Heilige Familje in een Landschap, krachtig op Doek geschilderd, door een dito [Italiaansch] Meester | *Mat:* op doek	H	(Sold) fl 1 Coclers

1808/11/28	AMSCH	0111	*Een Italiaansch Meester* | In een Landschap, vertoond zig de H. Maagd Maria, met het Kindje op haar Schoot, waar bij eenige Heilige Vrouwen en Engelen, kragtig op Doek, door een Italiaansch Meester | *Mat:* op doek	S	(Sold) fl 1 T Spaan
1809/07/19	AMSCH	0069	*Een Italiaansch Meester* | Eene boetvaardige Magdalena, met zaamgevouwe handen en de oogen hemelwaards, voor haar staat een Krusifix, een Doodshoofd en opengeslagen Boek. Teder en uitvoerig gepenceeld, door een Italiaansch Meester | *Mat:* op koper *Size:* hoog 9, breed 7 duim	[Wijkersloot?]	(Sold) fl 2:15 Zonnenberg
1810/03/23	HAVIN	0049	*Een Italiaan* | Een Manskop, fraai, door een Italiaan	Rudolf Hendrik de Wetstein [or others]	(Unknown)
1810/06/06	RMMUY	0094	*Een Italiaansch meester* | St. Jan den Dooper. Meesterlijk schoon geschilderd, door een Italiaansch meester | *Mat:* op doek		(Unknown) fl 6
1810/06/06	RMMUY	0168	*Een Italiaansch Meester* | Een Heilige op de Wolken, en Kindertjes. Door een Italiaansch Meester | *Mat:* op koper		(Unknown) fl 1
1810/06/06	RMMUY	0205	*Een Italiaansch Meester* | Een Historisch Onderwerp. Stout en krachtig geschilderd. Door een Italiaansch Meester | *Mat:* op doek		(Unknown) fl 4:10
1810/06/06	RMMUY	0206	*Een Italiaansch Meester* | Eene Groep met Vrugten. Door een Italiaansch Meester | *Mat:* op doek		(Unknown) fl 11:15
1810/06/06	RMMUY	0210	*Een Italiaansch Meester* | Een St. Paulus. Door een Italiaansch Meester | *Mat:* op doek		(Sold) fl 3 v Eijk
1810/06/20	AMSCH	0131	*Een Italiaansch Meester* | De Apostel Joannes; meesterlijk geschilderd door een Italiaansch Meester	S	(Sold) fl 1 Hodges
1810/06/20	AMSCH	0133	*Een Italiaansch Meester* | St. Sebastiaan aan een Boom gebonden, met pijlen doorschoten; meesterlijk op doek, door een Italiaansch Meester | *Mat:* op doek	S	(Sold) fl 3:15 Cassino
1810/10/11	AMSCH	0119	*Een Italiaansch Meester* | Het Afbeeldsel van eene bevallige Vrouw, voorstellende de Dichtkunst; zeer schoon geschilderd, door een Italiaansch Meester | *Mat:* op paneel *Size:* hoog 21, breed 17 duimen	M	(Sold) fl 10 de Vries

Italian (or Michelangelo)

1810/08/06	AMSCH	0136	*M. Angelo; Italiaansch Meester* | Zeven stuks, voorstellende de Werken van Barmhartigheid, ieder stuk eigenaardig met Beelden en toepasselijk bijwerk gestoffeerd en alle meesterlijk en breed geschilderd, door M. Angelo of een ander voornaam Italiaansch Meester | *Mat:* op doek *Size:* ieder is hoog 28, breed 38 duimen	A	(Sold) fl 40 J Spaan

Italian (copy after)

1802/09/06	AMSCH	0155	*een Italiaansch Meester* | Een Madona; naar een Italiaansch Meester, fix gepenceeld	Mevrouw Achtienhoven	(Sold) fl 2 J Yver

Italian (manner)

1805/07/10	AMSCH	0218	*Een Italiaansche Meester* | Een Historieele Ordinantie van verscheide Beelden; als door een Italiaansche Meester	Y[ver]	(Sold) fl 1:10 Geld

Italian – Venetian

1809/07/25	HGBSM	0080	*Een Venetiaans Meester* | Een zittende Vrouw, levensgroote met een Kind aan de borst, door een Venetiaans Meester | *Mat:* op doek *Size:* hoog 45 en een half, breed 35 en een half duim	D van der Aa [or] E B ten Dall	(Sold) fl 53 L Voerman

Swiss

1805/10/09	HGBSM	HH0033	*Een Zwitschers meester* | Een Zwitschers gezicht met stoffagie, door een Zwitschers meester | *Mat:* op paneel	T H van Willigen [or others]	(Sold) fl 1:2 van der Linden
1810/03/23	HAVIN	0052	*Een Zwitsers Meester* | Twee Gezigten aan de Boven-Rhijn, door een Zwitsers Meester	Rudolf Hendrik de Wetstein [or others]	(Unknown)

Index of Owners

1801–1810

A.
Anonymous 1801/03/16
Balen, H. (I) 1807/08/26
Brakenburg 1801/10/19
Brueghel, J. (I) 1805/12/16
Cok, J.M. 1802/06/28
Dame, A. 1809/06/13
Drielenburch, W. 1801/03/16
Ducq, Johan le 1801/10/19
Elliger, O. (II) 1807/08/26
Hoogsaat, J.C. 1810/03/26
Janson, J. 1801/10/19
Man 1804/04/28
Marseus, O. 1809/06/13
Matthieu, C. 1804/04/28
Meijer, Hend. (II) 1801/10/19
Mieris, W. 1801/10/19
Molenaer, Klaes 1808/08/23
Moreelse, P. 1810/03/26
Palamedesz., A. 1802/06/28
Schalcken 1802/06/28
Schalcken 1810/03/26
Schoute, Gilbert 1802/06/28
Seghers, D. 1802/06/28
Snyders, F. 1802/06/28
Steen, J. 1801/10/19
Teniers, D. (II) 1802/09/06
Tol, D. 1801/10/19
Vlieger, S. 1804/04/28
Vrancx 1802/06/28
Vroom, C. 1802/06/28
Waterloo, A. 1802/09/06
Wouwerman, P. 1804/04/28
Zeemann 1804/04/28

A. (1802, May 5)
Anonymous 1802/05/05
Asch, P.J. van 1802/05/05
Berckheyde, G. 1802/05/05
Blanckerhoff 1802/05/05
Brakenburg 1802/05/05
Brekelencam, Q. 1802/05/05
Brouwer, Adr. 1802/05/05
Brueghel, J. (I) 1802/05/05
Cappelle 1802/05/05
Dubois, J. 1802/05/05
Gelder, A. 1802/05/05
Grandjean, J. 1802/05/05
Janson, J. 1802/05/05
Lubienietski, C. 1802/05/05
Lundens 1802/05/05
Miereveld, M. 1802/05/05
Molenaer, J.M. 1802/05/05
Ommeganck, B. 1802/05/05
Ostade, A. 1802/05/05
Pynas, J. 1802/05/05
Snyders, F. 1802/05/05
Steen, J. 1802/05/05
Velde, W. 1802/05/05
Verschuring, H. 1802/05/05
Vrancx 1802/05/05
Weenix 1802/05/05
Wouwerman, Ph. 1802/05/05

A. (1802, December 13)
Aelst, W. 1802/12/13
Alcock 1802/12/13
Anonymous 1802/12/13
Asselyn 1802/12/13
Avercamp, H. 1802/12/13
Bega 1802/12/13
Bemmel, J. 1802/12/13
Berckheyde 1802/12/13
Berckheyde, G. 1802/12/13
Berninck, H. 1802/12/13
Bloemen, P. 1802/12/13
Borssom 1802/12/13
Brakenburg 1802/12/13
Brouwer, Adr. 1802/12/13
Brueghel, J. (I) 1802/12/13
Brueghel, P. (II) 1802/12/13
Camphuysen, R. 1802/12/13
Cappelle 1802/12/13
Carree, M. 1802/12/13
Compe, Jan ten 1802/12/13
Cuyp, A. 1802/12/13
Does 1802/12/13
Dubbels, H. 1802/12/13
Ducq, Johan le 1802/12/13
Ekels, Jan (I) 1802/12/13
Everdingen, A. 1802/12/13
Everdingen, Cesar 1802/12/13
Ferguson, Wm. 1802/12/13
Gael, B. 1802/12/13
Grasdorp, W. 1802/12/13
Hals, F. (I) 1802/12/13
Hansen, C.L. 1802/12/13
Heem, J.D. 1802/12/13
Heeremans, Thos. 1802/12/13
Helst, B. 1802/12/13
Heusch 1802/12/13
Honthorst, G. 1802/12/13
Italian 1802/12/13
Kessel, J. (III) 1802/12/13
Koller, J.J. 1802/12/13
Lauwers, J.J. 1802/12/13
Lingelbach 1802/12/13
Liss 1802/12/13
Lundens 1802/12/13
Maes, N. 1802/12/13
Molenaer, J.M. 1802/12/13
Molenaer, Klaes 1802/12/13
Molijn 1802/12/13
Mommers, H. 1802/12/13
Momper, J. (II) 1802/12/13
Myn, H. 1802/12/13
Neer, A. 1802/12/13
Netscher, Casp. 1802/12/13
Oolen, Adr. 1802/12/13
Os, Geo. 1802/12/13
Ostade, A. 1802/12/13
Regemorter, P. 1802/12/13
Rosa, S. 1802/12/13
Ruisdael, J. 1802/12/13
Ruysdael, S. 1802/12/13
Saftleven, H. 1802/12/13
Schellinks 1802/12/13
Simons, M. 1802/12/13
Soolmaker 1802/12/13
Sorgh, H.M. 1802/12/13
Storck, Abr. 1802/12/13
Thier, B.H. 1802/12/13
Velde, W. 1802/12/13
Vermeulen, A. 1802/12/13
Vitringa 1802/12/13
Vries, R. 1802/12/13
Wet, J.W. 1802/12/13
Wyck, T. 1802/12/13

A. (1803, April 27)
Albani, Fr. 1803/04/27
Amigoni, J. 1803/04/27
Andrea del Sarto 1803/04/27
Anna, Vito 1803/04/27
Anne, P. 1803/04/27
Anonymous 1803/04/27
Anonymous-Antique 1803/04/27
Anonymous-Modern 1803/04/27
Aquila, P. 1803/04/27
Bovette, Simone 1803/04/27
Caravaggio 1803/04/27
Carracci 1803/04/27
Carracci, L. 1803/04/27
Casanova, F. 1803/04/27
Cignani, C. 1803/04/27
Conca, S. 1803/04/27
Correggio 1803/04/27
David 1803/04/27
Domenichino 1803/04/27
Dughet 1803/04/27
Dyck, Anth. van 1803/04/27
Ferri, C. 1803/04/27
Flemal, B. (I) 1803/04/27
Giordano, L. 1803/04/27
Giorgione 1803/04/27
Giulio Romano 1803/04/27
Guercino 1803/04/27
Leonardo da Vinci 1803/04/27
Maratti 1803/04/27
Monbellian 1803/04/27
Moreelse, P. 1803/04/27
Novelli, P. 1803/04/27
Panini, G.P. 1803/04/27
Perugino 1803/04/27
Pichenelli 1803/04/27
Pietro da Cortona 1803/04/27
Polidoro da Caravag. 1803/04/27
Poussin, N. 1803/04/27
Raffaello Santi 1803/04/27
Reni 1803/04/27
Ribera 1803/04/27
Roos, P.P. 1803/04/27
Rosa, Fr. 1803/04/27
Rosa, S. 1803/04/27
Rubens 1803/04/27
Santafede, Fab. 1803/04/27
Schedoni 1803/04/27
Serenacio 1803/04/27
Serenado 1803/04/27
Settefano, M. 1803/04/27
Tiziano 1803/04/27

A. (1804, May 7)
identical with "F" on August 8, 1804
Anonymous 1804/05/07
Backhuysen 1804/05/07
Brouwer, Adr. 1804/05/07
Brueghel, J. (I) 1804/05/07
Carree, M. 1804/05/07
Compe, Jan ten 1804/05/07
Denies, I. 1804/05/07
Dolci, C. 1804/05/07
Ekels, Jan (I) 1804/05/07
Ekels, Jan (II) 1804/05/07
Essen, C. 1804/05/07
Faber, J.H. 1804/05/07
Goyen 1804/05/07
Hoorn, J. 1804/05/07
Huchtenburgh, Jan 1804/05/07
Italian 1804/05/07
Kruger, Jac. 1804/05/07
Laquy, W.J. 1804/05/07
Lingelbach 1804/05/07
Lubienietski, C. 1804/05/07
Maes, D. 1804/05/07
Metsu 1804/05/07
Mettenleiter, J.J. 1804/05/07
Mieris, W. 1804/05/07
Molenaer, J.M. 1804/05/07
Neer, A. 1804/05/07
Ouwater, Isaak 1804/05/07
Roedig, J.C. 1804/05/07
Roepel, C. 1804/05/07
Schouman, A. 1804/05/07
Schyndel 1804/05/07
Silo, A. 1804/05/07
Steen, J. 1804/05/07
Storck, Abr. 1804/05/07
Toorenburgh, G. 1804/05/07
Troost, C. 1804/05/07
Velde, A. 1804/05/07
Velde, W. 1804/05/07
Weenix, J.B. 1804/05/07
Wijnants 1804/05/07
Wit, Jacob de 1804/05/07
Witte, E. 1804/05/07

A. (1804, August 8)
Brakenburg 1804/08/08
Cuyp, J.G. 1804/08/08
Ducq, Johan le 1804/08/08
Goltzius, Hend. 1804/08/08
Hooch, P. 1804/08/08
Kessel, J. (III) 1804/08/08
Koninck, P. 1804/08/08
Lairesse, G. 1804/08/08
Lundens 1804/08/08
Marseus, O. 1804/08/08
Molijn 1804/08/08
Naiveu 1804/08/08
Velde, A. 1804/08/08
Velde, W. 1804/08/08
Victors, Jan 1804/08/08
Weenix 1804/08/08
Wijnants 1804/08/08
Wouwerman, P. 1804/08/08

A. (1807, August 26)
Anonymous 1807/08/26
Asch, P.J. van 1807/08/26
Bredael, J. 1807/08/26
Dujardin, K. 1807/08/26
Elliger, O. (II) 1807/08/26
Essen, C. 1807/08/26
Goyen 1807/08/26
Kalraet 1807/08/26
Molenaer, J.M. 1807/08/26
Monogrammist L.T. 1807/08/26
Romeyn 1807/08/26
Silo, A. 1807/08/26
Steen, J. 1807/08/26
Storck, Abr. 1807/08/26
Witte, E. 1807/08/26
Wouwerman, P. 1807/08/26
Wouwerman, Ph. 1807/08/26

A. (1809, April 17)
Anonymous 1809/04/17
Balen, H. (I) 1809/04/17
Bloot, P. 1809/04/17
Broeck, E. 1809/04/17
Brueghel, J. (I) 1809/04/17
Carree, Hend. (I) 1809/04/17
Decker, C. 1809/04/17
Heusch, Jacob 1809/04/17
Huchtenburgh, Jan 1809/04/17
Koninck, P. 1809/04/17
Looten, J. 1809/04/17
Miel 1809/04/17
Molenaer, J.M. 1809/04/17
Monogrammist L.B. 1809/04/17
Moucheron 1809/04/17
Os, Pieter G. 1809/04/17
Rombouts 1809/04/17
Saftleven, H. 1809/04/17
Savoye, D. 1809/04/17
Teniers, D. (II) 1809/04/17
Vermeer, Jan (III) 1809/04/17
Vermeulen, A. 1809/04/17
Vries, R. 1809/04/17
Wouwerman, P. 1809/04/17
Wouwerman, Ph. 1809/04/17

A. (1809, June 13)
Defrance, L. 1809/06/13
Koedijck 1809/06/13
Michaelis, G.J. 1809/06/13
Os, Geo. 1809/06/13
Pee, A. 1809/06/13
Steen, J. 1809/06/13
Verbeeck, P.C. 1809/06/13

A. (1810, June 20)
Alcock, E. 1810/06/20
Anonymous 1810/06/20
Appel 1810/06/20
Balen, H. (I) 1810/06/20
Beerstraten, J. 1810/06/20
Berchem, N.P. 1810/06/20
Bergh, R.V. 1810/06/20
Beyeren 1810/06/20
Bloemaert, A. 1810/06/20
Brakenburg 1810/06/20
Brekelencam, Q. 1810/06/20
Bruyn, T. 1810/06/20
Dalens, Dirck 1810/06/20
Ducq, Johan le 1810/06/20
Dyck, Anth. van 1810/06/20

Ekels, Jan (I) 1810/06/20
Ferguson, Wm. 1810/06/20
Glimes, P. de 1810/06/20
Goyen 1810/06/20
Hals, F. (I) 1810/06/20
Heemskerck 1810/06/20
Heeremans, Thos. 1810/06/20
Heusch, Jacob 1810/06/20
Hoet, G. (I) 1810/06/20
Hondecoeter, M. 1810/06/20
Horemans, J.J. (I) 1810/06/20
Huchtenburgh, Jan 1810/06/20
Koller, J.J. 1810/06/20
Koninck, P. 1810/06/20
Lairesse, Jan 1810/06/20
Lubienietski, C. 1810/06/20
Maes, D. 1810/06/20
Maes, N. 1810/06/20
Meijer, H. 1810/06/20
Miereveld, M. 1810/06/20
Mijts, J. 1810/06/20
Molenaer, J.M. 1810/06/20
Molenaer, Klaes 1810/06/20
Naiveu 1810/06/20
Ostade, A. 1810/06/20
Pothoven, H. 1810/06/20
Pynacker 1810/06/20
Schendel, B. 1810/06/20
Schyndel 1810/06/20
Smeesters 1810/06/20
Toorenvliet, A. 1810/06/20
Vermeulen, A. 1810/06/20
Verschuir 1810/06/20
Voorhout, J. (I) 1810/06/20
Withoos, M. 1810/06/20

A. (1810, August 6)
Bega 1810/08/06
Berchem, N.P. 1810/08/06
Berckheyde, G. 1810/08/06
Dou 1810/08/06
Dujardin, K. 1810/08/06
Gagneraux, Bén. 1810/08/06
Goyen 1810/08/06
Griffier, R. 1810/08/06
Hackert, J.P. 1810/08/06
Heusch, Wm. 1810/08/06
Heyden, J. 1810/08/06
Italian 1810/08/06
Kuster, J.K. 1810/08/06
Lairesse, G. 1810/08/06
Lingelbach 1810/08/06
Maes, D. 1810/08/06
Meincs, Gabriel 1810/08/06
Michelangelo 1810/08/06
Molenaer, Klaes 1810/08/06
Monogrammist G.G.F. 1810/08/06
Ruisdael, J. 1810/08/06
Steen, J. 1810/08/06
Teniers, D. (II) 1810/08/06
Vanloo, J.C.D. 1810/08/06
Velde, A. 1810/08/06
Vernet, C.J. 1810/08/06
Weenix 1810/08/06
Weenix, J.B. 1810/08/06
Wijnants 1810/08/06
Wüest, J.H. 1810/08/06
Zeemann 1810/08/06

A. (1810, October 11)
Anonymous 1810/10/11
Backer 1810/10/11
Bergen, D. 1810/10/11
Bloemaert 1810/10/11
Bloemaert, A. 1810/10/11
Boudewyns 1810/10/11
Brueghel, J. (I) 1810/10/11
Cabel, A. 1810/10/11
Carree 1810/10/11
Coelenbier, Jan 1810/10/11
Colonia, A. 1810/10/11
Cornelisz. van Haarlem 1810/10/11
Croos, W. 1810/10/11
Dyck, Anth. van 1810/10/11
Everdingen, A. 1810/10/11
Gelder, A. 1810/10/11
Goltzius, Hend. 1810/10/11
Goyen 1810/10/11
Hooch, P. 1810/10/11
Kalf 1810/10/11
Keirincx, Alex. 1810/10/11
Kips, J. 1810/10/11
Lairesse, Jan 1810/10/11
Lastman, P.P. 1810/10/11
Lingelbach 1810/10/11
Maes, N. 1810/10/11
Martszen, J. (II) 1810/10/11
Miereveld, M. 1810/10/11
Moeyaert, C. 1810/10/11
Molenaer, J.M. 1810/10/11
Molenaer, Klaes 1810/10/11
Monogrammist E.V.N. 1810/10/11
Neranus, A. 1810/10/11
Palamedesz., A. 1810/10/11
Potter, Paulus 1810/10/11
Roghman, R. 1810/10/11
Rubens 1810/10/11
Rynsoever, G. 1810/10/11
Saftleven, H. 1810/10/11
Schütz 1810/10/11
Storck, Abr. 1810/10/11
Storck, J. 1810/10/11
Teniers, D. (II) 1810/10/11
Tieling, C. 1810/10/11
Verkolje, N. 1810/10/11
Vinck, J. 1810/10/11
Vrancx 1810/10/11
Vrijmoet, J. 1810/10/11
Wit, Jacob de 1810/10/11

A, Van der, see Aa, van der

Aa, van der (relative of D. van der Aa)
buyer at the sale of Dirk van der Aa, July 25/26, 1809
Aa, Dirk 1809/07/25
Anonymous 1809/07/25
Backer 1809/07/25
Brakenburg 1809/07/25
Burch, Hendrick 1809/07/25
Cuyp, B. 1809/07/25
Flemish-Brabant 1809/07/25
Hals, F. (I) 1809/07/25
Hondecoeter, M. 1809/07/25
Hulst 1809/07/25
Keller, J.H. (II) 1809/07/25
Molenaer, J.M. 1809/07/25
Molijn 1809/07/25
Poel, E. 1809/07/25
Rubens 1809/07/25
Sibilla, G. 1809/07/25
Storck, Abr. 1809/07/25
Vermeulen, A. 1809/07/25
Wit, Jacob de 1809/07/25

Aa, Dirk van der
1731–1809; painter and dealer active in The Hague
Aa, Dirk 1809/07/25
Anonymous 1803/08/24
Anonymous 1809/07/25
Anonymous 1809/10/19
Anonymous-Modern 1809/07/25
Backer 1809/07/25
Backhuysen 1809/07/25
Beest, J. 1809/07/25
Begeyn 1809/07/25
Berckheyde, G. 1809/07/25
Bergen, D. 1809/07/25
Besanger, S. 1809/07/25
Besters, A.J. 1809/07/25
Blinkvliet, M. 1809/07/25
Bloemen 1809/10/19
Bloemen, P. 1805/10/09
Bloemen, P. 1809/07/25
Both, A. 1809/07/25
Brakenburg 1809/07/25
Brueghel 1809/07/25
Brueghel, P. (II) 1809/07/25
Burch, Hendrick 1809/07/25
Carree, Hend. (I) 1805/10/09
Carree, Hend. (I) 1809/07/25
Carree, M. 1809/07/25
Colyer, Edwaert 1809/07/25
Courtois, J. 1809/07/25
Cranach, L. (I) 1809/07/25
Crari, G.B. 1809/07/25
Crayer, G. 1803/08/24
Croos, A. 1809/07/25
Croos, N. 1809/07/25
Cuylenborch, A. 1809/07/25
Cuylenburg, C. 1809/07/25
Cuyp, A. 1809/07/25
Cuyp, B. 1809/07/25
Does 1809/07/25
Does, S. 1809/07/25
Dolci, C. 1809/07/25
Dongen, Dionys 1809/07/25
Droochsloot, J.C. 1809/07/25
Dujardin, K. 1809/07/25
Eeckhout, G. 1809/07/25
Ermels, J.F. 1807/06/10
Ermels, J.F. 1809/07/25
Fargue, P.C. 1809/07/25
Flemish-Brabant 1809/07/25
Francken 1809/07/25
French 1809/07/25
Gael, B. 1809/07/25
Gool, Jan 1809/07/25
Goyen 1809/07/25
Graat 1809/07/25
Hals, F. (I) 1809/07/25
Heeremans, Thos. 1809/07/25
Helmont, M. 1809/07/25
Hondecoeter 1809/07/25
Hondecoeter, M. 1809/07/25
Huchtenburgh, Jan 1809/07/25
Hulst 1809/07/25
Italian-Venetian 1809/07/25
Jansen, R. 1809/07/25
Jong, J. 1809/07/25
Kamper, Godaert 1809/07/25
Keller, J.H. (II) 1809/07/25
Koningh, L. 1809/07/25
Kuster 1809/07/25
Lambrechts, J.B. 1809/07/25
Laquy, W.J. 1809/07/25
Lens, A.C. 1809/07/25
Lin, H. 1809/07/25
Loren, S. 1809/07/25
Lust, D. 1809/07/25
Maes, N. 1809/07/25
Man, C. 1809/07/25
Mieris 1809/07/25
Molenaer, J.M. 1809/07/25
Molenaer, Klaes 1809/07/25
Molijn 1809/07/25
Monogrammist A.S.H. 1809/07/25
Monogrammist A.V.B. 1809/07/25
Monogrammist C.W.V.D.B. 1809/07/25
Monogrammist D.V.B. 1809/07/25
Monogrammist J.V.B. 1809/07/25
Monogrammist L. 1809/07/25
Moritz, Louis 1809/07/25
Neer, A. 1809/07/25
Netscher, Casp. 1809/07/25
Ostade, A. 1809/07/25
Ostade, I. 1809/07/25
Palamedesz., A. 1803/08/24
Palamedesz., A. 1809/07/25
Palamedesz., P. (I) 1809/07/25
Peeters, B. (I) 1809/07/25
Poel, E. 1809/07/25
Quast, P.J. 1809/07/25
Rembrandt 1809/07/25
Rode 1809/07/25
Roedig, J.C. 1809/07/25
Roepel, C. 1809/07/25
Romeyn 1809/07/25
Rubens 1809/07/25
Saftleven, H. 1809/07/25
Sant Acker, F. 1809/07/25
Savery, R. 1809/07/25
Schalcken 1809/07/25
Scheffer 1809/07/25
Schweickardt, H. 1809/07/25
Seghers, D. 1809/07/25
Sibilla, G. 1809/07/25
Soolmaker 1809/07/25
Steen, J. 1809/07/25
Stoop 1809/07/25
Storck, Abr. 1809/07/25
Tengeler, W. 1809/07/25
Thulden 1805/10/09
Thulden 1809/07/25
Troost, J.H. 1809/07/25
Ulft 1809/07/25
Valois, J.F. 1809/07/25
Vanloo, J. 1809/07/25
Velde, W. 1809/07/25
Verboom, A.H. 1809/07/25
Verbruggen, G. (II) 1809/07/25
Verelst, Joh. 1809/07/25
Vermeer, Jan (II) 1809/07/25
Vermeulen, A. 1809/07/25
Vernet, C.J. 1809/07/25
Verschuring, H. 1809/07/25
Vlieger, S. 1809/07/25
Vliet, H.C. 1803/08/24
Vonck, E. 1809/07/25
Voorhout, J. (I) 1809/07/25
Vrancx 1809/07/25
Wild, T. 1809/07/25
Wit, Jacob de 1809/07/25
Witmont, H. 1809/07/25
Wouwerman, Ph. 1809/07/25
Wst, G.D. 1809/07/25
Wulfraet 1809/07/25
Wyntrack, D. 1809/07/25

Abrahams, Bn.
Chalon, L. 1802/12/13

Abresch
Fargue, Maria la 1802/09/18

Achina, see Ackina

Achtienhoven, Weduwe, see Witt, Aldegonda Maria Theresia de

Ackermans, Pr.
Dattan 1802/05/10

Ackina
active until 1805; also spelled Achina and Agina
Aelst, W. 1805/07/10
Anonymous 1802/05/05
Anonymous 1802/06/16
Anonymous 1803/08/17
Anonymous 1805/07/03
Anonymous 1805/07/10
Asselyn 1803/08/17
Batist, Karel 1802/06/16
Berchem, N.P. 1802/06/16
Bisschop, J. 1802/06/16
Bol, F. 1802/05/05
Borch, G. ter (II) 1805/07/03
Brakenburg 1805/07/10
Bredael, J. 1805/07/03
Bredael, P. 1803/08/17
Bys, J.R. 1802/06/16
Carree 1805/07/03
Colaert, Johannes 1802/05/05
Cuyp, A. 1802/06/16
Dalens, Dirck (I) 1805/07/10
Delen 1805/07/10
Does, S. 1802/05/05
Dongen, Dionys 1802/06/16

Aelst, W. 1808/06/06
Bega 1802/09/18
Langendijk, D. 1808/06/06
Lingelbach 1810/03/26
Ommeganck, B. 1808/06/06
Ostade, A. 1810/03/26
Ruisdael, J. 1810/03/26
Thier, B.H. 1802/09/18
Wyck, T. 1802/09/18

Beeldsnijder, Wolfert, Mr.
1740–1806; iron merchant and alderman of Ijsselstein
Anonymous 1806/10/16
Balen 1806/10/16
Borch, G. ter (II) 1806/10/16
Bramer 1806/10/16
Brekelencam, Q. 1806/10/16
Bruegel, P. (I) 1806/10/16
Dalens, Dirck 1806/10/16
Denner, B. 1806/10/16
Dubbels, H. 1806/10/16
Ducq, Johan le 1806/10/16
Heemskerck, Jan 1806/10/16
Huchtenburgh, Jan 1806/10/16
Keyser, Thos. de 1806/10/16
Laer, P. 1806/10/16
Molenaer, J.M. 1806/10/16
Palamedesz., A. 1806/10/16
Saftleven, C. 1806/10/16
Storck, J. 1806/10/16
Vertangen 1806/10/16
Weenix 1806/10/16
Wouwerman, P. 1806/10/16

Beeldsnyder, see Beeldsnijder

Beer
Anonymous 1802/07/27
Ostade, A. 1802/07/27

Beijer, Charles
Anonymous 1802/02/23

Belaerts
Fargue, Maria la 1802/11/01

Beljaart, see Beljard

Beljard, Gerardus
d. ca.1806; resident of Middelburg
Anonymous 1802/10/18
Anonymous 1803/06/07
Anonymous 1803/06/27
Anonymous 1806/10/17
Backhuysen 1806/10/17
Brueghel 1806/10/17
Brueghel, P. 1806/10/17
Colyer, Edwaert 1806/10/17
Cort, H. 1806/10/17
Goyen 1806/10/17
Hondius, A. 1806/10/17
Hoogerheyden, E. 1806/10/17
Horemans, J.J. (I) 1806/10/17
Kleijne, David 1806/10/17
Monogrammist J.C.D. 1806/10/17
Monogrammist R.K.B. 1806/10/17
Ostade 1806/10/17
Roskam, H. 1806/10/17
Troost, C. 1806/10/17
Vermeulen 1806/10/17

Bendiks
Anonymous 1801/05/11

Bennekom, van
Wolfaerts, Artus 1802/09/21

Benthem, Salomon van
bookdealer and auctioneer in Middelburg
Anonymous 1802/10/18
Anonymous 1803/06/07
Anonymous 1803/11/30
Anonymous 1804/06/18
Anonymous 1807/10/12
Anonymous 1810/04/17
Anonymous 1810/09/17
Holsteijn, C. 1803/11/30

Berg, see also Bergh

Berg, Otto Willem Johan, Mr.
1752–1825; merchant and banker in Amsterdam, posthumously titled Heer van Dussen-Muilkerk en Middelburgh
Anonymous 1808/06/13
Beerstraten, A. 1808/06/13
Cuyp, J.G. 1808/06/13
Ekels, Jan (II) 1808/06/13
Gael, B. 1808/06/13
Lingelbach 1808/06/13
Rietschoof, H. 1808/06/13
Roghman, R. 1808/06/13
Storck, Abr. 1808/06/13

Bergen, van
Anonymous 1808/06/13
Poel, E. 1808/06/13
Witte, E. 1808/06/13

Bergen, van den (Gent)
Bergen, D. 1808/06/13

Bergh, van den
Anonymous 1803/12/12
Boonen, A. 1803/12/12
Eckhard, C. 1803/12/12

Bergh, van den (Gent)
Berchem, N.P. 1808/06/13
Metsu 1808/06/13
Poelenburgh, C. 1808/06/06
Steen, J. 1808/06/13

Bergh, Johannes Bernardus van den
1779–1831; dealer and gilder
Anonymous 1801/03/16
Horemans, J.J. (I) 1801/03/16
Martszen, J. (II) 1801/03/16
Vonck, E. 1801/03/16

Berghe, see Bergh

Bergveld
Nieulandt, A. (I) 1802/06/28
Titsinger 1802/06/28

Berkhaut
Steen, J. 1804/10/16

Bernard
Anonymous 1805/07/10
Troost, J.H. 1805/07/10

Bernard, Jan
1765–1833; amateur painter, draftsman, etcher and lithographer
Camsen, J. 1804/08/08
Myn, G. 1804/08/08

Bertin, see Burtin

Besançon
Sanders, G. 1801/03/31

Bicker, Jan Bernd
1746–1812; merchant, banker and politician in Amsterdam
Asselyn 1809/07/19
Berchem, N.P. 1809/07/19
Berckheyde, G. 1809/07/19
Borch, G. ter (II) 1809/07/19
Compe, Jan ten 1809/07/19
Dietrich, Chr. 1809/07/19
Does, S. 1809/07/19
Dubbels, H. 1809/07/19
Dujardin, K. 1809/07/19
Griffier, R. 1809/07/19
Heyden, J. 1809/07/19
La Haye, R. 1809/07/19
Lingelbach 1809/07/19
Metsu 1809/07/19
Mieris, F. (I) 1809/07/19
Molenaer, J.M. 1809/07/19
Netscher, Casp. 1809/07/19
Os, J. 1809/07/19
Ostade, A. 1809/07/19
Ouwater, Isaak 1809/07/19
Ruisdael, J. 1809/07/19
Slingeland, P.C. 1809/07/19
Steen, Antoon 1809/07/19
Steen, J. 1809/07/19
Teniers, D. (II) 1809/07/19
Velde, A. 1809/07/19
Velde, E. (I) 1809/07/19
Vrancx 1809/07/19
Wijnants 1809/07/19
Wouwerman, Ph. 1809/07/19

Bicker, Lambertus
1732–1801; professor of medicine
Anonymous 1802/05/22
Anonymous-Modern 1802/05/22
Beeldemaker 1802/05/22
Beerstraten 1802/05/22
Bloemaert, A. 1802/05/22
Both, J. 1802/05/22
Brueghel 1802/05/22
Glauber, J. 1802/05/22
Meijer, H. 1802/05/22
Moens, F. 1802/05/22
Monogrammist F.V.T. 1802/05/22
Romeyn 1802/05/22
Saftleven, H. 1802/05/22

Bie, de
Belgian dealer, probably from Antwerp
Apshoven 1803/04/20

Bierman, Gerrit Hendrik
Heem, C. 1802/09/21
Janson, J. 1802/09/21

Bijdals (widow)
active in Middelburg
Anonymous 1802/10/18

Blaauwpot, see Blauwpot

Blauwpot
Anonymous 1803/12/12
Eckhard, C. 1803/12/12
Kuster 1803/12/12

Bleuland, Jan
1756–1838; professor of medicine at Utrecht University
Janson, J. 1802/09/21

Blijk, Rafael van den
1768–1848; dealer in Dordrecht
Bout, P. 1810/07/23
Dubbels, H. 1802/11/01
Goyen 1810/07/23
Huchtenburgh, Jan 1802/11/01
Monogrammist A.S. 1810/07/23
Rombouts 1810/07/23
Verbuys, A. 1802/11/01

Blommers
Anonymous 1805/10/09
Beerstraten, A. 1805/10/09
Brouwer, Adr. 1805/10/09
Goyen 1805/10/09
Sorgh, H.M. 1805/10/09
Vries 1805/10/09
Zeemann 1805/10/09

Blussé, Pieter, Junior
bookdealer in Dordrecht, partner of Pieter van Braam, q.v.
Teniers, D. (II) 1810/07/23

Blyk, see Blijk

Bochaut
Cornelisz. van Haarlem 1810/10/11

Boelen
Anonymous 1801/03/16
Anonymous 1801/05/11
Anonymous 1801/08/19
Anonymous 1802/09/06
Anonymous 1803/08/01
Anonymous 1803/12/12
Anonymous 1805/07/10
Anonymous 1805/12/16
Anonymous 1806/05/05
Anonymous 1806/08/13
Anonymous 1808/08/23
Avercamp, H. 1802/02/16
Besters, A.J. 1805/07/10
Brakenburg 1805/07/10
Breenbergh 1801/05/11
Brekelencam, Q. 1802/09/06
Brouwer, Adr. 1802/06/16
Delen 1806/08/13
Does 1806/05/05
Dou 1802/09/06
Ekels, Jan (I) 1801/03/16
Elliger 1805/07/10
Fyt 1806/08/13
Hagen, Joris 1802/06/28
Heem 1802/09/06
Heemskerck 1802/06/28
Heusch, Wm. 1806/05/05
Hondecoeter, G. 1806/08/13
Honthorst, G. 1806/05/05
Jongh, L. 1805/07/10
Kessel, J. (III) 1808/06/13
Kruger, Jac. 1801/03/16
Laen, D.J. 1802/06/16
Molijn 1805/07/10
Momper, J. (II) 1802/09/06
Monogrammist A.B. 1806/08/13
Monogrammist J.A.H. 1802/06/28
Monogrammist P.S. 1802/06/28
Monogrammist R. 1802/06/16
Mutscher, A. 1801/05/11
Myn, H. 1801/08/19
Oolen, Adr. 1802/02/16
Oolen, Adr. 1806/05/05
Ostade 1802/09/06
Ostade, I. 1806/08/13
Rande, Abraham 1801/03/16
Roos, P.P. 1802/02/16
Rosa, S. 1802/02/16
Saftleven, C. 1802/06/28
Simons, M. 1806/05/05
Stuven 1801/03/16
Troyen, R. 1802/02/16
Velde, E. (I) 1806/05/05
Velde, E. (I) 1806/08/13
Velde, W. 1808/08/23
Verschuring, H. 1805/07/10
Vitringa 1806/05/05
Vrancx 1802/06/28
Waldorp, J.G. 1801/03/16
Wijnants 1802/06/28
Wit, Jacob de 1803/12/12
Wyck, T. 1806/05/05

Boelen, B.
Dubbels, H. 1802/12/13
Martszen, J. (II) 1802/12/13
Rubens 1808/06/13

Boelen, T.
Compe, Jan ten 1808/06/13
Haensbergen, J. van 1808/06/13
Lingelbach 1808/06/13

Ochtervelt 1808/06/13
Sam, Engel 1808/06/13
Wijnants 1808/06/13
Wyck, T. 1808/06/13

Boelhouwer
Anonymous 1806/05/05
Anonymous 1808/06/13
Anonymous 1808/08/23
Anonymous 1810/05/22
Anonymous 1810/10/11
Beyeren 1810/06/20
Brakenburg 1810/06/20
Bril, P. 1808/08/23
Brueghel, J. (I) 1808/08/23
Carracci, L. 1810/07/26
Dürer 1810/07/26
Goltzius, Hend. 1810/10/11
Goyen 1805/07/10
Goyen 1808/08/23
Hobbema 1810/06/20
Hondecoeter, M. 1810/06/20
Huysmans, C. 1806/08/13
Huysmans, C. 1810/07/26
Klomp 1810/10/11
Kuik, J. 1809/06/13
Molenaer, J.M. 1810/06/20
Molenaer, Klaes 1808/08/23
Ostade, I. 1809/06/13
Porcellis, Jan 1810/05/22
Pynacker 1810/07/26
Reni 1810/07/26
Rosa, S. 1810/07/26
Schepper 1810/10/11
Schouman, A. 1809/06/13
Teniers, D. (II) 1806/08/13
Tieling, C. 1810/08/06
Weenix, J.B. 1810/06/20
Wijnants 1810/05/22
Witte, E. 1806/05/05

Boercoert
Both, A. 1802/11/01
Diepraem 1802/11/01
Gelder, A. 1802/11/01

Boers
Anonymous 1809/07/25
Monogrammist L. 1809/07/25

Boerse, see Boersen

Boersen, Juffr.
Anonymous 1802/07/27
Brekelencam, Q. 1802/07/27
Dusart, Corn. 1802/07/27
Fris, Jan 1802/07/27
Neeffs, P. (I) 1802/07/27

Boerson, see Boersen

Bogaard
includes Bogard, Bogart and Bogaart
Anonymous 1807/06/10
Anonymous 1809/07/25
Backhuysen 1809/07/25
Baen, Jan de 1807/06/10
Cappelle 1807/06/10
Croos, S. 1808/06/11
Cuylenburg, C. 1809/07/25
Flinck 1807/06/10
Francken 1809/07/25
Kobell, Jan (II) 1808/06/11
Molijn 1810/07/23
Schouman, A. 1808/06/06
Vrancx 1809/07/25
Wit, Jacob de 1809/07/25

Bogaart, see Bogaard

Bogard, see Bogaard

Bogart, see Bogaard

Boldoot
Zeemann 1809/06/13

Bols, L.
Beijer, J. de 1810/08/06

Bolten, J.
Brekelencam, Q. 1804/05/07

Bomme, Leendert Haze, see Haze Bomme, Leendert

Bonte
Brekelencam, Q. 1809/04/22
Victors, Jan 1809/04/22

Bonvoije
Anonymous 1808/08/23

Booijmans, see Boymans

Boom, Dr.
Anonymous 1803/10/10

Bos, J. de
Bol, F. 1810/08/06
Lairesse, G. 1810/08/06
Wit, Jacob de 1810/08/06

Bosboom, Frans Johannes
dealer and auctioneer in The Hague
Anonymous 1809/07/25

Boscet
Anonymous 1802/05/24
Bruegel, P. (I) 1802/05/24

Bosch, de
Wouwerman, Ph. 1810/08/01

Bosch, van den
Beerstraten, A. 1806/11/24
Beschey, J. 1810/08/10
Dusart, Corn. 1806/11/24
Huchtenburgh, Jan 1806/11/24
Laquy, W.J. 1806/11/24
Pothoven, H. 1806/11/24

Bosch Jeronimozn. II, Bernardus de
1742–1816; auctioneer, son of Jeronimo de Bosch II, nephew of Bernardus de Bosch Jeronimozn. I, and brother-in-law of Jeronimo de Vries
Berckheyde, G. 1801/05/11
Borch, G. ter (II) 1801/05/11
Velde, A. 1801/05/11
Wijnants 1801/05/11

Bosse
Anonymous 1803/10/10

Bosset
Anonymous 1802/05/24
Velde, E. (I) 1802/05/24

Boulhouwer, see Boelhouwer

Bouman, Leonardus
d. ca.1802; Catholic priest in Leyden
Aelst, W. 1802/08/24
Anonymous 1802/08/24
Backhuysen 1802/08/24
Balen, H. (I) 1802/08/24
Beeldemaker 1802/08/24
Bent, J. 1802/08/24
Berchem, N.P. 1802/08/24
Bloos, P. 1802/08/24
Borch, G. ter (II) 1802/08/24
Brekelencam, Q. 1802/08/24
Brouwer, Adr. 1802/08/24
Coclers, J.B.B. 1802/08/24
Croos, N. 1802/08/24
Cuyp, A. 1802/08/24
Dalens, Dirck 1802/08/24
Denies, I. 1802/08/24
Does, S. 1802/08/24
Doornik, Jan 1802/08/24
Glauber, J. 1802/08/24
Goyen 1802/08/24
Graat 1802/08/24
Griffier, J. (I) 1802/08/24
Heemskerck 1802/08/24
Hoet, G. (I) 1802/08/24
Hoogstraten, S. 1802/08/24
Huchtenburgh, Jan 1802/08/24
Italian 1802/08/24
Janson, J. 1802/08/24
Janson, J.C. 1802/08/24
Janson, P. 1802/08/24
Jordaens, H. 1802/08/24
La Haye, R. 1802/08/24
Lelienbergh 1802/08/24
Man 1802/08/24
Maton, B. 1802/08/24
Meuleman, P. 1802/08/24
Mieris, F. (II) 1802/08/24
Mieris, W. 1802/08/24
Molenaer, J.M. 1802/08/24
Molenaer, Klaes 1802/08/24
Mommers, H. 1802/08/24
Moni, L. de 1802/08/24
Monogrammist C.B. 1802/08/24
Monogrammist H. 1802/08/24
Monogrammist V.H. 1802/08/24
Moor, C. 1802/08/24
Moucheron 1802/08/24
Naiveu 1802/08/24
Neer, A. 1802/08/24
Neer, E. 1802/08/24
Netscher, Casp. 1802/08/24
Ostade, A. 1802/08/24
Ostade, I. 1802/08/24
Palamedesz., A. 1802/08/24
Palamedesz., P. (I) 1802/08/24
Porcellis, Jan 1802/08/24
Pynacker 1802/08/24
Renard 1802/08/24
Reyers, R. 1802/08/24
Romeyn 1802/08/24
Rossen, Dirk 1802/08/24
Rubens 1802/08/24
Ruisdael 1802/08/24
Ruisdael, J. 1802/08/24
Ruysdael, S. 1802/08/24
Saenredam, P.J. 1802/08/24
Saftleven, H. 1802/08/24
Schaalje, C.J. 1802/08/24
Schalcken 1802/08/24
Seghers, D. 1802/08/24
Sluis, J. 1802/08/24
Soolmaker 1802/08/24
Sorgh, H.M. 1802/08/24
Steen, J. 1802/08/24
Storck, Abr. 1802/08/24
Swanevelt 1802/08/24
Teniers, D. (II) 1802/08/24
Tol, D. 1802/08/24
Toorenvliet, J. 1802/08/24
Veer, Abraham 1802/08/24
Velde 1802/08/24
Velde, A. 1802/08/24
Verkolje 1802/08/24
Vertangen 1802/08/24
Victors, Jan 1802/08/24
Vlieger, S. 1802/08/24
Vliet, H.C. 1802/08/24
Vries, R. 1802/08/24
Weenix 1802/08/24
Werff, A. 1802/08/24
Wet, J.W. 1802/08/24
Wouwerman, Ph. 1802/08/24
Wyck, T. 1802/08/24

Bourne, L. H. De Hare
Does, J. (I) 1802/05/10

Bout
Anonymous 1802/02/23

Bouwer, see Baur

Boymans, Frans Jacob Otto
d. 1847; judge at the Utrecht Court of Justice
Poelenburgh, C. 1801/10/19
Werff, A. 1801/10/19

Braam, Pieter van
1740–1817; bookseller, auctioneer, printer, and poet in Dordrecht; partner of Pieter Blussé Junior, q.v.
Anonymous 1802/11/01
Avercamp, H. 1810/07/23
Beerstraten, A. 1810/07/23
Duynen, I. 1802/11/01
Goyen 1802/11/01
Janson, J. 1802/11/01
Porcellis, Jan 1810/07/23
Verschuring, H. 1802/11/01
Vosmaer, Nic. 1802/11/01

Bracke, van den
Anonymous 1809/04/22
Bol, F. 1809/04/22
Hackaert, J. 1809/04/22
Lingelbach 1809/04/22
Rembrandt 1809/04/22

Brandwyk, see Randwijk

Brave
Balen, H. (I) 1802/09/06
Berchem, N.P. 1802/09/06
Both, J. 1802/09/06
Brueghel, P. 1802/09/06
Courtois, J. 1802/09/06
Cranach, L. (I) 1802/09/06
Neer, A. 1802/09/06
Ostade, I. 1802/09/06
Pynacker 1802/09/06
Saftleven, C. 1802/09/06
Seghers, D. 1802/09/06
Teniers, D. (II) 1802/09/06
Wouwerman, P. 1802/09/06

Bredius, Abraham
1781–1863; owner of a gunpowder factory in Amsterdam; often working in partnership with his father-in-law J. Remmers, q.v.
Anonymous 1809/04/22
Compe, Jan ten 1809/07/19
Defrance, L. 1809/06/13
Gossaert 1810/08/01
Hondecoeter, M. 1809/04/22
Janson, J. 1809/04/22
Lamme, A. 1809/04/22
Laquy, W.J. 1809/04/22
Lingelbach 1809/09/06
Michaelis, G.J. 1809/06/13
Moni, L. de 1809/09/06
Os, Pieter G. 1809/04/22
Ouwater, Isaak 1809/07/19
Palthe 1809/04/22
Silo, A. 1809/04/22
Steen, J. 1810/08/06
Teniers, D. (II) 1810/08/06
Thier, B.H. 1809/04/22
Velde, W. 1809/07/19
Verbeeck, P.C. 1809/06/13
Vries, R. 1809/04/22
Wouwerman, Ph. 1809/04/22
Zepp, C. 1809/06/13

Breemen, van
Ruisdael, J. 1807/06/10

Brendel
Anonymous 1802/05/24

Brender
Anonymous 1801/03/31

Brent, Carle Van
Vernet, C.J. 1801/04/23

Brerkhuis
Brakenburg 1804/10/16

Brink, van den
Anonymous 1803/04/27
Anonymous 1803/09/07
Aquila, P. 1803/04/27
Backhuysen 1805/07/10
Blanckerhoff 1804/02/27
Castiglione, G.B. 1803/09/07
Courtois, J. 1803/09/07
Dusart, Corn. 1804/02/27
Guercino 1803/04/27
Huchtenburgh, Jan 1804/02/27
Maratti 1803/04/27
Monogrammist J.D.S. 1804/02/27
Moucheron, F. 1804/02/27
Neer, A. 1804/02/27
Panini, G.P. 1803/04/27
Pietro da Cortona 1803/04/27
Poel, E. 1803/09/07
Rubens 1803/04/27
Tiziano 1803/04/27
Trautmann, J.G. 1803/09/07

Broek, van den
Anonymous 1805/10/09
Backer 1805/10/09
Croos 1805/10/09
Dalens, Dirck 1805/10/09
Poelenburgh, C. 1805/10/09
Schalcken 1805/10/09
Willegen, D. 1805/10/09

Broekhinkel, H.
resident of Delfshaven
Fredriks, J.H. 1810/03/26

Bron
Anonymous 1801/10/06
Laer, P. 1801/10/06

Bronsteede
Huysum, Justus van (I) 1801/04/23

Brouwer
Carree, M. 1802/07/27
Gaesbeeck, A. 1802/06/28
Monogrammist J.A.H. 1802/06/28
Rembrandt 1802/07/27
Steen, J. 1802/06/28
Troost, C. 1802/06/28
Verkolje, N. 1802/06/28
Vitringa 1802/07/27

Bruin, de
Aelst, W. 1809/04/22
Amers, Piters 1809/04/22
Anonymous 1809/04/22
Apshoven 1809/04/22
Balen 1809/04/22
Barbiers, P. 1809/04/22
Beerstraten, A. 1809/04/22
Begeyn 1809/04/22
Bent, J. 1809/04/22
Berchem, N.P. 1809/04/22
Berckheyde, G. 1809/04/22
Bergen, D. 1809/04/22
Bloot, P. 1809/04/22
Boonen, A. 1809/04/22
Borssom 1809/04/22
Both, J. 1809/04/22
Boursse, E. 1809/04/22
Bramer 1809/04/22
Brekelencam, Q. 1809/04/22
Brueghel, J. (I) 1809/04/22
Brussel, P. 1809/04/22
Camphuysen 1809/04/22
Carree, M. 1809/04/22
Compe, Jan ten 1809/04/22
Coques 1809/04/22
Cuyp, A. 1809/04/22
Cuyp, J.G. 1809/04/22
Decker, C. 1809/04/22
Dou 1809/04/22
Droochsloot, Abr. 1809/04/22
Dubbels, H. 1809/04/22
Ducq, Johan le 1809/04/22
Eckhardt 1809/04/22
Essen, C. 1809/04/22
Fargue, Maria la 1809/04/22
Gaesbeeck, A. 1809/04/22
Gool, Jan 1809/04/22
Goyen 1809/04/22
Greuze 1809/04/22
Hals, F. (I) 1809/04/22
Heda 1809/04/22
Heusch, Wm. 1809/04/22
Hobbema 1809/04/22
Hondecoeter, M. 1809/04/22
Huchtenburgh, Jan 1809/04/22
Hulft, T.M. 1809/04/22
Hulk, A. Pietersz. 1809/04/22
Janson, J. 1809/04/22
Klomp 1809/04/22
Lamme, A. 1809/04/22
Laquy, W.J. 1809/04/22
Lauwers, J.J. 1809/04/22
Lelienbergh 1809/04/22
Lundens 1809/04/22
Mansker 1809/04/22
Metsu 1809/04/22
Mettenleiter, J.J. 1809/04/22
Mieris, F. (I) 1809/04/22
Mieris, W. 1809/04/22
Molenaer, J.M. 1809/04/22
Molenaer, Klaes 1809/04/22
Moni, L. de 1809/04/22
Monogrammist J.P. 1809/04/22
Monogrammist S.H.K. 1809/04/22
Morel, Jan Evert 1809/04/22
Moucheron, F. 1809/04/22
Os, Pieter G. 1809/04/22
Ostade 1809/04/22
Ostade, A. 1809/04/22
Ostade, I. 1809/04/22
Oudendyck, A. 1809/04/22
Ouwater, J. 1809/04/22
Palamedesz., A. 1809/04/22
Palthe 1809/04/22
Pardanus, Abraham 1809/04/22
Pee 1809/04/22
Pee, T. 1809/04/22
Peeters, B. (I) 1809/04/22
Poel, E. 1809/04/22
Potter, Paulus 1809/04/22
Rembrandt 1809/04/22
Ruisdael, J. 1809/04/22
Ruysdael, S. 1809/04/22
Schmitt, J.C. 1809/04/22
Schyndel, J. 1809/04/22
Siberechts, J. 1809/04/22
Silo, A. 1809/04/22
Soolmaker 1809/04/22
Sorgh, H.M. 1809/04/22
Spaendonck, G. 1809/04/22
Steen, J. 1809/04/22
Storck, J. 1809/04/22
Teniers, D. (II) 1809/04/22
Thier, B.H. 1809/04/22
Tol, D. 1809/04/22
Toorenvliet, J. 1809/04/22
Uden, Lucas 1809/04/22
Velde, E. (I) 1809/04/22
Velde, W. 1809/04/22
Vermeulen, A. 1809/04/22
Vermeulen, Corn. (III) 1809/04/22
Versteeg 1809/04/22
Victors, Jan 1809/04/22
Vliet, H.C. 1809/04/22
Vries, R. 1809/04/22
Weenix, J.B. 1809/04/22
Wijnants 1809/04/22
Winter, Gillis 1809/04/22
Wit, Jacob de 1809/04/22
Wouwerman, Ph. 1809/04/22
Wyck, T. 1809/04/22
Zepp, C. 1809/04/22

Bruin de Neve, de
resident of Dordrecht
Carree, M. 1810/08/10
Cerquozzi 1810/08/10
Dou 1810/08/10
Molenaer, J.M. 1810/08/10
Wyntrack, D. 1810/08/10

Brunelli
Andrea del Sarto 1810/06/06
Anonymous 1810/06/06
Carree, M. 1810/06/06
Dyck, Anth. van 1810/06/06
Nijmegen, D. 1810/06/06
Poussin, N. 1810/06/06

Bruning, A.
Anonymous 1803/04/20

Brunis
Anonymous 1803/04/20
Verelst, S. 1803/04/20
Wigmana, G. 1803/04/20

Bruyn, de, see Bruin, de

Bruys
Knip, N.F. (I) 1802/07/27

Bryan
possibly the English dealer Michael Bryan, 1757–1821
Anonymous 1801/06/13
Cuyp, J.G. 1801/06/13
Neer, A. 1801/06/13

Bucerus
Marseus, O. 1802/07/27

Buck
Anonymous 1809/06/13
Bol, F. 1809/06/13
Defrance, L. 1809/06/13
Droochsloot, J.C. 1809/06/13
Koninck, P. 1809/06/13
Lundens 1809/06/13
Roos, K. 1809/06/13
Schütz 1809/06/13
Teniers, D. (II) 1809/06/13
Tol, D. 1809/06/13
Toorenvliet, A. 1809/06/13
Vermeulen, A. 1809/06/13
Vollerdt, J.C. 1809/06/13
Wouwerman, P. 1809/06/13
Wubbels, Jan 1809/06/13
Wulfraet 1809/06/13
Zegelaar, G. 1809/06/13

Buford, Abr.
Finjé, A. 1804/10/22
Monogrammist J.R.W. 1804/10/22

Buijs, see also Buys

Buijs, Cornelis
1746–1826; art teacher, draftsman, aquarellist and painter
Lairesse, G. 1809/09/06
Metsu 1801/05/11

Buike, see Buiker

Buiker
active in Dordrecht; also spelled Buike
Anonymous 1803/10/10

Bulhouwer, see Boelhouwer

Bunt, H.
Monogrammist D.V.B. 1809/07/27

Burch Wz., Franc van der, Mr.
d. ca.1804; mayor of Delft
Anonymous 1804/07/25
Backhuysen 1804/07/25
Bakken 1804/07/25
Beeldemaker, A.C. 1804/07/25
Bon, C. de 1804/07/25
Borch, G. ter (II) 1804/07/25
Boudewyns 1804/07/25
Brekelencam, Q. 1804/07/25
Brouwer, Adr. 1804/07/25
Brueghel 1804/07/25
Burg (Burgh) 1804/07/25
Carree, Hend. (I) 1804/07/25
Cuyp, A. 1804/07/25
Dou 1804/07/25
Droochsloot, J.C. 1804/07/25
Ducq, Johan le 1804/07/25
Goyen 1804/07/25
Haastert, I. 1804/07/25
Hals, F. (I) 1804/07/25
Heemskerck, M. 1804/07/25
Heemskerk, H. 1804/07/25
Heeremans, Thos. 1804/07/25
Heusch 1804/07/25
Hooch, P. 1804/07/25
Huchtenburgh, Jan 1804/07/25
Jonge, M. 1804/07/25
Koninck 1804/07/25
Lievens, J. (I) 1804/07/25
Molenaer, J.M. 1804/07/25
Monogrammist I.W. 1804/07/25
Monogrammist J.G. 1804/07/25
Monogrammist L.B. 1804/07/25
Monogrammist P. 1804/07/25
Monogrammist V.Z. 1804/07/25
Mortel 1804/07/25
Neter, L. 1804/07/25
O., Jaques 1804/07/25
Olis 1804/07/25
Ostade 1804/07/25
Ous, S. 1804/07/25
Palamedesz., A. 1804/07/25
Palamedesz., P. (I) 1804/07/25
Poel, E. 1804/07/25
Poelenburgh, C. 1804/07/25
Porcellis, Jan 1804/07/25
Rembrandt 1804/07/25
Ribera 1804/07/25
Rijnenburg, N. 1804/07/25
Ruisdael, J. 1804/07/25
Saenredam 1804/07/25
Saftleven, C. 1804/07/25
Saftleven, H. 1804/07/25
Steen, J. 1804/07/25
Steenwyck, Hend. 1804/07/25
Teniers, D. (II) 1804/07/25
Tol, D. 1804/07/25
Trytam, E. 1804/07/25
Verdonck, Corn. 1804/07/25
Vlieger, S. 1804/07/25
Zeemann 1804/07/25

Buren, J. van, Mr.
bailiff for Noordwijkerhout, Hillegom, Lisse and Voorhout
Anonymous 1808/11/12
Beham, H.S. 1808/11/12
Bloemaert, A. 1808/11/12
Carracci, Agost. 1808/11/12
Carriera 1808/11/12
Heeremans, Thos. 1808/11/12
Holbein, H. (II) 1808/11/12
Hooch, P. 1808/11/12
Janson, J. 1808/11/12
Janson, J.C. 1808/11/12
Janson, P. 1808/11/12
Kessel, J. (I) 1808/11/12

C. (1808, November 28)
Anonymous 1808/11/28
Borch, G. ter (II) 1808/11/28
Haag, T.P.C. 1808/11/28
Heem, J.D. 1808/11/28
Houckgeest, G. 1808/11/28
Limborch, H. 1808/11/28
Palamedesz., A. 1808/11/28
Vitringa 1808/11/28
Vries, R. 1808/11/28

C. (1809, April 17)
Anonymous 1809/04/17
Backhuysen 1809/04/17
Beerstraten, J. 1809/04/17
Bega 1809/04/17
Berchem, N.P. 1809/04/17
Bergen, D. 1809/04/17
Brekelencam, Q. 1809/04/17
Lingelbach 1809/04/17
Moucheron, F. 1809/04/17
Rubens 1809/04/17
Ruisdael, J. 1809/04/17
Vermeer, Jan (III) 1809/04/17

C. (1809, July 19)
Anonymous 1809/07/19
Compe, Jan ten 1809/07/19
Goyen 1809/07/19
Hondecoeter, M. 1809/07/19
Knupfer 1809/07/19
Lingelbach 1809/07/19
Rembrandt 1809/07/19
Storck, Abr. 1809/07/19
Voorhout, J. (I) 1809/07/19
Vosmaer, Daniel 1809/07/19
Vrancx 1809/07/19
Wit, Jacob de 1809/07/19
Wtewael, J. 1809/07/19

C. (1810, June 20)
Ekels, Jan (II) 1810/06/20
Schalcken 1810/06/20

C. (1810, August 6)
Anonymous 1810/08/06
Beerstraten, A. 1810/08/06
Berckheyde, G. 1810/08/06
Brakenburg 1810/08/06
Brueghel, J. (I) 1810/08/06
Coelenbier, Jan 1810/08/06
Dou 1810/08/06
Honthorst, G. 1810/08/06
Miereveld, M. 1810/08/06
Mignon, A. 1810/08/06
Molenaer, J.M. 1810/08/06
Momper, J. (II) 1810/08/06
Musscher, M. 1810/08/06
Ostade, I. 1810/08/06
Poel, E. 1810/08/06
Ruyven, P.J. 1810/08/06
Steen, J. 1810/08/06
Ulft 1810/08/06
Velde, E. (I) 1810/08/06
Vliet, H.C. 1810/08/06
Vois, Ary de 1810/08/06

C. (1810, October 11)
Anonymous 1810/10/11
Berchem, N.P. 1810/10/11
Both, J. 1810/10/11
Bril, P. 1810/10/11
Brueghel, J. (I) 1810/10/11
Brugman, N. 1810/10/11
Claude Lorrain 1810/10/11
Coninxloo, G. 1810/10/11
Cuyp 1810/10/11
Diepenbeeck, A.J. 1810/10/11
Does, S. 1810/10/11
Dou 1810/10/11
Elsheimer, A. 1810/10/11
Griffier, R. 1810/10/11
Jordaens, J. (I) 1810/10/11
Lauri, F. 1810/10/11
Leyden, J. 1810/10/11
Maes, D. 1810/10/11
Melder, G. 1810/10/11
Metsu 1810/10/11
Miereveld, M. 1810/10/11
Molenaer, J.M. 1810/10/11
Moor, C. 1810/10/11
Neer, A. 1810/10/11
Oolen, Jan 1810/10/11
Ostade, A. 1810/10/11
Potter, Paulus 1810/10/11
Pynacker 1810/10/11
Rembrandt 1810/10/11
Rubens 1810/10/11
Schalcken 1810/10/11
Slingeland, P.C. 1810/10/11
Steen, J. 1810/10/11
Teniers, D. (II) 1810/10/11
Tol, D. 1810/10/11
Vinne, V.L. (I) 1810/10/11
Vliet, H.C. 1810/10/11
Vrancx 1810/10/11
Vroom, H. 1810/10/11
Weenix, J.B. 1810/10/11
Zeemann 1810/10/11

CC. (1802, May 5)
Anonymous 1802/05/05

Calckberner, Johan Caspar
1721–1803; resident of Breda
Anonymous 1804/08/02
Balen, H. (I) 1804/08/02
Berchem, N.P. 1804/08/02
Bloemaert, A. 1804/08/02
Bosschaert 1804/08/02
Brueghel, J. (I) 1804/08/02
Carree 1804/08/02
Colyer, Edwaert 1804/08/02
Cossiers, J. 1804/08/02
Douien 1804/08/02
Droochsloot, J.C. 1804/08/02
Ducq, Johan le 1804/08/02
Erp 1804/08/02
Francken 1804/08/02
Hoecke, J. 1804/08/02
Holf, N. 1804/08/02
Huchtenburgh, Jan 1804/08/02
Jordaens, J. (I) 1804/08/02
Kessel, J. (I) 1804/08/02
Lingelbach 1804/08/02
Molenaer, J.M. 1804/08/02
Momper, J. (II) 1804/08/02
Monogrammist H.D.M. 1804/08/02
Monogrammist P.V.H. 1804/08/02
Neeffs, P. (I) 1804/08/02
Noot 1804/08/02
Palamedesz., P. (I) 1804/08/02
Poelenburgh, C. 1804/08/02
Quellinus, E. (II) 1804/08/02
Rubens 1804/08/02
Saftleven, C. 1804/08/02
Savery, R. 1804/08/02
Snyders, F. 1804/08/02
Stalbemt 1804/08/02
Vinckeboons, D. 1804/08/02
Vlieger, S. 1804/08/02
Vrancx 1804/08/02
Vries, R. 1804/08/02
Wijnants 1804/08/02
Willeboirts 1804/08/02
Wouters, F. 1804/08/02
Wouwerman 1804/08/02

Camphuijsen, see Camphuysen

Camphuysen
possibly the Amsterdam painter Jan Kamphuijsen, 1760–1841
Anonymous 1801/06/10
Anonymous 1803/04/27
Anonymous 1805/12/16
Backhuysen 1804/08/08
Dusart, Corn. 1802/06/28
Hackaert, J. 1803/08/17
Heem, C. 1804/08/08
Holbein, H. (II) 1803/09/07
Huysum, Jan 1803/09/07
Mieris, W. 1804/08/08
Moucheron, I. 1803/08/17
Tiziano 1803/04/27

Cannegieter, Herman, Mr.
1723–1804; professor of law at Franeker University
Anonymous 1805/09/24

Cannegieter, Johannes, Mr.
1731–1804; professor of law at Groningen University
Anonymous 1804/10/20
Bemmel 1804/10/20
Borch, G. ter (II) 1804/10/20
Croos 1804/10/20
Droochsloot, J.C. 1804/10/20
Koninck 1804/10/20
Monogrammist D.V.B. 1804/10/20
Rombouts 1804/10/20
Storck, Abr. 1804/10/20

Cannegieteri, see Cannegieter

Caré, see Carré

Caree, see Carré

Carli, B.
Anonymous 1801/08/19
Breenbergh 1801/04/13
Forman, L. 1801/04/13
Momas, G.F. 1801/03/16
Reni 1801/04/13

Carré, Jan Anthony Jacobus, Mr.
1772–1830; lawyer, secretary to the court of justice in The Hague, dealer and expert
Anonymous 1802/09/18
Anonymous 1803/08/24
Anonymous 1805/10/09
Anonymous 1806/08/20
Anonymous 1807/06/10
Anonymous 1807/08/27
Anonymous 1809/07/25
Bassen 1804/10/16
Bega 1802/05/24
Biset, J.A. 1805/10/09
Bredael 1803/08/24
Bril, P. 1805/10/09
Brueghel, J. (I) 1805/10/09
Burch, Hendrick 1805/10/09
Carree 1803/08/24
Compe, Jan ten 1807/06/10
Droochsloot, J.C. 1805/10/09
Droochsloot, J.C. 1807/06/10
Flemish-Brabant 1805/10/09
Hoet, G. (I) 1805/10/09
Honthorst, G. 1806/08/20
Horemans, J.J. (I) 1807/06/10
Italian 1803/08/24
Kessel, J. (III) 1808/06/13
Klomp 1807/06/10
Langendijk, D. 1803/08/24
Massys, Q. 1807/08/26
Momper, J. (II) 1805/10/09
Monogrammist D.V.B. 1809/07/25
Monogrammist M.C. 1807/06/10
Palamedesz., A. 1803/08/24
Palamedesz., P. (I) 1803/08/24
Poel, E. 1805/10/09
Poel, E. 1809/07/25
Schellinks, Daniel 1808/06/13
Schyndel, J. 1805/10/09
Strating, Jaco. 1807/06/10
Stuven 1807/06/10
Teniers, D. (II) 1802/09/18
Teniers, D. (II) 1804/04/28
Tol, D. 1805/10/09
Verbruggen, G. (II) 1809/07/25
Vinckeboons, D. 1805/10/09
Vitringa 1803/08/24
Vonck, E. 1809/07/25

Carree, Hendrik
1732–1814; painter and restorer in The Hague
Carree, F. 1802/05/24
Leemans, J. 1802/05/24
Wouwerman, P. 1802/05/24

Cassano
Anonymous 1810/08/06
Murillo 1810/08/06

Cassino
Anonymous 1810/07/26
Arthois 1810/07/26
Balen, H. (I) 1810/07/26
Bassano 1810/07/26
Berckheyde, G. 1810/07/26
Bergen, D. 1810/07/26
Bloemaert 1810/07/26
Bloemaert, A. 1810/07/26
Bloemen 1810/07/26
Boudewyns 1810/07/26
Bout, P. 1810/07/26
Bril, P. 1810/07/26
Bronzino, Agn. 1810/07/26
Brueghel, J. (I) 1810/07/26
Cabel, A. 1810/07/26
Canaletto 1810/07/26
Carracci 1810/07/26
Carracci, A. 1810/07/26
Carracci, L. 1810/07/26
Casanova, F. 1810/07/26
Champaigne, P. 1810/07/26
Cignani, C. 1810/07/26
Claude Lorrain 1810/07/26
Correggio 1810/07/26
Cranach, L. (I) 1810/07/26
Crayer, G. 1810/07/26
Deane 1810/07/26
Decker 1810/07/26
Decker, C. 1810/06/20
Decker, C. 1810/07/26
Dietrich, Chr. 1810/07/26
Dolci, C. 1810/07/26
Ducq, Johan le 1810/06/20
Dughet 1810/07/26
Dürer 1810/07/26
Dutch 1810/07/26
Ferg, F. 1810/07/26
Filippo Napoletano 1810/07/26
Genoels, Abr. 1810/07/26
German 1810/07/26
Guercino 1810/07/26
Hackaert, J. 1810/07/26
Hackert, J.P. 1810/07/26
Hals, F. (I) 1810/06/20
Hals, F. (I) 1810/07/26
Honthorst, G. 1810/07/26
Huysmans, C. 1810/06/20
Huysmans, C. 1810/07/26
Italian 1810/06/20
Jordaens, J. (I) 1810/07/26
Kalraet 1810/07/26
Lauri, F. 1810/07/26
Leonardo da Vinci 1810/07/26
Limborch, H. 1810/07/26
Lingelbach 1810/07/26
Locatelli, A. 1810/07/26
Lubienietski, C. 1810/06/20
Lucas van Leyden 1810/07/26
Meulen, A.F. 1810/07/26
Millet, J.F. (I) 1810/07/26

Avercamp, H. 1806/08/20
Berchem, N.P. 1806/08/20
Dyk, P. 1806/08/20
Mieris, F. (I) 1806/08/20

Coclaier, see Coclers

Coclair, see Coclers

Coclaire, see Coclers

Coclairs, see Coclers

Coclaur, see Coclers

Cocler, see Coclers

Coclers, Louis-Bernard
1741–1817; painter, engraver, restorer and dealer active in Amsterdam
Aelst, W. 1801/03/16
Aelst, W. 1807/08/26
Anonymous 1801/03/16
Anonymous 1801/04/13
Anonymous 1801/05/11
Anonymous 1801/10/06
Anonymous 1802/02/16
Anonymous 1802/05/05
Anonymous 1802/06/28
Anonymous 1802/09/29
Anonymous 1802/12/13
Anonymous 1803/04/20
Anonymous 1803/08/01
Anonymous 1803/12/12
Anonymous 1804/02/27
Anonymous 1804/05/07
Anonymous 1804/08/08
Anonymous 1804/12/10
Anonymous 1805/07/03
Anonymous 1806/05/05
Anonymous 1806/08/13
Anonymous 1806/08/20
Anonymous 1806/11/24
Anonymous 1807/08/26
Anonymous 1808/06/13
Anonymous 1808/08/23
Anonymous 1808/11/28
Anonymous 1809/04/22
Anonymous 1810/06/20
Anonymous 1810/08/06
Appelman, Bart. 1802/05/05
Asch, P.J. van 1804/02/27
Backhuysen 1801/04/13
Backhuysen 1804/12/10
Backhuysen 1806/08/13
Backhuysen 1807/08/26
Backhuysen 1808/06/13
Backhuysen 1808/08/23
Balen, H. (I) 1802/12/13
Balen, H. (I) 1803/07/18
Barbiers, P. 1804/02/27
Barbiers, P. (I) 1801/03/16
Beeldemaker 1806/05/05
Beeldemaker 1807/08/26
Beeldemaker, A.C. 1802/05/05
Beeldemaker, A.C. 1803/12/12
Beerstraten, J. 1810/06/20
Beesten, A.H. 1804/02/27
Bega 1801/10/19
Bega 1808/08/23
Begeyn 1801/03/16
Begeyn 1802/12/13
Bent, J. 1807/08/26
Berchem, N.P. 1801/04/13
Berchem, N.P. 1801/05/11
Berchem, N.P. 1801/06/10
Berchem, N.P. 1801/10/06
Berchem, N.P. 1802/06/16
Berchem, N.P. 1802/12/13
Berchem, N.P. 1808/08/23
Berckheyde, G. 1804/12/10
Bergen, D. 1801/10/06
Beyeren 1804/02/27
Beyeren 1808/08/23
Biset, C.E. 1804/08/08
Bisschop, Abr. 1806/05/05
Blanckerhoff 1801/03/16
Blanckerhoff 1801/05/11
Blanckerhoff 1808/06/13
Bloemaert 1807/08/26
Bloemaert, A. 1801/03/16
Bloemaert, A. 1808/08/23
Bloemen 1803/12/12
Bloemen, Nor. 1802/02/16
Bloemen, P. 1803/12/12
Bogdany 1808/06/06
Bol, F. 1809/04/22
Bol, F. 1810/08/01
Bolomey, B.S. 1804/08/08
Boonen, A. 1807/08/26
Borch, G. ter (II) 1806/05/05
Borch, G. ter (II) 1810/06/20
Borssom 1804/02/27
Both, A. 1801/06/10
Both, J. 1801/06/10
Both, J. 1808/06/06
Both, J. 1808/08/23
Boudewyns 1801/04/23
Brakenburg 1806/05/05
Bray, Jan 1808/08/23
Bray, S. 1805/07/03
Breenbergh 1804/12/10
Bril, P. 1802/06/28
Broeck, E. 1802/09/29
Broeck, E. 1807/04/13
Brouwer, Adr. 1807/08/26
Brueghel, J. (I) 1803/07/18
Brueghel, P. (II) 1804/08/08
Brugghen, Hendrick ter 1803/04/20
Camphuysen, G.D. 1802/06/28
Cappelle 1802/05/05
Cappelle 1803/12/12
Carree, M. 1801/03/16
Casanova, F. 1803/12/12
Compe, Jan ten 1804/12/10
Compe, Jan ten 1808/08/23
Corvi 1808/06/06
Cuyp, A. 1810/08/01
Dalens, Dirck 1807/08/26
Decker, C. 1808/10/28
Delen 1804/12/10
Dietrich, Chr. 1804/07/25
Does, J. (I) 1802/09/29
Does, S. 1808/08/23
Dongen, Dionys 1801/04/23
Dorne, F. 1806/05/05
Dou 1801/03/16
Dou 1802/06/16
Dou 1806/08/13
Dou 1808/08/23
Dou 1810/08/06
Droochsloot, J.C. 1802/02/16
Dujardin, K. 1801/05/11
Dujardin, K. 1804/02/27
Dujardin, K. 1807/08/26
Dujardin, K. 1808/10/28
Dujardin, K. 1809/07/19
Dusart, Corn. 1802/09/29
Dyck, Anth. van 1801/04/13
Dyck, Anth. van 1806/05/05
Dyck, Anth. van 1808/06/06
Dyck, Anth. van 1808/08/23
Dyck, Anth. van 1808/11/28
Dyk, P. 1804/12/10
Eeckhout, G. 1801/04/13
Eeckhout, G. 1809/09/06
Ekels, Jan (I) 1804/05/07
Ekels, Jan (I) 1808/08/23
Ekels, Jan (II) 1808/08/23
Elsheimer, A. 1801/04/13
Elsheimer, A. 1802/06/16
Fargue, Karel 1804/12/10
Ferguson, Wm. 1801/03/16
Filippo Napoletano 1803/12/12
Flinck 1801/04/13
Flinck 1802/05/05
Flinck 1802/12/13
Flinck 1803/04/20
Flinck 1806/08/13
Floris, F. (I) 1804/08/08
Francken 1801/03/16
Francken 1802/02/16
Francken, Amb. (I) 1805/07/03
Francken, Frans (II) 1803/07/18
Franks, J. 1802/06/16
French 1802/12/13
Fyt 1807/08/26
Gael, B. 1801/04/23
Gael, B. 1802/06/16
Gael, B. 1807/08/26
Gaesbeeck, A. 1801/06/10
Gagneraux, Bén. 1810/08/06
Gelder, A. 1802/05/05
Gelder, A. 1806/08/13
German 1802/06/28
Glauber, J. 1809/09/06
Goltzius, Hend. 1807/08/26
Gool, Jan 1807/08/26
Gool, Jan 1808/08/23
Goyen 1801/04/23
Goyen 1801/05/11
Goyen 1804/05/07
Goyen 1806/11/24
Goyen 1809/04/22
Goyen 1810/06/20
Graat 1803/08/17
Hackaert 1803/12/12
Hackert, J.P. 1810/08/06
Haensbergen, J. van 1807/08/26
Hagen, Joris 1808/06/11
Hals, D. 1803/04/20
Hals, F. (I) 1804/07/25
Hals, F. (I) 1806/08/13
Hals, F. (I) 1808/08/23
Heem, C. 1806/08/20
Heem, J.D. 1801/04/23
Heem, J.D. 1802/09/29
Heem, J.D. 1807/08/26
Heeremans, Thos. 1807/08/26
Heeremans, Thos. 1810/08/06
Helst, B. 1802/09/29
Helst, B. 1808/06/06
Heusch 1808/06/11
Heusch, Jacob 1802/02/16
Heusch, Wm. 1801/08/19
Heusch, Wm. 1808/06/06
Heusch, Wm. 1810/08/06
Heyden, J. 1802/12/13
Hobbema 1801/10/19
Hobbema 1808/08/23
Hoet, G. (I) 1803/12/12
Hondecoeter, G. 1802/02/16
Hondecoeter, M. 1801/03/16
Hondecoeter, M. 1801/04/13
Hondecoeter, M. 1801/06/10
Hondecoeter, M. 1808/06/13
Hondecoeter, M. 1808/08/23
Hondecoeter, M. 1810/08/06
Hooch, Gerrit 1802/05/05
Hooch, P. 1801/10/19
Hooch, P. 1804/12/10
Horemans, J.J. (I) 1804/08/08
Huchtenburgh, Jan 1801/10/06
Huchtenburgh, Jan 1801/10/19
Huchtenburgh, Jan 1807/08/26
Huchtenburgh, Jan 1808/06/13
Huysum, Jan 1801/03/16
Huysum, Jan 1801/06/10
Huysum, Jan 1807/08/26
Italian 1803/04/20
Italian 1804/08/08
Italian 1808/08/23
Italian 1808/11/28
Janson, J. 1804/12/10
Janson, J.C. 1804/12/10
Jordaens, J. (I) 1801/04/13
Jordaens, J. (I) 1808/11/28
Keirincx, Alex. 1802/05/05
Keirincx, Alex. 1804/02/27
Kessel, J. (III) 1806/08/13
Kipshaven, I. 1802/06/28
Klomp 1801/08/19
Klomp 1802/05/05
Klomp 1808/08/23
Kuster, J. 1803/08/17
Kuster, J.K. 1810/08/06
Lacroix 1803/12/12
Laen, D.J. 1801/03/16
Lairesse, G. 1806/05/05
Lairesse, G. 1806/11/24
Lairesse, G. 1810/08/06
Lancret 1804/12/10
Leclerc, S. (II) 1803/12/12
Leeuw 1801/03/16
Leeuw 1808/08/23
Lievens, J. (I) 1808/11/28
Lingelbach 1801/05/11
Lingelbach 1801/06/13
Lingelbach 1802/05/05
Lingelbach 1802/06/16
Lingelbach 1804/05/07
Lingelbach 1809/07/19
Loutherbourg 1803/12/12
Lundens 1802/02/16
Lundens 1802/09/29
Maat, N. 1807/08/26
Maes, D. 1807/08/26
Maes, N. 1801/03/16
Maes, N. 1803/12/12
Marseus, O. 1804/02/27
Martszen, J. (II) 1802/06/16
Maton, B. 1806/08/13
Metsu 1801/03/16
Metsu 1801/06/10
Mettenleiter, J.J. 1804/05/07
Meulen, A.F. 1804/08/08
Mieris, F. (I) 1801/10/19
Mieris, F. (I) 1803/04/20
Mieris, F. (I) 1804/12/10
Mieris, F. (II) 1804/12/10
Mieris, W. 1801/10/19
Mieris, W. 1804/12/10
Mieris, W. 1807/08/26
Mieris, W. 1808/06/06
Mignon, A. 1805/07/03
Mignon, A. 1808/06/11
Moeyaert, C. 1808/11/28
Molenaer, Bart. 1807/08/26
Molenaer, J.M. 1804/05/07
Molenaer, J.M. 1808/11/28
Molenaer, Klaes 1801/08/19
Molenaer, Klaes 1802/06/28
Molenaer, Klaes 1804/08/08
Molenaer, Klaes 1804/12/10
Molenaer, Klaes 1810/06/20
Molijn 1803/04/20
Mommers, H. 1801/03/16
Moni, L. de 1804/12/10
Monogrammist I.B. 1801/05/11
Monogrammist I.B. (1562) 1803/04/20
Monogrammist J.A.H. 1802/06/28
Monogrammist W.L. 1807/08/26
Moor, C. 1803/07/18
Mortel 1801/05/11
Moucheron, F. 1801/04/13
Moucheron, F. 1801/05/11
Moucheron, F. 1801/06/10
Moucheron, F. 1808/10/28
Moucheron, F. 1809/09/06
Moucheron, I. 1802/02/16
Moucheron, I. 1802/06/28
Moucheron, I. 1810/08/06
Murant 1801/06/10
Murant 1806/08/13
Murillo 1807/04/13
Musscher, M. 1804/08/08
Nason, P. 1807/08/26

Neeffs, P. (I) 1806/05/05
Neer, A. 1802/02/16
Neer, A. 1802/06/28
Neer, A. 1807/08/26
Neer, A. 1808/10/28
Netscher, Casp. 1802/02/16
Netscher, Casp. 1802/06/28
Netscher, Casp. 1810/06/20
Netscher, T. 1808/11/28
Nieulandt 1801/04/23
Os, J. 1804/02/27
Os, J. 1804/05/07
Os, J. 1804/12/10
Ostade, A. 1801/04/13
Ostade, A. 1803/04/20
Ostade, A. 1803/08/01
Ostade, A. 1803/12/12
Ouwater, Isaak 1804/02/27
Ouwater, Isaak 1804/12/10
Palamedesz., A. 1807/08/26
Palamedesz., P. (I) 1803/12/12
Palamedesz., P. (I) 1804/02/27
Palamedesz., P. (I) 1805/07/03
Palamedesz., P. (I) 1808/08/23
Palma 1803/04/20
Piemont 1807/08/26
Pimont, Jan 1808/06/06
Poel, E. 1804/02/27
Poel, E. 1808/08/23
Poelenburgh, C. 1803/04/20
Poelenburgh, C. 1805/07/03
Porcellis, Jan 1801/05/11
Porcellis, Jan 1803/12/12
Pothoven, H. 1810/06/20
Potter, Paulus 1802/06/16
Potuyl 1806/11/24
Pynacker 1801/06/10
Rembrandt 1801/04/13
Rembrandt 1803/08/17
Rembrandt 1806/08/13
Rembrandt 1807/08/26
Rembrandt 1808/11/28
Rembrandt 1809/09/06
Reni 1803/12/12
Rietschoof 1801/03/16
Roghman, R. 1802/05/05
Roghman, R. 1806/08/13
Romeyn 1801/03/16
Romeyn 1805/07/03
Romeyn 1808/06/11
Rubens 1806/08/13
Rubens 1808/11/28
Ruisdael, J. 1802/12/13
Ruisdael, J. 1804/05/07
Ruisdael, J. 1805/07/03
Ruisdael, J. 1807/08/26
Ruisdael, J. 1808/08/23
Ruisdael, J. 1810/08/01
Ruysch, R. 1802/06/16
Ruysch, R. 1807/08/26
Ruysdael, S. 1806/11/24
Saftleven, H. 1801/04/23
Saftleven, H. 1804/12/10
Saftleven, H. 1810/06/20
Sandrart, Joachim (I) 1806/08/20
Savery, R. 1804/12/10
Schalcke, C. 1801/05/11
Schalcken 1805/07/03
Schellinks, W. 1801/03/16
Schellinks, W. 1807/08/26
Schouman, A. 1804/02/27
Schouman, A. 1804/05/07
Schweickardt, H. 1804/05/07
Schweickardt, H. 1804/12/10
Slingeland, P.C. 1801/05/11
Smit, Aernout 1804/05/07
Smit, Aernout 1808/08/23
Snyders, F. 1802/05/05
Sorgh, H.M. 1801/06/10
Sorgh, H.M. 1802/06/28
Spaendonck, G. 1808/08/23
Staveren, J.A. 1802/05/05
Steen, J. 1801/05/11
Steen, J. 1803/07/18
Steen, J. 1804/05/07
Steen, J. 1805/07/03
Steen, J. 1808/06/06
Steenwyck, Hend. 1801/06/10
Steenwyck, Hend. 1801/10/19
Steenwyck, Hend. 1808/08/23
Stoop, J. 1801/06/10
Storck, Abr. 1801/03/16
Storck, Abr. 1801/05/11
Storck, Abr. 1802/06/28
Storck, Abr. 1804/02/27
Storck, Abr. 1804/08/08
Storck, Abr. 1807/08/26
Storck, Abr. 1808/06/11
Storck, Abr. 1808/08/23
Storck, J. 1801/03/16
Strij, J. 1808/06/13
Swanevelt 1801/06/10
Swanevelt 1806/11/24
Teniers, D. (II) 1802/02/16
Teniers, D. (II) 1806/08/13
Teniers, D. (II) 1808/08/23
Tol, D. 1801/06/10
Tol, D. 1802/05/05
Toorenburgh, G. 1802/06/28
Toorenburgh, G. 1807/08/26
Uden, Lucas 1809/04/22
Ulft 1810/08/06
Velde, A. 1801/04/13
Velde, A. 1801/06/10
Velde, A. 1802/06/16
Velde, A. 1803/04/20
Velde, A. 1809/09/06
Velde, E. (I) 1808/08/23
Velde, W. 1801/06/10
Velde, W. 1801/10/06
Velde, W. 1801/10/19
Velde, W. 1804/05/07
Velde, W. 1804/12/10
Velde, W. 1807/08/26
Verbeeck, P.C. 1801/08/19
Verbeeck, P.C. 1802/02/16
Verbeeck, P.C. 1807/08/26
Verboom, A.H. 1802/06/16
Verbruggen, G. (II) 1802/05/05
Verkolje, N. 1802/06/28
Vermeer, Jan 1803/12/12
Vermeer, Jan (III) 1802/06/16
Vermeer, Jan (III) 1808/08/23
Vermeulen, A. 1802/05/05
Vermeulen, A. 1802/12/13
Vermeulen, A. 1804/05/07
Vernet, C.J. 1807/08/26
Verschuring, H. 1808/08/23
Vertangen 1803/12/12
Vlieger, S. 1801/05/11
Vlieger, S. 1802/06/16
Vois, Ary de 1806/08/13
Vois, Ary de 1809/09/06
Vonck 1803/04/20
Vrancx 1801/03/16
Vrancx 1802/02/16
Vrancx 1802/06/28
Vries, R. 1801/05/11
Vries, R. 1802/02/16
Vries, R. 1802/06/16
Vucht, Jan 1803/04/20
Watteau, J.A. 1802/12/13
Watteau, J.A. 1803/12/12
Weenix 1801/04/13
Weenix 1801/06/10
Weenix 1809/09/06
Weenix, J.B. 1804/05/07
Weenix, J.B. 1807/08/26
Weenix, J.B. 1808/08/23
Werff, A. 1801/05/11
Werff, A. 1803/07/18
Werff, A. 1808/06/06
Wet, J.W. 1808/08/23
Wijnants 1801/10/06
Wijnants 1802/06/16
Wijnants 1804/05/07
Wils, Jan 1802/05/05
Wit, Jacob de 1806/08/13
Withoos, M. 1810/06/20
Witte, E. 1804/05/07
Witte, E. 1804/08/08
Witte, E. 1804/12/10
Wolfaerts, Artus 1802/06/28
Wolfsen, Aleijda 1808/08/23
Wouwerman 1803/12/12
Wouwerman, J. 1801/08/19
Wouwerman, P. 1804/08/08
Wouwerman, P. 1806/11/24
Wouwerman, P. 1808/08/23
Wouwerman, Ph. 1801/10/06
Wouwerman, Ph. 1802/02/16
Wouwerman, Ph. 1804/05/07
Wouwerman, Ph. 1810/08/06
Wouwerman, Pieter 1801/06/10
Wtewael, J. 1802/06/28
Wulfraet 1804/08/08
Wyck, J. 1801/06/10
Wyck, J. 1802/02/16
Wyck, T. 1801/04/13
Wyck, T. 1802/12/13
Wyck, T. 1807/04/13
Wyck, T. 1808/06/11
Wyck, T. 1808/08/23

Coehoorn, Menno, Baron van
d. 1800; magistrate in The Hague
Anonymous 1801/10/19
Anonymous 1801/12/01
Asselyn 1801/10/19
Backhuysen 1801/10/19
Bega 1801/10/19
Berchem, N.P. 1801/10/19
Berckheyde, G. 1801/10/19
Bergen, D. 1801/10/19
Bol, F. 1801/10/19
Boonen, A. 1801/10/19
Brakenburg 1801/10/19
Brekelencam, Q. 1801/10/19
Burg, Adriaan 1801/10/19
Cappelle 1801/10/19
Compe, Jan ten 1801/10/19
Cuyp, A. 1801/10/19
Does, S. 1801/10/19
Droochsloot, J.C. 1801/12/01
Ducq, Johan le 1801/10/19
Dusart, Corn. 1801/10/19
Gael, B. 1801/10/19
Griffier, R. 1801/10/19
Heem 1801/10/19
Heusch, Jacob 1801/10/19
Hobbema 1801/10/19
Hoet, G. (I) 1801/10/19
Hooch, P. 1801/10/19
Huchtenburgh, Jan 1801/10/19
Janson, J. 1801/10/19
Lingelbach 1801/10/19
Maes, D. 1801/10/19
Meijer, Hend. (II) 1801/10/19
Mieris, F. (I) 1801/10/19
Mieris, W. 1801/10/19
Molenaer, J.M. 1801/10/19
Moni, L. de 1801/10/19
Naiveu 1801/10/19
Neeffs, P. (I) 1801/10/19
Neer, A. 1801/10/19
Os, J. 1801/10/19
Ostade, A. 1801/10/19
Poelenburgh, C. 1801/10/19
Prins, J.H. 1801/10/19
Ravesteyn, J.A. 1801/10/19
Romeyn 1801/10/19
Ruisdael, J. 1801/10/19
Ruysch, R. 1801/10/19
Schalcken 1801/10/19
Steen, J. 1801/10/19
Steenwyck, Hend. 1801/10/19
Teniers, D. (II) 1801/10/19
Tol, D. 1801/10/19
Troost, C. 1801/10/19
Velde, A. 1801/10/19
Velde, W. 1801/10/19
Velde, W. (I) 1801/10/19
Verkolje, N. 1801/10/19
Versteeg 1801/10/19
Vrancx 1801/10/19
Weenix 1801/12/01
Werff, A. 1801/10/19
Werff, P. 1801/10/19
Wouwerman, J. 1801/10/19
Wouwerman, Ph. 1801/10/19
Wtewael, J. 1801/10/19

Colonbon
Anonymous 1807/06/10
Avercamp, H. 1807/06/10
Compe, Jan ten 1807/06/10
Jordaens, J. (I) 1807/06/10
Wijnants 1807/06/10

Contant
Molenaer, J.M. 1810/05/22

Cooth, C. van
Borch, G. ter (II) 1802/09/06
Goyen 1802/09/06
Holbein, H. (II) 1803/04/20
Huchtenburgh, Jan 1802/09/06
Palamedesz., P. (I) 1802/09/06

Cosoly
Dinter, G. 1802/05/10

Coste, la
Dou 1808/06/06
Moni, L. de 1808/06/06

Crabbendam
Zeemann 1803/09/07

Crajenschot, B.J.
Amsterdam bookdealer
Murant 1809/04/17
Staveren, J.A. 1809/04/17
Tieling, N. 1809/04/17
Wyck, T. 1809/04/17

Cramer
Anonymous 1804/08/08
Anonymous 1810/08/06
Schendel, B. 1807/06/10

Cremer, Thomas Theodoor
1743–1815; resident of Rotterdam
Brekelencam, Q. 1805/07/03
Groenewegen, G. 1808/06/06
Honthorst, G. 1810/08/01
Kessel, J. (III) 1808/06/06
Metsu 1810/08/01
Mieris, F. (I) 1805/07/03
Muys, Nic. 1808/06/06
Velde, A. 1805/07/03
Velde, A. 1808/06/06
Velde, A. 1810/08/01
Vermeer, Jan (III) 1805/07/03
Weenix 1810/08/01
Wijnants 1810/08/01
Wit, Jacob de 1808/06/06
Wouwerman, Ph. 1810/08/01

Croes, see Croese

Croese Edz., Hendrik
1762–1838; insurance broker, founde of the Brand- en Levensverzekerings Sociëteit in Amsterdam
Anonymous 1801/08/19
Borch, G. ter (II) 1810/08/01
Cappelle 1810/08/01

Anonymous 1806/05/05
Anonymous 1806/11/24
Anonymous 1808/11/28
Anonymous 1810/06/20
Anonymous 1810/07/26
Anonymous 1810/10/11
Backer 1810/08/06
Backhuysen 1802/06/16
Barbiers, P. 1802/12/13
Berckheyde, G. 1801/06/10
Besanger, S. 1802/09/29
Bloemaert, A. 1801/10/06
Bloemaert, A. 1803/12/12
Bloemaert, A. 1809/06/13
Bol, F. 1801/06/10
Bola, F. 1801/03/16
Borssom 1802/12/13
Brakenburg 1805/12/16
Bramer 1809/04/22
Breenbergh 1801/10/06
Brekelencam, Q. 1809/06/13
Buys, Jac. 1808/06/13
Crayer, G. 1802/12/13
Cuyp, A. 1806/05/05
Dalens, Dirck 1803/12/12
Does, S. 1802/12/13
Dujardin, K. 1802/12/13
Dusart, Corn. 1801/10/19
Dusart, Corn. 1806/11/24
Dyck, Anth. van 1802/09/06
Dyck, Anth. van 1803/08/17
Everbroeck, F. 1802/06/16
Ferguson, Wm. 1801/08/19
Flemish-Brabant 1801/08/19
French 1802/05/05
Goyen 1803/08/17
Goyen 1804/02/27
Goyen 1806/08/13
Goyen 1809/06/13
Haensbergen, J. van 1808/10/28
Hendriks, W. 1810/08/06
Honthorst, G. 1810/08/06
Huysum, Jan 1801/04/23
Italian 1802/09/06
Italian 1802/09/29
Italian 1802/12/13
Jordaens, J. (I) 1802/09/06
Kessel, J. (III) 1802/12/13
Klomp 1806/05/05
Koninck, P. 1803/08/17
Laer, P. 1802/12/13
Lairesse, G. 1804/07/25
Lairesse, G. 1805/12/16
Lairesse, G. 1807/08/26
Laquy, W.J. 1809/06/13
Lingelbach 1801/06/10
Lingelbach 1802/12/13
Maes, D. 1807/08/26
Manfredi, B. 1801/04/13
Meyling, J. 1802/02/16
Mignon, A. 1806/08/13
Molenaer, J.M. 1810/06/20
Molenaer, Klaes 1803/08/01
Moni, L. de 1806/05/05
Monogrammist J.D. 1802/09/29
Myn, G. 1801/04/13
Myn, G. 1804/12/10
Mytens, D. (I) 1801/04/13
Ochtervelt 1810/06/20
Peeters, B. (I) 1806/08/13
Piemont 1802/02/16
Rembrandt 1803/12/12
Rijck, C. de 1801/06/10
Roore 1803/08/01
Rubens 1801/08/19
Saftleven, C. 1801/08/19
Saftleven, C. 1802/12/13
Saftleven, C. 1810/06/20
Schut, C. (I) 1803/08/01
Storck, Abr. 1802/02/16
Straaten, Hend. 1801/08/19
Toorenvliet, J. 1802/09/06
Toorenvliet, J. 1810/06/20
Troost, C. 1808/11/28
Velde, E. (I) 1801/08/19
Verbeeck, P.C. 1801/08/19
Verboom, A.H. 1801/08/19
Verelst, S. 1809/09/06
Verschuring, H. 1802/12/13
Vliet, H.C. 1806/05/05
Vliet, H.C. 1809/04/22
Weenix 1806/08/13
Wit, Jacob de 1806/05/05
Wit, Jacob de 1808/10/28
Withoos, J. 1804/02/27
Witte, E. 1806/11/24
Wouwerman, J. 1801/06/10
Zegelaar, G. 1810/10/11

Dijll, see Dijl

Dirkse
Asselyn 1810/05/22
Dujardin, K. 1810/05/22
Ruysch, R. 1810/05/22
Slingeland, P.C. 1810/05/22
Velde, A. 1810/05/22

Disconi
Cuyp, A. 1810/07/23
Fabritius, Carel 1810/07/23

Does, C. van der
Schweickardt, H. 1806/05/05
Toorenburgh, G. 1806/05/05

Dongen, Dionys van
1748–1819; painter active primarily in Rotterdam
Anonymous 1802/10/18
Anonymous 1808/06/11
Anonymous 1809/07/25
Asselyn 1810/03/26
Bega 1810/06/06
Brekelencam, Q. 1808/06/11
Cornelisz. van Haarlem 1808/06/11
Hondecoeter, Gillis 1810/08/10
Janson, J.C. 1810/06/06
Klootwijk 1810/07/23
Kobell, H. 1808/06/06
Maton, B. 1807/06/10
Pynacker 1810/08/10
Sorgh, H.M. 1810/06/06
Verschuring, H. 1809/07/25
Vinckeboons, D. 1808/06/11
Wouwerman, Ph. 1810/06/06

Doralle
Anonymous 1805/07/10
Boonen, A. 1805/07/10
Dorasse, C. 1805/07/10
Essen, C. 1805/07/10
Os, Pieter G. 1805/07/10
Vernet, C.J. 1805/07/10

Doublet, Pieter
b. 1766; accountant and second husband of Louise Marie Ten Kate (van Loo)
Anonymous 1801/06/10
Beerstraten, J. 1801/06/10
Berckheyde, G. 1801/06/10
Beschey, J. 1801/06/10
Bloot, P. 1801/06/10
Bol, F. 1801/06/10
Bredael, P. 1801/06/10
Breenbergh 1801/06/10
Cappelle 1801/06/10
Coopse, P. 1801/06/10
Cuyp, J.G. 1801/06/10
Dubbels, H. 1801/06/10
Essen, C. 1801/06/10
Gael, B. 1801/06/10
Goyen 1801/06/10
Hooch, P. 1801/06/10
Keirincx, Alex. 1801/06/10
Kobell, H. 1801/06/10
Laen, D.J. 1801/06/10
Lairesse, Jan 1801/06/10
Lastman, P.P. 1801/06/10
Lingelbach 1801/06/10
Molenaer, J.M. 1801/06/10
Molenaer, Klaes 1801/06/10
Moucheron, I. 1801/06/10
Palamedesz., A. 1801/06/10
Potter, Paulus 1801/06/10
Saftleven, H. 1801/06/10
Sonje, J.G. 1801/06/10
Sorgh, H.M. 1801/06/10
Stoop, J. 1801/06/10
Velde, A. 1801/06/10
Velde, W. 1801/06/10
Verboom, A.H. 1801/06/10
Vries, R. 1801/06/10
Witte, E. 1801/06/10
Wyck, J. 1801/06/10
Wyck, T. 1801/06/10

Dreesen
Anonymous 1802/07/27

Drielst, Egbert van
1745–1818; landscape painter and restorer
Anonymous 1808/06/13
Carree, M. 1808/06/13
Eeckhout, G. 1808/06/13
Elfers, J. 1808/06/13
Hooch, P. 1808/06/13
Janson, J. 1808/06/13
Metsu 1808/06/13
Mignon, A. 1808/06/13
Molenaer, J.M. 1808/06/13
Mortel 1808/06/13
Ostade 1808/06/13
Vrancx 1808/06/13

Driesseler
Bisschop, Abr. 1806/05/05
Velde, E. (I) 1806/05/05

Dubach
Anonymous 1803/06/27

Dullev, van
Dongen, Dionys 1808/06/11

Dupré (Amsterdam)
most transactions probably attributable to the dealer F. Dupré, q.v.
Alcock, E. 1810/06/20
Amers, Piters 1809/04/22
Andrea del Sarto 1808/06/13
Anonymous 1802/12/13
Anonymous 1804/02/27
Anonymous 1805/12/16
Anonymous 1806/08/13
Anonymous 1807/06/10
Anonymous 1807/08/26
Anonymous 1807/08/27
Anonymous 1808/06/11
Anonymous 1808/06/13
Anonymous 1808/08/23
Anonymous 1808/11/28
Anonymous 1809/04/22
Anonymous 1809/06/13
Anonymous 1809/07/25
Anonymous 1810/05/22
Anonymous 1810/07/26
Anonymous 1810/08/01
Anonymous 1810/08/06
Anonymous 1810/10/11
Apshoven 1809/04/22
Arthois 1807/08/26
Asselyn 1806/11/24
Ast 1810/10/11
Balen 1809/04/22
Balen, H. (I) 1810/06/20
Balen, H. (I) 1810/07/26
Bassen 1806/08/13
Beer, J. 1805/12/16
Beerstraten, A. 1808/10/28
Begeyn 1806/11/24
Begeyn 1809/04/22
Berchem, N.P. 1808/08/23
Berchem, N.P. 1809/04/22
Berchem, N.P. 1809/06/13
Berckheyde, G. 1809/04/22
Bergen, D. 1809/04/22
Bloemaert 1810/10/11
Bloemen, Nor. 1804/02/27
Borkeloo, J. 1807/08/26
Borssom 1806/08/13
Borssom 1809/04/22
Both, J. 1808/08/23
Boudewyns 1810/07/26
Bout, P. 1810/07/26
Bouts, F. 1806/08/13
Brakenburg 1810/06/20
Bramer 1809/04/22
Breenbergh 1809/04/22
Brouwer, Adr. 1806/08/13
Brueghel, J. (I) 1806/08/13
Brueghel, J. (I) 1807/08/26
Brueghel, J. (I) 1808/08/23
Cappelle 1806/05/05
Cappelle 1806/11/24
Caravaggio 1810/10/11
Carree, Joh. 1806/08/13
Carree, M. 1809/04/22
Carree, M. 1810/06/20
Colaert, Johannes 1808/10/28
Compe, Jan ten 1806/05/05
Compe, Jan ten 1809/04/22
Courtois, J. 1810/06/20
Cuyp, A. 1809/04/22
Dalens, Dirck 1806/08/13
Decker, C. 1809/04/22
Delen 1808/06/13
Delen 1809/06/13
Diepenbeeck, A.J. 1810/08/06
Dietzsch, J.C. 1806/11/24
Dongen, Dionys 1808/06/11
Dou 1806/08/13
Dou 1808/08/23
Dou 1809/04/22
Dregt, J. 1810/10/11
Drielst, E. 1808/11/28
Dubbels, H. 1809/04/22
Dubordieu, P. 1808/06/06
Ducq, Johan le 1809/04/22
Ducq, Johan le 1810/06/20
Dujardin, K. 1810/06/20
Dürer 1808/06/06
Dusart, Corn. 1807/08/26
Eckhardt 1809/04/22
Elfers, J. 1808/06/13
Essen, C. 1809/04/22
Flinck 1806/08/13
Franck, J.W. 1808/08/23
Frey, Anna 1810/05/22
Gael, B. 1810/10/11
Gaesbeeck, A. 1806/11/24
Gerards 1809/04/22
Goltzius, Hend. 1804/02/27
Gool, Jan 1806/08/13
Gool, Jan 1807/06/10
Gool, Jan 1807/08/26
Gool, Jan 1808/08/23
Goyen 1807/08/26
Goyen 1809/04/22
Graat 1804/02/27
Grandjean, J. 1808/06/13
Grebber, A.C. 1810/10/11
Hackaert, J. 1810/07/26
Hals, F. (I) 1807/08/26
Hals, F. (I) 1808/11/28
Heem, J.D. 1808/11/28

Leeuw, Pieter 1809/06/13
Lelienbergh 1809/06/13
Locatelli, A. 1809/06/13
Molenaer, Klaes 1809/06/13
Momper, J. (II) 1809/06/13
Ostade, I. 1809/06/13
Poelenburgh, C. 1809/06/13
Porcellis, Jan 1809/06/13
Saftleven, H. 1809/06/13
Sanders, G. 1809/06/13
Schütz 1809/06/13
Storck, Abr. 1809/06/13
Tol, D. 1809/06/13
Toorenvliet, A. 1809/06/13
Utrecht, Adr. 1809/06/13
Verelst, S. 1809/06/13
Vertangen 1809/06/13
Vries, R. 1809/06/13
Willaerts, Adam 1809/06/13
Wouwerman, P. 1809/06/13
Wubbels, Jan 1809/06/13
Zegelaar, G. 1809/06/13

E. (1809, July 19)
Anonymous 1809/07/19
Does, S. 1809/07/19

Ebbens
Anonymous 1805/10/09
Peeters, B. (I) 1805/10/09

Ebersdyk, see Eversdyk

Eck, Johannes
Backhuysen 1808/06/06
Bergen, D. 1808/06/06
Brueghel, J. (I) 1808/06/06
Coninck, D. 1808/06/06
Dou 1808/06/06
Hackaert, J. 1808/06/06
Heem, J.D. 1808/06/06
Heyden, J. 1808/06/06
Hondecoeter, M. 1808/06/06
Koninck, P. 1808/06/06
Mignon, A. 1808/06/06
Ruisdael, J. 1808/06/06
Steen, J. 1808/06/06
Velde, A. 1808/06/06
Vermeer, Jan (III) 1808/06/06
Weenix, J.B. 1808/06/06
Wouwerman, Ph. 1808/06/06

Eekhof
Anonymous 1810/06/20
Lairesse, Jan 1810/06/20
Vermeulen, A. 1810/06/20

Eijk, see Eyk

Eijnden, see Eynden

Eik, see Eyk

Einden, see Eynden

Elias
Anonymous 1801/05/11
Backhuysen 1801/05/11
Beerstraten, J. 1801/05/11
Berckheyde, G. 1801/05/11
Borch, G. ter (II) 1801/05/11
Decker, C. 1801/05/11
Dujardin, K. 1801/05/11
Gael, B. 1801/05/11
Ghersi, T. 1801/05/11
Goyen 1801/05/11
Klomp 1801/05/11
Lastman, P.P. 1801/05/11
Lingelbach 1801/05/11
Metsu 1801/05/11
Molenaer, J.M. 1801/05/11
Molenaer, Klaes 1801/05/11
Monogrammist I.B. 1801/05/11
Neer, A. 1801/05/11
Poel, E. 1801/05/11
Potter, Paulus 1801/05/11
Ruisdael, J. 1801/05/11
Sandrart, Joachim (I) 1801/05/11
Steen, J. 1801/05/11
Storck, Abr. 1801/05/11
Velde, A. 1801/05/11
Velde, W. 1801/05/11
Verboom, A.H. 1801/05/11
Verkolje, N. 1801/05/11
Vermeer, Jan (III) 1801/05/11
Vertangen 1801/05/11
Victors, Jan 1801/05/11
Vlieger, S. 1801/05/11
Vliet, H.C. 1801/05/11
Vries, R. 1801/05/11
Wijnants 1801/05/11
Zeemann 1801/05/11

Elink, Anna, Mejuffrouw
1715–1802
Anonymous 1802/06/28
Bager, Johann 1802/06/28
Bassen 1802/06/28
Bega 1802/06/28
Berckheyde, G. 1802/06/28
Berckheyde, J. 1802/06/28
Beschey, J. 1802/06/28
Blaauw, J. 1802/06/28
Bloemaert, A. 1802/06/28
Bloot, P. 1802/06/28
Boonen, A. 1802/06/28
Brakenburg 1802/06/28
Brekelencam, Q. 1802/06/28
Bril, P. 1802/06/28
Brussel, P. 1802/06/28
Burg, M. 1802/06/28
Camphuysen, G.D. 1802/06/28
Chalon, L. 1802/06/28
Coclers, J.B.B. 1802/06/28
Compe, Jan ten 1802/06/28
Cuyp, A. 1802/06/28
Denner, B. 1802/06/28
Dongen, Dionys 1802/06/28
Dou 1802/06/28
Droman, F. 1802/06/28
Ducq, Johan le 1802/06/28
Dusart, Corn. 1802/06/28
Ekels, Jan (I) 1802/06/28
Elliger, O. (II) 1802/06/28
Fargue, Maria la 1802/06/28
Flemish-Brabant 1802/06/28
Franks, J. 1802/06/28
Gaesbeeck, A. 1802/06/28
Gerards 1802/06/28
German 1802/06/28
Goltzius, Hend. 1802/06/28
Goyen 1802/06/28
Griffier, R. 1802/06/28
Hagen, Joris 1802/06/28
Heemskerck 1802/06/28
Heeremans, Thos. 1802/06/28
Hendriks, W. 1802/06/28
Heyden, J. 1802/06/28
Hoet, G. (I) 1802/06/28
Huchtenburgh, Jan 1802/06/28
Huysum, Jan 1802/06/28
Janson, J. 1802/06/28
Keun, Hend. 1802/06/28
Kipshaven, I. 1802/06/28
Koller, J.J. 1802/06/28
Koninck 1802/06/28
Kruger, Jac. 1802/06/28
Laquy, W.J. 1802/06/28
Lastman, P.P. 1802/06/28
Lauwers, J.J. 1802/06/28
Lubienietski, C. 1802/06/28
Metsu 1802/06/28
Mettenleiter, J.J. 1802/06/28
Mieris, F. (II) 1802/06/28
Mieris, W. 1802/06/28
Molenaer, J.M. 1802/06/28
Molenaer, Klaes 1802/06/28
Moni, L. de 1802/06/28
Monogrammist A.B. 1802/06/28
Monogrammist F.F. 1802/06/28
Monogrammist G.B. 1802/06/28
Monogrammist H.B. 1802/06/28
Monogrammist J.A.H. 1802/06/28
Monogrammist P.S. 1802/06/28
Morgenstern, J.L.E. 1802/06/28
Moucheron, F. 1802/06/28
Myn, H. 1802/06/28
Naiveu 1802/06/28
Neeffs, P. (I) 1802/06/28
Neer, A. 1802/06/28
Netscher, Casp. 1802/06/28
Nicodemo, Aug. 1802/06/28
Nieulandt, A. (I) 1802/06/28
Ochtervelt 1802/06/28
Ostade, A. 1802/06/28
Ostade, I. 1802/06/28
Ouwater, Isaak 1802/06/28
Ouwater, J. 1802/06/28
Palamedesz., A. 1802/06/28
Pape, Abr. 1802/06/28
Pee, T. 1802/06/28
Peeters, B. (I) 1802/06/28
Poelenburgh, C. 1802/06/28
Roore 1802/06/28
Ruisdael, J. 1802/06/28
Ruysch, R. 1802/06/28
Saftleven, C. 1802/06/28
Schalcken 1802/06/28
Schütz, J.G. 1802/06/28
Schweickardt, H. 1802/06/28
Seppo 1802/06/28
Sorgh, H.M. 1802/06/28
Steen, J. 1802/06/28
Stoop 1802/06/28
Storck, Abr. 1802/06/28
Toorenburgh, G. 1802/06/28
Troost, C. 1802/06/28
Velde, A. 1802/06/28
Velde, E. (I) 1802/06/28
Verkolje, N. 1802/06/28
Vertangen 1802/06/28
Victors, Jan 1802/06/28
Vois, Ary de 1802/06/28
Voorhout, J. (I) 1802/06/28
Vrancx 1802/06/28
Waerdigh 1802/06/28
Waterloo, A. 1802/06/28
Wigmana, G. 1802/06/28
Wijnants 1802/06/28
Willaerts 1802/06/28
Witte, E. 1802/06/28
Wolfaerts, Artus 1802/06/28
Wtewael, J. 1802/06/28
Wulfraet 1802/06/28
Xavery, Frans 1802/06/28

Ellinkhuyzen, P.L.
Battem 1808/06/06

Endemann
Lelie, A. 1801/04/23

Enden, see Eynden

Engelan, see Engelen

Engelbert, see Engelberts

Engelberts, Engelbert Michaël
1773–1843; dealer and son of Engelbertus Matthias Engelberts, 1732–1807, q.v.
Anonymous 1808/06/13
Berckheyde, J. 1806/11/24
Borrekens, J.P. 1806/11/24
Carree, M. 1808/06/13
Fyt 1808/06/13
Heem, David 1808/06/13
Heeremans, Thos. 1808/06/13
Heerswijk, H.F. 1808/06/13
Heusch, Wm. 1808/06/13
Lingelbach 1808/06/13
Moucheron 1808/06/13
Neeffs, P. (I) 1806/11/24
Neer, A. 1808/10/28
Roghman, R. 1806/08/13
Schut, C. (I) 1808/06/13
Seghers, D. 1808/06/13
Vermeer, Jan (II) 1806/11/24
Vliet, H.C. 1808/06/13
Weenix 1809/07/19
Werff, P. 1808/06/13
Wijnants 1808/06/13
Wouwerman, P. 1810/05/22

Engelberts, Engelbertus Matthias
1732–1807; writer, amateur draftsman and Protestant minister in Hoorn
Anonymous 1808/06/13
Backer, J.A. 1808/06/13
Beerstraten, A. 1808/06/13
Begeyn 1808/06/13
Bent, J. 1808/06/13
Blanckerhoff 1808/06/13
Breenbergh 1808/06/13
Broeck, E. 1808/06/13
Cappelle 1808/06/13
Carree, M. 1808/06/13
Colonia, A. 1808/06/13
Compe, Jan ten 1808/06/13
Correggio 1808/06/13
Croos, P. 1808/06/13
Diepenbeeck, A.J. 1808/06/13
Does, S. 1808/06/13
Drielst, E. 1808/06/13
Droochsloot, J.C. 1808/06/13
Dubbels, H. 1808/06/13
Duynen, I. 1808/06/13
Dyck, Anth. van 1808/06/13
Everdingen, A. 1808/06/13
Fyt 1808/06/13
Gael, B. 1808/06/13
Graef, T. 1808/06/13
Heem, David 1808/06/13
Heeremans, Thos. 1808/06/13
Heerswijk, H.F. 1808/06/13
Heusch, Wm. 1808/06/13
Hondecoeter, M. 1808/06/13
Huchtenburgh, Jan 1808/06/13
Huysum, Jan 1808/06/13
Janson, J. 1808/06/13
Kessel, J. (III) 1808/06/13
Liender, Pieter van 1808/06/13
Lingelbach 1808/06/13
Lorme, A. 1808/06/13
Maes, D. 1808/06/13
Metsu 1808/06/13
Mignon, A. 1808/06/13
Molenaer, J.M. 1808/06/13
Mortel 1808/06/13
Moucheron 1808/06/13
Moucheron, F. 1808/06/13
Neeffs, P. (I) 1808/06/13
Nijmegen, G. 1808/06/13
Piemont 1808/06/13
Quellinus, E. (II) 1808/06/13
Rembrandt 1808/06/13
Roghman, R. 1808/06/13
Rombouts 1808/06/13
Romeyn 1808/06/13
Roskam, H. 1808/06/13
Royen, W.F. van 1808/06/13
Rubens 1808/06/13
Ruisdael, J. 1808/06/13
Ruysdael, S. 1808/06/13
Sam, Engel 1808/06/13
Schellinks, Daniel 1808/06/13
Schut, C. (I) 1808/06/13

Seghers, D. 1808/06/13
Steen, J. 1808/06/13
Storck, Abr. 1808/06/13
Stuven 1808/06/13
Tonderen, P. 1808/06/13
Toorenvliet, J. 1808/06/13
Velde, A. 1808/06/13
Verboom, A.H. 1808/06/13
Victors, Jan 1808/06/13
Vitringa 1808/06/13
Vliet, H.C. 1808/06/13
Walscapelle 1808/06/13
Werff, P. 1808/06/13
Wijnants 1808/06/13
Withoos, M. 1808/06/13
Wouwerman, Ph. 1808/06/13
Wouwerman, Pieter 1808/06/13
Wyck, T. 1808/06/13

Engelberts, R.
d. ca.1810; preacher in Oostsouburg, Zeeland
Anonymous 1810/09/17

Engelen, J.
d. ca.1809; active in Arnhem
Anonymous 1807/12/00
Goyen 1807/12/00
Hondecoeter 1807/12/00

Enschut
Anonymous 1809/10/16

Enst en Dijk, see Estendijk

Enstendijk, van
Haensbergen, J. van 1808/10/28
Ruysdael, S. 1808/10/28

Eps, van
Anonymous 1803/10/10

Esser, Margaretha Maria, see Laar, Margaretha Maria van

Esser, Wijnand
1779–1860; dealer and painter active in The Hague and Amsterdam
Albani, Fr. 1803/04/27
Anonymous 1803/04/27
Anonymous 1805/07/03
Anonymous-Antique 1803/04/27
Aquila, P. 1803/04/27
Beerstraten, A. 1805/07/03
Does, S. 1810/03/26
Monogrammist H.B. 1805/07/03
Vlieger, S. 1805/07/03

Eustein
Snyders, F. 1803/08/24

Eversdijk, see Eversdyk

Eversdyk
Anonymous 1809/06/13
Bassen 1809/06/13
Bergh, R.V. 1810/06/20
Hooch, P. 1809/06/13
Roghman, R. 1810/06/20
Ruysdael, S. 1808/10/28
Verboom, A.H. 1810/06/20
Vlieger, S. 1808/11/28
Willaerts, Adam 1809/06/13

Eyk, Johannes van
dealer in The Hague
Aa, Dirk 1809/07/25
Anonymous 1802/09/06
Anonymous 1802/09/29
Anonymous 1809/07/25
Anonymous 1810/03/26
Anonymous 1810/06/06
Anonymous 1810/07/23
Beerstraten, A. 1810/07/23
Begeyn 1809/07/25
Berckheyde, G. 1809/07/25
Bisschop, J. 1810/07/23
Blieck 1810/03/26
Both, A. 1809/07/25
Bout, P. 1810/07/23
Brekelencam, Q. 1810/03/26
Courtois, J. 1809/07/25
Croos, A. 1809/07/25
Croos, N. 1809/07/25
Cuyp, A. 1810/07/23
Decker, C. 1810/03/26
Does 1809/07/25
Does, S. 1809/07/25
Dujardin, K. 1810/03/26
Eeckhout, G. 1809/07/25
Fargue, P.C. 1809/07/25
Gael, B. 1809/07/25
Gool, Jan 1809/07/25
Goyen 1810/03/26
Goyen 1810/07/23
Hals, F. (I) 1809/07/25
Hondecoeter, M. 1809/07/25
Huchtenburgh, Jan 1809/07/25
Huysmans, C. 1805/12/16
Italian 1810/06/06
Keller, J.H. (II) 1809/07/25
Klomp 1802/09/29
Koningh, L. 1809/07/25
Koningh, L. 1810/07/23
Lairesse, G. 1810/03/26
Langendijk, D. 1810/03/26
Laquy, W.J. 1809/07/25
Lin, H. 1809/07/25
Man, C. 1809/07/25
Metsu 1810/07/23
Mieris 1809/07/25
Monogrammist A.V.B. 1810/07/23
Monogrammist J.V.B. 1809/07/25
Moritz, Louis 1809/07/25
Neer, A. 1809/07/25
Neer, E. 1810/03/26
Nickelen 1810/06/06
Os, Pieter G. 1802/09/29
Ostade, A. 1802/09/29
Ostade, A. 1809/07/25
Ostade, I. 1809/07/25
Ostade, I. 1810/07/23
Palamedesz., A. 1809/07/25
Peeters, B. (I) 1809/07/25
Potter, Paulus 1810/07/23
Rombouts, Johannes 1810/03/26
Romeyn 1809/07/25
Ruisdael, J. 1810/03/26
Schalcken 1809/07/25
Scheffer 1809/07/25
Schweickardt, H. 1809/07/25
Soolmaker 1809/07/25
Steen, J. 1810/03/26
Teniers, D. (II) 1810/07/23
Troost, J.H. 1809/07/25
Ulft 1809/07/25
Velde, E. (I) 1810/07/23
Verboom, A.H. 1809/07/25
Verbruggen, G. (II) 1809/07/25
Vermeulen, A. 1809/07/25
Vlieger, S. 1810/06/06
Voorhout, J. (I) 1809/07/25
Wigmana, G. 1810/07/23
Wit, Jacob de 1809/07/25
Wit, Jacob de 1810/07/23
Wouwerman, Ph. 1809/07/25
Wst, G.D. 1809/07/25
Wulfraet 1809/07/25

Eynde, see Eynden

Eynden, Roland van
1747–1819; writer and amateur painter in Dordrecht
Anonymous 1810/07/23
Backhuysen 1810/07/23
Beeldemaker, A.C. 1810/07/23
Nijmegen, G. 1810/06/06
Orley, J. 1802/11/01
Steen, J. 1810/07/23

F.
Backhuysen 1803/06/20
Does, J. (I) 1803/06/20
Tol, D. 1803/06/20
Vermeer, Jan 1803/06/20

F. (1801, August 19)
Anonymous 1801/08/19
Boudewyns 1801/08/19
Honthorst, G. 1801/08/19
Horemans, J.J. (I) 1801/08/19
Kessel, J. (I) 1801/08/19
Molenaer, Klaes 1801/08/19
Momper, J. (II) 1801/08/19
Peeters, B. (I) 1801/08/19
Storck, Abr. 1801/08/19
Verschuring, H. 1801/08/19
Wit, Jacob de 1801/08/19
Witte, E. 1801/08/19

F. (1802, February 16)
Ast 1802/02/16
Brassauw 1802/02/16
Hoffman, Martin 1802/02/16
Meyling, J. 1802/02/16
Rembrandt 1802/02/16
Verdonck, Corn. 1802/02/16
Vermeulen, A. 1802/02/16

F. (1802, May 5)
Kuik, J. 1802/05/05
Oolen, Adr. 1802/05/05
Soolmaker 1802/05/05

F. (1803, June 20)
Heusch, Wm. 1803/06/20
Italian 1803/06/20
Rosa, S. 1803/06/20

F. (1803, December 12)
Anonymous 1803/12/12
Boonen, A. 1803/12/12
Bredael, P. 1803/12/12
Gelder, A. 1803/12/12
Maes, G. 1803/12/12
Ochtervelt 1803/12/12
Rembrandt 1803/12/12
Silo, A. 1803/12/12
Verboom, W.H. 1803/12/12
Vries, R. 1803/12/12

F. (1804, August 8)
identical with "A" on May 7, 1804
Backhuysen 1804/08/08
Compe, Jan ten 1804/08/08
Dolci, C. 1804/08/08
Ekels, Jan (I) 1804/08/08
Metsu 1804/08/08
Neer, A. 1804/08/08
Toorenburgh, G. 1804/08/08
Velde, A. 1804/08/08
Vois, Ary de 1804/08/08

F. (1806, May 5)
Anonymous 1806/05/05
Peeters, B. (I) 1806/05/05
Vliet, H.C. 1806/05/05

F. (1806, August 13)
Anonymous 1806/08/13
Avercamp, H. 1806/08/13
Brussel, P. 1806/08/13
Camphuysen, D. 1806/08/13
Chalon, L. 1806/08/13
Dalens, Dirck 1806/08/13
Decker, C. 1806/08/13
Droochsloot, J.C. 1806/08/13
Dubbels, H. 1806/08/13
Dujardin, K. 1806/08/13
Everdingen, A. 1806/08/13
Hobbema 1806/08/13
Hondecoeter 1806/08/13
Lingelbach 1806/08/13
Lubienietski, C. 1806/08/13
Martszen, J. (II) 1806/08/13
Metsu 1806/08/13
Meulen, A.F. 1806/08/13
Molenaer, Klaes 1806/08/13
Mommers, H. 1806/08/13
Monogrammist C.W.M. 1806/08/13
Ochtervelt 1806/08/13
Ostade, I. 1806/08/13
Ouwater, Isaak 1806/08/13
Ouwater, J. 1806/08/13
Regemorter, P. 1806/08/13
Roos 1806/08/13
Smit, Aernout 1806/08/13
Storck, Abr. 1806/08/13
Thier, B.H. 1806/08/13
Verboom, A.H. 1806/08/13
Verdonck, Corn. 1806/08/13
Vries, R. 1806/08/13
Weenix, J.B. 1806/08/13
Witte, E. 1806/08/13
Wouwerman 1806/08/13
Wouwerman, P. 1806/08/13

F. (1808, November 28)
Backhuysen 1808/11/28
Dubourg, L. 1808/11/28
Fredriks, J.H. 1808/11/28
Lievens, J. (I) 1808/11/28
Ruysch, R. 1808/11/28
Troost, C. 1808/11/28

F. (1809, July 19)
Velde, W. 1809/07/19

F. (1810, May 22)
Anonymous 1810/05/22
Bega 1810/05/22
Berchem, N.P. 1810/05/22
Cranach, L. (I) 1810/05/22
German 1810/05/22
Glauber, J. 1810/05/22
Laer, P. 1810/05/22
Ostade, A. 1810/05/22
Porcellis, Jan 1810/05/22
Potter, Paulus 1810/05/22
Ruysdael, S. 1810/05/22
Schendel, B. 1810/05/22
Storck, Abr. 1810/05/22
Wiltens, C. 1810/05/22
Zeemann 1810/05/22

F. (1810, August 6)
Aelst, W. 1810/08/06
Anonymous 1810/08/06
Backer 1810/08/06
Bray, S. 1810/08/06
Bredael, J. 1810/08/06
Cuyp, J.G. 1810/08/06
Diepenbeeck, A.J. 1810/08/06
Everdingen, A. 1810/08/06
Heem, J.D. 1810/08/06
Heeremans, Thos. 1810/08/06
Honthorst, G. 1810/08/06
Miereveld, Jan 1810/08/06
Neer, A. 1810/08/06
Tieling, C. 1810/08/06
Troost, C. 1810/08/06
Vlieger, S. 1810/08/06
Zeemann 1810/08/06

Faessen
Bijlert 1802/11/01

Fagel, Hendrik III, baron
1765–1838; Dutch Greffier residing in England and Dutch ambassador from 1813–1824
Mieris, F. (I) 1802/09/29
Potter, Paulus 1802/09/29
Velde, A. 1802/09/29

Fahn, Jan
Droochsloot, J.C. 1802/05/10

Farret
Berchem, N.P. 1801/04/23
Huchtenburgh, Jan 1801/04/23

Feen, Tjetse van der, Mr.
lawyer active in Amsterdam
Monogrammist D.V.B. 1809/07/27
Monogrammist L.B. 1809/07/27
Salm, A. 1809/07/27

Ferguson
Anonymous 1804/05/07
Anonymous 1806/11/24
Fargue, P.C. 1804/05/07
Quellinus, E. (II) 1804/08/08
Troost, C. 1804/05/07

Flen
Helst, B. 1806/08/13

Flines, de
Anonymous 1806/11/24
Bloemaert, A. 1806/05/05

Florijn
Anonymous 1802/12/13
Chalon, L. 1802/12/13
Elliger, O. (II) 1802/12/13
Francken 1802/12/13
Heerschop, H. 1802/12/13
Jonkers 1802/12/13
Pothoven, H. 1802/12/13
Roos 1802/12/13
Steenwyck, Hend. 1802/12/13
Troost, J.H. 1802/12/13
Vrancx 1802/12/13
Werff, H.N. 1802/12/13
Willaerts 1802/12/13

Focken
Anonymous 1810/06/20
Ast 1810/06/20
Heeremans, Thos. 1810/06/20
Horemans, J.J. (I) 1810/06/20
Koller, J.J. 1810/06/20

Fokke
perhaps Jan Fokke, q.v., or his brother the dealer Arend Fokke Simonsz., 1755–1812
Anonymous 1810/08/06

Fokke, Jan
1742–1812; draftsman, etcher, writer and poet
Zegelaar, G. 1803/12/12

Foorn, van der
Janson, J.C. 1801/03/31

Foreest, van
presumably a member of the Alkmaar family of this name
Aertsen 1801/08/19
Anonymous 1801/08/19
Backhuysen 1801/08/19
Balen, H. (I) 1801/08/19
Brekelencam, Q. 1801/08/19
Brueghel, J. (I) 1801/08/19
Dubbels, H. 1801/08/19
Ferguson, Wm. 1801/08/19
Flemish-Brabant 1801/08/19
Goyen 1801/08/19
Heem 1801/08/19
Holbein, H. (II) 1801/08/19
Hooch, P. 1801/08/19
Hooren, J. 1801/08/19
Lingelbach 1801/08/19
Micker, J.C. 1801/08/19
Mieris 1801/08/19
Molenaer, J.M. 1801/08/19
Monogrammist B.H. 1801/08/19
Monogrammist J.R. 1801/08/19
Palamedesz., A. 1801/08/19
Poelenburgh, C. 1801/08/19
Pompe, Gerrit 1801/08/19
Rennet 1801/08/19
Rootius, Jan A. 1801/08/19
Ruysdael, S. 1801/08/19
Steen, J. 1801/08/19
Storck, Abr. 1801/08/19
Velde, E. (I) 1801/08/19
Velde, W. 1801/08/19
Vinne, V.L. (I) 1801/08/19
Vos 1801/08/19
Withoos, M. 1801/08/19
Wouwerman, J. 1801/08/19
Wyck, T. 1801/08/19

Forreest, van, see Foreest, van

Fortman
Maratti 1806/05/05

Fortuyn, Gerrit Hendrik
1731–1807; resident of Gouda
Anonymous 1808/04/26
Asselyn 1808/04/26
Backhuysen 1808/04/26
Beeldemaker 1808/04/26
Begeyn 1808/04/26
Berchem, N.P. 1808/04/26
Berckheyde, G. 1808/04/26
Bloot, P. 1808/04/26
Borch, G. ter (II) 1808/04/26
Both, J. 1808/04/26
Brekelencam, Q. 1808/04/26
Cappelle 1808/04/26
Colonia, A. 1808/04/26
Correggio 1808/04/26
Croos 1808/04/26
Cuylenborch, A. 1808/04/26
Cuyp, A. 1808/04/26
Cuyp, B. 1808/04/26
Decker 1808/04/26
Does, S. 1808/04/26
Dongen, Dionys 1808/04/26
Dou 1808/04/26
Ducq, Johan le 1808/04/26
Dürer 1808/04/26
Dusart, Corn. 1808/04/26
Eeckhout, G. 1808/04/26
Flinck 1808/04/26
Francken 1808/04/26
Goyen 1808/04/26
Hagen, Joris 1808/04/26
Hals, F. (I) 1808/04/26
Helt, F. 1808/04/26
Hobbema 1808/04/26
Hondecoeter, M. 1808/04/26
Houbraken, H. 1808/04/26
Houten, F. 1808/04/26
Huchtenburgh, Jan 1808/04/26
Janson, J. 1808/04/26
Jordaens, J. (I) 1808/04/26
Kalraet 1808/04/26
Klomp 1808/04/26
Kroost, C. 1808/04/26
Lairesse, G. 1808/04/26
Le Brun, Chas. 1808/04/26
Lingelbach 1808/04/26
Lubienietski, C. 1808/04/26
Maes, D. 1808/04/26
Maes, N. 1808/04/26
Marcelis, J.C. 1808/04/26
Metsu 1808/04/26
Meyer, A. de 1808/04/26
Mieris, W. 1808/04/26
Molenaer, J.M. 1808/04/26
Molenaer, Klaes 1808/04/26
Monogrammist P. 1808/04/26
Moor, C. 1808/04/26
Naiveu 1808/04/26
Nap, J. 1808/04/26
Neck, Jan 1808/04/26
Neeffs, P. (I) 1808/04/26
Neer, A. 1808/04/26
Neyburgh, B.J. 1808/04/26
Ostade 1808/04/26
Ostade, I. 1808/04/26
Palamedesz., A. 1808/04/26
Pepyn, M. 1808/04/26
Pierson, A. 1808/04/26
Poel, E. 1808/04/26
Potter, Paulus 1808/04/26
Pynacker 1808/04/26
Quast, P.J. 1808/04/26
Rembrandt 1808/04/26
Romeyn 1808/04/26
Rubens 1808/04/26
Ruisdael, J. 1808/04/26
Ruysdael, S. 1808/04/26
Saftleven, H. 1808/04/26
Schalcke, C. 1808/04/26
Seghers, D. 1808/04/26
Sibilla, G. 1808/04/26
Silo, A. 1808/04/26
Snyders, F. 1808/04/26
Sonje, J.G. 1808/04/26
Sorgh, H.M. 1808/04/26
Steen, J. 1808/04/26
Stoffer, H. 1808/04/26
Storck, Abr. 1808/04/26
Teniers, D. (II) 1808/04/26
Toorenvliet, J. 1808/04/26
Vaart, Jan 1808/04/26
Velde 1808/04/26
Velde, W. 1808/04/26
Vermeer, Jan (III) 1808/04/26
Verschuir 1808/04/26
Verschuring, H. 1808/04/26
Vertangen 1808/04/26
Vinckeboons, D. 1808/04/26
Vlieger, S. 1808/04/26
Vliet, H.C. 1808/04/26
Vrancx 1808/04/26
Waanen 1808/04/26
Waterloo, A. 1808/04/26
Weenix 1808/04/26
Werff, A. 1808/04/26
Wet, J.W. 1808/04/26
Wijnants 1808/04/26
Witte, E. 1808/04/26
Wolfaerts, Artus 1808/04/26
Wouwerman 1808/04/26
Wouwerman, P. 1808/04/26
Wouwerman, Ph. 1808/04/26
Wyck, T. 1808/04/26
Wyntrack, D. 1808/04/26

Fouquet, Pierre, Jr.
1729–1800; publisher, printseller and picture dealer
Aelst, W. 1801/04/13
Amigoni, J. 1801/04/13
Anonymous 1801/04/13
Backhuysen 1801/04/13
Berchem, N.P. 1801/04/13
Blom, P. 1801/04/13
Bol, F. 1801/04/13
Bourdon 1801/04/13
Breenbergh 1801/04/13
Brussel, P. 1801/04/13
Cornelisz. van Haarlem 1801/04/13
Coypel, Ant. 1801/04/13
Decker, C. 1801/04/13
Dou 1801/04/13
Doudijns, W. 1801/04/13
Dubbels, H. 1801/04/13
Dusart, Corn. 1801/04/13
Dyck, Anth. van 1801/04/13
Eeckhout, G. 1801/04/13
Elliger, O. (II) 1801/04/13
Elsheimer, A. 1801/04/13
Flinck 1801/04/13
Forman, L. 1801/04/13
Giordano, L. 1801/04/13
Hackaert, J. 1801/04/13
Hals, F. (I) 1801/04/13
Heyden, J. 1801/04/13
Hondecoeter, M. 1801/04/13
Honthorst, G. 1801/04/13
Hooch, P. 1801/04/13
Huchtenburgh, Jan 1801/04/13
Huysum, Jan 1801/04/13
Italian 1801/04/13
Jordaens, J. (I) 1801/04/13
Lauri, F. 1801/04/13
Le Brun, Chas. 1801/04/13
Lingelbach 1801/04/13
Maes, N. 1801/04/13
Manfredi, B. 1801/04/13
Metsu 1801/04/13
Miel 1801/04/13
Moor, C. 1801/04/13
Moucheron, F. 1801/04/13
Myn, G. 1801/04/13
Mytens, D. (I) 1801/04/13
Neeffs, P. (I) 1801/04/13
Neer, A. 1801/04/13
Ostade, A. 1801/04/13
Oudenrogge, J.D. 1801/04/13
Pel, A. 1801/04/13
Poel, E. 1801/04/13
Procaccini, Cam. 1801/04/13
Rembrandt 1801/04/13
Reni 1801/04/13
Ruisdael, J. 1801/04/13
Ryckaert, D. (III) 1801/04/13
Saftleven, C. 1801/04/13
Slingeland, P.C. 1801/04/13
Snyders, F. 1801/04/13
Steen, J. 1801/04/13
Steenwyck, Hend. 1801/04/13
Teniers, D. (II) 1801/04/13
Troost, J.H. 1801/04/13
Velde, A. 1801/04/13
Verboom, A.H. 1801/04/13
Vermeer, Jan (III) 1801/04/13
Victors, Jan 1801/04/13
Vliet, H.C. 1801/04/13
Vois, Ary de 1801/04/13
Weenix 1801/04/13
Weenix, J.B. 1801/04/13
Werff, A. 1801/04/13
Wijnants 1801/04/13
Wouwerman, Ph. 1801/04/13
Wyck, T. 1801/04/13
Zegelaar, G. 1801/04/13

Fraaienhove
Anonymous 1804/06/18

Frantsen, see Frantzen

Frantsz, see Frantzen

Frantszen, see Frantzen

Frantze, see Frantzen

Frantzen
probably the Amsterdam broker Gerhardus Frantzen, b.1764
Anonymous 1801/08/19
Anonymous 1801/10/06
Anonymous 1802/09/06

Limborch, H. 1810/07/26
Mieris, W. 1802/06/28
Molenaer, Klaes 1810/06/20
Moni, L. de 1802/06/28
Ochtervelt 1802/06/28
Ostade, A. 1810/05/22
Ouwater, Isaak 1802/06/28
Potter, Paulus 1804/10/22
Ruysch, R. 1802/06/28
Steen, J. 1802/06/28
Toorenvliet, J. 1810/10/11
Verburgh, Dionijs 1804/02/27
Voorhout, J. (I) 1810/06/20
Xavery, Frans 1802/06/28

Gelder, de
most transactions probably attributable to Adrianus de Gelder, Kamerbode der Kunst-Confrerie van Pictura in The Hague
Anonymous 1805/10/09
Anonymous 1807/06/10
Anonymous 1809/07/25
Anonymous-Modern 1807/06/10
Beeldemaker 1807/06/10
Bega 1807/06/10
Brekelencam, Q. 1805/10/09
Bruegel, P. (I) 1807/06/10
Brueghel, J. (I) 1807/06/10
Carree, M. 1809/07/25
Droochsloot, J.C. 1805/10/09
Ducq, Johan le 1807/06/10
Haensbergen, J. van 1807/06/10
Hochecker, Franz 1805/10/09
Jacobsz., Juriaen 1805/10/09
Lelienbergh 1805/10/09
Liss 1805/10/09
Liss 1807/06/10
Maes, N. 1809/07/25
Meyer 1805/10/09
Momper, J. (II) 1807/06/10
Parmigianino 1805/10/09
Penning, N.L. 1807/06/10
Poelenburgh, C. 1807/06/10
Rombouts 1805/10/09
Sorgh, H.M. 1805/10/09
Storck, Abr. 1805/10/09
Storck, Abr. 1809/07/25
Velde, W. 1809/07/25
Verbruggen, G. (II) 1807/06/10
Verschuring, H. 1805/10/09
Vinckeboons, D. 1805/10/09
Wit, Jacob de 1809/07/25
Wouwerman, Ph. 1809/07/25

Gelder, A. de
probably Adrianus de Gelder, Kamerbode der Kunst-Confrerie van Pictura in The Hague
Anonymous 1806/08/20
Maes, N. 1806/08/20
Terwesten, Mat. 1806/08/20

Gelder, J. de
Anonymous 1810/07/23

Gelder, R. de
Beschey, B. 1805/10/09
Rubens 1805/10/09
Wit, Jacob de 1805/10/09

Gesen, see Giesen

Gevaerts
active in Utrecht
Anonymous 1802/09/21
Hoet, G. (I) 1802/09/21
Molenaer, J.M. 1802/09/21
Snyders, F. 1802/09/21

Giese, see Giesen

Giesen, Valkert van
d. ca.1822; dealer
Aertsen 1810/06/06
Anonymous 1801/06/13
Anonymous 1802/09/18
Anonymous 1803/08/24
Anonymous 1805/07/03
Anonymous 1805/10/09
Anonymous 1807/06/10
Anonymous 1808/06/11
Anonymous 1810/03/26
Asselyn 1803/08/24
Bassen 1803/08/24
Battem 1802/09/18
Bega 1802/09/18
Bogaert, Hendrick H. 1804/10/16
Carpioni, G. (I) 1803/08/24
Carree, Abr. 1803/08/24
Coclers, J.B. 1807/06/10
Cornelisz. van Haarlem 1801/06/13
Cornelisz. van Haarlem 1803/08/24
Croos, P. 1805/07/03
Decker, C. 1808/06/11
Dongen, Dionys 1802/09/18
Dou 1802/09/18
Dou 1808/06/11
Douw, S. 1802/09/18
Douw, S. 1803/08/24
Dürer 1808/06/11
Dusart, Corn. 1803/08/24
Dyck, Abraham van 1808/06/11
Engels, B. 1803/08/24
Floris, F. (I) 1810/06/06
Francken, Frans 1807/06/10
Goyen 1802/09/18
Goyen 1803/08/24
Groot, Johannes 1807/06/10
Heem, C. 1805/10/09
Hennekyn 1802/05/24
Hoet, G. (I) 1803/08/24
Italian 1801/06/13
Janson, P. 1808/06/11
Jordaens, J. (I) 1804/10/16
Kessel, J. (I) 1802/05/24
Klomp 1804/10/16
Largillière 1803/08/24
Limborch, H. 1802/09/18
Looten, J. 1802/05/24
Maes, D. 1803/08/24
Michau 1804/10/16
Mieris, W. 1807/06/10
Molenaer, J.M. 1805/07/03
Molenaer, Klaes 1804/04/28
Monogrammist B.V.S. 1808/06/11
Monogrammist P.W. 1807/06/10
Moucheron, I. 1808/06/11
Neeffs, P. (I) 1804/10/16
Nieulandt, A. (I) 1802/05/24
Ostade, A. 1804/04/28
Ostade, A. 1807/06/10
Ostade, I. 1808/06/11
Palamedesz., A. 1805/10/09
Palamedesz., P. (I) 1802/09/18
Pynacker 1803/08/24
Rembrandt 1807/06/10
Rubens 1807/06/10
Ruisdael, J. 1805/10/09
Ruisdael, J. 1808/06/11
Saftleven, C. 1808/06/11
Schalcken 1807/06/10
Sorgh 1808/06/11
Steen, J. 1807/06/10
Steen, J. 1808/06/11
Tamm 1807/06/10
Tempel, A.L. van den 1807/06/10
Teniers, D. (II) 1807/06/10
Troost, J.H. 1803/08/24
Vitringa 1807/06/10
Weenix 1808/06/11
Werff, A. 1805/07/03

Giessen, see Giesen

Gieze, van, see Giesen, van

Giezen, see Giesen

Gillissen, Pieter
d. ca.1801; bookseller in Middelburg
Anonymous 1801/09/04
Avercamp, H. 1801/09/04
Beeldemaker 1801/09/04
Bloemaert, A. 1801/09/04
Craen, L. 1801/09/04

Glad
Anonymous 1808/06/13
Asselyn 1808/06/13
Bent, J. 1808/06/13
Bloemen, J.F. 1808/06/13
Bloemen, P. 1808/06/13
Gerards 1808/06/13
Heer, G. 1808/06/13
Heusch, Wm. 1808/06/13
Kessel, J. (III) 1808/06/13
Lingelbach 1808/06/13
Lorme, A. 1808/06/13
Mignon, A. 1808/06/13
Molenaer, Klaes 1808/06/13
Nieulandt 1808/06/13
Piemont 1808/06/13
Romeyn 1808/06/13
Schellinks, Daniel 1808/06/13
Tonderen, P. 1808/06/13
Verbruggen, G. (II) 1808/06/13
Victors, Jan 1808/06/13

Goor
Nieulandt, W. (II) 1802/07/27

Graffelman
perhaps Andries Graffelman, ca.1767–1843, an amateur draftsman
Cuyp, A. 1805/12/16
Dorne, M. 1806/05/05
Dubbels, H. 1805/12/16
Dujardin, K. 1804/08/08
Fock, Harm. 1804/08/08
Fournier 1806/05/05
Gool, Jan 1807/08/26
Goyen 1807/08/26
Hulsdonck, J. 1804/08/08
Keun, Hend. 1807/08/26
Molenaer, J.M. 1804/08/08
Moni, L. de 1804/08/08
Os, Pieter G. 1804/08/08
Romeyn 1807/08/26
Simons, M. 1804/08/08

Gram
Anonymous 1806/08/20
Bogaert, Iemant 1806/08/20
Brueghel, J. (I) 1806/08/20
Fargue 1806/08/20
Heemskerck, M. 1806/08/20
Huchtenburgh, Jan 1806/08/20
Lairesse, Jan 1806/08/20
Metsu 1806/08/20
Molenaer, J.M. 1806/08/20
Moor, C. 1806/08/20
Moucheron, F. 1806/08/20
Mytens, Aert 1806/08/20
Poel, E. 1806/08/20
Thomas, Jan 1806/08/20
Vinckeboons, D. 1806/08/20
Vlieger, S. 1806/08/20
Vrancx 1806/08/20
Winghen, B. 1806/08/20

Graun
Maes, N. 1806/08/13

Grauu
Bloemaert 1806/05/05
Heemskerck 1806/05/05
Molenaer, J.M. 1806/05/05

Grave (widow)
Anonymous 1802/09/06
Anonymous 1805/07/10
Baur, W. 1802/09/06
Berchem, N.P. 1805/07/10
Borch, G. ter (II) 1805/07/10
Brekelencam, Q. 1802/09/06
Decker 1802/09/06
Eeckhout, G. 1805/07/10
Essen, C. 1805/07/10
Goyen 1805/07/10
Heemskerck, B. 1802/09/06
Heeremans, Thos. 1802/09/06
Klomp 1802/09/06
Kuster, J. 1802/09/06
Liss 1802/09/06
Meer, N. 1802/09/06
Molenaer, J.M. 1802/09/06
Molenaer, J.M. 1805/07/10
Molenaer, Klaes 1802/09/06
Myer, L. de 1802/09/06
Neer, A. 1805/07/10
Sonje, J.G. 1802/09/06
Toorenvliet, J. 1805/07/10
Vermeer, Jan (III) 1805/07/10
Wijnants 1802/09/06
Wijnants 1805/07/10

Grimmond
Anonymous 1809/06/13
Schütz 1809/06/13

Grimpe, see Grimpen

Grimpen
also spelled Grimpe
Amigoni, J. 1803/04/27
Anonymous 1803/04/20
Anonymous 1803/04/27
Anonymous 1803/06/20
Assteyn, B.A. 1803/09/07
Beeldemaker 1803/04/20
Brueghel 1803/09/07
Cuyp, A. 1802/06/16
Elliger, O. (I) 1802/02/16
Francken, Frans (II) 1803/07/18
Heusch, Wm. 1803/06/20
Honthorst, G. 1803/04/27
Maes, G. 1803/07/18
Monogrammist cK. 1803/04/20
Rubens 1803/04/27
Schalcken 1803/09/07
Teniers, D. (II) 1803/04/20
Teniers, D. (II) 1803/09/07
Velde, E. (I) 1803/09/07

Groen, J.
Steen, J. 1802/07/27

Groend
Anonymous 1806/05/05

Groeneveld
perhaps the draftsman Cornelis Groeneveld, active ca.1795–1813
Anonymous 1802/09/06

Groot, Jan de
d. ca.1804; possibly the painter, engraver and bookseller of this name active in The Hague 1757–1776
Anonymous 1804/12/10
Backhuysen 1804/12/10
Beerstraten, J. 1804/12/10
Berchem, N.P. 1804/12/10
Berckheyde, G. 1804/12/10

Breenbergh 1804/12/10
Compe, Jan ten 1804/12/10
Delen 1804/12/10
Drielst, E. 1804/12/10
Dyk, P. 1804/12/10
Elliger, Ant. 1804/12/10
Everdingen, Cesar 1804/12/10
Fargue, Karel 1804/12/10
Gool, Jan 1804/12/10
Griffier 1804/12/10
Haag, T.P.C. 1804/12/10
Hendriks, W. 1804/12/10
Herrlein, J.A. 1804/12/10
Hoet, G. (I) 1804/12/10
Hondecoeter, M. 1804/12/10
Hooch, P. 1804/12/10
Janson, J. 1804/12/10
Janson, J.C. 1804/12/10
Keun, Hend. 1804/12/10
Lancret 1804/12/10
Laquy, W.J. 1804/12/10
Lauwers, J.J. 1804/12/10
Liender, Pieter van 1804/12/10
Meijer, H. 1804/12/10
Metsu 1804/12/10
Mieris, F. (I) 1804/12/10
Mieris, F. (II) 1804/12/10
Mieris, W. 1804/12/10
Molenaer, Klaes 1804/12/10
Mommers, H. 1804/12/10
Moni, L. de 1804/12/10
Monogrammist I.A.H. 1804/12/10
Moucheron, I. 1804/12/10
Myn, G. 1804/12/10
Os, J. 1804/12/10
Ouwater, Isaak 1804/12/10
Pothoven, H. 1804/12/10
Prins, J.H. 1804/12/10
Pynacker 1804/12/10
Ruysdael, S. 1804/12/10
Saftleven, H. 1804/12/10
Savery, R. 1804/12/10
Schweickardt, H. 1804/12/10
Thier, B.H. 1804/12/10
Toorenburgh, G. 1804/12/10
Velde, A. 1804/12/10
Velde, W. 1804/12/10
Verkolje, N. 1804/12/10
Vliet, H.C. 1804/12/10
Witte, E. 1804/12/10
Zegelaar, G. 1804/12/10

Gruijter, see Gruyter

Gruiter, see Gruyter

Grundel
Anonymous 1803/08/24

Grutte
Zepp, C. 1810/05/22

Gruyter, Willem, Senior
ca.1763–1831; dealer active in Amsterdam
Aelst, W. 1802/12/13
Aelst, W. 1804/05/07
Aelst, W. 1805/07/03
Aelst, W. 1809/04/17
Aelst, W. 1810/10/11
Amigoni, J. 1803/04/27
Amigoni, J. 1805/07/10
Anonymous 1801/03/16
Anonymous 1801/04/23
Anonymous 1801/05/11
Anonymous 1801/08/19
Anonymous 1801/10/06
Anonymous 1802/02/16
Anonymous 1802/05/05
Anonymous 1802/06/16
Anonymous 1802/06/28
Anonymous 1802/07/27
Anonymous 1802/09/06
Anonymous 1802/09/18
Anonymous 1802/12/13
Anonymous 1803/04/20
Anonymous 1803/04/27
Anonymous 1803/06/20
Anonymous 1803/08/01
Anonymous 1803/09/07
Anonymous 1803/12/12
Anonymous 1804/02/27
Anonymous 1804/05/07
Anonymous 1804/08/08
Anonymous 1804/12/10
Anonymous 1805/07/10
Anonymous 1806/05/05
Anonymous 1806/08/13
Anonymous 1807/04/13
Anonymous 1807/08/26
Anonymous 1807/08/27
Anonymous 1808/06/13
Anonymous 1808/08/23
Anonymous 1808/10/28
Anonymous 1808/11/28
Anonymous 1809/04/17
Anonymous 1809/06/13
Anonymous 1809/07/19
Anonymous 1809/07/25
Anonymous 1810/05/22
Anonymous 1810/06/20
Anonymous 1810/08/06
Anonymous 1810/10/11
Anonymous-Modern 1803/09/07
Anonymous-Modern 1808/11/28
Antonissen, H.J. 1804/08/08
Antonissen, H.J. 1805/07/10
Antonissen, H.J. 1809/06/13
Apshoven 1806/08/13
Apshoven 1808/11/28
Asch, P.J. van 1802/05/05
Asch, P.J. van 1805/07/10
Asch, P.J. van 1808/08/23
Asselyn 1808/11/28
Asselyn 1809/04/17
Asselyn 1809/07/19
Asselyn 1810/05/22
Asselyn 1810/10/11
Ast 1809/06/13
Avercamp, H. 1802/12/13
Avercamp, H. 1805/07/03
Backer 1810/10/11
Backer, A. 1804/08/08
Backhuysen 1802/12/13
Backhuysen 1804/05/07
Backhuysen 1804/08/08
Backhuysen 1808/11/28
Backhuysen 1809/09/06
Balen 1801/03/16
Balen, H. (I) 1802/09/29
Balen, H. (I) 1803/09/07
Balen, H. (I) 1804/08/08
Balen, H. (I) 1808/11/28
Balen, H. (I) 1809/04/17
Balen, H. (I) 1809/06/13
Balen, H. (I) 1810/10/11
Barbiers, P. 1808/11/28
Bassano 1802/06/16
Bassano 1803/04/20
Bassen 1802/06/28
Bassen 1803/04/20
Bassen 1806/08/13
Bassen 1810/10/11
Beerstraten, A. 1802/09/06
Beerstraten, A. 1807/08/26
Beerstraten, A. 1808/08/23
Beerstraten, A. 1809/06/13
Beerstraten, A. 1810/10/11
Beerstraten, J. 1806/05/05
Beest, Sybrand 1805/07/10
Beesten, J. 1804/05/07
Bega 1803/08/17
Bega 1809/06/13
Begeyn 1801/08/19
Begeyn 1804/02/27
Begeyn 1804/08/08
Begeyn 1808/06/13
Belanger, B. 1804/02/27
Bellevois 1808/08/23
Bellevois 1809/06/13
Bemmel 1804/08/08
Bemmel 1806/08/13
Bent, J. 1804/05/07
Bent, J. 1804/08/08
Bent, J. 1806/08/13
Bent, J. 1808/08/23
Bent, J. 1808/11/28
Bent, J. 1809/04/17
Berchem, N.P. 1801/05/11
Berchem, N.P. 1802/02/16
Berchem, N.P. 1805/07/10
Berchem, N.P. 1809/06/13
Berckheyde, G. 1802/12/13
Berckheyde, G. 1803/08/17
Berckheyde, G. 1810/08/06
Berckheyde, G. 1810/10/11
Berckheyde, J. 1802/02/16
Berckheyde, J. 1803/06/20
Berckheyde, J. 1808/08/23
Bergen, D. 1806/08/13
Bergen, D. 1808/08/23
Bergen, D. 1809/04/17
Bergen, D. 1810/05/22
Berkenkamp 1803/08/01
Berninck, H. 1802/05/05
Beschey 1803/06/20
Beschey, B. 1809/04/17
Besters, A.J. 1802/06/16
Bijlert 1803/04/20
Bisschop, Abr. 1806/05/05
Bleeker, A. 1804/05/07
Blieck 1805/07/10
Bloemaert 1801/05/11
Bloemaert, A. 1802/05/05
Bloemaert, A. 1802/06/28
Bloemaert, A. 1803/04/20
Bloemaert, A. 1803/08/17
Bloemaert, A. 1806/08/13
Bloemaert, A. 1809/04/17
Bloemaert, A. 1809/06/13
Bloemen, P. 1808/08/23
Bol, F. 1809/06/13
Bol, F. 1810/10/11
Bolomey, B.S. 1802/12/13
Bolomey, B.S. 1804/08/08
Boonen, A. 1804/08/08
Borch, G. ter (II) 1804/08/08
Borch, G. ter (II) 1806/08/13
Borch, G. ter (II) 1809/06/13
Borch, G. ter (II) 1809/09/06
Borssom 1801/08/19
Borssom 1802/02/16
Both, A. 1805/07/10
Both, J. 1805/07/10
Both, J. 1809/07/19
Boudewyns 1801/08/19
Boudewyns 1810/10/11
Bout, P. 1804/08/08
Bout, P. 1806/08/13
Bout, P. 1808/11/28
Bout, P. 1810/10/11
Brakenburg 1803/07/18
Brakenburg 1804/08/08
Brakenburg 1807/08/26
Brakenburg 1809/06/13
Bramer 1802/12/13
Bramer 1804/02/27
Bray, S. 1804/08/08
Bray, S. 1806/08/13
Bray, S. 1808/08/23
Bredael 1809/04/17
Bredael, J. 1802/09/06
Bredael, J. 1807/08/26
Breenbergh 1802/09/06
Breenbergh 1803/08/17
Brekelencam, Q. 1801/03/16
Brekelencam, Q. 1802/07/27
Brekelencam, Q. 1803/06/20
Brekelencam, Q. 1805/07/10
Brekelencam, Q. 1806/08/13
Brekelencam, Q. 1808/08/23
Brekelencam, Q. 1809/06/13
Brekelencam, Q. 1810/10/11
Bril, P. 1802/06/28
Broeck, E. 1805/07/10
Broeck, E. 1808/06/13
Brouwer, Adr. 1804/08/08
Brouwer, Adr. 1805/07/10
Brouwer, Adr. 1806/08/13
Brouwer, Adr. 1808/11/28
Brouwer, J. 1801/05/11
Bruegel, P. (I) 1807/08/26
Brueghel 1803/09/07
Brueghel 1806/05/05
Brueghel, J. (I) 1801/08/19
Brueghel, J. (I) 1802/09/06
Brueghel, J. (I) 1802/09/29
Brueghel, J. (I) 1803/09/07
Brueghel, J. (I) 1804/08/08
Brueghel, J. (I) 1806/08/13
Brueghel, J. (I) 1808/08/23
Brueghel, J. (I) 1809/04/17
Brueghel, J. (I) 1809/06/13
Brueghel, J. (I) 1810/10/11
Brueghel, P. (II) 1802/12/13
Brussel, P. 1802/05/05
Brussel, P. 1810/05/22
Bruyn, T. 1810/06/20
Bryer, C. 1803/09/07
Burg, Adriaan 1803/06/20
Buys, Jac. 1802/02/16
Camphuysen 1804/02/27
Camphuysen, R. 1802/12/13
Camphuysen, R. 1806/08/13
Canaletto 1805/12/16
Cappelle 1810/10/11
Carree 1809/04/17
Carree, Hend. (I) 1802/09/18
Carree, M. 1806/08/13
Carree, M. 1808/08/23
Cats, Jac. 1809/06/13
Cerquozzi 1804/07/25
Chalon, L. 1807/08/26
Chalon, L. 1810/10/11
Cleve, Joos van 1806/05/05
Codanelli, P. 1804/08/08
Coelenbier, Jan 1810/10/11
Colonia, A. 1808/06/13
Colyer, Edwaert 1809/07/25
Compe, Jan ten 1801/10/19
Compe, Jan ten 1802/12/13
Compe, Jan ten 1804/05/07
Compe, Jan ten 1806/08/13
Compe, Jan ten 1810/05/22
Coopse, P. 1801/06/10
Courtois, J. 1808/08/23
Coxie, Ant. 1806/08/13
Coxie, M. (I) 1803/04/20
Cranach, L. (I) 1803/04/20
Cranach, L. (I) 1803/09/07
Cranach, L. (I) 1808/11/28
Croos, P. 1805/07/10
Croos, P. 1809/06/13
Cuylenborch, A. 1801/03/16
Cuyp, A. 1802/06/28
Cuyp, A. 1804/08/08
Cuyp, A. 1806/05/05
Cuyp, A. 1808/11/28
Cuyp, A. 1809/04/17
Cuyp, A. 1809/06/13
Cuyp, B. 1802/09/06
Decker 1805/07/10
Decker, C. 1806/08/13
Decker, C. 1808/10/28
Decker, C. 1809/04/17
Decker, Frans 1804/08/08
Delen 1804/12/10
Delen 1805/07/10

Denner, B. 1802/06/28
Denner, B. 1803/09/07
Denner, B. 1804/04/28
Denner, B. 1808/08/23
Diepenbeeck, A.J. 1803/09/07
Diepenbeeck, A.J. 1804/08/08
Diepenbeeck, A.J. 1809/06/13
Diepenbeeck, A.J. 1810/10/11
Dietrich, Chr. 1804/07/25
Dietrich, Chr. 1805/07/03
Dietrich, Chr. 1807/08/26
Dietrich, Chr. 1808/10/28
Dietrich, Chr. 1809/07/19
Does, J. (I) 1803/09/07
Does, J. (I) 1804/08/08
Does, S. 1809/04/17
Does, S. 1809/06/13
Does, S. 1810/10/11
Dolci, C. 1804/08/08
Dolci, C. 1809/07/25
Domenichino 1802/06/16
Dongen, Dionys 1801/06/10
Dongen, Dionys 1802/05/05
Doomer, L. 1805/07/10
Dou 1803/08/17
Dregt, J. 1809/04/17
Drielst, E. 1808/06/13
Drielst, E. 1808/08/23
Drielst, E. 1808/11/28
Drielst, E. 1809/06/13
Droochsloot, J.C. 1808/08/23
Dubbels, H. 1802/12/13
Dubbels, H. 1808/10/28
Dubbels, H. 1808/11/28
Dubbels, H. 1809/04/17
Dubbels, H. 1809/06/13
Dubbels, H. 1810/10/11
Dubois, G. 1803/08/17
Dubois, G. 1804/08/08
Dubois, J. 1802/05/05
Dubourg, L. 1806/08/13
Dubourg, L. 1809/06/13
Ducq, Johan le 1801/08/19
Ducq, Johan le 1802/06/28
Ducq, Johan le 1805/07/03
Ducq, Johan le 1805/07/10
Ducq, Johan le 1806/08/13
Ducq, Johan le 1809/09/06
Dughet 1802/06/16
Dughet 1803/04/27
Dujardin, K. 1804/08/08
Dujardin, K. 1807/08/26
Dujardin, K. 1809/07/19
Dujardin, K. 1809/07/25
Dujardin, K. 1810/05/22
Dusart, Corn. 1802/09/06
Dusart, Corn. 1808/11/28
Dyck, Anth. van 1803/04/27
Dyck, Anth. van 1803/07/18
Dyck, Anth. van 1803/09/07
Dyck, Anth. van 1804/08/08
Dyck, Anth. van 1805/07/10
Dyck, Anth. van 1808/06/13
Dyck, Anth. van 1809/04/17
Dyck, Anth. van 1810/10/11
Eeckhout, G. 1801/05/11
Eeckhout, G. 1802/07/27
Eeckhout, G. 1803/08/01
Eeckhout, G. 1804/07/25
Eeckhout, G. 1806/08/13
Eeckhout, G. 1809/04/17
Eeckhout, G. 1809/06/13
Eeckhout, G. 1810/10/11
Ekels, Jan (I) 1806/08/13
Ekels, Jan (I) 1808/11/28
Ekels, Jan (I) 1809/06/13
Ekels, Jan (II) 1801/08/19
Ekels, Jan (II) 1810/06/20
Elliger, O. (II) 1803/12/12
Elsheimer, A. 1803/08/17
Elsheimer, A. 1808/08/23
Elsheimer, A. 1809/04/17
Elsheimer, A. 1810/08/06
Elsheimer, Joh. 1804/08/08
Esselens, Jacob 1802/09/06
Esselens, Jacob 1803/09/07
Essen, C. 1801/03/16
Essen, C. 1802/12/13
Essen, C. 1805/07/10
Essen, C. 1807/08/26
Essen, C. 1809/06/13
Everdingen, A. 1802/12/13
Everdingen, A. 1810/10/11
Ferguson, Wm. 1802/05/05
Ferguson, Wm. 1802/12/13
Flinck 1802/12/13
Flinck 1808/11/28
Floris, F. (I) 1803/09/07
Floris, F. (I) 1804/08/08
Floris, F. (I) 1809/04/17
Fock, Harm. 1804/08/08
Fragonard, J.H. 1803/12/12
Francken 1809/07/25
Francken, Frans (II) 1804/05/07
Franks, J. 1802/06/28
Fredriks, J.H. 1808/11/28
French 1809/04/17
Fyt 1803/06/20
Gael, B. 1801/05/11
Gael, B. 1802/07/27
Gael, B. 1802/12/13
Gael, B. 1805/07/10
Gael, B. 1808/11/28
Gelder, A. 1801/05/11
Gelder, A. 1803/12/12
Gerards 1802/06/28
Gerards 1805/07/10
Gerards 1807/08/26
German 1807/08/26
Gillig, Jakob 1803/04/20
Glauber, J. 1804/07/25
Glauber, J. 1808/08/23
Glauber, J. 1810/06/20
Goltzius, Hend. 1802/06/28
Goltzius, Hend. 1802/09/06
Goltzius, Hend. 1806/08/13
Goltzius, Hend. 1809/04/17
Gool, Jan 1809/06/13
Goyen 1804/08/08
Goyen 1805/07/10
Goyen 1806/08/13
Goyen 1808/08/23
Goyen 1808/11/28
Goyen 1809/04/17
Goyen 1809/06/13
Goyen 1810/10/11
Grandjean, J. 1802/05/05
Grandjean, J. 1804/02/27
Grandjean, J. 1808/06/13
Grasdorp, W. 1802/07/27
Grasdorp, W. 1802/12/13
Grasdorp, W. 1804/08/08
Grebber, F.P. 1804/08/08
Griffier, J. (I) 1804/07/25
Griffier, R. 1810/10/11
Grypmoed, G. 1801/03/16
Haag, T.P.C. 1804/12/10
Haensbergen, J. van 1801/03/16
Hagen, Joris 1803/09/07
Hagen, Joris 1808/11/28
Hals, F. (I) 1802/12/13
Hals, F. (I) 1804/08/08
Hals, F. (I) 1806/05/05
Hals, F. (I) 1806/08/13
Hals, F. (I) 1808/08/23
Hals, F. (I) 1810/10/11
Hansen, C.L. 1806/05/05
Heem, C. 1803/06/20
Heem, C. 1804/08/08
Heem, C. 1808/10/28
Heem, David 1810/10/11
Heemskerck 1803/09/07
Heeremans, Thos. 1805/07/10
Heeremans, Thos. 1807/08/26
Heeremans, Thos. 1808/08/23
Helmont, M. 1804/08/08
Helmont, M. 1808/08/23
Helst, B. 1802/12/13
Helst, B. 1804/08/08
Helst, B. 1808/08/23
Helst, B. 1810/10/11
Hendriks, W. 1801/10/06
Hendriks, W. 1802/06/28
Hendriks, W. 1808/08/23
Hendriks, W. 1809/04/17
Hendriks, W. 1809/06/13
Henning 1802/02/16
Heusch 1802/12/13
Heusch 1804/08/08
Heusch, Jacob 1808/10/28
Heusch, Wm. 1801/08/19
Heusch, Wm. 1804/05/07
Heusch, Wm. 1806/08/13
Heusch, Wm. 1808/08/23
Heusch, Wm. 1809/06/13
Heyden, J. 1809/09/06
Heyden, J. 1810/05/22
Hobbema 1809/06/13
Hoecke, J. 1803/07/18
Hoet, G. (I) 1801/08/19
Hoet, G. (I) 1803/09/07
Hoet, G. (I) 1809/06/13
Holsteijn, C. 1802/12/13
Hondecoeter 1801/04/23
Hondecoeter, G. 1803/09/07
Hondecoeter, G. 1805/07/10
Hondecoeter, M. 1803/12/12
Hondecoeter, M. 1806/08/13
Hondecoeter, M. 1808/11/28
Honthorst, G. 1805/07/10
Honthorst, G. 1809/06/13
Hooch, P. 1803/06/20
Hooch, P. 1806/08/13
Hooch, P. 1808/11/28
Hoogstraten, S. 1804/08/08
Hoogstraten, S. 1808/08/23
Hoorn, J. 1804/05/07
Horemans, J.J. (I) 1805/07/10
Houbraken, Arn. 1808/10/28
Huchtenburgh, Jan 1801/03/16
Huchtenburgh, Jan 1801/10/19
Huchtenburgh, Jan 1805/07/03
Huchtenburgh, Jan 1808/11/28
Huchtenburgh, Jan 1809/04/17
Huchtenburgh, Jan 1809/06/13
Hulswit, Jan 1804/02/27
Hulswit, Jan 1806/05/05
Hulswit, Jan 1808/08/23
Huysum 1801/04/23
Huysum, Jan 1802/06/28
Huysum, Jan 1802/12/13
Huysum, Jan 1807/08/26
Huysum, Mich. 1801/04/23
Italian 1801/04/13
Italian 1802/12/13
Italian 1803/06/20
Italian 1803/09/07
Italian 1803/12/12
Italian 1804/08/08
Italian 1805/07/10
Janson, J. 1809/06/13
Janson, J. 1809/09/06
Janson, J. 1810/05/22
Janson, J. 1810/10/11
Janson, J.C. 1804/12/10
Janson, P. 1809/04/17
Jongh, L. 1803/06/20
Jordaens, J. (I) 1802/11/01
Jordaens, J. (I) 1806/08/13
Jordaens, J. (I) 1809/04/17
Jordaens, J. (I) 1810/10/11
Kalf 1810/10/11
Keirincx, Alex. 1801/03/16
Keirincx, Alex. 1804/05/07
Keirincx, Alex. 1810/10/11
Kessel, J. (III) 1804/02/27
Kessel, J. (III) 1804/08/08
Kessel, J. (III) 1808/08/23
Kessel, J. (III) 1809/04/17
Keyser, H. 1807/08/26
Klomp 1801/08/19
Klomp 1802/11/01
Klomp 1803/08/17
Klomp 1808/08/23
Klomp 1810/10/11
Knupfer 1803/08/17
Koninck, P. 1801/05/11
Koninck, P. 1802/12/13
Koninck, P. 1804/08/08
Koninck, P. 1805/07/10
Koninck, P. 1806/08/13
Koninck, P. 1809/04/17
Kraft, J. 1804/08/08
Kuik, J. 1809/06/13
Kuster 1808/10/28
Laer, P. 1802/12/13
Laer, P. 1804/08/08
La Haye, R. 1808/11/28
La Haye, R. 1809/07/19
Lairesse, G. 1804/02/27
Lairesse, G. 1804/07/25
Lairesse, G. 1804/08/08
Lairesse, G. 1805/07/03
Lairesse, G. 1808/08/23
Lairesse, G. 1810/10/11
Lairesse, Jan 1806/08/13
Lapotteren 1809/04/17
Laquy, W.J. 1802/06/28
Laquy, W.J. 1808/08/23
Laquy, W.J. 1808/11/28
Lauri, F. 1801/04/13
Lauri, F. 1808/08/23
Lauwers, J.J. 1802/06/28
Lauwers, J.J. 1804/12/10
Leclerc, S. (II) 1803/12/12
Leen, Willem van 1802/05/05
Leeuw 1810/10/11
Leeuw, Govert van der 1808/08/23
Leeuw, Pieter 1803/08/01
Leeuw, Pieter 1807/08/26
Leeuw, Pieter 1809/06/13
Lelienbergh 1809/06/13
Lievens, J. (I) 1803/09/07
Limborch, H. 1801/05/11
Lingelbach 1802/07/27
Lingelbach 1802/09/06
Lingelbach 1804/05/07
Lingelbach 1804/08/08
Lingelbach 1806/08/13
Lingelbach 1807/08/26
Lingelbach 1808/08/23
Lingelbach 1808/11/28
Lingelbach 1809/04/17
Lingelbach 1809/06/13
Lingelbach 1809/07/19
Lingelbach 1809/09/06
Lingelbach 1810/05/22
Lingelbach 1810/10/11
Linthorst 1809/06/13
Loren, S. 1809/07/25
Lucas van Leyden 1803/09/07
Lundens 1801/03/16
Lundens 1801/08/19
Lundens 1802/12/13
Lundens 1803/06/20
Lundens 1805/07/03
Lundens 1806/08/13
Lundens 1807/08/26
Maas, P. 1801/04/23
Maes, D. 1805/07/03
Maes, G. 1803/12/12
Maes, N. 1802/12/13
Maes, N. 1803/04/20
Maes, N. 1804/05/07
Maes, N. 1806/08/13
Maes, N. 1810/10/11
Man, C. 1803/06/20
Man, C. 1809/06/13

Murant 1808/12/31
Myn, H. 1808/12/31
Neer, A. 1808/12/31
Ostade, I. 1808/12/31
Palamedesz., A. 1808/12/31
Porcellis, Jan 1808/12/31
Silo, A. 1808/12/31
Teniers, D. (II) 1808/12/31
Vliet, H.C. 1808/12/31
Wet, J.W. 1808/12/31

Haas, Casper de
ca.1721–1802; master bricklayer living in Rotterdam
Anonymous 1802/09/18
Ast 1802/09/18
Backhuysen 1802/09/18
Battem 1802/09/18
Bega 1802/09/18
Beschey, B. 1802/09/18
Both, J. 1802/09/18
Carree, Hend. (I) 1802/09/18
Dongen, Dionys 1802/09/18
Dou 1802/09/18
Douw, S. 1802/09/18
Fargue, Maria la 1802/09/18
Franck, J.W. 1802/09/18
French 1802/09/18
Goyen 1802/09/18
Italian 1802/09/18
Koormans 1802/09/18
Lairesse, G. 1802/09/18
Lancret 1802/09/18
Le Brun, Chas. 1802/09/18
Limborch, H. 1802/09/18
Lingelbach 1802/09/18
Mieris, F. (I) 1802/09/18
Mieris, W. 1802/09/18
Mignon, A. 1802/09/18
Monogrammist A.V.R. 1802/09/18
Mooy, C.P. 1802/09/18
Nijmegen, G. 1802/09/18
Nijmegen, T. 1802/09/18
Ommeganck, B. 1802/09/18
Os, J. 1802/09/18
Ostade, I. 1802/09/18
Palamedesz., P. (I) 1802/09/18
Penninks, J. 1802/09/18
Porcellis, Jan 1802/09/18
Potter, Paulus 1802/09/18
Ruisdael, J. 1802/09/18
Saftleven, H. 1802/09/18
Savery, J. 1802/09/18
Schalcken 1802/09/18
Schoevaerdts, M. 1802/09/18
Schweickardt, H. 1802/09/18
Steen, J. 1802/09/18
Teniers, D. (II) 1802/09/18
Thier, B.H. 1802/09/18
Veen, P. 1802/09/18
Velde, J. (II) 1802/09/18
Werff, P. 1802/09/18
Wyck, T. 1802/09/18

Haas, Hendrik de
d. 1810; bookdealer in Dordrecht
Anonymous 1810/06/04
Beeldemaker 1810/06/04
Begeyn 1810/06/04
Berchem, N.P. 1810/06/04
Cuyp, A. 1810/06/04
Gelder, A. 1810/06/04
Houbraken, Arn. 1810/06/04
Hulst, Fr. 1810/06/04
Keller, J.H. (II) 1810/06/04
Molenaer, Klaes 1810/06/04
Molijn 1810/06/04
Monogrammist J.B.S. 1810/06/04
Monogrammist Q.B. 1810/06/04
Poel, E. 1810/06/04
Potter, Paulus 1810/06/04
Schouman, A. 1810/06/04
Withoos, M. 1810/06/04

Haccon
Anonymous 1804/06/18
Utrecht, Adr. 1807/10/12

Hachefort
Gysels, P. 1810/06/06

Haffner
also spelled Hafner
Anonymous 1803/06/20
Anonymous 1803/08/01
Anonymous 1803/12/12
Anonymous 1804/02/27
Anonymous 1804/05/07
Anonymous 1805/07/10
Anonymous-Modern 1805/07/10
Apshoven 1806/08/13
Barocci 1805/07/10
Berckheyde, G. 1805/07/10
Berckheyde, J. 1803/08/01
Besters, A.J. 1805/07/10
Blieck 1803/07/18
Blieck 1804/05/07
Blieck 1805/07/10
Borch, G. ter (II) 1805/07/10
Boucher 1805/07/10
Brakenburg 1803/06/20
Brakenburg 1805/07/10
Brouwer, Adr. 1804/05/07
Brouwer, Adr. 1805/07/10
Cappelle 1806/08/13
Carree, M. 1804/05/07
Carree, M. 1805/07/10
Claude Lorrain 1805/07/10
Cuyp, A. 1803/08/17
Droochsloot, J.C. 1806/08/13
Ducq, Johan le 1804/05/07
Ducq, Johan le 1805/07/10
Everdingen, A. 1804/05/07
Franck, J.W. 1803/06/20
Fris 1804/05/07
Griffier 1804/05/07
Griffier, R. 1803/06/20
Heemskerck, B. 1803/08/17
Honthorst, G. 1803/09/07
Honthorst, G. 1805/07/10
Italian 1805/07/10
Jode, P. 1803/08/01
Jode, P. 1805/07/10
Keirincx, Alex. 1803/08/01
Klomp 1804/05/07
Leonardo da Vinci 1803/09/07
Leonardo da Vinci 1805/07/10
Lingelbach 1806/08/13
Martszen, J. (II) 1805/07/10
Molenaer, J.M. 1804/05/07
Moucheron, I. 1806/08/13
Naiveu 1804/05/07
Naiveu 1805/07/10
Neeffs, P. (I) 1803/07/18
Neeffs, P. (I) 1803/09/07
Neeffs, P. (I) 1804/05/07
Neeffs, P. (I) 1805/07/10
Neer, A. 1804/05/07
Neer, A. 1805/07/10
Oolen, Jan 1806/08/13
Ostade, A. 1804/05/07
Palamedesz., P. (I) 1803/09/07
Palthe, G.J. 1804/05/07
Pieneman, J.W. 1805/07/10
Rubens 1805/07/10
Ruisdael, J. 1803/09/07
Ruisdael, J. 1804/05/07
Saftleven, C. 1803/09/07
Schalcken 1806/08/13
Silo, A. 1803/06/20
Silo, A. 1804/05/07
Silo, A. 1805/07/10
Storck, Abr. 1805/07/10
Teniers, D. (II) 1803/07/18
Treu 1805/07/10
Treu, Nic. 1803/09/07
Treu, Nic. 1804/05/07
Verboom, A.H. 1804/05/07
Verboom, A.H. 1806/08/13
Vinckeboons, D. 1803/07/18
Vinckeboons, D. 1805/07/10
Vitringa 1805/07/10
Vlieger, S. 1805/07/10
Vrancx 1806/08/13
Witte, E. 1804/05/07
Wouwerman, Ph. 1804/05/07
Zeemann 1806/08/13

Hafner, see Haffner

Hagen, A. van der
Ceulen, J.J. 1804/05/07
La Haye, R. 1804/05/07

Hakoun
Anonymous 1808/06/06
Nijmegen, G. 1808/06/06
Wouwerman, Pieter 1808/06/06

Halingins
Heeremans, Thos. 1805/07/03
Molenaer, Klaes 1805/07/03
Poel, E. 1805/07/03
Wigmana, G. 1805/07/03
Xavery, Frans 1805/07/03

Hall, van
see also Teyler van Hall
Asselyn 1808/06/13

Ham, van der
Anonymous 1802/07/27
Monogrammist J.M. 1802/07/27
Poelenburgh, C. 1802/07/27

Hamer
Velde, A. 1804/12/10

Hankock
Draaijenburg, W. 1803/04/20

Hant, de
active in Dordrecht
Strij, A. 1810/07/23
Strij, J. 1810/07/23
Vlieger, S. 1810/07/23

Harbomé
Anonymous 1804/05/07
Anonymous 1808/08/23
Blaauw, J. 1804/05/07
Royen, W.F. van 1802/09/06
Rubens 1804/05/07

Harde Swart, Bd. de
d. ca.1847
Brekelencam, Q. 1804/08/08
Cuyp, B. 1804/08/08
Does, J. (I) 1804/08/08
Everdingen, A. 1804/08/08
Everdingen, Cesar 1804/08/08
Flinck 1804/08/08

Hardegai
Borch, G. ter (II) 1807/10/12
Stoop 1807/10/12

Hardenberg, Cornelis van
1755–1843; painter, teacher and dealer
Anonymous 1806/08/20
Boudewyns 1805/07/03
Essen, C. 1805/07/03
Ostade 1805/10/09
Pee, T. 1805/07/03
Vlieger, S. 1805/07/03
Wijnants 1805/07/03
Zeemann 1805/07/03

Hari, Johannes, Senior
1772–1849; painter
Netscher, Casp. 1809/07/25

Haring
Anonymous 1810/07/26

Harmeyer
Anonymous 1806/08/20

Hart, van der
perhaps the Amsterdam architect Abraham van der Hart, 1747–1820.
Schalcken 1808/06/06

Hassevoord
Bloemen, P. 1809/07/25
Goyen 1809/07/25
Poel, E. 1809/07/25
Sant Acker, F. 1809/07/25
Wyntrack, D. 1809/07/25

Havelaar, J.J.
Berckheyde, G. 1808/06/06
Muys, Nic. 1808/06/06

Haze Bomme, Leendert Huibrecht de, Mr.
1762–1837; regent and public office holder in Middelburg
Alcock, E. 1803/12/15
Anonymous 1803/06/27
Anonymous 1803/12/15
Asselyn 1803/12/15
Battem 1803/12/15
Beeldemaker 1803/12/15
Blieck 1803/12/15
Bloot, P. 1803/12/15
Compe, Jan ten 1803/12/15
Cuyp, A. 1803/12/15
Delen 1803/12/15
Diepraem 1803/12/15
Douw, S. 1803/12/15
Drielst, E. 1803/12/15
Dyk, P. 1803/12/15
Francken 1803/12/15
Fyt 1803/12/15
Goyen 1803/12/15
Griffier 1803/12/15
Hals, D. 1803/12/15
Heem, J.D. 1803/12/15
Heeremans, Thos. 1803/12/15
Hoet, G. (I) 1803/12/15
Horemans, J.J. (I) 1803/12/15
Houckgeest, G. 1803/12/15
Huchtenburgh, Jan 1803/12/15
Kleijne, David 1803/12/15
La Haye, R. 1803/12/15
Lamen, C. van der 1803/12/15
Lingelbach 1803/12/15
Maes 1803/12/15
Mignon, A. 1803/12/15
Molenaer, J.M. 1803/12/15
Molenaer, Klaes 1803/12/15
Monogrammist A.A. 1803/12/15
Monogrammist A.B. 1803/12/15
Monogrammist A.S. 1803/12/15
Moucheron, F. 1803/12/15
Moucheron, I. 1803/12/15
Nollekens, P. 1803/12/15
Ostade, I. 1803/12/15
Palthe 1803/12/15
Poelenburgh, C. 1803/12/15
Ring, P. 1803/12/15
Schalcken 1803/12/15
Sorgh, H.M. 1803/12/15
Storck, Abr. 1803/12/15
Teniers, D. (II) 1803/12/15
Troost, C. 1803/12/15
Verelst, P. 1803/12/15
Vitringa 1803/12/15
Vlieger, S. 1803/12/15
Vogelsang, I. 1803/12/15

Dughet 1803/04/27
Dyck, Anth. van 1809/06/13
Esselens, Jacob 1809/06/13
Goyen 1803/04/20
Guercino 1803/04/27
Heemskerck, B. 1803/08/17
Hendriks, W. 1809/06/13
Hondecoeter, M. 1803/08/17
Hondecoeter, M. 1803/12/12
Houbraken, Arn. 1803/08/17
Italian 1810/06/20
Jordaens, J. (I) 1809/06/13
Koninck, P. 1803/08/01
Lairesse, G. 1803/08/17
Lairesse, Jan 1803/04/20
Lingelbach 1803/07/18
Lingelbach 1803/08/01
Looten, J. 1810/06/20
Mettenleiter, J.J. 1803/06/20
Meulen, A.F. 1803/08/01
Meulen, A.F. 1803/12/12
Miel 1803/12/12
Miereveld, M. 1810/10/11
Mijts, J. 1810/06/20
Molenaer, Klaes 1803/06/20
Molenaer, Klaes 1810/06/20
Moreelse, P. 1803/04/27
Moucheron, F. 1803/12/12
Moucheron, I. 1803/08/01
Nickelen 1803/04/20
Novelli, P. 1803/04/27
Ochtervelt 1810/06/20
Pynas, J. 1803/04/20
Ravesteyn, Hub. 1803/12/12
Ravesteyn, J.A. 1803/04/20
Ribera 1803/04/27
Ribera 1809/06/13
Rijnenburg, N. 1803/06/20
Roghman, R. 1810/06/20
Saftleven, H. 1803/08/01
Schedoni 1803/04/27
Schellinks 1803/12/12
Schellinks, W. 1803/06/20
Serenacio 1803/04/27
Settefano, M. 1803/04/27
Slingeland, P.C. 1803/12/12
Smit, Aernout 1803/06/20
Steen, J. 1802/09/06
Steen, J. 1803/04/20
Steen, J. 1809/06/13
Storck, Abr. 1803/06/20
Tempel, A.L. van den 1803/04/20
Teniers, D. (II) 1803/06/20
Teniers, D. (II) 1803/08/01
Thulden 1810/08/06
Toorenvliet, J. 1803/07/18
Utrecht, Adr. 1803/04/20
Velde, E. (I) 1803/04/20
Verboom, A.H. 1803/08/01
Verschuring, H. 1810/06/20
Vlieger, S. 1803/04/20
Vlieger, S. 1803/12/12
Vlieger, S. 1810/06/20
Vrancx 1803/04/20
Witte, E. 1810/06/20
Wyck, T. 1802/09/06

Hodges, Parker
Berckheyde, G. 1805/07/10
Dyck, Anth. van 1805/07/10

Hoeft, G. de
Monogrammist D.V.B. 1809/07/27
Monogrammist L.B. 1809/07/27
Salm, A. 1809/07/27

Hoeve, ter
Anonymous 1802/02/23

Hofman (Dordrecht)
possibly the Dordrecht painter and decorator Pieter Hofman, 1755–1837
Heem, J.D. 1802/11/01

Hogguer, Anna Maria (Ebeling), Mevrouw
1767–1812; wife of Paul Iwan Hogguer, banker and mayor of Amsterdam, 1760–1816
Goyen 1801/08/19
Hackaert, J. 1801/08/19
Heem, J.D. 1801/08/19
Hooch, P. 1810/08/01
Ruysdael, S. 1801/08/19

Honstee, J.
Anonymous 1801/08/19

Hooft, A. t'
d. ca.1804; probably a resident of Rotterdam
Anonymous 1804/10/08
Brueghel 1804/10/08
Droochsloot, J.C. 1804/10/08
Elsheimer, A. 1804/10/08
Lundens 1804/10/08
Marseus, O. 1804/10/08
Molenaer, Klaes 1804/10/08
Monogrammist NR 1804/10/08
Monogrammist P.W. 1804/10/08
Ostade, I. 1804/10/08
Reyers 1804/10/08
Teniers, D. (II) 1804/10/08
Verkolje 1804/10/08
Wouwerman 1804/10/08

Hooft, Johannes
Anonymous 1807/08/26
Canaletto 1807/08/26
Dalens, Dirck 1807/08/26
Pynas, J. 1807/08/26
Rombouts 1807/08/26
Wet, J.W. 1807/08/26

Hoogers, Hendrik
1747–1814; painter and dealer from Nijmegen
Grandjean, J. 1808/06/13
Nijmegen, D. 1808/06/13
Voorhout, J. (I) 1808/06/13

Hooghuis
Anonymous 1802/10/18

Hoola van Nooten, Dirk, Mr.
1747–1808; burgomaster and alderman in Schoonhoven
Anonymous 1808/12/12
Lairesse, G. 1808/12/12
Palamedesz., P. (I) 1808/12/12
Quast, P.J. 1808/12/12
Roy, J.B. de 1808/12/12
Santvoort, Pieter 1808/12/12
Willaerts 1808/12/12
Wouwerman 1808/12/12

Hoop, van der
Leen, Willem van 1810/06/06

Hoop, Hendrik van der
1725–1800; Dutch Minister Plenipotentiary at the court of Liège
Anonymous 1801/03/31
Ast 1801/03/31
Janson, J.C. 1801/03/31
Monogrammist J.V.H. 1801/03/31
Moucheron 1801/03/31
Sanders, G. 1801/03/31

Hoop, J. van der
active in Rotterdam
Neer, A. 1810/03/26

Hoop, L.B. van der
Anonymous 1810/03/26
Wyck, T. 1810/03/26

Houten, A. van
active in Amsterdam
Anonymous 1801/10/06
Anonymous 1802/02/23
Berchem, N.P. 1802/02/23
Casteels, P. (III) 1801/10/06
Droochsloot, J.C. 1801/10/06
Horemans, J.J. (I) 1801/10/06

Houten, W. ten
Breenbergh 1802/09/06
Dusart, Corn. 1802/09/06
Goyen 1802/09/06
Ostade, A. 1802/09/06
Rembrandt 1802/09/06
Silo, A. 1802/09/06

Hoven, van
Cuyp 1803/08/24
Meulen, A.F. 1803/08/24
Monogrammist I.V.D. 1803/08/24
Poel, E. 1803/08/24
Soolmaker 1803/08/24

Hoven, van den
Saftleven, H. 1802/09/21

Huguer, see Hogguer

Huibrechts, see Huybrechts

Huijbregts, see Huybrechts

Huijgens, see Huyghens

Huisrand
Anonymous 1809/07/25

Hulk
Myn, H. 1802/05/05
Wulfraet 1802/06/28

Hulsewit, see Hulswit

Hulswit, Jan
1766–1822; painter and dealer
Anonymous 1801/06/10
Anonymous 1802/09/06
Anonymous 1802/09/29
Anonymous 1802/12/13
Anonymous 1803/04/20
Anonymous 1803/04/27
Anonymous 1803/08/01
Anonymous 1804/05/07
Anonymous 1807/08/26
Anonymous 1808/08/23
Anonymous 1810/08/06
Asselyn 1801/10/19
Backhuysen 1806/05/05
Backhuysen 1808/08/23
Balen, J. 1803/07/18
Bens 1802/05/05
Berchem, N.P. 1804/08/08
Berckheyde, J. 1802/05/05
Bergen, D. 1810/05/22
Bol, F. 1804/07/25
Bol, F. 1805/07/10
Bol, F. 1805/12/16
Boonen, A. 1810/05/22
Borch, G. ter (II) 1806/05/05
Borssom 1806/08/13
Both, A. 1803/06/20
Both, J. 1803/06/20
Bovette, Simone 1803/04/27
Bray, S. 1804/08/08
Breenbergh 1803/06/20
Breenbergh 1804/08/08
Brekelencam, Q. 1801/04/23
Cappelle 1801/10/19
Cappelle 1804/02/27
Cappelle 1805/07/03
Crayer, G. 1810/07/26
Croos, P. 1802/05/05
Does, J. (I) 1802/02/16
Does, S. 1810/05/22
Dubbels, H. 1802/12/13
Dubois, G. 1810/06/20
Dughet 1810/07/26
Dujardin, K. 1810/05/22
Eeckhout, G. 1801/04/13
Eeckhout, G. 1802/09/06
Ekels, Jan (II) 1802/09/06
Everdingen, A. 1804/08/08
Everdingen, A. 1809/06/13
Francken, Frans (II) 1804/05/07
Gelder, A. 1804/02/27
Goyen 1804/05/07
Hackaert 1802/09/06
Hackaert, J. 1810/08/01
Heem, C. 1806/11/24
Heem, David 1808/08/23
Heem, J.D. 1805/07/10
Hobbema 1802/06/16
Hoet, G. (I) 1805/07/03
Hondecoeter, M. 1804/05/07
Hondecoeter, M. 1804/12/10
Hondecoeter, M. 1810/06/20
Honthorst, G. 1801/05/11
Hooch, P. 1802/12/13
Hooch, P. 1810/06/20
Huchtenburgh, Jan 1804/08/08
Huchtenburgh, Jan 1808/06/13
Italian 1807/08/26
Kessel, J. (III) 1808/08/23
Koninck, P. 1805/07/10
Lairesse, G. 1809/09/06
Lingelbach 1805/07/10
Maes, D. 1801/10/19
Maes, D. 1804/07/25
Maes, N. 1803/04/20
Mieris 1801/08/19
Molenaer, J.M. 1803/08/01
Mommers, H. 1802/05/05
Mommers, H. 1806/05/05
Moni, L. de 1805/07/03
Monogrammist G.B. 1802/06/28
Moucheron, I. 1804/08/08
Neer, E. 1806/11/24
Netscher, Casp. 1802/09/06
Ostade, A. 1803/04/20
Ostade, A. 1809/09/06
Peeters, B. (I) 1803/12/12
Pel, A. 1801/04/13
Poelenburgh, C. 1803/06/20
Rembrandt 1802/02/16
Rembrandt 1808/10/28
Rombouts 1807/08/26
Romeyn 1803/07/18
Romeyn 1810/05/22
Royen, W.F. van 1802/02/16
Rubens 1803/04/20
Ruisdael, J. 1801/08/19
Ruisdael, J. 1806/08/13
Ruisdael, J. 1808/08/23
Ruysdael, S. 1804/08/08
Saftleven, C. 1802/06/28
Santvoort, D. 1803/04/20
Schut, C. (I) 1808/08/23
Schyndel, J. 1806/08/13
Seghers, G. 1802/12/13
Snyders, F. 1803/07/18
Snyders, F. 1808/08/23
Sonje, J.G. 1802/05/05
Staveren, J.A. 1809/09/06
Steen, J. 1808/10/28
Steen, J. 1809/06/13
Tol, D. 1810/05/22
Velde, A. 1802/12/13
Velde, A. 1810/08/01
Velde, W. 1801/05/11
Vermeer, Jan (II) 1807/08/26
Victors, Jan 1801/08/19
Vinckeboons, D. 1803/07/18
Vliet, H.C. 1802/05/05
Vliet, H.C. 1804/12/10
Vries, R. 1802/05/05

J. (1802, May 5)
Anonymous 1802/05/05
Begeyn 1802/05/05
Bens 1802/05/05
Bol, F. 1802/05/05
Borch, G. ter (II) 1802/05/05
Burg, Dirk 1802/05/05
Cappelle 1802/05/05
Carree 1802/05/05
Colaert, Johannes 1802/05/05
Croos, P. 1802/05/05
Delen 1802/05/05
Dongen, Dionys 1802/05/05
Dubbels, H. 1802/05/05
Ekels, Jan (I) 1802/05/05
Ferguson, Wm. 1802/05/05
Francken 1802/05/05
Glauber, J. 1802/05/05
Hackaert 1802/05/05
Haensbergen, J. van 1802/05/05
Hals, F. (I) 1802/05/05
Hansen, C.L. 1802/05/05
Heyden, J. 1802/05/05
Huysum, Mich. 1802/05/05
Jordaens, J. (I) 1802/05/05
Kessel, J. (III) 1802/05/05
Klomp 1802/05/05
Koninck, Jacob 1802/05/05
Lairesse, G. 1802/05/05
Leen, Willem van 1802/05/05
Lingelbach 1802/05/05
Lundens 1802/05/05
Maes, N. 1802/05/05
Man, C. 1802/05/05
Mieris 1802/05/05
Molenaer, J.M. 1802/05/05
Mommers, H. 1802/05/05
Morel, J. 1802/05/05
Myn, H. 1802/05/05
Naiveu 1802/05/05
Nickelen 1802/05/05
Ommeganck, B. 1802/05/05
Os 1802/05/05
Ouwater, Isaak 1802/05/05
Roos, J.H. 1802/05/05
Ruisdael, J. 1802/05/05
Snyders, F. 1802/05/05
Storck, Abr. 1802/05/05
Strij, J. 1802/05/05
Troost, C. 1802/05/05
Velde, A. 1802/05/05
Verbeeck, P.C. 1802/05/05
Verboom, A.H. 1802/05/05
Vermeulen, A. 1802/05/05
Victors, Jan 1802/05/05
Vitringa 1802/05/05
Vrancx 1802/05/05
Weenix 1802/05/05
Westhoven 1802/05/05
Willaerts 1802/05/05
Winter, Gillis 1802/05/05
Withoos, M. 1802/05/05
Wouwerman, Ph. 1802/05/05
Zegelaar, G. 1802/05/05

J. (1802, September 6)
Anonymous 1802/09/06
Asselyn 1802/09/06
Avercamp, H. 1802/09/06
Beerstraten, A. 1802/09/06
Bent, J. 1802/09/06
Bloemaert, C. (II) 1802/09/06
Borch, G. ter (II) 1802/09/06
Breenbergh 1802/09/06
Brekelencam, Q. 1802/09/06
Brueghel, J. (I) 1802/09/06
Burg, Dirk 1802/09/06
Carree, M. 1802/09/06
Cuyp, B. 1802/09/06
Decker, Frans 1802/09/06
Drielst, E. 1802/09/06
Dusart, Corn. 1802/09/06
Dyck, Anth. van 1802/09/06
Eeckhout, G. 1802/09/06
Gael, B. 1802/09/06
Goltzius, Hend. 1802/09/06
Goyen 1802/09/06
Hackaert 1802/09/06
Hals, F. (I) 1802/09/06
Hansen, C.L. 1802/09/06
Heem 1802/09/06
Heem, David 1802/09/06
Hendriks, W. 1802/09/06
Italian 1802/09/06
Jordaens, J. (I) 1802/09/06
Kessel, J. (III) 1802/09/06
Klomp 1802/09/06
Koninck, Jacob 1802/09/06
Lairesse, G. 1802/09/06
Lingelbach 1802/09/06
Molenaer, J.M. 1802/09/06
Molenaer, Klaes 1802/09/06
Mommers, H. 1802/09/06
Moucheron 1802/09/06
Moucheron, F. 1802/09/06
Netscher, Casp. 1802/09/06
Ochtervelt 1802/09/06
Ommeganck, B. 1802/09/06
Oolen, Jan 1802/09/06
Os, Pieter G. 1802/09/06
Ostade, A. 1802/09/06
Porcellis, Jan 1802/09/06
Potter, Paulus 1802/09/06
Ring, P. 1802/09/06
Roghman, R. 1802/09/06
Romeyn 1802/09/06
Royen, W.F. van 1802/09/06
Ruisdael, J. 1802/09/06
Ruysdael, S. 1802/09/06
Storck, Abr. 1802/09/06
Velde, A. 1802/09/06
Verboom, A.H. 1802/09/06
Vermeer, Jan (II) 1802/09/06
Vermeulen, A. 1802/09/06
Victors, Jan 1802/09/06
Voorhout, J. (I) 1802/09/06
Wit, Jacob de 1802/09/06
Wyck, T. 1802/09/06
Zeemann 1802/09/06
Zegelaar, G. 1802/09/06

J. (1803, August 1)
Apshoven 1803/08/01
Beerstraten, Jan 1803/08/01
Berchem, N.P. 1803/08/01
Eeckhout, G. 1803/08/01
Flinck 1803/08/01
Goyen 1803/08/01
Hondecoeter, M. 1803/08/01
Huchtenburgh, Jan 1803/08/01
Jode, P. 1803/08/01
Keirincx, Alex. 1803/08/01
Koninck, P. 1803/08/01
Lairesse, Jan 1803/08/01
Leeuw, Pieter 1803/08/01
Ludick, L. 1803/08/01
Molenaer, J.M. 1803/08/01
Molenaer, Klaes 1803/08/01
Moucheron, I. 1803/08/01
Neeffs, P. (I) 1803/08/01
Ostade, A. 1803/08/01
Roore 1803/08/01
Saftleven, H. 1803/08/01
Savery, R. 1803/08/01
Schut, C. (I) 1803/08/01
Schyndel 1803/08/01
Storck, Abr. 1803/08/01
Teniers, D. (II) 1803/08/01
Velde, W. 1803/08/01
Verboom, A.H. 1803/08/01
Wet, Gerrit de 1803/08/01
Witte, E. 1803/08/01

J. (1804, May 7)
Anonymous 1804/05/07
Becker, J.W. 1804/05/07
Beesten, J. 1804/05/07
Bent, J. 1804/05/07
Berckheyde, G. 1804/05/07
Brekelencam, Q. 1804/05/07
Carree, M. 1804/05/07
Craesbeeck 1804/05/07
Hooch, P. 1804/05/07
Keirincx, Alex. 1804/05/07
Leeuw, Pieter 1804/05/07
Molenaer, Klaes 1804/05/07
Molijn 1804/05/07
Os, Pieter G. 1804/05/07
Rubens 1804/05/07
Velde, J. (II) 1804/05/07
Verdonck, Corn. 1804/05/07
Vertangen 1804/05/07
Zeemann 1804/05/07

J. (1804, August 8)
Bloemaert, A. 1804/08/08
Glauber, J. 1804/08/08
Lairesse, G. 1804/08/08
Mieris, W. 1804/08/08

J. (1805, July 10)
Anonymous 1805/07/10
Backhuysen 1805/07/10
Berchem, N.P. 1805/07/10
Leeuw, Pieter 1805/07/10
Lingelbach 1805/07/10
Molenaer, J.M. 1805/07/10
Teniers, D. (II) 1805/07/10
Toorenburgh, G. 1805/07/10
Velde, W. 1805/07/10
Vinckeboons, D. 1805/07/10

J. (1806, August 13)
probably identical with "S" on July 3, 1805, and "K" on June 13, 1808
Anonymous 1806/08/13
Bouts, F. 1806/08/13
Brekelencam, Q. 1806/08/13
Brussel, P. 1806/08/13
Cuyp, A. 1806/08/13
Ekels, Jan (II) 1806/08/13
Elliger, O. (II) 1806/08/13
Goyen 1806/08/13
Heem, J.D. 1806/08/13
Heyden, J. 1806/08/13
Johnson, C. (I) 1806/08/13
Mieris, W. 1806/08/13
Molenaer, Klaes 1806/08/13
Morel, Jan Evert 1806/08/13
Moucheron, F. 1806/08/13
Neer, A. 1806/08/13
Os, J. 1806/08/13
Palthe, G.J. 1806/08/13
Peeters, B. (I) 1806/08/13
Ring, P. 1806/08/13
Tol, D. 1806/08/13
Vois, Ary de 1806/08/13
Vrancx 1806/08/13
Wouwerman, P. 1806/08/13

J. (1808, August 23)
Anonymous 1808/08/23
Backer, J.A. 1808/08/23
Backhuysen 1808/08/23
Barbiers, P. 1808/08/23
Blanckerhoff 1808/08/23
Donck, G. 1808/08/23
Goyen 1808/08/23
Heem, David 1808/08/23
Hulswit, Jan 1808/08/23
Kessel, J. (III) 1808/08/23
Klomp 1808/08/23
Leeuw, Govert van der 1808/08/23
Lingelbach 1808/08/23
Maes, N. 1808/08/23
Mieris, W. 1808/08/23
Molenaer, Klaes 1808/08/23
Monogrammist A.V.M. 1808/08/23
Neer, A. 1808/08/23
Ostade, A. 1808/08/23
Parmigianino 1808/08/23
Poelenburgh, C. 1808/08/23
Schellinks, W. 1808/08/23
Schut, C. (I) 1808/08/23
Snyders, F. 1808/08/23
Verspronck, Joh. 1808/08/23
Vliet, H.C. 1808/08/23

J. (1810, August 6)
Anonymous 1810/08/06

JJ. (1804, May 7)
Amigoni, J. 1804/05/07
Anonymous 1804/05/07
Bloemen, P. 1804/05/07
Borssom 1804/05/07
Ceulen, J.J. 1804/05/07
Decker, Jan 1804/05/07
Everdingen, A. 1804/05/07
Goyen 1804/05/07
Hobbema 1804/05/07
Hondecoeter, M. 1804/05/07
Italian 1804/05/07
Keller, J.H. (II) 1804/05/07
La Haye, R. 1804/05/07
Lingelbach 1804/05/07
Molijn 1804/05/07
Oolen, Adr. 1804/05/07
Smit, Aernout 1804/05/07
Steen, J. 1804/05/07
Steenwyk, J. 1804/05/07
Vries, R. 1804/05/07
Wijnants 1804/05/07

Jaak
Monogrammist A.B. 1802/06/28

Jacobs
Anonymous 1807/08/26

Jansen
Breenbergh 1806/08/13

Jansen, Hendrik
Anonymous 1807/08/26
Bloemen, P. 1807/08/26
Borch, G. ter (II) 1807/08/26
Bray, S. 1807/08/26
Does, J. (I) 1807/08/26
Hals, F. (I) 1807/08/26
Micker, J.C. 1807/08/26
Ostade, A. 1807/08/26
Ruisdael, J. 1807/08/26
Saftleven, C. 1807/08/26
Schweickardt, H. 1807/08/26
Victors, Jan 1807/08/26
Wit, Jacob de 1807/08/26

Janzen, B.
Wit, Jacob de 1806/08/13

Jarman
Storck, J. 1807/08/26

Jepren, van, see Iperen, van

Jongh, de (relative of Daniël de Jongh)
perhaps Erdwin Adrianus de Jongh, 1777–1833, son of Daniël de Jongh
Hoogsaat, J.C. 1810/03/26
Moreelse, P. 1810/03/26
Schalcken 1810/03/26

Jongh Adrszn., Daniël de
1745–1809; merchant in copper, nephew and heir of the collector Daniël de Jongh, 1721–1796

Withoos, M. 1803/08/24
Wittel 1803/08/24

Kate, Herman ten
1731–1800; cloth merchant and member of parliament
Anonymous 1801/06/10
Asselyn 1801/06/10
Avercamp, H. 1801/06/10
Backhuysen 1801/06/10
Beerstraten, A. 1801/06/10
Beerstraten, J. 1801/06/10
Bega 1801/06/10
Bemmel, J. 1801/06/10
Berchem, N.P. 1801/06/10
Berckheyde, G. 1801/06/10
Beschey, J. 1801/06/10
Blanckerhoff 1801/06/10
Bol, F. 1801/06/10
Both, A. 1801/06/10
Both, J. 1801/06/10
Breenbergh 1801/06/10
Brouwer, Adr. 1801/06/10
Brueghel, J. (I) 1801/06/10
Cappelle 1801/06/10
Compe, Jan ten 1801/06/10
Cornelisz. van Haarlem 1801/06/10
Decker, C. 1801/06/10
Does, J. (I) 1801/06/10
Dongen, Dionys 1801/06/10
Doudijns, W. 1801/06/10
Dubbels, H. 1801/06/10
Dujardin, K. 1801/06/10
Dusart, Corn. 1801/06/10
Eeckhout, G. 1801/06/10
Everdingen, A. 1801/06/10
Fargue, Maria la 1801/06/10
Flinck 1801/06/10
Gaesbeeck, A. 1801/06/10
Goyen 1801/06/10
Griffier, R. 1801/06/10
Haensbergen, J. van 1801/06/10
Heusch, Jacob 1801/06/10
Heyden, J. 1801/06/10
Hondecoeter, M. 1801/06/10
Honthorst, G. 1801/06/10
Hoogstraten, Jan 1801/06/10
Huchtenburgh, Jan 1801/06/10
Huysum, Jan 1801/06/10
Jacobsz., Juriaen 1801/06/10
Klomp 1801/06/10
Koninck, P. 1801/06/10
Laer, P. 1801/06/10
Lairesse, G. 1801/06/10
Lingelbach 1801/06/10
Maes, D. 1801/06/10
Metsu 1801/06/10
Mieris, W. 1801/06/10
Molenaer, J.M. 1801/06/10
Moor, C. 1801/06/10
Moucheron, F. 1801/06/10
Murant 1801/06/10
Neer, A. 1801/06/10
Nepveu, J. 1801/06/10
Nijmegen, G. 1801/06/10
Noort, J. 1801/06/10
Noort, Pieter van 1801/06/10
Ochtervelt 1801/06/10
Os, J. 1801/06/10
Ostade, A. 1801/06/10
Poelenburgh, C. 1801/06/10
Pynacker 1801/06/10
Rembrandt 1801/06/10
Rijck, C. de 1801/06/10
Roghman, R. 1801/06/10
Ruisdael, J. 1801/06/10
Ruysch, R. 1801/06/10
Saenredam, P.J. 1801/06/10
Saftleven, H. 1801/06/10
Steen, J. 1801/06/10
Steenwyck, Hend. 1801/06/10
Stoop, J. 1801/06/10
Storck, Abr. 1801/06/10
Swanevelt 1801/06/10
Tol, D. 1801/06/10
Troost, C. 1801/06/10
Vanloo, J. 1801/06/10
Velde, A. 1801/06/10
Velde, W. 1801/06/10
Verboom, A.H. 1801/06/10
Vermeer, Jan 1801/06/10
Verschuir 1801/06/10
Verschuring, H. 1801/06/10
Vlieger, S. 1801/06/10
Vrancx 1801/06/10
Weenix 1801/06/10
Weenix, J.B. 1801/06/10
Werff, P. 1801/06/10
Wijnants 1801/06/10
Wouwerman, J. 1801/06/10
Wouwerman, Ph. 1801/06/10
Wouwerman, Pieter 1801/06/10
Wyck, J. 1801/06/10

Kellerman
Italian 1805/07/10

Kempe, A.
Anonymous 1808/08/23

Kerber
Flemish-Brabant 1805/10/09
Ostade, A. 1805/10/09
Wyck, T. 1805/10/09

Kerkhoven, J.
dealer
Molenaer, Klaes 1808/08/23
Ruysch, R. 1808/08/23
Weenix 1808/08/23

Keser, de
Anonymous 1802/11/01

Keurvorst
Kuik, J. 1809/06/13
Molenaer, Klaes 1809/06/13

Kieboon
Anonymous 1807/12/00

Kip, Willem Frederick Taelman
1761–1800
Aelst, W. 1801/03/16
Anonymous 1801/03/16
Apshoven 1801/03/16
Backhuysen 1801/03/16
Barbiers, P. (I) 1801/03/16
Beeldemaker 1801/03/16
Bega 1801/03/16
Bent, J. 1801/03/16
Berckheyde 1801/03/16
Bloot, P. 1801/03/16
Brekelencam, Q. 1801/03/16
Carree, Hend. (I) 1801/03/16
Carree, Joh. 1801/03/16
Carree, M. 1801/03/16
Cuylenborch, A. 1801/03/16
Cuyp, A. 1801/03/16
Delen 1801/03/16
Dou 1801/03/16
Droochsloot, J.C. 1801/03/16
Dubbels, H. 1801/03/16
Ekels, Jan (I) 1801/03/16
Essen, C. 1801/03/16
Flinck 1801/03/16
Gaesbeeck, A. 1801/03/16
Goyen 1801/03/16
Haensbergen, J. van 1801/03/16
Heemskerck, B. 1801/03/16
Herp, Wm. (I) 1801/03/16
Hoogstraten, Jan 1801/03/16
Horemans, J.J. (I) 1801/03/16
Huchtenburgh, Jan 1801/03/16
Huysmans, C. 1801/03/16
Huysum, Jan 1801/03/16
Janson, J. 1801/03/16
Kessel, J. (I) 1801/03/16
Laer, P. 1801/03/16
Lundens 1801/03/16
Metsu 1801/03/16
Miel 1801/03/16
Molenaer, J.M. 1801/03/16
Momas, G.F. 1801/03/16
Mommers, H. 1801/03/16
Monogrammist J.V.H. 1801/03/16
Neer, A. 1801/03/16
Nickelen, Jan 1801/03/16
Ostade 1801/03/16
Ostade, A. 1801/03/16
Ostade, I. 1801/03/16
Peeters, B. (I) 1801/03/16
Poel, E. 1801/03/16
Potter, Paulus 1801/03/16
Romeyn 1801/03/16
Ruisdael, J. 1801/03/16
Saftleven, H. 1801/03/16
Silo, A. 1801/03/16
Slingeland, P.C. 1801/03/16
Stoffe 1801/03/16
Storck, J. 1801/03/16
Teniers, D. (II) 1801/03/16
Victors, Jan 1801/03/16
Vlieger, S. 1801/03/16
Weenix, J.B. 1801/03/16
Withoos, P. 1801/03/16
Wouwerman, P. 1801/03/16
Wouwerman, Ph. 1801/03/16
Xavery, Frans 1801/03/16

Kirderberg
Essen, C. 1802/05/24

Kits, A.
Dregt, J. 1808/11/28
Drielst, E. 1808/11/28
Kuster 1808/11/28
Lundens 1808/11/28

Kleijn
Anonymous 1802/05/24
Lingelbach 1802/05/24
Mignon, A. 1802/05/24
Moucheron, I. 1802/05/24
Palthe, G.J. 1802/05/24
Vogelsang, I. 1802/05/24
Wyckenburch 1802/05/24

Kleijne, David
1754–1805; painter active in Middelburg
Delen 1802/05/10

Klemans
Potter, Paulus 1810/05/22

Kleyn, J.
Anonymous 1802/07/27

Kleynefelden
Anonymous 1802/07/27

Klijnveld
Anonymous 1808/11/28
Drielst, E. 1808/11/28
Heeremans, Thos. 1808/11/28

Klint
Scheffer, J.B. 1810/06/06

Klittenberg
Anonymous 1802/10/18

Klyné, D., see Kleijne, David

Klynveld, see Klijnveld

Knoop, W.
Wit, Jacob de 1804/02/27

Kobell, Johannes Baptist
1778–1814; painter
Anonymous 1802/06/16
Anonymous 1802/09/21
Beerstraten, J. 1802/09/21
Bergen, D. 1802/09/21
Both, A. 1802/06/16
Both, J. 1802/06/16
Brekelencam, Q. 1802/09/21
Decker, C. 1802/06/16
Elsheimer, A. 1802/06/16
Mieris, F. (I) 1802/06/16
Mieris, F. (II) 1810/03/26
Palamedesz., P. (I) 1802/06/16
Velde, A. 1802/06/16
Wijnants 1802/06/16
Wouwerman, J. 1802/06/16
Wouwerman, Ph. 1802/09/21
Wyck, T. 1802/06/16
Wyck, T. 1802/09/21
Zeemann 1802/06/16

Kock, J.W. de
active in Rotterdam; also spelled Kok
Aelst, W. 1810/03/26
Dongen, Dionys 1808/06/11
Ruisdael, J. 1810/08/10

Kok, see Kock

Koning
Anonymous 1803/06/07
Beyeren 1808/06/11
Saftleven, H. 1808/06/11

Koning van Holland, see Louis Bonaparte, koning van Holland

Kooij, see also Kooy

Kooij, M.
Bestens, C. 1808/10/28
Huchtenburgh, Jan 1808/10/28
Laquy, W.J. 1804/12/10
Silo, A. 1808/10/28

Koopman
Anonymous 1801/03/16
Anonymous 1810/06/20
Backhuysen 1801/03/16
Beeldemaker 1801/03/16
Cuyp, A. 1801/03/16
Dou 1801/03/16
Droochsloot, J.C. 1801/03/16
Essen, C. 1801/03/16
Ferguson, Wm. 1810/06/20
Metsu 1801/03/16
Moeyaert, C. 1810/06/20
Ostade, A. 1801/03/16
Palthe, Jan 1810/05/22
Peeters, B. (I) 1801/03/16
Potter, Paulus 1801/03/16
Stoffe 1801/03/16
Victors, Jan 1801/03/16
Vitringa 1806/08/20

Koopman, H. (Utrecht)
probably the artist Wijnand Koopman, d. ca.1842
Ostade, I. 1810/08/01

Kooy, Barend
1750–1819; shopkeeper and trader in coffee and tea
Anonymous 1808/10/28
Asselyn 1804/07/25
Berchem, N.P. 1801/10/19
Beschey, J. 1803/04/20
Bloemen, P. 1804/07/25

Backer 1803/12/12
Backhuysen 1802/09/29
Balen, H. (I) 1802/09/29
Bega 1802/09/29
Berchem, N.P. 1802/09/29
Besanger, S. 1802/09/29
Broeck, E. 1802/09/29
Brueghel, J. (I) 1802/09/29
Carree, M. 1804/02/27
Coecke, Pauwels 1803/08/17
Does, J. (I) 1802/09/29
Dubbels, H. 1802/09/29
Ducq, Johan le 1802/09/29
Dujardin, K. 1802/09/29
Dusart, Corn. 1802/09/29
Heem, J.D. 1802/09/29
Heem, J.D. 1804/02/27
Helst, B. 1802/09/29
Italian 1802/09/29
Jordaens, J. (I) 1802/09/29
Klomp 1802/09/29
Lingelbach 1802/09/29
Lundens 1802/09/29
Mieris, F. (II) 1802/09/29
Mieris, W. 1802/09/29
Molenaer, J.M. 1803/08/17
Monogrammist B.R. 1802/09/29
Monogrammist J.D. 1802/09/29
Neer, A. 1802/09/29
Os, Pieter G. 1802/09/29
Ostade, A. 1802/09/29
Pynacker 1802/09/29
Ruisdael, J. 1802/09/29
Saftleven, C. 1802/09/29
Santvoort, Ph. 1804/08/08
Steen, J. 1802/05/24
Steen, J. 1802/09/29
Toorenvliet, J. 1802/09/29
Vermeer, Jan (II) 1802/09/29
Vermeulen, A. 1802/09/29
Vlieger, S. 1802/09/29
Weenix 1804/08/08
Weenix, J.B. 1802/09/29
Wijnants 1802/09/29
Wit, Jacob de 1804/08/08
Wouwerman, Ph. 1802/09/29

LaCourt
Dyck, Abraham van 1807/06/10
Lingelbach 1807/06/10
Wijnants 1807/06/10

Lafontaine, Pierre-Joseph
1758–1835; painter and picture dealer
Aelst, W. 1801/04/13
Anonymous 1805/07/10
Anonymous 1806/08/13
Backhuysen 1805/07/10
Balen, H. (I) 1805/07/03
Beerstraten, A. 1805/07/10
Begeyn 1806/08/20
Berchem, N.P. 1802/06/16
Berchem, N.P. 1806/08/20
Berckheyde, J. 1805/07/03
Blom, P. 1801/04/13
Boonen, A. 1805/07/03
Both, A. 1810/08/01
Both, J. 1806/08/20
Both, J. 1810/08/01
Broeck, E. 1805/07/10
Brouwer, Adr. 1805/07/10
Brueghel 1803/09/07
Brueghel, J. (I) 1805/07/10
Cappelle 1806/08/13
Carree, Hend. (I) 1805/07/03
Cornelisz. van Haarlem 1801/04/13
Cuylenborch, A. 1805/07/10
Cuyp, A. 1806/08/20
Dongen, Dionys 1802/06/16
Dubbels, H. 1801/04/13
Dubbels, H. 1802/06/16
Ducq, Johan le 1802/06/16
Dusart, Corn. 1802/06/16
Dusart, Corn. 1805/07/10
Dyck, Anth. van 1810/08/01
Dyk, P. 1806/08/20
Eeckhout, G. 1806/08/13
Ferg, F. 1803/09/07
Ferguson, Wm. 1806/08/20
Glauber, J. 1806/08/20
Goyen 1803/09/07
Goyen 1805/07/03
Gryef 1803/09/07
Hals, D. 1805/07/10
Helmont, M. 1803/09/07
Herrlein, J.A. 1803/09/07
Hobbema 1802/06/16
Hobbema 1810/08/01
Hooch, P. 1801/04/13
Huchtenburgh, Jan 1802/06/16
Klomp 1802/06/16
Kool, N. 1802/06/16
Lairesse, G. 1806/08/20
Lastman, P.P. 1806/08/13
Lingelbach 1801/04/13
Lingelbach 1805/07/03
Looten, J. 1805/07/10
Marseus, O. 1803/09/07
Martszen, J. (II) 1803/09/07
Metsu 1806/08/20
Miel 1801/04/13
Molenaer, J.M. 1805/07/10
Momper, J. (II) 1803/09/07
Momper, J. (II) 1805/07/10
Monogrammist J.G.L. 1805/07/10
Murant 1805/07/10
Neeffs, P. (I) 1801/04/13
Neeffs, P. (I) 1805/07/10
Neeffs, P. (I) 1806/08/20
Neer, A. 1801/04/13
Neer, A. 1805/07/10
Ochtervelt 1806/08/13
Oolen, Adr. 1805/07/10
Ostade, A. 1802/06/16
Ostade, A. 1810/08/01
Palamedesz., A. 1805/07/10
Potter, Paulus 1802/06/16
Rembrandt 1802/06/16
Rembrandt 1806/08/20
Rembrandt 1810/08/01
Ruysdael, S. 1803/09/07
Schinnagl 1803/09/07
Silo, A. 1803/09/07
Silo, A. 1805/07/10
Steen, J. 1801/04/13
Steen, J. 1805/07/10
Steen, J. 1806/08/20
Steenwyck, Hend. 1801/04/13
Storck, Abr. 1802/06/16
Teniers, D. (II) 1805/07/10
Velde, A. 1810/08/01
Velde, W. 1810/08/01
Verbeeck, P.C. 1802/06/16
Verboom, A.H. 1801/04/13
Verboom, A.H. 1802/06/16
Vermeer, Jan (II) 1802/06/16
Victors, Jan 1805/07/03
Vinckeboons, D. 1805/07/10
Vitringa 1802/06/16
Vitringa 1805/07/10
Vrancx 1803/09/07
Vries, R. 1805/07/03
Vries, R. 1805/07/10
Weenix 1805/07/03
Weenix, J.B. 1801/04/13
Werff, A. 1801/04/13
Wijnants 1805/07/10
Wouwerman, Ph. 1810/08/01
Wyck, T. 1802/06/16

La Maine, J.
Anonymous 1802/09/21
Dyck, Anth. van 1802/09/21
Eeckhout, G. 1802/09/21
Hoet, G. (I) 1802/09/21
Lairesse, G. 1802/09/21
Molijn 1802/09/21
Monogrammist D. 1802/09/21
Werff, A. 1802/09/21

Lambrechtsen
Hoogerheyden, E. 1803/11/30
Kleijne, David 1803/11/30

Lamme, Arnoldus
1771–1856; art dealer, auctioneer and painter
Anonymous 1802/11/01
Goyen 1802/11/01
Kalraet, Barend 1802/11/01
Monogrammist A.W.B. 1802/11/01
Orient, Josef 1803/09/07
Roos, P.P. 1803/09/07
Rosa, S. 1803/09/07
Schutz, S. 1803/09/07
Storck, Abr. 1802/11/01
Toorenburgh, G. 1804/12/10
Wyck, J. 1803/09/07

Lammen, see Lamme

Landa
Anonymous 1809/07/25

Landa, Jan
Anonymous 1804/04/28
Brekelencam, Q. 1804/04/28
Brueghel 1804/04/28
Goyen 1804/04/28
Honthorst, G. 1804/04/28
Palamedesz., A. 1804/04/28

Landers (widow)
Vervoort, J. 1805/07/10

Lange, Aarnoud de
1740–1803; dealer and auctioneer in Amsterdam
Anonymous 1803/12/12
Bloemaert, A. 1803/12/12
Borch, G. ter (II) 1803/12/12
Chalon, L. 1803/12/12
Droochsloot, J.C. 1803/12/12
Essen, C. 1803/12/12
Klomp 1803/12/12
Laer, P. 1803/12/12
Metsu 1803/12/12
Silo, A. 1803/12/12
Steen, J. 1803/12/12
Velde, W. 1803/12/12
Vermeer, Jan 1803/12/12
Wit, Jacob de 1803/12/12

Langenberg, Dk.
Anonymous 1802/05/05

Langendijk, Dirk
1748–1805; painter, draftsman and aquarellist active in Rotterdam
Anonymous 1806/01/30
Bloemen 1806/01/30
Borch, G. ter (II) 1806/01/30
Canaletto 1806/01/30
Lamme, A. 1806/01/30
Langendijk, D. 1806/01/30
Poel, E. 1806/01/30

Langendyk, see Langendijk

Lans, Cornelis van der Looy, see Looy Lans, Cornelis van der

Lauwers, Jacobus Johannes
1753–1800; painter from Bruges and active in Amsterdam
Anonymous 1802/12/13
Avercamp, H. 1802/12/13
Barbiers, P. 1802/12/13
Bega 1802/12/13
Berchem, N.P. 1802/12/13
Brueghel, J. (I) 1802/12/13
Buys, Jac. 1802/12/13
Crayer, G. 1802/12/13
Cuyp, A. 1802/12/13
Does, S. 1802/12/13
Dujardin, K. 1802/12/13
Dürer 1802/12/13
Gael, B. 1802/12/13
Hackaert, J. 1802/12/13
Heyden, J. 1802/12/13
Italian 1802/12/13
Laer, P. 1802/12/13
Lauwers, J.J. 1802/12/13
Lingelbach 1802/12/13
Monogrammist P. 1802/12/13
Ostade, A. 1802/12/13
Ovens, J. 1802/12/13
Saftleven, C. 1802/12/13
Sonje, J.G. 1802/12/13
Tintoretto, J. 1802/12/13
Velde, A. 1802/12/13
Vermeer, Jan (III) 1802/12/13
Verschuring, H. 1802/12/13
Vinne, V.L. (I) 1802/12/13
Vonck, J. 1802/12/13
Vries, R. 1802/12/13
Witte, E. 1802/12/13
Wyck, T. 1802/12/13

LeBrn, see Lebrun

Lebrun, Jean-Baptiste-Pierre
1748–1813; French painter and picture dealer
Anonymous 1810/03/26
Anonymous 1810/08/06
Appelman, Bart. 1810/03/26
Asselyn 1810/08/01
Backhuysen 1810/03/26
Backhuysen 1810/08/01
Bega 1810/08/06
Berchem, N.P. 1810/08/01
Brouwer, Adr. 1810/03/26
Dalens, Dirck 1810/03/26
Deuren, O. 1810/08/01
Dou 1810/03/26
Dou 1810/08/06
Dujardin, K. 1810/03/26
Dujardin, K. 1810/08/01
Dusart, Corn. 1810/08/01
Gelder, A. 1810/03/26
Goyen 1810/08/06
Hackert, J.P. 1810/08/01
Heusch, Wm. 1810/08/06
Metsu 1810/03/26
Molenaer, Klaes 1810/08/06
Monogrammist P.S. 1810/03/26
Moor, C. 1810/08/06
Neer, A. 1810/03/26
Netscher, Casp. 1810/08/01
Ostade, A. 1810/08/01
Ostade, I. 1810/08/01
Potter, Paulus 1810/03/26
Potter, Paulus 1810/08/01
Pynacker 1810/08/01
Romeyn 1810/03/26
Ruisdael, J. 1810/08/01
Ruysdael, S. 1810/03/26
Schouman, A. 1810/03/26
Silo, A. 1810/08/06
Slingeland, P.C. 1810/03/26
Tol, D. 1810/08/01
Velde, A. 1810/08/01
Velde, W. 1810/03/26
Vernet, C.J. 1810/08/06
Weenix 1810/08/01
Weenix, J.B. 1810/08/01
Wils, Jan 1810/03/26

Wouwerman, Ph. 1810/03/26
Wouwerman, Ph. 1810/08/01

Le Dantú, P.
dealer active in Amsterdam
Avercamp, H. 1801/08/19
Beerstraten, A. 1802/05/05
Berckheyde, G. 1801/05/11
Berckheyde, G. 1802/05/05
Carree, M. 1801/08/19
Elsheimer, A. 1801/08/19
Gael, B. 1801/08/19
Goyen 1801/08/19
Haensbergen, J. van 1802/05/05
Horemans, J.J. (I) 1801/08/19
Meijer, H. 1801/08/19
Micker, J.C. 1801/08/19
Minderhout, H. 1801/08/19
Molenaer, J.M. 1801/08/19
Monogrammist J.B.W. 1801/08/19
Naiveu 1802/05/05
Peeters, B. (I) 1801/08/19
Poussin, N. 1801/08/19
Rietschoof, H. 1802/05/05
Ruysdael, S. 1801/08/19
Ruyter, H. 1802/05/05
Sorgh, H.M. 1801/08/19
Verschuring, H. 1801/08/19
Weenix 1802/05/05

Ledrach
also spelled Ledragh; active in Middelburg
Anonymous 1804/06/18

Ledragh, see Ledrach

Leelie, de, see Lelie, de

Leen, Willem van
1753–1825; painter and dealer residing at Delfshaven
Anonymous 1802/11/01
Anonymous 1803/04/20
Anonymous 1808/06/06
Anonymous 1808/06/11
Anonymous 1810/08/06
Anonymous 1810/10/11
Asch, P.J. van 1808/06/11
Balen, H. (I) 1810/06/06
Beerstraten, A. 1810/08/06
Bega 1808/06/11
Borman, Joh. 1810/07/23
Bramer 1808/06/11
Brekelencam, Q. 1808/06/11
Brueghel, J. (I) 1810/06/06
Cappelle 1810/10/11
Carree, Hend. (I) 1802/09/18
Cuyp, A. 1810/07/23
Diepraem 1802/11/01
Dou 1810/03/26
Dujardin, K. 1810/08/06
Dusart, Corn. 1810/07/23
Everdingen, A. 1810/08/06
Haan, C. de 1802/11/01
Heemskerck 1808/06/11
Huysum, Jan 1810/08/06
Janson, J. 1810/10/11
Lingelbach 1808/06/06
Lingelbach 1810/10/11
Lundens 1810/10/11
Meulen, A.F. 1808/06/11
Moucheron, F. 1808/06/06
Moucheron, I. 1808/06/11
Palamedesz., A. 1810/10/11
Raffaello Santi 1808/06/06
Rembrandt 1810/06/06
Rubens 1810/06/06
Ruisdael, J. 1801/04/13
Ruisdael, J. 1810/10/11
Ruysdael, S. 1810/06/06
Saftleven, C. 1808/06/06
Sorgh, H.M. 1810/03/26
Storck, Abr. 1808/06/11
Storck, Abr. 1810/10/11
Streeck, J. 1808/06/11
Versteeg 1810/06/06
Vinne, J. 1810/10/11
Vries 1810/03/26
Werff, A. 1810/08/06
Wouwerman, P. 1810/08/06

Leenhof
Anonymous 1801/03/31

Leering, van
Porcellis, Jan 1801/10/06

Leeuwen, van
Ameron, van 1809/10/16
Anonymous 1803/08/24
Anonymous 1806/08/20
Goyen 1809/10/16
Monogrammist A.D. 1809/10/16
Poel, E. 1809/10/16
Porcellis, Jan 1801/10/06

Le Gran, see Lebrun

Leijden, van
Anonymous 1803/08/17
Ravesteyn, J.A. 1801/10/19
Witte, E. 1803/08/17

Lelie, Adriaan de
1755–1820; painter and dealer, agent for the Amsterdam collector J.A. Brentano
Anonymous 1804/02/27
Banthem, J. 1804/05/07
Cavedone 1803/08/17
Dyck, Anth. van 1804/07/25
Fris 1804/05/07
Huchtenburgh, Jan 1802/06/16
Huysum, Jan 1809/09/06
Italian 1802/06/16
Italian 1804/05/07
Italian 1808/08/23
Koedijck 1809/06/13
Laer, P. 1801/06/10
Lingelbach 1810/08/01
Os, J. 1810/05/22
Roos, P.P. 1802/06/16
Sorgh, H.M. 1810/08/01
Steen, J. 1801/06/10
Steen, J. 1801/10/19
Steen, J. 1809/06/13
Teniers, D. (II) 1809/04/22
Treu, Nic. 1804/05/07
Verelst, Joh. 1804/08/08
Werff, A. 1810/08/06
Wouwerman, Ph. 1810/08/01
Wyck, T. 1802/06/16

Lelij, de, see Lelie, de

Lely, de, see Lelie, de

Lemens
Thier, B.H. 1810/05/22

Lennep, Abraham Jacob van, Jhr.
1778–1841; ship owner, broker and equerry to Louis Bonaparte
Beerstraten, J. 1808/06/06
Does, S. 1808/06/06
Eyck, H. 1808/06/06
Eyck, J. 1808/06/06
Geel, Joost 1808/06/06
Hagen, Joris 1808/06/06
Hondecoeter, M. 1808/06/06
Lelie, A. 1808/06/06
Mieris, W. 1808/06/06
Ostade, A. 1808/06/06
Potter, Paulus 1808/06/06
Snyders, F. 1808/06/06

Lepelaar
active in Middelburg
Anonymous 1803/10/10
Anonymous 1804/06/18

Ler...
Molenaer, J.M. 1803/08/24

Lesscher, D.
Anonymous 1803/04/20
Balen, H. (II) 1803/04/20
Beschey, J. 1803/04/20
Molenaer, J.M. 1803/04/20
Monogrammist C.H. (1600) 1803/04/20

Levie, see Levy

Levij, see Levy

Levy, Gebroeders
Bassano, J. 1808/06/06
Vrancx 1808/06/06

Levy, Isaac
Anonymous 1803/04/27

Levy, P.M.
Anonymous 1801/05/11
Balen, H. (I) 1801/05/11
Brueghel, J. (I) 1801/05/11
Hals, F. (I) 1802/06/16
Kalraet 1802/12/13
Ommeganck, B. 1801/08/19
Palamedesz., P. (I) 1802/06/16
Roos, J.H. 1802/05/05
Vermeulen, A. 1801/08/19

Levy, S.M.
Apshoven 1808/11/28
Barbiers, P. 1808/11/28
Buys, Jac. 1802/02/16
Carree, Abr. 1807/08/26
Everdingen, Cesar 1807/08/26
Flinck 1807/08/26
Victors, Jan 1810/06/20

Levysohn
Moreelse, P. 1808/06/06

Leyster
Anonymous 1803/06/20

Librun, see Lebrun

Limmen, van
Laer, P. 1802/12/13
Saftleven, H. 1802/12/13

Linden, van der
Anonymous 1805/10/09
Bredael 1805/10/09
Breenbergh 1804/12/10
Cuyp, B. 1805/10/09
Netscher, Casp. 1805/10/09
Ring, P. 1805/10/09
Swiss 1805/10/09
Teniers, D. (II) 1805/10/09

Lingen, van
Anonymous 1802/02/23

Lit, van
Teniers, D. (II) 1803/08/24

Loef
Cuyp, J.G. 1806/08/20
Miereveld, M. 1806/08/20
Mytens, D. (I) 1806/08/20

Logger, Hendrik
Schouman, M. 1810/07/23

Lohuijs
Anonymous 1810/07/26
Arthois 1810/07/26
Brueghel, J. (I) 1810/07/26
Decker 1810/07/26
Dutch 1810/07/26
Rysbrack 1810/07/26

Lohuis, see Lohuijs

Lohuys, see Lohuijs

Loon, Stad
Heck, C. 1802/07/27

Looy Lans, Cornelis van der
d. 1808
Anonymous 1808/12/31
Colonia, A. 1808/12/31
Croos 1808/12/31
Ducq, Johan le 1808/12/31
Dusart, A. 1808/12/31
Hoet, G. (I) 1808/12/31
Lelienbergh 1808/12/31
Man, Joost 1808/12/31
Mart, van der 1808/12/31
Mooy, C.P. 1808/12/31
Murant 1808/12/31
Myn, H. 1808/12/31
Neer, A. 1808/12/31
Ostade, I. 1808/12/31
Palamedesz., A. 1808/12/31
Porcellis, Jan 1808/12/31
Silo, A. 1808/12/31
Teniers, D. (II) 1808/12/31
Vliet, H.C. 1808/12/31
Wet, J.W. 1808/12/31

Louis
Goyen 1805/07/10

Louis Bonaparte, koning van Holland
1778–1846; King of Holland from 1806–1809
Backhuysen 1808/06/06
Beerstraten, J. 1808/06/06
Bega 1808/06/06
Berchem, N.P. 1808/06/06
Berchem, N.P. 1809/07/19
Bergen, D. 1808/06/06
Both, J. 1808/06/06
Brekelencam, Q. 1808/06/06
Brueghel, J. (I) 1808/06/06
Coninck, D. 1808/06/06
Cuyp, A. 1808/06/06
Does, S. 1808/06/06
Does, S. 1809/07/19
Dou 1808/06/06
Dubbels, H. 1809/07/19
Dusart, Corn. 1808/06/06
Eyck, H. 1808/06/06
Eyck, J. 1808/06/06
Flinck 1808/06/06
Geel, Joost 1808/06/06
Goyen 1808/06/06
Hackaert, J. 1808/06/06
Hagen, Joris 1808/06/06
Heem, J.D. 1808/06/06
Helst, B. 1808/06/06
Heyden, J. 1808/06/06
Hondecoeter, M. 1808/06/06
Huysum, Jan 1808/06/06
Koninck, P. 1808/06/06
Lelie, A. 1808/06/06
Lingelbach 1808/06/06
Mieris, F. (I) 1808/06/06
Mieris, W. 1808/06/06
Mignon, A. 1808/06/06

Moor, C. 1808/06/06
Ostade, A. 1808/06/06
Ostade, I. 1808/06/06
Poelenburgh, C. 1808/06/06
Pynacker 1808/06/06
Ruisdael, J. 1808/06/06
Saftleven, H. 1808/06/06
Snyders, F. 1808/06/06
Steen, J. 1808/06/06
Teniers, D. (II) 1809/07/19
Velde, A. 1808/06/06
Velde, E. (I) 1809/07/19
Velde, W. 1808/06/06
Vermeer, Jan (III) 1808/06/06
Weenix, J.B. 1808/06/06
Wijnants 1809/07/19
Witte, E. 1808/06/06
Wouwerman, Ph. 1808/06/06

Luchtmans, Cornelis Jan, Dr.
1777–1860; physician and dealer active in Rotterdam
Anonymous 1802/05/24
Anonymous 1808/06/11
Anonymous 1810/03/26
Anonymous 1810/06/06
Brekelencam, Q. 1810/03/26
Cuyp, A. 1808/06/11
Cuyp, A. 1810/06/06
Dürer 1810/06/06
Hondecoeter, M. 1808/06/11
Jongh, L. 1808/06/11
Jongh, L. 1810/06/06
Kobell, H. 1808/06/06
Kobell, Jan (II) 1808/06/11
Lingelbach 1808/06/11
Lucas van Leyden 1810/06/06
Moeyaert, C. 1808/06/06
Neer, A. 1810/06/06
Neer, E. 1808/06/11
Neranus, A. 1808/06/11
Ostade, I. 1808/06/06
Schellinks 1808/06/11
Storck, Abr. 1808/06/11
Weenix 1810/08/10

Lugtmans, see Luchtmans

M. (1801, May 11)
Berchem, N.P. 1801/05/11
Blanckerhoff 1801/05/11
Bloemaert 1801/05/11
Cappelle 1801/05/11
Crayer, G. 1801/05/11
Hals, F. (I) 1801/05/11
Honthorst, G. 1801/05/11
Limborch, H. 1801/05/11
Matthieu, C. 1801/05/11
Molenaer, Klaes 1801/05/11
Mortel 1801/05/11
Neeffs, P. (I) 1801/05/11
Palthe, G.J. 1801/05/11
Porcellis, Jan 1801/05/11
Romeyn 1801/05/11
Ruisdael, J. 1801/05/11
Vermeer, Jan 1801/05/11
Vlieger, S. 1801/05/11
Vries, R. 1801/05/11
Weenix, J.B. 1801/05/11

M. (1801, October 6)
Anonymous 1801/10/06
Bergen, D. 1801/10/06
Bleeker, J. 1801/10/06
Bloemaert, A. 1801/10/06
Both, J. 1801/10/06
Bredael, J. 1801/10/06
Cagnacci 1801/10/06
Chalon, L. 1801/10/06
Compe, Jan ten 1801/10/06
Coopse, P. 1801/10/06
Dalens, Dirck 1801/10/06
Droochsloot, J.C. 1801/10/06
Elsheimer, A. 1801/10/06
Franks, J. 1801/10/06
Gerards 1801/10/06
Gool, Jan 1801/10/06
Hendriks, W. 1801/10/06
Hobbema 1801/10/06
Hondecoeter, M. 1801/10/06
Horemans, J.J. (I) 1801/10/06
Jordaens, J. (I) 1801/10/06
Kessel, J. (III) 1801/10/06
Laer, P. 1801/10/06
Lairesse, G. 1801/10/06
Lundens 1801/10/06
Miel 1801/10/06
Netscher, Casp. 1801/10/06
Peeters, B. (I) 1801/10/06
Poel, E. 1801/10/06
Porcellis, Jan 1801/10/06
Rietschoof, J.C. 1801/10/06
Schoevaerdts, M. 1801/10/06
Steen, J. 1801/10/06
Steenwyk, J. 1801/10/06
Teniers, D. (II) 1801/10/06
Velde, E. (I) 1801/10/06
Velde, W. 1801/10/06
Verburgh, Dionijs 1801/10/06
Vermeer, Jan (II) 1801/10/06
Vlieger, S. 1801/10/06
Willaerts 1801/10/06
Winter, Gillis 1801/10/06

M. (1804, August 8)
Anonymous 1804/08/08
Beeldemaker, A.C. 1804/08/08
Victors, Jan 1804/08/08

M. (1805, July 10)
Amigoni, J. 1805/07/10
Beerstraten, A. 1805/07/10
Begeyn 1805/07/10
Bloemen, P. 1805/07/10
Brekelencam, Q. 1805/07/10
Brueghel, J. (I) 1805/07/10
Dalens, Dirck 1805/07/10
Delen 1805/07/10
Everdingen, A. 1805/07/10
Gael, B. 1805/07/10
Goyen 1805/07/10
Hondecoeter, G. 1805/07/10
Honthorst, G. 1805/07/10
Hoogstraten, S. 1805/07/10
Molenaer, J.M. 1805/07/10
Mommers, H. 1805/07/10
Momper, J. (II) 1805/07/10
Oolen, Adr. 1805/07/10
Sluis, J. 1805/07/10
Smit, Aernout 1805/07/10
Sorgh, H.M. 1805/07/10
Steen, J. 1805/07/10
Velde, A. 1805/07/10
Victors, Jan 1805/07/10
Vitringa 1805/07/10
Vrancx 1805/07/10
Vree, N. de 1805/07/10
Vries, R. 1805/07/10

M. (1809, June 13)
Dubois, H. 1809/06/13
Ekels, Jan (I) 1809/06/13
Gérard, M. 1809/06/13
Lingelbach 1809/06/13
Molenaer, Klaes 1809/06/13
Palamedesz., P. (I) 1809/06/13
Steen, J. 1809/06/13
Storck, J. 1809/06/13
Wijnants 1809/06/13

M. (1810, October 11)
Anonymous 1810/10/11
Apshoven 1810/10/11
Bassano, J. 1810/10/11
Caravaggio 1810/10/11
Correggio 1810/10/11
Goltzius, Hend. 1810/10/11
Guercino 1810/10/11
Helst, B. 1810/10/11
Italian 1810/10/11
Monogrammist S.L. 1810/10/11
Moucheron, F. 1810/10/11
Parenti 1810/10/11
Poussin, N. 1810/10/11
Raffaello Santi 1810/10/11
Reni 1810/10/11

Maagd, de
Anonymous 1803/10/10

Maas
Anonymous 1802/07/27
Anonymous 1810/08/06
Berckheyde, J. 1808/08/23

Maas, M.
Anonymous 1810/08/06

Maasen, van den
Anonymous 1803/04/27

Maat, ter
Huysum, Jan 1805/12/16

Macalester Loup, Duncan
1751–1812; lieutenant-colonel in the Scottish brigade stationed in The Hague and agent for the West Indies colony
Aelst, W. 1806/08/20
Andrea del Sarto 1806/08/20
Anonymous 1806/08/20
Anonymous-Modern 1806/08/20
Antonissen, H.J. 1806/08/20
Asch, P.J. van 1806/08/20
Asselyn 1806/08/20
Avercamp, H. 1806/08/20
Baen, Jan de 1806/08/20
Balen, H. (I) 1806/08/20
Beeldemaker 1806/08/20
Begeyn 1806/08/20
Berchem, N.P. 1806/08/20
Bergen, D. 1806/08/20
Bloemaert, A. 1806/08/20
Bogaert, Iemant 1806/08/20
Bolomey, B.S. 1806/08/20
Boonen, A. 1806/08/20
Bosch, J.H. 1806/08/20
Both, J. 1806/08/20
Bredael, P. 1806/08/20
Brueghel, J. (I) 1806/08/20
Burg (Burgh) 1806/08/20
Chapman, J. 1806/08/20
Cuylenburg, C. 1806/08/20
Cuyp, A. 1806/08/20
Cuyp, J.G. 1806/08/20
Does, S. 1806/08/20
Dutch 1806/08/20
Dyck, Anth. van 1806/08/20
Dyk, P. 1806/08/20
Ekels, Jan (I) 1806/08/20
Elsheimer, A. 1806/08/20
Fargue 1806/08/20
Ferguson, Wm. 1806/08/20
Flemish-Brabant 1806/08/20
Flinck 1806/08/20
Francken 1806/08/20
Glauber, J. 1806/08/20
Goyen 1804/04/28
Goyen 1806/08/20
Heem, C. 1806/08/20
Heemskerck, M. 1806/08/20
Heusch, Wm. 1806/08/20
Holbein, H. (II) 1806/08/20
Hondecoeter, Gysb. 1806/08/20
Hondecoeter, M. 1806/08/20
Honthorst, G. 1806/08/20
Hoogstraten, S. 1806/08/20
Huchtenburgh, Jan 1806/08/20
Italian 1806/08/20
Kalf 1806/08/20
Keller, J.H. (II) 1806/08/20
Lairesse, G. 1806/08/20
Lairesse, Jan 1806/08/20
Looten, J. 1806/08/20
Maas, J. 1806/08/20
Maes, D. 1806/08/20
Maes, N. 1806/08/20
Maratti 1806/08/20
Metsu 1806/08/20
Miereveld, M. 1806/08/20
Mieris, F. (I) 1806/08/20
Mieris, W. 1806/08/20
Molenaer, J.M. 1806/08/20
Monogrammist E.J. 1806/08/20
Monogrammist P.V. 1806/08/20
Moor, C. 1806/08/20
Moritz, Louis 1806/08/20
Moucheron, F. 1806/08/20
Mytens, Aert 1806/08/20
Mytens, D. (I) 1806/08/20
Neeffs, P. (I) 1806/08/20
Netscher, Casp. 1806/08/20
Os, J. 1806/08/20
Ouwater, Jac. 1806/08/20
Poel, E. 1806/08/20
Poelenburgh, C. 1806/08/20
Prins, J.H. 1806/08/20
Pynacker 1806/08/20
Querfurt, A. 1806/08/20
Rembrandt 1806/08/20
Romeyn 1806/08/20
Rosenberg, F. 1806/08/20
Saftleven, H. 1806/08/20
Sandrart, Joachim (I) 1806/08/20
Schalcken 1806/08/20
Schütz 1806/08/20
Schweickardt, H. 1806/08/20
Sin, P. le 1806/08/20
Slabbaert, Karel 1806/08/20
Sorgh, H.M. 1806/08/20
Steen, J. 1806/08/20
Terwesten, Mat. 1806/08/20
Thomas, Jan 1806/08/20
Tol, D. 1806/08/20
Valken, H. 1806/08/20
Velde, A. 1806/08/20
Verbeeck, P.C. 1806/08/20
Verbruggen, G. (II) 1806/08/20
Vermeulen, A. 1806/08/20
Verschuring, H. 1806/08/20
Versteeg 1806/08/20
Vinckeboons, D. 1806/08/20
Vitringa 1806/08/20
Vlieger, S. 1806/08/20
Vois, Ary de 1806/08/20
Vrancx 1806/08/20
Wijnants 1806/08/20
Winghen, B. 1806/08/20
Wouwerman, Ph. 1806/08/20

Mahy
dealer in Antwerp
Blok, H. 1804/10/16
Cerquozzi 1804/10/16
Decker, C. 1804/10/16
Moucheron, I. 1804/10/16
Pynacker 1804/10/16
Staveren, J.A. 1804/10/16
Verelst, P. 1804/10/16
Wijnants 1804/10/16

Maijer, A.
Horemans, J.J. (I) 1801/04/23
Huysum, Jan 1801/04/23
Verburgh, Dionijs 1801/04/23

Maijkel, David
also spelled Mayken
Anonymous 1808/08/23
Backer, J.A. 1808/08/23
Berckheyde, J. 1808/08/23
Bloemaert, A. 1808/08/23
Borch, G. ter (II) 1808/08/23
Courtois, J. 1808/08/23
Droochsloot, J.C. 1808/08/23
Dyck, Anth. van 1808/08/23
Griffier, J. (I) 1808/08/23
Poel, E. 1808/08/23
Regemorter, P. 1808/08/23
Ruisdael, J. 1808/08/23
Steenwyck, Hend. 1808/08/23
Storck, Abr. 1808/08/23
Verspronck, Joh. 1808/08/23

Makai
active in Dordrecht
Anonymous 1810/07/23

Malapert, Pieter de, Mr.
1740–1806; canon at Utrecht cathedral
Anonymous 1806/10/16
Balen 1806/10/16
Borch, G. ter (II) 1806/10/16
Bramer 1806/10/16
Brekelencam, Q. 1806/10/16
Bruegel, P. (I) 1806/10/16
Dalens, Dirck 1806/10/16
Denner, B. 1806/10/16
Dubbels, H. 1806/10/16
Ducq, Johan le 1806/10/16
Heemskerck, Jan 1806/10/16
Huchtenburgh, Jan 1806/10/16
Keyser, Thos. de 1806/10/16
Laer, P. 1806/10/16
Molenaer, J.M. 1806/10/16
Palamedesz., A. 1806/10/16
Saftleven, C. 1806/10/16
Storck, J. 1806/10/16
Vertangen 1806/10/16
Weenix 1806/10/16
Wouwerman, P. 1806/10/16

Mann, Jult
Hals, D. 1805/07/10

Mansveld, Daniel
1726–1806; resident of Amsterdam
Anonymous 1806/08/13
Cappelle 1806/08/13
Eeckhout, G. 1806/08/13
Everdingen, A. 1806/08/13
Huchtenburgh, Jan 1806/08/13
Molenaer, J.M. 1806/08/13
Moucheron, F. 1806/08/13
Ruisdael, J. 1806/08/13
Schyndel, J. 1806/08/13
Toorenvliet, J. 1806/08/13
Velde, A. 1806/08/13
Velde, E. (I) 1806/08/13
Wijnants 1806/08/13
Wouwerman, Ph. 1806/08/13

Manul
Anonymous 1803/10/10

Margadont
Anonymous 1807/06/10
Droochsloot, J.C. 1807/06/10

Marree, de
Anonymous 1801/06/13

Mars
Anonymous 1802/06/28

Martens
Anonymous 1809/04/22

Martins, see Martens

Masse
Dorasse, C. 1810/05/22
Schendel, B. 1810/05/22

Mast, van der
Maes, D. 1802/09/21

Mayer, A.
Accama 1801/04/23
Maas, P. 1801/04/23
Poussin, N. 1801/04/23
Verburgh, Dionijs 1801/04/23
Vlieger, S. 1801/04/23

Maykel, see Maijkel

Mayken, see Maijkel

Maynzart, see Mensart

Meer, van der
Alewyn, Abr. 1805/10/09
Anonymous 1810/09/17
Meijer, H. (I) 1805/10/09
Vries, P. 1805/10/09

Meertens
active in Middelburg; possibly A. or H. Meertens, qq.v.
Anonymous 1804/06/18
Anonymous 1805/09/23
Heemskerck 1807/10/12

Meertens, A.
resident of Middelburg; perhaps the painter Abraham Meertens, 1757–1823
Anonymous 1802/10/18
Anonymous 1803/10/10

Meertens, H.
Lingelbach 1802/05/10

Meertense, see Meertens

Meij, Ph.
probably erroneous for Philippus van der Schley, q.v.
Aelst, W. 1805/10/09
Balen, H. (I) 1805/10/09
Bent, J. 1805/10/09
Bloemaert, A. 1805/10/09
Brekelencam, Q. 1805/10/09
Brueghel 1805/10/09
Brueghel, J. (I) 1805/10/09
Guichardino 1805/10/09
Heem, J.D. 1805/10/09
Juncker, Jus. 1805/10/09
Kalf 1806/08/20
Kleijne, David 1805/10/09
Leonardo da Vinci 1805/10/09
Looten, J. 1806/08/20
Monogrammist J.T. 1805/10/09
Ruysch, R. 1805/10/09
Saftleven, H. 1806/08/20
Seghers, D. 1805/10/09
Sorgh, H.M. 1805/10/09
Steen, J. 1805/10/09
Teniers, D. (II) 1805/10/09
Velde, E. (I) 1805/10/09

Meijer
Anonymous 1803/10/10
Appel, J. (I) 1809/06/13
Uppink 1810/06/20
Withoos, M. 1801/08/19

Meijer, de
Alcock 1802/12/13
Anonymous 1802/07/27
Anonymous 1802/09/21
Anonymous 1802/12/13
Anonymous 1803/08/01
Anonymous 1803/09/07
Beelt, C. 1802/07/27
Berchem, N.P. 1802/09/06
Brakenburg 1802/12/13
Brouwer, Adr. 1803/09/07
Burg, M. 1802/06/28
Caravaggio 1803/04/27
Coosemans 1806/08/13
Cuyp, J.G. 1804/08/08
Decker 1802/09/06
Dongen, Dionys 1802/06/28
Ducq, Johan le 1804/02/27
Ferguson, Wm. 1804/02/27
Gael, B. 1802/12/13
Glimes, P. de 1802/12/13
Heem, C. 1803/06/20
Heem, J.D. 1802/07/27
Heemskerck 1804/02/27
Heeremans, Thos. 1802/06/28
Jacobsz., L. 1802/07/27
Jelgersma, T.H. 1802/06/16
Keun, Hend. 1802/06/28
Keun, Hend. 1804/02/27
Kuster, J. 1802/09/06
Lauwers, J.J. 1802/06/28
Lubienietski, C. 1806/08/13
Marseus, O. 1802/09/06
Molenaer, J.M. 1802/06/28
Monogrammist J.A.H. 1802/06/28
Neer, A. 1802/09/06
Ommeganck, B. 1804/05/07
Os, Pieter G. 1804/02/27
Ouwater, Isaak 1802/06/28
Poussin, N. 1803/04/27
Regemorter, P. 1802/12/13
Ring, P. 1802/09/06
Saftleven, C. 1802/06/16
Saftleven, C. 1802/06/28
Schendel, B. 1802/07/27
Schut, C. (I) 1803/04/20
Seppo 1802/06/28
Verkolje, N. 1802/06/28
Vermeulen 1806/08/13
Verschuir 1804/08/08
Victors, Jan 1802/09/06

Meijer, A.
Anonymous 1801/08/19
Cappelle 1801/06/10
Nollekens 1801/08/19
Noort, Pieter van 1801/06/10
Roghman, R. 1801/06/10

Meijer, C.
Bega 1802/02/16

Meijer, P. de
Anonymous 1802/10/18

Meijer, Son
Broeck, E. 1802/07/27
Kerckhoff, Fr. 1802/07/27

Meijling
Staveren, Jacob 1803/07/18

Meinsmaa
Anonymous 1807/12/00
Goyen 1807/12/00
Hondecoeter 1807/12/00

Meloen
Gelder, A. 1802/11/01
Goltzius, Hend. 1802/11/01
Molenaer 1802/11/01

Menli, see Menlie

Menlie, C.
also spelled Menli or Meuli; apparently a dealer active in Amsterdam
Delff, Corn.J. 1806/11/24
Kalf 1803/07/18
Lairesse, Jan 1801/06/10

Mensaart, see Mensart

Mensard, see Mensart

Mensart, François Jules
dealer, also described as conservator of the Rijksmuseum
Anonymous 1801/03/16
Anonymous 1801/04/13
Anonymous 1801/05/11
Anonymous 1802/05/05
Anonymous 1802/06/28
Anonymous 1802/12/13
Anonymous 1803/04/20
Anonymous 1803/04/27
Anonymous 1803/08/01
Anonymous 1803/12/12
Anonymous 1805/07/10
Anonymous 1806/05/05
Anonymous 1810/10/11
Asselyn 1802/12/13
Backer, A. 1804/08/08
Bega 1802/05/05
Begeyn 1806/05/05
Bemmel 1804/08/08
Berchem, N.P. 1802/06/16
Blaauw, J. 1802/06/28
Blanckerhoff 1802/05/05
Bloemaert, A. 1810/10/11
Both, J. 1806/05/05
Broeck, E. 1804/05/07
Bronchorst, J.G. 1805/07/10
Brueghel, J. (I) 1803/04/20
Brueghel, J. (I) 1806/05/05
Chalon, L. 1802/06/28
Colonia, A. 1810/10/11
Cuyp, A. 1806/08/13
Cuyp, J.G. 1804/08/08
Decker, Frans 1804/08/08
Dietrich, Chr. 1804/07/25
Dou 1805/07/03
Dyck, Anth. van 1805/07/10
Elliger, O. (II) 1810/10/11
Giordano, L. 1810/10/11
Goyen 1801/03/16
Hackaert 1803/12/12
Hoet, G. (I) 1802/06/28
Honthorst, G. 1801/06/10
Hooch, P. 1803/12/12
Hooch, P. 1810/05/22
Hoogsaat, J.C. 1802/05/05
Huchtenburgh, Jan 1801/03/16
Huchtenburgh, Jan 1806/05/05
Huysum, Justus van (I) 1801/04/23
Kleur, S. 1803/06/20
Lairesse, G. 1805/07/10
Le Brun, Chas. 1801/04/13
Maes, N. 1802/05/05
Martszen, J. (II) 1802/05/05
Martszen, J. (II) 1802/06/28
Martszen, J. (II) 1805/07/03
Matthieu, C. 1801/05/11
Meulen, A.F. 1804/08/08
Meulen, A.F. 1806/08/13
Miereveld, M. 1810/10/11
Molenaer, J.M. 1801/03/16
Molenaer, J.M. 1810/10/11
Moni, L. de 1806/05/05
Musscher, M. 1805/07/10
Neer, A. 1802/05/05
Ostade 1801/03/16
Ostade 1805/07/10
Ostade, I. 1802/05/05
Palamedesz., A. 1806/05/05
Peeters, B. (I) 1801/03/16
Romeyn 1801/03/16
Rubens 1803/12/12
Sonje, J.G. 1801/03/16

Steen, J. 1802/06/28
Storck, J. 1810/10/11
Teniers, D. (II) 1806/05/05
Toorenvliet, J. 1805/07/10
Uden, Lucas 1803/12/12
Valck, A. 1802/12/13
Velde, J. (II) 1804/05/07
Verboom, A.H. 1804/08/08
Verschuring, H. 1804/08/08
Victors, Jan 1801/03/16
Vinck, J. 1810/10/11
Watteau, J.A. 1804/05/07
Werff, A. 1810/08/06
Werff, H.N. 1802/12/13
Wit, Jacob de 1806/05/05
Wolfaerts, J.B. 1810/10/11

Menzard, see Mensart

Menzart, see Mensart

Merrem
d. ca.1802; almost certainly a German residing in Amsterdam
Anonymous 1801/05/11
Anonymous 1802/06/16
Apshoven 1802/06/16
Asselyn 1802/06/16
Backhuysen 1802/06/16
Balen, H. (I) 1802/06/16
Bassano 1802/06/16
Batist, Karel 1802/06/16
Bega 1802/06/16
Berchem, N.P. 1802/06/16
Berckheyde, G. 1802/06/16
Berckheyde, J. 1802/06/16
Besters, A.J. 1802/06/16
Bisschop, J. 1802/06/16
Bloemen, P. 1802/06/16
Bloot, P. 1802/06/16
Bol, F. 1801/04/13
Bol, F. 1801/10/19
Bol, F. 1802/06/16
Borch, G. ter (II) 1802/06/16
Both, A. 1802/06/16
Both, J. 1802/06/16
Brekelencam, Q. 1802/06/16
Brouwer, Adr. 1802/06/16
Brueghel, J. (I) 1802/06/16
Bys, J.R. 1802/06/16
Cappelle 1802/06/16
Caravaggio 1802/06/16
Carpioni, G. (I) 1802/06/16
Cuyp, A. 1802/06/16
Decker, C. 1801/08/19
Decker, C. 1802/06/16
Does, J. (I) 1802/06/16
Domenichino 1802/06/16
Dongen, Dionys 1802/06/16
Dou 1802/06/16
Droochsloot, J.C. 1802/06/16
Dubbels, H. 1802/06/16
Ducq, Johan le 1802/06/16
Dughet 1802/06/16
Dujardin, K. 1802/06/16
Dusart, Corn. 1802/06/16
Eeckhout, G. 1802/06/16
Elsheimer, A. 1802/06/16
Everbroeck, F. 1802/06/16
Everdingen, A. 1802/06/16
Everdingen, Cesar 1802/06/16
Franks, J. 1802/06/16
Gael, B. 1802/06/16
Geel, N. 1802/06/16
Goyen 1802/06/16
Gryef 1802/06/16
Hackaert, J. 1801/08/19
Hackaert, J. 1802/06/16
Hals, F. (I) 1802/06/16
Heda, G.W. 1802/06/16
Helst, B. 1802/06/16
Helst, Jer. 1802/06/16
Heusch, Jacob 1802/06/16
Hobbema 1802/06/16
Hoet, G. (I) 1802/06/16
Huchtenburgh, Jan 1802/06/16
Huysum, Jan 1802/06/16
Italian 1802/06/16
Jelgersma, T.H. 1802/06/16
Keirincx, Alex. 1802/06/16
Kessel, J. (III) 1802/06/16
Klomp 1802/06/16
Koninck, P. 1802/06/16
Kool, N. 1802/06/16
Laen, D.J. 1802/06/16
Laer, P. 1802/06/16
Leeuw 1802/06/16
Lingelbach 1802/06/16
Martszen, J. (II) 1802/06/16
Metsu 1802/06/16
Meulen, A.F. 1802/06/16
Miel 1802/06/16
Mieris, F. (I) 1802/06/16
Molenaer, J.M. 1802/06/16
Molenaer, Klaes 1802/06/16
Moni, L. de 1802/06/16
Monogrammist R. 1802/06/16
Moucheron, F. 1802/06/16
Neer, A. 1802/06/16
Netscher, Casp. 1801/10/06
Netscher, Casp. 1802/06/16
Nickelen, Jan 1802/06/16
Ostade, A. 1801/10/19
Ostade, A. 1802/06/16
Palamedesz., P. (I) 1802/06/16
Poelenburgh, C. 1801/08/19
Poelenburgh, C. 1802/06/16
Potter, Paulus 1802/06/16
Pourbus, F. (II) 1802/06/16
Prins, J.H. 1802/06/16
Pynacker 1802/06/16
Quast, P.J. 1802/06/16
Rembrandt 1802/06/16
Ridinger, J.E. 1802/06/16
Rietschoof, H. 1802/06/16
Roepel, C. 1802/06/16
Roos, P.P. 1802/06/16
Rosa, S. 1802/06/16
Roy, N. 1802/06/16
Rubens 1802/06/16
Ruisdael, J. 1801/04/13
Ruisdael, J. 1802/06/16
Ruysch, R. 1802/06/16
Saenredam, P.J. 1802/06/16
Saftleven, C. 1802/06/16
Saftleven, H. 1802/06/16
Schellinks, W. 1802/06/16
Schumacher, N. 1802/06/16
Soolmaker 1802/06/16
Sorgh, H.M. 1802/06/16
Spranger, B. 1802/06/16
Staveren, J.A. 1802/06/16
Steen, J. 1802/06/16
Steenwyck, Hend. 1802/06/16
Stoffe 1802/06/16
Stoop, J. 1802/06/16
Storck, Abr. 1802/06/16
Swanevelt 1802/06/16
Swebach, J.F.J. 1802/06/16
Teniers, D. (II) 1801/04/13
Teniers, D. (II) 1802/06/16
Tol, D. 1802/06/16
Velde, A. 1801/04/13
Velde, A. 1802/06/16
Verbeeck, P.C. 1802/06/16
Verboom, A.H. 1802/06/16
Verkolje, N. 1802/06/16
Vermeer, Jan 1801/05/11
Vermeer, Jan 1802/06/16
Vermeer, Jan (II) 1802/06/16
Vermeer, Jan (III) 1801/04/13
Vermeer, Jan (III) 1802/06/16
Veronese 1802/06/16
Verschuring, H. 1802/06/16
Vinne, V.L. (I) 1802/06/16
Vitringa 1802/06/16
Vlieger, J. 1802/06/16
Vlieger, S. 1802/06/16
Volaire, P.J. 1802/06/16
Vrancx 1802/06/16
Vries, R. 1802/06/16
Waterloo, A. 1802/06/16
Weenix 1802/06/16
Weenix, J.B. 1802/06/16
Weirother, N. 1802/06/16
Werff, P. 1802/06/16
Wijnants 1801/04/13
Wijnants 1802/06/16
Wit, Jacob de 1802/06/16
Witte, E. 1801/08/19
Wouwerman, J. 1802/06/16
Wouwerman, P. 1802/06/16
Wouwerman, Ph. 1802/06/16
Wouwerman, Pieter 1802/06/16
Wyck, T. 1802/06/16
Wyntrack, D. 1802/06/16
Zeemann 1802/06/16

Mes
Aa, Dirk 1809/07/25
Hulst 1809/07/25
Keller, J.H. (II) 1809/07/25
Molijn 1809/07/25
Poel, E. 1809/07/25
Storck, Abr. 1809/07/25
Vermeulen, A. 1809/07/25

Messing
Maes, N. 1808/06/06

Mets
Gelder, A. 1804/02/27

Mettenbrink, J.
dealer active in Amsterdam
Monogrammist C.W.M. 1806/08/13
Moor, C. 1806/08/13
Ouwater, J. 1806/08/13

Metz, C.
Anonymous 1807/08/26
Ostade, I. 1807/08/26

Meulemans, J.
Droochsloot, Abr. 1802/11/01

Meulen, H. van der
Dame, A. 1802/09/06

Meulen, V., see Vermeulen

Meulie, see Menlie

Meurens, see Meurrens

Meurrens, J.
also spelled Meurens; active in Dordrecht
Anonymous 1810/07/23
Cuyp, A. 1810/07/23

Mey, see Meij

Meyer, see Meijer

Mieden, A. van der, Mejuffrouw
d. ca.1802; probably the daughter of Adriaan van der Mieden, 1702–1764, steward to the High Counsel in The Hague and advisor to the stadholders Van Oranje
Anonymous 1802/05/24
Bega 1802/05/24
Bruegel, P. (I) 1802/05/24
Brueghel, J. (I) 1802/05/24
Carree, F. 1802/05/24
Dujardin, K. 1802/05/24
Elsteijn 1802/05/24
Essen, C. 1802/05/24
Gael, B. 1802/05/24
Goyen 1802/05/24
Heeremans, Thos. 1802/05/24
Hennekyn 1802/05/24
Huchtenburgh, Jan 1802/05/24
Kessel, J. (I) 1802/05/24
Leemans, J. 1802/05/24
Lingelbach 1802/05/24
Looten, J. 1802/05/24
Marrel, Jacob 1802/05/24
Mignon, A. 1802/05/24
Molenaer, J.M. 1802/05/24
Molenaer, Klaes 1802/05/24
Monogrammist A.W. 1802/05/24
Monogrammist L.P. 1802/05/24
Moucheron, I. 1802/05/24
Netscher, Casp. 1802/05/24
Nieulandt, A. (I) 1802/05/24
Palm, J. 1802/05/24
Palthe, G.J. 1802/05/24
Sabaar, P. 1802/05/24
Schweickardt, H. 1802/05/24
Steen, J. 1802/05/24
Storck, J. 1802/05/24
Velde, E. (I) 1802/05/24
Vitringa 1802/05/24
Vogelsang, I. 1802/05/24
Willaerts, C. 1802/05/24
Wouwerman, P. 1802/05/24
Wyck, T. 1802/05/24
Wyckenburch 1802/05/24

mijn
Anonymous 1802/09/06
Dubourg, L. 1808/11/28
Lauwers, J.J. 1802/06/28

Milet, Johannes Henricus, Mr.
d. ca.1810; councillor at the Court of Justice for the province of Zeeland in Middelburg
Anonymous 1810/04/17

Modera
Anonymous 1802/10/18
Anonymous 1804/06/18

Moens, Maria Magdalena van Sluypwijk, gravin van
1710/11–1802; illegitimate daughter of Gerbrand, graaf van Moens
Anonymous 1803/04/20
Anonymous-Antique 1803/04/20
Apshoven 1803/04/20
Backer, A. 1803/04/20
Balen, H. (II) 1803/04/20
Bassano 1803/04/20
Bassen 1803/04/20
Beeldemaker 1803/04/20
Berchem, N.P. 1803/04/20
Beschey, J. 1803/04/20
Bijlert 1803/04/20
Bloemaert, A. 1803/04/20
Bray, S. 1803/04/20
Bredael, P. 1803/04/20
Brueghel, J. (I) 1803/04/20
Brugghen, Hendrick ter 1803/04/20
Coxie, M. (I) 1803/04/20
Cranach, L. (I) 1803/04/20
Croos, R. 1803/04/20
Cuylenburg, C. 1803/04/20
Dalens, Dirck 1803/04/20
Diepenbeeck, A.J. 1803/04/20
Dou 1803/04/20
Draaijenburg, W. 1803/04/20
Flinck 1803/04/20
Gillig, Jakob 1803/04/20
Goyen 1803/04/20
Grebber, P. 1803/04/20
Hals, D. 1803/04/20
Heda 1803/04/20
Holbein, H. (II) 1803/04/20
Hondecoeter, G. 1803/04/20

Honthorst, G. 1803/04/20
Horemans, J.J. (I) 1803/04/20
Italian 1803/04/20
Lairesse, Jan 1803/04/20
Maes, N. 1803/04/20
Massys, Q. 1803/04/20
Miereveld, M. 1803/04/20
Mieris, F. (I) 1803/04/20
Mieris, W. 1803/04/20
Moeyaert, C. 1803/04/20
Molenaer, J.M. 1803/04/20
Molijn 1803/04/20
Monogrammist C.H. (1600) 1803/04/20
Monogrammist cK. 1803/04/20
Monogrammist I.B. (1562) 1803/04/20
Monogrammist I.B.I.R. 1803/04/20
Moreelse, P. 1803/04/20
Nickelen 1803/04/20
Ostade, A. 1803/04/20
Palamedesz., P. (I) 1803/04/20
Palma 1803/04/20
Poelenburgh, C. 1803/04/20
Porcellis, Jan 1803/04/20
Pynas, J. 1803/04/20
Ravesteyn, J.A. 1803/04/20
Rembrandt 1803/04/20
Rubens 1803/04/20
Santvoort, D. 1803/04/20
Schut, C. (I) 1803/04/20
Staveren, J.A. 1803/04/20
Steen, J. 1803/04/20
Steenwyck, Hend. 1803/04/20
Tempel, A.L. van den 1803/04/20
Teniers, D. (II) 1803/04/20
Utrecht, Adr. 1803/04/20
Vallee, Louis 1803/04/20
Velde, A. 1803/04/20
Velde, E. (I) 1803/04/20
Verelst, S. 1803/04/20
Veronese 1803/04/20
Vertangen 1803/04/20
Victors, Jan 1803/04/20
Vinckeboons, D. 1803/04/20
Vlieger, S. 1803/04/20
Vonck 1803/04/20
Vrancx 1803/04/20
Vucht, Jan 1803/04/20
Werff, P. 1803/04/20
Werters 1803/04/20
Wet, J.W. 1803/04/20
Wigmana, G. 1803/04/20
Willaerts, A. 1803/04/20
Wouwerman, Ph. 1803/04/20
Zuccari, F. 1803/04/20

Molder
Storck, Abr. 1808/08/23

Molenyzer
active in Amsterdam
Saftleven, C. 1810/03/26

Moll, see Molles

Molles
Anonymous 1808/06/13
Decker, Jan 1804/05/07
Ekels, Jan (I) 1804/08/08
Eyk, Abraham 1808/06/13
Janson, J.C. 1804/12/10
Lauwers, J.J. 1804/12/10
Metsu 1804/08/08
Ouwater, Isaak 1804/12/10
Palamedesz., A. 1804/08/08
Vries, R. 1808/06/13

Monnick, see Munnick

Mook
Anonymous-Modern 1805/07/10

Moor van Immerzeel, B. de, Mr.
d. ca.1802; burgermeester of Gouda
Anonymous 1802/05/01
Rembrandt 1802/05/01
Steem, C. de 1802/05/01

Moses, Isaac
Anonymous 1803/04/27
Correggio 1803/04/27

Muilman, Hendrik
d. ca.1813
Velde, A. 1801/06/10
Weenix 1801/06/10
Wijnants 1801/06/10

Muis
Nijmegen, G. 1802/09/18
Thier, B.H. 1802/09/18

Mulder
Molenaer, Klaes 1810/08/10

Mulder, see also Muller

Muller
either Hendrik Anthonij Muller, 1745–1826, or his son Gerrit, 1779–1826, q.v.
Bloemaert, H. 1810/06/06
Brueghel, J. (I) 1805/12/16

Muller, Gerrit
1779–1826; banker and landscape painter, son of Hendrik Anthonij Muller, 1745–1826
Everdingen, A. 1804/04/28
Nijmegen, G. 1804/04/28

Munk, Hendrik
1764–1825; collector for the state lottery
Monogrammist D.V.B. 1809/07/27
Monogrammist L.B. 1809/07/27
Salm, A. 1809/07/27

Munnick, de
Anonymous 1802/09/21
Drielenburch, W. 1802/09/21
Goyen 1802/09/21
Neer, A. 1802/09/21
Schellinks, W. 1808/11/28
Steen, J. 1802/09/21
Venne, A.P. 1802/09/21
Wouwerman, P. 1802/09/21

Munnikhuizen, Frans
1742–1820; Lutheran minister living in Rotterdam and later in Amsterdam
Anonymous 1806/11/24
Asselyn 1806/11/24
Backhuysen 1806/11/24
Beerstraten, A. 1806/11/24
Begeyn 1806/11/24
Bent, J. 1806/11/24
Berchem, N.P. 1806/11/24
Berckheyde, J. 1806/11/24
Bloemaert, A. 1806/11/24
Borrekens, J.P. 1806/11/24
Bramer 1806/11/24
Bredael 1806/11/24
Cappelle 1806/11/24
Carree, M. 1806/11/24
Colonia, A. 1806/11/24
Correggio 1806/11/24
Cuyp, J.A. 1806/11/24
Decker, C. 1806/11/24
Delen 1806/11/24
Delff, Corn.J. 1806/11/24
Dietzsch, J.C. 1806/11/24
Dongen, Dionys 1806/11/24
Droochsloot, J.C. 1806/11/24
Fargue, P.C. 1806/11/24
Gael, B. 1806/11/24
Gaesbeeck, A. 1806/11/24
Goyen 1806/11/24
Hals, F. (I) 1806/11/24
Heem, C. 1806/11/24
Heeremans, Thos. 1806/11/24
Hooch, P. 1806/11/24
Huchtenburgh, Jan 1806/11/24
Huysum, Jan 1806/11/24
Jagt, M. 1806/11/24
Janson, J. 1806/11/24
Laer, P. 1806/11/24
Lairesse, G. 1806/11/24
Lairesse, Jan 1806/11/24
Langendijk, D. 1806/11/24
Metsu 1806/11/24
Molenaer, Klaes 1806/11/24
Molijn 1806/11/24
Monogrammist AX 1806/11/24
Monogrammist P.M. 1806/11/24
Neeffs, P. (I) 1806/11/24
Neer, E. 1806/11/24
Nijmegen, D. 1806/11/24
Nijmegen, G. 1806/11/24
Ommeganck, B. 1806/11/24
Ostade, A. 1806/11/24
Palamedesz., A. 1806/11/24
Pennus 1806/11/24
Poel, E. 1806/11/24
Poorter, W. 1806/11/24
Potter, Paulus 1806/11/24
Potuyl 1806/11/24
Prins, J.H. 1806/11/24
Regemorter, P. 1806/11/24
Roepel, C. 1806/11/24
Roestraeten 1806/11/24
Romeyn 1806/11/24
Ruisdael, J. 1806/11/24
Ruysdael, S. 1806/11/24
Saenredam, P.J. 1806/11/24
Sages 1806/11/24
Schenis, W. 1806/11/24
Sonje, J.G. 1806/11/24
Sorgh, H.M. 1806/11/24
Staveren, J.A. 1806/11/24
Storck, J. 1806/11/24
Swanevelt 1806/11/24
Tol, D. 1806/11/24
Verbeeck, P.C. 1806/11/24
Verelst 1806/11/24
Vermeer, Jan (II) 1806/11/24
Vitringa 1806/11/24
Vlieger, S. 1806/11/24
Vrancx 1806/11/24
Vries, Hans 1806/11/24
Weenix 1806/11/24
Werff, P. 1806/11/24
Wigmana, G. 1806/11/24
Witte, E. 1806/11/24
Wouwerman, P. 1806/11/24
Wyck, T. 1806/11/24

Mutters
Carree, Hend. (I) 1805/10/09

Myn, see mijn

N.
Beerstraten, J. 1803/12/12
Eeckhout, G. 1803/12/12
Morel, Jan Evert 1803/12/12
Voorhout, J. (I) 1803/12/12

N. (1804, August 8)
Horemans, J.J. (I) 1804/08/08

N. (1805, July 10)
Backhuysen 1805/07/10
Bronchorst, J.G. 1805/07/10
Dusart, Corn. 1805/07/10
Elliger, O. (II) 1805/07/10
Everdingen, A. 1805/07/10
Goltzius, Hend. 1805/07/10
Hackaert, J. 1805/07/10
Heem, J.D. 1805/07/10
Holbein, H. (II) 1805/07/10
Horemans, J.J. (I) 1805/07/10
Huysum, Jan 1805/07/10
Lairesse, G. 1805/07/10
Looten, J. 1805/07/10
Molenaer, J.M. 1805/07/10
Molenaer, Klaes 1805/07/10
Moucheron, I. 1805/07/10
Palamedesz., A. 1805/07/10
Savery, R. 1805/07/10
Stoffe 1805/07/10
Vleughels, N. 1805/07/10

N. (1810, June 20)
Anonymous 1810/06/20
Avercamp, H. 1810/06/20
Borch, G. ter (II) 1810/06/20
Goyen 1810/06/20
Heeremans, Thos. 1810/06/20
Martszen, J. (II) 1810/06/20
Molenaer, Klaes 1810/06/20
Netscher, Casp. 1810/06/20
Peeters, B. (I) 1810/06/20
Roghman, R. 1810/06/20
Ruysdael, S. 1810/06/20
Saftleven, C. 1810/06/20
Steen, J. 1810/06/20
Toorenvliet, J. 1810/06/20
Verboom, A.H. 1810/06/20

Nagtegaal
Potter, Paulus 1802/09/18
Thier, B.H. 1802/09/18

Neelmeyer
Dalens, Dirck 1810/05/22

Nes
Compe, Jan ten 1807/06/10

Netscher
perhaps the Rotterdam painter Wilhelm Adriaan Netscher, who, however, is supposed to have been baptized in 1791
Janson, J. 1808/06/06
Netscher, Casp. 1808/06/06

Neufville, de
Anonymous 1802/12/13

Neyt
Anonymous 1801/08/19

Nibbelinck, F.R.E.
d. ca.1804; preacher in Dubbeldam
Anonymous 1805/06/24
Backhuysen 1805/06/24
Both, J. 1805/06/24
Boucher 1805/06/24
Burg (Burgh) 1805/06/24
Cuypers (Kuypers) 1805/06/24
Droochsloot, J.C. 1805/06/24
Gulck, A. 1805/06/24
La Haye, R. 1805/06/24
Mieris, W. 1805/06/24
Poelenburgh, C. 1805/06/24
Savery, R. 1805/06/24
Storck, Abr. 1805/06/24
Toorenvliet, J. 1805/06/24

Niekerk, J.
resident of Utrecht
Anonymous-Modern 1802/09/21
Asch, P.J. van 1802/09/21
Bloemen 1802/09/21
Droochsloot, J.C. 1802/09/21
Janson, J. 1802/09/21

Kessel, J. (III) 1808/06/13
Monogrammist G.V.H. 1808/06/13
Moucheron, F. 1808/06/13
Rombouts 1808/06/13

Ostie
Anonymous 1802/09/21

Otte, see Otten

Otten, Theodorus van
dealer and auctioneer in Amsterdam
Cranach, L. (I) 1810/05/22
Jordaens, J. (I) 1810/05/22
Mytens, Jan 1810/05/22
Palamedesz., A. 1801/08/19
Vinckeboons, D. 1810/05/22
Wigmana, J. 1810/05/22
Wtewael, J. 1810/05/22

Ottens, see Otten

Overhorst
Anonymous 1803/04/20

Oyens, Hendrik
dealer active in Amsterdam, partner of Lourens Joukes, q.v.
Lingelbach 1808/10/28
Moni, L. de 1808/10/28
Schalcken 1808/10/28
Steen, J. 1808/10/28

P.
Breenbergh 1806/08/13

P. (1805, July 10)
Anonymous 1805/07/10
Brouwer, Adr. 1805/07/10
Croos, P. 1805/07/10
Honthorst, G. 1805/07/10
Martszen, J. (II) 1805/07/10
Molenaer, J.M. 1805/07/10
Pee 1805/07/10
Rietschoof, H. 1805/07/10
Sorgh, H.M. 1805/07/10
Vries, R. 1805/07/10

P. (1807, August 26)
supposedly a descendant of the painter Jan van Gool, 1685-1763/65
Gool, Jan 1807/08/26

P. (1808, November 28)
Anonymous 1808/11/28

P. (1809, June 13)
Ast 1809/06/13
Brekelencam, Q. 1809/06/13
Laquy, W.J. 1809/06/13

Pakker, G.
Goltzius, Hend. 1810/10/11

Pakker, Hijman
dealer active in Amsterdam
Anonymous 1803/12/12
Anonymous 1805/07/03
Anonymous 1805/07/10
Anonymous 1810/10/11
Anonymous-Modern 1803/04/27
Aquila, P. 1803/04/27
Brekelencam, Q. 1803/12/12
Brueghel, P. 1803/12/12
Camphuysen, R. 1805/07/03
Heeremans, Thos. 1803/12/12
Lingelbach 1810/10/11
Loutherbourg 1803/12/12
Martszen, J. (II) 1808/10/28
Molenaer, Klaes 1810/10/11
Moni, L. de 1803/12/12
Monogrammist E.V.N. 1810/10/11
Moucheron, F. 1810/10/11
Neer, A. 1803/12/12
Ochtervelt 1803/12/12
Ruysdael, S. 1803/12/12
Steen, J. 1810/10/11
Teniers, D. (II) 1805/07/03
Valck (Valk) 1810/10/11
Verboom, A.H. 1810/10/11
Wyck, T. 1805/07/03

Pakker, Levy
dealer active in Amsterdam
Andrea del Sarto 1803/04/27
Anonymous 1801/10/06
Anonymous 1802/02/16
Anonymous 1802/02/23
Anonymous 1802/05/05
Anonymous 1802/06/16
Anonymous 1802/06/28
Anonymous 1802/09/06
Anonymous 1802/09/29
Anonymous 1802/12/13
Anonymous 1803/04/20
Anonymous 1803/04/27
Anonymous 1803/06/20
Anonymous 1803/08/01
Anonymous 1803/08/17
Anonymous 1803/09/07
Anonymous 1803/12/12
Anonymous 1804/02/27
Anonymous 1804/05/07
Anonymous 1804/08/08
Anonymous 1804/12/10
Anonymous 1805/07/03
Anonymous 1805/07/10
Anonymous 1805/12/16
Anonymous 1806/05/05
Anonymous 1806/08/13
Anonymous 1806/11/24
Anonymous 1807/08/26
Anonymous 1807/08/27
Anonymous 1808/06/13
Anonymous 1808/08/23
Anonymous 1808/10/28
Anonymous 1808/11/28
Anonymous 1809/04/22
Anonymous 1809/06/13
Anonymous 1809/07/19
Anonymous 1810/05/22
Anonymous 1810/06/20
Anonymous 1810/07/26
Anonymous 1810/08/06
Anonymous 1810/10/11
Anonymous-Modern 1803/04/27
Apshoven 1805/07/10
Asch, P.J. van 1802/05/05
Asch, P.J. van 1809/06/13
Asselyn 1802/12/13
Asselyn 1810/06/20
Ast 1802/02/16
Ast 1810/10/11
Avercamp, H. 1802/09/06
Avercamp, H. 1807/08/26
Avercamp, H. 1810/06/20
Backer, J.A. 1807/08/26
Backhuysen 1802/09/29
Backhuysen 1805/07/10
Backhuysen 1808/08/23
Balen 1806/05/05
Bassen 1802/05/05
Beeldemaker, A.C. 1804/08/08
Beelds, J. 1809/06/13
Beer, J. 1804/05/07
Beerstraten 1805/07/10
Beerstraten, J. 1810/10/11
Bega 1809/06/13
Begeyn 1803/12/12
Bellevois 1806/05/05
Bellucci 1803/09/07
Bemmel 1806/08/13
Berchem, N.P. 1805/07/10
Berckheyde 1802/12/13
Berckheyde, G. 1810/08/06
Berckheyde, J. 1804/02/27
Berckheyde, J. 1805/07/10
Berckheyde, J. 1806/11/24
Berg (Bergh) 1804/02/27
Besanger, S. 1802/09/29
Beyeren 1804/02/27
Beyeren 1808/08/23
Bisschop, Abr. 1810/10/11
Blanckerhoff 1805/07/10
Bleeker, A. 1806/05/05
Blinkvliet, M. 1807/08/26
Bloemaert 1804/02/27
Bloemaert 1810/10/11
Bloemaert, A. 1806/05/05
Bloemaert, A. 1808/08/23
Bloemaert, A. 1810/06/20
Bloemen 1810/07/26
Bloemen, Nor. 1802/02/16
Bol, F. 1805/12/16
Borch, G. ter (II) 1804/08/08
Borch, G. ter (II) 1805/07/03
Borssom 1803/12/12
Borssom 1805/07/03
Boucher 1805/07/10
Boudewyns 1810/07/26
Bout, P. 1810/07/26
Brakenburg 1805/07/03
Brakenburg 1805/07/10
Brakenburg 1805/12/16
Bramer 1806/11/24
Brekelencam, Q. 1809/06/13
Bril, P. 1802/09/06
Broeck, E. 1809/06/13
Brouwer, Adr. 1807/08/26
Bruegel, P. (I) 1807/08/26
Brueghel 1805/12/16
Brueghel 1810/06/20
Brueghel, J. (I) 1802/12/13
Brueghel, J. (I) 1805/07/03
Brueghel, J. (I) 1808/08/23
Brueghel, J. (I) 1809/06/13
Brueghel, J. (I) 1810/10/11
Burg, Dirk 1802/09/06
Cabbaey 1806/05/05
Cabel, A. 1810/10/11
Camphuysen, D. 1806/08/13
Canaletto 1808/08/23
Carree, M. 1805/07/10
Casanova, F. 1803/04/27
Casanova, F. 1810/07/26
Cignani, C. 1803/04/27
Codanelli, P. 1804/08/08
Colonia, A. 1806/11/24
Coxie, Ant. 1806/08/13
Cranach, L. (I) 1802/09/06
Croos, A. 1806/08/13
Croos, P. 1802/05/05
Croos, P. 1805/07/03
Croos, W. 1810/06/20
Cuylenborch, A. 1806/08/13
Cuylenburg, C. 1803/04/20
Cuyp, J.A. 1806/11/24
Dalens, Dirck 1810/06/20
Delen 1809/06/13
Denner, B. 1808/08/23
Diepenbeeck, A.J. 1804/08/08
Diepenbeeck, A.J. 1810/10/11
Does 1802/12/13
Dregt, J. 1810/08/06
Dregt, J. 1810/10/11
Drielst, E. 1808/11/28
Droochsloot, J.C. 1803/12/12
Droochsloot, J.C. 1810/06/20
Droochsloot, J.C. 1810/08/06
Dubbels, H. 1806/08/13
Dubois, G. 1805/12/16
Dubois, G. 1810/06/20
Dujardin, K. 1806/08/13
Dyck, Anth. van 1805/12/16
Dyck, Anth. van 1806/08/13
Ekels, Jan (I) 1805/12/16
Elliger, O. (II) 1802/06/28
Elliger, O. (II) 1810/10/11
Essen, C. 1803/09/07
Essen, C. 1807/08/26
Everdingen, A. 1804/05/07
Everdingen, A. 1805/07/10
Everdingen, A. 1810/10/11
Fargue, Maria la 1805/07/10
Fargue, P.C. 1804/05/07
Fargue, P.C. 1809/06/13
Filippo Napoletano 1810/07/26
Flinck 1802/02/16
Francken, Frans (II) 1805/07/03
Fyt 1802/12/13
Gael, B. 1802/12/13
Gael, B. 1805/07/10
Gael, B. 1805/12/16
Gael, B. 1808/11/28
Genoels, Abr. 1810/07/26
German 1810/05/22
Goyen 1802/06/16
Goyen 1804/08/08
Goyen 1805/12/16
Goyen 1809/06/13
Goyen 1810/06/20
Graat 1802/09/06
Grebber, F.P. 1804/08/08
Hackaert, J. 1805/07/10
Hals, D. 1808/06/13
Hals, F. (I) 1806/11/24
Heda 1803/04/20
Heda, G.W. 1802/06/28
Heem 1807/08/26
Heem, David 1810/10/11
Heem, G. 1805/07/10
Heem, J.D. 1802/12/13
Heemskerck 1810/10/11
Heemskerck, B. 1802/09/06
Heemskerck, B. 1805/07/03
Heeremans, Thos. 1802/12/13
Heeremans, Thos. 1804/02/27
Heeremans, Thos. 1806/11/24
Heeremans, Thos. 1807/08/26
Helst, B. 1806/05/05
Heusch 1802/12/13
Heusch, Jacob 1810/06/20
Hoet, G. (I) 1805/07/03
Hoet, G. (I) 1807/08/26
Holbein, H. (II) 1804/02/27
Hondecoeter, G. 1805/07/10
Honthorst, G. 1802/12/13
Honthorst, G. 1806/08/13
Hooch, C. 1807/08/26
Hooch, P. 1806/05/05
Hoogerheyden, E. 1807/08/26
Hoogstraten, S. 1804/08/08
Horemans, J.J. (I) 1803/04/20
Horemans, J.J. (I) 1806/05/05
Huysmans, C. 1805/12/16
Italian 1802/09/29
Italian 1802/12/13
Italian 1804/05/07
Italian 1804/08/08
Italian 1805/12/16
Italian 1807/08/26
Italian 1808/11/28
Janson, J. 1809/09/06
Janson, J. 1810/10/11
Jordaens, J. (I) 1802/09/29
Jordaens, J. (I) 1806/08/13
Jordaens, J. (I) 1810/10/11
Keirincx, Alex. 1809/06/13
Keirincx, Alex. 1810/06/20
Kessel, J. (III) 1805/07/03
Kessel, J. (III) 1806/05/05
Keyser, Thos. de 1806/05/05
Kips, J. 1810/10/11
Kloet, J. 1805/07/10
Koller, J.J. 1802/12/13
Koninck, Jacob 1802/12/13
Kruger, Jac. 1804/05/07
La Baze 1803/12/12

La Croix, P. 1809/06/13
Laer, P. 1802/12/13
Laer, P. 1810/05/22
La Haye, R. 1810/10/11
Lairesse, Jan 1806/11/24
Lairesse, Jan 1807/08/26
Lastman, P.P. 1802/06/28
Leent 1802/12/13
Leeuw, Pieter 1805/07/10
Liender, Pieter van 1810/08/06
Liender, Pieter van 1810/10/11
Lingelbach 1805/07/03
Lingelbach 1806/05/05
Lingelbach 1809/09/06
Liss 1802/12/13
Lundens 1802/05/05
Lundens 1802/12/13
Lundens 1805/07/03
Maas, J. 1808/11/28
Maes, D. 1810/08/06
Maes, N. 1802/05/05
Maes, N. 1810/10/11
Marseus, O. 1802/06/28
Marseus, O. 1805/12/16
Marseus, O. 1807/04/13
Martszen, J. (II) 1802/05/05
Martszen, J. (II) 1803/09/07
Martszen, J. (II) 1805/07/10
Martszen, J. (II) 1806/05/05
Martszen, J. (II) 1810/06/20
Martszen, J. (II) 1810/10/11
Meulen, A.F. 1810/07/26
Miereveld, Jan 1804/02/27
Mieris, F. (I) 1802/09/06
Mieris, W. 1805/07/10
Mieris, W. 1808/08/23
Mij, H. 1806/05/05
Molenaer, J.M. 1802/06/28
Molenaer, J.M. 1802/09/06
Molenaer, J.M. 1802/12/13
Molenaer, J.M. 1803/04/20
Molenaer, J.M. 1803/08/01
Molenaer, J.M. 1803/08/17
Molenaer, J.M. 1806/08/13
Molenaer, J.M. 1807/08/26
Molenaer, J.M. 1810/10/11
Molenaer, Klaes 1805/07/10
Molenaer, Klaes 1806/08/13
Molenaer, Klaes 1806/11/24
Molenaer, Klaes 1810/06/20
Molijn 1802/12/13
Molijn 1803/06/20
Molijn 1805/12/16
Molijn 1806/11/24
Molijn 1810/06/20
Molijn 1810/10/11
Mommers, H. 1804/12/10
Mommers, H. 1805/07/10
Mommers, H. 1808/11/28
Momper, J. (II) 1808/08/23
Momper, J. (II) 1809/06/13
Monogrammist AX 1806/11/24
Monogrammist H.D.M. 1805/07/10
Monogrammist L.T. 1807/08/26
Monogrammist P. 1802/12/13
Monogrammist V.D. 1805/07/10
Moreelse, P. 1806/08/13
Moucheron 1810/10/11
Moucheron, F. 1809/06/13
Moucheron, F. 1810/06/20
Moucheron, F. 1810/10/11
Moucheron, I. 1805/07/10
Moucheron, I. 1809/09/06
Myn, H. 1802/12/13
Neeffs, P. (I) 1803/08/01
Neer, A. 1805/07/10
Neranus, A. 1810/10/11
Nicodemo, Aug. 1802/06/28
Oolen, Adr. 1802/12/13
Os, J. 1805/07/03
Ostade 1804/02/27
Ostade, A. 1806/11/24
Ostade, I. 1805/07/03
Ostade, I. 1810/05/22
Oudenrogge, J.D. 1807/08/26
Ouwater, J. 1802/06/28
Palamedesz., A. 1805/07/03
Palamedesz., P. (I) 1808/08/23
Palamedesz., P. (I) 1810/10/11
Pee 1805/07/03
Peeters, B. (I) 1805/07/03
Pennus 1806/11/24
Poel, E. 1805/12/16
Poelenburgh, C. 1803/12/12
Porcellis, Jan 1802/12/13
Porcellis, Jan 1809/06/13
Porcellis, Jan 1810/10/11
Prins, J.H. 1806/08/13
Pynacker 1810/06/20
Pynas, J. 1802/05/05
Raffaello Santi 1803/04/27
Redeker, J. 1802/09/06
Rembrandt 1807/08/26
Rembrandt 1810/10/11
Roghman, R. 1802/09/06
Roghman, R. 1804/05/07
Rombouts 1805/12/16
Romeyn 1807/08/26
Roos 1802/12/13
Roos 1806/08/13
Roos, P.P. 1802/02/16
Rosa, Fr. 1803/04/27
Rosa, S. 1802/02/16
Rubens 1804/02/27
Rubens 1804/05/07
Rubens 1805/12/16
Rubens 1808/11/28
Rubens 1810/10/11
Ruisdael, J. 1810/10/11
Ruysdael, S. 1804/02/27
Ruysdael, S. 1804/12/10
Ruysdael, S. 1805/07/10
Ruysdael, S. 1806/11/24
Ruysdael, S. 1807/04/13
Saftleven, C. 1803/09/07
Saftleven, H. 1805/07/03
Saftleven, H. 1805/12/16
Saftleven, H. 1806/05/05
Saftleven, H. 1809/06/13
Saftleven, H. 1810/10/11
Santvoort, Pieter 1806/08/13
Savery, R. 1804/08/08
Savery, R. 1805/07/10
Savery, R. 1806/08/13
Schellinks, Daniel 1809/06/13
Schendel, B. 1810/06/20
Schenis, W. 1806/11/24
Schütz 1809/06/13
Sibilla, G. 1805/07/03
Silo, A. 1803/09/07
Silo, A. 1803/12/12
Silo, A. 1804/05/07
Silo, A. 1805/07/10
Silo, A. 1806/08/13
Smit, Aernout 1809/06/13
Smit, Aernout 1810/06/20
Sonje, J.G. 1806/11/24
Sorgh, H.M. 1806/11/24
Spranger, B. 1804/02/27
Steen, J. 1805/07/03
Steen, J. 1806/05/05
Steenwyck, Hend. 1802/12/13
Stoffe 1804/02/27
Stoffe 1805/07/10
Stoffe 1806/08/13
Storck, Abr. 1802/12/13
Storck, Abr. 1805/07/03
Storck, Abr. 1805/07/10
Storck, Abr. 1806/05/05
Storck, J. 1806/11/24
Straaten 1810/06/20
Swanevelt 1804/08/08
Teniers, D. (II) 1805/12/16
Teniers, D. (II) 1806/05/05
Teniers, D. (II) 1807/08/26
Teniers, D. (II) 1808/10/28
Teniers, D. (II) 1810/06/20
Terwesten, Mat. 1802/12/13
Tieling, L. 1802/02/16
Tintoretto, J. 1802/12/13
Toorenvliet, A. 1807/08/26
Toorenvliet, A. 1809/06/13
Troost, J.H. 1805/07/10
Troost, J.H. 1807/08/26
Valck (Valk) 1810/10/11
Vas, P. 1804/08/08
Velde, E. (I) 1803/04/20
Velde, E. (I) 1806/08/13
Velde, W. 1802/02/23
Velde, W. 1802/12/13
Velde, W. 1805/12/16
Venne, A.P. 1805/07/03
Verbeeck, P.C. 1806/11/24
Verbeeck, P.C. 1807/08/26
Verboom, A.H. 1802/05/05
Verboom, W.H. 1803/12/12
Verelst, S. 1809/06/13
Veronese 1810/07/26
Verschuring, H. 1806/05/05
Verschuring, H. 1808/08/23
Verspronck, Joh. 1804/05/07
Vertangen 1808/08/23
Vertangen 1810/06/20
Victors, Jan 1806/05/05
Victors, Jan 1806/08/13
Victors, Jan 1808/11/28
Vinckeboons, D. 1809/06/13
Vinne, V.L. (I) 1802/09/06
Visscher, C. (II) 1805/07/03
Vitringa 1805/07/10
Vitringa 1806/11/24
Vlieger, S. 1805/12/16
Vlieger, S. 1806/05/05
Vlieger, S. 1806/08/13
Vliet, H.C. 1804/08/08
Vois, Ary de 1810/08/06
Vonck, J. 1803/04/27
Vrancx 1805/12/16
Vrancx 1806/11/24
Vrancx 1810/08/06
Vries, Hans 1806/11/24
Vries, R. 1802/12/13
Waldorp, J.G. 1809/09/06
Watteau, J.A. 1802/12/13
Weenix 1802/05/05
Weenix 1805/12/16
Weenix 1810/10/11
Weenix, J.B. 1802/09/06
Werff, P. 1806/11/24
Wet, Gerrit de 1803/08/01
Wet, J.W. 1802/12/13
Wet, J.W. 1805/07/10
Wet, J.W. 1807/08/26
Wiertz, H.F. 1810/10/11
Wigmana, G. 1802/12/13
Wigmana, G. 1809/06/13
Wijnants 1805/07/10
Wijnants 1805/12/16
Wijnants 1809/04/22
Willaerts 1802/05/05
Willaerts 1802/06/28
Willaerts, Adam 1802/12/13
Willaerts, C. 1810/10/11
Wit, Jacob de 1804/05/07
Wit, Jacob de 1804/08/08
Wit, Jacob de 1810/10/11
Withoos, M. 1802/05/05
Withoos, M. 1805/07/03
Witmont, H. 1804/08/08
Witte, E. 1806/11/24
Wolfaerts, J.B. 1806/08/13
Wouwerman 1806/05/05
Wouwerman, P. 1802/09/06
Wtewael, J. 1804/08/08
Wulfraet 1802/09/06
Wyck, T. 1804/02/27
Wyck, T. 1805/07/03
Wyck, T. 1806/05/05
Wyck, T. 1806/08/13
Wyck, T. 1807/04/13
Wyck, T. 1809/06/13
Zeemann 1805/07/10
Zeemann 1806/08/13

Palmhoff
Hondecoeter, G. 1803/04/20
Moucheron, I. 1804/08/08
Willaerts, A. 1803/04/20

Pals, Gerrit van der
1754–1839; amateur draftsman, etcher and dealer active in Rotterdam
Ulft 1810/03/26

Palthe
Palm, J. 1803/08/24

Palts, van der
Berckheyde, G. 1808/06/13

Panse, see Ponse

Pantijn
Anonymous 1810/06/20
Camphuysen, J. 1810/06/20
Molenaer, J.M. 1810/06/20
Palamedesz., P. (I) 1810/06/20
Vertangen 1810/06/20

Parees
Goyen 1802/11/01

Parker
Klomp 1804/04/28
Wit, Jacob de 1804/04/28

Parrach
Victors, Jan 1801/08/19

Pätte, see Putte

Peeters, see Pieterse

Peeterse, see Pieterse

Peetersen, Gerhardus Marinus
d. ca.1823; active in Middelburg
Anonymous 1803/10/10
Anonymous 1803/11/30
Anonymous 1804/06/18
Blieck 1803/11/30
Moni, L. de 1802/05/10

Pels
active in Middelburg
Anonymous 1803/10/10

Penning
probably the painter Nicolaas Lodewick Penning, 1764–1818
Jansen, R. 1809/07/25
Vlieger, S. 1809/07/25

Pérignon, Alexis-Nicolas
1785–1864; French painter, expert and dealer; son-in-law of A.J. Paillet
Velde, A. 1810/08/01
Wijnants 1810/08/01

Petersen, G.M., see Peetersen

Petit (Amsterdam)
Molenaer, J.M. 1803/04/20
Wigmana, G. 1803/04/20

Philip, L.
Velde, A. 1805/07/10

Philipse
Yong 1803/11/30

Pictura (Teekengenootschap)
drawing society, possibly the one in Dordrecht or The Hague
Hoogstraten, S. 1810/06/06
Scheffer, J.B. 1810/06/06

Pieterse
Anonymous 1804/08/08
Anonymous 1805/12/16
Anonymous 1807/08/26
Avont, P. 1807/08/26
Bruegel, P. (I) 1804/08/08
Glauber, J. 1804/08/08
Helst, B. 1804/08/08
Molenaer, J.M. 1807/08/26
Saftleven, H. 1804/08/08

Ploos (widow)
Graat 1802/05/05

Plucks, Johannes Antoni Augustinus
1786 or 1788–1837; miniaturist, copyist and lithographer
Anonymous 1803/06/20
Anonymous 1804/05/07
Bloot, P. 1803/06/20
Marseus, O. 1803/06/20
Molenaer, J.M. 1803/06/20

Plukkooy
Savery, R. 1803/08/24

Pluks, see Plucks

Plux, see Plucks

Poelman
Valken, H. 1806/08/20

Pompe van Meerdervoort
family residing near Dordrecht
Cuyp, A. 1806/08/20

Ponse
Besanger, S. 1809/07/25
Besters, A.J. 1809/07/25
Gool, Jan 1805/10/09
Gool, Jan 1809/07/25
Molenaer, Klaes 1809/07/25
Moritz, Louis 1809/07/25
Nieulandt, A. (I) 1802/05/24
Valois, J.F. 1809/07/25

Posthumus, Pieter
dealer and organizer of auctions in Amsterdam
Anonymous 1810/10/11
Berchem, N.P. 1810/10/11
Both, J. 1810/10/11
Bril, P. 1810/10/11
Brueghel, J. (I) 1810/10/11
Brugman, N. 1810/10/11
Coninxloo, G. 1810/10/11
Cuyp 1810/10/11
Diepenbeeck, A.J. 1810/10/11
Does, S. 1810/10/11
Dou 1810/10/11
Elsheimer, A. 1810/10/11
Griffier, R. 1810/10/11
Jordaens, J. (I) 1810/10/11
Maes, D. 1810/10/11
Melder, G. 1810/10/11
Metsu 1810/10/11
Miereveld, M. 1810/10/11
Molenaer, J.M. 1810/10/11
Moor, C. 1810/10/11
Neer, A. 1810/10/11
Oolen, Jan 1810/10/11
Potter, Paulus 1810/10/11
Pynacker 1810/10/11
Rubens 1810/10/11
Schalcken 1810/10/11
Slingeland, P.C. 1810/10/11
Teniers, D. (II) 1810/10/11
Tol, D. 1810/10/11
Vliet, H.C. 1810/10/11
Vrancx 1810/10/11
Vroom, H. 1810/10/11
Weenix, J.B. 1810/10/11

Pot, see also Pott

Pot, G. van der (relative of Gerrit van der Pot)
Nijmegen, G. 1808/06/06

Pot, Gerrit van der, Heer van Groeneveld
1732–1807; merchant and sugar refiner
Aelst, W. 1808/06/06
Anonymous 1807/10/29
Anonymous 1808/06/06
Backhuysen 1808/06/06
Bassano, J. 1808/06/06
Battem 1802/09/18
Battem 1808/06/06
Beerstraten, J. 1808/06/06
Bega 1808/06/06
Begeyn 1808/06/06
Berchem, N.P. 1808/06/06
Berckheyde, G. 1808/06/06
Bergen, D. 1808/06/06
Beyeren 1808/06/06
Bogdany 1808/06/06
Borch, G. ter (II) 1808/06/06
Both, J. 1802/09/18
Both, J. 1808/06/06
Brekelencam, Q. 1808/06/06
Brueghel, J. (I) 1808/06/06
Castiglione, G.B. 1808/06/06
Coclers, B. 1808/06/06
Coninck, D. 1808/06/06
Corvi 1808/06/06
Cuyp, A. 1808/06/06
Does, S. 1808/06/06
Dou 1808/06/06
Dubordieu, P. 1808/06/06
Ducq, Johan le 1808/06/06
Dujardin, K. 1808/06/06
Dürer 1808/06/06
Dusart, Corn. 1808/06/06
Dyck, Anth. van 1808/06/06
Eeckhout, G. 1808/06/06
Elliger, O. (II) 1808/06/06
Eyck, H. 1808/06/06
Eyck, J. 1808/06/06
Flinck 1808/06/06
Gael, B. 1808/06/06
Geel, Joost 1808/06/06
Goyen 1808/06/06
Groenewegen, G. 1808/06/06
Hackaert, J. 1808/06/06
Hagen, Joris 1808/06/06
Heem, J.D. 1808/06/06
Helst, B. 1808/06/06
Heusch, Wm. 1808/06/06
Heyden, J. 1808/06/06
Holbein, H. (II) 1808/06/06
Hondecoeter, M. 1808/06/06
Hooch, P. 1808/06/06
Huchtenburgh, Jan 1808/06/06
Huysum, Jan 1808/06/06
Janson, J. 1808/06/06
Kessel, J. (III) 1808/06/06
Kobell, H. 1808/06/06
Koninck, P. 1808/06/06
Langendijk, D. 1808/06/06
Lelie, A. 1808/06/06
Lingelbach 1808/06/06
Maes, N. 1808/06/06
Metsu 1808/06/06
Mieris, F. (I) 1808/06/06
Mieris, W. 1808/06/06
Mignon, A. 1808/06/06
Moeyaert, C. 1808/06/06
Molenaer, J.M. 1808/06/06
Moni, L. de 1808/06/06
Moor, C. 1808/06/06
Moreelse, P. 1808/06/06
Moucheron, F. 1808/06/06
Muys, Nic. 1808/06/06
Netscher, Casp. 1808/06/06
Nijmegen, G. 1808/06/06
Ochtervelt 1808/06/06
Ommeganck, B. 1808/06/06
Ostade, A. 1808/06/06
Ostade, I. 1808/06/06
Pimont, Jan 1808/06/06
Poel, E. 1808/06/06
Poelenburgh, C. 1808/06/06
Potter, Paulus 1802/09/18
Potter, Paulus 1808/06/06
Potter, Pieter de 1808/06/06
Pynacker 1808/06/06
Raffaello Santi 1808/06/06
Ribera 1808/06/06
Romeyn 1808/06/06
Ruisdael, J. 1808/06/06
Ruysdael, S. 1808/06/06
Saftleven, C. 1808/06/06
Saftleven, H. 1808/06/06
Schalcken 1808/06/06
Schellinks, W. 1808/06/06
Schouman, A. 1808/06/06
Schweickardt, H. 1808/06/06
Slingeland, P.C. 1808/06/06
Snyders, F. 1808/06/06
Sorgh, H.M. 1808/06/06
Steen, J. 1808/06/06
Steenwyck, Hend. 1808/06/06
Teniers, D. (II) 1808/06/06
Thier, B.H. 1802/09/18
Thier, B.H. 1808/06/06
Tischbein 1808/06/06
Valentin de Boulogne 1808/06/06
Velde, A. 1808/06/06
Velde, W. 1808/06/06
Verbeeck, P.C. 1808/06/06
Vermeer, Jan (III) 1808/06/06
Vrancx 1808/06/06
Weenix, J.B. 1808/06/06
Werff, A. 1808/06/06
Wijnants 1808/06/06
Wit, Jacob de 1808/06/06
Witte, E. 1808/06/06
Wouwerman, Ph. 1808/06/06
Wouwerman, Pieter 1808/06/06
Wtewael, J. 1808/06/06
Wyck, T. 1808/06/06

Pot, W. van der
Coclers, B. 1808/06/06
Metsu 1808/06/06

Pott, Rembertus
1772–1855; resident of Rotterdam
Anonymous 1808/06/06
Anonymous 1810/03/26
Anonymous 1810/08/06
Bassano 1810/06/06
Bega 1810/08/01
Brakenburg 1810/06/06
Castiglione, G.B. 1808/06/06
Cerquozzi 1810/08/10
Dusart, Corn. 1810/08/01
Gael, B. 1808/06/06
Geel, Joost 1808/06/06
Honthorst, G. 1810/06/06
Honthorst, G. 1810/08/06
Molenaer, J.M. 1810/08/01
Ostade, I. 1810/08/06
Sorgh, H.M. 1810/08/01
Steenwyck, Hend. 1808/06/06
Teniers, D. (II) 1810/06/06
Tischbein 1808/06/06
Tiziano 1810/08/06
Valentin de Boulogne 1808/06/06
Vliet, H.C. 1810/08/01
Werff, A. 1808/06/06
Wouwerman, Ph. 1810/06/06

Praine
Rembrandt 1807/06/10

Praison, see Praiston

Praiston
also spelled Preston, Priston and Praison
Anonymous 1806/08/20
Bloemaert, A. 1806/08/20
Holbein, H. (II) 1806/08/20
Hondecoeter, M. 1806/08/20
Maratti 1806/08/20
Moucheron, F. 1806/08/20
Querfurt, A. 1806/08/20
Rosenberg, F. 1806/08/20
Verschuring, H. 1806/08/20
Wijnants 1806/08/20

Pré, du, see Dupré

Pree, de, see Dupré

Preijer
Utrecht, Adr. 1809/06/13

Preijn
Storck, J. 1809/06/13

Priester
schoolmaster in Middelburg
Anonymous 1807/10/12
Poelenburgh, C. 1802/05/10

Pruijsenaar, see Pruyssenaar

Pruijsner, see Pruyssenaar

Pruijssenaar, see Pruyssenaar

Pruisenaar, see Pruyssenaar

Pruisse, see Pruyssenaar

Pruissenaar, see Pruyssenaar

Pruizenaar, see Pruyssenaar

Pruysenaar, see Pruyssenaar

Pruysnaar, see Pruyssenaar

Pruyssenaar, Roelof Meurs
active until 1804; organizer of auctions in the "Huis met de Hoofden" in Amsterdam; also amateur draftsman
Aelst, W. 1802/12/13
Alcock 1802/12/13
Anonymous 1801/03/16
Anonymous 1801/05/11
Anonymous 1801/08/19
Anonymous 1802/05/05
Anonymous 1802/06/16
Anonymous 1802/09/06
Anonymous 1802/12/13
Anonymous 1803/04/27
Anonymous 1803/08/01
Anonymous 1804/05/07
Anonymous 1804/08/08
Apshoven 1803/04/20
Asch, P.J. van 1801/05/11
Asselyn 1801/05/11

Asselyn 1802/12/13
Avercamp, H. 1802/12/13
Backhuysen 1801/03/16
Backhuysen 1801/10/06
Backhuysen 1801/10/19
Backhuysen 1802/05/05
Backhuysen 1802/12/13
Backhuysen 1804/05/07
Balen 1801/03/16
Balen, H. (I) 1802/06/16
Balen, H. (II) 1803/04/20
Beerstraten, J. 1801/06/10
Beerstraten, J. 1802/12/13
Beerstraten, Jan 1803/08/01
Beest, Sybrand 1803/08/01
Bega 1801/06/10
Bega 1802/12/13
Begeyn 1801/03/16
Begeyn 1801/08/19
Begeyn 1802/12/13
Begeyn 1803/08/17
Bemmel, J. 1802/12/13
Bent, J. 1802/02/16
Berchem, N.P. 1801/03/16
Berchem, N.P. 1801/05/11
Berchem, N.P. 1802/09/06
Berchem, N.P. 1803/08/01
Berckheyde 1801/03/16
Berckheyde 1802/12/13
Berckheyde, G. 1802/12/13
Berckheyde, G. 1804/05/07
Berckheyde, J. 1801/05/11
Bergen, D. 1801/05/11
Bergen, D. 1801/10/19
Berninck, H. 1802/12/13
Blaauw 1802/12/13
Blanckerhoff 1801/03/16
Blanckerhoff 1801/05/11
Bloemaert 1801/05/11
Bloemaert, A. 1801/03/16
Bloemen, P. 1802/09/29
Bloemen, P. 1802/12/13
Bol, F. 1801/04/13
Bol, F. 1801/06/10
Bol, F. 1803/08/17
Bola, F. 1801/03/16
Borch, G. ter (II) 1801/05/11
Borch, G. ter (II) 1803/06/20
Borch, G. ter (II) 1804/08/08
Borssom 1801/08/19
Borssom 1802/12/13
Both, A. 1801/06/10
Bout, P. 1803/08/01
Brakenburg 1802/05/05
Brakenburg 1802/12/13
Bramer 1802/12/13
Breenbergh 1801/05/11
Brekelencam, Q. 1801/08/19
Brekelencam, Q. 1804/05/07
Breydel, K. 1801/08/19
Broeck, E. 1802/12/13
Brouwer, Adr. 1802/12/13
Brouwer, J. 1801/05/11
Brueghel, J. (I) 1801/08/19
Brueghel, J. (I) 1802/06/16
Brueghel, J. (I) 1802/12/13
Brueghel, P. (II) 1802/12/13
Brussel, P. 1801/05/11
Camphuysen 1801/03/16
Camphuysen, R. 1802/12/13
Cappelle 1801/05/11
Cappelle 1801/06/10
Cappelle 1802/12/13
Caravaggio 1802/06/16
Carree 1804/08/08
Carree, Hend. (I) 1801/03/16
Carree, Hend. (I) 1802/12/13
Carree, M. 1802/12/13
Colaert, Johannes 1801/03/16
Compe, Jan ten 1802/12/13
Crayer, G. 1801/05/11
Cuylenborch, A. 1801/03/16
Cuyp, A. 1801/03/16
Cuyp, A. 1802/12/13
David 1803/04/27
Decker 1801/03/16
Decker, Frans 1801/03/16
Delen 1801/03/16
Denner, B. 1801/05/11
Does 1802/12/13
Domenichino 1803/04/27
Doudijns, W. 1801/06/10
Drielenburch, W. 1801/03/16
Drielst, E. 1801/03/16
Drielst, E. 1802/12/13
Dubbels, H. 1801/06/10
Dubbels, H. 1802/09/29
Dubbels, H. 1802/12/13
Dubois, J. 1802/05/05
Dubois, J. 1803/06/20
Ducq, Johan le 1801/08/19
Ducq, Johan le 1802/12/13
Dujardin, K. 1801/05/11
Dujardin, K. 1803/08/17
Dusart, Corn. 1801/06/10
Dusart, Corn. 1803/07/18
Eeckhout, G. 1801/05/11
Ekels, Jan (I) 1802/12/13
Ekels, Jan (II) 1801/08/19
Esselens, Jacob 1804/05/07
Essen, C. 1801/03/16
Essen, C. 1801/06/10
Essen, C. 1802/12/13
Essen, C. 1804/05/07
Everdingen, A. 1802/12/13
Everdingen, A. 1803/06/20
Everdingen, A. 1804/08/08
Everdingen, Cesar 1802/12/13
Fargue, Maria la 1801/03/16
Ferguson, Wm. 1801/03/16
Ferguson, Wm. 1802/12/13
Flinck 1802/12/13
Flinck 1804/08/08
Fock, Harm. 1801/08/19
Francken 1801/03/16
Fyt 1802/12/13
Gael, B. 1801/08/19
Gael, B. 1802/12/13
Gelder, A. 1801/05/11
Giorgione 1802/12/13
Giulio Romano 1803/04/27
Glimes, P. de 1802/12/13
Gool, Jan 1803/08/17
Goyen 1801/03/16
Goyen 1802/09/06
Goyen 1803/08/01
Grasdorp, W. 1802/12/13
Greenwood 1801/03/16
Grypmoed, G. 1801/03/16
Hackaert, J. 1801/04/13
Hackaert, J. 1801/08/19
Hals, F. (I) 1801/05/11
Hals, F. (I) 1802/12/13
Hansen, C.L. 1801/03/16
Hansen, C.L. 1802/12/13
Heem 1801/08/19
Heem 1801/10/19
Heem, J.D. 1802/09/29
Heem, J.D. 1802/12/13
Heem, J.D. 1803/06/20
Heeremans, Thos. 1802/12/13
Helst, B. 1801/08/19
Helst, B. 1802/12/13
Heusch 1802/12/13
Heusch, Jacob 1802/09/29
Heyden, J. 1801/04/13
Hobbema 1803/06/20
Hobbema 1804/05/07
Hoet, G. (I) 1802/06/16
Holsteijn, C. 1802/12/13
Hondecoeter, M. 1801/03/16
Hondecoeter, M. 1802/05/05
Hondecoeter, M. 1804/05/07
Honthorst, G. 1801/05/11
Honthorst, G. 1802/12/13
Hooch, P. 1801/08/19
Hooch, P. 1802/12/13
Hooch, P. 1804/05/07
Hoogstraten, Jan 1801/03/16
Horemans, J.J. (I) 1801/03/16
Huchtenburgh, Jan 1801/03/16
Huchtenburgh, Jan 1801/08/19
Huchtenburgh, Jan 1802/12/13
Huysmans, P.J. 1801/03/16
Huysum, Jan 1801/03/16
Huysum, Jan 1801/04/23
Huysum, Jan 1801/08/19
Huysum, Jan 1802/12/13
Huysum, Jan 1804/08/08
Italian 1802/12/13
Italian 1804/02/27
Janson, J. 1801/05/11
Janson, P. 1801/03/16
Jongh, W. 1801/03/16
Jordaens, J. (I) 1801/05/11
Jordaens, J. (I) 1802/05/05
Kalraet 1802/12/13
Keirincx, Alex. 1801/03/16
Keirincx, Alex. 1803/08/01
Kessel, J. (III) 1801/08/19
Kessel, J. (III) 1802/06/16
Kessel, J. (III) 1802/12/13
Keun, Hend. 1801/03/16
Klomp 1801/04/23
Klomp 1801/06/10
Klomp 1801/08/19
Klomp 1802/09/06
Koller, J.J. 1802/12/13
Koninck, Jacob 1802/12/13
Koninck, P. 1801/05/11
Kruger, Jac. 1801/03/16
Kuster 1801/08/19
Kuster, J. 1803/08/17
Laen, D.J. 1801/03/16
Lairesse, G. 1802/09/29
Lairesse, G. 1802/12/13
Lairesse, Jan 1802/05/05
Lastman, P.P. 1801/06/10
Lauwers, J.J. 1802/12/13
Leen, Willem van 1801/08/19
Leent 1802/12/13
Leeuw 1801/03/16
Limborch, H. 1801/05/11
Lingelbach 1801/04/13
Lingelbach 1801/05/11
Lingelbach 1801/06/10
Lingelbach 1801/08/19
Lingelbach 1802/12/13
Liss 1802/09/06
Liss 1802/12/13
Lubienietski, C. 1802/05/05
Ludick, L. 1803/08/01
Lundens 1801/08/19
Lundens 1802/12/13
Maes, D. 1802/02/16
Maes, D. 1804/05/07
Maes, D. 1804/08/08
Maes, N. 1801/03/16
Maes, N. 1801/05/11
Maes, N. 1802/12/13
Martelli 1801/03/16
Martszen, J. (II) 1801/03/16
Martszen, J. (II) 1802/12/13
Matthieu, C. 1801/05/11
Meijer, H. 1801/08/19
Metsu 1801/03/16
Metsu 1801/06/10
Metsu 1804/07/25
Mettenleiter, J.J. 1801/08/19
Meulen, A.F. 1801/08/19
Meyering, Alb. 1802/05/05
Miel 1801/03/16
Miereveld, M. 1802/05/05
Mieris, F. (I) 1802/09/29
Mieris, W. 1802/09/29
Mieris, W. 1803/04/20
Minderhout, H. 1801/08/19
Molenaer, J.M. 1801/03/16
Molenaer, J.M. 1801/05/11
Molenaer, J.M. 1801/08/19
Molenaer, J.M. 1802/05/05
Molenaer, J.M. 1802/12/13
Molenaer, J.M. 1803/08/17
Molenaer, Klaes 1801/03/16
Molenaer, Klaes 1801/05/11
Molenaer, Klaes 1801/06/10
Molenaer, Klaes 1802/12/13
Molijn 1801/03/16
Molijn 1802/12/13
Mommers, H. 1801/03/16
Mommers, H. 1802/12/13
Mommers, H. 1804/05/07
Mommers, H. 1804/08/08
Momper, J. (II) 1801/03/16
Momper, J. (II) 1802/12/13
Monogrammist G.V.L. 1801/03/16
Mortel 1801/05/11
Moucheron 1801/03/16
Moucheron, F. 1801/05/11
Moucheron, I. 1802/05/05
Mutscher, A. 1801/05/11
Myn, G. 1801/03/16
Myn, H. 1801/08/19
Myn, H. 1802/05/05
Myn, H. 1802/12/13
Neeffs, P. (I) 1801/05/11
Neer, A. 1801/03/16
Neer, A. 1802/05/05
Neer, A. 1802/12/13
Nepveu, J. 1801/06/10
Netscher, Casp. 1802/12/13
Nickelen 1801/08/19
Nickelen, Jan 1801/03/16
Nijmegen, G. 1801/06/10
Norblin, J.P. 1803/12/12
Ochtervelt 1802/09/06
Ommeganck, B. 1801/08/19
Oncker, H. 1802/05/05
Oolen, Adr. 1802/05/05
Oolen, Adr. 1802/12/13
Os, Geo. 1802/12/13
Os, Pieter G. 1801/03/16
Os, Pieter G. 1801/08/19
Ostade 1803/12/12
Ostade, A. 1801/03/16
Ostade, A. 1801/04/13
Ostade, A. 1801/05/11
Ostade, A. 1802/12/13
Ostade, I. 1801/08/19
Ouwater, Isaak 1801/08/19
Ouwater, J. 1801/08/19
Palamedesz., A. 1801/03/16
Palamedesz., A. 1801/08/19
Palthe, G.J. 1801/05/11
Parrocel 1801/08/19
Peeters, Cath. 1801/03/16
Perugino 1803/04/27
Poel, E. 1801/05/11
Poel, E. 1803/08/17
Porcellis, Jan 1801/05/11
Potter, Paulus 1801/05/11
Pourbus, F. (II) 1801/05/11
Quinkhard, J.M. 1801/03/16
Rande, Abraham 1801/03/16
Regemorter, P. 1802/12/13
Reigenbach, J. 1801/03/16
Rembrandt 1801/03/16
Rembrandt 1804/07/25
Rentinck, A. 1803/08/01
Ribera 1803/07/18
Rietschoof 1801/03/16
Ring, P. 1802/12/13
Roghman, R. 1801/08/19
Romeyn 1801/03/16
Romeyn 1801/05/11
Romeyn 1802/09/06
Roore 1801/08/19
Rosa, S. 1802/12/13

Wouwerman 1801/08/19
Wouwerman, Pieter 1801/08/19

Q. (1809, June 13)
Appel, J. (I) 1809/06/13
Bega 1809/06/13
Boucher 1809/06/13
Decker, C. 1809/06/13
Heeremans, Thos. 1809/06/13
Kessel, J. (III) 1809/06/13
Laquy, W.J. 1809/06/13
Linthorst 1809/06/13
Marseus, O. 1809/06/13
Smit, Aernout 1809/06/13
Thier, B.H. 1809/06/13
Velde, W. 1809/06/13
Zeemann 1809/06/13

Q. (1810, June 20)
Molenaer, J.M. 1810/06/20
Ochtervelt 1810/06/20
Porcellis, Jan 1810/06/20
Roghman, R. 1810/06/20
Verschuring, H. 1810/06/20
Vertangen 1810/06/20
Witte, E. 1810/06/20

Q. (1810, August 6)
Anonymous 1810/08/06
Lingelbach 1810/08/06
Wyntrack, D. 1810/08/06

Quin, see Quinting

Quinting (relative of Pieter Quinting)
Bisschop, Abr. 1810/07/23
Velde, E. (I) 1810/07/23

Quinting, Pieter
1770-ca.1810; merchant in Dordrecht
Anonymous 1810/07/23
Beeldemaker 1810/07/23
Bisschop, Abr. 1810/07/23
Borman, Joh. 1810/07/23
Bout, P. 1810/07/23
Brekelencam, Q. 1810/07/23
Croos 1810/07/23
Cuyp, A. 1810/07/23
Cuyp, B. 1810/07/23
Cuyp, J.G. 1810/07/23
Diepraem 1810/07/23
Does 1810/07/23
Dyck, Anth. van 1810/07/23
Everdingen, A. 1810/07/23
Gelder, A. 1810/07/23
Goyen 1810/07/23
Heem, J.D. 1810/07/23
Heeremans, Thos. 1810/07/23
Hofman, P. 1810/07/23
Holsteijn, C. 1810/07/23
Houbraken, Arn. 1810/07/23
Hulst 1810/07/23
Hulst, Fr. 1810/07/23
Jordaens, J. (I) 1810/07/23
Keller, J.H. (II) 1810/07/23
Lamme, A. 1810/07/23
Lelienbergh 1810/07/23
Maes, N. 1810/07/23
Marseus, O. 1810/07/23
Molijn 1810/07/23
Monogrammist A.S. 1810/07/23
Monogrammist A.V.B. 1810/07/23
Monogrammist J.P. 1810/07/23
Monogrammist W.G. 1810/07/23
Moucheron 1810/07/23
Ostade 1810/07/23
Ostade, I. 1810/07/23
Ponse, Joris 1810/07/23
Rembrandt 1810/07/23
Rombouts 1810/07/23
Saftleven, C. 1810/07/23
Saftleven, H. 1810/07/23
Schalcken 1810/07/23
Scheffer, J.B. 1810/07/23
Schellinks 1810/07/23
Schouman, A. 1810/07/23
Steen, J. 1810/07/23
Storck, Abr. 1810/07/23
Velde, E. (I) 1810/07/23
Venne, A.P. 1810/07/23
Verboom, A.H. 1810/07/23
Vermeulen, A. 1810/07/23
Vermeulen, E. 1810/07/23
Wanum, Ary 1810/07/23
Withoos, M. 1810/07/23

R.
Anonymous 1801/03/16
Anonymous 1801/05/11
Anonymous 1802/05/05
Anonymous 1802/06/16
Anonymous 1803/04/27
Asch, P.J. van 1801/05/11
Backhuysen 1801/03/16
Backhuysen 1801/10/06
Backhuysen 1802/05/05
Balen, H. (II) 1803/04/20
Brakenburg 1802/05/05
Camphuysen 1801/03/16
Dubois, J. 1802/05/05
Dujardin, K. 1801/05/11
Giorgione 1802/12/13
Hackaert, J. 1801/08/19
Hals, F. (I) 1801/05/11
Heem 1801/08/19
Hondecoeter, M. 1802/05/05
Horemans, J.J. (I) 1801/03/16
Huchtenburgh, Jan 1802/12/13
Italian 1804/02/27
Kessel, J. (III) 1802/06/16
Lairesse, Jan 1802/05/05
Leen, Willem van 1801/08/19
Lingelbach 1801/05/11
Lubienietski, C. 1802/05/05
Maes, N. 1801/05/11
Meulen, A.F. 1801/08/19
Meyering, Alb. 1802/05/05
Miel 1801/03/16
Mieris, W. 1803/04/20
Monogrammist J.R. 1801/08/19
Moucheron, I. 1802/05/05
Myn, H. 1802/05/05
Neer, A. 1802/05/05
Oncker, H. 1802/05/05
Oolen, Adr. 1802/05/05
Ostade, A. 1801/05/11
Parrocel 1801/08/19
Poel, E. 1801/05/11
Potter, Paulus 1801/05/11
Pourbus, F. (II) 1801/05/11
Ruisdael, J. 1802/05/05
Steen, J. 1802/05/05
Stella, Jac. 1803/04/27
Storck, Abr. 1801/08/19
Teniers, D. (II) 1801/05/11
Velde, W. 1801/05/11
Verelst, Joh. 1802/05/05
Versteeg 1801/08/19
Voorhout, J. (I) 1802/05/05
Vrancx 1803/04/20
Weenix 1801/08/19
Werff, A. 1801/05/11
Wijnants 1801/05/11
Witte, E. 1802/12/13
Wyntrack, D. 1802/06/16
Zuccari, F. 1803/04/20

R. (1802, May 5)
Berckheyde, J. 1802/05/05

R. (1803, August 1)
Dupré, Daniel 1803/08/01
Teniers, D. (II) 1803/08/01

R. (1808, August 23)
Anonymous 1808/08/23
Leeuw 1808/08/23
Wijnants 1808/08/23

R. (1809, April 17)
Anonymous 1809/04/17
Asselyn 1809/04/17
Dubbels, H. 1809/04/17
Juncker, Jus. 1809/04/17
Laer, P. 1809/04/17
Molenaer, J.M. 1809/04/17
Molijn 1809/04/17
Prins, J.H. 1809/04/17
Storck, Abr. 1809/04/17
Vermeulen, A. 1809/04/17
Vollerdt, J.C. 1809/04/17
Vries, R. 1809/04/17
Wijnants 1809/04/17

R. (1810, May 22)
Anonymous 1810/05/22
Bent, J. 1810/05/22
Besters, C. 1810/05/22
Honthorst, G. 1810/05/22
Koller, J.J. 1810/05/22
Molenaer, J.M. 1810/05/22
Molenaer, Klaes 1810/05/22
Monogrammist C.V.M. 1810/05/22
Mytens, Jan 1810/05/22
Ostade, A. 1810/05/22
Porcellis, Jan 1810/05/22
Sondervan, J. 1810/05/22
Torunia, R. 1810/05/22
Wijnants 1810/05/22

R., D. van
Anonymous 1801/06/13
Begeyn 1801/06/13
Borch, G. ter (II) 1801/06/13
Carree, Hend. (I) 1801/06/13
Cornelisz. van Haarlem 1801/06/13
Cuyp, J.G. 1801/06/13
Does, S. 1801/06/13
Dongen, Dionys 1801/06/13
Doomer, L. 1801/06/13
Dou 1801/06/13
Dyck, Anth. van 1801/06/13
Fargue, Maria la 1801/06/13
Gael, B. 1801/06/13
Goyen 1801/06/13
Griffier 1801/06/13
Griffier, J. (I) 1801/06/13
Hals, F. (I) 1801/06/13
Heusch, Wm. 1801/06/13
Honthorst, G. 1801/06/13
Italian 1801/06/13
Lingelbach 1801/06/13
Liss 1801/06/13
Lundens 1801/06/13
Man, Joost 1801/06/13
Mieris, F. (I) 1801/06/13
Mieris, F. (II) 1801/06/13
Mieris, W. 1801/06/13
Molenaer, J.M. 1801/06/13
Mommers, H. 1801/06/13
Mortel 1801/06/13
Moucheron 1801/06/13
Murillo 1801/06/13
Neer, A. 1801/06/13
Neer, E. 1801/06/13
Nellius, M. 1801/06/13
Netscher, Casp. 1801/06/13
Olis 1801/06/13
Os, J. 1801/06/13
Ostade, A. 1801/06/13
Ostade, I. 1801/06/13
Palamedesz., A. 1801/06/13
Potter, Paulus 1801/06/13
Rottenhammer, H. (I) 1801/06/13
Ruisdael, J. 1801/06/13
Slingeland, P.C. 1801/06/13
Sorgh, H.M. 1801/06/13
Steen, J. 1801/06/13
Stoffe 1801/06/13
Storck, Abr. 1801/06/13
Storck, J. 1801/06/13
Tempel, A.L. van den 1801/06/13
Teniers, D. (II) 1801/06/13
Weenix 1801/06/13
Wouwerman 1801/06/13
Wouwerman, P. 1801/06/13
Wyck, T. 1801/06/13

Raan, H.G. van
Aelst, W. 1809/04/22
Barbiers, P. 1809/04/22
Gool, Jan 1807/08/26
Janson, J. 1809/04/22

Rabe
Anonymous 1803/06/20

Rander
Gael, B. 1802/11/01

Randwijk
Anonymous 1802/11/01
Asselyn 1802/11/01
Burg, Adriaan 1802/11/01
Cuyp, B. 1802/11/01
Diepraem 1802/11/01
Gael, B. 1802/11/01
Goyen 1802/11/01
Honthorst, G. 1802/11/01
Janson, J. 1802/11/01
Jordaens, J. (I) 1802/11/01
Monogrammist J.S. 1802/11/01
Neer, A. 1802/11/01
Porcellis, Jan 1802/11/01
Saftleven, H. 1802/11/01
Storck, Abr. 1802/11/01
Verschuring, H. 1802/11/01

Randwyk, see Randwijk

Reeringh
Lingelbach 1801/08/19

Regters, see Rigters

Reigersman, Johan Pieter
d. ca.1803; military officer
Anonymous 1803/04/18
Brueghel, J. (I) 1803/04/18
Carree, Hend. (I) 1803/04/18
Hoecke, R. 1803/04/18
Molenaer, J.M. 1803/04/18
Monogrammist P.V.A. 1803/04/18
Netscher, Casp. 1803/04/18
Schweickardt, H. 1803/04/18
Steen, J. 1803/04/18

Reijdon, see Reydon

Reijers, see Rijers

Remmers, Johannes
b. 1741?; wallpaper manufacturer and dealer working in partnership with his son-in-law Abraham Bredius, q.v.
Anonymous 1809/04/22
Defrance, L. 1809/06/13
Gossaert 1810/08/01
Hondecoeter, M. 1809/04/22
Janson, J. 1809/04/22
Janson, J.C. 1804/12/10
Lamme, A. 1809/04/22
Laquy, W.J. 1809/04/22
Michaelis, G.J. 1809/06/13
Moni, L. de 1809/09/06
Os, Pieter G. 1809/04/22
Palthe 1809/04/22
Silo, A. 1809/04/22

Rijers, Willem
Teniers, D. (II) 1807/08/26

Rijfsnijder
Anonymous 1801/08/19
Anonymous 1802/12/13
Anonymous 1803/12/12
Anonymous 1804/02/27
Anonymous 1805/07/10
Anonymous 1809/04/22
Anonymous 1809/06/13
Anonymous-Antique 1803/04/27
Beesten, A.H. 1803/06/20
Berninck, H. 1802/12/13
Beschey 1803/06/20
Beschey, J. 1807/08/26
Bol, F. 1805/07/10
Brekelencam, Q. 1804/05/07
Brekelencam, Q. 1809/06/13
Broeck, E. 1802/12/13
Brueghel, J. (I) 1810/05/22
Compe, Jan ten 1805/07/10
Delen 1809/06/13
Fargue, Maria la 1802/06/28
Fargue, P.C. 1806/11/24
Fargue, P.C. 1809/06/13
Franck, J.W. 1804/02/27
Gool, Jan 1809/04/22
Gryef 1810/10/11
Heeremans, Thos. 1805/07/10
Hendriks, W. 1803/12/12
Herp, Wm. (I) 1801/03/16
Janson, J. 1802/05/05
Janson, J. 1805/12/16
Lastman, P.P. 1801/05/11
Lastman, P.P. 1810/10/11
Lauwers, J.J. 1809/04/22
Lundens 1809/06/13
Miereveld, M. 1803/12/12
Molijn 1804/05/07
Moni, L. de 1802/06/16
Nickelen, Jan 1806/05/05
Oolen, Adr. 1803/12/12
Ouwater, Isaak 1802/06/28
Palmer, Cornelis 1809/06/13
Poelenburgh, C. 1801/06/10
Ring, P. 1802/12/13
Roestraeten 1806/11/24
Schumacher, N. 1802/06/16
Silo, A. 1808/06/13
Silo, A. 1808/08/23
Silo, A. 1809/06/13
Smit, Aernout 1805/12/16
Storck 1809/06/13
Storck, Abr. 1809/06/13
Storck, J. 1804/08/08
Toorenburgh, G. 1810/05/22
Verbeeck, P.C. 1802/05/05
Vertangen 1803/09/07
Vois, Ary de 1804/08/08
Vrancx 1803/09/07
Weenix, J.B. 1808/08/23
Werff, P. 1801/03/16
Wet, J.W. 1802/09/06
Wigmana, G. 1809/06/13
Wijnants 1802/06/16
Wouwerman, P. 1802/12/13
Wouwerman, P. 1806/11/24
Wulfraet 1802/06/28
Zepp, C. 1809/06/13

Rijfsnyder, see Rijfsnijder

Rijnbergh
also spelled Rynbergh and Rynberg
Barbiers, P. 1806/05/05
Janson, J. 1806/08/13
Molenaer, J.M. 1806/08/13
Molenaer, Klaes 1806/05/05
Ostade, I. 1806/08/13
Ouwater, J. 1806/08/13
Strij, A. 1806/08/13
Velde, A. 1806/08/13
Vlieger, S. 1806/08/13

Rijnders, see Reynders

Rijp, Gebroeders van
Gerardus Constantinus and Petrus Eliza van Rijp, sons of Petrus Constantinus van Rijp, Rotterdam auctioneers
Anonymous 1810/03/26
Brugghen, Hendrick ter 1810/08/10
Honthorst, G. 1810/08/10
Kaukerk, P. 1810/08/10
Ruisdael, J. 1810/08/10
Vermeulen, A. 1808/06/11
Victors, Jac. 1810/08/10

Rijswijk, see Vos (Rijswijk)

Rijt
Coopse, P. 1801/10/06

Ringeling, J.H.
d. ca.1828; active in The Hague
Lorme, A. 1810/03/26

Ringhuysen, see Rinkhuijzen

Rinkhuijzen
spelling uncertain
Anonymous 1810/05/22
Bent, J. 1810/05/22
Koller, J.J. 1810/05/22
Os, Pieter G. 1810/05/22
Potter, Paulus 1810/05/22
Torunia, R. 1810/05/22
Zepp, C. 1810/05/22

Rinkhuizen, see Rinkhuijzen

Rinkhuyzen, see Rinkhuijzen

Risch
Keun, Hend. 1802/06/28

Rochussen, Hendrik
1779–1852; active in Rotterdam and later in The Hague
Berchem, N.P. 1810/03/26

Roe
Anonymous 1802/11/01

Roedig
probably J.W. Roedig
Bloot, P. 1805/10/09
Bredael, J. 1805/10/09
Courtois, J. 1805/10/09
Cuyp, A. 1805/10/09
Goyen 1805/10/09
Huchtenburgh, Jan 1805/10/09

Roelands, G.
Bol, F. 1802/09/21
Ducq, Johan le 1802/09/21

Roelfsema, Pieter
1745–1826; burgermeester of Groningen and amateur painter
Anonymous 1810/08/06
Beerstraten, A. 1810/08/06
Borch, G. ter (II) 1808/06/06
Bredael, J. 1810/08/06
Dou 1810/08/06
Flinck 1810/08/01
Langendijk, D. 1808/06/06
Lingelbach 1808/06/06
Neer, A. 1810/08/06
Nijmegen, G. 1808/06/06
Ochtervelt 1808/06/06
Potter, Paulus 1808/06/06
Potter, Pieter de 1808/06/06
Sorgh, H.M. 1808/06/06
Teniers, D. (II) 1808/06/06
Teniers, D. (II) 1810/08/06
Thier, B.H. 1808/06/06
Vliet, H.C. 1810/08/06
Wijnants 1808/06/06
Zeemann 1810/08/06

Roelfzema, see Roelfsema

Roeloffs, see Roelofs

Roelofs
includes Roeloffs; most transactions probably attributable to Jacobus Roelofs, q.v.
Anonymous 1801/03/16
Carree, M. 1801/03/16
Colaert, Johannes 1801/03/16
Compe, Jan ten 1804/12/10
Goyen 1801/03/16
Goyen 1804/05/07
Heemskerck, B. 1801/03/16
Janson, P. 1801/03/16
Klomp 1802/09/29
Laquy, W.J. 1804/05/07
Monogrammist J.V.H. 1801/03/16
Neer, A. 1802/09/29
Nickelen, Jan 1801/03/16
Pee, T. 1804/02/27
Toorenburgh, G. 1804/05/07
Toorenburgh, G. 1804/12/10
Vlieger, S. 1801/03/16
Vries, R. 1804/05/07

Roelofs, B.
Anonymous 1808/06/13

Roelofs, Jacobus
d. ca.1846; dealer
Apshoven 1803/08/01
Bemmel, J. 1801/06/10
Berchem, N.P. 1801/10/19
Brekelencam, Q. 1804/08/08
Buys, Jac. 1802/02/16
Dou 1802/02/16
Flinck 1801/06/10
Lingelbach 1803/09/07
Os, J. 1801/06/10
Ruisdael, J. 1801/10/19
Ryckaert, D. (III) 1801/04/13
Soolmaker 1802/02/16
Verkolje, N. 1801/10/19
Wouwerman, Ph. 1801/06/10
Wouwerman, Ph. 1801/10/19

Roelsema, see Roelfsema

Roelsma, see Roelfsema

Roelszema, see Roelfsema

Rohan, de
Anonymous 1808/06/11
Everdingen, A. 1808/06/11
Heemskerck 1808/06/11
Hondecoeter, M. 1808/06/11
Hooch, P. 1808/06/11
Janson, J. 1808/06/11
Metsu 1808/06/11
Neer, A. 1808/06/11
Ruysdael, S. 1808/06/06
Ruysdael, S. 1808/06/11
Schalcken 1808/06/11
Tol, P. 1808/06/11

Rohen, de, see Rohan, de

Roi d'Hollande, see Louis Bonaparte, koning van Holland

Roij, de, see Roy, de

Roijere, see Royers

Roijers, see Royers

Rombouts, Jan
1733–1805; amateur painter active in Dordrecht
Asselyn 1810/03/26

Rooijers, see Royers

Rookmans
Anonymous 1805/07/10
Anonymous 1805/12/16
Brueghel, J. (I) 1805/12/16
Italian 1805/07/10
Sorgh, H.M. 1805/07/10
Storck, Abr. 1806/05/05
Teniers, D. (II) 1805/12/16
Vernet, C.J. 1805/07/10
Vries, S.W. 1805/12/16

Roos, Cornelis Sebille
1754–1820; dealer and organizer of auctions in Amsterdam
Aelst, W. 1805/07/03
Aelst, W. 1805/07/10
Aelst, W. 1809/04/22
Agricola, Chr. Ludwig 1803/09/07
Anonymous 1801/03/16
Anonymous 1801/04/13
Anonymous 1801/05/11
Anonymous 1801/06/10
Anonymous 1801/08/19
Anonymous 1802/09/06
Anonymous 1803/04/20
Anonymous 1803/06/20
Anonymous 1803/08/01
Anonymous 1803/09/07
Anonymous 1803/12/12
Anonymous 1804/02/27
Anonymous 1804/05/07
Anonymous 1804/08/08
Anonymous 1805/07/03
Anonymous 1805/07/10
Anonymous 1805/12/16
Anonymous 1806/05/05
Anonymous 1806/08/13
Anonymous 1806/11/24
Anonymous 1807/08/26
Anonymous 1808/06/13
Anonymous 1809/04/22
Anonymous 1810/08/06
Anonymous 1810/10/11
Antonissen, H.J. 1804/08/08
Apshoven 1805/07/03
Apshoven 1806/08/13
Apshoven 1810/10/11
Arthois 1807/08/26
Asch, P.J. van 1801/05/11
Asch, P.J. van 1802/09/29
Asch, P.J. van 1807/08/26
Asselyn 1805/12/16
Asselyn 1808/06/13
Backer, J.A. 1806/05/05
Backhuysen 1804/05/07
Backhuysen 1804/08/08
Backhuysen 1805/07/10
Backhuysen 1805/12/16
Backhuysen 1806/05/05
Backhuysen 1806/08/13
Backhuysen 1808/06/13
Backhuysen 1810/08/01
Balen, H. (I) 1801/05/11
Balen, H. (I) 1805/07/03
Balen, H. (I) 1810/07/26
Banthem, J. 1804/05/07
Beeldemaker 1806/05/05
Beeldemaker, A.C. 1804/08/08
Beer, J. 1804/05/07

Beer, J. 1805/12/16
Beerstraten 1805/07/10
Beerstraten, A. 1801/06/10
Beerstraten, A. 1804/07/25
Beerstraten, A. 1805/07/03
Beerstraten, A. 1805/12/16
Beerstraten, J. 1802/12/13
Beerstraten, J. 1803/12/12
Beest, Sybrand 1805/07/10
Beesten, A.H. 1803/06/20
Bega 1805/07/10
Begeyn 1806/05/05
Begeyn 1806/08/13
Begeyn 1808/06/13
Beijer, J. de 1810/08/06
Bemmel, W. 1803/06/20
Bent, J. 1804/05/07
Bent, J. 1805/12/16
Bent, J. 1809/04/22
Berchem, N.P. 1803/04/20
Berchem, N.P. 1804/08/08
Berchem, N.P. 1805/12/16
Berchem, N.P. 1806/05/05
Berckheyde, G. 1801/06/10
Berckheyde, G. 1804/08/08
Berckheyde, G. 1806/08/13
Berckheyde, G. 1808/06/13
Berckheyde, J. 1805/07/03
Berckheyde, J. 1805/07/10
Bergen, D. 1808/06/13
Berninck, H. 1807/08/26
Beschey 1805/07/03
Beschey, J. 1803/09/07
Biset, C.E. 1804/08/08
Bisschop, Abr. 1806/05/05
Blanckerhoff 1801/06/10
Bloemaert, A. 1803/04/20
Bloemaert, A. 1804/08/08
Bloemaert, A. 1805/12/16
Bloemaert, A. 1806/05/05
Bloemaert, A. 1810/08/06
Bloemen, P. 1805/07/03
Bloot, P. 1803/06/20
Bol, F. 1801/06/10
Bol, F. 1805/07/10
Bol, F. 1805/12/16
Bol, F. 1806/08/13
Boonen, A. 1804/08/08
Boonen, A. 1805/07/03
Boonen, A. 1809/04/22
Borch, G. ter (II) 1803/08/17
Borch, G. ter (II) 1804/08/08
Borch, G. ter (II) 1805/07/03
Borch, G. ter (II) 1806/05/05
Borch, G. ter (II) 1806/08/13
Borkeloo, J. 1805/07/03
Borssom 1806/05/05
Borssom 1806/08/13
Borssom 1809/04/22
Bosch, A. 1804/07/25
Both, A. 1805/07/10
Both, A. 1808/06/13
Both, J. 1804/08/08
Both, J. 1805/07/10
Both, J. 1805/12/16
Both, J. 1806/05/05
Both, J. 1808/06/13
Both, J. 1809/04/22
Brakenburg 1803/06/20
Brakenburg 1804/08/08
Brakenburg 1805/07/10
Brakenburg 1805/12/16
Brakenburg 1806/05/05
Brakenburg 1806/08/13
Bramer 1801/08/19
Bray, S. 1804/08/08
Bray, S. 1807/08/26
Bredael, J. 1805/07/03
Bredael, J. 1807/08/26
Bredael, P. 1803/04/20
Breenbergh 1803/06/20
Breenbergh 1804/08/08
Brekelencam, Q. 1809/04/22
Bril, P. 1805/07/03
Bril, P. 1808/06/13
Broeck, E. 1804/08/08
Brouwer, Adr. 1804/05/07
Brouwer, Adr. 1804/08/08
Brouwer, Adr. 1806/08/13
Brouwer, Adr. 1808/06/13
Bruegel, P. (I) 1804/08/08
Brueghel 1805/12/16
Brueghel, J. (I) 1801/05/11
Brueghel, J. (I) 1801/08/19
Brueghel, J. (I) 1804/05/07
Brueghel, J. (I) 1805/07/03
Brueghel, J. (I) 1806/08/13
Brueghel, J. (I) 1809/04/22
Brueghel, J. (I) 1810/07/26
Brueghel, P. (II) 1804/08/08
Burch, Hendrick 1806/08/13
Camphuysen 1809/04/22
Canaletto 1805/12/16
Cappelle 1803/08/01
Carracci, A. 1801/08/19
Carracci, A. 1808/06/13
Carree 1805/07/03
Carree, Abr. 1807/08/26
Carree, Hend. (I) 1805/07/03
Carree, M. 1804/05/07
Carree, M. 1805/12/16
Carree, M. 1809/04/22
Carree, M. 1810/06/20
Cok, J.M. 1802/06/28
Cok, J.M. 1804/02/27
Cok, J.M. 1804/05/07
Compe, Jan ten 1801/06/10
Compe, Jan ten 1804/05/07
Compe, Jan ten 1804/07/25
Compe, Jan ten 1804/08/08
Compe, Jan ten 1805/07/10
Compe, Jan ten 1805/12/16
Coosemans 1806/08/13
Cornelisz. van Haarlem 1801/06/10
Cornelisz. van Haarlem 1808/06/13
Croos, A. 1806/08/13
Croos, R. 1803/04/20
Cuylenborch, A. 1806/08/13
Cuyp, A. 1806/05/05
Cuyp, A. 1806/08/13
Cuyp, B. 1804/08/08
Dalens, Dirck 1808/06/13
Decker, C. 1801/05/11
Decker, C. 1801/08/19
Delen 1804/08/08
Delen 1805/07/10
Delen 1806/08/13
Delen 1807/08/26
Denies, I. 1804/05/07
Dietrich, Chr. 1803/09/07
Dietrich, Chr. 1804/07/25
Dietrich, Chr. 1807/08/26
Does, J. (I) 1804/08/08
Does, J. (I) 1805/07/10
Does, S. 1801/10/19
Dolci, C. 1804/05/07
Dolci, C. 1804/08/08
Dou 1803/04/20
Dou 1806/08/13
Doudijns, W. 1801/04/13
Droochsloot, Abr. 1809/04/22
Dubbels, H. 1801/06/10
Dubbels, H. 1805/12/16
Dubois, G. 1805/12/16
Dubois, G. 1806/08/13
Dubois, J. 1803/06/20
Ducq, Johan le 1805/07/10
Dujardin, K. 1802/09/29
Dujardin, K. 1805/12/16
Dujardin, K. 1807/08/26
Dujardin, K. 1810/08/06
Dupré, Daniel 1806/05/05
Dusart, Corn. 1801/06/10
Dusart, Corn. 1802/09/29
Dusart, Corn. 1805/12/16
Dyck, Anth. van 1803/07/18
Dyck, Anth. van 1804/08/08
Dyck, Anth. van 1805/07/10
Dyck, Anth. van 1805/12/16
Dyck, Anth. van 1806/08/13
Eeckhout, G. 1801/06/10
Eeckhout, G. 1803/12/12
Eeckhout, G. 1804/07/25
Eeckhout, G. 1808/06/13
Ekels, Jan (I) 1804/05/07
Ekels, Jan (I) 1804/08/08
Ekels, Jan (I) 1805/12/16
Ekels, Jan (II) 1804/05/07
Ekels, Jan (II) 1806/05/05
Elliger, O. (II) 1807/08/26
Esselens, Jacob 1804/05/07
Essen, C. 1804/05/07
Essen, C. 1806/08/13
Essen, C. 1807/08/26
Essen, C. 1809/04/22
Everdingen, A. 1804/08/08
Faber, J.H. 1804/05/07
Flemish-Brabant 1803/09/07
Flinck 1801/03/16
Flinck 1806/08/13
Flinck 1807/08/26
Fournier 1806/05/05
Francken, Amb. (I) 1805/07/03
Francken, Frans (II) 1805/07/03
Fredriks, J.H. 1805/07/03
French 1806/05/05
Fyt 1806/08/13
Gael, B. 1805/12/16
Gael, B. 1807/08/26
Gaesbeeck, A. 1801/03/16
Gaesbeeck, A. 1801/06/10
Gaesbeeck, A. 1809/04/22
Galle, H. (I) 1803/09/07
Gerards 1804/08/08
Gerards 1805/07/10
Giordano, L. 1810/08/06
Glauber, J. 1804/08/08
Goltzius, Hend. 1805/07/03
Gool, Jan 1805/07/03
Gool, Jan 1807/08/26
Govaerts, J.B. 1803/09/07
Goyen 1804/05/07
Goyen 1804/08/08
Goyen 1805/07/10
Goyen 1805/12/16
Goyen 1806/05/05
Goyen 1807/08/26
Goyen 1809/04/22
Graat 1806/05/05
Grandjean, J. 1805/12/16
Griffier, J. (I) 1806/08/13
Griffier, R. 1801/06/10
Griffier, R. 1810/06/20
Hackaert, J. 1809/04/22
Hagen, Joris 1805/07/03
Hals, D. 1805/07/10
Hals, F. (I) 1805/12/16
Hals, F. (I) 1806/05/05
Hals, F. (I) 1806/08/13
Hals, F. (I) 1810/08/06
Hamilton, P.F. 1803/09/07
Heda 1809/04/22
Heem 1805/07/10
Heem, C. 1806/08/13
Heem, C. 1810/06/20
Heem, J.D. 1804/07/25
Heemskerck, B. 1805/07/03
Helmbreker 1806/08/13
Helst, B. 1806/08/13
Hendriks, W. 1805/07/10
Hendriks, W. 1808/06/13
Heusch, Jacob 1801/06/10
Heusch, Jacob 1804/07/25
Heusch, Jacob 1804/08/08
Heusch, Jacob 1805/07/03
Heusch, Wm. 1808/06/13
Heusch, Wm. 1810/08/06
Heussen, N. 1810/08/06
Heuvel, P. 1805/07/03
Heyden, J. 1808/06/13
Hobbema 1805/07/03
Hobbema 1806/05/05
Hoet, G. (I) 1805/07/03
Hoffmann, Sam. 1803/09/07
Holbein, H. (II) 1801/08/19
Hondecoeter, G. 1806/08/13
Hondecoeter, M. 1801/10/06
Hondecoeter, M. 1803/08/01
Hondecoeter, M. 1805/07/03
Hondecoeter, M. 1806/05/05
Hondecoeter, M. 1810/06/20
Hondecoeter, M. 1810/08/01
Hondecoeter, M. 1810/08/06
Honthorst, G. 1801/04/13
Honthorst, G. 1801/08/19
Honthorst, G. 1804/05/07
Honthorst, G. 1806/08/13
Hooch, P. 1803/07/18
Hooch, P. 1805/07/03
Hoogerheyden, E. 1807/08/26
Hoogstraten, S. 1804/08/08
Hoorn, J. 1804/05/07
Horemans, J.J. (I) 1804/08/08
Horemans, J.J. (I) 1805/12/16
Horemans, J.J. (I) 1808/06/13
Huchtenburgh, Jan 1801/03/16
Huchtenburgh, Jan 1801/06/10
Huchtenburgh, Jan 1804/05/07
Huchtenburgh, Jan 1804/07/25
Huchtenburgh, Jan 1804/08/08
Huchtenburgh, Jan 1805/07/03
Huchtenburgh, Jan 1805/12/16
Huchtenburgh, Jan 1806/08/13
Hulsdonck, J. 1804/08/08
Huysmans, C. 1805/07/10
Huysmans, C. 1805/12/16
Huysmans, C. 1806/08/13
Huysmans, C. 1810/06/20
Huysum, Jan 1801/06/10
Huysum, Jan 1802/06/16
Huysum, Jan 1807/08/26
Huysum, Jan 1809/09/06
Italian 1804/05/07
Italian 1804/08/08
Italian 1806/05/05
Italian 1808/06/13
Janson, J. 1804/08/08
Janson, J. 1805/07/03
Janson, J. 1805/12/16
Janson, J. 1806/08/13
Jongh, L. 1805/07/10
Jordaens, J. (I) 1804/07/25
Jordaens, J. (I) 1806/08/13
Jordaens, J. (I) 1808/06/13
Kalf 1803/09/07
Kalraet 1807/08/26
Keirincx, Alex. 1805/12/16
Kessel, J. (III) 1804/05/07
Kessel, J. (III) 1806/05/05
Kieft, P. 1805/12/16
Kleijne, David 1806/08/13
Kloet, J. 1805/07/10
Klomp 1809/04/22
Koninck, P. 1805/07/10
Koninck, P. 1806/05/05
Kraft, J. 1804/08/08
Kruger, Jac. 1804/05/07
Kuijper, J. 1808/06/13
Lairesse, G. 1801/10/06
Lairesse, G. 1804/08/08
Lairesse, G. 1805/12/16
Lairesse, G. 1806/05/05
Lamme, A. 1809/04/22
Laquy, W.J. 1804/05/07
Laquy, W.J. 1804/12/10
Laquy, W.J. 1805/12/16
Laquy, W.J. 1810/05/22
Lastman, P.P. 1806/08/13

Vertangen 1806/08/13
Vertangen 1807/08/26
Victors, Jan 1801/08/19
Victors, Jan 1804/08/08
Victors, Jan 1807/08/26
Vinckeboons, D. 1803/09/07
Vinne, V.L. (I) 1801/08/19
Vlieger, C. 1809/04/22
Vlieger, S. 1805/07/03
Vlieger, S. 1805/12/16
Vlieger, S. 1806/08/13
Vliet, H.C. 1801/04/13
Vliet, H.C. 1804/08/08
Vois, Ary de 1801/04/13
Vois, Ary de 1804/08/08
Vois, Ary de 1805/07/03
Voorhout, J. (I) 1803/12/12
Vos, S. 1805/07/03
Vrancx 1802/06/28
Vrancx 1803/09/07
Vrancx 1805/07/03
Vrancx 1806/08/13
Vree, N. de 1804/08/08
Vries, R. 1809/04/22
Vries, S.W. 1805/12/16
Vroom, C. 1802/06/28
Vroom, H. 1804/02/27
Waal, J. 1806/08/13
Wagner, J.G. 1806/08/13
Watteau, J.A. 1804/05/07
Weenix 1801/10/06
Weenix 1803/07/18
Weenix 1805/07/03
Weenix 1806/08/13
Weenix 1808/06/13
Weenix 1810/08/01
Weenix, J.B. 1804/05/07
Weenix, J.B. 1807/08/26
Weenix, J.B. 1810/08/06
Werff, A. 1805/07/03
Werff, A. 1810/08/06
Wet, J.W. 1804/08/08
Wigmana, G. 1803/04/20
Wigmana, G. 1805/07/03
Wijnants 1801/03/16
Wijnants 1804/05/07
Wijnants 1804/08/08
Wijnants 1805/07/03
Wijnants 1805/12/16
Wijnants 1806/05/05
Wijnants 1809/04/22
Willaerts, A. 1806/08/13
Wils, Jan 1801/10/06
Wiltschier, J. 1806/08/13
Wit, Jacob de 1801/05/11
Wit, Jacob de 1804/05/07
Wit, Jacob de 1804/07/25
Wit, Jacob de 1804/08/08
Wit, Jacob de 1805/07/10
Withoos, M. 1808/06/13
Witmont, H. 1804/08/08
Witmont, H. 1805/07/10
Witte, E. 1804/05/07
Witte, E. 1804/08/08
Witte, E. 1807/08/26
Witte, E. 1808/06/13
Witte, E. 1810/06/20
Wouwerman 1806/05/05
Wouwerman, P. 1804/08/08
Wouwerman, P. 1805/07/10
Wouwerman, P. 1806/05/05
Wouwerman, P. 1807/08/26
Wouwerman, Ph. 1801/03/16
Wouwerman, Ph. 1801/10/06
Wouwerman, Ph. 1804/08/08
Wouwerman, Ph. 1805/07/03
Wouwerman, Ph. 1807/08/26
Wouwerman, Ph. 1808/06/13
Wouwerman, Pieter 1808/06/13
Wtewael, J. 1804/07/25
Wulfraet 1804/08/08
Wyck, J. 1801/06/10
Wyck, T. 1804/07/25
Wyck, T. 1805/07/03
Wyck, T. 1805/07/10
Wyck, T. 1807/08/26
Wyck, T. 1808/06/13
Wyck, T. 1809/04/22
Xavery, Frans 1805/07/03
Zeemann 1805/07/10
Zeemann 1806/08/13

Roosendaal, Stephanies, Mr.
d. ca.1803; city official in Hertogenbosch
Barrey, J. 1803/10/25
Singleton, H. 1803/10/25
Ward, James 1803/10/25
Westall, R. 1803/10/25

Rooyers, see Royers

Rosekrans, see Rosenkrans

Roselli
Caravaggio 1803/04/27

Rosenkrans
Anonymous 1808/10/28
Kuster 1808/10/28
Vitringa 1808/06/13

Rosier
Anonymous 1809/07/25

Roy, François de
dealer from Brussels
Aelst, W. 1802/09/29
Berchem, N.P. 1802/09/29
Brueghel, J. (I) 1801/06/10
Carree, Hend. (I) 1801/06/13
Compe, Jan ten 1801/10/19
Doomer, L. 1801/06/13
Dou 1801/06/13
Man, Joost 1801/06/13
Pynacker 1801/06/10
Spranger 1802/09/29
Teniers, D. (II) 1801/06/13
Velde, W. 1801/06/10
Werff, P. 1801/10/19

Royer, see Royers

Royere, see Royers

Royers, Jb.
Anonymous 1802/09/06
Anonymous 1803/08/24
Anonymous 1805/07/10
Anonymous 1806/08/13
Anonymous 1809/06/13
Anonymous 1810/08/06
Anonymous 1810/10/11
Backhuysen 1808/11/28
Bemmel, J. 1810/06/20
Brekelencam, Q. 1802/02/16
Carracci 1802/06/28
Cuyp, A. 1802/06/28
Denner, B. 1802/06/28
Ducq, Johan le 1805/07/10
Elsheimer, A. 1802/02/23
Goyen 1810/06/20
Hoet, G. (I) 1802/06/28
Jongh, L. 1805/07/10
Leeuw 1802/06/16
Leeuw 1810/10/11
Lingelbach 1802/02/23
Meulener 1802/09/06
Mieris, F. (II) 1802/06/28
Monogrammist J.A.H. 1802/06/28
Moucheron, F. 1802/02/23
Moucheron, F. 1802/06/16
Neer, A. 1802/06/28
Nepveu, J. 1802/02/16
Poelenburgh, C. 1802/02/23
Saftleven, H. 1802/02/23
Schalcken 1802/06/28
Steen, J. 1802/06/28
Stoop 1802/06/28
Valentin de Boulogne 1805/07/10
Velde, A. 1806/08/13
Wigmana, G. 1802/06/28
Wijnants 1806/08/13
Wulfraet 1802/06/28

Rozekrans, see Rosenkrans

Ruel
Anonymous 1806/08/13
Molenaer, Klaes 1806/08/13

Ruloffs, Bartholomeus
1741–1801; organist, composer, teacher and poet
Alcock, E. 1801/12/22
Anonymous 1801/12/22
Avercamp, H. 1801/12/22
Beschey 1801/12/22
Bisraat 1801/12/22
Bloemen 1801/12/22
Boursse, E. 1801/12/22
Chalon, L. 1801/12/22
Dalens, Dirck 1801/12/22
Dubourg, L. 1801/12/22
Dyck, Anth. van 1801/12/22
Ekels, Jan (I) 1801/12/22
Ekels, Jan (II) 1801/12/22
Essen, C. 1801/12/22
Fargue, P.C. 1801/12/22
Grasdorp, J.G. 1801/12/22
Heemskerck 1801/12/22
Heeremans, Thos. 1801/12/22
Hoet, J. 1801/12/22
Hondecoeter 1801/12/22
Houtstrom 1801/12/22
Janson, P. 1801/12/22
Koller, J.J. 1801/12/22
Laquy, W.J. 1801/12/22
Martszen, J. (II) 1801/12/22
Molenaer, J.M. 1801/12/22
Molenaer, Klaes 1801/12/22
Mommers, C. 1801/12/22
Monogrammist A.V.O. 1801/12/22
Monogrammist H.C. 1801/12/22
Monogrammist J.K. 1801/12/22
Monogrammist J.R. 1801/12/22
Monogrammist J.V.M. 1801/12/22
Monogrammist T.V.B. 1801/12/22
Neeffs, P. (I) 1801/12/22
Ostade 1801/12/22
Ostade, A. 1801/12/22
Ostade, I. 1801/12/22
Pothoven, H. 1801/12/22
Redeker 1801/12/22
Renard 1801/12/22
Renars 1801/12/22
Rink, P.J. 1801/12/22
Ruisdael 1801/12/22
Schalcke, C. 1801/12/22
Seldron, E. 1801/12/22
Steen, J. 1801/12/22
Toorenvliet, J. 1801/12/22
Troost, C. 1801/12/22
Ulft 1801/12/22
Vermeer, Jan (II) 1801/12/22
Vermeulen, B. 1801/12/22
Vonck 1801/12/22
Wit, Jacob de 1801/12/22
Wyck, T. 1801/12/22

Rutgers, Abraham, Ds.
1751–1809; priest and co-compiler of a Protestant hymnbook
Anonymous 1810/11/29

Rutte, see Rutten

Rutten
probably identical with Grutte, q.v.
Goyen 1810/05/22
Janson, J.C. 1810/05/22
Ruysdael, S. 1810/05/22
Sondervan, J. 1810/05/22
Storck, Abr. 1810/05/22

Ruyd, de
Berchem, N.P. 1802/07/27

Ryers, see Rijers

Ryfsneyder, see Rijfsnijder

Ryfsnyder, see Rijfsnijder

Ryke, de
Anonymous 1804/06/18

Rynberg, see Rijnbergh

Rynbergh, see Rijnbergh

Rynders, see Reynders

Ryp, van, see Rijp, van

S.
Anonymous 1801/03/16
Cappelle 1806/05/05
Delen 1801/03/16
Drielst, E. 1801/03/16
Huchtenburgh, Jan 1801/04/13
Keun, Hend. 1801/03/16
Lingelbach 1803/12/12
Miereveld, M. 1806/05/05
Myn, G. 1801/03/16
Schalcken 1806/05/05
Silo, A. 1801/03/16
Storck, Abr. 1805/07/03

S. (1801, October 6)
Anonymous 1801/10/06
Avercamp, H. 1801/10/06
Backhuysen 1801/10/06
Bassano 1801/10/06
Berchem, N.P. 1801/10/06
Breenbergh 1801/10/06
Carracci, A. 1801/10/06
Dou 1801/10/06
Dubourg, L. 1801/10/06
Henstenburgh 1801/10/06
Huchtenburgh, Jan 1801/10/06
Huysum, Jan 1801/10/06
Lairesse, G. 1801/10/06
Netscher, Casp. 1801/10/06
Ostade, A. 1801/10/06
Potter, Paulus 1801/10/06
Pynacker 1801/10/06
Rembrandt 1801/10/06
Romeyn 1801/10/06
Rottenhammer, H. (I) 1801/10/06
Tiziano 1801/10/06
Wigmana, J. 1801/10/06
Wils, Jan 1801/10/06
Witte, E. 1801/10/06
Wouwerman, Ph. 1801/10/06

S. (1804, August 8)
Anonymous 1804/08/08
Bega 1804/08/08
Brekelencam, Q. 1804/08/08
Compe, Jan ten 1804/08/08
Cuyp, J.G. 1804/08/08
Diepenbeeck, A.J. 1804/08/08
Everdingen, Cesar 1804/08/08
Holbein, H. (II) 1804/08/08
Italian 1804/08/08
Keun, Hend. 1804/08/08
Mieris, F. (II) 1804/08/08
Molenaer, Klaes 1804/08/08
Mommers, H. 1804/08/08
Moni, L. de 1804/08/08
Moucheron, I. 1804/08/08

Neer, A. 1804/08/08
Ouwater, Isaak 1804/08/08
Sorgh, H.M. 1804/08/08
Storck, Abr. 1804/08/08
Storck, J. 1804/08/08
Velde, W. 1804/08/08
Verschuir 1804/08/08
Vliet, W. 1804/08/08
Vries, R. 1804/08/08
Wouwerman, P. 1804/08/08

S. (1805, July 3)
probably identical with "J" on Aug.13, 1806, and "K" on June 13, 1808
Borch, G. ter (II) 1805/07/03
Croos, P. 1805/07/03
Heyden, J. 1805/07/03
Molenaer, J.M. 1805/07/03
Venne, A.P. 1805/07/03
Vrancx 1805/07/03
Wouwerman, J. 1805/07/03

S. (1807, August 26)
Anonymous 1807/08/26
Anonymous 1807/08/27
Bent, J. 1807/08/26
Blinkvliet, M. 1807/08/26
Borch, G. ter (II) 1807/08/26
Brakenburg 1807/08/26
Brouwer, Adr. 1807/08/26
Bruegel, P. (I) 1807/08/26
Chalon, L. 1807/08/26
Droochsloot, J.C. 1807/08/26
Gerards 1807/08/26
Goyen 1807/08/26
Graef, T. 1807/08/26
Heeremans, Thos. 1807/08/26
Hooch, C. 1807/08/26
Italian 1807/08/26
Jordaens, J. (I) 1807/08/26
Keun, Hend. 1807/08/26
Lingelbach 1807/08/26
Lundens 1807/08/26
Matthieu, C. 1807/08/26
Molenaer, J.M. 1807/08/26
Molenaer, Klaes 1807/08/26
Moni, L. de 1807/08/26
Neer, A. 1807/08/26
Palamedesz., A. 1807/08/26
Rennel, S. 1807/08/26
Roghman, R. 1807/08/26
Rombouts 1807/08/26
Romeyn 1807/08/26
Schyndel, J. 1807/08/26
Vermeer, Jan (II) 1807/08/26
Wet, J.W. 1807/08/26
Wit, Jacob de 1807/08/26

S. (1808, August 23)
Anonymous 1808/08/23
Asselyn 1808/08/23
Beerstraten, A. 1808/08/23
Bent, J. 1808/08/23
Huchtenburgh, Jan 1808/08/23
Os, Pieter G. 1808/08/23
Palamedesz., P. (I) 1808/08/23
Schyndel 1808/08/23
Wijnants 1808/08/23

S. (1808, November 28)
Anonymous 1808/11/28
Beschey, B. 1808/11/28
Eeckhout, G. 1808/11/28
Ekels, Jan (I) 1808/11/28
Heemskerck 1808/11/28
Italian 1808/11/28
Maas, J. 1808/11/28
Marseus, O. 1808/11/28
Moeyaert, C. 1808/11/28
Molenaer, J.M. 1808/11/28
Silo, A. 1808/11/28
Uyttenbroeck, M. 1808/11/28
Witte, E. 1808/11/28

S. (1809, April 17)
Anonymous 1809/04/17
Bosman, Maria 1809/04/17
Hondecoeter, M. 1809/04/17
Oudendyck, E. 1809/04/17
Palamedesz., A. 1809/04/17
Peeters, B. (I) 1809/04/17
Silo, A. 1809/04/17
Storck, Abr. 1809/04/17
Victors, Jan 1809/04/17

S. (1810, May 22)
Anonymous 1810/05/22
Molenaer, J.M. 1810/05/22
Palthe, Jan 1810/05/22
Tol, D. 1810/05/22
Vermeer, Jan (II) 1810/05/22
Walscapelle 1810/05/22

S. (1810, June 20)
Anonymous 1810/06/20
Ast 1810/06/20
Courtois, J. 1810/06/20
Dalens, Dirck 1810/06/20
Droochsloot, J.C. 1810/06/20
Italian 1810/06/20
Lairesse, G. 1810/06/20
Lundens 1810/06/20
Molijn 1810/06/20
Moucheron, F. 1810/06/20
Savery, R. 1810/06/20
Uppink 1810/06/20
Weenix, J.B. 1810/06/20
Wtewael, J. 1810/06/20

S. (1810, October 11)
Anonymous 1810/10/11
Bassen 1810/10/11
Bemmel, J. 1810/10/11
Bloemen, P. 1810/10/11
Gael, B. 1810/10/11
Gryef 1810/10/11
Janson, J. 1810/10/11
Lastman, P.P. 1810/10/11
Moeyaert, C. 1810/10/11
Mommers, H. 1810/10/11
Ostade, I. 1810/10/11
Rubens 1810/10/11
Schepper 1810/10/11
Stuven 1810/10/11
Toorenvliet, J. 1810/10/11
Wiertz, H.F. 1810/10/11

Salcedo
also spelled Salsedo
Anonymous 1803/12/12
Cornelisz. van Haarlem 1803/12/12
Eckhard, C. 1803/12/12
Savery, R. 1803/12/12
Venne, A.P. 1803/12/12

Salomon, Abraham
dealer
Anonymous 1806/08/20
Chapman, J. 1806/08/20
Hondecoeter, Gysb. 1806/08/20
Maas, J. 1806/08/20

Salomon, Isaac
dealer
Anonymous 1801/03/16

Salomons, see Salomon

Salsedo, see Salcedo

Sande, Johannes Jacobus van de
bookseller and auctioneer in Middelburg
Anonymous 1802/10/18
Anonymous 1810/09/17
Puyster 1802/05/10

Santheuvel, Pieter van den, Mr.
1732–1799; councillor, provost marshal and burgomaster of Dordrecht
Aa, Dirk 1810/07/23
Anonymous 1810/07/23
Avercamp, H. 1810/07/23
Backhuysen 1810/07/23
Beeldemaker, A.C. 1810/07/23
Beerstraten, A. 1810/07/23
Bisschop, J. 1810/07/23
Bloemaert, A. 1810/07/23
Borch, G. ter (II) 1810/07/23
Both, A. 1810/07/23
Brekelencam, Q. 1810/07/23
Cuyp, A. 1810/07/23
Droochsloot, Abr. 1810/07/23
Dusart, Corn. 1810/07/23
Fabritius, Carel 1810/07/23
Gerards 1810/07/23
Goyen 1810/07/23
Heem, J.D. 1810/07/23
Kalraet, Abr. 1810/07/23
Klootwijk 1810/07/23
Koningh, L. 1810/07/23
Leeuw 1810/07/23
Lingelbach 1810/07/23
Maes, N. 1810/07/23
Metsu 1810/07/23
Mieris, F. (I) 1810/07/23
Molenaer, Klaes 1810/07/23
Molijn 1810/07/23
Monogrammist A.B.S. 1810/07/23
Moor, C. 1810/07/23
Neeffs, P. (I) 1810/07/23
Oosterwijck, M. 1810/07/23
Ostade, I. 1810/07/23
Porcellis, Jan 1810/07/23
Potter, Paulus 1810/07/23
Pynacker 1810/07/23
Rembrandt 1810/07/23
Savery, R. 1810/07/23
Schouman, M. 1810/07/23
Smak Gregoor, G. 1810/07/23
Steen, J. 1810/07/23
Strij, A. 1810/07/23
Strij, J. 1810/07/23
Teniers, D. (II) 1810/07/23
Velde, A. 1810/07/23
Velde, E. (I) 1810/07/23
Vermeulen, A. 1810/07/23
Versteeg 1810/07/23
Vlieger, S. 1810/07/23
Wigmana, G. 1810/07/23
Wit, Jacob de 1810/07/23
Wouwerman, Pieter 1810/07/23

Sappé
Hoffman, Martin 1802/02/16

Sardet
Brekelencam, Q. 1810/06/20
Maes, N. 1810/06/20
Porcellis, Jan 1810/06/20
Wtewael, J. 1810/06/20

Sardet, C.
dealer
Jordaens, J. (I) 1807/08/26
Neer, C. 1807/08/26
Ostade, A. 1807/08/26
Wit, Jacob de 1807/08/26

Sart, du, see Dusart

Sartin, van
active in Rotterdam
Hooch, P. 1806/06/07
Sorgh, H.M. 1806/06/07

Schagen, Regter
Ducq, Johan le 1802/07/27

Schalk
Anonymous 1802/11/01
Anonymous 1810/07/23
Goyen 1810/07/23
Klootwijk 1810/07/23
Monogrammist J.B. 1802/11/01
Ostade 1810/07/23

Scheepens
Anonymous 1804/12/10
Heem, J.D. 1806/08/13
Verschuring, H. 1804/08/08

Scheffer
perhaps the painter Jean-Baptiste Scheffer, 1765–1809
Anonymous 1803/09/07
Anonymous 1803/12/12
Bout, P. 1803/09/07
Carracci 1803/12/12
Faistenberger, Ant. 1803/09/07
Glauber, J. 1803/09/07
Langenhöffel, J.J.F. 1803/09/07
Piazzetta 1803/09/07
Rembrandt 1803/09/07
Roos, Jan (I) 1803/09/07

Scheffers, see Scheffer

Scheide
Maes, D. 1801/04/23
Meyering, J. 1801/04/23

Scheltema, Take Pieters
1760–1837; painter active in Rotterdam and Amsterdam
Anonymous 1806/08/20
Hoogstraten, S. 1806/08/20

Schenkel Senior
Anonymous 1804/06/18

Scheurleer, Bernardus
1754–1828; bookdealer and auctioneer in The Hague
Backhuysen 1806/05/05
Berchem, N.P. 1806/05/05
Dongen, Dionys 1806/11/24
Elsheimer, A. 1806/05/05
Gael, B. 1806/11/24
Goyen 1806/11/24
Savery, R. 1806/05/05
Six, Nicolaas 1806/05/05
Strij, J. 1806/05/05
Thier, B.H. 1806/05/05
Velde, E. (I) 1806/05/05
Wijnants 1806/05/05

Schimmelpenninck Gzn., Gerrit
1759–1818; merchant and amateur painter active in Amsterdam
Ostade, A. 1801/05/11
Palthe, G.J. 1801/05/11
Palthe, G.J. 1802/05/05
Zegelaar, G. 1802/05/05

Schimmelpenning, see Schimmelpenninck

Schinkel, de
Anonymous 1802/10/18

Schipperl, see Schippers

Schippers
active in Middelburg
Anonymous 1803/10/10

Schleij, see Schley

Schley, Philippus van der
1724–1817; dealer and organizer of auctions in Amsterdam; see also Meij
Aelst, W. 1804/05/07
Anonymous 1801/03/16
Anonymous 1801/05/11
Anonymous 1801/08/19

Anonymous 1802/02/16
Anonymous 1802/06/16
Anonymous 1802/06/28
Anonymous 1802/09/06
Anonymous 1802/12/13
Anonymous 1803/06/20
Anonymous 1803/09/07
Anonymous 1803/12/12
Anonymous 1804/02/27
Anonymous 1804/05/07
Anonymous 1804/07/25
Anonymous 1804/08/08
Anonymous 1805/07/10
Anonymous 1806/05/05
Anonymous 1807/08/26
Anonymous 1809/04/22
Anonymous 1809/06/13
Anonymous 1810/10/11
Anonymous-Antique 1803/04/27
Asselyn 1801/05/11
Asselyn 1801/06/10
Avercamp, H. 1801/10/06
Avercamp, H. 1802/12/13
Avont, P. 1807/08/26
Backhuysen 1802/06/16
Backhuysen 1803/06/20
Balen, H. (I) 1807/08/26
Barbiers, P. 1802/12/13
Beerstraten, A. 1804/05/07
Beesten, A.H. 1803/06/20
Bega 1802/12/13
Begeyn 1804/07/25
Beijer, J. de 1809/06/13
Berchem, N.P. 1802/12/13
Berckheyde, G. 1801/06/10
Berckheyde, J. 1803/06/20
Berninck, H. 1802/12/13
Beschey 1803/06/20
Beschey, J. 1807/08/26
Blaauw, J. 1804/05/07
Bloemaert, A. 1808/11/28
Bloot, P. 1802/06/16
Bol, F. 1801/04/13
Bol, F. 1801/10/19
Bol, F. 1805/07/10
Bol, F. 1809/06/13
Boonen, A. 1805/07/10
Borch, G. ter (II) 1803/06/20
Both, A. 1803/06/20
Both, J. 1803/06/20
Boudewyns 1801/08/19
Brakenburg 1801/10/19
Brakenburg 1804/08/08
Bramer 1803/06/20
Breenbergh 1806/05/05
Brekelencam, Q. 1802/06/16
Brekelencam, Q. 1803/06/20
Brekelencam, Q. 1804/05/07
Bril, P. 1803/06/20
Broeck, E. 1802/12/13
Broeck, E. 1804/05/07
Brueghel, J. (I) 1802/12/13
Brueghel, J. (I) 1804/05/07
Brueghel, J. (I) 1805/12/16
Brueghel, J. (I) 1806/08/13
Brueghel, J. (I) 1807/08/26
Brueghel, J. (I) 1809/04/22
Brueghel, J. (I) 1810/05/22
Brueghel, P. 1802/09/06
Burg, Adriaan 1803/06/20
Buys, Jac. 1802/02/16
Buys, Jac. 1802/12/13
Camsen, J. 1804/08/08
Cats, Jac. 1809/06/13
Compe, Jan ten 1801/05/11
Compe, Jan ten 1804/07/25
Compe, Jan ten 1805/07/10
Compe, Jan ten 1809/06/13
Coopse, P. 1801/10/06
Cranach, L. (I) 1808/11/28
Crayer, G. 1802/12/13
Cuyp, A. 1802/12/13
Cuyp, J.G. 1804/08/08
Dalens, Dirck (I) 1805/07/10
Dame, A. 1809/06/13
Decker, C. 1801/08/19
Delen 1801/03/16
Delen 1807/08/26
Dietrich, Chr. 1804/07/25
Does, J. (I) 1803/06/20
Does, S. 1802/12/13
Dorasse, C. 1805/07/10
Drielenburch, W. 1801/03/16
Drielst, E. 1801/03/16
Dubourg, L. 1806/08/13
Dubourg, L. 1807/08/26
Dubourg, L. 1808/11/28
Ducq, Johan le 1801/10/19
Ducq, Johan le 1802/09/06
Ducq, Johan le 1803/06/20
Ducq, Johan le 1804/08/08
Dujardin, K. 1802/09/06
Dujardin, K. 1802/12/13
Dujardin, K. 1803/09/07
Dujardin, K. 1804/05/07
Dujardin, K. 1804/08/08
Dupré, Daniel 1803/08/01
Dürer 1802/12/13
Eeckhout, G. 1802/06/16
Eeckhout, G. 1809/06/13
Eeckhout, G. 1810/06/20
Ekels, Jan (II) 1802/09/06
Elliger, O. (II) 1803/12/12
Elliger, O. (II) 1804/05/07
Elliger, O. (II) 1807/08/26
Elsheimer, A. 1802/06/16
Essen, C. 1805/07/10
Everdingen, A. 1803/06/20
Fargue, Maria la 1802/06/28
Fargue, P.C. 1806/11/24
Flemish-Brabant 1803/06/20
Flinck 1807/08/26
Franck, J.W. 1803/06/20
Franck, J.W. 1804/02/27
Fyt 1803/06/20
Gael, B. 1802/12/13
Gael, B. 1808/11/28
Gelder, A. 1810/10/11
Giordano, L. 1804/07/25
Goltzius, Hend. 1804/08/08
Goyen 1804/05/07
Goyen 1805/07/10
Goyen 1808/11/28
Goyen 1809/04/22
Grebber, A.C. 1804/07/25
Greuze 1809/04/22
Griffier, R. 1803/06/20
Gryef 1810/10/11
Hackaert, J. 1801/08/19
Hackaert, J. 1802/12/13
Hals, D. 1805/07/10
Heem 1807/08/26
Heem, C. 1803/06/20
Heem, J.D. 1803/06/20
Heeremans, Thos. 1805/07/10
Helst, B. 1804/07/25
Hendriks, W. 1802/06/28
Hendriks, W. 1803/12/12
Herp, Wm. (I) 1801/03/16
Heusch, Wm. 1803/06/20
Heyden, J. 1802/12/13
Hobbema 1803/06/20
Honthorst, G. 1801/08/19
Hooch, P. 1803/06/20
Hooch, P. 1804/08/08
Hoogstraten, Jan 1801/06/10
Horemans, J.J. (I) 1801/08/19
Huchtenburgh, Jan 1801/03/16
Huchtenburgh, Jan 1801/04/13
Huchtenburgh, Jan 1802/06/16
Huchtenburgh, Jan 1803/06/20
Italian 1802/12/13
Italian 1803/06/20
Janson, J. 1801/10/19
Janson, J. 1802/05/05
Janson, J. 1805/12/16
Jongh, L. 1803/06/20
Juweel, Nic. 1809/04/22
Kessel, J. (I) 1801/08/19
Kessel, J. (III) 1804/08/08
Keun, Hend. 1801/03/16
Keun, Hend. 1807/08/26
Kleur, S. 1803/06/20
Koninck, P. 1804/08/08
Kuik, J. 1809/06/13
Laer, P. 1802/12/13
Lairesse, G. 1804/07/25
Lairesse, G. 1804/08/08
Langendijk, D. 1806/05/05
Laquy, W.J. 1802/05/05
Laquy, W.J. 1802/09/06
Laquy, W.J. 1807/08/26
Lastman, P.P. 1801/05/11
Lastman, P.P. 1810/10/11
Lauwers, J.J. 1802/06/28
Lauwers, J.J. 1802/12/13
Lauwers, J.J. 1810/05/22
Leeuw, Pieter 1807/08/26
Lingelbach 1802/12/13
Lingelbach 1803/12/12
Lundens 1801/10/06
Lundens 1804/08/08
Maat, N. 1807/08/26
Man, C. 1803/06/20
Marseus, O. 1803/06/20
Marseus, O. 1804/08/08
Marseus, O. 1809/06/13
Meijer, Hend. (II) 1801/10/19
Metsu 1802/06/16
Metsu 1804/12/10
Mettenleiter, J.J. 1803/06/20
Miereveld, M. 1803/12/12
Mieris, W. 1801/06/10
Mieris, W. 1801/10/19
Mieris, W. 1802/05/05
Mieris, W. 1804/05/07
Molenaer, Bart. 1807/08/26
Molenaer, J.M. 1809/04/22
Molenaer, Klaes 1801/08/19
Molenaer, Klaes 1802/06/16
Molenaer, Klaes 1803/06/20
Molenaer, Klaes 1808/08/23
Molijn 1803/06/20
Molijn 1804/05/07
Molijn 1804/08/08
Mommers, H. 1804/05/07
Momper, J. (II) 1801/08/19
Momper, J. (II) 1807/08/26
Moni, L. de 1801/10/19
Moni, L. de 1802/06/16
Monogrammist M.B. 1803/06/20
Monogrammist P. 1802/12/13
Moucheron, F. 1801/05/11
Moucheron, F. 1804/07/25
Moucheron, F. 1809/06/13
Myn, G. 1801/03/16
Myn, G. 1804/08/08
Naiveu 1804/08/08
Neer, A. 1806/08/13
Netscher, Casp. 1801/10/06
Netscher, Casp. 1802/06/16
Nickelen, Jan 1806/05/05
Nicodemo, Aug. 1808/11/28
Ommeganck, B. 1803/12/12
Oolen, Adr. 1803/12/12
Os, Pieter G. 1804/08/08
Os, Pieter G. 1805/07/10
Ostade 1809/06/13
Ostade, A. 1801/03/16
Ostade, A. 1801/10/19
Ostade, A. 1802/12/13
Ouwater, Isaak 1802/06/28
Ouwater, Isaak 1803/06/20
Ovens, J. 1802/12/13
Ovens, J. 1808/11/28
Palamedesz., A. 1807/08/26
Palamedesz., P. (I) 1804/05/07
Peeters, B. (I) 1801/08/19
Plankman, J. 1804/05/07
Poelenburgh, C. 1801/06/10
Poelenburgh, C. 1801/08/19
Poelenburgh, C. 1807/08/26
Poelenburgh, C. 1809/04/22
Porcellis, Jan 1810/05/22
Potter, Paulus 1801/10/06
Potter, Paulus 1802/06/16
Pynacker 1804/05/07
Quellinus, E. (II) 1804/08/08
Ricci, S. 1804/07/25
Ring, P. 1802/12/13
Roestraeten 1806/11/24
Romeyn 1801/10/19
Roos, K. 1809/06/13
Rosa, S. 1803/06/20
Rubens 1802/06/16
Rubens 1804/07/25
Rubens 1806/08/13
Ruisdael, J. 1801/04/13
Ruisdael, J. 1802/06/16
Ruisdael, J. 1806/05/05
Ruysdael, S. 1803/06/20
Saftleven, C. 1802/12/13
Saftleven, C. 1803/06/20
Saftleven, H. 1802/06/16
Sandrart, Joachim (I) 1801/05/11
Savery, R. 1803/06/20
Schalcken 1804/07/25
Schellinks, Daniel 1803/06/20
Schellinks, W. 1801/03/16
Schellinks, W. 1802/06/16
Schellinks, W. 1803/06/20
Schumacher, N. 1802/06/16
Seghers, D. 1802/09/06
Seghers, D. 1803/06/20
Silo, A. 1801/03/16
Silo, A. 1802/09/06
Silo, A. 1803/06/20
Silo, A. 1805/07/10
Silo, A. 1808/06/13
Smit, Aernout 1803/06/20
Smit, Aernout 1805/12/16
Snyders, F. 1803/06/20
Snyders, F. 1804/07/25
Sonje, J.G. 1802/12/13
Sorgh, H.M. 1802/06/28
Sorgh, H.M. 1809/09/06
Steen, J. 1801/06/10
Steen, J. 1801/10/06
Steen, J. 1801/10/19
Steen, J. 1802/06/16
Stekelin 1802/02/16
Storck, Abr. 1801/03/16
Storck, Abr. 1801/08/19
Storck, J. 1804/08/08
Stuven 1804/07/25
Swebach, J.F.J. 1803/06/20
Teniers, D. (II) 1801/04/13
Teniers, D. (II) 1802/06/16
Teniers, D. (II) 1802/09/06
Teniers, D. (II) 1803/06/20
Teniers, D. (II) 1804/07/25
Teniers, D. (II) 1809/04/22
Tintoretto, J. 1802/12/13
Tol, D. 1801/10/19
Tol, D. 1803/06/20
Toorenburgh, G. 1810/05/22
Troost, J.H. 1802/12/13
Troost, J.H. 1805/07/10
Velde, A. 1801/04/13
Velde, A. 1801/06/10
Velde, A. 1801/10/19
Velde, A. 1802/12/13
Velde, A. 1804/07/25
Velde, A. 1804/08/08
Velde, W. 1804/08/08
Velde, W. 1806/08/13
Verbeeck, P.C. 1802/05/05
Verbeeck, P.C. 1807/08/26

Sneck
Molenaer, Klaes 1802/06/16
Schellinks, W. 1802/06/16

Snellen, Willem, Mr.
d. ca.1804; mayor of Dordrecht
Anonymous 1805/06/24
Backhuysen 1805/06/24
Both, J. 1805/06/24
Boucher 1805/06/24
Burg (Burgh) 1805/06/24
Cuypers (Kuypers) 1805/06/24
Droochsloot, J.C. 1805/06/24
Gulck, A. 1805/06/24
La Haye, R. 1805/06/24
Mieris, W. 1805/06/24
Poelenburgh, C. 1805/06/24
Savery, R. 1805/06/24
Storck, Abr. 1805/06/24
Toorenvliet, J. 1805/06/24

Sonnevelt
Anonymous 1802/07/27
Gulik, R. 1802/07/27
Verburgh, Rutger 1802/07/27
Visscher, C. (II) 1802/07/27

Spaan
Andrea del Sarto 1809/06/13
Anonymous 1802/06/28
Anonymous 1802/09/06
Anonymous 1805/07/10
Anonymous 1806/05/05
Anonymous 1808/08/23
Anonymous 1808/10/28
Anonymous 1810/07/26
Asselyn 1808/08/23
Asselyn 1809/04/17
Ast 1809/06/13
Bega 1802/09/06
Begeyn 1806/11/24
Bent, J. 1808/06/13
Bergen, D. 1808/08/23
Bloemaert, A. 1802/09/06
Brakenburg 1808/10/28
Brouwer, Adr. 1808/11/28
Carree, F. 1802/09/06
Correggio 1810/10/11
Cranach, L. (I) 1810/07/26
Deane 1810/07/26
Decker, C. 1809/04/17
Does, S. 1809/04/17
Dou 1810/03/26
Dujardin, K. 1805/12/16
Dusart, Corn. 1805/12/16
Ekels, Jan (I) 1807/08/26
Elliger, O. (II) 1802/09/06
Everdingen, A. 1810/06/20
Everdingen, Cesar 1802/06/16
Ferg, F. 1810/07/26
German 1810/07/26
Graat 1802/09/06
Heemskerck, B. 1802/09/06
Heeremans, Thos. 1808/08/23
Henning 1805/12/16
Himpel, A. 1802/09/06
Honthorst, G. 1801/06/13
Hoogsaat, J.C. 1802/09/06
Huysum, Jan 1805/12/16
Italian 1802/09/06
Jordaens, J. (I) 1810/07/26
Kieft, P. 1805/12/16
Lingelbach 1810/10/11
Maes, D. 1802/09/06
Mieris, W. 1802/09/06
Molijn 1808/10/28
Mommers, H. 1801/06/13
Monogrammist T.V.S. 1805/07/10
Moucheron, I. 1804/12/10
Neer, A. 1807/08/26
Neer, A. 1809/04/17
Oolen, Adr. 1804/05/07
Ostade, A. 1809/04/17
Palamedesz., A. 1806/11/24
Palamedesz., P. (I) 1808/08/23
Pee, T. 1802/06/28
Perrini 1810/07/26
Pieneman, J.W. 1805/07/10
Poel, E. 1802/09/06
Prins, J.H. 1806/05/05
Redeker, J. 1802/09/06
Robert, H. 1810/07/26
Rombouts 1805/12/16
Roos, P.P. 1802/09/06
Rosa, S. 1802/09/06
Rottenhammer, H. (I) 1810/07/26
Royen, W.F. van 1809/06/13
Rubens 1802/09/06
Rubens 1809/04/17
Ruisdael, J. 1810/07/26
Sanders, G. 1805/12/16
Scheffer, J.L. 1809/04/17
Schellinks, W. 1809/06/13
Schyndel, J. 1807/08/26
Silo, A. 1808/08/23
Sluis, J. 1805/07/10
Smeesters 1809/04/17
Smit, Aernout 1805/12/16
Snellinck, C. 1810/07/26
Sorgh, H.M. 1810/03/26
Steen, J. 1808/10/28
Storck, Abr. 1801/06/13
Straaten 1808/10/28
Teniers, D. (II) 1805/12/16
Toorenvliet, J. 1802/09/06
Vermeer, Jan (II) 1805/12/16
Vermeer, Jan (III) 1810/03/26
Vertangen 1802/09/06
Vinne, V.L. (I) 1802/09/06
Voorhout, J. (I) 1802/09/06
Vries, R. 1809/04/17
Weenix 1805/12/16
Wet, J.W. 1802/09/06
Witte, E. 1810/03/26
Wyck, T. 1805/07/10

Spaan, F.
Vitringa 1808/11/28

Spaan, Gelinus van
d. ca.1801; merchant and poet
Anonymous 1801/11/21
Brekelencam, Q. 1801/11/21
Flemish-Brabant 1801/11/21
Molenaer, J.M. 1801/11/21
Monogrammist J.P. 1801/11/21
Verboom, W.H. 1801/11/21
Winter, Gillis 1801/11/21
Wouwerman 1801/11/21

Spaan, Jan
dealer, probably the painter Jan Spaan, ca.1742–1828, and probably father of Theodorus Spaan, q.v.
Amigoni, J. 1804/05/07
Anonymous 1801/05/11
Anonymous 1801/08/19
Anonymous 1802/02/16
Anonymous 1802/05/05
Anonymous 1802/09/06
Anonymous 1802/12/13
Anonymous 1803/06/20
Anonymous 1803/08/01
Anonymous 1804/05/07
Anonymous 1804/12/10
Anonymous 1806/08/13
Anonymous 1808/06/13
Anonymous 1808/08/23
Anonymous 1810/08/06
Anonymous 1810/10/11
Bassano 1802/12/13
Beerstraten, A. 1808/08/23
Begeyn 1802/09/06
Begeyn 1802/12/13
Berchem, N.P. 1810/08/06
Berckheyde, G. 1801/06/10
Berckheyde, J. 1802/06/28
Besanger, S. 1802/09/29
Beschey, J. 1802/06/28
Blanckerhoff 1808/06/13
Bleeker, J. 1801/10/06
Bloemaert, A. 1802/09/06
Bloot, P. 1802/06/28
Bramer 1801/08/19
Bray, Jan 1808/08/23
Brekelencam, Q. 1803/09/07
Brekelencam, Q. 1810/08/06
Bril, P. 1803/06/20
Broeck, E. 1802/09/06
Brueghel, J. (I) 1806/08/13
Brueghel, J. (I) 1808/08/23
Carracci, A. 1801/10/06
Cornelisz. van Haarlem 1802/12/13
Croos, P. 1809/06/13
Cuyp, A. 1801/10/19
Decker, Jan 1804/05/07
Dietrich, Chr. 1804/07/25
Dou 1801/10/06
Dou 1803/04/20
Droochsloot, J.C. 1808/08/23
Dujardin, K. 1801/05/11
Dyck, Anth. van 1802/12/13
Ekels, Jan (I) 1808/08/23
Elfers, J. 1808/06/13
Flemish-Brabant 1802/06/28
Flinck 1801/08/19
Francken 1802/12/13
Francken, Frans (II) 1804/05/07
Gael, B. 1801/10/19
Goltzius, Hend. 1804/08/08
Gool, Jan 1804/12/10
Goyen 1802/09/06
Hendriks, W. 1808/06/13
Heusch, Jacob 1801/10/19
Hondecoeter, M. 1801/03/16
Hooch, P. 1804/05/07
Italian 1802/02/16
Italian 1802/09/06
Italian 1802/12/13
Italian 1810/08/06
Janson, J.C. 1804/12/10
Keller, J.H. (II) 1804/05/07
Kessel, J. (III) 1804/08/08
Kessel, J. (III) 1808/06/13
Kessel, J. (III) 1808/08/23
Keun, Hend. 1804/08/08
Klomp 1802/09/06
Lairesse, Jan 1803/08/01
Laquy, W.J. 1804/12/10
Lauri, F. 1808/08/23
Lingelbach 1808/08/23
Lundens 1804/08/08
Maes, D. 1802/02/16
Michelangelo 1810/08/06
Mieris, F. (I) 1802/09/29
Mieris, W. 1802/09/06
Molenaer, J.M. 1809/07/19
Molenaer, Klaes 1802/06/28
Molenaer, Klaes 1802/09/06
Mommers, H. 1808/06/13
Monogrammist B.R. 1802/09/29
Monogrammist W.K. 1808/08/23
Neer, A. 1802/02/16
Neer, A. 1804/08/08
Nepveu, J. 1808/06/13
Ostade, I. 1808/08/23
Pape, Abr. 1802/06/28
Peeters, Cath. 1801/03/16
Poel, E. 1802/09/06
Poel, E. 1810/08/06
Post, F.J. 1802/02/16
Prins, J.H. 1808/08/23
Quast, P.J. 1802/06/16
Rembrandt 1808/08/23
Rottenhammer, H. (I) 1801/10/06
Rottenhammer, H. (I) 1802/12/13
Rubens 1802/09/06
Rubens 1806/08/13
Ruysch, R. 1801/10/19
Ruysdael, S. 1802/12/13
Ryckaert, D. (III) 1806/08/13
Schellinks, Daniel 1803/06/20
Staveren, J.A. 1808/06/13
Steen, J. 1810/08/06
Stoop, D. 1802/09/06
Storck, Abr. 1804/08/08
Storck, Abr. 1808/08/23
Teniers, D. (II) 1802/09/06
Tol, D. 1802/09/06
Toorenburgh, G. 1802/06/28
Toorenburgh, G. 1804/05/07
Toorenvliet, J. 1802/09/06
Ulft 1810/08/06
Vallee, Louis 1803/04/20
Velde, E. (I) 1801/10/06
Velde, E. (I) 1802/02/16
Velde, W. 1803/08/01
Velde, W. 1804/08/08
Vermeulen, A. 1802/09/29
Vertangen 1808/08/23
Voorhout, J. (I) 1802/09/06
Vrancx 1802/12/13
Vries, R. 1801/05/11
Weenix 1801/06/10
Weenix, J.B. 1810/08/06
Wijnants 1804/08/08
Willaerts 1808/08/23
Winter, Gillis 1801/10/06
Wouwerman, Ph. 1803/04/20
Wtewael, J. 1804/07/25
Wyck, T. 1810/08/06
Zeemann 1802/02/16
Zeemann 1810/10/11
Zegelaar, G. 1804/12/10

Spaan, Theodorus
1780–1811; dealer and joint auctioneer in Amsterdam
Aelst, W. 1810/08/06
Anonymous 1801/05/11
Anonymous 1801/08/19
Anonymous 1802/05/05
Anonymous 1802/09/06
Anonymous 1802/12/13
Anonymous 1803/04/27
Anonymous 1803/06/20
Anonymous 1803/08/01
Anonymous 1803/12/12
Anonymous 1804/02/27
Anonymous 1806/11/24
Anonymous 1807/08/26
Anonymous 1808/06/13
Anonymous 1808/08/23
Anonymous 1808/11/28
Anonymous 1809/06/13
Anonymous 1809/07/19
Anonymous 1810/05/22
Anonymous 1810/06/20
Anonymous 1810/07/26
Anonymous 1810/08/06
Anonymous 1810/10/11
Anonymous-Antique 1803/07/18
Asch, P.J. van 1807/08/26
Asselyn 1802/02/16
Avercamp, H. 1806/08/13
Backhuysen 1801/05/11
Balen, H. (I) 1810/10/11
Bassano, J. 1810/10/11
Bassen 1810/08/06
Beerstraten, A. 1806/11/24
Beerstraten, A. 1809/06/13
Bega 1805/07/03
Bemmel, W. 1803/06/20
Bent, J. 1806/11/24
Bent, J. 1808/06/13
Berchem, N.P. 1810/06/20
Bergen, D. 1810/10/11
Beschey, B. 1810/05/22

Bloemaert, A. 1802/09/06
Bloemen, P. 1802/06/16
Borch, G. ter (II) 1808/11/28
Borch, G. ter (II) 1810/08/01
Brakenburg 1802/06/28
Breenbergh 1804/07/25
Breenbergh 1808/06/13
Brekelencam, Q. 1801/10/19
Brekelencam, Q. 1803/12/12
Brekelencam, Q. 1809/06/13
Brekelencam, Q. 1810/08/06
Broeck, E. 1808/06/13
Brueghel, J. (I) 1806/08/13
Brueghel, J. (I) 1810/10/11
Cabel, A. 1810/07/26
Cappelle 1810/08/01
Caravaggio 1803/04/27
Carracci, A. 1810/07/26
Carree 1810/10/11
Chalon, L. 1807/08/26
Champaigne, P. 1810/07/26
Coclers, J.B.B. 1802/06/28
Compe, Jan ten 1805/07/03
Correggio 1810/10/11
Cuyp, A. 1810/08/01
Cuyp, J.G. 1810/08/06
Decker, C. 1806/08/13
Decker, C. 1806/11/24
Dietrich, Chr. 1810/08/01
Does, S. 1809/06/13
Dolci, C. 1802/12/13
Drielst, E. 1808/11/28
Drielst, E. 1810/08/01
Droochsloot, J.C. 1801/10/06
Dubbels, H. 1801/03/16
Dubois, G. 1806/08/13
Dujardin, K. 1808/08/23
Dyck, Anth. van 1810/08/01
Eeckhout, G. 1802/09/06
Eeckhout, G. 1809/09/06
Ekels, Jan (I) 1808/11/28
Elfers, J. 1808/06/13
Essen, C. 1806/08/13
Everdingen, A. 1802/06/16
Everdingen, A. 1806/08/13
Ferg, F. 1810/07/26
Ferri, C. 1803/04/27
Flemal, B. (I) 1803/04/27
Flinck 1807/08/26
Fyt 1806/08/13
Gael, B. 1806/08/13
Gérard, M. 1806/08/13
Gerards 1807/08/26
Giordano, L. 1803/04/27
Giorgione 1803/04/27
Gool, Jan 1807/08/26
Graef, T. 1808/06/13
Griffier, J. (I) 1806/08/13
Griffier, R. 1810/06/20
Guercino 1803/04/27
Hackert, J.P. 1810/08/06
Hagen, Joris 1808/11/28
Heem, David 1808/08/23
Heemskerck 1810/06/20
Heeremans, Thos. 1810/06/20
Helst, B. 1810/08/01
Hendriks, W. 1808/06/13
Heusch, Jacob 1809/06/13
Heyden, J. 1802/06/28
Heyden, J. 1809/07/19
Hobbema 1806/08/13
Hondecoeter, M. 1802/05/05
Hondecoeter, M. 1802/12/13
Horstink, W. 1809/09/06
Houckgeest, G. 1808/11/28
Huchtenburgh, Jan 1808/11/28
Hulswit, Jan 1808/08/23
Huysum, Jan 1808/08/23
Italian 1802/09/06
Italian 1808/11/28
Janson, J. 1808/06/13
Janson, J. 1810/05/22
Kessel, J. (III) 1808/08/23
Keun, Hend. 1809/09/06
Knupfer 1809/07/19
Koninck, Jacob 1802/09/06
Kuik, J. 1809/06/13
La Haye, R. 1808/11/28
Laquy, W.J. 1809/06/13
Lauri, F. 1808/08/23
Leeuw, Govert van der 1808/08/23
Lievens, J. (I) 1810/06/20
Limborch, H. 1808/11/28
Lingelbach 1808/06/13
Lingelbach 1809/06/13
Lingelbach 1810/06/20
Lingelbach 1810/08/01
Lingelbach 1810/10/11
Lundens 1810/06/20
Maas, J. 1802/09/06
Maes, D. 1808/06/13
Maes, N. 1810/06/20
Man, L.D. 1809/06/13
Marseus, O. 1804/08/08
Maton, B. 1810/08/01
Matthieu, C. 1807/08/26
Meincs, Gabriel 1810/08/06
Metsu 1803/12/12
Metsu 1806/08/13
Metsu 1810/08/01
Miel 1801/10/06
Miel 1802/02/16
Miereveld, M. 1810/08/01
Mieris, F. (I) 1803/04/20
Mieris, F. (I) 1809/07/19
Mieris, W. 1810/05/22
Molenaer, J.M. 1806/08/13
Molenaer, J.M. 1809/07/19
Molenaer, J.M. 1810/06/20
Molenaer, Klaes 1802/05/05
Molenaer, Klaes 1806/08/13
Molenaer, Klaes 1807/08/26
Molijn 1806/08/13
Molijn 1810/06/20
Mommers, H. 1803/12/12
Momper, J. (II) 1808/11/28
Moni, L. de 1807/08/26
Moni, L. de 1810/05/22
Monogrammist I.B.I.R. 1803/04/20
Morel, Jan Evert 1808/08/23
Morel, Jan Evert 1810/08/06
Moucheron, F. 1809/06/13
Moucheron, F. 1810/08/01
Moucheron, I. 1808/10/28
Naiveu 1804/08/08
Neeffs, P. (I) 1805/07/10
Neer, A. 1808/08/23
Os 1808/08/23
Ostade, A. 1810/05/22
Ouwater, Isaak 1806/08/13
Ouwater, Isaak 1807/08/26
Palamedesz., A. 1802/06/28
Palamedesz., A. 1808/11/28
Parmigianino 1808/08/23
Piemont 1804/08/08
Piemont 1808/06/13
Poelenburgh, C. 1803/04/20
Poelenburgh, C. 1808/11/28
Poelenburgh, C. 1809/06/13
Porcellis, Jan 1806/08/13
Potter, Paulus 1802/09/29
Rembrandt 1810/08/01
Rennel, S. 1807/08/26
Roepel, C. 1806/11/24
Roghman, R. 1810/10/11
Roos, P.P. 1802/09/06
Rosa, S. 1802/09/06
Rosa, S. 1809/06/13
Roskam, H. 1808/06/13
Ruisdael, J. 1801/05/11
Ruisdael, J. 1802/09/29
Ruisdael, J. 1808/10/28
Ruisdael, J. 1810/08/01
Ruysch, R. 1801/08/19
Ruysdael, S. 1806/08/13
Schalcken 1810/06/20
Schedoni 1803/04/27
Schellinks, Daniel 1802/02/16
Silo, A. 1808/11/28
Silo, A. 1810/08/06
Smeesters 1810/06/20
Smit, Aernout 1808/08/23
Sorgh, H.M. 1805/07/10
Staveren, J.A. 1806/08/13
Staveren, J.A. 1809/09/06
Steen, J. 1808/06/13
Steen, J. 1808/11/28
Steen, J. 1809/06/13
Steen, J. 1809/07/19
Steen, J. 1809/09/06
Steenwyck, Hend. 1802/12/13
Storck, Abr. 1802/12/13
Storck, Abr. 1803/08/01
Storck, Abr. 1806/08/13
Storck, Abr. 1809/06/13
Swanevelt 1803/09/07
Teniers, D. (II) 1802/09/06
Toorenvliet, J. 1802/05/05
Velde, A. 1801/06/10
Velde, A. 1809/07/19
Velde, W. 1810/08/01
Verboom, A.H. 1808/06/13
Verdonck, Corn. 1806/08/13
Verkolje, N. 1809/09/06
Vermeer, Jan 1809/09/06
Vermeer, Jan (III) 1808/08/23
Vertangen 1809/06/13
Victors, Jan 1807/08/26
Victors, Jan 1808/06/13
Victors, Jan 1808/08/23
Vitringa 1808/06/13
Vlieger, S. 1806/08/13
Vlieger, S. 1810/08/06
Vliet, H.C. 1802/12/13
Vonck 1803/06/20
Vree, N. de 1805/07/10
Vries, R. 1809/06/13
Vries, R. 1810/10/11
Wagner, J.G. 1806/08/13
Walscapelle 1808/06/13
Weenix 1810/08/06
Weenix, Juffr. 1810/05/22
Wigmana, G. 1806/11/24
Wijnants 1801/06/10
Wijnants 1810/06/20
Willaerts, C. 1810/10/11
Winter, Gillis 1802/02/16
Withoos, M. 1808/06/13
Witte, E. 1808/11/28
Wolfsen, Aleijda 1808/08/23
Wouwerman, P. 1808/11/28
Wouwerman, Ph. 1809/09/06
Wulfraet 1807/08/26
Zeemann 1810/08/06
Zyl, G. 1806/08/13

Spakler
Rubens 1807/08/26

Spanjaart, Govert
1731–1807
Anonymous 1808/12/31
Colonia, A. 1808/12/31
Croos 1808/12/31
Ducq, Johan le 1808/12/31
Dusart, A. 1808/12/31
Hoet, G. (I) 1808/12/31
Lelienbergh 1808/12/31
Man, Joost 1808/12/31
Mart, van der 1808/12/31
Mooy, C.P. 1808/12/31
Murant 1808/12/31
Myn, H. 1808/12/31
Neer, A. 1808/12/31
Ostade, I. 1808/12/31
Palamedesz., A. 1808/12/31
Porcellis, Jan 1808/12/31
Silo, A. 1808/12/31
Teniers, D. (II) 1808/12/31
Vliet, H.C. 1808/12/31
Wet, J.W. 1808/12/31

Specht
Anonymous 1803/06/27

Spies
possibly the draftsman and aquarellist Hendrik Spies, 1775–1841, from Zutphen
Poel, E. 1806/11/24

Spillebout, Jacobus
1733–1807; resident of Haarlem
Anonymous 1808/03/03
Bierweiler 1808/03/03
Blanckerhoff 1808/03/03
Bray, Jan 1808/03/03
Bresser, A. 1808/03/03
Chalon, L. 1808/03/03
Delcloche, P.J. 1808/03/03
Dyck, Anth. van 1808/03/03
Essen, C. 1808/03/03
Heeremans, Thos. 1808/03/03
Hodges, C.H. 1808/03/03
Hondecoeter 1808/03/03
Huchtenburgh, Jan 1808/03/03
Jordaens, J. (I) 1808/03/03
Kessel, J. (III) 1808/03/03
Kraul, K.F. 1808/03/03
Lagoor 1808/03/03
Molenaer, J.M. 1808/03/03
Mommers, H. 1808/03/03
Nickelen 1808/03/03
Nieulandt 1808/03/03
Noorde, Corn. 1808/03/03
Post, F.J. 1808/03/03
Pynacker 1808/03/03
Rombouts 1808/03/03
Ruysdael, S. 1808/03/03
Storck, Abr. 1808/03/03
Utrecht, Adr. 1808/03/03
Verspronck, Joh. 1808/03/03
Vinne, J. 1808/03/03
Vinne, Jan (I) 1808/03/03
Vinne, V.L. (I) 1808/03/03
Weenix 1808/03/03
Wouwerman, J. 1808/03/03

Sprink
Anonymous 1802/07/27

Spruijt, see Spruyt

Spruit, see Spruyt

Spruyt, Charles Joseph François
1769–1851; painter, engraver, son of the dealer Philippe Lambert Joseph Spruyt, 1727–1801
Anonymous 1801/06/10
Anonymous 1801/06/13
Anonymous 1802/05/05
Anonymous 1806/08/13
Anonymous 1806/08/20
Anonymous 1807/06/10
Anonymous 1807/08/26
Anonymous 1808/08/23
Anonymous 1810/07/23
Asch, P.J. van 1802/05/05
Asch, P.J. van 1806/08/20
Asselyn 1806/08/13
Backhuysen 1801/06/10
Backhuysen 1802/05/05
Backhuysen 1807/08/26
Bassano 1801/10/06
Begeyn 1802/05/05
Berckheyde, J. 1802/05/05
Bloemaert, A. 1802/05/05

Bloemen, P. 1808/08/23
Bol, F. 1802/05/05
Both, A. 1807/08/26
Brakenburg 1808/08/23
Bramer 1802/05/05
Bray, S. 1807/06/10
Bray, S. 1808/08/23
Brekelencam, Q. 1801/10/19
Burg, Dirk 1802/05/05
Cornelisz. van Haarlem 1801/06/13
Cuylenburg, C. 1806/08/20
Cuyp, A. 1807/06/10
Cuyp, J.G. 1806/08/20
Dietrich, Chr. 1807/08/26
Dietrich, Chr. 1810/07/26
Dou 1807/06/10
Dubbels, H. 1802/05/05
Dujardin, K. 1801/06/10
Dusart, Corn. 1801/04/13
Dusart, Corn. 1801/06/10
Dusart, Corn. 1807/08/26
Dyck, Anth. van 1807/08/26
Dyk, P. 1806/08/20
Eeckhout, G. 1807/06/10
Everdingen, A. 1810/07/23
Flemish-Brabant 1806/08/20
Francken 1802/05/05
Gael, B. 1802/05/05
Genoels, Abr. 1810/07/26
Gerards 1801/10/06
Gerards 1810/07/23
Hals, F. (I) 1801/04/13
Heem, J.D. 1807/08/26
Helst, A. 1802/05/05
Hobbema 1801/10/06
Hobbema 1802/05/05
Hooch, P. 1801/04/13
Hoogstraten, S. 1806/08/20
Huchtenburgh, Jan 1808/08/23
Huysum, Jan 1807/08/26
Jacobsz., Juriaen 1801/06/10
Janson, J. 1802/05/05
Jordaens, J. (I) 1801/04/13
Kessel, J. (III) 1802/05/05
Klomp 1802/05/05
Klomp 1808/08/23
Kobell, H. 1801/06/10
Koninck, P. 1802/05/05
Lastman, P.P. 1807/06/10
Lauri, F. 1810/07/26
Lingelbach 1801/06/10
Lingelbach 1801/06/13
Lingelbach 1808/08/23
Lingelbach 1810/07/26
Lucas van Leyden 1808/08/23
Lundens 1802/05/05
Lundens 1808/08/23
Maat, N. 1807/08/26
Maddersteeg 1807/08/26
Maes, N. 1801/04/13
Maes, N. 1802/05/05
Maratti 1806/08/13
Martszen, J. (II) 1802/05/05
Mieris, F. (I) 1801/06/13
Mieris, F. (I) 1806/08/20
Moeyaert, C. 1802/05/05
Molenaer, J.M. 1801/06/10
Molenaer, Klaes 1801/06/10
Molijn 1802/05/05
Monogrammist E.J. 1806/08/20
Monogrammist P.L. 1802/05/05
Moor, C. 1801/04/13
Moor, C. 1801/06/10
Moor, C. 1810/07/23
Moucheron 1801/06/13
Murillo 1807/08/26
Murillo 1810/07/26
Neer, A. 1802/05/05
Oolen, Jan 1807/08/26
Ostade, A. 1801/04/13
Ostade, A. 1801/10/19
Ostade, A. 1802/05/05
Ostade, A. 1808/08/23
Ostade, I. 1808/08/23
Oudendyck 1802/05/05
Palamedesz., A. 1807/08/26
Paling, I. 1807/08/26
Peeters, B. (I) 1801/10/06
Poelenburgh, C. 1810/07/26
Potter, Paulus 1801/06/10
Rembrandt 1806/08/20
Rembrandt 1807/08/26
Romeyn 1807/06/10
Roos, P.P. 1803/09/07
Rosa, S. 1803/09/07
Ruisdael, J. 1802/05/05
Saftleven, C. 1807/08/26
Schellinks, W. 1808/08/23
Sin, P. le 1806/08/20
Slingeland, P.C. 1801/06/13
Snyders, F. 1801/04/13
Steen, J. 1807/08/26
Steen, J. 1808/08/23
Storck, Abr. 1802/05/05
Teniers, D. (II) 1807/08/26
Troost, C. 1801/06/10
Troost, C. 1807/06/10
Velde, A. 1802/05/05
Velde, A. 1806/08/20
Verboom, A.H. 1801/06/10
Vermeer, Jan (III) 1802/05/05
Vertangen 1807/08/26
Victors, Jan 1807/08/26
Vitringa 1802/05/05
Vliet, H.C. 1807/06/10
Vois, Ary de 1801/04/13
Vois, Ary de 1806/08/20
Vrancx 1802/05/05
Vrancx 1803/09/07
Weenix 1801/06/10
Weenix 1802/05/05
Weenix, J.B. 1801/04/13
Wijnants 1801/10/06
Witte, E. 1807/08/26
Wouwerman, P. 1806/08/13
Wouwerman, P. 1808/08/23
Wouwerman, Ph. 1801/10/19
Wouwerman, Ph. 1802/05/05
Wtewael, J. 1801/10/19
Zeemann 1808/08/23

Spyk, Paulus van der
d. ca.1802; official in Dordrecht
Anonymous 1802/11/01
Asselyn 1802/11/01
Bassen 1802/11/01
Bijlert 1802/11/01
Both, A. 1802/11/01
Brueghel, P. (II) 1802/11/01
Burg, Adriaan 1802/11/01
Cuyp, A. 1802/11/01
Cuyp, B. 1802/11/01
Decker 1802/11/01
Diepraem 1802/11/01
Does 1802/11/01
Douw, S. 1802/11/01
Droochsloot, Abr. 1802/11/01
Dubbels, H. 1802/11/01
Duynen, I. 1802/11/01
Gael, B. 1802/11/01
Gelder, A. 1802/11/01
Goltzius, Hend. 1802/11/01
Goyen 1802/11/01
Haan, C. de 1802/11/01
Hals, F. (I) 1802/11/01
Hardimé 1802/11/01
Heem, C. 1802/11/01
Heemskerck 1802/11/01
Heeremans, Thos. 1802/11/01
Honthorst, G. 1802/11/01
Houbraken, Arn. 1802/11/01
Huchtenburgh, Jan 1802/11/01
Janson, J. 1802/11/01
Jordaens, J. (I) 1802/11/01
Keller, J.H. (II) 1802/11/01
Kessel, J. (III) 1802/11/01
Klomp 1802/11/01
Lelienbergh 1802/11/01
Maes, N. 1802/11/01
Molenaer 1802/11/01
Molenaer, J.M. 1802/11/01
Molijn 1802/11/01
Molyn, C. 1802/11/01
Monogrammist A.S. 1802/11/01
Monogrammist C.V.E 1802/11/01
Monogrammist H.C. 1802/11/01
Monogrammist H.R. 1802/11/01
Monogrammist H.T. 1802/11/01
Monogrammist J.B. 1802/11/01
Monogrammist J.M.R. 1802/11/01
Monogrammist J.S. 1802/11/01
Neer, A. 1802/11/01
Ostade, A. 1802/11/01
Palamedesz., A. 1802/11/01
Poel, E. 1802/11/01
Porcellis, Jan 1802/11/01
Romyn, A. 1802/11/01
Saftleven, H. 1802/11/01
Schalcken 1802/11/01
Schendel, B. 1802/11/01
Storck, Abr. 1802/11/01
Velde, E. (I) 1802/11/01
Verbuys, A. 1802/11/01
Verschuring, H. 1802/11/01
Vos, M. 1802/11/01
Vosmaer, Nic. 1802/11/01
Withoos, M. 1802/11/01
Wouwerman, Pieter 1802/11/01

Stam, J.
Anonymous 1810/06/20
Heemskerck 1810/06/20

Stants, C.
Monogrammist H.B. 1802/06/28

Stategaart, Maria
d. ca.1802; resident of Alkmaar
Anonymous 1802/07/27
Beelt, C. 1802/07/27
Berchem, N.P. 1802/07/27
Beschey, Charles 1802/07/27
Bino, H. 1802/07/27
Brekelencam, Q. 1802/07/27
Broeck, E. 1802/07/27
Carree, F. 1802/07/27
Carree, M. 1802/07/27
Ducq, Johan le 1802/07/27
Dusart, Corn. 1802/07/27
Eeckhout, G. 1802/07/27
Fris, Jan 1802/07/27
Gael, B. 1802/07/27
Grasdorp, W. 1802/07/27
Gulik, R. 1802/07/27
Heck, C. 1802/07/27
Heem, J.D. 1802/07/27
Jacobsz., L. 1802/07/27
Kerckhoff, Fr. 1802/07/27
Knip, N.F. (I) 1802/07/27
Lingelbach 1802/07/27
Marseus, O. 1802/07/27
Metsu 1802/07/27
Meyering, Alb. 1802/07/27
Molenaer, J.M. 1802/07/27
Mommers, H. 1802/07/27
Monogrammist D.V.B. 1802/07/27
Monogrammist F.A.O. 1802/07/27
Monogrammist J.M. 1802/07/27
Monogrammist J.V.B. 1802/07/27
Neeffs, P. (I) 1802/07/27
Nieulandt, W. (II) 1802/07/27
Ostade, A. 1802/07/27
Palamedesz., A. 1802/07/27
Poelenburgh, C. 1802/07/27
Rembrandt 1802/07/27
Ruysch, J. 1802/07/27
Schaaven 1802/07/27
Schendel, B. 1802/07/27
Smit, Aernout 1802/07/27
Steen, J. 1802/07/27
Steen, J. (18th c.) 1802/07/27
Verburgh, Rutger 1802/07/27
Verelst, S. 1802/07/27
Visscher, C. (II) 1802/07/27
Vitringa 1802/07/27
Vogelsang, I. 1802/07/27
Wel, W.V. 1802/07/27

Stech
Anonymous 1802/12/13

Steeg, V., see Versteegh

Steegh, V., see Versteegh

Steenstra
also spelled Stinstra; active in Harlingen
Borch, G. ter (II) 1808/06/06
Helst, B. 1808/06/06

Steenstraat, see Steenstra

Stees
Anonymous 1809/07/25
Besanger, S. 1809/07/25
Besters, A.J. 1809/07/25
Gool, Jan 1809/07/25
Molenaer, Klaes 1809/07/25
Tengeler, W. 1809/07/25
Verelst, Joh. 1809/07/25

Stepraan, J. Van
Anonymous 1801/06/13

Sterk, Augustus Elink
1748–1815; dealer, related to Anna Elink, 1715–1802, q.v.
Anonymous 1801/10/06
Berchem, N.P. 1801/10/06
Both, J. 1801/10/06
Ostade, A. 1801/10/06
Ostade, A. 1801/10/19
Rembrandt 1801/10/06
Teniers, D. (II) 1801/10/19
Toorenvliet, J. 1801/10/06
Velde, W. 1801/10/19
Velde, W. (I) 1801/10/19

Stevens
Anna, Vito 1803/04/27
Anne, P. 1803/04/27
Anonymous 1801/03/16
Anonymous 1801/06/10
Anonymous 1801/06/13
Anonymous 1802/05/05
Anonymous 1802/12/13
Anonymous 1803/04/27
Bassen 1802/05/05
Bega 1801/03/16
Berckheyde, J. 1803/04/27
Beschey, J. 1801/06/10
Bloot, P. 1801/06/10
Bredael, P. 1801/06/10
Breenbergh 1801/06/10
Conca, S. 1803/04/27
Correggio 1803/04/27
Cuyp, A. 1801/03/16
Does, J. (I) 1801/06/10
Does, S. 1801/06/13
Dolci, C. 1803/04/27
Dongen, Dionys 1801/06/13
Dusart, Corn. 1801/06/10
Everdingen, A. 1802/05/05
Goyen 1801/03/16
Goyen 1801/06/13
Goyen 1803/04/27
Graat 1802/05/05

Everdingen, A. 1809/06/13
Kessel, J. (III) 1809/06/13
Moucheron, F. 1809/06/13
Ruysdael, S. 1809/06/13
Verbeeck, P.C. 1809/06/13
Vermeulen, A. 1809/06/13
Wijnants 1809/06/13
Wulfraet 1809/06/13

T. (1810, May 22)
Goyen 1810/05/22
Mieris, F. (I) 1810/05/22
Ochtervelt 1810/05/22
Ostade, I. 1810/05/22
Ruysdael, S. 1810/05/22
Schalcken 1810/05/22
Vries, R. 1810/05/22
Werff, A. 1810/05/22

T. (1810, June 20)
Balen, H. (I) 1810/06/20
Vlieger, S. 1810/06/20
Vos 1810/06/20

T., S.
Avercamp, H. 1807/06/10
Balen, H. (I) 1807/06/10
Brueghel, J. (I) 1807/06/10
Ducq, Johan le 1807/06/10
Goyen 1807/06/10
Laquy, W.J. 1807/06/10
Palamedesz., A. 1807/06/10

Taak
Anonymous 1802/06/28
Koninck 1802/06/28
Lubienietski, C. 1802/06/28
Victors, Jan 1802/06/28

Taijs, see Thijs

Taixeira, see Teixeira

Taixera, see Teixeira

Tak, Adn.
Backhuysen 1803/11/30
Brueghel 1803/11/30
Brueghel, P. 1803/11/30

Takel
Anonymous 1802/06/16

Takséra, see Teixeira

Tallée
Janson, J. 1807/06/10

Tamé, T.
d. ca.1801; medical doctor, perhaps Tieleman Tamé
Anonymous 1801/06/23
Besanger, S. 1801/06/23

Taxaira, see Teixeira

Taxera, see Teixeira

Tebbetman
Gool, Jan 1807/08/26

Tedeman, B.
Hooch, P. 1806/05/05

Teekengenootschap, see Pictura

Teengs, D.
Anonymous 1802/12/13
Anonymous 1803/08/01
Avercamp, H. 1802/12/13
Beerstraten, J. 1804/02/27
Beerstraten, Jan 1803/08/01
Bega 1805/07/10
Bloot, P. 1803/09/07
Carree, M. 1803/09/07
Chalon, L. 1803/07/18
Ducq, Johan le 1802/12/13
Dujardin, K. 1809/07/19
Everdingen, A. 1804/02/27
Faber, J.H. 1804/05/07
Hals, F. (I) 1806/08/13
Hamilton, P.F. 1803/09/07
Hooch, P. 1809/07/19
Huchtenburgh, Jan 1804/02/27
Molenaer, J.M. 1803/08/17
Molenaer, Klaes 1803/08/01
Molenaer, Klaes 1803/09/07
Mommers, H. 1803/12/12
Mommers, H. 1804/02/27
Neer, A. 1805/07/10
Netscher, Casp. 1803/07/18
Ostade, A. 1809/07/19
Ruysdael, S. 1802/12/13
Schalcken 1805/07/10
Schutz, S. 1803/09/07
Silo, A. 1803/12/12
Steen, J. 1803/12/12
Troost, C. 1804/02/27
Watteau, J.A. 1803/09/07
Weenix, J.B. 1806/08/13
Witte, E. 1804/05/07

Teerling
Beerstraten, J. 1810/06/20
Heeremans, Thos. 1810/06/20
Velde, E. (I) 1810/06/20

Teissier
probably the Hague painter J.G. Teissier, 1750–1821
Amigoni, J. 1801/04/13
Anonymous 1801/10/19
Anonymous 1803/08/17
Anonymous 1803/08/24
Anonymous 1803/09/07
Anonymous 1805/07/03
Anonymous 1810/08/06
Asselyn 1810/08/01
Backer 1803/08/24
Backhuysen 1804/08/08
Backhuysen 1807/06/10
Backhuysen 1810/08/01
Balen, H. (I) 1805/10/09
Bassen 1803/08/24
Beest, J. 1809/07/25
Bega 1802/09/06
Bega 1810/08/06
Berchem, N.P. 1807/06/10
Berchem, N.P. 1810/08/01
Berckheyde 1806/08/20
Berckheyde, G. 1801/10/19
Berckheyde, G. 1805/07/03
Berckheyde, J. 1805/10/09
Blanckerhoff 1808/08/23
Borch, G. ter (II) 1807/06/10
Bos, N. 1805/10/09
Boudewyns 1803/07/18
Brakenburg 1802/06/28
Brakenburg 1803/08/24
Bredael 1803/08/24
Brekelencam, Q. 1803/08/24
Bril, P. 1803/08/24
Bril, P. 1805/10/09
Brouwer, Adr. 1804/08/08
Brueghel 1805/10/09
Brueghel, J. (I) 1807/06/10
Brueghel, P. (II) 1809/07/25
Brussel, P. 1807/06/10
Burg (Burgh) 1806/08/20
Cappelle 1802/06/16
Carpioni, G. (I) 1802/06/16
Carpioni, G. (I) 1803/08/24
Carree 1803/08/24
Carree, Abr. 1803/08/24
Chalon, L. 1803/08/24
Compe, Jan ten 1802/06/28
Compe, Jan ten 1807/06/10
Cornelisz. van Haarlem 1803/08/24
Cranach, L. (I) 1809/07/25
Crayer, G. 1803/08/24
Cuyp, A. 1806/08/20
Dalens, Dirck 1803/04/20
Deuren, O. 1810/08/01
Dou 1802/06/28
Dou 1810/08/06
Droman, F. 1802/06/28
Ducq, Johan le 1805/10/09
Dujardin, K. 1810/08/01
Dusart, Corn. 1802/06/28
Dusart, Corn. 1802/09/06
Dusart, Corn. 1810/08/01
Dutch 1806/08/20
Dyck, Anth. van 1803/08/24
Elliger, O. (II) 1802/06/28
Elsheimer, A. 1805/10/09
Engels, B. 1803/08/24
Esselens, Jacob 1803/08/24
Fargue, Maria la 1803/08/24
Fargue, P.C. 1803/08/24
Ferguson, Wm. 1805/07/03
Flinck 1806/08/20
French 1809/07/25
Gael, B. 1802/09/06
Gael, B. 1803/08/24
Gael, B. 1809/07/25
Geel, N. 1802/06/16
Gerards 1803/08/24
Gool, Jan 1807/06/10
Goyen 1803/08/24
Goyen 1806/08/20
Goyen 1809/07/25
Goyen 1810/08/06
Griffier 1801/06/13
Griffier, R. 1802/06/28
Hackaert, J. 1802/06/16
Hackaert, J. 1803/08/24
Hackert, J.P. 1810/08/01
Heusch 1804/08/08
Heusch, Wm. 1808/08/23
Heusch, Wm. 1810/08/06
Heyden, J. 1803/08/24
Hoecke, R. 1803/08/24
Hoet, G. (I) 1803/08/24
Hoet, G. (I) 1805/10/09
Holbein, H. (II) 1803/08/24
Honthorst, G. 1803/08/24
Honthorst, G. 1806/08/20
Huchtenburgh, Jan 1802/06/28
Huchtenburgh, Jan 1803/07/18
Huchtenburgh, Jan 1803/08/24
Huchtenburgh, Jan 1806/08/20
Italian 1803/08/24
Italian 1803/09/07
Jacobsz., Juriaen 1803/08/24
Janson, J. 1805/07/03
Janson, J. 1807/06/10
Kessel, J. (III) 1810/08/06
Kleijne, David 1803/08/24
Kleijne, David 1807/06/10
Koninck, P. 1810/08/06
Kuster 1809/07/25
Lairesse, G. 1803/08/24
Lairesse, G. 1810/08/06
Langendijk, D. 1803/08/24
Largillière 1803/08/24
Lingelbach 1803/08/24
Lucas van Leyden 1803/08/24
Maes, D. 1807/06/10
Meijer, H. 1807/06/10
Metsu 1802/09/06
Miel 1808/08/23
Millet, J.F. (I) 1803/08/24
Molenaer, J.M. 1803/08/24
Molenaer, Klaes 1803/08/24
Molenaer, Klaes 1810/08/06
Molijn 1807/06/10
Mommers, H. 1804/08/08
Moor, C. 1810/08/06
Moritz, Louis 1809/07/25
Moucheron 1802/09/06
Moucheron, F. 1807/06/10
Mytens 1803/08/24
Neeffs, P. (I) 1805/10/09
Neer, A. 1807/06/10
Neer, E. 1803/07/18
Netscher, Casp. 1803/08/24
Netscher, Casp. 1810/08/01
Ochtervelt 1803/08/24
Olis 1801/06/13
Os, J. 1805/10/09
Ostade, A. 1803/08/24
Ostade, A. 1809/07/25
Ostade, A. 1810/08/01
Ostade, I. 1802/06/28
Ostade, I. 1807/06/10
Ostade, I. 1810/08/01
Palamedesz., A. 1802/06/28
Palamedesz., A. 1803/08/24
Palm, J. 1803/08/24
Peeters, B. (I) 1803/09/07
Poelenburgh, C. 1803/08/24
Potter, Paulus 1810/08/01
Prins, J.H. 1806/08/20
Pynacker 1810/08/01
Raoux, J. 1803/08/24
Rietschoof, H. 1802/06/16
Rietschoof, H. 1805/07/03
Rietschoof, H. 1806/08/20
Roepel, C. 1802/06/16
Romeyn 1806/08/20
Roore 1802/06/28
Rottenhammer, H. (I) 1805/10/09
Ruisdael, J. 1803/08/24
Ruisdael, J. 1808/08/23
Ruisdael, J. 1810/08/01
Ruisdael, J. 1810/08/06
Saftleven, C. 1801/04/13
Savery, R. 1802/06/28
Savery, R. 1803/08/24
Schalcken 1803/08/24
Schinnagl 1803/09/07
Schinnagl 1807/06/10
Schoevaerdts, M. 1803/07/18
Schütz 1806/08/20
Seghers, D. 1809/07/25
Silo, A. 1810/08/06
Snellinck 1803/08/24
Snyders, F. 1803/08/24
Sorgh, H.M. 1802/06/28
Sorgh, H.M. 1805/07/03
Sorgh, H.M. 1806/08/20
Steen, J. 1801/06/13
Steen, J. 1803/08/24
Storck, Abr. 1802/06/16
Teniers, D. (II) 1803/08/24
Teniers, D. (II) 1804/07/25
Teniers, D. (II) 1808/08/23
Tischbein 1808/06/06
Tol, D. 1802/06/28
Tol, D. 1810/08/01
Troost, J.H. 1803/08/24
Ulft 1803/08/24
Velde, A. 1810/08/01
Velde, E. (I) 1802/06/28
Velde, E. (I) 1803/08/24
Velde, W. 1803/08/24
Verboom, A.H. 1803/08/24
Verbruggen, G. (II) 1803/08/24
Verbruggen, G. (II) 1806/08/20
Vermeulen, A. 1806/08/20
Vernet, C.J. 1810/08/06
Verschuring, H. 1805/10/09
Vinckeboons, D. 1807/06/10
Vitringa 1803/08/24
Vleughels, N. 1803/08/24
Vlieger, S. 1803/08/24

Vlieger, S. 1810/08/06
Vonck 1807/06/10
Vries, R. 1804/08/08
Vroom, H. 1803/08/24
Weenix 1809/09/06
Weenix 1810/08/01
Weenix, J.B. 1803/09/07
Weenix, J.B. 1810/08/01
Wigmana, G. 1802/06/28
Wit, Jacob de 1803/08/24
Wit, Jacob de 1805/10/09
Withoos, M. 1803/08/24
Wittel 1803/08/24
Wouwerman, Ph. 1803/08/24
Wouwerman, Ph. 1810/08/01
Wyck, T. 1804/08/08
Wyntrack, D. 1807/06/10
Wyntrack, D. 1810/08/06
Zeemann 1803/09/07
Zeemann 1804/07/25
Zeemann 1804/08/08

Teixeira, A.
dealer
Asselyn 1805/12/16
Brueghel, J. (I) 1802/05/24
Molenaer, J.M. 1806/08/20
Molenaer, Klaes 1802/05/24
Molijn 1809/07/25
Neer, A. 1807/06/10
Netscher, Casp. 1803/08/24
Pothoven, H. 1804/12/10
Rembrandt 1809/07/25
Schalcken 1806/08/20
Schweickardt, H. 1806/08/20
Steen, J. 1805/12/16
Vanloo, J. 1809/07/25
Versteeg 1806/08/20

Teixera, see Teixeira

Temmick, see Temminck

Temminck
inspector of government buildings formerly belonging to the prince of Nassau during the French occupation
Anonymous 1805/07/10
Anonymous 1807/06/10
Blanckerhoff 1805/07/10
Broeck, E. 1805/07/10
Cuylenborch, A. 1805/07/10
Diest, W. van 1807/06/10
Goyen 1807/06/10
Honthorst, G. 1805/07/10
Hooch, P. 1805/07/10
Monogrammist J.G.L. 1805/07/10
Monogrammist T.V.S. 1805/07/10
Schellinks, W. 1805/07/10
Stoffe 1807/06/10
Vermeulen, A. 1809/07/25
Vlieger, S. 1806/08/20
Vonck 1807/06/10
Vries, R. 1805/07/10
Weenix 1805/07/10
Wet, J.W. 1805/07/10

Temmink, see Temminck

Ten Dall, E.B., see Dall, E.B. ten

Tersien
Wet, J.W. 1802/08/24

Tersmitten
Anonymous 1801/10/06
Avercamp, H. 1801/10/06
Compe, Jan ten 1801/10/06
Franks, J. 1801/10/06
Huysum, Jan 1801/10/06
Mieris, W. 1801/06/10
Potter, Paulus 1801/10/06
Rottenhammer, H. (I) 1801/10/06
Tiziano 1801/10/06
Vlieger, S. 1801/10/06
Wigmana, J. 1801/10/06
Witte, E. 1801/10/06
Wouwerman, Ph. 1801/10/06

Tersteeg, Jan
1750–1807; merchant, dealer and amateur artist
Andrea del Sarto 1808/06/13
Anonymous 1808/06/13
Backhuysen 1808/06/13
Berchem, N.P. 1808/06/13
Berckheyde, G. 1808/06/13
Bloemen, J.F. 1808/06/13
Bloemen, P. 1808/06/13
Brussel, H. 1808/06/13
Buys, Jac. 1808/06/13
Compe, Jan ten 1808/06/13
Drielst, E. 1808/06/13
Dubourg, L. 1808/06/13
Eeckhout, G. 1808/06/13
Ekels, Jan (II) 1808/06/13
Gerards 1808/06/13
Goyen 1808/06/13
Grandjean, J. 1808/06/13
Haensbergen, J. van 1808/06/13
Hendriks, W. 1808/06/13
Hooch, P. 1808/06/13
Huysum, Jan 1808/06/13
Kuijper, J. 1808/06/13
Laquy, W.J. 1808/06/13
Lingelbach 1808/06/13
Metsu 1808/06/13
Mieris, W. 1808/06/13
Mignon, A. 1808/06/13
Neer, A. 1808/06/13
Ochtervelt 1808/06/13
Quinkhard, J.M. 1808/06/13
Ruisdael, J. 1808/06/13
Schellinks, Daniel 1808/06/13
Steen, J. 1808/06/13
Strij, J. 1808/06/13
Velde, A. 1808/06/13
Wijnants 1808/06/13
Wouwerman, Pieter 1808/06/13
Wyck, T. 1808/06/13

Tessier, see Teissier

Tessiol
Mortel 1807/06/10

Texeira, see Teixeira

Texera, see Teixeira

Texier, see Teissier

Texier Gerbet en Comp., see Teissier

Teyler van Hall
see also van Hall
Beerstraten, J. 1801/06/10
Molenaer, Klaes 1801/06/10

Teyssier, see Teissier

Thaijs, see Thijs

Thais, see Thijs

Theben
Anonymous 1807/06/10
Velde, E. (I) 1807/06/10

Theengs, see Teengs

Theens, see Teengs

Theijs, see Thijs

Theins, see Teengs

Theys, see Thijs

Thijs, Pieter Joseph
1749–1825; painter, restorer and dealer active in Brussels
Aelst, W. 1803/07/18
Aelst, W. 1804/05/07
Aelst, W. 1806/08/20
Anonymous 1801/06/13
Anonymous 1801/10/06
Anonymous 1804/02/27
Anonymous 1804/05/07
Anonymous 1804/10/16
Asselyn 1801/06/10
Backhuysen 1804/05/07
Backhuysen 1808/06/13
Beck [Unid.] 1804/10/16
Beschey, J. 1803/04/20
Blinkvliet, M. 1804/10/16
Borch, G. ter (II) 1806/06/07
Bray, S. 1803/04/20
Breenbergh 1801/06/10
Breenbergh 1808/06/13
Brueghel, J. (I) 1803/07/18
Carree, M. 1804/05/07
Compe, Jan ten 1801/10/06
Coypel 1804/07/25
Croos, P. 1808/06/13
Cuyp, A. 1804/05/07
Dalens, Dirck 1801/10/06
Denies, I. 1804/05/07
Does, S. 1801/06/13
Does, S. 1803/07/18
Dou 1803/04/20
Dubourg, L. 1801/10/06
Ducq, Johan le 1804/10/16
Ducq, Johan le 1806/06/07
Dusart, Corn. 1801/06/10
Dyck, Anth. van 1804/07/25
Elliger, O. (II) 1803/07/18
Fargue, Maria la 1801/06/10
Gael, B. 1804/05/07
Goyen 1806/06/07
Griffier 1804/05/07
Hackaert 1804/02/27
Hackaert, J. 1804/05/07
Heeremans, Thos. 1804/02/27
Helst, B. 1806/08/13
Hendriks, W. 1804/02/27
Honthorst, G. 1803/04/20
Huchtenburgh, Jan 1801/06/10
Huchtenburgh, Jan 1801/10/06
Huchtenburgh, Jan 1803/07/18
Huchtenburgh, Jan 1804/02/27
Jordaens, J. (I) 1801/10/06
Kessel, J. (III) 1801/10/06
Kessel, J. (III) 1804/05/07
Klomp 1806/08/13
Laen, D.J. 1801/06/10
Lairesse, G. 1804/02/27
Lingelbach 1801/06/10
Lingelbach 1804/02/27
Lingelbach 1804/07/25
Lingelbach 1804/10/16
Lingelbach 1806/08/13
Lubienietski, C. 1804/05/07
Lundens 1801/10/06
Maes, D. 1801/06/10
Maes, N. 1803/04/20
Malo, V. (I) 1803/07/18
Miereveld, M. 1803/04/20
Mieris, W. 1801/06/13
Mieris, W. 1804/05/07
Moeyaert, C. 1803/04/20
Mola, P.F. 1804/07/25
Molenaer, J.M. 1801/06/13
Mommers, H. 1806/08/13
Moni, L. de 1804/07/25
Monogrammist J.L. 1806/06/07
Moreelse, P. 1803/04/20
Moucheron, F. 1801/06/10
Moucheron, F. 1804/07/25
Neer, A. 1801/06/10
Neer, A. 1808/06/13
Netscher, Casp. 1801/10/06
Netscher, Casp. 1806/08/20
Nijmegen, G. 1808/06/13
Ochtervelt 1804/02/27
Ostade, A. 1801/06/10
Ostade, I. 1806/06/07
Ouwater, Isaak 1804/05/07
Palamedesz., A. 1801/06/10
Palamedesz., A. 1801/06/13
Palamedesz., A. 1804/02/27
Palamedesz., A. 1804/10/16
Plankman, J. 1804/05/07
Poel, E. 1801/10/06
Rembrandt 1804/10/16
Rietschoof, J.C. 1801/10/06
Romeyn 1804/10/16
Rottenhammer, H. (I) 1801/10/06
Rottenhammer, H. (I) 1803/07/18
Rubens 1803/04/20
Saftleven, C. 1806/06/07
Schellinks, W. 1806/08/13
Snellinck 1804/10/16
Sorgh, H.M. 1803/07/18
Sorgh, H.M. 1804/05/07
Steenwyck, Hend. 1803/04/20
Steenwyck, Hend. 1803/07/18
Storck, Abr. 1801/06/10
Torelli, Felice 1804/07/25
Velde, A. 1801/06/10
Velde, A. 1804/05/07
Velde, A. 1806/08/13
Velde, E. (I) 1803/04/20
Vermeer, Jan 1801/06/10
Vertangen 1804/05/07
Vertangen 1806/08/13
Vlieger, S. 1801/10/06
Vlieger, S. 1804/10/16
Vonck, J. 1804/02/27
Vrancx 1801/06/10
Vrancx 1803/04/20
Werff, P. 1806/06/07
Wijnants 1801/06/10
Wijnants 1806/08/13
Willaerts 1801/10/06
Witte, E. 1801/06/10
Witte, E. 1804/10/16
Wouwerman, P. 1803/07/18
Wouwerman, Ph. 1801/06/10
Wtewael, J. 1804/02/27
Zeemann 1806/06/07

Thoen
referred to in one instance as "de Wed[uwe]"
Anonymous 1803/08/01
Beest, Sybrand 1803/08/01
Berckheyde, J. 1803/08/01
Molenaer, J.M. 1803/08/01
Rentinck, A. 1803/08/01
Sturtzenbach, S. 1803/08/01
Victors, Jan 1803/08/01

Thomas, see Thomasse

Thomasse
dealer in Leyden; also spelled Thomassen, Tomas, Tomassen, etc.
Anonymous 1801/06/13
Anonymous 1807/06/10
Anonymous 1808/05/17
Anonymous 1809/04/17
Berchem, N.P. 1808/05/17
Beschey, B. 1809/09/06
Boonen, A. 1809/09/06
Brakenburg 1809/09/06
Dyck, Anth. van 1801/06/13

Gool, Jan 1807/06/10
Goyen 1807/06/10
Heemskerck, Jan 1808/06/11
Holsteijn, C. 1807/06/10
Hulst, J. 1808/05/17
Janson, J. 1809/09/06
Janson, P. 1808/06/11
Mieris, W. 1809/09/06
Moni, L. de 1809/09/06
Poelenburgh, C. 1805/10/09
Ring, P. 1808/05/17
Schalcken 1809/09/06
Slingeland, P.C. 1809/09/06
Steen, J. 1808/05/17
Steen, J. 1810/07/23
Tol, D. 1809/09/06
Tol, D. 1810/03/26
Troost, C. 1807/06/10
Valckenburg, D. 1807/06/10
Wit, Jacob de 1807/06/10

Thomassen, see Thomasse

Thyes, see Thijs

Thys, see Thijs

Tiessier, see Teissier

Tijs, see Thijs

Tilyn
Backhuysen 1804/04/28

Toll, van
Breenbergh 1802/09/21

Tomas, see Thomasse

Tomasse, see Thomasse

Tomassen, see Thomasse

Topher
Anonymous 1810/05/22
Backhuysen 1810/05/22
Besters, C. 1810/05/22
Dorasse, C. 1810/05/22

Toselli, see Tozelli

Tozelli, Francesco
active 1747–1822; Italian painter residing in Amsterdam
Anonymous 1803/09/07
Anonymous 1805/07/10
Bloemaert, A. 1804/08/08
Bloemen, P. 1805/07/03
Brueghel, J. (I) 1805/07/10
Carree, M. 1803/09/07
Courtois, J. 1803/09/07
Ducq, Johan le 1803/09/07
Goltzius, Hend. 1805/07/10
Heem, C. 1803/09/07
Helmont, M. 1803/09/07
Koninck, P. 1804/08/08
Lairesse, G. 1804/08/08
Lastman, P.P. 1805/07/03
Liss 1803/09/07
Martszen, J. (II) 1805/07/10
Michelangelo 1803/09/07
Molenaer, J.M. 1804/08/08
Mommers, H. 1804/08/08
Momper, J. (II) 1804/08/08
Romeyn 1803/09/07
Rubens 1803/09/07
Ruysdael, S. 1804/08/08
Teniers, D. (II) 1803/09/07
Urlaub 1803/09/07
Vinckeboons, D. 1803/09/07
Willaerts 1803/09/07
Wyck, T. 1805/07/03

Traayerhaven
Goyen 1806/10/17

Tuffers
Vos 1810/06/20

Tulleken
Droochsloot, J.C. 1809/10/16

Twisk
Anonymous 1810/05/22
Brussel, P. 1810/05/22
Os, Pieter G. 1810/05/22
Porcellis, Jan 1810/05/22

Twisk Cornelisz., Jan
dealer and auctioneer in Amsterdam
Brekelencam, Q. 1808/10/28
Ekels, Jan (I) 1810/06/20
Glimes, P. de 1810/06/20
Hoet, G. (I) 1810/06/20
Lairesse, G. 1810/06/20
Laquy, W.J. 1808/06/13
Oolen, Jan 1810/06/20

Tys, see Thijs

Tythoff
Palamedesz., A. 1808/11/28

U. (1810, August 6)
Koninck, P. 1810/08/06
Thulden 1810/08/06

Udink, Marten
1748–1808; resident of Amsterdam
Anonymous 1808/10/28
Beerstraten, A. 1808/10/28
Bestens, C. 1808/10/28
Bosch, A. 1808/10/28
Brakenburg 1808/10/28
Brekelencam, Q. 1808/10/28
Buys, Jac. 1808/10/28
Colaert, Johannes 1808/10/28
Compe, Jan ten 1808/10/28
Decker, C. 1808/10/28
Defrance, L. 1808/10/28
Dietrich, Chr. 1808/10/28
Dubbels, H. 1808/10/28
Dujardin, K. 1808/10/28
Gaesbeeck, A. 1808/10/28
Griffier, R. 1808/10/28
Haensbergen, J. van 1808/10/28
Heem, C. 1808/10/28
Heem, J.D. 1808/10/28
Heusch, Jacob 1808/10/28
Houbraken, Arn. 1808/10/28
Huchtenburgh, Jan 1808/10/28
Jongh, W. 1808/10/28
Kessel, J. (III) 1808/10/28
Kuster 1808/10/28
Lingelbach 1808/10/28
Martszen, J. (II) 1808/10/28
Mieris, F. (II) 1808/10/28
Mieris, W. 1808/10/28
Molenaer, J.M. 1808/10/28
Molijn 1808/10/28
Moni, L. de 1808/10/28
Morgenstern, J.L.E. 1808/10/28
Moucheron, F. 1808/10/28
Moucheron, I. 1808/10/28
Mutscher 1808/10/28
Neeffs, P. (I) 1808/10/28
Neer, A. 1808/10/28
Os, J. 1808/10/28
Ouwater, Isaak 1808/10/28
Panini, G.P. 1808/10/28
Rembrandt 1808/10/28
Roos, P.P. 1808/10/28
Rosa, S. 1808/10/28
Ruisdael, J. 1808/10/28
Ruysch, R. 1808/10/28
Ruysdael, S. 1808/10/28
Schalcken 1808/10/28
Silo, A. 1808/10/28
Sorgh, H.M. 1808/10/28
Steen, J. 1808/10/28
Storck, J. 1808/10/28
Straaten 1808/10/28
Teniers, D. (II) 1808/10/28
Vliet, H.C. 1808/10/28
Wit, Jacob de 1808/10/28
Witte, E. 1808/10/28
Wyck, J. 1808/10/28
Wyck, T. 1808/10/28

Udink, Theunis
brother of Marten Udink, q.v.
Vliet, H.C. 1808/10/28

Uije, van
Anonymous 1803/10/10

Uijttenbogaard, see Uyttenbogaart

Uitbogert, see Uyttenbogaart

Uitenbogaard, see Uyttenbogaart

Uittenbogaart, see Uyttenbogaart

Uittenbogart, see Uyttenbogaart

Uselino
Anonymous 1803/12/12
Chalon, L. 1803/12/12
Vertangen 1803/12/12

Uylenburg
Hoogstraten, Jan 1801/06/10
Steen, J. 1801/06/10
Velde, A. 1801/06/10

Uytenbogart, see Uyttenbogaart

Uytenbogerd, see Uyttenbogaart

Uytenbogert, see Uyttenbogaart

Uyttenbogaart
also spelled Uitenbogert, Uijttenbogart, etc.; possibly the wallpaper painter Isaac Uytenbogaart, 1767–1831
Backhuysen 1805/10/09
Beerstraten, J. 1804/12/10
Goyen 1807/06/10
Goyen 1809/07/25
Maes, D. 1807/06/10
Molenaer, Klaes 1803/08/24
Schyndel, J. 1803/08/24
Steen, J. 1807/06/10
Velde, W. 1803/08/24
Vlieger, S. 1803/08/24

Uyttenbogerd, see Uyttenbogaart

V.
Domenichino 1803/04/27
Lingelbach 1808/06/11

V. (1801, May 11)
probably the dealer Jacobus Vinkeles
Ekels, Jan (II) 1801/05/11
Ouwater, Isaak 1801/05/11
Ruysch, R. 1801/05/11
Saftleven, H. 1801/05/11
Verkolje, N. 1801/05/11
Xavery, Frans 1801/05/11
Zegelaar, G. 1801/05/11

V. (1805, December 16)
Anonymous 1805/12/16
Backhuysen 1805/12/16
Bent, J. 1805/12/16
Brakenburg 1805/12/16
Brueghel 1805/12/16
Brueghel, J. (I) 1805/12/16
Cuyp, A. 1805/12/16
Fargue, J.C. 1805/12/16
Molijn 1805/12/16
Poel, E. 1805/12/16
Vermeer, Jan (II) 1805/12/16
Vrancx 1805/12/16

V. (1809, April 22)
Anonymous 1809/04/22

V. (1809, July 19)
Kessel, J. (III) 1809/07/19
Molenaer, J.M. 1809/07/19

V. (1810, June 20)
Eeckhout, G. 1810/06/20
Hondecoeter, M. 1810/06/20

Vaillant, Christiaan Everhard
d. ca.1830
Dou 1805/07/03

Valee, see Vallée

Valentijn
Anonymous 1801/03/16
Bent, J. 1801/03/16
Goyen 1801/03/16
Hansen, C.L. 1801/03/16
Verbeeck, P.C. 1801/03/16
Xavery, Frans 1801/03/16

Valet, see Vallette

Valette, see Vallette

Valk Fyko'sz., Hendrik de
dealer and auctioneer in Amsterdam
Apshoven 1802/06/16
Bol, F. 1802/06/16
Both, A. 1802/06/16
Both, J. 1802/06/16
Does, J. (I) 1802/06/16
Everdingen, A. 1802/06/16
Hals, F. (I) 1802/06/16
Lingelbach 1802/06/16
Rembrandt 1802/06/16
Rosa, S. 1802/06/16
Saftleven, H. 1802/06/16
Velde, A. 1802/06/16
Waterloo, A. 1802/06/16
Weenix, J.B. 1802/06/16
Wijnants 1802/06/16
Zeemann 1802/06/16

Valkenar
Anonymous 1805/07/01

Vallé, see Vallée

Vallée
dealer
Beerstraten, J. 1810/10/11
Bent, J. 1808/08/23
Bisschop, Abr. 1810/10/11
Elliger, O. (II) 1810/10/11
Heemskerck 1810/10/11
Huchtenburgh, Jan 1808/08/23
Molijn 1810/10/11
Tol, D. 1810/05/22
Wiltens, C. 1810/05/22
Wouwerman, P. 1810/08/06
Zepp, C. 1809/06/13

Vallet, see Vallette

Vallette, Joseph
d. ca.1807

Anonymous 1804/12/10
Anonymous 1805/07/10
Anonymous 1807/08/26
Avercamp, H. 1807/08/26
Bloemen, P. 1805/07/03
Bloemen, P. 1807/08/26
Borkeloo, J. 1805/07/03
Borkeloo, J. 1807/08/26
Bray, S. 1807/08/26
Canaletto 1805/10/09
Canaletto 1807/08/26
Cornelisz. van Haarlem 1805/10/09
Correggio 1807/08/26
Dalens, Dirck 1805/07/03
Dalens, Dirck 1807/08/26
Does, J. (I) 1807/08/26
Doudijns, W. 1805/10/09
Dujardin, K. 1807/08/26
Dusart, Corn. 1807/08/26
Elsheimer, A. 1807/08/26
Everdingen, Cesar 1804/12/10
Everdingen, Cesar 1807/08/26
Flinck 1807/08/26
Fyt 1807/08/26
Gael, B. 1805/07/10
Gael, B. 1807/08/26
Gerards 1805/10/09
Gerards 1807/08/26
German 1807/08/26
Goltzius, Hend. 1807/08/26
Goyen 1807/08/26
Griffier, R. 1801/10/19
Griffier, R. 1807/08/26
Haag, T.P.C. 1807/08/26
Hals, F. (I) 1807/08/26
Helmont, M. 1807/08/26
Herrlein, J.A. 1804/12/10
Hondecoeter, M. 1807/08/26
Huysmans, C. 1807/08/26
Italian 1802/12/13
Italian 1807/08/26
Laquy, W.J. 1807/08/26
Linthorst 1807/08/26
Maes, D. 1806/08/20
Maes, D. 1807/08/26
Massys, Q. 1807/08/26
Molijn 1807/08/26
Monogrammist A.W. 1803/08/24
Murillo 1805/10/09
Murillo 1807/08/26
Neer, A. 1805/07/03
Ochtervelt 1807/08/26
Ostade, A. 1807/08/26
Ouwater, Isaak 1805/07/03
Ouwater, Isaak 1807/08/26
Palamedesz., A. 1807/08/26
Peeters, Clara 1805/10/09
Potter, Paulus 1807/08/26
Prins, J.H. 1807/08/26
Querfurt, A. 1805/07/03
Rembrandt 1805/10/09
Rembrandt 1807/08/26
Rubens 1807/08/26
Saftleven, C. 1807/08/26
Savery, J. (I) 1805/10/09
Savery, R. 1803/12/12
Savery, R. 1807/08/26
Schweickardt, H. 1807/08/26
Storck, Abr. 1805/07/03
Storck, Abr. 1807/08/26
Teniers, D. (II) 1807/08/26
Vernet, C.J. 1803/12/12
Versteeg 1805/10/09
Versteeg 1807/08/26
Vertangen 1804/08/08
Victors, Jan 1805/10/09
Victors, Jan 1807/08/26
Weenix, J.B. 1807/08/26
Wit, Jacob de 1805/10/09
Wit, Jacob de 1807/08/26
Witte, E. 1805/07/03
Witte, E. 1807/08/26

Valois, Jean François
1778–1853; painter of landscapes and architectural scenes
Janson, J. 1807/06/10

Veer, de
Anonymous 1804/02/27
Chalon, L. 1804/02/27
Hals, F. (I) 1804/02/27

Veer, L.
Monogrammist D.V.B. 1802/07/27
Vogelsang, I. 1802/07/27
Wel, W.V. 1802/07/27

Velde, van de
Schweickardt, H. 1802/05/24

Veldhoven
possibly the amateur painter Johannes Veldhoven, 1743–1814
Honthorst, G. 1802/11/01

Veldwijk
Anonymous 1801/03/16
Anonymous 1801/10/06
Ostade, I. 1801/03/16
Teniers, D. (II) 1801/03/16

Venhouse
Bronchorst, J.G. 1802/09/21

Verbuyl
Dou 1804/10/16
Monogrammist A.S.H. 1804/10/16

Verheijen
possibly the painter Jan Hendrik Veheijen, 1778–1846
Storck, Abr. 1801/06/10

Verhoesen
Bol, F. 1806/08/13
Brakenburg 1806/08/13
Bray, S. 1806/08/13
Brekelencam, Q. 1806/08/13
Palthe, G.J. 1806/08/13
Rugendas, G.P. (I) 1806/08/13
Wtewael, J. 1806/08/13

Verhoude
Heemskerck 1802/09/21
Moni, L. de 1802/09/21
Naiveu 1802/09/21
Schoubroeck, P. 1802/09/21
Silo, A. 1802/09/21
Snellinck, J. (III) 1802/09/21
Swagers, L.F. 1802/09/21

Verlem
Anonymous 1804/05/07

Verlinden
Molenaer, Klaes 1804/10/16
Palamedesz., A. 1804/10/16

Vermeulen
Anonymous 1801/08/19
Anonymous 1802/05/05
Anonymous 1802/05/24
Anonymous 1802/06/28
Anonymous 1802/09/29
Anonymous 1802/12/13
Anonymous 1803/04/27
Anonymous 1803/08/01
Anonymous 1806/05/05
Anonymous 1806/08/13
Anonymous 1806/08/20
Anonymous 1807/06/10
Bager, Johann 1802/06/28
Beeldemaker, A.C. 1802/05/05
Berchem, N.P. 1806/05/05
Blaauw 1806/05/05
Both, A. 1810/06/06
Both, J. 1810/06/06
Bout, P. 1802/05/05
Brouwer, Adr. 1802/06/28
Croos, P. 1802/05/05
Cuyp, A. 1806/05/05
Cuyp, A. 1810/07/23
Ekels, Jan (I) 1802/06/28
Gelder, A. 1806/05/05
Gerards 1802/06/28
Goyen 1802/06/28
Heem 1803/04/27
Heeremans, Thos. 1802/06/28
Koller, J.J. 1802/05/05
Kuster, H. 1802/02/16
Lamme, A. 1810/07/23
Martszen, J. (II) 1803/04/27
Metsu 1802/06/28
Mieris, F. (I) 1810/06/06
Mieris, W. 1807/06/10
Molenaer, J.M. 1808/10/28
Molenaer, Klaes 1802/06/28
Molijn 1802/02/16
Molijn 1802/05/05
Molijn 1803/06/20
Monogrammist L.P. 1802/05/24
Os 1802/05/05
Peeters, B. (I) 1802/06/28
Seppo 1802/06/28
Steen, J. 1810/06/06
Storck, Abr. 1802/06/28
Terwesten, Mat. 1806/08/20
Vermeulen, A. 1807/06/10
Vertangen 1802/06/28
Victors, Jan 1803/04/20
Watteau, J.A. 1801/08/19
Wit, Jacob de 1807/06/10
Wouwerman, P. 1807/06/10
Wyck, T. 1802/05/24

Vermeulen, Andries
1763–1814; painter and dealer in Dordrecht
Anonymous 1802/09/06
Anonymous 1809/07/25
Bergen, D. 1809/07/25
Blinkvliet, M. 1809/07/25
Breenbergh 1802/09/06
Brueghel 1809/07/25
Cuyp, A. 1809/07/25
Francken 1809/07/25
Helst, Jer. 1802/06/16
Keller, J.H. (II) 1809/07/25
Klomp 1802/09/06
Mommers, H. 1802/09/06
Monogrammist A.V.B. 1809/07/25
Monogrammist M. 1802/09/06
Saftleven, H. 1802/06/16
Sliehe, J.H. 1802/09/06
Storck, Abr. 1802/09/06
Vermeer, Jan (II) 1809/07/25
Vermeulen, A. 1809/07/25
Vrancx 1809/07/25
Weirother, N. 1802/06/16
Weyerman, J.C. 1802/09/06
Wit, Jacob de 1809/07/25
Witmont, H. 1809/07/25

Vermunt
Bredael 1806/11/24

Verniker
Anonymous 1809/10/16

Versluys, Cornelis, Mr.
d. ca.1808; resident of Leyderdorp, near Leyden
Aelst, W. 1808/05/18
Anonymous 1808/05/18
Asselyn 1808/05/18
Beeldemaker 1808/05/18
Berchem, N.P. 1808/05/18
Brouwer, Adr. 1808/05/18
Dujardin, K. 1808/05/18
Fyt 1808/05/18
Gool, Jan 1808/05/18
Heusch 1808/05/18
Lingelbach 1808/05/18
Maes, D. 1808/05/18
Marseus, O. 1808/05/18
Mignon, A. 1808/05/18
Molenaer, Klaes 1808/05/18
Neeffs, P. (I) 1808/05/18
Os, J. 1808/05/18
Ostade 1808/05/18
Pynacker 1808/05/18
Randhorst 1808/05/18
Teniers, D. (II) 1808/05/18
Velde, W. 1808/05/18
Wijnants 1808/05/18
Wouwerman 1808/05/18
Zeemann 1808/05/18

Versonne
Anonymous 1803/06/27

Versteeg, see Versteegh

Versteegh
Anonymous 1801/06/13
Anonymous 1802/11/01
Anonymous 1803/12/12
Anonymous 1808/06/13
Both, J. 1805/12/16
Wyck, T. 1801/06/13

Versteegh, Dk.
Moreelse, P. 1803/04/27
Novelli, P. 1803/04/27
Vrancx 1801/10/19

Versteegh, J.
Monogrammist H.T. 1802/11/01
Ostade, A. 1802/11/01
Schalcken 1802/11/01

Versteegh, Michiel
1756–1843; painter and auctioneer
Cuyp, A. 1802/11/01
Gelder, A. 1802/11/01
Goyen 1802/11/01
Hals, F. (I) 1802/11/01
Heemskerck 1802/11/01
Schendel, B. 1802/11/01

Vervier, J.B.
d. ca.1829; doctor of medicine residing in Ghent
Slingeland, P.C. 1808/06/06
Wtewael, J. 1808/06/06

Verweij
dealer in Rotterdam
Anonymous 1802/09/18
Mignon, A. 1802/09/18
Penninks, J. 1802/09/18
Saenredam, P.J. 1810/03/26
Saftleven, H. 1802/09/18
Savery, J. 1802/09/18
Thier, B.H. 1802/09/18
Werff, P. 1802/09/18

Verwey, see Verweij

Vin, van der
Breenbergh 1805/10/09
Hoecke, J. 1805/10/09
Steenwyck, Hend. 1805/10/09
Vries 1805/10/09
Waerdigh 1805/10/09

Vink en Fitsing
Brassauw 1802/02/16

Chalon, L. 1802/02/16
Palamedesz., P. (I) 1802/02/16
Pynas, J. 1802/02/16
Velde, E. (I) 1802/02/16
Watteau, J.A. 1802/02/16

Vinkeles, Jacobus
dealer and auctioneer
Amigoni, J. 1805/07/10
Anonymous 1802/09/29
Anonymous 1803/04/27
Anonymous 1803/06/20
Anonymous 1803/12/12
Anonymous 1804/05/07
Anonymous 1804/08/08
Anonymous 1805/07/03
Anonymous 1805/07/10
Anonymous 1806/05/05
Anonymous 1806/08/13
Anonymous-Modern 1805/07/10
Antonissen, H.J. 1804/08/08
Antonissen, H.J. 1805/07/10
Apshoven 1805/07/10
Apshoven 1806/08/13
Asch, P.J. van 1805/07/10
Avercamp, H. 1806/08/13
Backer, A. 1804/08/08
Backhuysen 1801/08/19
Backhuysen 1804/05/07
Backhuysen 1804/08/08
Backhuysen 1805/07/10
Backhuysen 1806/08/13
Baeck, Johannes 1806/08/13
Balen 1806/05/05
Balen, H. (I) 1804/08/08
Barbiers, P. 1806/05/05
Barocci 1805/07/10
Bassen 1805/07/10
Bassen 1806/08/13
Becker, J.W. 1804/05/07
Beerstraten, A. 1805/07/10
Beerstraten, J. 1804/05/07
Beerstraten, J. 1805/07/03
Beerstraten, J. 1806/05/05
Beesten, J. 1804/05/07
Bega 1802/09/29
Bega 1804/08/08
Bega 1805/07/03
Bega 1805/07/10
Begeyn 1804/08/08
Begeyn 1805/07/10
Begeyn 1806/05/05
Bellevois 1806/05/05
Bemmel 1804/08/08
Bemmel 1806/08/13
Bent, J. 1804/05/07
Bent, J. 1804/08/08
Bent, J. 1805/07/10
Bent, J. 1806/08/13
Berchem, N.P. 1805/07/10
Berckheyde, G. 1804/05/07
Berckheyde, G. 1805/07/10
Berckheyde, G. 1806/08/13
Berckheyde, J. 1804/05/07
Bergen, D. 1806/05/05
Bergen, D. 1806/08/13
Besters, A.J. 1805/07/10
Beurs, Wm. 1806/05/05
Blanckerhoff 1805/07/10
Bleeker, A. 1804/05/07
Bleeker, A. 1806/05/05
Blieck 1804/05/07
Blieck 1805/07/10
Bloemaert 1806/05/05
Bloemaert, A. 1806/08/13
Bloemen, P. 1805/07/10
Bol, F. 1805/07/10
Bol, F. 1806/05/05
Bolomey, B.S. 1804/08/08
Borch, G. ter (II) 1804/08/08
Borch, G. ter (II) 1805/07/10
Borch, G. ter (II) 1806/05/05
Borch, G. ter (II) 1806/08/13
Borssom 1803/12/12
Borssom 1805/07/03
Both, J. 1803/12/12
Boucher 1805/07/10
Boudewyns 1805/07/03
Bout, P. 1804/08/08
Bout, P. 1806/08/13
Bouts, F. 1806/08/13
Brakenburg 1804/05/07
Brakenburg 1805/07/10
Brakenburg 1805/12/16
Bray, S. 1806/08/13
Breenbergh 1805/07/03
Brekelencam, Q. 1804/05/07
Brekelencam, Q. 1804/08/08
Brekelencam, Q. 1805/07/03
Brekelencam, Q. 1805/07/10
Brekelencam, Q. 1806/08/13
Broeck, E. 1805/07/10
Bronchorst, J.G. 1805/07/10
Brouwer, Adr. 1804/08/08
Brouwer, Adr. 1805/07/10
Brouwer, Adr. 1806/08/13
Brueghel 1803/12/12
Brueghel 1806/05/05
Brueghel, J. (I) 1802/09/29
Brueghel, J. (I) 1804/08/08
Brueghel, J. (I) 1805/07/03
Brueghel, J. (I) 1805/07/10
Brueghel, J. (I) 1806/08/13
Brussel, P. 1806/08/13
Camphuysen, D. 1806/08/13
Camphuysen, R. 1806/08/13
Cappelle 1806/05/05
Carree, Joh. 1806/08/13
Carree, M. 1804/05/07
Carree, M. 1805/07/10
Carree, M. 1806/08/13
Chalon, L. 1806/08/13
Claude Lorrain 1805/07/10
Codanelli, P. 1804/08/08
Compe, Jan ten 1804/05/07
Compe, Jan ten 1804/08/08
Compe, Jan ten 1806/05/05
Compe, Jan ten 1806/08/13
Coxie, Ant. 1806/08/13
Craesbeeck 1804/05/07
Croos, P. 1805/07/10
Cuyp, A. 1804/05/07
Cuyp, A. 1804/08/08
Cuyp, A. 1805/07/10
Cuyp, A. 1806/05/05
Cuyp, A. 1806/08/13
Cuyp, J.G. 1804/08/08
Dalens, Dirck 1805/07/10
Dalens, Dirck 1806/08/13
Decker 1805/07/10
Decker, C. 1806/08/13
Decker, Frans 1804/08/08
Decker, Jan 1804/05/07
Delen 1805/07/10
Diepenbeeck, A.J. 1804/08/08
Dietrich, Chr. 1806/05/05
Does 1806/05/05
Droochsloot, J.C. 1806/08/13
Dubbels, H. 1801/08/19
Dubbels, H. 1806/08/13
Dubois, G. 1804/08/08
Dubourg, L. 1806/08/13
Ducq, Johan le 1804/05/07
Ducq, Johan le 1804/08/08
Ducq, Johan le 1805/07/03
Ducq, Johan le 1805/07/10
Ducq, Johan le 1806/08/13
Dujardin, K. 1804/05/07
Dujardin, K. 1804/08/08
Dujardin, K. 1806/08/13
Dusart, Corn. 1805/07/10
Dyck, Anth. van 1805/07/10
Dyck, Anth. van 1806/08/13
Eeckhout, G. 1805/07/03
Eeckhout, G. 1806/08/13
Ekels, Jan (I) 1804/05/07
Ekels, Jan (I) 1806/08/13
Ekels, Jan (II) 1806/08/13
Elliger 1805/07/10
Elliger, O. (II) 1805/07/10
Elliger, O. (II) 1806/05/05
Elliger, O. (II) 1806/08/13
Elsheimer, A. 1806/05/05
Elsheimer, Joh. 1804/08/08
Everdingen, A. 1804/05/07
Everdingen, A. 1805/07/10
Everdingen, A. 1806/08/13
Everdingen, Cesar 1804/08/08
Fargue, P.C. 1804/05/07
Floris, F. (I) 1804/08/08
Fock, Harm. 1804/08/08
Francken 1806/05/05
Fris 1804/05/07
Gael, B. 1804/05/07
Gael, B. 1805/07/10
Gael, B. 1806/08/13
Gelder, A. 1806/05/05
Goltzius, Hend. 1805/07/10
Goltzius, Hend. 1806/08/13
Gool, Jan 1806/08/13
Goyen 1804/08/08
Goyen 1805/07/03
Goyen 1805/07/10
Goyen 1806/08/13
Grasdorp, W. 1804/08/08
Grebber, F.P. 1804/08/08
Grebber, P. 1804/05/07
Griffier 1804/05/07
Griffier, R. 1806/05/05
Hackaert, J. 1804/05/07
Hackaert, J. 1805/07/10
Hals, F. (I) 1804/08/08
Hals, F. (I) 1806/05/05
Hals, F. (I) 1806/08/13
Hansen, C.L. 1806/05/05
Heem, C. 1804/08/08
Heem, G. 1805/07/10
Heem, J.D. 1804/07/25
Heem, J.D. 1805/07/10
Heem, J.D. 1806/08/13
Heemskerck 1806/05/05
Heeremans, Thos. 1805/07/10
Helmont, M. 1804/08/08
Helst, B. 1804/08/08
Helst, B. 1806/05/05
Hendriks, W. 1806/05/05
Heusch 1804/08/08
Heusch, Wm. 1804/05/07
Heusch, Wm. 1806/05/05
Heusch, Wm. 1806/08/13
Heyden, J. 1804/07/25
Heyden, J. 1806/08/13
Hobbema 1805/07/10
Hobbema 1806/08/13
Holbein, H. (II) 1804/08/08
Holbein, H. (II) 1805/07/10
Hondecoeter 1806/08/13
Hondecoeter, G. 1805/07/10
Hondecoeter, M. 1806/08/13
Honthorst, G. 1805/07/10
Hooch, P. 1801/08/19
Hooch, P. 1804/05/07
Hooch, P. 1806/05/05
Hooch, P. 1806/08/13
Hoogstraten, S. 1804/08/08
Hoogstraten, S. 1805/07/10
Hoogstraten, S. 1806/05/05
Horemans, J.J. (I) 1805/07/10
Horemans, J.J. (I) 1806/05/05
Huchtenburgh, Jan 1804/05/07
Huchtenburgh, Jan 1804/08/08
Huchtenburgh, Jan 1806/05/05
Hulswit, Jan 1806/05/05
Huysum, Jan 1805/07/10
Italian 1803/12/12
Italian 1804/08/08
Italian 1805/07/03
Italian 1805/07/10
Italian 1806/05/05
Janson, J. 1804/08/08
Janson, J. 1805/07/10
Janson, J. 1806/05/05
Jode, P. 1805/07/10
Johnson, C. (I) 1806/08/13
Johnson, C. (I) 1808/06/13
Jongh, L. 1805/07/10
Jordaens, J. (I) 1806/08/13
Keirincx, Alex. 1804/05/07
Kessel, J. (III) 1804/05/07
Kessel, J. (III) 1804/08/08
Kessel, J. (III) 1805/07/03
Kessel, J. (III) 1806/05/05
Keun, Hend. 1804/08/08
Keyser, Thos. de 1806/05/05
Klomp 1804/05/07
Klomp 1806/05/05
Koedijck 1806/05/05
Koninck, P. 1804/08/08
Koninck, P. 1806/05/05
Koninck, P. 1806/08/13
Laer, P. 1804/08/08
Lairesse, G. 1803/08/17
Lairesse, G. 1804/05/07
Lairesse, G. 1805/07/10
Lairesse, Jan 1806/08/13
Laquy, W.J. 1806/05/05
Lastman, P.P. 1805/07/03
Leeuw, Pieter 1804/05/07
Leeuw, Pieter 1805/07/10
Leonardo da Vinci 1805/07/10
Lingelbach 1801/08/19
Lingelbach 1804/05/07
Lingelbach 1805/07/10
Lingelbach 1806/05/05
Lingelbach 1806/08/13
Looten, J. 1805/07/10
Lubienietski, C. 1806/08/13
Lundens 1806/08/13
Maes, N. 1804/05/07
Maes, N. 1806/08/13
Martszen, J. (II) 1804/08/08
Martszen, J. (II) 1805/07/10
Martszen, J. (II) 1806/08/13
Meijer, H. 1806/05/05
Metsu 1804/08/08
Metsu 1806/08/13
Meulen, A.F. 1806/08/13
Miereveld, Jan 1804/08/08
Miereveld, M. 1806/05/05
Miereveld, P. 1806/05/05
Mieris, F. (I) 1806/08/13
Mieris, F. (II) 1802/09/29
Mieris, F. (II) 1804/08/08
Mieris, W. 1805/07/10
Mieris, W. 1806/08/13
Molenaer, J.M. 1804/02/27
Molenaer, J.M. 1804/05/07
Molenaer, J.M. 1804/08/08
Molenaer, J.M. 1805/07/10
Molenaer, J.M. 1806/05/05
Molenaer, J.M. 1806/08/13
Molenaer, Klaes 1804/05/07
Molenaer, Klaes 1804/08/08
Molenaer, Klaes 1805/07/03
Molenaer, Klaes 1805/07/10
Molenaer, Klaes 1806/05/05
Molenaer, Klaes 1806/08/13
Molijn 1804/05/07
Molijn 1805/07/10
Molijn 1806/05/05
Mommers, H. 1804/05/07
Mommers, H. 1804/08/08
Mommers, H. 1805/07/10
Mommers, H. 1806/05/05
Mommers, H. 1806/08/13
Momper, J. (II) 1804/08/08
Momper, J. (II) 1805/07/10
Momper, J. (II) 1806/05/05

Moni, L. de 1804/08/08
Monogrammist C.W.M. 1806/08/13
Monogrammist D.B. 1805/07/10
Monogrammist D.V.B. 1806/05/05
Monogrammist G.E.M. 1805/07/10
Monogrammist V.D. 1805/07/10
Morel, J. 1806/05/05
Morel, Jan Evert 1804/05/07
Morel, Jan Evert 1806/08/13
Morgenstern, J.L.E. 1805/07/10
Moucheron, F. 1804/05/07
Moucheron, F. 1806/05/05
Moucheron, F. 1806/08/13
Moucheron, I. 1804/08/08
Moucheron, I. 1805/07/03
Moucheron, I. 1805/07/10
Murant 1804/08/08
Murant 1805/07/10
Murant 1806/05/05
Musscher, M. 1804/08/08
Musscher, M. 1805/07/10
Naiveu 1804/05/07
Naiveu 1805/07/10
Neeffs, P. (I) 1804/05/07
Neeffs, P. (I) 1805/07/10
Neeffs, P. (I) 1806/08/13
Neer, A. 1804/05/07
Neer, A. 1804/08/08
Neer, A. 1805/07/03
Neer, A. 1805/07/10
Neer, A. 1806/05/05
Neer, A. 1806/08/13
Neer, E. 1804/08/08
Netscher, Casp. 1804/08/08
Neustück, Max. 1806/08/13
Nickelen, Jan 1806/05/05
Ochtervelt 1806/08/13
Ommeganck, B. 1804/05/07
Ommeganck, B. 1804/08/08
Ommeganck, B. 1806/05/05
Ommeganck, M.J. 1808/06/13
Oolen, Adr. 1805/07/10
Oolen, Adr. 1806/05/05
Oolen, Jan 1804/08/08
Os, Geo. 1804/05/07
Os, J. 1804/05/07
Os, J. 1806/08/13
Os, Pieter G. 1804/05/07
Os, Pieter G. 1804/08/08
Os, Pieter G. 1806/05/05
Ostade, A. 1802/09/29
Ostade, A. 1804/05/07
Ostade, I. 1804/08/08
Ostade, I. 1806/08/13
Oudendyck 1806/08/13
Ouwater, Isaak 1804/08/08
Ouwater, Isaak 1806/05/05
Ouwater, Isaak 1806/08/13
Ouwater, J. 1806/05/05
Ouwater, J. 1806/08/13
Palamedesz., A. 1805/07/10
Palthe, G.J. 1804/05/07
Palthe, G.J. 1806/08/13
Pee 1805/07/10
Peeters, B. (I) 1806/05/05
Peeters, B. (I) 1806/08/13
Pieneman, J.W. 1805/07/10
Poelenburgh, C. 1805/07/03
Poelenburgh, C. 1806/05/05
Porcellis, Jan 1806/08/13
Prins, J.H. 1806/05/05
Prins, J.H. 1806/08/13
Pynacker 1804/05/07
Pynacker 1804/08/08
Ravesteyn, Hub. 1806/08/13
Regemorter, P. 1806/08/13
Reigenbach, J. 1806/05/05
Rembrandt 1805/07/10
Rietschoof, H. 1805/07/10
Ring, P. 1806/08/13
Roepel, C. 1804/07/25
Roghman, R. 1804/05/07
Rombouts 1803/09/07
Roos 1806/08/13
Rosa, S. 1806/05/05
Rubens 1804/05/07
Rubens 1805/07/10
Ruisdael 1805/07/10
Ruisdael, J. 1804/05/07
Ruisdael, J. 1804/08/08
Ruisdael, J. 1806/05/05
Ruysdael, S. 1804/08/08
Ruysdael, S. 1806/08/13
Saftleven, H. 1804/07/25
Saftleven, H. 1804/08/08
Saftleven, H. 1805/07/10
Saftleven, H. 1806/05/05
Salm, A. 1806/08/13
Santvoort, Ph. 1804/08/08
Santvoort, Pieter 1806/08/13
Savery, R. 1804/08/08
Savery, R. 1805/07/10
Savery, R. 1806/05/05
Savery, R. 1806/08/13
Schalcken 1805/07/10
Schalcken 1806/05/05
Schalcken 1806/08/13
Scheffer 1806/08/13
Schellinks, W. 1804/08/08
Schellinks, W. 1806/08/13
Schweickardt, H. 1804/05/07
Schweickardt, H. 1806/05/05
Silo, A. 1804/05/07
Silo, A. 1805/07/10
Silo, A. 1806/08/13
Simons, M. 1806/05/05
Sluis, J. 1805/07/10
Smit, Aernout 1805/07/10
Smit, Aernout 1806/08/13
Snyders, F. 1806/05/05
Soolmaker 1806/08/13
Sorgh, H.M. 1804/05/07
Sorgh, H.M. 1804/08/08
Sorgh, H.M. 1805/07/10
Spaendonck, G. 1806/05/05
Steen, J. 1803/12/12
Steen, J. 1804/08/08
Steen, J. 1805/07/10
Steen, J. 1806/08/13
Steenwyck, Hend. 1802/09/29
Steenwyck, Hend. 1805/07/10
Stoffe 1805/07/10
Stoffe 1806/08/13
Storck, Abr. 1804/08/08
Storck, Abr. 1805/07/03
Storck, Abr. 1805/07/10
Storck, Abr. 1806/05/05
Storck, Abr. 1806/08/13
Storck, J. 1804/08/08
Strij, A. 1806/08/13
Strij, J. 1806/05/05
Teniers, D. (II) 1805/07/10
Thier, B.H. 1806/05/05
Thier, B.H. 1806/08/13
Tol, D. 1806/08/13
Toorenburgh, G. 1805/07/10
Toorenburgh, G. 1806/05/05
Treu 1805/07/10
Treu, Nic. 1804/05/07
Troost, C. 1804/05/07
Velde, A. 1804/05/07
Velde, A. 1805/07/10
Velde, A. 1806/08/13
Velde, E. (I) 1805/07/10
Velde, E. (I) 1806/05/05
Velde, E. (I) 1806/08/13
Velde, J. (II) 1804/05/07
Velde, W. 1804/08/08
Velde, W. 1805/07/10
Verbeeck, P.C. 1804/08/08
Verboom, A.H. 1804/05/07
Verboom, A.H. 1806/08/13
Verdonck, Corn. 1804/05/07
Verdonck, Corn. 1806/08/13
Verelst, Joh. 1804/08/08
Vermeer, Jan (II) 1802/09/29
Vermeer, Jan (III) 1805/07/03
Vermeer, Jan (III) 1806/05/05
Vermeulen 1806/08/13
Vermeulen, A. 1804/08/08
Vermeulen, A. 1806/05/05
Verschuir 1804/08/08
Verschuir 1805/07/10
Verschuring, H. 1804/08/08
Verschuring, H. 1805/07/10
Verspronck, Joh. 1804/05/07
Versteeg 1804/05/07
Vertangen 1804/05/07
Vertangen 1805/07/10
Victors, Jan 1804/08/08
Victors, Jan 1805/07/03
Victors, Jan 1805/07/10
Victors, Jan 1806/05/05
Victors, Jan 1806/08/13
Vinckeboons, D. 1805/07/10
Vitringa 1805/07/10
Vitringa 1806/05/05
Vleughels, N. 1805/07/10
Vlieger, S. 1804/08/08
Vlieger, S. 1805/07/10
Vlieger, S. 1806/05/05
Vlieger, S. 1806/08/13
Vliet, W. 1804/08/08
Vois, Ary de 1806/08/13
Voorhout, J. (I) 1804/07/25
Voorhout, J. (I) 1806/05/05
Voorhout, J. (I) 1806/08/13
Vrancx 1805/07/10
Vrancx 1806/05/05
Vrancx 1806/08/13
Vree, N. de 1805/07/10
Vries, R. 1804/05/07
Vries, R. 1804/08/08
Vries, R. 1805/07/03
Vries, R. 1805/07/10
Vries, R. 1806/08/13
Weenix 1804/08/08
Weenix 1806/08/13
Weenix, J.B. 1806/08/13
Wet, J.W. 1806/05/05
Wigmana, G. 1806/08/13
Wijnants 1802/09/29
Wijnants 1804/08/08
Wijnants 1805/07/10
Wit, Jacob de 1804/08/08
Wit, Jacob de 1806/05/05
Wit, Jacob de 1806/08/13
Withoos, M. 1805/07/10
Witte, E. 1804/05/07
Witte, E. 1805/07/03
Witte, E. 1806/05/05
Witte, E. 1806/08/13
Wolfaerts, J.B. 1806/08/13
Wouwerman 1805/07/03
Wouwerman 1806/08/13
Wouwerman, P. 1804/05/07
Wouwerman, P. 1804/08/08
Wouwerman, P. 1806/08/13
Wouwerman, Ph. 1802/09/29
Wouwerman, Ph. 1804/05/07
Wouwerman, Ph. 1804/08/08
Wtewael, J. 1804/08/08
Wtewael, J. 1806/08/13
Wyck, T. 1804/05/07
Wyck, T. 1804/08/08
Wyck, T. 1805/07/03
Wyck, T. 1806/05/05
Wyck, T. 1806/08/13
Zeemann 1804/05/07
Zeemann 1804/08/08
Zegelaar, G. 1804/05/07
Zick, Jan. 1803/09/07

Vinne Jansz., Vincent van der
1736–1811; painter and dealer in Haarlem
Anonymous 1801/05/11
Anonymous 1802/05/05
Avercamp, H. 1801/06/10
Bega 1802/06/16
Bens 1802/05/05
Berckheyde, G. 1801/06/10
Berckheyde, G. 1802/06/16
Brekelencam, Q. 1801/08/19
Cappelle 1802/05/05
Dujardin, K. 1804/05/07
Glauber, J. 1802/05/05
Goyen 1801/08/19
Huysum, Jan 1801/04/13
Jordaens, J. (I) 1802/05/05
Kessel, J. (III) 1801/08/19
Lairesse, G. 1802/05/05
Lingelbach 1802/05/05
Lingelbach 1802/09/29
Molenaer, J.M. 1801/05/11
Molenaer, J.M. 1802/05/05
Monogrammist B.H. 1801/08/19
Monogrammist M.B. 1803/06/20
Nickelen 1802/05/05
Ostade, A. 1802/06/16
Oudenrogge, J.D. 1801/04/13
Rietschoof, H. 1802/05/05
Ruisdael, J. 1801/08/19
Seghers, D. 1803/06/20
Snyders, F. 1802/05/05
Sorgh, H.M. 1802/06/16
Steen, J. 1802/05/05
Steen, J. 1803/06/20
Velde, W. 1801/05/11
Wijnants 1803/06/20
Wouwerman 1801/08/19
Wouwerman, J. 1802/06/16

Vinnen, van der, see Vinne, van der

Visser
active in Dordrecht
Anonymous 1810/07/23
Cuyp, B. 1810/07/23
Heeremans, Thos. 1810/07/23
Hulst 1810/07/23
Lamme, A. 1810/07/23
Lelienbergh 1810/07/23
Molijn 1810/07/23
Moucheron 1810/07/23

Visser, de (Vrouw)
Brekelencam, Q. 1810/07/23
Holsteijn, C. 1810/07/23
Strij, A. 1810/07/23

Visser, Gysbert
d. ca.1804; dealer in Dordrecht
Anonymous 1805/06/24
Backhuysen 1805/06/24
Both, J. 1805/06/24
Boucher 1805/06/24
Burg (Burgh) 1805/06/24
Cuypers (Kuypers) 1805/06/24
Droochsloot, J.C. 1805/06/24
Gulck, A. 1805/06/24
La Haye, R. 1805/06/24
Mieris, W. 1805/06/24
Poelenburgh, C. 1805/06/24
Savery, R. 1805/06/24
Storck, Abr. 1805/06/24
Toorenvliet, J. 1805/06/24

Visser, J. de
Anonymous 1810/07/23
Heem, J.D. 1810/07/23
Savery, R. 1810/07/23
Wouwerman, Pieter 1810/07/23

Vlamink
Anonymous 1802/10/18

Vlymen, van
Anonymous 1810/08/06

Voerman, L.
Anonymous 1805/10/09

Anonymous 1806/08/20
Anonymous 1809/07/25
Beeldemaker 1806/08/20
Crari, G.B. 1809/07/25
Cuyp, B. 1805/10/09
Does, S. 1806/08/20
Droochsloot, J.C. 1809/07/25
Dyck, Anth. van 1806/08/20
Italian-Venetian 1809/07/25
Lust, D. 1809/07/25
Moritz, Louis 1809/07/25
Poel, E. 1805/10/09
Steen, J. 1809/07/25
Vermeulen, A. 1809/07/25
Werff, P. 1805/10/09

Voet
Weenix, Juffr. 1810/05/22

Voorden, van
Aa, Dirk 1809/07/25
Anonymous 1809/07/25
Keller, J.H. (II) 1809/07/25

Voort, van der
perhaps the dealer Gerrit Anthony van der Voort, 1784–1864
Asselyn 1806/08/13
Berckheyde, G. 1806/08/13
Bramer 1806/08/13
Breenbergh 1806/08/13
Cappelle 1806/08/13
Dujardin, K. 1806/08/13
Eeckhout, G. 1806/08/13
Gérard, M. 1806/08/13
Helst, B. 1806/08/13
Hooch, P. 1806/08/13
Klomp 1806/08/13
Kyckenburgh, D.N. 1806/08/13
Lingelbach 1806/08/13
Maratti 1806/08/13
Moeyaert, C. 1810/10/11
Molenaer, J.M. 1806/08/13
Moucheron, I. 1806/08/13
Oolen, Jan 1806/08/13
Ryckaert, D. (III) 1806/08/13
Schellinks, W. 1806/08/13
Velde, A. 1806/08/13
Vertangen 1806/08/13
Vries, R. 1806/08/13
Wijnants 1806/08/13
Wouwerman, P. 1806/08/13
Zyl, G. 1806/08/13

Vos, de
Bol, F. 1806/08/13
Snyders, F. 1806/08/13
Willaerts 1801/10/06

Vos (Rijswijk)
Heem, C. 1802/11/01
Monogrammist J.M.R. 1802/11/01

Vos, Jacob de
1735–1833; insurance broker
Ruisdael, J. 1809/07/19
Vrancx 1809/07/19

Vreesman, see Wreesman

Vries, Jeronimo de
1776–1853; art critic, butter merchant and joint organizer of auctions at the "Huis met de Hoofden" in Amsterdam
Anonymous 1807/08/26
Anonymous 1808/06/13
Anonymous 1809/04/22
Anonymous 1809/06/13
Anonymous 1810/06/20
Anonymous 1810/08/06
Anonymous 1810/10/11
Antonissen, H.J. 1807/08/26
Antonissen, H.J. 1810/05/22
Backer, J.A. 1807/08/26
Backhuysen 1807/08/26
Beeldemaker 1807/08/26
Beerstraten, A. 1807/08/26
Beerstraten, J. 1810/10/11
Berchem, N.P. 1810/08/01
Berckheyde, G. 1807/08/26
Berckheyde, G. 1809/07/19
Berckheyde, G. 1810/07/26
Bergen, D. 1810/07/26
Bloemaert 1807/08/26
Boonen, A. 1807/08/26
Boursse, E. 1809/04/22
Brekelencam, Q. 1809/04/22
Brueghel 1807/08/26
Casteels, P. (III) 1807/08/26
Chalon, L. 1807/08/26
Compe, Jan ten 1809/07/19
Dietrich, Chr. 1807/08/26
Dou 1810/08/06
Dubois, J. 1807/08/26
Dughet 1810/07/26
German 1810/05/22
Griffier, R. 1810/08/06
Gysels, P. 1807/08/26
Haensbergen, J. van 1807/08/26
Heeremans, Thos. 1810/06/20
Helst, B. 1810/06/20
Hendriks, W. 1809/06/13
Hendriks, W. 1810/08/06
Heusch, Wm. 1809/04/22
Heyden, J. 1810/08/06
Huysum, Jan 1810/08/01
Italian 1810/10/11
Jongh, W. 1808/10/28
Jongh, W. 1810/08/06
Kessel, J. (III) 1808/06/13
Kessel, J. (III) 1810/08/06
Koninck, P. 1810/06/20
Lingelbach 1810/06/20
Lingelbach 1810/08/06
Lingelbach 1810/10/11
Lucas van Leyden 1810/07/26
Lundens 1807/08/26
Maddersteeg 1807/08/26
Maes, D. 1807/08/26
Mettenleiter, J.J. 1807/08/26
Miereveld, M. 1807/08/26
Miereveld, M. 1809/06/13
Miereveld, M. 1810/06/20
Miereveld, M. 1810/10/11
Mieris, F. (I) 1810/08/01
Mieris, F. (II) 1808/10/28
Mieris, W. 1810/08/01
Molenaer, J.M. 1807/08/26
Molenaer, Klaes 1810/06/20
Molijn 1807/08/26
Moni, L. de 1808/10/28
Monogrammist W.L. 1807/08/26
Moucheron, I. 1807/08/26
Neer, A. 1810/08/06
Neer, C. 1807/08/26
Oolen, Jan 1807/08/26
Oudenrogge, J.D. 1807/08/26
Ouwater, Jac. 1807/08/26
Procaccini 1810/07/26
Pynas, J. 1807/08/26
Rembrandt 1807/08/26
Rissel, J. 1807/08/26
Rombouts 1807/08/26
Romeyn 1807/08/26
Rubens 1810/08/01
Ruisdael, J. 1807/08/26
Saenredam, P.J. 1810/08/01
Schalcken 1810/08/01
Schellinks, W. 1807/08/26
Snyders, F. 1806/08/13
Steen, J. 1810/08/01
Storck, Abr. 1808/06/13
Storck, Abr. 1810/08/06
Teniers, D. (II) 1807/08/26
Teniers, D. (II) 1810/08/06
Toorenvliet, A. 1807/08/26
Toorenvliet, A. 1810/06/20
Velde, A. 1809/07/19
Velde, A. 1810/08/06
Velde, E. (I) 1810/06/20
Velde, W. 1807/08/26
Verbeeck, P.C. 1807/08/26
Voorhout, J. (I) 1807/08/26
Vrancx 1809/04/22
Vrancx 1810/08/06
Weenix 1809/04/17
Werff, A. 1810/08/01
Wijnants 1808/06/13
Wijnants 1810/06/20
Wijnants 1810/08/06
Wijnants 1810/10/11
Wouwerman, P. 1807/08/26
Wouwerman, Ph. 1809/04/22
Wouwerman, Ph. 1810/08/01
Wouwerman, Ph. 1810/08/06
Wulfraet 1810/08/06
Wyck, T. 1809/04/22
Wyck, T. 1810/08/06
Zegelaar, G. 1810/10/11

Vriesman, see Wreesman

W.
Begeyn 1801/06/13
Borch, G. ter (II) 1801/06/13
Fargue, Maria la 1801/06/13
Griffier, J. (I) 1801/06/13
Heusch, Wm. 1801/06/13
Mieris, F. (II) 1801/06/13
Mieris, W. 1801/06/13
Mortel 1801/06/13
Ostade, A. 1801/06/13
Tempel, A.L. van den 1801/06/13
Weenix 1801/06/13
Wouwerman, P. 1801/06/13

W. (1803, December 12)
Anonymous 1803/12/12
Beer 1803/12/12
Brakenburg 1803/12/12
Cramer, Petrus 1803/12/12
Croos, P. 1803/12/12
Delen 1803/12/12
Elliger, O. (II) 1803/12/12
Hooch, P. 1803/12/12
Keller, J.H. (II) 1803/12/12
Keun, Hend. 1803/12/12
Lambrechts, J.B. 1803/12/12
Miereveld, M. 1803/12/12
Ostade, A. 1803/12/12
Palamedesz., P. (I) 1803/12/12
Poel, E. 1803/12/12
Porcellis, Jan 1803/12/12
Vertangen 1803/12/12
Wigmana, G. 1803/12/12
Wijnants 1803/12/12

W. (1804, May 7)
Asch, P.J. van 1804/05/07
Bol, F. 1804/05/07
Fargue, P.C. 1804/05/07
Francken, Frans (II) 1804/05/07
Hooch, P. 1804/05/07
Monogrammist J.V.G. 1804/05/07
Murant 1804/05/07
Ostade 1804/05/07
Steen, J. 1804/05/07
Teniers, D. (II) 1804/05/07
Victors, Jan 1804/05/07
Wouwerman 1804/05/07

W. (1804, August 8)
Brekelencam, Q. 1804/08/08
Cuyp, J.G. 1804/08/08
Decker, Frans 1804/08/08
Ducq, Johan le 1804/08/08
Goyen 1804/08/08
Huchtenburgh, Jan 1804/08/08
Janson, J. 1804/08/08
Martszen, J. (II) 1804/08/08
Molenaer, J.M. 1804/08/08
Moucheron, I. 1804/08/08
Murant 1804/08/08
Musscher, M. 1804/08/08
Neer, A. 1804/08/08
Netscher, Casp. 1804/08/08
Oolen, Jan 1804/08/08
Ostade, I. 1804/08/08
Ruisdael, J. 1804/08/08
Ruysdael, S. 1804/08/08
Steen, J. 1804/08/08
Verbeeck, P.C. 1804/08/08
Victors, Jan 1804/08/08
Vliet, W. 1804/08/08
Weenix 1804/08/08
Wijnants 1804/08/08
Wouwerman, Ph. 1804/08/08

W. (1808, June 13)
Both, A. 1808/06/13
Both, J. 1808/06/13
Hondecoeter, M. 1808/06/13
Ruisdael, J. 1808/06/13
Wouwerman, Ph. 1808/06/13

Wagenaar, A.
d. ca.1803; notary in Middelburg
Anonymous 1803/06/07

Wal, see Wall

Wall, van der
probably the Utrecht painter Wm. R. van der Wall, 1756–1813
Anonymous 1808/06/11
Heusch 1808/06/11
Vermeulen, A. 1808/06/11
Vermeulen, Corn. (III) 1804/10/16
Versteeg 1804/10/16

Walle, see Wall

Wallen, van
also spelled van Waller
Anonymous 1802/09/18
Bega 1802/09/18
Thier, B.H. 1802/09/18

Waller, van, see Wallen, van

Warem
Anonymous 1803/06/27

Waterlander
Kleijne, David 1802/05/10

Weddelink
Anonymous 1803/12/12

Weeber
Schütz, J.G. 1802/06/28

Weiden, van der
Anonymous 1802/11/01

Weiland
includes Wijland and Weyland
Aertsen 1801/08/19
Anonymous 1801/03/16
Anonymous 1801/08/19
Apshoven 1801/03/16
Berckheyde 1801/03/16
Bloot, P. 1801/03/16
Carracci, A. 1801/08/19
Decker 1801/03/16
Dou 1809/09/06
Dyck, Anth. van 1809/09/06
Essen, C. 1801/03/16
Goyen 1806/08/13
Molenaer, J.M. 1801/03/16
Mommers, H. 1801/03/16
Monogrammist P.W. 1801/08/19

Nickelen, Jan 1801/03/16
Tuling 1801/08/19
Victors, Jan 1801/08/19

Weksteen
Anonymous 1803/10/10

Well Az., Arnoldus van
1773–1818; painter from Dordrecht
Anonymous 1802/11/01
Houbraken, Arn. 1802/11/01
Lelienbergh 1802/11/01

Welmeer
perhaps the sculptor Christiaan Welmeer, 1742–1814
Drielst, E. 1808/11/28

Wennegers
Velde, E. (I) 1802/06/28

Wepner
Bloemaert, C. (II) 1802/09/06

Werland
Potter, Paulus 1810/08/10

Werumeus, Arnold Sicco
d. ca.1802; councillor in Groningen
Aelst, W. 1802/05/11
Anonymous 1802/05/11
Beckeringh, T. 1802/05/11
Berckheyde 1802/05/11
Bogaert, Hendrick H. 1802/05/11
Brekelencam, Q. 1802/05/11
Brouwer, Adr. 1802/05/11
Coelmans, J. 1802/05/11
Cuylenborch, A. 1802/05/11
Dusart 1802/05/11
Gael, B. 1802/05/11
Goyen 1802/05/11
Hauck, J.L. 1802/05/11
Heeremans, Thos. 1802/05/11
Kalf 1802/05/11
Maes, D. 1802/05/11
Marseus, O. 1802/05/11
Molenaer, Klaes 1802/05/11
Mommers, H. 1802/05/11
Neer, A. 1802/05/11
Oudenrogge, J.D. 1802/05/11
Poel, E. 1802/05/11
Ruytenbach 1802/05/11
Schendel, B. 1802/05/11
Schotanus, Petrus 1802/05/11
Schyndel 1802/05/11
Seghers, D. 1802/05/11
Steen, J. 1802/05/11
Storck, Abr. 1802/05/11
Venne, P. van de 1802/05/11
Vinckeboons, D. 1802/05/11
Wassenbergh, J.A. 1802/05/11
Wet, J.W. 1802/05/11
Wet, S. 1802/05/11
Wouwerman 1802/05/11
Wyck, T. 1802/05/11
Zeemann 1802/05/11

Westenberg
Anonymous 1810/08/06

Westerouen van Meeteren, Mattheus
1765–1807; merchant, councillor and alderman in Dordrecht
Anonymous 1807/09/28
Beeldemaker 1807/09/28
Berchem, N.P. 1807/09/28
Bisschop, Abr. 1807/09/28
Cuyp, A. 1807/09/28
Cuyp, B. 1807/09/28
Diepraem 1807/09/28
Douw, S. 1807/09/28
Duynen, I. 1807/09/28
Gael, B. 1807/09/28
Goyen 1807/09/28
Houbraken, Arn. 1807/09/28
Kalraet, Barend 1807/09/28
Lamme, Arie 1807/09/28
Meulemans 1807/09/28
Potter, Paulus 1807/09/28
Wouwerman 1807/09/28

Westhoff
Anonymous 1803/04/27
Anonymous-Antique 1803/04/27

Westreenen, van
Anonymous 1806/08/20

Wet, A. van
active in Dordrecht
Aa, Dirk 1810/07/23

Wetstein, Rudolf Hendrik de
d. ca.1809
Anonymous 1810/03/23
Bergen, D. 1810/03/23
Both, A. 1810/03/23
Delcloche 1810/03/23
Flinck 1810/03/23
Glauber, J. 1810/03/23
Goyen 1810/03/23
Graat 1810/03/23
Hondecoeter, Gysb. 1810/03/23
Horemans, J.J. (I) 1810/03/23
Italian 1810/03/23
Lairesse, G. 1810/03/23
Lingelbach 1810/03/23
Maes, D. 1810/03/23
Molenaer, J.M. 1810/03/23
Monogrammist F.B. 1810/03/23
Monogrammist F.M. 1810/03/23
Monogrammist H.P. 1810/03/23
Monogrammist M.B. 1810/03/23
Monogrammist P.V.B. 1810/03/23
Moucheron 1810/03/23
Ostade, I. 1810/03/23
Post, F.J. 1810/03/23
Rademaker 1810/03/23
Romeyn 1810/03/23
Rubens, A.F. 1810/03/23
Rugendas, G.P. (I) 1810/03/23
Ruisdael, J. 1810/03/23
Saftleven, H. 1810/03/23
Savery, R. 1810/03/23
Slingeland, P.C. 1810/03/23
Sorgh, H.M. 1810/03/23
Spruyt, P.L.J. 1810/03/23
Steen, J. 1810/03/23
Swiss 1810/03/23
Velde, W. 1810/03/23
Vernet, C.J. 1810/03/23
Vinne, J. 1810/03/23
Vlieger, S. 1810/03/23
Weenix, J.B. 1810/03/23
Wit, Jacob de 1810/03/23
Wouwerman 1810/03/23
Wulfraet 1810/03/23
Wulfraet, Marg. 1810/03/23
Zeemann 1810/03/23

Weyland, see Weiland

Wiere, A. van der
Anonymous 1803/10/10

Wiggers
Anonymous 1807/06/10
Stoop 1807/06/10
Storck, Abr. 1807/06/10
Thier, B.H. 1807/06/10

Wigmoore
Vermeulen, A. 1808/06/11

Wijkersloot, see Wijkerslooth

Wijkerslooth van Grevenmachern, Hendricus Theodorus van
1780–1823; member of the Amsterdam city counsel, 1808–1823
Both, J. 1809/07/19
Dujardin, K. 1809/07/19
Hooch, P. 1809/07/19
Italian 1809/07/19
Knupfer 1809/07/19
Lundens 1809/07/19
Molenaer, J.M. 1809/07/19
Potuyl 1809/07/19
Sala, Gabrielle 1809/07/19
Savery, R. 1809/07/19
Voorhout, J. (I) 1809/07/19
Weenix 1809/07/19
Wit, Jacob de 1809/07/19

Wijland, see Weiland

Wilkensohn
Anonymous 1804/05/07

Willigen, Adriaan van der
1766–1841; writer, joint organizer of art exhibitions, school inspector
Dürer 1808/09/13
Goyen 1808/09/13
Lucas van Leyden 1808/09/13
Wüest, J.H. 1808/09/13

Willigen, T.H. van
d. ca.1805; counselor to the Bavarian kurfurst; perhaps an error for Mr. Franciscus Antonius van Willigen, b.1738
Aelst, W. 1805/10/09
Alewyn, Abr. 1805/10/09
Anonymous 1805/10/09
Backer 1805/10/09
Backhuysen 1805/10/09
Balen, H. (I) 1805/10/09
Beerstraten, A. 1805/10/09
Bent, J. 1805/10/09
Berckheyde, J. 1805/10/09
Beschey, B. 1805/10/09
Biset, J.A. 1805/10/09
Bloemaert, A. 1805/10/09
Bloemen, P. 1805/10/09
Bloot, P. 1805/10/09
Bolff, C. 1805/10/09
Bos, N. 1805/10/09
Bredael 1805/10/09
Bredael, J. 1805/10/09
Breenbergh 1805/10/09
Brekelencam, Q. 1805/10/09
Bril, P. 1805/10/09
Brouwer, Adr. 1805/10/09
Brueghel 1805/10/09
Brueghel, J. (I) 1805/10/09
Burch, Hendrick 1805/10/09
Camphuysen, D. 1805/10/09
Canaletto 1805/10/09
Carree, Hend. (I) 1805/10/09
Cornelisz. van Haarlem 1805/10/09
Courtois, J. 1805/10/09
Croos 1805/10/09
Cuyp, A. 1805/10/09
Cuyp, B. 1805/10/09
Dalens, Dirck 1805/10/09
Doudijns, W. 1805/10/09
Droochsloot, J.C. 1805/10/09
Ducq, Johan le 1805/10/09
Dusart, Corn. 1805/10/09
Elsheimer, A. 1805/10/09
Flemish-Brabant 1805/10/09
Fyt 1805/10/09
Gerards 1805/10/09
Gool, Jan 1805/10/09
Goyen 1805/10/09
Guichardino 1805/10/09
Heem, C. 1805/10/09
Heem, J.D. 1805/10/09
Heemskerck, M. 1805/10/09
Hochecker, Franz 1805/10/09
Hoecke, J. 1805/10/09
Hoet, G. (I) 1805/10/09
Huchtenburgh, Jan 1805/10/09
Huysum, Jan 1805/10/09
Italian 1805/10/09
Jacobsz., Juriaen 1805/10/09
Juncker, Jus. 1805/10/09
Kleijne, David 1805/10/09
Lelienbergh 1805/10/09
Leonardo da Vinci 1805/10/09
Liss 1805/10/09
Meijer, H. (I) 1805/10/09
Meyer 1805/10/09
Momper, J. (II) 1805/10/09
Monogrammist J.T. 1805/10/09
Murillo 1805/10/09
Neeffs, P. (I) 1805/10/09
Neer, A. 1805/10/09
Netscher, Casp. 1805/10/09
Os, J. 1805/10/09
Ostade 1805/10/09
Ostade, A. 1805/10/09
Palamedesz., A. 1805/10/09
Parmigianino 1805/10/09
Peeters, B. (I) 1805/10/09
Peeters, Clara 1805/10/09
Poel, E. 1805/10/09
Poelenburgh, C. 1805/10/09
Rembrandt 1805/10/09
Ring, P. 1805/10/09
Rombouts 1805/10/09
Rottenhammer, H. (I) 1805/10/09
Rubens 1805/10/09
Ruisdael, J. 1805/10/09
Ruysch, R. 1805/10/09
Saftleven, C. 1805/10/09
Savery, J. (I) 1805/10/09
Schalcken 1805/10/09
Schyndel, J. 1805/10/09
Seghers, D. 1805/10/09
Sorgh, H.M. 1805/10/09
Steen, J. 1805/10/09
Steenwyck, Hend. 1805/10/09
Storck, Abr. 1805/10/09
Swagers, L.F. 1805/10/09
Swiss 1805/10/09
Teniers, D. (II) 1805/10/09
Terwesten 1805/10/09
Thulden 1805/10/09
Tol, D. 1805/10/09
Valentin de Boulogne 1805/10/09
Velde, E. (I) 1805/10/09
Verbruggen, G. (II) 1805/10/09
Verelst, P. 1805/10/09
Verschuring, H. 1805/10/09
Versteeg 1805/10/09
Victors, Jan 1805/10/09
Vinckeboons, D. 1805/10/09
Vrancx 1805/10/09
Vries 1805/10/09
Vries, P. 1805/10/09
Waerdigh 1805/10/09
Werff, P. 1805/10/09
Wigmana, G. 1805/10/09
Willaerts, Adam 1805/10/09
Willegen, D. 1805/10/09
Wit, Jacob de 1805/10/09
Wyck, T. 1805/10/09
Zeemann 1805/10/09

Wind, de, Dr.
Rubens 1803/11/30

Wind, Gerard de
1730–1800; physician and professor of medicine in Middelburg
Droochsloot, J.C. 1801/07/06

Wind, Samuel de
1742–1803; physician and surgeon in Middelburg
Anonymous 1803/11/30
Backhuysen 1803/11/30
Blieck 1803/11/30
Brueghel 1803/11/30
Brueghel, P. 1803/11/30
Holsteijn, C. 1803/11/30
Hoogerheyden, E. 1803/11/30
Kleijne, David 1803/11/30
Rubens 1803/11/30
Yong 1803/11/30

Winkel, Ganse, see Gansewinkel

Winkel, J.
Monogrammist J.V.B. 1802/07/27

Winter, Pieter Nicolaas van
1745–1807; Amsterdam merchant
Lingelbach 1801/04/23

Wistenberg
Ruisdael, J. 1808/08/23

Wit, J.J. de
Backhuysen 1808/06/06
Berchem, N.P. 1808/06/06
Both, J. 1808/06/06
Flinck 1808/06/06
Helst, B. 1808/06/06
Moor, C. 1808/06/06
Saftleven, H. 1808/06/06
Velde, W. 1808/06/06
Witte, E. 1808/06/06
Wouwerman, Ph. 1808/06/06

Witt, Aldegonda Maria Theresia de
d. after 1819; widow of Johannes Baptista Josephus Achtienhoven, d. 1801
Anonymous 1801/08/19
Anonymous 1802/09/06
Anonymous 1804/05/07
Balen, H. (I) 1801/08/19
Beerstraten 1802/09/06
Begeyn 1802/09/06
Berchem, N.P. 1802/09/06
Bredael, J. 1801/10/06
Bredael, P. 1802/09/06
Brekelencam, Q. 1801/08/19
Brekelencam, Q. 1802/09/06
Bril, P. 1802/09/06
Broeck, E. 1802/09/06
Brueghel, J. (I) 1801/08/19
Brueghel, J. (I) 1802/06/16
Brueghel, J. (I) 1802/09/06
Carree, Joh. 1806/08/13
Carree, M. 1804/05/07
Cuyp, A. 1806/08/13
Dou 1802/09/06
Esselens, Jacob 1802/09/06
Essen, C. 1802/09/06
French 1802/09/06
Gelder, A. 1806/08/13
Hackaert, J. 1802/09/06
Heyden, J. 1805/07/03
Hooren, J. 1801/08/19
Huchtenburgh, Jan 1805/07/03
Italian 1802/09/06
Laer, P. 1802/06/16
Lingelbach 1802/09/06
Lingelbach 1804/05/07
Maas, J. 1802/09/06
Marseus, O. 1802/09/06
Metsu 1802/09/06
Miel 1801/10/06
Miel 1802/06/16
Mieris, F. (I) 1802/09/06
Molenaer, J.M. 1802/06/16
Molenaer, J.M. 1806/08/13
Molenaer, Klaes 1806/08/13
Mommers, H. 1802/09/06
Momper, J. (II) 1802/09/06
Moucheron, F. 1804/05/07
Neck, Jan 1802/09/06
Nepveu, J. 1802/09/06
Oolen, Jan 1802/09/06
Ostade 1802/09/06
Ostade, I. 1801/08/19
Poelenburgh, C. 1802/06/16
Prins, J.H. 1802/06/16
Pynacker 1804/05/07
Royen, W.F. van 1802/09/06
Ruisdael, J. 1804/05/07
Ruysdael, S. 1801/08/19
Savery, R. 1802/09/06
Schoevaerdts, M. 1801/10/06
Schütz, Franz 1802/09/06
Silo, A. 1802/09/06
Sliehe, J.H. 1802/09/06
Sorgh, H.M. 1802/06/16
Steen, J. 1804/05/07
Steen, J. 1805/07/03
Steens, D. 1802/09/06
Stoffe 1802/06/16
Stoop, J. 1802/06/16
Storck, Abr. 1801/08/19
Storck, Abr. 1802/09/06
Storck, Abr. 1804/05/07
Velde, A. 1802/06/16
Velde, A. 1805/07/03
Vermeer, Jan (II) 1801/10/06
Verschuring, H. 1802/06/16
Verschuring, H. 1802/09/06
Vertangen 1801/08/19
Voorhout, J. (I) 1802/09/06
Vries, R. 1801/08/19
Waterloo, A. 1802/09/06
Wijnants 1802/06/16
Wouwerman, P. 1802/06/16
Wouwerman, P. 1802/09/06
Wouwerman, P. 1804/05/07

Woertman, Johan Jacob, Mr.
1753–1809; councillor and alderman in Utrecht
Anonymous 1810/03/07
Anonymous-Modern 1810/03/07
Bassen 1810/03/07
Berchem, N.P. 1810/03/07
Bloemaert 1810/03/07
Bloemaert, A. 1810/03/07
Borch, G. ter (II) 1810/03/07
Bramer 1810/03/07
Brekelencam, Q. 1810/03/07
Bronchorst, J.G. 1810/03/07
Cari, A. 1810/03/07
Cuyp, A. 1810/03/07
Does 1810/03/07
Does, S. 1810/03/07
Droochsloot, J.C. 1810/03/07
Ducq, Johan le 1810/03/07
Dusart 1810/03/07
Dyck, Anth. van 1810/03/07
Gael, B. 1810/03/07
Geelen, C. (I) 1810/03/07
Heem, C. 1810/03/07
Heusch 1810/03/07
Hondecoeter 1810/03/07
Hondecoeter, M. 1810/03/07
Klomp 1810/03/07
Lamen, C. van der 1810/03/07
Lingelbach 1810/03/07
Mignon, A. 1810/03/07
Molenaer, J.M. 1810/03/07
Molijn 1810/03/07
Monogrammist H.J. 1810/03/07
Monogrammist M. 1810/03/07
Moucheron 1810/03/07
Palamedesz., A. 1810/03/07
Poelenburgh, C. 1810/03/07
Rubens 1810/03/07
Saftleven, H. 1810/03/07
Savery, R. 1810/03/07
Snyders, F. 1810/03/07
Steen, J. 1810/03/07
Storck, Abr. 1810/03/07
Swagers, L.F. 1810/03/07
Velde 1810/03/07
Victors, Jan 1810/03/07
Wijnants 1810/03/07
Willaerts 1810/03/07
Wouwerman 1810/03/07
Wouwerman, J. 1810/03/07
Wouwerman, P. 1810/03/07

Wolf
Monogrammist P.W. 1801/08/19

Wolft, B.
Anonymous 1801/08/19
Backhuysen 1801/08/19
Bourdon 1801/04/13
Brueghel, J. (I) 1801/08/19
Cappelle 1802/12/13
Everdingen, A. 1801/06/10
Honthorst, G. 1801/08/19
Huysum, Jan 1801/08/19
Kessel, J. (III) 1802/06/16
Lairesse, G. 1801/06/10
Lairesse, G. 1802/09/06
Molenaer, J.M. 1801/08/19
Molenaer, Klaes 1801/08/19
Procaccini, Cam. 1801/04/13
Rennet 1801/08/19
Roghman, R. 1801/08/19
Rosa, S. 1802/12/13
Ruysdael, S. 1801/08/19
Ruysdael, S. 1802/12/13
Velde, W. 1801/05/11
Vos 1801/08/19

Wreesman Borgertzn., Warnaar
ca.1748–1814; wine merchant
Backhuysen 1801/06/10
Berckheyde, G. 1810/08/06
Both, J. 1810/03/26
Brouwer, Adr. 1801/06/10
Brussel, P. 1801/04/13
Cappelle 1810/08/01
Decker, C. 1801/06/10
Dujardin, K. 1810/08/06
Fourdrier 1810/03/26
Hackaert, J. 1810/08/01
Heyden, J. 1801/06/10
Kobell, Jan (II) 1810/08/01
Potter, Paulus 1810/03/26
Roedig, J.C. 1804/05/07
Steen, J. 1810/03/26
Velde, A. 1810/08/01

Wynen, W.
Anonymous 1801/08/19
Avercamp, H. 1801/08/19
Brueghel, J. (I) 1801/08/19
Carree, M. 1801/08/19
Ducq, Johan le 1801/08/19
Elsheimer, A. 1801/08/19
Flinck 1801/08/19
Francken 1801/08/19
Heusch, Wm. 1801/08/19
Hoet, G. (I) 1801/08/19
Molenaer, Klaes 1801/08/19
Monogrammist J.B.W. 1801/08/19
Nollekens 1801/08/19
Potter, Pieter de 1801/08/19
Poussin, N. 1801/08/19
Rottenhammer, H. (I) 1801/08/19
Ruisdael, J. 1801/08/19
Saftleven, C. 1801/08/19
Smit, Jan Borritsz. 1801/08/19
Straaten, Hend. 1801/08/19
Verbeeck, P.C. 1801/08/19
Vertangen 1801/08/19
Victors, Jan 1801/08/19
Vrancx 1801/08/19
Vries, R. 1801/08/19
Wulfraet 1801/08/19

Wyngaert, O.D., see Onderdewyngaart Canzius, J.H.

X. (1802, September 6)
Anonymous 1802/09/06
Begeyn 1802/09/06
Borch, G. ter (II) 1802/09/06
Ferguson, Wm. 1802/09/06
Huchtenburgh, Jan 1802/09/06
Keirincx, Alex. 1802/09/06
Palamedesz., P. (I) 1802/09/06
Weenix, J.B. 1802/09/06
Weyerman, J.C. 1802/09/06

X. (1804, May 7)
Decker, Jan 1804/05/07
Huchtenburgh, Jan 1804/05/07
Pynacker 1804/05/07
Versteeg 1804/05/07

X. (1808, August 23)
Backhuysen 1808/08/23
Both, J. 1808/08/23
Everdingen, A. 1808/08/23
Goyen 1808/08/23
Hobbema 1808/08/23
Lingelbach 1808/08/23
Poelenburgh, C. 1808/08/23
Prins, J.H. 1808/08/23

X. (1810, June 20)
Anonymous 1810/06/20
Camphuysen, J. 1810/06/20
Hooch, P. 1810/06/20
Keirincx, Alex. 1810/06/20
Molenaer, J.M. 1810/06/20
Palamedesz., P. (I) 1810/06/20
Porcellis, Jan 1810/06/20
Verboom, A.H. 1810/06/20
Vertangen 1810/06/20

Y. (1805, July 3)
Carree, Hend. (I) 1805/07/03
Dupré, Daniel 1805/07/03
Hillegaert, P. (I) 1805/07/03
Ouwater, Isaak 1805/07/03
Vertangen 1805/07/03
Wouwerman, P. 1805/07/03

Y. (1805, December 16)
Anonymous 1805/12/16
Backhuysen 1805/12/16
Francken 1805/12/16
Honthorst, G. 1805/12/16
Italian 1805/12/16
Vrancx 1805/12/16

Y. (1806, May 5)
Anonymous 1806/05/05
Backhuysen 1806/05/05
Honthorst, G. 1806/05/05

Y. (1808, August 23)
Anonymous 1808/08/23
Borch, G. ter (II) 1808/08/23
Brakenburg 1808/08/23
Canaletto 1808/08/23
Helst, B. 1808/08/23
Huchtenburgh, Jan 1808/08/23
Monogrammist W.K. 1808/08/23
Silo, A. 1808/08/23
Storck, Abr. 1808/08/23
Weenix 1808/08/23
Witte, E. 1808/08/23

Y. (1808, November 28)
Ovens, J. 1808/11/28

Index of Previous Owners

1801–1810